The Pocket MACQUARIE DICTIONARY

Second Edition

General Editor
JRL Bernard

First edition edited by
David Blair

The Jacaranda Press

First published 1982 by
THE JACARANDA PRESS
33 Park Road, Milton, Qld 4064

Offices also in Sydney and Melbourne

Second edition 1989

© Macquarie University NSW 1982, 1989

National Library of Australia
Cataloguing-in-Publication data

The Pocket Macquarie dictionary.

2nd ed.
ISBN 0 7016 2582 1.

1. English language — Dictionaries.
2. English language — Australia —
Dictionaries. I. Blair, David, 1942- .
II. Bernard, John, 1926- .

423

All rights reserved. No part of this publication
may be reproduced, stored in a retrieval system,
or transmitted in any form or by any means,
electronic, mechanical, photocopying, recording,
or otherwise, without the prior permission of
the publisher.

A number of words entered in this dictionary
are derived from trademarks. However, the
presence or absence of this indication of
derivation should not be regarded as affecting
the legal status of any trademark.

Printed and bound in Australia by
Australian Print Group, Maryborough, Vic.

10 9 8 7 6 5

Contents

Editorial staff vi
Preface to first edition vii
Preface to second edition x
How to use the dictionary xii
Key to structure of entries xvii
Abbreviations and symbols used in the dictionary xviii

A pocket dictionary of Australian English 1

Appendixes
  Grammar: tense and case 1199
  Metric conversion 1200
  Paper sizes 1202
  Military ranks 1202
  Roman numerals 1203
  Abbreviations for common academic qualifications 1204
  The Periodic Table 1206
  The International System of Units (SI) 1208
  Points of the compass 1209

Editorial staff

General Editor – Second Edition	JRL Bernard, BSc, BA, PhD, DipEd (Syd)
Consulting Editor	David Blair, MA (Syd)
Executive Editor	Richard Tardif
Senior Editor	Margaret McPhee
Editors	Ann Atkinson Leah Bloomfield Alison Moore Jessie Terry
Computer Systems	William E Smith Kris Burnet
Editorial Assistants	Maureen Leslie Collette Ryan Anne Teong
Editorial Committee, The Macquarie Dictionary	Editor in Chief: Arthur Delbridge, AO, MA (Lond), BA, DipEd (Syd), HonDLitt (Macq) John Bernard, BSc, BA, PhD, DipEd (Syd) David Blair, MA (Syd) Susan Butler, BA (Syd) Pamela Peters, BA (Melb), MA (Syd) Richard Tardif, BA (Syd), MGenStud (NSW)

Preface to the first edition

Dictionaries are like maps. They are intended to guide readers through the vocabulary of their language – through territory which is partly familiar but also, in part, unknown. And like maps, dictionaries can be written on a large scale or on a small scale. A large-scale map is able to show more landmarks, including many which are smaller or less important. Small-scale maps have to be more selective. They may not be able to show the more trivial aspects of their territory; but they must remain a reliable guide to the traveller as far as major features are concerned.

This *Pocket* edition of *The Macquarie Dictionary* is written on a smaller scale than its predecessor, but its purpose is the same: to make available to Australians an authoritative record of the words they use. The amount of detail differs, but the two works are based on the same principles: that our dictionaries should be written by Australians for Australians, and that they should be accurate in content, and clear and simple in style.

The *Pocket Macquarie* is based on the same research that produced *The Macquarie Dictionary*. It shares the same computer database; it has access to the same file of citations, and to the same body of editorial expertise. But it is not merely an abbreviation of the larger volume. We have believed it important to avoid a style which is too compact and complex – a common result of abbreviating a longer text. So all entries have been written in a way that will make the text easy to follow.

We have taken the view that definitions should not be harder to understand than the words they seek to explain. Accordingly, we have made every effort to explain hard words by easier ones – that is, by words which are more common and which the average reader is likely to use frequently. A list of words to be used in defining was drawn up by our editorial staff, based on published research into patterns of vocabulary use. This formed our basic defining strategy.

There were two significant variations to this strategy, however. The first occurs in some entries in scientific or technical fields. It is often the case that a total avoidance of technical words in a definition produces a longwinded entry which, although composed of simple words, is difficult to follow and wasteful of space. And sometimes by avoiding a technical term we can give a misleading impression of usage in that area. To say, for example, that tin is 'used in making *mixtures*' is not as helpful as saying that it is 'used in making *alloys*', despite the fact that *mixtures* is a simpler term.

The second departure from this principle arises from the wish to give more than just simple description of the meanings of words. Where possible, alternative terms, or synonyms, are given. This gives readers access to the wider resources of the Australian English lexicon and encourages vocabulary expansion. These synonyms, of course, cannot be restricted to the basic defining vocabulary.

In the selection of headwords to be treated, special consideration was given to the lists of specialist words which play such a major part in our technological society, and to terms which find their place in school curriculums across the country. In this process the editorial staff have had the benefit of advice from many consultants — from scientists, educationists, and professionals in many fields.

Words from what we call 'the general vocabulary' have had their own careful consideration, of course. They make up the bulk of our discourse, and our dialect owes its subtle but distinctive flavour to many of them. Some are 'world words' which would be recognised by speakers of any variety of English; others have a range of meanings that differ from the range they have in other parts of the world; still others form that class of obvious Australianisms by which we are often recognised. We have tried to do justice to the distinctiveness of Australian usage without giving undue weight to superficial and ephemeral Australianisms.

It can be assumed that all listed words are in use in Australia, unless they are labelled otherwise. We have included some which have no particular currency in Australia, because we judge that Australians might want to know of their usage in other parts of the world. These are marked with such labels as *Brit.* or *USA*. It may be thought useful for Australians to know, for instance, that *paddock* is a New Zealandism meaning 'a football field'.

Just as there are regional differences, so too there are differences in levels of formality. The general vocabulary is in this respect broadly divided into two classes, the formal on the one hand, and the informal (or colloquial) on the other. We have labelled as *colloquial* words which are appropriate to conversational speech or writing. Such words are characteristic of informal contexts where standard, conservative or polite words are thought not to be obligatory. Colloquialisms range from those words or phrases which are merely informal, to those regarded as slang or vulgar. We have, for the most part, left it to the reader's judgment as to where in the range a particular item lies, since individual judgments vary from one occasion to another. The occasional exceptions are those words where the type of usage is constant enough to warrant a label such as *disapproving* or *offensive*.

Any words without such a label are to be taken as acceptable in any context, formal or informal, though even here there is room for individual judgment.

Many standard abbreviations are included as headwords, and these pose something of a problem for dictionaries because modern usage is changing rapidly. It used to be universal that upper-case initials in abbreviations were separated by full-stops (as *A.B.C.*, *N.S.W.*).

It is now more common, however, to omit the punctuation (as *ABC*, *NSW*), and the *Pocket Macquarie* reflects this practice. But the fact that this dictionary gives only the one style is not intended to indicate that the use of full-stops is improper or even unusual.

Similarly, the dictionary does not always give the *-ize* variation for the *-ise* ending on verbs, although it is commonly used. Such forms as *standardize* and *finalize* are in frequent use within Australia and are generally accepted.

In the treatment of pronunciation, the *Pocket Macquarie* records the most common standard Australian pronunciations. Each word is presented in the symbols of the International Phonetic Alphabet; these characters are clear in print, are easy to use and form an internally consistent international standard. Their use has clear advantages over the use of an ad hoc respelling system.

Many readers have an interest in the derivation of words, and in response to this we have retained substantial etymologies in this *Pocket* edition. They have been designed to show the development of the meaning of a word rather than the change in its form and have been written in a simple style with the minimum of abbreviations.

In all these respects, we have endeavoured to present a record of the standard Australian vocabulary, as Australians speak it, in a form suitable for home, school or office. We trust that it will find a ready acceptance among those whose language it seeks to describe.

David Blair

Preface to the second edition

In the second edition of the *Pocket Macquarie Dictionary* it has been possible for the first time to include encyclopedic entries on a large scale. There are about five thousand of them.

In the main the headwords of the encyclopedic entries are proper nouns. Very often they are the names of persons or places of note, but some of them are the names of items which are more various — important organisations, constellations, mythical figures, events, and so on. Of whatever kind, all of them have been selected with the needs of Australian readers in mind. They refer to people or things that Australians will want to know about, the names of which they will want to be able to spell and to pronounce. An emphasis has been given to the number of entries with an Australian reference, in order to make sure that the local scene is especially well covered, but the treatment overall is global.

The encyclopedic entries are written in a style which makes them easy to follow, thereby continuing the sensible pattern established by the *Pocket Macquarie* in its first edition.

Inevitably the number of headwords which are foreign names has greatly increased in this edition and it will be noted that the pronunciations given for them are those which an educated Australian might use when speaking in his or her own form of English. Foreign pronunciations are not attempted.

Even so, a few extra sounds which are not as a rule thought of as being English have been included, because educated Australians can be heard to use them in this context. There are the local versions of two generalised nasal vowels, /ō/ as in *bon voyage* /bō vwaˈjaʒ/ and /æ̃/ as in *Rodin* /rouˈdæ̃/ neither of which have their true French values, and the vowel /y/, which is approximated by saying *Hugh* with rounded lips and which turns up in words like *Dürer* /ˈdyrə/.

Another change which this edition introduces is less immediately apparent. A few spellings of English words have been adopted which were not included in the first edition. For example, words ending in "-ise" now find beside themselves in the headword position their alternative in "-ize", with the implication that both are freely available for use. This is no more than the plain truth, since both are current in Australian writing, but the *Pocket Macquarie* continues to prefer the "-ise" forms, as for many years has the Australian Government *Style Manual*, because they imply fewer exceptions of pattern to be remembered. For example "advise" does not occur with an "-ize" spelling and if "-ize" is a general preference, "advise" must be remembered as an exception.

In the case of words ending in "-our" which have an alternative in "-or", the growing favor in which the "-or" forms now find themselves, especially in educational circles, has been acknowledged. Thus, beside "colour" in equal position will now appear "color" — or rather beside "color" in equal position will still appear "colour". The Macquarie editors of this edition regard the "-or" spellings as to be preferred, even if as yet they are not the more frequent. They have put them first in the headword position and have adopted them for their own use within definitions.

There is no question of such spellings being uniquely American. "Color", "honor", "favor" and the rest, occurred widely in written British English before American English was an established entity. The later British retreat to "colour", "honour" and even to the unsuccessful "terrour", was made in an attempt to be more "French". The "-or" spellings are old ones and they are easier for learners to handle since they simplify the pattern of derived and associated word sets. The pair "honour-honorary" is restored to unity if spelled "honor-honorary", etc.

A more important consideration than all this, however, is the simple fact that "-or" forms are now so frequent that the eye slides over them without registering them as in any way strange. This is the case also of those words in which the old digraphs "oe" and "ac" have become simplified by common usage. Few readers will have paused to reflect that the first sentences of this preface used the spelling "encyclopedic", not "encyclopaedic".

Both are of course still freely available, both are "correct", and the inclusion of both in cases like this for the first time in this edition of the *Pocket Macquarie* can only be an improvement, since it allows the dictionary more accurately to reflect the present condition of our vibrant and ever-changing language.

JRL Bernard

How to use the dictionary

You will find that entries in the dictionary are highly structured in form. In general, information about spelling and pronunciation comes first, meanings next, etymologies and run-ons last.

Not sure of the spelling?

THE HEADWORD
... is the word or words being defined in an entry, given in its standard or most common spelling. It appears in large bold-face type, slightly farther into the left margin than the usual line of text.

Australian /ɒsˈtreɪljən, əs-/, *adj.* **1.** of or relating to Australia. ◇*n.* **2.** person born or living in Australia. **3.** → **Australian English**.

Get as close as you can to the word you're looking for by following the letters you're sure about; then check several possibilities until you find the word you want.

Headwords are ordered strictly alphabetically, and can be found by taking each successive letter of the headword in alphabetical order. Word spaces, hyphens and apostrophes should be ignored. For example, **backblocks** and **back-burn** are found between **back** and **back country**.

Headwords which are spelt in exactly the same way but which have different histories are entered separately and distinguished by a small superscript number.

---

gibber[1] /ˈdʒɪbə/, *v.i.* **1.** to speak in a disjointed way; chatter. ◇*n.* **2.** gibbering speech. [? obs. *gib*, v., caterwaul, behave like a cat]

gibber[2] /ˈgɪbə/, *n.* a stone; boulder. [Aboriginal]

Alternative spellings are often given. They normally occur at the end of the entry, before the etymology.

---

emu /ˈimju/, *n.* a large, flightless, three-toed Australian bird closely related to the ostrich, but smaller. Also, **emeu**. [Pg *ema* ostrich, cassowary]

Sometimes, however, the variant spelling applies to only one of the senses of a word. When this is the case, the variant is placed directly in front of that definition, after the bold-face number.

> **beaut** /bjut/, *Colloq.* ◇*adj.* **1.** fine; good. ◇*n.* **2.** Also, **beauty.** someone or something pleasant or excellent. ◇*interj.* **3.** (exclamation of approval, delight, etc.).

Headwords include those prefixes and suffixes which are productive in word-formation.

> **ante-,** a prefix meaning 'before in space or time', as in *antediluvian*, *anteroom*. [L]

Not sure how to say it?

THE PRONUNCIATION
... follows the headword, and is contained within slant brackets.

> **alloy** /ˈælɔɪ/, *n.*; /əˈlɔɪ, ˈælɔɪ/, *v.* ◇*n.* **1.** a substance consisting of two or more metals mixed by fusion, electrolytic deposition, etc. **2.** a less costly metal mixed with more

A key to the symbols, which are characters of the International Phonetic Alphabet, is given inside the front and back covers of the dictionary.

What part of speech is it?

THE PARTS-OF-SPEECH LABELS
... tell whether a word is a noun (*n.*), adjective (*adj.*), etc. The label precedes each set of definitions to which it applies. Find the headword you want, look through the definitions to locate the sense you're interested in, and the previous part-of-speech label is the one that applies.

Wherever the part of speech changes within an entry, a diamond (◇) comes before the label to help make the change more obvious.

> **assent** /əˈsɛnt/, *v.i.* **1.** to agree (oft. fol. by *to*): *to agree to a statement.* ◇*n.* **2.** an agreement, as to a suggestion; acquiescence; concurrence. [ME, from L] – **assenter,** *n.*

Is it 'swum' or 'swam'?

INFLECTED FORMS
... are shown immediately after the pronunciation.

> **swim** /swɪm/, *v.*, **swam, swum, swimming,** *n.* ◇*v.i.* **1.** to move along or in water by movements of the limbs, fins, tail, etc. **2.**

For irregular *verbs* like **swim**, the past tense (I **swam**), past participle (I have **swum**) and present participle (I am **swimming**) are given.

Often the past tense and the past participle are identical; the form is not repeated on those occasions.

When verbs take regular inflections, i.e. *-ed* for past tense and past participle (**walked, have walked**), *-ing* for present participle (**am walking**), the forms are not given.

For *nouns* the plural form is given when it is not formed merely by the addition of *-s* or *-es*. **Dog** forms a regular plural **dogs**, and **class** a regular plural **classes**, but **ox** forms an irregular plural **oxen**.

For *adjectives* the comparative and superlative are given only when they are not formed by the addition of *-er* and *-est*. **Black** has the regular forms **blacker** and **blackest**, but **bony** has the irregular forms **bonier** and **boniest**.

In all the above cases, however, regular forms are given whenever there may be some doubt about the standard practice.

Who says it? . . . where? . . . when?

RESTRICTIVE LABELS

. . . give you information about how the usage of the word might be limited as to social context, region, time or subject. Such words might be marked as *Colloq*, *US*, *Obs*, *Sport*, etc.

Some labels apply to a whole entry: they stand *outside* the definition numbers.

---

abaft /ə'baft/, *Naut.* ◇*prep.* **1.** in the rear of; behind. ◇*adv.* **2.** at or towards stern (rear of ship); aft. [ME]

Others apply to only one definition: they stand immediately *after* the relevant definition number.

---

galah /gə'la/, *n.* **1.** a small Australian cockatoo, pale grey above and deep pink below. **2.** *Colloq.* a fool; simpleton. [Aboriginal]

What does it mean?

DEFINITIONS

. . . If you've heard or seen a word which is unknown to you, first find the appropriate headword. Then scan the definitions until you find the one that best fits the original context. Definitions are individually numbered in a single sequence. The central and usually the most common meaning is put first. Then come the figurative, specialised and rare meanings.

The use of a word is often shown by an illustrative phrase, printed in italic type and preceded by a colon.

---

forced /fɔst/, *adj.* **1.** enforced; compulsory: *forced labour.* **2.** strained or unnatural: *a forced smile.* **3.** caused by an emergency: *the forced landing of an aeroplane.*

The cross-reference arrow → indicates that the definition is not given in this place, but will be found under the headword that follows the arrow.

---

barbie /ˈbabi/, *n. Colloq.* → **barbecue**. Also, **barby**.

'See' indicates that more information is given under a related headword, perhaps an antonym (opposite) or a related species of animal, etc.

---

marl[2] /mal/, *n.* See **bandicoot**.

Some idiomatic phrases are listed alphabetically under main headwords, in smaller bold-face type. These are known as SECONDARY HEADWORDS: they are usually placed under the difficult or key word as headword.

---

edgeways /ˈɛdʒweɪz/, *adv.* **1.** with the edge forward. **2.** with a sideways movement. **3. get a word in edgeways**, to succeed in forcing one's way into a conversation.

Where did it come from?

ETYMOLOGIES

. . . give the origin of words. Placed towards the end of entries, in square brackets, they trace the progress of a word from one language to another and the development of its meaning.

---

filial /ˈfɪljəl, -iəl/, *adj.* **1.** of or relating to a son or daughter: *filial duty.* **2.** bearing the relation of a child to a parent. [LL, from L *filius* son, *filia* daughter]

In etymologies, a direction is sometimes given to another headword, and this is indicated by the fact that the word is printed in small capitals.

---

gigantic /dʒaɪˈgæntɪk/, *adj.* **1.** of, like, or suitable for a giant. **2.** very large; huge. [L: GIANT + IC]

What are the related words?

RUN-ONS

... are derived from the main headword, and don't need their own definition because they are simple extensions of the meaning. They appear at the end of the entry, in smaller boldface type, with a label saying what part of speech they are.

bushwalk /'buʃwɔk/, *v.i.* to walk through the bush for pleasure or sport. **—bushwalker**, *n.* **—bushwalking**, *n.*

Some of the most common formations are assumed: almost all adjectives can be turned into adverbs by the addition of *-ly*, and *-ness* turns adjectives into abstract nouns. These forms are normally not given.

Key to structure of entries

See 'How to Use the Dictionary' for explanation of terms

Headword — **petroleum** /pə'trouliəm/, *n.* **1.** Also, **rock-oil.** an oily, usu. dark-colored liquid (a mixture of various hydrocarbons), occurring naturally in various parts of the world, and commonly obtained by drilling. It is used (in its natural state or after certain treatment) as a fuel, or separated by distillation into petrol, paraffin products, etc. **2.** → **petrol.** [ML: rock oil] — **petrolic**, *adj.* — *Cross-reference* / *Inflected forms*

petty /'peti/, *adj.*, **-tier, -tiest. 1.** of small importance; trifling; trivial: *petty grievances*. **2.** of lesser or secondary importance, worth, etc. **3.** having or showing narrow ideas, interests, etc.: *petty minds*. **4.** mean or ungenerous in small or unimportant things: *a petty revenge*. [ME, from OF] — **pettily**, *adv.* — **pettiness**, *n.* — *Illustrative phrase*

Pronunciation in International Phonetic Alphabet

Petty /'peti/, *n.* **Bruce Leslie**, born 1929, Australian cartoonist and caricaturist. — *Restrictive label (social context)*

pew /pju/, *n.* **1.** (in a church) one of a group of fixed benchlike seats (with backs). **2.** *Colloq.* any chair; any place to sit down: *Take a pew.* [ME, from OF: balcony, from L: elevated place, balcony] — *Etymology*

phase /feɪz/, *n., v.*, **phased, phasing.** ◇*n.* **1.** any of the appearances in which a thing of varying states shows itself to the eye or mind. **2.** a stage of change or development. **3.** the particular appearance presented by the moon or a planet, etc., at a given time. **4.** *Biol.* an aspect of or stage in meiosis or mitosis. **5.** *Zool.* any of the stages of development of certain animals which take on a different color according to the breeding condition. **6.** *Chem, Phys.* a physically separate, homogeneous part of a mixed system: *the solid, liquid, and gaseous phases of a substance*. **7.** *Phys, Elect.* a particular stage or point of advancement of a wave cycle. **8. out of phase,** not working or happening together. ◇*v.t.* **9.** to plan or arrange in phases. **10.** to introduce (into a system or the like) in stages. ◇*v.* **11. phase in,** to introduce gradually and fit into a system or the like. **12. phase out,** to take out gradually from a system. [backformation from *phases*, pl. of Gk *phasis*] — **phaser**, *n.* — *Restrictive label (subject)* / *Run-on*

Secondary headword

philosophical /filə'sɒfɪkəl/, *adj.* **1.** of or relating to philosophy: *philosophical studies*. **2.** versed in or occupied with philosophy, as people. **3.** proper to or befitting a philosopher. **4.** rationally or sensibly calm in trying circumstances: *a philosophical acceptance of necessity*. **5.** (formerly) of or relating to natural philosophy or physical science. Also, **philosophic.** — *Secondary variant*

philosophise or **philosophize** /fə'lɒsəfaɪz/, *v.i.*, **-phised, -phising.** to reason, theorise or moralise. — **philosophiser**, *n.* — *Equal variant*

Abbreviations and symbols used in the dictionary

A'asia Australasia
abbrev. abbreviation
adj. adjective
adv. adverb
Aeron Aeronautics
AF Anglo-French
Agric Agriculture
Alg Algebra
Amer Ind American Indian
Anat Anatomy
Anc Hist Ancient History
Anglican Ch Anglican Church
Anthrop Anthropology
Ar Arabic
Aram Aramaic
Archaeol Archaeology
Archit Architecture
Astrol Astrology
Astron Astronomy
Aust Australia, Australian

b. blend of, blended
Biochem Biochemistry
Biol Biology
Bot Botany
Bldg Trades Building Trades
Brit British

c. cognate with
cap. capital
Carp Carpentry
Celt Celtic
Chem Chemistry
Class Myth Classical Mythology
Colloq Colloquial
Comm Commerce
conj. conjunction

d dialect, dialectical
D Dutch
Dan Danish

E English
eastn eastern
Ecol Ecology
Econ Economics
Educ Education
e.g. for example (*exempli gratia*)
Egypt Egyptian
Elect Electronics, Electrical
Eng Hist English History

Engin Engineering
esp. especially
etc. et cetera
Europ Hist European History

F French
fem. feminine
fig. figurative
Flem Flemish
fol. followed
Fr Hist French History
Fris Frisian

G German
Geog Geography
Geol Geology
Geom Geometry
Ger Hist German History
Gk Greek
Gmc Germanic
Goth Gothic
Govt Government
Gram Grammar
Gymn Gymnastics

Heb Hebrew
HG High German
Hind Hindustani
Hist History
Hung Hungarian

Icel Icelandic
i.e. that is (*id est*)
IE Indo-European
indic. indicative
Indust Law Industrial Law
interj. interjection
Internat Law International Law
It Italian

Jap Japanese
Jew Hist Jewish History
joc. jocular
Journal Journalism

L Latin
l.c. lower case
LG Low German
lit. literally
Lit Literature
LGk Late Greek (300–700)

LHeb	Late Hebrew
LL	Late Latin (390–700)

M 1. Middle
 2. Medieval
masc. masculine
ME Middle English (1100–1500)
Mech Mechanics
Med Medicine
Mediev Hist Medieval History
Metall Metallurgy
Mex Mexican
MF Middle French (1400–1600)
MGk Medieval Greek (700–1500)
Mil Military
Mineral Mineralogy
ML Medieval Latin (700–1500)
Mod Hist Modern History
Myth Mythology

n. noun
Naut Nautical
NL Neo-Latin (1500+)
Norw Norwegian
NSW New South Wales
NT Northern Territory
nth north
nthn northern
NZ New Zealand

O Old
obs. obsolete
OE Old English (before 1100)
OF Old French (before 1400)
oft. often
Old Test Old Testament
ONF Old North French
orig. origin, original, originally
OS Old Saxon

Parl Parliament
Parl Proc Parliamentary Procedures
Pers Persian
Pg Portuguese
Pharm Pharmacy
Philos Philosophy
Photog Photography
Phys Physics
pl. plural
Pol Polish
p.p. past participle
Pr Provençal
prep. preposition
pres. part. present participle
pron. pronoun

Psychiat Psychiatry
Psychol Psychology

Qld Queensland

R League Rugby League
Rom Romance, Romanic
Rom Cath Ch Rome-based Catholic Church
R Union Rugby Union
Russ Russian

SA South Australia
Scand Scandinavian
Scot Scottish
Shipbldg Shipbuilding
sing. singular
Skt Sanskrit
Sp Spanish
Stats Statistics
sth south
sthn southern
subj. subjunctive
Surf Surfing
Surg Surgery
Swed Swedish

Tas Tasmania
Tech Drawing Technical Drawing
Theat Theatre
Theol Theology
Turk Turkish

ult. ultimate, ultimately
uncert. uncertain
US United States of America
usu. usually

v. verb
var. variant
Vet Sci Veterinary Science
v.i. intransitive verb
Vic Victoria
VL Vulgar Latin
v.t. transitive verb

WA Western Australia
westn western
WGMc West Germanic
WInd West Indian

Zool Zoology

& and
? perhaps
* hypothetical form

Aa

A, a, *n., pl.* **A's, a's,** or **As. 1.** the first letter of the English alphabet. **2.** the first in any ordered group. **3.** the highest mark for school work, etc. **4.** *Music.* the sixth note in the scale of C major.

a[1] /eɪ/; *weak form* /ə/, *adj. or indef. article.* used in the following ways: **1.** before a noun that means a single but not a particular member of a general group: *She is a woman; Do you have a pen?* **2.** before a proper noun to mean a person or thing is in some way similar to that named: *He is quite a Romeo.* **3.** before nouns of plural, but not particular quantity: *a few; a great many.* **4.** to mean 'any', 'a single one': *He does not have a friend in the world.* **5.** to mean 'the same': *two of a kind.* Also, before a vowel, **an**[1]. [ME]

a[2] /eɪ/; *weak form* /ə/, *adj. or indef. article.* each; every: *three times a day.* [orig. *a*, *prep.*, OE *an, on*, confused with the indefinite article. See A-[1]]

a-[1], a prefix meaning 'on', 'in', 'into', 'to', 'towards' which, placed before some nouns, forms an adjective or adverb: *afoot, ashore, apart, aside.* [OE *an, on* at, on]

a-[2], a prefix, a reduced form of Old English *of*, as in *afresh, anew.* [ME *a-*, OE *of* (*prep.*) off, of]

a-[3], a prefix meaning **1.** 'up', 'out', or 'away', as in *arise, awake.* **2.** intensified action, as in *abide, amaze.* [ME *a-*, up, out, away, from OE *ā*]

a-[4], a prefix meaning 'off', 'away', 'from'; a variant of **ab-**, before *m, p,* and *v*, as in *aperient, avert.* [ME *a-*, from L *ab-*]

a-[5], variant of **ad-**, used: **1.** before *sc, sp, st,* as in *ascend.* **2.** in words of French origin, as in *amass.* [ME *a-*, from F, from L]

a-[6], a prefix meaning 'not', 'without', 'opposite to', as in *asocial, amoral, asymmetric.* [Gk]

A, *Symbol.* **1.** acre. **2.** ampere. **3.** answer.

Å, *Symbol.* angstrom.

AA /eɪ eɪ/ *Abbrev.* Alcoholics Anonymous.

AAP /eɪ eɪ 'pi/, *Abbrev.* Australian Associated Press.

aardvark /'ɑdvak/, *n.* a large African mammal active at night, which digs burrows, lives on termites, and has a long tongue and ears. [Afrikaans]

Aaron /'ɛərən/, *n. Bible.* the first high priest of the Hebrews and the brother of Moses. –**Aaronic,** *adj.* [See Exodus 4:14]

A'asia, *Abbrev.* Australasia.

AAT /eɪ eɪ 'ti/, *Abbrev.* Australian Antarctic Territory.

ab-[1], a prefix meaning 'off', 'away', 'from' as in *abduct, abnormal.* [L, representing *ab*, *prep.*, from, away]

abbreviation

ab-[2], a prefix indicating a c.g.s. electromagnetic unit of measurement: *an abvolt is equivalent to* 10^{-8} *volts.* [abbrev. of ABSOLUTE]

aback /ə'bæk/, *adv.* **1.** *Naut.* with wind blowing against the front (of a sail or ship), preventing forward movement. **2. taken aback, a.** *Naut.* caught by the wind in this way. **b.** surprised; disconcerted. [ME]

abacus /'æbəkəs/, *n., pl.* **-ci** /-saɪ/. a device for calculating, consisting of beads strung on rods set in a frame. [L, from Gk]

abaft /ə'baft/, *Naut. prep.* **1.** in the rear of; behind. ◇*adv.* **2.** at or towards the stern (rear of ship); aft. [ME]

abalone /æbə'louni/, *n.* a type of shellfish, the flesh of which is used for food and the shell for ornaments. [Sp.]

abandon[1] /ə'bændən/, *v.t.* **1.** to leave, not intending to return: *They abandoned their home.* **2.** to give up; relinquish: *Don't abandon hope; They had to abandon their position in the queue.* **3.** to give up (something begun) without finishing: *to abandon a cricket match because of rain.* **4.** to give (oneself) up completely (to strong feelings, etc.): *He abandoned himself to grief.* **5.** *Law.* to give up (partly damaged property) to insurer in order to make claim for total loss. [ME, from OF] –**abandonment,** *n.*

abandon[2] /ə'bændən/, *n.* freedom from care, worry, or restraint: *They danced with abandon.* [F]

abase /ə'beɪs/, *v.t.*, **abased, abasing.** to lower in rank, opinion of others, etc; humiliate. [b. BASE[2] and ME *abesse(n)* (from LL *bassus* low)] –**abasement,** *n.*

abashed /ə'bæʃt/, *adj.* ashamed or embarrassed. [ME, from OF: astonish]

abate /ə'beɪt/, *v.*, **abated, abating.** ◇*v.t.* **1.** to make less; diminish: *This medicine will abate the pain.* **2.** *Law.* to put an end to (nuisance, action, etc.); decrease: *The storm has abated.* [ME] –**abatement,** *n.*

abattoirs /'æbətwɑz, -tɔz/, *n.* a building or place where animals are killed for food. Also, **abattoir.** [F]

abb, /æb/ *n.* (a warp yarn made from) the inferior wool at the edges of a fleece.

abbess /'æbɛs/, *n.* the superior of nuns in a convent. [ME, from LL]

abbey /'æbi/, *n., pl.* **-beys.** the (buildings lived in by) religious establishment of monks or nuns; a monastery or convent. [ME *abbeye,* from OF *abaie,* from LL *abbātia*]

abbot /'æbət/, *n.* the superior of monks in a monastery. [ME, from LL, from Gk, from Aram. *abbā* father] –**abbacy,** *n.*

abbrev., *Abbrev.* abbreviation. Also, **abbr.**

abbreviate /ə'briviett/, *v.t.*, **-ated, -ating.** to make (a word or phrase) shorter by leaving out some letters. [L]

abbreviation /əbrivi'eɪʃən/, *n.* **1.** a shortened form of a word or phrase, used to mean the whole, e.g. *Mon* for *Monday.* **2.** reduction in length; abridgment. [L]

ABC

ABC[1] /ˌeɪ biː 'siː/, *Abbrev.* **1.** Australian Broadcasting Corporation. **2.** (formerly) Australian Broadcasting Commission.

ABC[2] /ˌeɪ biː 'siː/, *n.* **1.** the alphabet. **2.** the main or basic facts, etc. (of any subject).

abdicate /'æbdəkeɪt/, *v.i., v.t.,* **-cated, -cating.** to give up (a claim, right or position, esp. that of being king or queen): *He abdicated in 1936*; *She abdicated the throne.* [L *abdicātus,* pp.] —**abdication,** *n.*

abdomen /'æbdəmən/, *n.* **1.** (in vertebrates, including man) that part of the body that includes the stomach and most of the digestive organs; belly. **2.** *Insects.* (in arthropods) the last section of the body, behind the thorax. [L] —**abdominal,** *adj.*

abduct /əb'dʌkt/, æb-/, *v.t.* to carry (someone) off using deceit or force; kidnap. [L] —**abductor,** *n.* —**abduction,** *n.*

Abel /'eɪbəl/, *n. Bible.* the second son of Adam and Eve, slain by his brother, Cain. [See Genesis 4]

Abelard /'æbəlad/, *n.* **Peter,** 1079–1142, French philosopher, teacher, and theologian. His love affair with Héloïse is one of the famous romances of history.

Aberdeen /æbə'din/, *n.* **George Hamilton-Gordon, 4th Earl of,** 1784–1860, British statesman; prime minister 1852–55.

Aberdeen Angus, *n.* (one of) a breed of hornless beef cattle with smooth black hair, originally bred in Scotland.

Aberdeenshire /æbə'dinʃə, -ʃə/, *n.* a former county of north-eastern Scotland, now part of Grampian region. Also, **Aberdeen.**

aberration /æbə'reɪʃən/, *n.* **1.** a change or departure from what is right, normal, or true. **2.** a temporary fall from a healthy mental condition. [L] —**aberrant,** *adj.*

abet /ə'bet/, *v.t.,* **abetted, abetting.** to help or encourage (usu. something undesirable): *to abet a crime.* [ME, from OF]

abeyance /ə'beɪəns/, *n.* the state of being inactive or disused for a limited time. [AF: expectation, from OF: gape after]

abhor /əb'hɔ/, *v.t.,* **-horred, -horring.** to regard with hate or disgust; loathe. [late ME, from L] —**abhorrence,** *n.*

abhorrent /əb'hɒrənt/, *adj.* **1.** causing hate and disgust; detestable: *I find that idea abhorrent.* **2.** completely opposed (fol. by *to*): *That decision is abhorrent to justice.*

abide /ə'baɪd/, *v.,* **abode** /ə'boʊd/ or **abided, abiding.** ◇*v.i.* **1.** to remain; continue; stay: *abide with me.* **2.** *Archaic.* to live; reside. ◇*v.t.* **3.** *Colloq.* to put up with; tolerate: *I can't abide such people.* ◇*v.* **4.** **abide by, a.** to remain faithful to; stand by: *abide by your friends; I'll abide by what I said.* **b.** to wait for or accept; conform to: *I'll abide by the decision.* [OE *ābīdan.* See A-[3]] —**abidance,** *n.* —**abiding,** *adj.*

ability /ə'bɪləti/, *n., pl.* **-ties. 1.** the power to do or act. **2.** the skill in an activity or subject; talent; competence: *an ability in*

abode

maths; a person of great ability. [ME, from F, from L]

abiogenesis /ˌeɪbaɪoʊ'dʒɛnəsəs/, *n.* the theory or belief that living things can be produced from non-living matter. [A-[6] + BIO- + GENESIS]

abject /'æbdʒɛkt/, *adj.* **1.** completely miserable; humiliating: *abject poverty.* **2.** humble; servile: *an abject apology.* **3.** deserving contempt: *an abject liar.* [ME, from L] —**abjection,** *n.*

abjure /əb'dʒʊə/, *v.t.,* **-jured, -juring.** to promise or swear solemnly to give up (rights, loyalties, bad behavior, etc.). [L] —**abjuration,** *n.*

ablation /ə'bleɪʃən/, *n. Geol.* erosion (wearing away) of a solid body by a fluid. [L: a carrying away]

ablative /'æblətɪv/, *adj., n.* (relating to) the form of a noun (in Latin, etc.) which expresses place from which, time when, place in which, manner, agency, etc.: *ablative case.* [L *ablātīvus* expressing removal]

ablaze /ə'bleɪz/, *adj.* **1.** on fire. **2.** shining as if on fire. **3.** full of strong feeling: *ablaze with anger.*

able /'eɪbəl/, *adj.,* **abler, ablest. 1.** having enough power, skill, knowledge or opportunity: *He is able to drive a car; Are you able to go to the party?* **2.** having or showing special skills or knowledge: *an able teacher; an able performance.* [ME, from L *habilis* easy to handle, fit] —**ably,** *adv.*

-able, a suffix used to form adjectives, esp. from verbs, to mean something can be done (*obtainable*), should be done (*payable*), is worthy to be done (*forgivable*), is suitable for (*eatable*), is likely to happen (*perishable*). It is also attached to other parts of speech (esp. nouns) as in *comfortable, marriageable,* and even verb phrases, as in *get-at-able.* Also, **-ble, -ible.** [ME, from L *-ābilis*]

able-bodied /'eɪbəl-bɒdid/, *adj.* physically strong and healthy.

ablution /ə'bluʃən/, *n.* **1.** a ceremonial washing of hands, body, or holy objects. **2.** (*pl.*) the act of washing oneself: *to perform one's ablutions.* [ME, from L]

abnegate /'æbnəgeɪt/, *v.t.,* **-gated, -gating.** to refuse or give up (a right, etc.); renounce. [L] —**abnegation,** *n.*

abnormal /æb'nɔməl/, *adj.* different from the usual rule, type or standard (usu. not in desirable way). [L *abnormis* irregular + -AL[1]] —**abnormality,** *n.*

Abo /'æboʊ/, *Colloq. (oft. offensive) n.* (also *l.c.*) **1.** an Aborigine. **2.** Aboriginal. [shortened form of ABORIGINE]

aboard /ə'bɔd/, *adv.* **1.** on or in a ship, train, bus, etc.; on board: *All aboard!* ◇*prep.* **2.** on a (ship, etc.): *We went aboard the boat.*

abode /ə'boʊd/, *n.* **1.** a place where someone lives; habitation. ◇*v.* **2.** past tense and past participle of **abide.** [OE, pt. of *ābīdan* ABIDE]

abolish / abroad

abolish /əˈbɒlɪʃ/, *v.t.* to put an end to; annul: *to abolish slavery.* [F, from L: perish] —**abolishment**, *n.*

abolition /æbəˈlɪʃən/, *n.* the act of putting an end to something; destruction; annulment. [L] —**abolitionary**, *adj.*

abomasum /æbəˈmeɪsəm/, *n.* the fourth or true stomach of ruminants (cud-chewing animals, as the cow). [NL]

A-bomb /ˈeɪ-bɒm/, *n.* → **atomic bomb**.

abominable /əˈbɒmɪnəbəl, əˈbɒmnəbəl/, *adj.* **1.** causing hate or disgust; loathsome. **2.** *Colloq.* shocking; unpleasant. [ME, from L] —**abominably**, *adv.*

abominate /əˈbɒmənent/, *v.t.*, **-nate**, **-nating.** to regard with great hate or disgust; abhor. [L *abōminātus*, pp., having prayed against as an ill omen]

abomination /əbɒməˈneɪʃən/, *n.* **1.** a person, thing or action causing great hate or disgust. **2.** extreme dislike; detestation.

aboriginal /æbəˈrɪdʒənəl/, *adj.* **1.** (*usu. cap.*) of or relating to the Australian Aborigines. **2.** of or relating to an aborigine (def. 2); indigenous. ◇*n.* **3.** (*usu. cap.*) an Australian Aborigine.

Aboriginal reserve, *n.* land set aside for the Aboriginal people to live in.

aborigine /æbəˈrɪdʒəni/, *n.* (*usu. cap.*) **1.** one of a race of tribal peoples, the earliest known to live in Australia. **2.** (generally) one of a people living in a country or place from earliest known times. [L: from the beginning]

abort /əˈbɔt/, *v.i.* **1.** (esp. of a foetus) to fail to develop completely. **2.** *Colloq.* (of a military operation, test of a machine, etc.) to fail. ◇*v.t.* **3.** to cause (something) to abort. **4.** to cause (a foetus) to be born before it is developed enough to live. [L] —**abortive**, *adj.*

abortion /əˈbɔʃən/, *n.* **1.** the birth or removal of a foetus from the womb before it is developed enough to live. **2.** *Biol.* the stopping of development of an organ at early stage. **3.** anything which fails to develop successfully. [L: miscarriage]

abound /əˈbaʊnd/, *v.i.* **1.** to be in great numbers; be plentiful: *Gum trees abound in this valley.* **2.** to be rich (fol. by *in*): *Australia abounds in minerals.* **3.** to be filled; teem (fol. by *with*): *This river abounds with fish.* [ME, from L] —**abounding**, *adj.*

about /əˈbaʊt/, *prep.* **1.** of; concerning; relating to; in regard to: *to talk about secrets.* **2.** somewhere near or in: *He is about the house.* **3.** close to: *about my height.* **4.** on the point of (fol. by *infinitive*): *about to leave.* **5.** in various directions around: *to wander about the place.* **6.** concerned with; engaged in doing: *She is about her work.* **7.** on every side of; around: *the fence about the pool.* ◇*adv.* **8.** near in time, number, degree, etc.; approximately: *about 100 kilometres.* **9.** *Colloq.* nearly; almost: *about ready.* **10.** nearby: *He is somewhere about.* **11.** in various directions; around: *look about; to move things about.* **12.** half round; in the opposite direction: *to spin about.* **13.** *Naut.* on the opposite tack. **14.** in turn; in rotation: *We'll play turn and turn about.* **15.** around; at large: *There are a lot of colds about.* ◇*adj.* **16.** **up and about**, astir; active (after sleep or illness). [OE *on būtan* on the outside (of)]

about-face /əbaʊt-ˈfeɪs/, *n., v.*, **-faced**, **-facing.** ◇*n.* **1.** a complete, sudden change in position, opinion, etc.; volte-face. **2.** *Mil.* a command to turn to the opposite direction. ◇*v.i.* **3.** to turn in opposite direction. Also, **about-turn.**

above /əˈbʌv/, *adv.* **1.** in or to a higher place; overhead: *the blue sky above.* **2.** earlier, esp. in a book, etc.: *from what has been said above.* **3.** in heaven: *the angels above.* ◇*prep.* **4.** higher than in place, rank or power: *to fly above the earth; A general is above a captain.* **5.** more in quantity or number than: *The weight is above a tonne.* **6.** not capable of, or too good for: *He is above telling lies; above suspicion.* **7.** too difficult for: *This question is above me.* **8.** more than; in preference to: *to favor one child above another; I chose one above the other.* **9.** **above all**, most important of all. **10. above oneself**, having too high an opinion of oneself; conceited. ◇*adj.* **11.** said or written earlier: *the above explanation.* ◇*n.* **12. the above**, something which was said, mentioned, or written earlier. [OE from A-¹ + *bufan* above]

aboveboard /əbʌvˈbɔd/, *adv.* **1.** without tricks or deceit; openly. ◇*adj.* **2.** open; honest. Also, (*esp. after a verb*) **above board.**

abracadabra /æbrəkəˈdæbrə/, *n.* **1.** a word used in magic spells or written in a triangular form as a charm. **2.** meaningless talk; gibberish. [L]

abrade /əˈbreɪd/, *v.t., v.i.*, **abraded**, **abrading.** to scrape off or wear down by rubbing. [L: scrape off] —**abradant**, *n., adj.*

Abraham /ˈeɪbrəhæm/, *n. Bible.* the first of the great patriarchs, father of Isaac, and traditional founder of the Hebrew people. [See Genesis 11-25]

abrasion /əˈbreɪʒən/, *n.* an act or result of rubbing or scraping: *an abrasion on the knee.* [L]

abrasive /əˈbreɪsɪv, -zɪv/, *n.* **1.** any material or substance used for rubbing, grinding, polishing, etc., e.g. emery or sand. ◇*adj.* **2.** causing abrasion. **3.** (of a personality) annoying; irritating. —**abrasiveness**, *n.*

abreast /əˈbrɛst/, *adv.* **1.** side by side: *They walked three abreast.* **2.** alongside; not behind, in knowledge, etc. (fol. by *of* or *with*): *We must keep abreast of the news.*

abridge /əˈbrɪdʒ/, *v.t.*, **abridged**, **abridging.** **1.** to shorten (a book, interview, etc.) by leaving some parts out. **2.** to make less; diminish. [ME, from OF, from L: shorten] —**abridged**, *adj.* —**abridgment**, *n.*

abroad /əˈbrɔd/, *adv.* **1.** in or to a foreign country or countries, usu. overseas: *to live abroad.* **2.** out of doors: *The owl is abroad at night.* **3.** at large; in circulation; astir: *There's an evil spirit abroad.* **4.** in all directions; widely: *to throw seeds abroad.* [ME A-¹ + BROAD]

abrogate /ˈæbrəgeɪt/, *v.t.*, **-gated, -gating.** to bring (a law, etc.) officially to an end; abolish; repeal. [L] **—abrogation,** *n.*

Abrolhos Islands /əˈbrɒləs aɪləndz/, *n.pl.* → **Houtman Abrolhos.**

abrupt /əˈbrʌpt/, *adj.* **1.** sudden; without warning: *an abrupt entrance.* **2.** changing from one subject to another suddenly: *an abrupt style of writing.* **3.** brief and impolite in speech or manner; brusque. **4.** steep; precipitous: *an abrupt climb.* [L: broken off] **—abruptly,** *adv.* **—abruptness,** *n.*

abs-, a prefix meaning 'off', 'away', 'from', variant of **ab-,** before *c, q, t,* as in *abscond.*

Absalom /ˈæbsələm/, *n. Bible.* the third son of David, king of the Hebrews, who rebelled against his father and was killed. [See II Samuel 13-19]

abscess /ˈæbses, ˈæbsəs/, *n.* a collection of pus in a cavity of the body, often with swelling and inflammation, and usu. caused by bacteria. [L: a going away]

abscissa /æbˈsɪsə/, *n., pl.* **-scissas, -scissae** /-ˈsɪsi/. (in plane Cartesian coordinates) the *x*-coordinate of a point, i.e., its horizontal distance from the *y*-axis measured parallel to the *x*-axis. [L, short for *linea abscissa* line cut off]

abscond /æbˈskɒnd, əb-/, *v.i.* to run away secretly, esp. to avoid the law. [L: put away] **—absconder,** *n.*

abseil /ˈæbseɪl/, *v.i. Mountaineering.* to lower oneself with a double rope down a steep slope. [G]

absence /ˈæbsəns/, *n.* **1.** a state or period of being away: *I'll do his work during his absence.* **2.** a lack; non-existence: *the absence of proof.* [ME, from L]

absent /ˈæbsənt/, *adj.*; /əbˈsent/, *v.* ◇*adj.* **1.** not present; away. **2.** lacking: *Cooking is absent from my skills.* ◇*v.t.* **3.** to take or keep (oneself) away: *They absented themselves from school.* [ME, from L]

absentee /æbsənˈti/, *n.* **1.** a person who is not present. **2.** a person who habitually is away from his or her place of work, school, etc. **3.** (formerly) an escaped convict.

absenteeism /æbsənˈtiːɪzəm/, *n.* the practice of staying away from work, school, etc.

absent-minded /æbsənt-ˈmaɪndəd/, *adj.* not attentive; forgetful.

absinth /ˈæbsɪnθ/, *n.* **1.** a bitter, green-colored, very strong alcoholic drink made with wormwood, having a liquorice flavor. **2.** → **wormwood** (def. 1). Also, **absinthe.** [F, from L, from Gk: wormwood]

absolute /ˈæbsəluːt/, *adj.* **1.** complete; perfect; pure: *absolute truth.* **2.** not limited in any way; arbitrary: *an absolute monarch; absolute command.* **3.** not dependent on or relative to anything else: *an absolute moral value.* **4.** *Gram.* not grammatically connected with any other part of the sentence, as *It being Sunday* in *It being Sunday, the family went to church.* **5.** *Phys.* **a.** not dependent on or relative to an arbitrary value or any particular substance or system: *absolute zero of temperature.* **b.** relating to a system of units based on some primary or basic units, esp. units of length, mass, and time. **c.** relating to measurement based on an absolute zero or unit: *absolute pressure.* **6.** *Law.* (of a court order, decree, etc.) having full effect immediately; without conditions: *The convict was given an absolute pardon.* **7. the Absolute** (*sometimes l.c.*). *Philos.* that which is free from any restriction and is the origin of all things. [ME, from L: loosened from]

absolute alcohol, *n.* ethyl alcohol containing not more than one per cent by weight of water.

absolutely /ˈæbsəˌluːtli/; *emphatic* /ˌæbsəˈluːtli/, *adv.* **1.** completely; wholly; unconditionally. **2.** *Colloq.* yes; certainly.

absolute majority, *n.* the difference in number between the votes for the leading candidate and the (lower) total of all other votes cast. See **majority** (def. 2).

absolute temperature, *n.* temperature measured in kelvins from absolute zero; thermodynamic temperature.

absolute zero, *n.* the lowest possible theoretical temperature at which matter can exist; the temperature at which particles, whose movement is heat, would be at rest. Defined as zero kelvin or −273.15 degrees Celsius.

absolution /æbsəˈluːʃən/, *n.* **1.** the act of absolving. **2.** the condition of being absolved. **3.** *Church.* (a formal statement of) a forgiveness of sin and freedom from punishment. [L: an acquittal]

absolutism /ˈæbsəluːtˌɪzəm/, *n.* the principle or practice of absolute power in government; despotism. **—absolutist,** *n.*

absolve /əbˈzɒlv/, *v.t.*, **-solved, -solving.** **1.** to free (someone) from blame, punishment, duty, etc. (fol. by *from*). **2.** to pardon; acquit. **3.** *Church.* to give or pronounce forgiveness of sins to (someone). [L: loosen from]

absorb /əbˈsɔb, -ˈzɔb/, *v.t.* **1.** to suck up or drink in (liquids): *This cloth will absorb the milk.* **2.** to take in; assimilate: *The newcomers were quickly absorbed into the group; The student absorbed all the facts.* **3.** to take up or receive in by chemical or molecular action. **4.** to take in without echo or reaction: *to absorb sound.* [L]

absorbed /əbˈsɔbd, -ˈzɔbd/, *adj.* totally interested; engrossed.

absorbent /əbˈsɔbənt, -ˈzɔ-/, *adj.* able to absorb moisture. **—absorbency,** *n.*

absorbing /əbˈsɔbɪŋ, -ˈzɔ-/, *adj.* extremely interesting: *an absorbing book.*

absorption /əbˈsɔpʃən, -ˈzɔp-/, *n.* **1.** the act, process or result of absorbing: *absorption of substances into the blood.* **2.** interest; preoccupation. [L] **—absorptive,** *adj.*

abstain /əbˈsteɪn/, *v.i.* **1.** to stop oneself from doing or enjoying something (fol. by *from*): *to abstain from smoking.* **2.** to choose not to cast one's vote. [ME, from L]

abstemious /əb'stimiəs/, *adj.* careful or restrained in the use of food, drink, etc. [L]

abstention /əb'stenʃən/, *n.* an act of abstaining, esp. from voting. [L: abstained]

abstinence /'æbstənəns/, *n.* an act or practice of abstaining, esp. from drinking alcohol. [ME, from L] —**abstinent**, *adj.*

abstract /'æbstrækt/, *adj., n.;* /əb'strækt/ for defs 6, 7, /'æbstrækt/ for def. 8, *v.,* ⋄*adj.* **1.** thought of separately from matter, practice and particular examples; not concrete: *abstract numbers; abstract thought.* **2.** theoretical; not applied. **3.** difficult to understand; abstruse. ⋄*n.* **4.** a short account of an essay, speech, etc.; a summary. **5. in the abstract,** without relating to special examples or practical experience. ⋄*v.t.* **6.** to draw or take away; remove. **7.** to think of (something) generally, not in relation to particular examples: *to abstract the idea of beauty.* **8.** to make a short account of (an essay, etc.); summarise. [L: drawn away]

abstract art /ˌæbstrækt 'at/, *n.* an art style, popular in the 20th century, which values form and color, not the realistic representation of an object.

abstracted /əb'stræktəd/, *adj.* lost in thought; preoccupied.

abstract expressionism, *n.* abstract art of the 1950s and later, which does not use traditional styles and techniques, but is based on forms which are not figurative and not formal.

abstraction /əb'strækʃən/, *n.* **1.** an abstract or general idea or expression. **2.** an impractical idea. **3.** an act of abstracting. **4.** a state of being lost in thought; reverie. **5.** *Art.* a work of abstract art either without any relation to natural objects (**pure abstraction**) or with representation of them through geometrical or generalised forms (**near abstraction**). [L]

abstract noun /ˌæbstrækt 'naʊn/, *n.* a noun having an abstract (as opposed to *concrete*) meaning, e.g. *fear, love, size, beauty.*

abstruse /əb'strus/, *adj.* difficult to understand; esoteric: *abstruse questions.* [L: concealed]

absurd /əb'sɜd, -'zɜd/, *adj.* **1.** without reason or common sense; obviously false or foolish; ridiculous: *an absurd statement.* **2.** laughable; comical. [L] —**absurdity**, *n.*

abundance /ə'bʌndəns/, *n.* **1.** a plentiful amount or supply: *an abundance of love; food in abundance.* **2.** fullness: *in the abundance of my heart.* **3.** wealth. [ME, from L]

abundant /ə'bʌndənt/, *adj.* **1.** present in great amount; more than enough: *an abundant supply.* **2.** having in great quantity; abounding (fol. by *in*): *a river abundant in fish.* [ME, from L]

abuse /ə'bjuz/, *v.,* **abused, abusing**; /ə'bjus/, *n.* **1.** to use wrongly or improperly; misuse: *He abused his position of authority.* **2.** to do wrong to; injure. **3.** to speak insultingly to. ⋄*n.* **4.** wrong or improper use; misuse. **5.** insulting or violent language. **6.** ill treatment of a person. **7.** a dishonest or evil practice. [F, from L: misuse] —**abusive**, *adj.*

Abu Simbel /ˌæbu 'sɪmbəl/, *n.* a former village in southern Egypt, now covered by Lake Nasser; site of two temples of Ramses II, which were moved in 1966–67 to a level above the lake.

abut /ə'bʌt/, *v.i.,* **abutted, abutting.** to touch at one end; adjoin (oft. fol. by *on, upon,* or *against*): *This piece of land abuts upon a street.* [ME, from OF: join end to end] —**abuttal**, *n.*

abysmal /ə'bɪzməl/, *adj.* **1.** too great to measure: *abysmal ignorance.* **2.** very bad: *an abysmal performance.*

abyss /ə'bɪs/, *n.* **1.** a hole or space too deep to measure. **2. the abyss,** hell. [L *abyssus,* from Gk *ábyssos* without bottom]

Abyssinia /ˌæbə'sɪniə/, *n.* former name of **Ethiopia.** —**Abyssinian**, *adj., n.*

ac-, a prefix of direction or addition, variant of **ad-**, before *c* and *qu*, as in *accede, acquire.*

-ac, an adjective suffix meaning 'relating to', as in *elegiac, cardiac.* [representing Gk adj. suffix *-akos*]

Ac, *Chem. Symbol.* actinium.

AC, *Abbrev.* **1.** Companion of the Order of Australia. **2.** *Elect. Abbrev.* Also, **a.c.** alternating current.

acacia /ə'keɪʃə, ə'keɪsiə/, *n.* a tree or shrub, native to warm areas, and usu. known in Australia as wattle. [L, from Gk: a thorny Egyptian tree]

academic /ˌækə'dɛmɪk/, *adj.* **1.** relating to higher education, as at a college, university, or academy. **2.** theoretical or intellectual; not related to practical skills: *an academic subject; an academic question.* ⋄*n.* **3.** a member of college or university, esp. teacher.

academy /ə'kædəmi/, *n., pl.* **-mies. 1.** a society for encouragement of literature, science or art. **2.** a school for instruction in a particular art or science: *a military academy.* [L, from Gk: place sacred to *Akádēmos,* a Greek hero] —**academician**, *n.*

Academy Awards, *n.pl.* annual awards for all aspects of film-making; established 1929 and administered by the American Academy of Motion Picture Arts and Sciences. See **Oscar**.

Acadia /ə'keɪdiə/, *n.* a former French colony in south-eastern Canada; ceded to Great Britain 1713. French, **Acadie.**

acanthus /ə'kænθəs/, *n., pl.* **-thuses, -thi** /-θaɪ/. a herb found in the Mediterranean area and tropical and nearby regions, including Australia, having large spiny leaves. [L, from Gk: a thorny tree]

Acapulco /ˌækə'pʊlkoʊ/, *n.* a seaport and tourist resort in south-western Mexico. Pop. 301 902 (1980).

acc., *Abbrev.* **1.** accompanied (by). **2.** according (to). **3.** account. **4.** accusative.

accede /ək'sid/, *v.i.,* **-ceded, -ceding. 1.** to agree; consent; yield: *I accede to your demands.* **2.** to come (*to*) high office, etc.: *to accede to the throne.* **3.** *Internat. Law.* to

accede

become a party to a treaty, not as a signatory, but by a subsequent formal acceptance of its provisions, etc. [L: go to]

accelerando /əkselə'rændou, æk-/, adv. (musical direction) gradually increasing in speed. [It.]

accelerate /ək'seləreit, æk-/, v., -rated, -rating. ◇v.t. 1. to cause to move or advance faster: *to accelerate growth.* 2. to make happen sooner: *These events accelerated the fall of the government.* 3. *Phys.* to change the amount and/or direction of the velocity of (a body). ◇v.i. 4. to become faster; increase in speed. [L]

acceleration /əkselə'reiʃən, æk-/, n. 1. the act of accelerating; increase of speed. 2. *Phys.* a (measure of rate of) change in velocity.

accelerator /ək'seləreitə, æk-/, n. a device, usu. a pedal, which increases the speed of a vehicle by controlling the throttle.

accent /'æksent, n.; /æk'sent/, v. ◇n. 1. the degree or pattern of stress or pitch that forms the special character of a vowel or syllable. 2. *Gram.* a mark showing stress, pitch, or vowel quality etc. 3. *Poetry.* regularly repeated stress. 4. a characteristic style of pronunciation: *foreign accent.* 5. *Music.* **a.** (a mark showing) stress or emphasis given to certain notes. **b.** stress or emphasis regularly repeated as part of rhythm. 6. (*pl.*) words or tones expressing some emotion: *He spoke in the accents of love.* 7. a special character of something, as taste, style, etc. 8. particular attention or emphasis: *She puts a lot of accent on studying.* ◇v.t. 9. to pronounce with a particular accent. 10. to mark (writing, music) with an accent. 11. to stress; accentuate. [L: tone]
—**accentual**, adj.

accentuate /ək'sentʃueit/, v.t., -ated, -ating. to give importance to; emphasise. [ML] —**accentuation**, n.

accept /ək'sept/, v.t. 1. to take or receive (something offered) usu. with approval or agreement: *to accept a gift; accept an invitation.* 2. to agree to; admit as valid or satisfactory: *to accept an excuse; accept the report of a committee.* 3. to take responsibility for (duties of office, order for payment, etc.). 4. to put up with; accommodate oneself to: *I will have to accept the situation.* 5. to believe: *to accept a fact.* [ME, from L]

acceptable /ək'septəbəl/, adj. 1. worthy of being accepted; satisfactory. 2. pleasing to the receiver; agreeable; welcome. —**acceptability**, n.

acceptance /ək'septəns/, n. 1. the act of taking, receiving or agreeing to something. 2. approval; favorable reception. 3. the fact or condition of being accepted or acceptable. 4. an agreement to pay an order, bill, etc.

accepted /ək'septəd/, adj. according to custom; established; approved.

access /'ækses/, n. 1. the act or right of coming to; admittance; approach: *to gain access to a person.* 2. way or means of approach: *There is no access to the highway from this street.* 3. a parent's right to see a child. ◇v.t. 4. to find

accommodate

(information) in a computer. ◇adj. 5. *Radio, TV, etc.* run by, or open to, special-interest groups who wish to broadcast their own programs.

accessible /ək'sesəbəl/, adj. 1. easy to come near to; approachable. 2. open to the influence of (fol. by *to*): *accessible to reason.* 3. able to be gained: *accessible food supply.* —**accessibility**, n.

accession /ək'seʃən/, n. 1. the act of taking up a position or office: *accession to the throne.* 2. (an increase by) something added: *an accession of land; accession of books to the library.* 3. agreement: *accession to a demand.* 4. *Internat. Law.* formal acceptance of a treaty between states or countries. [L: increase]

accessory /ək'sesəri/, n., pl. -ries, adj. ◇n. 1. an additional part or object which adds to the attractiveness or convenience of an outfit or unit, e.g. a handbag, car radio, etc. 2. Also, **accessary**. *Law.* a person who is not the main party in a crime, nor present when it is carried out, but yet is in some way concerned in it. ◇adj. 3. added; extra. 4. *Geol.* (of a mineral) present in small amounts in a rock. [LL]

acciaccatura /əkætʃə'tjurə/, n. *Music.* a short ornamental note a semitone above or below, and struck just before, the main note. [It.]

accident /'æksədənt/, n. 1. an unwanted or unfortunate happening; casualty; mishap. 2. anything that happens unexpectedly, without planning: *It was an accident that we found the mistake.* 3. chance; fortune: *I met him by accident.* 4. a less important or irregular quality: *accidents of the landscape.* [ME, from L: happening]

accidental /æksə'dentl/, adj. 1. happening by chance or accident: *an accidental meeting.* 2. coming as a side-effect; incidental: *accidental gains.* ◇n. 3. a part or quality which is not central. 4. *Music.* any sign placed before a note showing a sharp, flat, or natural not in the key signature.

acclaim /ə'kleim/, v.t. 1. to praise or cheer with words or sounds of joy or approval; applaud. 2. to announce with (shouts of) praise: *They acclaimed him King.* ◇n. 3. a vote by voice, often unanimous. 4. strong approval or praise; unanimous applause. [L] —**acclamation**, n.

acclimatise or **acclimatize** /ə'klaimətaiz/, v.t., v.i. -tised, -tising. to make or become used to a new climate or environment: *to acclimatise a plant; He acclimatised slowly to the country.* [F] —**acclimatisation**, n.

acclivity /ə'klivəti/, n., pl. -ties. an upward slope, as of ground. (opposed to *declivity*). [L: steepness]

accolade /'ækəleid/, n. 1. the ceremonial touch of a sword on the shoulder, to award a knighthood. 2. any expression of praise; honor.

accommodate /ə'kɒmədeit/, v., -dated, -dating. ◇v.t. 1. to do a kindness to; oblige: *to accommodate a friend.* 2. to provide with housing or some other need: *He will accommo-*

accommodate

date me with money. **3.** to change (oneself or a situation); adapt: *We will accommodate ourselves to the new plan.* **4.** to bring into harmony; reconcile: *to accommodate differences.* **5.** to provide space for (something or someone): *This hotel accommodates 200 people.* ◇*v.i.* **6.** to become adjusted. [L: suited]

accommodating /əˈkɒmədeɪtɪŋ/, *adj.* easy to deal with; obliging.

accommodation /əkɒməˈdeɪʃən/, *n.* **1.** the act or process of people or things adapting to a situation or to each other. **2.** a room for a visitor to stay, esp. in hotel; lodgings. **3.** a willingness to help others.

accompaniment /əˈkʌmpnɪmənt/, *n.* **1.** something less important or added for ornament, balance, etc.: *That wine is a perfect accompaniment to the meal.* **2.** *Music.* a part written to provide musical backing for a melody.

accompanist /əˈkʌmpənəst/, *n.* someone who plays a musical accompaniment.

accompany /əˈkʌmpəni, əˈkʌmpni/, *v.t.*, **-nied, -nying. 1.** to go or be in company with: *to accompany a friend; Thunder accompanies lightning.* **2.** to put in company; associate (fol. by *with*): *She will accompany the talk with a film.* **3.** *Music.* to play or sing an accompaniment to. [ME, from F]

accomplice /əˈkʌmpləs, -ˈkɒm-/, *n.* a partner in a crime. [earlier *complice*, from F, from ML: companion; the phrase *a complice* became *accomplice* by failure to recognise it as made up of two words]

accomplish /əˈkʌmplɪʃ, -ˈkɒm-/, *v.t.* to carry out successfully; perform; finish. [ME, from LL]

accomplished /əˈkʌmplɪʃt, -ˈkɒm-/, *adj.* **1.** completed; done: *an accomplished fact.* **2.** highly skilled; expert: *She is an accomplished singer.* **3.** skilled in the ways of polite society.

accomplishment /əˈkʌmplɪʃmənt, -ˈkɒm-/, *n.* **1.** completion; fulfilment: *the accomplishment of our desires.* **2.** anything successfully done; achievement: *the accomplishments of scientists.* **3.** (*oft. pl.*) a social art, grace or skill.

accord /əˈkɔd/, *v.i.* **1.** to agree or be in harmony; conform (oft. fol. by *with*): *That accords with what he told me.* ◇*v.t.* **2.** to give; concede: *to accord due praise.* ◇*n.* **3.** similarity of opinions; agreement; harmony. **4.** an international agreement. **5. of one's own accord,** without being asked; voluntarily. **6. with one accord,** with total and immediate agreement. [LL] —**accordance,** *n.* —**accordant,** *adj.*

according /əˈkɔdɪŋ/, *adv.* **1. according to, a.** in keeping with; conforming to: *They must work according to the rules.* **b.** in proportion to: *They were paid according to their hours of work.* **c.** as stated by: *according to him, it was an accident.* ◇*adj.* **2.** agreeing.

accordingly /əˈkɔdɪŋli/, *adv.* **1.** in keeping with what has happened; correspondingly. **2.** in due course; therefore; so.

accordion /əˈkɔdiən/, *n. Music.* a portable box-shaped wind instrument with bellows, played with button-like keys. [ACCORD + -ION] —**accordionist,** *n.*

accumulate

accost /əˈkɒst/, *v.t.* to approach and speak to (someone) esp. in bold or offensive way. [F, from LL: put side by side]

account /əˈkaʊnt/, *n.* **1.** a list of particular events; narrative: *an account of everything as it happened.* **2.** a statement of reasons, causes, etc., explaining one's conduct, etc. **3.** reason; consideration: *on all accounts.* **4.** value; importance: *things of no account.* **5.** judgment; estimation: *I will take that into account.* **6.** profit; advantage: *She can turn anything to account* **7.** *Bookkeeping.* a formal record of money paid out and received by a person or business. **8.** *Economics.* **a.** a business arrangement with a bank, building society, etc., which gives a customer the use of certain banking services. See **savings bank, trading bank. b.** (a record of) money kept or deposited in a bank, etc. **9.** → **charge account. 10.** Some special uses are: **bring / call to account,** to demand an explanation of actions.
give a good account of (oneself), to do well.
on account of, because of.
on / to account, as a part payment: *I will pay $50 on account.*
◇*v.i.* **11.** to give an explanation (fol. by *for*): *That accounts for his disappearance.* **12.** to cause death, capture, etc. (fol. by *for*): *The plane crash accounted for twenty people.* ◇*v.t.* **13.** to count; consider as: *I account myself well paid.* [ME, from LL]

accountable /əˈkaʊntəbəl/, *adj.* **1.** in a position where one may be asked to explain; responsible (*to* a person, *for* an act, etc.): *I am not accountable to anyone for my deeds.* **2.** able to be explained. —**accountability,** *n.* —**accountably,** *adv.*

accountant /əˈkaʊntənt/, *n.* a person whose work is to examine and/or keep business accounts. —**accountancy,** *n.*

accounting /əˈkaʊntɪŋ/, *n.* the theory and system of setting up and looking after the books of a business, in order to examine its financial position and operating results. See **bookkeeping.**

accoutrements /əˈkuːtrəmənts/, *n.pl.* **1.** clothing; equipment; trappings. **2.** equipment of a soldier other than weapons and clothing.

accredit /əˈkrɛdət/, *v.t.* **1.** to give credit to (someone) (fol. by *with*): *We accredit her with the plan.* **2.** to consider as belonging; attribute: *They accredit this discovery to Edison.* **3.** to give credentials to (an official, agent, representative, etc.) **4.** to declare (something) as meeting official requirements. [F] —**accreditation,** *n.*

accretion /əˈkriʃən/, *n.* **1.** an increase in size by natural growth or by gradual addition. **2.** the growing together of separate parts into a single whole. [L]

accrue /əˈkruː/, *v.i.*, **-crued, -cruing. 1.** to happen or result as a natural growth. **2.** to come as a regular addition: *Interest accrues on money in the bank.* [from *accrue*, obs. n., from F: increase, from L] —**accrual,** *n.*

accumulate /əˈkjuːmjʊleɪt/, *v.*, **-lated, -lating.** ◇*v.t.* **1.** to heap up; gather; collect: *to accumulate wealth.* ◇*v.i.* **2.** to grow into a heap or mass: *Unpaid bills accumulate.*

accumulate

[L: heaped up] —**accumulative**, *adj.* —**accumulation**, *n.*

accumulator /əˈkjumjəleɪtə/, *n.* **1.** *Elect.* a storage battery for electrical energy. **2.** a device in computing machines where the arithmetic operations are performed. [L]

accurate /ˈækjərət/, *adj.* **1.** truthful; exact. **2.** free from error: *an accurate typist*. [L: cared for] —**accurateness**, **accuracy**, *n.*

accursed /əˈkɜsəd, əˈkɜst/, *adj.* **1.** under a curse; ruined. **2.** worthy of curses; detestable. Also, **accurst**.

accusation /ˌækjuˈzeɪʃən/, *n.* **1.** a charge of doing wrong. **2.** the wrong with which someone is charged: *The accusation is murder.* Also, **accusal** /əˈkjuzəl/. [L]

accusative case /əˈkjuzətɪv keɪs/, *n. Gram.* See **case**[1] and Appendix. [L, translation of Gk (*ptōsis*) *aitiātikē* (case) relating to that which is caused]

accuse /əˈkjuz/, *v.t.*, **-cused, -cusing. 1.** to bring a charge against; charge with the fault or crime (*of*). **2.** to blame. [L] —**accuser**, *n.* —**accusatory**, *adj.*

accused /əˈkjuzd/, *adj.* **1.** charged with a fault or crime. ◇*n.* **2.** the person charged in a criminal law case.

accustom /əˈkʌstəm/, *v.t.* to make (oneself) used (fol. by *to*); habituate: *He will accustom himself to the heat.* [OF *a* to + *costume* custom]

accustomed /əˈkʌstəmd/, *adj.* **1.** usual; habitual: *in their accustomed way*. **2.** in the habit (of); used (fol. by *to*): *accustomed to doing good*; *accustomed to good food*.

ac-dc /ˌeɪˌsiːˈdiːˌsiː/, *adj. Elect.* relating to an apparatus, as a radio, which can operate from either an alternating current or direct current power source.

ace /eɪs/, *n.* **1.** a playing card or die marked with a single spot. **2.** *Tennis, etc.* a successful serve which the opponent fails to touch. **3.** a very small quantity, amount, or degree: *within an ace of winning*. **4.** a highly skilled person; expert: *an ace at dancing*. **5.** a fighter pilot who has shot down five or more enemy aeroplanes. ◇*adj.* **6.** excellent; outstanding. [ME *as*, from L, supposedly from d. Gk, var. of Gk *heis* one]

-aceous, a suffix of adjectives used in scientific language to mean: **1.** relating to, as in *sebaceous*. **2.** of the nature of, or similar to, as in *herbaceous*. [NL *-aceus*, from L *-āceus* of a specific kind or group]

acerbate /ˈæsəbeɪt/, *v.t.*, **-bated, -bating. 1.** to make sour or bitter. **2.** to irritate; exasperate. [L]

acerbity /əˈsɜbəti/, *n., pl.* **-ties. 1.** sourness, with roughness or sharpness of taste. **2.** harshness or severity, of temper, words, etc. [F, from L] —**acerbic**, *adj.*

acetaldehyde /ˌæsəˈtældəhaɪd/, *n.* a volatile, colorless liquid, CH_3CHO, used commercially in the silvering of mirrors and in organic synthesis.

acetate /ˈæsəteɪt/, *n. Chem.* a salt formed from acetic acid. See **-ate**[2]. —**acetated**, *adj.*

Achilles

acetate fibre, *n.* a synthetic fibre made from cellulose (the chief part of plant cell walls). Also, **acetate**.

acetic /əˈsitɪk, əˈsɛtɪk/, *adj.* relating to, derived from, or producing vinegar or acetic acid.

acetic acid, *n.* a sour, colorless, acid, CH_3COOH, with a sharp smell, being the main compound in vinegar, used to make acetate fibre, etc.; ethanoic acid. —**acetous**, *adj.*

aceto-, a word part used to show the presence of acetic acid or the radical acetyl. Also, **acet-**. [combining form representing L *acētum* vinegar]

acetone /ˈæsətoʊn/, *n.* a colorless, volatile, flammable liquid, CH_3COCH_3, a ketone, used as a solvent and in varnishes, etc.

acetyl /ˈæsətl, əˈsitl/, *n.* a radical, CH_3CO-, as in acetic acid. —**acetylic**, *adj.*

acetylcholine /ˌæsətalˈkoʊlin, əˌsitl-/, *n.* an ester of acetic acid and choline, found in animals and some plants, thought to be responsible for the transmission of nerve impulses across synapses.

acetylene /əˈsɛtəlin, -lən/, *n.* a colorless gas, C_2H_2, first member of the alkyne series, made by the action of water on calcium carbide, used in metal welding and cutting, and in organic synthesis; ethyne.

acetylene series, *n.* →**alkyne series**.

Achaea /əˈkiə/, *n.* an ancient region of southern Greece, on the Gulf of Corinth.

Achaean League /əˈkiən ˌliɡ/, *n.* a political confederation of Achaean and other Greek cities, 281–146 BC.

Achaemenid /əˈkimənɪd, əˈkɛm-/, *n., pl.* **Achaemenids, Achaemenidae, Achaemenides.** a member of a dynasty of Persian kings, ruling from 549 to 331 BC; empire extended from the Aegean Sea to the Indus river.

ache /eɪk/, *v.*, **ached, aching**, *n.* ◇*v.i.* **1.** to suffer continous pain. **2.** to be eager; yearn. ◇*n.* **3.** a continuous pain. **4.** a longing. [OE *acan*, v., *æce*, n.]

Achebe /əˈtʃeɪbeɪ/, *n.* **Chinua** /ˈtʃɪnwɑ/, born 1930, Nigerian novelist concentrating on the changes in Africa brought about by Westernisation.

achene /əˈkin/, *n. Bot.* a small dry, one-seeded indehiscent fruit. [NL *achaenium*, from Gk *a-* A[6] + Gk *chainein* gape + *-ium* IUM]

Acheron /ˈækərɒn/, *n. Class Myth.* **1.** a river in Hades, over which Charon ferried the souls of the dead. **2.** the lower world; hell. —**Acherontic**, *adj.*

achieve /əˈtʃiv/, *v.t.*, **achieved, achieving. 1.** to bring to a successful end; accomplish: *to achieve the task*. **2.** to bring about, as by effort; gain: *to achieve victory*. [ME, from OF phrase (*venir*) *a chef* = LL *ad caput venīre* come to a head] —**achievable**, *adj.* —**achiever**, *n.* —**achievement**, *n.*

Achilles /əˈkɪliz/, *n. Gk Legend.* the hero of Homer's *Iliad*, the greatest Greek warrior in the Trojan war, who came to be the ideal of

Achilles Greek manhood. He died when Paris wounded him in the heel, where he was vulnerable. — **Achillean**, *adj.*

Achilles heel, *n.* a single major weakness or point open to attack. [See ACHILLES]

Achilles tendon, *n.* the tissue joining the calf muscles to the heelbone.

achromatic /ˌeɪkrəˈmætɪk/, *adj.* 1. without color, as neutral greys. 2. *Biol.* containing or consisting of achromatin. [Gk: colorless]

achromatin /əˈkroʊmətɪn/, *n.* that part of the nucleus of a cell which stains less easily than the rest.

acid[1] /ˈæsəd/, *n.* 1. *Chem.* a compound containing hydrogen which dissociates in water (or in other solvents) to produce positively-charged hydrogen ions. It reacts with a base (negatively charged) to form a salt and water. 2. a substance with a sour taste. ◇*adj.* 3. tasting sharp or sour: *acid fruits.* 4. sour; sharp; ill-tempered: *an acid remark.* 5. *Geol.* (of igneous rocks) containing 66% or more silica. [L: sour] —**acidic**, *adj.* —**acidity**, *n.*

acid[2] /ˈæsəd/, *n. Colloq.* 1. → LSD. 2. **drop acid,** to take LSD. [(*lysergic*) *acid* (*diethylamide*)]

acidify /əˈsɪdəfaɪ/, *v.t., v.i.,* **-fied, -fying.** to make or become acid; convert or change into an acid.

acid test, /- test /. *n.* 1. a test for gold using nitric acid. 2. the deciding test; final analysis.

-acious, an adjective suffix made by adding **-ous** to nouns ending in **-acity** (the *-ty* being dropped) meaning 'full of' or 'tending to' as in *vivacious.*

-acity, a suffix of nouns meaning 'quality' or 'a state of being', as in *vivacity*. [F, from L *-ācitas*]

acknowledge /əkˈnɒlɪdʒ/, *v.t.,* **-edged, -edging.** 1. to admit to be real or true; recognise the existence of: *to acknowledge the need for help.* 2. to show recognition of: *She acknowledged him with a wave.* 3. to recognise the authority or claims of: *to acknowledge his right to vote.* 4. to indicate thanks for: *I gratefully acknowledge your help.* 5. to admit the receipt of: *to acknowledge a letter.* [b. obs. *acknow* (OE *oncnāwan* confess) and *knowledge*, v., admit] —**acknowledgment,** *n.*

aclinic line /əˈklɪnɪk 'laɪn/, *n.* an imaginary line around the earth near the equator where the magnetic needle remains horizontal.

acme /ˈækmi/, *n.* the highest point; culmination. [Gk]

acne /ˈækni/, *n.* a condition caused by inflammation of the oil-secreting glands, resulting in pimples, esp. on the face. [orig. uncert.]

acolyte /ˈækəlaɪt/, *n.* 1. a minor helper in a church ceremony. 2. a helper; attendant. [ME, from ML, from Gk: follower]

Aconcagua /ˌækɒnˈkægwə/, *n.* a mountain in western Argentina, in the Andes; the highest peak in the Western Hemisphere. 6959 m.

acorn /ˈeɪkɔːn/, *n.* the fruit of the oak, a nut in a hardened scaly cup. [OE *æcern*]

acoustic /əˈkuːstɪk/, *adj.* 1. Also, **acoustical.** relating to hearing, or to the science of sound. 2. *Music.* relating to instruments whose sound is not electronically amplified. [F, from Gk] —**acoustically,** *adv.*

acoustics /əˈkuːstɪks/, *n.* 1. *Phys.* the science of sound. 2. (*treated as pl.*) properties of a building, esp. a concert hall, with respect to sounds produced in it.

acquaint /əˈkweɪnt/, *v.t.* 1. to make familiar (fol. by *with*): *to acquaint him with our plan.* 2. to provide with knowledge; inform: *She will acquaint him with the news.* [ME, from LL: make known]

acquaintance /əˈkweɪntəns/, *n.* 1. a person whom one knows, but not well enough to regard as a friend. 2. personal knowledge: *acquaintance with the fact.*

acquiesce /ˌækwiˈɛs/, *v.i.,* **-esced, -escing.** to agree, esp. in a quiet way; consent (oft. fol. by *in*): *to acquiesce in an opinion.* [L] —**acquiescence,** *n.* —**acquiescent,** *adj.*

acquire /əˈkwaɪə/, *v.t.,* **-quired, -quiring.** 1. to come into possession of; get as one's own: *to acquire property.* 2. to gain for oneself through one's actions or efforts: *to acquire learning.* [L]

acquired immune deficiency syndrome, *n.* a disease caused by a virus (HIV) which breaks down the body's natural defences resulting in severe infections, skin tumors and death. Also, **AIDS.**

acquisition /ˌækwəˈzɪʃən/, *n.* 1. the act of acquiring or gaining possession: *the acquisition of property.* 2. something acquired: *a precious acquisition.* ◇*v.t.* 3. to acquire (books for a library, etc.). [L]

acquisitive /əˈkwɪzətɪv/, *adj.* tending or eager to collect possessions: *an acquisitive society.*

acquit /əˈkwɪt/, *v.t.,* **-quitted, -quitting.** 1. to clear from a charge of fault or crime; pronounce not guilty (fol. by *of*). 2. to free (a person) from a responsibility. 3. to settle (a debt, claim, etc.). 4. **acquit oneself,** to behave; perform: *He will acquit himself well in battle.* [ME, from OF] —**acquittal,** *n.*

acre /ˈeɪkə/, *n.* 1. a unit of land measurement in the imperial system, equal to 4840 square yards, and approx. equivalent to 0.405 hectares. *Symbol:* ac 2. (*pl.*) land in general. 3. (*pl.*) *Colloq.* large quantities: *There were acres of cars.* [OE *æcer*]

acreage /ˈeɪkərɪdʒ/, *n.* acres collectively; range in acres.

acrid /ˈækrəd/, *adj.* 1. sharp and bitter to the taste. 2. sharp; stinging: *acrid remarks.* [L *ācer* sharp]

acrimony /ˈækrəməni/, *n., pl.* **-nies.** sharpness, harshness or bitterness of temper or speech. [L] —**acrimonious,** *adj.*

acro-, a word element meaning 'tip', 'top', or 'edge', as in *acronym.* Also, before vowels, **acr-.** [Gk *akro-*, combining form of *ákros* at the top or end]

acrobat /'ækrəbæt/, *n.* a skilled performer who can walk on a tightrope, perform on a trapeze, etc. [F, from Gk: walking on tiptoe] —**acrobatic**, *adj.* —**acrobatically**, *adv.*

acrobatics /ækrə'bætɪks/, *n.* **1.** (*treated as sing.*) the tricks of an acrobat; gymnastics. **2.** (*treated as pl.*) any tricks needing quick movement or thinking: *mental acrobatics*.

acronym /'ækrənɪm/, *n.* a word formed from the first letters of other words, as ANZAC (from *Australian and New Zealand Army Corps*). [ACR(O)- + Gk *ónyma* name]

acrophobia /ækrə'foubiə/, *n.* abnormal fear of being in high places.

acropolis /ə'krɒpəlɪs/, *n.* **1.** (*cap.*) the citadel of Athens; site of the Parthenon. **2.** the citadel of any ancient Greek city. [Gk *akrópolis* the upper city]

across /ə'krɒs/, *prep.* **1.** from side to side of: *a bridge across a river.* **2.** on the other side of: *across the sea.* **3.** unexpectedly into contact with: *We came across our friends.* ◇*adv.* **4.** from one side to another: *I came across in a boat.* **5.** on the other side: *We'll soon be across.* [A- + CROSS]

acrostic /ə'krɒstɪk/, *n.* a set of words or lines, as a poem, in which the first, last, or other particular letters form a word, phrase, of the alphabet, etc. [L, from Gk]

acrylic /ə'krɪlɪk/, *adj.* **1.** relating to fibres formed of a polymer of a compound of acrylic acid, or to materials made from such fibres. ◇*n.* **2.** such a material. [*acr(olein)* + -YL + -IC]

acrylic acid, *n.* one of a series of acids derived from the alkenes, with the general formula, $C_nH_{2n-2}O_2$. It is colorless, corrosive and easily polymerised.

acrylic resin, *n.* one of the group of resins formed by polymerising esters or amides of acrylic acid, used mainly when transparency is wanted. Perspex and plexiglas are in this group.

act /ækt/, *n.* **1.** anything done or performed; a doing; deed. **2.** the process of doing: *caught in the act* **3.** an order, law, judgment: *an act of Parliament.* **4.** one of the main divisions of a play or opera. **5.** an individual performance forming part of a variety program, etc.: *a singing act.* **6.** behavior which is a pretence: *He's not really an ocker — it's just an act.* **7.** a show of bad temper. ◇*v.i.* **8.** to do something; produce effect; perform: *His mind acts quickly; The medicine failed to act.* **9.** to work in a particular way; perform special duties: *to act as boss.* **10.** to behave: *to act well under pressure.* **11.** to pretend. **12.** to perform as an actor: *Did she ever act on the stage?* **13.** to serve or stand in (fol. by *for*): *The governor will act for the Queen.* ◇*v.t.* **14.** to represent (a character): *to act Macbeth.* **15.** to pretend: *to act deep interest.* **16.** to behave in keeping with: *act your age.* **17.** to behave as: *to act the fool.* ◇*v.* **18. act on/upon**, **a.** to act in keeping with; follow: *He acted upon my suggestion.* **b.** to affect: *Alcohol acts on the brain.* **19. act out**, to give expression to (an idea, feeling, etc.) by acting. **20. act up**, *Colloq.* to cause trouble. [ME, from L *actum* a thing done]

ACT /eɪ si 'tiː/, *Abbrev.* Australian Capital Territory.

acting /'æktɪŋ/, *adj.* **1.** temporary (as a replacement): *the acting Prime Minister.* **2.** working; functioning. ◇*n.* **3.** the occupation, performance, or art of an actor.

actinide /'æktənaɪd/, *n.* any of the series of elements with atomic numbers between 89 and 105.

actinium /æk'tɪniəm/, *n.* a radioactive chemical element, occurring in pitchblende and like the rare earths in chemical behavior and valency. *Symbol:* Ac; *at. no.* 89; *at. wt of most stable isotope:* 227; *radioactive half-life:* 21.7 years.

actinomycete /æktɪnoʊ'maɪsiːt/, *n.* any of a group of micro-organisms commonly thought of as filamentous bacteria.

action /'ækʃən/, *n.* **1.** the process or state of acting or of being active: *The machine is now in action.* **2.** something done; deed. **3.** (*pl.*) habitual or usual acts; conduct. **4.** energetic activity. **5.** effect: *the action of wind on a ship's sails.* **6.** manner of moving: *the action of a horse.* **7.** the moving parts of a machine, musical instrument, etc. **8.** *Phys.* the product of work or energy and time. See **Planck's constant. 9.** military combat. **10.** the main event(s) of a story or play. **11.** (the right of) taking legal steps against another person, company, etc. [L]

actionable /'ækʃənəbəl/, *adj.* providing grounds for legal action.

Actium /'æktiəm/, *n.* a promontory in north-western ancient Greece; Antony and Cleopatra were defeated by Octavian and Agrippa in a naval battle near here, 31 BC.

activate /'æktəveɪt/, *v.t.*, **-vated**, **-vating**. **1.** to make active or more active. **2.** *Phys.* to make radioactive. **3.** to quicken (reactions) by various means, such as heating. —**activation**, *n.*

activated complex, /ˌæktəveɪtəd 'kɒmpleks/ *n.* a short-lived state which appears during chemical reactions; when the molecules are not in their original form but are not yet products.

active /'æktɪv/, *adj.* **1.** in a state of action. **2.** continually doing or moving; busy: *an active life; an active market.* **3.** able to move quickly; nimble: *an active animal.* **4.** causing or initiating action. **5.** *Gram.* of or in the active voice. **6.** (of a volcano) capable of erupting. **7.** capable of acting or reacting, esp of chemicals. ◇*n.* **8.** *Gram.* the active voice. [L] —**actively**, *adv.*

active voice, *n.* a type of verb form which indicates that the subject of the verb is doing the action, and not having the action done to it, e.g. *sings* in *Cathy sings beautifully*, or *have seen* in *We have seen that film.* See **passive voice.**

activist /'æktəvəst/, *n.* an active worker for a cause, esp. a political cause. —**activism**, *n.*

activity /æk'tɪvəti/, *n., pl.* **-ties.** **1.** the state of being active. **2.** any particular deed, action or pastime. **3.** energy; liveliness. ◇*adj.*

activity / Addington

4. *Educ.* relating to provision made for slow learners, using methods of learning and teaching associated with activities: *activity class.*

act of God, *n.* the direct, uncontrollable action of a natural force, e.g. cyclone, earthquake.

actor /ˈæktə/, *n.* **1.** someone who acts the part of a character in a play. **2.** someone who acts; doer. [L] —**actress**, *n. fem.*

Acts of the Apostles, *n. Bible.* the fifth book in the New Testament. Also, **Acts.**

ACTU /ˌeɪ si ti ˈju/, *Abbrev.* Australian Council of Trade Unions.

actual /ˈæktʃuəl/, *adj.* **1.** existing in act or fact; real. **2.** now existing; present: *the actual position of the moon.* [LL: active, practical]

actuality /ˌæktʃuˈæləti/, *n., pl.* **-ties. 1.** actual existence; reality. **2.** (*pl.*) actual conditions or circumstances; facts.

actually /ˈæktʃuəli, ˈæktʃəli/, *adv.* as an actual or existing fact; really.

actuary /ˈæktʃuəri/, *n., pl.* **-ries.** *Econ.* someone who calculates risks, rates of payment, etc., based on statistics or recorded facts. [L] —**actuarial** /ˌæktʃuˈɛəriəl/, *adj.*

actuate /ˈæktʃueɪt/, *v.t.,* **-ated, -ating.** to move to action: *He was actuated by selfish feelings.* [ML] —**actuation**, *n.*

acuity /əˈkjuəti/, *n.* sharpness; acuteness: *acuity of sight; acuity of thought.* [ML]

acumen /ˈækjəmən/, *n.* quickness of understanding; keen judgment. [L]

acupuncture /ˈækjəpʌŋktʃə, ˈækə-/, *n.* a Chinese medical practice of puncturing particular areas of skin with long sharp needles, or applying heat, pressure or a laser beam to these points to treat disease or relieve pain. [L *acu(s)* needle + PUNCTURE] —**acupuncturist**, *n.*

acute /əˈkjut/, *adj.* **1.** ending in a sharp point. **2.** sharp in effect; intense: *acute sorrow.* **3.** severe; crucial: *an acute shortage.* **4.** (of disease, etc.) brief and severe (opposed to *chronic*). **5.** keen of mind; perceptive: *an acute observer.* **6.** sensitive and accurate: *acute eyesight.* **7.** *Geom., etc.* (of an angle) less than 90°. **8.** *Gram.* of or having a particular accent (´). [L: sharpened] —**acuteness**, *n.*

-acy, a suffix of nouns of quality, condition, office etc., as in *fallacy, primacy, accuracy, delicacy,* etc. [representing L *-ācia, -ātia,* and Gk *-áteia*]

acyclic /eɪˈsaɪklɪk, eɪˈsɪklɪk/, *adj.* not happening in cycles; not regular. [A-[6] + CYCLIC]

ad-, a prefix of direction, tendency, and addition, as in *advice, advent.* Also, **ac-, af-, ag-, al-, an-, ap-, ar-, as-, at-,** and **a-**[5]. [L, representing *ad*, prep., to, towards, at, about]

-ad, a suffix forming nouns meaning a collection of a certain number, as in *triad*. [Gk]

AD /ˌeɪ ˈdi/, *Abbrev.* since Christ was born: *From 20 BC to AD 50 is 70 years.* [L *annō Dominī* in the year of our Lord]

adage /ˈædɪdʒ/, *n.* a wise saying; proverb. [F, from L *adagium*]

adagio /əˈdɑʒioʊ, -dʒioʊ/, *adv.* (a musical direction) in an unhurried manner; slowly. [It.]

Adam /ˈædəm/, *n.* **1.** *Bible.* the name of the first man; progenitor of the human race. **2. not to know (someone) from Adam,** *Colloq.* not to know (someone) at all. [See Genesis 2:7]

adamant /ˈædəmənt/, *n.* **1.** a diamond or any hard substance unable to be broken. ◇*adj.* **2.** firm in purpose or opinion; unyielding. [L, from Gk] —**adamantine**, *adj.*

Adams /ˈædəmz/, *n.* **1. John**, 1735–1826, second president of the US, 1797–1801; leader in the American War of Independence. **2. John Couch**, 1819–92, English astronomer; calculated the existence of Neptune. **3. John Quincy** /ˈkwɪnsi/, 1767–1848, son of John (def. 1), sixth president of the US, 1825–29; secretary of state 1817–25.

Adam's apple, *n.* a projection of the thyroid cartilage at the front of the (male) throat.

adapt /əˈdæpt/, *v.t., v.i.* to make or become suitable to needs, conditions, etc.; adjust; modify: *to adapt a design for special uses; to adapt to a new country.* [L] —**adaptive**, *adj.* —**adaptable**, *adj.* —**adaptability**, *n.*

adaptation /ˌædəpˈteɪʃən, ˌædæp-/, *n.* **1.** the act or result of adapting; adjustment **2.** *Lit.* a work rewritten for a different presentation: *adaptation of a book for the stage.* **3.** *Biol.* alteration in the structure or work of organisms which enables them to live and multiply in changed conditions. **4.** Also, **adaption** /əˈdæpʃən/. a slow change of individual and social activity to fit surrounding customs.

adaptor *or* **adapter** /əˈdæptə/, *n.* **1.** a piece which fits together parts having different sizes or forms. **2.** an additional part to convert a machine, tool, etc., to a different use. **3.** *Geog.* a plant or animal that, by evolution, has developed ways of surviving through a certain set of conditions.

add /æd/, *v.t.* **1.** to unite or join so as to increase number, quantity, size or importance: *to add another stone to the pile.* **2.** to find the sum of (oft. fol. by *up*). **3.** to say or write further: *Let me add this.* **4.** to include (fol. by *in*). ◇*v.i.* **5.** to provide or be an extra part (fol. by *to*): *to add to his grief.* ◇*v.* **6. add up, a.** to amount (fol. by *to*): *It adds up to murder.* **b.** *Colloq.* to make sense: *The facts don't add up.* [ME, from L]

addendum /əˈdɛndəm/, *n., pl.* **-da** /-də/. something added, esp. an appendix to a book. [L]

adder /ˈædə/, *n.* a small poisonous snake, the common European viper. [var. of ME *nadder* (*a nadder* being taken as *an adder*), OE *nædre*]

addict /ˈædɪkt/, *n.* someone dependent on a practice or habit: *drug addict; a football addict.* [L: devoted] —**addiction**, *n.* —**addicted**, *adj.*

addictive /əˈdɪktɪv/, *adj.* (esp. of drugs) causing or tending to cause dependence or addiction.

Addington /ˈædɪŋtən/, *n.* **Henry (1st Viscount Sidmouth),** 1757–1844, English politician, prime minister 1801–04; celebrated for his mediocrity.

Addis Ababa

Addis Ababa /ˈædəs ˈæbəbə/, *n.* the capital of Ethiopia, situated on a central plateau. Pop. 1 423 111 (1984). Arabic, **Adis Abeba.**

addition /əˈdɪʃən/, *n.* **1.** the act, process or result of adding or uniting. **2.** the process of uniting two or more numbers into one sum, shown by the symbol +. **3. in addition to,** as well as; besides. [L *additio*] **–additional,** *adj.*

additive /ˈædətɪv/, *n.* a substance added, usu. in small amounts, esp. to preserve food, etc. [L]

addled /ˈædl/, *adj.* **1.** mentally confused; muddled. **2.** (of eggs) bad; rotten. [OE *adela* liquid filth]

address /əˈdrɛs, ˈædrɛs/, *n.*; /əˈdrɛs/, *v.* ◇*n.* **1.** a formal speech or writing directed to person or group: *an address on Australian politics.* **2.** a direction as to name and home shown on a letter, etc. **3.** a place where a person lives or may be reached. **4.** (*usu. pl.*) attentions paid by a lover; courtship. ◇*v.t.* **5.** to make formal speech to: *The leader addressed the crowd.* **6.** to direct (words) (fol. by *to*): *to address a warning to someone.* **7.** to direct for mail delivery: *to address a letter.* **8.** to direct the energy or force of (oneself) (fol. by *to*): *He addressed himself to his work.* [ME, from L *ad* to + *directus* straight]

adduce /əˈdjus/, *v.t.* **-duced, -ducing.** to bring forward in argument; give as proof; cite: *to adduce reasons.* [L: lead to] **–adducible,** *adj.*

-ade[1], **1.** a suffix found in nouns marking action, result of action, person(s) acting, as in *blockade, escapade, brigade.* **2.** a noun suffix indicating a drink made from a fruit, as in *lemonade.* [F, from Pr. *-ada,* from L *-āta*]

-ade[2], a collective suffix, variant of **-ad,** as in *decade.*

Adelaide /ˈædəleɪd/, *n.* **1.** the capital city of SA, on the Torrens River on the eastern side of Gulf St Vincent; founded 1836; university, 1874. Pop. 977 721 (1986). **2.** a river in the NT flowing from the mountains south of Darwin into Clarence Strait, north-east of Darwin. 180 km. [named after Queen *Adelaide,* wife of William IV]

adenoid /ˈædənɔɪd/, *n.* **1.** (*usu. pl.*) an enlarged mass of tissue in the upper pharynx, common in children, often preventing breathing. ◇*adj.* **2.** Also, **adenoidal.** /ædəˈnɔɪdl/. relating to the lymphatic glands. [Gk: glandular]

adenosine triphosphate /æˈdɛnəsin traɪˈfɒsfeɪt, ædəˈnousɪn/, *n.* the main source of chemical energy for all reactions in living cells. *Abbrev.:* ATP

adept /əˈdɛpt/, *adj.* highly skilled, proficient; expert. [L: having attained] **–adeptness,** *n.*

adequate /ˈædəkwət/, *adj.* satisfactory, suitable or fit (oft. fol. by *to* or *for*). [L: equalised] **–adequacy,** *n.*

adhere /ədˈhɪə/, *v.i.,* **-hered, -hering. 1.** to stick fast; cling (fol. by *to*). **2.** to be a follower or supporter (fol. by *to*): *to adhere to a party; a leader; a church.* **3.** to hold closely or firmly (fol. by *to*): *to adhere to a plan.* [L] **–adherence,** *n.*

adherent /ədˈhɪərənt, -ˈhɛrənt/, *n.* **1.** one who follows or supports a leader, cause, etc. (fol. by *of*). ◇*adj.* **2.** sticking; clinging.

adhesion /ədˈhiʒən/, *n.* the act of sticking together or the state of being stuck together; attachment. [L]

adhesive /ədˈhisɪv, -ˈhɪzɪv/, *adj.* **1.** clinging, tenacious. ◇*n.* **2.** a substance for sticking things together, e.g. gum, glue, etc. **–adhesively,** *adv.*

ad hoc /æd ˈhɒk/, *adj.* **1.** for this (special purpose). An **ad hoc committee** is one set up to deal with one subject only. **2.** impromptu. An **ad hoc decision** is one made with regard to urgent needs of the moment. [L]

ad hominem /æd ˈhɒmənəm/, *adv.* to the man; personal. An **ad hominem argument** appeals to a person's prejudices rather than to his reason. [L]

adiabatic /ˌædiəˈbætɪk/, *adj. Phys., Chem.* without gain or loss of heat (compare *isothermal*). [Gk *adiábatos* impassable + -IC]

ad infinitum /æd ˌɪnfəˈnaɪtəm/, forever; endlessly. [L]

adipose /ˈædəpoʊs/, *adj.* fatty; consisting of or containing fat. [NL: fatty, from L *adeps* fat] **–adiposity,** *n.*

adj., *Abbrev.* **1.** adjective. **2.** adjectival.

adjacent /əˈdʒeɪsənt/, *adj.* lying near, or close; adjoining; neighboring: *land adjacent to the main road.* [L] **–adjacency,** *n.*

adjacent angle, *n.* one of two angles having the same meeting point and a common side between them.

adjective /ˈædʒəktɪv/, *n. Gram.* a word used to describe or limit a noun, e.g. *red* in *red bag* or in *That bag is red.* [L] **–adjectival,** *adj.*

adjoin /əˈdʒɔɪn/, *v.t., v.i.* to be in contact with or next to (one another); touch: *His land adjoins the lake; The houses adjoin.* [ME, from L: join to] **–adjoining,** *adj.*

adjourn /əˈdʒɜn/, *v.t.* **1.** to put off the meeting of (a court, committee, etc.) until a future time or to another place. **2.** to put off; defer; postpone. ◇*v.i.* **3.** to put off a meeting, etc.: *We shall adjourn for an hour.* **4.** to move: *Shall we adjourn to the living room?* [ME, from OF phrase *a jorn nome* until an appointed day] **–adjournment,** *n.*

adjudicate /əˈdʒudəkeɪt/, *v.,* **-cated, -cating.** ◇*v.t.* **1.** to pronounce or pass judgment on; determine (a case) through court of law. ◇*v.i.* **2.** to sit in judgment (fol. by *upon*). **3.** to act as judge in a competition. [L] **–adjudicator,** *n.* **–adjudication,** *n.* **–adjudicative,** *adj.*

adjunct /ˈædʒʌŋkt/, *n.* **1.** something added to another thing. **2.** a secondary person in some duty or work; assistant. **3.** *Gram.* a modifying word, phrase, etc. [L]

adjure 13 Adonis

adjure /ə'dʒuə/, *v.t.*, **-jured, -juring**. to urge or command, seriously and solemnly, often under oath. [ME, from L]

adjust /ə'dʒʌst/, *v.t.* **1.** to fit (one thing to another); adapt: *to adjust things to a standard*. **2.** to put in working order or position; regulate: *to adjust an instrument*. **3.** to settle (differences, etc.) satisfactorily. **4.** *Insurance*. to fix (the sum to be paid on a claim) or settle (a claim). ◊*v.i.* **5.** to change oneself; adapt. [F (obs.) *adjuster*, from LL *adjuxtāre*] **–adjustable**, *adj.*

adjustment /ə'dʒʌstmənt/, *n.* **1.** the act of adapting to a given purpose. **2.** the state of being adjusted; orderly relation of parts or elements. **3.** a means of adjusting, e.g. a handle, button etc.: *the adjustment of a microscope*. **4.** a settlement of a disputed account or claim.

adjutant /'ædʒətənt/, *n. Mil.* a staff officer who assists the commanding officer. [L: aiding] **–adjutancy**, *n.*

ad lib /æd 'lɪb/, *adv.* **1.** freely; impromptu. ◊*adj.* **2.** spoken or done without preparation.

administer /æd'mɪnəstə, əd-/, *v.t.* **1.** to manage (affairs, a government, etc.); have charge of the proper use and the application of. **2.** to give; apply: *to administer medicine; to administer an oath*. **3.** *Law.* to manage or dispose of (an estate, etc.). ◊*v.i.* **4.** to provide assistance; bring aid or supplies (fol. by *to*): *to administer to the needs of the poor*. **5.** to act as an administrator. [L] **–administrable**, *adj.* **–administrant**, *adj., n.*

administrate /æd'mɪnəstreɪt, əd-/, *v.t.*, **-trated, -trating**. → **administer**.

administration /ədmɪnəs'treɪʃən/, *n.* **1.** the management or direction of the affairs of a business, government, etc. **2.** any group of people entrusted with this. **3.** *Law.* the management of property owned by someone else, by an executor, etc. **4.** the act of giving out, esp. formally or in a ceremony: *administration of holy communion, of medicine, of an oath*. **–administrative**, *adj.*

administrator /əd'mɪnəstreɪtə/, *n.* a person who directs or manages affairs of any kind. [L]

admirable /'ædmərəbəl/, *adj.* worthy of admiration, exciting approval, respect or liking; excellent. [L] **–admirably**, *adv.*

admiral /'ædmərəl/, *n.* **1.** *Mil.* the highest rank in the navy. See Appendix. **2.** any of various butterflies, e.g. **Australian admiral**. [var. of ME *amiral*, from OF, from Ar *amīr al* (chief of); var. *admiral* arose by association with L *admīrābilis* admirable] **–admiralship**, *n.*

Admiral's Cup /ædmərəlz 'kʌp/, *n.* **1.** a series of international yachting races held every two years off Cowes, England. **2.** the trophy for this event.

admiralty /'ædmərəlti/, *n., pl.* **-ties**. **1.** the office or charge of an admiral. **2.** *Brit. (cap.)* the government department having charge of naval affairs.

Admiralty Islands, *n.pl.* a group of islands north-east of PNG, forming part of the Bismarck Archipelago. 2072 km².

admiration /ædmə'reɪʃən/, *n.* **1.** a feeling of wonder, pleasure, and approval. **2.** the act of looking on or thinking of with pleasure: *admiration of a painting*. **3.** an object of wonder or great approval: *She was the admiration of everyone*.

admire /əd'maɪə/, *v.t.*, **-mired, -miring**. to regard with wonder, pleasure, and approval. [L: wonder at]

admirer /əd'maɪərə/, *n.* **1.** someone who admires: *I am an admirer of TS Eliot*. **2.** a lover.

admissible /əd'mɪsəbəl/, *adj. Law.* allowable or acceptable as court evidence.

admission /əd'mɪʃən/, *n.* **1.** the process of entering, dependent on permission or help given, or on the removal of problems: *My admission into hospital took three hours*. **2.** power or permission to enter: *to grant a person admission to the country*. **3.** the price paid for entrance, as to theatre, etc. **4.** the act or condition of being received or accepted in a position or office; appointment: *admission to practise law*. **5.** confession of a charge, error, or crime; acknowledgment: *His admission of the mistake solved the mystery*. **6.** a point or statement admitted; concession. [L]

admit /əd'mɪt/, *v.*, **-mitted, -mitting**. ◊*v.t.* **1.** to allow to enter: *to admit a student to college*. **2.** to give right or means of entrance to: *This ticket admits me to the theatre*. **3.** to allow as valid; concede: *to admit the force of an argument*. **4.** to have room for at the one time: *This bridge only admits one car*. **5.** to confess: *He admitted his guilt*. ◊*v.i.* **6.** to leave room for (fol. by *of*): *This problem admits of no other solution*. [L] **–admittance**, *n.*

admittedly /əd'mɪtədli/, *adv.* by one's own statement: *I was admittedly very nervous about the whole thing*.

admixture /'ædmɪkstʃə, əd'mɪkstʃə/, *n.* **1.** the act of mixing. **2.** the state of being mixed. **3.** anything added; any different element.

admonish /əd'mɒnɪʃ/, *v.t.* **1.** to advise against something; caution; warn. **2.** to tell of, or reprove for, a fault, duty, etc., esp. mildly: *to admonish someone as a brother*. [L] **–admonition**, *n.* **–admonitory**, *adj.*

ad nauseam /æd 'nɔziəm, -eɪ-/, *adv.* to the point of disgust or boredom. [L]

ado /ə'du/, *n.* **1.** activity; bustle; fuss. **2.** **much ado about nothing**, a great fuss about very little. [ME *at do* to do]

adobe /ə'doʊbi/, *n.* **1.** the sun-dried brick in common use in countries having little rainfall. **2.** a yellow sand or clay, left by rivers, and used to make bricks. [Sp]

adobe flat, *n.* a smooth plain of dark heavy clay soil, deposited by short-lived rainfall or thaw streams.

adolescence /ædə'lesəns/, *n.* the period between puberty and adulthood; youth. **–adolescent**, *n., adj.*

Adonis /ə'doʊnəs/, *n. Gk Myth.* a favorite of Aphrodite, killed by a wild boar, but permitted by Zeus to pass four months of every

Adonis | 14 | advantage

year in the lower world with Persephone, four with Aphrodite, and four wherever else he chose. In another account he spent half the year on earth and thus symbolically represented the vegetation cycle.

adopt /ə'dɒpt/, *v.t.* **1.** to take (a child) as one's own, by formal legal act. **2.** to choose (something) for oneself: *to adopt a name; to adopt an idea.* **3.** to vote to accept: *The House adopted the report.* [L] —**adoption**, *n.*

adoptive /ə'dɒptɪv/, *adj.* related by adoption: *an adoptive parent; an adoptive child.*

adorable /ə'dɔrəbəl/, *adj.* **1.** worthy of being adored, loved, etc. **2.** *Colloq.* attractive; delightful. —**adorably**, *adv.*

adoration /ædə'reɪʃən/, *n.* **1.** worship; homage. **2.** strong and faithful love.

adore /ə'dɔ/, *v.*, **adored, adoring.** ◇*v.t.* **1.** to regard with the greatest love and respect. **2.** to honor as divine; worship: *to be adored as gods; O come let us adore him.* **3.** *Colloq.* to like greatly. ◇*v.i.* **4.** to worship. [L: address, worship] —**adoring**, *adj.*

adorn /ə'dɔn/, *v.t.* to make (something) pleasing or more attractive; embellish; decorate: *Truth adorns beauty; New furniture adorned the room.* [L]

adornment /ə'dɔnmənt/, *n.* **1.** ornament: *adornments and furnishings of a room.* **2.** an adorning; ornamentation: *personal adornment.*

ADP /eɪ di 'pi/, *Abbrev.* automatic data processing.

adrenal /ə'drinəl/, *adj.* **1.** placed near or on the kidneys. **2.** of or produced by the adrenal glands. [AD- + L *rēnēs* kidneys + -AL[1]]

adrenalin /ə'drɛnəlɪn, -lɪn/, *n.* **1.** a hormone produced by the adrenal glands, which is sent into the blood when the body is undergoing stress or activity. It increases heart rate, blood pressure and blood sugar levels. **2.** this substance purified from animals and used as a drug for the above properties. Also, **adrenaline.**

Adrian /'eɪdriən/, *n.* **1.** name of six popes, including **Adrian I**, died 795, pope 772–795, and **Adrian IV** (*Nicholas Breakspear*), c. 1100–59, pope 1154–59, the only Englishman to become pope.

Adriatic Sea /ˌeɪdri'ætɪk 'si/, *n.* an arm of the Mediterranean Sea between Italy and Yugoslavia. About 800 km long.

adrift /ə'drɪft/, *adj.* **1.** not fastened by any kind of moorings; at mercy of winds and currents. **2.** influenced by any chance impulse. **3.** *Colloq.* confused; wide of the mark. [A-[1] + DRIFT]

adroit /ə'drɔɪt/, *adj.* skilful in using the hand or mind; clever; ingenious. [AF *à droit* rightly] —**adroitly**, *adv.* —**adroitness**, *n.*

adsorb /æd'sɔb/, *v.t.* to gather (a gas, liquid, or dissolved substance) on surface in a condensed layer, as is the case when charcoal adsorbs gases. [AD- + L *sorbēre* suck in, modelled on ABSORB] —**adsorbent**, *adj.* —**adsorption**, *n.*

adulate /'ædʒəleɪt, 'ædjuleɪt/, *v.t.*, **-lated, -lating.** to show pretended devotion; to praise too much. [L] —**adulation**, *n.* —**adulator**, *n.* —**adulatory**, *adj.*

adult /ə'dʌlt, 'ædʌlt/, *adj.* **1.** having reached full size and strength; grown-up; mature. **2.** relating to or designed for adults: *adult education.* ◇*n.* **3.** person who is grown up. **4.** full-grown animal or plant. **5.** *Law.* person who has reached 18 years of age. [L] —**adulthood**, *n.*

adulterate /ə'dʌltəreɪt, -tərɪt/, *v.t.*, **-rated, -rating;** /ə'dʌltərət, -tərɪt/, to reduce the quality of by adding inferior materials or substances; make impure: *to adulterate food.* [L: defiled] —**adulteration**, *n.*

adulterer /ə'dʌltərə/, *n.* a person who commits adultery. —**adulteress**, *n.fem.*

adultery /ə'dʌltəri/, *n., pl.* **-teries.** voluntary sexual relations between a married person and anyone other than his or her lawful partner. [L] —**adulterous**, *adj.*

adumbrate /'ædəmbreɪt/, *v.t.*, **-brated, -brating. 1.** to give a faint shadow or likeness of; outline. **2.** to darken or make unclear; overshadow. [L: shadowed] —**adumbration**, *n.*

adv., *Abbrev.* **1.** adverb. **2.** adverbial.

advance /əd'væns, -'vans/, *v.*, **-vanced, -vancing,** *n., adj.* ◇*v.t.* **1.** to move or bring forwards in place: *The general advanced his troops.* **2.** to bring to view or notice; propose: *to advance an argument.* **3.** to improve; further: *to advance one's interests.* **4.** to raise in rank; promote. **5.** to raise in rate: *to advance the price.* **6.** to bring forward in time; accelerate: *to advance growth.* **7.** to supply beforehand, or pay in expectation of being paid back: *to advance money on loan.* ◇*v.i.* **8.** to move or go forwards; proceed: *The troops advanced.* **9.** to improve or make progress; grow: *to advance in knowledge or rank.* **10.** to increase in quantity, value, price, etc.: *Shares advanced three points.* ◇*n.* **11.** a movement forwards; progress. **12.** a step forwards; actual progress in any course of action: *the advance of knowledge.* **13.** (*usu. pl.*) an effort to bring about friendship, understanding, etc. **14.** a rise in price. **15.** *Comm.* a giving of money on goods before payment is received. **16.** a loan. **17. in advance, a.** before; in front: *She is in advance of the other students.* **b.** beforehand; ahead of time: *He paid his rent in advance.* ◇*adj.* **18.** made or given in advance: *an advance payment; an advance copy.* **19.** going before: *The advance party set up camp.* [ME, from LL *abante* from before] —**advancer**, *n.* —**advancement**, *n.*

'Advance Australia Fair', *n.* the national anthem of Australia, 1974–76, and from 1984, replacing 'God Save the Queen'; composed about 1878.

advanced /əd'vænst, -'vanst/, *adj.* **1.** placed forward: *with foot advanced.* **2.** far on in progress; above average: *an advanced class in French.* **3.** far on in time: *an advanced age.*

advantage /əd'væntɪdʒ, -'van-/, *n., v.*, **-taged, -taging.** ◇*n.* **1.** something specially favorable to success in life or in a course of action: *the advantage of good education.* **2.** gain;

advantage benefit; profit: *It is to his advantage.* **3.** a better or stronger position (oft. fol. by *over* or *of*): *don't let him have the advantage of us.* **4.** *Tennis.* the first point after score of 40 each (deuce). **5. take advantage of, a.** to make use of: *to take advantage of the chance.* **b.** to make too many demands of (someone's kindness, etc.); impose upon. ◇*v.t.* **6.** to be of service to; benefit. [ME *avantage*, from OF *avant* before, forward, from LL]

advantageous /ˌædvənˈteɪdʒəs/, *adj.* of advantage; useful; profitable; beneficial. —**advantageously**, *adv.*

advantage rule, *n. Football, Basketball, etc.* the rule under which play may be allowed to continue after a faulty move, if the move has resulted in disadvantage to the offending team.

advent /ˈædvent/, *n.* **1.** a coming into place, view, or being; arrival: *advent of death.* **2.** (*cap.*) *Church.* **a.** the period of four weeks before Christmas. **b. Second Advent**, the second coming of Christ. [ME from L: arrival]

adventitious /ˌædvenˈtɪʃəs/, *adj.* accidentally obtained; added from outside; foreign. [L: coming from abroad]

adventure /ədˈventʃə/, *n., v.,* **-tured, -turing.** ◇*n.* **1.** a journey, activity, etc., of uncertain result and sometimes of danger. **2.** an exciting experience. **3.** a liking for exciting activities: *spirit of adventure.* ◇*v.t.* **4.** to risk or take chance of; dare. ◇*v.i.* **5.** to take part in an adventure. [ME from L (*rēs*) *adventūra*, future p., (a thing) about to happen]

Adventure Bay, *n.* an inlet on the eastern coast of Bruny Island, Tas; an anchoring place for many early navigators such as Abel Tasman and James Cook.

adventurer /ədˈventʃərə/, *n.* **1.** a person who looks for adventure; soldier of fortune. **2.** someone who undertakes any great business risk; speculator. —**adventuress**, *n. fem.*

adventurous /ədˈventʃərəs/, *adj.* **1.** Also, **adventuresome**. inclined or willing to take part in adventures. **2.** attended with risk; needing courage.

adverb /ˈædvɜb/, *n.* a word used to modify or limit a verb, adjective or another adverb, e.g. *well* in *She sings well.* An adverb expresses some relation of place, time, manner, degree, cause, result, condition, exception, purpose, etc. **2.** Also, **adverbial**. any word or phrase of similar function or meaning. [L] —**adverbial**, *adj.*

adversary /ˈædvəsri, -səri/, *n., pl.* **-saries.** an opponent; enemy. [ME, from L]

adverse /ˈædvɜs, ədˈvɜs/, *adj.* **1.** threatening or hostile; antagonistic: *adverse criticism.* **2.** opposing one's interests or desire: *adverse influences.* **3.** being or acting in an opposite direction: *adverse winds.* **4.** opposite; confronting. [ME from L: turned against]

adversity /ədˈvɜsəti/, *n., pl.* **-ties.** a condition marked by misfortune or distress: *That family lives in adversity.* [ME, from L: opposition]

advert /ədˈvɜt/, *v.i.* to call attention or refer (fol. by *to*): *He adverted briefly to the events of the day.* [L: turn to]

advertise /ˈædvətaɪz/, *v.,* **-tised, -tising.** ◇*v.t.* **1.** to give information to the public concerning; make public announcement of, by publication in magazines, by printed posters, by broadcasting over radio, television, etc.: *to advertise a reward.* **2.** to praise the good qualities of, in order to encourage the public to buy or invest in. **3.** to offer (something) for sale or to make known (a job vacancy) etc., by placing an advertisement in a newspaper, magazine, etc. ◇*v.i.* **4.** to draw public attention to things for sale, public events, etc.: *it pays to advertise.* **5.** to ask (*for*) by placing an advertisement in a newspaper, magazine, etc.: *to advertise for a baby-sitter.* [ME, from L] —**advertiser**, *n.*

advertisement /ədˈvɜtəsmənt/, *n.* any public notice, as in a newspaper, or on television or radio, intended to increase sales, fill jobs, etc. [ME, from MF]

Advertiser /ˈædvətaɪzə/, *n.* **The,** a major Australian newspaper published daily in Adelaide; founded in 1858. Also, *Colloq.,* **The 'Tiser** /ˈtaɪzə/.

advice /ədˈvaɪs/, *n.* **1.** an opinion suggested, or offered, as worth following. **2.** a message esp. from a distance, containing information: *advice from abroad.* **3.** a formal or professional opinion given by a lawyer, doctor, etc. [late ME, from L *ad-* AD- + *vīsum*, pp. neut., what seems best] —**adviser**, *n.*

advisable /ədˈvaɪzəbəl/, *adj.* sensible; to be recommended. —**advisability**, *n.*

advise /ədˈvaɪz/, *v.,* **-vised, -vising.** ◇*v.t.* **1.** to give advice to (someone); tell (someone) what should be done: *I advise you to be careful.* **2.** to give (a person, etc.) information or notice (fol. by *of*): *We advised the bank of our move.* ◇*v.i.* **3.** to give advice: *I shall act as you advise.* [LL]

advised /ədˈvaɪzd/, *adj.* considered: now chiefly in *ill-advised* or *well-advised*. —**advisedness**, *n.*

advisedly /ədˈvaɪzədli/, *adv.* after proper consideration; deliberately.

advisory /ədˈvaɪzəri/, *adj.* of, or giving, advice; having the power to advise: *an advisory council.*

advocacy /ˌædvəkəsi/, *n.* an act of pleading for, supporting, or recommending.

advocate /ˈædvəkeɪt/, *v.,* **-cated, -cating;** /ˈædvəkət, -kɛt/, *n.* ◇*v.t.* **1.** to plead in favor of; support, recommend publicly: *He advocated peace.* ◇*n.* **2.** someone who defends or upholds by argument (fol. by *of*): *an advocate of peace.* **3.** someone who pleads for, or on behalf of, someone; an intercessor. [L: one summoned to help another (in legal case)] —**advocator**, *n.*

adze /ædz/, *n.* a heavy chisel-like steel tool fastened at right angles to a wooden handle, used to prepare timber, etc. [OE *adesa*]

ae-, for words that begin with **ae-,** see also **e-**.

Aegean /əˈdʒiən/, *adj.* relating to the civilisation that preceded the historic Hellenic period and which flourished in various islands

Aegean | 16 | **afar**

Aegean in, and lands near to, the Aegean Sea, as Crete, etc.

Aegean Sea, *n.* an arm of the Mediterranean Sea between Greece and Asia Minor. About 560 km long and 320 km wide.

Aegeus /ə'dʒiəs, 'idʒiəs/, *n. Gk Legend.* king of Athens and father of Theseus.

aegis /'idʒəs/, *n.* protection; sponsorship: *under the aegis of the Australian government.* [L, from Gk: (a goatskin) the shield of Zeus]

-aemia, a suffix referring to state of blood, as in *toxaemia.* Also, **-emia, -haemia, -hemia.** [NL, from Gk *-aimia* (as in *anaimia* want of blood), from *haima* blood]

Aeneas /ə'niəs/, *n. Class. Myth.* the son of Anchises and Aphrodite (Venus); a Trojan hero, who became the founder of Rome. See **Aeneid.**

Aeneid /ə'niəd/, *n.* a Latin epic poem by Virgil, recounting the adventures of Aeneas after the fall of Troy.

aeolian /i'oulian, eɪ-/, *adj. Geol.* deposited or formed by wind as dunes or loess. [AEOLUS + -IAN]

aeolian harp, *n.* a box over which are stretched a number of strings sounded by the wind; wind harp. Also, **aeolian lyre.**

Aeolis /'iələs/, *n.* an ancient coastal region and Greek colony in north-western Asia Minor.

Aeolus /'iələs/, *n. Gk Myth.* the ruler of the winds.

aeon /'iən/, *n.* **1.** a long period of time; an age. **2.** *Geol.* the largest division of geological time, containing two or more eras. Also, **eon.** [L, from Gk: lifetime, age]

aerate /'ɛəreɪt/, *v.t.*, **-rated, -rating. 1.** to charge or treat with air or gas, esp. with carbon dioxide. **2.** to expose to the free action of air, esp. to freshen, or remove unpleasant smells. **– aeration,** *n.*

aerator /'ɛəreɪtə/, *n.* **1.** an apparatus for aerating water or other fluids. **2.** device used to bleach wheat, etc., and destroy fungi and insects. **3.** *Agric.* a substance, or mechanical process, which breaks up soil so that air may penetrate.

aerial /'ɛəriəl/, *n.* **1.** *Radio.* that part of a radio system which sends out or receives electromagnetic waves; antenna. ◇*adj.* **2.** of, in, or produced by the air: *aerial currents.* **3.** living in the air: *aerial creatures.* **4.** reaching high into the air; lofty: *aerial spires.* **5.** of the nature of air; airy: *aerial beings.* **6.** unreal; visionary: *aerial fancies.* **7.** *Biol.* growing in the air, as roots of some trees. [L: airy (from Gk) + -AL¹]

aero-, a word part indicating: **1.** air; atmosphere. **2.** gas. **3.** aeroplane. [Gk, combining form of *āēr* air]

aerobatics /ɛərə'bætɪks/, *n. pl.* **1.** stunts carried out by aircraft; aerial acrobatics. **2.** (*construed as sing.*) skill of giving aerobatic display. **– aerobatic,** *adj.*

aerobic /ɛə'roubɪk/, *adj.* (of organisms or tissues) living or active only in the presence of free oxygen (opposed to *anaerobic*).

aerobics /ɛə'roubɪks/, *n.pl.* physical exercises intended to improve and maintain physical fitness by strengthening the heart and lungs.

aerodrome /'ɛərədroum/, *n.* a landing field for aeroplanes with buildings, equipment, hangars, etc., but usu. smaller than airport.

aerodynamics /ˌɛəroudaɪ'næmɪks/, *n.* the study of air in motion and of forces acting on solids in motion relative to the air through which they move. **– aerodynamic,** *adj.*

aerofoil /'ɛərəfɔɪl/, *n.* any surface designed to help in lifting or controlling an aircraft, etc., by making use of the current of air through which it moves.

aeronautics /ɛərə'nɒtɪks/, *n.* the science or art of flight; aviation. [pl. of *aeronautic,* from NL: relating to sailing in the air. See -ICS] **– aeronautic, aeronautical,** *adj.*

aeroplane /'ɛərəpleɪn/, *n.* an aircraft, heavier than air, kept aloft by the upward force of the passing air on its fixed wings, and driven by propellers, jet propulsion, etc.

aerosol /'ɛərəsɒl/, *n.* **1.** a system consisting of colloidal particles dispersed in gas; a smoke or fog. **2.** a container from which pressurised liquids, such as household cleaner, paint, etc., can be sprayed. [AERO- + SOL²]

aerospace /'ɛərouspeɪs/, *n.* the earth's atmosphere and the space beyond it.

Aeschylus /'iskələs/, *n.* 525–456 BC, Greek tragic poet and dramatist; his plays include the *Oresteia* and *Prometheus Bound.* **– Aeschylean,** *adj.*

Aesop /'isɒp/, *n.* 620?–564? BC, Greek author of fables. **– Aesopian** /i'soupiən/, *adj.*

aesthete *or* **esthete** /əs'θit, 'isθit, 'ɛsθit/, *n.* someone very sensitive to the beauties esp. of art or nature. [Gk: one who perceives]

aesthetic *or* **esthetic** /əs'θɛtɪk, is-/, *adj.* **1.** relating to the sense of what is beautiful, or science of aesthetics. **2.** having a sense, or a love, of beauty. [Gk: perceptive]

aesthetics *or* **esthetics** /əs'θɛtɪks, is-/, *n.* **1.** *Philos.* the science which deduces from nature and taste the rules and principles of art; theory of the fine arts; science of the beautiful. **2.** *Psychol.* the study of mind and emotions in relation to the sense of beauty.

aestivate /'ɛstəveɪt/, *v.i.,* **-vated, -vating.** *Zool.* to pass summer in an inactive condition. See **hibernate.** **– aestivation,** *n.*

aetiology /iti'ɒlədʒi/, *n.* the study of the causes of anything, esp. of diseases. [L, from Gk *aitía* cause. See -LOGY] **– aetiologist,** *n.*

Aetolia /i'touliə/, *n.* a powerful federal state of ancient Greece.

Aetolian League /i'touliən lig/, *n.* a Greek political confederation which flourished in the third century BC in opposition to the Achaean League.

af-, variant of **ad-** (by assimilation) before *f,* as in *affect.*

afar /ə'fa/, *adv.* **1.** far away (usu. prec. by *from*): *He came from afar.* **2.** at or to a distance

afar (oft. fol. by *off*): *He saw the plane afar off.* [ME *a fer.* See A-¹, FAR]

affable /ˈæfəbəl/, *adj.* **1.** easy to talk to or to approach; polite; friendly. **2.** expressing friendliness; mild; benign: *an affable expression.* [F, from L: able to be spoken to] —**affability, affableness,** *n.* —**affably,** *adv.*

affair /əˈfeə/, *n.* **1.** anything done or to be done: *an affair of great importance; affairs of state.* **2.** (*usu. pl.*) matters of interest or concern: *put your affairs in order.* **3.** an event or particular action, operation, etc. **4.** a love affair. [F *à faire to do*]

affect¹ /əˈfekt/, *v.t.* **1.** to act on; produce an effect or change in: *Cold affects the body.* **2.** to move (in mind or feelings); impress: *Poetry affected me deeply.* ◇*n.* **3.** *Psychol.* feeling or emotion. [L: influenced]

affect² /əˈfekt/, *v.t.* **1.** to make a show of; pretend; feign: *to affect ignorance.* **2.** to use or take by preference; choose; prefer: *strange costume which he affected.* [F, from L]

affectation /ˌæfekˈteɪʃən/, *n.* **1.** a pretence or show (fol. by *of*): *an affectation of great wealth.* **2.** a manner or behavior which is not natural or real: *His affectations are unbearable.* [L: a pursuit after]

affected¹ /əˈfektəd/, *adj.* **1.** acted upon; influenced. **2.** attacked, as by weather or disease; impaired. **3.** moved; touched: *She was deeply affected by the music.* [pp. of AFFECT¹]

affected² /əˈfektəd/, *adj.* **1.** taken on artificially: *He has such affected speech.* **2.** pretending to possess qualities which are not natural: *an affected person.* [pp. of AFFECT²]

affection /əˈfekʃən/, *n.* **1.** a steady love; goodwill; attachment: *Parents have special affection for their children.* **2.** emotion or mental state. [L]

affectionate /əˈfekʃənət/, *adj.* having or showing great love or affection.

affective /əˈfektɪv/, *adj.* **1.** of the feelings; emotional. **2.** causing feelings; affecting.

afferent /ˈæfərənt/, *adj.* leading to a central point (opposed to *efferent*): *afferent nerves; afferent veins.* [L: bringing to]

affiance /ˈæfiəns, əˈfaɪəns/, *v.*, **-anced, -ancing,** *n.* ◇*v.t.* **1.** to engage to be married; betroth: *to affiance a daughter.* ◇*n.* **2.** the swearing of faith, esp. a marriage contract. **3.** trust; confidence; reliance. [ME, from LL: pledge]

affidavit /ˌæfəˈdeɪvət/, *n. Law.* a written statement sworn or affirmed which may be used as a substitute for oral evidence in court. [L: he has made oath]

affiliate /əˈfɪlieɪt/, *v.*, **-ated, -ating;** /əˈfɪliət/, *n.* ◇*v.t.* **1.** to connect as a branch or part; unite; associate (fol. by *with*): *affiliate the union with the ACTU.* **2.** to bring into association or close connection: *The two banks were affiliated.* ◇*v.i.* **3.** to connect or join oneself. ◇*n.* **4.** someone or something affiliated; associate. [LL: adopted as a son] —**affiliation,** *n.*

affinity /əˈfɪnəti/, *n., pl.* **-ties. 1.** a natural liking for, or attraction to, a person or thing. **2.** similarity or connection, esp. structural. **3.** relationship, esp. by marriage. **4.** *Chem.* that force by which atoms of different elements tend to hold together to form molecules. [ME, from L]

affirm /əˈfɜm/, *v.t.* **1.** to state positively; state as true: *to affirm loyalty to a country.* **2.** to establish; confirm; ratify. ◇*v.i.* **3.** to declare positively; assert solemnly. **4.** *Law.* to declare solemnly without swearing. [L] —**affirmation,** *n.*

affirmative /əˈfɜmətɪv/, *adj.* **1.** agreeing or stating to be true: *an affirmative answer.* ◇*n.* **2.** a positive statement: *two negatives make an affirmative.* **3.** an affirmative word or phrase, as *yes* or *I do.* [LL]

affix /əˈfɪks/, *v.*; /ˈæfɪks/, *n.*, ◇*v.t.* **1.** to fix; fasten or join (oft. fol. by *to*): *to affix stamps to a letter.* **2.** to stamp or press on (an official seal or stamp). ◇*n.* **3.** something joined or fixed on. **4.** *Gram.* a meaningful part (prefix, infix, or suffix) added to the stem or base of a word, e.g. *ed* added to *want* to form *wanted.* [L: fasten to] —**affixture,** *n.*

afflict /əˈflɪkt/, *v.t.* to cause pain to mind or body; trouble greatly: *to be afflicted with sickness.* [L: thrown down] —**afflictive,** *adj.*

affliction /əˈflɪkʃən/, *n.* **1.** a state of pain or grief: *They sympathised with us in our affliction.* **2.** any cause of continual pain of body or mind, as sickness, loss, etc. [ME, from L]

affluence /ˈæfluəns/, *n.* **1.** wealth: *to live in great affluence.* **2.** plentiful supply, as of thoughts, words, etc.; profusion. [F, from L]

affluent /ˈæfluənt/, *adj.* **1.** wealthy; rich: *an affluent person.* ◇*n.* **2.** a stream flowing into a river; tributary. [ME, from L: flowing to]

afford /əˈfɔd/, *v.t.* **1.** to have enough money (to do something) (usu. with *can* or *may*): *We can afford to eat well.* **2.** to have enough money to pay for; to be able to spare the price of (usu. with *can* or *may*): *He can't afford a car.* **3.** to be able to give or spare (usu. with *can* or *may*): *I can't afford the loss of a day.* **4.** to give; supply: *It affords me great pleasure.* [OE *geforthian* further, accomplish] —**affordable,** *adj.*

affray /əˈfreɪ/, *n.* a public fight; noisy quarrel; brawl. [ME, from LL *ex-* EX.¹ + *-fridāre*, from *fridus* peace]

affricative /əˈfrɪkətɪv/, *n.* a speech sound beginning with a stop and ending with a fricative, as the *ch* in *chop* (which begins like *t* and ends like *sh*). Also, **affricate.** [L: rubbed on or against]

affront /əˈfrʌnt/, *n.* **1.** an open insult. ◇*v.t.* **2.** to offend or insult openly. **3.** to meet face to face; confront: *to affront death.* [ME, from LL] —**affronter,** *n.* —**affrontingly,** *adv.*

Afghan /ˈæfɡæn/, *n.* **1.** Also, **Afghani.** a native or inhabitant of Afghanistan. **2.** (formerly) a camel driver from the north-west parts of India, employed in the outback of Australia, and sometimes self-employed as an itinerant merchant.

Afghan hound /'æfgæn haʊnd/, n. a breed of greyhound with very long silky hair.

Afghanistan /æf'gænəstæn/, n. a republic in central Asia, bounded by Turkmenia, Tadzhikistan, Iran, China and Pakistan; independent since 1919 and a republic since 1973. Pop. 14 366 434 (1984 est.); 652 225 km². *Languages:* mainly Pashtu and Dari. *Currency:* afghani. *Cap.:* Kabul.

aficionado /əfɪʃɪə'nɑdoʊ/, n. someone with a keen interest (in a sport, etc.); enthusiast: *an aficionado of football*. Also, **afficionado**. [Sp.]

afield /ə'fild/, adv. **1.** away; at a distance. **2.** off the usual course.

afloat /ə'floʊt/, adj. **1.** (supported) on the water; floating: *The ship is afloat*. **2.** on board ship; at sea. **3.** flooded: *The main deck was afloat*. **4.** moving without guide or control; adrift. **5.** going from place to place; in circulation: *A rumor is afloat*.

afocal /eɪ'foʊkəl/, adj. having no finite focal point, like a telescope.

A 4 /eɪ 'fɔ/, an international standard size of paper, 297 × 210mm.

afraid /ə'freɪd/, adj. **1.** feeling fear; frightened: *afraid of the lion*. **2.** sadly of the opinion; sorry; regretful (sometimes fol. by *that*): *I'm afraid you must go now*; *She is not here, I'm afraid*. [ME]

afresh /ə'frɛʃ/, adv. again; anew: *Start afresh*.

Africa /'æfrɪkə/, n. the second largest continent, south of Europe and between the Atlantic and Indian Oceans; about 30 300 000 km². – **African**, n., adj.

African National Congress, n. a South African political organisation, founded in 1912 and banned 1960–90, fighting for majority rule. *Abbrev.:* ANC

African violet, n. a tropical plant, with dark-green hairy leaves and purple, pink, or white flowers, usu. grown indoors.

Afrikaans /æfrɪ'kɑnz, -'kɑns/, n. a language of South Africa, developed out of the speech of the 17th-century settlers from Holland and still very like Dutch; South African Dutch; Taal. [var. spelling of D *Afrikaansch*]

Afrikaner /æfrɪ'kɑnə/, n. an Afrikaans-speaking South African born of white parents of Dutch, German, or Huguenot descent. Also **Afrikander**. [Afrikaans *Afrikaander*, b. *Afrikaans* and *Hollander*]

afro /'æfroʊ/, n. a hairstyle in which long, frizzy hair is cut to form a large rounded shape.

Afro-, combining form meaning 'African', 'Negro'. [L *Afer* African]

aft /ɑft/, adv. *Naut.* at, in, or towards the stern (back of a ship). [OE *æftan* from behind]

after /'ɑftə/, prep. **1.** behind; following. **2.** in search or pursuit of: *Run after him*. **3.** about; concerning: *to inquire after a person*. **4.** later in time than; at the end of. **5.** following and because of: *after what has happened I can never return*. **6.** below in rank or standard; next to. **7.** in the style of: *after Raphael; to make something after a model*. **8.** with name of: *He was named after his uncle*. **9.** according to: *arranged after the first letter of their names*. ◇*adv.* **10.** behind; in the rear: *Jill came tumbling after*. **11.** later in time; afterwards: *happy ever after*. ◇*adj.* **12.** later in time; next; following; subsequent: *in after years*. **13.** *Naut.* rear: *the after deck*. ◇*conj.* **14.** following the time that: *after the boys left*. [OE *æfter* (from *æf-* away from + *-ter*, comparative suffix)]

afterbirth /'ɑftəbɜθ/, n. the placenta and foetal membranes expelled from the uterus after the birth of offspring.

afterglow /'ɑftəgloʊ/, n. **1.** the glow frequently seen in the sky after sunset. **2.** a second or secondary glow. **3.** *Phys.* the persistence of radiation from a gas discharge or luminescent screen after the source of excitation has been removed.

afterlife /'ɑftəlaɪf/, n. **1.** life after death. **2.** later life.

aftermath /'ɑftəmæθ, -mɑθ/, n. conditions resulting from something, esp. a disaster: *the aftermath of the storm*. [AFTER + *math* a mowing (OE *mæth*)]

afternoon /ɑftə'nun/, n. **1.** the time from midday until evening. **2.** the later part: *the afternoon of life*. ◇*adj.* **3.** relating to the later part of the day.

afterthought /'ɑftəθɔt/, n. **1.** an idea after an act; answer or idea that comes to one's mind too late, or afterwards. **2.** an action, remark, etc. prompted by an afterthought.

afterwards /'ɑftəwədz/, adv. at a later time; subsequently. Also, **afterward** /'ɑftəwəd/. [OE]

Ag, *Chem. Symbol.* silver. [L *argentum*]

AG /eɪ 'dʒi/, *Abbrev.* **1.** Adjutant-General. **2.** Attorney-General.

again /ə'gɛn, ə'geɪn/, adv. **1.** once more; in addition; another time: *He did it all over again*. **2.** also; besides; moreover. **3.** on the other hand: *It might happen and then again it might not*. **4.** to the same place or person: *to return again*. **5. as much again**, twice as much. [OE *ongegn*, adv. and prep., opposite (to), towards, again, from *on* in + *gegn* straight]

against /ə'gɛnst, ə'geɪnst/, prep. **1.** in an opposite direction to, so as to meet; towards; upon: *to ride against the wind*; *The rain beats against the window*. **2.** touching or pressing on: *to lean against a wall*. **3.** in opposition to; hostile to: *twenty votes against ten*; *against reason*. **4.** in resistance to or defence from: *protection against burglars*. **5.** in preparation for; providing for: *He saved money against losing his job*. **6.** in exchange for; in return for: *to draw out money against a cheque*. **7.** compared to; as an alternative to; in contrast with (sometimes preceded by *as*): *the advantages of flying against going by train*. [AGAIN + *-(e)s*, adv. gen. suffix + *-t* added later]

Agamemnon /ægə'mɛmnɒn/, n. *Gk Legend.* a king of Mycenae, son of Atreus and

Agamemnon brother of Menelaus; leader of the Greeks against Troy. Upon his return he was slain by his faithless wife, Clytemnestra.

agapanthus /ˌægəˈpænθəs/, *n.* any of several African plants with rounded heads of blue or white flowers; African lily. [Gk *agápē* love + *ánthos* flower]

agape[1] /əˈgeɪp/, *adv.* **1.** showing wonder or eagerness, with mouth wide open. ◇*adj.* **2.** wide open.

agape[2] /ˈægəpeɪ, əˈgɑːpi/, *n. Relig.* **1.** a meal taken by early Christians in memory of the last supper. **2.** Christian or unselfish love. [Gk]

agar-agar /ˌeɪgɑːˈeɪgɑː/, *n.* a jelly-like product of certain seaweeds, used to thicken culture media (as for bacteria) and soups (esp. in Asia), etc. Also, **agar**. [Malay: jelly]

agate /ˈægət/, *n.* **1.** a type of quartz (chalcedony) showing colored stripes or other markings (cloudy, mosslike, etc.). **2.** a child's playing marble made of agate or of glass to look like agate. [F, from L, from Gk]

age /eɪdʒ/, *n., v.,* **aged, ageing** or **aging**. ◇*n.* **1.** the length of time someone or something has lived or existed: *His age is twenty years; a tree or building of unknown age.* **2.** a stage of human life, esp. one of a particular level of ability or legal responsibility: *age of consent.* **3. act/be your age,** *Colloq.* to behave in a manner expected of one's age. **4. of age,** *Law.* at an age, usu. 18, at which one gets certain legal rights, as the right to vote. **5.** a period or stage of human life: *person of middle age.* **6.** old age: *His eyes were dim with age.* **7.** (*usu. cap.*) a particular period of historical or geological time: *the Ice Age; the Stone Age; the Middle Ages.* **8.** *Colloq.* a long time: *I haven't seen you for an age or for ages.* **9.** *Psychol.* a person's level of development in an area expressed as the average age at which that level is reached: *She is only five, but has a reading age of seven.* **10.** any one of the stages in human history divided, according to Hesiod, into the golden, silver, bronze, heroic, and iron ages. The happiest and best was the first (or golden) age, and the worst the iron age. ◇*v.i.* **11.** to grow old or appear older: *He is ageing rapidly.* ◇*v.t.* **12.** to make old; cause to grow old or to seem old: *Fear aged her overnight.* **13.** to allow to mature or become fit for use: *to age wine.* [ME, from OF, from L] **—ageing, aging,** *n., adj.* **—aged,** *adj.* **—agedly,** *adv.*

-age, a noun suffix forming: **1.** collective nouns, as in *acreage.* **2.** nouns showing condition, rank, etc., as in *bondage.* **3.** nouns expressing a process or result, as in *breakage, postage.* [OF, from L *-āticum,* neut. adj. suffix]

Age, The, a major Australian newspaper published daily in Melbourne; founded in 1854.

ageism /ˈeɪdʒəsm/, *n.* discrimination against a person, esp. an elderly person, because of their age, without consideration of individual abilities. **—ageist,** *adj., n.*

agency /ˈeɪdʒənsi/, *n., pl.* **-cies. 1.** an organisation providing a service or acting as intermediary between people or organisations: *an employment agency.* **2.** the place of business of an agent. **3.** the job, position, or business of an agent. **4.** an action; doing: *the agency of Providence; by the agency of friends.*

agenda /əˈdʒɛndə/, *n., pl.* **-das.** a list, plan or program of things to be done, talked about, etc. [L]

agent /ˈeɪdʒənt/, *n.* **1.** a person authorised to act on behalf of another: *My agent has power to sign my name.* **2.** someone or something that acts or has the power to act: *a free agent.* **3.** something with an effect or used for a particular purpose: *a cleansing agent.* **4.** an active cause: *an agent of destruction.* **5.** an official or representative of a business firm, esp. a travelling salesperson. **6.** *Chem.* a substance which causes a reaction. ◇*adj.* **7.** acting (opposed to *patient* in the sense of being acted upon). [L: driving, doing] **—agential, agentive,** *adj.*

agent orange, *n.* a highly dangerous chemical, in military use as a defoliant.

agent provocateur /ˌaʒɒn prəvɒkəˈtɜː/, *n., pl.* **agents provocateurs** /ˌaʒɒn prəvɒkəˈtɜːz/. **1.** a secret agent hired to encourage persons or groups to break the law, riot, etc., so that they may be punished or discredited. **2.** any person who encourages dissatisfaction or law-breaking. [F]

age of consent, *n.* the age at which a person, esp. a female, is considered by law to be allowed to marry or have sexual intercourse.

Age of Reason, *n.* any period in history, esp. the 18th century in Europe, characterised by a critical approach to religious, social, and philosophical matters.

agglomerate /əˈglɒməreɪt/, *v.,* **-rated, -rating;** /əˈglɒmərət/, *adj., n.* ◇*v.t., v.i.* **1.** to collect or gather into a mass. **2.** gathered together into a lump or mass. ◇*n.* **3.** a mass of things clustered together. **4.** *Geol.* a type of rock made of large angular volcanic pieces. [L: wound into a ball] **—agglomeration,** *n.* **—agglomerative,** *adj.*

agglutinate /əˈgluːtɪneɪt/, *v.,* **-nated, -nating;** /əˈgluːtɪnət/, *adj.* ◇*v.t.* **1.** to cause to stick on or together, as if with glue. ◇*adj.* **2.** joined by or as if by glue. [L: pasted to]

agglutination /əˌgluːtɪˈneɪʃən/, *n.* **1.** the act or process of uniting by glue or other substance. **2.** the condition of being stuck together. **3.** something united or stuck together in a mass. **4.** *Chem.* the sticking together of small suspended particles making larger masses. **5.** *Immunol.* the clumping of bacteria, red blood cells, etc., due to an antibody. **6.** *Ling.* the process of simple words or word parts joining to form compound words. **—agglutinative,** *adj.*

aggrandise or **aggrandize** /əˈgrændaɪz/, *v.t.,* **-dised, -dising. 1.** to make larger or wider; extend. **2.** to make (something) greater or appear greater in power, wealth, or honor. [F, from L *ad-* AD- + *grandīre* make great] **—aggrandisement** /əˈgrændɪzmənt/, *n.* **—aggrandiser,** *n.*

aggravate /ˈægrəveɪt/, *v.t.,* **-vated, -vating. 1.** to make worse or more severe: *to aggravate guilt; Grief aggravated her illness.*

aggravate

2. *Colloq.* to irritate; provoke: *threats will only aggravate him.* [L: added to the weight of] —**aggravated**, *adj.* —**aggravating**, *adj.* —**aggravatingly**, *adv.* —**aggravation, aggravator**, *n.*

aggregate /ˈægrəgət/, *v., adj., n.;* /ˈægrəgeɪt/, *v.,* **-gated, -gating.** ◇*adj.* **1.** formed by adding together single things into a mass or sum; combined: *the aggregate mark for all six subjects.* ◇*n.* **2.** sum or collection of single things; total: *the aggregate of all past experience.* **3.** *Geol.* mixture of different mineral substances that can be separated mechanically, e.g. granite. **4.** any hard material added to cement to make concrete. **5. in the aggregate,** considered together; collectively. ◇*v.t., v.i.* **6.** to bring or come together; collect into one sum or mass. [L: added to] —**aggregation**, *n.* —**aggregately**, *adv.* —**aggregative**, *adj.*

aggression /əˈgrɛʃən/, *n.* **1.** any offensive action. **2.** the action of a country invading another or affecting it or its people by force. **3.** the making of attacks; offensive behavior. **4.** *Psychol.* the emotional desire or need to attack. [L]

aggressive /əˈgrɛsɪv/, *adj.* **1.** marked by or noted for aggression; tending to attack. **2.** active; energetic; vigorous. —**aggressively**, *adv.* —**aggressiveness**, *n.*

aggressor /əˈgrɛsə/, *n.* a person who attacks first; attacker or invader. [L]

aggrieved /əˈgriːvd/, *adj.* **1.** hurt; oppressed; wronged: *She felt herself aggrieved.* **2.** *Colloq.* feeling that one has been treated unjustly; hurt; resentful: *an aggrieved expression on his face.*

aggro /ˈægroʊ/, *adj. Colloq.* aggressive; violent.

aghast /əˈgɑːst/, *adj.* suddenly frightened and/or amazed; appalled: *They stood aghast at this unexpected disaster.* [ME: terrify]

agile /ˈædʒaɪl/, *adj.* quick and active; lively: *an agile gymnast; an agile mind.* [L] —**agilely**, *adv.*

agility /əˈdʒɪləti/, *n.* the ability to move quickly and easily; nimbleness: *agility of the body or mind.* [late ME, from L]

Agincourt /ˈæʒɪnkɔː, ˈædʒɪnkɔːt/, *n.* a village in northern France, near Calais; site of a decisive victory of the English under Henry V over the French, 1415.

agist /əˈdʒɪst/, *v.t. Farming.* to take in and feed or pasture (someone else's sheep, cattle, etc.) for payment. [ME, from OF *à* to + *giste* resting-place] —**agistor**, *n.*

agistment /əˈdʒɪstmənt/, *n. Farming.* **1.** the act of agisting: *His cattle are out on agistment because of the drought.* **2.** the price paid for agisting sheep, cattle, etc.

agitate /ˈædʒɪteɪt/, *v.,* **-tated, -tating.** ◇*v.t.* **1.** to move or shake about: *The wind agitates the sea.* **2.** to give regular motion to: *to agitate a fan.* **3.** to excite; disturb; perturb: *Her mind is agitated by emotion.* ◇*v.i.* **4.** to try to get public support for something: *to agitate for a change in the law.* [L: aroused, excited] —**agitative**, *adj.* —**agitator**, *n.*

agitation /ædʒəˈteɪʃən/, *n.* **1.** the act of agitating. **2.** a condition of being agitated: *He walked away in great agitation.*

AGM /eɪ dʒi ˈem/, *Abbrev.* Annual General Meeting.

agnate /ˈægneɪt/, *n.* **1.** a relative who is descended through males from a common male ancestor. **2.** any male relative on the father's side. ◇*adj.* **3.** related, esp. through males or on the father's side. [L: born to] —**agnatic**, *adj.* —**agnation**, *n.*

agnostic /ægˈnɒstɪk/, *n.* **1.** someone who believes that human knowledge is limited to experience and that God is unknowable. ◇*adj.* **2.** having to do with agnostics or their beliefs. **3.** claiming that all knowledge, or a particular question, is relative and uncertain. [A-[6] + Gk *gnōstikós* knowing. Coined by TH Huxley 1869] —**agnosticism**, *n.* —**agnostically**, *adv.*

ago /əˈgoʊ/, *adv.* in past time; past: *some time ago; long ago.* [OE *āgān* go by, pass]

agog /əˈgɒg/, *adj.* **1.** highly excited; eager: *agog with curiosity.* ◇*adv.* **2.** excitedly; eagerly. [F *en gogues* in a merry mood]

agonic line /əˈgɒnɪk laɪn/, *n. Geol., Geog.* an imaginary line on the earth's surface connecting places where the magnetic compass points true north as well as magnetic north.

agonise or **agonize** /ˈægənaɪz/, *v.,* **-nised, -nising.** ◇*v.i.* **1.** to suffer great pain; writhe in agony. **2.** to make great effort; struggle. ◇*v.t.* **3.** to cause great pain to; torture. [ML, from Gk: contend] —**agonisingly**, *adv.*

agony /ˈægəni/, *n., pl.* **-nies. 1.** great pain. **2.** intense mental excitement of any kind. **3.** the struggle before death: *mortal agony.* [ME, from Gk: contest, anguish]

agoraphobia /ægərəˈfoʊbiə/, *n. Psychol.* an abnormal fear of being in an open space. [Gk: market place + PHOBIA]

Agra /ˈɑːgrə/, *n.* a city in northern India, in Uttar Pradesh; site of the Taj Mahal. Pop. 694 191 (1981).

agrarian /əˈgrɛəriən/, *adj.* **1.** relating to land or the holding or owning of land: *agrarian laws.* **2.** relating to farming; rural. **3.** growing in fields; wild. ◇*n.* **4.** someone who believes in dividing land equally or more fairly. [L: pertaining to land] —**agrarianism**, *n.*

agree /əˈgriː/, *v.,* **agreed, agreeing.** ◇*v.i.* **1.** to say yes; consent (oft. fol. by *to*): *He agreed to go with the teacher; Do you agree to the conditions?* **2.** to have the same opinion (oft. fol. by *with*): *I don't agree with you.* **3.** to live in peace or without conflict; act in the same way. **4.** to come to one opinion: *to agree upon a course of action.* **5.** to be suitable or agreeable; match; be consistent (fol. by *with*): *The picture does not agree with the story.* **6.** to suit or be compatible (fol. by *with*): *The food does not agree with me.* **7.** *Gram.* to correspond in inflectional form, e.g. in number, case, gender, or person (fol. by *with*): *In French an adjective must agree with its noun.* ◇*v.t.* **8.** to admit; concede (fol.

agree

by noun clause): *I agree that she runs faster.* **9.** to arrange or determine: *We agreed that we should meet again.* [ME, from OF phrase *a gré* at pleasure]

agreeable /ə'griəbəl/, *adj.* **1.** pleasant; likeable: *agreeable manners.* **2.** willing or ready to agree: *Are you agreeable?* **3.** suitable (fol. by *to*). —**agreeableness**, *n.* —**agreeably**, *adv.*

agreed /ə'grid/, *adj.* arranged by general consent or agreement: *They met at the agreed time.*

agreement /ə'grimənt/, *n.* **1.** the act of coming to an arrangement. **2.** the arrangement itself. **3.** the condition of agreeing: *agreement among the members; agreement between the two stories; agreement of a verb with a noun.*

agric., *Abbrev.* agricultural.

agriculturalist /ægrə'kʌltʃərələst/, *n.* **1.** farmer. **2.** an expert in agriculture. Also, **agriculturist**.

agricultural pipe, /ægrə'kʌltʃərəl paip/, *n.* a pipe, usu. plastic, with ridges and slits, used for drainage in agriculture, landscaping, etc. Also, **ag pipe**.

agriculture /'ægrəkʌltʃə/, *n.* farming, including growing crops or trees, raising animals, etc. [L *agrī*, gen. of *ager* land + *cultūra* cultivation] —**agricultural**, *adj.*

Agrippa /ə'grɪpə/, *n.* **Marcus Vipsanius** /ˌmakəs vɪp'seɪniəs/, 63–12 BC, Roman statesman, general, engineer; victor over Antony and Cleopatra at Actium.

agro-, a word part meaning 'soil', 'field', as in *agrology.* [Gk, combining form of *agrós*]

agrology /ə'grɒlədʒi/, *n.* soil science as applied to farming. —**agrologic, agrological**, *adj.*

agronomy /ə'grɒnəmi/, *n.* **1.** soil science and plant science as applied to farming, esp. crops. **2.** → **agriculture**. —**agronomist**, *n.*

aground /ə'graund/, *adv.* **1.** on or onto the ground: *The ship ran aground.* ◇*adj.* **2.** stranded: *hard aground.*

ague /'eɪgju/, *n.* **1.** *Med.* a malarial fever marked by regularly returning fits of cold, heat, and sweating. **2.** a fit of shaking or shivering. [ME, from OF, from Pr., from L *acūta* (*febris*) acute (fever)] —**agued**, *adj.*

ah /a/, *interj.* (an exclamation of pain, surprise, pity, complaint, joy, etc.) [ME]

a.h., *Abbrev.* after hours. Also, **AH**

A.h, *Symbol.* ampere hour.

ahead /ə'hɛd/, *adv.* **1.** in front; before; forward; onward. **2. be ahead**, to be better off; be winning: *I was well ahead in the deal.* **3. get ahead of**, to pass or beat (someone) at something. [A-¹ + HEAD]

Ahern /ə'hɜn/, *n.* **Michael John**, born 1942, Australian state National Party politician; became premier of Qld in 1987.

Ahmedabad /'aməˌdəbæd/, *n.* a city in western India, in Gujarat state. Pop. 2 059 725 (1981). Also, **Ahmadābād**.

ahoy /ə'hɔɪ/, *interj.* (used in calling or greeting, esp. on ships). [*a*, interj. + HOY]

air

AI /eɪ 'aɪ/, *Abbrev.* **1.** artificial insemination. **2.** artificial intelligence. **3.** Amnesty International.

aid /eɪd/, *v.t.* **1.** to help, support or make easier. ◇*v.i.* **2.** to give help. ◇*n.* **3.** help; support; assistance. **4.** someone or something that helps; helper. **5. in aid of**, directed towards; intended to achieve. [ME, from L]

AID /eɪ aɪ 'di/, *Abbrev.* artificial insemination (by) donor.

aide-de-camp /eɪd-də-'kɒ̃/, *n., pl.* **aides-de-camp**. a personal assistant, esp. a military officer, to a general, governor, etc. Also, **aide**. [F: camp assistant]

AIDS /eɪdz/, *n.* → **acquired immune deficiency syndrome**.

AIF /eɪ aɪ 'ɛf/, *Abbrev.* Australian Imperial Force.

ail /eɪl/, *v.t.* **1.** to cause (someone) to feel pain or uneasiness: *My legs ail me.* ◇*v.i.* **2.** to feel pain or be ill (usu. not badly): *He is ailing.* [OE *eglan*]

aileron /'eɪlərɒn/, *n.* a movable flap of an aircraft wing, usu. on the trailing (back) edge, used to keep the aircraft level or to turn, roll, etc. [F, diminutive of *aile* wing]

ailing /'eɪlɪŋ/, *adj.* sickly: *an ailing child.*

ailment /'eɪlmənt/, *n.* an illness or disorder, esp. a mild one.

aim /eɪm/, *v.t.* **1.** to direct or point (something) at someone or something: *He aimed his gun carefully before shooting*; *That remark was aimed at you.* ◇*v.i.* **2.** to point or direct a gun or other weapon: *She aimed at his head.* **3.** to try; strive (fol. by *at* or *to*): *They aim to save something every month.* **4.** to direct efforts towards a goal: *to aim high.* ◇*n.* **5.** the act of aiming or directing something. **6. take aim**, to point a weapon. **7.** a thing or person aimed at or towards; purpose; target. [ME, from L: estimate]

aimless /'eɪmləs/, *adj.* without aim; purposeless. —**aimlessly**, *adv.* —**aimlessness**, *n.*

ain't /eɪnt/, (non-standard) contraction of *am not, are not, is not, have not,* or *has not: I ain't seen it.*

Ainu /'aɪnu/, *n.* a member of an aboriginal race of the northernmost islands of Japan, having Caucasian features, light skin, and hairy bodies.

air /ɛə/, *n.* **1.** a mixture of oxygen, nitrogen and other gases which surrounds the earth and forms its atmosphere. **2.** movement of the atmosphere; a light breeze. **3.** expression; publicity: *She loves to give air to her ideas.* **4.** general character or appearance. **5.** *Music.* **a.** a tune; melody. **b.** an aria. **6.** Some special uses are:
clear the air, to clear up a disagreement, settle a tense situation, etc.
give oneself airs / put on airs, to pretend importance; behave in a conceited or grand manner.
(up) in the air, **1.** without basis or reality; imaginary or uncertain. **2.** undecided or unsettled.

into thin air, completely out of sight or reach; without trace.
on the air, broadcasting or being broadcast.
walk on air, to feel very happy or delighted.
◇*v.t.* **7.** to let air into or put out in the open air, so as to dry or freshen; ventilate: *to air sheets; to air a room.* **8.** to show off or make public: *to air opinions.* [ME, from L, from Gk: air, mist]

air-bladder /'ɛə-blædə/, *n.* **1.** a sac (small bag) or cell containing air. **2.** an air-filled sac which regulates the buoyancy of fishes swimming at different depths.

airborne /'ɛəbɔn/, *adj.* **1.** carried or held up by air. **2.** in the air; flying.

air-brake /'ɛə-breɪk/, *n.* **1.** *Aeron.* a hinged flap or other part for slowing down an aircraft. **2.** a brake or system of brakes operated by compressed air.

air-brush /'ɛə-brʌʃ/, *n.* a small pencil-type spray gun used for very fine paint work or stencilling.

airbus /'ɛəbʌs/, *n.* a passenger aircraft operating over short distances.

air chief marshal, *n. Mil.* the highest rank in the air force. See Appendix.

air-conditioning /'ɛə-kəndɪʃənɪŋ/, *n.* the treating of air to control temperature, humidity, and dust.

aircraft /'ɛəkrɑft/, *n., pl.* **-craft.** any machine which can fly in the air, either by being lighter than air (such as balloons) or by the aerodynamic forces of its surfaces pushing against the air (such as aeroplanes, helicopters, and gliders).

aircraft-carrier /'ɛəkrɑft-,kæriə/, *n.* a large naval ship, designed to be used as an air base at sea, with a long deck for aircraft to land on and take off from.

aircraftman /'ɛəkrɑftmən/, *n.pl.,* **-men.** *Mil.* the lowest rank in the air force. See Appendix.

Airedale /'ɛədeɪl/, *n.* a large heavy dog with a rough brown or tan coat which is black or grizzled over the back; Airedale terrier. [from *Airedale* a city in England]

airfield /'ɛəfild/, *n.* an area where aircraft land and take off, usu. with runways, buildings, etc.

air force, *n.* the part of the armed forces of a country concerned with military aircraft.

airgun /'ɛəgʌn/, *n.* a gun operated by compressed air.

air hostess, *n.* a woman employed to look after passengers on aircraft.

airily /'ɛərəli/, *adv.* **1.** cheerfully. **2.** lightly; delicately.

airing /'ɛərɪŋ/, *n.* **1.** an exposure to air, to cool, dry or freshen. **2.** a making known (of proposal, ideas, etc.) to gain public reaction.

airlift /'ɛəlɪft/, *n.* **1.** the carrying of people, supplies, etc., by aircraft when roads, etc., are blocked. ◇*v.t.* **2.** to move by airlift.

airline /'ɛəlaɪn/, *n.* a system or company providing regular flights for passengers or goods.

airliner /'ɛəlaɪnə/, *n.* a large passenger aircraft operated by an airline.

airlock /'ɛəlɒk/, *n.* **1.** an airtight compartment at the entrance of a chamber that has air under pressure, as in a spacecraft, where the airlock prevents that air escaping into space. **2.** *Engineering.* an air bubble in a pipe which stops the flow of liquid.

airmail /'ɛəmeɪl/, *n.* **1.** the system of sending mail by aircraft. **2.** mail sent by aircraft.

airman /'ɛəmən/, *n., pl.* **-men.** an air pilot, esp. a member of an air force.

air-mass /'ɛə-mæs/, *n.* a body of air which does not vary horizontally in temperature.

airplay /'ɛəpleɪ/, *n.* the amount of time given to broadcasting a recording.

air-pocket /'ɛə-pɒkət/, *n.* **1.** *Aeron.* a downward current of air, usu. causing an aircraft suddenly to fall some distance. **2.** a pocket of air which holds back a flow of gas or liquid, as in a mine.

airport /'ɛəpɔt/, *n.* a large area where aircraft land and take off, usu. with a control tower, hangars, and buildings for arriving and departing passengers and goods.

air-pressure /'ɛə-prɛʃə/, *n.* **1.** the pressure of the atmosphere. **2.** the pressure of air, as inside a tyre.

air-raid /'ɛə-reɪd/, *n.* an attack by enemy aircraft, esp. for dropping bombs.

airs /ɛəz/, *n.pl.* See **air** (def. 6).

airship /'ɛəʃɪp/, *n.* a self-propelled lighter-than-air craft.

airspace /'ɛəspeɪs/, *n.* the part of the atmosphere above a country or state which is considered the property of that country.

airspeed /'ɛəspid/, *n.* the speed of an aircraft relative to the air around it. See **ground speed.**

airstream /'ɛəstrim/, *n.* **1.** a flow or current of air. **2.** a wind, esp. one at a high altitude.

airstrip /'ɛəstrɪp/, *n.* an area of prepared ground on which to land an aeroplane, esp. in a remote place.

air terminal, *n.* a building in which air passengers come together before or after a flight.

airtight /'ɛətaɪt/, *adj.* closed or close so that air cannot enter: *an airtight container.*

airwaves /'ɛəweɪvz/, *n.pl.* (in non-technical use) use the air seen as a substance through which radio and television signals go.

airy /'ɛəri/, *adj.* **airier, airiest. 1.** open to a free current of air; breezy: *airy rooms.* **2.** light in appearance; thin: *airy lace.* **3.** light in manner or movement; lively; graceful: *an airy walk.* **4.** light as air; insubstantial; imaginary: *airy dreams.* **5.** careless; superficial; flippant: *an airy wave goodbye.* —**airiness,** *n.*

airy-fairy

airy-fairy /ˌeəri-ˈfeəri/, *adj. Colloq. (oft. disapproving)* fanciful.

AIS /eɪ aɪ ˈes/, *Abbrev.* → **Australian Illawarra Shorthorn.**

aisle /aɪl/, *n.* **1.** a clear path between seats in a church, hall, etc. **2.** *Archit.* one of two passages along the length of a church, cut off from the nave by piers or columns. [var. of *isle*, translation of late ML *insula* aisle (in L island)]

aitch /eɪtʃ/; *non-standard* /heɪtʃ/, *n.* the letter H, h.

ajar /əˈdʒɑ/, *adv.* neither quite open nor shut; partly opened: *Leave the door ajar.* [ME *on char* on the turn]

Ajax /ˈeɪdʒæks/, *n. Gk Legend.* **1.** a mighty warrior of the Greeks in the siege of Troy. He killed himself in disappointment when Achilles' armor was won by Odysseus. **2. the lesser Ajax**, a Locrian king, a hero in the Trojan War, second in speed only to Achilles.

AJC /eɪ dʒeɪ ˈsi/, *Abbrev.* Australian Jockey Club.

AK /eɪ ˈkeɪ/, *Abbrev.* Knight of the Order of Australia.

akela /əˈkeɪlə/, *n.* the person in charge of a pack of cubs in the Scout movement. [named after *Akela*, leader of the wolf pack in the *Jungle Book* of Rudyard Kipling]

Akhenaten /ˌækəˈnɑtən/, *n.* died *c.* 1357 BC, king of Egypt *c.* 1375 – *c.* 1357 BC; worshipped a single god, Aten; founded new capital at Tell el Amarna. Original name, **Amenhotep IV.** Also, **Akhenaton, Ikhanaton, Ikhnaton.**

Akihito /ˌækəˈhitoʊ/, *n.* born 1933, became Emperor of Japan in 1989.

akimbo /əˈkɪmboʊ/, *adv.* with hands on hip: *to stand with arms akimbo.* [ME]

akin /əˈkɪn/, *adj.* **1.** related by blood. **2.** related by nature or kind: *Tennis balls and oranges are akin in shape.* [A-[2] + KIN]

al-, variant of **ad-** before *l*, as in *allure*.

-al[1], an adjective suffix meaning 'of or relating to', 'connected with', 'of the nature of', 'like', 'suiting', etc., occurring in many adjectives and in many nouns of adjectival origin, as *annual, choral, equal, regal.* [L *-ālis* (neut. *-āle*) pertaining to]

-al[2], a suffix forming nouns of action from verbs, as in *refusal, denial, recital, trial.* [L *-āle* (pl. *-ālia*), neut. of adj. suffix *-ālis*]

-al[3], a suffix showing that a chemical compound includes an aldehyde group, as in *chloral.* [short for AL(DEHYDE)]

Al, *Chem. Symbol.* aluminium.

ala /ˈeɪlə/, *n.*, *pl.* **alae** /ˈeɪli/. a wing-like part, as of a bone, shell, seed, stem, etc. [L: wing]

Alabama /ˌæləˈbæmə/, *n.* a state in the south-eastern US. Pop. 4 053 000 (1986 est.); 133 667 km[2]. *Cap.*: Montgomery. *Abbrev.*: Ala. —**Alabamian, Alabaman,** *adj.*, *n.*

alabaster /ˈæləbæstə/, *n.* **1.** a fine variety of gypsum, often white and translucent, used for ornamental objects such as lamp bases, small statues, etc. ◇*adj.* **2.** made of alabaster. **3.** like alabaster; smooth and white: *her alabaster throat.* [ME, from L, from Gk: an alabaster box]

à la carte /a la ˈkat/, *adj., adv.* according to a menu which gives a price for each dish: *dinner à la carte.* [F]

alacrity /əˈlækrəti/, *n.* **1.** energy; liveliness; briskness. **2.** cheerful willingness. [L] —**alacritous,** *adj.*

Aladdin /əˈlædən/, *n.* a character in *The Arabian Nights' Entertainment*, who becomes the possessor of a magic lamp and ring, with which he commands two genies.

Alamo /ˈæləmoʊ/, *n.* a mission building in San Antonio, Texas, which underwent a terrible siege by Mexicans in February 1836, was taken on 6 March, and its entire garrison of US rebels killed.

Alaric /ˈælərɪk/, *n.* AD *c.* 370–410, king of the Visigoths; captured Rome 410.

alarm /əˈlɑm/, *n.* **1.** a sudden fear or painful suspense caused by recognition of danger; apprehension; fright. **2.** any sound or message to warn of approaching danger: *a false alarm; to give the alarm.* **3.** (a sound from) a device of any kind used to call attention, wake from sleep, warn of danger, etc. ◇*v.t.* to fill with sudden fear or worry. [ME, from OF, from It.: tumult, fright, from *al l'arme* to arms]

alarm clock, /ˈ- klɒk/, *n.* a clock which can be set to make a noise at a particular time to wake people from sleep.

alarmist /əˈlɑmɪst/, *n.* a person who raises an alarm, esp. making the danger seem greater than it really is.

alas /əˈlæs, əˈlɑs/, *interj.* (an exclamation of sorrow, pity, concern, or recognition of evil.) [ME, from OF *a, ha* ah + *las* miserable, from L *lassus* weary]

alaska /əˈlæskə/, *n.* a baked ice-cream dessert, usu. made on a sponge cake base, with fruit or other flavoring, the whole enclosed in meringue.

Alaska /əˈlæskə/, *n.* a state of the US in north-western North America. Pop. 534 000 (1986 est.); 1 518 776 km[2]. *Cap.*: Juneau. *Abbrev.*: Alas. —**Alaskan,** *adj., n.*

alb /ælb/, *n.* a white linen robe, worn by priests. [OE, from L *alba* (*vestis*) white (garment)]

Albania /ælˈbeɪniə/, *n.* a republic in south-eastern Europe, bordered by Yugoslavia, Macedonia, Greece and the Adriatic and Ionian Seas; gained independence from Turkish rule in 1912; a socialist republic 1946–90; parliamentary democracy from 1991. Pop. 2 841 300 (1983 est.); 28 748 km[2]. *Language*: Albanian. *Currency*: lek. *Cap.*: Tirana. Official name, **People's Republic of Albania.** —**Albanian,** *adj., n.*

Albany /ˈælbəni/, *n.* **1.** a town in south-western WA, on King George Sound; a major port. Pop. 16 316 (1986).

albatross /ˈælbətrɒs/, *n.* any of various large web-footed seabirds related to the petrels, of the Pacific and southern waters, noted for

albatross   24   **Alexander**

their powers of flight. [var. of *algatross*, from Pg. *alcatraz* seafowl, cormorant; change of -*g*- to -*b*- ? by association with L *alba* white (the bird's color)]

albeit /ɔl'biːt,fflæl-/, *conj.* although: *a necessary albeit cowardly course.* [ME *al be it* although it be]

Albert /'ælbət/, *n.* Prince (*Francis Charles Augustus Albert Emmanuel, Prince of Saxe-Coburg-Gotha*), 1819–61, German prince, husband of Queen Victoria; known as Prince Consort.

Albert Edward /ælbət 'edwəd/, Mount, a mountain in PNG, in the Owen Stanley Ranges. 3990 m.

albino /æl'biːnoʊ/, *n., pl.* -**nos.** **1.** a person with a pale, milky skin, light hair, and pink eyes, resulting from an absence of pigmentation (coloring matter). **2.** an animal or plant with a marked absence of coloring. [Pg., from L: white] —**albino,** *adj.* —**albinism,** *n.*

Albion /'ælbiən/, *n. Poetic.* Britain. [L, said to be derived from *albus* white]

album /'ælbəm/, *n.* **1.** a book with blank leaves on which photographs, stamps, etc., can be fixed. **2.** a book of specially chosen things as songs, stories, etc. **3.** a folder for holding gramophone records. **4.** a long-playing recording on which there is a collection of songs or pieces. [L]

albumen /'ælbjəmən/, *n.* **1.** the white of an egg. **2.** *Bot.* the matter about the embryo in a seed which is its food. **3.** *Biochem.* → **albumin.** [L (def. 1), from *albus* white]

albumin /'ælbjəmən/, *n.* any of a class of water-soluble proteins found in milk, egg, blood and in animal and vegetable tissues. [L] —**albuminous,** *adj.*

Albuquerque /'ælbəkəːki/, *n.* **Afonso de**, 1453–1515, Portuguese navigator; founded the Portuguese empire in the Indian Ocean.

Albury-Wodonga /ˌɒlbəri-wə'dɒŋgə/, *n.* a regional urban growth centre on the Murray River, formed in 1974 by the cities of Albury, NSW, on the north bank and Wodonga, Vic, on the south bank. Pop. 58 082 (1986).

Alcazar /ælkə'zɑ/, *n.* the palace of the Moorish kings (later, of Spanish royalty) at Seville.

alchemy /'ælkəmi/, *n.* the medieval form of chemistry which tried to find ways of changing all metals into gold. [ME, from OF, from ML, from Ar.] —**alchemist,** *n.* —**alchemic, alchemical,** *adj.*

alcheringa /æltʃə'rɪŋgə/, *n.* → **Dreamtime.** Also, **alchera** /'æltʃərə/. [Aboriginal]

Alcibiades /ælsə'baɪədiz/, *n.* 450?–404 BC, Athenian politician and general.

Alcock /'ɔlkɒk/, *n.* **Sir John William**, 1892–1919, English aviator; made the first flight across the Atlantic with AW Brown in 1919.

alcohol /'ælkəhɒl/, *n.* **1.** a colorless, flammable liquid (**ethanol** or **ethyl alcohol**, C_2H_5OH), the intoxicating part of alcoholic drinks, formed from some sugars (esp. glucose) by fermentation, now usu. prepared by treating grain with malt and adding yeast. **2.** any drink containing this spirit. **3.** *Chem.* any of a class of chemical compounds having the formula ROH, where R represents an alkyl group, derived from the hydrocarbon by replacement of a hydrogen atom by the hydroxyl radical, OH. [ML: orig., fine powder; hence, essence, from Ar.: the powdered antimony, kohl]

alcoholic /ælkə'hɒlɪk/, *adj.* **1.** relating to or containing alcohol. **2.** caused by alcohol: *alcoholic poisoning.* **3.** suffering from alcoholism. ◇*n.* **4.** a person suffering from alcoholism.

alcoholism /'ælkəhɒlɪzəm/, *n.* a diseased condition resulting from long-term excessive use of alcoholic drinks.

Alcott /'ɔlkət, -kɒt/, *n.* **Louisa May**, 1832–88, US author, best known for her novel *Little Women* (1868).

alcove /'ælkoʊv/, *n.* **1.** a small area set back or receding from a room, often for a bed, for books in a library, etc. **2.** such a space, as for chairs, in a garden. [F, from Sp., from Ar.]

Ald., *Abbrev.* Alderman. Also, **ald.**

aldehyde /'ældəhaɪd/, *n.* one of a group of organic compounds with the formula R-CHO, which produce acids when oxidised and alcohols when reduced. See -**al**[3]. [NL: alcohol deprived of hydrogen]

alderman /'ɔldəmən/, *n., pl.* -**men.** a local government representative elected by people living in a municipality. [OE, from *ealdor* chief, elder + *mann* man]

Alderney /'ɔldəni/, *n.* one of a breed of cattle such as Jersey or Guernsey cattle. [named after *Alderney*, the northernmost of the islands in the English Channel]

alderwoman /'ɔldəwʊmən/, *n., pl.* -**men.** a female local government representative.

Aldrin /'ɔldrən/, *n.* **Edwin Eugene** ('*Buzz*'), born 1930, US astronaut; as a crew member of Apollo 11, the second person to walk on the moon.

ale /eɪl/, *n.* **1.** any of various English types of beer brewed by the top fermentation method. **2.** any beer. [OE]

aleph /'ɑləf/, *n.* the first letter in the Hebrew alphabet (×).

alert /ə'lɜt/, *adj.* **1.** very attentive: *an alert mind.* **2.** quick to react; nimble. ◇*n.* **3.** an air-raid warning. **4. on the alert,** ready for danger; watchful. **5. red alert,** state of being ready to meet an attack or emergency. ◇*v.t.* **6.** to warn of an attack or raid. [F, from It.: on the lookout] —**alerted,** *adj.* —**alertly,** *adv.* —**alertness,** *n.*

Aleutian Islands /ə'luʃən ˈaɪləndz/, *n.pl.* an archipelago extending west between the Bering Sea and the Pacific Ocean for about 1900 km; a part of Alaska. Also, **Aleutians.**

Alexander /ælɪg'zændə, -'zæn-/, *n.* name of eight popes, notably Alexander VI (*Roderigo Lanzol y Borgia*), 1431?–1503, pope 1492–1503.

Alexander the Great, *n.* 356–323 BC, king of Macedonia 336–323 BC; conqueror of Greek city-states and Persian Empire from Asia Minor and Egypt to India.

Alexandria /ˌælɡˈzændriə, -ˈzan-/, *n.* **1.** Arabic, **Al-Iskandariyah.** port in northern Egypt, on the Nile delta; founded by Alexander the Great, 332 BC; ancient seat of learning, famous for its library. Pop. 2 201 000 (1975). **2.** a cattle station in the eastern NT, on the Barkly Tableland. 16 400 km².

Alexandrine /ˌælɪɡˈzændrɪn, -drɪm/, *n.* **1.** *Poetry.* a verse or line of poetry of six iambic feet **2.** (in French poetry) a verse of alternate couplets of twelve and thirteen syllables. [F *alexandrin*, from poems in this metre about ALEXANDER THE GREAT]

alfalfa /ælˈfælfə/, *n.* *Chiefly US.* → lucerne.

al fine /æl ˈfiːni/, *adv.* (a musical direction) to the end. [It.]

Alfred the Great /ˈælfrəd/, *n.* AD 849–899, king of England, 871–899; defeated invading Danes and established the rule of the West Saxon royal house, built the first English fleet, encouraged education, and translated several Latin works into English.

alfresco /ælˈfrɛskoʊ/, *adv.* **1.** in the open air; out-of-doors: *to dine alfresco.* ◇*adj.* **2.** open-air: *an alfresco cafe.* [It.: in the cool]

alga /ˈælɡə/, *n.*, *pl.* **-gae** /-dʒiː/. any of the chlorophyll-containing one- or many-celled plants to which belong the sea-weed and various other forms which grow near the water. [L: seaweed] –**algal,** *adj.*

algebra /ˈældʒəbrə/, *n.* **1.** the branch of mathematics which uses letters to stand for numbers in order to generalise mathematical processes. **2.** any special system of notation (signs and symbols) adapted to the study of a special system of relationships. **3.** *Maths.* **a.** the study of mathematical systems having operations similar to those of addition and multiplication. **b.** the name given to particular systems of the above type: *vector algebra, matrix algebra.* [ML, from Ar.: bone-setting, reunification (referring to the solving of algebraic equations)] –**algebraist,** *n.*

algebraic /ˌældʒəˈbreɪk/, *adj.* **1.** relating to or occurring in algebra. **2.** *Maths.* (of a number) satisfying a polynomial equation with integral coefficients: $\sqrt{2}$ *is algebraic as it satisfies the equation* $x^2 - 2 = 0$. Also, **algebraical.** –**algebraically,** *adv.*

algebraic sum, *n.* the total of a number of quantities of the same kind, taking the sign into account: *The algebraic sum of 4, −6 and −1 is −3.*

Algeria /ælˈdʒɪəriə/, *n.* a republic in north-western Africa, on the Mediterranean sea; a French colony before independence in 1962. Pop. 22 971 558 (1987); 2 381 741 km². *Languages:* Arabic, also French and Berber. *Currency:* dinar. *Cap.:* Algiers. French, **Algérie.** –**Algerian, Algerine,** *n.*, *adj.*

-algia, a noun suffix meaning 'pain', as in *neuralgia.* [NL, from Gk]

Algiers /ælˈdʒɪəz/, *n.* a seaport in and the capital of Algeria, in the northern part. Pop. 1 483 000 (1987 est.). Arabic, **El Djazaïr.**

ALGOL /ˈælɡɒl/, *n.* a language in which computer programs are written, in algebraic notation. Also, **Algol.** [ALGO(RITHMIC) + L(ANGUAGE)]

algorism /ˈælɡərɪzəm/, **1.** the art of calculating with the Arabic figures, one to nine, plus the zero; arithmetic. **2.** →**algorithm.** [ME, from Ar. *al Khwārizmī* the native of *Khwārizm* Khiva (i.e. *Abū Ja'far Mohammed ibn Mūsā*, 9th C Arab mathematician, author of a famous treatise on algebra translated into ML]

algorithm /ˈælɡərɪðəm/, *n.* an effective method for solving a particular mathematical problem in a certain limited number of steps. Also, **algorism.** [var. of ALGORISM by association with ARITHMETIC] –**algorithmic** /ˌælɡəˈrɪðmɪk/, *adj.*

alias /ˈeɪliəs/, *adv.*, *n.*, *pl.* **aliases.** ◇*adv.* **1.** otherwise; also called. ◇*n.* **2.** a false name. [L: at another time or place]

Ali Baba /ˌæli ˈbɑːbə/, *n.* the poor woodcutter, hero of a tale in *The Arabian Nights' Entertainment*, who uses the magic words 'open sesame' to open the door to the wealth in the cave of the Forty Thieves.

alibi /ˈæləbaɪ/, *n.*, *pl.* **-bis.** **1.** *Law.* (evidence in) a defence by an accused person that he was elsewhere at the time the offence was committed. **2.** *Colloq.* an excuse. [L: elsewhere]

Alice Springs /ˌæləs ˈsprɪŋz/, *n.* a town in central Australia in the southern part of the NT; on the Todd River and on a plain in the MacDonnell Ranges; surveyed in 1888 and officially called Stuart until 1933. Pop. 22 759 (1986). Also, **the Alice.** [named after *Alice Todd*, wife of Sir Charles TODD]

alien /ˈeɪliən/, *n.* **1.** someone born in another country who has not acquired citizenship by naturalisation. **2.** a foreigner. **3.** someone who has been shut out or excluded; an outsider. ◇*adj.* **4.** belonging or relating to aliens: *alien property.* **5.** not belonging; foreign; strange: *alien speech.* **6.** opposed; incompatible; repugnant (fol. by *to*): *ideas alien to our way of thinking.* [ME, from L: belonging to another]

alienate /ˈeɪliəneɪt/, *v.t.*, **-nated, -nating.** **1.** to cause (someone) to be unfriendly. **2.** to turn away: *to alienate the affections.* **3.** *Law.* to hand over or convey, as title, property, or other right, to another: *to alienate lands.* [L: estranged] –**alienation,** *n.* –**alienator,** *n.*

alight[1] /əˈlaɪt/, *v.i.*, **alighted** or **alit** /əˈlɪt/, **alighting.** **1.** to get down from a horse or out of a vehicle; dismount. **2.** to settle or stay after descending: *a bird alights on a tree.* **3.** to come accidentally, or without design (fol. by *on* or *upon*): *Walking through the park you will alight upon places of great beauty.* [OE]

alight[2] /əˈlaɪt/, *adj.* lighted up; burning. [ME]

align /əˈlaɪn/, *v.t.* **1.** to lay out or regulate by line; form in line: *align the troops.* **2.** to

align

bring into line: *align the picture on the wall; align oneself with current practice.* [F] **—aligner,** *n.*

alignment /ə'laɪnmənt/, *n.* **1.** the act or result of arranging in a line: *the alignment of that picture is wrong.* **2.** a taking of sides; joining a group, party or cause: *His alignment is with the Labor Party.*

alike /ə'laɪk/, *adv.* **1.** in the same manner; equally: *known to treat all customers alike.* ◇*adj.* **2.** having a great deal in common; similar: *He thinks all politicians are alike.* [ME, from Scand.]

aliment /'æləmənt/, *n.*; /'æləment/, *v.* ◇*n.* **1.** food. **2.** support. ◇*v.t.* **3.** to support; sustain. [L: food] **—alimental,** *adj.* **—alimentally,** *adv.*

alimentary /ælə'mentri/, *adj.* relating to food or nutrition.

alimentary canal, *n.* the digestive passage in any animal from the mouth to the anus.

alimony /'æləməni/, *n.* →**maintenance** (def. 3).

A-line /'eɪ-laɪn/, *adj.* (of a dress, skirt, etc.) gradually widening from the shoulders or waist; flared.

aliphatic /ælə'fætɪk/, *adj.* having to do with those organic compounds which are open chains, as the alkanes. [Gk]

alive /ə'laɪv/, *adj.* **1.** in life or existence; living. **2.** in a state of action; in force or operation: *keep a memory alive.* **3.** full of life; lively: *alive with excitement.* **4.** filled as with living things; swarming; teeming: *The place was alive with ants.* **5. alive to,** aware of; recognising: *alive to the possibility of defeat.* [OE *on life* in life]

alkali /'ælkəlaɪ/, *n., pl.* **-lis, -lies. 1.** *Chem.* any of various bases, the hydroxides of Group I and II elements and of ammonia, which dissociate in water, etc., to provide hydroxyl ions (OH⁻), and neutralise acids to form salts and water. **2.** *Agric.* a soluble mineral salt, or a mixture of soluble salts, occurring in soils, etc., usu. damaging crops. [ME, from Ar.: ashes of certain beach plants] **—alkalify,** *v.* **—alkaline,** *adj.* **—alkalinity,** *n.*

alkali metal, *n.* a monovalent metal, one of the first group of the periodic table, including potassium, sodium, lithium, rubidium, caesium, and francium, whose hydroxides are alkalis.

alkaline-earth metal, /ˌælkəlaɪn-ɜθ 'metəl/ *n.* a bivalent metal, one of the second group of the periodic table including beryllium, magnesium, calcium, strontium, barium, and radium.

alkaloid /'ælkəlɔɪd/, *n.* **1.** one of a class of basic nitrogenous organic compounds found in plants, such as nicotine, atropine, morphine, or quinine. ◇*adj.* **2.** Also, **alkaloidal** /ælkə'lɔɪdl/. acting like an alkali; alkaline.

alkane /'ælkeɪn/, *n.* any member of the alkane series.

alkane series, *n.* a series of saturated hydrocarbons which are open chains and which have the general formula C_nH_{2n+2}, e.g.

allegation

methane (CH_4), ethane (C_2H_6), propane (C_3H_8), etc.; methane series.

alkene /'ælkin/, *n.* any member of the alkene series.

alkene series, *n.* a series of unsaturated hydrocarbons which are open chains with a double bond present, and which have the general formula C_nH_{2n}, e.g. ethene (C_2H_4), propene (C_3H_6), etc.

alkyl group /'ælkəl grʌp/, *n.* a univalent group or radical derived from an alkane by removal of a hydrogen atom, having the formula C_nH_{2n+1}. Also, **alkyl radical.** [ALK(ALI) + -YL]

alkyne /'ælkaɪn/, *n.* any member of the alkyne series. Also, **alkine.**

alkyne series, *n.* a series of unsaturated hydrocarbons which are open chains with one triple bond, which have the general formula C_nH_{2n-2}, e.g. ethyne (C_2H_2), propyne (C_3H_4), etc.

all /ɔl/, *adj.* **1.** the whole of (with reference to quantity, extent, duration, amount, or degree): *all Australian; all year round.* **2.** the whole number of: *all these books are mine.* **3.** a large number of; many (chiefly with *kind, sorts, manner*): *all kinds of people.* **4.** any; any whatever: *beyond all doubt.* **5.** greatest possible: *with all speed.* ◇*pron.* **6.** whole quantity or amount: *to eat all of something.* **7.** whole number: *all of us.* **8.** everything: *Is that all?* ◇*n.* **9.** a whole; everything; totality. **10.** Some special uses are: **above all,** before everything else.

after all, 1. after everything has been considered; not withstanding. **2.** in spite of everything that was done, said, etc.: *He lost the fight after all.*

all in all, (taking) everything together, as a whole.

at all, 1. in any degree: *not bad at all.* **2.** in any way: *no offence at all.*

for good and all, forever; finally.

in all, all included: *100 people in all.*

once (and) for all, for the final time.

◇*adv.* **11.** wholly; entirely; quite: *all alone.* **12.** only; exclusively: *He spent his income all on pleasure.* **13.** each; apiece: *the score was one all.* **14.** by so much; to that extent (fol. by *the* and a comparative adjective): *Rain made conditions all the worse.* [OE *all, eall*]

all-, variant of **allo-** before vowels.

Allah /'ælə/, *n.* the Muslim name for God. [Ar. *Allāh,* contraction of *al ilāh* the God]

Allan-a-Dale /ˌælən-ə-'deɪl/, *n.* (in English ballads) a youth, friend of Robin Hood, who stopped his sweetheart from marrying an aged knight and took her for his own bride.

allay /ə'leɪ/, *v.t.* **-layed, -laying. 1.** to put at rest; quiet (fear, suspicion, etc.). **2.** to make less bad; relieve; alleviate: *to allay pain.* [OE: put down, suppress, from *ā-* A-³ + *lecgan* lay] **—allayer,** *n.*

all clear, *n.* a signal which indicates that dangers or obstructions have been removed and that it is safe to start or continue a journey, etc.

allegation /ælə'geɪʃən/, *n.* **1.** a claim made without proof. **2.** a statement offered as a plea, excuse, or justification. **3.** a statement

allegation

made by a person or party in court which they attempt to prove. [ME, from L]

allege /əˈledʒ/, v.t., **-leged, -leging. 1.** to claim without proof. **2.** to declare positively; affirm; assert. **3.** to argue in support of; urge as reason or excuse. [ME, from L] —**alleger**, n. —**alleged**, adj.

allegiance /əˈlidʒəns/, n. **1.** the duty of subject or citizen to country or government; *He promised allegiance to the Queen.* **2.** faithfulness to person, thing or cause. [ME, from OF]

allegory /ˈæləgəri, -gri/, n., pl. **-ries.** a story, poem, etc., in which events and characters have symbolic meaning. [ME, from L, from Gk] —**allegorical**, adj.

allegretto /æləˈgrɛtoʊ/, adv. (musical direction) in rapid tempo (speed). [It., diminutive of *allegro* ALLEGRO]

allegro /əˈleɪgroʊ/, adv. (musical direction) in rapid tempo (speed). [It., from L: brisk]

allelomorph /əˈliləmɔf, əˈlɛlə-/, n. one of two or more genes at the same locus (position)of homologous chromosomes, causing contrasting Mendelian characters.

alleluia /æləˈlujə/, interj. **1.** praise to the Lord; hallelujah. ◇n. **2.** a song of praise to God. [L, from Gk, from Heb.: praise ye Jehovah]

Allen /ˈælən/, n. **Woody** (*Allen Stewart Konigsberg*), born 1935, US comedian, film director and actor; won Academy Award for *Annie Hall* (1977).

allergen /ˈælədʒən/, n. any substance which might cause an allergy. [ALLER(GY) + -GEN] —**allergenic**, adj.

allergy /ˈælədʒi/, n., pl. **-gies.** a state of physical sensitivity to certain things normally harmless, as pollens, food, fruits, etc. [NL, from Gk] —**allergic**, adj.

alleviate /əˈliviːeɪt/, v.t., **-ated, -ating.** to make (pain, punishment, etc.) easier to be accepted; lessen; mitigate: *to alleviate sorrow*. [LL] —**alleviator**, n. —**alleviation**, n.

alley¹ /ˈæli/, n., pl. **alleys. 1.** Also, **alleyway.** a narrow back street or walkway, usu. between or behind a row of buildings; lane. **2.** a long narrow enclosure with a smooth wooden floor for games such as bowling, etc. **3. up one's alley**, perfectly suited to one's tastes or skills. [ME, from OF: a going, passage, from *aler* go]

alley² /ˈæli/, n., pl. **alleys.** a large playing marble. [diminutive abbrev. of ALABASTER]

alliance /əˈlaɪəns/, n. **1.** the state of being allied or connected. **2.** a marriage, or union brought about between families through marriage. **3.** a formal agreement by two or more nations to work together for special purposes. **4.** a joining of efforts or interests by persons, families, states, or organisations: *an alliance between church and state*. [ME, from OF]

allied /ˈælaɪd/, adj. **1.** joined by treaty (political agreement). **2.** related: *allied species*. **3.** (*cap.*) relating to the Allies.

allied angles, n.pl. *Maths.* a pair of angles formed by the intersection of two parallel lines with a transversal, so that both angles lie on the same side of the transversal and are between the parallel lines; co-interior angles.

allies /ˈælaɪz/, n.pl. plural of **ally.**

Allies /ˈælaɪz/, n.pl. **1.** (in World War I) the nations of the Triple Entente (Great Britain, France, Russia) and the nations allied with them (Belgium, Serbia, Japan, Italy, etc., not including the US), as opposed to Germany and Austria-Hungary. **2.** (in World War II) the countries that fought against the Axis powers.

alligator /ˈæləgeɪtə/, n. **1.** a reptile like the crocodile, found in the south-eastern US. **2.** *Colloq.* a crocodile found elsewhere, as the Australian sea-going crocodile. [Sp. *el lagarto* the lizard, from L: lizard]

Alligator /ˈæləgeɪtə/, n. the name of three rivers in the north-western NT which all flow into Van Diemen Gulf. **1. East Alligator** flows north-west from Arnhem Land. 160 km. **2. South Alligator** flows northward from the region of Mount Stow. 160 km. **3. West Alligator** flows due north parallel to the South Alligator River. 80 km.

alliteration /əlɪtəˈreɪʃən/, n. **1.** the repeated use of one consonant, as in *suspicious signs*. **2.** the commencement of two or more words of a word group with the same letter, as in *apt alliteration's artful aid*. See **assonance.** [AL- + L *lītera* letter + -ATION] —**alliterative**, adj.

allo-, word part indicating difference or variation, as in *allotrope.* Also, **all-.** [Gk, combining form of *állos* other]

allocate /ˈæləkeɪt/, v.t., **-cated, -cating. 1.** to set apart for a particular purpose; assign; allot: *to allocate shares*. **2.** to fix the place of; locate. [ML, from L *al-* AL- + *locāre* place] —**allocation**, n.

all-ordinaries index, /ˌɔl-ˌɔdənəriz ˈɪndɛks/, n. a weighted average given by a stock exchange of ordinary share prices of a particular group of companies expressed in relation to a base period. Also, **all-ords.**

allot /əˈlɒt/, v.t., **-lotted, -lotting. 1.** to divide or distribute as by lot; hand out; distribute; apportion: *to allot shares*. **2.** to set apart for a special purpose: *to allot money for a new park*. **3.** to give as a share (*to*); appoint: *I will allot two hours to maths, two to English*. [MF *a to* + *loter* divide by lot]

allotment /əˈlɒtmənt/, n. **1.** a section, share, or thing allotted. **2.** a block of land: *vacant allotment*.

allotrope /ˈælətroʊp/, n. one of two or more forms of a chemical element: *Charcoal, graphite and diamond are allotropes of carbon*. —**allotropic**, adj.

all-out /ˈɔl-aʊt/, adj. using all one's resources; complete; total: *an all-out effort*.

allow /əˈlaʊ/, v.t. **1.** to give permission to or for; permit: *to allow students to be absent*. **2.** to give as one's share or as suited to one's needs; assign: *to allow someone $100 for spending money*. **3.** to permit (without meaning to) by neglect or mistake: *to allow an error to occur*. **4.** to admit; acknowledge; concede: *to allow a*

allow

claim. **5.** to take into account; set apart; deduct: *to allow an hour for changing trains.* ◇*v.* **6. allow for,** to take into consideration; make room; provide for: *to allow for breakage.* [ME, from OF: assign] —**allowed,** *adj.* —**allowable,** *adj.*

allowance /ə'laυəns/, *n.* **1.** a definite amount or share given or set apart; ration. **2.** acceptance; admission: *the allowance of a claim.* **3.** tolerance: *We made allowance for his youth.* **4.** *Mech.* a prescribed variation in dimensions (size). See **tolerance.**

alloy /'ælɔɪ, *n.*; /ə'lɔɪ, 'ælɔɪ/, *v.* ◇*n.* **1.** a substance consisting of two or more metals mixed by fusion, electrolytic deposition, etc. **2.** a less costly metal mixed with more valuable one. ◇*v.t.* **3.** to reduce the value of, by adding something; debase; impair. [OF, from L: combine]

all right, /ɔl 'raɪt / *adj.* **1.** safe and sound: *Are you all right?* **2.** satisfactory; acceptable: *His work is sometimes all right.* ◇*adv.* **3.** Also, **alright.** satisfactorily; acceptably; correctly: *He did his job all right.*

all-rounder /ɔl'raυndə/, *n.* **1.** a person able to do many things with equal competence (ability). **2.** *Sport.* someone skilled in all aspects of a game, as a cricketer who bowls, bats, and fields equally well.

All Saints' Day, *n.* a Christian festival celebrated on 1 November in honor of all the saints; Allhallows.

All Souls' Day, *n.* (in the Roman Catholic Church) a day of prayer for the souls of the dead, on 2 November.

allspice /'ɔlspaɪs/, *n.* a mildly sharp and sweet-smelling spice made from a tropical American berry; pimento.

allude /ə'lud/, *v.i.*, **-luded, -luding.** to speak of indirectly or casually (fol. by *to*). [L: play with]

allure /ə'lυə, ə'ljuə/, *v.*, **-lured, -luring.** *n.* ◇*v.t.* **1.** to attract or charm by an offer of some real or apparent good; tempt. ◇*n.* **2.** charm; fascination. [ME, from OF *a* to + *lurer* LURE] —**alluring,** *adj.*

allusion /ə'luʒən/, *n.* a passing or informal mention of something, often indirectly: *a classical allusion.* [L: playing with] —**allusive,** *adj.*

alluvial /ə'luviəl/, *adj.* **1.** relating to alluvium (a deposit of sand, mud, etc. by a river). **2.** relating to a mine, claim, diggings, etc., on alluvial soil. ◇*n.* **3.** gold-bearing alluvial ground. [L *alluvium* ALLUVIUM + -AL[1]]

alluvial fan, *n.* a fan-shaped alluvial deposit formed by a stream where its velocity is suddenly decreased, as at the mouth of a ravine or at the foot of a mountain. Also, **alluvial cone.**

alluvium /ə'luviəm/, *n., pl.* **-via** /-viə/, **-viums. 1.** a deposit of sand, mud, etc., formed by flowing water. **2.** sedimentary matter deposited in this way within recent times, esp. in valleys of large rivers. [L, neut. of *alluvius* washed towards]

ally /ə'laɪ/, *v.*, **-lied, lying.** /'ælaɪ/, *n., pl.* **-lies.** ◇*v.t.* **1.** to unite formally by marriage,

along

treaty, league, etc. (fol. by *to* or *with*). **2.** to bind together or relate, as by resemblance or friendship. ◇*v.i.* **3.** to enter into an agreement or alliance; join or unite. ◇*n.* **4.** someone or something united or associated with another, esp. a nation, by treaty. **5.** someone who helps or works with another; supporter; associate. [F, from L: bind to]

Alma-Ata /ælmə-'atə/, *n.* a city in the southern USSR in Asia; the capital of the Kazakh SSR. Pop. 1 088 000 (1986 est.). Formerly, **Verny.**

alma mater /ælmə 'meɪtə/, *n. Chiefly US.* (*sometimes caps*) the school, college, or university where one was taught. [L: fostering mother]

almanac /'ɔlmənæk, 'æl-/, *n.* a calendar giving the time of such events as sunrise and sunset, changes of the moon and tides, etc., or other special information. Also, **almanack.** [ME, from ML, from Sp., ? from Ar.]

almighty /ɔl'maɪti/, *adj.* **1.** possessing all power; omnipotent: *God Almighty.* **2.** having great power or authority: *the almighty power of the press.* **3.** *Colloq.* great; extreme: *He's in an almighty fix.* ◇*n.* **4. the Almighty,** God. [OE *ælmihtig, ealmihtig* all mighty] —**almightily,** *adv.* —**almightiness,** *n.*

almond /'amənd/, *n.* **1.** (a tree bearing) an edible nut. **2.** a delicate pale tan color. [ME, from L, from Gk]

almoner /'amənə/, *n.* **1.** a social worker with some medical training attached to a hospital. **2.** *Hist.* a person who dispenses (deals out) alms or charity. [ME, from LL *eleēmosyna* ALMS]

almost /'ɔlmoust/, *adv.* very nearly. [OE, *æl mæst* nearly]

alms /amz/, *n. sing. or pl.* that which is given to the poor or needy; charity. [OE, from LL, from Gk: compassion, alms]

aloe /'æloυ/, *n., pl.* **-oes.** an African plant which yields the drug (**aloes**) used as a purgative. [OE *aluwan*, from L, from Gk]

aloft /ə'lɔft/, *adv., adj.* **1.** high up; in or into the air; above ground. **2.** *Naut.* at or towards the masthead; in the upper rigging. [ME, from Scand.]

alone /ə'loυn/, *adj.* **1.** apart; by one's self: *to be alone.* **2.** only: *Man shall not live by bread alone.* **3. leave alone, a.** to allow (someone) to be by himself or herself. **b.** to not interfere with. ◇*adv.* **4.** apart from others. **5.** only; merely. **6. stand alone,** to be special because of one's ability, etc. [ME *al one* all (wholly) one] —**aloneness,** *n.*

along /ə'lɔŋ/, *prep.* **1.** through or for the length of; from one end to the other of: *to walk along a road.* **2.** by the length of: *a row of flowers along a path.* **3.** in agreement with: *along the lines suggested.* ◇*adv.* **4.** in a line; onwards. **5.** by the length; lengthways. **6.** in company, together (fol. by *with*): *I'll go along with you.* **7. all along,** all the time. **8. get along,** *Colloq.* **a.** to go; leave. **b.** to be on friendly terms. **c.** to manage successfully;

along 29 **alternate angles**

cope **9. go along with** to agree with. [OE *andland*]

alongside /əlɒŋˈsaɪd/, *adv.* **1.** along or by the side; at or to the side of anything: *We brought the boat alongside.* ◇*prep.* **2.** beside; by the side of.

aloof /əˈluːf/, *adv.* **1.** at a distance, but within view; withdrawn: *to stand aloof.* ◇*adj.* **2.** disinterested: unsympathetic; reserved. [A-¹ + *loof* LUFF, windward]

alopecia /æləˈpiːʃə/, *n.* loss of hair; baldness. [L, from Gk: mange of foxes]

aloud /əˈlaʊd/, *adv.* **1.** with the natural tone of voice: *to read aloud.* **2.** with a loud voice; loudly: *to cry aloud*

alp /ælp/, *n.* **1.** a high mountain. **2.** (*pl.*) a high mountain system, usu. covered with snow. **3. the Alps**, a mountain system in southern Europe, extending from France through Switzerland and Italy to Austria and Yugoslavia. Highest peak, Mont Blanc, 4807 m.

ALP /eɪ ɛl ˈpiː/, *Abbrev.* Australian Labor Party.

alpaca /ælˈpækə/, *n.* **1.** a domesticated South American animal related to the llama, having long, soft, silky hair or wool. **2.** the (fabric made from) hair of this animal. [Sp., from *paco*, Peruvian animal name (to which the Ar. article, *al*, has been prefixed)]

alpha /ˈælfə/, *n.* **1.** the first letter in the Greek alphabet (A, α), equal to A. **2.** the first; beginning. **3.** *Astron.* a star, usu. the brightest of a constellation.

alphabet /ˈælfəbɛt/, *n.* **1.** the letters of a language in their usual order. **2.** any system of characters or signs for representing sounds or ideas. [L, from Gk *álpha* A + *bêta* B]

alphabetical /ælfəˈbɛtɪkəl/, *adj.* **1.** in the order of the alphabet: *alphabetical arrangement.* **2.** relating to an alphabet. **–alphabetically**, *adv.*

alphabetise *or* **alphabetize** /ˈælfəbətaɪz/, *v.t.*, **-tised, -tising.** to arrange in order of the alphabet: *to alphabetise a list of names.* **–alphabetisation**, *n.*

Alpha Centauri /ælfə sɛnˈtɔːri/, *n.* the brightest star in the constellation Centaurus; second nearest star to the sun.

alpha decay, *n.* a radioactive disintegration in which alpha particles are emitted.

alphanumeric /ælfənjuˈmɛrɪk/, *adj.* (of a set of characters) conveying information by using both letters and numbers. Also, **alphanumerical.** [b. ALPHA(BET) + NUMERIC(AL)]

alpha particle, *n.* a positively charged particle made up of two protons and two neutrons (and therefore equivalent to the nucleus of a helium atom), given out by some radioactive substances when bombarded.

alpha radiation, *n.* radiation consisting of streams of alpha particles; alpha rays.

alpha ray, *n.* a stream of alpha particles.

alpine /ˈælpaɪn/, *adj.* **1.** relating to any high mountain. **2.** very high; elevated. **3.** *Bot.* (of plants etc.) growing on mountains, above the limit of tree growth. **4.** (*cap.*) *Geol.* concerned with the major mountain-building period which occurred in Europe and Northern Africa in the Tertiary period. [L *Alpīnus*, from the ALPS]

already /ɔlˈrɛdi/, *adv.* **1.** by or before this (or that) time: *Her bicycle had already been fixed.* **2.** sooner than expected: *You're not leaving already?* [ME *al redy* all ready]

Alsace-Lorraine /ælsæs-lɒˈreɪn/, *n.* an area in north-eastern France, including the regions, formerly provinces, of Alsace and Lorraine; a part of Germany 1871–1919 and 1940–44. 14 522 km². German, **Elsass-Lothringen.**

Alsatian /ælˈseɪʃən/, *n.* (*oft. l.c.*) → **German shepherd.**

also /ˈɔːlsoʊ/, *adv.* in addition; too; further. [OE *alswā, ealswā* all (wholly or quite) so]

also-ran /ˈɔːlsoʊ-ˌræn/, *n.* **1.** an unplaced horse in race. **2.** someone unimportant.

alt., *Abbrev.* **1.** alternate. **2.** altitude. **3.** alto.

Altamira /æltəˈmɪərə/, *n.* a cave in northern Spain famous for its Palaeolithic paintings of animals.

altar /ˈɔːltə, ˈɒl-/, *n.* **1.** an elevated place or structure, on which sacrifices are offered or on which religious ceremonies are performed. **2.** (in many Christian churches) a communion table. **3. lead to the altar**, to marry (a woman). [OE *altar(e)*, from LL]

Altdorf /ˈɑːltdɔːf/, *n.* a town in central Switzerland; the setting of the William Tell legend. Pop. 8647 (1970).

alter /ˈɔːltə, ˈɒl-/, *v.t.* **1.** to make different in some way; modify. ◇*v.i.* **2.** to become different in some respect. [F, from L: other]

alteration /ɔːltəˈreɪʃən, ɒl-/, *n.* **1.** the act of altering. **2.** the condition of being altered. **3.** a change; modification.

altercation /ɔːltəˈkeɪʃən, ɒl-/, *n.* a heated or angry argument; dispute; wrangle. **–altercative,** *adj.*

alter ego /æltər ˈiːgoʊ, ɒl-/, *n.* **1.** another side of oneself. **2.** a close friend. [L: lit., another I]

alternate /ˈɔːltəneɪt, ˈɒl-/, *v.*, **-nated, -nating;** /ɔlˈtɜːnət, ɒl-/, *adj.* ◇*v.i.* **1.** to follow one another in time or place (usu. fol. by *with*): *Day and night alternate with each other.* **2.** to change about by turns beween points, states, actions, etc.: *He alternates between hope and despair.* ◇*v.t.* **3.** to use or perform by turns, or one after another. ◇*adj.* **4.** arranged or following each after the other, in succession: *alternate winter and summer.* **5.** every other one of a series: *Read only alternate lines.* **6.** *Bot.* (of leaves, etc.) placed singly at different heights on the axis, on each side, in turn or at certain distances from one another. [L] **–alternately,** *adv.* **–alternation, alternateness,** *n.*

alternate angles, *n.pl. Maths.* a pair of equal angles formed by two parallel lines with a third line crossing both.

alternating current, /ˌɔltəneɪtɪŋ 'kʌrənt/ *n.* a current that reverses direction in regular cycles. *Abbrev.*: AC, a.c.

alternation of generations, *n. Biol.* an alternating in a single line of reproduction, between generations unlike and generations like a given ancestor, esp. the alternation of sexual with asexual reproduction.

alternative /ɔl'tɜnətɪv, ɒl-/, *n.* **1.** (a possibility of) one out of two or more things. **2.** a remaining course or choice. ◇*adj.* **3.** affording a choice between two things, or a possibility of one out of two. **4.** offering standards and types of behavior of a minority group within and opposed to an established Western society. [ML]

alternator /'ɔltəneɪtə, 'ɒl-/, *n.* a generator of alternating current.

although /ɔl'ðoʊ/, *conj.* even though. Also, **altho'**. [ME, from *al* even + THOUGH]

altimeter /'æltəmɪtə/, *n.* a sensitive type of barometer used in aircraft for recording altitude (height). — **altimetry,** *n.*

altitude /'æltətʃud/, *n.* **1.** the height above sea-level of any point on the earth's surface or in the atmosphere. **2. a.** *Astron.* the distance of a star, planet, etc., above the horizon. **b.** *Engin. etc.* the angle of elevation of any point above the horizon. **3.** *Geom.* (the length of) the perpendicular line from the base of a figure to its highest point. **4.** high point or region: *mountain altitudes.* [ME, from L: height]

alto /'æltoʊ/, *n., pl.* **-tos,** *adj.* ◇*n. Music.* **1.** a female singer in the lowest range; contralto. **2.** a particularly high male voice; countertenor. **3.** a musical part for an alto voice. ◇*adj.* **4.** in or relating to this range. [It., from L: high]

alto-, a word part meaning 'high'. Also, **alt-, alti-.** [combining form representing L *altus*]

alto clef, *n. Music.* a sign placing middle C on the third line of the stave.

altogether /ˌɔltə'geðə/, *adv.* **1.** wholly; entirely; completely; quite: *altogether bad.* **2.** in all: *His debt amounted to altogether to $20.* **3.** on the whole: *Altogether I'm glad it's over.* [ME *al* ALL, adj. + *togeder* TOGETHER]

alto-rilievo /ˌæltoʊ-rə'livoʊ/, *n., pl.* **-vos.** a sculpture in high relief, in which the figures stand out from the background by at least half their depth (opposed to *bas-relief*). Also, **alto-relievo.** [It.]

altruism /'æltruˌɪzəm/, *n.* the principle or practice of seeking the welfare of others (opposed to *egoism*). [F, from It.: of or to others] — **altruist,** *n.* — **altruistic,** *adj.*

alum /'æləm/, *n.* an astringent crystalline substance, a double sulphate of aluminium and potassium, and used in medicine, dyeing, and many technical processes. [ME, from L]

alumina /ə'lumənə/, *n. Mineral.* an oxide of aluminium, Al_2O_3. [NL, from L] — **aluminous,** *adj.*

aluminate /ə'lumənеɪt, əl'ju-/, *n.* **1.** *Chem.* the salt formed by the reaction of amphoteric aluminium hydroxide in an alkali, $Al(OH)_4^-$. See **-ate**[2]. **2.** *Mineral.* metallic oxide combined with alumina.

aluminium /ˌæljə'mɪniəm/, *n.* a silver-white light-weight metal that does not easily oxidise or tarnish, which is found in nature in igneous rocks, shales, clays, and most soils, and is often used in alloys. *Symbol:* Al; *at. wt:* 26.9815; *at. no.:* 13. [NL, from L *alūmen* alum]

alveolus /æl'viələs, ælvi'oʊləs/, *n., pl.* **-li** /-ˌlaɪ/. **1.** an air-cell of the lungs. **2.** a hollow inside of the jawbone in which the root of a tooth is set. [L, diminutive of *alveus* hollow] — **alveolar,** *adj.*

always /'ɔlweɪz, -wəz/, *adv.* **1.** all the time; without interruption. **2.** every time; on every occasion: *He always works on Saturday.* [ME]

alyssum /ə'lɪsəm/, *n.* a low-growing garden plant which has small yellow, blue, or white flowers. [NL, from Gk name of a plant, lit., curing (canine) madness]

Alzheimer's disease /'æltshaɪməz dəˌzɪz/, *n.* a progressive, organic disease involving degeneration of the brain, resulting in confusion and disorientation. [named after Alois *Alzheimer*, 1864–1915, German physician]

am /æm/, *weak forms* /əm, m/, *v.* 1st person singular present indicative of **be**. [OE *eom*]

a.m. /eɪ 'ɛm/, *Abbrev.* **1.** before noon. **2.** the period from 12 midnight to 12 noon. [L *ante merīdiem*]

Am, *Chem. Symbol.* americium.

AM /eɪ 'ɛm/, *Abbrev.* **1.** amplitude modulation. **2.** Member of the Order of Australia.

AMA /eɪ ɛm 'eɪ/, *Abbrev.* Australian Medical Association.

amalgam /ə'mælgəm/, *n.* **1.** a mixture or combination. **2.** an alloy of mercury mixed with another metal or metals. **3.** a rare mineral, an alloy of silver and mercury, occurring as silver-white crystals or grains. [ME, from L: poultice, from Gk]

amalgamate /ə'mælgəmeɪt/, *v.,* **-mated, -mating.** ◇*v.t.* **1.** to mix so as to make a combination; unite; combine: *to amalgamate two businesses.* **2.** *Metall.* to mix or alloy (a metal) with mercury. ◇*v.i.* **3.** to combine, unite, or grow together; coalesce. — **amalgamation,** *n.*

amanuensis /əˌmænju'ɛnsəs/, *n., pl.* **-ses** /-siz/. a person employed to take down what another dictates, etc.; secretary. [L: secretary, orig. adj., from (*servus*) ā *manū* secretary + *-ensis* belonging to]

amaranth /'æmərænθ/, *n.* **1.** *Poetic.* a flower that never fades. **2.** any of group of herbs or small shrubs which are grown for their showy flowers or colored leaves. [L, from Gk: unfading] — **amaranthine,** *adj.*

amass /ə'mæs/, *v.t.* **1.** to gather for oneself: *to amass a fortune.* **2.** to collect into a mass or pile; bring together. [F, from L: lump (of dough, etc.)] — **amassable,** *adj.* — **amasser,** *n.* — **amassment,** *n.*

amateur — amend

amateur /'æmətə, 'æmətʃə/, *n.* **1.** someone who cultivates any study or art or other activity for enjoyment instead of professionally or for gain. **2.** an athlete who has never competed for money. **3.** an unskilled person or one with only slight knowledge of the job. [F, from L: lover] —**amateurish**, *adj.* —**amateurism**, *n.*

amatory /'æmətri/, *adj.* relating to lovers or lovemaking; expressive of love: *amatory poems; an amatory look.* [L *amātōrius*]

amaze /ə'meɪz/, *v.t.* to fill with surprise; astonish. [OE *āmasian*] —**amazement**, *n.* —**amazing**, *adj.*

Amazon /'æməzən/, *n.* **1.** a river in northern South America, flowing from the Peruvian Andes east through northern Brazil to the Atlantic; the largest river in the world; about 6570 km. **2.** *Gk Legend.* one of a race of female warriors said to dwell near the Black Sea. **3.** one of a mythical tribe of female warriors in South America. **4.** (*l.c.*) a tall, physically strong woman. [(def. 2) ME, from L, from Gk, ult. orig. uncert.; the name of the river refers to female warriors seen in its vicinity] —**Amazonian**, *adj.*

ambassador /æm'bæsədə/, *n.* **1.** a diplomatic minister of the highest rank who represents his or her country's interests in another country. **2.** an acceptable messenger or representative. **3.** a person of some personal fame as an athlete, actor, etc., who wins goodwill for their country in another: *She was a real ambassador for Australia when she played in Sweden.* [ME, from F, from It. *ambasciatore*; probably of Celtic origin] —**ambassadorial**, *adj.*

amber /'æmbə/, *n.* **1.** a yellow, sometimes reddish or brownish, fossil resin of vegetable origin, not transparent, and able to gain a negative electrical charge by friction. **2.** a yellowish brown colour. **3.** an amber light used as a warning in traffic signals, etc. ◊*adj.* **4.** like or of amber. [ME, from ML, from Ar.]

ambergris /'æmbəgris, -gris/, *n.* an opaque, ash-colored substance, which comes from the intestines of a sperm whale, usu. found floating on the ocean or found ashore, used chiefly in perfumes. [late ME, from F *ambre gris* grey amber]

amberjack /'æmbədʒæk/, *n.* a sportfish of the Great Barrier Reef, closely related to the yellowtail kingfish.

ambi-, a word part meaning 'both', 'around', 'on both sides', as in *ambidextrous*. [combining form representing L *ambi-* around, or *ambo* both]

ambidextrous /æmbi'dekstrəs/, *adj.* **1.** able to use both hands equally well. **2.** unusually skilful; facile. —**ambidexterity**, *n.*

ambience /'æmbiəns/, *n.* **1.** the surrounding atmosphere; environment. **2.** the mood, character, quality, atmosphere, etc., as of a place or setting. [F]

ambient /'æmbiənt/, *adj.* completely surrounding: *ambient air.* [L *ambiens*, ppr., going around]

ambiguity /æmbə'gjuəti/, *n.*, *pl.* **-ties. 1.** a doubtfulness or uncertainty of meaning. **2.** an ambiguous word or expression. [ME *ambiguite*, from L *ambiguitas*]

ambiguous /æm'bɪgjuəs/, *adj.* **1.** open to interpretation; having double meaning; equivocal: *an ambiguous answer.* **2.** of doubtful or uncertain nature; difficult to understand, distinguish, or classify: *a jewel of ambiguous character.* **3.** lacking clearness; obscure; indistinct. [L: doubtful]

ambit /'æmbət/, *n.* **1.** boundary; limits; sphere. **2.** scope; extent. **3.** circumference. [ME, from L: scope]

ambition /æm'bɪʃən/, *n.* **1.** an eager desire for success, power, or fame; aspiration: *She is full of ambition.* **2.** the object desired or sought after: *The crown was his ambition.* [ME, from L: striving for honors] —**ambitious**, *adj.*

ambivalence /æm'bɪvələns/, *n.* **1.** the presence in a person of opposite and conflicting feelings towards a person or object. **2.** an uncertainty or ambiguity, esp. due to an inability to make up one's mind. —**ambivalent**, *adj.*

amble /'æmbəl/, *v.*, **-bled, -bling,** *n.* ◊*v.i.* **1.** (of a horse, etc.) to walk in such a way that it lifts first two legs on one side and then two on the other. **2.** to go at an easy rate. ◊*n.* **3.** an easy or gentle pace. [ME, from L: walk] —**ambling**, *adj.*

ambrosia /æm'brouziə/, *n.* **1.** the food of the gods of classical mythology. **2.** something especially delicious to taste or smell. **3.** a mild, originally Swedish, cheese. [L, from Gk: food of the gods] —**ambrosial**, *adj.*

ambulance /'æmbjələns/, *n.* a vehicle specially equipped for carrying sick or wounded persons. [F (*hôpital*) *ambulant* walking (hospital)]

ambulate /'æmbjəleɪt/, *v.i.*, **-lated, -lating.** to walk or move about. [L: walked] —**ambulation**, *n.* —**ambulatory, ambulant**, *adj.*

ambush /'æmbʊʃ/, *n.* **1.** the act of attacking unexpectedly from a hidden position. **2.** such a hidden position. ◊*v.t.* **3.** to attack from an ambush. [ME, from OF, from *bûche* bush, of Gmc orig.]

ameliorate /ə'miliəreɪt, ə'miljəreɪt/, *v.t.*, *v.i.*, **-rated, -rating.** to make or become better; improve. [F] —**amelioration**, *n.*

amen /a'men, eɪ-/, *interj.* it is so; so be it (used after a prayer, hymn, etc.). [OE, from LL, from Gk, from Heb.: certainty, truth]

Amen /'amən/, *n.* a minor Theban god with the head of a ram, symbolising fertility and life, later identified by the Egyptians with the sun-god, Amen-Ra, their principal deity. Also, **Amon.** [Egypt., explained as 'the one who hides his name']

amenable /ə'menəbəl, ə'min-/, *adj.* **1.** willing to listen, take suggestions, etc; cooperative. **2.** responsible (to legal authority, etc.). [F *à to* + *mener* bring, from L *mināre* drive + -ABLE]

amend /ə'mend/, *v.t.* **1.** to alter (a law, etc.) **2.** to change for the better; improve,

amend

correct: *amend your ways*. [ME, from L: correct] —**amendment**, *n*.

amends /ə'mendz/, *n. sing. or pl.* **1.** compensation; reparation. **2. make amends**, to make up for loss or injury of any kind; compensate. [ME, from OF: reparation]

amenity /ə'menəti, ə'min-/, *n., pl.* **-ties.** **1.** (*pl.*) the equipment or services of a house, area, etc., which make life comfortable and pleasant. **2.** the quality of being pleasant or agreeable: *the amenity of the climate*. [late ME, from L]

amenorrhoea /əmenə'riə, eɪ-/, *n.* absence of menstruation. [A-[6] + MENO- + -(R)RHOEA]

America /ə'merɪkə/, *n.* **1.** the United States of America. **2.** North, Central and South America together with the offshore islands. [named after AMERIGO VESPUCCI]

American /ə'merəkən/, *adj.* relating to. **1.** the United States of America. **2.** either North or South America. ◇*n.* **3.** someone born or living in America.

American Civil War, *n.* →**Civil War**.

American Indian, *n.* a member of the aboriginal race of America or of any of the aboriginal North and South American stocks, often excepting the Eskimos.

American Samoa, *n.* the islands of the Samoa group belonging to the US, including mainly Tutuila and the Manua islands. Pop. 28 000 (1977); 197 km[2]. *Cap.*: Pago Pago.

America's Cup, *n.* an international yacht racing competition. [named after the schooner *America*, which won the trophy (orig. called the One Hundred Guinea Trophy) in Britain in 1851]

americium /æmə'rɪsiəm/, *n.* a radioactive element, one product of the bombardment of uranium and plutonium by high energy helium ions. *Symbol*: Am; *at. no.*: 95. *At. wt*: 243. [AMERIC(A) + -IUM]

amethyst /'æməθɪst/, *n.* **1.** *Mineral*. a type of purple or violet quartz used in jewellery. **2.** a purple sapphire (**oriental amethyst**). **3.** a purplish color. [L, from Gk: lit., remedy for drunkenness] —**amethystine** /æmə'θɪstɪn, -taɪn/, *adj.*

amiable /'eɪmiəbəl/, *adj.* having or showing agreeable personal qualities, as good temper, kindheartedness, friendliness, etc. [ME, from L: friendly] —**amiability** /eɪmiə'bɪləti/, *n.*

amicable /'æmɪkəbəl/, *adj.* friendly: *an amicable settlement*. [L] —**amicability**, *n.*

amid /ə'mɪd/, *prep.* surrounded by; among; amidst. [OE *on middan* in the middle]

amide /'æmaɪd/, *n. Chem.* **1.** a compound formed by the reaction of ammonia with some metals, in which the NH[2] grouping is kept, as *potassium amide*, KNH[2]. **2.** a compound obtained by replacing the OH group in organic acids by the NH[2] radical. [AM(MONIA) + -IDE] —**amidic**, *adj.*

amido-, a prefix indicating the replacement of an OH group by the NH[2] radical. **2.** (*sometimes*) →**amino-**. [combining form of AMIDE]

amidst /ə'mɪdst/, *prep.* →**amid**. [ME]

amine /ə'min, 'æmɪn/, *n.* any of a class of compounds prepared from ammonia by replacing one, two, or all hydrogen atoms with organic radicals. [AM(MONIA) + -INE[2] (def. 3)]

amino-, a prefix indicating an amino group. [combining form of AMINE]

amino acid /ə'minou, 'æmənou 'æsəd/, *n.* any of a group of organic compounds containing an amino group and a carboxyl group. Many are considered to be the building blocks for proteins.

amino group, *n.* the basic radical, NH[2]. Also, **amino radical**.

amiss /ə'mɪs/, *adv.* **1.** wrongly; inappropriately: *to speak amiss*. **2. take amiss**, to be offended at: *Don't take my comments amiss*. **3. come amiss**, to be unwelcome: *Some new clothes wouldn't come amiss with me*. ◇*adj.* **4.** (only after a verb) wrong; out of order: *There is something amiss with it*. [ME A-[1] + *mis* wrong]

amitosis /æmə'tousəs/, *n.* a direct method of cell division in which the nucleus divides simply without formation of chromosomes. [A-[6] + MITOSIS] —**amitotic**, *adj.*

amity /'æməti/, *n., pl.* **-ties.** friendship; good relations, esp. between nations. [ME, from L: friend]

ammeter /'æmɪtə/, *n.* an instrument for measuring the strength of electric currents in amperes. [AM(PERE) + -METER[1]]

ammonia /ə'mouniə, -jə/, *n.* **1.** a colorless, strong smelling gas, NH[3], a compound of nitrogen and hydrogen, very soluble in water. **2.** Also, **ammonia water** or **aqueous ammonia**. this gas dissolved in water. [NL, obtained from *ammoniac*, a substance found near shrine of the Egyptian divinity Ammon, in Libya] —**ammoniate**, *v.t.*

ammonite /'æmənaɪt/, *n.* one of the coiled, chambered fossil shells of the extinct cephalopod molluscs. [NL *Ammōnītes*, from ML *cornū Ammōnis* horn of Ammon, an Egyptian divinity]

ammonium /ə'mouniəm, -njəm/, *n.* a radical, NH[4], which plays the part of a metal in the compounds formed when ammonia reacts with acids.

ammunition /ˌæmjə'nɪʃən/, *n.* **1.** material used in firing a gun or explosive weapon, such as powder, bullets, rockets, etc. **2.** any materials able to be used as weapons, such as bombs, chemicals, etc. **3.** *Colloq.* any means of attack and defence in general, as evidence used in argument. [F (obs.). See MUNITION]

amnesia /æm'niʒə, -ziə/, *n.* loss of memory. [NL, from Gk: forgetfulness] —**amnesiac** /æm'niziæk/, **amnesic** /æm'nisɪk, -zɪk/, *adj.*

amnesty /'æmnəsti/, *n., pl.* **-ties**, *v.*, **-tied**, **-tying.** ◇*n.* **1.** a general act of pardon, esp. for offences against a government. **2.** a time during which offenders against the law may admit their offences without action being taken

amnesty

against them. ◇v.t. **3.** to give amnesty to; pardon. [L, from Gk: forgetfulness]

Amnesty International, *n.* an international organisation formed in 1961 to help people imprisoned for their political or religious beliefs.

amniocentesis /ˌæmnioʊsenˈtisəs/, *n., pl.* **-ses** /-siz/. the removal of some amniotic fluid, esp. to test for abnormality in an unborn baby. [AMNIO(N) + *centesis* (from NL, from Gk *kéntēsis* a pricking]

amnion /ˈæmniən/, *n., pl.* **-nia** /-niə/. the innermost membrane containing the embryo of insects, reptiles, birds, and mammals. [NL, from Gk] **–amniotic,** *adj.*

amoeba /əˈmibə/, *n., pl.* **-bae** /-bi/, **-bas.** a microscopic, one-celled animal (a type of protozoan) which constantly changes shape as it moves and absorbs food. [NL, from Gk: change] **–amoebic,** *adj.*

among /əˈmʌŋ/, *prep.* **1.** surrounded by; in or into the midst of: *You are among friends.* **2.** one of; included in a group of: *That's among the things we must do.* **3.** from; out of (a group): *Choose among these; You are only one among many.* **4.** to, by, for or with (more than two people): *Divide these among you; Let them settle it among themselves.* [OE *on* (ge)*mang* in the crowd, in the midst of]

amongst /əˈmʌŋst/, *prep.* among. [ME]

amoral /eɪˈmɒrəl, æ-/, *adj.* without moral quality; neither moral nor immoral. [A-[6] + MORAL]

amorous /ˈæmərəs/, *adj.* **1.** willing or ready to love. **2.** feeling or showing love (esp. of sexual kind): *amorous looks.* **3.** relating to love: *amorous poetry.* [ME, from OF, from L: love]

amorphous /əˈmɔfəs/, *adj.* **1.** without fixed shape or form. **2.** of no particular kind or character: *an amorphous style of painting.* **3.** *Geol.* occurring in a mass without crystalline structure. **4.** *Chem.* non-crystalline. [Gk] **–amorphism,** *n.*

amortise *or* **amortize** /əˈmɔtaɪz, ˈæmətaɪz/, *v.t.,* **-tised, -tising.** to end (a debt, etc.) by regular part payments to a sinking fund. [ME, from OE: deaden, buy out, from *mort* death]

amount /əˈmaʊnt/, *n.* **1.** quantity or extent: *There was a large amount of laughter.* **2.** the value or importance: *the amount of the damage.* **3.** the sum total: *What amount do I owe?* ◇v.i. **4.** to be equal or add up in value, quantity, effect, etc. (fol. by *to*): *The costs amount to $100; Her advice didn't amount to much.* [ME, from OF phrase *a mont* to the mountain]

amount of substance, *n.* a basic physical quantity that is proportional to the number of specified particles of a substance. The Specific Particle may be an atom, molecule, ion, radical, electron, etc., or a group of such particles. The basic unit of amount of substance is the mole.

amour /əˈmʊə/, *n.* a love affair, esp. a secret one. [F, probably from Pr., from L: love]

amp., /æmp/ *Abbrev.* **1.** amperage. **2.** ampere.

amplitude modulation

amperage /ˈæmpərɪdʒ/, *n.* the strength of an electric current measured in amperes.

ampere /ˈæmpeə/, *n.* the base SI unit of electric current. *Symbol:* A [named after AM *Ampère*, 1775–1836, French physicist]

ampersand /ˈæmpəsænd/, *n.* the name of the character &, meaning *and.*

amphetamine /æmˈfetəmin, -maɪn/, *n.* a drug used to relieve nasal congestion or to stimulate the central nervous system.

amphi-, a word part meaning 'on both sides', 'of both kinds', 'around', as in *amphitheatre, amphibious.* [Gk]

amphibian /æmˈfɪbiən/, *n.* **1.** the class of vertebrate animals, as the frog, newt, etc., that live on land but breed in water, the young metamorphosing (changing) into adult form from early fish-like (tadpole) stage. **2.** an amphibious plant. **3.** an aeroplane that can take off from and land on either land or water. **4.** an amphibious vehicle. [NL, from Gk: living a double life] **–amphibian,** *adj.*

amphibious /æmˈfɪbiəs/, *adj.* **1.** able to live both on land and in water. **2.** able to operate on both land and water. **3.** of twofold or mixed nature. [Gk: living a dual life]

amphibole /ˈæmfəboʊl/, *n.* any of a complex group of hydrous silicate minerals, containing chiefly calcium, magnesium, sodium, iron, and aluminium, and occurring as important constituents of many rocks.

amphitheatre /ˈæmfɪθɪətə/, *n.* **1.** an oval or circular building with rows of seats rising around a central open area, as those of ancient Rome. **2.** any similarly shaped level area surrounded by rising ground. **3.** a place for public contests or games; arena. **4.** a semi-circular rising row of seats in a modern theatre. [L, from Gk]

amphoteric /æmfəˈterɪk/, *adj.* functioning as an acid or as a base.

ample /ˈæmpəl/, *adj.,* **-pler, -plest. 1.** of large size, measure or amount; abundant. **2.** more than enough. [ME, from L] **–ampleness,** *n.* **–amply,** *adv.*

amplifier /ˈæmpləfaɪə/, *n.* **1.** *Elect.* an instrument for increasing the strength of electric waves or impulses fed into it. **2.** such an instrument used to increase sound produced by a radio, record-player, or musical instruments, as the electric guitar.

amplify /ˈæmpləfaɪ/, *v.,* **-fied, -fying.** *v.t.* **1.** to make greater; enlarge. **2.** to expand (a story) by the addition of details, etc. **3.** *Elect.* to increase the strength of (impulses or waves). **4.** to make louder; magnify (the sound of). [ME, from L: enlarge] **–amplification,** *n.*

amplitude /ˈæmplətfud/, *n.* **1.** breadth; largeness; extent. **2.** large measure; abundance. **3.** *Elect.* the maximum strength of an alternating current during its cycle (different from the mean or effective strength). **4.** *Phys.* the distance or range from the maximum or minimum point of a wave pattern to the middle point or neutral value. [L]

amplitude modulation, *n.* a system of radio transmission in which the amplitude of

amplitude modulation the carrier wave is varied in accordance with the frequency of the signal. *Abbrev.*: AM

ampoule /'æmpul/, *n.* a sealed glass container used to hold liquids for injection. [F, from L: bottle]

ampulla /æm'pulə/, *n., pl.* **-pullae** /-'puli/. **1.** *Anat.* a widened part of a passage or tube in the body, esp. in the ear. **2.** *Church.* a container for wine and water used at the altar or for holy oil. **3.** a two-handled bottle used by the ancient Romans for oil, etc. [L] —**ampullary**, *adj.*

amputate /'æmpjəteɪt/, *v.t.*, **-tated**, **-tating.** to cut off (a limb, etc.) by medical operation. [L] —**amputation**, *n.*

Amritsar /æm'rɪtsə/, *n.* a city in northwestern India, in Punjab, site of the Golden Temple, the most important Sikh religious centre; site of the 1919 massacre of Mahatma Gandhi's followers by British troops. Pop. 594 844 (1981).

Amsterdam /'æmstədæm/, *n.* a seaport in and the parliamentary capital of the Netherlands, in North Holland, on the IJsselmeer. Pop. 679 140 (1986 est.).

amt, *Abbrev.* amount.

amuck /ə'mʌk/, *adv. in the phrase* **run amuck,** to rush about wildly, usu. intending to kill. Also, **amok.**

amulet /'æmjələt/, *n.* something (usu. jewellery) worn to protect against evil; charm. [L]

Amundsen /'amundsən/, *n.* **Roald** /'rouald/, 1872–1928, Norwegian explorer; first to reach the South Pole, December 1911.

Amur /a'muə/, *n.* a river in eastern Asia, forming most of the boundary between northern Manchuria and south-eastern Russia, flowing into the Sea of Okhotsk. About 4350 km.

amuse /ə'mjuz/, *v.t.*, **amused, amusing. 1.** to make time pass pleasantly for (someone); entertain. **2.** to make (someone) laugh or smile. [late ME, from MF *amuser* occupy with trifles, divert]

amusement /ə'mjuzmənt/, *n.* **1.** the condition of being amused; enjoyment. **2.** something which amuses; an entertainment, as cinema, concert, merry-go-round, etc. [F]

amygdale /ə'mɪgdeɪl/, *n.* an almond-shaped cavity in an igneous rock, formed by the expansion of steam and later filled with minerals. —**amygdaloidal**, *adj., n.*

amylase /'æməleɪz/, *n.* an enzyme found in digestive juices, etc., which changes starches to simple sugars such as glucose.

amytal /'æmətæl/, *n.* a colorless crystalline substance, $C_{11}H_{18}N_2O_3$, used esp. as a sedative drug.

an /æn/, *weak form* /ən/, *adj. or indefinite article.* the form of **a** before a vowel sound. See **a**[1]. [OE *ān*]

an-[1], a prefix meaning 'not', 'without', 'opposite to', variant of a-[2], before vowels and *h*, as in *anarchy*. Also, **a-**[6]. [Gk]

an-[2], a prefix of direction or addition, variant of **ad-** before *n*, as in *announce*.

-an, a suffix forming adjectives and nouns, meaning: **1.** 'belonging to', 'relating to', as *Australian, Elizabethan,* 'believing in', 'adhering to', as *Christian, republican,* 'specialising in' as *historian.* **2.** *Zool.* 'relating to a certain class', as in *mammalian.* [L *-ānus*]

An, *Chem. Symbol.* actinon.

ana-, a prefix meaning 'up', 'throughout', 'again', 'back', as in *anagram.* [Gk, representing *aná,* prep.]

-ana, noun suffix meaning collection of material relating to a given subject, as in *Australiana.* [L, neut. pl. of *-ānus* -AN]

Anabaptist /ænə'bæptəst/, *n.* (*also l.c.*) a member of a Christian sect, originating in 16th century, in which adult baptism is practised, and a form of Christian communism is attempted.

anabolism /ə'næbəlɪzəm/, *n.* See **metabolism.**

anabranch /'ænəbræntʃ/, *n.* a branch of a river which leaves the main stream and either enters it again or dries up. [short for *ana(stomosing) branch*]

anachronism /ə'nækrənɪzəm/, *n.* **1.** the mistake of placing something in the wrong (usu. earlier) period of time, as in *Captain Cook filmed the east coast of Australia.* **2.** something that is out of its proper time or out of date. [Gk] —**anachronistic**, *adj.*

anaconda /ænə'kɒndə/, *n.* a large South American snake of the boa family. [orig. unknown; ? from Singhalese]

anaemia *or* **anemia** /ə'nimiə/, *n.* a lack of red blood cells or their haemoglobin content, causing paleness and weakness. [NL, from Gk: want of blood] —**anaemic**, *adj.*

anaerobic /ænə'roʊbɪk/, *adj.* (of organisms or tissues) needing the absence of free oxygen or not needing its presence (opposed to *aerobic*).

anaesthesia *or* **anesthesia** /ænəs'θiʒə, -ziə/, *n.* **1.** *Med.* a general or local inability to feel (pain, etc.), brought about by certain drugs. **2.** *Pathol.* a general loss of ability to feel (pain, heat, cold, touch, etc.). [NL, from Gk: insensibility]

anaesthetic *or* **anesthetic** /ænəs'θɛtɪk/, *n.* a substance such as ether, chloroform, etc., that produces anaesthesia.

anaesthetise *or* **anaesthetize** *or* **anesthetise** *or* **anesthetize** /ə'nisθətaɪz/, *v.t.*, **-tised, -tising.** to make (someone) unable to feel pain, etc., as by an anaesthetic. —**anaesthetisation**, *n.* —**anaesthetist**, *n.*

anagram /'ænəgræm/, *n.* a word or sentence formed by changing the order of letters in another word or sentence, as *caned* is an anagram of *dance.* [NL, from Gk: transposition of letters]

anal /'eɪnəl/, *adj.* of, relating to, or near the anus.

analgesia /ænəl'dʒiziə/, *n.* inability to feel pain. [NL, from Gk]

analgesic /ˌænəlˈdʒɪzɪk, -sɪk/, n. 1. a medicine that relieves or removes pain. ◇adj. 2. having to do with or causing removal of pain.

analog /ˈænəlɒg/, adj. 1. Elect. measuring or representing by use of a continuously variable quantity, such as a voltage. 2. showing measurement by use of a continuously variable display, such as the needle on a car speedometer: *an analog watch*.

analog computer, n. a type of calculating machine in which numbers are represented by directly measurable quantities (as voltages, resistances, or rotations).

analogous /əˈnæləgəs, -dʒəs/, adj. 1. similar or comparable in some way. 2. Biol. similar in function but not evolved from similar organs, as the wings of a bee and those of a hummingbird. [L, from Gk: proportionate]

analogue /ˈænəlɒg/, n. 1. something analogous to something else. 2. Biol. an organ or part analogous to another. [F, from Gk *análogon*]

analogy /əˈnælədʒi/, n., pl. **-gies**. 1. a partial agreement, or likeness between two or more things, which forms the basis for a comparison: *It is possible to draw an analogy between the heart and a pump*. 2. Logic. a form of reasoning in which a known similarity between two or more things leads to idea that they are similar in other ways. [L, from Gk: orig., equality of ratios, proportion]

analyse /ˈænəlaɪz/, v.t., **-lysed**, **-lysing**. 1. to examine (something) in order to find out or show its basic elements, meaning, etc.: *to analyse an argument; to analyse a poem*. 2. to make a mathematical, chemical, grammatical, etc., analysis of. 3. → **psychoanalyse**. [backformation from ANALYSIS]

analysis /əˈnæləsəs/, n., pl. **-ses** /-siz/. 1. separation of something into its basic parts in order to discover its nature, meaning, etc.: *the grammatical analysis of a sentence*. 2. a short statement of results of this; outline or summary, as of a book. 3. *Chem.* **a.** separation of a substance into its elements to find their kind or quantity. **b.** the finding out of the kind or amount of one or more of the constituents of a substance, whether actually obtained in separate form or not. 4. → **psychoanalysis**. [ML, from Gk: a breaking up]

analyst /ˈænəlɒst/, n. 1. someone who is skilled in analysis. 2. → **psychoanalyst**.

analytic /ˌænəˈlɪtɪk/, adj. 1. relating to or using analysis. 2. Logic. (of a proposition) proved true by the meaning of words rather than by fact or experience, as *all fathers are men*. Also, **analytical**. [ML, from Gk]

analytical geometry, /ˌænəˌlɪtɪkəl dʒiˈɒmətri/, n. geometry that uses the methods of algebra.

Ananda Marga /əˌnændə ˈmɑgə/, n. a communalistic religious sect founded in India in 1955. [Skt: lit. joy way]

anandrous /ænˈændrəs/, adj. Bot. having no stamens (male organs). [Gk: without a man]

ananthous /ænˈænθəs/, adj. Bot. without flowers. [AN-[1] + Gk *ánthos* flower + -OUS]

anaphase /ˈænəfeɪz/, n. the stage in mitotic cell division after the splitting of the chromosomes, in which the chromosomes move away from each other to opposite ends of the cell.

anarchism /ˈænəkɪzəm/, n. 1. the belief that all forms of government should be ended and replaced by a system of free cooperation. 2. the method or practice of putting this into effect. — **anarchist**, n.

anarchy /ˈænəki/, n. 1. the condition of society without government or law. 2. political and social disorder due to lack of governmental control. 3. disorder in general; chaos. 4. the theory and practice of anarchism. [Gk: lack of a ruler] — **anarchic, anarchical**, adj.

anathema /əˈnæθəmə/, n., pl. **-mas**. 1. a formal curse of the Christian church, excommunicating someone or declaring something evil. 2. a person or thing so cursed. 3. a strong curse; execration. 4. someone or something hated or loathed: *She is anathema to me*. [LL, from Gk: something devoted (to evil)]

Anatolia /ˌænəˈtoʊliə/, n. a vast plateau between the Black Sea and the Mediterranean Sea; in ancient usage, synonymous with the peninsula of Asia Minor; in modern usage, applied to Turkey in Asia.

anatomy /əˈnætəmi/, n., pl. **-mies**. 1. the structure of an animal or plant, or of any of its parts. 2. the science of the structure of animals and plants. 3. the cutting up of animals or plants for study of their structure. 4. any detailed examination. 5. *Colloq.* the body; bodily form; figure. [LL, from Gk: dissection] — **anatomical**, adj. — **anatomist**, n.

ANC /eɪ en ˈsiː/, Abbrev. African National Congress.

-ance, a suffix of nouns meaning action, condition, or quality, as *brilliance, distance, assistance, defiance*. Cf. **-ence**. [ME *-ance*, from F, from L]

ancestor /ˈænsɛstə/, n. 1. someone from whom a person is descended, usu. more distant than a grandparent; forefather. 2. Biol. an earlier type from which an animal or plant is known or thought to have developed. [ME, from L: predecessor] — **ancestress**, n. fem., — **ancestral**, adj.

ancestry /ˈænsɛstri, -səs-/, n., pl. **-tries**. 1. ancestral descent, esp. when noble. 2. a line of ancestors: *He wants to trace his ancestry*.

anchor /ˈæŋkə/, n. 1. a heavy structure attached by cable to a boat, floating bridge, etc., and dropped into water to hold it in place. 2. any similar object for holding steady or for checking movement. 3. something that gives steadiness, esp. of the mind: *Hope is his anchor*. 4. **at anchor**, held still by an anchor. 5. **cast anchor**, to let down the anchor. 6. **weigh anchor**, to take up the anchor. ◇v.t. 7. to hold tightly by an anchor. 8. to fix or fasten firmly. [OE *ancor*, from L, from Gk]

anchorage /ˈæŋkərɪdʒ/, n. 1. a place for anchoring. 2. a charge for anchoring. 3. that to which anything is fastened. 4. something that can be depended upon.

anchorite /'æŋkəraɪt/, *n.* someone who lives alone in an isolated place for religious reasons; hermit. [ME, from ML]

anchorman /'æŋkəmæn/, 1. *Sport.* a person who is most heavily relied upon in a team, as the last runner in a relay race, etc. 2. *Radio, TV.* the person who links different parts of a program; compare.

anchovy /'æntʃəvi, æn'tʃoʊvi/, *n., pl.* **-vies**. *n.* a type of small, herring-like fish found in Australia and elsewhere, esp. southern Europe, oft. used in the form of a paste. [Sp. and Pg., probably from It. (Genoese), from LL, from Gk]

ancien régime /ˌɒnsiɒn reɪ'ʒim/, *n.* a former system of government, esp. that of France before the 1789 revolution. [F: the political and social system of France before the Revolution of 1789]

ancient /'eɪnʃənt, 'eɪntʃənt/, *adj.* 1. of or in time long past, esp. before the end of the Western Roman Empire, AD 476: *ancient history.* 2. very old; of great age: *an ancient monument; an ancient woman.* 3. *Law.* having existed for a particular period of time, often 20 years: *an ancient matter.* ◇*n.* 4. (*usu. pl.*) a person, esp. a classical writer, who lived in ancient times, as an ancient Greek, Roman, Hebrew, etc. [ME, from LL: former, old, from L *ante* before]

ancillary /æn'sɪləri/, *n., pl.,* **-aries**, *adj.* (someone or something) acting as help or support (to). [L: a handmaid]

-ancy, a variant of **-ance**, used mainly in nouns of condition or quality, as in *buoyancy.* [L *-antia*]

and /ænd/; *weak forms* /ənd, ən, n/, *conj.* (*connecting words, phrases or clauses*) 1. with; along with; also: *pens and pencils.* 2. as a result: *Concentrate and your work will improve.* 3. afterwards: *Do the shopping and come straight home.* 4. as well as: *nice and warm.* 5. *Colloq.* to (used between verbs): *try and do it.* [OE; akin to G *und*]

Andamooka /ændə'mʊkə/, *n.* a town in eastern central SA noted for opal mining. Pop. 402 (1986).

andante /æn'dænteɪ, -ti/, *adv.* (musical direction) fairly slowly and evenly. [It.: lit., walking]

Anderson /'ændəsən/, *n.* **Jessica Margaret**, born 1925, Australian novelist; author of *Tirra Lirra by the River* (1978).

Andes /'ændiz/, *n.pl.* a lofty mountain system in South America, extending about 7250 km from northern Colombia and Venezuela south to Cape Horn. Highest peak of the Western Hemisphere), Aconcagua, 6960 m.

Andorra /æn'dɔrə/, *n.* a principality in south-western Europe, in the eastern Pyrenees between France and Spain; administratively independent while under the joint sovereignty of the President of France and Spanish bishop of Urgel. Pop. 46 976 (1986); 467 km^2. *Languages:* Catalan, also French and Spanish. *Currency:* French franc and Spanish peseta. *Cap.:* Andorra la Vella. Official name, **Valleys of Andorra.** —**Andorran**, *n., adj.*

Andrew /'ændru/, *n.* 1. **Saint**, one of the twelve apostles of Jesus. Patron saint of Scotland and Russia. 2. **Prince** (*Andrew Albert Christian Edward*) (**Duke of York**), born 1960, the second son of Elizabeth II of Britain.

Androcles /'ændrəkliz/, *n. Rom. Legend.* a slave whose life was spared by a lion from whose foot he had years before extracted a thorn.

androgynous /æn'drɒdʒənəs/, *adj.* 1. *Bot.* having male and female flowers in the same cluster. 2. being both male and female; hermaphroditic. [L, from Gk: hermaphrodite]

Andromeda /æn'drɒmədə/, *n.* 1. *Gk Myth.* the daughter of Cassiopeia and wife of Perseus, by whom she was rescued from a sea-monster. 2. *Astron.* a northern constellation containing the Andromeda galaxy, the nearest spiral galaxy to the Milky Way; 2.2 million light years distant.

-ane, a noun suffix used to indicate saturated aliphatic hydrocarbons of the alkane series, as *decane, pentane, propane.*

anecdote /'ænəkdoʊt/, *n.* a short account of an amusing or interesting event, oft. connected with a particular person. [ML, from Gk: things unpublished] —**anecdotal**, *adj.*

anechoic chamber /ˌænɛˌkoʊɪk 'tʃɛmbə/, *n.* a room free from echo especially built for acoustic measurement and research.

anemometer /ænə'mɒmətə/, *n.* 1. an instrument for recording the speed and direction of wind. 2. instrument for measuring rate of flow of a liquid. —**anemometric**, *adj.* —**anemometry**, *n.*

anemone /ə'nɛməni/, *n.* 1. a type of plant, native to the Mediterranean area, with mostly red and blue flowers. 2. → **sea-anemone**. [L, from Gk: windflower]

aneroid barometer /ˌænərɔɪd bə'rɒmətə/, *n.* an instrument for measuring atmospheric pressure by recording the action of air pressure on the elastic top of a box emptied of air.

aneurism /'ænjərɪzəm/, *n.* an abnormal widening of the wall of a blood vessel weakened by disease. Also, **aneurysm**. [Gk: dilatation] —**aneurysmal, aneurismal**, *adj.*

anew /ə'nju/, *adv.* 1. again. 2. in a new way or form. [OE *ofniowe*]

Angas family /'æŋgəs ˌfæmli/, *n.* an Australian family notable in public life in SA since its foundation. 1. **George Fife**, 1789–1879, English-born philanthropist and one of the founders of SA. 2. his son, **George French**, 1822–86, Australian artist and naturalist, born in England. 3. **John Howard**, 1823–1904, son of George Fife, English-born philanthropist; preceded his father in settling in SA.

angel /'eɪndʒəl/, *n.* 1. *Theol.* one of group of spiritual beings, attendants and messengers of God. 2. the usual representation of such a being, in human form, with wings. 3. a person, esp. a woman, who is thought to be like an angel in beauty, kindliness, etc. 4. a protecting or guardian spirit. 5. *Colloq.* a person

angel / anguish

angel who gives money to help anything, esp. a theatrical play. [ME, from L, from Gk *ángelos*, orig., messenger] —**angelic, angelical,** *adj.*

angelfish /'eɪndʒəlfɪʃ/, *n., pl.* **-fishes,** (esp. collectively) **-fish. 1.** a type of small, brightly-colored fish found in tropical waters in Australia and elsewhere. **2.** a type of South American freshwater fish, oft. kept in aquariums.

angelica /æn'dʒɛlɪkə/, *n.* **1.** a tall plant found in both hemispheres, the sweet-smelling root and stalks of which are used in medicine and cooking. **2.** the preserved stalks of this plant, used as cake decoration. **3.** an essence made from this plant, used as flavoring, esp. in liqueurs. [ML: angelic (herb)]

angelus /'ændʒələs/, *n. Rom. Cath. Ch.* **1.** (*oft. cap.*) a prayer in memory of the Annunciation. **2.** the bell (**angelus bell**) heard in the morning, at noon, and in the evening, to tell the time when the angelus is to be said. [LL. See ANGEL]

anger /'æŋɡə/, *n.* **1.** a strongly felt displeasure caused by real or supposed wrongs; wrath; ire. ◇*v.t.* **2.** to excite to anger or violence. [ME, from Scand.]

angina /æn'dʒaɪnə/, *n.* **1.** an inflammatory disease in or near the throat, as quinsy, croup, mumps, etc. **2.** → **angina pectoris.** [L: quinsy, lit., strangling] —**anginal,** *adj.*

angina pectoris /æn'dʒaɪnə 'pɛktərəs/, *n.* a pain below the sternum, (breast bone) most often brought about by exertion or excitement and caused by lack of blood to the heart, usu. due to coronary artery disease. [NL: angina of the chest]

angio-, a word part meaning 'vessel', or 'container', as in *angiosperm*. [NL, from Gk: vessel]

angiogram /'ændʒiəɡræm/, *n.* an X-ray photograph, taken after an injection of special dyes into blood vessels.

angiosperm /'ændʒiəspɜm/, *n.* a plant having its seeds enclosed in an ovary (opposed to *gymnosperm*). —**angiospermous,** *adj.*

angle[1] /'æŋɡəl/, *n., v.,* **-gled, -gling.** ◇*n.* **1.** *Maths.* **a.** a space between two lines or three planes diverging (branching) from a common point, or within two planes extending from a common line. **b.** a figure so formed. **c.** the amount of rotation (turning) needed to bring one line or plane into coincidence with another. **2.** an angular shape or design; corner; recess: *an angle of a building*. **3.** a point of view: *new angle on a problem*. **4. at an angle,** sloping; not at a right angle (to). ◇*v.t.* **5.** to move, direct, bend or present at an angle. **6.** to put a slant or bias on (a question, statement, etc.). ◇*v.i.* **7.** to move or bend in an angle. [ME, from F, from L]

angle[2] /'æŋɡəl/, *v.i.,* **-gled, -gling. 1.** to fish with hook and line. **2. angle for,** to try to get something by underhand means or trickery: *to angle for a present*. [OE *angul* fishhook]

Angle /'æŋɡəl/, *n.* one of a West Germanic people that migrated from Schleswig to Britain in the 5th century AD and founded the kingdoms of East Anglia, Mercia, and Northumbria. As early as the 6th century their name was extended to all the Germanic inhabitants of Britain. [OE *Angle,* orig. the inhabitants of *Angel,* a district of what is now Schleswig, said to be named from its hooklike shape.]

angle of incidence, *n.* the angle that a line, ray of light, etc., meeting a surface makes with a perpendicular to that surface at the point of meeting.

angle of reflection, *n.* the angle that a ray of light, or the like, reflected from a surface, makes with a perpendicular to that surface at the point of reflection.

angle of refraction, *n.* the angle that a refracted ray of light makes with a perpendicular to the surface or interface at the point of refraction.

angler /'æŋɡlə/, *n.* **1.** someone who fishes for pleasure. **2.** any of various Australian fishes, variously colored, having a modified dorsal spine above the mouth forming a 'fishing rod' which can be moved to trap smaller fish.

Anglican /'æŋɡlɪkən/, *adj.* **1.** having to do with the Anglican Church. ◇*n.* **2.** a member of the Anglican Church. [ML]

Anglican Church, *n.* any church related to the Church of England, as the Anglican Church of Australia.

Anglo-, a word part meaning 'relating to England or English', as in *Anglo-Saxon*. [combining form representing ML *Anglus* Englishman, *Anglī* (pl.) the English]

Anglo-Saxon /ˌæŋɡloʊ-'sæksən/, *n.* someone who belongs to the English-speaking world. [ML *Anglo-Saxonēs* the English people]

Angola /æŋ'ɡoʊlə/, *n.* a republic in south-western Africa, on the Atlantic; a Portuguese colony before independence in 1975. Pop. 9 105 000 (1987 est.); 1 246 700 km². *Languages:* Portuguese, also African languages, esp. of the Bantu family. *Currency:* kwanza. *Cap.:* Luanda. —**Angolan,** *n., adj.*

angophora /æn'ɡɒfərə/, *n.* any of number of species of trees of eastern Australia related to the eucalyptus, some noted for their twisted pink branches or creamy white flowers in summer.

Angora /æŋ'ɡɔrə/, *n.* **1.** a type of goat or rabbit with long silky hair. **2.** → **mohair.** [from *Angora,* variant of *Ankara,* capital of Turkey]

angry /'æŋɡri/, *adj.,* **-grier, -griest. 1.** feeling or showing anger or resentment (*with* or *at* a person, *at* or *about* a thing). **2.** characterised by anger; wrathful: *angry words*. **3.** inflamed, as a sore; showing inflammation. [ME]

angstrom /'æŋstrəm/, *n.* a unit of length for measuring short wavelengths and distances between atoms in molecules, equal to 10^{-10} metres. *Symbol:* Å [named after AJ *Ångström,* 1814–74, Swedish physicist]

anguish /'æŋɡwɪʃ/, *n.* **1.** pain in either body or mind; severe suffering or distress: *anguish of grief*. ◇*v.t., v.i.* **2.** to affect with or suffer anguish. [ME: straits, distress]

angular /'æŋgjələ/, *adj.* **1.** having angle or angles. **2.** consisting of, found at, or forming an angle. **3.** of, relating to, or measured by an angle. **4.** acting or moving awkwardly. **5.** stiff in manner; unbending. [L] — **angularity,** *n.*

anhydride /æn'haɪdraɪd, -drəd/, *n.* a compound formed by the removal of water, or an oxide of a non-metal (**acid anhydride**) or of a metal (**basic anhydride**) which forms an acid or a base, respectively, with the addition of water. [Gk: without water]

anhydrous /æn'haɪdrəs/, *adj.* showing loss of all water, esp. water of crystallisation. [Gk: without water]

aniline /'ænələn/, *n.* an oily liquid, $C_6H_5NH_2$, the basis of many brilliant dyes, and used in the production of plastics, resins, etc.

animadversion /ænəmæd'vɜʒən/, *n.* a remark, usu. implying judgment; criticism. [L]

animal /'ænəməl/, *n.* **1.** any living thing not a plant, generally able to feel and move about, etc. **2.** any animal other than man. **3.** an inhuman, brutish, and beastlike person. ◇*adj.* **4.** of, relating to, or derived from animals: *animal life; animal fats.* **5.** concerned with the physical or carnal nature of man: *animal needs.* [L: living being]

animal husbandry, /–'hʌzbəndri/, *n.* the science of breeding, feeding and care of animals, esp. on a farm.

animalism /'ænəməlɪzəm/, *n.* **1.** an animal state; state of being influenced by physical desires and not by mental activity or moral forces; sensuality. **2.** the belief that human beings are without spiritual nature.

animal kingdom, /ænəməl 'kɪŋdəm/ *n.* the animals of the world thought of as a group (distinguished from *plant kingdom*).

animate /'ænəmeɪt/, *v.*, **-mated, -mating;** /'ænəmət/, *adj.* ◇*v.t.* **1.** to give life to; make alive. **2.** to make lively; vivacious; vigorous. **3.** to encourage. **4.** to move to action; actuate: *animated by religious faith.* ◇*adj.* **5.** alive; possessing life: *animate creatures.* [L]

animated /'ænəmeɪtəd/, *adj.* **1.** full of life, action, or spirit; lively. **2.** moving or made to move as if alive: *animated cartoons.*

animation /ænə'meɪʃən/, *n.* **1.** animated quality; liveliness; vivacity; spirit; life. **2.** the process of preparing animated cartoons.

animism /'ænəmɪzəm/, *n.* **1.** the belief that all natural objects and the universe itself possess a soul. **2.** belief in spirits. [L *anima* soul + -ISM] — **animist,** *n., adj.* — **animistic,** *adj.*

animosity /ænə'mɒsəti/, *n., pl.* **-ities.** a feeling of ill will or violent dislike; hostility. [late ME, from L: courage]

anion /'ænaɪən/, *n.* **1.** *Chem.* a negatively charged ion which is attracted to the anode in electrolysis. **2.** any negatively charged atom, radical, or molecule. [Gk: going up]

anise /'ænɪs, 'ænəs/, *n.* a herb-like plant yielding aniseed. [ME, from L, from Gk: dill, anise]

aniseed /'ænəsid/, *n.* the strong-smelling seed of anise, used in medicine, cookery, etc.

Ankara /'æŋkərə/, *n.* the capital of Turkey, in the central part. Pop. 2 235 000 (1985). Formerly (until 1930), **Angora.**

ankle /'æŋkəl/, *n.* the joint connecting the foot with the leg. [ME, from Scand.]

anklet /'æŋklət/, *n.* an ornament or support for the ankle, corresponding to a bracelet for the wrist or forearm.

ankylose /'æŋkəloʊz/, *v.*, **-losed, -losing.** ◇*v.t.* **1.** to join together, such as two hard tissues, as the bones of a joint. ◇*v.i.* **2.** to grow together or become joined by ankylosis, Also, **anchylose.**

ankylosis /æŋkə'loʊsəs/, *n.* abnormal adhesion or immobility of the bones in a joint, as by a direct joining of the bones. [NL, from Gk: stiffening of the joints] — **ankylotic,** *adj.*

ANL /eɪ ɛn 'ɛl/, *Abbrev.* Australian National Line.

annals /'ænəlz/, *n.pl.* **1.** history or relation of events recorded year by year. **2.** historical records generally. [L *annālēs* (*librī* books) yearly records] — **annalist,** *n.*

Annapurna /ænə'pɜnə/, *n.* a mountain massif in the Himalayas, in northern central Nepal. Highest peak 8078 m.

Anne /æn/, *n.* **1. Queen,** 1665-1714, queen of Great Britain and Ireland 1702-14 (daughter of James II of England). **2. Princess** (*Anne Elizabeth Alice Louise*), born 1950, daughter of Elizabeth II of Britain.

anneal /ə'nil/, *v.t.* to heat (glass, pottery, metals, etc.) to free from or prevent internal stress. [OE *an* on + *ælan* burn]

annelid /'ænəlɪd/, *n.* a group of worms including earthworms, leeches, various marine worms, etc., characterised by their ringed or segmented bodies. [F, from L: ring]

Anne of Cleves /'klivz/, *n.* 1515-57, the fourth wife of Henry VIII of England.

annex /'ænɛks, ə'nɛks/, *v.*; /'ænɛks/, *n.* ◇*v.t.* **1.** to join, or add, esp. to something larger or more important; unite; append. **2.** to take possession of: *Germany annexed Austria in World War II.* ◇*n.* **3.** Also, **annexure.** something annexed or added, esp. an addition to legal papers: *an annex to an agreement.* [ME, from L: joined] — **annexation,** *n.*

annexe /'ænɛks/, *n.* a building added or joined to larger building. [F]

annihilate /ə'naɪəleɪt/, *v.t.*, **-lated, -lating.** **1.** to reduce to nothing; destroy completely: *The bombing annihilated the city.* **2.** to destroy the form of: *to annihilate an army.* **3.** *Colloq.* to defeat, as in argument, competition, or like. [LL] — **annihilation,** *n.*

anniversary /ænə'vɜsəri/, *n., pl.* **-ries,** *adj.* ◇*n.* **1.** the day on which an event took place in an earlier year. **2.** the celebration of such a date. ◇*adj.* **3.** relating to an anniversary: *anniversary gift.* [L]

anno Domini /ænoʊ 'dɒmənaɪ, -ni/, in the year of our Lord. *Abbrev.:* AD [L]

annotate /'ænəteɪt/, *v.t.*, **-tated, -tating.** to supply with notes; make remarks upon: *to annotate works of Bacon.* [L] — **annotation**, *n.*

announce /ə'naʊns/, *v.t.*, **-nounced, -nouncing. 1.** to make known publicly; give notice of. **2.** to state the arrival or presence of: *to announce guests; announce dinner.* [ME, from OF, from L] — **announcement**, *n.*

announcer /ə'naʊnsə/, *n.* someone who announces, esp. one who reads news or introduces programs on radio or television.

annoy /ə'nɔɪ/, *v.t.* to bother; make rather angry. [ME, from OF: displease, from LL *in odiō* in hatred] — **annoying**, *adj.*

annoyance /ə'nɔɪəns/, *n.* **1.** that which annoys; nuisance: *Some visitors are an annoyance.* **2.** the act of annoying. **3.** the feeling of being annoyed.

annual /'ænjuəl/, *adj.* **1.** of, for, or relating to a year; yearly. **2.** taking place or returning once a year: *annual celebration.* **3.** *Bot.* living only one growing season, as beans or wheat. **4.** performed during one year: *annual course of the sun.* ◇*n.* **5.** a plant living only one year or season. **6.** a book or magazine published once a year. — **annually**, *adv.*

annuity /ə'njuəti/, *n., pl.* **-ties. 1.** a sum of money paid regularly (esp. once each year) to a person, often for life. **2.** the right to receive such income. [ME, from L: yearly]

annul /ə'nʌl/, *v.t.*, **annulled, annulling.** to put an end to; abolish (used esp. of laws, etc.): *to annul a marriage.* [ME, from LL] — **annulment**, *n.*

annulate /'ænjulət, -leɪt/, *adj.* **1.** formed of ringlike segments, as an annelid worm. **2.** having rings or ringlike bands. — **annulation**, *n.*

annulus /'ænjələs/, *n., pl.* **-li** /-laɪ/, **-luses. 1.** a ring; ringlike part, band, or space. **2.** an area or space between two circles that have the same centre. [L: ring]

annunciate /ə'nʌnsieɪt/, *v.t.*, **-ated, -ating.** to announce. [ME: announced, from ML]

annunciation /ənʌnsi'eɪʃən/, *n.* **1.** (*oft. cap.*) the announcement by the angel Gabriel to the Virgin Mary of the incarnation of Christ. **2.** (*cap.*) a festival (25 March) established by the church in memory of this.

anode /'ænoʊd/, *n.* **1.** a positively charged electrode which attracts emitted electrons as in a radio valve, etc. **2.** a positive electrode of a cell (defs 5 and 6) (opposed to a *cathode*). [Gk: way up]

anodyne /'ænədaɪn/, *n.* **1.** a medicine that relieves or removes pain. **2.** anything that lessens pain or distress. ◇*adj.* **3.** soothing to feelings. [L, from Gk: freeing from pain]

anoint /ə'nɔɪnt/, *v.t.* **1.** to put oil on; apply oily liquid to. **2.** to cover with any liquid. **3.** to make holy; consecrate: *God anointed his prophet.* [ME, from OF, from L] — **anointer**, *n.* — **anointment**, *n.*

anomalous /ə'nɒmələs/, *adj.* varying from the usual type or form; abnormal; irregular. [L, from Gk: irregular]

anomaly /ə'nɒməli/, *n., pl.* **-lies. 1.** a variation from what is normal. **2.** something anomalous: *an anomaly of human nature.* **3.** *Geol.* a noticeable local difference from average results, in a mineral exploration survey. [L, from Gk] — **anomalistic**, *adj.*

anon /ə'nɒn/, *adv. Archaic.* **1.** in short time; soon. **2.** at another time. [OE *on ān* into one, *on āne* in one, immediately]

anon. /ə'nɒn/, *Abbrev.* anonymous.

anonymous /ə'nɒnəməs/, *adj.* **1.** without any name stated, as that of author, writer etc.: *anonymous pamphlet.* **2.** of unknown name: *anonymous author.* **3.** lacking personal character. [Gk] — **anonymity, anonymousness**, *n.*

anopheles /ə'nɒfəliz/, *n., pl.* **-les.** the mosquito which, when carrying organisms causing malaria, may pass on the disease to human beings. [NL, from Gk: useless, hurtful]

anorexia /ænə'rɛksiə/, *n.* a lack of physical desire for food. Also, **anorexy.** [AN-[1] + Gk *órexis* longing]

anorexia nervosa /ænəˌrɛksiə nɜː'voʊsə/, *n.* a mental disease, most common in adolescent girls, causing strong dislike of food.

another /ə'nʌðə/, *adj.* **1.** second; further; additional: *another piece of cake.* **2.** different; of different kind: *at another time; another man.* ◇*pron.* **3.** one more; additional one: *Try another.* **4.** different one; something different: *going from one house to another.* [ME; orig. *an other*]

Ansett /'ænsɛt/, *n.* **1. Sir Reginald Myles,** 1909–81, Australian aviator and company director of transport and tourist enterprises. **2.** his son, **Robert Graham** ('**Bob**'), born 1933, Australian company director.

Ansett Airlines of Australia, *n.* an internal Australian airline, founded in 1936 by Reginald Ansett. Formerly (1936–57), **Ansett Airways Pty Ltd**; (1957–68), **Ansett-ANA.**

Anshan /æn'ʃæn/, *n.* a city in north-eastern China, in Liaoning province. Pop. 1 088 900 (1985 est.).

answer /'ænsə, 'an-/, *n.* **1.** a spoken or written reply to a question, request, letter, etc. **2.** an action as reply: *The answer was the sound of gunfire.* **3.** *Law.* a statement of facts in opposition to those stated in a charge. **4.** a solution to a problem, esp. in mathematics. **5.** a piece of work (written or otherwise) given to show knowledge or ability in a test or examination. ◇*v.i.* **6.** to make an answer; reply by word or act: *to answer with a nod.* **7.** to respond (to a direction, command, etc.); obey; acknowledge (fol. by *to*): *to answer to the whip; to answer to her name.* **8.** to state oneself publicly responsible (fol. by *for*): *I will answer for his safety.* **9.** to act or suffer because of (fol. by *for*): *to answer for his crimes.* **10.** to be satisfactory or serve (fol. by *for*): *to answer for a purpose.* ◇*v.t.* **11.** to act or speak in reply or response to: *to answer a bell; answer a question.* **12.** to

answer 40 **anthrax**

give as an answer: *to answer yes or no.* **13.** to make a defence against (a charge). **14.** to serve or suit: *This will answer my needs.* **15.** to match; correspond to: *He answers the police description.* ◇*v.* **16. answer back,** to make a rude or cheeky reply. [OE *and-* against + *swaru,* akin to *swerian* swear]

answerable /ˈænsərəbəl/, *adj.* **1.** accountable; responsible (*for* or *to* a person, act, etc.): *I am answerable for his safety; He is answerable to his employer.* **2.** able to be answered.

ant /ænt/, *n.* any of certain small insects widely found in many species, all of which have some degree of social organisation. [OE *æmete*]

-ant, 1. an adjective suffix, originally participial, as in *pleasant.* **2.** a noun suffix used in words of participial origin, as in *servant,* See **-ent.** [F, from L *-ant-,* nom. *-ans, -ant,* ppr. ending]

antacid /æntˈæsəd/, *n., adj.* (an agent or medicine) acting against acidity, esp. of the stomach.

antagonise *or* **antagonize** /ænˈtægənaɪz/, *v.t.,* **-nised, -nising.** to make angry; make an enemy of: *His tactless speech antagonised half the voters.*

antagonism /ænˈtægənɪzəm/, *n.* **1.** the activity or relation of opposing parties or conflicting forces; active opposition. **2.** an opposing force, principle, or tendency. [Gk]

antagonist /ænˈtægənəst/, *n.* someone who is opposed to or strives with another in any kind of contest; opponent; adversary. [Gk]

antagonistic /æn,tægəˈnɪstɪk/, *adj.* acting in opposition; mutually opposing.

antarctic /æntˈɑktɪk/, *adj.* **1.** of, at, or near the South Pole. **2.** *Colloq.* very cold. [L, from Gk: opposite the north]

Antarctica /æntˈɑktɪkə/, *n.* an ice-covered continent around the South Pole; no indigenous inhabitants but research stations belonging to twelve nations, including Australia, have been established; regulated by Antarctic Treaty of 1961. 13 900 000 km².

Antarctic Circle, *n.* an imaginary circle around the earth forming the northern boundary of the South Frigid Zone, at latitude 66°32′S.

Antarctic Ocean, *n.* the ocean south of the Antarctic Circle.

Antarctic Zone, *n.* the section of the earth's surface lying within the Antarctic Circle.

ante /ˈænti/, *n.* **1.** *Cards.* (in poker) money put into a pool by each player after seeing their hand but before taking new cards. **2.** the amount paid as one's share. **3. raise** *or* **up the ante,** to increase suddenly the price to be paid for goods or services. [L *ante* before]

ante-, a prefix meaning 'before in space or time', as in *antediluvian, anteroom.* [L]

anteater /ˈæntitə/, *n.* **1.** → **echidna. 2.** → **numbat. 3.** any of various animals of tropical America, e.g. the armadillo, which feed mainly on termites. **4.** → **aardvark.**

antecedent /æntəˈsidənt/, *adj.* **1.** going or being before; preceding; prior (oft. fol. by *to*): *antecedent event.* ◇*n.* **2.** (*pl.*) **a.** ancestry. **b.** someone's past history. **3.** a former happening, event, etc. **4.** *Gram.* a noun or phrase which is replaced by a following pronoun or other substitute in a sentence. [L]

antechamber /ˈæntɪtʃeɪmbə/, *n.* a room which leads to larger room. [F, from It., from L]

antechinus /æntəˈkaɪnəs/, *n.* See **marsupial mouse.**

antedate /ˈæntɪdeɪt, æntɪˈdeɪt/, *v.t.,* **-dated, -dating. 1.** to be of older date than; precede: *The Peruvian Empire antedates that of Mexico.* **2.** to fix an earlier date to.

antediluvian /ˌæntɪdəˈluviən/, *adj.* **1.** belonging to period before the Flood, recorded as having taken place in days of Noah. **2.** out of date; primitive; *antediluvian ideas.* **3.** old; outmoded. ◇*n.* **4.** someone who is old or old-fashioned. [ANTE- + L *dīluvi(um)* deluge + -AN]

antelope /ˈæntəloʊp/, *n., pl.* **-lopes,** (*esp. collectively*) **-lope.** a slightly built, hollow-horned ruminant related to cattle, sheep, and goats, found mainly in Africa and Asia. [ME, from ML, from LGk]

antenatal /æntiˈneɪtl/, *adj.* before birth; during pregnancy: *antenatal examination.*

antenna /ænˈtɛnə/, *n., pl.* **-tennae** /-ˈtɛni/ *for def. 1;* **-tennas** *for def. 2.* **1.** *Zool.* a jointed organ found in pairs on heads of insects, crustaceans, etc., often called feelers. **2.** a radio or television aerial. [L: a sailyard] **—antennal,** *adj.,* **antennary,** *adj.*

anterior /ænˈtɪəriə/, *adj.* **1.** placed before; situated more to the front (opposite of *posterior*). **2.** going before in time; preceding; earlier: *an anterior age.* [L: compar. adj. from *ante* before] **—anteriority,** *n.* **—anteriorly,** *adv.*

anteroom /ˈæntirum/, *n.* **1.** a smaller room which leads to the main room. **2.** a waiting room.

anthem /ˈænθəm/, *n.* **1.** a ceremonial song of praise, devotion, or patriotism (national pride). **2.** a piece of religious music, usu. with words taken from the Scriptures. [OE *antemn(e), antefn(e),* from VL, from LL, from Gk. See ANTIPHON]

anther /ˈænθə/, *n. Bot.* the pollen-bearing part of a stamen. [NL, from Gk: flowery]

ant hill, *n.* **1.** a mound of earth formed by a colony of ants when building their nest. **2.** a pillar of earth, typically one to two metres high, built up by termites in forming a nest. Also, **anthill.**

anthology /ænˈθɒlədʒi/, *n., pl.* **-gies.** a collection of writings, esp. poems, by various authors or from various books. [Gk: lit., a flower-gathering] **—anthologise,** *v.* **—anthologist,** *n.*

anthracite /ˈænθrəsaɪt/, *n.* a hard, black coal which burns almost without flame. See **coal** (def. 1).

anthrax /ˈænθræks/, *n., pl.* **-thraces** /-θrəsiz/. an infectious disease of cattle, sheep, etc., sometimes passed on to human beings. [L, from Gk: carbuncle, coal] **—anthracic,** *adj.*

anthropo-, a word part meaning 'human being', 'man', as in *anthropomorphic*. Also, **anthrop-**. [Gk, combining form of *ánthrōpos*]

anthropoid /'ænθrəpɔɪd/, *adj.* Also, **anthropoidal**. **1.** like a human being. ◊*n.* **2.** an anthropoid ape, as a gorilla, chimpanzee, etc. [Gk]

anthropologist /ænθrə'pɒlədʒəst/, *n.* someone who studies or is concerned with anthropology.

anthropology /ænθrə'pɒlədʒi/, *n.* the scientific study of the origin and development of mankind.

anthropomorphism /ænθrəpə'mɔːfɪzəm/, *n.* the attributing of human form or behavior to non-human beings or things, esp. gods or animals. — **anthropomorphic**, *adj.*

anti /'ænti/, *n., pl.* **-tis**, *adj. Colloq.* ◊*n.* **1.** someone who is opposed to a particular practice, party, action, etc. ◊*adj.* **2.** against; opposed to; antagonistic (to).

anti-, a prefix meaning 'against', 'opposed to', with the following particular meanings: **1.** opposed; in opposition: *anti-British*. **2.** not genuine; pseudo-: *anti-Christ*. **3.** opposite or reverse of: *antihero*. **4.** placed opposite: *antipole*. **5.** moving in reverse or opposite direction: *anticyclone*. **6.** *Med.* corrective; preventive; curative: *antihistamine*. Also, **ant-**. [Gk]

antibiotic /ˌæntibaɪ'ɒtɪk/, *n.* **1.** a chemical substance produced by micro-organisms, which is able to stop the growth of and destroy bacteria and other micro-organisms. **2.** such a substance, separated and purified (as penicillin, streptomycin) and used in treatment of infectious diseases. ◊*adj.* **3.** of or involving antibiotics.

antibody /'æntibɒdi/, *n., pl.* **-bodies.** any of various substances in the blood or developed in immunisation, which act against bacterial or viral poisons or destroy bacteria.

antic /'æntɪk/, *n.* **1.** (*oft. pl.*) odd or silly behavior; foolish and strange movements of the body. ◊*adj.* **2.** *Archaic.* foolish; odd; grotesque; ludicrous: *antic disposition*. [It. *antico* old (but used as if It. *grottesco* grotesque), from L]

Antichrist /'æntikraɪst/, *n. Theol.* a person or power seen as a mighty antagonist (opponent) of Christ. [Gk]

anticipate /æn'tɪsəpeɪt/, *v.t.*, **-pated, -pating. 1.** to foretaste; foresee; realise beforehand: *to anticipate pleasure*. **2.** to expect: *to anticipate an acquittal*. **3.** to be before (someone else) in doing something; forestall. **4.** to consider or mention before proper time: *to anticipate more difficult questions*. **5.** *Econ.* to spend (money) before it is really available for use. [L] — **anticipatory**, *adj.*

anticipation /ænˌtɪsə'peɪʃən/, *n.* **1.** the act of anticipating. **2.** foretaste; expectation; hope.

anticlimax /ænti'klaɪmæks/, *n.* **1.** a noticeable descent from what is high, serious or noble to what is unimportant or foolish. **2.** an inglorious or disappointing conclusion to what has gone before. — **anticlimactic**, *adj.*

anticlinal /ænti'klaɪnəl/, *adj.* **1.** sloping in opposite directions from a central axis. **2.** sloping downwards on both sides from a median plane (axial plane), as an upward fold of rock strata. [ANTI- + *-clinal*, adj. combining form indicating slope]

anticline /'æntiklaɪn/, *n.* an anticlinal rock structure.

anticlockwise /ænti'klɒkwaɪz/, *adv., adj.* (in a direction) opposite to the rotation of hands of clock.

anticyclone /ænti'saɪkloʊn/, *n.* a horizontal spiral movement of the atmosphere around a region of high barometric pressure. See **cyclone**. — **anticyclonic**, *adj.*

antidepressant /ˌæntidə'prɛsənt/, *n.* **1.** any of a class of drugs used in treating mental depression. ◊*adj.* **2.** of, relating to, or concerned with this class of drugs.

antidote /'æntidoʊt/, *n.* **1.** a medicine or other substance to stop the effects of poison, disease, etc. **2.** whatever prevents or counteracts the effects of something else. [L, from Gk: given against] — **antidotal**, *adj.*

antifebrile /ænti'fibraɪl/, *n., adj.* (a substance) effective against fever.

antifreeze /'æntifriz/, *n.* a substance added to the water in the radiator of a car's engine to stop the water freezing.

antigen /'æntɪdʒən, 'æntə-/, *n.* any substance which, when injected into animal tissue, will cause the production of antibodies. [ANTI(BODY) + -GEN] — **antigenic**, *adj.*

Antigone /æn'tɪgəni/, *n. Gk Legend.* a daughter of Oedipus by his mother, Jocasta. For performing funeral rites (forbidden by edict of Creon, King of Thebes) over her brother Polynices, she was condemned to be buried alive, and hanged herself.

antihero /'ænti,hɪəroʊ/, *n.* the main character, or hero, of a novel, film, etc., who does not possess the traditional heroic characteristics of bravery, strength, etc.

antihistamine /ænti'hɪstəmin, -maɪn/, *n.* any of certain drugs which decrease the effect of the histamine released in allergic conditions of the body, as in hay-fever, etc. — **antihistamine, antihistaminic**, *adj.*

Antill /'æntɪl/, *n.* **Sir John Henry**, 1904–86, Australian composer; best known for the ballet suite *Corroboree* (1944).

Antilles /æn'tɪliz/, *n.pl.* a chain of islands in the West Indies, divided into the **Greater Antilles** (Cuba, Hispaniola, Jamaica, and Puerto Rico), and, to the south-east, the **Lesser Antilles** (the Leeward Islands, the Windward Islands, Barbados, and the Netherlands Antilles).

antimacassar /ˌæntimə'kæsə/, *n.* an ornamental covering for backs and arms of chairs, etc., to keep them from being soiled. [ANTI- + *Macassar*, hair oil obtained from Macassar, a seaport in Indonesia]

antimatter /ˈæntimætə/, n. Phys. matter consisting of antiparticles. Contact between antimatter and matter results in destruction of both with the production of gamma radiation.

antimony /ˈæntəməni/, n. a brittle white metallic element used chiefly in alloys and (in compounds) in medicine. Symbol: Sb; at no.: 51; at. wt: 121.75. [late ME, from ML] —**antimonial**, adj., n.

antineutrino /ˌæntinjuˈtriːnoʊ/, n. the antiparticle of a neutrino.

antineutron /ˌæntiˈnjuːtrɒn/, n. the antiparticle of a neutron.

antinode /ˈæntinoʊd/, n. a point, line, or area in a vibrating medium at which the amplitude of variation of the disturbance is greatest, found halfway between two adjacent nodes. —**antinodal**, adj.

antinomy /ænˈtɪnəmi/, n., pl. -mies. opposition between two laws. [L, from Gk]

antinuclear /ˌæntiˈnjuːkliə/, adj. opposed to development of nuclear industry.

antiparticle /ˈæntiˌpɑːtɪkəl/, n. Phys. a particle matching a particular elementary particle with equal mass but opposite electric charge.

antipasto /ˌæntiˈpæstoʊ/, n. a small course of tasty foods such as smoked meat, fish, etc., usu. at the beginning of a meal; hors d'oeuvres. [It.]

antipathy /ænˈtɪpəθi/, n., pl. -thies. a natural or settled dislike; repugnance; aversion: *He had a strong antipathy to strangers.* [L, from Gk: having opposite feelings] —**antipathetic**, adj.

antiphon /ˈæntəfən/, n. Church. a psalm, hymn, or prayer sung in alternate parts. [ML, from Gk: sounding in answer]

antiphony /ænˈtɪfəni/, n., pl. -nies. a style of music sung turn-by-turn by a choir in two divisions.

antipodes /ænˈtɪpədiːz/, n.pl. 1. points diametrically opposite each other on the earth. 2. **the Antipodes**, Australia or Australasia as being directly opposite Britain. [L, from Gk: with feet opposite] —**antipodean**, adj., n.

antiproton /ˌæntiˈproʊtɒn/, n. the antiparticle of a proton.

antiquary /ˈæntəkwɔri/, n., pl. -quaries. an expert on ancient things; a student or collector of extremely old things. [L: of antiquity] —**antiquarian**, adj.

antiquated /ˈæntəkweɪtəd/, adj. 1. grown old; obsolete. 2. difficult to use in the present.

antique /ænˈtiːk/, adj., n., v., -tiqued, -tiquing. ◊adj. 1. of or dating from former times as opposed to modern. ◊n. 2. an object of art or a furniture piece of a former period. 3. the antique (usu. Greek or Roman) style, esp. in art. ◊v.t. 4. to make appear antique. [L: old]

antiquity /ænˈtɪkwəti/, n., pl. -ties. 1. the quality of being ancient; great age: *a family of great antiquity.* 2. ancient times; former ages, often before the Middle Ages. 3. (usu. pl.) something belonging to or remaining from ancient times.

anti-Semite /ˌænti-ˈsɛmaɪt/, n. a person who hates the Jews. —**anti-Semitic**, adj. —**anti-Semitism**, n.

antiseptic /ˌæntiˈsɛptɪk/, n. 1. a chemical substance that destroys poisonous microorganisms that produce disease. ◊adj. 2. relating to such a substance. —**antiseptically**, adv. —**antisepsis**, n.

antisocial /ˌæntiˈsoʊʃəl/, adj. 1. unwilling or unable to mix normally with people. 2. opposed or damaging to social order, or to the principles on which society is built. —**antisocially**, adv.

Antisthenes /ænˈtɪsθəniːz/, n. 444?–365? BC, Greek philosopher, founder of the Cynic school.

antithesis /ænˈtɪθəsəs/, n., pl. -ses /-siːz/. 1. opposition; contrast: *the antithesis of theory and fact.* 2. the direct opposite (fol. by *of*). 3. the setting of one clause or phrase against another to which it is opposed. [LL, from Gk: opposition] —**antithetic, antithetical**, adj.

antitoxin /ˌæntiˈtɒksən/, n. a substance formed in the body, which fights a particular poison, often used in treating or immunising (protecting) against certain infectious diseases.

antivenene /ˌæntivəˈniːn/, n. 1. an antitoxin produced in the blood by repeated injections of venom, as of snakes. 2. the cells or compounds obtained from such blood used for injection. Also, **antivenin**.

antler /ˈæntlə/, n. one of the solid periodically-shed horns, usually branched, of an animal of the deer family. [ME, from L: before eye]

Antony /ˈæntəni/, n. Mark (Marcus Antonius), 83?–30 BC, Roman general; friend of Caesar.

antonym /ˈæntənɪm/, n. a word opposed in meaning to another (opposed to *synonym*): *'Good' is the antonym of 'bad'.* [ANT(I)- + Gk ónyma name; modelled on SYNONYM]

Anubis /əˈnjuːbəs/, n. Egypt. Myth. a son of Osiris identified by the Greeks with Hermes, and represented as having the head of a dog. [L, from Gk from Egypt. *Anup* jackal]

anus /ˈeɪnəs/, n. the opening at the lower end of the alimentary canal, through which the solid refuse of digestion passes out. [L]

anvil /ˈænvəl/, n. a heavy iron block with a smooth surface, frequently of steel, on which red- or white-hot metals are hammered into desired shapes. [OE *anfilt(e)*]

anxiety /æŋˈzaɪəti/, n., pl. -ties. 1. tension or unease of mind caused by fear of danger or misfortune. 2. concerned desire; eagerness. 3. *Psychol.* a state of fear and tension found in some disorders of the mind. [L]

anxious /ˈæŋʃəs, ˈæŋk-/, adj. 1. full of anxiety: *to be anxious about someone's safety.* 2. eager (fol. by infinitive or *for*): *anxious to please.* 3. causing anxiety or worry; difficult: *an anxious business; an anxious time.* [L: troubled]

any /ˈɛni/, adj. 1. one, a, an, or (with a plural noun) some, whichever or whatever it may be: *Ask any politician.* 2. in whatever

any   43   **apiary**

quantity or number, great or small: *Have you any butter?* **3.** every: *any schoolboy knows that.* **4.** a great or unlimited (amount): *any number of things.* **5.** (with a negative) none at all: *She never gets any thanks.* ◇*pron.* **6.** (treated in grammar as *sing.*) any person or thing, or (*treated as pl.*) any persons or things: *He does better than any before him.* ◇*adv.* **7.** in any degree; at all: *Do you feel any better?* [OE *ænig*, from *ān* one]

anybody /ˈenibɒdi, -bədi/, *pron.* any person.

anyhow /ˈenihaʊ/, *adv.* **1.** in any case; at all events. **2.** in a careless manner.

anyone /ˈeniwʌn/, *pron.* any person; anybody.

anything /ˈeniθɪŋ/, *pron.* any thing whatever; something, no matter what.

anyway /ˈeniweɪ/, *adv.* in any case; anyhow.

anywhere /ˈeniweə/, *adv.* in, at, or to any place.

ANZAAS /ˈænzæs/, *n.* an association of scientific workers and scholars formed in 1888 as the Australasian Association for the Advancement of Science; present name since 1930. [*A*(*ustralian and*) *N*(*ew*) *Z*(*ealand*) *A*(*ssociation for the*) *A*(*dvancement of*) *S*(*cience*)]

Anzac /ˈænzæk/, *n.* **1.** a member of the Australian and NZ Army Corps during World War I. **2.** a soldier from Australia or NZ. [*A*(*ustralian and*) *N*(*ew*) *Z*(*ealand*) *A*(*rmy*) *C*(*orps*)]

ANZAC /ˈænzæk/, *Abbrev.* Australian and New Zealand Army Corps.

Anzac Cove, *n.* the cove on the western coast of the Gallipoli peninsula in Turkey where Australian and NZ troops landed in World War I.

Anzac Day, *n.* 25 April, the anniversary of the ANZAC landing at Gallipoli in 1915.

ANZUS /ˈænzəs/, *n.* Australia, NZ, and the US, esp. as associated in the formal agreement to defend each other (**ANZUS Pact** or **Treaty**) signed in 1951. [*A*(*ustralia*) *N*(*ew*) *Z*(*ealand and the*) *U*(*nited*) *S*(*tates*)]

AO /eɪ ˈoʊ/, *Abbrev.* Officer of the Order of Australia.

A1 /eɪˈwʌn/, *adj. Colloq.* **1.** first class; excellent. **2.** in good health. Also, **A-1, A-one.**

aorta /eɪˈɔːtə/, *n., pl.* **-tas, -tae** /-tiː/. *Anat.* the largest blood vessel taking blood away from the heart, leading from the left ventricle (chamber) to all of the body except the lungs. [NL, from Gk] **—aortic, aortal,** *adj.*

ap-, a variant of **ad-** before *p*, as in *appear.*

AP /eɪ ˈpiː/, *Abbrev.* Australia Party.

apace /əˈpeɪs/, *adv.* with speed; quickly; swiftly.

Apache /əˈpætʃi/, *n., pl.* **Apaches, Apache.** one of a group of Indian tribes in the south-western US.

apart /əˈpɑːt/, *adv.* **1.** separately or aside in movement, place, position or consideration: *Set something apart; Joking apart, what do you think?* **2.** in pieces, or to pieces: *to take a watch apart.* **3. apart from**, aside from: *apart from other considerations.* ◇*adj.* **4.** separate; independent: *a class apart.* [ME, from L *ad partem* to the side]

apartheid /əˈpɑːteɪt/, *n.* (esp. in South Africa) the separation of people according to their race. [Afrikaans]

apartment /əˈpɑːtmənt/, *n.* **1.** a single room in a building. **2.** (*pl.*) a set of furnished rooms, among others in a building. **3.** a home unit. [F, from It.]

apathy /ˈæpəθi/, *n., pl.* **-thies. 1.** lack of feeling; absence of any emotion. **2.** lack of interest in things which others find moving or exciting. [L, from Gk: insensibility] **—apathetic,** *adj.*

ape /eɪp/, *n., v.,* **aped, aping,** *adv.* ◇*n.* **1.** any of several types of monkey with either no tail or a very short one. ◇*v.t.* **2.** to copy, sometimes mindlessly; mimic. ◇*adv.* **3. go ape,** *Colloq.* to react with over-much and uncontrolled pleasure, excitement, etc. (fol. by *over*). [OE *apa*] **—apelike, apish,** *adj.*

Apennines /ˈæpənaɪnz/, *n.pl.* a mountain range traversing the length of the Italian peninsula. Highest peak, Monte Corno, 2912 m.

aperient /əˈpɪəriənt/, *n.* a medicine or something eaten that softens bowel contents; laxative. [L: opening]

aperitif /əˈperətɪf/, *n.* a small alcoholic drink often taken to heighten desire for a meal. [F]

aperture /ˈæpətʃə/, *n.* **1.** a hole, slit, crack, or other opening. **2.** *Optics.* an opening that limits the quantity of light that can enter a viewing instrument. [L]

apex /ˈeɪpeks/, *n., pl.* **apexes, apices** /ˈeɪpəsiːz/. **1.** the tip, point, or highest part of anything. **2.** fulfilment; climax. [L: point, summit]

aphasia /əˈfeɪʒə, -ziə/, *n.* loss of language and speech ability due to damage to the central nervous system. [NL, from Gk: speechlessness] **—aphasic,** *adj.*

aphelion /əˈfiːliən/, *n., pl.* **-lia** /-liə/. the point of a planet's (or other circling body's) orbit most distant from the sun. See **perihelion.** [NL]

aphid /ˈeɪfəd/, *n.* a type of plant-sucking insect. Also, **aphis.** [NL]

aphorism /ˈæfərɪzəm/, *n.* a short saying containing a general truth. [ML, from Gk: definition] **—aphoristic,** *adj.* **—aphorist,** *n.*

aphrodisiac /æfrəˈdɪziæk/, *n.* a drug or food that wakes or increases sexual desire. [Gk]

Aphrodite /æfrəˈdaɪti/, *n.* the Greek goddess of love and beauty, identified by the Romans with Venus.

Apia /ˈæpiə, ˈæpiə/, *n.* a seaport in and the capital of Western Samoa, on Upolu island. Pop. 33 170 (1981).

apiary /ˈeɪpiəri/, *n., pl.* **-ries.** a place in which bees are kept; a stand or shed containing a number of beehives. [L] **—apiarist,** *n.*

apical

apical /'æpɪkəl, 'eɪ-/, *adj.* of, at, or forming the top-most point. [L *apex* summit + -AL¹]

apiculture /'eɪpɪkʌltʃə/, *n.* the rearing of bees. [L *api(s)* bee + CULTURE]

apiece /ə'piːs/, *adv.* for each piece, or person; each: *an orange apiece; costing a dollar apiece*. [orig. two words, *a* to or for each + PIECE]

aplomb /ə'plɒm/, *n.* complete self-possession. [F]

apo-, a prefix meaning 'from', 'away', 'off', 'away from', as in *apostasy*. Also, **ap-**, **aph-**. [Gk. See AB-¹]

apocalypse /ə'pɒkəlɪps/, *n.* **1.** discovery; revelation; disclosure. **2.** (*cap.*) *Bible.* the last book of the New Testament; Revelation. [from writings, so named, Jewish and Christian, which appeared from about 200 BC to AD 350, assuming to make revelation of the ultimate divine purpose; Gk: revelation] –**apocalyptic**, *adj.*

apocrypha /ə'pɒkrəfə/, *n. pl.* (*now treated as sing.*) works whose author or truth is in question. [from Christian religious writings so named, of uncertain origin, regarded by some as inspired, but rejected by most authorities]

apocryphal /ə'pɒkrəfəl/, *adj.* **1.** of doubtful authorship. **2.** false; fictitious.

apogee /'æpədʒiː/, *n.* **1.** *Astron.* the point in the orbit of a heavenly body or artificial satellite most distant from the earth. See **perigee**. **2.** the highest or most distant point; climax. [F, from L, from Gk: distance from the earth] –**apogeal**, **apogean**, *adj.*

Apollo /ə'pɒloʊ/, *n.* **1.** a Greek (and Roman) deity, the god of light, healing, music, poetry, prophecy, youthful manly beauty, etc. **2.** an unusually good-looking young man. **3.** a US space program which aimed to explore the moon by landing a person land on its surface and return safely to earth; crew members of the spaceship Apollo 11 made the first lunar landing on 20 July 1969. [L, from Gk]

apologetic /əpɒlə'dʒɛtɪk/, *adj.* **1.** showing that one is sorry for a fault, failure, etc. **2.** defending in speech or writing. [LL, from Gk] –**apologetically**, *adv.*

apologetics /əpɒlə'dʒɛtɪks/, *n.* the science or method of defending in argument.

apologia /æpə'loʊdʒɪə/, *n.* a formal defence or support in speech or writing, as of a cause. Also, **apology**. [L, from Gk: a speech in defence] –**apologist**, *n.*

apologise or **apologize** /ə'pɒlədʒaɪz/, *v.i.*, **-gised, -gising. 1.** to offer excuses or regrets for some fault, hurtful statement, failure, or injury. **2.** to make a formal defence in speech or writing. –**apology**, *n.*

apology /ə'pɒlədʒi/, *n., pl.* **-gies. 1.** an expression of regret or sadness, offered for some fault or wrong. **2.** a poor example; something making do: *a sad apology for a hat*. [L, from Gk: speech in defence]

apoplexy /'æpəplɛksi/, *n.* marked loss of body function due to damage to brain blood-supply; stroke. [ME, from L, from Gk: disable by a stroke] –**apoplectic**, *adj.*

apostasy /ə'pɒstəsi/, *n., pl.* **-sies.** a total desertion of one's religion, principles, party, cause, etc. [ME, from L, from Gk: revolt] –**apostate**, *n., adj.* –**apostatise**, *v.*

apostle /ə'pɒsəl/, *n.* **1.** one of the twelve selected followers sent out by Christ to spread his teachings. **2.** an originator or committed supporter of any great reform, or cause. [OE *apostol*, from L, from Gk: one sent away]

apostle bird, *n.* a greyish-brown bird of the Australian interior which travels in groups; happy family bird; twelve apostle bird.

Apostles' Creed, *n.* a creed of virtually universal acceptance in the Christian Church, dating back to about 500 and traditionally ascribed to Christ's apostles.

apostolic /æpə'stɒlɪk/, *adj.* **1.** having to do with an apostle, esp. the twelve apostles. **2.** of the pope; papal. –**apostolically**, *adv.*

apostrophe¹ /ə'pɒstrəfi/, *n.* the sign (') used to show: **1.** the leaving out of one or more letters in a word, as in *o'er* for *over*, *they're* for *they are*. **2.** the possessive case, as in *lion's* (*sing.*), *lions'* (*pl.*). **3.** certain plurals, as in *mind your p's and q's*. [special use of APOSTROPHE²]

apostrophe² /ə'pɒstrəfi/, *n.* a departure from an address, esp. in the form of a personal word to someone not present. [L, from Gk: a turning away] –**apostrophic**, *adj.* –**apostrophise**, *v.*

apothecary /ə'pɒθəkri, -kəri/, *n., pl.* **-ries.** *Archaic.* a chemist, a mixer of drugs. [ME, from LL: shopkeeper]

apotheosis /əpɒθi'oʊsəs, /-siːz/, *n., pl.* **-ses 1.** the raising to the rank of a god. **2.** a perfect example; an ideal. [L, from Gk: deification] –**apotheose**, *v.*

appal /ə'pɔːl/, *v.t.*, **-palled, -palling. 1.** to strike with fear; fill with alarm and horror. **2.** *Colloq.* to shock; dismay; displease. [ME, from OF: become or make pale] –**appalling**, *adj.*

Appalachian Mountains /æpə,leɪʃən 'maʊntənz/, *n.pl.* a mountain system of eastern North America, extending from Quebec province in Canada to northern Alabama. Highest peak, Mt Mitchell, 2037 m. Also, **Appalachians**.

apparatus /æpə'rɑːtəs, -'reɪtəs/, *n., pl.* **-tus, -tuses. 1.** any equipment used for a particular purpose. **2.** a division of an organisation, esp. that part concerned with general management: *the apparatus of a political party*. [L: preparation]

apparel /ə'pærəl/, *n.* a person's outer clothing; raiment. [ME, from OF: make ready]

apparent /ə'pærənt/, *adj.* **1.** capable of being clearly seen or understood; plain or clear. **2.** seeming; ostensible: *the apparent motion of the sun*. **3.** having the right to claim a throne, title, or other estate, by reason of birth: *the heir apparent*. [L: appearing] –**apparently**, *adv.*

apparition /ˌæpəˈrɪʃən/, *n.* anything that appears, esp. something remarkable or out-of-the-ordinary, as a ghost. [L: See APPEAR] — **apparitional**, *adj.*

appeal /əˈpiːl/, *n.* **1.** a call for help, support, mercy, money, etc.: *The prisoners made an appeal for mercy;* a Red Cross appeal. **2.** a request to some person or group for support, decision, etc. **3.** *Sport.* a call from a player to the referee or umpire for a decision on a point of play. **4.** *Law.* a formal request for review by a higher court. **5.** the power to attract or to move the feelings: *The game has lost its appeal; sex appeal.* ◇ *v.i.* **6.** to make an appeal. [ME, from L: approach, summon] — **appealing**, *adj.*

appear /əˈpɪə/, *v.i.* **1.** to come into public view; become visible: *A cloud appeared on the horizon.* **2.** to have a certain look; seem: *to appear wise.* **3.** to be clear or made clear by evidence: *It appears to me that you are right.* **4.** *Law.* to come formally before a court, ruling body, etc. [ME, from L *appārēre* come forth]

appearance /əˈpɪərəns/, *n.* **1.** the act of fact of appearing, as to the eye, the mind, or the public. **2.** an outward look or aspect which may be different to what is the case; mien: *a man of noble appearance.* **3.** outward show or seeming; semblance: *to avoid the appearance of wanting money.* **4. to keep up appearances**, to keep up a (socially acceptable) outward show (often to hide an inner fault). **5. to all appearances**, seemingly; so far as can be seen. **6.** an apparition.

appease /əˈpiːz/, *v.t.*, **-peased, -peasing. 1.** to bring to a state of peace, quiet, or happiness: *to appease an angry king.* **2.** to satisfy: *I appease my hunger.* **3.** to agree to the unjust demands (of a country or government) in order to escape war. [ME, from OF *a* to + *pais* (from L *pax*) peace] — **appeasement**, *n.*

appellant /əˈpelənt/, *n.* **1.** *Law.* someone who appeals to a higher court. ◇ *adj.* **2.** appellate. [L: appealing]

appellate /əˈpelət/, *adj.* having to do with appeals. [L: appealed]

appellation /ˌæpəˈleɪʃən/, *n.* (the giving of) a name or title. [L: name]

append /əˈpend/, *v.t.* to add, as an extra part; annex. [L: hang (something) on] — **appendage**, *n.*, — **appendant**, *n.*, *adj.*

appendicectomy /əˌpendəˈsektəmi/, *n.*, *pl.* **-mies.** *Surg.* the removal of the vermiform appendix. Also, **appendectomy** /ˌæpənˈdektəmi/. [L *appendix* APPENDIX + -ECTOMY]

appendicitis /əˌpendəˈsaɪtəs/, *n.* the inflammation of the vermiform appendix. [L *appendix* APPENDIX + -*ītis* -ITIS]

appendix /əˈpendɪks/, *n.*, *pl.* **-dixes, -dices** /-dəsiz/. **1.** matter which is added to the main body of a book, giving explanation, figures and books used. **2.** *Anat.* **a.** a projection of tissue. **b.** the vermiform appendix. [L: appendage]

appertain /ˌæpəˈteɪn/, *v.i.* → pertain (def. 2). [ME, from LL]

appetiser *or* **appetizer** /ˈæpətaɪzə/, *n.* a food or drink that increases the desire for food.

appetising *or* **appetizing** /ˈæpətaɪzɪŋ/, *adj.* attractive to the appetite.

appetite /ˈæpətaɪt/, *n.* **1.** a desire for food, drink, or any bodily want: *to work up an appetite; the natural appetites.* **2.** a learned interest or want: *an appetite for reading.* [ME, from L: onset, desire for]

Appian Way /ˈæpiən weɪ/, *n.* an ancient Roman road extending from Rome to Brundisium (now Brindisi); begun 312 BC. About 560 km.

applaud /əˈplɔːd/, *v.i.* **1.** to express approval by clapping the hands, shouting, etc. ◇ *v.t.* **2.** to praise or show approval in any way: *to applaud an actor; He will applaud your conduct.* [L] — **applause**, *n.*

apple /ˈæpəl/, *n.* **1.** (a tree of temperate regions, bearing) a crisp edible fruit, usu. round and with thin red, yellow or green skin. **2.** any of various angophoras, thought to look like apple trees. **3. She's apples** *or* **She'll be apples**, *Colloq.* all is well. [OE *æppel*]

Appleton /ˈæpəltən/, *n.* **1. Sir Edward Victor,** 1892–1965, English scientist; his research into the ionosphere was important to the development of radar; Nobel prize for physics 1947.

appliance /əˈplaɪəns/, *n.* an instrument or machine, esp. one operated by electricity and made for use in the home. [APPLY + -ANCE]

applicable /əˈplɪkəbəl, ˈæp-/, *adj.* able to be used; suitable; relevant. — **applicability**, *n.* — **applicably**, *adv.*

applicant /ˈæplɪkənt/, *n.* someone who applies or asks; a candidate: *an applicant for a job.* [L]

application /ˌæpləˈkeɪʃən/, *n.* **1.** the act of putting to special use: *application of common sense to a problem.* **2.** the quality of being useable for a particular purpose; relevance: *This has no application to the case.* **3.** the act of applying: *application of paint to a wall.* **4.** the thing applied. **5.** (the act of making) a written or spoken request. **6.** close attention; continuous effort: *application to one's studies.* [L: a joining to]

applied /əˈplaɪd/, *adj.* put to practical use, as a science (distinguished from *theoretical*, or *pure* science).

appliqué /ˈæpləkeɪ/, *n.* (the ornamentation formed by) the sewing or attaching of one material to another. [F: put on]

apply /əˈplaɪ/, *v.*, **-plied, -plying.** ◇ *v.t.* **1.** to lay on; bring into physical closeness: *to apply a match to powder.* **2.** to bring to bear; put into practical operation, as a principle, law, rule, etc. **3.** to put to use, often with reference to some person or thing: *They know how to apply their labor; to apply the finding to the case.* **4.** to give with full attention; set: *I apply my mind to my lessons.* ◇ *v.i.* **5.** to have a bearing; be relevant: *The arguments apply to the case.* **6.** to make request; ask: *They can apply for a job.* [ME, from L: attach] — **applier**, *n.*

appoggiatura — April fool

appoggiatura /əpɒdʒə'tjurə/, *n. Music.* an ornamental note played before another note and taking a portion of its time. [It., from *appoggiare* lean]

appoint /ə'pɔɪnt/, *v.t.* **1.** to choose and put into a position; designate: *to appoint a new secretary.* **2.** to set up and fix by command or decision: *Laws appointed by God.* **3.** *Law.* to name (a person) who will receive property according to a will. **4.** to provide with what is necessary; equip. [ME, from OF *a-* A-⁵ + *pointer* POINT] **—appointment,** *n.*

apportion /ə'pɔʃən/, *v.t.* to divide and give out in just portions; share out in fair divisions: *to apportion costs.* [F *à* to + *portionner* PORTION, v.] **—apportionment,** *n.*

apposite /'æpəzɪt/, *adj.* suitable; well-adapted; pertinent: *an apposite answer.* [L: put to]

apposition /æpə'zɪʃən/, *n.* **1.** the act of placing together; juxtaposition. **2.** *Gram.* a relation between expressions in a sentence, which are used in the same way and have the same relation to other elements, the second expression adding to the first. For example: *Adam, the first man,* has *the first man* in apposition to *Adam*. **—appositional,** *adj.* **—appose,** *v.*

appraise /ə'preɪz/, *v.t.*, **-praised, -praising.** to judge as to quality, size, weight, etc.; estimate the value of. [b. *apprize* (from ME *aprise(n),* from OF *apriser,* from phrase *à pris* for sale) and PRAISE] **—appraisal,** *n.*

appreciable /ə'priʃəbəl/, *adj.* **1.** able to be seen or noticed; noticeable. **2.** fairly large.

appreciate /ə'priʃieɪt, ə'prisi-/, *v.*, **-ated, -ating.** ◇*v.t.* **1.** to place a high enough value on: *Her great ability was not appreciated.* **2.** to be fully conscious of; detect: *Can you appreciate the dangers?* **3.** to raise in value. ◇*v.i.* **4.** to increase in value. [L: appraised] **—appreciative,** *adj.* **—appreciation,** *n.*

apprehend /æprə'hɛnd/, *v.t.* **1.** to take into keeping; arrest by legal authority. **2.** to realise the meaning of; understand: *She will apprehend the situation.* **3.** to have fear of; anticipate: *I apprehend no violence.* [L: seize] **—apprehension,** *n.*

apprehensible /æprə'hɛnsəbəl/, *adj.* capable of being understood.

apprehensive /æprə'hɛnsɪv/, *adj.* uneasy or fearful about something that may happen: *apprehensive of* (or *for*) *her safety.*

apprentice /ə'prɛntəs/, *n., v.,* **-ticed, -ticing.** ◇*n.* **1.** someone who is bound for a fixed period of time to work for another in return for instruction in a trade. **2.** *Horseracing.* a jockey in training, under 21 years of age. ◇*v.t.* **3.** to bind to an employer for instruction in a trade. [ME, from OF *a(p)rendre* teach, learn, APPREHEND] **—apprenticeship,** *n.*

apprise /ə'praɪz/, *v.t.*, **-prised, -prising.** to inform; advise (oft. fol. by *of*). [F *a(p)pris,* pp. of *a(p)prendre* learn, teach. See APPRENTICE]

approach /ə'prəʊtʃ/, *v.t.* **1.** to come nearer or near to: *to approach the city; approaching Homer as a poet.* **2.** to make advances or a suggestion to: *to approach the minister with a plan.* ◇*v.i.* **3.** to come nearer; draw near: *the storm approaches.* ◇*n.* **4.** the act of drawing or being near: *the approach of a horseman; a fair approach to the truth.* **5.** any means of reaching: *the approach to a city; an approach to a problem.* **6.** (*sing.* or *pl.*) advances made to a person. **7.** (*pl.*) *Mil.* cover for protecting forces in an advance against a strong position. [ME *aproche(n),* from OF *aprochier,* from LL *appropiāre*]

approachable /ə'prəʊtʃəbəl/, *adj.* (of a person) easy to approach; friendly.

approbation /æprə'beɪʃən/, *n.* approval; praise.

appropriate /ə'prəʊpriət, *adj.;* /ə'prəʊpriɛɪt/, *v.,* **-ated, -ating.** ◇*adj.* **1.** suitable or fitting for a particular purpose, person, occasion, etc.: *Please wear appropriate dress.* ◇*v.t.* **2.** to set apart for some particular purpose or use: *Parliament appropriates funds for the university.* **3.** to take for oneself, esp. illegally or without permission. [L: made one's own] **—appropriation,** *n.*

approval /ə'pruvəl/, *n.* **1.** the act of approving; approbation. **2. on approval,** (of goods for sale) taken or sent for examination, with the choice of buying or returning.

approve /ə'pruv/, *v.,* **-proved, -proving.** ◇*v.t.* **1.** to declare or consider good, satisfactory, etc: *She approves the standard of his work.* **2.** to agree to officially; sanction. ◇*v.i.* **3.** to speak or think favorably (usu. fol. by *of*): *I approve of him.* [ME, from L]

approx. /ə'prɒks/, *Abbrev.* approximate(ly).

approximate /ə'prɒksəmət, *adj.;* /ə'prɒksəmeɪt/ *v.,* **-mated, -mating.** ◇*adj.* **1.** nearly exact, equal, or perfect: *That is an approximate kilo.* **2.** inaccurate; rough. **3.** near; close together. ◇*v.t.* **4.** to come near to; approach closely to. ◇*v.i.* **5.** to come near in position, quality, amount, etc. (usu. fol. by *to*): *His answer approximated to the truth.* [L] **—approximation,** *n.* **—approximately,** *adv.*

appurtenance /ə'pɜtənəns/, *n.* **1.** something that goes with another more important thing. **2.** (*pl.*) equipment; accessories: *the appurtenances of a house.* [ME, from AF, from L: belong to] **—appurtenant,** *adj.*

Apr., *Abbrev.* April.

après-ski /,æpreɪ'ski/, *adj., n.* (of or relating to) a party held, clothes worn, etc. at the end of a day of skiing. [F: after ski]

apricot /'eɪprɪkɒt, -prə-/, *n.* **1.** (a tree producing) a yellowish fruit, something like a small peach. **2.** a pinkish yellow or yellowish pink. ◇*adj.* **3.** of this color. [L *praecoqua* apricots]

April /'eɪprəl/, *n.* the fourth month of the year, having 30 days.

April fool, *n.* a person tricked on 1 April (**April Fools' Day**), when practical jokes are traditionally played.

a priori /ei pri'ɔri, a prai'ɔrai/, *adj., adv.* (reasoning) from cause to effect or from a general law to a particular example. [L: from something prior]

apron /'eiprən/, *n.* **1.** a piece of clothing, worn over other clothes, for covering and protecting the front of a person. **2.** *Civ. Eng.* concrete or other covering for protecting a surface of earth from the action of moving water. **3.** a hard-surfaced area around airfield buildings. **4.** the part of a stage in front of the curtain or arch. **5.** *Geol.* a deposit of gravel and sand in front of a moraine. **6.** *Mach.* that part of a lathe carriage containing the clutches and gears. **7. tied to someone's apron strings**, emotionally dependent on one's mother, wife, etc. [ME *napron* (*napron* being later taken as *an apron*), from OF, from L: napkin, cloth]

apropos /æprə'pou/, *adv.* **1.** to the purpose; appropriately. **2.** with reference or regard; in respect (fol. by *of*): *apropos of nothing.* **3.** by the way. ◇*adj.* **4.** well-suited; appropriate: *apropos remarks.* **5. apropos of**, relating to. [F]

apse /æps/, *n. Archit.* a semicircular or many-sided recess in a building with an arched roof, esp. at the east end of a church. [L *apsis*, from Gk: circle, arch, apse]

apsis /'æpsəs/, *n., pl.* **apsides** /æp'saidiz, 'æpsədiz/. *Astron.* **1.** either of the two points at the extremities of the eccentric orbit of a planet, satellite, etc. **2. line of apsides**, the line connecting two such points. [L. See APSE] —**apsidal**, *adj.*

apt /æpt/, *adj.* **1.** likely (to do something); inclined: *That dog is apt to run away.* **2.** quick to learn: *an apt pupil.* **3.** well-suited; appropriate: *an apt example.* [ME, from L: joined; fitted]

aptitude /'æptətʃud/, *n.* a quickness in learning; talent: *He has an aptitude for music.* [ML, from L]

aqua /'ækwə/, *n., pl.* **aquae** /'ækwi/. → **aquamarine** (defs 2 and 3). [L: water]

aqualung /'ækwəlʌŋ/, *n.* a cylinder of air, strapped on to a person's back, with a tube leading to a watertight mask over the mouth, for deep underwater swimming.

aquamarine /ˌækwəmə'rin/, *n.* **1.** a light-blue or greenish blue kind of beryl, used in jewellery. **2.** a light blue-green or greenish blue color. ◇*adj.* **3.** of this color. Also, **aqua**. [L *aqua marina* sea water]

aquanaut /'ækwənɔt/, *n.* **1.** a person working and living for a time underwater for research purposes. **2.** a skindiver. [L *aqua* water + (ASTRO)NAUT]

aquaplane /'ækwəpleɪn/, *n., v.,* **-planed, -planing**. ◇*n.* **1.** a single broad water-ski. ◇*v.i.* **2.** to ride an aquaplane. **3.** (of a car, etc.) to slide out of control over the wet surface of a road. [L *aqua* water + PLANE¹; modelled on AEROPLANE]

aqua regia /ˌækwə 'ridʒə/, *n.* a mixture of one part of nitric acid and three parts of hydrochloric acid.

aquarium /ə'kwɛəriəm/, *n., pl.* **aquariums, aquaria** /ə'kwɛəriə/. (a building containing) a pond or tank in which living fish and water plants are kept and shown. [L]

Aquarius /ə'kwɛəriəs/, *n.* a constellation and sign of the zodiac, represented by the Water-bearer. [L: water-bearer]

aquatic /ə'kwɒtɪk/, *adj.* **1.** living or growing in water. **2.** practised on or in water: *aquatic sports.* [L: watery]

aqueduct /'ækwədʌkt/, *n.* a structure carrying a channel for supplying water over a long distance, often built over a valley or river. [L *aquae ductus* conveyance of water]

aqueous /'ækwiəs, 'eɪkwi-/, *adj.* **1.** of, like, or containing water. **2.** (of rocks) formed of matter deposited in or by water.

aqueous humor *or* **aqueous humour**, *n.* the watery fluid in the space between the cornea and the lens of the eye.

aquifer /'ækwəfə/, *n.* a layer of rock which holds water and allows water to flow slowly through it. Also, **aquafer**.

aquiline /'ækwəlaɪn/, *adj.* **1.** of or like an eagle. **2.** (of the nose) curved like an eagle's beak; hooked. [L]

Aquinas /ə'kwaɪnəs/, *n.* **Saint Thomas** ('*the Angelic Doctor*'), 1225?–1274, Italian philosopher and one of the great theologians of the Roman Catholic Church.

Aquino /ə'kinoʊ/, *n.* **1. Benigno** /bə'niɲoʊ/, 1932–83, Philippine politician, chief opposition leader from 1965 until his assassination. **2.** his wife, **Corazon**, born 1933, Philippine politician; president 1986–92.

Aquitaine /ˌækwə'teɪn/, *n.* **1.** a region in south-western France, on the Bay of Biscay. **2.** an ancient Roman province in Gaul, and later a medieval duchy. Latin, **Aquitania.**

-ar¹, an adjective suffix meaning 'of or relating to', 'like', as in *linear, regular*. [L *-āris*]

-ar², a noun suffix, as in *vicar, scholar, collar.* [representing L *-ārius, -āris*, etc.]

-ar³, a noun suffix indicating an agent (replacing regular **-er¹**), as in *beggar, liar.* [special use of -AR²]

Ar, *Chem. Symbol.* argon.

Arab /'ærəb/, *n.* **1.** a member of the Arabic race (now widely spread in Asia and Africa, and formerly in southern Europe). **2.** a horse of graceful, intelligent breed native to Arabia and adjacent countries. [ME, from L *Arabs*, from Gk '*Araps*, from Arabic '*arab*] —**Arabic**, *n., adj.*

arabesque /ˌærə'bɛsk/, *n.* **1.** a position in ballet in which one leg is stretched behind and the body lowered forward. **2.** *Music.* a highly ornamented short composition. **3.** a kind of ornament with a fanciful pattern of flowers, leaves, vases, animals, etc. ◇*adj.* **4.** decorated in this style. [F: Arabian, from It.]

Arabia /ə'reɪbiə/, *n.* a peninsula in south-western Asia between the Red Sea and the Persian Gulf, including Saudi Arabia, Yemen, Oman, and other political divisions; divided in ancient time into **Arabia Deserta**, the northern part, **Arabia Felix**, the southern part (sometimes restricted to Yemen), and **Arabia Petraea**, the north-western part. About 2 600 000 km². — **Arabian**, *adj.*, *n.*

Arabian Desert /ə'reɪbɪən 'dezət/, *n.* a large desert in Egypt between the Nile valley and the Red Sea.

Arabian Nights' Entertainment, *n.* **The**, a collection of Eastern folk tales derived in part from Indian and Persian sources and dating from the 10th century AD. Also, **The Thousand and One Nights**.

Arabic numerals /'ærəbɪk/, *n. pl.* the characters 0, 1, 2, 3, 4, 5, 6, 7, 8, 9. Also, **Arabic figures**.

arable /'ærəbəl/, *adj.* (of land) able to be cultivated for production of crops. [L *arābilis* that can be ploughed]

Arachne /ə'rækni/, *n. Gk Myth.* a Lydian maiden who challenged Athene to a contest in weaving, and was turned into a spider. [L, from Gk: lit., spider]

arachnid /ə'ræknɪd/, *n.* a class of arthropods with eight legs, that includes spiders, scorpions, mites, etc. [NL *Arachnida*, from Gk: spider, spider's web] — **arachnidan**, *adj.*, *n.*

arachnoid /ə'ræknɔɪd/, *adj.*, *n. Anat.* (relating to) the middle one of the three membranes which cover the brain and spinal cord. [Gk: like a cobweb]

Arafat /'ærəfæt/, *n.* **Yasser**, born 1929, Palestinian revolutionary; became leader of the Palestinian Liberation Organisation in 1968.

Arafura Sea /ærə,fjurə 'si/, *n.* a sea lying between PNG, Indonesia, and the northern coast of Australia, including the Gulf of Carpentaria. [probably from Portuguese *Alfours* free men, as applied to the inland tribes of the Aru Islands]

Aranda /'ærəndə/, *n.* an Australian Aboriginal language still in use around the Finke River and in the Simpson Desert. Also, **Arunta**.

Ararat /'ærəræt/, *n.* a volcanic mountain with two peaks, in eastern Turkey, near the boundary with Iran and Armenia; 5089 m.

arbiter /'abətə/, *n.* **1.** a person in a position to decide points of disagreement; judge. **2.** someone who has complete control of something. [L: witness, judge]

arbitrary /'abətrəri, 'abətri/, *adj.* **1.** based on personal feeling or opinion rather than reason or a general rule: *an arbitrary interpretation of a novel*. **2.** of unlimited power; despotic: *an arbitrary government*. **3.** not laid down in written law and so decided by the court: *an arbitrary punishment*. **4.** selected at random or by convention. [L: uncertain]

arbitrate /'abətreɪt/, *v.t.*, *v.i.*, **-trated, -trating. 1.** to decide (a matter) as an arbiter or arbitrator; determine. **2.** to put forward (a matter) for settlement; settle by arbitration. [L] — **arbitrator**, *n.*

arbitration /abə'treɪʃən/, *n.* **1.** *Law*. the non-judicial settlement of a dispute by means of a hearing before an impartial umpire or tribunal. **2.** *Indust. Law*. the settlement of a dispute between parties (for whom conciliation has failed) by a government-appointed arbitrator who is empowered to make a binding decision. — **arbitral**, *adj.*

arbor[1] or **arbour** /'abə/, *n.* a shady place formed by trees, shrubs, or climbing plants. [ME, from L *herba* plant]

arbor[2] /'abə/, *n. Mach.* a beam, shaft, axis, or spindle.

arboreal /a'bɔriəl/, *adj.* **1.** relating to trees; treelike. **2.** living in or among trees.

arboriculture /ə'bbrɪkʌltʃə/, *n.* the cultivation of trees and shrubs. [*arbori-* (combining form representing L *arbor* tree) + CULTURE]

arc /ak/, *n.*, *v.*, **arced** /akt/, **arcing** /'akɪŋ/ or **arcked, arcking**. ◇*n.* **1.** any part of a circle or other curved line. **2.** *Elect.* the luminous bridge formed by the passage of a current across a gap between two conductors or terminals. **3. strike an arc**, in electric welding, to apply a rod to the material to be welded, thus causing an arc (def. 2). ◇*v.i.* **4.** to form an electric arc. [ME, from L *arcus* bow]

arcade /a'keɪd/, *n.* **1.** *Archit.* **a.** a series of arches supported on columns. **b.** a part of a building with an arched roof. **2.** a covered passageway, usu. arched, with shops on either side. [F, from It.: bow, arch, from L]

Arcadia /a'keɪdiə/, *n.* a mountainous district in Greece in the centre of the Peloponnesus, known from ancient times for its quiet rural simplicity. [L, from Gk]

Arcadian /a'keɪdiən/, *adj.* relating to an ideal simplicity of country life; pastoral.

arcane /a'keɪn/, *adj.* mysterious; secret; understood only by a few. [L: shut up, keep]

arch[1] /atʃ/, *n.* **1.** a curved structure resting on supports at both ends, used to support weight, or to bridge or roof an open space, etc. **2.** Also, **archway**. such a structure built as an ornamental gateway. **3.** something curved like an arch: *the arch of the foot; the arch of the heavens*. ◇*v.t.* **4.** to build an arch across (an opening). **5.** to make into the shape of an arch; curve: *A horse arches its neck*. [ME, from L *arcus* bow]

arch[2] /atʃ/, *adj.* **1.** chief; most important; principal: *the arch villain*. **2.** mischievous; roguish: *an arch smile*. [separate use of ARCH-]

arch-, a prefix meaning 'first', 'chief', as in *archbishop*. [OE *arce-*, *erce-*, from L, from Gk, combining forms of *archós* chief]

-arch, a suffix meaning 'chief', 'ruler', as in *monarch*. [see ARCH-]

arch., *Abbrev.* archaic.

Archaean /a'kiən/, *adj.*, *n.* (relating to) the early Pre-Cambrian era or series of rocks. [Gk *archaio-* meaning 'ancient, primitive' + -AN]

archaeology or **archeology** /akɪ'blədʒi/, *n.* the scientific study of any culture, esp. a very ancient one, by digging up and describing its remains. [Gk: knowledge of ancient things] — **archaeologist**, *n.*, — **archaeological**, *adj.*

archaeopteryx /akɪ'bptərɪks/, *n.* a fossil bird, the oldest known type, with teeth and a long, feathered, vertebrate tail. [NL, from *archaeo-* ARCHAEO- + Gk *ptéryx* wing, bird]

Archaeozoic /ˌakiəˈzouɪk/, *adj., n.* (relating to) the most ancient period of the earth's history (preceding the Proterozoic), during which the earliest forms of life probably appeared.

archaic /aˈkeɪɪk/, *adj.* belonging to a much earlier period; old-fashioned. [Gk: antique]

archaism /ˈakeɪɪzəm/, *n.* 1. something archaic, as a word or style of writing. 2. the use of something that is archaic, as in literature. [Gk] —**archaist**, *n.* —**archaistic**, *adj.*

archangel /ˈakeɪndʒəl/, *n.* one of highest order of angels. [ME, from L, from Gk: chief angel] —**archangelic**, *adj.*

archbishop /atʃˈbɪʃəp/, *n.* a bishop of the highest rank. [OE *arcebiscop* (representing *hēahbiscop* high bishop)]

archeology /akiˈɒlədʒi/, *n.* →**archaeology**. —**archeological, archeologist**, *n.*

archer /ˈatʃə/, *n.* someone who shoots with a bow and arrow. [ME, from L *arcus* bow]

Archer[1] /ˈatʃə/, *n.* **Robyn**, born 1948, Australian performer, singer, and writer; interpreter of the works of Brecht.

Archer[2], *n.* an Australian racehorse, the winner of the first two Melbourne Cups (1861, 1862).

archerfish /ˈatʃəfɪʃ/, *n.* a type of small tropical fish of north-eastern Queensland and South-East Asia, which catches insects by spitting water at them.

archery /ˈatʃəri/, *n.* 1. the practice, art, or skill of an archer. 2. archers or their weapons collectively.

archespore /ˈakəspɔ/, *n.* one of the primitive cell, or group of cells, which give rise to spores. —**archesporial**, *adj.*

archetype /ˈakətaɪp/, *n.* a typical example or original model; prototype: *He was the archetype of all great rulers.* [L, from Gk: first-moulded, original] —**archetypal**, *adj.*

Archibald /ˈatʃəbɔld/, *n.* **Jules François** (*John Feltham Archibald*), 1856–1919, Australian journalist; one of the founders of the *Bulletin* (1880); his will provided for the Archibald Memorial and the Archibald Prize.

Archibald Prize, *n.* an art prize awarded annually since 1921 for an oil or watercolor portrait, generally of a public figure. [named after JF ARCHIBALD]

Archimedes /akəˈmidɪz/, *n.* 287?–212 BC, Greek mathematician, physicist, and inventor; discovered the principles of specific gravity and of the lever. —**Archimedean**, *adj.*

Archimedes' principle, *n.* the principle that the weight of the liquid displaced by a floating object is equal to the weight of the object.

archipelago /akəˈpɛləgou/, *n., pl.* **-gos, -goes.** 1. a large body of water with many islands. 2. the island groups in such a body of water. [It. *arcipelago*, lit., chief sea]

architect /ˈakətɛkt/, *n.* 1. someone who designs buildings and directs their construction. 2. the designer or maker of anything: *architect of an idea.* [L, from Gk: chief builder]

architecture /ˈakətɛktʃə/, *n.* 1. the art or science of planning and constructing buildings. 2. the style of a building or buildings collectively. 3. the action of building; construction. [L] —**architectural**, *adj.*

architrave /ˈakətreɪv/, *n. Archit.* 1. a beam resting directly on tops of columns (of a classical temple, etc.). 2. an ornamented band around a doorway, window, etc. [It. *architrave*, ARCHI- + *trave* (from L: beam)]

archives /ˈakaɪvz/, *n.pl.* (a place for keeping) public records or other historical documents relating to a family, company, country, etc. [F, from L, from Gk: public building, pl., records] —**archival**, *adj.* —**archivist**, *n.*

-archy, a word part meaning 'rule', 'government', as in *monarchy*. [Gk *-archía*]

arc light, *n.* a lamp in which the source of the bright white light is an electric arc, usu. between carbon rods. Also, **arc lamp**.

arctic /ˈaktɪk/, *adj.* 1. of, at, or near the North Pole. 2. *Colloq.* extremely cold. ◇*n.* 3. (*cap.*) the area north of the Arctic Circle. [L, from Gk: of the Bear (constellation), northern]

Arctic Circle, *n.* an imaginary circle around the earth forming the southern boundary of the North Frigid Zone, at latitude 66°32′.

Arctic Ocean, *n.* an ocean north of North America, Asia, and the Arctic Circle. About 14 090 000 km^2.

Arctic Zone, *n.* the section of the earth's surface lying within the Arctic Circle.

-ard, a noun suffix, oft. disapproving in tone, marking a person as having a particular quality as in *drunkard, wizard.* Also, **-art**. [OF *-ard, -art*, from G *-hart*, hard, hardy]

ardent /ˈadnt/, *adj.* full of feeling or enthusiasm; fervent: *ardent promises, an ardent believer.* [L: burning] —**ardency**, *n.*

ardor or **ardour** /ˈadə/, *n.* warmth of feeling; fervor; enthusiasm. [ME, from OF, from L]

arduous /ˈadʒuəs/, *adj.* 1. requiring great effort; strenuous; difficult: *arduous work.* 2. hard to climb; steep: *an arduous path.* 3. causing hardship: *arduous living conditions.* [L]

are[1] /a/; *weak form* /ə/, *v.* the present indicative pl. of the verb **be**. [dialect OE (Northumbrian) *aron*]

are[2] /ɛə/, *n.* a non-SI metric measure of area equal to 100 square metres. [F, from L: AREA]

area /ˈɛəriə/, *n., pl.* **areas, areae** /ˈɛəriˌi/. 1. a particular part of the earth's surface; region: *the area around Broome.* 2. a section or part: *an area of the body; the reception area of a hotel.* 3. the range or scope of a subject: *the whole area of science.* 4. *Maths.* a measure of surface (plane or curved). The SI unit of area is the square metre (m^2). [L: piece of level ground, open space]

arena /ə'rinə/, *n.* **1.** the oval space in an ancient Roman amphitheatre for games and fights. **2.** an enclosed place for sports contests, shows, etc. **3.** any field of competitive activity: *the arena of politics*. [L: sand, sandy place]

arenaceous /ærə'neɪʃəs/, *adj.* **1.** of or relating to sand. **2.** relating to sedimentary rock of sand particles and others down to 0.002 mm in diameter. [L: sandy]

aren't /ant/, *v.* **1.** short form of *are not*. **2.** short form of *am not* (as a question).

areola /ə'rɪələ/, *n.*, *pl.* **-lae** /-li/. **1.** a small ring of color, as around a nipple. **2.** a small space, as between fibres of connective tissue. [L diminutive of *āreā* AREA]

Areopagus /æri'ɒpəgəs/, *n.* **1.** a hill in Athens, to the west of the Acropolis. **2.** *Gk Hist.* the council which met on this hill. [L, from Gk: hill of ARES]

Ares /'ɛəriz/, *n.* the Greek god of war, identified by the Romans with Mars. [L, from Gk]

argent /'adʒənt/, *n.* **1.** *Archaic.* silver (color). ◇*adj.* **2.** like silver; silvery white. [F, from L: silver]

Argentina /adʒən'tinə/, *n.* a republic in southern South America, on the Atlantic and bounded by the Andes mountains to the west; a Spanish colony before independence in 1816; a republic since 1852. Pop. 31 030 000 (1986 est.); 2 766 889 km². *Language:* Spanish. *Currency:* peso. *Cap.:* Buenos Aires. Also, **the Argentine**. – **Argentine** /'adʒəntaɪn/, **Argentinean** /adʒən'tɪnɪən/, *n., adj.*

Argentine ant /'adʒəntin ænt/, *n.* a very destructive small brown ant, originating in South America, now spread widely throughout the world.

argentum /a'dʒɛntəm/, *n. Chem.* silver. [L]

argillaceous /adʒə'leɪʃəs/, *adj.* relating to sedimentary rock consisting of particles less than 0.002 mm in diameter.

argon /'agɒn/, *n.* a colorless, odorless, chemically inactive, gaseous element. *Symbol:* Ar; *at. no.:* 18; *at. wt:* 39.948. [NL, from Gk: idle]

Argonaut /'agənɔt/, *n. Gk Legend.* a member of the band that sailed to Colchis with Jason in the ship Argo in search of the Golden Fleece. [L from Gk *Argó* Argo + *naútēs* sailor]

argon-welding /agən'wɛldɪŋ/, *n.* a form of electric welding in which argon is used as a shield around the weld to keep out air.

Argos /'agɒs/, *n.* an ancient city in southeastern Greece, the centre of Argolis; a powerful rival of Sparta, Athens, and Corinth.

argot /'agoʊ/, *n.* the peculiar language or slang of any class or group, formerly that of thieves. [F; orig. unknown]

arguable /'agjuəbəl/, *adj.* **1.** able to be supported by argument; plausible. **2.** open to argument; doubtful.

argue /'agju/, *v.*, **-gued**, **-guing**. ◇*v.i.* **1.** to state reasons for or against something in opposition to someone else: *argue for change*; *argue with a friend*. **2.** to quarrel: *They argue all the time*. ◇*v.t.* **3.** to support by giving reasons: *The lawyer argued the case*; *He argued that it was true*; *Her letter argues patience*. **4.** to persuade by reasoning: *She argued him into doing it*. **5.** to show; imply: *His looks argue disappointment*. [ME, from L *argūtāre*, frequentative of *arguere* show]

argument /'agjəmənt/, *n.* **1.** a disagreement; quarrel. **2.** a discussion in which reasons for and against something are stated. **3.** a fact or series of reasons, stated in support of something. **4.** a summary of the subject matter of a book, etc. [ME, from L: proof]

argumentation /agjəmən'teɪʃən/, *n.* **1.** debate. **2.** (the stating of) reasons together with the conclusion drawn from them.

argumentative /agjə'mɛntətɪv/, *adj.* **1.** fond of argument: *an argumentative person*. **2.** marked by argument; controversial: *an argumentative matter*.

argus /'agəs/, *n.* **1.** a keen-eyed or watchful person. **2.** a type of pheasant found in SE Asia, marked with eyelike spots. [Gk: *Argus*, a giant with 100 eyes]

Argyle /'agaɪl/, *n.* **Lake**, a major reservoir about 40 km south of Kununurra, in WA; formed by the damming in 1970–72 of the Ord River; the main reservoir of the Ord River Irrigation Scheme.

Argyle apple, *n.* a medium-sized tree of eastern Australia, oft. cultivated for the pleasant appearance of its blue-grey leaves.

Argyll /a'gaɪl/, *n.* a former county of western Scotland, now largely part of Strathclyde region. Also, **Argyllshire**.

aria /'ɑrɪə/, *n.* an air or melody for a single voice, with accompaniment, in an opera, oratorio, etc. [It, from L: air]

Ariadne /æri'ædni/, *n. Gk Legend.* a daughter of Minos and Pasiphaë; she gave Theseus the thread whereby he escaped from the Labyrinth.

-arian, a suffix of adjectives and nouns, usu. meaning that a person believes or practises something, as in *humanitarian*, *librarian*. [-ARY + -AN]

arid /'ærɪd/, *adj.* **1.** dry and hot; without rain; barren. **2.** uninteresting; dull; uncreative. [L: dry] – **aridity,** *n.*

Aries /'ɛəriz/, *n.* the Ram, a constellation and sign of the zodiac. [L: a ram]

arise /ə'raɪz/, *v.i.*, **arose**, **arisen**, **arising**. **1.** to come into being; appear: *New questions may arise in your mind*. **2.** to result (fol. by *from*): *A problem arises from this decision*. **3.** to rise; move upwards. [OE *ā-* up + *rīsan* rise]

Aristides /ærəs'taɪdiz/, *n.* ('the Just'), 530?–467? BC, Athenian statesman and general; important in Greek victories over the Persians at Marathon (490) and Salamis (480).

Aristippus /ærəs'tɪpəs/, *n.* 435?–356? BC, Greek philosopher who founded a school at Cyrene, and formed the philosophy of hedonism.

aristocracy — armchair

aristocracy /ˌærəˈstɒkrəsi/, *n., pl.* **-cies.**
1. a government or a state in which power is held by a privileged upper class, usu. of noble birth. 2. such a class of people. 3. a class of people regarded as the best in any activity: *an aristocracy of ability*. [L, from Gk: rule of the best]

aristocrat /ˈærəstəkræt/, *n.* 1. a member of the aristocracy; a noble. 2. someone having the tastes, manners, etc., of an aristocrat. 3. someone who supports the aristocracy as a form of government. —**aristocratic**, *adj.*

Aristophanes /ˌærəˈstɒfəniz/, *n.* 448?–385? BC, Athenian poet and writer of comedy, as *The Birds* (414) and *Lysistrata* (411).

Aristotelian /ˌærɪstəˈtiliən/, *adj.* 1. of or relating to Aristotle or his teaching. ◇*n.* 2. someone who thinks in particulars and facts based on experience as opposed to the abstract theories of Platonism. Also, **Aristotelean.**

Aristotle /ˈærəˌstɒtl/, *n.* 384–322 BC, Greek philosopher, pupil of Plato, tutor of Alexander the Great; influenced Islamic philosophers as Averroës, and Catholic theologians as Thomas Aquinas.

arithmetic /əˈrɪθmətɪk/, *n.*; /ˌærəθˈmɛtɪk/, *adj.*, ◇*n.* 1. the branch of mathematics concerned with calculating with numbers. 2. Also, **theoretical arithmetic.** the theory of numbers, including the study of the divisibility of whole numbers, etc. ◇*adj.* 3. Also, **arithmetical.** of or relating to arithmetic. [L, from Gk: of or for reckoning] —**arithmetician,** *n.*

arithmetic mean /ˌærɪθmɛtɪk ˈmin/, *n.* *Maths.* the average value of several quantities obtained by adding them together and dividing the sum by the number of quantities, e.g., the arithmetic mean of 1, 5, 2, 8 is 4.

arithmetic progression /ˌærɪθmɛtɪk prəˈɡrɛʃən/, *n.* the series in which each quantity is obtained by the addition of one constant number to the quantity before it, e.g., 1, 4, 7, 10, 13. Also, **arithmetic series.**

Arizona /ˌærəˈzoʊnə/, *n.* a state in the south-western US. Pop. 3 317 000 (1986 est.); 295 024 km². *Cap.*: Phoenix. *Abbrev.*: Ariz.

Arjuna /əˈdʒunə/, *n. Hindu Myth.* the chief hero of the Bhagavad-gita.

ark /ak/, *n.* 1. *Bible.* the large, covered, floating vessel built by Noah for safety during the Flood. 2. any similar vessel. 3. Also, **ark of the covenant.** a chest or box sacred to Jews as representing the presence of God, carried by them on their journey to the Promised Land and kept in the temple in Jerusalem. 4. Also, **holy ark.** a wooden chest kept in the synagogue to hold writings of Jewish law. [OE *arc, earc,* from L *arca* a chest, coffer]

Arkansas /ˈakənsɔ/, *n.* a state in the southern central US. Pop. 2 372 000 (1986 est.); 137 539 km². *Cap.*: Little Rock. *Abbrev.*: Ark.

Arkwright /ˈakraɪt/, *n.* **Sir Richard,** 1732–92, English inventor of the spinning jenny.

Arles /alz, al/, *n.* a town in south-eastern France on the river Rhône; Roman amphitheatre. Pop. 50 345 (1975).

arm[1] /am/, *n.* 1. the upper limb of the human body from the shoulder to the hand. 2. the equivalent limb of any vertebrate. 3. a covering for the arm, as a sleeve. 4. any arm-like part, as the support of the side of a chair, a lake forming an inlet from sea, etc. 5. a branch of an organisation. 6. power; strength: *the arm of the law*. 7. Some special uses are:
arm in arm, with the arm of one person linked with the arm of another.
at arm's length, at a distance, such as to avoid familiarity, etc.
in arms, so young as to be carried in the arms, as a baby.
with open arms, with warmth and enthusiasm. [OE *arm, earm*]

arm[2] /am/, *n.* 1. (*usu. pl.*) weapon. ◇*v.i.* 2. to prepare for war by making or supplying arms. ◇*v.t.* 3. to supply (a person, military unit, etc.) with arms. 4. to provide (a person or thing) with something that gives strength or protection: *She armed herself with answers to his questions.* [ME, from L]

armada /aˈmadə/, *n.* 1. a large number of boats, war ships or aircraft. 2. (*cap.*) the fleet sent by Spain against England in 1588, which was broken up and scattered by storms. Also, the **Spanish** or **Invincible Armada.** [Sp., from L: armed forces]

armadillo /amaˈdɪloʊ/, *n., pl.* **-los.** a type of burrowing mammal, mostly active at night. Its body has a protective covering of bony plates. Found throughout South America and north as far as Texas. [Sp., diminutive of *armado* armed, from L]

Armageddon /amaˈɡɛdn/, *n.* 1. *Bible.* the place where the final battle between the forces of good and evil will be fought at the end of the world. 2. any war of great importance, esp. World War I. [LL, from G, from Heb. *har megiddōn,* the mountain region of *Megiddo,* site of several great battles in the Old Testament. See Revelation 16:16]

Armagh /aˈma/, *n.* a town in a county of the same name in Northern Ireland; Saint Patrick is said to have founded the first mission settlement here. Pop. 12 297 (1971).

armament /ˈaməmənt/, *n.* 1. weapon equipment, esp. that of an aeroplane, vehicle, or warship. 2. a military force equipped for war. 3. preparation for war by making and supplying arms. [L: equipment, ship's tackle]

armature /ˈamətʃə/, *n.* 1. *Biol.* the protective covering of an animal or plant. 2. *Elect.* **a.** the iron or steel placed across the poles of a permanent magnet to close it, or to the poles of an electromagnet to carry mechanical force. **b.** the part of an electrical machine which includes the coils carrying the current. **c.** a part of an electrical machine that vibrates when activated by a magnetic field. [L: armor]

armchair /ˈamtʃɛə/, *n.* 1. a chair with supports at the side for the forearms or elbows. ◇*adj.* 2. basing ideas on theory or reading, rather than practical experience: *an armchair critic*; *an armchair traveller*.

armed /amd/, *adj.* **1.** having weapons. **2.** prepared and ready.

armed services, *n.pl.* the principal military forces of a country or countries including army, navy, air force, etc. Also, **armed forces**.

Armenia /a'miniə/, *n.* **1.** a republic in western Asia, bordered by Georgia, Azerbaijan, Iran and Turkey; a member of the CIS; a constituent republic of the Soviet Union 1922–91, known as the **Armenian Soviet Socialist Republic**. Pop. 3 288 000 (1989 est.); 29 785 km². *Language*: Armenian. *Cap*.: Yerevan. **2.** a region of western Asia, including this republic and parts of Turkey and Iran; the traditional home of the Armenians, an ancient Indo-European people. **– Armenian**, *n.*, *adj.*

Armidale /'amədeil/, *n.* a city in the New England district of NSW; wool studs; university, 1954. Pop. 19 525 (1986).

armistice /'aməstəs/, *n.* an agreement by warring parties to stop fighting so as to discuss peace; truce. [NL, from L: *armi*- (combining form of *arma* arms) + *-stitium* (from *sistere* stop)]

Armistice Day, *n.* the anniversary of the end of World War I on 11 November 1918, when the armistice was signed.

armor *or* **armour** /'amə/, *n.* **1.** a defensive covering, usu. of metal, worn to protect the body during fighting. **2.** protective metal plates used on warships, tanks, aeroplanes, etc. **3.** any protective covering, as the scales of a fish. ◇*v.t.* **4.** to provide with armor. [ME, from L] **– armored**, *adj.*

armorer *or* **armourer** /'amərə/, *n.* **1.** a maker or repairer of arms and armor. **2.** a person in charge of small arms in a military unit.

armorial /a'mɔriəl/, *adj.* belonging to heraldry or coats of arms.

Armorican /a'mɒrikən/, *adj. Geol.* relating to the period of mountain-building in Europe in the Upper Carboniferous and Permian periods.

armory *or* **armoury** /'aməri/, *n.*, *pl.* **-ries**. **1.** a place for storing weapons. **2.** armor collectively. [ME *armurie*]

armpit /'ampɪt/, *n.* the hollow part under the arm at the shoulder.

arms /amz/, *n.pl.* **1.** weapons. **2.** a pictorial design used as a symbol by a family, town, nation, etc.; heraldic bearing. **3.** Some special uses are:

bear arms, to serve as a soldier.
take (up) arms, to prepare to fight.
under arms, armed.
(up) in arms, **1.** armed and prepared to fight. **2.** angry or indignant (fol. by *at*). [ME, from L]

Armstrong /'amstrɒŋ/, *n.* **1. Gillian May**, born 1950, Australian film director; films include *My Brilliant Career* (1979). **2. Helen Porter** → Dame Nellie **Melba**. **3. Louis** ('Satchmo'), 1900–71, US jazz trumpeter and composer. **4. Neil**, born 1930, US astronaut; first human being to walk on the moon.

army /'ami/, *n.*, *pl.* **-mies**. **1.** (*cap.* or *l.c.*) the military land forces of a nation. **2.** a unit in a large army, consisting of two or more corps, etc. **3.** a large group of people organised for a particular cause. **4.** a large number; multitude: *an army of insects*. [ME, from L: armed forces]

Arnhem Land /'anəm lænd/, *n.* **1.** one of Australia's largest Aboriginal reserves, lying east and south-east of Darwin. About 97 000 km². **2.** (formerly) an area comprising the northern part of the NT from the Roper River west to the Victoria River. [named after the Dutch ship *Arnhem*, from which the first European sighting of this region was made, in 1623]

Arnold /'anəld/, *n.* **1. Matthew**, 1822–88, English poet, essayist and literary critic; author of *Culture and Anarchy* (1869).

aroma /ə'roumə/, *n.* **1.** a smell, esp. an agreeable one; fragrance. **2.** a quality or atmosphere that seems typical (of something). [L, from Gk: spice, sweet herb]

aromatic /ærə'mætɪk/, *n.*, *adj.* (a plant, drug or medicine) having an aroma.

aromatic compound, *n.* any of a class of organic compounds including benzene, naphthalene, anthracene, and their derivatives, which contain an unsaturated ring of carbon atoms. Many have an agreeable smell.

arose /ə'rouz/, *v.* past tense of **arise**.

around /ə'raʊnd/, *adv.* **1.** in a circle on every side: *A crowd gathered around*; *The land is mine for 20 km around*. **2.** here and there; about: *to travel around*. **3.** somewhere about or near: *to wait around*. **4.** with a circular movement: *The wheels go around*. **5.** *Colloq.* active; in circulation: *That singer has been around for a long time*. ◇*prep.* **6.** on all sides of; surrounding: *a belt around her waist*. **7.** on the other side of: *the house around the corner*. **8.** here and there, in, or near: *to drive around the country*; *stay around the house*. **9.** *Colloq.* near to in time, amount, etc.; approximately: *around ten o'clock*. [A-¹ + ROUND]

arouse /ə'raʊz/, *v.t.*, **aroused**, **arousing**. **1.** to cause to become active; bring into being: *I aroused him to action*; *Don't arouse suspicion*. **2.** to wake from sleep. **3.** to make (someone) sexually excited. [ROUSE¹, modelled on ARISE] **– arousal**, *n.*

Arp /ap/, *n.* **Jean** /ʒɒ̃/ or **Hans** /hans/, 1887–1966, French sculptor, painter, and poet; one of the founders of Dada.

arpeggio /a'pedʒiou/, *n.*, *pl.* **-os**. *Music.* **1.** the sounding of the notes of a chord one after the other instead of together. **2.** (esp. on keyboard instruments and harp) the playing of a chord so that the notes are sounded very rapidly one after the other and finally all together. **3.** such a chord. [It.: play on the harp]

arr., *Abbrev.* **1.** arranged. **2.** arrival.

arraign /ə'reɪn/, *v.t.* **1.** *Law*. to bring (a prisoner) before a court to answer to a charge. **2.** to charge (someone) with faults; accuse. [ME, from ML: call to account] **– arraignment**, *n.*

arrange /ə'reɪndʒ/, *v.*, **-ranged**, **-ranging**. ◇*v.t.* **1.** to put in order: *to arrange books on a shelf*. **2.** to come to an agreement about; settle:

arrange / **artery**

to arrange a sale. **3.** to prepare or plan: *to arrange a wedding; to arrange to meet a friend.* **4.** *Music.* to change (a composition) to make it suitable for a particular kind of performance, esp. for different instruments or voices. ◊*v.i.* **5.** to make preparations or arrangements: *I arranged for her to come early.* [ME, from OF *a-* A.⁵ + *rangier* RANGE, v.]

arrangement /ə'reɪndʒmənt/, *n.* **1.** act of arranging. **2.** manner or result of arranging: *an arrangement of flowers; a musical arrangement for two voices.* **3.** settlement or agreement. **4.** (usu. pl.) plan; preparation: *Are the arrangements for your trip completed?* [F]

arrant /'ærənt/, *adj.* complete; thorough; utter: *an arrant fool; arrant nonsense.* [var. of ERRANT]

arras /'ærəs/, *n.* a (weave of) rich tapestry, esp. as a wall hanging. [named after *Arras*, a town in N France]

array /ə'reɪ/, *v.t.* **1.** to place in position for battle, as soldiers, etc. **2.** to dress, esp. with show; bedeck. ◊*n.* **3.** a regular order, as of soldiers ready for battle. **4.** a group of things on show: *The shop had a good array of books.* **5.** clothing. [ME, from OF *a* to + *rei* order, of Gmc origin]

arrear /ə'rɪə/, *n.* **1.** (usu. pl.) something that is owed or overdue. **2. in arrear** or **in arrears**, behind in payments, etc. [ME, from L *ad-* AD- + *retrō* backwards]

arrest /ə'rɛst/, *v.t.* **1.** to seize or capture by legal authority: *The police arrested the criminal.* **2.** to catch and fix: *The shouting arrested her attention.* **3.** to stop the movement or growth of (something): *to arrest the current of a river; arrest a disease.* ◊*n.* **4.** the act of arresting (a person, etc.): *The police have made an arrest.* **5.** the state of being arrested: *The criminal was put under arrest.* **6.** a stopping of movement or growth: *cardiac arrest.* **7.** anything used for stopping the motion of a machine. [ME, from L *ad-* AD- + *restāre* stop]

arrival /ə'raɪvəl/, *n.* **1.** the act of arriving: *time of arrival.* **2.** the reaching of any object or condition: *arrival at a decision.* **3.** a person or thing that arrives: *a new arrival at the school.*

arrive /ə'raɪv/, *v.i.*, **-rived, -riving. 1.** to come to the end of a journey or stage of journey: *The train has arrived.* **2.** to reach (fol. by *at*): *to arrive at a conclusion; arrive at the age of 30.* **3.** (of time) to come: *The moment has arrived.* **4.** to reach a position of success. [ME, from LL: come to shore]

arrogant /'ærəgənt/, *adj.* having or showing too high an opinion of one's importance or rights; very proud: *an arrogant teacher; arrogant behavior.* [ME, from L: assuming] —**arrogance**, *n.*

arrogate /'ærəgeɪt/, *v.t.*, **-gated, -gating. 1.** to claim for oneself without right. **2.** to state or think (something) about another without just reason. [L: assumed, asked of]

arrow /'æroʊ/, *n.* **1.** a thin, pointed, wooden weapon made to be shot from a bow, usu. with feathers at the end to balance it. **2.** anything like an arrow in form, such as a sign used to show direction. [ME and OE *arwe*]

arrowroot /'ærərut/, *n.* (a starch for cooking obtained from) a type of tropical American plant with white flowers.

arse /as/, *n., v.*, **arsed, arsing.** *Colloq.* (*offensive*) ◊*n.* **1.** the bottom; buttocks. ◊*v.* **2. arse around**, to act like a fool; waste time. [ME; OE *ears*]

arsenal /'asənəl/, *n.* a place for keeping or making arms and military stores of all kinds. [It.: dock]

arsenic /'asənɪk/, *n.* **1.** a greyish-white element having a metallic lustre, and forming poisonous compounds. Symbol: As; *at. no.*: 33; *at. wt*: 74.9216. **2.** arsenic trioxide or white arsenic, As₂O₃, which is used in medicine and painting, and in poison for vermin. ◊*adj.* **3.** of or containing arsenic. [ME, from L, from Gk] —**arsenic, arsenical**, *adj.*

arson /'asən/, *n.* the intentional and unlawful burning of a building or other property. [AF, from LL: a burning] —**arsonist**, *n.*

art¹ /at/, *n.* **1.** the production or expression of what is beautiful or visually attractive. **2.** the products of human visual creativity, such as drawing, painting, sculpture, architecture. **3.** Also, **fine arts.** any branch of these arts, esp. painting. **4.** (*pl.*) Also, **liberal arts.** creative or non-scientific branches of learning collectively, esp. as a course of university study. **5.** the skill or work of humans (oft. opposed to *nature*). **6.** skilled practice: *the art of making speeches.* **7.** a studied action; cunning: *She is full of art; He knows the arts of politics.* [ME, from OF, from L: skill, art]

art² /at/, *v. Archaic.* 2nd person singular, present indic., of the verb **be.** [ME; OE *eart*]

Art Deco /at 'dɛkoʊ, 'deɪkoʊ/, *n.* a style of ornament, originating in the 1920s and 1930s, marked by geometrical forms and the use of such materials as plastic, glass, etc. Also, **art deco.** [F *Art Déco*, shortened form of *Exposition Internationale des Arts Décoratifs*, Paris, 1925]

artefact /'atəfækt/, *n.* **1.** an object made by a human, e.g. a tool, work of art, etc. **2.** *Biol.* a substance, etc., not naturally present in tissue, but formed by death or reagent. Also, **artifact.** [L]

Artemis /'atəməs/, *n. Gk Myth.* a goddess, sister of Apollo, represented as a virgin huntress and associated with the moon; identified by the Romans with Diana. [L, from Gk]

arterial /a'tɪəriəl/, *n.* of, relating to, or like an artery or arteries.

arteriosclerosis /a,tɪəriouskləˈroʊsəs/, *n. Med.* a disease, usu. in elderly people, marked by loss of elasticity and thickening of the arterial walls. [NL, from Gk: *artērio-* artery + *sklērōsis* hardening]

artery /'atəri/, *n., pl.* **-teries. 1.** *Anat.* a blood vessel which carries blood from the heart to various parts of the body. **2.** a main channel in a system of communications or transport. [ME, from L, from Gk]

artesian basin /ɑˌtiːʒən ˈbeɪsən/, *n. Geol.* a series of rocks formed in such a way that water is held in an aquifer under pressure.

artesian bore /ɑˌtiːʒən ˈbɔː/, *n.* a well sunk through an aquifer in which pressure rather than pumping keeps water rising above ground. Also, **artesian well**. [F *artésien* pertaining to *Artois*, former province of France where such wells were bored]

artful /ˈɑtfəl/, *adj.* clever in getting what one wants; cunning: *artful plans*.

arthritis /ɑˈθraɪtəs/, *n. Med.* swelling and pain in a joint of the body, as in gout. [L, from Gk: joint disease] —**arthritic**, *adj., n.*

arthro-, *Anat.* a word part meaning joint, as in *arthropod*. Also, **arthr-**. [Gk]

arthropod /ˈɑθrəpɒd/, *n.* one of the group of invertebrates, having jointed legs and a segmented body, as the insects, arachnids, crustaceans, etc.

Arthur[1] /ˈɑθə/, *n.* a legendary king in post-Roman Britain; leader of the Knights of the Round Table and the subject of much European literature, as Sir Thomas Malory's *Morte d'Arthur*. —**Arthurian**, *adj.*

Arthur[2] /ˈɑθə/, *n.* **1. Chester Alan**, 1830–86, 21st president of the US 1881–85. **2. Sir George**, 1784–1854, Scottish-born administrator in Australia; lieutenant-governor of Tasmania 1823–37.

artichoke /ˈɑtətʃoʊk, ˈɑtɪtʃoʊk/, *n.* **1.** a thistle-like plant with a flower head of leaf-like scales used as a vegetable; globe artichoke. **2.** this vegetable. **3.** →**Jerusalem artichoke**. [It., from Pr., from Ar.]

article /ˈɑtɪkəl/, *n., v.,* **-cled, -cling.** ◇*n.* **1.** a piece of writing on a particular subject, complete in itself but forming part of a book, newspaper, magazine, etc. **2.** a particular or separate thing: *an article of food or dress*. **3.** a thing in general: *What is that article?* **4.** (in some languages) any word, as the English words *a* or *an* (**indefinite article**) and *the* (**definite article**), which come before nouns to indicate their particularity, etc. **5.** a separate section, clause, item in an agreement, contract, law, etc. ◇*v.t.* **6.** to bind by contract, etc.: *to article an apprentice; an articled clerk in a lawyer's office*. [ME, from F, from L *articulus*, diminutive of *artus* joint]

articles of association, *n.pl.* (a document containing) the rules and constitution of a registered company.

articulate /ɑˈtɪkjʊleɪt/, *v.,* **-lated, -lating**; /ɑˈtɪkjʊlət/, *adj.* ◇*v.t.* **1.** to speak (words, etc.) clearly. **2.** *Phonet.* to make the movements of the speech organs necessary to produce (speech). **3.** to unite with joints. ◇*v.i.* **4.** to speak with clearly pronounced syllables or words: *He articulates well*. **5.** to form a joint. ◇*adj.* **6.** clear; distinct. **7.** able to express ideas clearly: *She is very articulate on that subject*. **8.** having the power of speech. **9.** Also, **articulated**. having joints or segments. [L]

articulation /ɑˌtɪkjʊˈleɪʃən/, *n.* **1.** *Phonet.* the act of articulating speech. **2.** the degree of clearness of speech. **3.** the act of joining. **4.** a joint. **5.** *Bot.* a place between two parts where separation happens naturally, as the joint between a leaf and stem.

artifact /ˈɑtəfækt/, *n.* →**artefact**.

artifice /ˈɑtəfəs/, *n.* **1.** a clever trick or device. **2.** trickery; deception. **3.** a skilful way of doing something. [F, from L]

artificer /ɑˈtɪfəsə/, *n.* **1.** a skilful worker or craftsman. **2.** *Mil.* a person in military services who does repairs to machinery, etc.

artificial /ɑtəˈfɪʃəl/, *adj.* **1.** made by humans (opposed to *natural*): *artificial flowers*. **2.** copying what is natural; not genuine; affected: *artificial sorrow; artificial manners*. [ME, from L] —**artificiality**, *n.*

artificial insemination, *n.* the placing of sperm into the vagina or uterus by methods other than sexual intercourse, in order to bring about pregnancy.

artificial kidney, *n.* →**kidney machine**.

artificial respiration, *n.* a method for restarting someone's breathing, as by rhythmic pressure on the rib cage, or mouth-to-mouth breathing.

artillery /ɑˈtɪləri/, *n.* **1.** large guns fitted on wheels, as cannon, etc. **2.** the branch of an army concerned with such guns. [ME, from OF: implements of war]

artisan /ˈɑtəzən/, *n.* someone skilled in a craft. [F, from It. *arte* guild]

artist /ˈɑtəst/, *n.* **1.** someone who practises one of the fine arts, esp. painting. **2.** someone who practises one of the performing arts, as acting or singing. **3.** someone who uses the skills of art in their work, etc.: *a commercial artist; an artist with words*. [F, from It., from LL] —**artistic**, *adj.*

artiste /ɑˈtist/, *n.* (*oft. used to make fun of a person's pretensions*) **1.** an entertainer, esp. an actor, singer or dancer. **2.** someone who shows skill and taste in some activity: *a cooking artiste*.

artistry /ˈɑtəstri/, *n., pl.* **-tries.** artistic skill, quality or activities.

artless /ˈɑtləs/, *adj.* free from pretence; natural; simple: *an artless manner; artless beauty*.

Art Nouveau /ɑt nu'voʊ/, *n.* a style of art, architecture and ornament of the 1890s, marked by patterns of twisting flower and vegetable forms, based on ideas of naturalistic representation. Also, **art nouveau**. [F: new art]

art union, *n.* a lottery, usu. with non-cash prizes.

arty /ˈɑti/, *adj.,* **-tier, -tiest.** *Colloq.* making an obvious show of artistic awareness or ability.

Aru Islands /ˌɑru ˈaɪləndz/, *n.pl.* an island group in Indonesia, south-west of the island of New Guinea. About 8500 km^2.

arvo /ˈɑvoʊ/, *n. Colloq.* afternoon. [modified shortened form of AFTERNOON + -O]

-ary, **1.** an adjective suffix meaning 'relating to', as in (*honorary, voluntary*). **2.** a noun suffix meaning 'a place for' (*dictionary, aviary*), or marking the office of a person (*missionary, secretary*), or other relations (*adversary*). [L -*ārius*, neut. -*ārium*]

Aryan /'eəriən/, *n.* **1.** *Ethnol.* a member or descendant of the prehistoric people who spoke Indo-European. **2.** (in Nazi doctrine) a non-Jewish Caucasian, esp. one of Nordic physical type.

aryl /'æril/, *adj.* of or pertaining to any of the organic radicals obtained from the aromatic hydrocarbons by removing a hydrogen atom, as phenyl (C_6H_5) from benzene (C_6H_6).

as /æz/; *weak form* /əz/, *adv.* **1.** to the same degree (fol. by the conjunction *as*): *as good as gold.* ◇*conj.* **2.** used in the expressions *as* (or *so*) *... as, same ... as*, etc., to mean degree, manner, etc. (*as good as gold, in the same way as before*), or in the expressions *so as, such as,* to mean purpose or result (fol. by *to*): *to listen so as to hear.* **3.** in the degree, manner, etc., of or that: *quick as thought; speak as he does; as I hear it.* **4.** though: *Bad as it is, it could be worse.* **5.** when or while. **6.** since; because. **7.** for instance. **8.** Some special uses are: **as for** or **as to**, with regard to. **as if** or **as though**, as it would be if. **as it were**, in a way; so to speak. **as yet**, **1.** up to now. **2.** for the moment; just yet. ◇*rel. pron.* **9.** that; who; which (esp. after *such* and *the same*): *the same film as we saw before.* **10.** (of) which fact (referring to previous statement): *I may fail you, as you realise.* ◇*prep.* **11.** in the character or capacity of: *to appear as Othello; to serve as a warning.* [OE *alswā, ealswā* all so, quite so]

as-, prefix of direction or addition, variant of **ad-** before *s*, as in *assert*.

As, *Chem. Symbol.* arsenic.

asbestos /əs'bestəs, æs-/, *n.* **1.** a fibrous amphibole, used for making heat-resistant or fireproof articles. **2.** a fire-resistant material made from asbestos fibres. [L, from Gk: unquenchable]

asbestosis /æsbes'tousəs/, *n.* a disease of the lungs caused by breathing in asbestos particles.

ascend /ə'send/, *v.i.* **1.** to climb or go upwards: *The road started to ascend; The smoke is ascending from the chimney.* **2.** *Music.* to go from lower to higher notes. ◇*v.t.* **3.** to go up; climb: *to ascend a hill; to ascend a ladder.* [ME, from L: climb up]

ascendant /ə'sendənt/, *n.* **1.** a position of power or control: *to be in the ascendant.* **2.** *Astrol.* (a sign of the zodiac containing) the point of the ecliptic rising above the horizon at time of birth, etc. ◇*adj.* **3.** more powerful; predominant. **4.** rising. Also, **ascendent.** – **ascendancy**, *n.*

ascension /ə'senʃən/, *n.* **1.** an act of ascending; ascent. **2.** (*usu. cap.*) *Church.* the rising of Christ from earth to heaven. **3.** (*usu. cap.*) *Islam.* the rising of Mohammed. [ME, from L]

Ascension /ə'senʃən/, *n.* a British island in the southern Atlantic. Pop. 1200 (1977); 88 km².

Ascension Day /– 'deɪ/, *n.* the fortieth day after Easter, commemorating the ascension of Christ.

ascent /ə'sent/, *n.* **1.** an act of ascending; upward movement. **2.** an upward slope; gradient. [from ASCEND, modelled on DESCENT]

ascertain /æsə'teɪn/, *v.t.* to find out by examination, or testing, so as to know as certain; determine. [ME, from OF: make certain] – **ascertainable**, *adj.* – **ascertainment**, *n.*

ascetic /ə'setɪk/, *n.* **1.** a person who chooses to follow a strict (usu. religious) code of self-denial. **2.** (in the early Christian Church) a man living apart; hermit. ◇*adj.* **3.** self-denying. [Gk: monk, hermit (orig. athlete)] – **ascetically**, *adv.* – **asceticism**, *n.*

ascorbic acid /ə'skɔbɪk 'æsəd/, *n.* vitamin C, found in citrus fruits, tomatoes, etc., and also made industrially.

ascribe /ə'skraɪb/, *v.t.*, **ascribed**, **ascribing**. **1.** to consider as connected, as to a cause or origin; assign: *The alphabet is usually ascribed to the Phoenicians.* **2.** to consider to belong: *to ascribe wisdom to old age.* [L: add to a writing] – **ascription**, *n.*

asdic /'æzdɪk/, *n.* an instrument to determine the position of objects under water by measuring the direction and return time of a sound echo. [acronym from *Allied Submarine Detection Investigation Committee*]

ASEAN /'æziæn, 'æs-/, *n.* a treaty grouping consisting of Indonesia, Malaysia, the Philippines, Singapore, Thailand, and Brunei, dating from 1967; Australia is one of six 'dialogue partners'. [*A(ssociation of) S(outh-)E(ast) A(sian) N(ations)*]

aseptic /eɪ'septɪk/, *adj.* free from the living germs of disease, fermentation, or rotting. – **aseptically**, *adv.* – **asepsis**, *n.*

asexual /eɪ'sekʃuəl/, *adj.* **1.** not sexual. **2.** having no sex or no sexual organs. – **asexuality**, *n.*

ash[1] /æʃ/, *n.* **1.** (*oft. pl.*) the powdery leftover matter that remains after burning: *hot ashes; soda ash.* **2.** *Geol.* the finely crushed lava thrown out by a volcano. **3.** (*pl.*) ruins, as from destruction by burning: *the ashes of an ancient empire.* **4.** (*pl.*) the remains of the human body after cremation (burning). **5. the Ashes**, the trophy, a wooden urn containing a cremated cricket stump, kept permanently in England, played for by England and Australia in test cricket. [OE *asce, æsce*]

ash[2] /æʃ/, *n.* **1.** a tree of the Northern Hemisphere producing valuable, tough wood. **2.** any Southern Hemisphere tree whose wood or leaves resemble that of the ash. [OE *æsc*]

ashamed /ə'ʃeɪmd/, *adj.* **1.** feeling shame; upset by guilt. **2.** unwilling through fear or shame: *ashamed to speak.* **3.** unwilling to admit (fol. by *of*): *ashamed of her misdeeds.*

ashen /'æʃən/, *adj.* **1.** ash-colored; grey. **2.** consisting of ashes. [ASH[1] + -EN[2]]

ash flow, *n.* (a deposit from) a fall of volcanic ash, generally a highly-heated mixture of vol-

ash flow

canic gases and ash produced by a sudden explosion.

Ashmore and Cartier Islands /ˈæʃmɔ ən ˈkatiə/, *n.pl.* a group of four uninhabited islands (Cartier Island and the three Ashmore Islands) more than 500 km off the WA coast north of Derby; under Australian government jurisdiction.

ashram /ˈæʃræm, ˈɒʃrəm/, *n.* a group of people living together for spiritual development, as through yoga, meditation, etc. [Skt *ā* towards, near to + *s'rama* fatigue, exertion, religious exercise]

Ashton /ˈæʃtən/, *n.* **Julian Rossi**, 1851–1942, born in England, landscape painter; founded the influential Sydney Art School (now the Julian Ashton Art School) in 1896.

Ash Wednesday, *n.* **1.** the first day of Lent. **2.** 16 February, 1983, which marked the start of three days of bushfires in Vic and SA, which claimed 71 lives.

ashy /ˈæʃi/, *adj.*, **ashier, ashiest. 1.** ash-colored; pale. **2.** sprinkled or covered with ashes.

Asia /ˈeɪʒə/, *n.* the largest continent, bounded by Europe and the Pacific, Arctic, and Indian oceans; separated from Europe by the Ural Mountains, Black Sea and Mediterranean Sea, and from Africa by the Red Sea. Pop. 2 405 300 000 (1980); 44 418 500 km^2.

Asia Minor, *n.* a peninsula in western Asia between the Black Sea and the Mediterranean Sea, including most of Asiatic Turkey. See **Anatolia**.

Asian /ˈeɪʒən, ˈeɪʃən/, *adj.* **1.** of or relating to Asia. ◇*n.* **2.** someone born or living in Asia. Also, **Asiatic.**

aside /əˈsaɪd/, *adv.* **1.** on or to one side, apart: *to turn aside; He put his cares aside.* ◇*n.* **2.** words spoken softly, so as not to be heard by some of the people present, as in a theatre where only the audience is meant to hear. **3.** a remark which is separate from the main subject.

Asimov /ˈæzəmɒf/, *n.* **Isaac**, 1920–92, Russian-born biochemist and science-fiction author; works include *I, Robot* (1950) and *The Gods Themselves* (1972).

asinine /ˈæsənaɪn/, *adj.* stupid; obstinate. [L: ass] —**asininity,** *n.*

ASIO /ˈeɪzioʊ/, *n.* a statutory body formed in 1949 responsible for counterespionage and for the collecting of information on subversive or terrorist activity. [*A(ustralian) S(ecret) I(ntelligence) O(rganization)*]

ASIS /ˈeɪsəs/, *n.* an agency for the secret collection of information on the intentions of foreign countries. [*A(ustralian) S(ecret) I(ntelligence) S(ervice)*]

ask /ask/, *v.t.* **1.** to put a question to: *She will ask him.* **2.** to try to find information about: *to ask the way;* (or, with a double object) *to ask him the way.* **3.** to attempt by words to obtain; request: *to ask advice; ask a favor.* **4.** to request of (with a personal object, and with or without *for* before the thing desired): *I ask you a great favor.* **5.** to demand; expect: *to ask a price for something.* **6.** to invite: *to ask guests.* ◇*v.i.* **7.** to make inquiry; inquire: *She asked after him.* **8.** to request (fol. by *for*): *ask for bread.* ◇*v.* **9. ask for trouble / it,** *Colloq.* to behave so as to invite trouble. **10. I ask you,** (a phrase showing surprise, disapproval, etc.). **11. if you ask me,** (a phrase for effect meaning 'in my opinion'). [OE *āscian*]

askance /əˈskæns/, *adv.* **1.** with mistrust or disapproval: *He looked askance at my offer.* **2.** sideways. Also, **askant** /əˈskænt/. [orig. uncert.]

askew /əˈskju/, *adv.* **1.** to one side; out of line; obliquely; awry. ◇*adj. (used after a verb)* **2.** slanting. [A-^{1} + SKEW]

Askin /ˈæskən/, *n.* **Sir Robert William** (*Robin William Askin*), 1909–81, Australian state Liberal Party politician; premier of NSW 1965–75.

asleep /əˈslip/, *adv.* **1.** in or into a state of sleep. ◇*adj. (used after a verb)* **2.** sleeping. **3.** inactive. **4.** (of a body part) numb, without sensation.

asocial /eɪˈsoʊʃəl/, *adj.* Psychol., etc. avoiding or refusing people's company.

asp /æsp/, *n.* any of several poisonous snakes, esp. the Egyptian cobra. [L, from Gk]

asparagus /əˈspærəgəs/, *n.* **1.** a plant with long green shoots. **2.** the young shoots used as a table vegetable. [L, from Gk]

aspect /ˈæspɛkt/, *n.* **1.** the way a thing appears to the eye or mind; look: *the physical aspect of the country; both aspects of a question.* **2.** the side or surface facing a given direction: *the dorsal aspect of a fish.* **3.** view; direction; exposure: *The house has a southern aspect.* **4.** *Gram.* (in some languages) the part of the sense of a verb's meaning which shows the relation of the action of the verb to the passage of time, as in continuous aspect (e.g. *was eating*), completed aspect (e.g. *had eaten*), etc. [ME, from L: look at]

aspen /ˈæspən/, *n.* any of various species of poplar, with leaves that tremble in the slightest breeze. [ME, from OE *æspe*]

asperity /æsˈpɛrəti, əs-/, *n., pl.* **-ties.** roughness or harshness; severity: *asperity in her tone of voice.* [L: roughness]

aspersion /əˈspɜʒən, əspəʃən/, *n.* a damaging remark or criticism: *to cast aspersions on one's character.*

asphalt /ˈæsfɔlt, ˈæsfɛlt/, *n.* **1.** any of various dark-colored, solid substances containing bitumen composed mostly of mixtures of hydrocarbons, occurring in various parts of the earth. **2.** a similar substance, one of the products of petroleum-cracking operations. **3.** a mixture of such a substance with crushed rock, etc., used for roads, etc. [LL, from Gk]

asphyxia /əsˈfɪksiə/, *n. Med.* the extreme condition caused by lack of oxygen and too much carbon dioxide in the blood, caused by interruption to breathing, as in choking. [Gk: stopping of the pulse] —**asphyxiant,** *n.* —**asphyxiate,** *v.*

aspic /'æspɪk/, *n.* a savory jelly made from meat or fish stock sometimes with added gelatine. [F]

aspidistra /ˌæspə'dɪstrə/, *n.* a plant bearing large evergreen leaves, once widely grown as a house plant. [NL, from Gk: shield]

aspirate /'æspəreɪt/, *v.*, **-rated, -rating;** /'æspərət/, *n.* ◇*v.t.* **1.** *Phonet.* to let go (a stop) in such a way that the breath escapes with friction that is heard, as in *title* where the first *t* is aspirated, the second is not. **2.** to draw or remove (fluids) by suction, as with an aspirator. ◇*n.* **3.** *Phonet.* a stop consonant which is aspirated. [L: breathed on] — **aspiration,** *n.*

aspirator /'æspəreɪtə/, *n.* **1.** an instrument employing suction. **2.** a jet pump used in laboratories to produce a partial vacuum.

aspire /ə'spaɪə/, *v.i.* **-spired, -spiring.** **1.** to desire, aim, or seek eagerly, esp. for something great or far-reaching (fol. by *to, after,* or an infinitive): *to aspire after truth; to aspire to be a leader among men.* **2.** *Archaic or Poetic.* to rise up; soar; mount. [ME, from L: breathe on] — **aspirant,** *n.* — **aspiration,** *n.*

aspirin /'æsprən/, *n.* a white crystalline derivative of salicylic acid, used to relieve the pain of headache, rheumatism, gout, etc. and reduce fevers. [G (orig. trademark)]

Asquith /'æskwəθ/, *n.* **Herbert Henry** (*1st Earl of Oxford and Asquith*), 1852-1928, British statesman; prime minister 1908-16.

ass /æs/, *n.* **1.** a long-eared mammal, related to the horse, serving as a slow, patient, sure-footed carrier; the donkey. **2.** a fool. [OE, from OWelsh *asyn* ass, from L]

assail /ə'seɪl/, *v.t.* **1.** to set upon with violence; assault. **2.** to attack with arguments, requests, insults, etc. [ME, from VL, from L *ad-* AD- + *salire* leap] — **assailant,** *n.*

assassin /ə'sæsən/, *n.* someone who sets out to murder, esp. for religious or political reasons or for a reward. [named after one of an order of Muslim fanatics, active in Persia and Syria from about 1090 to 1272, whose chief object was to assassinate Crusaders; F, from ML, from Ar.: hashish eaters]

assassinate /ə'sæsəneɪt/, *v.t.* **-nated, -nating.** **1.** to kill by sudden or secret, pre-planned attack, esp. for political or religious reasons. **2.** to ruin or destroy disloyally: *to assassinate a person's character.* [ML] — **assassination,** *n.*

assault /ə'sɔlt, -'sɒlt/, *n.* **1.** the act of attacking; onslaught. **2.** *Mil.* the stage of close fighting in an attack. **3.** *Law.* an unlawful (attempt at) bodily attack upon another, with or without a weapon as by holding a stone or club in a threatening manner. **4.** →**indecent assault.** ◇*v.t.* **5.** to make an assault upon; attack; assail. **6.** to (attempt to) attack sexually. [ME, from OF: ASSAIL] — **assaulter,** *n.*

assay /ə'seɪ, 'æseɪ/, *v.*, /ə'seɪ/, *n.,* ◇*v.t.* **1.** to examine by trial, evaluate or put to test: *to assay his ability; to assay a drug for its strength.* **2.** to determine (the proportions of metals in ores) by smelting. **3.** to attempt; endeavor. ◇*n.* **4.** *Metall.* (a record of) an examination of a mineral ore or alloy to determine what is in it. **5.** *Pharm., etc.* the determination of the strength, purity, etc., of a drug, etc. **6.** a substance being analysed. **7.** an examination; trial; attempt. [ME, from OF, from LL: weighing] — **assayer,** *n.* — **assayable,** *adj.*

assemblage /ə'sɛmblɪdʒ/, *n.* **1.** a number of persons or things collected together; a group. **2.** *Art.* a method of forming a three-dimensional work of art by combining different elements, on a hanging surface or in a free position. [F]

assemble /ə'sɛmbəl/, *v.,* **-bled, -bling.** ◇*v.t.* **1.** to bring together; gather into one place, company, body or whole. **2.** to put or fit (parts) together, as of a machine. ◇*v.i.* **3.** to come together; gather; meet. [ME, from OF, from LL: compare, imitate] — **assembler,** *n.*

assembly /ə'sɛmbli/, *n., pl.* **-blies. 1.** a company of people gathered together, usu. for the same purpose. **2.** (*cap.*) *Govt.* a law-making body, esp. a lower house of a parliament. **3.** the putting together of parts to make machines, as aeroplanes. [ME, from OF]

assembly line, *n.* an arrangement of machines, tools, and workers in which each worker performs a special operation on an incomplete unit.

assent /ə'sɛnt/, *v.i.* **1.** to agree (oft. fol. by *to*): *to assent to a statement.* ◇*n.* **2.** agreement, as to a suggestion; acquiescence; concurrence. [ME, from L] — **assenter,** *n.*

assert /ə'sɜt/, *v.t.* **1.** to state as true; affirm; declare: *She will assert her innocence.* **2.** to defend (claims, rights, etc.). **3.** to put (oneself) forward boldly. [L: joined to] — **asserter, assertor,** *n.*

assertion /ə'sɜʃən/, *n.* **1.** a positive statement; declaration. **2.** the act of asserting.

assertive /ə'sɜtɪv/, *adj.* given to asserting; positive; dogmatic.

assess /ə'sɛs/, *v.t.* **1.** to estimate officially the value of (property, income, etc.) as a basis for taxation (fol. by *at*): *The property was assessed at two million dollars.* **2.** to fix or determine the amount of (damages, a tax, a fine, etc.). **3.** to place a tax or other charge on. [ME, from LL: fix a tax] — **assessable,** *adj.* — **assessment,** *n.*

assessor /ə'sɛsə/, *n.* **1.** someone who makes assessments, as of damage for insurance purposes, or of property, etc., for taxation purposes. **2.** someone who advises a court on questions which involve special knowledge. [L: assistant judge, ML assessor of taxes] — **assessorial,** *adj.*

asset /'æsɛt/, *n.* **1.** a useful thing or quality: *Neatness is an asset.* **2.** a single item of property: *Your best asset is the house.*

assets /'æsɛts/, *n.pl.* **1.** *Comm.* the possessions of a person or business consisting of such items as property, machinery, moneys promised, cash, etc. **2.** any property available for paying debts, etc. [ME, from OF: enough, from L *ad-* AD- + *satis* enough]

assiduous /ə'sɪdjuəs/, *adj.* **1.** continual; unremitting: *assiduous reading.* **2.** faithful in

assiduous

application; attentive; devoted. [L: sitting down to]

assign /əˈsaɪn/, v.t. **1.** to make over or give, as in distribution; allot: *to assign rooms at a hotel*. **2.** to appoint, as to a post or duty: *assign to stand guard*. **3.** to choose and name; specify: *to assign a day*. **4.** to consider as belonging; attribute: *to assign a reason*. **5.** *Law*. to transfer: *to assign the benefits of a contract*. ◇v.i. **6.** *Law*. to transfer property, esp. in trust for payment of debts. ◇n. **7.** (usu. pl.) *Law*. a person to whom the property or interest of another is or may be given over: *my heirs and assigns*. [ME, from OF, from L] **–assigner**; *Chiefly Law*, **assignor**, n. **–assignable**, adj.

assignation /ˌæsɪgˈneɪʃən/, n. **1.** an appointment for a meeting, now esp. a forbidden love-meeting. **2.** the act of assigning; assignment.

assignee /əsaɪˈniː/, n. **1.** *Law*. **→assign** (def. 7). **2.** (formerly) a convict assigned as a servant.

assignment /əˈsaɪnmənt/, n. **1.** something assigned, as a particular task or duty. **2.** the act of assigning. **3.** *Law*. the giving over of a right, interest, or title, or the written record of this. **4.** a task set for a student to do as part of a course.

assignment system, n. (formerly) a system under which convicts in Australia were assigned to settlers as servants and laborers, stopped in 1841.

assimilate /əˈsɪməleɪt/, v., -lated, -lating. ◇v.t. **1.** to take in and include as part of one's own; absorb (fol. by *to* or *with*). **2.** to make like; cause to resemble (fol. by *to* or *with*). **3.** to compare; liken (fol. by *to* or *with*). ◇v.i. **4.** to be or become absorbed. **5.** to become or be like; resemble (fol. by *to* or *with*). [L: likened] **–assimilable**, adj.

assimilation /əˌsɪməˈleɪʃən/, n. **1.** the act or process of assimilating. **2.** the state or condition of being assimilated. **3.** *Biol*. the absorption and transformation of food, etc. into tissue. **4.** *Zool*. the similarity of an animal to its surroundings, in both shape and color. **5.** the process in which individuals or groups of differing origins take on the basic attitudes, habits and life-styles of another culture. **6.** the changing of a sound to one more like, or the same as, another sound near it. **–assimilative**, adj. **–assimilatory**, adj.

Assisi /əˈsiːzi, -ˈsiːsi/, n. a town in central Italy, in Umbria; birthplace of St Francis. Pop. 24 500 (1976).

assist /əˈsɪst/, v.t. **1.** to give support, help, or aid to in some activity, or in time of trouble. **2.** to be associated with as a helper. ◇v.i. **3.** to give aid or help. [F, from L: stand by] **–assistance,** n.

assistant /əˈsɪstənt/, n. **1.** someone who helps or is associated with a higher-ranking person in some position or work; helper. ◇adj. **2.** assisting; helpful.

assize /əˈsaɪz/, n. *Brit*. (usu. pl.) (formerly, in England and Wales) a court session, held at regular times in particular places by a judge travelling through the English counties. [ME, from OF: session, from L: sit by]

assurance

associate /əˈsoʊʃieɪt, ˈsoʊsieɪt/, v., -ated, -ating; /əˈsoʊʃiət, -siət/, n., adj. ◇v.t. **1.** to connect, as in thought: *I associate camping with discomfort*. **2.** to join as a companion, or partner: *I associated myself with the group*. **3.** to unite; combine: *Coal is associated with shale*. ◇v.i. **4.** to enter into an association or group; unite. **5.** to keep company: *to associate only with wealthy people*. ◇n. **6.** a partner in some interest or someone who shares a common purpose. **7.** a companion: *my closest associate*. **8.** anything usu. associated with another. **9.** someone with a lower rank of membership in an association. ◇adj. **10.** associated, esp. as a companion or partner: *an associate partner*. **11.** having lower rank of membership. [ME, from L: joined to]

Associated Press /əˈsoʊʃieɪtəd ˈprɛs/, n. a business organisation of newspapers throughout the US together with correspondents abroad for the reporting and distribution of news. *Abbrev*.: AP

association /əˌsoʊsiˈeɪʃən/, n. **1.** an organisation of people with a common purpose. **2.** the act of associating. **3.** companionship or partnership. **4.** connection or combination. **5.** the connection of ideas in thought. **6.** *Ecol*. a group of plants living together under uniform environmental conditions and having a uniform and particular appearance. **–associative**, adj.

assonance /ˈæsənəns/, n. **1.** similarity of sounds. **2.** a type of rhyme, using the same vowel sounds, though with different consonants, as *valley* and *happy*. See **alliteration**. [F, from L: sounding to] **–assonant**, adj., n.

assorted /əˈsɔːtəd/, adj. **1.** arranged in sorts or varieties. **2.** consisting of various kinds; miscellaneous. **3.** matched; suited.

assortment /əˈsɔːtmənt/, n. **1.** the act of sorting; classification. **2.** an assorted collection.

asst, *Abbrev*. assistant.

assuage /əˈsweɪdʒ/, v.t., -suaged, -suaging. **1.** to make less severe; ease: *to assuage grief*. **2.** to fill the needs of; satisfy: *to assuage appetite, thirst, etc*. **3.** to calm; pacify. [ME, from OF, from L *ad-* AD- + *suāvis* sweet]

assume /əˈsjuːm/, v.t., -sumed, -suming. **1.** to take for granted: *Can you assume it will work?* **2.** to agree to do; undertake: *to assume office, a responsibility, etc*. **3.** to take on: *to assume new habits of life*. **4.** to pretend to have or be; feign: *to assume a false modesty*. **5.** to take over: *to assume a right to oneself*. [late ME, from L: take up]

assumption /əˈsʌmʃən, əˈsʌmpʃən/, n. **1.** the act of assuming. **2.** something taken for granted; a supposition. **3.** an overbearing manner; presumption. **4. a.** (oft. cap.) the bodily taking up into heaven of the Virgin Mary after her death. **b.** (cap.) a feast in memory of it on 15 August.

assurance /əˈʃɔːrəns, -ˈʃʊə-/, n. **1.** a declaration intended to give confidence or guarantee. **2.** full confidence or trust; cer-

assurance   59   **asylum**

tainty. **3.** freedom from fearfulness; self-reliance. **4.** forwardness; impudence. **5.** insurance (now usu. only life insurance).

assure /ə'ʃɔ/, *v.t.*, **-sured, -suring. 1.** to declare earnestly to. **2.** to make sure or certain; convince, as by a promise or declaration. **3.** to make (an event or position) sure: *This assures the success of our work.* **4.** to give confidence to; encourage. **5.** to insure, esp. against death. [ME, from L[L]] **–assured,** *adj.*

Assyria /ə'sɪriə/, *n.* an ancient empire in south-western Asia; greatest extent (750–612 BC) from Egypt to the Tigris River and Persian Gulf.

Astaire /ə'steə/, *n.* **Fred** (*Frederick Austerlitz*), 1899–1987, US dancer and film actor; co-starred with Ginger Rogers in a series of musical comedies.

astatine /'æstətin, -taɪn/, *n. Chem.* a rare element of the halogen family. *Symbol:* At; *at. no.:* 85.

aster /'æstə/, *n.* **1.** *Bot.* a plant which bears flowers with petals arranged around a yellow centre. **2.** *Biol.* either of two star-shaped structures formed in a cell during division. [L, from Gk: star]

asterisk /'æstərɪsk/, *n.* the figure of a star (*), used in writing and printing to indicate reference to a footnote, something left out, etc. [LL, from Gk: star]

astern /ə'stɜn/, *adv. Naut.* **1.** to the rear (of); behind. **2.** in the rear; in a position behind.

asteroid /'æstərɔɪd/, *n.* **1.** *Astron.* one of several hundred planetary bodies with orbits lying mostly between those of Mars and Jupiter. ◇*adj.* **2.** like a star. [Gk: starlike]

asthenosphere /əs'θɪnəsfɪə, -'θɛn-/, *n.* a relatively weak layer of the earth beneath the crust, 80–150 km below the earth's surface.

asthma /'æsmə/, *n.* a disorder that causes difficulties in breathing. [Gk: panting]

astigmatic /ˌæstɪg'mætɪk/, *adj.* to do with, having, or correcting astigmatism.

astigmatism /ə'stɪgmətɪzəm/, *n.* a defect of the eye or of a lens in which rays of light from an outer point converge at different points, thus causing imperfect vision or images. [A-[6] + Gk *stigma* point + -ISM]

astir /ə'stɜ/, *adj.* (*used after a verb*) **1.** in motion. **2.** up and about; out of bed.

Astley /'æstli/, *n.* **Thea,** born 1925, Australian novelist; author of *Girl with a Monkey* (1958).

Aston /'æstən/, *n.* **Matilda Ann** ('*Tilly*'), 1873–1947, Australian writer and teacher of the blind.

astonish /ə'stɒnɪʃ/, *v.t.* to strike with sudden and great wonder; amaze. [OE *stunian* resound] **–astonishing,** *adj.* **–astonishment,** *n.*

Astor /'æstə/, *n.* **Nancy, Viscountess,** 1879–1964, member of a US and British family involved in commerce and politics; first woman to take a seat in the British House of Commons.

astound /ə'staʊnd/, *v.t.* to overcome with amazement. [pp. of obs. *astone, astun.* See ASTONISH, STUN] **–astounding,** *adj.*

Astraea /æs'triːə/, *n. Gk Myth.* the goddess of justice, daughter of Zeus and Themis, the last of the immortals to leave mankind.

astrakhan /'æstrəkæn, æstrə'kæn/, *n.* **1.** a type of fur of young lambs, with closely curled wool. **2.** a fabric with a curled pile similar to it. [named after *Astrakhan*, a city in the USSR]

astral /'æstrəl/, *adj.* having to do with or coming from the stars; starry; stellar. [L: star, from Gk]

astray /ə'streɪ/, *adv.* out of the right way; straying; wandering.

astride /ə'straɪd/, *adv.* **1.** in a position with legs spread wide or on either side of. ◇*prep.* **2.** with a leg on each side of.

astringent /ə'strɪndʒənt/, *adj.* **1.** (as affecting the skin) refreshing, tightening, drying: *an astringent after-shave lotion.* **2.** severe, sharp, harsh: *an astringent style.* **3.** (of tastes) unpleasantly dry, hard. ◇*n.* **4.** an astringent agent (esp. cosmetic). [L] **–astringency,** *n.*

astro-, a word part meaning 'star', as in *astrology*. [Gk, combining form of *ástron*]

astrology /əs'trɒlədʒi/, *n.* a study which accepts, and claims to explain, the influence of the heavenly bodies on human affairs. [ME, from L *astrologia*, from Gk] **–astrologer,** *n.* **–astrological,** *adj.* **–astrologically,** *adv.*

astronaut /'æstrənɔt/, *n.* a person trained as a pilot, etc., to take part in the flight of a spacecraft; cosmonaut. [backformation from ASTRONAUTICS]

astronautics /ˌæstrə'nɔtɪks/, *n.* the science of flight outside earth's atmosphere.

astronomical /ˌæstrə'nɒmɪkəl/, *adj.* **1.** of or connected with astronomy. **2.** very large, like the numbers used in astronomy. Also, **astronomic.**

astronomical unit, *n.* the mean (average) distance between the centre of the earth and the centre of the sun, about 149.6×10^9 metres, used as a unit of distance within the solar system. *Symbol:* AU

astronomy /əs'trɒnəmi/, *n.* the science of the heavenly bodies, their movements, positions, distances, sizes, etc. [ME, from L, from Gk] **–astronomer,** *n.*

astute /əs'tjut/, *adj.* of keen understanding; shrewd; cunning. [L: adroitness, cunning] **–astuteness,** *n.*

asunder /ə'sʌndə/, *adv.* **1.** in or into pieces: *to tear asunder.* **2.** apart or widely separated: *as wide asunder as the poles.* [OE *on sundran* apart]

Aswan High Dam /æs'wæn/, *n.* a large dam across the Nile near Aswan, completed in 1970, and forming the reservoir Lake Nasser; 109 m high.

asylum /ə'saɪləm/, *n.* **1.** *Obs.* a home for the care of the insane, the blind, children without parents or the like. **2.** a sanctuary, as

asylum   60   **atmosphere**

formerly for criminals and debtors. **3.** *Internat. Law.* a refuge granted political refugees: *political asylum.* **4.** any shelter offering safety. [L, from Gk: inviolable]

asymmetric /eɪəˈmetrɪk/, *adj.* lacking symmetry. Also, **asymmetrical.** —**asymmetry**, *n.*

asymptote /ˈæsɪmtoʊt/, *n. Maths.* a straight line which is approached more and more closely by a point moving along a curved line but which is not touched by that point however far it moves. —**asymptotic, asymptotical**, *adj.*

at /æt; *weak form* ət/, *prep.* **1.** a particle specifying a point occupied, reached, sought, or otherwise concerned, as in place, time, order, experience, etc.: *at home; at hand; at noon; at zero; at work; at ease; at length; at risk.* **2.** Some special uses are:
at it again, acting in a characteristic manner.
at sea, a. on the ocean; sailing. **b.** confused.
at that, as things stand: *Let it go at that.* [OE *æt*]

at-, different form of **ad-** before *t*, as in *attend.*

At, *Chem. Symbol.* astatine.

atavism /ˈætəvɪzəm/, *n.* **1.** *Biol.* the reappearance after many generations of characteristics of some far-removed ancestor. **2.** a return to an earlier type. [L *atavus* ancestor + -ISM] —**atavist**, *n.* —**atavistic**, *adj.*

ataxia /əˈtæksiə/, *n.* a disorder in which muscles are not co-ordinated. [NL, from Gk: disorder] —**ataxic, atactic**, *adj.*

ate /eɪt, ɛt/, *v.* past tense of **eat.**

-ate¹, a suffix forming: **1.** nouns indicating esp. persons having some duty or special office, as in *advocate, candidate, curate.* **2.** nouns indicating result of action, as in *mandate* (lit., a thing commanded). **3.** verbs from any Latin or other stem, as in *actuate, agitate.* [L -*ātus, -āta, -ātum*]

-ate², *Chem.* a suffix forming the name of a salt made by the action of an acid on a base, esp. where the name of the acid ends in -*ic*, as in *acetate*, formed from *acetic acid.* [L -*ātum* neut. of -*ātus* -ATE¹]

-ate³, a suffix forming nouns meaning condition, estate, office, etc., as in *consulate, senate.* [L -*ātus*, suffix making nouns of 4th declension]

a tempo /a ˈtempoʊ/, *adv.* (a musical direction) returning to the original speed. [It.]

Aten /ˈɑtən/, *n.* a sun-god introduced into Egyptian religion by Amenhotep IV as the only god. Also, **Aton.**

atheism /ˈeɪθi,ɪzəm/, *n.* the principle or belief that there is no God. [Gk *átheos* without a god + -ISM] —**atheist**, *n.* —**atheistic**, *adj.*

Athena /əˈθinə/, *n.* the Greek goddess of wisdom, arts, industries, and prudent warfare, identified by the Romans with Minerva. Also, **Athene** /əˈθini/.

Athens /ˈæθənz/, *n.* the capital of Greece, in the south-eastern part near the Saronic Gulf; in the 5th century BC, an important artistic, intellectual and political centre. Pop. 885 737 (1981). Greek, **Athínai.** —**Athenian**, *adj., n.*

atherosclerosis /ˌæθəroʊsklɪəˈroʊsəs/, *n.* the thickening of the artery wall due to the laying down of a fat-like substance. [NL, from Gk *athēr* chaff + SCLEROSIS]

Atherton /ˈæθətn/, *n.* a town and shire on the Atherton Tableland, Qld. Pop. 4639 (1986). [named after John Atherton, 1837–1913, pastoralist who settled in N Qld]

Atherton Tableland, *n.* a plateau in the Great Dividing Range in northern Qld west of Cairns; tobacco and maize production. 32 000 km².

athlete /ˈæθlit/, *n.* **1.** someone trained in exercises of physical skill and strength. **2.** someone trained for track and field events only. [L, from Gk: contestant in games]

athlete's foot, *n.* a skin disease of the feet, caused by a fungus.

athletic /æθˈlɛtɪk/, *adj.* **1.** physically active and strong. **2.** of an athlete or athletics.

athletics /æθˈlɛtɪks/, *n.* **1.** (*usu. treated as pl.*) athletic sports, as running, rowing, boxing, etc. **2.** (*usu. treated as sing.*) track and field events only.

athwart /əˈθwɔt/, *adv.* **1.** from side to side: transversely. ◇*prep.* **2.** from side to side of; across. **3.** in opposition to. [A-¹ + THWART, adv.]

-ation, a suffix forming nouns signalling action, process, condition, or result, or something producing a result as in *migration, separation, starvation.* See **-ion, -tion.** [L -*ātio* = -ATE¹ + -ION]

-ative, an adjective suffix expressing tendency, bearing, connection, etc., as in *affirmative, demonstrative, talkative.* See **-ive.** [L -*ātivus* = -ATE¹ + -IVE]

Atkinson /ˈætkɪnsən/, *n.* **Sir Harry Albert,** 1831–92, NZ politician, born in England; prime minister 1876–77, 1883–84, 1884, 1887–91.

Atlantic Ocean /ətˌlæntɪk ˈoʊʃən/, *n.* an ocean bordered by North and South America in the Western Hemisphere, and Europe and Africa in the Eastern Hemisphere, divided by the equator into the **North Atlantic** and the **South Atlantic.** About 81 662 700 km²; with connecting seas, about 106 450 000 km²; greatest known depth, 8381 m.

Atlantis /ətˈlæntəs/, *n.* a mythical island in the Atlantic Ocean, first mentioned by Plato, supposedly west of Gibraltar, said to have finally sunk into the sea.

atlas /ˈætləs/, *n.* **1.** a bound collection of maps. **2.** a book of photographs or tables covering any subject. **3.** (*usu. cap.*) the demigod in classical mythology, condemned to support the sky on his shoulders.

Atlas Mountains, *n.pl.* a mountain range in north-western Africa, extending for about 2414 km through Morocco, Algeria, and Tunisia. Highest peak, Mt Tizi, 4165 m.

ATM /eɪ ti ˈɛm/, *Abbrev.* automatic teller machine.

atmosphere /ˈætməsfɪə/, *n.* **1.** the air surrounding the earth. **2.** this air at any given place: *The atmosphere is damp after the rain.*

atmosphere   61   **attaché**

3. *Astron.* the mixture of gases surrounding any of the heavenly bodies. **4.** a feeling or mood: *an atmosphere of freedom.* **5.** *Chem.* any gaseous medium. [NL, from Gk *atmó(s)* vapor + *sphaîra* SPHERE] **—atmospheric,** *adj.*

at. no., *Abbrev.* atomic number.

A to D, *Abbrev.* analog to digital.

atoll /'ætɒl/, *n.* a coral island enclosing a salt-water lake. [Maldive *atol*]

atom /'ætəm/, *n.* **1.** the smallest unit of an element that can take part in chemical reactions. Each consists of protons, neutrons and electrons, whose number and arrangement determine the element and its properties. **2.** (esp. formerly) a theoretical or imagined particle of matter so tiny that it cannot be divided. [L, from Gk: indivisible]

atomic /ə'tɒmɪk/, *adj.* **1.** of atoms. **2.** driven by atomic energy. **3.** using atomic weapons. **4.** *Chem.* existing as free uncombined atoms. **—atomically,** *adv.*

atomic bomb, *n.* a bomb whose strength is derived from splitting the nuclei of atoms, changing part of their mass into energy. Also, **atom bomb, A-bomb.** See **hydrogen bomb.**

atomic clock, *n.* a highly accurate clock in which an electric oscillator, as a crystal, is regulated by the vibration of an atomic system.

atomic energy, *n.* **1.** the energy obtained from changes within the atomic nucleus, chiefly from the splitting or melting together of nuclei. **2.** this energy used for power, as in industry.

atomic heat, *n.* the product of the specific heat and the atomic weight of an element.

atomic mass, *n.* the mass of an isotope of an element measured in atomic mass units.

atomic mass unit, *n.* a unit for expressing the mass of a single isotope of an element, equal to one twelfth of the mass of the common neutral isotope of carbon, $^{12}_{6}C$. Equal to $1.660\ 53 \times 10^{-27}$ kg. *Symbol:* u

atomic number, *n.* the number of protons in the nucleus of an atom of a given element. *Abbrev.:* at. no.

atomic power, *n.* energy released in nuclear reactions.

atomic theory, *n.* **1.** the modern theory of the atom having a complex internal structure and electrical properties. **2.** *Phys.* the mathematical and geometrical description of the motions of the electrons in the atom about the nucleus. **3. →Dalton's atomic theory. 4.** *Philos.* **—atomism.**

atomic weight, *n.* the average weight of the atoms of an element, measured in atomic mass units. *Abbrev.:* at. wt; a.w.

atomise or **atomize** /'ætəmaɪz/, *v.t.*, **-mised, -mising. 1.** to reduce to atoms. **2.** to reduce to fine particles or spray. **—atomisation,** *n.*

atomiser or **atomizer** /'ætəmaɪzə/, *n.* an apparatus for reducing liquids to a fine spray.

atomism /'ætəmɪzəm/, *n.* the theory that extremely small elements are the basic material of all matter, and that all observable change is due to change in the relation of such elements to one another. **—atomist,** *n.* **—atomistic,** *adj.*

atonal /eɪ'toʊnəl, ə-/, *adj. Music.* having no key or tonal centre. [A-[6] + TONAL] **—atonality,** *n.* **—atonally,** *adv.*

atone /ə'toʊn/, *v.i.*, **atoned, atoning.** to make up or make amends, as for an offence or error (fol. by *for*). [backformation from ATONEMENT] **—atoner,** *n.*

atonement /ə'toʊnmənt/, *n.* **1.** satisfaction or making up for a wrong; amends. **2.** *Theol.* the healing of the relationship between God and man by means of the sufferings and death of Christ. [phrase *at one* in accord + -MENT]

ATP /eɪ ti 'pi/, *Abbrev.* **→adenosine triphosphate.**

Atreus /'eɪtriəs/, *n. Gk Legend.* a king of Mycenae, and a son of Pelops. His evil deeds and those of his house gave many themes to the Greek dramatists.

atrium /'eɪtriəm, 'eɪ-/, *n., pl.* **-tria** /-triə/. **1.** *Archit.* the central main room of an ancient Roman private house. **2.** *Anat.* either of the two upper cavities of the heart into which blood enters from the veins. [L]

atrocious /ə'troʊʃəs/, *adj.* **1.** shockingly wicked or cruel; heinous; ruthless: *atrocious crimes.* **2.** very bad or lacking in taste; execrable: *She shows atrocious taste in clothes.* **3.** *Colloq.* very bad. [ATROCI(TY) + -OUS] **—atrociousness,** *n.*

atrocity /ə'trɒsəti/, *n., pl.* **-ties. 1.** the quality of being atrocious. **2.** a cruel or wicked act or behavior. [L]

atrophy /'ætrəfi/, *n., v.,* **-phied, -phying.** ◊*n.* **1.** *Med.* wasting away of all or part of body as from poor nutrition or other cause. **2.** degeneration; reduction in size and strength through lack of use. ◊*v.t., v.i.* **3.** to affect with or undergo atrophy. [L, from Gk: lack of nourishment] **—atrophic,** *adj.*

atropine /'ætrəpən, -in/, *n.* a poisonous crystalline alkaloid, obtained from belladonna (deadly nightshade), which blocks parasympathetic nerve stimulation. It is used medicinally as an antispasmodic, to dilate the pupil of the eye, or with anaesthetics. [NL *Atropa,* the belladonna genus (from Gk *Atropos,* in Gk mythology, one of the Fates who cut off the thread of life) + -INE[2]]

attach /ə'tætʃ/, *v.t.* **1.** to fasten; affix; join; connect: *to attach a cable.* **2.** to join in action or function: *He attached himself to the team.* **3.** to place on duty with an organisation for a short time only, esp. a military unit. **4.** to assign or attribute: *to attach importance to an expression.* **5.** to bind by ties of affection, love, or regard (fol. by *to*): *She is attached to her mother.* **6.** *Law.* to seize a person or property with legal approval. [ME, from OF *a-* AD- + word akin to TACK[1]] **—attachable,** *adj.*

attaché /ə'tæʃeɪ/, *n.* a person appointed to an official staff, as a government representative, esp. an ambassador in a foreign country. [F *attacher* ATTACH]

attaché case, *n.* → **briefcase.**

attachment /ə'tætʃmənt/, *n.* **1.** the act of attaching, or state of being attached. **2.** the feeling that binds someone to another person or thing; regard; affection. **3.** something extra that attaches or is attached, esp. a fastening, or an accessory for an electrical appliance.

attack /ə'tæk/, *v.t.* **1.** to set upon with force or weapons; begin war against: *attack the enemy.* **2.** to direct unfavorable argument, etc., against; blame violently. **3.** to set about (a task) or go to work on (a thing) forcefully. **4.** (of disease, destructive agencies, etc.) to begin to affect. ◇*v.i.* **5.** to make an attack; begin war. ◇*n.* **6.** a military operation with the aim of overcoming an enemy and destroying its forces and will to resist. **7.** the initial (offensive) movement in a contest; onset. **8.** the act or manner of presenting a musical work; vigor; precision; flair. [F, from It.: attack, ATTACH] —**attacker,** *n.*

attain /ə'teɪn/, *v.t.* **1.** to reach or complete by continued effort; accomplish; achieve: *to attain the opposite side of a beach.* ◇*v.* **2. attain to,** to arrive at; succeed in reaching or obtaining. [ME, from L: touch upon] —**attainable,** *adj.* —**attainment,** *n.*

attainder /ə'teɪndə/, *n. Law.* (formerly) the loss of a person's civil rights and property following a judge's sentence of death. [ME, from OF *ataindre* ATTAIN; later associated with F *taindre* stain, from L *tingere*]

attar /'ætə/, *n.* a perfume or essential oil obtained from flowers or petals, esp. of damask roses. [Pers., from Ar.]

attempt /ə'tɛmpt, ə'tɛmt/, *v.t.* **1.** to make an effort at; try; undertake; seek: *to attempt conversation; to attempt to study.* **2.** to attack; make an effort against: *to attempt a person's life.* ◇*n.* **3.** effort to complete something; trial or essay. **4.** an attack; assault: *an attempt upon a person's life.* [L: try]

attend /ə'tɛnd/, *v.t.* **1.** to be present at: *to attend school; to attend a meeting.* **2.** to accompany as a result: *a cold attended with fever.* **3.** to look after; serve. ◇*v.i.* **4.** to apply oneself: *to attend to our work.* **5.** to take care or charge of: *to attend to a task.* **6.** to wait (*on*) with service. [ME, from L: stretch towards]

attendance /ə'tɛndəns/, *n.* **1.** the act of attending. **2.** (the number of) persons present. **3.** the number of times (out of a maximum) that a person is present.

attendant /ə'tɛndənt/, *n.* **1.** someone who attends another, as for service or company: *a cloakroom attendant.* **2.** someone who is present, as at a meeting. ◇*adj.* **3.** being present or in attendance; accompanying. **4.** existing together; consequent: *attendant evils.*

attention /ə'tɛnʃən/, *n.* the act of attending. **2.** the fixing of the mind upon an object. **3.** politeness; consideration; notice: *Your letter will receive our early attention.* **4.** *Mil.* **a.** a command to stand straight and still. **b.** state of so standing: *at attention.* [ME, from L]

attentive /ə'tɛntɪv/, *adj.* **1.** giving or paying attention; observant. **2.** polite; courteous. —**attentiveness,** *n.*

attenuate /ə'tɛnjueɪt/, *v.,* -ated, -ating. ◇*v.t.* **1.** to make thin or fine; rarefy. **2.** to weaken or reduce in force, quantity, or value. ◇*v.i.* **3.** to become thin or fine. **4.** to grow less; weaken. [L: made thin] —**attenuation,** *n.*

attest /ə'tɛst/, *v.t.* **1.** to bear witness to; certify; declare to be correct, true, genuine: *to attest the truth of a statement.* **2.** to give proof of; manifest: *His works attest his industry.* [L: bear witness] —**attestor, attester,** *n.* —**attestation,** *n.*

attic /'ætɪk/, *n.* the part of a building, esp. a house, directly under the roof, and often used for storage. [F, from L *Atticus* Attic (orig., as applied to a square column in building)]

Attica /'ætɪkə/, *n.* the region around Athens, in south-eastern Greece.

Attila /ə'tɪlə/, *n.* ('Scourge of God'), died AD 453, king of the Huns who invaded Europe; defeated at Châlons, 451, by the Romans and Visigoths.

attire /ə'taɪə/, *v.,* -tired, -tiring, *n.* ◇*v.t.* **1.** to dress, esp. for special occasions, ceremonials, etc. ◇*n.* **2.** (rich or splendid) clothes. [ME, from OF: put in order]

attitude /'ætətjud/, *n.* **1.** manner of behavior, or disposition, with regard to a person or thing: *a menacing attitude.* **2.** position of body suitable for an action, feeling, etc. [F, from It., from ML: aptitude] —**attitudinal,** *adj.*

Attlee /'ætli/, *n.* **Clement Richard, 1st Earl,** 1883–1967, British statesman; prime minister 1945–51; his government instituted many social welfare programs, as the National Health Service.

attorney /ə'tɜni/, *n., pl.* **-neys. 1.** a person appointed by another to conduct any business on their behalf (**attorney in fact**). **2. power of attorney,** a legal right or document by which one person is allowed to act for another. [ME, from OF: assign]

attorney-general /ə,tɜni-'dʒɛnrəl/ *n., pl.* **attorneys-general, attorney-generals.** the chief law officer of government, and minister responsible for organisation of justice.

attract /ə'trækt/, *v.t.* to draw or win by behavior, appearance, influence, or force: *to attract attention; to attract admirers.* [L: drawn to]

attraction /ə'trækʃən/, *n.* **1.** the act or power of attracting. **2.** that which charms. **3.** *Phys.* a force which pulls two or more bodies together, or causes them to revolve around one centre. **4.** an entertainment offered to the public.

attractive /ə'træktɪv/, *adj.* **1.** appealing to one's liking or admiration; pleasing. **2.** pleasing to the eye; handsome.

attribute /ə'trɪbjut/, *v.,* -uted, -uting; /'ætrəbjut/, *n.* ◇*v.t.* **1.** to consider as belonging; regard as owing, as an effect to cause (oft. fol. by *to*). ◇*n.* **2.** something considered

attribute   63   **august**

as belonging; quality, character, characteristic, or property: *Wisdom is one of his attributes*. [ME, from L: assigned] **–attribution**, *n*. **–attributive**, *adj*.

attrition /əˈtrɪʃən/, *n*. **1.** a rubbing against; friction. **2.** a wearing down or away by friction; abrasion. **3.** *Mil*. a reduction of effectiveness of force caused by loss of people and material: *a war of attrition*. [L]

attune /əˈtjun, əˈtʃun/, *v.t.*, **-tuned, -tuning.** to adjust to tune; bring into accord: *His ideas are not attuned to ours*. [AT- + TUNE]

at. wt, *Abbrev.* atomic weight.

atypical /eɪˈtɪpɪkəl/, *adj*. not typical; irregular; abnormal. Also, **atypic.** [A-⁶ + TYPICAL] **–atypically**, *adv*.

Au, *Chem. Symbol.* gold. [L *aurum*]

AU, *Symbol.* astronomical unit.

aubergine /ˈoʊbədʒin/, *n*. →**eggplant**. [F]

auburn /ˈɔbən/, *n*. **1.** a reddish-brown or golden-brown color. ◊*adj*. **2.** having auburn color: *auburn hair*. [ME, from L *alburnus* whitish, from *albus* white]

Auckland /ˈɔklənd/, *n*. a city in the northern part of the North Island of NZ. Pop. 144 000 (1983).

auction /ˈɔkʃən, ˈɒkʃən/, *n*. **1.** a public sale at which property or goods are sold to the highest bidder. ◊*v.t.* **2.** to sell by auction (sometimes fol. by *off*). [L: an increasing]

auctioneer /ɔkʃəˈnɪə, ɒk-/, *n*. a person who conducts sales by auction.

audacious /ɔˈdeɪʃəs/, *adj*. **1.** bold or daring; spirited; adventurous: *audacious fighter*. **2.** reckless or bold in wrongdoing; impudent; presumptuous. [AUDACI(TY) + -OUS]

audacity /ɔˈdæsəti/, *n*. **1.** boldness or daring, esp. careless boldness. **2.** cheek; effrontery; insolence. [L *audācia* daring + -TY²]

Auden /ˈɔdn/, *n*. **W(ystan) H(ugh)** /ˈwɪstən/, 1907–73, US poet born in England, noted for his lyrical technique.

audible /ˈɔdəbəl/, *adj*. able to be heard; loud enough to be heard. [ML, from L: hear] **–audibility**, *n*.

audience /ˈɔdiəns/, *n*. **1.** an assembly of listeners or spectators (viewers): *the audience at a film*. **2.** persons reached by book, radio broadcast, etc.; public. **3.** a chance or opportunity of being heard or of speaking with someone; formal interview: *to have an audience with the queen*. [ME, from L: attention, hearing]

audio /ˈɔdioʊ/, *n*. **1.** an electronic apparatus using audible frequencies. ◊*adj*. **2.** relating to sound reproduction apparatus.

audio-, a word part meaning 'hear', 'of or for hearing', as in *audiometer*. [combining form representing L *audīre* hear]

audiology /ɔdiˈɒlədʒi/, *n*. the study of the hearing mechanism, esp. diagnosis and measurement. **–audiological**, *adj*. **–audiologist**, *n*.

audiometer /ɔdiˈɒmətə/, *n*. an instrument for measuring and recording hearing. **–audiometric**, *adj*. **–audiometry**, *n*.

audio system, *n*. a combination of turntable, tapedeck, amplifier, loudspeakers, etc.

audiovisual /ɔdioʊˈvɪʒuəl/, *adj*. involving at the same time the faculties of seeing and hearing: *an audiovisual aid to teaching*.

audit /ˈɔdət/, *n*. **1.** an official examination of accounts and records, esp. of financial accounts. ◊*v.t.* **2.** to make audit of; examine (accounts, etc.) officially. ◊*v.i.* **3.** to examine and verify an account or accounts by reference to vouchers. [ME, from L: a hearing]

audition /ɔˈdɪʃən/, *n*. **1.** the act, sense, or power of hearing. **2.** a hearing given to a musician, speaker, etc., to test voice qualities, performance, etc. ◊*v.t.* **3.** to give (someone) an audition. ◊*v.i.* **4.** to be tested or to perform in an audition. [L: a hearing]

auditor /ˈɔdətə/, *n*. **1.** a person appointed and authorised to examine accounts and accounting records. **2.** a hearer; listener.

auditorium /ɔdəˈtɔriəm/, *n., pl.* **-toriums, -toria** /-ˈtɔriə/. **1.** the space for the audience in a concert hall, theatre, etc. **2.** a large building or room for meetings, etc. [L]

auditory /ˈɔdətri, -təri/, *adj*. relating to hearing, to the sense of hearing, or to the organs of hearing: *auditory nerve*. [L]

auditory canal, *n*. the tubelike passage leading from the outer section of the ear to the eardrum. Also, **ear canal**.

auditory nerve, *n*. the nerve that transmits the sensation of sound from the internal ear towards the brain.

Aug, *Abbrev.* August.

Augean stables /ɔˈdʒiən ˈsteɪbəlz/, *n.pl. Gk Myth*. the stables in which a king (**Augeas**) kept 3000 oxen and which had not been cleaned for thirty years. Hercules accomplished the task in a single day by turning the river Alpheus through the stable.

auger /ˈɔgə/, *n*. a carpenter's tool, larger than a gimlet, with a spiral groove for drilling holes in wood or in the ground. [ME, var. of *nauger* (a *nauger* being taken as *an auger*), OE *nafogār*]

aught /ɔt/, *n*. anything whatever; any part: *for aught I know*. [OE *ā, ō* ever + *wiht* thing]

augment /ɔgˈment/, *v.t.* **1.** to make larger; enlarge in size or length; increase. ◊*v.i.* **2.** to become larger. [ME, from L: increase] **–augmentation**, *n*.

augmented /ɔgˈmentəd/, *adj. Music.* (of an interval) greater by one semitone than the corresponding perfect or major interval.

augur /ˈɔgə/, *n*. **1.** (in ancient Rome) one of a body of officials charged with observing and explaining omens for guidance in public affairs. ◊*v.i.* **2.** to be a sign; bode (well or ill). [L] **–augural**, *adj*. **–augurship**, *n*.

august /ɔˈgʌst/, *adj*. **1.** causing feelings of reverence or admiration; of awe-inspiring respect; majestic: *an august scene*. **2.** deserving

august

of respect because of age; venerable: *your august father*. [L *augustus*]

August /'ɔgəst/, *n.* the eighth month of the year, containing 31 days. [named after AUGUSTUS Caesar]

Augustan /ɔ'gʌstən/, *adj.* having some of the characteristics of the Augustan period of literature (17th and 18th centuries), esp. classicism, correctness, brilliance, nobility.

Augustine /ɔ'gʌstən/, *n.* Saint, died 604, Roman monk; headed the group of missionaries that landed in England in 597 and began the conversion of the English to Christianity; first archbishop of Canterbury.

Augustus /ɔ'gʌstəs/, *n.* (*Gaius Julius Caesar Octavianus, Augustus Caesar*), 63 BC–AD 14, first Roman emperor, 27 BC–AD 14; reformer, patron of arts and literature; heir and successor to Julius Caesar. Before 27 BC, called **Octavian**. – **Augustan**, *adj.*

auk /ɔk/, *n.* any of certain short-winged, three-toed diving birds found in northern seas. [Scand.]

au lait /oʊ 'leɪ/, *adj.* prepared or served with milk. [F]

au naturel /oʊ nætʃə'rɛl/, *adj.* **1.** in natural state; naked. **2.** cooked plainly. **3.** uncooked. [F]

aunt /ant/, *n.* **1.** the sister of one's father or mother. **2.** the wife of one's uncle.

aura /'ɔrə/, *n., pl.* **auras, aurae** /'ɔri/. a distinctive air; atmosphere; character: *an aura of culture*. [L, from Gk: breath of air]

aural /'ɔrəl/, *adj.* relating to the ears, or to hearing.

Aurelius /ɔ'riliəs/, *n.* **Marcus** (*Marcus Aurelius Antoninus*), AD 121–180, emperor of Rome 161–180; Stoic philosopher and writer. – **Aurelian**, *adj.*

aureole /'ɔrioʊl, '-ɔ-/, *n.* **1.** any encircling ring of light or color; halo. **2.** *Astron.* → **corona** (defs 1 and 2). **3.** *Geol.* a zone surrounding an igneous mass within which metamorphic changes have taken place; contact zone. Also, **aureola** /ɔri'oʊlə, ɔ'riələ/. [L: golden]

auricle /'ɔrɪkəl, 'ɒr-/, *n.* **1.** *Anat.* **a.** the projecting outer portion of the ear; pinna. **b.** → **atrium** (def. 2). **2.** *Bot., Zool.* a part like or likened to the ear. [L: ear] – **auricled**, *adj.*

auricular /ɔ'rɪkjələ/, *adj.* **1.** of or relating to organs of hearing. **2.** understood by or addressed to the ear: *auricular confession*. **3.** dependent on hearing; aural.

auriferous /ɔ'rɪfərəs/, *adj.* yielding or containing gold. [L *aurifer* gold-bearing + -OUS]

aurora /ɔ'rɔrə/, *n.* **1.** an atmospheric display in the sky of moving streamers or bands of light, usu. green, red or yellow, probably caused by streams of charged particles from the sun passing into the Earth's magnetic field. **2.** (*cap.*) *Class. Myth.* dawn, often personified by the Romans and by others as a goddess (Eos).

Australasia

aurora australis /ə'rɔrə ɒs'trɑləs/, *n.* the aurora of the Southern Hemisphere; southern lights. [NL]

aurora borealis /ə'rɔrə bɔri'ɑləs/, *n.* the aurora of the Northern Hemisphere; northern lights. [NL]

aurum /'ɔrəm/, *n. Chem.* gold. [L]

Auschwitz /'aʊʃvɪts/, *n.* a town in south-western Poland; site of Nazi concentration camp during World War II. Pop. 42 700 (1975). Polish, **Oświęcim**.

auscultation /ɒskəl'teɪʃən/, *n.* the act of listening, esp. to movement of the heart. [L: listening]

auspice /'ɔspəs/, *n., pl.* **auspices** /'ɔspəsəz/. **1.** (*usu. pl.*) favoring influence; patronage: *under the auspices of the Australian Red Cross Society*. **2.** a favorable circumstance. **3.** a sign; omen. [L *auspicium*] – **auspicial**, *adj.*

auspicious /ɔ'spɪʃəs, ə-/, *adj.* **1.** indicating success; favorable: *an auspicious moment*. **2.** favored by fortune; prosperous; fortunate.

AUSSAT /'ɒz,sæt/, *n.* an organisation formed in 1981 by the federal government and Telecom Australia to own and operate Australia's domestic satellite communications system; first satellite launched 1985. [*Aus*(*tralia's National*) *Sat*(*ellite System*)]

Aussie /'ɒzi/, *n., adj. Colloq.* (an) Australian.

Aust, *Abbrev.* Australia(n).

Austcare /'ɒstkɛə/, *n.* an Australian organisation formed in 1960 to aid refugees around the world; current name adopted in 1967. [*Aust*(*ralians*) *Care* (*for Refugees*)]

Austen /'ɒstən/, *n.* **Jane**, 1775–1817, English novelist; her works include *Pride and Prejudice* (1813) and *Emma* (1816).

austere /ɒs'tɪə/, *adj.* **1.** disagreeable in manner; stern; forbidding. **2.** severe in self-discipline; strict. **3.** grave; sober; serious. **4.** severely simple; without ornament: *austere writing*. **5.** sour to the taste or flavor; harsh; rough. [ME, from L, from Gk]

austerity /ɒs'tɛrəti/, *n., pl.* **-ties. 1.** austere quality; severity of manner, life, etc.; lack of wealth or ornament. ◊*adj.* **2.** showing austerity; adopted for the sake of, or because of, austerity.

Austerlitz /'ɔstəlɪts/, *n.* a town in the Czech Republic in the eastern part, in Moravia; Napoleon defeated the combined Russian and Austrian armies here in 1805.

austral /'ɒstrəl/, *adj.* **1.** southern. **2.** (*cap.*) Australian. **3.** (*cap.*) Australasian. [L *austrālis*]

Austral /'ɒstrəl/, *n.* **Florence Mary** (*Florence Wilson*), 1894–1968, Australian opera and concert singer; noted internationally as a dramatic soprano.

Australasia /,ɒstrə'leɪʒə, -ʃə/, *n.* Australia, New Zealand, and neighboring islands of the South Pacific Ocean. – **Australasian**, *adj., n.*

Australia /ɒsˈtreɪljə/, *n.* **1.** the country consisting of the federated states of New South Wales, Queensland, South Australia, Tasmania, Victoria, and Western Australia, together with the territories, the Australian Capital Territory and the Northern Territory. It is an independent member of the Commonwealth. Pop. 15 602 156 (1986); 7 682 300 km^2. *Languages:* English, and various Aboriginal languages. *Currency:* Australian dollar. *Cap.:* Canberra. Official name: **Commonwealth of Australia**. **2.** the continent south-east of Asia, lying between the Indian and Pacific Oceans; the smallest continent in the world. 7 614 500 km^2. [L *Terra Australis* southern land]

Australia Council, *n.* a statutory authority established in 1975 to encourage the development of the arts in Australia; formerly the Australian Council for the Arts, an advisory body formed in 1968.

Australia Day, *n.* an Australian national day, 26 January, commemorating the landing of Governor Phillip at Sydney Cove in 1788.

Australia Felix, *n.* the term applied by explorer Thomas Mitchell to a region south of the Murray River (present-day Victoria).

Australia First Movement, *n.* a nationalist organisation formed in Sydney in 1941 to support the defence of Australia by recalling Australian forces from overseas.

Australian[1] /ɒsˈtreɪljən, əs-/, *adj.* **1.** of or relating to Australia. ◇*n.* **2.** a person born or living in Australia. **3.** → **Australian English**.

Australian[2] /ɒsˈtreɪljən/, *n.* **The. 1.** Australia's first independent newspaper, published 1824–48. **2.** an Australian daily newspaper, published nationally, started in 1964 by News Ltd.

Australiana /ɒˌstreɪliˈɑːnə, əs-/, *n.pl.* objects, esp. of historical interest, originating in or relating to Australia, as early books, furniture, paintings, etc.

Australian Airlines, *n.* an internal airline established by the Australian government in 1946. Formerly (1946–86), **Trans-Australia Airlines (TAA)**.

Australian Alps, *n.pl.* the highest section of the Great Dividing Range, extending from south-eastern NSW to southern central Vic; site of the Snowy Mountains Hydro-electric Scheme. Highest peak, Mount Kosciusko, 2228 m.

Australian and New Zealand Army Corps, *n.* an army corps formed in 1914–15 in Egypt, from a mixture of Australian and NZ divisions. *Abbrev.:* ANZAC

Australian Antarctic Territory, *n.* a region in eastern Antarctica claimed as a territory of Australia 1933–59.

Australian Broadcasting Corporation, *n.* a statutory authority formed in 1983 which operates a national television network, domestic and overseas radio services, is a major concert organisation and a book-publishing company. Formerly (1932–1983), **Australian Broadcasting Commission**. *Abbrev.:* ABC

Australian Capital Territory, *n.* an Australian federal territory, created in 1911 as an enclave within south-eastern NSW; contains Canberra, the country's capital city. The area around Jervis Bay, on the east coast, is also included. Pop. 249 407 (1986). 2330 km^2 (Canberra and surrounding area); 72.5 km^2 (Jervis Bay and surrounding area). *Abbrev.:* ACT

Australian Council of Trade Unions, *n.* a national body formed in 1927 which acts as the coordinator of the Australian trade union movement, oversees the management of each trade union and controls disputes within unions. *Abbrev.:* ACTU

Australian crawl, *n.* → **crawl** (def. 6).

Australian Defence Force Academy, *n.* an academy for officer cadets of the three armed forces, established 1986 in the ACT; offers tertiary training previously provided at Point Cook, Duntroon Military College, and Jervis Bay.

Australian Democrats, *n.pl.* a liberalist political party formed in 1977 by Donald Chipp.

Australian Derby, *n.* a horserace run annually at Ascot, Perth, on Boxing Day; first run 1972.

Australian English, *n.* that dialect of English which is spoken by native-born Australians.

Australian Federal Police, *n.* the major law enforcement body of the Australian Commonwealth, created in 1979 with the incorporation of the former Commonwealth and ACT police forces. *Abbrev.:* AFP

Australian Flying Corps, *n.* a military flying organisation which operated in World War I, prior to the formation of the RAAF. *Abbrev.:* AFC

Australian Illawarra Shorthorn /ɪləˈwɒrə/, *n.* a breed of horned dairy cattle with a thick smooth coat, usu. deep red, developed in the Illawarra district of NSW.

Australian Imperial Force, *n.* a special army of volunteers for overseas service which began enlistment in 1914; formed again in World War II. *Abbrev.:* AIF

Australian Inland Mission, *n.* an organisation which developed in 1912, offering support to people in remote parts of the country; first director John Flynn.

Australian Labor Party, *n.* → **Labor Party**.

Australian Light Horse, *n.* an Australian mounted division, consisting of several brigades, which served in the Middle East in World War I.

Australian magpie, *n.* → **magpie** (def. 1).

Australian National Line, *n.* the trading name of the Australian Shipping Commission, set up by the Commonwealth Government in 1956 to operate coastal and overseas cargo shipping; also operates one passenger ship. *Abbrev.:* ANL

Australian Red Cross Society, *n.* a body founded in 1941 which gives assistance to the

Australian Red Cross Society — sick and wounded; its services include the Blood Transfusion Service.

Australian Rules, *n.pl.* a type of football which originated in Australia and which is most popular in southern and western states. It has its origins in Gaelic football and is played by two teams of eighteen players. Also, **Australian National Football, Australian Football, Aussie Rules**.

Australian Secret Intelligence Service, *n.* →ASIS.

Australian Security Intelligence Organization, *n.* →ASIO.

Australian silky terrier, *n.* a small, lightly built dog of medium length with erect ears, docked tail and long, silky, blue or grey-blue coat with tan markings. Also, **Sydney silky**.

Australind /ˈɒstrəlɪnd/, *n.* a town on the south-west coast of WA, north of Bunbury; originally the site of an unsuccessful agricultural settlement on the English model. Pop. 2864 (1986).

australite /ˈɒstrəlaɪt/, *n.* a tektite found in Australia.

Australoid /ˈɒstrələɪd/, *adj.* relating to a racial group which includes the Australian Aborigines. [AUSTRAL(IAN) + -OID]

australopithecine /ˌɒstrəlouˈpɪθəsin/, *n.* a primate of the Pleistocene epoch, found first in southern Africa, with jaws like a man and a skull like an ape.

Australorp /ˈɒstrəlɔp/, *n.* one of the Australian breed of Orpington fowl, usu. black in color and kept mainly for egg production.

australwink /ˈɒstrəlˌwɪŋk/, *n.* a type of small shellfish, similar to the periwinkle, found in great numbers on the Australian coast.

Austria /ˈɒstriə/, *n.* a republic in central Europe, containing part of the Alps and the Danube basin; the centre of the Austro-Hungarian Empire until the end of World War I (1918). Pop. 7 554 000 (1987); 83 855 km². *Language:* German. *Currency:* schilling. *Cap.:* Vienna. German, **Österreich**. —**Austrian**, *n., adj.*

Austria-Hungary /ˌɒstriə-ˈhʌŋgəri/, *n.* a former monarchy in central Europe, including the empire of Austria, kingdom of Hungary and various crownlands; dissolved 1918. —**Austro-Hungarian**, *adj.*

Austro-, a word part, meaning 'southern', as *Austro-Asian*. [L: the south]

Austronesia /ˌɒstrəˈniʒə/, *n.* the islands of the central and south Pacific.

autarchy /ˈɔtəki/, *n., pl.* **-chies**. *n.* 1. →**autocracy**. 2. self-government. [Gk: self-rule] —**autarchic**, *adj.*

autarky /ˈɔtəki/, *n., pl.* **-kies**. the condition of being self-supporting, esp. economically. [Gk]

auth., *Abbrev.* 1. author. 2. authorised.

authentic /ɔˈθɛntɪk/, *adj.* 1. entitled to acceptance or belief; reliable; trustworthy: *an authentic story*. 2. of authorship or origin stated; genuine: *authentic documents*. 3. *Law*. carried out with all due formalities: *an authentic deed*. [LL, from Gk: warranted] —**authentically**, *adv.*

authenticate /ɔˈθɛntəkeɪt/, *v.t.*, **-cated, -cating**. to establish as genuine, sound or valid. —**authentication**, *n.*

authenticity /ˌɔθɛnˈtɪsəti/, *n.* the quality of being authentic; reliability; genuineness.

author /ˈɔθə/, *n.* 1. a person who writes a literary work, esp. a novel, poem, essay, etc. 2. the creator of anything. ◇*v.t.* 3. to be the author of; write. [ME, from L *auctor* originator] —**authoress**, *n. fem.*

authorise *or* **authorize** /ˈɔθəraɪz/, *v.t.*, **-rised, -rising**. 1. to give authority or legal power to; empower (to do something). 2. to give authority for; formally approve (an act or proceeding). 3. to establish through usage: *authorised by custom*. 4. to provide ground for; warrant; justify. —**authoriser**, *n.* —**authorised**, *adj.* —**authorisation**, *n.*

authoritarian /ɔˌθɒrəˈtɛəriən, ə-/, *adj.* 1. favoring principle of subjection to authority contrasted with that of personal freedom. ◇*n.* 2. a person who favors authoritarian principles. [AUTHORITY(Y) + -ARIAN] —**authoritarianism**, *n.*

authoritative /ɔˈθɒrətətɪv, ə-/, *adj.* 1. having the right or weight of authority: *an authoritative opinion*. 2. having an air of authority; positive; peremptory; dictatorial.

authority /ɔˈθɒrəti, ə-/, *n., pl.* **-ties**. 1. (of a person) the right to determine, judge or settle; right to control, command; warrant. 2. an accepted source of information, advice, etc.; testimony; witness. 3. (the writings of) an expert on a subject. 4. a statute, court rule, or legal decision which establishes a rule or principle of law; ruling. [ME, from L]

autism /ˈɔtɪzəm/, *n. Psychiat.* a condition of unknown cause, characterised by an inability to relate to people and by inappropriate or obsessive behavior. [AUTO + -ISM] —**autistic**, *adj.*

auto¹ /ˈɔtou/, *n. US*. an automobile.

auto² /ˈɔtou/, *n.* automatic control.

auto-¹, a word part meaning 'self', 'same', as in *autograph*. Also, **aut-**. [Gk, combining form of *autós*]

auto-², a combining form of **automobile**.

autobiography /ˌɔtəbaɪˈɒgrəfi/, *n., pl.* **-phies**. an account of person's life written by himself or herself. —**autobiographical**, *adj.* —**autobiographically**, *adv.*

autochthon /ɔˈtɒkθən/, *n., pl.* **-thons, -thones** /-θəniz/. an aboriginal inhabitant; native. [Gk: lit., sprung from the land itself]

autocracy /ɔˈtɒkrəsi/, *n., pl.* **-cies**. (a country ruled by a person having) unlimited authority over others; absolute rule. [Gk]

autocrat /ˈɔtəkræt/, *n.* absolute ruler; someone who rules without regard for other people. [Gk: ruling by oneself] —**autocratic**, *adj.*

autograph /ˈɔtəgræf, -graf/, *n.* 1. a person's own handwriting, esp. a signature.

autograph / Ave Maria

◇*v.t.* **2.** to write one's name on or in: *to autograph a book.* [L, from Gk. See AUTO-[1], -GRAPH] —**autographic, autographical,** *adj.*

automatic /ˌɔtəˈmætɪk/, *adj.* **1.** having the power of self-motion; self-moving or self-acting; mechanical. **2.** *Med.* occurring unconsciously, as certain muscular actions. **3.** (of a firearm, pistol, etc.) using part of the force of the explosion to remove the used cartridge shell, introduce a new one, and fire repeatedly. **4.** done unconsciously or from force of habit, mechanical (opposed to *voluntary*). ◇*n.* **5.** a machine which in some way operates by itself, as a motor car with automatic gears. [Gk *autómatos* self-acting + -IC] —**automatically,** *adv.*

automatic data processing, *n.* the use of machines such as computers, etc., to store, organise, and perform calculations on large quantities of data with a minimum of human activity.

automatic pilot, *n.* an automatic steering apparatus in aircraft. *n.* computerised equipment provided in a public place by a bank, building society etc., which allows customers to withdraw money, transfer funds, etc.; autobank, automatic teller.

automatic teller machine, *n.* computerised equipment located outside banks, in shopping centres, etc., offering basic banking facilities, operated by a plastic card with a magnetised stripe and the keying in of a PIN.

automatic transmission, *n.* a transmission system on a motor vehicle in which gearchanging is operated automatically in accordance with the car or engine speed rather than manually by the driver.

automation /ɔtəˈmeɪʃən/, *n.* **1.** the science of applying automatic control to industrial processes; replacement of manpower by complex machinery. **2.** the process or act of making a mechanical process automatically controlled. [b. AUTOM(ATIC) + (OPER)ATION]

automaton /ɔˈtɒmətən/, *n., pl.* **-tons, -ta** /-tə/ a machine with its own power source, which appears to move or work independently.

automobile /ˈɔtəməbɪl/, *n.* a car. [F]

automotive /ɔtəˈmoʊtɪv/, *adj.* **1.** driven by a self-contained power plant. **2.** relating to motor vehicles.

autonomous /ɔˈtɒnəməs/, *adj.* self-governing; independent; subject to its own laws only. [Gk] —**autonomy,** *n.*

autopsy /ˈɔtɒpsi/, *n., pl.* **-sies.** inspection and examination of a body after death, to determine the cause of death; post-mortem. [Gk: seeing with one's own eyes]

autosome /ˈɔtəsoʊm, -zoʊm/, *n.* any chromosome other than the sex chromosome in species having both types.

autosuggestion /ˌɔtəsəˈdʒɛstʃən, ˌɔtoʊ-/, *n. Psychol.* suggestion arising from within a person rather than from outside.

autotomy /ɔˈtɒtəmi/, *n.* the spontaneous casting off of a damaged or trapped body part, such as tails by lizards or legs by spiders and crabs, etc.

autotrophic /ɔtəˈtroʊfɪk/, *adj.* (of plants) building their own nutritive substances.

autumn /ˈɔtəm/, *n.* **1.** the season of the year between summer and winter; in the Southern Hemisphere, March, April and May. **2.** a period of maturity passing into decline. [L] —**autumnal,** *adj.*

aux., *Abbrev.* auxiliary. Also, **auxil.**

auxiliary /ɔgˈzɪljəri, ɒg-/, *adj., n., pl.* **-ries.** ◇*adj.* **1.** giving support; helping; aiding; assisting. **2.** additional; subsidiary: *auxiliary soldiers.* **3.** used as a reserve: *auxiliary engine.* ◇*n.* **4.** someone or something that gives aid of any kind; helper. **5.** → **auxiliary verb.** [L: aid]

auxiliary verb, *n.* a verb usu. found before infinitives and participles, and expressing time, aspect, voice, etc. (I *will* go; we *have* spoken).

avail /əˈveɪl/, *v.i.* **1.** to have force; be of use; serve. **2.** to be of value or profit. ◇*v.t.* **3.** to be of use or value to; profit; advantage. ◇*v.* **4.** avail oneself of, to give oneself advantage of; make use of. [ME, from L: be strong, have effect]

available /əˈveɪləbəl/, *adj.* **1.** suitable or ready for use; at hand; of use or service: *available resources.* **2.** having sufficient power or effectiveness; valid. —**availability,** *n.*

avalanche /ˈævəlænʃ, -lɑnʃ/, *n., v.*, **-lanched, -lanching.** ◇*n.* **1.** a large mass of snow, ice, etc., separated from a mountain slope and sliding or falling suddenly downwards. **2.** anything like an avalanche in suddenness and destructiveness: *an avalanche of misfortunes.* ◇*v.i.* **3.** to come down in, or like, an avalanche (from F: b. d. *avaler* go down (from L *ad-* AD- + *vallis* valley) and F (Swiss) *lavenche* of pre-Latin orig.]

Avalon /ˈævəlɒn/, *n. Arthurian Legend.* an island represented as an earthly paradise in the western seas, to which King Arthur and other heroes were carried at death. [ML *insula Avallōnis* island of Avalon]

avant-garde /ˌævɒnˈgɑd/, *n.* **1.** the vanguard; leaders in progress in any field, esp. the arts; new ideas or thinkers. ◇*adj.* **2.** relating to avant-garde. **3.** modern; experimental. [F: vanguard]

avarice /ˈævərəs/, *n.* an insatiable greed for riches; desire to gain and collect wealth. [ME, from OF, from L: greed]

avaricious /ævəˈrɪʃəs/, *adj.* characterised by avarice; greedy; covetous.

avatar /ævəˈtɑ/, *n. Hinduism.* the descent of a god to earth in bodily form; the incarnation of a god. [Skt: descent]

ave /ˈaveɪ/, *interj.* hail! welcome! [L: be or fare well]

Ave, *Abbrev.* avenue. Also, **ave.**

Avebury /ˈeɪvbəri/, *n.* a village in Wiltshire, near Stonehenge; site of a large system of prehistoric megaliths.

Ave Maria /ˌaveɪ məˈriə/ *n.* **1.** the 'Hail, Mary', a prayer in the Roman Catholic Church, based on the greeting of the angel Gabriel to

Ave Maria — away

the Virgin Mary. **2.** the bead or beads on a rosary used to count off each prayer as spoken. [L: hail, Mary]

avenge /ə'vendʒ/, *v.*, **avenged, avenging.** ◇*v.t.* **1.** to take revenge on or satisfaction for: *avenge a death.* ◇*v.i.* **2.** to take vengeance. [ME, from L: punish] —**avenger**, *n.* —**avengement**, *n.*

avenue /'ævənju/, *n.* **1.** a street, esp. one lined with trees. **2.** a way or opening for entrance or exit: *avenue to India; avenue of escape.* [F, from L: come to]

aver /ə'vɜ/, *v.t.*, **averred, averring.** to declare in a positive manner; affirm. [ME, from L *ad-* AD- + *vērus* true]

average /'ævərɪdʒ, -vrɪdʒ/, *n., adj., v.,* **-raged, -raging.** ◇*n.* **1.** an arithmetic mean; the result of dividing the sum of two or more quantities by the number of quantities. **2.** the ordinary, normal, or typical amount, rate, quality, kind, etc. ◇*adj.* **3.** relating to an average; calculated by average; forming an average. **4.** *Colloq.* only fair in quality or performance; mediocre: *It was only an average show.* ◇*v.i.* **5.** to have or show an average: *to average as expected.* ◇*v.* **6. average down,** to purchase more of a business stock, etc., at a lower price so as to reduce the average cost of one's shares. **7. average up,** to purchase more of a stock, etc., at a higher price to take advantage of a possible rise in prices. **8. average out,** *Colloq.* to divide or sort out, more or less evenly. [cf. F: customs duty, etc., c. It., from Ar.: damages]

averse /ə'vɜs/, *adj.* not willing; disinclined; reluctant; opposed (to): *averse to flattery.* [L: turned away]

aversion /ə'vɜʒən, -'vɜʃən/, *n.* **1.** a strong dislike; repugnance; antipathy (usu. fol. by *to*). **2.** an object of such dislike: *My pet aversion is exams.*

avert /ə'vɜt/, *v.t.* **1.** to turn away or aside: *avert one's eyes.* **2.** to prevent; ward off: *avert evil.* [ME, from L: turn away]

aviary /'eɪvəri, 'eɪvjəri/, *n., pl.* **-ries.** a large cage or enclosure in which birds are kept. [L *avis* bird]

aviation /ˌeɪvi'eɪʃən/, *n.* the act, art, or science of flying by mechanical means, esp. with heavier-than-air craft. [F]

aviator /'eɪvieɪtə/, *n.* the pilot of an aeroplane or other aircraft; flier. —**aviatrix, aviatress,** *n. fem.*

avid /'ævəd/, *adj.* **1.** eager; greedy (oft. fol. by *for*): *avid for pleasure or power.* **2.** keen: *avid hunger.* [L: eager]

Avignon /avi'njõ/, *n.* a town in south-eastern France, on the river Rhône; papal residence 1309–77. Pop. 90 900 (1975).

avocado /ævə'kadoʊ/, *n., pl.* **-dos.** a tree bearing) a pear-shaped tropical fruit, usu. eaten raw, esp. as salad fruit. [Sp., from Nahuatl: lit., testicle]

Avogadro's hypothesis /ævəˌgædroʊ haɪ'pɒθəsəs/, *n.* the hypothesis which states that equal volumes of gases under the same conditions of temperature and pressure contain equal numbers of molecules. [named after Count Amedeo *Avogadro,* 1776–1856, Italian physicist and chemist]

Avogadro's number, /ævəˌgædroʊz 'nʌmbə/ *n.* the number of atoms or molecules in a mole of substance; $6.022\ 52 \times 10^{23}$ per mole. Also, **Avogadro's constant.**

avoid /ə'vɔɪd/, *v.t.* **1.** to keep away from; keep clear of; shun; evade: *avoid a person; avoid danger.* **2.** *Law.* to make void or of no effect; invalidate. [ME, from OF: empty out] —**avoidance**, *n.* —**avoidable**, *adj.*

avoirdupois /ˌævwadju'pwa, ævədə'pɔɪz/, *n.* **1.** a former system of weights (**avoirdupois weight**) used for goods other than gems, precious metals, and drugs. **2.** *Colloq.* weight; heaviness. [ME, from OF: goods sold by weight, lit., to have weight]

Avon /'eɪvən, 'eɪvɒn/, *n.* **1.** a river in central England, flowing south-east through Stratford-on-Avon to the Severn. 129 km. **2.** a river in south-western WA; the upper course of the Swan.

avow /ə'vaʊ/, *v.t.* **1.** to admit or acknowledge frankly or openly; own; confess. **2.** to state; assert; affirm; declare. [ME, from L: summon] —**avowal**, *n.* —**avowed**, *adj.*

avuncular /ə'vʌŋkjələ/, *adj.* like an uncle: *avuncular regard.* [L: uncle]

a.w., *Abbrev.* atomic weight.

await /ə'weɪt/, *v.t.* **1.** to wait for; look for or expect. **2.** to be in store for; be ready for. ◇*v.i.* **3.** to wait, as in expectation. [ME, from ONF *a-* A-[5] + *waitier* watch]

awake /ə'weɪk/, *v.,* **awoke** or **awaked, awoken, awaking,** *adj.* ◇*v.t.* **1.** to rouse (someone) from sleep; wake up. **2.** to stir the interest of; excite: *to awake them to the realities of life.* **3.** to stir, disturb (the memories, fears, etc.). ◇*v.i.* **4.** to wake up; come out of sleep. ◇*adj.* **5.** waking, not sleeping. **6.** watchful; alert: *awake to a danger.* [OE *awacen*]

awaken /ə'weɪkən/, *v.t., v.i.* →**waken.** [OE]

awakening /ə'weɪkənɪŋ/, *n.* **1.** the act of awaking from sleep. **2.** a revival of interest or attention; a waking up, as from indifference, ignorance, etc.

award /ə'wɔd/, *v.t.* **1.** to grant (as reward for achievement); assign; bestow: *to award prizes.* **2.** to give as a result of a legal decision by a law court or arbitrator. ◇*n.* **3.** something awarded, e.g. payment or a medal. [ME, from AF: observe, decide, from L]

aware /ə'weə/, *adj.* conscious (*of*); informed: *aware of danger.* [OE *gewær* watchful] —**awareness**, *n.*

awash /ə'wɒʃ/, *adj. Naut.* just level with surface of water, so that waves break over. **2.** flooded with water. **3.** washing about; thrown about by waves.

away /ə'weɪ/, *adv.* **1.** from any place; off: *to go away* **2.** apart; at a distance: *to stand away from the wall.* **3.** aside: *turn your eyes away.* **4.** from one's possession: *to give money away.* **5.** without hesitation: *fire away.* **6.** at once;

away   69   **azure**

forthwith: *right away.* **7. do away with**, to get rid of; kill. **8. make away with**, to run off with; steal. ◇*adj.* **9.** absent: *away from home.* **10.** from here; distant: *six kilometres away.* **11.** *Sport.* (played) on an opponents' ground. ◇*interj.* **12.** go away! depart! [OE *aweg*, earlier *on weg* on way]

awe /ɔ/, *n., v.*, **awed, awing.** ◇*n.* **1.** mixed feelings of respect or reverential fear, etc., inspired by what is grand or sublime: *in awe of God.* ◇*v.t.* **2.** to inspire or influence with awe. [ME, from Scand.] **—awesome,** *adj.*

awful /'ɔfəl/, *adj.* **1.** *Colloq.* extremely bad; unpleasant; ugly. **2.** inspiring fear; dreadful; terrible. **3.** inspiring awe; solemnly impressive. [ME, from AWE + -FUL]

awkward /'ɔkwəd/, *adj.* **1.** lacking skill; clumsy. **2.** ungraceful; ungainly; uncouth: *awkward gestures.* **3.** difficult to handle; dangerous: *an awkward customer.* **4.** embarrassing or trying: *an awkward moment.* **5.** deliberately difficult; perverse; obstructive. [*auk* backhanded (from Scand.) + -WARD]

awl /ɔl/, *n.* a small pointed instrument for making holes in leather, wood, etc. [OE *æl*]

awn /ɔn/, *n.* the bristle-like fibres on a plant, esp. on a head of wheat, barley, etc. [ME, from Scand.]

awning /'ɔnɪŋ/, *n.* **1.** a rooflike shelter of canvas, metal, etc., in front of a window or door, over a deck, etc., as for protection from the sun. **2.** a shelter.

awoke /ə'wouk/, *v.* past tense of **awake.**

AWOL /eɪ ˌdʌbəlju ou 'ɛl, 'ɛrwɒl/, *Abbrev. Chiefly US Mil.* absent without leave.

awry /ə'raɪ/, *adv.* **1.** with a turn or twist to one side; askew: *to glance or look awry.* **2.** away from reason or the truth. **3.** wrong; amiss: *Our plans went awry.* [ME *on wry*]

axe /æks/, *n., pl.* **axes**, *v.* **axed, axing.** ◇*n.* **1.** a tool with a bladed head on a long handle used for chopping wood, etc. **2. have an axe to grind,** to have a private purpose or selfish end to reach. **3. the axe,** *Colloq.* **a.** a severe cutting down (of spending). **b.** dismissal from a job or position; the sack. ◇*v.t.* **4.** to cut, shape or trim with, or as if with, an axe. **4.** *Colloq.* to dismiss from a position. [OE *æx*]

axes /'æksiz/, *n.* plural of **axis.**

axial /'æksiəl/, *adj.* **1.** of, relating to, or forming an axis. **2.** found on axis.

axil /'æksəl/, *n.* the angle between the upper side of a leaf or stem and the supporting stem or branch. [L: armpit]

axiom /'æksiəm/, *n.* **1.** a recognised truth. **2.** an established and universally accepted principle or rule. **3.** *Philos., Maths., etc.* a statement that needs no proof as it is accepted as true. [L, from Gk: a requisite] **—axiomatic,** *adj.*

axis /'æksəs/, *n., pl.* **axes** /'æksiz/. **1.** the real or imaginary line about which a (rotating) body, such as the earth, turns. **2.** the central line of any symmetrical body: *the axis of the cylinder, of the eye, etc.* **3.** a fixed line used as a reference, as in plotting a curve on a graph. **4.** *Bot.* the longitudinal support on which organs or parts are arranged; the stem, root; the central line of any body. **5.** an agreement between two or more nations to coordinate their foreign and military plans, and to include with them a group of dependent or supporting powers. [L: axle, axis, board. See AXLE]

axis of symmetry, *n. Maths.* a line exactly through the middle of a symmetrical figure.

axle /'æksəl/, *n. Mech.* a bar or shaft, on which or with which a wheel or pair of wheels rotate (turn). [OE *eaxl*(*e*) shoulder]

axolotl /æksə'lɒtl/, *n.* a type of Mexican salamander which breeds in the larval stage.

axon /'æksɒn/, *n. Anat.* an appendage of a neuron which carries impulses away from the cell. Also, **axone** /'æksoun/. [Gk: axis]

ayatollah /aɪə'tɒlə/, *n.* the title of a high-ranking religious leader in the Shiite sect of Islam, official religion of Iran.

aye /aɪ/, *adv., n., pl.* **ayes.** ◇*adv.* **1.** yes. ◇*n.* **2.** an affirmative vote or voter: *The ayes have it.* Also, **ay.** [OE *gī* YEA]

Ayers Rock /ˌɛəz 'rɒk/, *n.* → **Uluru.** [named after Sir Henry Ayers, a premier of SA]

Ayr /ɛə/, *n.* a town in northern Qld at the mouth of the Burdekin River; sugar mills. Pop. 8639 (1986).

azalea /ə'zeɪljə/, *n.* a type of shrub, usu. deciduous, with showy flowers, of the rhododendron genus. [NL, from Gk: (fem. adj.) dry; so named as growing in dry soil]

azan /æ'zan/, *n.* (in Muslim countries) a call to prayer, proclaimed by the muezzin (crier) from the minaret of the mosque five times daily. [Ar.: invitation]

Azerbaijan /ˌæzəbaɪ'dʒan/, *n.* a republic in western Asia on the Caspian Sea; a member of the CIS; a constituent republic of the Soviet Union 1922–91, known as the **Azerbaijan Soviet Socialist Republic.** Pop. 7 029 000 (1989 est.); 86 600 km². *Language:* Azerbaijani. *Cap.:* Baku. **—Azerbaijani,** *n., adj.* **—Azeri,** *n., adj.*

azimuth /'æzəməθ/, *n. Astron., Navig.* an arc of the horizon from the celestial meridian to the foot of the great circle passing through the zenith, nadir, and point of the celestial sphere in question. [ME *azimut*, from Ar *as* (=*al*) the + *sumūt*, pl. of *samt* way] **—azimuthal,** *adj.*

Azoic /ə'zouɪk/, *adj., n.* (relating to) the geological time before life appeared. [Gk *ázōos* lifeless + -IC]

Aztec /'æztɛk/, *n.* **1.** a member of an Indian people dominant in Central Mexico at the time of the Spanish invasion (1519). **2.** a Uto-Aztecan language of the Nahuatl subgroup, Still extensively spoken in Mexico; Nahuatl. **—Aztecan,** *adj.*

azure /'eɪʒə/, *adj.* **1.** of a sky blue color. ◇*n.* **2.** the blue of an unclouded sky. **3.** a blue pigment, now esp. cobalt blue. **4.** the sky. [ME, from Ar., from Pers.: lapis lazuli]

Bb

B, b, *n., pl.* **B's** or **Bs**, **b's** or **bs**. **1.** the second letter of the English alphabet. **2.** the second in any ordered group: *plan B*. **3.** the second highest mark for school work, etc. **4.** *Music.* the seventh note in the scale of C major.

b., *Abbrev.* **1.** born. **2.** *Music.* bass. **3.** *Cricket.* bowled. **4.** breadth. **5.** brother.

B, *Symbol.* **1.** *Chem.* boron. **2.** (of pencils) black. ◇*Abbrev.* **3.** bay. **4.** Bible **5.** British.

Ba, *Chem. Symbol.* barium.

baa /ba/, *v.,* **baaed**, **baaing**, *n.* ◇*v.i.* **1.** (of a sheep) to cry; bleat. ◇*n.* **2.** the crying of a sheep. [imitative]

Baader-Meinhof /badə-'maɪnhɔf/, *n.* a group of West German anticapitalist guerillas, led by Andreas Baader (1943–77) and Ulrike Meinhof (1934–76).

Baal /bal/, *n.* any local deity among the ancient Semitic peoples, esp. the chief god of the Phoenicians.

baba /'babə/, *n.* sponge cake, soaked in alcoholic spirits, usu. rum, and served as dessert.

Babbage /'bæbɪdʒ/, *n.* **1. Benjamin Herschel**, 1815–78, Australian explorer and engineer, born in England; led expeditions to SA in the 1850s. **2. Charles**, 1792–1871, English mathematician; pioneer of calculating machines.

babbitt metal /,bæbɪt 'metl/, *n.* an alloy of tin, antimony, lead and copper, used to reduce friction in bearings, etc. [named after Isaac *Babbitt*, 1799–1862, US inventor]

babble /'bæbəl/, *v.,* **-led**, **-ling**, *n.* ◇*v.i.* **1.** to speak words quickly and unclearly. **2.** to talk foolishly or without purpose; chatter. **3.** to make a continuous soft sound; murmur: *a babbling stream.* ◇*v.t.* **4.** to speak (words) quickly and unclearly. **5.** to tell thoughtlessly: *He babbled the whole secret.* ◇*n.* **6.** unclear speaking, as when many are talking at once. **7.** foolish talk; chatter. **8.** a soft, gentle sound. [ME; imitative]

babbler /'bæblə/, *n.* any of several noisy, insect-eating birds, common in bushland and the open forest of Australia, as the **grey-crowned babbler**.

babe /beɪb/, *n.* **1.** a baby. **2.** an inexperienced person. **3.** *Colloq.* a young woman. [ME]

babel /'beɪbəl/, *n.* **1.** a scene of noise and confusion. **2.** *Bible.* (*cap.*) an ancient city (Babylon) where the building of a tower intended to reach heaven was begun and a confounding of the language of the people took place. [See Gen.II]

baboon /bæ'bun, bə-/, *n.* a type of large monkey, found in Africa and Arabia, with a doglike mouth, large cheeks and short tail. [ME, from OF: stupid person]

baby /'beɪbi/, *n., pl.* **-bies**, *adj., v.,* **-bied**, **-bying**. ◇*n.* **1.** a very young child of either sex. **2.** a young animal. **3.** the youngest member of a family, group, etc. **4.** a childish person. **5.** *Colloq.* an invention or idea of which a person is particularly proud. **6.** *Colloq.* a girl. ◇*adj.* **7.** of, like, or suitable for a baby: *baby clothes; a baby face.* **8.** small of its kind: *a baby grand (piano).* ◇*v.t.* **9.** to treat like a young child. [ME] —**babyish**, *adj.*

Babylon /'bæbələn/, *n.* **1.** an ancient city of south-western Asia, on the river Euphrates, noted for its magnificence and culture; the capital of Babylonia and later of the Chaldean Empire. **2. Hanging Gardens of**, its gardens, probably built in the form of a tower or pyramid; one of the Seven Wonders of the World. [L, from Gk, from Akkadian: the gate of the god]

Babylonia /bæbə'loʊniə/, *n.* an ancient empire in south-western Asia, in the lower Tigris-Euphrates valley; period of greatness c. 1900–539 BC.

baby-sit /'beɪbi-sɪt/, *v.,* **-sat**, **-sitting**. ◇*v.i.* **1.** to take charge of a child or children while the parents are out. ◇*v.t.* **2.** to mind (a child). —**baby-sitter**, *n.*

baccarat /'bækəra, bækə'ra/, *n.* a card game played for money. Also, **baccara**. [F; orig. unknown]

bacchanal /'bækənəl/, *n.* **1.** a follower of Bacchus. **2.** a wild, drunken party; orgy. **3.** a person taking part in this. ◇*adj.* **4.** Also, **bacchic**. relating to Bacchus. [L. See BACCHUS]

bacchanalia /bækə'neɪliə, -'neɪ-/, *n.pl.* **1.** an ancient Roman festival in honor of Bacchus. **2.** any drunken parties. [L] —**bacchanalian**, *adj.*

Bacchus /'bækəs/, *n.* (in Roman mythology) the god of wine. See **Dionysus**. [L, from Gk]

Bacchus Marsh /,bækəs 'maʃ/, *n.* a town and shire in Vic, north-west of Melbourne on the Werribee River. Pop. 7640 (1986).

bach /bætʃ/, *v.i. Colloq.* (usu. of a man) to do one's own housekeeping when not used to it. Also, **batch**. [abbrev. of BACHELOR]

bachelor /'bætʃələ/, *n.* **1.** an unmarried man. **2.** a person with a first or lowest degree at university: *Bachelor of Arts.* [ME, from OF, from ML: small dairy farmer]

Bach family /bak/, *n.* a family of German composers and musicians including **1. Johann Sebastian**, 1685–1750, the greatest and most prolific composer and musician of the baroque era whose work profoundly influenced later composers Haydn, Mozart and Beethoven. **2.** his son **Johann Christian**, 1735–82, composer; known as the 'English' Bach.

bacillus /bə'sɪləs/, *n., pl.* **-cilli** /-'sɪli/. any of the group of aerobic, rod-shaped bacteria. [LL: small rod]

back[1] /bæk/, *n.* **1.** the rear part of the human body from neck to end of spine. **2.** the

similar part of the body of animals. **3.** the spine. **4.** the rear part of anything: *the back of the head*. **5.** the area farthest from the front: *the back of a hall*. **6.** any rear part of an object serving to support, protect, etc.: *the back of a book/chair*. **7.** *Football, etc.* a defending player behind the forwards. ◇**8.** Some special uses are:
behind someone's back, in secret; without someone's knowledge.
be/get on someone's back, *Colloq.* to urge constantly to further action; nag.
break the back of, to deal with or finish the most difficult part of (a job, etc.).
get one's back up, to become annoyed.
put (someone's) back up, *Colloq.* to annoy (someone).
put one's back into, to do (something) with all one's strength.
see the back of, to be rid of (a person, job, etc.).
turn one's back on, to disregard, neglect, or be uncaring; ignore.
◇*v.t.* **9.** to support as with power, influence or money: *We backed the new theatre company.* **10.** to cause to move backwards: *to back a car.* **11.** to bet on: *to back a horse in a race.* **12.** to provide with a back or backing. **13.** to be at the back of; form a background for: *Sandhills back the beach.* ◇*v.i.* **14.** to go backwards. **15.** *Naut.* (of wind) to change direction anticlockwise. ◇*v.* **16.** Some special uses are:
back down, to give up a position in an argument, etc.
back out of, to avoid fulfilling (an agreement, etc.).
back up, 1. to support; encourage: *She will back up my demands.* **2.** to go or cause to move backwards. **3.** *Computers.* to make a copy of data on tape, disk, etc., as a safety measure.
back water, *Naut.* to move a boat backwards.
◇*adj.* **17.** being of the rear: *a back door.* **18.** away from the front position; remote: *back country.* **19.** relating to the past: *back pay.* **20.** coming or going back; backward: *back current.* [OE *bæc*]

back² /bæk/, *adv.* **1.** at, to, or towards the rear; backwards: *to step back.* **2.** in or towards a former place, condition or time: *We are back in our old home; I like to look back on my youth.* **3.** in reply; in return: *I will pay back what I owe.* **4.** in reversal of the usual course: *to take back a gift.* **5. back and forth,** first in one direction and then the other. [var. of ABACK]

backbench /'bækbentʃ/, *n.* the parliamentary members of a particular political party who are not ministers or shadow ministers. —**backbencher,** *n.*

backbite /'bækbaɪt/, *v.i.* **-bit, -bitten** or (*Colloq.*) **-bit, -biting.** to attack the character of an absent person.

backblocks /'bækblɒks/, *n. pl.* **1.** inland country areas, usu. with small populations. **2.** *Colloq.* the outer suburbs of a town.

backbone /'bækboʊn/, *n.* **1.** the spine. **2.** something like a backbone in appearance, position, or purpose, esp. the main support of something. **3.** strength of character; courage, etc.

back-burn /'bæk-bɜn/, *v.t.* **1.** to clear (land) by burning into or against the wind. ◇*v.i.* **2.** to control a fire by burning off an area in advance of it.

back country, *n.* country areas with small populations.

backdate /'bækdeɪt/, *v.t.,* **-dated, -dating.** to date (something) earlier; apply retrospectively: *We shall backdate the pay rise.*

backdrop /'bækdrɒp/, *n.* the curtain at the back of a stage, oft. with a painted scene. Also, **backcloth.**

backer /'bækə/, *n.* **1.** someone who bets on the results of a race. **2.** someone who provides money to support a business, theatrical production, etc.

backfill /'bækfɪl/, *n.* **1.** material used to refill a hole that has been dug for mining or building purposes. ◇*v.t., v.i.* **2.** to fill with backfill.

backfire /bæk'faɪə/, *n., v.,* **-fired, -firing.** ◇*n.* **1.** the too early burning of petrol in the engine of a car, etc., causing loss of power and a loud explosive sound. ◇*v.i.* **2.** (of an engine) to produce a backfire. **3.** to bring results opposite to those planned: *The idea backfired.*

backformation /'bækfɔmeɪʃən/, *n.* a new word formed by shortening another, in reverse of the usual order of formation, as *edit* from *editor.*

backgammon /'bækgæmən, bæk'gæmən/, *n.* a board game for two people with pieces moved after throws of a dice. [BACK¹, *adj.* + OE *gamen* game; game so called because the pieces often go back and re-enter]

background /'bækgraʊnd/, *n.* **1.** the part of a view or scene situated in the rear or the distance, esp. in a picture. **2.** the events, conditions, etc., that lead up to and explain something: *the background of the war.* **3.** a person's social origin, experience and education. **4.** *Computers.* a program which can be interrupted by a more important task. **5. in the background,** out of sight or notice.

backhand /'bækhænd/, *n.* **1.** a stroke, as in tennis, by a right-handed player from the left of the body (or the reverse for a left-handed player), with the back of the hand turned forwards. **2.** writing which slopes backwards or to the left.

backhanded /bæk'hændəd/, *adj.* **1.** performed with a backhand. **2.** having a double meaning: *a backhanded compliment.*

backhoe /'bækhoʊ/, *n.* a small tractor with a scoop at the back for digging.

backing /'bækɪŋ/, *n.* **1.** something which forms, or is placed at, the back of anything to give it support. **2.** support of any kind. **3.** the people giving support. **4.** a musical background for a singer.

backlash /'bæklæʃ/, *n.* **1.** any sudden, violent, or unexpected backward movement, as of a wave, wheels of a machine, etc. **2.** a strong political or social movement, sometimes sudden and violent, against a previous development.

backlog /'bæklɒg/, n. a build-up (of work, letters, etc.) needing attention.

back of beyond/Bourke, Colloq. ◇n. 1. any far, distant or remote place; the outback. ◇adv. 2. in or to the outback.

back passage, n. → **rectum**.

back-pedal /'bæk-pedl/, v.i., **-alled, -alling. 1.** to press the pedals of a bicycle backwards, as in slowing down. **2.** to slow down or move backwards, as to avoid danger. **3.** to give up one's position in an argument.

backroom /'bækrum/, adj. doing important work without public notice or in secret: backroom boys in the lab.

backscatter /'bækskætə/, n. the bending of the direction of waves or alpha particles through angles greater than 90° caused by electromagnetic force, etc. Also, **backscattering**.

back-seat driver, n. a passenger in a car who offers unwanted advice about driving.

backsight /'bæksaɪt/, n. the reading on a levelling rod that is held on a point of known elevation, used in calculating the elevation of the levelling instrument.

backslide /'bækslaɪd, bæk'slaɪd/, v.i., **-slid, -slidden** or **-slid, -sliding.** to return to former bad behavior. – **backslider,** n.

backstab /'bækstæb/, v.t., **-stabbed, -stabbing.** to do harm to (somebody) secretly, esp. a friend. – **backstabber,** n.

backstage /bæk'steɪdʒ, adv.; /'bæksteɪdʒ/, adj. out of view of the audience in a theatre, as behind the scenes or in the dressing rooms.

backstairs /'bæksteəz/, adj. secret; underhand: backstairs gossip. Also, **backstair**.

backstitch /'bækstɪtʃ/, n. **1.** a type of stitch in which the thread doubles back each time on the stitch before it. ◇v.i., v.t. **2.** to sew (something) by such stitches.

backstop /'bækstɒp/, n. **1.** Sport. a person or fence placed to prevent the ball going too far. **2.** someone who or something that is relied on for help when all else fails: I have $500 as a backstop.

backstroke /'bækstroʊk/, n., v., **-stroked, -stroking.** ◇n. **1.** a backhand stroke. **2.** Swimming. a stroke in which the swimmer is on their back moving their arms backwards in turn. ◇v.i. **3.** Swimming. to perform backstroke.

back-to-front /,bæk-tə-'frʌnt/, adj. opposite to the correct position; disordered.

backtrack /'bæktræk/, v.i. **1.** to return over the same course. **2.** to change one's mind about an agreement, plan, opinion, etc. – **backtracker,** n.

backup /'bækʌp/, n. **1.** support or help: His plan received a lot of backup. **2.** something kept for use when needed; a second way of support. **3.** a build-up, esp. of a liquid: the backup of floodwater.

backward /'bækwəd/, adj. **1.** Also, **backwards.** turned or moving towards the back or opposite direction: backward look; backward step. **2.** behind in development: a backward child. **3.** shy; hesitating. ◇adv. **4.** → **backwards.** [ME]

backwards /'bækwədz/, adv. **1.** towards the back. **2.** with the back first. **3.** opposite to the usual or right way: to spell backwards. **4.** towards the past. **5.** towards a less advanced condition: My work is going backwards. **6. backwards and forwards,** first in one direction and then the other. **7. bend/lean/fall over backwards,** Colloq. to try hard to please, help, etc. Also, **backward.** [ME]

backwash /'bækwɒʃ/, n. **1.** Naut. the water thrown back by a motor, oars, etc. **2.** Aeron. the air which flows back from the propellers. **3.** a condition lasting after the event which caused it. **4.** water running down the beach towards the surf after a wave has broken.

backwater /'bækwɒtə/, n. **1.** Naut. water held or forced back, as by a dam, flood or tide. **2.** a body of still, stale water connected to a river but not reached by its current. **3.** a place where there is considered to be little development.

backwoods /'bækwʊdz/, n.pl. **1.** → **back country. 2.** any little known area: the backwoods of English literature.

backyard /bæk'jɑd/, n. **1.** an enclosure behind a building, usu. a house. ◇adj. **2.** relating to a tradesman who operates a small or part-time business from his home: a backyard motor mechanic. **3.** operating outside the law: a backyard abortionist.

bacon /'beɪkən/, n. the meat from the back and sides of a pig, salted and dried or smoked. [ME, from OF, from Gmc]

Bacon /'beɪkən/, n. **Francis (Baron Verulam, Viscount St Albans),** 1561–1626, English essayist, philosopher and politician.

bacteria /bæk'tɪəriə/, n., pl. of **bacterium.** the group of one-celled, usu. nongreen, micro-organisms, which multiply by simple division and of which various types are concerned in fermentation, decay, production of disease, etc. [NL, from Gk: little stick] – **bacterial,** adj. – **bacteroid,** adj.

bactericide /bæk'tɪərəsaɪd/, n. anything that can kill bacteria.

bacteriology /bæk,tɪəri'ɒlədʒi/, n. the science that deals with bacteria. – **bacteriological,** adj. – **bacteriologically,** adv. – **bacteriologist,** n.

Bactrian camel /,bæktriən 'kæməl/, n. a two-humped camel native to central Asia.

bad /bæd/, adj., **worse, worst,** n., adv. ◇adj. **1.** not good: bad behavior. **2.** of poor quality; not fit for its purpose: a bad coin; a bad shot; bad heating; bad pronunciation. **3.** unskilful; incompetent (fol. by at): bad at tennis. **4.** not effective under the law; invalid: a bad claim. **5.** having a harmful effect: bad air; bad for him. **6.** in ill health; sick: to feel bad. **7.** sorry; upset: to feel bad about a mistake. **8.** unpleasant; unwelcome; disagreeable: bad news; bad weather; a bad temper. **9.** severe: a bad accident; a bad mistake. **10.** decayed; rotten. **11. go bad,** decay. **12. not bad,**

Colloq. **a.** fair; not very good. **b.** excellent. ◇*n.* **13.** bad events, conditions, qualities in general: *There is a lot of bad in the world.* ◇*adv.* **14.** badly. [ME *badde;* ? backformation from OE *bæddel* effeminate person] —**badness**, *n.*

bad apple, *n. Colloq.* **1.** an immoral or dishonest person. **2.** one of a group, worse than the rest. Also, **bad egg.**

bade /bæd/, *v.* past tense of **bid.**

Baden-Powell /beɪdn-'paʊl, -'poʊəl/, *n.* **Robert Stephenson Smyth, 1st Baron,** 1857–1941, British general; founded the Boy Scouts in 1908 and (with his sister Agnes Baden-Powell) the Girl Guides in 1909.

badge /bædʒ/, *n.* **1.** an object, usu. of metal or designed cloth, worn as a sign of loyalty, membership, rank, etc. **2.** any mark that shows a particular condition or quality. [ME *bage, bagge;* orig. unknown]

badger /'bædʒə/, *n.* **1.** a type of burrowing, flesh-eating mammal found in Europe and America. ◇*v.t.* **2.** to annoy; nag at. [? from BADGE (with allusion to white mark on head) + -ARD]

badinage /'bædənaʒ, -adʒ/, *n.* light, playful talk; banter. [F: fool, from Pr: gape, from LL]

badly /'bædli/, *adv.* **1.** in a bad manner. **2.** very much: *to need something badly.* **3. badly off**, lacking in money etc.; poor.

badminton /'bædmɪntən/, *n.* a game in which a shuttlecock is batted across a high net. [named after *Badminton*, village in Gloucestershire, England]

Baedeker /'beɪdəkə/, *n.* any of the series of guidebooks for travellers issued by the German publisher Karl Baedeker, 1801–59, and his successors.

baffle /'bæfəl/, *v.*, **-fled, -fling,** *n.* ◇*v.t.* **1.** to confuse; puzzle. **2.** to prevent (somebody) from doing something; impede. ◇*n.* **3.** a wall, screen or plate for controlling the flow of gases, sounds, liquids, etc. [orig. uncert.] —**bafflement**, *n.*

bag /bæg/, *n., v.,* **bagged, bagging.** ◇*n.* **1.** a container of leather, cloth, paper, etc. for carrying articles, e.g. a suitcase, handbag. **2.** (a measure of) the contents of a bag. **3.** *Hunting.* the amount of game caught or killed by a sportsman. **4.** (*pl.*) *Colloq.* a lot; plenty: *She's got bags of money.* **5.** something like a bag, as a cow's udder, or loose skin under the eyes. **6.** Also, **old bag.** *Colloq.* an unpleasant and unattractive woman. ◇**7.** Some special uses are:

bag and baggage, *Colloq.* with all one's possessions.

bag of bones, a very thin animal or person.

bag of tricks, *Colloq.* a collection of many varied articles; everything needed.

in the bag, certain to be obtained or to succeed.

◇*v.i.* **8.** to swell. **9.** to hang loosely. ◇*v.t.* **10.** to put into a bag. **11.** to kill or catch, as in hunting. **12.** *Colloq.* to grab; seize; steal. [ME *bagge*, probably from Scand]

bagatelle /bægə'tel/, *n.* **1.** something of little value. **2.** a game similar to billiards. **3.** → **pinball. 4.** a short, light musical composition, usu. for the piano. [F, from It: little berry]

baggage /'bægɪdʒ/, *n.* **1.** Also, **luggage.** all the bags, etc., of a person travelling. **2.** the equipment that is carried with an army. **3.** *Colloq.* a pert young woman.

bagging /'bægɪŋ/, *n.* the strong woven material used for making bags.

baggy /'bægi/, *adj.*, **-gier, -giest.** baglike; hanging loosely in folds.

Baghdad /'bægdæd/, *n.* the capital of Iraq, in the central part of the country, on the Tigris River. Pop. 4 648 609 (1985). Also, **Bagdad.**

bagman /'bægmən/, *n., pl.* **-men.** (formerly) a swagman; tramp.

bagpipes /'bægpaɪps/, *n.pl.* a musical instrument with pipes coming out of a windbag into which air is blown, usu. by the mouth.

bags /bægz/, *v.t.* **1.** to claim as one's right. ◇*interj.* **2.** Also, **bags I.** (exclamation by which someone, usu. a child, establishes first claim to something): *Bags I have first ride.*

Baha'i /bə'haɪ, 'bahaɪ/, *n.* (a follower of) the Baha'i Faith, a religion, originally derived from Islam, which emphasises the spiritual unity of all mankind and of all religions. [Pers *Baha'(u'llah)* splendor (of God), title of the founder]

Baha'i Faith *n.* a religion founded in 1863 by Mirza Husain Ali, titled Baha'u'llah (Glory of God); the world centre is in Haifa, Israel.

Bahamas /bə'haməz/, *n.pl.* **the,** a parliamentary state consisting of about 700 islands (29 inhabited) in the West Indies; main islands are New Providence and Grand Bahama; British colony before independence in 1973. Pop. 209 505 (1980). 13 939 km². *Language:* English. *Currency:* Bahamian dollar. *Cap.:* Nassau. Also, **Bahama Islands.**

Bahasa Indonesia /bə,hazə ɪndə'nizə/, *n.* the official language of the Republic of Indonesia, based mainly on Malay.

Bahrain /ba'reɪn/, *n.* an Arab state consisting of about 35 islands in the mid-Persian Gulf; a British Protected State before independence in 1971. Pop. 481 433 (1987 est.). 678 km². *Languages:* Arabic, also English. *Currency:* dinar. *Cap.:* Manama. Also, **Bahrein.** —**Bahraini, Bahreini,** *n., adj.*

Baikal /baɪ'kæl/, *n.* **Lake,** a lake in Russia in south-eastern Siberia; the deepest freshwater lake in the world. About 31 494 km²; about 1620 m deep.

bail¹ /beɪl/, *n.* **1.** property left with a court so that a person charged with a crime may be freed until the time for trial. **2.** the condition of being thus freed: *He is on bail.* **3.** the person or persons giving bail: *I will go bail for her.* **4. jump bail**, to fail to appear in court at the appointed time and thus lose one's bail. ◇*v.t.* **5.** Also, **bail out. a.** to obtain the freedom of (someone) by giving bail. **b.** to help (someone)

bail *out of trouble.* **6.** to deliver possession of (goods, etc.) for storage, hire, etc., without change of ownership. [ME, from L: carry]

bail² /beɪl/, *v.t., v.i., n.* →**bale²**.

bail³ /beɪl/, *n.* **1.** *Cricket.* either of the two small pieces of wood laid across the top of the stumps to form the wicket. **2.** a bar for separating horses in a stable. **3.** a framework for holding a cow's head during milking. ◇*v.* **bail up, a.** to put (a cow) in a bail. **b.** to hold up and rob. **c.** to delay (someone) with conversation. [ME, from OF: barrier; of obscure origin]

Bail /beɪl/, *n.* **Murray,** born 1941, Australian novelist; works include *Homesickness* (1980).

Bailey bridge, *n.* a bridge of steel sections that can be taken apart and carried, used esp. in military operations. [named after Sir Donald Bailey, 1901–85, its English inventor]

bailiff /'beɪlɪf/, *n.* a law officer employed by a sheriff to deliver court orders, collect payments of debts, etc. [ME, from OF: govern]

bailiwick /'beɪlɪwɪk/, *n.* the office or area of a bailiff. [ME bailie bailiff + OE *wice* office]

bain-marie /ˌbæn-məˈri/, *n.* a pan of hot water into which another vessel is placed to cook its contents gently. [F: bath of Mary or Miriam, ref. to Miriam the sister of Moses, in the Middle Ages considered an alchemist]

Baird /bɛəd/, *n.* **John Logie** /'lougi/, 1888–1946, Scottish inventor; demonstrated the first television transmitter in 1926.

bairn /bɛən/, *n. Chiefly Scot.* a child. [Scot]

Bairnsdale /'bɛənzdeɪl/, *n.* a town in eastern Vic, on the Mitchell River. Pop. 10 328 (1986). [corruption of *Bernisdale*, a village on the Isle of Skye]

bait /beɪt/, *n.* **1.** food, etc., used on a hook or trap to catch fish or animals. **2.** food containing poison, etc., used to kill or drug animals. **3.** anything that is used to attract or tempt. ◇*v.t.* **4.** to put bait on (a hook or trap). **5.** to add harmful substances to (food) to kill or drug animals. **6.** to set dogs upon (an animal) for sport. **7.** to make (someone) angry for amusement by making rude remarks, etc. [ME, from Scand]

baize /beɪz/, *n.* a soft, usu. green, woollen cloth, used for tops of card tables, etc. [F: bay-colored, from L]

bake /beɪk/, *v.,* **baked, baking.** ◇*v.t.* **1.** to cook by dry heat, esp. in oven. **2.** to harden by heat. ◇*v.i.* **3.** to bake bread, etc. **4.** to become baked. **5.** *Colloq.* to be very hot. [OE *bacan*]

bakelite /'beɪkəlaɪt/, *n.* a type of plastic used for making radio cabinets, telephone receivers, etc. [Trademark; named after its inventor, LH *Baekeland,* 1863–1944, Belgian-US chemist]

baker /'beɪkə/, *n.* someone whose business is to make and sell bread, cake, etc.

Baker /'beɪkə/, *n.* **1. Reginald Leslie** ('Snowy'), 1884–1953, Australian all-round sportsman and film star; lived in the US from 1920. **2. Sidney John,** 1912–76, Australian linguist and writer, born in NZ; author of *The Australian Language* (1945).

baker's dozen, *n.* thirteen.

bakery /'beɪkəri/, *n., pl.* **-ries.** a place where bread, etc., is baked or sold.

Bakery Hill /ˌbeɪkəri 'hɪl/, *n.* a hill in the Ballarat goldfields, Vic; site of mass meetings of miners in 1854 during the unrest leading to the Eureka Stockade.

baking powder, *n.* any of various powders used in baking to make dough rise, made of sodium bicarbonate and an acid substance (such as cream of tartar), which together react with water to give out carbon dioxide.

baking soda, *n.* → **sodium bicarbonate.**

baklava /bəˈklava, 'bækləvə/, *n.* a very thin pastry filled with nuts and honey, made orig. in Greece, Turkey, etc. [Turk]

baksheesh /'bækʃiʃ, bæk'ʃiʃ/, *n.* (in Middle Eastern countries) money given as a gift or tip. [Pers: give]

bal., *Abbrev.* balance.

Balaclava /bæləˈklavə/, *n.* **1.** Also, **Balaklava.** a seaport on the Black Sea; scene of the charge of the Light Brigade in the Crimean War, 1854. Pop. 1 365 (1986). **2.** Also, **balaclava helmet.** (*l.c.*) a knitted woollen covering for the head that leaves only the face uncovered.

balalaika /bæləˈlaɪkə/, *n.* a Russian musical instrument like a triangular guitar. [Russ]

balance /'bæləns/, *n., v.,* **-anced, -ancing.** ◇*n.* **1.** an instrument for weighing, usu. a swaying bar with scales (pans) hanging at the ends. **2.** a condition in which all parts are equal in weight, amount, etc.; equilibrium. **3.** the habit of calm behavior, judgment, etc. **4.** a pleasing arrangement of elements in a work of art. **5.** something used to produce balance. **6.** what remains or is left over. **7.** *Comm.* **a.** equality between totals of two sides of an account. **b.** the difference between the totals of money received and paid out in an account. ◇*v.t.* **8.** to weigh in a balance. **9.** to compare the weight or importance of: *Let's balance these arguments.* **10.** to serve as equal weight or force to; counterbalance: *Your calmness balances my temper.* **11.** to put or hold in a state of balance: *balance a book on your head; balance the shapes in a design.* **12.** *Comm.* to find or equalise the difference between the two sides of an account. ◇*v.i.* **13.** to be equal in weight, parts, etc.; to be in equilibrium: *The account doesn't balance; Do these scales balance?* **14.** *Comm.* to arrange accounts in order to make the totals of both sides equal. [ME, from LL: having two scales]

balance of nature, *n.* that natural state in which plants, insects, animals, etc., live together and feed on each other without endangering the existence of any species.

balance of payments, *n.* the difference between a nation's total payments (debits) to and total receipts (credits) from other countries.

balance of power, 1. (of a political or military power) a position in which power is more or less evenly divided between two or more groups. **2. to hold the balance of power,** to be able to make one side the most powerful by supporting it.

balance of trade, *n.* the difference between the value of goods going out of a country (exports) and those coming in (imports).

balance sheet, *n.* a statement of money received by and paid out of a business, set out in such a way that the two totals are equal.

Balboa /bæl'bouə/, *n.* **Vasco Núñez de** /væskou 'nunjez deɪ/, 1475?–1517, Spanish adventurer and explorer; discovered the Pacific Ocean in 1513.

balcony /'bælkəni/, *n., pl.* **-nies. 1.** a railed platform coming out from the wall of a building. **2.** the highest floor of seats in a theatre, etc. [It: scaffold, from OHG]

bald /bɔld/, *adj.* **1.** lacking hair (on the head): *bald head; bald person.* **2.** lacking some natural growth or covering: *bald mountain.* **3.** (of tyres) having the outer rubber worn off. **4.** bare; plain; unadorned: *bald style of writing.* **5.** open; undisguised: *bald lie.* **6.** *Zool.* having white on the head: *bald eagle.* [ME from obs. *ball* white spot] – **balding,** *adj.* – **baldness,** *n.*

Balder /'bɔldə/, *n.* (*'the Good'*) *Scand Myth.* the son of Odin, and one of the chief deities; god of the summer sun. Also, **Baldr.**

balderdash /'bɔldədæʃ/, *n.* foolish talk; nonsense.

Baldwin /'bɔldwən/, *n.* **1. Stanley** (*Earl Baldwin of Bewdley*), 1867–1947, British politician; prime minister 1923–24, 1924–29, 1935–37. **2. James Arthur,** 1924–87, US novelist and essayist; noted for his involvement in the civil rights movement.

bale[1] /beɪl/, *n., v.,* **baled, baling.** ◇*n.* **1.** a large supply of goods for storage, shipping, etc., tightly tied up with cords or wires, etc.: *bale of wool.* ◇*v.t.* **2.** to make into bales. [ME, from Flem, from OF, from Gmc]

bale[2] /beɪl/, *v.,* **baled, baling,** *n.* ◇*v.t.* **1.** to remove (water) from boat, as with a bucket or a can (usu. fol. by *out*). ◇*v.i.* **2.** to bale water ◇*v.* **3. bale out, a.** to jump from a plane with a parachute. **b.** *Colloq.* to give up a dangerous position or course. ◇*n.* **4.** a bucket, etc., for baling. Also, **bail.** [ME, from OF: bucket, from VL: vessel]

baleen /bə'lin/, *n. Zool.* → **whalebone** (def. 1). [ME, from L: whale]

baleful /'beɪlfəl/, *adj.* full of harm or hate. [OE]

Balfour /'bælfə/, *n.* **Arthur James,** (*1st Earl of Balfour*), 1848–1930, British conservative politician and writer; prime minister 1902–05.

Balfour Declaration, *n.* a statement by the British Government in 1917 of its support for the establishment of 'a national home' in Palestine for the Jewish people, providing that the rights of existing non-Jewish communities be safeguarded.

Bali /'bali/, *n.* an island province of Indonesia, east of Java. Pop. 2 709 200 (1986); 5560 km^2. *Cap.:* Denpasar.

Balkan /'bɔlkən/, *n.* **the Balkans,** the Balkan States or the Balkan Peninsula.

Balkan Peninsula, *n.* a peninsula in southern Europe, bordered by the Adriatic, Ionian, Aegean and Black Seas.

Balkan States, *n.pl.* the countries in the Balkan Peninsula: Yugoslavia, Romania, Bulgaria, Albania, Greece, and the European part of Turkey. Also, **the Balkans.**

ball[1] /bɔl/, *n.* **1.** a round or roundish object; sphere. **2.** such an object for use in various games. **3.** a throw, play, action, movement, etc., of a ball: *a low or high ball; a good ball.* **4.** *Mil.* a solid missile that does not explode, usu. round, for firing from a cannon, gun, etc. **5.** a rounded part of the body: *the ball of the thumb.* **6.** (*pl.*) *Colloq.* the testicles. ◇**7.** Some special uses are:

ball of muscle / strength, *Colloq.* a person who is very healthy and strong.

have the ball at one's feet, to be on the way to success.

have the ball in one's court, *Colloq.* to have the chance or responsibility of acting.

on the ball, *Colloq.* quick to learn, understand, or take action.

start / keep the ball rolling, *Colloq.* to start / keep something going. [ME, from Scand]

ball[2] /bɔl/, *n.* **1.** a formal social gathering at which people dance. **2.** *Colloq.* an enjoyable occasion. [F, from LL]

ballad /'bæləd/, *n.* **1.** a simple poem with short stanzas, which tells a story. **2.** a light, simple song, oft. sentimental, in which all stanzas have the same tune. **3.** a pop song, usu. slow and sentimental. [ME, from Pr: dance, from LL]

Ballance /'bæləns/, *n.* **John,** 1839–93, NZ Liberal politician, born in Northern Ireland; prime minister 1891–93.

ball and chain, *n.* **1.** a heavy iron ball fastened by a chain to prisoner's leg. **2.** anything that limits movement.

ball-and-socket joint, *n.* a joint formed by a ball or knob in a close-fitting cup, which allows a degree of movement in all directions.

Ballarat /'bæləræt/, *n.* a city in southern Vic, west of Melbourne; site of extensive goldfields after 1851 discovery of gold; site of the Eureka Stockade in 1854. Pop. 63 802 (1986). Official name, **Ballaarat.** [Aboriginal: resting place]

Ballarat Reform League, *n.* a league formed by miners on the Ballarat goldfields in 1854 to work for the abolition of the licensing system and other Chartist reforms.

ballast /'bæləst/, *n.* **1.** heavy material carried by a ship to keep it steady, or by a balloon to control height. **2.** anything that gives mental, moral, or political steadiness. **3.** broken stone, etc., placed under railway sleepers for support and drainage. ◇*v.t.* **4.** to supply

ballast 76 **banana**

with ballast: *to ballast a ship*. **5.** to give steadiness to. [MLG *bal* bad + *last* load]

ball-bearing /bɔl-'beəriŋ/, *n.* (a ball in) a bearing in which moving parts turn or run on rolling steel balls.

ballcock /'bɔlkɒk/, *n.* a device for controlling the supply of water to a tank, toilet cistern, etc., by a valve which shuts and opens with the rise and fall of a floating ball connected to it.

ballerina /bælə'rinə/, *n., pl.* **-nas.** a female ballet dancer. [It]

ballet /'bæleɪ/, *n.* **1.** a style of European formal dancing, often designed to tell a story, using graceful, precise movement. **2.** a performance in this style of dancing. **3.** a company of dancers. [F, from It: little ball]

Ballina /'bælənə/, *n.* a town and shire on the north coast of NSW at the mouth of the Richmond River. Pop. 12 398 (1986).

ballistic /bə'lɪstɪk/, *adj.* **1.** relating to (the motion of) missiles or projectiles, as bullets and rockets, propelled and guided only at the start of flight and continuing under no power, acted on only by gravity and the resistance of air, etc., through which they pass. **2.** relating to ballistics.

ballistics /bə'lɪstɪks/, *n.* the study of the motion of ballistic missiles or projectiles. —**ballistician**, *n.*

balloon /bə'lun/, *n.* **1.** a bag, usu. round or roundish, filled with a lighter-than-air gas, designed to rise and float in the atmosphere. It may have a basket for passengers, etc. **2.** a blow-up rubber bag, usu. brightly colored, used as a children's toy or party decoration. **3.** something shaped like a balloon. **4.** a balloon shape containing words said by speaker shown in a comic strip picture. ◇*v.i.* **5.** to go up or ride in a balloon. **6.** to swell like a balloon. ◇*v.t.* **7.** to inflate with air. [It *balla* ball] —**balloonist**, *n.*

ballot /'bælət/, *n., v.,* **-loted, -loting.** ◇*n.* **1.** a ticket or paper used in voting. **2.** the number of votes placed or recorded: *a large ballot*. **3.** Also, **secret ballot**. secret voting with printed or written ballots or voting machines. **4.** the right to vote: *to give the ballot to 18 year-olds*. **5.** a little ball used in voting or drawing lots as (formerly) in the Australian conscription system. ◇*v.i.* **6.** to vote by ballot. **7.** to draw lots: *to ballot for places*. [It *balla* ball] —**ballotter**, *n.*

ballot-paper /'bælət-peɪpə/, *n.* a piece of paper listing the names of candidates for election, on which the voter records a vote.

ballpoint pen, *n.* a pen whose point is a small ball-bearing. Also, **ballpoint, biro.**

Balls Pyramid /'bɔlz/, *n.* a basalt pinnacle rising from the Tasman Sea off the eastern coast of Australia, near Lord Howe Island. 552 m. [named after Lieutenant Henry *Ball*, its discoverer]

ballyhoo /bæli'hu/, *n.* **1.** noise, confusion or uproar. **2.** advertising that is exciting or sensational. [orig. obscure]

balm /bam/, *n.* **1.** any of various oily, sweet-smelling, resinous substances, often of medicinal value, got from certain tropical plants; balsam. **2.** any of various sweet-smelling plants, esp. the lemon-scented perennial herb, lemon balm. **3.** a sweet-smelling ointment. **4.** anything which heals, soothes, or makes something less painful. [ME, from L: balsam]

Balmain bug /bæl,meɪn 'bʌg/, *n.* an eatable, flattened crustacean first discovered in Port Jackson (Sydney harbor). [named after *Balmain*, a suburb of Sydney, NSW]

Balmoral /bæl'mɒrəl/, *n.* a castle in Scotland, near Braemar; a royal summer residence.

balmy /'bami/, *adj.,* **balmier, balmiest. 1.** pleasant; mild: *balmy weather*. **2.** like balm, sweet-smelling; soothing: *balmy leaves*. —**balmily**, *adv.* —**balminess**, *n.*

baloney /bə'louni/, *n. Colloq.* nonsense. Also, **boloney.**

balsa /'bɔlsə/, *n.* **1.** (a tree of tropical America with) a very lightweight wood used for rafts, etc. **2.** a raft, esp. one made of balsa. [Sp]

balsam /'bɔlsəm, 'bɒl-/, *n.* **1.** any of various sweet-smelling resins from certain trees; balm. **2.** any tree or plant yielding balsam. **3.** a kind of garden plant, with red, pink or white flowers. **4.** balm (def. 3 and 4). [OE, from L, from Gk]

Baltic Sea /,bɔltɪk 'si/, *n.* a sea in northern Europe, bounded by Sweden, Finland, Latvia, Lithuania, Estonia, Poland, Germany, and Denmark. About 420 000 km^2.

Baltic States, *n.pl.* the republics of Estonia, Latvia, and Lithuania, sometimes including Finland.

baluster /'bæləstə/, *n.* one of a row of short pillars (usu. stone) supporting a rail or coping. [F, from It, from L, from Gk: pomegranate flower]

balustrade /bælə'streɪd/, *n.* a rail or coping and the row of balusters supporting it.

bamboo /bæm'bu/, *n., pl.* **-boos. 1.** any of certain woody or treelike tropical and semitropical grasses. **2.** the hollow woody stem of this plant, used for building, making furniture, poles, etc. [D, from Malay *mambu*]

bamboozle /bæm'buzəl/, *v.t.,* **-zled, -zling.** to deceive or confuse. [? of cant orig.] —**bamboozlement**, *n.* —**bamboozler**, *n.*

ban^1 /bæn/, *v.,* **banned, banning**, *n.* ◇*v.t.* **1.** to forbid; prohibit: *to ban a book*. ◇*n.* **2.** prohibition. [ME, from Scand]

ban^2 /bæn/, *n.* a public announcement; proclamation; edict. See **banns.** [OE]

Banaba /'banabə/, *n.* an island in western Kiribati; the largest coral island in the world. 321 km^2. Formerly, **Ocean Island.**

banal /bə'nal, 'beɪnəl/, *adj.* ordinary; unoriginal; trite. [F, from Gmc: proclamation] —**banality**, *n.* —**banally**, *adv.*

banana /bə'nanə/, *n.* **1.** (a tropical plant with bunches of) a long, curved, yellow-skinned fruit. **2.** (*pl.*) **go bananas**, *Colloq.* to go mad. [Pg, Sp, from native name in Guinea]

banana republic, *n.* any small tropical country considered backward, politically unstable, etc., and dependent on the trade of rich foreign nations.

Bancks /bæŋks/, *n.* **James Charles**, 1889-1952, Australian cartoonist; creator of the comic strip *Ginger Meggs*.

band[1] /bænd/, *n.* **1.** a group of people acting together; company; troop. **2.** a group of musicians: *dance band; rock band; brass band.* ◇*v.t., v.i.* **3.** to unite in a group. [F, from Gmc]

band[2] /bænd/, *n.* **1.** a strip contrasting with its surroundings in color, material, etc. **2.** a thin, flat strip of material for tying, binding, decorating, etc.: *hat band; rubber band.* **3.** *Mining.* a layer of stone containing ore or a similar valuable material, esp. opal. **4.** (*pl.*) a collar from which hang two square-ended strips of white linen, often part of academic, legal or clerical dress. **5.** *Radio.* a defined range of frequencies. ◇*v.t.* **6.** to mark or fasten with a band or bands. [ME, from F] **—banded**, *adj.*

bandage /'bændɪdʒ/, *n., v.,* **-daged, -daging.** *n.* **1.** a strip of material used to bind a wound, hold a dressing in place, etc. **2.** anything used to bind or tie together. ◇*v.t.* **3.** to bind or cover with a bandage. [F] **—bandager**, *n.*

bandanna /bæn'dænə/, *n.* a large colored handkerchief or scarf. Also, **bandana**. [apparently from Hind *bandhnu*, mode of dyeing in which the cloth is tied so as to prevent parts from receiving the dye]

Bandaranaike /bændərə'naɪəkə/, *n.* **Sirimavo** /sɪrɪ'mavoʊ/, born 1916, prime minister of Sri Lanka (Ceylon) 1960-65, 1970-77; the world's first woman prime minister.

Banda Sea /ˌbændə 'si/, *n.* a sea between Sulawesi and the island of New Guinea, south of Maluku and north of Timor.

banded anteater, *n.* →**numbat**.

bandicoot /'bændikut/, *n.* **1.** any of various small rat-like Australian marsupials, active at night, and feeding on insects, worms, plant roots, etc. They are of two main types: **a.** the **long-eared** or **rabbit-eared bandicoot**, or **bilby**, with silky hair, living in dry areas. **b.** the **short-eared bandicoot**, e.g. the **barred bandicoot** or **marl**, a long-nosed bandicoot of dry southern Australia, the common **long-nosed bandicoot**, of eastern rainforests, and the **brindled bandicoot**, a short-nosed bandicoot of western NSW to WA. **2. lousy as a bandicoot**, mean; miserly. ◇*v.t.* **3.** *Colloq.* to dig up (roots, etc.), without disturbing the top of the plant. [Telugu *pandikokku* pig-rat of India and Sri Lanka]

bandit /'bændət/, *n.* an armed robber or outlaw. [It *bandito*, from *bandire* proscribe]

Bandler /'bændlə/, *n.* **Faith**, born 1918, Australian author; co-founder of the Aboriginal Australian Fellowship in 1956; author of *Welou, My Brother* (1984).

bandolier /bændə'lɪə/, *n.* a broad belt worn over a soldier's shoulder, with small loops or pockets for cartridges. Also, **bandoleer**. [F, from Sp: band, sash, from It, of Gmc orig.]

bandsaw /'bændsɔ/, *n.* a power saw consisting of an endless toothed steel band driven by two wheels.

band spectrum, *n.* an emission or absorption spectrum consisting of a number of bands or lines, as produced by molecules.

Bandung /bæn'dʊŋ/, *n.* a city in Indonesia, in western Java. Pop. 1 462 637 (1980).

bandwagon /'bændwægən/, *n. in the phrase* **climb/jump on the bandwagon**, to join the winning side; follow the crowd.

bandy /'bændi/, *v.,* **-died, -dying,** *adj.* ◇*v.t.* **1.** to pass from one to another, or back and forth; give and take: *to bandy blows or words.* ◇*adj.* **2.** (of legs) bending outward at knees. **3.** →**bandy-legged**. [orig. obscure]

bandy-legged /'bændi-lɛgəd, -lɛgd/, *adj.* having crooked legs; bowlegged.

bane /beɪn/, *n.* **1.** someone or something that ruins, destroys or kills. **2.** a deadly poison. **3.** ruin; destruction; death. [OE *bana* slayer] **—baneful**, *adj.*

Banfield /'bænfild/, *n.* **E(dmund) J(ames)**, 1852-1923, Australian writer and naturalist, born in England; author of *The Confessions of a Beachcomber* (1908).

bang[1] /bæŋ/, *n.* **1.** a loud, sudden explosive noise. **2.** a knock or blow. ◇*v.t.* **3.** to strike, knock or slam (something). ◇*v.i.* **4.** to strike noisily: *to bang on the door.* **5.** to make a loud noise. **6.** to slam: *The door banged.* ◇*adv.* **7.** exactly: *bang in the middle.* [probably from Scand]

bang[2] /bæŋ/, *n.* **1.** (*oft. pl.*) a fringe of hair. ◇*v.t.* **2.** to cut (hair) to form a fringe over the forehead. **3.** to dock (the tail of a horse, etc.) [short for BANGTAIL]

Bangalore /'bæŋgəlɔ/, *n.* a city in southern India, the capital of Karnataka (formerly Mysore) state, in the south-eastern part. Pop. 2 476 355 (1981).

bangalow /'bæŋgəloʊ/, *n.* a slender palm tree of NSW and Qld, sometimes growing in clumps near the coast. Also, **bangalow palm**. [Aboriginal]

Bangeta /ban'geta/, *n.* **Mount**, a mountain in eastern PNG, in Morobe District. 4121 m.

Bangkok /bæŋkɒk/, *n.* the capital and principal port of Thailand, on the Chao Phraya River. Pop. (with suburbs) 5 018 327 (1983 est.). Thai, **Krung Thep**.

Bangladesh /bæŋglə'dɛʃ/, *n.* a republic in southern Asia, on the Bay of Bengal and mainly surrounded by Indian territory; was the province of East Pakistan from 1947 until Indian-backed secession in 1971. Pop. 100 468 000 (1985 est.). 143 998 km². *Language:* Bengali. *Currency:* taka. *Cap.:* Dacca. **—Bangladeshi**, *n., adj.*

bangle /'bæŋgəl/, *n.* a ring-shaped metal or plastic ornament worn round the wrist or ankle. [Hind: bracelet of glass]

bangtail /ˈbæntˌeɪl/, *n.* **1.** an animal with a docked tail, esp. a horse. ◊*adj.* **2. bangtail muster**, **a.** a round-up of cattle for counting. **b.** a carnival or sports day in a country town. [*bang* (nasal var. of *bag* cut) + TAIL] **—bangtailed**, *adj.*

banish /ˈbænɪʃ/, *v.t.* **1.** to send from a country or place by official order; condemn to exile. **2.** to drive or put away: *to banish sorrow*. [ME, from LL: ban, of Gmc orig.] **—banisher**, *n.* **—banishment**, *n.*

banister /ˈbænəstə/, *n.* **1.** one of the supports of a stair rail. **2.** (*oft. pl.*) a stair rail and its supports. Also, **bannister**. [var. of BALUSTER]

banjo /ˈbændʒoʊ/, *n., pl.* **-jos**. **1.** a musical instrument of the guitar family, with a round body covered in front with parchment. **2.** *Colloq.* any banjo-shaped object; e.g. a spade, frying pan. [var. of *bandore*, from LL, from Gk: musical instrument with three strings] **—banjoist**, *n.*

bank[1] /bæŋk/, *n.* **1.** a pile, mass, or slope: *bank of earth; bank of clouds*. **2.** the land along the side of a river, stream, etc. **3.** *Geog.* a raised shelf of ground under the sea. ◊*v.t.* **4.** to form into a bank or mass (usu. fol. by *up*): *to bank up the snow*. **5.** to tip or slope (an aeroplane) sideways. **6.** to cover (a fire) with ashes, fuel, etc., to make it burn slowly. ◊*v.i.* **7.** to rise in or form a bank, as clouds or snow. **8.** to tip or slope sideways, like turning an aeroplane, road, etc. [ME, probably from Scand]

bank[2] /bæŋk/, *n.* **1.** an organisation which stores and lends money and does other financial business, as supplying paper money, changing foreign money, etc. **2.** the office or building of a bank. **3.** a store; reserve: *blood bank*. ◊*v.i.* **4.** to operate as a bank. **5.** to keep money in, or have account with, a bank. **6.** *Colloq.* to rely (fol. by *on*): *I'm banking on you to help*. ◊*v.t.* **7.** to deposit in a bank. ◊*v.* **8. bank up**, to gather; accumulate: *The line of cars banked up*. [ME, from F, from It *banca*, orig. bench; table; of Gmc orig.]

bank[3] /bæŋk/, *n.* **1.** a line of objects. **2.** *Music.* a row of keys in an organ. **3.** a row of oars. [ME, LL, from Gmc source of BENCH]

bankbook /ˈbæŋkbʊk/, *n.* a small book showing a record of a person's bank account; passbook.

bank-draft /ˈbæŋk-drɑːft/, *n.* a draft drawn by one bank on another, payable on demand or at a specified future date.

banker[1] /ˈbæŋkə/, *n.* **1.** someone who manages a bank or works in banking. **2.** someone who holds or supplies money for another.

banker[2] /ˈbæŋkə/, *n.* **1.** a bank-high flood. **2. run a banker**, to be flowing up to the top of the banks.

banking /ˈbæŋkɪŋ/, *n.* the business of a bank or a banker.

banknote /ˈbæŋknoʊt/, *n.* paper money issued by a bank.

Bank of New South Wales, *n.* an Australian bank, founded in 1817; first bank in Australia; now called Westpac.

bankrupt /ˈbæŋkrʌpt/, *n., adj.* **1.** *Law.* (a person) judged insolvent by a court, whose property is managed for and divided among creditors, under bankruptcy law. **2.** (any person) unable to pay money owed to others. **3.** (a person) completely lacking some human quality: *a moral bankrupt; creatively bankrupt*. ◊*v.t.* **4.** to make bankrupt. [F, from It *banca* bank + *rotta*, broken, from L] **—bankruptcy**, *n.*

Banks /bæŋks/, *n.* **Sir Joseph**, 1743–1820, born in England, explorer and botanist in Australia; accompanied James Cook on the *Endeavour* 1768–71; personal collection of journals known as **Banks Papers**.

banksia /ˈbæŋksiə/, *n.* any of various Australian shrubs and trees with leathery leaves and dense cylindrical heads of yellow flowers. [NL, named after Sir Joseph BANKS]

Banks Strait, *n.* a narrow passage of water between north-eastern Tas and Clarke Island. About 21 km wide. [named after Sir Joseph BANKS]

Bankstown /ˈbæŋkstaʊn/, *n.* a city in NSW in the Sydney metropolitan area; important industrial centre. Pop. 151 570 (1986).

bank-up /ˈbæŋk-ʌp/, *n.* a collected mass; accumulation: *The strike caused a bank-up of mail.*

banner /ˈbænə/, *n.* **1.** a flag; pennant. **2.** a strip of material with a design or message on it, e.g. as carried in demonstrations. **3.** something representing beliefs or principles: *the banner of freedom*. **4.** *Journalism.* a headline across the width of a page of a newspaper, esp. the front page. [ME, from LL: standard, of Gmc orig.]

Banner /ˈbænə/, *n.* **Tim**, Australian runner; won World Championship 1926.

Bannister /ˈbænəstə/, *n.* **Roger Gilbert**, born 1929, English athlete; first person to run a mile in under four minutes (1954).

Bannon /ˈbænən/, *n.* **John Charles**, born 1943, Australian state Labor politician; became premier of SA in 1982.

banns /bænz/, *n.pl. Church.* the public announcement of an intended marriage, formerly required by English law. [var. of *bans*, pl. of BAN[2], *n.*]

banquet /ˈbæŋkwət/, *n., v.,* **-queted, -queting.** ◊*n.* **1.** a formal and ceremonious meal, often for a special occasion. ◊*v.i.* **2.** to take part in a banquet. ◊*v.t.* **3.** to give (someone) a banquet. [F, from It: table, sumptuous meal, diminutive of *banco* bench]

banshee /ˈbænʃi, bænˈʃi/, *n.* a spirit in Irish and Scottish folklore supposed to warn of death by its wailing. [Irish *bean sídhe* woman of the fairies]

bantam /ˈbæntəm/, *n.* **1.** (*oft. cap.*) any of certain very small domestic fowls. **2.** a small person, esp. a quarrelsome one. [from *Bantam*, a village in W Java from where the fowls are said to have originated]

bantamweight /'bæntəmweɪt/, n. a boxer weighing between 51 and 54 kg (amateur).

banter /'bæntə/, n. **1.** playful teasing. ◇v.t., v.i. **2.** to tease. [orig. unknown]

Bantu /'bæntu, 'bantu/, n., pl. **-tu, -tus**, adj. ◇n. **1.** a group of African languages which includes Swahili, Tswana, Zulu, Ganda, and Kongo. **2.** any of the negroid peoples who speak these languages. ◇adj. **3.** relating to the Bantu languages or peoples.

banyan /'bænjæn/, n. any of various trees of the fig family whose branches send out roots to the ground, sometimes making it spread over wide area. Also, **banian**. [orig. a particular tree under which Hindu Banian traders had built a pagoda]

baobab /'beɪoʊˌbæb/, n. a large tropical tree with a very thick trunk, native to Africa and northern Australia; sour gourd. [native African]

Baotou /baʊˈtoʊ/, n. a city in northern China in Nei Monggol on the Huang He. Pop. 866 200 (1985 est.). Formerly, **Paotow** or **Pao-t'ou**.

baptise or **baptize** /bæpˈtaɪz/, v.t., **-tised, -tising. 1.** to dip in water, sprinkle or pour water on; in a Christian ceremony to accept someone, usu. a baby, into the church; christen. **2.** to clean of sin; initiate or dedicate by purifying. [ME, from LL, from Gk: immerse]

baptism /'bæptɪzəm/, n. **1.** the act of baptising. **2. baptism of fire, a.** a soldier's first battle. **b.** any severe test; crucial ordeal. —**baptismal**, adj.

Baptist /'bæptəst/, n. Relig. a member of a Christian group which claims that baptism (usu. with immersion) should follow only upon a personal statement of Christian faith.

bar¹ /ba/, n., v., **barred, barring**, prep. ◇n. **1.** a long, evenly shaped solid object, esp. one of wood or metal used as a guard or barrier for some mechanical purpose: the bars of a fence. **2.** any oblong piece of solid material: bar of soap; bar of silver. **3.** a band or stripe: bar of light. **4.** Mining. a band of rock or gravel which traps gold in a stream. **5.** an offshore ridge of sand or gravel lying across the mouth of a bay or river or parallel to the shore. **6.** anything which prevents movement or gets in the way; an obstacle; barrier: a bar to entry. **7.** Music. **a.** Also, **bar-line**. a vertical line across the stave to separate the rhythmic groups. **b.** the part between two bar-lines. Each bar contains the same number of beats. **8.** a table, counter or room where drinks are served. **9.** any counter or shop selling one type of goods: tobacco bar. **10.** barristers considered as a group. **11.** the legal profession. **12.** a division in a courtroom separating the public from the judges, jury, barristers, solicitors, etc. **13.** the place in court where prisoners stand or sit. **14.** a strip of silver or other metal added to a medal as further honor: DSO and bar. **15. not to have a bar (of)**, not to put up with: I won't have a bar of it. ◇v.t. **16.** to shut in or out. **17.** to block or prevent. **18.** to forbid; exclude. **19.** to mark with bars, stripes, or bands. ◇prep. **20.** except; omitting; but: bar none. [ME, from LL barra, of disputed origin]

bar² /ba/, n. a non-SI unit of pressure equal to 10^5 newtons per square metre. [Gk: weight]

bar³ /ba/, adj. **1.** (in children's games) not to be caught or hurt; inviolate: Don't touch me, I'm bar. ◇n. **2.** (in games) a safe position where one cannot be caught. ◇interj. **3.** an appeal to be treated as bar. [from barley appeal for respite]

Barabbas /bəˈræbəs/, n. Bible. a condemned robber released by Pilate instead of Jesus. [See Mark 15:6–11; John 18:40]

Barassi /bəˈræsi/, n. **Ron(ald Dale)**, born 1936, Australian Rules footballer and coach; first life member of the VFL.

barb /bab/, n. **1.** a sharp point sticking out backwards from a main point, as on a fishhook, arrowhead, or fence wire. **2.** a sharp or unkind remark. **3.** Biol. a beardlike growth or part. **4.** Birds. any of the fine hairlike parts joined to the shaft of a feather. ◇v.t. **5.** to furnish with a barb. [ME, from L: beard] —**barbed**, adj.

Barbados /baˈbeɪdɒs, -doʊs/, n. a parliamentary state, an island in the West Indies north-east of Trinidad; a British colony before independence in 1966. Pop. 248 983 (1980). 430 km². Language: English. Currency: East Caribbean dollar. Cap.: Bridgetown. —**Barbadian**, n., adj.

barbarian /baˈbɛəriən/, n. **1.** a person belonging to a culture which has no form of writing and is regarded as uncivilised, esp. used of ancient European people other than the Greeks and Romans. **2.** a person with little knowledge and bad manners. ◇adj. **3.** of or like a barbarian. [F, from L: barbarous country] —**barbarianism**, n.

barbaric /baˈbærɪk/, adj. **1.** Also, **barbarous** /'babərəs/. relating to or like barbarians; uncivilised, rude or cruel. **2.** (of art and culture) crude and lively. [ME, from L, from Gk: foreign, barbaric] —**barbarically**, adv.

barbarism /'babərɪzəm/, n. **1.** the condition of being barbarian or barbarous. **2.** a barbarian act or product. Also, **barbarity**.

Barbary Coast /'babəri koʊst/, n. the Mediterranean coastline of North Africa, including the present states of Morocco, Algeria, Tunisia and Libya; once infested with pirates who harassed Mediterranean trade.

barbecue /'babəkju/, n., v., **-cued, -cuing**. ◇n. **1.** a fireplace or metal frame for cooking meat, etc., over open fire. **2.** meat cooked in this way. **3.** a rack or spit on which whole animals, as pig or lamb, are roasted. **4.** a party, usu. outdoor, where barbecued food is served. ◇v.t. **5.** to cook on barbecue. Also, **barbeque, bar-b-q**. [Sp, from Haitian barboka]

barbed wire, n. steel wire with barbs at short intervals, used for fences.

barbel /'babəl/, n. a thin feeler at the mouth of certain fishes.

barbell /ˈbabel/, *n.* (in weight-lifting) a steel bar, about two metres long, to which disc-shaped weights are attached.

barber /ˈbabə/, *n.* someone whose job is to cut and style men's hair and to shave or trim the beard. [ME, from L *barba* beard]

barbie /ˈbabi/, *n. Colloq.* → **barbecue**. Also, **barby**.

barbiturate /baˈbɪtʃərət, -eɪt/, *n.* any of various derivatives of barbituric acid. Short-acting barbiturates are used as anaesthetics and long-acting barbiturates as sedatives and to control epilepsy. They can be addictive, if taken regularly.

Barbizon School /ˈbabəzon skul/, *n.* a group of French landscape painters of the late 19th century, including Théodore Rousseau, who worked chiefly at Barbizon, a village in northern France.

Barcelona /basəˈloʊnə/, *n.* a large seaport in north-eastern Spain, on the Mediterranean. Pop. 1 699 231 (1986 est.).

barchan /ˈbakæn/, *n.* a crescent-shaped sand-dune. Also, **barchane, barkhan**.

Barcoo /baˈku/, *n.* one of a network of rivers in inland south-western Qld; flows from north-east of Barcaldine 550 km in a south-westerly direction; joins with the Thomson River to form Cooper Creek. [Aboriginal]

Barcoo salute, *n.* → **salute** (def. 5). [*Barcoo* River, Qld]

bard /bad/, *n.* **1.** a Celtic poet, esp. ancient or medieval. **2.** *Archaic.* a poet. **3. the bard**, Shakespeare. [ME, from Celtic] —**bardic**, *adj.*

bare /beə/, *adj.* **barer, barest**, *v.*, **bared, baring**. ◇*adj.* **1.** uncovered; naked: *bare knees; bare walls.* **2.** unornamented; plain: *the bare facts.* **3.** worn smooth; threadbare. **4.** only just enough. ◇*v.t.* **5.** to make bare. [OE *bær*] —**bareness**, *n.*

bareback /ˈbeəbæk/, *adv.* without a saddle: *to ride bareback.*

barebelly /ˈbeəbeli/, *n.* any sheep with bare belly and legs; rosella. Also, **bluebelly**. —**barebellied**, *adj.*

barefaced /ˈbeəfeɪst/, *adj.* **1.** with the face uncovered. **2.** boldly open; undisguised. **3.** shameless: *a barefaced lie.*

barely /ˈbeəli/, *adv.* only; just; no more than: *She is barely 16.*

Barents Sea /ˌbeərənts ˈsi/, *n.* a part of the Arctic Ocean between north-eastern Europe and the islands of Spitsbergen, Franz Josef Land, and Novaya Zemlya. [named after Willem *Barents*, died 1597, Dutch navigator and explorer]

bargain /ˈbagən/, *n.* **1.** a trade agreement; deal. **2.** something bought cheaply. **3. into the bargain**, more than what is stated or agreed; moreover; besides. **4. strike a bargain**, to agree on a deal. ◇*v.i.* **5.** to argue terms or prices; haggle. **6.** to agree; make a bargain. ◇*v.* **7. bargain for**, to be prepared for; expect: *He got more than he bargained for.* **8. bargain on**, to count on; rely on. [ME, from OF] —**bargainer**, *n.*

barge /badʒ/, *n., v.,* **barged, barging**. ◇*n.* **1.** a large flat-bottomed boat, usu. towed, used for moving goods. **2.** a ceremonial vessel used for state occasions. ◇*v.t.* **3.** to carry by barge. ◇*v.i.* **4.** to move by pushing or shoving: *to barge through a crowd.* ◇*v.* **5. barge in**, to push in or interrupt. **6. barge into**, to bump into. [ME, from L, from Gk: (Egyptian) boat or barge]

baritone /ˈbærətoʊn/, *n.* **1.** (a singer with) a medium deep male voice between a tenor and a bass. **2.** any music or instrument within such a range. [Gk: deep sounding]

barium /ˈbeəriəm/, *n.* a whitish, active, divalent metallic element. Symbol: Ba; *at. wt*: 137.34; *at. no.*: 56. [NL; from BAR(YTES) + -IUM]

barium enema, *n.* an injection of barium sulfate into the rectum before an X-ray to show up any abnormality in the large intestine or rectum.

barium meal, *n.* preparation of barium sulfate swallowed before an X-ray to show up any abnormality of the stomach or duodenum.

bark[1] /bak/, *n.* **1.** the harsh cry of a dog. **2.** a similar sound made by another animal or by a person. ◇*v.i.* **3.** to make the sound of a bark or barks. **4.** *Colloq.* to advertise a show at the entrance. ◇*v.t.* **5.** to speak with a bark: *He barked an order.* ◇*v.* **6. bark up the wrong tree**, to misdirect effort. [OE *beorcan*]

bark[2] /bak/, *n.* **1.** the outer covering of woody stems, branches, and roots of plants. **2.** → **tanbark**. ◇*v.t.* **3.** to pull bark from; peel. **4.** to remove a circle of bark from; ring-bark. **5.** to tan. **6.** to rub skin from; graze: *She barked her shins.* [ME, from Scand] —**barker**, *n.*

bark[3] /bak/, *n.* → **barque**.

Barkly Tableland /ˌbakli ˈteɪbəllænd/, *n.* a plateau region in the north-east of the NT extending across the border into Qld; cattle stations. About 130 000 km². [named after Sir Henry *Barkly*]

barley /ˈbali/, *n.* **1.** any of various grasses with short leaves and tightly bunched bristly flower spikes. **2.** the grain of these plants, used as food, and in making beer and whisky. Also, **barleycorn**. [OE *bærlic*]

barmaid /ˈbameɪd/, *n.* a woman who serves drinks in a hotel bar. —**barman**, *n. masc.*

bar mitzvah, *n. Judaism.* **1.** a boy aged 13, when he acquires religious duties. **2.** a ceremony and feast marking this. [Heb.: son of the commandment]

barmy /ˈbami/, *adj.,* **barmier, barmiest**. *Colloq.* mad; stupid; silly. [orig. full of froth, from *barm* froth of yeast]

barn /ban/, *n.* a building for storing hay, grain, etc., and often for housing cattle, etc. [OE *bere* barley + *ærn* place, house]

barnacle /ˈbanəkl/, *n.* **1.** any of certain shellfish which cling to ship bottoms, floating timber, and rocks. **2.** someone or something that clings tight. [late ME *bernacle*, of obscure orig.] —**barnacled**, *adj.*

Barnard /'banəd/, *n.* **1. Christiaan Neethling** /ˌkrɪstiən 'niθlɪŋ/, born 1922, South African surgeon; performed the first human heart transplant, in 1967. **2. Marjorie Faith**, 1897–1987, Australian writer and historian. See **Barnard Eldershaw**.

Barnard Eldershaw /ˌbanəd 'ɛldəʃɔ/, *n.* **M.** the pseudonym used by Marjorie Barnard and Flora Eldershaw for the works they wrote together, as *A House is Built* (1929) and *Tomorrow and Tomorrow* (1947).

Barnardo /bə'nadoʊ/, *n.* **Dr Thomas John**, 1845–1905, British philanthropist who founded homes for destitute children in England.

Barnardo's Australia, *n.* a publicly-funded organisation in NSW and the ACT which houses and cares for destitute children.

barney /'bani/, *Colloq.* ◇*n.* **1.** an argument or fight. **2.** cheating. ◇*v.i.* **3.** to argue or fight. [Brit d.]

barnstorm /'banstɔm/, *v.i.* to tour country areas, stopping often and making political speeches. [orig. US theatrical colloq., to take a show through rural districts; lit. to storm the barns]

Barnum /'banəm/, *n.* **Phineas Taylor** /'fɪniəs/, 1810–91, US showman; created 'The Greatest Show on Earth' (1871) and, with JA Bailey, founded the Barnum and Bailey Circus.

baro-, a word part meaning 'weight', 'pressure', as in *barometer*. [combining form representing Gk *báros* weight]

barometer /bə'rɒmətə/, *n.* **1.** an instrument for measuring atmospheric pressure, so as to determine height, weather changes, etc. **2.** anything that shows changes: *barometer of public opinion*. —**barometric**, *adj.* —**barometry**, *n.*

baron /'bærən/, *n.* **1.** a man holding a peerage of (in UK) the lowest titled rank. **2.** a feudal lord holding lands directly from the king, etc. **3.** a rich and powerful man: *squatter baron*. [ME, from ML: man, free man] —**baronial**, *adj.* —**baronage**, *n.* —**baroness**, *n. fem.*

baronet /'bærənət, -nɛt/, *n.* a member of the British hereditary rank of commoners.

baroque /bə'rɒk, bə'roʊk/, *adj.* **1.** *Art.* in or relating to a style of heavily ornamented art and architecture developed in Italy in the 16th century. **2.** *Music.* in or relating to the ornamented style of the 17th and early 18th centuries. **3.** heavily ornamented. ◇*n.* **4.** baroque style or period. [F, from Pg: irregular]

Barossa Valley /bəˌrɒsə 'væli/, *n.* a grape growing district in SA north-east of Adelaide; about 30 km long and 8 km wide.

barque /bak/, *n.* **1.** *Naut.* a type of three-masted sailing ship. **2.** *Poetic.* any boat. Also, **bark**. [ME, from L]

barrack[1] /'bærək/, *n.* (*usu. pl.*) **1.** a building or group of buildings for lodging soldiers. **2.** any large, plain building housing many people. ◇*v.t.* **3.** to lodge in barracks. [F, from It]

barrack[2] /'bærək/, *v.i.* to shout encouragement and support (fol. by *for*). [? N Ireland d. *barrack* to brag, boast of fighting powers] —**barracker**, *n.*

barracouta /ˌbærə'kutə/, *n.* a long, cold-water, southern fish, caught for sport and food. Also, **couta**. [from BARRACUDA]

barracuda /ˌbærə'kudə/, *n.* any of various fierce warm-water fishes, some of which are caught for food. Also, **sea-pike**. [Sp, from W Ind]

barrage /'bæraʒ, -adʒ/, *n., v.*, **-raged**, **-raging**. ◇*n.* **1.** *Mil.* heavy gunfire used to provide a barrier before enemy forces. **2.** any long heavy attack: *barrage of questions*. ◇*v.t.* **3.** to cut off by or attack with a barrage. [F *barrer*, v., bar]

barramundi /ˌbærə'mʌndi/, *n.* → **giant perch**. [Aboriginal]

barrel /'bærəl/, *n., v.*, **-relled**, **-relling**. ◇*n.* **1.** a cylindrical container made of strips of wood banded together, with bulging sides and flat ends. **2.** a unit of volume in the imperial system, equal to 35 gallons. **3.** any cylindrical container or part; tube. **4.** the tube of a gun. **5. over a barrel**, at a disadvantage. ◇*v.t.* **6.** to put in a barrel. [ME, from OF]

barrel organ, *n.* a musical instrument in which air from a bellows is let into a set of pipes by pins in a revolving barrel.

barren /'bærən/, *adj.* **1.** unable to produce offspring; infertile; sterile: *a barren woman*. **2.** unproductive: *barren land*. **3.** uninteresting or unattractive. **4.** mentally unproductive; stupid. **5.** lacking (usu. fol. by *of*): *barren of feeling*. [ME, from OF, of pre-L orig.] —**barrenness**, *n.*

barricade /'bærəkeɪd, ˌbærə'keɪd/, *n., v.*, **-caded**, **-cading**. ◇*n.* **1.** a defensive wall hastily put up. **2.** any barrier or blockage: *a barricade of rubbish*. ◇*v.t.* **3.** to block or defend with a barricade. [F, probably from Pr *barricada* a barricade, orig. made of casks filled with earth, from *barrica* cask] —**barricader**, *n.*

Barrie /'bæri/, *n.* **Sir J(ames) M(atthew)**, 1860–1937, Scottish playwright, novelist and short-story writer; author of *Peter Pan* (1904).

barrier /'bæriə/, *n.* **1.** anything barring or blocking things or people from passing: *road barrier; mountain barrier; trade barrier*. **2.** a limit; boundary: *the barriers of social class*. **3.** (*oft. cap.*) *Geog.* the part of the southern polar icecap reaching out beyond land, resting in places on the ocean bottom. **4.** *Geog.* a bar formed offshore by waves and currents, separated from the mainland by lagoons or marshes. [ME, from AF: bar]

Barrier Range, *n.* a range in the far west of NSW, 160 km long, parallel to the SA border. Highest peak, 430 m.

barrier reef, *n.* a long narrow offshore ridge of coral close to or above the surface of the sea.

barring /'bɑrɪŋ/, *prep.* excepting; except for: *Barring accidents, I'll be there.*

Barrington /'bærɪŋtən/, *n.* **George** (*George Waldron*), 1755?–1804, British pickpocket, transported to Australia in 1790; pardoned in 1796 to become chief constable of Parramatta.

Barrington Tops, *n.* a large plateau on the southern edge of Mount Royal Range, northwest of Dungog, NSW. Highest peak, 1555 m.

barrister /'bærəstə/, *n.* a lawyer whose main work is presenting cases in court; a lawyer admitted to the bar. [*barri-* (combining form of BAR¹) + -STER]

barrow¹ /'bæroʊ/, *n.* **1.** a cart for selling goods, esp. fruit and vegetables, in the street. **2.** →**wheelbarrow**. [OE *bearwe*]

barrow² /'bæroʊ/, *n.* an ancient or prehistoric burial mound. [OE *beorg* hill, mound]

Barrow Island, *n.* an island off the central coast of WA; rich oilfield.

Barry /'bæri/, *n.* **Sir Redmond**, 1813–80, Australian judge, born in Ireland; became first chancellor of the University of Melbourne, in 1853.

bar sinister, *n.* condition, evidence, or proof of bastard birth.

barter /'bɑtə/, *v.i., v.t.* **1.** to trade or swap rather than buy with money. ◇*n.* **2.** the act of bartering or a thing bartered. [ME, from OF: exchange, cheat] —**barterer**, *n.*

Bartók /'bɑtɒk/, *n.* **Béla** /'beɪlə, 'belə/, 1881–1945, Hungarian composer whose music was influenced by Hungarian folk songs.

Barton /'bɑtn/, *n.* **Sir Edmund**, 1849–1920, Australian politician; first prime minister 1901–03.

Barwick /'bɑwɪk/, *n.* **Sir Garfield Edward John**, born 1903, Australian lawyer and Liberal politician; federal Attorney-General 1958–64, Chief Justice of Australia 1964–81.

Barwon /'bɑwən/, *n.* a river in NSW which is part of the Darling River and forms a section of the border between NSW and Qld.

baryon /'bæriɒn/, *n.* an elementary particle which is a nucleon or a hyperon.

barysphere /'bærəsfɪə/, *n.* →**centrosphere**. [Gk *barys* heavy + SPHERE]

barytes /bə'raɪtiz/, *n.* a common mineral, barium sulfate, $BaSO_4$ in crystal form, the principal ore of barium; heavy spar. [Gk: weight]

basal /'beɪsəl/, *adj.* **1.** of, at, or forming a base. **2.** basic; fundamental.

basalt /'bæsɒlt/, *n.* a dark, dense, volcanic rock, often with columnar structure. [L *basaltes* a dark, hard marble of Ethiopia] —**basaltic**, *adj.*

bascule /'bæskjul/, *n.* **1.** a lever or seesaw apparatus. **2. bascule bridge,** a kind of drawbridge in which the rising section is counterbalanced by a weight. [F: a seesaw]

base¹ /beɪs/, *n., v.,* **based, basing.** ◇*n.* **1.** the bottom of anything, on which it stands or rests; support. **2.** a principle; foundation; basis. **3.** the main element or ingredient. **4.** a starting point. **5. a.** a defended or protected centre for army, navy or airforce activities. **b.** a centre for operation or supply. **6.** *Baseball.* any of the four fixed points to which players run and must touch. **7.** *Maths.* **a.** the number of units on which a counting system is based, as ten in the decimal system, where each digit position is worth ten times that on its right. In base two (binary) each digit position is worth twice that on its right: *9 is written 101 in base two.* **b.** a number that when raised to certain power has a logarithm (based on that number) equal to that power: *The logarithm to base 10 of 10 000 is 4.* **8.** *Geom.* the side or face of geometric figure from which the altitude is drawn. **9.** *Chem.* a compound which reacts with acid to form a salt, e.g. metallic oxides and hydroxides, amines, alkaloids and ammonia. See **alkali.** ◇*v.t.* **10.** to establish; ground: *to base a theory on experience.* [ME, from L, from Gk: a stepping, a step, pedestal, base]

base² /beɪs/, *adj.,* **baser, basest. 1.** morally low; mean; selfish; cowardly. **2.** of little value: *base metals.* **3.** debased or counterfeit: *base coin.* **4.** *Archaic.* low, short or poor. [ME, from LL *bassus* low]

baseball /'beɪsbɔl/, *n.* **1.** a game played with a wooden bat and a hard ball, by two teams of nine players, on a diamond field of four bases around which the batter must run. **2.** the ball used in this game.

basement /'beɪsmənt/, *n.* **1.** a storey of a building below ground level. **2.** the bottom part of a structure supporting the upper parts.

basement complex, *n.* metamorphic igneous rocks, esp. pre-Cambrian, under sedimentary rocks.

bases¹ /'beɪsəz/, *n.* plural of **base**¹.

bases² /'beɪsiz/, *n.* plural of **basis**.

bash /bæʃ/, *v.t.* **1.** to hit or beat. ◇*n.* **2.** a hit or blow. **3.** *Colloq.* drinking spree. **4.** *Colloq.* a try: *Give it a bash; Have a bash at it.*

bashful /'bæʃfəl/, *adj.* shy or very modest; diffident. [See ABASHED]

Basho /'bɑʃoʊ/, *n.* (*Matsuo Munefusa*), 1644–94, Japanese poet; often considered the greatest writer of Haiku.

basic /'beɪsɪk/, *adj.* **1.** of, relating to, or forming a base; fundamental: *basic principle, ingredient, etc.* **2.** *Chem.* **a.** of, relating to, or containing a base (def. 8). **b.** (of a compound) accepting all possible hydrogen ions, and so able to attract more protons. **c.** alkaline. ◇*n.* **3.** something basic or essential.

BASIC /'beɪsɪk/, *n.* a relatively simple computer programming language. Also, **Basic.** [*B*(*eginner's*) *A*(*ll-purpose*) *S*(*ymbolic*) *I*(*nstruction*) *C*(*ode*)]

basic wage, *n.* the minimum wage, determined by an Arbitration Commission in some states, that can be paid to an adult worker employed under an award or agreement.

basidium /bə'sɪdiəm/, *n., pl.* **-sidia** /-'sɪdiə/. a special form of spore-bearing

basidium   83   **bastion**

organ in fungi, in which spores form at the tips of stalks, as in mushrooms. [BAS(IS) + -IDIUM] —**basidial**, *adj.*

basil /'bæzəl/, *n.* a herb used in cooking; sweet basil. [ME, from L, from Gk: royal]

basilica /bə'sılıkə, -'zı-/, *n.* **1.** an oblong building, esp. a church with the nave higher than the aisles. **2.** *Rom Cath Ch.* a church with special ceremonial rights. [L, from Gk: royal; in ancient Rome, a large oblong building near the Forum, used as a hall of justice and public meeting place.

basilisk /'bæsəlısk, 'bæz-/, *n. Class. Myth.* a serpent with deadly breath and look. [L, from Gk: king]

basin /'beısən/, *n.* **1.** a container, usu. round and less deep than wide, used mainly to hold water, esp. for washing. **2.** a sink or washbasin. **3.** a cooking bowl. **4.** a protected area where ships are docked. **5.** *Geog.* **a.** a hollow in the earth's surface, wholly or partly surrounded by higher land: *ocean basin; lake basin; river basin.* **b.** an area of country drained by a river. [ME, from LL: water vessel]

basis /'beısəs/, *n., pl.* **-ses** /-sız/. **1.** the bottom or base of anything, or that on which it stands or rests. **2.** a basic principle. **3.** the main part; principal ingredient. [L, from Gk. See BASE¹]

bask /bask/, *v.i.* **1.** to lie in or enjoy warmth: *to bask in the sunshine.* **2.** to enjoy something pleasant: *to bask in popularity.* [ME, from Scand]

basket /'baskət/, *n.* **1.** a container made of cane, thin wood, plastic, etc., woven together, often having handles. **2.** anything like a basket in shape or use. [ME; orig. unknown]

basketball /'baskətbɔl/, *n.* (a large ball used in) a game played by two teams of five men (or six women), in which points are scored by throwing the ball through a horizontal hoop on the top of a pole at the opponent's end of the court.

baso-, variant of **basi-**.

basophil /'beısəfıl/, *n.* a cell, esp. a white blood cell, having an attraction to basic dyes.

basque /bask/, *n.* **1.** (*cap.*) one of a people of unknown origin inhabiting the western Pyrenees region of Spain and France. **2.** (*cap.*) their language, historically connected only with Iberian. **3.** a woman's close-fitting top, sometimes with a part reaching over hips. **4.** this part or skirt hanging from the waist of a garment. **5.** a tightly knitted band on the lower edge and cuffs of a jumper, etc. [F]

bas-relief /ba-rə'lif/, *n.* a carving on a flat surface, in which the figures are raised only slightly from the background; sculpture in low relief. [F, from It *basso-rilievo* low relief]

bass¹ /beıs/, *adj.* **1.** deep-sounding; low(est) in pitch or range. ◇*n.* **2.** (a singer with) the lowest adult male voice. **3.** a bass part or instrument. **4.** →**double bass**. [ME *bas* low]

bass² /bæs/, *n.* an Australian freshwater fish. [var. of d. E *barse*, OE *bærs*]

Bass /bæs/, *n.* **George**, 1771–1803?, English naval surgeon, explorer and naturalist in Australia; with Matthew Flinders, explored the south-eastern coastline, discovering Bass Strait and circumnavigating Tasmania.

bass clef /beıs 'klef/, *n. Music.* a sign (like a backwards C) on a stave to show that the fourth line from the bottom is the F below middle C; F clef.

basset /'bæsət/, *n.* a long-bodied, shortlegged dog resembling a dachshund but larger and heavier. Also, **basset hound**. [F, orig. diminutive of *bas* low]

basset horn, *n.* an instrument of the clarinet family, no longer used.

bass guitar, *n.* (a player of) a four-stringed electric guitar, the bass instrument in rock groups.

bassinette /bæsə'net/, *n.* a basket in which a baby sleeps. Also, **bassinet**. [F]

bassoon /bə'sun/, *n.* a double-reed woodwind instrument, the bass of the oboe family.

basso profundo, *n.* (a singer with) a very deep bass voice. [It: deep bass]

Bass Strait, *n.* the stretch of ocean separating Tas from mainland Australia; about 210 km wide. [named after George BASS]

bast /bæst/, *n.* the inner bark of the lime and other trees, used in making matting, etc. [OE *bæst*]

bastard /'bastəd/, *n.* **1.** a person whose parents were not married; an illegitimate child. **2.** *Colloq.* (*offensive*) an unpleasant or hateful person. **3.** *Colloq.* any person (without offensive meaning). [ME, from OF: probably from *bast* saddle used for carrying goods + *-ard* -ARD] —**bastardly**, *n.*

bastardise or **bastardize** /'bastədaız/, *v.t.*, **-dised**, **-dising**. **1.** *Archaic.* to declare a bastard. **2.** to reduce the quality or value of. **3.** to shame, as part of a cruel introduction to school, the army, etc. —**bastardisation**, *n.*

bastardry /'bastədri/, *n.* unpleasant or cruel behavior.

baste¹ /beıst/, *v.t.*, **basted**, **basting**. *Sewing.* to tack. [ME, from OG]

baste² /beıst/, *v.t.*, **basted**, **basting**. to moisten (meat, etc.) while cooking, with hot fat, etc. [? F]

Bastille /bæs'til/, *n.* a famous fortress in Paris, used as a prison, built in the 14th century and destroyed 14 July 1789. [ME, from F, from *bastir* build]

Bastille Day, *n.* 14 July, a national holiday of the French republic commemorating the fall of the Bastille.

bastinado /bæstə'nadoʊ/, *n., pl.* **-does**. **1.** a blow or beating with a stick, etc. **2.** an Asian form of punishment by hitting the soles of the feet or the buttocks with a stick. [Sp: stick]

bastion /'bæstıən/, *n.* **1.** a fortified place. **2.** any person or thing which supports or defends. [F, from It: build] —**bastioned**, *adj.*

bat¹ /bæt/, *n., v.*, **batted, batting.** ◇*n.* **1.** the club or stick used in games, esp. cricket and baseball, to hit the ball. **2.** a batsman. **3.** a stick or club. **4.** →**batt. 5. off one's own bat,** on one's own, without help or advice. ◇*v.t.* **6.** to hit with or as if with a bat. [OE *batt* cudgel] –**batter,** *n.*

bat² /bæt/, *n.* **1.** a small mouselike winged mammal, active at night. **2. have bats in the belfry,** to have mad ideas; to be crazy or peculiar. **3. like a bat out of hell,** very fast. [var. of ME *bakke,* from Scand]

bat³ /bæt/, *v.t.,* **batted, batting. 1.** to wink or flutter (the eyelids). ◇*v.* **2. not bat an eye/eyelid,** to show no feelings or surprise.

Bataán /bə'tæn, -'tan/, *n.* a peninsula in the Philippines, in western Luzon, where the US and Philippine forces surrendered to the Japanese during World War II.

Batavia /bə'teɪviə/, *n.* **1.** a former Dutch name of **Jakarta. 2.** a Dutch ship wrecked in 1629 on a reef of the Houtman Abrolhos; commanded by François Pelsaert.

batch /bætʃ/, *n.* **1.** a quantity or number taken together; group: *a batch of prisoners.* **2.** a quantity of bread, cakes, etc., baked at once. [OE *bacan* bake]

bate /beɪt/, *v.t.,* **bated, bating.** to hold (breath): *to wait with bated breath.* [aphetic var. of ABATE]

Bates /beɪts/, *n.* **Daisy May,** 1863–1951, Australian social worker, born in Ireland; noted for her work with Aboriginals.

bath /baθ/, *n., pl.* **baths** or (esp. def. 5) /baðz/; /baθ/, *v.,* ◇*n.* **1.** the washing, esp. of a body, in water, other liquid, steam, etc. **2.** the water or other liquid used for a bath. **3.** a container for this liquid, etc., esp. a large metal or plastic one for bathing the body. **4.** (*oft. pl.*) a building with rooms or equipment for washing or bathing. **5.** (*pl.*) a public swimming pool. **6.** (*usu. pl.*) a town or place visited for medical treatment by bathing, etc.; spa. ◇*v.t.* **7.** to put or wash in a bath. [OE *bæth*]

Bath¹ /baθ/, *n.* a city in south-western England, in Avon county; mineral springs; Roman remains. Pop. 79 965 (1981)

Bath² /baθ/, *n.* **Order of the,** an order of knighthood founded in 1725.

bathe /beɪð/, *v.,* **bathed, bathing,** *n.* ◇*v.t.* **1.** to dip or soak in water or other liquid to clean, etc. **2.** to wash. **3.** to moisten or wet with any liquid. ◇*v.i.* **4.** to have a bath. **5.** to swim for pleasure. ◇*n.* **6.** *Chiefly Brit.* the act of bathing, as in the sea. [OE *bæth* bath] –**bather,** *n.*

bathers /'beɪðəz/, *n.pl.* →**swimsuit.**

batho-, a word part meaning 'deep', as in *batholith.* [combining form representing Gk *báthos* depth]

batholith /'bæθəlɪθ/, *n.* a large mass of igneous rock, esp. granite, formed very deep below the surface. Also, **batholite** /'bæθəlaɪt/, **bathylith.** –**batholithic, batholitic,** *adj.*

bathos /'beɪθɒs/, *n.* **1.** a comical drop from high to common level; anticlimax. **2.** ordinariness or unimportance. **3.** insincere emotion; sentimentality. [Gk: depth] –**bathetic,** *adj.*

Bathurst /'bæθəst/, *n.* a city in central eastern NSW, on the Macquarie River; former goldmining centre; oldest Australian inland town. Pop. 22 280 (1986). [named after Henry, 3rd Earl *Bathurst*]

Bathurst Bay Hurricane, *n.* a cyclone which caused coastal waters to rise 15 m and sweep into Bathurst Bay, Qld, in 1899, drowning 300. Also, **Cyclone Mahina.**

Bathurst burr, *n.* a plant with burrs that stick in sheep's wool. [from BATHURST]

Bathurst Island, *n.* an island 80 km north of Darwin, NT, west of Melville Island; an Aboriginal reserve, owned by the Tiwi Land Council. 2600 km². [See BATHURST]

bathyscaphe /'bæθəskeɪf/, *n.* a small submarine for deep-sea exploration and study. Also, **bathyscaph.**

bathysphere /'bæθəsfɪə/, *n.* a ball-shaped diving apparatus from which to study deep-sea life. [Gk *bathý(s)* deep + -SPHERE]

batik /'batɪk, 'bætɪk/, *n.* (a cloth with a pattern made by) a method of marking with wax before dyeing. [Malay (Javanese)]

batman /'bætmən/, *n., pl.* **batmen.** an army officer's servant.

Batman /'bætmən/, *n.* **John,** 1801–39, Australian pioneer; explored and settled the Port Phillip area.

baton /'bætn/, *n.* **1.** a stick or club, esp. as sign of an official position. **2.** *Music.* the thin stick used by a conductor. **3.** *Sport.* a short stick handed by one runner to the next in a relay race. [F, from LL *bastum;* orig. uncert.]

batsman /'bætsmən/, *n., pl.* **-men.** *Cricket, etc.* a person who specialises in batting, or whose turn it is to bat.

batt /bæt/, *n.* a rectangular sheet of matted fibreglass, cottonwool, etc., used for insulation. Also, **bat.**

battalion /bə'tæljən/, *n.* **1.** *Army.* a unit of three or more companies or similar units. **2.** an army arranged for battle. **3.** (*oft. pl.*) a large number or force. [F, from It]

batten¹ /'bætn/, *v.i.* **1.** to become fat. **2.** to live well, esp. at the expense of others (fol. by *on*). [Scand]

batten² /'bætn/, *n.* **1.** a light flat strip of wood used to fasten the main parts of a structure together. ◇*v.t.* **2.** *Naut.* to fasten with battens and tarpaulins: *to batten down the hatches.* [var. of BATON]

batter¹ /'bætə/, *v.t.* **1.** to beat repeatedly or hard. **2.** to damage by beating or misuse. ◇*v.i.* **3.** to give out heavy repeated blows: *to batter on the door.* [ME frequentative of BAT¹]

batter² /'bætə/, *n.* **1.** a mixture of flour, milk or water, eggs, etc., beaten together. ◇*v.t.* **2.** to coat with batter. [late ME use of BATTER¹]

battering ram, *n.* an ancient military machine with a heavy beam for battering down walls, etc.

battery /'bætəri, -tri/, *n., pl.* **-ries. 1.** *Elect.* a series of cells for producing or storing electricity. **2.** a set of guns, machines, instruments, or other things to be used together. **3.** a large number of cages in which chickens, etc., are reared. **4.** the act of beating or battering. [F: beat]

battle /'bætl/, *n., v.* **battled, battling.** ◇*n.* **1.** a fight or struggle, esp. between armed forces; contest. ◇*v.i.* **2.** to fight or struggle. ◇*v.t.* **3.** to fight or struggle with or against: *to battle cancer.* **4.** to force: *He battled his way.*

battleaxe /'bætəlæks/, *n.* **1.** an axe used as a weapon of war. **2.** *Colloq.* a tough or aggressive woman.

battledore /'bætldɔ/, *n.* **1.** a bat like a small racquet, for hitting a shuttlecock. **2.** Also, **battledore and shuttlecock.** the game played with a battledore and shuttlecock. [ME *bater* BATTER[1] + *dore* beetle]

battlement /'bætlmənt/, *n.* a wall or parapet with indentations or openings, orig. for shooting through. [ME, ? from OF: fortify]

battler /'bætlə/, *n.* **1.** someone who struggles long and hard against difficulties. **2.** a hard-working person, esp. if poor.

battleship /'bætlʃɪp/, *n.* a warship with the heaviest armor and most powerful guns.

batty /'bæti/, *adj.,* **-ier, -iest.** *Colloq.* silly; crazy. [BAT[2] + -Y[1]]

bauble /'bɔbl/, *n.* **1.** a cheap ornament; trinket. **2.** a jester's staff. [ME, from OF: toy, probably from L *bellus* pretty]

Baudin /boʊ'dæ/, *n.* **Thomas Nicolas** /nikoʊ'la/, c.1754–1803, French navigator and explorer; led a French expedition to survey the coastline of Australia (New Holland) 1800–03.

Bauer /'baʊə/, *n.* **Ferdinand Lukas**, 1760–1826, Austrian painter; botanical artist on Matthew Flinders' expedition to Australia in 1801.

Bauhaus /'baʊhaʊs/, *n.* a school of design established in Weimar in 1918 by Walter Gropius to create buildings which utilised all the resources of art, science, and technology. [G: building house]

baulk /bɔk/, *v.i.* **1.** to stop or pull up as if barred or blocked: *He baulked at making the speech.* ◇*v.t.* **2.** to block; hinder; thwart: *baulked in my plans.* **3.** to miss; let slip; fail to use: *to baulk a chance; to baulk a catch.* ◇*n.* **4.** a defeat or disappointment. **5.** a block; a hindrance. **6.** a cross-beam in the roof of a house which unites and supports the rafters. [OE *balca* ridge]

bauxite /'bɔksaɪt/, *n.* a rock which is the principal ore of aluminium. [Les *Baux*, in southern France + -ITE[1]]

Bavaria /bə'vɛəriə/, *n.* a state in southern Germany; formerly a kingdom. *Cap.*: Munich. German, **Bayern.** Pop. 11 023 000 (1987 est.); 70 549 km².

bawd /bɔd/, *n. Archaic.* **1.** a woman who runs a brothel. **2.** a prostitute. [ME, ? from F *baud* gay, from WGmc] —**bawdry,** *n.*

bawdy /'bɔdi/, *adj.* **-dier, -diest.** containing sexual talk or jokes. —**bawdily,** *adv.* —**bawdiness,** *n.*

bawdy house, *n.* →**brothel** (def. 1).

bawl /bɔl/, *v.i.* **1.** to cry or weep noisily. **2.** to cry out loudly and strongly. ◇*v.t.* **3.** to shout out. **4.** *Orig. US.* to scold (fol. by *out*). ◇*n.* **5.** a loud shout; wail; outcry. [ME, probably from ML *baulāre* bark as a dog]

bay[1] /beɪ/, *n.* a wide opening in the shore of a sea or lake. [ME, from LL]

bay[2] /beɪ/, *n.* **1.** a space in a projecting part of a wall, esp. containing a window. **2.** *Archit.* a space or division of a wall, building, etc., between two vertical architectural features (as pillars). **3.** a space between parallel shelvings, as in a library or shop. **4.** a section or space in an aircraft: *bomb bay; engine bay.* **5.** an area set back from the flow of traffic: *parking bay.* [ME, from LL: gape]

bay[3] /beɪ/, *n.* **1.** a deep, long bark, esp. of dogs in hunting. **2. at bay,** forced to turn and face an enemy or a hunter. **3. bring to bay,** to force into a position where escape is impossible. ◇*v.i., v.t.* **4.** to bark or howl (at), esp. deep and long, like dog in hunting. [ME, from OF]

bay[4] /beɪ/, *n.* **1.** the European laurel, whose leaves are used as a herb in cooking; sweet bay. **2.** a crown or wreath of bay leaves given for victory or excellence. [ME, from L: berry]

bay[5] /beɪ/, *n.* **1.** a reddish brown. **2.** a horse of such a color. ◇*adj.* **3.** (of horses, etc.) of the color bay. [ME, from L]

Bayeux tapestry /beɪˌjɜ 'tæpestri/, *n.* a strip of embroidered linen 70.4 m long and 50.8 cm wide, dating from the 12th century, preserved in Bayeux, a town in north-western France; depicts events leading to the Norman conquest of England.

Baynton /'beɪntən/, *n.* **Barbara Jane** (*Janet Ainsleigh*), 1857–1929, Australian author; wrote *Bush Studies* (1902).

Bay of Islands, *n.* a bay containing 149 islands on the eastern coast of northern North Island, NZ; site of NZ's first permanent white settlement, formed by Samuel Marsden in 1814. [named by James COOK in 1769]

bayonet /'beɪnət/, *n., v.,* **-neted, -neting.** ◇*n.* **1.** a blade for stabbing that can be joined to the end of a rifle. ◇*v.t.* **2.** to kill or wound with a bayonet. [F, from *Bayonne*, in France, where such weapons were first manufactured]

bay whaling, *n.* whaling from stations based on land.

bazaar /bə'za/, *n.* **1.** a marketplace or area of shops, esp. in Asia. **2.** any place where a variety of goods is sold. **3.** a sale, esp. to raise money for charity; a fete. [F, from Ar, from Pers]

bazooka /bə'zukə/, *n.* a cylindrical weapon that fires a rocket to destroy tanks, etc.

bazooka

[fanciful coinage, orig. applied to an invented musical instrument]

BBC /ˌbi bi 'si/, *Abbrev.* British Broadcasting Corporation. Also, *Colloq.*, the **Beeb**.

BBQ, *Abbrev.* barbecue.

BC /ˌbi 'si/, *Abbrev.* before Christ: *From 20 BC to AD 50 is 70 years.*

BCA /ˌbi si ei/, *Abbrev.* Bush Church Aid Society.

BCOF, *Abbrev.* British Commonwealth Occupation Force.

b/d, *Abbrev. Accounting.* brought down.

bdellium /'dɛliəm/, *n.* (a plant yielding) a sweet-smelling gum resin. [L, from Gk, translating Heb]

be /bi/, *v. pres. indic. sing.* I **am**; you **are**; he, she, it **is**; *pl.* we, you, they **are**; *past indic. sing.* I **was**; you **were**; he, she, it **was**; *pl.* we, you, they **were**; *pres. subj.* **be**; *past subj.* **were**; *past part.* **been**; *pres. part.* **being**; *old forms* thou **art**; thou **wast** or **wert**. **1.** to exist; have reality; live: *He is no more.* **2.** to take place; happen: *The wedding was last week.* **3.** a word connecting a subject either with a predicate or with adjectives, in statements, questions, and commands: *You are late; Tomorrow is Thursday; Is he here?; Be good at school today.* **4.** a word serving to form certain phrases, as in **a.** infinitive phrases: *(I wanted) to be a dancer.* **b.** participial phrases: *(the art of) being agreeable.* **5.** a word used as an auxiliary verb with a present participle of another verb, to form the continuous tenses: *I am waiting; She was running.* **6.** a word used as an auxiliary verb with a past participle, in passive forms of transitive verbs: *The date was fixed.* [ME *been*, OE *beon*, from IE *bheu-* become]

be-, a prefix meaning 'about', 'around', 'all over', used to form verbs, adding the idea of 'all over', 'thoroughly', e.g. in *becloud, besmear, bepraise*, or to form transitive verbs from intransitives or from nouns or adjectives, e.g. in *begrudge, belabor, befriend, belittle*. [OE, unstressed form of *bī* by]

Be, *Chem. Symbol.* beryllium.

beach /bitʃ/, *n.* **1.** a sandy or pebbly shore of a sea, lake, or river. ◇*v.t.* **2.** to run or pull up (a ship or boat) on a beach. [? from OE *bece* brook, with sense 'pebbly course of stream', hence 'shingle']

beachcomber /'bitʃkoumə/, *n.* **1.** someone who lives on or near a beach, gathering things thrown up by the sea. **2.** a long rolling wave.

beachhead /'bitʃhɛd/, *n. Mil.* an area held on an enemy shore where soldiers and equipment are landed.

beacon /'bikən/, *n.* **1.** a guiding or warning signal, e.g. a fire, esp. on a tower, hill, etc. **2.** a lighthouse. **3.** anything that warns or guides. [OE *b'eac(e)n*]

bead /bid/, *n.* **1.** a small ball of glass, pearl, wood, etc., with a hole through it for stringing. **2.** (*pl.*) a necklace. **3.** (*pl.*) *Rom Cath Ch.* a rosary. **4.** any small round object. **5.** a drop of liquid: *beads of sweat*. ◇*v.t.* **6.** to ornament with beads. ◇*v.i.* **7.** to form beads or drops.

[ME *bede* prayer, rosary bead, var. of *ibed*, OE *gebed* prayer] —**beaded**, *adj.*

beadle /'bidl/, *n. Anglican Ch.* (formerly) a minor parish officer. [OE *bydel* herald, warrant officer, etc.]

beady /'bidi/, *adj.*, **beadier**, **beadiest**. **1.** small, round and shiny like a bead: *beady eyes*. **2.** covered with or full of beads.

beagle /'bigəl/, *n.* (one of) a breed of small dogs with short legs and long hanging ears, used esp. in hunting. [ME *begle*; orig. uncert.]

Beagle /'bigəl/, *n.* HMS, a British ship much used for surveying in the Southern Hemisphere; used in the investigation of Australia's north-western coastline, and Bass Strait; Charles Darwin was the official scientist.

beak¹ /bik/, *n.* **1.** the hard horny mouth of a bird. **2.** similar horny head part in other animals, e.g. the turtle, platypus, etc. **3.** *Colloq.* the nose. **4.** anything shaped like a beak, e.g. the lip of jug. [ME, from L *beccus*, of Celtic orig.] —**beaked**, *adj.*

beak² /bik/, *n. Colloq.* **1.** a magistrate or judge. **2.** a schoolteacher. [orig. unknown]

beaker /'bikə/, *n.* **1.** a large drinking cup with a wide mouth; a mug. **2.** a container, usu. glass, with a flat bottom, straight sides and a pouring lip, used in laboratories. [var. (influenced by BEAK¹) of d. E *bicker*, ME *biker*, from Scand]

Beaker Folk /'bikə fouk/, *n.* a prehistoric people of western Europe during the third millennium BC. [named after the characteristic beakers found among their remains]

beam /bim/, *n.* **1.** a long thick piece of timber, metal, stone, etc. **2.** *Bldg Trades.* one of the main horizontal supports in a building. **3.** *Shipbldg.* a strong piece of timber or metal across a ship to support the deck, hold the sides, etc. **4.** *Naut.* **a.** the side of ship or the direction at right angles to the keel, with reference to the wind, sea, etc. **b.** the width of a ship at its widest part. **5.** the widest part. **6.** the crossbar of a balance from the ends of which hang scales or pans. **7.** a ray, or group of parallel rays, of light or other radiation. **8.** the cone-shaped range of effective use of a microphone or loudspeaker. **9.** *Radio., Aeron.* a signal transmitted along a narrow course, used to guide pilots through darkness, bad weather, etc. **10. on (the) beam. a.** on the course shown by a radio beam. **b.** *Colloq.* just right; correct; in touch. **11. off (the) beam, a.** not on the course shown by a radio beam. **b.** *Colloq.* wrong; incorrect; out of touch. **c.** *Colloq.* crazy. ◇*v.t.* **12.** *Radio.* to broadcast (a signal) on a narrow beam. ◇*v.i.* **13.** to send out beams, esp. of light. **14.** to smile broadly. [OE *bēam* tree, piece of wood, ray of light]

bean /bin/, *n.* **1.** a plant of the legume family with long pods containing smooth seeds eaten fresh or dried. **2.** the seed or pod of such a plant. **3.** a similar seed of another plant: *coffee bean*. **4. full of beans**, *Colloq.* lively; energetic. **5. spill the beans**, *Colloq.* to give away information. [OE *bēan*]

beanbag /'binbæg/, *n.* **1.** a small cloth bag filled with beans, used as a toy. **2.** a large cushion filled with pellets and used as a chair.

beancurd /'binkɜd/, *n.* a curd made from white soya beans, usu. formed into small blocks; used in Asian cookery.

beanfeast /'binfist/, *n. Colloq.* a feast; a celebration. Also, **beano.**

beanie /'bini/, *n. Colloq.* a small close-fitting knitted cap.

bean shoot, *n.* a bean and its very young shoot, esp. a mung bean or a soya bean. Also, **bean sprout.**

bear[1] /beə/, *v.,* **bore** /bɔ/, or (*old form*) **bare, borne,** or **born, bearing.** ◇*v.t.* **1.** to hold up; support: *to bear the weight of the roof.* **2.** to carry; transmit: *to bear gifts; bear gossip.* **3.** to guide or take: *They bore him to the king.* **4.** to push: *We were borne along by the crowd.* **5.** to put up with; tolerate; endure: *I can't bear that man; I can bear the pain.* **6.** to accept responsibility of: *to bear the cost.* **7.** to hold up under; sustain: *Her claim doesn't bear close examination.* **8.** to be fit for or worthy of: *The story doesn't bear repeating.* **9.** to have a right to: *to bear title.* **10.** to have or show: *to bear signs of damage.* **11.** to carry in one's mind: *to bear love; to bear ill feeling.* **12.** to hold or behave (oneself): *He bears himself with dignity.* **13.** to give birth to: *to bear a child.* **14.** to produce by natural growth: *Plants bear leaves.* ◇*v.i.* **15.** to hold or remain firm (fol. by *up*). **16.** to be patient (fol. by *with*). **17.** to press or weigh (fol. by *on, against, down,* etc.). **18.** to relate: *This remark bears on the subject.* **19.** to lie, point or move in a certain direction: *The ship is bearing due west; The harbor bears due east from here.* **20.** to produce offspring, fruit, etc. ◇*v.* **21.** Some special uses are:
bear a hand, to help.
bear away, to change course away from the wind.
bear down, 1. to press or push downwards. **2.** of ship, car, etc., to draw near, usu. fast.
bear out, to prove right: *The facts bear me out.*
bear witness, to be or give evidence or proof.
bring to bear, to cause to have effect. [OE *beran*]

bear[2] /beə/, *n.* **1.** a large heavy mammal with coarse fur and a very short tail. **2.** a clumsy or rude person. **3.** someone who sells shares on a stock exchange, expecting to buy them later at lower prices. See **bull**[1] (def. 3:). [OE *bera*] —**bearish,** *adj.*

beard /bɪəd/, *n.* **1.** the hair growing on the lower part of a man's face. **2.** *Biol.* any beard-like growth or tuft, e.g. on a goat's jaw, below bird's beak, on wheat, etc. ◇*v.t.* **3.** to oppose boldly; defy. [OE *beard*] —**bearded,** *adj.*

bearded dragon /bɪədəd 'drægən/, *n.* **1.** → **bearded lizard.** **2.** → **frill-necked lizard.**

bearded lizard, *n.* an Australian dragon lizard with a frill it can raise around its neck; frilled lizard; Jew lizard. Also, **bearded dragon.**

beardie /'bɪədi/, *n.* → **ling.**

Beardsley /'bɪədzli/, *n.* **Aubrey Vincent,** 1872–98, English artist and illustrator, noted for his black-and-white Art Nouveau style drawings.

bearer /'beərə/, *n.* **1.** someone or something that bears, carries, or supports. **2.** (in India and Africa, formerly) a native servant of a European. **3.** someone presenting a cheque, etc., for money or goods. **4.** → **pallbearer.**

bearing /'beərɪŋ/, *n.* **1.** the manner in which someone carries or behaves himself: *a man of dignified bearing.* **2.** the ability to stand something unpleasant; endurance. **3.** relation; relevance (fol. by *on*): *some bearing on the problem.* **4.** a supporting part. **5.** (*oft. pl.*) (sense of) direction or relative position. **6.** *Geog.* a horizontal angle measured from 0° to 90° fixing the direction of a line relative to (true or magnetic) north or south. **7.** *Heraldry.* any single figure or design on a coat of arms.

bear market, *n. Stock Exchange.* a period of depressed trading during and after a fall in share prices, when traders consider there is little chance of quick recovery.

bearskin /'beəskɪn/, *n.* **1.** the skin or fur of a bear. **2.** a tall black fur cap worn esp. by soldiers.

beast /bist/, *n.* **1.** any animal except humans, but esp. a large four-legged one. **2.** animal nature shared by humans and other animals. **3.** a person who is dirty, cruel, etc. [ME, from LL]

beastly /'bistli/, *adj.,* **beastlier, beastliest. 1.** of or like a beast; bestial. **2.** *Colloq.* nasty; disagreeable. —**beastliness,** *n.*

beat /bit/, *v.,* **beat, beaten** or **beat, beating,** *n., adj.* ◇*v.t.* **1.** to strike repeatedly and usu. violently. **2.** to hit with a stick or whip, as punishment. **3.** to whip in order to thicken or aerate: *to beat cream.* **4.** to attack so as to hurt or break (usu. fol. by *up*). **5.** to move up and down; flap: *a bird beats its wings.* **6.** to shape by hammering (usu. fol. by *out*). **7.** to make (a path) by repeated use. **8.** *Music.* to mark (time) by waving a hand, tapping, etc. **9.** to drive (hunted animals) out of cover. **10.** to defeat or do better than: *She beat him in the race.* **11.** to break (a habit, etc.). **12.** to be too difficult for; puzzle: *It beats me how he managed it.* ◇*v.i.* **13.** to strike repeated blows. **14.** to make any regular and repeated movement; throb or pulsate: *Her heart beat strongly.* **15.** to strike or fall strongly: *The sun beat down on his head.* **16.** to sound when hit: *a drum beating loudly.* **17.** to play, as on a drum. **18.** to hunt through bushes, etc., for game. ◇*v.* **19.** Some special uses are:
beat about the bush, to avoid coming to the point.
beat a retreat, to run away; withdraw.
beat down, *Colloq.* to get lower price from.
beat up, to attack and hurt or damage.
◇*n.* **20.** (the sound made by) a stroke or blow. **21.** a regular movement; throb. **22.** a habitual path, esp. of policeman. **23.** *Music.* **a.** any unit of time within a bar: *Common time has four beats to the bar.* **b.** a stroke of hand, etc., marking a beat of music. **24.** *Poetry.* the stress

in a foot or rhythmical unit of poetry. **25.** *Phys.* a repeated throb or pulse caused by the interference of two waves, currents, or sounds of slightly different frequency. ◇*adj.* **26.** *Colloq.* tired out. **27.** relating to young people, esp. in 1950s, who turned away from conventional behavior, clothes, etc. [OE *bēatan*] —**beaten**, *adj.* —**beating**, *n.*

beater /'biːtə/, *n.* **1.** someone or something that beats. **2.** a device for beating something: *an egg-beater.* **3.** a person who rouses wild game from forests or other cover.

beatific /biə'tɪfɪk/, *adj.* **1.** joyful; blissful: *a beatific smile.* **2.** giving blessedness. [LL]

beatify /bi'ætəfaɪ/, *v.t.*, **-fied**, **-fying**. **1.** to make very happy. **2.** *Rom Cath Ch.* to declare (a dead person) among the blessed in heaven, therefore worthy of special religious honor. [F, from L: make happy]

beatitude /bi'ætə,tjud/, *n.* **1.** highest blessedness or happiness. **2.** (*oft. cap.*) *Theol.* any one of the declarations of blessedness made by Christ in the Sermon on the Mount, e.g. 'Blessed are the poor'. [L]

Beatles /'biːtlz/, *n.pl.* **the**, British band, formed in 1959, generally considered the most popular and influential of pop groups. See **John Lennon, Paul McCartney, George Harrison** and **Ringo Starr.**

beatnik /'biːtnɪk/, *n. Colloq.* a member of the beat generation. See **beat** (def. 27).

Beaton /'biːtn/, *n.* **Sir Cecil Walter Hardy**, 1904–80, English photographer and designer.

beau /boʊ/, *n., pl.* **beaus, beaux** /boʊz/. **1.** a suitor. **2.** someone too concerned with his clothes and appearance; a dandy. [ME, from OF, n. use of *beau* (earlier *bel*) handsome, from L]

Beau Brummell /boʊ 'brʌməl/, *n.* → **Brummell.**

Beaufort scale /'boʊfət ˌskeɪl/, *n.* a scale of numbers for showing the force or speed of wind, from 0 for calm to 12 for hurricane, or speeds over 120 km/h. [named after Sir Francis *Beaufort*, 1774–1857, British admiral who devised it]

Beaumarchais /boʊmɑ'ʃeɪ/, *n.* **Pierre Augustin Caron de** /pjɛə ougy'stæ ka'rɔ̃ də/, 1732–99, French dramatist, best known for *The Barber of Seville* and *The Marriage of Figaro.*

Beaurepaire /'boʊrəpɛə/, *n.* **Sir Frank** (*Francis Joseph Edmund*), 1891–1956, Australian Olympic swimmer and industrialist.

beaut /bjut/, *Colloq.* ◇*adj.* **1.** fine; good. ◇*n.* **2.** Also, **beauty.** someone or something pleasant or excellent. ◇*interj.* **3.** (an exclamation of approval, delight, etc.).

beauteous /'bjutiəs/, *adj. Poetic.* beautiful. —**beauteousness,** *n.*

beautician /bju'tɪʃən/, *n.* a worker in or manager of a beauty salon.

beautiful /'bjutəfəl/, *adj.* **1.** having or showing beauty. **2.** very pleasant: *a beautiful meal.* **3.** perfect: *a beautiful example.* —**beautifully,** *adv.*

beautify /'bjutəfaɪ/, *v.t.*, **-fied, -fying.** to decorate or make more beautiful: *a plan to beautify the city.* [BEAUTY + -FY] —**beautification,** *n.* —**beautifier,** *n.*

beauty /'bjuti/, *n., pl.* **beauties. 1.** that quality which causes pleasure or admiration or delights the aesthetic sense. **2.** something or someone beautiful. **3.** a particular advantage: *The beauty of this job is the long holidays.* ◇*interj.* **4.** (an exclamation of approval, delight, etc.). [ME, from OF *beau*. See BEAU]

beauty spot, *n.* **1.** a patch worn on face or elsewhere to set off the fairness of the skin. **2.** a mole or other mark on the skin. **3.** a place or feature of beauty, esp. scenic.

Beauvoir /boʊ'vwɑ/, *n.* **Simone de**, 1908–86, French existentialist novelist, essayist and feminist.

beaux /boʊz/, *n.* plural of **beau.**

beaver /'bivə/, *n.* **1.** a rodent of Europe, Asia and North America, with soft brown fur and webbed back feet, which builds dams in streams. **2.** a flat, round hat made of beaver fur or similar fabric. ◇*v.i.* **3.** to work hard and steadily (fol. by *away*). [OE *beofor*]

Beaver /'bivə/, *n.* **Bruce**, born 1928, Australian poet and novelist; collections of poems include *Letters to Live Poets* (1966) and *Lauds and Plaints* (1967–72).

Beaverbrook /'bivəbrʊk/, *n.* **William Maxwell Aitken**, 1879–1964, (*1st Baron Beaverbrook*), Canadian-born British newspaper proprietor and conservative politician.

bebop /'bibɒp/, *n.* a style of jazz with complex rhythms and harmonies and odd instrumental effects. Also, **bop, rebop.** [fanciful coinage] —**bebopper,** *n.*

becalmed /bə'kɑmd/, *adj.* (of a sailing ship) stopped or still because of lack of wind.

became /bə'keɪm/, *v.* past tense of **become.**

because /bɪ'kɒz, -'kɔz, bə-/, *conj.* **1.** for the reason that; due to the fact that: *The game was abandoned because it rained.* ◇*adv.* **2.** by reason; on account (fol. by *of*): *The game was abandoned because of rain.* [ME *bi cause* by cause]

beche-de-mer /ˌbɛʃ-də-'mɛə/, *n.* any of several kinds of slug-like sea animal. [from the name of the language of its original fishers]

beck /bɛk/, *n.* in the phrase **at one's beck and call,** at one's service. [short for BECKON]

Becker /'bɛkə/, *n.* **Boris**, born 1967, German tennis player; Wimbledon singles champion 1985, 1986, 1989, 1990; the first unseeded player and the youngest (17 years, 7 months) male to win at Wimbledon.

Becket /'bɛkət/, *n.* **Saint Thomas (à)**, c. 1118–70, archbishop of Canterbury; murdered because of his opposition to Henry II's policies towards the Church.

Beckett /'bɛkət/, *n.* **Samuel**, 1906–89, Irish author and playwright, writing in French and English; wrote *Waiting for Godot* (1952); awarded Nobel prize for literature 1969.

beckon /ˈbɛkən/, *v.t., v.i.* **1.** to signal or direct (towards one) by a wave of the hand, etc. **2.** to attract. [OE *bēacen* sign] —**beckoner**, *n.*

become /bəˈkʌm/, *bi-* /, *v.*, **became**, **become**, **becoming**. ◇*v.i.* **1.** to come into being; come or grow to be: *He became tired.* **2.** to be the fate (*of*): *What will become of her?* ◇*v.t.* **3.** to look good on; suit: *That dress becomes you.* [OE *becuman* come about, happen]

becoming /bəˈkʌmɪŋ, bi-/, *adj.* **1.** attractive; flattering: *a becoming dress.* **2.** suitable; proper.

Becquerel /bɛkəˈrɛl/, /ˈbɛkərəl/, *n.* **Antoine Henri**, 1852–1908, physicist who discovered radioactivity; shared Nobel prize for physics (1903) with Marie and Pierre Curie.

bed /bɛd/, *n., v.*, **bedded, bedding**. ◇*n.* **1.** a piece of furniture for sleeping on or in, often including the mattress, sheets, etc. **2.** the use of a bed; sleeping accommodation. **3.** any resting place. **4.** a piece of ground (in a garden) in which plants are grown. **5.** the ground under a sea, river, etc. **6.** the base; foundation. **7.** *Geol.* a layer of sedimentary rock. **8. a bed of roses**, a very pleasant position. **9. put to bed**, to help (someone) to go to bed or place (a child) in bed. ◇*v.t.* **10.** to provide with a bed (fol. by *down*). **11.** to fix or plant in a bed (of earth, etc.). **12.** to have sexual intercourse with. ◇*v.i.* **13.** to go to bed (fol. by *down*). [OE *bedd*]

bedbug /ˈbɛdbʌg/, *n.* a small flat, wingless, bloodsucking insect, that lives in houses and esp. beds.

bedding /ˈbɛdɪŋ/, *n.* **1.** any materials for a bed, as blankets for people, dried grass for animals. **2.** *Bldg Trades.* a foundation or bottom layer of any kind. **3.** *Geol.* arrangement of rocks in layers.

Bede /biːd/, *n.* **Saint** ('*the Venerable Bede*'), 673?–735, English monk, historian, and theologian; wrote earliest history of England. Also, **Baeda.**

bedeck /bəˈdɛk/, *v.t.* to decorate.

bedevil /bəˈdɛvəl, bi-/, *v.t.*, **-illed, -illing. 1.** to torment or treat badly. **2.** to confuse; muddle: *That question will bedevil him.* —**bedevilment**, *n.*

Bedivere /ˈbɛdɪvɪə/, *n. Arthurian Legend.* **Sir**, the knight who brought the dying King Arthur to the barge in which the three queens bore him to the Isle of Avalon.

bedlam /ˈbɛdləm/, *n.* a scene of wild confusion. [ME *bedlem*, alteration of *Bethlehem*, from the former Royal Bethlehem Hospital, a lunatic asylum in SE London]

bedouin /ˈbɛduən/, *n.* **1.** (*cap.*) Also **Beduin**. a member of any of the nomadic tribes of Arabs that inhabit the deserts of Asia or Africa. **2.** a wanderer. [F, from Ar: desert dweller]

bedpan /ˈbɛdpæn/, *n.* a toilet pan for use by people ill in bed.

bedraggled /bəˈdrægəld, bi-/, *adj.* limp, wet and dirty.

bedridden /ˈbɛdrɪdn/, *adj.* forced to stay in bed. [OE, lit., bed-rider]

bedrock /ˈbɛdrɒk/, *n.* **1.** *Geol.* unbroken solid rock, usu. under soil or rock pieces. **2.** any firm foundation. **3. get down to bedrock**, *Colloq.* to come to the important things.

bedside /ˈbɛdsaɪd/, *n.* **1.** the side of a bed. ◇*adj.* **2.** attending a sick person: *a good bedside manner.*

bed-sitting room, *n.* a furnished room for both night and daytime living.

bedsore /ˈbɛdsɔː/, *n.* a sore due to continuous lying in bed, as in a long illness.

bedspread /ˈbɛdsprɛd/, *n.* an outer cover for a bed.

bedstead /ˈbɛdstɛd/, *n.* the framework of a bed supporting the springs and mattress.

bed-wetting /ˈbɛd-wɛtɪŋ/, *n.* →**enuresis**.

bee /biː/, *n.* **1.** a stinging insect which collects pollen and nectar from flowers and makes honey, as the bumblebee, honeybee, etc. **2.** a contest: *a spelling bee.* **3.** a local gathering for work, etc.: *a working bee.* **4. bee in one's bonnet**, a fixed idea, sometimes slightly silly. [OE *bēo*]

Beeb /biːb/, *n. Colloq.* **the**, the BBC.

beech /biːtʃ/, *n.* any of various trees of temperate areas, with smooth grey bark and small edible triangular nuts. [OE *bēce*]

beef /biːf/, *n.* **1.** (the meat from) a bull or cow. **2.** *Colloq.* strength; brawn. **3.** *Colloq.* a complaint. ◇*v.i.* **4.** *Colloq.* to complain; grumble. [ME, from OF *boef*, from L: ox]

beefeater /ˈbiːfiːtə/, *n.* a guard at the Tower of London.

beefwood /ˈbiːfwʊd/, *n.* any of various Australian trees with red-colored timber.

beefy /ˈbiːfi/, *adj.*, **beefier, beefiest.** fleshy; brawny; solid. —**beefiness**, *n.*

Bee Gees /ˌbiː ˈdʒiːz/, *n.pl.* **the**, pop group formed in the 1950s by three British-born Australian brothers, Barry, Maurice and Robin Gibb.

beehive /ˈbiːhaɪv/, *n.* **1.** a place for bees to live. **2.** a crowded, busy place.

beeline /ˈbiːlaɪn/, *n.* a direct line, like the course of bees returning to a hive: *The children made a beeline for the food.*

Beelzebub /biˈɛlzɪbʌb/, *n.* **1.** the devil. **2.** (in Milton's *Paradise Lost*) one of the fallen angels, second only to Satan himself. [orig. with ref. to Beelzebub, 'the prince of the devils'. See Matt 12:24]

been /biːn/; *weak form* /bən/, *v.* past participle of **be**.

Beenleigh /ˈbiːnli/, *n.* a town in southeastern Qld; rum distilling, sugar cane industry. Pop. 10 344 (1986).

beep /biːp/, *n.* **1.** the sound made by a horn on a car or other vehicle. **2.** a short, high-pitched sound often electronically produced. ◇*v.t., v.i.* **3.** to (cause to) produce a beep.: *to beep the horn; It beeped loudly.*

beer /bɪə/, *n.* **1.** an alcoholic drink brewed and fermented from malted barley and flavored with hops. **2.** a type of drink made from roots, or sugar, yeast, etc.: *ginger beer*; *root beer*. **3.** a glass, can, etc., of beer. [OE *bēor*]

beestings /'bistɪŋz/, *n. pl.* colostrum, esp. of a cow. Also, **beastings, biestings.**

beeswax /'bizwæks/, *n.* the wax made by bees, from which they build their honeycomb.

beeswing /'bizwɪŋ/, *n.* a thin film formed on wines, esp. port, after long keeping.

beet /bit/, *n.* any of various plants whose varieties include the red beet, which has a fleshy edible root, and the sugar beet, which yields sugar. [OE, from L]

Beethoven /'beɪt,hoʊvən/, *n.* **Ludwig van** /'lʊdvɪg væn/, 1770–1827, German composer.

beetle /'bitl/, *n., v.,* **-tled, -tling.** ◇*n.* **1.** an insect whose front wings are hard, horny structures covering the thin, rear, flying wings. **2.** *Colloq.* any of various insects like beetles, e.g. the cockroach. ◇*v.i.* **3.** *Colloq.* to move swiftly (oft. fol. by *off* or *along*). [OE *bitula* lit., biter]

Beeton /'bitn/, *n.* **Isabella Mary,** 1836–65, English cookery writer, best known for *Mrs Beeton's Book of Household Management* (1859–60).

beetroot /'bitrut/, *n.* the root of the red beet, used as a vegetable.

befall /bə'fɔl, bi-/, *v.t., v.i.,* **-fell, -fallen, -falling.** to happen (to): *How could that have befallen?*; *What will befall her next?* [OE]

befit /bə'fɪt, bi-/, *v.t.,* **-fitted, -fitting.** to be fitting for; be suited to: *His clothes befit the occasion.* —**befitting,** *adj.*

before /bə'fɔ, bi-/, *adv.* **1.** in front; ahead. **2.** at an earlier time; previously. **3.** earlier or sooner: *Begin at midday, not before.* ◇*prep.* **4.** in front of; in advance of: *before the house*; *before the army.* **5.** earlier than: *before the war.* **6.** ahead of; in the future of: *Great promise is before our country.* **7.** rather than: *They would die before yielding.* **8.** ahead of; as in order or rank: *We put freedom before fame.* **9.** in the presence or sight of: *before an audience.* **10.** under consideration of: *before a judge.* **11. before the wind,** *Naut.* blown along by the wind. ◇*conj.* **12.** earlier than the time when: *Before we go, we will eat.* **13.** rather than: *I will die before I submit.* [OE *be* by + *foran* before]

beforehand /bə'fɔhænd, bi-/, *adv.* in advance; ahead of time.

befuddle /bə'fʌdl, bi-/, *v.t.,* **-dled, -dling. 1.** to make stupidly drunk. **2.** to confuse, as with smooth-sounding argument.

beg /bɛg/, *v.,* **begged, begging.** ◇*v.t.* **1.** to ask for, in the hope of receiving as a gift. **2.** to ask for, or of, esp. humbly or as a favor: *to beg forgiveness*; *to beg him to forgive me.* **3.** to demand permission (to say or do something): *I beg to differ, I beg to point out a mistake.* ◇*v.i.* **4.** to ask for money; to live by asking for gifts. **5.** to ask humbly or sincerely: *to beg for help.* ◇*v.* **6. beg off,** to excuse oneself from. **7. beg the question, a.** to take for granted the very point raised in a question. **b.** to evade the point at issue. **8. go begging,** to be unwanted; be unclaimed: *This land is going begging.* [OE *bedecian*]

Bega /'bigə/, *n.* a town on the coast of southern NSW; agricultural and dairy industry, particularly cheese manufacturing. Pop. 4294 (1986). [Aboriginal: beautiful or large camping ground]

began /bə'gæn, bi-/, *v.* past tense of **begin.**

beget /bə'gɛt, bi-/, *v.t.,* **begot, begotten** or **begot, begetting. 1.** to produce (a child) (used mainly of the male parent). **2.** to cause: *Jealousy begets unhappiness.* [ME]

beggar /'bɛgə/, *n.* **1.** one who begs or lives by begging. **2.** someone with no money. **3.** (in playful or sympathetic use) a person: *a dear little beggar*; *You poor beggar!* **4. beggar for punishment,** someone who always works hard. ◇*v.t.* **5.** to reduce to poverty; impoverish. **6.** to make seem powerless: *Her beauty beggars description.* [ME]

beggarly /'bɛgəli/, *adj.* **1.** as of a beggar; desperately poor. **2.** mean; miserly —**beggarliness,** *n.*

begin /bə'gɪn/, *v.,* **began, begun, beginning.** ◇*v.i.* **1.** to take the first step of an action; start. **2.** to come into existence; arise; originate. ◇*v.t.* **3.** to take the first step in (something); start; commence. **4.** to bring (something) into existence; create; found. [OE] —**beginner,** *n.*

beginning /bə'gɪnɪŋ/, *n.* **1.** the act or fact of entering upon an action or state. **2.** the point of time or space at which anything begins: *the beginning of the Christian age.* **3.** (*oft. pl.*) the first stage of anything: *the beginnings of science.*

begone /bə'gɒn, bi-/, *v.i.* (*usu. command*) to go away, depart.

begonia /bə'goʊniə, -jə/, *n.* any of various tropical plants popular for their handsome, often many-colored leaves and waxy flowers. [named after Michel *Bégon*, 1638–1710, French patron of science]

begot /bə'gɒt, bi-/, *v.* past tense and past participle of **beget.**

begotten /bə'gɒtn, bi-/, *v.* past participle of **beget.**

begrudge /bə'grʌdʒ, bi-/, *v.t.,* **-grudged, -grudging. 1.** to be discontented at seeing (someone) have (something): *to begrudge a man his good luck.* **2.** to be unwilling to give or allow: *The bosses begrudge her the money she earned.*

beguile /bə'gaɪl, bi-/, *v.t.,* **-guiled, -guiling. 1.** to charm. **2.** to influence by deceit; mislead; delude. **3.** to take away from by cleverness (fol. by *of*). **4.** to pass (time) pleasantly.

beguine /bə'gin/, *n.* a South American dance. [Creole F: flirtation]

begum /'bigəm/, *n.* (in India) a Muslim woman of high rank. [Hind]

begun /bə'gʌn, bi-/, v. past participle of **begin**.

behalf /bə'haf, bi-/, n. side or interest (preceded by *on*): *He fought on behalf of his country*. [ME *behalve* beside, in OE a phrase, *be healfe (him) by (his) side*]

behave /bə'heɪv, bi-/, v., **-haved, -having**. ◇v.i. **1.** to bear oneself or itself; act: *She behaved with generosity*; *The ship behaves well*. **2.** to act in a socially acceptable manner: *Did the child behave?* ◇v. **3. behave oneself**, to act in a socially acceptable manner. [late ME, apparently from BE- + HAVE hold oneself a certain way]

behavior or **behaviour** /bə'heɪvjə, bi-/, n. **1.** the manner of behaving or acting. **2.** *Psychol.* the actions or activities of any organism as basis for study. **-behavioral**, adj.

behaviorism or **behaviourism** /bə'heɪvjə,rɪzəm, bi-/, n. *Psychol.* the study in humans and animals of observable responses as reactions to the outer environment with little reference to states of mind. **-behaviorist**, n., adj.

behead /bə'hɛd, bi-/, v.t. to cut off the head of; decapitate.

beheld /bə'hɛld, bi-/, v. past tense and past participle of **behold**.

behest /bə'hɛst, bi-/, n. command. [OE *behǽs* promise]

behind /bə'haɪnd, bi-/, prep. **1.** at the back of: *behind the house*. **2.** after; later than: *behind schedule*. **3.** less advanced than: *behind his class in science*. **4.** on the far side of; beyond: *behind the mountain*. **5.** supporting; promoting: *The council is behind the idea*. **6.** hidden by: *Bitterness lay behind her smile*. ◇adv. **7.** at or towards the back: *She pushed him behind*. **8.** in a place, state or stage already passed: *He left his wallet behind*. **9.** late: *behind with the rent*. **10.** slow, as a watch or clock. ◇n. **11.** the buttocks. **12.** *Aust. Rules*. A score of one point, achieved by putting the ball between a goal post and an outer post. [OE]

behold /bə'hoʊld, bi-/, v.t., **-held, -holding**. to look at; see: *You will behold a child*. [OE *behaldan* keep] **-beholder**, n.

beholden /bə'hoʊldn, bi-/, adj. bound to feel grateful; indebted.

behove /bə'hoʊv, bi-/, v.t., **-hoved, -hoving**. to be necessary or proper for (now only in impersonal use): *It behoves me to see him*. [OE *behōfian* need]

beige /beɪʒ/, n., adj. very light brown, as of natural wool. [F]

Beijing /beɪ'dʒɪŋ/, n. the capital of the People's Republic of China, in the north-eastern part; forms a separate municipality. Pop. 4 983 000 (1987 est.). Formerly, **Peking**.

being /'biɪŋ/, n. **1.** existence; life: *What is the purpose of our being?* **2.** nature; self: *She threw her whole being into the task*. **3.** something that lives or exists: *beings on a strange planet; a human being*. **4.** *Philos*. **a.** that which has reality either materially or in idea. **b.** absolute existence in a complete or perfect state, lacking no necessary characteristic; essence.

Beirut /beɪ'rut/, n. a seaport in and the capital of Lebanon. Pop. 1 500 000 (1985 est.).

belabor or **belabour** /bə'leɪbə, bi-/, v.t. **1.** to beat severely. **2.** to attack continually, as by making fun of.

Belarus /bɛlə'rus/, n. a republic in eastern Europe bordered by Russia, Latvia, Lithuania, Poland and Ukraine; a member of the CIS; a constituent republic of the Soviet Union 1922–91, known as the **Byelorussian Soviet Socialist Republic**. Pop. 10 200 000 (1989 est.); 207 600 km². *Language*: Belarusian. *Cap.*: Minsk. Also, **Byelorussia, Belorussia**. **-Belarusian**, n., adj.

belated /bə'leɪtəd, bi-/, adj. coming or being late or too late: *to give belated thanks*.

belay /bə'leɪ, bi-/, v., **-layed, -laying**. ◇v.t. **1.** *Navig*. to fasten (a rope) by winding around a pin or short rod. **2.** *Mountaineering*. to secure (a rope or person) by a turn of rope round a steady object. ◇v.i. **3.** *Naut. Colloq*. to stop (usu. as a command). **4.** to make a rope tight. [OE *belecgan* cover]

belch /bɛltʃ/, v.i. **1.** to pass wind noisily from the stomach through the mouth; burp. **2.** to throw out contents violently, as a volcano. ◇v.t. **3.** to throw out (something) violently. ◇n. **4.** the noise or action of belching; burp. [ME]

beleaguer /bə'ligə, bi-/, v.t. to surround: *beleaguered with annoyances; beleaguered with enemies*. [D *be-* about + *leger* camp] **-beleaguered**, adj.

Belfast /'bɛlfast, bɛl'fast/, n. a seaport in and the capital of Northern Ireland; the centre of Irish Protestantism; shipbuilding and linen industry. Pop. 354 400 (1981).

belfry /'bɛlfri/, n., pl. **-fries**. **1.** a tower which contains a bell. **2.** the part of any structure in which a bell is hung. [ME, from OF, from Gmc]

Belg, *Abbrev*. **1.** Belgian. **2.** Belgium.

Belgium /'bɛldʒəm/, n. a kingdom in north-western Europe, on the North Sea; independent since 1830; a leader of post-war European international cooperation. Pop. 9 858 895 (1986 est.). 30 519 km². *Languages*: Dutch and French. *Currency*: franc. *Cap.*: Brussels.

Belgrade /bɛl'greɪd/, n. the capital of Yugoslavia, on the Danube; capital of Serbia. Pop. 1 087 915 (1981). Serbian, **Beograd**.

belie /bə'laɪ, bi-/, v.t., **-lied, -lying**. **1.** to give a false account of: *His face belied his thoughts*. **2.** to show to be false: *Her trembling belied her calm words*. **3.** to prove false to; fail to justify: *His exam results belie his earlier promise*. [OE *be-* BE- + *lēogan* LIE¹]

belief /bə'lif, bi-/, n. **1.** something which is believed; an accepted opinion. **2.** acceptance of the truth or reality of a thing, without complete proof: *Your story is not worthy of belief*. **3.** confidence; faith; trust: *a child's belief in his*

belief

parents. **4.** a system of religious principles: *the Christian belief.* [ME]

believe /bə'liv, bi-/, v., **-lieved, -lieving.**
◇v.i. **1.** to have confidence (*in*); trust: *You must believe in me, if the plan is to work.* **2.** to be persuaded of the truth of anything; accept a principle, system, etc. (fol. by *in*): *Do you believe in life after death?*; *to believe in co-ed schools.* ◇v.t. **3.** to accept as true; credit: *to believe a person; to believe a story.* **4.** to think: *I believe the Opposition is lying.* [ME, from OE *lēfan*] — **believable,** adj. — **believer,** n.

belittle /bə'lɪtl, bi-/, v.t., **-tled, -tling.** to make little or less important; depreciate; disparage.

bell[1] /bel/, n. **1.** a sounding instrument, usu. of metal, cup-shaped with a wide mouth, rung by the clapper hanging within it. **2.** any instrument, esp. electrical, giving out a continuous ringing sound, e.g. a doorbell. **3.** a stroke, sound, or signal made by a bell. **4.** anything shaped like a bell. **5.** *Naut.* the half-hourly divisions of a watch marked by strokes of a bell. **6. ring a bell,** *Colloq.* to sound familiar. [OE *belle*]

bell[2] /bel/, v.i. (esp. of a stag) to bellow or roar. [ME *belle(n)*, OE *bellan* roar, c. G *bellen* bark]

Bell /bel/, n. **1. Alexander Graham,** 1847–1922, US scientist, born in Scotland; invented the telephone. **2. Sir Francis Henry Dillon,** 1851–1936, NZ politician, prime minister 1925.

belladonna /belə'dɒnə/, n. (a drug obtained from) deadly nightshade. See **atropine**. [It: lit., fair lady]

bellbird /'belbɜd/, n. a yellowish-green honeyeater, with a piping, bell-like call. Also, **bell-miner.**

belle /bel/, n. a woman or girl admired for her beauty. [F]

Bellenden Ker Range /beləndən 'kɜ/, n. a mountain range in north-eastern Qld south of Cairns. Highest peak, Bartle Frere, 1657 m.

Bellerophon /bə'lerəfən/, n. *Gk Myth.* a hero of Corinth who, on the winged horse Pegasus, slew the monster Chimera.

belles-lettres /bel-'letrə/, n.pl. the finer or more elegant forms of literature. [F] — **belletrist,** n. — **belletristic,** adj.

bellicose /'belɪkoʊs/, adj. keen to fight; warlike; pugnacious. [L: war] — **bellicosity,** n.

belligerent /bə'lɪdʒərənt/, adj. **1.** warlike; given to fighting or quarrelling. **2.** of war or those involved in war. ◇n. **3.** a party to war or quarrel. [L] — **belligerence,** n.

bell jar, n. a bell-shaped glass cover, for holding gases in chemical operations.

Belloc /'belək, -ɒk/, n. **Hilaire** /hɪ'leə/, 1870–1953, British author and poet, born in France.

Bellona /bə'loʊnə/, n. *Rom Myth.* the goddess of war (sister or wife of Mars).

bellow /'beloʊ/, v.i. **1.** to make a hollow, loud, animal cry, as a bull or cow. **2.** to roar; bawl: *bellowing with anger.* ◇v.t. **3.** to express

92

belt

with a loud, deep voice: *to bellow an answer.* ◇n. **4.** The act or sound of bellowing. [ME, apparently b. OE *bellan* BELL[2] and *bylgan* bellow]

Bellow /'beloʊ/, n. **Saul,** born 1915, US novelist and playwright, born in Canada; awarded Nobel prize for literature 1976.

bellows /'beloʊz/, n. *sing. and pl.* an instrument or machine for producing a strong current of air when it is pumped, as for a fire or an organ. [OE]

belly /'beli/, n., pl., **-ies,** v., **-ied, -ying.**
◇n. **1.** the front or underneath part of a vertebrate animal from the chest to the thighs, containing the stomach, bowel, etc; the abdomen. **2.** the stomach. **3.** appetite for food; gluttony. **4.** the inside of anything: *the belly of a ship.* **5.** a raised section of anything, as of a bottle, etc. **6.** the front, inner, or underneath part (opposed to *back*). ◇v.t., v.i. **7.** to make or become swollen: *The wind bellied the sails; The sails bellied in the wind.* [OE: bag, skin]

belly-ache /'beli-eɪk/, n. *Colloq.* **1.** a pain in the stomach, esp. colic. **2.** a complaint. ◇v.i. **3.** to complain.

bellybutton /'belibʌtn/, n. *Colloq.* the navel.

belong /bə'lɒŋ, bi-/, v.i. **1.** to have a rightful place; to be connected with (oft. fol. by *to*): *It just doesn't belong here; He belongs to Sydney.* ◇v. **2. belong to, a.** to be the property of: *The book belongs to him.* **b.** to be part of: *That cover belongs to this jar.* [ME BE- + *longen* belong, from OE *gelang* belonging to]

belonging /bə'lɒŋɪŋ, bi-/, n. **1.** relationship; affinity: *a sense of belonging.* **2.** (*pl.*) possessions; goods.

beloved /bə'lʌvəd, -'lʌvd, bi-/, adj. **1.** greatly loved. ◇n. **2.** someone who is greatly loved.

below /bə'loʊ, bi-/, adv. **1.** in or to a lower place; beneath. **2.** on or to a lower floor; downstairs. **3.** at a later point on a page or in writing: *See below for further notes.* **4.** in a lower rank or grade: *the class below.* ◇prep. **5.** lower than: *below the knee; below the usual cost.* **6.** unworthy of. [ME *biloogħe* by low]

Belsen /'belsən/, n. a village in north-western Germany; the site of a Nazi concentration camp during World War II. Also, **Bergen-Belsen.**

belt /belt/, n. **1.** a band of material, as leather, worn around the waist to support clothing, for ornament, etc. **2.** *Sport.* such a band as a token of honor or success. **3.** any encircling band, strip, or strips. **4.** a large strip of land having special characteristics: *the wheat belt.* **5.** *Mach.* a band or cord connecting and pulling about each of two or more wheels, etc., to continue or change the direction of movement. **6. below the belt,** against the rules; unfairly. ◇v.t. **7.** to dress or surround with a belt. **8.** to fasten on (a sword, etc.) by means of a belt. **9.** to beat with a belt, etc. **10.** *Colloq.* to give a blow to. **11.** to sing very loudly and often roughly (fol. by *out*): *They belted out the school song.* ◇v.i. **12.** *Colloq.* to move quickly: *to belt along.* ◇v. **13. belt up,**

belt 93 **benign**

Colloq. **a.** be quiet; shut up. **b.** to fasten a safety belt. [OE, ? from L]

BEM, /ˌbi i 'em/ *Abbrev.* British Empire Medal.

bemoan /bəˈmoʊn, bi-/, *v.t.* to grieve over; bewail; lament.

bemused /bəˈmjuzd, bi-/, *adj.* **1.** unable to think clearly; confused; muddled; stupefied. **2.** lost in thought; preoccupied.

Benaud /ˈbenoʊ/, *n.* **Richie** (*Richard Benaud*), born 1930, Australian Test cricketer and journalist.

bench /bentʃ/, *n.* **1.** a long seat with or without a back. **2. a.** a seat for members of parliament, judges in court or people in other official positions. **b.** a court of law: *a High Court bench.* **3.** the position of a judge: *appointed to the bench.* **4.** the group of people sitting as judges. **5.** the strong work-table of a carpenter or other mechanic. **6.** *Geog.* a flat section of land on a valley slope above the stream bed, or along a coast above the level of the sea or lake. [OE *benc*]

benchmark /ˈbentʃmak/, *n.* **1.** a point of known height, usu. a mark cut into some lasting material, to serve as a reference point in running a line of levels for the determination of other heights. **2.** a standard from which quality or excellence is measured.

bend /bend/, *v.*, **bent** or (*old form*) **bended, bending,** *v.t.* **1.** to bring (a bow, etc.) into a state of tension by curving it. **2.** to force into a different or particular, esp. curved, shape, by pressure. **3.** to cause to give in: *He will bend them to his will.* **4.** to turn (energy, mind, etc.) in a particular direction: *She must bend her energy to the job at hand.* **5.** *Naut.* to fasten. ◊*v.i.* **6.** to become curved or bent. **7.** to take on a bent position; stoop. **8.** to bow to indicate one's lesser rank or position; yield; submit. **9.** to turn in a particular direction: *At the bridge, the road bends.* ◊*v.* **10. bend over backwards,** to try as hard as one can. ◊*n.* **11.** an act or result of bending. **12.** a bent thing or part; curve; crook. **13.** *Naut.* a knot by which a rope is fastened to another rope or to something else. **14. round the bend,** *Colloq.* mad. **15. the bends,** a dangerous disorder where nitrogen bubbles form in the blood because of a too rapid decrease in surrounding pressure, found esp. in divers who have surfaced too quickly. [OE *bendan* bind, bend (a bow)] —**bendable,** *adj.*

bender /ˈbendə/, *n. Colloq.* a period of heavy drinking. [Brit]

Bendigo /ˈbendəɡoʊ/, *n.* a city in central Vic; major commercial centre; pastoral and manufacturing industries. Pop. 53 944 (1986).

Bendigo pottery, *n.* **1.** a pottery works at Bendigo; the oldest in Australia. **2.** the pottery made there.

bene-, a word part meaning 'well', as in *benediction.* [L, combining form of *bene,* adv.]

beneath /bəˈniθ, bi-/, *adv.* **1.** below; in a lower place, position, state, etc. **2.** underneath: *the heaven above and the earth beneath.* ◊*prep.*

3. below; under: *beneath the same roof.* **4.** further down than; underneath. **5.** lower in position, power, etc., to: *A captain is beneath a general.* **6.** unworthy of; below the level of: *beneath your notice.* [OE *be* by + *neothan* below]

Benedictine /benəˈdɪktʃn/, *n.* **1.** *Eccles.* a member of an order of monks founded at Monte Cassino, between Rome and Naples, by St Benedict about AD 530, or of various congregations of nuns following his rule. The rules of the order (**Benedictine rule**) are silence and useful employment when not in divine service. —*adj.* **2.** pertaining to St Benedict or to an order following his rule.

benediction /benəˈdɪkʃən/, *n. Church.* **1.** the act of pronouncing a blessing. **2.** the form of blessing given at the close of a church service, etc. [ME, from L] —**benedictory,** *adj.*

benefactor /ˈbenəfæktə, benəˈfæktə/, *n.* **1.** someone who gives help or does good. **2.** someone who makes a gift of money, as in a will. [L] —**benefactress,** *n. fem.*

benefice /ˈbenəfəs/, *n.* **1.** a position providing a living for a church minister. **2.** the income provided. [ME, from L: benefit, favor]

beneficent /bəˈnefəsənt/, *adj.* doing good or causing good to be done, often by giving gifts. —**beneficence,** *n.*

beneficial /benəˈfɪʃəl/, *adj.* giving benefit; advantageous; helpful.

beneficiary /benəˈfɪʃəri/, *n.*, pl. **-aries**. **1.** one who receives benefits or advantages. **2.** *Law.* a person named as the one receiving income or property under a will, insurance policy, etc.

benefit /ˈbenəfət/, *n., v.,* **-fited, -fiting**. ◊*n.* **1.** an act of kindness. **2.** anything that is for the good of a person or thing. **3.** any public performance to raise money for a worthy purpose. **4.** payment or other assistance given by an insurance company, public agency, etc. ◊*v.t.* **5.** to do good to: *The holiday will benefit her.* ◊*v.i.* **6.** to gain advantage: *He will benefit from the will.* [L *bene* BENE- + *factum* thing done]

benevolent /bəˈnevələnt/, *adj.* **1.** wishing to do good for others. **2.** intended for doing good rather than making profit: *a benevolent organisation.* [L: well-wishing] —**benevolence,** *n.*

Bengal /benˈɡɔl, benˈɡɑl/, *n.* **1.** a former province in north-eastern India; in 1947 divided into **East Bengal** (now Bangladesh) and **West Bengal** (in India). **2. Bay of,** a part of the north-eastern Indian Ocean between Burma and India. 2 172 000 km². —**Bengalese,** *n., adj.*

Ben-Gurion /ben-ˈɡuriən/, *n.* **David,** 1886–1973, Israeli politician; prime minister 1949–53, 1955–63.

benighted /bəˈnaɪtəd/, *adj.* backward in learning or in morals. [pp. of *benight, v.,* from BE- + NIGHT]

benign /bəˈnaɪn/, *adj.* **1.** kind or showing kindness or gentleness: *a benign smile.* **2.** favorable; propitious. **3.** *Med.* causing little or

no harm: *a benign growth*. [ME, from L: kind]
—**benignity**, *n*.

Benjamin[1] /ˈbendʒəmən/, *n. Bible.* the youngest and favorite son of Jacob by Rachel, and brother of Joseph.

Benjamin[2] /ˈbendʒəmən/, **Phyllis Jean**, born 1907, Australian Labor politician in Tas; first woman in Australia to lead an Upper House.

Ben Lomond /ben ˈloumənd/, *n.* **1.** a mountain in western Scotland, east of Loch Lomond. 973 m. **2.** a mountain in central north-eastern Tas. 1573 m. **3.** a mountain and town in the New England Range in northern NSW; highest railway station in Australia (1363 m above sea level). 1519 m.

Bennelong /ˈbenəlɒŋ/, *n.* 1764?–1813, an Aboriginal captured by Governor Phillip in 1789 and installed with his family in a hut in Sydney; he was taken to England by Phillip; on his return he was unable to fit back into Aboriginal society.

Bennelong Point, *n.* a small tract of land between Farm Cove and Sydney Cove NSW; now the site of the Sydney Opera House. [originally the site of the hut in which BENNELONG lived]

Bennett /ˈbenət/, *n.* **1. Agnes Elizabeth Lloyd**, 1872–1960, Australian medical practitioner in NZ; during World War I became the first female commissioned officer in the British Army. **2. (Enoch) Arnold**, 1867–1931, English novelist.

Ben Nevis /ben ˈnevəs/, *n.* a peak in western Scotland in the Grampians; the highest point in the British Isles. 1343 m.

Benny /ˈbeni/, *n.* **Jack**, 1894–1974, US comedian.

bent[1] /bent/, *adj.* **1.** curved; crooked. **2.** set; determined (fol. by *on*): *bent on evil*. **3.** *Colloq.* stolen: *to sell bent goods*. **4.** *Colloq.* dishonest; corrupt: *a bent cop*. **5.** *Colloq.* different from what is considered to be normal behaviour, as by taking illegal drugs, being homosexual, etc. **6.** *Music.* (of a note) slightly changed from the pitch of the scale. ◇*n.* **7.** a direction followed; inclination; bias: *a bent for painting*. **8.** *Eng.* a bent form, as a frame placed across a building, to give support. [pp. of BEND]

bent[2] /bent/, *n.* a type of fine-stalked grass used for lawns. [OE *beonet*]

Bent /bent/, *n.* **1. Ellis**, 1783–1815, English barrister in Australia; judge-advocate of NSW under Governor Macquarie, with whom he clashed over the right of emancipists to practise law. **2.** his brother, **Jeffery Hart**, 1780–1852, English judge in Australia; like his brother, clashed with Macquarie and was dismissed from office in 1816.

benumb /bəˈnʌm, bɪ-/, *v.t.* **1.** to make numb: *benumbed by cold*. **2.** to deaden (the mind, the senses, etc); stupefy. [OE *benumen* deprived]

Benz /benz, bents/, *n.* **Karl Friedrich**, 1844–1929, German engineer who pioneered the development of the internal-combustion engine and the car.

benzene /ˈbenzin, benˈzin/, *n.* a colorless, volatile, flammable, aromatic hydrocarbon, C_6H_6, obtained chiefly from coal tar, and used as a solvent for resins, fats, etc., and in the production of dyes, etc.

benzene ring, *n.* (the picture of) the structure of benzene as a hexagon with a carbon atom at each of its points, each of which has a hydrogen atom bonded to it. One or more of these hydrogen atoms may be replaced, forming benzene ring derivatives.

benzine /ˈbenzin, benˈzin/, *n.* a colorless, volatile, flammable liquid, a mixture of various hydrocarbons, obtained in the purification of petroleum, and used in cleaning, dyeing, etc.

benzo-, a word part meaning 'having to do with or made from benzene'. Also, **benz-**.

benzol /ˈbenzɒl/, *n.* untreated industrial benzene. Also, **benzole**.

benzyl /ˈbenzəl/, *n.* a univalent organic radical, $C_6H_5CH_2-$, from a benzene hydrocarbon.

Beowulf /ˈbeɪəwʊlf/, *n.* an Old English epic poem of the early eighth century; the best known example of Old English literature.

bequeath /bəˈkwɪð, -ˈkwɪθ/, *v.t.* **1.** *Law.* to leave (property etc.) to another by will. **2.** to hand down; pass on. [OE BE- + *cwethan* say]
—**bequeathal**, *n*.

bequest /bəˈkwest, bɪ-/, *n.* **1.** *Law.* an arrangement in a will concerning personal property, esp. money. **2.** →**legacy**. [OE]

berate /bəˈreɪt/, *v.t.*, **-rated, -rating.** to scold.

Berber /ˈbɜbə/, *n.* a member of a group of North African tribes living in Barbary and the Sahara.

bereave /bəˈriv, bɪ-/, *v.t.*, **-reaved** or **-reft, -reaving. 1.** to cause to suffer loss (*usu. in passive*): *He had been recently bereaved by the death of his wife.* **2. the bereaved**, people suffering loss of their relatives. [OE BE- + *rēafian* rob]
—**bereavement**, *n*.

bereft /bəˈreft/, *v.* **1.** past participle of **bereave**. ◇*adj.* **2.** suffering loss: *bereft of family; bereft of hope; bereft of land*. **3.** lacking: *bereft of meaning*.

Beresford /ˈberəsfəd/, *n.* **Bruce**, born 1940, Australian film director.

beret /ˈbereɪ/, *n.* a soft round cap that fits closely. [F, from Béarn dialect, from LL: cloak]

Bergman /ˈbɜgmən/, *n.* **1. Ingmar**, born 1918, Swedish film director; films include *The Seventh Seal* (1956). **2. Ingrid**, 1915–82, Swedish stage and film actress in Hollywood and Europe; films include *Casablanca* (1943) and *Anastasia* (1956).

beri-beri /ˈberi-beri/, *n.* a disease of nerves outside the central nervous system caused by deficiency in vitamin B_1. [Singhalese, reduplication of *beri* weakness]

Bering Sea /ˌbɛrɪŋ ˈsi, ˌbɪərɪŋ/, a part of the northern Pacific north of the Aleutian Islands. About 2 274 020 km². [named after Vitus

Bering Sea

Bering, 1681-1741, Danish navigator and explorer of the northern Pacific for Russia]

Bering Strait, *n.* the strait between Alaska and Russia in Asia, connecting the Bering Sea and the Arctic Ocean. 58 km wide.

berkelium /bə'kiliəm/, *n.* an artificial, radioactive, metallic element, *Symbol:* Bk; *at. no.:* 97; *at. wt:* 247. [*Berkel(ey)*, California, where first identified + -IUM]

Berkshire /'bɑkʃɪə -ʃə/, *n.* **1.** a county in southern England; 1878 km²; Pop. 734 100 (1986 est.). *Administrative Centre:* Reading. **2.** a breed of black pigs with white markings on the feet (orig. from southern England).

berley /'bɜli/, *n.* **1.** any bait, spread on the water by fisherman to attract fish. **2.** *Colloq.* *leg-pulling; good humored deceit.* [orig. uncert.]

Berlin[1] /bɜ'lɪn/, *n.* **Irving** (*Israel Isidore Baline*), born 1888 in Russia, US songwriter.

Berlin[2] /bɜ'lɪn/, *n.* the capital and largest city of Germany, in the eastern central part; capital of the former kingdom of Prussia, and of the unified Germany 1871-1945; divided 1945-90 into US, British, and French sectors (**West Berlin**) and a Soviet sector (**East Berlin**); in 1991 became the capital of the reunified Germany, with administration gradually being transferred from Bonn. Pop. 3 352 848 (1989 est.).

Bermuda /bə'mjudə/, *n.* a group of islands in the Atlantic, about 930 km east of North Carolina, US; British colony since 1684. Pop. 54 050 (1986); 52 km². *Cap.:* Hamilton. Also, the **Bermudas**. —**Bermudan, Bermudian,** *adj., n.*

Bermuda Triangle, *n.* an area of the Atlantic Ocean enclosed by imaginary lines from Florida to Bermuda to Puerto Rico and back to Florida; unexplained disappearance of ships and aircraft.

Bern /bɜn/, *n.* the capital of Switzerland, in the north-western part. Pop. 138 574 (1986 est.).

Bernhardt /'bɜnhɑt, 'bɛənhɑt/, *n.* **Sarah** (*Rosine Bernard*), 1845-1923, French tragic actress.

Bernini /bɜ'nini, bɛə-/, *n.* **Giovanni Lorenzo** /dʒə'vɑni lou'rɛntsoʊ/, 1598-1680, Italian sculptor, architect and painter of the baroque era.

Bernstein /'bɜnstaɪn/, *n.* **Leonard**, 1918-90, US conductor and composer; works include *West Side Story* (1957).

Berri /'bɛri/, *n.* **1.** a town and irrigation district in south-eastern SA on the Murray River; winery, distillery, canneries. Pop. 3 502 (1986). **2.** —**Berry**[2] (def.2).

berry /'bɛri/, *n., pl.* **-ries. 1.** any small, (usu.) stoneless and juicy fruit, e.g. the gooseberry, strawberry, etc. **2.** a dry seed, e.g. a coffee bean. **3.** *Bot.* a simple fruit having a soft wall in which the seeds are fixed, e.g. the grape, gooseberry, tomato, etc. [¼OE *berie*]

berserk /bə'zɜk/, *adj.* violently and destructively wild or insane.

berth /bɜθ/, *n.* **1.** a shelf-like space, bunk, or whole room given to a traveller on a ship or a train as a sleeping space. **2.** *Navig.* a space for a ship to tie up at a dock. **3. give a wide berth to,** to avoid; keep away from. ◊*v.t.* **4.** to give space to (a ship) to lie in dock. ◊*v.i.* **5.** to come to a dock. [probably from BEAR[1]]

beryl /'bɛrəl/, *n.* **1.** the mineral group which includes the emerald. **2.** a pale bluish green. [ME, from L, from Gk]

beryllium /bə'rɪliəm/, *n.* a grey, divalent, hard, light, metallic element, used in copper alloys for springs and contacts. *Symbol:* Be; *at. no.:* 4; *at. wt:* 9.0122. [BERYL + -IUM]

Berzelius /bɜ'ziliəs/, *n.* **Baron Jöns Jakob** /jɒns 'jakɒb/, 1779-1848, Swedish chemist who introduced the present system of chemical symbols.

beseech /bə'sitʃ, bi-/, *v.t.* **-sought** or **-seeched, -seeching. 1.** to beg urgently: *I beseech you, help me!* **2.** to beg for; solicit: *I beseech help.* [OE *sēcan* seek]

beset /bə'sɛt, bi-/, *v.t.*, **-set, -setting. 1.** to attack on all sides; assail; harass (*usu.* *in pass.*): *beset by enemies; beset by difficulties.* **2.** to surround. [OE, from BE- + *settan* SET] —**besetment,** *n.* —**besetting,** *adj.*

beside /bə'saɪd, bi-/, *prep.* **1.** by or at the side of; near: *Sit down beside me.* **2.** compared with: *Beside her, he is tall.* **3.** apart from; not connected with: *beside the point.* **4. beside oneself,** out of one's mind through strong feelings. ◊*adv.* **5.** in addition; besides. [OE *be sīdan* by side]

besides /bə'saɪdz, bi-/, *adv.* **1.** moreover: *Besides, you are too ill.* **2.** in addition. **3.** otherwise; else. ◊*prep.* **4.** in addition to. **5.** other than; except. [BESIDE + adv. *-s*]

besiege /bə'sidʒ, bi-/, *v.t.*, **-sieged, -sieging. 1.** to surround with armed forces. **2.** to crowd round. **3.** to attack, as with questions, etc. —**besieger,** *n.*

besom /'bizəm/, *n.* **1.** brush or twigs bound together as a broom. **2.** a broom of any kind. [OE *besema*]

besotted /bə'sɒtəd, bi-/, *adj.* **1.** filled with foolish love: *He was besotted with her.* **2.** made stupid, or drunk.

besought /bə'sɔt, bi-/, *v.* past tense and past participle of **beseech.**

bespeak /bə'spik, bi-/, *v.*, **-spoke** or (*old form*) **-spake, -spoken** or **-spoke, -speaking.** ◊*v.t.* **1.** to ask for in advance: *to bespeak the reader's patience.* **2.** to show, indicate: *This bespeaks a kindly heart.* [OE *besprecan* speak of]

Bessemer process /'bɛsəmə/, *n.* the removal of impurities in steel production by blasting air through molten iron. [named after Sir Henry **Bessemer** (1813-98), its English inventor]

best /bɛst/, *adj.* (*superlative of* **good**). **1.** of the highest quality, excellence, or standing. **2.** most advantageous, suitable, or desirable: *best way.* **3.** largest; most: *She's been lost for the best part of a day now.* **4.** favorite: *best friend.* ◊*adv.* **5.** (*superlative of* **well**) with most advantage or success. **6. had best,** would be wiser,

best

safer, etc., to. ◇*n.* **7.** the utmost thing, quality, state or part. **8.** one's finest clothing. **9. all the best,** (an expression of good will). **10. at best,** in the most favorable circumstances. **11. for the best, a.** having an unexpectedly good result. **b.** with good intentions or motives. **12. make the best of,** to manage as well as one can (in unfavorable or difficult circumstances). [OE *betst*]

bestial /ˈbestiəl/, *adj.* **1.** relating to a beast; savage. **2.** inhuman; irrational; brutal. [ME, from L] —**bestially,** *adv.* —**bestialise,** *v.t.*

bestiality /besti'æləti/, *n.* **1.** bestial character or conduct; beastliness. **2.** the sexual relations of a human with an animal; sodomy.

bestir /bəˈstɜː, bɪ-/, *v.t.* (*generally reflexive*), **-stirred, -stirring.** to stir to action; rouse. [ME *bestiren*, from OE *bestyrian* heap up]

best man, *n.* the chief attendant of the bridegroom at a wedding.

bestow /bəˈstoʊ, bɪ-/, *v.t.* **1.** to present as a gift; give; confer. **2.** to put; stow; deposit; store. —**bestowal, bestowment,** *n.*

bet /bet/, *n., v.,* **bet** or **betted, betting.** ◇*n.* **1.** an agreement that something, esp. money, will be given, in case one is wrong, to another who has a different opinion. **2.** that which is promised. **3.** someone or something on which to place one's hopes: *He's a bad bet.* ◇*v.t.* **4.** to risk (money, etc.) as part of a bet; pledge; wager; stake. ◇*v.i.* **5.** to make a bet. **6.** to make a habit of betting. **7. you bet,** *Colloq.* you may be sure; certainly. [orig. uncert.] —**better, bettor,** *n.*

beta /ˈbitə/, *n.* **1.** the second letter of the Greek alphabet (B, β). **2.** (in examinations, etc.) the second highest mark or grade.

betake /bəˈteɪk, bɪ-/, *v.t.* (*generally reflexive*), **-took, -taken, -taking.** to go: *She betook herself to market.*

beta particle, *n.* an electron or positron emitted by some radioactive substances.

beta ray, *n.* stream of beta particles.

betel nut /ˈbitl/, *n.* the fruit of a type of palm, chewed in New Guinea and in many parts of tropical Asia.

bête noire /bet ˈnwɑː/, *n.* someone or something one especially dislikes; bugbear. [F: black beast]

Bethesda /bəˈθezdə/, *n. Bible.* a pool in Jerusalem, believed to have healing powers. [See John 5:2-4]

bethink /bəˈθɪŋk, bɪ-/, *v.t.,* **-thought, -thinking.** *Archaic* (*generally reflexive*) **1.** to remember; recall. **2.** to think; consider. [OE BE- + *thencan* consider]

Bethlehem /ˈbeθləhəm, -lihɛm/, *n.* a town on the west bank of the river Jordan, near Jerusalem; birthplace of Jesus and of David. Pop. 15 000 (1965).

betide /bəˈtaɪd, bɪ-/, *v.,* **-tided, -tiding.** *Archaic.* ◇*v.t.* **1.** to happen to; befall; come to: *Woe betide the villain!* ◇*v.i.* **2.** to come to pass. [OE *tidan* betide]

Betjeman /ˈbetʃəmən/, *n.* **John,** 1906-84, English poet and writer; poet laureate 1972-84.

betoken /bəˈtoʊkən, bɪ-/, *v.t.* to give a sign of; indicate.

betook /bəˈtʊk, bɪ-/, *v.* past tense of **betake.**

betray /bəˈtreɪ, bɪ-/, *v.t.* **1.** to be disloyal to (one's country, friends, etc.). **2.** to be unfaithful in keeping or upholding: *to betray a trust.* **3.** to reveal or disclose on purpose: *to betray a secret.* **4.** to reveal unknowingly (something secret). ◇*v.* **5.** betray oneself, to reveal one's real character, plans, etc. [ME, from OF, from L *trādere* give over] —**betrayal,** *n.* —**betrayer,** *n.*

betroth /bəˈtroʊð, -ˈtroʊθ, bɪ-/, *v.t.* to promise to marry or give in marriage. [OE *trēowth* pledge] —**betrothal,** *n.* —**betrothed,** *n., adj.*

better /ˈbetə/, *adj.* (*comparative of* **good**). **1.** of higher quality or excellence; superior: *better position.* **2.** of more value, use, fitness, etc.: *a better time for action.* **3.** larger; greater: *the better part of a lifetime.* **4.** improved in health; recovered. ◇*adv.* (*comparative of* **well**). **5.** in a more excellent manner: *to behave better.* **6. had better,** would be wiser, safer, etc., to. **7. better off,** in better conditions. **8. think better of,** to reconsider and decide more wisely. ◇*v.t.* **9.** to make better; improve; increase the good qualities of. ◇*v.* **10. better oneself,** to improve one's social position, education, etc. ◇*n.* **11.** (*pl.*) those people with more wisdom, rank, etc. than oneself. [OE *betera*]

bettong /beˈtɒŋ/, *n.* See **rat-kangaroo.** [Aboriginal]

between /bəˈtwin, bɪ-/, *prep.* **1.** within the space, time, degree, etc., separating (two or more points, objects, etc.). **2.** connecting: *a link between parts.* **3.** involving; concerning; of: *war between nations; choice between things.* **4.** by joint action or possession of: *to own land between them.* **5. between you and me** or **between ourselves,** in secret. ◇*adv.* **6.** in the intervening space or time: *visits far between.* [OE *be* by + *-twēonan, -twēonum,* from *twā* two]

betwixt /bəˈtwɪkst, bɪ-/, *prep., adv.* **1.** *Archaic.* between. **2. betwixt and between,** neither one nor other; in a middle position. [OE *betweox*]

bevel /ˈbevəl/, *n., v.,* **-elled, -elling.** ◇*n.* **1.** the slope that one line or surface makes with another when not at right angles. **2.** a woodworking tool used to make such a slope. ◇*v.t., v.i.* **3.** to cut or slope at an angle. [orig. obscure] —**beveller,** *n.*

bevel gear, *n.* gearwheels with sloping edges, made so that they work at an angle to each other.

beverage /ˈbevrɪdʒ, ˈbevərɪdʒ/, *n.* a drink of any kind: *alcoholic beverages.* [ME, from L: drink]

bevy /ˈbevi/, *n., pl.* **bevies.** **1.** a flock of birds, esp. of quail. **2.** a group, esp. of girls or women. [ME *bevey*; orig. uncert.]

bewail /bə'weɪl, bi-/, *v.t., v.i.* to express deep sorrow (for); lament.

beware /bə'wɛə, bi-/, *v.i. (now only used as imperative or infinitive)* to be wary, cautious, or careful (fol. by *of* or a clause): *beware of the dog.*

bewilder /bə'wɪldə, bi-/, *v.t.* to confuse or puzzle completely; perplex. [BE- + *wilder* to cause to lose one's way] **—bewilderment**, *n.*

bewitch /bə'wɪtʃ, bi-/, *v.t.* to affect by or as by magic; enchant.

Beynon /'beɪnən/, *n.* **Richard**, born 1925, Australian playwright and actor; known esp. for *The Shifting Heart* (1956).

beyond /bə'jɒnd, bi-/, *prep.* **1.** farther on than; more distant than: *beyond the horizon; beyond the house.* **2.** later than: *They stayed beyond the time limit.* **3.** outside the limits or reach of; past: *beyond human understanding.* **4.** more than; in excess of; over and above: *They live beyond their means.* ◇*adv.* **5.** further on or away: *as far as the house and beyond.* ◇*n.* **6.** *(oft. caps)* life after death: *the Great Beyond.* [OE *be* by + *geondan* beyond]

b/f, *Comm. Abbrev.* brought forward.

Bhoodan /bu'dan/, *n.* (in India) a socio-agricultural reform movement, in which landowners gave land to the community, founded by Vinoba Bhave (1895–1982), in 1951.

Bhopal /boʊ'pal/, *n.* the capital of Madhya Pradesh, in the central part of India; site of a gas leak at Union Carbide Corp plant in 1984 which killed over 2000. Pop. 671 018 (1981).

BHP /bi eɪtʃ 'pi/, *Abbrev.* The Broken Hill Proprietary Company Limited.

Bhutto /'butoʊ/, *n.* **1. Zulfikar Ali** /ˌzulfɪkɑr 'ali/, 1928–79, president of Pakistan 1971–77; sentenced to death following seizure of power by General Zia. **2.** his daughter, **Benazir** /'bɛnəzɪə/, born 1953; prime minister of Pakistan 1988–90.

bi-, prefix meaning 'twice, doubly, two', as in *bilateral, binocular.* [L, combining form of *bis* twice, doubly]

Bi, *Chem. Symbol.* bismuth.

Biafra /bi'æfrə/, *n.* the eastern region of Nigeria; independent 1967–70; overthrown by Nigerian government forces.

biannual /baɪ'ænjuəl/, *adj.* taking place twice a year.

bias /'baɪəs/, *n., adv., v.,* **biased, biasing.** ◇*n.* **1.** a diagonal line of direction, esp. across woven fabric: *to cut cloth on the bias.* **2.** an opinion which prevents a fair consideration of a subject. ◇*adv.* **3.** slantingly; obliquely. ◇*v.t.* **4.** to influence, usu. unfairly; prejudice; warp. [F: slant, probably from L *biaxius* having two axes]

bias binding, *n.* a binding for cloth, cut on the bias (def. 1), used esp. in hems.

bib /bɪb/, *n.* **1.** an article of clothing worn under the chin by a child, esp. while eating, to protect its clothes. **2.** the upper part of an apron. [ME; orig. uncert., ? from L *bibere* drink]

bibl., *Abbrev.* **1.** biblical. **2.** bibliographical.

Bible /'baɪbəl/, *n.* **1.** (a copy of) the sacred writings of the Christian religion, consisting of the Old and New Testaments. **2.** *Judaism.* the Old Testament only. **3.** *(l.c.)* any book accepted as authoritative or as favorite reading: *His Bible was his book of orchids.* [ME, from ML, from Gk: book] **—biblical,** *adj.*

Bible Belt, *n.* an area, orig. of the southern US, noted for religious beliefs which claim the literal truth of the Bible in every detail.

biblio-, a word part meaning: **1.** book, as in *bibliography.* **2.** Bible. [Gk, combining form of *biblion* book]

bibliography /bɪbli'ɒgrəfi/, *n., pl.* **-phies. 1.** a list of source materials used or consulted in the preparation of a book, an essay, etc. **2.** a complete or selective list of literature on a particular subject or by a given author. **3.** an ordered description, history, classification, etc., of books and other written or printed works. **—bibliographic, bibliographical,** *adj.* **—bibliographer,** *n.*

bibulous /'bɪbjələs/, *adj.* having the habit of drinking too much alcohol. [L: freely drinking] **—bibulousness,** *n.*

bicameral /baɪ'kæmərəl/, *adj.* having two branches, chambers, or houses, as a government body.

bicarbonate /baɪ'kɑbənət, -neɪt/, *n.* a salt of carbonic acid, containing the HCO_3^- ion.

bicarbonate of soda, *n.* → **sodium bicarbonate.**

bicentenary /baɪsən'tinəri, -'tɛnəri/, *adj., n., pl.* **-naries.** ◇*adj.* **1.** of or relating to a 200th anniversary. ◇*n.* **2.** a 200th anniversary or its celebration. **—bicentennial,** *adj.*

biceps /'baɪsɛps, -sɛps/, *n.* a muscle having two points of origin, esp. the muscle on the front of the upper arm. [L: two-headed]

bicker /'bɪkə/, *v.i.* to take part in senseless argument; wrangle. [ME] **—bickerer,** *n.*

bicuspid /baɪ'kʌspɪd/, *adj.* **1.** having two points or cusps, as certain teeth. ◇*n.* **2.** *Anat.* one of eight such teeth in humans. [BI- + L *cuspis* point]

bicycle /'baɪsɪkəl/, *n.* a vehicle with two wheels, one in front of the other, steered by handlebars and driven by pedals. [F, from *bi-* BI- + Gk *kýklos* circle, wheel] **—bicyclist,** *n.*

bicyclic /baɪ'saɪklɪk, -'sɪklɪk/, *adj.* **1.** consisting of or having two circles, cycles, etc. **2.** *Bot.* in two whorls, as the stamens of flower.

bid /bɪd/, *v.,* **bade** /bæd/ (or **bid** (*for defs 3–5*), **bidden** or **bid, bidding,** *n.* ◇*v.t.* **1.** to command; order; direct: *to bid them depart.* **2.** to say as a greeting or a farewell: *to bid goodbye.* **3.** *Comm.* to offer (a price) at an auction or (terms) in competition to secure a contract. **4.** *Cards.* to enter a bid: *to bid two no-trumps.* ◇*v.i.* **5.** to make an offer to purchase at a price. ◇*n.* **6.** the act of someone who bids. **7.** an offer, as at auction. **8.** *Cards.* **a.** the points or tricks a player offers to make. **b.** the turn of a person to bid. **9.** an attempt to achieve a goal or purpose: *a bid for power*. [OE (*ge*)*bidden* beg, ask, pray] –**bidder**, *n*.

biddable /'bɪdəbəl/, *adj*. willing to do what is asked; obedient; docile.

bidding /'bɪdɪŋ/, *n*. **1.** a command; order. **2.** bids collectively in cards or auction.

biddy /'bɪdi/, *n*., *pl*. **-dies**. *Colloq*. a woman, esp. one who is old. [orig. uncert.]

bide /baɪd/, *v. in the phrase* **bide one's time**, to wait for a favorable chance. [OE *bīdan*]

bidet /'biːdeɪ/, *n*. a small low basin, with running water, for washing the genital area. [F]

biennale /biə'nɑːli/, *n*. a major exhibition, as of art, held every two years. [It]

biennial /baɪ'ɛniəl/, *adj*. **1.** happening every two years. **2.** *Bot*. completing the normal term of life in two years. ◇*n*. **3.** any event occurring once in two years. **4.** a biennial plant. [L *biennium* two-year period + *-AL*¹]

bier /bɪə/, *n*. a frame or stand on which a dead body, or a coffin containing it, is laid before burial. [OE *bēr*, *bær*]

bifid /'baɪfəd/, *adj*. having two parts or lobes separated by a cleft. [L] –**bifidity**, *n*.

bifocal /baɪ'foʊkəl/, *adj*. **1.** *Chiefly Optics*. having two foci. **2.** (of glass lenses) having two sections, one for close and the other for distant vision. ◇*n*. **3.** (*pl*.) glasses with bifocal lenses.

bifoliate /baɪ'foʊliət, -eɪt/, *adj*. having two leaves.

bifurcate /'baɪfəkeɪt, -kɜːt/, *v*., **-cated, -cating**; /'baɪfəkət, -kɜːt/, *adj*. ◇*v.t*. **2.** divided into two branches. [L *bi-* BI- + *furca* fork] –**bifurcation**, *n*.

big /bɪg/, *adj*., **bigger, biggest**, *adv*. ◇*adj*. **1.** large in size, noise, amount, etc. **2.** elder: *her big brother*. **3.** important in influence, standing, wealth, etc.: *big business*. ◇*adv*. **4.** *Colloq*. boastfully: *to talk big*. **5.** *Colloq*. on a grand scale; liberally: *to think big*. **6. big on**, knowledgeable and enthusiastic (eager) about: *big on wine*. [ME; orig. uncert.]

bigamy /'bɪgəmi/, *n*. the crime of marrying again while having a legal wife or husband still living. [ME, from OF] –**bigamist**, *n*. –**bigamous**, *adj*.

Big Ben /bɪg 'bɛn/, *n*. **1.** the bell in the clock tower of the Houses of Parliament in London. **2.** the clock. **3.** the tower. [named after Sir *Ben*jamin Hall, First Commissioner of Works at the time of building]

Big Brother, *n*. a ruler, esp. one who tries to control people's private lives and thoughts. [from a character in the novel '*1984*', by George ORWELL]

Big Brother Movement, *n*. a private organisation founded in 1925 to encourage migration of boys from England to Australia.

Big Dipper *n. Chiefly US Astron*. → **plough** (def. 3).

big end, *n. Motor Vehicles*. the larger end of a connecting rod in an engine, which bears on a crankshaft. [short for *big end bearing*]

Big Five *n*. the US, UK, France, Italy, and Japan, in World War I and at the Paris Peace Conference, 1919.

Big Four *n*. the US, UK, USSR, and France in the United Nations following World War II.

big game, *n*. **1.** large animals, esp. when hunted for sport. **2.** an important prize or goal.

Bigge /bɪg/, *n*. **John Thomas**, 1780–1843, English judge; King's Commissioner in NSW 1819–21.

bight /baɪt/, *n*. **1.** a loop or bent part of rope. **2. a.** a bend or curve in shore of sea or river. **b.** a body of water bounded by such a bend; bay. ◇*v.t*. **3.** to fasten with a bight of rope. [OE *byht* a bend]

bigot /'bɪgət/, *n*. a person unreasonably convinced of the rightness of a particular opinion, practice etc. [F; orig. uncert.] **bigoted**, *adj*. –**bigotry**, *n*.

big top, *n*. the main tent in a circus.

bigwig /'bɪgwɪg/, *n*. *Colloq*. a very important person.

bike /baɪk/, *n*. *Colloq*. a bicycle, tricycle, or motorcycle.

bikini /bə'kiːni/, *n*. a very brief two-piece swimming costume. [from *Bikini Atoll* in the Marshall Islands in the N Pacific, prominent as a site for US nuclear bomb tests, 1946–58]

bilabial /baɪ'leɪbiəl/, *Linguistics*. ◇*adj*. **1.** pronounced with two lips brought close together or touching. In the English bilabial consonants *p*, *b*, and *m*, the lips touch; in bilabial *w*, they do not. ◇*n*. **2.** a bilabial speech sound.

bilateral /baɪ'lætrəl/, *adj*. **1.** relating to, involving, or affecting two sides or parties. **2.** *Law. etc.* (of a contract) binding the parties to returning obligations. **3.** arranged on opposite sides of an axis; two-sided. –**bilateralism**, **bilateralness**, *n*.

bilby /'bɪlbi/, *n*. See **bandicoot**. [Aboriginal]

bile /baɪl/, *n*. **1.** a bitter yellow or greenish liquid secreted by the liver and helping in digestion. **2.** ill nature; peevishness. [F, from L]

bilge /bɪldʒ/, *n*. *Naut*. **a.** either of the rounded parts at either side of a ship's hull. **b.** the lowest part of a ship's hold. **c.** Also, **bilge water**, bad water that collects in a ship's bilge. **2.** *Colloq*. nonsense; rubbish. [orig. unknown]

bilingual /baɪ'lɪŋgwəl/, *adj*. **1.** able to speak two languages. **2.** of or contained in two languages. ◇*n*. **3.** a bilingual person. [L: speaking two languages] –**bilingualism**, *n*.

bilious /'bɪljəs/, *adj*. **1.** *Med*. relating to bile or to an excess secretion of bile. **2.** *Med*. suffering from, caused by, or attended by trouble with bile or the liver. **3.** *Med*. suffering from, or caused by, an upset stomach. **4.** bad-tempered. [L: full of bile] –**biliousness**, *n*.

-bility, a suffix forming nouns from adjectives ending in *-ble*, as in *nobility*. [ME, from F, from L *bilitas*]

bilk /bɪlk/, *v.t.* **1.** to avoid payment of (a debt). **2.** to cheat; defraud. **3.** to escape from; elude. [orig. unknown] **—bilker,** *n.*

bill[1] /bɪl/, *n.* **1.** an account of money owed for goods or services supplied: *bill of charges*. **2.** *Govt.* a form or draft of a proposed Act of Parliament. **3.** a written or printed public notice or advertisement. **4. —bill of exchange. 5.** a printed theatre program or similar. ◇*v.t.* **6.** to announce by bill or public notice: *A new actor was billed for this week*. **7.** to include as part of a program. **8.** to send (someone) a bill (def. 1). [ME, from Anglo-F *billa*, var. of ML *bulla* seal]

bill[2] /bɪl/, *n.* **1.** a bird's beak. **2. bill and coo,** (of doves, etc.) to join beaks and make soft murmuring sounds. [OE *bile* beak]

billabong /ˈbɪləbɒŋ/, *n.* a waterhole, orig. part of a river, formed by the drying up of the channel connecting it to the river. [Aboriginal]

billet[1] /ˈbɪlət/, *n.*, *v.*, **-eted, -eting.** ◇*n.* **1. a.** a lodging for a soldier, esp. in a private house. **b.** private, usu. unpaid, short-term lodgings for members of a group or team. **2.** *Mil.* an official order (to a householder) to provide such lodging. **3.** a job; appointment; position. ◇*v.t.* **4.** *Mil.* to direct (a soldier) by note, or spoken order, where to lodge. **5.** to provide lodging for; quarter. [ME, from OF]

billet[2] /ˈbɪlət/, *n.* **1.** a small thick stick of wood, esp. one cut for fuel. **2.** *Metall.* a bar or slab of iron or steel, esp. when obtained from an ingot by forging. **3.** *Archit.* one of series of short rods forming part of a moulding. [ME *billette*, from OF *billete*, diminutive of *bille* log]

billfish /ˈbɪlfɪʃ/, *n. pl.* **-fishes,** (*esp. collectively*) **-fish.** any of various large game fish, e.g. marlin or sailfish.

billiards /ˈbɪljədz/, *n.* a game played by two or more people on a rectangular table, with hard balls hit by means of cues. [F *bille* log] **—billiardist,** *n.*

billion /ˈbɪljən/, *n.* **1. a.** a thousand times a million, or 10^9. **b.** (*becoming rare*) a million times a million, or 10^{12}. **2.** *Colloq.* a large amount. ◇*adj.* **3.** amounting to a billion in number. [F, from bi- BI- + (*mi*)*llion*, i.e. the second power of one million] **—billionth,** *adj.*, *n.*

Billiton /ˈbɪlətən, bɪˈlɪtən/, *n.* an island in Indonesia, south-west of Borneo in the Java Sea; 4833 km[2]. Also, **Belitong.**

bill of exchange, *n.* a written permission or order to pay a certain sum of money to a particular person.

bill of fare, *n.* a list of foods served; menu.

bill of health, *n.* **1.** a certificate as to the health of ship's company before that ship leaves port. **2. a clean bill of health,** *Colloq.* proof of the good health of (a person, animal, etc.) or the good condition of (a piece of machinery, equipment, etc.).

bill of rights, *n.* a formal statement of the basic rights of the people of a nation.

bill of sale, *n.* an official statement giving title in personal property from one person to another, as security against a loan or debt (**conditional bill of sale**), or permanently (**absolute bill of sale**).

billow /ˈbɪloʊ/, *n.* **1.** a great wave or rush of sea. **2.** any large, swelling mass: *billows of smoke*. ◇*v.i.* **3.** to rise or roll in or like billows; surge. [Scand] **—billowy,** *adj.*

billy /ˈbɪli/, *n.*, *pl.* **billies. 1.** a cylindrical container for liquids, usu. with a close-fitting lid. **2.** any container, for boiling water, making tea, etc. **3. boil the billy,** to make tea. [probably from Scot d. *bally* a milk-pail]

billygoat /ˈbɪligoʊt/, *n.* a male goat.

billyo /ˈbɪlioʊ/, *n. Colloq.* in the phrases **1. like billyo.** with great speed: *He rode like billyo*. **2. off to billyo,** off course; astray; in error. Also, **billyoh.**

Bimberi /bɪmˈbɛri/, *n.* Mount, the highest peak in the ACT in the **Bimberi Range** southwest of Canberra. 1910 m. Also, **Bimberi Peak.**

bin /bɪn/, *n.*, *v.*, **binned, binning.** ◇*n.* **1.** a box or enclosed space used for storing grain, wool when shorn, coal, refuse, etc. **2.** a bin used by a winemaker for storing wine and bottles. **3.** (of wine) a particular bottling, usu. of above average quality. ◇*v.t.* **4.** to store in a bin. [OE *binn(e)* crib]

binary /ˈbaɪnəri/, *adj.* **1.** consisting of, or involving two. **2.** using, involving, or expressed in binary number system. **3.** *Maths.* having two variables. [L: consisting of two things]

binary digit, *n.* a single digit in a binary number.

binary fission, *n.* **1.** (of a cell) reproduction by splitting into two equal parts. **2.** *Phys.* (of an atom) the splitting of nucleus into two roughly equal parts. See **fission.**

binary number, *n.* a number stated in the binary number system.

binary number system, *n.* a number system which uses only the digits 0 and 1, based on rules $1 + 0 = 1$, $1 + 1 = 10$. Also, **binary system, binary notation.**

binary star, *n.* a system of two stars which revolve round a common centre of gravity.

bind /baɪnd/, *v.*, **bound, binding,** *n.* ◇*v.t.* **1.** to tie up or fasten with a band or bond, as hair, a person, sheaves of grain, etc. **2.** to cover or bandage (oft. fol. by *up*): *to bind up her arm*. **3.** to cause to harden or cohere. **4.** to sew the edges of (fabric) with stitching or binding. **5.** to unite by legal or moral tie. **6.** (*usu. pass.*) to place under an obligation. See **bound**[1] (def. 3). **7.** *Law.* to put under a legal obligation (fol. by *over*): *to bind a man over to keep the peace*. **8.** *Med.* to restrain (the bowels) from their natural working; constipate. **9.** to fasten or secure (a book) within a cover. ◇*n.* **10.** something that binds. **11.** *Colloq.* annoyance; nuisance; bore. [OE *bindan*]

binder /ˈbaɪndə/, n. 1. someone or something that binds. 2. a removable cover for loose papers. 3. an informal contract in force while a more formal one is being written. 4. *Bldg Trades.* a material, e.g. cement, used to join bricks etc.

bindi-eye /ˈbɪndi-aɪ/, n. a weed with a fruit which breaks into small spiky pieces.

binding /ˈbaɪndɪŋ/, n. 1. anything that binds, as the covering around pages of a book, the band along edge of cloth, etc. ◇*adj.* 2. having the power to bind (someone to do something): *a binding agreement.*

binding energy, n. the energy needed to split the nucleus of an atom into the nucleons of which it is made.

bindweed /ˈbaɪndwid/, n. → **convolvulus**.

bine /baɪn/, n. 1. a climbing plant stem, as of the hop. 2. → **bindweed**. [var. of BIND]

Binet test /ˈbiːneɪ test/, n. a test for finding out the comparative development of the intelligence of children, etc. [named after Alfred Binet, 1857-1911, French psychologist]

binge /bɪndʒ/, n. *Colloq.* a period of too much eating, drinking or spending; spree. [Lincolnshire d. *binge* (v.) to soak]

binghi /ˈbɪŋi/, n. *Colloq.* an Aboriginal. [Aboriginal: brother]

binocular /bəˈnɒkjələ/, adj. 1. using two eyes: *binocular sight.* ◇*n.* 2. (*pl.*) double magnifying glasses used by both eyes at once.

binomial /baɪˈnoʊmiəl/, n. *Maths.* an expression which is a sum or difference of two terms, as $3x + 2y$ or $x^2 - 4x$. [LL: having two names]

binomial distribution, n. *Stats.* a distribution giving the probability of obtaining a particular number of successes in a set of tests each of which can end in either a success or failure.

binomial theorem, n. a formula for expanding a binomial in sum form.

bio-, a word part meaning 'life', 'living things', as in *biology*. [Gk, combining form of *bíos* life]

biochemistry /baɪoʊˈkɛməstri/, n. that branch of chemistry concerned with living matter. *Abbrev.:* biochem. — **biochemical**, *adj.* — **biochemist**, n.

biodegradable /ˌbaɪoʊdəˈɡreɪdəbəl/, adj. able to be broken down by the action of living organisms, esp. of bacteria: *a biodegradable detergent.*

biogenesis /ˌbaɪoʊˈdʒɛnəsəs/, n. 1. the theory that living organisms come from other living organisms only. Also, **biogeny** /baɪˈɒdʒəni/. 2. the development of living organisms from earlier living organisms. — **biogenetic**, *adj.*

biogeographical realm /baɪoʊdʒiə ˌɡræfɪkəl ˈrɛlm/, n. a region of the world marked by distinctive flora and fauna. The realms are: Holarctic, Ethiopian, Madagascan, Oriental, Neotropical, Australian, New Zealand, Polynesian.

biogeography /baɪoʊdʒiˈɒɡrəfi/, n. the study of the geographical distribution of living things. — **biogeographical**, *adj.*

biography /baɪˈɒɡrəfi/, n., *pl.* -phies. 1. an account or a study of a person's life, written by another. 2. the branch of literature consisting of such writings. [Gk] — **biographical**, *adj.* — **biographer**, n.

biological /baɪəˈlɒdʒɪkəl/, adj. 1. relating to biology. 2. of or relating to the products and operations of applied biology.

biological clock, n. a system built into living organisms, which controls the timing of the cycle of biological processes (biorhythms) and which is not dependent on outside time.

biological warfare, n. warfare which uses living organisms, such as bacteria, or poisons produced from them to harm man, domestic animals, or food crops. Also, **germ warfare**.

biology /baɪˈɒlədʒi/, n. the science of living matter in all its forms, esp. origin, growth, reproduction, structures, etc. — **biologist**, n.

biolysis /baɪˈɒləsəs/, n. the destruction of a living thing, esp. the chemical breaking down of organic matter; death. — **biolytic**, *adj.*

biome /ˈbaɪoʊm/, n. an ecological community of plants and animals spread over large natural areas, as a coral reef, tropical rain forest, etc.

bionic /baɪˈɒnɪk/, adj. 1. of or relating to bionics. 2. *Colloq.* having body parts replaced by electronic equipment so as to give superhuman strength.

bionics /baɪˈɒnɪks/, n. the study of biological systems to help in the development of such equipment as electronic limbs. [BI(O)- + (ELECTR)ONICS]

biophysics /baɪoʊˈfɪzɪks/, n. that branch of biology concerned with the study of biological structures and actions using the principles of physics. — **biophysical**, *adj.*

biopsy /ˈbaɪɒpsi/, n. *Med.* the removal of a piece of tissue from a living body and the examination of it for signs of disease, etc.

biorhythm /ˈbaɪoʊrɪðəm/, n. 1. the theory that human energy is based on three separate, in-built cycles, those of the body, the emotions, and the mind. 2. the pattern of one such cycle.

biosphere /ˈbaɪəsfɪə/, n. that part of the earth where living organisms are to be found.

biot /ˈbaɪɒt/, n. an electromagnetic unit of current equal to 10 amperes.

biotechnology /ˌbaɪoʊtɛkˈnɒlədʒi/, n. → **ergonomics**.

biotin /ˈbaɪətən/, n. a crystalline acid, one of the vitamin B complex factors, found in liver, eggs, yeast, and other foods; vitamin H.

biotite /ˈbaɪətaɪt/, n. a very common mineral of the mica group, an important ingredient of igneous rocks. [named after JB *Biot*, French physicist]

biotype /ˈbaɪətaɪp/, n. a group of organisms with the same hereditary characteristics; genotype. — **biotypic**, *adj.*

bipartisan /baɪˈpætɪzæn, -zən/, *adj.* of or supported by two (otherwise opposing) parties, esp. political parties.

bipartite /baɪˈpɑtaɪt/, *adj.* **1.** being in two parts. **2.** concerning two parties; bilateral. [L: divided into two parts]

biped /ˈbaɪpɛd/, *n., adj.* (an animal) with two feet. [L: two-footed] —**bipedal**, *adj.*

biplane /ˈbaɪpleɪn/, *n.* an aircraft with two pairs of wings, one above the other.

bipolar /baɪˈpoʊlə/, *adj.* having or relating to two poles. —**bipolarity**, *n.*

birch /bɜtʃ/, *n.* **1.** a type of tree or shrub of the Northern Hemisphere with smooth outer bark and close-grained wood. **2.** the timber from it. **3.** a birch rod, or a bunch of birch cuttings, used as a whip. [OE *bierce*]

bird /bɜd/, *n.* **1.** one of a class of warm-blooded, egg-laying, vertebrates with two legs, a body covered with feathers, and wings with which most types fly. **2.** *Colloq.* a person, esp. one with some peculiarity: *He's a funny old bird.* **3.** *Colloq.* a girl, esp. a girlfriend. **4. bird in the hand**, that which is sure though perhaps not entirely satisfactory. **5. birds of a feather**, *Colloq.* people of similar character. **6. (strictly) for the birds**, not worth doing. [OE *brid(d)* young bird, chick]

birdie /ˈbɜdi/, *n.* *Golf.* a score of one stroke under par on a hole.

birdlime /ˈbɜdlaɪm/, *n.* sticky material spread on branches to catch small birds.

bird of paradise, *n.* **1.** a type of song bird found in Australia and the island of New Guinea, noted for the fine, brightly colored feathers of the male. **2.** a tropical plant with purple stems opening out into orange flowers similar in shape to birds' heads.

bird of passage, *n.* **1.** a bird that migrates seasonally. **2.** a person who keeps travelling from one place to another.

bird of prey, *n.* any flesh-eating bird such as the eagle, hawk, vulture, owl, etc., usu. with a strong beak and claws for catching, killing or eating animals or other birds.

bird's-eye /ˈbɜdz-aɪ/, *adj.* **1.** seen from above: *a bird's-eye view of a city.* **2.** giving an account of the main points (of a subject): *a bird's-eye view of history.* **3.** having markings like birds' eyes.

bird's-foot delta, *n.* a delta formed by the outgrowth of fingers or pairs of natural banks at the mouth of the river making a bird's-foot shape, e.g. the Mississippi delta.

bird's-nest fern, *n.* a type of fern of Australia, India and Polynesia, having large leaves thought to be like a bird's nest.

Birdsville /ˈbɜdzvɪl, -vəl/, *n.* a cattle-droving and tourist centre in south-western Qld. Pop. 52 (1961).

Birdsville Track, *n.* a historic stockroute from Birdsville in south-western Qld to Marree in eastern central SA. 500 km.

Birdwood /ˈbɜdwʊd/, *n.* **William Riddell** (*Baron of Anzac and Totnes*), 1865–1951, British soldier; officer commanding the Australian and New Zealand Army Corps during World War I.

birefringence /baɪrəˈfrɪndʒəns/, *n.* the double bending of light by mineral crystals, causing, in some cases (esp. calcite), two images of any object seen through the mineral.

biretta /bəˈrɛtə/, *n.* a stiff square cap with four pieces projecting at the top, worn by some Roman Catholic priests.

Birmingham /ˈbɜmɪŋəm/, *n.* a city in central England, in West Midlands; industrial centre. Pop. 1 008 000 (1985 est.).

biro /ˈbaɪroʊ/, *n.* → **ballpoint pen**. [Trademark]

birth /bɜθ/, *n.* **1.** the act of being born: *the day of his birth.* **2.** the act of bringing forth a baby: *an easy birth.* **3.** origin; lineage; descent: *of Italian birth.* **4.** a natural ability supposedly inherited: *a musician by birth.* **5.** any beginning or origin: *the birth of a nation.* **6. give birth to, a.** to bring forth (a baby). **b.** to be the origin of. [ME, from Scand]

birth control, *n.* the control of the number of births a woman has by methods of contraception.

birthday /ˈbɜθdeɪ/, *n.* (the anniversary of) the day of a person's birth or a thing's beginning.

birthrate /ˈbɜθreɪt/, *n.* a number of births for every 100 or 1000 people in a given area during a given time.

birthright /ˈbɜθraɪt/, *n.* any right or property to which a person is entitled by birth.

bis /bɪs/, *adv.* twice: used in music to mean that a part is to be repeated. [L. See BI-]

Biscay /ˈbɪskeɪ/, *n.* **Bay of**, a large bay of the Atlantic between western France and northern Spain. 223 000 km².

biscuit /ˈbɪskət/, *n.* **1.** a stiff mixture of flour, liquid, fat, etc., sweetened or unsweetened, shaped into small thin pieces and baked until crisp. **2.** a pale brown color. **3.** pottery after the first baking and before glazing. ◇*adj.* **4.** pale brown. [ME, from L *bis* twice + *coquere* cook]

bisect /baɪˈsɛkt/, *v.t.* **1.** to cut or divide into two parts. **2.** *Geom.* to cut or divide into two equal parts. —**bisection**, *n.*

bisector /baɪˈsɛktə/, *n.* *Geom.* a line or plane bisecting an angle or section of a line.

bisexual /baɪˈsɛkʃuəl/, *n.* **1.** *Biol.* a plant, animal or human with both male and female reproductive organs; hermaphrodite. **2.** a person sexually attracted to both sexes.

bishop /ˈbɪʃəp/, *n.* **1.** a member of the highest order in the ministry of some Christian churches, having charge of a diocese. **2.** *Chess.* a piece which moves only diagonally. [OE, from VL, from Gk: overseer]

bishopric /ˈbɪʃəprɪk/, *n.* the diocese or office of a bishop. [OE *bisceop* bishop + *rīce* dominion]

Bismarck /ˈbɪzmɑk/, *n.* **Otto von** /ˈɒtoʊ fɒn/ (*Prince Otto Eduard Leopold von Bismarck*

Schönhausen, 'The Iron Chancellor'), 1815-98, German politician; first chancellor of the modern German Empire, 1871-90.

Bismarck Archipelago, *n.* a group of islands in the south-western Pacific, north-east of PNG, including the Admiralty Islands, New Hanover, New Ireland and adjacent islands.

bismuth /ˈbɪzməθ/, *n.* a brittle, metallic element, having compounds used in medicine. Symbol: Bi; at. no.: 83; at. wt: 208.98. [G *Wismut;* orig. uncert.]

bison /ˈbaɪsən/, *n., pl.* **-son.** *Zool.* a large North American buffalo with high, long-haired shoulders. [L, from Gmc]

bisque /bɪsk, bisk/, *n.* a thick, creamy soup, oft. made of shellfish or game. [F]

bistro /ˈbɪstrou/, *n.* **1.** a wine bar. **2.** a small restaurant.

bisulfate /baɪˈsʌlfeɪt/, *n.* a salt of sulfuric acid, containing the radical -HSO₄. See **dibasic acid.**

bisulfite /baɪˈsʌlfaɪt/, *n.* a salt of sulfurous acid, containing the radical -HSO₃. See **dibasic acid.**

bit[1] /bɪt/, *n.* **1.** a metal bar placed in a horse's mouth and attached to the reins, used to control a horse. **2.** anything that controls or holds back. **3.** *Mach.* a cutting or hole-making part of various tools. See **brace and bit. 4. take the bit between one's teeth, a.** to throw off control. **b.** to throw all one's energies into something. [OE *bite* action of biting]

bit[2] /bɪt/, *n.* **1.** a small piece or quantity of anything: *a bit of string; a bit of sense.* **2.** a short time: *Wait a bit.* **3.** *Archaic.* a small coin: *threepenny bit.* **4.** a share or part of a duty, job, etc.: *Do your bit.* **5. bit by bit,** slowly; gradually; in stages. [OE *bita* bit, morsel]

bit[3] /bɪt/, *n.* a single, basic unit of information, used in connection with computers, etc. [short for B(INARY DIG)IT]

bitch /bɪtʃ/, *n.* **1.** a female dog, fox, wolf, etc. **2.** *Colloq.* *(offensive)* a woman, esp. an unpleasant or bad-tempered one. ◇*v.i.* **3.** *Colloq.* to complain. [OE *bicce*] **– bitchy,** *adj.* **– bitchiness,** *n.*

bite /baɪt/, *v.,* **bit, bitten** or **bit, biting,** *n.* ◇*v.t.* **1.** to cut, seize, or wound with the teeth. **2.** to cut into: *The knife bit his flesh.* **3.** to hurt or sting: *Mosquitoes are biting tonight.* **4.** (of an acid) to eat into or corrode. **5.** *Colloq.* to trouble; worry: *What's biting you?* **6.** *Colloq.* to borrow from (someone) (oft. fol. by *for*). **7.** to take hold of (a person's interest, etc.): *The fitness craze has bitten her; He is bitten by love.* ◇*v.i.* **8.** to press the teeth (*into, on,* etc.). **9.** *Angling.* (of fish) to take the bait. **10.** to be deceived by a trick, etc. ◇*v.* **11. bite back,** to hold back: *She bit back her angry words.* **12. bite the dust.** *Colloq.* **a.** to fall dead. **b.** to fail. ◇*n.* **13.** the act of biting. **14.** a wound made by biting. **15.** *Dentistry.* the angle at which the upper and lower teeth meet. **16.** a sharp effect, feeling or taste. **17.** the quantity bitten off. **18.** a quantity of food. **19.** *Mach.* a tight hold or grip, as of a tool. [OE *bītan*]

biting /ˈbaɪtɪŋ/, *adj.* **1.** keen; piercing: *biting cold.* **2.** cutting; sarcastic: *a biting remark.*

bitser /ˈbɪtsə/, *n. Colloq.* a dog, etc., of mixed breed; mongrel. Also, **bitzer.**

bitten /ˈbɪtn/, *v.* **1.** past participle of **bite.** ◇*adj.* **2.** *Colloq.* tricked; cheated.

bitter /ˈbɪtə/, *adj.* **1.** having a sharp, disagreeable taste. **2.** hard to accept or bear: *a bitter lesson; bitter sorrow.* **3.** bitingly cold: *a bitter wind.* **4.** filled with sour feeling; resentful: *He is bitter towards his family; bitter words.* **5.** sharp; harsh: *bitter cold; a bitter landscape.* ◇*n.* **6.** something bitter; bitter things in general. **7.** *Chiefly Brit.* a bitter type of beer. [OE *biter;* akin to BITE] **– bitterness,** *n.*

bittern /ˈbɪtən/, *n.* a small or medium-sized bird of the heron family, such as the **brown bittern** of southern Australia, New Caledonia and NZ. [ME, from OF]

bitters /ˈbɪtəz/, *n.pl.* a drink, usu. alcoholic, containing bitter herbs or roots.

bittersweet /ˈbɪtəˈswit/, *adj.* **1.** both bitter and sweet to the taste. **2.** both pleasant and painful.

bitumen /ˈbɪtʃəmən/, *n.* **1.** a substance, such as asphalt or tar, used in road-making, painting, etc. **2.** a tarred or sealed road or other surface. [L] **– bituminous,** *adj.*

biuret /ˈbaɪjurɛt/, *n.* an alkaline solution of a protein, urea, etc., which gives a violet color on the addition of a copper sulfate (the biuret test for proteins, etc.).

bivalent /baɪˈveɪlənt, ˈbɪvələnt/, *adj.* **1.** *Chem.* **a.** having a valency of 2. **b.** having 2 valencies, as mercury, which has valencies 1 and 2. **2.** *Biol.* relating to pairs or sets of similar or identical chromosomes. ◇*n.* **3.** *Biol.* a bivalent pair or set of chromosomes. **– bivalency,** *n.*

bivalve /ˈbaɪvælv/, *adj., n. Zool.* (relating to) a shell-fish with two shells jointed together, such as the oyster.

bivouac /ˈbɪvuæk/, *n., v.,* **-acked, -acking.** ◇*n.* **1.** a camp, esp. a military one, set up for a short time out in the open. ◇*v.i.* **2.** to camp out. [F, probably from d. G]

bizarre /bəˈzɑ/, *adj.* very strange in appearance, style, or general character. [F: odd, from Sp: brave, ? from Basque *bizar* beard]

Bjelke-Petersen /ˌbjɛlkɪˈpitəsən/, *n.* **Sir Joh(annes)** /dʒouˈhænəs/, born 1911 in NZ, Australian National Party politician; premier of Qld 1968-87.

bk, *Abbrev.* **1.** bank. **2.** book.

blab /blæb/, *v.,* **blabbed, blabbing,** *n.* ◇*v.t.* **1.** to tell (a secret) thoughtlessly. ◇*v.i.* **2.** to talk or chatter thoughtlessly. **3.** to tell a secret. ◇*n.* **4.** foolish talk. **5.** Also, **blabbermouth.** a person who blabs. Also, **blabber.** [orig. uncert.]

black /blæk/, *adj.* **1.** without brightness or color, owing to the taking in of all, or nearly all, the light rays from a source; the opposite of white. **2.** *Anthrop.* relating or belonging to a people with dark skin, as the Australian

Aborigines, Negroes, etc. **3.** dirty. **4.** completely dark: *a black night*. **5.** sad; dismal: *a black outlook*. **6.** angry; forbidding: *a black look*. **7.** evil; wicked: *a black deed*. **8.** meaning disapproval or dishonor: *a black mark*. **9.** (of coffee or tea) without milk or cream. **10. be in someone's black books,** to be out of favor with someone. ◇*n*. **11.** a black color. **12.** (*sometimes cap.*) a member of a dark-skinned people, as a Negro, an Australian Aborigine, etc. **13.** anything black, as soot, shoe polish, a dark-colored chessman, etc. **14.** black clothing: *to be in black*. **15. in the black,** not owing money; in credit. ◇*v.t.* **16.** to make black; put black on: *He blacked his shoes*. **17.** (of a trade union) to bring normal working in (a factory, industry, etc.) to a stop. ◇*v.* **18. black out, a.** (during war) to put out or cover the lights of (a city, etc.) as a defence against attack by enemy aircraft. **b.** to hide (news, etc.) from the public. **c.** to lose consciousness. [OE *blæc*]

black-and-blue /ˌblæk-ən-ˈbluː/, *adj.* discolored, as by bruising. Also (*esp. after a verb*), **black and blue.**

Black and Tan, *n.* a member of an armed force of about 6000 men sent by the British government to Ireland in June 1920, to suppress revolutionary activity; so called from the color of their uniforms.

black and white, *n.* **1.** a drawing or picture done without color. **2. in black and white, a.** in print or writing. **b.** in clear opposites: *He sees things in black and white,.* **c.** in simple and clear terms: *Tell her in black and white,.*

black-and-white /ˌblæk-ən-ˈwaɪt/, *adj.* **1.** of or relating to a film, television program, or photograph which is not in color. **2.** of or relating to a television set which does not receive programs in color. **3.** with clear oppositions and choices.

blackball /ˈblækbɔːl/, *v.t.* **1.** to keep (someone) out of a group, club etc. **2.** to vote against (someone). ◇*n.* **3.** a negative vote.

black ban, *n.* a refusal by a group, as of producers, trade unions, buyers, etc., to supply or buy goods or services.

black belt, *n. Judo.* (a person entitled to wear) a belt given as sign of a particular rank.

blackberry /ˈblækbəri, -bri/, *n., pl.* **-ries. 1.** a prickly plant which grows in tangled bushes; bramble. **2.** its black or purple edible fruit.

blackbird /ˈblækbɜːd/, *n.* a European songbird of the thrush family, now introduced into Australia.

blackbirding /ˈblækbɜːdɪŋ/, *n.* (formerly) the kidnapping of South Pacific islanders (Kanakas) to provide slave labor in Australia.

blackboard /ˈblækbɔːd/, *n.* a smooth dark board, used for writing or drawing on with chalk.

black boy, *n.* a small Australian grasstree with a tall, thin, flowering head, thought to look like a grass-skirted native figure with a spear; xanthorrhoea.

Blackburn /ˈblækbɜːn/, *n.* **1. Sir Charles Bickerton,** 1874–1972, Australian physician, born in England. **2. James,** 1803–54, Australian architect and engineer, born in England; transported to Tasmania 1833, granted free pardon 1841.

blackbutt /ˈblækbʌt/, *n.* a type of Australian gum tree with dark bark at the base of the trunk.

black coal, *n.* ordinary coal containing more than 80 per cent of carbon, such as bituminous coal and anthracite.

black comedy, *n.* comedy dealing with a sad, bitter or horrifying subject.

blackcurrant /blækˈkʌrənt/, *n.* (a shrub bearing) a small, edible black fruit.

blacken /ˈblækən/, *v.,* **-ened, -ening.** ◇*v.t.* **1.** to make black; darken. **2.** to speak evil of (someone's character); defame. ◇*v.i.* **3.** to grow or become black.

Blacket /ˈblækət/, *n.* **Edmund Thomas,** 1817–83, Australian architect, born in England; noted for his Sydney churches and buildings at the University of Sydney, esp. the Great Hall.

black eye, *n.* bruising round the eye, resulting from a blow, etc.

black-eyed Susan, *n.* one of many different types of plants, whose brightly-colored flowers have dark centres.

blackfellow /ˈblækfɛloʊ, -fɛlə/, *n.* (*esp. in Aboriginal pidgin*) an Aborigine. Also, **blackfella, blackfeller.**

Black Forest /blæk ˈfɒrəst/, *n.* a forest-covered mountainous region in south-western Germany. Highest peak, Feldberg, about 1433 m. German, **Schwarzwald.**

black gold, *n.* **1.** coal. **2.** oil.

blackguard /ˈblækgɑːd/, *n.* **1.** a dishonorable person; scoundrel. ◇*v.t.* **2.** to use insulting language about or to (someone). [BLACK + GUARD]

blackhead /ˈblækhɛd/, *n.* **1.** a small, black-tipped pimple usu. on the face. **2.** *Vet Sci.* an infectious disease of turkeys, chickens, and many wild birds.

black hole, *n.* a region thought to arise from the collapse of a star under its own gravity and from which no radiation or matter can escape.

Black Hole of Calcutta, *n.* a dungeon in which the Nawab of Bengal in 1756 confined 146 English prisoners, of whom only 23 survived.

blackjack /ˈblækdʒæk/, *n.* **1.** *Hist.* a large cup or jug for beer, etc., orig. made of leather covered with tar. **2.** the black flag of a pirate ship. **3.** *Mineral.* a dark, iron-rich variety of sphalerite; blende. **4.** *Colloq.* treacle or other dark sweet substance. **5.** *Cards.* → pontoon².

blackleg /ˈblæklɛg/, *n., v.,* **-legged, -legging.** ◇*n.* **1.** → scab (def. 3). **2.** a cheat, esp. in racing or gambling. **3.** *Vet. Sci.* an infectious, usu. fatal disease of cattle and sheep with painful swellings in the legs. ◇*v.i.* **4.** to scab (def. 6).

black list, *n.* a list of people, etc., considered fit for punishment, disapproval, etc.

black magic, *n.* magic used for evil purposes.

blackmail /'blækmeɪl/, *n.* **1.** *Law.* **a.** an act of demanding payment, as by threats of making known damaging information. **b.** such a payment. ◇*v.t.* **2.** to demand such a payment from (someone). [BLACK + *mail* coin, rent (ME, from OF)] —**blackmailer**, *n.*

Blackman /'blækmən/, *n.* **Charles Raymond**, born 1928, Australian artist; noted for his figure paintings of children.

black market, *n.* an illegal market which does not keep to price controls, rationing, etc. —**black marketeer**, *n.*

black mass, *n.* an irreverent imitation of the Mass, performed by devil-worshippers.

blackout /'blækaʊt/, *n.* **1.** the putting out or covering of all lights that might be seen by enemy aircraft, etc., during war. **2.** an electrical power failure, resulting in loss of the lights, etc. **3.** *Theat.* the putting out of all stage lights for a change of scene, etc. **4.** the loss of consciousness, memory or sight for a short time.

Black Poll /blæk 'poʊl/, *n.* → **Aberdeen Angus**.

black power, *n.* **1.** a movement, originating in the US, for the gaining of equality by blacks through violence or politics. **2.** a similar movement elsewhere.

black prince, *n. Colloq.* **1.** a large Australian cicada colored black with some green markings on its back. **2. the**, 1330–76, Edward, Prince of Wales (the son of Edward III).

black pudding, *n.* a dark sausage made of blood, suet, etc.

Black Sea, *n.* an inland sea south of eastern Europe, bounded by Moldovia, Ukraine, Russia, Georgia, Turkey, Romania, and Bulgaria; about 435 120 km². Greatest depth, about 2195 m. Also, **Euxine Sea**. Ancient name, **Pontus Euxinus**.

black sheep, *n.* someone thought to be not as good as the rest of their family, etc.

blacksmith /'blæksmɪθ/, *n.* a person who works in iron, esp. making and fitting horseshoes. [BLACK (in ref. to iron or black metal) + SMITH]

black snake, *n.* → **red-bellied black snake**.

black spot, *n.* a fungus infection causing black spots on leaves.

Black Sunday, *n.* the name given to 6 February 1938, when Australia's greatest surf rescue occurred at Bondi Beach, Sydney, NSW; 180 rescued, 5 died.

Black Thursday, *n.* the name given to 6 February 1851, the day of a devastating bushfire in Vic.

Blacktown /'blæktaʊn/, *n.* a city within the western metropolitan area of Sydney, NSW. Pop. 192 442 (1986). [from *Black Town*, a settlement established by Governor Macquarie for the purpose of 'civilising the blacks']

blacktracker /'blæktrækə/, *n.* an Aboriginal tracker employed by the police.

black wattle, *n.* a small tree of eastern Australia with creamy-yellow flowers and a bark which gives tannin.

Black Wednesday /blæk 'wɛnzdeɪ/, *n.* the name given to 9 January 1878, the day when a large number of public servants were dismissed in Vic. [a parody on BLACK THURSDAY]

bladder /'blædə/, *n.* **1.** *Anat., Zool.* **a.** a sac in the body formed by membranes and muscles, which expands in order to store urine. **b.** any similar bodily sac for liquid or gas. **2.** *Bot.* a sac containing air, as in some seaweeds. **3.** any expanding bag, e.g. the inner bag of a football. [OE *blædre* bladder, blister]

blade /bleɪd/, *n.* **1.** the flat cutting part of a sword, knife, etc. **2.** (*pl.*) a hand-held tool like scissors for shearing sheep. **3.** a leaf of a plant, esp. of grass. **4.** *Bot.* the broad part of a leaf, not including the stem, etc. **5.** a cut of beef from the shoulder. **6.** a thin, flat part of something, as of a bone, oar, etc. **7.** an attractive, carefree young man. [OE]

Blainey /'bleɪni/, *n.* **Geoffrey Norman**, born 1930, Australian historian; noted for *The Tyranny of Distance* (1966).

Blair /blɛə/, *n.* **Harold**, 1924–76, Australian tenor and music teacher.

Blake /bleɪk/, *n.* **William**, 1757–1827, English mystical poet and artist.

Blake Prize, *n.* a prize awarded annually in Australia for a work of religious art. [named after William BLAKE]

blame /bleɪm/, *v.*, **blamed, blaming**, *n.* ◇*v.t.* **1.** to place the responsibility for (a fault, mistake, etc.) on someone or something: *He blamed the accident on a broken wheel.* **2.** to place such responsibility on (someone or something): *I blame you for this trouble.* ◇*v.* **3. to blame**, responsible for a fault or mistake: *He is to blame.* ◇*n.* **4.** the finding of fault: *Lazy people bring blame on themselves.* **5.** responsibility for a fault, mistake, etc.: *You will get the blame.* [ME, from OF from LL: BLASPHEME] —**blameless**, *adj.* —**blameworthy**, *adj.*

Blamey /'bleɪmi/, *n.* **Sir Thomas Albert**, 1884–1951, Australian soldier; Commander, Allied Land Forces in the south-west Pacific under General MacArthur in World War II; first Australian field-marshal (1950).

Blanc /blɒ̃/, *n.* **Mont**, a mountain on the French-Italian border; the highest peak of the Alps. 4810 m.

blanch /blænʃ, blanʃ/, *v.t.* **1.** to make white by removing color. **2.** *Hort.* to make white or prevent from becoming green by keeping out light. **3.** to put (vegetables, meat, nuts, etc.) in boiling water for a very short time, in order to preserve color, remove skins, etc.; scald. ◇*v.i.* **4.** to become pale, as with sickness or fear. [ME, from OF *blanc* white]

blancmange /blə'mɒnʒ, -'mɒndʒ/, *n.* a sweet jelly-like dessert made with thickened and flavored milk. [ME, from OF: lit., white food]

bland /blænd/, *adj.* **1.** agreeable or pleasant but often lacking in character: *a bland manner; a bland style of decoration.* **2.** mild; easily digested: *a bland diet.* [L]

Bland /blænd/, *n.* **William**, 1789–1868, Australian medical practitioner, born in England; active in gaining representative government for NSW.

blandish /'blændɪʃ/, *v.t.* to please (someone) with admiring words or actions; flatter. [ME, from L: flatter] —**blandishment**, *n.*

blank /blæŋk/, *adj.* **1.** not written or printed on: *blank paper.* **2.** not filled in: *a blank cheque.* **3.** lacking ornament or opening: *a blank wall.* **4.** showing no attention, feeling or understanding: *a blank face; a blank look.* **5.** complete; utter: *blank stupidity.* ◇*n.* **6.** a place where something is lacking; an empty space: *a blank in one's memory; a blank on an exam paper.* **7.** a printed form containing spaces to be filled in. **8.** a mark, such as a dash, put in the place of a letter or word. **9.** *Mach.* a piece of metal prepared to be stamped or cut into a finished object, such as a coin or key. **10.** → **blank cartridge**. **11. draw (a) blank**, to get no results; fail. [ME, from OF *blanc* white, from Gmc]

blank cartridge, *n.* a cartridge containing powder only, without a bullet.

blank cheque, *n.* **1.** a cheque bearing a signature but no stated amount. **2.** a free hand; carte blanche.

blanket /'blæŋkət/, *n.* **1.** a large rectangular piece of soft fabric, usu. wool, used esp. as a bed covering. **2.** any layer or covering that hides something: *a blanket of clouds.* ◇*v.t.* **3.** to cover with or as if with a blanket. ◇*adj.* **4.** covering or intended to cover a group or class of things, conditions, etc.: *blanket approval.* [ME, from OF *blanc* white]

blank verse, *n.* **1.** unrhymed verse. **2.** unrhymed iambic pentameter verse.

blare /blɛə/, *v.*, **blared**, **blaring**. ◇*v.i.* **1.** to make a loud sound. ◇*v.t.* **2.** to sound loudly; proclaim noisily. [ME, from MD]

blarney /'blani/, *n.*, *v.*, **-neyed**, **-neying**. ◇*n.* **1.** flattering talk; cajolery. ◇*v.t.* **2.** to use blarney; wheedle. [from the BLARNEY STONE]

Blarney stone, *n.* a stone in Blarney Castle near Cork, Ireland, said to confer skill in flattery to anyone who kisses it.

blasé /bla'zeɪ, 'blazeɪ/, *adj.* indifferent to and bored by the pleasures of life. [F: exhausted, satiated]

blaspheme /blæs'fim/, *v.*, **-phemed**, **-pheming**. ◇*v.t.* **1.** to speak without respect of (God or sacred things). **2.** to speak evil of; abuse. ◇*v.i.* **3.** to use words considered irreverent or disrespectful of God or what is held sacred. [LL, from Gk: speak ill] —**blasphemer**, *n.*

blasphemy /'blæsfəmi/, *n.*, *pl.* **-mies**. **1.** words or actions showing disrespect for God or sacred things. **2.** *Theol.* the crime of taking to oneself the rights or qualities of God. **3.** a lack of respect towards anything held sacred. [LL, from Gk: slander] —**blasphemous**, *adj.*

blast /blast/, *n.* **1.** a sudden blowing of air or gust of wind. **2.** (the sound of) blowing of a horn, whistle, etc. **3.** *Metall.* air under pressure directed into blast furnace to support combustion. **4.** an act of exploding; explosion. **5.** a movement of air, or a shock wave, caused by an explosion. **6.** severe criticism. ◇*v.t.* **7.** to blow (a horn, etc.). **8.** to affect with any bad influence; ruin; destroy: *It blasted their hopes.* **9.** to tear (rock, etc.) to pieces with an explosive. **10.** to criticise (someone) severely. ◇*v.i.* **11.** to set off explosions: *The army is blasting near the caves.* ◇*interj.* **12.** (an exclamation of anger or irritation). [OE *blæst*] —**blaster**, *n.*

-blast, a combining form meaning 'embryo', 'sprout', 'germ'. [Gk]

blast furnace, *n.* an upright, steel cylindrical furnace using a forced blast of air to produce molten iron which may be made into steel or formed into pig-iron.

blast-off /'blast-ɒf/, *n. Aerospace*. → **lift-off**.

blatant /'bleɪtnt/, *adj.* **1.** (of actions, etc.) intentionally obvious or undisguised: *blatant mistake; blatant lie.* **2.** (of people) attracting attention by (bad) behavior; brazen; barefaced. [coined by Spenser. Cf. L *blatire* babble] —**blatancy**, *n.*

blather /'blæðə/, *n.* **1.** foolish talk. ◇*v.i.*, *v.t.* **2.** to talk or speak foolishly. Also, **blether**. [ME, from Scand]

Blaxland /'blækslənd/, *n.* **Gregory**, 1778–1853, Australian explorer and pioneer farmer, born in England; leader of the first expedition to cross the Blue Mountains.

blaze¹ /bleɪz/, *n.*, *v.*, **blazed**, **blazing**. ◇*n.* **1.** a bright flame or fire. **2.** a bright, hot gleam or glow: *a blaze of sunshine.* **3.** a sparkling brightness: *a blaze of jewels.* **4.** a sudden passion or fury. ◇*v.i.* **5.** to burn brightly. **6.** to shine like flame. **7.** (of guns) to fire continuously. [OE *blase* torch, flame] —**blazing**, *adj.*

blaze² /bleɪz/, *n.*, *v.*, **blazed**, **blazing**. ◇*n.* **1.** a spot or mark made on a tree to point out a path, etc., in a forest. **2.** a white patch on the face of a horse, cow, etc. ◇*v.* **3. blaze a trail**, **a.** to mark out a trail with blazes. **b.** to break new ground; pioneer. [LG *bläse* a white mark on the head of a horse or steer]

blazer /'bleɪzə/, *n.* a jacket, oft. brightly colored or embroidered with a crest, worn by sportsmen or school children.

blazon /'bleɪzən/, *v.t.* **1.** to show publicly; proclaim. **2.** to represent (a coat of arms) in proper form and color. ◇*n.* **3.** a coat of arms. [ME, from OF: shield]

bldg, *Abbrev.* building.

bleach /blitʃ/, *v.t.*, *v.i.* to make or become white, pale, or colorless. ◇*n.* a substance used for bleaching. [OE *blæcean*]

bleachers /'blitʃəz/, *n.pl.* uncovered seats or stands for sports spectators.

bleak /blik/, *adj.* **1.** bare; desolate: *a bleak plain.* **2.** cold and piercing: *a bleak wind.*

bleak 3. empty; dreary: *a bleak hope*. [ME *bleke* pale, from OE] **–bleakness**, *n*.

blear /blɪə/, *v.t.* **1.** to make (the eyes or sight) dim, as with tears or tiredness. ◇*n.* **2.** a blur; *a bleared state*. [ME; orig. uncert.] **–bleary**, *adj.* **–blearily**, *adv*.

bleat /blit/, *v.i.* **1.** to cry as a sheep, goat, etc. **2.** to speak with a bleating sound. **3.** to complain; moan. ◇*n.* **4.** the cry of a sheep, goat, etc. [OE *blætan*]

bleed /blid/, *v.,* **bled** /bled/, **bleeding**. ◇*v.i.* **1.** to lose blood, from the body or internally from the vascular system. **2.** to die, as in battle: *He bled for the cause.* **3.** (of blood, etc.) to flow out. **4.** (of color) to run. **5.** to give out sap, juice, etc. **6.** to feel pity, sorrow: *The nation bleeds for its dead soldiers.* ◇*v.t.* **7.** to cause to lose blood, esp. from surgery. **8.** to drain, draw sap, liquid, air, etc., from: *to bleed the brakes of a car.* **9.** to extort money from: *They bled him white.* [OE *blōd* blood] **–bleeding**, *n*.

bleeder /'blidə/, *n.* **→haemophiliac.**

bleep /blip/, *v.i.* **1.** to give out a high-pitched broken sound, or a radio signal. ◇*n.* **2.** a single short high-pitched sound. [imitative]

blemish /'blemɪʃ/, *v.t.* **1.** to destroy the perfection of. ◇*n.* **2.** a spot or stain; defect; disfigurement. [ME, from OF: make livid]

blench /blentʃ/, *v.i.* to draw away; flinch; quail. [OE *blencan* deceive]

blend /blend/, *v.,* **blended, blending**, *n*. ◇*v.t.* **1.** to mix or combine: *He blended the flour and water.* **2.** to mix (various sorts or grades) so as to obtain a particular kind or quality. **3.** to prepare (food) using a blender. ◇*v.i.* **4.** to mix or combine: *Those substances blend well.* **5.** to go with or suit: *The chairs blend well with the wallpaper.* **6.** to have no apparent separation: *Sea and sky seemed to blend.* ◇*n.* **7.** a mixture produced by blending. **8.** *Linguistics.* a word made up from parts of others, e.g. *smog*, a blend of *smoke* and *fog*. [OE]

blende /blend/, *n.* sphalerite or certain other sulfides. [G, from *blenden* blind, deceive]

blender /'blendə/, *n.* an electric device, used for chopping or mixing food.

blenny /'bleni/, *n., pl.* **-ies.** a small sea fish. [L, from Gk: *blenny*, orig. slime]

bless /bles/, *v.t.,* **blessed** or **blest**, **blessing**. **1.** to make sacred; pronounce holy; glorify; consecrate. **2.** to give good things to: *a nation blessed with peace.* **3.** to feel thankful or grateful for (something) or to (someone). **4.** to protect or guard from evil. **5.** *Church.* to make the sign of the cross over. **6.** to approve: *Do you bless this marriage?* [OE: consecrate, orig. with blood, from *blōd* blood]

blessed /'blesəd, blest/, *adj.* **1.** holy; consecrated; sacred. **2.** fortunate; happy. ◇*n.* **3. the blessed**, people thought to have gone to Heaven. **–blessedness**, *n*.

blessing /'blesɪŋ/, *n.* **1.** the act or words of someone who blesses. **2.** a special favor, mercy, or gift, esp. from God. **3.** a prayer for God's favor; benediction. **4.** praise; devotion; worship.

blest /blest/, *v.* **1.** past tense and past participle of **bless.** ◇*adj.* **2.** blessed.

blew /blu/, *v.* past tense of **blow.**

Bligh /blaɪ/, *n.* **William**, 1754–1817, English-born naval officer and governor of NSW, 1806–1808; captain of HMS *Bounty* in 1787.

blight /blaɪt/, *n.* **1.** a widely found plant disease, such as tomato blight. **2.** anything that ruins, destroys, etc. **3.** **→sandy blight.** ◇*v.t.* **4.** to destroy; ruin; frustrate. [orig. unknown]

blimp /blɪmp/, *n.* a small airship or dirigible, used chiefly for observation. [orig. uncert.]

blind /blaɪnd/, *adj.* **1.** lacking the sense of sight. **2.** unwilling or unable to try to understand; unreasonable: *blind to all arguments.* **3.** lacking awareness or reason: *blind stupor; blind anger.* **4.** *Colloq.* drunk. **5.** hidden from view. **6.** closed at one end: *blind street.* **7.** done without seeing: *blind flying.* **8.** made without knowledge in advance: *blind date.* **9.** relating to blind people: *blind school.* ◇*v.t.* **10.** to make blind, as by hurting, dazzling or bandaging the eyes, etc. **11.** something that blocks the vision or keeps out light, e.g. a shade for a window. **12.** a cover for hiding an action or a purpose; decoy: *His business was a blind for his crimes.* **13. the blind**, sightless people. ◇*adv.* **14.** without being able to see one's way: *to fly blind.* **15.** without proper consideration: *to enter into a deal blind.* [OE] **–blinding**, *adj.* **–blindness**, *n*.

blindfold /'blaɪndfoʊld/, *v.t.* **1.** to prevent sight by covering (the eyes); cover the eyes of. ◇*n.* **2.** a cover over the eyes. ◇*adj.* **3.** with the eyes covered: *blindfold test.* [BLIND + FOLD¹ wrap up]

blindman's buff, *n.* game in which a blindfolded player tries to catch and name another player. [LG *buff*, a blow or slap]

blind spot, *n.* **1.** *Anat.* a small area on the retina, insensitive to light, at which the optic nerve leaves eye. **2.** a matter about which someone is ill-informed or prejudiced. **3.** a place where the view is blocked, as by a window column in a car.

blind staggers, *n.* any of various forms of brain and spinal disease in horses, cattle and other animals. Also, **staggers.**

blink /blɪŋk/, *v.i.* **1.** to shut and open the eyes, esp. rapidly and repeatedly. **2.** to shine unsteadily or dimly; twinkle. ◇*v.t.* **3.** to cause (the eyes, light) to blink. **4.** to shut the eyes to; evade, shirk. ◇*n.* **5.** a blinking. **6.** a gleam; glimmer. **7. on the blink**, *Colloq.* not working properly. [ME: blench]

blinker /'blɪŋkə/, *n.* **1. →indicator** (def. 1). **2.** *(pl.)* a pair of flaps on a bridle to prevent a horse from seeing sideways.

blip /blɪp/, *n.* a spot of light on a radar screen showing the position of an aeroplane, submarine, etc.

bliss /blɪs/, *n.* **1.** a lightness of heart; gladness. **2.** the greatest happiness or delight. **3.** *Theol.* the joy of heaven. [OE *blīthe* BLITHE] —**blissful**, *adj.*

blister /'blɪstə/, *n.* **1.** a bubble-like swelling under the skin, containing watery matter esp. from a burn or other injury. **2.** any similar swelling. ◇*v.t.* **3.** to raise blisters on. ◇*v.i.* **4.** to form blisters; become blistered. [ME, ? from OF: clod, lump] —**blistery**, *adj.*

blistering /'blɪstərɪŋ/, *adj.* harsh; biting: *blistering wind; blistering attack.*

blithe /blaɪð/, *adj.* happy; merry; cheerful. Also, **blithesome**. [OE *blīthe* kind, joyous]

blithering /'blɪðərɪŋ/, *adj.* stupid; jabbering.

blitz /blɪts/, *n.* **1.** *Mil.* a war waged by surprise, swiftly and violently. **2. the Blitz**, night air-raids by German bombers in World War II on London and elsewhere, esp. in the period 1940-41. **3.** a swift, sudden attack: *a blitz on litterbugs.* ◇*v.t.* **4.** to attack with a blitz. [G: lightning (war)]

blizzard /'blɪzəd/, *n.* a violent snow storm. [var. of d. *blizzer* blaze, flash, blinding flash of lightning]

bloat /bloʊt/, *v.t.* **1.** to make bigger, as with air, water, etc.; cause to swell. **2.** to puff up, as with pride. **3.** to cure (fishes) by soaking in salt water and smoking. ◇*n.* **4.** *Vet Sci.* Also, **bloating.** (in cattle, sheep, horses, etc.) an enlargement of the abdomen, caused by too much eating of green fodder, esp. legumes. [ME *blout* puffy, from Scand]

blob /blɒb/, *n.* **1.** a drop of liquid; bubble. **2.** a small lump or drop. [? imitative]

bloc /blɒk/, *n.* a group of states, parties, etc., united by similar political systems, etc. [F. See BLOCK]

block /blɒk/, *n.* **1.** a solid mass of wood, stone, metal etc. **2.** a child's building brick. **3.** a mould on which something is shaped, e.g. a hat block. **4.** *Qld.* one of the wooden supports for a house built above ground. **5.** a piece of wood used for engraving. **6.** *Print.* a letterpress printing plate mounted on base. **7.** a (wooden) bench or board for chopping, beheading, etc. **8.** *Mech.* **a.** a device consisting of one or more grooved pulleys mounted in the casing or shell, to which a hook or the like is attached, used for transmitting power, changing the direction of motion, etc. **b.** a casing or shell holding a pulley. **9.** *Pathol.* an obstruction, as of a nerve. **10.** *Sport.* the stopping of an opponent's actions or course. **11.** a quantity, portion, or section taken as unit: *block of tickets.* **12.** a section of land, oft. in a suburb, for building a house on, etc.: *a block of land; a building block.* **13.** a group of city or town buildings enclosed by intersecting streets. **14.** a row of buildings, or one large building, divided into separate houses, flats, etc. **15.** *Athletics.* Also, **starting block.** one of a pair of supports for the feet, used by a sprinter to give more power from a crouching start. **16.** *Colloq.* **lose** or **do one's block,** to become very angry. ◇*v.t.* **17.** to fit, shape or prepare with blocks; mount on blocks. **18.** to cut into blocks. **19.** to draw or outline roughly, without details (fol. by *out* or *in*). **20.** to obstruct (a space, movement, etc.); stop or delay (a person, etc.) by placing obstacles in the way. **21.** to hide from view (fol. by *out*): *Smoke blocked out the sun.* **22.** *Pathol, Physiol.* to stop movement along (a nerve, etc.). ◇*v.i.* **23.** to act so as to stop an opponent (as in football, boxing, etc.). [ME, apparently from OF *bloc* block, mass, from Gmc] —**blockage**, *n.*

blockade /blɒ'keɪd/, *n.*, *v.*, **-kaded, -kading.** ◇*n.* **1.** *Navy, Mil.* the closing of a port, harbor, etc., by enemy ships or soldiers to prevent entrance or exit. ◇*v.t.* **2.** to close (a port, etc.), in this way.

block and tackle, *n.* pulley blocks and ropes used for lifting heavy things.

blockbuster /'blɒkbʌstə/, *n.* **1.** an aerial bomb containing high explosives used in World War II to destroy large areas. **2.** *Colloq.* anything large and exciting, as a lavish theatrical production, successful political campaign, etc.

block diagram, *n.* **1.** *Elect, Eng.* a diagram which shows the relationships between the parts of a system. **2.** *Geol.* a drawing in three dimensions to show the structural relationships between rocks below the surface.

blockhouse /'blɒkhaʊs/, *n. Mil.* a fortlike structure with openings in the walls from which guns are fired.

block letter, *n.* a plain typelike capital letter. Also, **block capital.**

bloke /bloʊk/, *n. Colloq.* a man; fellow; guy.

blond /blɒnd/, *adj.* **1.** light-colored. **2.** having light-colored hair and skin. ◇*n.* **3.** a blond person. Also, (of a female) **blonde.** [F, from ML *blondus* yellow]

blood /blʌd/, *n.* **1.** the fluid that circulates in arteries and veins or the main vascular system of animals. **2.** the body fluids spilled out with injury; gore. **3.** the vital principle; life. **4.** murder; bloodshed; slaughter: *blood on his hands.* **5.** the juice or sap of plants, esp. if red. **6.** temper or state of mind: *person of hot blood.* **7.** descent from a common ancestor: *related by blood.* **8.** *Stock Breeding.* a recorded and respected background; pure-bred breeding. **9. in cold blood,** calmly, coolly, and deliberately. ◇*v.t.* **10.** to cause to bleed. **11.** to initiate. [OE *blōd*]

bloodbath /'blʌdbɑθ/, *n.* → **massacre.**

blood brother, *n.* someone who has sworn lifelong brotherhood to, and joined his blood with that of, another.

blood count, *n.* a count of the number of red or white blood cells in a certain volume of blood.

bloodcurdling /'blʌd,kɜdlɪŋ/, *adj.* frightening; terrifying.

blooded /'blʌdəd/, *adj.* **1.** having a certain type of blood: *warm-blooded animals.* **2.** initiated.

blood feud, *n.* → **vendetta.**

blood group, *n.* one of several sections into which blood may be grouped according to its clotting reactions. Also, **blood type.**

bloodhound /'blʌdhaʊnd/, *n.* one of breed of large, powerful dogs with a strong sense of smell, used for tracking animals, etc.

bloodless /'blʌdləs/, *adj* **1.** without blood; pale. **2.** free from bloodshed: *bloodless victory.* **3.** cold-hearted: *bloodless charity.*

blood money, *n.* **1.** a fee paid to a hired murderer. **2.** compensation paid to the relatives of a murdered person.

blood plasma, *n.* the liquid part of human blood oft. stored for transfusions.

blood-poisoning /'blʌd-pɔɪznɪŋ/, *n.* a morbid condition of the blood due to the presence of poisonous matter or microorganisms; toxaemia; septicaemia.

blood pressure, *n.* the pressure of blood against the inner walls of blood vessels.

blood relation, *n.* someone related by birth. Also, **blood relative**.

bloodshed /'blʌdʃed/, *n.* the taking of life; slaughter.

bloodshot /'blʌdʃɒt/, *adj.* (of the eyes) red from enlarged blood vessels.

blood sports, *n.pl.* sports involving bloodshed, e.g. hunting.

bloodstock /'blʌdstɒk/, *n.* thoroughbred stock, esp. stud horses.

bloodstream /'blʌdstrim/, *n.* the blood flowing through the circulatory system.

bloodsucker /'blʌdsʌkə/, *n.* **1.** any animal that sucks blood, esp. the leech. **2.** → **waratah anemone**. **3.** an extortionist.

bloodthirsty /'blʌdθɜsti/, *adj.* cruel; murderous.

blood vessel, *n.* any of vessels (arteries, veins, capillaries) through which blood circulates.

bloodwood /'blʌdwʊd/, *n.* any of several kinds of gum trees esp. those with red sap.

bloody /'blʌdi/, *adj.*, **bloodier**, **bloodiest**, *v.*, **bloodied**, **bloodying**, *adv.* ◇*adj.* **1.** stained with blood: *bloody handkerchief.* causing bloodshed: *bloody battle.* **2.** of the nature of, or relating to blood. **3.** *Colloq.* (a word indicating approval or disapproval): *bloody miracle; bloody idiot.* ◇*v.t.* to stain with blood. ◇*adv.* **4.** *Colloq.* very; extremely: *bloody awful.* [OE *blōdig*]

bloom /blum/, *n.* **1.** the flower of a plant. **2.** the state of having the buds opened. **3.** a glowing, healthy condition: *bloom of youth.* **4.** a state of full development; prime; perfection. **5.** *Bot.* a whitish powdery coating on the surface of certain fruits and leaves. ◇*v.i.* **6.** to produce or yield flowers. **7.** to be in a state of healthy beauty and vigor; flourish. [ME, from Scand] —**blooming**, *adj.*

bloomers /'bluməz/, *n.pl.* **1.** loose trousers gathered at the knee, formerly worn by women. **2.** woman's pants similar to these. [named after a Mrs Amelia *Bloomer* of New York, about 1850]

blossom /'blɒsəm/, *n. Bot.* **1.** the flower of a plant, esp. of a fruit tree: *apple blossom.* ◇*v.i.* **2.** *Bot.* (of a tree) to produce or yield blossoms. **3.** to develop; flourish (oft. fol. by *out*). [OE *blōs(t)m(a)* flower] —**blossomy**, *adj.*

blot /blɒt/, *n., v.*, **blotted**, **blotting**. ◇*n.* **1.** a spot or stain, esp. ink on paper. **2.** a blemish on character or reputation. ◇*v.t.* **3.** to darken; make dim. **4.** to remove, destroy (fol. by *out*): *to blot out a bad memory.* **5.** to dry with absorbent paper or the like. ◇*v.i.* **6.** (of ink, etc.) to spread in a stain. [ME; orig. uncert.]

blotch /blɒtʃ/, *n.* **1.** a large irregular spot or blot. ◇*v.t.* **2.** to mark with blotches; blot, spot, or blur. [b. BLOT and BOTCH] —**blotchy**, *adj.*

blotting paper, *n.* soft, absorbent paper used esp. for soaking up ink.

blouse /blaʊz/, *n, v.*, **bloused**, **blousing**. ◇*n.* **1.** a light, loosely fitting shirt, esp. one gathered or held in at the waist. ◇*v.i.* **2.** to hang loose and full. ◇*v.t.* **3.** to drape loosely. [F, ? from Pr (*lano*) *blouso* short (wool)]

blouson /'bluzɒn, 'blaʊzɒn/, *adj.* (of a dress, jacket, etc.) having a loose-fitting top gathered in at the waist. [F]

blow[1] /bloʊ/, *n.* **1.** a sudden stroke with hand or weapon. **2.** a sudden shock; calamity. **3.** the first and longest stroke made in shearing sheep. **4. come to blows**, to start to fight. [northern ME *blaw*; orig. uncert.]

blow[2] /bloʊ/, *v.*, **blew** /blu/, **blown**, **blowing**, *n.* ◇*v.i.* **1.** (of the wind or air) to be in motion. **2.** to move along, carried by wind: *Dust was blowing.* **3.** to produce a current of air, as with the mouth, bellows, etc.: *to blow on your hands.* **4.** *Music.* (of a horn, trumpet, etc.) to give out sound. **5.** to make a blowing sound; whistle. **6.** to breathe hard or quickly; pant. **7.** *Zool.* (of a whale) to spout. **8.** (of a fuse, gasket, light bulb, valve, tyre, etc.) to burn out or burst; become unusable (oft. fol. by *out*). **9.** (of a candle, etc.) to be put out, as by wind (fol. by *out*). ◇*v.t.* **10.** to drive by means of a current of air. **11.** to put out (a flame, etc.) with a puff of air (fol. by *out*). **12.** to clear or empty by forcing air through. **13.** to shape (glass, etc.) with a current of air. **14.** to cause to explode (fol. by *up, to bits*, etc.). **15.** *Photog.* to enlarge a photograph (fol. by *up*). **16.** *Colloq.* to waste; squander: *to blow one's money.* **17.** *Colloq.* to fail in something: *to blow an exam.* ◇*v.* **18.** Some special uses are:

blow in, *Colloq.* to make an unexpected visit; drop in.

blow out, *Econ.* to exceed the limits of a budget.

blow over, **1.** to cease, as a storm. **2.** to be forgotten.

blow (someone) up, *Colloq.* to scold or abuse (someone).

blow up, **1.** to come into being: *A storm blew up.* **2.** to explode.

◇*n.* **19.** (a storm with) a strong wind. **20.** a discolored quartz-rich rock, sometimes thought to indicate mineral deposits below. [OE *blāwan*]

blow³ /bloʊ/, *v.i.* **blew, blown, blowing.** to blossom; bloom; flower. [OE *blōan*]

Blowering Dam /ˈblaʊərɪŋ dæm/, *n.* a dam on the Tumut River in southern NSW; used for hydro-electricity and irrigation.

blowfish /ˈbloʊfɪʃ/, *n.* → **toado.**

blowfly /ˈbloʊflaɪ/, *n., pl.* **-flies.** any of various true flies which lay eggs or larvae on meat, or sores, wounds, etc., esp. the **blue blowfly.**

blowfly strike, *n.* an infestation of the flesh of a living sheep by the maggots of a blowfly, esp. the blue blowfly.

blowhole /ˈbloʊhoʊl/, *n.* **1.** an opening for letting out air or gas. **2.** either of two nostrils in the head of whales through which they breathe. **3.** a hole in the ice to which whales or seals come to breathe. **4.** a hole in the coastal rock formation up through which sea water is forced violently by tide or wave.

blowlamp /ˈbloʊlæmp/, *n.* a small portable apparatus which gives a hot flame by forcing kerosene under pressure through a small nozzle and burning it in air.

blown¹ /bloʊn/, *adj.* **1.** swollen; distended. **2.** out of breath; exhausted. **3.** → **flyblown. 4.** formed by blowing: *blown glass.* [see BLOW²]

blown² /bloʊn/, *adj.* (of a flower) fully opened. [see BLOW³]

blow-out /ˈbloʊ-aʊt/, *n.* **1.** the bursting of a car tyre. **2.** the burning out of an electrical fuse. **3.** a sudden or violent escape of air, steam, oil or gas from a well, or the like. **4.** an excess on the limits of a budget.

blowpipe /ˈbloʊpaɪp/, *n.* **1.** a pipe or tube through which pellets, darts, etc., are blown by the breath. **2.** a tube for forcing a stream of air or gas into a flame to increase its heat. **3.** *Glass-blowing.* a long iron pipe used to gather and blow glass.

blow-up /ˈbloʊ-ʌp/, *n.* **1.** an explosion or other violent happening. **2.** an outburst of temper. **3.** *Photog.* an enlargement.

blubber /ˈblʌbə/, *n.* **1.** *Zool.* the fat found between the skin and muscle of whales, etc., from which oil is made. ◇*v.i.* **2.** to weep, usu. noisily. ◇*v.t.* **3.** to speak while weeping. ◇*adj.* **4.** swollen. [ME; apparently imitative] —**blubbery,** *adj.*

bludge /blʌdʒ/, *v.,* **bludged, bludging,** *n. Colloq.* ◇*v.i.* **1.** to avoid responsibilities. **2.** to take unfair advantage of others (fol. by *on*). ◇*v.t.* **3.** to borrow without intention of repaying; cadge. ◇*n.* **4.** a job which involves almost no work. [short for BLUDGEON] —**bludger,** *n.*

bludgeon /ˈblʌdʒən/, *n.* **1.** a short, heavy club. ◇*v.t.* **2.** to strike or hit with a bludgeon. **3.** to force (someone) into something; bully. [orig. unknown] —**bludgeoner,** *n.*

blue /bluː/, *n., adj.,* **bluer, bluest.** ◇*n.* **1.** the pure color of clear sky; deep azure (between green and violet in the spectrum). **2. the blue, a.** the sky. **b.** the sea. **c.** the unknown; nowhere: *out of the blue.* **3.** Also, **washing blue.** a substance used to whiten clothes in washing them. **4.** (a badge, colors, etc. awarded to) a sportsperson who represents their university in a contest with another. **5.** (*pl.*) → **blues. 6.** *Colloq.* a fight; dispute. **7.** *Colloq.* a mistake. **8.** *Colloq.* (a nickname for a red-headed person). ◇*adj.* **9.** of or colored with blue. **10.** (of the skin) discolored by cold, fear, or rage. **11.** depressed in spirits; dismal: *I'm feeling blue.* **12.** obscene: *blue movie.* **13. once in a blue moon,** rarely. **14. true blue,** loyal; faithful; genuine. [ME, from Gmc]

Blue /bluː/, *n.* Billy, 1737?–1834, a NSW boatman thought to have been born in the West Indies; transported to Sydney in 1801, he ran the first ferry service between his own land grant, Blues Point, and Millers Point.

blue asbestos, *n.* → **crocidolite.**

blue baby, *n.* a baby born with cyanosis.

Bluebeard /ˈbluːbɪəd/, *n.* **1.** (in folklore) a nickname of the Chevalier Raoul, whose seventh wife found in a forbidden room the bodies of the other six. **2.** any man alleged to have murdered a number of his wives or other women.

bluebell /ˈbluːbel/, *n.* any herb or plant with blue bell-shaped flowers e.g. the harebell, campanula, wood hyacinth.

blueberry /ˈbluːbəri/, *n., pl.* **-ries.** the blue edible berry of various small North American shrubs.

blueberry ash, *n.* a tree of eastern Australia with bell-like flowers and blue berries.

bluebird /ˈbluːbɜːd/, *n.* a type of small North American songbird.

blue blood, *n.* **1.** descent from nobility. **2.** a person of noble descent. —**blue-blooded,** *adj.*

bluebottle /ˈbluːbɒtl/, *n.* **1.** a small sea animal, a type of coelenterate, found in warm seas and having a long, blue, gas-filled sac with tentacles which give a painful sting. **2.** a type of large, blue and green fly.

blue-collar /ˈbluː-kɒlə/, *adj.* belonging or relating to industrial workers (opposed to *white-collar*).

blue-faced honeyeater, *n.* a honeyeater, olive-green with white underparts, with a large blue eye-patch of bare skin, found in northern and eastern Australia. Also, **blue-eye.**

blue flier, *n.* a fully-grown female of the red kangaroo. See **kangaroo.**

blue grass, *n.* **1.** a type of grass, such as Kentucky blue grass,. **2.** folk music of the southeastern US using instruments such as the guitar, banjo and fiddle. Also, **bluegrass.**

blue gum, *n.* a type of gum tree with smooth and often bluish-colored bark.

blue heeler, *n.* a type of purebred Australian cattle dog. Also, **Queensland blue heeler, Australian blue speckle cattle dog.**

Blue Lake, *n.* a lake at Mt Gambier in south-eastern SA; in summer changes from grey to bright blue; source of the water supply for city of Mount Gambier. 71 ha.

blue metal, *n.* crushed dark igneous rock used in road-making, etc.

Blue Mountains, *n.pl.* **1.** a part of the Great Dividing Range in NSW, extending from Emu Plains to Mt Victoria. Highest peak, Mt Bindo, 1362 m. **2. City of the,** a local government administrative area including Katoomba, Wentworth Falls, Leura and Blackheath. Pop. 63 866 (1986). 1400 km². [from their blue color when viewed from a distance]

blue peter, *n.* a blue flag with a white square in the centre, raised by a ship as a signal that it is ready to leave port. [BLUE + *peter*, orig. REPEATER]

blue pointer, *n.* →**mako**.

blueprint /'bluprɪnt/, *n.* **1.** a photographic copy in which the print is white on a blue ground, used in making copies of building plans, etc. **2.** any detailed plan which serves as a model for later practice. ◇*v.t.* **3.** to make a blueprint of.

blue-ribbon /'blu-rɪbən/, *adj.* **1.** *Politics.* relating to an electorate, sure to be held by a particular party; safe. **2.** of or relating to a prize-winner.

blue-ringed octopus, *n.* a small octopus of eastern Australia with blue to purple bands on the tentacles and a highly poisonous bite.

blues /bluz/, *n.pl.* **1.** a state of unhappiness; depression. **2.** a type of song, of American Negro origin, often slow and sad and used in jazz. [short for *blue devils*]

bluestocking /'blustɒkɪŋ/, *n.* (*usu. offensive.*) a woman who is strongly interested in literature or other kinds of learning as opposed to practical or social activities. [so called because members of a certain mid-18th C London literary circle wore blue woollen instead of formal black silk stockings]

blue-tongue /'blu-tʌŋ/, *n.* a type of large, harmless Australian lizard with a broad blue tongue. Also, **blue-tongue lizard.**

blue vein, *n.* a type of cheese with blue-green veins of cultured mould.

blue whale, *n.* a whale of northern and southern oceans, with yellowish underparts, the largest known mammal.

bluey /'blui/, *n.* **1.** →**swag** (def. 1). **2.** *Colloq.* (a name for a red-headed person). **3.** *Colloq.* (a name for anything colored blue). **4.** *Colloq.* a summons in hand.

bluff¹ /blʌf/, *adj.* **1.** rough but friendly in manner; hearty. **2.** with a broad and very steep front, as a ship, etc. ◇*n.* **3.** a broad, steep cliff, hill, etc. [probably from LG *blaf* flat]

bluff² /blʌf/, *v.t.*, **1.** to trick (someone) by showing a bold front. **2.** to gain by bluffing: *He bluffed his way through the situation.* ◇*v.i.* **3.** to show a bold front in order to deceive. ◇*n.* **4.** an act of bluffing. **5.** someone who bluffs. **6. call someone's bluff,** to show someone up as only pretending. [orig. uncert.]

blunder /'blʌndə/, *n.* **1.** a stupid mistake. ◇*v.i.* **2.** to move or act blindly. **3.** to make a stupid mistake. ◇*v.t.* **4.** to do (something) wrongly; bungle. **5.** to say (something) thoughtlessly (usu. fol. by *out*). [ME, from Scand]

blunt /blʌnt/, *adj.* **1.** having a dull edge or point; not sharp. **2.** plain in speech or manner; straightforward. **3.** slow in understanding; dull. ◇*v.t.* **4.** to make blunt. **5.** to weaken the effect of. [ME; orig. unknown]

blur /blɜ/, *v.*, **blurred, blurring**, *n.* ◇*v.t.* **1.** to make (something) unclear or confused: *This pen blurs my writing; That noise blurs my mind.* ◇*v.i.* **2.** to become unclear. ◇*n.* **3.** a mark which blurs. **4.** something that is blurred. [? akin to BLEAR] —**blurry**, *adj.*

blurb /blɜb/, *n.* information or advertisement usu. giving praise, on the cover of book or record. [coined by Gelett Burgess, 1866–1951, American humorist and illustrator]

blurt /blɜt/, *v.t.* to tell (something) suddenly or thoughtlessly (usu. fol. by *out*). [? imitative]

blush /blʌʃ/, *v.i.* **1.** to become red in the face from embarrassment, shame, etc. **2.** to feel shame (*at*, *for*, etc.). **3.** (of flowers, etc.) to become pink. ◇*n.* **4.** a reddening of the face. **5.** a pinkish color. ◇*adj.* **6.** pale pink. [OE *blyscan* redden]

bluster /'blʌstə/, *v.i.* **1.** (of the wind, etc.) to be loud and violent. **2.** to act or speak in a noisy and unnecessarily forceful manner. ◇*v.t.* **3.** to force by blustering. ◇*n.* **4.** a violent noise. **5.** blustering speech or behavior. [ME, ? from LG] —**blustery**, *adj.*

Blyton /'blaɪtn/, *n.* **Enid (Mary)**, 1896–1968, English author, esp. of children's stories.

BMX /bi ɛm 'ɛks/, *adj.* **1.** of or relating to the racing of small, strongly-built bicycles over specially made rough tracks. ◇*n.* any bicycle made for such a use.

B'nai B'rith /bəneɪ bə'riθ, 'brɪθ/, *n.* a fraternal organisation of Jewish men. [Heb *bæn‘e bærith* sons of the covenant]

BO /bi 'oʊ/, *n. Colloq.* body odor.

boa /'boʊə/, *n.*, *pl.* **boas. 1.** a type of non-poisonous snake that kills by coiling around prey and crushing. **2.** a long, snake-shaped garment of feathers, etc., worn about the neck by women. [L]

boa constrictor, *n.* a boa of Central and South America, up to four metres long.

Boadicea /boʊədɪ'siə/, *n.* died AD 62, queen of the Iceni who led an unsuccessful revolt against the Roman government of Britain. Also, **Boudicca.**

Boake /boʊk/, *n.* **Barcroft Henry Thomas**, 1866–92, Australian poet; works collected and published under the title, *Where the Dead Men Lie, and other Poems* (1897).

boar /bɔ/, *n.* an uncastrated male pig. [OE *bār*]

board /bɔd/, *n.* **1.** a flat piece of wood cut thin and long. **2.** (*pl.*) *Theat.* the stage. **3.** Also, **shearing board. a.** the floor of a woolshed. **b.** the shearers employed in a woolshed. **4.** a flat, thin piece of wood, or other material, for some special use: *chess board*;

board 111 **body corporate**

ironing-board; *noticeboard*. **5.** →**blackboard. 6.** the stiff covered cardboard used to form the binding of a book. **7. a.** a table, esp. for meals. **b.** meals provided for payment: *bed and board*. **8.** an official group of people who control some activity: *board of directors*; *board of trade*. **9.** the side or edge of anything, as in *sea-board*. **10. across the board,** including all groups or levels. **11. on board,** on or in a ship, aeroplane, or vehicle. ◇*v.t.* **12.** to cover or close with boards (sometimes fol. by *up*). **13.** to provide with meals, or with meals and room, esp. for payment. **14.** to get on or enter (a ship, train, etc.). ◇*v.i.* **15.** to be provided with a room, or with meals and a room in return for payment. [OE *bord* board, table, shield]

boarder /'bɔdə/, *n.* **1.** someone who is supplied with meals and a room in return for payment. **2.** a pupil at a boarding school.

boarding school, *n.* a school where pupils live and are provided with meals.

Boardman /'bɔdmən/, *n.* **Norman Keith,** born 1926, Australian biochemist.

boast /boʊst/, *v.i.* **1.** to speak with too much pride, esp. about oneself. ◇*v.t.* **2.** to be proud in the possession of: *The town boasts a new school.* ◇*n.* **3.** something boasted of. **4.** speech used in boasting. [ME; orig. unknown] —**boastful,** *adj.* —**boaster,** *n.*

boat /boʊt/, *n.* **1.** a small, usu. open vessel for travel on water. **2.** *Colloq.* a ship. **3.** an open dish shaped like a boat: *a gravy boat.* **4. in the same boat,** in the same situation, usu. an unfortunate one. ◇*v.i.* **5.** to go in a boat. [OE *bāt*] —**boating,** *n.*

boater /'boʊtə/, *n.* a straw hat with a flat hard brim.

boat people, *n.* people escaping from South-East Asia, setting out for Australia or other countries by boat.

boatswain /'boʊsən/, *n.* an officer on a ship in charge of a deck crew and equipment. Also, **bo's'n, bosun.** [OE *bātswegen* boatman]

bob[1] /bɒb/, *n., v.,* **bobbed, bobbing.** ◇*n.* **1.** a short jerky movement: *a bob of the head.* **2.** a quick curtsy. ◇*v.t.* **3.** to move quickly down and up: *bob the head.* **4.** to show (something) with such a movement: *bob a greeting.* **5.** to curtsy quickly. **6.** to move with jerky movements, usu. up and down. **7.** to rise to the surface or appear suddenly (fol. by *up*): *A cork always bobs up in water.* [ME; orig. uncert.]

bob[2] /bɒb/, *n., v.,* **bobbed, bobbing.** ◇*n.* **1.** a style of short haircut for women and children. **2.** a horse's tail cut short. **3.** a small object hanging at the end of something, e.g. the weight on a pendulum. ◇*v.t.* **4.** to cut short; dock. [ME: bunch, cluster, knob; orig. obscure]

bob[3] /bɒb/, *n. Colloq.* (formerly) a shilling.

bobbin /'bɒbən/, *n.* a cylindrical object upon which thread is wound, as used in spinning, machine sewing, etc. [F: wind up]

bobble /'bɒbəl/, *n.* a small ball, usu. of wool, which hangs from hats, etc., for ornament.

bobby-dazzler /bɒbi-'dæzlə/, *n. Colloq.* an excellent thing or person.

bobby pin, *n.* a metal hairpin which closes tightly on itself to hold the hair.

bobcat /'bɒbkæt/, *n.* **1.** a North American wildcat. **2.** a small four-wheeled vehicle used for digging trenches, etc.

bobsleigh /'bɒbsleɪ/, *n.* a racing sledge with two sets of runners, one behind the other. [BOB[2] + SLEIGH]

bobuck /'boʊbʌk/, *n.* See **brush-tailed possum.**

Boccherini /bɒkə'rini/, *n.* **Luigi** /lu'idʒi/, 1743–1805, Italian cellist and composer.

bod /bɒd/, *n. Colloq.* a person. [short for BODY]

Boddy /'bɒdi/, *n.* **Michael,** born 1934, Australian playwright; major work *The Legend of King O'Malley* (1970).

bode /boʊd/, *v.,* **boded, boding.** ◇*v.t.* **1.** to be a sign or omen of (something in the future). ◇*v.* **2. bode ill/well,** to be a bad/good omen. [OE *bode* messenger]

bodgie[1] /'bɒdʒi/, *adj. Colloq.* **1.** worthless or badly done. **2.** (of names, etc.) false. [Obs. Brit. *bodge* to patch or mend clumsily]

bodgie[2] /'bɒdʒi/, *n. Colloq.* esp. in the 1950s, one of a group of young men with unusual dress and wild behavior.

bodice /'bɒdəs/, *n.* **1.** the fitted upper part of a woman's dress. **2.** a woman's outer garment covering the waist and chest. [var. of *bodies*, pl. of BODY]

bodily /'bɒdəli/, *adj.* **1.** of or relating to the body; corporeal. ◇*adv.* **2.** as a whole; not in parts.

boding /'boʊdɪŋ/, *n., adj.* →**foreboding.**

bodkin /'bɒdkən/, *n.* **1.** a small pointed instrument for making holes in cloth, etc. **2.** a blunt needle for drawing cord, etc., through a hem, etc. **3.** a long hairpin. [ME: dagger; orig. unknown]

Bodoni /bə'doʊni/, *n.* a style of type. [named after Giambattista *Bodoni*, 1740–1813]

body /'bɒdi/, *n., pl.* **bodies,** *v.,* **bodied, bodying.** ◇*n.* **1.** the complete physical structure of a person or animal (or sometimes, of a plant). **2.** a dead person or animal; corpse. **3.** the physical structure of person or animal (not including the limbs and head); trunk. **4.** the central structure or main part of a thing: *the body of a vehicle; the body of a speech; the body of the population.* **5.** a mass of matter: *a body of water.* **6.** any of the larger objects in space, as a sun, moon, or planet. **7.** *Colloq.* a person. **8.** a number of things or people taken as a whole: *a governing body; a large body of friends.* **9.** strength of flavor, etc.: *wine of a good body.* **10.** flesh or physical substance (as opposed to *spirit* or *soul*). **11.** *Agric.* the quality possessed by woollen fibre when it appears full and thick. **12. keep body and soul together,** to remain alive. ◇*v.t.* **13.** to represent in bodily form (usu. fol. by *forth*). [OE *bodig*]

body corporate, *n. Law.* a body, equivalent to a company, consisting of the owners of a

body corporate

block of home units under a strata title, acting as its governing body.

bodyguard /'bɒdigad/, *n.* a person or a group of people acting as a personal guard for a high official, etc.

body language, *n.* communication through body movement, facial expression, etc., rather than through words.

body politic, *n.* the people of a nation considered as forming a single political body under an organised government.

bodywork /'bɒdiwɜk/, *n.* the outer shell of a car body.

Boer /bɔ/, *n.* 1. a South African of Dutch extraction. ◇*adj.* 2. of or pertaining to the Boers. [D: peasant, countryman]

Boer War, *n.* 1. a war in which Great Britain fought against the Transvaal and Orange Free State, 1899-1902. 2. a war between Great Britain and the Transvaal, 1880-81.

bog /bɒg/, *n., v.*, **bogged, bogging.** ◇*n.* 1. (an area of) wet, spongy ground, with soil formed mainly of decayed vegetable matter. 2. *Colloq.* a toilet. ◇*v.t., v.i.* 3. to make or become stuck (oft. fol. by *down*): *This homework is bogging me down; The car bogged down in mud.* [Irish or Gaelic: soft] —**boggy,** *adj.*

Bogan /'bougən/, *n.* a river which rises near Parkes in western NSW and flows in a north-westerly direction to join the Barwon River near Bourke. 590 km.

Bogart /'bougat/, *n.* **Humphrey De Forest,** 1899-1957, US film actor, esp. noted for his anti-hero roles in gangster and detective films such as *The Maltese Falcon* (1941) and *The Big Sleep* (1946).

bogey /'bougi/, *n., pl.* **bogeys.** *Golf.* a score of one over par. [from *The Bogey Man,* a popular song c. 1908, thought of as a feared and invincible opponent]

boggle /'bɒgəl/, *v.i.*, **-gled, -gling.** 1. to show or feel fear, surprise, etc.: *Her eyes boggled at his words.* 2. to be unwilling to go on, as from fear: *The horse boggled at the jump.* [var. of *bug* BUGBEAR]

bogie[1] /'bougi/, *n.* 1. a low truck or trolley. 2. one of a pair of trucks supporting a railway engine, carriage, etc. [? var. of BOGY]

bogie[2] /'bougi/, *n.* 1. a swim. 2. a swimming hole. [Aboriginal]

Bogong /'bougɒŋ/, *n.* 1. **Mount,** a mountain in north-eastern Victoria; the state's highest peak; popular ski resort. 1986 m. 2. (*l.c.*) Also, **bugong.** a large, dull-colored Australian moth sometimes used as food. [Aboriginal: high plains]

bogus /'bougəs/, *adj.* false; counterfeit. [orig. uncert.]

bogy /'bougi/, *n., pl.* **bogies.** 1. an evil spirit; hobgoblin. 2. anything that frightens or continually annoys one. [from obs. *bog*]

bohemian /bou'himiən/, *n.* 1. a person, esp. an artist or a writer, who lives and acts without regard for convention. ◇*adj.* 2. relating to or typical of bohemians. —**bohemianism,** *n.*

Bohr theory /bɔ θɪəri/, *n.* the theory of atomic structure in which the electrons are described as moving in separate orbits about a central nucleus. [named after Niels *Bohr,* 1885-1962, Danish physicist; Nobel prize for physics 1922]

boil[1] /bɔɪl/, *v.i.* 1. to change from liquid to gas by being heated, bubbling as gas rises to the surface of the liquid. 2. to be stirred up like boiling liquid: *The sea was boiling.* 3. to be stirred up by angry feeling. 4. to contain, or be contained in, a liquid that boils: *The billy is boiling; The potatoes are boiling.* 5. to feel very hot. ◇*v.t.* 6. to cause to boil. 7. to cook by boiling. ◇*v.* 8. **boil down, a.** to reduce by boiling. **b.** to shorten. 9. **to boil down to,** to have as the basic element: *The question boils down to this.* 10. **to boil over, a.** to overflow while boiling. **b.** to be unable to control excitement, anger, etc. ◇*n.* 11. the act or condition of boiling. [ME, from L]

boil[2] /bɔɪl/, *n.* a painful, pus-filled, inflamed sore, caused by infection. [OE *bȳ*]

boiler /'bɔɪlə/, *n.* 1. a closed vessel in which water, etc., is heated to produce steam or other vapor for heating or for driving engines, etc. 2. a tank for supplying or storing hot water in the home. 3. a chicken which is fit to be eaten only when boiled.

boilermaker /'bɔɪləmeɪkə/, *n.* a person who makes boilers or other industrial metal objects.

boilersuit /'bɔɪləsut/, *n.* a one-piece garment of strong material for rough work.

boiling point, *n.* 1. the temperature at which a liquid boils at a given pressure. 2. a high state of excitement or emotion.

boisterous /'bɔɪstrəs/, *adj.* 1. rough and noisy. 2. (of waves, weather, wind, etc.) rough and stormy. [ME; orig. unknown]

Bo Ju'i /bou dʒu'i/, *n.* AD 772-846, Chinese poet, who established many literary reforms such as using everyday language to write poetry or social protest. Formerly, **Po Chü-i.**

bold /bould/, *adj.* 1. without fear; ready to take risks. 2. without shame or modesty. 3. rude or disrespectful. 4. standing out clearly to the eye: *bold handwriting.* 5. *Print.* (of type, etc.) with heavy lines in bold face. [OE *b(e)ald*]

bold face, *n. Print.* type that has thick, heavy lines, as the headwords in this dictionary. —**bold-face,** *adj.*

Boldrewood /'bouldəwud/, *n.* **Rolf** (*Thomas Alexander Browne*), 1826-1915, English-born Australian novelist; major work *Robbery Under Arms* published in three volumes in 1888.

bole /boul/, *n.* the stem or trunk of a tree. [ME, from Scand]

bolero /bə'lɛərou, bə'lɪərou/, *n., pl.* **-ros.** 1. (the music for) a Spanish dance in triple time. 2. a short jacket ending above or at the waistline. [Sp]

Boleyn /bə'lɪn, 'bʊlɪn/, *n.* **Anne,** 1507-36, second wife of Henry VIII of England; mother of Elizabeth I.

Bolingbroke /ˈbɒlɪŋbrʊk/, n. surname of **Henry IV** of England.

Bolivia /bəˈlɪviə/, n. an inland republic in central South America, bordered by Chile, Peru, Brazil, Paraguay and Argentina; a Spanish colony before independence in 1825. Pop. 6 429 000 (1985 est.). 1 098 581 km². Languages: Spanish, Quechua and Aymará. Currency: peso. Cap.: Sucre (legal), La Paz (administrative). — **Bolivian**, n., adj.

boll /boʊl/, n. the rounded seed vessel or pod of a plant, as of flax or cotton. [var. of BOWL¹]

bollard /ˈbɒlɑd/, n. **1.** a strong post to prevent vehicles from going up on footpaths or traffic islands. **2.** Naut. a post on which a ship's ropes are tied. [? BOLE + -ARD]

Bolshevik /ˈbɒlʃəvɪk/, n., pl. **Bolsheviks, Bolsheviki. 1.** (in Russia, 1903-17) a member of the more radical majority of the Social Democratic Party, advocating abrupt and forceful seizure of power by the proletariat. **2.** a member of a communist party. **3.** (offensive) any person with radical socialist ideas. Also, **bolshevik**. [Russ, from *bolshe* greater, more, with allusion to the majority (Russ *bolshinstvo*) of the Russian Social Democratic Party at the 1903 congress] — **bolshevism**, n.

Bolshoi Ballet /ˌbɒlʃɔɪ ˈbæleɪ/, n. the principal ballet company of Moscow. [from the *Bolshoi* Theatre, Moscow]

bolster /ˈboʊlstə/, n. **1.** a long, ornamental pillow. **2.** something like a bolster in shape or use. **3.** a support. ◇v.t. **4.** to support with or as if with a pillow (something weak, unworthy, etc.) (oft. fol. by *up*): *This success will bolster up your pride.* [OE *bolster*]

bolt /boʊlt/, n. **1.** a sliding bar which fastens a door, gate, etc. **2.** the part of a lock which slides out with the action of the key to fasten a door, etc. **3.** a strong, threaded, metal pin, oft. with a head, which, with a nut, holds things together. **4.** a length of cloth woven at one time. **5.** a sudden movement or escape; dash. **6.** an arrow, esp. one for a crossbow. **7.** a flash of lightning; thunderbolt. **8. bolt out of/from the blue**, a sudden and unexpected happening. ◇v.t. **9.** to fasten with a bolt. **10.** to swallow (food) quickly or without chewing. ◇v.i. **11.** to run away suddenly, oft. because of fear. ◇adv. **12. bolt upright**, stiffly and completely upright. [OE] — **bolter**, n.

Bolte /ˈbɒlti/, n. **Sir Henry Edward**, 1908-90, Australian state politician; premier of Victoria 1955-72.

Boltzmann's constant /ˌboʊltsmænz ˈkɒnstənt/, n. Phys. fundamental constant relating macroscopic and microscopic thermodynamics, equal to the ratio of the gas constant to Avogadro's number or 1.380 622 x 10⁻²³ joule per kelvin. Symbol: k [named after Ludwig Boltzmann, 1844-1906, Austrian physicist]

bolus /ˈboʊləs/, n. Med. **1.** a round mass of medicine, larger than an ordinary pill. **2.** a lump of chewed food, swallowed all at once.

Bomaderry /ˈbɒmədɛri/, n. a town on the Shoalhaven River south of Wollongong in NSW; railway terminus of the Illawarra line. Pop. (with Nowra) 19 553 (1986).

bomb /bɒm/, n. **1.** a hollow container filled with an explosive charge, for dropping, throwing or setting off with a timing device. **2.** Colloq. an old car. **3. go like a bomb**, Colloq. to go successfully or rapidly. ◇v.t. **4.** to attack or destroy with a bomb or bombs. **5.** Colloq. to fail; perform badly at: *He bombed the exam.* ◇v.i. **6.** to fail (oft. fol. by *out*): *She bombed out in the test.* [F, from It, from L: booming sound, from Gk]

bombard /bɒmˈbɑd/, v.t. **1.** to attack with heavy guns or bombs. **2.** Phys. to direct a stream of high-speed particles towards. **3.** to attack continuously: *to bombard someone with questions*. [ME, from OF: cannon, from L: loud noise] — **bombardment**, n.

bombast /ˈbɒmbæst/, n. high-sounding and oft. insincere words; verbiage. [F, from L *bombyx* silkworm, silk, from Gk] — **bombastic**, adj.

Bombay /bɒmˈbeɪ/, n. a port in western India on the Arabian Sea; the capital of Maharashtra state and the largest city in India. Pop. 8 243 504 (1981).

bomber /ˈbɒmə/, n. **1.** a person who throws or places bombs. **2.** an aeroplane which carries and drops bombs.

bombora /bɒmˈbɔrə/, n. (a dangerous current over) a hidden reef of rocks. [Aboriginal]

bombshell /ˈbɒmʃɛl/, n. **1.** a bomb. **2.** something causing surprise and shock: *His death was a bombshell.* **3.** a very attractive woman.

bona fide /ˌboʊnə ˈfaɪdi/, adj. **1.** Also, **bona-fide**. without falseness; genuine. ◇n. **2. bona-fides**, something that proves genuine intention or position. [L]

bonanza /bəˈnænzə/, n. an occasion bringing wealth or good luck. [Sp: fair weather, prosperity, from L *bonus* good]

Bonaparte family /ˈboʊnəpɑt/, n. a Corsican family who rose to prominence through the influence of Napoleon I, Emperor of France. **1. Joseph**, 1768-1844, king of Naples and Spain; brother of Napoleon I. **2. → Napoleon I. 3. Lucien**, 1775-1840, Prince of Canino; brother of Napoleon I. **4. Louis**, 1778-1846, king of Holland; brother of Napoleon I and father of Napoleon III. **5. Jérôme**, 1784-1860, king of Westphalia; brother of Napoleon I. **6. → Napoleon III**. Italian, **Buonaparte**.

bonbon /ˈbɒnbɒn/, n. **1.** a type of small sweet or lolly. **2.** a paper roll twisted at each end and containing a gift, joke, etc., which makes a small explosion when pulled. Also, **bon bon, bon-bon**. [F]

bond /bɒnd/, n. **1.** something that binds, fastens, or holds together: *a bond of feeling*; *the bonds of a prisoner*. **2.** any binding written agreement, such as a promise to work for a certain time made when accepting a scholarship. **3.** Law. **a.** a written admittance of an amount owed. **b.** a written agreement in which someone released by a court promises to be of good behavior or avoid a certain kind of behavior for a specified period. **4.** the state of taxable goods kept in storage until tax is paid: *goods in bond*. **5.** a certificate of government debt to an individual, usu. at a fixed rate of interest. **6.** → **bond money. 7.** a substance that causes particles to stick; binder. **8.** *Chem.* any connection between atoms in any molecule, or between atoms and molecules in any substance. See **ionic, covalent, hydrogen, dative bond. 9.** → **bond paper. 10.** *Bldg Trades.* an arrangement of stones or bricks in a wall, etc., made by overlapping them in order to bind them strongly. ◇*v.t.* to hold or join with a bond. **11.** to put (goods, a person) in or under bond. **12.** *Finance.* to place a bonded debt on; mortgage. **13.** *Bldg Trades.* to cause (bricks, etc.) to hold together firmly by overlapping them. ◇*v.i.* **14.** to hold together by being bonded, as bricks in wall. [ME]

Bond /bɒnd/, *n.* **Alan**, born 1938 in England, Australian businessman; leader of the syndicate which issued the successful America's Cup challenge in 1983.

bondage /'bɒndɪdʒ/, *n.* **1.** slavery; unfree servitude. **2.** the condition of being under the control of an outside force.

Bondaian /bɒn'daɪən/, *n.* a cultural period of Aboriginal development recognised in eastern Australia and reaching a climax about 1600 years ago (it follows the Capertian but overlaps to some extent). [from BONDI]

bonded /'bɒndəd/, *adj.* **1.** secured by or consisting of bonds: *a bonded debt*. **2.** placed in bond: *bonded goods*. **3.** (of textiles) bound by fibres onto a prepared backing material.

bond energy, *n.* the energy needed to separate two atoms joined by a bond.

Bondi /'bɒndaɪ/, *n.* a beach and suburb in Sydney, NSW; tourist attraction. [Aboriginal *Boondi* sound of waves breaking on the beach *or* sound of tumbling waters]

Bondi point /'bɒndaɪ/, *n. Archaeol.* a sharpened stone flake typical of the Bondaian period of Aboriginal development. Also, **Bondai point**.

bondman /'bɒndmən/, *n., pl.* **-men. 1.** a male slave. **2.** *Old Eng Law.* a villein. Also, **bondsman, bondservant**.

bond money, *n.* money additional to rent which a person pays when first renting a property and which is held as security against damage or failure to pay rent.

bond paper, *n.* a type of white paper of high quality.

bond store, *n.* a building for the storage of goods on which tax has not yet been paid.

bone /boʊn/, *n., v.,* **boned, boning.** ◇*n.* **1.** *Anat., Zool.* any of the separate pieces of hard tissue skeleton of which a vertebrate consists. **2.** any similar substance, such as ivory, whalebone, etc. **3.** a piece of a bone with meat on it, as food. **4.** something made of bone. ◇**5.** Some special uses are:
bare bones, the most important parts or facts in the most simple form: *the bare bones of an argument*.

bone of contention, a matter which causes disagreement.
have a bone to pick, to have a matter to complain about.
feel in one's bones, to have a strong feeling without any apparent reason.
make no bones about, to be absolutely honest about.
point the bone at, 1. *Colloq.* to wish bad luck upon. **2.** *Anthrop.* (among tribal Aborigines) to cause the death of (a guilty person) by pointing a bone at him.
◇*v.t.* **6.** to take out the bones of: *to bone a fish*.
◇*v.* **7. bone up**, *Colloq.* to study hard; get information (fol. by *on*). [OE *bān*]

bone china, *n.* a type of fine china in which ash from burned bones is used.

bonfire /'bɒnfaɪə/, *n.* a large fire in an open place. [earlier *bonefire*; heaps of wood and bones were burned at certain old festivals]

bongo /'bɒŋgoʊ/, *n., pl.* **-gos, -goes**. one of pair of small drums, played by beating with the fingers. [Amer Sp]

bonhomie /bɒn'ɒmi/, *n.* friendliness; sociable behavior. [F: good man]

bonkers /'bɒŋkəz/, *adj. Colloq.* mad, crazy.

Bonn /bɒn/, *n.* a city in western Germany, in North Rhine-Westphalia, on the Rhine; capital of West Germany 1949–90; replaced as capital of the reunified Germany by Berlin in 1991; remains as seat of government, with administration gradually being transferred to Berlin. Pop. 291 439 (1987 est.).

Bonnard /bɒ'na/, *n.* **Pierre**, 1867–1947, French impressionist painter.

Bonner /'bɒnə/, *n.* **Neville Thomas**, born 1922, Australian politician; first Aboriginal to hold a seat in Federal Parliament; resigned from Liberal Party 1983 and stood unsuccessfully as an independent.

bonnet /'bɒnət/, *n.* **1.** a woman's outdoor head covering, tied under the chin. **2.** any of other types of hoods or protective coverings, esp. the metal cover over the engine of a motor vehicle. [ME, from OF: cap]

bonny /'bɒni/, *adj.,* **-ier, -iest. 1.** looking healthy and pretty. **2.** *Scot.* fine (oft. used ironically). Also, **bonnie**. [ME]

bonsai /'bɒnsaɪ/, *n.* **1.** the practice, orig. Japanese, of growing very small examples of trees and shrubs by skilful cutting back of roots and branches. **2.** a tree or shrub so grown. [Jap. *bon* bowl, pot + *sai* to plant]

bonus /'boʊnəs/, *n.* **1.** something given or paid in addition to what is due or expected. **2.** a sum of money paid to a shareholder, employee, etc. in addition to a regular dividend or pay. **3.** *Stock Exchange.* also, **bonus issue**, a free issue of shares to shareholders of a company. **4.** *Insurance.* dividend. [L: (adj.) good]

bon voyage /ˌbɒ vwaˈjaʒ, vɔɪˈjaʒ/, *interj.* pleasant trip. [F]

bony /'boʊni/, *adj.,* **bonier, boniest. 1.** of or like bone. **2.** full of bones: *a bony fish*. **3.** (of a person) thin, or having large bones.

Bonynge /ˈbɒnɪŋ/, n. **Richard**, born 1930, Australian pianist and conductor; appointed Musical Director of the Australian Opera in 1976; husband of Joan Sutherland.

bonzer /ˈbɒnzə/, adj. Colloq. excellent or pleasing. Also, **bonza**.

boo /buː/, interj., v., **booed**, **booing**. ◇interj. **1.** (an exclamation used to express disapproval, etc., or to frighten). ◇v.i., v.t. **2.** to cry 'boo' (at someone).

boob /buːb/, n. Colloq. **1.** a foolish person. **2.** Also, **boo-boo**. a foolish mistake. **3.** Colloq. a woman's breast. ◇v.i **4.** to make a mistake. [See BOOBY]

boobook /ˈbuːbʊk/, n. a small brownish owl with white-spotted back and wings, widespread in Australia and NZ.

booby /ˈbuːbi/, n., pl. **-bies**. **1.** a foolish person. **2.** a large seabird with long wings and a wedge-shaped tail as the **brown booby**, of tropical seas and northern Australian coastline. [probably from Sp. *bobo* fool]

booby prize, n. a prize given in fun to the worst performer in a game or competition.

booby trap, n. **1.** an object so placed as to fall on or trip up a person who is off guard. **2.** *Mil.* a hidden bomb or mine placed so that it will be set off by an unknowing person.

boodie rat /ˈbuːdi ræt/, n. See **rat-kangaroo**.

boogie-woogie /ˌbʊɡi-ˈwʊɡi, ˌbuːɡi-ˈwuːɡi/, n. a piano style using jazz and blues melodic variations over a continuously repeated bass pattern. Also **boogie**.

book /bʊk/, n. **1.** a written or printed work of some length, on sheets of paper, fastened or bound together. **2.** a number of sheets of writing paper bound together and used for making notes, keeping accounts, etc. **3.** a main division of a literary work. **4. the (Good) Book**, the Bible. **5.** a record of bets, as on a horserace. **6.** a set of tickets, cheques, stamps, etc., bound together like a book. **7. bring to book**, to demand an explanation from. **8. by (the) book**, with formal correctness. **9. in someone's good / bad books**, in / out of favor with someone. **10. take a leaf out of someone's book**, to follow someone else's example. **11. throw the book at**, Colloq. **a.** to bring all possible charges against (an offender). **b.** to punish severely. ◇v.t. **12.** to make an advance order for (tickets, rooms, etc;); reserve. **13.** to engage the services of (a performer, etc.) **14.** to record the name of (someone) in order to charge him with an offence: *The police booked him for speeding*. ◇v.i. **15.** to record one's name at a hotel, etc. (fol. by *in*). **16.** to make an advance order for tickets, services, etc. [OE *bōc*]

bookcase /ˈbʊkkeɪs/, n. a set of shelves for books.

Booker Prize /ˈbʊkə praɪz/, n. a UK literary award made annually for a work of fiction by a resident of the UK or the Commonwealth, including former Commonwealth countries.

booking /ˈbʊkɪŋ/, n. **1.** an advance order for rooms, tickets, etc. **2.** an engagement to perform.

bookish /ˈbʊkɪʃ/, adj. **1.** much given to reading or study. **2.** based on books rather than real life; academic: *bookish language; a bookish viewpoint*. **—bookishness**, n.

bookkeeping /ˈbʊkkiːpɪŋ/, n. the work or skill of keeping records of business accounts. **—bookkeeper**, n.

bookmaker /ˈbʊkmeɪkə/, n. a person who takes the bets of others, as on horses in racing. **—bookmaking**, n.

Book of Common Prayer, the service book of the Church of England, essentially adopted but changed in details by other churches of the Anglican communion.

book value, n. *Econ.* an amount which a trader shows in the accounts as the value of something.

bookworm /ˈbʊkwɜːm/, n. **1.** a small insect that eats books. **2.** a person who is exceptionally interested in reading or study.

boom[1] /buːm/, v.i. **1.** to make a deep, resounding noise. **2.** to develop, progress or flourish, as a business, city, etc. ◇v.t. **3.** to give forth with booming sound (usu. fol. by *out*): *The clock boomed out 12*. ◇n. **4.** a loud, deep sound as of waves or distant guns. **5.** a rapid increase in business activity, etc. ◇adj. **6.** caused by a boom (def. 5): *boom prices*. [imit.]

boom[2] /buːm/, n. **1.** *Naut.* a long pole or spar, used to extend the foot of certain sails. **2.** a pole or spar used to guide or lift weights from a derrick. **3.** a chain or cable, etc., used to confine floating timber, etc. **4.** (in a television or film studio) a movable arm supporting a camera, microphone or floodlight above the actors. **5. lower the boom on**, to refuse; prohibit: *He lowered the boom on further discussion*. [D: tree, beam]

boomer /ˈbuːmə/, n. any large male kangaroo, esp. the great grey or forester. [Warwickshire d.]

boomerang /ˈbuːməræŋ/, n. **1.** a curved piece of wood used as a missile by the Aborigines, one form of which can be thrown so as to return to the thrower. ◇v.i. **2.** to return or spring back: *The argument boomeranged; The cheque boomeranged.* [Aboriginal]

boon /buːn/, n. an advantage enjoyed; something to be thankful for; blessing. [ME, from Scand]

Boone /buːn/, n. **Daniel**, 1735–1820, US pioneer, esp. in Kentucky.

boor /bɔː, bʊə/, n. **1.** a rude or bad-mannered person. **2.** a peasant, esp. uneducated; rustic. [D *boer* peasant] **—boorish**, adj. **—boorishly**, adv. **—boorishness**, n.

boost /buːst/, v.t. **1.** to lift, raise, or increase: *to boost prices*. **2.** *Aeron., Motor Vehicles*. → **supercharge** (def. 1). ◇n. **3.** an upward push. **4.** an aid that helps a person to succeed. [b. BOOM[1] and HOIST]

booster /ˈbustə/, *n.* **1.** *Elect.* a device for increasing or decreasing circuit voltage. **2.** *Astronautics.* **a.** a rocket engine used as the main supply of thrust in a missile flight. **b.** any stage of a missile containing this engine. **3.** *Pharm.* a substance, usu. injected, for maintaining a person's immunity to a particular infection.

boot[1] /but/, *n.* **1.** a heavy shoe, reaching up to, or above the ankle. **2.** a place for baggage, usu. at the rear of a car or bus. **3.** a kick. [ME, from OF; of Gmc orig.]

boot[2] /but/, *n.* **1. to boot**, into the bargain, in addition. ◇*v.i.* **2.** *Obs.* or *Poetic.* to be of profit; advantage: *It boots not to complain.* [OE *bōt* advantage]

boot[3] /but/, *v.t.* to put a computer into an operational state. Also, **boot up**.

booth /buð, buθ/, *n.* **1.** a stall or lightweight structure for use at a market or fair. **2.** a small compartment for a telephone, film projector, etc. [ME, from Scand]

Booth /buð, buθ/, *n.* **1. John Wilkes**, 1838–65, member of a British family of US stage actors; assassin of Abraham Lincoln. **2. William**, 1829–1912, English preacher; founder of the Salvation Army.

bootleg /ˈbutleg/, *n., v.,* **-legged, -legging**, *adj. Chiefly US.* ◇*n.* **1.** an alcoholic drink secretly and unlawfully made, sold, or carried. ◇*v.t., v.i.* **2.** to make, sell, or carry (spirits or other goods) illegally. ◇*adj.* **3.** made, sold, or carried unlawfully. [arose from the practice of concealing illegal spirits in the leg of the boot] **–bootlegger**, *n.*

bootstrap /ˈbutstræp/, *n.* **1.** a loop sewn on the side of a boot to assist in pulling it on. **2.** *Computers.* a program by which a computer can be made to translate more difficult programs.

booty /ˈbuti/, *n., pl.* **-ties.** anything stolen in war by violence and robbery; plunder. [late ME]

booze /buz/, *n., v.,* **boozed, boozing**. *Colloq.* ◇*n.* **1.** an alcoholic drink. ◇*v.i., v.t.* **2.** to drink too much. [ME, from MD] **–boozer**, *n.* **–boozy**, *adj.*

bora /ˈbɔrə/, *n.* a sacred piece of ground where special initiation ceremonies are performed by Aborigines. [Aboriginal]

borage /ˈbɒrɪdʒ, ˈbɔ-/, *n.* a plant with hairy leaves and stems, used in salads. [ME, from OF: stuff, from ML: wool]

borate /ˈbɔreɪt/, *n. Chem.* See **-ate**[2].

borax /ˈbɔræks/, *n. Chem.* a white, crystalline sodium borate, used in the manufacture of glass, etc. [ML, from Ar, from Pers]

Bordeaux /bɔˈdoʊ/, *n.* a seaport in southwestern France, in Gironde department, on the river Garonne; famous wine centre. Pop. 201 965 (1982).

border /ˈbɔdə/, *n.* **1.** an edge; side; margin. **2.** a boundary line that separates one country, state, region or district from another. **3.** an ornamental trimming or design around the edge of a printed page, garment, etc. **4.** a narrow piece of ground in a garden, oft. enclosing a special section. ◇*v.t.* **5.** to make a border about; adorn with a border. **6.** to form a border or boundary to. **7.** to lie on the border of; adjoin. [ME, from OF: side, edge; of Gmc orig.]

Border Leicester /ˌbɔdə ˈlestə/, *n.* a popular British long-wool sheep highly valued in Australia for cross breeding with the merino.

borderline /ˈbɔdəlaɪn/, *adj.* **1.** on or near the edge or boundary. **2.** uncertain; indeterminate. **3.** (in an examination, etc.) qualifying or failing to qualify by narrow margin: *Her final result was a borderline pass.* **4.** on the verge of madness or indecency. ◇*n.* **5.** a boundary.

Border Ranges, *n.pl.* the mountain ranges on the eastern border between Qld and NSW.

bore[1] /bɔ/, *v.,* **bored, boring**, *n.* ◇*v.t.* **1.** to pierce (a solid substance) or make (a round hole, etc.) with an auger, drill, or other similar instrument. **2.** to force by persistent forward movement. ◇*n.* **3.** a hole made by boring, or as if by boring. **4.** a deep but small hole bored out of the earth to tap underground water supplies, esp. in dry country areas. **5.** the inside diameter of hollow cylindrical object, as of the barrel of a gun. [OE *borian*] **–borer**, *n.*

bore[2] /bɔ/, *v.,* **bored, boring**, *n.* ◇*v.t.* **1.** to weary by tedious repetition, dullness, unwelcome attentions, etc. ◇*n.* **2.** a dull, tiresome person. **3.** a person or job which annoys. [orig. unknown] **–boredom**, *n.* **–boring**, *adj.*

bore[3] /bɔ/, *v.* past tense of **bear**[1].

Boreas /ˈbɔriəs/, *n. Gk Myth.* the north wind, as personified or deified by the Greeks.

boree /bɔˈri/, *n.* → **myall**. [Aboriginal *booreah* fire]

borer /ˈbɔrə/, *n.* **1.** → **auger**. **2.** an insect that bores into wood.

Borg /bɔg/, *n.* **Björn** /bjɔn/, born 1956, Swedish tennis player, Wimbledon champion.

Borgia family /ˈbɔdʒə/, *n.* noble family originally from Valencia, Spain of considerable influence in church and political life in Renaissance Italy. **1. Alfonso de**, 1378–1458, founder of family in Italy; became Pope Callistus III; uncle of Rodrigo. **2. Rodrigo Lanzol**, 1431–1503, appointed cardinal by Alfonso de Borgia; later became Pope Alexander VI; father of Cesare and Lucrezia. **3. Cesare**, 1476–1507, Italian cardinal, military leader and politician; apparently the model for Machiavelli's *Prince*. **4. Lucrezia**, 1480–1519, notorious political intriguer and patron of culture; Duchess of Ferrara.

boric acid /ˈbɔrɪk ˈæsəd/, *n.* any of a group of acids derived from boron trioxide used as an antiseptic, preservative, and in fireproofing compounds, cosmetics, cements and enamels.

boride /ˈbɔraɪd/, *n.* a hard, heat-resistant compound. See **-ide**.

born /bɔn/, *adj.* **1.** brought into independent being or life, as from the womb. **2.** begun; founded; established. **3.** having from birth special qualities or character: *a born fool.* ◇*v.i.* **4.** past participle of **bear**[1], now normally replaced in all senses by **borne**.

borne /bɔn/, v. past participle of **bear**.

Borneo /'bɔniou/, n. an island in the western Pacific in the Malay Archipelago, divided into Kalimantan (Indonesian Borneo), the Malaysian states of Sabah and Sarawak, and Brunei. Pop. 10 920 606 (1985 est.); 751 100 km^2.

bornite /'bɔnaɪt/, n. a common mineral, copper iron sulfide, Cu$_5$FeS$_4$, an important ore of copper. [after I von *Born*, 1742–91, Austrian mineralogist. See -ITE^1]

boron /'bɔrɒn/, n. a non-metallic element present in borax, etc. *Symbol:* B; *at. no.:* 5; *at. wt:* 10.8.

boron carbide, n. a black crystalline solid, B$_4$C, the hardest known substance after the diamond, and used to form control rods in nuclear reactors. See -**ide**.

boronia /bə'rounɪə/, n. any of various Australian shrubs with small brown or pink flowers. [after It botanist Francesco *Borone*, 1769–94]

borough /'bʌrə/, n. 1. *Vic.* an area of land similar to a municipality in the other States of Australia. 2. *Brit.* an urban community incorporated by royal charter. [OE *burg* stronghold]

Borromini /borou'mini/, n. **Francesco** /fræn'tʃeskou/, 1599–1667, Italian architect.

borrow /'bɔrou/, v.t. 1. to take or obtain (a thing) on the promise to return it later. 2. to get from another, esp. a foreign, source; adopt: *English has borrowed words from many languages*. ◇v.i. 3. to borrow something: *Do not beg or borrow*. [OE *borg* a pledge] –**borrower**, n.

borsch /bɔʃ/, n. a Russian soup containing beetroot, served hot or cold. [Russ]

borstal /'bɔstl/, n. *Brit.* a home or reform centre for young offenders between ages of 16 and 21. [named after *Borstal*, village in Kent, where the first such reformatory is situated]

borzoi /'bɔzɔɪ/, n., pl. -**zois**. a large swift dog with a soft coat and a long, pointed nose; Russian wolfhound. [Russ: swift]

Bosch /bɔʃ/, n. **Hieronymus** /hɪə'rɒnəməs/, 1450?–1516, Dutch painter of bizarre allegorical works.

bosh /bɒʃ/, n. *Colloq.* complete nonsense; absurd or foolish talk or opinions. [Turk: empty, vain]

Bosnia-Herzegovina /bɒznɪə-heətsəgou.vinə/, n. a republic in south-eastern Europe; a constituent republic of Yugoslavia from 1946 until secession in 1991–92; a part of Serbia within Yugoslavia 1918–46; a part of Austria–Hungary 1908–18 and previously a Turkish province. Pop. 4 441 000 (1988 est.); 51 564 km^2. *Cap.:* Sarajevo. Also, **Bosnia-Hercegovina**, **Bosnia**.

bosom /'buzəm/, n. 1. the human breast, esp. of a woman. 2. the part of a garment which covers the breast. 3. the breast seen as representing feelings. 4. an enclosure formed by the breast and the arms: *She hugged him to her bosom*. ◇adj. 5. personal; intimate: *bosom friend*. [OE *bōsm*]

Bosporus /'bɒspərəs/, n. a strait between Europe and Asia, connecting the Black Sea and the Sea of Marmara. 29 km long. Also, **Bosphorus**.

boss^1 /bɒs/, n. *Colloq.* 1. a person who employs or superintends others; foreman; manager. 2. someone who controls a political or other group. ◇v.t. 3. to be master of or over; manage; direct; control. ◇v.i. 4. to be boss. [D *baas* master]

boss^2 /bɒs/, n. 1. *Bot, Zool.* a raised part on the body or on some organ of an animal or plant. 2. *Geol.* a knob-like mass of rock. 3. a small projection, ornamental in character. [ME, from OF]

bossy /'bɒsi/, adj., **bossier**, **bossiest**. *Colloq.* acting like a boss; domineering. [BOSS^1 + -Y^1]

Boston /'bɒstən/, n. a city in the US, capital of Massachusetts, in the eastern part; the largest city and seaport in New England. Pop. 573 600 (1986 est.). –**Bostonian**, adj., n.

Boston Tea Party, n. *US Hist.* a raid on British ships in Boston Harbor on 16 December 1773, in which colonists of Boston, disguised as Indians, threw tea into the harbor as a protest against British taxes on tea.

bosun /'bousən/, n. → **boatswain**.

Boswell /'bɒzwəl/, n. **James**, 1740–95, Scottish author; biographer of Samuel Johnson. –**Boswellian**, adj.

botanical /bə'tænɪkəl/, adj. relating to plants or the study of plants. [ML *botanicus* (Gk *botanikós*) + -AL^1]

botanical garden, n. (*oft. pl.*) a large garden, usu. open to public, where trees, shrubs and plants from many lands are grown and studied.

botany /'bɒtəni/, n., pl. -**nies**. 1. the science of plants; the branch of biology that deals with plant life. 2. the plant life of an area: *the botany of the Simpson Desert*. [ML *botanicus*, from Gk] –**botanist**, n.

Botany Bay, n. 1. a bay on the eastern coast of Australia, 8 km south of Sydney; site of James Cook's first landing in Australia; original destination of the First Fleet. ◇adj. 2. (formerly) of or pertaining to New South Wales. [named in recognition of the unique plants collected near the bay by Sir Joseph Banks]

botch /bɒtʃ/, v.t. 1. to spoil by poor work; bungle. 2. to do or say in a bungling manner. ◇n. 3. Also, **botch-up**. a clumsy or poor piece of work; a bungle: *His carpentry was a complete botch*. [ME *bocchen*; orig. uncert.] –**botcher**, n. –**botchery**, n.

both /bouθ/, adj., pron. 1. the one and the other; two together: *Give both dates*; *Both had been there*. ◇conj., adv. 2. alike; equally: *both men and women*; *He is both ready and willing*. [ME, from Scand]

bother /'bɒðə/, v.t. 1. to give trouble to; annoy; pester; worry. 2. to confuse; bewilder. ◇v.i. 3. to bother oneself. 4. to cause annoyance or trouble. ◇n. 5. a worried or perplexed state. ◇interj. 6. (a mild exclamation.) [orig. unknown]

bothersome /'bɒðəsəm/, adj. annoying; troublesome.

bo tree /ˈbou tri/, *n.* the sacred fig tree under which the Buddha is said to have originally reached enlightenment.

Botswana /bɒtˈswanə/, *n.* an inland republic in southern Africa, bordered by South Africa, Zimbabwe, Namibia and Zambia; a British protectorate before independence in 1966. Pop. 1 051 000 (1984 est.). 582 000 km². *Languages:* English and Setswana. *Currency:* pula. *Cap.:* Gaborone. Formerly, Bechuanaland.

Botticelli /bɒtəˈtʃɛli/, *n.* Sandro (*Alessandro di Mariano dei Filipepi*), 1447–1510, Florentine Renaissance painter.

bottle /ˈbɒtl/, *n., v.,* **-tled, -tling.** ◇*n.* **1.** a portable vessel with a neck or mouth, now commonly made of glass or plastic, used for holding liquids. **2.** the contents of a bottle: *a bottle of wine.* **3.** bottled milk for babies (opposed to *the breast*): *raised on the bottle.* ◇*v.t.* **4.** to put into or seal in a bottle; to preserve (fruit or vegetables) in bottles. ◇*v.* **5. bottle up**, to shut in or restrain closely: *to bottle up one's feelings.* [ME, from LL: BUTT⁴]

bottlebrush /ˈbɒtlbrʌʃ/, *n.* any species of the Australian plant callistemon, whose flower has spikes like a cylindrical brush.

bottled gas, *n.* → **liquefied petroleum gas.**

bottleneck /ˈbɒtlnɛk/, *n.* **1.** a narrow entrance or passage way. **2.** a place, or stage in a process, where progress becomes slow. **3.** a narrow part of road between two wide sections, esp. a place where traffic is likely to be held up. **4.** a slide made from the neck of a bottle and used for stopping the strings of a steel guitar.

bottler /ˈbɒtlə/, *n. Colloq.* something that excites admiration or approval: *You little bottler!*

bottom /ˈbɒtəm/, *n.* **1.** the lowest or deepest part of anything, opposite to the top: *the bottom of a hill; the bottom of the sea.* **2.** the place of least honor or achievement: *the bottom of the class.* **3.** the lowest gear of a motor; first gear. **4.** the underside: *the bottom of an iron.* **5.** *Naut.* the keel of a ship. **6.** *Colloq.* the buttocks. **7.** the basic part: *the bottom of my heart.* **8. at bottom**, in reality; fundamentally. ◇*v.t.* **9.** to provide with a bottom. **10.** to base or found (fol. by *on* or *upon*). **11.** to get to the bottom of; fathom. ◇*v.i.* **12.** to reach the bottom. ◇*adj.* **13.** lowest. **14.** fundamental: *the bottom cause.* [OE *botm*]

botulism /ˈbɒtjʊlɪzəm/, *n.* a disease of the nervous system caused by a toxin developed esp. in spoiled preserved and other foods, often causing death. [L *botulus* sausage + -ISM]

bouclé /ˈbukleɪ/, *n.* a yarn with loops, which produces a woven or knitted fabric with a rough appearance. [F]

boudoir /ˈbudwɑ/, *n.* a woman's private room. [F: pout, sulk]

bouffant /ˈbufɒ/, *adj.* puffed out; full, as sleeves, a hairstyle, or curtains. [F]

Bougainville /ˈbougənvɪl/, *n.* the largest of the Solomon Islands in the southern Pacific. Pop. 144 200 (1984 est.); 10 567 km². Chief town: Kieta. [named after Louis Antoine de *Bougainville*, 1729–1811, French scientist and explorer of the Pacific]

bougainvillea /bougənˈvɪliə/, *n.* a tropical plant with brightly colored bracts (leaves), widely grown in tropical and subtropical Australia. [See BOUGAINVILLE]

bough /bau/, *n.* a branch of a tree, esp. one of the larger, main branches. [OE: shoulder, bough]

bought /bɔt/, *v.* past tense and past participle of **buy.**

bouillon /ˈbujɒn/, *n.* a plain, clear stock or broth. [F: boil]

boulder /ˈbouldə/, *n.* a large, rounded rock worn smooth by weather. [short for *boulder stone*, ME *bulder-*, from Scand]

Boulder /ˈbouldə/, *n.* a town in southern WA, adjoining Kalgoorlie; mining. Pop. (with Kalgoorlie) 22 232 (1986). [named after the Great *Boulder*, an early mine]

boulevard /ˈbuləvad/, *n.* a broad avenue or street of a city, often lined with trees. [F, from MLG]

bounce /bauns/, *v.,* **bounced, bouncing,** *n.* ◇*v.i.* **1.** to move with a bound, and a rebound, as a ball: *The ball bounced back from the wall.* **2.** to burst cheerfully (*into* or *out of*): *to bounce into and out of a room.* **3.** *Colloq.* (of cheques) to be dishonored; to be returned unpaid. ◇*v.t.* **4.** to cause to bound or rebound: *to bounce a ball; to bounce a child up and down.* **5.** to persuade or convince (someone) by bluff. ◇*n.* **6.** a rebound or bound: *Catch the ball on the first bounce.* **7.** a sudden jump or leap. **8.** the ability to bounce; resilience. [ME: thump, from LG, *bums!* thump!]

bouncer /ˈbaunsə/, *n.* **1.** anything which bounces. **2.** *Colloq.* a person employed in a club, etc., to throw out disorderly people. **3.** *Cricket.* → **bumper.**

bouncing /ˈbaunsɪŋ/, *adj.* big, strong, or healthy: *a bouncing baby.*

bound¹ /baund/, *adj.* **1.** tied; in bonds: *a bound prisoner.* **2.** fastened within a cover, as a book. **3.** under an obligation, legally or morally: *bound to help.* **4.** determined or sure: *It is bound to happen.* **5.** constipated. [pp. of BIND]

bound² /baund/, *v.i.* **1.** to move by leaps; leap; jump; spring. **2.** to rebound, as a ball. ◇*n.* **3.** a jump; leap. [F: leap, orig., resound]

bound³ /baund/, *n.* **1.** (usu. *pl.*) limiting line, or boundary: *the bounds of space and time.* **2. out of bounds,** not to be entered; forbidden. ◇*v.t.* **3.** to limit as by bounds or boundaries. ◇*v.i.* **4.** to have boundaries (*on*); abut. [ME, from LL]

bound⁴ /baund/, *adj.* going or intending to go; destined (fol. by *for*): *This train is bound for Bathurst.*

-bound, a suffix used to mean: **1.** headed in the direction of: *westbound, homeward-bound.* **2.** kept in; restrained: *housebound.*

boundary /'baundri/, *n., pl.* **-ries,** *adj.* ◇*n.* **1.** something that indicates the bounds or limits: *the boundary of a property.* **2.** *Cricket.* **a.** the marked limits of a field used for a game. **b.** a stroke which sends the ball beyond those limits. ◇*adj.* **3.** *Phys.* surrounding the outside of a solid or liquid body.

bounteous /'bauntiəs/, *adj.* freely given; plentiful; abundant. [*bounte* (earlier var. of BOUNTY) + -OUS] —**bounteousness,** *n.*

bountiful /'bauntəfəl/, *adj.* **1.** generous in giving gifts or favors. **2.** abundant; ample: *a bountiful supply.*

bounty /'baunti/, *n., pl.* **-ties. 1.** whatever is given generously. **2.** a reward. **3.** a sum paid for killing animals said to be pests: *a dingo bounty.* [ME, from L: goodness]

Bounty /'baunti/, *n.* **HMS,** the ship captained by William BLIGH, on which the crew mutinied in 1789.

bounty system, *n.* (formerly) a system in which money was given as a bounty by the governor of a colony to a settler who helped a skilled person to come to live in the colony.

bouquet /bu'keɪ, bou'keɪ/, *n.* **1.** a bunch of flowers; nosegay. **2.** a smell typical of wine, brandy, etc; aroma. [F: bunch, clump of trees, from OF: wood]

bouquet garni /gɑ'ni, 'gani/, *n.* a bunch of herbs, usu. including bayleaf, thyme and parsley, used to give flavor to sauces, stews, etc.

bourbon /'bɜbən/, *n.* a type of whisky distilled from corn. [orig. the whisky produced in *Bourbon* County, Kentucky]

Bourbon /'bɔːbn/, *n.* a member of the last house of the French royalty, or of any of its branches, as the former royal family of Spain.

bourgeois /'buəʒwa, 'bu-/, *n., pl.* **-geois,** *adj.* ◇*n.* **1.** a member of the social class between the wealthy and the working class; middle class. ◇*adj.* **2.** belonging to or consisting of the middle class. [F]

bourgeoisie /buəʒwa'zi/, *n.* **1.** the bourgeois class. **2.** (in Marxism) the class opposed to the proletariat or working class. [F]

Bourke /bɜk/, *n.* a town and shire in north-western NSW, on the Darling River; a wool railhead. Pop. 3018 (1986). Formerly, **Eighteen Mile Point, Fort Bourke.** [named after Sir Richard *Bourke,* governor of NSW 1831–37]

bourn /bɔn/, *n.* **1.** a bound; limit. **2.** a destination; goal. **3.** a realm; domain. Also, **bourne.** [F *borne*]

bout /baut/, *n.* **1.** a contest, esp. a boxing or wrestling match; trial of strength. **2.** a period; spell: *a bout of illness.* [var. of obs. *bought* bend, turn, from BOW[1]]

boutique /bu'tik/, *n.* a small shop selling fashionable or luxury articles. [F]

bouzouki /bə'zuki/, *n.* a stringed musical instrument from Greece, related to the mandolin, played by plucking. [Modern Gk]

bovine /'bouvaɪn/, *adj.* **1.** relating to a genus of ruminant animals, both domestic and wild, with large stocky bodies and hollow, curved horns on top of the head. **2.** dull; stolid; ox-like. [L *bōs* ox]

bow[1] /bau/, *v.i.* **1.** to bend or curve downwards; stoop: *The trees bowed low.* **2.** to yield; submit: *to bow to the inevitable.* **3.** to bow in worship, reverence, respect, etc. **4.** to bend the head or body in greeting, etc. ◇*v.t.* **5.** bend or incline in respect, shame, or agreement: *to bow one's head.* **6.** to cause to stoop: *Age had bowed his head.* ◇*v.* **7. bow and scrape,** to be servant-like. **8. bow out,** to retire; leave the scene. ◇*n.* **9.** the inclination of the head or body in greeting, assent, or thanks. [OE *būgan*]

bow[2] /bou/, *n.* **1.** a piece of wood or other material easily bent by a string stretched between its ends, used for shooting arrows. **2.** a bend or curve: *a bow in the road.* **3.** a knot, as of ribbon, consisting of one or two loops and two ends. **4.** *Music.* a device, orig. curved, but now almost always straight, with horse hairs stretched upon it, designed for playing any stringed instrument. ◇*adj.* **5.** curved; bent like a bow: *bow legs.* ◇*v.t.* **6.** *Music.* to perform by means of a bow upon a stringed instrument. ◇*v.i.* **7.** *Music.* to play with a bow. [OE *boga*]

bow[3] /buə, bou/, *n.* **1.** (*sometimes pl.*) the front or forward part or end of a ship, boat, airship, etc. **2.** the rower nearest the bow. [LG or D]

bow compass, *n. Tech. Drawing.* one of set of compasses whose legs are joined by a bow-shaped piece.

bowel /'bauəl/, *n.* **1.** (*usu. pl.*) the parts of the alimentary canal below the stomach; intestines or entrails. **2.** the inner parts: *the bowels of a ship.* [ME, from L *botulus* sausage]

Bowen /'bouən/, *n.* a town and port in northern Qld on Port Denison. Pop. 7705 (1986).

Bowen Basin, *n.* a coal-bearing area in central Qld, stretching from Collinsville 650 km south to Moura; about 100 km wide.

bower /'bauə/, *n.* **1.** a leafy shelter; arbor. **2.** *Archaic.* a country house; cottage. **3.** *Poetic.* a woman's private room; chamber; boudoir. ◇*v.t.* **4.** to enclose in bower. [OE *būan* dwell]

bowerbird /'bauəbɜd/, *n.* **1.** any of various birds of Australia and the island of New Guinea, related to the birds of paradise, which build bower-like structures to conduct their courtship. **2.** a person who collects useless objects.

Bowes-Lyon /'bouz-laɪən/, *n.* **Elizabeth Angela Marguerite,** born 1900, wife of George VI; mother of Elizabeth II.

Bowie /'boui/, *n.* **David** (*David Robert Jones*), born 1947, British pop singer and composer; an important influence in experimental rock music.

bowie knife, *n.* a heavy sheath-knife having a long, single-edged blade. [named after James *Bowie,* 1796–1836, US pioneer]

bowl[1] /boul/, *n.* **1.** a rather deep, round dish or basin, used mainly for holding liquids, food, etc. **2.** the contents of a bowl. **3.** anything shaped like a bowl: *the bowl of a pipe*. [ME *bolle*, from OE, c. Icel *bolli*]

bowl[2] /boʊl/, *n*. **1.** a heavy biased or weighted ball used in the game of bowls. **2.** a delivery of a ball in bowling. ◊*v.i.* **3.** to roll a bowl, as in a game of bowls. **4.** *Cricket*. to deliver a ball with a straight arm in such a way that it bounces once before reaching the bat. ◊*v.t.* **5.** to throw or roll (a ball, hoop, etc.). **6.** to upset; disconcert (fol. by *over*). **7.** *Cricket*. to dismiss (a batsman) by delivering a ball which breaks the batsman's wicket. [ME *boule*, from OF: ball, from L *bulla* bubble]

bowleg /ˈboʊleg/, *n*. a leg curved or bowed outwards below knee. — **bow-legged**, *adj*.

bowler[1] /ˈboʊlə/, *n*. a hard felt hat with rounded crown and a narrow brim. [BOWL[1] + -ER[2]]

bowler[2] /ˈboʊlə/, *n*. someone who bowls.

bowline /ˈboʊlɪn, ˈboʊlən/, *n*. a knot which forms a non-slipping loop. Also, **bowline knot**.

bowls /boʊlz/, *n*. **1.** → **lawn bowls**. **2.** Also, **carpet bowls**. a game similar to lawn bowls, but played indoors. **3.** skittles, ninepins, or tenpin bowling.

bowyang /ˈboʊjæŋ/, *n. Colloq*. a string or strap tied around a trouser leg below the knee. [Brit d. *bowy-yanks* leather leggings]

box[1] /bɒks/, *n*. **1.** a case or receptacle, usu. rectangular, of wood, metal, cardboard, etc., with a lid or removable cover. **2.** a quantity contained in a box. **3.** a present or gift: *a Christmas box*. **4.** a collection of money for charity, etc. **5.** a semi-private compartment in a theatre, opera house, etc. **6.** (in a court of law) a stand or pew reserved for a witnesses, the accused or the jury. **7.** a driver's seat on a horse-drawn carriage. **8.** a stall for horses. **9.** a page of a book divided by lines, a border, or white space. **10.** *Mach*. an enclosing, protecting, or hollow part; casing; chamber; bush; socket. **11.** *Baseball*. the space where the batter stands (or, less often, the pitcher or coach). **12. one out of the box**, an outstanding person or thing. **13. the box**, *Colloq*. a television set. **14. the whole box and dice**, the whole; the lot. ◊*v.t.* **15.** to put into a box. **16.** to enclose or confine as if in a box (oft. fol. by *up* or *in*). **17.** to mix (separate mobs of sheep) (fol. by *up*). ◊*v*. **18. box in**, **a.** to build a box around. **b.** to surround; imprison: *to be boxed in by traffic*. [special use of BOX[3]]

box[2] /bɒks/, *n*. **1.** a blow as with the hand or fist. ◊*v.t.* **2.** to strike with the hand or fist, esp. on the ear. ◊*v.i.* **3.** to fight with the fists; spar. [ME; orig. unknown] — **boxing**, *n*.

box[3] /bɒks/, *n*. **1.** an evergreen shrub or small tree much used for ornamental borders, hedges, etc., and yielding a hard, durable wood. See **boxwood**. **2.** any type of gum tree with a characteristic close, short-fibred bark. **3.** any of various other species of shrubs or trees. [ME and OE, from L *buxus*, from Gk *pyxos*]

boxer /ˈbɒksə/, *n*. **1.** a person who boxes; pugilist; prize fighter. **2.** a smooth-coated, medium-sized brown dog related to the bulldog and the terrier.

Boxer Rebellion, *n*. an unsuccessful rebellion in Peking (Beijing) in 1900 of members of a nationalistic Chinese secret society (the **Boxers**) against foreign interests in China.

box-frame /ˈbɒks-freɪm/, *n. Bldg Trades*. a fixed, unmovable frame, usu. of steel, used as basis for certain structures.

box girder, *n*. a hollow girder which is square or rectangular in cross-section.

Boxing Day /ˈbɒksɪŋ deɪ/, *n*. the day after Christmas Day, observed as a holiday. [traditionally the day on which Christmas boxes or presents were given to employees]

box jellyfish, *n*. a type of jellyfish found in tropical seas, the common Australian species being highly poisonous; sea wasp. Also, **box jelly**.

box number, *n*. **1.** the number of a box at a post office, used as a postal address. **2.** the number given in a newspaper advertisement as the address to which replies may be directed, care of the newspaper office.

box office, *n*. **1.** an office in which tickets are sold at a theatre, etc. **2.** the ability of an entertainment or a performer to attract an audience: *This show will be good box office*. ◊*adj*. **3.** relating to the sales of tickets: *a box office success*.

box spanner, *n*. a hollow tube shaped at one or both ends to fit a nut, and turned by a bar through the diameter.

boxwood /ˈbɒkswʊd/, *n*. a hard, fine-grained wood much used for wood engravers' blocks, musical and mathematical instruments, etc.

boy /bɔɪ/, *n*. **1.** a male child, from birth to the beginning of youth. **2.** an immature young man. **3.** a young servant. [ME; orig. uncert.] — **boyish**, *adj*.

boycott /ˈbɔɪkɒt/, *v.t.* **1.** to join together in preventing dealings with, so as to frighten or force: *to boycott a person, foreign goods, etc.* **2.** to stop buying or using: *to boycott a commercial product*. ◊*n*. **3.** an act or instance of boycotting. [from Captain Charles C *Boycott*, 1832–97, land agent for the Earl of Erne, County Mayo, Ireland, ostracised by the tenants]

Boyd[1] /bɔɪd/, *n*. **Benjamin**, 1803?–51, Australian banker, whaler and pastoralist, born in England; established whaling station at Twofold Bay, NSW.

Boyd[2] /bɔɪd/, *n*. a ship seized and burnt by Maoris at Whangaroa, NZ, in 1809; 60 people killed; known as the **Boyd Massacre**.

Boyd family, *n*. a family of Australians distinguished in the arts; members include **1. Arthur Merric**, 1862–1940, Australian watercolor painter, born in NZ. **2.** his fourth son, **Martin à Beckett**, 1893–1972, writer, born in Switzerland, settled in England; author of *A Difficult Young Man* (1955) and *The Cardboard Crown* (1952). **3. Arthur Merric Bloomfield**, grandson of Arthur Merric, born 1920, painter,

Boyd Family   121   **braid**

sculptor and potter. **4. Guy Martin à Beckett**, grandson of Arthur Merric, 1923–88, sculptor.

Boydtown /'bɔɪdtaʊn/, *n.* a township set up by Benjamin Boyd at Twofold Bay, NSW, in 1843; only ruins remain.

Boyle /bɔɪl/, *n.* **1. Raelene Ann**, born 1951, Australian sprinter; Commonwealth Games gold medallist. **2. Robert**, 1627–91, English chemist and physicist; known for his work on the physical properties of gases.

Boyle's law /'bɔɪlz lɔ/, *n.* the principle that, at a constant temperature, the volume taken up by a given quantity of ideal gas is inversely proportional to the pressure upon the gas. See **gas laws**. [named after Robert BOYLE]

Boyne /bɔɪn/, *n.* **1.** a river in eastern Ireland, near which William III defeated James II (1690). 113 km. **2.** a river in central coastal Qld, rising north of Monto and flowing north to enter the sea near Gladstone. About 120 km.

boy scout, *n.* →**scout**.

boysenberry /'bɔɪzənbɛri, -bri/, *n., pl.* **-ries.** a blackberry-like fruit with a flavor similar to raspberries. [named after R *Boysen*, US botanist]

Br, *Chem. Symbol.* bromine.

bra /bra/, *n.* →**brassiere**. [abbrev.]

Brabham /'bræbəm/, *n.* **Sir Jack** (*John Arthur Brabham*), born 1926, Australian racing car driver and designer; triple world champion.

brace /breɪs/, *n., v.*, **braced, bracing.** ◇*n.* **1.** something that holds parts together or in place, e.g. a clamp. **2.** anything that makes steady. **3.** *Mach.* a device for holding and turning tools for boring or drilling. **4.** *Bldg Trades.* a piece of timber, metal, etc., used to support or position another piece or section of framework. **5.** (*oft. pl.*) *Dentistry.* a round or flat metal wire placed against the surfaces of teeth, used to straighten them. **6.** *Med.* an appliance for supporting a weak joint or joints. **7.** (*pl.*) straps or bands worn over the shoulders for holding up trousers. **8.** one of two characters, { or }, for connecting written or printed lines. ◇*v.t.* **9.** to furnish, fasten, or strengthen with a brace. **10.** to fix firmly; make steady. [ME *brase(n)* from OF *bracier* embrace]

brace and bit, *n.* a boring tool consisting of a bit and a handle for rotating it.

bracelet /'breɪslət/, *n.* an ornamental band for the wrist or arm. [ME, from L: arm]

brachio-, a word part meaning 'arm', as in *brachiopod*. Also, (before a vowel), **brachi-**. [NL, combining form representing L *brāchium*, or its source, Gk *brachiōn*]

brachiopod /'breɪkiəpɒd, 'bræk-/, *n.* a mollusc-like marine animal with dorsal and ventral shells.

brachy-, a word part meaning 'short'. [Gk, combining form of *brachýs*]

brachycome /bræki'koʊmi/, *n.* an Australian daisy with blue to purple flowers, cultivated as a garden plant.

bracing /'breɪsɪŋ/, *adj.* strengthening; invigorating.

bracken /'brækən/, *n.* **1.** a large, coarse fern, which is widespread throughout higher rainfall areas of Australia. **2.** a clump of ferns. [ME, from Scand]

bracket /'brækət/, *n.* **1.** a support of wood, metal, etc., oft. in the shape of a right angle, placed under a shelf or the like. **2.** *Archit.* an ornamental support for a statue, etc. **3.** either of two sets of signs [or], (or) used to group words or figures together. **4.** a grouping of persons, musical items, etc.: *low income bracket; a bracket of songs.* ◇*v.t.* **5.** to furnish with or support by a bracket or brackets. **6.** to place within brackets; enclose. **7.** to group together; classify. [F, from Pr, or Sp, from L: breeches, of Celtic orig.]

brackish /'brækɪʃ/, *adj.* slightly salty; having a salty flavor. [D *brak* + -ISH¹]

bract /brækt/, *n.* a specialised leaf or leaflike part, usu. found at the base of a flower.

Bradfield /'brædfild/, *n.* **John Job Crew**, 1867–1943, Australian civil engineer; supervising engineer of the Sydney Harbor Bridge.

Bradfield Plan, *n.* a water conservation scheme, conceived by JJC Bradfield, involving the damming of the Burdekin and other northern Qld rivers on the coastal side of the Great Dividing Range, and transporting the water to inland areas by tunnel.

Bradley /'brædli/, *n.* **William**, 1757–1833, British naval officer; in Australia, assisted in surveying Port Jackson and Broken Bay; surveyed Norfolk Island.

Bradman /'brædmən/, *n.* **Sir Donald George**, born 1908, Australian cricketer; Test captain 1936–48; regarded as Australia's greatest batsman.

Brady /'breɪdi/, *n.* **Matthew**, 1799–1826, English-born bushranger in Van Diemen's Land.

brag /bræg/, *v.*, **bragged, bragging**, *n.* ◇*v.i.* **1.** to use boastful language; boast. ◇*n.* **2.** a boast. [Scand] —**bragger, braggart**, *n.*

Bragg /bræg/, *n.* **1. Sir William Henry**, 1862–1942, British physicist, in Australia 1885–1908; noted for study of crystal structure. **2.** his Australian-born son, **Sir (William) Lawrence**, 1890–1971, British physicist; shared Nobel prize for physics (1915) with his father.

Brahma /'bramə/, *n.* **1.** (in philosophical Hinduism) the Supreme Being, Source and final Goal of all being; Atman, the World Soul. **2.** (in later Hinduism) the first member of the trinity, also known as 'The Creator'. See **Vishnu** and **Shiva**. [Skt]

Brahman /'bramən/, *n., pl.* **-mans. 1.** a member of the highest, or priestly, caste among Hindus. **2.** a breed of cattle originating in India and used widely in Australia for crossbreeding. Also, **Brahmin**. [Skt] —**Brahmanic, Brahmanical**, *adj.*

Brahms /bramz/, *n.* **Johannes** /joʊ'hænəs/, 1833–97, German composer.

braid /breɪd/, *v.t.* **1.** to weave together strips or strands of; plait. ◇*n.* **2.** a braided length of hair; plait. **3.** a narrow band or tape, formed by weaving together silk, cotton, wool, or other material, used as a trimming for garments, etc. [OE *bregdan* move to and fro, weave]

braille /breɪl/, *n.* a system of printing using raised points which can be felt and interpreted by blind people, thus enabling them to read. [named after Louis *Braille*, 1809-52, its inventor]

brain /breɪn/, *n.* **1.** (*sometimes pl.*) the soft mass of greyish and whitish nerve substance which fills the cranium of man and vertebrates; centre of sensation, body coordination, thought, emotion, etc. **2.** (*usu. pl.*) understanding; intelligence. **3.** *Colloq.* a highly intelligent or well-informed person. **4. pick someone's brains**, to use another person's work or ideas to one's own advantage. [OE *bregen*] **–brainy**, *adj.*

brainstorm /ˈbreɪnstɔːm/, *n.* **1.** a sudden, violent attack of madness. **2.** *Colloq.* a sudden idea, answer to a problem, etc.

brainwash /ˈbreɪnwɒʃ/, *v.t.* to indoctrinate so intensely that beliefs, esp. political, are changed. **–brainwashing**, *n.*

braise /breɪz/, *v.t.*, **braised, braising.** to cook (meat or vegetables) by frying in fat and then cooking slowly in very little liquid. [F: hot charcoal; of Gmc orig.]

brake[1] /breɪk/, *n., v.*, **braked, braking.** ◇*n.* **1.** (*sometimes pl.*) any mechanical device for stopping the motion of a wheel, motor, or vehicle, mainly by means of friction or pressure. **2.** a tool or machine for breaking up flax or hemp, to separate the fibre. ◇*v.t.* **3.** to slow or stop the motion of (a wheel, motor vehicle, etc.) as by a brake. **4.** to process (flax or hemp) by crushing it in a brake. ◇*v.i.* **5.** to use or apply a brake. **6.** to slow down. [ME, from MLG and/or MD; akin to BREAK]

brake[2] /breɪk/, *n.* a place densely covered with bushes, shrubs, brambles, or cane; thicket. [cf. MLG *brake*]

brake drum, *n.* the steel or cast-iron drum on the wheel of a motor vehicle, against which a **brake shoe** is pressed to stop the wheel.

bramble /ˈbræmbəl/, *n.* any rough prickly plant such as the common blackberry. [OE *brōm* broom] **–brambly**, *adj.*

bran /bræn/, *n.* the ground husk of wheat or other grain, after separation from flour. [ME, from OF]

branch /brɑːntʃ/, *n.* **1.** *Bot.* a division or subdivision of the stem of a tree, shrub, etc. **2.** a limb, offshoot, etc.: *the branches of a deer's horns*. **3.** any member or part of a body or system; section; subdivision: *various branches of learning*. **4.** a local division of a company, store, library, etc. **5.** a particular line of family descent. **6.** *Geog.* a (tributary) stream. ◇*v.i.* **7.** to put forth branches; spread in branches. **8.** to separate into branches; diverge. **9. branch out**, to develop in a new direction. ◇*v.t.* **10.** to divide as if into branches. [ME, from LL *branca* paw, claw]

Brancusi /brænˈkuːzi, brɒnˈkuːʃi/, *n.* **Constantin**, 1876-1957, French sculptor born in Romania, noted for the simplicity of his abstract forms.

brand /brænd/, *n.* **1.** a trademark or trade name to identify a product. **2.** a kind, grade, or make, as shown by a brand, stamp, etc. **3.** a mark made by burning, etc., to indicate the ownership of cattle. **4.** any mark of disgrace; stigma. **5.** an iron for branding. **6.** *Archaic or Poetic.* a sword. ◇*v.t.* **7.** to mark with a brand. **8.** to name as being disgraceful; stigmatise. [OE; akin to BURN] **–brander**, *n.*

Brand /brænd/, *n.* **Mona**, born 1915, Australian playwright and poet.

Brandenburg Gate /ˌbrændənbɜːg ˈgeɪt/, *n.* a triumphal arch in Berlin standing on the border between East and West Berlin.

brandish /ˈbrændɪʃ/, *v.t.* to shake or wave, as a weapon; flourish. [ME, from OF *brand* sword; of Gmc orig.]

Brando /ˈbrændoʊ/, *n.* **Marlon**, born 1924, US film actor; films include *A Streetcar Named Desire* (1951), *On the Waterfront* (1954), and *The Godfather* (1972).

Brandt /brɑnt/, *n.* **Willi** /ˈvɪli/, 1913-92, German politician; chancellor of West Germany 1969-74; Nobel Peace prize 1971.

brandy /ˈbrændi/, *n., pl.* **-dies.** a spirit distilled from the fermented juice of grapes or, sometimes, of apples, peaches, plums, etc. [short for *brandywine*, from D *brandewijn* burnt (i.e. distilled) wine]

Braque /brɑk, bræk/, *n.* **Georges** /ʒɔːʒ/, 1881-1963, French painter; founder of cubism with Picasso.

Brasch /bræʃ/, *n.* **Reverend Rabbi Rudolph**, born 1912, Australian rabbi and writer.

brash /bræʃ/, *adj.* **1.** bold; impudent; forward. **2.** hasty; rash. [orig. obscure]

brass /brɑs/, *n.* **1.** an alloy of copper and zinc which is long-lasting and easily worked. **2.** an article made of brass. **3.** a collective term for musical instruments of the trumpet and horn families, blown through a funnel or cup mouthpiece, and not having a reed. **4.** a memorial plaque. **5.** a metallic yellow color. **6.** Also, **top brass**. *Colloq.* high-ranking people in an organisation, esp. in the army. **7.** *Colloq.* too much confidence; impudence; effrontery. **8.** *Colloq.* money. ◇*adj.* **9.** of brass or brass instruments. [OE *bræs*] **–brassy**, *adj.*

brassiere /ˈbræziə, -siə/, *n.* a woman's undergarment which supports the breasts. [F]

brat /bræt/, *n.* a child (used usu. in annoyance). [cf. d. *brat* rag, trash, OE *bratt* cloak]

bravado /brəˈvɑdoʊ/, *n.* a show of confidence and boldness, often pretended. [Sp See BRAVE]

brave /breɪv/, *adj.*, **braver, bravest**, *n., v.*, **braved, braving**. ◇*adj.* **1.** possessing or showing courage. **2.** making a fine appearance: *a brave new world*. ◇*n.* **3.** a North American Indian or other fierce warrior. ◇*v.t.* to meet or face courageously: *to brave misfortunes*. **4.** to dare; defy: *to brave the storm*. ◇*v.* **5. brave it out**, to ignore or resist all opposition. [F,

brave from It *bravo* brave, from Sp: vicious (first applied to bulls)] **—bravery, braveness,** *n.*

bravo /'bra:vou/, *interj.*, *n.*, *pl.* **-vos.** ◇*interj.* **1.** well done! good! ◇*n.* **2.** a shout of 'bravo!' [It, properly adj. See BRAVE]

bravura /brə'vurə, -'vju:-/, *n.* **1.** *Music.* a showy passage or piece, requiring great skill. **2.** a display of daring. [It: bravery, spirit]

brawl /brɔ:l/, *n.* **1.** a noisy quarrel. ◇*v.i.* **2.** to quarrel angrily and noisily; wrangle. **3.** to make a noise, as water flowing over a rocky bed. [OE *brōthan* go to ruin]

brawn /brɔ:n/, *n.* **1.** well-developed muscles. **2.** muscular strength. **3.** meat, esp. of a pig, boiled, and pressed. [ME, from OF, from Gmc] **—brawny,** *adj.*

bray /breɪ/, *n.* **1.** a rough, breathy cry, as of the donkey. **2.** any similar sound, as a human laugh. ◇*v.i.* **3.** (of a donkey, trumpet, etc.) to make a loud, harsh cry or sound. [ME, from OF]

braze /breɪz/, *v.t.*, **brazed, brazing.** to join (pieces of brass, steel, etc.) by heating and applying a high melting solder. [? F *braser,* from *braise* live coals. See BRAISE]

brazen /'breɪzən/, *adj.* **1.** made of or like brass. **2.** shameless or cheeky: *His brazen conduct will lose him the job.* ◇*v.t.* **3.** to face with boldness (fol. by *out*): *She must brazen out his questions.* [OE *bræs* brass]

brazier /'breɪziə/, *n.* a metal container for holding burning fuel, as for heating a room. [F *braise* live coals]

Brazil /brə'zɪl/, *n.* a republic in central and north-eastern South America, the fifth largest country in the world; a Portuguese colony before independence in 1822. Pop. 141 302 000 (1987 est.); 8 511 965 km². *Language:* Portuguese. *Currency:* cruzeiro. *Cap.:* Brasília. Portuguese, **Brasil.** **—Brazilian,** *n.*, *adj.*

brazil nut, *n.* the triangular seed of a Brazilian tree, a popular eating nut.

breach /briːtʃ/, *n.* **1.** the act or result of breaking; a break. **2.** a gap made in a wall, etc.; rift; fissure. **3.** a failure to observe or keep (a law, trust, faith, promise, etc.) **4.** a breaking of a friendship. ◇*v.t.* **5.** to make a breach or opening in. [ME, from OF, from Gmc]

bread /bred/, *n.* **1.** a food baked from flour, water or milk and usu. yeast. **2.** food; means of support; livelihood. **3.** *Colloq.* money; earnings. **4. break bread,** to share food. [OE *brēad*]

bread-and-butter /,bred-ən-'bʌtə/, *adj.* **1.** providing the means of living. **2.** *Colloq.* matter-of-fact. **3.** expressing thanks, as a letter or telephone call to a host.

breadfruit /'bredfru:t/, *n.* a large, round, starchy fruit yielded by a tree of the Pacific islands, baked for food.

breadline /'bredlaɪn/, *n.* **1.** a line of poor people waiting to receive free food. **2. on the breadline,** living at the barest level, usu. supported by public help.

breadth /bredθ/, *n.* **1.** *Maths.* the measure across a surface or solid, as opposed to its length and (in the case of a solid) thickness; width. **2.** a piece of something as measured by its width: *a breadth of cloth.* **3.** a freedom from narrowness; liberality: *breadth of understanding.* **4.** size in general; extent. [OE *brædu* + -TH¹]

breadwinner /'bredwɪnə/, *n.* one who earns a living for a family.

break /breɪk/, *v.*, **broke** (old form **brake**), **broken** (old form **broke**), **breaking,** *n.* ◇*v.t.* **1.** to divide into parts violently. **2.** to dishonor: *to break a law or promise.* **3.** to fracture a bone of: *to break a leg.* **4.** to tear; wound: *to break the skin.* **5.** to discontinue abruptly: *to break the silence.* **6.** to destroy the regularity or arrangement of: *to break the timetable; to break ranks.* **7.** to put an end to; overcome: *The army will break the king's rule.* **8.** to interrupt: *to break the monotony.* **9.** to do better than; outdo: *to break a record.* **10.** to make known: *to break the news.* **11.** to disable, destroy or ruin, often financially. **12.** to train away from a habit (fol. by *of*). **13.** *Cricket.* to strike so as to knock the bails from (a wicket) **14.** *Elect.* stop the flow of (an electric current). ◇*v.i.* **15.** to separate into pieces; esp. suddenly and violently; become broken; burst. **16.** to end relations (fol. by *up* or *with*): *She will break with him; They will break up.* **17.** *Law.* to open or force one's way into a house, store, etc.: *to break and enter.* **18.** (of a wave) to fall forward after reaching a peak. **19.** to free oneself (oft. fol. by *away*): *to break away from the police.* **20.** (of a news item) to appear in print: *The story will break tomorrow.* **21.** to force a way (fol. by *in, through, out* etc.). **22.** to burst (fol. by *in, forth, from,* etc.). **23.** to come suddenly into notice. **24.** (of a dawn, day, etc.) to begin. **25.** to change a state or activity (fol. by *into*): *to break into song.* **26.** to give way under pressure (oft. fol. by *down*). **27.** (of the heart) to be crushed esp. by grief: *He thought his heart would break.* **28.** (of the voice) to vary between two registers, esp. in grief or during adolescence. **29.** (in a race) to start before the signal to do so has been given. ◇**30.** Some special uses are:

break away, 1. (in racing) to start too early. **2.** *Football.* to outrun the defending players and run towards the opposing goal. **3.** to move and keep away from another person. **4.** → secede.

break camp, to pack up tents and continue a march.

break down, 1. to destroy by breaking. **2.** overcome. **3.** to analyse. **4.** to collapse. **5.** to stop working. **6.** to dilute.

break even/square, to have one's profits equal to one's losses.

break in, 1. to interrupt. **2.** to make suitable by using: *break in a new pair of shoes.* **3.** to make (a horse) used to being handled. **4.** to enter a house or the like by force.

break into, 1. to interrupt. **2.** to enter (a house or the like) by force.

break new ground, to attempt a new area of activity.

break off, 1. to separate by breaking. **2.** to put a stop to; discontinue. **3.** to stop suddenly.

break out, 1. *Pathol.* (of certain diseases) to appear in eruptions. **2.** (of prisoners, etc.) to escape.

break service, *Tennis.* to win a game when receiving the service.

break up, **1.** to separate; finish; disband. **2.** (of a school, etc.) to finish a term, for holidays. **3.** *Colloq.* to explode into laughter. ◊*n.* **31.** a separation of parts; a breaking; a fracture, rupture, or bursting. **32.** an opening made by breaking; a gap. **33.** an attempt to escape: *a break for freedom.* **34.** an interruption of continuity; suspension. **35.** a sudden change, as in sound or direction. **36.** *Colloq.* an opportunity; chance. **37.** a short rest, as from work. **38.** an instrumental solo in jazz and rock music. **39.** any continuous run, esp. of good fortune. **40.** a premature start in racing. **41.** *Cricket, etc.* change in direction of a ball when it bounces. **42. give (someone) a break**, *Colloq.* to give (someone) a fair chance. **43. those are the breaks**, *Colloq.* that is how life is. [OE *brecan*] —**breakable**, *adj.*

breakage /ˈbreɪkɪdʒ/, *n.* **1.** an act of breaking. **2.** an allowance for loss or damage of articles broken.

breakaway /ˈbreɪkəweɪ/, *n.* **1.** the act of breaking away, as of a political or similar group. **2.** *Rugby Union.* either of two players who pack down on either side of the back row in a scrum. **3.** a panic rush of a mob of cattle, horses, etc. ◊*adj.* **4.** of that which has broken away.

breakdown /ˈbreɪkdaʊn/, *n.* **1.** a ceasing to work properly, as of a machine. **2.** a failure of health. **3.** an analysis of statistical figures. **4.** *Chem.* → **decomposition**.

breaker /ˈbreɪkə/, *n.* a wave that breaks or dashes into foam. [BREAK + -ER¹]

breakfast /ˈbrekfəst/, *n.* **1.** the first meal of the day. ◊*v.i.* **2.** to eat breakfast. [ME *brek* break + *fast* FAST²]

break-in /ˈbreɪk-ɪn/, *n.* the unlawful entry of a building, usu. by force.

breakneck /ˈbreɪknek/, *adj.* dangerous; hazardous: *breakneck speed.*

breakthrough /ˈbreɪkθru/, *n.* **1.** *Mil.* an advance through a defence into the unorganised areas in the rear. **2.** any development, as in science, technology, or political relations, which allows further progress.

breakwater /ˈbreɪkwɔtə/, *n.* a structure built to break the force of waves, as before a harbor.

bream /brim/, *n.* **1.** in Australia, any of various sea fishes, popular as food and for sport, as the **black** or **silver bream**, of eastern Australian waters. **2.** elsewhere, any of various freshwater fishes with a flat, deep body. [ME, from OF, of Gmc orig.]

breast /brest/, *n.* **1.** *Anat., Zool.* the upper front part of the body; the chest. **2.** *Anat., Zool.* a milk gland, esp. of a woman, or of female animals. **3.** that part of a garment which covers the chest. **4.** the breast, thought of as the base of thoughts and feelings. **5.** *Mining.* the face or heading at which the working is going on. **6. make a clean breast of**, to make a full confession of. ◊*v.t.* **7.** to face; meet boldly or advance against: *The ship breasted the waves.* [OE *brēost*]

breastbone /ˈbrestboʊn/, *n.* → **sternum**.

breastfeed /ˈbrestfid/, *v.t., v.i.,* **-fed, -feeding.** to feed (a child) on milk from the breast.

breastplate /ˈbrestpleɪt/, *n.* armor for the breast.

breast stroke, *n. Swimming.* a stroke in which both hands move forwards, outwards and back from the chest while the legs move in a frog-like manner.

breath /breθ/, *n.* **1.** *Anat.* the air taken in and breathed out in respiration. **2.** respiration (breathing) or a single respiration: *There was no breath in the body; She took a deep breath.* **3.** the ability to breathe, esp. freely: *He was short of breath.* **4.** a whisper. **5.** a light current of air. **6.** the moisture produced by the condensation of breath. **7.** breath carrying some odor. **8. below** or **under one's breath**, in a whisper. **9. out of breath**, short of breath, as after exercise; breathless. **10. take one's breath away**, to surprise; astound. [OE *brǣth* smell, exhalation]

breathalyser /ˈbreθəlaɪzə/, *n.* device to determine the amount of alcohol in the breath.

breathe /brið/, *v.,* **breathed** /brɪðd/, **breathing.** ◊*v.i.* **1.** to draw in and give out air; respire. **2.** to speak softly. **3.** to pause, as for breath; take rest (only in the infinitive): *Give me a chance to breathe.* **4.** to blow lightly. **5.** to live; exist. **6. breathe freely**, to be freed from anxiety or fear; relax. ◊*v.t.* **7.** to inhale and exhale (air) in respiration. **8.** to say softly; whisper: *She breathed her promises.* **9.** to express; manifest: *The valley breathed contentment.* **10.** to exhale: *dragons breathing fire.*

breather /ˈbriðə/, *n.* a pause for rest.

breathless /ˈbreθləs/, *adj.* **1.** out of breath: *The blow left him breathless.* **2.** with the breath held, as in expectancy: *breathless listeners.* **3.** without movement, as the air.

breathtaking /ˈbreθteɪkɪŋ/, *adj.* causing extreme excitement: *a breathtaking performance.*

Brecht /brekt/, *n.* **Bertolt** /ˈbeətɒlt/, 1898–1956, German dramatist and poet; noted for his style of epic theatre and themes of greed and corruption in capitalist society; in 1949 founded East Germany's **Berliner Ensemble** theatre company.

bred /bred/, *v.* past tense and past participle of **breed**.

breech /britʃ/, *n.* **1.** the lower part of anything, as the buttocks of the human body. **2.** the metal behind the bore of a cannon, or the barrel of a gun. [OE *brēc*, pl.]

breech birth, *n.* a birth in which the baby's buttocks, instead of its head, appear first.

breeches /ˈbrɪtʃəz/, *n.pl.* trousers covering the hips and thighs. [BREECH + -ES]

breed /brid/, *v.,* **bred, breeding,** *n.* ◊*v.t.* **1.** to produce (offspring). **2.** to obtain (offspring) by the mating of parents. **3.** to raise (livestock, etc.). **4.** to bring about; produce: *Dirt breeds disease.* ◊*v.i.* **5.** to produce

breed offspring. **6.** to be produced; grow; develop: *They will breed under perfect conditions.* ◇*n.* a relatively similar group within a species, developed by man. **7.** race; strain. **8.** sort; kind. [OE *brōd* brood] —**breeder**, *n.*

breeding /'briːdɪŋ/, *n.* **1.** the rearing of animals to improve their quality. **2.** the production of new plant forms by selection and crossing. **3.** the results of training seen in behavior; good manners.

breeze /briːz/, *n., v.,* **breezed, breezing.** ◇*n.* **1.** a wind or current of air. **2.** *Colloq.* an easy task: *It's a breeze.* ◇*v.i.* **3.** *Colloq.* to move in an easy-going manner (oft. fol. by *along, in*). ◇*v.* **4. breeze through,** *Colloq.* to perform without effort. [Sp (and Pg) *briza*]

breezy /'briːzi/, *adj.,* **breezier, breeziest.** **1.** windy. **2.** fresh; sprightly; cheerful. —**breezily**, *adv.* —**breeziness**, *n.*

Bremen /'breɪmən, 'bremən/, *n.* **1.** a small state in northern West Germany. Pop. 654 600 (1987 est.); 404 km². **2.** the capital of this state; a port on the river Weser; a member of the Hanseatic League. Pop. 521 976 (1987 est.).

Brennan /'brenən/, *n.* **Christopher John**, 1870–1932, Australian symbolist poet and scholar; works include the collections *Poems 1913* (1914) and *A Chant of Doom, and Other Verses* (1918).

Brent of Bin Bin /ˌbrent əv 'bɪn bɪn/, *n.* pseudonym used by Miles Franklin, Australian novelist, for six of her novels.

brethren /'breðrən/, *n.pl.* **1.** *Archaic.* plural of **brother**. **2.** fellow members.

Breton /'bretn/, *n.* **1.** a native or inhabitant of Brittany. **2.** the Celtic language of Brittany. —*adj.* **3.** relating to Brittany, the Bretons, or their language. [F. See BRITON]

breve /briːv/, *n.* **1.** a mark (ˇ) placed over a vowel to show that it is pronounced short, as in *bŭt*. **2.** *Music.* the longest modern note, equal to two semibreves. [It, from L *brevis* short]

brevi-, a word part meaning 'short'. [L, combining form of *brevis*]

brevity /'brevəti/, *n., pl.* **-ties. 1.** shortness of time; briefness: *the brevity of human life.* **2.** shortness and clearness of speech; conciseness. [L *brevis* short]

brew /bruː/, *v.t.* **1.** to make (beer, etc.) from malt, etc., by soaking, boiling, and fermentation. **2.** to make (tea) (oft. fol. by *up*). **3.** to bring about; cause: *to brew mischief.* ◇*v.i.* **4.** to brew beer, etc. **5.** (of tea, etc.) to be in preparation: *The tea is brewing now.* **6.** to be forming or gathering (oft. fol. by *up*): *Trouble was brewing.* ◇*n.* **7.** a quantity brewed in a single process. **8.** a drink prepared by brewing. [OE *brēowan*] —**brewer**, *n.*

brewery /'bruːəri/, *n., pl.* **-ries.** an establishment for brewing beer, etc.

Brezhnev /'brɛʒnɛf/, *n.* **Leonid Ilyich** /liːəniːd 'ɪlitʃ/, 1906–82, Soviet politician, born in Ukraine; first secretary of the Soviet Communist Party, 1964–82; president of the Soviet Union 1977–82.

briar /'braɪə/, *n.* **1.** a white heath, of southern Europe, whose woody root is used for making tobacco pipes. **2.** such a pipe. [F: heath, from LL derivative of Gallic *brūcus* heather]

bribe /braɪb/, *n., v.,* **bribed, bribing.** ◇*n.* **1.** a payment given or promised for illegal behavior (often to an official person). **2.** anything given to persuade. ◇*v.t.* **3.** to give or promise a bribe to. **4.** to influence by bribing. ◇*v.i.* **5.** to give bribes. [ME] —**bribable**, *adj.* —**bribery**, *n.* —**briber**, *n.*

Bribie Island /braɪbi 'aɪlənd/, *n.* an island in Moreton Bay, Qld, north of Brisbane; 30 km long and 8 km wide; a popular seaside resort. Pop. 4789 (1981).

bric-a-brac /'brɪk-ə-bræk/, *n.* various articles of old-fashioned, ornamental, or other interest. Also, **bric-à-brac**. [F]

brick /brɪk/, *n.* **1.** a rectangular block of clay, usu. hardened and dried in a kiln, and used for building, etc. **2.** such blocks collectively. **3.** any similar block. **4.** *Colloq.* a helpful person. ◇*v.t.* **5.** to lay, line, wall, or build with brick (oft. fol. by *up*). [ME, from MD]

Brickfield Hill /ˌbrɪkfiːld 'hɪl/, *n.* an area of southern inner Sydney, NSW. [former site of brickfields]

brick veneer, *n.* (a building with) a single layer of bricks facing a timber framework.

bridal /'braɪdl/, *adj.* relating to a bride or a wedding. [OE *brȳd* bride + *ealo* ale, feast]

bride /braɪd/, *n.* a woman just married, or about to be married. [OE *brȳd*]

bridegroom /'braɪdgrum/, *n.* a man just married, or about to be married. [OE *brȳd* bride + *guma* man (c. L *homo*)]

bridesmaid /'braɪdzmeɪd/, *n.* a young woman who attends the bride at a wedding.

bridge¹ /brɪdʒ/, *n., v.,* **bridged, bridging.** ◇*n.* **1.** a structure standing over a river, road, etc., providing a way of passage for cars, etc. **2.** *Naut.* a raised platform on a ship for the officer in charge. **3.** *Anat.* the upper line of the nose. **4.** *Dentistry.* a replacement for a missing tooth or teeth, which may be fixed or removable. **5.** *Music.* a thin support across which the strings of a stringed instrument are stretched. **6.** *Elect.* an instrument for measuring electrical resistance. ◇*v.t.* **7.** to make a bridge over; span. [OE *brych*]

bridge² /brɪdʒ/, *n. Cards.* a game, based on whist, in which the whole pack of 52 cards is dealt among two pairs of players, each bidding to win a number of tricks. The two types are **auction bridge** and **contract bridge.** [orig. uncert.]

Bridge of Sighs, *n.* a bridge in Venice through which prisoners are said to have been led for trial in the ducal palace.

Bridges /'brɪdʒɪz/, *n.* **Robert**, 1844–1930, English poet; poet laureate 1913–30.

Bridget /'brɪdʒət/, *n.* **Saint**, 453–523, Irish abbess; a patron saint of Ireland. Also, **Bride, Brigid, Brigit.**

Bridgewater /ˈbrɪdʒwɒtə/, n. a town in south-eastern Tas on the Derwent River, near Hobart. Pop. 4485 (1986).

bridging finance /ˈbrɪdʒɪŋ ˌfaɪnæns/ n. a short-term loan at high interest.

bridle /ˈbraɪdl/, n., v., **-dled, -dling.** ◇n. 1. leather strapping around the head of a horse, consisting usu. of a head strap, bit, and reins, and used to control the animal. 2. anything that constrains or pulls back. ◇v.t. 3. to put a bridle on. 4. to control as with a bridle; restrain; curb. ◇v.i. 5. to draw up the head and draw in the chin, as in annoyance; to be resentful (oft. fol. by *at*). [OE *brīdel*]

brie /briː/, n. a soft cheese, ripened through bacterial action, as made in Brie, a district in northern France.

brief /briːf/, adj. 1. taking little time. 2. using few words; concise; succinct. 3. angrily short in speech. 4. close-fitting and short in length: *a brief dress*. ◇n. 5. a short outline. 6. *Law*. a summary prepared by a solicitor for a barrister containing all the information and documents relevant to the presentation of a case in court. 7. **hold a brief for,** to support. 8. **in brief,** in short. ◇v.t. 9. to instruct by a brief: *The solicitor will brief the barrister.* [F, from L] **—briefness,** n.

briefcase /ˈbriːfkeɪs/, n. a flat, rectangular, case used for carrying books, etc.

briefs /briːfs/, n. pl. close-fitting, legless underpants.

brig /brɪɡ/, n. *Naut.* a two-masted vessel with square sails on both masts. [shortened form of BRIGANTINE]

Brig, *Abbrev. Mil.* 1. Brigade. 2. Brigadier.

brigade /brəˈɡeɪd/, n. 1. a large body of troops. 2. a group organised for a special purpose: *a fire brigade*. [F, from It: troop, from *brigare* strive, contend]

brigadier /ˌbrɪɡəˈdɪə/, n. *Mil.* See Appendix. [F, from *brigade* BRIGADE. See -IER]

brigalow /ˈbrɪɡəloʊ/, n. 1. a type of acacia growing over large areas of northern NSW and Qld. 2. **the brigalow,** country where brigalow forms the main plant-life. [Aboriginal]

brigand /ˈbrɪɡənd/, n. one of a gang of robbers in mountain or forest regions. [ME, from OF, from It. See BRIGADE]

brigantine /ˈbrɪɡəntiːn/, n. a two-masted sailing ship, with fewer sails than a brig. [F, from It]

bright /braɪt/, adj. 1. radiating or reflecting light; luminous; shining. 2. filled with lights. 3. (of a colour) strong, clear and vivid. 4. glorious or splendid. 5. clever or witty. 6. lively; cheerful, as a person. 7. favorable or hopeful: *bright prospects*. [OE *brhyt, beorht*] **—brighten,** v.

brightness /ˈbraɪtnəs/, n. 1. a bright quality. 2. the amount of light given off apart from hue, pure white having the most brightness and pure black having none. 3. *Phys.* the luminous intensity per unit area of broad source of light, measured in candelas per square metre.

brilliance /ˈbrɪljəns/, n. 1. great brightness; splendor; lustre. 2. excellent intellectual ability. 3. brightness (def.2).

brilliant /ˈbrɪljənt/, adj. 1. shining brightly; sparkling; glittering; lustrous. 2. outstanding; illustrious: *a brilliant achievement*. 3. having or showing great intelligence. 4. (of a style in playing music) lively; vivacious. ◇n. 5. a diamond (or other gem) of a particular cut, typically round in outline and with many surfaces on its slopes. [F, ? from L *bēryllus* BERYL]

brim /brɪm/, n., v., **brimmed, brimming.** ◇n. 1. the upper edge of anything hollow; rim: *the brim of a cup*. 2. the wide flat part of a hat which shades the eyes. ◇v.i. 3. to be full to flowing over: *Her eyes would brim with tears.* [OE *brim* sea]

brimstone /ˈbrɪmstoʊn/, n. → **sulfur.** [ME *brinn(en)* burn + *ston* stone]

brindled /ˈbrɪndld/, adj. grey or brownish-yellow with darker streaks or spots.

brine /braɪn/, n. 1. strongly salted water. 2. (the water of) the sea. [OE *brȳne*]

bring /brɪŋ/, v.t., **brought** /brɔːt/, **bringing.** 1. to cause to come with oneself; carry; convey: *I'll bring the book to the meeting*. 2. to cause (something or someone) to come: **a.** to a receiver or owner: *Working at night brings me good money; That painting will bring $500*. **b.** to the mind or knowledge: *That brings an idea*. **c.** to a particular position or state: *The divorce brought him low*. **d.** to a particular opinion or decision: *Deep consideration brings me to say 'no'*. **e.** into existence, view, action, or effect: *Money cannot bring happiness; Night brings the stars*. 3. to lead; persuade: *He couldn't bring himself to do it.* 4. *Law*. to put forward before a court: *He will bring the case to court.* ◇5. Some special uses are:

bring about, 1. to cause; accomplish. **2.** *Naut.* to turn (a ship) on to the opposite tack.
bring back, to remind one of.
bring down, 1. to cause (a plane, animal, footballer, etc.) to fall. **2.** to reduce (a price). **3.** to humble or subdue. **4.** to introduce a proposed law: *to bring down a bill*.
bring in, 1. to introduce: *The new boss may bring in new ideas*. **2.** to yield (an income, cash, etc.)
bring on, 1. to cause: *Too much eating can bring on discomfort*. **2.** to cause to advance: *The warmth of summer will bring on the plants*.
bring out, 1. to encourage (a timid person): *Acting will bring her out*. **2.** to publish. **3.** to formally introduce (a girl) into society.
bring round, 1. to persuade of an opinion. **2.** to restore to consciousness.
bring to, 1. to bring back to consciousness. **2.** *Naut.* to head a ship close to the wind and stop her with helm and sails.
bring up, 1. to care for during childhood; rear. **2.** to introduce to notice or consideration: *I must bring up this problem at the meeting*. **3.** to cause to advance, as troops: *bring up the rear*. **4.** to vomit. [OE *bringan*]

brink /brɪŋk/, n. the edge, esp. of a steep place or of land near water. [ME, from Scand]

brinkmanship /ˈbrɪŋkmənʃɪp/, *n. Colloq.* the practice of risking disaster, esp. war, to gain one's ends.

Brinsmead /ˈbrɪnzmiːd/, *n.* **Hesba** (*Hesba Fay Brinsmead-Hungerford, 'Pixie'*), born 1922, Australian children's novelist; author of *Pastures of the Blue Crane* (1964).

briny /ˈbraɪni/, *adj.*, **brinier, briniest**, *n.* ◇*adj.* **1.** of or like brine; salty. ◇*n.* **2. the briny**, *Colloq.* the sea. – **brininess**, *n.*

bri-nylon /braɪ-ˈnaɪlɒn/, *n.* nylon orig. made in Britain. [Trademark]

briquette /brɪˈket/, *n.* a shaped block of pressed coal dust for use as fuel. Also, **briquet**. [F]

Brisb, *Abbrev.* Brisbane.

Brisbane /ˈbrɪzbən/, *n.* **1.** the capital of Qld, in the south-east of the state, on the Brisbane River, some 20 km inland from Moreton Bay. Pop. 1 149 401 (1986). **2.** a river in south-eastern Qld, rising east of Kingaroy and flowing south-east to Moreton Bay. 344 km. [named after Sir Thomas *Brisbane*, governor of NSW 1821-25]

Brisbane Line, *n.* **the**, a strategic line of defence planned in World War II in the event of a Japanese invasion; running from Brisbane to Melbourne, it was drawn up for the defence of Australia's most populated areas.

brisk /brɪsk/, *adj.* **1.** quick and active; lively: *a brisk breeze; a brisk walk.* **2.** sharp and invigorating: *brisk weather.* [? akin to BRUSQUE]

brisket /ˈbrɪskət/, *n.* (the meat from) the breast of an animal. [ME, from OF, from Gmc]

bristle /ˈbrɪsəl/, *n., v.*, **-tled, -tling**. ◇*n.* **1.** one of the short, stiff, hairs of certain animals, esp. pigs, used in making brushes, etc. **2.** any short, stiff hair or hairlike piece. ◇*v.i.* **3.** to stand or rise stiffly, like bristles: *The dog's hair bristled.* **4.** to raise the bristles, as a fearful animal: *The dog bristled.* **5.** to be thickly covered with something suggestive of bristles: *The plain bristled with guns.* **6.** to be clearly angry, hostile, etc: *He bristled with annoyance.* [ME] – **bristly**, *adj.*

Brit, *Abbrev.* **1.** Britain. **2.** British.

Britain /ˈbrɪtn/, *n.* **1.** → **Great Britain**. **2. Battle of**, a series of heavy bombing attacks on Britain by the German air force in August to October 1940, repulsed by a small force of Royal Air Force fighters.

Britannia /brəˈtænjə/, *n.* **1.** *Chiefly Poetic.* England, Scotland, and Ireland. **2.** the feminine personification of Great Britain or the British Empire. [L]

britches /ˈbrɪtʃəz/, *n.pl. Colloq.* **1.** trousers. **2. too big for one's britches**, conceited. [var. OF BREECHES]

British /ˈbrɪtɪʃ/, *adj.* **1.** relating to Britain or the British Commonwealth. **2.** relating to the English language as spoken in Britain, esp. the standard English language as spoken in southern England. **3. best of British (luck)**, (a wish for good fortune, often where there is little chance of success). ◇*n.* **4.** the British people. [OE *Bryttas, Brettas* Britons, from Celtic] – **Britisher**, *n.*

British Antarctic Territory, *n.* a colony in the south Atlantic created in 1962 from certain of the Falkland Islands Dependencies and comprising the South Shetland Islands, the South Orkney Islands and Graham Land.

British Commonwealth of Nations, *n.* former name of the **Commonwealth of Nations**.

British Empire, *n.* **1.** (formerly) the dominions, colonies, protectorates, dependencies, trusteeships, etc., collectively, under the control of the British Crown. **2. Order of the**, a military and civil order of knighthood.

British Isles, *n.pl.* a group of islands in western Europe, comprising Britain, Ireland, the Isle of Man and adjacent islands.

Briton /ˈbrɪtn/, *n.* **1.** a native or inhabitant of Britain, or (sometimes) of the Commonwealth. **2.** one of the Celtic people who in early times occupied the southern part of the island of Britain. [ML *Brito*; replacing ME *Breton*, from OF, from L *Bretto*]

Brittany /ˈbrɪtəni/, *n.* an administrative region of north-western France forming a peninsula between the English Channel and the Bay of Biscay. Pop. 3 165 200 (1986 est.). 28 334 km². French, *Bretagne*.

Britten /ˈbrɪtn/, *n.* **Benjamin**, 1913-76, English composer, pianist, and conductor, noted especially for his operas and choral works.

brittle /ˈbrɪtl/, *adj.* **1.** breaking easily. **2.** tense; irritable. [OE *brēotan* break] – **brittleness**, *n.*

broach /broʊtʃ/, *n.* **1.** *Mech.* a long, tapering tool with a notched edge which enlarges a hole as the tool is pulled through. **2.** a spit for roasting meat. **3.** a boring tool for tapping wine containers. ◇*v.t.* **4.** to enlarge and finish with a broach. **5.** to tap or pierce. **6.** to mention for the first time: *to broach a subject.* [ME, from L *brocc(h)us* projecting]

broad /brɔd/, *adj.* **1.** of great breadth: *a broad river.* **2.** of great size; large: *the broad ocean.* **3.** widely spread; open; full: *broad daylight.* **4.** not limited or narrow; liberal: *broad experience; broad sympathies.* **5.** main or general: *the broad outlines of a subject.* **6.** plain or clear: *a broad hint.* **7.** bold; plain-spoken. **8.** (of conversation) rough; coarse. **9.** (of an accent) having the characteristics of a dialect strongly emphasised. ◇*n.* **10.** the broad part of anything. **11.** *Colloq.* a woman. [OE *brād*]

Broad Australian, *n.* that pronunciation of Australian English in which the characteristics of Australian pronunciation are most emphasised.

broad bean, *n.* an annual plant grown for its large seeds, which are used as a vegetable.

broadcast /ˈbrɔdkɑst/, *v.*, **-cast** or **-casted, -casting**, *n., adv.* ◇*v.t.* **1.** to send (messages, speeches, music, etc.) by radio. **2.** to scatter (seed). **3.** to spread (information, gossip, etc.). ◇*v.i.* **4.** to send radio messages, speeches, etc. ◇*n.* **5.** *Radio.* **a.** the sending out

broadcast of radio messages, speeches, etc. **b.** a radio program. ◇*adv.* **6.** so as to spread far and wide. **–broadcaster,** *n.*

broadcloth /'brɔdklɒθ/, *n.* **1. cotton broadcloth,** a cotton shirt or dress material resembling fine poplin. **2. rayon broadcloth,** a spun rayon fabric similar to cotton broadcloth. **3. woollen broadcloth,** woollen dress goods with the nap laid parallel to the selvedge.

broaden /'brɔdn/, *v.i., v.t.* to become or make broad; widen.

broad jump, *n.* → **long jump.**

broad-minded /brɔd-'maɪndəd/, *adj.* free from prejudice or bigotry; liberal; tolerant.

broadsheet /'brɔdʃit/, *n.* **1.** a sheet of paper, usu. large, printed on one side only, for handing out or posting. **2.** a ballad, song, etc., printed, or orig. printed, on a broadsheet. **3.** a newspaper printed on the standard sheet size of paper.

broadside /'brɔdsaɪd/, *n.* **1.** *Naut.* the whole side of a ship above the waterline. **2.** *Navy.* (the firing of) all the guns on one side of a ship. **3.** an abusive attack. **4.** → **broadsheet** (def. 1). **5.** any broad surface or side, as of a house.

broadsword /'brɔdsɔd/, *n.* a straight, broad, flat sword.

Broadway /'brɔdweɪ/, *n.* a street in New York City, famous for its theatres.

brocade /brə'keɪd/, *n., v.,* **-caded, -cading.** ◇*n.* **1.** a fabric woven with a rich design. The right side has a raised effect. ◇*v.t.* **2.** to weave with a design or figure. [Sp: interweave with gold or silver, from L] **–brocaded,** *adj.*

broccoli /'brɒkəli, -laɪ/, *n.* a plant of the mustard family, like the cauliflower, the flowering head of which is used as a vegetable. [It, pl. of *broccolo* sprout, from L: projecting]

brochure /'brəʊʃə, brə'ʃʊə/, *n.* → **pamphlet** (def. 2). [F: stitch]

brogue[1] /broʊɡ/, *n.* a broad accent, esp. Irish, in the pronunciation of English. [special use of BROGUE[2]]

brogue[2] /broʊɡ/, *n.* a strongly made, comfortable shoe. [Irish, Gaelic *brōg* shoe]

broil /brɔɪl/, *v.t.* **1.** *US.* to cook by direct heat; grill. **2.** to make very hot. ◇*v.i.* **3.** to be made very hot. **4.** to burn (with impatience, etc.). [ME, ? from OF: burn, from LL]

broke /broʊk/, *v.* **1.** past tense of **break. 2.** *Archaic or Colloq.* past participle of **break.** ◇*adj.* **3.** *Colloq.* out of money; bankrupt.

broken /'broʊkən/, *adj.* **1.** torn; ruptured; fractured. **2.** not complete; fragmentary: *a broken set.* **3.** disregarded or disobeyed; infringed; violated: *a broken law.* **4.** interrupted or discontinuous: *broken sleep.* **5.** uneven; (of ground) rough; (of water) with a disturbed surface as choppy water, surf, etc.; (of weather) patchy, unsettled. **6.** weakened in strength, spirit, etc. **7.** tamed: *The horse was not yet broken to the saddle.* **8.** imperfectly spoken, as language: *He spoke broken English.* **9.** ruined; bankrupt. **–brokenness,** *n.*

Broken Bay, *n.* an inlet just north of Sydney, NSW; consists of three main branches, Brisbane Water, Pittwater and the entrance to the Hawkesbury River.

broken chord, *n. Music.* a chord whose notes are played one after the other rather than together.

broken-hearted /broʊkən-'hatəd/, *adj.* crushed by grief.

Broken Hill, *n.* a city in far western NSW; major mining area for lead, silver and zinc. Pop. 24 460 (1986).

Broken Hill Proprietary Company Limited, The, an Australian public company incorporated in 1885, involved mainly in mining and iron and steel production; Australia's largest manufacturing organisation. *Colloq.* **the Big Australian.** *Abbrev.:* BHP

broker /'broʊkə/, *n.* an agent who buys or sells (property, shares, etc.) for another. [ME from AF: broacher (of casks), tapster (hence retailer)] **–brokerage,** *n.*

brolga /'brɒlɡə/, *n.* a large, silvery-grey bird, a crane, of northern and eastern Australia which dances, perhaps as part of its courtship; native companion. [Aboriginal]

brolly /'brɒli/, *n. Colloq.* umbrella.

brome /broʊm/, *n.* a grass, existing in about 40 species, esp. one used for pasture. Also, **brome grass.** [L, from Gk: kind of oats]

bromic acid /'broʊmɪk æsəd/, *n.* an acid, $HBrO_3$, containing bromine and oxygen, used as an oxidising agent.

bromide /'broʊmaɪd/, *n.* **1.** *Chem.* See **-ide. 2.** silver bromide, esp. in photography. **3.** *Colloq.* a sedative.

bromine /'broʊmin, -aɪn/, *n.* an element, a dark-reddish fuming liquid, like chlorine and iodine in chemical properties. *Symbol:* Br; *at. no.:* 35; *at. wt:* 9.909. See **halogen.**

bronchi /'brɒŋkaɪ/, *n.* plural of **bronchus.**

bronchial /'brɒŋkiəl/, *adj.* relating to the bronchi.

bronchial tubes, *n.pl.* the bronchi, or the bronchi and their branches.

bronchitis /brɒŋ'kaɪtəs/, *n.* an inflammation of the membrane lining of the bronchial tubes. [NL; from BRONCH(US)- + -ITIS] **–bronchitic,** *adj.*

bronchus /'brɒŋkəs/, *n., pl.* **-chi** /-kaɪ/. *n.* either of the two main branches of the trachea (windpipe). [NL from Gk *brónchos* windpipe]

bronco /'brɒŋkoʊ/, *n., pl.* **-cos.** *US.* a wild or half-tamed pony; mustang. [Sp: rough, rude]

Bronhill /'brɒnhɪl/, *n.* **June** (*June Gough*), born 1929, Australian soprano; star of musicals, operettas and operas. [from BRO(KE)N HILL, her home town]

Brontë family /'brɒnti/, *n.* a family of three sisters, all English novelists. **1. Charlotte** (*'Currer Bell'*), 1816–55; best known for *Jane Eyre* (1847). **2. Emily Jane** (*'Ellis Bell'*), 1818–48, author of *Wuthering Heights*

(1848). **3. Anne** (*'Acton Bell'*), 1820–49, author of *The Tenant of Wildfell Hall* (1848).

brontosaurus /brɒntə'sɔrəs/, *n.* a large plant-eating dinosaur with a long neck and tail. [*bronto-*, combining form from Gk *bronté* thunder + -SAURUS]

bronze /brɒnz/, *n., adj., v.,* **bronzed, bronzing.** ◇*n.* **1.** *Metall.* a strong and long-lasting brown alloy, of copper and tin. **2.** a metallic brownish color. **3.** a work of art, as a statue, medal, etc., made of bronze. ◇*adj.* **4.** of the color of bronze. ◇*v.t.* **5.** (of the sun) to make (a person's skin) brown: *He is bronzed after his holiday.* [F, from It]

Bronze Age, *n.* **1.** the age in the history of mankind (between the Stone and Iron Ages) marked by the use of bronze tools. **2.** (*l.c.*) See **age** (def. 10).

bronze-wing /'brɒnz-wɪŋ/, *n.* **1.** any of various Australian birds whose wings have a golden metallic sheen, as the **bronze-wing pigeon, bronze-wing cuckoo. 2.** *NT, WA Colloq.* a half-caste Aboriginal.

brooch /broʊtʃ/, *n.* an ornament made to be fastened to clothing with a pin. [var. of BROACH, *n.*]

brood /brud/, *n.* **1.** a number of young creatures produced or hatched at one time; a family of offspring or young. **2.** a breed or kind: *the devil and his brood.* ◇*v.t.* **3.** (of a bird) to sit over (eggs or young); incubate. ◇*v.i.* **4.** (of a bird) to sit over eggs to be hatched. **5.** to meditate moodily; worry (usu. fol. by *on*/*over*). ◇*adj.* **6.** kept for breeding purposes: *a brood mare.* [OE *brōd*]

broody /'brudi/, *adj.,* **broodier, broodiest. 1.** likely or tending to brood or sit on eggs: *a broody hen.* **2.** moody.

brook¹ /brʊk/, *n.* a small, natural stream of fresh water; creek. [OE *brōc* stream]

brook² /brʊk/, *v.t.* to bear; suffer; tolerate (usu. in a negative sentence): *He will brook no delay.* [OE *brūcan*]

Brooke /brʊk/, *n.* **Rupert,** 1887–1915, English lyric poet.

broom /brum/, *n.* **1.** a sweeping implement consisting of a flat brush of bristles, nylon, etc., on a long handle. **2.** a sweeping implement consisting of a bunch of twigs or plant stems on a handle; besom. **3.** any of the shrubby plants common in western Europe, which grow on uncultivated ground and have long, thin branches bearing yellow flowers. [OE *brōm*]

Broome /brum/, *n.* a town and port on the north-western coast of WA on Roebuck Bay; pearling. Pop. 5778 (1986).

bros., *Abbrev.* brothers. Also, **Bros**

broth /brɒθ/, *n.* a thin soup of meat or fish stock. [OE]

brothel /'brɒθəl/, *n.* **1.** a house of prostitution. **2.** *Colloq.* any house, room, etc., in a disorderly state.

brother /'brʌðə/, *n., pl.* **brothers, brethren. 1.** a male child of the same parents as another, (**full brother** or **brother-german**); male sibling. **2.** a male child of only one of one's parents (**half-brother**). **3.** a male member of the same kinship group, nationality, profession, etc.; an associate; a fellow countryman, fellow man, etc. **4.** *Eccles.* a male member of a religious organisation not, or not yet, in holy orders. [OE *brōthor*]

brotherhood /'brʌðəhʊd/, *n.* **1.** the state or quality of being a brother or brotherly. **2.** a society or organisation of men formed for mutual aid or benefit. **3.** all those working in a particular trade or profession: *the medical brotherhood.*

Brotherhood of St Lawrence, *n.* a social welfare organisation and religious order of the Anglican Church founded in Australia in 1930; government assisted from 1971.

brother-in-law /'brʌðər-ɪn-lɔ/, *n., pl.* **brothers-in-law. 1.** one's husband's or wife's brother. **2.** one's sister's husband. **3.** the husband of one's wife's or husband's sister.

brotherly /'brʌðəli/, *adj.* **1.** of or like a brother; fraternal. **2.** kind; loyal. **–brotherliness,** *n.*

brought /brɔt/, *v.* past tense and past participle of **bring.**

brouhaha /'bruhɑhɑ/, *n.* an uproar; turmoil. [F, probably onomatopoeic]

brow /braʊ/, *n.* **1.** the ridge over the eye. **2.** the hair growing on that ridge; eyebrow. **3.** (*sing.* or *pl.*) the forehead: *to knit one's brows.* **4.** the expression of the face; countenance: *a brow of care.* **5.** the edge of a steep place. [OE *brū*]

browbeat /'braʊbit/, *v.t.,* **-beat, -beaten, -beating.** to frighten by fierce looks or words; bully; intimidate.

brown /braʊn/, *n.* **1.** the color of earth, a mixture of red, yellow and black. ◇*adj.* **2.** of the color brown: *a brown horse.* **3.** having skin of that color: *The Polynesians are a brown people.* **4.** sunburned or tanned. ◇*v.t., v.i.* **5.** to make or become brown. [OE *brūn*]

Brown /braʊn/, *n.* **1. Bryan,** born 1948, Australian film actor. **2. Ford Madox,** 1821–93, English historical painter. **3. Robert,** 1773–1858, Scottish botanist; travelled with Matthew Flinders on board the *Investigator*; first to observe Brownian motion.

brown coal, *n.* → **lignite.**

Brownian motion /,braʊniən 'moʊʃən/, *n.* irregular random movements, as of microscopic particles suspended in a liquid, smoke particles in air, etc. Also, **Brownian movement.** [first noticed (in 1827) by Robert BROWN]

brownie /'braʊni/, *n.* **1.** (in folklore) a little brown goblin, esp. one who helps secretly in household work. **2.** (*cap.*) a member of the junior division of the Girl Guides. **3.** a fruit loaf baked in a camp oven. **4.** a type of thick brown biscuit.

Browning /'braʊnɪŋ/, *n.* **1. Elizabeth Barrett** /'bærət/, 1806–61, English poet; author of *Sonnets from the Portuguese* (1850). **2.** her husband, **Robert,** 1812–89, English

Browning poet; author of *The Ring and the Book* (1868–69).

Brownlow Medal /ˌbraʊnloʊ 'medl/, n. a trophy awarded annually by the Victorian Football League to the best and fairest player of the season.

brown owl, n. the woman in charge of a group of Brownies.

brown rice, n. unpolished rice.

Brownshirt /'braʊnʃɜːt/, n. 1. a member of Hitler's storm-troopers. 2. (loosely) any Nazi.

brown snake, n. any of certain venomous Australian snakes, brownish or olive in color, e.g. the **common brown snake**, or the **gwardar**.

brown sugar, n. unrefined or partially refined sugar.

browse /braʊz/, v., browsed, browsing, n. ◇v.i. 1. (of cattle, deer, etc.) to feed or graze 2. to glance at random through a book, a shop, etc. ◇n. 3. a casual look through a book, a shop, etc. [MF: young sprout, from Gmc] — **browser**, n.

Bruce /bruːs/, n. 1. **Robert the** (*Robert I, Robert Bruce*), 1274–1329, king of Scotland 1306–29; preserved the independence of Scotland by victory over the English at Bannockburn in 1314. 2. **Stanley Melbourne, 1st Viscount**, 1883–1967, Australian Nationalist-Country Party politician; prime minister 1923–29.

brucellosis /bruːsə'loʊsəs/, n. an infection often causing abortions in animals and a type of fever in man. [NL from *Brucella* genus name (named after Sir David Bruce, 1855–1931, Australian physician)]

Brueghel family /'brɔɪɡəl/, n. a Flemish family of genre and landscape painters. 1. **Pieter** (*The Elder*), c. 1525–69, best known for his scenes of peasant life. 2. his son, **Pieter** (*The Younger*), 1564–1637, noted for his horrific images of hell. 3. **Jan**, 1568–1625, son of Pieter the Elder, known for his miniaturist style. Also **Bruegel, Breughel**.

bruise /bruːz/, v., bruised, bruising. n. ◇v.t. 1. to cause a discoloration by striking or pressing, without breaking the skin or drawing blood. 2. to hurt on the surface: *to bruise feelings; to bruise fruit.* 3. to crush (drugs or food) by beating or pounding. ◇v.i. 4. to develop a discolored spot on the skin as the result of a blow, fall, etc. 5. to be hurt: *His feelings bruise easily.* ◇n. 6. an injury due to bruising; contusion. [OE *brȳsan* crush]

bruiser /'bruːzə/, n. 1. a boxer. 2. *Colloq.* a tough fellow; bully.

brumby /'brʌmbi/, n. a wild horse, esp. one descended from runaway stock. [Aboriginal]

Brummell /'brʌməl/, n. **Beau** /boʊ/ (*George Bryan Brummell*), 1778–1840, a leader of fashion in Regency England.

brunch /brʌntʃ/, n. a midmorning meal that serves as both breakfast and lunch. [b. BR(EAK-FAST and L)UNCH]

Brunei /'bruːnaɪ/, n. a sultanate in the western Pacific, on the north-west coast of the island of Borneo, bordered by the Malaysian State of Sarawak; a British protectorate before independence in 1984. Pop. 215 900 (1984 est.). 5765 km². *Languages:* Malay, also Chinese and English. *Currency:* Brunei dollar. *Cap.:* Bandar Seri Begawan.

Brunel /bruː'nɛl/, n. **Isambard Kingdom** /'ɪzəmbad/, 1806–59, English civil engineer and steamship designer.

Brunelleschi /brunə'lɛski/, n. **Filippo** /fi'lipou/, 1377?–1446, Florentine architect, designed the dome of the cathedral in Florence.

brunette /bruː'nɛt/, adj. 1. (of the skin, eyes, or hair) dark; brown. 2. (of a person) having dark or brown hair, eyes, or skin. ◇n. 3. a woman or girl with dark hair, skin, and eyes.

Brunette Downs, n. a pastoral property in the NT on the Barkly Tableland; 12 000 km².

Brunhild /'brʊnhɪld/, n. 1. (in the *Nibelungenlied*) a legendary queen of Iceland, wife of King Gunther, for whom she is won by Siegfried. 2. *Scand Legend*. a Valkyrie, won by Sigurd for Gunnar. Also, **Brynhild**. [G. cf. Icel *Brynhildr*]

Brünnhilde /brʊn'hɪldə, bryn-/, n. 1. heroine of Wagner's music-drama *The Valkyrie*. 2. *Colloq.* any large woman thought to resemble the full-figured sopranos commonly associated with this role.

Brunswick Bay /ˌbrʌnzwɪk 'beɪ/, n. a bay with many islands on the northern coast of WA, north of Yampi Sound.

brunt /brʌnt/, n. the shock or force of an attack, etc.; the main stress, force, or violence: *to bear the brunt of their criticism.* [ME; orig. uncert.]

brush¹ /brʌʃ/, n. 1. an instrument consisting of bristles, hair, or the like, set in or attached to a handle, used for painting, cleaning, polishing, etc. 2. an act of brushing; an application of a brush. 3. the bushy tail of an animal, esp. of a fox. 4. a slight touch or contact. 5. a brief hostile encounter; argument; skirmish. ◇v.t. 6. to sweep, rub, clean, paint, etc., with a brush: *to brush paint on smoothly.* 7. to touch lightly in passing: *The grass brushed her legs as she ran.* 8. to remove by brushing or by lightly passing over (usu. fol. by *aside*).: *He brushed her remarks aside.* 9. **brush up, a.** to polish up; smarten. **b.** to revise and renew or improve one's skill in: *He is going to brush up his French.* [ME, from OF, from Gmc]

brush² /brʌʃ/, n. 1. a dense growth of bushes, shrubs, etc.; scrub; thicket. 2. a thinly settled region covered with scrub. 3. → **scrub²** (def. 3). [ME, from OF *broce*]

brush box, n. a tall evergreen forest tree of eastern Australia, often grown as an ornamental and street tree.

Brushmen of the Bush, n.pl. a group of painters formed at Broken Hill, NSW, in 1973 with interest in works depicting the local area; includes Pro Hart and Jack Absalom.

brush-tailed possum /ˌbrʌʃ-teɪld ˈpɒsəm/, n. any of various medium-sized, strongly-built possums with bushy tail, e.g. the common **brush possum**, found through most of Australia, which often lives in roofs and eats garden plants, and the **bobuck**, of eastern Australian mountain areas.

brush turkey, n. a large mound-building bird of the wooded parts of eastern Australia. Also, **scrub turkey**.

brushwood /ˈbrʌʃwʊd/, n. 1. branches of trees cut or broken off. 2. densely growing small trees and shrubs. 3. small branches bound with wire and used to make fences. [BRUSH² + WOOD]

brushwork /ˈbrʌʃwɜːk/, n. 1. the skill, style, or manner in which a painter uses his brush. 2. painting or other work done with a brush.

brusque /brʌsk, brʊsk/, adj. abrupt in manner; blunt; rough: *a brusque welcome*. [F, from It: rude, sharp from L: broom] – **brusqueness**, n.

Brussels /ˈbrʌsəlz/, n. the capital of Belgium, in the central part; headquarters of Common Market and of NATO. Pop. 976 536 (1986 est.). French, **Bruxelles**.

brussels sprout, n. → sprout (def. 6).

brutal /ˈbruːtl/, adj. 1. cruel; savage; inhuman: *a brutal blow*. 2. crude; harsh: *the brutal truth*.

brutality /bruːˈtæləti/, n., pl. **-ties**. 1. the quality of being brutal. 2. a brutal act.

brute /bruːt/, n. 1. a non-human animal; beast. 2. a brutal person. 3. *Colloq*. a selfish or unsympathetic person. 4. the animal qualities, desires, etc., of man: *The brute in him came out*. ◇*adj*. 5. lacking reason, consciousness or intelligence; inhuman; irrational: *brute strength*; *the brute mind*. [F, from L: dull]

Brutus /ˈbruːtəs/, n. **Marcus Junius** /ˈmɑːkəs ˈdʒuːniəs/, 85?–42 BC, Roman provincial administrator; one of the assassins of Julius Caesar.

Bryant /ˈbraɪənt/, n. 1. **Mary**, 1765–?, English convict of the First Fleet who, with her husband and children, absconded and sailed from Sydney to Timor. 2. **William**, 1759?–91, English convict, husband of Mary.

B3 /bi ˈθriː/, n. an international standard size of paper. See Appendix.

btu /bi ti ˈjuː/ *Abbrev*. British thermal unit.

bubble /ˈbʌbəl/, n., v., **-bled, -bling**. ◇*n*. 1. **a.** a small ball of gas in or rising through a liquid. **b.** a small ball of gas in a thin liquid envelope. 2. a cavity filled with air or gas, in amber, glass, etc. 3. something that is not real or firm, or does not last; a delusion. ◇*v.i*. 4. to send up bubbles; effervesce. 5. to be full of good humor or high spirits (oft. fol. by *over*): *She bubbled over with enthusiasm*. 6. to flow or run with a gurgling noise; gurgle: *a bubbling pot*. [ME]

bubble-and-squeak /ˌbʌbəl-ən-ˈskwiːk/, n. left-over vegetables, or meat and vegetables, fried together.

bubbler /ˈbʌblə/, n. → **drinking fountain**.

bubbly /ˈbʌbli/, adj. 1. containing bubbles; bubbling. 2. of or like bubbles: *a bubbly personality*. ◇*n*. 3. *Colloq*. champagne.

bubonic plague /bjuːˌbɒnɪk ˈpleɪɡ/, n. a contagious epidemic disease with chills, fevers, and inflamed swellings, which is carried by fleas from rats.

buccaneer /ˌbʌkəˈnɪə/, n. 1. a pirate. ◇*v.i*. 2. to act like, or lead the life of, a buccaneer. [F *boucan* frame for curing meat, from Tupi] – **buccaneering**, n., adj.

Buccaneer Archipelago, n. four groups of islands in the north of WA at the entrance to King Sound.

Bucephalus /bjuːˈsɛfələs/, n. the warhorse of Alexander the Great.

Buchan /ˈbʌkən/, n. **John** (*Baron Tweedsmuir*), 1875–1940, Scottish novelist and historian; author of *The Thirty-Nine Steps* (1915); governor-general of Canada 1935–40.

Buchanan /bjuːˈkænən/, n. **Nathaniel**, 1826–1901, Australian explorer and farmer, born in Ireland; pioneered many Qld and NT stock-routes.

Bucharest /ˌbukəˈrɛst, bjuː-/, n. the capital and largest city of Romania, in the southern part. Pop. 1 975 808 (1985 est.).

Buchenwald /ˈbukənvald/, n. a former Nazi concentration camp in central Germany, near Weimar, infamous for atrocities perpetrated there.

buck¹ /bʌk/, n. 1. the male of certain animals, as the deer or rabbit. 2. a young man. [ME]

buck² /bʌk/, v.i. 1. (of a saddle or pack animal) to jump with an arched back and come down with the head low and forelegs stiff, usu. in order to throw off a rider or a pack. 2. *Colloq*. to resist obstinately: *to buck at improvements*. ◇*v.t*. 3. to throw or try to throw (a rider) by bucking. 4. *Colloq*. to resist obstinately; object strongly to: *to buck the system*. ◇*n*. 5. an act of bucking. [special use of BUCK¹]

buck³ /bʌk/, n. *in the phrase* **pass the buck**, *Colloq*. to shift the responsibility or blame to another person. [orig. uncert.]

buck⁴ /bʌk/, n. *US. Colloq*. 1. a dollar. 2. **a fast buck**, money earned with little effort, often by dishonest means. [shortened form of *buckskin*, an accepted form of exchange in the US frontier.]

Buck /bʌk/, n. **Pearl S**(*ydenstricker*), 1892–1973, US novelist, best known for her novels set in China; Nobel prize for literature 1938.

bucket /ˈbʌkət/, n., v., **-eted, -eting**. ◇*n*. 1. a vessel, usu. round with flat bottom and a handle, for carrying water, sand, etc. 2. anything like this in shape or use, esp. on a conveyor belt. 3. the amount contained in a bucket. 4. a small container of ice-cream; dixie. 5. **kick the bucket**, *Colloq*. to die.

bucket 132 **buffalo**

◇*v.t.* **6.** to lift, carry, or handle in a bucket (oft. fol. by *up* or *out*). **7.** to shake or toss jerkily (fol. by *about*): *The wind bucketed the ship about.* ◇*v.i.* **8.** to be shaken or tossed jerkily (fol. by *about*): *The ship bucketed about violently.* **9.** (of rain), to pour down heavily (fol. by *down*). [ME, from OF *bucket* pail, tub] —**bucketful**, *n.*

bucket seat, *n.* (in a car, etc.) a seat with a rounded back, to hold one person.

Buckingham Palace /ˈbʌkɪŋəm ˈpæləs/, *n.* the London residence of the British sovereign, at the west end of St James's Park.

buckjump /ˈbʌkdʒʌmp/, *v.i.* (of a horse) to buck. [BUCK² + JUMP]

buckjumper /ˈbʌkdʒʌmpə/, *n.* **1.** a horse which bucks. **2.** a rider of such a horse. **3.** a small damper or bunion.

buckle /ˈbʌkl/, *n., v.,* **-led, -ling.** ◇*n.* **1.** a clasp with a movable tongue for fastening a belt or strap. **2.** a bend or bulge, as in a sheet of metal. ◇*v.t.* **3.** to fasten with a buckle. **4.** to cause to bend or shrivel, through heat or pressure; warp; curl. ◇*v.i.* **5.** to set to work with energy (fol. by *to* or *down to*). **6.** to bend, warp, or give way suddenly, as with heat or pressure. **7. buckle under**, to yield; give way. [ME, from F: buckle, boss of a shield, from L *bucca* cheek; mouth]

buckler /ˈbʌklə/, *n.* a small round shield. [ME, from OF: shield, orig., one with a boss.]

Buckley /ˈbʌkli/, *n.* **William**, 1780?–1856, British-born convict, escaped and lived with Aboriginal people 1803–35, after which he was employed as liaison officer with them.

Buckley's chance /ˈbʌkliz tʃæns/, *n.* Also, **Buckley's, Buckley's hope. 1.** a very slim chance; forlorn hope. **2. Buckley's and none**, (*joc.*) two chances amounting to next to no chance. [probably pun on *Buckley and Nunn*, a Melbourne store]

buckshot /ˈbʌkʃɒt/, *n.* a large size of lead shot used on big game.

buckskin /ˈbʌkskɪn/, *n.* **1.** the skin of a buck or deer. **2.** a strong, soft, yellowish or greyish leather, orig. from deerskin, now usu. from sheepskin. **3.** (*pl.*) US. breeches made of buckskin.

bucks party, *n.* a party held on the eve of a wedding for the bridegroom by his male friends. Also, **bucks' party.**

bucktooth /ˈbʌktuθ/, *n., pl.* **-teeth** /-ˈtiθ/. (usu. in pl.) an upper tooth that sticks out.

buckwheat /ˈbʌkwit/, *n.* **1.** (a grain with) triangular seeds which are used as a food for animals, and in the US made into a flour for cakes, etc. **2.** buckwheat flour. [*buck* (OE *bōc* beech) + WHEAT; so called from its beechnut-shaped seed]

bucolic /bjuˈkɒlɪk/, *adj.* Also, **bucolical. 1.** relating to shepherds; pastoral. **2.** agricultural; rustic; rural: *bucolic isolation.* ◇*n.* **3.** a pastoral poem: *the bucolics of Virgil.* [L, from Gk: rustic] —**bucolically**, *adv.*

bud /bʌd/, *n., v.,* **budded, budding.** ◇*n.* **1.** *Bot.* a small shoot or growth on the stem of a plant containing the first stages of a leaf, flower, or both. **2.** *Zool.* (in certain simple animals) a prominence which develops into a new individual, sometimes permanently attached to the parent and sometimes becoming detached; gemma. **3.** *Anat.* any small rounded part. **4. nip in the bud**, to stop (something) before it gets under way. ◇*v.i.* **5.** to put forth or produce buds, as a plant. **6.** to begin to grow and develop. ◇*v.t.* **7.** to cause to bud. **8.** *Bot.* to graft by inserting a single bud into the stock. [ME *budde*; orig. uncert.]

Budapest /ˈbudəpɛst/, *n.* the capital of Hungary, on the Danube; formed by the union of the cities of Buda and Pest (1872). Pop. 2 076 000 (1986 est.).

Buddha /ˈbudə/, *n.* 'The Enlightened One', a title applied especially to the great religious teacher, variously known as Siddhartha and Gautama (or Gotama), or Sakyamuni, who flourished in India about the sixth century BC, regarded by his followers as the latest of a series of teachers (Buddhas) possessing perfect enlightenment and wisdom. [Skt: wise, enlightened]

Buddhism /ˈbudɪzəm/, *n.* a world religion, founded by the teacher Buddha, which teaches that life is full of suffering and that supreme happiness and peace (Nirvana) is gained by destroying greed, hatred, and delusion. —**Buddhist**, *n., adj.*

buddy /ˈbʌdi/, *n., pl.* **-dies.** *Colloq.* a comrade; mate.

budge /bʌdʒ/, *v.i., v.t.* **budged, budging.** to move, or cause to move, slightly; (cause to) give way (usu. with negative): *Don't budge; You can't budge him.* [F, from L: to boil]

budgerigar /ˈbʌdʒərɪˌgɑ/, *n.* a small yellow and green parakeet of the inland regions of Australia, widely domesticated and bred in many colored varieties. Also, **budgerygah.** [Aboriginal]

budget /ˈbʌdʒət/, *n., adj., v.,* **-eted, -eting.** ◇*n.* **1.** a plan or list of expected income and spending for some future period. **2.** specifically, a plan of government income and spending. ◇*adj.* **3.** for a person with a small income; cheap: *a budget car.* ◇*v.i., v.t.* **4.** to plan (for) an allotment of (time, time, etc.). [late ME, from F *bouge* bag, from L] —**budgetary**, *adj.*

Buenos Aires /bweɪnəs ˈaɪriz, ˈɛərɪz/, *n.* a seaport in and the capital of Argentina, in the eastern part, on the river Plate. Pop. 2 922 829 (1980).

buff /bʌf/, *n.* **1.** a thick light yellow leather, orig. made of buffalo skin. **2.** *Colloq.* an enthusiast; expert: *a wine buff.* **3.** (from the buff uniforms worn by New York volunteer firemen in the 1820s) ◇*adj.* **3.** made of buff (leather). **4.** buff colored. ◇*v.t.* **5.** to polish (metal) or to give a smooth, shiny lustre to (other surfaces). [F: buffalo, from It]

buffalo /ˈbʌfəloʊ/, *n., pl.* **-loes, -los**, (*esp. collectively*) **-lo.** any of several kinds of bovine animal, wild or domesticated, as the Indian buffalo, now widespread in the north of Australia. [It *bufalo*, from d. L]

buffalo grass, *n.* a lawn grass, introduced orig. from America, rough and springy with thick growth of runners, usu. grown in warm districts.

buffer /'bʌfə/, *n.* **1.** a large, flat knob, as those at each end of a railway carriage, for absorbing the shock of a collision. **2.** anything which absorbs the shock of opposing forces. [from *buff*, to blow or slap, + -ER¹]

buffer solution, *n.* a solution whose acidity or alkalinity remains almost unchanged by dilution or by the addition of acid or alkali.

buffer state, *n.* a smaller state lying between two larger states which are likely to go to war. Also, **buffer zone**.

buffet¹ /'bʌfət/, *n., v.,* **-feted, -feting.** ◇*n.* **1.** a blow, as with the hand: *the buffets of fortune.* ◇*v.t.* **2.** to strike, esp. with the hand. **3.** to shake; jostle (*usu. in passive*): *The ship was buffeted by strong winds.* [ME, from OF *buffe* a blow]

buffet² /'bʌfeɪ, 'bufeɪ/, *n.* **1.** a counter where light food is served. **2.** a low cupboard for holding cups and plates; sideboard. ◇*adj.* **3.** (of a meal) spread on tables or buffets from which guests serve themselves. [F: chair, table]

buffet car, *n.* a train carriage in which drinks and light meals are served.

buffoon /bə'fun/, *n.* **1.** someone who amuses people by tricks, odd facial expressions, jokes, etc.; clown. **2.** someone who acts the fool: *What a buffoon!* [F, from It *buffone* jester, from *buffa* a jest] **— buffoonery**, *n.* **— buffoonish**, *adj.*

bug /bʌg/, *n., v.,* **bugged, bugging.** ◇*n.* **1.** loosely, any insect, esp. one with the forewings thickened at the base. Sucking mouth parts allow them to suck plant juices or to feed on animals, including man. **2.** → **bedbug**. **3.** *Colloq.* an illness due to an infection. **4.** (*oft. pl.*) *Colloq.* something that is wrong; defect: *getting rid of the bugs in a computer program.* **5.** *Colloq.* an idea or subject with which one is obsessed: *He has a bug about the unions.* **6.** *Colloq.* a microphone hidden to record conversation. ◇*v.t.* **7.** *Colloq.* to hide or put a microphone in (a room, etc.). **8.** *Colloq.* to annoy (someone). [ME *bugge*]

bugbear /'bʌgbɛə/, *n.* **1.** any cause, real or imaginary, of needless fear or annoyance. **2.** *Obs.* a goblin thought to eat up naughty children. [*bug* a bogey + BEAR²]

bugger /'bʌgə/, *n.* **1.** one who practises bestiality or sodomy. **2.** *Colloq.* **a.** (*joc.*) any person. **b.** (*offensive*) a hateful person. ◇*v.t.* **3.** to practise bestiality or sodomy on. **4.** *Colloq.* to cause damage, annoyance, etc., to (usu. fol. by *up*). ◇*interj.* **5.** (a strong expression of annoyance, disgust, etc.): *Oh, bugger!* [F, from ML *Bulgarus* a Bulgarian, a heretic; certain Bulgarian heretics were charged with this activity] **— buggery,** *n.*

buggy /'bʌgi/, *n., pl.* **-gies. 1.** a two-wheeled horse-drawn carriage. **2.** *Colloq.* a motor vehicle: *beach buggy.* [orig. uncert.]

bugle /'bjugəl/, *n., v.,* **-gled, -gling. 1.** a cornet-like military wind instrument, usu. metal, used for sounding signals. ◇*v.i.* **2.** to sound a bugle. [ME, from OF, from L: ox] **— bugler**, *n.*

build /bɪld/, *v.,* **built** (*old form* **builded**), **building**, *n.* ◇*v.t.* **1.** to make (a structure) by joining parts together; construct: *to build a house.* **2.** to establish, increase, and strengthen (oft. fol. by *up*): *to build a business up.* **3.** to base; construct: *to build one's hopes on promises.* **4.** to fill with houses (usu. fol. by *up*): *They will build up this area soon.* **5.** to block the view from (a building) by putting up another building close to it (fol. by *out*). ◇*v.i.* **6.** to be in the business of building. **7.** to add a room or rooms to a house (fol. by *on*): *We are building on next year.* **8. build up to**, to prepare for: *The music was building up to a climax.* ◇*n.* **9.** type of bodily structure: *a person's build.* [OE *bold* dwelling, house] **— builder**, *n.*

building /'bɪldɪŋ/, *n.* **1.** a structure built for people to live or work in. **2.** the act, business, or art of constructing houses, etc.

building alignment, *n.* A boundary set on either side of a street by a planning authority, beyond which buildings may not project. Also, **building line**.

building covenant, *n.* a limitation on the form or position of a building by the local authority or the previous owner of the site.

building society, *n.* an organisation that uses money deposited as savings by its members as a fund for lending money to members to buy or build a house.

build-up /'bɪld-ʌp/, *n.* **1.** any gradual increase. **2.** *Mil.* (a gathering of) large numbers of troops, etc., for an attack. **3.** an advertising campaign for a person or a product.

built /bɪlt/, *v.* past tense and past participle of **build**.

built-up area /'bɪlt-ʌp ɛəriə/, *n.* an area of high population density where speed-limits apply to traffic.

Bukharin /bu'karən/, *n.* **Nikolai Ivanovich** /ˌnɪkəlaɪ ɪ'vanəvɪtʃ/, 1888–1938, Soviet editor, writer and communist leader, executed in one of Stalin's purges.

bulb /bʌlb/, *n.* **1.** *Bot.* **a.** a very short underground stem with fleshy white overlapping leaves, e.g. onion, lily. A bulb stores food and water, and may produce both flowering stems and roots. **b.** a plant growing from a bulb. **2.** any round, enlarged part: *the bulb of a thermometer; an electric light bulb.* [L, from Gk] **— bulbar,** *adj.*

bulbous /'bʌlbəs/, *adj.* **1.** bulb-shaped; bulging. **2.** having, or growing from, bulbs. Also, **bulbaceous** /bʌl'beɪʃəs/.

bulbul /'bulbul/, *n.* a small Asian bird with a black crest and red patch below the eye, introduced into Australia in the early 1900s. [Pers]

Bulgaria /bʌl'gɛəriə, bul-/, *n.* a republic in south-eastern Europe, in the eastern Balkans and on the Black Sea; a monarchy before 1946; a socialist republic 1946–91; parliamentary democracy from 1991. Pop. 8 949 618 (1986 est.). 110 912 km². *Languages*: Bulgarian, also Turkish and Macedonian. *Currency*: lev. *Cap.*: Sofia.

bulge /bʌldʒ/, *n.*, *v.*, **bulged, bulging.** ◇*n.* **1.** a rounded part that swells out; protuberance; hump. **2.** (*cap.*) **Battle of the**, the final German offensive of World War II, begun 16 December 1944 and thrusting deep into Allied territory in northern and eastern Belgium; repulsed January 1945. ◇*v.i.* **3.** to form a bulge; be protuberant. ◇*v.t.* **4.** to swell (something) out. [ME, from L: bag, of Celtic orig.] –**bulgy**, *adj.*

bulk /bʌlk/, *n.* **1.** size in regard to height, depth and width: *a ship of great bulk.* **2.** the main part of something: *They spend the bulk of their income on rent.* **3.** unpackaged goods or cargo. **4. in bulk, a.** unpackaged. **b.** in large quantities. ◇*v.i.* **5.** to be of bulk, weight, or importance. [ME *bolke* heap, from Scand]

bulkhead /ˈbʌlkhed/, *n.* **1.** one of the upright structures dividing a ship, an aircraft, etc., into parts. **2.** an upright structure built across an underground passage to prevent the passage of air, water, or mud.

bulky /ˈbʌlki/, *adj.*, **bulkier, bulkiest. 1.** of large and often awkward size. **2.** of or relating to wool of good substance, length and thickness. –**bulkily**, *adv.*

bull[1] /bʊl/, *n.* **1.** an uncastrated male animal of the bovine family. **2.** the male of certain other animals, as the elephant, whale, etc. **3.** *Stock Exchange.* someone who buys in the belief that rising prices will enable a quick profit to be made on resale. See **bear**[2] (def. 3). **4. bull in a china shop,** a clumsy person in a situation needing care. ◇*adj.* **5.** male. **6.** bull-like; large. [OE *bula*]

bull[2] /bʊl/, *Rom Cath Ch.* a formal written order or letter from the Pope, bearing his seal. [ME, from ML: seal, document, from L: bubble, knob]

bull[3] /bʊl/, *n. Colloq.* **1.** nonsense. **2.** dishonest or boastful talk. [shortened form of BULLSHIT]

Bullamakanka /bʊləməˈkæŋkə/, *n.* an imaginary and remote town.

bull ant, *n.* a type of large, attacking ant with powerful jaws and a very painful sting. Also, **bulldog ant.**

bull-bar /ˈbʊl-ba/, *n.* See **kangaroo bar.**

bulldog /ˈbʊldɒɡ/, *n.* a large-headed, short-haired type of dog, of fairly small size, but very powerful.

bulldoze /ˈbʊldoʊz/, *v.t.*, **-dozed, -dozing. 1.** to move with a bulldozer. **2.** *Colloq.* to force someone to do something, oft. with violence or threats. **3.** *Colloq.* to force or push: *They bulldozed their way through the crowd; He bulldozed the act through parliament.* [BULL¹ + *doze* (southern US d. var. of DOSE), i.e., give a dose fit for a bull]

bulldozer /ˈbʊldoʊzə/, *n.* a powerful tractor with a vertical blade at the front end for moving earth, rocks, etc.

bullet /ˈbʊlət/, *n.* **1.** a small metal object, for shooting from a small firearm. **2.** something like a bullet in shape, effect or movement. [F: little ball]

bulletin /ˈbʊlətən/, *n.* **1.** a short account or statement, as of news or events. **2.** a regular publication, as of a society. **3.** (*cap.*) **The Bulletin,** an Australian weekly news magazine, founded as a literary magazine in 1880 by J Archibald and J Haynes; taken over in 1962 by Australian Consolidated Press with completely new editorial policy. [F, from It. See BULL²]

bullfight /ˈbʊlfaɪt/, *n.* a form of entertainment in which a person fights with and usu. kills a bull. –**bullfighter,** *n.* –**bullfighting,** *n.*

bullfrog /ˈbʊlfrɒɡ/, *n.* a type of large, loud-voiced frog, as the Australian marsh frog.

bull-headed /bʊl-ˈhedəd/, *adj.* blindly determined; obstinate.

bullion /ˈbʊljən/, *n.* gold or silver in the mass or in the form of bars, etc. [ME, from AF: mint, from *bouillir* boil, from L]

bull market, *n. Stock Exchange.* a period of busy trading during and after a rise in share prices when traders consider that further price rises are likely.

bullock /ˈbʊlək/, *n.* **1.** a castrated male animal of the bovine family; steer. ◇*v.i.* **2.** to work very hard. [OE *bulluc*]

bullock dray, *n.* a wagon drawn by bullocks formerly used for carrying heavy loads of wool, timber, etc.

bullocky /ˈbʊləki/, *n.* **1.** a driver of a bullock team. **2.** violent language.

bullring /ˈbʊlrɪŋ/, *n.* a round enclosed area for bullfights.

bullroarer /ˈbʊlrɔrə/, *n.* a long, thin piece of wood on a string which is whirled in the air to make a roaring sound, used for religious ceremonies by Australian Aborigines, etc., and as a children's toy; thunder stick; churinga.

bullseye /ˈbʊlzaɪ/, *n.* **1.** a central spot, usu. black, of a target for shooting, etc. **2.** a shot that strikes the bullseye. **3.** a small circular opening or window. **4.** a thick, round piece of glass in a ship's deck, etc., to let in light. **5.** the central boss in a sheet of blown glass. **6.** a round, hard sweet.

bullshit /ˈbʊlʃɪt/, *n. Colloq. (offensive)* nonsense.

bull-terrier /bʊl-ˈterɪə/, *n.* a strongly built, short-haired breed of dog produced by crossing the bulldog and the terrier.

bully[1] /ˈbʊli/, *n.*, *pl.* **-lies,** *v.*, **-lied, -lying,** *adj.* ◇*n.* **1.** a person who likes frightening or ordering about smaller or weaker people. ◇*v.i., v.t.* **2.** to act as a bully (towards). ◇*adj.* **3.** *Colloq.* fine; excellent. [D *boele* lover]

bully[2] /ˈbʊli/, *n. Hockey.* a method by which play is started or restarted. Two opposing players with the ball between them strike the ground and the opponent's stick alternately three times, and then try to hit the ball first.

bully beef, *n. Colloq.* corned beef.

bulrush /ˈbʊlrʌʃ/, **1.** *Bible.* papyrus. **2.** a type of tall rushlike plant from which mats, seats of chairs, etc., are made. Also, **bull-rush**. [*bull* large + RUSH²]

bulwark /ˈbulwək/, *n.* **1.** a wall of earth or other material situated round a place as a defence; rampart. **2.** anything serving as a protection or defence. **3.** (*usu. pl.*) *Naut.* a solid part of a ship's side reaching up above the level of the deck. [ME]

bum /bʌm/, *n. v.*, **bummed, bumming**, *adj. Colloq.* ◇*n.* **1.** the buttocks. **2.** a lazy and irresponsible person. ◇*v.t.* **3.** to get (something) for nothing or borrow (something) without intending to return it. ◇*v.i.* **4.** to live as a bum (oft. fol. by **around**). ◇*adj.* **5.** of poor quality; [akin to BUMP]

bumble /ˈbʌmbl/, *v.*, **bumbled, bumbling**. *Colloq.* ◇*v.i.* **1.** to move, perform, or speak clumsily: *She bumbled through her speech.* ◇*v.t.* **2.** to manage badly.

bumblebee /ˈbʌmblbi/, *n.* a type of large, hairy social bee. Also, **humble bee**. [*bumble* BUZZ + BEE]

bummer /ˈbʌmə/, *n. Colloq.* a failure or disappointment.

bump /bʌmp/, *v.t.* **1.** to hit more or less heavily against; collide with. **2.** to cause (something) to hit: *I bumped my head on the ceiling.* ◇*v.i.* **3.** to hit; collide: *The cars bumped; He bumped into the wall.* **4.** to move with jerks: *The car bumped about on the rough ground.* ◇*v.* **5. bump into**, to meet (someone) by chance. **6. bump off**, *Colloq.* to kill. **7. bump up**, *Colloq.* to increase. ◇*n.* **8.** a light hit or blow. **9.** the act of hitting together; a collision. **10.** a swelling caused by a blow. **11.** a small area raised above the level of the surrounding surface, as on skull, road, etc. [imitative] –**bumpy**, *adj.*

bumper /ˈbʌmpə/, *n.* **1.** → **bumper bar**. **2.** a cup or glass completely filled. **3.** *Colloq.* something unusually large or full. **4.** *Colloq.* a cigarette end. **5.** *Cricket.* a ball which is so bowled that it bounces high; bouncer. ◇*adj.* **6.** unusually large or full: *a bumper crop.*

bumper bar, *n.* a bar fixed across the front or rear of a vehicle to give it protection if hit.

bumpkin /ˈbʌmpkɪn/, *n.* an awkward, clumsy person, oft. from the country. [MD: little barrel]

bumptious /ˈbʌmpʃəs/, *adj.* unpleasantly self-important: *I don't like that bumptious young man.* [BUMP + -*tious*, modelled on FRACTIOUS, etc.] –**bumptiousness**, *n.*

bun /bʌn/, *n.* **1.** a kind of bread roll, sweetened or savory, and round-shaped. **2.** hair arranged at the back of the head in the shape of a bun. [ME; orig. uncert.]

Bunbury /ˈbʌnbəri/, *n.* a city and major port in south-western WA, south of Perth. Pop. 23 031 (1986). [named after Lieutenant *Bunbury*, an explorer of the area in 1836]

bunch /bʌntʃ/, *n.* **1.** a group of things connected or gathered together; cluster: *a bunch of bananas; a bunch of flowers.* **2.** *Colloq.* a group of people. ◇*v.t., v.i.* **3.** to gather into folds or into a fold (oft. fol. by *up*): *She bunched her dress up; The children were told to bunch together.* [ME; orig. uncert.] –**bunchy**, *adj.*

Bundaberg /ˈbʌndəbɜg/, *n.* a city in south-eastern Qld, on the Burnett River; major sugar cane growing area. Pop. 33 368 (1986).

Bundesrat /ˈbʊndəsrat/, *n.* **1.** (formerly) a federal legislative council of representatives from the 26 states of the German Empire. **2.** (formerly) the upper house of the federal West German parliament. [G]

Bundestag /ˈbʊndəstak/, *n.* (formerly) the lower house of the federal West German parliament.

bundle /ˈbʌndl/, *n., v.*, **-dled, -dling**. ◇*n.* **1.** a group of things loosely held together: *a bundle of hay.* **2.** something wrapped for carrying; package. **3.** *Biol.* a collection of strands of specialised tissue. **4. drop one's bundle**, *Colloq.* to lose mental control, hope, etc. ◇*v.t.* **5.** to dress warmly (fol. by *up*). **6.** to send away hastily (fol. by *off, out,* etc.). ◇*v.i.* **7.** to leave hastily (fol. by *off, out,* etc.). **8.** to dress warmly (fol by *up*). [ME, from MD; akin to OE *byndele* binding together]

bundy /ˈbʌndi/, *n. Colloq.* a clock which marks the arrival and departure times of employees on a card pushed into it. [Trademark]

bung /bʌŋ/, *n.* **1.** a stopper for the hole of a cask, etc. **2.** → **bunghole**. ◇*v.t.* **3.** to close with a bung (oft. fol. by *up*). **4.** to block (oft. by *up*). **5.** *Colloq.* to throw; toss. **6.** to arrange hastily. ◇*adj.* **7.** *Colloq.* in poor working order. [ME, from MD]

bungalow /ˈbʌŋɡəloʊ/, *n.* a house of one storey. [Hind: of Bengal]

Bungaree /ˈbʌŋɡəri/, *n.* died 1830, an Australian Aboriginal guide and interpreter who sailed around Australia with Matthew Flinders in 1801–02 and accompanied Phillip Parker King's expedition.

bunger /ˈbʌŋə/, *n.* a firework which produces a loud bang.

bunghole /ˈbʌŋhoʊl/, *n.* a hole in a cask through which it is filled.

bungle /ˈbʌŋɡəl/, *v.*, **-gled, -gling**, *n.* ◇*v.i., v.t.* **1.** to do (something) awkwardly or incorrectly. ◇*n.* **2.** the act of bungling. **3.** something which is bungled. [? imitative]

bunion /ˈbʌnjən/, *n.* a swelling of a joint on the foot, esp. on the big toe. [orig. obscure]

bunk /bʌŋk/, *n.* **1.** a built-in bed like a shelf, as on a ship. **2.** one of pair of beds built one above the other. **3.** *Colloq.* any bed. ◇*v.i.* **4.** *Colloq.* to lie down in a place for sleep, esp. in rough conditions (oft. fol. by *down*). [orig. unknown]

bunker¹ /ˈbʌŋkə/, *n.* **1.** a large holder for fuel, etc. **2.** *Golf.* an area, usu. at the side of a green, which has been dug out and nearly filled with sand to form a hazard. ◇*v.t.* **3.** *Golf.* to hit (a ball) into a bunker [orig. uncert.]

bunker² /ˈbʌŋkə/, *n.* a shelter, oft. underground, for protection against air attack, bombs, etc. [G]

bunkum /ˈbʌŋkəm/, *n.* insincere talk. Also, **bunk**. [alteration of *Buncombe*, a county in the

US, in North Carolina, from its Congressional representative's phrase, 'talking for Buncombe']

bunny /'bʌni/, *n., pl.* **-nies.** *Colloq.* **1.** a rabbit. **2.** a foolish or unlucky person, esp. someone left with the responsibility for a situation.

Bunny /'bʌni/, *n.* **Rupert Charles Wulsten**, 1864–1947, Australian artist who worked mainly in France.

Bunsen /'bʌnsən/, *n.* **Robert Wilhelm** /'vɪlhɛlm/, 1811–99, German chemist; discovered caesium and rubidium; developed spectrum analysis with Gustav Kirchhoff.

Bunsen burner, *n.* a type of gas burner with a very hot, blue flame, used widely in laboratories. [named after RW BUNSEN]

bunt /bʌnt/, *v.t.* **1.** to push (something) with the horns or head. **2.** *Baseball.* to bat (the ball) gently so that it moves a short distance. ◊*n.* **3.** *Baseball.* the act of bunting. [nasalised var. of BUTT[3]]

bunting /'bʌntɪŋ/, *n.* **1.** a coarse open cloth used for flags, signals. **2.** flags or other decorations made from long pieces of bunting. [cf. G *bunt* of various colors]

bunya-bunya /'bʌnjə-bʌnjə/, *n.* a tall, cone-bearing tree of Australia, the seeds of which can be eaten. [Aboriginal]

Bunyan /'bʌnjən/, *n.* **John**, 1628–88, English preacher and author of *The Pilgrim's Progress* (1678).

bunyip /'bʌnjəp/, *n.* an imaginary creature of Aboriginal legend, said to live in swamps and streams. [Aboriginal]

buoy /bɔɪ/, *n. Naut.* **1.** an anchored floating object, marking a channel, hidden rocks, etc. **2.** → lifebuoy. ◊*v.t.* **3.** to keep afloat: *She used a piece of wood to buoy her up.* **4.** to lift the spirits of; encourage: *Hope buoyed them up.* **5.** *Naut.* to mark with a buoy. [ME, from MD: buoy, from L: fetter]

buoyancy /'bɔɪənsi/, *n.* **1.** the power to float or rise in a liquid. **2.** the power of supporting something so that it floats. **3.** cheerfulness. —**buoyant**, *adj.*

Burarra /bu'rarə/, *n.* an Australian Aboriginal language of the Blyth River, NT. Also, **Burera, Barera**.

burble /'bɜbəl/, *v.,* **-bled, -bling,** *n.* ◊*v.t.* **1.** to make a bubbling sound. **2.** to speak quickly and unclearly. ◊*n.* **3.** a bubbling, gentle sound. **4.** a flow of excited, unclear speech. [probably imitative]

Burchett /'bɜtʃət/, *n.* **Wilfred Graham**, 1911–83, Australian journalist; the first Western journalist in Hiroshima after the 1945 atom bomb.

Burdekin /'bɜdəkən/, *n.* a major river system in coastal north-eastern Qld, rising inland from Ingham and flowing south-east, then north, to form a delta near Ayr. Over 720 km.

burden /'bɜdn/, *n.* **1.** something which is carried; load. **2.** something which is borne with difficulty: *burden of responsibilities.* **3.** the weight that a ship is able to carry. ◊*v.t.* **4.** to load heavily. [OE *byrthen*] —**burdensome**, *adj.*

bureau /'bjurou, bju'rou/, *n., pl.* **-eaus, -eaux** /-ouz/. **1.** a desk with drawers for papers. **2.** a government or independent office for giving out information, administration, etc. [F: desk, office, OF: cloth-covered table, kind of woollen cloth, from L: woollen cloth]

bureaucracy /bju'rɒkrəsi/, *n., pl.* **-cies.** **1.** a system of administration marked by centralisation of authority, a hierarchical structure, specialisation of function, and strictly prescribed rules and procedures. **2.** unnecessary official rules and procedures. **3.** a body of administrative officials, e.g. in the public service; the public service as a whole. **4.** (government by) unelected officials who are not directly responsible to the public. **5.** the unnecessary widening of the number and power of government departments and bureaus. [F. See BUREAU, -CRACY]

bureaucrat /'bjurəkræt/, *n.* an official of a bureaucracy, esp. one who follows rules without exercising intelligent judgment. —**bureaucratic**, *adj.*

burette /bju'rɛt/, *n.* a glass tube marked with units of measurement, with a tap at the bottom, used for measuring small quantities of liquid. [F: cruet, diminutive of *buire* vessel for wine, etc.]

burg /bɜg/, *n. Hist.* a fortified town. [var. of *burgh* borough]

burgeon /'bɜdʒən/, *v.i.* **1.** to begin to grow by putting out buds, shoots, as a plant (oft. fol. by *out, forth*). **2.** to grow rapidly: *The population of the town burgeoned.* Also, **bourgeon**. [ME, from OF, ? from Gmc]

burgess /'bɜdʒəs/, *n. Hist.* a representative of a borough, corporate town, or university in Parliament. [ME, from LL: a citizen]

Burgess /'bɜdʒəs/, *n.* **1. Anthony**, born 1917, English satirical novelist and essayist; author of *A Clockwork Orange* (1962). **2. Guy**, 1911–63, British spy, defected to the Soviet Union in 1951.

burgher /'bɜgə/, *n. Hist.* a citizen of a town, esp. a trader in a medieval city.

burglar /'bɜglə/, *n.* someone who commits a burglary. [AF *burgur* burglar, from *burgier* pillage]

burglary /'bɜgləri/, *n., pl.* **-ries.** the crime of breaking into and entering a building intending to commit a robbery or other wrongdoing.

burgle /'bɜgəl/, *v.i., v.t.,* **-gled, -gling.** to perform a burglary (in). [backformation from BURGLAR]

burgundy /'bɜgəndi/, *n., pl.* **-dies. 1.** a type of wine, red or white, which is usu. still and dry, produced in the Burgundy (def. 3) region. **2.** a dull bluish red (color). **3.** (*cap.*) an administrative region in south-eastern France. Pop. 1 607 300 (1986 est.); 31 779 km^2. **4.** (*cap.*) a medieval European monarchy (1384–1477) which included most of present-day Belgium and the Netherlands.

burial /ˈberiəl/, *n.* an act of burying, esp. a dead body. [BURY + -AL² (cf. FUNERAL)]

burin /ˈbjuərən/, *n.* **1.** a pointed steel rod, used for engraving in metal or marble. **2.** a stone tool used formerly by the Aborigines of eastern NSW. [F, probably of Gmc orig.]

Burke /bɜk/, *n.* **Robert O'Hara**, 1821–61, Australian explorer, born in Ireland; with William Wills led the expedition that first crossed Australia south to north 1860–61; died during return trip.

burl /bɜl/, *Colloq.* ◇*n.* **1.** a try. ◇*v.i.* **2.** to move quickly. (fol. by *along*). [northern Brit d. *birl* to spin]

burlap /ˈbɜlæp/, *n.* →**hessian**.

burlesque /bɜˈlɛsk/, *n., adj., v.,* **-lesqued, -lesquing.** ◇*n.* **1.** a literary or theatrical work which amuses by treating serious material with ridicule or ordinary material with pretended seriousness. **2.** any comic imitation; caricature. ◇*adj.* **3.** of or relating to burlesque. ◇*v.i.* **4.** to make a comic imitation. ◇*v.t.* **5.** to make (someone or something) ridiculous by doing this. [F, from It *burlesco*, from *burla* jest, mockery]

burly /ˈbɜli/, *adj.,* **-lier, -liest.** large in bodily size; stout. [ME; orig. uncert.]

Burma /ˈbɜmə/, *n.* a socialist republic in South-East Asia, bordered by Bangladesh, India, China, Laos and Thailand; part of British India until 1937, then a separate British dependency until independence in 1948; military rule (since 1988) adopted official name of Myanmar in 1989. Pop. 35 307 913 (1983); 676 552 km². Language: Burmese. Currency: kyat. Cap.: Rangoon. —**Burmese**, *adj., n.*

Burma Road, *n.* a mountainous road extending from Lashio in Burma through China to Kunming in Yunnan province; used in World War II for supplying Jiang Jie-shi's forces in China.

burn /bɜn/, *v.,* **burnt** or **burned, burning,** *n.* ◇*v.i.* **1.** to be on fire: *The wood is burning.* **2.** to feel extreme heat or similar: *His face burned in the wind.* **3.** to give light or extreme heat: *The lights burn all night; This sand burns.* **4.** to feel strongly: *She was burning with anger.* **5.** to undergo combustion. **6.** to become discolored, tanned, or blackened through heat: *The meat is burning.* ◇*v.t.* **7.** to destroy, partly or wholly, with fire. **8.** to cause to feel heat. **9.** to damage, discolor, or treat with heat: *The sun burnt her back; Don't burn your fingers.* **10.** to form by fire or heat: *to burn a hole.* **11.** *Chem.* to cause to undergo combustion. **12.** to pass through or over quickly (fol. by *up*): *This car burns up the kilometres.* **13.** to clear or improve land by burning the cover (oft. fol. by *off*). ◇*v.* **14. burn one's fingers,** to suffer through having interfered. ◇*n.* **15.** *Pathol.* a wound produced by heat or extreme cold, wind, chemicals, poison gas, electricity, or lightning. **16.** an act of burning or baking, as in brickmaking. **17.** Also, **burn-off.** the action or result of clearing land by fire. [OE]

burn-back /ˈbɜn-bæk/, *n.* the burning of undergrowth, etc., to prevent bush fires.

burner /ˈbɜnə/, *n.* that part of a gas stove, lamp, etc., from which flame comes.

Burnet /ˈbɜːnɛt/, *n.* **Sir (Frank) Macfarlane**, 1899–1985, Australian medical scientist; joint winner of the Nobel prize for medicine (1960) for his work in immunology.

Burnett /ˈbɜːnɛt/, *n.* a river in coastal south-eastern Qld, rising near Burnett Heads and flowing into Hervey Bay. About 430 km.

Burnie /ˈbɜni/, *n.* a town, municipality and port on the north-western coast of Tas. Pop. 20 665 (1986).

burning /ˈbɜnɪŋ/, *adj.* of great importance and interest: *a burning question.*

burnish /ˈbɜnɪʃ/, *v.t.* **1.** to polish (a surface) by rubbing. ◇*n.* **2.** brightness; gloss. [ME, from OF: make brown, polish, from *brun* brown, from Gmc]

Burns /bɜnz/, *n.* **1. George** (*Nathan Birnbaum*), born 1896, US comic entertainer. **2. Robert**, 1759–96, Scottish lyric poet whose works include *Auld Lang Syne.*

Burns, Philp and Co Ltd /fɪlp/, *n.* an Australian company operating as a wholesale and retail merchant, importer, shipping and general travel agent, steel, glass and liquor merchant, etc.; incorporated in 1883, public status since 1896.

burnt /bɜnt/, *v.* past tense and past participle of **burn.**

burnt sienna, *n.* See **sienna.**

burp /bɜp/, *n. Colloq.* **1.** → **belch** (def. 4). ◇*v.i.* **2.** → **belch** (def. 1). ◇*v.t.* **3.** to cause (a baby) to belch, by patting on the back after feeding. [imitative]

burr¹ /bɜ/, *n.* **1.** *Bot.* a rough, prickly case around the seeds of certain plants, such as the chestnut. **2.** something or someone that sticks like a burr. [ME, from Scand] —**burry,** *adj.*

burr² /bɜ/, *n.* **1.** a type of tool for cutting or drilling. **2.** a rough area left on metal after cutting, drilling, etc. [var. of BURR¹]

burr³ /bɜ/, *n.* **1.** a certain pronunciation of the letter *r* that marks some English dialects. **2.** a whirring sound. ◇*v.i.* **3.** to make a whirring sound. [apparently imitative; ? associated with idea of roughness in BURR¹]

Burragorang /ˈbʌrəɡəræŋ/, *n.* **Lake,** a large reservoir in eastern NSW, created by the Warragamba dam; forming part of the water supply for Sydney and Wollongong.

Burrinjuck Dam /ˌbʌrəndʒʌk ˈdæm/, *n.* a dam on the Murrumbidgee River, NSW, used for irrigation and hydro-electricity.

burramys /ˈbʌrəməs/, *n.* a small mountain possum, which is very rare and lives only at Mt Hotham, Vic.

burrawang /ˈbʌrəwæŋ/, *n.* a palm-like plant of Australia, the nuts of which were once eaten by Aborigines. [Aboriginal]

burren /ˈbʌrən/, *n. Archaeol.* a type of stone flake worn away on both edges.

burr medic, *n.* a type of pasture herb with pods bearing small hooks. Also, **burr medick.**

burro — Bush Nursing Association

burro /'bʌroʊ, 'bʊroʊ/, *n., pl.* **-ros.** a donkey, esp. one used to carry loads. [Sp: small horse, from L]

burrow /'bʌroʊ/, *n.* **1.** a hole in the ground made by a small animal, such as a rabbit, to live and shelter in. **2.** any similar place of shelter. ◊*v.i.* **3.** to make a burrow. **4.** to live or hide in a burrow. **5.** to search with a digging movement: *She burrowed into her bag.* ◊*v.t.* **6.** to make a burrow in (hill, etc.). **7.** to make (a hole) by burrowing. [ME]

bursar /'bɜsə/, *n.* **1.** an officer in charge of money, etc., esp. of college or university. **2.** a student holding a bursary. [ML: purse]

bursary /'bɜsəri/, *n., pl.* **-ries.** a grant of money to a school or university student. [ML]

burst /bɜst/, *v.,* **burst, bursting,** *n.* ◊*v.i.* **1.** to break open with sudden violence; explode. **2.** to come or go suddenly and forcibly: *He burst out of the room; The idea burst into my mind.* **3.** to give way to an expression of violent emotion: *to burst into speech; to burst into tears.* **4.** to be very full, as if ready to break open: *The bag was bursting with shopping; I am bursting with anger.* ◊*v.t.* **5.** to cause (something) to burst. ◊*n.* **6.** an act or result of bursting. **7.** a sudden action or effort: *a burst of clapping; a burst of speed.* **8.** a sudden expression of emotion, etc. [OE *berstan*]

bury /'bɛri/, *v.t.,* **buried, burying.** **1.** to put in the ground and cover with earth. **2.** to put (a dead body) into the ground, a tomb, or the sea. **3.** to cause (something) to sink in: *He buried the knife in her chest.* **4.** to cover in order to hide: *She buried her face in her hands.* **5.** to occupy (oneself) completely: *He buried himself in his work.* **6.** to put out of mind: *to bury a disagreement.* [OE *byrgan*]

bus /bʌs/, *n., pl.* **buses** or **busses,** *v.,* **bussed, bussing** or **bused, busing.** ◊*n.* **1.** a vehicle with a long body containing seats for passengers, usu. operating as part of a regular service; omnibus. **2.** *Colloq.* a motor car or aeroplane. **3.** *Computers.* a circuit or group of circuits which provide a communication path between two or more devices. **4. miss the bus,** to miss one's only chance. ◊*v.i.* **5.** to travel by bus. ◊*v.t.* **6.** to transport (people) by bus. [short for OMNIBUS]

busby /'bʌzbi/, *n., pl.* **-bies.** **1.** a tall fur hat, worn by some divisions in the British Army. **2.** → **bearskin** (def. 2). [? akin to obs. *buzz wig*]

Busby /'bʌzbi/, *n.* **1. James,** 1801–71, Scottish viticulturist and administrator in Australia and New Zealand. **2.** his father, **John,** 1765–1857, English-born Australian civil engineer; constructed **Busby's Bore** which served Sydney with water 1830–58.

bush[1] /bʊʃ/, *n.* **1.** a woody plant with many branches which usu. arise from or near the ground. **2.** *Bot.* a small group of shrubs appearing as a single plant. **3.** something suggesting this, as a thick head of hair, or an animal's tail. **4.** an area of land covered with bushy growth or trees. **5.** the countryside in general, as opposed to the towns. **6. beat about the bush,** to avoid coming to the point in a conversation, etc. **7. go bush, a.** to take up a way of life close to nature. **b.** Also, **take to the bush.** to disappear suddenly from one's normal surroundings. ◊*v.i.* **8.** to be or become like a bush. ◊*adj.* **9.** uncivilised; rough. [ME; unexplained var. of *busk,* from Scand] —**bushy,** *adj.*

bush[2] /bʊʃ/, *n. Mech.* **1.** a metal lining put into a hole to prevent wearing. **2.** a metal lining, usu. removable, used as a bearing. ◊*v.t.* **3.** to provide with a bush. [MD]

Bush /bʊʃ/, *n.* **George Herbert,** born 1924, US Republican politician; vice-president 1980–89; 41st president of the US 1989–93.

bush ballad, *n.* a poem in ballad metre dealing with life in the Australian bush.

bush band, *n.* a band which performs Australian folk music, usu. with such instruments as the accordion, tea-chest bass, guitar, etc.

Bush Brotherhood, *n.* (*also l.c.*) a society of Anglican clergy and lay people formed in 1897 which conducts the ministry of the church in the remote areas of Australia.

bushcraft /'bʊʃkrɑft/, *n.* a knowledge of how to live in and travel through the bush.

Bush Church Aid Society, *n.* an organisation formed in Sydney, NSW, in 1919 by Anglican clergy and lay people to provide missionary and medical services to outback Australia. *Abbrev.:* BCA

bushed /bʊʃt/, *adj.* **1.** lost. **2.** very tired; exhausted. **3.** confused.

bushel /'bʊʃəl/, *n.* a unit of dry measure in the imperial system equal to $36.36872 \times 10^{-3} m^3$ (eight gallons). [ME, from OF, from Gallic word meaning hollow of the hand]

bushfire /'bʊʃfaɪə/, *n.* a fire in forest or bush country.

bush fly, *n.* a type of small, black fly, large numbers of which fly about humans and animals in the bush.

bush house, *n.* a small garden shelter in which plants being cultivated are protected from the weather.

bushido /bʊ'ʃidoʊ/, *n.* a code of behavior of warriors of feudal Japan, based on unselfish loyalty and courage. [Jap: lit. the way of the warrior]

bushie /'bʊʃi/, *n.* a person, usu. uncultivated, who lives in the bush.

Bush Inn /bʊʃ ɪn/, *n.* a hotel in New Norfolk, Tasmania, which claims to be the oldest hotel still operating in Australia; now known as the **Bush Hotel.**

bush-lawyer /bʊʃ-'lɔjə/, *n. Colloq.* a person who pretends to knowledge of the law. Also, **bush lawyer.**

bushman /'bʊʃmən/, *n.* **1.** a person who lives in the bush. **2.** someone skilled in bushcraft. —**bushmanship,** *n.*

Bush Nursing Association, *n.* one of the autonomous organisations established in the various states of Australia to provide a district nursing service to isolated communities and out-

bushranger /'buʃreɪndʒə/, n. 1. (formerly) a person who hid in the bush and lived by robbing travellers. 2. (formerly) someone knowing how to live in rough country; bushman. —**bushranging**, n.

bush rat, n. a type of Australian native rodent.

bush sickness, n. the loss of strength and weight leading to death in sheep, cattle and goats, due to lack of minerals in pastures. —**bush-sick**, adj.

bush telegraph, n. 1. a system of sending messages over wide distances among primitive peoples, by drumbeats, etc. 2. Colloq. an unofficial method of sending messages and spreading information quickly, as by word of mouth. Also, **bush wireless**.

bushwalk /'buʃwɔk/, v.i. to walk through the bush for pleasure or sport. —**bushwalker**, n. —**bushwalking**, n.

bush week, n. Colloq. 1. an imaginary holiday time when country people come to town. 2. a time when people are taken advantage of.

bushwhacker /'buʃwækə/, n. Colloq. someone who lives in the bush; bushie. —**bushwhacking**, n.

busily /'bɪzəli/, adv. in a busy manner.

business /'bɪznəs/, n. 1. someone's work or trade. 2. Econ. the buying and selling of goods in order to make a profit. 3. Comm. a person or company doing this. 4. something with which a person is rightfully concerned. 5. affair; matter. 6. **mean business**, to have serious intentions. [OE (North) bisignes]

businessman /'bɪznəsmən/, n., pl. **-men** /-mən/ a man who works in commercial business or trade.

businesswoman /'bɪznəswumən/, n., pl. **-women** /-wɪmən/. a woman who works in commercial business or trade.

busker /'bʌskə/, n. an entertainer who gives performances in streets, parks, markets, etc. —**busk**, v.

buskin /'bʌskən/, n. 1. (formerly) an outer covering for the foot and leg reaching to the calf. 2. the high shoe worn by tragic actors of ancient Greece and Rome. [orig. uncert.]

buss /bʌs/, n., v.t., v.i. Archaic. kiss. [cf. d. G Buss]

Bussell /'bʌsəl/, n. **Grace**, 1860–1935, Australian woman who, with stockman Sam Isaacs, rescued the passengers of the wrecked steamer Georgette in 1876 near Busselton, WA.

Busselton /'bʌsəltən/, n. a town and shire on Geographe Bay in southern WA; holiday and tourist resort. Pop. 7784 (1986).

bust[1] /bʌst/, n. 1. a sculpture of the head and shoulders of a person. 2. the chest or breast, esp. of a woman. [F, from It busto, of unknown orig.]

bust[2] /bʌst/, Colloq. ◇v.i. 1. to burst. 2. (of friends, etc.) to quarrel and part (fol. by up).
◇v.t. 3. to burst (oft. fol. by in). 4. to break (oft. fol. by up). 5. to interrupt violently and cause (a meeting, etc.) to break up (fol. by up). 6. (of police) to raid and arrest. ◇n. 7. a complete failure; bankruptcy. 8. a drunken party. 9. a police raid. ◇adj. 10. Also, **busted**. broken; ruined. 11. bankrupt. [d. or colloq. var. of BURST]

bustard /'bʌstəd/, n. a large, heavy bird living in the grassy plains and open scrub country of Australia. Also, **plains turkey**. [ME, from OF, from L avis tarda slow bird]

buster /'bʌstə/, n. 1. Colloq. (a term of address to man or boy). 2. → **southerly buster**.

bustle[1] /'bʌsəl/, v., **-tled, -tling**, n. ◇v.i. 1. to move or act with a great show of energy (oft. fol. by about). ◇v.t. 2. to cause (someone) to bustle. ◇n. 3. energetic activity; commotion. [? var. of obs. buskle]

bustle[2] /'bʌsəl/, n. (formerly) a pad or wire framework worn by women at the back to fill out the skirt. [? from BUSTLE[1]]

bust-up /'bʌst-ʌp/, n. a fight or quarrel, leading to a parting between friends, etc.

busy /'bɪzi/, adj., **busier, busiest**, v., **busied, busying**. ◇adj. 1. actively occupied: He is busy with his work; She is too busy to come. 2. full of or marked by activity: a busy time of the day. 3. → **engaged** (def.4). ◇v.t. 4. to make or keep busy: I am going to busy myself writing letters. [OE bysig busy] —**busyness**, n.

busybody /'bɪzibɒdi/, n., pl. **-bodies**. a person who interferes in the affairs of others.

but /bʌt/; weak form /bət/, conj. 1. on the contrary: They all went, but I didn't. 2. except that (oft. fol. by that): Nothing would please him but that I should sing. 3. without it also being the case that: It never rains but it pours. 4. other than: I can do nothing but go. 5. **but for**, except for; were it not for: She would have died but for you. ◇prep. 6. except; save: No one replied but me. ◇adv. 7. only: There is but one correct answer. 8. though; however: But this was not the end of the story. 9. **all but**, almost: It is all but finished. ◇n. 10. an objection: Let us have no buts about it. [OE b(e)ūta(n) on the outside, without]

butane /'bjuten, bju'teɪn/, n. an aliphatic hydrocarbon, C_4H_{10}, having two isomeric forms and used as a fuel. See **-ane**. [BUT(YL) + -ANE]

butch /butʃ/, adj. Colloq. with a notably masculine appearance or manner. [? from BUTCHER]

butcher /'butʃə/, n. 1. someone who sells meat. 2. someone who kills animals, or prepares their flesh for food or market. 3. a cruel and violent murderer. ◇v.t. 4. to kill (animals) for food or market. 5. to murder violently. 6. to make a mess of: to butcher a job. [ME, from OF boc he-goat, from Gmc] —**butchery**, n.

butcherbird /'butʃəbɜd/, n. a type of shrike-like Australian bird which hangs its dead prey on spikes or thorns.

butler /'bʌtlə/, *n.* the head male servant of a household. [ME, from AF *bouteille* bottle]

Butler /'bʌtlə/, *n.* **Samuel**, 1835–1902, English novelist, author of *The Way of All Flesh* (1903).

butt[1] /bʌt/, *n.* **1.** the thick, large or blunt end of anything, as of a gun, fishing rod, arrow, etc. **2.** an end which is not used up, as of a cigarette. **3.** a hind leg of beef on the bone. [ME; apparently short for BUTTOCK]

butt[2] /bʌt/, *n.* **1.** a person or thing that is an object of humor, ridicule, etc: *He is always the butt of their jokes.* **2.** (in rifle or archery practice) a wall of earth behind the targets which stops bullets or arrows. **3.** (*pl.*) an area with targets for rifle or archery practice. ◇*v.i.* **4.** →**abut**. ◇*v.t.* **5.** to join the ends of (two things) together. [ME, from OF: end, extremity, of Gmc orig.]

butt[3] /bʌt/, *v.t.* **1.** to strike with the head or horns. ◇*v.i.* **2.** to strike something or at something with the head or horns. **3.** to stick out. **4.** *Colloq.* to interrupt or interfere. (fol. by *in*). ◇*n.* **5.** a push with head or horns. [ME, from OF, strike, thrust, abut, touch, from *bout* end, of Gmc orig.]

butt[4] /bʌt/, *n.* **1.** a large cask or barrel, esp. for wine or beer. **2.** *Wool.* a package and measure of greasy wool. [ME]

butte /bjut/, *n.* *US and Canada.* a single hill or mountain rising suddenly above the surrounding land. [F: hill, properly, mound for target]

butter /'bʌtə/, *n.* **1.** a soft, yellowish solid formed from the fatty part of milk during churning and used for eating and cooking. **2.** any food substance used similarly for spreading: *peanut butter.* **3.** any of certain butter-like substances, as some metallic chlorides and vegetable oils which are solid at ordinary temperatures. ◇*v.t.* **4.** to put butter on. **5.** *Colloq.* to try to please by praising (oft. fol. by *up*). [OE *butere*, from L, from Gk] –**buttery**, *adj.*

buttercup /'bʌtəkʌp/, *n.* →**ranunculus**.

butter-fingers /'bʌtə-fɪŋɡəz/, *n.* *Colloq.* a person who drops things easily.

butterfly /'bʌtəflaɪ/, *n.*, *pl.* **-flies. 1.** a type of insect, active during the day, with joined antennae and large, broad wings, oft. brightly colored and marked. **2.** (*pl.*) a nervous feeling in the stomach. **3.** *Swimming.* Also, **butterfly stroke.** a stroke in which both arms are lifted together from the water and thrown forward. [OE *buttorflēoge*, ? orig. used of a butter-colored (yellow) species]

Butterley /'bʌtəli/, *n.* **Nigel Henry**, born 1935, Australian pianist and composer.

buttermilk /'bʌtəmɪlk/, *n.* the sour liquid remaining after butter has been separated from milk or cream.

butternut pumpkin /ˌbʌtənʌt 'pʌmpkən/, *n.* a type of pumpkin, long in shape, with orange flesh and skin, which is widely used as a vegetable.

butterscotch /'bʌtəskɒtʃ/, *n.* a kind of toffee or flavoring made with butter, brown sugar, vanilla extract, etc.

buttery /'bʌtəri/, *n.*, *pl.* **-ries. 1.** a room in which the wines and provisions of a household are kept; pantry. **2.** a room in universities, etc., in which food and drink are supplied to students. [ME, from OF: cask]

buttock /'bʌtək/, *n.* *Anat.* either of the two rounded parts of the body at the base of the back. [OE *buttuc*]

button /'bʌtn/, *n.* **1.** a small solid object, usu. round, used as a fastening or ornament on clothing. **2.** anything like a button in shape and size, as a young mushroom or a small knob pressed to ring a bell, etc. **3.** *Bot.* a bud or other outgrowth of a plant. ◇*v.t.* **4.** to fasten with a button or buttons. **5.** *Colloq.* to complete (business, etc.) successfully (fol. by *up*). [ME, from OF: thrust]

buttonhole /'bʌtnhoʊl/, *n.*, *v.*, **-holed, -holing.** ◇*n.* **1.** a hole through which a button is passed in order to fasten. **2.** a small flower or group of flowers worn in buttonhole in the lapel of a coat. ◇*v.t.* **3.** to make buttonholes in. **4.** to hold (someone) up with conversation.

buttonhole stitch, *n.* a type of stitch used to strengthen the edge of material, as in a buttonhole.

buttress /'bʌtrəs/, *n.* **1.** *Archit.* a structure built against a wall or building for the purpose of giving it support. **2.** any support; prop. ◇*v.t.* **3.** *Archit.* to support by a buttress. **4.** to support; prop up: *He buttressed his argument with examples.* [OF *bouterez*, pl., from *bouter* thrust; abut]

buttress root, *n.* a flattened growth from the root and trunk of certain trees, esp. of the rain forest.

butyl /'bjutəl/, *n.* a univalent radical, C_4H_9-, derived from butane. See **alkyl group**.

Buvelot /'buvəloʊ/, *n.* **Abram-Louis**, 1814–88, Swiss artist in Australia; noted for his Australian landscapes.

buxom /'bʌksəm/, *adj.* (of a woman) **1.** large-breasted. **2.** healthily plump, attractive and cheerful. [OE *būgan* bend, bow]

buy /baɪ/, *v.*, **bought, buying**, *n.* ◇*v.t.* **1.** to gain possession of, or right to, by paying money. **2.** to gain by giving other kind of payment or reward: *He tried to buy her love with flattery.* **3.** *Colloq.* to accept (an idea, explanation, etc.). ◇*v.i.* **4.** to be or become a buyer. ◇*v.* **5. buy off,** to get rid of (claim, opposition, etc.) by payment; bribe. **6. buy out,** to buy all of the shares, or interest of (a partner or owner of company, etc.). **7. buy up,** to buy as much as one can of. **8. buy into, a.** to buy shares in (a company, etc.). **b.** *Colloq.* to choose to become involved in (an argument, etc.). ◇*n.* **9.** the act of buying or the thing bought: *Those shoes were a good buy.* [OE *bycgan*]

buyer /'baɪə/, *n.* **1.** someone who buys. **2.** someone whose work is to buy stock for a department store, etc.

Buzo /'bjuzoʊ/, *n.* **Alexander John**, born 1944, Australian playwright; plays include *The*

buzz /bʌz/, *n.* **1.** a low, humming sound, as of bees or many people speaking. **2.** *Colloq.* a telephone call. **3.** *Colloq.* a pleasant bodily feeling, as from drugs. ◇*v.i.* **4.** to make a low, humming sound. **5.** to move busily from place to place (usu. fol. by *about*). **6.** *Colloq.* to go; leave (usu. fol. by *off*). ◇*v.t.* **7.** to make a buzzing sound with: *The fly buzzed its wings.* **8.** *Colloq.* to call (someone) by telephone or buzzer. **9.** *Aeron. Colloq.* to fly an aeroplane very low over: *to buzz a field.* [imitative]

buzzard /'bʌzəd/, *n.* a heavily-built bird of the hawk family. [ME, from OF, from L: kind of hawk]

buzzer /'bʌzə/, *n.* an electrical device which signals with a buzz.

buzz-saw /'bʌz-sɔ/, *n.* a small circular saw, so named because of the noise it makes.

B/W, *Abbrev.* black and white.

by /baɪ/, *prep.* **1.** near to: *a house by the river.* **2.** using as a way; via: *He came by the main road*; *They travelled by car.* **3.** past (a point near): *She went by the church.* **4.** during: *by day; by night.* **5.** not later than: *Be home by 2 o'clock.* **6.** to the amount of: *dearer by 20 cents.* **7.** according to: *by his own account*; *by any standards.* **8.** with the participation of: *missed by us all.* **9.** in the name of: *to swear by the Bible.* **10.** through the action of: *The tree was planted by the queen*; *It was done by force.* **11.** in serial order after: *piece by piece.* **12.** combined with (in multiplication or relative measurements): *5 by 6 equals 30; The room measures 4 metres by 5 metres.* **13.** using as a unit of measure: *beef by the kilogram.* ◇*adv.* **14.** near: *It is close by.* **15.** past a point near something: *The car drove by.* **16.** aside: *Put it by for the moment.* **17.** over; past: *in times gone by.* **18. by and by,** before long; presently. **19. by and large,** in general. [OE *bī*]

by-, a prefix meaning **1.** secondary; incidental, as in *by-product.* **2.** out of the way; removed, as in *byway.* **3.** near, as in *bystander.* Also, **bye-**.

bye /baɪ/, *n.* **1.** *Sport.* a state of having no opponent in a contest where competitors are in pairs, bringing the right to compete in the next round. **2.** *Cricket.* a run made on a ball not struck by the batsman. **3. by the bye.** Also, **by the by,** by the way; incidentally. [var. spelling of BY, *prep.*, in noun use]

bye-bye /baɪ-'baɪ/, *interj.* /'baɪ-baɪ/, *n., pl.* **bye-byes.** *Colloq.* ◇*interj.* **1.** goodbye. ◇*n.* **2.** (*pl.*) (*in children's speech*) sleep.

by-election /'baɪ-əlekʃən/, *n.* a parliamentary election held between general elections, to fill the seat of a member who has died, retired, etc. Also, **bye-election.**

bygone /'baɪgɒn/, *adj.* **1.** past; gone by: *bygone days.* ◇*n.* **2.** something which is past.

by-law /'baɪ-lɔ/, *n.* a rule of a local government authority with legal effect only within the area covered by that authority. [ME *by* town from Scand]

BYO /bi waɪ 'oʊ/, *adj.* **1.** of a party, dinner, etc., to which one brings one's own alcoholic drinks. ◇*n.* **2.** a restaurant which allows people to bring their own alcoholic drinks. Also, **BYOG.** [short for *b*(*ring*) *y*(*our*) *o*(*wn grog*)]

bypass /'baɪpas/, *n.* **1.** a road enabling motorists to avoid towns and other heavy traffic points on the main road. **2.** a secondary pipe or other channel connected with the main passage for carrying liquid or gas around a fixed object. ◇*v.t.* **3.** to avoid (something) by using a bypass. **4.** to go ahead without asking or informing (someone in charge, etc.)

bypass operation, *n. Med. Colloq.* a surgical operation to divert the passage of blood around a blocked blood vessel, esp. in the heart.

by-product /'baɪ-prɒdʌkt/, *n.* something produced in addition to the main product or result of an operation, as in manufacture.

Byrd Land /'bɜd lænd/, *n.* a part of Antarctica, south-east of the Ross Sea; discovered and explored by Richard E Byrd; claimed by the US. Formerly, **Marie Byrd Land.**

byre /'baɪə/, *n.* a cowhouse or shed. [OE]

Byrne /bɜn/, *n.* **Joseph,** 1857–1880, Australian bushranger; a member of Ned Kelly's gang.

Byron[1] /'baɪrən/, *n.* **George Gordon, Lord** (*6th Baron Byron*), 1788–1824, English Romantic poet; major works include *Don Juan* (1819–24).

Byron[2] /'baɪrən/, *n.* **Cape,** a cape on the northern coast of NSW; easternmost point of the Australian mainland.

byronic /baɪ'rɒnɪk/, *adj.* darkly passionate or sad. [from Lord BYRON, whose personality, esp. as reflected in his poetry, was of this nature]

bystander /'baɪstændə/, *n.* a person present at but not taking part in some action.

byte /baɪt/, *n.* a unit of information, usu. eight bits, stored by a computer.

byway /'baɪweɪ/, *n.* **1.** a little-used road. **2.** an area of study, activity, etc., that is not of main importance.

byword /'baɪwɜd/, *n.* **1.** the name of a person or thing which is thought of as representing some quality or idea: *His name is a byword for courage.* **2.** a common saying; proverb. [OE *bīword*]

Byzantine /'bɪzəntin, -taɪn, bə'zæntaɪn, -tən/, *adj.* of or relating to the style of art or architecture of the Byzantine Empire, esp. of the fifth and sixth centuries, characterised by the rich use of mosaics, domes, decoration, etc.

Byzantine Empire, *n.* the Eastern Roman Empire after the fall of the Western Empire in AD 476, having Constantinople as its capital.

Byzantium /bə'zæntiəm/, *n.* an ancient Greek city on the Bosporus, commanding the entrance to the Black Sea; Constantine I built the city of Constantinople on this site, AD 330; now **Istanbul.**

Cc

C, c, *n., pl.* **C's** or **Cs, c's** or **cs. 1.** the third letter of the English alphabet. **2.** the third in any series. **3.** *Music* **a.** the first note of the C major scale. **b.** middle C.

c, *Symbol.* **1.** cent; cents. **2.** cycle.

c/-, care of.

c., *Abbrev.* **1.** Also, **c** about: *c. 50 BC* [L *circa, circiter, circum*] **2.** *Cricket.* caught.

C, *Symbol.* **1.** *Elect.* capacitance. **2.** *Chem.* carbon. **3.** 100. [L *centum*] See **Roman numerals. 4.** Celsius. **5.** Centigrade. **6.** century: *19th C.* **7.** *Music.* (as a time signature) → **common time. 8.** *Elect.* coulomb. **9.** *Phys.* the velocity of light in a vacuum, 2.997925×10^8 metres/sec.

ca, *Abbrev.* about: *ca AD 476*. [L *circa*]

Ca, *Chem. Symbol.* calcium.

cab /kæb/, *n.* **1.** → **taxi. 2.** (formerly) any of various one-horse vehicles for public hire, e.g. the hansom. **3.** the covered part of a truck where the driver sits. [short for *cabriolet*, a type of horse-drawn carriage, from F: caper (with reference to its movement)]

cabal /kəˈbal, kəˈbæl/, *n.* **1.** a small group of people making secret plans. **2.** the plans of such a group; intrigue. [ML]

cabaret /ˈkæbəreɪ/, *n.* **1.** a show usu. consisting of singing, dancing and comedy, at a restaurant, nightclub, etc. **2.** a club, etc., that provides such a show. [F: cellar, orig. uncert.]

cabbage /ˈkæbɪdʒ/, *n.* a common type of green vegetable with thick leaves wrapped tightly around a short stem. [ME, from F, probably from Pr *cap* head, from L]

cabbage butterfly, *n.* a large, white butterfly, whose larvae feed on cabbage. Also, **cabbage white butterfly.**

cabbage tree, *n.* a tall palm tree with large leaves, of the coast of eastern Australia, the buds of which can be eaten. Also, **cabbage tree palm.**

cabbage tree hat, *n.* a wide-brimmed hat made from leaves of the cabbage tree, common in the early days of the colony and later seen as a symbol of national pride.

cabbala /kəˈbalə/, *n.* **1.** (among certain Jewish rabbis and medieval Christians) a system of ideas based on a mystical interpretation of the Scriptures. **2.** any occult or secret system of ideas. Also, **cabala.** [ML, from Heb: tradition] —**cabbalism,** *n.* —**cabbalist,** *n.* —**cabbalistic,** *adj.*

Cabernet Sauvignon, /ˌkæbəneɪ ˈsouvɪnjɒ/, *n.* (a grape widely used in making) a claret-style wine. [F]

cabin /ˈkæbən/, *n.* **1.** a small house; hut: *a log cabin.* **2.** a room in a ship, for passengers, etc. **3.** *Aeron.* an enclosed place in an aircraft for the pilot, passengers, or cargo. [ME, from F, from Pr, from LL]

cabinet /ˈkæbənət, ˈkæbnət/, *n.* **1.** (*also cap.*) a group of ministers from the ruling political party who advise the leader and are responsible for the government of a state or nation. See **shadow cabinet. 2.** a piece of furniture with shelves, drawers, etc., for storage or display. **3.** a private room. ◇*adj.* **4.** relating to a political cabinet: *a cabinet meeting.* [F, from It]

cabinet-maker /ˈkæbənət-meɪkə/, *n.* someone who makes fine furniture.

cable /ˈkeɪbəl/, *n., v.,* **-bled, -bling.** ◇*n.* **1.** a thick, strong rope, now usu. made of several wires twisted together. **2.** *Naut.* a ship's anchor chain. **3.** *Elect.* a bundle of insulated wires through which an electric current can flow. **4.** a telegram sent to another country, esp. by cable under the sea. ◇*v.t.* **5.** to send (a message) by submarine cable. **6.** to send a message to (someone) in this way. ◇*v.i.* **7.** to send a message by undersea cable. [ME]

cable car, *n.* a car hanging from overhead moving cables which draw it up and down steep hills, across valleys, etc.

cable length, *n.* a unit of length, $\frac{1}{10}$ of a nautical mile. Also, **cable's length.**

cable stitch, *n.* a knitting pattern where one set of stitches is crossed over another to produce a rope-like effect.

Caboolture /kəˈbultʃə/, *n.* a town and shire north of Brisbane, Qld, on the **Caboolture River.** Pop. 8915 (1986). [Aboriginal: carpet snake]

caboose /kəˈbus/, *n.* **1.** the kitchen on a ship's deck; galley. **2.** *US.* a guard's van on a goods train. [LG]

cac-, variant of **caco-.**

cacao /kəˈkeɪoʊ, -ˈkaʊ/, *n., pl.* **-caos. 1.** a small evergreen tropical American tree grown for its seeds, from which cocoa and chocolate are made. **2.** the seeds of this tree. [Sp., from Nahuatl]

cachalot /ˈkæʃəlɒt/, *n.* → **sperm whale.** [F, from Pg, from L: pot]

cache /kæʃ/, *n., v.,* **cached, caching.** ◇*n.* **1.** a hiding or storing place, esp. one in the ground, for supplies, treasure, etc. **2.** the store of food, etc., that is hidden there. ◇*v.t.* **3.** to put in a cache; conceal; hide. [F: hide]

cachet /ˈkæʃeɪ, kæˈʃeɪ/, *n.* **1.** a seal, as on a letter. **2.** a mark or sign of high quality, etc. **3.** high social position; prestige; kudos. [F: hide]

cackle /ˈkækəl/, *v.,* **-led, -ling,** *n.* ◇*v.i.* **1.** to make a shrill, broken sound, as a hen after laying an egg. **2.** to laugh or chatter noisily: *He cackled with glee.* ◇*n.* **3.** a sound of cackling. [ME *cackelen*; imitative]

caco-, combining form meaning 'bad', 'deformed', or 'unpleasant'. [Gk *kako-*, combining form of *kakós* bad]

cacophony /kəˈkɒfəni/, *n., pl.* **-nies.** a harsh sound; dissonance. [NL, from Gk] —**cacophonous**, *adj.*

cactoblastis /ˌkæktəˈblæstəs/, *n.* a small moth, whose larvae feed on the prickly-pear.

cactus /ˈkæktəs/, *n., pl.* **-ti** /-ti, -tar/, **-tuses.** any of various thick-stemmed desert plants, which store water, are usu. leafless and spiny, often produce showy flowers, and are mostly native to hot, dry areas of America. [L, from Gk: kind of prickly plant]

cad /kæd/, *n.* a man who, though a gentleman by birth, does not behave like one. —**caddish**, *adj.*

cadastral survey /kəˈdæstrəl ˌsɑːveɪ/, *n.* a survey of boundaries and subdivision of land.

cadaver /kəˈdævə, -ˈdɑːvə/, *n.* a dead body, esp. of a human being; corpse. [L]

cadaverous /kəˈdævərəs/, *adj.* **1.** of or like a corpse. **2.** pale and thin; gaunt.

caddie /ˈkædi/, *n., v.*, **-died, -dying.** ◇*n.* **1.** *Golf.* a person hired to carry the player's clubs, find the ball, etc. ◇*v.i.* **2.** to work as a caddie. Also, **caddy.** [F *cadet* CADET]

caddy /ˈkædi/, *n., pl.* **-ies.** a small box or tin, esp. for holding tea. [Malay]

Cadell /kəˈdɛl/, *n.* **Francis,** 1822–79, Scottish-born Australian navigator, shipowner and merchant.

cadence /ˈkeɪdəns/, *n.* **1.** rhythmic movement, as of poetry. **2.** a fall in the pitch of the voice, esp. in speaking poetry. **3.** *Music.* a set of notes or chords which indicates the end of a composition, phrase, etc. [ME, from F, from It *cadenza*, from L: falling]

cadenza /kəˈdɛnzə/, *n. Music.* an elaborate passage, for the voice or a solo instrument, usu. near the end of a concerto. [It. See CADENCE]

cadet /kəˈdɛt/, *n.* **1.** a person being trained in the armed services, police, public service, journalism, etc. **2.** a member of a military training unit in a secondary school. **3.** a younger son. [F: chief, from L: head] —**cadetship**, *n.*

cadge /kædʒ/, *v.* **cadged, cadging.** ◇*v.t.* **1.** to borrow or get (something), esp. from a friend, usu. with no intent to repay: *May I cadge a cigarette?* ◇*v.i.* **2.** to beg: *I don't like to cadge; He cadges for ice-creams every time we go out together.* [orig. unknown]

Cadman /ˈkædmən/, *n.* **John,** 1757?–1848, English-born superintendent of government boats in Australia 1827–45.

cadmium /ˈkædmiəm/, *n. Chem.* a white, ductile, divalent metallic element which looks like tin, used in electroplating and in making certain alloys. It is also used in control rods of nuclear reactors. *Symbol:* Cd; *at. no.:* 48; *at. wt:* 112.410. See **transition element.** [NL, from L, from Gk] —**cadmic**, *adj.*

Cadmus /ˈkædməs/, *n. Gk Legend.* a Phoenician prince who planted the teeth of a dragon he had slain, from which sprang up many warriors who fought each other until only five survived. These five, led by Cadmus, founded Thebes.

cadre /ˈkɑːdə/, *n.* a key group of people needed to establish and train a new military, political or other unit. [F: frame, from It., from L: a square]

CAE /si eɪ ˈi/, *Abbrev.* **1.** College of Advanced Education. **2.** *Vic.* Council for Adult Education.

caecum /ˈsikəm/, *n., pl.* **-ca** /-kə/. a small sac, esp. the one at the beginning of the large intestine. [L *caecus* blind] —**caecal**, *adj.*

caeno-, variant of **caino-**.

Caesar /ˈsizə/, *n.* **1. Gaius Julius** /ˌgaɪəs ˈdʒuliəs/, c. 100–44 BC, Roman general, statesman and historian; conqueror of Gaul (58–50) and Britain (55–54); dictator of the Roman Empire (49–44). **2.** the title of Roman emperors from Augustus to Hadrian. **3.** any emperor or dictator.

caesarean section /səˌzɛəriən ˈsɛkʃən/, *n.* an operation for delivering a baby, in which the womb and walls of the abdomen are cut through (supposedly performed at the birth of Julius Caesar). Also, **caesarian.**

caesium /ˈsiziəm/, *n. Chem.* a rare, extremely active, soft, monovalent metallic element. *Symbol:* Cs; *at. no.:* 55; *at. wt:* 132.91. The radioactive isotope, **caesium-137,** is used in radiotherapy. Also, **cesium.** [L: bluish grey]

caesura /səˈʒurə/, *n., pl.* **-ras, -rae** /-ri/. *Poetry.* a pause (a mark indicating) a pause in a line of poetry. [L: a cutting] —**caesural**, *adj.*

cafe /ˈkæfeɪ/; (*joc.*) /keɪf/, *n.* **1.** a shop where coffee and light refreshments are served. **2.** a restaurant, usu. low-priced. Also, **café.** [F. See COFFEE]

cafeteria /ˌkæfəˈtɪəriə/, *n.* a reasonably cheap restaurant or snack-bar, usu. self-service. [Amer Sp: coffee shop]

caffeine /ˈkæfin/, *n.* a bitter crystalline alkaloid, found in coffee, tea, etc., and used as a stimulant, diuretic, etc. [F *café* coffee]

caftan /ˈkæftæn/, *n.* **1.** a man's long garment, with long sleeves and tied at the waist, worn under a coat in the Middle East. **2.** a similar garment, worn by women (and men) in western countries. [Turk, Pers *qaftān*]

cage /keɪdʒ/, *n., v.t.*, **caged, caging.** ◇*n.* **1.** a box-shaped enclosure made with wires, bars, etc., where birds or animals are kept. **2.** anything that confines or imprisons; prison. **3.** any cage-like framework, esp. some lifts. ◇*v.t.* **4.** to put in, or as if in, a cage. [ME, from L: enclosure]

cagey /ˈkeɪdʒi/, *adj.*, **cagier, cagiest.** *Colloq.* careful; secretive; wary: *His cagey replies revealed little.* Also, **cagy.** —**cagily**, *adv.* —**caginess**, *n.*

cahoot /kəˈhut/, *n. in the phrase* **in cahoot** or **cahoots,** in partnership; in conspiracy. [? F: hut, cabin]

Cain[1] /keɪn/, *n. Bible.* the first son of Adam and Eve, who murdered his brother Abel. Genesis 4.

Cain² /keɪn/, *n.* **John**, born 1931, Australian state Labor politician; became premier of Victoria in 1982.

caino-, a prefix meaning 'new', 'recent', as in *Cainozoic*. Also, **ceno-, caeno-**. [See -CENE]

Cainozoic /ˌkaɪnoʊˈzoʊɪk, ˌkeɪ-/, *adj., n.* (relating to) the geological era of rocks of most recent age, up to the present. [CAINO- + ZO(O)- + -IC]

cairn /kɛən/, *n.* a heap of stones set up as a landmark, monument, etc. [Scot, from Gaelic *carn* pile of stones] — **cairned**, *adj.*

cairngorm /ˈkɛəngɔːm/, *n.* a yellow or brown type of quartz. [so called from the *Cairngorms*, a range of mountains in Scotland]

Cairns¹ /kɛənz/, *n.* **Jim** (*James Ford Cairns*), born 1914, Australian federal Labor politician; regarded as the leader of the Labor Party's left wing in the 1960s and early 1970s.

Cairns² /kænz, kɛənz/, *n.* a town in north-eastern Qld, on the western shore of Trinity Bay; commercial centre for the surrounding sugar cane district. Pop. 54 862 (1986). [named after William Wellington *Cairns*, governor of Qld 1875–77]

Cairo /ˈkaɪroʊ/, *n.* the capital of Egypt, in the northern part, on the eastern bank of the Nile. Pop. 6 325 000 (1986 est.). Arabic, **Al-Qahirah**.

caisson /ˈkeɪsən/, *n.* **1.** an airtight box-like structure in which people can work underwater, on river beds, etc. **2.** an ammunition box (usu. on two wheels). [F]

cajole /kəˈdʒoʊl/, *v.i., v.t.*, **-joled, -joling.** to persuade by compliments or promises; wheedle; coax. [F *cajoler*, ? b. *caresser* caress and *enjôler* capture] — **cajolery**, *n.*

Cajun /ˈkeɪdʒən/, *n.* (in Louisiana, US) a descendant of the exiles from Acadia; Acadian. Also, **Cajian**. [var. of *Acadian*. See ACADIA.]

cake /keɪk/, *n., v.,* **caked, caking.** ◇*n.* **1.** a sweet baked food made usu. with butter or margarine and flour, sugar, eggs, etc., often decorated with icing. **2.** a flat, thin mass of (unleavened) bread. **3.** a shaped mass of other food: *fish cakes for tea.* **4.** a shaped or solid mass: *a cake of soap.* **5. piece of cake**, *Colloq.* something easily done or obtained. **6. take the cake**, to win the prize (used ironically): *This rudeness takes the cake.* **7. to have one's cake and eat it**, to have the advantages of something without any of the disadvantages. ◇*v.t., v.i.* **8.** to form, or become formed, into a cake or solid crust: *She caked the make-up on; Mud caked on his shoes.* [ME, from Scand]

cal, *Symbol.* calorie (def. 1a).

Cal, *Symbol.* calorie (def. 1b).

calabash /ˈkæləbæʃ/, *n.* **1.** *Bot.* (a plant bearing) any of various gourds. **2.** the dried hollow shell of the calabash used as a drinking or cooking vessel. **3.** a bottle, kettle, tobacco-pipe bowl, drum, etc., made from it. [F, from Sp: gourd, ? from Pers: melon]

Calabria /kəˈlæbriə/, *n.* **1.** a region in south-western Italy. Pop. 2 131 412 (1986 est.); 1509 km². *Main town:* Reggio di Calabria. **2. Battle of**, a Mediterranean World War II sea battle, in 1940, between ships of the Australian and British navies and the Italian fleet, which withdrew.

Calais /ˈkæleɪ/, *n.* a seaport in northern France on the Straits of Dover; the nearest French port to England. Pop. 76 935 (1982).

calamari /kæləˈmɑːri/, *n.* → **squid**. [It]

calamine /ˈkæləmaɪn/, *n.* a liquid soothing to the skin, prepared from mixture of zinc oxide with ferric oxide. [F, from ML]

calamity /kəˈlæmɪti/, *n., pl.* **-ties. 1.** great trouble; adversity; misery. **2.** a great misfortune; disaster. [late ME, from L] — **calamitous**, *adj.*

calcareous /kælˈkɛəriəs/, *adj.* of, coated with, containing, or like calcium carbonate; chalky: *calcareous earth.* [L: relating to lime]

calcify /ˈkælsəfaɪ/, *v.t., v.i.*, **-fied, -fying.** *Med., Geol.* to make or become hardened by the deposit of calcium salts or lime, as in body tissues or rocks. [L *calx* lime + -(I)FY] — **calcification**, *n.*

calcine /ˈkælsaɪn, -sən/, *v.t., v.i.*, **-cined, -cining.** to change into calx or a friable (easily powdered) substance by heat. [F, from L *calx* lime] — **calcination**, *n.*

calcite /ˈkælsaɪt/, *n.* a common crystalline mineral, calcium carbonate, CaCO₃. Limestone, marble and chalk consist largely of calcite. [L *calx* lime + -ITE¹]

calcium /ˈkælsiəm/, *n.* *Chem.* a silver-white divalent metal, occurring as salts in limestone, chalk, marble, etc. *Symbol:* Ca; *at. no.:* 20; *at. wt:* 40.08. [NL, from L *calx* lime + -IUM]

calcium carbonate, *n.* a crystalline compound, CaCO₃, known as calcite, chalk, whiting, dripstone, etc. See -ate².

calculate /ˈkælkjəleɪt/, *v.*, **-lated, -lating.** ◇*v.t.* **1.** to work out (something) by mathematical methods; compute: *to calculate the average speed of the car.* **2.** to estimate: *He wrongly calculated that his actions would inspire confidence.* ◇*v.i.* **3.** to plan or rely (fol. by *on* or *upon*): *I have calculated on having two weeks to study.* [L: counted]

calculated /ˈkælkjəleɪtəd/, *adj* **1.** undertaken after considering the probability of success or failure: *a calculated risk.* **2.** planned deliberately or cold-bloodedly: *a calculated insult.*

calculating /ˈkælkjəleɪtɪŋ/, *adj.* **1.** able to perform mathematical calculations: *a calculating machine.* **2.** (of a person) very careful; shrewd. **3.** (of a person) selfishly planning; scheming.

calculation /kælkjəˈleɪʃən/, *n.* **1.** the act or result of calculating; computation. **2.** an opinion based on various facts in a case; forecast. **3.** careful planning.

calculator /ˈkælkjəleɪtə/, *n.* a machine, usu. small and electronic, that performs mathematical operations. [L]

calculus /ˈkælkjələs/, *n., pl.* **-luses** (*def. 1*) **-li** /-laɪ/ (*def. 2*). **1.** *Maths.* the branch of mathematics concerned with the measurement of quantities which are continually changing, by treating continuous change as if it were made up of many small parts. **Differential calculus** can be used to calculate rate of change, as in the slope of a curve. **Integral calculus** can be used to calculate the end result of a continuous change, such as the area under a curve. **2.** *Med.* a stone (def. 8) found in the gall bladder, kidneys, or other parts of the body. [L: stone used in counting, diminutive of *calx* small stone, lime]

Calcutta /kæl'kʌtə/, *n.* a seaport in northeastern India, capital of West Bengal state, on the river Hooghly. Pop. 3 305 006 (city), 9 194 018 (urban agglomeration) (1981).

Calder /'kɔldə/, *n.* **Alexander**, 1898-1976, US sculptor, famous esp. for his mobiles.

Caledonia /kælə'dounɪə/, *n. Chiefly Poetic.* Scotland.

calendar /'kæləndə/, *n.* **1.** any of various systems of counting time, esp. fixing the beginning, length, and divisions of the year: *the Chinese calendar.* **2.** an arrangement in table or chart form of the days of each month and week in a year. **3.** an official listing, of cases to be tried in a court, events and courses of a university year, etc. [L: account book]

calender /'kæləndə/, *n.* **1.** a machine with rollers in which cloth, paper, etc., is pressed, smoothed, made glossy, etc. ◇*v.t.* **2.** to press in a calender. [F, probably from Pr, from L: cylinder]

calendula /kə'lɛndʒələ/, *n. Bot.* the common marigold, whose flowers are used medicinally, esp. in a healing cream. [NL]

Caley /'keɪli/, *n.* **George**, 1770-1829, English-born botanist and explorer in Australia.

calf[1] /kaf/, *n., pl.* **calves.** **1.** the young of the cow or ox (usu. under one year). **2.** the young of some other animals, as the elephant, seal and whale. **3. kill the fatted calf,** to prepare a feast of welcome. [OE]

calf[2] /kaf/, *n., pl.* **calves.** the fleshy part of the back of the human leg below the knee. [ME, from Scand]

calibrate /'kæləbreɪt/, *v.t.,* **-brated, -brating.** **1.** to measure the calibre of. **2.** to work out, check, or correct the scale of (any measuring instrument). **– calibrator,** *n.* **– calibration,** *n.*

calibre /'kæləbə/, *n.* **1.** the diameter of something cylindrical, esp. a bullet, or of the inside of a tube, as the bore of gun. **2.** personal ability or character: *a man of fine calibre.* **3.** the quality of something. [F, from It, from Ar: mould]

calico /'kælɪkoʊ/, *n., pl.* **-coes, -cos.** white or unbleached coarse cotton cloth. [named after *Calicut,* a city on the coast of Malabar, India]

California /kælə'fɔnjə, -'fɔnɪə/, *n.* a state in the western United States, on the Pacific coast. Pop. 25 981 000 (1986 est.); 411 015 km[2]. *Cap.:* Sacramento. *Abbrev.:* Calif. **– Californian,** *adj., n.*

californium /kælə'fɔniəm/, *n.* an artificial, radioactive, metallic element. *Symbol:* Cf; *at. no.:* 98; *at. wt:* 251. [(University of) *Californ*(*ia*), where first identified, + -IUM]

Caligula /kə'lɪgjələ/, *n.* **Gaius Caesar** /gaɪəs 'sizə/, AD 12-41, Roman emperor 37-41; noted for his autocratic nature and cruelty.

caliph /'keɪləf/, *n.* **1.** a successor (usu. of Mohammed, as head of Islam). **2.** the title for the head of a Muslim state. Also, **calif, kaliph, khalif.** [ME, from ML, from Ar: successor]

call /kɔl/, *v.t.* **1.** to cry out in a loud voice. **2.** (of a bird or other animal) to give its own particular cry. **3.** to order or announce; proclaim: *to call a halt; call a strike.* **4.** to read out aloud (a roll or list). **5.** to attract the attention of (someone) by shouting. **6.** to attract (someone's attention) to something: *She called the policeman's attention to the trouble.* **7.** to wake (someone) up by a call: *Call me at 8 o'clock.* **8.** to command or ask (someone) to come; summon: *to call a cab; call a witness.* **9.** to organise (a meeting). **10.** to telephone (oft. fol. by *up*): *I'll call her on her birthday.* **11.** *Econ.* to ask for payment of all or part of the unpaid part of a company's share capital. **12.** to give a name to; name: *They call him Jim.* **13.** to describe as something particular: *He called me a liar.* **14.** *Cards.* → **bid** (def. 4). **15.** to describe (a horserace, etc.) as it is being run. ◇*v.i.* **16.** to speak loudly; shout; cry: *Who calls so loudly?* **17.** (of a bird or animal) to give its own call. **18.** to make a short visit: *He called at the shop to pick up the groceries.* **19.** to telephone a person: *I will call tomorrow.* ◇**20.** Some special uses are:

call attention (to oneself), to behave so that people will take notice.

call back, 1. to bring or ask back; recall. **2.** to telephone again or in return.

call for, 1. to go and get (something). **2.** to need; require; demand: *The occasion calls for a celebration.*

call forth, to bring into action.

call in, 1. to collect: *to call in debts.* **2.** to withdraw from circulation: *to call in gold; call in notes.* **3.** to bring; invite: *time to call in the doctor.*

call in(to) question, to throw doubt upon.

call it a day, to bring an activity to an end.

call off, 1. to order to stop: *Call off your dog.* **2.** to cancel or postpone: *They called off the picnic.*

call on, 1. to ask (a person) usu. for something: *to call on a person for a song.* **2.** to make a short visit to: *to call on friends.*

call out, 1. to say in a loud voice. **2.** to order into service: *to call out the army.*

call up, 1. to demand payment of. **2.** to send for (someone) for military service. **3.** to bring to the mind: *to call up my sorrows again.*

◇*n.* **21.** a cry or shout. **22.** the cry of a bird or other animal. **23.** a signal sounded by a bugle, bell, etc. **24.** a short visit: *to make a call on someone.* **25.** a telephone conversation: *That was a long call.* **26.** an invitation; summons. **27.** a sense of attraction, or divine appointment, to a job or service: *She felt the call to the ministry.* **28.** need; occasion: *He had no call to* say that. **29.** a demand or claim. **30.** demand esp. for a product: *In winter, there is not much call for swimwear.* **31.** *Cards.* → **bid** (def. 8). **32.** *Stock Exchange.* the option of claiming stock at or before a given date. **33. on call, a.** *Comm.* payable or subject to return without advance notice. **b.** (of doctors, etc.) available for duty at short notice. ◇*adj.* **34.** *Comm.* repayable on demand: *call money; a call loan.* [ME *calle(n)*]

Callaghan /ˈkæləhæn/, *n.* (**Leonard**) **James**, born 1912, British Labour statesman; prime minister 1976–79.

Callas /ˈkæləs/, *n.* **Maria**, 1923–77, Greek operatic soprano, born in the US.

caller /ˈkɔlə/, *n.* **1.** someone who calls. **2.** someone who makes a short visit. [CALL + -ER¹]

callgirl /ˈkɔlgəl/, *n.* a prostitute who makes appointments by telephone.

calli-, a word part meaning 'beauty'. [Gk *kalli-*, combining form of *kállos*]

calligraphy /kəˈlɪgrəfi/, *n.* (the art of doing) beautiful handwriting. [Gk] —**calligrapher**, **calligraphist**, *n.* —**calligraphic**, *adj.*

calling /ˈkɔlɪŋ/, *n.* **1.** a job, profession, or trade. **2.** an inner urge to do something, esp. work; vocation.

calliper /ˈkæləpə/, *n.* **1.** (*usu. pl.*) a tool with two hinged legs, used for measuring short distances. **2.** *Med.* a metal splint used to support a limb. Also, **caliper**. [var. of CALIBRE]

calliper rule, *n.* a measuring tool with two parallel legs, one fixed and one sliding along a marked scale.

callistemon /kəˈlɪstəmən/, *n.* → **bottlebrush**.

callisthenics /ˌkælɪsˈθɛnɪks/, *n.* **1.** (*treated as sing.*) the practice or art of exercising muscles to make oneself healthy, strong, and graceful. **2.** (*as pl.*) such exercises. Also, **calisthenics**. [Gk *kállos* beautiful + *sthénos* strength + -ICS] —**callisthenic**, *adj.*

Callisto /kəˈlɪstoʊ/, *n.* Gk Myth. a nymph loved by Zeus and so punished by Hera, who changed her into a bear; Zeus set her in the sky as the constellation Ursa Major.

callous /ˈkæləs/, *adj.* **1.** hardened, esp. of skin. **2.** insensitive, hard-hearted. [L: hardskinned] —**callousness**, *n.*

callow /ˈkæloʊ/, *adj.* young and inexperienced: *a callow youth.* [OE *calu, calw-*] —**callowness**, *n.*

callus /ˈkæləs/, *n., pl.* **-luses**, *v.* ◇*n.* **1.** *Med.* **a.** a hardened or thickened part of the skin. **b.** the new growth joining a broken bone. **2.** *Bot.* a healing growth over a wound of a plant. ◇*v.i.* **3.** to make a callus. [L: hardened skin]

calm /kam/, *adj.* **1.** without rough movements; still: *calm sea.* **2.** (of weather) not windy. **3.** free from excitement or emotion: *a calm face; a calm mood.* ◇*n.* **4.** freedom from movement, excitement, etc.; stillness. ◇*v.t., v.i.* **5.** to make or become calm (oft. fol. by *down*): *to calm an excited dog; to calm down after a quarrel.* [ME *calme*, from OF, from It *calma* (as if orig., heat of the day, hence, time for resting, quiet)] —**calmness**, *n.*

caloric /kəˈlɒrɪk, keɪ-/, *adj.* relating to heat. [F, from L: heat] —**caloricity** /ˌkæləˈrɪsəti/, *n.*

calorie /ˈkæləri/, *n.* **1.** *Phys.* **a.** Also, **gram calorie** or **small calorie**. a non-SI unit of measurement for heat, usu. defined as the quantity of heat needed to raise the temperature of one g of water one degree C at 15°C. *Symbol:* cal **b. kilocalorie** or **large calorie**, (*usu. cap.*) a quantity of heat equal to 1000 gram calories. *Symbol:* kcal or Cal. **2.** a non-SI unit equal to the kilocalorie, used to express the heat output of an organism or energy value of food. The SI unit is the kilojoule; 1 calorie = 4.1868 kJ. [F, from L: heat]

calorimeter /ˌkæləˈrɪmətə, keɪ-/, *n.* an instrument for measuring quantities of heat. [L *calor* heat + -I- + -METER¹]

Caloundra /kəˈlaʊndrə/, *n.* a resort on the Sunshine Coast in southern Qld. Pop. 16 215 (1986).

calumet /ˈkæljəmɛt/, *n.* a long, ceremonial tobacco pipe used by North American Indians, esp. as sign of peace. [F, from L: little reed]

calumny /ˈkæləmni/, *n., pl.* **-nies**. a false statement designed to hurt someone or give him or her a bad name; slander. [L]

Calvary /ˈkælvəri/, *n.* Golgotha, the place where Jesus was crucified. [L *calvāria* skull, used to render Aram. *goghaltā*, from Heb. *gulgoléth* skull]

calve /kav/, *v.i.*, **calved**, **calving**. (of a cow) to give birth to young. [ME]

Calvert /ˈkælvət/, *n.* **James Snowden**, 1825–84, Australian explorer and botanist, born in England; accompanied Leichhardt on his 1844 expedition to northern Australia.

calves /kavz/, *n.* plural of **calf**.

Calvin /ˈkælvən/, *n.* **John**, 1509–64, religious reformer and theologian, born in France; leader of the Protestant Reformation in Geneva, Switzerland.

Calvinism /ˈkælvənɪzəm/, *n.* *Theol.* the teachings of John Calvin. —**Calvinist**, *n., adj.* —**Calvinistic**, *adj.*

Calwell /ˈkɔlwəl/, *n.* **Arthur Augustus**, 1896–1973, Australian Labor parliamentarian; leader of the ALP and the federal opposition 1960–67.

calx /kælks/, *n., pl.* **calces** /ˈkælsiz/, **calxes**. the oxide or ash which remains after metals, minerals, etc., have been burnt. [L: small stone, lime]

calypso /kəˈlɪpsoʊ/, *n., pl.* **-sos**. **1.** a West Indian song, usu. about a subject of current interest, and with syncopated rhythm. **2.** music in such a style.

Calypso /kəˈlɪpsoʊ/, *n.* Gk Legend. a seanymph who for seven years detained Odysseus on the island of Ogygia.

calyx /ˈkeɪlɪks, ˈkæl-/, *n., pl.* **calyces** /ˈkæləsiz, ˈkeɪ-/, **calyxes**. *Bot.* the outermost

calyx parts of a flower, usu. green; sepals. [L, from Gk: covering, husk, calyx]

cam /kæm/, n. a machine part used to change revolving motion into irregular, up-and-down or sideways motion. [D or LG: cog]

camaraderie /kæməˈradəri/, n. close friendship; mateship. [F, from comrade]

camber /ˈkæmbə/, v.t., v.i. 1. to bend or curve upwards in middle. ◇n. 2. a slight upwards curve, as of a road surface. [F: bent, from L]

Camberwell /ˈkæmbəwel/, n. a city within the metropolitan area of Melbourne, Victoria. Pop. 83 792 (1986).

cambium /ˈkæmbiəm/, n. Bot. a cylindrical layer of plant cells which divide and differentiate to form more cells, making the stem or root thicker. [LL: exchange]

Cambodia /kæmˈboudiə/, n. a republic in south-east Asia, occupying the south-western part of the Indochinese peninsula, on the Gulf of Thailand; part of French Indochina before independence in 1953; a republic since 1970. Pop. 7 688 000 (1987 est.). 181 035 km². *Language:* Khmer, also French. *Currency:* riel. *Cap.:* Phnom-Penh. Also, **Kampuchea.**

Cambrian /ˈkæmbriən/, adj., n. Geol. (relating to) the first period of the Palaeozoic era.

cambric /ˈkeimbrɪk/, n. a cotton or linen fabric of fine close weave. [Flem *Kameryk* Cambrai, a city in N France]

Cambridge /ˈkeimbrɪdʒ/, n. 1. a city in eastern England. Pop. 90 440 (1981). 2. the university situated there, founded 1209.

Camden /ˈkæmdən/, n. a town in eastern NSW, south-west of Sydney; formerly, the site of John Macarthur's properties where he carried out important sheep breeding experiments. Pop.10 065 (1986). [named after Lord *Camden*, 1759–1840, English secretary of state for the colonies from 1804]

came /keim/, v. past tense of **come.**

camel /ˈkæməl/, n. 1. a large mammal with a humped back, used to carry people and loads in deserts. The **Arabian camel**, or dromedary, has one hump, and the **Bactrian camel** has two humps. 2. → **camelhair.** 3. a pale brown color. [ME and OE, from L, from Gk *kámˉelos*; of Semitic orig.]

camelhair /ˈkæməlheə/, n. 1. a fabric made of hair of camel, usu. mixed with wool, etc., used for coats. ◇ adj. 2. (of an artist's brush) made from the tail hairs of squirrels.

camellia /kəˈmiljə/, n. one of several shrubs or trees native to Asia, with glossy evergreen leaves and white, pink, or red, waxy, roselike flowers. [named after GJ *Kamel*, 1661–1706, Moravian Jesuit missionary]

Camelot /ˈkæmələt/, n. the legendary site of King Arthur's palace and court.

camembert /ˈkæməmbeə/, n. a rich, creamy, soft, ripened cheese, usu. made in small flat rounds, covered with a thin greyish-white mould. [named after *Camembert*, a town in Normandy, France]

cameo /ˈkæmiou/, n., pl. **-os.** 1. a layered gem or stone carved in relief so that the design and background are different colors. 2. a short piece of literary writing. [It; probably of oriental orig.]

camera /ˈkæmrə, ˈkæmərə/, n., pl. **-eras** *for defs 1 and 2,* **-erae** /-əri/ *for def. 3.* 1. a photographic apparatus in which an image is formed by a lens on sensitive plates or film. 2. *TV.* a machine in which a picture is formed and changed into electrical signals. 3. **in camera, a.** *Law.* in a judge's private room. **b.** privately. [L: arch, vault, ML chamber, treasury. See CHAMBER]

camisole /ˈkæmɪsoul/, n. 1. a woman's decorative undergarment, orig. to cover the corset. 2. a woman's simple top with narrow shoulder straps. [F, from Sp: little shirt]

camouflage /ˈkæməflaʒ, -fladʒ/, n., v., **-flaged, -flaging.** ◇n. 1. the act, method, or result of making something hard to see against its background. 2. a covering up or deceiving; disguise. ◇v.t. 3. to hide or disguise by camouflage: *The tank is well camouflaged.* [F: disguise]

camp¹ /kæmp/, n. 1. (a place for) a group of tents, caravans, or other temporary shelters. 2. the people staying in a camp. 3. an (overnight) resting place for sheep or cattle. 4. a place where soldiers are housed, in tents, huts, etc. 5. a group of people with the same ideas: *the socialist camp.* ◇v.i. 6. to set up camp. 7. to live temporarily in a tent (oft. fol. by *out*). 8. (of sheep or cattle) to gather to rest. [F, from It. *campo* field, from L] — **camper,** n.

camp² /kæmp/, adj. n. 1. (in) an exaggerated or unnatural style, often amusing or effeminate. 2. homosexual. ◇v. 3. **camp it up, a.** to make (something) showy or unnatural. **b.** to show off homosexuality. [? d. *camp* impetuous, uncouth person, hence objectionable, effeminate]

campaign /kæmˈpein/, n. 1. a series of military operations in a particular region and having one major objective. 2. a course of activities for a special purpose: *a sales campaign; an election campaign.* [F, from L *campus* plain] — **campaigner,** n.

Campaign for Nuclear Disarmament, n. a movement formed in Britain in 1958 to protest against the increased production, testing, etc., of nuclear weapons. *Abbrev.:* CND

campanology /kæmpəˈnɒlədʒi/, n. the study or skill of ringing bells. [L *campāna* bell + -O- + -LOGY] — **campanologist, campanologer,** n.

Campaspe /kæmˈpæspi/, n. a river in Victoria, rising in the Great Dividing Range west of Macedon and flowing north to join the Murray. 240 km.

Campbell /ˈkæmbəl/, n. 1. **David,** 1915–79, Australian lyric poet; author of *The Man in the Honeysuckle* (1980). 2. **Donald,** 1921–67, English water speed record-holder. 3. **Robert,** 1769–1846, Australian pioneer settler and merchant, born in Scotland; co-founder of Australia's first savings bank.

Campbell-Bannerman /ˈkæmbəlˈbænəmən/, n. Sir Henry, 1836–1908, British Liberal Party politician; prime minister 1905–08.

Campbelltown /ˈkæmbəltaʊn/, n. a city in the metropolitan area of Sydney, NSW. Pop. 121 297 (1986). [named by Lachlan Macquarie for his wife Elizabeth *Campbell*]

Camp David Agreement, n. a peace treaty signed in 1978 by Egyptian President Sadat and Israeli Prime Minister Begin, negotiated also by US President Carter. [from *Camp David*, official country residence of the US president, where the treaty was signed]

campervan /ˈkæmpəvæn/, n. a motor van with beds, kitchen, etc. Also, **camper**.

camphor /ˈkæmfə/, n. a whitish, translucent, crystalline, pleasant-smelling substance, obtained from the camphor laurel and used in medicine, production of celluloid, etc. [ML, from Ar, from Malay *kāpūr*]

camphor ball, n. →**mothball**.

camphor laurel, n. a tree, orig. of eastern Asia, yielding camphor.

campus /ˈkæmpəs/, n. the grounds of a university, technical college, etc. [L: field]

CAMS, Confederation of Australian Motor Sports.

camshaft /ˈkæmʃɑft/, n. a revolving shaft with cams.

Camus /kaˈmy/, n. **Albert** /alˈbɛə/, 1913–60, French existentialist novelist and playwright; works include *L'Étranger* (1942) and *La Peste* (1947); Nobel prize for literature 1957.

can[1] /kæn/; *weak forms* /kən, kn/ (or (if followed by k or g) /kŋ/), v., *pres. sing.* **can**; *past* **could**; *old form* thou **canst**. ◊*aux.* **1.** to be able to; have the ability, power, right, knowledge, qualifications, or means to: *You can lift the box.* **2.** *Colloq.* may; have permission to: *can I speak to you a moment?* [OE *cann, can*]

can[2] /kæn/, n., v., **canned, canning**. ◊n. **1.** a container, usu. for liquid, made of sheet metal. **2.** a tin (def. 4). **3. carry the can**, *Colloq.* to take the blame. ◊v.t. **4.** to put in a container, usu. sealed for preservation. [OE *canne*]

Canaan /ˈkeɪnən/, n. **1.** the ancient region, included in modern Palestine (now Israel and Jordan), lying between Jordan, the Dead Sea, and the Mediterranean; the land promised by God to Abraham. [Heb *kana'an*] —**Canaanite**, n.

Canada /ˈkænədə/, n. a federal parliamentary state in the northern part of North America, bordering on the US to the south; the second largest country in the world; a British colony before independence in 1867; origin, settled by both Britain and France; French-speaking separatist movement remains. Pop. 25 857 000 (1987 est.). 9 976 139 km². *Languages:* English and French. *Currency:* Canadian dollar. *Cap.:* Ottawa. —**Canadian**, n., adj.

canal /kəˈnæl/, n. **1.** a waterway dug for shipping, drainage, irrigation, etc. **2.** *Biol.* a tubular passage for food, air, etc.; duct. [late ME, from L: pipe, groove]

Canaletto /kænəˈlɛtoʊ/, n. **Antonio**, 1697–1768, Italian painter, noted for his accurately detailed Venetian scenes.

canapé /ˈkænəpeɪ/, n. a thin piece of bread, toast, etc., topped with fish, cheese, etc., and served as an appetiser.

canary /kəˈnɛəri/, n., *pl.* **-ries**. **1.** Also, **canary bird**. a small, yellow songbird, a kind of finch, often kept in a cage. **2.** Also, **canary yellow**. a bright, clear yellow color. **3.** Also, **canary bird**. (formerly) a convict. [named after the CANARY ISLANDS]

Canary Islands, *n.pl.* a group of mountainous islands in the Atlantic, near the northwestern coast of Africa, forming two provinces of Spain. Pop. 1 444 626 (1981); 7495 km². Also, **Canaries**. [F *Canarie* (the principal island), from Sp *Canaria*, in L *canāria insula* isle of dogs]

canasta /kəˈnæstə/, n. a card game similar to rummy. [Sp: ? *canasta* kind of basket]

Canaveral /kəˈnævərəl/, n. **Cape**, a cape on an island off eastern Florida; site of the US Air Force Missile Test Centre. Formerly (1963–73), **Cape Kennedy**.

Canberra /ˈkænbrə, -bərə/, n. **1.** the capital city of Australia, in the ACT, on the southern tablelands of NSW; area established as the capital in 1912, after which the city was gradually built. Pop. 248 441 (1986). **2. HMAS**, an Australian cruiser used during World War II; attacked and sunk by a Japanese cruiser in August 1942 with a loss of 78 lives. [from *Canberry, Kembery*, or *Gnabra*, versions of the Aboriginal name for the area]

cancan /ˈkænkæn/, n. a high-kicking dance, performed on stage by women, which came into fashion about 1830 in Paris. [F]

cancel /ˈkænsəl/, v., **-celled, -celling**. ◊v.t. **1.** to cross out (writing, etc.) by drawing a line through. **2.** to make (something) no longer legal or effective. **3.** to mark or make a hole in (a postage stamp, bus ticket, etc.) so it cannot be used again. **4.** to call off (something arranged): *to cancel a picnic.* **5.** *Maths.* to cross out (a factor common to both terms of a fraction, equal terms on opposite sides of an equation, etc.). ◊v. **6. cancel out**, to make up for; counterbalance. [late ME, from L: to make like a lattice, to strike out a writing] —**cancellation**, n.

cancer /ˈkænsə/, n. **1.** *Med.* an abnormal growth which uses nutrients needed by the body, and tends to spread and to reappear after surgery. **2.** anything evil that spreads and destroys. **3.** (*cap.*) *Astrol.* the fourth sign of the zodiac, represented by a crab. **4. Tropic of Cancer**, see **tropic** (def. 1a). [L: crab, tumor] —**cancerous, cancroid, Cancerian**, *adj.*

candela /kænˈdilə, -ˈdeɪlə/, n. the basic SI unit of luminous intensity. *Symbol:* cd [L: candle]

candelabrum /kændəˈlɑbrəm/, n., *pl.* **-bra** /-brə/. an ornamental branched candlestick. [L: candle]

candid /'kændəd/, *adj.* **1.** open and sincere. **2.** fair; honest. **3.** informal or taken without the subject's knowledge: *a candid photograph.* [L *candidus* white, sincere]

candidate /'kændədeɪt, -dət/, *n.* **1.** someone who applies or is chosen to be considered for a job, award, etc. **2.** a person taking a test or examination. **3.** *Colloq.* a suitable subject: *That fruit is a candidate for the rubbish bin.* [L *candidātus* clad in white, as a Roman candidate for office] **– candidacy, candidature, candidateship,** *n.*

candied /'kændid/, *adj.* **1.** cooked in sugar: *candied fruits.* **2.** crystallised. **3.** honeyed or sweet; flattering.

candle /'kændl/, *n.* **1.** a piece of tallow, wax, etc., with a wick through it, burnt to give light. **2. international candle,** a unit of luminous intensity, now replaced by **candela**. **3. burn the candle at both ends,** to try to do too much, wearing oneself out. **4. can't hold a candle to,** *Colloq.* to be not nearly as good as. [OE *candel*, from L]

candle bark, *n.* **1.** bark which hangs in strips from some gum trees. **2.** a smooth-barked gum tree of eastern Australia.

candlestick /'kændlstɪk/, *n.* a holder for a candle.

candor *or* **candour** /'kændə/, *n.* **1.** openness; sincerity; honesty. **2.** fairness; impartiality. [L: radiance, purity, candor]

candy /'kændi/, *n., pl.* **-dies, -dies, -died, -dying.** ◇*n.* **1.** a sweet made of sugar crystallised by boiling. **2.** *US.* any sweet. ◇*v.t.* **3.** to cook in sugar syrup to preserve. **4.** to reduce (sugar, etc.) to crystals, usu. by boiling. [F *sucre candi* candied sugar (*candi* from Ar *qand* sugar, from Pers]

cane /keɪn/, *n., v.,* **caned, caning.** ◇*n.* **1.** a long, thin, jointed, woody stem of certain plants, such as bamboo. **2.** a stick used for punishing school children. **3.** a walking stick. **4.** rattan used in weaving chairs, etc. ◇*v.t.* **5.** to beat with a cane. **6.** to make or fit with cane: *to cane chairs.* [ME, from OF, from Pr or It, from L, from Gk: reed]

cane toad, *n.* a toad, introduced into Australia, now a widespread pest in Qld.

canine /'keɪnaɪn/, *adj.* **1.** of or like dog(s). ◇*n.* **2.** *Anat., Zool.* a pointed tooth on each side of each jaw. **3.** *Zool.* any animal of the dog family, including wolves, jackals, and foxes. [L: of a dog]

Canis Major /keɪnɪs 'meɪdʒə/, *n. Astron.* a southern constellation containing Sirius, the brightest of the stars. Also, the **Great Dog**. [L: the greater dog]

canister /'kænəstə/, *n.* a small box, usu. of metal: *a tea canister.* [L, from Gk: wicker basket]

canker /'kæŋkə/, *n.* **1.** *Med., Vet Sci.* ulcerous sore or disease. **2.** *Bot.* a stem disease. **3.** anything that rots, infects, or destroys. ◇*v.t.* **4.** to infect; corrupt. ◇*v.i.* **5.** to become cankered. [OE *cancer*, from L: gangrene]

cankerworm /'kæŋkəwɜm/, *n.* a striped green caterpillar which damages fruit trees, etc.

cannabis /'kænəbəs/, *n.* the (dried flowers of) indian hemp; marijuana. [L: hemp]

canned /kænd/, *adj.* **1.** preserved in a can or tin. **2.** *Colloq.* recorded: *canned laughter.*

cannelloni /kænə'louni/, *n.* tubular or rolled pieces of pasta usu. filled with a mixture of meat, cheese, etc., and served with tomato or cream sauce. [It]

Cannes /kæn, kan, kænz/, *n.* a seaport in south-eastern France, in Alpes-Maritimes department, on the Mediterranean; coastal resort; film festival. Pop. 72 787 (1982).

cannibal /'kænəbəl/, *n.* **1.** a person who eats human flesh. **2.** any animal that eats its own kind. [Sp *Caribe* Carib] **– cannibalism,** *n.*

Canning[1] /'kænɪŋ/, **George,** 1770–1827, British statesman; prime minister 1827.

Canning[2] /'kænɪŋ/, *n.* a river in south-western WA, flowing north-west from the Darling Range to the Swan River; the **Canning Reservoir**, about halfway along the river, supplies much of Perth's water. [named after George Canning]

Canning Stock-route, *n.* Australia's longest stock-route, no longer used, which extended 1400 km in WA from Halls Creek to Wiluna. [named after Alfred Canning, surveyor who pioneered the route in 1906]

cannon /'kænən/, *n., pl.* **-nons,** (*esp. collectively*) **-non,** *v.* ◇*n.* **1.** a large ancient gun fixed on wheels and used for firing heavy balls, etc. **2.** a powerful automatic gun for firing explosive shells. **3.** Also, **cannon bit, canon bit.** the part of a bit which is in a horse's mouth. **4.** any strike and springing back, e.g. a ball hitting a wall and bouncing off. ◇*v.i.* **5.** to crash; collide with (fol. by *into*). [F, from It: large tube, from L]

cannot /'kænɒt, kæ'nɒt/, *v.* a form of **can not**.

canny /'kæni/, *adj.,* **-nier, -niest. 1.** not taking risks; careful; wary. **2.** wise; shrewd; astute. [apparently from CAN[1]] **– canniness,** *n.*

canoe /kə'nu/, *n., v.i.,* **-noed, -noeing.** ◇*n.* **1.** a light narrow boat moved by paddle(s). ◇*v.i.* **2.** to go in a canoe. [Sp, from Carib] **– canoeing,** *n.* **– canoeist,** *n.*

canon[1] /'kænən/, *n.* **1.** the law or body of laws of a church. **2.** any rule, law, principle, or standard. **3.** an officially accepted set of holy books. **4.** a list of works of a writer generally accepted as genuine. **5.** *Rom Cath Ch.* a list of recognised saints. **6.** *Music.* a piece in which the same tune is played or sung by two or more parts overlapping each other. [ME and OE, from L: rule, canon, from Gk: straight rod, rule, standard]

canon[2] /'kænən/, *n.* a member of a cathedral chapter. [ME, from ML] **– canonry,** *n.*

canonical /kə'nɒnɪkəl/, *adj.* **1.** conforming to church law. **2.** included in the canon of the

Bible. **3.** recognised or accepted. ◇*n.* **4.** (*pl.*) the clothes of the clergy. [L, from Gk]

canonise *or* **canonize** /'kænənaɪz/, *v.t.*, **-nised**, **-nising**. **1.** *Church.* to place in the canon of saints. **2.** to glorify. **– canonisation**, *n.*

canoodle /kə'nudl/, *v.i.*, **-dled**, **-dling**. *Colloq.* to kiss and cuddle.

canopy /'kænəpi/, *n., pl.* **-pies**. **1.** a covering hung or held over a throne, bed, holy object, etc. **2.** an overhanging protection or shelter. **3.** the sky. **4.** the fabric part of a parachute. **5.** the highest part of a forest, consisting of the upper branches of tall trees. [ME, from L: net curtains, from Gk: mosquito net]

cant[1] /kænt/, *n.* **1.** insincere expressions of goodness or high morals. **2.** words, phrases, etc., used by a particular group of people; jargon: *thieves' cant; sociological cant.* [L: song]

cant[2] /kænt/, *n.* **1.** a slope; slant. **2.** a sudden movement that tilts or overturns something. ◇*v.t., v.i.* **3.** to slope or slant; tilt. [MD, or MLG *kant*, both probably from ONF, from L: corner, side]

can't /kant/, *v.* contraction of *cannot*.

Cantab., of Cambridge. [ML *Cantabrigiensis*]

cantaloupe /'kæntəlup/, *n.* → **rockmelon**. Also, **cantaloup**. [F, from It *Cantalupo*, a former estate of the Pope near Rome, where it was first grown in Europe]

cantankerous /kæn'tæŋkərəs/, *adj.* bad-tempered; quarrelsome. [? from ME *contek* contention]

cantata /kæn'tɑtə/, *n. Music.* a work for soloist(s) and choir with words or story set to music but not acted; short oratorio. [It: sing, from L]

canteen /kæn'tin/, *n.* **1.** a restaurant, cafeteria, or sandwich shop connected with factory, office, school, etc. **2.** a cutlery box. **3.** a small container for carrying drinking water. [F, from It *cantina* cellar, wine cellar, from L]

canter /'kæntə/, *n.* an easy gallop. [short for *Canterbury gallop* (as of pilgrims to Canterbury, England)]

Canterbury /'kæntəbri, -bəri/, *n.* **1.** a city in south-eastern England, in Kent; famous cathedral; medieval pilgrimages to the tomb of St Thomas à Becket; its archbishop is primate of all England. Pop. (district) 116 829 (1981).

Canterbury Plains, *n.* an area of rich farmland along the eastern coast of South Island, NZ. About 10 360 km².

cantilever /'kæntəlivə/, *n.* **1.** *Archit.* **a.** the free horizontal part of a structure projecting beyond its support. **b.** a bracket projecting from a wall to support a balcony, etc. **2.** either of two arms reaching towards each other from opposite banks or piers, forming a span of a bridge (**cantilever bridge**) when joined. [orig. uncert.]

canto /'kæntoʊ/, *n., pl.* **-tos**. **1.** a main division of a long poem. **2.** *Music.* a song or tune. [It, from L: song]

canton /'kæntɒn, kæn'tɒn/, *n.* **1.** an area of land being part of a country, esp. a state of Switzerland. **2.** a division or part. [F: corner, from L] **– cantonal**, *adj.*

Canton /kæn'tɒn/, *n.* former name of Guangzhou.

Cantonese /kæntə'niz/, *n.* a Chinese language of southern China.

cantor /'kæntə/, *n.* **1.** a church choir leader. **2.** the Jewish religious official singing the liturgy. [L: singer]

Canuck /kə'nʌk/, *n. Colloq.* a Canadian, esp. a French Canadian.

Canute /kə'njut, -'nut/, *n.* AD 994?–1035, Danish king of England 1017–35, of Denmark 1018–35, and of Norway 1028–35. Also, **Cnut, Knut**.

canvas /'kænvəs/, *n.* **1.** a closely woven, heavy cloth of cotton or other fibres, used for tents, sails, etc. **2.** a piece of canvas on which an oil painting is done. **3.** tent(s): *campers living under canvas.* **4.** sails collectively: *a ship under full canvas.* **5.** a fabric, usu. stiff, of coarse loose weave, used as a base for embroidery, etc. [ME, from L *cannabis* hemp]

canvass /'kænvəs/, *v.t.* **1.** to try to get votes, support, etc., from (an area, group of people, etc.). **2.** to examine carefully; discuss; debate. [var. of CANVAS *n.*; orig. meaning to toss (someone) in a canvas sheet] **– canvasser**, *n.*

canyon /'kænjən/, *n.* a deep valley with steep sides. [Sp: tube, from L: reed]

cap /kæp/, *n., v.t.*, **capped**, **capping**. ◇*n.* **1.** a small hat, esp. a soft, close-fitting one with a peak. **2.** an item of flat headgear, with a peak, brim, or visor at the front, worn by soldiers, policemen, etc. **3.** special headgear showing rank, job, etc.: *nurse's cap.* **4.** → **mortarboard**. **5.** *Sport.* (cap given to show) membership of a team, esp. a national team. **6.** a protective top or lid: *lens cap.* **7.** a top or upper surface: *the cap of a wave.* **8.** *Bot.* the top of a mushroom. **9.** a small explosive used in toy guns to make the sound of a shot. **10.** → **diaphragm** (def. 3). **11. cap in hand**, humbly. ◇*v.t.* **12.** to put a cap on; cover. **13.** to complete. **14.** to outdo; excel. [OE *cæpe*, from LL: cap, hooded cloak, cape, apparently from *caput* head]

cap., *Abbrev.* (*pl.* **caps**) a capital letter.

capability /keɪpə'bɪləti/, *n., pl.* **-ties**. **1.** the quality of being capable; capacity; ability. **2.** (*usu. pl.*) a quality, ability, etc., that can be developed or used.

capable /'keɪpəbəl/, *adj.* **1.** having the ability, esp. to get things done; competent: *a capable instructor.* **2. capable of**, **a.** having ability, strength, etc., to; qualified or fitted for: *capable of judging art.* **b.** open to the influence or effect of: *an arrangement capable of improvement.* **c.** tending to; inclined to: *capable of murder.* [LL]

capacious /kə'peɪʃəs/, *adj.* able to hold a lot: *a capacious bag.* [CAPACI(TY) + -OUS] **– capaciousness**, *n.*

capacitance /kə'pæsətəns/, n. the property of a system which enables it to store an electrical charge, measured in farads; electrical capacity. [CAPACIT(Y) + -ANCE]

capacitor /kə'pæsətə/, n. an apparatus for accumulating and holding an electric charge, consisting of two conducting surfaces separated by an insulator; condenser.

capacity /kə'pæsəti/, n., pl. **-ties**. 1. the ability to contain, absorb, or hold. 2. volume; content. 3. mental ability: *the capacity of a student*. 4. power, ability, or possibility of doing something (fol. by *of, for,* or infinitive): *capacity for self-protection; capacity to act quickly*. 5. position; function: *in the capacity of a legal adviser*. 6. maximum output: *factory working at capacity*. [ME, from L]

cape[1] /keɪp/, n. a sleeveless garment fastened round the neck and hanging over the shoulders. [F, from Sp, from LL]

cape[2] /keɪp/, n. a piece of land extending out into the sea, a lake, etc. [ME, from F, from Pr., from L *caput* head]

Cape /keɪp/, n. the →**Cape of Good Hope.**

Cape Barren goose, n. a rare Australian bird of the duck family, greyish with pink legs and a black bill. [named after CAPE BARREN ISLAND]

Cape Barren Island, n. an island off the north-eastern tip of Tasmania in Bass Strait, the second largest of the Furneaux Group.

Cape Horn, n. a headland on a small island at the southern extremity of South America. Also, **the Horn.**

Cape of Good Hope, n. a cape near the southern extremity of Africa.

caper[1] /'keɪpə/, v.i. 1. to jump or dance about. ◇n. 2. a foolish action; prank. [fig. use of L *caper* he-goat]

caper[2] /'keɪpə/, n. a Mediterranean shrub with a flower bud used pickled in sauces, etc. [ME *caperis,* from L *capparis,* from Gk *kápparis*]

Capertian /kæpə'tiən/, n. a cultural period of Aboriginal development recognised in eastern Australia, beginning about 6000 years BP and ending about 2000 years BP. [named after *Capertee,* NSW]

Cape Town, n. a seaport in the Republic of South Africa, near the Cape of Good Hope; seat of the legislature of South Africa; capital of Cape Province. Pop. 776 617 (1986).

Cape York Peninsula, n. a peninsula in Qld; its tip is the northernmost point of mainland Australia.

capillary /kə'pɪləri/, n., pl. **-laries,** adj. ◇n. 1. *Anat.* one of the tiny blood vessels between the ends of the arteries and the beginnings of the veins. 2. Also, **capillary tube.** a thin tube with a small opening. ◇adj. 3. relating to or occurring in a capillary. 4. *Phys.* **a.** relating to the property of surface tension. **b. capillary action,** the raising or lowering of liquids in thin tubes, etc., due to forces between molecules, such as surface tension, and between molecules of the liquid and the tube, etc. **c. capillary attraction or repulsion,** the pulling together or pushing apart which seems to take place between a liquid and a tube, etc. 5. *Bot.* like hair in the manner of growth or in shape. [L: relating to the hair]

capital[1] /'kæpɪtl/, n. 1. a city or town which is the official seat of government in a country, state, etc. 2. a capital (upper case) letter. 3. the wealth, in money or property, owned by an individual, firm, etc. 4. any form of wealth used to produce more wealth. 5. the ownership interest in a business. 6. any source of profit, advantage, power, etc.: *He tried to make capital out of a chance situation.* 7. (oft. *cap.*) capitalists as a group or class. ◇*adj.* 8. relating to capital: *capital stock.* 9. highly important. 10. chief, esp. as being the seat of government. 11. excellent or first-rate. 12. (of letters) of the large size used at the beginning of a sentence or as the first letter of a proper name. 13. involving the loss of life, usu. as punishment: *a capital offence.* [ME, from L *capitālis* relating to the head or to life, chief]

capital[2] /'kæpɪtl/, n. *Archit.* the head, or top part, of a pillar, etc. [ME, from L *caput* head]

capital accounts, *n.pl. Comm.* accounts showing the final financial position as assets minus liabilities.

capital appreciation, n. the increase in the value of an asset over a period of time.

capital assets, n. pl. →**fixed assets.**

capital distribution, n. the giving out of free shares to shareholders in a company.

capital gains, n. pl. profits from the sale of capital assets, such as property, etc.

capital goods, n. pl. goods used in the production of other goods.

capital-intensive /'kæpɪtl-ɪn,tensɪv/, adj. relating to an industry which, while needing little man-power, requires a large amount of capital (opposed to *labor-intensive*).

capitalise or **capitalize** /'kæpətəlaɪz/, v.t., **-lised, -lising.** 1. to print in capital letters, or to begin with a capital. 2. to supply with capital. 3. to estimate the value of (a stock or an enterprise). 4. to take advantage of (oft. fol. by *on*): *to capitalise on one's opportunities.*

capitalism /'kæpətəlɪzəm/, n. 1. the system under which the means of production, distribution, and exchange are mostly privately owned and directed. 2. system favoring such an economy and its resulting wealth structure.

capitalist /'kæpətəlɪst/, n. 1. someone who has capital employed in business enterprises. ◇*adj.* 2. founded on or believing in capitalism. –**capitalistic,** *adj.*

capital stock, n. the total shares issued by a company.

Capitol /'kæpɪtl/, n. 1. the building at Washington, DC, used by the Congress of the US for its sessions. 2. the ancient temple of Jupiter at Rome, on the Capitoline. [ME, from L: head]

Capitoline /kə'pɪtəlaɪn/, n. one of the Seven Hills of ancient Rome.

capitulate /kə'pɪtʃəleɪt/, v.i., **-lated, -lating.** to surrender without conditions, or on particular terms. [ML: arrange in chapters, from L: head] **—capitulation,** n.

Capone /kə'poʊn/, n. **Al(phonse),** 1899-1947, US gangster.

cappuccino /kæpə'tʃinoʊ/, n. coffee made on a machine which forces steam through the milk to make it frothy. [It: hood]

Capri /kə'pri, 'kæpri/, n. a rocky island off the Bay of Naples, in western Italy; famous for its scenery and grottoes. Pop. 7489 (1981); 14 km².

capriccio /kə'prɪtʃioʊ/, n., pl. **-cios, -ci** /-tʃi/. Music. a lively work in a free style. [It *capro* goat, from L]

caprice /kə'pris/, n. **1.** a sudden change of mind without apparent reason; whim. **2.** a tendency to change one's mind without apparent reason; capriciousness. **3.** Music. → **capriccio.** [F, from It *capriccio* CAPRICCIO] **—capricious,** adj. **—capriciousness,** n.

Capricorn /'kæprəkɔn/, n. **1.** Also, **Capricornus.** a group of fixed stars and the tenth sign of the zodiac, represented by a goat. **2. Tropic of Capricorn,** see tropic (def. 1a). [L: goat-horned] **—Capricornian,** n., adj.

caps, Abbrev. capital letters.

capsicum /'kæpsəkəm/, n. any of a number of pepper plants yielding fruits ranging in taste from mild to extremely hot, used in salads, pickles and curries. [L *capsa* box]

capsize /kæp'saɪz/, v.i., v.t., **-sized, -sizing.** to turn over: *The boat capsized*; *They capsized the boat.* [orig. unknown]

capstan /'kæpstən/, n. a cylindrical apparatus turned by hand or motor, onto which a rope is wound, used for raising weights (as an anchor) or drawing things closer (as a ship to its jetty). [ME, from Pr, from L: halter]

capsulate /'kæpsələnt, -lət/, adj. enclosed in or formed into a capsule. Also, **capsulated.**

capsule /'kæpʃul, -ʃəl/, n. **1.** a small case, envelope, or covering, as that containing a dose of medicine. **2.** Bot. **a.** a dry fruit containing at least two carpels (seed-producing structures). **b.** the spore case of various non-flowering plants. **3.** Anat., Zool. a membranous sac. **4.** the area of a spaceship containing the crew or instruments, which separates from the engines after take-off. **5.** anything in shortened form, as a story or news item. [L: little box] **—capsular,** adj.

Capt, Abbrev. Captain.

captain /'kæptn/, n. **1.** a person who is in authority over others; leader. **2.** Mil. See Appendix. ◇v.t. **3.** to lead or command as a captain. [ME, from OF: chief, from L: head] **—captaincy,** n.

Captain Moonlite, n. → Captain Moonlite.

caption /'kæpʃən/, n. **1.** a heading or title, as of a picture, article, or page. **2.** Films. the title of a scene, words of a speech, etc., shown on the screen. ◇v.t. **3.** to provide with a caption. [L]

captious /'kæpʃəs/, adj. **1.** making much of unimportant faults; difficult to please. **2.** coming from a fault-finding tendency: *captious remarks*. [L] **—captiousness,** n.

captivate /'kæptəveɪt/, v.t., **-vated, -vating.** to charm by beauty or excellence; enchant. [LL: taken captive] **—captivation,** n. **—captivator,** n.

captive /'kæptɪv/, n. **1.** a prisoner. ◇adj. **2.** made or held prisoner. **3.** enslaved by love, etc.; captivated. [L] **—captivity,** n.

captor /'kæptə/, n. a person who captures.

capture /'kæptʃə/, v., **-tured, -turing.** ◇v.t. **1.** to take by force or trickery; take prisoner; seize. ◇n. **2.** the act of seizing. **3.** a thing or person captured. **4.** Phys. the process by which an atom or nucleus gains an extra particle. **5.** Geog. the process by which one river acquires the tributaries of another. [F, from L]

car /ka/, n. **1.** → **motor car. 2.** Poetry. a chariot, as of war or triumph. **3.** a railway carriage or wagon. **4.** the part of a lift, etc., in which passengers, etc., are carried. [ME, from L, of Celtic orig.]

Caracalla /kærə'kælə/, n. (*Marcus Aurelius Antonius Bassianus*), AD 188-217, Roman emperor AD 211-217; assassinated following a reign marked by cruelty and economic mismanagement.

Caractacus /kə'ræktəkəs/, n. fl. AD c. 50, chieftain who opposed the Romans in Britain. Also, **Caradoc** /kə'rædək/.

carafe /kə'raf, -'ræf, 'kærəf/, n. the (contents of) a glass bottle for water, wine, etc. [F, from It, from Ar: drinking vessel]

caramel /'kærəməl/, n. **1.** burnt sugar, used for coloring and flavoring food, etc. **2.** a type of sweet, made from sugar, butter, milk, etc. **3.** the light brown color of caramel. ◇adj. **4.** of the color of caramel. [F, from Sp]

carapace /'kærəpeɪs/, n. a protective plate or shell covering the back of an animal. [F, from Sp]

carat /'kærət/, n. **1.** Also, **metric carat.** a unit of weight in gemstones, 0.2 grams. *Abbrev.:* CM **2.** a twenty-fourth part (used as a measure of pureness of gold, pure gold being 24 carats fine). [F, from It: light weight, from Gk: carob bean, carat, diminutive of *kéras* horn]

Caravaggio /kærə'vadʒioʊ/, n. **Michelangelo Merisi da** /mɪkəl,andʒəloʊ mə'rizi da/, 1573-1610, Italian baroque painter of mainly religious subjects.

caravan /'kærəvæn/, n., v. **-vanned, -vanning.** ◇n. **1.** a vehicle which can be pulled by a car, and in which people can live. **2.** a similar vehicle, horse-drawn, once lived in by gipsies and circus folk, etc. **3.** Also, **caravanserai.** a group of people travelling together, oft. with camels, tents, etc., over deserts in Asia or Africa. ◇v.i. **4.** to live, as for a holiday, in a caravan. [F, from Pers]

caraway /ˈkærəweɪ/, n. a herb, bearing unusual-tasting, seedlike fruit (**caraway seeds**) used in cookery. [late ME, from ML, from Ar]

carbide /ˈkɑːbaɪd/, n. See **-ide**.

carbine /ˈkɑːbaɪn, ˈkɑːbiːn/, n. a light rifle with a short barrel, for use in situations where free movement is difficult. [F]

carbo-, word part meaning 'carbon', as in *carbonate*. Also, **carb-**. [combining form of CARBON]

carbohydrate /kɑːbəˈhaɪdreɪt/, n. any of a class of organic compounds containing oxygen, hydrogen and carbon, including sugars, starch, and cellulose.

carbon /ˈkɑːbən/, n. **1.** *Chem.* a common element which forms organic compounds with hydrogen, oxygen, etc., and which has diamond, graphite and charcoal as allotropes. *Symbol:* C; *at. no.:* 6; *at. wt:* 12.011. **2.** *Elect.* the carbon electrode through which the current is conducted in arc lighting or welding. **3.** a sheet of carbon paper. **4.** a copy made by using carbon paper. **5.** the isotope **carbon 14** used in radiocarbon dating. [F, from L: coal, charcoal]

Carbonari /kɑːbəˈnɑːri/, n.pl., sing. **-ro**. the members of a 19th-century secret political society, of revolutionary aims, in Italy, France, and Spain. [It, pl. of *carbonaro* charcoal-burner] — **Carbonarism**, n.

carbonate /ˈkɑːbəneɪt, -nət/ n.; /ˈkɑːbəneɪt/, v., **-nated, -nating**. ○n. **1.** *Chem.* See **-ate**². ○v.t. **2.** to form into a carbonate. **3.** to treat (soft drinks, etc.) with carbon dioxide so as to make them bubbly. [NL] — **carbonation**, n.

carbon cycle, n. **1.** *Biol.* the circulation on earth of carbon atoms, from the atmosphere through plants and animals back into the atmosphere. **2.** *Phys.* cycle of nuclear changes inside stars, giving out atomic energy, and gradually changing hydrogen into helium.

carbon dating, n. →**radiocarbon dating**.

carbon dioxide, n. a colorless, odorless, non-flammable gas, CO_2, used widely in industry as dry ice, and in fizzy drinks, etc. It is present in the atmosphere and is formed during respiration.

Carboni /kɑːˈboʊni/, n. **Raffaello**, 1820–75, Australian writer, poet and goldminer, born in Italy; one of the leaders of the Ballarat Reform League.

carbonic acid, n. the weak acid, H_2CO_3, formed when carbon dioxide dissolves in water.

Carboniferous /kɑːbəˈnɪfərəs/, adj. **1.** of that part of the Palaeozoic period in which much coal was formed between the Devonian and Permian. **2.** (l.c.) producing coal. — n. **3.** a late Palaeozoic period or system next following the Devonian. [CARBON + -I- + -FEROUS]

carbonisation or **carbonization** /kɑːbənaɪˈzeɪʃən/, n. **1.** *Chem.* formation of carbon from organic matter. **2.** coal distillation, as in coke ovens. **3.** treatment of wool or wool fabric to remove vegetable matter.

carbonise or **carbonize** /ˈkɑːbənaɪz/, v.t., **-nised, -nising**. **1.** to burn until black, forming carbon. **2.** to coat or enrich with carbon. **3.** to treat (wool) chemically to remove burrs, seeds, etc.

carbon monoxide, n. a colorless, odorless, poisonous gas, CO, formed when carbon burns in too little oxygen.

carbon paper, n. paper coated usu. with a carbon preparation, used between sheets of writing paper to make copies.

carbon tetrachloride, n. a non-flammable, colorless liquid, CCl_4, used in medicine and as a fire-extinguisher, cleaning fluid, solvent, etc.

carborundum /kɑːbəˈrʌndəm/, n. *Chem.* silicon carbide, SiC, used as a grinding material, for sharpening knives, etc. [CARBO- + (CO)RUNDUM]

carboxyl group, n. a univalent radical —COOH, present in all organic acids. [CARB(O)- + OX(YGEN) + -YL]

carboxylic acid, n. an organic acid (as acetic acid, benzoic acid), marked by the presence of one or more carboxyl groups.

carbuncle /ˈkɑːbʌŋkəl/, n. **1.** a painful boil-like swelling under the skin resulting in the formation of pus. **2.** a garnet cut in a convex rounded form without facets. [ME, from ONF, from L *carbunculus*, diminutive of *carbo* (live) coal] — **carbuncled**, adj. — **carbuncular**, adj.

carburettor /kɑːbəˈretə/, n. an apparatus in an internal-combustion engine for mixing fuel with the correct proportion of air to form explosive gas.

carcass /ˈkɑːkəs/, n. **1.** the dead body of an animal or (now offensively) of a human being. **2.** (*in fun*) a living body: *Get your carcass over here.* **3.** an unfinished framework, as of house or ship. Also, **carcase**. [F, from It]

carcinogen /kɑːˈsɪnədʒən/, n. any substance which tends to produce a cancer in a body. — **carcinogenic**, adj.

carcinoma /kɑːsəˈnoʊmə/, n., pl. **-mata** /-mətə/, **-mas**. a growth which is not regulated by normal body controls and which often spreads; a cancer. [L, from Gk: a cancer]

card¹ /kɑːd/, n. **1.** a piece of stiff paper or thin pasteboard, usu. rectangular: *a business card; computer card.* **2.** →**postcard**. **3.** a piece of cardboard usu. with a picture and verse, bearing a greeting: *a Christmas card.* **4.** one of a set of cards used in playing various games, in telling the future, etc. **5.** (pl.) a game or games played with such a set. **6.** *Colloq.* a plan, idea, approach to a problem, etc.: *He has a card up his sleeve.* **7.** a program of events, as at horseraces. **8.** *Colloq.* an amusing or strange person. **9. put one's cards on the table**, to speak plainly, openly. **10. on the cards**, likely to happen. [ME, from L *charta* (see CHART)]

card² /kɑːd/, n. **1.** a comblike device used to clear knots from wool, etc., before spinning. ○v.t. **2.** to prepare (wool, etc.) with a card. [late ME, from L: thistle] — **carder**, n. — **carding**, n.

cardamom /'kadəməm/, n. a sweet-smelling seed of various Asian plants, used as a spice. [L, from Gk]

cardboard /'kadbod/, n. **1.** a thick, stiff, paper-like material. ◇adj. **2.** made of or like cardboard. **3.** in appearance only; insubstantial: *a cardboard prime minister; a cardboard empire*.

card-carrying /'kad-kæriŋ/, adj. possessing full membership, as of a trade union.

cardi-, variant of **cardio-** before vowels, as in *cardiology*.

cardiac /'kadiæk/, adj. relating to the heart. [L *cardiacus* of the heart, from Gk *kardiakós*]

cardiac arrest, n. a serious disorder in which the heart stops pumping blood through the body.

Cardiff /'kadəf/, n. the capital of Wales; an important seaport located in the south-east. Pop. 266 267 (1981).

cardigan /'kadɪgən/, n. a knitted jacket usu. with buttons down the front. [named after the 7th Earl of *Cardigan*, 1797-1868]

cardinal /'kadənəl/, adj. **1.** of first importance; chief; principal; fundamental: *a cardinal point to remember*. **2.** a deep rich red. ◇n. **3.** one of the members of the Sacred College of the Roman Catholic Church, ranking next to the pope. **4.** a deep rich red color. [ME, from L: chief]

cardinal number, n. Maths. a number such as *1, 2, 3*, which indicates how many things are in a given set, but not their order. See *ordinal*.

cardio-, word part meaning 'heart'. Also, **cardi-**. [Gk *kardio-*, combining form of *kardía*]

cardiology /kadi'ɒlədʒi/, n. the study of the heart and the work it does. —**cardiologist**, n.

cardiovascular /,kadiou'væskjələ/, adj. relating to the heart and blood vessels.

cardsharp /'kadʃap/, n. a person who cheats at card games, esp. for a living. Also, **cardsharper**. —**cardsharping**, n.

care /keə/, n., v., **cared**, **caring**. ◇n. **1.** worry; anxiety; concern: *Care had aged him.* **2.** a cause of worry, anxiety, distress, etc.: *free from care.* **3.** serious attention; solicitude; heed; caution: *He will give great care to work.* **4.** protection; charge: *under the care of a doctor.* **5.** an object of concern or attention. **6.** care of. Also, **c/o**, **c/-**. at the address of. ◇v.i. **7.** to be troubled or concerned: *She cares too much.* **8.** to have a liking or taste (fol. by *for*): *I don't care for cabbage.* **9.** to have a fondness (fol. by *for*): *He cares greatly for her.* **10.** to look after (fol. by *for*): *The state must care for the needy.* **11.** to be inclined: *I don't care to do it today.* ◇v. **12. (someone) couldn't care less**, Colloq. (someone) doesn't care at all. [OE *caru* (*cearu*)]

careen /kə'rin/, v.t. to cause (a ship) to lie on its side, as for repairing. [F, from L: keel] —**careenage**, n. —**careener**, n.

career /kə'rɪə/, n. **1.** the general course of action of a person through life. **2.** the occupation, profession, etc., followed throughout one's life: *a career in law*. ◇v.i. **3.** to run or move rapidly along. [F, from It, from L]

carefree /'keəfri/, adj. without anxiety or worry.

careful /'keəfəl/, adj. **1.** avoiding hasty action; cautious. **2.** taking pains in one's work; exact; thorough. **3.** (of things) done or performed with exactness: *a careful job*. **4.** kindly aware (fol. by *of, about, in*): *He is careful of their feelings*. **5.** Colloq. mean; parsimonious.

careless /'keələs/, adj. **1.** not paying enough attention to what one does. **2.** not exact or thorough: *careless work*. **3.** done or said without thinking; unconsidered: *a careless remark*. **4.** not caring or troubling; unconcerned (fol. by *of, about, in*): *careless of his health*.

carer /'keərə/, n. a person who looks after other people, esp. aged or disabled relatives.

caress /kə'rɛs/, n. **1.** an act expressing fondness, as an embrace, kiss, etc. ◇v.t. **2.** to touch or stroke gently to show fondness. [F, from It, from L: dear] —**caressingly**, adv.

caret /'kærət/, n. a mark (∧) made in written or printed material to show where something is to be added. [L: there is lacking]

caretaker /'keəteɪkə/, n. **1.** a person who takes care of a thing or place, esp. a building. ◇adj. **2.** holding office for a short time only, until a new appointment, etc., can be made: *caretaker governor*.

Carey /'keəri/, n. **Peter**, born 1943, Australian novelist and short-story writer; works include the collection of stories, *The Fat Man in History* (1974) and the novel *Oscar and Lucinda* (1988); awarded 1990 Booker Prize.

cargo /'kagou/, n., pl. **-goes**, **-gos**. **1.** the goods carried on a ship. **2.** load. [Sp: load]

Caribbean /kærə'biən, kə'rɪbiən/, adj. **1.** pertaining to the Caribs, the Lesser Antilles, or the Caribbean Sea. **2.** —**Caribbean Sea**. **3.** the islands collectively of the Caribbean Sea.

Caribbean Sea, n. a sea between Central America, the West Indies, and South America. About 2 500 000 km²; greatest known depth 7239 m.

caribou /'kærəbu/, n., pl. **-bou**. any of several kinds of reindeer from North America. [Canadian F, from Algonquian *xalibu* pawer, scratcher]

caricature /'kærəkətʃʊə/, n., v., **-tured**, **-turing**. ◇n. **1.** a picture, description, etc., making a special point of the peculiarities or individual features of people or things. **2.** the art or process of making such pictures, etc. **3.** any imitation so inferior as to be laughable. ◇v.t. **4.** to make a caricature of. [F, from It: (over)load, exaggerate] —**caricaturist**, n.

caries /'keəriz/, n. decay, as of bone or teeth. [L] —**carious**, adj.

carillon /kə'rɪljən/, n. **1.** a set of bells hung in a tower and sounded by hand, pedal or machinery. **2.** a melody played on such bells. [F: chime of (orig. four) bells, from L *quattuor* four] —**carillonist**, n.

Carl XVI Gustaf /kal 'gustav/, n. born 1946, became king of Sweden in 1973.

Carlyle /ka'laɪl/, n. **Thomas**, 1795–1881, Scottish essayist and historian; writer of *The French Revolution* (1837).

Carmel /'kaməl/, n. **Mount**, a ridge in north-western Israel, near the Mediterranean coast. About 23 km long; highest point, about 550 m.

Carmelite /'kaməlaɪt/, n. *Rom Cath Ch.* **1.** a mendicant friar belonging to a religious order founded on Mt Carmel in the 12th century; a White Friar. **2.** a nun belonging to this order. [LL, from Gk: inhabitant of Mt CARMEL]

Carmichael /'kaɪmaɪkəl/, n. **Stokely**, born 1941, US activist for black rights, born in Trinidad.

carminative /'kamənətɪv/, n., adj. a (drug causing) passing of gas from the body, relieving flatulence. [L *carmīnātus*, pp., carded + -IVE]

carmine /'kamɪn/, n. **1.** a crimson or purplish red color. **2.** a crimson coloring obtained from cochineal. ◇adj. **3.** crimson or purplish red. [ML, from Sp: crimson]

carnage /'kanɪdʒ/, n. the killing of a great number, as in battle; butchery; massacre. [F, from It: meat, from L: flesh]

carnal /'kanəl/, adj. **1.** not spiritual; only human; temporal; worldly. **2.** relating to the flesh or the body; sensual. **3.** sexual. [ME, from L: flesh] —**carnality**, n.

carnal knowledge, n. sexual intercourse, esp. with one under the age of consent.

Carnarvon /ka'navən/, n. a town and shire on the central western coast of WA, at the mouth of the Gascoyne River; important port. Pop. 6847 (1986).

carnation /ka'neɪʃən/, n. **1.** any of numerous cultivated varieties of pinks with clove-smelling flowers of various colors. **2.** pink; light red. ◇adj. **3.** colored a light red. [L: fleshiness]

carnelian /ka'niliən/, n. a red or reddish variety of stone used in jewellery, etc. Also, **cornelian**. [ME, from OF]

carnival /'kanəvəl/, n. **1.** an occasion of merrymaking, usu. with much movement and noise, processions, etc. **2.** a procession, usu. for a special occasion. **3.** a fair or amusement show, esp. a travelling show. **4.** a series of sporting events: *a surfing carnival; sports carnival*. **5.** a period set aside for a carnival, esp. the season immediately before Lent. [It: stop (eating) meat]

Carnivale /kanə'vali/, n. a multicultural festival held annually in Sydney, NSW, since September 1981.

carnivore /'kanəvɔ/, n. **1.** *Zool.* one of the Carnivora, the order of mammals, chiefly flesh-eating, that includes the cats, dogs, bears, etc. **2.** *Bot.* a flesh-eating plant.

carob /'kærəb/, n. a Mediterranean tree, bearing a long, dry pod containing hard seeds in a sweet pulp, used as animal fodder, and in cookery as a substitute for chocolate. [F, from Ar]

carol /'kærəl/, n., v., -**rolled**, -**rolling**. ◇n. **1.** a joyful song, esp. a Christmas song or hymn. ◇v.t., v.i. **2.** to sing (a song) in a lively, joyful manner. [ME, from OF] —**caroller**, n.

Carolina /kærə'laɪnə/, the Carolinas, North Carolina and South Carolina.

Caroline /'kærəlaɪn/, adj. relating to the time of Charles I or Charles II, kings of England: *Caroline theatre*.

carotid /kə'rɒtəd/, adj. relating to either of the two large arteries, one on each side of the neck, which carry blood to the head. [Gk: stupor (thought to be caused by compression of these arteries)] —**carotidal**, adj.

carousal /kə'raʊzəl/, n. a noisy or drunken feast or other social gathering.

carouse /kə'raʊz/, n., v., -**roused**, -**rousing**. ◇n. **1.** a noisy or drunken feast. ◇v.i. **2.** to engage in a carouse; drink deeply. [G *gar aus* (drink a cup) wholly out]

carousel /kærə'sɛl/, n. **1.** → **merry-go-round** (def. 1). **2.** a continuously circulating belt by which bags are returned to travellers after a journey by plane, ship, bus, etc. [F, from It, from L: cart]

carp¹ /kap/, v.i. to find fault; complain unreasonably: *to carp at small mistakes*. [ME, from Scand]

carp² /kap/, n., pl. **carp**. a large, freshwater food fish, commonly bred in ponds and introduced into Australia. [ME, from Pr, from LL *carpa*; of Gmc orig.]

-**carp**, a noun ending meaning 'fruit', used in botanical terms, as *pericarp*. [combining form representing Gk *karpós*]

Carpathian Mountains /ka'peɪθiən/, n.pl. a mountain system in central Europe, extending about 1300 km from northern Slovakia to central Romania. Highest peak, Gerlachovka, 2663 m. Also, **Carpathians**.

carpel /'kapəl/, n. simple seed-bearing organ of a flower. [NL, from Gk: fruit]

Carpentaria /kapən'tɛəriə/, n. **Gulf of,** a large inlet on the northern coast of Australia, between Arnhem Land and Cape York Peninsula; extends about 650 km south to the shores of the Gulf country. About 500 km wide.

carpenter /'kapəntə/, n. a person who puts up and fixes the wooden parts, etc., in buildings. [ME, from LL: wagon-maker, from L *carpentum* wagon]

carpentry /'kapəntri/, n. → **woodwork**.

carpet /'kapət/, n. **1.** a heavy fabric for covering floors. **2.** any covering of or like a carpet. **3. on the carpet**, being or about to be blamed. ◇v.t. **4.** to cover or furnish with, or as with, a carpet. [ME, from L: card (wool)]

carpetbagger /'kapətbægə/, n. **1.** a person who moves to a place, seeking profit or advantage for himself. **2.** (in US history) (*offensive*) a North American who went to the South after the Civil War to seek advantages in the disorganised political situation.

carpet shark, n. → **wobbegong**.

carpet snake, *n.* a large, non-poisonous Australian snake that kills by crushing, often used in barns to control rats, mice, etc.

-carpic, a word part related to -carp. [-CARP + -IC]

carpo-, a word part meaning 'fruit'. [Gk *karpo-*, combining form of *karpós*]

-carpous, combining form related to -carp. [-CARP + -OUS]

carpus /'kɑpəs/, *n., pl.* **-pi** /-pi/. the wrist, or its bones.

Carrara /kə'rɑrə/, *n.* a town in north-western Italy; famous for its marble. Pop. 65 687 (1981).

carrel /kə'rel, 'kærəl/, *n.* (in a library) a small area used by students for individual study. [OF, from ML]

carriage /'kærɪdʒ/, *n.* **1.** a wheeled vehicle, usu. horse-drawn, for carrying people, esp. one made for comfort and style. **2.** a passenger-carrying unit on trains. **3.** a wheeled support, for moving something heavy, as a cannon. **4.** a part, as of a machine, designed for carrying something. **5.** a manner of carrying the head and body; bearing: *the carriage of a soldier*. **6.** the act of carrying; conveyance: *the expenses of carriage*. **7.** the cost of carrying. [ME, from ONF]

carriageway /'kærɪdʒweɪ/, *n.* that part of a road which carries vehicles.

carrier /'kæriə/, *n.* **1.** a person or thing that carries. **2.** a person, company, etc., which takes people or goods to a destination. **3.** a frame or part for carrying something, as on a bicycle. **4.** *Med.* a person, carrying but usu. not affected by, particular organisms, who may pass a disease to others. **5.** *Radio.* Also, **carrier wave.** a wave whose amplitude, frequency or phase is varied in order to send a signal. **6.** → **aircraft-carrier.**

carrier pigeon, *n.* a pigeon trained to fly home from great distances and used to carry messages; a homing pigeon.

carrion /'kæriən/, *n.* **1.** dead and decaying flesh. ◊*adj.* **2.** feeding on carrion **3.** of or like carrion. [ME, OF, from L *caro* flesh]

Carroll /'kærəl/, *n.* Lewis (*Charles Lutwidge Dodgson*), 1832–98, English writer and mathematician; wrote *Alice in Wonderland* (1865).

carrot /'kærət/, *n.* **1.** a plant whose orange-red root is used as a vegetable. **2.** *Colloq.* something meant to tempt: *to hold out a carrot*. [F, from L, from Gk]

Carruthers /kə'rʌðəz/, *n.* Jimmy (*James William Carruthers*), 1929–90, Australian bantamweight boxer; first Australian boxing world champion.

carry /'kæri/, *v.,* **-ried, -rying,** *n., pl.* **-ries.** ◊*v.t.* **1.** to take from one place to another in a vehicle, ship, pocket, hand, etc. **2.** to take or bring: *The wind carries sounds.* **3.** to hold (oneself) in a certain manner: *She carries herself proudly.* **4.** to take, esp. by force; capture; win: *The army will carry the town.* **5.** to succeed in electing (a candidate) or in having accepted (a motion or bill). **6.** (of a newspaper or magazine) to print: *The paper will carry the story.* **7.** to extend: *to carry the war into enemy territory.* **8.** to have as a quality, etc.: *His opinion carries great weight.* **9.** *Maths.* to move (a number) from one column to the next, as from units to tens, tens to hundreds, etc. **10.** *Comm.* to keep on hand or in stock. **11.** to be pregnant with: *She is carrying her third child.* ◊*v.i.* **12.** to act as a bearer. **13.** to be able to cover an area: *My voice carries farther than his.* **14.** to bear the head in a particular manner, as a horse. ◊**15.** Some special uses are:

carry away, 1. to influence (too) greatly: *The music carries me away; She was carried away by the excitement.* **2.** *Naut.* (of a mast, sail, etc.), to break away from its fastenings.

carry forward, 1. to go ahead in (some activity). **2.** *Bookkeeping.* to transfer (an amount, etc.) to the next column, page, etc.

carry off, 1. to win (the prize, honor, etc.). **2.** to handle (a situation) boldly and successfully: *He carried it off well.* **3.** to cause the death of: *It was cancer that finally carried him off.*

carry on, 1. to manage; conduct: *to carry on a business.* **2.** to behave in an excited or foolish manner. **3.** to continue.

carry out, to complete (a plan, etc.).

carry over, to put off until later.

carry through, 1. to complete. **2.** to support: *She will carry them through.*

◊*n.* **16.** the range, as of a gun, golf ball, etc. **17.** a carrying. [ME, from LL: convey by wagon, from L]

Carstensz /'kɑstənz/, *n.* Jan /jan/, Dutch navigator; explored part of the Gulf of Carpentaria in 1623 in the *Pera* and the *Arnhem,* after which Arnhem Land was named. Also, **Carstenzoon.**

cart /kɑt/, *n.* **1.** (formerly) a heavy horse-drawn vehicle, usu. for the carrying of heavy goods. **2.** any small vehicle moved by hand. **3. put the cart before the horse,** to confuse the correct order. ◊*v.t.* **4.** to carry in or as in a cart. [OE *cræt*]

carte blanche, /kɑt 'blɒntʃ/ *n., pl.* **cartes blanches** /kɑts 'blɒntʃ/. full power or freedom to act, make decisions, etc.

cartel /kɑ'tel/, *n.* a group formed of various firms to fix prices, etc., in some field of business. [F, from It, from L *charta* paper]

Carter /'kɑtə/, *n.* **1.** Howard, 1873–1939, English Egyptologist, discovered the tomb of King Tutankhamen in 1922. **2.** Jimmy (*James Earl Carter*), born 1924, 39th president of the US, 1977–81.

Cartesian /kɑ'tiʒən/, *adj.* relating to Descartes, to his mathematical methods, or to his philosophy which began wuth the famous phrase *Cogito, ergo sum* (I think therefore I am), which viewed physical nature mechanically and which in science emphasised rationalism and logic. [from *Cartesius,* Latinised form of the name of René DESCARTES] —**Cartesianism,** *n.*

Cartesian coordinates, *n.pl. Maths.* numbers given to a point to identify its position, being the perpendicular distances of the point from two (or three) axes.

Carthage /'kaθɪdʒ/, *n.* an ancient city-state in northern Africa, near modern Tunis; destroyed by the Romans, 146 BC. —**Carthaginian** /kaθə'dʒɪnɪən/, *adj.*, *n.*

cartilage /'katəlɪdʒ, 'kætlɪdʒ/, *n. Anat., Zool.* a firm, elastic, flexible substance, whitish or yellowish in color, consisting of connective tissue; gristle. [F, from L *cartilāgo* gristle] —**cartilaginous**, *adj.*

cartography /ka'tɒgrəfi/, *n.* making of maps or charts. Also, **chartography**. [ML *carta* chart, map + -GRAPHY] —**cartographic**, *adv.*

carton /'katən/, *n.* a cardboard box, esp. one in which food, such as eggs, milk, etc., is packaged and sold. [F. See CARTOON]

cartoon /ka'tun/, *n.* **1.** a humorous or satirical drawing as in a newspaper, etc., on some subject or person of current interest. **2.** *Art.* a sample drawing, for a fresco, mosaic, tapestry, etc., from which the final work is copied. **3.** a comic strip. **4.** a film consisting of many slightly different drawings run through a projector, to give the impression of movement. ◊*v.t.* **5.** to represent by a cartoon. [F, from It: pasteboard, cartoon, from L: paper] —**cartoonist**, *n.*

cartridge /'katrɪdʒ/, *n.* **1.** Also, **cartridge case.** cylindrical case of pasteboard, metal, etc. for holding a complete charge of powder, and often also a bullet or shot, for a rifle, machine-gun, etc. **2.** a container for: **a.** ink for some types of fountain pen. **b.** a recording or magnetic tape for computer, tape recorder, etc.

cartridge paper, *n.* unbleached drawing or printing paper.

cartwheel /'katwil/, *n.* **1.** a wheel of a cart, usu. large, wooden, with spokes and metal tyres. **2.** a somersault, performed sideways, with legs and arms outstretched.

caruncle /'kærəŋkəl, kə'rʌŋkəl/, *n. Zool.* a fleshy growth, as on the head of a bird; fowl's comb. [L: little flesh] —**caruncular, carunculous**, *adj.*

Caruso /kə'rusou/, *n.* **Enrico** /en'rikou/, 1873–1921, Italian operatic tenor.

carve /kav/, *v.*, **carved, carving.** ◊*v.t.* **1.** to fashion by cutting: *to carve a block of stone into a statue.* **2.** to produce by cutting: *to carve a design in wood.* **3.** to cut into slices or pieces, as meat. **4.** to make by one's own efforts (oft. fol. by *out*): *He carved out a good career for himself.* **5.** *Colloq.* to slash (someone) with knife, etc. (fol. by *up*). ◊*v.i.* **6.** to decorate by cutting figures, designs, etc. **7.** *Colloq.* to divide profits, illegal gain, an estate, etc. (fol. by *up*). [OE *ceorfan* cut] —**carver**, *n.*

Cary /'kɛəri/, *n.* **(Arthur) Joyce (Lunel)**, 1888–1957, English novelist; author of *The Horse's Mouth* (1944).

caryatid /kæri'ætəd/, *n., pl.* **-ids, -ides** /-ədiz/. *Archit.* a carved figure of a woman used as a supporting column. [L, from Gk: women of Caryae (site of a temple to Artemis)] —**caryatidal**, *adj.*

cas., *Abbrev.* casual.

Casablanca /kæsə'blæŋkə/, *n.* a seaport in north-western Morocco. Pop. 2 139 204 (1982). Arabic, **Dar-el-Beida.**

Casanova /kæsə'nouvə, kæzə-/, *n.* **Giovanni Jacopo** /dʒəvani 'jakəpou/, 1725–98, Italian amorous adventurer and writer.

cascade /kæs'keɪd/, *n., v.,* **-caded, -cading.** ◊*n.* **1.** a waterfall over steep rocks or something looking like this. ◊*v.i.* **2.** to fall in or like a cascade. [F, from It, from L: fall]

case[1] /keɪs/, *n.* **1.** an example of occurrence, existence, etc., of something: *a case of forgetfulness.* **2.** the actual state of things: *That is not the case.* **3.** a question or problem: *a case of conscience.* **4.** a situation; condition; plight. **5.** a statement of facts, reasons, etc.: *a strong case for the proposed law.* **6.** a disease, etc., needing medical treatment. **7.** *Law.* a proceeding in a court of law. **8.** *Gram.* **a.** the form of a noun, pronoun or adjective, which shows the relation these words have to other words in the sentence. **b.** the relationship shown by such a form. There are three such relations shown in English: subjective (or nominative) case, marking the subject of a verb; objective (or accusative) case, marking the object of a verb; and possessive (or genitive) case, marking possession, ownership, origin, etc. See Appendix. **9. in any case,** under any circumstances; anyhow. [ME, from L: a falling, occurrence]

case[2] /keɪs/, *n., v.,* **cased, casing.** ◊*n.* **1.** a container, as a box, sheath, etc. **2.** →**suitcase. 3.** the contents of a case. **4.** *Print.* a tray, of wood or metal, with divisions for holding types and case. arranged in set of two, the **upper case** for capitals, etc. and **lower case** for small letters, etc. ◊*v.t.* **5.** to put or enclose in a case. [ME, from L: box, receptacle]

casein /'keɪsɪn, -sin/, *n.* the major group of proteins in milk, which forms the basis of cheese and certain plastics. [L *cāseus* cheese + -IN[1]]

casement /'keɪsmənt/, *n.* **1.** a hinged window which opens like a door. **2.** *Poetic.* any window. [CASE[2] + -MENT]

case study, *n.* a study of a person, family or situation, which may be used to illustrate or prove a theory.

Casey /'keɪsi/, *n.* **1. Gavin**, 1907–64, Australian journalist, novelist and short-story writer; author of *It's Harder for Girls* (1942). **2. Richard Gardiner**, (*Baron Casey of Berwick, Victoria, and of the City of Westminster*), 1890–1976, diplomat, administrator, and Liberal party politician; governor-general of Australia 1965–69.

Casey Station, *n.* an Australian meteorological and scientific research station established in Antarctica in 1969. [named after Lord RG CASEY]

cash /kæʃ/, *n.* **1.** money, esp. actual notes, as opposed to a cheque. **2.** money paid to make a purchase, as opposed to credit. ◊*v.t.* **3.** to give or obtain cash for: *to cash a cheque.* ◊*v.*

cash 158 **cast**

4. cash in on, *Colloq.* to gain return or advantage from. [F, from Pr, from L: box]

Cash /kæʃ/, *n.* **1. Johnny**, born 1932, US country and western singer, composer and guitarist. **2. Martin**, 1810–77, Australian bushranger, born in Ireland. **3. Pat**, born 1965, Australian tennis player; Wimbledon singles champion 1987.

cash crop, *n.* a crop which, when harvested, gives a quick return of money.

cashew /ˈkæʃuː/, *n.* **1.** a tropical American tree whose bark yields medicinal gum. **2.** Also **cashew nut.** a small, edible, kidney-shaped nut. [F, from Brazilian Pg, from Tupi]

cash flow, *n.* the amount of cash coming in and out of a company in a given period.

cashier /kæˈʃɪə/, *n.* a person who has charge of cash or money, esp. in a bank. [F: cash box]

cashmere /ˈkæʃmɪə/, *n.* **1.** the fine wool growing under the coarse outer hair of Kashmir goats of India, often used for clothing. **2.** a soft twilled wool fabric.

Cashmere /ˈkæʃmɪə/, *n.* →**Kashmir**.

cash register, *n.* a machine or till for recording amounts of sales, etc.

casing /ˈkeɪsɪŋ/, *n.* **1.** a case or protective covering, as round a motor car tyre. **2.** a framework, esp. around a door, window etc. **3.** an iron pipe or tube, esp. as used in oil and gas wells. **4.** a strip of material sewn into a garment to hold elastic, a drawstring, etc.

casino /kəˈsiːnoʊ/, *n., pl.* **-nos.** a building or large room for meetings, amusements, gambling, etc. [It: little house, from L: cottage]

Casino /kəˈsiːnoʊ/, *n.* a town in north-eastern NSW; important air, rail and road junction. Pop. 10 067 (1986).

cask /kɑːsk/, *n.* **1.** a barrel-like container, used for holding liquids, etc. **2.** the contents of such a container. [F, from Sp: skull, helmet, cask for wine, etc.), from LL: break, shake]

casket /ˈkɑːskət/, *n.* **1.** a small chest or box, as for jewels. **2.** →**coffin**. [orig. uncert.]

Caspian Sea /ˈkæspiən siː/, *n.* a salt lake between south-eastern Europe and Asia; the largest inland body of water in the world. About 370 300 km²; 26 m below sea-level.

Cassab /ˈkæsæb/, *n.* **Judy**, born 1920 in Vienna, Australian painter, noted esp. as a portraitist; Archibald Prize winner 1961, 1968.

Cassandra /kəˈsændrə/, *n. Class. Legend.* a prophetess, daughter of Priam and Hecuba of ancient Troy, who was fated never to be believed.

cassava /kəˈsɑːvə/, *n.* **1.** any of several tropical plants cultivated for their tuberous roots, which yield important food products. **2.** starch from the roots, a source of tapioca. Also, **manioc**. [Sp, from Haitian]

casserole /ˈkæsəroʊl/, *n., v.,* **-roled, -roling.** ◇*n.* **1.** a baking dish of glass, pottery, etc., usu. with a cover. **2.** any food, usu. a mixture, baked in such a dish. ◇*v.t.* **3.** to bake in a casserole. [F *casse* pan, ladle, from LL, from Gk: little cup]

cassette /kəˈset, kæˈset/, *n.* **1.** *Photog.* the film-holder in certain types of camera; magazine. **2.** (in video and tape recorders) a plastic container enclosing a recording tape.

cassette recorder, *n.* a tape recorder that uses cassettes.

cassia /ˈkæsiə/, *n.* **1.** (a tree producing) a variety of cinnamon (cassia bark). **2.** any herbs, shrubs, and tropical trees, some of whose pods yield senna while others can be pulped to produce a mild laxative. [OE, from L, from Gk, from Heb]

Cassius Longinus /ˌkæsiəs lɒnˈdʒaɪnəs/, *n.* **Gaius** /ˈɡaɪəs/, died 42 BC, Roman politician and general, who led a conspiracy against Julius Caesar.

cassock /ˈkæsək/, *n.* a long, close-fitting garment worn by clergymen, etc. [F, from It]

cassowary /ˈkæsəwɒri/, *n., pl.* **-ries.** any of several large, three-toed, flightless, Australasian birds not unlike the ostrich, but smaller. [Malay]

cast /kɑːst/, *v.,* **cast, casting,** *n., adj.* ◇*v.t.* **1.** to throw; fling; hurl (oft. fol. by *away, off, out,* etc.) **2.** to direct (the eye, a glance, the mind, etc.) **3.** to cause (light, etc.) to fall upon something or in a certain direction. **4.** to throw out (a fishing line, anchor, etc.). **5.** to throw down; throw (an animal) on its back or side. **6.** to part with; lose: *A snake casts its skin.* **7.** to shed or drop (hair, fruit, etc.), esp. prematurely. **8.** to send off (a swarm), as bees do. **9.** *Theat.* to allot parts (of a play) to actors; select (actors) for a play: *We're casting Macbeth this week*; *They cast him as the lead*. **10.** *Metall.* to form (molten metal, etc.) into a particular shape by pouring into a mould; to produce (an object or article) by such a process. **11.** to compute; add, as a row of figures. **12.** to calculate (a horoscope); forecast. **13.** *Naut.* to let go or let loose, as a vessel from a mooring (fol. by *loose, off,* etc.). ◇*v.i.* **14.** to throw a fishing line or similar (oft. fol. by *about*). **15.** to calculate or add. ◇**16.** Some special uses are:

cast a vote, to vote (def. 6).

cast about, (fol. by *for* or an infinitive) **1.** to search with the mind, as for a reason. **2.** to scheme.

cast back, to refer to something past.

cast down, to make unhappy; discourage.

cast off, **1.** to get rid of; reject. **2.** *Knitting.* to make the final row of stitches.

cast on, *Knitting.* to make the first row of stitches.

◇*n.* **17.** an act of casting or throwing. **18.** a throw of dice or a fishing line. **19.** the sweep or encircling movements a sheepdog makes when rounding up sheep. **20.** *Theat.* actors to whom parts in a play are given. **21.** *Metall.* **a.** the act of casting (def. 10). **b.** the quantity of metal cast at one time. **22.** any impression or mould. **23.** *Med.* a surgical dressing usu. made of plaster of Paris. **24.** outward form; appearance. **25.** sort; kind; style: *different cast of person.* **26.** a permanent twist or turn, esp. squint: *to have a cast in the eye.* **27.** a bend or twist; warp. **28.** a slight tinge of some color;

cast   159   **catacomb**

hue; shade. **29.** *Geol.* a fossil showing only surface features of an organism. **30.** a mass of feathers, furs, bones, etc., discharged from the stomach by a hawk or other birds. ◇*adj.* **31.** lost; discarded: *We found the cast shoe of a horse.* **32.** (of a sheep) fallen, and not able to rise. [ME, from Scand] **—caster,** *n.*

castanets /ˌkæstəˈnets/, *n. pl.* a pair of shells of ivory or hard wood held in the palm of the hand and struck together in time to music and dancing. [Sp, from L: chestnut]

castaway /ˈkɑːstəweɪ/, *n.* **1.** a ship-wrecked person. **2.** an outcast. ◇*adj.* **3.** cast adrift.

caste /kɑːst/, *n.* **1. a.** one of the divisions or social classes into which Hindus are rigidly separated and of which privileges or disadvantages are carried by inheritance. **b.** the system or basis of this division. **2.** any rigid system of social distinctions. [Sp, Pg *casta* breed, race, from L: pure, CHASTE]

caster sugar, *n.* finely ground white sugar. Also, **castor sugar.**

castigate /ˈkæstəgeɪt/, *v.t.,* **-gated, -gating.** to punish in order to correct; criticise. [L] **—castigation,** *n.* **—castigator,** *n.*

casting /ˈkɑːstɪŋ/, *n.* **1.** that which is cast; any article which has been cast in a mould. **2.** the selection of actors for play, film, etc.

casting vote, *n.* the deciding vote of the chairman, used when votes are equally divided.

cast iron, *n.* an alloy of iron, carbon, and other elements made by casting in a mould.

cast-iron /ˈkɑːst-aɪən/, *adj.* **1.** made of cast iron. **2.** strong; hardy. **3.** unyielding; rigid; inflexible.

castle /ˈkɑːsəl, ˈkæsəl/, *n., v.,* **-tled, -tling.** ◇*n.* **1.** a strongly-built fort-like building, as the home of a prince in former times. **2.** a kind of fort strongly protected against military attack. **3.** a large and stately home. **4.** *Chess.* the rook. ◇*v.t.* **5.** to place or enclose in or as if in a castle. [ME, from L: fortress]

Castle Hill Rising, *n.* a rebellion of Irish convicts at Castle Hill, NSW, in 1804; Australia's first rebellion.

Castlemaine /ˈkæsəlmeɪn, ˈkɑːsəl-/, *n.* a city in central Vic, north-west of Melbourne; a fruit-growing and farming centre; an important manufacturing town. Pop. 7656 (1986).

Castlereagh /ˈkɑːsəlreɪ, ˈkæsəl-, ˌkɑːsəlˈreɪ, ˌkæsəl-/, *n.* **1.** a town in central eastern NSW, west of Sydney, on the Nepean River; early settlement. **2.** a river in northern central NSW, rising in the Warrumbungle Range, flowing east then west to Gilgandra. [named after Lord *Castlereagh,* 1769–1822, British foreign secretary 1812–22.]

castor[1] /ˈkɑːstə/, *n.* a brownish substance taken from certain glands of the beaver, used in medicine and perfumes. [L, from Gk: beaver]

castor[2] *or* **caster** /ˈkɑːstə/, *n.* **1.** a small wheel set under furniture, etc., to help in moving it. **2.** a bottle or cruet with holes in top, for holding salt, sugar etc.

Castor and Pollux /ˌkɑːstər ən ˈpɒləks/, *n. Gk Myth.* twin sons of Leda and brothers of Helen (called the Dioscuri or sons of Zeus), famous for protection of sailors, and for brotherly affection. Pollux, who was immortal, spent alternate days with the gods and with his mortal brother in Hades.

castor oil, *n.* a sticky oil taken from the seeds of an Indian plant, used as a cathartic, lubricant, etc.

castor sugar, *n.* →**caster sugar.**

castrate /ˈkæstreɪt, kæsˈ-/, *v.t.,* **-trated, -trating.** to deprive of testicles; emasculate. [L] **—castration,** *n.*

Castro /ˈkæstroʊ/, *n.* **Fidel** /fiˈdel/ (*Fidel Castro Ruz*), born 1927, Cuban communist revolutionary leader; became prime minister in 1959.

casual /ˈkæʒuəl/, *adj.* **1.** happening by chance: *a casual meeting.* **2.** offhand; without any definite thought: *a casual remark, etc.* **3.** careless; unconcerned: *a casual attitude.* **4.** informal: *casual clothes.* **5.** employed only irregularly: *a casual worker.* ◇*n.* **6.** a worker employed only irregularly. **7.** (*pl.*) comfortable, informal clothes, shoes, etc. [LL *cāsuālis* by chance]

casualty /ˈkæʒuəlti/, *n., pl.* **-ties. 1.** *Mil.* a soldier missing in action, or killed, wounded, or captured as result of enemy action. **2.** a person hurt or killed in an accident. **3.** Also, **casualty ward.** the section of a hospital to which accident or emergency cases are taken.

casuarina /ˌkæzjəˈriːnə/, *n.* any of a group of Australian trees and shrubs with jointed stems and no real leaves; she-oak.

casuistry /ˈkæzjuɪstri/, *n., pl.* **-tries.** clever but false use of general moral principles in particular cases of conscience. **—casuistic,** *adj.*

cat[1] /kæt/, *n.* **1.** a small furry animal often kept as a pet. **2.** any animal of the group which includes the lion, tiger, etc. **3.** a spiteful woman. **4.** → **cat-o'-nine-tails. 5.** → **catfish. 6. let the cat out of the bag,** to disclose information, usu. unintentionally. **7. rain cats and dogs,** to rain heavily. **8. the cat's pyjamas (whiskers),** *Colloq.* an excellent person, idea, etc. [OE *cat, catte*] **—catty,** *adj.*

cat[2] /kæt/, *n.* a catamaran.

cata-, prefix meaning 'down', 'against', 'back'. [Gk]

catabolism /kəˈtæbəlɪzəm/, *n. Biol.* See **metabolism.** [Gk *katabolē* a throwing down + -ISM] **—catabolic,** *adj.*

cataclysm /ˈkætəklɪzəm/, *n.* **1.** any violent upheaval, esp. one of social or political nature. **2.** *Geol.* a sudden and violent physical action producing changes in the earth's surface. [L, from Gk: deluge] **—cataclysmic, cataclysmal,** *adj.*

catacomb /ˈkætəkoʊm, -kʌm/, *n.* **1.** (*usu. pl.*) an underground cemetery, esp. one with many tunnels, rooms, etc. **2.** any series of underground tunnels and caves. [OE *catacumbe,* from LL]

Catalan /ˈkætələn, -lən/, *adj.* relating to Catalonia, its inhabitants, or their language.

catalogue /ˈkætəlɒg/, *n., v.,* **-logued, -loguing.** ◇*n.* **1.** a list, usu. in alphabetical order, with brief notes on names, articles, etc., entered. **2.** a record of books and other resources of a library or collection, shown on cards, or in book form, etc. **3.** any list or register. ◇*v.t.* **4.** to make a catalogue of; enter in catalogue. [F, from LL, from Gk: a list] –**cataloguer, cataloguist,** *n.*

Catalonia /kætəˈloʊnjə/, *n.* a region in north-eastern Spain, formerly a province. *Regional Centre:* Barcelona. Spanish, **Catalun.**

catalyse *or* **catalyze** /ˈkætəlaɪz/, *v.t.,* **-lysed, -lysing.** *Chem.* to cause, or increase the rate of, a chemical reaction by adding a substance (catalyst) which is not itself changed permanently by the reaction. –**catalysis,** *n.* –**catalytic,** *adj.*

catalyst /ˈkætəlɒst/, *n.* **1.** *Chem.* a substance that causes catalysis. **2.** a person or thing that acts as an agent in stimulating or causing change. –**catalytic,** *adj.*

catamaran /ˈkætəmərӕn/, *n. Naut.* **1.** a float or raft, usu. of several logs or pieces of wood tied together. **2.** any sea craft with twin parallel hulls. [Tamil: tied tree or wood]

catapult /ˈkætəpʌlt/, *n.* **1.** a Y-shaped stick with an elastic strip between the prongs for propelling stones, etc. **2.** an ancient military engine for throwing darts, stones, etc. **3.** a device for launching a plane from the deck of a ship, esp. a ship not equipped with flight deck. ◇*v.t.* **4.** to throw as from a catapult. **5.** to hit (an object) by means of a catapult. ◇*v.i.* **6.** to shoot forth from or as if from a catapult. [L, from Gk]

cataract /ˈkætərækt/, *n.* **1.** a rush of water over a steep surface; waterfall, esp. a large one. **2.** any furious rush or downpour of water; deluge. **3.** a disease of the eye in which the lens becomes clouded causing loss of sight. [ME, from L: waterfall, from Gk: down rushing]

catarrh /kəˈta/, *n.* an inflammation of the mucous membrane, resulting in over-secretion of mucous, esp. in the respiratory tract. [L, from Gk: running down] –**catarrhal,** *adj.*

catastrophe /kəˈtæstrəfi/, *n.* **1.** a sudden disaster. **2.** a disastrous event or end. **3.** a sudden violent disturbance, esp. of the earth's surface; cataclysm. [Gk: overturning] –**catastrophic,** *adj.*

Catastrophe /kəˈtæstrəfi/, *n.* **Cape,** the point on the western side of the entrance to Spencer Gulf, SA.

catatonia /kætəˈtoʊniə/, *n. Psychol., Psychiatry.* abnormal behavior showing unusual limitations of movement and speech, as well as resistance to suggestions from others. [CATA- + Gk *tónos* tension] –**catatonic,** *adj., n.*

catbird /ˈkætbɜd/, *n.* a rainforest bird with a call like that of a cat.

catcall /ˈkætkɔl/, *n.* **1.** a sound used to express disapproval at a theatre, meeting, etc. ◇*v.i* **2.** to make catcalls. ◇*v.t.* **3.** to express disapproval of by catcalls.

catch /kætʃ/, *v.,* **caught, catching,** *n.* ◇*v.t.* **1.** to capture, esp. after pursuit; take captive. **2.** to lay hold of, grasp; seize; snatch: *to catch a ball.* **3.** to entrap, or deceive. **4. a.** to be in time to reach (a train, boat, etc.). **b.** to board; travel on. **5.** to come upon suddenly; surprise or detect, as in some action: *I caught him stealing.* **6.** to strike; hit: *The blow caught him on the head.* **7.** *Cricket.* to dismiss (a batsman) by catching the ball before it touches the ground. **8.** to get, receive, or contract (oft. used figuratively): *to catch cold; I caught the spirit of the occasion.* **9.** to allow or cause to be caught: *to catch a finger in the door.* **10.** to get by attraction or impression: *to catch the eye, attention, etc.* **11.** to hear or see: *Did you catch that program on the Great Barrier Reef?* ◇*v.i.* **12.** to become fastened or entangled: *The balloon caught in the trees.* **13.** to stick: *This door catches.* **14.** to become lit, take fire: *The wood caught instantly.* **15.** to be successful in catching: *This bait catches well.* ◇**16.** Some special uses are:
catch it, *Colloq.* to get into trouble.
catch on, *Colloq.* **1.** to become popular. **2.** to understand.
catch one's breath, 1. to gasp in surprise, fear, etc. **2.** to return to normal breathing: *I need a moment to catch my breath.*
catch out, 1. to trap (somebody), as into revealing a secret or displaying ignorance. **2.** to surprise.
catch up, 1. to seize quickly: *He caught up the child in his arms.* **2.** to become involved in: *They were caught up in the crowd.* **3.** Also, **catch up with, catch up to.** to follow and reach, become level with, or overtake: *He caught her up by running; He caught up with the rest of the class by hard work.*
catch up on, to make up: *She caught up on her sleep.*
◇*n.* **17.** the act of catching. **18.** that which is caught, as a quantity of fish. **19.** anything worth getting: *It was a great catch.* **20.** a fragment: *catches of song.* **21.** *Cricket.* the catching and holding of the ball after it has been batted and before it touches ground. **22.** a difficulty, usu. unseen: *What's the catch?* [ME, from ONF, from L: take]

catcher /ˈkætʃə/, *n. Baseball, Softball.* the player who stands behind the bat or home base to catch the pitched ball.

catchment area, *n.* **1.** Also, **catchment basin.** *Geog.* the drainage area, esp. of a reservoir or river. **2.** the area from which people may come to a school, hospital etc.

Catchpole /ˈkætʃpoʊl/, **Margaret,** 1762–1819, Australian convict and pioneer settler, born in England.

catchword /ˈkætʃwɜd/, *n.* **1.** a word or phrase repeated for effect, esp. by a political party. **2.** a word printed at the top of a page in a dictionary or other reference book to point to the first or last article on that page.

catchy /ˈkætʃi/, *adj.,* **catchier, catchiest.** *adj.* **1.** pleasing and easily remembered: *a catchy tune.* **2.** tricky; deceptive: *a catchy question.*

catechise or **catechize** /ˈkætəkaɪz/, v.t., **-chised, -chising.** to instruct using a catechism. [LL, from Gk: teach orally]

catechism /ˈkætəkɪzəm/, n. **1.** *Church.* an elementary book containing a summary of the principles of the Christian religion, esp. as those of a particular church, in the form of questions and answers. **2.** contents of a catechism. [LL]

catechist /ˈkætəkəst/, n. **1.** a person who catechises. **2.** *Church.* a person appointed to instruct others in the principles of religion as preparation for baptism, confirmation, etc. — **catechistic, catechistical,** adj.

catecholamine /kætəˈkoʊləmɪn/, n. any of a group of compounds, as adrenalin, which have important effects on the central nervous system.

categorical /kætəˈgɒrɪkəl/, adj. **1.** direct; explicit; allowing of no dispute: *a categorical answer.* **2.** *Logic.* (of a proposition) unconditional, straightforwardly true or false.

categorise or **categorize** /ˈkætəgəraɪz/, v.t., **-rised, -rising.** to put in a category. — **categorist,** n.

category /ˈkætəgəri, -təgri/, n., pl. **-ries. 1.** a division in any field of knowledge. **2.** a class or division in a scheme of classification. [L, from Gk: assertion]

cater /ˈkeɪtə/, v.i. **1.** to provide food and service, etc. at functions (fol. by *for*). **2.** to provide that which is desired: *to cater for popular demand.* **3.** to go out of one's way to please or provide for (fol. by *to*): [ME *catour,* buyer of provisions, from OF: buyer] — **caterer,** n.

caterpillar /ˈkætəpɪlə/, n. the wormlike larva of a butterfly or moth. [ME, of uncert. orig.]

caterwaul /ˈkætəwɔl/, v.i. **1.** to cry or howl like a cat. **2.** to quarrel like cats. [ME, *cater* (cf. G *Kater* tomcat) + *wrawen* howl]

catfish /ˈkætfɪʃ/, n., pl. **-fishes,** (esp. collectively) **-fish.** in Australia, any of various species of fresh water and marine fishes such as **fork-tail catfish, eel-tailed catfish.**

catgut /ˈkætgʌt/, n. the intestines of sheep or other animals, used in surgery as ligatures, and as strings for musical instruments, etc.

cath-, variant of **cata-** before *h,* as in *cathode.*

catharsis /kəˈθɑsəs/, n. **1.** a getting rid of troublesome feelings, esp. under the influence of art, drugs or psychotherapy. **2.** *Med.* purgation, esp. of bowels. [NL, from Gk: a cleansing]

cathartic /kəˈθɑtɪk/, adj. **1.** Also, **cathartical.** relating to or inducing catharsis. ◇n. **2.** a very strong laxative. [L, from Gk: fit for cleansing, purgative]

Cathay /kæˈθeɪ/, n. *Archaic* or *Poetic.* China.

cathedra /kəˈθidrə/, n., pl. **-drae** /-dri/. the official chair, as of a professor in a university. See **ex cathedra.** [L, from Gk: chair]

cathedral /kəˈθidrəl/, n. the main church of a diocese, containing the bishop's throne.

Catherine /ˈkæθrən/, n. **Saint,** died AD 307, Christian martyr of Alexandria who was tortured on a spiked wheel and beheaded.

Catherine II, n. (*'the Great'*), 1729–96, consort of Tsar Peter III, and empress of Russia 1762–96.

Catherine de Medici /ˈmɛˈditʃi/, n. → Catherine de' **Medici.**

Catherine of Aragon /ˈærəgən/, n. 1485–1536, first wife of Henry VIII of England and mother of Mary I of England.

catherine-wheel /ˈkæθrən-wil/, n. a firework which spins as it burns, throwing out colored lights.

catheter /ˈkæθətə/, n. *Med.* a hollow tube used to drain fluids from body cavities, esp. urine from the bladder. [LL, from Gk: let down]

cathode /ˈkæθoʊd/, n. **1.** a negatively-charged electrode which sends out electrons, as in a radio valve, etc. **2.** the negative electrode of a cell (defs. 5 and 6) (opposed to *anode*). [Gk: way down]

cathode ray, n. a stream of electrons generated at the cathode during an electric discharge in a vacuum tube.

cathode-ray oscilloscope, n. *Phys.* an instrument which displays the shape of a voltage or current wave on a cathode-ray tube. Also, **cathode-ray oscillograph.** *Abbrev.:* CRO

cathode-ray tube, n. *Electronics.* a vacuum tube in which is generated a beam of electrons which can be centred on a sensitised screen, so as to reproduce pictures in television receivers, etc.

catholic /ˈkæθlɪk, -əlɪk/, adj. **1.** relating to the whole Christian body or Church. **2.** (*cap.*) of or relating to the Catholic Church. **3.** universal; involving all, of interest to all. **4.** broad-minded; liberal: *to be catholic in one's tastes, interests, etc.* ◇n. **5.** (*cap.*) a member of a Catholic Church, most commonly the Catholic Church (def.2). [L, from Gk] — **Catholicism, catholicism** n.

Catholic Church, n. **1.** the whole Christian body or Church. **2.** a Christian Church maintaining apostolic succession, with a hierachy of priests and bishops, the pope as head, and administrative headquarters in the Vatican. Also, **Roman Catholic Church, Church of Rome. 3.** (among Anglicans) the Church as comprising all orthodox churches maintaining the apostolic succession of bishops.

cation /ˈkætaɪən/, n. *Phys., Chem.* **1.** a positively-charged ion which is attracted to the cathode in electrolysis. **2.** any positively-charged ion, radical, or molecule. [Gk *katión,* ppr. neut., going down]

catkin /ˈkætkən/, n. *Bot.* a hanging spike of unisexual flowers, as on the pussy willow. [D: little cat]

catmint /ˈkætmɪnt/, n. a plant, of the mint family, with strongly scented leaves, which cats like. Also, **catnip.** [CAT¹ + MINT¹]

catnap /ˈkætnæp/, *n.* **1.** a short, light nap or sleep, esp. one taken in the daytime. ◇*v.i.* **2.** to take a nap; doze.

Cato /ˈkeɪtoʊ/, *n.* **1. Marcus Porcius** /ˈpɔːʃɪəs/ ('*the Elder*' or '*the Censor*'), 234–149 BC, Roman statesman, soldier, and writer. **2.** his great-grandson, **Marcus Porcius** ('*the Younger*'), 95–46 BC, Roman statesman, soldier, and Stoic philosopher. **3. Nancy Fotheringham**, born 1917, Australian writer of historical novels, short stories, poetry, and non-fiction works.

cat-o'-nine-tails /ˌkæt-ə-ˈnaɪn-ˌteɪlz/, *n., pl.* **-tails.** a whip, usu. having nine knotted cords fastened to a handle, formerly used to beat criminals.

CAT scanner /ˈkæt skænə/, *n.* a machine which produces a series of X-rays, and is often used for medical investigation.

cat's-eye /ˈkæts-aɪ/, *n.* **1.** any of certain gems which reflect light, esp. the **oriental** or **precious cat's-eye**. **2.** a small reflector marking the centre or the side of a road.

cat's-paw /ˈkæts-pɔ/, *n.* **1.** a person used by another to serve his or her purpose; a tool. **2.** *Naut.* a light breeze gently moving across the surface of water. Also, **catspaw.**

cattle /ˈkætl/, *n.* farm animals, esp. cows, bulls, oxen, referred to collectively without stating age, breed or sex. [ME, from L: wealth, stock. See CAPITAL[1], *n.*]

cattlegrid /ˈkætlgrɪd/, *n.* a pit covered by a grid set in a roadway, designed to prevent the passage of animals while allowing people and vehicles to cross. Also, **cattleramp.**

cattle-run /ˈkætl-rʌn/, *n.* a property on which cattle are grazed for meat production. Also, **cattle station.**

Catullus /kəˈtʊləs/, *n.* **Gaius Valerius** /ɡaɪəs vəˈlɪərɪəs/, 84?–54? BC, Roman lyric poet.

catwalk /ˈkætwɔk/, *n.* **1.** any narrow walking space or platform as on a bridge, above the stage of a theatre, or in an aircraft. **2.** a long, narrow platform on which fashion models parade clothes.

Caucasian /kɔˈkeɪʒən/, *adj.* **1.** relating to so-called 'white race', the peoples of Europe, south-western Asia, and northern Africa, so named because native peoples of the Caucasus were considered typical. **2.** having the characteristics of the Caucasian race. **3.** relating to the Caucasus mountain range. ◇*n.* **4.** someone belonging to the Caucasian race. Also, **Causasoid.** See **Mongoloid, Negroid.**

Caucasus /ˈkɔkəsəs/, *n.* a mountain range between southern Russia and Georgia. Highest peak, Mt Elbrus (highest in Europe), 5633 m.

caucus /ˈkɔkəs/, *n.* a meeting of the parliamentary members of a political party to make decisions. [Amer Ind *caucuasa*, adviser]

caudal /ˈkɔdl/, *adj. Zool.* **1.** of, at, or near the tail. **2.** tail-like: *caudal additions.* [NL, from L: tail]

caught /kɔt/, *v.* past tense and past participle of **catch.**

caul /kɔl/, *n.* **1.** part of a membrane sometimes covering the head of a child at birth. **2.** a membrane covering the lower intestines of various animals, formerly used to make sausage skins. **3.** *Carp.* a sheet of thin plywood or aluminium. [ME, from F: kind of cap]

cauldron /ˈkɔldrən/, *n.* a large kettle or boiler, usu. rounded, with a lid and handles. Also, **caldron.** [ME, from L: hot]

Caulfield /ˈkɔfild/, *n.* a city in the metropolitan area of Melbourne, Victoria; site of Caulfield racecourse. Pop. 67 718 (1986).

Caulfield Cup, *n.* an annual horse race, first run in the 1860s, held in Caulfield, Victoria.

cauliflower /ˈkɒlɪflaʊə/, *n.* a cultivated plant with a white fleshy head used as a vegetable. [half adoption, half translation of NL *cauliflōra*, lit., cabbage-flower]

caulk /kɔk/, *v.t.* **1.** to make (a vessel, window, etc.) watertight or airtight by filling its seams or cracks with tar, etc. **2.** to fill or close (seams or cracks) so as to make watertight, airtight, etc. Also, **calk.** [ME, from L: tread, press]

causal /ˈkɔzəl/, *adj.* of, constituting, or suggesting a cause.

causality /kɔˈzælətɪ/, *n.pl.*, **-ties. 1.** the relation of cause and effect. **2.** the quality of being a cause.

causation /kɔˈzeɪʃən/, *n.* **1.** the action of causing or producing. **2.** the relation of cause to effect. **3.** anything that produces an effect; cause.

causative /ˈkɔzətɪv/, *adj.* **1.** acting as a cause; productive (fol. by *of*). **2.** *Gram.* expressing causation, as the verb *fell* (to cause to fall). ◇*n.* **3.** *Gram.* a causative word.

cause /kɔz/, *n., v.,* **caused, causing.** ◇*n.* **1.** that which produces an effect; the thing, person, etc., from which something results. **2.** the ground of any action or result; reason; motive. **3.** good or sufficient reason: *to complain without cause.* **4.** *Law.* a ground of legal action; matter over which someone goes to law. **5.** any subject, question, etc. which a person or party supports: *to fight for a cause.* ◇*v.t.* **6.** to be a cause of; bring about. [ME, from L *causa*]

cause célèbre /kɔz səˈlebrə/, *n.* an issue causing public debate and interest. [F: a celebrated legal case]

causeway /ˈkɔzweɪ/, *n.* a raised road or path, as across low or wet ground. [var. of *causey* way, from ME, from LL *calciāta* paved road]

caustic /ˈkɒstɪk/, *adj.* **1.** capable of burning, eating away, or destroying living tissue: *caustic soda.* **2.** critical or sarcastic: *a caustic remark.* ◇*n.* **3.** a caustic substance. [L, from Gk: capable of burning] **–caustically**, *adv.* **–causticity**, *n.*

caustic soda, *n.* sodium hydroxide, NaOH, used in metallurgy and photography.

cauterise or **cauterize** /'kɔtəraɪz/, *v.t.* **-rised, -rising.** to burn with a hot iron, or with fire or caustic, esp. to sterilise: *to cauterise a wound* —**cauterisation**, *n.*

caution /'kɔʃən/, *n.* **1.** care in regard to danger or evil; prudence; wariness: *Go forward with caution.* **2.** a warning (esp. in law) to a person, that his words or actions may be used against him. **3.** *Colloq.* someone or something unusual, odd, amazing, etc. ◇*v.t.* **4.** to give a warning to; suggest or urge to take heed. **5.** *Law.* to warn (someone) that his words may be used against him. [L] —**cautionary**, *adj.* —**cautious**, *adj.*

cavalcade /'kævəlkeɪd/, *n., v.*, **-caded, -cading.** ◇*n.* **1.** a procession esp. of people on horseback or in horse-drawn carriages. ◇*v.i.* **2.** to ride in procession. [F, from It, from LL: ride on horseback]

cavalier /kævə'lɪə/, *n.* **1.** a horseman, esp. a mounted soldier; knight. **2.** a courtly gentleman; gallant. ◇*adj.* **3.** haughty, disdainful, or supercilious. **4.** offhand towards matters of some importance; casual. [F, from It, from L]

cavalry /'kævəlri/, *n., pl.* **-ries. 1.** *Mil.* army combat units formerly mounted on horseback, and now often equipped with armored vehicles. **2.** horsemen, horses, etc., collectively. [F, from It: knighthood] —**cavalryman**, *n.*

cave /keɪv/, *n., v.,* **caved, caving.** ◇*n.* **1.** a hollow in the earth, esp. one opening more or less horizontally into a hill, mountain, etc. ◇*v.t.* **2.** to explore caves, as a sport. **3.** to cause to fall (fol. by *in*): *They caved in the roof with their weight.* ◇*v.i.* **4.** to fall or sink, as the ground (fol. by *in*): *The roof caved in under their weight.* **5.** *Colloq.* to give, yield, or submit (fol. by *in*). [ME, from L *cava* hollow (places)]

Cavell /'kævəl/, *n.* **Edith Louisa,** 1865–1915, English nurse, executed by the Germans in World War I.

caveman /'keɪvmæn/, *n.* **1.** a cave-dweller; man of Palaeolithic era. **2.** a person who lived in the Palaeolithic era.

cavern /'kævən/, *n.* a cave, esp. a large cave. [ME, from L *caverna* cave]

cavernous /'kævənəs/, *adj.* **1.** like a cavern; deep set; hollow. **2.** full of small cavities; porous. **3.** of or like a cavern: *cavernous darkness.*

caviar /'kæviɑ, kævi'ɑ/, *n.* salted eggs of sturgeon and other large fish, considered a delicacy. [F, from It, from Turk]

cavil /'kævəl/, *v.*, **-illed, -illing,** *n.* ◇*v.i.* **1.** to raise stupid and trivial objections; find fault unnecessarily. ◇*n.* **2.** a trivial and annoying objection. [F, from L: a jeering] —**caviller**, *n.*

Cavill family /'kævəl/, *n.* a family of notable Australian swimmers credited with developing the swimming stroke known as the Australian crawl. **1. Frederick,** 1839–1927 English-born Australian swimming coach. **2. Charles,** 1871–97, son of Frederick, Australian swimmer; first man to swim the Golden Gate crossing in San Francisco. **3. Sydney St Leonards,** 1880–1945, son of Frederick, Australian swimmer; originator of the butterfly stroke. **4. Richard Theophilus,** 1884–1938, son of Frederick, Australian swimmer; winner of NSW and Australian championships; first to use the crawl in competition swimming.

cavitation /kævə'teɪʃən/, *n. Engineering.* the rapid formation and collapse of vapor pockets in a flowing liquid in regions of very low pressure, a frequent cause of serious structural damage to propellers, pumps, etc. [F, from LL: hollowness]

cavity /'kævəti/, *n., pl.* **-ties.** any empty space; hollow. [F, from LL: hollowness]

cavity wall, *n. Bldg Trades.* a type of double wall esp. of brick with an air space between which is designed to keep out noise, cold, etc.

Cawley /'kɔli/, *n.* **Evonne Fay** (*Evonne Fay Goolagong*), born 1951, Australian tennis player; twice winner of Wimbledon singles title.

Caxton /'kækstən/, *n.* **William,** 1422?–91, first English printer; translator and author.

cay /keɪ, ki/, *n.* a small island; key. [Sp]

cayenne /keɪ'en/, *n.* a hot, biting spice consisting of the ground pods and seeds of any of several varieties of capsicum; red pepper. Also, **cayenne pepper.** [named after *Cayenne,* in French Guiana]

Cayley /'keɪli/, *n.* **Neville William,** 1886–1950, Australian ornithological artist; specialised in Australian birds.

Cazaly /kə'zeɪli/, *n.* **Roy,** 1893–1963, Australian Rules footballer.

Cazneaux /'kæznou/, *n.* **Harold,** 1878–1953, Australian pictorialist photographer.

Cb, *Chem. Symbol.* columbium.

CB /si 'bi/, *Abbrev.* **1.** Companion of the (Order of the) Bath. **2.** citizen's band (radio).

CBE /si bi 'i/, *Abbrev.* Commander of the (Order of the) British Empire.

CB radio, *n.* citizen's band radio. Also, **CB.**

cc, *Abbrev.* **1.** cubic capacity. **2.** cubic centimetre or centimetres. **3.** carbon copy.

C clef, *n. Music.* the sign of middle C on the stave.

Cd, *Chem. Symbol.* cadmium.

Ce, *Chem. Symbol.* cerium.

CE, in the Common Era (as a replacement of AD).

cease /sis/, *v.*, **ceased, ceasing.** ◇*v.i.* **1.** to stop (doing something): *She ceased crying.* **2.** to come to an end. ◇*v.t.* **3.** to put a stop or end to; discontinue: *to cease work.* [ME, from L: go, yield]

cease-fire /sis-'faɪə/, *n.* **1.** an order to stop firing. **2.** a ceasing of active warfare; truce.

Cebú /'sibu, ser'bu/, *n.* one of the Philippine Islands, in the central part of the group. Pop. 1 634 200 (1970); 4411 km^2.

cedar /'sidə/, *n.* **1.** a type of Old World coniferous (cone-bearing) tree with fine-grained wood, as **cedar of Lebanon**. **2.** any of various American juniper trees used for making lead pencils, etc. **3.** any of various non-coniferous trees of Australia or NZ, often referred to as cedar and used in furniture making. [OE, from L, from Gk]

cede /siːd/, *v.t.*, **ceded, ceding.** to yield or formally resign and give over to another, as by treaty: *to cede land or country*. [L: go, withdraw, yield, grant]

cedilla /səˈdɪlə/, *n.* a mark placed under *c* before *a, o,* or *u,* as in *façade,* to show that it has the sound of *s*. [Sp: the mark (orig. a *z* written after *c*), from diminutive of L *zēta,* from Gk: name of letter *z*]

ceiling /ˈsiːlɪŋ/, *n.* **1.** the overhead interior lining of a room; the surface of a room opposite the floor. **2.** top limit: *price ceiling on rent*. **3.** *Naut.* flooring, usu. wooden, covering double-bottom tanks, at the bottom of a ship's hold. **4.** *Aeron.* the maximum height to which a particular aircraft can rise under certain conditions. ◇*adj.* **5.** *Colloq.* maximum. [ME *ceil*]

-cele[1], a word part meaning 'tumor', as in *varicocele*. [combining form representing Gk *kēlē*]

-cele[2], variant of **-coele**.

Celebes /ˈsɛləbiːz, səˈliːbɪz/, *n.* → **Sulawesi.**

Celebes Sea, *n.* a part of the Pacific Ocean which separates Sulawesi from the Philippines. Also, **Sulawesi Sea.**

celebrant /ˈsɛləbrənt/, *n.* **1.** the priest who performs religious rites. **2.** Also, **marriage celebrant.** a secular official who conducts a civil marriage.

celebrate /ˈsɛləbreɪt/, *v.*, **-brated, -brating.** ◇*v.t.* **1.** to observe (a day or an event) with ceremonies or festivities. **2.** to praise publicly; honor. **3.** to perform with special rites and ceremonies; solemnise: *to celebrate mass*. ◇*v.i.* **4.** *Colloq.* to engage in a festive activity; have a party. [L] —**celebrator,** *n.* —**celebration,** *n.* —**celebrated,** *adj.*

celebrity /səˈlɛbrəti/, *n., pl.* **-ties. 1.** a famous or well-known person. **2.** fame; renown.

celerity /səˈlɛrəti/, *n.* great speed; swiftness. [ME, from L]

celery /ˈsɛləri/, *n.* a plant, of the parsley family, whose stalks are used as a vegetable. [F, from d. It, from LL, from Gk: parsley]

celery cabbage, *n.* → **Chinese cabbage.**

celesta /səˈlɛstə/, *n.* a keyboard instrument consisting mainly of steel plates struck by hammers. Also, **celeste** /səˈlɛst/. [F: heavenly]

celestial /səˈlɛstiəl/, *adj.* **1.** of the spiritual or invisible heaven; heavenly; divine: *celestial joy*. **2.** of the sky or heavens. [ME, from L *caelestis* heavenly]

celestial equator, *n. Astron., Navig.* the great circle of a celestial sphere, the plane of which is at right angles to the axis of earth.

celestial guidance, *n.* a system of guiding missiles or spacecraft which uses the positions of celestial bodies as points of reference.

celestial sphere, *n. Astron.* the imaginary spherical shell formed by the sky, usu. represented as an infinite sphere with the observer's position as the centre.

celibacy /ˈsɛləbəsi/, *n., pl.* **-cies. 1.** the unmarried state, esp. of priests, etc., under vows. **2.** sexual chastity.

celibate /ˈsɛləbət/, *n.* **1.** someone who remains unmarried, esp. for religious reasons. ◇*adj.* **2.** unmarried. **3.** chaste. [L: unmarried]

cell /sɛl/, *n.* **1.** a small room in a convent, prison, etc. **2.** a small group acting as a unit within a larger organisation. **3.** *Biol.* **a.** a plant or animal structure, usu. microscopic, containing nuclear and cytoplasmic material, enclosed by a membrane (animal) or cell wall (plant); structural unit of plant and animal life. **b.** a tiny cavity as in animal or plant tissue. **4.** *Bot.* the pollen sac of an anther. **5.** *Elect.* a generator of electricity which forms all, or part of a voltaic battery, consisting in simple form of two plates, each of different metal, placed in a jar containing dilute acid or other electrolyte (**voltaic cell**). **6.** *Chem.* an apparatus for producing electric current from chemical energy, consisting of the electrolyte, its container, and electrodes (**electrolytic cell**). [OE *cell,* from L: room]

cellar /ˈsɛlə/, *n.* **1.** an underground room or store; basement. **2.** a supply or stock of wines. [L: pantry]

cell-division /ˈsɛl-dəvɪʒən/, *n. Biol.* the division of a cell in reproduction or growth.

cellist /ˈtʃɛləst/, *n.* someone who plays the cello. Also, **'cellist, violoncellist.**

cello /ˈtʃɛloʊ/, *n., pl.* **-los, -li.** a four-stringed instrument of the violin family with a pitch between that of the viola and the double bass, which stands upright on the floor between the player's knees. Also, **'cello, violoncello.** [short form of VIOLONCELLO]

cellophane /ˈsɛləfeɪn/, *n.* a transparent paper-like product of viscose, impervious to moisture, used to wrap sweets, tobacco, etc. [Trademark: CELLUL(OSE) + -O- + -PHANE]

cellular /ˈsɛljələ/, *adj.* **1.** of or relating to cells, esp. tiny sections or cavities. **2.** *Textiles.* loosely woven, with open airholes. [L: little room]

cellulite /ˈsɛljəlaɪt/, *n.* fatty deposits, giving a dimply appearance to the skin, which apparently cannot be removed by dieting or exercise.

celluloid /ˈsɛljəlɔɪd/, *n.* **1.** *Chem.* a plastic consisting mainly of a cellulose salt and camphor, used for toys, toilet articles, photographic film, etc. **2.** films; cinema. ◇*adj.* **3.** relating to films: *celluloid hero*. **4.** unreal; synthetic. [Trademark: CELLUL(OSE) + -OID]

cellulose /ˈsɛljəloʊs/, *n. Chem.* a carbohydrate, the chief material forming cell walls of plants, and the main part of wood, cotton, hemp, paper, etc. [L *cellula* little cell + -OSE[2]]

Celsius /ˈsɛlsɪəs/, *adj.* **1.** relating to the scale of temperature in degrees Celsius (°C) with 0°C set at the melting point of ice, and 100°C set at the boiling point of water. ◇*n.* **2.** Celsius scale. *Symbol:* C [named after A *Celsius*, 1701–44, Swedish astronomer]

Celt /kɛlt, sɛlt/, *n.* a member of an Indo-European people now represented chiefly by the Irish, Gaels, Welsh, and Bretons. Also, **Kelt**. [L *Celtae*, pl., from Gk *Keltoí*]

Celtic /ˈkɛltɪk, ˈsɛltɪk/, *n.* **1.** a group of Indo-European languages including Irish, Scottish, Gaelic, Welsh, Breton, etc., surviving now in Ireland, the Scottish Highlands, Wales, and Brittany. ◇*adj.* **2.** of the Celts or their language. Also, **Keltic**. —**Celticism**, *n.*

cement /səˈmɛnt/, *n.* **1.** a material (oft. called **Portland cement**) commonly formed by burning a mixture of clay and limestone, used for making concrete. **2.** *Geol.* the firm groundmass surrounding and binding together pieces of rocks. **3.** *Dentistry.* a glue-like plastic substance used to fill cavities (holes) in teeth. **4.** a solvent used for joining film, plastic models, etc. **5.** *Colloq.* → **concrete**. ◇*v.t.* **6.** to unite by, or as by, cement: *Their friendship was cemented by time.* **7.** to coat or cover with cement. ◇*v.i.* **8.** to become cemented; join together or unite; cohere. [L: rough stone] —**cementation**, *n.*

cemetery /ˈsɛmətri/, *n.*, *pl.* **-teries.** a burial ground, esp. one not attached to a church; graveyard. [ME, from LL, from Gk]

-cene, a word part meaning 'recent', 'new', as in *Pleistocene*. [combining form representing Gk *kainós*]

ceno-[1], variant of **caino-**

ceno-[2], variant of **coeno-**. Also, before vowels, **cen-**.

cenotaph /ˈsɛnətɑːf/, *n.* a municipal, civic or national memorial to those killed in war. [L, from Gk: an empty tomb] —**cenotaphic**, *adj.*

Cenozoic /ˌsiːnəˈzoʊɪk/, *adj. Chiefly US.* → **Cainozoic**.

censer /ˈsɛnsə/, *n.* a container in which incense is burned. [ME, from OF]

censor /ˈsɛnsə/, *n.* **1.** an official who examines books, news reports, films, etc., to determine those parts considered unsuitable or dangerous on moral, political, military, or other grounds. **2.** a critic; faultfinder. ◇*v.t.* **3.** to examine and act upon as a censor. **4.** to remove (words, etc.) as in censorship. [L] —**censorial**, *adj.* —**censorious**, *adj.*

censorship /ˈsɛnsəʃɪp/, *n.* **1.** the act or practice of censoring. **2.** the office or power of censor.

censure /ˈsɛnʃə/, *n.*, *v.*, **-sured, -suring.** ◇*n.* **1.** an expression of disapproval; blaming ◇*v.t.* **2.** to find fault with; disapprove; condemn. [ME, from L: censorship; judgment]

census /ˈsɛnsəs/, *n.* **1.** an official counting of population, with details as to age, sex, job, etc. **2.** (in ancient Rome) the registration of citizens and their property, for purposes of taxation. [L]

cent /sɛnt/, *n.* **1.** $\frac{1}{100}$ of a dollar. **2.** a coin of this value. [L: short for *centēsimus* hundredth]

cent- /sɛnt-/, → **centi-**.

cent., *Abbrev.* **1.** centigrade. **2.** central. **3.** centum (in *per cent*). **4.** century.

centaur /ˈsɛntɔː/, *n. Gk Legend.* one of a race of monsters having the head, trunk, and arms of a man, and the body and legs of a horse. [ME, from L, from Gk]

Centaurus /sɛnˈtɔːrəs/, *n. Astron.* a southern constellation containing the first magnitude stars Alpha Centauri (the star nearest the solar system) and Beta Centauri.

centenary /sɛnˈtiːnəri, -ˈtɛn-/, *n.*, *pl.* **-ries. 1.** 100th anniversary. **2.** period of 100 years; century. [L *centēnārius* of or containing 100] —**centenarian**, *n.*

centennial /sɛnˈtɛnɪəl/, *adj.* **1.** marking the end of 100 years. **2.** lasting 100 years. **3.** taking place every 100 years. [L *centennium* 100 years + -AL[1]; modelled on BIENNIAL]

centesimal /sɛnˈtɛsəməl/, *adj.* hundredth; divided into hundredths. [L *centēsimus* hundredth + -AL[1]]

centi- /ˈsɛnti-/, a prefix indicating $\frac{1}{100}$ of a given unit, as in *centigram*. Also, before vowels, **cent-**. *Symbol:* c [L, combining form of *centum*]

Centigrade /ˈsɛntɪɡreɪd/, *adj.* → **Celsius**. [F. See CENTI-, -GRADE]

centigram /ˈsɛntɪɡræm/, *n.* $\frac{1}{10}$ of a gram. *Symbol:* cg

centimetre /ˈsɛntɪmiːtə/, *n.* $\frac{1}{100}$ of a metre. *Symbol:* cm

centipede /ˈsɛntɪpiːd/, *n.* a small insect-like creature having a long, thin body with a single pair of legs to each segment. [L: hundred-footed insect]

centr-, variant of **centro-** before vowels.

central /ˈsɛntrəl/, *adj.* **1.** of or forming a centre. **2.** in, at, or near the centre. **3.** chief; principal; dominant: *the central idea; central character in a play.* [L]

Central America, *n.* continental North America south of Mexico, comprising Guatemala, Honduras, El Salvador, Nicaragua, Costa Rica, Panama, and Belize. About 520 000 km².

Centralia /sɛnˈtreɪljə/, *n. Colloq.* the inland region of continental Australia. —**Centralian**, *adj.*, *n.*

Central Intelligence Agency, *n.* the US federal government agency that coordinates intelligence, espionage, etc. *Abbrev.:* CIA

centralise *or* **centralize** /ˈsɛntrəlaɪz/, *v.*, **-lised, -lising.** ◇*v.t.* **1.** to bring under one control, esp. in government. **2.** to come together at a centre. —**centralisation**, *n.*

centralism /ˈsɛntrəlɪzəm/, the principle or system of centralisation, esp. in government. —**centralist**, *n.*, *adj.*

centrality /sɛnˈtrælɪti/, *n.* central position or state.

Central Mount Stuart /'stjuət/, *n.* a hill north of Alice Springs, NT. 845 m. [discovered and named Mt Sturt by J McDouall STUART in honor of Charles STURT; name later changed to honor Stuart himself]

central nervous system, *n.* the brain and spinal cord considered together.

central processing unit, *n.* the arithmetical and logical computing part of a computer considered separately from input/output devices. Also, **central processor unit.**

centre /'sentə/, *n., v.* **-tred, -tring.** ◇*n.* **1.** *Geom.* the middle point, esp. the point within a circle or sphere at an equal distance from all points of the circumference or surface, or the point within a regular many-sided figure at an equal distance from the vertices. **2.** the point, pivot, axis, etc., round which anything turns. **3.** a place or group of buildings set aside as an area for a particular activity: *a shopping centre.* **4.** the middle of anything. **5.** (*often cap.*) a political party or position, midway between conservative and socialist. **6.** *Sport.* the player in a central position. **7.** *Med.* a group of nerve cells controlling a particular body process. **8. the (Red) Centre,** the desert area in the middle of Australia. ◇*v.t.* **9.** to place in or on a centre: *He centred the photograph on the page.* **10.** to collect at a centre; concentrate; focus (fol. by *on, around,* etc.): *We centred our attention on the new car.* ◇*v.i.* **11.** to be at or come to a centre (fol. by *on, around,* etc.): *Attention centred on the sick woman.* [ME, from L, from Gk: sharp point, centre]

centreboard /'sentəbɔd/, *n.* a movable keel in a boat that can be pulled up in shallow water; dogger plate. Also, **centreplate.**

centrefold /'sentəfould/, *n.* folded pages in the centre of a magazine, designed to be lifted out and usu. containing a large photograph.

centre of attraction, *n.* **1.** the point towards which bodies are attracted by the force of gravity. **2.** a person or thing on which attention is focused.

centre of buoyancy, *n.* the point in a floating body through which the forces of buoyancy act.

centre of gravity, *n.* the point through which the resultant of gravitational forces acts on a body in any position. Same as **centre of mass** in a uniform gravitational field.

centre of mass, *n.* that point of a body (or system of bodies) at which its whole mass could be concentrated without changing its linear inertia in any direction. For ordinary bodies near the earth, this point is the same as **centre of gravity.**

centrepiece /'sentəpis/, *n.* **1.** an ornament, vase of flowers, etc., placed in the centre of a table. **2.** the most important or most easily seen item in a display.

centre-punch /'sentə-pʌntʃ/, *n.* **1.** a tool used to mark the centre of holes to be drilled, consisting of a punch with a cone-shaped point. ◇*v.t.* **2.** to mark with this tool.

centri-, variant of **centro-,** as in *centrifugal.*

centrifugal /sen'trɪfjəgəl, sentrə'fjugəl/, *adj.* **1.** moving or directed outwards from the centre. **2.** relating to or worked by centrifugal force: *a centrifugal pump.* [NL *centrifugus* centre-fleeing + -AL[1]]

centrifugal force, *n.* the outward force acting on a body moving in a curved path.

centrifuge /'sentrəfjudʒ, -fjuʒ/, *n.* a machine consisting of a rotating container, in which substances of different densities, as cream and milk, may be separated by centrifugal force, or in which animals, instruments etc. are subjected to prolonged accelerations. [F: centrifugal] **–centrifugation,** *n.*

centripetal /sen'trɪpətl/, *adj.* **1.** moving or directed inwards; towards the centre. **2.** working by centripetal force. [NL *centripetus* centre-seeking + -AL[1]]

centripetal force, *n.* a force acting on a body, which causes it to move in a circle or curve by pulling it towards the centre.

centro-, a word part meaning 'centre'. Also, **centr-, centri-.** [combining form representing L *centrum* and Gk *kéntron*]

centroid /'sentrɔɪd/, *n. Maths, Mech., etc.* (of a curve, surface, body, etc.) that point whose coordinates are the mean values of the coordinates of all points in the given object.

centromere /'sentrəmɪə/, *n. Biol.* the part of a chromosome to which the spindle is attached during mitosis. **–centromeric,** *adj.*

centrosome /'sentrəsoum/, *n. Biol.* a very small protoplasmic body thought of by some people to be the active centre of cell division in mitosis. [CENTRO- + -SOME[3]]

centrosphere /'sentrəsfɪə/, *n. Biol.* **1.** the central part of an aster, containing the centrosome. **2.** *Geol.* the interior or centre of earth; barysphere.

centuple /'sentjəpəl/, *adj.* a hundred times as great; hundredfold. [F, from LL: hundredfold]

centurion /sen'tjuriən/, *n.* (in the Roman Army) the leader of one hundred men. [ME, from L]

century /'sentʃəri/, *n., pl.* **-ries. 1.** any period of 100 years, esp. one reckoned forwards or backwards from an historical epoch, as from the birth of Jesus. **2.** any group or collection of 100, e.g. 100 runs in cricket. [L *centuria* a division of a hundred things]

cephalic /sə'fælɪk/, *adj.* of or relating to the head. [L, from Gk: of the head]

-cephalic, a word part meaning 'head'.

cephalo-, a word part meaning 'head', as in *cephalopod.* Also, **cephal-.** [Gk]

cephalopod /'sefələpɒd/, *n.* one of a class of molluscs, including the cuttlefish, squid, octopus, etc., which have tentacles attached to the head. [CEPHALO- + -POD] **–cephalopodan,** *adj., n.*

cephalous /'sefələs/, *adj.* having a head. [CEPHAL(O)- + -OUS]

-cephalous, a word part meaning 'head', as in *hydrocephalous.* [CEPHAL(O)- + -OUS]

-ceptor, a word part meaning 'taker', 'receiver', as in *preceptor*. [L]

cer-, variant of **cero-**, used before vowels, as in *ceraceous*.

CER, *n.* a trade agreement between Australia and NZ. [C(*loser*) E(*conomic*) R(*elations*)]

Ceram /sə'ræm/, *n.* an island of the Moluccas in Indonesia west of New Guinea. Pop. 300 000 (1961). 18 625 km².

ceramic /sə'ræmɪk/, *adj.* relating to things made from clay, etc. or to their manufacture: *ceramic art.* Also, **keramic**. [Gk: pottery]

ceramics /sə'ræmɪks/, *n.* 1. (*treated as sing.*) the art and method of making clay products, etc. 2. (*treated as pl.*) articles of earthenware, porcelain, etc. [pl. of CERAMIC. See -ICS] —**ceramist**, **ceramicist**, *n.*

cerato-, *Zool.* a word part meaning 'horn', 'horny', or 'hornlike'. [Gk *keráto-*, combining form of *kéras* horn]

ceratoid /'serətɔɪd/, *adj.* hornlike; horny. [Gk: hornlike]

Cerberus /'sɜːbərəs/, *n.* 1. a frightening or unfriendly keeper or guard. 2. *Class. Myth.* a dog, usu. represented as having three heads, which guarded the entrance of the underworld. —**Cerberian**, *adj.*

cereal /'sɪərɪəl/, *n.* 1. a grain plant, such as wheat, rye, oats, rice, maize, etc. 2. the grain itself. 3. food made from grain, esp. a breakfast food. [L *Cereālis* pertaining to Ceres, ancient Italian goddess of agriculture and corn]

cerebellum /,serə'beləm/, *n., pl.* **-bella** /-'belə/. the back part of the brain, controlling voluntary movements, posture, and balance. [L] —**cerebellar**, *adj.*

cerebral /'serəbrəl/, *adj.* 1. of or relating to the cerebrum, or the brain. 2. requiring thought; intellectual. [NL]

cerebral palsy, *n.* a form of paralysis caused by brain damage. Sufferers are called spastics.

cerebrate /'serəbreɪt/, *v.i.*, **-brated**, **-brating**. to use the brain. —**cerebration**, *n.*

cerebro-, a word part meaning 'cerebrum'. Also (before a vowel), **cerebr-**.

cerebrospinal /,serəbrou'spaɪnəl/, *adj.* 1. relating to or affecting both the brain and the spinal cord. 2. relating to the central nervous system (distinguished from *autonomic*).

cerebrum /'serəbrəm/, *n., pl.* **-bra** /-brə/. the largest and upper part of the brain, consisting of two hemispheres, partly separated, but connected by a broad band of fibres, and controlling voluntary and conscious thoughts and processes. [L: brain]

ceremonial /,serə'mounɪəl/, *adj.* 1. relating to, used for or marked by, ceremonies or a ceremony; ritual; formal. ◇*n.* 2. a system of ceremonies for a particular occasion; rite or ceremony: *the ceremonial of death.* —**ceremonialism**, *n.* —**ceremonialist**, *n.*

ceremonious /,serə'mounɪəs/, *adj.* 1. carefully observing ceremony; formally or elaborately polite. 2. relating to, marked by, or consisting of ceremony; formal.

ceremony /'serəmənɪ/, *n., pl.* **-monies**. 1. a formal action or set of actions performed on a solemn or important religious, public or state occasion: *a wedding ceremony.* 2. any formal act or gesture, esp. a meaningless one: *He made a ceremony out of his departure.* 3. formal actions or gestures as a whole; formality: *The new bridge was opened with great ceremony.* 4. **stand on ceremony**, to be too formal or polite. [L: sacred rite]

Ceres /'sɪəriːz/, *n.* 1. *Class. Myth.* an ancient Italian goddess of tillage and corn, under whose name the Romans adopted the worship of the Greek goddess Demeter. 2. *Astron.* the first asteroid discovered (1801), and the largest, with a diameter of about 785 km. [L]

cerise /sə'riːs, -'riːz/, *adj., n.* cherry red. [F]

cerium /'sɪərɪəm/, *n.* a grey, ductile, metallic element of the rare-earth group, occurring in compounds. *Symbol*: Ce; *at. no.*: 58; *at. wt*: 140.12.

CERN /sɜːn/, *n.* a European organisation for nuclear research, with a research centre in Geneva. [C(*onseil*) E(*uropéen pour la*) R(*echerche*) N(*ucléaire*)]

cero-, word part meaning 'wax', as in *cerography.* Also, **cer-**. [Gk *kēro-*, combining form of *kērós*]

cerography /sɪə'rɒgrəfɪ/, *n.* the art of engraving on wax.

cert., *Abbrev.* 1. certificate. 2. certified.

certain /'sɜːtn/, *adj.* 1. having no doubt; confident; assured (oft. fol. by *of* before a noun, verbal noun or pronoun): *I am certain of being able to finish today; He was certain she was the one.* 2. sure; inevitable; bound to come (fol. by an infinitive verb): *It is certain to happen.* 3. established as true or sure; unquestionable; indisputable: *It is certain that he tried.* 4. agreed upon; fixed: *on a certain day.* 5. definite or particular, but not named: *certain people.* 6. some, though not much: *a certain reluctance.* [ME, from L: fixed, certain]

certainly /'sɜːtnlɪ/, *adv.* 1. with certainty; without doubt; assuredly. ◇*interj.* 2. yes! of course!

certainty /'sɜːtntɪ/, *n., pl.* **-ties**. 1. the condition of being certain. 2. something certain; an assured fact. 3. *Colloq.* something seen as certain to happen, or to do something, as to win a race: *That horse is an absolute certainty.*

certificate /sə'tɪfɪkət/, *n.*; /sə'tɪfɪkeɪt/, *v.*, **-cated**, **-cating**. ◇*n.* 1. a written paper stating the truth of certain facts, or verifying status, qualifications, ownership, etc. 2. a document given to someone who passes a particular examination, as proof of passing. 3. an examination for which a certificate is awarded. ◇*v.t.* 4. to witness to (the truth of something) by a certificate. [ME, from ML]

certified /'sɜːtɪfaɪd/, *adj.* 1. having, or proved by, a certificate: *a certified tradesman.* 2. (of a product) guaranteed. 3. officially declared insane.

certify /'sɜːtɪfaɪ/, *v.*, **-fied**, **-fying**. *v.t.* 1. to give reliable information of; guarantee as

certain. 2. to state in writing that (something) is true. **3.** to state officially that (someone) is insane. ◇*v.i.* **4.** to give assurance; testify. [ME, from F, from ML] —**certifier,** *n.* —**certification,** *n.*

certitude /'sətətjud/, *n.* total belief; certainty.

cerumen /sə'rumən/, *n.* a yellowish waxlike substance from certain glands in the ear canal, which keeps it moist and stops the entrance of dust, insects, etc.; earwax. [NL, from L: wax]

Cervantes Saavedra /sə,væntiz sa'veɪdrə/, *n.* **Miguel de** /mi'gel deɪ/, 1547–1616, Spanish novelist, dramatist, and poet; author of *Don Quixote* (1605), a major influence on the development of the novel.

cervic-, combining form of **cervical.** Also, **cervico-.**

cervical /'səvɪkəl, sə'vaɪkəl/, *adj.* relating to the cervix or to the neck. [L *cervix* neck + -AL¹]

cervical smear, *n.* → **Pap smear.**

cervix /'səvɪks/, *n., pl.* **cervixes, cervices** /sə'vaɪsiz/. *Anat.* the neck of the uterus. [L]

cesium /'siziəm/, *n. Chem.* → **caesium.**

cessation /sɛ'seɪʃən/, *n.* a stopping or ceasing; pause: *cessation of war.* [L]

cession /'sɛʃən/, *n.* the act of ceding; a giving up (of rights, territory, etc.) to another by treaty or agreement. [L]

Cessnock /'sɛsnɒk/, *n.* a city in central eastern NSW, north of Sydney; coal mining. Pop. (with Bellbird) 17 506 (1986). [named after *Cessnock* Castle, Scotland]

cesspit /'sɛspɪt/, *n.* a pit containing a cesspool.

cesspool /'sɛspul/, *n.* **1.** a pit or cistern for holding the drainage or sewerage from a house. **2.** any filthy receptacle or place: *a cesspool of iniquity; His mind is a cesspool.*

cet-, a word part meaning 'whale'. [combining form representing L *cētus* and Gk *kētos* whale]

cetacean /sə'teɪʃən/, *adj.* **1.** belonging to the class of marine mammals that includes the whales, dolphins, porpoises, etc. ◇*n.* **2.** a cetacean mammal. [NL *Cetācea*] —**cetaceous,** *adj.*

Ceylon /sə'lɒn/, *n.* the former name of **Sri Lanka.** —**Ceylonese,** *adj.*

Cézanne /seɪ'zan/, *n.* **Paul,** 1839–1906, French post-impressionist painter.

cf., *Abbrev.* compare. [L *confer*]

c/f., *Abbrev.* (in accounting) carry forward; carried forward.

cg, *Symbol.* centigram; centigrams.

c.g.s. /si dʒi 'ɛs/, *n. Abbrev.* centimetregram-second (system). Also, **CGS**

chablis /'ʃæbli, 'ʃabli/, *n.* a very dry white table wine, originally from the Burgundy wine area in France. [*Chablis,* town in N central France]

Chad /tʃæd/, *n.* **1.** a republic in northern central Africa, bordered by Libya, the Central African Republic, Niger, Cameroon and Sudan; a territory within French Equatorial Africa before independence in 1960. Pop. 5 265 000 (1987); 1 284 000 km². *Languages:* French, also Arabic and African tribal languages. *Currency:* franc. *Cap.:* Ndjamena. French, **Tchad.**

chador /'tʃadə/, *n.* full, dark-colored garment which covers the body and hides the face below the eyes, worn by Moslem women as an outer garment. Also, **chadur.** [Pers, from Hind: square piece of cloth]

Chadwick /'tʃædwɪk/, *n.* **Sir James,** 1891–1974, English physicist; discovered the neutron; Nobel prize for physics 1935.

chafe /tʃeɪf/, *v.,* **chafed, chafing,** *n.* ◇*v.t.* **1.** to warm by rubbing: *They chafed his cold feet.* **2.** to wear down or make sore by rubbing: *This saddle chafes my horse.* **3.** to annoy; irritate: *Her words chafed him.* ◇*v.i.* **4.** to become worn or sore by rubbing: *This kind of leather chafes easily.* **5.** to be annoyed or irritated: *He chafed at her words.* **6.** to become impatient; fret: *She chafed at the delay.* ◇*n.* **7.** a sore caused by rubbing. [ME, from LL contraction of L *calefacere* make hot]

chafer /'tʃeɪfə/, *n.* any beetle of the scarab family. [OE *ceafor*]

chaff¹ /tʃaf/, *n.* **1.** the husks (outer coverings) of grains and grasses separated from the seed. **2.** straw cut small for animal feed. **3.** worthless matter; rubbish. [OE *ceaf*] —**chaffy,** *adj.*

chaff² /tʃaf/, *v.t., v.i.* **1.** to tease (someone) good-naturedly. ◇*n.* **2.** good-natured teasing; banter; raillery. [? special use of CHAFF¹] —**chaffer,** *n.*

Chaffey /'tʃeɪfi/, *n.* **George,** 1848–1932, and his brother, **William Benjamin,** 1856–1926, Canadian-born Australian pioneers of irrigation.

chaffinch /'tʃæfɪntʃ/, *n.* a small, common European bird with a pleasant short song, often kept as a pet in a cage. [OE *ceaffinc*]

chafing dish /'tʃeɪfɪŋ/, *n.* a dish over a flame for cooking or keeping food warm at the table.

Chagall /ʃə'gal/, *n.* **Marc,** 1887–1985, Russian painter in France and the US, noted for his use of color and fantastic themes.

chagrin /'ʃægrɪn, ʃə'grin/, *n.* **1.** a feeling of annoyance, disappointment or humiliation. ◇*v.t.* **2.** to make angry by disappointment or humiliation. [F. See SHAGREEN]

chain /tʃeɪn/, *n.* **1.** a connected series of links or rings, made of metal or other material, used for joining things together, confining, restraining, etc., or for ornament. **2.** (*usu. pl.*)something that binds and restrains: *the chains of desire.* **3.** (*pl.*) **a.** bonds or fetters. **b.** bondage. **4.** a series of things connected or following in order: *a mountain chain; a chain of events.* **5.** a number of similar businesses, as banks, theatres, hotels, etc., under one ownership. **6.** *Chem.* the bonding of atoms of the same element, as carbon to carbon. **7.** a unit of measurement in the imperial system (66 feet or 20.1168 metres). **8. drag the chain,** *Colloq.* to shirk or fall behind in one's share of work or responsibility. ◊*v.t.* **9.** to fasten or secure with a chain. **10.** to tie up; fetter; confine: *chained to his desk.* [ME, from L]

chain-drive /'tʃeɪn-draɪv/, *n.* **1.** the transmission of power by means of an endless chain moving between sprocket-wheels. **2.** the endless chain itself.

chain-gang /'tʃeɪn-gæŋ/, *n.* a group of convicts chained together for hard labour.

chain-reaction /tʃeɪn-rɪ'ækʃən/, *n.* **1.** *Phys.* nuclear reaction which produces enough neutrons to continue the reaction. **2.** *Chem.* a reaction which results in a product necessary for the continuing of the reaction. **3.** *Colloq.* a series of reactions brought about by one event: *A pay-increase for railwaymen would cause a chain-reaction of wage claims.*

chainsaw /'tʃeɪnsɔː/, *n.* a power-driven saw with teeth set on a revolving chain.

chain-smoke /'tʃeɪn-smoʊk/, *v.t., v.i.,* **-smoked, -smoking.** to smoke (cigarettes) continually, esp. when lighting the next from the butt of the previous one. —**chain-smoker,** *n.*

chain-stitch /'tʃeɪn-stɪtʃ/, *n.* **1.** a kind of ornamental stitching in which each stitch is a loop linked to the loop before. ◊*v.t.* **2.** to sew with a chain-stitch.

chain-store /'tʃeɪn-stɔː/, *n.* one of a group of shops under the same ownership.

chair /tʃɛə/, *n.* **1.** a seat with a back and legs or other support, often with arms, usu. for one person. **2.** a seat of office. **3.** an official position, as that of a professor. **4.** the person occupying the chair, esp. the chairman of a meeting: *Madam chair will open the discussion.* **5. take the chair,** to act as chairman at a meeting. ◊*v.t.* **6.** to conduct as chairman: *He will chair the meeting.* [ME, from L: seat, from Gk *kathédra*]

chairlift /'tʃɛəlɪft/, *n.* a line of chairs hung from a motor-driven, revolving cable, for carrying people up or down mountains.

chairperson /'tʃɛəpɜːsən/, *n.* someone who controls a meeting, committee, etc. Also, **chairman,** *n. masc.,* **chairwoman,** *n. fem.*

chaise /ʃeɪz/, *n.* a light, open carriage, esp. a one-horse, two-wheeled carriage. [F]

chaise longue /ʃeɪz 'lɒŋ/, *n.* a kind of couch long enough to provide full-length leg room. [F: long chair]

chalcedony /kæl'sɛdəni/, *n., pl.* **-nies.** a variety of quartz, often milky or greyish. [ME, from L (Vulgate), from Gk]

chalcocite /'kælkəsaɪt/, *n.* a common mineral, cuprous sulfide, Cu_2S, an important ore of copper.

chalcopyrite /kælkə'paɪraɪt/, *n.* a very common mineral, copper iron sulfur, $CuFeS_2$, an important ore of copper.

Chaldea /kæl'dɪə/, *n.* an ancient region in southern Babylonia.

chalet /'ʃæleɪ/, *n.* **1.** (orig.) the hut of a person caring for animals in the Swiss mountains. **2.** a mountain cottage, low and with wide eaves. **3.** a dwelling for holiday use, esp. in snow regions. [F (Swiss)]

chalice /'tʃælɪs/, *n.* **1.** *Church.* a cup for the wine at Mass or Holy Communion. **2.** *Poetry.* a drinking cup. [ME, from L *calix* cup]

chalk /tʃɔːk/, *n.* **1.** *Geol.* soft, white, limestone consisting of fossilised remains of very small water organisms. **2.** a prepared piece of chalk or chalk-like substance, esp. calcium sulfate, for marking on blackboards, etc. **3. like chalk and cheese,** *Colloq.* complete opposites. **4. by a long chalk,** by far. ◊*v.t.* **5.** to mark or write with chalk: *He chalked his name on the board.* ◊*v.* **6. chalk up, a.** to score: *They chalked up 360 runs.* **b.** to credit (to): *We can chalk it up to experience.* [OE *cealc,* from L: lime]

challenge /'tʃælɪndʒ/, *n., v.,* **-lenged, -lenging.** ◊*n.* **1.** a call to take part in a test of skill, strength, etc. **2.** a call to fight, as to a duel, etc. **3.** something that makes demands upon one's skills, etc.: *This job is a challenge.* **4. a.** a calling into question (as of rights to join in, be present at, etc.). **b.** *Mil.* a demand by a guard for someone to show who they are. **c.** *Law.* a formal objection to a juror or to an entire jury. ◊*v.t.* **5.** to invite (someone) to compete in a test of skill, strength, etc. **6.** to make demands upon: *This job will challenge your abilities.* **7.** *Mil.* to stop (someone) and demand identification or a password. **8.** *Law.* to make formal objection to (a juror or jury). [ME, from L *calumnia* CALUMNY]

Challenger /'tʃælɪndʒə/, *n.* a manned orbiter used in the US space shuttle program of the 1980s.

chamber /'tʃeɪmbə/, *n.* **1.** (formerly) a private room, esp. a bedroom. **2.** (the meeting hall of) a law-making body: *They are meeting in the chamber; The upper chamber is discussing his request.* **3.** (*pl.*) a place where a judge hears matters not requiring action in court. **4.** (*pl.*) the rooms of barristers and others. **5.** a closed-in space; cavity: *a chamber of the heart.* **6.** that part of the barrel of a gun which receives the charge. [ME, from L]

chamberlain /'tʃeɪmbəlɪn/, *n.* the official in charge of the household of a sovereign or member of the nobility. [ME, from OF, from OG]

Chamberlain /'tʃeɪmbəlɪn/, *n.* **1. Lindy** (*Alice Lynne Chamberlain*), born 1948, Australian woman convicted in 1982 for the murder of her daughter, Azaria, at Ayers Rock in 1980; released from prison 1986; conviction quashed 1988. **2. (Arthur) Neville,** 1869–1940, UK Conservative prime minister 1937–40; tried to avoid war with a policy of appeasement towards Nazi Germany.

chamber magistrate, *n.* a solicitor employed in a Court of Petty Sessions, who gives free legal advice.

chambermaid /'tʃeɪmbəmeɪd/, *n.* a female servant who takes care of bedrooms.

chamber music, *n.* music suited for performance in a room or a small concert hall, esp. using a small number of instruments.

chamber of commerce, *n.* an association, mainly of business people, to protect and improve business in an area.

chamber orchestra, *n.* a small orchestra of twenty to thirty players.

chamber-pot /'tʃeɪmbə-pɒt/, *n.* a portable vessel used in bedrooms as a toilet.

Chambers Pillar /tʃeɪmbəz 'pɪlə/, *n.* a sandstone monolith in the southern NT, south of Alice Springs. About 34 m high and 6 m wide. [named by J McDouall STUART after James *Chambers*, one of his patrons]

chameleon /kəˈmiːliən, fə-/, *n.* **1.** any of a group of lizards, found mainly in Africa and Madagascar, which have a greatly developed power of changing skin color to blend into the background. **2.** a changeable person. [ME, from L, from Gk: ground lion] **– chameleonic**, *adj.*

chamfer /'tʃæmfə/, *n.* **1.** a slope cut into the edge or corner of a solid, so that its angle is no longer 90°. ◇*v.t.* **2.** to cut so as to form a chamfer. **3.** to cut grooves in (a column). **4.** to improve the appearance of; smarten (fol. by *up*). [F *chant* side + *fraindre* (from L: break)]

chamois /'ʃæmwɑː/, *for def. 1*; /'ʃæmi/, *for def. 2*., *n., pl.* **-ois. 1.** a goatlike antelope, of the high mountains of Europe and southwestern Russia. **2.** Also, **chammy.** soft leather made from various skins or synthetics (originally chamois skin) treated with oil. [F, from LL *camox*]

chamomile /'kæməmaɪl/, *n.* a herb with strongly scented leaves, the flowers of which are used in teas and medicines. Also, **camomile.** [LL, from Gk: earth apple]

champ[1] /tʃæmp/, *v.t.* **1.** to bite upon, esp. impatiently: *Horses champ the bit.* **2.** to chew noisily; munch. ◇*v.i.* **3.** to make strong chewing or biting movements. ◇*v.* **4. to champ at the bit,** to be anxious to begin. [? nasalised var. of *chop* bite at, from *chap*, *chop* jaw]

champ[2] /tʃæmp/, *n. Colloq.* champion.

champagne /ʃæm'peɪn/, *n.* **1.** a bubbly white wine orig. produced in Champagne, France. **2.** a very pale yellow or cream color. ◇*adj.* **3.** having the color of champagne.

champignon /'ʃæmpɪnjɒn/, *n.* a mushroom, picked when very small, while the cap still meets the stem. [F, from L *campus* field]

champion /'tʃæmpiən/, *n.* **1.** a person or animal who holds first place in any sport. **2.** someone who fights for or defends any person or cause: *a champion of the needy.* ◇*v.t.* **3.** to act as champion of; defend; support. ◇*adj.* **4.** first among all competitors: *He is champion material.* **5.** *Colloq.* first-rate. [ME, from L *campus* field (of battle)] **– championship**, *n.*

Champs Élysées /ʃɒz eɪli'zeɪ/, *n.* a famous boulevard in Paris; cafes, shops, and theatres; a tourist centre. [F: lit. Elysian Fields]

Chan /tʃæn/, *n.* Sir Julius, born 1940, PNG politician; prime minister 1980–82.

chance /tʃæns, tʃɑːns/, *n., v.,* **chanced, chancing,** *adj.* ◇*n.* **1.** the absence of any known reason for an event to turn out one way rather than another, spoken of as if it had real power of action: *She believes that chance will decide it.* **2.** fortune; fate; luck: *If by chance we find the treasure, we will be rich.* **3.** the possibility of anything happening: *The chances are two to one against us.* **4.** an opportunity: *Now is your chance.* **5.** a risk: *Take a chance.* **6. half a chance,** any opportunity at all. **7. the main chance,** the opportunity to further one's own interests: *He had an eye to the main chance.* ◇*v.i.* **8.** to happen unexpectedly: *It may chance that the king will die.* **9.** to come by chance (fol. by *on* or *upon*): *They chanced upon some welcome shade.* ◇*v.t.* **10.** *Colloq.* to take a risk (usu. fol. by impersonal *it*): *I will chance it.* ◇*v.* **11. chance one's arm,** to make an attempt, despite possible failure. ◇*adj.* **12.** due to chance: *a chance occurrence.* [ME, from LL *cadentia* a falling out]

chancel /'tʃænsəl, 'tʃɑːnsəl/, *n.* the space around the church altar, usu. fenced in, for the priest, choir, etc. [ME, from L *cancellī* (pl.) bars, lattice (which enclosed the chancel)]

chancellery /'tʃænsəlri, 'tʃɑːns-/, *n., pl.* **-ries. 1.** the position of a chancellor. **2.** the office or department of a chancellor. **3.** the building or room occupied by a chancellor's department. Also, **chancellory, chancelry.** [ME, from OF]

chancellor /'tʃænsələ, 'tʃɑːnsələ/, *n.* **1.** *Chiefly Brit.* the title of various legal and other high officials. **2.** the chief minister of state in German-speaking countries, as present-day West Germany. **3.** the honorary head of a university. [ME, from LL *cancellārius*, orig. officer stationed at a tribunal] **– chancellorship,** *n.*

chancery /'tʃænsəri/, *n., pl.* **-ceries. 1.** the office of a chancellor. **2.** (*cap.*) *Brit.* the Lord Chancellor's court, now a division of the High Court of Justice. **3. in chancery,** *Brit.* in a helpless position. [ME, var. of CHANCELLERY]

chancre /'ʃæŋkə/, *n. Med.* a sore with a hard base, the first sign of syphilis. [F, from L *cancer* crab, cancer] **– chancrous,** *adj.*

chandelier /ʃændə'lɪə/, *n.* an ornamental branched support hanging from the ceiling, holding a number of lights. [F]

chandler /'tʃændlə/, *n.* **1.** a dealer or trader: *a ship's chandler.* **2.** someone who makes or sells candles. [ME, from OF: candle-seller]

Changchun /tʃʌŋ'tʃuən/, *n.* a city in north-eastern China; the capital of Jilin province. Pop. 1 424 500 (1985 est.). Formerly, **Hsinking.**

change /tʃeɪndʒ/, *v.,* **changed, changing,** *n.* ◇*v.t.* **1.** to make different; alter in condition, appearance, etc.: *You must change your habits.* **2.** to exchange for something else: *To change your boy would be silly.* **3.** to give or get money of smaller pieces or different currency in exchange for: *to change a dollar note; to change dollars for francs*. **4.** to give and take one with another; exchange: *to change places with someone*. **5.** to replace the coverings of: *to change a baby; to change clothes*. **6.** to select a higher or lower (gear of a car). ◇*v.i.* **7.** to become different; alter (sometimes fol. by *to* or *into*). **8.** to make a change or an exchange. **9.** to change trains or other forms of transport. **10.** to change one's clothes. **11.** to change gear (fol. by *up* or *down*): *The idea is to change down on hills*. ◇*v.* **12. change hands,** to pass from one possessor to another. **13. change one's mind,** to go back on an earlier decision. **14. change one's tune,** to take on a different, usu. humbler, attitude. ◇*n.* **15.** variation; alteration; modification; deviation; transformation. **16.** the replacing of one thing with another. **17.** variety: *A holiday would provide some change*. **18.** that which is or may be used instead of another: *a change of plans*. **19.** a fresh set of clothing. **20.** money returned when the amount given is larger than the amount due. **21.** small coins. **22.** (*oft. cap.*) *Comm.* a place where traders meet to do business; an exchange. **23.** any of the various orders in which a set of bells may be rung. **24. ring the changes,** to ring bells according to one of the orders of change. [ME, from LL]

changeable /ˈtʃeɪndʒəbəl/, *adj.* likely to change or to be changed; variable. —**changeability, changeableness,** *n.*

changeling /ˈtʃeɪndʒlɪŋ/, *n.* a child supposedly exchanged secretly for another, esp. by fairies; an elfchild.

change of life, *n.* → **menopause.**

change of state, *n. Phys., Chem.* the change of a substance from one physical state (solid, liquid, or gas) into another.

Changi /ˈtʃæŋi/, *n.* an area in eastern Singapore; site of Singapore's international airport and a prison used as a Japanese prisoner-of-war camp during World War II.

channel /ˈtʃænəl/, *n., v.,* **-nelled, -nelling.** ◇*n.* **1.** the bed and banks of a river, stream, creek or gully. **2.** the deeper part of a river, ocean passage, etc. **3.** a wide strait, as between a continent and an island. **4.** a sea passage which ships can use to travel between two larger bodies of water such as the English Channel. **5.** a means of approach. **6.** a course into which something may be directed: *He will put his energy into better channels when he is older*. **7.** a way through which anything passes: *channels of communication*. **8.** a frequency band for one-way communication, its width depending on the type of transmission (as telephone, radio, television, etc.). **9.** a tube for passing through liquids or fluids. **10.** a groove. ◇*v.t.* **11.** to make pass through a channel. **12.** to direct towards some course: *to channel interests*. **13.** to form a channel in; groove. [ME, from L *canālis* CANAL]

Channel Country *n.* a large area in the arid south-west of Qld crossed by many river channels, esp. those of the Georgina and Diamantina Rivers and Cooper Creek.

Channel Islands, *n.pl.* a group of islands in the English Channel, near the coast of France, consisting of Alderney, Guernsey, Jersey, Sark, and smaller islands; British Crown dependency. Pop. 130 000 (1985 est.); 194 km².

chant /tʃænt, tʃant/, *n.* **1.** a song; singing. **2.** a short, simple melody, with single notes to which a varying number of syllables are sung, used in singing psalms, etc. **3.** a chant-like quality of the voice in speaking. ◇*v.t.* **4.** to sing to a chant, or in the manner of a chant, esp. in a church service. ◇*v.i.* **5.** to sing a chant. [ME, from L: sing] —**chanter,** *n.*

chaos /ˈkeɪɒs/, *n.* **1.** total confusion or disorder. **2.** (*usu. cap.*) the endless space or formless matter supposed to have been before the beginning of the ordered universe. [L, from Gk] —**chaotic,** *adj.*

chap[1] /tʃæp/, *v.,* **chapped, chapping,** *n.* ◇*v.t.* **1.** to cause to open in small cracks. **2.** (of cold) to crack, roughen, and redden (the skin). ◇*v.i.* **3.** to become chapped. ◇*n.* **4.** a crack, esp. in the skin. [ME; orig. uncert.]

chap[2] /tʃæp/, *n. Colloq.* a fellow; man or boy. [short for *Chapman* pedlar]

chap., *Abbrev.* **1.** chaplain. **2.** chapter. Also, **Chap**

chapel /ˈtʃæpəl/, *n.* **1.** a separate part of a church, used for special services. **2.** a room or building for worship in a college or school, country house, royal court, etc. **3.** *Brit.* a place of worship of a religious body outside the established Church. **4.** a religious service in a chapel. **5.** (a meeting of) members of a trade union in a printing or publishing house. [ME, from LL *cappella* sanctuary for relics (such as the cape of St Martin), diminutive of *capa, cappa* cape]

chaperone /ˈʃæpəroʊn/, *n.* **1.** an older person, usu. a married woman, who accompanies and is responsible for an unmarried woman or a group of young people. ◇*v.t.* **2.** to attend or accompany as chaperone. Also, **chaperon.** [F: hood] —**chaperonage,** *n.*

chaplain /ˈtʃæplən/, *n.* a clergyman attached to a college, school, etc., or to a military unit. [ME, from LL *capella* CHAPEL] —**chaplaincy,** *n.*

chaplet /ˈtʃæplət/, *n.* **1.** an ornamental band for the head. **2.** a string of beads. [ME, from OF: little headdress] —**chapleted,** *adj.*

Chaplin /ˈtʃæplən/, *n.* **Charles Spencer** ('*Charlie*'), 1889–1977, British comedian, film actor, and film director. —**Chaplinesque,** *adj.*

Chappell family /ˈtʃæpəl/, *n.* an Australian family of cricketers. **1. Ian Michael,** born 1943, Australian Test cricket captain 1971–75, captain in World Series Cricket in 1977–78. **2.** his brother, **Gregory Stephen,** born 1948, Australian cricketer; Test captain 1975–77, 1979–83; one of Australia's most noted batsmen. **3.** their brother, **Trevor,** born 1952, Australian Test cricketer.

chapter /ˈtʃæptə/, *n.* **1.** a main division, usu. numbered, of a book, etc. **2.** a meeting of clergy or priests of a church. **3.** chapter

and verse, full detail. **4. chapter of accidents**, a series of closely following misfortunes. [ME, from L: small head, capital of column, chapter]

char[1] /tʃɑ/, *v.*, **charred, charring.** ◇*v.t.* **1.** to burn or reduce to charcoal. **2.** to burn slightly; scorch. ◇*v.i.* **3.** to become charred. [? short for CHARCOAL]

char[2] /tʃɑ/, *n., v.*, **charred, charring.** *Colloq.* ◇*n.* **1.** →**charwoman.** ◇*v.i.* **2.** to do housework by the hour or day for money. [OE *cerr, cyrr* turn, time, occasion, affair]

character /ˈkærəktə/, *n.* **1.** the sum of qualities that sets one person or thing apart from others. **2.** the moral quality of a person or people: *The Australian character is not without failings.* **3.** good moral quality or standing: *He is a person of character.* **4.** the idea held of a person's character, either good or bad. **5.** a reference (def. 6). **6.** a position: *in the character of a friend rather than teacher.* **7.** a person: *a strange character.* **8.** *Colloq.* an odd or interesting person: *He's a real character!* **9.** a person represented in a play, story, etc. **10.** any characteristic of an organism resulting from the action of a gene or genes sometimes acting together with the environment. **11.** a significant visual mark or symbol. **12.** a sign as used in a writing system, as a letter of the alphabet. **13. in character**, in keeping with previous character, behavior, etc. **14. out of character**, not in keeping with previous character, behavior, etc. [L, from Gk: instrument for marking, mark]

characterise *or* **characterize** /ˈkærəktəraɪz/, *v.t.*, **-rised, -rising. 1.** to be a characteristic or quality of. **2.** to describe the particular quality of. —**characterisation**, *n.*

characteristic /kærəktəˈrɪstɪk/, *adj.* relating to, being, or showing the character or special quality; typical; distinctive. ◇*n.* **2.** a feature or quality that is distinctive. **3.** *Maths.* the integral part of a logarithm, indicating the size of the number involved: *The characteristic of 3.5014 is 3.*

charade /ʃəˈrɑd/, *n.* **1.** a game in which players act out a word or phrase which others guess. **2.** stupid or pointless pretence. [F, from Pr: entertainment]

charcoal /ˈtʃɑkoʊl/, *n.* **1.** a form of carbon obtained by the incomplete burning of wood or other organic substances. **2.** a drawing pencil of charcoal. **3.** a drawing made with charcoal. ◇*v.t.* **4.** to blacken, write or draw with charcoal. [ME; orig. uncert.]

charge /tʃɑdʒ/, *v.*, **charged, charging,** *n. v.t.* **1.** to fill or furnish (a thing) with the quantity it is made to receive: *I ask you to charge your glasses.* **2.** to supply with electrical energy: *to charge a battery.* **3.** to fill (air, water, etc.) with other matter: *water charged with carbon dioxide.* **4.** to load (the mind, heart, etc.). **5.** to lay a command or duty on. **6.** to blame; accuse (usu. fol. by *with*): *Charge him with murder.* **7.** to hold or record a debt against (a person). **8.** to record as a debt. **9.** to put off payment on (a service or purchase) by recording it on a charge account. **10.** to ask as a price. **11.** to attack by rushing violently against: *They will charge the town.* ◇*v.i.* **12.** to make a rush, as to an attack: *They will charge to the field.* ◇*n.* **13.** the quantity of anything used to fill something. **14.** *Elect.* →**electric charge. 15.** a quantity of explosive to be set off at one time. **16.** a responsibility given to one, as of care, etc. **17.** anything or anybody given over to one's care. **18.** a command; exhortation. **19.** *Law.* an address of instruction by a judge to a jury at the close of a trial. **20.** an accusation of guilt: *He was arrested on a charge of murder.* **21.** price or cost. **22.** an entry in an account or something due. **23.** an onset or attack, as of soldiers. **24.** a signal for a military charge. **25.** the quantity of energy stored in an electrical storage battery. **26.** *Colloq.* a thrill; a kick. **27. in charge**, in command. **28. in charge of**, having the care of: *in charge of the class.* **29. in the charge of**, in the care of. [ME, from LL *carricāre* load]

charge account, *n.* an arrangement with a department store, etc., by which the cost of goods purchased is recorded for payment at a later date.

chargé d'affaires /ˌʃɑʒeɪ dəˈfɛə/, *n., pl.* **chargés d'affaires. 1.** an official placed in charge during the temporary absence of the ambassador or minister. **2.** an official sent to a state to which a diplomat of higher grade is not sent. Also, **chargé.** [F: lit., entrusted with affairs]

charger /ˈtʃɑdʒə/, *n.* **1.** a horse intended to be ridden in battle. **2.** *Elect.* an apparatus which charges storage batteries.

chariot /ˈtʃærɪət/, *n.* **1.** a two-wheeled vehicle used in ancient times for war, racing, processions, etc. **2.** any stately carriage. [ME, from OF. See CAR]

charisma /kəˈrɪzmə/, *n., pl.* **-mata** /-mətə/. **1.** Also, **charism** /ˈkærɪzəm/. a gift or power (such as healing) given by the Holy Spirit to a Christian. **2.** the ability to influence or impress people through special personal qualities, esp. as in public figures. [Gk: gift] —**charismatic**, *adj., n.*

charitable /ˈtʃærətəbəl/, *adj.* **1.** generous in gifts to help in the needs of others. **2.** kindly or not severe in judging others. **3.** relating to charity: *a charitable institution.* [ME, from OF] —**charitableness**, *n.*

charity /ˈtʃærəti/, *n., pl.* **-ties. 1.** (an act of) private or public help to needy people; benevolence. **2.** something given to people in need; alms. **3.** (an institution for) a charitable collection of money. **4.** generous feeling, esp. towards those in need. **5.** Christian love. **6.** (*cap.*) (in Greek and Roman mythology) one of the three Graces, daughters of Zeus. ◇*adj.* **7.** relating to organisations, money-raising activities, etc., of a charitable nature. [ME, from L *cāritas* affection]

charlatan /ˈʃɑlətən/, *n.* someone who pretends to more knowledge or skill than they possess; a quack. [F, from It: chatter]

Charlemagne /ˈʃɑləmeɪn, ʃɑləˈmɑnjə/, *n.* ('*Charles the Great*'), AD 742–814, king of the

Charlemagne Franks AD 768–814; as Charles I, emperor of the Holy Roman Empire AD 800–814.

Charles¹ /tʃalz/, n. (*Charles Philip Arthur George, Prince of Wales*), born 1948, son of Queen Elizabeth II, heir apparent to the throne of Great Britain and Northern Ireland.

Charles² /tʃalz/, n. (*Ray Charles Robinson*), born 1930, US singer, composer and pianist; influential in jazz, blues and rock music.

Charles I /tʃalz/, n. 1. →**Charlemagne**. 2. (*Charles Stuart*) 1600–49, king of England and Ireland from 1625 until executed in 1649 after his defeat in the Civil War (son of James I).

Charles II, n. 1630–85, king of England and Ireland 1660–85 after the Restoration (1660) (son of Charles I of England).

Charles's law /tʃalzɪz/, n. *Phys.* the law which states that, for an ideal gas at constant pressure, a rise in temperature of 1°C will cause gas to increase by $\frac{1}{273}$ of its volume. See **gas laws**. [named after JAC *Charles*, 1746–1823, French physicist]

charleston /tʃalstən/, n. a type of dance, of Negro origin, popular in the 1920s. [from *Charleston*, a seaport in the US, in Carolina]

Charlotte Waters /ʃalət ˈwɔtəz/, n. the site of water springs in NT near the SA border; formerly a small settlement and station on the Overland Telegraph. [named after Lady *Charlotte* Bacon, daughter of the 6th Earl of Oxford]

Charlton /tʃaltən/, n. **Andrew** ('*Boy*'), 1907–75, Australian swimmer; Olympic gold medallist 1924.

charm /tʃam/, n. 1. (a quality of having) the power to please and attract. 2. an ornament to be worn on a chain around the wrist. 3. any action done, object worn or verse recited which is supposed to have magical power. 4. **like a charm**, successfully; perfectly. ◇v.t. 5. to attract powerfully by beauty, etc. 6. to act upon with or as with a charm; enchant. [ME, from L *carmen* song, incantation] –**charmer**, n. –**charming**, adj.

charnel-house /ˈtʃanəl-haus/, n. a place in which the bodies or bones of the dead are put. [See CARNAL]

Charon /ˈkɛərən/, n. *Class. Myth.* the ferryman who conveyed souls of the dead across the Styx.

chart /tʃat/, n. 1. a sheet giving information, often in table or graph form. 2. a map, esp. one showing sea and waterways. 3. an outline map showing special information: *a weather chart*. 4. (*usu. pl.*) a list of the best-selling popular records for a particular period. ◇v.t. 5. to make a chart of. 6. to plan a course of action. [F, from L *c(h)arta* paper, from Gk: leaf of paper]

charter /tʃatə/, n. 1. a written instrument or contract, esp. relating to land transfers. 2. **a.** a written undertaking, given by a ruler or law-making body, giving certain rights, etc. **b.** a written grant by a governing power creating a university, company, etc. ◇v.t. 3. to establish by charter. 4. to hire or make available for hire. ◇adj. 5. founded or protected by a charter. 6. hired for a particular purpose or journey: *a charter plane*. [ME, from L]

chartered accountant, n. an accountant who is a member of an institute of accountants given a royal charter.

Charters Towers /tʃatəz ˈtauəz/, n. a city in north eastern Qld, south-west of Townsville; centre of a pastoral and dairying district. Pop. 7208 (1986).

Chartism /ˈtʃatɪzəm/, n. a movement of political reformers active in England from 1838 to 1848, whose principles and demands were set out in the People's Charter. [L *charta* charter + -ISM] –**Chartist**, n., adj.

Chartres /ˈʃatrə/, n. a city in northern France; famous Gothic cathedral. Pop. 77 795 (1985).

chartreuse /ʃaˈtrɜz/, n., adj. clear, light green with a yellowish tinge. [F]

charwoman /ˈtʃawumən/, n., pl. **-women**. a woman hired to do household work. [CHAR² + WOMAN]

chary /ˈtʃɛəri/, adj., **charier**, **chariest**. 1. careful; wary. 2. shy. 3. not giving freely (oft. fol. by *of*): *chary of his praise*. [OE *cearig* sorrowful] –**charily**, adv.

chase¹ /tʃeɪs/, v., **chased**, **chasing**, n. ◇v.t. 1. to follow after quickly in order to seize, overtake, etc. 2. to hunt. 3. to put to flight. ◇v.i. 4. to follow closely: *to chase after someone*. ◇n. 5. the act of chasing; pursuit. 6. the sport of hunting. 7. an area of open land set aside for plants and animals. [ME, from OF, from L: seize]

chase² /tʃeɪs/, n., v., **chased**, **chasing**. ◇n. 1. Also, **chasing**. a groove; lengthened hollow. ◇v.t. 2. to groove. [F, from L: box]

chase³ /tʃeɪs/, v.t., **chased**, **chasing**. to ornament (metal) by engraving or embossing. [F: shrine] –**chaser**, n.

chaser /ˈtʃeɪsə/, *Colloq.* a mild drink taken after a drink of high alcohol content.

chasm /ˈkæzəm/, n. 1. a very deep crack in the earth's surface. 2. a wide difference of feeling, interest, etc., between people, groups, nations. [L, from Gk] –**chasmal**, adj.

chassis /ˈʃæzi/, n., pl. **chassis** /ˈʃæziz/. the frame, wheels, and sometimes machinery of a motor vehicle, on which the body is supported. [F: frame]

chaste /tʃeɪst/, adj. 1. not having had sexual intercourse; virtuous; pure. 2. free from offensiveness; decent: *chaste language*. 3. pure in style; subdued; simple. [ME, from L: pure] –**chastity**, n.

chasten /ˈtʃeɪsən/, v.t. 1. to punish (someone) so as to bring about improvement; chastise. 2. to keep in check; subdue. [OF *chastier*, from L] –**chastener**, n.

chastise or **chastize** /tʃæsˈtaɪz/, v.t., **-tised**, **-tising**. 1. to punish esp. by beating. 2. to find fault with; scold. [ME] –**chastisement**, n. –**chastiser**, n.

chat /tʃæt/, v., **chatted**, **chatting**, n. ◇v.i. 1. to talk together in a familiar or informal

chat 174 **cheek**

manner. ◇v.t. **2.** *Colloq.* to talk persuasively to or flirt with (fol. by *up*): *to chat up a girl.* ◇n. **3.** informal conversation. **4.** (in Australia) any of several small, ground-feeding, insect-eating birds, some of which have metallic call notes. **5.** (elsewhere) any of several birds known for their harsh chattering cries. [short for CHATTER]

chateau /'ʃætou/, *n., pl.* **-teaus, -teaux** /-'touz/. a French castle, or a similar large house. [F, from L]

Chatham Islands /'tʃætəm 'ailəndz/, *n.pl.* an island group in the South Pacific, about 805 km east of and belonging to NZ. Pop. 770 (1983); 963 km².

chattel /'tʃætl/, *n.* **1.** a movable article of property. **2.** (esp. formerly) a slave. [ME, from OF. See CATTLE]

chatter /'tʃætə/, *v.i.* **1.** to make continual, quick sounds, speechlike but meaningless: *the chatter of a monkey.* **2.** to talk rapidly and to little purpose; jabber. **3.** to make a rapid clicking noise by striking together, as the teeth from cold. ◇n. **4.** senseless or foolish talk. **5.** the act or sound of chattering: *the chatter of the machines.* [ME; imitative]

chatterbox /'tʃætəbɒks/, *n.* a very talkative person.

chatty /'tʃæti/, *adj.,* **-tier, -tiest.** given to or full of chat or familiar talk; conversational: *a chatty letter.* **-chattily,** *adv.* **-chattiness,** *n.*

Chaucer /'tʃɔsə/, *n.* **Geoffrey,** 1340?-1400, English poet; described 14th-century life in *The Canterbury Tales.* **-Chaucerian,** *adj., n.*

chauffeur /'ʃoufə, ʃou'fɜ/, *n.* a person employed to drive a private car. [F: stoker, from *chauffer* heat]

Chauvel /ʃɔ'vɛl/, *n.* **1. Charles Edward,** 1897-1959, Australian film producer and director. **2.** his wife, **Elsa** (*Elsie Wilcox*), 1898-1983, Australian film actor, scriptwriter, and producer. **3. Sir Henry George,** ('*Harry*'), 1865-1945, Australian general; a commander in World War I.

chauvinism /'ʃouvənɪzəm/, *n.* **1.** blind and aggressive loyalty to military ideals. **2.** unthinking support of any cause or group: *male chauvinism.* [F; from Nicolas Chauvin, an old soldier and overenthusiastic admirer of Napoleon I] **-chauvinist,** *n., adj.* **-chauvinistic,** *adj.*

cheap /tʃip/, *adj.* **1.** of a relatively low price. **2.** charging low prices: *a very cheap shop.* **3.** of poor quality: *That material is cheap and nasty.* **4.** of small value: *Talk is cheap.* **5.** mean: *cheap conduct.* **6.** obtainable at low interest: *when money is cheap.* ◇adv. **7.** at a low price. ◇n. **8. on the cheap,** *Colloq.* at a low price. [OE *cēap* bargain]

cheapen /'tʃipən/, *v.t.* **1.** to make cheap or cheaper. **2.** to lay open to a charge of worthlessness, esp. of behavior: *to cheapen oneself.*

cheapskate /'tʃipskeit/, *n.* (*offensive*) a mean person.

cheat /tʃit/, *n.* **1.** a deceitful act; swindle; deception. **2.** a person who cheats. ◇v.t. **3.** to take from (somebody) by trickery; swindle (fol. by *of, out of*). **4.** to mislead. **5.** to avoid by or as if by tricks: *to cheat death.* ◇v.i. **6.** to practise trickery: *She would always cheat.* ◇v. **7. cheat on,** *Colloq.* **a.** to deceive. **b.** to be sexually unfaithful to (one's spouse or lover). [ME, var. of *escheat*, from OF: fall to one's share] **-cheater,** *n.*

check /tʃɛk/, *v.t.* **1.** to stop the movement of; suddenly or forcibly. **2.** to hold back or control. **3.** to find out the correctness of; verify. **4.** to leave in someone's care for a short time (fol. by *in*): *You must check in your coat.* **5.** to mark in a pattern of squares. **6.** *Aust Rules.* to keep close watch on one's opposite number, so as to stop them getting or effectively kicking the ball. ◇v.i. **7.** to match accurately: *The reprint checks with the original, item for item.* **8.** to make an inquiry for correctness, etc. (usu. fol. by *up* or *on*): *I'll check up on the matter.* **9.** to make a stop; pause. ◇v. **10. check in,** to record one's arrival, as at a hotel, etc. **11. check out, a.** to leave, as a hotel, etc. **b.** *Colloq.* to have a look at. ◇n. **12.** a person or thing that checks or holds back. **13.** a sudden stoppage; repulse; rebuff. **14.** a control or test with a view to examining the correctness of performance or preventing error. **15.** a means or standard to insure against error, etc. **16.** a pattern formed of squares. **17.** fabric having a check pattern. **18.** *Chess.* the position of the king open to direct attack. **19. in check, a.** under control. **b.** *Chess.* (of a player) having a king which is open to direct attack, or (of the king) being open to direct attack. ◇adj. **20.** serving to check, control, verify, etc. **21.** ornamented with a check pattern; chequered. ◇interj. **22.** *Chess.* (a call to inform one's opponent that his king is in check.) [ME, from OF *eschec*]

checked /tʃɛkt/, *adj.* having a pattern of squares; chequered.

checkers /'tʃɛkəz/, *n.* US. draughts.

checkmate /'tʃɛkmeɪt/, *n., v.,* **-mated, -mating,** *interj.* ◇n. **1.** *Chess.* the act of putting the opponent's king into an inescapable check, thus ending the game. **2.** defeat; overthrow. ◇v.t. **3.** *Chess.* to put (a king) into checkmate. ◇interj. **4.** *Chess.* (the call announcing checkmate). [ME *chek mat*, from Ar *shāh māt* the king is dead]

checkout /'tʃɛkaʊt/, *n.* the cash desk in a supermarket.

checkpoint /'tʃɛkpɔɪnt/, *n.* a place where traffic is stopped for inspection.

checkup /'tʃɛkʌp/, *n.* **1.** an examination as to accuracy, comparison, etc. **2.** a routine overall examination.

cheddar /'tʃɛdə/, *n.* **1.** a smooth white or yellow cheese, with a firm texture. **2. hard** or **stiff cheddar,** *Colloq.* **-- cheese** (def. 3). [*Cheddar*, a town in Somerset, England]

cheek /tʃik/, *n.* **1.** either side of the face below eye level. **2.** a buttock. **3.** one side of the head of a hammer. **4.** *Mach.* either of the sides of a pulley or block. **5.** *Colloq.* boldness;

impudence. **6. cheek by jowl,** close together. **7. turn the other cheek,** to ignore an insult, attack, etc. **8. with one's tongue in one's cheek,** mockingly; insincerely. ◇*v.t.* **9.** *Colloq.* to address rudely. [OE *cēace*]

cheeky /'tʃiki/, *adj.,* **cheekier, cheekiest.** *Colloq.* without respect; insolent: *a cheeky fellow; cheeky behavior.* — **cheekily,** *adv.* — **cheekiness,** *n.*

cheep /tʃip/, *v.i.* **1.** to make weak, high sounds, as a chicken; peep. ◇*n.* **2.** a small, weak sound. [imitative]

cheer /tʃɪə/, *n.* **1.** a shout of encouragement, approval, etc. **2.** joy or gladness; encouragement; comfort: *Her success gave him cheer.* **3. three cheers,** three collective shouts of hooray, to show approval for someone. ◇*v.t.* **4.** to greet with shouts of approval, etc. **5.** to gladden (oft. fol. by *up*): *The news will cheer him up.* **6.** to encourage (oft. fol. by *on*): *We will cheer the team on.* ◇*v.i.* **7.** to utter cheers of approval, etc. **8.** to become cheerful (oft. fol. by *up*). ◇*interj.* **9.** (*pl.*) *Colloq.* to your health. [ME, from OF: face, from LL]

cheerful /'tʃɪəfəl/, *adj.* **1.** in good spirits: *a cheerful person.* **2.** bringing or giving cheer; pleasant; bright: *cheerful surroundings.* **3.** arising from good spirits: *cheerful song.*

cheerio¹ /tʃɪəri'oʊ/, *interj., n., pl.* **-os.** *Colloq.* goodbye.

cheerio² /'tʃɪərioʊ/, *n.* a cocktail frankfurt.

cheery /'tʃɪəri/, *adj.,* **-rier, -riest. 1.** in good spirits; blithe; gay. **2.** too obviously cheerful; over-hearty. **3.** bringing about cheer; enlivening. — **cheerily,** *adv.* — **cheeriness,** *n.*

cheese /tʃiz/, *n.* **1.** the curd of milk separated from the whey and prepared in any of many ways as a food. **2.** a cake or definite mass of this substance. **3. hard or stiff cheese,** *Colloq.* **a.** bad luck. **b.** (a sharp reply to an appeal for sympathy). [OE *cēse*]

cheesecake /'tʃizkeɪk/, *n.* **1.** a kind of open pie filled with a custard-like preparation containing cheese. **2.** *Colloq.* photographs of women displaying their bodies.

cheesecloth /'tʃizklɒθ/, *n.* a coarse cotton material of open weave, originally used in cheese-making.

cheesed-off /tʃizd-'ɒf/, *adj. Colloq.* bored; fed up; annoyed. Also (esp. after the verb), **cheesed off, cheesed.**

cheeseparing /'tʃizpɛərɪŋ/, *adj.* **1.** saving money to a mean degree; parsimonious. ◇*n.* **2.** mean economy.

cheesy¹ /'tʃizi/, *adj.,* **-sier, -siest.** like cheese in taste or texture. — **cheesiness,** *n.*

cheesy² /'tʃizi/, *adj.* forced, usu. insincere: *a cheesy grin.* [from *cheese,* spoken to induce a smile while being photographed]

cheetah /'tʃitə/, *n.* an animal of the cat family, of south-western Asia and Africa, similar to the leopard, and the fastest four-legged animal. Also, **cheetah.** [Hind]

chef /ʃɛf/, *n.* a cook, esp. a head cook. [F. See CHIEF]

chef-d'oeuvre /ʃɛf-'dɜvrə/, *n., pl.* **chefs-d'oeuvre** /ʃɛf-'dɜvrə/. a best work, esp. of an author, painter, etc.

Che Guevara /tʃeɪ gə'varə/, *n.* → Guevara.

cheiro-, different form of **chiro-.**

Chekhov /'tʃɛkɒf/, *n.* **Anton Pavlovich,** 1860-1904, Russian short-story writer and dramatist; wrote *The Three Sisters* (1901) and *The Cherry Orchard* (1904). Also, **Tchekhoff.** — **Chekhovian,** *adj.*

chem-, a word part meaning 'chemical' used before vowels. Also (esp. before a consonant), **chemo-.**

chemical /'kɛmɪkəl/, *adj.* **1.** of or concerned with the science of chemistry. ◇*n.* **2.** a substance produced by or used in a chemical process.

chemical engineering, *n.* the science concerned with the development and use of chemical processes in industry.

chemical equation, *n.* a representation of a chemical reaction in symbols.

chemical reaction, *n.* a process involving two or more substances in which their molecular constitution is changed.

chemical warfare, *n.* warfare with poisonous gases, defoliants, etc.

chemise /ʃə'miz/, *n.* a woman's loose-fitting shirt-like undergarment or shift. [F, from LL *camisia* shirt (prob. from Celtic)]

chemist /'kɛmɪst/, *n.* **1.** a scientist whose particular area of study and research is chemistry. **2.** a shop where medicines and cosmetics, etc., are sold. **3.** someone trained in pharmacy. [var. of ALCHEMIST]

chemistry /'kɛmɪstri/, *n., pl.* **-tries. 1.** the science concerned with the composition of substances, the basic forms of matter and the interactions between them. **2.** chemical properties of a substance, etc.: *chemistry of carbon; chemistry of food.* [CHEMIST + -RY]

chemo-, variant of **chem-** used esp. before a consonant.

chemosynthesis /kɛmoʊ'sɪnθəsəs/, *n. Bot.* the production by plants of food substances from carbon dioxide and water with energy from other chemical reactions. — **chemosynthetic,** *adj.*

chemotaxis /kɛmoʊ'tæksəs/, *n.* the property in a cell or organism, showing attraction or repulsion to chemical substances.

chemotherapy /kɛmoʊ'θɛrəpi/, *n.* the treatment of disease using chemicals, esp. in treating cancer. — **chemotherapist,** *n.*

chemurgy /'kɛmədʒi/, *n.* a branch of applied chemistry concerned with the industrial use of organic substances, esp. farm products. — **chemurgic, chemurgical,** *adj.*

Chengdu /tʃɛŋ'du/, *n.* a walled city in central China, the capital of Sichuan province. Pop. 1 523 400 (1985 est.). Formerly, **Chengtu.**

chenille /ʃə'nil/, *n.* **1.** (a fabric with weft of) velvety yarn, used in embroidery, fringes,

chenille

etc. **2.** usu. unbleached cotton, where lines of short tufts of cotton have been added to form a pattern; used for bedspreads, etc.

cheongsam /tʃɒŋˈsæm/, *n*. a straight dress with a slit skirt, oft. made of silk, and originally worn by Chinese women. [Chinese *ch'ang shan* long jacket]

Cheops /ˈkiːɒps/, *n*. fl. c. 2700 BC, king of Egypt, of the fourth dynasty; builder of great pyramid at Al Jizah. Also, **Khufu**.

cheque /tʃek/, *n*. *Banking*. a written order, usu. on a standard printed form, asking a bank to pay a certain amount of money to a particular person. It may be either *crossed* (payable only through a bank account), or *uncrossed* (payable on demand). [altered spelling of CHECK]

cheque account, *n*. a bank account from which money may be withdrawn by cheque at any time by the customer.

chequer /ˈtʃekə/, *n*. a pattern of squares. [ME, from AF: chessboard]

chequered /ˈtʃekəd/, *adj*. **1.** marked in squares. **2.** marked by many changes in character or fortune: *a chequered career*.

Chequers /ˈtʃekəz/, *n*. the British prime minister's official country house, situated near Aylesbury in Buckinghamshire.

cherish /ˈtʃerɪʃ/, *v.t*. **1.** to hold or treat (something) as dear: *She cherished her freedom*. **2.** to care for tenderly; nurture. **3.** to cling to (ideas, etc.). [ME, from F *cher* dear, from L *cārus*]

Chernobyl /ˈtʃənɒbɪl, tʃəˈnoʊbəl/, *n*. a city in Ukraine, near Kiev; site of an accident at a nuclear plant in 1986, resulting in a large amount of radiation being released into the atmosphere.

Cherokee /ˈtʃerəki, ˌtʃerəˈkiː/, *n*., *pl*. **-kee**, **-kees**. **1.** a member of an important tribe of North American Indians of Iroquoian family whose present centre is Oklahoma. **2.** an Iroquoian language.

cheroot /ʃəˈruːt/, *n*. a cigar with cut ends. [F, from Tamil: a roll]

cherry /ˈtʃeri/, *n*., *pl*. **-ries**, *adj*. ◇*n*. **1.** a type of small, round, juicy, stone fruit varying in color from pink to black. **2.** (the wood of) the tree bearing this fruit. **3.** a bright red color. ◇*adj*. **4.** bright red. [ME, backformation from OE *ciris* (the -s being taken for plural sign), from VL from L: cherry tree, from Gk *kerasós*]

cherub /ˈtʃerəb/, *n*., *pl*. **cherubim** /ˈtʃerəbɪm, ˈkeː-/ for def. 1; **cherubs** for def. 2. **1.** *Bible*. a powerful spiritual being or angel, shown in later art as a child with wings. **2.** a child with a chubby, innocent face. [OE *cherubin*, pl., ult. from Heb: sing.] —**cherubic**, *adj*.

chess /tʃes/, *n*. a game played by two people, each with 16 pieces called chessmen, on a chequered board. [ME, from OF]

chest /tʃest/, *n*. **1.** the part of the body from the neck to the stomach, enclosed by ribs and diaphragm; thorax. **2.** a box, usu. a large, strong one, with hinges and a lock for the safekeeping of valuables. **3.** a box for the

176

chiasma

storage of certain goods: *medicine chest*; *tea-chest*. **4. get (something) off one's chest**, to talk about something that is worrying one. [OE *cest, cist*, from L, from Gk: box]

Chesterton /ˈtʃestətən/, *n*. **G(ilbert) K(eith)**, 1874–1936, English essayist, critic, and novelist; author of the *Father Brown* detective stories.

chestnut /ˈtʃesnʌt/, *n*. **1.** (the edible nut of) a tree of the beech family. **2.** any of various fruits or trees like the chestnut, esp. the horse chestnut. **3.** a reddish brown color. **4.** a horse of this color. **5.** *Colloq*. an old or stale joke, anecdote, etc. ◇*adj*. **6.** reddish brown. [obs. *chesten* chestnut (OE *cisten-*, from WGmc, from L, from Gk *kastanéa*) + NUT]

chevalier /ˌʃevəˈlɪə, ʃəˈvæljeɪ/, *n*. **1.** a member of certain orders of honor: *chevalier of the Legion of Honor of France*. **2.** a knight; cavalier. [ME, from OF *chevalier*, from *cheval* horse, from L]

chevon /ˈʃevɒn/, *n*. the meat of the goat used as food. [F *chèvre* goat]

chevron /ˈʃevrən/, *n*. a badge with V-shaped stripes, worn on the sleeve of a police or armed forces uniform, etc., to show rank, etc. [F: rafter, chevron, from F: goat, from L]

chew /tʃuː/, *v.t*. **1.** to bite and crush with the teeth; masticate. **2.** to damage or destroy by or as if by chewing (fol. by *up*): *This machine has chewed up the carpet*. **3.** to think about; consider deliberately (fol. by *over*): *I'll chew this idea over*. ◇*v.i*. **4.** to perform the act of crushing or grinding with the teeth. ◇*n*. **5.** the act of chewing. [OE *cēowan*]

chewing gum, *n*. a sticky substance for chewing, usu. made of sweetened and flavored chicle. Also, *Colloq*. **chewie**.

chewy /ˈtʃuːi/, *adj*. needing much chewing; tough: *This steak is very chewy*.

Cheyenne /ʃaɪˈæn/, *n*., *pl*. **-enne**, **-ennes**. a member of a plains tribe of Algonquian linguistic stock; now divided between Montana (**Northern Cheyenne**) and Oklahoma (**Southern Cheyenne**).

chez /ʃeɪ/, *prep*. at the home of. [F]

chg., *Abbrev*. *Comm*. charge.

chiack /ˈtʃaɪæk/, *Colloq*. *v.t*. **1.** to make fun of (someone); taunt; deride; tease. ◇*n*. **2.** cheek; jeering. Also, **chyack**. [Brit *chi-hike*, a salute, exclamation]

Chiang Kai-shek /ˌtʃæŋ kaɪˈʃek/, *n*. → **Jiang Jie-shi**.

Chiang Mai /tʃæŋ ˈmaɪ/, *n*. a city in north-western Thailand. Pop. 100 000 (1975). Also, **Chiengmai**.

chiaroscuro /kiˌɑːrəˈskjʊəroʊ/, *n*., *pl*. **-ros**. the treatment of light and shade in a picture or sketch to give a feeling of depth, often without colors. [It *chiaro-oscuro* bright-dark]

chiasma /kaɪˈæzmə/, *n*., *pl*. **-mata** /-mətə/. *Biol*. a crossing point in chromosomes which are conjugating (joining). [NL from Gk: arrangement in the form of the Greek letter *chi* (X)] —**chiasmal**, **chiasmic**, *adj*.

chic /ʃik/, *adj.* **1.** cleverly attractive in style; stylish. ◇*n.* **2.** cleverly attractive style, esp. in dress. [F]

Chicago /ʃəˈkagoʊ/, *n.* a city in the US, in north-eastern Illinois; a port on Lake Michigan. Pop. 3 009 530 (1986 est.). —**Chicagoan**, *n.*

chicanery /ʃəˈkeɪnəri/, *n., pl.* **-ries.** the (use of) legal tricks or misleading arguments. See **sophistry**.

chick /tʃɪk/, *n.* **1.** a young chicken or other bird. **2.** a child. **3.** *Colloq.* a young woman.

chicken /ˈtʃɪkən/, *n.* **1.** a young hen or rooster (or the young of certain other birds). **2.** a hen or rooster of any age, or its flesh. **3.** *Colloq.* a young person. **4.** *Colloq.* a coward. **5. play chicken,** to do something dangerous because of a dare. **6. count one's chickens before they are hatched,** *Colloq.* to act on the basis of something which has not yet happened. ◇*adj.* **7.** *Colloq.* lacking courage. ◇*v.* **8. chicken out,** to withdraw because of lack of courage, etc. [OE *cicen, ciken*]

chickenfeed /ˈtʃɪkənfid/, *n. Colloq.* **1.** a small or almost worthless sum of money. **2.** anything or anybody almost worthless.

chickenpox /ˈtʃɪkənpɒks/, *n. Med.* a viral disease, commonly of children, which causes fever and small blisters.

chicken wire, *n.* light wire netting used as fencing for chickens, for protecting vegetable gardens, etc. Also, **chicken mesh.**

chickpea /ˈtʃɪkpi/, *n.* **1.** a plant of the legume family, bearing pods with pealike seeds used for food. **2.** its seeds. [earlier *chich (pease)*, from F *(pois) chiche*, from L *cicer* vetch]

chickweed /ˈtʃɪkwid/, *n.* a common weed with small, white flowers.

chicle /ˈtʃɪkəl/, *n.* a sticky substance made from the juice of a tropical American tree, used to make chewing gum, etc. Also, **chicle gum.** [Amer Sp, from Nahuatl]

chicory /ˈtʃɪkəri/, *n., pl.* **-ries.** a blue-flowered herb, the leaves of which may be used in salads, while the roasted, powdered roots are added to coffee. [F, from L, from Gk]

chide /tʃaɪd/, *v.i.* **chided** or **chid; chided, chid** or **chidden; chiding.** to scold; find fault. [OE *cīdan*] —**chidingly**, *adv.*

chief /tʃif/, *n.* **1.** the head or ruler of a group of people, tribe, organisation, etc. **2.** *Colloq.* boss. ◇*adj.* **3.** highest in rank or authority. **4.** most important: *his chief merit; the chief difficulty.* [ME, from L: head]

chiefly /ˈtʃifli/, *adv.* **1.** above all; principally. **2.** mainly; mostly.

chieftain /ˈtʃiftən/, *n.* the leader of a clan or a tribe. [ME, from LL] —**chieftaincy, chieftainship,** *n.*

chiffon /ʃəˈfɒn, ˈʃɪfɒn/, *n.* **1.** a sheer light material made of silk, nylon, or rayon. ◇*adj.* **2.** (of food) made light, usu. by adding beaten egg-whites. [F *chiffe* rag]

chiffonier /ʃɪfəˈnɪə/, *n.* a high chest of drawers. [F]

Chifley /ˈtʃɪfli/, *n.* **(Joseph) Ben(edict)**, 1885–1951, Australian Labor politician; federal treasurer 1941–49, prime minister 1945–49.

chignon /ˈʃɪnjɒn/, *n.* a large coil of hair, worn at the back of the head by women. [F, from L: chain]

chihuahua /tʃəˈwawə, ʃəˈwawə/, *n.* a Mexican breed of very small dog.

chil-, another form of **chilo-,** used before vowels.

chilblain /ˈtʃɪlbleɪn/, *n.* (*usu. pl.*) *Med.* a swelling on the hands or feet caused by being too long exposed to cold conditions. [CHIL(L) + *blain* swelling, from OE]

child /tʃaɪld/, *n., pl.* **children. 1.** a boy or girl; infant. **2.** *Law.* a young person under a certain age determined by statute. Depending upon the purpose, this age may be set at 17, 18, or 21 years. **3.** a childish person. **4.** a son or daughter. **5.** any descendant. **6.** any person or thing seen as the product of a particular influence, etc.: *Satan's followers are the children of darkness.* **7. with child,** pregnant. [ME *child*, pl. *childre(n)*, OE *cild*, pl. *cild(ru)*]

Child /tʃaɪld/, *n.* **Joan**, Australian federal Labor politician; first ALP woman to be elected to the House of Representatives (1974).

child abuse, *n.* physical or emotional ill-treatment of a child, esp. by a parent.

childbirth /ˈtʃaɪldbɜθ/, *n.* → **parturition.**

Childe /tʃaɪld/, *n.* **Vere Gordon** /vɪə/, 1892–1957, Australian archaeologist, working mainly in Britain.

childhood /ˈtʃaɪldhʊd/, *n.* **1.** the time of being a child. **2. second childhood,** childishness in old age; senility.

childish /ˈtʃaɪldɪʃ/, *adj.* **1.** of, or like a child. **2.** stupid; silly; immature. [OE *cildisc*]

childproof /ˈtʃaɪldpruf/, *adj.* made so that it cannot be opened or damaged by children.

children /ˈtʃɪldrən/, *n.* plural of **child.**

Chile /ˈtʃɪli/, *n.* a republic in South America, extending along the Pacific coast from Peru and Bolivia to Cape Horn, bounded by the Andes mountains to the east; a Spanish colony before independence in 1818. Pop. 12 475 000 (1987 est.); 756 626 km². *Language:* Spanish. *Currency:* peso. *Cap.:* Santiago. —**Chilean,** *n., adj.*

chili /ˈtʃɪli/, *n., pl.* **-ies.** → **chilli.**

chiliad /ˈkɪliæd/, *n.* one thousand. **2.** a thousand years. [Gk *chēlioi* thousand]

chill /tʃɪl/, *n.* **1.** coldness, esp. a moderate but penetrating coldness. **2.** a feeling of cold, usu. with shivering. **3.** a cold stage, as a first sign of illness. **4.** a discouraging feeling. **5.** coldness of manner, lack of friendliness. ◇*adj.* **6.** chilly. ◇*v.i.* **7.** to become cold. ◇*v.t.* **8.** to affect with cold; make chilly. **9.** to make cool, but not freeze: *to chill wines.* **10.** to harden (metal) by sudden cooling. **11.** to discourage; depress: *chill his hopes.* [OE *ciele, cile* coolness] —**chilled,** *adj.*

chilli /ˈtʃɪli/, *n., pl.* **-ies. 1.** the fruit of some varieties of capsicum, usu. small and hot

chilli to the taste. **2.** capsicum having such a fruit, sometimes grown as a decorative plant. Also, **chili, chilli pepper.** [Amer Sp, from Nahuatl]

chilly /'tʃɪli/, *adj.*, **-ier, -iest**, *adv.* ◇*adj.* **1.** producing a feeling of cold; causing shivering. **2.** feeling cold; sensitive to cold. **3.** without warmth of feeling; unfriendly: *a chilly look*. —**chilliness**, *n.*

chilo-, word part meaning 'lip', 'labial'. [Gk *cheilo-*, combining form of *cheilos* lip]

Chimbu /'tʃɪmbu/, *n.* a province in central PNG. Pop. 186 400 (1986 est.); 6100 km^2. *Administrative Centre:* Kundiawa. Also, **Simbu**.

chime /tʃaɪm/, *n.*, *v.*, **chimed, chiming**. ◇*n.* **1.** an arrangement for striking a bell or bells to make a musical sound and the sound so made: *a door chime; the chime of Big Ben.* **2.** a set of upright metal tubes struck with a hammer, and the sound so made. **3.** → **carillon**. ◇*v.i.* **4.** to sound in harmony like a set of bells. **5.** to make a musical sound by striking a bell, etc.; ring chimes. **6.** to agree. ◇*v.t.* **7.** to make (music, etc.), as a bell or bells. **8.** to strike (a bell, etc.), so as to produce a musical sound. **9.** to show (the hour, etc.) by chiming. ◇*v.* **10. chime in**, to break suddenly into a conversation, esp. to show agreement. [OE, from L *cymbalum* cymbal]

chimera /kɪ'mɪərə, kə-/, *n.*, *pl.* **-ras**. **1.** *Greek Mythology.* (oft. *cap.*) a fire-breathing monster, with a lion's head, goat's body, and serpent's tail. **2.** an impossible, wild idea. [L, from Gk *chimaira* lit., she-goat]

chimerical /kaɪ'merɪkəl, kə-/, *adj.* **1.** unreal; imaginary; visionary. **2.** wildly fanciful. Also, **chimeric**.

chimney /'tʃɪmni/, *n.*, *pl.* **-neys**. **1.** a structure, usu. vertical, containing a passage or flue through which the smoke, gases, etc. of a fire or furnace escape. **2.** that part of such a structure which rises above a roof. **3.** a glass tube, around the flame of a lamp. **4.** *Mountaineering.* a narrow opening in a rock face. [ME, from L: furnace, from Gk]

chimneysweep /'tʃɪmniswɪp/, *n.* someone whose job it is to clean out chimneys.

chimpanzee /tʃɪmpæn'zi/, *n.* a small, clever ape of equatorial Africa. Also, **Colloq. chimp**. [a Bantu language in Angola, W Africa]

chin /tʃɪn/, *n.* **1.** the lower part of the face, below the mouth. **2.** the point of the lower jaw. **3. keep one's chin up**, to remain cheerful under trying conditions. **4. take it on the chin**, to take suffering or punishment bravely. [OE *cin*]

Chin, Chinese.

china /'tʃaɪnə/, *n.* **1.** porcelain (orig. from China) used for making dishes, etc. **2.** plates, cups, etc., collectively: *Bring out the best china.* ◇*adj.* **3.** made of china.

China /'tʃaɪnə/, *n.* a republic in eastern Asia, bordering many countries including Russia to the north and with a long Pacific coast; the most populous and the third largest country in the world; a republic since 1911; a socialist republic since 1949 when the previous nationalist government retreated to the island of Taiwan. Pop. 1 064 135 000 (1987 est.); 9 561 000 km^2. *Language:* Chinese (many dialects, chiefly Mandarin). *Currency:* yuan. *Cap.:* Beijing. Chinese, **Zhongguo**. Official name, **People's Republic of China**. **2. Republic of**, the name adopted by the Nationalist Chinese for **Taiwan**.

China Sea /tʃaɪnə 'si/, *n.* a western part of the Pacific, divided by Taiwan Strait into the South and East China Seas.

chinchilla /tʃɪn'tʃɪlə/, *n.* **1.** a small South American rodent whose skin is used as a fur. **2.** a thick, woollen fabric. [Sp: little bug]

chine /tʃaɪn/, *n.* **1.** (a cut of meat from) the backbone. **2.** a ridge of land. ◇*v.t.* **3.** to cut along or across the backbone. [ME, from OF, from Gmc]

Chinese cabbage, /tʃaɪˌniz 'kæbɪdʒ/ *n.* a tall, yellow-white, closely-leaved vegetable, like a head of celery but more leafy; celery cabbage.

Chinese gooseberry, *n.* a (vine bearing) round, hairy fruit about 7 cm long with a gooseberry-like flavor; Kiwi fruit.

Chinese Revolution, *n.* **1.** the nationalist revolt, 1911–12, which overthrew the Manchu dynasty and created a Chinese republic. **2.** the period during which, under Mao Zedong, China became a communist republic, esp. the 1940s and early 1950s. **3.** → **Cultural Revolution**.

chink[1] /tʃɪŋk/, *n.* **1.** a crack; fissure. **2.** a narrow opening. [OE *cinu, cine* crack, fissure + *-k*, suffix. See **-OCK**]

chink[2] /tʃɪŋk/, *v.i., v.t.* **1.** to make, or cause to make, a short, sharp, ringing sound, as of coins or glasses striking together. ◇*n.* **2.** a chinking sound. [imitative]

Chino-, combining form meaning 'Chinese'.

Chinook /tʃə'nuk, -'nuk/, *n.*, *pl.* **-nook, -nooks**. **1. Lower Chinook** and **Upper Chinook**, (*pl.*) North American Indian tribes of the Columbia River. **2.** a member of these tribes.

chintz /tʃɪnts/, *n.*, *pl.* **chintzes**. printed cotton material, usu. shiny, used esp. for curtains and furniture coverings. [Hind *chīnt*] —**chintzy**, *adj.*

chip /tʃɪp/, *n.*, *v.*, **chipped, chipping**. ◇*n.* **1.** a small piece, as of wood or china, separated by chopping, cutting, or breaking. **2.** a very small piece, as of food, etc.: *chocolate chips*. **3. a.** a deep-fried finger of potato. **b.** a very thin slice of potato fried and eaten cold as a snack; crisp. **4.** a gap made by chipping: *There's a chip in this cup*. **5.** *Games.* a flat plastic object used as a counter in certain card games, etc. **6.** *Elect.* a tiny square of semiconductor material, with an electrical circuit etched on it, used in computers, etc. **7.** wood, straw, etc., in thin strips for weaving into hats, baskets, etc. **8. cash in one's chips**, *Colloq.* to die. **9. have had one's chips**, *Colloq.* to be finished, beaten. **10. a chip off the old block**, *Colloq.* a person much like one or both parents. **11. a chip on the shoulder**, *Colloq.* a long-standing resentment; grievance. **12. the chips are down**, *Colloq.* the point of decision has been

chip

reached. ◇*v.t.* **13.** to cut with an axe, chisel, etc. **14.** *Agric.* to use a hoe, etc., to weed without disturbing the soil surface. **15.** to cut or break off (a bit of something). **16.** to make a mark by breaking off a bit of (something). **17.** to cut potatoes into chips. **18.** to shape or produce by cutting away pieces. **19.** to taunt, poke fun at. ◇*v.i.* **20.** to break off in small pieces; to become chipped. ◇*v.* **21. chip in**, *Colloq.* **a.** to put in money, help, etc. **b.** to interrupt, enter uninvited into another's conversation. [OE *cippian*]

chipboard /'tʃɪpbɔd/, *n.* **1.** a board made from waste wood, sawdust, resin etc., used in sheets for light structural work. **2.** a board, usu. made of wastepaper, used in box-making, etc. Also, **particle board.**

chip heater, *n.* a water heater which burns wood chips.

chipmunk /'tʃɪpmʌŋk/, *n.* any of various small striped squirrels from North America and Asia. [N Amer Ind: squirrel]

Chipp /tʃɪp/, *n.* **Don(ald Leslie)**, born 1925, Australian federal politician; one of the founders of the Australian Democrats party and its parliamentary leader 1977–86.

Chippendale /'tʃɪpəndeɪl/, *n.* **Thomas**, 1718?–79, English cabinet-maker and furniture designer.

Chirico /'kirikoʊ/, *n.* **Giorgio de**, 1888–1978, Greek-born metaphysical painter working mainly in Italy; important forerunner of surrealism.

chiro-, a word part meaning 'hand', as in *chiropractic*. [Gk *cheiro-*, combining form of *cheír*]

chirography /kaɪ'rɒgrəfi/, *n.* → **handwriting**.

chiropody /kə'rɒpədi/, *n.* the treatment of minor foot problems, such as corns, bunions, etc. [CHIRO- + Gk *-podia*, from *poús* foot] –**chiropodist**, *n.*

chiropractic /kaɪrə'præktɪk/, *n.* a body-healing system based upon the idea that disease is caused by something being wrong with the nerves in the spine, and can therefore be cured by adjustments to the segments of the spinal column. [CHIRO- + Gk *praktikós* practical]

chiropractor /'kaɪrəpræktə/, *n.* someone who practises chiropractic.

chirp /tʃɜp/, *v.i.* **1.** to make a short, sharp sound, as small birds and certain insects. ◇*v.t.* **2.** to sound or talk in a chirping manner. ◇*n.* **3.** a chirping sound.

chirpy /'tʃɜpi/, *adj. Colloq.* cheerful; lively; gay. –**chirpily**, *adv.*

chirrup /'tʃɪrəp/, *v.*, **-ruped, -ruping**, *n.* → **chirp**. [var. of CHIRP]

chisel /'tʃɪzəl/, *n., v.*, **-elled, -elling.** ◇*n.* **1.** a long, thin, steel tool, with a cutting edge at one end, used to cut or shape wood, stone, etc. ◇*v.t.* **2.** to cut, shape, etc., with a chisel. **3.** *Colloq.* **a.** to cheat; swindle. **b.** to get by cheating. ◇*v.i.* **4.** to work with a chisel. **5.** *Colloq.* to use trickery; cheat. [ME, from L: cut] –**chiseller**, *n.* –**chiselled**, *adj.*

chloroform

Chisholm /'tʃɪzəm/, *n.* **Caroline**, 1808–77, English-born welfare worker and philanthropist in Australia; best known for her work with immigrant women.

chit[1] /tʃɪt/, *n.* **1.** a voucher showing money owed for food, drink, etc. **2.** a voucher allowing admittance to a restricted area, as a military base. **3.** a note; short memorandum. [Hind *chitthi*]

chit[2] /tʃɪt/, *n.* a young person, esp. an impudent girl: *She's a chit of a girl*. [? akin to KITTEN]

chitchat /'tʃɪttʃæt/, *n.* **1.** small talk. **2.** gossip. [varied reduplication of CHAT]

chitin /'kaɪtɪn/, *n. Biol.* a horny organic substance which is in the outer surface of insects and some shellfish, etc. [F, from Gk: tunic] –**chitinous**, *adj.*

chiton /'kaɪtən, -tɒn/, *n.* a small, round mollusc, which sticks to rocks. [Gk]

Chittagong /'tʃɪtəgɒŋ/, *n.* a seaport in eastern Bangladesh, near the Bay of Bengal. Pop. 1 388 476 (1981).

chivalry /'ʃɪvəlri/, *n. Europ Hist.* **1.** the ideal characteristics of a knight, such as courtesy, generosity, bravery, etc. **2.** the rules and customs of the system of medieval knighthood. [ME, from OF *chevalier* CHEVALIER] –**chivalrous**, *adj.*

chive /tʃaɪv/, *n.* a small bulbous plant, of the leek and onion family, with long, thin leaves which are used as a herb in cookery. Also, **chive garlic**. [ME, from L: onion]

chivvy /'tʃɪvi/, *v.t.*, **-ied, -ying**. to worry; nag. [? short for 'Chevy Chase' in a Scot ballad]

chlor-[1], a word part meaning 'green', as in *chlorine*. Also, **chloro-**[1]. [Gk, combining form of *chlōrós*]

chlor-[2], a combining form indicating 'chlorine'. Also, **chloro-**[2].

chloride /'klɔraɪd/, *n.* a compound of two elements only, one of which is chlorine. See **-ide**.

chlorinate /'klɔrəneɪt, 'klɒ-/, *v.t.*, **-nated, -nating**. **1.** *Chem.* to combine or treat with chlorine. **2.** to disinfect (water) by using chlorine. –**chlorination**, *n.* –**chlorinator**, *n.*

chlorine /'klɔrin/, *n.* a greenish-yellow gaseous non-burning element, poisonous and very irritating to the nose and lungs. It is used as a powerful bleach used in industry. *Symbol:* Cl; *at. no.:* 17; *at. wt:* 35.453. [CHLOR-[1] + -INE[2]]

chlorite /'klɔraɪt/, *n.* one of a group of minerals consisting of hydrous silicates of aluminium, ferrous iron, and magnesium, occurring in green platelike crystals or scales, and common in some metamorphic rocks. [Gk *chlōrítis* kind of green stone]

chloro-[1], another form of **chlor-**[1], used before consonants, as in *chlorophyll*.

chloro-[2], another form of **chlor-**[2], used before consonants, as in *chloroform*.

chloroform /'klɒrəfɔm/, *n.* **1.** a colorless volatile liquid, $CHCl_3$, used as a solvent and formerly as an anaesthetic. ◇v.t. **2.** to anaesthetise with chloroform. [CHLORO-² + FORM(YL)]

chlorophyll /ˈklɒrəfil/, n. Bot, Biochem. the green coloring substance of leaves and plants, which traps the energy of sunlight. It is necessary for the production of carbohydrates by photosynthesis, and is used as a dye for cosmetics and oils. [CHLORO-¹ + -PHYLL]

chloroplast /ˈklɒrəplæst/, n. a complex cell mass containing chlorophyll, where photosynthesis (in a plant) takes place.

chock /tʃɒk/, n. **1.** a block or piece of wood, etc., for filling in a space, esp. one placed under a wheel to prevent movement. ◇v.t. **2.** to furnish with or secure by a chock or chocks. ◇adv. **3.** as close or tight as possible: *chock against the edge*. [ONF *choque* log or block of wood]

choco /ˈtʃoʊkoʊ/, n. Colloq. member of the Australian militia or a conscripted soldier in World War I. Also, **chocko**. [from *The Chocolate Soldier*, operetta by Oscar Strauss]

chocolate /ˈtʃɒklət, ˈtʃɒkələt/, n. **1.** a preparation of cacao seeds husked, roasted, and ground (without removing any fat), often sweetened and flavored with vanilla, etc. **2.** a drink or sweet made from this. **3.** a dark brown color. ◇adj. **4.** made with or from chocolate. **5.** having the color of chocolate. [Sp, from Nahuatl *chocolatl* bitter water]

Choctaw /ˈtʃɒktɔː/, n., pl. **-taw, -taws.** (pl.) a large Muskhogean tribe of North American Indians, formerly living chiefly in southern Mississippi, now in Oklahoma.

CHOGM /ˈtʃɒgəm/, n. Commonwealth Heads of Government Meeting; the meeting of the Commonwealth of Nations leaders, held every two years.

choice /tʃɔɪs/, n., adj., **choicer, choicest.** ◇n. **1.** the act of choosing; selection. **2.** the power of choosing; option. *What I decide to do is my choice.* **3.** the person or thing chosen: *This book is my choice.* **4.** a great number and variety from which to choose: *a wide choice of candidates.* **5.** that which is liked more; the best part of anything. **6.** an alternative. **7.** a well-chosen supply. ◇adj. **8.** worthy of being chosen; excellent; superior: *a choice apple.* **9.** carefully chosen: *delivered in choice words.* **10. choice language,** Colloq. colorfully rude language. [ME, from OF *choisir* choose, of Gmc orig.]

choir /ˈkwaɪə/, n. **1.** an organised group of singers, esp. used in a church service. **2.** any large group or band, or a part of one: *a string choir.* **3.** that part of a church used by the singers. [ME, from L *chorus.* See CHORUS]

choke /tʃoʊk/, v., **choked, choking,** n. ◇v.t. **1.** to stop the breath of, by squeezing or blocking the windpipe; strangle; stifle; suffocate. **2.** to stop the breath or speech, etc., by or as by strangling or stifling. **3.** to stop the growth or action of: *to choke off discussion.* **4.** to stop by filling; obstruct; congest. **5.** to fill to the top. **6.** (in internal-combustion engines) to enrich the fuel mixture by decreasing the air to the carburettor to help in starting a motor, etc. **7. choke down,** to swallow with difficulty. ◇v.i. **8.** to suffer strangling or suffocation. **9.** to be blocked or clogged. **10.** to be temporarily overcome with emotion. ◇n. **11.** the act or sound of choking. **12.** (in internal-combustion engines) the device by which the air supply to a carburettor is decreased or stopped. **13.** Mach. any device which, by blocking a passage, controls the flow of air, etc. [OE *acēocian*]

choker /ˈtʃoʊkə/, n. **1.** a close-fitting necklace or band. **2.** Colloq. a high, tight collar.

choko /ˈtʃoʊkoʊ/, n. a (perennial vine bearing) pear-shaped green fruit used as a vegetable. Also, **chayote.**

chol-, a word part meaning 'gall' or 'bile'. Also, **chole-, cholo-.** [Gk, combining form of *cholē* bile]

cholecystectomy /ˌkɒləsɪsˈtɛktəmi/, n., pl. **-mies.** the removal of the gall bladder.

choler /ˈkɒlə/, n. anger; wrath; irritability. [LL *cholera* bile, from Gk: name of the disease]

cholera /ˈkɒlərə/, n. any of several diseases of the digestive tract, esp. Asian cholera, marked by diarrhoea, vomiting, cramp, etc., which can lead to death. [L, from Gk] —**choleraic,** adj.

choleric /ˈkɒlərɪk/, adj. showing a quick temper; angry.

cholesterol /kəˈlɛstərɒl/, n. Biochem. an organic compound found in the liver, blood and brain, the yolk of eggs, and elsewhere. A high level of cholesterol in the bloodstream has been linked to a greater risk of heart and artery disease. [CHOL(E)- + Gk *ster(eós)* solid]

cholo-, variant of **chol-** before consonants.

Chomsky /ˈtʃɒmski/, n. **Noam,** born 1928, US linguist and political observer and critic; put forward the influential theory of syntactic structure known as transformational, or generative, grammar.

Chongqing /tʃʊŋˈtʃɪŋ/, n. a long-established city (third millenium BC) in south-western China in Sichuan province at the meeting of the Chang and Jialing rivers. Pop. 2 030 800 (1985 est.). Formerly, **Ch'ung-ch'ing, Chungking, Pahsien.**

chook /tʃʊk/, n. Colloq. domestic fowl. Also, **chookie, chooky.** [Brit d., imitative]

choose /tʃuːz/, v., **chose, choosing.** ◇v.t. (old form) **1.** to select from a number of things or persons. **2.** to prefer and decide (to do something): *He chose to stand for election.* **3.** to want; desire. ◇v.i. **4.** to make a choice. [OE *cēosan*] —**chooser,** n.

choosy /ˈtʃuːzi/, adj. Colloq. hard to please; particular, esp. in making a choice: *choosy about food.* Also, **choosey.**

chop¹ /tʃɒp/, v., **chopped, chopping,** n. ◇v.t. **1.** to cut with a quick, heavy blow or blows, using an axe, etc. **2.** to make by so cutting. **3.** to cut in pieces. **4.** *Tennis, Cricket, etc.* to hit (a ball) downwards with bat or racquet at an angle. **5.** Colloq. to dismiss; give the sack to; fire. ◇v.i. **6.** to make a quick heavy

chop

stroke or strokes, as with an axe. ◇v. **7. chop off**, *Colloq.* to finish suddenly. ◇n. **8.** the act of chopping. **9.** a short, downward cutting blow. **10.** *Colloq.* a share, cut (def. 41): *in for one's chop*. **11.** a piece chopped off. **12.** a slice of mutton, lamb, veal, pork, etc. containing some bone. **13.** the short, irregular, broken motion of waves. **14.** a stretch of water with this wave formation. **15. get the chop,** *Colloq.* **a.** to be killed. **b.** to be put off from work. [var. of CHAP[1]]

chop[2] /tʃɒp/, *v.i.*, **chopped, chopping.** to turn, shift, or change suddenly, as the wind: *to chop and change*. [OE *cēapian*]

chop[3] /tʃɒp/, *n. (pl.)* the jaw. [? special use of CHOP[1]]

chop[4] /tʃɒp/, *n. in the phrase* **not much chop**, *Colloq.* no good. [Hind: impression, stamp]

Chopin /ˈʃoʊpæ̃/, *n.* **Frédéric François**, 1810–49, Polish-French pianist and composer of chiefly piano works; noted for his lyric compositions.

chopper /ˈtʃɒpə/, *n.* **1.** someone or something that chops. **2.** a short axe with a large blade used for cutting up meat, etc.; a butcher's cleaver. **3.** *(pl.) Colloq.* the teeth. **4.** *Colloq.* a helicopter. **5.** a bike with wide, high handlebars.

choppy /ˈtʃɒpi/, *adj.*, **-pier, -piest. 1.** (of the sea, etc.) forming short, irregular, broken waves. **2.** (of the wind) changing suddenly or irregularly; variable.

chopstick /ˈtʃɒpstɪk/, *n.* one of a pair of thin sticks, of wood or ivory, used by the Chinese, etc., to bring food to the mouth. [Pidgin English *chop* quick + STICK[1]]

chop suey /ˈsuːi/, *n.* a dish consisting of small pieces of meat or chicken cooked with bean sprouts or other vegetables, commonly served in Chinese restaurants. [Chinese: mixed bits]

choral /ˈkɔːrəl/, *adj.* of, sung by, or written for, a chorus or a choir [ML, from L *chorus.* See CHORUS] **—chorally**, *adv.*

chorale /kɒˈrɑːl/, *n.* a simple slow hymn-like tune usu. sung by a choir and congregation together.

chord[1] /kɔːd/, **1.** *Geom.* that part of a straight line between two of its intersections with a curve. **2.** *Civ. Eng.* one of the main members (beams) which lie along the top or bottom edge of a truss framework. **3.** feeling or emotion. **4.** *Anat.* → **cord** (def. 3). [L: cord, string, from Gk: gut, string of a musical instrument. See CORD] **—chordal, chorded**, *adj.*

chord[2] /kɔːd/, *n. Music.* a combination of three or more notes, sounded either simultaneously or in quick succession. [var. spelling (influenced by CHORD[1]) of *cord*, short form of ACCORD, n.]

chordate /ˈkɔːdeɪt/, *adj.* **1.** *Zool.* belonging or relating to the phylum which includes animals with a backbone or with a rudimentary form of one. ◇n. **2.** *Zool.* a chordate animal. [NL: having a chord. See CHORD[1]]

Christchurch

chore /tʃɔː/, *n.* **1.** a small or odd job, usu. domestic. **2.** *(pl.)* regular and dull work around a house or farm. **3.** a hard or unpleasant job. [OE *cyrr*]

choreography /ˌkɒriˈɒɡrəfi/, *n.* **1.** the art of writing ballets, etc., and arranging separate dances. **2.** the art of representing the various movements in dancing by a system of symbols. **3.** the art of dancing. Also, **choreography** /kəˈrɛɡrəfi/. [*choreo-* (combining form representing Gk *choreía* dance) + -GRAPHY] **—choreographer**, *n.* **—choreographic**, *adj.* **—choreograph**, *v.*

chorister /ˈkɒrəstə/, *n.* a singer in a choir. [ML *chorista* chorister + -ER[1]]

chortle /ˈtʃɔːtl/, *v.*, **-tled, -tling,** *n.* ◇v.i. **1.** to laugh with glee. ◇n. **2.** a gleeful laugh. [b. CHUCKLE and SNORT; coined by Lewis CARROLL in *Through the Looking-Glass* (1871)] **—chortler**, *n.*

chorus /ˈkɔːrəs/, *n., pl.* **-ruses,** *v.,* **-rused, -rusing.** ◇n. **1. a.** a group of people singing together. **b.** a piece of music for several people to sing together. **c.** a part of a song in which others join the main singer or singers. **d.** any part of a song that is repeated. **2.** the sounds spoken or sung. **3.** (in musical shows) **a.** the group of dancers and singers. **b.** the singing or song of such a group. **4. in chorus,** speaking or singing at the same time. ◇v.i. **5.** to sing or speak in chorus. ◇v.t. **6.** to perform in chorus. [L, from Gk *chorós* dance, band of dancers, chorus]

chose /tʃoʊz/, *v.* past tense and obsolete past participle of **choose.**

chosen /ˈtʃoʊzən/, *v.* **1.** past participle of **choose.** ◇adj. **2.** picked from a number; preferred. ◇n. **3.** → **elect.**

Chou En-lai /ˌtʃoʊ ɛnˈlaɪ/, *n.* former name of **Zhou Enlai.**

chough /tʃʌf/, *n.* a black bird with white wing patches, found in eastern Australia. [ME]

chow /tʃaʊ/, *n.* **1.** Also, **chow-chow.** one of a Chinese breed of dogs with a thick, even coat of brown or black hair and a black tongue. **2.** *Colloq.* food.

chowder /ˈtʃaʊdə/, *n.* a kind of soup or stew made of shellfish, fish, or vegetables, with potatoes, onions and seasoning. [probably from F: cauldron, from LL *caldus, calidus* hot]

chow mein /tʃaʊ ˈmeɪn/, *n.* a dish of noodles mixed with chopped vegetables and small amounts of meat and/or poultry. [Chinese: fried flour]

chq., *Abbrev.* cheque.

chrism /ˈkrɪzəm/, *n.* an oil used in religious ceremonies. [OE *crisma*, from L, from Gk: unguent, unction] **—chrismal,** *adj.*

Christ /kraɪst/, *n.* **1.** the Anointed; the Messiah expected by the Jews. **2.** Jesus of Nazareth, as fulfilling this expectation. [OE *Crist*, from L *Christus*, from Gk, trans. of Heb: anointed]

Christchurch /ˈkraɪstʃɜːtʃ/, *n.* a city in NZ, near the eastern coast of South Island. Pop. 168 200 (1986).

christen /'krɪsən/, *v.t.* **1.** to give a name to at baptism. **2.** to name and dedicate; give a name to; name: *We christened the boat Freda.* **3.** *Colloq.* to make use of for the first time: *We christened the new sail yesterday.* [OE *cristnian* make Christian (by baptism)]

Christendom /'krɪsəndəm/, *n.* **1.** Christians as a whole. **2.** the Christian world. [OE *cristen* Christian + -DOM]

christening /'krɪsənɪŋ, 'krɪsnɪŋ/, *n.* the ceremony of baptism.

Christian[1] /'krɪstʃən/, *adj.* **1.** relating to or coming from Jesus Christ: *Christian teachings.* **2.** believing in Jesus Christ or belonging to the religion of Jesus Christ. **3.** *Colloq.* decent or humane: *a Christian gentleman.* ◇*n.* **4.** someone who believes in Jesus Christ or belongs to the Christian religion. **5.** *Colloq.* a decent or humane person: *He's a real Christian!* [L]

Christian[2] /'krɪstʃən/, *n.* **Fletcher**, English senior master's mate who led the mutiny on HMS *Bounty* in 1789.

Christianity /krɪsti'ænəti/, **1.** the Christian religion. **2.** Christian beliefs or practices; Christian quality or character.

Christian name, *n.* the name given at baptism or at birth as opposed to the family name; personal name.

Christian Science /krɪstʃən 'saɪəns/, *n.* a system of religious teaching, based on the Scriptures, the most notable application of which is the treatment of disease by mental and spiritual means; founded in the US about 1866 by Mrs Mary Baker Eddy. — **Christian Scientist**, *n.*

Christie /'krɪsti/, *n.* **Agatha Mary Clarissa**, 1891–1976, British writer of thrillers, often featuring the Belgian detective character Hercule Poirot.

Christmas /'krɪsməs/, *n.* **1.** church festival of the birth of Jesus, celebrated on 25 December. **2.** 25 December (**Christmas Day**), a holiday for giving gifts, greetings, etc. **3.** period or season around Christmas: *I shall be away next Christmas.* ◇*adj.* **4.** given on, held on, or connected with Christmas: *a Christmas present.* [OE *Cristes mæsse* mass of Christ]

Christmas beetle, *n.* a beetle with rainbow colors on its wings, usu. seen in Australia in mid-summer.

Christmas bell, *n.* a plant of eastern Australia with hanging red and yellow flowers.

Christmas bush, *n.* an Australian shrub or small tree with white flowers and red sepals, flowering at Christmas and used for decoration.

Christmas Island, *n.* **1.** an Australian territory in the Indian Ocean, about 350 km south of Java; phosphate deposits. About 135 km[2]. **2.** an island in the Line Islands in the central Pacific; the largest atoll in the world.

Christmas tree, *n.* **1.** a tree, usu. pine or fir, hung with decorations at Christmas. **2.** a tree of the mistletoe family, native to western Australia.

Christopher /'krɪstəfə/, *n.* **Saint**, died AD 250?, a legendary martyr of early Christianity; protector of travellers.

-chroic, an adjectival word part indicating color (of skin, plants, etc.). See **-chroous**. [Gk *chrōikós* colored]

chrom-, **1.** a word part referring to color. **2.** a word part referring to chromium. **3.** a combining form in chemistry used to distinguish a colored compound from its colorless form. Also, **chromo-**. [def. 1, see -CHROME; def. 2, see CHROMIUM]

-chrom-, a word part, the same as **chrom-**, as in *polychromatic.*

chromat-, a variant of **chromato-** before vowels.

chromatic /krə'mætɪk/, *adj.* **1.** relating to color or colors. **2.** *Music.* **a.** involving a change to the diatonic scale by the use of accidentals. **b.** progressing by semitone(s). [L, from Gk: relating to color (chiefly in musical sense)] — **chromatically**, *adv.*

chromatid /'kroumətɪd/, *n.* one of two identical chromosomal strands into which a chromosome splits lengthwise before cell division.

chromatin /'kroumətɪn/, *n.* that part of the animal or plant cell nucleus which easily takes on chemical stains under analysis. [CHROMAT- + -IN[1]]

chromato-, **1.** a word part referring to color. **2.** a word part meaning 'chromatin'. [Gk, combining form of *chrōma* color]

chromatography /kroumə'tɒɡrəfi/, *n. Chem.* the method of separating mixtures into their constituents using their different rates of absorption by solids such as silica, paper etc. [CHROMATO- + -GRAPHY] — **chromatographic**, *adj.*

chromatolysis /kroumə'tɒləsəs/, *n.* the dissolution and disintegration of chromatin.

chromatoplasm /'kroumətəplæzəm/, *n. Biol.* the colored part of protoplasm. Also, **chromoplasm**.

chrome /kroum/, *n.* → **chromium**. [Gk: color]

-chrome, a word part meaning 'color', as in *polychrome*. [Gk *chrōma*]

chrome alum, *n.* a dark violet double sulfate of chromium and potassium, $KCr(SO_4)_2 \cdot 12H_2O$, crystallising like common alum, and used in dyeing.

chrome steel, *n.* steel of great hardness and strength, containing chromium, carbon, and other elements. Also, **chromium steel**.

chromite /'kroumaɪt/, *n.* **1.** *Chem.* See **-ite**[1]. **2.** a common mineral, which is the main ore of chromium.

chromium /'kroumiəm/, *n.* a shiny, hard, brittle metallic element found in compounds used for making pigments and also in corrosion-resisting chromium plating. *Symbol:* Cr; *at. no.:* 24; *at. wt:* 51.996. [Gk *chrōm(a)* COLOR + -IUM]

chromolithography /,kroumoulə'θɒɡrəfi/, *n.* the process of lithographing in colors. — **chromolithographer**, *n.* — **chromolithographic**, *adj.*

chromomere /ˈkroʊməmɪə/, n. one of the chromatin granules of a chromosome. —**chromomeric**, adj.

chromophore /ˈkroʊməfɔː/, n. 1. any chemical group which produces color in a compound, as the azo group −N = N−. 2. the structural layout of atoms which is found in many colored organic compounds.

chromosome /ˈkroʊməsoʊm/, n. one of the set of thread-shaped bodies in the cell nucleus which carry the genes. [CHROM(O) + -SOME³] —**chromosomal**, adj.

chromosome number, n. the characteristic number of chromosomes of any biological species.

chron-, a word part meaning 'time', as in *chronometer*. Also, **chrono-**. [Gk, combining form of *chrónos*]

chronic /ˈkrɒnɪk/, adj. 1. habitual; inveterate; constant: *a chronic smoker*. 2. continuing a long time: *chronic civil war; chronic depression*. 3. having long had a disease or habit, etc.: *a chronic invalid*. 4. *Colloq.* very bad; deplorable: *a chronic sense of humor*. [L, from Gk] —**chronically**, adv.

chronicle /ˈkrɒnɪkəl/, n., v., **-cled, -cling**. ◇n. 1. a record or account of events; a history. ◇v.t. 2. to record in or as in a chronicle. [ME, from OF *cronique*, from ML, from Gk: annals] —**chronicler**, n.

Chronicles /ˈkrɒnɪkəlz/, n.pl. two historical books of the Old Testament, following Kings.

chronological /krɒnəˈlɒdʒɪkəl/, adj. 1. arranged in order according to time: *chronological tables*. 2. relating to or in accordance with chronology: *chronological character*. Also, **chronologic**.

chronology /krəˈnɒlədʒi/, n., pl. **-gies**. 1. the science of arranging time in periods and giving dates to events. 2. the arrangement of past events according to their order in time. —**chronologer, chronologist**, n.

chronometer /krəˈnɒmətə/, n. a very accurate clock for measuring time, used esp. at sea. —**chronometric, chronometrical**, adj. —**chronometrically**, adv.

chronoscope /ˈkrɒnəskoʊp/, n. an instrument for measuring accurately very small intervals of time, as in determining the speed of projectiles.

-chroous, → **-chroic**. [suffix formed from the stem of Gk *chróa* surface, color + -OUS]

chrysalis /ˈkrɪsəlɪs/, n., pl. **chrysalises, chrysalids, chrysalides** /krəˈsælədiːz/. the hard-shelled pupa of a moth or butterfly. [L, from Gk: gold-colored sheath of butterflies]

chrysanthemum /krəˈsænθəməm, krəˈzænθ-/, n. a perennial plant with big, showy flowers. [L, from Gk: golden flower]

chrysolite /ˈkrɪsəlaɪt/, n. → **olivine**. [ME, from ML, from Gk: a bright yellow stone (probably topaz)]

chrysoprase /ˈkrɪsəpreɪz/, n. a green chalcedony, much used in jewellery. [L, from Gk: gold leek]

CHU, *Abbrev.* centigrade heat unit.

chub /tʃʌb/, n., pl. **chubs**, (*esp. collectively*) **chub**. a common European freshwater fish. [ME]

chubby /ˈtʃʌbi/, adj., **-bier, -biest**. round and plump: *a chubby face; chubby cheeks*.

chuck¹ /tʃʌk/, v.t. 1. to throw with a quick movement, usu. a short distance. 2. to pat or tap lightly, as under the chin. 3. *Colloq.* to eject (fol. by *out*): *They chucked him out of the nightclub*. 4. *Colloq.* to resign from (oft. fol. by *in*): *He's chucked in his job*. 5. *Colloq.* to do; perform, usu. with some flamboyance: *to chuck a U-ie*. 6. to contribute (fol. by *in*): *I'll chuck ten dollars in*. ◇v.i. 7. *Colloq.* to vomit (sometimes fol. by *up*). ◇v. 8. **chuck it (in)**, to stop doing something; give up (something begun) without finishing. 9. **chuck off**, *Colloq.* to speak sarcastically or critically about (fol. by *at*). 10. **chuck one's hand in**, to give up; refuse to go on. ◇n. 11. a light pat or tap, as under the chin. 12. a short throw; toss. [imitative]

chuck² /tʃʌk/, n. 1. Also, **chuck steak**. a cut of beef between the neck and the shoulder-blade. 2. a block or log used as a chock. 3. a device like a clamp for holding tools or work in a machine: *lathe chuck*. [var. of CHOCK]

chuckle /ˈtʃʌkəl/, v., **chuckled, chuckling**, n. ◇v.i. 1. to laugh in a soft, amused way. ◇n. 2. a soft, amused laugh. —**chuckler**, n.

chuditch /ˈtʃʊdɪtʃ/, n. See **native cat**.

chuff /tʃʌf, tʃʊf/, n. 1. a puff of gas, steam, etc., from an engine. 2. the sound produced by this puff. ◇v.i. 3. to move while blowing out smoke: *The train chuffed into the station*. ◇v. 4. **chuff off**, *Colloq.* to go away. Also, **choof**. [? b. CHUG + PUFF]

chug /tʃʌɡ/, n., v., **chugged, chugging**. ◇n. 1. a short, dull explosive sound: *the steady chug of an engine*. ◇v.i. 2. to make this sound: *The motor chugged quietly*. 3. to move while making this sound: *The train chugged along the track*. [imitative]

chukka /ˈtʃʌkə/, n. (in polo) one of the periods of play. Also, **chukker**. [Hind]

chum /tʃʌm/, n., v., **chummed, chumming**. ◇n. 1. a close friend or companion: *boyhood chums*. 2. an Englishman. See **new chum**. ◇v. 3. **chum up with**, to meet and become friendly with. [orig. uncert.]

chummy /ˈtʃʌmi/, adj., **-mier, -miest**. friendly; intimate; sociable.

chump /tʃʌmp/, n. 1. *Colloq.* a stupid person. 2. *Meat Industry*. the section of lamb, between the leg and the loin, which is cut into chops.

chunder /ˈtʃʌndə/, v.i. *Colloq.* to vomit.

chunk /tʃʌŋk/, n. a thick mass or lump of anything: *a chunk of bread*. [nasalised var. of CHUCK², n.]

chunky /ˈtʃʌŋki/, adj., **-kier, -kiest**. thick, stout or bulky; thickset; stocky: *a chunky boy; a chunky sweater*. —**chunkiness**, n.

church /tʃɜːtʃ/, n. 1. a building for public Christian worship. 2. the public worship of

God in a church: *He goes to church twice on Sundays.* **3.** (*cap.*) **a.** the whole body of Christian believers: *The church is united in prayer.* **b.** any part of this body with the same particular beliefs and the same authority; Christian denomination: *the Uniting Church.* **4.** the church as a political power: *the history of church and state.* **5.** the clerical profession: *The third son went into the church.* [OE *cir(i)ce, cyrice* from Gk *kȳriakón (dôoma)* Lord's (house)]

Churchill /'tʃɜːtʃɪl/, *n.* **Sir Winston (Leonard Spencer)**, 1874–1965, British Conservative statesman and writer; prime minister 1940–45, 1951–55; noted for his leadership during World War II.

Churchill Fellowship, *n.* a fellowship awarded by the Winston Churchill Memorial Trust, established in Australia in 1965, to finance both investigative projects and study overseas.

Church Missionary Society of Australia, *n.* a Church of England body, established in Australia in 1825.

Church of England, *n.* a Christian Church, the established church in England, with the Queen or King as its head. See **Anglican**.

Church of England in Australia, *n.* until 1981, former title of the Anglican Church of Australia.

Church of Rome, *n.* → **Catholic Church** (def. 2).

churinga /tʃəˈrɪŋɡə/, *n.* a sacred representation of an aboriginal totemic object, usu. made of wood or stone; bullroarer. Also, **tjuringa**. [Aboriginal]

churl /tʃɜːl/, *n.* **1.** a rude, boorish, or surly person. **2.** *Archaic.* a peasant; a rustic. [OE *ceorl* freeman of the lowest rank] —**churlish**, *adj.*

churn /tʃɜːn/, *n.* **1. a.** a container or machine in which cream or milk is shaken to make butter. **b.** something similar for making ice cream, etc. **2.** a large metal container for milk. ◇*v.t.* **3.** to shake or stir in order to make into butter: *to churn cream.* ◇*v.i.* **4.** to move about with a rough or violent motion: *The sea churned around the ship; His stomach churned at the thought of it.* [OE *cyrin*]

chute /ʃuːt/, *n.* **1.** a sloping channel for sending water, grain, coal, rubbish, etc., to a lower level; shoot. **2.** a waterfall; steep descent, as in a river; rapid. **3.** a sloping board, with sides, down which a swimmer may slide into the water. **4.** a parachute. **5.** *Agric.* a narrow passage, often sloping steeply, through which animals are moved for branding, drenching or loading, or as an exit from a woolshed for shorn sheep. [b. F *chute* a fall (from L *cadere*) and E SHOOT]

chutney /'tʃʌtni/, *n., pl.* **-neys.** a relish of Indian origin which consists of fruit or vegetable cooked with sugar, spices, vinegar, etc. [Hind]

Ci, *Abbrev.* curie.

CIA /siː aɪ 'eɪ/, *US. Abbrev.* Central Intelligence Agency.

CIB /siː aɪ 'biː/, *Abbrev.* **1.** Criminal Investigation Branch. **2.** *Brit.* Criminal Investigation Bureau.

cicada /səˈkɑːdə, səˈkeɪdə/, *n., pl.* **-dae** /-diː/, **-das.** a large, winged insect which appears in summer and makes a loud, shrill sound in hot weather. [L]

cicatrix /'sɪkətrɪks/, *n., pl.* **cicatrices** /sɪkəˈtraɪsiːz/, **cicatrixes**. the scar left by a wound. Also, **cicatrice** /'sɪkətrəs/. [L] —**cicatricial**, *adj.* —**cicatricose**, *adj.*

Cicero /'sɪsərəʊ/, *n.* **Marcus Tullius**, 106–43 BC, Roman statesman, orator, and writer; worked to preserve the principles of republicanism.

cichlid /'sɪklɪd/, *n.* a tropical, freshwater fish, often kept in home aquariums. [NL, from Gk: kind of sea fish] —**cichloid**, *n., adj.*

Cid /sɪd, θɪð/, *n.* **El (the)** ('*El Cid Campeador'*, **Rodrigo Diaz de Vivar**), 1040?–99, Spanish soldier and hero of the wars against the Moors. [Sp, from Ar *sayyid* lord]

CID /siː aɪ 'diː/, *Abbrev.* Criminal Investigation Department.

-cidal, adjective form of **-cide**. [-CIDE + -AL¹]

-cide, a word part meaning 'killer' or 'act of killing'. [L: to kill]

cider /'saɪdə/, *n.* **1.** a drink, fermented or unfermented, made from apples. **2. cider vinegar**, vinegar made from cider. [ME, from LL, from Gk, from Heb: strong drink]

cider-press /'saɪdə-prɛs/, *n.* a press for crushing apples to make cider.

CIF /siː aɪ 'ɛf/, *Abbrev.* cost, insurance, and freight (included in price quoted). Also, **c.i.f.**, **c.f.i.**

cigar /səˈɡɑː/, *n.* a small, shaped roll of tobacco leaves prepared for smoking. [Sp ? from *cigarra* grasshopper, from L]

cigarette /sɪɡəˈrɛt/, *n.* a roll of finely cut tobacco for smoking, usu. enclosed in thin paper. [F: little cigar]

Cilento family /səˈlɛntoʊ/, *n.* an Australian family noted for medical service and other activities. **1. Sir Raphael West**, 1893–1985, medical practitioner; president of the Medical Board of Qld 1939–45. **2.** his wife, **Lady Phyllis Dorothy**, 1894–1987, medical practitioner, journalist, and author. **3. (Elizabeth) Diane**, daughter of Sir Raphael and Lady Cilento, born 1932, actor, author and film producer.

cilia /'sɪliə/, *n.pl., sing.* **cilium** /'sɪliəm/. **1.** eyelashes. **2.** *Zool.* tiny hairlike projections from the surface of cells, responsible for locomotion, feeding, etc. **3.** *Bot.* very small, hairlike growths. [L] —**ciliate, ciliated**, *adj.*

ciliary /'sɪljəri/, *adj.* **1.** of or relating to a delicate ring of tissue in the eye from which the lens is suspended by means of fine ligaments. **2.** relating to cilia.

Cimabue /tʃiːməˈbueɪ/, *n.* **Giovanni** /dʒəˈvɑːni/, 1240?–1302?, Florentine painter and mosaicist in the Byzantine style.

cinch /sɪntʃ/, *n.* **1.** a strong girth for a saddle or pack. **2.** *Colloq.* something certain or easy: *This exam's a cinch.* [Sp, from L: girdle] — **cinchy**, *adj.*

cincture /'sɪŋktʃə/, *n.* a belt or girdle, esp. that worn by priests during religious ceremonies. [L: girdle]

cinder /'sɪndə/, *n.* **1.** a burnt-out or partly burnt piece of coal, wood, etc. **2.** (*pl.*) any kind of ashes. **3.** (*pl.*) *Geol.* coarse lava thrown out by volcanoes. [OE *sinder* cinder, slag] — **cindery**, *adj.*

cinderella /sɪndə'relə/, *n.* a neglected, ignored or despised person or thing: *Research is the cinderella of this university.* [from *Cinderella*, heroine of a well-known fairy-tale]

cine-, a word part meaning 'motion'. [combining form from Gk *kīneîn* move]

cinema /'sɪnəmə/, *n.* **1.** a theatre where films are shown; picture theatre. **2. the cinema**, films considered together. [short for CINEMATOGRAPH] — **cinematic**, *adj.* — **cinematically**, *adv.*

cinemascope /'sɪnəməskoʊp/, *n.* a film process which enables wide screen projection so that the image on the screen is twice its usual length. [Trademark]

cinematograph /sɪnə'mætəgræf/, *n.* a film projector or camera. [Gk *kīnēma* motion + -GRAPH] — **cinematographer**, *n.* — **cinematographic**, *adj.* — **cinematography**, *n.*

cineraria /sɪnə'rɛəriə/, *n.* a garden plant, native to the Canary Islands, with heart-shaped leaves and clusters of flowers with white, blue, purple, red, or variegated rays. [L *cinerārius* pertaining to ashes (with reference to the soft white down on the leaves)]

cinerarium /sɪnə'rɛəriəm/, *n., pl.* -**raria** /-'rɛəriə/. a place for keeping the ashes of the dead after cremation. [L] — **cinerary**, *adj.*

Cinesound /'sɪnisaʊnd/, *n.* an Australian film studio formed as a subsidiary of the Greater Union Organisation in 1932; ceased production of feature films in 1940.

cinnabar /'sɪnəba/, *n.* **1.** a mineral, mercuric sulfide, HgS, often vermilion colored, the principal ore of mercury. **2.** red mercuric sulfide, used as a pigment. **3.** bright red; vermilion. [L, from Gk *kinnábari*, of oriental orig.]

cinnamon /'sɪnəmən/, *n.* **1.** an aromatic bark used as a spice, or medicinally. **2.** yellowish or reddish brown. [LL, from Gk]

Cinque Ports /sɪŋk/, *n.pl.* an ancient association of maritime towns in south-eastern England, orig. (1278) numbering five (Hastings, Romney, Hythe, Dover, and Sandwich), and later including Winchelsea, Rye, and several others, receiving special privileges for their part in the naval defence of England.

-cion, a suffix having the same function as **-tion**, as in *suspicion*. [L *-cio*]

cipher /'saɪfə/, *n.* **1.** the arithmetical symbol (0) meaning nought, or no quantity or magnitude. **2.** any of the Arabic numbers 1 to 9. **3.** a person or thing of no value or importance. **4. a.** a secret (method of) writing; code: *The enemy's cipher was broken by our experts.* **b.** the key to this. **5.** combination initials in a design; monogram. ◇ *v.i.* **6.** to use figures or numerals arithmetically. ◇ *v.t.* **7.** to calculate numerically; figure. **8.** to write in, or as in, code or cipher. Also, **cypher**. [ME, from ML, from Ar: empty]

cir., *Abbrev.* about. Also, **circ.** [L *circa, circiter, circum*]

circa /'sɜkə, 'sɜsə/, *prep., adv.* about (used esp. in approximate dates): *The old map was dated circa 1400.* Abbrev.: c., c, ca [L]

circadian /sɜ'keɪdiən/, *adj.* (of physiological activity) occurring approximately every 24 hours. [L: round about]

Circe /'sɜsi/, *n. Gk Legend.* the enchantress represented by Homer as turning the companions of Odysseus into swine by a magic drink. — **Circean** /sɜ'siən/, *adj.*

circle /'sɜkəl/, *n., v.,* -**cled**, -**cling**. ◇ *n.* **1.** (a flat round area enclosed by) a curved line which is everywhere equally distant from a fixed point within it, called the centre. **2.** anything with the shape of a circle: *a circle of trees / buildings; She has dark circles under her eyes from too much work; A circle of gold sat on the king's head.* **3.** the upper section of seats in a theatre: *the dress circle.* **4.** the area within which something acts, has influence, etc.: *She is well-known in political circles.* **5.** a series ending where it began, and forever repeated: *This kind of thinking is just a vicious circle.* **6.** a complete series forming a connected whole; cycle: *the circle of the seasons.* **7.** a number of people bound by a common tie; coterie: *John's little circle has such interesting people in it.* **8.** *Geog.* a parallel of latitude: *the Antarctic circle.* ◇ *v.t.* **9.** → **encircle**. **10.** to move in a circle or circuit around: *He circled the house cautiously.* ◇ *v.i.* **11.** to move in a circle. [L: little circle, ring]

circlet /'sɜklət/, *n.* **1.** a small circle. **2.** a ring. **3.** a ringshaped ornament, esp. for the head.

circuit /'sɜkət/, *n.* **1.** the act of going or moving round: *The circuit of the enemy's position was nearly complete.* **2.** any circular or roundabout journey; a round: *The tour made a circuit of the city.* **3.** a circular racing track. **4.** a journey from place to place, made at regular periods, to perform certain duties, etc.: *The district judge's circuit.* **5.** way followed, places visited, or area covered by such a journey: *The travelling theatre has a new circuit this year.* **6.** a street which is circular or roughly so (usu. as street name). **7.** a number of races of a season or series. **8.** *Elect.* the complete path of an electric current. ◇ *v.t.* **9.** to go or move round; make the circuit of: *They circuited the city.* [ME, from L]

circuit-breaker /'sɜkət-breɪkə/, *n.* a device for interrupting an electric circuit.

circuitous /sə'kjuətəs/, *adj.* roundabout; not direct: *They took a circuitous route to the house.*

circuitry /'sɜkətri/, *n.* a system of electrical circuits.

circular /'sɜkjələ/, *adj.* **1.** of or relating to a circle. **2.** having the form of a circle; round. **3.** moving in or forming a circle or a circuit: *Their path through the bush was circular.* **4.** moving or occurring in a cycle or round. **5.** circuitous; roundabout; indirect: *He gives such circular explanations that I don't know where to go.* **6.** (of a letter, etc.) addressed and sent to a number of people. ◇*n.* **7.** a letter, notice, etc. sent round to a number of people. [L: circle] —**circularity,** *n.* —**circularly,** *adv.*

circularise or **circularize** /'sɜkjələraɪz/, *v.t.*, **-rised, -rising. 1.** to send circulars to. **2.** to circulate (a letter, pamphlet, etc.). **3.** to make circular. —**circularisation,** *n.*

Circular Quay, *n.* the water transport terminus of Sydney Harbor, NSW, situated on Sydney Cove.

circular saw, *n.* a power-driven saw consisting of a circular disc with a toothed edge, which turns round at high speed.

circulate /'sɜkjəleɪt/, *v.*, **-lated, -lating.** ◇*v.i.* **1.** to move in a circle or circuit, as the blood in the body. **2.** to pass from place to place, from person to person, etc.; be disseminated or distributed: *The rumor circulated quickly.* **3.** *Colloq.* to move amongst the guests at a party. ◇*v.t.* **4.** to make something go from place to place, person to person, etc: *to circulate a rumor.* [L: gathered into a circle] —**circulative,** *adj.* —**circulator,** *n.* —**circulatory,** *adj.*

circulation /sɜkjə'leɪʃən/, *n.* **1.** the act of circulating or moving in a circle or circuit. **2.** the continuous movement of the blood, sap, etc., through a body or system. **3.** the sending or passing of anything from place to place, person to person, etc.: *the circulation of ideas / money.* **4.** the distribution of copies of a publication among readers: *Circulation of this morning's newspaper has been delayed.* **5.** the number of copies of each issue of a newspaper, magazine, etc., distributed: *The magazine has a circulation of 2000.* **6.** *Colloq.* (of a person) **a. in circulation,** socially active. **b. out of circulation,** socially inactive.

circum-, a prefix referring to movement round or about, on all sides, as in *circumvent, circumcise, circumference.* [L]

circumcise /'sɜkəmsaɪz/, *v.t.*, **-cised, -cising. 1.** to remove the foreskin of (males), sometimes as a religious rite. **2.** to remove part of the clitoris of (females). [ME, from L: cut around] —**circumcision,** *n.*

circumference /sə'kʌmfərəns/, *n.* **1.** the outer boundary, esp. of a circular area. **2.** the length of such a boundary. [L] —**circumferential,** *adj.*

circumflex /'sɜkəmfleks/, *n.* **1.** a mark (ˆ) used over a vowel in certain languages to show pronunciation. ◇*adj.* **2.** marked with a circumflex. [L: bent round] —**circumflexion,** *n.*

circumlocution /sɜkəmlə'kjuʃən/, *n.* **1.** a roundabout way of speaking; use of too many words. **2.** a roundabout expression: *He used a circumlocution to hide his embarrassment.* [L] —**circumlocutory,** *adj.*

circumnavigate /sɜkəm'nævɪgeɪt/, *v.t.*, **-gated, -gating.** to sail round (the earth, an island). —**circumnavigation,** *n.* —**circumnavigator,** *n.*

circumscribe /'sɜkəmskraɪb, sɜkəm'skraɪb/, *v.t.*, **-scribed, -scribing. 1.** to surround; encircle. **2.** to limit; confine, esp. narrowly (usu. in passive): *Their knowledge is strictly circumscribed.* **3.** *Geom.* to draw (a figure) round another figure so as to touch as many points as possible: *to circumscribe a square.* [L: draw a line round, limit] —**circumscriber,** *n.* —**circumscription,** *n.*

circumspect /'sɜkəmspekt/, *adj.* **1.** watchful on all sides; cautious; prudent: *circumspect in behavior.* **2.** well-considered: *circumspect ambition.* [late ME, from L: considerate, wary] —**circumspection,** *n.*

circumstance /'sɜkəmstæns/, *n.*, *v.*, **-stanced, -stancing.** ◇*n.* **1.** the condition, concerning time, place, manner, etc., which goes together with or changes a fact or event. **2.** (*usu. pl.*) the state of affairs surrounding and influencing a person or thing: *forced by circumstances to do a thing.* **3.** (*pl.*) the condition or state of a person's material affairs: *a lady in reduced circumstances.* **4.** a happening; occurrence: *His arrival was a fortunate circumstance.* **5. in** or **under no circumstances,** never; regardless of events. **6. in** or **under the circumstances,** considering the conditions; such being the case. **7. pomp and circumstance,** stately and ceremonious display. ◇*v.t.* **8.** to place in particular circumstances or relations, (usu. in passive): *He is fortunate in being well circumstanced for public life.* [ME, from L: surrounding conditions]

circumstantial /sɜkəm'stænʃəl/, *adj.* **1.** of, having to do with, or coming from circumstances. **2.** secondary; incidental. **3.** dealing with or giving circumstances or details; detailed; particular: *He gave a highly circumstantial account of his journey.*

circumstantial evidence, *n. Law.* facts offered as evidence from which the existence of other facts is to be understood, where direct evidence is not available.

circumvent /sɜkəm'vent/, *v.t.* **1.** to get the better of by cleverness; outwit: *circumvent the law.* **2.** to go round; avoid: *circumvent the bridge.* [L *circumventus,* pp., surrounded]

circus /'sɜkəs/, *n.* **1.** a travelling company of performers, animals, etc. **2.** the performance itself. **3.** (in ancient Rome) an open enclosure, surrounded by tiers of seats, for the chariot races, public games, etc. **4.** *Brit.* a place, originally circular, with several streets leading from it: *Piccadilly Circus.* **5.** noisy and rough behavior or activity; uproar: *Last Saturday's match was just a circus.* [L, from Gk *kirkos* ring]

cirrhosis /sɪ'roʊsəs, sə-/, *n.* a serious disease which alters the make-up of the liver. [NL, from Gk *kirrhós* tawny + *-osis* -OSIS] —**cirrhotic,** *adj.*

cirro-, combining form of **cirrus.**

cirrus /'sɪrəs/, *n.*, *pl.* **cirri** /'sɪri/. **1.** *Bot.* a tendril. **2.** *Zool.* a threadlike outgrowth

cirrus serving as a barbel, tentacle, foot, arm, etc. **3.** a high, fleecy or feathery cloud, consisting of very small ice crystals. [L: curl, tuft, fringe]

CIS. *n.* → **Commonwealth of Independent States.**

cissy /'sɪsi/, *n. Colloq.* → **sissy.**

Cistercian /səs'tɜːʃən/, *n.* **1.** a member of an order of monks and nuns founded in 1098 at Cîteaux, near Dijon, France, under the rule of St Benedict. *–adj.* **2.** belonging to this order.

cistern /'sɪstən/, *n.* a container or tank for holding water or other liquid. [ME, from L: box]

citadel /'sɪtədel/, *n.* **1.** a fort in or near a city, to control it or to form a final point of defence. **2.** any strongly defended place; stronghold. [F, from It: city]

cite /saɪt/, *v.t.*, **cited, citing. 1. a.** to quote (a passage, book, etc.), esp. as an authority. **b.** to mention in support, or as proof; refer to as an example. **2.** to call offically to appear in court. **3.** *Mil.* to mention (a soldier, unit, etc.), as for bravery. [ME, from L: move, excite, call] *–citable, citeable, adj. –citation, n.*

citizen /'sɪtəzən/, *n.* **1.** a member, native or naturalised, of a state or nation (as distinguished from *alien*). **2.** someone who lives in a particular city or town: *the citizens of Tamworth.* [ME, from OF *citeain*, from *cite* CITY]

citizen band radio, *n.* radio communication with transmitters and receivers suitable for individual use, as by truck drivers, etc.

Citizen Military Forces, *n.pl.* an Australian military force, established in 1948; a component of the larger Army Reserve. *Abbrev.:* CMF

citric acid /ˌsɪtrɪk 'æsəd/, *n.* an organic acid occurring in small amounts in almost all living cells as part of the citric acid cycle, and in greater amounts in many fruits, esp. in limes and lemons.

citron /'sɪtrən/, *n.* **1.** a pale yellow fruit like the lemon but larger and with thicker rind. ◇*adj.* **2.** pale yellow: [F, from It, from L: citron tree]

citronella /sɪtrə'nelə/, *n.* a fragrant grass, of southern Asia, cultivated as the source of an oil (**citronella oil**) used in making liniment, perfume, and soap. [NL, named from its citron-like smell]

citrus /'sɪtrəs/, *n.* **1.** any tree or shrub of the group which includes the citron, lemon, lime, orange, grapefruit, etc. ◇*adj.* **2.** Also, **citrous.** of or relating to such trees or shrubs. [L]

city /'sɪti/, *n., pl.* **cities. 1. a.** a large or important town. **b.** an area within a large, widespread city, as the City of Parramatta within Greater Sydney or the City of Nunawading within Greater Melbourne. **c.** the central business area of a city. **2.** a city-state, esp. in ancient Greece. **3.** the people of a city: *The city was in revolt.* [ME, from OF, from L *cīvitas* citizenship, the state, a city]

city hall, *n.* (in some cities) the building housing the administrative offices of a city; town hall.

city-state /ˌsɪti-'steɪt/, *n.* an independent state consisting of a self-governing city with its dependencies, esp. in ancient Greece.

civet /'sɪvət/, *n.* **1.** a yellow, oily substance with a strong musklike smell, obtained from civet cats and used in perfumery. **2.** Also, **civet cat.** a catlike, meat-eating mammal of southern Asia and Africa that has glands in the genital area that secrete civet. [F, from It, from Ar]

civic /'sɪvɪk/, *adj.* **1.** of or relating to a city; municipal: *civic problems.* **2.** of or relating to citizenship: *civic duties.* [L *cīvis* citizen]

civic centre, *n.* the part of a town or city where public buildings are closely grouped.

civil /'sɪvəl/, *adj.* **1.** of or consisting of citizens: *civil life/society.* **2.** of the commonwealth or state: *civil affairs.* **3.** of the citizen as an individual: *civil liberty.* **4.** civilised or polite; courteous. [ME, from L]

civil defence, *n.* emergency measures organised by citizens against natural disaster or enemy attack.

civil disobedience, *n.* a refusal, usu. for political reasons, to obey laws, pay taxes, etc.

civil engineer, *n.* an engineer concerned with the design and building of public works, such as roads, bridges, etc. *–civil engineering, n.*

civilian /sə'vɪljən/, *n.* **1.** a person in ordinary life (as different from a soldier, etc.) ◇*adj.* **2.** relating to non-military life and activities.

civilisation *or* **civilization** /sɪvəlaɪ'zeɪʃən/, *n.* **1.** an advanced state of human society, showing a high level of art, science, religion, etc. **2.** those people or nations that have reached such a state. **3.** the type of culture, society, etc., of a specific group: *Greek civilisation.* **4.** the act or process of civilising.

civilise *or* **civilize** /'sɪvəlaɪz/, *v.t.*, **-lised, -lising.** to bring out of a savage state; refine. [ML]

civilised *or* **civilized** /'sɪvəlaɪzd/, *adj.* **1.** having an advanced culture, society, etc. **2.** polite; well-bred; refined.

civility /sə'vɪləti/, *n., pl.* **-ties. 1.** politeness; courtesy. **2.** (*usu. pl.*) polite conversation: *The two men exchanged civilities.*

civil law, *n.* **1.** the laws of a state or nation regulating ordinary private matters (as different from criminal, military, or political matters). **2.** the systems of law coming from Roman law (as different from *common law, canon law*). **3.** the law of a state (as different from other kinds of law, as *international law*).

civil liberty, *n.* freedom of opinion, movement, etc., limited only by the public good.

civilly /'sɪvəli/, *adv.* **1.** politely, considerately, gently. **2.** in accordance with civil law.

civil marriage, *n.* a marriage performed by a state official rather than a clergyman.

civil rights, *n.pl.* the personal rights of the citizen in society.

civil war, *n.* war between parties, areas, etc., within one country.

Civil War, *n.* **1.** Also, the **Great Rebellion**. the war in England between the Parliamentarians and Royalists (1642-52). **2.** the American war between the North and the South (1861-65). **3.** → **Spanish Civil War**.

civvies /'sɪvɪz/, *n.pl. Colloq.* civilian clothes.

CJ, *Abbrev.* Chief Justice.

ck, *Abbrev.* creek.

clack /klæk/, *v.i.* **1.** to make a quick, sharp sound. **2.** to talk rapidly and continuously; chatter (oft. fol. by *on*). ◊*v.t.* **3.** to cause to clack. ◊*n.* **4.** a clacking sound. [ME imitative] **—clacker**, *n.*

clad /klæd/, *v.* past tense and past participle of **clothe**.

cladding /'klædɪŋ/, *n.* a covering of any kind fixed to a structure, esp. a building.

clado-, a word part meaning 'sprout', 'branch'. Also, before vowels, **clad-**. [combining form representing Gk *kládos* sprout]

cladode /'klædoʊd/, *n.* a leaf-like flattened branch or stem. Also, **cladophyll**.

claim /kleɪm/, *v.t.* **1.** to demand by or as a right. **2.** to declare as fact. **3.** to need or require: *Her plight claims our attention.* ◊*n.* **4.** a demand for something as due. **5.** an assertion of something as fact. **6.** a right to something. **7.** something claimed, as a piece of land for mining purposes, or a payment in accordance with an insurance policy, etc. [ME, from L: call] **—claimable**, *adj.* **—claimer**, *n.*

clairvoyant /klɛəˈvɔɪənt/, *adj.* **1.** having the power of seeing objects or actions beyond the natural range of the senses. ◊*n.* **2.** a clairvoyant person. [F *clair* clear + *voyant*, seeing] **—clairvoyance**, *n.*

clam /klæm/, *n.* **1.** a mollusc with two shells which can be tightly closed. **2.** *Colloq.* a secretive or silent person. ◊*v.* **clam up**, *Colloq.* to be silent; to refuse to talk. [OE: band, bond]

clamber /'klæmbə/, *v.i., v.t.* to climb, using both feet and hands; climb with effort or difficulty. [ME *clambren*] **—clamberer**, *n.*

clammy /'klæmi/, *adj.*, **-mier**, **-miest**. covered with cold, sticky moisture; cold and damp. [? Flem *klammig* sticky] **—clamminess**, *n.*

clamor or **clamour** /'klæmə/, *n.* **1.** loud and continued noise and shouting. **2.** a strong expression of desire or complaint. ◊*v.i.* **3.** to make a clamor; raise an outcry. ◊*v.t.* **4.** to express noisily. [ME, from L: a cry, shout] **—clamorer**, *n.* **—clamorous**, *adj.*

clamp /klæmp/, *n.* **1.** a tool used for strengthening or supporting objects or fastening them tightly together, usu. with movable ends connected by a screw. ◊*v.t.* **2.** to fasten with or fix in a clamp. **3.** to press firmly. ◊*v.* **4. clamp down**, *Colloq.* to become more strict. [MD]

clan /klæn/, *n.* **1.** a group of families or households, esp. among the Scots, the heads of which claim descent from a common ancestor. **2.** *Anthrop.* an association of lineages which have certain interests in common, as the organisation of marriage, land, common territory, ceremony, etc. [Gaelic *clann* family, stock]

Clancy of the Overflow /'klænsi/, *n.* an Australian folklore hero, featuring in the bush ballads 'The Man from Snowy River' and 'Clancy of the Overflow' by AB Paterson.

clandestine /klænˈdɛstɪn/, *adj.* secret; private; concealed: *a clandestine marriage.* [L]

clang /klæŋ/, *v.i.* **1.** to give out a loud, bell-like sound, as metal when struck; ring loudly or harshly. ◊*v.t.* **2.** to cause to resound or ring loudly. ◊*n.* **3.** a clanging sound. [imitative]

clanger /'klæŋə/, *n. Colloq.* a noticeable error or mistake, as an embarrassing remark: *to drop a clanger.*

clangor or **clangour** /'klæŋə, 'klæŋgə/, *n.* **1.** a loud, echoing sound, as of pieces of metal struck together. ◊*v.i.* **2.** to make a clangor; clang. [L] **—clangorous**, *adj.*

clank /klæŋk/, *n.* **1.** a sharp, hard, metallic sound: *clank of chains.* **2.** to move with or make such sounds. ◊*v.t.* **3.** to cause to resound sharply, as metal clanking together. [D]

clannish /'klænɪʃ/, *adj.* (of a group) like a clan, esp. showing (overly) close association of its members.

clap[1] /klæp/, *v.*, **clapped**, **clapping**. *n.* ◊*v.t.* **1.** to strike with a quick, smart blow, producing a short, sharp sound; slap; pat. **2.** to strike (the hands) together loudly. **3.** to show approval of, by clapping; applaud. **4.** to put, place, apply, etc., quickly and effectively: *clapped into jail.* ◊*v.i.* **5.** to make a sudden, sharp sound, as of two bodies being struck together. **6.** to clap one's hands, as in applause. ◊*n.* **7.** the act or sound of clapping. **8.** a loud, sudden noise, as of thunder. **9.** a sudden stroke or blow: *a clap on the back.* **10.** an expression of approval by clapping; applause. [OE *clæppan*]

clap[2] /klæp/, *n. Colloq.* venereal disease, esp. gonorrhoea (usu. preceded by *the*). [MF: brothel]

clapper /'klæpə/, *n.* something that claps, esp. the tongue of a bell.

clapperboard /'klæpəbɔd/, *n.* (in film-making) a board showing details of a scene and having a clapper to mark the sound track clearly, filmed at the beginning of each scene.

Clapton /'klæptən/, *n.* **Eric** (*Eric Patrick Clapp*), born 1945, British guitarist, singer and composer; one of the most influential of rock musicians; bands include the Yardbirds and Cream.

Clare /klɛə/, *n.* Irish, **An Clár**. a county in western Republic of Ireland, in Munster province. Pop. 91 343 (1986); 3188 km^2. *County Town:* Ennis.

Clarence /'klærəns/, *n.* a river in north-eastern NSW, rising in the McPherson Range and flowing south-east to the Pacific Ocean near Maclean. About 400 km.

Clarence Colliery, *n.* the largest underground mine in Australia, in central eastern NSW, west of Lithgow.

Clare of Assisi /klɛə əv ə'sisi/, *n.* Saint, 1194-1253, Franciscan nun; founder of the Poor Clares; patron saint of television.

claret /'klærət/, *n.* **1.** the red (orig. light red or yellowish) table wine of Bordeaux, France. **2.** a similar wine made elsewhere. ◇*adj.* **3.** deep purplish red. [ME, from OF: somewhat clear, light-colored, from L]

clarify /'klærəfaɪ/, *v.t., v.i.,* **-fied, -fying. 1.** to make or become understandable. **2.** to make or become clear by removal of sediment or rubbish, often over slow heat: *She clarified the butter.* [ME, from OF, from LL] **–clarification,** *n.* **–clarifier,** *n.*

clarinet /ˌklærə'nɛt/, *n.* one of the woodwind musical instruments, tube-like, with a single reed. Also, **clarionet** /ˌklæriə'nɛt/. [F: little clarion] **–clarinettist,** *n.*

clarion /'klæriən/, *adj.* **1.** clear and ringing. **2.** inspiring, rousing. ◇*n.* **3.** an old type of trumpet used for high-sounding passages. **4.** *Poetic.* the sound of the clarion. **5.** a clear, sharp call. [ME, from ML, from L *clārus* clear]

clarity /'klærəti/, *n.* clearness. [L]

Clark /klak/, *n.* **(Charles) Manning (Hope)**, born 1915, Australian historian.

Clarke, 1. Marcus Andrew Hislop, 1846-81, Australian writer, born in England; recorder of early Melbourne bohemia and author of the novel *For the Term of His Natural Life* (1874). **2. William Branwhite**, 1798-1878, Australian geologist and clergyman, born in England; one of the first discoverers of gold, 1841.

clash /klæʃ/, *v.i.* **1.** to make a loud, harsh noise. **2.** to collide, esp. noisily. **3.** to disagree; conflict. **4.** to coincide unfortunately (esp. of events). ◇*n.* **5.** a loud, harsh noise. **6.** conflict; opposition, esp. of views or interests. [b. CLAP¹ and DASH]

clasp /klasp, klasp/, *n.* **1.** a device, usu. of metal, for fastening things or parts together; any fastening or connection; anything that clasps. **2.** a firm hold; embrace. ◇*v.t.* **3.** to fasten with a clasp. **4.** to take hold of; grasp: *clasping hands.* [ME *claspe(n)*]

class /klas/, *n.* **1.** a number of people, things, etc., regarded as forming one group through possession of similar qualities; kind; sort. **2.** any division of people or things according to rank or grade. **3. a.** a group of pupils taught together. **b.** the period or year during which they are taught. **4.** a section of society sharing essential economic, political or cultural characteristics, and having the same social position: *middle class.* **5.** a social rank, esp. high rank. **6.** an admired style in manner or dress: *She has real class.* **7.** (in travel) a grade or standard in ships, planes, etc.: *to travel first class.* **8.** *Zool., Bot.* a major subdivision of phylum, usu. consisting of many different orders, as gastropods, mammals, angiosperms. ◇*v.t.* **9.** to put into a class; rate. ◇*adj.* **10.** relating to class. [F, from L *classis* class (of people, etc.), army, fleet] **–classable,** *adj.* **–classer,** *n.*

class action, *n.* a legal action brought by a group of people all with the same complaint or claim against the same defendant.

classic /'klæsɪk/, *adj.* **1.** of first or highest class or rank. **2.** serving as a standard, model, or guide: *a classic example.* **3.** of ancient Greek and Roman times, esp. relating to literature and art; classical. **4.** relating to an established set of artistic or scientific standards and methods. ◇*n.* **5.** someone or something of the highest class, as a writer or a work of art. **6.** (*pl.*) the literature and languages of ancient Greece and Rome. **7.** someone or something whose behavior conforms to the expected. [L: of the first or highest class]

classical /'klæsɪkəl/, *adj.* **1.** classic. **2.** (*sometimes cap.*) in accordance with the classics, esp. ancient Greek and Roman models in literature or art, or with later systems of principles modelled upon them. **3.** conforming to established taste or critical standards; relating to traditional forms. **4.** (of music) said to be serious or of special worth, often taking one of several traditional forms, as sonata, symphony, etc., and different from simpler and more widely popular music. **5.** (of music) following strict rules of style and form, esp. as composed before 1800 (opposed to *romantic*). **–classicality,** *n.*

classicism /'klæsəsɪzəm/, *n.* **1.** the (use of) principles of classical literature or art. **2.** the classical style in literature or art, characterised esp. by attention to form, with general effect of regularity, simplicity, balance, proportion, and controlled emotion. **–classicist,** *n.*

classification /ˌklæsəfə'keɪʃən/, *n.* **1.** the act or result of classifying. **2.** the placement of plants and animals into groups according to structure, origin, etc. The usual series of categories is phylum (in zoology) or division (in botany), class, order, family, genus, species, and variety. **3.** one of several degrees (restricted, top secret, etc.) of security protection for government papers, etc. **4.** (in libraries, etc.) a system for arranging books, etc., according to fields of knowledge and certain subjects within each field. **–classificatory,** *adj.*

classified advertisement, /ˌklæsəfaɪd əd'vɜtəsmənt/. a small newspaper advertisement, usu. single-column, esp. one advertising a job, object for sale, etc.

classify /'klæsəfaɪ/, *v.t.,* **-fied, -fying. 1.** to arrange in classes; place according to class. **2.** to mark or declare (a document, paper, etc.) of value to an enemy, and limit its handling and use. **–classifiable,** *adj.* **–classified,** *adj.*

class war, *n.* (in Marxist thought) the struggle for political and economic power carried on between capitalists and workers.

classy /'klasi/, *adj. Colloq.* of high class, rank, or grade; stylish; fine.

clastic /'klæstɪk/, *adj.* **1.** *Biol.* breaking or dividing up into parts: *clastic cell.* **2.** relating to an anatomical model made up of movable pieces. **3.** consisting of fragments of pre-existing rocks. [Gk *klastós* broken + -IC]

clatter /ˈklætə/, *v.i.*, *v.t.* **1.** to make or cause to make a rattling sound, as of hard bodies striking quickly together. ◇*n.* **2.** clattering noise; disturbance. [OE *clatrian*, of imitative orig.]

Claudius I /ˈklɔːdiəs/, *n.* 10 BC–AD 54, Roman emperor AD 41–54; invaded Britain in AD 43.

clause /klɔz/, *n.* **1.** *Gram.* a group of words containing a subject and a predicate, forming a sentence or part of sentence. **2.** a section of a (legal) document, complete in itself. [ME, from ML] – **clausal**, *adj.*

claustrophobia /klɒstrəˈfoʊbiə, klɔs-/, *n.* the fear of being enclosed in a small space. [NL, from L *claustrum* enclosure + *-phobia* -PHOBIA] – **claustrophobic**, *adj.*

claves /kleɪvz/, *n.pl.* a musical instrument consisting of two wooden sticks which are struck together.

clavichord /ˈklævəkɔd/, *n.* an early type of piano, in which strings were softly struck with metal blades standing out from the rear ends of the keys. [ML, from L *clāvi(s)* key + *chord(a)* string]

clavicle /ˈklævɪkəl/, *n.* either of two slender bones each connecting the breastbone with the shoulder blade and forming the front part of the shoulder; collarbone. [L: little key] – **clavicular**, *adj.*

clavier /ˈklæviə, kləˈvɪə/, *n.* any stringed instrument with a keyboard, such as the harpsichord, clavichord, piano or organ. [G, from F: keyboard, from L: key]

claw /klɔ/, *n.* **1.** a sharp, usu. curved, nail on foot of animal. **2.** a foot with such nails. **3.** anything that looks like a claw. **4.** the pincers of some shellfish and insects. ◇*v.t.* **5.** to tear, scratch, seize, pull, etc., with or as with claws. ◇*v.i.* **6.** to tear or scratch (fol. by *at*). [OE *clawian*]

claw hammer, *n.* a hammer having a head with one end curved and split for pulling out nails.

clay /kleɪ/, *n.* **1.** a natural earthy material which is easily shaped when wet, used for making bricks, pottery, etc. **2.** earth; mud. **3.** the human body. [OE *clǣg*] – **clayey**, **clayish**, *adj.*

Clay /kleɪ/, *n.* **Cassius** → **Muhammad Ali**.

claypan /ˈkleɪpæn/, *n.* a depression in the ground which retains water.

-cle, variant of **-cule**. [L *-culus*, *-cula*, *-culum*; in some words, from F]

clean /klin/, *adj.* **1.** free from dirt or filth; unsoiled; unstained. **2.** free from foreign matter or obstruction: *a clean harbor.* **3.** free of radioactivity. **4.** free from imperfection: *clean timber.* **5.** morally pure; upright; honorable. **6.** sportsmanlike: *a clean fight.* **7.** even; with smooth edge or surface: *a clean cut.* **8.** complete; perfect: *a clean sweep.* ◇*adv.* **9.** in a clean manner. **10.** wholly; completely; quite. **11.** *Cricket.* (bowled) by a ball which breaks the wicket without touching the batsman or bat. **12. come clean**, to make a full confession. ◇*v.t.* **13.** to make clean. ◇*v.* **14. cleanout**, to empty or rid (something) of rubbish and dirt: *to clean out the pantry.* **15. clean up, a.** to put in order; tidy up. **b.** to finish up; reach the end of. **c.** *Colloq.* to make (money); succeed. **d.** *Sport, etc.* to defeat crushingly: *Carlton cleaned up Richmond last Saturday.* [ME *clene*, OE *clǣne* pure, clear, c. D and G *klein* small]

cleanliness /ˈklɛnlinəs/, *n.* personal neatness and cleanness.

cleanse /klɛnz/, *v.t.*, **cleansed**, **cleansing**. **1.** to make clean, pure, etc. **2.** to remove by, or as by, cleaning: *His leprosy was cleansed.* [OE, from *clǣne* clean] – **cleanser**, *n.*

cleanskin /ˈklinskɪn/, *n.* **1.** an unbranded animal. **2.** someone who is free from blame, or has no record of police conviction. **3.** → **cleanskin nobby**.

cleanskin nobby, *n.* an opal found in an abandoned mine, not noticed by previous miners.

clear /klɪə/, *adj.* **1.** free from darkness, or cloudiness; light. **2.** bright, shining. **3.** transparent. **4.** free of blemishes: *a clear complexion.* **5.** easily seen, heard or understood. **6.** free from confusion, or doubt; certain: *My mind is quite clear about the matter.* **7.** free from guilt or blame; innocent. **8.** free from obstructions or obstacles; open. **9.** without obligation or liability; free from debt. ◇*adv.* **10.** in a clear manner; clearly; distinctly; entirely. ◇*v.t.* **11.** to make clear; free from darkness, indistinctness, confusion, uncertainty, obstruction, obligation, etc. **12.** to pay (a debt) in full. **13.** to pass (cheques, etc.) through a clearing house. **14.** to gain as clear profit; to earn, after (tax) deductions: *to clear $1000 per month.* [ME, from L]

clearance /ˈklɪərəns/, *n.* **1.** the act of clearing. **2.** a clear space; a clearing. **3.** official authority to see classified or secret material. **4.** *Naut.* the official certificate or papers (**clearance papers**) which allow a ship to enter or leave port.

clearing /ˈklɪərɪŋ/, *n.* **1.** a piece of cleared land, as in a forest. **2.** the mutual exchange between banks of cheques and drafts, and the settlement of the differences.

clearing house, *n.* **1.** a place or office where claims and accounts are settled, as between banks. **2.** a central office for receiving and giving out information.

clearway /ˈklɪəweɪ/, *n.* a stretch of road, esp. in a built-up area, on which, between stated times, motorists may stop only in emergencies.

Cleary /ˈklɪəri/, *n.* **Jon Stephen**, born 1917, Australian author; major works include *The Sundowners* (1948).

cleat /klit/, *n.* a small wedge-shaped block of wood or metal fastened to something for support. [ME *clete* wedge]

cleavage /ˈklivɪdʒ/, *n.* **1.** (in rocks) a tendency to split in certain directions. **2.** the state of being cleft or split; division. **3.** *Biol.* the total or partial division of a fertilised egg into

cleavage 191 **climate**

smaller cells. **4.** *Colloq.* the cleft between a woman's breasts.

cleave[1] /kliv/, *v.i.*, **cleaved, cleaving. 1.** to stick; cling or hold fast (fol. by *to*). **2.** to be attached or faithful (fol. by *to*). [OE *cleofian*]

cleave[2] /kliv/, *v.t.*, **cleft** or **cleaved** or **clove, cleft** or **cleaved** or **cloven, cleaving. 1.** to divide or part by a cutting blow, esp. along the grain or any other natural line of division. **2.** to make by or as by cutting: *to cleave a path through the wilderness*. **3.** to separate or sever by, or as by, splitting. [OE *cleofan*]

cleaver /'klivə/, *n.* a heavy knife or long-bladed chopper used by butchers for cutting up meat.

Cleese /kliz/, *n.* **John Marwood**, born 1939, British comic writer and actor; noted for television series such as *Monty Python's Flying Circus* and *Fawlty Towers*.

clef /klɛf/, *n.* (in music) the symbol placed upon the stave to show the name and pitch of notes in the lines and spaces. [F, from L: key]

cleft[1] /klɛft/, *n.* a space, opening or division made by cleaving; split. [ME *clift*, OE *geclyft* split, crack, fissure]

cleft[2] /klɛft/, *v.* **1.** past tense and past participle of **cleave**[2]. ◇*adj.* **2.** cloven; split; divided.

cleft palate, *n.* a congenital problem of the palate in which the roof of the mouth is split lengthwise.

Cleisthenes /'klaɪsθəniz/, *n.* fl. 508 BC, Athenian statesman; important in the founding of Athenian democracy.

clematis /klə'meɪtɪs, 'klɛmətəs/, *n.* any of flowering vines or shrubs, as traveller's joy of eastern Australia, which are found also in Europe and western Asia. [L, from Gk: little vine branch]

Clemenceau /klɛmɒ̃'sou/, *n.* **Georges Eugène Benjamin** /ʒɔʒ/, 1841–1929, French statesman, journalist, and physician; prime minister of France 1906–09 and 1917–20.

clemency /'klɛmənsi/, *n.* **1.** mercy or kind understanding, esp. as shown towards an enemy. **2.** mildness of weather. **3.** mildness of personal manner, etc. [ME, from L] – **clement,** *adj.*

Clement /'klɛmənt/, *n.* the name adopted by 14 popes, notably: **1. V** (*Bertrand de Got*), 1264–1314, pope 1305–14, who transferred the papacy to Avignon. **2. VII** (*Giulio de' Medici*), 1478?–1534, pope 1523–34 (nephew of Lorenzo de' Medici).

clench /klɛntʃ/, *v.t.* **1.** to close (the hands, teeth, etc.) tightly. **2.** to grasp firmly; grip. **3.** to settle clearly; clinch. ◇*n.* **4.** the act of clenching. **5.** a tight hold; grip. **6.** that which holds fast or clenches; clamp. [OE *beclencan* hold fast]

Cleopatra /kliə'patrə, -'pætrə/, *n.* 69?–30 BC, queen of Egypt 47–30 BC. She saved her kingdom by winning the love of Julius Caesar and Mark Antony, but was defeated by Octavian. After her death by suicide, Egypt became a Roman province.

clergy /'klɜdʒi/, *n., pl.* **-gies.** those ordained for ministering in the Christian Church, as distinct from the laity. [ME, from LL *clēricus* CLERIC]

clergyman /'klɜdʒimən/, *n., pl.* **-men.** a male member of the clergy.

cleric /'klɛrɪk/, *n.* a member of the clergy. [LL, from Gk: clergy, orig., lot, allotment]

clerical /'klɛrɪkəl/, *adj.* **1.** relating to clerks or to office workers: *a clerical mistake*. **2.** of, relating to, or characteristic of the clergy or the clergyman. [LL]

clerk /klak/, *n.* **1.** a person employed to keep records or accounts, attend to letters, etc. **2.** the chief executive of city or municipal councils: *town clerk*. **3.** a builder's representative, responsible for the quality of work on a building site: *clerk of works*. [OE *clerc, cleric,* from LL: CLERIC]

clever /'klɛvə/, *adj.* having quick intelligence; bright; able. [ME *cliver*; orig. uncert.] – **cleverness,** *n.*

clew /klu/, *n.* **1.** a ball or skein of thread, yarn, etc. **2.** *Naut.* the lower corner of a sail. ◇*v.t.* **3.** *Naut.* to haul the (lower corners of a sail) up to the yard (fol. by *up*). [OE *cleowen*]

clianthus /kli'ænθəs/, *n.* a plant bearing scarlet flowers, as Sturt's desert pea of inland Australia.

cliché /'kliʃeɪ/, *n., pl.* **-chés** /-eɪz/. an expression, idea, practice, etc., used so often it has lost its force. [F, pp. of *clicher* to stereotype. Cf. G *Klitsch* doughy mass] – **clichéd,** *adj.*

click /klɪk/, *n.* **1.** a slight, sharp sound: *the click of a door latch*. **2.** a speech sound produced by sucking air into a partial vacuum in the mouth. ◇*v.i.* **3.** to make a click or series of clicks. **4.** to fall into place or be understood: *His story suddenly clicked.* ◇*v.t.* **5.** to cause to click; strike with a click. [imitative] – **clicker,** *n.*

client /'klaɪənt/, *n.* **1.** a person who applies to a lawyer, accountant, etc. for advice or help. **2.** a customer. [ME, from L *cliens* retainer] – **cliental,** *adj.*

clientele /kliən'tɛl/, *n.* the customers, clients, etc. (of a lawyer, businessman, etc.) as a whole. [L]

cliff /klɪf/, *n.* a high, steep face of a rocky mass; precipice. [OE *clif*]

cliff-hanger /'klɪf-hæŋə/, *n.* **1.** a contest, election, etc., so closely matched that the outcome is uncertain until the end. **2.** a particularly suspenseful play, novel, serial, etc.

climacteric /klaɪ'mæktərɪk, klaɪmək'tɛrɪk/, *adj.* **1.** relating to a critical period; crucial. **2.** *Physiol.* the period of decrease of reproductive activity, esp. in women at menopause. [L, from Gk]

climate /'klaɪmət/, *n.* **1.** the general weather conditions of a region, averaged over a series of years. **2.** an area with a particular kind of climate: *We're moving to a warmer climate.* **3.** the general attitude and opinions of a group of people. [ME, from LL, from Gk:

clime, zone, lit., slope (of the earth from equator to pole)] **—climatic,** adj. **—climatically,** adv.

climax /'klaɪmæks/, n. **1.** the highest point of anything; culmination. **2.** an important point in a drama; turning point of the action in a play. **3.** Ecol. that stage of a plant-animal community which is stable within existing environmental conditions. **4.** sexual climax; orgasm. ◇v.i. **5.** to reach a climax. ◇v.t. **6.** to bring to a climax. [L, from Gk *klîmax* ladder, staircase, climax] **—climactic,** adj.

climb /klaɪm/, v.i. **1.** to move upwards; ascend. **2.** to rise slowly by, or as by, continued effort. **3.** (of ground) to slope upward. **4.** (of plants) to ascend by twining or by means of tendrils, etc.: *a climbing rose*. **5.** to rise, or attempt to rise, in social position. **6.** to go down (a ladder, pole, etc.), esp. by using both hands and feet (fol. by *down*). ◇n. **7.** an ascent by climbing. **8.** a place to be climbed. [OE *climban*]

clime /klaɪm/, n. *Poetic.* **1.** a region of the earth. **2.** climate. [LL *clima* CLIMATE]

clinch /klɪntʃ/, v.t. **1.** to secure (a driven nail, etc.) by bending down the point. **2.** to fasten (work) together thus. **3.** to settle (a matter) with great certainty. **4.** Naut. to secure overlapping plates on the side of a ship. ◇v.i. **5.** Boxing, etc. to engage in a clinch (def. 7). ◇n. **6.** the act of clinching. **7.** Boxing. a close hold which hinders the opponent's punches. **8.** Colloq. an embrace. [later var. of CLENCH] **—clincher,** n.

cline /klaɪn/, n. a continuous, graded variation in the members of a species across wide geographical or ecological range.

cling /klɪŋ/, v.i., **clung, clinging. 1.** to stick closely; adhere. **2.** to hold fast; cleave. **3.** to be or remain close. **4.** to remain attached (to an idea, hope, memory, etc.). [OE *clingan* stick or draw together, shrivel] **—clinger,** n. **—clingy,** adj.

clinic /'klɪnɪk/, n. **1.** a class of practical instruction for medical students which takes place with patients in a hospital ward. **2.** the out-patient section of a hospital. **3.** a medical centre used for such treatments as X-rays, child care, vaccinations, etc. **4.** a hospital for private patients. [LL: of a bed, from Gk]

clinical /'klɪnɪkəl/, adj. **1.** relating to a clinic, sick room or hospital. **2.** concerned with the observation and personal treatment of disease in a patient. **3.** scientific; detached, unemotional: *He has a clinical attitude to death.*

clink¹ /klɪŋk/, v.i. **1.** to make a light, sharp, ringing sound, as of glasses hitting together. ◇n. **2.** the rather piercing cry of some birds. [ME]

clink² /klɪŋk/, n. *Colloq.* prison; gaol. [apparently from *Clink* prison in Clink St, Southwark, London]

clinker /'klɪŋkə/, n. **a.** a hard brick, used for paving, etc. **b.** an overburnt face brick. **2.** a scale of oxide formed on iron during forging. **3.** a mass of non-burnable matter joined together, as that left after burning coal. ◇v.i. **4.** to form clinkers in burning. [D: kind of brick]

Clinton /'klɪntən/, n. **Bill** (*William Jefferson Clinton*), born 1946, US Democratic politician; became 42nd president of the US in 1993.

clip¹ /klɪp/, v., **clipped, clipping,** n. ◇v.t. **1.** to cut, or cut off or out, as with shears; trim by cutting. **2.** to cut or trim the hair or fleece of; shear. **3.** to punch a hole in (a ticket). **4.** to pronounce (words) in a brisk and precise manner. **5.** *Colloq.* to hit with a sharp, glancing blow: *The punch clipped his shoulder.* **6.** *Colloq.* to cheat. ◇v.i. **7.** to clip or cut something; make the motion of clipping something. ◇n. **8.** the act of clipping. **9.** → **woolclip. 10.** an extract from a film. **11.** *Colloq.* rate; pace: *at a rapid clip*. [ME, from Scand] **—clipping,** n.

clip² /klɪp/, n. **1.** a small device for gripping and holding tightly; metal clasp, esp. one for papers, letters, hair, etc. **2.** a holder for ammunition ready for putting into the magazine of certain weapons. [OE *clyppan* embrace]

clip³ /klɪp/, n. *Colloq.* a video clip.

clipper /'klɪpə/, n. **1.** (*oft. pl.*) a cutting tool, esp. shears, used to cut grass, hair, etc. **2.** a swiftly moving horse, etc. **3.** a sailing ship built for great speed.

clique /klik/, n. a small group of people, esp. one that is snobbishly exclusive. [F, *claque*, hired applauders in a theatre]

clitoris /'klɪtərəs, 'klaɪ-/, n. the small, erectile organ of the vulva. [NL, from Gk: shut]

Clive /klaɪv/, n. **Robert** (*Baron Clive of Plassey*), 1725–1774, British general and statesman in India. His victory in the Battle of Plassey in 1757 was important in giving Great Britain control of India.

cloaca /kloʊ'eɪkə/, n., *pl.* **-cae** /-kiː/. *Zool.* **1.** a cavity in the pelvic region of birds, reptiles, amphibians, many fishes and certain mammals, into which intestinal, urinary and generative canals open. **2.** a similar cavity in invertebrates. [L: sewer] **—cloacal,** adj.

cloak /kloʊk/, n. **1.** a loose outer garment. **2.** something which covers or conceals; disguise; pretext. ◇v.t. **3.** to cover with, or as with a cloak. **4.** to hide; conceal. [ME, from ML: cloak, orig. bell; ? of Celtic orig]

cloak-and-dagger /kloʊk-ən-'dægə/, adj. (of a play, event, etc.) melodramatic; concerned with spies, intrigue, etc.

cloakroom /'kloʊkrum/, n. a room where cloaks, overcoats, etc., may be left for a short time.

clock /klɒk/, n. **1.** an instrument for measuring and indicating time, oft. having pointers (hands) which move round on a dial to mark the hour, etc. **2.** *Colloq.* a piece of measuring equipment having a dial, as a tachometer. **3.** the dial itself. **4.** *Elect.* a circuit producing regular pulses which control the speed of operation of a system. ◇v.t. **5.** to time, test, or measure by clock, esp. of races. ◇v. **6. clock in** or **on,** to register the time of arrival at work. **7. clock out** or **off,** to register the time of departure from work. [ME, from MD: instrument for measuring time]

clockwise /'klɒkwaɪz/, *adv., adj.* in the same direction as the hands of a clock rotate.

clockwork /'klɒkwɜk/, *n.* **1.** the mechanism of a clock, or similar mechanism. **2. like clockwork,** with perfect regularity or precision.

clod /klɒd/, *n.* **1.** a lump or mass, esp. of earth, soil or clay. **2.** a stupid person; dolt. [OE *clodd*] **−cloddish,** *adj.*

clodhopper /'klɒdhɒpə/, *n.* **1.** a clumsy, stupid person; rustic; bumpkin. **2.** (*pl.*) strong, heavy shoes.

clog /klɒg/, *v.*, **clogged, clogging,** *n.* ◇*v.t.* **1.** to hold back; hamper; hinder. ◇*v.i.* **2.** to become blocked, or choked up. ◇*n.* **3.** anything that stops movement or action; encumbrance; hindrance. **4.** a heavy block, as of wood, fastened to a man or beast to slow down movement. **5.** a kind of shoe with a thick sole, usu. made of wood. [ME *clog, clogge*; orig. uncert.] **−cloggy,** *adj.*

cloister /'klɔɪstə/, *n.* **1.** a covered walk, esp. at the side of a building, as a church, college, etc. **2.** a place of religious seclusion; monastery; nunnery; convent. ◇*v.t.* **3.** to confine as if in a cloister; seclude. [ME, from OF, b. *cloison* partition and L *claustrum* enclosed place] **−cloistral,** *adj.*

clone /kloʊn/, *v.t.,* **cloned, cloning.** ◇*v.t.* **1.** to reproduce (an individual) asexually, by implanting one of its body cells into an egg cell from which the nucleus has been removed, and allowing the egg cell to develop. The resulting individual is an exact replica of the donor and has no relationship with the female providing or nurturing the egg cell. ◇*n.* **2.** an organism produced in this way. **3.** *Hort.* a group of plants originating as parts of the same individual, from buds or cuttings. Also, **clon** /klɒn, kloʊn/. [Gk: slip; twig]

close /kloʊz/, *v.*, **closed, closing;** /kloʊs/, *adj.,* **closer, closest,** *adv;* /kloʊz/ *for defs 24-25;* /kloʊs/ *for defs 26-27,* n. ◇*v.t.* **1.** to stop or block up (a gap, entrance, opening, etc.). **2.** to shut. **3.** to shut in or surround on all sides; enclose (fol. by *in*): *to close in with a fence.* **4.** to refuse entry to: *Lifesavers closed the beach because of sharks.* **5.** to bring together; join up: *to close the ranks of troops.* **6.** to end; to shut down, either temporarily or permanently: *to close debate.* ◇*v.i.* **7.** to become closed; shut. **8.** to come to an end, finish; terminate. **9.** *Stock Exchange.* to be worth at the end of a trading period: *Gold closed at a higher level than yesterday.* ◇*v.* **10. close in,** to surround and approach (a place) gradually, as in making a capture. **11. close with,** *Naut.* **a.** to come close to. **b.** to fight; engage in close encounter. **c.** to come to terms. ◇*adj.* **12.** shut; shut tight; not open. **13.** shut in; enclosed. **14.** narrow; confined: *close quarters.* **15.** lacking fresh air: *a close room.* **16.** practising secrecy; secretive; reticent: *She is very close about her income.* **17.** stingy; parsimonious: *close with his money.* **18.** having the parts near together; compact: *fabric of close weave.* **19.** near, or near together, in space, time, or relation: *in close contact.* **20.** *Ball Games.* noted for short passes and cautious methods: *They played a close game.* **21.** based upon a strong uniting feeling of love, honor, etc: *a close friendship.* **22.** strict; searching; minute: *close study.* ◇*adv.* **23.** in a close manner; closely. ◇*n.* **24.** the act of closing. **25.** the end or conclusion. **26.** an enclosed place; any piece of private land. **27.** a narrow entry leading to a courtyard; cul-de-sac. [ME, from F, from L *clausum* enclosed place] **−closeness,** *n.* **−closer,** *n.*

closed /kloʊzd/, *adj.* restricted in any of various ways; exclusive.

closed circuit, *n.* an electrical circuit which has been completed so that a current can flow along it.

closed-circuit television, *n.* a television system in which cameras and receivers are linked by wires, used to view events in another part of a building, for security, monitoring of production operations, etc.

closed set, *n. Maths.* a set (def. 38) having a particular number of elements.

closed shop, *n.* **1.** a workshop, factory, etc., in which the employer must call on a particular trade union to provide employees. ◇*adj.* **2.** inflexible: *closed shop mentality.*

close quarters, *n.pl.* **1.** a small, cramped place or position. **2.** direct and close contact.

closet /'klɒzət/, *n.* **1.** a small room, enclosed recess, or cabinet, for clothing, food, utensils, etc. **2.** a water closet; toilet. ◇*adj.* **3.** secret: *a closet drinker.* ◇*v.t.* **4.** to shut up in a private room for a conference, interview, etc. [ME, from OF: little enclosed place, from L]

closure /'kloʊʒə/, *n.* **1.** the act of closing or shutting. **2.** the state of being closed. **3.** a bringing to an end; conclusion. **4.** Also, **closure motion.** *Parl. Proc.* the method of closing debate and causing an immediate vote to be taken on a question under discussion. [ME, from L: shut]

clot /klɒt/, *n., v.*, **clotted, clotting.** ◇*n.* **1.** a mass or lump, as of blood. **2.** *Colloq.* a stupid person. ◇*v.i.* **3.** to form into clots; coagulate. ◇*v.t.* **4.** to cause to clot; cover with clots. [OE *clott* lump]

cloth /klɒθ/, *n., pl.* **cloths** /klɒθs/, *adj.* ◇*n.* **1.** fabric formed by weaving, felting, etc., from wool, hair, silk, flax, cotton, or other fibre, used for garments, upholstery, and many other purposes. **2. the cloth,** the clergy. **3.** *Naut.* one of several lengths of canvas stitched together to make a sail. ◇*adj.* **4.** made of, covered with, or relating to cloth. [OE *clath*]

clothe /kloʊð/, *v.t.,* **clothed** or **clad, clothing. 1.** to provide with clothing. **2.** to cover with, or as with, clothing. **3.** to provide; endow (as with meaning). [OE *clāthian*]

clothes /kloʊðz/, *n.pl.* **1.** garments for the body; articles of dress. **2.** bedclothes. [orig., pl. of CLOTH]

clothing /'kloʊðɪŋ/, *n.* **1.** garments collectively; clothes; apparel. **2.** a covering.

cloud /klaʊd/, *n.* **1.** a visible collection of particles of water or ice suspended in air, usu.

cloud at an elevation above the earth's surface. **2.** any similar mass, esp. of smoke, dust, steam, etc. **3.** anything that obscures, darkens, or causes gloom, trouble, suspicion, disgrace, etc. **4.** a great number of insects, birds, etc., flying together: *a cloud of locusts.* **5. on cloud nine**, *Colloq.* in a state of great happiness or bliss. ◇*v.t.* **6.** to overspread or cover with, or as with, a cloud or clouds. **7.** to overshadow; obscure; darken. **8.** to cover with gloom, disgrace, etc. ◇*v.i.* **9.** to grow cloudy; become clouded. [OE *clūd* rock, hill]

cloudburst /ˈklaʊdbɜst/, *n.* a sudden and very heavy rainfall.

cloud chamber, *n. Phys.* an instrument for making tracks of ionising particles visible as a row of droplets which condense from a saturated vapor.

cloudy /ˈklaʊdi/, *adj.*, **cloudier, cloudiest. 1.** full of or overcast with clouds: *a cloudy sky.* **2.** of or like cloud or clouds; relating to clouds. **3.** obscure; not clear or transparent: *cloudy liquid; cloudy ideas.* **4.** darkened by gloom, trouble, etc.: *cloudy looks.* **5.** under suspicion, disgrace, etc.: *cloudy reputation.* **–cloudily**, *adv.* **–cloudiness**, *n.*

clout /klaʊt/, *n.* **1.** *Colloq.* a blow, esp. with hand; cuff. **2.** Also, **clout nail.** a short flat-headed nail. **3.** force; effectiveness: *The committee has no political clout.* ◇*v.t.* **4.** *Colloq.* to strike, esp. with hand; cuff. [OE *clūt* piece of cloth or metal]

clove[1] /kloʊv/, *n.* the dried flower bud of a tropical tree, used whole or ground as spice. [ME, from OF *clou de girofle* nail of clove, so called from the shape]

clove[2] /kloʊv/, *n.* one of the small bulbs formed in the axils of the scales of a mother bulb, as in garlic. [OE *clufu* clove, bulb, tuber]

clove[3] /kloʊv/, *v.* past tense of **cleave**[2].

cloven /ˈkloʊvən/, *v.* past participle of **cleave**[2]. ◇*adj.* **2.** cleft, split, divided: *cloven feet or hoofs.*

cloven-hoofed /kloʊvən-ˈhʊft/, *adj.* **1.** having split hoofs, once assumed to represent halves of single undivided hoof, as in cattle. **2.** devilish; satanic.

clover /ˈkloʊvə/, *n.* **1.** any of various herbs with leaves with three leaflets and dense flower heads, many species of which are grown as forage plants. **2. in clover**, in comfort or luxury. [OE *clāfre*]

cloverleaf /ˈkloʊvəlif/, *n., pl.* **-leaves. 1.** a leaf of a clover. **2.** a road junction consisting of overpasses, underpasses, etc., forming the pattern of a four-leaf clover.

clown /klaʊn/, *n.* **1.** a jester or buffoon in a circus, pantomime, etc. **2.** *Colloq.* a fool; idiot. **3.** *Archaic.* a peasant; rustic. **4.** a coarse, ill-bred person; boor. ◇*v.i.* **5.** to act like a clown. [orig. uncert.] **–clownish**, *adj.* **–clownery**, *n.*

cloy /klɔɪ/, *v.t.* **1.** to weary by too much food, sweetness, pleasure, etc.; surfeit; satiate. ◇*v.i.* **2.** to cause to feel satiated. [from obs. *acloy* to stop up, drive in a nail, ? from MF, from L *clāvus* nail] **–cloying**, *adj.*

club /klʌb/, *n., v.,* **clubbed, clubbing.** ◇*n.* **1.** a heavy stick, usu. thicker at one end than the other, suitable for weapon; cudgel. **2.** the butt end of a rifle. **3.** a stick or bat used to drive a ball, etc., in various games. **4.** a stick with a crooked head used in golf, etc. **5.** a group of people organised for social, literary, sporting, political, or other purpose. **6.** a building or rooms owned by or associated with such a group, sometimes lavishly decorated and furnished, and offering dining, gambling, theatrical and other facilities to members. **7.** (a playing card bearing) a black figure like a clover-leaf (♣). **8.** (*pl.*) the suit of cards so marked. ◇*v.t.* **9.** to beat with, or as with, a club. **10.** to unite; combine; join together. ◇*v.i.* **11.** to join together as for a common purpose. [ME, from Scand]

club foot, *n.* **1.** a deformed or distorted foot, often clublike. **2.** the condition of such a foot. **–clubfooted**, *adj.*

cluck /klʌk/, *v.i.* **1.** to utter the cry of a hen brooding or calling her chicks. ◇*v.t.* **2.** to call or utter as by clucking: *clucking her sympathy.* [var. of *clock* (now Scot and d.), from OE *cloccian*]

clucky /ˈklʌki/, *adj. Colloq.* feeling a sentimental desire to have children.

clue /klu/, *n., v.,* **clued, cluing.** ◇*n.* **1.** anything that serves to guide or direct in the solution of a problem, mystery, etc. ◇*v.* **2. clue (someone) up**, to give (someone) the facts. [var. of CLEW]

clump /klʌmp/, *n.* **1.** a group (of trees, shrubs, grasses, etc.) growing thickly together. **2.** lump or mass. ◇*v.i.* **3.** to walk heavily and carelessly. **4.** to gather or be gathered into clumps. ◇*v.t.* **5.** to gather or form in clumps. [OE *clympre*] **–clumpy, clumpish**, *adj.*

clumsy /ˈklʌmzi/, *adj.*, **-sier, -siest.** awkward in movement or action; without skill or grace: *a clumsy workman.* [from obs. v. *clumse* be benumbed with cold, from Scand] **–clumsily**, *adv.* **–clumsiness**, *n.*

Clunes /klunz/, *n.* a town in Victoria north-west of Melbourne; site of one of Victoria's first goldfields. Pop. 817 (1986).

clung /klʌŋ/, *v.* past tense and past participle of **cling**.

Clunies-Ross /kluniz-ˈrɒs/, *n.* **John**, founded a settlement on the Cocos (Keeling) Islands in 1827, establishing hereditary rule on the islands, which lasted until 1978.

cluster /ˈklʌstə/, *n.* **1.** a number of things of the same kind, growing or held together; bunch: *a cluster of poppies.* **2.** *Astron.* a group of stars which move together. ◇*v.t.* **3.** to gather into a cluster. ◇*v.i.* **4.** to form clusters. [OE *cluster* bunch]

clutch[1] /klʌtʃ/, *v.t.* **1.** to seize with, or as with, the hands or claws; grasp. **2.** to grip or hold tightly or firmly. **3.** to try to seize (fol. by *at*). ◇*n.* **4.** (*usu. pl.*) power or control; mastery: *in the clutches of the enemy.* **5.** the act of clutching; a snatch; a grasp. **6.** a tight hold; grip. **7.** (of a motor) a device which engages

clutch and disengages the engine from transmission, or the pedal which operates this device. [OE *clyccan* crook or bend, close (the hand), clench]

clutch² /klʌtʃ/, *n.* **1.** the number of eggs produced or incubated at one time. **2.** a brood of chickens. ◇*v.t.* **3.** to hatch (chickens). [var. of d. *cletch*, akin to *cleck* hatch, from Scand]

clutch-start /'klʌtʃ-stat/, *v.t.* to start (the engine of a motor vehicle) by having it in gear with the clutch disconnected while it is rolled forward, and then quickly re-engaging the clutch.

Clutha /'kluːðə/, *n.* a river in southern South Island, NZ, flowing south-east to the Pacific Ocean. 338 km.

clutter /'klʌtə/, *v.t.* **1.** to fill (a place) with litter, disorder. ◇*n.* **2.** disorderly heap; litter. **3.** confusion; disorder. [var. of *clotter*, from CLOT]

Clyde /klaɪd/, *n.* **Firth of**, an inlet of the Atlantic, in south-western Scotland. 103 km long.

Clydesdale /'klaɪdzdeɪl/, *n.* one of a breed of strong, active draught horses originally raised in Clydesdale, Scotland.

Clytemnestra /klaɪtəm'nɛstrə/, *n.* Gk Legend. the daughter of Tyndareus and Leda, wife of Agamemnon. See **Agamemnon, Aegisthus, Orestes.** Also, **Clytaemnestra.**

cm, *Symbol.* centimetre; centimetres.

cmdr, *Abbrev.* commander.

CMF /siː ɛm 'ɛf/, *Abbrev.* Citizen Military Forces.

CND, Campaign for Nuclear Disarmament.

Cnossus /'nɒsəs/, *n.* →**Knossos.**

co-, **1.** a prefix signifying association and accompanying action, occurring mainly before vowels and *h* and *gn*, as in *coalition*, *cohabit*, *cognate.* **2.** a prefix signifying partnership, joint responsibility or ownership, as in *co-producer*, *co-writer*. [L, var. of *com-* COM-]

c/o., *Abbrev.* **1.** care of. **2.** carried over. Also, **c.o.**

Co, **1.** *Chem. Symbol.* cobalt. **2.** *Abbrev.* company.

CO /siː 'oʊ/, *Abbrev.* commanding officer.

coach /koʊtʃ/, *n.* **1.** a large, enclosed, four-wheeled carriage, used esp. on state occasions. **2.** →**stagecoach. 3.** a bus, esp. a single-decker, used for long journeys or for sightseeing. **5.** a railway carriage. **5.** a person who trains athletes for games, contests, etc. **6.** a private teacher who prepares a student for an examination. ◇*v.t.*, *v.i.* **7.** to teach, instruct or train (athletes, etc.). [F, from Hung]

coachwood /'koʊtʃwʊd/, *n.* a tree with light, easily worked timber, found in gullies in eastern Australia.

coagulate /koʊ'ægjəleɪt/, *v.t.*, *v.i.*, **-lated, -lating.** to change from a fluid into a thickened mass; curdle; congeal. [L: curdled] —**coagulation**, *n.* —**coagulator**, *n.* —**coagulative**, *adj.*

coal /koʊl/, *n.* **1.** a black or dark brown colored organic rock used as fuel, as **hard coal** (anthracite), **soft coal** (bituminous coal), **brown coal** (lignite). **2.** *Obs.* charcoal. **3. coals of fire, a.** good actions in return for bad, giving rise to feelings of remorse: *His smiles heaped coals of fire on my head.* **b.** reproaches. **4. coals to Newcastle**, anything supplied unnecessarily. **5. haul, (someone) over the coals**, to scold; reprimand. **6. add coals to the fire**, to make a bad situation worse. [OE *col* live coal]

coalesce /koʊə'lɛs/, *v.i.*, **-lesced, -lescing. 1.** to grow together or into one body. **2.** to unite so as to form one mass, community, etc. [L] —**coalescence**, *n.* —**coalescent**, *adj.*

coalface /'koʊlfeɪs/, *n.* **1.** part of a coal seam from which coal is cut. **2. work at the coalface**, *Colloq.* to play an active part in a project, organisation, etc.

coal gas, *n.* **1.** gas produced by burning coal. **2.** gas used for lighting and heating.

coalition /koʊə'lɪʃən/, *n.* **1.** union into one body or mass; fusion. **2.** a combination or alliance, esp. a temporary one between people, political parties, states, etc. [ML, from L: coalesce] —**coalitionist**, *n.*

coalmine /'koʊlmaɪn/, *n.* a mine or pit from which coal is obtained. —**coalminer**, *n.* —**coalmining**, *n.*, *adj.*

Coal River, *n.* the original name for the Hunter River, NSW, which officially changed in 1797.

Coalsack /'koʊlsæk/, *n.* one of two dark areas in space, the **Southern Coalsack**, a large dark space near the Southern Cross, and the **Northern Coalsack**, a dark space in the Milky Way in the northern constellation Cygnus.

coalscuttle /'koʊlskʌtl/, *n.* a bucket in which coal is carried into a room.

coal tar, *n.* the thick, black liquid formed during distillation of coal, which yields benzene, phenol, etc. (from which are derived many dyes), and **coal tar pitch**, used in making pavements, etc.

coarse /kɔːs/, *adj.*, **coarser, coarsest. 1.** of inferior or faulty quality, not pure or choice; common; base: *coarse manners; a coarse lad.* **2.** consisting of relatively large parts or particles: *coarse sand.* **3.** lacking in fineness of texture, structure, etc. **4.** harsh. **5.** lacking feeling, manner, etc.; not refined. **6.** (of screws) having the threads widely spaced. **7.** (of metals) unrefined. [adjectival var. of COURSE, *n.*, with the sense of ordinary]

coast /koʊst/, *n.* **1.** the land beside the sea; the seashore. **2. the coast is clear**, the danger has gone. ◇*v.i.* **3.** to keep going on momentum already gained. **4.** to descend a hill, on a bicycle without using the pedals, or in a car which is not in gear. ◇*v.* **5. coast along**, to act or perform with minimal effort. [ME, from L *costa* rib, side] —**coastal**, *adj.*

coastal plain, *n.* **1.** a broad low plain between a mountain range and the sea. **2.** lowland bordering the sea coast, formed usu. by erosion and deposition.

coaster /ˈkoustə/, *n.* **1.** a ship which trades from port to port along a coast. **2.** a small dish or mat placed under glasses, etc., to protect the table from moisture or heat.

coastguard /ˈkoustgad/, *n.* **1.** a police force responsible for patrolling a coastline, watching for ships in danger, etc. **2.** a member of a coastguard.

coast rosemary, *n.* a grey-green shrub with white flowers found on sea cliffs in NSW and often planted as an ornamental.

Coastwatchers /ˈkoustwɒtʃəz/, *n.* an Australian intelligence organisation formed in 1919 and being a vital source of information during World War II; consisted of civilians appointed by the Royal Australian Navy who were stationed on the mainland, PNG and the Solomons whose duty it was to report any suspicious occurrences.

coat /kout/, *n.* **1.** an outer garment with sleeves, as an overcoat, dress coat, etc. **2.** a natural covering, as hair, fur, or wool of animal, the bark of a tree, or the skin of a fruit. **3.** anything that covers or conceals: *a coat of paint.* ◇*v.t.* **4.** to cover or provide with a coat or coating. [ME, from OF, from Gmc]

Coates /kouts/, *n.* **Joseph Gordon**, 1878–1943, NZ statesman; prime minister 1925–28.

coat of arms, *n.* **1.** a tunic or tabard (jacket) covered with heraldic designs, worn by medieval knights over their armor. **2.** the heraldic bearings of a person; escutcheon. [translation of F *cotte d'armes*]

coat of mail, *n.* a suit of armor; garment made of interlinked metal rings, overlapping metal plates, etc.

coax /kouks/, *v.t.* **1.** to persuade by gentle urging, wheedling, etc. **2.** to get or win by coaxing: *He coaxed the money out of her.* ◇*v.i.* **3.** to use gentle persuasion, etc. [from obs. *cokes*, *n.*, fool; of doubtful orig.] **— coaxer**, *n.* **— coaxingly**, *adv.*

coaxial /kouˈæksiəl/, *adj.* **1.** having a common axis. **2.** (of a cable) consisting of an insulated central conductor with tubular stranded conductors laid over it and separated by layers of insulation. Also, **coaxal** /kouˈæksəl/.

cob /kɒb/, *n.* **1.** → **corncob**. **2.** a male swan. **3.** a short-legged, thickset horse. **4.** a small lump of coal, ore, etc. **5.** a roundish mass, lump, or heap. [ME]

cobalt /ˈkoubɒlt, -bəlt/, *n.* **1.** *Chem.* a silver-white metallic element which, when occurring as the silicate gives important blue coloring substances for ceramics. Symbol: Co; at. no.: 27; at. wt: 58.9332. **2.** a blue pigment containing cobalt. **3.** the isotope, cobalt 60, used in treatment of cancer. [G: goblin]

cobalt bloom, *n.* the mineral erythrite, hydrated cobalt arsenate, usu. of a peach-red color, used for coloring glass and ceramics.

Cobar /ˈkoubə/, *n.* a town and shire in north-western NSW; principal producer of copper in NSW. Pop. 4287 (1986).

Cobb and Co /ˈkɒb ən kou/, *n.* an Australian coach company established in 1853 by four Americans and purchased by James Rutherford and partners in 1859; operated until 1924 when it was superseded by the service car.

cobber /ˈkɒbə/, *n. Colloq.* a friend; mate. [Brit d. *cob* to form a friendship with]

cobble /ˈkɒbəl/, *n., v.,* **-bled, -bling.** ◇*n.* **1.** → **cobblestone. 2.** (*pl.*) → **cob** (def. 4). **3.** a badly completed job of sewing, mending, etc. **4.** *Geol.* a rock fragment between 64 and 256 mm in diameter, rounded by erosion. ◇*v.t.* **5.** to mend (shoes, etc.); patch. **6.** to put together roughly or clumsily. **7.** to pave with cobblestones. [? COB, def. 5]

cobbler[1] /ˈkɒblə/, *n.* **1.** a person who mends shoes. **2.** a clumsy workman. **3.** an iced drink made of wine, fruit, sugar, etc. **4.** a fruit pie with a biscuit dough topping, usu. made in a deep dish. **5.** one of the Australian eel-tailed catfishes.

cobbler[2] /ˈkɒblə/, *n.* a wrinkled sheep that is difficult to shear, often left till last; snob. [? pun on *cobbler's last*]

cobblestone /ˈkɒbəlstoun/, *n.* a rounded stone used in paving.

cobia /ˈkoubiə/, *n.* a dark-brown to blackish eastern Australian sport fish.

COBOL /ˈkoubɒl/, *n.* a language for writing computer programs for commercial use. Also, **Cobol.** [*Co(mmon) B(usiness) O(riented) L(anguage)*]

Cobourg Peninsula /ˈkoubəg/, *n.* a narrow extension of land in the north-western extremity of Arnhem Land, NT. About 96 km long.

cobra /ˈkɒbrə, ˈkoubrə/, *n.* a venomous snake noted for its ability to spread out the skin of its neck so that it looks like a hood. [short for Pg *cobra* (from L *colubra* serpent) *de capello* hood snake]

cobweb /ˈkɒbweb/, *n.* **1.** a web or net spun by a spider to catch its prey. **2.** a single thread spun by spider. **3.** anything fine-spun or flimsy. [ME *coppe* spider + WEB]

cocaine /kouˈkeɪn/, *n.* a bitter crystalline alkaloid, taken from leaves of the South American **coca** shrubs, formerly used as local anaesthetic, but now mainly as a stimulant. Also, **cocain.**

coccus /ˈkɒkəs/, *n., pl.* **-ci** /-saɪ/. a spherical bacterial organism. [NL, from Gk: grain, seed] **— coccoid**, *adj.*

coccyx /ˈkɒksɪks, ˈkɒkɪks/, *n., pl.* **coccyges** /kɒkˈsaɪdʒiz/. a small triangular bone forming the lower end of the spinal column in humans. [L, from Gk: coccyx, orig., cuckoo] **— coccygeal**, *adj.*

cochineal /kɒtʃəˈnil, ˈkɒtʃənil/, *n.* **1.** an insect which lives on cacti of Mexico and other warm regions of Central America. **2.** (crimson color of) dye produced from the dried bodies of this insect. [F, from Sp.: slater, from *cochino* pig]

cochlea /ˈkɒkliə/, *n., pl.* **-leae** /-lii/. a spiral shaped part of the internal ear, in

cochlea   197   **COD**

man and most other mammals. [L, from Gk: snail, something spiral] **—cochlear**, *adj.* **—cochleate**, *adj.*

cock[1] /kɒk/, *n.* **1. a.** the male of the domestic fowl; rooster. **b.** the male of certain other birds: *cock robin.* **2. → weathercock. 3. → stopcock. 4.** the hammer of a firearm. **5.** *Colloq. (offensive)* the penis. ◇*v.t.* **6.** to pull back and set the hammer of (a firearm) so that it is ready to fire. [OE *cocc*]

cock[2] /kɒk/, *v.t.* **1.** to set or turn up or to one side, often in a jaunty, or significant manner: *He wore his hat cocked on one side.* ◇*v.i.* **2.** to stand or stick up noticeably. [probably special use of COCK[1]]

cockade /kɒ'keɪd/, *n.* a knot of ribbon, rosette, feather, etc., worn on a hat as a badge or part of a uniform. [F *cocarde*, from *coq* cock] **—cockaded**, *adj.*

cockatiel /kɒkə'tiːl/, *n.* a small, crested, long-tailed parrot, common in inland areas of Australia. [D]

cockatoo /kɒkə'tuː/, *n.* **1.** any of various crested parrots of Australia, the Malay archipelago, etc. **2.** a small-scale farmer. [D, from Malay]

Cockatoo Island, *n.* **1.** an island in the Buccaneer Archipelago, Yampi Sound, WA; iron deposits. 31 km². **2.** an island in the mouth of the Parramatta River, in Sydney Harbor, NSW; shipbuilding, early colonial prison. 16 ha.

cockatrice /'kɒkətrəs, -traɪs/, *n.* **1.** a mythical snake with a deadly glance, said to be hatched by a serpent from a cock's egg, and usu. shown with the head, legs, and wings of a cock and the body and tail of a snake. **2. → basilisk.** [ME, from L]

Cockburn Sound /'koʊbən saʊnd/, *n.* a large sheltered harbor in WA, south of Fremantle. About 15 km long.

cockerel /'kɒkərəl, 'kɒkrəl/, *n.* a young domestic cock. [diminutive of COCK[1]]

cocker spaniel, /kɒkə 'spænjəl/ *n.* one of a breed of small spaniels trained for use in hunting or kept as pets.

cockeyed /'kɒkaɪd/, *adj.* **1.** having a squinting eye; cross-eyed. **2.** *Colloq.* twisted to one side; crooked. **3.** *Colloq.* foolish; absurd, illogical. **4.** *Colloq.* drunk.

cockfight /'kɒkfaɪt/, *n.* a fight between gamecocks, usu. with metal spurs attached to their legs, on the outcome of which spectators place bets. **—cockfighting**, *n.*

cockle /'kɒkəl/, *n., v.*, **-led**, **-ling.** ◇*n.* **1.** an edible bivalve mollusc with somewhat heart-shaped, radially ribbed shells, found in Europe. **2. → cockleshell. 3. cockles of the heart**, the inmost parts of the heart; depths of one's emotions or feelings: *That film warmed the cockles of my heart.* ◇*v.t., v.i.* **4.** to contract, or cause to contract, into wrinkles; pucker: *a book cockled by water.* [ME, from F, from Gk: little mussel or cockle]

cockleshell /'kɒkəlʃɛl/, *n.* **1.** the shell of a cockle. **2.** the shell of some other molluscs, as a scallop. **3.** a small, light boat.

cockney /'kɒkni/, *n., pl.* **-neys**, *adj.* ◇*n. (oft. cap.)* **1.** a native of London, esp. of the East End. **2.** the special form of language spoken by cockneys. ◇*adj.* **3.** of cockneys or their speech. [ME *cockeney* cock's egg (i.e. malformed egg)]

cockpit /'kɒkpɪt/, *n.* **1.** (in some aeroplanes) an enclosed space containing seats for the pilot and copilot. **2.** the driver's seat in a racing car.

cockroach /'kɒkroʊtʃ/, *n.* any of various insects, usu. nocturnal, which have a flattened body and long feelers, and are common household pests. [popular rendition of Sp *cucaracha*]

cockscomb /'kɒkskoʊm/, *n.* **1.** the fleshy growth on the head of a cock; comb (def. 3). **2. → coxcomb** (def. 2).

cocksure /'kɒkʃɔː/, *adj.* too certain; arrogantly overconfident.

cocktail /'kɒkteɪl/, *n.* **1.** a short mixed alcoholic drink, usu. chilled and often sweetened. **2.** an appetiser of fruit or tomato juice. ◇*adj.* **3.** small; able to be eaten with the fingers: *cocktail sausage.* [orig. unknown]

cocky[1] /'kɒki/, *adj.*, **cockier**, **cockiest**. *Colloq.* overly smart; self-assertive; conceited: *a cocky fellow; a cocky answer.* **—cockily**, *adv.* **—cockiness**, *n.*

cocky[2] /'kɒki/, *n. Colloq.* **1.** a cockatoo, parrot. **2.** a farmer, esp. one who farms on a small scale. [abbrev. COCKATOO]

coco /'koʊkoʊ/, *n., pl.* **-cos**. a tall, slender tropical palm which produces the coconut; coconut palm. [Sp, Pg: grinning face]

cocoa /'koʊkoʊ/, *n.* **1.** the roasted, husked, and ground seeds of cacao from which most fat has been removed. **2.** a drink made from cocoa powder. **3.** a brown or reddish brown color. [var. of CACAO]

cocoa bean, *n.* the seed of the cacao tree.

coconut /'koʊkənʌt/, *n.* a large, hard-shelled seed of the coconut palm, lined with white edible meat, and containing a milky liquid.

cocoon /kə'kuːn/, *n.* **1.** a silky envelope spun by the larvae of many insects such as silkworms, serving as a covering while they are in the chrysalis or pupal state. **2.** a similar protective coverings, as the silky case in which certain spiders enclose their eggs. ◇*v.t.* **3.** to enclose within a protective covering. [F *coque* shell]

Cocos Islands /koʊkəs 'aɪləndz/, *n.pl.* a group of 27 islands in the Indian Ocean, 3685 km almost due west of Darwin, NT. Also, **Cocos (Keeling) Islands.**

cod /kɒd/, *n.* **1.** any of a number of often unrelated fishes, both freshwater and marine, as the Murray cod, etc. **2.** any of a number of marine fishes of Southern Australia belonging or related to the European cod family, esp. the rock cod and the ling. [ME]

cod., *Abbrev.* **1.** codex. **2.** codicil. **3.** codification.

COD /si oʊ 'di/, *Abbrev.* cash on delivery.

coda /'koudə/, *n.* the passage at the end of a musical composition, introduced to bring it to a satisfactory close. [It, from L *cauda* tail]

coddle /'kɒdl/, *v.t.*, **-dled, -dling. 1.** to cook (eggs, fruit, etc.) slowly in water just below boiling point. **2.** to treat tenderly; pamper. [from *caudle* kind of gruel, from ONF, from L *calidus* hot]

code /koud/, *n., v.,* **coded, coding.** ◇*n.* **1.** any ordered collection of existing laws of a country, or of those relating to a particular subject: *Civil code of France.* **2.** any system or collection of rules and regulations: *code of honor.* **3.** a system of symbols into which messages can be translated, for communication by telegraph, etc., or for secrecy: *Morse code; secret code.* **4.** a symbol (made up of signs, numbers, letters, sounds, etc.) in such a system. **5.** a system of symbols for giving information or instructions to an electronic computer. ◇*v.t.* **6.** to arrange in code; enter in code. **7.** to translate into code. [ME, from F, from L *cōdex*. See CODEX]

codeine /'koudin/, *n.* a white, crystalline, slightly bitter alkaloid taken from opium, used in medicine to reduce pain, to calm and to induce sleep. Also, **codein, codeia** /kou'diə/. [Gk *kōdeia* head, poppyhead + -INE²]

codex /'koudɛks/, *n., pl.* **codices** /'koudəsiz, 'kɒdə-/. a manuscript volume, esp. of an ancient classic, Scriptures, etc. [L: tree trunk, book]

codger /'kɒdʒə/, *n.* an odd or peculiar (old) person; eccentric: *a lovable old codger.* [? var. of CADGER]

codicil /'kɒdəsɪl/, *n.* a supplement to a will, containing an addition, change, explanation, etc. [L: little codex] —**codicillary,** *adj.*

codify /'koudəfaɪ, 'kɒdə-/, *v.t.*, **-fied, -fying.** to arrange (laws, etc.) in a code. —**codifier,** *n.* —**codification,** *n.*

cod-liver oil, /,kɒd-lɪvə 'ɔɪl/ *n.* an oil used in medicine as a source of vitamins A and D.

codpiece /'kɒdpis/, *n.* (in 15th- and 16th-century male costume) a bag or flap fastened to the front of tight-fitting hose or trousers to cover the genitals. [*cod* scrotum + PIECE]

coeducation /,kouɛdʒə'keɪʃən/, *n.* joint education, esp. of both sexes in the same institution and classes. —**coeducational,** *adj.*

coefficient /kouə'fɪʃənt/, *n.* **1.** something that acts together with another thing to produce a result. **2.** *Maths.* a number in an algebraic expression by which a quantity is multiplied: *3 is the coefficient of x in 3x.* **3.** *Phys.* a quantity, constant for a given substance, body, or process under particular conditions, used as the measure of one of its properties: *the coefficient of friction.*

-coele, *Abbrev.* a word part relating to some small cavity of the body. Also, **-cele, -coel.** [combining form representing Gk *koilía* belly and *koîlos* hollow]

coelenterate /sə'lɛntərert, -tərət/, *n.* one of a group of invertebrate animals that includes the hydras, jellyfishes, sea-anemones, corals, etc., marked by a single internal cavity serving for digestion, excretion, and other functions.

coeno-, a word part meaning 'common'. Also, **ceno-,** (before a vowel) **coen-**. [Gk *koino-*, combining form of *koinós*]

coenobite /'sinəbaɪt/, *n.* a member of a religious order living in a convent or community. Also, **cenobite.** [LL *coenobīta*, from *coenobium*, from Gk *koinóbion* convent, neut. of *koinóbios* living in a community]

coenzyme /kou'ɛnzaɪm/, *n. Biochem.* → **cofactor.**

coerce /kou'ɜs/, *v.t.*, **-erced, -ercing.** to force or compel to do something. [L: hold together] —**coercer,** *n.* —**coercible,** *adj.* —**coercion,** *n.* —**coercive,** *adj.*

coercive force /kou'ɜsɪv/, *n.* the strength of the magnetic field needed to annul residual magnetism in a ferromagnetic substance. Also, **coercivity** /kouɜ'sɪvəti/.

Coeur de Lion /kɜ də li'ɒ̃/, *n.* a name given to Richard I of England. [F: lion heart]

coeval /kou'ivəl/, *adj.* **1.** of the same age, date, or duration; equally old. **2.** occurring at the same time; contemporary. [L *coaevus* of the same age + -AL¹]

coexist /kouəg'zɪst/, *v.i.* to exist together or at same time. —**coexistence,** *n.* —**coexistent,** *adj.*

cofactor /'koufæktə/, *n.* **1.** an accompanying factor. **2.** *Biochem.* an organic compound combining with enzymes necessary for many reactions.

C of E, *Abbrev.* Church of England.

coffee /'kɒfi/, *n.* **1.** a drink made from roasted and ground or crushed seeds (**coffee beans**) from the two-seeded fruit (**coffee berry**) of *Coffea arabica* and other species of trees and shrubs of tropical regions. **2.** the berries or seeds of such plants before grinding. **3.** the color of coffee; light brown. [Turk, from Ar]

coffer /'kɒfə/, *n.* **1.** a box or chest, esp. one for valuables. **2.** (*pl.*) a treasury; funds. **3.** → **caisson.** [ME, from OF: chest, from L: basket]

coffin /'kɒfən/, *n.* a box or case in which a dead body is placed to be buried. [ME, from OF: small basket, coffin, from L, from Gk: basket]

Coffs Harbour /kɒfs 'habə/, *n.* a town, shire and port on the north coast of NSW. Pop. 18 074 (1986).

cog /kɒg/, *n.* **1.** *Mech.* one of a series of toothlike parts sticking out of a gearwheel for giving motion to or receiving motion from a corresponding part on another wheel. **2.** a person of little importance in a large organisation: *He is only a cog in the machine.* [ME]

cogent /'koudʒənt/, *adj.* forcing agreement or belief; convincing: *a cogent argument.* [L: forcing] —**cogency,** *n.*

cogitate /'kɒdʒəteɪt/, *v.i., v.t.,* **-tated, -tating.** to think hard (about); ponder. [L] —**cogitation,** *n.* —**cogitative,** *adj.*

cognac /'kɒnjæk/, *n.* a high-quality brandy, esp. one made in France.

cognate /'kɒgneɪt/, *adj.* 1. related by birth or origin; of the same parentage, descent, etc.: *cognate languages; a cognate species.* ◇*n.* 2. someone or something cognate with another. [L] —**cognation**, *n.*

cognisance /'kɒgnəzəns, 'kɒnə-/, *n.* knowledge; notice: *to take cognisance of a fact.* [ME, from L: come to know] —**cognisant**, *adj.*

cognition /kɒg'nɪʃən/, *n.* 1. the act or process of knowing; perception. 2. product of cognition; something known. [ME, from L] —**cognitive**, *adj.*

cognomen /kɒg'noumən/, *n., pl.* **-nomens, -nomina** /-'nɒmənə, -'noumənə/. 1. a surname. 2. any name, esp. a nickname. 3. *Hist.* the third, usu. last name of a Roman citizen, being that of his house or family, as in 'Caius Julius *Caesar*'. [L] —**cognominal**, *adj.*

cohabit /kou'hæbət/, *v.i.* to live together in a sexual relationship. [LL: dwell with] —**cohabitation**, *n.*

cohere /kou'hɪə/, *v.i.*, **-hered, -hering.** 1. to stick together firmly. 2. to be connected naturally or logically. [L: stick together]

coherent /kou'hɪərənt/, *adj.* 1. cohering; sticking together. 2. having natural or a well reasoned connection of parts; consistent: *a coherent argument.* 3. *Phys.* (of electromagnetic radiation, esp. light) having its waves in phase. —**coherence**, *n.*

cohesion /kou'hiʒən/, *n.* 1. the act or state of cohering or sticking together. 2. *Phys.* the state or process by which particles of a body or substance are bound together, esp. the attraction between molecules of liquid. —**cohesive**, *adj.*

cohort /'kouhɔt/, *n.* 1. one of the ten divisions of a legion in an ancient Roman army. 2. a group or company, esp. of soldiers or fighters. 3. a supporter or helper; ally. [L: enclosure]

coiffure /kwʌ'fjuə/, *n.* 1. a style of arranging the hair. 2. a head covering; headdress. [F: furnish with a coif]

coil /kɔɪl/, *v.t.* 1. to wind (rope, etc.) into loops one above another. ◇*v.i.* 2. to form continuous loops, or spirals: *The snake coiled, ready to attack.* ◇*n.* 3. a connected series of loops or spirals into which rope, etc., is wound. 4. a single such loop. 5. *Elect.* **a.** a conductor, such as a copper wire, wound up in a series of loops or spirals. **b.** a device formed mainly of such a conductor. 6. *Med.* a spiral-shaped device placed into the uterus to prevent conception. [F: gather, from L]

coin /kɔɪn/, *n.* 1. a piece of metal stamped and sent out by the government for public use as money. 2. such money in general. ◇*v.t.* 3. to form (money) by stamping metal. 4. to stamp (metal) in order to form money. 5. *Colloq.* to earn or gain (money) rapidly. 6. to invent: *to coin a new word.* [L *cuneus* wedge] —**coinage**, *n.*

coincide /kouən'saɪd/, *v.i.*, **-cided, -ciding.** 1. to be in the same position in time or space. 2. to happen at the same time or period in time. 3. to agree or be the same (in opinion, etc.). [L *co-* CO- + *incidere* fall on] —**coincident**, *adj.* —**coinciding**, *adj.*

coincidence /kou'ɪnsədəns/, *n.* 1. the condition or fact of coinciding. 2. a striking fact of two or more events happening at one time by chance: *It is a coincidence that we have the same birthday; We met by sheer coincidence.* —**coincidental**, *adj.*

co-interior angles, *n.pl. Maths.* → **allied angles.**

coir /'kɔɪə/, *n.* the prepared fibre of the coconut, used in making rope, matting, etc. [Malayalam: cord]

coitus /'kouətəs/, *n.* → **sexual intercourse.** Also, **coition** /kou'ɪʃən/. [L: go together, meet]

coke /kouk/, *n.* the solid product formed by removing gases from coal by heating, and used as fuel. [ME *colk* core]

col /kɒl/, *n.* 1. *Geog.* a pass between two higher-standing parts of mountain range. 2. *Weather.* an area of comparatively low pressure between two anticyclones. [L *collum* neck]

col-, a prefix meaning 'with', 'jointly', variant of **com-**, before *l*, as in *collateral*.

col., *Abbrev.* 1. color(ed). 2. column.

Col, *Abbrev.* colonel.

cola /'koulə/, *n.* a soft drink containing an extract prepared from the cola nut. [Latinisation of *Kola, Kolla, Goora,* in Negro languages of W Africa]

Colac /'koulæk/, *n.* a city (on the edge of a lake of the same name) in the Western District, Victoria, south-east of Camperdown. Pop. 10 545 (1986). [Aboriginal]

colander /'kʌləndə, 'kɒl-/, *n.* a vessel with many small holes for draining off liquids, used esp. in cookery. Also, **cullender.** [L *cōlāre* strain]

cola nut, *n.* a brownish seed produced by a tree of western tropical Africa, the West Indies and Brazil, which contains caffeine and is used in soft drinks. Also, **kola nut.**

cold /kould/, *adj.* 1. having a temperature lower than the normal body temperature: *cold hands.* 2. having or feeling a lack of warmth: *I am cold; It is cold today.* 3. dead. 4. *Colloq.* unconscious because of a blow, shock, etc. 5. lacking in feeling, enthusiasm, friendliness, etc.: *cold reason; a cold smile.* 6. faint; weak: *a cold scent.* 7. unprepared: *He started cold in the race.* 8. (of colors) suggesting cold, as tones of blue: *a cold picture.* ◇9. Some special uses are: **cold comfort**, almost no comfort.
cold feet, the loss of courage for carrying out something.
in cold blood, purposefully and without feeling.
leave (someone) cold, to fail to move someone's feelings.
throw cold water on, to discourage.
◇*n.* 10. the absence of heat. 11. the feeling produced by the loss of heat from the body.

12. Also, **the common cold**. an illness caused by a virus, marked by a blocked nose, coughing, etc. **13. catch/take cold**, to suffer from such an illness. **14. the cold**, cold weather. **15. in the cold**, left out, ignored. [OE *cald*]

cold-blooded /ˈkoʊld-blʌdəd/, *adj.* **1.** without feeling, esp. of pity: *a cold-blooded murder*. **2.** (of a person) sensitive to cold. **3.** of or relating to animals whose blood temperature ranges from freezing point upwards in accordance with the temperature of the surroundings, as fishes and reptiles.

cold front, *n. Weather.* a surface where a cool air mass meets a warmer air mass, into which it is advancing.

cold-shoulder /ˌkoʊld-ˈʃoʊldə/, *v.t.* to act coldly towards; ignore. [from the phrase *give (someone) the cold shoulder*]

cold sore, *n.* a blister-like sore on the face, oft. appearing during a cold (def. 11); herpes simplex.

cold storage, *n.* the storage of food, furs, etc., in a specially cooled place.

cold war, *n.* a serious economic and political conflict between nations, etc., stopping just short of military action.

Colebee /ˈkoʊlbi/, *n.* one of the two Aboriginals (the other being Bennelong) captured by Governor Arthur Phillip in 1789.

coleopterous /ˌkɒliˈɒptərəs/, *adj.* belonging or relating to the order of insects that includes beetles. [Gk: sheath-winged]

Coleridge /ˈkoʊlrɪdʒ/, *n.* **Samuel Taylor**, 1772–1834, English poet, critic, and philosopher; well-known for poems such as *The Rime of the Ancient Mariner* (1798) and *Kubla Khan* (1816).

coleslaw /ˈkoʊlslɔ/, *n.* a salad of finely sliced white cabbage. Also, **slaw**. [D *koolsla*, from *kool* cabbage + *sla*, from *salade* salad]

coleus /ˈkoʊliəs/, *n.* a plant of tropical Asia and Africa, some kinds of which are cultivated for their bright, colored leaves. [Gk: sheath (so called from the union of the filaments about the style)]

colic /ˈkɒlɪk/, *n.* a severe pain in the stomach or bowels. [ME, from L, from Gk: relating to the colon] —**colicky**, *adj.*

colitis /kɒˈlaɪtəs, kə-/, *n.* an inflammation of the bowel. [NL; see COLON², -ITIS]

coll., *Abbrev.* **1.** collection. **2.** collective. **3.** college.

collaborate /kəˈlæbəreɪt/, *v.i.*, **-rated, -rating. 1.** to work, one with another: *They collaborated in producing the book.* **2.** to work together with an enemy within one's country: *He was accused of collaborating with the Nazis.* [LL] —**collaboration**, *n.* —**collaborator, collaborationist**, *n.* —**collaborative**, *adj.*

collage /kəˈlɑʒ/, *n.* an art work made from pieces of various materials, as newspaper, cloth, etc., pasted to a surface.

collagen /ˈkɒlədʒən/, *n.* a protein contained in connective tissue and bones which gives gelatine when boiled. [F *collagène*, from Gk *kólla* glue + *géne* -GEN]

collapse /kəˈlæps/, *v.*, **-lapsed, -lapsing**, *n.* ◇*v.i.* **1.** to fall in or down suddenly: *The roof collapsed in the storm; The old man collapsed from the heat.* **2.** to be made so that parts can be folded flat together: *This chair collapses.* **3.** to fail suddenly; break down: *The project collapsed; His strength has collapsed.* ◇*v.t.* **4.** to cause (something) to collapse. ◇*n.* **5.** the act of falling in or down. **6.** a sudden, complete failure; breakdown. [L: fallen together] —**collapsible, collapsable**, *adj.*

collar /ˈkɒlə/, *n.* **1.** something worn or placed round the neck, esp. part of a garment such as a shirt, coat, etc. **2.** a leather or metal band put round an animal's neck to hold or identify it. **3.** the part of a harness round a horse's neck. **4.** *Mach.* an enlargement around a rod or shaft, serving usu. as a holding or bearing piece. ◇*v.t.* **5.** to put a collar on. **6.** to seize by the collar or neck. **7.** *Colloq.* to seize, take or gain control of. [L: neckband, collar, from *collum* neck]

collarbone /ˈkɒləboʊn/, *n.* → clavicle.

collate /kəˈleɪt, kɒ-/, *v.t.*, **-lated, -lating. 1.** to compare writings, statements, etc., in order to note points of agreement or disagreement. **2.** to put together (a book, etc.) by sorting its pages into correct order ready for binding. [L: brought together] —**collator**, *n.*

collateral /kəˈlætərəl/, *adj.* **1.** positioned at the side. **2.** running side by side; parallel. **3.** accompanying or supporting the main thing; secondary: *collateral security*. **4.** descended from the same ancestor, but through a different line; not directly related. ◇*n.* **5.** property, etc., pledged as additional security for the payment of a loan. [ME, from ML. See COL-, LATERAL]

collation /kəˈleɪʃən/, *n.* **1.** the act, process, or result of collating. **2.** a light meal. [ME, from L: a bringing together]

colleague /ˈkɒliɡ/, *n.* one of two or more people working together in an office, profession, etc.; associate. [F, from L: one chosen with another]

collect¹ /kəˈlɛkt/, *v.t.* **1.** to gather together; assemble: *Please collect all the books in the room*. **2.** to gather and keep examples of (something): *He collects stamps as a hobby.* **3.** to gather (money) for rent, debts, winnings, gifts, etc. **4.** to regain control of (oneself, one's thoughts, etc.). **5.** to call for and take away: *I'll collect it tomorrow*. **6.** *Colloq.* to run into or hit, esp. in a car, etc. ◇*v.i.* **7.** to gather together; assemble: *A crowd collected to watch the fire.* **8.** to build up in amount; accumulate: *Rainwater is collecting in the drainpipe.* [L: gathered together] —**collectable, collectible**, *adj.*

collect² /ˈkɒlɛkt/, *n.* any of certain short prayers used as part of a service in Western Churches. [ME, from ML *collecta* short prayer, orig., a gathering together]

collected /kəˈlɛktəd/, *adj.* having control of oneself; self-possessed.

collection /kəˈlɛkʃən/, *n.* **1.** the act of collecting: *There is a regular mail collection here.* **2.** something which is collected: *a stamp collection*. [ME, from L]

collective /kə'lɛktɪv/, *adj.* **1.** relating to a group of individuals taken together as a whole; combined: *collective ownership; the collective intelligence of a group.* ◇ *n.* **2.** → **collective noun**. **3.** a collective organisation, such as a group of people working together for the common good, rather than competing with each other. **4.** *Govt.* a unit of organisation in a system of collectivism.

collective bargaining, *n.* an unofficial system of reaching agreement in an industrial dispute between employers and employees, through discussions held by representatives of both sides.

collective noun, *n.* a noun that is singular in form but expresses a grouping of individual objects or people, as *family, jury,* and *clergy.*

collectivism /kə'lɛktəvɪzəm/, *n.* the principle of control by the people as a whole, or by the state, of all production or economic activities. — **collectivist**, *n., adj.*

collector /kə'lɛktə/, *n.* **1.** a person employed to collect debts, tickets, taxes, etc. **2.** someone who collects books, paintings, stamps, etc., as a hobby. [ME, from LL]

college /'kɒlɪdʒ/, *n.* **1.** an educational institution, attended usu. after high school, which gives certificates, diplomas and degrees in technical, professional and academic areas. **2.** an institution set up by members of a profession, as the *Royal Australian College of Surgeons.* **3.** a residence within a university, oft. established for students by churches. **4.** any of certain large private schools. **5.** an organised association of people having certain powers and duties: *an electoral college.* [ME, from L *collēgium* association, a society] — **collegian**, *n.* — **collegiate**, *adj.*

College of Cardinals, *n. Rom Cath Ch.* the Sacred College which comprises all the cardinals and which elects and advises the Pope. Official name, **Sacred College of Cardinals**.

collide /kə'laɪd/, *v.i.*, **-lided, -liding. 1.** to come together with force; crash: *The cars collided.* **2.** to be opposed; conflict: *Their opinions on the matter collide.* [L]

collie /'kɒli/, *n.* any of various intelligent dogs much used for guarding sheep, esp. one of Scottish breed, with long thick hair and bushy tail. Also, **colly**.

Collie /'kɒli/, *n.* a town and shire in south-western WA on the **Collie River**. Pop. 7829 (1986).

collier /'kɒliə/, *n.* **1.** (a sailor in) a ship for carrying coal. **2.** a coal-miner.

colliery /'kɒljəri/, *n., pl.* **-ries.** a coal mine, including all buildings and equipment.

collimate /'kɒləmeɪt/, *v.t.*, **-mated, -mating. 1.** to make parallel. **2.** to adjust the line of sight of (a telescope etc.). **3.** to limit the beam of radiation to the required dimensions. [L: brought into line with] — **collimation**, *n.*

collinear /kɒ'lɪniə/, *adj.* lying in the same straight line. [COL- + LINEAR]

Collins /'kɒlənz/, **1. David,** 1756–1810, British administrator in Australia; first lieutenant-governor of Tasmania. **2. Tom.** See Joseph Furphy.

collision /kə'lɪʒən/, *n.* **1.** the act of colliding; crash. **2.** a conflict of opinions, interests, etc. [ME, from L: collide]

collocation /kɒlə'keɪʃən/, *n.* **1.** the act or result of placing things together or in proper order. **2.** *Linguistics.* the joining together of particular words, as *green as grass.* — **collocate**, *v.t.*

colloid /'kɒlɔɪd/, *n. Chem.* a substance in solution of particle size between 10^{-5} and 10^{-7} cm, i.e. between a true solution and a coarse suspension. [Gk *kólla* glue + -OID] — **colloidal**, *adj.*

colloq., *Abbrev.* **1.** colloquial(ly). **2.** colloquialism.

colloquial /kə'loʊkwiəl/, *adj.* **1.** suitable for or marked by conversational speech or writing, in which the speaker or writer feels free to choose words from the informal, slang, or vulgar elements of the language. **2.** conversational.

colloquialism /kə'loʊkwiə,lɪzəm/, *n.* **1.** a colloquial word or expression. **2.** colloquial style or usage.

colloquium /kə'loʊkwiəm/, *n., pl.* **-iums, -ia.** *n.* an informal conference or group discussion.

colloquy /'kɒləkwi/, *n., pl.* **-quies. 1.** a speaking together; conversation or discussion. **2.** a literary work in the form of conversation. [L: conversation] — **colloquist**, *n.*

collusion /kə'luʒən/, *n.* a secret agreement for the purpose of deceiving or doing wrong; conspiracy. [ME, from L: a playing together] — **collusive**, *adj.*

cologne /kə'loʊn/, *n.* a perfumed, scented toilet water; eau de Cologne. Also, **Cologne water**. [for *Cologne* water (made at *Cologne,* Germany, since 1709)]

Colombia /kə'lʌmbiə, kə'lɒmbiə/, *n.* a republic in north-western South America, on the Caribbean Sea and the Pacific Ocean; a Spanish colony before independence in 1819; a republic since 1886. Pop. 28 655 000 (1987 est.). 1 138 914 km². *Language:* Spanish. *Currency:* peso. *Cap.:* Bogotá. — **Colombian**, *adj.*

Colombo /kə'lʌmboʊ/, *n.* a seaport in and the capital of Sri Lanka, on the west coast; one of the world's largest artificial harbors. Pop. 643 000 (1984 est.).

Colombo Plan, *n.* a plan for economic development in southern and south-eastern Asia, established in 1950 by seven Commonwealth countries in the area; US and Japan joined later.

colon¹ /'koʊlən/, *n.* a point of punctuation (:) marking off the main part of a sentence from a following example, quotation, etc. [L, from Gk: limb, clause]

colon² /ˈkoʊlən/, n., pl. **-lons, -la** /-lə/. the part of bowel between the caecum and the rectum. [ME, from L, from Gk: food, colon] — **colonic,** adj.

colonel /ˈkɜːnəl/, n. Mil. See Appendix. [F, from It: little column]

colonial /kəˈloʊniəl/, adj. **1.** of or relating to a colony or colonies. **2. a.** relating to the six British colonies in Australia before they federated in 1901, or to their period. **b.** relating to the 13 British colonies which became the United States of America. ◇n. **3.** a person who lives in a colony.

colonialism /kəˈloʊniəˌlɪzəm/, n. the idea or practice of one nation seeking to extend or keep its control over other peoples or lands.

colonise or **colonize** /ˈkɒlənaɪz/, v., **-nised,** or **-nising.** ◇v.t. **1.** to establish a colony in or form into a colony: *England colonised Australia.* ◇v.i. **2.** to form or settle in a colony. — **colonisation,** n. — **coloniser, colonist,** n.

colonnade /kɒləneɪd, kɒləˈneɪd/, n. **1.** a series of columns set at a regular distance apart, and usu. supporting a roof, series of arches, etc. **2.** a long row of trees. [F, from It, from L *columna* column]

colony /ˈkɒləni/, n., pl. **-nies. 1.** a group of people who leave their native country to form a settlement in a new land ruled by, or connected with, the parent state. **2.** the area thus settled. **3.** any of several settlements in Australia before the achievement of responsible government. **4.** a group of people from a particular foreign country or with a common occupation living in a city or country, esp. close together. **5.** a group of bacteria growing together as descendants of a single cell. **6.** *Ecol.* group of animals or plants of the same kind, existing close together. [ME, from L]

color or **colour** /ˈkʌlə/, n. **1.** a sensation produced in the eyes by light of different wavelengths being reflected or transmitted by a substance. The most obvious property of a color is its hue, the basic ones being *red, orange, yellow, green, blue, indigo* and *violet.* **2.** color of the face, esp. as showing health; complexion. **3.** color of the skin of a person; racial complexion. **4.** striking characteristics that make something interesting: *a novel of great color.* **5.** an appearance of truth or realism given by including details of an event, place or period: *This description lends color to the story.* **6.** a substance used for coloring, as pigment, paint or dye. **7.** (*pl.*) a symbol, badge, flag, etc., with distinctive colors showing membership of a school, team, military unit, etc. **8.** kind; variety; general character. **9.** the distinctive tone of a musical sound. **10.** a particle of a valuable mineral, esp. gold, found by washing certain gravel. **11. with flying colors,** very successfully. **12. off color,** not well; ill. **13. show one's true colors,** to show one's true nature, opinions, etc. ◇v.t. **14.** to give or apply color to. **15.** to cause (something) to appear different from the reality: *Some newspapers color the news.* **16.** to influence or change: *Personal feelings colored his account.* ◇v.i. **17.** to take on or change color. **18.** to become red in the face. [ME, from OF, from L]

Colorado /kɒləˈrɑːdoʊ/, n. a state in the western United States. Pop. 3 267 000 (1986 est.); 269 619 km². *Cap.*: Denver. *Abbrev.*: Colo.

coloratura /kɒlərəˈtjʊərə/, n. **1.** (a vocal music marked by) runs, trills, and other such decorations. **2.** a soprano singer who specialises in such music. Also, **colorature** /ˈkɒlərətjʊə/. [It: to color, from L]

color-bar or **colour-bar** /ˈkʌləbɑː/, n. economic, political, or social restrictions separating peoples of different color, esp. non-whites from whites.

color-blindness or **colour-blindness** /ˈkʌləblaɪndnəs/, n. an inability to tell the difference between certain colors, as red and green, or to perceive color at all. — **color-blind,** adj.

colored or **coloured** /ˈkʌləd/, adj. **1.** having color. **2.** belonging wholly or in part to a non-white race. **3.** influenced or biased: *a colored statement.* ◇n. **4.** any person of a non-white race.

colorful or **colourful** /ˈkʌləfəl/, adj. **1.** having a lot of color. **2.** having a striking and interesting style, character, appearance, etc.: *a colorful personality.*

coloring or **colouring** /ˈkʌlərɪŋ/, n. **1.** the act or method of applying color. **2.** Also, **coloration.** appearance as to color. **3.** a false appearance; show. **4.** a substance used to color something.

colossal /kəˈlɒsəl/, adj. **1.** of great size; huge. **2.** *Colloq.* splendid; marvellous.

Colosseum /kɒləˈsiəm/, n. an amphitheatre in Rome, the greatest in antiquity, begun by Vespasian and inaugurated (AD 80) by Titus. [L, properly neut. of *colosseus* colossal. Cf. COLOSSUS]

colossus /kəˈlɒsəs/, n., pl. **-lossi** /-ˈlɒsaɪ/, **-lossuses. 1.** (*cap.*) a bronze statue of Apollo which, according to legend, stood across the entrance to the harbor at Rhodes. See **Seven Wonders of the World. 2.** any huge statue. **3.** a thing or person of great size or importance. [ME, from L, from Gk]

colostomy /kəˈlɒstəmi/, n. a surgical operation to form an artificial anus or opening from the bowel through the stomach wall.

colostrum /kəˈlɒstrəm/, n. → **beestings.**

colt /koʊlt/, n. **1.** a male horse not past its fourth birthday. **2.** a young or inexperienced man, esp. a sportsman. [OE] — **coltish,** adj.

Columbia /kəˈlʌmbiə/, n. America, or the United States, esp. as a feminine personification.

columbine /ˈkɒləmbaɪn/, n. a kind of plant having colorful flowers with five petals. [ME, from LL: dovelike; from the resemblance of the inverted flower to a cluster of doves]

Columbus /kəˈlʌmbəs/, n. **Christopher** (Spanish, *Cristóbal Colón*; Italian, *Cristoforo Colombo*), 1446?–1506, Italian navigator in

Spanish service; commonly said to be the discoverer of America, 1492.

column /ˈkɒləm/, n. 1. *Archit.* an upright, usu. cylindrical, structure of greater length than thickness, usu. used as a support; pillar. 2. any column-like object, mass, or formation: *a column of smoke; a column of troops*. 3. *Geol.* a sequence of rock units deposited through various periods of geological time. 4. *Geol.* a cylindrical formation made by the union of a stalactite and stalagmite. 5. one of two or more rows of printed matter going down a page. 6. a vertical row of numbers. 7. a regular article in a newspaper, etc., usu. signed, and oft. dealing with a particular subject: *a political column*. [ME, from OF, from L: pillar, post] — **columned, columnar,** *adj.*

columnist /ˈkɒləməst, ˈkɒləmnəst/, n. a writer or organiser of a special column in a newspaper, etc.

column shift, n. a gear lever fitted on the steering column of a motor vehicle.

com-, a prefix meaning 'with', 'jointly', 'in combination' and 'completely', as in *compare, command*. See **co-** (def. 1). Also, **con-, col-, cor-**. [L: combining form of *cum* with]

Com, *Abbrev.* 1. commander. 2. commodore.

coma /ˈkoʊmə/, n., pl. **-mas.** a state of deep, long-lasting unconsciousness due to disease, injury, poison, etc. [Gk: deep sleep] — **comatose,** *adj.*

Comanche /kəˈmæntʃi/, n., pl. **-ches, -che.** (pl.) a tribe of the Shoshonean group of North American Indians, formerly ranging from the Mexican border to the River Platte; now living in Oklahoma.

comb /koʊm/, n. 1. a piece of plastic, metal, etc., with teeth for arranging or cleaning hair, or for holding it in place. 2. a card for dressing wool, etc. 3. a fleshy comb-shaped growth on the head of a domestic fowl. 4. → **honeycomb.** ◇v.t. 5. to tidy or arrange (the hair, etc.) with a comb. 6. to remove or separate as with a comb (oft. fol by *out*). 7. to search thoroughly: *She combed the desk for the missing letter*. ◇v.i. 8. (of a wave) to roll over or break. [OE]

combat /ˈkɒmbæt, kəmˈbæt/, v., **-bated, -bating;** /ˈkɒmbæt/, n. ◇v.t. 1. to fight or oppose strongly: *to combat poverty*. ◇n. 2. a fight between two men, armies, etc. [F, from L *com-* COM- + *batt(u)ere* beat] — **combative,** *adj.*

combatant /ˈkɒmbətənt/, n. 1. a person or group that fights. ◇*adj.* 2. fighting or ready to fight.

comber /ˈkoʊmə/, n. a long breaking wave.

combination /kɒmbəˈneɪʃən/, n. 1. the act or result of combining. 2. something formed by combining a number of things. 3. a group of people or parties with a common purpose. 4. a set or series of numbers or letters used in operating a **combination lock,** used on safes, etc. 5. *Maths.* the selection of a particular number of different objects from a given larger number of different objects without regard to the order of their selection. [LL] — **combinational,** *adj.*

combine /kəmˈbaɪn/, v., **-bined, -bining;** /ˈkɒmbaɪn/, n. ◇v.t. 1. to bring or join into a close union or whole. ◇v.i. 2. to unite; join together. 3. to enter into chemical union. ◇n. 4. a combination of people or groups to help their common political or commercial interests. 5. → **combine harvester.** [ME, from LL: join together]

combine harvester, n. a machine that combines the operations of reaping, threshing, and winnowing grain.

combing /ˈkoʊmɪŋ/, n. a process in the preparation of worsted yarn, which makes the longer fibres parallel and removes short fibres, broken ends, etc.

combining form, n. a special form of a word used only in compounds, as *Anglo-* in *Anglo-Saxon*.

combo /ˈkɒmboʊ/, n. *Colloq.* any small band of musicians.

combustible /kəmˈbʌstəbəl/, *adj.* 1. able to catch fire and burn easily; flammable. ◇n. 2. a combustible substance. [L: burned up] — **combustibility,** n.

combustion /kəmˈbʌstʃən/, n. 1. the act or process of burning. 2. *Chem.* rapid oxidation accompanied by heat and usu. light. — **combustive,** *adj.*

come /kʌm/, v., **came, come, coming.** ◇v.i. 1. to move towards the speaker or a particular place; approach. 2. to arrive in the course of time, process, succession etc.: *Christmas comes every year*. 3. to move into view; appear: *The light comes and goes*. 4. to reach; extend: *The dress comes to her knees*. 5. to take place; happen: *Happiness comes to everyone sometime*. 6. to take place at a certain point in an order, series, etc.: *Age comes after youth*. 7. to be produced, offered, etc.: *Toothpaste comes in tubes*. 8. to happen in the mind: *I hope the answer will come to me*. 9. to originate; be derived: *This dog comes from a good breed*. 10. to be born in or live in: *I come from France*. 11. to arrive or appear as a result: *This comes of carelessness*. 12. to enter or be brought into a particular state or condition: *to come into use*. 13. to become: *to come untied*. ◇v.t. 14. *Colloq.* to produce; cause: *Don't come that rubbish*. 15. *Colloq.* to play the part of: *to come the big chief*. ◇16. Some special uses are:
come about, 1. to happen in due course; occur.
come across, 1. to meet with, esp. by chance. 2. *Colloq.* to pay or give. 3. to be understood.
come along, to hurry.
come at, 1. to rush at and attack. 2. *Colloq.* to agree to do.
come by, 1. to obtain; acquire. 2. to stop for a visit.
come down, 1. to lose wealth, rank, etc. 2. to be handed down by tradition or inheritance.
come down on, to blame; scold.
come down with, to become ill with (a disease).
come good, *Colloq.* to improve after a bad beginning.

come in, 1. to enter. 2. to become useful, fashionable, etc. 3. to finish in a race, etc.

come into, to inherit.

come off, 1. to happen; occur. 2. to reach the end: *to come off with honors*. 3. to become unfastened.

come off it, *Colloq.* to stop acting or talking in a particular way.

come on, 1. to develop; make progress. 2. to appear onstage.

come out, 1. to happen; make known. 2. to appear in print, etc. 2. to be made known; show itself. 3. to make one's first entry into society, onto the stage, etc.

come out with, to tell, make known.

come over, to happen to; affect: *What's come over him?*

come round, 1. to regain consciousness. 2. to change (opinion, direction, etc.).

come through, to reach an end (of something) successfully.

come to, 1. to regain consciousness. 2. to amount to; equal.

come to light, to be found after a period of time.

come undone/unstuck, *Colloq.* to break down; collapse.

come up, to arise; present itself (for discussion, etc.).

come upon, to meet by chance.

come up to, 1. to equal. 2. to reach.

come up with, to produce; supply. [OE *cuman*]

comeback /'kʌmbæk/, *n.* **1.** *Colloq.* a return to a former position of success, etc. **2.** *Colloq.* a quick reply or return action. **3. a.** a sheep bred for wool or mutton by breeding a half-breed sheep to a sheep of one of the parent breeds, either merino or meat-producing. **b.** the wool from such a sheep. **4.** a type of rust-resistant wheat.

comedian /kə'midiən/, *n.* **1.** a performer or writer of comedy. **2.** a very amusing person. **—comedienne**, *n. fem.*

comedy /'kɒmədi/, *n., pl.* **-dies. 1.** a play, film, novel, etc., of a light and humorous character, usu. with a happy or cheerful ending. **2.** a humorous element of literature or, generally, of life. **3.** any humorous event or series of events. [ME, from L, from Gk *kômos* mirth + *ōidós* singer]

comely /'kʌmli/, *adj.*, **-lier, -liest.** pleasant in appearance; attractive. [OE *cymlic*] **—comeliness**, *n.*

comestible /kə'mɛstəbəl/, *n.* (*usu. pl.*) an article of food. [ME, from L: eaten up]

comet /'kɒmət/, *n.* a heavenly body orbiting about the sun, usu. consisting of a central solid nucleus surrounded by a misty mass (the **coma**) which forms a tail in the direction away from the sun. [ME, from L, from Gk: long-haired] **—cometary**, *adj.*

comeuppance /kʌm'ʌpəns/, *n. Colloq.* a well-deserved punishment; retribution.

comfort /'kʌmfət/, *v.t.* **1.** to lighten the sorrow or anxiety of (someone); console. ◊*n.* **2.** relief in sorrow or anxiety; consolation; solace. **3.** a person or thing that gives such relief. **4.** a state of pleasant freedom from pain or anxiety and of satisfaction of bodily wants. **5.** something which brings about such a state. [ME, from OF, from L: strengthen] **—comforting**, *adj.*

comfortable /'kʌmftəbəl, 'kʌmfətəbəl/, *adj.* **1.** giving comfort, support, or consolation. **2.** being in a state of comfort. **3.** enough to satisfy: *a comfortable income.*

comforter /'kʌmfətə/, *n.* **1.** someone who or something which comforts. **2.** (*cap.*) *Bible.* the Holy Spirit. **3.** a thick woollen scarf.

comfrey /'kʌmfri/, *n., pl.* **-freys.** a kind of plant of Europe and Asia, having blue, purplish or white flowers, used in making herbal tea, etc. [ME, from L *conferva* healing plant]

comfy /'kʌmfi/, *adj. Colloq.* comfortable.

comic /'kɒmɪk/, *adj.* **1.** of or relating to comedy. **2.** humorous; funny; laughable. ◊*n.* **3.** *Colloq.* a comic actor. **4.** a magazine containing comic strips. [L, from Gk]

comical /'kɒmɪkəl/, *adj.* **1.** amusing, funny. **2.** *Colloq.* odd; strange. **—comicality**, *n.*

comic strip, *n.* a series of cartoon drawings, telling a funny story, adventure story, etc.

coming /'kʌmɪŋ/, *n.* **1.** arrival; advent. ◊*adj.* **2.** next approaching: *this coming week.* **3.** on the way to fame or success: *up and coming.*

Comintern /'kɒmɪntən/, *n.* the Third Communist International, dissolved 1943; the organisation of the Soviet Communist Party, headed by its Politburo, for extending world revolution. Also, **Komintern.** [*Com(munist) Intern(ational)*]

comma /'kɒmə/, *n.* a mark of punctuation (,) used to show small breaks in the continuity of a sentence. [L, from Gk: short clause]

command /kə'mænd, -'mand/, *v.t.* **1.** to order, direct or demand, usu. with the right to be obeyed: *She commanded him to go home*; *He commanded silence.* **2.** to have charge of or control over. **3.** to overlook: *a hill commanding the sea.* **4.** to deserve and get: *His position commands respect.* ◊*v.i.* **5.** to give orders or be in charge. ◊*n.* **6.** the act of commanding or ordering. **7.** an order; direction. **8.** *Mil.* **a.** an order given by an officer to a person of lower military rank. **b.** a body of soldiers, etc., or area, station, etc., under a commander. **9.** power to command or control; mastery. [ME from OF, from L *com-* COM- + *mandāre* enjoin] **—commanding**, *adj.*

commandant /'kɒməndænt, -dant/, *n. Mil.* a commanding officer of a place, group, etc. [F: commanding]

commandeer /kɒmən'dɪə/, *v.t.* **1.** to order or force into active military service. **2.** to seize (private property) for military or other public use. **3.** *Colloq.* to seize without permission or by force. [Afrikaans, from F: command]

commander /kə'mændə, -'mand-/, *n.* **1.** someone who has power to direct; leader; chief officer. **2.** the chief commissioned officer (regardless of rank) of a military unit. **3.** *Mil.* See Appendix. **4.** a rank in certain modern orders of knighthood. **—commandership**, *n.*

commander-in-chief /kə,mændər-ɪn-'tʃif/, *n., pl.* **commanders-in-chief.** 1. an officer in overall command of an army or armed forces. 2. an officer in command of a particular part of an army or navy.

commandment /kə'mændmənt, kə'mand-/, *n.* 1. a command. 2. *Bible.* a holy command, such as one of the Ten Commandments given by God to Moses.

commando /kə'mændou, -'man-/, *n., pl.* **-dos, -does.** a (member of) a small specially trained fighting force used for making quick attacks inside enemy areas. [Afrikaans, from Pg]

commemorate /kə'memərert/, *v.t.*, **-rated, -rating.** 1. to keep alive the memory of. 2. to honor the memory of by a ceremony, etc. [L: brought to remembrance] **—commemoration**, *n.* **—commemorative**, *adj.*

commence /kə'mens/, *v.t., v.i.* **-menced, -mencing.** to begin; start. [ME, from OF, from LL *com-* COM- + *initiāre* begin] **—commencement**, *n.*

commend /kə'mend/, *v.t.* 1. to suggest as worthy of trust, notice, kindness, etc.; recommend. 2. to entrust; give in care of. [ME, from L: commit] **—commendable**, *adj.* **—commendation**, *n.* **—commendatory**, *adj.*

commensal /kə'mensəl/, *n., adj.* (an animal or plant) living with, on, or in another, but with neither one dependent on the other (opposed to *parasite*). [ML, from L *com-* COM- + *mensālis* belonging to the table] **—commensalism**, *n.* **—commensality**, *n.*

commensurable /kə'menʃərəbəl/, *adj.* 1. having a common measure or divisor. 2. suitable in measure; proportionate. [LL: having a common measure] **—commensurability**, *n.*

commensurate /kə'menʃərət/, *adj.* 1. having the same measure or size. 2. **commensurable.** [L *com-* COM- + *mensūrātus*, measured] **—commensuration**, *n.*

comment /'kɒment/, *n.* 1. a note in explanation or criticism of a passage in a writing, book, etc.; annotation. 2. a remark that gives an opinion or criticism. ◇*v.i.* 3. to make written or spoken comments. [ME, from LL *commentum* exposition, L: contrivance, invention]

commentary /'kɒməntəri, -tri/, *n., pl.* **-taries.** 1. a series of written comments, oft. in the form of an essay. 2. something that illustrates a point; comment. 3. a series of spoken comments, such as a description of a broadcast or televised public event. **—commentarial**, *adj.*

commentator /'kɒmənteɪtə/, *n.* a writer or broadcaster who makes remarks that explain or comment on news and events, or who describes sporting events, etc.

commerce /'kɒmɜs/, *n.* 1. buying and selling of goods or commodities, esp. on a large scale between different countries or between different parts of the same country; trade; business. 2. social relations. [F, from L: trade]

commercial /kə'mɜʃəl/, *adj.* 1. of or relating to commerce. 2. likely to be sold in great numbers: *Is the invention commercial?* 3. setting profits or immediate gains above artistic considerations. 4. not completely or chemically pure: *commercial soda.* 5. *Radio, TV.* dependent on the income from advertising. ◇*n.* 6. *Radio, TV.* an advertisement.

commercialism /kə'mɜʃəlɪzəm/, *n.* 1. the principles, practices and spirit of commerce. 2. a commercial custom or expression. 3. (*oft. disapproving*) the giving of undue importance to profits or immediate gains. **—commercialist**, *n.* **—commercialistic**, *adj.*

commercial traveller, *n.* a travelling representative of a firm, who tries to gain orders for goods, etc.

commiserate /kə'mɪzəreɪt/, *v.*, **-rated, -rating.** ◇*v.i.* 1. to sympathise (fol. by *with*). ◇*v.t.* 2. to feel or express sorrow or sympathy for. [L] **—commiseration**, *n.* **—commiserative**, *adj.*

commissar /'kɒməsɑ/, *n.* formerly, the head of a government department in the Soviet Union. [Russ, from F]

commissariat /kɒmə'sɛəriət, -riæt/, *n.* 1. the department of an army charged with supplying provisions, etc. 2. (formerly) one of the departments of government of the USSR. [F]

commissary /'kɒməsəri/, *n., pl.* **-saries.** 1. *Mil.* an officer of the commissariat. 2. someone to whom some charge is given by a higher power; deputy. 3. **→commissar.** [ME, from L: committed] **—commissarial**, *adj.*

commission /kə'mɪʃən/, *n.* 1. the act of giving in charge. 2. an order, charge, or direction, given by someone in authority. 3. a document giving power to perform certain duties or giving a particular rank, as to an officer in the army or navy. 4. a group of people officially charged with particular duties. 5. the condition of anything in active service or use: *My car is out of commission today.* 6. a duty or matter given to one's charge. 7. the right to act for another or others in commercial transactions. 8. the performing of a crime, error, etc. 9. a sum of money or a percentage given to a representative, salesman, etc., for services. 10. an amount or percentage charged for exchanging money, etc. 11. *Navy.* the condition of a ship ordered to active service, and supplied with a captain and crew. ◇*v.t.* 12. to give a commission to. 13. to charge with a duty. 14. to put (a ship, etc.) in commission. [ME, from L]

commissionaire /kəmɪʃə'nɛə/, *n.* a uniformed messenger or doorkeeper at a hotel, office, theatre, etc.

commissioner /kə'mɪʃənə/, *n.* 1. a member of an official commission (def. 4). 2. a government official in charge of a department.

commit /kə'mɪt/, *v.t.*, **-mitted, -mitting.** 1. to give in trust or charge; entrust; consign. 2. to commit for preservation: *to commit to writing, memory, etc.* 3. to hand over custody of to an institution, as a gaol, etc. 4. (of a magistrate) to send (an accused) to trial by jury: *to commit for trial.* **5.** to hand over for treatment, removal, etc.: *to commit papers to the flames.* **6.** to do; perform; perpetrate: *to commit murder;* **7.** to bind as by promise; pledge. [ME, from L: bring together, join, entrust] —**committable**, *adj.* —**committal**, *n.*

commitment /kə'mɪtmənt/, *n.* **1.** a committing or being committed. **2.** something to which one has committed oneself; a pledge. **3.** *Law.* a court order directing that someone be imprisoned.

committee /kə'mɪti/, *n.* **1.** a group of people directed to investigate, report, or act in special cases. **2. standing committee**, a permanent committee, intended to consider all matters relating to a particular subject. [AF: committed]

commo /'kɒmoʊ/, *n. Colloq.* a communist.

commode /kə'moʊd/, *n.* a chair containing a chamber-pot. [F, from L *commodus* fit, convenient, useful]

commodious /kə'moʊdiəs/, *adj.* convenient and roomy; spacious: *a commodious house.* [ME, from ML. See COMMODE]

commodity /kə'mɒdəti/, *n., pl.* **-ties. 1.** a thing that is of use. **2.** an article of trade or commerce.

commodore /'kɒmədɔ/, *n.* **1.** *Mil.* See Appendix. **2.** the senior captain of a line of commercial vessels. **3.** the president of a yacht or boat club. [possibly from D, from F: command]

common /'kɒmən/, *adj.* **1.** belonging equally to, or shared by a number of people: *common property.* **2.** joint; united: *a common effort against the enemy.* **3.** belonging to the whole community; public: *common land.* **4.** widespread; general; ordinary: *common knowledge.* **5.** happening often; familiar; usual: *a common event, common salt.* **6.** of very ordinary quality; mean; low. **7.** coarse; vulgar: *common manners.* **8.** ordinary; having no rank, etc.: *a common soldier, the common people.* **9. in common**, in joint possession, use, etc.; jointly. [ME, from OF, from L: common, general]

commonalty /'kɒmənəlti/, *n., pl.* **-ties. 1.** the common people as opposed to the nobility, etc. **2.** the members of an official body.

common brown snake, *n.* a medium sized, poisonous snake, found mainly in dry areas of Australia. Also, **brown snake, mallee snake.**

common chord, *n.* (in music) a chord consisting of the first, third and fifth notes of a scale.

common denominator, *n.* **1.** *Maths.* a whole number able to be divided with no remainder by all the denominators of a set of fractions. **2.** an interest, belief, etc., shared by a group of people.

commoner /'kɒmənə/, *n.* one of the common people.

common factor, *n. Maths.* a whole number which divides exactly into two or more given whole numbers.

common fraction, *n. Maths.* a fraction having the numerator above and the denominator below a straight line (as opposed to a *decimal fraction*).

common gender, *n.* the gender of a noun or pronoun which may be either masculine or feminine, or both: for example, *child, person, they.*

common law, **1.** the system of law originating in England as distinct from the civil or Roman law and the canon or ecclesiastical law. **2.** the unwritten law, esp. of England, based on custom or court decision, as distinct from statute law. **3.** the law administered through the system of writs, as distinct from equity, etc. —**common-law**, *adj.*

commonly /'kɒmənli/, *adv.* **1.** usually; generally; ordinarily. **2.** in a common manner.

common market, *n.* **1.** a group of countries agreeing to trade with one another without the taxing of goods. **2.** (*caps.*) the European Economic Community.

common multiple, *n. Maths.* a whole number able to be divided by two or more given whole numbers.

common noun, *n. Gram.* a noun which can be used of any one or all the members of a class, and can follow an article, as *man, men, city, cities,* in contrast to *Shakespeare, Hobart.* See **proper noun.**

commonplace /'kɒmənpleɪs/, *adj.* **1.** ordinary; without special characteristics: *a commonplace person.* **2.** used or said too often; hackneyed: *a commonplace remark.* ◇ *n.* **3.** a well-known, customary, or obvious remark. **4.** anything common, ordinary, or uninteresting. [translation of L *locus commūnis,* Gk (*koinós*) *topós* a stereotyped topic, argument, or passage in literature]

common room, *n.* (in schools, universities, etc.) a sitting room for the use of the teaching staff and sometimes the students.

commons /'kɒmənz/, *n.pl.* **1.** the common people as opposed to a ruling class. **2.** (*cap.*) the elective house of the parliament of Britain and other countries.

commonsense /kɒmən'sɛns/, *n.* sound, practical understanding. Also, **common sense.** —**commonsense**, *adj.* —**commonsensical**, *adj.*

common time, *n. Music.* a rhythm having four beats to each bar.

commonweal /'kɒmənwil/, *n.* public good.

commonwealth /'kɒmənwɛlθ/, *n.* **1.** the whole body of people of a nation or state. **2.** (*cap.*) a federation of states and territories with powers and responsibilities divided between a central government and a number of smaller governments. **3.** (*cap.*) a loose political grouping consisting of the United Kingdom, and countries which are or have been controlled by Britain. **4.** any body of people united by some common interest.

Commonwealth Banking Corporation, *n.* a bank established in 1911 which acted as Australia's central bank up until the foundation of the Reserve Bank in 1959; controls the Commonwealth Trading Bank of Australia, the Commonwealth Savings Bank of Australia and the Commonwealth Development Bank of Australia. Formerly (1911-60), **Commonwealth Bank of Australia.**

Commonwealth Day, *n.* the official birthday of Queen Elizabeth II, 11 June; until 1966, celebrated on 24 May, Queen Victoria's birthday. Formerly, **Empire Day.** Also, **Queen's Birthday holiday.**

Commonwealth Games, *n.pl.* international meetings of athletes from the members of the Commonwealth of Nations; modelled on the Olympic Games and similarly held at four-yearly intervals. Formerly (1930-54), **British Empire Games;** (1954-66), **British Empire and Commonwealth Games;** (1966-74), **British Commonwealth Games.**

Commonwealth of Independent States, *n.* a confederation of 11 independent republics in eastern Europe and western, central and northern Asia, formed in 1991 by most of the constituent republics of the former Soviet Union, the largest member being Russia. Pop. 273 345 000 (based on 1989 Soviet Union figures); 22 183 321 km^2. *Languages:* Russian and more than 100 local languages. *Cap.:* Minsk. *Abbrev.:* CIS. See **Soviet Union.**

Commonwealth of Nations, *n.* a loose political community including Great Britain and independent nations which were formerly British dominions or colonies, along with their dependencies; each recognises the British monarch as head of the Commonwealth.

Commonwealth Scientific and Industrial Research Organization, *n.* →CSIRO.

Commonwealth Serum Laboratories, *n.* an Australian institute established in 1916 by the federal government to manufacture and provide research for sera, vaccines, etc.

Commonwealth star, *n.* the large seven-pointed star on the flag of the Commonwealth of Australia, approved in 1908.

commotion /kə'mouʃən/, *n.* **1.** a violent or wild and noisy motion; agitation. **2.** a political or social upset; sedition; insurrection.

communal /kə'mjunəl, 'kɒmjənəl/, *adj.* **1.** relating to a commune or a community. **2.** relating to the people of a community: *communal land.* –**communality,** *n.*

communalism /kə'mjunəlɪzəm, 'kɒmjən-/, *n.* a system of government in which each commune rules itself, and the nation is only a union of such states. –**communalist,** *n.* –**communalistic,** *adj.*

commune[1] /kə'mjun/, *v.i.,* **-muned, -muning.** to talk together, share thoughts or feelings. [ME, from OF: share, from *comun* common]

commune[2] /'kɒmjun/, *n.* **1.** any group of like-minded people choosing to live in a self-sufficient way, often following ideas differing from those held by most: *hippy commune.* **2.** (*cap.*) a revolutionary committee which took the place of the municipality of Paris in the French Revolution of 1789, and soon overthrew the supreme authority in the state. It was suppressed by the Convention in 1794. **3.** (*cap.*) →**Paris Commune.** [F, fem. of *commun* common]

communicable /kə'mjunɪkəbəl/, *adj.* able to be passed on from person to person. [ML]

communicant /kə'mjunɪkənt/, *n.* someone who receives Holy Communion.

communicate /kə'mjunɪkeɪt/, *v.,* **-cated, -cating.** ◇*v.t.* **1.** to pass on to another; impart; transmit. **2.** to make known: *We will communicate the news to her.* ◇*v.i.* **3.** to share thoughts: *They communicate well with each other.* **4.** to have or form a joining passage. **5.** to receive Holy Communion. [L: shared] –**communicator,** *n.*

communication /kəmjunə'keɪʃən/, *n.* **1.** the act or fact of communicating; transmission. **2.** the passing on or sharing of thoughts, opinions, or information. **3.** something which is communicated. **4.** an official paper or message containing views, information, etc. **5.** the passage or a means of passage between places. **6.** the science or process of sending information, esp. by electronic or mechanical means. **7.** (*pl.*) the means of passing on information by telephone, radio, television, etc. –**communicative,** *adj.*

communion /kə'mjunjən/, *n.* **1.** the act of sharing, esp. of thoughts, interests, etc. **2.** association; fellowship. **3.** *Church.* a group of people having one common religious faith; a religious denomination. **4.** →**Holy Communion.** [ME, from L: fellowship]

communiqué /kə'mjunəkeɪ/, *n.* an official report, as of war news, etc., usu. to the press or public. [F]

communism /'kɒmjənɪzəm/, *n.* **1.** a theory or system of social organisation based on the holding of all property in common. **2.** a system of social organisation in which all economic activity is run by a government or by a single all-powerful political party. [F. See COMMON]

communist /'kɒmjənəst/, *n.* **1.** a follower of communism. **2.** (*oft. cap.*) someone who belongs to a political party which supports communism. ◇*adj.* **3.** relating to communists or communism. –**communistic,** *n.*

Communist Manifesto, *n.* a pamphlet (1848) by Karl Marx and Friedrich Engels; first statement of the principles of modern communism.

community /kə'mjunəti/, *n., pl.* **-ties. 1.** a social group of any size whose members live in one area, share government, and often share a common background. **2.** a group of organisms, both plant and animal, living together in an ecologically related fashion in a particular region. **3.** similar character; agreement; identity: *community of interests.* [L]

commutation /kɒmju'teɪʃən/, *n.* **1.** the act of exchanging one thing for another. **2.** the

commutation ... changing of a punishment, etc., for another less severe. —**commutative**, *adj.*

commutative law /'kɒmju,teɪtɪv lɔː/, *n. Maths.* a law stating that the order in which certain operations are performed makes no difference, as in the addition and multiplication of numbers.

commutator /'kɒmjuteɪtə/, *n.* a device for changing the direction of an electric current.

commute /kə'mjuːt/, *v.*, **-muted**, **-muting**. ◇*v.t.* 1. to exchange (a thing, esp. a payment) for another or something else. 2. to change (a punishment, etc.) for one less severe: *The death sentence was commuted to life imprisonment.* ◇*v.i.* 3. to travel regularly between home (usu. distant) and work. [L: change wholly]

commuter /kə'mjuːtə/, *n.* someone who regularly travels some considerable distance to work from his home, esp. by public transport.

comp., *Abbrev.* comparative.

compact[1] /kəm'pækt, 'kɒmpækt/, *adj.*; /kəm'pækt/, *v.*; /'kɒmpækt/, *n.*, ◇*adj.* 1. joined or packed closely together; dense; solid. 2. arranged within a relatively small space. 3. expressed in a few words. ◇*v.t.* 4. to join or pack closely together; consolidate; condense. ◇*n.* 5. a small case containing a mirror, face powder, etc. [L: joined together]

compact[2] /'kɒmpækt/, *n.* an agreement between people; a contract. [L: having agreed with]

companion /kəm'pænjən/, *n.* 1. someone who associates with another. 2. a person, usu. a woman, employed to be with or help another. 3. someone or something that matches or goes with another. 4. an information booklet: *The Golfer's Companion.* 5. a member of the lowest rank in an order of knighthood. [LL, from L *com-* COM- + *pānis* bread] —**companionship**, *n.*

companionable /kəm'pænjənəbəl/, *adj.* fitted to be a companion; sociable.

companionway /kəm'pænjən,weɪ/, *n. Naut.* (the space occupied by) the steps leading down from a deck to a cabin.

company /'kʌmpəni/, *n., pl.* **-nies**. 1. a number of people grouped together, often for social purposes. 2. companionship. 3. a guest or guests. 4. a number of people united for a common purpose, esp. for business or trade. 5. a number of people associated for the purpose of presenting theatrical productions, etc. 6. *Mil.* a smaller group within a regiment or battalion. 7. *Naut.* a ship's crew, including officers. 8. **bear** or **keep company**, to associate or go with. 9. **part company, a.** to cease an association or friendship with. **b.** to leave or separate from (each other). [ME, from OF. See COMPANION]

company tax, *n.* a tax based on the profits of limited companies.

company title, *n. Law.* a form of interest in a property, where the whole of a building is owned by a company, shares in which are held by people living in the building.

compar., *Abbrev.* comparative.

comparable /'kɒmprəbəl, -pərəbəl/, *adj.* 1. able to be compared. 2. worthy of comparison. —**comparableness**, *n.*

comparative /kəm'pærətɪv/, *adj.* 1. relating to or based on comparison. 2. judged by comparison; relative. 3. *Gram.* of the second degree of the comparison of adjectives and adverbs. ◇*n.* 4. *Gram.* **a.** the comparative degree. **b.** a form in it, as English *lower* in contrast to *low* and *lowest, more skilful* in contrast to *skilful* and *most skilful*.

compare /kəm'peə/, *v.*, **-pared**, **-paring**, *n.* ◇*v.t.* 1. to represent as similar; liken (fol. by *to*). 2. to note the similarities and differences of (fol. by *with*): *to compare one sample with another.* ◇*v.i.* 3. to bear comparison; be held equal. 4. to match in quality, etc: *The views of this country compare with any in the world.* ◇*v.* 5. compare notes, to exchange views, ideas, etc. ◇*n.* 6. comparison: *joy beyond compare.* [ME, from F, from L: bring together]

comparison /kəm'pærəsən/, *n.* 1. the act or result of comparing. 2. a likening; estimate or statement of the similarities and differences between certain things. [ME, from OF, from L]

compartment /kəm'pɑːtmənt/, *n.* 1. a part or space marked off. 2. a separate room, section, etc.: *the compartment of a railway carriage; a watertight compartment in a ship.* [F, from It, from LL: divide] —**compartmental**, *adj.*

compass /'kʌmpəs/, *n.* 1. an instrument for determining directions, the chief part of which is a freely moving magnetised needle pointing to magnetic north and south. 2. a line enclosing any area; measurement round. 3. the space within limits; area; extent; range; scope. 4. the total range of notes of a voice or musical instrument. 5. (usu. pl.) an instrument for drawing circles, measuring distances, etc., consisting of two legs hinged together at one end. ◇*v.t.* 6. to go or move round: *The sun compassed the earth.* 7. to extend around. 8. to understand. [ME, from OF: divide exactly, from L: equal step]

compassion /kəm'pæʃən/, *n.* a feeling of sorrow or pity for another; sympathy. [ME, from LL: sympathy]

compassionate /kəm'pæʃənət/, *adj.* 1. having or showing compassion. 2. given on the basis of compassion: *compassionate leave.*

compass rose, *n.* a pattern on a map, sometimes presented artistically, which shows the direction of true north and magnetic north.

compatible /kəm'pætəbəl/, *adj.* 1. able to exist together in agreement. 2. able to be used together efficiently with other elements in a system. [ML, from LL: suffer with] —**compatibility**, *adv.*

compatriot /kəm'peɪtriət/, *n.* another person of one's own country; fellow countryman or countrywoman. [L] —**compatriotism**, *n.*

compel /kəm'pɛl/, *v.t.*, **-pelled**, **-pelling**. 1. to force or drive, esp. to a course of action: *They can compel him to attend school.* 2. to

compel bring about by force. [ME, from L] —**compellable**, *adj.* —**compeller**, *n.*

compelling /kəm'pelɪŋ/, *adj.* (of a person, writer, actor, etc.) attracting strong interest or respect.

compendious /kəm'pendɪəs/, *adj.* containing the main information about a subject in brief form; concise.

compendium /kəm'pendɪəm/, *n., pl.* **-diums, -dia** /-dɪə/. a shortened account of a complete subject. [L: a saving, a short way]

compensate /'kɒmpənseɪt/, *v.*, **-sated, -sating.** ◇*v.t.* **1.** to make up for: *We will compensate your losses.* **2.** to make up (for something) to (a person); recompense: *He will compensate them for the damage to their ship.* **3.** *Mech.* to offset the effects of (a force or the like). ◇*v.i.* **4.** to provide or be an equivalent. **5.** make up (fol. by *for*). [L: counterbalanced] —**compensator**, *n.* —**compensatory**, *adj.*

compensation /kɒmpən'seɪʃən/, *n.* **1.** the act of compensating. **2.** something given or received as making up for services, debt, loss, suffering, etc.; indemnity. **3.** *Biol.* the development or action of a bodily structure in response to the lack of effectiveness of another one. **4.** *Psychol.* exaggerated behavior which compensates for some weak aspect of personality. —**compensational**, *adj.*

compere /'kɒmpeə/, *n., v.*, **-pered, -pering.** ◇*n.* **1.** a person who introduces the acts in a show. ◇*v.i., v.t.* **2.** to act as a compere. [F]

compete /kəm'piːt/, *v.i.*, **-peted, -peting.** to set oneself against another for a prize, profit, etc.; vie: *to compete in a race, in business, etc.* [L: contend for]

competence /'kɒmpətəns/, *n.* **1.** the quality of being capable or competent; adequacy. **2.** sufficiency, esp. of money to live on. **3.** *Law.* the quality or position of being legally competent (which includes such things as being above a certain age, having soundness of mind, citizenship, etc.). Also, **competency.**

competent /'kɒmpətənt/, *adj.* **1.** having ability or skill in an area. **2.** fitting, suitable, or enough for the purpose; adequate. **3.** *Law.* (of a witness, etc.) being legally fit. [L: being fit]

competition /kɒmpə'tɪʃən/, *n.* **1.** the act of competing; rivalry. **2.** a test between people to win some prize or advantage, as a struggle between shops to attract buyers, or between organisms for food, space, etc. **3.** person(s) against whom another competes: *The competition is outstanding.* [L]

competitive /kəm'petətɪv/, *adj.* of, relating to, involving, or decided by competition: *competitive examination.* Also, **competitory.**

competitor /kəm'petətə/, *n.* someone who competes; rival.

compile /kəm'paɪl/, *v.t.*, **-piled, -piling.** **1.** to put together (information, etc.) in one book or work. **2.** to make (a book, etc.) from information, illustrations, etc., from various sources. [ME, from OF, from L: snatch together and carry off] —**compilation**, *n.*

compiler /kəm'paɪlə/, *n.* *Computers.* a computer program which translates programming languages into the basic commands acted upon by the computer.

complacency /kəm'pleɪsənsi/, *n., pl.* **-cies.** a feeling of quiet pleasure, esp. with oneself; self-satisfaction. —**complacent**, *adj.*

complain /kəm'pleɪn/, *v.i.* **1.** to express grief, pain, uneasiness, or dissatisfaction, etc.; find fault. **2.** to tell of one's pains, illnesses, etc. **3.** to make a formal accusation. [ME, from OF, from LL: lament] —**complainer**, *n.* —**complaining**, *adj.*

complainant /kəm'pleɪnənt/, *n.* someone who makes a complaint, as in a legal action.

complaint /kəm'pleɪnt/, *n.* **1.** an expression of grief, regret, pain, blame or discontent; lament. **2.** a cause of complaint. **3.** a cause of bodily pain; malady. **4.** *Law.* the first statement of the party bringing an action in court. [ME, from OF]

complaisant /kəm'pleɪsənt, -zənt/, *adj.* tending to please; obliging; agreeable; gracious; compliant. [F: pleasing, from L]

complement /'kɒmpləmənt/, *n.*; /'kɒmpləˌment/, *v.*, ◇*n.* **1.** something which completes or makes perfect. **2.** the quantity or amount that completes anything. **3.** either of two parts or things needed to make the other whole. **4.** the full quantity or amount. **5.** the full number of officers and crew required to man a ship. **6.** *Gram.* the words used to complete a grammatical structure, esp. in the predicate, as an object (*man* in *He saw the man*), predicate adjective (*tall* in *The tree is tall*), or predicate noun (*John* in *His name is John*). **7.** *Geom.* the angle needed to bring a given angle to a right angle. **8.** *Maths.* all members of any set, class or space of elements, that are not in a given subset. ◇*v.t.* **9.** to complete; form a complement to. [ME, from L: that which fills up, (later) fulfilment]

complementary /kɒmplə'mentəri, -tri/, *adj.* **1.** forming a complement; completing. **2.** complementing each other.

complementary angle, *n.* the angle which, together with the given angle, adds to 90°.

complete /kəm'pliːt/, *adj., v.*, **-pleted, -pleting.** ◇*adj.* **1.** having all its parts or elements; whole; entire; full. **2.** finished; ended; concluded. **3.** perfect in kind or quality; consummate. **4.** total; absolute: *I've been a complete fool.* ◇*v.t.* **5.** to make complete; make whole or entire. **6.** to make perfect. **7.** to bring to an end; finish; fulfil. [ME, from L: filled up, completed]

completion /kəm'pliːʃən/, *n.* **1.** the act or result of completing. **2.** the end; fulfilment: *the completion of a task.*

complex /'kɒmpleks, kəm'pleks/, *adj.*; /'kɒmpleks/, ◇*adj.* **1.** made up of parts connected with each other; compound; composite. **2.** difficult to understand or explain; complicated: *Maths is too complex for me.* **3.** *Maths.*

complex

relating to a number of the form $z = x + iy$, where x and y are real numbers and $i = \sqrt{-1}$. ◇*n.* **4.** a complex whole or system: *a shopping complex; a complex of ideas.* **5.** *Psychol.* a group of related ideas, feelings, memories, etc. which operate together. **6.** *Colloq.* a fixed idea, often of concern: *He has a complex about his height.* [L: having embraced]

complexion /kəm'plekʃən/, *n.* **1.** the natural color and appearance of the skin, esp. of the face. **2.** appearance; aspect; character. [ME, from LL: constitution, L combination]

complexity /kəm'pleksəti/, *n., pl.* **-ties.** the state or quality of being complex; intricacy.

complex sentence, *n.* a sentence containing a main clause and one or more dependent clauses, e.g. *When the clock strikes* (dependent clause), *it will be 3 o'clock* (main clause).

compliance /kəm'plaɪəns/, *n.* **1.** the act of agreeing. **2.** the state of being too willing to agree. **3. in compliance with,** in keeping with. – **compliant,** *adj.*

complicate /'komplɪkeɪt/, *v.t.,* **-cated, -cating. 1.** to make more difficult to understand or deal with. **2.** to increase the number of parts of; make more complex. [L: folded together]

complicated /'komplɪkeɪtəd/, *adj.* **1.** composed of many related parts; not simple; complex; intricate. **2.** difficult to understand, explain, etc.

complication /kɒmplɪ'keɪʃən/, *n.* **1.** (the bringing about of) a complicated state or condition. **2.** a complicating element: *Her refusal to attend is a complication.* **3.** *Med.* a disease or condition which exists alongside and may worsen the original disease.

complicity /kəm'plɪsəti/, *n., pl.* **-ties.** the state of being a partner (in wrongdoing): *complicity in a crime.*

compliment /'komplɪmənt/; /'komplɪˌment/, *v.* ◇*n.* **1.** an expression of praise or admiration: *He paid you a great compliment.* **2.** a formal act or expression of respect or regard: *the compliments of the season.* **3.** polite, esp. insincere, praise; flattery. ◇*v.t.* **4.** to pay a compliment to: *to compliment a woman on her new hat.* **5.** to congratulate: *to compliment a student on examination success.* [F, from It, from Sp: fulfil, from L]

complimentary /kɒmplɪ'mentri/, *adj.* **1.** of the nature of, giving, or addressing a compliment. **2.** free: *a complimentary ticket.*

comply /kəm'plaɪ/, *v.i.,* **-plied, -plying.** to act in keeping (with wishes, requests, commands, requirements, conditions, etc.) [It: fulfil, complete, from Sp, from L: complete]

compo /'kompoʊ/, *n. Colloq.* a payment to cover a hurt suffered at or in connection with one's work. Also, **comp.** [COMPENSATION]

component /kəm'poʊnənt/, *adj.* **1.** being part of; constituent: *A turntable is a component part of a record-player.* ◇*n.* **2.** a part of a whole. **3.** *Phys.* (of a vector quantity such as a force, velocity, etc.) one of the parts which

compound

when combined together make up the vector. **4.** *Elect.* one of the parts of an electronic circuit, e.g. resistor, capacitor, inductor, etc. [L: composing]

comport /kəm'pɔt/, *v.t.* **1.** to bear or carry (oneself); behave: *She does comport herself well.* ◇*v.i.* **2.** to agree; suit (fol. by *with*): *That comports with our facts.* [F: bear, behave, from L: carry together] – **comportment,** *n.*

compose /kəm'poʊz/, *v.,* **-posed, -posing.** ◇*v.t.* **1.** to make by uniting parts or elements of. **2.** to be the parts or elements of. **3.** to make up; constitute. **4.** to put in proper form or order. **5.** to arrange the parts or elements of (a picture, etc.). **6.** to create (a literary or musical production). **7.** to arrange or settle, as a quarrel, etc. **8.** to bring (the body or mind) to a condition of calmness, etc.; calm; quiet. **9.** *Print.* to set (type). ◇*v.i.* **10.** to create, esp. musical works. [ME, from OF. See COMPOSITE] – **composer,** *n.*

composed /kəm'poʊzd/, *adj.* calm; tranquil; serene. – **composedly,** *adv.*

composite /'kɒmpəzət/, *adj.* **1.** made up of various parts or elements; compound. **2.** (*cap.*) *Archit.* relating to a classical style combining features of the Corinthian and Ionic styles. ◇*n.* **3.** something composite; a compound. [L *compōnere* put together, compound, compose]

composite number, *n. Maths.* a whole number greater than one which is able to be divided with no remainder by a whole number other than itself and one.

composition /kɒmpə'zɪʃən/, *n.* **1.** the act of combining parts to form a whole, as in the composition of works of music and literature. **2.** the resulting state or product, as musical works, etc. **3.** make-up; constitution. **4.** a compound substance. **5.** a short essay written as a school exercise. **6.** *Print.* the setting up of type for printing.

composition of forces, *n.* the combination of two or more forces, velocities, etc., (*components*), into a single equivalent force, velocity, etc., (the *resultant*).

compositor /kəm'pɒzətə/, *n. Print.* a person who puts together the type for a printed page.

compos mentis /kɒmpəs 'mentəs/, *adj.* able to think clearly. [L]

compost /'kɒmpɒst/, *n.* a mixture of various kinds of decaying organic matter, as dung, dead leaves, etc., used for fertilising land. [ME, from OF, from L: compounded]

composure /kəm'poʊʒə/, *n.* a calm state of mind; tranquillity.

compote /'kɒmpɒt/, *n.* a dish of fruit cooked in sugar and water. [F, from L. See COMPOSITE]

compound[1] /kɒm'paʊnd/, *adj., n.;* /kəm'paʊnd/, *v.,* ◇*adj.* **1.** made of two or more parts or elements, or involving two or more actions, etc.; composite. **2.** *Gram.* (of a word) consisting of two or more parts which are also words, e.g. *housetop, blackberry,* historically also *cupboard, breakfast.* ◇*n.* **3.** something

compound 211 **comrade**

formed by combining parts, elements, etc. **4.** *Chem.* a substance made up of two or more elements, joined chemically in a fixed proportion, whose properties, when so joined, are different from those of the original elements. **5.** *Gram.* a compound word. ◇*v.t.* **6.** to put together into a whole; combine. **7.** to make by combining parts, etc.; construct. **8.** to settle by agreement, esp. for a reduced amount, as a debt. **9.** *Law.* to agree, for a fee or benefit, not to punish a wrongdoer for: *to compound a crime or felony.* **10.** to increase or make worse: *The rain compounded their problems.* ◇*v.i.* **11.** to make a bargain; compromise. **12.** to settle a debt, etc., by agreement. [ME, from OF, from L: put together] **—compoundable,** *adj.*

compound² /'kɒmpaʊnd/, *n.* **1.** any place where a group of people live who may share common interests, occupation or race. **2.** a closed-off area to which people are sometimes confined. **3.** an area in which animals are held. [Malay *kampong* enclosure]

compound eye, *n.* an eye divided into many individual light-receiving elements.

compound fracture, *n.* a break in a bone which lies beneath an open wound, increasing the risk of infection.

compound interest, *n.* interest paid both on the principal (original amount) and remaining unpaid interest.

compound sentence, *n.* a sentence with two or more independent clauses, usu. joined by one or more conjunctions, e.g. *The lightning flashed* (independent clause) *and* (conjunction) *the rain fell* (independent clause).

comprehend /kɒmprə'hend/, *v.t.* **1.** to understand the meaning or nature of; conceive; know. **2.** to take in; include; comprise. [ME, from L *comprehendere* seize] **—comprehensible,** *adj.* **—comprehendingly,** *adv.*

comprehension /kɒmprə'henʃən/, *n.* **1.** the act or fact of comprehending. **2.** inclusion; comprehensiveness; perception or understanding. **3.** (in schools) a formal exercise in reading and understanding, usu. tested with a set of short questions. [L]

comprehensive /kɒmprə'hensɪv/, *adj.* **1.** including much; inclusive. **2.** having a wide understanding. **—comprehensiveness,** *n.*

comprehensive school, *n.* a large secondary school providing a wide range of courses for children of all levels of ability.

compress /kəm'pres/, *v.*; /'kɒmpres/, *n.* ◇*v.t.* **1.** to press together; force into less space. ◇*n.* **2.** *Med.* a soft pad of linen, or the like, held in place by a bandage, used to give pressure, cold, heat, etc. [ME, from L] **—compressible,** *adj.* **—compressibility,** *n.* **—compressed,** *adj.*

compression /kəm'preʃən/, *n.* **1.** the act of forcing into a small space. **2.** the state of being pressed together. **3.** (in some internal-combustion engines) the decrease in volume and increase of pressure of the air or firing mixture in the cylinder before it starts burning, produced by the movement of the piston towards the cylinder head.

compressor /kəm'presə/, *n.* any machine, as a pump, in which a gas is forced into a small space so that its expansion may be used as a source of power. [L]

comprise /kəm'praɪz/, *v.t.*, **-prised, -prising. 1.** to include; contain. **2.** to be made up of; be composed of. [ME, from F, from L: seize] **—comprisal,** *n.*

compromise /'kɒmprəmaɪz/, *n., v.,* **-mised, -mising.** ◇*n.* **1.** the settlement of differences by a giving way on both sides; arbitration. **2.** anything resulting from a compromise. **3.** something intermediate between two different things. ◇*v.t.* **4.** to settle by a compromise. **5.** to lay open to danger, dishonor, suspicion, scandal, etc.: *To cheat would compromise your standing in the class.* ◇*v.i.* **6.** to make a compromise. [ME, from F, from L: a mutual promise to abide by a decision] **—compromiser,** *n.*

comptroller /kən'troʊlə, kɒmp-/, *n.* the financial officer and controller of a household, esp. of a royal household. [variant spelling of *controller*]

compulsion /kəm'pʌlʃən/, *n.* **1.** the act of forcing; constraint; coercion. **2.** the state of being compelled. **3.** *Psychol.* a strong, unexplained urge to carry out a given act. [ME, from L]

compulsive /kəm'pʌlsɪv/, *adj.* **1.** → **compulsory. 2.** *Chiefly Psychol.* relating to compulsion. **3.** unable to break a given habit: *She is a compulsive eater.* **4.** forcing one to continue, esp. of pleasurable activities: *compulsive reading.*

compulsory /kəm'pʌlsəri/, *adj.* **1.** using force; compelling; constraining: *compulsory measures.* **2.** forced; obligatory. **—compulsoriness,** *n.* **—compulsorily,** *adv.*

compunction /kəm'pʌŋkʃən, -'pʌnʃən/, *n.* uneasiness of conscience or feelings; contrition; remorse. [ME, from LL: remorse]

computation /ˌkɒmpju'teɪʃən/, *n.* **1.** the act, process, or method of calculating. **2.** the amount calculated.

compute /kəm'pjut/, *v.*, **-puted, -puting.** ◇*v.t.* **1.** to determine by calculation; reckon; calculate: *to compute the distance of the moon from the earth.* ◇*v.i.* **2.** to calculate. [L: reckon] **—computability,** *n.*

computer /kəm'pjutə/, *n.* an apparatus for performing mathematical calculations electronically according to a set of stored instructions called a program.

computer program, *n.* → **program** (def. 6).

computer terminal, *n.* a device for receiving or giving information, connected to a computer but at a distance from it.

comrade /'kɒmreɪd, 'kɒmrəd/, *n.* **1.** a close companion; friend; mate. **2.** a fellow member of a political party (esp. the Communist Party), etc. [F, from Sp *camarada*, lit., group living in one room, from L *camera* CHAMBER] **—comradeship,** *n.*

con¹ /kɒn/, *adv.* against an opinion, etc.; not pro (for). [short for L *contrā*, as adv.; in opposition, as prep., against]

con² /kɒn/, *v.t.*, **conned, conning.** to learn; study; examine carefully. Also, **con up**. [var. of CAN¹, OE *can, con,* a finite form of *cunnan* know]

con³ /kɒn/, *n. Colloq.* → **convict.**

con⁴ /kɒn/, *adj., n., v.,* **conned, conning.** ◇*adj.* 1. relating to the gaining of someone's confidence in order to swindle them: *a con game; con man.* ◇*n.* 2. a con trick; swindle. ◇*v.t.* 3. to trick; defraud. [short for CONFIDENCE TRICK or MAN]

con⁵ /kɒn/, *n. Colloq.* → **conservatorium.**

con-, variant of **com-,** before consonants except *b, h, l, p, r, w,* as in *convene, condone,* and, by assimilation, before *n,* as in *connection.* See **co-** (def. 1).

Conan Doyle /ˈkoʊnən ˈdɔɪl/, *n.* → Sir Arthur Conan **Doyle.**

concatenate /kɒnˈkætəneɪt/, *v.,* **-nated, -nating,** *adj.* ◇*v.t.* 1. to unite in a set or chain. ◇*adj.* 2. joined together as in a chain. [L *concatēnātus,* pp.] —**concatenation,** *n.*

concave /ˈkɒnkeɪv/, *adj.* curved like the inside of a circle; hollow and curved, esp. of optical lenses and mirrors. See **convex.** [L] —**concavity,** *n.*

conceal /kənˈsiːl/, *v.t.* 1. to hide; cover or keep from sight. 2. to refuse to disclose; keep (something) secret. [ME, from OF, from L: hide] —**concealable,** *adj.* —**concealer,** *n.* —**concealment,** *n.*

concede /kənˈsiːd/, *v.,* **-ceded, -ceding.** ◇*v.t.* 1. to admit as true, fair or proper. 2. to grant as a right; yield. ◇*v.i.* 3. to admit defeat (in an election). 4. to give in; yield. [L]

conceit /kənˈsiːt/, *n.* 1. an unreasonably high estimate of one's own ability, importance, etc. 2. something which is born in the mind; a thought; an idea. 3. a fanciful thought, idea or expression, esp. of a far-fetched nature. [ME]

conceited /kənˈsiːtəd/, *adj.* having too high an opinion of one's abilities, importance, etc.

conceive /kənˈsiːv/, *v.,* **-ceived, -ceiving.** ◇*v.t.* 1. to form (an opinion, purpose, etc.): *He conceived the plan yesterday.* 2. to form an idea of; imagine: *She must conceive the house to be grand.* 3. to understand: *Can you conceive their unhappiness?* 4. to become pregnant with: *to conceive a baby.* ◇*v.i.* 5. to form an idea; think (fol. by *of*): *I can't conceive of that ever happening here.* 6. to become pregnant. [ME, from OF, from L: take in] —**conceiver,** *n.* —**conceivable,** *adj.*

concentrate /ˈkɒnsəntreɪt/, *v.,* **-trated, -trating,** *n.* ◇*v.t.* 1. to bring to bear on one point; direct towards one object; focus: *She concentrated the light on his face.* 2. to make stronger or purer by removing or reducing what is foreign. 3. *Chem.* to increase the strength of a solution, as by evaporation. ◇*v.i.* 4. to bear on a centre. 5. to become stronger or purer. 6. to direct one's thoughts or actions towards one subject. ◇*n.* 7. a concentrated form of something. [CON- + L *centrum* centre + -ATE¹]

concentration /kɒnsənˈtreɪʃən/, *n.* 1. the act of concentrating. 2. a concentrated state. 3. total attention to one object. 4. something concentrated. 5. *Chem.* the amount of a particular substance in a given space or a stated unit of a mixture, solution, or ore, expressed as per cent by weight or by volume, weight per unit volume, normality, molality, etc.

concentration camp, *n.* a guarded enclosure for the holding of political prisoners, racial minority groups, etc., esp. any of the camps run by the Nazis before and during World War II for the imprisonment and mass killing of Jews, etc.

concentric /kənˈsɛntrɪk/, *adj.* (of circles, spheres, etc.) having the same centre. Also, **concentrical.** —**concentricity,** *n.*

concept /ˈkɒnsɛpt/, *n.* a general idea, understanding of something: *your concept of love.* [L: a conceiving] —**conceptual,** *adj.*

conception /kənˈsɛpʃən/, *n.* 1. the act of conceiving. 2. the state of being conceived. 3. the beginning of pregnancy; fertilisation. 4. a beginning. 5. an idea; concept. —**conceptional,** *adj.* —**conceptive,** *adj.*

conceptualise or **conceptualize** /kənˈsɛptʃuəlaɪz/, *v.t., v.i.,* **-lised, -lising.** to form an idea of.

concern /kənˈsɜːn/, *v.t.* 1. to relate to; be of interest or importance to; affect: *The problem concerns us all.* 2. to interest or involve (oft. fol. by *with* or *in*). 3. to disquiet or trouble (used in the passive): *to be concerned about a person's health.* ◇*n.* 4. a matter of interest, care, or importance; affair: *It's no concern of mine.* 5. anxiety; solicitude. 6. a business. [L *con-* CON- + *cernere* separate, have respect to]

concerned /kənˈsɜːnd/, *adj.* 1. interested. 2. involved. 3. troubled or anxious: *a concerned look.*

concerning /kənˈsɜːnɪŋ/, *prep.* relating to; regarding; about.

concert /ˈkɒnsət/ *for def. 1;* /ˈkɒnsɜːt/ *for def. 2, n.;* /kənˈsɜːt/, *v.* ◇*n.* 1. **a.** a public performance, by one or more musicians. **b.** a performance of different acts not necessarily all musical, as in a school concert. 2. the agreement of two or more in a plan; accord; harmony. ◇*v.t.* 3. to do or arrange by agreement. 4. to plan; devise. ◇*v.i.* 5. to plan or act together. [F, from It: be in accord, from L: contend]

concerted /kənˈsɜːtəd/, *adj.* 1. arranged by agreement; prearranged; planned: *concerted action.* 2. *Music.* arranged in parts for several voices or instruments.

concertina /kɒnsəˈtiːnə/, *n., v.,* **-naed, -naing.** ◇*n.* 1. a musical instrument like an accordion but hexagonal in section. 2. *Colloq.* a side of lamb. ◇*v.i.* 3. to fold up or collapse like a concertina. [CONCERT + *-ina,* diminutive suffix]

concertmaster /'kɒnsətmɑːstə/, *n.* the first violinist of an orchestra; leader.

concerto /kən'tʃɛətoʊ, kən'tʃɜːtoʊ/, *n., pl.* **-tos, -ti** /-tiː/. *Music.* a piece of music for one or more solo instruments and orchestra. [It]

concession /kən'sɛʃən/, *n.* **1.** the act of conceding or yielding. **2.** a thing or point yielded, esp. after a disagreement. **3.** something yielded by a controlling or governing authority, e.g. land, franchise. [L]

conch /kɒntʃ, kɒŋk/, *n., pl.* **conchs** /kɒŋks/, **conches**, /'kɒntʃəz/. **1.** the spiral shell of a gastropod, which makes a sound when blown. **2.** any of several sea gastropods. [L, from Gk: mussel or cockle, shell-like part or thing, external ear]

conchology /kɒn'kɒlədʒi, kɒŋ-/, *n.* the branch of zoology dealing with molluscs. [*concho-* (from Gk *koncho-*, combining form of *kónchē* mussel) + -LOGY]

conciliate /kən'sɪliˌeɪt/, *v.t.*, **-ated, -ating. 1.** to overcome the distrust or hostility of, by calming; placate; reconcile. **2.** to win or gain (regard or favor). **3.** to attempt to bring disputing parties into voluntary agreement. [L: brought together] **—conciliator,** *n.* **—conciliatory,** *adj.*

conciliation /kənsɪli'eɪʃən/, *n.* **1.** the act of conciliating. **2.** the method of working out arguments, esp. industrial disputes by arbitration.

concise /kən'saɪs/, *adj.* expressing much in few words; brief and comprehensive; succinct: *a concise account.* [L: cut up or off] **—conciseness, concision,** *n.*

conclave /'kɒnkleɪv, 'kɒŋ-/, *n.* **1.** any private meeting. **2.** a (place of) private meeting of the cardinals of the Roman Catholic Church for the election of a pope. [ME, from L: lockable place]

conclude /kən'kluːd, kəŋ-/, *v.*, **-cluded, -cluding.** ◇*v.t.* **1.** to bring to an end; finish; terminate: *to conclude a speech.* **2.** to bring to a decision; settle or arrange finally: *to conclude a treaty.* **3.** to decide by reasoning; deduce; infer. ◇*v.i.* **4.** to come to an end; finish. **5.** to arrive at an opinion or judgment; come to a decision; decide. [ME, from L: shut up]

conclusion /kən'kluːʒən, kəŋ-/, *n.* **1.** the end or close; last part. **2.** the last main division of a speech, book, etc., containing a summing up of the points. **3.** a result; outcome: *a foregone conclusion.* **4.** a final arrangement; settlement. **5.** a final decision. **6.** an opinion or thought reached from the facts available; deduction; inference. **7. in conclusion,** finally. [ME, from L]

conclusive /kən'kluːsɪv, kəŋ-/, *adj.* serving to settle or decide a question; decisive; convincing: *conclusive evidence.*

concoct /kən'kɒkt, kəŋ-/, *v.t.* **1.** to make by combining parts, esp. in cookery: *to concoct a soup or a dinner.* **2.** to make up; contrive: *to concoct a story.* [L: cooked together, digested] **—concoction,** *n.*

concomitant /kən'kɒmətənt, kəŋ-/, *adj.* **1.** happening together; concurrent. ◇*n.* **2.** a concomitant quality, condition, person, or thing. [LL: accompanying] **—concomitance, concomitancy,** *n.*

concord /'kɒnkɔːd, 'kɒŋ-/, *n.* **1.** agreement between people; unanimity; accord. **2.** peace. **3.** a treaty. **4.** *Music.* **→consonance.** [ME, from F, from L: agreement]

concordance /kən'kɔːdns, kəŋ-/, *n.* **1.** the state of being in agreement; harmony. **2.** an alphabetical index of the main words of a book, as of the Bible, with a reference to the part in which each is found. **—concordant,** *adj.*

Concorde /'kɒnkɔːd/, *n.* the first civil supersonic aircraft, capable of flying at 2125 km/h; constructed by Great Britain and France.

concourse /'kɒnkɔːs, 'kɒŋ-/, *n.* **1.** a coming together of people; assembly. **2.** an open space or main hall in a public building, esp. in a railway station or airport. **3.** grounds for racing, athletic sports, etc. **4.** a running or coming together (of water, etc.); confluence. [ME, from OF, from L: running together]

concrete /'kɒnkriːt, 'kɒŋ-/, *adj., n., v.*, **-creted, -creting.** ◇*adj.* **1.** existing as an actual thing or instance; real. **2.** concerned with realities or actual examples rather than abstractions; particular (as opposed to general): *a concrete idea.* **3.** *Gram.* representing an actual thing rather than a quality, state etc.: *a concrete noun.* **4.** made of concrete (def. 6): *a concrete pavement.* ◇*n.* **5.** a material used in building, etc., made by mixing cement, sand, and small broken stones, etc., with water, and allowing the mixture to harden. ◇*v.i., v.t.* **6.** to use, or treat with, concrete. **7.** to unite, or form, into a mass; harden; solidify. [L: grown together, hardened]

concretion /kən'kriːʃən, kəŋ-/, *n.* **1.** the act or process of concreting. **2.** a solidified mass. **3.** *Med.* **→calculus** (def. 2). **4.** an adhesion or union of two parts. **5.** *Geol.* a rounded mass of mineral matter occurring in sandstone, clay, etc., often in concentric layers around a solid centre.

concubine /'kɒŋkjubaɪn/, *n.* **1.** (in societies where marriage to more than one person at one time is permitted) a secondary wife. **2.** a woman who lives with a man without being married to him. [ME, from L] **—concubinage,** *n.*

concupiscence /kɒn'kjuːpəsəns/, *n.* **1.** sexual desire; lust. **2.** eager or unlawful desire. **—concupiscent,** *adj.*

concur /kən'kɜː/, *v.i.*, **-curred, -curring. 1.** to agree (oft. fol. by *with*). **2.** to act together; cooperate; combine. **3.** to happen at the same time. [ME, from L: run together]

concurrent /kən'kʌrənt/, *adj.* **1.** occurring or existing together or side by side. **2.** acting together; cooperating. **3.** in agreement; accordant. **4.** *Geom.* passing through the same points: *four concurrent lines.* **—concurrence,** *n.*

concuss /kən'kʌs, kəŋ-/, *v.t.* **1.** to hurt the brain of (someone) by a heavy blow or fall; to knock out. **2.** to strike or shake violently.

concussion /kən'kʌʃən, kəŋ-/, n. **1.** (the shock caused by) a blow, collision, etc. **2.** *Med.* a jarring of the brain, spinal cord, etc., from a blow, fall, etc. [L: shock] —**concussive**, *adj.*

Condamine /'kɒndəmaɪn/, n. a river in south-eastern Qld, rising on the western side of the Great Dividing Range and flowing west to join Dogwood Creek to form the Balonne. About 690 km.

condemn /kən'dɛm/, v.t. **1.** to express strong disapproval of; censure. **2.** to judge (a person) to be guilty; sentence to punishment. **3.** to judge (something) to be unfit for use or service: *The old ship was condemned.* **4.** to force into a certain state or action: *The injury condemned him to a life of inactivity.* [ME, from OF, from L]

condemnation /ˌkɒndɛm'neɪʃən/, n. **1.** the act of condemning. **2.** strong disapproval; reproof. **3.** the condition of being condemned. **4.** the cause or reason for condemning. —**condemnatory**, *adj.*

condensation /ˌkɒndɛn'seɪʃən/, n. **1.** the act of changing a gas or vapor usu. to a liquid, or to a solid form. **2.** a condensed state or form. **3.** *Chem.* the reaction between two or more organic molecules, leading to the formation of a larger molecule and the splitting out of a simple molecule such as water or alcohol.

condense /kən'dɛns/, v., **-densed**, **-densing**. ◇v.t. **1.** to make more dense; reduce the volume of. **2.** to change to another and denser form, as a gas or vapor to a liquid or solid state. **3.** to put (a book, etc.) into fewer words; abridge. ◇v.i. **4.** to become liquid or solid, as a gas or vapor. [ME, from L: make thick]

condenser /kən'dɛnsə/, n. **1.** someone or something that condenses. **2.** *Chem.* an apparatus for reducing gases to liquid or solid form. **3.** *Optics.* a lens or combination of lenses, used to gather and concentrate rays of light and direct them upon an object. **4.** *Elect.* → **capacitor.**

Conder /'kɒndə/, n. **Charles**, 1868–1909, Australian painter, born in London, noted for his watercolor paintings on silk; earlier identified with the Heidelberg School.

condescend /kɒndə'sɛnd/, v.i. **1.** to agree or stoop (to do something), below one's social level: *The general condescended to eat with the soldiers.* **2.** to act as if one is from a higher position, rank, etc.: *I dislike people who condescend.* [ME, from F, from LL: stoop] —**condescending**, *adj.* —**condescension**, n.

condiment /'kɒndəmənt/, n. something used to give an extra taste to food, e.g. a sauce or seasoning. [L: spice]

condition /kən'dɪʃən/, n. **1.** the particular state of being of someone or something, esp. in relation to circumstances: *a condition of weightlessness in space.* **2.** state of health: *Doctor said his condition was bad.* **3.** state of physical fitness: *He is out of condition.* **4.** *Agric.* the degree of fatness of a beast or carcass. **5.** a limiting or modifying circumstance: *Business conditions aren't good at the moment.* **6.** a circumstance which is necessary for some result; prerequisite. **7.** something demanded as a necessary part of an agreement. **8. on condition that**, if; provided that. ◇v.t. **9.** to put in a fit or proper state: *The athlete conditioned himself by running four kilometres a day.* **10.** to subject to particular conditions; affect; influence: *School conditions our ideas on life.* [ME, from L *condicio* (erroneously *conditio*) agreement, stipulation, circumstances]

conditional /kən'dɪʃənəl/, *adj.* **1.** containing or depending on a condition or conditions; not absolute: *a conditional agreement.* **2.** *Gram.* (of a sentence, clause, or mood) expressing a condition, e.g. *If the suit is dear* (conditional clause), *don't buy it.* —**conditionality**, n.

conditional pardon, n. (formerly) a pardon granted to a convict, who was then called an emancipist, but who could not leave the penal colony to which he or she had been transported until the original sentence had expired.

conditioned response, n. *Psychol.* a learnt response caused by a stimulus, object or situation (**conditioned stimulus**) other than the one to which it is the natural response (**unconditioned stimulus**). When a dog salivates at the sound of a bell instead of at the sight of food, it is a conditioned response,. Also, **conditioned reflex.**

condole /kən'doʊl/, v.i., **-doled**, **-doling**. to express sympathy with a person in sorrow; grieve (fol. by *with*). [LL *condolēre* suffer greatly] —**condolatory**, *adj.* —**condolence**, n. —**condolingly**, *adv.*

condom /'kɒndəm/, n. a thin sheath, usu. of rubber, worn over the penis during intercourse, used as a contraceptive and to prevent venereal infection. [? named after *Condom*, 18th C English physician said to have devised it]

condominium /kɒndə'mɪniəm/, n. *Internat. Law.* joint rule over a territory by several foreign states. [NL, from L: *con-* CON- + *dominium* lordship]

condone /kən'doʊn/, v.t., **-doned**, **-doning**. to pardon or overlook (an offence). [L: give up]

condor /'kɒndə/, n. a large vulture, as the **Andean condor** and **California condor**. [Sp, from South American Indian]

conducive /kən'djusɪv/, *adj.* leading; contributive (fol. by *to*): *Exercise is conducive to fitness.*

conduct /'kɒndʌkt/, n.; /kən'dʌkt/, v., ◇n. **1.** personal behavior; way of acting: *good conduct.* **2.** direction or management; execution: *the conduct of a business.* ◇v.t. **3.** to behave (oneself). **4.** to carry on; manage; direct: *to conduct a campaign.* **5.** to direct as leader: *to conduct an orchestra.* **6.** to lead or guide; escort. **7.** to serve as a channel or medium for (heat, electricity, sound, etc.). ◇v.i. **8.** to lead. **9.** to act as a conductor. [L: bring together] —**conductible**, *adj.* —**conductibility**, n.

conductance /kən'dʌktəns/, n. *Elect.* the conducting power of a conductor. Equal to the

conductance reciprocal of resistance for direct current and the resistance divided by the square of impedance for alternating currents. The derived SI unit of conductance is the siemens. *Symbol:* S.

conduction /kənˈdʌkʃən/, *n. Phys.* **1.** the conducting of heat, electricity, sound, etc. through something. **2.** → **conductivity**.

conductivity /ˌkɒndʌkˈtɪvəti/, *n., pl.* **-ties.** the ability of a substance to conduct heat, electricity, or sound: *Copper has a high conductivity.*

conductor /kənˈdʌktə/, *n.* **1.** someone who conducts; a leader, guide, director, or manager. **2.** a person on a train, bus, etc., who collects fares. **3.** a person who directs the playing of an orchestra or chorus, esp. with a baton. **4.** a substance, body, or device that easily conducts heat, electricity, sound, etc. — **conductorship**, *n.* — **conductress**, *n. fem.*

conduit /ˈkɒndɪt, ˈkɒndʒuət/, *n.* **1.** a pipe, tube, etc., for carrying water, gas, etc. **2.** *Elect.* a pipe that encloses electrical wires to protect them from damage. [ME, from OF, from LL: brought together]

Condy's crystals, /ˌkɒndiz ˈkrɪstlz/ *n.pl. Chem.* potassium permanganate, $KMnO_4$, a powerful oxidant, formerly used as a disinfectant, etc. [named after Henry Bollman *Condy*, 19th C English physician]

cone /koun/, *n.* **1.** *Geom.* a solid with a round base, the sides of which meet at the top in a point. **2.** any object shaped like this: *an ice-cream cone.* **3.** *Bot.* the cone-like fruit of the pine, fir, etc., consisting of partly separated seed-bearing scales overlapping each other. **4.** *Zool.* a light-sensitive nerve-cell present in the retina of the eye. [L, from Gk]

Coney Island /ˌkouni ˈaɪlənd/, *n.* an island off New York; seaside resort and amusement centre. 8 km long.

confection /kənˈfekʃən/, *n.* **1.** the process of mixing or preparing. **2.** a sweet preparation (liquid or dry) of fruit, etc. [ME, from L: a making ready]

confectionery /kənˈfekʃənri/, *n., pl.* **-eries. 1.** confections or sweets. **2.** the work or business of a person who makes or sells sweets, cakes, etc.

confederacy /kənˈfedərəsi, -ˈfedrəsi/, *n., pl.* **-cies. 1.** a group of people, parties, or states united for some common purpose. **2.** a combination for unlawful purposes; a conspiracy.

confederate /kənˈfedərət/, *adj., n.;* /kənˈfedəreɪt/, *v.,* **-rated, -rating.** ◇*adj.* **1.** united in a league or alliance, or a conspiracy. ◇*n.* **2.** someone united with others in a confederacy; an ally. **3.** an accomplice. **4.** (*cap.*) a supporter of the Confederate States of America during the American Civil War. ◇*v.t., v.i.* **5.** to form (a group) into a confederacy or conspiracy. [ME, from LL: united in a league] — **confederation**, *n.*

Confederate States of America, *n.pl.* the name assumed by the 11 Southern states (Alabama, Arkansas, Florida, Georgia, North Carolina, South Carolina, Texas, Virginia, Tennessee, Louisiana, and Mississippi) which seceded from the American Union in 1860–61.

confer /kənˈfɜ/, *v.,* **-ferred, -ferring.** ◇*v.t.* **1.** to give as a gift, favor, honor, etc. (fol. by *on* or *upon*): *We confer this medal on you.* ◇*v.i.* **2.** to talk together; consult with others. [L: bring together]

conference /ˈkɒnfərəns/, *n.* **1.** a meeting for consultation or discussion. **2.** the act of conferring or consulting together; consultation, esp. on a serious matter. — **conferential**, *adj.*

confess /kənˈfes/, *v.t.* **1.** to acknowledge or admit: *to confess a secret; to confess a crime; I must confess that I haven't read it.* **2.** *Church.* **a.** to make known (one's sins), esp. to a priest. **b.** (of a priest) to hear the confession of. ◇*v.i.* **3.** to make a confession; plead guilty (fol. by *to*). [ME from L]

confession /kənˈfeʃən/, *n.* **1.** an admission; concession: *a confession of guilt.* **2.** the admission of sins to a priest to obtain forgiveness. **3.** something confessed. **4.** Also, **confession of faith**, a formal declaration of religious beliefs. [ME, from L]

confessional /kənˈfeʃənəl/, *adj.* **1.** of or like a confession. ◇*n.* **2.** a place set apart for the hearing of confessions by a priest.

confessor /kənˈfesə/, *n.* **1.** Also, **confesser**. someone who confesses. **2.** someone to whom one confesses.

confetti /kənˈfeti/, *n.pl., sing.* **-fetto** /-ˈfetou/. small pieces of colored paper, thrown at carnivals, weddings, etc. [It, pl. of *confetto* comfit]

confidant /ˈkɒnfəˌdænt, ˈkɒnfədənt/, *n.* someone to whom secrets or personal matters are confided or told. [F, from It, from L: trusting] — **confidante**, *n. fem.*

confide /kənˈfaɪd/, *v.,* **-fided, -fiding.** ◇*v.i.* to show trust by telling secrets, personal matters, etc. (fol. by *in*). ◇*v.t.* **1.** to tell, as a secret. **2.** to entrust (something) to the care, knowledge, or good faith of another person. [ME, from L: trust altogether] — **confider**, *n.*

confidence /ˈkɒnfədəns/, *n.* **1.** full trust; faith in someone. **2.** *Politics.* the wish to retain the government in office, as shown by a vote on a particular issue: *The future of the government rests on a vote of confidence.* **3.** belief in one's ability. **4.** certainty; assurance. **5.** a secret. **6. in confidence**, as a secret or private matter: *I told him in confidence.*

confidence man, *n.* someone who cheats by a confidence trick.

confidence trick, *n.* a swindle in which the victim's trust is gained and used to persuade them to part with their money.

confident /ˈkɒnfədənt/, *adj.* **1.** having strong belief; sure: *confident of victory.* **2.** sure of oneself; bold: *a confident bearing.* **3.** overbold.

confidential /ˌkɒnfəˈdenʃəl/, *adj.* **1.** spoken or written in confidence; secret: *a confidential letter.* **2.** showing confidence or intimacy; telling private matters: *a confidential tone.*

confidential

3. entrusted with secrets or private matters: *a confidential secretary.* —**confidentiality**, *n.*

confiding /kən'faɪdɪŋ/, *adj.* trustful.

configuration /kənfɪgə'reɪʃən, -fɪgju-/, *n.* **1.** the arrangement of the parts of something. **2.** the shape or outline resulting from this; conformation. **3.** *Astron.* the relative position or arrangement of the stars, planets, etc. **4.** *Chem.* the relative position in space of the atoms in a molecule. [L: shape after some pattern] —**configurational, configurative**, *adj.*

confine /kən'faɪn/, *v.t.*, -**fined**, -**fining**; /'kɒnfaɪn/, *n.* ◇*v.t.* **1.** to enclose within limits; limit or restrict: *Quick action confined the epidemic to the boarders in the school.* **2.** to shut or keep in; imprison. **3.** to keep in bed. ◇*n.* **4.** (*usu. pl.*) a boundary or bound. [F, from It: bordering, from L]

confinement /kən'faɪnmənt/, *n.* **1.** the act of confining; imprisonment. **2.** a period of being confined, esp. of a woman in childbirth.

confirm /kən'fɜm/, *v.t.* **1.** to make certain or sure; corroborate; verify: *This confirms my suspicions.* **2.** to make certain or definite, oft. by some legal act; ratify: *to confirm an agreement, appointment, etc.* **3.** to make firm or more firm; add strength to: *The news confirmed my ideas.* **4.** *Church.* to administer the religious ceremony that admits a person as a full member of a church. [L: make firm] —**confirmable**, *adj.* —**confirmation**, *n.*

confirmed /kən'fɜmd/, *adj.* firmly settled in a habit or condition: *a confirmed drunkard; a confirmed bachelor.*

confiscate /'kɒnfəskeɪt/, *v.t.*, -**cated**, -**cating**. **1.** to seize (private property) for the public treasury. **2.** to seize as by authority; appropriate summarily: *The teacher confiscated the student's radio.* [L: put away in a chest] —**confiscation**, *n.*

conflagration /kɒnflə'greɪʃən/, *n.* a large and destructive fire. [L]

conflict /kən'flɪkt/, *v.*; /'kɒnflɪkt/, *n.* ◇*v.i.* **1.** to be in opposition to one another; disagree; clash. ◇*n.* **2.** a fight or struggle. **3.** disagreement of ideas; a quarrel: *conflict between church and state.* **4.** an emotional disagreement; antagonism: *There is often conflict in marriage.* [L: struck together] —**confliction**, *n.* —**conflictory**, *adj.*

confluence /'kɒnfluəns/, *n.* **1.** the flowing together of two or more streams. **2.** the place of junction. **3.** the body of water so formed. **4.** a coming together of people or things; crowd. —**confluent**, *n. adj.*

conform /kən'fɔm/, *v.i.* **1.** to act in accordance with certain rules; comply (fol. by *to*). **2.** to become similar in form or character. ◇*v.t.* **3.** to make similar in form or character. **4.** to bring into agreement. [ME, from F, from L: fashion, shape after] —**conformable**, *adj.* —**conformist**, *n.* —**conformity**, *n.*

conformation /kɒnfə'meɪʃən/, *n.* —**configuration**.

confound /kən'faʊnd/, *v.t.* **1.** to mix so that the elements cannot be separated. **2.** to treat or regard mistakenly as the same; confuse. **3.** to surprise or perplex. **4.** to damn: *Confound it!* [ME, from OF, from L: pour together, mix, confuse] —**confounded**, *adj.*

confront /kən'frʌnt/, *v.t.* **1.** to meet face to face (either a person or danger); stand in the way of. **2.** to oppose boldly; defy. [F, from L *con*- CON- + *frons* forehead] —**confrontation**, *n.*

Confucius /kən'fjuʃəs/. → **Kongfuzi**.

confuse /kən'fjuz/, *v.t.*, -**fused**, -**fusing**. **1.** to mix up or throw into disorder. **2.** to fail to tell the difference between; confound: *to confuse dates.* **3.** to perplex or bewilder. **4.** to disconcert. [ME, from L: confounded] —**confused**, *adj.* —**confusing**, *adj.*

confusion /kən'fjuʒən/, *n.* **1.** the state of being confused. **2.** disorder. **3.** lack of clearness. **4.** embarrassment. **5.** perplexity; bewilderment. **6.** *Psychol.* a troubled mental state; disorientation. [ME, from L]

confute /kən'fjut/, *v.t.*, -**futed**, -**futing**. to prove (a person, argument) to be false; disprove: *to confute an argument.* [L] —**confutation**, *n.*

conga /'kɒŋgə/, *n.* **1.** a lively Latin-American dance where dancers form a long winding line holding on to each other by the waist. **2.** a large cylindrical drum of Afro-American origin.

congeal /kən'dʒil/, *v.i.* **1.** to solidify, as by freezing or cooling. **2.** to thicken; coagulate, as blood. ◇*v.t.* **3.** to cause to solidify or coagulate. [ME, from L: cause to freeze together] —**congealment**, *n.* —**congelation**, *n.*

congeneric /kɒndʒə'nɛrɪk/, *adj.* of the same kind or genus. Also, **congenerous**.

congenial /kən'dʒiniəl/, *adj.* **1.** (of people) similar in feeling, interests, etc.: *congenial companions.* **2.** agreeable or pleasing; agreeing or suited in character: *a congenial job.* [CON- + L *genius* spirit] —**congeniality**, *n.*

congenital /kən'dʒɛnətl/, *adj.* existing at or from birth: *a congenital defect.* [L: born together with]

conger /'kɒŋgə/, *n.* a type of large edible eel. [ME, from L, from Gk]

congest /kən'dʒɛst/, *v.t.* **1.** to fill too much; overcrowd. **2.** *Med.* to cause an unnatural build-up of blood or mucus in (the vessels of) an organ or part. ◇*v.i.* **3.** to become congested. [L: brought together] —**congestive**, *adj.* —**congestion**, *n.*

conglomerate /kən'glɒmərət, 'kɒn-/, *n., adj.*; /kən'glɒmərert/, *v.*, -**rated**, -**rating**. ◇*n.* **1.** anything made of various materials or elements. **2.** *Geol.* a rock consisting of small round stones held together by clay, etc. **3.** a company which controls production of a wide range of different products, oft. created by the merging of different businesses. ◇*adj.* **4.** gathered into (or consisting of) a rounded mass; clustered. **5.** *Geol.* of the nature of a conglomerate. ◇*v.t., v.i.* **6.** to make (something) into or cause to become a ball or rounded mass. [L: rolled together] —**conglomeration**, *n.*

Congo /'kɒŋgoʊ/, *n.* **1.** a republic in western central Africa; a territory within French Equatorial Africa before independence in 1960. Pop. 1 909 248 (1984); 342 000 km^2. *Languages:* French, also Kilongo, Lingala, Monokutuba, Sanga, and local Bantu dialects. *Currency:* franc. *Cap.:* Brazzaville. Formerly, **Middle Congo, Congo-Brazzaville, the Congo. 2.** Also, **Zaire.** A river in central Africa, rising in south-eastern Zaire and flowing in a northerly arc to the Atlantic. 4800 km. − **Congolese,** *n., adj.*

congolli /kən'gouli/, *n.* a small marine and freshwater fish, entering southern and eastern Australian rivers; marble fish; freshwater flathead; sand trout. [Aboriginal]

congratulate /kən'grætʃəleɪt, kəŋ-/, *v.t.*, **-lated, -lating. 1.** to express joy to (a person), as on a happy event; express praise for something well-done. **2.** to consider (oneself) happy or fortunate. [L] − **congratulation,** *n.* − **congratulatory,** *adj.*

congregate /'kɒŋgrəgeɪt/, *v.*, **-gated, -gating,** *adj.* ◇*v.i.* **1.** to come together; assemble, esp. in large numbers. ◇*v.t.* **2.** to bring (people) together in a crowd; assemble; collect. ◇*adj.* **3.** assembled. **4.** collective. [ME, from L: collected into a flock]

congregation /kɒŋgrə'geɪʃən/, *n.* **1.** the act of congregating. **2.** a group of people gathered together, esp. for religious purposes, usu. in a church. **3.** *Rom Cath Ch.* a committee of cardinals.

congregational /kɒŋgrə'geɪʃənəl/, *adj.* **1.** of or relating to a congregation: *congregational singing.* **2.** (*oft. cap.*) relating to a form of church government in which each congregation or local church is a self-governing body, while remaining linked to other like congregations.

congress /'kɒŋgrɛs/, *n.* **1.** a formal meeting of representatives, as of societies, countries, etc., to exchange opinions on some matter of common interest. **2.** the national legislative body of the US, consisting of the Senate (upper house) and the House of Representatives (lower house). **3.** (*cap.*) an Indian political party established in 1885; now split into **Congress (I),** and **Congress (S),** a socialist party. [L: a meeting]

congruent /'kɒŋgruənt/, *adj.* **1.** agreeing; corresponding; congruous. **2.** *Geom.* being exactly the same size and shape, as of triangles. **3.** *Maths.* of or relating to two or more numbers which have the same remainder when divided by a given number called the modulus: *5 and 12 are congruent to the modulus 7.* − **congruence,** *n.*

congruous /'kɒŋgruəs/, *adj.* **1.** agreeing in character; accordant; harmonious; consistent (fol. by *with* or *to*). **2.** fitting; appropriate. [L: fit] − **congruity,** *n.*

conic /'kɒnɪk/, *adj.* having the form of, or relating to a cone. Also, **conical.** [Gk: cone-shaped]

conifer /'kɒnəfə, 'koʊ-/, *n.* any of the (mostly evergreen) cone-bearing trees and shrubs such as pine, spruce and fir, called the gymnosperms. [L: cone-bearing] − **coniferous,** *adj.*

conj., *Abbrev.* **1.** conjugation. **2.** conjunction. **3.** conjunctive.

conjecture /kən'dʒɛktʃə/, *n., v.*, **-tured, -turing.** ◇*n.* **1.** the formation or expression of an opinion without enough information. **2.** an opinion so formed or expressed; a guess. ◇*v.t.* **3.** to conclude or suppose without enough information to be reliable. [ME, from L: a throwing together, inference] − **conjectural,** *adj.*

conjoin /kən'dʒɔɪn/, *v.t., v.i.* to join or become joined together; unite; combine. [ME, from L: join together] − **conjoint,** *adj.*

conjugal /'kɒndʒəgəl, -dʒu-/, *adj.* concerning husband and wife; marital. [L *conjunx* husband or wife] − **conjugality,** *n.*

conjugate /'kɒndʒəgeɪt/, *v.*, **-gated, -gating;** /'kɒndʒəgət, -geɪt/, *adj.* ◇*v.t.* **1.** *Gram.* to give various forms of (a verb), depending on person, tense, number, etc. ◇*v.i.* **2.** *Biol.* (in the sexual reproduction of single-celled animals and plants) to unite temporarily to exchange nuclear material at the point of joining. ◇*adj.* **3.** joined together, esp. in a pair or pairs; coupled. **4.** (of words) having a common origin. [L: joined together, yoked] − **conjugative,** *adj.* − **conjugation,** *n.*

conjugate pair, *n. Chem.* an acid-base pair.

conjunct /kən'dʒʌŋkt, 'kɒndʒʌŋkt/, *adj.* **1.** joined together; associate. **2.** formed by conjunction. [ME, from L: joined together]

conjunction /kən'dʒʌŋkʃən/, *n.* **1.** the act of joining together; combination. **2.** the state of being joined together; union; association. **3.** a combination of events or circumstances. **4.** *Gram.* **a.** (in some languages) one of the main 'parts of speech', consisting of words used to join together words, phrases, clauses, or sentences. **b.** such a word, as English *and* or *but.* **5.** *Astron.* **a.** the meeting or passing of two or more planets in the same longitude or right ascension. **b.** the position of two or more planets when their longitudes are the same. − **conjunct,** *adj.* − **conjunctional,** *adj.*

conjunctiva /ˌkɒndʒʌŋk'taɪvə/, *n., pl.* **-vas, -vae** /-vi/. the very fine transparent skin that covers and helps to protect the surface of the eyelid and the surface of the eye. [NL, short for *membrāna conjunctīva* membrane serving to connect] − **conjunctival,** *adj.*

conjunctive /kən'dʒʌŋktɪv/, *adj.* **1.** connective. **2.** joined together; joint. ◇*n.* **3.** *Gram.* a conjunctive word; a conjunction.

conjunctivitis /kənˌdʒʌŋktə'vaɪtəs/, *n. Med.* a painful disease of the conjunctiva with redness and swelling. [NL. See CONJUNCTIVA, -ITIS]

conjuncture /kən'dʒʌŋktʃə/, *n.* **1.** a combination of events; a particular state of affairs. **2.** a serious state of affairs; a crisis. [CON- + JUNCTURE]

conjure /'kʌndʒə/, *v.*, **-jured, -juring.** ◇*v.t.* **1.** to call upon or command (a devil or spirit) by a spell, etc. **2.** to produce, bring about, etc., by, or as by, magic. ◇*v.i.* **3.** to call upon or command a devil or spirit by a spell. **4.** to practise magic. **5.** to practise sleight of hand. ◇*v.* **6. conjure up, a.** to call, raise up,

conjure

or bring into existence by magic. **b.** to bring to mind or recall. [ME, from L: swear together] **–conjuration,** *n.* **–conjurer,** *n.*

conk /kɒŋk/, *n. Colloq.* **1.** a nose. **2.** a blow; violent stroke. ◇*v.t.* **3.** *Colloq.* to hit or strike, esp. on the head. ◇*v.* **4. conk out,** *Colloq.* **a.** (of an engine) to break down; stop. **b.** to become tired suddenly; collapse. [probably alteration of CONCH]

con man, *n. Colloq.* → **confidence man.**

connect /kə'nekt/, *v.t.* **1.** to bind or fasten together; join or unite; link. **2.** to think of as related: *the pleasures connected with music.* ◇*v.i.* **3.** to become connected; join or unite. **4.** *Baseball, Tennis, etc., Colloq.* to hit the ball. [L: join, tie] **–connectedly,** *adv.* **–connecter, connector,** *n.*

Connecticut /kə'netɪkət/, *n.* a state in the north-eastern US. Pop. 3 189 000 (1986 est.); 12 973 km². *Cap.:* Hartford. *Abbrev.:* Conn

connection /kə'nekʃən/, *n.* **1.** the act of joining. **2.** the state of being joined. **3.** anything that joins; a connecting part: *telephone connection.* **4.** an association; relationship. **5.** a meeting of one means of transport with another, as a bus system with a railway. **6.** (*usu. pl.*) influential friends, relatives, etc. **7.** (*pl.*) *Horse-racing, etc.* the owners of a horse or dog, or the people close to it such as the trainer, jockey, etc. Also, **connexion.** [L]

connective /kə'nektɪv/, *adj.* **1.** serving or tending to join. ◇*n.* **2.** something that joins.

connective tissue, *n.* tissue which connects, supports, or surrounds other tissues, organs, etc.

Connellan /kə'nelən/, *n.* Edward John, founder of Connellan Airways, providing transport to remote districts of the NT, recognised as the 'flying mailman' of northern-central Australia.

Conner /'kɒnə/, *n.* Mount, a mass of rock, south-west of Alice Springs, NT; 3 km long and 1200 m wide.

conning tower, /'kɒnɪŋ taʊə/ *n.* **1.** a raised structure on a submarine which is the main entrance and lookout. **2.** an enclosed place on the deck of a warship for steering gear and pilot.

connive /kə'naɪv/, *v.i.*, **-nived, -niving. 1.** to avoid noticing or reporting that which one should oppose (fol. by *at*): *The policeman connived at the prisoner's escape.* **2.** to work together secretly (fol. by *with*). [L: shut the eyes] **–connivance,** *n.*

connoisseur /kɒnə'sɜ/, *n.* someone who is experienced and discriminating in a field (fine arts, wines, etc.). [F, from L: come to know]

Connors /'kɒnəz/, *n.* Jimmy (*James Scott Connors*), born 1952, US tennis player; Wimbledon champion 1974, 1982.

connote /kə'noʊt/, *v.t.*, **-noted, -noting.** to suggest a meaning in addition to the main meaning; imply. [L *con-* CON- + *notāre* mark] **–connotation,** *n.* **–connotative,** *adj.*

conscript

connubial /kə'njubiəl/, *adj.* of marriage; matrimonial; conjugal. [L: marriage] **–connubiality,** *n.*

conquer /'kɒŋkə/, *v.t.* **1.** to overcome by force; subdue: *to conquer an enemy.* **2.** to get control of by force of arms; win in a war: *to conquer the border area.* **3.** to gain victory over; surmount: *to conquer a problem.* ◇*v.i.* **4.** to gain a victory; win. [ME, from L: seek for] **–conqueror,** *n.* **–conquerable,** *adj.*

Conqueror /'kɒŋkərə/, *n.* the, William I of England.

conquest /'kɒŋkwest, 'kɒn-/, *n.* **1.** the act of conquering. **2.** the act of capturing someone's love or affection. **3.** the condition of being conquered; vanquishment. **4.** lands acquired by conquering. **5.** a person whose love or feelings have been captured. **6.** (*cap.*) **the Conquest,** the conquering of England by William, in 1066. [ME, from OF, from L: seek for]

conquistador /kɒn'kwɪstədɔ, kɒŋ-/, *n.*, *pl.* **-dors.** one of the Spanish conquerors of Mexico and Peru in the 16th century. [Sp]

Conrad /'kɒnræd/, *n.* Joseph (*Teodor Jozef Konrad Korzeniowski*), 1857–1924, British novelist, born of Polish parents; author of *Lord Jim* (1900).

consanguineous /kɒnsæŋ'gwɪniəs/, *adj.* related by birth; akin. Also, **consanguine** /kɒn'sæŋgwən/. [L] **–consanguinity,** *n.*

conscience /'kɒnʃəns/, *n.* **1.** the sense of right and wrong as regards one's own actions and motives. **2. in (all) conscience,** in (all) reason and fairness; in truth. [ME, from OF, from L *conscientia* joint knowledge]

conscientious /kɒnʃi'enʃəs/, *adj.* controlled by or done according to conscience; scrupulous: *a conscientious judge; conscientious conduct.*

conscientious objector, *n.* a person who, on moral or religious grounds, refuses to take part in military service.

conscious /'kɒnʃəs/, *adj.* **1.** aware of one's own existence, sensations, reasonings, etc.; provided with consciousness. **2.** inwardly aware or awake to something: *conscious of one's own faults; conscious of one's feelings.* **3.** intentional: *a conscious liar.* **4.** aware of oneself; self-conscious. **5.** deliberate or intentional. [L: knowing]

consciousness /'kɒnʃəsnəs/, *n.* **1.** the state of being conscious. **2.** the inward understanding of something; knowledge of one's own existence, sensations, reasonings, etc. **3.** the totality of thoughts and feelings of an individual, or of a number of people: *the moral consciousness of a nation.* **4.** mental awareness: *to regain consciousness after an operation.* **5. raise one's consciousness,** to raise the level of one's understanding and awareness of cultural and social issues.

conscript /'kɒnskrɪpt/, *adj.*, *n.*; /kən'skrɪpt/, *v.* ◇*adj.* **1.** enrolled or formed by conscription: *a conscript soldier; a conscript army.* ◇*n.* **2.** a recruit obtained by conscription. ◇*v.t.* **3.** to enrol compulsorily for service in the armed forces. [L: enrolled]

conscription /kənˈskrɪpʃən/, *n.* compulsory enrolment in the armed forces.

consecrate /ˈkɒnsɪkreɪt/, *v.t.*, **-crated, -crating. 1.** to make or declare sacred; set apart as holy. **2. a.** to place (someone) formally into high office by means of a religious ceremony; induct. **b.** to ordain (priests, etc.). **3.** to devote to some purpose; dedicate. **4.** to make an object of reverence: *a custom consecrated by time.* [ME, from L: dedicated] —**consecration**, *n.*

consecutive /kənˈsɛkjətɪv/, *adj.* **1.** following one another in uninterrupted succession. **2.** marked by logical order. **3.** *Music.* of or relating to a succession of similar harmonic intervals. [F, from L: having followed after]

consensus /kənˈsɛnsəs/, *n.* **1.** general agreement. **2.** an opinion held by all or most. [L: agreement]

consent /kənˈsɛnt/, *v.i.* **1.** to agree; assent; yield (fol. by *to* or infinitive). ◇*n.* **2.** permission; assent; acquiescence; compliance. **3.** agreement in feeling, opinion, course of action, etc.: *by common consent.* **4. age of consent**, the age at which consent to certain acts, esp. sexual intercourse and marriage, is valid in law. [ME, from OF, from L: feel together]

consequence /ˈkɒnsəkwəns/, *n.* **1.** the act or fact of following as an effect or result of something before it. **2.** something that so follows; an effect or result. **3. in consequence**, as a result. **4.** importance or significance: *a matter of no consequence.* **5.** importance in rank or position: *a man of consequence.*

consequent /ˈkɒnsəkwənt/, *adj.* **1.** following as an effect or result; resulting. **2.** logically consistent. **3.** *Geol.* (of a river) having a course or direction dependent on, or controlled by, geological structure or by the form and slope of the surface. [L]

consequential /kɒnsəˈkwɛnʃəl/, *adj.* of the nature of a consequence; following as an effect or result, or as a logical conclusion or inference; consequent; resultant.

conservation /kɒnsəˈveɪʃən/, *n.* **1.** the act of conserving, esp. of natural resources; preservation. **2.** care for and preservation of rivers, forests, etc. [L] —**conservational**, *adj.* —**conservationist**, *n.*

conservative /kənˈsɜːvətɪv/, *adj.* **1.** tending to preserve existing conditions, institutions, etc. **2.** cautious or moderate: *a conservative opinion.* **3.** traditional in style or manner. ◇*n.* **4.** a person of conservative principles. —**conservatism**, *n.*

Conservative Party, *n.* a UK political party, characterising itself chiefly as moderately progressive in policy. Official name, **Conservative and Unionist Party**.

conservatorium /ˌkɒnsəvəˈtɔːriəm/, *n.* a place for instruction in music and theatrical arts; school of music. Also, **con, conservatoire**.

conservatory /kənˈsɜːvətri/, *n., pl.* **-tries.** a glass-covered house or room into which plants in bloom are brought from a greenhouse.

conserve /kənˈsɜːv/, *v.,* **served, -serving;** /ˈkɒnsɜːv, kənˈsɜːv/, *n.* ◇*v.t.* **1.** to keep in a safe or sound state; preserve from loss, decay, waste, or injury, keep unimpaired. ◇*n.* **2.** (*oft. pl.*) fruit preserved in a jam. [ME, from L: preserve] —**conserver**, *n.*

consider /kənˈsɪdə/, *v.t.* **1.** to think about; meditate; reflect. **2.** to regard as or think to be: *I consider the test to be reasonable.* **3.** to think; suppose. **4.** to make allowance for. **5.** to pay attention to; regard: *He always considers others.* **6.** to think about (a position, purchase, etc.): *to consider buying.* ◇*v.i.* **7.** to think deliberately or carefully; reflect. [ME, from L: examine closely]

considerable /kənˈsɪdrəbəl/, *adj.* **1.** worthy of consideration; important. **2.** (of an amount, extent, etc.) fairly large or great.

considerate /kənˈsɪdərət/, *adj.* showing regard for another's circumstances, feelings, etc.

consideration /kənsɪdəˈreɪʃən/, *n.* **1.** the act of considering; meditation; deliberation. **2.** regard or account; something taken, or to be taken, into account. **3.** a thought; reflection. **4.** a payment for service given, etc.; compensation. **5.** thoughtful or sympathetic regard or respect; thoughtfulness for others. **6. take into consideration**, to consider; take into account. **7. under consideration**, being considered.

considering /kənˈsɪdərɪŋ/, *prep.* **1.** taking into account; in view of. ◇*adv.* **2.** with all things considered (used after the statement it modifies). ◇*conj.* **3.** taking into consideration that: *Considering he is so young, he has achieved a great deal.*

consign /kənˈsaɪn/, *v.t.* **1.** to hand over or deliver formally; commit (fol. by *to*). **2.** to entrust. **3.** to set apart; assign. **4.** to send; as by public carrier. [F, from L: furnish or mark with a seal] —**consignable**, *adj.* —**consignation**, *n.*

consignment /kənˈsaɪnmənt/, *n.* **1.** the act of consigning. **2.** something consigned. **3. on consignment**, (of goods) sent to an agent for sale.

consist /kənˈsɪst/, *v.i.* **1.** to be made up or composed (fol. by *of*). **2.** to be contained (fol. by *in*). **3.** to exist in harmony (fol. by *with*). [L: place oneself]

consistency /kənˈsɪstənsi/, *n., pl.* **-cies. 1.** agreement, harmony, or compatibility. **2.** firmness of material; solidity. **3.** the degree of density or viscosity: *the consistency of cream.* Also, **consistence**.

consistent /kənˈsɪstənt/, *adj.* **1.** agreeing; compatible. **2.** constantly keeping to the same principles, course, etc.

consolation /kɒnsəˈleɪʃən/, *n.* someone or something that consoles: *Her kindness was a consolation to him.* [ME, from L]

console[1] /kənˈsoʊl/, *v.t.,* **-soled, -soling.** to lessen the grief or sorrow of; comfort; solace; cheer. [L: comfort] —**consolable**, *adj.* —**consoler**, *n.* —**consolingly**, *adv.*

console[2] /ˈkɒnsoʊl/, *n.* **1.** a desk-like structure containing the keyboards, pedals, etc., of an organ, from which it is played. **2.** the con-

console

trol panel for an electrical or electronic system. **3.** a floor-model cabinet holding a radio, television, etc. **4.** *Computers.* a computer operator's control panel or terminal. [F; orig. uncert.]

consolidate /kən'sɒlɪdeɪt/, *v.,* **-dated, -dating.** ◇*v.t.* **1.** to make solid or firm; solidify; strengthen: *to consolidate gains.* **2.** to bring together; unite; combine: *to consolidate two companies of troops.* ◇*v.i.* **3.** to unite or combine. **4.** to become solid or firm. [L: made solid] **—consolidator,** *n.* **—consolidation,** *n.*

consolidated revenue, *n.* funds which a government receives by way of taxes, duties, etc.

consomme /'kɒnsɒmeɪ, kən'sɒmeɪ/, *n.* a clear soup made from meat or vegetable stock. Also, **consommé.** [F, from L: finish]

consonance /'kɒnsənəns/, *n.* harmony of sounds, esp. musical sounds.

consonant /'kɒnsənənt/, *n.* **1.** *Linguistics.* any speech sound which partly or completely stops the breath stream, as p, f or ʒ (opposed to *vowels*). **2.** a letter which usu. represents a consonantal sound. ◇*adj.* **3.** in agreement; agreeable; consistent (fol. by *to* or *with*). **4.** harmonious, as sounds. **5.** *Music.* constituting a consonance. [ME, from L: sounding together] **—consonantal,** *adj.*

consort /'kɒnsɔt, *n.;* kən'sɔt/, *v.* ◇*n.* **1.** a husband or wife; a spouse, esp. of a reigning monarch. **2.** a vessel or ship that travels with another. **3.** a group of instruments or voices in harmony. ◇*v.i.* **4.** to associate; keep company. **5.** to agree. [ME, from F: mate, from L *consors* partner, sharer]

consortium /kən'sɔtiəm, -ʃiəm/, *n., pl.* **-tia, -ʃə/. 1.** an association of business institutions, etc., for carrying into effect some special operation needing large amounts of capital. **2.** an association or union. [L: partnership]

conspicuous /kən'spɪkjuəs/, *adj.* **1.** easy to be seen. **2.** readily attracting the attention. [L: visible, striking]

conspiracy /kən'spɪrəsi/, *n., pl.* **-cies. 1.** the act of conspiring. **2.** a group of people meeting for an evil or unlawful purpose; plot. [CONSPIR(E) + -ACY] **—conspirator,** *n.*

conspire /kən'spaɪə/, *v.i.,* **-spired, -spiring. 1.** to agree together, esp. secretly, to do something wrong or illegal; join together for an evil or unlawful purpose. **2.** to act together; contribute jointly to a result. [ME, from L: breathe together]

constable /'kʌnstəbəl/, *n.* **1.** a police officer of the lowest rank. **2.** *Hist.* an officer of high rank in medieval monarchies, usu. the commander of all armed forces, particularly in the absence of the ruler. **3.** the keeper or governor of a royal castle. [ME, from OF, from LL *comes stabuli* count of the stable, master of the horse]

Constable /'kʌnstəbəl/, *n.* **John,** 1776–1837, English landscape painter; works include *The Hay Wain* and *Hadleigh Castle.*

constitutional

constabulary /kən'stæbjələri/, *n., pl.* **-ries. 1.** the body of constables of a district, etc. **2.** *Colloq.* the police. [ML]

constant /'kɒnstənt/, *adj.* **1.** uniform; invariable; always present. **2.** continuing without interruption. **3.** continual; persistent. **4.** faithful; steadfast. ◇*n.* **5.** something constant, invariable, or unchanging. **6. a.** *Maths, Phys.* a numerical quantity expressing a relation or value that remains unchanged under certain conditions. **b.** *Phys.* → **fundamental constant.** [ME, from L: standing firm] **—constancy,** *n.*

Constantine I /'kɒnstəntin/, *n.* **1.** ('*the Great*'), AD 280?–337, Roman emperor AD 324–37; built Constantinople as his new capital; made Christian worship lawful.

Constantinople /kɒnstæntə'noʊpəl/, *n.* a city built on the site of ancient Byzantium by Constantine the Great, AD 330; capital of the Eastern Roman Empire and later of the Ottoman Empire. See **Istanbul.**

constellation /kɒnstə'leɪʃən/, *n.* **1.** *Astron.* any of various groups of stars to which definite names have been given, as the Southern Cross. **2.** any brilliant gathering or collection; cluster; assemblage. [ME, from LL *constellātio* group of stars]

consternation /kɒnstə'neɪʃən/, *n.* amazement and dread causing a person to feel shock or fear. [L]

constipation /kɒnstə'peɪʃən/, *n.* a condition marked by difficulty in emptying bowels. **—constipate,** *v.*

constituency /kən'stɪtjuənsi/, *n., pl.* **-cies. 1.** → **electorate** (def. 1). **2.** any body of supporters; clientele.

constituent /kən'stɪtjuənt/, *adj.* **1.** serving to make up a thing; component: *constituent parts.* **2.** having the power to frame or alter a political constitution (rather than law-making power): *a constituent assembly.* ◇*n.* **3.** *Gram.* an element that forms part of a construction (sentence, clause, phrase, etc.). [L]

constitute /'kɒnstətjut/, *v.t.,* **-tuted, -tuting. 1.** (of elements, etc.) to compose; form. **2.** to appoint to an office or function; make or create. **3.** to set up or found (an institution, etc.) in legal form. [L: set up, established] **—constituter, constitutor,** *n.*

constitution /kɒnstə'tjuʃən/, *n.* **1.** the way in which anything is made: *the physical constitution of the sun.* **2.** the physical character of the body as to strength, health, etc.: *a strong constitution.* **3.** the act or state of constituting; establishment. **4.** a system of fundamental laws and principles of a government, state or society: *the Australian constitution.* [ME, from L]

constitutional /kɒnstə'tjuʃənəl/, *adj.* **1.** basic to or inherent in: *a constitutional weakness.* **2.** of a person's constitution. **3.** relating to, in accordance with, or subject to the constitution of a state, etc.: *constitutional monarchy; constitutional government.* ◇*n.* **4.** a walk or other exercise.

constrain /kənˈstreɪn/, v.t. **1.** to persuade forcibly; compel; oblige: *to constrain to agree.* **2.** to repress or restrain. [ME, from OF, from L: draw together]

constraint /kənˈstreɪnt/, n. **1.** confinement or restriction. **2.** repression of natural feelings and impulses. **3.** a forced or unnatural manner; embarrassment. **4.** something that constrains. [ME, from OF: constrained]

constrict /kənˈstrɪkt/, v.t. **1.** to draw together; compress. **2.** to restrict; inhibit. [L: drawn together]

constriction /kənˈstrɪkʃən/, n. **1.** the act of constricting. **2.** a feeling of tightness or pressure. **3.** something that constricts. —**constrictive**, *adj.*

constrictor /kənˈstrɪktə/, n. **1.** a snake that crushes its prey in its coils. **2.** someone or something that constricts. [NL]

construct /kənˈstrʌkt/, v.; /ˈkɒnstrʌkt/, n. ◇v.t. **1.** to form by putting together parts; build; frame; devise. **2.** *Geom., etc.* to draw, as a figure, so as to meet given conditions. ◇n. **3.** something constructed. **4.** an image or idea made up from several sources. [L: constructed, piled or put together] —**constructor, constructer**, n.

construction /kənˈstrʌkʃən/, n. **1.** the act or art of constructing. **2.** the way in which something is put together; structure: *objects of similar construction.* **3.** *Geom.* **a.** the process of drawing a figure so as to satisfy certain conditions. **b.** extra parts added to show a proof. **4.** *Gram.* the arrangement of two or more forms in a grammatical unit. **5.** the explanation of a law or text, etc. —**constructional**, *adj.*

constructive /kənˈstrʌktɪv/, adj. serving a useful purpose; helpful: *constructive suggestions; constructive criticism.*

construe /kənˈstruː/, v.t., **-strued, -struing. 1.** to show the meaning or intention of; explain; interpret; put a particular interpretation on. **2.** to deduce by construction or interpretation; infer. **3.** to explain the syntax of (a sentence); parse. **4.** to arrange or join (words, etc.) syntactically. [ME, from L: build up, pile together]

consul /ˈkɒnsəl/, n. **1.** an agent appointed by a state to live in a foreign country and discharge certain duties. **2.** either of the two chief magistrates of the ancient Roman republic. —**consular**, *adj.* —**consulship**, n.

consulate /ˈkɒnsjələt/, n. the offices officially occupied by a consul. [L]

consult /kənˈsʌlt/, v.t. **1.** to seek counsel from; ask advice of. **2.** to refer to for information. **3.** to have regard for (a person's interest, etc.) in making plans. ◇v.i. **4.** to consider or deliberate; take counsel; confer (fol. by *with*). [L: deliberate, take counsel]

consultant /kənˈsʌltənt/, n. **1.** a person who consults. **2.** a person who gives professional or expert advice. **3.** *Med.* a medical or surgical specialist.

consultation /ˌkɒnsəlˈteɪʃən/, n. **1.** the act of consulting; conference. **2.** a meeting to discuss or plan something. **3.** an application for professional advice, esp. to a doctor. —**consultative**, *adj.*

consume /kənˈsjuːm/, v.t., **-sumed, -suming. 1.** to destroy or expend by use; use up. **2.** to eat or drink up; devour. **3.** to destroy, as by decaying or burning. **4.** to spend (money, time, etc.) wastefully. [ME, from L: take up completely] —**consumable**, *adj., n.*

consumer /kənˈsjuːmə/, n. a person who buys and uses goods or services (opposed to *producer*).

consumer goods, n. pl. goods that satisfy personal needs, as clothing, food, etc.

consumerism /kənˈsjuːmərɪzəm/, n. **1.** a movement which aims at making consumers aware of their rights and also protecting their interests from dishonest trading practices. **2.** a theory that the economy of a capitalist society needs an ever increasing consumption of goods.

consumer price index, n. the weighted average cost of a standard basket of retail goods expressed in relation to a base period.

consummate /ˈkɒnsjumeɪt/, v., **-mated, -mating**; /ˈkɒnsjumət, kənˈsʌmət/, adj. ◇v.t. **1.** to bring to completion or perfection. **2.** to fulfil (a marriage) through sexual intercourse. ◇adj. **3.** complete or perfect. [late ME, from L: brought to the highest degree] —**consummative**, *adj.* —**consummation**, n.

consumption /kənˈsʌmpʃən/, n. **1.** the act of being consumed; decay. **2.** *Econ.* using up of goods and services having an exchangeable value. **3.** *Med.* a wasting disease, esp. tuberculosis of the lungs. [ME, from L: a wasting] —**consumptive**, *adj.*

contact /ˈkɒntækt/, n.; /ˈkɒntækt, kənˈtækt/, v. ◇n. **1.** the state or fact of touching or meeting. **2.** closeness; proximity; association. **3.** *Elect.* the moving part of a switch or relay which completes or breaks the circuit. **4.** a person who is useful as part of a network: *a business contact.* **5.** *Med.* someone who has been exposed to an infected person. **6. make contact**, to contact. ◇v.t. **7.** to get in touch with (a person). ◇v.i. **8.** to enter into or be in contact. [L: a touching] —**contact**, *adj.*

contact lens n. a device to aid poor sight consisting of small usu. plastic lens that fits closely over the eye and is held in place by eye fluid.

contagion /kənˈteɪdʒən/, n. **1.** the spreading of disease by contact. **2.** a contagious disease. **3.** the spreading of any influence or emotion from one person to another. [ME, from L: a contact]

contagious /kənˈteɪdʒəs/, adj. **1.** (of disease) able to be spread from one individual to another by close contact. **2.** carrying or spreading disease. **3.** tending to spread from one to another: *Panic is contagious.* [ME, from LL]

contain /kənˈteɪn/, v.t. **1.** to have within itself; hold or include within fixed limits. **2.** to be capable of holding; have the capacity for. **3.** to keep within proper bounds; restrain: *to contain oneself or one's feelings.* **4.** be equal to:

A centilitre contains ten millilitres. [ME, from OF, from L: hold together, hold back] —**containable**, *adj.*

container /kən'teɪnə/, *n.* **1.** anything that contains or can contain, as a carton, box, crate, tin, etc. **2.** a large, box-shaped unit for carrying goods on ships, trucks, etc., usu. of a standardised size for easy transport.

containment /kən'teɪnmənt/, *n.* the act or policy of limiting or stopping the expansion (beyond certain limits) of an opposing power, etc.

contaminate /kən'tæmɪneɪt/, *v.t.*, **-nated, -nating. 1.** to make impure by contact or mixture. **2.** to cause to become harmful or unusable by adding radioactive material to. [L] —**contaminative**, *adj.* —**contaminator**, *n.* —**contamination**, *n.*

contemplate /'kɒntəmpleɪt/, *v.*, **-plated, -plating.** ◇*v.t.* **1.** to look at or view with marked attention; view thoughtfully. **2.** to consider; think about; study. **3.** to have as a purpose; intend. **4.** to plan as a future event. ◇*v.i.* **5.** to think deeply; meditate. [L: having surveyed] —**contemplator**, *n.* —**contemplation**, *n.*

contemplative /'kɒntəm,pleɪtɪv, kən'templətɪv/, *adj.* **1.** given to or characterised by contemplation; meditative. ◇*n.* **2.** a person devoted to religious contemplation.

contemporaneous /kəntempə'reɪnɪəs/, *adj.* taking place at the same time; in the present. [L]

contemporary /kən'tempəri, -pri/, *adj., n., pl.* **-raries.** ◇*adj.* **1.** belonging to or existing at the same time. **2.** *Colloq.* in the most modern style; up-to-date. ◇*n.* **3.** a person or thing belonging to the same time or period as another: *Shakespeare was a contemporary of Bacon.* **4.** a person of the same age as another. [CON- + TEMPORARY]

contempt /kən'tempt/, *n.* **1.** the condition of being despised; dishonor; disgrace: *She holds him in contempt.* **2.** the feeling with which one regards anything considered mean, vile, or worthless: *She feels contempt for him.* **3.** *Law.* (an act showing) open disrespect of rules or orders of a court of law. [ME, from L: scorn]

contemptible /kən'temptəbəl/, *adj.* deserving of or held in contempt; despicable.

contemptuous /kən'temptʃuəs/, *adj.* showing or expressing contempt; scornful. [L *contemptu(s)* scorn + -OUS]

contend /kən'tend/, *v.i.* **1.** to fight in opposition; compete. **2.** to struggle; strive: *I have a lot to contend with.* ◇*v.t.* **3.** to maintain seriously: *I contend that he's lying.* [L: stretch out] —**contender**, *n.*

content[1] /'kɒntent/, *n.* **1.** the amount contained; capacity; volume. **2.** (*usu. pl.*) (a list of) chapters or chief topics of a book or document. **3.** (*usu. pl*) that which is contained: *He poured the contents of the bottle on the floor.* [ML *contentum* that which is contained]

content[2] /kən'tent/, *adj.* **1.** having one's desires limited to what one has; satisfied. ◇*v.t.* **2.** to make content. ◇*n.* **3.** Also, **content-ment.** the condition or feeling of being contented. [ME, from L: satisfied]

contented /kən'tentəd/, *adj.* satisfied.

contention /kən'tenʃən/, *n.* **1.** strife; rivalry; dispute. **2.** a competition; contest. [ME, from L: strife]

contentious /kən'tenʃəs/, *adj.* **1.** given to argument: *a contentious crew.* **2.** characterised by argument: *contentious issues.* [L]

contest /'kɒntest/, *n.*; /kən'test/, *v.* ◇*n.* **1.** a struggle for victory; fight, competition or argument. ◇*v.t.* **2.** to struggle or fight for. **3.** to argue against; dispute. ◇*v.i.* **4.** to dispute; contend; compete. [F, from L: call to witness, bring a legal action]

contestant /kən'testənt/, *n.* a person who takes part in contest or competition. [F]

context /'kɒntekst/, *n.* **1.** the parts of a sentence, paragraph or writing which come before or after a given passage or word: *to quote in context.* **2.** the circumstances or facts that surround a particular situation, event, etc. [ME, from L: connection] —**contextual**, *adj.*

contiguous /kən'tɪgjuəs/, *adj.* **1.** touching; in contact. **2.** very close without actually touching; near. [L touching] —**contiguousness, contiguity**, *n.*

continence /'kɒntənəns/, *n.* **1.** self-restraint, esp. in regard to sexual activity; moderation. **2.** Also, **continency.** the ability to control natural functions, esp. urination and defecation. [ME, from L]

continent /'kɒntənənt/, *n.* **1.** one of the main land masses of world, usu. considered as seven in number (Europe, Asia, Africa, North America, South America, Australia and Antarctica). **2. the Continent,** the mainland of Europe (as separate from the British Isles). ◇*adj.* **3.** exercising restraint in relation to desires or passions; temperate. **4.** able to control natural functions. [ME, from L: holding together]

continental divide, *n. Geog.* the watershed between river systems that flow into opposite sides of a continent as, in eastern Australia, the Great Dividing Range.

continental drift, *n.* the movement of continents away from the original single land mass to their present position.

continental shelf, *n.* that portion of a continent found under a shallow sea, in contrast with the deep ocean basins from which it is separated by the fairly steep **continental slope.**

contingency /kən'tɪndʒənsi/, *n., pl.* **-cies. 1.** a chance event, conditional on something uncertain. **2.** uncertainty; dependence on chance.

contingent /kən'tɪndʒənt/, *adj.* **1.** dependent for existence, occurrence, character, etc., on something not yet certain; conditional (oft. fol. by *on* or *upon*). **2.** happening by chance or without known cause; fortuitous; accidental. ◇*n.* **3.** a group of people with a single purpose, as troops sent on a particular mission. [ME, from L: touching, bordering on, reaching, befalling]

continual / contrary

continual /kən'tɪnjuəl/, *adj.* **1.** of regular or frequent recurrence; often repeated; very frequent. **2.** proceeding without interruption or cessation. [ML]

continuation /kəntɪnju'eɪʃən/, *n.* **1.** the act or fact of continuing or prolonging. **2.** the state of being continued. **3.** a part going or carrying on to a further point: *the continuation of a road*. **4.** a sequel, as to a story; supplement. –**continuance**, *n.* –**continuative**, *adj.*

continue /kən'tɪnju/, *v.*, **-ued**, **-uing**. ◊*v.i.* **1.** to go forwards; keep on. **2.** to go on after an interruption. **3.** to last; endure. **4.** to remain in a place or condition; abide; stay: *He'll continue in his ignorance*. ◊*v.t.* **5.** to go on with: *to continue action*. **6.** to extend from one point to another; prolong. **7.** to carry on; keep going: *to continue a narrative*. [ME, from L: make continuous]

continuity /kɒntə'njuəti/, *n., pl.* **-ties**. **1.** the condition or quality of being continuous. **2.** a continuous or connected whole.

continuo /kən'tɪnjuoʊ/, *n.* **1.** the bass part, usu. for a keyboard accompaniment, in baroque music. ◊*adj.* **2.** of such a part or the instruments which play it. [It]

continuous /kən'tɪnjuəs/, *adj.* **1.** having parts in immediate connection; unbroken. **2.** uninterrupted in time; without ceasing. **3.** *Gram.* indicating the verb aspect which shows progressive action, or a condition going on, e.g. *'is doing'* in *'he is doing it'*. See Appendix. [L: hanging together]

continuum /kən'tɪnjuəm/, *n., pl.* **-tinuums, -tinua** /-'tɪnjuə/. **1.** a continuous extent, series, or whole. **2. four-dimensional continuum,** *Phys.* (in the theory of relativity) the three dimensions of space and the dimension of time considered together.

contort /kən'tɔːt/, *v.t.* to twist; bend or draw out of shape; distort. [L: twisted] –**contortion**, *n.*

contortionist /kən'tɔːfənəst/, *n.* a person who performs difficult gymnastic feats involving contorted postures.

contour /'kɒntɔː, -tʊə/, *n.* **1.** the outline of a figure or body; the line that defines or bounds anything. **2.** → **contour line**. ◊*v.t.* **3.** to mark with contour lines. **4.** to make or form the contour or outline of. [F, from It, from L *con-* CON- + *tornāre* turn]

contour line, *n.* (in mapping) a line joining points of equal elevation.

contour map, *n.* a map on which uneven aspects of land surface are shown by contour lines, the relative spacing of the lines showing the relative slope of the surface.

contour ploughing, *n.* a system of ploughing along the contour lines of land to minimise the erosion of topsoil by rain.

contra-, a prefix meaning 'against', 'opposite', or 'opposing'. [L, prefix use of *contrā*, adv. and prep.]

contraband /'kɒntrəbænd/, *n.* **1.** goods imported or exported illegally. ◊*adj.* **2.** prohibited from export or import. [Sp]

contrabass /kɒntrə'beɪs/, *n.* **1.** (in any family of musical instruments) the member below the bass. **2.** (in the violin family) the double bass. –**contrabassist**, *n.*

contraception /kɒntrə'sɛpʃən/, *n.* the deliberate prevention of conception; birth control. [CONTRA- + (CON)CEPTION]

contraceptive /kɒntrə'sɛptɪv/, *adj.* **1.** tending or serving to prevent conception. **2.** relating to contraception. ◊*n.* **3.** a contraceptive agent or device, as a pill, foam, condom, etc.

contract /'kɒntrækt/, *n.*; /'kɒntrækt, kən'trækt/, *v.* ◊*n.* **1.** (a document containing) an agreement, esp. one enforceable by law. ◊*v.t.* **2.** to draw together or make smaller: *to contract a muscle*. **3.** to shorten (a word, etc.) by combining or omitting some of its parts. **4.** to acquire; incur: *to contract a disease; to contract debts*. **5.** to settle or establish by agreement: *to contract a marriage*. ◊*v.i.* **6.** to become smaller; shrink. **7.** to enter into an agreement. [ME, from L: agreement] –**contraction**, *n.* –**contractual**, *adj.* –**contractible**, *adj.*

contractor /'kɒntræktə, kən'træktə/, *n.* someone who contracts to supply or do something at a certain price or rate. [LL]

contradict /kɒntrə'dɪkt/, *v.t.* **1.** to assert the opposite of (something); deny: *Don't contradict what I say*. **2.** to deny the words or assertion of (a person): *Don't contradict me*. **3.** (of a statement, action, etc.) to be directly contrary to. ◊*v.i.* **4.** to utter a contrary statement. [L: said against] –**contradiction**, *n.*

contradictory /kɒntrə'dɪktəri/, *adj., n., pl.* **-ries**. ◊*adj.* **1.** asserting the contrary or opposite: *a contradictory reply*. **2.** contradicting each other: *contradictory statements*. **3.** (of a person) given to contradiction. **4.** (of a person) inconsistent; unpredictable. ◊*n.* **5.** *Logic.* an idea so related to another that it is impossible for both to be true or both to be false.

contradistinction /kɒntrədəs'tɪŋkʃən/, *n.* distinction by opposition or contrast. –**contradistinctive**, *adj.*

contralto /kən'træltoʊ, -'trɑːl-/, *n. Music.* the lowest female voice or voice part, between soprano and tenor. [It]

contraption /kən'træpʃən/, *n.* a device; contrivance.

contrapuntal /kɒntrə'pʌntl/, *adj.* **1.** (of music) composed of two or more relatively independent melodies sounded together. **2.** of or relating to counterpoint. [It *contrappunto* counterpoint + -AL[1]]

contrariwise /'kɒntrəriwaɪz/ *for defs 1, 2*; /kən'trɛəriwaɪz/ *for def. 3.*, *adv.* **1.** in the opposite way. **2.** on the contrary. **3.** perversely; obstinately.

contrary /'kɒntrəri/; *for def. 4 also* /kən'trɛəri/, *adj., n., pl.* **-ries**, *adv.* ◊*adj.* **1.** opposite in nature or character; mutually opposed: *contrary to fact; contrary ideas*. **2.** opposite in direction or position. **3.** unfavorable: *contrary winds*. **4.** self-willed; perverse: *a contrary child*. ◊*n.* **5.** that which is

contrary or opposite: *to prove the contrary.* **6.** either of two contrary things. **7.** *Logic.* an idea so related to another that it is impossible for both to be true, though both may be false, e.g.: *All judges are male* is the contrary of *No judges are male.* **8. on the contrary,** in opposition to what has been stated. **9. to the contrary,** to opposite or different effect. ◇*adv.* **10.** contrarily; contrariwise. [ME, from AF, from L: opposite, hostile] —**contrarily,** *adv.* —**contrariness,** *n.*

contrast /kən'trast/, *v.;* /'kontrast/, *n.* ◇*v.t.* **1.** to set in opposition in order to show unlikeness; compare by observing differences: *contrast these two paintings.* ◇*v.i.* **2.** to supply or form a contrast; set off: *This shirt contrasts well with your skirt.* **3.** to show unlikeness when compared; form a contrast: *He contrasts with his brother.* ◇*n.* **4.** the act of contrasting. **5.** the condition of being contrasted. **6.** something strikingly unlike: *She's quite a contrast to her brother.* [F, from It, from LL: withstand, oppose]

contravene /kontrə'vin/, *v.t.,* **-vened, -vening. 1.** to come or be in conflict with; go or act counter to; oppose. **2.** to violate, infringe, or transgress: *to contravene the law.* [L: oppose] —**contravention,** *n.*

contribute /kən'trɪbjut/, *v.t., v.i.,* **-uted, -uting. 1.** to give to a common stock or for a common purpose: *He contributed $40 to the fund; I haven't contributed yet.* **2.** to give (stories, etc.) to a magazine or newspaper. [L: brought together] —**contributor,** *n.* —**contribution,** *n.* —**contributory,** *adj.*

contrite /'kontraɪt, kən'traɪt/, *adj.* feeling or showing sorrow or sadness, esp. from guilt; penitent: *contrite sinner; contrite tears.* [ME, from L: ground, worn down]

contrition /kən'trɪʃən/, *n.* **1.** sincere penitence. **2.** *Theol.* sorrow for sin with the promise to amend bad ways. [ME, from L]

contrivance /kən'traɪvəns/, *n.* **1.** a device, esp. a mechanical one. **2.** the act or manner of contriving. **3.** the ability or power of contriving.

contrive /kən'traɪv/, *v.,* **-trived, -triving.** ◇*v.t.* **1.** to plan with cleverness; devise; invent. **2.** to bring about or effect by a device or plan; manage (to do something): *I'll contrive to be there.* ◇*v.i.* **3.** to form schemes or designs; plan; plot. [ME, from OF *con-* CON- + *trover* find] —**contrivable,** *adj.*

control /kən'troʊl/, *v.,* **-trolled, -trolling,** *n.* ◇*v.t.* **1.** to exercise restraint or direction over; dominate; command: *to control your dog; to control your feelings.* **2.** to direct the working of (a machine, vehicle, etc.). **3.** to hold in check; curb: *to control population growth.* **4.** to test or verify (a scientific experiment) by a parallel experiment or other standard of comparison. ◇*n.* **5.** the act or power of controlling; domination; command: *Keep your dog under control.* **6.** a check or restraint: *the control of population growth.* **7.** a standard of comparison in a scientific experiment. **8.** (*pl.*) a system of knobs, levers, etc., for controlling a machine, etc. **9.** a place at or from which officials control or regulate an event or system: *Send a message to control.* [F, from OF *contre-* COUNTER- + *rolle* ROLL] —**controllable,** *adj.* —**controller,** *n.*

control group, *n.* an experimental group which acts as a control (def. 7) in research.

control rod, *n.* **1.** *Phys.* a rod or tube, made from material which absorbs neutrons, used to control the rate of reaction in a nuclear reactor. **2.** *Radio.* an electrode in a radio valve, lying between the cathode and the anode, which controls the flow of current through the valve.

control unit, *n.* the part of a digital computer which causes it to perform its program in correct sequence.

controversial /kontrə'vɜʃəl/, *adj.* **1.** subject to different points of view; debatable. **2.** given to arguing; disputatious. —**controversialist,** *n.*

controversy /'kontrəvɜsi, kən'trɒvəsi/, *n., pl.* **-sies.** a dispute, debate, or contention concerning a matter of opinion. [L *controversia* debate, contention]

contumely /'kontjuməli, kən'tjuməli/, *n., pl.* **-lies. 1.** a show of contempt in words or actions; humiliating treatment. **2.** an insult; humiliation. [ME, from L] —**contumelious,** *adj.*

contuse /kən'tjuz/, *v.t.,* **-tused, -tusing.** to hurt as by a blow with a blunt instrument, without breaking the skin; bruise. [L: beaten together] —**contusive,** *adj.*

contusion /kən'tjuʒən/, *n.* a bruise.

conundrum /kə'nʌndrəm/, *n.* **1.** a riddle, the answer to which involves a pun or play on words. **2.** anything puzzling. [orig. unknown]

conurbation /konɜ'beɪʃən/, *n.* a large heavily populated area formed by growth and the gradual merging of formerly separate towns. [CON- + L *urbs* city + -ATION]

convalesce /konvə'lɛs/, *v.i.,* **-lesced, -lescing.** to grow stronger after illness; make progress towards recovery of health. [L: grow strong]

convalescence /konvə'lɛsəns/, *n.* **1.** the gradual recovery of health and strength after illness. **2.** the period during which a person is convalescing.

convalescent /konvə'lɛsənt/, *adj.* **1.** convalescing: *a convalescent patient.* **2.** of or relating to convalescence or convalescents: *a convalescent home.* ◇*n.* **3.** a convalescent person.

convection /kən'vɛkʃən/, *n.* **1.** *Phys.* the spreading of heat by circulation or the movement of the heated parts of a liquid or gas. **2.** *Geog.* a mechanical process, thermally produced, involving the upward or downward transfer of a limited part of the atmosphere. [LL, from L: carry together] —**convectional,** *adj.* —**convective,** *adj.*

convector /kən'vɛktə/, *n.* a heating device, esp. a room-heater, distributing heat by convection.

convene /kən'vin/, *v.,* **-vened, -vening.** ◇*v.i.* **1.** to come together or assemble, usu. for some public purpose. ◇*v.t.* **2.** to cause to assemble; convoke: *to convene a meeting.* **3.** to summon to appear, as before a judicial officer. [ME, from L: come together] —**convener,** *n.*

convenience /kən'viniəns/, *n.* **1.** the quality of being convenient; suitability. **2.** a situation or time convenient for someone: *I'll await your convenience.* **3.** personal advantage or use: *shelter for the convenience of travellers.* **4.** anything which makes life easier, e.g. a car, appliance, utensil, etc. **5.** (as a euphemism) a toilet.

convenient /kən'viniənt/, *adj.* **1.** favorable, easy, or comfortable for use. **2.** at hand; easily accessible. [ME, from L: agreeing, suiting]

convent /'kɒnvənt/, *n.* **1.** a (building occupied by) a community of persons, esp. nuns, devoted to religious life. **2.** a Roman Catholic or other school run by nuns. [L: meeting, assembly, company]

convention /kən'vɛnʃən/, *n.* **1.** a formal meeting or assembly, for discussion and action on particular matters. **2.** an agreement or contract. **3.** an international agreement, esp. one dealing with a specific matter, as postal service, copyright, arbitration, etc. **4.** general agreement or consent; accepted usage, esp. as a standard of operation. [L: a meeting]

conventional /kən'vɛnʃənəl/, *adj.* **1.** relating to accepted standards, established by general consent or usage: *conventional symbols; conventional greetings.* **2.** *Law.* resting on consent, stated or implied. **3.** (of weapons, warfare, etc.) not nuclear. —**conventionalist,** *n.* —**conventionalism,** *n.* —**conventionality,** *n.*

converge /kən'vɜdʒ/, *v.,* **-verged, -verging.** ◇*v.i.* **1.** to move towards each other, as lines which are not parallel. **2.** to tend to a common result, conclusion, etc. **3.** *Maths.* (of an infinite sequence of numbers) to approach a single number, called the limit of sequence. ◇*v.t.* **4.** to cause to converge. [LL: incline together]

convergence /kən'vɜdʒəns/, *n.* **1.** the act or result of converging. **2.** a point of convergence. **3.** *Biol.* similarity of form or structure caused by the environment rather than heredity. Also, **convergency** for defs. 1 and 2. —**convergent,** *adj.*

convergent evolution, /kən,vɜdʒənt evə'luʃən/ *n.* the appearance of apparently similar structures in organisms of different lines of descent.

conversant /kən'vɜsənt, 'kɒnvəsənt/, *adj.* familiar by use or study (fol. by *with*): *I'm not conversant with law terms.* [ME, from L: associating with] —**conversance, conversancy,** *n.*

conversation /kɒnvə'seɪʃən/, *n.* an interchange of thoughts by spoken words; talk; colloquy. [ME, from OF, from L: frequent use, intercourse] —**conversational,** *adj.* —**conversationalist,** *n.*

converse[1] /kən'vɜs/, *v.i.,* **-versed, -versing.** to talk with another; hold a conversation. [ME, from OF, from L: associate with]

converse[2] /'kɒnvɜs/, *adj.* **1.** turned about; opposite or contrary in direction or action. ◇*n.* **2.** a thing which is the opposite or contrary of another. [L: turned about]

conversion /kən'vɜʒən, -'vɜʃən/, *n.* **1.** the act or result of being converted. **2.** a change in character, form, or purpose. **3.** a change from one religion, political belief, etc., to another. **4.** *Maths.* a change in the form or units of expression. **5.** *Rugby.* **a.** the act of converting a try. **b.** the try so converted. **6.** *Phys.* the process of changing fertile material into fissile material in a nuclear reactor. —**conversional, conversionary,** *adj.*

convert /kən'vɜt/, *v.;* /'kɒnvɜt/, *n.* ◇*v.t.* **1.** to change into something of different form or properties; transmute; transform. **2.** *Chem.* to cause (a substance) to undergo chemical change: *to convert sugar into alcohol.* **3.** to cause to adopt a different religion, political belief, purpose, etc. **4.** *Rugby.* to add a goal to (a try) by kicking the ball over the crossbar of the goalposts. **5.** to exchange for an equivalent: *to convert banknotes into gold.* ◇*n.* **6.** a person who has been converted, as to religion or opinion. [ME, from L: turn about, change]

converter /kən'vɜtə/, *n.* **1.** *Elect.* **a.** a device which changes alternating current to direct current or vice versa. **b.** a device which changes the frequency of signals. **2.** *Electronics.* a translator from one electrical representation to another as an analog-to-digital converter. **3.** Also, **converter reactor.** *Phys.* a nuclear reactor which produces fissile material. Also, **convertor.**

convertible /kən'vɜtəbəl/, *adj.* **1.** able to be converted. **2.** (of a motor car) having a removable top. **3.** (of currency) able to be exchanged at a fixed price. **4.** (of paper currency) able to be exchanged for gold on demand to its full value at the issuing bank. ◇*n.* **5.** *Colloq.* a convertible motor car. —**convertibility, convertibleness,** *n.*

convex /'kɒnvɛks/, *adj.* **1.** (esp. of optical lenses and mirrors) curved outwards; bulging. ◇*n.* **2.** a convex surface, part, or thing. See **concave.** [L: vaulted, arched] —**convexity,** *n.*

convey /kən'veɪ/, *v.t.* **1.** to carry or transport from one place to another. **2.** to lead or conduct; transmit. **3.** to make known; impart; communicate. **4.** *Law.* to transfer; pass the title (of real property) to someone. [ME, from OF (from L *via* way, journey)] —**conveyable,** *adj.*

conveyance /kən'veɪəns/, *n.* **1.** the act of conveying; transmission; communication. **2.** a means of conveyance, esp. a vehicle; carriage; motor car. **3.** *Law.* the transfer of real property from one person to another. **b.** the instrument or document by which this takes place.

conveyancing /kən'veɪənsɪŋ/, *n.* that branch of legal practice concerned with examining titles, giving opinions as to their validity, and preparing deeds, etc., for transfer

conveyancing

of real property from one person to another. —**conveyancer**, *n.*

conveyor or **conveyer** /kənˈveɪə/, *n.* a device for moving material, as from one part of building to another.

conveyor belt, *n.* a flexible band passing around two or more wheels, etc., used to move objects from one place to another.

convict /kənˈvɪkt/, *v.*; /ˈkɒnvɪkt/, *n.* ◇*v.t.* **1.** to prove or declare guilty of an offence, esp. after a legal trial: *to convict a prisoner of a crime*. ◇*n.* **2.** a person proved or declared guilty of an offence. **3.** a person serving a prison sentence. **4.** (formerly) a person sent to the British colonies to serve a sentence. [ME, from L: overcome, convicted]

conviction /kənˈvɪkʃən/, *n.* **1.** *Law.* a finding that an accused is guilty of the crime charged: *He has many convictions for assault*. **2.** the act of convicting. **3.** the condition of being convinced; strong belief.

convince /kənˈvɪns/, *v.t.*, **-vinced, -vincing.** to persuade by argument or proof; cause to believe in the truth of what is said (oft. fol. by *of*): *to convince someone of his errors*. [L: overcome by argument or proof, convict of error or crime, prove] —**convincible**, *adj.* —**convincingly**, *adv.*

convivial /kənˈvɪviəl/, *adj.* **1.** fond of feasting, drinking, and merry company; jovial. **2.** of or suitable for a feast; festive. **3.** agreeable; sociable; merry. [L: of a feast] —**convivialist**, *n.* —**conviviality**, *n.*

convoke /kənˈvoʊk/, *v.t.*, **-voked, -voking.** to call together; assemble by summons. [L: call together]

convolute /ˈkɒnvəlut/, *v.*, **-luted, -luting.** *adj.* ◇*v.t.* **1.** to coil up; form into a twisted shape. ◇*adj.* **2.** rolled up together, or one part over another. [L: rolled together]

convolution /kɒnvəˈluʃən/, *n.* **1.** a rolled up or coiled state. **2.** a rolling or coiling together. **3.** a turn of anything coiled; whorl: *the convolutions of the brain*.

convolve /kənˈvɒlv/, *v.t.*, *v.i.*, **-volved, -volving.** to roll or wind (something) together; coil; twist. [L: roll together]

convolvulus /kənˈvɒlvjələs/, *n.*, *pl.* **-luses, -li** /-laɪ/. any of several kinds of climbing or creeping plants with trumpet-shaped flowers; bindweed; morning glory.

convoy /ˈkɒnvɔɪ/, *v.t.* **1.** to accompany or escort, usu. for protection: *The merchant ship was convoyed by a destroyer*. ◇*n.* **2.** the act of convoying. **3.** a protecting escort, as for ships or troops. **4.** a train of ships, vehicles, etc., travelling under escort. [ME, from F: convey]

convulse /kənˈvʌls/, *v.t.*, **-vulsed, -vulsing.** **1.** to shake violently; agitate. **2.** to cause to suffer violent muscular spasms: *to convulse with laughter*. [L: shattered]

convulsion /kənˈvʌlʃən/, *n.* **1.** *Med.* a twisting of the body caused by violent muscular contractions. **2.** a violent disturbance; commotion. **3.** a violent fit of laughter: *We were in convulsions over his story*.

convulsive /kənˈvʌlsɪv/, *adj.* marked or accompanied by convulsions or spasms: *convulsive rage; convulsive laughter*.

coo /ku/, *v.*, **cooed, cooing**, *n.* ◇*v.i.* **1.** to make the soft, murmuring sound of pigeons or doves. **2.** to murmur or talk fondly: *to bill and coo.* ◇*v.t.* **3.** to say by cooing. ◇*n.* **4.** a cooing sound. [imitative]

Coober Pedy /ˌkubə ˈpidi/, *n.* a settlement in northern SA; one of Australia's major producers of opals. Pop. 2103 (1986). [Aboriginal: hole in the ground]

cooee /ˈkui, kuˈi/, *n.*, *v.*, **-cooeed, -cooeeing.** ◇*n.* **1.** a long clear call rising at the end, used esp. in the bush as a signal. **2. within cooee**, within calling distance. **3. not within cooee**, far from achieving a given goal. ◇*v.i.* **4.** to make the call 'cooee'. Also, **cooey**. [Aboriginal]

cooee bird, *n.* → **koel** (def. 1).

cook /kʊk/, *v.t.* **1.** to prepare (food) by heating, as by boiling, baking, roasting, etc. **2.** to subject (something) to the action of heat: *This weather is cooking me.* **3.** *Colloq.* to invent falsely; concoct; falsify (oft. fol. by *up*): *to cook the books; cook up a story.* **4.** *Colloq.* to ruin; spoil. **5. cook one's goose**, to spoil one's plans. ◇*v.i.* **6.** to prepare food by heating. **7.** (of food) to undergo cooking: *This fish cooks well.* ◇*n.* **8. a.** a person who cooks. **b.** a person whose occupation is cooking. [OE *cōc*, from LL]

Cook[1] /kʊk/, *n.* **1. Captain James**, 1728–79, English navigator; first European to explore the east coast of Australia in the *Endeavour* in 1770. **2. Sir Joseph**, 1860–1947, Australian federal Liberal politician, born in England; prime minister 1913–14. **3. Kenneth**, 1929–87, Australian writer; works include the novel *Wake in Fright* (1961). **4. Patrick**, born 1949, Australian cartoonist and satirist.

Cook[2] /kʊk/, *n.* **Mount**, a mountain in NZ, in the central part of the South Island; the highest point in NZ. Also, **Aorangi**. 3764 m.

cookery /ˈkʊkəri/, *n.*, *pl.* **-eries**. the art, practice, or study of cooking.

cookhouse /ˈkʊkhaʊs/, *n.* a kitchen standing apart from the main building, as in gaols, army camps, early farm houses.

cookie /ˈkʊki/, *n.*, *pl.* **cookies**. **1.** *Chiefly US.* biscuit. **2.** *Colloq.* a person: *a smart cookie.* **3. that's the way the cookie crumbles**, *Colloq.* that's how things are. Also, **cooky**. [D: little cake]

Cook Islands, *n.pl.* a group of islands in the South Pacific, belonging to NZ. 256 km².

Cook Strait, *n.* a strait between North and South Islands in NZ. About 24 km wide at the narrowest point.

Cooktown /ˈkʊktaʊn/, *n.* a coastal town at the mouth of the Endeavour River in north-eastern Qld; a former goldmining centre. Pop. 964 (1986).

Cooktown orchid, *n.* an attractive, purple orchid found on rocks and trees in far northern Qld; the floral emblem of Qld.

cool /kul/, *adj.* **1. a.** pleasantly cold: *cool weather.* **b.** giving a feeling of pleasant coldness: *a cool dress.* **2. a.** calm; unexcited. **b.** not enthusiastic; unfriendly: *a cool reception.* **3.** without shame; unperturbed: *a cool villain.* **4.** *Colloq.* (of a number or sum) without exaggeration: *a cool thousand.* **5.** (of colors) with mostly green, blue, or violet. **6.** (of jazz) controlled, subtle, and relaxed. **7.** *Colloq.* **a.** attractive; excellent. **b.** smart; up-to-date; fashionable. ◇*n.* **8. a.** the condition of being cool. **b.** a cool time, place, etc: *the cool of the evening; Put it in the cool over there.* **9.** *Colloq.* calmness of manner; composure: *to keep/lose his cool.* ◇*v.t., v.i.* **10.** to make or become cool. ◇*v.* **11. cool off** or **down**, *Colloq.* **a.** to become cool. **b.** to stop being angry; become calmer or more reasonable. **12. cool one's heels,** to be kept waiting. [OE *cōl*]

coolabah /ˈkulabə/, *n.* a gumtree of inland Australia, with short and twisted branches, often found on waterways in flood areas. Also, **coolibah**. [Aboriginal]

coolamon /ˈkuləmɒn/, *n.* a wooden dish made and used by the Aborigines. [Aboriginal]

Coolangatta /kulənˈgætə/, *n.* the southernmost town of the Gold Coast in Qld; major tourist resort. [Aboriginal: beautiful lookout]

coolant /ˈkulənt/, *n.* **1.** a substance, usu. a liquid or gas, used to reduce heat in an engine, etc. **2.** a lubricant used to reduce heat caused by friction. [COOL + -ANT]

Coolgardie /kulˈgɑdi/, *n.* a town and shire in southern WA; early goldmining town. Pop. 989 (1986).

Coolgardie safe, *n.* → **cool safe.** Also, **Coolgardie cooler.** [from COOLGARDIE]

Coolidge /ˈkulɪdʒ/, *n.* **1. (John) Calvin,** 1872–1933, 30th president of the US 1923–29.

coolie /ˈkuli/, *n.* (in India, China, etc.) an unskilled native laborer. [Hindi]

cool safe, *n.* a cabinet for keeping food, which cools by allowing a breeze to blow through wet material, such as hessian.

Cooma /ˈkumə/, *n.* a town in the Monaro district in southern NSW; headquarters of the authority controlling the Snowy Mountains Hydro-Electric Scheme. Pop. 7406 (1986). [Aboriginal]

coomb /kum/, *n.* a narrow valley or deep hollow. Also, **combe, comb.** [OE *cumb* valley]

Coombs /kumz/, *n.* **Herbert Cole** ('*Nugget*'), born 1906, Australian economist; government economic adviser; chairman of the Reserve Bank 1959–68.

coon /kun/, *n.* **1.** (*offensive*) a dark-skinned person. **2.** a raccoon.

co-op /ˈkoʊ-ɒp/, *n.* a cooperative shop, store, society, etc.

coop /kup/, *n.* **1.** a cage or pen for keeping or carrying fowls. **2.** any small or narrow place. ◇*v.t.* **3.** to place in, as in a coop; confine narrowly (oft. fol. by *up* or *in*): *I'm sick of being cooped up here.* [OE *cȳpe* basket]

cooper /ˈkupə/, *n.* **1.** a person who makes or repairs casks or barrels. ◇*v.t.* **2.** to make or repair (casks, barrels, etc.). ◇*v.i.* **3.** to work as a cooper. [ME, from MD or MLG from VL, from L *cūpa* cask] —**cooperage**, *n.*

Cooper /ˈkupə/, *n.* **1. Gary** (*Frank James Cooper*), 1901–61, US film actor; won Academy Awards for *High Noon* (1952) and *Sergeant York* (1941).

cooperate /koʊˈɒpəreɪt/, *v.i.,* **-rated, -rating. 1.** to work or act together or jointly. **2.** to act willingly; stop resisting: *Why don't you cooperate for once?* [LL: having worked together] —**cooperator,** *n.* —**cooperation,** *n.*

cooperative /koʊˈɒpərətɪv, -ˈɒprətɪv/, *adj.* **1.** cooperating. **2.** showing a willingness to cooperate; helpful. **3.** having cooperation as a feature: *a cooperative plan.*

cooperative society, *n.* a business owned and controlled by its members, and formed to provide them with work or with goods at advantageous prices; a **consumers' cooperative** is owned by its customers, and **producers' cooperative** by its workers.

Cooper Creek /ˌkupə ˈkrik/, *n.* a river which runs from the junction of the Thomson and Barcoo Rivers across the south-western corner of Qld into the north-east of SA, and then in a westerly direction to Lake Eyre. 800 km. Formerly, **Cooper's Creek.**

coopt /koʊˈɒpt/, *v.t.* to elect into a body by the votes of the existing members. [L]

coordinate /koʊˈɔdəneɪt/, *v.,* **-nated, -nating;** /koʊˈɔdənət, -neɪt/, *adj., n.* ◇*v.t.* **1.** to place or arrange in due order or proper relative position; combine harmoniously: *to coordinate the work of different people; He must learn to coordinate his hands on the piano.* ◇*v.i.* **2.** to go together with; match. **3.** to act or work together with; cooperate. ◇*adj.* **4.** equal in rank or importance; matching. **5.** *Maths.* using or having to do with systems of coordinates. ◇*n.* **6.** an equal. **7.** (*oft. pl.*) clothes that match or go together. **8.** *Maths.* any of the magnitudes which define the position of a point, line, etc. by reference to a fixed figure, system of lines, etc. —**coordinative,** *adj.* —**coordinator,** *n.*

coordinate bond, *n. Chem.* → **dative bond.**

coordinate clause, *n.* one of two or more clauses of the same kind, which are linked by the coordinating conjunctions *and, but, or.* See **subordinate clause.**

coordinate covalent bond, *n. Chem.* → **semipolar bond.**

coordinated /koʊˈɔdəneɪtəd/, *adj.* showing coordination.

coordination /koʊˌɔdəˈneɪʃən/, *n.* **1.** the act or result of coordinating. **2.** the ability to coordinate the movements of one's body: *Balletdancers have good coordination.* **3.** due ordering or proper relation; harmonious combination.

coordination compound, *n.* a class of compounds consisting of a central transition element ion surrounded by a set (2 to 9) of other atoms, negative ions or small molecules called ligands.

coordination number, *n.* the number of outer, or ligand, atoms bonded to the central ion in a coordination compound.

coori /'kuri/, *n., adj.* → **koori**.

Coorong /'kurɒŋ/, *n.* **the,** a shallow salt lagoon in south-eastern SA which extends south-east from the mouth of the Murray River. 145 km. [Aboriginal: neck]

coot /kut/, *n.* **1.** a water bird with lobed toes and short wings and tail, as the Australian coot, a large black bird with a round white patch on its head and a white bill. **2.** Also, **bald coot.** → **swamphen.** *Colloq.* **a.** a man. **b.** a fool; simpleton. [? D *koet*]

Coot-tha /'ku-ðə/, *n.* **Mount,** a mountain in south-eastern Qld, overlooking Brisbane and Moreton Bay. 226 m.

cop /kɒp/, *n., v.,* **copped, copping.** *Colloq.* ◇*n.* **1. a.** a policeman. **b.** → **silent cop. 2.** something advantageous, or profitable, as in the phrases: **a. sweet cop,** an easy job. **b. sure cop,** something certain. **c. not much cop,** not worthwhile. ◇*v.t.* **3.** to steal. **4.** to receive in payment. **5.** to accept; put up with: *Would you cop a deal like that?* **6.** to be dealt, receive: *He copped more than his fair share.* ◇**7.** some special uses are:

cop a load, to contract venereal disease.
cop it, to be punished.
cop it sweet, to take punishment without complaint.
cop the lot, to suffer great misfortune.
cop out, 1. to choose not to do (something); opt out of (something). **2.** to fail completely.
cop this! look at this! [OE *coppian* lop, steal]

cope[1] /koup/, *v.i.,* **coped, coping.** to succeed in putting up with, or in handling something difficult (oft. fol. by *with*): *They cannot cope with the increased work; She is impossible to cope with.* [ME, from F: strike]

cope[2] /koup/, *n.* **1.** a long cloak-like garment worn by clergy for special ceremonies or in processions. **2.** any cloak-like or canopy-like covering: *the cope of heaven.* [OE *cāp,* from ML: cope]

Copenhagen /koupən'heigən/, *n.* a seaport in and the capital of Denmark, on the eastern coast of Zealand. Pop. 1 358 540 (1985). Danish, **Kobenhavn.**

Copernicus[1] /kə'pɜːnɪkəs/, *n.* **Nicolaus** /nɪkə'leɪəs/, 1473–1543, Polish astronomer who promulgated the now accepted theory that the earth and the planets move about the sun (the **Copernican system**). Polish, **Kopernik.** – **Copernican,** *adj.*

Copernicus[2] /kə'pɜːnɪkəs/, *n.* a large crater on the moon, over 4000 m deep; source of a system of rays.

Copeton Dam /ˌkoʊpətən 'dæm/, *n.* a dam in northern NSW, on the Gwydir River; source of water for domestic, stock and irrigation purposes. About 113 m in height and 1484 m in length.

copha /'koufə/, *n.* a white waxy solid derived from coconut flesh used as a shortening in cooking; coconut butter. Also, **copha butter.** [Trademark]

copier /'kɒpɪə/, *n.* **1.** a person who copies; a copyist. **2.** a photostat machine; photocopier.

coping /'koupɪŋ/, *n.* a brick or stone covering on top of a wall, usu. made sloping or pitched, so as to carry off water.

coping stone, *n.* **1.** the top stone of a wall. **2.** a stone used for or in a coping. **3.** the finishing touch. Also, **copestone.**

copious /'koupɪəs/, *adj.* **1.** plentiful; abundant: *a copious supply of milk.* **2.** having or giving an abundant supply: *a copious vegetable garden.* **3.** showing abundance or fullness, as of thoughts or words: *a copious writer.* [ME, from L: plentiful]

cop-out /'kɒp-aut/, *n. Colloq.* an irresponsible way out of a difficult situation.

copper[1] /'kɒpə/, *n.* **1.** *Chem.* a reddish-brown malleable, ductile metallic element. Symbol: Cu; at. no. 29; at. wt: 63.54. **2.** a copper coin, as the English penny or the US cent. **3.** a container made of copper. **4.** a large vessel (formerly of copper) for boiling clothes. **5.** a metallic reddish-brown color. ◇*v.t.* **6.** to cover or coat with copper. ◇*adj.* **7.** made of copper. **8.** copper-colored. **9.** relating to copper: *copper smelting.* [OE *coper, copor* from L *aes Cyprium* Cyprian metal]

copper[2] /'kɒpə/, *n. Colloq.* a policeman. [See COP]

copperhead /'kɒpəhed/, *n.* a venomous Australian snake that lives in marshy areas, brown to black above with a coppery red band behind the head, and about two metres long.

copperplate /'kɒpəpleɪt/, *n.* **1.** a plate of polished copper on which writing, a picture, or a design is made by engraving or etching. **2.** a print or impression from such a plate. **3.** an engraving or printing of this kind. **4.** a formal, rounded, heavily sloping style of handwriting, formerly much used in engravings. ◇*adj.* **5.** (of handwriting) sloping, rounded and formal; in the style of copperplate.

coppice /'kɒpəs/, *n.* **1.** Also, **copse.** a wood or thicket of small trees or bushes. ◇*v.t.* **2.** to cut (trees) to encourage a number of thin trunks to grow from the root-stock. [OF *couper* cut]

Coppola /'kɒpələ/, *n.* **Francis Ford,** born 1939, US film director and screenwriter; films include *The Godfather* (1971) and *Apocalypse Now* (1979).

copra /'kɒprə/, *n.* the dried flesh of the coconut, from which coconut oil is pressed. [Pg, from Indian]

copro-, a prefix meaning 'dung' or 'excrement', as in *coprophagous.* [combining form of Gk *kópros* dung]

coprophagous /kɒp'rɒfəgəs/, *adj.* feeding on dung, as certain beetles. [COPRO- + -PHAGOUS]

copse /kɒps/, *n.* → **coppice** (def. 1).

Coptic /'kɒptɪk/, *n.* the extinct language of Egypt which developed from ancient Egyptian, used liturgically by Egyptian Christians. [from *Copt*]

copula /'kɒpjələ/, *n., pl.* **-lae** /-liː/. something that connects or links together. [L: a band, bond] – **copular**, *adj.*

copulate /'kɒpjuleɪt/, *v.i.*, **-lated, -lating**. to unite in sexual intercourse. [L: coupled]

copulation /kɒpju'leɪʃən/, *n.* **1.** sexual union or intercourse. **2.** a joining together or coupling.

copulative /'kɒpjulətɪv/, *adj.* **1.** serving to unite or couple: *a copulative verb.* **2.** having the nature of a copula: *This verb has a copulative function.* **3.** of or relating to copulation.

copy /'kɒpi/, *n., pl.* **copies**, *v.*, **copied, copying**. ◇*n.* **1.** something made to be exactly like another: *We need four copies of the letter.* **2.** one of the various examples of the same book, magazine, etc. **3.** written, typed, or printed matter, or artwork, intended to be printed. ◇*v.t.* **4.** to make a thing exactly like another; transcribe; reproduce: *to copy a set of figures.* **5.** to follow as a pattern or model; imitate: *She copied her sister in everything.* ◇*v.i.* **6.** to make a copy or copies. **7.** to use unfairly another person's written work: *James is always copying from me in history class.* [ME, from L: plenty, ML: transcript]

copybook /'kɒpibʊk/, *n.* **1.** a book in which examples of handwriting are printed for learners to imitate. **2. blot one's copybook**, to spoil or hurt one's reputation or record. ◇*adj.* **3.** (esp. in some sports) according to the rules; excellent.

copycat /'kɒpikæt/, *n., v.*, **-catted, -catting**. *Colloq.* ◇*n.* **1.** someone who imitates another's acts or behavior. ◇*v.i.* **2.** to imitate in this way.

copyist /'kɒpiɪst/, *n.* **1.** a person who writes copies of manuscripts and documents by hand; scribe; transcriber. **2.** an imitator.

copyright /'kɒpiraɪt/, *n.* **1.** the exclusive right, given by law for a fixed period of time, to make and sell copies of, and to control in other ways, a book, play or film, or a musical or artistic work. ◇*adj.* **2.** protected by copyright. ◇*v.t.* **3.** to have a copyright put on something.

copywriter /'kɒpiraɪtə/, *n.* someone who writes the words for advertisements or publicity releases.

coquet /koʊ'kɛt, kɒ'kɛt/, *v.*, **-quetted, -quetting**, *adj.* ◇*v.i.* **1.** to trifle in love; flirt. **2.** to act without seriousness; trifle; dally. ◇*adj.* **3.** coquettish. [F: little cock] – **coquetry**, *n.*

coquette /koʊ'kɛt, kɒ'kɛt/, *n.* a woman who tries to gain the admiration and affections of men just for self-gratification without having any sincere feeling for them; a flirt. [F. See COQUET] – **coquettish**, *adj.*

cor-, a variant of **com-** before *r*, as in *corrupt*.

coral /'kɒrəl/, *n.* **1.** the hard, limy skeletons of small marine animals, the individual polyps of which come forth by budding. **2.** such skeletons collectively, forming reefs, islands, etc. **3.** an individual coral animal. **4.** a pinkish or reddish-orange color. ◇*adj.* **5.** made of coral: *a coral reef; a coral necklace.* **6.** like coral, esp. in color: *a coral dress.* [ME, from OF, from L, from Gk: red coral]

coralfish /'kɒrəlfɪʃ/, *n.* any of various small, brightly colored marine fish of coral reefs.

coral island, *n.* an island formed by the building-up of coral sand (from destroyed coral reef), bird droppings, etc.

coral reef, *n.* a reef or bank formed by the growth and deposit of coral polyps.

Coral Sea, *n.* **1.** a part of the South Pacific, partially enclosed by north-eastern Australia, PNG, the Solomon Islands and Vanuatu; includes the waters of the Great Barrier Reef and Torres Strait. **2. Battle of the**, a battle between the Allied forces and the Japanese during World War II, on 7–8 May 1942, which prevented the establishment of a Japanese base at Port Moresby.

coral snake, *n.* a small, venomous, but unaggressive snake of eastern Australia, red with black and yellow banding.

coral tree, *n.* a thorny tree with showy bright red flowers, introduced from India, now widely cultivated in Australia. Also, **coxcomb coral tree**.

coral trout, *n.* an important commercial food fish of the Great Barrier Reef.

Corangamite /kə'ræŋgəmaɪt/, *n.* **Lake**, a large salt lake in south-western Vic. 140 km^2.

cor anglais /kɔr 'ɒŋleɪ/, *n.* the alto of the oboe family, richer in sound and a fifth lower than the oboe. Also, **English horn**.

Corbusier /kɔ'bjuzjeɪ/, *n.* See **Le Corbusier**.

cord /kɔd/, *n.* **1.** a string or small rope made of several strands twisted or woven together. **2.** → **flex**. **3.** *Anat.* a cord-like structure: *the spinal cord.* **4. a.** a cord-like rib on the surface of cloth. **b.** a ribbed fabric, esp. corduroy. **5.** any influence acting as a tie or bond on someone: *tied by a cord of family love.* ◇*v.t.* **6.** to bind or fasten with cords. [ME, from L, from Gk: gut]

cordate /'kɔdeɪt/, *adj.* heart-shaped, as a shell. [NL, from L *cor* heart]

corded /'kɔdəd/, *adj.* **1.** provided with, made of, having, or in the form of cords. **2.** ribbed, as a fabric. **3.** bound with cords.

cordial /'kɔdiəl/, *adj.* **1.** hearty; warmly friendly. ◇*n.* **2. a.** *Obs.* a stimulating medicine; a tonic. **b.** anything that invigorates, enlivens and stimulates. **3. a.** a fruit-flavored concentrated syrup to be mixed with water as a drink. **b.** *Tas, Qld.* → **soft drink**. [ME, from L *cor* heart]

cordiality /ˌkɔdi'æləti/, *n., pl.* **-ties**. (an expression of) a cordial quality or feeling.

cordillera /kɔdɪl'jeərə/, *n.* **1.** a connected mountain chain. **2.** a series of more or less parallel ranges of mountains together with the plateaux and basins between them. [Sp: mountain chain, from L: rope] – **cordilleran**, *adj.*

cordon /'kɔdn/, *n.* **1. a.** a cord or braid worn for ornament or as a fastening. **b.** a ribbon worn, usu. diagonally across the breast, as a badge of a knightly or honorary order.

cordon

2. a line of police, military posts, or the like, enclosing or guarding a particular area. ◇*v.t.* **3.** to enclose or cut off with a cordon (oft. fol. by *off*). [F]

cordon bleu /ˌkɔdɒn 'blɜ/, *n.* **1.** the sky-blue ribbon worn as a badge by knights of the highest order of French knighthood under the Bourbons. **2.** some similar high distinction, esp. in cookery. ◇*adj.* **3.** (of cooking) excellent.

corduroy /'kɔdʒərɔɪ, 'kɔdərɔɪ/, *n.* **1.** a cotton pile fabric with lengthwise cords or ridges. **2.** (*pl.*) Also, **cords**. trousers made of this. ◇*adj.* **3.** of or like corduroy. **4.** built of logs laid together crosswise, as a road across swampy ground. [obs. *duroy*, a kind of coarse woollen fabric]

core /kɔ/, *n.*, *v.*, **cored, coring**. ◇*n.* **1.** the central part of a fleshy fruit. **2.** the central, innermost, or most important part of anything: *the core of a curriculum*. **3.** a cylinder of rock, soil, etc., cut out by boring. **4.** *Elect.* a piece of iron, bunch of iron wires, etc., forming the central or inner part of an electromagnet, induction coil, etc. **5.** *Phys.* the inner part of a nuclear reactor consisting of the fuel and the moderator. **6.** *Geol.* the central mass of the earth, inside the mantle. ◇*v.t.* **7.** to remove the core of (fruit). **8.** to cut from the central part. [ME; orig. unknown]

corella /kəˈrɛlə/, *n.* either of two large Australian parrots, the **little corella**, which is white tinged with pink or red, and the **long-billed corella**, which is white with orange-red markings. [Latinised form of Aboriginal *carall*]

Corfu /kɔˈfu/, *n.* one of the Ionian Islands, off the north-west coast of Greece. Pop. 99 477 (1981); 593 km². Ancient name, **Corcyra**. Modern Greek, **Kérkyra**.

corgi /'kɔgi/, *n.* a small dog of either of two ancient Welsh breeds, with short legs, squat body, and erect ears. Also, **Welsh corgi**.

coriander /ˌkɒriˈændə/, *n.* **1.** a herbaceous plant with strong-smelling seedlike fruit (**coriander seeds**) used in cookery and medicine. **2.** the fruit or seeds. [ME, from L, from Gk]

Corinth /'kɒrɪnθ/, *n.* **1.** an ancient city in Greece, strategically situated on the Isthmus of Corinth; notorious for its luxury. **2. Isthmus of**, a narrow isthmus connecting the Peloponnesus with central Greece; crossed by a ship canal.

Corinthian /kəˈrɪnθiən/, *adj.* **1.** *Archit.* referring to one of the three Greek pillars, distinguished by a bell-shaped capital with rows of acanthus leaves and a continuous frieze. ◇*n.* **2.** (*pl.*) the two books or epistles of the New Testament addressed by St Paul to the Christian community at Corinth.

Corio Bay /ˌkɒriou 'beɪ/, *n.* the western arm of Port Phillip Bay, Vic, on which Geelong is situated.

Coriolanus /ˌkɒriəˈleɪnəs/, *n.* **Gaius** (or **Gnaeus**) **Marcius** /ˌgaɪəs/ or /ˌnaɪəs 'maːsiəs/, a legendary Roman general of the fifth century BC who, in revenge for being exiled, led an army against Rome, but was turned back by the appeals of his mother and his wife.

Coriolis force /ˌkɒriˌoʊləs 'fɔːs/, *n. Maths, Phys.* an abstract mathematical force that seems to act on objects moving relative to the rotating earth, and causes the direction of the trade winds and the deflection of projectiles.

cork¹ /kɔk/, *n.* **1.** the outer bark of a tree (the **cork oak**), used for making stoppers of bottles, floats, etc. **2.** a piece of cork, or other material (as rubber), used as a stopper for a bottle, etc. **3.** a small float to buoy up a fishing line or to show when a fish bites. **4.** (*cap.*) a county in southern Republic of Ireland, in Munster province. Pop. 412 623 (1981); 7462 km². ◇*v.t.* **5.** to stop with, or as with, a cork (oft. fol. by *up*). [Sp *alcorque* shoe with cork, from Ar, from L: oak]

cork² /kɔk/, *v.i.* to receive a hit on: *to cork your knee*.

corkage /'kɔkɪdʒ/, *n.* a charge made by a restaurant, etc., for serving liquor brought in by the customer.

corker /'kɔkə/, *n.* **1.** something striking or astonishing. **2.** something very good of its kind: *That new boat's a corker*.

corkscrew /'kɔkskru/, *n.* **1.** a spiral instrument with a sharp point and a handle, for pulling corks from bottles. ◇*adj.* **2.** looking like a corkscrew; helical; spiral: *a corkscrew dive*. ◇*v.i.* **3.** to move in a spiral or zigzag course.

corm /kɔm/, *n. Bot.* a short, swollen upright stem-base in which food is stored, as in the gladiolus. [NL *cormus*, from Gk *kormós* tree trunk with boughs lopped off]

cormorant /'kɔmərənt/, *n.* **1.** a large, waterbird with webbed toes, which is believed to have a big appetite. **2.** a greedy person. ◇*adj.* **3.** greedy; rapacious; insatiable. [ME, from OF *corp* raven + *marenc* marine]

corn¹ /kɔn/, *n.* **1.** the seed of various grain plants, esp. wheat in England, oats in Scotland and Ireland, and maize in North America and Australia. **2.** a grain plant. **3.** a single seed of the grain plants. **4.** *Colloq.* a trite or sentimental writing or style. ◇*v.t.* **5.** to preserve with salt or pickle in brine: *corned beef*. [OE]

corn² /kɔn/, *n.* **1.** a hard, painful growth of skin, esp. on the toes or feet. **2. tread on someone's corns**, to hurt someone's feelings. [OF: horn, from L *cornū*]

corncob /'kɔnkɒb/, *n.* **1.** the elongated woody core of an ear of maize. **2.** a tobacco pipe with a bowl made of this.

cornea /'kɔniə/, *n., pl.* **-neas** /-niəz/, **-neae** /-nii/. the transparent outer covering of the eye, covering the iris and the pupil. [L: horny] **— corneal**, *adj.*

cornelian /kɔˈniliən/, *n.* → **carnelian**.

corner /'kɔnə/, *n.* **1.** a place where two lines or surfaces meet and form an angle. **2.** the space between these lines or surfaces; angle: *the corner of a room; The boxer went to his corner to rest*. **3.** a projecting angle: *This table has sharp corners*. **4.** the place where two streets meet. **5.** a remote or secret place: *to whisper*

corner *in corners.* **6.** an awkward or difficult position: *a tight corner.* **7.** a region; quarter: *all corners of the earth.* **8.** *Soccer, Hockey, etc.* a free kick or hit from the corner of the field. ◇**9.** Some special uses are:
cut corners, 1. to do something with as little time, effort, or money as possible: *Don't cut corners if you want to do it well.* **2.** to bypass an official procedure, or the like: *You can cut corners if you go straight to the manager.*
the Corner, Also, **Corner country.** the land where the borders of Qld, SA, and NSW meet.
turn the corner, to begin to get well; improve.
round the corner, very close; within walking distance.
◇*v.t.* **10.** to place in or drive into, or as into, a corner: *The police cornered the man; Lack of money will corner him in the end.* **11.** to get control of (a stock, etc.): *to corner the market.* ◇*v.i.* **12.** (of a car), to turn a corner, esp. at speed: *This car corners well at 60 km/h.* ◇*adj.* **13.** situated at a junction of two roads: *a corner shop.* **14.** made to be fitted or used in a corner: *a corner table.* [ME, from L: horn, corner]

cornerstone /ˈkɔnəstoʊn/, *n.* **1.** a stone built into a corner of the foundation of an important building as the official start of building, usu. laid with formal ceremonies. **2.** someone or something of basic importance.

cornet /ˈkɔnət/, *n.* **1.** a wind instrument similar to the trumpet, but smaller and with a mellower sound. **2.** a little cone of paper twisted at the end, used for holding sweets, etc. **3.** a cone, as for ice-cream. [ME, from OF, from L: horn]

cornflour /ˈkɔnflaʊə/, *n.* a starch, or starchy flour, made from maize, rice, or other grain, used as a thickening agent in cooking.

Cornforth /ˈkɔnfəθ/, *n.* **Sir John Warcup**, born 1917, Australian scientist working in England; shared 1975 Nobel prize for chemistry.

cornice /ˈkɔnəs/, *n., v.,* **-niced, -nicing.** ◇*n.* **1.** *Archit.* a horizontal moulded projection which crowns or finishes a wall, building, etc. **2.** a moulding between the walls and ceiling of a room. [F, from It, from MGk: summit, Gk: anything curved or bent]

Corn Law, *n. Eng Hist.* any one of a series of laws regulating the home and foreign grain trade, the last of which was repealed in 1846.

cornstalk /ˈkɔnstɔk/, *n.* **1.** the stalk or stem of corn. **2.** *Colloq.* a person native to or living in NSW. **3.** *Colloq.* a tall, thin person. **4.** *Obs. Colloq.* a native-born Australian, usu. thought of as taller and thinner than the immigrant.

cornucopia /ˌkɔnjəˈkoʊpiə/, *n.* **1.** (a representation of) the mythical horn of the goat Amalthaea, which suckled Zeus, represented as overflowing with flowers, fruit, etc., and symbolising plenty. **2.** an overflowing supply of anything. [L *cornū cōpiae* horn of plenty] **– cornucopian,** *adj.*

Cornwall /ˈkɔnwəl/, *n.* a county in southwestern England; includes the Scilly Isles. Pop. 448 200 (1986); 3515 km². Administrative Centre: Truro.

corny /ˈkɔni/, *adj.,* **-nier, -niest. 1.** hackneyed; lacking subtlety: *a corny joke.* **2.** sentimental; mawkish.

corolla /kəˈrɒlə/, *n.* the petals of a flower collectively. [L: garland, little crown]

corollary /kəˈrɒləri/, *n., pl.* **-ries. 1.** a proposition that follows, without needing further proof, from one that has already been proved. **2.** something that follows naturally from something else; natural consequence or result. [ME, from LL: corollary, L: gift, orig. garland]

corona /kəˈroʊnə/, *n., pl.* **-nas, -nae** /-ni/. **1.** a colored circle of light seen round the sun or moon, caused by the diffraction of light by water drops in the earth's atmosphere. See **halo** (def. 3). **2.** the outer part of the sun's atmosphere, seen as a shining circle around the sun during an eclipse. **3.** *Bot.* a crownlike part, esp. on the inner side of a corolla, as in the narcissus. **4.** *Elect.* a discharge often visible at the surface of a conductor. [L: garland]

coronary /ˈkɒrənri/, *adj.* **1.** of or like a crown. **2.** *Anat.* **a.** encircling like a crown, as certain blood vessels. **b.** relating to the arteries which supply the heart tissues and which originate in the root of the aorta. ◇*n.* **3.** a heart attack. [L]

coronary occlusion, *n.* → **coronary thrombosis.**

coronary thrombosis, *n.* the blocking of a coronary arterial branch by a blood clot within the vessel, usu. at a place narrowed by arteriosclerosis.

coronation /kɒrəˈneɪʃən/, *n.* the act or ceremony of crowning a king or queen.

coroner /ˈkɒrənə/, *n.* an officer whose chief duty is to investigate by inquest (often before a **coroner's jury**) any death not clearly due to natural causes. [ME, from AF: officer of the crown]

coronet /ˈkɒrənət/, *n.* **1.** a small crown worn by peers or members of the nobility. **2.** a crownlike ornament for the head, as of gold or jewels. [OF: little crown]

coronial /kəˈroʊniəl/, *adj.* of or relating to a coroner: *a coronial court.*

Corot /kɒˈroʊ/, *n.* **Jean Baptiste Camille** /ʒɒ batist kaˈmijə/, 1796–1875, French landscape painter.

Corp, *Abbrev.* **1.** corporal. **2.** corporation. Also, **corp.**

corpora /ˈkɔpərə/, *n.* plural of **corpus.**

corporal[1] /ˈkɔpərəl/, *adj.* of the human body; bodily; physical: *corporal punishment.* [ME, from L *corporālis*] **– corporality,** *n.*

corporal[2] /ˈkɔpərəl, -prəl/, *n. Mil.* See Appendix. [F, from It *caporale,* from L: head]

corporate /ˈkɔpərət, -prət/, *adj.* **1.** of or forming a corporation: *a corporate body.* **2.** united in one body. **3.** shared by all persons in a group: *corporate ownership.* [L: formed into a body]

corporation /kɔpəˈreɪʃən/, *n.* **1.** an association of individuals, created by law or under authority of law, having a continuous existence apart from that of its members, and powers and liabilities distinct from those of its members. **2.** any group of people united, or regarded as united, in one body. **3.** *Colloq.* a large pot belly.

corporeal /kɔ'pɔriəl/, *adj.* **1.** having the nature of the physical body; bodily. **2.** having the nature of matter; material; tangible: *corporeal property.* [L *corporeus* of the nature of body + -AL¹] – **corporeality, corporealness,** *n.*

corps /'kɔ:/, *n., pl.* **corps** /kɔz/. **1.** a military unit of ground combat forces consisting of two or more divisions and other troops. **2.** a group of people associated or acting together: *the press corps; the diplomatic corps.* [F]

corpse /'kɔps/, *n.* a dead body, usu. of a human being.

corpulence /'kɔpjələns/, *n.* bulkiness or largeness of body; fatness. Also, **corpulency.** [ME, from F, from L] – **corpulent,** *adj.*

corpus /'kɔpəs/, *n., pl.* **-pora** /-pərə/. **1.** a large or complete collection of writings, laws, etc. **2.** the main part; the bulk. [L]

corpuscle /'kɔpəsəl/, *n.* **1.** one of the very small bodies in the blood (**blood corpuscles,** both red and white), the lymph (**lymph corpuscles,** white only), etc. **2.** a very small particle. Also, **corpuscule** /kɔ'pʌskjul/. [L: a little body] – **corpuscular,** *adj.*

corpus delicti /kɔpəs də'lɪktaɪ/, *n.* the group of facts which together make up a criminal offence. [L: body of the transgression]

corral /kɔ'ral/, *n., v.,* **-ralled, -ralling.** ◇*n.* **1.** a pen or enclosure for horses, cattle, etc. **2.** a defensive enclosure formed by a ring of wagons. ◇*v.t.* **3.** to confine in, or as in, a corral. [Sp: enclosed yard, from *corro* a ring]

correct /kə'rekt/, *v.t.* **1.** to set right; remove the mistakes or faults of: *Susan corrected her sums in class; to correct the wheel alignment.* **2.** to point out the errors in: *to correct someone's manners.* **3.** to scold (a child, etc.) in order to improve behavior. **4.** to counteract the working or effect of (something hurtful). **5.** *Phys.* to change or adjust so as to make conform with a standard or some desired condition: *to correct a reading to allow for zero error, atmospheric pressure, etc.* ◇*adj.* **6.** agreeing in fact or truth; free from error, accurate: *a correct statement.* **7.** agreeing with an accepted standard; proper: *correct behavior.* [ME, from L: made straight, directed] – **corrective,** *adj.*

correction /kə'rekʃən/, *n.* **1.** the act of correcting. **2.** something used to replace what is wrong; emendation: *The corrections covered the page.* **3. a.** a rebuke; chastisement; discipline; reproof. **b.** (*as a euphemism*) punishment (of prisoners, etc.). **4.** *Phys.* a number or quantity added to or subtracted from a calculation or reading to make it more accurate. – **correctional,** *adj.*

Correggio /kɔ'redʒoʊ/, *n.* **Antonio Allegri da** /an,tounjou a'leɪgri da/, 1494-1534, Italian painter.

correlate /'kɔrəleɪt/, *v.,* **-lated, -lating,** *n.* ◇*v.t.* **1.** to place in or bring into a mutual relationship; establish in orderly connection: *to correlate one set of figures with another.* ◇*v.i.* **2.** to have a mutual relation; stand in correlation: *These figures do not correlate easily with those.* ◇*n.* **3.** either of two related things, esp. when one implies the other: *Lung cancer is thought to be a correlate of smoking.* [COR- + RELATE]

correlation /kɔrə'leɪʃən/, *n.* **1.** (the bringing into) mutual relation of two or more things, parts, etc. **2.** *Stats.* the degree of relationship of two attributes or measurements on the same group of elements.

correlative /kɔ'relətɪv/, *adj.* mutually related, so that each suggests or adds meaning to the other.

correspond /kɔrə'spɒnd/, *v.i.* **1.** to be in agreement or conformity (oft. fol. by *with* or *to*): *His words and actions do not correspond.* **2.** to match; be similar or analogous; be equivalent in function, position, amount, etc. (fol. by *to*): *Our Australian bush corresponds to the European woodland.* **3.** to communicate by exchange of letters. [L *cor-* COR- + *rēspondēre* answer] – **corresponding,** *adj.*

correspondence /kɔrə'spɒndəns/, *n.* Also, **correspondency. 1.** the act or fact of corresponding. **2.** agreement; conformity. **3.** relation, similarity or analogy. **4.** communication by exchange of letters. **5.** (a series of) letters between correspondents.

correspondent /kɔrə'spɒndənt/, *n.* **1.** someone who communicates by letters. **2.** a person employed to contribute news, etc., regularly from a distant place. **3.** one who has regular business relations with another, esp. at a distance. **4.** a thing that corresponds to something else. ◇*adj.* **5.** matching.

corresponding angles, *n.pl.* a pair of equal angles formed by the intersection of two parallel lines with a transversal, such that both angles lie on the same side of the transversal and are similarly placed with respect to the parallel lines.

corridor /'kɔrədɔ/, *n.* **1.** a passage connecting parts of a building. **2.** a passage into which several rooms, apartments, or railway compartments open. **3.** a narrow strip of land owned by an inland country, giving it an outlet to the sea: *the Polish corridor.* [F: long passageway, from It *corridore* covered way, from Sp, from L: run]

Corriedale /'kɔrədeɪl/, *n.* a white-faced breed of sheep, orig. developed in NZ. [from *Corriedale,* the property where it was developed]

corroborate /kə'rɒbəreɪt/, *v.t.,* **-rated -rating.** to make more certain; confirm: *The witness's story corroborates what the policeman said.* [L: strengthened] – **corroborative, corroboratory,** *adj.* – **corroborator,** *n.*

corroboration /kərɒbə'reɪʃən/, *n.* **1.** the act of corroborating. **2.** a corroboratory fact, statement, etc. **3.** *Law.* independent evidence which connects an accused person with a crime.

corroboree /kə'rɒbəri/, *n.* **1.** an Aboriginal gathering, mostly functioning as a social, informal occasion for dancing and

corroboree

singing, but also as an elaborate religious ceremony. 2. *Colloq.* any large or noisy gathering. [Aboriginal]

corrode /kə'roud/, v., **-roded, -roding.**
◇v.t. 1. to eat away gradually. 2. *Chem.* to eat away the surface of (metal) by chemical action. ◇v.i. 3. to become corroded. [L: gnaw away] —**corrodible**, adj.

corrosion /kə'rouʒən/, n. the act, process, or product of corroding. [L]

corrosive /kə'rousɪv/, n., adj. (something) having the quality of corroding or eating away.

corrugate /'kɒrəgeɪt/, v.i., v.t., **-gating.** to wrinkle; fold in ripples. [L: wrinkled] —**corrugation**, n.

corrugated iron, /ˌkɒrəgeɪtəd 'aɪən/, n. sheet iron or steel formed into wavy ridges.

corrupt /kə'rʌpt/, adj. 1. dishonest; guilty of dishonesty, esp. involving bribery: *a corrupt judge*. 2. of low character; wicked; evil. 3. infected or rotting. 4. inaccurate; containing mistakes or changes: *a corrupt text of Shakespeare*. 5. *Computers.* (of data or programs) damaged by errors or electrical interference. ◇v.t. 6. to make dishonest, disloyal, or unfair, esp. by bribery. 7. to lower the morals of. 8. to infect, spoil or rot. 9. to change (a language, text, etc.) for the worse; debase. [ME, from L: broken in pieces, destroyed] —**corrupter**, n. —**corruptive**, adj.

corruptible /kə'rʌptəbəl/, adj. able to be corrupted.

corruption /kə'rʌpʃən/, n. 1. the act or result of corrupting. 2. the condition of being corrupt; depravity. 3. bribery. 4. decay.

corsage /kɔ'sɑʒ/, n. a small bunch of flowers, esp. worn pinned to a dress. [F: body]

corsair /'kɔseə/, n. a pirate or pirate ship. [F, from F: runner, from L: course]

corset /'kɔsət/, n. 1. (*oft. pl.*) a tight, stiffened undergarment worn by women to give shape and support to the body; stays. 2. a similar garment worn by either sex for support, as of an injured spine. [ME, from F] —**corsetry**, n.

Corsica /'kɔsɪkə/, n. an island in the Mediterranean, south-east of and forming, with a number of islets, a region of France. Pop. 248 700 (1986 est.); 8682 km². *Cap.*: Ajaccio. French, **Corse**. —**Corsican**, adj., n.

cortege /kɔ'teɪʒ, -'teɪʒ/, n. 1. a procession. 2. a group of attendants; retinue. Also, **cortège**. [F, from It: court]

Cortés /'kɔtez/, n. **Hernando** /eə'nandoʊ/ or **Hernán** /eə'nan/, 1485–1547, Spanish conqueror of Mexico. Also, **Cortez**.

cortex /'kɔteks/, n., pl. **-tices** /-təsiz/. 1. *Bot.* the inner bark. 2. *Anat., Zool.* the outer layer of some organs, esp. that of the grey matter of the brain. [L: bark, rind, shell] —**cortical**, adj.

corticate /'kɔtəkət, -keɪt/, adj. *Bot.* having a cortex. Also, **corticated**. [L: having bark]

cortisone /'kɔtəzoʊn/, n. a hormone from the adrenal cortex used in treating shock, inflammation, arthritic disease, etc.

corundum /kə'rʌndəm/, n. a hard mineral, aluminium oxide, Al_2O_3, including types such as the ruby and sapphire, valuable as gems, and other types used as powder for polishing. [Indian (Tamil) *kurundam*, from Skt: ruby]

coruscate /'kɒrəskeɪt/, v.i., **-cated, -cating.** to flash light; sparkle. [L: moved quickly, flashed] —**coruscation**, n.

corvée /'kɔveɪ/, n. 1. *Hist.* labor owed to a feudal lord. 2. forced labor; unpaid work done as tax. [F, from L: bring together by entreaty]

corvette /kɔ'vet/, n. *Navy.* small, fast, lightly armed, escort vessel. [F, from L: ship of burden]

cos¹ /kɒs/, n. kind of lettuce with long, coarse, crisp leaves.

cos² /kɒz/, n. *Maths.* the sine of the complement of a given angle. [abbrev.]

Cosa Nostra /ˌkoʊzə 'nɒstrə/, n. a criminal organisation in the US, the structure of which is based on the Sicilian Mafia. [It: our thing]

cosec /'koʊsek/, n. *Maths.* the secant of the complement of a given angle. [abbrev. from *cosecant*]

coset /'koʊset/, n. *Maths.* a set that when added to another set produces a specified larger set.

cosh /kɒʃ/, n. 1. a blunt weapon. ◇v.t. 2. to hit with a cosh.

cosine /'koʊsaɪn/, n. *Maths.* → **cos²**.

cosmetic /kɒz'metɪk/, n., adj. (a substance) meant to improve the health or beauty of the face or skin. [Gk: relating to adornment] —**cosmetically**, adv.

cosmic /'kɒzmɪk/, adj. 1. of or relating to the cosmos. 2. universal; infinite. 3. forming part of the physical universe, esp. beyond Earth. 4. orderly; harmonious. [Gk: of the world] —**cosmically**, adv.

cosmo-, a word part meaning 'cosmos'. Also, **cosm-**.

cosmography /kɒz'mɒgrəfi/, n., pl. **-phies.** a description or picture of the world or universe. [Gk: description of the world] —**cosmographer**, n. —**cosmographic, cosmographical**, adj.

cosmology /kɒz'mɒlədʒi/, n. *Philos.* the study or theory of the origin, structure, workings of the universe. —**cosmological, cosmologic**, adj. —**cosmologist**, n.

cosmonaut /'kɒzmənɔt/, n. → **astronaut**. [COSMO- + Gk *nautēs* sailor]

cosmopolitan /ˌkɒzmə'pɒlətn/, adj. 1. belonging to all parts of the world. 2. *Bot., Zool.* found worldwide. 3. free from local or national ideas or loyalties; at home all over world.

cosmos /'kɒzmɒs/, n. 1. the physical universe. 2. the world or universe in order and harmony. See **chaos** (def. 2). 3. a complete and ordered system. [NL, from Gk *kósmos* order, form, the world or universe as an ordered whole, ornament]

Cossack /'kɒsæk/, *n.* one of a people now living mainly in the coastal areas of the Black and Azov seas, noted as horsemen, who served under the Russian tsars.

cosset /'kɒsət/, *v.t.* to treat as a pet; pamper. [cf. OE *cossetung* kissing]

cossie /'kɒzi/, *n. Colloq.* → **swimsuit**. Also, **cozzie**.

cost /kɒst/, *n., v.,* **cost** (or (def. 8) **costed**, **costing**. ◇*n.* 1. the price paid to get, make, do, or maintain something. 2. loss; expense: *managed at great cost to her health.* 3. the spending of money, time, labor, trouble, etc. 4. (*pl.*) *Law.* the expenses of legal action, esp. when ordered to be paid by the loser to the winner. 5. **at all costs**, or **at any cost**, whatever the cost. ◇*v.t.* 6. to require the spending of money, time, labor, etc., for; be got for price of: *It cost 50 cents.* 7. to result in a particular loss: *It may cost him his life.* 8. to find out or guess the costs of. [ME, from OF, from L: stand together]

costal /'kɒstl/, *adj.* relating to the ribs or side of body: *the costal nerves.* [LL]

Costa Rica /ˌkɒstə 'rikə/, *n.* a republic in Central America, on the Pacific Ocean and the Caribbean Sea; a Spanish colony before independence in 1821. Pop. 2 416 809 (1984). 50 700 km². *Language:* Spanish. *Currency:* colón. *Cap.:* San José. — **Costa Rican**, *n., adj.*

costermonger /'kɒstəmʌŋɡə/, *n. Brit.* someone who sells fruit, fish, etc., esp. from a barrow. Also, **coster**.

costive /'kɒstɪv/, *adj.* constipated. [OF, from L]

costly /'kɒstli/, *adj.,* **-lier, -liest. 1.** of high price. **2.** *Archaic.* splendid; lavish. — **costliness**, *n.*

costo-, a word part meaning 'rib'. [combining form representing L *costa*]

cost of living, *n.* the average retail prices of food, clothing, and other needs, paid by a person, family, etc., in order to live at their usual standard.

cost price, *n.* 1. the price at which goods are bought for resale. 2. the cost of production.

cost-push inflation, *n.* inflation caused by higher costs, as for wages or raw materials. See **demand-pull inflation**.

costume /'kɒstium/, *n., v.,* **-tumed, -tuming.** ◇*n.* 1. a style of clothing, etc., esp. of a particular nation, group of people, period of history, etc.: *Greek national costume.* 2. clothing or an outfit representing an animal, character, theme, etc.: *a gorilla costume; a clown's costume.* 3. clothes for a particular time or activity: *a swimming costume.* ◇*v.t.* 4. to dress; provide costumes for: *to costume a play.* [F, from It: habit, fashion, from L: custom]

costume jewellery, *n.* decorative jewellery of little monetary value.

cosy /'kouzi/, *adj.,* **-sier, -siest,** *n., pl.* **-sies.** ◇*adj.* 1. comfortable; snug. ◇*n.* 2. a cover for keeping something warm: *tea cosy.* [orig. Scot; probably from Scand] — **cosily**, *adv.* — **cosiness**, *n.*

cot[1] /kɒt/, *n.* 1. a child's bed with enclosed sides. 2. a light or folding bed, esp. of canvas. [Anglo-Ind, from Hindi]

cot[2] /kɒt/, *n. Poet.* 1. a cottage; hut. 2. → **cote.** [OE]

cot[3] /kɒt/, *n. Maths.* → **cotan.** [abbrev.]

cotan /'koutæn/, *n. Maths.* the tangent of the complement of a given angle. Also, **cot** [abbrev. from *cotangent*]

cot case, *n. Colloq.* someone tired, drunk, or ill, and fit only for bed.

cot death, *n.* → **sudden infant death syndrome**.

cote /kout/, *n.* a shelter for doves, pigeons, sheep, etc. [OE]

Côte d'Ivoire /kout di'vwa/, *n.* a republic on the west coast of Africa, bordered by Ghana, Liberia, Guinea, Mali and Burkina Faso. Pop. 9 810 000 (1985 est.); 322 462 km². *Languages:* French, also local dialects such as Akan, Mossi, Dyola and Malinke. *Currency:* franc. *Cap.:* Abidjan (legislative). *Cap. designate:* Yamoussoukro (administrative). Formerly, **the Ivory Coast**.

coterie /'koutəri/, *n.* a close group of friends or people with common interests; clique. [F: set, association of people]

Cotopaxi /ˌkɒtə'pæksi/, *n.* a volcano in central Ecuador, in the Andes; the highest known active volcano in the world. 5943 m.

cottage /'kɒtɪdʒ/, *n.* a small one-storey house.

cottage cheese, *n.* a soft white lumpy cheese made from skimmed milk.

cottage industry, *n.* an industry, e.g. knitting, pottery, or weaving, done in the home of the worker.

cotter pin /'kɒtə pɪ/, *n.* a pin with a split end which is spread after being pushed through a hole, to prevent it from coming loose.

cotton /'kɒtn/, *n.* 1. the soft white hairs of fibres on the seeds of certain plants. 2. a plant yielding cotton. 3. cloth, thread, etc., made of cotton. ◇*v.i.* 4. *Colloq.* to understand; grasp idea (oft. fol. by *on*): *She cottons on quickly.* [ME, from OF, from It, from Ar]

cotton bud, *n.* a small thin stick with the ends wound with cottonwool, used for applying eye make-up, etc. [Trademark]

cottonbush /'kɒtnbʊʃ/, *n.* any of several unrelated plants bearing cotton-like hairs, esp. when used for cattle feed.

cottonwood /'kɒtnwʊd/, *n.* 1. a shrub of eastern Australia, with downy leaves. 2. → **poplar**.

cottonwool /ˌkɒtn'wʊl/, *n.* 1. raw cotton with the natural wax removed, used for dressing wounds, removing make-up, etc. 2. raw cotton.

cotyledon /ˌkɒtə'lidn/, *n. Bot.* the first or primitive leaf of the embryo of seed (flowering) plants. [L: *navelwort* (a plant), from Gk: any cup-shaped hollow]

couch[1] /kautʃ/, *n.* 1. an upholstered seat for two or more people, usu. with a back and arm-

couch /kʊtʃ/, *n.* **1.** to force air from the lungs suddenly and noisily. ◊*v.t.* **1.** to put into words; express: *couched in official terms.* **5.** to lay or put down. ◊*v.i.* **6.** to lie at rest. **7.** to lie in hiding; lurk. [ME, from L: lay in its place]

couch² /kutʃ/, *n.* any of various lawn grasses with long creeping roots. [var. *quitch*, from OE *cwice*; akin to QUICK, *adj.*]

cougar /ˈkuːɡə/, *n.* → **puma.** [F, from NL, from SAmer Indian]

cough /kɒf/, *v.i.* **1.** to force air from the lungs suddenly and noisily. ◊*v.t.* **2.** to drive out by coughing (fol. by *up* or *out*): *to cough up blood.* ◊*v.* **3. cough up,** *Colloq.* to give; hand over. ◊*n.* **4.** the act or sound of coughing. **5.** an illness marked by coughing. [OE *cohhetan* cough]

could /kʊd/, *v.* past tense of **can¹.** [OE]

couldn't /ˈkʊdnt/, *v.* contraction of **could not.**

coulomb /ˈkuːlɒm/, *n.* the derived SI unit of electric charge, defined as the quantity of electricity transported in 1 ampere in 1 second. *Symbol:* C [named after CA de *Coulomb*, 1736–1806, French physicist]

Coulomb's Law, *n. Phys.* the principle that the force pulling together or pushing apart two electrically charged bodies is proportional to the product of the charges, and inversely proportional to the square of the distance between them.

council /ˈkaʊnsəl/, *n.* **1.** a gathering of people called or meeting to discuss, decide, or advise on certain matters. **2.** the local government of a city, town, or other area. [ME, from OF, from L: assembly]

Council for Civil Liberties, *n.* an Australian non-government body established in 1963 to provide information and discussion on legal matters and to work to ensure the upholding of such matters as freedom of speech.

councillor /ˈkaʊnsələ/, *n.* a member of a council.

council of war, *n.* **1.** a meeting of high-ranking military or naval officers to talk about war problems and plans. **2.** any meeting to make important plans.

counsel /ˈkaʊnsəl/, *n., v.,* **-selled, -selling.** ◊*n.* **1.** advice. **2.** an exchange of opinions to decide or plan something: *to take counsel with a friend.* **3.** a purpose; plan. **4.** a barrister; barristers (collectively). **5. keep one's own counsel,** to keep secret one's opinion or plans. ◊*v.t.* **6.** to advise. **7.** to encourage the doing of; recommend (a plan, etc.) [ME, from OF, from L: consultation, plan]

counsellor /ˈkaʊnsələ/, *n.* someone who counsels or advises, esp. a psychologist: *school counsellor; marriage guidance counsellor.*

count¹ /kaʊnt/, *v.t.* **1.** to check over one by one (the objects of a group, etc.) to find out how many there are; add up. **2.** to calculate; compute. **3.** to list or name the numbers up to. **4.** to include. **5.** to believe to be: *He counts himself lucky.* ◊*v.i.* **6.** to name numbers or objects in order. **7.** to depend or rely (fol. by *on* or *upon*). **8.** to have importance or value. **9.** to be worth; amount to (oft. fol. by *for*). ◊*v.* **10. count out,** to leave out; disregard: *Count me out.* ◊*n.* **11.** the act of counting; numbering; adding up. **12.** the sum or total. **13. on all counts,** in every way. [ME, from OF, from L: calculate, reckon]

count² /kaʊnt/, *n.* (in some European countries) a nobleman corresponding in rank to a British earl. [AF, from L: companion]

countdown /ˈkaʊntdaʊn/, *n.* the final backwards count of time before the firing of a rocket, letting off an explosive, etc., ending with the firing or explosion at zero.

countenance /ˈkaʊntənəns/, *n., v.,* **-nanced, -nancing.** ◊*n.* **1.** appearance, esp. the look or expression of a face. **2.** the face; visage. **3.** encouragement; support. **4. in countenance,** unembarrassed. **5. out of countenance,** disconcerted. ◊*v.t.* **6.** to encourage; support. **7.** to put up with; permit. [ME, from OF: bearing, from ML: demeanor, L: restraint]

counter¹ /ˈkaʊntə/, *n.* **1.** a shelf, bar or other surface at which goods are sold, people eat or drink, etc. **2. under the counter, a.** not on show; available only on request. **b.** secretly. **3.** anything used in keeping count, as in games. **4.** an imitation coin; token. [ME, from AF: counting house, counting table, from OF: count]

counter² /ˈkaʊntə/, *n.* someone or something that counts.

counter³ /ˈkaʊntə/, *adv.* **1.** in the wrong way; in the opposite direction. **2.** in opposition: *to run counter to the rules.* ◊*adj.* **3.** opposite; opposed. ◊*n.* **4.** something opposite to, against or in response to something else. ◊*v.t.* **5.** to go against; oppose. **6.** to meet or answer (a move, blow, etc.) by another in return. ◊*v.i.* **7.** to make an answering or opposing move. [F, from L *contrā*, in opposition, against]

counter-, a combining form of **counter³,** as in *counteract.*

counteract /kaʊntərˈækt/, *v.t.* to act against; prevent the effect of by opposite action. **–counteraction,** *n.* **–counteractive,** *adj.*

counterattack /ˈkaʊntərətæk/, *n.;* /kaʊntərəˈtæk/, *v.* ◊*n.* **1.** an attack made in response or opposition to another attack. ◊*v.i., v.t.* **2.** to make a counterattack (against).

counterbalance /ˈkaʊntəbæləns/, *n.;* /kaʊntəˈbæləns/, *v.,* **-anced, -ancing.** ◊*n.* **1.** a weight balancing another. ◊*v.t.* **2.** to weigh or act against with equal force.

counter culture, *n.* a small group within a society which is opposed to that society's values and lifestyle.

counterespionage /ˌkaʊntərˈɛspiənaʒ, -nadʒ/, *n.* action against enemy espionage.

counterfeit /ˈkaʊntəfət, -fit/, *adj.* **1.** made to imitate something else, so as to deceive; not

counterfeit genuine: *counterfeit coins.* **2.** pretended: *counterfeit grief.* ◇*n.* **3.** an imitation; forgery. ◇*v.t.* **4.** to look like or imitate. ◇*v.i.* **5.** to pretend. [ME from OF: imitated, from *contre* CONTRA- + *faire* do (from L)] —**counterfeiter**, *n.*

counterintelligence /ˌkaʊntərɪn'telədʒəns/, *n.* the use of codes, censorship, etc., to prevent an enemy getting information.

countermand /ˌkaʊntə'mænd, -'mɑnd/, *v.t.* **1.** to cancel (a command, order, etc.). **2.** to recall or stop by another order. ◇*n.* **3.** a command or order cancelling an earlier one. [ME, from OF *contre* CONTRA- + *mander* command, (from L: enjoin)]

counterpane /'kaʊntəpeɪn/, *n.* a bedspread. [var. of obs. *counterpoint* cover, from OF]

counterpart /'kaʊntəpɑt/, *n.* one of two things or people that fit, suit, look like, or match each other.

counterpoint /'kaʊntəpɔɪnt/, *n. Music.* **1.** the art of combining different tunes in harmony. **2.** a melody composed to be combined with another melody. [F *contrepoint*, from ML (*cantus*) *contrā punctus* (song) pointed against]

counterproductive /ˌkaʊntəprə'dʌktɪv/, *adj.* reducing success or effectiveness.

counter-revolution /ˌkaʊntə-revə'luʃən/, *n.* a revolution against a government recently established by a revolution. —**counter-revolutionary**, *adj.*, *n.*

countersign /'kaʊntəsaɪn/, *n.*; /'kaʊntəsaɪn, kaʊntə'saɪn/, *v.* ◇*n.* **1.** *Mil.* a password or signal given in order to pass a guard. ◇*v.t.* **2.** to sign (a document) in addition to another signature, esp. in confirmation. [OF, from It] —**countersignature**, *n.*

countertenor /'kaʊntətɛnə/, *n.* (a singer with) an adult male voice higher than the tenor.

counterweight /'kaʊntəweɪt/, *n.* a counterbalance. —**counterweighted**, *adj.*

countess /'kaʊntɪs/, *n.* **1.** the wife or widow of a European count or British earl. **2.** a woman whose rank is equal to a count or earl. [ME, from OF, from LL: companion (female)]

countless /'kaʊntləs/, *adj.* too many to count.

country /'kʌntri/, *n., pl.* -**tries**, *adj.* ◇*n.* **1.** an area of land; region. **2.** a large land area separated by geographical conditions or by a particular population. **3.** the land area or people of a nation or state. **4.** the land of which a person is a citizen or where a person was born. **5.** land in its natural condition, or with forests, farms, small towns, etc., as opposed to large towns or cities. **6. go to the country**, to call an election. ◇*adj.* **7.** unsophisticated: *country manners.* [ME, from OF, from LL: what lies opposite, from L]

countryman /'kʌntrimən/, *n., pl.* -**men**. **1.** a person from one's own country. **2.** a man who lives in the country.

Country Party, *n.* former name of the **National Party**.

countryside /'kʌntrisaɪd/, *n.* the country (def. 5) or the people who live there.

Country Women's Association, *n.* an organisation without political or religious affiliations, first established in NSW in 1922, and now operating in all states; provides services for country women and children. Also, **CWA**

county /'kaʊnti/, *n.* **1.** one of the larger divisions of local government. **2.** the people living in a county, esp. (in Britain) land-owning gentry. [ME, from OF, from LL: COUNT²]

County Court, *n.* (in Vic) an intermediate court, superior to a magistrate's court and inferior to the Supreme Court.

coup /ku/, *n., pl.* **coups** /kuz/. a plan carried out suddenly and successfully. [F, from LL: blow, from Gk]

coup de grâce /ku də 'gras/, *n.* **1.** a death-blow, e.g. a bullet in the head to make sure the executed person is dead. **2.** a finishing stroke. [F: stroke of mercy]

coup d'état /ku deɪ'tɑ/, *n.* a sudden takeover of government, esp. illegally or by force. [F: stroke of state]

coupe /ku'peɪ/, *n.* (a fruit dessert served in) a shallow glass or bowl. [OF, from LL *cuppa* cup]

coupé /'kupeɪ/, *n.* **1.** a two-door car often with front seats only. **2.** a short four-wheeled closed horse-drawn carriage. [F: cut]

Couperin /kupə'ræ̃/, *n.* **François** /frɒ̃'swɑ/, 1668-1733, French composer; noted for his organ and harpsichord works.

couple /'kʌpəl/, *n., v.,* -**led**, -**ling**. ◇*n.* **1.** a combination of two; a pair. **2.** two people who live together: *a married couple.* **3.** *Mech.* a pair of equal, parallel forces acting in opposite directions and tending to produce a circular movement. ◇*v.t., v.i.* **4.** to join; connect; link together (in a pair). [ME, from L: band, bond]

couplet /'kʌplət/, *n.* **1.** a pair of lines of poetry, esp. rhyming and of the same length. **2.** a pair; couple. [F: little couple]

coupling /'kʌplɪŋ/, *n.* **1.** the act of someone or something that joins or connects. **2.** a mechanical device joining parts or things together.

coupon /'kupɒn/, *n.* **1.** a ticket or card with some value, as allowing the holder to exchange it for goods or money. **2.** an order form for goods, esp. one cut from an advertisement. **3.** an entry form for competitions, etc. [F]

courage /'kʌrɪdʒ/, *n.* the ability to meet difficulties and danger firmly or without fear; bravery. [ME, from OF: heart, from L] —**courageous**, *adj.*

courgette /kɔ'ʒɛt/, *n.* →**zucchini**.

courier /'kʊriə/, *n.* **1.** a messenger. **2.** a person who makes arrangements for, or travels with, a group of tourists. **3.** a person who works for a courier service. [F, from It: runner, from L: run]

courier service, *n.* a company which provides a service collecting and delivering letters and parcels.

course /kɔs/, *n., v.*, **coursed, coursing.** ◇*n.* **1.** an onward movement. **2.** a path, way or channel along which anything moves: *the course of a stream; the course of a ship.* **3.** the ground, water, etc., on which a race is run, sailed, etc. **4.** a passing through time or stages; progress: *in the course of a year; during the course of a battle.* **5.** the usual order of events: *The disease must take its course; a matter of course.* **6.** a particular way of doing something. **7.** a set series: *a course of injections; the science course.* **8.** the part of a meal served at one time: *The main course was steak.* **9.** a horizontal row of stones, bricks, etc. in a wall. **10. in due course**, in order; at the right time. **11. of course**, certainly; obviously. ◇*v.t.* **12.** to run through or over. **13.** to chase; pursue. ◇*v.i.* **14.** to hunt (game) with dogs, esp. by sight and not by smell. **15.** to race greyhounds. **16.** to follow a course. **17.** to run; race. [F]

coursing /'kɔsɪŋ/, *n.* Brit. the sport of hunting hares, etc., with dogs that follow by sight rather than by smell.

court /kɔt/, *n.* **1.** an open space wholly or partly enclosed by a wall, buildings, etc. **2.** a short street. **3.** an area for playing tennis, etc. **4.** the palace of a king, queen, duke, etc. **5.** the family, advisers, etc., of a king, queen, etc. **6.** a formal gathering held by a king, etc. **7.** attention paid to someone to get favor, approval, etc.: *to pay court to a pretty woman.* **8.** *Law.* **a.** a place where trials are held, etc. **b.** the people officially gathered to decide a case. **c.** judge(s) sitting in court. **9. out of court**, without a hearing; privately. ◇*v.t.* **10.** to try to win the favor or love of. **11.** to try to get: *to court favor.* **12.** to encourage or lay oneself open to: *to court insults.* ◇*v.i.* **13.** to try to win someone's love; woo. [ME, from OF, from L: enclosure]

court card, *n.* a king, queen, or knave (jack) in a pack of playing cards.

courteous /'kɜtɪəs/, *adj.* well-mannered; polite. [ME, from OF: court]

courtesan /'kɔtəzæn/, *n.* **1.** a mistress (def. 4) of a king, nobleman, etc. **2.** a prostitute. [F, from It: woman of the court]

courtesy /'kɜtəsɪ/, *n., pl.* **-sies. 1.** (an instance of) good manners; politeness. **2.** permission or favor: *reprinted by courtesy of the author.* [ME, from OF: courteous]

courthouse /'kɔthaʊs/, *n.* a building in which courts of law are held.

courtier /'kɔtɪə/, *n.* someone in attendance at the court of a king, etc.

courtly /'kɔtlɪ/, *adj.*, **-lier, -liest.** polite; elegant; refined. **–courtliness**, *n.*

court martial, *n., pl.* **court martials, courts martial.** a court of naval, army, or airforce officers which tries charges under military law. **–court-martial**, *v.*

Court of Petty Sessions, *n.* (in ACT, WA and Tas) a magistrate's court.

Court of St James's, *n.* the official name of the British royal court, so called from St James's Palace, the former scene of royal receptions.

Court of Summary Jurisdiction, *n.* (in SA and NT) a magistrate's court.

courtroom /'kɔtrum/, *n.* a room in which a law court is held.

courtship /'kɔtʃɪp/, *n.* the act or period of courting.

court shoe, *n.* a woman's low-cut heeled shoe, without straps or laces.

courtyard /'kɔtjad/, *n.* an open space enclosed by walls or building.

cousin /'kʌzən/, *n.* **1.** the son or daughter of one's uncle or aunt. **2.** someone related through a shared ancestor. Cousins (def. 1) are also called **first cousins, full cousins**, or **cousins-german; second cousins** are the children of one of one's parents' first cousins, etc. The child of one's own first cousin is **(first) cousin once removed**, sometimes loosely called second cousin. **3.** any relation. **4.** a person or thing related to another by similarity, language, etc.: *our Canadian cousins.* [F, from L: mother's sister's child]

couture /ku'tjʊə/, *n.* dressmaking and design.

couturier /ku'tʊrɪə/, *n.* a person who designs, makes, and sells high-fashion clothes for women. [F: sewing] **–couturière**, *n.fem.*

covalency /koʊ'veɪlənsɪ/, *n.* the number of electron pairs that an atom can share with those which surround it. Also, **covalence** /koʊ'veɪəns/. **–covalent**, *adj.*

covalent bond, *n. Chem.* the bond formed by the sharing of electrons between two atoms, each of which gives an equal number of electrons. In the single covalent bond, two electrons are shared, in the double four, and in the triple six.

cove[1] /koʊv/ *n.* **1.** a small bay or inlet. **2.** a sheltered corner or hole, as in a mountain or cliffs. [OE *cofa* chamber]

cove[2] /koʊv/, *n.* **1.** *Colloq.* man: *an odd sort of cove.* **2.** the boss (def. 1), esp. the manager of a sheep station. [said to be from Romany *kova* creature]

coven /'kʌvən/, *n.* a gathering of witches. [var. of CONVENT]

covenant /'kʌvənənt/, *n.* **1.** an agreement between people; contract. **2.** *Theol.* an agreement made by God with man, as recorded in the Bible. **3.** *Law.* a formal sealed contract. ◇*v.t., v.i.* **4.** to promise by covenant. [ME, from OF, from L: agree] **–covenanter**, *n.*

Covent Garden /'kɒvənt, 'kʌv-/, *n.* a district in central London, noted for its former vegetable and flower market; site of the Royal Opera House (home of the Royal Ballet).

Coventry /'kɒvəntrɪ, 'kʌv-/, *n.* a city in England, in West Midlands; industrial centre; modern cathedral, built after the original was gutted in an air-raid during World War II. Pop. 322 573 (1981).

cover /'kʌvə/, *v.t.* **1.** to put something on or over a thing to protect or hide it. **2.** to lie over; occupy the surface of. **3.** to bring upon (oneself): *He covered himself with glory.* **4.** to shelter; protect. **5.** *Mil.* to protect (a person, military position, etc.) by taking a position from which one can shoot at any attackers. **6.** to hide. **7.** to spread over. **8.** to aim a gun, etc., at. **9.** to include; provide for; take in: *The book covers the whole French course.* **10.** to be enough to make up for or pay for: *This cheque should cover the costs.* **11.** to get news, pictures, etc., of: *He's covering the flood for a television station.* **12.** to pass or travel over: *We covered 600 kilometres today.* **13.** (of a male animal) to mate with. ◇*v.i.* **14.** to do the work of (someone absent): *She covered for me while I was ill.* ◇*v.* **15. cover up, a.** to cover completely. **b.** to try to hide, esp. a crime or mistake. ◇*n.* **16.** something that covers, e.g. the lid of a box, the jacket or binding of a book, etc. **17.** protection; shelter. **18.** insurance against the risk of loss, damage, etc. **19.** something which hides; concealment. **20.** *Stamps.* an envelope or wrapping for mail, with a stamp and postmark. **21. break cover,** to come out, esp. suddenly, from hiding. **22. take cover,** to hide or shelter oneself. **23. under cover,** secret(ly). [ME, from OF, from L: *cover over*] —**coverer,** *n.* —**coverless,** *adj.* —**coverage,** *n.* —**covering,** *n.*

cover charge, *n.* an extra amount added to a charge for food and drink by a restaurant, nightclub, etc.

coverlet /ˈkʌvələt/, *n.* a bedspread. [ME, from OF *covre* COVER + *lit* bed]

cover note, *n.* a document providing temporary insurance until a policy is prepared.

covert /ˈkʌvət, ˈkoʊvət/, *adj.* **1.** covered; sheltered. **2.** hidden; secret; disguised. ◇*n.* **3.** a shelter; disguise; hiding place. [ME, from OF: covered]

cover-up /ˈkʌvər-ʌp/, *n.* **1.** an attempt to hide something. **2.** a made-up excuse. **3.** a garment worn over a swimsuit.

covet /ˈkʌvət/, *v.t.* **1.** to desire too much or unfairly. **2.** to wish for, esp. eagerly. [ME, from L: desire] —**covetous,** *adj.* —**covetable,** *adj.* —**coveter,** *n.*

covey /ˈkʌvi/, *n., pl.* **-eys.** a group of partridges or similar birds. [ME, from OF: incubate, from L: lie]

cow[1] /kaʊ/, *n., pl.* **cows,** (*old form*) **kine.** **1.** the adult female of cattle. **2.** the female of various other large animals, e.g. the elephant, whale. **3.** *Colloq.* an ugly or bad-tempered woman. **4. poor cow,** *Colloq.* (expressing sympathy) unfortunate person. **5. till the cows come home,** for a long time; for ever. [OE *cu*]

cow[2] /kaʊ/, *v.t.* to frighten or subdue with threats, etc. [Scand]

Cowan /ˈkaʊən/, *n.* **Edith Dircksey,** 1861–1932, Australian state politician and social worker; first woman in Australia to be elected a member of parliament, when elected to the WA Legislative Assembly in 1921.

coward /ˈkaʊəd/, *n.* someone who lacks courage. [ME, from OF: tail, from L, through comparison with an animal with its tail between its legs] —**cowardice,** *n.* —**cowardly,** *adj.*

Coward /ˈkaʊəd/, *n.* **Sir Noël Pierce,** 1899–1973, English author, actor, and composer; noted for comedies such as *Blithe Spirit* (1941).

cowboy /ˈkaʊbɔɪ/, *n.* a person employed, esp. in the US, to herd cattle, usu. on horseback; stockman.

cower /ˈkaʊə/, *v.i.* to bow down in fear or shame; cringe. [ME, from Scand]

cowl /kaʊl/, *n.* **1.** the (hood of) the garment worn by monks. **2.** a hood-shaped covering for a chimney. **3.** a cowling. ◇*v.t.* **4.** to cover with, or as if with, a cowl. [OE *cūle, cug(e)le,* from LL: cowl, L: hood] —**cowled,** *adj.*

Cowley /ˈkaʊli/, *n.* **John Maxwell,** born 1923, Australian physicist.

cowlick /ˈkaʊlɪk/, *n.* a tuft of hair turned up, usu. over the forehead.

cowling /ˈkaʊlɪŋ/, *n.* a cover for an aircraft engine.

cowpat /ˈkaʊpæt/, *n.* a rounded lump of cow dung.

cowpox /ˈkaʊpɒks/, *n.* a virus disease of cows marked by spots on the teats and udders. The virus is used for vaccinating humans against smallpox.

Cowra /ˈkaʊrə/, *n.* a town and shire in eastern central NSW on the Lachlan River. Pop. 8207 (1986).

cowry /ˈkaʊri/, *n., pl.* **-ries.** the shell of various sea snails, used as money or ornament. Also, **cowrie.** [Hind *kaurī*]

cowslip /ˈkaʊslɪp/, *n.* an English primrose with yellow flowers.

cox /kɒks/, *n.* a coxswain.

Cox /kɒks/, *n.* **William,** 1764–1837, Australian pioneer landowner and road-builder, born in England; supervised the building of a road over the Blue Mountains 1814–15.

coxcomb /ˈkɒkskoʊm/, *n.* **1.** →**cockscomb** (def. 1). **2.** a conceited dandy. —**coxcombry,** *n.*

coxswain /ˈkɒksən, -sweɪn/, *n.* the person steering a boat, esp. in rowing. [ME *cock* ship's boat + SWAIN servant]

coy /kɔɪ/, *adj.* **1.** shy; bashful. **2.** pretending shyness. [ME, from F, from L: at rest]

Coy, *Abbrev.* Company.

coyote /kɔɪˈoʊti/, *n.* a wild, wolf-like animal of the dog family, of western North America, that howls at night. [Mex Sp, from S Amer Indian]

cozen /ˈkʌzən/, *v.t. Obs.* to cheat; deceive. [orig. obscure] —**cozener,** *n.* —**cozenage,** *n.*

cozzie /ˈkɒzi/, *n. Colloq.* →**swimsuit.** Also, **cossie.**

cP, *Phys. Symbol.* centipoise.

CP /siˈpi/, *Abbrev.* **1.** Communist Party. **2.** Country Party.

CPA /si pi ˈeɪ/, *Abbrev.* Communist Party of Australia.

CPI /si pi ˈaɪ/, *Abbrev.* Consumer Price Index.

cpl, *Abbrev.* corporal.

cps /si pi 'ɛs/, *Abbrev.* **1.** cycles per second. **2.** characters per second.

CPU /si pi 'ju/, *Computers. Abbrev.* central processing unit.

cr., *Abbrev.* credit.

Cr, *Chem. Symbol.* chromium.

crab[1] /kræb/, *n., v.*, **crabbed, crabbing.** ◇*n.* **1.** any of various usu. saltwater crustaceans with eight legs, two pincers and a flattish shell over the body. **2.** a machine for pulling or lifting heavy weights. **3.** → **crablouse.** ◇*v.i.* **4.** to move sideways. **5.** to fish for crabs. [OE *crabba*]

crab[2] /kræb/, *n. Colloq.* an ill-tempered person. [ME *crabbe*, ? var. of d. *scrab* crab-apple] — **crabby,** *adj.*

crab-apple /'kræb-æpəl/, *n.* any of various types of small sour apple, used for making jelly, etc.

crabbed /kræbd/, *adj.* **1.** cramped and hard to read: *crabbed handwriting.* **2.** crabby.

crabby /'kræbi/, *adj.*, **-bier, -biest.** irritable.

crablouse /'kræblaʊs/, *n.* a body louse that infects the pubic area and causes itching. Also, **crab.**

crack /kræk/, *v.i.* **1.** to make a sudden, sharp breaking sound. **2.** to break, usu. without the parts separating; split. **3.** (of the voice) to make a rough sound or change pitch suddenly. **4.** to fail; give way. ◇*v.t.* **5.** to cause to make a sharp sound: *He cracked the whip.* **6.** to break or split. **7.** *Colloq.* to break into or open: *They cracked the safe last night.* **8.** *Colloq.* to solve: *to crack a code.* **9.** to tell (a joke). **10.** *Chem., Engin.* to process by cracking (def. 1). ◇*v.* **11. crack down on,** *Colloq.* to become strict with. **12. crack up,** *Colloq.* **a.** to break down, esp. mentally: *He cracked up when his wife died.* **b.** to praise: *It's not all it's cracked up to be.* **13. get cracking,** *Colloq.* to start; get going. ◇*n.* **14.** a sudden, sharp noise. **15.** a (rifle) shot. **16.** a hard or loud blow. **17.** a break without the parts separating; split. **18.** a slight opening: *The door was only open a crack.* **19.** a broken or changing tone of voice. **20.** *Colloq.* a try: *Have a crack at it.* **21.** an expert. **22.** *Colloq.* a joke. **23. crack of dawn,** the first light of day. **24. crack of doom,** the end of the world. ◇*adj.* **25.** *Colloq.* first-rate: *a crack rider.* [OE *cracian resound*] — **cracked,** *adj.*

crackdown /'krækdaʊn/, *n.* the enforcing of strict rules, esp. suddenly: *a police crackdown on drink driving.*

cracker /'krækə/, *n.* **1.** a thin, crisp, plain biscuit. **2.** a firework. **3.** → **bonbon.** (def. 2). **4.** something first-rate: *This model is a cracker.*

crackers /'krækəz/, *adj. Colloq.* mad; crazy. Also, **cracked.**

cracking /'krækɪŋ/, *n.* **1.** the process of breaking down hydrocarbons by heat, pressure, etc., to produce petrol. ◇*adj.* **2.** fast; vigorous: *a cracking pace.* **3.** *Colloq.* fine; excellent.

crackle /'krækəl/, *v.* **-led, -ling,** *n.* ◇*v.t., v.i.* **1.** to (cause to) make slight, sharp sounds; snap or rustle. ◇*n.* **2.** the act or sound of crackling. [frequentative of CRACK]

crackling /'kræklɪŋ/, *n.* crisp cooked pork skin.

crackpot /'krækpɒt/, *n., adj. Colloq.* (a person who is) odd or mad.

-cracy, a noun ending meaning 'rule', 'government', 'governing body', as in *democracy*, *bureaucracy*. [F *-cratie*, from Gk *-kratia*, from *krátos* rule, strength]

cradle /'kreɪdəl/, *n., v.*, **-dled, -dling.** ◇*n.* **1.** a little bed or cot for a baby, usu. on rockers. **2.** the place of early growth of something: *Greece was the cradle of democracy.* **3.** a framework for support or protection. **4.** a kind of box on rockers used to wash gold-bearing gravel or sand to separate the gold. ◇*v.t.* **5.** to place, hold, or rock (something) as if in a cradle: *cradled in her arms.* [OE *cradol*]

cradle cap, *n.* a scaly condition of a baby's scalp.

Cradle Mountain, *n.* a mountain in north-western Tasmania, near the Huskisson River. 1545 m.

cradle-snatcher /'kreɪdl-snætʃə/, *n.* someone romantically involved with a much younger person.

Crafers-Bridgewater /kreɪfəz-'brɪdʒwɒtə/, *n.* an urban centre in south-eastern SA, near Adelaide, in the Mount Lofty Ranges; comprises the four townships of Crafers, Stirling, Aldgate and Bridgewater. Pop. 11 222 (1986).

craft /kraft/, *n., pl.* **-s** (defs 1-3), **craft** (def. 5). **1.** skill; dexterity. **2.** skill used for bad purposes; cunning. **3.** an art, or job needing special skill, esp. with the hands; handicraft. **4.** the members of a skilled trade, thought of as a group. **5.** a boat, ship or aircraft. ◇*v.t.* **6.** to make skilfully by hand. [OE *cræft*]

craftsman /'kraftsmən/, *n., pl.* **-men. 1.** someone who practises a craft; artisan. **2.** → **artist. 3.** *Mil.* a private in the Royal Australian Electrical and Mechanical Engineers. See Appendix. — **craftsmanship,** *n.*

crafty /'krafti/, *adj.*, **-tier, -tiest.** clever, esp. in deceiving; cunning. — **craftily,** *adv.* — **craftiness,** *n.*

crag /kræg/, *n.* a steep rough rock sticking out. [ME, from Celtic; see Welsh *craig* rock] — **cragged,** *adj.* — **craggy,** *adj.*

crake /kreɪk/, *n.* a small lake and swamp bird of the rail family. [ME, from Scand]

cram /kræm/, *v.*, **crammed, cramming.** ◇*v.t.* **1.** to overfill (something) by force. **2.** to force or stuff (fol. by *into, down*, etc.). **3.** to overfill with food. ◇*v.i.* **4.** to study for an examination by hastily memorising facts. [OE *crammian,* from *crimman* insert]

cramp[1] /kræmp/, *n.* a sudden painful contraction of a muscle. [ME, from MD]

cramp[2] /kræmp/, *n.* **1.** a metal bar with bent ends, for holding together wood, stone,

cramp etc. **2.** → **clamp**. **3.** anything that holds or ties. ◇*v.t.* **4.** to hold or tie tightly, preventing free movement; confine; restrict. ◇*v.* **5. cramp one's style**, *Colloq.* to prevent someone from showing ability, etc. [MD: hook, clamp]

cramped /kræmpt/, *adj.* **1.** contracted; narrow. **2.** crowded and hard to read: *cramped handwriting*.

cranberry /ˈkrænberi, -bri/, *n., pl.* **-ries.** a sour red berry used for a sauce, jelly, etc. [LG]

Cranbourne /ˈkrænbən/, *n.* a town and shire in southern central Vic, south-east of Melbourne. Pop. 14 005 (1986).

crane /kreɪn/, *n., v.,* **craned, craning.** ◇*n.* **1.** a large wading bird with very long legs, bill and neck. **2.** a machine, usu. with an upright post and moving arm, for lifting and lowering heavy weights and moving them from place to place. ◇*v.t., v.i.* **3.** to stretch (the neck), esp. to see something. [OE *cran*]

cranio-, a combining form of **cranium**. Also, **crani-**.

cranium /ˈkreɪniəm/, *n., pl.* **-nia** /-niə/. **1.** the skull of a vertebrate. **2.** the part of the skull which encloses the brain. [ML, from Gk] —**cranial**, *adj.*

crank /kræŋk/, *n.* **1.** a handle or arm at right angles to the shaft of a machine, to transmit movement or change it from a turning movement to movement back and forward, or vice versa. **2.** *Colloq.* an odd person, or one who holds peculiar opinions. ◇*v.t.* **3.** to cause (a shaft) to turn by a crank. **4.** to start (an engine, a car) by a crank. ◇*v.i.* **5.** to bend. [OE *cranc*, in *crancstæf* weaving implement, crank]

crankcase /ˈkræŋkkeɪs/, *n.* (in an internal-combustion engine) a part enclosing the crankshaft, connecting rods, etc.

crankshaft /ˈkræŋkʃɑft/, *n.* a shaft driving or driven by a crank, esp. the main shaft of an engine carrying cranks to which the connecting rods are joined.

cranky /ˈkræŋki/, *adj.,* **-kier, -kiest. 1.** bad-tempered. **2.** peculiar; odd. **3.** shaky; out of order. —**crankiness**, *n.*

cranny /ˈkræni/, *n., pl.* **-nies.** a small, narrow opening (in a wall, rock, etc.); chink; crevice. [ME, from F: fissure (from *crener* cut away, from L)]

crap /kræp/, *n., v., crapped, crapping. Colloq.* ◇*n.* **1.** (*offensive*) excrement; faeces. **2.** nonsense; rubbish. **3.** junk; odds and ends. ◇*v.i.* **4.** (*offensive*) to defecate. [ME *crappe* chaff, from MD] —**crappy**, *adj.*

craps /kræps/, *n.* a gambling game played with two dice.

crapulous /ˈkræpjələs/, *adj.* (sick from) drinking or eating too much. Also, **crapulent**. [L: intoxication] —**crapulousness, crapulence**, *n.*

crash /kræʃ/, *v.t.* **1.** to fall, hit something or break in pieces noisily. **2.** to force or drive with violence and noise. **3.** *Colloq.* to come uninvited or without permission to: *to crash a party*. **4.** to damage in a fall or by running into something: *He's crashed his car*. ◇*v.i.* **5.** to break or fall to pieces noisily. **6.** to make the noise of something breaking or falling. **7.** to fail suddenly: *The company crashed*. **8.** to move, go or hit with a crash. **9.** (of aircraft) to fall to the ground. **10.** *Colloq.* to fall asleep when tired out. ◇*n.* **11.** a breaking or falling to pieces with a loud noise. **12.** the shock of hitting something and breaking. **13.** a sudden and violent falling to ruin. **14.** *Computers.* a system failure which destroys the content of the computer memory. **15.** the sudden failure of a company, etc. **16.** a sudden loud crashing noise. ◇*adj.* **17.** *Colloq.* using full speed and effort: *a crash course*. [ME; b. CRAZE and MASH] —**crasher**, *n.*

crass /kræs/, *adj.* **1.** stupid; gross: *crass ignorance*. **2.** coarse; rude. [L: solid, thick, dense, fat]

-crat, a noun ending meaning 'ruler', 'member of ruling body', 'supporter of particular form of rule', as in *aristocrat, bureaucrat, democrat*. See **-cracy**. [F *-crate*, from Gk *kratḗs* ruler]

crate /kreɪt/, *n., v., crated, crating.* ◇*n.* **1.** a box, usu. wooden, for packing fruit, furniture, etc. **2.** *Colloq.* a worn-out old car, aircraft, etc. ◇*v.t.* **3.** to pack in a crate. [L: wicker-work]

crater /ˈkreɪtə/, *n.* **1.** the cup-shaped opening at the top of a volcano. **2.** (in the surface of the earth, moon, etc.) a rounded hole formed by a meteorite. **3.** a hole in the ground where a bomb, etc., has exploded. **4.** a bowl used by ancient Greeks and Romans, orig. for mixing wine and water. [L, from Gk: orig. bowl for mixing wine and water] —**craterous**, *adj.* —**cratering**, *n.*

cravat /krəˈvæt/, *n.* an oblong scarf worn round the neck, esp. by men. [F *cravate*; so called because adopted from the Croats (F *Cravates*)]

crave /kreɪv/, *v., craved, craving.* ◇*v.t.* **1.** to desire eagerly. **2.** to need greatly. **3.** to ask or beg for. ◇*v.i.* **4.** to long (fol. by *for* or *after*). [OE *crafian*] —**craving**, *n.*

craven /ˈkreɪvən/, *n., adj.* coward(ly). [ME, from OF, b. *crav(anté)* overthrown and *(recre)ant* RECREANT]

craw /krɔ/, *n.* **1.** → **crop** (def. 8). **2.** the stomach of an animal. **3. stick in one's craw**, to be unacceptable. [ME]

Crawford /ˈkrɔfəd/, *n.* **1. Dorothy**, born 1911, radio and television producer; with Hector, formed the production company, Crawfords, in 1945. **2.** her brother, **Hector**, 1913–91, television producer.

crawl /krɔl/, *v.i.* **1.** to move, by dragging the body along the ground like a worm, or on hands and knees, like a baby. **2.** to move slowly: *The day crawled by*. **3.** to behave humbly, trying to win favor. **4.** to be, or feel as if, overrun with crawling things: *crawling with ants*. ◇*n.* **5.** the act of crawling. **6.** Also, **Australian crawl.** *Swimming.* a stroke done with the face to the water, using each arm in turn and with continuous up and down kicking; freestyle. [ME, from Scand]

crawler /ˈkrɔlə/, *n.* **1.** someone or something that crawls. **2.** any device as a tank, truck, tractor, etc., moving on endless belt tracks.

crayfish /ˈkreɪfɪʃ/, *n., pl.* **-fishes** (*esp. collectively*) **-fish. 1.** any of various freshwater crustaceans with eight legs and large claws, e.g. yabby, marron. **2.** →**lobster** (def. 1). **3.** any similar crustacean of the Northern Hemisphere. [ME *crevice*, from OF, from OHG: crab]

crayon /ˈkreɪɒn/, *n., v.,* **-oned, -oning.** ◇*n.* **1.** a stick of colored wax, chalk, etc., used for drawing. **2.** a crayon drawing. ◇*v.t.* **3.** to draw with crayon. [F, from L: chalk]

craypot /ˈkreɪpɒt/, *n.* a crayfish trap.

craze /kreɪz/, *v.,* **crazed, crazing,** *n.* ◇*v.t., v.i.* **1.** to (cause to) go mad. **2.** to break; shatter. ◇*n.* **3.** a short-lived fashion, or sudden keenness; fad. **4.** a tiny crack in the glaze of pottery, etc. [ME *crase(n)* break, from Scand]

crazy /ˈkreɪzi/, *adj.,* **-zier, -ziest. 1.** mad; insane. **2.** peculiar **3.** unrealistic; impractical: *a crazy plan.* **4.** *Colloq.* very keen or excited. **5.** likely to fall to pieces. —**craziness,** *n.*

creak /krik/, *v.i.* **1.** to make a sharp, rough, or squeaking sound: *The rusty hinges creak.* **2.** to move with creaking. ◇*v.t.* **3.** to cause to creak. ◇*n.* **4.** a creaking sound. [ME *creken,* compare OE *crācettan* CROAK]

cream /krim/, *n.* **1.** the fatty part of milk, which rises to the surface. **2.** any food made with cream or like cream. **3.** any creamlike substance: *face cream.* **4.** the best part. **5.** a yellowish white color. ◇*v.i.* **6.** to form cream. **7.** to foam. ◇*v.t.* **8.** to beat until creamy: *to cream butter and sugar.* **9.** to put cream in or on. [ME, from F, from LL: chrism]

cream of tartar, *n.* an acid powder used in baking; potassium hydrogen tartrate.

creamy /ˈkrimi/, *adj.,* **-mier, -miest. 1.** containing cream. **2.** cream in color, feel or taste. —**creaminess,** *n.*

crease /kris/, *n., v.,* **creased, creasing.** ◇*n.* **1.** a line or mark produced by folding. **2.** a sharp ridge ironed into a trouser leg. **3.** *Cricket.* one of three lines near the wicket marking the limits of movement of the bowler or the batsman. ◇*v.t., v.i.* **4.** to fold or wrinkle. [orig. unknown]

create /kriˈeɪt/, *v.,* **-ated, -ating.** ◇*v.t.* **1.** to make; cause to exist; produce. **2.** to design or invent. **3.** to make into; appoint: *to create someone a peer.* ◇*v.i.* **4.** *Colloq.* to make a fuss or an uproar. [L: brought into being] —**creation,** *n.*

creatine /ˈkriətɑn/, *n. Biochem.* an amino acid, a major source of chemical energy in muscle, found mainly as **creatine phosphate** in the tissues of all vertebrates and some invertebrates.

creation /kriˈeɪʃən/, *n.* **1.** the act or result of creating. **2. the Creation,** the bringing into being of the universe by God. **3.** the world; universe. **4.** an original design or invention. —**creational,** *adj.*

creative /kriˈeɪtɪv/, *adj.* **1.** able to create. **2.** original. **3.** productive. —**creativeness,** *n.* —**creativity,** *n.*

creature /ˈkritʃə/, *n.* **1.** anything created. **2.** a living being. **3.** a person: *you poor creature.* **4.** a person dependent on or influenced by another. [ME, from OF, from LL: a thing created]

creche /kreɪʃ, krɛʃ/, *n.* a day nursery for babies and small children. [F, from OHG: crib]

credence /ˈkridns/, *n.* belief: *to give credence to a statement.* [ME, from ML: belief, from L: believing]

credential /krəˈdɛnʃəl/, *n.* **1.** something which gives the right to belief or trust. **2.** (*usu. pl.*) a letter or certificate showing the holder's right to a position of trust or authority. [ML *crēdentia* belief + -AL²]

credibility gap, *n.* a difference between what is said and the actual facts.

credible /ˈkrɛdəbəl/, *adj.* **1.** believable. **2.** worthy of belief or trust. [ME, from L] —**credibility, credibleness,** *n.*

credit /ˈkrɛdɪt/, *n.* **1.** belief; trust. **2.** influence or power resulting from the trust of others. **3.** trustworthiness; credibility. **4.** reputation. **5.** a favorable opinion. **6.** approval or acknowledgement of some action, quality, etc.: *Give her credit for her ability.* **7.** a source of approval or honor. **8.** (*pl.*) a list at the start or end of a film, in a theatre program, etc., showing the names of the people who helped. **9.** time allowed for payment. **10.** trust in someone's ability to pay. **11.** a reputation as a person who can be trusted to pay back money. **12.** the power to buy or borrow on trust. **13.** a sum of money due to a person. **14.** the balance in one's favor in an account. **15.** *Bookkeeping.* **a.** an entry of payments or value received, in an account. **b.** the (right-hand) side of an account, where credit entries are made. See **debit** (def. 2). **16. on credit,** with agreement to pay later. ◇*v.t.* **17.** to believe; trust. **18.** to give honor to; do credit to. **19.** to describe (someone) as having (fol. by *with*): *to credit him with great ability.* **20.** *Bookkeeping.* to enter on the credit side of an account. **21.** to award to: *I was credited with three points in history.* [F, from It, from L: believed]

creditable /ˈkrɛdətəbəl/, *adj.* bringing credit, honor, or approval.

credit card, *n.* a card enabling the holder to obtain goods and services on credit. Also, **credit plate.**

creditor /ˈkrɛdətə/, *n.* **1.** a person or company that gives credit in business dealings. **2.** someone to whom money is owed (opposed to *debtor*).

credo /ˈkridoʊ, ˈkrɪdoʊ/, *n., pl.* **-dos. 1.** → **creed. 2.** (a musical setting of) a creed (def. 2). [L: I believe, the first word of the Apostles' and the Nicene Creeds in Latin]

credulity /krəˈdjulətɪ/, *n.* a tendency to believe too readily. [late ME *credulite,* from L *crēdulitas*]

credulous /ˈkrɛdʒələs/, *adj.* **1.** ready to believe things, esp. without good reasons. **2.** marked by or arising from credulity. [L: apt to believe] **– credulousness,** *n.*

Cree /kriː/, *n., pl.* **Cree, Crees.** (*pl.*) an American Indian tribe belonging to the Algonquian linguistic stock, and situated in Manitoba, Saskatchewan, etc. [short for F *Kristinaux*, from *Kinistenoag*, given as one of their own names]

creed /kriːd/, *n.* **1.** any system of belief. **2.** a formal statement of a religious belief. [OE *crēda*, from L *crēdo* I believe. See CREDO] **– creedal, credal,** *adj.* **– creedless,** *adj.*

creek /kriːk/, *n.* **1.** a small stream. **2.** *Brit.* a narrow inlet or bay. **3. up the creek,** *Colloq.* in trouble. [ME, from Scand]

Creek /kriːk/, *n.* (*pl.*) a powerful confederacy of Muskhogean Indians which once occupied the greater part of Alabama and Georgia. [so called because of numerous streams in Creek territory]

creel /kriːl/, *n.* a wickerwork basket or trap for fish, etc. [ME, from L: wickerwork]

creep /kriːp/, *v.,* **crept, creeping** *n.* ◇*v.i.* **1.** to move with the body close to the ground; crawl. **2.** to move slowly or so as not to be seen. **3.** (of a plant) to grow along the ground. ◇*v.* **4. make (one's) flesh creep,** to frighten or disgust. ◇*n.* **5.** the act of creeping. **6.** *Colloq.* an unpleasant person. **7. the creeps,** a feeling of fear or disgust. [OE *crēopan*]

creeper /ˈkriːpə/, *n. Bot.* a plant which grows along the ground, etc., sending out rootlets from the stem, e.g. ivy.

creepy /ˈkriːpi/, *adj.,* **-pier, -piest. 1.** creeping. **2.** having or causing fear or disgust: *a creepy silence.* **3.** *Colloq.* (of a person) unpleasant, obnoxious or insignificant. **– creepiness,** *n.*

cremate /krɪˈmeɪt/, *v.t.,* **-mated, -mating.** to burn (a dead body) to ashes. [L: consumed by fire] **– cremation,** *n.*

crematorium /ˌkrɛməˈtɔːriəm/, *n., pl.* **-riums** or **-ria.** an establishment for cremating dead bodies.

crème /krɛm/, *n.* **1.** cream. **2.** a rich liqueur. [F]

crenation /krəˈneɪʃən/, *n.* a rounded tooth or part sticking out, as on edge of a leaf. Also, **crenature.**

crenellated /ˈkrɛnəleɪtəd/, *adj.* having square indentations or battlements. [F: little notch] **– crenellation,** *n.*

creole /ˈkriːoʊl/, *n.* **1.** someone born in the West Indies, Spanish America, or US, but of European, usu. Spanish or French, parentage. **2.** a person of mixed creole and Negro descent. **3.** a pidgin which has become the first language of a group of people. ◇*adj.* **4.** (of people, animals or plants) born or growing in a country, but of foreign origin. Also, **Creole.** [F, from Sp: native to the locality, from Pg: bring up, from L: create]

Creon /ˈkriːɒn/, *n. Gk Legend.* king of Thebes, after the fall of Oedipus. See **Antigone**

creosote /ˈkriːəsoʊt/, *n., v.,* **-soted, -soting.** ◇*n.* **1.** an oily liquid with a strong smell distilled from wood tar or coal tar; used as an antiseptic and to preserve wood. ◇*v.t.* **2.** to treat with creosote. [*creo-* (combining form representing Gk *kréas* flesh) + Gk *sōtḗr* savior] **– creosotic,** *adj.*

crepe /kreɪp/, *n.* **1.** a light fabric of silk, cotton, or other fibre, with a finely crinkled surface. **2.** Also, **crepe paper.** a thin paper wrinkled like crepe. **3.** black crepe used for mourning armbands, etc. **4.** a thin pancake. [F, from L: curled]

crepe rubber, *n.* rubber pressed into ridged sheets, used esp. for shoe soles.

crept /krɛpt/, *v.* past tense and past participle of **creep.**

crepuscular /krɪˈpʌskjələ/, *adj.* like, or relating to twilight. [L *crepusculum*]

crescendo /krəˈʃɛndoʊ/, *n.* a gradual increase in force or loudness. [It: increasing, from L]

crescent /ˈkrɛsənt, ˈkrɛzənt/, *n.* **1.** the shape of the moon in its first or last quarter. **2.** anything of a similar shape, esp. a street. [L: increasing]

cress /krɛs/, *n.* a plant related to mustard whose fast-growing seed leaves are used for salad and as a garnish. [OE *cresse*]

crest /krɛst/, *n.* **1.** a tuft or other natural growth on top of the head of a bird or other animal. **2.** anything like such a tuft. **3.** a (feather) ornament on a helmet. **4.** (the top of) a helmet. **5.** part of a coat of arms, used for badges, etc.: *a school crest.* **6.** the head or top of anything. ◇*v.t.* **7.** to provide with a crest. **8.** to reach the crest of. ◇*v.i.* **9.** to form or reach a crest. [ME, from OF, from L: tuft] **– crested,** *adj.* **– crestless,** *adj.*

crestfallen /ˈkrɛstfɔːlən/, *adj.* disappointed or sad.

Cretaceous /krəˈteɪʃəs/, *adj.* **1.** *Geol.* the third and latest of the periods included in the Mesozoic era. **2.** (*l.c.*) of, like, or containing chalk. – *n.* **3.** *Geol.* the system of strata deposited during the Cretaceous period.

Crete /kriːt/, *n.* a mountainous Greek island in the Mediterranean; centre of Minoan civilisation c. 2500– c. 1100 BC; archaeological sites. Pop. 502 165 (1981); 8260 km². *Cap.:* Canea. Modern Greek, **Kríti.** **– Cretan,** *adj.*

cretin /ˈkrɛtn/, *n.* **1.** a person suffering from cretinism. **2.** *Colloq.* a very stupid person. [F, from d. F *crestin*, from L *Christiānus* Christian] **– cretinous,** *adj.*

cretinism /ˈkrɛtnɪzəm/, *n.* a condition due to lack of the thyroid hormone, marked by dwarfism and idiocy.

cretonne /krəˈtɒn/, *n.* a heavy cotton material in printed designs, used esp. for curtains and loose covers. [F, from *Creton*, village in Normandy]

crevasse /krəˈvæs/, *n.* a deep crack in the ice of a glacier. [F. See CREVICE]

crevice /'krevəs/, *n.* a crack forming an opening; cleft; rift; fissure. [ME, from OF: burst, from L: crack] —**creviced,** *adj.*

crew[1] /kru/, *n.* **1.** a group of people working at something together; gang. **2.** a group of people operating a ship, boat, or aircraft. ◇*v.i.* **3.** to act as (a member of) a crew. ◇*v.t.* **4.** to provide with a crew. [ME, from ONF: increase, from L: grow]

crew[2] /kru/, *v.* past tense of **crow**[2].

crew cut, *n.* a very short haircut.

crewel /'kruəl/, *n.* a fine woollen yarn used for embroidery, etc. [ME *crule,* of unknown orig.] —**crewelwork,** *n.*

crewel needle, *n.* a needle with a sharp point and large eye.

crew neck, *n.* a plain ribbed neckband fitting closely around the neck.

crib /krɪb/, *n., v.,* **cribbed, cribbing.** ◇*n.* **1.** a child's cot. **2.** a cattle stall or pen. **3.** a rack or box for food for cattle, horses, etc. **4.** a framework used in construction. **5.** a packed meal. **6.** *Colloq.* **a.** the copy(ing) of another's work; plagiarism. **b.** a translation or other aid used by students, often dishonestly. ◇*v.t., v.i.* **7.** *Colloq.* **a.** to copy (another's work); plagiarise. **b.** to use a crib. [OE *crib(b)*]

cribbage /'krɪbɪdʒ/, *n.* a card game. [CRIB + -AGE]

crick /krɪk/, *n.* **1.** a muscle cramp, e.g. of the neck or back. ◇*v.t.* **2.** to cause a crick in: *I've cricked my neck.* [orig. uncert.]

Crick /krɪk/, *n.* **Francis Harry Compton,** born 1916, English physicist and biochemist; shared Nobel prize for physiology or medicine (1962) with James Watson and Maurice Wilkins for work in determining the structure of DNA.

cricket[1] /'krɪkət/, *n.* a leaping, chirping insect related to the grasshopper and locust. [ME, from OF *criquet;* imitative]

cricket[2] /'krɪkət/, *n.* **1.** an outdoor game played with a ball, bats, and wickets, by two teams of 11 players. **2.** *Colloq.* fair play: *His behavior was not cricket.* [See OF *criquet* stick] —**cricketer,** *n.*

crier /'kraɪə/, *n.* **1.** a person who cries. **2.** (formerly) a person who shouts out public announcements.

crime /kraɪm/, *n.* **1.** an act which breaks the law. **2.** crimes collectively: *the problem of crime.* **3.** any wrongdoing, esp. serious. **4.** *Colloq.* something wrong or unfortunate: *It's a crime to have to work so hard.* [ME, from L: offence]

Crimea /kraɪ'mɪə/, *n.* a large peninsula in Ukraine, separating the Black Sea from the Sea of Azov. About 26 000 km². Russian, **Krim, Krym.**

Crimean War /kraɪ,mɪən 'wɔ/, *n.* a war between Great Britain, France, Turkey, and Sardinia on one side, and Russia on the other, fought chiefly in the Crimea, 1853–56.

criminal /'krɪmənəl/, *adj.* **1.** of or relating to crime or its punishment: *criminal law.* **2.** of, guilty of, or involving crime. ◇*n.* **3.** a person convicted of a crime. [L] —**criminality,** *n.*

criminology /ˌkrɪmə'nɒlədʒi/, *n.* the science dealing with the causes of crime and the treatment of criminals. [L *crimen* crime + -O- + -LOGY] —**criminologist,** *n.*

crimp /krɪmp/, *v.t.* **1.** to press into small regular folds; corrugate; make wavy. **2.** to curl (hair), esp. with a hot iron. ◇*n.* **3.** a crimped condition or form. **4.** something crimped. [OE *gecrympan* curl (from *crump* crooked)] —**crimper,** *n.* —**crimpy,** *adj.*

crimson /'krɪmzən/, *n.* **1.** a deep purplish red color. ◇*adj.* **2.** bloody. ◇*v.t., v.i.* **3.** to make or become crimson. [ME, from It or from Sp, both from Ar]

cringe /krɪndʒ/, *v.,* **cringed, cringing,** *n.* ◇*v.i.* **1.** to bend or bow down, esp. from fear or humility; shrink; cower. **2.** to act too humbly, in the hope of favor. ◇*n.* the act of cringeing. [OE *cringan* yield, fall (in battle)]

crinkle /'krɪŋkəl/, *v.,* **-kled, -kling,** *n.* ◇*v.i.* **1.** to wrinkle; ripple. **2.** to rustle. ◇*v.t.* **3.** to cause to crinkle. ◇*n.* **4.** a wrinkle. **5.** a crinkling sound. [OE *crincan* bend, yield] —**crinkly,** *adj.*

crinoline /'krɪnəlɪn/, *n.* **1.** a petticoat of stiff material, worn by women under a full skirt, esp. in the 19th century. **2.** a hoop skirt. [F, from It]

cripple /'krɪpəl/, *n., v.,* **-pled, -pling.** ◇*n.* **1.** someone partly or wholly without the use of one or more limbs. **2.** a person or animal disabled in any way: *an emotional cripple.* ◇*v.t.* **3.** to disable. [OE *crypel;* akin to CREEP]

crisis /'kraɪsəs/, *n., pl.* **-ses** /-siz/. **1.** a turning point in course of anything. **2.** a time of trouble or danger. **3.** a turning point in a disease, leading to recovery or death. [L, from Gk: decision]

crisp /krɪsp/, *adj.* **1.** hard but dry and easily breakable; brittle: *crisp toast.* **2.** firm and fresh: *crisp lettuce.* **3.** sharp; brisk; decided: *a crisp manner; a crisp reply.* **4.** lively. **5.** cool, dry and refreshing: *crisp air.* **6.** clean and neat: *a crisp uniform.* **7.** wrinkled or curly: *crisp hair.* ◇*v.t.* **8.** to make crisp. **9.** to curl. ◇*v.i.* **10.** to become crisp. ◇*n.* **11.** → **chip** (def. 3b.). **12.** something crisp: *burnt to a crisp.* [OE, from L: curled] —**crispy,** *adj.* —**crispness,** *n.*

crisscross /'krɪskrɒs/, *adj.* **1.** crossing or with crossing lines. **2.** a crisscross mark or pattern. ◇*adv.* **3.** in a crisscross manner. ◇*v.t., v.i.* **4.** to mark with or form crossing lines. [var. of *christcross* Christ's cross]

criterion /kraɪ'tɪəriən/, *n., pl.* **-teria** /-'tɪəriə/, **-terions.** a standard, rule, or principle for testing anything. [Gk *kritērion* test, standard]

critic /'krɪtɪk/, *n.* **1.** a person skilled in judging the qualities of some class of things: *an art critic; a literary critic.* **2.** someone who judges severely or finds fault. [L, from Gk: skilled in judging]

critical /'krɪtɪkəl/, *adj.* **1.** tending to find fault or judge severely. **2.** of, involving, or

critical related to criticism: *a critical article; critical analysis*. **3.** relating to or with the quality of a crisis or turning point: *the critical moment*. **4.** dangerous: *a critical shortage of water*. **5.** serious; severe: *in a critical condition*.

critical angle, *n. Phys.* the angle of incidence below or above which light rays are totally internally reflected.

critical constants, *n.pl. Phys.* the critical temperature, pressure, density, and volume of a substance.

critical mass, *n. Nuclear Phys.* the minimum quantity of fissile material needed for a chain-reaction to take place.

critical pressure, *n. Phys.* the pressure of the saturated vapor of a substance at the critical temperature.

critical state, *n. Phys.* the state of a substance where its gas and liquid forms have the same density, being at the critical temperature, pressure, and volume.

critical temperature, *n. Phys.* (of a gas) the temperature above which a gas cannot be made liquid by pressure alone.

critical velocity, *n.* the velocity at which the flow of a fluid becomes disturbed or rough.

critical volume, *n.* the volume taken up by one mole or unit mass of substance while in a critical state.

criticise *or* **criticize** /'krɪtəsaɪz/, *v.t., v.i.,* **-cised, -cising. 1.** to analyse and make judgments about the faults and good qualities (of). **2.** to find fault (with). **–criticiser**, *n.*

criticism /'krɪtəsɪzəm/, *n.* **1.** an analysis and judging of the quality of something: *literary criticism*. **2.** disapproval; fault-finding. **3.** a critical remark, article, or essay.

critique /krə'tik, krɪ-/, *n.* **1.** an article or essay criticising something. **2.** the art or practice of criticism. [F, from Gk: the critical art]

croak /kroʊk/, *v.i.* **1.** to make a low, hoarse sound, like a frog. **2.** to speak with a low, rough voice. **3.** to talk hopelessly; grumble. **4.** *Colloq.* to die. ◇*n.* **5.** the act or sound of croaking. [OE *crācettan*] **–croaker**, *n.* **–croaky**, *adj.*

Croatia /kroʊ'eɪʃə/, *n.* a republic in southeastern Europe; a constituent republic of Yugoslavia from 1918 until secession in 1991–92; a medieval kingdom before annexation by the Hungarians, Turks and Austrians; formerly the Austrian crownland of **Croatia and Slavonia**. Pop. 4 679 000 (1989); 56 538 km². *Cap.*: Zagreb. *Language*: Croatian. **Hrvatska.** **–Croatian,** *n., adj.*

crochet /'kroʊʃə, 'kroʊʃeɪ/, *n., v.,* **-cheted** /-ʃəd, -ʃeɪd/, **-cheting** /-ʃəɪŋ, -ʃeɪɪŋ/. ◇*n.* **1.** the craft of making lace or fabric by using a hook to draw yarn into interlocked loops. ◇*v.t., v.i.* **2.** to form by crochet. [F: hooked implement, from OF: little hook]

crocidolite /kroʊ'sɪdəlaɪt/, *n.* a mineral of the amphibole group, basically a sodium iron silicate, occurring in fibres in **blue asbestos**, and appearing in altered form, as the **tiger's eye**, which is golden brown, or **hawk's eye**, which is dark blue. [*crocido-* (combining form representing Gk *krokís* wool) + -LITE]

crock¹ /krɒk/, *n.* (a piece of) earthenware pot or jar. [OE *croc(c), crocca* pot]

crock² /krɒk/, *n.* **1.** an old worn-out horse or ewe. **2.** *Colloq.* a broken-down old person. [akin to CRACK, *v.*]

crockery /'krɒkəri/, *n.* china dishes, pottery, etc., in general.

Crockett /'krɒkət/, *n.* **David** ('Davy'), 1786–1836, American frontiersman and political figure, killed in the Texan defence of the Alamo.

crocodile /'krɒkədaɪl/, *n.* **1.** a large, lizard-like reptile living in the waters of tropical Africa, Asia, Australia, and America. **2.** crocodile skin, used for shoes, handbags, etc. [L, from Gk: lizard] **–crocodilian,** *adj.*

crocodile tears, *n.pl.* false or insincere tears or sorrow.

crocus /'kroʊkəs/, *n., pl.* **crocuses. 1.** a garden plant of the iris family with single showy flowers, grown from a bulb. **2.** a deep yellow color; saffron. [L, from Gk: saffron]

Croesus /'krisəs/, *n.* died 546 BC, king of Lydia 560–546 BC, noted for his great wealth.

croft /krɒft/, *n.* a small piece of enclosed ground next to a house, used for crops or animals, esp. in Scotland. [OE] **–crofter,** *n.*

croissant /krwʌsɒ̃/, *n.* a roll of yeast dough or puff pastry, shaped into a crescent and baked.

Cro-Magnon /kroʊ-'mægnən, -'mænjən/, *adj.* of or relating to the prehistoric race *Homo sapiens*, an early type of modern man, characterised by a very long head, low face and eye sockets and tall stature. [from Cro-Magnon, a cave in SW France, where in 1868 remains were first found]

Cromwell /'krɒmwel, -wəl/, *n.* **Oliver,** 1599–1658, English general, Puritan statesman, and Lord Protector of the Commonwealth 1653–58.

crone /kroʊn/, *n.* an old woman. [MD *croonje,* from ONF *carogne* carcass]

cronk /krɒŋk/, *adj. Colloq.* **1.** dishonest. **2.** sick; ailing. [Brit d. *crank*]

crony /'kroʊni/, *n., pl.* **-nies.** a close friend. [? from Gk: longlasting, from *chrónos* time]

crook¹ /krʊk/, *n.* **1.** a bent or curved object, part, or tool; hook. **2.** a hooked or curved stick, e.g. a shepherd's staff or bishop's crosier. **3.** a bend or curve. **4.** *Colloq.* a dishonest person. ◇*v.t., v.i.* **5.** to bend or curve. [ME, from Scand]

crook² /krʊk/, *Colloq.* ◇*adj.* **1.** sick; disabled. **2.** bad; inferior. **3.** unpleasant; difficult: *a crook job.* ◇*adv.* **4. go crook at** or **on,** to scold.

crooked /'krʊkəd/, *adj.* **1.** bent. **2.** deformed. **3.** dishonest. [OE *gecrōcod*]

croon /krun/, *v.t., v.i.* **1.** to sing, hum, or murmur. **2.** to sing in a sentimental manner. [ME, from MD: murmur] **–crooner,** *n.*

crop /krɒp/, *n., v.,* **cropped, cropping.** ◇*n.* **1.** the cultivated produce of the ground, e.g. grain or fruit, growing or gathered. **2.** the yield of produce for a particular season or place. **3.** a collection or group: *a crop of lies.* **4.** the handle of a whip. **5.** a short riding whip with a loop. **6.** the act or result of cropping. **7.** a short haircut. **8.** the enlargement of a bird's gullet in which food is held before digestion. ◇*v.t.* **9.** to cut off or remove the tops or ends of. **10.** to cut short. **11.** to clip the ears, hair, etc., of. **12.** to grow or gather as a crop. ◇*v.i.* **13.** to yield a crop. ◇*v.* **14. crop up,** to appear, esp. unexpectedly. [OE]

crop-dust /'krɒp-dʌst/, *v.t.* to spray crops, usu. from an aircraft, to kill insects or disease. —**crop-duster,** *n.* —**crop-dusting,** *n.*

cropper /'krɒpə/, *n.* **1.** someone or something that crops. **2.** a plant which yields a crop: *This variety is a good cropper.* **3. come a cropper,** *Colloq.* **a.** to fall heavily. **b.** to fail or to meet with an accident.

crop rotation, *n.* the system of growing different crops in the same piece of ground in turn, to keep the soil fertile.

croquet /'kroʊkeɪ, -ki/, *n.* an outdoor game played with mallets to knock wooden balls through a series of metal arches. [d. F: hockey stick]

croquette /kroʊ'kɛt/, *n.* a small mass of chopped or mashed meat, fish, potato, etc., often crumbed and deep-fried. [F: crunch]

Crosby /'krɒzbi/, *n.* **Bing** (*Harry Lillis Crosby*), 1904–77, US singer and actor; noted for his 'crooning' style of singing.

crosier /'kroʊziə/, *n.* a hooked stick carried as a symbol of his position by a bishop or abbot.

cross /krɒs/, *n.* **1.** any object, figure, or mark in shape of two intersecting lines, such as + or X. **2.** the mark (X) made instead of a signature by a person who cannot write. **3.** a crossing. **4.** something opposing. **5.** the mixing of breeds of animals or plants. **6.** an animal, plant, etc., produced by crossing; crossbreed. **7.** something between two things in character: *a cross between a book and a magazine.* **8.** a structure made of an upright post with a bar across it on which people were formerly put to death. **9. the Cross,** the cross upon which Jesus died. **10.** the cross as the sign of Christianity. **11.** a structure or monument in the form of a cross. **12.** any of various images of the Christian cross as used for ornament, in art, etc., such as the Latin, Greek, St. George's, or Maltese cross. **13.** any trouble, hardship, duty, etc.: *He has his cross to bear.* ◇*v.t.* **14.** to mark with a cross. **15.** to place in the form of a cross: *to cross the fingers.* **16.** to draw a line across. **17.** to lie or pass across; intersect. **18.** to go or reach from one side to the other: *to cross the river.* **19.** to meet and pass. **20.** to oppose; thwart. **21.** to cause (members of different breeds, etc.) to produce offspring; crossfertilise. ◇*v.i.* **22.** to lie across; intersect. **23.** to go or reach from one side or place to another. **24.** to meet and pass. **25.** to interbreed. ◇*v.* **26. cross one's mind,** to come as an idea; occur to one. **27. cross the floor,** in parliament, to vote with the opposing party. ◇*adj.* **28.** lying or passing across; crossed. **29.** involving interchange; reciprocal. **30.** opposite; contrary. **31.** unfavorable. **32.** bad-tempered; irritable. **33.** of mixed breed; crossbred; hybrid. [OE *cros*, from OIrish, from L *crux*] —**crossness,** *n.*

cross-, the first part of compounds, modifying the second part, meaning **1.** going across: *crossroad.* **2.** counter: *cross-examination.* **3.** cross-shaped: *crossbones.*

Cross /krɒs/, *n.* **Zora Bernise May,** 1890–1964, Australian journalist, novelist and poet.

crossbar /'krɒsbɑ/, *n.* **1.** a bar, line, or stripe across another. **2.** *Gymn.* a horizontal bar used for jumping over, etc.

crossbench /'krɒsbɛntʃ/, *n. Parl.* **1.** a seat for those who belong to neither government nor opposition. ◇*adj.* **2.** independent. —**crossbencher,** *n.*

crossbones /'krɒsboʊnz/, *n.pl.* two bones placed crosswise, usu. below a skull, as a symbol of death.

crossbow /'krɒsboʊ/, *n. Mediev. Hist.* a weapon consisting of a bow fixed across a piece of wood with a groove to direct an arrow. —**crossbowman,** *n.*

crossbreed /'krɒsbrid/, *v.,* **-bred, -breeding,** *n.* ◇*v.t., v.i.* **1.** to produce (a hybrid) within a species, using two breeds or varieties. ◇*n.* **2.** a person of mixed race. **3.** an animal produced by crossbreeding. —**crossbred,** *adj.*

crosscheck /krɒs'tʃɛk, 'krɒstʃɛk/, *v.t.* to make sure of the truth or accuracy of (something) by checking from other sources.

cross-country /'krɒs-kʌntri/, *adj.;* /krɒs'kʌntri/, *adv.* across open country; not following roads.

crosscut /'krɒskʌt/, *adj., n., v.,* **-cut, -cutting.** ◇*adj.* **1.** made or used for cutting across: *a crosscut saw.* **2.** cut across. ◇*n.* **3.** a cut or course across. ◇*v.t., v.i.* **4.** to cut across.

cross-examine /krɒs-əg'zæmən/, *v.t.,* **-ined, -ining. 1.** to question closely. **2.** *Law.* to question (a witness called by the opposing side) to check the truth or accuracy of his or her story. —**cross-examination,** *n.* —**cross-examiner,** *n.*

cross-eyed /'krɒs-aɪd/, *adj.* having both eyes turned towards the nose.

cross-fertilise or **cross-fertilize** /krɒs-'fɜtəlaɪz/, *v.t.,* **-lised, -lising. 1.** *Biol.* to fertilise by fusion of the egg of one individual with the sperm (or male gamete) of another. **2.** *Bot.* to fertilise one flower or plant with pollen from another (opposed to *self-fertilise*). —**cross-fertilisation,** *n.*

cross-fire /'krɒs-faɪə/, *n.* **1.** *Mil.* line(s) of fire from two or more positions, crossing one another. **2.** a lively exchange of words or opinions.

crossing /'krɒsɪŋ/, *n.* **1.** the act of someone or something that crosses. **2.** a place where lines, tracks, etc., cross; intersection. **3.** a place at which a road, river, railway, etc., may be crossed.

crossing over, *n.* **1.** any instance of crossing or exchanging. **2.** *Biol.* an exchange of corresponding parts between homologous chromosomes, esp. during meiosis.

crossover /ˈkrɒsouvə/, *n.* **1.** the act of crossing over. **2.** *Biol.* a genotype resulting from crossing over during meiosis.

crossover network, *n. Elect.* an audio circuit device in a radio or record player which sorts impulses received and channels them into high- or low-frequency loudspeakers.

crosspatch /ˈkrɒspætʃ/, *n. Colloq.* a cross person.

cross-pollinate /krɒs-ˈpɒləneɪt/, *v.t.*, **-nated, -nating.** → **cross-fertilise.** – **cross-pollination,** *n.*

cross-purpose /krɒs-ˈpɜːpəs/, *n.* **1.** an opposing or contrary purpose. **2. be at cross-purposes,** to talk or act on the basis of a wrong opinion of the other's intention; misunderstand (each other).

cross-reference /krɒs-ˈrefrəns/, *n.* a reference from one part of a book, index, etc., to another. – **cross-refer, cross-reference,** *v.*

crossroad /ˈkrɒsroud/, *n.* **1.** a road that crosses another. **2.** a road connecting main roads. **3. a.** Also, **crossroads.** the place where roads meet. **b.** (*usu. pl.*) a point where one must decide between different courses of action.

cross-section /ˈkrɒs-sekʃən/, *n.* **1.** a cutting across anything, esp. at right angles to its length. **2.** a piece cut off in this way. **3. a.** a drawing of the surface that would be shown by this cutting: *a cross-section of the leg showing skin, nerves, muscles and bone.* **4.** a typical selection; sample showing all characteristic parts: *a cross-section of Australian opinion.* ◊*v.t.* **5.** to cut or make into a cross-section. – **cross-sectional,** *adj.*

cross-stitch /ˈkrɒs-stɪtʃ/, *n.* **1.** (a style of embroidery using) stitch made by crossing two straight stitches in an X shape. ◊*v.t., v.i.* **2.** to sew or work with a cross-stitch.

crosswise /ˈkrɒswaɪz/, *adv.* **1.** across; transversely. **2.** in the form of a cross. Also, **crossways.**

crossword /ˈkrɒswɜːd/, *n.* a puzzle in which words are to be worked out from clues and fitted, running across or down, into an arrangement of numbered squares. Also, **crossword puzzle.**

crotch /krɒtʃ/, *n.* a forked piece, part, etc., as of the human body or a pair of trousers where the two legs join. [var. of CRUTCH] – **crotched,** *adj.*

crotchet /ˈkrɒtʃət/, *n.* **1.** *Music.* a note with the time value of one beat, i.e., $\frac{1}{4}$ of the value of a semibreve. **2.** an odd idea or fancy. **3.** a hooklike part or object. [ME, from OF. See CROCHET]

crotchety /ˈkrɒtʃəti/, *adj.* **1.** given to odd fancies. **2.** *Colloq.* bad-tempered or difficult.

crouch /krautʃ/, *v.i.* **1.** (of people) to lower the body with legs bent, leaning forward. **2.** (of animals) to lie low as when about to spring. **3.** to bend or hunch the body. **4.** to bend in a humble or slavish way; cringe. ◊*n.* **5.** the act or position of crouching. [ME, from OF: become bent, from *croche* hook]

croup[1] /kruːp/, *n. Med.* inflammation of the larynx (throat), esp. in children, marked by a hoarse cough and difficulty in breathing. [use of *croup,* *v.* (now dial.), cry hoarsely, b. CROAK and WHOOP]

croup[2] /kruːp/, *n.* the rump or buttocks of certain animals, esp. the horse. Also, **croupe.** [ME *croupe,* from F, from Gmc]

croupier /ˈkruːpiə/, *n.* an attendant who collects and pays money at a gambling table. [F; orig.: someone who rides behind on the croup of another's horse]

crouton /ˈkruːtɒn/, *n.* a small piece of fried or toasted bread served in soup, etc. [F]

crow[1] /krou/, *n.* **1.** any of various black, shiny birds with a rough-sounding call. **2. as the crow flies,** in a straight line. **3. stone the crows,** *Colloq.* (an expression of surprise). [OE *crawe*]

crow[2] /krou/, *v.,* **crowed** (or **crew** for def. 1), **crowing, crowing,** *n.* ◊*v.i.* **1.** to make the sound of a cock. **2.** to make a wordless cry of pleasure, like a baby. **3.** to talk loudly of one's success; boast. ◊*n.* **4.** a crowing sound. [OE *crāwen*; imitative]

Crow /krou/, *n.* a North American Indian tribe, belonging to the Siouan linguistic stock, living in eastern Montana. [translation of their own name, *Absaroke* crow, sparrowhawk, or bird people]

crowbar /ˈkroubɑː/, *n.* an iron bar, often with a wedge-shaped end, for use as a lever, etc.

crowd /kraud/, *n.* **1.** a large number of people or things gathered closely together. **2.** people in general. **3.** a group or set of people; clique: *I can't get on with your crowd.* ◊*v.i.* **4.** to gather in large numbers. **5.** to press forward; push. ◊*v.t.* **6.** to press closely together; force into a confined space. **7.** to overfill. [OE *crūdan*] – **crowded,** *adj.*

croweater /ˈkrouiːtə/, *n. Colloq.* a South Australian.

crown /kraun/, *n.* **1.** an ornamental headdress worn by a king, queen, etc., as a symbol of position, usu. made of gold and precious stones, etc. **2. a.** the power or position of a king, queen, etc. **b.** the governing power of a state under a monarchical government. **3.** a crownlike symbol or design, used in crests, as a badge of rank, etc. **4.** a wreath worn on the head as a mark of victory or honor. **5.** an honor or reward. **6.** a coin of several countries, usu. with a crown or crowned head on it; in UK and Australia formerly a five shilling piece. **7.** a pre-metric paper size, 15 x 20 inches. **8.** something crown-shaped, e.g. the corona of a flower. **9.** the top or highest part of anything, as of a head, hat, or mountain. **10.** the highest or best part or quality: *the crown of his achievements.* **11. a.** the part of a tooth above the gum, covered by enamel. **b.** an artificial replacement for this. ◊*v.t.* **12.** to place a crown or wreath on the head of. **13.** to install a king, queen, etc., in office by crowning. **14.** to honor; reward. **15.** to top, or be the top part of: *Snow crowned the mountain.* **16.** *Colloq.* to hit on the head. **17.** to complete well or successfully. [ME, from AF, from L: garland, crown]

crown cap, *n.* →**crown seal.**

crown land, *n.* land belonging to the government.

crown-of-thorns starfish, *n.* a starfish with sharp, stinging spines, found widely in tropical waters, esp. on the Great Barrier Reef, where it destroys coral.

crown seal, *n.* a metal cap for sealing fizzy drink, crimped over the rim of a bottle.

crown wheel, *n.* the larger of two wheels in a bevel gear.

crow's-foot /'krouz-fut/, *n., pl.* **-feet.** (*usu. pl.*) a wrinkle at the outer corner of the eye.

crow's-nest /'krouz-nɛst/, *n. Naut.* **1.** a lookout box or shelter near the top of a ship's mast. **2.** a similar lookout ashore.

crucial /'kruʃəl/, *adj.* of the greatest importance; decisive; critical: *a crucial experiment.* [L, combining form of *crux* cross]

crucible /'krusəbəl/, *n.* **1.** a container used for heating substances to high temperatures. **2.** a severe test. [ML: night lamp, melting pot]

crucifix /'krusəfiks/, *n.* **1.** a cross with the figure of Jesus on it. **2.** a Christian cross. [ME, from LL: fixed to a cross]

crucifixion /krusə'fikʃən/, *n.* **1.** the act of crucifying. **2.** (*cap.*) (a picture, etc., of) the death of Jesus on the cross.

cruciform /'krusəfɔrm/, *adj.* cross-shaped.

crucify /'krusəfaɪ/, *v.t.,* **-fied, -fying. 1.** to put to death by nailing or binding the body to a cross. **2.** to treat cruelly; torment. [ME, from OF, from LL: fix to a cross]

crude /krud/, *adj.,* **cruder, crudest. 1.** in a raw or natural state; unrefined: *crude oil; crude sugar.* **2.** not carefully done. **3.** lacking grace, style, or politeness: *crude behavior.* [ME, from L: raw, crude, rough] **—crudeness,** *n.* **—crudity,** *n.*

cruel /'kruəl/, *adj.* **1.** tending or liking to cause suffering; harsh: *a cruel person.* **2.** causing pain or distress: *a cruel remark.* [ME, from OF, from L: hard, cruel, akin to *crudus* CRUDE]

cruelty /'kruəlti/, *n., pl.* **-ties. 1.** the condition or quality of being cruel. **2.** cruel nature or behavior. **3.** a cruel act.

cruet /'kruət/, *n.* **1.** a set, on a stand, of containers for salt, pepper, and mustard or for vinegar and oil. **2.** one such container. [ME, from OF: little pitcher, from Gmc]

cruise /kruz/, *v.,* **cruised, cruising,** *n.* ◇*v.i.* **1.** to sail from place to place, as when looking for enemy ships, etc. **2.** (of a car, aircraft, etc.) to move easily at moderate speed. ◇*n.* **3.** a cruising voyage. [D: cross, cruise]

cruiser /'kruzə/, *n.* **1.** a fast warship of medium size. **2.** a ship for pleasure trips.

crumb /krʌm/, *n.* **1.** a small piece broken or fallen off something, esp. bread, cake, etc. **2.** the soft inner part of bread (opposed to crust). ◇*v.t.* **3.** to cover with breadcrumbs. **4.** to break into crumbs. [OE *cruma*]

crumble /'krʌmbəl/, *v.t., v.i.,* **-bled, -bling.** to break into small pieces or crumbs. [OE *gecrymman* crumble (from *cruma* crumb)] **—crumbly,** *adj.*

crummy /'krʌmi/, *adj.,* **-mier, -miest.** *Colloq.* of poor quality or in poor condition. Also, **crumby.**

crumpet /'krʌmpət/, *n.* a kind of soft, moist, flat yeast cake with holes on top, usu. served toasted and buttered. [short for *crumpet cake* curled cake, ME *crompid*, crimped]

crumple /'krʌmpəl/, *v.t., v.i.,* **-pled, -pling. 1.** to crush together into wrinkles. **2.** to break down; collapse. [ME *crimplen* wrinkle]

crunch /krʌntʃ/, *v.t.* **1.** to chew (crisp food) with the teeth. **2.** to crush or grind noisily. ◇*v.i.* **3.** to make a crunching sound. ◇*n.* **4.** the act or sound of crunching. **5.** *Colloq.* a moment of crisis. [b. *craunch* and CRUSH] **—crunchy,** *adj.*

crupper /'krʌpə/, *n.* **1.** the leather strap on the back of a saddle or harness, passing under a horse's tail to prevent the saddle from slipping forward. **2.** a horse's rump. [ME, from OF]

crusade /kru'seɪd/, *n., v.,* **-saded, -sading.** ◇*n.* **1.** (*oft. cap.*) any of the military expeditions of European Christians in the 11th, 12th, and 13th centuries to regain the Holy Land from Muslims. **2.** a strong group movement to defend or advance some idea or cause. ◇*v.i.* **3.** to go on, run, or join in a crusade. [b. OF and Sp: bear the cross, from L *crux* cross] **—crusader,** *n.*

crush /krʌʃ/, *v.t.* **1.** to press between hard surfaces so as to break or compress. **2.** to break into small pieces. **3.** to crush stone. **3.** to press (fruit, etc.) in order to force out juice, etc. **4.** to put down or overpower: *to crush a rebellion.* ◇*v.i.* **5.** to become crushed. **6.** to press or crowd. ◇*n.* **7.** the act of crushing. **8.** the state of being crushed. **9.** *Colloq.* a crowd. **10.** a drink made by crushing fruit: *orange crush.* **11.** *Colloq.* a great fondness, often short-lived. [ME, from OF: break, crush] **—crusher,** *n.*

Crusoe /'krusoʊ/, *n.* **Robinson**, the shipwrecked seaman in Defoe's novel *Robinson Crusoe* (1719), who lives adventurously for years on a small uninhabited island.

crust /krʌst/, *n.* **1.** (a piece of) the hard surface of a roll or loaf of bread. **2.** the pastry covering of a pie. **3.** any hard outer surface or covering. **4.** *Colloq.* a living: *to earn a crust.* [ME, from L: rind]

crustacean /krʌs'teɪʃən/, *n.* one of a class of arthropods with hard shells, usu. living in water, e.g. prawns, crabs, barnacles, slaters, etc.

crusty /'krʌsti/, *adj.,* **crustier, crustiest. 1.** like or having a crust. **2.** rough or sour-tempered; gruff or surly: *a crusty old man; a crusty remark.* **—crustiness,** *n.*

crutch /krʌtʃ/, *n*. **1.** a stick or support to help an injured or old person walk, usu. with a piece at the top to fit under the armpit. **2.** a forked support or part. **3.** the part where the legs meet in the body or trousers. **4.** *Colloq.* anything leaned on or relied on. ◇*v.t.* **5.** to shear (wool) from a sheep's hindquarters. **6.** to support on a crutch. [OE *crycc*]

crux /krʌks/, *n., pl.* **cruxes, cruces** /ˈkruːsiːz/. a vital, basic, or decisive point. [L: cross, torment, trouble]

cry /kraɪ/, *v*., **cried, crying,** *n., pl.* **cries.** ◇*v.i.* **1.** to make wordless sounds, esp. of unhappiness or suffering, usu. with tears. **2.** to weep; shed tears. **3.** to call loudly; shout. ◇*v.t.* **4.** to shout out. **5.** to sell by shouting. **6.** to beg for. ◇*v.* **7. cry down, a.** to speak poorly of. **b.** to prevent (someone) from speaking, esp. by talking loudly: *He cried down any opposition*. **8. cry off,** to break (a promise, agreement, etc.). **9. cry up,** to praise. ◇*n*. **10.** a shout or scream. **11.** a noise or shouting out. **12.** an urgent request; appeal. **13.** a call of goods for sale, as by a street seller. **14.** a battle cry; rallying call: *The cry went up.* **15.** a fit of weeping: *Have a good cry.* **16.** (a characteristic) sound or call of an animal. **17. a far cry, a.** long distance. **b.** very different. [ME, from L: wail]

crying /ˈkraɪɪŋ/, *adj.* demanding attention or improvement: *a crying shame*.

cryo-, a word part meaning 'icy cold', 'frost', 'low temperature'. [Gk *kryo-,* combining form of *krýos*]

cryogen /ˈkraɪədʒən/, *n*. a substance for producing low temperatures; a freezing mixture. —**cryogenic,** *adj.*

cryolite /ˈkraɪəlaɪt/, *n*. a white or clear mineral, sodium aluminium fluoride, Na$_3$AlF$_6$, used in the production of aluminium.

cryonics /kraɪˈɒnɪks/, *n*. the practice of storing a dead body at a very low temperature in the hope that it may be possible to bring it back to life in future. —**cryonic,** *adj.*

cryophyte /ˈkraɪəfaɪt/, *n*. a plant, esp. an alga, growing on ice and snow.

crypt /krɪpt/, *n*. an underground room or hole, esp. beneath the main floor of a church, used as a burial place, etc. [L, from Gk: hidden] —**cryptal,** *adj.*

cryptic /ˈkrɪptɪk/, *adj.* **1.** hidden; secret. **2.** mysterious; obscure: *a cryptic message*.

crypto-, a word part meaning 'hidden', as in *cryptogram*. Also, before vowels, **crypt-.** [combining form representing Gk *kryptós*]

cryptogram /ˈkrɪptəgræm/, *n*. something written in code. —**cryptogrammic,** *adj.*

cryptograph /ˈkrɪptəgræf, -grɑːf/, a system of secret writing; code. —**cryptography,** *n*. —**cryptographer, cryptographist,** *n*. —**cryptographic,** *adj.*

crystal /ˈkrɪstl/, *n*. **1.** a clear mineral or glass which looks like ice. **2.** clear crystallised quartz. **3.** *Chem., Mineral.* a substance with a particular geometric form due to the regular arrangement of atoms, ions, or molecules in it. **4.** a single grain or piece of crystalline substance. **5.** clear, brilliant glass. **6.** cut glass. **7.** →**quartz crystal.** ◇*adj.* **8.** of or like crystal. [ME, from OF] —**crystalline,** *adj.*

crystal ball, *n*. a ball into which a fortune-teller looks, supposedly to foresee distant or future events.

crystallise or **crystallize** /ˈkrɪstəlaɪz/, *v*., **-lised, -lising.** ◇*v.t.* **1.** to form into crystals. **2.** to (make something) take an actual or particular form. **3.** to coat with sugar. ◇*v.i.* to form crystals. —**crystallisation,** *n*.

crystallo-, a word part meaning 'crystal', as in *crystallography*. Also, before vowels, **crystall-.** [Gk *krystallo-,* combining form of *krystállos*]

crystallography /krɪstəˈlɒgrəfi/, *n*. the science dealing with the form and structure of crystals. —**crystallographer,** *n*. —**crystallographic,** *adj.*

crystal oscillator, *n*. a source of electrical oscillations of very constant frequency determined by the physical features of a quartz crystal.

c/s, *Symbol.* cycles per second. See **hertz.**

Cs, *Chem. Symbol.* caesium.

CSIRO /ˌsiː ɛs aɪ ɑːr ˈoʊ/, *n*. Commonwealth Scientific and Industrial Research Organisation; an Australian statutory body established in 1949 carrying out research on behalf of the Commonwealth; the largest scientific research organisation in Australia.

CSM /ˌsiː ɛs ˈɛm/, *Abbrev.* Chief Stipendiary Magistrate.

CST /ˌsiː ɛs ˈtiː/, *Abbrev.* Central Standard Time.

cu., *Abbrev.* cubic.

Cu, *Chem. Symbol.* copper. [L *cuprum*]

cub /kʌb/, *n*. **1.** the young of certain animals, as the lion and bear. **2.** *Colloq.* an awkward or uncivilised youth. **3.** a junior member of Boy Scouts (aged 8–11). ◇*adj.* **4.** trainee: *a cub reporter*. [var. of COB] —**cubbish,** *adj.* —**cubbishness,** *n*.

Cuba /ˈkjuːbə/, *n*. a republic consisting of a group of islands in the Caribbean Sea, south of Florida, US; an independent republic since 1902 but under US influence until establishment of Castro's government in 1960. Pop. 10 290 000 (1987 est.); 110 922 km^2. *Language:* Spanish. *Currency:* peso. *Cap.:* Havana. —**Cuban,** *n., adj.*

cubby /ˈkʌbi/, *n., pl.* **-bies.** a children's playhouse or other small room or enclosed area. Also, **cubbyhole, cubbyhouse.** [obs. *cub* shed]

cube /kjuːb/, *n*. **1.** a solid with six equal square sides. **2.** a piece of anything in this shape: *a sugar cube*. **3.** the result of multiplying something by itself twice; the third power of a quantity: *The cube of 4 is 4 × 4 × 4, or 64. The cube of x is x^3*. [L, from Gk: die, cube]

cube root, *n*. the quantity of which a given quantity is the cube (def. 3): *4 is the cube root of 64*.

cubic /'kjubɪk/, *adj.* **1.** solid or relating to solid content; of three dimensions: *cubic metre* (the volume of cube with edges each one metre long). **2.** Also, **cubical, cubiform,** cube-shaped. **3.** *Maths.* of the third power or degree.

cubicle /'kjubɪkəl/, *n.* a small space or partly enclosed tiny room: *a changing cubicle; toilet cubicle.* [L: bedchamber]

cubism /'kjubɪzəm/, *n. Art.* a movement, started in France in 1907, which used the arrangements of lines and geometrical shapes to show solidity and volume of objects on a flat surface. —**cubist,** *n.* —**cubistic,** *adj.*

cubit /'kjubət/, *n.* an ancient linear unit based on the length of the forearm, usu. between 45 and 55 cm. [ME, from L *cubitum* elbow, ell]

cuckold /'kʌkəld/, *n.* **1.** a man whose wife has had sexual intercourse with another man. ◇*v.t.* **2.** to make a cuckold of (a husband). [ME *cokewold*; orig. uncert.] —**cuckoldry,** *n.*

cuckoo /'kuku/, *n.* **1.** any of a number of migratory birds noted for their habit of laying eggs in the nests of other birds. **2.** (the sound of) the typical two-note call of the cuckoo. **3.** *Colloq.* fool. ◇*adj.* **4.** *Colloq.* mad or foolish. [ME *cucu* (imitative of its call)]

cuckoo-shrike /'kuku-fraɪk/, *n.* any of various mainly tropical birds, as the **black-faced cuckoo-shrike,** which is blue-grey in color with a black face.

cuckoo-spit /'kuku-spɪt/, *n.* a frothy substance found on plants, produced by the larvae of certain insects.

cucumber /'kjukʌmbə/, *n.* (a creeping plant bearing) a fruit, which is usu. long and thin with green skin and white flesh and is used for salads and for pickling. [F, from L]

cucurbit /kju'kɜbət/, *n.* a plant of the gourd family, including pumpkins, melons, and zucchini. [ME, from L: gourd]

cud /kʌd/, *n.* **1.** food which cattle, etc., return from the first stomach to the mouth to chew a second time. **2. chew the cud,** to think over something; ponder. [OE *cudu*]

cuddle /'kʌdl/, *v.*, **-dled, -dling,** *n.* ◇*v.t.* **1.** to draw or hold close fondly; hug gently. ◇*v.i.* **2.** to lie or curl up close. ◇*n.* **3.** a hug; embrace. [obs. *couth,* friendly + *-le,* frequentative suffix] —**cuddlesome, cuddly,** *adj.*

cudgel /'kʌdʒəl/, *n., v.,* **-elled, -elling.** ◇*n.* **1.** a short thick stick used as a weapon; club. ◇*v.t.* **2.** to beat. ◇*v.* **3. cudgel one's brains,** to think hard. [OE *cycgel*]

cudgerie /'kʌdʒəri/, *n.* any of several large Australian rainforest trees. [Aboriginal]

cue[1] /kju/, *n., v.,* **cued, cueing.** ◇*n.* **1.** *Theat.* anything said or done that serves as a signal for subsequent words or action: *An offstage door slam was his cue to enter.* **2.** a hint; guiding suggestion. ◇*v.t.* **3.** to give a cue to. [? spelling of abbrev. *q.* or *qu.* for L *quando* when]

cue[2] /kju/, *n., v.,* **cued, cueing.** ◇*n.* **1.** a long tapered stick with a leather tip, used to hit the ball in billiards, etc. **2.** → **queue** (def. 2).

◇*v.t.* **3.** to hit with a cue. [var. of *queue,* from F]

cue ball, *n.* (in billiards, etc.) the ball struck by the cue, as distinguished from the other balls on the table.

cuff[1] /kʌf/, *n.* **1.** a fold, band, piece of lace, etc., at the wrist of a sleeve. **2.** a trouser turn-up. **3.** → **handcuff. 4. off the cuff,** without preparation; on the spur of the moment: *to speak off the cuff.* [ME *cuffe* glove]

cuff[2] /kʌf/, *v.t.* **1.** to hit with the open hand; beat. ◇*n.* **2.** a blow with the fist or open hand. [cf. Swed *kuffa* thrust, push]

cuisenaire rods /kwizə,nɛə 'rɒdz/, *n.pl.* colored wooden blocks of different lengths, used in teaching numbers to children. [named after the inventor, Georges *Cuisenaire,* Belgian educationalist]

cuisine /kwə'zin/, *n.* style of cooking; cookery. [F, from L: kitchen]

cul-de-sac /'kʌl-də-sæk/, *n.* a street, lane, etc., closed at one end. [F: bottom of sack]

-cule, a noun ending meaning 'small', as in *animalcule, molecule.* Also, **-cle.** [F, or from L *-culus, -cula, -culum*]

Culgoa /kʌl'goʊə/, *n.* a river which is a continuation of the Balonne River in southern Qld, flowing in a south-westerly direction to join the Darling River north of Bourke in NSW. 320 km. [Aboriginal: running through, or returning]

culinary /'kʌlənri, -ənəri/, *adj.* relating to the kitchen or cookery; used in cooking. [L: kitchen]

cull /kʌl/, *v.t.* **1.** to choose; pick out the best from. **2.** to collect; gather. **3.** to remove animals of a lower quality from a (herd or flock). ◇*n.* **4.** the act of culling. **5.** something culled, esp. an animal taken from a herd or flock. [ME, from OF, from L: collect]

Culloden /kʌ'lɒdn/, *n.* a moor in Scotland, near Inverness; decisive victory of the English over the Jacobites under Prince Charles Edward Stuart, 1746.

culminate /'kʌlmənеɪt/, *v.i.,* **-nated, -nating.** to reach the highest point (usu. fol. by *in*). [LL: crowned] —**culmination,** *n.*

Culotta /kə'lɒtə/, *n.* Nino /'ninoʊ/ → John O'Grady.

culottes /kə'lɒts/, *n.pl.* trousers cut wide to look like a skirt. [F]

culpable /'kʌlpəbəl/, *adj.* deserving blame. [L: blameworthy] —**culpability, culpableness,** *n.*

culprit /'kʌlprət/, *n.* someone guilty of or responsible for an offence or fault. [orig. uncert.; traditionally explained as from L *cul(pābilis),* guilty + AF *pri(s)t* ready, i.e. the prosecution is ready to prove guilt]

cult /kʌlt/, *n.* **1.** any particular system of religious worship, esp. with reference to its rites and ceremonies. **2.** → **sect. 3.** an intense, almost religious devotion to a person or thing: *a cult of Napoleon.* **4.** a popular fashion; craze. [L: care, worship] —**cultism,** *n.* —**cultist,** *n.* —**cultic,** *adj.*

cultivar /'kʌltəvɑ/, *n.* a variety of a plant that has been produced only under cultivation. [CULTI(VATED) + VAR(IETY)]

cultivate /'kʌltəveɪt/, *v.t.*, **-vated**, **-vating**. **1.** to work (land) in raising crops. **2.** to dig; turn over (earth). **3.** to encourage the growth or development of. **4.** to grow. **5.** to develop or improve by education; train; refine: *to cultivate the mind.* **6.** to work at or encourage: *to cultivate a friendship.* **7.** to try to make friends with (someone). [ML: tilled, from L: till] **–cultivated**, *adj.* **–cultivation**, *n.*

Cultivated Australian /,kʌltəveɪtəd əs'treɪljən/, *n.* that pronunciation of Australian English which serves as a prestige form. See **spectrum of Australian English**.

cultivator /'kʌltəveɪtə/, *n.* a tool or machine for loosening the earth around plants.

Cultural Revolution /,kʌlʃərəl revə'luʃən/, *n.* a movement in China, 1966–68, intended to preserve ideological and revolutionary enthusiasm, esp. among the young, for Mao Zedong's revolution.

culture /'kʌltʃə/, *n., v.,* **-tured**, **-turing**. ◇*n.* **1.** the state or stage of civilisation of a particular people at a certain time: *Greek culture.* **2.** the skills, arts, beliefs, and customs of a group of people, passed on from one generation to another. **3.** development or improvement by education or training. **4.** the cultivation of soil. **5.** the raising of plants or animals, esp. to improve or develop them. **6.** *Biol.* the growing of cells, e.g. bacteria or human tissue, for scientific studies, medicinal use, etc. ◇*v.t.* **7.** to cultivate. [ME, from F, from L: tending, cultivation] **–cultural**, *adj.*

cultured /'kʌltʃəd/, *adj.* **1.** grown by cultivation. **2.** civilised; refined.

cultured pearl, *n.* a pearl made to grow around a tiny object put inside the shell of an oyster or clam.

culture shock, *n.* confusion and unhappiness caused by difficulty in getting used to a culture different from one's own.

culvert /'kʌlvət/, *n.* a drain or channel crossing under a road, etc.; conduit. [orig. uncert.]

cum /kʌm, kʊm/, *prep.* (used between two nouns to describe object with two functions): *a bedroom-cum-living room.* [L]

Cumberland Islands /,kʌmbələnd 'aɪləndz/, *n.pl.* a group of islands which extends along the coast of northern Qld between Mackay and the Whitsunday Passage. Also, the **Whitsunday Group**.

cumbersome /'kʌmbəsəm/, *adj.* **1.** troublesome; burdensome. **2.** awkward; unwieldy. Also, **cumbrous**.

cumin /'kʌmən/, *n.* (a small plant with) a seedlike fruit used as a spice in cooking. Also, **cummin**. [ME, from L, from Gk]

cummerbund /'kʌməbʌnd/, *n.* a sash worn round a man's waist with a tail coat or dress shirt. [Hind, from Pers]

Cummings /'kʌmɪŋz/, **Edward Estlin** (*e e cummings*), 1894–1962, US poet, writer, and painter; noted for his experimental use of punctuation, typography and verse form.

cumquat /'kʌmkwɒt/, *n.* → **kumquat**.

cumulative /'kjumjələtɪv/, *adj.* **1.** increasing, growing, or formed by repeated additions; accumulated. **2.** *Law.* (of gaol sentences) to be served one after another (opposed to *concurrent sentences*).

cumulonimbus /,kjumjəloʊ'nɪmbəs/, *n.* a mass of cloud rising in the form of mountains or towers, typical of thunderstorms.

cumulus /'kjumjələs/, *n., pl.* **-li** /-li/. **1.** a heap; pile. **2.** *Weather.* a cloud with a flat base topped with rounded heaps, usu. white with a clear outline and seen in fair weather. **–cumulous**, *adj.*

cuneiform /'kjunəfɔm/, *adj.* **1.** wedge-shaped. ◇*n.* **2.** the characters used in writing in ancient Persia, Assyria, etc. [L *cuneus* wedge + -I- + -FORM]

cunjevoi /'kʌndʒəvɔɪ/, *n.* **1.** a plant with arrow-shaped leaves, growing in Asia, Pacific Islands, and Australia in rainforest and along coastal rivers. Its roots (poisonous when raw) were cooked and eaten by Aborigines. **2.** Also, **cunje**. a common Australian primitive seashore animal, used as fish bait. [Aboriginal]

cunnilingus /,kʌnə'lɪŋgəs/, *n.* oral stimulation of female genitals.

cunning /'kʌnɪŋ/, *n.* **1.** ability; skill. **2.** the skill used in a clever plan, or in deceiving. ◇*adj.* showing or done with cunning; crafty. [OE *cunnung*, from *cunnan* know (how)]

Cunningham /'kʌnɪŋhəm, 'kʌnɪŋəm/, *n.* **Allan**, 1791–1839, Australian botanist and explorer, born in England.

cup /kʌp/, *n., v.,* **cupped**, **cupping**. ◇*n.* **1.** a small, round, open container, made of china, plastic, metal, etc., used mainly to drink from. **2.** the contents of a cup. **3.** a unit of volume, formerly 8 fl. oz, now 250 ml. **4.** a cup-shaped part of something. **5.** (*oft. cap.*) **a.** an ornamental cup or other article, offered as a prize. **b.** a contest in which a cup is the prize: *the Melbourne Cup; Davis Cup.* **6.** *Church.* the wine used for communion. **7. in one's cups**, drunk; inebriated. ◇*v.t.* **8.** to take or put in (or as if in) a cup. **9.** to form into the shape of a cup. [OE *cuppe*, from LL: cup, from L: tub, cask]

cupboard /'kʌbəd/, *n.* a piece of furniture or built-in space with door(s), usu. with shelves, used for storage. [ME, from CUP + BOARD]

Cupid /'kjupəd/, *n.* **1.** the Roman god of love, son of Venus, commonly represented as a winged boy with bow and arrows. See **Eros**[1]. **2.** (*l.c.*) an image or representation of this god. [ME from L *Cupīdo*, lit., desire, passion]

cupidity /kju'pɪdəti/, *n.* an eager or unreasonable desire, esp. to possess something. [L: passionate desire]

cupola /'kjupələ/, *n.* a rounded roof or ceiling, or a dome upon a roof. [It: dome, from LL: little tub, cask]

cupr-, a word part meaning 'copper'. Also, before consonants, **cupri-**, **cupro-**. [L, combining form of *cuprum*]

cupric /'kjuprɪk/, *adj. Chem.* of or containing copper, esp. in the divalent state as *cupric oxide*, CuO.

cuprite /'kjuprait/, *n.* cuprous oxide, Cu_2O, an ore of copper.

cuprous /'kjuprəs/, *adj.* containing monovalent copper: *cuprous oxide*.

cur /kɜ/, *n.* **1.** a fierce or worthless dog. **2.** a low, hateful person. [ME *curre*; imitative]

curable /'kjurəbəl/, *adj.* able to be cured. **–curability, curableness,** *n.*

curaçao /kjurə'seɪoʊ/, *n.* a liqueur flavored with bitter orange peel. [from *Curaçao*, main island of Netherlands Antilles, off the coast of Venezuela]

curacy /'kjurəsi/, *n., pl.* **-cies.** the position or work of a curate.

curare /kju'rari/, *n.* a blackish resin-like substance containing the poison strychnine, which stops the action of motor nerves. Also, **curari**. [Carib (S Amer Indian)]

curate /'kjurət/, *n.* a clergyman employed as an assistant of a rector or vicar. [ME, from ML]

curative /'kjurətɪv/, *n., adj.* (something used for) curing or healing.

curator /kju'reɪtə/, *n.* the person in charge of a museum, art collection, etc. [L: overseer, guardian] **–curatorial,** *adj.* **–curatorship,** *n.*

curb /kɜb/, *n.* **1.** anything that holds back or controls. **2.** an enclosing framework or edge. ◇*v.t.* **3.** to control or hold back. [ME, from F: curved, from L: bent, crooked]

curd /kɜd/, *n.* **1.** (*oft. pl.*) a jellied or solidified substance formed from milk by the action of an acid or rennet, either eaten fresh (see **junket**) or made into cheese. **2.** any similar substance: *beancurd.* ◇*v.t., v.i.* **3.** to turn into curd. [ME] **–curdy,** *adj.*

curdle /'kɜdl/, *v.i., v.t.*, **-dled, -dling. 1.** to form into curd; coagulate. **2.** (of a substance containing milk) to (cause to) go grainy due to curd forming. [frequentative of CURD]

cure /kjuə, 'kjuə/, *n., v.*, **cured, curing.** ◇*n.* **1.** a medicine or treatment to heal or remove disease. **2.** successful treatment; healing. **3.** *Church.* responsibility for the spiritual welfare of people in a certain area. ◇*v.t.* **4.** to restore (someone) to health. **5.** to get rid of (illness, a bad habit, etc.) **6.** to preserve (meat, fish, etc.) by salting, drying, etc. **7.** to prepare, preserve, or finish (a substance) by a chemical or physical process. [ME, from OF, from L: care, treatment, concern] **–curer,** *n.*

curette /kju'ret/, *n., v.*, **-retted, -retting.** ◇*n.* a spoon-shaped surgical instrument used for removing tissue from body cavities such as the womb. ◇*v.t.* to scrape with a curette. [F: cleanse, from L] **–curettage,** *n.*

curfew /'kɜfju/, *n.* **1.** *Hist.* the ringing of a bell in the evening as a signal to put out fires and lights. **2.** (a rule or law setting) a time after which people may not move about on the streets. [ME, from OF *cuevre-feu* cover-fire]

curia /'kjurɪə/, *n., pl. curiae* /'kjurii/. **1.** the senate house in ancient Rome. **2.** *Rom Cath Ch* (*usu. cap.*). Also, **Curia Romana**. the papal court and government. [L] **–curial,** *adj.*

Curie /'kjuri/, *n.* **1. Marie**, 1867–1934, Polish-born physicist and chemist in France; with her husband **Pierre**, 1859–1906, discovered radium in 1898; shared Nobel prize for physics (1903) with her husband and Henri Becquerel; won Nobel prize for chemistry (1911). **2.** (*l.c.*) the non-SI unit of measurement of activity of the nuclide of a radioactive atom, equal to 37 x 10^9 becquerels.

curie point, *n.* the temperature at which a ferromagnetic substance becomes merely paramagnetic.

Curie's law /,kjuriz 'lɔ/, *n.* the law stating that the magnetic susceptibility of a substance (i.e. how easily it can be magnetised) is inversely proportional to the absolute temperature. [named after Pierre CURIE]

curio /'kjurioʊ/, *n., pl. curios.* an unusual article or art object. [short for CURIOSITY]

curiosity /kjuri'ɒsəti/, *n., pl.* **-ties. 1.** the desire to learn or know about anything; inquisitiveness. **2.** a curious or interesting quality or thing. [L]

curious /'kjurɪəs/, *adj.* **1.** wanting to learn or know; inquiring. **2.** taking interest in others' affairs; prying. **3.** interesting because strange or new. [ME, from OF, from L: careful, inquiring, inquisitive]

curium /'kjurɪəm/, *n.* an element produced from plutonium, though not found in nature. *Symbol:* Cm; *at. no.:* 96 [named after Marie and Pierre CURIE]

curl /kɜl/, *v.t., v.i.* **1.** to form into curves, rings, or coils. ◇*v.* **2. curl one's lip,** to express scorn. **3. curl up, a.** to curl. **b.** to sit or lie with legs drawn up. ◇*n.* **4.** a ringlet of hair. **5.** anything of spiral, curved, or twisted shape. [ME, from MD or MFlem] **–curly,** *adj.*

curler /'kɜlə/, *n.* a roller, pin, etc., used to curl hair.

curlew /'kɜlju/, *n.* any of various shorebirds with long legs and a long, thin, downcurved bill. [ME, from OF; imitative]

curlicue /'kɜlikju/, *n.* an ornamental curl or twist. Also, **curlycue**.

curling /'kɜlɪŋ/, *n.* the Scottish game of sliding large round stones on ice towards a mark called the tee.

currajong /'kʌrədʒɒŋ/, *n.* **–kurrajong.**

currant /'kʌrənt/, *n.* **1.** a small seedless raisin. **2.** the small, acid, round fruit or berry of certain shrubs, such as **redcurrant**, **white currant**, and **blackcurrant**. [ME, from AF (*raisins de*) *Corauntz* (raisins of) Corinth]

currawong /'kʌrəwɒŋ/, *n.* any of several large black and white or greyish Australian birds with solid bodies, large pointed bills, yellow eyes, and loud, ringing calls. **2.** a small tree, of the wattle family. [Aboriginal]

currency /'kʌrənsi/, *n., pl.* **-cies,** *adj.* ◇*n.* **1.** the money in current use in a country. **2.** the fact or quality of being used, passed on, or generally accepted. ◇*adj.* **3.** *Obs.* born in Australia; not an immigrant: *a currency lad; a currency lass.*

current /'kʌrənt/, *adj.* **1.** belonging to the present time; in progress: *the current month.* **2.** generally used or accepted. ◇*n.* **3.** the flow, as of a river. **4.** part of a large body of water or air moving in one direction. **5.** *Phys.* **a.** the flow of an electric charge. **b.** a measure of the rate of flow. The SI unit of current is the ampere. **6.** a general course or tendency. [L: running]

current account, *n.* → **cheque account.**

curriculum /kə'rɪkjələm/, *n., pl.* **-lums, -la** /-lə/. **1.** the range of courses of study given in a school, college, university, etc. **2.** a particular course. [L: running, course] —**curricular,** *adj.*

curriculum vitae /kə,rɪkjuləm 'vitaɪ/, *n.* a short account of a person's education and work history. Also, **CV.**

curry[1] /'kʌri/, *n., pl.* **-ries,** *v.,* **-ried, rying.** ◇*n.* **1.** an Asian, esp. Indian, sauce or dish of meat or vegetables, cooked with a mixture of powdered spices, usu. hot to the taste. ◇*v.t.* **2.** to prepare (food) with a curry sauce or powder. [Tamil *kari* sauce]

curry[2] /'kʌri/, *v.,* **-ried, -rying.** ◇*v.t.* **1.** to rub and clean (a horse, etc.) with a brush or comb. **2.** to prepare (tanned leather) by soaking, scraping, beating, coloring, etc. **3.** to beat; thrash. ◇*v.* **4. curry favor,** to try to gain favor by kindness, politeness, flattery, etc. [ME, from OF: put in order, from *con-* CON- + *-reder* make ready (from Gmc)]

curse /kɜs/, *n., v.,* **cursed** or **curst, cursing.** ◇*n.* **1.** the expression of a wish that evil things will happen to someone. **2.** swearing; a blasphemous or obscene oath. **3.** an evil that has been called upon someone. **4. the curse,** *Colloq.* menstruation. ◇*v.t.* **5.** to wish or call evil, accident, or injury upon. **6.** to swear at. **7.** to cause to suffer from. ◇*v.i.* **8.** to swear; utter curses. [OE *curs,* from *cūrsian,* v., curse, reprove, from OIrish *cūrsagim* I blame] —**cursed,** *adj.*

cursive /'kɜsɪv/, *n., adj.* (writing or print) in a flowing style with letters joined together. [ML, from L: a running]

cursor /'kɜsə/, *n.* **1.** the sliding part of a measuring tool such as a slide rule. **2.** a moving dot or line, as on a computer video screen showing where the next words will appear.

cursory /'kɜsəri/, *adj.* short and rapid, without noticing details; superficial: *a cursory inspection.* [L: of a runner or a race] —**cursoriness,** *n.*

curt /kɜt/, *adj.* **1.** short. **2.** rudely short in speech, manner, etc. [L: cut short, clipped]

curtail /kɜ'teɪl/, *v.t.* to cut short. [obs. *curtal,* v., dock, from F: short, from L] —**curtailer,** *n.* —**curtailment,** *n.*

curtain /'kɜtn/, *n.* **1.** a hanging piece of material used to cover a window, decorate a room, etc. **2.** *Theat.* **a.** a hanging cloth used to hide all or part of the stage from the audience. **b.** (the time of) the opening of the curtain at the start of a performance. **c.** (the time of) the close of the curtain at the end of a scene or act. **3.** anything that shuts off, covers, or hides. ◇*v.t.* **4.** to provide or shut off with, or as if with, a curtain. [ME, from OF, from LL: curtain]

curtain call, *n.* the appearance of performers on stage at the end of a performance to acknowledge the clapping, etc., of the audience.

Curtin /'kɜtn/, *n.* **John Joseph,** 1885-1945, Australian Labor politician; prime minister of Australia 1941-45.

curtsy /'kɜtsi/, *n., pl.* **-sies,** *v.,* **-sied, -sying.** ◇*n.* **1.** a respectful bow made by women by bending the knees and lowering the body. ◇*v.i.* **2.** to make a curtsy. [var. of COURTESY]

curvaceous /kɜ'veɪʃəs/, *adj. Colloq.* (of a woman) having a full and shapely figure; curvy. [CURVE + -ACEOUS]

curvature /'kɜvətʃə/, *n.* **1.** the act of curving. **2.** a curved condition, often abnormal: *curvature of the spine.*

curve /kɜv/, *n., v.,* **curved, curving.** ◇*n.* **1.** a continuously bending line without angles. **2.** any curved outline, form, thing, or part. ◇*v.t., v.i.* **3.** to bend in a curve. [L *curvus* bent, curved] —**curved,** *adj.* —**curvedness,** *n.* —**curvy,** *adj.*

curvi-, a combining form of **curve.**

curvilinear /kɜvə'lɪniə/, *adj.* formed or marked by curved lines. Also, **curvilineal.**

Cusack /'kjuzæk/, *n.* **(Ellen) Dymphna** /'dɪmfnə/, 1902-81, Australian author; major works include the play *Red Sky at Morning* (1942).

cuscus /'kʌskʌs/, *n.* a type of marsupial with a round head, small ears, thick, woolly fur and a long grasping tail, which lives in trees in NG and nearby islands and rainforest areas of northern Qld. The cuscus is a phalanger, and closely related to the brush-tailed possum.

cusec /'kjusɛk/, *n.* a unit of measurement in the imperial system, equal to one cubic foot per second or about $0.028 \, m^3/s$ (as rate of flow).

cushion /'kuʃən/, *n.* **1.** a soft bag or pad used to sit, kneel, or lie on. **2.** anything similar in appearance or use. **3.** something to absorb or protect from shock or pressure. ◇*v.t.* **4.** to place on or support with a cushion. **5.** to provide with a cushion or cushions. **6.** to lessen or soften the force or effect of. [ME, from OF, ? from L *culcita* cushion]

cushy /'kuʃi/, *adj.,* **cushier, cushiest.** *Colloq.* easy; comfortable: *a cushy job.* [Anglo-Indian, from Hind: excellent]

cusp /kʌsp/, *n.* **1.** a point; pointed end. **2.** *Anat., Zool., Bot.* a point sticking out or up, as on the crown of a tooth. **3.** the point of a crescent, esp. of the moon. **4.** *Astrol.* the period of change from one sign to the next: *to be born on the cusp*. [L *cuspis* point] — **cusped, cuspate, cuspidate,** *adj.*

cuspid /'kʌspəd/, *n.* a tooth with a single point; canine tooth.

cuss /kʌs/, *n. Orig. US Colloq.* **1.** a curse. **2.** a person or animal: *a queer but likeable cuss.* [early var. of CURSE]

cussed /'kʌsəd/, *adj. Colloq.* stubborn or difficult.

custard /'kʌstəd/, *n.* **1.** Also, **egg custard.** a mixture of eggs, milk, and sugar, baked gently until set. **2.** a sweet sauce made from milk, cornflour, and flavoring, usu. with yellow coloring or egg. [earlier *crustarde* a kind of patty, from OE *croste* CRUST]

custard-apple /'kʌstəd-æpəl/, *n.* the soft-fleshed fruit of any of several tropical trees.

Custer /'kʌstə/, *n.* **George Armstrong,** 1839-76, US general; died in defeat at the battle with the Sioux at Little Bighorn.

custodian /kʌs'toudiən/, *n.* a keeper; guardian.

custody /'kʌstədi/, *n., pl.* **-dies. 1.** keeping; guardianship; care: *The car was held in police custody.* **2.** arrest or imprisonment: *He was taken into custody.* [L] — **custodial,** *adj.*

custom /'kʌstəm/, *n.* **1.** habitual practice; the usual way of acting. **2.** usual actions in general; convention. **3.** a long-continued habit so well-established that it has the force of law. **4.** *Sociol.* a pattern of habitual activity usu. passed on from one generation to another; tradition. **5.** a habit of doing business or shopping at a particular place: *The shopkeeper valued their custom.* **6.** (*pl.*) **a.** a tax, toll, duty, esp. one imposed on goods coming into the country. **b.** the government department that collects these taxes. [ME, from OF, from L: custom]

customary /'kʌstəməri, -təmri/, *adj.* **1.** according to custom; usual. **2.** of or established by custom rather than law. [ML, from OF: custom]

custom-built /'kʌstəm-bɪlt/, *adj.* made to individual order: *a custom-built car.*

customer /'kʌstəmə/, *n.* **1.** someone who buy goods or services from another. **2.** *Colloq.* a person; fellow: *a queer customer.*

custom-made /'kʌstəm-meɪd/, *adj.* made to individual order: *custom-made shoes.*

customs duties, *n.pl.* taxes paid on imported or, sometimes, exported goods.

cut /kʌt/, *v.,* **cut, cutting,** *adj., n.* ◇*v.t.* **1.** to make an opening or wound in with a sharp-edged instrument: *He cut his finger.* **2.** to strike sharply with a whip, etc. **3.** to hurt severely the feelings of: *Her angry words cut him.* **4.** to divide with a sharp-edged instrument; sever: *to cut a rope.* **5.** to saw down (trees, etc.); fell. **6.** to reap; mow: *to cut grain*; *to cut hay.* **7.** to make shorter by removing a part with a sharp-edged instrument: *to cut the hair.* **8.** to cross; intersect: *One line cuts another at right angles.* **9.** to stop the running of: *He cut the engine of the car.* **10.** to make shorter by leaving out a part: *to cut a speech* **11.** (sometimes fol. by *down*) to lower; reduce: *to cut wages.* **12.** *Radio, TV.* to stop recording (a scene, broadcast, etc.). **13.** *Films, TV., etc.* to prepare (filmed material) by cutting and rearranging pieces of film. **14.** to make by cutting, as a statue, jewel, garment, etc. **15.** to dig out: *to cut a ditch.* **16.** *Colloq.* to give up. **17.** *Colloq.* to refuse to recognise socially. **18.** to perform or make: *to cut a caper.* **19.** *Colloq.* to stay away from. **20.** *Cards.* to divide (a pack of cards) into two or more parts before dealing. **21.** *Sport.* to hit (a ball) so as to change its course and cause it to spin. **22.** *Cricket.* **a.** to strike (a ball) with a bat held horizontally, sending it to the off side. **b.** to bowl (a ball) so that it changes course on bouncing. **23.** to record a song, etc., on (a record). ◇*v.i.* **24.** to perform the action of cutting: *These scissors cut well.* **25.** to be able to be cut: *Butter cuts easily.* **26.** to pass, go, or come, esp. in the most direct way (fol. by *across, through, in,* etc.): *to cut across a field.* **27.** to strike or hurt sharply. **28.** *Cards.* to cut the cards. **29.** *Radio, TV.* to stop filming or recording. **30.** *Colloq.* to run away. **31.** *Cricket.* to cut in batting. ◇**32.** Some special uses are:

be cut out for, to be suitable for.

cut back, 1. to shorten; reduce. **2.** (in a novel, film, etc.) to return suddenly to earlier events.

cut down, to reduce, esp. costs, etc.

cut in, 1. to interrupt. **2.** to pull in between other cars too soon after overtaking. **3.** *Elect.* to switch on. **4.** to begin to shear sheep.

cut it fine, to leave oneself only a small amount of time, etc.

cut it out, *Colloq.* to stop.

cut no ice, to have no effect on (fol. by *with*).

cut off, 1. to stop (somebody or something) before a certain point is reached; intercept. **2.** to interrupt. **3.** to bring to a sudden end. **4.** to shut out. **5.** to leave out of a will, etc.

cut out, 1. to leave out; omit. **2.** to remove and take the place of (esp. a rival). **3.** to stop; cease. **4.** to form or make by cutting. **5.** (of an electrical device) to switch off, as when overloaded. **6.** to remove sheep or cattle from a herd or flock.

cut teeth, to have teeth grow through the gums.

cut up, 1. to cut into pieces. **2.** *Colloq.* to upset.

◇*adj.* **33.** divided or separated by cutting: *cut flowers.* **34.** *Bot.* incised; cleft. **35.** made by cutting: *cut glass.* **36.** reduced: *cut prices.* **37. cut and dried, a.** fixed or settled beforehand. **b.** lacking freshness or interest. **38. cut out,** (of shearing) finished. ◇*n.* **39.** the act of cutting; a stroke or blow as with a knife, whip, etc. **40.** a piece cut off, esp. of meat. **41.** *Colloq.* a share of profits, etc. **42.** the quantity cut, as wool or timber. **43.** the result of cutting, such as a wound, dug out passage, etc. **44.** the manner or fashion in which anything is cut. **45.** a passage or course straight across: *a short cut.* **46.** a certain number of sheep or cattle cut out from the herd. **47.** the leaving out of a part. **48.** a reduction. **49.** an act, speech, etc., which hurts the feelings. **50.** a blow from a cane as punishment. **51.** *Sport.* **a.** the act of cutting a ball. **b.** the spin of the ball. **52.** *Films, TV., etc.* a quick change from one shot to another. **53. a cut above,** *Colloq.* better than another in some way. [ME *cutten, kytten, kitten*]

cutback /'kʌtbæk/, *n.* the reduction to an earlier rate, as in production.

cute /kjut/, *adj.*, **cuter, cutest. 1.** *Colloq.* pleasingly pretty. **2.** clever; shrewd. [var. of ACUTE] **—cuteness,** *n.*

cut glass, *n.* glass ornamented or shaped by cutting or grinding. **—cutglass,** *adj.*

Cuthbert /'kʌθbət/, *n.* **Betty,** born 1938, Australian sprinter; winner of three Olympic gold medals in 1956, and one in 1964.

cuticle /'kjutɪkəl/, *n.* **1.** → **epidermis. 2.** the non-living skin surrounding the edges of a fingernail or toenail. **3.** *Bot.* the very thin transparent film covering the surface of plants, formed from the outer surfaces of epidermal cells. [L: skin] **—cuticular,** *adj.*

cutlass /'kʌtləs/, *n.* a short, heavy, slightly curved sword. [F, from L: small knife]

cutlery /'kʌtləri/, *n.* cutting instruments in general, esp. those for dinner-table use. [F]

cutlet /'kʌtlət/, *n.* **1.** a small cut of meat, containing a rib, and cut from the neck. **2.** a small, flat piece of fish prepared for eating. [F: little rib, from L]

cut-off /'kʌt-ɒf/, *n.* **1.** a set limit. **2.** the stopping of the passage of steam or liquid through an engine, etc.

cut-out /'kʌt-aʊt/, *n. Elect.* a device for breaking an electric circuit when the current goes above the safety level.

cut-price /'kʌt-praɪs/, *adj.* **1.** (of goods), for sale at a lower than standard price. **2.** (of a shop, etc.) dealing in such goods.

cutter /'kʌtə/, *n.* **1.** someone whose work is cutting, as in a clothing factory. **2.** a small sailing boat with one mast. **3.** a medium-sized boat for rowing or sailing, esp. that belonging to a warship. **4.** *Cricket.* a ball which suddenly changes direction after striking the ground.

cutthroat /'kʌtθroʊt/, *n.* **1.** a murderer. **2.** a razor with long, open blade. ◇*adj.* **3.** merciless; relentless: *cutthroat competition.* **4.** relating to a game played by three or more people, each acting and scoring as an individual.

cutting /'kʌtɪŋ/, *n.* **1.** something cut off. **2.** *Hort.* a piece cut from a plant, usu. a root, shoot, or leaf, in order to reproduce a new plant. **3.** a piece cut out of a newspaper; clipping. **4.** something produced by cutting, as a passage cut through high ground. **5.** (*pl.*) *Geol.* small pieces of rock broken or torn off during drilling. ◇*adj.* **6.** that cuts. **7.** sharply cold, as a wind. **8.** hurting the feelings severely; sarcastic: *a cutting remark.*

cuttlebone /'kʌtlboʊn/, *n.* the chalky inside shell or plate of true cuttlefishes, used to make powder for polishing, and in bird food.

cuttlefish /'kʌtlfɪʃ/, *n., pl.* **-fishes,** (*esp. collectively*) **-fish.** any of various cephalopod molluscs, with two gills, ten sucker-bearing arms and the power of sending out a black, ink-like liquid when attacked. Also, **cuttle.** [OE *cudele*]

Cutty Sark /kʌti 'sak/, *n.* a famous three-masted tea clipper built in 1869 and now docked permanently at Greenwich, England.

cutworm /'kʌtwɜm/, *n.* any of various caterpillars which feed at night on young plants of corn, cabbage, etc., cutting them off near the ground.

CV /si 'vi/, *n.* → **curriculum vitae.** [abbrev.]

CWA /,si dʌbəlju 'eɪ/, *n.* → **Country Women's Association.** [abbrev.]

cwt, *Abbrev.* hundredweight.

-cy, a suffix of nouns, meaning **1.** condition, as *accuracy, lunacy, vacancy.* **2.** rank or dignity, as *captaincy, magistracy.* [representing F -*cie,* -*tie,* L -*cia,* -*tia,* Gk -*kia,* -*keia,* -*tia,* -*teia*]

cyanide /'saɪənaɪd/, *n.* a highly poisonous salt. See **-ide.** Also, **cyanid.**

cyanine /'saɪənin/, *n.* any of various dyes used to make photographic plates sensitive to a color range. Also, **cyanin** /'saɪənən/.

cyano-, a word part referring to the cyanide group, **—CN.** Also **cyan-** before vowels. [Gk *kyano,* combining form of *Kyanos,* dark blue]

cyanosis /saɪə'noʊsəs/, *n.* blueness of the skin, as from lack of oxygen in the blood. Also, **cyanopathy** /saɪə'nɒpəθi/. [NL, from Gk: dark blue color]

cybernetics /saɪbə'nɛtɪks/, *n.* the scientific study of those methods of control and communication which are shared by living organisms and machines, esp. as relating to the operations of computers. [Gk *kybernētēs* helmsman + -ICS] **—cybernetic,** *adj.*

cycad /'saɪkæd/, *n.* any of a group of plants, in appearance halfway between ferns and palms, many having a thick unbranched trunk bearing a crown of large feathery leaves. [NL *Cycas* the typical genus, from Gk: kind of palm]

cycl-, a word part meaning 'cycle', used esp. in chemistry in relation to cyclic compounds and also in regard to wheel turns. Also, **cyclo-** before consonants. [Gk *kykl-,* combining form of *kýklos* ring, circle, wheel]

Cyclades /'sɪklədiz/, *n. pl.* a group of Greek islands in the southern Aegean. Pop. 88 458 (1981); 2650 km².

cyclamate /'saɪkləmeɪt, -mət/, *n.* any of a group of artificial sweeteners.

cyclamen /'saɪkləmən, 'sɪk-/, *n.* any of various plants with nodding white, purple, pink, or red flowers, the petals of which fold backwards. [NL, from Gk]

cycle /'saɪkəl/, *n., v.,* **-cled, -cling.** ◇*n.* **1.** a period of time in which certain events repeat themselves in the same order and at the same time apart. **2.** any complete series of operations or events. **3.** any long period of years; an age. **4.** a series of poems, songs or stories about the same event, person, etc. **5.** a bicycle, tricycle, etc. **6.** *Phys.* any series of changes in or operations performed by a system which brings it back to its original state, as in alternating electric current. ◇*v.i.* **7.** to ride a bicycle, etc. **8.** to move or happen in cycles. [L, from Gk: ring, circle]

cycle per second, *n.* → **hertz.** *Symbol:* c/s

cyclic /'saɪklɪk, 'sɪklɪk/, *adj.* **1.** of or relating to a cycle or cycles; happening in cycles. **2.** *Geom.* (of a figure) able to be inscribed in a circle: *a cyclic quadrilateral*. **3.** *Chem.* of or indicating a compound whose structural formula contains a closed chain or ring of atoms. **4.** *Bot.* having the parts of a flower, etc., arranged in circular growths around the same point on the stem. [L, from Gk: circular] –**cyclical,** *adj.*

cyclist /'saɪklɪst/, *n.* someone who rides a bicycle, tricycle, etc.

cycloid /'saɪklɔɪd/, *adj.* **1.** like a circle; circular. **2.** (of fishes' scales) smooth-edged and more or less circular in form. ◇*n.* **3.** a fish with such scales. **4.** *Geom.* a curve described by a point on the circumference of a circle as it rolls on a straight line in its plane. [Gk: like a circle] –**cycloidal,** *adj.*

cyclone /'saɪkloʊn/, *n.* **1.** an atmospheric pressure system marked by relatively low pressure at its centre with strong surrounding wind movement. See **anticyclone. 2.** a tropical hurricane. [Gk: moving in a circle] –**cyclonic,** *adj.*

Cyclone Tracy, *n.* a cyclone which hit Darwin, NT, on 25 December 1974 resulting in the loss of fifty lives; wind speeds of up to 300 km per hour caused extensive damage to the city's buildings and more than half of the population were evacuated.

Cyclops /'saɪklɒps/, *n. Gk Myth.* one of a race of giants with only one circular eye in the middle of the forehead. [L, from Gk: round-eyed]

cyclostome /'saɪkləstoʊm, 'sɪklə-/, *adj.* **1.** belonging or relating to a group or class of aquatic vertebrates including the lampreys and hagfishes, marked by pouch-like gills and a circular sucking mouth. **2.** having a circular mouth. [CYCLO- + Gk *stóma* mouth]

cyclostyle /'saɪkləstaɪl/, *n.* **1.** a device for making copies, consisting of a kind of pen with a small toothed wheel at the end which cuts holes in specially prepared paper to form a stencil. ◇*v.t.* **2.** to copy using a cyclostyle.

cyclotron /'saɪklətrɒn/, *n.* an accelerator for giving very high speed to charged particles by repeated electric impulses at high frequency, with particles moving in spiral paths in a strong magnetic field.

cyder /'saɪdə/, *n.* → **cider.**

cygnet /'sɪgnət/, *n.* a young swan. [ME, from L *cygnus* swan (from Gk) + -ET]

cylinder /'sɪləndə/, *n.* **1.** *Geom.* **a.** a solid figure with a circular cross-section which remains the same in size for the whole length of the figure. **b.** the curved surface of a cylinder. **2.** any object shaped like a cylinder, whether solid or hollow. **3.** the body of a pump. **4.** the part of an engine in which the piston moves. [L, from Gk: cylinder] –**cylindrical,** *adj.*

cylinder head, *n.* a removable part of an internal-combustion engine fastened to the cylinder block and containing all or part of the combustion chamber.

cymbal /'sɪmbəl/, *n.* one of a pair of curved plates, usu. of brass, which are used as a musical instrument, being struck together to produce a sharp ringing sound. [OE, from L, from Gk: cup, bowl] –**cymbalist,** *n.*

cymbidium /sɪm'bɪdiəm/, *n.* any of various types of orchid found widespread in Africa, Asia and Australia.

cyme /saɪm/, *n.* the flowering part of a plant in which the first flower grows on the main stem and following flowers grow on secondary and other stems. [L: sprout, from Gk]

Cymru /'kʊmri/, *n.* → **Wales.**

cynic /'sɪnɪk/, *n.* **1.** someone who does not believe in the goodness of people or events and often expresses this by sneering, etc. **2.** (*cap.*) one of group of ancient Greek philosophers who developed the teachings of Socrates and were scornful of the need for worldly pleasures. ◇*adj.* **3.** of or like a cynic. [L, from Gk: doglike, churlish, Cynic] –**cynical,** *adj.*

cynicism /'sɪnəsɪzəm/, *n.* **1.** a cynical way of thinking or character. **2.** a cynical remark. **3.** (*cap.*) the beliefs or practices of the Cynics.

cynocephalus /saɪnoʊ'sɛfələs/, *n., pl.* **-cephali** /-'sɛfəlaɪ/. **1.** → **thylacine. 2.** a mythical dog-headed man.

cynosure /'sɪnəʃʊə/, *n.* something that strongly attracts attention by its brightness, etc. [L, from Gk: dog's tail]

cypher /'saɪfə/, *n., v.i., v.t.,* → **cipher.**

cypress /'saɪprəs/, *n.* (the wood of) any of various evergreen, cone-bearing trees with dark green scale-like, overlapping leaves. [from Gk]

cypress pine, *n.* a cone-bearing tree producing valuable softwood timber.

cyprinoid /'sɪprənɔɪd, sə'praɪnɔɪd/, *adj.* **1.** similar to or belonging to a group of fishes including the carps, suckers, loaches, etc. ◇*n.* **2.** cyprinoid fish.

Cyprus /'saɪprəs/, *n.* an island republic in the eastern Mediterranean, south of Turkey; a British colony before independence in 1960; territory and power disputed by the Greek and Turkish sections of the population; northern third of the island unilaterally declared a separate Turkish republic (the **Turkish Republic of Northern Cyprus**) in 1983 but not recognised internationally. Pop. 719 000 (1987 est.); 9251 km². *Languages:* Greek and Turkish. *Currency:* pound. *Cap.*: Nicosia.

Cyrano de Bergerac /sɪranoʊ də 'bɛəʒəræk, səranoʊ də 'bɜʒəræk/, *n.* **Savinien** /savi'njæ/, 1619-55, French soldier, duellist, and romantic writer; hero of a play by Rostand.

Cyrillic /sə'rılık/, *adj.* relating to an old Slavic alphabet said to have been invented by St Cyril, now used for the writing of Russian and Bulgarian. [from St *Cyril*]

Cyrus /'saırəs/, *n.* ('*the Elder*' or '*the Great*'), died 529 BC, king of Persia 558?–529 BC; founder of the Persian Empire.

cyst /sıst/, *n.* **1.** *Med.* a closed sac formed in animal tissues, often containing liquid. **2.** a bladder, sac, or vesicle. **3.** *Zool.* a sac, usu. round, containing an animal that has passed into a dormant condition. [NL, from Gk: bladder, bag, pouch] – **cystic**, *adj.*

cystitis /sıs'taıtəs/, *n.* inflammation of the urinary bladder.

-cyte, a word part meaning cell or cells, as in *leucocyte*. [combining form representing Gk *kýtos* container]

cyto-, a word part meaning cell or cells, as in *cytogenesis*. Also, before, vowels, **cyt-**. [Gk *kyto-*, combining form of *kýtos* container]

cytogenesis /ˌsaıtou'dʒɛnəsəs/, *n.* the origin and development of cells.

cytogenetics /ˌsaıtoudʒə'nɛtıks/, *n.* the study of the part played by cells in heredity, mutation, and evolution.

cytology /saı'tɒlədʒi/, *n.* the scientific study of cells, esp. their formation, structure, and functions. – **cytologist**, *n.*

cytoplasm /'saıtəplæzəm/, *n.* the living substance of a cell not including the nucleus. Also, **cytoplast** /'saıtəplæst/. – **cytoplasmic**, *adj.*

czar /za/, *n.* → **tsar**.

Czechoslovakia /ˌtʃɛkəslə'vakiə/, *n.* formerly, a republic in central Europe; formed in 1918 as a nation for the Czechs and Slovaks of the collapsed Austro-Hungarian Empire; a federal republic 1948–92; on 1 January 1993 divided into two nations. See **Czech Republic** and **Slovakia**. – **Czechoslovakian**, *n., adj.*

Czech Republic /ˌtʃɛk rə'pʌblık/, *n.* a republic in central Europe, bordered by Germany, Poland, Slovakia and Austria; a constituent republic of Czechoslovakia before becoming an independent nation in 1993. Pop. 10 298 731 (1991); 79 232 km². *Language*: Czech. *Currency*: koruna. *Cap*.: Prague. Czech, **Ceská Republika**.

Dd

D, d, /n., pl./ **D's** or **Ds, d's** or **ds**. **1.** the fourth letter of the English alphabet. **2.** /Music./ the second note of the scale of C major.

d., /Abbrev./ **1.** daughter. **2.** delete. **3.** penny, pence. [L /denarius/] **4.** died. **5.** dialect. **6.** diameter. **7.** density. **8.** detective.

'd, short form of **had** or **would**.

D, **1.** Roman numeral for 500. **2.** /Chem. Symbol./ deuterium.

D /di/, /n./ detective. Also, **d.** / → / **DA** /di 'eɪ/, /n. US/ → **district attorney**. [Abbrev.]

DA /di 'eɪ/, /n. US/ → **district attorney**. [abbrev.]

dab /dæb/, /v./, **dabbed, dabbing,** /n./ ◇/v.t./ **1.** to touch or tap gently, esp. with a soft or moist substance. **2.** to apply (a substance) with light strokes: /to dab ointment on a sore./ ◇/v.i./ **3.** to touch lightly. ◇/n./ **4.** a quick or light tap, as with the hand or something soft. **5.** a small quantity, esp. of something moist. [ME]

dabble /'dæbəl/, /v./, **-bled, -bling.** ◇/v.t./ **1.** to dip in and out of a liquid; splash. ◇/v.i./ **2.** to play in water, as with the hands or feet. **3.** to do anything without serious interest: /to dabble in literature./ [Flem] —**dabbler**, /n./

dabchick /'dæbtʃɪk/, /n./ any of various Australian or European grebes.

dab hand, /n. Colloq./ a person particularly skilled (usu. fol. by /at/).

da capo /da 'kapoʊ/, /adv./ (a musical direction) from the beginning. [It]

Dacca /'dækə/, /n./ the capital of Bangladesh, in the eastern central part. Pop. 3 458 602 (1981).

Dachau /'dækaʊ/, /n./ a town in southern Germany, in Bavaria; site of a Nazi concentration camp, the scene of mass murders during World War II. Pop. 33 400 (1983 est.).

dachshund /'dæksənd, 'dæʃhənd/, /n./ a German breed of small dog with a long body and very short legs. [G /Dachs/ badger + /Hund/ dog]

dactyl /'dæktɪl, -tl/, /n./ **1.** /Zool./ a finger or toe. **2.** /Poetry./ a foot (def. 6) of three syllables, one long followed by two short, or in modern verse, one accented followed by two unaccented, as in 'Géntly ănd hūmănlў'. [ME, from L, from Gk: finger or toe] —**dactylic**, /adj./

dad /dæd/, /n. Colloq./ **1.** Also, **daddy.** father. **2.** (a form of address to an older man). [earlier /dadde/, nursery substitute for FATHER]

dada /'dadə/, /n./ a movement in art and literature from about 1915 to 1922, which deliberately offended by going against traditional artistic and social standards. [F /dada/ hobbyhorse, symbol of the movement] —**dadaism**, /n./ —**dadaist**, /n./

Daintree

daddy-long-legs /ˌdædi-'lɒŋ-legz/, /n. sing. and pl./ a small spider with long, thin legs, often found indoors.

dado /'deɪdoʊ/, /n., pl./ **-dos, -does. 1.** the part of a pedestal between the base and the cap. **2.** the lower broad part of an inside wall finished in wallpaper, fabric, paint, etc. [It: die, cube, pedestal, from L]

Daedalus /'dɪdələs/, /n. Gk Myth./ an Athenian architect who built the labyrinth for Minos and made wings for himself and his son Icarus. [L, from Gk: the cunning worker]

daemon /'dimən, 'daɪ-/, /n./ **1.** /Gk Myth./ **a.** a secondary god. **b.** a guardian spirit of a place or person. **2.** → **demon**. [L, from Gk] —**daemonic**, /adj./

DAF, /Abbrev./ delayed auditory feedback.

daffodil /'dæfədɪl/, /n./ **1.** a plant with yellow, bell-shaped flowers. **2.** a light or pale yellow color. [unexplained var. of ME /affodille/, from Gk /asphódelos/]

daft /daft/, /adj./ **1.** simple or foolish. **2.** mad; insane. Also, **daffy.** [OE /gedǣte/ mild, meek]

dag[1] /dæg/, /n./ wool, usu. dirty, from a sheep's hindquarters.

dag[2] /dæg/, /n. Colloq./ an odd or amusing person.

dag[3] /dæg/, /n. Colloq./ **1.** an untidy or dirty person. **2.** a person lacking in style. —**daggy**, /adj./

da Gama /də 'gamə/, /n./ **Vasco**. See **Gama**.

dagger /'dægə/, /n./ **1.** a weapon with a short pointed blade, like a small sword. **2.** /Print./ a mark (†) used for references, etc.; obelisk. **3. look daggers,** to look angrily or threateningly. [ME]

dagger orchid, /n./ a type of orchid often forming large masses on trees in coastal forests of NSW and southern Qld.

dago /'deɪgoʊ/, /n., pl./ **-gos, -goes.** /Colloq. (offensive)/ a person of Latin race, esp. an Italian, Spaniard or Portuguese. Also, **Dago.** [? Sp /Diego/ James]

dahlia /'deɪljə/, /n./ a type of plant, native to Mexico and Central America, widely cultivated for its showy flowers. [NL; named after A /Dahl/, died 1789, Swedish botanist]

daily /'deɪli/, /adj., n., pl./ **-lies,** /adv./ ◇/adj./ **1.** done, happening or appearing each day or each weekday. ◇/n./ **2.** a newspaper appearing each day or each weekday. **3.** a woman employed to come and do housework every day. ◇/adv./ **4.** every day; day by day: /She phoned the hospital daily./

Daimler /'deɪmlə/, /n./ **Gottlieb** /'gɒtlib/, 1839–90, German engineer and motor-car manufacturer.

Daintree /'deɪntri/, /n./ a coastal river in north-eastern Qld, rising north-west of Mossman and flowing north then south-east to the Pacific Ocean south of Cape Tribulation. About 108 km.

dainty /'deɪnti/, *adj.*, **-tier, -tiest**, *n., pl.* **-ties.** ◊*adj.* **1.** delicately pleasing in appearance or movement. **2.** pleasing to the taste; delicious. **3.** having particular tastes; fastidious. ◊*n.* **4.** something pleasing to the taste; a delicacy. [ME, from OF, from L: worthiness] —**daintily**, *adv.*

dairy /'dɛəri/, *n., pl.* **dairies**, *adj.* ◊*n.* **1.** a place where milk and cream are kept and made into butter and cheese. **2.** a shop or company that sells milk, butter, etc. **3.** (the cows on) a farm which is mainly devoted to the production of milk and milk products. ◊*adj.* **4.** relating to or made in a dairy. [ME *dei* female servant + *-erie* -ERY] —**dairying**, *n.*

dais /'deɪəs/, *n.* a raised platform at the end of a room, for seats of honor, a speaker's desk, etc. [ME, from OF, from LL: table]

daisy /'deɪzi/, *n., pl.* **-sies. 1.** a type of plant whose flower heads have a yellow centre and white rays. **2.** any similar shaped flower of different colors. **3. push up daisies**, *Colloq.* to be dead and buried. [OE *daegeseage* day's eye]

Dakota /də'koʊtə/, *n.* North Dakota or South Dakota.

daks /dæks/, *n.pl. Colloq.* trousers. [Trademark]

Dalai Lama /ˌdælaɪ 'lamə/, *n.* **1.** (until 1959) the chief pontiff and governmental ruler of Tibet, believed to be a reincarnation of previous Dalai Lamas. **2.** the 14th Dalai Lama, born 1935, who fled to India in 1959 following the Chinese occupation of Tibet; Nobel Peace prize 1989. [Tibetan]

Dalby /'dɒlbi/, *n.* a town in south-eastern Qld in the northern Darling Downs; one of Australia's major stock-selling centres. Pop. 8338 (1986).

dale /deɪl/, *n.* a small open valley. [OE *dæl*]

Dali /'dali/, *n.* **Salvador**, 1904–89, Spanish surrealist painter.

Dallas /'dæləs/, *n.* a city in the US, in north-eastern Texas; President Kennedy assassinated here in 1963. Pop. 1 003 530 (1986 est.).

dally /'dæli/, *v.i.*, **-lied, -lying. 1.** to waste time. **2.** to make love playfully. **3.** to play carelessly; flirt: *to dally with danger*. [ME, from OF: talk] —**dalliance**, *n.*

Dalmatia /dæl'meɪʃə/, *n.* a region in western Yugoslavia along the east coast of the Adriatic. Pop. 622 000 (1985 est.).

Dalmatian /dæl'meɪʃən/, *n.* a breed of dog having a white color with many small dark-colored spots.

dal segno /dæl 'sɛnjoʊ/, *adv.* (a musical direction) go back to the sign and repeat. [It]

Dalton's atomic theory, *n.* the early theory that matter is made up of particles called atoms, the atoms of any particular element being the same, but differing from those of other elements in their weight. Compounds are formed by combination of different elements in simple numerical proportions. Still useful as a basis for chemistry. [named after John Dalton, 1766–1844, English chemist and physicist]

Daly /'deɪli/, *n.* a large river in the NT, flowing from south-west of Katherine north-west to Anson Bay. 320 km; wildlife sanctuary.

dam[1] /dæm/, *n., v.*, **dammed, damming.** ◊*n.* **1.** a wall of earth, stone, etc., built to hold back the flow of water. **2.** the body of water held back in this way. ◊*v.t.* **3.** to provide with a dam; hold back with a dam. **4.** to stop or block up. [ME]

dam[2] /dæm/, *n.* a female parent (used esp. of four-legged animals). [ME var. of DAME]

damage /'dæmɪdʒ/, *n., v.*, **-aged, -aging.** ◊*n.* **1.** an injury or harm that lowers the value or usefulness of something. **2.** (*pl.*) *Law.* an amount of money judged equal to the cost of an injury. **3.** *Colloq.* cost; expense. ◊*v.t.* **4.** to cause damage to. [ME, from OF]

Damascus /də'mæskəs/, *n.* the capital of Syria, in the south-western part; reputed to be the oldest continuously existing city in the world. Pop. 1 292 000 (1987 est.).

damask /'dæməsk/, *n.* **1.** a fabric of linen, silk, cotton, or wool, woven with wavy patterns, often used as table linen. **2.** a deep pink color. ◊*adj.* **3.** made of or like damask. **4.** deep pink. ◊*v.t.* **5.** to ornament with a wavy design, as in damask cloth. [ME, from L, from Gk: Damascus]

dame /deɪm/, *n.* **1.** a form of address to any woman of high rank. **2.** the title of the wife of a knight or baronet. **3.** (*cap.*) the title of a woman who holds one of a number of orders, as Dame of the Order of Australia. **4.** *Colloq.* a woman. **5.** the part of a comic old woman in a pantomime, usu. played by a man. [ME, from L: mistress, lady]

dame school, *n.* (formerly) a small school usu. run by one woman. In Australia, dame schools were often run by convicts for the children of soldiers and convicts.

damn /dæm/, *v.t.* **1.** to declare (something) to be bad, unfit, wrong, or illegal. **2.** to condemn to ruin, or eternal punishment in hell. **3.** to declare or prove (someone) to be guilty. ◊*n.* **4.** a very small amount: *It's not worth a damn.* ◊*interj.* **5.** (an expression of anger or annoyance.) [ME, from L: condemn, doom] —**damning**, *adj.*

damnation /dæm'neɪʃən/, *n.* **1.** the act of damning or the state of being damned. ◊*interj.* **2.** (an expression of anger, disappointment, etc.).

damned /dæmd/, *adj.* **1.** condemned, esp. to eternal punishment in hell. **2.** hateful. ◊*adv.* **3.** extremely.

Damocles /'dæməkliz/, *n. Class. Legend.* a flatterer, who, having extolled the happiness of Dionysius, tyrant of Syracuse, was placed at a banquet with a sword suspended over his head by a single hair, to show him the perilous nature of that happiness. —**Damoclean** *adj.*

damp /dæmp/, *adj.* **1.** slightly or fairly wet; moist. ◊*n.* **2.** moisture in the air or an

damp object. **3.** a feeling of sadness or discouragement. ◇*v.t.* **4.** to make damp; moisten. **5.** to stop or slow down the action, etc., of. **6.** to put out; choke; extinguish. **7.** *Acoustics, Music.* to stop or slow down the action of (a vibrating string, etc.); dull; deaden. **8.** to provide (esp. pianos) with a damper or dampers. **9.** *Phys.* to make the amplitude of (a wave) smaller. [ME, from MFlem: vapor] **—dampness,** *n.*

dampcourse /'dæmpkɔs/, *n.* a layer of material laid in a wall to stop moisture rising. Also, **damp-proof course.**

dampen /'dæmpən/, *v.t.* **1.** to make damp; moisten. **2.** to dull or deaden. ◇*v.i.* **3.** to become damp. **—dampener,** *n.*

damper[1] /'dæmpə/, *n.* **1.** a movable plate for controlling the draught in a stove, etc. **2.** *Music.* **a.** a device in pianos, etc., to deaden the vibration of the strings. **b.** a device on a brass instrument to soften the tone. **3.** *Elect.* a device to keep the indicator of a measuring instrument from swinging too much. **4. put a damper on,** *Colloq.* to discourage.

damper[2] /'dæmpə/, *n.* bread made from a simple flour and water dough, cooked in coals or wood ashes. [Brit d.]

Dampier[1] /'dæmpiə/, *n.* **William,** 1651–1715, English navigator, explorer, writer and pirate; landed in north-western Australia in 1688 and 1699.

Dampier[2] /'dæmpiə/, *n.* a town and port on the central western coast of WA, west of Port Hedland. Pop. 2201 (1986). [named after William DAMPIER]

damsel /'dæmzəl/, *n. Archaic.* a young unmarried woman; girl. [ME, from L: mistress, lady]

Dan, 1. *Bible.* Daniel. **2.** Danish.

Danaë /'dæneɪi/, *n. Gk Legend.* a maiden imprisoned by her father Acrisius, King of Argos, because of an oracle's prophecy. Visited by Zeus in the form of a shower of gold, she became the mother of Perseus.

dance /dæns, dans/, *v.*, **danced, dancing,** *n.* ◇*v.i.* **1.** to move the feet or body rhythmically, esp. to music. **2.** to move about quickly as from excitement or emotion. ◇*v.t.* **3.** to perform or take part in (a dance): *to dance a jig.* **4. dance attendance on,** to wait upon continually or humbly. ◇*n.* **5.** a specially arranged group of rhythmical movements, generally done to music. **6.** a social gathering for dancing; ball. **7.** a piece of music suitable for dancing to. [ME, from OF; probably of Gmc origin.] **—dancer,** *n.*

D and C /di ən 'si/, *n.* dilatation and curettage, a surgical method for the removal of tissue from the uterus by scraping.

dandelion /'dændilaɪən, -də-/, *n.* a plant, common as a weed, marked by deeply toothed leaves and golden yellow flowers. [F *dent de lion* lion's tooth (with allusion to the toothed leaves)]

Dandenong /'dændənɒŋ/, *n.* a city within the metropolitan area of Melbourne, Vic. Pop. 56 461 (1986).

Dandenong Ranges, *n.pl.* a low-lying range of hills, east of Melbourne, Vic. Highest peak, Mt Dandenong, 634 m.

dandle /'dændəl/, *v.t.*, **-dled, -dling.** to move lightly up and down, as a child on the knees or in the arms. [? from Scand]

dandruff /'dændrəf, -rʌf/, *n.* scales which form from dead skin under the hair. Also, **dandriff.** [orig. unknown]

dandy /'dændi/, *n., pl.* **-dies,** *adj.*, **-dier, -diest.** ◇*n.* **1.** a man who is too concerned about clothes and appearance; fop. ◇*adj.* **2.** *Colloq.* fine; very good. [? special use of *Dandy,* var. of *Andy* (Andrew)]

Dane /deɪn/, *n.* **1.** a native or inhabitant of Denmark. **2.** *Hist.* any of the Northmen or Vikings who invaded and occupied England in the ninth to eleventh centuries. **—Danish,** *adj.*

danger /'deɪndʒə/, *n.* **1.** a situation in which harm or injury is likely to happen; peril. **2.** a possible cause of pain or damage: *He is a danger to other drivers.* [ME, from LL: lordship]

dangerous /'deɪndʒərəs/, *adj.* full of or causing danger or risk.

dangle /'dæŋgəl/, *v.*, **-gled, -gling.** ◇*v.i.* **1.** to hang loosely, moving backwards and forwards. ◇*v.t.* **2.** to hold or carry (something) so that it hangs loosely. [Scand]

Daniel /'dænjəl/, *n. Bible.* **1.** a Jewish captive and prophet living in Babylon. **2.** a book in the Old Testament.

Daniell cell /'dænjəl sɛl/, *n.* a primary cell producing 1.1 volts, consisting of a zinc anode standing in dilute sulfuric acid in a porous pot, and a copper cathode standing in copper sulfate. [named after John *Daniell,* 1790–1845, English physicist]

dank /dæŋk/, *adj.* unpleasantly or unhealthily moist. [ME]

Dante /'danteɪ, 'dænteɪ/, *n.* (*Dante Alighieri*), 1265–1321, Italian poet; author of *The Divine Comedy.*

danthonia /dæn'θoʊniə/, *n.* a type of Australian and NZ grass; wallaby grass.

Danube /'dænjub/, *n.* a river in Europe, flowing from the Black Forest in south-western Germany east to the Black Sea. 2776 km.

Danzig /'dænsɪg/, *n.* German name of **Gdansk.**

daphne /'dæfni/, *n.* **1.** a small shrub, some types of which are cultivated for their sweet-smelling flowers. **2.** (*cap.*) *Gk Myth.* a nymph who, pursued by Apollo, was saved by being changed into a laurel tree. [L, from Gk: laurel]

dapper /'dæpə/, *adj.* **1.** neat; trim; smart. **2.** small and active. [ME: pretty; elegant]

dapple /'dæpəl/, *n.* **1.** spotted marking, as of an animal's skin or coat. **2.** an animal with a spotted skin or coat. ◇*adj.* **3.** Also, **dappled.** spotted: *a dapple horse.* [orig. uncert.]

Darcy /'dasi/, *n.* **(James) Les(lie),** 1895–1917, Australian champion boxer.

Dardanelles /dadə'nɛlz/, *n.pl.* the strait between European and Asiatic Turkey, connecting the Aegean with the Sea of Marmara; 64 km long; 2.4 km wide. Formerly, **Hellespont**.

dare /deə/, v., **dared** or **durst**, **dared**, **daring**, n. ◇v.i. **1.** to have the necessary courage or boldness for something. ◇v.t. **2.** to have the necessary courage for. **3.** to meet defiantly: *She dared his anger.* **4.** to move to action, esp. suggesting someone lacks courage; challenge: *I dare you to fight* ◇v. **5. dare say**, to think something probable. ◇n. **6.** *Colloq.* a challenge, as to some dangerous act. [OE *durran*] **−darer**, n.

daredevil /'deədevəl/, n. **1.** a very daring person. ◇adj. **2.** daring; reckless.

darg /dag/, n. **1.** a day's work. **2.** a production quota. [ME *dawerk*, OE *dægweorc* day-work]

dargawarra /dagə'wɔrə/, n. See **hopping-mouse**. [Aboriginal]

daring /'deərɪŋ/, n. **1.** adventurous courage; boldness. ◇adj. **2.** willing to take bold risks; intrepid.

Darius III /də'raɪəs/, n. died 330 BC; king of Persia 336–330 BC; defeated by Alexander the Great.

Darjeeling /da'dʒilɪŋ/, n. a city in north-eastern India, in the foothills of the Himalayas; famous for its tea. Pop. 63 600 (1984).

dark /dak/, adj. **1.** with very little or no light: *a dark room.* **2.** radiating little light: *a dark color.* **3.** not pale or fair: *a dark complexion.* **4.** cheerless; gloomy: *a dark atmosphere.* **5.** angry-looking; sullen: *a dark look.* **6.** evil; wicked: *dark thoughts.* **7.** hard to understand; obscure: *a dark comment.* ◇n. **8.** the absence of light. **9.** night. **10. in the dark**, lacking knowledge; ignorant. [OE *deorc*] **−darkness**, n.

Dark /dak/, n. **Eleanor**, 1901–85, Australian author; her works include the historical trilogy *The Timeless Land* (1941), *Storm of Time* (1948), and *No Barrier* (1953).

Dark Ages, n.pl. **1.** the time in history from about AD 476 to about AD 1000. **2.** (loosely) the whole of the Middle Ages, the period preceding the Renaissance.

darken /'dakən/, v.t., v.i. **1.** to make or become dark or darker. **2.** to make or become sad.

dark horse, n. **1.** an unexpected winner in a race, competition, etc. **2.** a person whose abilities may be greater than they are known to be.

darkroom /'dakrum/, n. a room from which light has been shut out, used in developing photographic film, etc.

darling /'dalɪŋ/, n. **1.** a person dearly loved by another. **2.** a person or thing in great favor. ◇adj. **3.** very dear; much loved. [OE *déore* dear + -LING¹]

Darling¹ /'dalɪŋ/, n. **Sir Ralph**, 1775–1858, English-born army officer and administrator in Australia; governor of NSW 1825–31.

Darling² /'dalɪŋ/, n. a river rising in Qld, near Stanthorpe, flowing south-west through NSW to the Murray River near Wentworth. Its course is known by several names: Dumaresq, Macintyre, Barwon, and Darling. From its source to the Murray, about 2700 km.

Darling clover, n. a sweet-smelling, clover-like plant which is found in inland areas of Australia and is useful food for cattle, etc. [from DARLING River]

Darling Downs, n.pl. a fertile area in south-eastern Qld about 160 km west of Brisbane. [named by their discoverer, Allan Cunningham, after Sir Ralph DARLING]

Darling lily, n. a handsome, sweet-smelling lily, found along inland watercourses of northern and central Australia. [from DARLING River]

Darling pea, n. any of a number of herbs with red-purple flowers, widespread esp. in inland areas of Australia and often the cause of poisoning of cattle, etc. [from DARLING River]

Darling Range, n. a scarp east of Perth, WA, running roughly parallel to the coast for about 300 km, from the Moore River in the north to Brunswick Junction in the south. Highest peak, 582 m.

Darling shower, n. →**dust storm**. [from DARLING River]

darn¹ /dan/, v.t. **1.** to mend (clothes, etc.) with crossing rows of stitches, filling up the hole. ◇n. **2.** a darned place in a garment, etc. [OE *dernan* hide]

darn² /dan/, *Colloq.* ◇adj., adv. **1.** damned. ◇v.t. **2.** to damn; curse. ◇interj. **3.** (a mild expression of anger, etc.) [var. of DAMN]

Darnley /'danli/, n. **Lord** (*Henry Stewart* or *Stuart*), 1545–67, Scottish nobleman; the second husband of Mary, Queen of Scots; father of James I of England.

dart /dat/, n. **1.** a small, thin, pointed weapon, usu. thrown by the hand. **2.** a sudden, quick movement. **3.** (pl.) a game in which darts are thrown at a board marked as a target. **4.** a seam where a wedge-shaped piece has been cut out to help shape a garment. ◇v.i., v.t. **5.** to move or throw quickly and suddenly. [ME, from OF, from Gmc]

darter /'datə/, n. any of various fish-eating birds having small heads, long, thin necks, and long, pointed bills, widespread in Australia and elsewhere.

Darwin¹ /'dawən/, n. **Charles**, 1809–82, English naturalist; explained his theory of evolution by natural selection in *On the Origin of Species* (1859).

Darwin² /'dawən/, n. a city on the north-western coast of the NT, on **Darwin Harbor**; administrative capital of the NT; settlement established 1869. Pop. 72 937 (1986). [named after Charles DARWIN]

Darwinism /'dawənɪzəm/, n. the theory of Charles Darwin which holds that all species evolved from parent forms, with selection of those with variations best fitted to survive in the struggle for existence. [See Charles DARWIN] **−Darwinist**, n., adj.

dash /dæʃ/, v.t. **1.** to strike violently, esp. so as to break to pieces. **2.** to throw violently or suddenly: *He dashed a cup to the floor.* **3.** to ruin (hopes, plans, etc.). **4.** to cause to lose hope, happiness, etc. **5.** to write, make, etc., hastily (usu. fol. by *off* or *down*): *to dash off a letter.* ◇v.i. **6.** to strike with violence: *The waves dash against the rocks.* **7.** to move with speed; rush. ◇n. **8.** a small quantity: *a dash of salt.* **9.** a horizontal line (—) used in writing to indicate a break or pause in a sentence. **10.** a sudden movement; rush. **11.** a short race: *a 100-metre dash.* **12.** spirited action or style. **13.** → **dashboard. 14.** (in Morse code, etc.) a signal longer than a dot, used in groups of dots, dashes and spaces to represent letters. **15. cut a dash**, to make a fine impression. **16. do one's dash**, to use up one's energies. [ME]

dashboard /'dæʃbɔd/, n. the instrument board of a motor car or of an aeroplane.

dashing /'dæʃɪŋ/, adj. **1.** spirited; lively. **2.** showy; stylish.

dastard /'dæstəd/, n., adj. (a person who is) mean, underhand and cowardly. [ME] — **dastardly**, adj.

dasyure /'dæzijuə/, n. See **native cat**. [NL *Dasyurus*, from *dasy*- (combining form of Gk: shaggy) + *-ūrus* (from Gk: tail)]

data /'deɪtə, 'dɑːtə/, n. **1.** plural of **datum**. **2.** (*treated as sing. or pl.*) information known or available, esp. numbers, measurements, etc.

database /'deɪtəbeɪs, 'dɑːtə-/, n. **1.** information stored in a computer, organised to make it easy to find a particular part. **2.** any large collection of information. Also, **databank**.

date[1] /deɪt/, n., v., **dated, dating.** ◇n. **1.** (a set of figures showing) a particular point or period of time when something happens or happened. **2.** a written date on a building, coin, etc., that shows the time of its making. **3.** the time or period to which anything belongs: *The digging has found objects of an earlier date.* **4.** *Colloq.* an appointment made for a particular time. **5.** *Colloq.* a person, usu. of the opposite sex, with whom one has a social appointment. **6. to date**, to the present time. ◇v.i. **7.** to belong to a particular period or bear the date of a particular time. **8.** *Colloq.* to go out with a person of the opposite sex. ◇v.t. **9.** to mark with a date: *to date a letter.* **10.** to give a date or time to. **11.** to find out the age of: *to date a fossil.* **12.** to show to be of a certain age, often old: *That dress dates you.* **13.** *Colloq.* to go out with (a person of the opposite sex). [ME, from F, from L: things given]

date[2] /deɪt/, n. a fleshy oblong fruit obtained from a type of palm. [ME, from OF, from L, from Gk: date, orig. finger]

date line, n. **1.** a line in a letter, newspaper article, etc., giving the date (and often the place) of origin. **2.** Also, **International Date Line.** an imaginary line running approximately along the meridian 180° from Greenwich, England, the areas on either side of which are counted as differing by one calendar day.

dative /'deɪtɪv/, adj., n. *Gram.* (relating to) the form of a noun which indicates that it is the indirect object of the verb. [ME, from L: of giving]

dative bond, n. a chemical bond of the covalent type in which the electrons forming the bond are supplied by a single atom; coordinate bond.

datum /'deɪtəm, 'dɑːtəm/, n., pl. **-ta** /-tə/. **1.** any given statement which forms a basis for further reasoning. **2.** (*oft. pl.*) any fact taken to be a matter of direct observation. [L: something given]

daub /dɔb/, v.t., v.i. **1.** to cover or coat (something) with soft, sticky matter, such as oil, mud, etc. **2.** to paint unskilfully. ◇n. **3.** material for daubing walls, etc. **4.** anything daubed on. **5.** a badly-done painting. [ME, from OF, from L: whiten, plaster]

daughter /'dɔtə/, n. **1.** a female child or person in relation to her parents. **2.** any female descendant. **3.** someone whose relationship is as that of a daughter to a parent: *a daughter of the church.* [OE *dohtor*]

daughter-in-law /'dɔtər-ɪn-lɔ/, n., pl. **daughters-in-law.** the wife of one's son.

daughter product, n. a radioactive decay product.

Daumier /doumi'eɪ/, n. **Honoré** /ɒnɒ'reɪ/, 1808–79, French lithographer, painter, and sculptor best known for his social and political caricatures.

daunt /dɔnt/, v.t. **1.** to overcome with fear; intimidate. **2.** to lessen the courage of; dishearten. [ME, from OF, from L: tame, subdue]

dauntless /'dɔntləs/, adj. fearless; bold.

dauphin /'dɔfən, 'doʊfæn/, n. the title of the eldest son of the king of France, from 1349 to 1830. [F, apparently orig. a proper name used as a surname; often identified with L *delphinus* dolphin]

Dauphiné /doʊfi'neɪ/, n. a historic province in south-eastern France; its former rulers assumed the title of *dauphin*.

David /'deɪvəd/, n. **1.** fl. c. 1000 BC, the second king of the Hebrews, successor to Saul; united the tribes of Israel into a nation with the capital at Jerusalem. **2. Saint** (*Saint Dewi*), died AD 601?, Welsh bishop, patron saint of Wales.

Davidson /'deɪvədsən/, n. **Alan Keith** ('*Davo*'), born 1929, Australian Test cricketer; noted all-rounder.

da Vinci /də 'vɪntʃi/, n. See **Leonardo da Vinci.**

Davis[1] /'deɪvəs/, n. **1. Bette** /'bɛti/, 1908–89, US film actor; films include *All About Eve* (1950). **2. Jack**, born 1918, Australian poet, playwright, and Aboriginal activist; works include the poetry collection *The First-Born and Other Poems* (1970). **3. Jefferson**, 1808–89, US politician; president of the Confederate States of America 1861–65. **4. John King**, 1884–1967, Australian Antarctic explorer and navigator, born in England. **5. Judy**, born 1956, Australian film and stage actor; films include *My Brilliant Career* (1979). **6. Sammy** (Sammy Davis Jr), 1925–90, US singer and actor.

Davis² /ˈdeɪvəs/, *n.* an Australian research base in Antarctica, established in 1957. [named after JK DAVIS]

Davis Cup, *n.* **1.** an annual men's lawn tennis competition between national teams. **2.** the trophy for this competition.

davit /ˈdævət/, *n.* a curved structure (often one of two) on the side of a vessel, used for raising or lowering boats, goods, etc. [ME, from AF, apparently diminutive of *Davi* David]

Davy /ˈdeɪvi/, *n.* **Edward**, 1806–85, Australian physician and inventor, born in England; one of the inventors of the electric telegraph.

dawdle /ˈdɔdəl/, *v.i.*, **-dled, -dling. 1.** to waste time; idle; trifle. **2.** to walk slowly. [? var. of *daddle* TODDLE]

Dawe /dɔ/, *n.* **Bruce**, born 1930, Australian poet; wrote the collections *Condolences of the Season* (1971) and *Sometimes Gladness: Collected Poems 1954–1982* (1983).

Dawes /dɔz/, *n.* **William**, 1762–1836, English soldier, astronomer, and surveyor in Australia.

dawn /dɔn/, *n.* **1.** the first appearance of daylight. **2.** the beginning of anything; advent. ◇*v.i.* **3.** to begin to grow light in the morning. **4.** to begin to open or develop. **5.** to begin to be understood by (fol. by *on* or *upon*): *The idea may dawn on him.* [ME *dawening* dawn, apparently from Scand]

dawn parade, *n.* a memorial ceremony held at dawn on Anzac Day. Also, **dawn service.**

Dawson¹ /ˈdɔsən/, *n.* **Peter Smith,** 1882–1961, Australian baritone.

Dawson² /ˈdɔsən/, *n.* a river in central eastern Qld rising in the Carnarvon Range and flowing east and north to meet the Fitzroy. 640 km.

day /deɪ/, *n.* **1.** the time between sunrise and sunset; the period of light between two nights. **2.** the light of day; daylight. **3.** the period during which the earth makes one complete turn on its axis. **4.** the part of a day given to working: *an 8-hour day.* **5.** a day of competition or struggle: *to win the day.* **6.** (*oft. pl.*) a particular time or period: *the present day; in days of old.* **7.** a period of power or influence: *Every man has his day.* **8. call it a day,** to bring an activity to a close. **9. day by day,** daily. **10. day in, day out,** all day, every day for a period of time. [OE *dæg*]

Day /deɪ/, *n.* **Doris** (*Doris Kappelhoff*), born 1924, US singer and film actor; noted esp. for light romantic comedy roles.

daybook /ˈdeɪbʊk/, *n.* *Bookkeeping.* a book in which the sales of the day are entered.

daybreak /ˈdeɪbreɪk/, *n.* the first appearance of light in the morning; dawn.

day centre, *n.* a place where children and elderly or disabled people may go for social activities during the day.

daydream /ˈdeɪdrim/, *n.* **1.** a dreamlike period enjoyed while awake; reverie. ◇*v.i.* **2.** to spend time in daydreams.

daylight robbery, *n.* a shameless attempt to rob, overcharge or cheat someone.

daylight-saving /ˌdeɪlaɪt-ˈseɪvɪŋ/, *n.* a system of advancing clocks during the summer months to give more hours of daylight at the end of the average working day.

daze /deɪz/, *v.*, **dazed, dazing,** *n.* ◇*v.t.* **1.** to stun (someone) with a blow, shock, etc. **2.** to confuse; bewilder; dazzle. ◇*n.* **3.** a dazed condition: *She is in a daze.* [ME, from Scand]

dazzle /ˈdæzəl/, *v.*, **-zled, -zling,** *n.* ◇*v.t.* **1.** to overpower or lessen (the vision) by strong light. **2.** to cause wonder to (someone) by a display of any kind: *He dazzled us with his knowledge.* ◇*v.i.* **3.** to overpower by light: *That torch dazzles.* ◇*n.* **4.** the act or fact of dazzling. **5.** confusing brightness. [from DAZE] **–dazzlingly,** *adv.*

dB, *Symbol.* decibel.

DBE /di bi ˈi/, *Abbrev.* Dame (Commander of the Order) of the British Empire.

DC /di ˈsi/, *Abbrev.* **1.** *Music.* da capo. **2.** direct current. **3.** District of Columbia.

DCM /di si ˈem/, *Abbrev.* Distinguished Conduct Medal.

D-day /ˈdi-deɪ/, *n.* the day set for the beginning of a previously planned attack, esp. the day (6 June 1944) of the Allied entry into Normandy.

DDR /di di ˈa/, *Abbrev.* German Democratic Republic; East Germany. Also, **GDR** [G D(*eutsche*) D(*emokratische*) R(*epublik*)]

DDT /di di ˈti/, *n. Abbrev.* a very powerful insecticide, dichloro-diphenyl-trichloroethane.

de-, a prefix meaning **1.** removal, as in *debug, dethrone.* **2.** negation, as in *demerit, derange.* **3.** descent, as in *degrade, deduce.* **4.** reversal, as in *deactivate.* [ME, from L]

deacon /ˈdikən/, *n.* **1.** (orig.) an officer of the early Christian Church. **2.** *Rom Cath Ch.* a member of a major order. **3.** *Anglican Ch.* the rank held before becoming a priest. **4.** (in other churches) an appointed or elected officer with various duties. [OE *dēacon, diacon,* from LL, from Gk: servant, minister, deacon]

deactivate /diˈæktəveɪt/, *v.t.*, **-vated, -vating. 1.** to treat a bomb, shell, etc., so that it cannot explode. **2.** *Phys., Chem.* to return (an activated substance, esp. a catalyst) to its normal state. **3.** *Phys.* to lose radioactivity. **–deactivation,** *n.*

dead /dɛd/, *adj.* **1.** no longer living. **2.** not having life; inanimate: *dead matter.* **3.** deathlike: *a dead sleep.* **4.** having no feeling; insensible; numb: *dead to all sense of shame.* **5.** no longer in existence or use: *dead languages.* **6.** *Colloq.* very tired; exhausted. **7.** unproductive: *dead capital.* **8.** not glossy, bright, or brilliant: *a dead color.* **9.** complete; absolute: *a dead loss; dead silence.* **10.** sure; unerring: *He's a dead shot with a rifle.* **11.** *Sport.* out of play: *a dead ball.* **12.** *Elect.* free from electric current. **13. dead**

dead   263   **dear**

to the world, *Colloq.* asleep, esp. deeply. ◇*n.* **14. the dead, a.** dead people. **b.** a period of greatest darkness, coldness, etc.: *the dead of night; the dead of winter.* ◇*adv.* **15.** absolutely; completely: *dead right; dead broke.* **16.** with a sudden and complete stopping of movement, etc.: *He stopped dead.* **17.** directly; exactly; diametrically: *The wind was dead ahead.* [OE *dēad*]

dead centre, *n.* **1.** (in a piston-driven engine or pump) either of two positions of the crank in which the connecting rod has no power to turn it, occurring when the piston is at the top or bottom of its stroke. **2.** → **Dead Heart.**

deaden /ˈdɛdən/, *v.t.* **1.** to make less sensitive, active or strong; dull; weaken: *to deaden sound; deaden the senses.* **2.** to treat (a floor, etc.) so that sound will be prevented from coming through it.

Dead Heart, *n.* the central area of Australia; Dead Centre.

dead heat, *n.* a race in which two or more competitors finish together.

dead letter, *n.* **1.** a law, etc., which has lost its force, but is not formally done away with. **2.** a letter which lies unclaimed at a post office, usu. because of incorrect address, etc. —**deadletter,** *adj.*

deadline /ˈdɛdlaɪn/, *n.* the latest time for finishing something.

deadlock[1] /ˈdɛdlɒk/, *n.* **1.** a state of affairs in which it is impossible to move forward. **2.** *Parl.* an equal vote with no chance of breaking the tie. ◇*v.t., v.i.* **3.** to bring or come to a deadlock.

deadlock[2] /ˈdɛdlɒk/, *n.* a lock with a bolt which can be fixed in place after the door is shut. It is more secure than a springloaded bolt.

deadly /ˈdɛdli/, *adj.*, **-lier, -liest,** *adv.* ◇*adj.* **1.** causing or tending to cause death; fatal: *a deadly poison.* **2.** aiming to kill or destroy: *a deadly enemy.* **3.** leading to spiritual death: *a deadly sin.* **4.** like death: *deadly paleness.* ◇*adv.* **5.** in a manner suggesting death: *deadly pale.* —**deadliness,** *n.*

deadly nightshade, *n.* a plant with poisonous black berries and purple flowers. Also, **belladonna.**

dead man's handle, *n.* a handle used to control the speed of an electric train, etc., which cuts off the power supply if the pressure of the driver's hand is removed.

deadpan /ˈdɛdpæn/, *adj. Colloq.* **1.** (of a person, esp. the face or voice) completely lacking expression, esp. when telling jokes. ◇*adv.* **2.** in a deadpan manner; without expression.

dead reckoning, *n.* **1.** (in navigation) the calculation of position by means of distances travelled, taking into account drift, etc., rather than using the stars as a guide. **2.** a position as so calculated.

Dead Sea, *n.* a salt lake between Israel and Jordan; the lowest lake in the world. 74 km long; 16 km wide; 394 m below sea-level.

Dead Sea scrolls, *n.pl.* a collection of ancient Hebrew and Aramaic manuscripts dating from the second century BC to AD 70, found in caves north-west of the Dead Sea in 1947 and 1952.

dead weight, *n.* **1.** the heavy weight of anything lifeless. **2.** a responsibility, etc., which weighs heavily. —**deadweight,** *adj.*

deadwood /ˈdɛdwʊd/, *n.* **1.** dead branches or trees. **2.** a person or thing regarded as useless.

deaf /dɛf/, *adj.* **1.** lacking the sense of hearing, wholly or partly. **2.** refusing to listen; heedless; inattentive: *deaf to advice.* ◇*n.* **3. the deaf,** people unable to hear. [OE *dēaf*]

deafen /ˈdɛfən/, *v.t.* **1.** to make deaf. **2.** to make (someone) senseless with noise. **3.** to make (a sound) unable to be heard, esp. by a louder sound. —**deafening,** *adj.*

Deakin /ˈdikən/, *n.* **Alfred,** 1856–1919, Australian politician; prime minister 1903–04, 1905–08 and 1909–10.

deal[1] /dil/, *v.*, **dealt, dealing,** *n.* ◇*v.i.* **1.** to be concerned (fol. by *with* or *in*): *to deal with the first question; Botany deals with the study of plants.* **2.** to take action with a thing or person (usu. fol. by *with*): *Law courts must deal with lawbreakers.* **3.** to conduct oneself towards people: *to deal fairly.* **4.** to do business: *to deal with a firm.* **5.** to give out, esp. cards required in a game: *Will you deal?* ◇*v.t.* **6.** to give shares of; apportion (oft. fol. by *out*). **7.** to share out among a number of people, as cards required in a game. **8.** to deliver: *to deal a blow.* ◇*n.* **9.** *Colloq.* a business agreement: *We did a good deal with the builder.* **10.** an arrangement, as in politics or commerce, often made secretly, which is of profit to all concerned. **11.** treatment; arrangement: *a raw deal; a fair deal.* **12.** quantity, amount, extent, or degree: *They make a great deal of noise.* **13.** *Cards.* **a.** the giving out to the players of the cards in a game. **b.** the turn of a player to deal. **14. a big deal,** *Colloq.* a serious matter. **15. big deal!** *Colloq.* (a sarcastic exclamation of contempt). [OE *dǣlan* divide, share]

deal[2] /dil/, *n.* (a board of) fir or pine wood. [ME, from MLG or MD]

dealer /ˈdilə/, *n.* **1.** someone who buys and sells articles: *a dealer in antiques.* **2.** *Cards.* the player giving out the cards.

dealing /ˈdiliŋ/, *n.* **1.** (usu. pl.) relations; trading: *business dealings.* **2.** behavior in relation to others; treatment: *honest dealing.*

dealt /dɛlt/, *v.* past tense and past participle of **deal**[1].

dean /din/, *n.* **1.** *Educ.* the head of a university faculty. **2.** *Church.* the head of a cathedral, division of a diocese, etc. [ME, from OF, from LL: chief of ten]

Dean /din/, *n.* **James,** 1931–55, US actor; became a symbol of rebellious youth after such films as *Rebel Without a Cause* (1955).

dear /dɪə/, *adj.* **1.** beloved or loved: *a dear friend of mine.* **2.** (in a letter) highly respected: *Dear Sirs.* **3.** precious: *dear to his heart.* **4.** high-priced; expensive. **5.** charging high

dear 264 **debut**

prices. ◇*n.* **6.** someone who is loved or precious: *my dear.* ◇*adv.* **7.** fondly: *I loved her dear.* **8.** at a high price. ◇*interj.* **9.** (an exclamation of surprise, upset, etc.). [OE *dēore*]

dearth /dɜθ/, *n.* **1.** a very small supply; lack. **2.** insufficiency and dearness of food; famine. [OE *dēor*, hard, rigorous]

death /deθ/, *n.* **1.** the act of dying; end of life. **2.** (*oft. cap.*) the power of death, thought of as a person, usu. a skeleton. **3.** the condition of being dead: *to lie still in death.* **4.** the end; destruction: *It will mean the death of our hopes.* **5.** a condition like death, as a loss of spiritual life. **6.** a cause of death: *You'll be the death of me.* ◇**7.** Some special uses are:
at death's door, gravely ill.
do to death, **1.** to kill. **2.** to repeat (something) till it seems to lose meaning.
in at the death, **1.** present when a hunted animal is caught and killed. **2.** present at the climax of a situation.
like death (warmed up), *Colloq.* appearing or feeling extremely ill or exhausted.
like grim death, firmly: *He hung on like grim death.*
put to death, to kill; execute.
sick to death of, *Colloq.* bored and annoyed with. [OE *dēath*]

death adder, *n.* a venomous snake of Australia and PNG with a thick body and broad head. Also, **deaf adder**.

death certificate, *n.* an official paper signed by a doctor, declaring a person dead and stating the cause if known.

death duty, *n.* (*usu. pl.*) a tax paid on property received through a will.

deathly /'deθli/, *adj.* **1.** causing death; deadly; fatal. **2.** like death. ◇*adv.* **3.** in the manner of death: *deathly pale.* **4.** very; utterly: *deathly afraid.* [OE *dēathlīc*]

death mask, *n.* a copy in wax of a person's face taken after death.

death row, *n. Colloq.* a group of cells in which prisoners who are to be executed are kept, esp. in prisons in the US.

death warrant, *n.* **1.** an official order directing a person's death. **2.** anything which ends hope, etc.

death-wish /'deθ-wɪʃ/, *n.* a desire, esp. unconscious, for one's own death.

deb /dɛb/, *n.* → **debutante**.

debacle /deɪ'bakəl, də-/, *n.* a sudden break-up, overthrow or collapse; crushing disaster. [F *dé-* DIS-[1] + *bâcler* bar (from L: stick, rod)]

debar /di'ba, də-/, *v.t.* **-barred, -barring.** **1.** to prevent (someone) from being present or involved. **2.** to prevent or disallow (an action, etc.). [OF *des-* DIS-[1] + *barrer* bar]

debase /də'beɪs/, *v.t.* **-based, -basing.** **1.** to reduce in quality; adulterate. **2.** to lower in rank. **—debasement**, *n.*

debatable /də'beɪtəbəl/, *adj.* **1.** open to being debated. **2.** under question. Also, **debateable**.

debate /də'beɪt/, *n., v.,* **-bated, -bating.** ◇*n.* **1.** a discussion, esp. of a public question. **2.** a formal discussion in which two opposing views are put forward in turn by two teams of speakers. ◇*v.i.* **3.** to take part in a discussion, esp. in a law-making or public assembly. **4.** to discuss or argue; consider. **5.** to take part in a debate (def. 2). ◇*v.t.* **6.** to discuss or argue (a question). [ME, from OF]

debauch /də'bɔtʃ/, *v.t.* **1.** to corrupt by exposing to debauchery. ◇*v.i.* **2.** to take part in a debauch. ◇*n.* **3.** a period of debauchery. [OF: seduce from duty] **—debauched**, *adj.* **—debauchment**, *n.*

debauchery /də'bɔtʃəri/, *n., pl.* **-eries.** a complete yielding to sensual pleasures; intemperance.

debenture /də'bɛntʃə/, *n.* **1.** a note admitting a debt. **2.** money lent to a business which bears interest at a fixed rate and for which repayment is guaranteed. [L: there are owing]

debilitate /də'bɪlɪteɪt/, *v.t.* **-tated, -tating.** to make weak; weaken; enfeeble. [L: weakened] **—debilitation**, *n.*

debility /də'bɪləti/, *n., pl.* **-ties.** the condition of being weak or feeble; weakness. [ME, from L: weakness]

debit /'dɛbət/, *n.* **1.** the recording of a debt in an account. **2. a.** a recorded item of debt. **b.** any entry, or the total shown, on the debit (left) side of an account. ◇*v.t.* **3.** to charge with a debt: *The shop will debit her for the purchase.* **4.** to enter upon the debit side of an account. [L: something owed]

debonair /dɛbə'nɛə/, *adj.* (esp. of a man) suave; stylish. Also, **debonaire, debonnaire**. [ME, from OF phrase *de bon aire* of good disposition]

debrief /di'brif/, *v.t. Orig. US.* to question (a soldier, astronaut, diplomat, etc.) after a mission. **—debriefing**, *n.*

debris /'dɛbri, 'deɪbri, də'bri/, *n.* the remains of anything broken down or destroyed; ruins; fragments; rubbish. [OF]

debt /dɛt/, *n.* **1.** that which is owed. **2.** (the condition of being under) an obligation to pay something. **3. bad debt**, a debt which will not be paid. [ME, from OF *dete*, from L: thing owed]

debt of honor or **debt of honour** *n.* a debt which is not able to be recovered legally, as a gambling debt.

debtor /'dɛtə/, *n.* someone who is in debt.

debug /di'bʌg/, *v.t.,* **-bugged, -bugging.** *Colloq.* **1.** to find and remove faults in (an electronic system). **2.** to remove electronic listening devices from (a room, etc.).

debunk /di'bʌŋk/, *v.t. Colloq.* to show up the falseness of; make fun of.

Debussy /də'busi, dəbu'si/, *n.* **Claude Achille** /kloud a'ʃil/, 1862–1918, French impressionist composer.

debut /'deɪbju, -bu, də'bu/, *n.* **1.** a first appearance in public, on stage, etc. **2.** a formal introduction and entrance into society. [F:

make the first stroke in a game, make one's first appearance]

debutante /ˈdebjətɒnt/, *n.* a girl making her debut into society. [F] —**debutant**, *n. masc.*

dec- → **deka-**.

Dec, *Abbrev.* December.

deca- → **deka-**.

decade /ˈdekeɪd/, *n.* 1. a period of ten years. 2. a set or series of ten. [F, from L, from Gk: a group of ten] —**decadal**, *adj.*

decadence /ˈdekədəns/, *n.* the act or process of falling into a lower state; decay; deterioration. Also, **decadency**. [F, from L *dē* DE- + *cadere* fall] —**decadent**, *adj., n.*

decagon /ˈdekəgɒn, -gən/, *n.* a closed figure having ten angles and ten sides. [ML. DECA- + -GON]

decahedron /dekəˈhiːdrən/, *n., pl.* **-drons, -dra** /-drə/. a solid figure having ten faces.

decamp /dɪˈkæmp/, *v.i.* 1. to depart from a camp; break camp. 2. to depart quickly and secretly. [F *dé*- DIS-¹ + *camper* encamp]

decant /dəˈkænt/, *v.t.* 1. to pour off gently, as liquor, without disturbing the matter at the bottom. 2. to pour from one container into another. [ML. See DE-, CANT²] —**decantation**, *n.*

decanter /dəˈkæntə/, *n.* a vessel from which wine, water, etc., are served

decapitate /dəˈkæpəteɪt, di-/, *v.t.*, **-tated, -tating**. to cut off the head of; behead. [ML, from L *caput* head] —**decapitation**, *n.* —**decapitator**, *n.*

decapod /ˈdekəpɒd/, *n.* 1. any crustacean with five pairs of walking legs, including crabs, lobsters, crayfish, prawns, etc. 2. any cephalopod with ten arms and two gills, as the cuttlefish, squid, etc.

de Castella /di kæsˈtelə/, *n.* **Robert**, born 1957, Australian marathon runner; Commonwealth Games gold medallist.

decathlon /dəˈkæθlɒn, dəˈkæθlən/, *n.* an athletic competition comprised of ten different events. [DECA- + Gk *āthlon* contest]

decay /dɪˈkeɪ, də-/, *v.i.* 1. to fall away from a state of excellence, health, etc.; deteriorate; decline. 2. to become decomposed; rot. 3. *Phys.* **a.** (of a radioactive substance) to break down by giving out alpha, beta, or gamma rays. **b.** (of an elementary particle) to change into a more stable particle. 4. *Electronics.* (of a current or voltage) to fall away after the source of energy has been removed from the circuit. ◊*v.t.* 5. to cause to decay. ◊*n.* 6. a gradual falling into a poorer condition. 7. the act of rotting; decomposition. 8. *Phys.* **a.** the breaking down of a radioactive substance. **b.** the change of an elementary particle into a more stable one. [ME, from OF *de-* DE- + *cair* (from L: fall)]

decease /dəˈsiːs/, *n., v.*, **-ceased, -ceasing**. ◊*n.* 1. departure from life; death. ◊*v.i.* 2. to die. [ME, from OF, from L: departure, death] —**deceased**, *adj.*

deceased estate, *n.* →**estate** (def. 2b).

deceit /dəˈsiːt/, *n.* 1. the act or practice of deceiving. 2. an act or device meant to deceive; a trick; stratagem. 3. deceiving quality; falseness. [ME, from OF: deceive] —**deceitful**, *adj.* —**deceitfulness**, *n.*

deceive /dəˈsiːv/, *v.t.*, **-ceived, -ceiving**. 1. to mislead by a false appearance or statement; delude. 2. to be unfaithful to; commit adultery against. [ME, from OF, from L: catch, deceive]

decelerate /diˈselərеɪt/, *v.i., v.t.*, **-rated, -rating**. to reduce the velocity or speed (of). [DE- + (AC)CELERATE] —**deceleration**, *n.*

December /dəˈsembə/, *n.* the 12th month of the year, containing 31 days. [L: the tenth month of the early Roman year]

Decembrist /dəˈsembrəst/, *n. Russian Hist.* a participant in the unsuccessful revolt against the Tsar Nicholas I on his accession in December 1825.

decency /ˈdiːsənsi/, *n., pl.* **-cies**. 1. the condition or quality of being decent. 2. a keeping to the accepted standards of good taste, modesty, etc. 3. (*pl.*) the requirements of respectable life or conduct.

decennial /dəˈseniəl/, *adj.* 1. of or for ten years. 2. happening every ten years. ◊*n.* 3. the day ten years after a particular event.

decent /ˈdiːsənt/, *adj.* 1. fitting; appropriate. 2. keeping to recognised standards of behavior, good taste, modesty, etc. 3. respectable; worthy: *a decent family*. 4. fair; tolerable; passable: *a decent wage*. 5. *Colloq.* kind; obliging: *Thanks, that's decent of you.* [L: fitting]

decentralise or **decentralize** /diˈsentrəlaɪz/, *v.t.*, **-lised, -lising**. 1. to spread out (industry, population, etc.) from an area of density, esp. from large cities to less developed areas. 2. to spread more evenly the administration of (an organisation, government, etc.). —**decentralisation**, *n.*

deception /dəˈsepʃən/, *n.* 1. the act of deceiving. 2. the condition of being deceived. 3. something that deceives; a cheat. [ME, from LL: deceive]

deceptive /dəˈseptɪv/, *adj.* tending to deceive. [NL]

deci-, a prefix meaning $\frac{1}{10}$ of a given unit, as in *decigram*. *Symbol:* d [combining form representing L *decem* ten, *decimus* tenth]

decibel /ˈdesəbel/, *n.* a unit expressing difference in power, usu. between electric or sound signals, or between some particular signal and a standard reference level. *Symbol:* dB

decide /dəˈsaɪd/, *v.*, **-cided, -ciding**. ◊*v.t.* 1. to settle (a question, struggle, etc.) by giving victory to one side. 2. to settle (anything in question or doubt). 3. to bring (a person) to a decision: *His warning decided me. I would not go.* ◊*v.i.* 4. to settle something in question or doubt. 5. to come to a conclusion. [ME, from L: cut off, determine]

decided /dəˈsaɪdəd/, *adj.* 1. settled. 2. completely clear and obvious; unquestionable;

unmistakable. **3.** free from uncertainty; resolute; determined.

deciduous /dəˈsɪdjuəs/, *adj.* **1.** losing the leaves every year, as trees, etc. **2.** falling off at a particular season, stage of growth, etc., as leaves, horns, teeth, etc. [L: falling down]

decile /ˈdesaɪl/, *n. Stats.* one of the values of a variable which divides the distribution of the variable into ten groups having equal frequencies. Thus, there are ten deciles, each having the same numbers of people, things, etc., but a varying range of scores. [L *dec(em)* ten + -ILE]

decimal /ˈdesəməl/, *adj.* **1.** relating to tenths, or to the number ten. **2.** proceeding by tens: *a decimal system.* ◇*n.* **3.** → **decimal fraction. 4.** → **decimal number.** [L *decimus* tenth + -AL¹]

decimal classification, *n.* See **Dewey decimal classification.**

decimal currency, *n.* a money system in which units are based on powers of ten: *1 dollar × 10⁻² becomes $0.01.*

decimal fraction, *n.* a fraction whose denominator (lower figure) is some power of ten. It is usu. shown by a dot (the **decimal point**) written before the numerator (upper figure) as $0.4 = \frac{4}{10}$.

decimalise or **decimalize** /ˈdesəməlaɪz/, *v.t.*, **-lised, -lising.** to reduce to a decimal system. — **decimalisation,** *n.*

decimal number, *n. Maths.* any string of digits containing a decimal point: *1.0, 5.23, 3.14159 . . .* are decimal numbers.

decimal place, *n.* the position of a digit to the right of a decimal point: *In 9.623, 3 is in the third decimal place.*

decimal point, *n.* (in the decimal system) the dot going before the non-whole part of a number.

decimal system, *n.* any system of counting or measurement whose units are powers of ten.

decimate /ˈdesəmeɪt/, *v.t.*, **-mated, -mating. 1.** to destroy a great number or amount of. **2.** to kill every tenth person of. [L] — **decimation,** *n.* — **decimator,** *n.*

decipher /dəˈsaɪfə/, *v.t.* **1.** to make out the meaning of (poor or partly destroyed writing, etc.). **2.** to discover the meaning of (anything difficult to understand, as a code). — **decipherable,** *adj.*

decision /dəˈsɪʒən/, *n.* **1.** the act of deciding. **2.** a judgment, as one formally made by a court. **3.** that which is decided; a resolution. **4.** the quality of being decided (def. 3); firmness, as of character: *a woman of decision.* [L: a cutting down; decision]

decisive /dəˈsaɪsɪv/, *adj.* **1.** having the power of deciding; ending controversy: *a decisive fact; a decisive test.* **2.** showing decision; resolute; determined.

deck /dek/, *n.* **1.** a horizontal wooden floor reaching from side to side of a ship or part of a ship. **2.** any surface like this, as the top surface of a surfboard or the platform of a bus or bridge. **3.** a horizontal stand on or in a tape recorder, record-player, etc., above which the turntable or spools turn around. **4. clear the decks, a.** *Naut.* to prepare for battle, as by removing from the deck all unnecessary gear. **b.** *Colloq.* to prepare for action of any kind. **5. hit the deck,** *Colloq.* to fall to the ground or floor. **6. on deck,** *Colloq.* on duty; present at the time. ◇*v.t.* **7.** to clothe in something ornamental; array (oft. fol. by *out*). [MD: cover]

deckchair /ˈdektʃeə/, *n.* a light folding chair with a back and seat of canvas or similar material.

-decker, a combining form indicating a certain number of levels, as in *double-decker bus.*

deckhand /ˈdekhænd/, *n.* any sailor who works on the deck.

deckle edge, *n.* the irregular edge of handmade paper, formerly much used for ornamental effect in fine books.

declaim /dəˈkleɪm/, *v.i.* **1.** to make a formal speech. **2.** to speak violently (fol. by *against*). **3.** to speak or write for effect, without sincerity. [ME, from L: cry aloud] — **declamation,** *n.* — **declamatory,** *adj.*

declarable /dəˈkleərəbəl/, *adj.* (of goods, etc.) required by law to be declared at customs; dutiable.

Declaration of Independence, *n. US.* (the document recording) the public proclamation on 4 July 1776, which declared the thirteen Colonies to be free and independent of Great Britain.

Declaration of Rights, *n. Eng Hist.* the statement of the rights and liberties of the people accepted by William and Mary on taking the throne in 1688.

declare /dəˈkleə/, *v.*, **-clared, -claring.** ◇*v.t.* **1.** to make known, esp. in formal terms. **2.** to state officially; proclaim: *The government declared war.* **3.** to make a statement of (goods, etc.) that are taxable. ◇*v.i.* **4.** *Cricket.* to close an innings before all ten wickets have fallen. [ME, from L: make clear] — **declaration,** *n.* — **declaratory,** *adj.*

declared /dəˈkleəd/, *adj.* acknowledged; professed: *He's a declared enemy of mine.*

declassify /diˈklæsəfaɪ/, *v.t.*, **-fied, -fying.** to remove a classification (def. 3) from (government documents, etc.); make available to the public.

declension /dəˈklenʃən/, *n.* **1.** *Gram.* **a.** the form (inflection) of a noun, pronoun or adjective that shows its case, number or gender, e.g. *who, whose, whom.* **b.** a class of such words having similar sets of forms, as the second declension in Latin. **2.** a bending, sloping, or moving downward. [L: a bending aside, inflection]

declination /deklə'neɪʃən/, *n.* **1.** *Astron.* the angular distance of a planet or star north or south of the celestial equator. **2.** Also, **magnetic declination/variation.** the horizontal angle between the direction of true north and magnetic north at any place. **3.** *Obs.* a polite refusal.

decline /dəˈklaɪn/, v., **-clined, -clining**. /dəˈklaɪn, ˈdɪklaɪn/, n. ◇v.t. **1.** to refuse, usu. politely: *He declined to say more about it; He declined the offer with thanks.* **2.** to cause to slope downward. **3.** *Gram.* to say or give the inflected forms of (a noun, pronoun, or adjective). ◇v.i. **4.** to refuse politely: *He declined, saying he was busy.* **5.** to bend or move downward; descend. **6.** to draw towards the close, as the day. **7.** to decrease in strength, character, value, etc.; deteriorate: *The price of gold declined recently.* ◇n. **8.** a downward slope. **9.** a gradual loss, as in strength, health, character, value, etc.; deterioration. **10.** the last part or phase. [ME, from L: bend from, avoid, inflect]

declivity /dəˈklɪvəti/, n., pl. **-ties**. a downward slope, as of ground (opposed to *acclivity*). [L: slope]

decoction /dəˈkɒkʃən/, n. **1.** the act of extracting the essence of a substance by boiling in water. **2.** a substance obtained by this method.

decode /diˈkoʊd/, v.t., **-coded, -coding**. to translate from code into the original language or form.

décolleté /deɪˈkɒlətei/, adj. **1.** (of a dress) low-necked. **2.** wearing a low-necked dress. [F: with neck bared]

decompose /ˌdikəmˈpoʊz/, v., **-posed, -posing**. ◇v.t. **1.** to break up or separate into simple parts or elements; disintegrate. ◇v.i. **2.** to rot; putrefy. [F *dé-* DIS-¹ + *composer* COMPOSE] —**decomposable**, adj. —**decomposition**, n.

decompress /ˌdikəmˈprɛs/, v.t. **1.** to reduce the pressure in. **2.** to return (a person) to the normal pressure of the atmosphere in a decompression chamber. —**decompression**, n.

decompression chamber /ˌdikəmˈprɛʃən ˈtʃeɪmbə/, n. a room in which pressure can be changed slowly so that people who have been under high pressure (as divers, etc.) can gradually be returned to atmospheric pressure; hyperbaric chamber.

decongestant /ˌdikənˈdʒɛstənt/, n., adj. (a drug) relieving congestion.

decor /ˈdeɪkɔː, ˈdɛkɔː/, n. **1.** decoration in general. **2.** the decoration of a room, stage, etc. [F, from L: decorate]

decorate /ˈdɛkəreɪt/, v., **-rated, -rating**. ◇v.t. **1.** to furnish or provide with something attractive or ornamental; embellish: *They decorated the streets for Christmas.* **2.** to plan and carry out the painting, wall-papering and sometimes furnishing of (a house, room, etc). **3.** to honor with a badge, medal, etc. ◇v.i. **4.** to decorate a house, etc. [L] —**decorator**, n.

decoration /ˌdɛkəˈreɪʃən/, n. the act of decorating. **2.** something that decorates: *party decorations.* **3.** the style in which a house, room, etc., is decorated. **4.** a badge, medal, etc., given and worn as a mark of honor.

decorative /ˈdɛkərətɪv, ˈdɛkrətɪv/, adj. **1.** serving or used to decorate. **2.** attractive but superficial.

decorum /dəˈkɔrəm/, n. **1.** correctness of behavior, speech, dress, etc. **2.** that which is proper; fitness; propriety. [L: something decorous] —**decorous**, adj.

decoy /ˈdikɔɪ/, n.; /dəˈkɔɪ/, v. ◇n. **1.** someone or something that entices, as into a trap, danger, etc. ◇v.t. **2.** to entice into a trap by a decoy; lure. [var. of *coy* (now d.), both from D (*de*) *kooi* (the) cage, from L *cavea* CAGE]

decrease /dəˈkris/, v., **-creased, -creasing**; /ˈdikris, dəˈkris/, n. ◇v.i. **1.** to lessen gradually in extent, quantity, strength, power, etc. ◇v.t. **2.** to make less; cause to diminish. ◇n. **3.** a process of growing less, or the resulting condition. **4.** the amount by which a thing is lessened. [ME, from OF, from L: grow less]

decree /dəˈkri/, n., v., **-creed, -creeing**. ◇n. **1.** an official command or decision by a government or other authority. **2.** *Law.* a judgment. ◇v.t. **3.** to order by decree; ordain. ◇v.i. **4.** to give a decree. [ME, from OF, from L: decree]

decrepit /dəˈkrɛpət/, adj. broken down or weakened by old age; feeble; infirm. [L: noiseless] —**decrepitude**, n.

decrescendo /ˌdikrəˈʃɛndoʊ/, adv. *Music*. gradually reducing force or loudness; diminuendo (opposed to *crescendo*). [It: DECREASE]

decriminalise *or* **decriminalize** /diˈkrɪmənəlaɪz/, v.t., **-lised, -lising**. to declare by legislation that a form of behavior is not criminal.

decry /dəˈkraɪ/, v.t., **-cried, -crying**. to speak badly of. [F *dé-* DIS-¹ + *crier* CRY] —**decrial**, n.

dedicate /ˈdɛdəkeɪt/, v.t., **-cated, -cating**. **1.** to set apart and give to a god or to a holy purpose. **2.** to give up totally, as to some person or end: *He dedicated his life to medicine.* **3.** to address (a book, piece of music, etc.) to a friend, etc., as a mark of respect, affection, etc.: *I dedicate this book to my mother.* [L: proclaimed, devoted] —**dedication**, n. —**dedicated**, adj. —**dedicatory**, adj.

deduce /dəˈdjus/, v.t., **-duced, -ducing**. to reach a conclusion from known or supposed facts; infer by logical reasoning. [L: lead down, derive] —**deducible**, adj. —**deductive**, adj.

deduct /dəˈdʌkt/, v.t. to take away, as from a sum or amount. [L: led down, withdrawn] —**deductable, deductible**, adj.

deduction /dəˈdʌkʃən/, n. **1.** an act of deducting; subtraction. **2.** an amount deducted. **3.** (the process of drawing) a conclusion from something known or assumed.

deed /did/, n. **1.** something done; an act: *a good deed.* **2.** a notable act; feat; exploit. **3.** *Law.* a signed agreement, usu. concerning ownership of land or property. [OE *dēd*]

deed poll, n. (a deed showing) a formal declaration of a person's act and intention, esp. to change his or her name.

deem /dim/, v.i. **1.** to have an opinion; judge; think. ◇v.t. **2.** to hold as an opinion; think; regard. [OE *dēman*]

deep /dip/, *adj.* **1.** going far down, in or back: *a deep sea; a deep wound; a deep cupboard.* **2.** being a certain distance down, in or back: *a tank two metres deep.* **3.** going far from side towards the centre; broad: *a deep border.* **4.** coming or going from far down: *a deep breath.* **5.** hard to understand; abstruse: *Maths is too deep for me.* **6.** not superficial; profound: *a deep relationship; deep sorrow.* **7.** great in amount; intense: *deep sleep.* **8.** (of colors) intense; dark and vivid: *a deep red.* **9.** low in pitch: *a deep voice.* **10.** very cunning: *He's a deep one.* **11.** much involved: *deep in debt.* **12.** *Cricket.* relatively far from the wicket: *the deep field.* **13.** *Tennis.* (of a shot) played from baseline to baseline. **14. go off the deep end**, *Colloq.* to become angry, excited or hysterical. **15. in deep water**, *Colloq.* in trouble or difficulties. ◇*n.* **16.** the deep part(s) of the sea, a river, etc. **17.** any deep space or place. **18.** the part of greatest intensity, as of winter. ◇*adv.* **19.** to or at a great or particular depth. **20.** profoundly; intensely: *He thought deep on the matter.* [OE *dēop*]

deepen /'dipən/, *v.t., v.i.* to make or become deep or deeper.

deep freeze, *n.* (a section of) a refrigerator in which food can be quickly frozen and stored at a very low temperature; freezer. [Trademark] – **deep-freeze**, *v.*

deep structure, *n. Gram.* See **transformational grammar**.

deepwater /'dipwɔtə/, *adj.* **1.** (of a port) being able to accommodate relatively large ships. **2.** (of a ship, etc.) ocean-going. **3.** living in deep, as opposed to shallow, waters.

deer /dɪə/, *n., pl.* **deer.** any of several types of mainly large, hoofed, grass-eating animals, the males of which have wide branching horns or antlers. [OE *dēor*]

deerstalker /'dɪəstɔkə/, *n.* **1.** someone who hunts deer. **2.** a soft hat, pointed at the back and front, and having ear coverings.

de-escalate /di-'ɛskəleɪt/, *v.t.*, **-lated, -lating**. to reduce one's involvement in (a war, campaign, program, etc.). – **de-escalation**, *n.*

def., *Abbrev.* definition.

deface /də'feɪs/, *v.t.*, **-faced, -facing**. to damage the appearance of; disfigure. [ME, from F] – **defacement**, *n.*

de facto /di 'fæktoʊ, də, deɪ/, *adj.* **1.** in fact; in reality. **2.** actually existing, whether with or without right, as in a de facto relationship in which a man and woman living together are not married but are known as de facto husband and wife. [L: from the fact]

defame /dɪ'feɪm, də-/, *v.t.*, **-famed, -faming**. to damage the good name or reputation of (a person or group); slander; libel. [ME, from ML] – **defamatory**, *adj.* – **defamation**, *n.*

default /də'fɔlt/, *n.* **1.** failure to act; neglect. **2.** failure to pay debts. **3.** *Law.* failure to perform an act legally required, esp. failure to appear in a law court when required, or failure to pay a debt. **4.** failure to take part in or finish something, as a competition. **5.** want; lack; absence: *owing to default of water.* ◇*v.i.* **6.** to fail in fulfilling or satisfying an engagement, claim, or obligation. **7.** to fail to pay debts, or to account properly for money, etc., in one's care. **8.** *Law.* to fail to appear in court. **9. a.** to fail to take part in or finish anything, as a match. **b.** to lose a match by default. ◇*v.t.* **10.** to fail to do or pay. **11.** *Law.* to lose by failure to appear in court. **12. a.** to fail to take part in (a game, race, etc.). **b.** to lose (a game, etc.) by default. [ME from OF]

defeat /də'fit/, *v.t.* **1.** to overcome in a contest, battle, etc.; win or achieve victory over; vanquish. **2.** to cause to fail; thwart; frustrate. ◇*n.* **3.** the act of overcoming in a contest, etc.: *Our defeat of the other team meant that we played in the finals.* **4.** a condition of being defeated; vanquishment: *Their defeat was total.* **5.** a bringing to nothing; frustration. **6.** undoing; destruction; ruin. [ME, from OF: undone]

defecate /'dɛfəkeɪt/, *v.i.*, **-cated, -cating**. to pass waste material from the bowel. [L: cleansed from dregs] – **defecation**, *n.*

defect /'difɛkt, də'fɛkt/, *n.*; /də'fɛkt/, *v.* ◇*n.* **1.** a fault; imperfection. **2.** a want or lack, esp. of something necessary for perfection or completeness; deficiency. ◇*v.i.* **3.** to desert a country, cause, etc. [L: want, defect] – **defector**, *n.* – **defection**, *n.*

defective /də'fɛktɪv/, *adj.* **1.** having a defect; faulty; imperfect. **2.** *Psychol.* having well below average intelligence or behavior.

defence /də'fɛns/, *n.* **1.** protection against attack. **2.** something that defends, as a strong wall, etc. **3.** the defending of a cause, etc., by speech, argument, etc.: *He gave a strong defence.* **4.** *Law.* **a.** the argument(s) in answer to the charge made against a defendant. **b.** a legally recognised justification or excuse. **c.** a defendant and the lawyers of the defence. **5.** *Sport.* **a.** the practice or art of defending oneself or one's goal. **b.** the players in a team who defend the goal, etc. [ME, from OF, from LL: prohibition, from L: ward off]

defence mechanism, *n.* **1.** *Med.* a defensive activity within the body, such as the production of an antitoxin. **2.** *Psychol.* a process which opposes the entry into consciousness or the acting out of unacceptable or painful ideas and desires.

defend /də'fɛnd/, *v.t.* **1.** to keep safe from harm (oft. fol. by *from* or *against*). **2.** to support by argument, etc.; uphold. **3.** to act as lawyer for (an accused person). ◇*v.i.* **4.** *Law.* to contest (a criminal charge or civil claim). [ME, from OF, from L: ward off]

defendant /də'fɛndənt/, *n. Law.* a person against whom a charge is brought in court.

defensible /də'fɛnsəbəl/, *adj.* **1.** able to be defended against attack. **2.** able to be defended in argument; justifiable. – **defensibility**, *n.*

defensive /də'fɛnsɪv/, *adj.* **1.** serving to defend; protective: *defensive armor.* **2.** made or carried on for the purpose of resisting attack. **3.** acting as if being attacked or expecting attack: *a defensive attitude.* ◇*n.* **4.** a defensive attitude or position.

defer /dəˈfɜ/, *v.t.*, *v.i.*, **-ferred**, **-ferring**. to put off (action, etc.) to a future time. [ME, from L: delay] —**deferment**, *n.* —**deferral**, *n.* —**deferred**, *adj.*

defer² /dəˈfɜ/, *v.i.*, **-ferred**, **-ferring**. to give way in judgment, opinion or will, esp. with respect (fol. by *to*). [F from L: carry from or down, report, accuse]

deference /ˈdefərəns/, *n.* **1.** an act of giving way to the opinion, will, etc., of another. **2.** respectful or courteous regard: *in deference to his wishes.* —**deferential**, *adj.*

deferred share /dəˌfɜd ˈʃɛə/, *n.* a share sold on the understanding that buyers must accept a delay in payment if necessary. See **share** (def. 2).

defiance /dəˈfaɪəns/, *n.* a daring or antagonistic resistance to authority or to any opposing force. —**defiant**, *adj.*

deficiency /dəˈfɪʃənsi/, *n., pl.* **-cies**. **1.** the condition or fact of lacking something; lack; incompleteness; insufficiency. **2.** the amount lacked; deficit. —**deficient**, *adj.*

deficit /ˈdefəsət/, *n.* the amount by which a sum of money falls short of the required amount. [L: there is wanting]

defile¹ /dəˈfaɪl/, *v.t.*, **-filed**, **-filing**. **1.** to make dirty or unclean; pollute; taint. **2.** to destroy the purity of; make unclean. [OE *befylan* make foul] —**defilement**, *n.*

defile² /dəˈfaɪl, ˈdifaɪl/, *n., v.*, **-filed**, **-filing**. ◇*n.* **1.** any narrow passage, esp. between mountains. ◇*v.i.* **2.** to march in a line, or by files; file off. [F: file off]

define /dəˈfaɪn/, *v.t.*, **-fined**, **-fining**. **1.** to give the meaning of (a word, phrase, etc.). **2.** to explain the nature of; describe. **3.** to fix the limits of. **4.** to make clear the outline or form of. [ME, from F, from L: limit, determine, explain, terminate]

definite /ˈdefənət/, *adj.* **1.** clearly stated; not vague or general; fixed; precise; exact. **2.** having fixed limits. **3.** *Colloq.* certain; sure: *He was quite definite about his intentions.* [L: limited, determined]

definite article, *n. Gram.* an article, as in English *the*, which specifies a particular example of the noun it modifies.

definition /defəˈnɪʃən/, *n.* **1.** the act of defining or making definite or clear. **2.** a formal statement of the meaning of a word, phrase, etc. **3.** clearness of shape, color or sound: *The photograph lacks definition.*

definitive /dəˈfɪnətɪv/, *adj.* **1.** deciding or settling; conclusive; final. **2.** serving to fix definitely. **3.** most accurate and complete; final.

deflate /dəˈfleɪt/, *v.t.*, **-flated**, **-flating**. **1.** to let the air or gas out of (a balloon, tyre, etc.). **2.** to reduce (prices, currency, etc.). **3.** to make (a person) feel less important: *That comment deflated him.*

deflation /dəˈfleɪʃən/, *n.* **1.** the act of deflating. **2.** a general reduction in the prices of goods and services, esp. when production costs are not similarly reduced. **3.** *Geol.* the removal of material from a beach, etc., by wind action. —**deflationary**, *adj.*

deflect /dəˈflɛkt/, *v.i.* **1.** to bend or turn aside; swerve. ◇*v.t.* **2.** to cause to turn from a true course or right line. [L] —**deflector**, *n.* —**deflective**, *adj.*

deflection /dəˈflɛkʃən/, *n.* **1.** the act or result of deflecting. **2.** *Phys.* **a.** the difference or the swing of the indicator of an instrument from the position taken as zero. **b.** the amount of such movement. **3.** *Phys.* the bending of light rays from a straight line. Also, **deflexion**.

deflower /diˈflaʊə/, *v.t.* **1.** to take the virginity of. **2.** to rob of beauty, freshness, sanctity, etc. —**defloration**, *n.*

Defoe /dəˈfoʊ/, *n.* **Daniel**, 1661?–1731, English novelist and essayist, best known for *Robinson Crusoe* (1719).

defoliant /dəˈfoʊliənt/, *n.* a chemical used to strip a tree, etc., of leaves.

defoliate /dəˈfoʊlieɪt/, *v.*, **-ated**, **-ating**, *adj.* ◇*v.t.* **1.** to strip (a tree, etc.) of leaves. ◇*v.i.* **2.** to lose leaves. ◇*adj.* **3.** having lost its leaves, as a tree; defoliated. [ML, from L *folium* leaf] —**defoliation**, *n.*

deform /dəˈfɔm/, *v.t.* **1.** to put out of shape; disfigure; spoil. [ME, from L: disfigure] —**deformation**, *n.* —**deformed**, *adj.*

deformity /dəˈfɔməti/, *n., pl.* **-ties**. **1.** the quality or condition of being disfigured or misshapen. **2.** a disfigured part of the body, etc.

defraud /dəˈfrɔd/, *v.i.* to deceive someone so as to get their money, etc.; cheat. [ME, from L]

defray /dəˈfreɪ/, *v.t.* to bear or pay (costs, etc.). [F, OF: pay costs, from *des-* DIS-¹ + *frai* cost] —**defrayal**, *n.* —**defrayment**, *n.*

Defries /dəˈfriz/, *n.* **Colin**, Australian aviator; born in England; the first to attempt to fly a powered heavier-than-air craft, on 9 December 1909.

defrost /diˈfrɒst, də-/, *v.t.* **1.** to remove ice from. **2.** to cause (food, etc.) to thaw, as by removing from a refrigerator. ◇*v.i.* **3.** to become unfrozen; thaw.

deft /dɛft/, *adj.* skilful; nimble; dexterous. [ME; var. of DAFT]

defunct /dəˈfʌŋkt/, *adj.* **1.** dead; extinct. **2.** no longer in use; not operative. [L: discharged, finished]

defuse /diˈfjuz/, *v.t.*, **-fused**, **-fusing**. **1.** to remove the fuse from (a bomb). **2.** to calm (a situation).

defy /dəˈfaɪ/, *v.t.*, **-fied**, **-fying**. **1.** to show no fear or respect for; resist boldly or openly: *Criminals defy the law*; *His son defied him by answering back.* **2.** to provide a good defence against: *a fort which defies attack.* **3.** to dare (someone) to do something thought to be impossible. [ME, from OF *de-* DE- + *fier* (from L: trust)]

Degas /ˈdeɪɡɑ/, *n.* **Hilaire Germain Edgar** /iˌleə ʒɛˌmæ edˈɡa/, 1834–1917, French painter; known esp. for his studies of ballet dancers.

de Gaulle /dəˈgɔl, ˈgoul/, n. **Charles André Joseph Marie** /ʃal ɔ̃,drei ʒou,zef maˈri/, 1890-1970, French general and politician; president of France 1959-69.

degenerate /dəˈdʒɛnəreɪt/, v., **-rated, -rating**; /dəˈdʒɛnərət/, adj. ◇v.i. **1.** to become worse in physical, mental, or moral qualities; decline; deteriorate. **2.** Biol. to change back to a simpler type. ◇adj. **3.** having become worse in physical or moral qualities; deteriorated; degraded: *a degenerate king.* **4.** Phys., Astron. (of a gas) having its atomic nuclei and electrons packed too closely together to permit production of nuclear energy, as in white dwarf stars. ◇n. **5.** someone who has gone below a normal type or standard, as in morals or character. [L: departed from its race] **—degeneracy**, n. **—degenerative**, adj.

degeneration /dədʒɛnəˈreɪʃən/, n. **1.** the process of degenerating. **2.** the condition of being degenerate. **3.** Biol. a change back to a simpler type. **4.** Biol. the process by which a tissue breaks down and may be made into or replaced by other kinds of tissue.

degrade /dəˈgreɪd/, v.t., **-graded, -grading**. **1.** to reduce from a higher to a lower rank, degree, etc. **2.** to lower in character or quality; debase. **3.** to reduce in amount, strength, intensity, etc. **4.** Geog. to wear down by erosion. **5.** Chem. to break down a compound into a simpler one. [ME, from ecclesiastical LL: reduce in rank, from L *gradus* grade] **—degradation**, n. **—degraded**, adj. **—degrading**, adj.

degree /dəˈgri/, n. **1.** a step or stage in a scale or course. **2.** Biol., Law, etc. a single stage in a line of descent. **3.** a stage in a scale of rank, station, etc.: *a man of high degree.* **4.** a stage in a scale of intensity or amount: *to the last degree.* **5.** a unit of measurement of angles shown as °, one degree equalling $\frac{1}{360}$ of the circumference of a circle. **6.** Alg. the sum (total) of the exponents (def. 3) of the variables in an algebraic expression: x^3 and $2x^2y$ are *terms of degree three.* **7.** a unit of measurement of temperature. **8. a.** Geog. a unit of measurement of latitude or longitude. **b.** Astron. the position or point of the celestial sphere fixed by its angular distance measured from the equator (equinoctial) or a given meridian. **9.** a title given by a university for successful work, or as recognition of achievement. **10.** Gram. one of the three forms (positive, comparative and superlative) of adjectives and adverbs, comparing quality, quantity or intensity, as in English *low, lower, lowest.* **11.** US. the classification of certain crimes according to their seriousness: *first degree murder.* **12. by degrees**, gradually. **13. to a degree**, to an uncertain but considerable amount. [ME, from OF, from L *gradus* step, degree]

de Groot /də ˈgrut/, n. **Francis Edward**, 1888-1969, Irish-born member of the New Guard known for his disruption of the official opening of the Sydney Harbor Bridge in 1932 as a public protest against Premier JT Lang.

de Havilland /də ˈhævələnd/, n. **Sir Geoffrey**, 1882-1965, British aircraft designer and manufacturer.

dehisce /dəˈhɪs/, v.i., **-hisced, -hiscing**. to burst open, as the seed pods of plants. [L *dehiscere*] **—dehiscence**, n. **—dehiscent**, adj.

dehydrate /ˈdihaɪdreɪt/, v., **-drated, -drating**. ◇v.t. **1.** to deprive of water. **2.** to remove water from (vegetables, etc.), for preservation. ◇v.i. **3.** to lose water or become dry. [DE- + HYDR-[1] + -ATE[1]] **—dehydration**, n.

deify /ˈdiəfaɪ, ˈdeɪə-/, v.t., **-fied, -fying**. **1.** to make a god of. **2.** to look upon or worship as a deity: *to deify money.* [ME, from OF, from LL] **—deific**, adj. **—deification**, n.

deign /deɪn/, v.i. to see as fit; condescend: *He deigned to reply.* [ME, from OF, from L: deem worthy]

deity /ˈdiəti, ˈdeɪ-/, n., pl. **-ties**. **1.** a god or goddess. **2.** divine character or nature. **3. the Deity**, God. [ME, from OF, from LL]

deject /dəˈdʒɛkt/, v.t. to lower the spirits of; dispirit; dishearten. [L: thrown down] **—dejected**, adj. **—dejection**, n.

deka- /ˈdɛkə-/, a prefix indicating ten times a given unit, as in *dekametre.* Also, **deca-**, before vowels, **dec-, dek-**. Symbol: da [Gk *deka-*, combining form of *déka* ten]

Delacroix /dələˈkrwɑ/, n. **Ferdinand Victor Eugène** /fɛədiˌnɔ̃ vik,tɔ ɜˈʒɛn/, 1798?-1863, French romantic painter.

de la Mare /də la ˈmɛə/, n. **Walter John**, 1873-1956, English poet and novelist, known esp. for his children's verse.

Delaware /ˈdɛləwɛə/, n. a state in the eastern US on the Atlantic coast. Pop. 633 000 (1986 est.); 5328 km². *Cap.* Dover.

delay /dəˈleɪ, di-/, v.t. **1.** to put off until later; defer; postpone. **2.** to stop for a time; retard; hinder: *What delayed you?* ◇v.i. **3.** to move or act slowly; linger; loiter: *Don't delay.* ◇n. **4.** an act of delaying; procrastination; loitering. **5.** an occasion on which one is delayed. [ME, from OF, from L: loosen]

delectable /dəˈlɛktəbəl/, adj. delightful; very pleasing; delicious. [ME, from L] **—delectably**, adv.

delectation /ˌdilɛkˈteɪʃən/, n. → **delight**.

delegate /ˈdɛləgət, -geɪt/, n.; /ˈdɛləgeɪt/, v., **-gated, -gating**. ◇n. **1.** someone representing a person or group, as at a conference, etc.; deputy; representative. ◇v.t. **2.** to send or appoint (a person) to act for others. **3.** to give (powers, functions, etc.) to another as an agent or deputy. [L: sent, deputed] **—delegacy**, n.

delegation /dɛləˈgeɪʃən/, n. **1.** an act of delegating. **2.** a group of people officially appointed to represent another, or others.

delete /dəˈlit/, v.t., **-leted, -leting**. to strike out or take out (anything written or printed); cancel; erase; expunge. [L: done away with, destroyed] **—deletion**, n.

deleterious /dɛləˈtɪəriəs/, adj. harmful to health; hurtful; injurious. [NL, from Gk]

Delhi /'deli/, *n.* a city in northern India, on the Jumna River, comprising **Old Delhi**, the former capital of the old Mogul Empire and administrative centre of British India, 1912-29, and **New Delhi**, the capital of the Republic of India. Pop. 5 729 283 (1981).

deli /'deli/, *n. Colloq.* →**delicatessen**.

Delian League /'diliən lig/, *n.* an alliance of ancient Greek states, established in 478 BC to carry on the war against Persia.

deliberate /də'libərət/, *adj.*; /də'libəreɪt/, *v.*, **-rated, -rating.** ◇*adj.* **1.** carefully considered; purposeful; intentional. ◇*v.t.* **2.** to consider carefully: *to deliberate a question.* ◇*v.i.* **3.** to think carefully; reflect. **4.** to meet for formal discussion. [L: weighed well] – **deliberator,** *n.* – **deliberation,** *n.* – **deliberative,** *adj.*

Delibes /də'lib/, *n.* **Clément Philibert Léo** /kleɪ,mõ fili,beə leɪ'ou/, 1836-91, French composer, best known for his ballet music.

delicacy /'deləkəsi/, *n., pl.* **-cies. 1.** the quality of being delicate. **2.** something tasty to eat that is rare or costly.

delicate /'deləkət/, *adj.* **1.** finely-made: *delicate lace.* **2.** soft or faint, as color: *a delicate shade of pink.* **3.** so fine or slight that it can hardly be seen; subtle: *a delicate distinction.* **4.** easily damaged; fragile. **5.** needing great care, caution, or tact: *a delicate situation.* **6.** sensitive; fine: *a delicate instrument.* **7.** very sensitive in perception or feeling; fastidious. [ME, from L: delightful, luxurious, soft]

delicatessen /ˌdeləkə'tesən/, *n.* a shop selling cooked or prepared goods, such as salamis. [G: delicacies, from F, from It: delicate]

delicious /də'lɪʃəs/, *adj.* **1.** very pleasing to the taste or smell. **2.** very enjoyable; delightful. ◇*n.* **3.** (*cap.*) certain types of eating apples. [ME, from OF, from L: delight]

delight /də'laɪt/, *n.* **1.** great pleasure or enjoyment; joy; rapture. **2.** something that gives great pleasure. ◇*v.t., v.i.* **3.** to give or have great pleasure: *Your gift delights me; I delight in your song.* [L: allure] – **delighted,** *adj.* – **delightful,** *adj.*

Delilah /də'laɪlə/, *n. Bible.* Samson's mistress, who betrayed him to the Philistines. [See Judges 16]

delimit /di'lɪmət/, *v.t.* to fix or mark the limits of; demarcate. [F, from L] – **delimitation,** *n.* – **delimitative,** *adj.*

delineate /də'lɪnieɪt/, *v.t.,* **-ated, -ating. 1.** to draw the outline or shape of. **2.** to show in words; describe. [L: sketched out] – **delineable,** *adj.* – **delineation,** *n.*

delinquent /də'lɪŋkwənt/, *adj.* **1.** failing in a duty; guilty of a misdeed or offence. **2.** of or relating to delinquents. ◇*n.* **3.** someone, esp. a young person, who is delinquent and uncontrollable: *a juvenile delinquent.* [L] – **delinquency,** *n.*

deliquesce /delɪ'kwes/, *v.i.,* **-quesced, -quescing. 1.** to melt away. **2.** to become liquid by taking up water from the air, as certain salts. [L: melt away] – **deliquescent,** *adj.* – **deliquescence,** *n.*

delirious /də'lɪriəs/, *adj.* **1.** suffering from delirium. **2.** of or like delirium. **3.** wildly excited.

delirium /də'lɪriəm/, *n., pl.* **-liriums, -liria** /-'lɪriə/. **1.** a more or less temporary disorder of the mind, as in fevers, mental disturbances or intoxication, marked by restlessness, excitement, hallucinations, etc. **2.** a wildly excited or emotional state. [L: be deranged, lit., go out of the furrow]

delirium tremens /dɪ,lɪriəm 'treməns/, *n. Med.* violent delirium (def. 1) resulting from chronic alcoholism and marked by trembling, etc. [NL: trembling delirium]

Delius /'diliəs/, *n.* **Frederick**, 1862-1934, English composer.

deliver /də'lɪvə/, *v.t.* **1.** to give into another's keeping. **2.** to carry and hand over (letters, goods, etc.) **3.** to cause to move in a certain direction: *The bowler delivered a fast ball.* **4.** to strike: *to deliver a blow.* **5.** to produce: *Our mines are still delivering 192 million tonnes of coal each year.* **6.** to pronounce: *to deliver a verdict.* **7.** to assist at the birth of: *The doctor delivered the baby yesterday.* **8.** (usu. in passive) to assist (a female) in giving birth (fol. by *of*): *She was delivered of a healthy baby girl.* **9.** to set free or save: *Deliver us from evil.* ◇*v.i.* **10.** to give birth. **11.** to deliver goods, etc.; make deliveries. [ME, from F, from LL: set free] – **deliverance,** *n.*

delivery /də'lɪvəri/, *n., pl.* **-eries. 1.** the delivering of letters, goods, etc. **2.** a giving up or handing over; surrender. **3.** a manner of speaking: *He has a clear delivery.* **4.** an act or manner of delivering, as of a ball by the bowler in cricket. **5.** the act of being set free. **6.** the act of giving birth to a child; parturition. **7.** something delivered. ◇*adj.* **8.** of or relating to someone or something that makes deliveries: *delivery truck; delivery man.*

dell /del/, *n.* a small valley, esp. a wooded one. [OE *dell*]

della Robbia /,delə 'robjə/, *n.* → **Robbia family.**

Delltones /'deltounz/, *n.pl.* **the,** Australian rock'n'roll vocal group, formed in 1959.

Delos /'dilos/, *n.* a tiny Greek island in the Cyclades, in the south-western Aegean; the site of an oracle of Apollo. Pop. 16 (1971); 3.4 km².

Delphi /'delfi, -faɪ/, *n.* an ancient city in central Greece, on the slopes of Mt Parnassus; site of the most famous oracle of Apollo.

Delphic oracle /ˌdelfɪk 'brəkəl/, *n. Gk Legend.* the oracle of the temple of Apollo at Delphi which often gave ambiguous answers.

delphinium /del'fɪniəm/, *n.* any of many garden plants having spikes of irregular, blue flowers. [NL, from Gk: dolphin; so called from the shape of the nectar-secreting organ]

delta /'deltə/, *n.* **1.** the fourth letter (Δ, φ, = English *D*, *d*) of the Greek alphabet. **2.** anything triangular, like the Greek capital Δ. **3.** a nearly flat plain of soil between out-spreading

delta branches of a river at its mouth, often triangular: *the Nile delta.* —**deltaic**, *adj.*

delta ray, *n. Phys.* an electron knocked out of an atom by a fast-moving ionised particle.

deltoid /'dɛltɔɪd/, *n.* **1.** *Anat.* a large triangular muscle covering the shoulder joint and used to lift the arm up sideways. ◇*adj.* **2.** triangular. [Gk: delta-shaped]

delude /də'lud, -'ljud/, *v.t.,* **-luded, -luding.** to mislead the mind or judgment of; deceive. [L: play false]

deluge /'dɛljudʒ/, *n., v.,* **-uged, -uging.** ◇*n.* **1.** a great overflowing of water; inundation; flood; downpour. **2.** anything that pours over like a flood: *a deluge of words.* **3. the Deluge**, *Bible.* the great flood in the days of Noah. ◇*v.t.* **4.** to flood; inundate. **5.** to overrun; overwhelm. [ME, from OF, from L]

delusion /də'luʒən, -'ljuʒən/, *n.* **1.** a false belief or opinion. **2.** *Psychiatry.* a false belief which cannot be changed by reasoning or by an explanation of the facts. When continuing, it indicates psychosis. See **illusion** (def. 4), **hallucination.** —**delusive, delusory**, *adj.*

deluxe /də'lʌks/, *adj.* of very fine quality; sumptuous. Also, **de luxe.** [F: of luxury]

delve /dɛlv/, *v.i.,* **delved, delving.** to search thoroughly for information, etc. [OE *delfan*]

demagogue /'dɛməgɒg/, *n.* **1.** a leader who uses the emotions of the population for his or her own interests; an unprincipled popular orator. **2.** (historically) a leader of the people. [Gk *dēmos* people + *agōgós* leader] —**demagogic**, *adj.* —**demagoguery**, *n.* —**demagogy**, *n.* —**demagoguism**, *n.*

de Maistre /də 'mɛstrə/, *n.* **Roy** (*Leroy Leveson Laurent Joseph de Maistre*), 1894–1968, Australian artist; pioneer of post-impressionism and cubism in Australia.

demand /də'mænd, -'mand/, *v.t.* **1.** to ask for with force; claim as a right: *to demand award wages.* **2.** to call for or need: *a job which demands patience.* **3.** *Law.* to lay formal legal claim to. ◇*v.i.* **4.** to make a demand; inquire or ask. ◇*n.* **5.** the act of demanding. **6.** that which is demanded. **7.** an inquiry or question. **8.** a requisition; legal claim. **9.** the condition of being demanded for purchase or use: *an article in great demand.* **10.** *Econ.* **a.** the desire to purchase and possess, together with the power of purchasing. **b.** the quantity of any goods which buyers will take at a particular price. See **supply.** **11. on demand**, *Comm.* liable to be payed upon presentation and demand. [F, from ML: demand, from L: give in charge, entrust]

demand-pull inflation, *n. Econ.* a situation where prices are forced higher because the demand for a product is much greater than the producer's ability to supply it. See **cost-push inflation.**

demarcate /'dɛməkeɪt/, *v.t.,* **-cated, -cating.** **1.** to mark off boundaries of. **2.** to separate clearly. [backformation from DEMARCATION]

demarcation /dimə'keɪʃən/, *n.* **1.** the marking off of the boundaries of something. **2.** a division between things, esp. between types of work carried out by members of different trade unions. **3.** separation by clear boundaries. [Sp: mark out the bounds of]

demean /də'min/, *v.t.* to lower in dignity or standing; debase: *That behavior demeans you.* [DE- + MEAN², modelled on DEBASE]

demeanor or **demeanour** /də'minə/, *n.* behavior; bearing; conduct. [ME, from OF, from DE- + *mener* lead]

demented /də'mɛntəd/, *adj.* of unbalanced mind; mad; suffering from dementia. —**dementedly**, *adv.* —**dementedness**, *n.*

dementia /də'mɛnʃiə, -ʃə/, *n. Psychiatry.* a disorder of the mind marked by loss of mental powers, commonly a result of continued mental or other diseases. [L: madness]

demerit /di'mɛrət/, *n.* **1.** a failing (in behavior); fault. **2.** a mark against a person for bad behavior or a deficiency. [ML: fault, from L: deserve]

demesne /də'meɪn/, *n.* **1.** possession of land in one's own right. **2.** land attached to a manor house, kept for the owner's use. **3.** a district; region. [ME, from AF. See DOMAIN]

Demeter /də'mitə/, *n. Gk Myth.* the goddess of the fruitful earth, protector of social order and marriage; Roman counterpart, Ceres. [L, from Gk]

demi-, a prefix meaning **1.** half, as in *demimonde.* **2.** less than usual, as in *demigod.* [F, from L *dīmidius* half]

demigod /'dɛmigɒd/, *n.* **1.** someone partly divine and partly human; a minor deity. **2.** a person considered to be a god.

demilitarised zone or **demilitarized zone** /di'mɪlətəraɪzd ˌzoʊn/, *n. Mil.* an area in which the gathering of, or control by, military forces is not allowed.

demimonde /ˌdɛmi'mɒnd/, *n.* the world of people on the fringes of respectability. [F: half-world]

demise /də'maɪz/, *n.* **1.** death. **2.** *Law.* a death resulting in the transfer of property. [OF: sent or put away]

demister /di'mɪstə/, *n.* an apparatus that blows air, usu. heated, onto the windscreen of a car to clear it of mist.

demo /'dɛmoʊ/, *n. Colloq.* →**demonstration.**

demo-, a word part meaning 'people', 'common people'. [Gk, combining form of *dēmos* district, people]

demobilise or **demobilize** /di'moʊbəlaɪz/, *v.t, v.i.,* **-lised, -lising.** to disband (an army, etc.) or become disbanded. —**demobilisation**, *n.*

democracy /də'mɒkrəsi/, *n., pl.* **-cies.** **1.** government by the people, or by their elected representatives. **2.** a state having such a government. **3.** the principle that all people should have equal political rights. [F, from

democracy   273   **-dendron**

Gk *dēmokratía* popular government, from *dēmo-* DEMO- + *-kratía* rule, authority] —**democratic**, *adj.*

democrat /'deməkræt/, *n.* **1.** someone who supports or practises Democracy. **2.** (*cap.*) *US.* a member of the Democratic Party.

Democratic Party /demə'krætɪk ˌpɑːti/, *n. US.* one of the two major national political parties in the US; orig. the Democratic-Republican party in 1832, renamed in 1840. See **Republican Party**.

democratise *or* **democratize** /dəˈmɒkrətaɪz/, *v.t., v.i.,* **-tised, -tising.** to make or become democratic. —**democratisation**, *n.*

demography /dɪˈmɒgrəfi/, *n.* the science of population statistics, as of births, deaths, diseases, marriages, etc. —**demographer**, *n.* —**demographic**, *adj.* —**demographics**, *n.*

demolish /dəˈmɒlɪʃ/, *v.t.* **1.** to pull down (a building, etc.). **2.** to put an end to; destroy; ruin totally. [F, from L: throw down, destroy] —**demolishment, demolition**, *n.*

demon /'diːmən/, *n.* **1.** an evil spirit; devil. **2.** a person of great energy, enthusiasm, etc.: *He's a demon for work.* [ME, from LL: evil spirit, L: spirit, from Gk: divine power, fate, god] —**demonic**, *adj.* —**demonism**, *n.*

demon-, a word part meaning 'demon'. Also, **demono-** before consonants. [Gk, combining form of *daímōn*]

demonetise *or* **demonetize** /diːˈmʌnətaɪz/, *v.t.,* **-tised, -tising. 1.** to take away the value of (money); devalue. **2.** to withdraw from use as money. —**demonetisation**, *n.*

demoniac /dəˈmoʊniæk/, *adj.* Also, **demoniacal** /deməˈnaɪəkəl/. **1.** of, relating to, or like a demon. **2.** (seemingly) possessed by a demon; raging; frantic. ◇*n.* **3.** a demoniac person. [ME, from LL, from Gk] —**demoniacally**, *adv.*

demonology /diːməˈnɒlədʒi/, *n.* the study of demons or of beliefs about demons. —**demonologist**, *n.*

demonstrate /'demənstreɪt/, *v.,* **-strated, -strating.** ◇*v.t.* **1.** to show by arguments or reasoning; prove. **2.** to describe and explain with examples or by experiment. **3.** to show (feelings). ◇*v.i.* **4.** to make, give, or take part in, a demonstration. [L: showed, proved] —**demonstrable**, *adj.*

demonstration /demənˈstreɪʃən/, *n.* **1.** the act of demonstrating. **2.** a proof, description or explanation. **3.** the act of showing and explaining a product, in order to advertise it. **4.** a public show of opinion, as a march or mass meeting.

demonstrative /dəˈmɒnstrətɪv/, *adj.* **1.** characterised by or given to open showing of feelings, etc. **2.** serving to demonstrate; explanatory or illustrative. **3.** serving to prove the truth of anything. **4.** *Gram.* (of a word) pointing out the thing referred to. ◇*n.* **5.** *Gram.* a demonstrative word, as *this* or *these*.

demonstrator /'demənstreɪtə/, *n.* **1.** a person or thing that demonstrates. **2.** someone who explains, teaches, or advertises by practical demonstrations. **3.** a new car used only for demonstration.

demoralise *or* **demoralize** /dɪˈmɒrəlaɪz/, *v.t.,* **-lised, -lising. 1.** to lower the morals or morale of (a person, group, etc.). **2.** to reduce (an army, etc.) to a weak or disordered state. [F] —**demoralisation**, *n.*

Demosthenes /dəˈmɒsθəniːz/, *n.* 384?—322 BC, Athenian politician and orator, famous for his speeches against Philip II of Macedonia.

demote /dəˈmoʊt, di-/, *v.t.,* **-moted, -moting.** to reduce to a lower class (opposed to *promote*). [DE- + *mote*, modelled on PROMOTE] —**demotion**, *n.*

demotic /dəˈmɒtɪk/, *adj.* of or relating to the people; popular (def. 2). [Gk: popular, plebeian]

demur /dəˈmɜː/, *v.,* **-murred, -murring,** *n.* ◇*v.i.* **1.** to object; take exception. ◇*n.* **2.** an objection raised. [ME, from OF, from L: linger] —**demurral**, *n.*

demure /dəˈmjʊə, -ˈmjɔː/, *adj.,* **-murer, -murest. 1.** unnaturally modest, coy, or prim. **2.** quiet; serious; sedate; reserved. [ME, from OF: grave, ripe, from L: mature]

demurrage /dɪˈmʌrɪdʒ/, *n. Comm.* (a charge payable for) a delay beyond the time agreed upon in the loading or unloading of a vessel or railway truck.

demystify /diːˈmɪstəfaɪ/, *v.t.,* **-fied, -fying.** to remove the air of mystery from. —**demystification**, *n.*

den /den/, *n.* **1.** a cave or hole used as shelter by a wild animal. **2.** a hiding place or shelter, esp. of thieves. **3.** a squalid or wretched place: *den of misery.* **4.** a quiet, cosy room for personal use. [OE *denn*]

denarius /dəˈnɛəriəs/, *n., pl.* **-narii** /-ˈnɛəriiː/. an ancient Roman silver coin. [L: containing ten (smaller coins). See DENARY]

denary /'diːnəri/, *adj.* containing or increasing by ten; tenfold; or decimal. [L: containing ten, from *dēnī* ten at a time]

denature /diːˈneɪtʃə/, *v.t.,* **-tured, -turing. 1.** to change the nature of. **2.** to make (alcohol, etc.) unfit for drinking. **3.** *Chem.* to change (a protein) chemically or physically, causing loss of its biological activity. —**denaturant**, *n.* —**denaturation**, *n.*

dendrite /'dendraɪt/, *n.* **1.** *Geol.* a branching figure or mark, like a tree in form, occurring on or in certain stones or minerals, etc. **2.** *Anat., Med.* the branching part of a neurone which picks up the stimulus. [Gk: of a tree]

dendro-, a word part meaning 'tree', as in *dendrology.* Also, **dendr-** before vowels. [Gk, combining form of *déndron*]

dendrobium /denˈdroʊbiəm/, *n.* an orchid type found in Asia and Australia; rock lily.

dendrology /denˈdrɒlədʒi/, *n.* that part of botany that deals with trees and shrubs.

-dendron, a word part meaning 'tree', as in *rhododendron.* [representing Gk *déndron* tree]

dengue /'dengi/, *n. Med.* an infectious, tropical disease, marked by pain in the joints and muscles. [Sp, from African (Swahili) *dinga* cramp]

Deng Xiaoping /dʌŋ ʃaʊˈpɪŋ/, *n.* born 1904, Chinese politician; appointed a vice-chairman of the Communist Party in 1977.

denial /dəˈnaɪəl/, *n.* **1.** an act of denying. **2.** → **self-denial**.

denigrate /'denəgreɪt/, *v.t.*, **-grated, -grating.** to devalue the importance or worth of; defame. [L: blackened] **— denigration,** *n.* **— denigrator,** *n.*

Deniliquin /dəˈnɪləkwən/, *n.* a town in southern NSW on the Edward River; important sheep grazing area and the centre of the largest area under irrigation in Australia. Pop. 7566 (1986).

denim /'denəm/, *n.* **1.** a heavy cotton material used for overalls, trousers, etc. **2.** (*pl.*) *Colloq.* denim trousers or overalls. [F, short for *serge de Nîmes* serge of Nîmes]

denizen /'denəzən/, *n.* **1.** a person who lives in a particular place. **2.** anything put into a new place, condition, etc. [ME, from AF, from L: from within]

Denmark /'denmak/, *n.* a kingdom in northern Europe, consisting of the peninsula of Jutland and the nearby islands. Pop. 5 124 794 (1987 est.); 43 080 km². *Language:* Danish. *Currency:* krone. *Cap.:* Copenhagen. Danish, **Danmark**.

denominate /dəˈnɒmɪneɪt/, *v.t.*, **-nated, -nating.** to give a name to. [L]

denomination /dənɒməˈneɪʃən/, *n.* **1.** a name, esp. one for a class of things. **2.** an authorised religious group, esp. one within the Christian church. **3.** the act of denominating. **4.** the class of units of quantity, weight, value, etc.: *money of small denominations.*

denominational /dənɒməˈneɪʃənəl/, *adj.* of or relating to a particular religious body.

denominator /dəˈnɒməneɪtə/, *n. Maths.* (of a fraction) the number under the line, which shows the number of equal parts into which the unit is divided; a divisor.

denotation /dinoʊˈteɪʃən/, *n.* **1.** the exact meaning of a word, opposed to *connotation.* **2.** an act or fact of denoting; indication. **3.** something that denotes; a mark; symbol. **4.** *Logic.* the class of particulars to which a word can be applied. **— denotative,** *adj.*

denote /dəˈnoʊt/, *v.t.*, **-noted, -noting. 1.** to be a mark or sign of; indicate: *A quick pulse often denotes fever.* **2.** to be a name for. **3.** to represent by a symbol: *to denote dollars by '$'.* [F, from L: mark out] **— denotable,** *adj.*

denouement /deɪˈnumɒ̃/, *n.* the end of the story, where everything is explained. [F DE- + *nouer*, from L: knot, tie]

denounce /dəˈnaʊns/, *v.t.*, **-nounced, -nouncing. 1.** to speak or write against; censure. **2.** to give formal notice of the end of (a treaty, etc.). [ME, from L: threaten] **— denouncement,** *n.*

dense /dens/, *adj.*, **denser, densest. 1.** having parts that are closely packed together; compact: *a dense forest; a dense population.* **2.** stupid; obtuse; thickheaded. **3.** *Photog.* (of a developed negative (def. 12)) showing little light; relatively opaque. [L: thick, thickly set]

density /'densəti/, *n., pl.* **-ties. 1.** the state or quality of being dense (def. 1); compactness; a closely set or crowded condition. **2.** *Phys.* **a.** the mass per unit of volume. **b.** the amount per unit volume or area of any physical quantity: *energy density; current density.* **3.** *Photog.* the amount of light that any medium, esp. a photographic plate or negative (def. 12), lets through, usu. expressed logarithmically.

dent /dent/, *n.* **1.** a small hollow in a surface, as from a blow. ◊*v.t.* **2.** to make a dent in or on; indent. ◊*v.i.* **3.** to become indented. [ME]

dental /'dentl/, *adj.* **1.** of or relating to teeth or dentistry. **2.** *Phonetics.* with tongue tip touching or near upper front teeth, as θ in *thin.* ◊*n.* **3.** *Linguistics.* a dental sound. [L *dens* tooth]

dental technician, *n.* a person whose job is to make false teeth, caps for teeth, etc.

dentate /'denteɪt/, *adj.* having a toothed margin, or toothlike projections or processes. [L] **— dentation,** *n.*

denti-, a word part meaning 'tooth', as in *dentifrice.* Also, before vowels, **dent-.** [L, combining form of *dens*]

dentine /'dentin/, *n. Anat.* the hard calcareous tissue beneath the enamel, forming the greatest part of a tooth. [DENT(I)- + -INE²] **— dentinal,** *adj.*

dentist /'dentəst/, *n.* a person whose profession is dentistry. [F]

dentistry /'dentəstri/, *n.* the profession dealing with the prevention and treatment of diseases of the teeth and mouth.

dentition /denˈtɪʃən/, *n.* **1.** the growing of teeth; teething. **2.** the type, number, and arrangement of the teeth of any animal, including man. [L: teething]

D'Entrecasteaux /'dɒntrəkæs,toʊ/, *n.* **Joseph-Antoine Raymond de Bruni** /ʒoʊsɛfɒ̃,twan reɪ,mɒ̃ də bruˈni/, 1739–93, French-born navigator and explorer of the Australian Pacific waters.

denture /'dentʃə/, *n.* an artificial replacement for one or more teeth. [F]

denude /dəˈnjud/, *v.t.*, **-nuded, -nuding.** to make naked or bare; strip: *Trees were denuded of leaves.* [L: lay bare] **— denudation,** *n.*

denunciate /dəˈnʌnsieɪt/, *v.t.*, **-ated, -ating.** to accuse; denounce; condemn openly. [L] **— denunciator,** *n.* **— denunciatory,** *adj.*

denunciation /dənʌnsiˈeɪʃən/, *n.* **1.** a denouncing as evil; open and harsh condemnation. **2.** an announcement of coming evil; threat; warning.

deny /dəˈnaɪ/, *v.t.*, **-nied, -nying. 1.** to declare not to be true: *I deny the charge.* **2.** to refuse to believe (a teaching, etc.); regard as false

deny | 275 | **deprecate**

or mistaken. **3.** to refuse to grant (a claim, request, etc.): *He denied me my rights.* **4.** to refuse to recognise; disown; repudiate. **5. deny oneself,** to exercise self-denial. [ME, from F, from L] **—deniable,** *adj.*

deodorant /di'oudərənt/, *n.* a substance which destroys or prevents unpleasant smells.

deodorise or **deodorize** /di'oudəraız/, *v.t.*, **-rised, -rising.** to remove an unpleasant smell from.

deoxyribonucleic acid /di,ɒksi,raɪbounju,kliːk 'æsɪd/, *n.* → DNA.

depart /də'paːt/, *v.i.* **1.** to go away, as from a place; take one's leave. **2.** to turn aside or away; diverge (fol. by *from*). ◇*v.t.* **3.** *Rare.* to go away from or leave: *to depart this life.* [ME, from OF *de-* DE- + *partir* leave, divide (from L)]

departed /də'paːtəd/, *adj.* **1.** dead; deceased. **2.** gone; past.

department /də'paːtmənt/, *n.* **1.** a division or separate part of a complex whole or organised system, esp. in government or business. **2.** a section of a school, college, or university dealing with a particular field of knowledge: *department of English.* **3.** a section of a retail store selling a particular kind of goods. **—departmental,** *adj.*

department store, *n.* large retail shop selling a range of goods in different departments.

departure /də'paːtʃə/, *n.* **1.** a going away; a setting out or starting. **2.** a divergence or deviation.

depend /də'pend/, *v.i.* **1.** to rely: *You may depend on his report.* **2.** to rely for support, help, etc.: *Children depend on their parents.* **3.** to be decided or influenced (by). [ME, from OF, from L: hang upon] **—dependable,** *adj.*

dependant /də'pendənt/, *n.* **1.** someone who depends on or looks to another for support, favor, etc. **2.** a person to whom one gives financial support. **3.** a servant; retainer. Also, **dependent.**

dependence /də'pendəns/, *n.* **1.** the state of being dependent for aid, support, etc. **2.** trust; reliance; confidence. **3.** subjection; subordination: *dependence of church upon state.*

dependency /də'pendənsi/, *n., pl.* **-cies. 1.** the state of being dependent; dependence. **2.** a small country ruled by another.

dependent /də'pendənt/, *adj.* **1.** depending on something else for help, support, etc. **2.** conditioned (by); contingent (on): *Whether we play is dependent on the weather.* **3.** subject; subordinate. **4.** *Maths.* (of a quantity or variable) depending upon another for value.

dependent clause, *n.* → **subordinate clause.**

depersonalise or **depersonalize** /di-'pɜːsənəlaɪz/, *v.t.*, **-lised, -lising.** to make impersonal. **—depersonalisation,** *n.*

depict /də'pɪkt/, *v.t.* **1.** to represent by or as by a picture; portray. **2.** to represent in words; describe. [L: portrayed] **—depicter,** *n.* **—depiction,** *n.* **—depictive,** *adj.*

depilatory /də'pɪlətri/, *n., pl.* **-ries,** *adj.* (a substance for) removing hair.

deplete /də'pliːt/, *v.t.*, **-pleted, -pleting.** to reduce; lessen; decrease. [L: emptied out] **—depletion,** *n.* **—depletive, deplitory** (?)

deplorable /də'plɔːrəbəl/, *adj.* **1.** causing grief or regret; lamentable. **2.** worthy of blame; wretched.

deplore /də'plɔː/, *v.t.*, **-plored, -ploring.** to feel or express deep grief for or about; regret deeply: *We deplore this accident.* [L: bewail] **—deploringly,** *adv.*

deploy /də'plɔɪ/, *v.t.* **1.** to spread out (troops or military units) to form a wide front. **2.** make careful or effective use of (mineral resources, arguments, etc.). [F, from L: fold] **—deployment,** *n.* **—deployable,** *adj.*

deponent /də'pounənt/, *n. Law.* someone who testifies under oath, esp. in writing. [L: laying aside, depositing, ML: testifying]

deport /də'pɔːt/, *v.t.* **1.** to take forcibly, as to prison or a place of exile. **2.** to expel (an undesirable alien) from a country; banish. **3.** to bear, conduct, or behave (oneself) in a particular manner. [F, from L: carry away, transport, banish] **—deportation,** *n.* **—deportee,** *n.*

deportment /də'pɔːtmənt/, *n.* **1.** the manner of bearing; carriage: *stately deportment.* **2.** behavior; demeanor; conduct.

depose /də'pouz/, *v.*, **-posed, -posing.** ◇*v.t.* **1.** to remove from high office or position. **2.** to declare or testify, esp. under oath, usu. in writing. ◇*v.i.* **3.** to bear witness; give testimony under oath, esp. in writing. [ME, from OF: put down] **—deposable,** *adj.* **—deposer,** *n.*

deposit /də'pɒzət/, *v.t.* **1.** to put or lay down; place; put. **2.** to place for safekeeping or in trust: *He deposited his money in a bank.* ◇*n.* **3.** a coating of metal deposited by electric current. **4.** something entrusted to another for safekeeping. **5.** money placed in a bank. **6.** anything given as security or in part payment. [L: put away or down, deposited, ML testified] **—depositor,** *n.*

deposition /depə'zɪʃən, dipə-/, *n.* **1.** *Law.* **a.** the giving of testimony under oath. **b.** a statement under oath, taken down in writing, which may be used in a court in place of the witness. **2.** the removal from office or position; a deposing. **3.** the act of depositing.

depository /də'pɒzətri, -ətəri/, *n., pl.* **-ries. 1.** a place where anything is deposited or stored for safekeeping; storehouse. **2.** trustee.

depot /'depou/, *n.* **1.** a depository; storehouse. **2.** a garage where buses or trams are kept. [F, from L: a deposit]

depraved /də'preɪvd/, *adj.* morally bad; corrupt. [ME, from L: pervert] **—depravation,** *n.*

depravity /də'prævəti/, *n., pl.* **-ties. 1.** the state of being depraved; wickedness. **2.** a depraved act or practice.

deprecate /'deprəkeɪt/, *v.t.*, **-cated, -cating.** to state earnest disapproval of; urge

deprecate

reasons against; protest against (a scheme, purpose, etc.). [L: having prayed against] —**deprecatory**, adj. —**deprecation**, n.

depreciate /dəˈpriʃieɪt, dəˈprisieɪt/, v., **-ated, -ating.** ◇v.t. **1.** to reduce the buying power of (money). **2.** to lessen the value of; belittle. ◇v.i. **3.** to go down in value. [LL: undervalued] —**depreciatingly**, adv. —**depreciator**, n. —**depreciatory**, n.

depreciation /dəpriʃiˈeɪʃən, -prisi-/, n. **1.** a decrease in the value of goods, property, etc., due to wear and tear, decay, decline in price, etc. **2.** a decrease in the buying power or exchange value of money. **3.** a belittling; disparagement.

depredation /deprəˈdeɪʃən/, n. **1.** a robbery. **2.** a destruction.

depress /dəˈpres/, v.t. **1.** to lower in spirits; deject; dispirit. **2.** to press down; lower. **3.** to lower in force, energy, etc.; weaken; make dull. **4.** to lower in amount or value: *to depress the market.* [ME, from OF, from L: pressed down] —**depressed**, adj. —**depressor**, n.

depressant /dəˈpresənt/, n., adj. (a substance) having the quality of lowering bodily activities; sedative.

depression /dəˈpreʃən/, n. **1.** an act of depressing. **2.** the state of being depressed. **3.** a sunken place; a hollow. **4.** *Psychol.* a state of despondency marked by feelings of inadequacy, reduced activity, sadness, etc. **5.** a time of reduced economic activity and high unemployment. **6.** (*cap.*) **the Depression.** Also, **the Great Depression,** the worldwide economic slump of the 1930s, resulting in mass unemployment. **7.** *Weather.* an area of low air pressure. [ME, from L] —**depressive**, adj.

deprive /dəˈpraɪv/, v.t., **-prived, -priving. 1.** to take away something possessed or enjoyed; dispossess; strip; bereave: *to deprive a man of his money.* **2.** to keep (a person, etc.) from possessing or enjoying something withheld: *to deprive a man of freedom.* [ME, from OF, from L: deprive] —**deprivation**, n.

deprived /dəˈpraɪvd/, adj. without certain advantages of money or social class; lacking educational opportunities, affection, etc.

dept, *Abbrev.* department.

depth /depθ/, n. **1.** a measure or distance downwards, inwards, or backwards. **2.** the state or quality of being deep. **3.** deepness, as of water. **4.** complexity, as of a subject. **5.** seriousness; gravity. **6.** intensity, as of color, feelings, etc. **7.** (*usu. pl.*) the deepest part, place or condition, as of the sea. **8. beyond** or **out of one's depth, a.** in water so deep one cannot touch the bottom. **b.** beyond one's ability or understanding. **9. in depth,** intensively; thoroughly. [ME, from *dep-* (OE *dēop* DEEP) + -TH[1]]

depth charge, n. a bomb dropped or thrown into the sea from a ship or plane, which explodes on reaching a certain depth, used to destroy submarines, etc.

deputation /depjuˈteɪʃən/, n. **1.** an appointment to represent or act for or on behalf of another or others. **2.** → delegation.

depute /dəˈpjut/, v.t., **-puted, -puting. 1.** to appoint as one's substitute or agent. **2.** to hand over (a charge, etc.) to another. [ME, from OF, from LL: destine, allot, L: count as, reckon]

deputise or **deputize** /ˈdepjətaɪz/, v., **-tised, -tising.** ◇v.t. **1.** to appoint as deputy. ◇v.i. **2.** to act as deputy.

deputy /ˈdepjəti/, n., *pl.* **-ties,** adj. ◇n. **1.** a person appointed or given permission to act for another. **2.** a member of a lower house in certain parliaments. ◇adj. **3.** acting as deputy for another. [ME, from OF: deputed] —**deputyship**, n.

der., *Abbrev.* **1.** derivation. **2.** derivative. **3.** derived.

derail /dɪˈreɪl/, v.t. **1.** to cause a (train, etc.) to run off the rails. ◇v.i. **2.** (of a train, etc.) to run off rails or track. —**derailment**, n.

derange /dəˈreɪndʒ/, v.t., **-ranged, -ranging. 1.** to throw into disorder. **2.** to disturb the condition, action, or functions of. **3.** to make insane. [F, from OF] —**deranged**, adj. —**derangement**, n.

derby /ˈdabi, ˈdɜbi/, n., pl. **-bies.** an important race, esp. of horses. [named after a horserace at Epsom Downs, England, founded 1780 by the Earl of *Derby*]

Derby /ˈdabi/, n. **Edward George Geoffrey Smith Stanley, 14th Earl of,** 1799–1869, British conservative politician; prime minister 1852, 1858–59, 1866–68.

Derbyshire /ˈdabiʃɪə, -ʃə/, n. a county in central England. Pop. 916 800 (1986 est.); 2606 km². *Administrative Centre:* Matlock. Also, **Derby.**

derelict /ˈderəlɪkt/, adj. **1.** left or deserted, esp. of a ship abandoned at sea. **2.** neglected; dilapidated. ◇n. **3.** property, esp. a ship, left by the owner. **4.** a destitute person. [L: forsaken utterly]

dereliction /derəˈlɪkʃən/, n. **1.** culpable neglect, as of duty; delinquency; fault. **2.** the act of abandoning.

deride /dəˈraɪd/, v.t., **-rided, -riding.** to laugh at with disrespect; scoff; jeer; mock. [L: laugh] —**derider**, n.

derision /dəˈrɪʒən/, n. the act of making fun of someone; ridicule; mockery. [L] —**derisible**, adj. —**derisive**, adj.

derivation /derəˈveɪʃən/, n. **1.** the act of deriving or the state of being derived. **2.** origination or origin. **3.** that which is derived; derivative. **4.** *Gram.* **a.** the process of composing new words by the addition of prefixes or suffixes to already existing root words as *atomic* from *atom, hardness* from *hard.* **b.** the history (of a word) from its earliest known form. —**derivational**, adj. —**derivate**, n.

derivative /dəˈrɪvətɪv/, adj. **1.** coming from something else; derived. **2.** not original or first; secondary. ◇n. **3.** something derived. **4.** *Chem.* a substance or compound

derivative   277   **desert oak**

obtained from, or structurally related to, another compound. **5.** *Maths.* the instantaneous rate of change of a function in relation to a variable.

derive /dəˈraɪv/, *v.*, **-rived, -riving.** ◇*v.t.* **1.** to receive, obtain, take, or trace (something) from a source or origin: *He derives his good looks from his father.* **2.** to obtain by reasoning; deduce. **3.** *Chem.* to make (a compound) from another one by chemical substitution, etc. ◇*v.i.* **4.** to come or originate (fol. by *from*): *His good looks derive from his father.* [F, from L: lead off]

-derm, a word part meaning 'skin', as in *endoderm*. [Gk -*dermos*, etc., having skin, skinned]

dermal /ˈdɜməl/, *adj.* of or relating to skin.

dermatitis /dɜməˈtaɪtəs/, *n.* an inflammation of the skin.

dermato-, a word part meaning 'skin', as in *dermatology*. Also, **derm-, dermat-, dermo-.** [Gk, combining form of *dérma*]

dermatology /dɜməˈtɒlədʒi/, *n.* the study of the skin and its diseases. —**dermatological**, *adj.* —**dermatologist,** *n.*

derog., *Abbrev.* **1.** derogative **2.** derogatory.

derogatory /dəˈrɒgətri, -ətəri/, *adj.* showing or causing lack of respect; disparaging; depreciatory. Also, **derogative.**

De Rougemont /də ˈruːʒmɒnt/, *n.* Louis, 1847–1921, Australian adventurer and lecturer, probably born in Paris; on his own admission reputed to have been 'the greatest liar on earth'.

derrick /ˈdɛrɪk/, *n.* **1.** a type of crane for lifting and moving heavy weights. **2.** a towerlike framework over an oil-well. [named after *Derrick*, a hangman at Tyburn, London, about 1600]

dervish /ˈdɜvɪʃ/, *n.* a member of any of various Muslim groups, some of which use violent whirling dances or energetic chanting as part of their religious practices. [Turk, from Pers: religious mendicant]

Derwent /ˈdɜwənt/, *n.* **1.** a river in southeastern Tas, rising in Lake St Clair in central Tas and flowing in a south-easterly direction entering the sea at Storm Bay. 190 km.

desalination /ˌdiːsæləˈneɪʃən/, *n.* the removal of salt from sea water so that it becomes suitable for drinking or for irrigation. Also, **desalinisation.**

descant /ˈdɛskænt, *n.*; /dɛsˈkænt, dəs-/, *adj., v.* ◇*n.* **1.** *Music.* an additional melody accompanying a simple musical theme and usu. played or sung at a higher pitch. ◇*adj.* **2.** *Music.* (of an instrument) the smallest and highest pitched in the range in common use: *descant recorder.* ◇*v.i.* **3.** to make comments; discourse. Also, **discant.** [ME, from ONF (from L *cantus* song)] —**descanter,** *n.*

Descartes /deɪˈkɑt/, *n.* **René** /rəˈneɪ/, 1596–1650, French philosopher and mathematician.

descend /dəˈsɛnd/, *v.i.* **1.** to move or pass from a higher to a lower place; go or come down; fall; sink. **2.** to pass from the earlier to later times, or from the general to the particular. **3.** to slope or tend downward. **4.** to approach with haste and oft. anger (fol. by *on* or *upon*): *The teacher descended upon the boys who were smoking.* ◇*v.t.* **5.** to move or lead downward. [ME, from OF, from L] —**descendent,** *adj.*

descendant /dəˈsɛndənt/, *n.* a person descended from an ancestor; offspring. [F: descending]

descent /dəˈsɛnt/, *n.* **1.** the act or fact of descending. **2.** a downward slope, passage or stairway. **3.** ancestry: *of noble descent.* [ME, from OF]

describe /dəˈskraɪb/, *v.t.*, **-scribed, -scribing. 1.** to state the characteristics of in written or spoken words; give an account of (a scene, person, etc.). **2.** *Geom.* to draw the outline of. [L: copy off, sketch off, describe] —**describer,** *n.*

description /dəˈskrɪpʃən/, *n.* **1.** a representation by written or spoken words: *Can you give a description of the thief?* **2.** sort; kind; variety: *people of that description.* **3.** *Geom.* the act of describing a shape. [ME, from L]

descriptive /dəˈskrɪptɪv/, *adj.* **1.** serving as a description, esp. a good one. **2.** marked by much description. **3.** *Gram.* seeking to describe language as it is used, rather than state what it should be. —**descriptiveness,** *n.*

descriptive clause, *n.* a relative clause, in English writing usu. set off in commas, which describes but does not identify the antecedent. In 'This year, *which has been dry,* is bad for crops' the italicised part is a descriptive clause (opposed to *restrictive clause*).

descry /dɛsˈkraɪ/, *v.t.*, **-scried, -scrying. 1.** to make out (something distant or unclear) by looking closely; discern; espy. **2.** to perceive; distinguish; detect. [ME, apparently from OF: proclaim] —**descrier,** *n.*

desecrate /ˈdɛsəkreɪt/, *v.t.*, **-crated, -crating.** to use (a holy thing or place) in an unworthy way; profane. [DE- + *-secrate*, modelled on CONSECRATE] —**desecrater,** **desecrator,** *n.* —**desecration,** *n.*

desert¹ /ˈdɛzət/, *n.* **1.** a sandy or stony area, so lacking in rainfall that it can support few forms of plant life, or none at all. ◇*adj.* **2.** of, relating to, or like a desert; desolate; barren. [ME, from OF from L: abandoned]

desert² /dəˈzɜt/, *v.t.* **1.** to leave (a person, place, etc.) without intending to return; abandon; forsake: *He deserted his wife.* **2.** (of a soldier or sailor) to leave or run away from (service, duty, etc.) with no intention of returning. ◇*v.i.* **3.** (esp. of a soldier or sailor) to forsake one's duty, etc. [F, from L: abandon] —**deserter,** *n.*

desert³ /dəˈzɜt/, *n.* (usu. pl.) something which is deserved; reward or punishment: *He got his just deserts.* [ME, from OF: deserved]

desertion /dəˈzɜʃən/, *n.* the act of deserting.

desert oak, *n.* **1.** a termite-resistant tree of central and north-western Australia. **2.** any

desert oak

other tree of dry areas, with oak-like timber, as the acacia.

desert pea, *n.* → Sturt's desert pea.

desert rat, *n.* **1.** → jerboa (def. 2). **2.** *Mil. Colloq.* a member of various Allied forces who fought in desert campaigns in North Africa, 1941–42. [named after the divisional sign, a jerboa, of the British 7th armored division]

deserve /dəˈzɜːv/, *v.t.*, **-served, -serving.** to be worthy of (merit, reward, punishment, esteem, etc.). [ME, from OF, from L: serve zealously] **–deserving,** *adj.* **–deserved,** *adj.*

de-sex /di-ˈseks/, *v.t. Colloq.* to spay or castrate (an animal).

desiccate /ˈdesəkeɪt/, *v.*, **-cated, -cating.** ◇*v.t.* **1.** to dry thoroughly; dry up. **2.** to preserve (food, etc.) by taking away moisture. ◇*v.i.* **3.** to become dry. [L: completely dried] **–desiccation,** *n.* **–desiccated,** *adj.*

design /dəˈzaɪn/, *v.t.* **1.** to prepare sketches or plans for (work to be undertaken): *to design a house.* **2.** to plan or fashion artistically or skilfully. **3.** to intend (something) for a purpose: *designed for use in the home.* **4.** to form or conceive in the mind; contrive: *to design a new card game.* ◇*n.* **5.** an outline, sketch, or plan, as for a painting, building, engine, etc., to be done or built. **6.** the art of designing things: *a school of design.* **7.** intention; purpose. **8.** (*usu. pl.*) an evil or selfish intention: *to have designs on (or against) a person.* **9. by design,** deliberately. [F: designate, from L: mark out] **–designedly,** *adv.* **–designer,** *n.*

designate /ˈdezɪɡneɪt/, *v.*, **-nated, -nating.** /ˈdezɪɡnət, -neɪt/, *adj.* ◇*v.t.* **1.** to mark or point out; indicate; show; specify. **2.** to entitle; give a name to. **3.** to suggest appointment for duty, office, purpose, etc. ◇*adj.* **4.** appointed to office but not yet in possession of it; designated: *the ambassador designate.* [L: marked out] **–designative,** *adj.* **–designator,** *n.* **–designation,** *n.*

desirable /dəˈzaɪrəbəl/, *adj.* **1.** worthy of being desired; pleasing, excellent, or fine. **2.** (of a person or thing) exciting desire: *a desirable woman; a desirable car.* ◇*n.* **3.** a person or thing considered desirable. **–desirability, desirableness,** *n.* **–desirably,** *adv.*

desire /dəˈzaɪə/, *v.*, **-sired, -siring,** *n.* ◇*v.t.* **1.** to wish or long for; crave; want. **2.** to express a wish for, implying a request: *The king desires your presence.* ◇*n.* **3.** a strong need; craving. **4.** a request. **5.** something desired. **6.** sexual appetite; lust. [ME, from OF, from L: want] **–desirer,** *n.* **–desirous,** *adj.*

desist /dəˈzɪst/, *v.i.* to cease (as from some action); stop: *You must desist from this behavior.* [OF, from L: leave off]

desk /desk/, *n.* **1.** a type of table with a flat or sloping top used for writing, oft. with drawers or pigeonholes. **2.** that section of a hotel, office, building, etc., from which public services are provided: *reception desk; information desk.*

desktop /ˈdesktɒp/, *adj.* (of computers, office equipment, etc.) small enough to be used at a desk. See **laptop.**

desolate /ˈdesələt, ˈdez-/, *adj.*; /ˈdesəleɪt, ˈdez-/, *v.*, **-lated, -lating.** ◇*adj.* **1.** barren or laid waste; devastated. **2.** deserted; lonely. **3.** hopeless; helpless. **4.** very sad; dreary; dismal. ◇*v.t.* **5.** to lay waste; devastate. **6.** to make unhappy or disconsolate. **7.** to forsake or abandon. [ME, from L: left alone, forsaken] **–desolation,** *n.*

despair /dəˈspeə/, *n.* **1.** a loss of hope; hopelessness. **2.** something which causes hopelessness or of which there is no hope. ◇*v.i.* **3.** to lose or give up hope; to be without hope (oft. fol. by *of*): *to despair of success.* [ME, from OF, from L: be without hope] **–despairing,** *adj.*

despatch /dəˈspætʃ/, *v.t., v.i., n.* → dispatch. **–despatcher,** *n.*

desperado /despəˈrɑːdoʊ/, *n., pl.* **-does, -dos.** a desperate or reckless criminal. [probably a refashioning of *desperate* after Sp words in *-ado*]

desperate /ˈdesprət, -pərət/, *adj.* **1.** ready to run any risk; reckless with despair: *desperate villain.* **2.** leaving little or no hope; serious or dangerous; very bad: *desperate illness.* **3.** having no hope; despairing. **4.** undertaken as a last resort: *a desperate remedy.* [late ME, from L: given up, despaired of] **–desperation,** *n.*

despicable /dəˈspɪkəbəl/, *adj.* deserving to be hated or despised; contemptible. [LL, from L: despise]

despise /dəˈspaɪz/, *v.t.*, **-spised, -spising.** to look down upon, as with hate or contempt; scorn; disdain. [ME, from OF, from L: look down upon, despise]

despite /dəˈspaɪt/, *prep.* **1.** in spite of; notwithstanding. ◇*n.* **2.** contemptuous treatment; disrespect; insult. **3.** *Archaic.* hatred; malice. **4. in despite of,** in contempt or defiance of. [ME, from OF, from L: a looking down upon]

despoil /dəˈspɔɪl/, *v.t.* to take away possessions from; rob; plunder; pillage. [ME, from OF, from L: plunder, rob] **–despoilment, despoliation,** *n.*

despondent /dəˈspɒndənt/, *adj.* having lost heart, courage or hope; depressed. **–despondency,** *n.*

despot /ˈdespɒt/, *n.* a ruler with total power, esp. one who is unjust and cruel. [Gk *despótēs* master] **–despotic,** *adj.* **–despotically,** *adv.*

despotism /ˈdespətɪzəm/, *n.* **1.** the rule of a country by a despot; exercise of complete authority. **2.** total power or control; tyranny.

dessert /dəˈzɜːt/, *n.* the last course of a meal, usu. fruit or a sweet dish. [F: clear the table]

dessertspoon /dəˈzɜːtspuːn/, *n.* a spoon, between a tablespoon and teaspoon in size, often used to eat dessert.

destination /destəˈneɪʃən/, *n.* **1.** the planned end of journey or voyage. **2.** the final

destination   279   **determine**

purpose or end for which something is designed.

destine /'destɪn/, *v.t.*, **-tined, -tining. 1.** to set apart for a particular use, purpose, etc.; design; intend. **2.** to appoint beforehand; predetermine. [ME, from OF, from L: make fast, establish, appoint] —**destined**, *adj.*

destiny /'destɪni/, *n., pl.* **-nies. 1.** a predetermined course of events esp. as relating to a person's life; fate. **2.** a power or agency believed to determine this course of events. [ME, from OF]

destitute /'destɪtjut, -tʃut/, *adj.* **1.** without the necessary things of life. **2.** completely without (something) (fol. by *of*). [ME, from L: put away, abandoned] —**destitution**, *n.*

destroy /dəˈstrɔɪ/, *v.t.* **1.** to spoil completely; ruin; demolish. **2.** to put an end to; extinguish; kill. [ME, from OF, from L: pull down, destroy]

destroyer /dəˈstrɔɪə/, *n.* **1.** a person or thing which destroys. **2.** a small, fast warship, orig. designed to destroy torpedo boats.

destruct /dəˈstrʌkt/, *v.t.* **1.** to blow up or destroy (a missile that has failed to operate properly). ◇*v.i.* **2.** (of such a missile) to destroy itself automatically. ◇*n.* **3.** the destruction of a rocket or the like before the completion of its mission. [backformation from DESTRUCTION]

destruction /dəˈstrʌkʃən/, *n.* **1.** destroying or being destroyed; demolition; annihilation. **2.** the cause or means of destroying. [ME, from L]

destructive /dəsˈtrʌktɪv/, *adj.* **1.** tending to destroy; causing destruction (fol. by *of* or *to*). **2.** having a negative effect (opposed to *constructive*): *destructive remarks.*

desuetude /'deswətjud, dəˈsjuətjud/, *n.* the state of being no longer used or practised. [F, from L]

desultory /'desəltri, -təri, 'dez-/, *adj.* **1.** moving from one thing to another; disconnected; unmethodical: *desultory conversation.* **2.** without plan: *desultory thought.* [L: of a leaper; superficial]

detach /dəˈtætʃ/, *v.t.* **1.** to unfasten and separate; disengage. **2.** to send (sailors, ships, etc.) on a special voyage: *Men were detached to defend the base.* [F, from OF: nail] —**detachable**, *adj.*

detached /dəˈtætʃt/, *adj.* **1.** standing apart; separate; unattached (usu. applied to houses). **2.** not interested; unconcerned; aloof. **3.** objective; unbiased.

detachment /dəˈtætʃmənt/, *n.* **1.** the act of detaching or separating. **2.** the state of being unconcerned, or distant; aloofness. **3.** the quality of not holding biased or prejudiced views. **4.** a force of troops or naval ships.

detail /'diteɪl/, *n.* **1.** a small, single part. **2.** such small parts regarded together; minutiae. **3.** fine, delicate ornamentation: *Notice the detail of his painting.* **4.** a part or section of something, esp. a work of art, oft. enlarged. **5.** *Mil.* (an officer or small force chosen for) a special service or duty. **6. in detail**, giving many facts. ◇*v.t.* **7.** to relate or report fully: *detail the plans.* **8.** *Mil.* to order or appoint for some particular duty, as a guard, etc. **9.** to ornament with fine, delicate patterns. **10.** to improve the appearance of (a motor vehicle, plane, etc.) before sale by finishing and decorating it, inside and out. [F: cut in pieces]

detain /dəˈteɪn/, *v.t.* **1.** to stop from taking action; keep waiting; delay. **2.** to keep under control or in custody; restrain. [ME, from OF, from L: keep back] —**detainment**, *n.* —**detainee**, *n.*

detect /dəˈtɛkt/, *v.t.* to discover or notice (a fact or action): *to detect someone in a dishonest act; detect an untruth.* [L: discovered, uncovered] —**detectable, detectible**, *adj.* —**detection**, *n.*

detective /dəˈtɛktɪv/, *n.* **1.** a person, usu. a member of a police force, whose work is to make enquiries and gather information, esp. to find out who committed a crime. ◇*adj.* **2.** relating to detection or detectives: *a detective story.*

detector /dəˈtɛktə/, *n.* **1.** a person or thing that discovers something. **2.** *Radio.* a device for finding electric oscillations or waves. [LL]

détente /deɪˈtɒnt/, *n.* an easing of tension between nations. [F]

detention /dəˈtɛnʃən/, *n.* **1.** a keeping under guard; confinement. **2.** the keeping in (of a pupil) after school hours as a punishment.

deter /dəˈtɜ/, *v.t.*, **-terred, -terring.** to discourage or stop (someone) from acting or continuing. [L: frighten from] —**determent**, *n.*

detergent /dəˈtɜdʒənt/, *adj.* **1.** cleansing; purging. ◇*n.* **2.** any cleaning product, esp. one which, unlike soap, is not made from fats or oils.

deteriorate /dəˈtɪəriəreɪt/, *v.t., v.i.*, **-rated, -rating.** to make or become worse or lower in character or quality. [LL] —**deterioration**, *n.*

determinant /dəˈtɜmənənt/, *adj.* **1.** determining; defining. ◇*n.* **2.** a determining agent or factor. **3.** *Maths.* an algebraic expression of the elements of a square matrix. —**determinantal**, *adj.*

determination /dətɜməˈneɪʃən/, *n.* **1.** the act of deciding; fixing or settling of purpose. **2.** a decision made, esp. after consideration. **3.** a result brought about; solution. **4.** an official settlement of a problem, quarrel, etc. **5.** the quality of being determined or resolute; firmness of purpose: *He showed great determination.* **6.** *Biol.* the fixing of the nature of structured differences in a group of cells before actual, visible differentiation.

determine /dəˈtɜmən/, *v.t.*, **-mined, -mining. 1.** to settle or decide (an argument, question, etc.) by an official decision. **2.** to reach a decision as after reasoning, examining, etc. **3.** *Geom.* to fix the position of. **4.** to fix or decide causally; condition: *Demand deter-*

determine — **deviate**

mines supply. [ME, from OF, from L: limit] **—determiner,** *n.*

determined /dɪˈtɜːmənd/, *adj.* **1.** firm; resolute; unflinching: *a determined person.* **2.** having made up one's mind; decided; resolved: *determined to go through with it.*

determinism /dɪˈtɜːmənɪzəm/, *n.* the belief that all human events are the results of former conditions, physical or psychological. **—determinist,** *n., adj.* **—deterministic,** *adj.*

deterrent /dɪˈterənt, -ˈtɜːr-/, *n.* something that has a discouraging effect: *They are making nuclear weapons as a deterrent to invaders.* **—deterrence,** *n.*

detest /dɪˈtest/, *v.t.* to feel distaste for; hate; dislike intensely. [F, from L: curse while calling a deity to witness] **—detestable,** *adj.* **—detestation,** *n.*

detonate /ˈdetəneɪt/, *v.i., v.t.,* **-nated, -nating.** to explode, or cause to explode, esp. with great noise, suddenness, or violence. [L: thundered forth] **—detonation,** *n.*

detonator /ˈdetəneɪtə/, *n.* **1.** an explosive, set off by either percussion or ignition, used to make other substances explode. **2.** something that explodes.

detour /ˈdiːtʊə, -tuə, -tɔː/, *n.* **1.** a roundabout way or course, esp. one used temporarily while a main road is closed. ◇*v.i.* **2.** to go by way of a detour. ◇*v.t.* **3.** to send by way of a detour. [F: turn aside, from]

detract /dɪˈtrækt/, *v.t.* **1.** to draw away or turn aside. ◇*v.i.* **2.** to take away part, as from quality, value, or regard: *That remark detracts from my opinion of him.* [L: drawn away or down] **—detractor,** *n.* **—detraction,** *n.*

detriment /ˈdetrəmənt/, *n.* **1.** loss, damage, or physical hurt: *He spoke to the detriment of his friends.* **2.** a cause of loss or damage. [L: loss, damage] **—detrimental,** *adj.*

detritus /dɪˈtraɪtəs/, *n.* **1.** particles worn or broken away from rock by water or glacial ice. **2.** any broken up material; debris. [L: a rubbing away]

Detroit /dɪˈtrɔɪt/, *n.* **1.** a port in the US, in south-eastern Michigan, on the Detroit River; car manufacturing centre. Pop. 1 086 220 (1986 est.).

Deucalion /djuːˈkeɪliən/, *n. Gk Legend.* a son of Prometheus. He survived the deluge with his wife Pyrrha, and became the ancestor of the renewed human race.

deuce /djuːs/, *n.* **1.** a card, or side of a dice, having two pips. **2.** *Tennis.* the stage in a game at which both players have won an equal number of points, and one must win two in succession to win the game. [OF: two]

Deut, *Abbrev. Bible.* Deuteronomy.

deuterium /djuːˈtɪəriəm/, *n.* an isotope of hydrogen, having twice the mass of ordinary hydrogen; heavy hydrogen. *Symbol:* D; *at. no.:* 1; *at. wt.:* 2.01. [NL, from Gk: having second place]

Deuteronomy /ˌdjuːtəˈrɒnəmi/, *n. Bible.* the fifth book of the Pentateuch, containing a second statement of the Mosaic law. [LL, from Gk: the second law]

Deutsche Demokratische Republik /ˈdɔɪtʃə deməˈkrɑːtɪʃə reɪpuˈblɪk/, *n.* → **East Germany.**

Deutschland /ˈdɔɪtʃlʌnt, -lænd/, *n.* → **Germany.**

Deutschmark /ˈdɔɪtʃmɑːk/, *n.* the unit of currency of Germany.

De Valera /də vəˈlɪərə, -ˈleərə/, *n.* Eamon /ˈeɪmən/, 1882–1975, Irish politician; president of Sinn Fein (1917); formed Fianna Fail party (1927); prime minister of Ireland 1937–48, 1951–54, 1957–59; president 1959–73.

devaluation /ˌdiːvæljuˈeɪʃən/, *n.* **1.** an official lowering of the legal exchange value of a country's currency or money in circulation. **2.** any reduction in value, importance, etc.

devalue /diːˈvæljuː/, *v.t.,* **-valued, -valuing. 1.** to decrease the worth or value of (something). **2.** to lower the legal value of (a currency).

devastate /ˈdevəsteɪt/, *v.t.,* **-stated, -stating.** to lay waste; ravage; make desolate. [L] **—devastation,** *n.*

develop /dɪˈveləp/, *v.t.* **1.** to bring to a more advanced or effective state. **2.** to cause to grow or become larger. **3.** to enlarge upon the detail or idea: *develop one's ideas.* **4.** to bring into being or activity; generate; evolve. **5.** to build on (land). **6.** *Biol.* to cause to go through the process of natural evolution. **7.** *Photog.* to treat (a photographic plate, etc.) with chemical agents so as to bring out the picture. ◇*v.i.* **8.** to grow into a more mature or advanced state; advance; expand. **9.** to come gradually into existence or operation; be evolved. **10.** *Biol.* to undergo differences in ontogeny or progress in phylogeny. [F *dé-* DIS-[1] + *voluper* wrap]

developed /dɪˈveləpt/, *adj.* (of a nation, region, etc.) industrialised.

developer /dɪˈveləpə/, *n.* **1.** a person (or company) which buys land for development projects. **2.** *Photog.* a photographic solution used to develop film or plate.

developing /dɪˈveləpɪŋ/, *adj.* (of a country) in the early stages of building an industrial economy. Also, **less-developed, underdeveloped.**

development /dɪˈveləpmənt/, *n.* **1.** the act, process or result of developing. **2.** a developed state, form, or product. **3.** evolution, growth, expansion. **4.** a building project, usu. large, as office block, housing estate, shopping complex, etc. **5.** *Music.* the part of a movement or composition in which a theme or themes are developed. **—developmental,** *adj.*

deviant /ˈdiːviənt/, *adj.* **1.** departing from what is accepted as normal. ◇*n.* **2.** someone who is deviant, usu. in sexual behavior. **—deviance, deviancy,** *n.*

deviate /ˈdiːvieɪt/, *v.,* **-ated, -ating;** /ˈdiːviət/, *n.* ◇*v.i.* **1.** to turn aside (from a way or course); swerve; digress. **2.** to depart (from acceptable behavior). ◇*n.* **3.** → **deviant.** [L *de-* DE- + *via* way] **—deviator,** *n.*

deviation /divi'eɪʃən/, n. **1.** the act of deviating; divergence. **2.** *Stats.* the difference between one of a set of values and the mean of the set.

device /də'vaɪs/, n. **1.** an invention or contraption. **2.** a crafty scheme; trick. **3.** a design or emblem on a coat of arms. **4.** a motto. **5. leave to one's own devices,** to allow (someone) to act without interference. [ME, from OF, from L: divided]

devil /'devəl/, n. **1.** *Theol.* **a.** (*sometimes cap.*) the chief spirit of evil; Satan. **b.** any evil spirit. **2.** a person of great cleverness or energy: *He's a devil for organising.* **3.** an unfortunate person: *poor devil.* **4.** a wicked person: *The young devil stole the cake.* **5.** an errand boy or the youngest boy in a printing office: *printer's devil.* **6. between the devil and the deep blue sea,** faced with two equally unpleasant possibilities. **7. give the devil his due,** to do justice to or give deserved praise to an unpleasant or disliked person. **8. speak** or **talk of the devil,** here comes the person who has been the subject of recent conversation. ◊*v.t.* **9.** *Cookery.* to grill, esp. with hot spices. [OE *deofol*, from L, from Gk: Satan, orig. slanderer]

devilment /'devəlmənt/, n. devilish action or conduct; mischief.

devilry /'devəlri/, n., pl. **-ries. 1.** extreme wickedness. **2.** mischievous or wicked behavior. **3.** demonology. Also, **deviltry.**

devil's advocate, n. a person who supports an opposing or bad cause, esp. for the sake of argument: *I'll play devil's advocate.* [translation of NL *advocātus diabolī*, in the Cath Church the official appointed to present the arguments against a proposed canonisation]

Devil's Island, n. a former French penal colony, off the coast of French Guiana. French, **Île du Diable.**

Devil's Marbles n.pl. an unusual collection of granite boulders south of Tennant Creek in the NT; of spiritual significance to local Aborigines.

devious /'diviəs/, adj. **1.** departing from the direct way; circuitous. **2.** not straightforward; tricky; deceptive; deceitful. [L: out of the way]

devise /də'vaɪz/, v., **-vised, -vising.** ◊*v.t.* **1.** to order or arrange a plan of; think out; plan; contrive; invent. **2.** *Law.* to assign or transmit (property, esp. real property) by will. ◊*v.i.* **3.** to form a plan; contrive. [ME, from OF, from L: separate]

devitrify /di'vɪtrəfaɪ/, v.i., **-fied, -fying.** *Geol.* (of glassy, igneous rocks) to change into rocks composed of definite and distinct crystals. —**devitrification,** n.

devoid /də'vɔɪd/, adj. empty of or free from (fol. by *of*). [from OF *desvuidier* empty out]

devolution /divə'luʃən/, n. **1.** the act or fact of devolving. **2.** *Biol.* backwards evolution (opposed to *evolution*); degeneration. **3.** the passing on or delegation of power or authority. —**devolutionary,** adj.

devolve /də'vɒlv/, v., **-volved, -volving.** ◊*v.t.* **1.** to transfer or delegate (a duty, responsibility, etc.) to or upon another; pass on. **2.** *Law.* to pass by inheritance or legal succession. ◊*v.i.* **3.** to fall as a duty or responsibility on a person: *The job of addressing envelopes devolved on me.* [L: roll down] —**devolvement,** n.

devon /'devən/, n. **1.** a large, smooth sausage, usu. sliced and eaten cold. **2.** (*cap.*) Formerly, also **Devonshire.** a county in southwestern England. Pop. 999 000 (1986 est.); 6765 km². *Administrative Centre:* Exeter.

Devonian /də'vouniən/, adj., n. (relating to) a geological period following the Silurian and preceding the Carboniferous.

Devonport /'devənpɔt/, n. a city and port in northern Tas on the Mersey River; agricultural and dairying area. Pop. 22 645 (1986).

devote /də'vout/, v.t., **-voted, -voting.** to set apart or appropriate (oneself, time, money, etc.) for a particular purpose, cause, person, etc.: *to devote oneself to science*; *She devotes her evenings to her children.* [L: vowed]

devoted /də'voutəd/, adj. **1.** loving and loyal: *a devoted friend.* **2.** dedicated; consecrated.

devotee /devə'ti/, n. a person particularly devoted to anything, esp. religion; an enthusiast.

devotion /də'vouʃən/, n. **1.** dedication; consecration. **2.** a serious attachment to a cause, person, etc. **3.** *Theol.* a readiness to perform what belongs to the service of God. **4.** (*oft. pl.*) *Eccles.* religious worship; a form of prayer for special use. [ME, from L]

devour /də'vauə/, v.t. **1.** to swallow or eat up hungrily or voraciously. **2.** to destroy, as by fire. **3.** to take in greedily with the senses or intellect. **4.** to absorb or engross wholly: *devoured by fears.* [ME, from OF, from L: swallow down]

devout /də'vaut/, adj. **1.** devoted to religious worship or service; pious; religious. **2.** expressing devotion or piety: *devout prayer.* **3.** sincere; heartfelt. [ME, from OF, from L: devoted]

dew /dju/, n. **1.** moisture condensed from the atmosphere, esp. at night, and left in the form of small drops upon any cool surface. **2.** moisture in small drops on a surface, as tears, perspiration, etc. ◊*v.t.* **3.** to wet as with dew. [OE *dēaw*]

Dewar /djuə/, n. **Sir James,** 1842–1923, Scottish chemist and physicist; invented the vacuum flask.

dewclaw /'djuklɔ/, n. an inner claw or digit in the foot of some dogs, which does not reach the ground in walking.

Dewey decimal classification /'djui/, n. (in libraries) a system of classifying and arranging books into ten main subject classes. Also **decimal classification.** [named after Melvil *Dewey,* 1851–1931, US librarian]

De Witts Land /də 'wɪts lænd/, n. **1.** a district in WA, inland from Roeburn. **2.**

De Witts Land (formerly) the name given on early Dutch charts to an area of land on the western coast of Australia.

dewlap /'djulæp/, n. a loose fold of skin under the throat, esp. of cattle. [from *dew*, of uncert. meaning + *lap*, OE *læppa* pendulous piece]

dewpoint /'djupɔɪnt/, n. the temperature of air at which dew begins to form; the temperature at which a given sample of air will have a relative humidity of 100 per cent.

dewy /'djui/, adj., dewier, dewiest. 1. having the quality of dew: *dewy tears*. 2. *Poetic*. falling gently or refreshingly, like dew: *dewy sleep*. —**dewily**, adv. —**dewiness**, n.

dexter /'dɛkstə/, adj. 1. on the right-hand side. 2. *Heraldry*. (on a coat of arms) on the right side, from the view-point of the bearer, and thus on left to a viewer. [L: right, favorable]

dexterity /dɛks'tɛrəti/, n. a cleverness or skill in using the hands, body or mind.

dexterous /'dɛkstrəs, -tərəs/, adj. 1. mentally or physically skilful. 2. right-handed. Also, **dextrous**.

dextral /'dɛkstrəl/, adj. relating to the right-hand side; right (opposed to *sinistral*). —**dextrality**, n.

dextro-, a word part meaning 'right'. [L, combining form of *dexter* right]

dhal /dɑl/, n. the Indian name for lentils or a dish made of lentils. [Hind]

dharma /'dɑmə/, n. (in Hinduism and Buddhism) 1. basic quality or character. 2. the doctrine or teaching of the Buddha. 3. (obedience to) a law, esp. a religious law. [Skt: decree, custom]

dhow /daʊ/, n. an Arab sailing vessel. [Ar]

di-[1], prefix meaning 'twice', 'doubly', 'two', as in *dicotyledon*. [Gk, representing *dis* twice, doubly]

di-[2], a variant of **dis-[1]**.

di-[3], a variant of **dia-**.

Di, *Chem. Symbol.* didymium.

dia-, a prefix meaning 1. passing through, as in *diarrhoea*. 2. thoroughly; completely, as in *diagnosis*. 3. in different directions, as by separation, as in *dialysis*. [Gk, representing *diá*, prep., through; between, across, by, of]

diabase /'daɪəbeɪs/, n. a dark, igneous rock consisting mainly of augite and felspar; an altered dolerite. [F] —**diabasic**, adj.

diabetes /daɪə'bitiz/, n. any of several diseases in which the ability of the body to use sugar is reduced, esp. those in which sugar appears abnormally in the urine (**diabetes mellitus**) or there is excessive production of urine (**diabetes insipidus**). [NL, from Gk: a passer through]

diabolic /daɪə'bɒlɪk/, adj. 1. of or like a devil; fiendish: *a diabolic plot*. 2. *Colloq*. difficult; unpleasant; very bad. Also, **diabolical**. [LL, from Gk]

diacid /daɪ'æsɪd/, adj. (of an acid or a salt) having two replaceable hydrogen ions.

diacritic /daɪə'krɪtɪk/, n. a mark added to a letter or character to distinguish it from a similar one. [Gk: that separates or distinguishes] —**diacritical**, adj.

diadem /'daɪədɛm/, n. a crown, or similar ornament. [L, from Gk: fillet, band]

diagnosis /daɪəg'noʊsəs/, n., pl. -**ses** /-siz/. 1. *Med*. **a**. the process of identifying a disease by examination of the patient. **b**. the result of this process: *His diagnosis was cancer*. 2. the process of testing to identify other problems, esp. learning difficulties. 3. *Biol*. a description which allows an organism to be placed in a classification (def. 2). [NL, from Gk: a distinguishing] —**diagnose**, v. —**diagnostic**, adj. —**diagnostics**, n.

diagnostician /ˌdaɪəgnɒs'tɪʃən/, n. an expert in making diagnoses.

diagonal /daɪ'ægənəl/, adj. 1. *Maths*. (of a straight line) connecting two non-adjacent angles or vertices of a quadrilateral, polygon, or polyhedron. 2. having a sloping direction. ◇n. 3. a diagonal line. [L, from Gk: from angle to angle]

diagram /'daɪəgræm/, n., v., -**grammed**, -**gramming**. ◇n. 1. a figure, or set of lines, marks, etc., to explain a geometrical idea, give the outlines of an object, show the course or results of a process, etc. 2. a drawing, plan or chart that explains the parts, operation, etc., of something. ◇v.t. 3. to make a diagram of. [L, from Gk: that which is marked out by lines] —**diagrammatic**, adj.

diagraph /'daɪəgræf, -grɑf/, n. 1. an instrument used in reproducing outlines, plans, etc., on any desired scale. 2. a combined protractor and scale. [F, from Gk: mark out by lines]

dial /'daɪəl/, n., v., **dialled**, **dialling**. ◇n. 1. the face of a clock, watch, gauge, etc. 2. a rotating knob or disc used for tuning a radio, making telephone connections, etc. 3. *Colloq*. the human face. ◇v.t. 4. to measure, select, show or tune in by means of a dial. 5. to call (a number or person) on a telephone. [ME, from ML: daily, from L: day]

dial., *Abbrev*. 1. dialect. 2. dialectal.

dialect /'daɪəlɛkt/, n. a variety of a language spoken in a particular district or by a social group. [L, from Gk: discourse, language, dialect] —**dialectal**, adj.

dialectic /daɪə'lɛktɪk/, adj. 1. of, or relating to, logical argument or discussion. ◇n. 2. the examination of ideas by or as if by a debate between the opposing points of view. 3. any formal system of reasoning or thought. 4. → **Hegelian dialectic**. [L, from Gk *dialektikḗ (technē)* argumentative (art)]

dialectical materialism /daɪə'lɛktɪkəl mə'tɪərɪəlɪzəm/, n. a theory developed mainly by Karl Marx, combining parts of traditional materialist philosophy with the method of Hegelian dialectic. —**dialectical materialist**, n.

dialectician /ˌdaɪəlɛk'tɪʃən/, n. 1. someone skilled in dialectic; logician. 2. a person who studies dialects.

dialogue /ˈdaɪəlɒg/, n. 1. a conversation between two or more people, esp. characters in a novel, play, etc. 2. an exchange of ideas or opinions on a particular issue. 3. (esp. in diplomacy) a discussion between parties, countries, etc., usu. with the aim of agreement: *We need dialogue with China*. [F, from L, from Gk]

dialysis /daɪˈæləsəs/, n., pl. **-ses** /-siz/. 1. *Chem.* the separation of smaller molecules from larger ones in a solution by selective diffusion through a semipermeable membrane. 2. *Med.* (in cases of defective kidney function) the removal of waste products from the blood by causing them to diffuse through a semipermeable membrane; haemodialysis. [Gk: separation, dissolution] — **dialyse**, v.

diamanté /daɪəˈmɒnti, diə-/, n., adj. (a fabric) covered with glittering particles. [F]

Diamantina /daɪmənˈtinə/, n. a river which rises near the Selwyn Range in south-western Qld and flows in a south-westerly direction into Lake Eyre in SA. 900 km.

diameter /daɪˈæmətə/, n. 1. *Geom.* a straight line passing through the centre of any figure or body (esp. circle or sphere) to the circumference or surface at each side. 2. the length of such a line; thickness of a body. [ME, from L, from Gk: diagonal, diameter]

diametrical /daɪəˈmɛtrɪkəl/, adj. 1. relating to a diameter. 2. (of opposite sides, viewpoints, etc.) direct; absolute: *diametrical opposites*. Also, **diametric**. — **diametrically**, adv.

diamond /ˈdaɪəmənd, ˈdaɪmənd/, n. 1. an extremely hard, and nearly pure form of carbon, used in industry, or as a precious stone. 2. a tool with an uncut diamond, used for cutting glass. 3. (a playing card showing) a red rhombus-shaped figure (♦). 4. a baseball field. ◇adj. 5. indicating the 75th, or sometimes the 60th, event of a series, as a wedding anniversary: *diamond wedding*. [ME, from L *adamas* adamant, diamond]

diamond drill, n. *Geol.* a drill having a hollow, cylindrical bit (def. 4b) set with diamonds, used for collecting cores of rock samples for geological study.

diamond snake, n. *Zool.* a large Australian python, greenish-black in color with yellow diamond spots on its sides.

Diana /daɪˈænə/, n. 1. Roman goddess of the moon and of hunting, and protector of women; Greek counterpart, Artemis. 2. (**Princess of Wales**), born 1961, wife of Prince Charles.

dianthus /daɪˈænθəs/, n. any of several plants including the carnation and sweet william. [NL, from Gk]

diapason /daɪəˈpeɪzən, -sən/, n. either of the two principal stops of a pipe organ. [L, from Gk: (concord) through all (notes of the scale)] — **diapasonic**, adj.

diaper /ˈdaɪəpə, ˈdaɪpə/, n. US. a baby's nappy. [ME, from OF, from MGk: pure white]

diaphanous /daɪˈæfənəs/, adj. transparent or translucent. [ML, from Gk]

diaphragm /ˈdaɪəfræm/, n. 1. *Anat.* a partition between the thoracic (chest) cavity and the abdominal cavity in mammals. 2. a vibrating membrane or disc, as in a telephone or microphone. 3. a contraceptive device covering the cervix. 4. *Optics.* a ring or plate used to control the amount of light entering an instrument such as a camera or telescope. [LL, from Gk: midriff, barrier]

diarrhoea /daɪəˈriə/, n. an intestinal disorder marked by frequency and fluidity of bowel movements. Also, **diarrhea**. [Gk: a flowing through] — **diarrhoeal, diarrhoeic**, adj.

diary /ˈdaɪəri/, n., pl. **-ries**. 1. a daily record, esp. of the writer's own experiences or thoughts. 2. a book for keeping such a record, or for entering appointments. [L: daily allowance, journal] — **diarist**, n.

Dias /ˈdiæs/, n. Bartholomeu /bɑtɒlouˈmeɪou/ c. 1450–1500, Portuguese navigator and discoverer of the Cape of Good Hope. Also, **Diaz**.

Diaspora /daɪˈæspərə/, n. 1. the whole body of Jews scattered among the Gentiles after the Babylonian captivity. 2. (among the early Jewish Christians) the body of Jewish Christians outside Palestine. 3. the dispersion of the Jews. [Gk: a scattering]

diaster /daɪˈæstə/, n. *Biol.* the stage in mitosis at which the chromosomes, after their division and separation, are grouped near the poles of the spindle. — **diastral**, adj.

diastole /daɪˈæstouli/, n. the normal rhythmical relaxation of the heart. See **systole**. [LL, from Gk: lengthening] — **diastolic**, adj.

diastrophism /daɪˈæstrəfɪzəm/, n. 1. the movements which cause the earth's crust to be deformed, producing continents, mountains, etc. 2. any deformation caused in this way. [Gk: distortion] — **diastrophic**, adj.

diatom /ˈdaɪətəm, -tɒm/, n. *Biol.* any of a number of single-celled water plants. [NL *Diatoma*, genus of diatoms, from Gk: cut through]

diatomaceous earth /daɪətəˈmeɪʃəs ˈɜθ/, n. *Geol.* fine earth chiefly made up of the cell walls of diatoms, used in swimming-pool filters. Also, **diatomite** /daɪˈætəmaɪt/.

diatomic /daɪəˈtɒmɪk/, adj. *Chem.* having two atoms in the molecule.

diatonic /daɪəˈtɒnɪk/, adj. *Music.* involving only the tones, intervals, or harmonies of a major or minor scale without chromatic change. [LL, from Gk] — **diatonically**, adv.

diatribe /ˈdaɪətraɪb/, n. a bitter and violent attack or criticism. [L, from Gk: pastime, study, discourse]

dibasic acid /daɪˌbeɪsɪk ˈæsəd/, n. an acid containing two replaceable hydrogen ions and so able to form two series of salts, normal and acid salts, as carbonates and bicarbonates.

dibs /dɪbz/, n.pl. *Colloq.* 1. → **marbles** (def. 4b). 2. a stake in a game. 3. funds or money: *in the dibs*. 4. winnings. [from *dibstones*, formerly a children's game played with small stones; var. of DAB]

dice /daɪs/, *n.pl., sing.* **die**, *v.*, **diced, dicing.** ◇*n.* **1.** small cubes marked on each side with a different number of spots (one to six), used in games of chance or in gambling. **2.** (*treated as sing.*) any of several games, esp. gambling games, played by shaking and throwing the dice. **3.** any small cubes. **4. no dice**, *Colloq.* of no use; unsuccessful; out of luck. **5.** to cut into small cubes. **6.** *Colloq.* to throw away, reject. ◇*v.t.* **7.** to play at dice. [see DIE²] —**dicer**, *n.*

dicey /'daɪsi/, *adj. Colloq.* dangerous; risky.

dicho-, a word part meaning 'in two parts', 'in pairs'. [Gk, combining form of *dícha* in 2, asunder]

dichotomy /daɪ'kɒtəmi/, *n., pl.* **-mies.** a division into two parts. [Gk: a cutting in two]

dichroism /'daɪkroʊˌɪzəm/, *n.* (of many doubly refracting crystals) the property of showing different colors when viewed from different directions. [Gk: of two colors]

dichromate /daɪ'kroʊmeɪt, -mət/, *n.* a salt of a hypothetical acid, $H_2Cr_2O_7$, such as potassium dichromate, $K_2Cr_2O_7$, a powerful oxidising agent.

dick¹ /dɪk/, *n. Colloq.* a detective. [shortened form of DETECTIVE; ? influenced by DICK²]

dick² /dɪk/, *n. Colloq.* (*offensive*) the penis.

dickens /'dɪkənz/, *n., interj.* (preceded by *the*) devil; deuce: *What the dickens are you doing?*

Dickens /'dɪkənz/, *n.* Charles (John Huffam), 1812-70, English novelist. —**Dickensian**, *adj.*

Dickinson /'dɪkənsən/, *n.* Emily, 1830-86, US poet.

dicky¹ /'dɪki/, *n., pl.* **-ies. 1.** a detachable shirt front or apron. Also, **dicky-seat.** **2.** a small seat at the outside or back of a vehicle; rumble seat. Also, **dickie.** [application of *Dicky*, diminutive of *Dick*, proper name]

dicky² /'dɪki/, *adj. Colloq.* **1.** unsteady, in bad health: *dicky heart*. **2.** difficult: *a dicky position*.

dicotyledon /ˌdaɪkɒtə'lidn/, *n. Bot.* a plant with two cotyledons. —**dicotyledonous**, *adj.*

dictaphone /'dɪktəfoʊn/, *n.* a machine, like a small tape recorder, that records and replays dictation. [Trademark; from DICTA(TE) + -PHONE]

dictate /dɪk'teɪt/, *v.*, **-tated, -tating;** /'dɪkteɪt/, *n.* ◇*v.t., v.i.* **1.** to say or read aloud (something) to be written down or mechanically recorded. **2.** to order (something), or give orders, with authority. ◇*n.* **3.** a powerful order or command. **4.** a guiding or ruling principle. [L: pronounced, dictated]

dictation /dɪk'teɪʃən/, *n.* **1.** the act of dictating for someone else to write down, etc. **2.** words, or a passage, letter, etc., dictated. **3.** the act of ordering with authority.

dictator /dɪk'teɪtə, 'dɪkteɪtə/, *n.* **1.** a person with total power, esp. in a government not freely chosen by the people. **2.** (in ancient Rome) a person who by law had total authority in time of trouble but for no longer. **3.** a domineering person. [L]

dictatorial /ˌdɪktə'tɔriəl/, *adj.* **1.** of or relating to a dictator or a dictatorship. **2.** tending to dictate or command; imperious.

dictatorship /dɪk'teɪtəʃɪp/, *n.* a country, government or form of government in which one person has total power.

diction /'dɪkʃən/, *n.* **1.** a style of spoken or written expression: *good diction; a Latin diction.* **2.** clearness in speech. [L: a saying]

dictionary /'dɪkʃənri, 'dɪkʃənəri/, *n., pl.* **-aries. 1.** a book with an alphabetical collection of the words of a language, with their meanings, pronunciations, etymologies, etc. **2.** a book giving alphabetically arranged information on particular subjects, classes of words, names, etc: *a biographical dictionary*. [ML: a word-book, from LL: word]

dictum /'dɪktəm/, *n., pl.* **-ta** /-tə/, **-tums. 1.** a command; pronouncement. **2.** a saying; maxim. [L: something said, a saying, a command]

did /dɪd/, *v.* past tense of **do.**

didactic /daɪ'dæktɪk, də-/, *adj.* **1.** meant to teach; instructive: *didactic poetry*. **2.** wanting to teach or lecture others too much: *a didactic old lady*. [Gk: apt at teaching] —**didactically**, *adv.* —**didacticism**, *n.*

diddle /'dɪdl/, *v.t.*, **-dled, -dling.** *Colloq.* to cheat; swindle. [orig. uncert.] —**diddler**, *n.*

didgeridoo /ˌdɪdʒəri'du/, *n.* a long, pipe-shaped, Aboriginal wind instrument made of wood. [Aboriginal]

didn't /'dɪdnt/, *v.* contraction of *did not.*

die¹ /daɪ/, *v.i.*, **died, dying. 1.** to stop living. **2.** (of non-living things) to cease to exist: *The secret died with him*. **3.** to lose force or strength. **4.** to stop working: *The engine died*. **5.** to pass or fade slowly (usu. fol. by *away, out,* or *down*): *The storm slowly died down*. **6.** to suffer as if dying: *I die in this heat*. **7.** *Colloq.* to desire or want keenly or greatly (fol. by *for*): *I'm dying for a drink*. ◇*v.* **8. die off**, to die one after another until the number is greatly reduced. **9. die out**, to become extinct. [ME *deghen*]

die² /daɪ/, *n., pl.* **dies** for def. *1*, **dice** for def. *2; v.*, **died, dieing.** ◇*n.* **1.** any of several tools for cutting, pressing, stamping, etc. metal, coins, etc. **2.** singular of **dice.** **3. the die is cast**, the decision can no longer be changed. ◇*v.t.* **4.** to impress, shape, or cut with a die. [ME, from OF, from L: given (apparently in sense of given by fortune)]

dieback /'daɪbæk/, *n.* a plant disease resulting in gradual death from the leaf tips downwards.

die-casting /'daɪkɑstɪŋ/, *n.* (something made by) a process in which metal is forced into metallic moulds under hydraulic pressure.

diehard /'daɪhad/, *n.* someone who strongly opposes change.

dielectric /ˌdaɪə'lɛktrɪk/, *Elect.* ◇*adj.* **1.** non-conducting. ◇*n.* **2.** a dielectric substance;

dielectric   285   **diffusion**

insulator. [DI-³ + ELECTRIC] —**dielectrically**, *adv*.

Dien Bien Phu /djen bjen 'fu/, *n*. a village in north-eastern Vietnam; the site of a French military post besieged and captured by the Vietminh in 1954.

dieresis /daɪ'erəsəs/, *n*., *pl*. **-ses** /-sɪz/. **1.** *Linguistics*. the separation of two adjacent vowels. **2.** a sign (¨) placed over the second of two adjacent vowels to show separate pronunciation, as in *Noël*. [L, from Gk: separation, division]

diesel /'dizəl/, *n*. **1.** →**diesel engine**. **2.** a locomotive, truck, ship or the like, driven by a diesel engine.

diesel engine, *n*. an ignition-compression type of internal-combustion engine. [named after Rudolf *Diesel*, 1859–1913, German inventor]

diesel oil, *n*. the oil left after petrol and kerosene have been taken from crude petroleum; used in diesel engines. Also, **dieseline, gas oil**.

diet¹ /'daɪət/, *n.*, *v.*, **-eted, -eting**. ◇*n*. **1.** food, as seen in terms of its types, qualities, and effects on health. **2.** a particular selection of food, chosen to improve health. **3.** the food a person usually eats. **4.** anything used or taken by habit. ◇*v.i*. **5.** to choose or limit the food one eats to improve one's health, appearance, etc. [ME, from L, from Gk: way of living, diet] —**dieter**, *n*., —**dietary**, *adj*.

diet² /'daɪət/, *n*. a formal assembly, esp. for discussing state or church affairs. [ME, from ML: public assembly]

dietetic /daɪə'tetɪk/, *adj*. relating to diet, or to control of the use of food. —**dietetics**, *n*.

dietitian /daɪə'tɪʃən/, *n*. someone trained to give dietary advice. Also, **dietician**.

Dietrich /'ditrɪk/, *n*. **Marlene** /ma'leɪnə/, 1901–92, US actor and singer, born in Germany.

Dieu et mon droit /ˌdjɜ eɪ mɔ̃ 'drwa/, *n*. God and my right; motto of the Royal Arms of Great Britain.

differ /'dɪfə/, *v.i*. **1.** to be unlike, or not the same. **2.** to disagree in opinion, belief, etc. (oft. fol. by *with* or *from*). [F, from L: bear apart, put off, be different]

difference /'dɪfrəns/, *n*. **1.** the state, instance, or relation of being different; dissimilarity. **2.** a marked change in a situation. **3.** an identifying quality; distinguishing characteristic. **4.** a disagreement in opinion; quarrel. **5.** *Maths*. the amount by which one quantity is greater or less than another. **6. split the difference, a.** to compromise. **b.** to divide the remainder equally. [OE, from L]

different /'dɪfrənt/, *adj*. **1.** having unlike qualities; dissimilar. **2.** separate or distinct. **3.** various; several: *It comes in different colors*. **4.** not ordinary; striking. [ME, from L. See DIFFER]

differential /dɪfə'renʃəl/, *adj*. **1.** of or relating to difference. **2.** distinguishing; distinctive: *a differential feature*. **3.** depending upon a difference. **4.** relating to or using the difference of two or more motions, forces, etc.: *a differential gear*. ◇*n*. **5.** *Mach*. an epicyclic train of gears designed to permit two or more shafts to revolve at different speeds when driven by a third shaft, esp. a set of gears in a motor car which permit the driving wheels to revolve at different speeds when the car is turning. **6.** *Maths*. the linear function which best approximates changes in a given function in the neighborhood of a given point. [ML, from L: difference]

differential calculus, *n*. the branch of mathematics which studies the properties and uses of derivatives and differentials. See **calculus**.

differential coefficient, *n*. *Maths*. →**derivative** (def. 5).

differential equation, *n*. *Maths*. an equation involving differentials or derivatives.

differentiate /dɪfə'renʃieɪt/, *v*., **-ated, -ating**. ◇*v.t*. **1.** to mark off by differences: *His hair differentiates him from his brother*. **2.** to see the difference in or between; discriminate: *I can differentiate him from his brother*. **3.** *Maths*. to obtain the derivative of. ◇*v.i*. **4.** to change in character. **5.** to make a distinction; discriminate: *I can differentiate between the two*. **6.** *Biol*. (of cells or tissues) to develop from generalised to specialised kinds. —**differentiation**, *n*.

difficult /'dɪfəkəlt/, *adj*. **1.** hard to do, perform, understand, etc. **2.** hard to deal with. **3.** hard to please. [backformation from DIFFICULTY]

difficulty /'dɪfəkəlti/, *n*., *pl*. **-ties**. **1.** the fact or condition of being difficult. **2.** (*oft. pl.*) an embarrassing situation, esp. of financial affairs. **3.** (a cause of) trouble. **4.** unwillingness; reluctance. **5.** something which is hard to do, understand, etc.: *English is my difficulty*. [ME, from L]

diffident /'dɪfədənt/, *adj*. **1.** lacking confidence in one's own ability, timid, etc. **2.** reserved in manner, etc. [L: mistrusting] —**diffidence**, *n*.

diffraction /də'frækʃən/, *n*. **1.** the effect on light or other radiation when it passes by the edge of an opaque body, or is sent through small holes, resulting in the formation of a series of light and dark bands, color, spectra, etc. It is caused by interference due to the wave nature of radiation. **2.** a similar effect on soundwaves when passing by the edge of a building or other large body. —**diffractive**, *adj*.

diffuse /də'fjuz/, *v*., **-fused, -fusing**; /də'fjus/, *adj*. ◇*v.t*., *v.i*. **1.** to pour out or spread (something). **2.** *Phys*. to mix, move, or spread by diffusion. ◇*adj*. **3.** widely spread or scattered. **4.** marked by unnecessary length in speech or writing; wordy. [ME, from L: poured out]

diffusion /də'fjuʒən/, *n*. **1.** the act of diffusing. **2.** the state of being diffused. **3.** a lengthiness of speech or writing. **4.** *Phys*. **a.** filling of any space by fluid, or mixing of fluids due to free movement of their particles or molecules. **b.** the process of being scattered.

diffusion   286   dilettante

See **scatter** (def. 3). **5.** *Anthrop., Sociology.* the spreading of elements from one culture to another.

dig /dɪg/, *v.*, **dug, digging**, *n.* ◇*v.i.* **1.** to break up, turn over, or remove earth, etc., with a spade, the hands, etc. **2.** to make one's way by, or as by, digging. ◇*v.t.* **3.** to break up, turn over, or remove (earth) with a spade, the hands, etc. (oft. fol. by *up*). **4.** to make (a hole, tunnel, etc.) in this way. **5.** to obtain or remove in this way (oft. fol. by *up* or *out*): *He dug up an old coin.* **6.** to find by study or search: *They dug the information out.* **7.** to push; thrust: *He dug his hands into his pockets; He dug her in the ribs.* **8.** *Colloq.* to understand or like: *I really dig old movies.* ◇*v.* **9. dig in**, **a.** to dig trenches for defence in battle. **b.** to hold to one's position or opinion firmly. **10. dig into**, *Colloq.* to begin (work, eating, etc.) actively. ◇*n.* **11.** a push; poke: *She gave him a dig in the ribs.* **12.** a cutting remark. **13.** an archaeological excavation. **14.** *Colloq.* → **digger** (def. 4). **15.** *Colloq.* (*pl.*) living quarters where one pays rent or board. [ME, probably from F, of Gmc orig.]

digest /dəˈdʒɛst, daɪ-/, *v.*; /ˈdaɪdʒɛst/, *n.* ◇*v.t.* **1.** to prepare (food) in the stomach and intestines for use by the body. **2.** to take in mentally; think over: *to digest information.* **3.** to shorten systematically; summarise. ◇*v.i.* **4.** to digest food. **5.** to be digested as food. ◇*n.* **6.** a collection of written matter, oft. summarised, as a group of laws. [ME, from L: separated, arranged, dissolved] —**digestible**, *adj.*

digestion /dəˈdʒɛstʃən, daɪ-/, *n.* **1.** the act or process by which food is digested. **2.** the power of digesting food. —**digestive**, *adj.*

digger /ˈdɪgə/, *n.* **1.** a tool, part of a machine, etc., for digging. **2.** a miner, esp. a gold-miner. **3.** *Colloq.* an Australian soldier, esp. one who served in World War I. **4.** (a term of friendly address among men) mate.

digger's speedwell /ˌdɪgəz ˈspidwɛl/, *n.* a soft-wooded shrub with purplish-blue flowers and leaves that wrap around the stem, common esp. in tableland areas of eastern Australia. Also, **digger's delight**. [from the mistaken idea that it grows only on gold-bearing soil]

diggings /ˈdɪgɪŋz/, *n.pl.* **1.** a place where digging or mining is carried on. **2.** something which is dug out. **3.** *Colloq.* → **dig** (def. 15).

digging stick /ˈdɪgɪŋ stɪk/, *n.* (among tribal Aborigines) a specially shaped stick used for digging up roots, yams, etc.

digit /ˈdɪdʒɪt/, *n.* **1.** a finger or toe. **2.** any of the numerals 0, 1...9. [L: finger, toe]

digital /ˈdɪdʒɪtl/, *adj.* **1.** of, like, or having a digit or digits. **2.** *Elect.* of or relating to information represented by patterns made up from qualities existing in two states only, on and off, as pulses: *digital signals.* **3.** (of clocks, gauges, etc.) displaying the time, amount, etc., as numbers. See **analog**.

digital computer, *n.* a type of computer in which the numbers are represented by patterns of on-off states of voltages.

digitalis /ˌdɪdʒəˈtaləs/, *n.* **1.** any of various plants with long spikes, esp. the common foxglove. **2.** the dried leaves of the common foxglove, used in medicine, esp. as a heart stimulant. [NL: of the finger (after G name *Fingerhut* thimble)]

digital-to-analog converter /ˌdɪdʒətl-tu-ˌænəlɒg kənˈvɜːtə/, *n.* an electronic device for changing digital signals to analog signals. —**digital-to-analog conversion**, *n.*

dignified /ˈdɪgnəfaɪd/, *adj.* marked by dignity of appearance or manner: *dignified conduct.*

dignify /ˈdɪgnəfaɪ/, *v.t.*, **-fied, -fying**. to give honor or dignity to; ennoble. [L]

dignitary /ˈdɪgnətri, -nətəri/, *n.*, *pl.* **-taries**. a person who holds high rank or office, esp. in government or the church.

dignity /ˈdɪgnəti/, *n.*, *pl.* **-ties**. **1.** nobleness of manner or style; stateliness. **2.** nobleness of mind; worthiness. **3.** high rank or title. **4.** degree of excellence or rank. **5.** sense of self-importance or self-respect. [L: worthiness, rank]

digraph /ˈdaɪgræf, -graf/, *n.* a pair of letters representing a single speech sound, as *ea* in *meat*.

digress /daɪˈgrɛs/, *v.i.* to wander away from the main subject in speaking or writing. [L: having departed] —**digression**, *n.* —**digressive**, *adj.*

dihedral /daɪˈhidrəl/, *adj. Maths.* **1.** having, or formed by, two planes: *a dihedral angle.* **2.** relating to or having a dihedral angle or angles. **3.** (of an aircraft) having the wings sloping, esp. upwards. See **anhedral**. ◇*n.* **4.** Also, **dihedral angle, dihedron**. *Maths.* an angle made by two planes which intersect. **5.** *Aeron.* the slope, esp. upwards, of the wings of an aeroplane. [DI-[1] + Gk *hédra* seat, base + -AL[1]]

dike /daɪk/, *n.* → **dyke**[1].

dilapidated /dəˈlæpədeɪtəd/, *adj.* fallen into a state of ruin, decay or disrepair. —**dilapidation**, *n.*

dilate /daɪˈleɪt, də-/, *v.*, **-lated, -lating**. ◇*v.t.* **1.** to make (something) wider or larger. ◇*v.i.* **2.** to become wider or larger; expand: *Her pupils dilated.* **3.** to speak at length (sometimes fol. by *upon* or *on*) [L: spread out] —**dilation, dilatation**, *n.* —**dilator**, *n.*

dilatory /ˈdɪlətri, -təri/, *adj.* **1.** tending to delay; slow; tardy: *a dilatory person.* **2.** intended to bring about delay: *a dilatory strategy.* [L: delayer] —**dilatoriness**, *n.*

dilemma /dəˈlɛmə, daɪ-/, *n.* **1.** a situation in which a choice must be made between equally undesirable alternatives. **2.** any very difficult problem. [LL, from Gk: double proposition] —**dilemmatic**, *adj.*

dilettante /ˌdɪləˈtænti, ˈdɪlətænt/, *n.*, *pl.* **-ti** /-ti/, **-tes**, *adj.* ◇*n.* **1.** someone who takes an interest in an art or science for amusement only; dabbler. **2.** a lover of the fine arts. ◇*adj.* **3.** of or relating to dilettantes. [It, from L: delight]

Dili /'dɪli/, *n.* a seaport in Indonesia; capital of East Timor, in the northern part. Pop. 6730 (1970).

diligent /'dɪlədʒənt/, *adj.* **1.** constant and careful in doing something: *He's a diligent worker.* **2.** done with careful attention; painstaking: *diligent work.* [ME, from L: choosing, liking] **—diligence,** *n.*

dill[1] /dɪl/, *n.* **1.** a plant bearing a seedlike fruit used in medicine and cooking. **2.** its seeds or leaves. [OE *dile-*]

dill[2] /dɪl/, *n. Colloq.* a fool. Also, **dillpot.**

dillybag /'dɪlibæg/, *n.* **1.** any small bag for carrying food or personal belongings. **2.** a bag of twisted grass or fibre used by Aborigines. Also, **dilly.** [Aboriginal *dilly* + BAG]

dillydally /'dɪlidæli/, *v.i.*, **-dallied, -dallying.** to waste time, esp. by indecision; loiter. [from DALLY]

dilute /daɪ'lut, -'ljut/, *v.*, **-luted, -luting,** *adj.* ◇*v.t.* **1.** to make thinner or weaker by the addition of water, etc. ◇*adj.* **2.** reduced in strength, as a chemical with water added; weak: *a dilute solution.* [L: washed to pieces, dissolved, diluted]

dilution /daɪ'luʃən/, *n.* **1.** the act of diluting. **2.** something diluted. **3.** *Chem.* the volume of solvent (usu. in litres) in which a unit quantity (usu. a gram-molecule) of solute is dissolved.

diluvial /daɪ'luviəl, də-/, *adj.* **1.** relating to a flood, esp. that described in Genesis. **2.** *Geol.* relating to or consisting of diluvium. Also, **diluvian.** [L]

diluvium /daɪ'luviəm, də-/, *n., pl.* **-via** /-viə/. a coarse surface deposit formerly thought to be the result of a general flood but now regarded as glacial drift. [L: deluge]

dim /dɪm/, *adj.*, **dimmer, dimmest,** *v.*, **dimmed, dimming.** ◇*adj.* **1.** not bright; lacking in light: *a dim room.* **2.** not clearly seen or heard; indistinct: *a dim object.* **3.** not clear to the mind; vague: *a dim idea.* **4.** not brilliant; dull: *a dim color.* **5.** not seeing clearly: *eyes dim with tears.* **6.** disapproving: *to take a dim view of something.* **7.** *Colloq.* (of a person), lacking in understanding; stupid. ◇*v.t., v.i.* **8.** to make or become dim. [OE *dim(m)*] **—dimness,** *n.*

dim., *Abbrev.* **1.** diminuendo. **2.** diminutive. Also, **dimin.**

Dimboola /dɪm'bulə/, *n.* a town and shire in central eastern Vic.; salt refining and general pastoral area. Pop. 1514 (1986). [Singhalese *dimula* land of figs]

dime /daɪm/, *n. US.* a silver coin with a value of ten cents. [ME, from OF, from L: tenth part, tithe]

dimension /də'mɛnʃən/, *n.* **1.** size measured in a particular direction. **2.** (*usu. pl.*) measurement; extent; scope: *a room dimension*; *a problem of huge dimensions.* **3.** aspect: *The discussion took on a new dimension.* **4.** *Maths.* the number of coordinates needed to represent the points on a line, shape or solid. [L: a measuring] **—dimensional,** *adj.*

dimer /'daɪmə/, *n.* a substance made of molecules formed from two molecules of a monomer, e.g. a disaccharide.

diminish /də'mɪnɪʃ/, *v.t.* **1.** to make smaller; lessen; reduce. **2.** to reduce in importance, authority, etc.; disparage. ◇*v.i.* **3.** to become less; decrease.

diminished responsibility, *n. Law.* limitation of a person's criminal responsibility in killing another on the ground of mental weakness or abnormality.

diminishing returns, *n. pl.* the theory that constant increases in production will result, after a certain point, in smaller and smaller increases in output, profit, etc.

diminuendo /də,mɪnju'ɛndoʊ/, *adv. Music.* gradually reducing in force or loudness; descrescendo. [It]

diminutive /də'mɪnjətɪv/, *adj.* **1.** small; tiny: *a diminutive house.* **2.** *Gram.* relating to a form denoting smallness, familiarity, etc., as the suffix *-let* in *droplet.* ◇*n.* **3.** *Gram.* (a word formed with) a diminutive suffix. [ME, from L: lessened]

dimmer /'dɪmə/, *n.* a device by which the strength of lighting is varied.

dimorphism /daɪ'mɔfɪzəm/, *n.* **1.** *Zool.* the appearance of two forms separate in structure, coloration, etc., among animals of the same species. **2.** *Bot.* an appearance of two different forms of flowers, leaves, etc., on the same plant. **3.** *Chem.* the property of some substances that enables them to exist in two chemically identical but crystallographically distinct forms. **—dimorphous, dimorphic,** *adj.*

dimple /'dɪmpəl/, *n., v.*, **-pled, -pling.** ◇*n.* **1.** a small natural hollow on the human body, esp. one formed in the cheek by smiling. ◇*v.i., v.t.* **2.** to form dimples (in). [ME, related to MHG: pool]

dim sim /dɪm 'sɪm/, *n.* a food of Chinese origin, made of meat wrapped in thin dough and steamed or fried. [? Cantonese *tim-sam* snack]

dimwit /'dɪmwɪt/, *n. Colloq.* a stupid or slow-thinking person. **—dimwitted,** *adj.*

din /dɪn/, *n., v.*, **dinned, dinning.** ◇*n.* **1.** a loud, continued and confused noise. ◇*v.t.* **2.** to sound or utter with noisy repetition. ◇*v.i.* **3.** to make a din. [OE *dyne, dynn*]

dine /daɪn/, *v.i.*, **dined, dining.** to eat the main meal of the day; have dinner.

diner /'daɪnə/, *n.* **1.** one who dines. **2.** a restaurant car on a train. **3.** a cafeteria or small, cheap restaurant.

ding /dɪŋ/, *v.i.* **1.** to strike or beat. **2.** to sound, as a bell; ring, esp. repeatedly. ◇*v.t.* **3.** to cause to ring, as by striking. **4.** *Colloq.* to smash; damage. ◇*n.* **5.** a blow or stroke. **6.** the sound of bell, etc. **7.** *Colloq.* a minor accident with a car, bike, etc. **8.** *Colloq.* an argument. [imitative]

dingbat /'dɪŋbæt/, *n. Colloq.* **1.** a stupid or peculiar person. **2. the dingbats,** a fit of madness or rage.

ding-dong /'dɪŋ-dɒŋ/, *n.* **1.** the sound of a bell. **2.** a loud and heated argument. ◇*adj.* **3.** *Colloq.* hard fought: *a ding-dong contest*; *a ding-dong argument*. [imitative]

dinghy /'dɪŋi/, *n., pl.* **-ghies. 1.** a small rowing or sailing boat, esp. one that belongs to a ship. **2.** an inflatable rubber boat carried by aircraft for use in emergency. [Hind]

dingo /'dɪŋgoʊ/, *n., pl.* **-goes, gos,** *v.* ◇*n.* **1.** an Australian wild dog, introduced by the Aborigines, oft. brownish-yellow in color, with pointed ears, bushy tail, and with a call more like a howl or yelp than a bark. **2.** a worthless person; coward. ◇*v.i.* **3.** to act in a cowardly manner. ◇*v.* **4. dingo on (someone),** to be disloyal to (someone); betray. [Aboriginal]

dingy /'dɪndʒi/, *adj.,* **-gier, -giest.** of a dark, dull, or dirty color; lacking brightness or freshness; shabby; disreputable. [orig. uncert.] —**dinginess,** *n.*

dink /dɪŋk/, *v.t. Colloq.* →**double** (def. 17).

dinkum /'dɪŋkəm/, *Colloq.* ◇*adj.* **1.** Also, **dinky-di.** true; honest; genuine: *dinkum Aussie.* ◇*adv.* **2.** truly. See **fair dinkum.** [Brit d.]

dinky /'dɪŋki/, *n.* a small tricycle. [Brit d.]

dinner /'dɪnə/, *n.* **1.** the main meal of the day, taken either about noon or in the evening. **2.** a formal meal in honor of some person or occasion. [ME, from F]

dinosaur /'daɪnəsɔː/, *n.* any of various extinct reptiles, many of which were very large. [NL: terrible lizard]

dint /dɪnt/, *n.* **1.** force; power: *by dint of argument.* **2.** a dent. ◇*v.t.* **3.** to make a dint in. [OE *dynt*]

diocese /'daɪəsəs/, *n., pl.* **dioceses** /'daɪəsəsəz, 'daɪəsiːz/. a district, with its population, that comes under the care of a bishop. [ME, from OF, from L: district, from Gk: housekeeping, administration, province]

Diocletian /daɪə'kliːʃən/, *n.* AD 245-313, Roman emperor, AD 284-305.

diode /'daɪoʊd/, *n.* →**valve** (def. 5). [DI-¹ + -ODE²]

dioecious /daɪ'iːʃəs/, *adj.* (esp. of plants) having the male and female organs in separate individuals. [NL, from Gk]

Diogenes /daɪ'ɒdʒəniːz/, *n.* c. 412-c. 323 BC, Greek philosopher.

Dionysia /daɪə'nɪziə/, *n.pl.* (in ancient Greece) the drama festivals in honor of Dionysus, out of which Greek comedy and tragedy developed. [L, from Gk]

dionysian /daɪə'nɪsiən, -'nɪz-/, *adj.* wild; orgiastic. [named after DIONYSUS]

Dionysius Exiguus /daɪə,nɪsiəs ɛg'zɪgjuəs/, *n.* fl. AD 530, Scythian monk and scholar; believed to have founded the system of reckoning dates as before or after the birth of Christ.

Dionysus /daɪə'naɪsəs/, *n. Gk Myth.* the youthful and beautiful god of wine and the drama; Roman counterpart, Bacchus. Also, **Dionyso.**

dioptre /daɪ'ɒptə/, *n.* the unit of power of a lens. [L, from Gk: kind of levelling instrument]

dioxide /daɪ'ɒksaɪd/, *n.* an oxide containing two atoms of oxygen per molecule, as *manganese dioxide,* MnO_2. [DI-¹ + OXIDE]

dip /dɪp/, *v.,* **dipped, dipping,** *n.* ◇*v.t.* **1.** to put into a liquid for a short time. **2.** to raise or take up (liquid) by repeatedly filling a small container: *to dip water out of a boat.* **3.** to lower and raise: *to dip a flag in salute.* **4.** to dip (sheep, etc.) in a disinfectant solution in order to kill mites, etc., in their wool. **5.** to direct (motor-car headlights) downwards. ◇*v.i.* **6.** to plunge into a liquid and come out quickly. **7.** to put a hand, container, etc., into something in order to remove an object: *She dipped in her bag for a hanky; They dipped into their savings.* **8.** to sink or drop down. **9.** to slope downwards. ◇*v.* **10. dip into, a.** to study (a subject) without serious interest. **b.** to read here and there in (a book). **11. dip out,** *Colloq.* **a.** to choose to miss out; avoid (fol. by *on*): *I'll dip out on this round.* **b.** to miss out; fail: *He dipped out at exam time.* ◇*n.* **12.** the act of dipping. **13.** something which is taken up by dipping. **14.** a liquid into which something is dipped. **15.** →**sheep dip. 16.** a momentary lowering; a sinking down. **17.** a soft savory mixture into which biscuits, etc., are dipped before being eaten. **18.** a downward slope. **19.** a hollow in the land. **20.** *Geol., Mining.* the downward slope of a stratum, vein, fault, joint, etc., in relation to a horizontal plane. **21.** *Survey.* the angular amount by which the horizon lies below the level of the eye. **22.** the angle which a freely swinging magnetic needle makes with the plane of the horizon. **23.** *Colloq.* a short swim. **24.** a candle made by dipping a wick into melted wax. [OE *dyppan*; akin to DEEP]

dip., *Abbrev.* diploma.

diphtheria /dɪf'θɪəriə/, *n.* an infectious disease marked by high fever and the formation of a false membrane in the air passages, esp. in the throat. [NL, from Gk *diphthéra* skin, leather + -ia, -IA]

diphthong /'dɪfθɒŋ/, *n.* **1.** a speech sound consisting of a glide from one vowel to another within one syllable, as *ei* in *vein.* **2.** →**digraph. 3.** a combination of two letters representing a vowel, as æ or œ. [LL, from Gk: having two sounds] —**diphthongal,** *adj.*

diploid /'dɪplɔɪd/, *Biol.* ◇*adj.* **1.** having two similar sets of chromosomes. ◇*n.* **2.** an organism or cell with chromosomes that have paired in preparation for cell-division. See **haploid.**

diploma /də'ploʊmə/, *n., pl.* **-mas.** a document stating success in an examination or some other educational qualification, usu. at a lower level or in a more specialised subject than a degree. [L, from Gk: paper folded double, letter of recommendation, licence, etc.]

diplomacy /də'ploʊməsi/, *n., pl.* **-cies. 1.** the conducting by government officials of relations between states. **2.** the science of

diplomacy   289   **dirge**

conducting such relations. **3.** skill in managing relations between people; tact. [F] —**diplomat, diplomatist,** *n.* —**diplomatic,** *adj.*

diplomatic corps /ˌdɪpləˈmætɪk kɔː/, *n.* a body of diplomats officially attached to a state or capital. Also, **diplomatic body.**

diplomatic immunity, *n.* the freedom from local court action, taxation, etc., which is the right of official representatives of a foreign state.

diplosis /dəˈplousəs/, *n. Biol.* the doubling of the chromosome number by the union of the haploid sets during the fusion of gametes. [Gk: a doubling]

dipole /ˈdaɪpoul/, *n.* **1.** a pair of equal and opposite electric charges or magnetic poles, forces, etc., as on the surfaces of a body or in a molecule. **2.** a molecule where the centres of positive and negative charges are separated. —**dipolar,** *adj.*

dipole moment, *n.* a physical quantity which determines the moment or rotation of a dipole when placed in an electric or magnetic field.

dipper /ˈdɪpə/, *n.* a container with a handle, used for taking up liquids.

dipsomania /ˌdɪpsəˈmeɪniə/, *n.* an irresistible desire for alcoholic drink. [NL, from Gk *dípso(s)* thirst + *manía* MANIA] —**dipsomaniac,** *n.*

dipterous /ˈdɪptərəs/, *adj.* **1.** *Entomol.* belonging or relating to an order of insects, including the common houseflies, gnats, mosquitoes, etc., which have a single pair of membranous wings. **2.** *Bot.* (of seeds, stems, etc.) having two winglike appendages. Also, **dipteral.** [NL *dipterus* two-winged, from Gk *dípteros*]

diptych /ˈdɪptɪk/, *n.* **1.** a hinged two-leaved writing tablet used in the ancient world. **2.** a pair of pictures on two panels hinged together. [LL: double-folded, from Gk]

dire /daɪə/, *adj.,* **direr, direst. 1.** causing great fear or suffering; dreadful. **2. in dire straits,** in great difficulty or danger. [L]

direct /dəˈrɛkt, daɪ-/, *v.t.* **1.** to guide; conduct; manage. **2.** to give instructions to; command; order: *I directed him to do it.* **3.** to tell or show (a person) the way to a place, etc. **4.** to organise and control the production of a play or film. **5.** to point or aim towards a place or object. **6.** to address (words, a letter, etc.) to a person. ◊*v.i.* **7.** to act as a guide or director. **8.** to give commands or orders. ◊*adj.* **9.** going in a straight line or by the shortest course; straight: *a direct route.* **10.** in an unbroken line of descent; lineal. **11.** without anything or anyone in between; immediate. **12.** going straight to the point; straightforward: *a direct insult.* **13.** (of opposites, contrasts, etc.) complete; exact. **14.** *Gram.* (of a quotation or speech) consisting exactly of the words originally used (opposed to *reported*). **15.** *Elect.* of or relating to direct current. ◊*adv.* **16.** in a direct manner. [ME, from L] —**directness,** *n.*

direct action, *n.* any method of using the strength of organised workers or any other large group directly against employers or government, as by strikes, working strictly to rule, etc., rather than negotiations.

direct current, *n. Elect.* a relatively steady current in one direction in a circuit. Also, **DC, d.c.** See **alternating current.**

direct evidence, *n. Law.* evidence of a fact or transaction perceived by a witness at first hand. See **circumstantial evidence.**

direction /dəˈrɛkʃən, daɪ-/, *n.* **1.** the act of directing, pointing, aiming, etc. **2.** the line along which anything lies, faces, moves, etc., towards a certain point or area. **3.** the point or area itself. **4.** a line of action, tendency, etc. **5.** guidance; instruction; management. **6.** an order; command. **7.** a name and address on a letter, etc. **8.** the decisions of the director in a stage or film production.

directional /dəˈrɛkʃənəl, daɪ-/, *adj.* **1.** of or relating to direction in space. **2.** *Radio.* able to be used for determining the direction of signals received, or for sending signals in a particular direction: *a directional antenna.*

direction-finder /dəˈrɛkʃən-faɪndə/, *n.* a device on a radio receiver which determines the direction of incoming radio waves.

directive /dəˈrɛktɪv, daɪ-/, *adj.* **1.** serving to direct. ◊*n.* **2.** an instruction or order.

directly /dəˈrɛktli, daɪ-/, *adv.* **1.** in a direct line, way, or manner. **2.** without delay; immediately. **3.** exactly; precisely. ◊*conj.* **4.** as soon as: *Directly he arrived, he mentioned the subject.*

direct object, *n.* (in English and some other languages) a word denoting the person or thing towards which the action of a transitive verb is directed. For example: *He hit the horse* has *the horse* as the direct object.

director /dəˈrɛktə, daɪ-/, *n.* **1.** someone who directs. **2.** *Comm.* one of a group of people chosen to control or govern the affairs of a company or corporation. **3.** a person in charge of the production of a play or film. —**directorship,** *n.*

directory /dəˈrɛktəri, -tri/, *n., pl.* **-ries,** *adj.* ◊*n.* **1.** a book containing an alphabetical list of names and addresses, maps, subject headings, etc.: *a telephone directory; a directory.* **2.** (*cap.*) *French Hist.* **the Directory.** Also, **Directoire** /dɪrɛkˈtwɑː/. the body of five directors forming the executive of France from 1795 to 1799. ◊*adj.* **3.** serving to direct. [L: that directs]

directrix /dəˈrɛktrɪks/, *n., pl.* **-trices** /-trəsiːz/. *Maths.* a fixed line used in the description of certain curves or surfaces. [NL]

direct speech, *n.* (in writing) the recording of speech giving the exact words used. See **reported speech.**

direct tax, *n.* a compulsory government tax levied directly on the people who will pay it, e.g. income tax. See **indirect tax.**

dirge /dɜːdʒ/, *n.* a funeral song or tune, or one expressing grief. [L: direct, first word of the antiphon sung in the L office of the dead]

dirigible /ˈdɪrɪdʒəbəl, dəˈrɪdʒəbəl/, n. 1. → **airship**. ◇adj. 2. that may be directed or steered. [L: direct + -IBLE]

dirk /dɜk/, n. a short dagger, esp. as used in the Scottish Highlands. [orig. uncert.]

Dirk Hartog Island /dɜk ˈhatɒg/, n. a long narrow island in the Indian Ocean off the coast of WA at the entrance to Shark Bay. 77 km long.

dirt /dɜt/, n. 1. earth or soil, esp. when loose. 2. any unclean substance, as excrement, mud, etc. 3. something nasty, mean, or worthless. 4. bad language. 5. unpleasant gossip. 6. *Mining*. crude broken ore or waste. ◇adj. 7. made of dirt: *a dirt road*. [ME *drit*, from Scand]

dirty /ˈdɜti/, adj., **dirtier, dirtiest**, v., **dirtied, dirtying**, n., adv. ◇adj. 1. covered with dirt; unclean. 2. nasty; mean. 3. morally unclean; indecent. 4. *Sport*. marked by rough, unfair play: *a dirty fight*. 5. (of nuclear devices) producing unwanted radioactive waste products. 6. stormy, as the weather. 7. appearing to be unclean; dingy: *dirty green color*. 8. *Colloq*. angry: *a dirty look*. ◇v.t., v.i. 9. to make or become dirty. ◇n. 10. **do the dirty on**, *Colloq*. to behave unfairly or wrongly towards. ◇adv. 11. *Colloq*. very; extremely: *a dirty great lie*. – **dirtiness**, n.

dis-¹, a prefix meaning 'apart', 'away', or having negative or reversing force (See **de-** and **un-²**), as in *disability, disbelief, dishearten, disinfect, disown*. Also, **di-**. [L]

dis-², a variant of **di-¹**, as in *dissyllable*.

Dis /dɪs/, n. *Rom Myth*. the god of the lower world; Pluto.

disability /dɪsəˈbɪləti/, n., pl. **-ties**. 1. a lack of power, strength, or physical or mental ability; incapacity. 2. anything which disables, as an illness.

disable /dɪsˈeɪbəl/, v.t., **-bled, -bling**. 1. to make unable; cripple; incapacitate. 2. to make legally unable. – **disablement**, n.

disabuse /dɪsəˈbjuz/, v.t., **-bused, -busing**. to free from deception or mistake.

disaccharide /daɪˈsækəraɪd/, n. any of a group of carbohydrates whose molecules each consist of two bonded monosaccharides, e.g. sucrose.

disadvantage /dɪsədˈvæntɪdʒ/, n., v., **-taged, -taging**. ◇n. 1. an unfavorable situation or condition; handicap. 2. harm to interest, character, profit, etc. ◇v.t. 3. to place under a disadvantage. – **disadvantageous**, adj.

disadvantaged /dɪsədˈvæntɪdʒd/, adj. 1. low in social or economic rank or background: *a disadvantaged area*. 2. lacking a reasonable standard of living, education, etc.

disaffect /dɪsəˈfɛkt/, v.t. to lose the affection of; make discontented or disloyal. – **disaffection**, n.

disagree /dɪsəˈgri/, v.i., **-greed, -greeing**. 1. to fail to agree; differ (fol. by *with*): *The conclusions disagree with the facts*. 2. to have different opinions; dissent. 3. to quarrel. 4. to have a bad effect: *That food disagrees with me*. – **disagreement**, n.

disagreeable /dɪsəˈgriəbəl/, adj. 1. not to one's taste or liking; unpleasant. 2. unpleasant in manner or nature; unfriendly. – **disagreeableness**, n.

disallow /dɪsəˈlaʊ/, v.t. 1. to refuse to allow. 2. to refuse to admit the truth or legality of. – **disallowance**, n.

disappear /dɪsəˈpɪə/, v.i. 1. to cease to appear or be seen: *My pen has disappeared*. 2. to cease to exist or be known: *Her anxiety disappeared when she saw him*. – **disappearance**, n.

disappoint /dɪsəˈpɔɪnt/, v.t. 1. to fail to satisfy the expectations or wishes of (a person): *His behavior disappointed us*. 2. to defeat (hopes, plans, etc.); thwart; frustrate. [OF] – **disappointment**, n.

disapprobation /ˌdɪsæprəˈbeɪʃən/, n. disapproval; censure.

disapprove /dɪsəˈpruv/, v., **-proved, -proving**. ◇v.t. 1. to refuse to approve. ◇v.i. 2. to have an unfavorable opinion (fol. by *of*): *She disapproved of their behavior*. – **disapproval**, n. – **disapprovingly**, adv.

disarm /dɪsˈam/, v.t. 1. to remove weapons or other means of attack from. 2. to take away the anger, suspicion, etc., of; make friendly: *Her smile disarmed him*. ◇v.i. 3. to reduce the size of armed forces, weapon supplies, etc. [OF] – **disarmament**, n.

disarming /dɪsˈamɪŋ/, adj. removing or likely to remove anger, suspicion, etc.; winning: *a disarming smile*.

disarray /dɪsəˈreɪ/, v.t. 1. to put out of order; disorder. ◇n. 2. disorder; confusion. 3. disorderly dress.

disassemble /dɪsəˈsɛmbəl/, v.t., **-bled, -bling**. to take apart. – **disassembly**, n.

disassociate /dɪsəˈsoʊʃieɪt, -siˌeɪt/, v.t., **-ated, -ating**. → **dissociate**. – **disassociation**, n.

disaster /dəˈzastə/, n. 1. any sudden or great misfortune; calamity. 2. *Colloq*. a total failure, as a person, machine, plan, etc.: *The new dishwasher has been a complete disaster*. [It: not having a (lucky) star] – **disastrous**, adj.

disavow /dɪsəˈvaʊ/, v.t. to refuse to admit knowledge of, connection with, or responsibility for. [ME, from OF] – **disavowal**, n.

disband /dɪsˈbænd/, v.t., v.i. to break up (a band, company, military force, etc.). [MF] – **disbandment**, n.

disbar /dɪsˈba/, v.t., **-barred, -barring**. to remove the right to practise law from (a lawyer). – **disbarment**, n.

disbelieve /dɪsbəˈliv/, v., **-lieved, -lieving**. ◇v.t. 1. to refuse to believe: *I disbelieve your statement*. ◇v.i. 2. to have no faith (fol. by *in*): *I disbelieve in man-made solutions*. – **disbelief**, n.

disburse /dɪsˈbɜs/, v.t., **-bursed, -bursing**. to pay out (money); expend. [OF *des-* DIS.¹ + *bourse* purse (from LL)] – **disbursement**, n.

disc /dɪsk/, *n.* **1.** any thin, flat, circular plate or object. **2.** *Computers.* →**disk. 3.** a gramophone record. **4.** *Bot., Zool., etc.* any of various roundish, flat structures or parts, as a plate of tissue between parts of a flower. **5.** *Anat., Zool.* **a. interarticular disc,** a plate of cartilage between joints of the body. **b. intervertebral disc,** a plate of cartilage between vertebrae. [L *discus* DISCUS]

discard /dɪsˈkad/, *v.*; /ˈdɪskad/, *n.* ◇*v.t.* **1.** to throw aside; cease to use. **2.** *Cards.* to throw out or play (an unwanted card or cards). ◇*v.i.* **3.** *Cards.* to discard a card or cards. ◇*n.* **4.** the act of discarding. **5.** someone or something that is discarded.

disc brake, *n.* a brake, commonly used on the road wheels of motor vehicles and the landing wheels of aircraft, in which pads rub on a flat disc joined on to the rotating part to be slowed down.

discern /dəˈsɜn/, *v.t.* **1.** to see, recognise, or understand clearly. **2.** to recognise as separate or different; discriminate: *He can discern good from bad.* [ME, from F, from L: separate, set apart] —**discernible,** *adj.* —**discernment,** *n.*

discerning /dəˈsɜnɪŋ/, *adj.* having good powers of discernment, esp. in matters of taste; discriminating: *a discerning critic.*

discharge /dɪsˈtʃadʒ/, *v.*, **-charged, -charging;** /ˈdɪstʃadʒ/, *n.* ◇*v.t.* **1.** to unload (a ship, etc.). **2.** to fire; shoot: *to discharge a gun.* **3.** to give out; emit: *The pipe discharged water.* **4.** to fulfil or perform (a duty, responsibility, etc.). **5.** to dismiss from office, employment, service, etc. **6.** to send away or allow to go (fol. by *from*). **7.** to pay (a debt). **8.** *Law.* **a.** to terminate (an obligation): *to discharge a debt by payment.* **b.** to release (someone) from an obligation. **9.** *Elect.* to rid (something) of a charge of electricity: *A short circuit may discharge a battery.* ◇*v.i.* **10.** to get rid of a charge or load. **11.** to give out liquid, etc.: *The wound was discharging.* **12.** to go off; explode: *The gun discharged.* **13.** *Elect.* to lose, or give up, a charge of electricity. ◇*n.* **14.** the act of discharging a ship, load, etc. **15.** the act of firing a weapon. **16.** a sending or coming out, as of water from a pipe; emission. **17.** something discharged. **18.** *Law.* **a.** the freeing of someone held by police or in prison. **b.** the termination of an obligation. **19.** the payment of a debt. **20.** dismissal from office, employment, service, etc. **21.** a certificate of release, as from service, responsibility, etc. **22.** *Elect.* **a.** the withdrawing or transferring of an electric charge. **b.** the equalisation of potential difference between two terminals, etc. [ME, from OF]

disc harrow, *n.* a harrow with a number of sharp-edged discs that break up and turn the soil and destroy weeds as the machine is drawn along. Also, **disc plough.**

disciple /dəˈsaɪpəl/, *n.* **1.** any follower of Christ, esp. one of the first 12. **2.** a follower of any set of ideas. [ME, from OF, from L] —**discipleship,** *n.*

disciplinarian /ˌdɪsəpləˈnɛəriən/, *n.* **1.** someone who believes in or uses strict discipline. ◇*adj.* **2.** using punishment to control.

discipline /ˈdɪsəplən/, *n., v.*, **-plined, -plining.** ◇*n.* **1.** training designed to teach proper conduct or behavior in accordance with rules. **2.** punishment given to correct and train. **3.** the training effect of experience, trouble, etc.: *The army will be good discipline for him.* **4.** a state of order kept by training and control: *to keep good discipline in an army.* **5.** a set or system of rules. **6.** a branch of learning: *the discipline of mathematics.* ◇*v.t.* **7.** to bring to a state of order and obedience by training and control. **8.** to punish; correct; chastise: *I shall have to discipline him severely.* [ME, from L: instruction] —**discipliner,** *n.* —**disciplinary,** *adj.*

disc jockey, *n.* someone who presents radio programs of recorded music.

disclaim /dɪsˈkleɪm/, *v.t.* **1.** to claim no interest in or connection with; disavow; disown: *She will disclaim all knowledge.* **2.** *Law.* to give up a claim or right to. [AF *des-* DIS-[1] + *clamer* CLAIM]

disclaimer /dɪsˈkleɪmə/, *n.* **1.** the act of disclaiming; repudiation or denial of a claim. **2.** someone who disclaims. **3.** a clause or document disclaiming something, as in a contract, etc.

disclimax /dɪsˈklaɪmæks/, *n. Geog.* a previously stable plant community which has been made unstable by some new factor, e.g. grassland put under pasture. Also, **plagioclimax.**

disclose /dəsˈkloʊz/, *v.t.*, **-closed, -closing. 1.** to allow to be seen or known; reveal: *He may disclose the plan.* **2.** to uncover. [ME, from OF from L: close] —**disclosure,** *n.*

disco /ˈdɪskoʊ/, *n.* **1.** →**discotheque.** ◇*adj.* **2.** of or relating to music written for use in discotheques.

discolor or **discolour** /dɪsˈkʌlə/, *v.t.* **1.** to change or spoil the color of; stain. ◇*v.i.* **2.** to change color; become faded or stained. —**discoloration,** *n.*

discomfit /dɪsˈkʌmfət/, *v.t.* **1.** to throw into confusion and unease; disconcert. **2.** to upset the plans of; thwart; foil. **3.** *Archaic.* to defeat completely; rout. [ME, from OF *des-* DIS-[1] + *confire* make, accomplish (from L)] —**discomfiture,** *n.*

discomfort /dɪsˈkʌmfət/, *n.* **1.** the absence of comfort or pleasure; uneasiness; pain. ◇*v.t.* **2.** to disturb the comfort or happiness of. [ME, from OF]

discompose /ˌdɪskəmˈpoʊz/, *v.t.*, **-posed, -posing. 1.** to bring into disorder; unsettle. **2.** to disturb the calm of; agitate; perturb. —**discomposure,** *n.*

disconcert /ˌdɪskənˈsɜt/, *v.t.* **1.** to upset the self-possession of; confuse; perturb. **2.** to throw into disorder or confusion. —**disconcerting,** *adj.* —**disconcerted,** *adj.*

disconformity /ˌdɪskənˈfɔməti/, *n., pl.* **-ties.** *Geol.* the surface between two nearly

disconformity

horizontal layers of rock representing a long time-period between the laying-down of the lower and upper beds.

disconnect /dɪskəˈnɛkt/, *v.t.* to break the connection of or between; detach. —**disconnection**, *n*.

disconnected /ˌdɪskəˈnɛktəd/, *adj.* 1. not connected; disjointed; broken. 2. not making sense; incoherent. —**disconnectedness**, *n*.

disconsolate /dɪsˈkɒnsələt/, *adj.* unable to be comforted in trouble; inconsolable. [ML]

discontent /ˌdɪskənˈtɛnt/, *adj.* 1. Also, **discontented**. not content; dissatisfied. ◇*n*. 2. Also, **discontentment**. lack of contentment; dissatisfaction. ◇*v.t.* 3. to cause to lose contentment; dissatisfy; displease.

discontinue /ˌdɪskənˈtɪnju/, *v.*, **-tinued, -tinuing**. ◇*v.t.* 1. to cause to finish. 2. to stop taking, using, etc.: *to discontinue a newspaper.* ◇*v.i.* 3. to come to an end or stop; cease; desist. —**discontinuer**, *n*. —**discontinuation, discontinuity**, *n*.

discontinuous /ˌdɪskənˈtɪnjuəs/, *adj.* not continuous; broken; interrupted; intermittent.

discord /ˈdɪskɔd/, *n*. 1. a lack of agreement between persons or things. 2. (in music) a combination of musical notes sounded together, which is not pleasant to the ear. 3. any confused or unpleasant noise; dissonance. [ME, from OF, from L: be at variance] —**discordance**, *n*. —**discordant**, *adj*.

discotheque /ˈdɪskətɛk/, *n*. a place or club in which people dance, esp. to recorded music. Also, **discothèque, disco**. [F]

discount /ˈdɪskaʊnt/ for defs 1-3, /dɪsˈkaʊnt/ for def 4, *v.*; /ˈdɪskaʊnt/, *n*., *adj*. ◇*v.t.* 1. to make a reduction of: *He discounted 3% off the price.* 2. to sell (goods) at a discount. 3. to buy or sell (a bill or note) before maturity, at a reduction based on the interest for the time it still has to run. 4. to leave out of account; disregard. ◇*n*. 5. an amount taken off for quick payment or other special reason: *They give a 3% discount here.* 6. any deduction from the normal value. 7. **at a discount**, *Comm*. below par. ◇*adj.* 8. giving or having a discount: *a discount store; a discount price*. [OF *des-* DIS.[1] + *conter* COUNT[1]] —**discountable**, *adj*.

discourage /dɪsˈkʌrɪdʒ/, *v.t.*, **-raged, -raging.** 1. to cause to lose courage; dishearten; dispirit. 2. to persuade (someone) to turn aside (fol. by *from*): *He will discourage her from attempting the climb.* 3. to stop by opposition or difficulty; hinder: *Low prices discourage industry.* 4. to express disapproval of: *They are silly to discourage new ideas*. [OF] —**discouragement**, *n*. —**discouragingly**, *adv*.

discourse /ˈdɪskɔs, dɪsˈkɔs/, *n*.; /dɪsˈkɔs/, *v.*, **-coursed, -coursing**. ◇*n*. 1. a sharing of thought by words; talk; conversation. 2. a formal discussion of a subject in speech or writing. ◇*v.i.* 3. to take part in talking; converse. 4. to discuss a subject formally in speech or writing. [ME, from F, from L]

discourteous /dɪsˈkɜtiəs/, *adj.* lacking politeness; impolite; uncivil; rude. —**discourteousness, discourtesy**, *n*.

discover /dɪsˈkʌvə/, *v.t.* to get knowledge of, learn of, or find out, esp. for the first time. [ME, from OF *des-* DIS.[1] + *covrir* COVER] —**discovery**, *n*. —**discoverer**, *n*.

Discovery Bay /dɪsˌkʌvri ˈbeɪ/, *n*. a large bay on the southern coast of Australia which straddles the border between Victoria and SA. 80 km wide.

discredit /dɪsˈkrɛdət/, *v.t.* 1. to lower the regard in which (a person) is held: *His drinking habits will discredit him.* 2. to show to be undeserving of belief; destroy confidence in: *The new findings discredit our early theories.* 3. to give no belief to; disbelieve: *They discredit the report.* ◇*n*. (something that leads to) loss or lack of belief or regard: *That behavior is to his discredit.* [DIS.[1] + CREDIT, *v*.] —**discreditable**, *adj*.

discreet /dəsˈkrit/, *adj.* 1. showing sound judgment in avoiding mistakes or faults; prudent; circumspect. 2. not given to careless talk; restrained. [ME, from OF, from L: separated]

discrepancy /dɪsˈkrɛpənsi/, *n*., *pl.* **-cies**. 1. the state of differing or disagreeing; difference; inconsistency: *There is discrepancy in the unemployment figures of the two departments.* 2. an example of this: *One discrepancy involves school leavers*. [OF, from L: dissimilarity] —**discrepant**, *adj*.

discrete /dɪsˈkrit/, *adj.* 1. separate from others; distinct. 2. having individual parts; discontinuous: *discrete data*. [L: separated]

discretion /dɪsˈkrɛʃən/, *n*. 1. the power or right of deciding or acting according to one's own judgment. 2. the quality of being discreet: *You can trust his discretion.* 3. **at one's discretion**, as one wishes or decides. —**discretionary**, *adj*.

discriminate /dəsˈkrɪmənɛɪt/, *v.*, **-nated, -nating**; /dəsˈkrɪmənət/, *adj*. ◇*v.i.* 1. to take an unfair or biased attitude (fol. by *against*): *The government discriminates against the poor.* 2. to note or observe a difference; distinguish: *I can discriminate between the twins.* ◇*v.t.* 3. to make or be a difference in or between; differentiate: *John's big ears discriminate him from his twin.* 4. to note as different; distinguish: *to discriminate the colors.* ◇*adj.* 5. able to see fine differences. [L: divided, distinguished] —**discriminator**, *n*.

discriminating /dəsˈkrɪmənɛɪtɪŋ/, *adj.* having skill in seeing and weighing differences, esp. in matters of taste: *a discriminating man*.

discrimination /dəsˌkrɪməˈneɪʃən/, *n*. 1. the act of discriminating. 2. the making of a difference in particular cases, as in favor of or against a person or thing: *discrimination against the poor.* 3. the power of making fine distinctions; discriminating judgment.

discriminatory /dəsˈkrɪmənətəri, -tri/, *adj.* showing prejudice or unfair preference for one person or group over another.

discursive /dɪsˈkɜsɪv/, *adj.* passing rapidly or irregularly from one subject to another;

discursive

rambling; digressive. **—discursiveness**, *n.* **—discursion**, *n.*

discus /ˈdɪskəs/, *n., pl.* **discuses, disci** /ˈdɪsaɪ/. a circular plate for throwing in athletic contests, used by the ancient Greeks and Romans and by modern athletes. [L, from Gk: discus, disc, DISC]

discuss /dəsˈkʌs/, *v.t.* to examine the considerations for and against by conversation; debate; talk over. [ME, from L: struck asunder] **—discussion**, *n.*

disdain /dɪsˈdeɪn/, *v.t.* **1.** to look down on or treat as lesser; despise; scorn. ◇*n.* **2.** a feeling of contempt for anything regarded as unworthy; scorn. [ME, from OF *des-* DIS-¹ + *deignier* DEIGN] **—disdainful**, *adj.*

disease /dəˈziz/, *n., v.,* **-seased, -seasing.** ◇*n.* **1.** a sick condition of a part or the whole of an organism. **2.** any situation which is not as it normally is, as of the mind, affairs, etc. ◇*v.t.* **3.** to affect with disease; make ill. [ME, from OF *des-* DIS-¹ + *aise* EASE]

diseconomy /dɪsəˈkɒnəmi/, *n.* **1.** the lack of economy; a faulty economy. **2. diseconomies of scale**, a situation where a manufacturer finds that any increase in capital outlay in plant and machinery results in higher costs per unit of production.

disembark /dɪsəmˈbɑk/, *v.t.* **1.** to unload (passengers) from a ship, aircraft, etc. ◇*v.i.* **2.** (of passengers) to leave a ship, aircraft, etc. **—disembarkation**, *n.*

disembodied /dɪsəmˈbɒdɪd/, *adj.* free of the body: *a disembodied spirit.*

disembowel /dɪsəmˈbaʊəl/, *v.t.,* **-elled, -elling.** to remove the intestines from; eviscerate. **—disembowelment**, *n.*

disenchant /dɪsənˈtʃænt/, *v.t.* to free from enchantment; disillusion. **—disenchantment**, *n.*

disengage /dɪsənˈgeɪdʒ/, *v.,* **-gaged, -gaging.** ◇*v.t.* **1.** to free (from attachment, duty, etc.): *to disengage a clutch.* **2.** to break off action with (an enemy). ◇*v.i.* **3.** to become disengaged; free oneself. **—disengagement**, *n.*

disentangle /dɪsənˈtæŋgəl/, *v.t.,* **-gled, -gling.** to free from knots, tangles, etc.; untangle; extricate (fol. by *from*). **—disentanglement**, *n.*

disestablishmentarian /ˌdɪsəsˌtæblɪʃmənˈtɛəriən/, *n.* someone who favors the separation of the church from the state. **—disestablishmentarianism**, *n.*

disfavor *or* **disfavour** /dɪsˈfeɪvə/, *n.* **1.** unfavorable regard; displeasure: *The government views tax avoiders with disfavor.* **2.** a lack of favor; the state of being regarded unfavorably: *in disfavor at the royal court.* ◇*v.t.* **3.** to regard or treat with disfavor.

disfigure /dɪsˈfɪgə/, *v.t.,* **-ured, -uring.** to spoil the appearance or beauty of; deform; deface. [ME, from OF] **—disfigurement**, *n.*

disfranchise /dɪsˈfræntʃaɪz/, *v.t.,* **-chised, -chising.** to take certain rights from (persons), esp. the right to vote. **—disfranchisement**, *n.*

dishonorable

disgorge /dɪsˈgɔdʒ/, *v.,* **-gorged, -gorging.** ◇*v.t.* **1.** to throw out from or as if from the throat: *He disgorged his meal; The train disgorged its passengers.* ◇*v.t.* **2.** to disgorge something. [ME, from OF]

disgrace /dəsˈgreɪs/, *n., v.,* **-graced, -gracing.** ◇*n.* **1.** the state of being in dishonor; ignominy; shame. **2.** a cause of shame or reproach; something which dishonors. **3.** the state of being out of favor. ◇*v.t.* **4.** to bring shame upon. [F, from It *disgrazia*] **—disgraceful**, *adj.*

disgruntle /dɪsˈgrʌntl/, *v.t.,* **-tled, -tling.** to make discontented. [DIS-¹ + GRUNT] **—disgruntlement**, *n.* **—disgruntled**, *adj.*

disguise /dəsˈgaɪz/, *v.,* **-guised, -guising,** *n.* ◇*v.t.* **1.** to change the appearance of, so as to hide identity. **2.** to conceal or cover up the real state or character of: *She may disguise her intentions.* ◇*n.* **3.** a covering, condition, manner, etc., that serves for concealment of character or quality. **4.** the make-up, mask or costume of an entertainer. **5.** the act of disguising. **6.** the state of being disguised. [ME, from OF *des-* DIS-¹ + *guise* GUISE]

disgust /dəsˈgʌst/, *v.t.* **1.** to cause complete dislike in (someone). **2.** to offend the moral sense of (someone). ◇*n.* **3.** a strong dislike caused by something which offends. [MF] **—disgustedly**, *adv.* **—disgusting**, *adj.*

dish /dɪʃ/, *n.* **1.** an open, more or less shallow container, used for serving food. **2.** a particular preparation of food. **3.** anything like a dish in form or use. **4.** *Colloq.* an attractive person. ◇*v.t.* **5.** to serve in a dish, as food (usu. fol. by *up*): *Time to dish up the dinner.* ◇*v.* **6. dish out,** to share out. [OE *disc* dish, plate, bowl, from L *discus* dish, discus]

disharmony /dɪsˈhɑməni/, *n., pl.* **-nies.** a lack of agreement between persons or things; discord. **—disharmonious**, *adj.*

dishcloth /ˈdɪʃklɒθ/, *n.* a cloth for washing dishes. Also, **dishrag.**

dishearten /dɪsˈhɑtn/, *v.t.* to lower the spirits of; discourage. **—dishearteningly**, *adv.*

dishevelled /dɪˈʃɛvəld/, *adj.* **1.** hanging loosely or in disorder; unkempt: *dishevelled hair.* **2.** untidy; disordered: *a dishevelled appearance.*

dishonest /dɪsˈɒnəst/, *adj.* **1.** not honest; tending to lie, cheat, or steal: *a dishonest person.* **2.** proceeding from or showing a lack of honesty; fraudulent: *a dishonest business.* **—dishonesty**, *n.*

dishonor *or* **dishonour** /dɪsˈɒnə/, *n.* **1.** lack of honor or respect: *His actions show dishonor to his country.* **2.** shame; ignominy; disgrace: *His actions brought dishonor on his country.* ◇*v.t.* **3.** to bring shame on; disgrace: *His actions dishonor his country.* **4.** to fail or refuse to honor (a cheque, etc.) by payment. [ME, from OF, from L]

dishonorable *or* **dishonourable** /dɪsˈɒnrəbəl, -ərəbəl/, *adj.* **1.** showing lack of honor; shameful: *a dishonorable act.* **2.** having no honor: *a dishonorable man.*

disillusion /dɪsə'luːʒən/, *v.t.* **1.** to free from false ideas; disenchant. ◇*n.* **2.** a freeing or being freed from false ideas; disenchantment. —**disillusionment**, *n.*

disincline /ˌdɪsɪn'klaɪn/, *v.t.*, **-clined, -clining.** to make unwilling: *The rain disinclines me to go.* —**disinclination**, *n.* —**disinclined**, *adj.*

disinfect /ˌdɪsɪn'fɛkt/, *v.t.* to free (rooms, clothing, etc.) from infection or the possibility of infection. —**disinfector**, *n.*

disinfectant /dɪsən'fɛktənt/, *n.* **1.** any chemical substance that destroys bacteria. ◇*adj.* **2.** disinfecting.

disinformation /dɪsɪnfə'meɪʃən/, *n.* false information spread deliberately so as to mislead (an enemy, etc.).

disingenuous /ˌdɪsɪn'dʒɛnjuəs/, *adj.* lacking straightforwardness or sincerity; insincere. —**disingenuousness**, *n.*

disinherit /ˌdɪsɪn'hɛrət/, *v.t.* to cut out from a will (def. 6) (one who was to receive property, etc.): *She disinherited her grandson.* —**disinheritance**, *n.*

disintegrate /dɪs'ɪntəgreɪt/, *v.t., v.i.* **-grated, -grating.** to reduce or separate to particles or parts; break up: *He disintegrated the model*; *The model disintegrated*. —**disintegration**, *n.*

disinter /dɪsɪn'tɜː/, *v.t.*, **-terred, -terring.** to take out of a place of burial; exhume; unearth. —**disinterment**, *n.*

disinterested /dɪs'ɪntrəstəd/, *adj.* **1.** not influenced by selfish considerations. **2.** *Colloq.* (*not formally correct*) uninterested.

disjoint /dɪs'dʒɔɪnt/, *v.t.* **1.** to disconnect at the joints. **2.** to put out of order; derange. ◇*adj.* **3.** *Maths.* (of two sets) having no elements in common. [OF, from L: disconnect]

disjointed /dɪs'dʒɔɪntəd/, *adj.* **1.** having the joints or connections separated: *a disjointed fowl.* **2.** not fitting together; incoherent: *a disjointed story.*

disjunctive /dɪs'dʒʌŋktɪv/, *adj.* **1.** serving or tending to separate; dividing. **2.** *Gram.* setting two or more expressions in opposition to each other, as *but* in *poor but happy*, or expressing a choice, as *or* in *this or that*. ◇*n.* **3.** *Gram.* a disjunctive word.

disk /dɪsk/, *n.* a memory unit for computers consisting of a rapidly spinning magnetic disc on which information is recorded by magnetising the surface. Also, **disc.**

dislike /dɪs'laɪk/, *v.*, **-liked, -liking.** ◇*v.t.* **1.** not to like; feel distaste for: *I dislike potatoes.* ◇*n.* **2.** the feeling of disliking; distaste: *I have taken a strong dislike to him.*

dislocate /'dɪslakeɪt/, *v.t.*, **-cated, -cating.** **1.** to put out of joint or out of position, as a limb or an organ. **2.** to throw out of order; derange; upset; disorder. [ML, from L] —**dislocation**, *n.*

dislodge /dɪs'lɒdʒ/, *v.t., v.i.* **-lodged, -lodging.** to remove or go from a place of rest. —**dislodgment**, *n.*

disloyal /dɪs'lɔɪəl/, *adj.* not loyal; faithless; treacherous. [OF *des-* DIS-¹ + *loial* law-abiding (from L)] —**disloyalty**, *n.*

dismal /'dɪzməl/, *adj.* feeling or causing deep sadness; gloomy; dreary. [ME *dismall*; orig. uncert.]

dismantle /dɪs'mæntl/, *v.t.*, **-tled, -tling.** **1.** to pull down; take apart. **2.** to take the covering, etc., from. [F (obs.). See DIS-¹, MANTLE] —**dismantlement**, *n.*

dismay /dɪs'meɪ/, *v.t.* **1.** to cause to feel strong disappointment. **2.** to break down the courage of, as by sudden danger or trouble; daunt. ◇*n.* **3.** a sudden disappointment or loss of courage. [ME, probably from OF]

dismember /dɪs'mɛmbə/, *v.t.* **1.** to divide limb from limb. **2.** to separate into parts. [ME, from OF] —**dismemberment**, *n.*

dismiss /dɪs'mɪs/, *v.t.* **1.** to direct or allow to leave. **2.** to remove, as from office or service. **3.** *Cricket.* to cause (a batsman or team) to be out. **4.** to discard or reject. **5.** to lay aside, esp. to put aside from consideration. **6.** *Law.* to put out of court, as a complaint or appeal. [ML: sent away] —**dismissal**, *n.* —**dismissive**, *adj.*

Dismissal, *n.* **the**, the dismissal of the Australian federal government by the governor-general in 1975, resulting from an unprecedented blocking of supply by the Senate.

dismount /dɪs'maʊnt/, *v.i.* **1.** to get off a horse, bicycle, etc. ◇*v.t.* **2.** to bring or throw down, as from a horse. **3.** to remove (a thing) from its support, setting, etc. **4.** to take (machinery, etc.) to pieces.

Disney /'dɪzni/, *n.* **Walt(er E)**, 1901–66, US film producer, esp. of animated cartoons; best known for his characters Mickey Mouse and Donald Duck.

Disneyland /'dɪznilænd/, *n.* an amusement park in Anaheim, California, created by Walt Disney.

disobedience /dɪsə'biːdiəns/, *n.* lack of obedience; refusal to obey. —**disobedient**, *adj.*

disobey /dɪsə'beɪ/, *v.t.* **1.** to fail or refuse to obey (an order, person, etc.). ◇*v.i.* **2.** to be disobedient. [ME, from OF]

disoblige /dɪsə'blaɪdʒ/, *v.t.*, **-bliged, -bliging.** **1.** to refuse or fail to be helpful in some way. **2.** to give offence to; affront. —**disobliging**, *adj.* —**disobligingly**, *adv.*

disorder /dɪs'ɔːdə/, *n.* **1.** a lack of order or regular arrangement; confusion. **2.** something which is different from usual, esp. in physical or mental health. **3.** a public disturbance. ◇*v.t.* **4.** to destroy the order of. **5.** to upset the physical or mental health of. —**disordered**, *adj.*

disorderly /dɪs'ɔːdəli/, *adj.* **1.** in a state of disorder; irregular; untidy; confused. **2.** hard to control; unruly. **3.** *Law.* opposed to public order. —**disorderliness**, *n.*

disorganise *or* **disorganize** /dɪs'ɔːgənaɪz/, *v.t.*, **-nised, -nising.** to destroy the organisa-

disorganise

tion or arrangement of; throw into confusion or disorder.

disorientate /dɪsˈɔːrɪəntɛɪt/, v.t., -tated, -tating. to confuse esp. geographically. Also, **disorient**. – **disorientation**, n.

disown /dɪsˈoun/, v.t. to refuse to admit that (something or someone) belongs to oneself; repudiate; renounce.

disparage /dəsˈpærɪdʒ/, v.t., -raged, -raging. to speak of or treat as of little value; depreciate; belittle. [ME, from OF *des-* DIS-[1] + *parage* equality (from L)] – **disparagingly**, adv. – **disparagement**, n.

disparate /ˈdɪspərət/, adj. different in kind; dissimilar; unlike. [L: separated] – **disparity**, n.

dispassionate /dɪsˈpæʃənət/, adj. free from or unaffected by strong feeling or bias; impartial; calm: *a dispassionate witness*.

dispatch /dɪsˈpætʃ/, v.t., -patched, -patching. 1. to send off; put under way: *He will dispatch a telegram*. 2. to put to death; kill. 3. to carry through (business, etc.) speedily; settle quickly. ◇n. 4. the sending off of a messenger, letter, etc. 5. a putting to death; killing. 6. efficient performance or speed: *Proceed with all possible dispatch*. 7. a state or military communication sent by special messenger. 8. mentioned in dispatches, named in military reports for special bravery. 9. a news account sent by a reporter to a newspaper. 10. a telegram. Also, **despatch**. [It or Sp, from OF: set free, from L]

dispel /dɪsˈpɛl/, v.t., -pelled, -pelling. to drive off in various directions; scatter: *He will dispel your fears*. [L: drive asunder]

dispensable /dɪsˈpɛnsəbəl/, adj. that may be done without; unimportant. – **dispensability**, n.

dispensary /dɪsˈpɛnsəri, -sri/, n., pl. -saries. a place where medicines and medical advice are given.

dispensation /ˌdɪspɛnˈseɪʃən/, n. 1. the act of giving out; distribution: *the dispensation of justice*. 2. that which is given out: *a judge's dispensation*. 3. a doing away with something. 4. *Rom Cath Ch.* the relaxation of a Church law for a particular occasion. – **dispensational**, adj.

dispense /dɪsˈpɛns/, v., -pensed, -pensing. ◇v.t. 1. to deal out; distribute: *The courts must dispense justice*. 2. to direct the giving out of (laws, etc.). 3. *Pharm.* to make up and give out (medicine), esp. on prescription. ◇v. 4. **dispense with, a.** to do without; forgo. **b.** to do away with; get rid of. [ME, from OF, from L: weigh out] – **dispenser**, n.

dispersal /dɪsˈpɜːsəl/, n. → **dispersion** (def. 1).

disperse /dəsˈpɜːs/, v., -persed, -persing. ◇v.t. 1. to scatter abroad; spread. 2. to cause to vanish: *The wind has dispersed the fog*. ◇v.i. 3. to separate and move apart in different directions without order or regularity: *The crowd dispersed at 10 o'clock*. 4. to be scattered out of sight; vanish. [F, from L: scattered]

dispose

dispersion /dəsˈpɜːʒən, -ʃən/, n. 1. the act of dispersing. 2. the state of being dispersed. 3. *Phys.* **a.** a variation of the refractive index of a medium according to the wavelength of electromagnetic radiation passing through it. **b.** the separation of light into colors, produced in this way. 4. *Stats.* the scattering of scores of a distribution around an average score. 5. *Chem.* a system of particles suspended in a fluid; colloid.

dispirit /dɪsˈpɪrət/, v.t. to lower the spirits of; discourage; dishearten. – **dispirited**, adj. – **dispiriting**, adj.

displace /dɪsˈpleɪs/, v.t., -placed, -placing. 1. to put out of the usual or proper place: *War can displace families*. 2. to take the place of; replace. 3. to remove from a position, office, etc. – **displaceable**, adj.

displaced person, n. someone who has been forced to leave their country, esp. by war or revolution.

displacement /dɪsˈpleɪsmənt/, n. 1. the act of displacing. 2. the state of being displaced. 3. *Phys.* the displacing or replacing of one thing by another, e.g. of water by something dipped, sunk, or floating in it. 4. *Phys.* **a.** the weight of fluid displaced by a floating body, equivalent to the weight of the body: *The ship has a displacement of 10 000 tonnes*. **b.** the volume of fluid displaced by a body dipped or sunk in it, equivalent to the volume of the body. 5. *Geol.* the distance of rocks from their original position, caused by movement along a fault. 6. *Psychol.* the transference of feeling or attachment from one object to another.

display /dɪsˈpleɪ/, v.t. 1. to show; exhibit: *The ship will display a flag; His face displayed fear*. ◇n. 2. the act of displaying; exhibition; show: *a display of goods; a display of skill*. 3. an ostentatious display: *a display of wealth*. 4. behavior used by birds in communication, often before mating. [ME, from OF: deploy]

displease /dɪsˈpliːz/, v., -pleased, -pleasing. ◇v.t. 1. to cause dissatisfaction to; offend; annoy. ◇v.i. 2. to be unpleasant. – **displeasingly**, adv. – **displeasure**, n.

disport /dɪsˈpɔːt/, v.t., v.i. to amuse (oneself). [ME, from OF from L]

disposable /dəsˈpoʊzəbəl/, adj. able to be disposed of or thrown away.

disposable income, n. that part of a person's income which remains after tax, etc. has been taken out.

disposal /dəsˈpoʊzəl/, n. 1. the act of putting in a particular way; arrangement. 2. a disposing of as by gift or sale. 3. the power or right to deal with a thing; control: *left to his disposal*.

dispose /dəsˈpoʊz/, v., -posed, -posing. ◇v.t. 1. to put in a particular order: *The captain will dispose the army for battle*. 2. to give a tendency to; incline (*usu. in p.p.*): *I feel disposed to have a quiet weekend*. ◇v.i. 3. to arrange or decide matters: *Man proposes, God disposes*. ◇v. 4. **dispose of, a.** to get rid of. **b.** to make over or part with, as by gift or sale. [ME, from OF]

disposition /dɪspəˈzɪʃən/, *n.* **1.** a general quality of mind: *an unhappy disposition.* **2.** a mental or physical tendency; willingness. **3.** an arrangement, as of soldiers or buildings. **4.** the final settlement of a matter. **5.** a giving away or selling: *disposition of property.* **6.** the power to dispose of a thing; control: *left under his disposition.* [L]

dispossess /dɪspəˈzɛs/, *v.t.* to put (a person) out of possession, esp. of real property; oust. —**dispossession**, *n.* —**dispossessor**, *n.*

disprin /ˈdɪsprən/, *n.* (*also cap.*) a soluble form of aspirin. [Trademark]

disproportion /dɪsprəˈpɔʃən/, *n.* **1.** lack of proportion. **2.** something out of proportion. —**disproportionate**, *adj.*

disprove /dɪsˈpruv/, *v.t.*, **-proved**, **-proving.** to prove (a claim, argument, etc.) to be false or wrong; refute; invalidate. [ME, from OF] —**disprovable**, *adj.*

disputable /dɪsˈpjutəbəl, ˈdɪspjətəbəl/, *adj.* likely to be called into question; questionable.

disputation /dɪspjuˈteɪʃən/, *n.* **1.** an argument or discussion. **2.** a formal debate based on a thesis. —**disputatious**, *adj.*

dispute /dəsˈpjut/, *v.*, **-puted**, **-puting**, *n.* ◇*v.i.* **1.** to take part in an argument or discussion. **2.** to argue fiercely; quarrel. ◇*v.t.* **3.** to argue about; discuss: *They will dispute that question at the conference.* **4.** to argue against: *I must dispute your claim.* **5.** to struggle against; oppose: *The army will dispute any advance by the enemy.* ◇*n.* **6.** an argument or quarrel. [ME, from L]

disqualify /dɪsˈkwɒləfaɪ/, *v.t.*, **-fied**, **-fying. 1.** to make or declare unsuitable: *His poor health may disqualify him from holding a pilot's licence.* **2.** *Sport.* to declare (someone) unable to compete in a match because the rules have been broken. —**disqualification**, *n.*

disquiet /dɪsˈkwaɪət/, *v.t.* **1.** to make uneasy; disturb. ◇*n.* **2.** lack of quiet; disturbance; unrest; uneasiness. —**disquieting**, *adj.* —**disquietude**, *n.*

Disraeli /dɪzˈreɪli/, *n.* **Benjamin** (*Earl of Beaconsfield*), 1804–81, British Conservative politician and novelist; prime minister 1868, 1874–80.

disregard /dɪsrəˈgad/, *v.t.* **1.** to pay no attention to; leave out of consideration. **2.** to treat without due regard or respect. ◇*n.* **3.** lack of attention; neglect. **4.** lack of due regard.

disrepair /dɪsrəˈpɛə/, *n.* the state of being out of repair or neglected: *The shed fell into disrepair.*

disreputable /dɪsˈrɛpjətəbəl/, *adj.* **1.** having a bad name: *a disreputable company.* **2.** not respectable: *disreputable clothes.*

disrepute /dɪsrəˈpjut/, *n.* the loss or lack of good opinion; discredit (usu. prec. by *in*, *into*): *That idea is in disrepute now.*

disrespect /dɪsrəˈspɛkt/, *n.* lack of respect; rudeness: *He showed disrespect to the old man.* —**disrespectful**, *adj.*

disrobe /dɪsˈroʊb/, *v.i.*, *v.t.* **-robed**, **-robing.** to undress.

disrupt /dɪsˈrʌpt/, *v.t.* to interrupt; disturb: *The children may disrupt the meeting.* [L] —**disruption**, *n.* —**disruptive**, *adj.*

dissatisfaction /dɪsætəsˈfækʃən/, *n.* lack of satisfaction; state of not being satisfied.

dissatisfy /dɪsˈsætəsfaɪ/, *v.t.*, **-fied**, **-fying.** to make ill-satisfied or discontented. —**dissatisfied**, *adj.*

dissect /dəˈsɛkt, daɪ-/, *v.t.* **1.** to cut apart (an animal body, plant, etc.) for examination. **2.** to examine closely; analyse. [L: cut asunder] —**dissector**, *n.* —**dissection**, *n.*

dissected /dəˈsɛktəd, daɪ-/, *adj.* **1.** *Bot.* deeply scored into many parts, as a leaf. **2.** *Geog.* (of a land surface) cut by erosion into hills and valleys or into flat upland areas separated by valleys.

dissemble /dəˈsɛmbəl/, *v.*, **-bled**, **-bling.** ◇*v.i.* **1.** to hide one's true feelings. ◇*v.t.* **2.** to hide the real nature of. **3.** to put on the appearance of; feign. [DIS-¹ + *-semble*, (See SEMBLANCE) modelled on RESEMBLE]

disseminate /dəˈsɛmənɛɪt/, *v.t.*, **-nated**, **-nating.** to scatter, as seed in sowing; spread abroad; promulgate: *to disseminate information.* [L] —**dissemination**, *n.* —**disseminator**, *n.*

dissension /dəˈsɛnʃən/, *n.* a difference in opinion; disagreement, esp. violent.

dissent /dəˈsɛnt/, *v.i.* **1.** to differ in opinion; disagree (oft. fol. by *from*): *She dissents from the chairwoman's ruling.* **2.** to refuse to accept the authority of an established church. ◇*n.* **3.** a difference in opinion. **4.** separation from an established church; nonconformity. [ME, from L: differ in opinion] —**dissenting**, *adj.* —**dissenter**, *n.*

dissertation /dɪsəˈteɪʃən/, *n.* **1.** a written essay, or thesis. **2.** a formal talk. —**dissertational**, *adj.*

disservice /dɪsˈsɜvəs/, *n.* harm; injury; an ill turn: *He did her a disservice, though he meant to be kind.* —**disserviceable**, *adj.*

dissident /ˈdɪsədənt/, *adj.* **1.** differing; disagreeing; dissenting. ◇*n.* **2.** someone who differs; a dissenter, esp. against a particular political system. [L: differing, sitting apart] —**dissidence**, *n.*

dissimilar /dɪˈsɪmələ/, *adj.* not similar; unlike; different. —**dissimilarity**, *n.*

dissimulate /dəˈsɪmjəleɪt/, *v.*, **-lated**, **-lating.** ◇*v.t.* **1.** to disguise or hide (one's feelings, etc.) under a false appearance; dissemble. ◇*v.i.* **2.** to feign; pretend; dissemble. [L] —**dissimulator**, *n.* —**dissimulation**, *n.*

dissipate /ˈdɪsəpeɪt/, *v.t.*, *v.i.*, **-pated**, **-pating. 1.** to scatter, or become scattered, in various directions; disperse; disintegrate. **2.** to scatter, or become scattered wastefully or extravagantly: *She dissipated her fortune in gambling.* [L: scattered, demolished] —**dissipater**, *n.* —**dissipative**, *adj.*

dissipated /ˈdɪsəpeɪtəd/, *adj.* **1.** given to or marked by excessive seeking of pleasure;

dissipated intemperate; dissolute. **2.** scattered; dispersed; dispelled. **–dissipatedness,** *n.*

dissipation /ˌdɪsəˈpeɪʃən/, *n.* **1.** the act of dissipating. **2.** the state of being dissipated; dispersing; disintegration. **3.** a wasting by misuse. **4.** a corrupt or wasteful way of living; intemperance; debauchery.

dissociate /dɪˈsoʊʃieɪt, -ˈsoʊsieɪt/, *v.t., v.i.,* **-ated, -ating. 1.** to withdraw from the association of; disunite; separate. **2.** *Chem.* to subject to or to undergo dissociation. Also, **disassociate.** [L] **–dissociative,** *adj.*

dissociation /dɪˌsoʊsiˈeɪʃən/, *n.* **1.** the act of dissociating or state of being dissociated. **2.** *Phys., Chem.* the decomposition of a compound due to either dissolution in a solvent forming ions (electrolytic dissociation) or heating (thermal dissociation). See **electrolyte**.

dissoluble /dɪˈsɒljəbəl/, *adj.* able to be dissolved. **–dissolubility,** *n.*

dissolute /ˈdɪsəlut/, *adj.* immoral; given to dissipation; licentious. [L: loosened] **–dissoluteness,** *n.*

dissolution /ˌdɪsəˈluʃən/, *n.* **1.** the breaking down of a thing into its parts. **2.** the state of being broken into parts. **3.** the undoing or breaking up of a tie, bond, assembly, etc. **4.** *Govt.* an order issued by the head of state terminating a parliament and making a new election necessary. **5.** decay, death, or destruction. **6.** *Chem.* the act of dissolving in a liquid.

dissolve /dəˈzɒlv/, *v.,* **-solved, -solving.** ◇*v.t.* **1.** to make a solution of in a solvent: *to dissolve sugar in water.* **2.** to undo (a tie or bond); break up (a connection, union, assembly, etc.). **3.** *Govt.* to order the termination of a parliament, usu. at a regular interval, or in the event of the government being defeated. **4.** to bring to an end; destroy; dispel. ◇*v.i.* **5.** to become dissolved, as in a solvent: *Sugar dissolves in water.* **6.** to break up; disperse. **7.** to disappear gradually: *The figure dissolved into the mist.* [ME, from L: loosen, disunite] **–dissolvable,** *adj.*

dissonance /ˈdɪsənəns/, *n.* **1.** an inharmonious or harsh sound; discord. **2.** *Music.* a combination of notes usually thought of as being in a state of unrest and needing resolution (opposed to *consonance*). **3.** disagreement; incongruity. Also, **dissonancy. –dissonant,** *adj.*

dissuade /dɪˈsweɪd/, *v.t.,* **-suaded, -suading.** to advise or persuade not to do something (fol. by *from*): *We dissuaded him from leaving home.* [L: advise against] **–dissuasion,** *n.* **–dissuasive,** *adj.*

dissymmetric /ˌdɪsəˈmɛtrɪk/, *adj.* **1.** lacking symmetry. **2.** of or relating to two objects which are symmetrically arranged in opposite directions, as the two hands of the human body. **–dissymmetrical,** *adj.* **–dissymmetry,** *n.*

distaff /ˈdɪstaf/, *n.* a stick with a split end, either hand-held or part of a machine, used for holding wool, flax, etc., from which the thread is drawn in spinning. [OE *distæf*]

distance /ˈdɪstns, ˈdɪstəns/, *n., v.,* **-tanced, -tancing.** ◇*n.* **1.** the amount of space between things or points: *the distance between Sydney and Perth; We travelled a great distance.* **2.** the condition or fact of being distant; remoteness: *The distance of Sydney from Perth makes communication difficult.* **3.** any kind of gap or space: *the distance between ideas and action; The business has covered a lot of distance in a year.* **4.** the far part of a landscape, etc.: *The distance was covered in haze.* **5. go the distance,** to complete something. **6. keep one's distance,** to be reserved or aloof. ◇*v.t.* **7.** to leave far behind, as in a race. **8.** to make distant, esp. in feelings: *She distanced herself from them.*

distant /ˈdɪstənt/, *adj.* **1.** far off or apart in space or time; remote: *a distant town.* **2.** separate or apart in space: *a place a kilometre distant.* **3.** far apart in any way: *a distant relative.* **4.** not friendly; reserved; aloof. **5.** to a distance: *a distant journey.* [F, from L: being distant, standing apart]

distasteful /dɪsˈteɪstfəl/, *adj.* **1.** causing dislike. **2.** unpleasant to the taste.

distemper[1] /dɪsˈtɛmpə/, *n.* **1.** *Vet Sci.* an infectious viral disease of young dogs. **2.** a disordered condition of mind or body; bad humor; discontent. ◇*v.t.* **3.** to derange physically or mentally. [ME, from ML. See DIS-[1], TEMPER]

distemper[2] /dɪsˈtɛmpə/, *n.* **1.** a water paint used on interior walls and ceilings, esp. one containing glue or casein. ◇*v.t.* **2.** to paint with distemper. [OF, from L]

distend /dəsˈtɛnd/, *v.i., v.t.* to make or become stretched or bloated; swell. [L] **–distension,** *n.* **–distensible,** *adj.*

distil /dəsˈtɪl/, *v.,* **-tilled, -tilling.** ◇*v.t.* **1.** to purify and concentrate (a liquid) by heating it to vapor, and then changing it back to liquid by condensation. **2.** to extract by distillation. **3.** to separate (*off* or *out*) by distillation: *to distil salt out of water.* **4.** to let fall or give forth in or as if in drops: *to distil wisdom.* ◇*v.i.* **5.** to undergo distillation. **6.** to fall in drops; trickle; exude. [ME, from L: drip down] **–distillable,** *adj.* **–distilled,** *adj.*

distillate /ˈdɪstələt, -leɪt/, *n.* **1.** a product obtained by distillation. **2.** → **diesel oil.**

distillation /ˌdɪstəˈleɪʃən/, *n.* **1.** the process of distilling. **2.** the purification or concentration of a substance. **3.** something reduced to a pure state, leaving only what is essential: *The book contains the distillation of his thought.* **4.** product of distilling; distillate. **–distillatory,** *adj.*

distillery /dəsˈtɪləri/, *n., pl.* **-eries.** a place where distilling, esp. of alcoholic spirits, is carried on.

distinct /dəsˈtɪŋkt/, *adj.* **1.** not the same; separate (oft. fol. by *from*): *Could you move into two distinct groups?; That group is distinct from the other.* **2.** different in nature or qualities; dissimilar: *This new method is quite distinct from the old.* **3.** clear; definite; unmistakable: *a distinct sense that something is wrong.* **4.** clearly seen or heard: *a distinct movement on the horizon.* **–distinctness,** *n.*

distinction /dəs'tɪŋkʃən/, *n.* **1.** a marking of something as different: *The distinction between the two sets of marks is plain.* **2.** the recognising or noting of differences; discrimination: *The distinction made between black and white peoples has had some sad results.* **3.** difference: *The distinction between psychology and psychiatry is not always fully understood.* **4.** a distinguishing characteristic: *He has the distinction of being the only one who always comes late.* **5.** a mark of special favor: *She was given the distinction of appearing on the platform with the leaders.* **6.** marked superiority; note; eminence: *a writer of distinction.* **7.** (in some universities, colleges, etc.) the highest grade awarded.

distinctive /dəs'tɪŋktɪv/, *adj.* noticeable, and therefore serving to distinguish; characteristic.

distinguish /dəs'tɪŋgwɪʃ/, *v.t.* **1.** to mark off as different (fol. by *from*): *Spots on the leaf distinguish this plant from its nearest relative.* **2.** to recognise as distinct or different; discriminate: *I can distinguish this plant by the spots on its leaves.* **3.** to see or hear clearly; make out; discern: *to distinguish a faint speck on the horizon.* **4.** to be a quality of; characterise: *Huge ears distinguish the African elephant.* **5.** to make prominent, conspicuous, or eminent: *to distinguish oneself in battle.* ◇*v.i.* **6.** to recognise or indicate a difference; discriminate (fol. by *between*): *The exam marks will distinguish between the good and lazy students; I can distinguish between right and wrong.* [L: separate, distinguish]

distinguished /dəs'tɪŋgwɪʃt/, *adj.* **1.** noted; eminent; famous: *a distinguished musician.* **2.** having an air of superiority: *a distinguished gentleman.*

distort /dəs'tɔt/, *v.t.* **1.** to twist out of shape; deform: *to distort a wheel rim.* **2.** to represent wrongly; pervert: *to distort her ideas; distort the truth.* [L] –**distorted**, *adj.*

distortion /dəs'tɔʃən/, *n.* **1.** the act of distorting: *The distortion of their arguments can only lead to trouble.* **2.** the state of being distorted. **3.** anything distorted: *The resulting distortion was very ugly.* **4.** *Elect.* a change in the waveform of a signal which reduces the clarity or quality of the information. –**distortional**, *adj.*

distract /dəs'trækt/, *v.t.* **1.** to draw away or divert the mind or attention of: *The music outside the window distracted the class.* **2.** to amuse; entertain; divert: *Games distracted them for a whole week.* **3.** to disturb or trouble greatly in the mind (*usu.* as *p.p.*): *She was distracted and nervous.* [L: pulled asunder] –**distraction**, *n.* –**distracted**, *adj.* –**distracting**, *adj.*

distraught /dəs'trɔt/, *adj.* **1.** distracted; greatly troubled in mind; bewildered. **2.** driven mad; crazed. [var. of *Obs. distract*, adj.]

distress /dəs'trɛs/, *n.* **1.** great pain, anxiety, or sorrow; acute suffering; affliction. **2.** the state of suffering caused by lack of money, housing, etc. **3.** a state of great danger or difficulty: *a ship in distress.* ◇*v.t.* **4.** to cause (someone) pain, anxiety, or sorrow; trouble sorely; worry; bother. [ME, from OF, from L: drawn tight] –**distressing, distressful**, *adj.* –**distressingly**, *adv.*

distress call, *n.* **1.** an international code sign meaning that the sender is in danger or difficulty, as *Mayday* or *SOS.* **2.** any communication indicating distress: *The Red Cross sent out a distress call for blood donors.*

distress signal, *n.* a signal by people in danger calling for help and showing their position by radio, flag, etc.

distribute /dəs'trɪbjut/, *v.t.*, **-uted, -uting. 1.** to divide and give out in shares; deal out; allot: *to distribute presents to children.* **2. a.** to scatter or spread; disperse: *to distribute manure over a field.* **b.** (usu. in passive) to occur; be found; be dispersed: *The Sydney red gum is distributed over a large area; These plants are distributed into 22 classes.* [L] –**distributable**, *adj.*

distribution /dɪstrə'bjuʃən/, *n.* **1.** the act of distributing: *The distribution of presents made everyone happy.* **2.** the state or manner of being distributed: *an unfair distribution of wealth; the distribution of coniferous forests.* **3.** arrangement; classification: *distribution into types.* **4.** anything distributed: *a distribution to the poor.* **5.** the process by which goods reach consumers; process of selling a product: *Some quality is lost in distribution.* **6.** *Econ.* **a.** the division of the total income of any society among its members, or among the factors of production. **b.** the system of dispersing goods throughout a community. **7.** *Stats.* → **frequency distribution.** –**distributional**, *adj.*

distribution curve, *n.* a curve or line on a graph whose axes or data are based upon a specific frequency distribution. See **frequency distribution.**

distributive /dəs'trɪbjətɪv/, *adj.* **1.** characterised by or relating to distribution. **2.** *Gram.* treating the members of a group individually, as the adjectives *each* and *every.* **3.** *Maths.* allowing a number to be multiplied separately by each term in a set, as in $a(b+c)$.

distributor /dəs'trɪbjətə/, *n.* **1.** someone or something that distributes. **2.** *Comm.* a person whose work is in the marketing of goods. **3.** *Mech.* a device in a multicylinder engine which sends electric current to the spark plugs in a definite order. **4.** a main road, usu. a freeway, designed to take traffic quickly from the centre of the city towards the outer suburbs. Also, **distributer.**

district /'dɪstrɪkt/, *n.* **1.** a region or locality. **2.** an area of land marked out for some administrative or other purpose: *the Brisbane postal district.* **3.** *SA.* → **shire** (def. 1). [ML: territory under jurisdiction, special use of L: constrained]

district attorney, *n. US.* a public prosecutor for a specific district. Also, **DA**.

District Court, *n.* **1.** (in NSW, Qld and WA) an intermediate court, superior to the lowest level of courts presided over by magistrates, and inferior to the Supreme Court. See **County Court. 2.** (in NZ) a court with jurisdiction over limited civil matters and less serious

District Court   299   **diversion**

criminal offences, as well as summary and committal proceedings.

District of Columbia /kə'lʌmbiə/, *n.* an area in the eastern US coextensive with the federal capital, Washington; governed by the US Congress. Pop. 626 000 (1986 est.); 179 km². *Abbrev.:* DC

distrust /dɪs'trʌst/, *n.* **1.** lack of trust; doubt; suspicion. ◇*v.t.* **2.** to feel distrust of; regard with doubt or suspicion. —**distrustful**, *adj.*

disturb /də'stɜb/, *v.t.* **1.** to interrupt the quiet, rest, or peace of: *The children's noise disturbed their father.* **2.** to interfere with; interrupt; hinder: *to disturb the working of a program; disturb someone's sleep.* **3.** to throw into commotion or disorder; agitate; disorder; unsettle: *to disturb water by throwing in stones.* **4.** to perplex; trouble: *Horror films always disturb him.* [L: throw into disorder, disturb] —**disturbingly**, *adv.*

disturbance /də'stɜbəns/, *n.* **1.** the act of disturbing: *The disturbance of the water brought mud to the surface.* **2.** the state of being disturbed: *Horror films always cause me disturbance.* **3.** an instance of this; commotion: *A disturbance in the clouds.* **4.** something that disturbs: *Her mere presence was a disturbance.* **5.** an outbreak of disorder; breach of public peace: *The rioters caused a disturbance.* **6.** *Geol.* the bending or faulting of rock from its original position.

disunite /dɪsju'naɪt/, *v.t.*, *v.i.*, **-nited**, **-niting.** to separate; divide. —**disunity**, *n.*

disuse /dɪs'jus/, *n.*; /dɪs'juz/, *v.*, **-used**, **-using.** ◇*n.* **1.** a stopping of use or practice: *The old house fell into disuse.* ◇*v.t.* **2.** to stop using.

ditch /dɪtʃ/, *n.* **1.** a long, narrow hollow dug in the earth, as for draining or irrigating land; trench. **2.** any open passage or trench, as a natural channel or waterway. **3.** *last ditch*, *Colloq.* the last defence; utmost extremity. ◇*v.t.* **4.** to dig a ditch or ditches in. **5.** *Colloq.* to get rid of: *They ditched their old car; She ditched her boyfriend.* [OE *dīc*]

dither /'dɪðə/, *n.* **1.** *Colloq.* a state of nervous excitement or confused hesitancy. ◇*v.i.* **2.** to be nervously hesitant and confused: *They dithered over which route to take.* [var. of *didder*, ME *diddir*; orig. obscure] —**dithering**, **dithery**, *adj.*

ditto /'dɪtoʊ/, *n.*, *pl.* **-tos**, *adv.*, *v.*, **-toed**, **-toing.** ◇*n.* **1.** the same (used in accounts, lists, etc., to avoid repetition). *Symbol:* "; *Abbrev.:* do ◇*adv.* **2.** as already stated; likewise. ◇*v.t.* **3.** to duplicate; copy. [It: said, aforesaid, from L: said]

ditty /'dɪti/, *n.*, *pl.* **-ties. 1.** a poem intended to be sung. **2.** a short, simple song. [ME, from OF, from L: thing composed or recited]

diuretic /,daɪju'rɛtɪk/, *n.*, *adj.* (a substance) causing an increased flow of urine. [LL: promoting urine, from Gk]

diurnal /daɪ'ɜnəl/, *adj.* **1.** daily. **2.** of or belonging to the daytime. **3.** active or out by day, as certain birds, insects, flowers, etc. (opposed to *nocturnal*). [LL: daily]

div., *Abbrev.* **1.** dividend. **2.** division.

diva /'divə/, *n.*, *pl.* **-vas**, **-ve** /-vi/. a distinguished female singer; prima donna. [It, from L: goddess]

divalent /daɪ'veɪlənt, 'daɪvɛlənt/, *adj.* having a valency of two, as the ferrous ion, Fe^{++}

divan /də'væn/, *n.* **1.** a low bed or sofa. **2.** a long, cushioned seat against a wall, as in Middle Eastern countries. **3.** (formerly) (a room used for) a council of state in Turkey and other Middle Eastern countries. [Turk, from Pers]

dive /daɪv/, *v.*, **dived**, **diving**. ◇*v.i.* **1.** to plunge, esp. head first, into water, etc. **2.** to go below the surface of the water, as a submarine. **3.** (of an aeroplane) to descend steeply. **4.** to penetrate suddenly into anything, as with the hand: *She dived into the box and brought out a pair of shoes; He dived into his work.* **5.** to dart; go out of sight: *The thief dived behind the cupboard.* ◇*n.* **6.** the act of diving. **7.** *Colloq.* a disreputable place, as for drinking, gambling, etc. **8.** a sharp drop or fall: *Profits took a dive this week.* [OE *dȳfan*, dip]

dive-bomb /'daɪv-bɒm/, *v.t.* **1.** *Aeron.* to bomb by diving at a steep angle so that the pilot sights the target through the gun sights and releases the bombs just before pulling out. ◇*v.i.* **2.** *Colloq.* to jump into water with the knees tucked under the chin.

diver /'daɪvə/, *n.* **1.** a person or thing that dives. **2.** a person who makes a business of diving, as for pearl oysters, to examine sunken vessels, etc. **3.** any of various birds which habitually dive, as loons, grebes, etc.

diverge /daɪ'vɜdʒ/, *v.i.*, **-verged**, **-verging. 1.** to move or lie in different directions from a common point; branch off. **2.** to differ in opinion or character; deviate. **3.** to digress from a plan, discussion, etc. **4.** *Maths.* (of an infinite sequence of numbers) to not converge. [NL, from L] —**divergence**, *n.* —**divergent**, *adj.*

divers /'daɪvəz/, *adj.* several, sundry (sometimes used as a pronoun): *in divers ways; divers of them.* [ME, from OF, from L *diversus*, pp., lit., turned different ways]

diverse /daɪ'vɜs, 'daɪvɜs/, *adj.* **1.** different; unlike. **2.** of various kinds or forms; multiform. [var. of DIVERS] —**diverseness**, *n.*

diversify /daɪ'vɜsəfaɪ, də-/, *v.*, **-fied**, **-fying.** ◇*v.t.* **1.** to make diverse, as in form or character; give variety or diversity to; variegate. **2.** to vary (investments); invest in different types of (securities). ◇*v.i.* **3.** to extend one's activities, esp. in business, over more than one field. [F, from ML, from L *diversi*- diverse + *-ficāre* make] —**diversification**, *n.* —**diversified**, *adj.* —**diversifiable**, *adj.*

diversion /də'vɜʒən, daɪ-/, *n.* **1.** a turning aside from a course. **2.** a compulsory detour on a road or motorway, to avoid an obstacle,

diversion

roadworks, etc. **3.** a distraction from business, care, etc.; recreation; entertainment; amusement; a pastime. **4.** *Mil.* an action intended to draw attention away from the point of main attack. **—diversionary**, *adj.*

diversity /dəˈvɜːsəti, daɪ-/, *n., pl.* **-ties. 1.** the state or fact of being diverse; difference. **2.** variety; multiformity.

divert /dəˈvɜːt, daɪ-/, *v.t.* **1.** to turn aside or from a path or course; deflect: *to divert a river.* **2.** to set (traffic) on a detour. **3.** to draw off to a different object, purpose, etc.: *I'll divert their attention.* **4.** to entertain or amuse; distract. [OF, from L: turn aside, separate] **—divertible**, *adj.*

diverticulum /daɪvəˈtɪkjələm/, *n., pl.* **-la** /-lə/. *Anat.* a blind tubular sac or growth, branching off from a canal or cavity, as in the intestine. [L: byway] **—diverticular**, *adj.*

diverting /dəˈvɜːtɪŋ, daɪ-/, *adj.* entertaining; amusing.

divest /daɪˈvɛst/, *v.t.* **1.** to take off the clothing, etc., of; disrobe (fol. by *of*). **2.** to strip or deprive of anything; dispossess (fol. by *of*). [ML, from OF]

divide /dəˈvaɪd/, *v.*, **-vided, -viding,** *n.* ◇*v.t.* **1.** to separate into parts; split up: *A river divides the city; All that backbiting has divided the staff.* **2.** to separate or part from each other or from something else; sunder; cut off. **3.** to deal out in parts; share; apportion: *to divide a cake; divide an estate; to divide time between work and play.* **4.** to separate in opinion or feeling; cause to disagree: *The tax issue divided Parliament.* **5.** to classify: *Zoologists divide animals into families.* **6.** *Maths.* to separate into equal parts by the process of division: *to divide 16 by 4.* **7.** *Parl. Proc.* to separate (a legislature, etc.) into two groups to find out the vote on a question. ◇*v.i.* **8.** to become divided or separated: *to divide into four parts; The staff divided over the issue.* **9.** to branch; diverge; fork: *The road divides 3 km out of town.* **10.** *Maths.* to do division. **11.** *Parl. Proc.* to vote by separating into two groups. ◇*n.* **12.** *Geog.* a watershed: *the Great Divide.* [ME, from L: force asunder] **—divided**, *adj.*

dividend /ˈdɪvədɛnd/, *n.* **1.** *Maths.* a number to be divided by another number (the divisor). **2.** *Finance.* **a.** a pro rata share in an amount to be distributed, as of a company's profits to shareholders. **b.** interest payable on public funds. **3.** a payment to creditors and shareholders in a liquidated company. **4.** a share of anything divided. **5.** the totalisator payout on a racing bet. **6.** *Colloq.* a good result or advantage: *The way I'm doing it is paying dividends.* [L: thing to be divided]

divider /dəˈvaɪdə/, *n.* **1.** a person or thing that divides. **2.** (*pl.*) a pair of compasses as used for dividing lines, measuring, etc.

divination /dɪvəˈneɪʃən/, *n.* **1.** the discovering of what is unknown or the foretelling of future events, as by supernatural means. **2.** a prophecy; augury. [L] **—divinatory**, *adj.*

divine /dəˈvaɪn/, *adj., v.,* **-vined, -vining.** ◇*adj.* **1.** of or relating to God or a god. **2.**

divisive

addressed or belonging to God; religious; sacred: *divine service.* **3.** coming from God: *the divine right of kings.* **4.** supremely good, great, etc.: *a person of divine beauty.* **5.** *Colloq.* excellent: *What a divine dress!* ◇*v.t., v.i.* **6.** to discover (water, metal, etc.) by a divining rod. **7.** to discover or tell (something unknown or the future), as by supernatural means; prophesy. **8.** to guess or make out (something) by conjecture: *to divine someone's intentions.* [ME, from L] **—diviner**, *n.*

divine right of kings, *n.* the belief that a king's right to rule comes directly from God, not from the people, and that he should therefore be obeyed in all things.

diving bell, *n.* a hollow vessel filled with air under pressure, in which people may work under water.

diving board, *n.* a plank projecting over a swimming pool from which swimmers may dive. See **springboard**.

diving suit, *n.* a heavy watertight garment with an attached air-supply line, worn by divers.

divining rod, *n.* a rod or forked stick, commonly of hazel, said to tremble or move when held over a spot where water, metal, etc., is underground.

divinity /dəˈvɪnəti/, *n., pl.* **-ties. 1.** the quality of being divine; divine nature. **2.** a divine being; a god. **3.** the science of divine things; theology. **4.** godlike character; supreme excellence.

divisibility /dəvɪzəˈbɪləti/, *n.* **1.** the capability of being divided. **2.** *Maths.* the capacity of being exactly divided, without remainder.

divisible /dəˈvɪzəbəl/, *adj.* able to be divided. **—divisibleness**, *n.* **—divisibly**, *adv.*

division /dəˈvɪʒən/, *n.* **1.** the act of dividing or the state of being divided; partition: *the division of a country after war.* **2.** a distribution; a sharing-out: *a just division of wealth.* **3.** *Maths.* the opposite process to multiplication; the finding of a quantity (the quotient) which, when multiplied by a given quantity (the divisor), gives another given quantity (the dividend). Symbol: ÷. **4.** something that divides; a dividing line or mark: *the division between NSW and Qld.* **5.** a section, grouping or category: *All the players under 15 will be in A division.* **6.** a separation by difference of opinion or feeling; disagreement; dissension: *The divisions in our society are alarming.* **7.** *Govt.* the separation of the members of a legislature, etc., into two groups, in taking a vote. **8.** a semi-independent administrative unit in industry or government. **9.** a major military unit, larger than a regiment or brigade and smaller than a corps, usu. commanded by a major general. [L] **—divisional, divisionary,** *adj.* **—divisionally,** *adv.*

division sign, *n.* the symbol (÷) placed between two expressions, denoting division of the first by the second.

divisive /dəˈvɪzɪv, -ˈvaɪsɪv/, *adj.* creating division or discord.

divisor /dǝ'vaɪzǝ/, *n. Maths.* the number by which another number (the dividend) is divided.

divorce /dǝ'vɔs/, *n., v.,* **-vorced, -vorcing.** ◊*n.* **1.** the legal dissolution (def. 3) of marriage. **2.** a complete separation of any kind. ◊*v.t.* **3.** to separate, esp. by legal dissolving of marriage. [ME, from F, from L: separation, dissolution]

divorcee /dǝvɔ'si/, *n.* a divorced person.

divulge /daɪ'vʌldʒ, daɪ-/, *v.t.,* **-vulged, -vulging.** to disclose or reveal (something private, secret, or unknown). [L: make common] —**divulger**, *n.* —**divulgence**, *n.*

divvy /'dɪvi/, *n., pl.* **-vies,** *v.,* **-vied, -vying.** *Colloq.* ◊*n.* **1.** → **dividend. 2.** (*pl.*) rewards; profits; gains. ◊*v.t.* **3.** to share out (fol. by *up*). **4.** to share with (fol. by *with*). [shortened form of DIVIDEND]

dixie /'dɪksi/, *n.* **1. a.** a large iron pot in which a stew, tea, etc., is made. **b.** a portable metal dish, used as a plate, cup, and cooking utensil by a soldier in the field. **2.** a small container of ice-cream; bucket. [Hind]

Dixie /'dɪksi/, *n.* the southern US.

dizzy /'dɪzi/, *adj.,* **-zier, -ziest,** *v.,* **-zied, -zying.** ◊*adj.* **1.** having an unpleasant feeling of spinning around, with a tendency to fall; giddy; vertiginous. **2.** bewildered; confused. **3.** causing a giddy feeling: *a dizzy height.* **4.** *Colloq.* foolish or stupid. ◊*v.t.* **5.** to make dizzy. [OE *dysig* foolish] —**dizzily**, *adv.* —**dizziness**, *n.*

DJ /di 'dʒeɪ/, *n.* → **disc jockey.**

Djakarta /dʒǝ'katǝ/, *n.* former spelling of **Jakarta.**

dL, *Abbrev.* decilitre.

DLP /di ɛl 'pi/, *Abbrev.* Democratic Labor Party.

DMZ /di ɛm 'zɛd/, *Abbrev.* Demilitarised Zone.

DNA /di ɛn 'eɪ/, *n.* one of a class of large molecules which consist of nucleotides in a double helix structure and are found in the nuclei of cells and viruses. Responsible for passing on genetic characteristics. Also, **deoxyribonucleic acid.** [abbrev.]

Dnieper /'dnipǝ/, *n.* a river rising in western Russia and flowing south through Belarus and Ukraine to the Black Sea. About 2253 km. Russian, **Dnepr.**

D-notice /'di-noʊtǝs/, *n.* a classification for books, films, etc., which are considered to be dangerous to national security.

do[1] /du/, *v. pres. indic. sing.* I **do;** you **do;** he, she, it **does;** *pl.* we, you, they **do;** *past indic. sing. and pl.* I, you, he, she, it, we, you, they **did;** *past part.* **done;** *pres. part.* **doing;** *old forms* thou **doest** or **dost;** he **doeth** or **doth;** *n., pl.* **dos** or **do's.** ◊*v.t.* **1.** to perform (an act, duty, etc.). **2.** to carry out (a piece or amount of work, etc.). **3.** to put forth; exert: *do your best.* **4.** to be the cause of (good, harm, credit, etc.); bring about; effect. **5.** to render (homage, justice, etc.). **6.** to deal with (anything) as the case may require: *do the meat; do the dishes.* **7.** to cover; traverse: *We did 14 kilometres today.* **8.** to travel at a specified speed: *The car was doing 65 kilometres per hour.* **9.** *Colloq.* to serve (a period of time) in prison. **10.** to study: *He is doing German.* **11.** *Colloq.* to visit as a tourist or sightseer: *They did Spain last year.* **12.** *Colloq.* to serve; suffice for: *This will do us for the present.* **13.** *Colloq.* to provide; prepare: *This pub does lunches.* **14.** *Colloq.* to cheat or swindle. **15.** *Colloq.* to use up; expend: *He did his money at the races.* ◊*v.i.* **16.** to act, esp. effectively; be in action. **17.** to behave or proceed (wisely, etc.). **18.** to get along or fare (well or ill); manage (with; without, etc.). **19.** to be enough; suffice: *Will this do?* **20.** to deal; treat (fol. by *by*): *to do well by a man.* ◊*aux. v.* **21.** (used without special meaning in the forming of some questions, negatives, and commands): *Do you think so? I don't agree.* **22.** (used to lend emphasis to a principal verb): *Do come.* **23.** (used to avoid repetition of a full verb or verb expression): *I think as you do; Did you see him? I did.* ◊**24.** Some special uses are:
can or **could do with,** to require or be likely to benefit from: *I could do with more sleep.*
do away with, 1. to put an end to; abolish. **2.** to kill.
do for, 1. to accomplish the defeat, ruin, death, etc., of. **2.** *Colloq.* to cook and keep house for. **3.** to provide or manage for.
do in, *Colloq.* **1.** to kill; murder. **2.** to exhaust; tire out. **3.** to ruin.
do one's thing, *Colloq.* to act according to one's own self-image.
do or die, to make a supreme effort.
do over, 1. to redecorate; renovate: *to do over a room.* **2.** to beat up; assault.
do up, to renovate.
have to do with, to be connected with: *Smoking has a lot to do with cancer.*
make do, to get along with the resources available.
◊*n.* **25.** *Colloq.* a festivity or party: *We're having a big do next week.* **26.** (*pl.*) rules, customs, etc.: *dos and don'ts.* **27.** *NZ.* a success: *make a do of something.* [OE *dōn*]

do[2] /doʊ/, *n. Music.* See **solfa** and **solfège.** [see GAMUT]

do[3], *Abbrev.* ditto.

dob /dɒb/, *v.,* **dobbed, dobbing.** *Colloq. in the phrases* **1. dob in, a.** to betray; report (someone), as for a misdeed. **b.** to name (someone absent) for an unpleasant task. **c.** to contribute. **2. dob on,** to inform against; betray. —**dobber**, *n.*

dobbin /'dɒbǝn/, *n.* a horse, esp. a workhorse. [var. of *Robin,* familiar var. of *Robert,* man's name]

Dobell /doʊ'bɛl/, *n.* **Sir William,** 1899–1970, Australian artist noted for his portraits; winner of the Archibald Prize 1943, 1948 and 1959; a controversy followed the 1943 award.

Doberman pinscher /doʊbǝmǝn 'pɪntʃǝ/, *n.* a breed of large, smooth-coated terriers, usu. black and tan or brown, with long forelegs, and wide hindquarters. Also, **Doberman.**

Dobson /'dɒbsən/, *n.* **Rosemary de Brissac**, born 1920, Australian poet; author of the collection *Ship of Ice* (1948).

doc /dɒk/, *n. Colloq.* a doctor.

docile /'dousail/, *adj.* **1.** easily trained or taught; teachable. **2.** easily managed or handled; tractable. [ME, from L] **—docility**, *n.*

dock[1] /dɒk/, *n.* **1.** a wharf; pier. **2.** a waterway between two wharves, for receiving a ship while in port. **3.** (*pl.*) the area of a city where the docks are situated: *The cafe is down in the docks.* **4. →dry dock. 5.** a partly enclosed structure which a plane, truck, etc., can enter for the purpose of loading, repair, etc. **6.** *Colloq.* **in dock, a.** (of equipment, etc.) out of order and being fixed. **b.** (of a person) ill; laid up. ◇*v.t.* **7.** to bring into a dock; lay up in a dock. **8.** to put into a dry dock for repairs, etc. ◇*v.i.* **9.** to come or go into a dock or dry dock: *The ship docks at 3 o'clock today.* [orig. uncert.]

dock[2] /dɒk/, *n.* **1.** the solid or fleshy part of an animal's tail. **2.** The part of a tail left after cutting. ◇*v.t.* **3.** to cut off the end of (a tail, etc.) **4.** to deduct a part from (wages, etc.): *to dock $100 from her wages.* [OE *-docca*, in *fingerdocca* finger muscle]

dock[3] /dɒk/, *n.* the part of a courtroom where the accused is placed during trial. [Flem *dok* cage]

dock[4] /dɒk/, *n.* a tall, broad-leafed weed with a long taproot. [OE *docce*]

docket /'dɒkət/, *n.* **1.** a carrier's note stating the contents of a parcel, etc.; consignment note; freight note; ticket. **2.** a warrant certifying payment of customs duty. **3.** a note acknowledging receipt of goods or services. **4.** a receipt: *Have you kept the docket for the clothes you bought?* [ME *doket*; orig. obscure]

dockyard /'dɒkjad/, *n.* a naval establishment containing docks, shops, warehouses, etc., where ships are built, fitted out, and repaired.

doctor /'dɒktə/, *n.* **1.** a person licensed to practise medicine, or some branch of medicine; a physician or medical practitioner other than a surgeon. **2.** a person who has received the highest degree given by a university. **3.** (*cap.*) an academic title or title of respect for such a person. **4.** *Colloq.* a person who repairs or fixes things: *tree doctor.* **5.** a strong, fresh breeze: *Albany doctor; Fremantle doctor; Esperance doctor.* **6.** *Colloq.* a cook. ◇*v.t.* **7.** to treat medicinally. **8.** *Colloq.* to repair or mend. **9.** *Colloq.* to tamper with; falsify; adulterate. **10.** *Colloq.* to castrate or spay. [L: teacher] **—doctoral**, *adj.*

doctorate /'dɒktərət/, *n.* the degree of doctor.

doctrinaire /ˌdɒktrə'neə/, *n., adj.* (a person) applying principles or theories inflexibly, with no regard for circumstances. [F]

doctrine /'dɒktrən/, *n.* **1.** a particular principle taught or advocated: *the doctrine of original sin.* **2.** that which is taught; teachings collectively: *Christian doctrine; Marxist doctrine.* [ME, from F, from L: teaching, learning] **—doctrinal**, *adj.*

document /'dɒkjəmənt/, *n.*; /'dɒkju,ment/, *v.* ◇*n.* **1.** a written or printed paper giving information or evidence. ◇*v.t.* **2.** to provide with documents, evidence, or the like. **3.** to support by documentary evidence: *to document a case.* [ME, from L: lesson, example]

documentary /ˌdɒkju'mentəri, -tri/, *adj., n., pl.* **-ries.** ◇*adj.* **1.** Also, **documental.** relating to, consisting of, or derived from documents: *documentary evidence.* ◇*n.* **2.** a factual presentation of a real event, person's life, etc., in a television or radio program, film, etc.

documentation /ˌdɒkjumen'teɪʃən/, *n.* **1.** the use of documentary evidence. **2.** a furnishing with documents. **3.** the recording of an event, as by the media.

dodder /'dɒdə/, *v.i.* to shake; tremble; totter. [See DITHER] **—doddery**, *adj.*

dodeca-, a word part meaning '12'. Also, before vowels, **dodec-**. [Gk *dōdeka-*]

dodecagon /dou'dekəgən/, *n.* a polygon with 12 angles and 12 sides. [Gk. See DODECA-, -GON] **—dodecagonal**, *adj.*

dodecahedron /ˌdoudekə'hidrən/, *n., pl.* **-drons, -dra** /-drə/. a solid figure with 12 faces. [Gk] **—dodecahedral**, *adj.*

dodge /dɒdʒ/, *v.,* **dodged, dodging,** *n.* ◇*v.i.* **1.** to move aside or change position suddenly, as to avoid a blow or to get behind something. **2.** to use tricks or evasions; prevaricate. ◇*n.* **3.** a spring aside. **4.** *Colloq.* a shifty trick; clever expedient. [orig. uncert.]

dodgem /'dɒdʒəm/, *n.* a small electric car driven on a special rink at carnivals, shows, etc. Also, **dodgem car.** [? b. DODGE + (TH)EM]

dodger /'dɒdʒə/, *n.* **1.** a person who dodges. **2.** a shifty person. **3.** a small handbill.

dodgy /'dɒdʒi/, *adj.* **1.** crafty; artful. **2.** *Colloq.* difficult; awkward; tricky.

dodo /'doudou/, *n., pl.* **-does, -dos. 1.** a clumsy flightless bird about the size of a goose, formerly inhabiting the islands of Mauritius, Reunion, and Rodriguez, but now extinct. **2.** *Colloq.* a silly or slow-witted person. **3. dead as a dodo**, *Colloq.* defunct or inanimate beyond possibility of revival. [Pg *doudo* silly]

doe /dou/, *n.* **1.** the female of the deer and antelope. **2.** the female of certain other animals, as the kangaroo, goat, and rabbit. [ME, OE *dā*]

Doe /dou/, *n.* **John** or **Jane,** a fictitious name used esp. in 19th century actions of ejectment when the plaintiff's real name could not be revealed.

Doenitz /'dɒnɪts/, *n.* **Karl,** 1892–1980, German admiral, succeeded Hitler as German Head of State; surrendered to Allies 7 May 1945, thus ending World War II. Also, **Dönitz.**

does /dʌz/; *weak form* /dəz/, *v.* **1.** third person singular present indicative of **do**[1]. **2. that does it!** (exclamation showing exasperation, defeat, etc.).

doesn't /'dʌzənt/, *v.* short form of *does not.*

doff /dɒf/, *v.t.* **1.** to put or take off, as dress. **2.** to remove (the hat) in greeting. [contraction of *do off*. See DON²]

dog /dɒg/, *n., v.,* **dogged, dogging.** ◇*n.* **1.** any of various four-legged, flesh-eating mammals, either wild, such as wolves, foxes, etc., or domesticated, such as poodles, German shepherds, etc. **2.** the male of such an animal (opposed to *bitch*). **3.** a mean despicable fellow. **4.** a fellow or person: *a gay dog; lucky dog.* **5.** any of various mechanical devices, as for holding something. **6.** (*pl.*) *Colloq.* greyhound racing. **7.** *Colloq.* an informer. **8. go to the dogs,** *Colloq.* to go to ruin. **9. lead a dog's life,** to have a difficult existence. **10. let sleeping dogs lie,** to leave alone things that may cause trouble. ◇*v.t.* **11.** to follow closely like a dog. **12.** to trouble; plague: *Bad luck dogged his life.* [OE *docga*]

dogbox /'dɒgbɒks/, *n.* a box-like compartment in a train opening into a corridor.

dog-collar /'dɒg-kɒlə/, *n.* **1.** a collar worn by a dog. **2.** *Colloq.* a stiff collar, worn back-to-front by certain clergymen. **3.** → **choker** (def. 2).

doge /doʊdʒ/, *n. Europ Hist.* the chief magistrate of the old republics of Venice and Genoa. [It, from L: leader]

dog-ear /'dɒg-ɪə/, *n.* **1.** a turned-down corner of a page in a book as from careless use, or to mark a place. ◇*v.t.* **2.** to mark with dog-ears. – **dog-eared,** *adj.*

dogfight /'dɒgfaɪt/, *n.* **1.** a fight between dogs. **2.** combat between two fighter planes. **3.** any rough fight with no rules.

dogfish /'dɒgfɪʃ/, *n., pl.* **-fishes,** (*esp. collectively*) **-fish.** any of various small sharks.

dogged /'dɒgəd/, *adj.* not giving in easily; determined; obstinate.

doggerel /'dɒgərəl/, *adj.* **1.** (of poetry) comic and usu. irregular in measure. **2.** rude; crude; poor. ◇*n.* **3.** doggerel poetry. [ME; orig. uncert.]

doggo /'dɒgoʊ/, *adv. Colloq.* **1.** out of sight. **2. lie doggo,** to hide.

doghouse /'dɒghaʊs/, *n.* **1.** a kennel. **2. in the doghouse,** in disfavor.

dogleg /'dɒglɛg/, *n.* **1.** a sharp bend in a road, race-track, golf course, etc. ◇*adj.* **2.** Also, **doglegged.** having such a bend.

dogma /'dɒgmə/, *n., pl.* **-mas, -mata** /-mətə/. **1.** a system of principles, as of a church. **2.** an opinion; belief; principle. [L, from Gk]

dogmatic /dɒg'mætɪk/, *adj.* **1.** of, relating to, or of the nature of a dogma or dogmas; doctrinal. **2.** giving opinions without proof and expecting people to accept them; positive; opinionated. Also, **dogmatical.** – **dogmatically,** *adv.*

dogmatism /'dɒgmətɪzəm/, *n.* dogmatic (def. 2) character; arrogant assertion of opinions. – **dogmatist,** *n.*

Dog on the Tuckerbox, *n.* a bronze monument of a dog on a marble pedestal situated near Gundagai, NSW, on the Hume Highway.

dog paddle, *n.* a simple swimming stroke in which the legs are kicked and the hands paddle.

Dog Star, *n.* → **Sirius.**

dogwatch /'dɒgwɒtʃ/, *n.* **1.** a short early evening watch on board ship. **2.** the night shift, as in a coal mine.

doh /doʊ/, *n. Music.* Also, **do.** See **solfa.**

doily /'dɔɪli/, *n., pl.* **-lies.** a small ornamental mat, as of embroidery or lace, paper or plastic, often placed under cakes on a plate etc. [named after a 17th C draper of London]

doing /'duɪŋ/, *n.* **1.** action; performance; execution: *It's all in the doing.* **2.** (*pl.*) deeds; proceedings. **3.** *Colloq.* a beating. **4. nothing doing,** (an exclamation meaning no). **5. take a bit of** or **a lot of** or **some doing,** to need a lot of effort.

Dolby system /'dɒlbi sɪstəm/, *n.* a method of reducing noise in recording and playback of magnetic tapes. [Trademark]

doldrums /'dɒldrəmz/, *n.pl.* **1.** an area of calm near equator. **2. in the doldrums,** period of inactivity, depression, etc. [orig. uncert.]

dole /doʊl/, *n., v.,* **doled, doling.** ◇*n.* **1.** a giving out in small amounts, esp. to those in need. **2.** a payment by government to an unemployed person. **3. go** or **be on the dole,** to receive such payments. ◇*v.t.* **4.** to give out in small quantities (fol. by *out*). [OE *dāl* part, portion]

dole bludger, *n. Colloq.* (*offensive*) someone who is unemployed and lives on the dole without trying to find employment.

dolerite /'dɒləraɪt/, *n. Geol.* a coarse-grained variety of igneous rock, esp. basalt or rocks like it. [Gk *dolerós* deceptive + -ITE¹] – **doleritic,** *adj.*

doll /dɒl/, *n.* **1.** a toy representing a child or other human being; a child's toy baby. **2.** a pretty but unintelligent woman. **3.** *Colloq.* an attractive woman, esp. one who is young. ◇*v.i.* **4.** *Colloq.* to dress smartly (fol. by *up*). ◇*v.t.* **5.** to dress (oneself) up too much (fol. by *up*). [from *Doll, Dolly,* for *Dorothy,* woman's name]

dollar /'dɒlə/, *n.* **1.** the unit of Australian money, equal to 100 cents. *Symbol:* $. **2.** any of various units elsewhere, as in the US, Hong Kong, etc. **3. bottom dollar,** the last of a person's money: *down to his bottom dollar.* [HG *Thaler*, for *Joachimsthaler* coin of Joachimsthal, town in Bohemia where they were coined]

dollar bird, *n.* a bird with a large white spot on each wing, which breeds in summer in Australia and migrates to PNG.

dollop /'dɒləp/, *n. Colloq.* a shapeless lump; a blob.

dolly /'dɒli/, *n., pl.* **dollies.** **1.** a child's name for a doll. **2. a.** a low truck with small wheels for moving heavy objects. **b.** *Films, TV,* a small, movable platform for carrying cameras, directors, etc. **3.** any of various devices thought to look like a doll, used for washing clothes, scouring wool, and washing gold ore. **4.** (in panel beating, etc.) a hand tool with one end made very heavy as by lead, and used to form sheet metal, reshape a dented pipe, etc. **5.** Also, **dolly bird.** *Colloq.* a young, pretty girl who is not very intelligent.

dolmen /'dɒlmən/, *n.* an ancient structure of two large upright stones holding up a horizontal stone.

dolomite /'dɒləmaɪt/, *n.* **1.** a very common mineral, calcium magnesium carbonate. **2.** a rock consisting largely of this mineral. [named after DG de *Dolomieu*, 1750–1801, French geologist] **– dolomitic**, *adj.*

dolorous /'dɒlərəs/, *adj.* full of, expressing, or causing pain or sorrow; mournful. **– dolour**, *n.*

dolphin /'dɒlfɪn/, *n.* **1.** any of various large, intelligent sea mammals, some of which are commonly called porpoises, which have a long, sharp nose. **2.** either of two fishes noted for their fast color changes when dying. **3.** *Naut.* a post, pile cluster, or buoy to which to moor a vessel. [ME, from OF, from L, from Gk *delphīs*]

dolt /doʊlt/, *n.* a dull, stupid person; a blockhead. **– doltish**, *adj.*

-dom, a noun suffix meaning: **1.** domain, as in *kingdom*. **2.** collection of persons, as in *officialdom*. **3.** rank, as in *earldom*. **4.** general condition, as in *freedom*. [OE *-dōm*, suffix, representing *dōm*, n. See DOOM]

dom., *Abbrev.* **1.** domestic. **2.** domicile. **3.** dominant.

domain /də'meɪn/, *n.* **1.** *Law.* ownership and control over the use of land. **2.** a field of activity, knowledge, etc.: *the domain of commerce; the domain of science.* **3.** a region with specific characteristics, types of growth, animal life, etc. **4.** (*cap.*) **the**, a park in Sydney, NSW, next to the Botanic Gardens on the eastern side of the city; a traditional forum for public speaking. 40 ha. **5.** *Phys.* a small region of ferromagnetic substance in which its atoms or molecules have a common direction of magnetisation. **6.** *Maths.* (of a function) the set of values of the independent variables for which the function is defined. [F, from L: that belonging to a lord]

dome /doʊm/, *n.* **1.** *Archit.* a large, hemispherical roof. **2.** anything shaped like a dome. **3.** *Geol.* a roughly symmetrical upfold, with beds dipping in all directions, more or less equally, from a point. **4.** *Geol.* a smoothly-rounded, rock-capped mountain summit, roughly resembling the dome or cupola of a building. [L *domus* house] **– domed**, *adj.* **– domical**, *adj.*

Domesday Book /'duːmzdeɪ bʊk/, *n.* a record of a survey of the lands of England made by order of William the Conqueror about 1086, giving ownership, extent, value, etc., of the properties. Also, **Doomsday Book.**

domestic /də'mɛstɪk/, *adj.* **1.** of or relating to the home, the household, or family. **2.** enjoying home life or matters. **3.** living with humans; tame: *domestic animals*. **4.** belonging, existing, or produced within a country; not foreign. ◇*n.* **5.** a hired household servant. **6.** *Colloq.* an argument with one's spouse. [L: belonging to the household] **– domestically**, *adv.*

domesticate /də'mɛstəkeɪt/, *v.t.*, **-cated**, **-cating. 1.** to train (an animal) to live with man; tame. **2.** to cause to enjoy home life. **– domestication**, *n.* **– domesticity**, *n.*

domicile /'dɒməsaɪl/, *n.*, *v.*, **-ciled**, **-ciling.** ◇*n.* **1.** someone's home; a place of residence; an abode. **2.** *Law.* the country deemed by law to be a person's permanent place of residence. **3.** *Comm.* the place at which a bill of exchange is made payable, other than the acceptor's private or business address. ◇*v.i.* **4.** to have one's domicile; dwell (fol. by *at*, *in*, etc.). [F, from L: habitation, dwelling] **– domiciliary**, *adj.*

dominant /'dɒmənənt/, *adj.* **1.** ruling; controlling; most influential. **2.** having a commanding position: *the dominant points of the globe.* **3.** main; major; chief: *Steel production is the dominant industry in Newcastle.* **4.** *Biol.* relating to or showing a dominant. ◇*n.* **5.** *Biol.* a hereditary character resulting from a gene with a greater biochemical activity than another, called the recessive. The dominant is stronger than the recessive. See **recessive**. **6.** *Music.* the fifth note of a scale. [F, from L] **– dominance**, *n.*

dominate /'dɒməneɪt/, *v.*, **-nated**, **-nating.** ◇*v.t.* **1.** to rule; control. **2.** to tower above; overshadow. ◇*v.i.* **3.** to rule over; exercise control; predominate. **4.** to have a commanding position. [L] **– dominator**, *n.* **– dominative**, *adj.* **– domination**, *n.*

domineer /dɒmə'nɪə/, *v.i.* to govern or command without considering the wishes of others; tyrannise. [D, from F, from L: rule] **– domineering**, *adj.*

Dominic /'dɒmənɪk/, *n.* **Saint** (*Domingo de Guzmán*), 1170–1221, Spanish priest; founder of the Dominican order.

Dominican /də'mɪnɪkən/, *adj.* **1.** relating to St Dominic or to the religious order founded by him. **2.** relating to the Dominican Republic.

Dominican Republic, *n.* a republic in the West Indies, between Cuba and Puerto Rico; a Spanish colony before independence in 1844; occupied by US military forces 1916–24. Pop. 6 077 710 (1987 est.); 48 422 km². *Language:* Spanish. *Currency:* peso. *Cap.:* Santo Domingo. Formerly, **Santo Domingo.**

dominion /də'mɪnjən/, *n.* **1.** rule, or power to rule; control or influence. **2.** the lands ruled by one person or government. [ME, from F (obs.), from L: lordship, ownership]

domino /'dɒmənoʊ/, *n.*, *pl.* **-noes**. **1.** (*pl. treated as sing.*) a game played with flat, oblong pieces, usu. of wood, the faces of which are divided in halves, each either blank or marked with dots, from one to six. **2.** one of these pieces. [orig. unknown]

domino theory, *n.* the theory that a particular political event in one country will lead to its repetition in others, as a Communist

domino theory

takeover of one SE Asian country leading to a similar takeover of countries near it.

Domitian /dəˈmɪʃən/, n. AD 51-96, Roman emperor AD 81-96.

don[1] /dɒn/, n. 1. (cap.) a Spanish title showing high rank. 2. a Spanish lord or gentleman. 3. (in British universities) a tutor of a college. [Sp, from L: master, lord]

don[2] /dɒn/, v.t., **donned, donning**. to put on (clothing, etc.). [contraction of *do on*. See DOFF]

Don /dɒn/, n. a river flowing from central European Russia south through a wide arc to the Sea of Azov. About 2090 km.

Donar /ˈdɒnə/, n. German Myth. the god of thunder. [OHG. c. OE *thunor*, Icel *Thōr*, G *Donner*]

donate /douˈneɪt/, v.t., **-nated, -nating**. to present as a gift, as to a fund or cause. —**donator**, n. —**donation**, n. —**donative**, adj.

Donatello /dɒnəˈtɛloʊ/, n. (*Donato di Betto Bardi*), c. 1386-1466, pre-eminent Florentine sculptor. Also, **Donato** /dɒˈnɑtoʊ/.

Doncaster and Templestowe /ˌdɒŋkæstər ən ˈtɛmpəlstoʊ/, n. a city within the metropolitan area of Melbourne, Victoria, north-west of its centre. Pop. 99 269 (1986).

done /dʌn/, v. 1. past participle of *do*[1]. 2. **have** or **be done with**, to have finished with. ◊adj. 3. completed; finished; settled. 4. worn out; used up. 5. socially acceptable: *Wearing thongs isn't done*.

Donegal /ˈdɒnɪɡɔl/, n. a county in the north-western Republic of Ireland on the Atlantic coast. Pop. 129 428 (1986); 4830 km². *County town*: Lifford. *Irish*, **Dún na nGall**.

dong /dɒŋ/, v.t. 1. *Colloq*. to hit, punch. ◊v.i. 2. (of a bell, etc.) to ring. ◊n. 3. *Colloq*. a heavy blow.

donga /ˈdɒŋɡə/, n. 1. a shallow gully or dried-out watercourse. 2. a makeshift shelter. [Afrikaans: watercourse, from Zulu]

Donizetti /dɒnəˈzɛti, dɒnəˈtsɛti/, n. **Gaetano** /ɡeɪˈtɑnoʊ/, 1797-1848, Italian operatic composer.

Don Juan /dɒn ˈdʒuən, ˈwɑn/, n. a legendary Spanish nobleman of dissolute habits.

donkey /ˈdɒŋki/, n., pl. **-keys**, adj. ◊n. 1. a domesticated ass. 2. a stupid, silly or obstinate person. 3. **donkey's years**, a long time. ◊adj. 4. *Mech*. auxiliary: *a donkey pump*. [? familiar var. of *Duncan*, man's name]

donkey vote, n. a vote cast unthinkingly, giving the order of preferences from the top to bottom on the ballot paper.

Donleavy /dʌnˈlivi/, n. **J(ames) P(atrick)**, born 1926, US-born writer and dramatist living in Ireland; best known for *The Ginger Man* (novel, 1955); play, 1959).

donna /ˈdɒnə/, n. 1. a lady. 2. (cap.) a title of respect for a lady. [It, from L: lady, mistress]

Donne /dʌn/, n. **John**, 1573-1631, English metaphysical poet and clergyman.

dope

donnybrook /ˈdɒnibrʊk/, n. a fight or argument; brawl. Also, **donneybrook**. [orig. with ref. to a fair held annually until 1855 at *Donnybrook*, Dublin, and famous for rioting and dissipation]

Donnybrook /ˈdɒnibrʊk/, n. a town and shire in south-western WA south-east of Bunbury. Pop. 1352 (1986).

Donohoe /ˈdɒnəhu/, n. **John** ('*Bold Jack*'), 1806?–1830, Australian bushranger, born in Dublin; became a folk hero, his exploits being the subject of several songs and ballads. Also, **Donahue, Donohue, Donahoo, Donohoo, Donahoe**.

donor /ˈdoʊnə/, n. 1. someone who gives or donates something. 2. *Med*. **a**. a person or animal giving blood for transfusion. **b**. a person giving body organs, as a kidney or heart, for transplant surgery. 3. *Chem*. an atom which gives both electrons in a dative bond. 4. *Elect*. an imperfection or impurity in a semiconductor which causes conduction by electrons. [ME, from AF, L: give]

Don Quixote /dɒn ˈkwɪksət, kiˈhoʊtɛɪ/, n. the hero of a romance (1605 and 1615) by Cervantes, who was inspired by lofty and chivalrous but impractical ideals.

don't /doʊnt/, v. shortened form of *do not*.

doodle /ˈdudl/, v., **-dled, -dling**, n. ◊v.t., v.i. 1. to draw (a pattern, etc.) or scribble while preoccupied. ◊n. 2. the pattern, figure, etc., so drawn.

doom /dum/, n. 1. a terrible fate. 2. ruin; death. 3. a judgment or sentence, esp. an unfavorable one. ◊v.t. 4. to destine, esp. to a terrible fate. 5. to pronounce judgment against; condemn. [OE *dōm* judgment, sentence, law]

doomsday /ˈdumzdeɪ/, n. Judgment Day, at the end of the world. [OE *dōmes dæg* day of judgment]

Doomsday Book, n. → **Domesday Book**.

door /dɔ/, n. 1. a movable flat piece of wood, etc., used for closing and opening an entrance to a building, room, cupboard, etc. 2. a doorway. 3. a building, etc., to which a door belongs: *two doors down the street*. 4. **lay at the door of**, to blame someone for. 5. **next door to**, **a**. in the next house to. **b**. very near. 6. **out of doors**, outside. [OE *duru*]

doorjamb /ˈdɔdʒæm/, n. one of the two upright posts forming the sides of a doorway.

doorknock /ˈdɔnɒk/, v.i. 1. to go from house to house asking for money for some charity, support for some political party, etc. ◊n. 2. a campaign of doorknocking: *The Heart Foundation is holding a doorknock*. ◊adj. 3. of or relating to such a campaign: *a doorknock appeal*.

dopa /ˈdoʊpə/, n. an amino acid, naturally present in the body. [d(ihydr)o(xy)p(henyl)a(l-anine)]

dope /doʊp/, n., v., **doped, doping**. *Colloq*. ◊n. 1. any drug, esp. a narcotic. 2. information. 3. a stupid person. ◊v.t. 4. to affect with dope or drugs (oft. fol. by *up*): *They*

dope 306 **double**

doped the horses before the race. [D *doop* a dipping, sauce]

dopey /'doupi/, *adj.*, **dopier, dopiest.** *Colloq.* **1.** affected by or as if by a depressant drug; sluggish. **2.** stupid; slow-witted. Also, **dopy.**

doppelgänger /'dɒpəlgɛŋə/, *n.* a ghostly double of a living person. Also, **doubleganger.** [G: double-goer]

Doppler effect /'dɒplə ə,fɛkt/, *n. Phys.* a change which seems to occur in the frequency and wavelength of sound or light waves perceived as the distance between the source and receiver changes. [named after CJ *Doppler*, 1803–53, Austrian physicist]

Doric /'dɒrɪk/, *adj. Archit.* describing or relating to the simplest of the three Greek columns, distinguished by low proportions, a shaft without a base, and a saucer-shaped capital. [L, from Gk *Dōrikós*]

dormant /'dɔmənt/, *adj.* **1.** lying asleep or as if asleep. **2.** in a state of rest or inactivity; quiescent; in abeyance: *dormant buds; a dormant volcano.* [ME, from OF, from L: sleep, be inactive] — **dormancy,** *n.*

dormer /'dɔmə/, *n.* **1.** Also, **dormer window.** an upright window in a projection built out from a sloping roof. **2.** the projecting structure. [orig., a sleeping chamber] — **dormered,** *adj.*

dormitory /'dɔmətri/, *n., pl.* **-tories.** a room for sleeping, usu. large and containing many beds, for the inmates of a school or other institution. [L]

dormouse /'dɔmaʊs/, *n., pl.* **-mice** /-maɪs/. *Zool.* any of several small, furry-tailed rodents of Europe, Asia and Africa, which look like small squirrels. [? DOR(MANT) + MOUSE]

Dorrigo Range /dɒrɪgoʊ 'reɪndʒ/, *n.* a ridge extending from the highest point in the New England Range in northern NSW almost to the sea near Coffs Harbor. Highest peak, 1600 m.

dorsal /'dɔsəl/, *adj.* **1.** *Zool.* of, relating to, or found on the back, as an organ or part: *dorsal nerves; a dorsal fin.* **2.** *Bot.* relating to the surface away from the axis, as of a leaf. [L *dorsum* back]

Dorset /'dɔsət/, *n.* a county in southern England on the English Channel. Pop. 638 200 (1986 est.); 2520 km². *Administrative centre:* Dorchester. Also, **Dorsetshire.**

dorsi-, combining form of **dorsal, dorsum.** Also, **dorso-.**

dorsum /'dɔsəm/, *n., pl.* **-sa** /-sə/. the back, as of the body, or an organ, part, etc. [L]

dory /'dɔri/, *n., pl.* **-ries. 1.** a flattened, deep-bodied, spiny-rayed, food fish (the **John Dory**), found in both European and Australian seas. **2.** any similar fish. [ME, from F: gilded]

dose /doʊs/, *n., v.,* **dosed, dosing.** ◇*n.* **1.** a quantity of medicine to be taken at one time. **2.** a definite quantity of anything like medicine, esp. of something unpleasant or disagreeable: *We've had a dose of bad weather lately.* **3.** *Phys.* the amount of ionising radiation absorbed by a given quantity of material, usu. measured in rads; dosage. ◇*v.t.* **4.** to give doses to (oft. fol. by *up*): *The doctor dosed him (up) with cough medicine.* [F, from ML, from Gk: giving, portion, dose] — **dosage,** *n.*

doss /dɒs/, *Colloq.* ◇*n.* **1.** a place to sleep, esp. in a cheap lodging house. ◇*v.i.* **2.** to make a temporary sleeping place for oneself (oft. fol. by *down*). [F *dos* back, from L]

dossier /'dɒsiə/, *n.* a bundle of papers on the same subject, esp. containing information about a particular person. [F: a bundle of papers with a label on the back]

Dostoevski /dɒstɔɪ'ɛfski/, *n.* **Feodor Mikhailovich** /fɪ,odə mɪ'keɪlɒvɪtʃ/, 1821–81, Russian novelist and short-story writer. Also, **Dostoyevsky.** — **Dostoevskian,** *adj.*

dot /dɒt/, *n., v.,* **dotted, dotting.** ◇*n.* **1.** a small spot; speck: *The car soon became a dot on the horizon.* **2.** a small, roundish mark made with or as if with a pen. **3.** *Music.* **a.** a point placed after a note or rest showing that its length is to be increased one half. **b.** a point placed under or over a note showing that it is to be shortened. **4.** (in Morse code, etc.) a signal shorter than a dash, used in groups of dots, dashes, and spaces, to represent letters. **5. in the year dot,** *Colloq.* long ago. **6. on the dot,** *Colloq.* exactly on time; punctual. ◇*v.t.* **7.** to mark or cover with or as with a dot or dots. **8. dot one's i's and cross one's t's,** *Colloq.* to give attention to all the details. [OE *dott* head of a boil]

dote /doʊt/, *v.i.,* **doted, doting. 1.** to give too much love or fondness (fol. by *on* or *upon*): *His grandmother doted on him.* **2.** to be weak-minded, esp. from old age. [ME] — **dotage,** *n.*

dotterel /'dɒtərəl/, *n.* any of several small wading birds related to the English plover, found on temperate and tropical coasts of Australia. Also, **dottrel.** [DOTE + -REL]

dotty /'dɒti/, *adj.,* **-tier, -tiest. 1.** *Colloq.* mad; eccentric; crazy. **2.** *Colloq.* overly fond. **3.** marked with dots.

double /'dʌbəl/, *adj., n., v.,* **-led, -ling,** *adv.* ◇*adj.* **1.** twice as great, heavy, strong, etc.: *double pay; a double portion.* **2.** twofold in form, size, amount, extent, etc.; of extra size or weight: *a double blanket; a double bed.* **3.** made of two like parts; paired: *a double cherry.* **4.** *Bot.* (of flowers) having a greatly increased number of petals. **5.** (of musical instruments) producing notes an octave lower: *double bass.* **6.** twofold in character, meaning, or conduct (sometimes one good and one bad); ambiguous: *a double interpretation; a double life.* ◇*n.* **7.** anything doubled. **8.** a duplicate; counterpart. **9.** *Films, etc.* a stand-in who takes another's place if necessary. **10.** *Tennis.* two serving faults in a row. **11.** (*pl.*) a game in which there are two players on each side. **12.** a bet on two horses, in different races, any winnings and the money from the first bet being placed on the second horse: *feature double; daily double.* **13. at** or **on the double, a.** in double time. **b.** *Colloq.* fast; quickly; at a run. ◇*v.t.* **14.** to make double or twice as great: *to double your income.* **15.** *Films, etc.* to act as a double for another actor. **16.** to bend or fold with one part upon another (oft. fol. by *over, up, back,* etc.). **17.** to carry a second person on a horse, bicycle, etc. ◇*v.i.* **18.** to become double. **19.** to double a stake in gambling or the like (oft. fol. by *up*). **20.** to bend or fold (oft. fol. by *up*). **21.** to turn back on a course (oft. fol. by *back*). **22.** to serve in two ways. ◇*adv.* **23.** twofold; doubly. [ME, from OF, from L *duplus*]

double agent, *n.* a secret agent working at the same time for two opposed employers, as countries, governments, etc., usu. without either of them knowing of the association with the other.

double bar, *n.* a double vertical line on a stave showing the end of a piece or section of music.

double-barrelled /'dʌbəl-bærəld/, *adj.* **1.** having two barrels, as a gun. **2.** serving a double purpose. **3.** (of a surname) having two elements hyphenated.

double bass, *n.* the largest instrument of the violin family, which has four strings and is played resting upright on the floor.

double bond, *n.* two covalent bonds joining two atoms of a molecule together, oft. common in unsaturated organic compounds, as in the alkene series.

double-breasted /'dʌbəl-brestəd/, *adj.* (of a coat, jacket, etc.) having one side overlapping the other, with two rows of buttons and one row of buttonholes.

double chin, *n.* a fold of fat beneath the chin.

doublecross /dʌbəl'krɒs/, *v.t. Colloq.* to deceive by pretending friendship; betray.

double-dealing /dʌbəl-'dilɪŋ/, *n.* **1.** deception. ◇*adj.* **2.** deceitful; treacherous. —**double-dealer,** *n.*

double decomposition, *n. Chem.* a chemical reaction between two compounds in which each decomposes and recombines with its opposite from the other compound, forming two new compounds.

double dissolution, *n. Govt.* an order given by a governor-general dissolving both houses of parliament and causing a new election for all senators and members to be called.

double-dutch /dʌbəl-'dʌtʃ/, *n. Colloq.* nonsense; gibberish; incomprehensible speech.

double entendre /dʌbəl ɒn'tɒndrə/, *n.* a word or expression with two meanings, esp. when one of the meanings is indelicate. [F (obs.)]

double exposure, *n.* (a photograph made by) the taking of two photographs on one frame of film.

double helix, *n.* any two interlocking spirals, esp. the structure of DNA where two spiral chains are held together by hydrogen bonds.

double-jointed /dʌbəl-'dʒɔɪntəd/, *adj.* (of a person) having joints which enable the limbs to bend in extraordinary ways.

double refraction, *n. Phys.* the separation of a ray of light into two unequally refracted rays, as in passing through certain crystals.

double salt, *n. Chem.* a compound which is formed by crystallisation of two salts out of a solution, and which, when redissolved, ionises separately, e.g. potassium aluminium sulfate.

double standard, *n.* any principle, moral code, etc., which permits greater freedom to one person or group than to another, esp. that which imposes stricter sexual morals on women than men.

doublet /'dʌblət/, *n.* **1.** a close-fitting outer body garment, with or without sleeves, formerly worn by men. **2.** a pair of like things; couple. **3.** one of a pair of like things; a duplicate. **4.** a false gem made by welding together two pieces of a different nature, as a thin bar of opal covering a quartz or plastic dome. [ME, from OF]

doublethink /'dʌbəlθɪŋk/, *n.* the ability to accept two inconsistent facts at the same time and to ignore the conflict between them. [coined by George Orwell in *Nineteen Eighty-Four* (1949)]

double time, *n.* **1.** double wages paid to people who work at unpopular times, such as public holidays, etc. **2.** a slow running pace used by troops in step. **3. in double time,** with speed; quickly.

doubloon /dʌb'lun/, *n.* a former Spanish gold coin. [L: double]

doubt /daʊt/, *v.t.* **1.** to be uncertain in opinion about; hold questionable; hesitate to believe: *I doubt the validity of that argument.* **2.** to distrust: *I doubt that argument.* ◇*v.i.* **3.** to feel uncertain; be undecided. ◇*n.* **4.** undecidedness of opinion or belief; feeling of uncertainty. **5.** distrust; suspicion. **6. beyond a shadow of doubt,** for certain; definitely. **7. no doubt, a.** probably. **b.** certainly. **8. without doubt,** without question; certainly. [ME, from L: hesitate, doubt] —**doubtingly,** *adv.*

doubtful /'daʊtfəl/, *adj.* **1.** causing doubt; uncertain; ambiguous: *a doubtful argument.* **2.** uncertain; hesitating: *He feels doubtful about his future.* **3.** questionable, as of character.

douche /duʃ/, *n., v.,* **douched, douching.** ◇*n.* **1.** (an instrument for forcing) a stream of water into or onto any part of the body to wash or medicate it. ◇*v.t.* **2.** to give a douche to. [F, from It: conduit, shower, from L: lead]

dough /doʊ/, *n.* **1.** flour, mixed with water, milk, etc., used for baking into bread, cake, etc. **2.** *Colloq.* money. [OE *dā*]

doughnut /'doʊnʌt/, *n.* a small ring-shaped deep-fried cake. Also, **donut.** [DOUGH + NUT, in allusion to the original shape]

doughty /'daʊti/, *adj.,* **-tier, -tiest.** strong; hardy; valiant. [OE: be good, avail] —**doughtily,** *adv.* —**doughtiness,** *n.*

Douglas /'dʌɡləs/, *n.* **1. Donald Wills,** born 1892, US aircraft designer whose company developed the Douglas (DC) series of aircraft.

2. Sir James ('*the Black Douglas*'), c. 1286-1330, Scottish military leader. **3. Kirk** (*Yssur Danilovitch Demsky*), born 1916, US film actor and producer. **4. Michael**, born 1945, son of Kirk, US actor, won Academy Award for *Wall Street* (1988).

Douglas-Home /ˌdʌɡləs-'hjuːm/, *n.* **Sir Alexander Frederick** (*Alec*), formerly **14th Earl of Home**, born 1903, British politician; renounced his title to sit in House of Commons; prime minister 1963-64.

dour /'dauə, duə/, *adj.* **1.** sour; sullen; gloomy. **2.** hard; severe; stern. [Scot d., from L: hard]

douse /daus/, *v.t.*, **doused, dousing. 1.** to put into water, or throw water over; drench. **2.** *Colloq.* to put out (a light). [orig. obscure]

dove /dʌv/, *n.* **1.** any bird of the pigeon family. **2.** (*cap.*) the Holy Spirit. **3.** an innocent or gentle person. **4.** a politician or political adviser who favors peaceful policies. [OE *dūfe-*, akin to DIVE, v.] — **dovish**, *adj.*

dovecot /'dʌvkɒt/, *n.* a small house or box for domestic pigeons. Also, **dovecote** /'dʌvkoʊt/.

dover /'douvə/, *n.* **1.** a pocket knife. **2.** hand shears. [orig. from brand name on blade of both knife and shears]

Dover /'douvə/, *n.* **1.** a seaport in south-eastern England, in eastern Kent, nearest to the coast of France. Pop. 100 751 (1981). **2. Straits of**, a strait between England and France, connecting the English Channel with the North Sea. Least width, 32 km. French, **Pas de Calais**.

dovetail /'dʌvteɪl/, *n.* **1.** *Carp.* a joint or fastening formed by tenons (projections) and mortices (cavities) made to fit into one another. ◊*v.t., v.i.* **2.** to join or fit together with or as if with a dovetail.

dowager /'dauədʒə/, *n.* **1.** a woman of rank who holds some title or property from her dead husband. **2.** *Colloq.* a dignified elderly lady. [MF: woman with a dower, from L: dowry]

dowdy /'daudi/, *adj.* badly dressed; not smart or stylish. [ME *doude*; orig. obscure] — **dowdiness**, *n.*

dowel /'dauəl/, *n.* **1.** Also, **dowel pin**. a pin, usu. round, fitting into corresponding holes in two pieces of wood, etc., to join them or to prevent slipping. **2.** Also, **dowelling**. long, thin wooden rods suitable for this purpose. [compare G *Döbel* peg, plug, pin]

dower /'dauə/, *n.* **1.** (formerly) that part (a third) of a dead husband's property allowed by law to his widow for her life. **2.** →**dowry**. **3.** a natural gift or endowment. ◊*v.t.* **4.** to provide with a dower or dowry; endow. [ME, from OF, from L: dowry]

down[1] /daun/, *adv.* **1.** from higher to lower; in descending direction or order; into or in a lower position or condition: *to climb down quickly*. **2.** on or to the ground: *He fell down*. **.** to a point of quietness, inactivity, etc.: *to calm down; My business is winding down*. **4.** to or in a position spoken of as lower: *They've moved down from Sydney*. **5.** to or at a low point, degree, rate, pitch, volume, etc. **6.** from an earlier to a later time: *The song had come down from the Middle Ages*. **7.** from a greater to a lesser bulk, consistency, strength, etc.: *to boil down syrup*. **8.** in cash; at once: *to pay $40 down*. **9.** *Colloq.* to a lower or worse condition of life, etc.: *to come down in the world*. **10.** *Boxing.* touching the ring floor with some part of the body other than the feet. **11. down to earth**, practical, realistic. **12. down with**, let us be rid of: *Down with the tyrant!* ◊*prep.* **13.** to, towards, at or at a lower place on or in: *down the stairs; down the social ladder*. **14.** in the same course or direction as: *to sail down the river*. **15. down south**, *Colloq.* in the south. ◊*adj.* **16.** downwards; going or directed downwards: *From here the way is down for about three km*. **17.** travelling away from a terminus: *the down train*. **18.** in bed through illness: *He is down with measles*. **19.** inactive; quiet: *The wind is down*. **20.** losing or having lost money at gambling: *He was $10 down*. **21.** *Games.* losing or behind an opponent by a certain number of points, holes, etc. **22.** unhappy; depressed: *He's feeling a bit down these days*. **23. down and out, a.** *Colloq.* without friends, money, or prospects; destitute. **b.** *Boxing.* touching the ring floor with some part of the body other than the feet and not able to rise again. **24. down at heel**, poor; shabby; seedy. **25. down in the mouth**, discouraged; depressed. **26. down on**, over-severe; unnecessarily ready to find faults and punish harshly. ◊*n.* **27.** a period of depression: *the ups and downs of a business*. **28.** *Colloq.* a grudge; feeling of hostility: *He has a down on me*. ◊*v.t.* **29.** to put or throw down; subdue; overcome: *We downed the other side easily*. **30.** to drink: *to down a glass of beer*. ◊*v.* **31. down tools**, (of workers) to stop working, as in starting a strike. ◊*interj.* **32.** (a command, esp. to a dog, to stop jumping, etc.): *Down, Blue!* **33.** (a command to take cover, or duck). [OE *of dūne* from (the) hill]

down[2] /daun/, *n.* **1.** fine soft feathers. **2.** any fine soft hairy growth, as on the human face or limbs, or on some plants. [ME, from Scand] — **downy**, *adj.*

down[3] /daun/, *n.* (usu. *pl.*) open, rolling, upland country usu. covered with grass. [OE *dūn* hill]

Down /daun/, *n.* a county in south-eastern Northern Ireland on the Irish Sea. Pop. 53 600 (1982); 2466 km². *County town*: Downpatrick. Irish, **An Dún**.

down-and-out /daun-ən-'aut/, *n. Colloq.* a person, usu. of disreputable appearance, without friends, money, or prospects.

downcast /'daunkast/, *adj.* **1.** directed downwards, as the eyes. **2.** depressed; dejected in spirit.

downer /'daunə/, *n. Colloq.* **1.** a tranquilliser, e.g. valium. **2.** a depressing experience.

downfall /'daunfɔl/, *n.* **1.** a going down to a lower position or standing; overthrow; ruin. **2.** a cause of this: *Gambling will be his downfall*. **3.** a fall, as of rain or snow. — **downfallen**, *adj.*

downgrade /daʊnˈgreɪd/, v., **-graded, -grading**, n., adj., adv. ◇v.t. **1.** to give (a person, job, etc.) a lower status. **2.** to speak ill of; denigrate; belittle. ◇n. **3.** a downward slope. **4. on the downgrade**, heading for poverty, ruin, etc. ◇adj., adv. **5.** downhill.

downhill /daʊnˈhɪl/, adv.; /ˈdaʊnhɪl/, adj. ◇adv. **1.** down the slope of a hill. **2.** downwards into a worse position, condition, etc.: *Her business is going downhill fast*. ◇adj. **3.** going downwards on or as on a hill: *The path from now on is mainly downhill*.

Downing Street, n. **1.** a short street in Westminster, London; usual residence of the British prime minister at No. 10; other important government offices here. **2.** *Colloq.* the British prime minister and cabinet.

down-market /ˈdaʊn-makət/, adj. of or relating to goods and commercial services of inferior status, quality and price. See **up-market**.

down payment, n. a deposit on a purchase made on an instalment plan or mortgage.

downpipe /ˈdaʊnpaɪp/, n. a pipe for leading rainwater from roofs to a drain or the ground.

downpour /ˈdaʊnpɔ/, n. a heavy fall of rain.

downright /ˈdaʊnraɪt/, adj. **1.** complete; thorough; absolute; out-and-out: *a downright lie*. **2.** direct; straightforward: *a downright character*. ◇adv. **3.** completely or thoroughly; straightforwardly: *He is downright rude*.

downstage /daʊnˈsteɪdʒ/, adv.; /ˈdaʊnsteɪdʒ/, adj. at, towards or relating to the front of the stage in a theatre.

downstairs /daʊnˈstɛəz/, adv.; /ˈdaʊnstɛəz/, adj., n. ◇adv. **1.** down the stairs: *to walk downstairs*. **2.** to or on a lower floor: *The kitchen has been moved downstairs*. ◇adj. **3.** Also, **downstair**. relating to or situated on a lower floor. ◇n. **4.** the lower floor of a house.

downstream /daʊnˈstrim/, adv.; /ˈdaʊnstrim/, adj., adv. ◇adv. **1.** with or in the direction of the current of a stream. ◇adj. **2.** farther down a stream.

Down syndrome, n. a chromosomal abnormality which results in mental retardation and certain physical characteristics, such as slanting eyes; mongolism. Also, **Down's syndrome**. [from John Langdon-*Down*, 1828–96, English physician]

down-to-earth /ˈdaʊn-tu-əθ/, adj. sensible; without pretensions; realistic: *a down-to-earth person*; *a down-to-earth attitude*.

downtown /daʊnˈtaʊn/, adv.; /ˈdaʊntaʊn/, adj. to or in the business section of a city.

downtrodden /ˈdaʊntrɒdn/, adj. trodden down; trampled upon; tyrannised over. Also, **downtrod**.

down-under /daʊn-ˈʌndə/, n. *Colloq.* Australia, NZ, and nearby Pacific islands, esp. as viewed from the Northern Hemisphere.

downward /ˈdaʊnwəd/, adj. **1.** moving or tending to a lower place or condition; descending: *a downward path*; *a downward trend*. ◇adv. **2.** downwards.

downwards /ˈdaʊnwədz/, adv. **1.** from a higher to a lower place or condition. **2.** from earlier times to the present day. Also, **downward**.

downwind /daʊnˈwɪnd/, adv.; /ˈdaʊnwɪnd/, adj. **1.** in the direction in which the wind is blowing; with the wind. **2.** *Naut.* towards or at the leeward side.

dowry /ˈdaʊəri, ˈdaʊri/, n., pl. **-ries**. property that a woman brings to her husband at marriage. [ME, from AF. See DOWER]

dowse /daʊs/, v.t., v.i., **dowsed, dowsing**. →**douse**.

doxology /dɒkˈsɒlədʒi/, n., pl. **-gies**. a hymn or form of words praising God. [ML, from Gk: a praising] —**doxological**, adj.

doyen /ˈdɔɪən/, n. the senior member of a body, class, profession, etc. [F. See DEAN] —**doyenne**, n. fem.

Doyle /dɔɪl/, n. **Sir Arthur Conan**, 1859–1930, British author of detective stories and historical romances; creator of Sherlock Holmes.

doz., *Abbrev.* dozen; dozens.

doze /doʊz/, v., **dozed, dozing**, n. ◇v.i. **1.** to sleep lightly or fitfully. **2.** to fall into such a sleep without meaning to (oft. fol. by *off*). ◇n. **3.** a light or fitful sleep. [OE *dwæsian* become stupid]

dozen /ˈdʌzən/, n., pl. **dozen, dozens**. **1.** a group of 12 units or things. **2. daily dozen**, daily physical exercises. [ME, from OF: twelve, from L]

dpt, *Abbrev.* department.

Dr, *Abbrev.* **1.** Doctor. **2.** debtor. **3.** Drive (in street names).

drab /dræb/, adj., **drabber, drabbest**, n. ◇adj. **1.** having a dull grey or brown color. **2.** dull; cheerless. ◇n. **3.** a dull brownish or yellowish grey. [F *drap* cloth]

drachma /ˈdrækmə/, n., pl. **-mas, -mae** /-mi/. **1.** the main silver coin of the ancient Greeks, varying in weight and value. **2.** the monetary unit of modern Greece. [L, from Gk: handful]

draconian /drəˈkoʊniən/, adj. severe; harsh; rigorous. Also, **draconic** /drəˈkɒnɪk/. [from *Draco*, Athenian statesman of 7th century BC noted for the severity of his code of laws] —**draconically**, adv.

Dracula /ˈdrækjələ/, n. **Count**, a vampire who feeds on human blood in the novel *Dracula* (1897) by Bram Stoker.

draft /drɑft/, n. **1.** a preliminary plan, sketch, or design. **2.** a rough form of any writing, intended to be revised or copied. **3.** →**conscription**. **4.** a written order for the payment of money; bill of exchange. **5.** an animal or animals chosen and separated from the herd or flock. ◇v.t. **6.** to draw the outlines or plan of; sketch. **7.** to write as a draft. **8.** to conscript. **9.** to separate animals from the herd or flock for a particular purpose, such as branding. [OE *dragan* draw]

draftsman

draftsman /'drɑːftsmən/, n. → **draughtsman** (def. 1)

draft dodger, n. Colloq. someone who avoids or tries to avoid conscription into the armed forces.

drag /dræg/, v., **dragged**, **dragging**, n. ◇v.t. **1.** to draw with force, effort, or difficulty; pull heavily or slowly along; haul: *He has to drag the truck out of the mud*; *He dragged himself out of bed*. **2.** to search with a drag (def. 11): *The police dragged the river for the body*. **3.** to introduce (something uninteresting or not to the point) (fol. by *in*): *He used to drag in the same old arguments*. **4.** to make something go on for too long or in an uninteresting way (oft. fol. by *out* or *on*): *They dragged the meeting out for two more hours*. ◇v.i. **5.** to trail on the ground. **6.** to move heavily or with effort: *The motor is dragging*. **7.** to pass with uninteresting slowness: *The play dragged in the last act*. **8.** to use a drag or dragnet; dredge: *The police dragged the dam without success*. ◇v. **9. drag one's feet**, to be deliberately slow to act; be recalcitrant. **10. drag the chain**, Colloq. to hinder others by doing something slowly. ◇n. **11.** something used by or for dragging, as a dragnet or a dredge. **12.** a heavy harrow. **13.** a four-horse sporting and passenger coach with seats inside and on top. **14.** a metal shoe to receive a wheel of heavy wagons and serve as a wheel lock on steep gradients. **15.** anything that holds up progress. **16.** heaviness; weight; resistance. **17.** a slow, laborious movement; retardation. **18.** a force due to the relative airflow exerted on an aeroplane or other body tending to reduce its forward movement. **19.** Colloq. somebody or something that is very uninteresting: *The party was a drag, so we left early*. **20.** Colloq. women's clothes worn by men. **21.** Colloq. → **drag race**. [ME]

dragnet /'drægnet/, n. **1.** a net to be drawn along the bottom of a river, pond, etc., or along the ground, to catch fish, find a dead body, etc. **2.** anything that serves to catch or drag in, as a police system.

dragon /'drægən/, n. **1.** a mythical monster variously represented, generally as a huge winged reptile with a crested head and terrible claws, and often spouting fire. **2.** a fierce, violent person. **3.** a formidable woman, esp. one who watches the behavior of others. **4.** any of various lizards, as the frill-necked lizard of northern Australia. [ME, from OF, from L, from Gk: serpent]

dragonfly /'drægənflaɪ/, n., pl. **-flies**. a large, harmless insect with a long thin body and two pairs of gauze-like wings.

dragoon /drə'guːn/, n. **1.** a cavalryman of certain regiments. ◇v.t. **2.** to force by severe and oppressive measures; coerce. [F: kind of gun, 'fire-breather', decorated with dragon]

drag race, n. a car race, the winner being the car that can accelerate fastest from a standstill. Also, **drag**.

dragster /'drægstə/, n. **1.** a car designed for drag racing. **2.** a bicycle with high handlebars, small wheels, and a long saddle.

dramatise

drain /dreɪn/, v.t. **1.** to draw off water from (soil, a road etc.) by ditches, pipes, etc. **2.** to draw (water) away. **3.** to make (food, dishes, etc.) dry by allowing liquid to run off. **4.** to empty (a cup, etc.) by drinking its contents. **5.** to deprive of possessions, money, strength, etc., by gradual withdrawal; exhaust (oft. in pass.): *That wedding has drained me of money*. ◇v.i. **6.** to flow off gradually: *The water drained away through the sand*; *The blood drained from her face*. **7.** to become empty or dry by the gradual flowing off of moisture: *The pool took hours to drain*. ◇n. **8.** something by which anything is drained, as a pipe, tube or conduit. **9.** something which uses up or exhausts: *a drain on my bank balance*; *a drain on my nerves*. **10. go down the drain**, Colloq. **a.** to be wasted. **b.** to become worthless. [OE *drēnian*, *drēahnian* drain, strain out]

drainage /'dreɪnɪdʒ/, n. **1.** the act or process of draining. **2.** a system of drains, artificial or natural. **3.** something which is drained off.

drainage basin, n. the whole area drained by a river and all its tributaries. Also, **drainage area**.

drainpipe /'dreɪnpaɪp/, n. a pipe for carrying water or waste, usu. from buildings.

drake /dreɪk/, n. a male duck or similar bird. [ME]

Drake /dreɪk/, n. **Sir Francis**, c. 1540–96, English buccaneer, circumnavigator of the globe, and admiral.

dram /dræm/, n. **1.** a unit of measurement in the imperial system, equal to $\frac{1}{16}$ ounce avoirdupois weight (27.34 grains) or approx. 1.772 g. **2.** a small drink of liquor. **3.** a small quantity of anything. [ME, from OF, from L: drachma]

drama /'drɑːmə/, n. **1.** a story or short piece in dialogue, intended to be acted on stage, radio or television, and usu. involving conflict or contrast of characters. **2.** plays as a branch of literature: *the drama of the Elizabethan age*. **3.** the branch of art which deals with plays from their writing to their final production: *a school of drama*. **4.** any exciting, important or fast moving series of events: *the drama surrounding his resignation*. [LL: a play, from Gk: deed, play]

dramatic /drə'mætɪk/, adj. **1.** of or relating to drama: *dramatic art*. **2.** using the form or manner of drama: *the dramatic structure of a novel*. **3.** full of excitement or conflict.

dramatic irony, n. → **irony** (def. 1).

dramatics /drə'mætɪks/, n. **1.** (treated as sing. or pl.) the art of producing or acting in dramas. **2.** (treated as pl.) dramatic productions, esp. by amateurs. **3.** (treated as pl.) dramatic behavior; histrionics.

dramatise or **dramatize** /'dræmətaɪz/, v.t., **-tised**, **-tising**. **1.** to put into dramatic form, esp. from another form of literature or from history. **2.** to express or represent dramatically: *He dramatises his sorrows*. —**dramatisation**, n.

dramatis personae /ˌdræmətəs pəˈsouniː/, *n.pl.* **1.** the characters in a drama. **2.** *Colloq.* the most important people in any situation. [L]

dramatist /ˈdræmətəst/, *n.* a writer of dramas or dramatic poetry; playwright.

drank /dræŋk/, *v.* past tense and former past participle of **drink**.

drape /dreɪp/, *v.*, **draped, draping**, *n.* ◇*v.t.* **1.** to cover or hang with cloth or some fabric, esp. in graceful folds. **2.** to arrange (hangings, clothing, etc.) in graceful folds. **3.** *Colloq.* to place in a casual manner: *He draped his legs over the arm of the chair.* ◇*v.i.* **4.** to fall in folds, as drapery. ◇*n.* **5.** (*pl.*) curtains. [F: cloth, from LL]

draper /ˈdreɪpə/, *n.* a dealer in textiles, cloth goods, etc. [ME, from AF]

drapery /ˈdreɪpəri/, *n., pl.* **-peries. 1.** cloths or textile fabrics taken as a whole. **2.** the business of a draper. **3.** coverings, hangings, clothing, etc., of some fabric, esp. as arranged in loose, graceful folds.

drastic /ˈdræstɪk/, *adj.* **1.** acting with force or violence; harsh. **2.** extreme: *drastic measures.* [Gk *drastikós* efficacious] —**drastically**, *adv.*

draught /draft/, *n.* **1.** a current of air, esp. in a room, chimney, etc. **2.** a device for controlling the flow of air in a stove, fireplace, etc. **3.** the act of drawing or pulling, or that which is drawn. **4.** the drawing of a liquid from its container, as of beer from a barrel. **5.** a drink, or an amount drunk as a continuous act: *He downed the lot at a draught.* **6.** a dose of medicine. **7.** a catch of fish. **8. a.** the action of displacing water by a ship or boat. **b.** the depth of water a ship or boat needs to float it. **9. a.** (*pl. treated as sing.*) a game played by two people, each with 12 pieces, on a chequered board. **b.** one of the pieces in this game. **10.** → **draft** (esp. defs 1 and 2). ◇*adj.* **11.** drawn as required: *draught beer.* **12.** used or suited for pulling loads. [ME *draht*. See DRAFT]

draughtboard /ˈdraftbɔd/, *n.* a board marked off into 64 squares of two alternating colors, on which draughts and chess are played. Also, **draughtsboard**.

draughthorse /ˈdrafthɔs/, *n.* a strong, heavily built horse, 15 hands or over in height, used for pulling heavy loads.

draughtsman /ˈdraftsmən/, *n., pl.* **-men. 1.** a person who draws sketches, plans, or designs. **2.** a piece used in a game of draughts, usu. a small colored disc.

draughty /ˈdrafti/, *adj.*, **draughtier, draughtiest**. characterised by or causing draughts of air. —**draughtiness**, *n.*

draw /drɔ/, *v.*, **drew** /druː/, **drawn, drawing**, *n.* ◇*v.t.* **1.** to cause to move in a particular direction by pulling; pull; drag; lead: *to draw a cart; He drew his hand away.* **2.** to bring or take out, as from a container or source: *to draw blood; to draw money.* **3.** to attract: *to draw a crowd.* **4.** to pick or choose at random: *to draw cards.* **5.** to sketch in lines or words; delineate; depict: *to draw a picture.* **6.** to take in, as by sucking or breathing: *to draw breath.* **7.** to get; derive; deduce: *to draw a conclusion.* **8.** to disembowel. **9.** to drain (a pond, etc.) by a channel, etc. **10.** to pull out to full or greater length; make by stretching, as wire. **11.** to write or sign an order, draft, or bill of exchange. **12.** *Naut.* (of a boat) to displace (a certain depth of water). **13.** *Sport.* to leave (a contest) undecided. ◇*v.i.* **14.** to put into action a pulling, moving, or attracting force: *A sail draws by being filled with wind and properly trimmed.* **15.** to move as or as if under a pulling force: *The ship draws near.* **16.** to take out a sword, pistol, etc., for action. **17.** to use or practise the art of tracing figures; practise drawing. **18.** to shrink or contract: *The crowd drew together.* **19.** (of tea) to infuse. **20.** to produce or have a draught of air, etc., as in a pipe or flue. **21.** *Games.* to leave a contest undecided. ◇**22.** Some special uses are:
draw a blank, to be unsuccessful, esp. when looking for someone or something.
draw out, 1. to extract. **2.** to make longer; lengthen; prolong. **3.** to encourage or persuade somebody to talk.
draw stumps, *Cricket.* to pull up the stumps as a sign that the day's play has ended.
draw up, 1. to bring or come to a halt. **2.** to prepare or set out (a document, plan, etc.). **3.** to arrange, esp. in military formation.
◇*n.* **23.** the act of drawing. **24.** something that draws or attracts attention, audiences, etc. **25.** that which is drawn, as a lot: *a lucky draw.* **26.** the distance from the bottom of a mine pit to the top. **27.** *Sport.* a drawn or undecided contest: *The match ended in a draw.* [OE *dragan*]

drawback /ˈdrɔbæk/, *n.* **1.** a disadvantage or hindrance. **2.** the taking of tobacco smoke fully into the lungs.

drawbridge /ˈdrɔbrɪdʒ/, *n.* a bridge of which the whole or a part may be raised, lowered or drawn aside.

drawcard /ˈdrɔkad/, *n.* a person, entertainment, occasion, etc., that is likely to produce a large attendance.

drawer /drɔ/ *for defs 1 and 2;* /ˈdrɔə/ *for defs 3 and 4, n.* **1.** a sliding compartment, as in a piece of furniture, that may be drawn out. **2.** (*pl.*) → **underpants. 3.** a person or thing that draws. **4.** *Finance.* a person who draws an order, draft, or bill of exchange.

drawing /ˈdrɔɪŋ, ˈdrɔrɪŋ/, *n.* **1.** the act of a person or thing that draws. **2.** a sketch, plan, or design, esp. one made with a pen, pencil, or crayon.

drawing-pin /ˈdrɔɪŋ-pɪn/, *n.* a short broad-headed tack designed to be pushed in by the thumb. Also, **thumbtack**.

drawing room, *n.* a room where guests are entertained, esp. after dinner. [obs. *drawing* withdrawing + ROOM]

drawl /drɔl/, *v.t., v.i.* **1.** to say or speak slowly, with vowels lengthened. ◇*n.* **2.** the manner of speaking in this way. [from DRAW]

drawn /drɔn/, *v.* **1.** past participle of **draw.** ◇*adj.* **2.** tired; haggard; tense.

drawstring /'drɔstrɪŋ/, n. a string, cord, etc., which tightens or closes an opening, as of a bag, clothing, etc., when one or both ends are pulled.

dray /dreɪ/, n. 1. a low, strong cart without fixed sides, for carrying heavy loads. 2. a sledge. [ME *draye* sledge without wheels]

dread /drɛd/, v.t. 1. to fear greatly: *to dread death*. ◇n. 2. terror or great fear. 3. a deep awe or reverence. ◇adj. 4. greatly feared; frightful; terrible. 5. held in awe; revered. [OE *drǣdan*]

dreadful /'drɛdfəl/, adj. 1. causing great dread, fear, or terror; terrible: *a dreadful fate*. 2. awe-inspiring. 3. *Colloq.* extremely bad, unpleasant, ugly, etc.: *a dreadful film*.

dreadnought /'drɛdnɔt/, n. 1. (formerly) a type of battleship. 2. *Colloq.* a large, powerful vehicle, as a truck, tram, etc. 3. a person who fears nothing.

dream /drim/, n., v., **dreamed** or **dreamt**, **dreaming**. ◇n. 1. a succession of images or ideas passing through a sleeping person's mind. 2. a daydream; reverie. 3. a state of constant absent-mindedness: *She lives in a dream*. 4. something or somebody of an unreal beauty or charm: *a dream of a girl*. 5. a hope; aim: *a dream of building his own house*. ◇v.i. 6. to have a dream or dreams: *I dream every night*. 7. to indulge in daydreams or reveries: *Instead of studying he was dreaming*. 8. to imagine; suppose; fancy (fol. by *of*): *How could you dream of such a thing?* ◇v.t. 9. to see or imagine in sleep or in a vision. 10. to imagine; suppose; fancy: *I never dreamt such a thing*. 11. to pass or spend (time, etc.) in dreaming (oft. fol. by *away*). 12. **dream up**, *Colloq.* to invent; to form or plan an idea in the imagination. [OE *drēam* mirth, noise]

dreaming /'drimɪŋ/, n. 1. an Aborigine's awareness and knowledge of the Dreamtime. 2. (*cap.*) **the Dreaming**, → **Dreamtime**. [from the Aboriginal notion that in a dreaming state one is receptive to this form of awareness]

dreamt /drɛmt/, v. a past tense and past participle of **dream**.

Dreamtime /'drimtaɪm/, n. (in Aboriginal mythology) the time in which the earth received its present form and in which the patterns and cycles of life and nature were begun.

dreamy /'drimi/, adj., **dreamier**, **dreamiest**. 1. full of or causing dreams. 2. like, or as in, dreams; visionary. 3. vague; abstracted: *a dreamy manner*. 4. quiet; soothing; gentle: *dreamy music*. 5. *Colloq.* wonderful; extremely pleasing: *a dreamy new dress*. — **dreamily**, adv. — **dreaminess**, n.

dreary /'drɪəri/, adj., **drearier**, **dreariest**. 1. causing sadness or gloom. 2. dull; boring. [OE *drēorig* gory, cruel, sad] — **drearily**, adv. — **dreariness**, n.

dredge /drɛdʒ/, n., v., **dredged**, **dredging**. ◇n. 1. a dragnet or other device for gathering material or objects from the bed of a river, etc. ◇v.t. 2. to clear out with a dredge; remove sand, silt, mud, etc., from the bottom of: *to dredge a harbor*. ◇v.i. 3. to use a dredge: *to dredge for the body*. 4. to find, usu. with some difficulty (fol. by *up*): *to dredge up an idea*. [late ME *dreg*, akin to OE *dragan* DRAW]

dregs /drɛgz/, n. 1. the sediment of wine or other drink; lees; grounds. 2. any waste or worthless residue: *the dregs of society*. [ME, from Scand]

drench /drɛntʃ/, v.t. 1. to wet thoroughly; steep; soak: *The rain drenched my clothes*. 2. *Vet Sci.* to give a dose of medicine to, esp. by force: *to drench a horse*. ◇n. 3. something that drenches: *a drench of rain*. 4. a dose of medicine for an animal. [OE *drencan*, make drink]

Dresden /'drɛzdən/, n. a city in southern East Germany, on the Elbe. Pop. 519 769 (1986 est.).

dress /drɛs/, n., adj., v., **dressed**, **dressing**. ◇n. 1. the chief outer garment worn by women, covering the body from shoulders to legs; frock. 2. clothing; apparel; garb: *the dress of the Middle Ages*. 3. fine clothes; formal costume: *full dress*. ◇adj. 4. of or for a dress or dresses: *a dress shop*; *dress material*. 5. of or for a formal occasion: *a dress suit*; *a dress uniform*. ◇v.t. 6. to put clothes, ornaments, etc., on; deck; attire. 7. to arrange, adorn (a shop window, the hair, etc.). 8. to prepare for use: *He dressed the chicken*; *The farmer dressed the land*. 9. to treat (wounds or sores) by disinfecting, bandaging, etc. 10. to make straight; bring (troops) into line: *to dress ranks*. 11. *Colloq.* to scold severely; upbraid; rebuke (fol. by *down*). ◇v.i. 12. to put on clothes, esp. formal or evening clothes: *She is dressing for dinner*. 13. to come into line, as troops. ◇v. 14. **dress up**, **a.** to put on best clothes. **b.** to put on fancy dress, costume, or disguise. [ME, from OF: arrange, from L: straight]

dressage /'drɛsaʒ/, n. the art of training a horse in obedience, deportment, and responses.

dress circle, n. a curved gallery in a theatre, cinema, etc., originally set apart for spectators in evening dress.

dresser /'drɛsə/, n. a sideboard with shelves and drawers for dishes, etc. [ME, from OF]

dressing /'drɛsɪŋ/, n. 1. the act of a person or thing that dresses: *Dressing takes him hours*. 2. a type of sauce for food: *salad dressing*. 3. stuffing for a chicken. 4. a bandage, etc., for a wound. 5. → **top dressing**.

dressing-table /'drɛsɪŋ-teɪbəl/, n. a table or chest of drawers, usu. with a mirror.

dress rehearsal, n. a rehearsal of a play in costume, with scenery, properties, and lights arranged and operated as for a performance.

dressy /'drɛsi/, adj. 1. smart; stylish; showy. 2. suitable for formal occasions.

drew /dru/, v. past tense of **draw**.

Dreyfus /'dreɪfəs, 'draɪ-/, n. 1. **Alfred**, 1859–1935, French army officer (Jewish), convicted of treason in 1894 and 1899, but proved innocent in 1906. 2. **George**, born 1928 in Germany, Australian musician, composer and conductor.

dribble /'drɪbəl/, v., **-bled, -bling,** n. ◇v.i. **1.** to fall or flow in drops or small quantities; trickle. **2.** to let saliva flow from the mouth; drivel; slaver. **3.** (in certain sports) to move a ball along by a series of rapid kicks, bounces, or pushes. ◇v.t. **4.** to let fall in drops. **5.** *Sport.* to move (the ball) along by a quick succession of kicks, bounces, pushes, or hits. ◇n. **6.** a small trickling stream. **7.** a small quantity of anything. [obs. *drib* drip] —**dribbler,** n.

dribs and drabs /drɪbz ən 'dræbz/, n.pl. small and often irregular amounts.

dried /draɪd/, v. past tense and past participle of **dry.**

drier /'draɪə/, adj. **1.** comparative of **dry.** ◇n. Also, **dryer. 2.** something which dries. **3.** something added to paints, varnishes, etc., to make them dry quickly. **4.** a machine for removing moisture (from clothes, hair, etc.).

driest /'draɪəst/, adj. superlative of **dry.**

drift /drɪft/, n. **1.** a driving movement or force; impetus. **2.** *Aeron.* the deviation of an aircraft, ship, etc., from a set course, due to currents. **3.** a tendency or trend: *the drift to the cities; the drift of public opinion towards improved conservation.* **4.** the course of anything; tenor; general meaning: *the drift of an argument.* **5.** a heap of any matter driven together: *a drift of sand.* **6.** *Mech.* a round, pointed piece of steel for enlarging holes in metal, or for bringing holes in line to receive rivets, etc. ◇v.i. **7.** to be carried along by currents of water or air, or by the force of circumstances. **8.** to wander aimlessly. **9.** to collect into heaps: *drifting sand.* ◇v.t. **10.** to carry along: *The current drifted the boat out to sea.* **11.** to drive into heaps: *drifted snow.* [ME *drift* act of driving]

drifter /'drɪftə/, n. **1.** someone or something that drifts. **2.** *Colloq.* a person who wanders aimlessly through life, continually moving, changing jobs, etc.

driftwood /'drɪftwʊd/, n. wood floating on, or cast ashore by, the water.

drill[1] /drɪl/, n. **1.** a tool or machine for boring cylindrical holes. **2.** *Mil.* training in formal marching or other precise military or naval movements. **3.** any strict, methodical training or exercise: *fire drill.* **4.** *Colloq.* the correct procedure; routine: *They showed the new man the drill.* **5.** a shellfish which attacks oysters. ◇v.t. **6.** to pierce or bore (a hole). **7.** *Mil.* to train (soldiers) in formation marching, etc. **8.** train (someone) in new work or procedure. ◇v.i. **9.** to use a drill (def. 1). **10.** to go through an exercise in military or other training. [D *drillen* bore, drill]

drill[2] /drɪl/, n. **1.** a small furrow made in the soil in which to sow seeds. **2.** a machine for sowing seeds in such furrows. **3.** a row of seeds or plants thus sown. ◇v.t. **4.** to sow (seed) or raise (crops) in drills. [orig. uncert.]

drily /'draɪli/, adv. dryly.

drink /drɪŋk/, v., **drank, drunk, drinking,** n. ◇v.i. **1.** to swallow liquid; imbibe. **2.** to drink alcohol, esp. habitually or too much. **3.** to drink in someone's honor (fol. by *to*). ◇v.t. **4.** to swallow (a liquid). **5.** to take in (a liquid) in any manner; absorb. **6.** to take in (words, music, etc.) eagerly (fol. by *in*). **7.** to swallow the contents of. **8.** to drink in honor of: *to drink someone's health.* ◇n. **9.** any liquid suitable for swallowing. **10.** alcohol; beer, spirits, etc. **11.** the habit of drinking too much alcohol. **12. the drink,** *Colloq.* the sea or a large lake. [OE *drincan*]

drink-driving /drɪŋk-'draɪvɪŋ/, n. driving a car whilst under the influence of alcohol.

drinking fountain, n. a fountain (def. 4) which sends up water suitable for drinking. Also, **bubbler.**

drip /drɪp/, v., **dripped** or **dript, dripping,** n. ◇v.i. **1.** to let fall drops; shed drops: *A tap drips if the washer is worn out.* **2.** to fall in drops, as a liquid: *Water drips from a tap.* ◇v.t. **3.** to let fall in drops: *The tap drips water.* ◇n. **4.** the act or sound of dripping. **5.** *Med.* a continuous slow infusion of liquid into a blood vessels of a patient. **6.** *Colloq.* a boring or dull person. [ME, from Scand]

drip-dry /'drɪp-draɪ/, adj., v., **-dried, -drying.** ◇adj. **1.** (of clothing) able to dry smooth without the need of ironing, when hung dripping wet. ◇v.i., v.t. **2.** to dry or let dry in this way.

dripolator /'drɪpəleɪtə/, n. a coffee-making machine in which boiling water is allowed to pass down slowly through finely ground coffee beans.

dripping /'drɪpɪŋ/, n. **1.** fat that has dripped from meat in cooking. ◇adj., adv. **2.** soaking: *I am dripping; My clothes are dripping wet.*

dripstone /'drɪpstoʊn/, n. calcium carbonate, $CaCO_3$, occurring in stalactites and stalagmites.

drive /draɪv/, v., **drove, driven, driving,** n., adj. ◇v.t. **1.** to send, force, drive, away, off, in, out, back, etc., by force: *to drive the mice away; You drive me crazy.* **2.** to force to work: *He drives himself too hard.* **3.** to control the movement of (an animal, vehicle, etc.). **4.** to take someone in a car, etc.: *to drive someone to the station.* **5.** to carry (business, a bargain, etc.) vigorously through. **6.** *Mining, etc.* to excavate horizontally (or nearly so). **7.** *Sport.* to hit or throw (the ball) quickly and strongly. ◇v.i. **8.** to go along before a strong force; be impelled: *The ship drove before the wind.* **9.** to rush or dash violently: *The ship drove against the rocks.* **10.** to make an effort to reach or obtain; aim (fol. by *at*): *What is he driving at?* **11.** to act as driver. **12.** to go or travel in a driven vehicle: *to drive away; to drive back.* ◇n. **13.** the act of driving. **14.** a sending along by force, as of game, cattle, or floating logs, in a particular direction. **15.** animals, logs, etc., thus driven. **16.** *Psychol.* a source of motivation: *the sex drive.* **17.** *Sport.* a powerful stroke or action. **18.** a vigorous onset or onward course, esp. of an army, etc. **19.** a united effort to get something done: *a membership drive; a fund-raising drive.* **20.** energy and initiative: *That man has real drive.* **21.** a trip in a driven vehicle: *to go for a drive.*

drive   314   **drott**

22. a road for driving, esp. a private road to a private house. 23. *Mining.* a horizontal tunnel or shaft. 24. *Mach.* a driving mechanism: *a gear drive; a chain drive.* 25. *Motor Vehicles.* a point or points of power application to the roadway: *front drive, four-wheel drive.* ◇*adj.* 26. relating to a part of a machine used in its propulsion: *a drive shaft.* [OE *drīfan*]

drive-in /'draɪv-ɪn/, *n.* 1. an outdoor cinema where people can watch films while remaining in their cars. ◇*adj.* 2. (of a shop, etc.) that serves customers in their cars.

drivel /'drɪvəl/, *v.*, **-elled, -elling**, *n.* ◇*v.i.* 1. to let saliva flow from the mouth. 2. to talk childishly or stupidly. ◇*n.* 3. childish or silly talk; nonsense; twaddle. [OE *dreflian*]

driven /'drɪvən/, *v.* 1. past participle of **drive**. ◇*adj.* 2. piled up by the wind: *pure as the driven snow.*

driver /'draɪvə/, *n.* 1. someone who drives an animal, vehicle, etc. 2. a golf club for hitting the ball long distances.

drive shaft, *n.* any turning shaft (bar) that sends power from an engine to that part which is to be driven, as wheels, etc.

driveway /'draɪvweɪ/, *n.* a passage along which vehicles may be driven.

driving /'draɪvɪŋ/, *adj.* 1. (of a person) able to make others work; energetic. 2. violent; having great force. 3. passing on or transmitting power. 4. relating to the control of vehicles, esp. cars: *a driving test.* 5. rhythmic; urgent; in a fast tempo.

drizzle /'drɪzəl/, *v.*, **-zled, -zling**, *n.* ◇*v.i.* 1. to rain gently and steadily in fine drops; sprinkle. ◇*n.* 2. a very light rain. [OE *drēosan* fall] –**drizzly**, *adj.*

droll /droʊl/, *adj.* amusingly odd; comical. [F, from MD: little man] –**drollness**, *n.* –**drolly**, *adv.* –**drollery**, *n.*

dromedary /'drɒmədəri, -dri/, *n., pl.* **-daries**. the one-humped or Arabian camel. [ME, from L: dromedary, from Gk: running]

drone[1] /droʊn/, *n.* 1. the male of bees, stingless and making no honey. 2. someone who is lazy; idler. [OE *drān*]

drone[2] /droʊn/, *v.*, **droned, droning**, *n.* ◇*v.i.* 1. to speak in or make a dull, continued sound. ◇*n.* 2. *Music.* a continuous low tone produced by various forms of bagpipes or bass strings of some other musical instruments. 3. a continuous low sound; hum; a buzzing. [See DRONE[1]] –**droningly**, *adv.*

drongo[1] /'drɒŋgoʊ/, *n., pl.* **-gos**. a tropical insect-eating bird, usually black with a long forked tail, such as the **spangled drongo** of Australia. [Malagasy]

drongo[2] /'drɒŋgoʊ/, *n. Colloq.* a slow-witted stupid person. [? from *Drongo*, name of racehorse in early 1920s which never won a race]

drool /druːl/, *v.i.* 1. → **drivel**. 2. to have a greedy interest in (fol. by *over*).

droop /druːp/, *v.i.* 1. to bend, or hang down, as from weakness. 2. to lose spirit or courage. ◇*n.* 3. the act or condition of drooping. [ME, from Scand] –**drooping**, *adj.* –**droopy**, *adj.*

drop /drɒp/, *n., v.*, **dropped** or **dropt, dropping**. ◇*n.* 1. a small rounded quantity of liquid which falls. 2. the quantity of liquid contained in such a mass. 3. a tiny quantity of anything. 4. (*usu. pl.*) a liquid medicine given drop by drop. 5. the distance, amount or depth to which anything drops or falls. 6. a fall in degree, amount, value, etc.: *a drop in price.* 7. something that drops or looks like a drop in size, shape, etc. 8. a. the total number of lambs from a flock of sheep. b. the lambing season. ◇*v.i.* 9. to fall in drops: *Rain drops from the clouds.* 10. to fall, sink down. 11. to come to an end: *There the matter dropped.* 12. to withdraw; disappear (fol. by *out*). 13. to fall lower in condition, degree, etc.; sink: *The prices dropped sharply.* 14. to pass easily into a different state: *to drop asleep.* 15. to fall or move (back, behind, etc.). 16. to visit informally (fol. by *in, by, across*, etc.): *He drops in on us occasionally.* ◇*v.t.* 17. to let fall: *to drop anchor.* 18. to give birth to (young). 19. to express casually, as a hint. 20. to send or post: *Drop me a line.* 21. to bring to the ground by a blow, etc. 22. to set down, as from a car, etc. (fol. by *off*). 23. to leave out (a letter or syllable): *He dropped his h's.* 24. to lower (the voice). 25. to dismiss (someone, something). 26. *Colloq.* to stop, cease: *Drop it!* 27. **drop off, a.** to decrease: *Sales have dropped off.* **b.** to fall asleep. [OE *dropa*] –**droppable**, *adj.*

drop kick, *n. Football.* a kick given the ball just as it rises from ground after being dropped by the kicker. –**drop-kick**, *v.*

droplet /'drɒplət/, *n.* a small drop.

drop-out /'drɒp-aʊt/, *n.* 1. someone who decides to leave college or university, or to leave ordinary society and practise another life-style. 2. *Computers.* the loss of information stored on magnetic tape files.

dropper /'drɒpə/, a glass tube with a rubber cap at one end and a small hole at the other, for drawing in liquid and releasing it in drops. Also, **eye-dropper**.

droppings /'drɒpɪŋz/, *n.pl.* the dung of animals.

drop shot, *n. Tennis.* a stroke which causes the ball to fall suddenly after clearing the net.

dropsy /'drɒpsi/, *n.* an illness where a large amount of fluid collects in a certain tissue or body cavity. [ME, from OF, from L *hydrōpsis*, from Gk] –**dropsied**, *adj.*

drosophila /drəˈsɒfələ/, *n., pl.* **-lae** /-liː/. a fruit fly which is widely used in laboratory studies of heredity. [NL, from Gk]

dross /drɒs/, *n.* 1. a waste product taken off molten metal during smelting. 2. waste matter. [OE *drōs*]

drott /drɒt/, *n.* 1. a tool with several uses such as digging, pushing or lifting earth, which can be fixed to an excavator. 2. an excavator with such a tool. [Trademark]

drought

drought /draʊt/, *n.* **1.** dry weather; lack of rain. **2.** scarcity: *a petrol drought*. [OE *drūgath*, akin to *drȳge* dry] —**droughty**, *adj.*

drove[1] /droʊv/, *v.* past tense of **drive**.

drove[2] /droʊv/, *n., v.,* **droved, droving**. ◇*n.* **1.** a number of cattle, sheep, etc., driven in a group; herd; flock. **2.** a large crowd of people, esp. on the move. ◇*v.t.* **3.** to drive cattle or sheep, usu. over long distances. [OE *drāf* act of driving, herd, company]

drover /'droʊvə/, *n.* someone who drives cattle, sheep, etc., to market, usu. over long distances.

drown /draʊn/, *v.i.* **1.** to be suffocated by being under water or other liquid for too long. ◇*v.t.* **2.** to suffocate (a person, etc.) by holding under water or other liquid. **3.** to destroy; get rid of: *to drown your sorrows*. **4.** to flood. **5.** to overpower (sound) by a louder sound (fol. by *out*). [OE *druncnian*]

drowse /draʊz/, *v.,* **drowsed, drowsing**, *n.* ◇*v.i.* **1.** to be sleepy. ◇*n.* **2.** a sleepy condition. [OE *drūsian* droop, become sluggish] —**drowsy**, *adj.*

drub /drʌb/, *v.t.,* **drubbed, drubbing**. **1.** to beat with stick, etc.; flog. **2.** to defeat completely. [? Ar *darb* stroke] —**drubbing**, *n.*

drudge /drʌdʒ/, *n., v.,* **drudged, drudging**. ◇*n.* **1.** someone who works at uninteresting tasks. ◇*v.i.* **2.** to work at uninteresting tasks. [OE *Drycg*- bearer (in proper name)]

drudgery /'drʌdʒəri/, *n., pl.* **-eries**. dull, hard, or uninteresting work.

drug /drʌg/, *n., v.,* **drugged, drugging**. ◇*n.* **1.** a chemical given to prevent or cure mental or physical disease. **2.** a habit-forming medicinal substance; a narcotic. ◇*v.t.* **3.** to mix (food or drink) with a drug (esp. to produce unconsciousness). **4.** to poison with a drug. [ME, from OF, ? from D *drog* dry thing]

drugstore /'drʌgstɔ/, *n.* US. a chemist's shop where cigarettes, light meals, etc., are also sold.

Druid /'druəd/, *n.* **1.** (*oft. l.c.*) one of an order of priests or ministers of religion among the ancient Celts of Gaul, Britain, and Ireland. **2.** a member of one of several modern movements to revive druidism, which meet seasonally in special costume to conduct their ceremonies. [F, from L] —**druidic, druidical**, *adj.* —**druidism**, *n.*

drum /drʌm/, *n., v.,* **drummed, drumming**. ◇*n.* **1.** a musical instrument with a hollow body covered at one or both ends with a tightly stretched membrane (skin), which is struck with the hand or stick(s). **2.** the sound made by a drum. **3.** *Biol.* a natural organ by which an animal produces a loud or deep sound. **4.** something like a drum in shape or structure, or in the noise it produces. **5.** *Anat.* → **eardrum**. **6.** → **brake drum**. **7.** a drum-like cylindrical container for oil, etc. **8.** *Colloq.* confidential news or advice: *to give someone the drum*. ◇*v.i.* **9.** to beat or play a drum. **10.** to beat on anything continuously: *She drummed on the desk with her fingers*. ◇*v.t.* **11.** to beat (something) continuously. **12.** to force by repeated effort (fol. by *into*): *to drum an idea into someone*. **13.** to dismiss in disgrace (fol. by *out*): *Drum him out of the Army*. **14.** to get (trade, customers, etc.) (oft. fol. by *up*): *to drum up business*. [16th C E *drumslade* drummer, from LG: drumbeat]

drummer /'drʌmə/, *n.* **1.** someone who plays a drum. **2.** a learner, or the slowest shearer, in a shearing gang. **3.** a common fast-swimming fish found in the shallow coastal waters of southern Australia.

drumstick /'drʌmstɪk/, *n.* **1.** a stick for beating a drum. **2.** the lower part of the leg of a cooked chicken, duck, etc.

drunk /drʌŋk/, *adj.* **1.** under the influence of alcohol. **2.** controlled by strong feeling (fol. by *with*): *drunk with joy; drunk with success*. ◇*n.* **3.** *Colloq.* someone who is drunk. ◇*v.* **4.** past participle of **drink**. —**drunken**, *adj.*

drunkard /'drʌŋkəd/, *n.* someone who is often drunk.

drupe /drup/, *n. Bot.* a fruit, e.g. the peach, cherry, plum, etc., having a soft juicy layer around a hard central stone usu. enclosing a single seed. [NL: drupe, L: overripe olive, from Gk]

dry /draɪ/, *adj.,* **drier, driest,** *v.,* **dried, drying**, *n.* ◇*adj.* **1.** not wet or damp. **2.** having little or no rain: *a dry climate; a dry season*. **3.** not under, in, or on water: *dry land*. **4.** not giving water or other liquid: *a dry well*. **5.** not yielding milk: *a dry cow*. **6.** free from tears: *dry eyes*. **7.** thirsty or causing thirst: *dry work*. **8.** without butter, etc.: *dry toast*. **9.** (of wines) not sweet. **10.** plain; simple: *dry facts*. **11.** dull; uninteresting: *a dry subject*. **12.** humorous or sarcastic in an impersonal way: *dry humor*. **13.** characterised by lack of alcohol: *a dry party*. ◇*n.* **14. the dry**, (*sometimes cap.*) the rainless season in central and northern Australia, from May to November. ◇*v.t.* **15.** to make dry; to free from moisture. ◇*v.i.* **16.** to become dry; lose moisture. ◇*v.* **17. dry out,** (of alcoholics, drug addicts, etc.) to stop using a drug and gradually rid the body of its effects. **18. dry up, a.** to become completely dry. **b.** to become unable to think clearly. **c.** to stop talking. [OE *drȳge*] —**dryly, drily**, *adv.* —**dryness**, *n.*

dry cell, *n.* a battery, as used in torches, radios, etc., in which the electrolyte exists in the form of a paste to keep it from spilling.

dry-clean /draɪ-'klin/, *v.t.* to clean (garments, etc.) with chemical solvents, etc., rather than water. —**dry-cleaning**, *n.*

Dryden /'draɪdn/, *n.* **John**, 1631–1700, English Augustan poet, dramatist, and critic.

dry dock, *n.* **1.** a basin-like structure from which water can be emptied, used when repairing ships. **2.** a floating structure which may be raised to lift a ship out of the water for repairs.

dryer /'draɪə/, *n.* → **drier**.

dry ice, *n.* solid carbon dioxide, used to keep things cold.

dry measure, *n.* a system of units of volume formerly used in Britain, Australia and the US for measuring grain, fruits, etc.

dry rot, *n.* **1.** the decay of ageing timber causing it to crumble, due to various fungi. **2.** any of various diseases of vegetables in which dead tissue becomes dry.

dry run, *n.* a test exercise or practice.

Drysdale /ˈdraɪzdeɪl/, *n.* **Sir (George) Russell**, 1912–81, Australian artist, born in England; noted for his paintings of the harsh Australian outback.

dry socket, *n.* a painful tooth socket which has become infected and sore after removal of the tooth.

DSC /ˌdi ɛs ˈsi/, *Abbrev.* Distinguished Service Cross.

DSM /ˌdi ɛs ˈɛm/, *Abbrev.* Distinguished Service Medal.

DSO /ˌdi ɛs ˈoʊ/, *Abbrev.* Distinguished Service Order.

D to A /ˌdi tu ˈeɪ/ *Abbrev. Computers.* digital to analog.

d.t.'s /ˌdi ˈtiz/, *n.* → delirium tremens. Also, **d.t.**

dual /ˈdjuəl/, *adj.* **1.** of or relating to two. **2.** made or consisting of two parts; double: *dual controls on a plane.* [L: containing two] – **dually**, *adv.*

dualism /ˈdjuəlɪzəm/, *n.* **1.** the state of being in two parts; division into two. **2.** *Philos.* a theory stating that there are two, and only two, totally basic principles, such as mind and body. – **dualist**, *n.* – **dualistic**, *adj.*

duality /djuˈælɪti/, *n.* a dual state or quality.

dub[1] /dʌb/, *v.t.*, **dubbed, dubbing. 1.** to strike lightly with a sword in the ceremony of giving a knighthood: *The king dubbed him knight.* **2.** to strike, cut, rub, etc., in order to make smooth, or of an equal surface: *to dub leather; to dub timber.* [OE *dubbian*]

dub[2] /dʌb/, *v.t.*, **dubbed, dubbing.** to change the soundtrack of (a film or videotape), as in replacing a dialogue in another language. [short for DOUBLE]

Dubbo /ˈdʌboʊ/, *n.* a city in eastern central NSW, on the Macquarie River. Pop. 25 796 (1986).

dubious /ˈdjubiəs/, *adj.* **1.** doubtful; uncertain. **2.** of doubtful quality; questionable: *a dubious compliment.* [L: doubtful] – **dubiousness**, *n.*

Dublin /ˈdʌblən/, *n.* the capital of the Republic of Ireland, in the eastern part on the river Liffey. Pop. 502 337 (1986). Irish, **Baile Átha Cliath.**

ducal /ˈdjukəl/, *adj.* of or relating to a duke. [LL: leader. See DUKE]

ducat /ˈdʌkət/, *n.* a gold coin formerly in wide use in European countries. [ME, from F, from It *ducato* a coin (orig. one issued in 1140 by Roger II of Sicily as Duke of Apulia)]

Duchamp /dyˈʃõ/, *n.* **Marcel**, 1887–1968, French pioneer of modern art.

duchess /ˈdʌtʃɛs, ˈdʌtʃəs/, *n.* **1.** the wife or widow of a duke. **2.** *Hist.* a woman who holds (in her own right) the rule or titles of a duchy. ◇*v.t.* **3.** *Colloq.* to give (someone) an exaggerated welcome, with a hidden purpose in mind. [ME, from F]

duchy /ˈdʌtʃi/, *n.*, *pl.* **duchies.** the territory ruled by a duke or duchess. [ME, from OF]

duck[1] /dʌk/, *n.* **1.** any of several types of swimming bird with a flat bill, short legs, and webbed feet. **2.** the female duck, as opposed to the male (or **drake**). **3.** the flesh of a duck, eaten as food. [OE *dūce* diver]

duck[2] /dʌk/, *v.i., v.t.* **1.** to lower (the head, etc.) suddenly; bob. **2.** to push (the whole body or the head) for a moment under water. **3.** to avoid (a blow, job, etc.). ◇*v.* **4. duck out / off,** to go away for a short time. ◇*n.* **5.** the act of ducking. [ME *douke*]

duck[3] /dʌk/, *n.* an amphibious military vehicle. [from *DUKW*, its code name in World War II]

duck[4] /dʌk/, *n. Cricket.* a batsman's score of zero.

duckbill /ˈdʌkbɪl/, *n.* → platypus. Also, **duck-billed platypus.**

duckling /ˈdʌklɪŋ/, *n.* a young duck.

duco /ˈdjukoʊ/, *n.* **1.** a type of paint, esp. as applied to the bodywork of a motor vehicle. ◇*v.t.* **2.** to spray or otherwise coat (a vehicle) with duco. [Trademark]

duct /dʌkt/, *n.* **1.** any tube, canal, etc., by which various substances are carried. **2.** *Anat., Zool.* a tube carrying a body fluid: *a tear duct.* **3.** a pipe which carries electrical wiring. [L: leading, conduct, conduit]

ductile /ˈdʌktaɪl/, *adj.* **1.** able to be hammered out thin, as certain metals. **2.** able to be drawn out into wire or threads, as gold. **3.** easily influenced; compliant; tractable. [ME, from L: that may be led] – **ductility**, *n.*

ductless gland /dʌktləs ˈglænd/ *n. Biol.* a gland producing hormones which flow directly into the blood or lymph, etc.; endocrine gland.

dud /dʌd/, *Colloq.* ◇*n.* **1.** someone or something that proves a failure. ◇*adj.* **2.** useless. [orig. uncert.]

dudgeon /ˈdʌdʒən/, *n.* a feeling of annoyance; anger: *We left in high dudgeon.* [orig. unknown]

Dudley /ˈdʌdli/, *n.* **Robert (Earl of Leicester)**, 1532?–88, English politician and favorite of Queen Elizabeth I.

duds /dʌdz/, *n.pl. Colloq.* **1.** trousers. **2.** clothes, esp. old or ragged clothes. [ME, akin to LG: coarse sackcloth]

due /dju/, *adj.* **1.** payable now, or at some future time. **2.** rightful; proper; adequate: *in due time; due care.* **3.** owing, as to a cause: *a delay due to an accident.* **4.** expected to be ready, be present, or arrive. **5.** that which is due or owed. **6.** (*usu. pl.*) payment due, as a charge, fee, etc. **7. give a person their due,**

due   317   **dump**

to give proper credit to. ◇*adv.* **8.** directly or straight: *He sailed due east.* [ME, from OF, from L: owe]

duel /ˈdjuəl/, *n., v.,* **-elled, -elling.** ◇*n.* **1.** a prearranged fight between two persons, using deadly weapons and having special rules of action. **2.** any contest between two people or parties. ◇*v.i.* **3.** to fight in a duel. [ML: a combat between two] —**dueller, duellist,** *n.*

duet /djuˈet/, *n.* a musical piece for two voices or performers. [It: two] —**duettist,** *n.*

duff[1] /dʌf/, *n. Brit.* a flour pudding, boiled or steamed, in a bag. [var. of DOUGH]

duff[2] /dʌf/, *v.t.* **1.** to steal (cattle, sheep, etc.), usu. changing brands. **2.** to change the appearance of (esp. old or stolen goods). [back-formation from Brit thieves' slang *duffer* seller of stolen goods]

duffer /ˈdʌfə/, *n.* **1.** a stupid person. **2.** an unprofitable mine, claim, etc. [? Scot *duffar* a stupid, inactive fellow]

Dufy /dyˈfi/, *n.* **Raoul** /raˈul/, 1877–1953, French Fauvist artist.

dug /dʌɡ/, *v.* past tense and past participle of **dig**.

dugong /ˈduɡɒŋ/, *n.* a tropical plant-eating water mammal, having flipper-like forelimbs. [Malay]

dugout /ˈdʌɡaʊt/, *n.* **1.** a rough shelter dug into the ground or the face of a bank. **2.** a boat made by hollowing out a log.

duke /djuk/; /duk/ *for def. 3, n.* **1.** a ruling prince; ruler of a small state called a duchy. **2.** a nobleman of highest rank after that of a prince. **3.** (*usu. pl.*) *Colloq.* the hand or fist. [ME *duc*, from OF, from L *dux* leader]

Duke of Edinburgh's Award, *n.* one of the awards presented as part of a scheme set up by Prince Philip, Duke of Edinburgh, in 1956 to promote the development of young people; scheme launched in Australia in 1962.

dulcet /ˈdʌlsət/, *adj.* (esp. of sounds) pleasing; soothing. [ME, from OF, from L: sweet]

dulcimer /ˈdʌlsəmə/, *n. Music.* a musical instrument with metal strings struck with light hammers. [ME, from OF]

dull /dʌl/, *adj.* **1.** slow of understanding; stupid. **2.** lacking sharpness in the senses or feelings; unfeeling. **3.** not sharply felt: *a dull pain.* **4.** low in spirits; listless. **5.** boring, uninteresting: *a dull talk.* **6.** not sharp; blunt: *a dull knife.* **7.** not bright, or clear; dim: *a dull day; a dull sound.* ◇*v.t., v.i.* **8.** to make or become dull. [ME *dul, dull*; akin to OE *dol* foolish, stupid] —**dullish,** *adj.* —**dullness,** *n.* —**dully,** *adv.*

dullard /ˈdʌləd/, *n.* a dull or stupid person. [DULL, *adj.* + -ARD]

duly /ˈdjuli/, *adv.* **1.** in a due manner; properly. **2.** in due season; on time.

Dumaresq /djuˈmerɪk/, *n.* a river which forms part of the NSW-Qld border; rises in the Great Dividing Range and flows west to join the Macintyre River. [named in 1827 by its discoverer Allan Cunningham after the *Dumaresqs*, a family prominent in the early days of the colony of NSW]

Dumas /dyˈma/, *n.* **1. Alexandre** /alɛkˈsɔ̃drə/ (*Dumas père*), 1802–70, French novelist and dramatist best known for historical novels including *The Three Musketeers* (1844) and *The Count of Monte Cristo* (1844). **2. Alexandre** (*Dumas fils*), 1824–95, French dramatist and novelist; son of Alexandre; best known for *La Dame aux Camélias* (novel, 1848; play, 1852).

Du Maurier family /dju ˈmɒriɛɪ/, *n.* English literary and theatrical family. **1. George Louis Palmella Busson,** 1834–96, Paris-born illustrator and novelist. **2.** his son, **Sir Gerald,** 1873–1934, actor and theatrical manager. **3. Daphne,** 1903–89, granddaughter of George, romantic novelist best known for *Rebecca* (1938) and *My Cousin Rachel* (1951).

dumb /dʌm/, *adj.* **1.** unable to speak. **2.** silent. **3.** stupid; dull-witted. [OE]

dumbbell /ˈdʌmbɛl/, *n.* a weight used for exercises, consisting of two balls joined by a barlike handle.

dumbfound /ˈdʌmfaʊnd/, *v.t.* to make speechless, esp. with amazement. Also, **dumfound.** [b. DUMB and CONFOUND]

dumb waiter, *n.* **1.** a small stand placed near a dining table. **2.** a lift made of a framework with shelves, drawn up and down in a shaft, for carrying food, etc.

dummy /ˈdʌmi/, *n., pl.* **-mies,** *adj., v.,* **-mied, -mying.** ◇*n.* **1.** a copy of something, used for display, to indicate appearance, show off clothing, etc. **2.** *Colloq.* a stupid person. **3.** someone who has nothing to say or who takes no active part in things. **4.** (esp. in buying land) someone secretly acting for another. **5.** *Cards.* the person whose hand is laid face-up on the table and is usu. played by his partner. **6.** a rubber teat given to a baby to suck. **7.** *Football.* Also, **dummy pass.** a pretended move. ◇*adj.* **8.** imitation; counterfeit. ◇*v.i.* **9.** *Football.* to make a dummy pass.

dummy run, *n.* a trial; practice; first attempt.

Dumont d'Urville /ˌdjumɒnt ˈdɜvɪl/, *n.* **Jules Sébastien César** /dʒulz sə,bæstiən seɪˈza/, 1790–1842, French navigator and naval officer; carried out expeditions in the area of Australia and NZ.

dump[1] /dʌmp/, *v.t.* **1.** to throw down in a large pile; drop heavily. **2.** to empty out, unload from a container, truck, etc. **3.** to get rid of; hand over to somebody else. **4.** (of a wave) to hurl a body-surfer down heavily. ◇*v.i.* **5.** to fall or drop down suddenly. **6.** to unload. **7.** to offer for sale at a low price. ◇*n.* **8.** a place for dumping. **9.** *Mil.* a supply of ammunition or other material, stored for later use. **10.** *Colloq.* a place, house, etc., that is poorly kept. [ME, from Scand]

dump[2] /dʌmp/, *n.* (formerly) a round piece cut from the centre of a silver dollar, and used as a coin. See **holey dollar.** [orig. uncert.]

dumper /'dʌmpə/, *n. Surfing.* a wave which breaks onto and dumps surfers to the bottom.

dumpling /'dʌmplɪŋ/, *n.* **1.** a rounded mass of steamed dough often served with stewed meat, etc. **2.** a boiled or baked pudding made of a wrapping of dough covering an apple or other fruit. [? orig. *lumpling* little lump]

dumps /dʌmps/, *n.pl. Colloq.* an unhappy state of mind: *down in the dumps.* [Brit obs. *dump* a slow dance, sad tune]

dun[1] /dʌn/, *v.,* **dunned, dunning,** *n.* ◇*v.t.* **1.** to make repeated and insistent demands upon, esp. for payment of a debt. ◇*n.* **2.** a demand for payment, esp. a written one. [special use of obs. *dun* din, from Scand; see Icel *duna* boom, roar]

dun[2] /dʌn/, *adj.* **1.** dull or greyish brown. **2.** dark; gloomy. [OE *dunn*]

Dunbar /'dʌnbə/, *n.* a ship bound for Sydney from Plymouth, wrecked at the entrance to Sydney Harbor in 1857, with 120 lives lost.

Duncan /'dʌŋkən/, *n.* **Isadora,** 1878–1927, US dancer and choreographer whose free style, based on natural movements, influenced the development of modern dance.

Duncan I, *n.* died 1040, king of Scotland 1034–40, murdered by Macbeth.

dunce /dʌns/, *n.* a dull-witted or stupid person. [from John *Duns* Scotus, c. 1265–c. 1308, scholastic theologian; his system was attacked as foolish by the humanists]

dunderhead /'dʌndəhɛd/, *n.* a dunce; stupid person.

dune /djun/, *n.* a hill of sand formed by wind, usu. in desert areas or near lakes and oceans. [OE *dūn*]

Dunedin /dʌn'idɪn/, *n.* a town in southeastern South Island, NZ. Pop. 74 500 (1985 est.).

dung /dʌŋ/, *n.* manure; excrement, esp. of animals. [OE *dung*] –**dungy,** *adj.*

dungaree /dʌŋgə'ri/, *n.* **1.** a coarse cotton cloth used esp. for sailors' clothing. **2.** (*pl.*) work clothes, overalls, etc., made of this fabric. [Hind]

dung beetle, *n.* any of several beetles that feed upon or breed in dung, as the sacred Egyptian scarab.

dungeon /'dʌndʒən/, *n.* any dark, small prison or cell, esp. underground. [ME, from OF, from LL: dominion, tower, from L: master, lord]

dunite /'dʌnaɪt/, *n. Geol.* an igneous rock made almost totally of olivine. [named from Mt *Dun* near Nelson, NZ, where it was first identified]

dunk /dʌŋk/, *v.t.* **1.** to place completely in water. **2.** to dip (biscuits, etc.) into coffee, milk, etc. [G: dip]

Dunkirk /dʌn'kɜk/, *n.* a seaport in northern France; scene of the evacuation under German fire of the British expeditionary force of over 330 000 men, 29 May–4 June 1940. Pop. 73 618 (1982). French, **Dunkerque.**

Dunlop /'dʌnlɒp/, *n.* **1. Sir (Ernest) Edward,** born 1907, Australian surgeon. **2. John Boyd,** 1840–1921, Scottish veterinary surgeon; manufactured the first pneumatic tyres.

dunnart /'dʌnat/, *n.* See **marsupial mouse.** [Aboriginal]

dunny /'dʌni/, *n. Colloq.* a toilet, especially an outside one in an unsewered area. [Brit d. *danna* dung + *ken* place]

Duntroon Military College /dʌn'trun/, *n.* a military training college at Duntroon, ACT, established 1911. Also, **Royal Military College.** See **Australian Defence Force Academy.**

duo /'djuou/, *n., pl.* **duos, dui** /'djui/. **1.** *Music.* a duet. **2.** a pair of singers, entertainers, etc. [It, from L: two]

duo-, a word part meaning 'two'. [L, combining form of *duo*]

duodecimal /djuou'dɛsəməl/, *adj.* **1.** relating to 12ths, or to number 12. ◇*n.* **2.** one of a system of numerals the base of which is 12. [L: twelfth]

duodenum /djuə'dinəm/, *n.* the first part of the small intestine lying below the stomach. [ML, from L: 12 each; so called from its length, about 12 finger breadths] –**duodenal,** *adj.*

dup., *Abbrev.* duplicate.

Dupain /dju'peɪn/, *n.* **Max,** born 1911, Australian painter, photographer, writer, and critic.

dupe /djup/, *n., v.,* **duped, duping.** ◇*n.* **1.** someone who is tricked or deceived. ◇*v.t.* **2.** to trick; deceive. [L *upupa* stupid bird] –**dupable,** *adj.*

duple /'djupəl/, *adj.* **1.** double; twofold. **2.** *Music.* having two beats to the bar. [L: double]

duplet /'djuplət/, **1.** *Music.* a group of two notes which are to be played in the time of three notes. **2.** *Chem.* a pair of electrons, shared between two atoms, forming a covalent bond.

duplex /'djuplɛks/, *adj.* **1.** double; twofold. ◇*n.* **2.** a two-storey block of flats or home units, one flat occupying each floor.

duplicate /'djupləkət/, *adj., n.;* /'djupləkeɪt/, *v.,* **-cated, -cating.** ◇*adj.* **1.** exactly like another. **2.** double. ◇*n.* **3.** a copy exactly like an original. **4. in duplicate,** in two copies, exactly alike. ◇*v.t.* **5.** to make an exact copy of; repeat. **6.** to double; make twofold. [L: doubled] –**duplicable,** *adj.* –**duplication,** *n.*

duplicity /dju'plɪsəti/, *n., pl.* **-ties. 1.** the quality or state of being double. **2.** deceitfulness in speech or action; double-dealing. [LL: doubleness, from L: twofold]

durable /'djurəbəl/, *adj.* **1.** having the quality of lasting or enduring. ◇*n.* **2.** (*pl.*) goods which are able to last. [ME, from L: lasting] –**durability,** *n.*

Durack[1] /'djuræk/, *n.* **Fanny** (*Sarah Durack*), 1889–1956, Australian swimmer; first

Durack Australian woman to win an Olympic gold medal (1912).

Durack² /'djuræk/, *n.* a river in northern WA in the Kimberley region which rises in the central plateau and flows first northward and then north-east into Cambridge Gulf. 230 km. [named after the *Durack* family, pioneer pastoralists]

Durante /dju'rænti/, *n.* **Jimmy** (*Jimmy Francis*), 1893-1980, US film comedian and nightclub performer.

duration /dju'reɪʃən/, *n.* **1.** the length of time anything continues or exists. **2. for the duration**, for a long time. [ME, from L: last]

Durban /'dɜbən/, *n.* a seaport in the eastern part of the Republic of South Africa, in Natal. Pop. 886 000 (1976).

Dürer /'djʊrə/, *n.* **Albrecht** /'ælbrext/ or **Albert**, 1471-1528, German painter and engraver, noted esp. for his woodcuts and copper engravings.

duress /dju'res/, *n.* **1.** the use of threats or force. **2.** the loss of freedom by force; imprisonment. [ME, from L: hardness]

during /'djʊrɪŋ/, *prep.* **1.** throughout the whole course of: *It is hot during the day.* **2.** at some time in the course of: *He visited me during the day.* [ME, from F, from L: endure]

Durrell /'dʌrəl/, *n.* **Lawrence (George)**, 1912-90, English novelist and poet.

durst /dɜst/, *v.* a past tense of **dare**.

dusk /dʌsk/, *n.* a state between light and darkness; the darker stage of twilight. [var. of OE *dux, dox* dark, c. L *fuscus* dark brown]

dusky /'dʌski/, *adj.,* **duskier, duskiest**. **1.** somewhat dark-colored. **2.** lacking in light; dim. —**duskiness**, *n.*

dust /dʌst/, *n.* **1.** earth or other matter in fine, dry particles. **2.** a cloud of finely powdered earth or other matter in the air. **3.** the remains of something that has decayed, as the human body. **4.** a low or humble condition. **5.** anything worthless. **6.** confusion; turmoil. **7. bite the dust**, to fall, or to be killed or wounded. **8. throw dust in someone's eyes**, to trick or mislead someone. ◇*v.t.* **9.** to free from dust by wiping, etc.: *to dust the table.* **10.** to cover lightly with dust or powder: *to dust the body with powder.* **11.** to spread lightly as dust: *to dust powder over the body.* ◇*v.i.* **12.** to wipe dust from furniture, etc. [OE *dūst*] —**dusty**, *adj.*

dust bowl, *n. Geog.* **1.** an area of very little vegetation where dust storms happen frequently. **2.** (*cap.*) **the Dustbowl**, popular name for an area of the US, in the southern central part, that was denuded of topsoil during the droughts of the mid 1930s. About 388 500 km².

duster /'dʌstə/, *n.* **1.** a cloth, brush, etc., for removing dust. **2.** a felt pad on a wooden block, used for cleaning blackboards.

dust jacket, *n.* a jacket (def. 2) for a book. Also, **dust cover**.

dustpan /'dʌstpæn/, *n.* a pan with a short handle into which dust is swept for removal.

dust storm, *n.* a storm of wind which raises thick masses of dust into the air, as in a desert area.

dust-up /'dʌst-ʌp/, *n. Colloq.* a noisy quarrel or fight.

Dusty /'dʌsti/, *n.* **Slim** (*David Gordon Kirkpatrick*), born 1927, Australian country and western singer, guitarist, and composer.

Dutch /dʌtʃ/, *adj.* **1.** of or relating to the people of the Netherlands or Holland, or their country or language. —*n.* **2.** the people of Netherlands or Holland.

Dutch courage, *n.* courage that comes from drinking alcohol.

Dutch East Indies, *n.pl.* former name of the Republic of **Indonesia**.

Dutch New Guinea, *n.* former name of **Irian Jaya**.

Dutch oven, *n.* **1.** a large, heavy pot with a close-fitting lid used for slow cooking. **2.** a metal container, open in front, for roasting meat, etc., before an open fire.

Dutch treat, *n.* a meal or outing in which each person pays for their own costs. Also, **Dutch shout**.

Dutch uncle, *n.* someone who corrects or scolds another severely and openly.

Dutch West Indies, *n.pl.* former name of **Netherlands Antilles**.

duteous /'djutiəs/, *adj.* obedient; dutiful.

dutiable /'djutiəbəl/, *adj. Comm.* (of imported goods, etc.) on which tax or duty is payable.

dutiful /'djutəfəl/, *adj.* **1.** performing one's duties; obedient: *a dutiful student.* **2.** resulting from or showing a sense of duty: *dutiful attention.* —**dutifulness**, *n.*

duty /'djuti/, *n., pl.* **-ties. 1.** what one is morally or legally bound to do. **2.** the force that binds one to what is morally right. **3.** an action called for by someone's position or office; function: *the duties of a soldier.* **4.** a tax placed by law on the import, export, sale, or production of goods, exchange of property, legal recognition of documents, etc. **5. off duty**, not at work. **6. on duty**, at work. [ME, from AF: due]

duumvir /'djuəmvɪə/, *n.pl.* **-virs, -viri** /-vɪəri/. one of two men holding a joint office, as in ancient Rome. [L: two men] —**duumvirate**, *n.*

duvet /'duveɪ, dju'veɪ/, *n.* a large bag filled with feathers, used as a quilt. [F: down]

dux /dʌks/, *n.* the top student in a school. [L: leader]

Dvořák /'dvɔʒak/, *n.* **Antonin** /'antɒnjin/, 1841-1904, Czech composer; best known for his Symphony No 9 *From the New World* (1893).

dwarf /dwɔf/, *n.* **1.** a person, animal or plant much below the ordinary height or size. ◇*adj.* **2.** of unusually small height or size; diminutive. ◇*v.t.* **3.** to cause to seem small: *The tower dwarfed the surrounding buildings.* **4.**

dwarf   320   **dysprosium**

to prevent the proper growth or development of. [OE *dweorg*] **—dwarfish**, *adj.*

dwarfism /'dwɔfɪzəm/, *n.* a condition marked by abnormal smallness of (part of) the body.

dwell /dwel/, *v.*, **dwelt** or **dwelled**, **dwelling**, *n.* ◇*v.i.* **1.** to live (in a particular place or condition): *They dwell in Ipswich; She dwells in sorrow.* ◇*v.* **2. dwell on/upon**, to continue thinking, speaking or writing about. ◇*n.* **3.** *Mach.* a pause happening regularly when a machine is in operation. **4.** the flat part on a cam. [OE *dwellan, dwelian* lead astray, hinder, delay]

dwelling /'dwelɪŋ/, *n.* the place where someone lives; residence.

dwindle /'dwɪndl/, *v.*, **-dled, -dling.** ◇*v.i.* **1.** to become smaller or less; shrink: *His fortune has dwindled away.* ◇*v.t.* **2.** to make smaller or less; cause to shrink: *Gambling dwindles his income.* [OE *dwīnan* languish]

Dy, *Chem. Symbol.* dysprosium.

dyad /'daɪæd/, *n.* **1.** a group of two; couple. **2.** *Chem.* element, atom, or radical having a valency of two. [Gk: the number two]

Dyak /'daɪæk/, *n.* a member of an inland people of Borneo, once notorious as headhunters, of the same stock as the Malays. Also, **Dayak.**

dye /daɪ/, *n.*, *v.*, **dyed, dyeing.** ◇*n.* **1.** a coloring material or matter. **2.** a liquid containing a dye, for coloring cloth, etc. **3.** a color or hue, esp. as produced by dyeing. **4. of the deepest/blackest dye**, of the worst kind. ◇*v.t., v.i.* **5.** to color or stain, or become colored, with a dye: *to dye a cloth red; This cloth dyes easily.* [OE *dēagian*] **—dyer**, *n.* **—dyeing**, *n.*

dying /'daɪɪŋ/, *adj.* **1.** nearing death: *a dying man.* **2.** happening just before death: *his dying words.* **3.** coming to an end: *the dying year.* ◇*n.* **4.** death.

dyke[1] /daɪk/, *n.*, *v.*, **dyked, dyking.** ◇*n.* **1.** a bank built to hold back the waters of the sea or a river. **2.** a ditch. **3.** a wall or bank of earth as thrown up in digging. **4.** *Geol.* a sheet-like body of igneous rock which cuts across the layers or structure of other rocks, formed by the intrusion of magma. See **sill** (def. 3). **5.** *Colloq.* a toilet. ◇*v.t.* **6.** to provide or protect with a dyke. [ME, from Scand]

dyke[2] /daɪk/, *n. Colloq.* a lesbian. [orig. unknown]

Dylan /'dɪlən/, *n.* **Bob** (*Robert Allen Zimmerman*), born 1941, US folk and rock composer, singer and musician; one of the most influential of pop figures, esp. as a protest singer during the 1960s.

dyna-, a word part meaning power, as in *dynamite.* Also, **dynam-.** [Gk, combining form of *dýnamis* power]

dynamic /daɪ'næmɪk/, *adj.* **1.** of or relating to a force causing movement (opposed to *static*) or to a force in any state. **2.** relating to dynamics. **3.** relating to or marked by energy or effective action: *a dynamic person; a dynamic movement.* [Gk: powerful]

dynamics /daɪ'næmɪks/, *n. pl.* **1.** *Phys.* the branch of mechanics concerned with the forces which cause or affect the movement of objects. **2.** (*treated as pl.*) the forces, physical or moral, at work in any field. **3.** *Music.* variations in volume of sound.

dynamism /'daɪnəmɪzəm/, *n.* **1.** the force or active principle on which a thing, person or movement operates. **2.** *Philos.* the theory that all things are basically active.

dynamite /'daɪnəmaɪt/, *n.*, *v.*, **-mited, -miting.** ◇*n.* **1.** a powerful explosive consisting of nitroglycerine mixed with some absorbent substance. **2.** *Colloq.* anything or anyone likely to be dangerous or to cause trouble. ◇*v.t.* **3.** to destroy with dynamite.

dynamo /'daɪnəmoʊ/, *n.*, *pl.* **-mos.** **1.** any rotating machine in which mechanical energy is changed into electrical energy, esp. a direct current generator. **2.** *Colloq.* a forceful, energetic person.

dynasty /'dɪnəsti/, *n.*, *pl.* **-ties.** the (historical period of) a succession of rulers from the same family. [L, from Gk: lord, chief] **—dynastic, dynastical**, *adj.*

dyne /daɪn/, *n.* a unit of force in the centimetre-gram-second system, equal to 10^{-5} newtons. [F, from Gk: force]

dys-, a prefix, esp. medical, meaning 'difficulty', 'poor condition', as in *dyslexia.* [Gk: hard, bad, unlucky]

dysentery /'dɪsəntri/, *n.* an infectious disease marked by an inflammation of the lower bowels, and diarrhoea with mucus and blood. [L, from Gk] **—dysenteric**, *adj.*

dysfunction /dɪs'fʌŋkʃən/, *n.* poor functioning, esp. of a part of the body.

dyslexia /dɪs'leksiə/, *n.* a disorder in reading ability, often associated with difficulty in writing and co-ordination. **—dyslectic, dyslexic**, *n., adj.*

dysmenorrhoea /dɪsˌmenə'riə/, *n. Med.* painful menstruation.

dyspepsia /dɪs'pepsiə/, *n. Med.* **→indigestion.** Also, **dyspepsy** /dɪs'pepsi/. [L, from Gk] **—dyspeptic**, *adj.*

dysphemism /'dɪsfəmɪzəm/, *n.* an expression which uses a harsh or offensive word instead of a mild one: *'Dead meat ticket' is a dysphemism for 'identity disc'.*

dysprosium /dɪs'proʊsiəm/, *n.* a rare-earth metallic element. *Symbol:* Dy; *at. no.*: 66; *at. wt*: 62.50.

Ee

E, e, *n., pl.* **E's** or **Es, e's** or **es. 1.** the fifth letter of the English alphabet. **2.** *Music.* the third note in the scale of C major.

e, *Symbol. Maths.* the constant, 2.718 2818..., used as the base of natural logarithms.

e-, variant of **ex-**[1], used in words of Latin origin before consonants except *c, f, p, q, s,* and *t,* as in *emit*.

E, *Abbrev.* **1.** east. **2.** eastern. **3.** English.

each /itʃ/, *adj.* **1.** every, of two or more considered one by one: *each stone in the building.* ◇*pron.* **2.** each one: *Each went his way.* ◇*adv.* **3.** apiece; individually: *They cost a dollar each.* [OE ǣlc, from ā ever + (ge)līc like]

each other, *n.* each the other (used to describe the action or relation between two or more people, objects, etc.): *They hit each other.*

eager /ˈigə/, *adj.* keen in desire or feeling; impatiently longing: *eager to go; eager for fame; an eager student.* [ME, from OF, from L: sharp] **—eagerness,** *n.*

eagle /ˈigəl/, *n.* **1.** a bird of prey noted for its size, strength, powerful flight and keenness of vision. **2.** *Golf.* a score two below par on any but par-three holes. [ME, from OF, from L]

eaglehawk /ˈigəlhɔk/, *n.* a large brown eagle with a broad wing-span and wedge-shaped tail; wedge-tailed eagle.

Eaglehawk Neck, *n.* a narrow isthmus east of Hobart, Tas, which joins the Tasman Peninsula to the Forestier Peninsula. Also, *Colloq.*, **the Neck.**

eaglet /ˈiglət/, *n.* a young eagle. [F]

ear[1] /iə/, *n.* **1.** the organ of hearing, usu. consisting of three parts (external, middle and inner ear). **2.** the external part alone. **3.** the sense of hearing. **4.** the ability to hear differences of sound, esp. quality and correctness of musical sounds: *an ear for music.* **5.** attention: *gain a person's ear.* **6. be all ears,** to listen attentively. **7. by ear,** without reference to written music. **8. have an ear to the ground,** to be well informed about a topic. **9. turn a deaf ear,** to refuse to help. [OE ēare]

ear[2] /iə/, *n.* the part of a cereal plant which contains the flowers and then the fruit, grains, or kernels. [OE ēar]

ear canal, *n.* →**auditory canal.**

eardrum /ˈiədrʌm/, *n.* →**tympanic membrane.**

Earhart /ˈɛəhat/, *n.* **Amelia,** 1898–1937, US pilot; first woman to make a solo flight over the Atlantic Ocean; her plane disappeared while on a round-the-world flight in 1937.

earth

earl /ɜl/, *n.* a British nobleman ranked below a marquess and above a viscount. [ME *erl,* OE *eorl* man, warrior] **—earldom,** *n.*

Earle /ɜl/, *n.* **1. Augustus,** 1793–1838, British-born artist in Australia; specialised in landscapes and portraits. **2. John,** 1865–1932, Australian politician; first Labor premier of Tas 1914–16.

early /ˈɜli/, *adv.,* **-lier, -liest,** *adj.* ◇*adv.* **1.** in or during the first part of some division of time, or of some course or series: *early in the year.* **2.** before the usual or appointed time: *Come early.* **3. early on,** after very little time has passed: *They came early on in the days of the colony.* ◇*adj.* **4.** taking place early: *an early appointment.* **5.** belonging to a period far back in time: *early English buildings.* **6.** occurring soon: *an early reply.* **7. early days,** too soon to form an opinion or see a result: *It's early days yet.* [OE ærlīce (from ær soon + -līce -LY)] **—earliness,** *n.*

earmark /ˈiəmak/, *n.* **1.** a mark made on an animal's ear to show who owns it. **2.** any identifying mark. ◇*v.t.* **3.** to mark with an earmark. **4.** to set aside for a particular use: *That money is earmarked for the flood victims.*

earmuff /ˈiəmʌf/, *n.* one of a pair of coverings for warming ears.

earn /ɜn/, *v.t.* **1.** to gain by labor or service: *He must earn his living.* **2.** to get or deserve as a result of something done: *You will earn a name for being dishonest.* **3.** to gain as due return or profit: *Those bonds earn good interest.* [OE *earnian*] **—earner,** *n.*

earnest[1] /ˈɜnəst/, *adj.* **1.** serious in intention, purpose, or effort: *an earnest worker.* **2.** showing depth and sincerity of feeling: *earnest words.* [OE *eornost*] **—earnestness,** *n.*

earnest[2] /ˈɜnəst/, *n.* part of something, given or done in advance as a pledge of the remainder. [OF]

earnings /ˈɜnɪŋz/, *n.pl.* money earned; wages; profits. [OE *earnung*]

earphone /ˈiəfoʊn/, *n.* a small device for changing electric signals into soundwaves, fitted into or held close to the ear.

earring /ˈiəˌrɪŋ/, *n.* a ring or other ornament worn in or on the lobe of the ear.

earshot /ˈiəʃɒt/, *n.* reach or range of hearing: *within earshot.*

earth /ɜθ/, *n.* **1.** (*oft. cap.*) the planet on which we live, the third in order from the sun. **2.** those living on this planet: *The whole earth rejoiced.* **3.** this world, as opposed to heaven and hell. **4.** dry land; the ground. **5.** the softer part of the land, as opposed to rock; soil. **6.** the hole of a ground-living animal. **7.** *Chem.* any of several metallic oxides which are not easily reduced, as alumina, etc. **8.** *Elect.* **a.** a conducting connection between an electric circuit or equipment and the ground or other large conducting body. **b.** a terminal to which the earthing connection is attached. **9. the earth,** everything or a great deal: *to cost the earth; want the earth.* **10. down to earth,** practical; plain; blunt. **11. run to earth,** to hunt down. ◇*v.t.*

earth 12. *Elect.* to establish an earth (def. 8) for (a device, circuit, etc.). [OE *eorthe*]

earthbound /'ɜθbaʊnd/, *adj.* 1. firmly fixed or tied to the earth. 2. heading towards the earth. 3. having only earthly interests.

earthenware /'ɜθənwɛə/, *n., adj.* (pots, etc.) made of baked or earthened clay.

earthling /'ɜθlɪŋ/, *n.* someone living on earth; a mortal.

earthly /'ɜθli/, *adj.*, **-lier, -liest.** 1. of the earth, esp. as opposed to heaven; worldly. 2. possible: *no earthly use.* [OE *eorthlīc*]

earthquake /'ɜθkweɪk/, *n.* a shaking of the ground caused by movements in the earth's crust resulting from a build-up of pressure, causing rocks to break and sending out shock waves (earthquake waves).

earthworm /'ɜθwɜm/, *n.* any one of many segmented worms that burrow in soil and feed on decaying organic matter.

earthy /'ɜθi/, *adj.*, **earthier, earthiest.** 1. of, consisting of or like earth or soil: *an earthy smell.* 2. coarse. 3. direct; robust. 4. sensual in a natural way. —**earthiness**, *n.*

ear trumpet, *n.* a trumpet-like device for collecting and amplifying sounds to help poor hearing.

earwig /'ɪəwɪg/, *n.* a harmless insect with pincers, which was once thought to hurt the human ear. [OE *ēarwicga* ear insect]

ease /iz/, *n., v.*, **eased, easing.** ◇*n.* 1. freedom from labor, pain, or physical annoyance of any kind; comfort: *The job was finished with ease.* 2. freedom from stiffness or formality: *ease of manner.* 3. **at ease, a.** *Mil.* a position in which soldiers may relax, but may not talk or leave. **b.** in a state of freedom from concern or anxiety. ◇*v.t.* 4. to give rest or relief to: *The news will ease her mind.* 5. to mitigate, lighten, or lessen: *This pill will ease the pain.* 6. to reduce the pressure, tension, etc., of (a rope, bandage, etc.). 7. to make less difficult; facilitate. 8. to move (a person or thing) slowly and with great care: *They eased the victim onto a stretcher.* ◇*v.i.* 9. to reduce in severity, tension, etc. (oft. fol. by *off* or *up*): *The rain should ease off soon.* 10. to move slowly and with great care (oft. fol. by *along*): *He eased along the ledge; It took time to ease into the new job.* [ME, from OF, from LL: near]

easel /'izəl/, *n.* a triangular frame for supporting an artist's canvas, a blackboard, etc. [D *ezel*, c. G *Esel* easel, lit., ass; akin to ASS]

easement /'izmənt/, *n.* 1. something that gives ease; a convenience. 2. *Law.* a right held by one person to make use of the land of another.

easily /'izəli/, *adv.* 1. in an easy manner; without trouble. 2. beyond question: *easily the best.* 3. probably; likely: *It could easily rain.*

east /ist/, *n.* 1. the point of the compass (90 degrees right of north) corresponding to the point where the sun rises. 2. the direction in which this point lies. 3. (*l.c.* or *cap.*) a land situated in this direction. 4. **the East,** → **orient** (def. 1). ◇*adj., adv.* 5. in, towards or coming from the east: *east wind; east side; He was walking east.* [OE *ēast*]

East Anglia /ist 'æŋgliə/, *n.* an early English kingdom in south-eastern Britain; modern Norfolk and Suffolk.

East Bengal, *n.* the part of the former Indian province of Bengal which became East Pakistan in 1947 and then Bangladesh in 1971.

East Berlin, *n.* formerly, the capital of East Germany, formed by the eastern part of Berlin (the former Soviet sector). See **Berlin.**

East China Sea, *n.* a part of the northern Pacific, bounded by China, Korea, Japan, the Ryukyus, and Taiwan.

Easter /'istə/, *n.* 1. a yearly Christian festival celebrating the resurrection of Jesus Christ, observed on the first Sunday after the full moon on or following 21 March. 2. Also, **Easter Day, Easter Sunday.** the day on which this festival is celebrated. [OE *ēastre*, pl. *ēastron*, orig., name of dawn goddess]

Easter Island, *n.* an island in the southern Pacific about 3700 km west of and belonging to Chile; noted for gigantic prehistoric statues. 166 km^2. Also, **Rapa Nui.**

easterly /'istəli/, *adj., adv.* towards or from the east.

eastern /'istən/, *adj.* 1. lying in, moving towards or coming from the east: *eastern seaboard; eastern passage; eastern wind.* 2. (*usu. cap.*) of or relating to the East: *the Eastern Church.* [OE *ēasterne*] —**easternmost,** *adj.*

Eastern Church, *n.* any body of Christians following the Orthodox Church and from countries originally part of the Eastern Roman Empire.

Eastern Hemisphere, *n.* the part of the world lying east of the Greenwich Meridian, including Asia, Africa, Australia, and Europe.

Eastern Roman Empire, *n.* the eastern division of the Roman Empire and, after AD 476, the Roman Empire with its capital at Constantinople. Also, **Eastern Empire.**

eastern spinebill, *n.* a small eastern Australian nectar-feeding bird, with a long, slim, downward-curving bill.

Eastern Standard Time, *n.* a time zone lying on the 150th meridian and including Qld, NSW, Vic and Tas, a half-hour ahead of *Central Standard Time* and two hours ahead of *Western Standard Time.*

East Germany, *n.* formerly, a republic in northern central Europe, on the Baltic Sea; formed in 1949 from the USSR-occupied zone of Germany; granted sovereignty in 1954; became part of reunified Germany in 1990. Official name, **German Democratic Republic.** German, **Deutsche Demokratische Republik.** *Abbrev.:* GDR or DDR —**East German,** *n., adj.*

East India Company, *n.* 1. a company chartered by the British government to trade between India and Britain, 1600–1874. 2. any

East India Company of several similar companies of other European countries: Dutch (1602–1798); French (1664–1769); Danish (1729–1801).

East Indiaman /ist 'ɪndiəmæn/ n. a large armed sailing vessel of the East India Company.

East Indies /ist 'ɪndiz/, n. a collective name of the two large peninsulas (India and Indochina) of South-East Asia, together with the Malay Archipelago.

East Timor, n. a territory comprising the eastern part of the island of Timor; became a Portuguese colony; invaded by Indonesia in 1975 and annexed 1976; annexation not recognised by the UN. *Cap.:* Dili.

East Prussia, n. a former province in northeastern Germany; until 1939 separated from Germany by the Polish Corridor; now divided between Poland and the USSR. German name, **Ostpreussen**.

eastward /'istwəd/, adj. **1.** moving, bearing, facing, or situated towards the east. ◇adv. **2.** eastwards. —**eastwardly**, adj., adv.

eastwards /'istwədz/, adv. towards the east. Also, **eastward**.

easy /'izi/, adj., **easier**, **easiest**, adv. ◇adj. **1.** not difficult; requiring no great effort: *easy to read*; *an easy victory*. **2.** free from pain, discomfort, worry, or care: *easy in one's mind*. **3.** providing ease or comfort: *an easy standing position*. **4.** not formal or stiff: *an easy manner*. **5.** not harsh; lenient: *an easy master*. **6.** not difficult to influence; compliant. **7.** *Colloq.* having no firm feelings in a matter: *I'm easy*. **8.** moderate: *an easy pace*; *an easy slope*. **9.** *Comm.* **a.** (of an item) not difficult to obtain. **b.** (of the market) not showing eager demand. **10. easy on the eyes**, attractive. **11. on easy street**, with plenty of money. ◇adv. **12.** *Colloq.* in an easy manner: *Take it easy*. **13. go easy**, *Colloq.* (fol. by on or with): *Go easy on the children*; *Go easy with that valuable vase*. **b.** to use sparingly (fol. by on or with): *Go easy on the honey*. [ME, from OF] —**easiness**, n.

eat /it/, v., **ate** /eɪt, ɛt/ **eaten** /'itn/ **eating**; n. ◇v.t. **1.** to take into the mouth and swallow. **2.** to destroy as if by eating; waste away; corrode (oft. fol. by *away*, *up*): *The sea will eat away the rock wall*. **3.** *Colloq.* to cause to worry; trouble: *What's eating you?* ◇v.i. **4.** to take a meal. **5.** to make a way by or as if by corrosion: *The rust has eaten through the metal*; *Gambling has eaten through his money*. ◇v. **6. eat one's heart out**, to waste away with longing. **7. eat one's words**, to take back what one has said. **8. eat out**, to dine at a restaurant, etc. rather than at home. ◇n. **9.** (*pl.*) *Colloq.* food. [OE *etan*] — **eatable**, adj.

eau de Cologne /oʊ də kəˈloʊn/, n. → **cologne**. [Trademark]

eaves /ivz/, n.pl. the overhanging lower edge of a roof. [OE *efes*]

eavesdrop /'ivzdrɒp/, v.i., **-dropped**, **-dropping**. to listen secretly. [lit., be on the *eavesdrop* (of a house), earlier *eavesdrip* ground on which falls the drip from the eaves, OE *yfesdrype*] —**eavesdropper**, n.

ebb /ɛb/, n. **1.** the falling of the tide (opposed to *flow*). **2.** a flowing backwards or away; a decline or decay. ◇v.i. **3.** to flow back or away, as the water of a tide (opposed to *flow*). **4.** to waste or fade away: *His life is ebbing*. [OE *ebba*]

ebony /'ɛbəni/, n., pl. **-onies**, adj. ◇n. **1.** a hard, heavy, long-lasting wood, most highly prized when black, from various tropical trees. ◇adj. **2.** made of ebony. **3.** black like ebony: *ebony eyes*. [ME, from L, from Gk]

ebullient /ə'bʊliənt, ə'bʌl-, ə'bjul-/, adj. **1.** overflowing with eagerness, excitement, etc. **2.** boiling; bubbling like a boiling liquid. [L: boiling out or up] —**ebullience**, n. —**ebullition**, n.

EC, *Abbrev.* European Community.

eccentric /ək'sɛntrɪk/, adj. **1.** differing from the recognised or usual character, practice, etc.; irregular; peculiar: *eccentric conduct*; *an eccentric person*. **2.** (of two circles or spheres) not having the same centre (opposed to *concentric*). **3.** (of an axis) not situated in the centre. ◇n. **4.** someone or something which is unusual, peculiar or odd. [LL, from Gk: out of the centre] —**eccentrically**, adv.

eccentricity /ɛksən'trɪsəti/, n., pl. **-ties**. **1.** an oddity or peculiarity, as of conduct. **2.** the quality or degree of being eccentric.

Eccl, *Bible. Abbrev.* Ecclesiastes. Also, **Eccles**.

Eccles /'ɛkəlz/, n. **Sir John (Carew)**, born 1903, Australian neurophysiologist at the US; shared the Nobel prize for medicine in 1963 for work on the nervous system.

Ecclesiastes /əkliːziˈæstiz/, n. a book of the Old Testament traditionally ascribed to Solomon. [LL, from Gk: lit., preacher]

ecclesiastic /əkliːziˈæstɪk/, n. **1.** a clergyman. ◇adj. **2.** ecclesiastical. [LL, from Gk: of the assembly or church]

ecclesiastical /əkliːziˈæstəkəl/, adj. of or relating to the church or the clergy; clerical: *ecclesiastical discipline*; *ecclesiastical affairs*.

ECG /i si 'dʒi/, *Abbrev.* **1.** electrocardiogram. **2.** electrocardiograph.

echelon /'ɛʃəlɒn/, n. **1.** a level of command: *in the higher echelons*. **2.** *Mil.* a steplike formation of troops, ships, planes, etc. [F: lit., ladder rung, from L: SCALE³]

echidna /ə'kɪdnə/, n., pl. **-nas**, **-nae** /-ni/. a spine-covered insect-eating monotreme with claws and a slender snout, found in Australia and the island of NG; spiny anteater. [NL, from Gk: viper]

echinoderm /ə'kaɪnədɜːm, ə'kɪnə-/, n. any of a phylum of sea animals such as starfishes, sea-urchins, etc. [NL]

echo /'ɛkoʊ/, n., pl. **echoes**, v., **echoed**, **echoing**. ◇n. **1.** a repetition of sound, produced by soundwaves bouncing back from a surface. **2.** a sound heard again near its source, after reflection. **3.** any repetition or close imitation, as of ideas or opinions of

echo   324   **Ecumenical Council**

another. **4.** *Elect.* the reflection of a radio wave such as is used in radar, etc. **5.** (*cap.*) *Gk Legend.* a mountain nymph who pined away for love of the beautiful youth Narcissus until only her voice remained. ◇*v.i.* **6.** to resound with an echo. **7.** to be repeated by or as if by an echo: *Her words echoed in my mind for years.* ◇*v.t.* **8.** to repeat by or as by an echo: *The hall will echo even faint sounds; His followers merely echoed his ideas.* **9.** to repeat the words, etc., of (a person etc.): *The children echo the teacher.* [L, from Gk: sound, echo]

Echuca /ə'tʃukə/, *n.* a city in northern central Vic at the junction of the Murray and Campaspe Rivers. Pop. 8409 (1986). [Aboriginal: meeting of the waters]

eclair /eɪ'kleə, ə-/, *n.* a light, finger-shaped cake made of choux pastry, filled with cream and coated with chocolate. [F: lit., lightning]

eclat /eɪ'klaː/, *n.* **1.** brilliance of success, etc.: *the eclat of a great achievement.* **2.** showy or complicated display. [F: fragment, also burst (of light, etc.)]

eclectic /ɛ'klɛktɪk/, *adj.* **1.** choosing from various sources. **2.** made up of what is chosen from different sources. ◇*n.* **3.** someone who follows an eclectic method, as in philosophy. [Gk: selective] —**eclectically**, *adv.* —**eclecticism**, *n.*

eclipse /ə'klɪps, i-/, *n., v.*, **eclipsed**, **eclipsing**. ◇*n.* **1.** *Astron.* **a.** the darkening of the light of a satellite when its primary planet stands between it and the sun, as in a **lunar eclipse** when the moon is within the earth's shadow. **b. solar eclipse**, the cutting out of the light of the sun by the moon being between it and the observer. **2.** any overshadowing; loss of brilliance or splendor. ◇*v.t.* **3.** to cause to suffer eclipse: *The moon eclipses the sun.* **4.** to make dim by comparison; surpass. [ME, from OF, from L, from Gk: a failing]

ecliptic /ə'klɪptɪk, i-/, *n.* **1.** the apparent yearly path of the sun in the heavens. ◇*adj.* **2.** Also, **ecliptical**. relating to an eclipse of the sun. See ECLIPSE. [L, from Gk: of or caused by an eclipse.

ecology /ə'kɒlədʒi/, *n.* the branch of biology which is concerned with relations between organisms and their environment. [Gk *oîko(s)* house + -LOGY] —**ecologist**, *n.* —**ecological**, *adj.*

economic /ɛkə'nɒmɪk, ikə-/, *adj.* **1.** relating to the production, distribution, and use of income and wealth. **2.** relating to the science of economics. **3.** relating to the means of living; utilitarian: *economic botany, etc.* [L, from Gk. See ECONOMY]

economical /ɛkə'nɒmɪkəl, ikə-/, *adj.* avoiding waste; thrifty: *an economical buy; an economical person.*

economics /ɛkə'nɒmɪks, ikə-/, *n.* **1.** (*treated as sing.*) the science of the production, distribution, and use of income and wealth. **2.** (*treated as pl.*) economically important points. —**economist**, *n.*

economise or **economize** /ə'kɒnəmaɪz/, *v.*, **-mised**, **-mising**. ◇*v.t.* **1.** to manage economically; use sparingly. ◇*v.i.* **2.** to practise economy (def. 1); avoid waste. —**economisation**, *n.*

economy /ə'kɒnəmi/, *n., pl.* **-mies**. **1.** the careful mangement of money, materials, etc. **2.** an act or means of careful saving; a saving. **3.** the management of the resources of a country, etc., with a view to productiveness and avoidance of waste: *national economy.* **4.** the efficient and sparing use of something: *economy of effort.* [L, from Gk: management of a household or of the state]

ecosphere /'ikousfɪə, 'ɛk-/, *n.* that part of the atmosphere of a planet which can support life.

ecosystem /'ikou,sɪstəm, 'ɛk-/, *n.* a community of organisms plus the environment in which they live and interact, as a pond, forest, etc.

ecotype /'ikoutaɪp, 'ɛk-, -kə-/, *n.* a subspecies which has become specially suited to certain environmental conditions.

ecstasy /'ɛkstəsi/, *n., pl.* **-sies**. **1.** a sudden overpowering feeling. **2.** a state of rapture. [ME, from OF, from ML, from Gk: distraction of mind] —**ecstatic**, *adj.*

ECT /i si 'ti/, *Abbrev.* electroconvulsive therapy.

ecto-, a prefix (chiefly in biological words) meaning 'outside', 'outer', 'external', 'lying upon' as in *ectoderm.* [Gk *ekto-*, combining form of *ektós* outside]

ectoderm /'ɛktoudəm, 'ɛktə-/, *n.* the outer cell layer in the embryo of many-celled organisms. —**ectodermal**, **ectodermic**, *adj.*

-ectomy, a combining form attached to the name of a body part and producing a word meaning an operation for the cutting out of that part, as in *appendicectomy.* [*ec-* (from Gk *ek-*, prefix form of *ek, ex* out of) + -TOMY]

ectopic pregnancy /ɛk,tɒpɪk 'prɛgnənsi/, *n. Med.* a pregnancy in which the fetus is in an abnormal place, i.e. outside the womb.

ectoplasm /'ɛktouplæzəm, 'ɛktə-/, *n.* **1.** *Biol.* the outer layer of the cytoplasm in certain cells. **2.** a substance supposed to come from the body of a medium (def. 10) during trances. —**ectoplasmic**, *adj.*

Ecuador /'ɛkwədɔː/, *n.* a republic on the Pacific coast of South America, bordered by Colombia and Peru; a former Spanish colony. Pop. 9 923 000 (1987 est.); 270 670 km². *Languages:* Spanish, also Quechua. *Currency:* sucre. *Cap.:* Quito. —**Ecuadorian**, **Ecuadoran**, *n., adj.*

ecumenical /ikjə'mɛnəkəl, ɛk-/, *adj.* **1.** universal, esp. including or involving the whole Christian Church. **2.** tending or intended to work towards unity among all Christian Churches: *the ecumenical movement.* Also, **ecumenic**. [LL, from Gk: general, universal] —**ecumenicalism**, *n.*

Ecumenical Council, *n. Rom Cath Ch.* an assembly of the bishops convened by the Pope to consider important questions of dogma and practice and to reach conclusions binding upon the entire Church.

eczema — educate

eczema /'ɛksəmə/, *n.* an inflammatory disease in which the skin becomes itchy and occasionally weeps. [NL, from Gk: a cutaneous eruption] — **eczematous**, *adj.*

-ed[1], a suffix forming the past tense, as in *He crossed the river.* [OE *-de, -ede, -ode, -ade*]

-ed[2], a suffix forming: **1.** the past participle, as in *He has crossed the river.* **2.** participial adjectives describing the result of the action of the verb, as *inflated balloons*. [OE *-ed, -od, -ad*]

-ed[3], a suffix forming adjectives from nouns, as *bearded, moneyed, tenderhearted*. [OE *-ede*]

ed. /ɛd/, *Abbrev.* **1.** edited. **2.** edition. **3.** *pl.* **eds.** editor.

edam /'idəm, 'ɛdəm/, *n.* a hard, round, yellow cheese, with a red wax rind. [named after *Edam*, in Holland, where it originated]

eddy /'ɛdi/, *n., pl.* **eddies**, *v.,* **eddied, eddying**. ◇*n.* **1.** (in a liquid or gas) a current not moving with the main current esp. one having a circular movement. ◇*v.i.* **2.** to move in eddies. [OE *ed-* turning + *ēa*, stream]

Edel Land /'idl lænd/, *n.* formerly, the Dutch name of part of the western coast of Australia from Geraldton north to Shark Bay.

edelweiss /'eɪdəlvaɪs/, *n.* a small plant with white woolly leaves and flowers, growing in the European Alps. [G, from *edel* noble + *weiss* white]

Eden[1] /'idn/, *n.* **(Robert) Anthony** (*Earl of Avon*), 1897–1977, British foreign minister 1935–38, 1940–45, 1951–55; Conservative prime minister 1955–57; resigned following the controversial British and French occupation of the Suez Canal zone (1956).

Eden[2] /'idn/, *n.* **1.** *Bible.* the garden where Adam and Eve lived. **2.** any delightful place or state. [Heb: lit., pleasure, delight]

edge /ɛdʒ/, *n., v.,* **edged, edging**. ◇*n.* **1.** the border or part beside a line of division: *the horizon's edge*. **2.** a brink, or a steep, rock face. **3.** one of the narrow surfaces of a thin, flat object: *a book with gold edges*. **4.** the line in which two surfaces of a solid object meet: *the edge of the box*. **5.** (the sharpness of) the thin, cutting edge of a cutting instrument: *That knife has a good edge*. **6.** sharpness or keenness (of language, argument, appetite, desire, etc.): *The walk gave an edge to their appetite.* **7. have the edge**, *Colloq.* to have the advantage (usu. fol. by *over*). **8. on edge**, **a.** nervous and excited; uncomfortable: *He was on edge about the interview.* **b.** annoyed; irritable: *The squeaking hinges set him on edge.* ◇*v.t.* **9.** to put an edge on. **10.** to trim or neaten the edges of: *edge a lawn.* **11.** to force or move gradually: *Can you edge your way through the crowd?* **12.** *Cricket.* to play the ball from the edge of the bat, usu. without meaning to; snick. ◇*v.i.* **13.** to move sideways; advance gradually. [OE *ecg*] — **edged**, *adj.* — **edger**, *n.*

edgeways /'ɛdʒweɪz/, *adv.* **1.** with the edge forward. **2.** with a sideways movement. **3. get a word in edgeways**, to succeed in forcing one's way into a conversation.

edging /'ɛdʒɪŋ/, *n.* something that serves for or decorates an edge.

edgy /'ɛdʒi/, *adj.,* **-ier, -iest**. on edge; irritable; nervous. — **edginess**, *n.*

edible /'ɛdəbəl/, *adj.* **1.** fit to be eaten as food; eatable. ◇*n.* **2.** (*usu. pl.*) anything edible; food. [L: eat] — **edibility**, *n.*

edict /'idɪkt/, *n.* an order given by a ruler or other authority. [L: declared, proclaimed]

edifice /'ɛdəfəs/, *n.* a building, esp. one of large size or showy appearance. [F, from L: building]

edify /'ɛdəfaɪ/, *v.t.,* **-fied, -fying**. to build up or increase the faith, morality, etc., of. [ME, from OF, from L: build] — **edification**, *n.* — **edifying**, *adj.*

Edinburgh[1] /'ɛdnbərə, -brə/, *n.* **1. Alfred Ernest Albert, Duke of**, 1844–1900, second son of Queen Victoria; wounded at Clontarf, Sydney, in 1868 by Henry James O'Farrell. **2. Prince Philip, Duke of**, born 1921, husband of Queen Elizabeth II.

Edinburgh[2] /'ɛdnbərə, -brə/, *n.* the capital of second largest city in Scotland; on the Firth of Forth. Pop. 420 200 (1982).

Edison /'ɛdəsən/, *n.* **Thomas Alva**, 1847–1931, US inventor, esp. of electrical devices.

edit /'ɛdət/, *v.t.* **1.** to direct the preparation of (a newspaper, magazine, etc.). **2.** to collect, prepare, and arrange (materials) for producing a newspaper, etc. **3.** to revise and correct. **4.** to make (a film or sound recording) by cutting and arranging first prints, sound track, etc.

edition /ə'dɪʃən/, *n.* **1.** one of a number of printings of the same book, newspaper, etc., later ones often having additions and changes made. **2.** the form in which a work of literature is published: *a one-volume edition of Shakespeare.* **3.** the total number of copies of a book, newspaper, etc., printed from one set of type at one time. **4.** *Colloq.* any similar form; version: *She's a young edition of yourself.* [L]

editor /'ɛdətə/, *n.* **1.** someone who prepares written material for publication, sometimes in one particular area. **2.** someone who is responsible for the content of a newspaper, etc., usu. someone who presents his or her opinion in the name of the paper. **3.** someone who edits films, recordings, etc. [L] — **editorship**, *n.*

editorial /ɛdə'tɔriəl/, *n.* **1.** an article, in a newspaper or similar, presenting an opinion or comment of an editor in the name of the paper; leader. ◇*adj.* **2.** of or relating to an editor.

EDP /i di 'pi/, *Abbrev.* electronic data processing.

educable /'ɛdʒəkəbəl/, *adj.* able to be educated. — **educability**, *n.*

educate /'ɛdʒəkeɪt/, *v.t.,* **-cated, -cating**. **1.** to develop the intellectual powers of (someone) by teaching, instruction, or schooling; qualify by instruction or training for a particular calling, practice, etc.; train. **2.** to provide education for; send to school. **3.** to develop or train (the ear, taste, etc.). [L: brought up, trained, educated] — **educator**, *n.*

educated /'edʒəkeɪtɪd/, *adj.* **1.** having undertaken education. **2.** displaying qualities of culture and learning.

education /edʒə'keɪʃən/, *n.* **1.** the act or process of educating; the passing on or gaining of knowledge, skill, etc. **2.** the result produced by instruction, training, or study: *He has a good education.* **3.** the science or art of teaching; pedagogics: *He is studying education.* —**educative, educational,** *adj.* —**educationalist,** *n.*

Edward /'edwəd/, *n.* **1.** ('*the Black Prince*') Prince of Wales 1330–76; English military commander (son of Edward III). **2. Prince** (*Edward Antony Richard Louis*), born 1964, youngest son of Queen Elizabeth II.

Edward III, *n.* 1312–77, king of England 1327–77; began the Hundred Years War against France.

Edward VII, *n.* (*Albert Edward*) 1841–1910, king of England 1901–10 (son of Queen Victoria).

Edward VIII, *n.* (*Duke of Windsor*) 1894–1972, king of England in 1936 (son of George V and brother of George VI); the only British monarch to abdicate.

Edwardian /ed'wodiən/, *adj.* relating to the time of Edward VII, now thought of as ornate, wealthy and leisurely.

Edward the Confessor /'edwəd ðə kən'fesə/, *n.* c. 1004–66, king of England 1042–66; founder of Westminster Abbey.

-ee, a suffix added to nouns to indicate someone who is the object of some action, or undergoes or receives something, as in *employee*. [F *-é*, pp. ending, from L *-ātus* -ATE¹]

EEC /i i 'si/, *Abbrev.* European Economic Community.

EEG /i i 'dʒi/, *Abbrev.* **1.** electroencephalogram. **2.** electroencephalograph.

eel /il/, *n.* a type of snakelike freshwater or sea fish noted for its slipperiness. [OE *ēl*]

e'en¹ /in/, *adv. Poetic.* even.

e'en² /in/, *n. Poetic.* evening.

Eendracht Land /'indrakt lænd/, *n.* formerly, the Dutch name of part of the west coast of Australia including Shark Bay and a section to the north. [named after the *Eendracht,* the ship commanded by Dirck HARTOG]

e'er /ɛə/, *adv. Poetic.* ever.

-eer, a suffix of nouns indicating someone who is concerned with, or employed in connection with something, as in *auctioneer, engineer, profiteer*. Also, **-ier**. [F *-ier*, from L *-ārius*. See -ARY and -ER²]

eerie /'ɪəri/, *adj.*, **eerier, eeriest.** weird or strange; mysterious; unnatural. Also, **eery.** [OE *earg* cowardly] —**eerily,** *adv.* —**eeriness,** *n.*

ef-, variant of **ex-¹** before *f*, as in *effluent*.

efface /ə'feɪs/, *v.t.*, **effaced, effacing. 1.** to wipe out; destroy: *It is hard to efface a memory.* **2.** to make not noticeable: *There is no need to efface yourself.* [ME, from F, *ef-* (from L *ex-* EX-¹) + *face* FACE] —**effacement,** *n.*

effect /ə'fekt, i-/, *n.* **1.** something that is produced by some cause; a result. **2.** power to produce results; force; weight: *of no effect; The law takes effect from Tuesday.* **3.** the state of being operative: *The plan was brought into effect.* **4.** the result intended: *He wrote to that effect.* **5.** (*usu. pl.*) (in theatre, films, etc.) a sight, sound, etc. produced to give a particular impression: *special effects.* **6.** (*pl.*) personal property; goods. **7. for effect,** for the sake of a desired impression. **8. in effect, a.** in fact or reality. **b.** in operation, as a law. ◇*v.t.* **9.** to produce as an effect; bring about; accomplish: *effect a change.* [ME, from L: brought about]

effective /ə'fektɪv, i-/, *adj.* **1.** producing the intended or expected result: *effective steps towards peace.* **2.** actually in effect: *The law becomes effective at midnight.* **3.** producing a striking reaction: *an effective picture.* —**effectiveness,** *n.*

effector /ə'fektə, i-/, *n.* an organ, tissue or cell that carries out a response to a nerve impulse. [L]

effectual /ə'fektʃuəl, i-/, *adj.* **1.** producing an intended effect; adequate. **2.** binding, as an agreement; valid. [LL]

effeminate /ə'femənət, i-/, *adj.* (of a man) soft or delicate to an unmanly degree in tastes, habits, etc.; womanish. [L: made womanish] —**effeminateness, effeminacy,** *n.*

effervesce /efə'vɛs/, *v.i.*, **-vesced, -vescing. 1.** to give off bubbles of gas, as fermenting liquors. **2.** to show excitement, liveliness, etc. [L: boil up] —**effervescence,** *n.* —**effervescent,** *adj.*

effete /ə'fit/, *adj.* **1.** having lost its energy; exhausted; worn out. **2.** unable to produce; sterile. [L: exhausted]

efficacy /'efəkəsi/, *n., pl.* **-cies.** ability to produce effects; effectiveness. [L] —**efficacious,** *adj.*

efficiency /ə'fɪʃənsi, i-/, *n., pl.* **-cies. 1.** the fact or quality of being efficient. **2.** the ratio of work done or energy developed by a machine, etc., to the energy supplied to it.

efficient /ə'fɪʃənt, i-/, *adj.* **1.** having and using the necessary knowledge, skill, and industry; competent; capable. **2.** producing an effect; causative. [L: accomplishing]

effigy /'efədʒi/, *n., pl.* **-gies. 1.** a representation or image, as on a coin. **2.** a doll or rough representation of a person, esp. one made for expressing feelings of hatred, as by witchcraft. **3. burn** or **hang in effigy,** to burn or hang an image of a person to express hatred, etc. [F, from L]

effloresce /eflɔ'rɛs/, *v.i.*, **-resced, -rescing. 1.** to burst into bloom; blossom. **2.** (of a crystal) to become powdery on the surface upon exposure to air, as a result of the loss of some water of crystallisation. **3.** (of a rock or mineral) to become covered with fine-grain crystals. [L *efflōrescere* blossom] —**efflorescence,** *n.* —**efflorescent,** *adj.*

effluent /'ɛfluənt/, *adj.* **1.** flowing out. ◇*n.* **2.** something that flows out, as liquid waste from industry, sewage works, etc. **3.** a stream flowing out of another stream, lake, etc. [L] —**effluence**, *n.*

effluvium /ə'fluviəm/, *n., pl.* **-via** /-viə/, **-viums.** an unpleasant or foul smell or vapor, usu. invisible. [L: a flowing out] —**effluvial**, *adj.*

effort /'ɛfət/, *n.* **1.** the use of power, physical or mental; exertion. **2.** an attempt. **3.** something done by trying; an achievement. [F, from OF *es-* (from L *ex-* EX-[1]) + *force* strength]

effrontery /ə'frʌntəri, i-/, *n., pl.* **-teries.** shameless or cheeky boldness. [F, from OF: shameless]

effusion /ə'fjuʒən, i-/, *n.* **1.** the act of pouring out. **2.** something poured out. **3.** the expression of feelings, etc., without holding back.

effusive /ə'fjusɪv, -zɪv, i-/, *adj.* unduly expressive of feeling: *effusive emotion; an effusive person.* —**effusiveness**, *n.*

e.g. /i 'dʒi/, *Abbrev.* for example. [L *exempli gratia*]

egalitarian /əgælə'tɛəriən, i-/, *adj.* **1.** expressing or believing in the equality of all people. ◇*n.* **2.** someone who expresses or believes in the equality of all people. [F *égal* EQUAL] —**egalitarianism**, *n.*

egg[1] /ɛg/, *n.* **1.** a roundish reproductive object or cell produced by female animals, protected by albumen jelly, membranes or shell, according to species. **2.** the above produced by birds, esp. by the domestic hen, covered with shell, and often used as food. **3.** anything like a hen's egg in shape, oval with one end broader than the other. [Scand]

egg[2] /ɛg/, *v.t.* to urge or encourage (usu. fol. by *on*). [Scand]

eggplant /'ɛgplænt/, *n.* (a plant with) a large, usu. dark purple, more or less egg-shaped fruit, used as a vegetable; aubergine.

eggwhite /'ɛgwaɪt/, *n.* the white of an egg; albumen.

eglantine /'ɛgləntin, -aɪn/, *n.* a wild rose of the Northern Hemisphere, with hooked prickles and pink flowers.

Egmont /'ɛgmɒnt/, *n.* **Mount**, an extinct volcano in Egmont National Park in the south-western part of the North Island, NZ. 2518 m.

ego /'igoʊ/, *n., pl.* **egos. 1.** the 'I' or self of any person; a person as an individual who thinks, feels, and wills, and is distinguished from others. **2.** *Colloq.* conceit; egotism. **3.** (in Freudian theory) the part of the personality which deals with the opposing demands of the conscience and the id. [L: I]

egocentric /igoʊ'sɛntrɪk, ɛgoʊ-/, *adj.* self-centred. —**egocentricity**, *n.*

egoism /'egoʊɪzəm, 'igoʊ-/, *n.* **1.** selfishness or self-centredness. **2.** → **egotism** (def. 1). **3.** *Philos.* the teaching that the person and his or her own self-interest are the (proper) goal of all action. [EGO + -ISM] —**egoist**, *n.* —**egoistic, egoistical**, *adj.*

egotism /'egətɪzəm, 'igoʊ-, 'igə-/, *n.* **1.** the habit of talking too much about oneself; boastfulness. **2.** selfishness; self-importance. —**egotist**, *n.* —**egotistic, egotistical**, *adj.*

ego trip, *n. Colloq.* behavior meant to attract attention and admiration.

egregious /ə'grɪdʒiəs, -dʒəs/, *adj.* remarkably bad; flagrant: *an egregious lie.* [L: distinguished, lit., (standing) out from the herd]

egress /'igrɛs/, *n.* **1.** the act of going out. **2.** a way out; an exit. **3.** the right to go out. [L: go out] —**egression**, *n.*

egret /'igrət/, *n.* any of various herons found throughout the world and bearing long plumes in breeding season. [ME, from OF]

Egypt /'idʒəpt, 'idʒɪpt/, *n.* **1.** a republic in north-eastern Africa, on the Mediterranean and Red seas; gained independence as a kingdom in 1922; a republic since 1953. Pop. 49 143 000 (1987 est.); 997 738 km². *Language:* Arabic, also English and French. *Currency:* Egyptian pound. *Cap.:* Cairo. Official name, **Arab Republic of Egypt. 2.** a former kingdom in north-eastern Africa; divided into **Lower Egypt** (the Nile Delta) and **Upper Egypt** (from near Cairo south to the Sudan).

eh /eɪ/, *interj.* (a questioning sound, sometimes expressing surprise or doubt): *Wasn't it lucky, eh?*

EHF /i eɪtʃ 'ɛf/, *Abbrev. Radio.* extremely high frequency.

Eichmann /'aɪkmən/, *n.* **Adolf**, 1906–62, German Nazi official who supervised the extermination of the Jews in World War II; he was captured and executed in Israel.

eider /'aɪdə/, *n.* any of several large seaducks of the Northern Hemisphere, usu. black and white. Also, **eider duck**. [Icel., from Old Norse]

eiderdown /'aɪdədaʊn/, *n.* **1.** down or soft feathers from the breast of the eider duck. **2.** a thick quilt, esp. one filled with eiderdown. [Icel]

Eiffel Tower /aɪfəl 'taʊə/, *n.* a tower of skeletal iron construction in Paris; built for the exhibition of 1889. 300 m high. [named after its designer, AG *Eiffel*]

Eiger /'aɪgə/, *n.* a mountain in Switzerland, in the Bernese Alps. 3975 m.

eight /eɪt/, *n.* **1.** a cardinal number, seven plus one (7 + 1). **2.** the symbol for this number, e.g. 8 or VIII. **3.** a set of eight people or things esp. a rowing crew. ◇*adj.* **4.** amounting to eight. [OE *eahta*] —**eighth**, *adj.*

eighteen /eɪ'tin/, *n.* **1.** a cardinal number, ten plus eight (10 + 8). **2.** the symbol for this number, e.g. 18 or XVIII. **3.** a team in Australian Rules football. ◇*adj.* **4.** amounting to 18. [OE *eahtatēne*] —**eighteenth**, *adj.*

eighty /'eɪti/, *n., pl.* **eighties**, *adj.* ◇*n.* **1.** a cardinal number, ten times eight (10 × 8). **2.** the symbol for this number, e.g. 80 or LXXX. **3.** (*pl.*) the numbers from 80 to 89 of a series, esp. someone's age or years of a century: *a man in his eighties.* ◇*adj.* **4.** amounting to eighty. [OE *eahtatig*] —**eightieth**, *adj., n.*

Einstein /'aɪnstaɪn/, *n.* **Albert**, 1879–1955, German-born physicist who formulated the theory of relativity; won Nobel prize for physics, 1921; became a US citizen in 1940.

einsteinium /aɪn'staɪniəm/, *n.* a radioactive, metallic element not found naturally, but produced from plutonium. *Symbol:* Es; *at. no:* 99; *at. wt:* 254. [EINSTEIN + -IUM]

Éire /'ɛərə/, *n.* former name of the Republic of **Ireland**; still its official Gaelic name.

Eisenhower /'aɪzənhaυə/, *n.* **Dwight D(avid)**, 1890–1969, 34th president of the US, 1953–61; US general, supreme commander of Allied Expeditionary Forces 1943–45.

Eisenstein /'aɪzənstaɪn/, *n.* **Sergei Mikhailovich** /sɛə,gjeɪ mɪk'heɪləvɪtʃ/, 1898–1948, Soviet film director; his major film was *The Battleship Potemkin* (1925).

eisteddfod /aɪ'stɛdfəd /, *n*, *pl.* **-fods -fodau** /-fədaɪ/. a competitive festival of music, poetry, etc. [Welsh: session, from *eistedd* sit]

either /'aɪðə, 'iðə/, *adj.* **1.** one or other of two: *Sit at either table.* **2.** each of two; both one and the other: *There were trees on either side.* ◇*pron.* **3.** one or other but not both: *Take either.* ◇*conj.* **4.** (used together with *or* to indicate one of two coordinate alternatives): *Either come or write.* ◇*adv.* **5.** (used after negative clauses joined by *and, or, nor*): *He is not fond of parties and I am not either;* (after a negative subordinate clause): *If you do not come, she will not come either.* [OE *ā* always + *gehwæther* each of two]

ejaculate /ə'dʒækjəleɪt, i-/, *v.,* **-lated, -lating.** ◇*v.t.* **1.** to say or shout suddenly and shortly; exclaim. **2.** to throw or send out suddenly and quickly; discharge. ◇*v.i.* **3.** to discharge semen. [L: having cast out] –**ejaculator**, *n.* –**ejaculation**, *n.* –**ejaculatory**, *adj.*

eject /ə'dʒɛkt, i-/, *v.t.* to drive, throw or force out. [L: thrown out] –**ejection**, *n.* –**ejective**, *adj.*

eke /ik/, *v.t.*, **eked, eking. 1.** to make (something) enough by adding to it or using it carefully (fol. by *out*): *to eke out the last of the butter.* **2.** to make (a living, etc.) with difficulty (fol. by *out*): *They eked out an existence in the barren land.* [OE *ēcan*]

elaborate /ə'læbərət, *adj.; /*ə'læbəreɪt, i-/, *v.,* **-rated, -rating.** ◇*adj.* **1.** worked in great detail; complicated. ◇*v.t.* **2.** to work out carefully or in detail. **3.** to produce or develop by labor. ◇*v.i.* **4.** to give (added) detail (fol. by *on* or *upon*): *to elaborate on an idea.* **5.** to become elaborate. [L: worked out] –**elaborateness**, *n.* –**elaborative**, *adj.* –**elaboration**, *n.*

El Alamein /ɛl 'æləmeɪn/, *n.* a town on the northern coast of Egypt, about 113 km west of Alexandria; site of a decisive British victory over the German Afrika Korps, October 1942. Also, **Alamein**. Arabic, **Al-'Alamayn**.

elan /eɪ'læn/, *n.* strong lively style. Also, **élan**. [F, from *élancer*, hurt, rush forth]

eland /'ilənd/, *n.* either of two large, heavily built African antelopes with spirally twisted horns. [Afrikaans, special use of D *eland* elk, from G, from Lithuanian]

elapse /ə'læps, i-/, *v.i.,* **elapsed, elapsing.** (of time) to slip by or pass. [L]

elastic /ə'læstɪk, i-/, *adj.* **1.** (of solids) having the property of recovering shape after being pushed, pulled, etc. **2.** (of gases) expanding spontaneously. **3.** flexible, yielding, or adaptable. **4.** (of a person) readily recovering from depression or tiredness. ◇*n.* **5.** a band or fabric made elastic with strips or threads of rubber. [NL, from Gk: propulsive]

elastic band, *n.* → **rubber band**.

elate /ə'leɪt, i-/, *v.t.,* **elated, elating.** to put in high spirits; make proud. [ME, from L: brought out, raised, exalted] –**elated**, *adj.* –**elation**, *n.*

Elba /'ɛlbə/, *n.* an Italian island in the Mediterranean between Corsica and Italy; the scene of Napoleon's first exile, 1814–15. Pop. 10 755 (1981); 223 km².

Elbe /ɛlb, 'ɛlbə/, *n.* a river flowing from the western part of the Czech Republic north-west through Germany into The North Sea near Hamburg. 1167 km.

elbow /'ɛlboυ/, *n.* **1.** a bend or joint between the upper and lower arm. **2.** something bent like an elbow, such as a turn in a road or river, or a piece of pipe. ◇*v.t., v.i.* **3.** to push with or as if with an elbow; jostle. [OE *elneboga*]

elbow grease, *n. Colloq.* hard physical work.

Elcho Island /,ɛlkoυ 'aɪlənd/, *n.* a narrow island in the Arafura Sea, north of north-eastern Arnhem Land in the NT. 48 km long and up to 14 km wide.

elder[1] /'ɛldə/, *adj.* **1.** older. **2.** higher in rank; senior. ◇*n.* **3.** a person older than oneself: *You should be polite to your elders.* **4.** an older and more powerful person in a tribe or social group. **5.** *Church.* (in some Protestant churches) a governing officer, often with teaching or pastoral duties. [OE *eldra*, etc. (comparative of *ald, eald* OLD)] –**eldership**, *n.*

elder[2] /'ɛldə/, *n.* a northern hemisphere shrub or small tree with small white flowers and red, purple or black berries.

elderberry /'ɛldəbɛri/, *n., pl.* **-ries. 1.** the fruit of the elder tree, used in making wine, jelly, etc. **2.** → **elder**[2].

elderly /'ɛldəli/, *adj.* (of people) old, or approaching old age. –**elderliness**, *n.*

Eldershaw /'ɛldəʃɔ/, *n.* **Flora**, 1897–1956, Australian historian and novelist. See **Barnard Eldershaw**.

eldest /'ɛldəst/, *adj., n.* oldest; firstborn. [OE *eldest(a)*, superlative of *ald, eald* OLD]

El Dorado /,ɛl dɔ'radoυ/, *n.* a legendary treasure city of South America, sought by the early Spanish explorers. [Sp.: the gilded]

Eleanor of Aquitaine /,ɛlənə əv 'ækwɪteɪn/, *n.* 1122?–1204, queen of Louis VII of France (1137–52); queen of Henry II of England (1154–89); mother of King Richard I and King John of England.

elect /əˈlekt, i-/, v.t. **1.** to choose by vote, esp. for a job or position: *to elect a president*. **2.** to decide in favor of: *to elect to do something*. **3.** to pick out or choose. ◇*adj.* **4.** chosen for a position, but not yet acting in it (usu. after noun): *president elect*. **5.** chosen. **6.** *Relig.* chosen by God, esp. for everlasting life. ◇*n.* **7.** a person or group chosen or worthy to be chosen, esp. by God. [ME, from L: chosen, picked out]

election /əˈlekʃən, i-/, n. the choosing by vote of person(s) for position(s).

electioneer /əˌlekʃəˈnɪə, i-/, v.i. to work for the success of a person, party, etc., in an election. —**electioneering**, *adj., n.*

elective /əˈlektɪv, i-/, *adj.* **1.** appointed by election. **2.** filled by an election: *elective position*. **3.** having the power to choose. **4.** not required; optional: *an elective subject; an elective course*. ◇*n.* **5.** a course or subject chosen; optional study.

elector /əˈlektə, i-/, n. **1.** someone who elects or may elect, esp. a qualified voter. **2.** *Hist. (often cap.)* one of the German princes who elected the Holy Roman Emperor.

electoral /əˈlektərəl, -trəl, i-/, *adj.* relating to electors or election.

electorate /əˈlektərət, -trət, i-/, n. **1.** (a group of voters in) an area represented by a member of parliament. **2.** the body of people who may vote in an election.

electr-, → **electro-**.

Electra /əˈlektrə/, n. *Gk Legend.* the daughter of Agamemnon and Clytemnestra. She persuaded her brother Orestes to avenge the murder of their father by their mother.

electric /əˈlektrɪk/, *adj.* **1.** of, relating to, or produced by electricity: *electric current; electric shock*. **2.** producing, carrying, or operated by electricity: *electric bell*. **3.** exciting; electrifying. **4.** (of musical instruments) amplified by a built-in electronic device: *electric guitar*. [NL, from L, from Gk: amber (as a substance that develops electricity under friction)] —**electrical**, *adj.*

electrical storm, n. → **thunderstorm**.

electric charge, n. **1.** a property of matter which determines its behavior in electric and magnetic fields. **2.** a quantity of electricity; the SI unit of electric charge is the coulomb.

electric current, n. a flow of electricity. See **current** (def. 5).

electric eye, n. → **photoelectric cell**.

electric field, n. a condition of space near an electric charge, varying electric current, or moving magnet, which shows itself as a force on the electric charge within that space.

electrician /əlekˈtrɪʃən, elek-, ilek-/, n. a person who sets up, operates, or repairs electrical equipment.

electricity /əlekˈtrɪsəti, elek-, ilek-/, n. **1.** a form of energy producing various physical effects, such as attraction and repulsion, light and heat, shock to the body, chemical decomposition, etc., due to the presence and movement of electrons, and other electrically charged particles. **2.** the science dealing with electricity. **3.** electric current or charge.

electrify /əˈlektrəfaɪ, i-/, v.t., **-fied, -fying**. **1.** to charge with, or subject to, electricity. **2.** to equip for the use of electric power: *to electrify a railway line*. **3.** to excite; thrill: *to electrify an audience*. —**electrifiable**, *adj.* —**electrification**, n. —**electrifier**, n.

electro-, a word part meaning 'relating to or caused by electricity', as in *electromagnet, electrograph*. Also, **electr-**. [Gk *ēlektro-*, combining form of *ēlektron* amber]

electrocardiogram /əˌlektroʊˈkadiəgræm, i-/, n. a record drawn or produced by an electrocardiograph. *Abbrev.:* ECG Also, **cardiogram**.

electrocardiograph /əˌlektroʊˈkadiəgræf, i-/, n. a machine which picks up and records the electrical activity of the heart. *Abbrev.:* ECG Also, **cardiograph**. —**electrocardiographic**, *adj.* —**electrocardiographically**, *adv.* —**electrocardiography**, n.

electrochemical series, n. *Chem.* → **electromotive series**.

electrocute /əˈlektrəkjut, i-/, v.t., **-cuted, -cuting**. to kill by electricity. [ELECTRO- + *-cute* in EXECUTE]. —**electrocution**, n.

electrode /əˈlektroʊd, i-/, n. a conductor through which an electric current enters or leaves an electrolytic cell, electric arc, or electronic valve or tube. [ELECTR(O)- + -ODE²]

electroencephalogram /əˌlektroʊenˈsefələgræm, i-/, n. a record drawn or produced by an electroencephalograph. *Abbrev.:* EEG

electroencephalograph /əˌlektroʊenˈsefələgræf, i-/, n. a machine which picks up and records the electrical activity of the brain. *Abbrev.:* EEG —**electroencephalographic**, *adj.*

electrograph /əˈlektrəgræf, i-/, n. an automatically traced curve which forms a record of the indications of an electrometer. —**electrographic**, *adj.* —**electrographically**, *adv.* —**electrography**, n.

electrolyse /əˈlektrəlaɪz, i-/, v.t., **-lysed, -lysing**. to decompose (break up) by electrolysis. —**electrolysation**, n. —**electrolyser**, n.

electrolysis /əlekˈtrɒləsəs, i-, ˌelekˈtrɒləsəs/, n. **1.** the chemical separation by an electric current of a compound, resulting in **a.** ion formation. **b.** the conduction of electricity. **c.** the deposition or liberation of the ions as their elements at the electrodes. **2.** *Surg.* the destroying of growths, hair roots, etc., by an electric current.

electrolyte /əˈlektrəlaɪt, i-/, n. *Chem.* any substance, as an acid, base, or salt, which separates into ions when dissolved in water, etc., or when melted, therefore becoming a conductor of electricity.

electrolytic /əlektrəˈlɪtɪk, i-/, *adj.* **1.** relating to or obtained by electrolysis. **2.** relating to an electrolyte. —**electrolytically**, *adv.*

electromagnet /əˌlektrou'mægnət, i-/, *n.* a magnet consisting of an iron or steel core with wire coiled round it through which an electric current is passed.

electromagnetic /əˌlektrouˈmægˈnetɪk, i-/, *adj.* relating to an electromagnet or electromagnetism. —**electromagnetically**, *adv.*

electromagnetic field, *n.* the field produced by the radiation of electromagnetic waves through space (or a conducting substance), marked by an electric and magnetic field varying in both time and space.

electromagnetic spectrum, *n.* the whole range of frequencies of electromagnetic waves, from radio waves through light to cosmic rays.

electromagnetic wave, *n.* a moving disturbance in space produced by the acceleration of an electric charge. It consists of an electric field and a magnetic field moving at right angles to each other, and to the direction of propagation of the wave.

electromagnetism /əˌlektrouˈmægnəˌtɪzəm, i-/, *n.* 1. magnetism produced by an electric current. 2. the science dealing with the relation between electric currents and magnetism.

electrometer /ɛlakˈtrɒmətə, əlek-, ilek-/, *n.* an instrument for picking up or measuring a potential difference by means of the mechanical forces between electrically charged bodies. See **electrograph**. —**electrometric**, **electrometrical**, *adj.* —**electrometrically**, *adv.*

electromotive force /əˌlektrou,moutiv 'fɔs/, *n.* a measure of the strength of the source of electrical energy which produces an electric current in a circuit. The SI unit is the volt. *Abbrev.:* e.m.f., EMF

electromotive series, *n. Chem.* the metals arranged in the order in which they will replace each other from their salts. Hydrogen is also included and metals above it in the series will displace it from acids. Also, **electrochemical series**.

electron /əˈlɛktrɒn, i-/, *n.* an elementary particle orbiting the nucleus in all atoms, with a mass of 9.1083×10^{-28} g. It has a negative electric charge of about 1.6×10^{-19} coulombs. [ELECTR(IC) + (I)ON]

electronegative /əˌlektrouˈnɛgətɪv, i-/, *adj.* 1. having a negative charge. 2. tending to attract electrons, forming anions or polar bonds.

electronic /ɛlakˈtrɒnɪk, əlek-, i-/, *adj.* of or relating to electrons or electronics.

electronic data processing, *n.* the use of computers to handle information. *Abbrev.:* EDP

electronic funds transfer, *n.* a computerised banking system for the transfer of money from one account to another.

electronics /əlekˈtrɒnɪks, i-, ɛlək-/, *n.* the study and application of the effects of the movement of electrons in valves and semiconductors.

electron microscope, *n.* a microscope using beams of electrons instead of light rays, forming an image on a screen or photographic plate.

electronvolt /əlektrɒnˈvoult/, *n.* a unit of energy used in X-rays, gamma rays, atomic and nuclear physics; 1 electronvolt is about 1.6×10^{-19} joules. *Symbol:* eV

electroplate /əˈlektrəpleɪt, i-/, *v.*, **-plated**, **-plating**, *n.* ◇*v.t.* 1. to plate or coat with metal by electrolysis. ◇*n.* 2. electroplated articles.

electropositive /əˌlektrouˈpɒzətɪv, i-/, *adj.* 1. having a positive charge. 2. tending to give up electrons, forming cations or polar bonds.

electrostatic /əlektrouˈstætɪk, i-/, *adj.* of or relating to static electricity.

electrovalency /əlektrouˈveɪlənsi, i-/, *n. Chem.* the valency of an ion, equal to the number of electrons lost or gained by an atom becoming an ion. —**electrovalent**, *adj.*

electrovalent bond, /əlektrou,veɪlənt 'bɒnd/, *n.* a type of chemical bond formed by one or more electrons passing from one atom to another, the resulting ions being held together by electrostatic attraction. Also, **ionic bond, polar bond.**

elegant /ˈɛləgənt, 'ɛli-/, *adj.* 1. tasteful or luxurious in dress, manners, etc. 2. graceful or dignified in tastes, habits, writing style, etc. 3. cleverly simple: *an elegant solution to a problem.* [L: fastidious, nice, fine, elegant] —**elegance**, *n.*

elegy /ˈɛlədʒi/, *n.*, *pl.* **-gies.** 1. a sorrowful poem, esp. a funeral song or lament for the dead. 2. *Music.* a sad or funeral composition. [L, from Gk: lament] —**elegise**, *v.* —**elegist**, *n.* —**elegiac**, *adj.*

element /ˈɛləmənt/, *n.* 1. a thing or quality that is part of a whole. 2. *Chem.* one of a class of substances each consisting totally of atoms of the same atomic number. 3. one of the simple substances, usu. earth, water, air, and fire, once thought to make up all matter. 4. the natural or ideal surroundings of any person or thing: *He's in his element.* 5. (*pl.*) atmospheric forces; weather: *protected from the elements.* 6. (*pl.*) the basic principles of an art, science, etc.: *the elements of grammar.* 7. *Elect.* **a.** a resistance wire, etc., making up the heating unit of an electric heater, cooker, etc. **b.** one of the electrodes of a cell or radio valve. 8. *Maths.* **a.** a member of a set. **b.** part of a geometric figure. [ME, from L: a first principle, rudiment]

elemental /ɛləˈmɛntl/, *adj.* 1. simple or basic, unable to be further divided. 2. of or like forces of nature; basic or powerful. 3. relating to the four elements (def. 3). 4. relating to chemical elements. —**elementally**, *adv.*

elementary /ɛləˈmɛntri, -təri/, *adj.* 1. of or relating to elements or first principles: *elementary education.* 2. simple or basic, unable to be further divided.

elementary particle, *n.* any of a class of particles which used to be thought to be the indivisible units of which matter is made up.

elephant /ˈɛləfənt/, *n.* 1. a very large plant-eating mammal with thick, almost hair-

elephant

less skin, a long grasping trunk, and long curved tusks. The African elephant is larger than the Indian elephant and has larger ears. **2.** See **white elephant**. [L, from Gk: elephant, ivory] —**elephantoid**, *adj.*

elephantiasis /ˌɛləfənˈtaɪəsəs, -fæn-/, *n.* a disease marked by huge enlargement of the legs, etc.

elephantine /ˌɛləˈfæntaɪn/, *adj.* **1.** of or like an elephant. **2.** huge, heavy or clumsy.

Eleusinian mysteries /ˌɛljuˈsɪnɪən ˈmɪstriz/, *n.pl.* (in ancient Greece) a religious festival orig. celebrated at Eleusis, near Athens, in honor of Demeter (Ceres), Persephone, and Dionysus.

elevate /ˈɛləveɪt/, *v.t.*, **-vated, -vating. 1.** to lift up. **2.** to raise in rank or position. **3.** to raise spirits of; cheer. [ME, from L] —**elevated**, *adj.*

elevation /ˌɛləˈveɪʃən/, *n.* **1.** height above sea or ground level. **2.** a high or raised place. **3.** grandeur or dignity; nobleness. **4.** the act of lifting. **5.** the state of being raised. **6.** *Archit.* **a.** a scale drawing of an object or structure, esp. the face of a building, showing it without perspective, every point being drawn as if looked at horizontally. **b.** the front, side, or back of a building. **7.** *Survey.* the angle between the line from an observer to an object above the observer and a horizontal line.

elevator /ˈɛləveɪtə/, *n.* **1.** someone or something that lifts or raises. **2.** a machine for lifting things. **3.** *US.* → **lift** (def. 12). **4.** a building for storing grain. **5.** *Aeron.* a hinged horizontal flap used to control the up and down movement of aeroplane. [LL]

eleven /əˈlɛvən/, *n.* **1.** a cardinal number, ten plus one (10 + 1). **2.** the symbol for this number, e.g. 11 or XI. **3.** a set of eleven people or things. **4.** a team of eleven players, as in soccer, cricket, hockey, etc. ◊*adj.* **5.** amounting to eleven. [OE *ellefne, endleofan*, etc., lit., one left (after counting ten)] —**eleventh**, *adj., n.*

eleventh hour /əlɛvənθ ˈaʊə/, *n.* the last possible moment for doing something. [from the parable (Matthew 20: 1-16) in which the workers hired at the eleventh hour received the same wages as those hired earlier] —**eleventh-hour**, *adj.*

elf /ɛlf/, *n., pl.* **elves** /ɛlvz/. **1.** in folklore and fairy tales, a being with magical powers, usu. like a small human in form, and occasionally concerned with humans or playing tricks on them. **2.** a small mischievous child or person. [OE *elfen* nymph (feminine elf)] —**elfin, elfish, elvish**, *adj.*

Elgar /ˈɛlgə/, *n.* **Sir Edward William**, 1857–1934, English composer; works include the *Pomp and Circumstance* marches and cello concertos.

Elgin marbles /ɛlgən ˈmabəlz/, *n.pl.* Greek sculpture of the fifth century BC, orig. on the Parthenon in Athens, and subsequently sculptured under the direction of Phidias; now in the British Museum in London. [after Thomas Bruce, 7th Earl of *Elgin* (1766–1841),

331

Elizabeth I

who arranged for the collection to be brought from Athens to London]

El Giza /ɛl ˈgizə/, *n.* a town in northern Egypt, near Cairo; the pyramids and the Sphinx are situated nearby. Pop. 1 670 800 (1986 est.). Also, **El Gi'zeh, Giza**, or **Gizeh**. Arabic, **Al-Jizah**.

El Greco /ɛl ˈgrɛkoʊ/, *n.* (*Domenikos Theotocopoulos, 'the Greek'*), 1541–1614, Spanish painter, born in Crete; noted for his abstract and exaggerated forms and dramatic use of color.

elicit /əˈlɪsət/, *v.t.* to draw or bring out: *to elicit the truth.* [L] —**elicitation**, *n.*

elide /əˈlaɪd, i-/, *v.t.*, **elided, eliding.** to leave out (vowel, consonant or syllable) in pronunciation.

eligible /ˈɛlədʒəbəl/, *adj.* **1.** suitable to be chosen. **2.** qualified. **3.** desirable, esp. as a husband or wife: *an eligible bachelor.* [F, from L: pick out] —**eligibly**, *adv.* —**eligibility** *n.*

Elijah /əˈlaɪdʒə/, *n.* a great Hebrew prophet of the ninth century BC. [I Kings 17, II Kings 2]

eliminate /əˈlɪməneɪt, i-/, *v.t.*, **-nated, -nating. 1.** to get rid of; remove: *to eliminate mistakes.* **2.** to leave out; ignore. **3.** *Biol., Med.* to expel from the body; excrete. **4.** *Maths.* to remove (an unknown quantity) from two or more simultaneous equations. [L: turned out of doors] —**elimination**, *n.* —**eliminative**, *adj.* —**eliminator**, *n.* —**eliminatory**, *adj.*

Eliot /ˈɛliət/, *n.* **1. George** (*Mary Ann Evans*), 1819–80, English realist novelist; her works include *Silas Marner* (1861), and *Middlemarch* (1872). **2. T(homas) S(tearns)**, 1888–1965, British poet, critic, and essayist, born in the US; his poetry includes *The Waste Land* (1922); his verse plays include *Murder in the Cathedral* (1935).

elision /əˈlɪʒən, i-/, *n.* the act or result of eliding.

elite /əˈlit, eɪ-, i-/, *n.* **1.** (*sometimes treated as pl.*) a group of people with the most power, money, education, etc. ◊*adj.* **2.** of or related to an elite; exclusive. [F: choose, from L]

elitism /əˈlitɪzəm, eɪ-, i-/, *n.* **1.** (belief in) rule by an elite. **2.** consciousness of or pride in belonging to a chosen or favored group. **3.** *Colloq.* snobbery. —**elitist**, *n., adj.*

elixir /əˈlɪksə, ɛ-, i-/, *n.* **1.** an alchemic preparation formerly believed to be able to change base metals into gold, or to increase the length of life: *elixir vitae* (*elixir of life*). **2.** a cure-all remedy; a panacea. **3.** a sweetened alcoholic liquid containing medicine. [ME, from ML, from Ar *el, al* the + *iksīr* philosopher's stone, probably from LGk: a drying powder for wounds]

Elizabeth /əˈlɪzəbəθ/, *n.* a city in South Australia, within the Adelaide metropolitan area, north-east of the city centre. Pop. 30 687 (1986).

Elizabeth I, *n.* 1533–1603, queen of England 1558–1603; successor of Mary I; daughter of Henry VIII and Anne Boleyn.

Elizabeth II, *n.* born 1926, became queen of England in 1952; daughter of George VI.

Elizabethan /əlɪzə'biθən, i-/, *adj.* **1.** relating to Elizabeth I, queen of England, 1558–1603, or to her times. ◇*n.* **2.** someone, esp. a poet or writer, who lived in England during the Elizabethan period.

Elizabeth Farm, *n.* the oldest house in Australia, built in 1793 by John Macarthur at Parramatta, NSW; Australia's merino wool industry began here in 1797.

elk /ɛlk/, *n., pl.* **elks** or **elk.** the largest existing European and Asiatic deer, closely related to the moose, having a large head and large antlers. [OE *ealh* elk]

Elkin /'ɛlkən/, *n.* **Adolphus Peter**, 1891–1979, Australian anthropologist and writer.

ell /ɛl/, *n.* a former measure of length, usu. about 115 cm. [OE *eln*, orig. meaning arm, forearm]

Ellice Islands /ɛləs 'aɪləndz/, *n.pl.* former name of **Tuvalu.**

Elliott /'ɛliət/, *n.* **1. Herb(ert James)**, born 1938, Australian middle-distance runner; won Olympic gold medal for 1500 m in 1960. **2. Sumner Locke**, born 1917, Australian novelist and playwright; author of *Careful, He Might Hear You* (1963).

ellipse /ə'lɪps, i-/, *n. Geom.* a plane curve shaped so that the sums of the distances of each point on it from two fixed points (the foci) are equal. [L]

ellipsis /ə'lɪpsəs, i-/, *n., pl.* **-ses** /-siz/. **1.** *Gram.* the omission from a sentence of a word or words which would make it more complete or clear. **2.** *Print.* a mark or marks as —— or . . . or * * *, to show an omission of letters or words. [L, from Gk: omission]

ellipsoid /ə'lɪpsɔɪd, i-/, *n. Geom.* a solid figure all plane sections of which are ellipses or circles. –**ellipsoidal**, *adj.*

elliptical /ə'lɪptɪkəl, i-/, *adj.* **1.** of or having the form of an ellipse. **2.** relating to or marked by grammatical ellipses. **3.** particularly short or shortened. Also, **elliptic.** –**elliptically**, *adv.*

elm /ɛlm/, *n.* any of several large trees, mostly deciduous, of the northern temperate regions and mountains of tropical Asia. [OE]

elocution /ɛlə'kjuʃən/, *n.* **1.** manner of speaking or reading in public. **2.** the study and practice of good, clear speaking including the management of voice and body movement. [L: a speaking out] –**elocutionary**, *adj.* –**elocutionist**, *n.*

elongate /i'lɒŋgeɪt/, *v.,* **-gated, -gating.** ◇*v.t.* **1.** to draw out to greater length; lengthen; extend. ◇*v.i.* **2.** to increase in length. [LL: removed, prolonged] –**elongation**, *n.*

elope /ə'loʊp, i-/, *v.i.* **eloped, eloping.** to run away with a lover, usu. in order to marry without permission from parents. [ME *a-*[3] + *lopen* LOPE] –**elopement**, *n.* –**eloper**, *n.*

eloquent /'ɛləkwənt/, *adj.* **1.** (of a person) able to use flowing, powerful and effective speech: *an eloquent orator.* **2.** (of words) suitable and effective: *an eloquent speech.* **3.** emotional or expressive: *eloquent looks.* [ME, from L: speaking out] –**eloquence**, *n.*

elouera /ɛ'laʊərə/, *n.* a stone tool possibly used as a scraper, often with a shiny surface, and typical of the Eloueran period of Aboriginal development.

Eloueran /ɛ'laʊərən/, *n.* a cultural period of Aboriginal development recognised in eastern Australia, which follows the Bondaian period and extends to the present.

El Salvador /ɛl 'sælvədɔ/, *n.* a republic on the Pacific coast of central America, bordered by Guatemala and Honduras; a Spanish colony before independence in 1841; a republic since 1856. Pop. 4 974 000 (1987 est.); 21 393 km². *Language:* Spanish. *Currency:* colón. *Cap.:* San Salvador.

else /ɛls/, *adv.* **1.** (in apposition to an indef. or interrog. pronoun). **a.** other than the person or the thing mentioned; instead: *somebody else; who else?* **b.** in addition: *What else shall I do? Who else is going?* **2.** (following an indef. or interrog. pronoun and forming with it an indef. or compound pronoun with an inflection at the end): *somebody else's child; nobody else's business.* **3.** otherwise: *Run, or else you will be late.* [OE *elles*]

elsewhere /'ɛlswɛə, ɛls'wɛə/, *adv.* somewhere else; in or to some other place.

Elsey /'ɛlsi/, *n.* a cattle station in the northern NT; the setting for *We of the Never Never* by Mrs Aeneas Gunn. 5350 km².

Eltham /'ɛlθəm/, *n.* an outer north-eastern suburb of Melbourne, Vic, in the Dandenong Ranges; former orchard area. Pop. 39 784 (1986).

elucidate /ə'lusədeɪt, i-/, *v.t., v.i.,* **-dated, -dating.** to make (something) understandable or clear; explain. [LL: made light] –**elucidation**, *n.* –**elucidatory**, *adj.*

elude /ə'lud, i-/, *v.t.,* **eluded, eluding. 1.** to avoid or escape, esp. by skill or trickery; evade: *to elude the guard; to elude the law.* **2.** to escape the mind; baffle. [L: finish play, deceive] –**eluder**, *n.* –**elusion**, *n.*

elusive /ə'lusɪv, i-/, *adj.* **1.** hard to express or define. **2.** hard to catch or find; evasive. Also, **elusory.** –**elusiveness**, *n.*

eluvium /ə'luviəm, i-/, *n., pl.* **-via** /-viə/. a deposit of soil, dust, etc., originating in the same place as it is found, as through decomposition of rock (distinguished from *alluvium*). [NL, from L *ēluere* wash out] –**eluvial**, *adj.*

elves /ɛlvz/, *n.* plural of **elf.**

em /ɛm/, *n.* **1.** the letter M, m. **2.** *Printing.* the square of the body size of any type (orig. the part of a line occupied by the letter M). [name of the letter M]

em-[1], variant of **en-**[1], before *b, p,* and sometimes *m,* as in *embalm.* See **im-**[1].

em-[2], variant of **en-**[2], before *b, m, p, ph,* as in *emphasis.*

emaciate /ə'meɪsieɪt, i-/, *v.t.,* **-ated, -ating.** to make thin or lean by gradual

emaciate

emaciate wasting away of flesh, esp. by starvation. [L] —**emaciation**, *n.*

emanate /'emoneɪt/, *v.i.*, **-nated, -nating.** to flow or come out; originate. [L] —**emanation**, *n.*

emancipate /ə'mænsəpeɪt, i-/, *v.t.*, **-pated, -pating. 1.** to free from checks of any kind, esp. from the inhibitions of society and tradition. **2.** to set free (a slave). [L] —**emancipation**, *n.* —**emancipator**, *n.* —**emancipative**, *adj.* —**emancipatory**, *adj.*

emancipist /ə'mænsəpɪst/, *n.* (formerly) a freed convict, esp. one who received a pardon from a colonial governor in Australia as a reward for good behavior.

emasculate /ə'mæskjʊlət, i-/, *v.t.*, **-lated, -lating. 1.** →**castrate. 2.** to take away the strength or energy from; weaken. [L] —**emasculation**, *n.*

embalm /ɛm'bam/, *v.t.* to treat (a dead body) with oils, spices, etc., or (now usu.) with drugs or chemicals, in order to preserve from decay. [ME, from F *em*- EM-¹ + *baume* BALM]

embankment /ɛm'bæŋkmənt,/, *n.* a bank, mound, dyke, etc., raised to hold back water, carry a road, etc.

embargo /ɛm'bagoʊ/, *n., pl.* **-goes**, *v.*, **-goed, -going.** ◇*n.* **1.** a government order forbidding movement of trading vessels from or into its ports. **2.** any limitation imposed upon business, esp. by law; restraint; prohibition. ◇*v.t.* **3.** to put an embargo on. [Sp: restrain, from Rom: BAR¹]

embark /ɛm'bak/, *v.i.* **1.** to come onto a ship, plane, etc., as for a voyage. **2.** to become involved in a profession, business, etc.: *to embark on a law career.* ◇*v.t.* **3.** to put or receive on board ship. [F] —**embarkation**, *n.*

embarrass /ɛm'bærəs/, *v.t.* **1.** to make (someone) uncomfortable, self-conscious, etc.; confuse. **2.** to place in financial difficulties: *The company was embarrassed by its debts.* **3.** to make difficult; complicate. **4.** to put difficulties in way of; impede. [F: block, obstruct] —**embarrassment**, *n.* —**embarrassing**, *adj.*

embassy /'ɛmbəsi/, *n., pl.* **-sies. 1.** a group of people officially representing their government in a foreign country; ambassador and staff. **2.** the official headquarters of an ambassador. [MF, from LL: office]

embattled /ɛm'bætld/, *adj.* involved in a battle or argument.

embed /ɛm'bɛd/, *v.t.*, **-bedded, -bedding. 1.** to fix firmly in or as if in a surrounding mass: *The stones were embedded in the garden; That day is embedded in my memory.* **2.** Linguistics. to put (a relative clause, etc.) within a main clause.

embellish /ɛm'bɛlɪʃ/, *v.t.* **1.** to make beautiful as by ornamentation; ornament; adorn. **2.** to heighten (a statement or tale) with imaginary additions; broider. [ME, from OF] —**embellisher**, *n.* —**embellishment**, *n.*

ember /'ɛmbə/, *n.* **1.** a small live piece of coal, wood, etc., as in a dying fire. **2.** (*pl.*) the last remains of a fire. [OE *æmerge*]

embroidery

embezzle /ɛm'bɛzəl/, *v.t.*, **-zled, -zling.** to unlawfully take (money, etc., entrusted to one's possession) for one's own use. [ME, from AF *en*- EM-¹ + *beseler* destroy, dissipate] —**embezzlement**, *n.* —**embezzler**, *n.*

embitter /ɛm'bɪtə/, *v.t.* to make bitter or more bitter.

emblazon /ɛm'bleɪzən/, *v.t.* **1.** to draw or write (something) on, or as if on, a heraldic shield: *The family name was emblazoned on the shield.* **2.** to declare publicly; proclaim. —**emblazonment**, *n.*

emblem /'ɛmbləm/, *n.* **1.** an object, or representation of it, as a sign of quality, state, class of persons, etc.; symbol. **2.** a symbolic drawing or picture, often with explanatory writing. [L: inlaid work, ornamentation, from Gk: an insertion] —**emblematic**, *adj.*

embodiment /ɛm'bɒdɪmənt/, *n.* that in which something is embodied; an incarnation: *She was the embodiment of goodness.*

embody /ɛm'bɒdi/, *v.t.*, **-bodied, -bodying. 1.** to provide with a body, as a spirit; give bodily form to. **2.** to give definite form to; express or use as example of (ideas, etc.) in concrete form. **3.** to include in a body; organise; incorporate: *Newest ideas are embodied in the course.*

embolism /'ɛmbəlɪzəm/, *n.* Med. the obstruction of a blood vessel by an embolus. [LL: intercalation, from Gk: throw in] —**embolismic**, *adj.*

embolus /'ɛmbələs/, *n., pl.* **-li** /-laɪ/. any material such as tissue fragments, bacteria, etc., carried by the blood stream and lodged in the vascular system. [L: piston, from Gk: peg, stopper]

emboss /ɛm'bɒs/, *v.t.* **1.** to raise (a design) on the surface of a fabric, metal, etc., so that it stands out from the background. **2.** to decorate (a fabric, metal, etc.) in such a manner. **3.** to cause to swell or bulge. [ME, from OF: swell in protuberances] —**embosser**, *n.* —**embossment**, *n.*

embouchure /'ɒmbʊʃʊə/, *n. Music.* the position of player's mouth and lips in relation to the mouthpiece of a wind instrument, esp. a flute. [F: put into the mouth, discharge by a mouth or outlet]

embrace /ɛm'breɪs/, *v.*, **-braced, -bracing**, *n.* ◇*v.t.* **1.** to take or hold in the arms; hug. **2.** to take or receive (an idea, etc.) gladly or eagerly. **3.** to make use of (an opportunity, etc.). **4.** to encircle; surround; enclose. **5.** to include. ◇*v.i.* **6.** to join in an embrace. ◇*n.* **7.** the act of embracing; a hug. [ME, from OF *em*- EM-¹ + *bras* arm (from L)] —**embraceable**, *adj.*

embroider /ɛm'brɔɪdə/, *v.t.* **1.** to decorate (a fabric) with ornamental needlework. **2.** to improve (a story), esp. with imagination.

embroidery /ɛm'brɔɪdəri, -dri/, *n., pl.* **-deries. 1.** the art of working ornamental designs on fabric, leather, etc., with needle and thread. **2.** embroidered work. **3.** *Colloq.* improvement by invented or overstated detail.

embroil /em'brɔɪl, əm-/, *v.t.* **1.** to involve, as in a fight, strife, etc.: *embroiled in an argument.* **2.** to throw into confusion; complicate. [F *em-* EM-¹ + *brouiller* disorder] —**embroilment**, *n.*

embryo /'embriou/, *n.*, *pl.* **-os. 1.** an organism in its earlier stages of development. **2.** (among mammals, etc.) a young animal during its earlier stages within the mother's body (including, in man, developmental stages up to the end of the seventh week. **3.** the first simple plant usu. contained in the seed. **4.** the beginning or early stage of anything. ◇*adj.* **5.** embryonic. [ML, from Gk]

embryol., *Abbrev.* embryology.

embryology /ˌembri'ɒlədʒi/, *n.* the science of the embryo, its beginnings, development, etc. —**embryological, embryologic,** *adj.* —**embryologist**, *n.*

embryonic /ˌembri'ɒnɪk/, *adj.* **1.** relating to or in the state of an embryo. **2.** coming first; rudimentary; undeveloped. Also, **embryonal** /'embriənəl/.

emend /ə'mend, i-/, *v.t.* **1.** to free from faults or errors; correct. **2.** to correct or change (text) by removing errors. [L: correct] —**emendable,** *adj.* —**emendation,** *n.*

emerald /'emrəld, 'emərəld/, *n.* **1.** a rare green variety of beryl, highly valued as a gem. **2.** clear bright green. ◇*adj.* **3.** having a clear, bright green color. [ME, from OF, from L: a green precious stone, from Gk]

Emerald Isle, *n. Poetic.* Ireland.

emerge /ə'mɜdʒ, i-/, *v.i.*, **emerged, emerging. 1.** to rise or come forth from or as from water, etc.: *The whale emerged from the deep.* **2.** to come forth into view or notice: *He emerged as a strong, new leader.* **3.** to come up or arise, as a question or concern: *Some difficulties began to emerge.* [L: rise out] —**emergence,** *n.*

emergency /ə'mɜdʒənsi, i-/, *n.*, *pl.* **-cies. 1.** a sudden and urgent occasion for action. **2.** a person who stands by in case of emergency. [ML: a coming up]

emergent /ə'mɜdʒənt, i-/, *adj.* **1.** emerging. **2.** (of a nation) recently independent and generally in an early stage of development.

emeritus /ə'merətəs, i-/, *n.*, *pl.* **-ti** /-tɪ/. *adj.* (a person) retired from active duty but keeping rank or title: *a professor emeritus*. [L: having served out one's time]

emery /'eməri/, *n.* a granular mineral substance, consisting typically of corundum mixed with magnetite or haematite, used for grinding and polishing. [F *émeri*, from Gk *smēris*]

emetic /ə'metɪk/, *n.*, *adj.* (a medicine or substance) causing vomiting. [L, from Gk]

e.m.f. /i em 'ef/, *Abbrev.* electromotive force. Also, **EMF**

-emia, variant of **-aemia**.

emigrate /'eməgreɪt, i-/, *v.i.*, **-grated, -grating.** to leave one country or region to settle in another; migrate. [L] —**emigrant,** *n.* —**emigrating,** *adj.*

eminence /'emənəns/, *n.* **1.** a high place, station, or rank. **2.** a high place or part; hill or elevation; height. **3.** (*cap.*) *Rom Cath Ch.* the title of honor of a cardinal: *your Eminence*.

eminent /'emənənt/, *adj.* **1.** high in station or rank; distinguished. **2.** lofty; high. [L: standing out]

emir /ɛ'mɪə, 'emɪə/, *n.* **1.** a Muslim or Arabic chieftain or prince. **2.** a title of honor of the descendants of Mohammed. Also, **emeer**. [Ar *amīr* commander]

emissary /'eməsəri, -əsri/, *n.*, *pl.* **-saries.** someone sent on mission; a representative. [L: scout]

emission /ə'mɪʃən, i-/, *n.* **1.** that which is emitted; discharge; emanation. **2.** *Electronics*. a measure of the number of electrons emitted by a heated filament or cathode of a vacuum tube. **3.** a discharge of fluid from the body, esp. semen. [L] —**emissive,** *adj.*

emit /ə'mɪt, i-/, *v.t.*, **emitted, emitting. 1.** to send forth; give out or forth (liquid, light, heat, sound, etc.); discharge. **2.** to issue (an order, decree, etc.). **3.** to utter (opinions, etc.). [L: send out]

emitter /ə'mɪtə, i-/, *n. Electronics*. an electrode that emits charge, esp. in a transistor.

Emmy /'emi/, *n. US.* one of the statuettes awarded annually for excellence in television performance and production. [from *Immy*, a popular name for *image orthicon tube*]

emollient /ə'mɒliənt, -'moʊ-/, *n.*, *adj.* (a medicine or substance) having the power of softening or soothing living tissues, esp. the skin. [L]

emolument /ə'mɒljəmənt/, *n.* profit arising from office or employment, such as salary or fees, etc. [L: profit]

emotion /ə'moʊʃən, i-/, *n.* **1.** a state of consciousness in which joy, sorrow, fear, hate, or similar, is experienced. **2.** any of the feelings of joy, sorrow, fear, hate, love, etc. [F: excite, from L] —**emotionless,** *adj.*

emotional /ə'moʊʃənəl, i-/, *adj.* **1.** relating to or affected by the emotions. **2.** appealing to the emotions: *It was an emotional request to the judge.* **3.** effected or determined by emotion rather than reason: *an emotional decision.* **4.** overwrought; displaying excessive emotion. —**emotionally,** *adv.* —**emotionalism,** *n.*

emotive /ə'moʊtɪv, i-/, *adj.* **1.** marked by or relating to emotion. **2.** exciting emotion.

empanel /em'pænəl/, *v.t.*, **-elled, -elling.** to enter on a panel or list for jury duty.

empathy /'empəθi/, *n.* emotional or mental understanding of the feelings or spirit of someone: *She has an empathy with children.* [Gk] —**empathic,** *adj.* —**empathically,** *adv.* —**empathise,** *v.*

emperor /'empərə/, *n.* **1.** the supreme ruler of an empire. **2.** any of various Australian fishes similar to bream, but having pointed heads and scaleless cheeks. [ME, from OF, from L: ruler]

emperor gum moth

emperor gum moth, *n.* a large moth of eastern Australia, with fawn to reddish-brown coloring.

emperor penguin, *n.* the largest of the Antarctic penguins, noted for its habit of holding its egg or young between its feet in a fold of skin like a pouch.

emphasis /'emfəsəs/, *n., pl.* **-ses** /-siz/. **1.** special force given to something to show its importance: *The leader placed great emphasis on the need for help.* **2.** stress laid on particular words or syllables in speaking. **3.** force of expression, action, etc. [L, from Gk]

emphasise or **emphasize** /'emfəsaiz/, *v.t.,* **-sised, -sising.** to give emphasis to; lay stress upon; stress.

emphatic /em'fætik/, *adj.* **1.** uttered, or to be uttered, with emphasis; strongly expressive. **2.** using emphasis in speech or action. **3.** forcibly significant; strongly marked; striking. [Gk: expressive] **— emphatically,** *adv.*

emphysema /emfə'simə/, *n. Med.* the abnormal swelling of an organ with air or other gas, esp. **pulmonary emphysema** which causes severe difficulty in breathing. [NL, from Gk: inflation]

empire /'empaiə/, *n.* **1.** a group of nations or peoples ruled over by an emperor or other powerful sovereign or government: *the Roman empire.* **2.** government under an emperor: *the first French empire.* **3.** supreme power or control; sovereignty. **4.** a large and powerful business group controlled by a single person or group of people. [ME, from F, from L *imperium* a command, authority, realm]

Empire Day, *n.* the former name for **Commonwealth Day.**

Empire Games, *n.pl.* See **Commonwealth Games.**

Empire State Building, *n.* the tallest building in the world until 1974; built in New York City in 1930–31. 449 m.

empirical /em'pirikəl/, *adj.* **1.** taken from or guided by experience or experiment. **2.** depending upon experience or observation rather than using science or theory. **— empirically,** *adv.*

empirical formula, *n.* **1.** *Chem.* the simplest kind of chemical formula giving the proportion of each element in a molecule: CH_2O *is the empirical formula of sugars.* **2.** any mathematical or engineering formula which is obtained on the basis of experimental results rather than pure theory.

empiricism /em'pirəsizəm/, *n.* **1.** the search for knowledge by empirical method or practice. **2.** *Philos.* the theory that all knowledge is gained from experience. **— empiricist,** *n., adj.*

employ /em'plɔi/, *v.t.* **1.** to use the services of (a person); have or keep in one's service; keep busy or at work: *This factory employs many men.* **2.** to make use of (an instrument, means, etc.); use; apply. **3.** to occupy or give (time, energies, etc.): *I employ my spare time in reading.* ◇*n.* **4.** employment;

en-

service: *to be in someone's employ.* [F, from L: enfold] **— employable,** *adj.* **— employment,** *n.*

employee /em'plɔii, emplɔi'i/, *n.* someone working for another person or a business firm for pay.

employer /em'plɔiə/, *n.* someone who employs other people, esp. for wages.

emporium /em'pɔriəm/, *n., pl.* **-poriums, -poria** /-'pɔriə/. a large store selling a great variety of goods. [L, from Gk: a trading place]

empower /em'pauə/, *v.t.* **1.** to give power or lawful right to; authorise: *I empowered him to make the deal for me.* **2.** to allow or permit.

empress /'emprəs/, *n.* **1.** a woman ruler of an empire. **2.** the consort of an emperor, usu. his wife. [ME, from OF, from L]

empty /'empti, 'emti/, *adj.,* **-tier, -tiest,** *v.,* **-tied, -tying,** *n., pl.* **-ties.** ◇*adj.* **1.** containing nothing; void; without usual contents or load: *an empty bottle; an empty truck.* **2.** not used; vacant; unoccupied: *an empty house.* **3.** lacking some quality; devoid (fol. by *of*): *a life empty of happiness.* **4.** *Colloq.* hungry. **5.** without knowledge or sense; frivolous; foolish. ◇*v.t.* **6.** to make empty: *to empty a bucket.* **7.** to discharge (contents): *to empty water out of a bucket.* ◇*v.i.* **8.** to become empty: *The room emptied quickly after the lesson.* ◇*n.* **9.** *Colloq.* something empty, as a bottle, can, or similar. [OE *æmtig,* from *æmetta* leisure + *-ig* -Y¹] **— emptily,** *adv.* **— emptiness,** *n.*

empyrean /empai'riən/, *n.* **1.** the highest heaven, formerly thought to contain the pure element of fire. **2.** the visible heavens; the sky. [LL, from Gk: fire] **— empyreal,** *adj.*

emu /'imju/, *n.* a large, flightless, three-toed Australian bird, closely related to the ostrich, but smaller. [Pg *ema* ostrich, cassowary]

emulate /'emjuleit, -jə-/, *v.t.,* **-lated, -lating. 1.** to try to equal or do better than. **2.** to imitate (someone respected or admired). **3.** to compete with successfully. [L: having rivalled] **— emulative,** *adj.* **— emulator,** *n.* **— emulation,** *n.*

emulsion /ə'mʌlʃən/, *n.* **1.** a milk-like mixture formed by the suspension of one liquid in another. **2.** *Pharm.* a medicine consisting of an oily, fatty, or other substance held in suspension in an aqueous fluid. **3.** *Photog.* a light-sensitive layer on a photographic film, plate, or paper, consisting of one or more silver salts in gelatine. [NL *ēmulsio,* from L *ēmulsus,* pp., milked out] **— emulsive,** *adj.*

en /en/, *n.* **1.** the letter N, n. **2.** *Print.* half of the width of an em.

en-¹, a prefix meaning primarily 'in', 'into', often serving to form transitive verbs from nouns or adjectives, as in *enable, enact, endear, engulf.* Also, **em-¹.** See **in-¹, im-¹.** [F, from L *in-,* representing *in,* prep., in, into, on, to]

en-², a prefix representing Greek *en-,* corresponding to **en-¹** and occurring chiefly in combinations already formed in Greek, as *energy, enthusiasm.* Also, **em-².**

-en¹, a suffix forming transitive and intransitive verbs from adjectives, as in *fasten, harden, sweeten*, or from nouns, as in *heighten, lengthen, strengthen*. [abstracted from old verbs like *fasten* (contrast *listen*, where *-en* has kept its non-morphemic character)]

-en², a suffix of adjectives indicating 'material', 'appearance', as in *ashen, golden, oaken*. [OE]

-en³, a suffix used to mark the past participle in many strong and some weak verbs, as in *taken, proven*. [OE]

-en⁴, a suffix forming plural of some nouns, as in *brethren, children, oxen*, and other words, now mostly archaic, as *eyen, hosen*. [OE *-an*, case ending of weak nouns, as in *oxan*, oblique sing. and nom. and acc. pl. of *oxa* ox]

-en⁵, a diminutive suffix, as in *maiden, kitten*, etc. [OE]

enable /ɛn'eɪbəl, ən-/, v.t., **-bled, -bling**. **1.** to make able; authorise: *This will enable him to do it.* **2.** to make possible or easy.

enabling /ɛn'eɪblɪŋ, ən-/, adj. *Law.* (of an act, statute, or bill) allowing a person, company or government to take action.

enact /ɛn'ækt, ən-/, v.t. **1.** to make into an act or statute. **2.** to order; ordain; decree. **3.** to act the part of: *to enact Hamlet*. —**enactment**, n.

enamel /ə'næməl/, n., v., **-elled, -elling**. ◇n. **1.** a glassy substance, usu. opaque, applied by fusion to a surface of metal, pottery, etc., as an ornament or for protection. **2.** any of various enamel-like varnishes, paints, etc. **3.** *Anat., Zool.* the hard, glossy, outer structure of the crowns of teeth. ◇v.t. **4.** to inlay, cover, or ornament with enamel. [ME, from AF] —**enameller**, n. —**enamelwork**, n. —**enamelling**, n.

enamor or **enamour** /ɛn'æmə, ən-/, v.t. to fill with love; charm; delight (usu. passive fol. by *of*): *to be enamored of a lady*. [ME, from OF *en-* EN.¹ + *amour* (from L *amor* love)]

encapsulate /ɛn'kæpsjəleɪt, ən-, -fə-/, v., **-lated, -lating**. **1.** to enclose in or as in a capsule. **2.** to put in shortened form; condense; abridge. —**encapsulation**, n.

-ence, a noun suffix equivalent to **-ance**, and corresponding to **-ent** in adjectives, as in *abstinence, consistence, dependence, difference*. [F, alteration of *-ance* -ANCE by etymological association with L *-entia*, noun suffix]

encephalin /ɛn'sɛfəlɪn/, n. a substance found in the brain which has properties like those of narcotics.

encephalitis /ɛnsɛfə'laɪtɪs, ɛnkɛf-, ən-/, n. inflammation of the brain. [NL; see ENCEPHAL(O)-, -ITIS] —**encephalitic**, adj.

encephalo-, a word element meaning 'brain', as in *encephalogram*. Also, **encephal-**. [Gk *enkephalo-*, combining form of *enképhalos*]

encephalogram /ɛn'sɛfələgræm, ɛnkɛf-/, n. an X-ray photograph of the brain.

enchant /ɛn'tʃænt, ən-, -'tʃɑnt/, v.t. **1.** to subject to magical influence; cast a spell over; bewitch. **2.** to delight greatly; charm. [ME, from OF, from L: chant a magic formula against] —**enchanter**, n. —**enchanting**, adj. —**enchantment**, n.

enchantress /ɛn'tʃæntrəs, ən-, -'tʃɑnt-/, n. **1.** a woman who enchants; sorceress. **2.** a charming woman.

encircle /ɛn'sɜkəl, ən-/, v.t., **-cled, -cling**. to enclose in a circle; surround: *The enemy encircled the hill*.

enclave /'ɛnkleɪv/, n. a country, or an outlying portion of it, completely surrounded by foreign land. [F, from Rom]

enclose /ɛn'kloʊz, ən-/, v.t., **-closed, -closing**. **1.** to shut in; close in on all sides, as with a fence or wall: *to enclose land*. **2.** to put in the same envelope, parcel, etc., as the main letter, etc.: *He enclosed a cheque*. [OF]

enclosure /ɛn'kloʊʒə, ən-/, n. **1.** the act or result of enclosing: *The horses were in a large enclosure*. **2.** (formerly) the practice of taking common land by setting up a fence around it. **3.** that which is enclosed, e.g. paper, money, etc., sent in a letter.

encode /ɛn'koʊd/, v.t., **-coded, -coding**. to put into coded form, as of a message, computer program, etc.

encompass /ɛn'kʌmpəs, ən-/, v.t. **1.** to form a circle about; encircle; surround. **2.** to enclose; contain.

encore /'ɒŋkɔ, 'ɒŋkɔ/, interj., n., v., **-cored, -coring**. ◇interj. **1.** again; once more (used by an audience in calling for a repetition of a song, etc., or for an additional item.) ◇n. **2.** a demand, as by applause, for a song, music, etc., to be presented again. **3.** that which is given in response to such demand. ◇v.t. **4.** to call for an encore from (a performer). [F: still, yet, besides, from L: within this hour]

encounter /ɛn'kaʊntə, ən-/, v.t. **1.** to come upon; meet with, esp. unexpectedly. **2.** to meet with or struggle against (difficulties, opposition, etc.). **3.** to meet (a person, military force, etc.) in conflict. ◇n. **4.** a meeting with a person or thing, esp. by chance. **5.** a meeting in conflict or opposition; battle; combat. [ME, from OF, from L *in-* IN-² + *contrā* against]

encourage /ɛn'kʌrɪdʒ, ən-/, v.t., **-raged, -raging**. **1.** to inspire with courage, confidence, or trust. **2.** to support by giving help, approval, etc. [ME, from OF *en-* EN-¹ + *corage* COURAGE] —**encouraging**, adj. —**encouragement**, n.

encroach /ɛn'kroʊtʃ, ən-/, v.i. **1.** to advance beyond proper limits. **2.** to illegally extend one's boundaries, buildings, or natural features onto the land of another, esp. stealthily or by gradual advances: *You're encroaching on my territory*. [ME, from OF *en-* EN-¹ + *croc* hook] —**encroachment**, n.

encumber /ɛn'kʌmbə, ən-/, v.t. **1.** to hold back; retard; impede. **2.** to block up or fill with what is obstructive or unnecessary. **3.** to weigh down; burden: *to encumber with debts; to encumber with parcels*. [ME, from OF *en-* EN-¹ + *combre* barrier (from LL, from Gallic *comberos* a bringing together)]

encumbrance /en'kʌmbrəns, ən-/, *n.* **1.** something useless which encumbers; burden; hindrance. **2.** a dependent person, esp. a child. **3.** *Law.* a claim on property, as a mortgage. Also, **incumbrance**.

encyclical /en'sıklıkəl, ən-/, *n.* **1.** a letter addressed by the pope to his bishops. ◊*adj.* **2.** for wide or general circulation. Also, **encyclic**. [LL, from Gk: circular, general]

encyclopedia *or* **encyclopaedia** /en-,saıklə'pidıə, ən-/, *n.* a book, or series of books giving information on general or special branches of knowledge, usu. arranged alphabetically: *a general encyclopedia; a medical encyclopedia*. [LL, from pseudo-Gk *enkyklopaideía*, for *enkýklios paideía* general education, complete round or course of learning] —**encyclopedic**, *adj.*

end /end/, *n.* **1.** the finishing point of anything that is longer than it is broad: *the end of a street; the end of a rope.* **2.** the furthest part of anything: *the ends of the earth.* **3.** the line or edge at which something finishes; limit; boundary. **4.** a coming to an end; termination; conclusion. **5.** a purpose, aim or object: *to gain one's end; What have you in mind in doing this?* **6.** a result; conclusion: *the end of the discussion was a decision to act.* **7.** death: *His end was sudden.* **8.** (*usu. pl.*) remains; remnant: *odds and ends.* **9.** a part or share of something: *her end of the work; my end of the house.* **10.** *Football, etc.* the half of the field which one team defends from attack by the other team. **11. at a loose end**, Also, **at loose ends**. not busy enough; having nothing to do. **12. make (both) ends meet**, to keep one's spending within one's income. **13. on end**, **a.** upright. **b.** continuously. ◊*v.t.*, *v.i.* **14.** to bring or come to an end; finish; cease: *He ended the discussion by leaving; Hostilities ended last year.* ◊*adj.* **15.** of or relating to an end: *end product; an end section.* [OE *ende*] —**ender**, *n.*

endanger /en'deındʒə, ən-/, *v.t.* to put in danger; imperil.

endear /en'dıə, ən-/, *v.t.* to make dear or beloved: *He endeared himself to his friends.* —**endearing**, *adj.* —**endearment**, *n.*

endeavor *or* **endeavour** /en'devə, ən-/, *v.i.* **1.** to make an effort; strive. ◊*v.t.* **2.** to attempt; try (fol. by infinitive): *He endeavors to keep things nice about his place.* ◊*n.* **3.** an effort; attempt: *His endeavor was in vain.* [ME *putten en deveren* to make it one's duty]

Endeavour, *n.* **HM Bark**, the ship commanded by James Cook when he charted the eastern Australian coast in 1770.

Endeavour Reef, *n.* a section of the Great Barrier Reef, Qld, east of Cooktown; believed to be where Captain Cook ran aground in 1770.

endemic /en'demık/, *adj.* **1.** Also, **endemical**. limited to a particular group or place, as a disease. ◊*n.* **2.** an endemic disease or plant. [Gk *éndēmos* belonging to a people + -IC] —**endemically**, *adv.* —**endemism, endemicity**, *n.*

ending /'endıŋ/, *n.* **1.** a bringing or coming to an end; termination; close. **2.** the final or finishing part: *The film had a sad ending.* **3.** (in popular use) any final word part, as *-ow* of *widow.* [OE *endung*]

endive /'endaıv/, *n.* a herb, probably of Indian origin with its leaves now widely used in salads and as a cooked vegetable. [ME, from L]

endless /'endləs/, *adj.* having or seeming to have no end: *an endless chain; an endless speech.* —**endlessness**, *n.*

endo-, a word part meaning 'internal', as in *endocrine*. Also, **end-**. [Gk, combining form of *éndon* within]

endocrine gland, /'endəkrən, -krın glænd/ *n.* any of various glands or organs, e.g. the thyroid gland, producing certain important secretions (hormones) which are carried by the blood to other parts of the body, where they regulate organ functions.

endocrinology /,endoukrə'nɒlədʒi/, *n.* the science that deals with the endocrine glands, esp. in their relation to bodily changes. —**endocrinologist**, *n.*

endoderm /'endoudəm/, *n.* the inner cell layer in the embryo of many-celled organisms.

endogamy /en'dɒgəmi/, *n.* a marriage within a tribe or social unit (opposed to *exogamy*). —**endogamous**, *adj.*

endometrium /,endou'mitriəm/, *n., pl.* **-tria** /-triə/. the mucous membrane lining the uterus.

endoplasm /'endouplæzəm/, *n.* the inner portion of the cytoplasm in the cell of a protozoan or vegetable cell (opposed to *ectoplasm*). —**endoplasmic**, *adj.*

endorse /en'dɔs, ən-/, *v.t.*, **-dorsed, -dorsing. 1.** to add a modifying statement to (a document, licence, etc.). **2.** to sign one's name to (a commercial document, cheque, etc.) as to transfer money, acknowledge receipt, etc. **3.** to give support to; approve: *I don't endorse that sort of behavior.* **4.** (of a branch of a political party) to select (someone) as a candidate for election: *Labor has endorsed him as its candidate.* Also, **indorse**. [ME, from OF *en-* on + *dos* (from L *dorsum* back)] —**endorsable**, *adj.* —**endorser**, *n.*

endorsement /en'dɔsmənt, ən-/, *n.* **1.** approval or sanction. **2.** the act of endorsing. **3.** a signature, etc. endorsing a document. **4.** a clause or statement added as a modification to a document, etc.

endothelium /endou'θiliəm/, *n., pl.* **-lia** /-liə/. the tissue which lines blood vessels, lymphatic vessels, etc. [NL, from Gk]

endothermic /endou'θɜmık/, *adj.* relating to a chemical change which is accompanied by an absorption of heat (opposed to *exothermic*).

endotoxin /,endou'tɒksən/, *n.* the toxic protoplasm of a micro-organism which is released when the organism dies or disintegrates.

endow /en'dau, ən-/, *v.t.* **1.** to provide with a lasting source of income: *to endow a college.* **2.** to provide as with some gift, power, or quality; equip: *Nature has endowed him with*

endow

great ability. [ME, from OF *en-* EN-[1] + *douer*, (from L: endow)] **—endower**, *n.*

endowment /ɛn'daʊmənt, ən-/, *n.* **1.** the act of endowing. **2.** money or property with which an organisation, person, etc., is endowed. **3.** (*usu. pl.*) natural qualities of mind or body; gift of nature.

endpaper /'ɛndpeɪpə/, *n.* (*oft. in pl.*) (in books) thick paper forming the inside cover and flyleaves.

endue /ɛn'dju, ən-/, *v.t.*, **-dued**, **-duing**. to provide with some gift, quality, or power: *endued with life and vigor.* [ME, from L: lead into]

endurance /ɛn'djʊərəns, ən-/, *n.* **1.** the fact or power of enduring or bearing anything. **2.** lasting quality; duration. **3.** something endured, as a hardship.

endure /ɛn'djʊə/, *v.*, **-dured**, **-during**. ◇*v.t.* **1.** to hold out against; undergo: *They endured the famine for three years.* **2.** to bear patiently or without resistence; tolerate: *I don't know how you endure that music.* ◇*v.i.* **3.** to continue to exist; last; remain: *Happiness can endure only so long.* [ME, from L: harden]

endways /'ɛndweɪz/, *adv.* **1.** on end. **2.** with an end upwards or forwards. **3.** towards the ends or end; lengthways. **4.** with ends touching; end to end. Also, **endwise** /'ɛndwaɪz/.

-ene, **1.** a noun suffix used to indicate unsaturated aliphatic hydrocarbons with one double bond, of the alkene series, as *ethene*, *propene*, etc. **2.** a generalised suffix used in trademarks for substances, oft. showing synthetic manufacture, as in *terylene*. [special use of *-ene*, adj. suffix (as in *terrene*), from L *-ēnus*]

ENE, east-north-east. See Appendix.

enema /'ɛnəmə/, *n.*, *pl.* **enemas, enemata** /ə'nɛmətə, i-/. *Med.* a fluid injected into the rectum to empty the bowels. [Gk: injection]

enemy /'ɛnəmi/, *n.*, *pl.* **-mies.** ◇*n.* **1.** someone who hates another, or has harmful designs against them; adversary; opponent. **2.** an armed foe; opposing military force. **3.** a hostile nation, state, or its people. **4.** something harmful. ◇*adj.* **5.** belonging to a hostile power or to its people: *enemy property.* [ME, from OF, from L: unfriendly, hostile]

energetic /ɛnə'dʒɛtɪk/, *adj.* having or showing energy; effective; vigorous. [Gk: active] **—energetically**, *adv.*

energy /'ɛnədʒi/, *n.*, *pl.* **-gies.** **1.** (habitual) capacity for vigorous activity: *You need a lot of energy to run a kindergarten.* **2.** actual exertion or use of power; operation; activity: *That machine uses too much energy.* **3.** a strong or forceful expression: *The energy of his words caught our attention.* **4.** *Physics.* the capacity for doing work, existing in various forms, e.g. kinetic energy, nuclear energy. The derived SI unit of energy is the joule. [LL, from Gk: agency, force]

enervate /'ɛnəveɪt/, *v.t.*, **-vated**, **-vating**. to take away the energy, force, or strength of; weaken: *This hot weather completely enervates*

engender

me. [L] **—enervation**, *n.* **—enervator**, *n.* **—enervative**, *adj.*

enfant terrible /ˌɒ̃fɒ̃ tə'riːblə/, *n.* **1.** a child who is rude or uncontrollable. **2.** a talented person whose ideas or behavior appear strange or threatening to others of his or her profession. [F]

enfeeble /ɛn'fibəl, ən-/, *v.t.*, **-bled**, **-bling**. to make feeble; weaken. [ME, from OF] **—enfeeblement**, *n.*

enfold /ɛn'foʊld, ən-/, *v.t.* **1.** to wrap up; envelop: *enfolded in a magic mantle.* **2.** to hold lovingly; embrace. **3.** to surround with or as if with folds.

enforce /ɛn'fɔs, ən-/, *v.t.*, **-forced**, **-forcing**. **1.** to put or keep in force; ensure obedience to: *to enforce laws; to enforce rules.* **2.** to obtain (payment, obedience, etc.) by force. **3.** to force (a course of action) upon a person. **4.** to impress, state or urge (an argument, point of view, etc.) forcibly. [ME, from OF, from L *in-* IN-[1] + *fortis* strong] **—enforceable**, *adj.* **—enforcedly**, *adv.* **—enforcer**, *n.* **—enforcement**, *n.*

enfranchise /ɛn'fræntʃaɪz, ən-/, *v.t.*, **-chised**, **-chising**. **1.** to grant a franchise to; admit to citizenship, esp. to the right of voting. **2.** *Law.* to give the right of being represented in Parliament. **3.** to set free; liberate, as from slavery. [MF *en-* EN-[1] + *franc* free, FRANK] **—enfranchisement**, *n.*

eng., *Abbrev.* **1.** an engine. **2.** engineering.

engage /ɛn'ɡeɪdʒ, ən-/, *v.*, **-gaged**, **-gaging**. ◇*v.t.* **1.** to obtain the attention or efforts of (a person, etc.): *He engaged her in conversation.* **2.** to obtain for aid, employment, use, etc.; hire: *to engage a workman; to engage a room.* **3.** to attract and hold fast: *to engage attention, interest, etc.* **4.** to bind as by a promise, contract, oath, etc.: *He engaged to do it in writing.* **5.** to promise in marriage; betroth (usu. used in passive). **6.** to bring (troops) into conflict; enter into battle with: *Our army engaged the enemy.* **7.** *Mech.* to cause to become interlocked: *to engage first gear.* ◇*v.i.* **8.** to occupy oneself; become involved: *to engage in business; to engage in politics.* **9.** to pledge one's word; assume an obligation. **10.** to enter into battle. **11.** *Mech.* to interlock. [F *en-* EN-[1] + *gage* pledge, GAGE[1]] **—engagement**, *n.*

engaged /ɛn'ɡeɪdʒd, ən-/, *adj.* **1.** busy or occupied; involved. **2.** under agreement to marry. **3.** *Mech.* **a.** interlocked. **b.** (of wheels) in gear with each other. **4.** (of a telephone line) inaccessible because already in use.

engaging /ɛn'ɡeɪdʒɪŋ, ən-/, *adj.* winning; attractive; pleasing. **—engagingly**, *adv.*

Engels /'ɛŋɡəlz/, *n.* **Friedrich**, 1820–95, German socialist writer in England, associated with Karl Marx; together they wrote *The Communist Manifesto* (1848); Engels' own works included *Condition of the Working Classes in England* (1844).

engender /ɛn'dʒɛndə, ən-/, *v.t.* **1.** to produce, cause, or give rise to: *Hatred engenders violence.* ◇*v.i.* **2.** to be produced or caused;

engender — enough

come into existence. [ME, from L: beget] —**engenderer**, n. —**engenderment**, n.

engine /'endʒən/, n. **1.** any mechanism or machine designed to convert energy into mechanical work: *a steam engine; internal-combustion engine*. **2.** a railway locomotive. [ME, from L: invention]

engineer /endʒə'nɪə/, n. **1.** someone trained in the design, construction, and use of engines or machines, or in any of the various branches of engineering: *a mechanical engineer; an electrical engineer*. **2.** a skilful manager. ◇v.t. **3.** to plan, construct, or manage as an engineer. **4.** to arrange, manage or carry through by skilful, clever means.

engineering /endʒə'nɪərɪŋ/, n. **1.** the art or science of applying knowledge of pure sciences such as physics, chemistry, biology, etc. in a practical way. **2.** the action, work, or profession of engineer. **3.** skilful or clever methods; manoeuvring.

England /'ɪŋɡlənd/, n. a country in north-western Europe, part of the United Kingdom; the largest division of Great Britain, bordered by Wales and Scotland. Pop. 47 254 500 (1986 est.); 130 441 km². *Cap.*: London.

English /'ɪŋɡlɪʃ/, adj. **1.** of, relating to, or characteristic of England, its people, etc. ◇n. **2.** the people of England. **3.** the Germanic language of the British Isles, widely spoken throughout the world. [ME]

English Channel, n. an arm of the Atlantic between England and France, connected with the North Sea by the Strait of Dover. About 563 km long; 32–160 km wide.

engorge /en'ɡɔdʒ, ən-/, v.t., **-gorged**, **-gorging**. **1.** to fill (oneself) up with food. **2.** *Med.* to fill up with blood. [F *engorger*, from *en-* EN.[1] + *gorge* GORGE] —**engorgement**, n.

engrave /en'ɡreɪv, ən-/, v.t., **-graved**, **-graving**. **1.** to cut (letters, designs, etc.) into a hard surface, as of metal, stone, or wood. **2.** to print from such a surface. **3.** to mark or ornament with such letters, designs, etc. **4.** to fix firmly (in the mind or memory). —**engraver**, n.

engraving /en'ɡreɪvɪŋ, ən-/, n. **1.** the act or art of someone or something that engraves. **2.** the design engraved. **3.** (a print made from) an engraved plate or block.

engross /en'ɡrous, ən-/, v.t. **1.** to occupy the mind or attention of completely; absorb: *That book engrossed her for days*. **2.** to write or copy (a document, etc.) in large and clear letters. **3.** to obtain all of (a commodity) in order to control the market; monopolise. [ME, from AF: write large] —**engrossing**, adj.

engulf /en'ɡʌlf, ən-/, v.t. to swallow up or surround completely: *Water engulfed the bridge; Sorrow engulfed them.*

enhance /en'hæns, -'hans, ən-/, v.t., **-hanced**, **-hancing**. **1.** to raise to a higher degree; intensify; magnify. **2.** to raise the value or price of. [ME, from OF *en-* EN.[1] + *haucier* raise] —**enhancement**, n.

enharmonic /ˌenhɑ'mɒnɪk/, adj. *Music*. having the same pitch in the tempered scale (as on a piano) but written in different notation, as G-sharp and A-flat. [LL: in accord, from Gk] —**enharmonically**, adv.

enigma /ə'nɪɡmə/, n. **1.** somebody or something puzzling or unable to be explained. **2.** a saying, question, picture, etc., containing a hidden meaning; riddle. [L, from Gk: riddle] —**enigmatic, enigmatical**, adj.

enjoy /en'dʒɔɪ, ən-/, v.t. **1.** to experience with joy or pleasure. **2.** to have and use with satisfaction: *She enjoys good health*. **3.** to find or experience pleasure for (oneself): *He enjoyed himself at the party*. [ME, from OF *en-* EN.[1] + *joir* JOY, v.] —**enjoyable**, adj. —**enjoyment**, n.

enlarge /en'lɑdʒ, ən-/, v., **-larged**, **-larging**. ◇v.t. **1.** to make larger; increase in size, quantity or capacity; expand. **2.** *Photog.* to make (a print) larger than the negative. ◇v.i. **3.** to grow larger; increase; expand. **4.** to speak or write at length and with more detail: *to enlarge upon a point in a discussion*. [ME, from OF *en-* EN.[1] + *large* LARGE] —**enlargement**, n.

enlighten /en'laɪtn, ən-/, v.t. to give knowledge or understanding to; instruct.

enlightened /en'laɪtnd, ən-/, adj. free from superstition; having knowledge or understanding.

enlightenment /en'laɪtnmənt, ən-/, n. **1.** the act of being enlightened. **2. the Enlightenment**, an 18th-century philosophical movement marked by a belief in human reason.

enlist /en'lɪst, ən-/, v.i. **1.** to enter into an agreement to serve in the armed forces. **2.** to enter into some cause, activity, etc.: *I enlisted for the football team*. ◇v.t. **3.** to cause to enlist for military service. **4.** to obtain (a person, services, etc.) for some cause, activity etc.: *I enlisted his help to move the furniture*. —**enlistment**, n.

en masse /ɒn 'mæs/, adv. in a mass or body; all together: *They left the theatre en masse*. [F]

enmity /'ɛnmətɪ/, n., pl. **-ties**. the feeling or condition of being hostile; antagonism; animosity. [ME, from F: enemy]

ennoble /ɛ'noubəl, ə-/, v.t., **-bled**, **-bling**. **1.** to raise in degree, excellence, or respect; dignify. **2.** to give a title of nobility to. —**ennoblement**, n.

ennui /ɒn'wi/, n. a feeling of weariness and discontent resulting from lack of interest; boredom. [F]

enormity /ə'nɒmətɪ, i-/, n., pl. **-ties**. **1.** greatness of size, extent, etc. **2.** great wickedness; atrociousness: *They were shocked by the enormity of his offences*. **3.** a very wicked act; atrocity. [L: hugeness, irregularity]

enormous /ə'nɒməs, i-/, adj. much larger than the common size, extent, etc.; huge; immense. [L: huge]

enough /ə'nʌf, i-/, adj. **1.** as much as is wanted or needed: *I've had enough food; Are there enough people to make a team?* ◇n. **2.** the amount or quantity wanted or needed;

enough sufficiency. ◇*adv.* **3.** in a quantity or degree that fulfils a need or desire; sufficiently. **4.** fully or quite: *ready enough.* **5.** fairly; tolerably: *He sings well enough.* [OE *genōh*]

enquire /ɪnˈkwaɪə, ən-, ɛn-/, *v.t., v.i., -quired, -quiring.* to try to gain (information) by asking. Also, **inquire.** —**enquirer,** *n.*

enquiry /ɪnˈkwaɪri, ən-, ɛn-/, *n., pl.* **-quiries. 1.** a looking for truth, information, or knowledge. **2.** a question or query. Also, **inquiry.**

enrage /ɛnˈreɪdʒ, ən-/, *v.t.,* **-raged, -raging.** to make very angry; infuriate. [MF]

enrapture /ɛnˈræptʃə, ən-/, *v.t.,* **-tured, -turing.** to cause to feel great delight. —**enrapt,** *adj.*

enrich /ɛnˈrɪtʃ, ən-/, *v.t.* **1.** to supply with riches, wealth, etc.: *Commerce enriches a nation.* **2.** to supply with large amounts of anything desirable or valuable: *Knowledge enriches your life.* **3.** to make finer in quality, taste, appearance, etc.: *Minerals enrich the soil; Herbs enrich the flavor of food.* [ME, from OF *en-* EN.[1] + *riche* RICH] —**enrichment,** *n.*

enrol /ɛnˈroʊl, ən-/, *v.,* **-rolled, -rolling.** ◇*v.t.* **1.** to write (a name) or put the name of (a person) on a list or in a record. ◇*v.i.* **2.** to enrol oneself: *to enrol in a course.* [ME, from OF *en-* EN.[1] + *rolle* ROLL, *n.*] —**enrolment,** *n.*

en route /ɒn ˈruːt/, *adv.* on the way: *She is en route to Brisbane.* [F]

ensconce /ɛnˈskɒns, ən-/, *v.t.,* **-sconced, -sconcing.** to settle comfortably or firmly: *I ensconced myself in an armchair.* [EN.[1] + *sconce* shelter]

ensemble /ɒnˈsɒmbəl/, *n.* **1.** all the parts of a thing taken together as a whole. **2.** a whole set of clothing: *She was wearing a green ensemble.* **3. a.** the united performance of the full number of singers, musicians, etc. **b.** the group so performing: *a string ensemble.* [ME, from F, from LL: at the same time]

ensign /ˈɛnsaɪn/; *Naval* /ˈɛnsən/, *n.* **1.** a flag or banner, as of a nation. **2.** a sign of office, power, etc., as a badge. **3.** (formerly) the lowest commissioned rank in the British infantry. [ME, from OF, from L: insignia]

ensue /ɛnˈsjuː, ən-/, *v.i.,* **-sued, -suing. 1.** to follow in order; come immediately afterwards. **2.** to follow as a result. [ME, from OF, from L: follow close upon]

en suite /ɒn ˈswiːt/, *n.* a small bathroom joined on to a bedroom. [F]

ensure /ɛnˈʃə, ən-/, *v.t.,* **-sured, -suring. 1.** to make sure or certain; guarantee: *We must take measures to ensure the success of the project.* **2.** to make safe, as from harm. [ME, from AF *en-* EN.[1] + OF *seur* SURE]

-ent, a suffix meaning the same as **-ant,** in adjectives and nouns, as in *ardent, dependent, different.* [L, present participle ending of some verbs]

ENT /iː ɛn ˈtiː/, *Abbrev. Med.* Ear, Nose, and Throat.

entail /ɛnˈteɪl, ən-/, *v.t.* **1.** to bring on by necessity or as a result: *That idea will entail a lot of work.* **2.** *Law.* (formerly) to cause (property) to be inherited by a fixed line of heirs. **3.** to involve (a proposition) as a logical deduction: *Being a bachelor entails being unmarried.* ◇*n.* **4.** property which is entailed. **5.** the order of descent settled for entailed property. [EN.[1] + *tail* entail, from OF: tax]

entangle /ɛnˈtæŋgəl, ən-/, *v.t.,* **-gled, -gling. 1.** to make tangled or twisted: *Don't entangle that string.* **2.** to catch in anything like a tangle: *The rope entangled my feet.* **3.** to put (someone) or get (oneself) into difficulties: *He entangled himself in crime.* —**entanglement,** *n.*

entente /ɒnˈtɒnt/, *n.* an understanding, as between nations. [F]

enter /ˈɛntə/, *v.i.* **1.** to come or go in. **2.** to make an entrance, as on the stage. ◇*v.t.* **3.** to come or go into: *She entered the room; The bullet entered the flesh.* **4.** to put in; insert: *She entered another definition into the dictionary.* **5.** to become a member of, or join: *They entered primary school.* **6.** to cause to be admitted, as into a school, competition, etc.: *She entered him for the race.* **7.** to begin upon (a career, etc.). **8.** to record or write on a list. **9.** *Law.* **a.** to place in regular form before a court, as a writ. **b.** to make an entrance on (lands) in order to claim a right to possession. **10.** to put forward formally; submit: *to enter an objection.* **11. enter into, a.** to take an interest or part in; engage in. **b.** to begin to consider (a subject, etc.). **c.** to sympathise with (a person's feelings, etc.). **d.** to form a part of: *Lead enters into the composition of pewter; This idea should enter into your plans.* [ME, from OF, from L: go into]

enteric /ɛnˈtɛrɪk/, *adj.* relating to the intestines. [Gk: intestine]

enteritis /ɛntəˈraɪtəs/, *n.* inflammation of the intestines.

enterprise /ˈɛntəpraɪz/, *n.* **1.** an undertaking, esp. an important, difficult or dangerous one. **2.** boldness or readiness in carrying out new projects. **3.** a company organised for commercial purposes. [ME, from OF *entre* INTER- + *prendre* seize, take (from L)]

enterprising /ˈɛntəpraɪzɪŋ/, *adj.* bold and energetic in carrying out new, important, or difficult projects.

entertain /ɛntəˈteɪn/, *v.t.* **1.** to hold the attention of agreeably; divert; amuse. **2.** to receive as a guest. **3.** to have in the mind; consider: *He entertained ideas of growing rich.* ◇*v.i.* **4.** to entertain guests. [ME, from F from *entre-* INTER- + *tenir* (from L: hold)] —**entertainment,** *n.*

entertainer /ɛntəˈteɪnə/, *n.* someone who entertains, esp. a singer, dancer, etc.

entertaining /ɛntəˈteɪnɪŋ/, *adj.* interesting and amusing; diverting.

enthalpy /ˈɛnθəlpi, ɛnˈθælpi, ən-/, *n.* a thermodynamic property of a substance or system equal to the sum of energy inside it and the product of its pressure and volume; heat content; total heat.

enthral /ɛnˈθrɒl, ən-/, *v.t.,* **-thralled, -thralling.** to hold the whole attention of;

enthral enchant: *Her beauty enthrals him; The story enthralled us.*

enthuse /ɛn'θuz, -'θjuz, ən-/, v., **-thused, -thusing.** ◇v.i. 1. to show enthusiasm. ◇v.t. 2. to cause to become enthusiastic. [back-formation from ENTHUSIASM]

enthusiasm /ɛn'θuziæzəm, -'θjuz-, ən-/, n. a strong feeling of eager interest. [LL *enthūsiasmus*, from Gk *enthousiasmós*] **—enthusiast**, n. **—enthusiastic**, adj.

entice /ɛn'taɪs, ən-/, v.t., **-ticed, -ticing.** to attract by exciting hope or desire. [ME, from OF: incite, from L: firebrand]

entire /ɛn'taɪə, ən-/, adj. 1. having all the parts or elements; whole: *The entire class came to the lecture.* 2. not broken or decayed; intact. 3. being wholly of one piece; undivided; continuous. 4. complete; thorough: *entire freedom of choice.* 5. not castrated: *an entire horse.* [ME from L: untouched, whole] **—entirety**, n.

entitle /ɛn'taɪtl, ən-/, v.t., **-tled, -tling.** 1. to give (a person or thing) a title, right, or claim to something. 2. to call by a particular title or name. [ME, from OF, from L *in-* IN-² + *titulus* TITLE]

entity /'ɛntəti/, n., pl. **-ties.** 1. something that has a real existence; thing. 2. being or existence. [LL]

entomology /ɛntə'mɒlədʒi/, n. a branch of zoology that deals with insects. **—entomological**, adj. **—entomologist**, n.

entourage /ɒntu'rɑdʒ, -rɑʒ/, n. a group of people attending and helping someone, esp. a person of rank; attendants. [F: surround]

entrails /'ɛntreɪlz/, n. pl. 1. the intestines or bowels. 2. the inner parts of anything. [ME, from F, from LL: intestines, from L: within]

entrance[1] /'ɛntrəns/, n. 1. the act of entering, as into a place or upon new duties. 2. a point or place of entering, as a door, opening, passage, etc. 3. the power or right of entering; admission. [OF]

entrance[2] /ɛn'træns, -'trans, ən-/, v.t., **-tranced, -trancing.** 1. to fill with delight or wonder; enrapture. 2. to put into a trance.

entrant /'ɛntrənt/, n. someone who enters, as into a university, competition, etc. [F]

entreat /ɛn'trit, ən-/, v.t. 1. to beg (a person); beseech; implore: *I entreated them for help.* 2. to beg for (something): *I entreated help from them.* ◇v.i. 3. to make a serious request. Also, **intreat.** [ME, from OF *en-* EN-¹ + *traitier* TREAT]

entreaty /ɛn'triti, ən-/, n., pl. **-treaties.** a serious request; supplication.

entree /'ɒntreɪ/, n. 1. a dish served at dinner before the main course. 2. the right of entering. Also, **entrée.** [F]

entrepreneur /ˌɒntrəprə'nɜ/, n. *Comm.* 1. someone who organises and manages any business undertaking, esp. one with considerable risk (oft. used in relation to theatrical enterprises). 2. an employer of productive labor; contractor. [F: undertake] **—entrepreneurial**, adj.

entropy /'ɛntrəpi/, n. 1. a measure of energy unavailable for work in a thermodynamic system. 2. a measure of the state of disorder of a system, e.g. the universe, as it moves towards inertness. [Gk *en-* EN-² + *tropḗ* transformation]

entrust /ɛn'trʌst, ən-/, v.t. 1. to give a trust or responsibility to: *I entrusted him with her care.* 2. to give (something) with trust for care, use, etc: *She entrusted her fortune to him; He entrusted his life to a thin rope.*

entry /'ɛntri/, n., pl. **-tries.** 1. the act of entering; entrance. 2. a way or place of entering. 3. permission or right of entering; access. 4. the act of recording something in a book, list, etc. 5. the statement, name, etc., so recorded. 6. someone entered in competition. 7. *Music.* a point in a musical performance where a member of an orchestra or choir or a soloist begins to play or sing after being silent for some time. [ME, from F]

enumerate /ə'njumərɛɪt, i-/, v.t., **-rated, -rating.** 1. to name one by one; specify as in a list. 2. to find the number of; count. [L: counted out] **—enumerable**, adj. **—enumerative**, adj. **—enumerator**, n. **—enumeration**, n.

enunciate /ə'nʌnsiɛɪt, i-/, v., **-ated, -ating.** ◇v.t. 1. to speak or pronounce (words, etc.), esp. in a particular manner: *He enunciates his words clearly.* 2. to state definitely, as a theory. 3. to declare; announce. ◇v.i. 4. to pronounce words, esp. in a clear manner. [L] **—enunciation**, n.

enuresis /ˌɛnju'risəs/, n. *Med.* lack of control over the passing of urine; bed-wetting. [NL, from Gk: make water in] **—enuretic**, adj.

envelop /ɛn'vɛləp, ən-/, v.t. 1. to wrap up in a covering. 2. to serve as a wrapping or covering for. 3. to surround completely. 4. to hide: *Mist enveloped the mountains; Mystery enveloped his actions.* [ME, from OF *en-* EN-¹ + *voluper* wrap] **—envelopment**, n.

envelope /'ɛnvəloʊp, 'ɒn-/, n. 1. a folded paper cover for a letter or the like. 2. something which envelops, such as a wrapper or surrounding cover. 3. an airtight glass or metal container of a vacuum tube. [F]

enviable /'ɛnviəbəl/, adj. worthy to be envied; highly desirable.

envious /'ɛnviəs/, adj. feeling or expressing envy: *He is envious of her success.* [ME, from OF: envy]

environment /ɛn'vaɪrənmənt, ən-/, n. 1. the surroundings or conditions which influence the life and work of a person or community of people. 2. *Ecol.* all the conditions amongst which an organism lives and which influence its behavior and development. 3. *Geog.* all the geographical features of an area, such as trees, land, water, etc., and the system connecting these. **—environmental**, adj.

environmentalism /ɛnˌvaɪrən'mɛntəlɪzəm, ən-/, n. 1. the theory that the development and behavior of animals and humans is mainly influenced by their environment. 2. belief

environmentalism

environmentalism in and support for the protection and conservation of the natural environment. —**environmentalist**, n.

environs /ɛnˈvaɪrənz, ən-/, n.pl. immediate neighborhood; surrounding parts or districts, as of a city. [F]

envisage /ɛnˈvɪzədʒ, -zɪdʒ, ən-/, v.t., **-aged, -aging**. to form a mental image of, esp. a future event. [F en- EN-¹ + visage VISAGE]

envoy /ˈɛnvɔɪ/, n. an agent of a government sent on an official mission, representing that government on a specific matter. [F: one sent]

envy /ˈɛnvi/, n., pl. **-vies**, v., **-vied, -vying**. ◇n. 1. a feeling of discontent, usu. with ill will, at seeing another's possessions, success, etc. 2. the desire for something possessed by another. 3. someone or something regarded with envy. ◇v.t. 4. To regard with envy. [ME, from OF, from L]

enzyme /ˈɛnzaɪm/, n. any protein able to act as a catalyst in a biochemical reaction. [MGk: leavened] —**enzymic, enzymatic**, adj.

eo-, a word part meaning 'early', 'primeval', as in eolith. [Gk, combining form of ēōs dawn]

Eocene /ˈiːousiːn, ˈiə-/, adj., n. Geol. (relating to) the second main division of the Tertiary period or system, coming after Palaeocene and before Oligocene.

Eogene /ˈiːoudʒiːn, ˈiə-/, adj. Geol. relating to a division of the Tertiary period or system that comprises Palaeocene, Eocene and Oligocene.

eolith /ˈiːoulɪθ, ˈiə-/, n. a simple flint tool characteristic of the earliest stage of human culture, shaped by, rather than for, use.

eolithic /iːouˈlɪθɪk, iə-/, adj. referring to the earliest stage of human culture, marked by the use of simple stone tools.

eon /ˈiːɒn/, n. →aeon.

Eos /ˈiːɒs/, n. the Greek goddess of the dawn; Roman counterpart, Aurora.

-eous, a suffix meaning 'full of', 'like', etc.; a variant of **-ous**. [L -eus]

Eozoic /iːouˈzouɪk, iə-/, adj., n. Geol. a division of Pre-Cambrian time during which life first appeared on earth, or rocks formed in this period. [EO- + ZO(O)- + -IC]

EP /i ˈpi/, adj., n. (referring to) a gramophone record with a double set of microgrooves that revolves at 45 r.p.m. [initials of extended play]

epacris /əˈpækrəs/, n. a shrub of Australia and NZ with bell-shaped or cylindrical flowers. Also, **epacrid**.

epaulet /ˈɛpələt, -lət/, n. an ornamental shoulder piece worn on uniforms, chiefly by officers of the armed forces. Also, **epaulette**. [F: shoulder, from L]

epeirogeny /ɛpəˈrɒdʒəni/, n. Geol. a movement of the earth's crust affecting the formation of broad areas of continents or ocean basins. [Gk épeiro(s) land, mainland, continent + -GENY] —**epeirogenic**, adj.

epigastrium

ephedrine /ˈɛfədrɪn, -draɪn/, n. a crystalline alkaloid used esp. for colds, asthma, and hay fever. Also, **ephedrin** /ˈɛfədrən/. [L: horsetail, a plant, from Gk]

ephemeral /əˈfɛmərəl, i-/, adj. 1. lasting only a day or a very short time; transitory. ◇n. 2. an ephemeral thing, as certain insects.

epi-, a prefix meaning 'on', 'to', 'against', 'above', 'near', 'after', 'in addition to', as in epicentre, epidermis. Also, **ep-, eph-**. [Gk, representing epí, prep. and adv., ep- before vowel, eph- before aspirate]

epic /ˈɛpɪk/, adj. Also, **epical**. 1. referring to poetry in which a series of heroic deeds or events is dealt with in a long continuous narrative: Homer's 'Iliad' is an epic poem. 2. grand; heroic: an epic event. ◇n. 3. an epic poem. 4. a novel, play, or film like an epic, esp. one dealing with the adventures and deeds of a single person. [L, from Gk: epos]

epicene /ˈɛpisin, -ˈepə-/, adj. 1. belonging to, or having the characteristics of, both sexes. ◇n. 2. an epicene person. [L, from Gk: common]

epicentre /ˈɛpisɛntə/, n. the point from which earthquake waves seem to go out, directly above the true centre of the disturbance. Also, **epicentrum**. [NL, from Gk: on the centre] —**epicentral**, adj.

epicure /ˈɛpɪkjuə, ˈɛpə-/, n. 1. someone who has a cultivated taste, as in food, drink, art, music, etc. 2. someone who enjoys luxury and sensuous pleasures. [orig. anglicised form of EPICURUS] —**epicurean**, adj., n.

Epicurus /ɛpəˈkjurəs/, n. 342?–270 BC Greek philosopher, who held that the external world resulted from a lucky combination of atoms, and that the highest good in life is pleasure, which consists in freedom from disturbance or pain.

epicyclic train /ɛpiˈsaɪklɪk treɪn/, n. Mach. any train of gears, the axes of the wheels of which revolve around a common centre. Also, **epicyclic gear**.

epidemic /ɛpəˈdɛmɪk/, adj. 1. Also, **epidemical**. (of a disease) attacking at the same time a large number of people in a locality where it is not permanently found, and spreading from person to person. ◇n. 2. a temporary but widespread presence of disease. [LL, from Gk: prevalence of an epidemic]

epidermis /ɛpiˈdɜːməs, ɛpəˈdɜːməs/, n. 1. Anat. the outer, non-sensitive layer of the skin. 2. Zool. the outermost living layer of an animal, usu. formed of one or more layers of cells. 3. Bot. the outer cell layer of vascular plants. [LL, from Gk: outer skin] —**epidermal**, adj.

epidural anaesthetic /ɛpiˌdjuərəl ænəsˈθɛtɪk/, n. an injection of an agent into the outer covering of the spinal cord to deaden feeling in the lower part of the body, esp. in childbirth. Also, **epidural**.

epigastrium /ɛpiˈɡæstriəm/, n. Anat. the upper and middle part of the abdomen, lying over the stomach. [NL, from Gk: over the belly]

epigene /ˈεpidʒin/, *adj. Geol.* formed or originating on the earth's surface (opposed to *hypogene*). [F, from Gk: growing after or later]

epiglottis /ˌεpiˈglɒtəs, ˈεpiglɒtəs/, *n.* a thin piece of cartilage that covers the opening to the larynx during swallowing, preventing the entrance of food and drink. [NL, from Gk] – **epiglottal, epiglottic,** *adj.*

epigram /ˈεpigræm, ˈεpə-/, *n.* 1. any witty or clever saying that is short and to the point. 2. a short poem dealing with a single subject, usu. with a witty or clever ending. [L, from Gk: an inscription] – **epigrammatic,** *adj.*

epigraph /ˈεpigræf, -grɑf, ˈεpə-/, *n.* 1. an inscription, esp. on a building, statue, etc. 2. a well-expressed quotation at the beginning of a book, chapter, etc. [Gk]

epilepsy /ˈεpəlεpsi/, *n.* a nervous disease usu. marked by convulsions (fits) and loss of consciousness. [LL, from Gk: a seizure]

epileptic /ˌεpəˈlεptɪk/, *adj.* 1. relating to epilepsy. ◇*n.* 2. someone who has epilepsy. – **epileptically,** *adv.*

epilogue /ˈεpilɒg, ˈεpə-/, *n.* 1. a speech by an actor at the end of a play. 2. a concluding part added to a book, etc. [F, from L, from Gk: a conclusion]

epiphany /əˈpɪfəni/, *n.* (*usu. cap.*) 1. an appearance, revelation, etc., of a divine being. 2. the Christian festival on 6 January, celebrating the appearance of Christ to the Magi. [Gk: appearance, manifestation]

epiphyte /ˈεpifaɪt, ˈεpə-/, *n.* a plant which grows upon another but does not get food, water, or minerals from it.

episcopacy /əˈpɪskəpəsi/, *n., pl.* **-cies.** government of the church by bishops. – **episcopal,** *adj.*

episcopalian /əˌpɪskəˈpeɪliən/, *adj.* relating to or keeping to the episcopal form of church government.

episcopate /əˈpɪskəpət, -peɪt/, *n.* 1. the position of a bishop; bishopric. 2. an order or body of bishops.

episiotomy /əˌpɪziˈɒtəmi/, *n.* a surgical cut made at the opening of the vagina during labor to minimise tearing and aid delivery. [Gk *epision* pubic area]

episode /ˈεpəsoʊd/, *n.* 1. one particular event in the course of a person's life or experience, etc. 2. an incidental section in the course of a story, play, etc. 3. any of a number of loosely connected scenes or stories making up a book, etc. 4. (in radio, television, etc.) any of the separate programs making up a serial. [Gk: coming in besides] – **episodic,** *adj.*

epistemology /əˌpɪstəˈmɒlədʒi/, *n.* the branch of philosophy which is concerned with the origin, nature, methods, and limits of human knowledge. [Gk: knowledge] – **epistemological,** *adj.* – **epistemic,** *adj.*

epistle /əˈpɪsəl/, *n.* 1. a letter, esp. a formal one. 2. (*usu. cap.*) one of the letters of the Apostles found in the New Testament. [OE *epistol,* from L, from Gk: message, letter] – **epistler,** *n.* – **epistolary, epistolatory,** *adj.*

epitaph /ˈεpitɑf, ˈεpə-/, *n.* 1. the words written on a tomb, stone, etc., in memory of a dead person. 2. any brief writing of a similar nature. [ME, from L, from Gk: funeral oration]

epithelium /ˌεpiˈθiliəm, ˌεpə-/, *n., pl.* **-liums, -lia** /-liə/. *Biol.* any tissue which covers a surface, or lines a cavity, etc., and which has protective, secreting or other functions, etc. as the epidermis, the lining of blood vessels, etc. [NL, from Gk *thēlē* nipple]

epithet /ˈεpəθεt, ˌεpi-, -θət/, *n.* 1. an adjective or phrase used to describe a person or thing, as in Alexander *the* Great. 2. an insulting word or phrase: *She hurled choice epithets at his departing figure.* [L, from Gk: added] – **epithetic, epithetical,** *adj.*

epitome /əˈpɪtəmi/, *n.* 1. a shortened account, esp. of a book, etc.; a summary or precis; an abstract. 2. a representation or typical example of something: *His words were the epitome of rudeness.* [L, from Gk: cut into, abridge]

epitomise *or* **epitomize** /əˈpɪtəmaɪz/, *v.t.,* **-mised, -mising.** to make or be an epitome of.

epizootic /ˌεpɪzoʊˈɒtɪk/, *adj. Vet Sci.* 1. (of diseases) temporarily common in animals. ◇*n.* 2. Also, **epizooty.** an epizootic disease. – **epizootically,** *adv.*

epoch /ˈipɒk, ˈεpɒk/, *n.* 1. a particular period of time noted for its character, events, state of affairs, etc. 2. the beginning of any important period in the history of anything. 3. *Geol.* the main division of a geological period. [ML, from Gk: check, pause, position, epoch] – **epochal** *adj.*

eponym /ˈεpənɪm/, *n.* a person, real or imaginary, from whom a tribe, place, etc., takes or is supposed to take, its name, as *Britons* from *Brut* (supposed to be the grandson of Aeneas). [Gk: named after]

epoxy /ɪˈpɒksi, ə-/, *adj., n., pl.* **epoxies.** ◇*adj.* 1. *Chem.* containing an oxygen atom that connects two atoms. ◇*n.* 2. Also, **epoxy** or **epoxide resin.** any of a class of organic substances made by polymerisation, used chiefly in adhesives, solder mix, etc. and in experimental sculpture. [EPI- + OXY-]

Epsom salts /ˌεpsəm ˈsɒlts/, *n.pl.* hydrated magnesium sulfate, used as a cathartic, etc. [so called because first prepared from the water of the mineral springs at *Epsom,* England]

equable /ˈεkwəbəl/, *adj.* 1. (of motion, temperature, etc.) free from change; uniform. 2. uniform in operation etc., as laws. 3. calm; even; tranquil or not easily disturbed, as the mind. [L: that can be made equal]

equal /ˈikwəl/, *adj., n., v.,* **equalled, equalling.** ◇*adj.* 1. as great as another (fol. by *to* or *with*). 2. of the same or similar quantity, degree, value, ability, etc. 3. evenly proportioned or balanced: *an equal mixture; an equal contest.* 4. just enough in quantity or

equal degree: *The supply is equal to the demand.* **5.** having enough powers, ability, or means: *He was equal to the task.* ◇*n.* **6.** someone who or something which is equal: *He has met his equal in chess.* ◇*v.t.* **7.** to be or become equal to; match: *two plus two equals four.* **8.** to make or do something equal to: *He equalled his previous long jump record.* **9.** to make up for fully: *He will equal your losses.* [L: like, equal] —**equalise,** *v.*

equality /ɪˈkwɒləti, ə-/, *n., pl.* **-ties. 1.** the condition of being equal; the same in quality, degree, value, rank, ability, etc. **2.** uniform character, as of motion or surface.

equals sign, *n.* the symbol =, used to show that two things are equal. Also, **equal sign.**

equanimity /ˌikwəˈnɪməti, ˌɛkwə-/, *n.* evenness of mind or temper; calmness; composure. [L: of an even mind]

equate /ɪˈkweɪt, ə-/, *v.t.*, **equated, equating. 1.** to state the equality of, or between, as in an equation. **2.** to regard, treat, or represent as equal: *He equates money with happiness.* [L: made equal]

equation /ɪˈkweɪʒən, ə-, -ʃən/, *n.* **1.** the act of making equal. **2.** an equally balanced state; equilibrium. **3.** *Maths.* an expression stating the equality of two quantities, using the sign = between them. **4.** *Chem.* a symbolic representation of a reaction. —**equational,** *adj.*

equator /əˈkweɪtə, ɪ-/, *n.* **1.** an imaginary circle going around the earth, lying halfway between the North and South poles. **2.** *Maths.* a circle separating a surface into two parts of the same shape and size. [ME, from LL: equaliser (of day and night, as when the sun is on the equator)] —**equatorial,** *adj.*

equatorial climate /ˌɛkwəˌtɔriəl ˈklaɪmət/, *n.* the type of climate characterised by consistently high temperatures and rainfall throughout the year, roughly between latitudes 5° N and 5° S.

equestrian /əˈkwɛstriən, ɪ-/, *adj.* **1.** of or relating to horses and horseriding. **2.** mounted on horseback. ◇*n.* **3.** a rider or performer on horseback. [L: horseman] —**equestrienne,** *n. fem.* —**equestrianism,** *n.*

equi-, a word part meaning 'equal', as in *equidistant, equivalent.* [combining form representing L *aequus* equal]

equilateral /ˌikwəˈlætərəl/, *n., adj. Geom.* (a figure) having all the sides equal. [LL]

equilibrant /əˈkwɪləbrənt, ɪ-/, *n. Phys.* a force or system of forces balancing another.

equilibrium /ˌikwəˈlɪbriəm, ɛ-/, *n., pl.* **-iums, -ia. 1.** a state of rest or balance due to the action of opposing forces. **2.** an equal balance between any powers, influences, etc. **3.** mental or emotional balance. **4.** *Chem.* a state of balance in a chemical reaction where the substances produced break down at the same rate as they are being formed.

equilibrium constant, *n.* a number, which for a given chemical reaction in equilibrium at a stated temperature and pressure, expresses the proportion of concentrations of original chemicals in solution to the concentrations of the end products. *Symbol:* K

equine /ˈɛkwaɪn, ˈi-/, *adj.* of or like a horse [L *equus* horse] —**equinity,** *n.*

equinoctial /ˌikwəˈnɒkʃəl, ɛ-/, *adj.* **1.** relating to an equinox or equinoxes, or to the equality of day and night. **2.** relating to the celestial equator. **3.** *Bot.* (of a flower) opening regularly at a certain hour. [ME, from L: equinox]

equinox /ˈikwənɒks, ˈɛ-/, *n.* the time when the sun is directly over the earth's equator, making night and day all over the earth of equal length, occurring about 21 March and 22 September. [L: equality between day and night]

equip /əˈkwɪp, ɪ-/, *v.t.*, **equipped, equipping.** to furnish or provide with whatever is needed for services or any task. [OF, probably from Scand]

equipment /əˈkwɪpmənt, ɪ-/, *n.* anything used to equip for a job, etc., esp. a collection of tools, machines, resources, skills, etc.

equitable /ˈɛkwətəbəl/, *adj.* fair; reasonable; just.

equity /ˈɛkwəti/, *n., pl.* **-ties. 1.** the quality of being fair; fairness; impartiality. **2.** anything which is fair and just. **3.** *Law.* **a.** a body of law (orig. English), serving to correct and make up for the limitations and inflexibility of common law. **b.** an equitable right or claim. **4.** (*pl.*) a company's ordinary shares not bearing fixed interest. **5.** (*cap.*) the actors' trade union. [L: equality, justice]

equiv., *Abbrev.* equivalent.

equivalent /əˈkwɪvələnt, ɪ-/, *adj.* **1.** equal in value, measure, force, effect, importance, etc. **2.** corresponding in position, function, etc. ◇*n.* **3.** anything which is equivalent. [ME, from LL: having equal power] —**equivalence,** *n.*

equivalent weight, *n. Chem.* the weight of an element, radical, or compound which will combine with, or replace, one gram of hydrogen or eight grams of oxygen.

equivocal /əˈkwɪvəkəl, ɪ-/, *adj.* **1.** uncertain; not determined: *an equivocal attitude.* **2.** of doubtful character; questionable; dubious. **3.** having two or more meanings; ambiguous. [ME, from LL: ambiguous]

equivocate /əˈkwɪvəkeɪt, ɪ-/, *v.i.*, **-cated, -cating.** to use words having more than one meaning, esp. in order to mislead; prevaricate. —**equivocatingly,** *adv.* —**equivocator,** *n.* —**equivocatory,** *adj.* —**equivocation,** *n.*

er /ə, ɜ/, *interj.* (the word representing the sound made by a speaker when hesitating.)

-er¹, a suffix: **1.** forming nouns naming people according to the work they do as in *hatter, tiler, tinner,* or their place of origin, as in *southerner, villager,* or naming either people or things from some special characteristic, as in *two-seater, teetotaller, fiver, tenner.* **2.** serving as a regular English formative of agent nouns from verbs as in *bearer, creeper, employer, harvester, teacher.* [OE *-ere*]

-er², a suffix of nouns showing persons or things according to what they are concerned or connected with, as in *butler, grocer, officer, gardener*. [ME, from AF, OF *-er, -ier*, from L *-ārius*]

-er³, an ending of certain nouns showing action or process, as in *dinner, rejoinder, remainder*. [F]

-er⁴, a suffix forming the comparative degree of adjectives, as in *harder, smaller*. [OE *-ra, -re*]

-er⁵, a suffix forming the comparative degree of adverbs, as in *faster*. [OE *-or*]

-er⁶, a suffix forming frequentative verbs, as *flicker, flutter, glimmer, patter*. [OE *-r*]

Er, *Chem. Symbol.* erbium.

ER, *Abbrev.* Queen Elizabeth. [L *Elizabeth Regina*]

era /ˈɪərə/, *n.* **1.** a period of time marked by a particular character, events, etc.: *an era of progress*. **2.** the period of time to which anything belongs. **3.** a period where years are counted from a given date: *the Christian era*. **4.** a date or event forming the beginning of any distinctive period. **5.** a major division of geological time: *the Palaeozoic era*. [LL: number or epoch by which reckoning is made]

eradicate /əˈrædəkeɪt, i-/, *v.t.*, **-cated, -cating. 1.** to remove or destroy totally; extirpate. **2.** to pull up by the roots. [L: rooted out] **—eradication,** *n.* **—eradicator,** *n.* **—eradicable,** *adj.*

erase /əˈreɪs, i-/, *v.t.*, **erased, erasing. 1.** to rub out (words, letters, etc.); efface. **2.** to wipe off (material recorded on tape) by demagnetising. [L: scratched out] **—erasable,** *adj.* **—erasure,** *n.*

eraser /əˈreɪzə, i-/, *n.* an instrument, as a piece of rubber, etc., for rubbing out marks made with a pen, pencil, chalk, etc.

erbium /ˈɜbiəm/, *n. Chem.* a rare-earth metallic element, having pink salts. *Symbol:* Er; *at. no.:* 68; *at. wt:* 167.3. [NL]

Erebus /ˈɛrəbəs/, *n. Class Myth.* **1.** the god of darkness, son of Chaos and brother of Night. **2.** a place of darkness between earth and Hades; the lower world.

Erechtheum /əˈrɛkθiəm/, *n.* a temple of the Ionic order on the Acropolis of Athens, built c. 420 BC; one of the most perfect examples of Greek architecture, notable for its porches of different height, supported by caryatids.

erect /əˈrɛkt, i-/, *adj.* **1.** upright in position or posture: *to stand or sit erect.* **2.** raised or directed upwards: *a dog with ears erect; erect penis.* **3.** *Bot.* upright throughout; not spreading, etc.: *an erect stem; an erect leaf.* ◇*v.t.* **4.** to build or set up; construct; raise: *to erect a house; to erect social barriers.* **5.** to raise and set in an upright position: *to erect a telegraph pole.* **6.** to set up or establish, as an institution; found. [ME, from L: set upright, built] **—erective,** *adj.*

erectile /əˈrɛktaɪl, i-/, *adj.* **1.** able to be erected or set upright. **2.** *Med.* able to be filled with blood and become rigid, as tissue.

erection /əˈrɛkʃən, i-/, *n.* **1.** the act of erecting. **2.** the condition of being erected. **3.** something erected, as a building, etc. **4. a.** a distended and rigid condition of an organ or part containing erectile tissue. **b.** an erect penis.

erg¹ /ɜg/, *n. Phys.* a unit of work or energy in the c.g.s. system, equal to 10^{-7} joules. *Symbol:* erg [Gk: work]

erg² /ɜg/, *n. Geog.* any large area covered deeply with sand in the form of shifting dunes, as parts of the Sahara Desert. [F, from Hamitic]

ergo /ˈɜgoʊ/, *conj., adv.* therefore; consequently. [L]

ergonomics /ɜgəˈnɒmɪks, ɜgoʊ-/, *n.* the study of the engineering aspects of the relationship between workers and their working environment.

erica /ˈɛrɪkə/, *n.* any of various shrubs related to the heaths, grown for their showy flowers.

Ericsson /ˈɛrɪksən/, *n.* **Leif** /liːf/, fl. AD 1000, a Scandinavian navigator (son of Eric the Red); probable discoverer of 'Vinland' or Nova Scotia.

Eric the Red /ˈɛrɪk/, *n.* born about AD 950, Norseman who discovered Greenland about AD 982 and later colonised it. Also, **Eric.**

Erin /ˈɛrɪn, ˈɛərɪn, -ən/, *n. Poetic* Ireland. [OIrish *Erinn*, dative of *Eriu*, later *Eire* Ireland]

eriostemon /ɛriˈɒstəmən/, *n.* a shrub found in temperate Australia, having white or pink waxy flowers; waxflower.

Eritrea /ɛrəˈtreɪə/, *n.* a republic in north-eastern Africa on the Red Sea; federated with Ethiopia in 1952; civil war led to international recognition of independence in 1991-92; formerly an Italian colony. Pop. 3 127 492 (1999 est.); 117 400 km². *Languages:* Tigrinya, also English and Arabic. *Currency:* Ethiopian birr. *Cap.:* Asmara. **— Eritrean,** *n., adj.*

ermine /ˈɜmən/, *n., pl.* **-mines,** (*esp. collectively*) **-mine.** **1.** the name given to a stoat when its fur turns white in winter. **2.** the white winter fur of the ermine, having a black tail tip. [ME, from OF, from Gmc]

Ernst /ɜnst/, *n.* **Max,** 1891–1976, German painter; a founder of surrealism.

erode /əˈroʊd, i-/, *v.t.*, **eroded, eroding. 1.** to eat out or away; destroy slowly: *Misfortune eroded his confidence.* **2.** to form (a channel, etc.) by eating or wearing away (used esp. in geology, when referring to the wearing away of soil, etc., by wind and water, etc. [L: gnaw off] **—erodent, erosive,** *adj.*

erogenous /əˈrɒdʒənəs, ɛ-, i-/, *adj.* **1.** tending to arouse sexual desire. **2.** sensitive to sexual stimulation: *erogenous zones.* Also, **erogenic** /ɛrəˈdʒɛnɪk/. **—erogeneity,** *n.*

eros /ˈɪərɒs, ˈɛrɒs/, *n.* **1.** earthly or sexual love. **2.** *Psychol.* self-preserving instincts as opposed to self-destructive instincts. **3.** sexual drive; libido. **4.** (*cap.*) the Greek god of love; Roman counterpart, Cupid. [L, from Gk: lit., love]

erosion /əˈroʊʒən, i-/, *n.* **1.** the act of eroding. **2.** the state of being eroded. **3.** the

erosion

process by which the earth's surface is worn away by the action of water, glaciers, winds, waves, etc.

erotic /ə'rɒtɪk, ε-, i-/, *adj.* **1.** of or relating to sexual love; amatory. **2.** arousing or satisfying sexual desire. **3.** marked by strong sexual desires. [Gk]

err /ɜ/, *v.i.* **1.** to be mistaken; be incorrect. **2.** to do wrong (morally); sin. **3.** to move away from the true course, aim, or purpose. [ME, from L: wander] —**erring**, *adj.*

errand /'erənd/, *n.* **1.** a short trip for a particular purpose: *He was sent on an errand.* **2.** the purpose of any trip or journey: *His errand was to tell his mother his father was coming.* [OE *ærende*]

errant /'erənt/, *adj.* **1.** travelling, as in search of adventure: *a knight errant.* **2.** deviating from the regular course. **3.** itinerant. [ME, from OF: travel (from VL: journey)]

erratic /ə'rætɪk, i-/, *adj.* **1.** irregular in movement and conduct; not fixed: *erratic winds; erratic behavior.* **2.** *Geol.* (of large rocks, etc.) moved to an unusual place as by glacial action. ◇*n.* **3.** *Geol.* an erratic block of rock; erratic boulder. [ME, from L: wander, err] —**erratically**, *adv.*

erratum /ə'rɑːtəm, ε-/, *n., pl.* -**ta** /-tə/. a mistake in writing or printing. [L: erred]

erroneous /ə'roʊniəs/, *adj.* containing a mistake; mistaken; incorrect. [ME, from L: straying]

error /'erə/, *n.* **1.** a mistake, as in action, speech, etc. **2.** the condition of having mistaken ideas or opinions: *in error about the date.* **3.** wrongdoing; a moral offence. **4.** *Phys., etc.* the difference between the observed (approximate) value and the true value of a quantity. [L]

ersatz /'ɜsæts, 'ɜsɑts/, *adj.* acting as a substitute: *an ersatz meat dish made of aubergine and oatmeal.* [G]

erstwhile /'ɜstwaɪl/, *adj.* former: *erstwhile enemies.*

erudite /'erədaɪt/, *adj.* characterised by erudition; learned or scholarly: *an erudite professor.* [L: instructed] —**eruditely**, *adv.* —**eruditeness**, *n.*

erudition /erə'dɪʃən/, *n.* learned knowledge, esp. in literature, history, etc.; learning; scholarship.

erupt /ə'rʌpt, i-/, *v.i.* **1.** to explode and pour out, as volcanic matter. **2.** (of teeth) to break through tissues and come up in the mouth. **3.** to break out suddenly or violently, as if from being held back. **4.** to break out with or as with a skin rash. [L: burst forth] —**eruptible**, *adj.* —**eruptive**, *adj.*

eruption /ə'rʌpʃən, i-/, *n.* **1.** a bursting forth suddenly and violently; outburst; outbreak. **2.** *Geol.* the ejection of molten rock, water, etc., as from a volcano, geyser, etc. **3.** that which is erupted or ejected, as molten rock, etc. **4.** *Med.* (the breaking out of) a rash, acne, etc. [L] —**eruptional**, *adj.*

-ery, a suffix of nouns showing the type of job, business, place, products, things grouped, qualities, actions, etc., as in *archery, bakery, cutlery, fishery, pottery, prudery, trickery.* [ME, from OF]

es-, for words with prefix **es-**, see **aes-** and **oes-**.

-es, a variant of **-s²** and **-s³** after *s, z, ch, sh*, and in those nouns ending in *-f* which have *-v-* in the plural. See **-ies**.

Esau /'iːsɔː/, *n. Bible.* a son of Isaac, the elder twin brother of Jacob, to whom he sold his birthright. [Genesis 25:21–25]

escalate /'eskəleɪt/, *v.t., v.i.,* -**lated**, -**lating**. to make or become larger or more intense: *to escalate a war; Prices will escalate.* [backformation from ESCALATOR] —**escalation**, *n.*

escalator /'eskəleɪtə/, *n.* a continuously moving staircase for carrying people up or down. [L: ladder]

escapade /'eskəpeɪd, eskə'peɪd/, *n.* a reckless proceeding; a wild prank. [F, from Sp, or from It]

escape /əs'keɪp/, *v.,* -**caped**, -**caping**, *n.* ◇*v.i.* **1.** to get away from or avoid capture, restraint, danger, evil, etc.: *to escape from prison; They escaped with their lives.* **2.** (of fluid, etc.) to leak or flow out from a container. **3.** *Bot.* (of an introduced plant) to grow wild. ◇*v.t.* **4.** to succeed in getting free from or avoiding (prison, capture, danger, evil, etc.): *to escape the police; to escape death.* **5.** to not be noticed or remembered by (a person): *His name escapes me.* **6.** to slip from (someone) by accident: *A sigh escaped her.* **7.** the act of escaping. **8.** a means of escaping: *a fire escape.* **9.** avoidance of reality. **10.** leakage, esp. of water, gas, etc. [ME, from ONF, from L: cloak] —**escapable**, *adj.* —**escaper, escapee**, *n.*

escapement /əs'keɪpmənt/, *n.* the part of a watch or clock which measures beats and controls the speed of the pendulum or balance wheel.

escape velocity, *n.* the minimum velocity that a body needs in order to escape from the gravitational field of a planet, etc.

escapism /əs'keɪpɪzəm/, *n.* the avoiding of reality through entertainment, imagination, etc. —**escapist**, *adj., n.*

escapology /eskə'pɒlədʒi/, *n.* the art of escaping from chains, ropes, etc. —**escapologist**, *n.*

escarpment /əs'kɑːpmənt/, *n.* **1.** a long, cliff-like ridge of rock usu. formed by faulting or fracturing of the earth's crust. **2.** ground cut into a steep slope around a fortification, castle, etc.

-esce, a suffix of verbs meaning to begin to be or do something, become, grow, as in *convalesce, deliquesce.* [L]

-escence, a suffix of nouns indicating action or process, change, state, or condition, etc., and corresponding to verbs ending in *-esce* or adjectives ending in *-escent*, as in *convalescence, deliquescence.* [L]

-escent, a suffix of adjectives meaning beginning to be or do something, becoming or being somewhat (as indicated), as in *convalescent, deliquescent,* often associated with verbs ending in *-esce* or nouns ending in *-escence*. [L]

eschatology /ɛskəˈtɒlədʒi/, *n.* (theology relating to) the doctrines of the end of the world, death, judgment, etc. [Gk: last] — **eschatological,** *adj.* — **eschatologist,** *n.*

eschew /əsˈtʃu, ɛsˈ-/, *v.t.* to avoid; shun: *to eschew evil.* [ME, from OF, from Gmc] — **eschewal,** *n.*

Escoffier /ɛsˈkɒfieɪ/, *n.* **(Georges) Auguste** /oʊˈgyst/, 1846–1935, French chef; awarded the Legion of Honor in 1920.

escort /ˈɛskɔt/, *n.*; /əsˈkɔt, ɛsˈ-/, *v.* ◇*n.* **1.** person(s), ship(s), etc., going with other(s) to give protection, guidance, or honor. **2.** someone going with another to a dance, party, etc.; partner. ◇*v.t.* **3.** to go with (someone) as an escort. [F, from It: guide, from L]

escutcheon /əsˈkʌtʃən/, *n.* **1.** a shield or shield-shaped surface, on which a coat of arms is drawn. **2. blot on the escutcheon,** a stain on one's honor or reputation. [AF, from L: shield] — **escutcheoned,** *adj.*

-ese, a noun and adjective suffix referring to place, nationality, language, writing style, etc., as in *Japanese, journalese.* [OF, from L]

ESE, *Abbrev.* east-south-east. See Appendix.

Eskimo /ˈɛskəmoʊ, ˈɛski-/, *n.*, *pl.* **-mos, -mo.** (one of) a race or people, with short stature, muscular build, light brown skin, and broad, flat face, living in areas of Greenland, northern Canada, Alaska, and north-eastern Siberia. [Dan, from F *Esquimaux* (pl.), from Algonquian name for the people, meaning eaters of raw flesh]

esky /ˈɛski/, *n.* a portable box for keeping food and drink cool. [Trademark]

esoteric /ɛsəˈtɛrɪk, esoʊ-/, *adj.* understood by, meant for, or belonging to a select few or to a special field of study; recondite. [Gk: inner] — **esoterically,** *adv.* — **esotericism, esotery,** *n.*

esp., *Abbrev.* especially.

ESP /i ɛs ˈpi/, *n. Abbrev.* extrasensory perception; perception or communication outside normal sensory activity, as in telepathy and clairvoyance. Also, **e.s.p.**

especial /əsˈpɛʃəl/, *adj.* **1.** special; exceptional; outstanding. **2.** of a particular kind. [ME, from OF, from L: pertaining to a particular kind] — **especially,** *adv.*

Esperance /ˈɛspərəns/, *n.* a coastal town and shire in southern central WA, about 200 km south of Norseman; port and tourist centre. Pop. 6440 (1986).

Esperanto /ɛspəˈræntoʊ/, *n.* an artificial language invented in 1887 by LL Zamenhof and intended for international auxiliary use. It is based on the commonest words in the most important European languages. [Sp *esperanza* hope, used by Zamenhof as a pseudonym]

espionage /ˈɛspiənəʒ, -nadʒ/, *n.* **1.** the practice of spying on others. **2.** the organised use of spies by governments to discover the secrets of other nations. [F: spy upon, from *espion* spy, from It, from Gmc]

esplanade /ˈɛspləneɪd, -nad/, *n.* any open level space for public walks, etc., esp. one by the sea. [F, from Sp, from L: level]

espouse /əsˈpauz, ɛsˈ-/, *v.t.,* **-poused, -pousing. 1.** to make (an idea, cause, etc.) one's own; adopt; embrace. **2.** to take in marriage; marry. [MF, from L: betroth, espouse] — **espousal,** *n.* — **espouser,** *n.*

espresso /ɛsˈprɛsoʊ/, *n.* coffee made by forcing steam through ground coffee beans. [It: expressed (coffee)]

esprit /əsˈpri, ɛsˈ-/, *n.* wit; sprightliness; lively intelligence. [F, from L: spirit]

espy /əsˈpaɪ, ɛsˈ-/, *v.t.,* **-pied, -pying.** to see at a distance; catch sight of; detect. [ME, from OF, from Gmc] — **espier,** *n.*

Esq, *Abbrev.* Esquire.

-esque, an adjective suffix indicating style, manner, or distinctive character, as in *arabesque, picturesque, statuesque.* [F, from It *-esco;* of Gmc orig.]

esquire /əsˈkwaɪə, ˈɛs-/, *n.* **1.** a polite title (usu. shortened to *Esq*) after a man's last name (*Mr* or *Dr* is left out when it is used): *John Smith, Esq* **2.** *Brit.* a member of the order of gentry next below a knight. [ME *esquier,* from OF, from LL *scūtārius* shield-bearer, from L *scūtum* shield]

-ess, a suffix forming feminine nouns, as in *countess, hostess, lioness.* [F, from L, from Gk]

essay /ˈɛseɪ/ *for def. 1,* /ˈɛseɪ, ɛˈseɪ/ *for def. 2, n.;* /ɛˈseɪ/, *v.* ◇*n.* **1.** a short piece of writing on a particular subject, often to argue a point of view. **2.** an effort (sometimes hesitant) to do or achieve something; attempt. ◇*v.t.* **3.** to try; attempt. [MF, from LL: a weighing]

essence /ˈɛsəns/, *n.* **1.** the basic character of a thing; intrinsic nature. **2.** a substance containing the characteristic properties of a plant, drug, etc., in concentrated form: *vanilla essence.* **3.** perfume. [ME, from L]

essential /əˈsɛnʃəl/, *adj.* **1.** totally necessary; indispensable: *Discipline is essential in an army.* **2.** relating to or forming the essence of something. ◇*n.* **3.** the main part; an indispensable element: *Concentrate on essentials rather than details.* See ESSENCE. [ME, from LL *essentiālis*] — **essentiality,** *n.*

essential amino acid, *n.* any amino acid which cannot be produced by the body, but must be supplied in the diet.

essential oil, *n.* any of a class of volatile oils obtained from plants, used in making perfumes, flavors, etc.

Essex[1] /ˈɛsəks/, *n.* **Robert Devereux** /ˈdɛvəru/, **Earl of,** 1566–1601, a favorite of Queen Elizabeth I who led an unsuccessful rebellion against the officials of her government in 1601 and was later executed for treason.

Essex[2] /ˈɛsəks/, *n.* a county in south-eastern England. Pop. 1 512 100 (1986 est.);

3957 km². *Administrative Centre:* Chelmsford. **2.** an Anglo-Saxon kingdom in the early seventh century.

-est, a suffix forming the superlative degree of adjectives and adverbs, as in *warmest, fastest, soonest*. [OE *-est, -ost*]

est., *Abbrev.* **1.** established. **2.** estimated.

establish /əsˈtæblɪʃ/, *v.t.* **1.** to set up on a firm or permanent basis; institute; found: *to establish a business*; *to establish a university*. **2.** to settle or install (someone) in a position, business, etc. **3.** to settle (oneself) as if permanently. **4.** to cause to be accepted: *to establish a custom*; *to establish a precedent*. **5.** to show (a fact, claim, etc.) to be valid; prove. **6.** to appoint or ordain (a law, etc.). **7.** to bring about: *to establish peace*. **8.** to make (a church) a state institution. [ME, from OF, from L: make stable]

establishment /əsˈtæblɪʃmənt, es-/, *n.* **1.** the act of establishing. **2.** something established, esp. an organisation or institution. **3. the Establishment,** those people collectively, whose opinions are said to have influence in society and government. **4.** office or home and everything connected with it (as furniture, grounds, employees, etc.).

estate /əˈsteɪt, es-/, *n.* **1.** an area (esp. large) of landed property: *to have an estate in the country*. **2.** *Law.* **a.** an interest in land, either as freehold or as leasehold. **b.** the total extent of the property of a person: *the estate of a deceased person*. **3.** a housing or industrial development. **4.** a period or condition of life or circumstances (sometimes with ref. to worldly prosperity or rank): *to attain to man's estate*. **5.** a political or social group or class: *The lords spiritual, lords temporal and the commons are the three estates of the realm*. **6.** *Archaic.* pomp or state. [ME, from OF, from L]

estate agent, *n.* someone who sells or manages properties, esp. houses, as an agent for the owners.

estate duty, *n.* → **death duty.**

esteem /əsˈtiːm/, *v.t.* **1.** to regard as valuable; respect: *I esteem him highly*. **2.** to consider (something) as being of a certain value: *I esteem it worthless*. ◇*n.* **3.** favorable opinion or judgment; respect or regard: *to hold her in high esteem*. [ME, from MF, from L]

ester /ˈɛstə/, *n.* an organic compound formed by the reaction between an organic acid and an alcohol, with water also being produced. See **salt.** [coined by L Gmelin, 1788–1853, German chemist] —**esterify,** *v.*

estimable /ˈɛstəməbəl/, *adj.* **1.** deserving respect or esteem. **2.** able to be estimated.

estimate /ˈɛstəmeɪt/, *v.*, **-mated, -mating;** /ˈɛstəmət/, *n.* ◇*v.t.* **1.** to approximately calculate (the value, size, weight, etc.). **2.** to form an opinion of; judge. ◇*n.* **3.** an approximate calculation of the value, amount, possible cost, etc., of something. **4.** a judgment or opinion. [L: valued, rated] —**estimative,** *adj.*

estimation /ɛstəˈmeɪʃən/, *n.* **1.** a judgment or opinion: *in my estimation*. **2.** esteem; respect: *to hold in high estimation*. **3.** an approximate calculation; estimate: *to make an estimation of one's resources*.

Estonia /esˈtoʊniə/, *n.* a republic in northern Europe on the Baltic Sea, south of the Gulf of Finland; a constituent republic of the Soviet Union 1940–91, known as the **Estonian Soviet Socialist Republic.** Pop. 1 573 000 (1989 est.); 47 397 km². *Language:* Estonian. *Cap.:* Tallinn. Also, **Esthonia.** —**Estonian,** *n., adj.*

estrange /əˈstreɪndʒ/, *v.t.*, **estranged, estranging. 1.** to lose the affection of (someone); alienate. **2.** to remove to or keep (usu. oneself) at a distance. [ME, from MF, from L: foreign] —**estrangement,** *n.*

estuary /ˈɛstʃuəri, ˈɛstʃəri/, *n., pl.* **-aries.** that part of the mouth or lower course of a river in which its current meets the sea's tides, and is subject to their effects. [L: a heaving motion, surge, tide] —**estuarial, estuarine,** *adj.*

-et, a noun suffix orig. indicating smallness (now lost in many words), as in *islet, bullet, facet, midget*. [OF *-et* masc., *-ette* fem.]

ETA /i ti ˈeɪ/, *Abbrev.* estimated time of arrival.

et al. /et ˈæl/, *Abbrev.* and others. [L *et alii*]

etc., *Abbrev.* → **et cetera.**

et cetera /ət ˈsɛtrə/, and others; and so forth; and so on (used to show that more of the same sort might have been mentioned, but for shortness are left out). *Abbrev.:* etc. [L *et cētera* and the rest]

etceteras /ətˈsɛtrəz, ɛt-, -ərəz/, *n.pl.* **1.** other things or persons unspecified. **2.** extras or sundries.

etch /etʃ/, *v.t.* **1.** to cut, bite, or corrode with acid; engrave (metals, etc.) with acid, esp. to form a design which when inked will give an impression on paper. **2.** to produce or copy (a design) by this method. **3.** to portray or outline clearly (a character, features, etc.). **4.** to fix in the memory; to root firmly in the mind. [D, from G: feed, corrode, etch] —**etcher,** *n.*

etching /ˈɛtʃɪŋ/, *n.* **1.** a process of making designs or pictures on a metal plate, glass, etc., by corrosion of acid instead of by burin. **2.** an impression taken from an etched plate. **3.** a plate on which such a design is etched.

eternal /əˈtɜːnəl, i-/, *adj.* **1.** lasting throughout eternity; without beginning or end: *eternal life*. **2.** perpetual; ceaseless: *eternal quarrelling*; *eternal chatter*. **3.** enduring; immutable: *eternal principles*. **4. the Eternal,** God.

eternal triangle, *n. Colloq.* the relationship of husband, wife, and mistress or lover, considered to be a common social situation.

eternity /əˈtɜːnəti, i-/, *n., pl.* **-ties. 1.** infinite time, continuing without beginning or end. **2.** eternal existence, esp. as contrasted with or following mortal life. **3.** (seemingly) endless period of time: *The doctor took an eternity to arrive*. [ME, from OF, from L]

-eth¹, the ending of the third person singular present indicative of verbs, now occurring only in old forms of English or used in serious or poetic language, as in *doeth* or *doth, hath, hopeth, sitteth*. [OE *-eth, -ath, -oth, -th*]

-eth[2], the form of *-th*, the ordinal suffix, after a vowel, as in *twentieth, thirtieth, etc.* See **-th**[2].

ethanal /'iθənæl, 'eθ-/, *n. Chem.* → **acetaldehyde**. See **-al**[3].

ethane /'iθeɪn/, *n.* an odorless, gaseous hydrocarbon, C_2H_6, an alkane, present in crude petroleum, etc. [ETH(ER) + -ANE]

ethanoic acid /εθə'noʊɪk/, *n.* → **acetic acid**.

ethanol /'εθənɒl, 'εθ-/, *n. Chem.* → **alcohol**. [ETHAN(E) + -OL[1]]

Ethelbert /'εθəlbət/, *n.* 552–616, king of Kent 560–616; issued the earliest known code of English laws. Also, **Aethelbert**.

ethene /'εθin/, *n. Chem.* → **ethylene**. See **-ene**.

ether /'iθə/, *n.* **1.** *Chem.* **a.** a highly volatile and flammable colorless liquid (**ethyl ether**), $(C_2H_5)_2O$, obtained by the action of sulfuric acid on alcohol, and used as a solvent and formerly as an anaesthetic. **b.** one of a class of organic compounds in which any two organic radicals are attached directly to oxygen, having the general formula R_2O. **2.** the upper regions of space; clear sky; heavens. [L, from Gk: upper air, sky]

ethereal /ə'θɪəriəl, i-/, *adj.* **1.** light; airy. **2.** extremely delicate or refined: *ethereal beauty.* **3.** heavenly.

etherise or **etherize** /'iθəraɪz/, *v.t.*, **-rised, -rising.** to put under the influence of ether. —**etherisation**, *n.* —**etheriser**, *n.*

ethic /'εθɪk/, *adj.* relating to morals; ethical. [L, from Gk: of morals, moral]

ethical /'εθɪkəl/, *adj.* **1.** relating to or dealing with morals or right or wrong conduct. **2.** in agreement with the rules or standards for (professional) right conduct or practice: *It is not ethical for doctors to advertise.*

ethics /'εθɪks/, *n.pl.* **1.** a system of moral principles, used to judge human action. **2.** the rules of conduct of a person, group etc.: *medical ethics.*

Ethiopia /iθi'oʊpiə/, *n.* a republic in northeastern Africa, on the Red Sea; an empire before the deposing of Emperor Haile Selassie in 1974; in 1952 federated with Eritrea which became independent in 1991–92 after civil war. Pop. 45 568 586 (based on 1989 est.); 1 106 100 km[2]. *Languages:* Amharic, also English and Arabic. *Currency:* birr. *Cap.:* Addis Ababa. Formerly, **Abyssinia**.

ethnic /'εθnɪk/, *adj.* **1.** relating to a population or particular group and their history, customs, language etc. **2.** of or relating to members of the community who are migrants or children of migrants and whose original language is not English. **3.** coming from a particular culture: *ethnic music.* ◇*n.* **4.** a member of an ethnic group. [ME, from LL, from Gk: national, gentile, heathen] —**ethnically**, *adv.*

ethno-, a word part meaning 'race', 'nation', as in *ethnology.* [Gk, combining form of *éthnos*]

ethnocentrism /εθnoʊ'sεntrɪzəm/, *n.* the belief that one's own group or culture is better than all others, having with it a feeling of scorn for other groups and cultures. —**ethnocentric**, *adj.*

ethnography /εθ'nɒɡrəfi/, *n.* the scientific description or study of cultures and races. —**ethnographer**, *n.*

ethnology /εθ'nɒlədʒi/, *n.* the study of the groups of mankind, their history, speech, etc. —**ethnological, ethnologic**, *adj.* —**ethnologist**, *n.*

ethos /'iθɒs/, *n.* **1.** character. **2.** *Sociol.* the basic spiritual character of a culture. [NL, from Gk: character]

ethyl /'εθəl, 'iθaɪl/, *n.* **1.** *Chem.* a univalent radical, C_2H_5, from ethane. **2.** a type of antiknock fluid, containing lead tetraethyl and other ingredients for a more even combustion. **3.** petrol to which this fluid has been added. [ETH(ER) + -YL] —**ethylic**, *adj.*

ethyl acetate, *n. Chem.* a colorless liquid ester with a fruity smell, used as solvent for paints, etc., as a flavoring and in perfume.

ethyl alcohol, *n.* See **alcohol**.

ethylene /'εθəlin/, *n. Chem.* a colorless, flammable gas, C_2H_4, an alkene, with an unpleasant smell, the first member of the alkene series. Also, **ethene**.

ethylene group, *n.* the bivalent radical, -CH_2CH_2-, derived from ethylene (ethene) or ethane.

ethylene series, *n. Chem.* → **alkene series**.

ethyl ether, *n.* See **ether** (def. 1a).

ethyne /'εθaɪn/, *n. Chem.* → **acetylene**.

etiolate /'itioʊleɪt/, *v.t.*, **-lated, -lating.** *Bot.* to cause (a plant) to whiten by removing light. [F: blanch] —**etiolation**, *n.*

etiquette /'εtɪkət/, *n.* the established code of behavior in a social class, community or profession for any occasion. [F, in OF: of Gmc orig.]

Etna /'εtnə/, *n.* **Mount**, an active volcano in eastern Sicily. 3279 m. Also, **Aetna**.

Eton College /itn 'kɒlɪdʒ/, *n.* a British non-government boys' school founded in 1440 by Henry VI.

Etruscan /ə'trʌskən/, *adj.* relating to Etruria, an ancient country in western Italy, its inhabitants, civilisation, art, or language. [L]

et seq., *pl.* **et seqq., et sqq.** and the following. [L *et sequens*]

-ette, a noun suffix, feminine form of **-et**, to show **a.** something made small as in *cigarette.* **b.** the feminine form of a word as in *usherette.* **c.** goods made as imitation of some more expensive material, as in *leatherette.* [F, fem. of *-et* -ET]

etym., *Abbrev.* **1.** etymological. **2.** etymology. Also, **etymol**.

etymology /εtə'mɒlədʒi/, *n., pl.* **-gies.** *Linguistics.* **1.** the study of historical linguistic change, esp. in individual words. **2.** an explanation of the history of a particular word. **3.** the analysis of the parts (prefixes, etc.) which make up a word. [L, from Gk] —**etymological, etymologic**, *adj.* —**etymologist**, *n.*

eu-, a prefix meaning 'good', 'well'. [Gk]

Eu, *Chem. Symbol.* europium.

eucalypt /'jukəlɪpt/, *n.* a gum tree. See **gum**[1] (def. 4).

eucalyptus /jukə'lɪptəs/, *n., pl.* **-tuses, -ti** /-taɪ/, *adj.* ◇*n.* **1.** *Bot.* evergreen tree commonly found in Australia, used for timber and oil. ◇*adj.* **2.** of or relating to a preparation, sweet, etc., containing eucalyptus oil. [NL, from *eu-* EU- + Gk *kalyptós* covered (with allusion to the cap covering the buds)]

Eucharist /'jukərəst/, *n. Church.* the (bread and wine) of the Lord's Supper. [LL, from Gk: gratefulness, thanksgiving, the eucharist] —**Eucharistic**, *adj.*

euchre /'jukə/, *n. Cards.* a game played by two, three, or four people, with the 32 (or 28 or 24) highest cards in the pack. [orig. uncert.]

Euclid /'juklɪd/, *n.* **1.** fl. c. 300 BC, Greek geometrician of Alexandria; his *Elements* of the principles of geometry is still a widely-used text. **2.** the works of Euclid, esp. his treatise on geometry. —**Euclidean, Euclidian**, *adj.*

Eucumbene /'jukəmbin/, *n.* **Lake**, a lake in south-eastern NSW, near Cooma; the main regulating storage of the Snowy Mountains Hydro-Electric Scheme. About 145 km².

eugenic /ju'dʒinɪk, -'dʒen-/, *adj.* of, bringing about, or showing improvement in the type of offspring produced. [Gk: well born] —**eugenically**, *adv.*

eugenics /ju'dʒinɪks, -'dʒen-/, *n.* the science of improving qualities of the human race, esp. by the careful choice of parents. —**eugenicist**, *n.*

euglena /ju'glinə/, *n. Zool.* a green type of protozoan with one flagellum and a red eyespot, oft. used for class and experimental study.

Eugowra /ju'gaʊrə/, *n.* a town in central NSW, east of Forbes; site of the only escorted gold coach robbery by bushrangers, in 1862. Pop. 579 (1986).

Euler /'ɔɪlə/, *n.* **Leonhard** /'leɪɒnhat/, 1707–1783, Swiss mathematician; founder of modern mathematical analysis.

eulogy /'julədʒi/, *n., pl.* **-gies**. **1.** a speech or writing in praise of a person or thing, esp. one to honor a dead person. **2.** high praise. [ML, from Gk: praise] —**eulogise**, *v.*

eunuch /'junək/, *n.* a castrated man. [ME, from L, from Gk: chamber attendant]

euph., *Abbrev.* **1.** euphemism. **2.** euphemistic.

euphemism /'jufəmɪzəm/, *n.* a mild word or phrase chosen to replace one that is more direct but less pleasant: *'To pass away' is a euphemism for 'to die'.* [Gk: use fair words]

euphonium /ju'foʊniəm/, *n. Music.* a tenor tuba mainly used in brass bands. [NL, from Gk: well-sounding]

euphony /'jufəni/, *n., pl.* **-nies**. pleasing quality of sound, esp. of speech sounds. [LL, from Gk: well-sounding] —**euphonious**, *adj.*

euphoria /ju'fɔriə/, *n.* a feeling or state of well-being, esp. one of unnatural joy. [NL, from Gk: bearing well] —**euphoric**, *adj.*

Euphrates /ju'freɪtiz/, *n.* a river flowing from eastern Turkey through Syria and Iraq, joining the Tigris to form the Shatt-al-Arab near the Persian Gulf. 2736 km.

euplastic /ju'plæstɪk/, *adj. Physiol.* capable of being changed into organised tissue. [Gk: easy to mould]

Eur., *Abbrev.* **1.** Europe. **2.** European.

eurabbie /ju'ræbi/, *n.* a type of eucalyptus tree found in eastern Australia with waxy bluish young leaves and white flowers; blue gum.

Eurasian /ju'reɪʒən/, *adj.* **1.** relating to Europe and Asia taken together. **2.** of mixed European and Asian descent. ◇*n.* **3.** a person one of whose parents is European and the other Asian.

eureka /ju'rikə/, *interj.* (a cry of victory at a supposed discovery). [Gk: I have found (it)]

Eureka flag, *n. Hist.* a blue flag bearing a white cross, with a star at the end of each arm, first raised at the Eureka Stockade in 1854 and more recently associated with the move to make Australia a republic.

Eureka Stockade, *n.* an armed rebellion of goldminers in Vic in 1854; arose out of a number of grievances including a 30 shillings tax on miners, lack of political representation, difficulties with land tenure and competition from the Chinese.

eurhythmics /ju'rɪðmɪks/, *n.* the art of expressing in bodily movements the rhythm of musical pieces. —**eurhythmic**, *adj.*

Euripides /ju'rɪpədiz/, *n.* 480?–406? BC, Athenian tragic poet and dramatist; plays include *Alcestis, Medea,* and *Electra.*

euro /'juroʊ/, *n. Zool.* see **kangaroo**.

Euro-, (*sometimes l.c.*) a prefix meaning 'European'. Also, *before a vowel*, **Eur-**.

eurodollar /'juroʊdɒlə/, *n.* a US dollar held in European banks and used to finance trade.

Europa /ju'roʊpə/, *n. Gk Myth.* a Phoenician princess taken to Crete by Zeus (who was disguised in the form of a white bull); the mother by him of Rhadamanthys, Minos, and Sarpedon.

Europe /'jurəp/, *n.* the continent which is the western part of the Eurasian landmass.

European /jurə'piən/, *adj.* **1.** relating to Europe or its inhabitants. **2.** coming from Europe. ◇*n.* **3.** someone born or living in Europe.

European Community, *n.* an association of European countries orig. established as three distinct communities, the European Coal and Steel Community (formed 1951), the European Economic Community (formed 1957) and the European Atomic Energy Community (formed 1957), supervised by a single commission since 1967; original members, Belgium, France, West Germany, Italy, Luxembourg and the Netherlands, were joined by the UK, Denmark and

Ireland in 1973, Greece in 1981, and Portugal and Spain in 1986; in 1990 West German membership was replaced by that of the reunited Germany. *Abbrev.*: EC

European Economic Community, *n.* an association created in 1957 to abolish internal tariffs among member countries and establish a common external tariff. See **European Community.** Also, the **Common Market.** *Abbrev.*: EEC

europium /ju'roupiəm/, *n.* a rare-earth metallic element with light pink salts. *Symbol:* Eu; *at. no.:* 63; *at. wt:* 151.96. [NL, from L *Europa* Europe]

eury-, a word part meaning 'broad'. [Gk, combining form of *eurýs*]

Eurydice /ju'rɪdəsi, ju-/, *n. Gk Myth.* the wife of Orpheus, permitted by Pluto to follow her husband out of Hades, but lost to him because he disobediently looked back at her. See **Orpheus.**

Eustachian tube /ju'steɪʃən tjub/, *n.* a canal leading from the middle ear to the pharynx (at the back of the mouth); auditory canal. [from Bartolommeo *Eustachio* fl. 1574, Italian anatomist]

eustatic movement /ju'stætɪk ˌmuvmənt/, *n. Geol.* the world-wide change in sea-level due to increase or decrease in the volume of water in seas, which may be caused by melting of icesheets.

euthanasia /juθə'neɪʒə/, *n.* **1.** painless death. **2.** the putting of a person to death painlessly, esp. a person suffering from an incurable and painful disease. [NL, from Gk: an easy death]

eV, *Symbol.* electronvolt.

evacuate /ə'vækjueɪt/, *v.t.,* **-ated, -ating. 1.** to leave (a town, etc.) empty; vacate. **2.** to move (people or things) from a disaster area, etc., to a safer place. **3.** to discharge (wastes) esp. from the bowels. [L: emptied out] —**evacuator,** *n.* —**evacuation,** *n.*

evacuee /əvækju'i/, *n.* someone who is removed from a place of danger.

evade /ə'veɪd, i-/, *v.t.,* **evaded, evading. 1.** to get round or escape from by trickery or cleverness: *to evade the law; to evade pursuit.* **2.** to avoid doing: *to evade a duty.* **3.** to keep from answering directly: *to evade a question.* [L: pass over, go out]

evaluate /ə'væljueɪt, i-/, *v.t.,* **-ated, -ating. 1.** to test and find the value, quality, etc. of; appraise. **2.** *Maths.* to find the numerical value of. [F, from OF: be worth, from L] —**evaluation,** *n.*

evangelical /ivæn'dʒɛləkəl/, ◇*adj. Church.* **1.** relating to the gospel and its teachings. **2.** relating to those Christian groups which place importance on the teachings and power of the Scriptures, rather than of the church itself, or of reason. **3.** evangelistic. ◇*n.* **4.** a follower of evangelical teachings or a member of an evangelical church.

evangelist /ə'vændʒələst, i-/, *n.* **1.** a preacher of the gospel. **2.** (*cap.*) any of the writers (Matthew, Mark, Luke, and John) of the four Gospels. **3.** one of a class of teachers in the early church, next in rank after apostles and prophets. [Gk: good messenger] —**evangelistic,** *adj.*

Evans /'ɛvənz/, *n.* **1. Sir Arthur John,** 1851–1941, English archaeologist. **2. Dame Edith,** 1888–1976, English actress. **3. George Essex,** 1863–1909, Australian poet, born in England; best-known work, *The Women of the West.* **4. George William,** 1780–1852, Australian explorer, born in England; explored the Blue Mountains and Bathurst districts of NSW and accompanied John Oxley's 1817–18 expeditions to the western plains; government surveyor in Tasmania.

evaporate /ə'væpəreɪt, i-/, *v.i., v.t.,* **-rated, -rating. 1.** to turn or change to vapor. **2.** to give off moisture, or take moisture from. **3.** to disappear or cause to disappear; fade. [LL: dispersed in vapor] —**evaporator,** *n.* —**evaporation,** *n.*

evasion /ə'veɪʒən, i-/, *n.* **1.** the act or means of escaping something by trickery or cleverness: *evasion of one's duty.* **2.** the avoiding of an argument, question, etc. **3.** a way of evading; subterfuge. [ME, from LL] —**evasive,** *adj.*

Evatt family /'ɛvət/, *n.* an Australian family prominent in the fields of law and politics. **1. Herbert Vere,** 1894–1965, federal Labor politician, judge and writer; leader of the Federal Opposition 1951–60. **2.** his brother, **Clive Raleigh,** born 1900, lawyer and state politician. **3. Elizabeth Andreas,** born 1933, daughter of Clive, lawyer; chief judge of the Family Court of Australia 1976–88; the first Australian woman to preside in a Federal court.

eve /iv/, *n.* **1.** the evening, or the day before any date or event: *Christmas eve.* **2.** the period just before any event, etc.: *the eve of a revolution.* [var. of EVEN²]

Eve /iv/, *n. Bible.* the first woman. [See Genesis 3:20. ME; OE, from L *Eva,* from Gk, from Heb explained as 'mother of the living']

even¹ /'ivən/, *adj.* **1.** level; flat; smooth: *an even surface.* **2.** on the same level: *even with the ground.* **3.** free from variations; regular; uniform: *even motion.* **4.** equal in measure: *even quantities.* **5.** divisible by two, thus, 2, 4, 6, 8, etc. are *even* numbers (opposed to *odd,* as 1, 3, etc.). **6.** marked by such a number: *the even pages of a book.* **7.** exactly expressible in whole numbers, or in tens, hundreds, etc., without fractional parts: *an even hundred.* **8.** exactly balanced on each side. **9.** not easily excited or angered; calm; placid: *an even temper.* **10.** fair; impartial: *an even bargain.* ◇*adv.* **11.** evenly. **12.** still; yet: *even more suitable.* **13.** (used to suggest the idea of something unusual or not expected): *The slightest noise, even, disturbs him.* **14.** just: *even now.* **15.** indeed (used as an intensive): *He is willing, even eager, to do it.* **16. break even,** to have one's profits and losses equal. **17. get even,**

even to get one's revenge. ◇*v.t., v.i.* **18.** to make or become even, level or smooth (oft. fol. by *out* or *off*). [OE *efen*]

even² /'ivən/, *n. Archaic.* evening. [OE *ēfen*]

evening /'ivnɪŋ/, *n.* **1.** the later part of the day and the early part of the night. **2.** any ending or weakening period: *the evening of life.* **3.** *Qld.* (esp. in rural areas) the period of the day after midday. ◇*adj.* **4.** relating to evening. [OE *æfnung*, from *æfnian* draw towards evening]

evening star, *n.* a bright planet, esp. Venus, seen in the west after sunset.

event /ə'vɛnt, i-/, *n.* **1.** anything that happens or is understood as happening, esp. something of importance. **2.** the fact of happening (esp. in the phrase *in the event of*): *In the event of rain, we will not be able to go.* **3.** the outcome, or result of anything (esp. in the phrase *after the event*). **4.** *Sport.* each of the items in a program of sport(s). **5. at all events** or **in any event**, whatever happens; in any case. [L: occurrence, issue] **—eventless,** *adj.*

eventual /ə'vɛntʃəl, -tʃuəl/, *adj.* **1.** resulting, or happening in the end; ultimate: *Who was the eventual winner?* **2.** depending upon uncertain or possible events.

eventuality /əvɛntʃu'æləti/, *n., pl.* **-ties.** a possible event or circumstance.

eventually /ə'vɛntʃəli, -tʃuəli/, *adv.* finally; ultimately.

eventuate /ə'vɛntʃueɪt/, *v.i.*, **-ated, -ating. 1.** to result: *The delay eventuated in our missing the plane.* **2.** to come about; happen: *Did your promotion eventuate?*

ever /'ɛvə/, *adv.* **1.** at all times: *He is ever ready to help.* **2.** continuously: *ever since then.* **3.** at any time: *Did you ever see anything like it?* **4.** (with emphatic force) by any chance; at all: *How ever did you manage?* **5. ever so,** to whatever degree; greatly: *ever so long.* [OE *æfre*, probably akin to *ā* ever]

Everage /'ɛvrɪdʒ/, *n.* **Dame Edna,** Moonee Ponds housewife-superstar, a character created by Barry Humphries.

Everest /'ɛvərəst/, *n.* **Mount,** a peak of the Himalayas, on the border between Nepal and the Xizang AR (Tibet); highest mountain in the world. 8848 m. Tibetan, **Chomolungma** ('mother goddess of the earth').

Everglades /'ɛvəgleɪdz/, *n.pl.* a swampy and partly forested region in the US, southern Florida, mostly south of Lake Okeechobee. Over 12 950 km².

evergreen /'ɛvəgrin/, *adj.* **1.** (of trees, shrubs, etc.) having living leaves all year long (opposed to *deciduous*). **2.** still popular, or seemingly youthful: *an evergreen song; an evergreen tennis player.* ◇*n.* **3.** an evergreen plant.

everlasting /ɛvə'lastɪŋ/, *adj.* **1.** always; forever: *everlasting God.* **2.** lasting or continuing for a long time. **3.** constantly happening; incessant: *I seem to have everlasting worries.* ◇*n.* **4.** eternity. **5.** Also, **everlasting flower.** any of various plants or flowers which keep their shape, color, etc., when dried.

Evert /'ɛvət/, *n.* **Chris(tine),** born 1954, US tennis player; ranked top woman player in the world 1974–1977.

every /'ɛvri/, *adj.* **1.** each (referring one by one to all the members of a group): *We go there every day.* **2.** all possible: *He has every chance of success.* **3. every bit,** *Colloq.* in all respects: *every bit as good.* **4. every now and then** or **every now and again** or **every once in a while,** from time to time; occasionally. **5. every other,** every second; every alternate: *The cleaner came every other day.* [OE *æfre ælc* EVER EACH]

everybody /'ɛvribɒdi/, *pron.* every person.

everyday /'ɛvrideɪ/, *adj.* **1.** of or relating to every day; daily. **2.** of or for ordinary days; as contrasted with special occasions: *everyday clothes.* **3.** ordinary; commonplace: *an everyday scene.*

everyone /'ɛvriwʌn/, *pron.* every person; everybody. Also, **every one.**

everything /'ɛvriθɪŋ/, *pron.* **1.** every thing or detail of a group or total; all. **2.** something very important: *This news means everything to us.*

evict /ə'vɪkt, i-/, *v.t.* to dispossess (an occupier), lawfully or unlawfully, from land, a building, etc. [L: overcome completely, (property) recovered by judicial decision] **—eviction,** *n.* **—evictor,** *n.*

evidence /'ɛvədəns/, *n., v.,* **-denced, -dencing.** ◇*n.* **1.** anything which tends to prove or disprove something; proof. **2.** that which makes something clear; sign. **3.** *Law.* the information, spoken or written, or objects (such as a photograph, a revolver, etc.) recognised by witnesses, and offered to the court or jury in proof of the facts being argued. **4. in evidence,** able to be easily seen; conspicuous. ◇*v.t.* **5.** to make evident or clear; show clearly: *The flowers evidenced an early spring.* **6.** to support by evidence: *He evidenced his claim with documents.*

evident /'ɛvədənt/, *adj.* plain or clear to the sight or understanding: *an evident mistake.* [L]

evidently /'ɛvədəntli/, *adv.* according to given information; apparently; obviously: *They were evidently caught stealing; He is evidently upset.*

evil /'ivəl/, *adj.* **1.** breaking the moral law; wicked: *an evil life; an evil person.* **2.** harmful; injurious: *evil laws.* **3.** marked by misfortune or suffering; disastrous: *The drought was an evil time for us.* **4. the evil one,** the devil; Satan. ◇*n.* **5.** anything which is evil; evil quality, conduct, etc.: *to choose the lesser of two evils.* **6.** harm; mischief; misfortune: *to wish one evil.* **7.** anything causing injury or harm. [OE *yfel*]

evil eye, *n.* the supposed power of certain people of causing injury or bad luck by a look. **—evil-eyed,** *adj.*

evince /ə'vɪns, i-/, *v.t.,* **evinced, evincing.** to show the possession of (a quality, trait, etc.): *She evinces pleasure in her new horse.* [L: overcome completely, prove, demonstrate]

eviscerate /ə'vɪsəreɪt, ɪ-/, *v.t.*, **-rated, -rating.** →**disembowel**. [L: disembowelled] —**evisceration**, *n.*

evocative /ə'vɒkətɪv/, *adj.* tending to evoke (memories): *That old song is evocative of my childhood.*

evoke /ə'voʊk, ɪ-/, *v.t.*, **evoked, evoking.** 1. to call up or produce (memories, feelings, etc.): *The music evoked calmness.* 2. to provoke; elicit: *That discussion evoked a response.* [L: call forth] —**evoker**, *n.*

evolution /ɛvə'luːʃən, ivə-/, *n.* 1. any process of formation or growth; development: *the evolution of man.* 2. something evolved; a product. 3. *Biol.* **a.** the gradual continuous genetic change of plants and animals to adapt to the environment. **b.** see **Darwinism**. 4. a motion incomplete in itself, but combining with other similar motions to produce a single action, as in a machine. 5. an evolving or giving off of gas, heat, etc. —**evolutionary**, *adj.* —**evolutionist**, *n.*

evolve /ə'vɒlv, ɪ-/, *v.*, **evolved, evolving.** ◇*v.t.* 1. to develop gradually: *to evolve a theory.* 2. *Biol.* to develop to a more complex condition. 3. to give off (smells, vapors, etc.) ◇*v.i.* 4. to come gradually into being; develop. [L: roll out, unroll, unfold] —**evolvement**, *n.*

ewe /juː/, *n.* a female sheep. [ME and OE]

ewer /'juːə/, *n.* a jug with a wide spout. [ME, from AF, from L: vessel for water]

ex /ɛks/, *prep.* 1. *Finance.* without, not including, or with no right to: *ex interest.* 2. *Comm.* out of; free out of: *ex warehouse, ex ship, etc.* (free of charges until time of removal from warehouse, ship, etc.). ◇*n.* 3. *Colloq.* one's former husband or wife. [L]

ex-[1], a prefix meaning 'out of', 'from', 'thoroughly' or 'former', used before vowels and *c, p, q, s, t,* as in *expatriot, exterminate, ex-wife.* Also, **e-, ef-**. [L]

ex-[2], variant of **exo-**.

Ex, *Abbrev. Bible.* Exodus.

exacerbate /ɛk'sæsəbeɪt/, *v.t.*, **-bated, -bating.** to increase the strength or violence of (disease, ill feeling, etc.); aggravate. [L: irritated] —**exacerbation**, *n.*

exact /əg'zækt, ɛg-/, *adj.* 1. strictly correct or accurate: *an exact likeness.* 2. completely right; precise: *the exact date.* 3. (of laws, discipline, etc.) strict: *He expects exact manners.* ◇*v.t.* 4. to call for or demand, sometimes by force: *to exact obedience; to exact money.* [L: forced out, required, measured by a standard] —**exacter, exactor**, *n.* —**exactness**, *n.*

exacting /əg'zæktɪŋ, ɛg-/, *adj.* 1. (of a person) severe or rigid in demands. 2. (of a task, etc.) needing complete attention or hard work.

exaction /əg'zækʃən, ɛg-/, *n.* 1. the act of exacting; extortion. 2. something exacted, esp. a tax, etc.

exactitude /əg'zæktətjuːd, ɛg-/, *n.* quality of being exact; exactness; accuracy.

exactly /əg'zæktli, ɛg-/, *adv.* 1. in an exact manner; precisely, according to rule, measure, fact, etc.; accurately. 2. *Colloq.* just: *She does exactly as she likes.* ◇*interj.* 3. quite so; that's right.

exaggerate /əg'zædʒəreɪt, ɛg-/, *v.*, **-rated, -rating.** ◇*v.t.* 1. to speak of (something) as greater than it is; overstate: *to exaggerate one's importance.* 2. to increase or enlarge abnormally. ◇*v.i.* 3. to use exaggeration, as in speech or writing: *a person who always exaggerates.* [L: heaped up] —**exaggeration**, *n.* —**exaggerated**, *adj.*

exalt /əg'zɔlt, ɛg-/, *v.t.* 1. to raise in rank, honor, power, character, etc.: *They exalted him to the position of president.* 2. to praise: *to exalt someone to the skies.* [L: lift up] —**exaltation**, *n.*

exalted /əg'zɔltəd, ɛg-/, *adj.* 1. raised, as in rank or character: *an exalted personage.* 2. uplifted, as in language; lofty: *an exalted style; exalted thoughts.* 3. very greatly excited.

examination /əgzæmə'neɪʃən, ɛg-/, *n.* 1. the act of examining; inspection; inquiry; investigation. 2. the act or process of testing students, etc., as by questions. 3. the test itself; list of questions asked. 4. the statements, etc., made by one examined. 5. *Law.* formal questioning. [L]

examine /əg'zæmən, ɛg-/, *v.t.*, **-ined, -ining.** 1. to inspect or look at carefully. 2. to test the knowledge, reactions, or abilities of (a student, etc.), esp. with questions or tasks. 3. *Law.* to question (someone) about actions or knowledge of facts; interrogate: *to examine a witness.* [ME, from F, from L: weigh accurately, test] —**examiner**, *n.*

example /əg'zæmpəl, ɛg-/, *n.* 1. one of several things, or a part of something, taken to show the character of the whole. 2. something to be followed; a pattern or model: *to set a good example.* 3. a model used to show one of a type; specimen. 4. something used to explain a rule or method, as a mathematical problem to be solved. 5. a case, esp. of punishment, used as a warning. [ME, from OF, from L]

exasperate /əg'zæspəreɪt, ɛg-/, *v.t.*, **-rated, -rating.** to annoy extremely; vex. [L: roughened] —**exasperation**, *n.*

exc., *Abbrev.* except.

Excalibur /ɛks'kæləbə/, *n.* the magic sword of King Arthur.

ex cathedra /ɛks kə'θiːdrə/, *adv.* from the seat of power; with authority, used esp. of those statements of the pope which are considered infallible. [L: from the chair] —**ex-cathedra**, *adj.*

excaudate /ɛks'kɔdeɪt/, *adj.* (of animals) tailless.

excavate /'ɛkskəveɪt/, *v.t.*, **-vated, -vating.** 1. to make hollow by removing the inner part; make a hole or cavity in. 2. to make (a hole, tunnel, etc.) by removing material. 3. to dig or scoop out (earth, etc.). 4. to lay bare or uncover by digging; unearth: *to excavate an ancient city.* [L *excavātus*, pp., hollowed out] —**excavation**, *n.* —**excavator**, *n.*

exceed /ək'siːd, ɛk-/, *v.t.* 1. to go beyond (a limit, measure) in quantity, degree etc.: *to exceed*

exceed

one's power; *to exceed the speed limit.* **2.** to be superior to; surpass. [ME, from F, from L: go out] **—exceedingly,** *adv.*

excel /ək'sel, ek-/, *v.,* **-celled, -celling.** ◇*v.t.* **1.** to be superior to; outdo: *She excels him at sport.* ◇*v.i.* **2.** to be superior in some respect: *She excels at sport.* [L]

excellence /'eksələns/, *n.* **1.** the fact or state of excelling; superiority. **2.** an excellent quality or feature. **3.** (*usu. cap.*)→**excellency** (def. 1).

excellency /'eksələnsi/, *n., pl.* **-cies. 1.** (*usu. cap.*) a title of honor given to certain high officials, as governors and ambassadors. **2.** (*usu. cap.*) a person so named. **3.** →**excellence** (defs. 1 and 2). [L]

excellent /'eksələnt/, *adj.* remarkably good; having superior quality. [ME, from L]

except[1] /ək'sept, ek-/, *prep.* **1.** leaving or taking out; excluding: *They were all there except me.* ◇*conj.* **2.** with the exception (that): *The houses were the same, except that they had different colored bricks.* **3.** otherwise than; but (fol. by an adv., phrase, or clause): *The room was well lit except in the corner.* [L: taken out]

except[2] /ək'sept, ek-/, *v.t.* to leave out; exclude: *present company excepted.* [ME, from F, from L]

excepting /ək'septɪŋ, ek-/, *prep.* excluding; barring; saving; except.

exception /ək'sepʃən, ek-/, *n.* **1.** the act or result of excepting. **2.** something excepted, or something outside a general rule. **3.** objection; opposition of opinion: *a statement liable to exception.* **4. take exception,** to make objection (usu. fol. by *to*): *I take exception to those words.* [L]

exceptional /ək'sepʃənəl, ek-/, *adj.* forming an exception; unusual; extraordinary.

excerpt /'eksɜpt, *n.;* /ek'sɜpt/, *v.* ◇*n.* **1.** a passage taken out of a book etc.; an extract. ◇*v.t.* **2.** to take out (a passage) from a book etc.; extract. [L: picked out]

excess /ək'ses, 'ek-/, *n.,* /ək-/, /'ekses/, *adj.* ◇*n.* **1.** the fact of exceeding (going beyond) something else in amount or degree. **2.** the amount or degree by which one thing exceeds another. **3.** an extreme amount or degree: *to have an excess of energy; He drank to excess.* **4.** a going beyond ordinary or proper limits, esp. in eating and drinking. ◇*adj.* **5.** more than is necessary, or usual; extra: *excess baggage.* [ME, from L: a departure] **—excessive,** *adj.*

exchange /əks'tʃeɪndʒ, ek-/, *v.,* **-changed, -changing,** *n.* ◇*v.t.* **1.** give up (something) in return for something else, usu. of equal value, quantity, etc.: *to exchange dollars for pounds.* **2.** to replace by another or something else: *to exchange a faulty tool.* **3.** (of two or more people) to each give and receive; interchange: *to exchange blows; to exchange gifts.* ◇*v.i.* **4.** to make an exchange: *We'll exchange with you.* **5.** to pass or be taken as an equivalent. ◇*n.* **6.** the act or process of exchanging: *an exchange of gifts.* **7.** something given or received in exchange for something else: *The car was a fair exchange.* **8.** a central office or station where incoming calls, letters, etc., are sorted, and redirected: *a telephone exchange.* **9.** a method or system by which debits and credits in different places are settled without the actual sending of money, by means of documents representing money values. **10.** the equal interchange of equivalent sums of money, as in the currencies of two countries. **11.** *Econ.* the varying rate or sum, in one country's money, given for a fixed sum in another; rate of exchange. [ME, from AF, from LL]

exchange rate, *n.* in international money markets, the rate at which one currency can be exchanged for another.

exchequer /əks'tʃekə/, *n.* **1.** a treasury, esp. of a state or nation. **2.** *Brit.* (*oft. cap.*) the government department controlling public money. [ME, from OF: chess board (so called with reference to the table-cover marked with squares on which accounts were reckoned with counters). See CHEQUER]

excise[1] /'eksaɪz/, *n.;* /ek'saɪz/, *v.,* **-cised, -cising.** ◇*n.* **1.** a tax or duty on certain locally made goods etc.: *an excise on tobacco.* **2.** a tax payable for a licence to carry on certain forms of work, to play certain sports, etc. ◇*v.t.* **3.** to place an excise on. [MD, from OF: a tax, from LL: tax] **—excision,** *n.*

excise[2] /ek'saɪz/, *v.t.,* **-cised, -cising. 1.** to cut out (a passage) from a book, article, etc. **2.** to cut out or off (a body part, tumor, etc.). [L: cut out] **—excision,** *n.*

excitable /ək'saɪtəbəl, ek-/, *adj.* able to be excited; easily excited.

excite /ək'saɪt, ek-/, *v.t.,* **-cited, -citing. 1.** to stir up the feelings of (someone). **2.** to cause; awaken: *to excite interest.* **3.** to stir to action: *to excite a dog.* **4.** to make restless, nervous, or eager. **5.** *Physiol.* to stimulate: *to excite a nerve.* **6.** *Physics.* to raise (an atom, nucleus, or molecule) to a higher energy state than the normal. [ME, from L: call forth, rouse] **—excitation,** *n.* **—excited,** *adj.*

excitement /ək'saɪtmənt, ek-/, *n.* **1.** the state of being stirred up or excited. **2.** something that excites: *Christmas is a great excitement for the children.*

exciting /ək'saɪtɪŋ, ek-/, *adj.* producing excitement; stirring.

excl., *Abbrev.* **1.** excluding. **2.** exclusive.

exclaim /əks'kleɪm, eks-/, *v.i., v.t.* to cry out or speak suddenly and with feeling, as in surprise, etc. [L: call out] **—exclaimer,** *n.* **—exclamatory,** *adj.*

exclamation /eksklə'meɪʃən/, *n.* **1.** the act of exclaiming. **2.** a loud complaint or protest; outcry; interjection.

exclamation mark, *n.* a punctuation mark (!) used after an exclamation. Also, **exclamation point.**

exclude /əks'klud, eks-/, *v.t.,* **-cluded, -cluding. 1.** to shut or keep out; prevent the entrance of. **2.** to shut out from consideration, advantages, etc. [ME, from L] **—exclusion,** *n.*

exclusive /əks'klusɪv, eks-/, *adj.* **1.** not including or admitting of something else; incompatible: *The idea of masculine is exclusive of the idea of feminine.* **2.** excluding from consideration or account: *100 to 121 exclusive* (excluding 100 and 121, but including from 101 to 120). **3.** limited to a given object or objects: *He pays exclusive attention to business.* **4.** shutting out all others from a part or share: *exclusive interview.* **5.** single or sole: *A horse was his exclusive means of transport.* **6.** (of a club, group, etc.) having limited membership; elitist. **7.** *Colloq.* fashionable: *an exclusive club.* [ML: excluded]

excommunicate /ekskə'mjunəkeɪt/, *v.*, **-cated, -cating**, *n., adj.* ◇*v.t.* **1.** to cut off from communion or membership, esp. of the church. ◇*n.* **2.** excommunicated person. ◇*adj.* **3.** excommunicated. [LL: put out of the community] —**excommunicator**, *n.* —**excommunication**, *n.*

excrement /'ekskrəmənt/, *n.* waste matter from the body, esp. the faeces. [L: what is evacuated] —**excremental**, *adj.*

excrescence /eks'kresəns/, *n.* **1.** an abnormal outgrowth, usu. harmless, on an animal or vegetable body. **2.** a normal outgrowth such as hair. —**excrescent**, *adj.*

excreta /əks'kritə, eks-/, *n.pl.* excreted matter, as sweat, urine, etc. [L: things separated] —**excretal**, *adj.*

excrete /əks'krit, eks-/, *v.t.*, **-creted, -creting**. to separate and discharge (waste or harmful matter) from the body. [L: sifted out, discharged] —**excretion**, *n.* —**excretive**, **excretory**, *adj.*

excruciating /əks'kruʃieɪtɪŋ, eks-/, *adj.* very painful; causing great suffering.

excursion /ək'skɜʃən, ek-/, *n.* **1.** a short journey or trip for a special purpose: *a pleasure excursion*; *a scientific excursion.* **2.** a trip in a bus, train, etc., at a reduced rate. **3.** a temporary departure from one's normal activities, work, etc: *He made a short excursion into teaching.* [L: a running out] —**excursionist**, *n.*

excursive /ək'skɜsɪv, ek-/, *adj.* of the nature of an excursion; wandering; digressive. —**excursiveness**, *n.*

excuse /ək'skjuz, ek-/, *v.*, **-cused, -cusing**; /ək'skjus/, *n.* ◇*v.t.* **1.** to pardon or forgive; overlook (a fault, etc.): *We'll excuse your behavior.* **2.** to try to remove the blame of; apologise for. **3.** to serve as a reason for (a fault, etc.); justify: *His youth does not excuse his behavior.* **4. a.** to free from duty, punishment, etc: *He excused her from the washing up.* **b.** to allow to leave: *She excused him from the room.* ◇*n.* **5.** something which is offered as, or serves as, a reason for being excused. **6.** the act of excusing. **7.** a pretended reason; pretext. **8.** a bad example of a particular thing: *She was wearing a poor excuse for a hat.* [ME, from L: allege in excuse]

exec. /əg'zek/, *Abbrev.* **1.** executive. **2.** executor.

execrable /'eksəkrəbəl/, *adj.* deserving to be hated; detestable; dreadful: *This is execrable weather.* —**execrably**, *adv.*

execrate /'eksəkreɪt/, *v.t.*, **-crated, -crating**. **1.** to hate completely; detest; abhor. **2.** to wish evil upon; curse. [L: having cursed] —**execration**, *n.* —**execrative**, **execratory** *adj.*

execute /'eksəkjut/, *v.t.*, **-cuted, -cuting**. **1.** to carry out; accomplish: *to execute a plan or order.* **2.** to perform or do: *to execute a dance movement*; *to perform a tune on the piano.* **3.** to put to death according to law. **4.** to produce in accordance with a plan or idea: *to execute a statue*; *to execute a picture.* **5.** *Law.* **a.** to give effect or force to (a law, sentence of a court, etc.). **b.** to carry out the instructions of (a will). **c.** to complete and make legal (a deed, etc.) as by signing, sealing, etc. [ME, from L: having followed out] —**executer**, *n.*

execution /eksə'kjuʃən/, *n.* **1.** the act of executing. **2.** a putting to death as a legal punishment. **3.** the manner or style of performance, as in music.

executioner /eksə'kjuʃənə/, *n.* a person appointed to carry out executions (def. 2).

executive /əg'zekjətɪv, eg-/, *adj.* **1.** suited for putting things into effect, practical performance or direction: *a person with executive ability.* **2.** responsible for or relating to the execution of laws or the administration of business affairs. ◇*n.* **3.** a person or group of people responsible for administration, as in a business company. **4.** a government body consisting of members of the party in power, which forms policy and controls government departments and instrumentalities.

executive council, *n.* a body consisting of the ministry and governor or governor-general, which gives formal approval to government decisions, etc.

executor /əg'zekjətə, eg-/, *n. Law.* the person named in a will to carry out its provisions. [ME, from L: one who follows out] —**executrix**, *n. fem.* —**executorial**, *adj.* —**executorship**, *n.*

exegesis /eksə'dʒisəs/, *n., pl.* **-ses** /-siz/. an explanation or interpretation of a written work, esp. the Bible. [NL, from Gk: explanation] —**exegetic**, **exegetical**, *adj.*

exemplary /əg'zempləri, eg-/, *adj.* **1.** worthy of being copied; commendable: *exemplary conduct.* **2.** serving as a warning: *an exemplary penalty.* **3.** serving as a model or pattern. **4.** serving as an example; typical. —**exemplariness**, *n.*

exemplify /əg'zempləfaɪ, eg-/, *v.t.*, **-fied, -fying**. **1.** to show or make clearer by example: *He exemplified his point with a diagram.* **2.** to serve as an example of: *This mistake exemplifies the whole problem.* [ME, from L *exemplificāre* example + *ficāre* make] —**exemplification**, *n.* —**exemplificative**, *adj.*

exempt /əg'zempt, eg-/, *v.t.* **1.** to free from duty or rule to which others are bound: *to exempt someone from military service.* ◇*adj.* **2.** freed from or not bound by a duty, rule,

exempt etc.: *He is exempt from taxes.* [ME, from L] —**exemptible**, *adj.* —**exemption**, *n.*

exequies /ˈɛksəkwiz/, *n.pl.*, *sing.* **-quy** /-kwi/. funeral ceremonies. [ME, from OF, from L: funeral procession] —**exequial**, *adj.*

exercise /ˈɛksəsaɪz/, *n.*, *v.*, **-cised, -cising.** ◇*n.* **1.** bodily or mental activity, esp. for training or improvement. **2.** something done or performed as practice or training in a particular skill: *French grammar exercises; piano exercises.* **3.** a putting into use or operation: *the exercise of care; the exercise of willpower.* **4.** a literary, musical or artistic work done for practice or to show a particular technical point. ◇*v.t.* **5.** to put through exercises, or forms of practice in order to train, develop, etc.: *to exercise soldiers; to exercise a horse; to exercise the voice.* **6.** to put into action, practice, or use: *to exercise care; to exercise patience; to exercise judgment.* **7.** to have as an effect: *to exercise influence on someone.* **8.** to worry; make uneasy: *His poor health exercised his mind.* ◇*v.i.* **9.** to do exercises; take bodily exercise. [ME, from OF, from L]

exert /əɡˈzɜt, ɛɡ-/, *v.t.* **1.** to use (power, ability, influence); put into energetic action. **2. exert oneself**, to make an energetic effort. [L] —**exertion**, *n.* —**exertive**, *adj.*

exeunt /ˈɛksiʊnt/, (a stage direction meaning that the actors named go out or off stage). [L]

exfoliate /ɛksˈfoʊlieɪt/, *v.i.*, **-ated, -ating. 1.** to throw off scales; to peel off in thin pieces, as bark or skin. **2.** *Geol.* **a.** to split or swell into a scaly aggregate, as certain minerals when heated. **b.** to separate into roughly concentric layers, as certain rocks during weathering. [LL: stripped of leaves] —**exfoliation**, *n.* —**exfoliative**, *adj.*

ex gratia /ɛks ˈɡreɪʃə/, *adj.* (given or done) as a favor and not because legally necessary. [L: out of grace]

exhale /ɛksˈheɪl/, *v.t.*, *v.i.*, **-haled, -haling.** to breathe out or give off (air, vapor, etc.). [ME, from F, from L: breathe out] —**exhalation**, *n.*

exhaust /əɡˈzɔst, ɛɡ-/, *v.t.* **1.** to wear out, or tire greatly (a person): *I have exhausted myself working.* **2.** to empty by drawing out the contents; drain off completely. **3.** to make a vacuum in. **4.** to use up completely: *I have exhausted my patience.* **5.** to treat or study thoroughly (a subject, etc.). ◇*n.* **6.** *Mach.* **a.** the escape of gases from the cylinder of an engine after ignition and expansion. **b.** the steam or gases given off. **c.** the parts of an engine through which the exhaust is ejected. [L: drained out] —**exhausted**, *adj.*

exhaustion /əɡˈzɔstʃən, ɛɡ-/, *n.* **1.** the act or process of exhausting. **2.** the state of being exhausted.

exhaustive /əɡˈzɔstɪv, ɛɡ-/, *adj.* covering a subject, etc., in detail; thorough: *an exhaustive treatment of the subject.*

exhibit /əɡˈzɪbət, ɛɡ-/, *v.t.* **1.** to show; display: *to exhibit anger; to exhibit shopping bags for inspection.* **2.** to place on public show: *to exhibit paintings.* ◇*v.i.* **3.** to present (works of art, etc.) to public view. ◇*n.* **4.** a show; exhibition: *art exhibit.* **5.** an object or collection of objects exhibited. **6.** *Law.* an object exhibited in court to illustrate or make clearer verbal evidence. [L] —**exhibitor, exhibiter**, *n.*

exhibition /ˌɛksəˈbɪʃən/, *n.* **1.** a public show or display, as of works of art or athletic skill. **2.** an act of exhibiting or presenting to view: *an exhibition of bad behavior.* **3.** an allowance of money made to a student at a university. **4. make an exhibition of oneself**, to behave foolishly in public.

exhibitionism /ˌɛksəˈbɪʃənɪzəm/, *n.* **1.** the tendency to try to attract attention to oneself or one's abilities. **2.** *Psychiat.* an abnormal tendency to attract attention to oneself, particularly by public showing of the sexual organs. —**exhibitionist**, *n.* —**exhibitionistic**, *adj.*

exhilarate /əɡˈzɪləreɪt, ɛɡ-/, *v.t.*, **-rated, -rating. 1.** to make cheerful or glad. **2.** to fill with energy or excitement; stimulate. [L] —**exhilarating**, *adj.* —**exhilaration**, *n.*

exhort /əɡˈzɔt, ɛɡ-/, *v.t.*, *v.i.* to urge, advise, or ask (someone) urgently. [ME, from L: urge, encourage] —**exhortation**, *n.* —**exhortative, exhortatory**, *adj.*

exhume /ɛksˈhjum/, *v.t.*, **-humed, -huming.** to dig (something buried, esp. a dead body) out of the earth; disinter. [L *ex-* EX.[1] + *humus* earth, ground] —**exhumation**, *n.*

exigency /əɡˈzɪdʒənsi, ɛɡ-, ˈɛksədʒənsi/, *n.*, *pl.* **-cies. 1.** a state of urgency. **2.** (*usu. pl.*) urgent need or demand of a particular occasion: *the exigencies of the times.* **3.** a situation which demands immediate action; an emergency. Also, **exigence**. —**exigent**, *adj.*

exile /ˈɛɡzaɪl, ˈɛksaɪl/, *n.*, *v.*, **-iled, -iling.** ◇*n.* **1.** long separation from one's country or home, oft. enforced. **2.** someone separated from his country or home. ◇*v.t.* **3.** to force (someone) to leave his country, home, etc.; banish. [ME, from OF, from L: banishment]

exist /əɡˈzɪst, ɛɡ-, ɪɡ-/, *v.i.* **1.** to have actual being; be: *That situation exists only in his mind.* **2.** to have life; live: *Dinosaurs existed long ago.* **3.** to continue to be or to live: *We cannot exist without water.* [L: stand forth, arise, be] —**existent**, *adj.*

existence /əɡˈzɪstəns, ɛɡ-, ɪɡ-/, *n.* **1.** the state or fact of existing; being: *That house is no longer in existence.* **2.** continuance in being or life; life: *a struggle for existence.* **3.** the manner of existing: *He has a strange existence.* **4.** all that exists. **5.** something that exists; an entity.

existential /ˌɛɡzɪsˈtɛnʃəl/, *adj.* **1.** relating to existence. **2.** *Philos.* **a.** of or relating to existentialism. **b.** (of a logical proposition) based on the actual existence of the objects concerned.

existentialism /ˌɛɡzɪsˈtɛnʃəlɪzəm/, *n.* any of a group of modern philosophical ideas, which teach the importance of human existence and the freedom and responsibility of the individual

existentialism   357   **expectorate**

to make decisions based on personal experience. —**existentialist**, *adj., n.*

exit /'ɛgzɪt, -zɪt, 'ɛksɪt, -sɪt/, *n.* **1.** a way or passage out. **2.** a going out or away; departure: *to make an exit.* **3.** the departure of a player from the stage as part of the action of a play. ◇*v.i.* **4.** to depart; go away. **5.** (a stage direction meaning that the actor named goes out or off stage). [special use of stage direction *exit* he goes out, influenced by association with L *exitus* a going out]

Exmouth /'ɛksməθ/, *n.* a town and shire on the north-western coast of WA, near North-West Cape; constructed as a residential and service centre for a US naval communications station in 1963. Pop. 3514 (1986).

exnuptial /ɛks'nʌpʃəl/, *adj.* born outside marriage.

exo-, a prefix meaning 'outside', 'external'. Also, **ex-**. [Gk: outside]

exocrine /'ɛksoʊkraɪn, -rɪn/, *adj.* **1.** relating to a gland, organ, etc. that secretes its products onto an outside surface. **2.** relating to such secretions.

Exod, *Abbrev. Bible.* Exodus.

exodus /'ɛksədəs/, *n.* **1.** a going out; departure or emigration, usu. of a large number of people. **2.** (*cap.*) the departure of the Israelites from Egypt under Moses. **3.** (*cap.*) the second book of the Old Testament, containing an account of this departure. [ME, from L, from Gk *éxodos* a going out]

exogamy /ɛk'sɒgəmi/, *n.* the custom of marrying outside the tribe or other social unit (opposed to *endogamy*). —**exogamous**, **exogamic**, *adj.*

exonerate /əg'zɒnəreɪt, ɛg-/, *v.t.*, **-rated**, **-rating**. **1.** to clear of a charge, etc.; free from blame. **2.** to free from a responsibility, duty, etc. [L: disburdened] —**exoneration**, *n.*

exorbitant /əg'zɔbətənt, ɛg-/, *adj.* going beyond what is normal, right, or reasonable: *an exorbitant price; exorbitant demand.* [LL: going out of the track] —**exorbitance**, *n.*

exorcise or **exorcize** /'ɛksɔsaɪz/, *v.t.*, **-cised**, **-cising**. **1.** to try to drive out (an evil spirit) by prayer or religious ceremonies. **2.** to free (a person, place, etc.) from evil spirits or influences. [LL, from Gk] —**exorcist**, *n.* —**exorcism**, *n.*

exoskeleton /ˌɛksoʊ'skɛlətən/, *n.* an outside protective covering, esp. when hard, such as the shell of crustaceans, the scales and plates of fishes, etc. (opposed to *endoskeleton*). —**exoskeletal**, *adj.*

exosphere /'ɛksoʊsfɪə/, *n.* the outermost part of the earth's atmosphere.

exothermic /ɛksoʊ'θɜmɪk/, *adj.* showing or having to do with a chemical change which causes release of heat (opposed to *endothermic*).

exotic /əg'zɒtɪk, ɛg-/, *adj.* **1.** of foreign origin or character; not native. **2.** strikingly unusual, colorful, or beautiful; strangely exciting. ◇*n.* **3.** anything exotic, as a plant. [L, from Gk: foreign, alien] —**exoticism**, *n.*

exotica /əg'zɒtɪkə, ɛg-/, *n.pl.* possessions, customs, etc., that are foreign, unusual or exotic.

expand /ək'spænd, ɛk-/, *v.t.*, *v.i.* **1.** to increase in size, volume, scope, etc.: *Heat expands metal; Most metals expand with heat.* **2.** to spread or stretch out; unfold: *A bird expands its wings; The buds had not yet expanded.* **3.** to express in greater detail; develop: *He expanded his talk; Let me expand on that idea.* [L: spread out]

expanse /ək'spæns, ɛk-/, *n.* **1.** something which is spread out, esp. over a large area. **2.** an uninterrupted space or area; wide extent: *an expanse of water; an expanse of land.* **3.** expansion; extension.

expansion /ək'spænʃən, ɛk-/, *n.* **1.** the act of expanding. **2.** the state of being expanded. **3.** the amount or degree of expanding. **4.** an expanded part or form of a thing: *expansion of a speech; expansion of a company.* [LL]

expansionism /ək'spænʃənɪzəm, ɛk-/, *n.* the policy of expansion, esp. of a nation's territory or influence. —**expansionist**, *n.*

expansive /ək'spænsɪv, ɛk-/, *adj.* **1.** tending to or able to expand. **2.** causing expansion. **3.** having a wide range; comprehensive. **4.** (of a person, mood, etc.) talkative; open; unrestrained: *He was in an expansive frame of mind.* —**expansiveness**, *n.*

expatiate /əks'peɪʃieɪt, ɛk-/, *v.i.*, **-ated**, **-ating**. to enlarge in speech or writing (fol. by *on* or *upon*): *to expatiate upon an idea.* [L: extended, spread out] —**expatiation**, *n.*

expatriate /ɛks'pætrieɪt/, *v.*, **-ated**, **-ating**; /ɛks'pætriət, -rieɪt/, *adj., n.* ◇*v.t.* **1.** to force (a person) to leave his native country; banish. **2.** to remove (oneself) from living in or being a citizen of one's native country. ◇*adj.* **3.** expatriated; exiled. ◇*n.* **4.** an expatriated person. [LL] —**expatriation**, *n.*

expect /ək'spɛkt, ɛk-/, *v.t.* **1.** to regard as likely to happen or come: *I expect to do it; I expect him to come.* **2.** to look for with reason: *We cannot expect obedience; Don't expect him to do that.* ◇*v.i.* **3.** *Colloq.* to suppose. **4.** *Colloq.* to be pregnant. [L: look for]

expectancy /ək'spɛktənsi, ɛk-/, *n., pl.* **-cies**. **1.** the quality or state of expecting; expectation; anticipation. **2.** the state of being expected. **3.** something expected: *a long life expectancy.* Also, **expectance**.

expectant /ək'spɛktənt, ɛk-/, *adj.* **1.** having expectations; expecting. **2.** expecting the birth of a child: *an expectant mother.* **3.** expected; anticipated; prospective.

expectation /ˌɛkspɛk'teɪʃən/, *n.* **1.** the act of expecting. **2.** the state of expecting: *He waits in expectation.* **3.** the state of being expected. **4.** something expected; a thing looked forward to. **5.** (*oft. pl.*) a prospect of future good, success, or profit: *to have great expectations.*

expectorant /ək'spɛktərənt/, *n.* a medicine that breaks up phlegm in the lungs.

expectorate /ək'spɛktəreɪt, ɛk-/, *v.*, **-rated**, **-rating**. ◇*v.t.* **1.** to cough or spit out

expectorate

(phlegm, etc.) from the throat or lungs. ◇v.i. **2.** to spit. [L: banished from the breast] —**expectoration**, n.

expediency /ək'spidiənsi, ek-/, n., pl. **-cies. 1.** the quality of being expedient or advantageous. **2.** a regard for what is useful or advantageous rather than for what is right or just; self-interest. **3.** something expedient. Also, **expedience**.

expedient /ək'spidiənt, ek-/, adj. **1.** fit or suitable for a particular purpose or situation: *It is expedient that you go.* **2.** based on consideration of advantage or interest, rather than right. **3.** acting in accordance with what is expedient. ◇n. **4.** something expedient. **5.** something used in an urgent situation; resource: *He resorted to bribery as an expedient.* [ME, from L: dispatching]

expedite /'ekspədaɪt/, v.t., **-dited, -diting. 1.** to speed up the progress of; hasten: *We must expedite this matter.* **2.** to do quickly: *He expedited his work.* [L: extricated, helped forwards, sent off or dispatched]

expedition /ekspə'dɪʃən/, n. **1.** a journey or voyage made for a particular purpose, such as war or exploration. **2.** a group of people or ships, etc., taking part in an expedition. **3.** speed in doing something. —**expeditionary**, adj.

expeditious /ekspə'dɪʃəs/, adj. quick and efficient. —**expeditiousness**, n.

expel /ək'spel, ek-/, v.t., **-pelled, -pelling. 1.** to drive or force out or away; eject: *to expel air from the lungs; to expel an invader from a country.* **2.** to cut off from membership or relations: *to expel a pupil from a school.* [ME, from L: drive out]

expend /ək'spend, ek-/, v.t. **1.** to use up: *to expend energy; to expend time; to expend care on something.* **2.** to pay out; spend. [L: weigh out, pay out]

expendable /ək'spendəbəl, ek-/, adj. **1.** able to be expended. **2.** not of essential importance; able to be sacrificed for a purpose: *Those soldiers were considered expendable.*

expenditure /ək'spendətʃə, ek-/, n. **1.** the act of expending. **2.** something which is expended, such as time, money, etc.

expense /ək'spens, ek-/, n. **1.** a cost or charge: *the expense of our holiday.* **2.** spending; expenditure: *We dined out at his expense; The job involved a great expense of time.* **3.** a cause or occasion of spending: *Owning a car is a great expense.* **4.** (pl.) Comm. **a.** costs met with in the course of one's work. **b.** money paid to cover such costs: *to receive a salary and expenses.* **5. at the expense of**, involving the loss or injury of: *They chose quantity at the expense of quality.* [ME, from AF, from LL: paid or weighed out]

expensive /ək'spensɪv, ek-/, adj. of great expense; costly.

experience /ək'spɪəriəns, ek-/, n., v., **-enced, -encing.** ◇n. **1.** a particular act of doing, seeing or living through something personally: *a strange experience.* **2.** the process or

expletive

fact of doing, seeing, or living through something personally: *You need more business experience; People learn best from experience.* **3.** knowledge or practical skill gained from what one has personally done, seen, or lived through: *We only want women with experience for this job.* ◇v.t. **4.** to have experience of; meet with; undergo: *He experienced a lot on his travels.* [ME, from OF, from L: trial, proof, knowledge]

experienced /ək'spɪəriənst, ek-/, adj. **1.** having had experience. **2.** wise or skilful through experience: *an experienced teacher; an experienced general.*

experiment /ək'sperəmənt, ek-/, n.; /ək'sperəment, ek-/, v. ◇n. **1.** an act or operation for the purpose of discovering or testing something: *a chemical experiment; an experiment in new teaching methods.* **2.** the carrying out of such operations; experimentation: *a product that is the result of long experiment.* ◇v.i. **3.** to try or test to find something out: *to experiment with drugs in order to find a cure.* [ME, from L: a trial, test] —**experimentation**, n. —**experimental**, adj.

expert /'ekspɜt/, n. **1.** someone who has special skill or knowledge in a particular field; specialist: *You need more business an expert on mining.* **2.** *Shearing.* the person who sharpens the shearers' cutters. ◇adj. **3.** possessing special skill or knowledge (oft. fol. by *in* or *at*): *an expert driver; to be expert at driving a car.* **4.** relating to or coming from an expert: *expert work; expert advice.* [ME, from L: having tried]

expertise /ekspɜ'tiz/, n. expert skill or knowledge.

expiate /'ekspieɪt/, v.t., **-ated, -ating.** to make up for (sin or wrongdoing) by repayment, accepting punishment, etc. [L] —**expiator**, n. —**expiation**, n. —**expiable**, adj. —**expiatory**, adj.

expire /ək'spaɪə, ek-/, v.i., **-pired, -piring. 1.** to breathe out air from the lungs. **2.** to give out the last breath; die. **3.** to come to an end; terminate. [ME, from F, from L: breathe out] —**expiration**, n.

expiry /ek'spaɪri/, n., pl. **-ries.** a coming to an end; termination: *expiry of a driving licence.*

explain /ək'spleɪn, ek-/, v.t. **1.** to make plain, clear, or understandable: *to explain a problem; to explain how to do something.* **2.** to give the meaning of; interpret: *to explain a word; to explain a poem.* **3.** to make clear the cause or reason of; account for: *Please explain your behavior.* ◇v.i. **4.** to give an explanation: *Let me explain.* **5. explain away**, to give excuses or reasons for: *He tried to explain away his absence.* [L: make plain, flatten out] —**explanatory**, adj.

explanation /eksplə'neɪʃən/, n. **1.** the act or process of explaining. **2.** a statement, etc., which explains. **3.** a meaning or interpretation: *to find the explanation of a mystery.* [L]

expletive /ək'splitɪv, ek-/, n. **1.** a violent exclamation or swearword. **2.** a syllable, word, or phrase added only to fill out a sentence or line. [LL: serving to fill out]

explicable /ɑksˈplɪkəbəl, ɛk-/, *adj.* able to be explained.

explicate /ˈɛkspləkeɪt/, *v.t.*, **-cated, -cating.** to make plain or clear; explain; interpret. [L: unfolded] **–explication**, *n.* **–explicative, explicatory**, *adj.*

explicit /əkˈsplɪsət, ɛk-/, *adj.* **1.** clearly and fully expressed: *an explicit statement or instruction.* **2.** clearly developed or thought out: *explicit knowledge; explicit belief.* **3.** definite in expression; outspoken: *He was quite explicit on that point.* [L: unfolded]

explode /əkˈsploʊd, ɛk-/, *v.*, **-ploded, -ploding.** ◇*v.i.* **1.** (of a gas, gun powder, etc.) to expand with force and noise because of rapid chemical change. **2.** to burst, fly into pieces, or break up violently with a loud noise as a result of inner pressure. **3.** to burst forth violently, esp. with noise, laughter, violent emotion, etc.: *She exploded with laughter.* ◇*v.t.* **4.** to cause (something) to explode. **5.** to prove to be false; discredit or disprove: *to explode a theory.* [L: drive out by clapping]

exploit[1] /ˈɛksplɔɪt/, *n.* a striking or notable deed; feat: *He told us of his exploits.* [ME, from OF, from L: unfolded]

exploit[2] /əkˈsplɔɪt, ɛk-/, *v.t.* **1.** to turn to practical or profitable use, esp. natural resources. **2.** to use (unfairly) for one's own purposes: *The company exploited their labor; She exploits her little brother.* [ME, from OF, from L: unfold] **–exploitation**, *n.* **–exploitative**, *adj.*

explore /əkˈsplɔ, ɛk-/, *v.*, **-plored, -ploring.** ◇*v.t.* **1.** to travel over (an area, etc.) for the purpose of discovery. **2.** to look into closely; examine: *I will explore your suggestion; The doctor explored the inside of the ear.* ◇*v.i.* **3.** to take part in exploring: *She explored in Africa.* [L] **–exploration**, *n.* **–exploratory**, *adj.* **–explorer**, *n.*

explosion /əkˈsploʊʒən, ɛk-/, *n.* **1.** the act of exploding. **2.** the noise of something exploding. **3.** a violent outburst of laughter, anger, etc. **4.** any sudden, rapid, or large increase: *the population explosion.* [L: a driving off by clapping]

explosive /əkˈsploʊzɪv, ɛk-, -sɪv/, *adj.* **1.** tending or serving to explode: *an explosive substance.* **2.** relating to or of the nature of an explosion. ◇*n.* **3.** an explosive substance such as dynamite. → **plosive.**

exponent /əkˈspoʊnənt, ɛk-/, *n.* **1.** someone or something that explains, or interprets. **2.** someone or something that supports and promotes (an idea, principle, etc.): *an exponent of free trade.* **3.** *Maths.* a symbol placed above and at the right of another symbol (the base), to show the power (def. 12) it is to be raised to, as in x^3. [L: putting forth]

exponential /ˌɛkspəˈnɛnʃəl/, *adj.* **1.** of or relating to an exponent. **2.** *Maths.* having the unknown quantity or variable as an exponent. ◇*n.* **3.** *Maths.* an exponential quantity or function.

export /əkˈspɔt, ɛk-, ˈɛkspɔt/, *v.*; /ˈɛkspɔt/, *n., adj.* ◇*v.t.* **1.** to send (goods, etc.) to other countries, esp. for sale, exchange, etc. ◇*n.* **2.** the act of exporting; exportation. **3.** something which is exported. ◇*adj.* **4.** of, relating to, or for export: *export income; export beef; of export quality.* [L: carry away] **–exportation**, *n.* **–exporter**, *n.*

expose /əkˈspoʊz, ɛk-/, *v.t.*, **-posed, -posing.** **1.** to lay open to danger, attack, harm, etc.: *to expose soldiers to gunfire; to expose one's feelings to laughter; to expose one's head to the rain.* **2.** to lay open to the influence of something: *They exposed their children to art at an early age.* **3.** to present to view; exhibit; display: *He exposed his wound to the doctor.* **4.** to make known; reveal: *She exposed her real intentions; They exposed his crimes.* **5.** to leave (a child, etc.) in an unsheltered or open place to die. **6.** *Photog.* to lay open (a plate, film or paper) to the action of light, etc. **7. expose oneself,** (of a man) to show the sexual organs in public. [OF *ex-* EX-[1] + *poser* put]

exposé /ˌɛkspoʊˈzeɪ/, *n.* **1.** a formal explanation or exposition. **2.** a public exposure of some wrongdoing. [F]

exposition /ˌɛkspəˈzɪʃən/, *n.* **1.** a large public show of products of art, manufacture, etc. **2.** a detailed statement or explanation, either spoken or written. **3.** the act of presenting to view; display. **4.** *Music.* a part of a fugue or a sonata form, in which the subject or main themes are first stated.

expostulate /əkˈspɒstʃuleɪt, ɛk-/, *v.i.*, **-lated, -lating.** to reason seriously with a person against something he intends to do or has done: *They expostulated with him on the foolishness of his actions.* [L] **–expostulation**, *n.* **–expostulatory**, *adj.*

exposure /əkˈspoʊʒə, ɛk-/, *n.* **1.** the act of making known or revealing, esp. something private, secret, or criminal. **2.** presentation to view, esp. in an open or public manner. **3.** a laying open to the action or influence of something: *exposure to the weather; exposure to danger; exposure to ridicule.* **4.** *Photog.* **a.** the act of presenting sensitive material such as film, plate, or paper, to light, etc. **b.** the length of time of this exposure. **5.** the state caused by being exposed to the weather for a long time: *She was suffering from hunger and exposure.* **6.** a situation with regard to sunlight or wind; aspect: *a house with a southern exposure.* [EXPOS(E) + -URE]

expound /əkˈspaʊnd, ɛk-/, *v.t.* **1.** to set forth or state in detail: *He expounded his new theory.* **2.** to explain; interpret. [ME, from OF, from L: put out, expose, set forth, explain]

express /əkˈsprɛs, ɛk-/, *v.t.* **1.** to put (thought) into words: *to express an idea clearly.* **2.** to show or make known; reveal: *Her actions expressed her feelings; He expressed his ideas in his painting.* **3.** to set forth the thoughts, feelings, etc., of (oneself): *He expresses himself in his work; She finds it hard to express herself in English.* **4.** to represent: *The painting in this painting expresses sadness.* **5.** to press out: *to express the juice of a fruit.* ◇*adj.* **6.** clearly stated; definite; explicit. **7.** special; particular; definite: *an express purpose.* **8.** exactly formed

express

or represented: *an express image.* **9.** sent by express (def. 15): *an express letter.* **10.** specially direct or fast: *an express train.* ◇*adv.* **11.** by express; unusually fast. **12.** specially; for a particular purpose. ◇*n.* **13.** an express train, bus, etc. **14.** a messenger or message specially sent. **15.** a system or method for sending parcels, money, etc. quickly: *to send a parcel by express.* [ME, from L: pressed out, described] —**expressly**, *adv.*

expression /ək'spreʃən, ek-/, *n.* **1.** the act of setting forth in words: *the expression of opinions; the expression of facts.* **2.** a particular word, phrase, or form of words: *a polite expression.* **3.** the manner or form in which a thing is expressed in words. **4.** the showing of feeling, character, etc., on the face, in the voice, in a work of art, etc: *Her loneliness found expression in her writing; She reads with a lot of expression.* **5.** a look or tone of voice that expresses feeling, etc.: *a sad expression.* **6.** the quality or power of expressing feeling, etc.: *a face that lacks expression.* **7.** the act of representing by symbols, etc. **8.** *Maths.* a combination of numbers or symbols with no equals sign, which represents a number or mathematical entity. **9.** the act of pressing out.

expressionism /ək'spreʃənɪzəm, ek-/, *n.* a theory of art, literature, etc., esp. the one originating in Europe about the time of World War I, in which free expression of the artist's emotional reactions is more important than natural or realistic representation. —**expressionist**, *n., adj.* —**expressionistic**, *adj.*

expressive /ək'spresɪv, ek-/, *adj.* **1.** serving to express: *a look expressive of gratitude.* **2.** full of expression or meaning: *an expressive smile.* —**expressiveness**, *n.*

expressway /ək'spreswei, ek-/, *n.* a road for high speed traffic. Also, **freeway**.

expropriate /eks'prouprient/, *v.t.*, **-ated, -ating. 1.** to take (property) from a private owner, esp. for public use. **2.** to dispossess (a person) of property. [LL: deprived of property] —**expropriation**, *n.*

expulsion /ək'spʌlʃən, ek-/, *n.* **1.** the act of driving out or expelling. **2.** the state of being expelled. [L] —**expulsive**, *adj.*

expunge /ək'spʌndʒ, ek-/, *v.t.*, **-punged, -punging.** to rub out; erase; obliterate: *expunge guilt.* [L: prick out, strike out] —**expunction**, *n.*

expurgate /'ekspəgeɪt, -pɜgeɪt/, *v.t.*, **-gated, -gating.** to remove parts thought to be offensive from (a book, etc.). [L: purged] —**expurgation**, *n.* —**expurgator**, *n.*

exquisite /'ekskwəzət, ək'skwɪzət, ek-/, *adj.* **1.** of fine and delicate beauty or charm. **2.** delicately and finely made. **3.** sharp, or keen: *exquisite pain; exquisite pleasure.* **4.** keenly or delicately sensitive: *an exquisite ear for music; exquisite taste.* [ME, from L: sought out]

extant /ek'stænt, 'ekstənt/, *adj.* still in existence; not destroyed or lost. [L: standing out]

exterior

extemporaneous /ɛkstempə'remiəs, ek-/, *adj.* done or spoken extempore: *an extemporaneous speech.* Also, **extemporary**. [LL]

extempore /ək'stempəri, ek-/, *adv., adj.* without preparation; impromptu: *to speak extempore; an extempore performance.* [L: out of the time]

extend /ək'stend, ek-/, *v.t.* **1.** to stretch out; draw out to the full length. **2.** to cause to reach or stretch: *He extended his soldiers along the front line.* **3.** to stretch forth or hold out: *She extended her hand.* **4.** to lengthen; prolong: *They extended the time of play.* **5.** to spread out in area, scope, etc.; expand: *They extended their operations interstate.* **6.** to offer; grant; give: *She extended me an invitation.* ◇*v.i.* **7.** to be or become extended. **8.** to reach or stretch: *This road extends for miles.* **9.** to increase in length, area, scope, etc. [ME, from L] —**extendible, extendable, extensible**, *adj.*

extended family, *n.* a family group or unit consisting not only of parents and children, but also immediate relatives, and sometimes people not related to the group. See **nuclear family**.

extensile /ek'stensaɪl/, *adj. Chiefly Zool., Anat.* able to be extended; adapted for stretching out.

extension /ək'stenʃən, ek-/, *n.* **1.** an extending or being extended. **2.** something extended; an extended object, time or space: *an extension to a house; an extension of time.* **3.** range of extending; extent. **4.** an extra telephone connected to the same line as a main telephone. **5.** *Comm.* a written agreement by someone who is owed a debt to give extra time to the person who owes it. **6.** *Anat.* the act of straightening a limb, or its resulting position. **7.** *Philos.* the class of things to which a term applies; denotation: *The extension of the term 'man' includes individuals as 'Socrates', 'Plato', 'Aristotle', etc.* ◇*adj.* **8.** of or relating to a course, service, etc., which is outside the normal work of an organisation: *The agriculture department offers an extension service to farmers.* [L] —**extensional**, *adj.*

extensive /ək'stensɪv, ek-/, *adj.* **1.** of great extent; wide; broad; large in amount: *an extensive forest.* **2.** far-reaching; comprehensive; thorough: *extensive knowledge; extensive enquiries.* —**extensiveness**, *n.*

extensor /ək'stensə, ek-, -sɔ/, *n.* a muscle which serves to straighten a part of the body. [LL: one who or that which stretches]

extent /ək'stent, ek-/, *n.* **1.** the space or degree to which a thing extends; length, area, or volume: *the extent of a line; to the full extent of his power.* **2.** something extended; a particular length, area, or volume. [ME, from AF, from L: extend]

extenuate /ək'stenjueɪt, ek-/, *v.t.*, **-ated, -ating. 1.** to represent (a fault, offence, etc.) as less serious. **2.** to serve to make (a fault, offence, etc.) seem less serious: *extenuating circumstances.* [L: made thin] —**extenuatory, extenuative**, *adj.* —**extenuation**, *n.*

exterior /ək'stɪəriə, ek-/, *adj.* **1.** outer; being on the outer side: *the exterior surface; exterior decorations.* **2.** situated or being out-

exterior side: *the exterior possessions of a country.* **3.** *Geom.* (of an angle) outer, as an angle formed outside two parallel lines when cut by a third line. ◇*n.* **4.** the outer surface or part; outside. [L, comparative of *exter, exterus* outer, outward]

exterminate /ək'stɜːməneɪt, ek-/, *v.t.*, **-nated, -nating.** to get rid of by destroying; destroy totally; extirpate. [L: pp., driven beyond the boundaries] —**extermination**, *n.* —**exterminator**, *n.*

external /ək'stɜːnəl, ek-/, *adj.* **1.** of or relating to the outside or outer part; outer. **2.** (of a cream, etc.) to be applied to the outside of a body. **3.** acting or coming from without. **4.** relating to outward appearance or show: *external acts of worship*. **5.** relating to what is outside or foreign: *external commerce*. **6.** *Philos.* belonging to the world of things, considered as separate from the mind. **7.** *Educ.* studying or studied outside a university, etc.: *an external degree*. ◇*n.* **8.** (*pl.*) things that are external and not absolutely necessary: *the externals of religion*. [L *extern(us)* outward + -AL¹] —**externality**, *n.*

external ear, *n.* that section of the ear which is made up of its visible outer part and the canal (passage) into the head.

extinct /əks'tɪŋkt, ek-/, *adj.* **1.** (of a volcano) no longer active; extinguished; quenched. **2.** (of an organisation, etc.) no longer working. **3.** having come to an end; (of a species) without a living representative. [ME, from L: destroyed, put out] —**extinction**, *n.*

extinguish /ək'stɪŋgwɪʃ, ek-/, *v.t.* **1.** to put out (a fire, light, etc.). **2.** to put an end to or bring to an end: *This news will extinguish all hope.* [L *ex(s)tinguere* put out, quench, destroy + -ISH²] —**extinguishment**, *n.* —**extinguisher**, *n.*

extirpate /'ekstəpeɪt, -stə-/, *v.t.*, **-pated, -pating. 1.** to remove completely; destroy totally; exterminate; do away with. **2.** to pull up by the roots; root up. [L: rooted out] —**extirpation**, *n.*

extol /ək'stoʊl, ek-/, *v.t.*, **-tolled, -tolling.** to praise highly; laud; eulogise. Also, **extoll.** [L: lift out or up] —**extoller**, *n.* —**extolment**, *n.*

extort /ək'stɔːt, ek-/, *v.t.* **1.** to take (something) from a person by violence, threats, etc. **2.** to take illegally under cover of office. [L: twisted or wrested out] —**extortive**, *adj.*

extortion /ək'stɔːʃən, ek-/, *n. Law.* the crime of obtaining money, etc., under cover of office. [ME, from L] —**extortionary**, *adj.* —**extortioner, extortionist**, *n.*

extortionate /ək'stɔːʃənət, ek-/, *adj.* **1.** excessively high: *extortionate prices*. **2.** characterised by extortion, as persons.

extra /'ekstrə/, *adj.* **1.** beyond or more than what is usual, expected, or necessary; additional: *an extra edition of a newspaper; an extra lecture.* **2.** better than usual: *extra fineness.* ◇*n.* **3.** something extra or additional. **4.** an additional expense. **5.** an edition of a newspaper other than the regular edition or editions. **6.** *Films.* a person hired by the day to play a small part. **7.** (*usu. pl.*) *Cricket.* a score or run not made from the bat, as a bye or a wide; a sundry. ◇*adv.* **8.** in excess of the usual or specified amount: *an extra high price.* **9.** beyond the ordinary degree; unusually; uncommonly: *done extra well.* [probably orig. short for EXTRAORDINARY]

extra-, a prefix meaning 'outside', 'beyond', 'besides', freely used to form compounds, which are mostly self-explanatory, as *extrajudicial*, etc. Also, **extro-.** [L, combining form of *extrā*, *adv.* and prep., outside (of), without]

extract /ək'strækt, ek-/, *v.; /*'ekstrækt/, *n.* ◇*v.t.* **1.** to draw forth or get out by force or effort: *The dentist must extract the tooth.* **2.** to draw out (a doctrine, principle, etc.). **3.** to obtain (pleasure, comfort, etc.) from a person, event, etc. **4.** to copy out (passages, etc.), as from a book, etc. **5.** to take by force (information, money, etc.). **6.** to separate or obtain (a juice, ingredient, etc.) from a mixture by pressure, distillation, etc. **7.** *Metall.* to separate (a metal) from an ore by any process. ◇*n.* **8.** something extracted, as the substance from a drug, plant, etc. **9.** a passage taken from a book, etc. [L: drawn out] —**extractable, extractible**, *adj.*

extraction /ək'strækʃən, ek-/, *n.* **1.** an extracting or being extracted. **2.** descent or lineage: *He is of German extraction.*

extracurricular /ˌekstrəkə'rɪkjələ/, *adj.* outside the regular course of study.

extradition /ˌekstrə'dɪʃən/, *n.* the giving up of a prisoner by one state or authority to another. [F, from L *ex-* EX-¹ + *trāditio* a giving over] —**extradite**, *v.* —**extraditable**, *adj.*

extramarital /ˌekstrə'mærətl/, *adj.* of or relating to sexual relations with someone other than one's husband or wife.

extraneous /ək'streɪniəs, ek-/, *adj.* introduced or coming from without; not belonging or proper to a thing; external; foreign. [L: that is without, foreign] —**extraneously**, *adv.* —**extraneousness**, *n.*

extraordinary /ək'strɔːdənri, ek-/, *adj.* **1.** beyond what is ordinary; out of the regular order: *extraordinary power.* **2.** unusual in character, amount, degree, etc.; remarkable: *extraordinary weather; an extraordinary book.* **3.** (usu. follows noun) (of officials, etc.) outside of, additional to, or ranking below an ordinary one: *a professor extraordinary.* [L: out of the common order] —**extraordinarily**, *adv.* —**extraordinariness**, *n.*

extrapolate /ek'stræpəleɪt/, *v.*, **-lated, -lating.** ◇*v.t.* **1.** *Stats.* to calculate a quantity which depends on one or more variables by extending the variables beyond their established ranges. **2.** to guess (what is not known) from that which is known; conjecture. ◇*v.i.* **3.** to perform extrapolation. [EXTRA- + *-polate* of INTERPOLATE] —**extrapolation**, *n.*

extrasensory /ˌekstrə'sensəri/, *adj.* outside the normal senses. See **ESP**.

extraterrestrial /ˌɛkstrətəˈrɛstriəl/, adj. outside or originating outside the earth.

extravagance /əkˈstrævəgəns, ɛk-/, n. 1. (a single example of) a wasteful outlaying of money. 2. (a single example of) any behavior taken to extremes.

extravagancies /əkˈstrævəgənsiz, ɛk-/, n., pl. **-cies**. extravagance.

extravagant /əkˈstrævəgənt, ɛk-/, adj. 1. spending more than is wise or necessary; wasteful: *an extravagant person.* 2. too high; exorbitant: *extravagant expenses; extravagant prices.* 3. (of actions, demands, opinions, etc.) going beyond the bounds of reason. 4. very elaborate; flamboyant: *an extravagant dress.* [ME, from ML: wander beyond, from L]

extravaganza /əkˌstrævəˈɡænzə, ɛk-/, n. an artistic production, as a comic opera or musical comedy, marked by wild and irregular form and feeling with detailed staging and costume. [b. EXTRAVAGANCE and It *stravaganza* queer behavior]

extreme /əkˈstriːm, ɛk-/, adj., **-tremer**, **-tremest**, n. ◇adj. 1. of a character or kind most removed from the ordinary or average: *an extreme case; extreme measures.* 2. very great in degree: *extreme joy.* 3. outermost: *at the extreme edge of the forest.* 4. farthest, or very far in any direction. 5. going to the utmost lengths: *extreme fashions; extreme politics.* ◇n. 6. the highest degree, or a very high degree: *showy in the extreme; to an extreme.* 7. one of two things as different from each other as possible: *the extremes of joy and grief.* 8. the farthest length, beyond the ordinary or average: *extreme in dress.* [ME, from L *extrēmus*, superl. of *exter* outer, outward] **—extremely**, adv.

extreme unction n. Rom Cath Ch. (formerly) a ceremonial act in which a seriously ill person is anointed with oil by a priest (now called **anointing of the sick**).

extremism /əkˈstriːmɪzəm, ɛk-/, n. a tendency to go to extremes, esp. in politics. **—extremist**, n.

extremity /əkˈstrɛmətiː, ɛk-/, n., pl. **-ties**. 1. the extreme point, limit, or part of something. 2. a limb of the body. 3. (chiefly pl.) the end part of a limb, as a hand or foot. 4. (oft. pl.) a condition, or times, of very great need, distress, etc. 5. the utmost degree: *the extremity of joy.*

extricate /ˈɛkstrəkeɪt/, v.t., **-cated, -cating**. to free; disengage; disentangle: *He will extricate the butterfly from the web; Can you extricate them from this unhappy situation?* [L: disentangled] **—extrication**, n.

extro-, a variant of **extra-** (used to contrast with **intro-**).

extrovert /ˈɛkstrəvɜːt/, n. 1. a person whose interests are directed chiefly to objects and considerations outside the self. See **introvert**. 2. a lively person who is interested in other people. ◇adj. 3. related to behavior typical of an extrovert. [EXTRO- + L *vertere* turn] **—extroversion**, n.

extrude /ɛkˈstruːd/, v., **-truded, -truding**. ◇v.t. 1. to force or press out; expel. 2. (in making metals, plastics, etc.) to form into a desired shape by forcing through a shaped opening; *to extrude tubing.* ◇v.i. 3. to jut out. [L: thrust out] **—extrusion**, n.

extrusive /ɛkˈstruːsɪv, -sɪv/, adj. Geol. 1. (of rocks) having been forced out in a plastic condition at the surface of the earth. 2. relating to volcanic rocks.

exuberant /əɡˈzjuːbərənt, ɛɡ-/, adj. 1. with great warmth of feeling; effusive: *an exuberant welcome.* 2. full of high spirits: *The soldiers were exuberant after their victory.* 3. rich in growth or production; luxuriant: *exuberant vegetation.* [L: being fruitful] **—exuberance**, n.

exude /əɡˈzjuːd, ɛɡ-/, v.i., v.t., **-uded, -uding**. to come or send out gradually in drops like sweat through pores or small openings. [L]

exult /əɡˈzʌlt, ɛɡ-/, v.i. to show or feel a lively or victorious joy; rejoice greatly (fol. by *in, at, over*, or an infinitive): *He exulted to find that he had won.* [L: leap out or up] **—exultant**, adj. **—exultantly**, adv. **—exultation**, n.

-ey[1], a variant of **-y**[1], used esp. after y, as in *clayey.*

-ey[2], a variant of **-y**[2], used esp. after y.

Eyck /aɪk/, n. 1. **Hubert** /ˈhuːbət/, or **Huybrecht Van** /ˈhɔɪbrɛkt vɒn/, 1366–1426, Flemish painter. 2. his brother, **Jan Van** /jɒn/ (*Jan van Brugge*), 1385?–1440, Flemish painter.

eye /aɪ/, n., pl. **eyes**; v., **eyed, eyeing** or **eying**. ◇n. 1. the organ of sight or vision. 2. all the structures within or near the orbit (eye socket) which assist the organ of vision. 3. this organ with respect to the color of the iris: *blue eyes.* 4. the area around the eye: *a black eye.* 5. sight; vision. 6. the power of using sight to particular advantage: *an eye for color.* 7. (oft. pl.) look, glance, or gaze: *Cast your eye over here.* 8. (oft. pl.) close observation or watch: *The teacher keeps an eye on the class.* 9. regard, respect, view, or aim: *with an eye to winning favor.* 10. (oft. pl.) the manner or way of looking at a thing: *in the eyes of the law.* 11. something similar to the eye in appearance, shape, etc., as the bud of a potato, the lens of a camera, etc. 12. *Weather.* the low pressure centre in a tropical hurricane, where calm conditions are found. 13. *Naut.* the exact direction from which the wind is blowing. ◇ 14. Some special uses are:

an eye for an eye, repayment given in the same form as an injury received.

catch someone's eye, to attract someone's attention.

cry one's eyes out, to weep greatly.

easy on the eye, attractive to look at.

get one's eye in, 1. (in cricket and other ball games) to be able, through practice, to follow the movement of the ball. 2. *Colloq.* to adapt oneself to a situation; become accustomed.

have an eye for, to be a good judge of.

have eyes only for, 1. to look at nothing else but. 2. to desire nothing else but.

in the public eye, well-known.

keep an eye on, to watch carefully; mind.

keep an eye out for, to be on the lookout for.

eye

make eyes at, to look flirtatiously at.
open the eyes of, to make (a person) aware of the truth of something.
pick the eyes out of, to choose the best parts, pieces, etc., of (a collection).
see eye to eye, to have the same opinion; agree.
shut or **close one's eyes to,** to refuse to see; disregard.
sight for sore eyes, a welcome sight or surprise.
turn a blind eye on or **to,** to pretend not to see; ignore.
up to the eyes in, very busy with.
with one's eyes open, fully understanding possible risks.
◇*v.t.* **15.** to fix the eyes upon. [OE *ēge*]

eyeball /'aɪbɔl/, *n.* **1.** the ball or globe of the eye. **2. eyeball to eyeball,** angrily face to face.

eyebrow /'aɪbraʊ/, *n.* (the hair on) the arch above the eye.

eye-dropper /'aɪ-drɒpə/, *n.* → **dropper.**

eyeglass /'aɪglas/, *n.* **1.** the eyepiece of an optical instrument. **2.** → **glass** (def. 4).

eyelash /'aɪlæʃ/, *n.* one of the short, thick, curved hairs growing on the edge of an eyelid.

eyelet /'aɪlət/, *n.* **1.** a small, typically round hole, as in cloth or leather, for passing a lace or cord through. **2.** a metal ring for lining a small hole. [ME, from F: little eye]

eyelid /'aɪlɪd/, *n.* the movable lid of skin which serves to cover and uncover the eyeball.

eyeliner /'aɪlaɪnə/, *n.* a chemical, pencil, etc., used cosmetically to apply dark lines to the edges of the eyelids.

eye shadow, *n.* material applied to the eyelids, to heighten beauty.

eyesight /'aɪsaɪt/, *n.* **1.** the power of seeing. **2.** the range of the eye.

eyesore /'aɪsɔ/, *n.* something unpleasant to look at: *The broken window was an eyesore to the neighbors.*

eyetooth /'aɪtuθ/, *n., pl.* **-teeth** /-tiθ/. **1.** a canine tooth, esp. of the upper jaw (so named from its position under the eye) **2. cut one's eyeteeth,** to become experienced enough to understand things. **3. give one's eyeteeth for,** *Colloq.* to desire greatly.

eyewash /'aɪwɒʃ/, *n.* **1.** Also, **eyewater.** a liquid preparation for the eyes. **2.** *Colloq.* anything done to mislead a person into thinking something is good or correct. **3.** *Colloq.* nonsense.

eyewitness /'aɪwɪtnəs/, *n.* **1.** a person who actually sees some act or occurrence. ◇*adj.* **2.** given by an eyewitness: *an eyewitness account of an accident.*

Eyre[1] /ɛə/, *n.* **Edward John,** 1815–1901, Australian explorer, born in England; explored south-western and central Australia.

Eyre[2] /ɛə/, *n.* **Lake,** the largest of the salt lakes of SA in the north-eastern part; rarely filled with water. It has two basins: **Lake Eyre North,** 145 km long and up to 64 km wide, and **Lake Eyre South,** 64 km long and 29 km wide. [named after explorer EJ EYRE]

eyrie /'ɪəri, 'ɛəri/, *n.* **1.** the high nest of a bird of prey, as an eagle, or of any large bird. **2.** a house, etc. built high. Also, **aerie, aery, eyry.** [*aerie,* from L: level ground]

Ezek, *Bible. Abbrev.* Ezekiel.

Ezekiel /ə'zikiəl/, *n. Bible.* **1.** fl. sixth century BC, one of the major Hebrew prophets. **2.** the 26th book of the Old Testament, written by him.

Ff

F, f, *n.*, *pl.* **F's** or **Fs**, **f's** or **fs**. **1.** the sixth letter of the English alphabet. **2.** the sixth in a series. **3.** *Music.* the fourth note in the scale of C major.

f., *Abbrev.* **1.** *Music.* forte. **2.** (*pl.* **ff.**) folio. **3.** following.

F, **1.** *Symbol.* Fahrenheit. **2.** *Abbrev.* female. **3.** *Elect. Symbol.* farad. **4.** *Genetics.* (with a number following) the offspring from a given parent, F_1 is the first generation of offspring, F_2 is the second, etc. **5.** *Chem. Symbol.* fluorine. **6.** *Abbrev.* French.

fa /fa/, *n. Music.* See **solfège** and **solfa**.

Fabian /'feɪbɪən/, *adj.* **1.** avoiding battle; purposely delaying: *Fabian policy.* **2.** favoring the gradual spread of socialism by peaceful means. ◇*n.* **3.** a person who holds Fabian ideals. [from Quintus *Fabius* Maximus, d. 203 BC, Roman general who harassed Hannibal's army without risking battle]

Fabian Society, *n.* a socialist society founded in England in 1884 favoring the gradual spread of socialism by peaceful means.

fable /'feɪbəl/, *n.* **1.** a short tale, oft. about animals, to teach a lesson about how a person should behave: *the fable of the tortoise and the hare.* **2.** a story not founded on fact. **3.** a story about supernatural people and happenings; legend. **4.** an untruth. [ME, from L: narrative]

fabled /'feɪbəld/, *adj.* **1.** celebrated in fable; legendary: *the fabled goddess of the wood.* **2.** having no real existence; fictitious: *a fabled chest of gold.*

fabric /'fæbrɪk/, *n.* **1.** a cloth made by weaving, knitting, or pressing fibres together: *woollen fabric.* **2.** the texture of the material: *cloths of different fabric.* **3.** framework; structure: *fabric of society.* **4.** *Geol.* the texture and arrangement of the elements of which a rock is composed. [ME, from L: workshop, art, fabric]

fabricate /'fæbrəkeɪt/, *v.t.*, **-cated, -cating. 1.** to make by art and labor; construct. **2.** to make by fitting together standard parts or sections. **3.** to invent (a legend, lie, etc.). [L: having made] –**fabricator**, *n.* –**fabrication**, *n.*

fabulous /'fæbjʊləs/, *adj.* **1.** almost unbelievable: *a fabulous price.* **2.** *Colloq.* wonderful; exceptionally pleasing. **3.** told about in or based on fables: *the fabulous travels of Hercules.* [L]

facade /fə'sad, fæ-/, *n.* **1.** *Archit.* a face or front, or the main face, of a building. **2.** an appearance, esp. a misleading one: *Behind his facade of generosity he hides a cruel nature.* Also, **façade**. [F]

facia

face /feɪs/, *n.*, *v.*, **faced, facing.** ◇*n.* **1.** the front part of the head, from the forehead to the chin. **2.** a look or expression on the face: *a sad face.* **3.** an expression, indicating annoyance, complaint, etc.: *He made faces behind her back.* **4.** *Colloq.* boldness; impudence: *How does she have the face to ask?* **5.** outward appearance: *old problems with new faces.* **6.** general appearance (of a land surface). **7.** a side of a hill, mountain, etc.: *The sheep were on the southern face.* **8.** a surface: *face of the earth; A cube has six faces.* **9.** the side upon which the use of a thing depends: *the face of a playing card; face of a watch,* etc. **10.** the most important side; front: *the face of a building,* etc. **11.** *Mining.* the front of an excavation, where the material is being or was last mined. **12.** *Printing.* **a.** the working surface of a type, plate, etc. **b.** the style or appearance of type; typeface: *broad face; narrow face.* ◇**13.** Some special uses are:

face to face, 1. opposite. **2.** confronted (fol. by *with*): *to come face to face with death.*

in (the) face of, despite: *in the face of many dangers.*

look someone in the face, to meet without fear or embarrassment.

lose / save face, to have one's dignity or social position damaged / restored.

show one's face, to make an appearance; be seen.

to someone's face, in someone's presence; openly.

◇*v.t.* **14.** to look towards: *face the light.* **15.** to have the front towards: *The statue faces the park.* **16.** to meet face to face; confront: *faced with a problem.* **17.** to oppose confidently or with courage: *They would face fearful odds.* **18.** (of a building, garment, etc.) to cover with a different material. **19.** to dress or smooth the surface of (a stone, etc.). **20.** to cause (soldiers) to turn to the right, left, or in the opposite direction. ◇*v.i.* **21.** to be turned (oft. fol. by *to, towards*). ◇**22. face it out**, to ignore or stand up to blame, etc. **23. face up to**, to meet courageously; acknowledge. [ME, from F, from VL: form, face]

facelift /'feɪslɪft/, *n.* **1.** plastic surgery on the face for removing age lines, etc. **2.** any improvement in appearance: *a facelift for an old building.*

facet /'fæsət/, *n.* **1.** one of the small plane polished surfaces of a cut gemstone. **2.** a side; aspect: *a facet of the mind.* **3.** *Zool.* one of the lenses of a compound arthropod eye. [F: little face]

facetious /fə'siʃəs/, *adj.* **1.** intended to be amusing: *His facetious remarks are often merely offensive.* **2.** trying to be amusing: *a facetious person.* [L: witticisms]

face value, *n.* **1.** the value stated on the face of a financial or legal document. **2.** apparent value: *to accept promises at face value.*

Facey /'feɪsi/, *n.* **A(lbert) B(arnett)**, 1894–1982, Australian writer; author of the autobiography *A Fortunate Life* (1981).

facia /'feɪʃə/, *n.* a panel on which instruments, control knobs, etc., are mounted, as in a motor car.

facial /ˈfeɪʃəl/, *adj.* **1.** of the face: *facial expression.* **2.** for the face: *a facial cream.* ◇*n.* **3.** *Colloq.* a beauty treatment for the face.

-facient, a suffix forming adjectives meaning 'that makes or causes (something)' and nouns meaning 'one that makes or causes (something)'. [L *faciens*, ppr., doing, making]

facies /ˈfeɪʃiiz/, *n.* **1.** the general appearance of something naturally occurring, such as a particular flora, fauna or ecosystem. **2.** *Med.* the facial expression accompanying a particular illness. **3.** *Geol.* the total properties of a series of rocks, including mineral composition, texture, type of bedding, animal content, indicating the conditions of formation. [L]

facile /ˈfæsaɪl/, *adj.* **1.** moving, acting, working, etc., with ease: *a facile hand; a facile tongue.* **2.** easily done, performed, used, etc.: *a facile victory; a facile method.* **3.** (of manners or people) agreeable or easily influenced. **4.** smooth but shallow; glib: *a facile expression.* [L: easy to do, easy]

facilitate /fəˈsɪləteɪt/, *v.t.*, **-tated, -tating.** to make easier or less difficult. **– facilitation**, *n.*

facility /fəˈsɪlɪti/, *n.*, *pl.* **-ties. 1.** something that makes possible the easier performance of any action; advantage: *They will provide every facility for the undertaking.* **2.** freedom from difficulty; ease: *facility of understanding.* **3.** readiness because of skill or practice; dexterity: *He has a facility with tools; to have a facility with words.* **4.** (*pl.*) Also, **toilet facilities.** bathroom and toilet. **5.** a building or buildings designed for a particular purpose, as for the holding of sporting events. [L]

facing /ˈfeɪsɪŋ/, *n.* **1.** a covering in different material on a building front, for ornament, protection, etc. **2.** material applied on the edge of a garment for ornament or protection.

facsimile /fækˈsɪməli/, *n.* **1.** an exact copy. **2.** → **fax.** [L *fac*, impv., make + *simile* (neut.) like]

fact /fækt/, *n.* **1.** what has really happened or is the case; truth; reality: *in fact rather than fable.* **2.** a truth known by actual experience or observation: *scientists working with facts.* **3.** something said to be true or supposed to have happened: *The facts are as follows.* **4.** an evil deed (now only in certain legal phrases): *before the fact* ; *after the fact.* **5. in fact,** really; indeed. [L: thing done]

faction /ˈfækʃən/, *n.* a smaller group of people within, but often opposed to the aims of, a larger group. [L: a doing or making, action, party] **– factional**, *adj.* **– factionalism**, *n.* **– factionalise**, *v.*

factious /ˈfækʃəs/, *adj.* **1.** acting only in the interests of a group or faction: *factious opposition.* **2.** caused by factional spirits or strife: *factious quarrels.* [L]

factitious /fækˈtɪʃəs/, *adj.* artificial; not occurring naturally: *factitious enthusiasm.* [L: made by art] **– factitiousness**, *n.*

fact of life, *n.* **1.** an event, development, situation, etc., which must be faced as unchangeable in life: *Sickness is a fact of life.* **2. facts of life,** information about sexual behavior and reproduction, esp. as explained to children.

factor /ˈfæktə/, *n.* **1.** one of the elements that brings about any given result. **2.** *Maths.* one of two or more numbers, etc., which when multiplied together produce a given product: *6 and 3 are factors of 18.* **3.** someone who acts, sometimes in business matters, for another. [L: doer, maker]

factorial /fækˈtɔriəl/, *n.* **1.** *Maths.* the product of an integer multiplied by all integers lower than itself: *The factorial of 4 (written 4!) is 4 x 3 x 2 x 1 = 24.* ◇*adj.* **2.** *Maths.* of or relating to factors or factorials.

factory /ˈfæktri, -tɔri/, *n.*, *pl.* **-ries.** a building or group of buildings where goods are made. [ML, from L *factor*]

factory floor, *n.* an industrial workplace or the people who work there, when viewed as separate from management, administration, etc.

factotum /fækˈtoʊtəm/, *n.* someone employed to do all kinds of work for another. [ML, from L *fac*, impv., do + *tōtum* (neut.) all]

factual /ˈfæktʃuəl/, *adj.* relating to facts; real.

faculty /ˈfækəlti/, *n.*, *pl.* **-ties. 1.** an ability, natural or learned, for a particular kind of action. **2.** one of the powers of the mind, as memory, reason, speech, etc.: *He is in full possession of all his faculties.* **3.** *Educ.* **a.** one of the branches of learning, as arts, law, or medicine, in a university. **b.** the teaching body in any of these branches. [ME, from L: ability, means]

FA Cup /ˌɛf eɪ ˈkʌp/, *n.* (in the UK) a cup awarded annually to the winners of a knock-out soccer competition, open to all member clubs of the British Football Association.

fad /fæd/, *n.* the short-term following by numbers of people of some action that excites attention, as a fashion, etc. [n. use of d. *fad, v.*, be busy about trifles] **– faddish**, *adj.*

Fadden /ˈfædn/, *n.* Sir Arthur William, 1895–1973, Australian accountant and politician; leader of the Country Party 1941–58; prime minister from August to October in 1941.

fade /feɪd/, *v.*, **faded, fading.** ◇*v.i.* **1.** to lose freshness, strength, or health: *The flowers faded.* **2.** (of light or color) to lose brightness. **3.** to disappear or die gradually (oft. fol. by *away* or *out*): *Her smile faded; That fashion just faded out.* **4.** *TV, Radio, Films.* to cause sound and / or image gradually to become clearer (fol. by *in* or *up*) or become less clear (fol. by *out*). **5.** (of radio signals) to lose strength. ◇*v.t.* **6.** to cause to fade: *Sunshine will fade curtains.* [ME, from OF: pale, weak, from b. L *vapidus* flat and *fatuus* insipid] **– fader**, *n.*

faeces *or* **feces** /ˈfisiz/, *n.pl.* waste matter discharged from the intestines; excrement. [L: dregs] **– faecal**, *adj.*

fag /fæg/, *v.*, **fagged, fagging**, *n.* ◇*v.i.* **1.** to work till wearied. ◇*v.t.* **2.** to exhaust (oft. fol. by *out*): *The work will fag him out.* ◇*n.* **3.** tiresome work; toil. **4.** *Brit.* a

fag younger boy at a public school required to perform certain services for an older pupil. **5.** *Colloq.* cigarette.

faggot /'fægət/, *n.* a bundle of sticks, etc., bound together and used for fuel, etc. [ME, from OF; orig. uncert.]

fah /fɑ/, *n. Music.* See **solfa**.

Fahrenheit /'færənhaɪt/, *adj.* **1.** relating to a thermometric scale in which the melting point of ice is 32 degrees above zero (32°F) and the boiling point of water is 212 degrees above zero (212°F). The relation of the degree Fahrenheit to the degree Celsius (°C) is expressed by the formula $°F = \frac{9}{5} °C + 32$. ◇*n.* **2.** the Fahrenheit scale. [named after Gabriel *Fahrenheit*, 1686–1736, German physicist, who devised this scale and introduced the use of mercury in thermometers]

fail /feɪl/, *v.i.* **1.** to fall short of or be wanting in action, detail, or result. **2.** to be insufficient or absent: *Our supplies may fail.* **3.** to fall off; dwindle. ◇*v.t.* **4.** to neglect to perform: *Despite her promise, she failed to help.* **5.** to prove of no use or help to: *Words fail me.* **6.** to take (an examination, etc.) without passing: *He failed maths this year.* **7.** to declare (a person) unsuccessful in a test, course of study, etc.: *The teacher failed him in maths.* ◇*n.* **8. without fail**, for certain; with certainty. [ME, from OF, from L: deceive, disappoint]

failing /'feɪlɪŋ/, *n.* **1.** a weakness; shortcoming: *Laziness is his main failing.* ◇*prep.* **2.** in the absence of: *Failing payment, we shall take him to court.*

fail-safe /'feɪl-seɪf/, *adj.* providing safety in the event of failure or accident: *a fail-safe system.*

failure /'feɪljə/, *n.* **1.** an act of failing; lack of success: *His effort ended in failure.* **2.** non-performance of something due or required: *a failure to do as promised.* **3.** a running short; insufficiency: *failure of crops; failure of supplies.* **4.** loss of strength, etc.: *the failure of health.* **5.** inability to meet financial commitments. **6.** someone or something that proves unsuccessful. [OF *faillir* FAIL]

fain /feɪn/, *adv. Archaic.* gladly; willingly (only with *would*, fol. by simple infinitive): *I would fain be with you.*

faint /feɪnt/, *adj.* **1.** lacking brightness, clearness, loudness, strength, etc.: *a faint light; a faint sound; a faint similarity.* **2.** half-hearted: *faint resistance; faint praise.* **3.** feeling weak, dizzy, or exhausted: *faint with hunger.* ◇*v.i.* **4.** to lose consciousness for a short time; swoon. ◇*n.* **5.** short loss of consciousness; a swoon. [ME, from OF: feigned, hypocritical, sluggish, spiritless]

fair¹ /feə/, *adj.* **1.** free from bias, dishonesty, or injustice: *a fair decision; a fair judge.* **2.** proper under the rules: *fair game; a fair hit.* **3.** moderately good, large, or satisfactory: *a fair income; fair appearance.* **4.** *Weather.* (of the sky) bright; sunny; cloudless to half-cloudy. **5.** free from anything that spoils the appearance, quality, or character. **6.** of a light color; not dark: *fair skin; fair hair.* **7.** pleasing in appearance; attractive. ◇**8.** Some special uses are: **fair and square**, honest; just; straightforward. **fair crack of the whip**, *Colloq.* (a request for fairness or reason). **fair to middling**, *Colloq.* reasonably good; so-so. **in a fair way to**, likely to; on the way to. ◇*adv.* **9.** in a fair manner: *He doesn't play fair.* **10.** straight; directly, as in aiming or hitting. **11.** *Colloq.* completely: *I was fair taken in.* **12. fair and square, a.** directly; accurately: *fair and square on the chin.* **b.** honestly; justly; straightforwardly. **13. fair's fair** (an exclamation asking for fair play). [OE *fæger*] —**fairness**, *n.*

fair² /feə/, *n.* **1.** an amusement show, usu. travelling from place to place, with sideshows, merry-go-rounds, etc. **2.** a periodic gathering of buyers and sellers, as of cattle, books, etc., in an appointed place: *the June book fair.* **3.** a display, often international, of a country's industrial and other achievements: *International Trade Fair.* [ME, from OF, from LL: holiday]

fair dinkum, *Colloq. adj.* **1.** true, genuine: *Are you fair dinkum?* ◇*interj.* **2.** Also, **fair dink.** (a declaration of or genuineness).

fair enough, *Colloq. adj.* **1.** acceptable; passable. ◇*interj.* **2.** (a statement of agreement).

Fairfax family /'feəfæks fæməli/, *n.* an Australian family of newspaper proprietors. **1. John**, 1804–77, newspaper proprietor and company director, born in England; purchased and developed the *Sydney Morning Herald* into an influential newspaper. **2.** his son, **Sir James Reading**, 1834–1919, newspaper proprietor and company director, born in England; revolutionised the *Herald* production with telegraphic communication. **3. Sir Warwick Oswald**, 1901–87, grandson of Sir James, Australian company chairman, author, playwright and grazier.

Fairfield /'feəfild/, *n.* a city in the west of the metropolitan area of Sydney, NSW. Pop. 153 522 (1986).

fair game, *n.* a fair, suitable, or likely object of attack: *The new pupils were fair game,.*

fair go, *Colloq. n.* **1.** a fair or reasonable course of action: *Do you think that's a fair go?* ◇*interj.* **2.** (a request for fairness or reason).

fairly /'feəli/, *adv.* **1.** in a fair manner; justly; impartially. **2.** moderately; tolerably: *fairly good.* **3.** actually; completely: *The wheels fairly spun.*

fairway /'feəweɪ/, *n.* **1.** *Golf.* that part of a golf course between tees and greens where the grass is kept short. **2.** *Naut.* (in a harbor, river, etc.) a channel which vessels can pass through.

fair-weather /'feə-weðə/, *adj.* **1.** for fair weather only. **2.** weakening or failing in time of trouble: *fair-weather friends.*

Fairweather /'feəweðə/, *n.* **Ian**, 1891–1974, Australian artist, born in Scotland; figurative and abstract art.

fairy /'feəri/, *n., pl.* **-ries. 1.** a tiny supernatural being said to have magical powers. **2.** *Colloq.* a male homosexual. [ME, from OF *faerie*, from *fae* FAY]

fairytale /'feəriteɪl/, *n.* **1.** a story usu. concerning fairies and folklore, as told to children.

fairytale 367 **fallen**

2. a statement or account of something imaginary or extraordinary. 3. an imaginary or untrue story; lie; fabrication. ◇*adj.* 4. relating to or likely to occur in a fairytale; unreal.

fait accompli /feɪt əkɒm'pliː/, *n.* an already completed fact; something already done. [F]

faith /feɪθ/, *n.* 1. confidence or trust in someone or something. 2. belief which is not based on proof. 3. belief in the teachings of religion. 4. a system of religious belief: *Christian faith; Jewish faith*. 5. a duty or obligation of loyalty (to a person, promise, engagement, etc.): *to keep or break faith with; to act in good faith; act in bad faith*. [ME, from OF, from L *fides*]

faithful /'feɪθfəl/, *adj.* 1. strict or thorough in performance of duty; conscientious: *She was a faithful worker*. 2. true to one's word, promises, vows, etc. 3. showing loyalty. 4. true to fact or an original: *a faithful account; a faithful copy*. ◇*n.* 5. **the faithful**, the body of loyal members or believers. —**faithless**, *adj.*

faith-healing /'feɪθ-hiːlɪŋ/, *n.* the practice of attempting to cure disease by prayer and religious faith. —**faith-healer**, *n.*

fake /feɪk/, *v.*, **faked**, **faking**, *n.*, *adj.* *Colloq.* ◇*v.t.* 1. to prepare, or make (something) deceptive, or fraudulent: *to fake money*. 2. to pretend; simulate: *to fake illness*. ◇*n.* 3. someone who fakes: *You can tell he's a fake*. 4. something faked or not genuine: *That diamond's a fake*. ◇*adj.* 5. designed to deceive or cheat: *He sold fake watches*. [orig. obscure] —**faker**, *n.*

fakir /'feɪkɪə/, *n.* 1. a Hindu holy man who practises self-denial and lives by begging. 2. a member of any Islamic religious order. Also, **fakeer**. [Ar: poor]

Falange /fəˈlændʒ/, *n.* the Spanish Fascist party founded in 1933 by José Antonio Primo de Rivera and subsequently united by General Franco with other right-wing groups into a single political party. —**Falangist**, *n.*

falcon /'fælkən, 'fɒlkən, 'fɔːkən/, *n.* 1. any of various birds of prey having long, pointed wings and a notched bill, and taking its quarry as it moves. 2. any of various hawks used in falconry, and trained to hunt other birds and game (properly the female only, the male being known as a tercel). [L *falx* sickle]

Falkland Islands /ˌfɔːklənd 'aɪləndz/, *n.pl.* a group of about 200 islands in the southern Atlantic about 480 km east of the Strait of Magellan; British crown colony. Pop. 1813 (1980); 12 173 km². *Cap.*: Stanley. Spanish, **Islas Malvinas**.

Falklands War /ˌfɔːkləndz 'wɔː/, *n.* an armed conflict between the UK and Argentina from March 1982 until the Argentine surrender in June; resulting from the Argentine claim to sovereignty of the Falkland Islands.

fall /fɔːl/, *v.*, **fell**, **fallen**, **falling**, *n.* ◇*v.i.* 1. to drop from a higher to a lower place or position through loss of balance or support. 2. to come down suddenly from a standing or upright position: *to fall on one's knees*. 3. to become less or lower: *The temperature will fall ten degrees*. 4. to hang down: *Her hair falls from the shoulders*. 5. to be cast down, as the eyes. 6. to yield to temptation: *to fall into sin*. 7. to lose high position, dignity, character, etc.: *to fall from power*. 8. to give in to attack: *The city fell to the enemy*. 9. (of a government) to be dismissed. 10. to be hurt or killed: *to fall in battle*. 11. to pass into a certain condition: *to fall asleep; to fall in love*. 12. to become: *to fall sick; to fall due*. 13. (of night, silence, etc.) to come as if dropping. 14. to come by chance into a particular position: *to fall among thieves*. 15. to take place; occur; happen: *Christmas falls on a Monday this year*. 16. to come by right: *The property will fall to the only living relative*. 17. (of the face) to lose animation or expression. 18. (of land) to slope. 19. to be directed, as light, sight, etc., on something. ◇*v.t.* 20. to fell (trees, etc.). ◇21. Some special uses are: **fall away**, 1. to withdraw support or loyalty. 2. to lose weight, strength, etc.; decline.
fall back on, 1. *Mil.* to go back to. 2. to seek help from.
fall behind, to slow down or fail to keep up with; lag: *to fall behind in work, payments, etc.*
fall down, *Colloq.* to fail: *to fall down on the job*.
fall flat, to fail to have the desired effect: *His jokes fell flat*.
fall for, *Colloq.* 1. to be deceived by. 2. to fall in love with.
fall foul, 1. (of ships) to come into collision. 2. to have trouble with.
fall in, 1. to fall to pieces. 2. to take one's proper place in line, as a soldier. 3. to agree.
fall in with, 1. to meet or join up with. 2. to agree to.
fall off, to decrease in number, amount, strength, etc.; diminish.
fall on or **upon**, to attack; assault.
fall on one's feet, to come out from a difficult state of affairs without serious harm.
fall out, 1. to drop out of line, as a soldier. 2. to quarrel. 3. to happen.
fall short, to fail to reach a particular goal.
fall through, to come to nothing; miscarry.
fall to, to begin: *to fall to work, argument, etc.*
fall under, to be classed as; be included in.
◇*n.* 22. the act of falling, or dropping from higher to lower, as of rain, snow, etc. 23. the quantity that descends: *a large fall of snow*. 24. a becoming less; a sinking to a lower level. 25. the distance through which anything falls. 26. (*usu. pl.*) a waterfall. 27. downward direction; slope. 28. a falling by accident, as to the ground: *to have a bad fall*. 29. *Chiefly US.* autumn. 30. a giving into temptation. 31. a defeat as of a city. 32. proper place: *the fall of an accent on a syllable*. 33. *Wrestling.* throwing and holding an opponent on his back. [OE *feallan*]

fallacy /'fæləsi/, *n.*, *pl.* **-cies**. 1. a deceptive, misleading, or false idea, belief, etc.: *a popular fallacy*. 2. a misleading or unsound argument. [ME *falacye*, from L *fallācia* deceit; replacing ME *fallace*, from OF] —**fallacious**, *adj.*

fallen /'fɔːlən/, *v.* 1. past participle of **fall**. ◇*adj.* 2. having dropped or come down from a higher place or level, or from an upright

fallen 368 **famine**

position. **3.** on the ground; prostrate; down flat. **4.** degraded: *a fallen woman*. **5.** destroyed: *a fallen city*. **6.** dead: *fallen in battle*.

fallible /ˈfæləbəl/, *adj.* **1.** subject to being deceived or mistaken; liable to err. **2.** tending to be mistaken or false. [ML, from L: deceive] —**fallibility, fallibleness**, *n.* —**fallibly**, *adv.*

falling star, *n.* → **meteor**.

Fallopian tubes /fəˈloupiən ˈtjubz/, *n.pl.* the uterine tubes, a pair of slender oviducts leading from the ovaries to the uterus, for the transport and fertilisation of ova. [named after Gabriello *Fallopio*, 1523–62, Italian anatomist]

fallout /ˈfɔlaut/, *n.* **1.** the descent of airborne particles of dust, soot, or, more particularly, of radioactive materials resulting from a nuclear explosion. **2.** the radioactive particles themselves.

fallow[1] /ˈfælou/, *adj.* (of land) ploughed and left unseeded for a season or more; uncultivated. [OE *fealga*, pl., fallow land]

fallow[2] /ˈfælou/, *adj.* pale yellow or light brown; dun: *a fallow deer*. [OE *fealu*]

false /fɔls, fɒls/, *adj.*, **falser, falsest**, *adv.* ◇*adj.* **1.** not true or correct; erroneous: *a false statement*. **2.** declaring what is untrue: *false prophets; false witness*. **3.** faithless; treacherous: *a false friend*. **4.** used to deceive or mislead; deceptive: *false weights; to give a false impression*. **5.** not genuine: *a false signature; false teeth*. **6.** *Biol.* not properly so called: *false acacia*. **7.** not properly adjusted, as a balance. ◇*adv.* **8. play (a person) false**, to behave disloyally. [OE *fals*, from L: feigned, deceptive, false]

falsehood /ˈfɔlshud/, *n.* **1.** lack of conformity to truth or fact. **2.** something false; an untrue idea, belief, etc.

false pretences, *n.pl.* the use of false records or misrepresentation, or similar illegal devices to obtain one's own ends.

falsetto /fɔlˈsɛtou/, *n.*, *pl.* **-tos**, *adj.*, *adv.* ◇*n.* **1.** (a man who sings with) an unnaturally high-pitched voice or range. ◇*adj.* **2.** of, or having the quality and range of such a voice. ◇*adv.* **3.** in a falsetto: *to speak falsetto*. [It., diminutive of *falso* FALSE]

falsify /ˈfɔlsəfaɪ/, *v.t.*, **-fied, -fying**. **1.** to make false or incorrect, esp. so as to deceive. **2.** to change unlawfully. **3.** to show or prove to be false; disprove. [ME, from L: that acts falsely] —**falsification**, *n.* —**falsifier**, *n.*

falsity /ˈfɔlsəti/, *n.*, *pl.* **-ties**. **1.** the quality of being false; incorrectness; untruthfulness; treachery. **2.** something false; falsehood. [L]

Falstaff /ˈfɔlstɑf/, *n.* the jovial fat knight in Shakespeare's *Henry IV* and *Merry Wives of Windsor*. —**Falstaffian**, *adj.*

falter /ˈfɔltə/, *v.i.* **1.** to waver in action, purpose, etc.; give way. **2.** to walk or speak hesitatingly or brokenly. **3.** (of a person or animal) to become unsteady in movement, of legs, steps, etc.: *with faltering steps*. ◇*v.t.* **4.** to say hesitatingly. [ME, ? from Scand] —**falteringly**, *adv.* —**falter**, *n.*

fame /feɪm/, *n.*, *v.*, **famed, faming**. ◇*n.* **1.** a widely-known reputation, esp. of favorable character: *literary fame; to seek fame*. **2.** reputation; common view; opinion generally held. ◇*v.t.* **3.** to spread the fame of; make famous: *The place is famed throughout the world*. [ME, from obs. F, from L: report, fame]

familial /fəˈmɪliəl/, *adj.* **1.** of or relating to a family. **2.** appearing in individuals by heredity: *a familial disease*.

familiar /fəˈmɪljə/, *adj.* **1.** well-known: *a familiar sight*. **2.** well-acquainted: *to be familiar with a subject*. **3.** easy; informal: *to write in familiar style*. **4.** close; intimate: *a familiar friend; to be on familiar terms*. **5.** unduly intimate; taking liberties; presuming. ◇*n.* **6.** a close friend.

familiarise *or* **familiarize** /fəˈmɪljəraɪz/, *v.t.*, **-rised, -rising**. **1.** to make (a person) familiar with. **2.** to make (something) well known; bring into common knowledge or use. —**familiarisation**, *n.*

familiarity /fəmɪliˈærəti/, *n.*, *pl.* **-ties**. **1.** close acquaintance; thorough knowledge of (a thing, subject, etc.). **2.** undue intimacy; freedom of behavior allowed only in the most intimate relations. **3.** absence of formality or ceremony.

family /ˈfæməli, ˈfæmli/, *n.*, *pl.* **-lies**, *adj.* **1.** parents and their children, whether living together or not. **2.** one's children as distinct from one's husband or wife. **3.** any social group of persons closely related by blood, as parents, children, uncles, aunts, and cousins; a group descended from a common ancestor. See **extended family**. **4.** *Biol.* the usual subdivison of an order, commonly consisting of several genera, as horses, ants, orchids. **5.** any group of related things: *We belong to the human family*. **6.** (in the classification of languages) a number of languages closely related to each other which form part of a major grouping: *English is of the Indo-European family*. ◇*adj.* **7.** of, relating to, or used by a family. **8.** (of a film, television program, etc.) suitable for all members to see: *a good family film*. **9. in the family way**, *Colloq.* pregnant. [ME, from L *familia* the servants of a household, household, family]

family court, *n.* **1.** a court which administers family law. **2. Family Court of Australia**, the federal court exercising jurisdiction over family law since 1976.

family law, *n.* that body of federal law which is concerned with the rights of parents and their children, esp. at the time of break-up of the family unit.

family planning, *n.* → **birth control**.

family tree, *n.* a genealogical chart showing ancestry, descent, and relationship of the members of a family, as of people, animals, languages, etc.

famine /ˈfæmən/, *n.* **1.** a severe and general shortage of food. **2.** any extreme and

famine 369 **Faraday**

general scarcity. **3.** extreme hunger; starvation. [ME, from F, from L]

famished /'fæmɪʃt/, *adj.* very hungry.

famous /'feɪməs/, *adj.* **1.** having fame; renowned; well-known: *a famous victory.* **2.** *Colloq.* first-rate; excellent. [ME, from AF, from L: fame]

fan[1] /fæn/, *n., v.,* **fanned, fanning.** ◇*n.* **1.** any device for causing a current of air, esp. a rotating device with a series of radiating blades attached to and revolving with a central hub. **2.** a device of feathers, leaves, paper, cloth, etc., usu. in a quarter or half circle when fully opened, for making a cooling current of air. **3.** anything like a fan, as the tail of a bird. **4.** *Geol.* a fan-shaped shingle, deposit, etc. ◇*v.t.* **5.** to move or agitate (the air) with, or as if with, a fan. **6.** to cool or refresh (a person) with, or as if with, a fan. **7.** to stir to activity: *to fan a flame, emotions, etc.* **8.** to spread out like a fan. [OE *fann*, from L *vannus* fan for winnowing grain] **—fanlike,** *adj.*

fan[2] /fæn/, *n. Colloq.* an enthusiastic follower: *football fan; film fan.* [short for FANATIC]

fanatic /fə'nætɪk/, *n.* a person with an extreme and unreasoning enthusiasm or zeal, esp. in religious matters. [L *fānāticus* relating to a temple, inspired by a divinity, frantic] **—fanatical,** *adj.* **—fanaticism,** *n.*

fancier /'fænsiə/, *n.* someone who has a special liking for or interest in something, as some animals or plants: *He is a dog fancier.*

fanciful /'fænsəfəl/, *adj.* **1.** being unusual or odd in appearance; quaint: *a fanciful design.* **2.** imaginary; unreal.

fancy /'fænsi/, *n., pl.* **-cies,** *adj.,* **-cier, -ciest,** *v.,* **-cied, -cying,** *interj.* ◇*n.* **1.** something imagined: *It was only a fancy.* **2.** imagination. **3.** a sudden impulse; whim: *She had a fancy for ice-cream.* **4.** a liking or fondness: *to take a fancy to something.* ◇*adj.* **5.** high quality: *fancy goods, fruits, etc.* **6.** ornamental: *fancy hat.* **7.** imaginative. **8.** depending on fancy or whim. **9.** bred to develop points of excellence, as an animal: *fancy breed.* ◇*v.t.* **10.** to form an idea of; imagine: *He fancied himself as an expert.* **11.** to believe without being sure or certain: *to fancy something's right.* **12.** to take a liking to: *to fancy swimming.* **13.** to place one's hopes or expectations on: *I fancy him to win the race.* ◇*interj.* **14.** (an expression of mild surprise). [contraction of FANTASY]

fancy dress, *n.* a special dress (costume), usu. characteristic of a particular period, place or idea for wear at a ball, party, etc.

fan delta, *n.* a partly submerged alluvial fan at the mouth of a river.

fanfare /'fænfeə/, *n.* a loud, showy piece of music, usu. short, played on trumpets or similar. [F]

fang /fæŋ/, *n.* **1.** one of the long, sharp, hollow, or grooved teeth of a snake, by which poison is injected. **2.** a canine tooth or something shaped like one. ◇*v.t.* **3.** to borrow money from; to beg from: *He fanged a loan.* [OE]

fanlight /'fænlaɪt/, *n.* a fan-shaped window above a door or other opening.

fantail /'fænteɪl/, *n.* **1.** a tail, end, or part shaped like a fan. **2.** a fancy breed of domestic pigeons with fan-shaped tail. **3.** any of various small birds having fanlike tails, as the Willie wagtail. **4.** an additional sail on a windmill for turning it into the wind.

fantasia /fæn'teɪziə, -'teɪʒə/, *n. Music.* **1.** a musical or literary composition in no fixed form or style. **2.** a medley of well-known tunes. [It., from L]

fantasise *or* **fantasize** /'fæntəsaɪz/, *v.i.,* **-sised, -sising.** to daydream.

fantastic /fæn'tæstɪk/, *adj.* **1.** peculiar or strange in character, design, movement, etc.: *fantastic ornaments.* **2.** fanciful or unexpected, as persons or their ideas, actions, etc. **3.** imaginary; groundless; not real: *fantastic fears.* **4.** very fanciful; irrational: *fantastic reasons.* **5.** *Colloq.* large, great: *a fantastic sum of money.* **6.** *Colloq.* very good; fine; wonderful. Also, **fantastical.** [ME, from ML: imaginary, from Gk]

fantasy /'fæntəsi, -zi/, *n., pl.* **-sies.** **1.** imagination or fancy. **2.** the forming of strange, often pleasing mental images; daydream. **3.** a mental image, esp. when grotesque. **4.** **→ hallucination. 5.** an unusual or odd thought, design, or invention. [ME, from OF, from L: idea, fancy, from Gk: impression, image]

FAO /ɛf eɪ 'oʊ/, *Abbrev.* Food and Agriculture Organisation.

FAQ /ɛf eɪ 'kju/, *Abbrev.* of reasonable or average quality, esp. applied to products as wheat, meat, etc. Also, **faq.**

far /fa/, *adv., adj.,* **further** *or* (esp. defs 1, 3, 4) **farther, furthest** *or* (esp. defs 1, 3, 4) **farthest.** ◇*adv.* **1.** at or to a great distance, long way off, or remote point or time: *to see far into the future.* **2.** Some special uses are:
as far as, to the distance, extent, or degree that.
by far, very much.
far and away, very much.
far and near/wide, over great distances.
far be it from me, I do not wish or dare.
far gone, in an advanced or extreme state.
far out, *Colloq.* **1.** (an exclamation showing surprise, admiration, etc.). **2.** out of the ordinary.
few and far between, rare; infrequent.
in so far, to such an extent.
so far, up to now.
so far so good, no trouble yet.
◇*adj.* **3.** at or to a great distance; remote in place. **4.** more distant of the two: *the far side.* **5.** remote in time, degree, scope, purpose, etc. **6. a far cry,** very different. [OE *feor*]

farad /'færəd/, *n.* the derived SI unit of electric capacitance that exists between two conductors when the transfer of an electric charge of one coulomb from one to the other changes the potential difference between them by one volt. *Symbol:* F [named after Michael FARADAY. See FARADAY'S LAW]

Faraday /'færədeɪ/, *n.* **Michael,** 1791–1867, English physicist and chemist; discovered electromagnetic induction and researched the principles of electrolysis.

Faraday's law /ˈfærədeɪz ˌlɔː/, *n.* either of two laws relating to electrolysis which state that **a.** the chemical action of an electric current is in proportion to the quantity of electricity passing through. **b.** the weight of substances set free or deposited by a given quantity of electricity is in proportion to their chemical equivalents. [named after Michael FARADAY]

faraway /ˈfɑːrəweɪ/, *adj.* **1.** distant; remote. **2.** dreamy, abstracted: *a faraway look.*

farce /fɑːs/, *n.* **1.** a (genre of) light, humorous play in which the story depends upon the situation rather than character. **2.** a foolish show; mockery. [ME, from F, from L: stuff] —**farcical**, *adj.*

fare /feə/, *n., v.,* **fared, faring.** ◇*n.* **1.** the price of travelling on a bus, plane, etc.: *Fares have risen.* **2.** food. ◇*v.i.* **3.** to be entertained, esp. with food and drink. **4.** to experience good or bad fortune, treatment, etc.: *He fared well.* **5.** to go; turn out; happen (used impersonally): *It fared ill with him.* [OE *faran*]

Far East /fɑːr ˈiːst/, *n.* the countries of eastern and south-eastern Asia, as China, Japan, Korea, Thailand, etc.

farewell /feəˈwel/, *interj.* **1.** goodbye; adieu; may you fare well. ◇*n.* **2.** good wishes at parting. **3.** leave-taking; departure: *a fond farewell.* ◇*adj.* **4.** parting; valedictory: *a farewell speech.* ◇*v.t.* **5.** to say goodbye to. [orig. two words, *fare well.* See FARE, *v.*]

far-fetched /fɑː-fetʃt/, *adj.* removed from everyday life; exaggerated: *a far-fetched story.*

farinaceous /færəˈneɪʃəs/, *adj.* (of a food) consisting or made of flour or starch.

farm /fɑːm/, *n.* **1.** land devoted to agriculture. **2.** a farmhouse and out buildings. **3.** a section of land or water used for some other industry, esp. raising of livestock, fish, etc.: *a chicken farm; an oyster farm.* **4.** a fixed amount accepted from a person in place of taxes or similar which he is authorised to collect. ◇*v.t.* **5.** to cultivate (land). **6.** to raise (livestock, fish, etc.) on a farm (def. 3). **7.** to take the proceeds or profits of (a tax, undertaking, etc.) on paying a fixed sum. **8.** to let or lease (taxes, revenues, an enterprise, etc.) to another for a fixed sum or a percentage (oft. fol. by *out*). **9.** to let or lease the labor or services of (a person) for hire. **10.** to contract for the maintenance of (a person, institution, etc.). **11.** to distribute (responsibilities, duties, etc.) (usu. fol by *out*): *He farmed out the difficult questions to the supervisor.* ◇*v.i.* **12.** *Geol.* to make an area available to another company for mineral exploration, particularly drilling, in return for a share of profits in any discoveries (fol. by *out*). **13.** to cultivate the soil; operate a farm. [ME, from F: fix, from L] —**farmer**, *n.* —**farming**, *n.*

farmstead /ˈfɑːmsted/, *n.* a farm with its buildings.

Farnham /ˈfɑːnəm/, *n.* **John Peter**, born 1949 in England, Australian pop and rock singer.

farrago /fəˈrɑːɡoʊ/, *n., pl.* **-goes.** a confused mixture; hotchpotch; medley: *a farrago of doubts, fears, hopes, wishes.* [L: mixed fodder, medley]

Farrer /ˈfærə/, *n.* **William James**, 1845–1906, Australian wheat-breeder, born in England; pioneered the scientific breeding of wheats resistant to rust and other diseases.

farrier /ˈfæriə/, *n.* **1.** a blacksmith who shoes horses. **2.** a doctor for horses; veterinary surgeon. **3.** *Mil.* an officer specially trained in shoeing horses and minor veterinary duties. [MF, from L: iron]

farrow /ˈfæroʊ/, *n.* **1.** a litter of pigs. ◇*v.i., v.t.* **2.** (of swine) to give birth to (a litter of pigs). [OE *fearh*]

fart /fɑːt/, *Colloq.* ◇*n.* **1.** an emission of wind from the anus, esp. an audible one. ◇*v.i.* **2.** to emit wind from the anus.

farther /ˈfɑːðə/, *compar. of* **far.** ◇*adv.* **1.** at or to a greater distance, degree, point. **2.** additionally; further. ◇*adj.* **3.** more distant or remote. **4.** additional; further. [ME *ferther*]

farthest /ˈfɑːðɪst/, *superl. of* **far.** ◇*adj.* **1.** most distant or remote. **2.** longest. ◇*adv.* **3.** to or at the greatest distance. [ME *ferthest*]

farthing /ˈfɑːðɪŋ/, *n.* **1.** a former British coin of bronze, worth one quarter of a penny, which ceased to be legal tender from 1 Jan 1961. **2.** something of very small value. [OE *fēorthung*]

fascia /ˈfeɪʃə/; (def. 3) /ˈfæʃiə/, *n., pl.* **fasciae** /ˈfæʃiiː/. **1.** a band or fillet. **2.** *Archit.* a long, flat member or band. **3.** *Anat., Zool.* a band or covering of connective tissue surrounding, supporting, or binding together internal organs or parts of the body. **4.** *Chiefly Zool.* a distinctly marked band of color. **5.** → **facia.** [L: band] —**fascial**, *adj.*

fasciate /ˈfæʃieɪt/, *adj.* **1.** bound with a band or bandage. **2.** *Zool.* consisting of or bound together in bundles. **3.** marked with band or bands. Also, **fasciated.** [L: enveloped with bands] —**fasciation**, *n.*

fascinate /ˈfæsəneɪt/, *v.t.,* **-nated, -nating. 1.** to attract and hold completely by delightful or interesting qualities. **2.** to take away the power of resistance or movement, as through terror. [L: enchanted] —**fascinating**, *adj.* —**fascination**, *n.*

fascism /ˈfæʃɪzəm/, *n.* **1.** (oft. cap.) a government system with strong centralised power, permitting no opposition, controlling all affairs of the nation (industrial, commercial, etc.), together with an aggressive nationalism; first established in Italy by Mussolini in 1922. **2.** *Colloq.* (*disapproving*) any extreme right-wing ideology, esp. one involving racism. [It *Fascismo*, from *fascio* group, bundle, from L *fascis* a bundle of rods containing an axe, a Roman emblem of official power, later adopted by the Italian Fascist party] —**fascist**, *n.*

fashion /ˈfæʃən/, *n.* **1.** the custom or style of dress, manners, etc. of a particular time: *latest fashion in clothes.* **2.** acceptable usage in dress, manners, etc., esp. of polite society: *principles of fashion.* **3.** manner; way; mode: *in warlike fashion.* **4.** a kind; sort: *fashions of furniture change with periods.* ◇*v.t.* **5.** to give shape or

fashion form to; make. **6.** to make to suit; adapt: *doctrines fashioned to today's needs.* ◊*adj.* **7.** relating to or displaying new fashions in clothes, etc.: *a fashion show.* [ME, from OF, from L: a doing or making]

fashionable /ˈfæʃənəbəl/, *adj.* **1.** of or in the fashion. **2.** of, or characteristic of, the world of fashion. —**fashionably,** *adv.*

fast[1] /fast/, *adj.* **1.** able to move quickly; swift; rapid: *a fast horse.* **2.** completed in short time: *a fast race; fast work.* **3.** in advance of the correct time: *His clock is fast.* **4.** characterised by energy or seeking of pleasure, as a way of life. **5.** firmly fixed in place; not able to escape: *to make fast.* **6.** firmly tied, as a knot. **7.** closed and made secure, as a door. **8.** lasting; permanent: *a fast color.* **9.** deep or sound, as sleep. **10.** *Photog.* allowing very short exposure, as by having a wide shutter opening or high film sensitivity: *a fast lens or film.* **11.** (of the surface of a cricket pitch, racecourse, etc.) hard and dry, and therefore not impeding fast movement. **12. pull a fast one,** *Colloq.* to act unfairly or deceitfully. ◊*adv.* **13.** tightly: *to hold fast.* **14.** soundly: *fast asleep.* **15.** quickly, swiftly, or rapidly. **16.** in quick succession. **17. play fast and loose with,** to behave in an inconsiderate, inconstant, or irresponsible manner towards. [OE *fæst*]

fast[2] /fast/, *v.i.* **1.** to eat no food. ◊*n.* **2.** a fasting; limiting of one's food either in kind or quantity, often as religious custom. **3.** a day or period of fasting. [OE *fæstan*]

fasten /ˈfasən/, *v.t.* **1.** to make fast; fix firmly in place or position; attach tightly to something else. **2.** to make secure, as an article of dress with buttons, clasps, etc., or a door with a lock, bolt, etc. **3.** to enclose securely, as a person or an animal (fol. by *in*). **4.** to attach by any connecting agency: *to fasten a crime upon someone.* **5.** to direct (the eyes, thoughts, etc.) intently. ◊*v.i.* **6.** to become fast, fixed, or firm. **7.** to take firm hold; seize (usu. fol. by *on*). **8.** (of the eyes, thoughts, etc.) to be directed intently. [OE *fæstnian*] —**fastener, fastening,** *n.*

fastidious /fæsˈtɪdiəs/, *adj.* hard to please; fussy: *a fastidious taste.* [L *fastīdiōsus*, from *fastīdium* loathing, disgust]

fat /fæt/, *adj.*, **fatter, fattest,** *n.*, *v.*, **fatted, fatting.** ◊*adj.* **1.** having more flesh than muscle; fleshy; corpulent; obese. **2.** having much edible flesh; well-fattened: *to kill a fat lamb.* **3.** consisting of, resembling, or containing fat; greasy. **4.** fertile, as land. **5.** thick; broad; extended. **6. a fat chance,** *Colloq.* little or no chance. **7. a fat lot,** *Colloq.* little or nothing. ◊*n.* **8.** a white or yellowish greasy substance serving as storage material in animals and plants. When pure, the fats are odorless, colorless, tasteless, insoluble in water but soluble in organic solvents. They are esters, formed by the reaction of various fatty acids with glycerol, and are called glycerides; lipid. **9.** animal tissue containing much of this substance. **10.** the richest or best part of anything. **11.** (*pl.*) livestock fattened for sale. **12. the fat is in the fire,** an unchangeable (and often disastrous) step has been taken. **13. the** **fat of the land,** great luxury. ◊*v.t.* **14.** to make fat; fatten. ◊*v.i.* **15.** to become fat. [OE *fætt*] —**fatness,** *n.*

Fatah /fəˈtɑ/, *n.* **Al,** a Palestinian terrorist organisation founded in 1956.

fatal /ˈfeɪtl/, *adj.* **1.** causing death: *a fatal accident.* **2.** causing destruction or ruin: *an action that is fatal to the success of a project.* **3.** clearly important; fateful: *The fatal day finally arrived.* **4.** proceeding from or decided by fate; inevitable. [ME, from L: belonging to fate]

fatalism /ˈfeɪtəlɪzəm/, *n.* the belief that all events are influenced by fate and therefore inevitable. —**fatalist,** *n.* —**fatalistic,** *adj.*

fatality /fəˈtæləti/, *n., pl.* **-ties. 1.** a disaster resulting in death; calamity; misfortune. **2.** someone who is killed in an accident, etc. **3.** the quality of causing death or disaster; deadliness; a fatal influence. **4.** a predetermined tendency to disaster. **5.** the quality of being subject to fate.

fate /feɪt/, *n.* **1.** (a supernatural power which supposedly designs) an unchangeable and unavoidable plan for the course of a human life; fortune; lot; destiny. **2.** death, destruction, or ruin. [ME, from L: a prophetic declaration, fate]

fated /ˈfeɪtəd/, *adj.* **1.** subject to, guided by, or predetermined by fate. **2.** destined. **3.** doomed.

fateful /ˈfeɪtfəl/, *adj.* **1.** involving momentous consequences; decisively important. **2.** fatal, deadly, or disastrous. **3.** controlled by irresistible destiny. **4.** prophetic; ominous.

Fates /feɪts/, *n. pl. Class Myth.* the three goddesses of destiny; Clotho spins the thread of life, Lachesis measures it, and Atropos severs it.

father /ˈfɑðə/, *n.* **1.** a male parent. **2.** the male founder of a race, family, or line. **3.** *Colloq.* a father-in-law, stepfather, or adoptive father. **4.** someone who has paternal care over another: *a father to the poor.* **5.** a title of respect for an old man. **6.** one of the leading men of a city, etc. **7.** someone or something that originates or establishes something: *James Watt was the father of the steam engine.* **8.** (*cap.*) *Theol.* the Supreme Being and Creator; God. **9.** *Eccles.* (oft. *cap.*) a title of respect, as for Church officers, monks, confessors, and priests. **10. the Father,** the first person of the Trinity. ◊*v.t.* **11.** to beget; be the father of. **12.** to originate; be the author of. **13.** to act as a father towards. [OE *fæder*] —**fatherhood,** *n.* —**fatherly,** *adj.*

Father Christmas, *n.* → **Santa Claus.**

father-in-law /ˈfɑðər-ɪn-lɔ/, *n., pl.* **fathers-in-law.** the father of one's husband or wife.

fatherland /ˈfɑðəlænd/, *n.* **1.** the country of one's birth or origin. **2.** the land of one's ancestors.

fathom /ˈfæðəm/, *n., pl.* **fathoms,** (esp. collectively) **fathom,** *v.* ◊*n.* **1.** a unit of depth in the imperial system equal to six ft or 1.8288m, used in nautical measurements. *Symbol:* fm

fathom 372 **fawn**

◇*v.t.* **2.** to reach in depth by measurement in fathoms; sound; try the depth or bottom of. **3.** to get to the bottom of; understand completely. [OE *fæthm*]

fatigue /fə'tiːg/, *n., v.,* **-tigued, -tiguing.** ◇*n.* **1.** (a cause of) weariness from bodily or mental exertion. **2.** *Physiol.* a temporary lessening of the proper functioning of organs, tissues, cells, etc., after too much use. **3.** *Mech.* the weakening of material subjected to stress. **4.** *Mil.* Also, **fatigue duty.** labor of a generally non-military kind such as cleaning or cooking. ◇*v.t.* **5.** to weary with bodily or mental effort; drain. [F, from L: tire]

fat lamb, *n.* a very young lamb, about four months old and still a suckling.

fatted /'fætəd/, *adj.* **1.** fattened. **2. kill the fatted calf,** to make grand preparations, esp. of food, for a guest.

fatten /'fætn/, *v.t.* **1.** to make fat. **2.** to feed for slaughter. **3.** to enrich; make fruitful. — **fattener,** *n.*

fatty /'fæti/, *adj.,* **-tier, -tiest,** *n.* ◇*adj.* **1.** consisting of, containing, or resembling fat: *fatty tissue.* ◇*n.* **2.** *Colloq.* a fat person. — **fattiness,** *n.*

fatty acid, *n.* any of a class of long-chain aliphatic carboxylic acids, involved in the formation of glycerides (fats).

fatuity /fə'tjuːəti/, *n., pl.* **-ties. 1.** foolishness; stupidity. **2.** something foolish. [L] — **fatuitous,** *adj.*

fatuous /'fætjuəs/, *adj.* foolish, esp. in an unconscious, self-satisfied manner; silly. [L] — **fatuousness,** *n.*

faucet /'fɔːsət/, *n.* any device for controlling the flow of liquid from a pipe or similar by opening or closing it; a tap; cock. [ME, from OF: force in, damage, from L: falsify]

Faulkner /'fɔːknə/, *n.* **William,** 1897–1962, US novelist, short-story writer, and poet; noted for *The Sound and the Fury* (1929) and *As I Lay Dying* (1930); Nobel prize for literature 1949. Also, **Falkner.**

fault /fɔlt, fɒlt/, *n.* **1.** something that fails; defect; flaw. **2.** an error or mistake. **3.** a misdeed or sin; transgression. **4.** delinquency; culpability; cause for blame. **5.** *Geol., Mining.* a break in the continuity of a body of rock or vein, with a dislocation along the plane of fracture. **6.** *Tennis, etc.* failure to serve the ball properly within the rules of the game. **7.** *Showjumping.* a scoring unit used in recording incorrectness of jumps in contests. **8. at fault,** open to blame. **9. find fault,** to find something wrong. **10. to a fault,** to a marked degree: *He was generous to a fault.* ◇*v.i.* **11.** *Geol.* to undergo a fault or faults. **12.** to commit a fault. ◇*v.t.* **13.** *Geol.* to cause fault in. **14.** to find fault with; blame. [ME, from OF, from L: deceive] — **faultless,** *adj.*

fault plane, *n. Geol.* a plane of fracture in a fault.

faulty /'fɔːlti/, *adj.,* **faultier, faultiest.** having faults; imperfect: *faulty workmanship.*

faun /fɔn/, *n.* (in Roman mythology) one of a class of rural gods represented as men with the ears, horns, and tail, and later also the hind legs of a goat. [ME, from L]

fauna /'fɔnə/, *n., pl.* **-nas, -nae.** *Zool.* the animals of a certain place or period, taken as a group (as distinguished from the plants or *flora*). [NL, special use of *Fauna,* name of sister of *Faunus,* in Roman mythology a woodland deity identified with Pan] — **faunal,** *adj.*

Fauré /fɔːˈreɪ/, *n.* **Gabriel Urbain** /gabriˌel yəˈbæ/, 1845–1924, French composer and teacher.

Faust /faʊst/, *n.* the chief character in a famous German story; he is represented as selling his soul to the devil for power or knowledge. — **Faustian,** *adj.*

faux pas /foʊˈpa, ˈfoʊ pa/, *n., pl.* **faux pas** /ˈfoʊ paz, -pa/. a slip in manners; a social blunder. [F]

favor or **favour** /'feɪvə/, *n.* **1.** a kind act; something done or granted out of goodwill, rather than from justice or for payment: *Can I ask a favor of you.* **2.** kindness; approval: *He's in the king's favor.* **3.** the state of being approved, or held in regard: *in favor; out of favor.* **4.** too much kindness; unfair concern: *show undue favor to someone.* **5.** a gift given as a token of goodwill, kind regard, love, etc. **6. in favor of, a.** in support of; on the side of. **b.** to advantage of. **c.** (of a cheque, etc.) payable to. ◇*v.t.* **7.** to regard favorably. **8.** to prefer unfairly. **9.** to show favor to; oblige. **10.** to help or support. [ME, from OF, from L]

favorable or **favourable** /'feɪvərəbəl, -vrəbəl/, *adj.* **1.** affording aid, advantage: *a favorable position.* **2.** approving. **3.** (of an answer) helpful. **4.** promising well: *The signs are favorable.* — **favorably,** *adv.*

favored or **favoured** /'feɪvəd/, *adj.* **1.** regarded or treated with favor. **2.** enjoying special advantages. **3.** having a certain appearance, used in combination, as in *ill-favored.*

favorite or **favourite** /'feɪvərət, -vrət/, *n.* **1.** someone or something regarded with special favor. **2.** *Sport.* a competitor regarded likely to win. **3.** *Racing.* the horse, dog, etc., which is most heavily backed. **4.** a person treated with special (esp. unfair) favor, as by a king. ◇*adj.* **5.** given preference: *a favorite child.* [F, from It *favorito,* from L]

favoritism or **favouritism** /'feɪvərətɪzəm, -vrə-/, *n.* **1.** the favoring of one person or group over others having equal claims: *The favoritism shown to one student made him unpopular.* **2.** the state of being a favorite.

Fawkes /fɔks/, *n.* **Guy,** 1570–1606, English conspirator and leader in the Gunpowder Plot to blow up the Houses of Parliament.

fawn[1] /fɔn/, *n.* **1.** a young deer, esp. less than a year old **2.** a fawn color. ◇*adj.* **3.** pale yellowish brown. ◇*v.i.* **4.** (of deer) to bring forth young. [ME, from OF, from L: offspring, young]

fawn[2] /fɔn/, *v.i.* **1.** (of people) to seek notice or favor by insincere praise; flatter. **2.** (of dogs) to show fondness by wagging the tail, etc. [OE *fægnian* rejoice, fawn] — **fawning,** *adj.*

fax /fæks/, *n.* Also, **facsimile**. **1.** a method of transmitting documents or pictures along a telephone line. **2.** a document or picture so transmitted. ◊*v.t.* **3.** to send (a document, picture, etc.) by fax. ◊*v.i.* **4.** to send a fax. [a respelling of the first part of FACS(IMILE)]

fay /feɪ/, *n.* →**fairy** (def. 1). [ME, from OF, from L *fāta* the Fates]

faze /feɪz/, *v.t.*, **fazed, fazing.** *Colloq.* to worry or disturb; discomfort; daunt: *The size of his opponent fazed him.* [var. of obs. *feeze* disturb, worry]

FBI /ɛf biˈaɪ/, *Abbrev. US.* Federal Bureau of Investigation.

Fe, *Chem. Symbol.* iron. [L *ferrum*]

fealty /ˈfiːəlti/, *n., pl.* **-ties.** *Hist.* faithfulness or loyalty, esp. as owed by a vassal to his feudal lord. [ME, from OF, from L: fidelity]

fear /fɪə/, *n.* **1.** a feeling of danger, evil, trouble, etc., about to happen. **2.** a specific fear: *fear of water; fear of heights; fear of spiders.* **3.** reverential awe, esp. towards God. **4.** likelihood or danger: *There's no fear of missing your train if you hurry.* **5. for fear of,** in order to avoid or prevent. **6. no fear!** *Colloq.* certainly not. ◊*v.t.* **7.** to regard with fear; be afraid of. **8.** to have reverential awe of. ◊*v.i.* **9.** to feel concern or anxiety for something: *I fear for your safety.* [OE *fǣr* sudden attack, sudden danger] **—fearless,** *adj.*

fearful /ˈfɪəfəl/, *adj.* **1.** causing, or likely to cause, fear: *a fearful height.* **2.** feeling fear, dread, or solicitude: *I am fearful of going alone.* **3.** full of awe or reverence. **4.** showing or caused by fear: *fearful trembling.* **5.** *Colloq.* extremely bad, large, etc.: *a fearful mess; a fearful burden.*

fearsome /ˈfɪəsəm/, *adj.* **1.** causing fear: *a fearsome weapon.* **2.** afraid; timid.

feasible /ˈfiːzəbəl/, *adj.* **1.** able to be done or carried out: *a feasible plan.* **2.** likely; probable: *a feasible theory, a feasible excuse.* [ME, from OF, from L: do, make] **—feasibility, feasibleness,** *n.* **—feasibly,** *adv.*

feast /fiːst/, *n.* **1.** a periodical celebration or festival having special religious or other significance. **2.** a rich and elaborate meal or entertainment esp. one for many or important guests; banquet. **3.** an abundant quantity of anything eaten or giving pleasure: *a feast of oysters; a feast of music.* **4.** something highly agreeable: *a feast for the eyes.* ◊*v.i.* **5.** to have or eat a feast (def. 2); eat sumptuously: *to feast for a week.* **6.** to look with delight at something pleasing: *to feast on someone's beauty.* ◊*v.t.* **7.** to provide or entertain with a feast. **8.** to delight; gratify. [ME, from OF, from L: festal] **—feasting,** *n.*

feat /fiːt/, *n.* an act or deed showing unusual boldness, strength or skill. [ME, from OF, from L: thing done]

feather /ˈfɛðə/, *n.* **1.** one of the growths from a bird's skin which together make the plumage, consisting of a central shaft fringed with long narrow barbs. **2.** condition, as of health, spirits, etc.: *in fine feather.* **3.** kind or character: *Birds of a feather flock together.* **4.** a tuft or fringe of hair resembling a feather. **5.** *Archery.* a feather or feathers attached to the rear end of an arrow to direct its flight. **6.** something very light, weak, or small. **7. a feather in one's cap,** mark of distinction; honor. **8. make the feathers fly,** to cause confusion; create disharmony. **9. show the white feather,** to show cowardice. ◊*v.t.* **10.** to provide (an arrow, etc.) with feathers. **11.** to clothe or cover with, or as with, feathers. **12.** *Rowing.* to turn (the blade of an oar) horizontally between strokes. **13.** *Aeron.* to stop (an engine) and hold its propeller in a position that offers least wind resistance. **14.** to touch the controls of (a machine) lightly so as to cause it to respond gently and evenly. **15. feather one's nest,** to provide for or enrich oneself. ◊*v.i.* **16.** to grow feathers. **17.** to be or become feathery in appearance. **18.** (of a wave off the shore) to break very slowly, developing a white cap. [ME and OE *fether*] **—feathered,** *adj.*

featherbed /ˈfɛðəbɛd/, *n., v.,* **-bedded, -bedding.** ◊*n.* **1.** a mattress filled with feathers. **2.** luxury; a pampered state generally. ◊*v.t.* **3.** to pamper; shield from hardship. **4.** to subsidise. **5.** to limit the work done in (a factory, industry, etc.) in order to avoid dismissing redundant workers. **—featherbedder,** *n.*

featherbrain /ˈfɛðəbreɪn/, *n.* a scatty or weak-minded person. Also, **featherhead.** **—featherbrained,** *adj.*

Feathertop /ˈfɛðətɒp/, *n.* Mount, the second highest peak in the Australian Alps in Victoria. 1924 m.

featherweight /ˈfɛðəweɪt/, *n.* **1.** (in amateur boxing) a boxer who weighs between 54 and 57 kg. **2.** a very light or insignificant person or thing. ◊*adj.* **3.** slight; trifling.

feathery /ˈfɛðəri/, *adj.* **1.** clothed or covered with feathers; feathered. **2.** like feathers; light; airy; unsubstantial.

feature /ˈfiːtʃə/, *n., v.,* **-tured, -turing.** ◊*n.* **1.** any part of the face: *His eyes are his worst feature.* **2.** an outstanding part or quality: *Good surfing beaches are a feature of the Australian coast.* **3.** the main film in a cinema program, usu. more than sixty minutes long. **4.** a special article, column, cartoon, etc., in a newspaper or magazine. **5.** a non-fiction radio or television program designed to entertain and inform. ◊*v.t.* **6.** to present or give prominence to: *to feature a new series of plays*; *to feature a special range of goods.* ◊*v.i.* **7.** to be a feature or distinctive mark of: *Fine lines feature very largely in Aboriginal painting.* **8.** to be prominent (fol. by *in*): *The Minister features often in the news.* [ME, from OF, from L: making, formation] **—featured,** *adj.*

Feb, *Abbrev.* February.

febri-, a word part meaning 'fever'. [L, combining form of *febris*]

febrile /ˈfɛbraɪl, -fi-/, *adj.* of or caused by fever; feverish. [L: pertaining to fever]

February /ˈfɛbruəri/, *n.* the second month of the year, containing 28 days, but 29 in leap years. [L *Februārius,* from *februa,* pl., the

February   374   **feel**

Roman festival of purification, celebrated 15 Feb]

feckless /ˈfɛkləs/, *adj.* lacking purpose or resource; ineffective; careless. [Scot]

fecund /ˈfɛkənd, ˈfik-/, *adj.* abundantly fertile or fruitful; productive. [L: fruitful]

fecundity /fəˈkʌndəti/, *n.* **1.** the capacity, esp. of female animals, to produce young in great numbers. **2.** fruitfulness or fertility, as of the earth. **3.** capacity of abundant production: *fecundity of imagination.*

fed /fɛd/, *v.* **1.** past tense and past participle of **feed.** ◇*adj.* **2. fed up**, *Colloq.* annoyed; tired of; frustrated (fol. by *with*): *I'm fed up with this nonsense.* Also, **fed up to the back teeth.**

Fed /fɛd/, *Abbrev.* Federal.

federal /ˈfɛdərəl, ˈfɛdrəl/, *adj.* **1.** of or relating to a federation (def. 2). **2. a.** relating to or of the nature of a union of states under a central government, distinct from the individual governments of the separate states: *the federal government of Australia.* **b.** favoring a strong central government in such a union. **c.** relating to such a central government: *federal offices; federal police.* ◇*n.* **3.** someone who favors federation or federalism. [L: compact, league]

federalism /ˈfɛdərəlɪzəm, ˈfɛdrə-/, *n.* **1.** the principle of federal government. **2.** Also, **new federalism**. the belief that the rights and powers of individual states in a federation should not be lessened or taken over by a central government. **—federalist,** *n. adj.*

Federal Bureau of Investigation, *n.* a US federal agency charged with investigation for the attorney general of the US and safeguarding national security. *Abbrev.:* FBI

federal court, *n.* **1.** a court created by the Commonwealth parliament in accordance with the Constitution to exercise the judicial power of the Commonwealth. The federal courts are the High Court of Australia, the Federal Court of Australia and the Family Court of Australia. **2. Federal Court of Australia**, a court, established in 1976, with an Industrial Division and a General Division.

federal system, *n.* a system of government in which responsibilities are divided between several parliaments one of which has responsibility for the nation as a whole, the others having responsibility for prescribed areas within the nation.

federate /ˈfɛdəreɪt/, *v.*, **-rated, -rating**; /ˈfɛdərət, ˈfɛdrət/, *adj.* ◇*v.t., v.i.* **1.** to join in a league or federation. ◇*adj.* **2.** allied; federated: *federate nations.* **—federator,** *n.*

federation /fɛdəˈreɪʃən/, *n.* **1.** the formation of a political unity with a central government, from a number of separate states, etc., each of which keeps control of its own internal affairs. **2.** the political unity so formed. **3.** (*cap.*) the uniting of the six self-governing colonies of Australia to form a union of states under a central federal government on 1 January 1901. ◇*adj.* **4.** of the style of architecture, etc., common at the time of the federation of the six Australian states: *a federation house.*

Federation Cup, *n.* an international lawn tennis trophy; the women's equivalent of the Davis Cup; first played in 1963.

Federation wheat, *n.* a variety of early-maturing, drought-resistant wheat developed by William Farrer. [first made available to farmers in 1902–03, just after the federation of the states of Australia]

fee /fi/, *n.* **1.** a sum paid for professional services, admissions, licences, tuition, etc. **2. hold in fee, a.** *Law.* to have full ownership of (land, etc.). **b.** *Poetic.* to have absolute mastery over. [ME, from AF; of Gmc orig.]

feeble /ˈfibəl/, *adj.*, **-bler, -blest**. **1.** weak in body, mind or moral sense. **2.** lacking in loudness, brightness, distinctness, etc.: *a feeble voice; feeble light.* **3.** lacking in force, strength, or effectiveness: *feeble resistance; feeble arguments.* [ME, from OF, from L: lamentable] **—feebleness,** *n.*

feed /fid/, *v.*, **fed, feeding,** *n.* ◇*v.t.* **1.** to give food to; nourish. **2. →breastfeed. 3.** to provide with material for growth or normal operation: *to feed a fire; Two creeks feed the river.* **4.** to serve as food for: *One chicken will feed several people.* **5.** to provide or supply (food, etc.): *to feed oats to a horse; to feed information to someone.* **6.** to satisfy; gratify: *Music feeds the spirit.* **7.** to let out slowly (fol. by *out*): *Feed the rope out to me.* **8.** to supply (material) to be operated upon, as to a machine: *to feed fuel into a furnace; to feed meat into a mincer.* ◇*v.i.* **9.** (usu. of animals) to take food; eat; graze. **10.** to flow steadily: *The stream feeds into the river.* ◇*n.* **11.** food, esp. for cattle, etc. **12.** milk, or other liquid preparations, for an unweaned baby. **13.** *Colloq.* a meal. **14.** a feeding mechanism: *petrol feed.* [OE *fēdan*]

feedback /ˈfidbæk/, *n.* **1.** the use as input of a part of the output of any system, esp. a mechanical, electronic, or biological one. **2.** an indication of the reaction of a recipient, as of an audience or market; response. **3.** the input of a signal into a microphone from the output of the same system, usu. causing a high-pitched screech. ◇*adj.* **4.** of, involving, or indicating a feedback.

feeder /ˈfidə/, *n.* **1.** someone or something that feeds an animal, machine, etc. **2.** someone or something that takes food or nourishment. **3.** a tributary stream, secondary road, branch of a railway or airline system, etc. **4. → bib** (def. 1).

feel /fil/, *v.*, **felt, feeling,** *n.* ◇*v.t.* **1.** to perceive or examine by touch: *Feel the roughness of this cloth; Feel how sharp this knife is.* **2.** to have a sensation (other than sight, hearing, taste, and smell) of: *She felt rather than saw him come into the room; They felt the cold.* **3.** to find or pursue (one's way) by touching, or cautious moves: *to feel a way round a room; feel a way round a difficulty.* **4.** to try and gauge the possibilities or reactions of (a situation, person, etc.) (fol. by *out*). **5.** to be emotionally affected by: *She feels his disgrace keenly.* **6.** to experience the effects of: *The whole region felt the storm.* **7.** to have a particular sensation or impression of (fol. by an adjunct or complement): *He felt himself accepted.* **8.** to have a general or

feel thorough conviction of: *I feel that you are in the wrong.* ◇*v.i.* **9.** to perceive things by touch or by any nerves of sensation other than those of sight, hearing, taste, and smell: *If you feel carefully, you will find that the edge has been worn away.* **10.** to make an examination by touch; grope: *She felt under the cupboard for the knife.* **11.** to have mental sensations or emotions: *She feels deeply about injustice; to feel happy; to feel angry.* **12.** to have sympathy or compassion (fol. by *with* or *for*): *We feel for you in your sorrow.* **13.** (of a particular state, situation, etc.) to affect one; seem to one: *How does it feel to be rich.* ◇*v.* **14. feel like,** to have a desire or inclination for: *I feel like a walk.* **15. feel oneself,** to be in one's usual mental or physical state; to be free from illness: *I just don't feel myself today.* **16. feel up to,** *Colloq.* to be well enough to be capable of; to be able to cope with. ◇*n.* **17.** the quality of an object that is sensed by feeling or touching: *a soapy feel; the feel of soap.* **18.** the act of feeling: *Let me have a feel of that wool.* **19.** quality: *Her actions have a nasty feel about them.* **20.** knowledge of how to handle a tool, job, etc.: *You'll soon get the feel of it.* **21.** the sense of touch: *soft to the feel.* [OE *fēlan*]

feeler /'filə/, *n.* **1.** someone or something that feels. **2.** a remark or hint designed to bring out the opinions or purposes of others. **3.** *Zool.* an organ of touch, as an antenna or tentacle.

feeling /'filɪŋ/, *n.* **1.** the sense of touch. **2.** a particular sensation, emotion or impression: *a feeling of warmth; a feeling of joy; a feeling of inferiority.* **3.** *Psychol.* consciousness itself. **4.** an intuition; premonition: *a feeling that something is going to happen.* **5.** capacity for emotion; pity: *She has no feeling.* **6.** sentiment; opinion: *The general feeling was in favor of the proposal.* **7.** Also, **bad feeling, ill feeling.** bitterness; collective or mutual hostility or ill will: *There was bad feeling over his promotion.* **8.** (*pl.*) sensibilities: *to hurt one's feelings.* **9.** fine emotional endowment: *a person of feeling.* **10.** *Music, etc.* **a.** emotional or sympathetic perception shown by an artist in his work. **b.** the general impression given by a work. **c.** sympathetic appreciation: *to play with feeling.* ◇*adj.* **11.** that feels; sentient; sensitive, as nerves. **12.** open to emotion; sympathetic: *a feeling person.* **13.** showing emotion: *a feeling look.*

feet /fit/, *n.* plural of **foot.**

Fehling's solution /ˌfeɪlɪŋz sə'luʃən/, *n.* a solution containing copper sulfate in alkali, which is used to detect and measure the quantity of certain sugars and other reducing agents. [named after Hermann *Fehling*, 1812–85, German chemist]

feign /feɪn/, *v.t.* **1.** to invent (a story, excuse, etc.). **2.** to pretend to have; put on an appearance of: *to feign sickness.* **3.** to imitate in order to deceive: *to feign another's voice.* ◇*v.i.* **4.** to make believe; pretend: *She feigns to be ill.* [ME, from OF, from L: form, conceive, devise] —**feigned,** *adj.*

feint /feɪnt/, *n.* **1.** a feigned attack meant to deceive an opponent. **2.** feigned appearance. ◇*v.i.* **3.** to make a feint. [F: feign]

feldspar /'fɛldspɑ, 'fɛlspɑ/, *n.* → **felspar.**

felicitation /fəˌlɪsə'teɪʃən/, *n.* an expression of good wishes; congratulation: *I send my felicitations on your birthday.*

felicitous /fə'lɪsətəs/, *adj.* happy or apt; well-chosen: *a felicitous word in a poem; He is a most felicitous choice for the job.*

felicity /fə'lɪsəti/, *n., pl.* **-ties. 1.** the state of happiness; bliss. **2.** aptness; skilfulness of expression. [ME, from L: happiness]

feline /'filaɪn/, *adj.* **1.** of or relating to the cat family. **2.** catlike in some way, esp. graceful, spiteful or stealthy. **3.** sly; spiteful; stealthy; treacherous. ◇*n.* **4.** animal of the cat family. [L: of a cat] —**felineness, felinity,** *n.*

fell[1] /fɛl/, *v.* past tense of **fall.**

fell[2] /fɛl/, *v.t.* to cause to fall; knock, strike, or cut down: *to fell a tree; He felled him with one blow.* [OE *fellan*]

fell[3] /fɛl/, *adj.* **1.** fierce; cruel; dreadful: *a fell blow.* **2.** destructive; deadly: *a fell poison; a fell disease; one fell swoop.* [ME, from OF: base]

fell[4] /fɛl/, *n.* the skin or hide of an animal; pelt. [ME and OE]

fellatio /fə'leɪʃioʊ/, *n.* oral stimulation of the male genitals.

feller /'fɛlə/, *n. Colloq.* a fellow. Also, **fella.**

fellow /'fɛloʊ/, *n.* **1.** *Colloq.* a man; boy. **2.** a friend; companion; comrade: *my dear fellow.* **3.** someone belonging to the same class; equal; peer: *the equal of his fellows.* **4.** one of a pair; mate or match: *Put the glove with its fellow.* **5.** (*usu. cap.*) a member of a learned or professional society: *a Fellow of the Royal Australian College of Surgeons.* **6.** *Educ.* a scholar or postgraduate student in a college or university, who is engaged in research rather than teaching. ◇*adj.* **7.** having the same position, work, condition, etc.: *fellow students.* [late OE *fēolaga,* from Scand]

fellowship /'fɛloʊʃɪp/, *n., v.,* **-shipped, -shipping.** ◇*n.* **1.** a sharing or unity of interest, feeling, etc.: *He feels fellowship with other workers.* **2.** companionship, esp. between members of the same church. **3.** an association of people with similar tastes, interests, etc. **4. a.** the position or salary of a fellow of a university, esp. in Britain. **b.** a foundation for the support of a fellow in a college or university.

felon /'fɛlən/, *n.* **1.** *Law.* someone who has committed a felony; criminal. **2.** → **convict.** [ME, from OF, ? from L: gall, bile]

felony /'fɛləni/, *n., pl.* **-nies.** *Law.* a serious criminal offence, as murder, burglary, etc. —**felonious,** *adj.*

felsic /'fɛlsɪk/, *adj.* of or relating to light colored rocks containing an abundance of such minerals as felspar and silica or the minerals themselves. [b. FELSPAR + SILICA]

felsite /'fɛlsaɪt/, *n.* a dense, igneous rock consisting typically of felspar and quartz. [FELS(PAR) + -ITE[1]] —**felsitic,** *adj.*

felspar /'fɛlspɑ/, *n.* any of a group of glassy minerals, principally aluminosilicates of potassium, sodium, and calcium, which are among the most important constituents of igneous rocks. Also, **feldspar**. [G *Feldspath*] —**felspathic**, *adj.*

felt[1] /felt/, *v.* past tense and past participle of **feel**.

felt[2] /felt/, *adj., n.* **1.** (made of) non-woven fabric of wool, fur, or hair, matted together by pressure. **2.** to make into felt; mat or press (fibres) together. **3.** to cover with, or as with felt. ◇*v.i.* **4.** to become matted together. [OE]

fem., *Abbrev.* **1.** female. **2.** feminine.

female /'fimeɪl/, *n.* **1.** a human being of the sex which conceives and brings forth young; a woman or girl. **2.** any animal of corresponding sex. **3.** *Bot.* a pistillate plant. ◇*adj.* **4.** belonging to the female sex. **5.** relating to this sex; feminine. **6.** composed of females: *a female cricket team.* **7.** *Bot.* **a.** indicating or relating to a plant or its reproductive structure which produces or contains elements that need fertilisation. **b.** (of seed plants) pistillate. **8.** *Mech.* indicating some part, etc., into which a corresponding part fits: *a female outlet; a female plug.* [ME, from OF, from L: woman] —**femaleness**, *n.*

Female Factory, *n. Hist.* a temporary gaol and place of employment for convict women in NSW, established at Parramatta in 1804; in 1821 a factory for weaving, with a hospital attached, was established nearby.

feminine /'femənən/, *adj.* **1.** relating to a woman. **2.** belonging to the female sex. **3.** marked by qualities thought to be possessed by women, as sympathy, gentleness, etc. **4.** effeminate. **5.** *Gram.* indicating or relating to a gender usu. indicating female sex. **6.** *Poetry.* **a.** (of a line) ending with an extra unaccented syllable. **b.** (of rhyming words) having a stressed first syllable followed by one or more unaccented syllables, as in *motion, notion.* ◇*n.* **7.** *Gram.* **a.** the feminine gender. **b.** a noun of that gender. [ME, from L: woman] —**femininity**, *n.*

femininity /femə'nɪnəti/, *n.* the quality of being feminine; womanliness.

feminism /'femənɪzəm/, *n.* advocacy of equal rights and opportunities for women, esp. the extension of their activities in social and political life. —**feminist**, *n., adj.*

femme fatale /fem fə'tal, fʌm/, *n.* a dangerously attractive woman. [F]

femto-, a prefix indicating 10^{-15} of a given unit, as in *femtogram*. Symbol: f. [Dan]

femur /'fimə/, *n., pl.* **femurs**, **femora** /'femərə/. *Anat.* the bone of the thigh, the longest bone in the body. [L: thigh]

fen /fen/, *n. Brit.* low land covered wholly or partially with water; boggy land; marsh. [ME and OE]

fence /fens/, *n., v.,* **fenced**, **fencing**. ◇*n.* **1.** an enclosure or barrier, of wire or wood, around or along a field, garden, etc. **2.** skill in argument, repartee, etc. **3.** *Colloq.* a person who receives and disposes of stolen goods. **4.** (in showjumping) an obstacle to be jumped by a horse. **5. over the fence**, not reasonable; immoderate. **6. sit on the fence**, to remain neutral; to avoid a conflict. ◇*v.t.* **7.** to enclose by some barrier, thus asserting exclusive right to possession: *to fence a garden.* **8.** to separate or protect by a fence (foll. by *off*). ◇*v.i.* **9.** to fight with a sword, foil, etc., as a sport. **10.** to try to avoid giving direct answers. **11.** *Colloq.* to receive stolen goods. [aphetic var. of DEFENCE] —**fencer**, *n.*

fencing /'fensɪŋ/, *n.* **1.** the act, practice, or art of using a sword, foil, etc., for defence and attack. **2.** an evading of direct answers; a parrying of arguments. **3.** an enclosure or railing. **4.** fences collectively. **5.** material for fences.

fend /fend/, *v.t.* **1.** to keep or ward off (oft. fol. by *off*): *to fend off blows.* ◇*v.i.* **2.** to parry. **3.** *Colloq.* to provide for: *to fend for oneself.* [var. of DEFEND]

fender /'fendə/, *n.* **1.** something which wards something off. **2.** a guard or screen before an open fireplace, to keep back falling coals or to prevent children falling in. **3.** *Chiefly US.* → **bumper bar**. [var. of DEFENDER]

Fenian /'finiən/, *n.* **1.** a member of an Irish revolutionary organisation founded in New York in 1858, which had for its aim the establishment of an independent Irish republic. **2.** (in Irish legend) a member of a roving band of warriors.

fennel /'fenəl/, *n.* **1.** an umbelliferous plant with yellow flowers, and bearing aromatic fruits used in cookery and medicine and also eaten as a vegetable. **2.** the fruits (**fennel seed**) of this plant. [OE *fenol*, from L: fennel]

Fens /fenz/, *n.pl.* **the**, a low-lying area in eastern England.

feoff /fif/, *n.* (in the feudal system) land owned by a lord, and held (by inheritance) by a vassal, in return for military service; fief. [ME, from OF: fee]

-fer, a noun suffix meaning 'bearing', 'producing', with a corresponding adjective in *-ferous*, as in *conifer* (a coniferous tree). [L: bearing]

feral /'ferəl, 'fɪərəl/, *adj.* **1.** (of animals or plants) wild. **2.** (of animals which were previously domesticated) gone wild: *feral cats.* **3.** of or characteristic of wild animals: *the feral state.* [L: wild beast]

ferment /'fəment/, *n.;* /fə'ment, fɜ-/, *v.,* ◇*n.* **1.** an agent or substance which causes fermentation. **2.** excitement; agitation; tumult: *a ferment of activity.* ◇*v.t.* **3.** to act upon as a ferment: *Yeast will ferment beer.* **4.** to cause to undergo fermentation: *We are going to ferment the apple juice.* **5.** to excite; agitate; foment. ◇*v.i.* **6.** to be fermented; undergo fermentation: *The apple juice has been there so long it has fermented.* **7.** to seethe with agitation or excitement. [L: agitation]

fermentation /fəmen'teɪʃən/, *n.* **1.** the act or process of fermenting. **2.** *Biochem.* the breakdown of complex molecules brought about by a ferment, as in the changing of grape sugar

fermentation   377   **festival**

into ethyl alcohol by yeast enzymes. **3.** excitement; agitation. —**fermentative**, *adj.*

Fermi /'feəmi/, *n.* **Enrico** /en'rikou/, 1901–54, Italian nuclear physicist, in the US from 1939; Nobel prize for physics 1938.

fermium /'fɜmiəm/, *n.* a synthetic, radioactive element. Symbol: Fm; *at. no.*: 100; *at. wt.*: 257. [from Enrico *Fermi*, 1901–54, Italian physicist, + -IUM]

fern /fɜn/, *n.* a pteridophytic plant with few leaves, large in proportion to the stems, and bearing sporangia on the undersurface or margin. [OE *fearn*] —**ferny**, *adj.*

Fernández /fɜ'nændeθ/, *n.* **Juan** /'hwan/, c. 1536–1602, Spanish navigator and explorer of the western coast of South America and islands of the Pacific.

ferocious /fə'rouʃəs/, *adj.* (of a person, action, etc.) savagely fierce, like a wild beast; violently cruel.

ferocity /fə'rɒsəti/, *n.* savage fierceness.

-ferous, an adjective suffix meaning 'bearing', 'producing', as in *auriferous, coniferous.*

Ferrari /fə'rari/, *n.* **Enzo**, 1898–1988, Italian racing car designer.

Ferrel's law /fɜrəlz 'lɔ/, *n.* a law stating that all bodies moving on the earth's surface are are deflected to the right in the northern hemisphere and to the left in the southern hemisphere. [named after William *Ferrel*, 1817–91, US meteorologist]

ferret /'ferət/, *n.* **1.** an animal of the weasel family with long slender body, used to hunt rabbits, etc. **2.** to search out or bring to light (oft. fol. by *out*): *to ferret out the facts.* ◇*v.i.* **3.** to search about. [ME, from OF, from L: thief] —**ferreter**, *n.* —**ferrety**, *adj.*

ferri-, a word part meaning 'iron', implying esp. combination with ferric iron. [var. of FERRO-]

ferric /'ferɪk/, *adj.* of or containing iron, esp. in the trivalent state.

ferro-, a word part meaning 'iron', in chemistry implying esp. combination with ferrous iron as opposed to ferric iron. Also, **ferri-**. [combining form representing L: iron]

ferromagnetic /ˌferoumæg'netɪk/, *adj.* (of a substance, such as iron) having magnetic properties in the absence of a magnetic field produced outside it. —**ferromagnetism**, *n.*

ferrous /'ferəs/, *adj.* of or containing iron, esp. in the divalent state.

ferrule /'ferul, -rəl/, *n.* a metal ring or cap on the end of a post, stick, handle, etc., for strength or protection. [late ME, from OF, from L: bracelets]

ferry /'feri/, *n.*, *pl.* **-ries**, *v.*, **-ried**, **-rying.** ◇*n.* **1.** a service which carries people across a river, harbor, etc., by boat. **2.** Also, **ferryboat.** one of the boats used in such a service. ◇*v.t.* **3.** to carry (something) over water in a boat or plane. **4.** to deliver (goods, people, etc.) from one place to another. [OE *ferian*]

fertile /'fɜtaɪl/, *adj.* **1.** capable of bearing abundantly: *fertile soil; fertile land.* **2.** abundantly productive or inventive: *a fertile imagination.* **3.** (of animals, plants, or people) able to produce offspring: *Mules are not fertile.* See **sterile**. **4.** *Biol.* fertilised, as an egg or ovum. **5.** *Phys.* (of an isotope) able to be converted into fissile material in a nuclear reactor. [ME, from L: fruitful] —**fertility**, *n.*

Fertile Crescent, *n.* an area in the Middle and Near East, once fertile but now partly desert, in which it is believed that man first practised agriculture; site of the Sumerian, Babylonian, Assyrian, Phoenician and Hebrew civilisations.

fertilise or **fertilize** /'fɜtəlaɪz/, *v.t.*, **-lised, -lising.** **1.** *Biol.* **a.** to make (an egg, ovum, or female cell) capable of development by union with the male element, or sperm. **b.** to make fertile, or impregnate (an animal or plant). **2.** to make fertile; enrich (soil, etc.) for crops, etc. **3.** to make productive. —**fertilisable**, *adj.* —**fertilisation**, *n.*

fertiliser /'fɜtəlaɪzə/, *n.* material used to fertilise the soil, esp. a commercial or chemical manure.

fertility cult, *n.* a primitive form of worship based on the performance of magical rituals to ensure the growth of crops, livestock, etc.

ferule /'ferul, -rəl/, *n., v.*, **-ruled, -ruling.** ◇*n.* **1.** a rod, cane, or flat piece of wood used for punishing children. Also **ferula**. ◇*v.t.* **2.** to punish with a ferule. [OE *ferele*, from L: rod, giant fennel]

fervent /'fɜvənt/, *adj.* **1.** very warm and earnest in feeling; ardent: *a fervent admirer; a fervent plea.* **2.** hot; burning; glowing. [ME, from L: boiling, glowing] —**fervency**, **ferventness**, *n.*

fervid /'fɜvəd/, *adj.* **1.** heated or vehement in spirit, enthusiasm, etc.: *a fervid orator.* **2.** burning; glowing; hot. [L: burning]

fervor or **fervour** /'fɜvə/, *n.* **1.** great warmth and earnestness of feeling: *to speak with fervor.* **2.** intense heat. [ME, from OF, from L: heat, passion]

fescue /'feskju/, *n.* a grass cultivated for pasture or lawns. [ME, from OF, from L: stalk, straw]

-fest, a suffix indicating a period of festive or enthusiastic activity in something: *musicfest, filmfest.*

festal /'festl/, *adj.* **1.** of or suitable for a feast, festival, or gala occasion: *festal music.* **2.** of or relating to academic dress for formal occasions: *a festal gown.* [late ME, from OF, from L: a festival, feast]

fester /'festə/, *v.i.* **1.** (of a wound) to form pus; suppurate. **2.** (of a foreign body, poison, resentment, etc.) to cause irritation; rankle. ◇*v.t.* **3.** to cause to fester. ◇*n.* **4.** ulcer; rankling sore. [ME, from OF, from L: ulcer]

festival /'festəvəl/, *n.* **1.** a periodic religious or other feast: *the festival of Christmas.* **2.** any time of feasting. **3.** a public celebration, with performances of music, processions, exhibitions, etc: *Moomba festival; festival of Sydney.* **4.** a series of musical, dramatic, or other

festival *performances: film festival.* **5.** *Archaic.* merry-making; revelry. ◇*adj.* **6.** festal: *They're in a festival mood.* [ME, from L: festive]

festive /ˈfɛstɪv/, *adj.* **1.** of or suitable for a feast or festival. **2.** joyful; merry: *festive mood.* [L: merry, lively] —**festively**, *adv.* —**festiveness**, *n.*

festivity /fɛsˈtɪvəti/, *n., pl.* **-ties. 1.** a festival. **2.** (*pl.*) festive proceedings. **3.** festive gaiety or pleasure.

festoon /fɛsˈtuːn/, *n.* **1.** a string or chain of flowers, leaves, ribbon, etc., hung in a curve between two points. **2.** any decoration in this form, as in architectural work or on pottery. ◇*v.t.* **3.** to adorn or drape: *to festoon a tree with lights.* [F, from It: festival, FEAST] —**festoonery**, *n.*

feta /ˈfɛtə/, *n.* →**fetta**.

fetch /fɛtʃ/, *v.t.* **1.** to go after and bring back: *to fetch a book from another room; to fetch a doctor.* **2.** to bring; cause to come: *His remark fetched blood to her cheeks.* **3.** to realise or bring in (a price, etc.): *That should fetch a good price.* **4.** to take (a breath) or utter (a sigh, etc.). **5.** to deal or deliver (a stroke, blow, etc.). ◇*v.i.* **6.** *Naut.* to move, go, or take a course. ◇*v.* **7. fetch and carry,** to do small menial jobs. **8. fetch up,** *Colloq.* **a.** to reach; end up. **b.** to vomit. **c.** to bring or come to a sudden stop: *The car swerved, fetching up against a tree.* ◇*n.* **9.** the act or distance of fetching. **10.** the reach or stretch of a thing (esp. the uninterrupted distance travelled by a wave on the sea). **11.** a trick; a dodge. [OE *feccan*]

fetching /ˈfɛtʃɪŋ/, *adj.* charming; captivating.

fete /feɪt/, *n., v.,* **feted, feting.** ◇*n.* **1.** a bazaar or fair held to raise money for a charity, church, school, etc. **2.** a feast or festival. ◇*v.t.* **3.** to make much of or entertain (someone); celebrate the presence of; lionise: *The committee feted the visitors with champagne.* Also, **fête.** [F. See FEAST]

fetid /ˈfɛtəd, ˈfiːtəd/, *adj.* stinking, esp. of decay. Also, **foetid.** [L] —**fetidness, fetidity**, *n.*

fetish /ˈfɛtɪʃ, ˈfiːt-/, *n.* **1.** an object believed to have magical powers or to be the dwelling place of a powerful spirit. **2.** any object of blind reverence. **3.** an obsession or fixation, usu. expressed in ritualistic behavior. **4.** *Psychol.* a non-sexual object (e.g. a lock of hair, garment, etc.), action or part of the body, which gives sexual stimulation. Also, **fetich.** [F, from Pg, from L: factitious]

fetishism /ˈfɛtɪʃɪzəm, ˈfiːt-, -təʃ-/, *n.* **1.** the belief in or use of fetishes. **2.** *Psychol.* the compulsive use of a fetish (def. 4) in attaining sexual gratification. **3.** blind devotion. Also, **fetichism.** —**fetishist**, *n.*

fetlock /ˈfɛtlɒk/, *n.* **1.** the part of a horse's leg situated behind the joint between the cannon bone and the great pastern bone, and bearing a tuft of hair. **2.** this tuft of hair. [ME; orig. obscure]

fetta /ˈfɛtə/, *n.* a soft, ripened white cheese, from Greece, made originally from goat's or ewe's milk and now from cow's milk, and cured in brine. Also, **feta.** [Modern Gk, from It, from L: mouthful, bite]

fetter /ˈfɛtə/, *n.* **1.** a chain or shackle placed on the feet. **2.** (*usu. pl.*) anything that confines or restrains. ◇*v.t.* **3.** to put fetters on; confine; restrain. [OE *feter*; akin to FOOT]

fettle /ˈfɛtl/, *n.* state; condition: *in fine fettle.* [ME, from OE *fetel* belt]

fettler /ˈfɛtlə/, *n.* a person responsible for maintaining the condition of a railway line.

feud[1] /fjuːd/, *n.* **1.** bitter, continuous hostility, esp. between two families, clans, etc. **2.** a quarrel; contention. ◇*v.i.* **3.** to conduct a feud. [ME, from OF, from OHG]

feud[2] /fjuːd/, *n.* →**feoff**. [ML]

feudal /ˈfjuːdl/, *adj.* **1.** of, relating to, or of the nature of a feoff: *a feudal estate.* **2.** of or relating to the holding of land in a feoff. **3.** of or relating to the feudal system: *feudal law.*

feudalism /ˈfjuːdəlɪzəm/, *n.* the feudal system, or its principles and practices. Also, **feudality.** —**feudalist**, *n.* —**feudalistic**, *adj.*

feudal system, *n.* the economic and social organisation used in Europe during the Middle Ages, based on the holding of lands in return for work or military service, and on the resulting relations between lord, vassal and serf.

fever /ˈfiːvə/, *n.* **1.** an unhealthy condition of the body marked by rise of temperature, quickening of the pulse, and disturbance of various bodily functions. **2.** any of a group of diseases in which a high temperature is an important symptom: *scarlet fever.* **3.** intense nervous excitement. **4. fever pitch**, the height of excitement (esp. of crowds): *His speech raised them to a fever pitch.* ◇*v.t.* **5.** to affect with or as with fever. [OE, from L] —**fevered**, *adj.*

feverish /ˈfiːvərɪʃ/, *adj.* **1.** excited or restless, as if from fever. **2.** having a fever, esp. a slight one. **3.** of or like fever. **4.** causing fever, as food. Also, **feverous.** —**feverishness**, *n.*

few /fjuː/, *adj.* **1.** not many; a small number (of). ◇*n.* **2. the few,** the minority: *Education used to be only for the few.* **3. a few,** a small number. **4. quite a few, a good few, some few,** *Colloq.* a fairly large number. [OE *fēawe*] —**fewness**, *n.*

fey /feɪ/, *adj.* **1.** having or showing magical or supernatural qualities, such as second sight, etc. **2.** light-headed; eccentric; slightly crazy. **3.** in the state of heightened awareness said to presage death. [OE *fǣge* doomed to die; timid]

fez /fɛz/, *n., pl.* **fezzes.** a felt cap, usu. red with a long black tassel, formerly the national headdress of the Turks. [Turk; named after the town of *Fez*, in Morocco]

ff., *Music. Abbrev.* →**fortissimo**.

fiancée /fiˈɒnseɪ/, *n.* the woman to whom a man is engaged. [F: betroth, from L] —**fiancé,** *n. masc.*

Fianna Fail /fiənə ˈfɔɪl, faɪl/, *n.* an Irish nationalist party, organised in 1927 by Eamon De Valera, advocating the establishment of

Fianna Fáil

Fianna Fáil an Irish Republic. [Irish: from *Fianna* Fenians + *Fáil* sod]

fiasco /fiˈæskoʊ/, *n., pl.* **-cos.** a shameful or ridiculous failure. [It: bottle; sense development obscure]

fiat /ˈfiæt, ˈfiət/, *n.* an order issued by an authority; sanction. [L: let it be done, or made]

fib /fɪb/, *n., v.,* **fibbed, fibbing.** ◇*n.* **1.** a lie about an unimportant matter. ◇*v.i.* **2.** to tell a fib. [short for *fibble-fable*, reduplication of FABLE]

fibr-, a word part meaning 'fibre', as in *fibrin*. Also, **fibri-, fibro-**. [combining form representing L *fibra*]

fibre /ˈfaɪbə/, *n.* **1.** a fine threadlike piece, as of cotton, or asbestos; filament. **2.** filaments collectively. **3.** matter made from such threads either natural or man-made: *muscle fibre; cloth fibre.* **4. moral fibre**, strength of character. **5. a.** fibrous matter from plants, used in industry, etc. **b.** this matter as an essential part of the diet; roughage. [ME, from L: fibre, filament]

fibreglass /ˈfaɪbəglɑːs/, *n.* material made of glass filaments, used as an insulator or fixed into plastic as a building material for boats, light car bodies, etc.; glass fibre. [Trademark]

fibre optics, *n.* Optics. the process of passing light along bundles of very fine glass or plastic fibres.

fibril /ˈfaɪbrəl, ˈfɪb-/, *n.* a small or fine fibre. [NL: little fibre, from L] **– fibrillar,** *adj.*

fibrin /ˈfaɪbrən/, *n.* **1.** *Biochem, Physiol.* a white, rough, fibrous protein, formed in the clotting of blood. **2.** *Bot.* a similar substance found in some plants; gluten. [FIBR- + -IN¹] **– fibrinous,** *adj.*

fibro /ˈfaɪbroʊ/, *adj., n.* (of or relating to) a material made of asbestos and cement used in building: *a fibro house.* Also, **fibrocement.** [Trademark]

fibrositis /faɪbrəˈsaɪtəs/, *n.* painful inflammation in fibrous tissue, as muscle.

fibrous /ˈfaɪbrəs/, *adj.* containing or like fibres.

fibula /ˈfɪbjulə, -jələ/, *n., pl.* **-lae** /-liː/, **-las. 1.** *Anat.* the outer and thinner of the two bones of the lower leg. **2.** *Zool.* a similar bone of the leg or hind limb of other animals. [L: clasp, buckle, pin] **– fibular,** *adj.*

-fic, an adjective suffix meaning 'making', 'producing', 'causing', as in *horrific, pacific*. [L: making]

-fication, a suffix of nouns of action or state meaning a 'making', 'producing', as in *pacification*. [L]

fiche /fiːʃ/, *n.* →**microfiche.**

fickle /ˈfɪkəl/, *adj.* changeable in friendship, interest, etc. [OE: deceitful, treacherous] **– fickleness,** *n.* **– fickly,** *adv.*

fiction /ˈfɪkʃən/, *n. Lit.* **1.** stories or works of the imagination, esp. in prose form as novels or short stories. **2.** something invented or imagined; a made-up story. [ME, from L: a making, fashioning] **– fictional,** *adj.*

fictitious /fɪkˈtɪʃəs/, *adj.* **1.** false; not genuine: *fictitious names.* **2.** relating to fiction; created by the imagination: *a fictitious hero.* [L: artificial]

-fid, an adjective suffix meaning "divided', as in *bifid, trifid, multifid, pinnatifid.* [L: cleave]

fiddle /ˈfɪdl/, *n., v.,* **-dled, -dling.** ◇*n.* **1.** *Music.* a stringed musical instrument of the viol class, esp. a violin. **2.** *Naut.* a small railing to prevent things from rolling off the table in bad weather. **3. fit as a fiddle,** in excellent health. **4. play second fiddle,** to take a minor part. ◇*v.i.* **5.** to make aimless movements, as with the hands. ◇*v.i.* **6.** *Colloq.* to play (a tune) on a fiddle. **7.** to waste: *to fiddle time away.* **8.** to plan by illegal means; to arrange dishonestly. [ME]

fiddle bow, *n. Music.* a bow strung with horsehair used for playing a violin or similar instrument.

fiddler /ˈfɪdlə/, *n.* **1.** someone who plays the fiddle. **2.** someone who makes aimless movements, etc. **3.** *Colloq.* a cheat. [ME and OE]

fiddlesticks /ˈfɪdlstɪks/, *interj.* **1.** nonsense. ◇*n.pl.* **2.** a game of skill, usu. for children, in which small sticks are removed separately from a disordered pile without moving the rest.

fiddly /ˈfɪdli/, *adj. Colloq.* difficult and taking time, as something small done with the hands.

fidelity /fəˈdɛləti/, *n., pl.* **-ties. 1.** the strict carrying out of promises, duties, etc. **2.** loyalty. **3.** faithfulness in marriage. **4.** strict holding to truth or fact; (of persons) honesty, truthfulness; (of descriptions, etc.) likeness to the original. **5.** *Elect.* the ability of an amplifier, transmitter, radio, etc., to reproduce a high quality sound. [L: faithfulness]

fidget /ˈfɪdʒət/, *v.i.* **1.** to move about restlessly; be uneasy. ◇*v.t.* **2.** to cause to fidget; make uneasy. ◇*n.* **3.** (*oft. pl.*) a condition of restlessness or uneasiness. **4.** someone who fidgets. [obs. *fidge*, var. of d. *fitch*] **– fidgety,** *adj.*

fief /fiːf/, *n. Hist.* →**feoff.** [F]

field /fiːld/, *n.* **1.** a piece of open or cleared ground, esp. one suitable for raising animals or growing crops. **2.** a piece of ground used for sports or contests. **3.** *Sport.* **a.** all those in a competition, esp. a race. **b.** the runners in a race other than the leaders. **c.** those players who are fielding. **4.** *Mil.* a battlefield. **5.** any region characterised by a certain feature or product: *a gold field; a field of ice.* **6.** the background of a painting, shield, flag, etc. **7.** a range of activity, interest, study, etc.: *My field of work is law.* **8.** a place of study, work, etc., away from the office, laboratory, etc., esp. one where basic material is gathered for later study. **9.** *Phys.* an area or space influenced by some force or thing: *electric field; magnetic field; gravitation field.* **10.** *Phys.* the whole area which can be seen through or projected by an

field   380   **figurative**

optical instrument at one time. **11.** *Computers.* a specified area of a record. ◇*v.t.* **12.** *Cricket, etc.* to place (a player) into the field to play. **13.** to deal with: *He fielded difficult questions.* ◇*v.i.* **14.** to act as a fielder. ◇*adj.* **15.** *Sport, etc.* of, or happening on, a field rather than a track: *Pole vault and long jump are field events.* **16.** of, or conducted in, open air: *We'll have a field study.* [ME and OE]

field day, *n.* **1.** a day spent in outdoor activities or sports. **2.** a day when explorations, investigations, etc., are carried on in the field. **3.** an occasion of total enjoyment, amusement, etc.

fielder /ˈfiːldə/, *n. Sport.* any member of the fielding team, as opposed to the one which is batting.

field goal, *n.* (in Rugby Football, etc.) a goal scored by drop-kicking the ball over the opponent's goal during play; drop goal.

Fielding /ˈfiːldɪŋ/, *n.* **Henry,** 1707-54, English novelist, best known for *Tom Jones* (1749) and *Joseph Andrews* (1742).

field marshal, *n. Mil.* an officer of the highest rank (above a general) in many armies.

fieldmouse /ˈfiːldmaʊs/, *n.* any of various short-tailed mice living in fields.

field of force, *n. Phys.* → **field** (def. 9).

Fields /fiːldz/, *n.* **1. Gracie** (*Grace Stansfield*), 1898-1979, English popular singer and comic actress. **2. WC** (*William Claude Dukenfield*), c. 1879-1946, US comic film actor.

fieldsman /ˈfiːldzmən/, *n., pl.* **-men.** (in cricket) a fielder.

field umpire, *n.* (in Australian Rules) the umpire in control of the game; central umpire.

fiend /fiːnd/, *n.* **1.** Satan; the devil. **2.** any evil spirit. **3.** a very cruel or wicked person. **4.** *Colloq.* a person or thing that is annoying or troublesome. **5.** *Colloq.* someone who spends a great amount of time playing some game, sport, etc.: *a bridge fiend.* [OE *fēond*] —**fiendish,** *adj.*

fierce /fɪəs/, *adj.,* **fiercer, fiercest. 1.** wild in temper, appearance, or action: *fierce animals; fierce looks.* **2.** violent in force, strength, etc.: *fierce winds.* **3.** furiously eager: *fierce competition.* **4.** *Colloq.* unreasonable; extreme: *the prices are fierce.* [ME, from OF, from L: wild, fierce, cruel] —**fiercely,** *adv.* —**fierceness,** *n.*

fiery /ˈfaɪəri/, *adj.,* **fierier, fieriest. 1.** consisting of, with, or containing fire: *a fiery furnace.* **2.** like or suggestive of fire: *a fiery heat; a fiery red color.* **3.** having strong feelings; passionate: *a fiery speech.* —**fierily,** *adv.* —**fieriness,** *n.*

fiesta /fiˈɛstə/, *n.* **1.** a religious celebration; a saint's day. **2.** a holiday or festival. [Sp, from L: festive]

fife /faɪf/, *n.* a high-pitched flute much used in military music. [G: pipe]

Fife /faɪf/, *n.* a former county of eastern Scotland. Also, **Fifeshire.**

fifteen /fɪfˈtiːn/, *n.* **1.** a cardinal number, ten plus five (10 + 5). **2.** a symbol for this number, as 15 or XV. **3.** a set or group of 15, as a rugby union team. ◇*adj.* **4.** amounting to 15 in number. [OE *fīf* FIVE + *-tēne* -TEEN] —**fifteenth,** *adj., n.*

fifth /fɪfθ/, *adj.* **1.** next after the fourth. **2.** being one of five equal parts. ◇*n.* **3.** a fifth part, esp. of one ($\frac{1}{5}$). **4.** the fifth member of a series. **5.** *Music.* a note on the fifth degree from a given note (counted as the first). [OE *fīfta*] —**fifthly,** *adv.*

Fifth Amendment, *n.* the section of the US Constitution concerning certain criminal proceedings, etc., which is sometimes invoked by witnesses at legislative hearings to avoid giving self-incriminating testimony.

fifth column, *n.* a group of persons living in a country who are in sympathy with its enemies, and who are serving enemy interests or are ready to help in an enemy attack. —**fifth columnist,** *n.*

fifty /ˈfɪfti/, *n., pl.* **-ties,** *adj.* ◇*n.* **1.** a cardinal number, ten times five (10 × 5). **2.** a symbol for this number, as 50 or L. **3.** a set of fifty persons or things. **4.** (*pl.*) the numbers from 50 to 59 of a series, esp. years of person's age or the years of a century. ◇*adj.* **5.** amounting to fifty in number. [OE *fīf* FIVE + *-tig* -TY[1]] —**fiftieth,** *adj., n.*

fifty-fifty /ˈfɪftiˈfɪfti/, *adv. Colloq.* **1.** with profits, responsibilities, etc., equally shared. ◇*adj.* **2.** in equal quantities: *a fifty-fifty mixture.*

fig /fɪɡ/, *n.* **1.** (a tree or shrub found in south-western Asia, having) a pear-shaped fruit. **2.** something of little value: *It is not worth a fig.* [ME, from OF, from L]

fig., *Abbrev.* **1.** figurative. **2.** figuratively. **3.** figures.

fight /faɪt/, *n., v.,* **fought, fighting.** ◇*n.* **1.** a battle or combat. **2.** any quarrel, contest, or struggle. **3.** the ability or desire to fight: *There was no fight left in him.* ◇*v.i.* **4.** to take part in battle or to try to defeat an opponent. ◇*v.t.* **5.** to struggle with or against in any manner: *to fight feelings of hunger.* **6.** to carry on (a battle, duel, quarrel, cause etc.). ◇*v.* **7. fight it out,** to struggle till a clear result is obtained. **8. fight off,** to struggle against; drive away. **9. fight shy of,** to keep carefully apart from (a person, affair, etc.). [OE *fe(o)htan*]

fighter /ˈfaɪtə/, *n.* **1.** someone who fights. **2.** *Mil.* An aircraft designed to seek out and destroy enemy aircraft in the air, and to protect bomber aircraft.

figment /ˈfɪɡmənt/, *n.* only a product of the imagination; an invention of the mind, as a story, theory, idea, etc. [L *figmentum* image, fiction, anything made]

figuration /fɪɡjəˈreɪʃən, fɪɡə-/, *n.* **1.** the act of shaping into a particular figure. **2.** the resulting figure or shape. **3.** the act of marking with designs.

figurative /ˈfɪɡjərətɪv, ˈfɪɡə-/, *adj.* **1.** involving a figure of speech, esp. a metaphor; metaphorical; not literal: *figurative expression.* **2.** representing by means of a figure or likeness,

figurative   381   **fillet**

as in drawing or sculpture. **3.** representing by a figure or emblem.

figure /'figə/, *n., v.,* **-ured, -uring.** ◇ *n.* **1.** a numerical number symbol, esp. an Arabic numeral. **2.** an amount or value expresssed in numbers. **3.** (*pl.*) the use of numbers in calculating: *poor at figures.* **4.** the bodily form or frame: *a graceful figure.* **5.** a person as he appears before the eyes of the world: *political figures.* **6.** a diagram or picture in a book, esp. a textbook. **7.** a representation, in sculptured or pictured form of something, esp. human. **8.** an emblem or type: *The dove is a figure of peace.* **9.** → **figure of speech. 10.** a pattern, as in cloth. **11.** a movement, or series of movements, in dancing or skating. **12.** *Music.* a short succession of musical notes, which produces a single impression. **13.** *Geom.* a combination of geometrical elements arranged in a particular form or shape: *The circle and square are plane figures; the sphere and cube are solid figures.* ◇ *v.t.* **14.** to calculate, compute. **15.** to express in figures. **16.** to mark with figures, or with a pattern or design. **17.** to show by a pictured or sculptured form, a diagram, or the like. **18.** to decide, judge, reason: *He figured that was the right path.* **19.** to solve; understand (oft. fol. by *out*). ◇ *v.i.* **20.** to work with numbers. ◇ *v.* **21. figure on,** *Colloq.* to count or rely on. [ME, from F, from L: form, shape] —**figureless,** *adj.* —**figurer,** *n.* —**figured,** *adj.*

figured bass, *n. Music.* the bass part in a musical score with numbers added under the notes to show the chords to be played.

figurehead /'figəhed/, *n.* **1.** a person who is seen as the head of a society, community, etc., but has no real power or responsibility. **2.** *Naut.* an ornamental figure, as a statue or bust, placed at the front of a ship.

figure of speech, *n. Lit.* an expression, e.g. a metaphor, simile, etc., in which words are used out of their usual sense, to suggest a picture or image, or for other special effect.

figurine /'figjurin/, *n.* a small ornamental figure of pottery, metalwork, etc. [F, from It: little figure]

Fiji /fi'dʒi/, *n.* a republic from October 1987 (formerly a parliamentary state) consisting of several hundred islands in the south-western Pacific, chiefly Viti Levu and Vanua Levu; a British colony before independence in 1970 Pop. 726 000 (1987); 18 376 km². *Languages:* Fijian and Hindi, also English. *Currency:* Fiji dollar. *Cap.:* Suva.

filament /'filəmənt/, *n.* **1.** a very fine thread or threadlike structure; a fibre or fibril. **2.** single element of textile fibre (as silk), or machine produced fibre (as rayon or nylon). **3.** *Bot.* a. stalklike part of a stamen, supporting the anther. b. a long fine cell or group of cells, as in some algae, fungi, etc. **4.** *Elect.* the threadlike wire in the bulb which when heated by passage of electric current gives off light. **5.** *Electron.* the heating element of a radio valve. [LL, from L: thread] —**filamentary,** *adj.* —**filamentous,** *adj.*

filch /filtʃ/, *v.t.* to steal (esp. something of small value); pilfer. [orig. unknown] —**filcher,** *n.*

file¹ /fail/, *n., v.,* **filed, filing.** ◇ *n.* **1.** folder or box, in which papers, etc., are arranged for easy reference. **2.** any orderly collection of papers, etc. **3.** *Computers.* a memory storage device, other than a core store, as a disk file, magnetic tape file, etc. **4. on file,** in orderly arrangement for convenient use. **5.** a line of persons or things arranged one behind another. ◇ *v.t.* **6.** to place or arrange in a file. **7.** to place on record (a petition, etc.). **8.** *Law.* to cause to be placed on the files of a court registry. **9.** *Journalism.* to send (newspaper copy) to a newspaper or news agency. ◇ *v.i.* **10.** to march in a file, one after another, as soldiers. [F: thread, string from L] —**filer,** *n.*

file² /fail/, *n., v.,* **filed, filing.** ◇ *n.* **1.** a metal (usu. steel) tool of varying size and form, with many small cutting teeth on its surface, for smoothing or cutting metal and other materials. ◇ *v.t.* **2.** to reduce, smooth, cut, or remove with a file. [d. OE *fíl*] —**filer,** *n.*

filial /'filjəl, -iəl/, *adj.* **1.** of or relating to a son or daughter: *filial duty.* **2.** bearing the relation of a child to a parent. [LL, from L *filius* son, *filia* daughter]

filibuster /'filəbʌstə/, *Orig US.* ◇ *v.i.* **1.** to delay the business in a parliament by making long speeches. ◇ *n.* **2.** such a speech [Sp., from D: freebooter] —**filibusterer,** *n.*

filiform /'filəfɔm, 'filə-/, *adj.* threadlike; filamentous. [L: thread + -FORM]

filigree /'filəgri/, *n., adj., v.,* **-greed, -greeing.** ◇ *n.* **1.** ornamental work of fine wires, esp. of a lace-like design. **2.** anything very delicate. ◇ *adj.* **3.** made of or like filigree. ◇ *v.t.* **4.** to pattern with or form into filigree. Also, **filagree, fillagree.** [F, from It. See FILE¹, GRAIN] —**filigreed,** *adj.*

fill /fil/, *v.t.* **1.** to make full; put as much as can be held into. **2.** to occupy to fullness: *Water filled the basin.* **3.** to supply to fullness: *to fill a house with furniture.* **4.** to satisfy, as food does. **5.** to extend throughout: *The perfume filled the room.* **6.** to have and perform the duties of (a position, post, etc.). **7.** to supply (a blank space) with written matter, etc. **8.** to meet (a need, etc.) satisfactorily: *The book fills a long-felt want.* **9.** to stop up or close: *to fill a tooth.* **10.** *Civ Eng.* to fill low ground with gravel, sand, or earth. ◇ *v.i.* **11.** to become full: *Her eyes filled with tears.* ◇ *v.* **12. fill in, a.** to fill (a hole, hollow, blank, etc.) with something. **b.** to complete (a paper, design, etc.) by filling blank spaces. **c.** to replace. **13. fill out, a.** to stretch (sails, etc.). **b.** to become larger, grow fat, as the figure, etc. **c.** to complete the details of (a plan, design, etc.). ◇ *n.* **14.** a mass of earth, stones, etc., used to fill a hollow, etc. [OE *fyllan*]

filler /'filə/, *n.* **1.** someone or something that fills. **2.** a liquid, paste, etc., used to fill in holes or cracks before painting. **3.** *Journalism.* something used to fill an empty space.

fillet /'filət/, *n.* **1.** a narrow strip, as of ribbon, wood, or metal. **2.** a strip of any

fillet material used for binding. **3.** *Cookery.* **a.** a strip or long (flat or thick) boned piece of fish. **b.** a standard cut of beef or pork, containing little fat and no bone. **4.** *Cookery.* to cut or prepare (meat or fish) as a fillet. [ME, from F: little thread, from L]

filling /'filɪŋ/, *n.* **1.** that which is put in to fill something: *the filling of a pie.* **2.** a substance used to fill in a tooth. **3.** the act of someone or something that fills.

fillip /'filəp/, *v.t.* **1.** to strike with the nail of a finger snapped from the end of the thumb. ◇*n.* **2.** the act or movement of filliping. **3.** anything that tends to stir up or excite; stimulus. [apparently imitative]

filly /'fili/, *n., pl.* **-lies. 1.** a female horse not past its fourth birthday; a young mare. **2.** *Colloq.* a girl. [Scand]

film /film/, *n.* **1.** a thin layer or coating. **2.** a thin sheet of any material. **3.** *Photog.* **a.** a sensitive coating, as of gelatine and silver bromide, used on photographic plate or film (def. 3b). **b.** a strip of cellulose material covered with this substance, used in cameras. **4.** *Films.* **a.** a film strip containing an ordered set of pictures or photographs of objects in motion projected on to a screen so rapidly as to give the appearance that the objects or actors are moving. **b.** such a film strip representing an event, play, story, etc. ◇*v.t.* **5.** to cover with a film, or thin skin. **6.** *Films.* **a.** to photograph with a film camera. **b.** to reproduce in the form of a film or films: *to film a novel.* ◇*v.i.* **7.** to become covered by a film. **8.** to be reproduced in a film: *This story films easily.* [OE *filmen*]

film-maker /'film-meɪkə/, *n.* a person who organises the making of a film, esp. by arranging finance; producer. Cf. **director**.

filmy /'filmi/, *adj.*, **filmier, filmiest.** of the nature of, like, or covered with a thin layer or film; semi-transparent. – **filmily,** *adv.* – **filminess,** *n.*

filo pastry /'filoʊ ˌpeɪstri/, *n.* paper-thin pastry made from flour and water, oft. used in Greek cookery.

filter /'filtə/, *n.* **1.** any device through which liquids are strained to remove unwanted particles or to recover solids. **2.** any of various similar devices, used for removing dust from air, unwanted elements from tobacco smoke, or blocking certain kinds of light rays. **3.** *Colloq.* a filter tip on a cigarette. **4.** *Phys.* a device for picking out waves or currents of certain frequencies. ◇*v.t.* **5.** to remove by the action of a filter. **6.** to act as a filter for. **7.** to pass through a filter. ◇*v.i.* **8.** to pass through or as through a filter. [ME, from OF, from ML: felt (used as a filter), from Gmc] – **filterer,** *n.*

filth /filθ/, *n.* **1.** decayed matter; offensive or disgusting dirt. **2.** an extremely dirty condition. **3.** moral uncleanliness, corruption; obscenity. [OE: foul]

filthy /'filθi/, *adj.*, **filthier, filthiest. 1.** characterised by, or having the nature of filth; disgustingly dirty. **2.** vile; obscene. **3.** *Colloq.* very unpleasant: *filthy weather.* ◇*adv.* **4. filthy rich,** very rich. – **filthiness,** *n.*

filtrate /'filtreɪt/, *v.*, **-trated, -trating,** *n.* ◇*v.t., v.i.* **1.** → **filter.** ◇*n.* **2.** liquid which has been passed through a filter. – **filtration,** *n.*

filum /'faɪləm/, *n., pl.* **-la /-lə/.** a thread-like structure or part; filament. [L]

fin /fin/, *n.* **1.** any of several wing- or paddle-like organs on the body of a fish, used for propelling, steering or balancing. **2.** *Naut.* a fin-shaped plane on a submarine or boat. **3.** a small, fin-shaped attachment underneath the rear of a surfboard. **4.** → **flipper. 5.** any part of a machine, etc., like a fin. [OE *finn*] – **finless,** *adj.* – **finlike,** *adj.*

fin., *Abbrev.* financial.

final /'faɪnəl/, *adj.* **1.** relating to or coming at the end; last in place, order, or time. **2.** bringing something to an end; conclusive or decisive: *a final argument.* ◇*n.* **3.** that which is last; that which forms an end of a series. **4.** (*oft. pl.*) something final, as a last game or contest in a series. **5.** (*pl.*) an examination at the end of a course. [ME, from L: end] – **finality,** *n.*

finale /fə'nɑli/, *n.* **1.** the last piece, division, or movement of a concert, opera, or musical composition. **2.** the last part of any performance. [It]

finalise *or* **finalize** /'faɪnəlaɪz/, *v.t.*, **-lised, -lising.** to put into final form; conclude. – **finalisation,** *n.*

finalist /'faɪnəlɪst/, *n.* someone who is allowed to take part in the final trial or round, as of an athletic contest.

finance /'faɪnæns, fə'næns/, *n., v.*, **-nanced, -nancing.** ◇*n.* **1.** the management of public money, as in the fields of banking and investment. **2.** (*pl.*) money supplies, as of a king, state, company, or an individual; revenue. ◇*v.t.* **3.** to supply with means of payment. **4.** to manage money supplies. ◇*v.i.* **5.** to manage finances. [ME, from OF: ending, payment, revenue] – **financial,** *adj.*

finance company, *n.* a company which arranges loans.

financial year /fəˌnænʃəl 'jɪə/, *n.* any 12-monthly period at the end of which a government, company, etc., balances its accounts and determines its financial condition. Also, **fiscal year.**

financier /fə'nænsɪə, faɪ-/, *n.* someone skilled in financial operations. [F: finance]

finch /fɪntʃ/, *n.* any of a number of small, often highly colored birds of eastern Australia including linnets, etc. [OE *finc*]

find /faɪnd/, *v.*, **found, finding,** *n.* ◇*v.t.* **1.** to come upon by chance; meet. **2.** to learn, or obtain by effort. **3.** to discover. **4.** to recover (something lost). **5.** to gain or regain the use of: *to find one's tongue.* **6.** to gain by effort: *to find safety in hiding.* **7.** to discover by experience: *to find something to be true.* **8.** *Law.* to determine after legal enquiry: *to find a person guilty.* ◇*v.* **9.** Some special uses are: **find fault,** to find cause of blame.
find oneself, to learn one's abilities.
find one's feet, 1. to be able to stand and

walk. **2.** to be able to act without the help of others.

find out, to discover in the course of time or experience; discover by search or inquiry; ascertain by study.
◇*n.* **10.** the act of finding; a discovery. **11.** something found; a discovery, esp. of value: *Our cook was a real find.* [OE *findan*] **—finder,** *n.* **—finding,** *n.*

fine[1] /faɪn/, *adj.*, **finer, finest,** *v.*, **fined, fining.** ◇*adj.* **1.** of the highest quality. **2.** free from imperfections. **3.** (of weather) **a.** sunny. **b.** without rain. **4.** excellent; admirable: *a fine sermon.* **5.** consisting of tiny particles: *fine sand.* **6.** very thin; slender: *fine thread.* **7.** (of a tool) sharp. **8.** delicate: *fine linen.* **9.** highly skilled: *a fine musician.* **10.** in good health; well: *I'm feeling fine.* ◇*v.i.* **11.** to become fine or finer. ◇*v.t.* **12.** to make fine or finer. **13.** (of weather) to become fine (fol. by *up*). [ME, from OF, from L: finish]

fine[2] /faɪn/, *n., v.*, **fined, fining.** ◇*n.* **1.** a sum of money paid as penalty for an offence. ◇*v.t.* **2.** to punish by a fine. [ME, from OF, from L: boundary, end, ML: settlement, fine]

fine[3] /ˈfiːneɪ/, *n. Music.* the end of a repeated section of a musical composition. [It: end]

fine arts, *n.pl.* those arts, such as architecture, sculpture, painting, music, etc. which aim to express qualities of beauty.

fine leg, *n. Cricket.* (the player in) the leg-side fielding position almost directly behind the wickets.

fineness /ˈfaɪnnəs/, *n.* **1.** the state or quality of being fine. **2.** *Metall.* the amount of pure metal (gold or silver) in an alloy, oft. expressed by the number of parts in 1000.

finery /ˈfaɪnəri/, *n.* fine or showy clothes, ornaments, etc. [FINE[1] + -ERY]

finesse /fəˈnɛs/, *n.* **1.** fine skill; subtlety. **2.** clever management; strategy. [F]

finetuner /faɪnˈtjuːnə/, *n.* **1.** a device which makes very small changes to the tuning of a radio, television, etc. **2.** *Music.* (of stringed instruments) a device having a metal screw whereby a string may be tuned more finely than by turning its peg.

finger /ˈfɪŋɡə/, *n.* **1.** any of the end parts of the hand, esp. one other than the thumb. **2.** a part of a glove made to cover a finger. **3.** (as a measurement) the width or length of a finger. **4.** something like a finger, or serving that purpose. ◇**5. burn one's fingers,** to get hurt by or suffer loss from a given action. **6. keep one's fingers crossed,** to wish for good luck. **7. not lift a finger,** to do nothing. ◇*v.t.* **8.** to touch with the fingers; handle. **7.** *Music.* to play on (an instrument) with the fingers. ◇*v.i.* **8.** to touch or handle something with the fingers. [OE]

finger cherry, *n.* an Australian tropical tree, with highly poisonous fruit.

fingernail /ˈfɪŋɡəneɪl/, *n.* the nail at the end of a finger.

fingerpick /ˈfɪŋɡəpɪk/, *n.* →**plectrum.**

fingerprint /ˈfɪŋɡəprɪnt/, *n.* **1.** an impression of the markings of the inner surface of the last joint of the thumb or finger. **2.** such an impression made with ink used to identify a person. ◇*v.t.* **3.** to take the fingerprints of.

fingerstall /ˈfɪŋɡəstɔːl/, *n.* a covering used to protect a finger.

fingertip /ˈfɪŋɡətɪp/, *n.* **1.** the tip of a finger. **2. at one's fingertips,** within easy reach.

finicky /ˈfɪnɪki/, *adj.* **1.** very particular; fussy. **2.** (of things) having too much unimportant detail.

finis /ˈfiːnɪs/, *n.* the end; the conclusion (often used at the end of a book). [L]

finish /ˈfɪnɪʃ/, *v.t.* **1.** to bring (action, speech, work, etc.) to an end. **2.** to come to the end of (a period of time, etc.). **3.** to use up completely (oft. fol. by *up* or *off*): *to finish a plate of food.* **4.** to destroy or kill (oft. fol. by *off*). **5.** to put the last treatment on (wood, metal, etc.). ◇*v.i.* **6.** to come to an end. **7.** to complete a course, etc. ◇*n.* **8.** the end; conclusion. **9.** a decisive ending; *a fight to the finish.* **10.** the quality of being finished with smoothness, elegance, etc. **11.** the manner in which a thing is finished in preparation: *a soft or dull finish, as of wood, metal, etc.* **12.** woodwork, panelling, etc., esp. in the inside of a building, used for purposes of neatness, etc. **13.** a final coat of plaster or paint. [ME, from F, from L: bound, end]

Finisterre /fɪnəsˈtɛə/, *n. Cape,* a headland in north-western Spain; the westernmost point of Spain.

finite /ˈfaɪnaɪt/, *adj.* **1.** having limits; able to be measured. **2.** (of space, time, etc.) subject to limitations or conditions: *finite existence.* [L: bounded]

finite verb, *n.* a verb limited by person, number, tense, mood, etc. (opposed to the infinite forms, participle, infinitive, etc.).

fink /fɪŋk/, *n. Colloq.* a contemptible person, esp. someone who goes back on a promise.

Finke /fɪŋk/, *n.* a river in southern central NT, rising about 150 km south of Alice Springs and flowing south-east, in the wet season, towards Lake Eyre. Over 600 km.

Finland /ˈfɪnlænd/, *n.* a republic in northern Europe, on the Baltic Sea, bordered by Norway, Sweden and Russia. Pop. 942 000 (1987 est.); 338 145 km². Languages: Finnish, also Swedish. *Currency:* markka. *Cap.:* Helsinki. Finnish, **Suomi.**

fiord /ˈfiɔːd/, *n.* (esp. on the coast of Norway) a narrow arm of the sea, with steep cliffs on each side. Also, **fjord.** [Norw]

Fiordland /ˈfiɔːdlænd/, *n.* a tourist area in south-western South Island, NZ; containing the largest national park in NZ, 1 223 405 ha.

fir /fɜː/, *n.* (the wood of) any of the coniferous (cone-bearing), pyramid-shaped trees, as the **balsam fir.** [OE *fyrh*]

fire /ˈfaɪə/, *n., v.*, **fired, firing.** ◇*n.* **1.** the heat and light of burning or combustion. **2.** (in a fireplace, furnace, etc.) a burning mass of material. **3.** the destructive burning of a

building, forest, etc.; conflagration. **4.** flashing light or luminous appearance. **5.** burning passion; enthusiasm. **6.** liveliness of imagination. **7.** fever; inflammation. **8.** severe trial or trouble. **9.** the shooting of guns: *to open fire*. ◇**10.** Some special uses are:
catch fire, to start burning.
on fire, **1.** burning. **2.** eager; ardent; zealous.
play with fire, to play carelessly with a dangerous matter.
set fire to or **set on fire**, **1.** to make burn. **2.** to excite violently; inflame.
under fire, **1.** exposed to enemy fire. **2.** under attack or criticism.
◇*v.t.* **11.** to set on fire. **12.** to supply (a furnace, boiler, etc.) with fuel or fire. **13.** *Pottery.* to apply heat to, in a kiln for baking or glazing; burn. **14.** to excite or inspire. **15.** to light, or cause to glow as if on fire. **16.** to shoot (a gun, missile, etc.). **17.** to direct or throw with force or speed: *to fire questions*. **18.** to dismiss from a job. ◇*v.i.* **19.** to start burning; be kindled. **20.** to glow as if on fire. **21.** to become excited, esp. with passion. **22.** to do with enthusiasm. **23.** (of a gun) to go off. **24.** to shoot a gun, missile, etc. **25. fire away**, *Colloq.* (usu. command) to begin speaking. [OE *fȳr*]

firearm /ˈfaɪəram/, *n.* any type of gun; rifle, etc.

fireball /ˈfaɪəbɔl/, *n.* **1.** a ball filled with explosive material, used as a projectile, to injure an enemy by an explosion, etc. **2.** a ball of fire, esp. the sun. **3.** a bright meteor. **4.** lightning with the appearance of a ball of fire. **5.** *Mil.* the very bright sphere of hot gases which forms at the explosion of a nuclear weapon. **6.** a ball of flaming gas (from eucalyptus tree oil), flying through the air in a bush fire.

firebrand /ˈfaɪəbrænd/, *n.* **1.** a piece of burning wood, etc. **2.** someone who causes unrest or trouble.

firebreak /ˈfaɪəbreɪk/, *n.* a strip of cleared land made to stop the spreading of fire.

fire brigade, *n.* a group of firefighters.

firecracker /ˈfaɪəkrækə/, *n.* → **firework** (def. 1).

firedamp /ˈfaɪədæmp/, *n.* a gas composed mainly of methane, which forms in mines and is dangerously explosive when mixed with air.

fire-escape /ˈfaɪər-əskeɪp/, *n.* a fire-proof staircase, etc., used to escape from a burning building.

firefighter /ˈfaɪəfaɪtə/, *n.* a person employed to put out or prevent fires, esp. bushfires.

firefly /ˈfaɪəflaɪ/, *n.*, *pl.* **-flies.** a soft-bodied, nocturnal beetle with light-producing organs; lightning bug. The luminous larvae or wingless females are called **glow-worms**.

fire irons, *n.pl.* tools used for tending a fire at home, e.g. tongs, poker, etc.

fireman /ˈfaɪəmən/, *n.*, *pl.* **-men. 1.** a person employed to put out or prevent fires; firefighter. **2.** a person employed to tend fires; stoker.

fireplace /ˈfaɪəpleɪs/, *n.* **1.** that part of a chimney which opens into a room, where wood, etc., is burnt. **2.** any open structure, usu. of concrete, for cooking, fires, etc., esp. at a camp site.

fireproof /ˈfaɪəpruf/, *adj.* **1.** resistant to catching fire. ◇*v.t.* **2.** to make fireproof.

firescreen /ˈfaɪəskrin/, *n.* a protective or decorative screen placed in front of fireplace.

fire station, *n.* a building where fire-fighting equipment is kept, and oft. firefighters are housed.

firestick /ˈfaɪəstɪk/, *n.* (formerly) a lighted stick carried from camp to camp by Aboriginals, esp. those in Tas, for lighting fires.

firestone /ˈfaɪəstoʊn/, *n.* a fire-resisting stone, esp. a kind of sandstone used in fireplaces, furnaces, etc. [OE *fȳr* fire + *stān* stone]

firestorm /ˈfaɪəstɔm/, *n.* an atmospheric phenomenon caused by a large fire, esp. after the mass bombing of a city, in which a rising column of air above the fire draws in strong winds and often rain.

firetail /ˈfaɪəteɪl/, *n.* a small grass finch with crimson upper tail-coverts, found in south-eastern Australia and Tas.

fire trail, *n.* a track cleared through the bush so that firefighters can get to bushfires.

firewheel tree, *n.* a tree, native to rainforests in NSW and Qld, which has whorls of bright red flowers.

firework /ˈfaɪəwɜk/, *n.* **1.** (usu. *pl.*) a small container filled with a chemical powder that burns to produce an explosion and a show of colored sparks and light. **2.** (*pl.*) a firework show. **3.** (*pl.*) an outburst of anger or bad temper.

firing /ˈfaɪərɪŋ/, *n.* **1.** the act of someone or something that fires. **2.** material for a fire; fuel. **3.** the act of baking pottery or glass.

firing line, *n.* **1.** (troops in) positions to fire upon enemy, etc. **2.** the forefront of any activity.

firing squad, *n.* soldiers, etc., with the duty of putting a condemned person to death by shooting.

firm¹ /fɜm/, *adj.* **1.** relatively solid, hard or stiff: *firm ground; firm texture.* **2.** securely fixed in place. **3.** steady; not shaking or trembling: *a firm hand; a firm voice.* **4.** (of a belief, decree, agreement, etc.) fixed, settled, or unchangeable. **5.** (of people or principle) steadfast or unwavering. **6.** (of prices, the market, etc.) not fluctuating or falling. ◇*v.t.*, *v.i.* **7.** to make or become firm. ◇*adv.* **8.** in a firm manner: *stand firm*. [L *firmus*]

firm² /fɜm/, *n.* a business company or the name under which it does business: *the firm of Jones and Co.* [It, Sp: signature, from L: confirm]

firmament /ˈfɜməmənt/, *n. Poetic.* the sky; heaven (def. 4). [ME, from LL: firmament, L: a support, prop]

first /fɜst/, *adj.* **1.** being before all others in time, order, rank, importance, etc. (used as the ordinal number of *one*); 1st. **2.** *Music.* the

first   385   **fissile**

highest or most important among several voices or instruments of same class: *first alto; first horn*. **3.** *Motor Vehicles.* of or relating to the lowest gear ratio. **4. at first hand,** from the first or original source. **5. first thing,** before anything else; at once; early. ◇*adv.* **6.** before all others or anything else in time, order, rank, etc. **7.** for the first time: *She first met him at a party.* **8.** rather than something else; sooner. **9.** at or in the beginning. **10. first up,** at the first attempt. ◇*n.* **11.** anyone or anything which is first in time, order, rank, etc. **12.** the beginning: *We liked her from the first.* **13.** first place in a race, etc. **14.** (*pl.*) the best quality of certain goods. [OE *fyrst*]

first aid, *n.* emergency treatment given to people hurt in an accident, etc., until a doctor can be obtained.

first base, *n.* **1.** *Baseball.* the first of the bases from home plate. **2. get to first base,** *Colloq.* to start making progress.

first class, *n.* the most luxurious type of accommodation for passengers on a ship, train, aircraft, etc.

first cousin, *n.* See **cousin.**

first-day cover /ˈfɜːst-deɪ ˈkʌvə/, *n.* an envelope with a newly-issued stamp, posted and franked on the day of issue.

first-degree /ˈfɜːst-dəgriː/, *adj.* of a degree which is at the extreme end of a scale, either as the lowest (*first-degree burn*) or highest (*first-degree murder*).

First Fleet *n.* the ships which brought the first white settlers (convicts, civilians and marines) to Australia in 1788.

First Fleeter, *n.* a person whose family can be traced back to someone who came to Australia with the First Fleet in 1788.

first-hand /ˈfɜːst-ˈhænd/, *adv.*; /ˈfɜːst-hænd/, *adj.*, from, or relating to, the first or original source.

firstly /ˈfɜːstli/, *adv.* in the first place; first.

first name, *n.* Christian name.

first officer, *n.* → **mate** (def. 5).

first-past-the-post /ˌfɜːst-past-ðə-ˈpoʊst/, *adj.* of or relating to a voting system in which the person who gets the largest number of votes wins.

first person, *n.* the class of a pronoun or verb in which the speaker is the subject. See **person** (def. 6) and Appendix.

first principle, *n.* any law or concept, etc., which represents the highest degree of generalisation and which depends on basic principles.

first string, *n.* **1.** → **first violinist. 2.** the best player in a sporting team. **3. the first string in one's bow,** a person's chief skill, ability, etc.

first violinist, *n.* **1.** the person playing first violin who is also the leader of the orchestra. **2.** any player of a first violin part.

First World War, *n.* → **World War I.**

fiscal /ˈfɪskəl/, *adj.* **1.** of or relating to the public treasury or revenues. **2.** relating to financial matters in general. [L: belonging to the state treasury]

fish /fɪʃ/, *n.*, *pl.* **fishes,** (*esp. collectively*) **fish.** ◇*n.* **1.** any of various cold-blooded, backboned animals living in water, with gills and usu. fins and long body covered with scales. **2.** any of various other water animals. **3.** the flesh of fish used as food. **4.** *Colloq.* (with adj.) a person: *a queer fish; a poor fish.* ◇**5.** Some special uses are:
drink like a fish, to drink too much (alcohol).
fish out of water, out of one's proper surroundings.
neither fish nor fowl, not anything particular or recognisable.
other fish to fry, other matters needing attention.
a fine/pretty kettle of fish, trouble; confusion. ◇*v.t.* **6.** to try to catch fish in (a stream, etc.). **7.** to feel or look for and find (fol. by *up, out,* etc.): *He fished a coin out of his pocket.* ◇*v.i.* **8.** to catch or try to catch fish. **9.** to feel or look (for something): *He fished in his pocket for a coin.* **10.** to try to get something indirectly: *to fish for compliments; to fish for information.* [OE *fisc*]

Fisher /ˈfɪʃə/, *n.* **Andrew,** 1862–1928, Australian Labor politician, born in Scotland; prime minister 1908–09, 1910–13, 1914–15.

fisherman /ˈfɪʃəmən/, *n.*, *pl.* **-men. 1.** a man fishing, whether as job or for pleasure. **2.** a vessel used in fishing.

fishery /ˈfɪʃəri/, *n.*, *pl.* **-ries. 1.** the job or industry of catching or breeding fish or other water animals. **2.** a place where fish, etc., are caught or bred.

fish-eye lens, /fɪʃ-aɪ ˈlɛnz/ *n.* a camera lens, shaped like fish's eye, which can take in view of almost 180°, but distorts the image.

fishing rod, *n.* a long rod with line, hook, and usu. reel, used in fishing.

fishmeal /ˈfɪʃmiːl/, *n.* dried and ground fish used as animal feed and fertiliser.

fishmonger /ˈfɪʃmʌŋɡə/, *n.* *Chiefly Brit.* a shopkeeper who sells fish.

fish-net /ˈfɪʃ-nɛt/, *adj.* (of fabric) made in loose, open weave like fishing net: *fish-net stockings.*

fishplate /ˈfɪʃpleɪt/, *n.* a plate bolted onto two separate pieces of metal (esp. railway tracks) to hold them together.

fishy /ˈfɪʃi/, *adj.*, **fishier, fishiest. 1.** fishlike in smell, taste, etc. **2.** *Colloq.* odd or questionable. **3.** dull and expressionless: *fishy eyes.*

Fisk /fɪsk/, *n.* **Sir Ernest Thomas,** 1886–1965, Australian pioneer of radio communication, born in England; established the first voice contact with England in 1924.

fissi-, a word part meaning 'split'. [L, combining form of *fissus*, pp.]

fissile /ˈfɪsaɪl/, *adj.* **1.** able to be split or divided. **2.** *Phys.* (of an atom, isotope, or nucleus) able to undergo nuclear fission, used esp. of an isotope which can undergo fission when hit by a slow neutron. Also, **fissionable.** [L]

fission /'fɪʃən/, *n.* **1.** a splitting into parts. **2.** *Biol.* the division of an organism into new organisms as a process of reproduction. **3.** *Phys.* the splitting of the nucleus of a heavy atom, such as uranium, to form the nuclei of lighter atoms. [L: a cleaving]

fissure /'fɪʃə/, *n., v.,* **-sured, -suring.** ◇*n.* **1.** a crack or split; cleft. **2.** a breaking or dividing. ◇*v.t., v.i.* **3.** to crack or split. [F, from L: a cleft]

fist /fɪst/, *n.* **1.** the hand with fingers closed tightly into the palm. **2. make a good/poor fist of,** to do (something) well/badly. [OE *fȳst*]

fisticuff /'fɪstɪkʌf/, *n.* **1.** a blow with the fist. **2.** (*pl.*) a fight with the fists.

fistula /'fɪstʃulə/, *n., pl.* **-las, -lae** /-li/. *Med.* an opening due to disease or a wound, leading from one hollow organ to another or to the surface of the skin. [L: pipe, tube, reed, ulcer] —**fistulous, fistular,** *adj.*

fit[1] /fɪt/, *adj.,* **fitter, fittest,** *v.,* **fitted, fitting,** *n.* ◇*adj.* **1.** suitable: *fit to be eaten.* **2.** right or proper. **3.** good enough; worthy; deserving. **4.** in good physical condition; healthy. ◇*v.t.* **5.** to be suitable for. **6.** to be of the right size or shape for. **7.** to make or change so as to fit something. **8.** to place closely or make space for (fol. by *in, into, on, over, together,* etc.). **9.** to provide; equip: *to fit a door with a new handle.* ◇*v.i.* **10.** to be suitable or proper. **11.** to be of the right size or shape. ◇*v.* **12. fit in,** to be well suited (to surroundings, companions, etc.). **13. fit out** or **up,** to provide with clothing, equipment, etc. ◇*n.* **14.** the way in which something fits: *a perfect fit.* **15.** the process of fitting. [ME *fyt*; orig. uncert.] —**fitness,** *n.*

fit[2] /fɪt/, *n.* **1.** a sudden attack: *a fit of coughing; a fainting fit.* **2.** a short period or burst of feeling or activity, etc. **3.** *Med.* the sudden loss of a part of brain function, marked by convulsions and/or unconsciousness. **4. by** or **in fits (and starts),** irregularly stopping and starting. [OE *fitt* fight, struggle]

fit[3] /fɪt/, *n. Archaic.* (a section of) a song or story. [OE *fitt*]

fitful /'fɪtfəl/, *adj.* stopping and starting; irregular; intermittent. [FIT[2] + -FUL]

fitter /'fɪtə/, *n.* **1.** someone who fits garments. **2.** someone who fits together or adjusts the parts of machinery.

fitting /'fɪtɪŋ/, *adj.* **1.** suitable or proper. ◇*n.* **2.** the act of adjusting or trying on clothes for proper fit. **3.** (of shoes or clothes) size. **4.** anything provided as equipment, a part, etc., or used to join parts. **5.** (*pl.*) furnishings, fixed equipment, etc.

Fitzgerald /fɪts'dʒɛrəld/, *n.* **1. Ella,** born 1918, US jazz singer. **2. F(rancis) Scott (Key),** 1896–1940, US novelist and short-story writer.

FitzGerald /fɪts'dʒɛrəld/, *n.* **R(obert) D(avid),** 1902–87, influential Australian poet of intellectual themes; poems include 'The Face of the Waters', 'Fifth Day', and 'The Wind at Your Door'.

Fitzroy /'fɪtsrɔɪ/, *n.* **1.** a river in northern WA, rising in the Kimberleys and flowing west to King Sound. About 644 km. **2.** a river in north-eastern Qld, starting where the Dawson and Mackenzie rivers meet and flowing north then south-east to Keppel Bay. About 480 km. **3.** an inner northern suburb of Melbourne, Vic. Pop. 18 163 (1986).

five /faɪv/, *n.* **1.** a cardinal number, four plus one (4 + 1). **2.** the symbol for this number, e.g. 5 or V. **3.** a set of five persons or things. ◇*adj.* **4.** amounting to five in number.

five hundred, *n.* a card game, usu. for four players, with bidding for trumps, rounds of tricks, and a winning total of 500 points.

fiver /'faɪvə/, *n. Colloq.* a five dollar note.

Five Towns, *n.pl.* the towns of Windsor, Richmond, Wilberforce, Castlereagh and Pitt Town on the Hawkesbury River, NSW; in 1810 Governor Macquarie selected these towns as places of refuge in times of flood.

fix /fɪks/, *v.,* **fixed, fixing,** *n.* ◇*v.t.* **1.** to make firm; secure. **2.** to put in a particular place, esp. permanently. **3.** to settle or determine: *to fix a price.* **4.** to direct steadily: *She fixed her eyes on the ball.* **5.** to make set or hard. **6.** to place or direct: *to fix the blame on someone.* **7.** to repair. **8.** to arrange or put in order. **9.** to provide with: *How are you fixed for money?* **10.** *Colloq.* to arrange or influence unfairly: *to fix a jury; to fix a game.* **11.** *Colloq.* to get even with or punish: *I'll fix him.* **12.** *Chem.* to change nitrogen from the air into nitrates, as bacteria in legumes or soil. **13.** *Photog.* to make a print permanent. **14.** *Biol.* to kill, harden, and preserve for study under a microscope. ◇*v.i.* **15.** to become fixed. **16.** to become set; take on a firm or solid form. **17.** to become permanent. **18.** to settle down. ◇*v.t.* **19. fix on/upon,** to decide on. **20. fix up, a.** to arrange, organise, or decide on. **b.** to put right; solve or repair.

21. fix (someone) up, to attend to (someone's) needs.

◇*n.* **22.** *Colloq.* a difficult position; predicament. **23.** (the determining of) an exact position, esp. of aircraft. **24.** *Colloq.* a shot of heroin or other drug. **25.** *Colloq.* an unfair arrangement or bribe. [ME, from L: fix] —**fixable,** *adj.* —**fixer,** *n.*

fixated /'fɪkseɪtəd, fɪk'seɪtəd/, *adj.* **1.** *Psychol.* stopped at an early stage of emotional development. **2.** *Colloq.* abnormally keen or interested; obsessed (fol. by *on*).

fixation /fɪk'seɪʃən/, *n.* **1.** the act or result of fixing. **2.** *Psychol.* a stopping of the emotional development of personality at early stage. [ME, from L: fix]

fixative /'fɪksətɪv/, *adj.* **1.** causing to be fixed or permanent. ◇*n.* **2.** a fixative substance, esp. one used to harden, preserve, prevent fading, etc.

fixed /fɪkst/, *adj.* **1.** made firm, secure, or permanent. **2.** set or directed on something: *a fixed stare.* **3.** set; established: *a fixed style.* **4.** put in order. **5.** *Colloq.* arranged.

fixed assets, *n.pl.* any long-term assets which are held solely for use and not for conversion into cash, e.g., land, buildings, machinery, etc. Also, **capital assets.**

fixed capital, *n.* capital (money) which has been used to buy property, build permanent constructions, or erect plant and machinery to be kept and used in running a business. (as opposed to *circulating capital*).

fixed costs, *n.pl. Comm.* costs that do not vary with output (e.g. rent, rates); overheads.

fixed deposit, *n.* a deposit placed in a bank or other financial institution for a fixed period of time and at a fixed interest rate.

fixed interest, *n.* an interest rate which is payable on a loan and which does not change for the entire period of the loan.

fixed point, *n. Phys.* an unvarying temperature, e.g. freezing point, boiling point, used to determine a thermometer scale.

fixity /ˈfɪksəti/, *n., pl.* **-ties.** the condition of being fixed; permanence.

fixture /ˈfɪkstʃə/, *n.* 1. something fixed in place, esp. in a house, etc.: *an electric-light fixture.* 2. *Colloq.* someone or something long established in the same position. 3. a sporting event to be held on a date arranged in advance.

fizz /fɪz/, *v.i.* 1. to make a hissing or bubbling sound. 2. to give off bubbles of gas; effervesce. ◇*n.* 3. a fizzing sound. 4. a bubbly drink. [backformation from FIZZLE]

fizzer /ˈfɪzə/, *n. Colloq.* 1. a firecracker which fails to explode. 2. a failure or disappointment.

fizzle /ˈfɪzəl/, *v.,* **-zled, -zling,** *n.* ◇*v.t.* 1. to make a hissing or sputtering sound. 2. *Colloq.* to fail after a good start (oft. fol. by *out*). ◇*n.* 3. a fizzling sound. [obs. *fise* from Scand]

fizzy /ˈfɪzi/, *adj.,* **-zier, -ziest.** 1. fizzing. 2. (of a drink) bubbly, either naturally sparkling or carbonated.

fjord /ˈfiɔd/, *n.* →**fiord.**

fl., *Abbrev.* flourished. [L *floruit*]

flab /flæb/, *n. Colloq.* fat on the body; flabbiness.

flabbergast /ˈflæbəɡæst, -ɡɑst/, *v.t.* to overcome (someone) with surprise; astound. [? FLABB(Y) + AGHAST]

flabby /ˈflæbi/, *adj.,* **-bier, -biest.** 1. hanging loosely; limp: *flabby muscles.* 2. having flabby flesh. 3. lacking firmness; weak. [cf. earlier *flappy* (from FLAP + -Y[1]) in same sense] —**flabbily,** *adv.* —**flabbiness,** *n.*

flaccid /ˈflæsəd/, *adj.* soft and hanging loosely; limp: *flaccid muscles.* [L] —**flaccidity,** *n.*

flag[1] /flæɡ/, *n., v.,* **flagged, flagging.** ◇*n.* 1. a piece of cloth with a particular color, design, etc., used as a symbol of a country, organisation, etc., or as a signal or decoration. 2. a printed or other copy of a flag. 3. a marker to draw attention to something. 4. part of a meter of a taxi that falls to show the taxi is hired. 5. **keep the flag flying,** to appear brave and cheerful in difficulty. 6. **strike** or **lower the flag,** to surrender (command). ◇*v.t.* 7. to place a flag or flags on. 8. to signal, mark, or warn with, or as if with, a flag. [apparently b. FLAP, *n.,* and obs. *fag,* n., flap, flag]

flag[2] /flæɡ/, *v.i.,* **flagged, flagging.** 1. to hang loosely; droop. 2. to grow weak or tired. [late ME *flagge* turf, probably from Scand]

flag[3] /flæɡ/, *n., v.,* **flagged, flagging.** ◇*n.* 1. a flagstone. ◇*v.t.* 2. to pave with flagstones.

flagellate /ˈflædʒəleɪt/, *v.,* **-lated, -lating;** /ˈflædʒələt/, *adj.* ◇*v.t.* 1. to whip; flog; lash. ◇*adj.* 2. Also, **flagellated.** *Biol.* having flagella. See **flagellum.** [L: whipped] —**flagellation,** *n.* —**flagellator,** *n.*

flagellum /fləˈdʒɛləm/, *n., pl.* **-gella, -gellums.** a long whiplike 'tail' that certain bacteria, protozoans, sperm, etc., use to swim with. [L: whip; scourge]

flageolet /flædʒəˈlɛt/, *n.* a small flute similar to a recorder; tin whistle.

flagging[1] /ˈflæɡɪŋ/, *adj.* drooping; weakening; failing. [FLAG[2] + -ING[2]]

flagging[2] /ˈflæɡɪŋ/, *n.* flagstones. [FLAG[3] + -ING[1]]

flag of convenience, *n.* the flag of a country in which a ship has been registered only to gain some financial or legal advantage.

flagon /ˈflæɡən/, *n.* 1. a large fat bottle for wine, etc. 2. a container for liquids, esp. with a handle, spout, and usu. a lid. [ME, from OF]

flagrant /ˈfleɪɡrənt/, *adj.* openly bad; glaring; notorious: *a flagrant crime.* [L: blazing, burning]

flagship /ˈflæɡʃɪp/, *n.* a ship which carries the commander of a fleet, squadron, etc., and flies his flag.

flagstone /ˈflæɡstoʊn/, *n.* a large, flat, thick piece of stone used for a path, floor, road, etc.

flail /fleɪl/, *n.* 1. a tool for threshing grain, consisting of a handle with a free-swinging stick. ◇*v.t.* 2. to thresh with a flail. 3. to hit or whip. ◇*v.i.* 4. to flap about. [OE *flygel*]

flair /flɛə/, *n.* 1. a natural ability; talent. 2. stylishness; dash. [F: smell, from L]

flak /flæk/, *n.* 1. anti-aircraft fire. 2. heavy criticism; abuse. [from G, abbrev. of *Fl(ieger-)A(bwehr-)K(anone)* anti-aircraft gun]

flake[1] /fleɪk/, *n., v.,* **flaked, flaking.** ◇*n.* 1. a small, flat, thin piece of anything. 2. a small piece split off something. ◇*v.t., v.i.* 3. to peel off or separate in flakes. 4. to form into flakes. ◇*v.* 5. Also, **flake out.** *Colloq.* to lie down or fall asleep or unconscious, as through fatigue. [OE *flac-,* which occurs in *flacor* flying (said of arrows)] —**flaky,** *adj.*

flake[2] /fleɪk/, *n.* shark meat sold for food.

flambé /flɒmˈbeɪ/, *adj.* (of food) served with a flaming sauce, esp. with brandy. [F: flamed]

flamboyant /flæmˈbɔɪənt/, *adj.* 1. flaming; brilliant. 2. showy; ornate. [F, from OF: small flame] —**flamboyance, flamboyancy,** *n.*

flame /fleɪm/, *n., v.,* **flamed, flaming.** ◇*n.* **1.** burning gas or vapor from a fire. **2.** (*oft. pl.*) the state of burning with a blaze of light: *to burst into flames.* **3.** a bright light or color. **4.** a strong emotion. **5.** *Colloq.* a person loved; sweetheart. ◇*v.i.* **6.** to burn with a flame or flames; blaze. **7.** to shine brightly; flash. **8.** to grow red or hot, or become very excited (oft. fol. by *up*). ◇*v.t.* **9.** to set on fire. [ME, from OF, from L]

flamenco /fləˈmɛŋkoʊ/, *n., pl.* **-cos.** a type of Spanish music or dance, esp. of gipsy style.

flameproof /ˈfleɪmpruːf/, *adj.* **1.** not easily burnt. **2.** (of cooking vessels) safe for use over an open flame.

flame test, *n. Chem.* a test to find whether certain elements are present in substances by noting the color they give to a flame.

flamethrower /ˈfleɪmθroʊə/, *n.* a weapon that throws a stream of burning fuel.

flame-tree /ˈfleɪm-triː/, *n.* an ornamental Australian tree with scarlet, bell-shaped flowers. Also, **Illawarra flame-tree.**

flaming /ˈfleɪmɪŋ/, *adj.* **1.** giving out flames; blazing. **2.** glowing. **3.** violent; vehement: *We had a flaming row.* **4.** *Colloq.* (a euphemism for various expletives): *Stone the flaming crows.*

flamingo /fləˈmɪŋɡoʊ/, *n., pl.* **-gos, -goes.** **1.** any of various water birds with very long neck and legs, webbed feet, bills bent downwards, and pinkish to red feathers. **2.** a dark shade of pinkish orange. [Pg, from Sp, from Pr]

flammable /ˈflæməbəl/, *adj.* easily set on fire.

flan /flæn/, *n.* an open pastry or sponge tart containing fruit, etc. [F]

Flanders /ˈflændəz, ˈflɑːn-/, *n.* a medieval country in western Europe, extending along the North Sea from the Straits of Dover to the mouth of the river Scheldt.

flange /flændʒ/, *n.* an edge, rim, or ridge on an object for keeping it in place, strengthening it, etc. [OF: bend]

flank /flæŋk/, *n.* **1.** the side of an animal between its ribs and hip. **2.** the thin piece of flesh of flank. **3.** the side of anything. **4.** *Mil, Navy.* the far right or left side of an army or fleet. **5.** *Aust Rules.* an outside position, as half-forward flank. ◇*v.t.* **6.** to be at the side of. **7.** to defend or guard at a flank. **8.** to pass round the flank of. [OE *flanc*, from OF, from Gmc]

flannel /ˈflænəl/, *n.* **1.** a warm, soft fabric, usu. of wool or a wool blend with a slight nap. **2.** → **washer** (def. 3). **3.** (*pl.*) trousers, etc., made of flannel. [orig. uncert.]

flannelette /flænəˈlɛt/, *n.* a cotton fabric, plain or printed, napped on one side to look like flannel.

flannel flower, *n.* an Australian plant with grey felt-like leaves and white-to-cream daisy-like flowers.

flap /flæp/, *v.,* **flapped, flapping,** *n.* ◇*v.i.* **1.** to swing about loosely, esp. with a noise: *a curtain flaps in the wind.* **2.** to move up and down like wings. **3.** *Colloq.* to become nervous or excited; panic. ◇*v.t.* **4.** to move (arms, wings, etc.) up and down. **5.** to cause to swing loosely, esp. with a noise. **6.** to slap. ◇*n.* **7.** a flapping movement. **8.** a flapping noise. **9.** a slap. **10.** something broad and bendable, or flat and thin, that hangs loosely, joined at one side only. **11.** *Aeron.* a hinged part of a wing, that can be lifted in flight to change lift and drag. **12.** *Colloq.* a state of nervous excitement: *in a flap.* [ME *flappe(n)*, probably of imitative orig.]

flapjack /ˈflæpdʒæk/, *n.* **1.** → **pikelet.** **2.** a thick, chewy, sweet, oat biscuit.

flapper /ˈflæpə/, *n.* a young woman in the 1920's, esp. one thought bold and unconventional.

flare /flɛə/, *v.,* **flared, flaring.** *n.* ◇*v.i.* **1.** to burn unsteadily. **2.** to blaze suddenly. (oft. fol by *up*). **3.** to burst out in sudden activity, emotion, etc. (sometimes fol. by *up* or *out*). **4.** to curve outwards like the end of a trumpet, or a wide skirt. ◇*v.t.* **5.** to show off. ◇*n.* **6.** an unsteady flame. **7.** a sudden blaze. **8.** (something used to make) a blaze of light used as a signal, etc. **9.** a sudden burst of activity or emotion. **10.** an outwards curve. [orig. meaning spread out, display; b. FLY¹ and BARE]

flash /flæʃ/, *n.* **1.** a sudden short burst of flame or light. **2.** a sudden, short outburst or show of joy, wit, etc. **3.** a short moment; an instant. **4.** a showy display. **5.** an identifying mark, as on a soldier's uniform. **6.** *Journal.* a short, urgent item of news on radio or television. **7.** → **flashgun. 8. flash in the pan,** something brilliant but short-lived. ◇*v.i.* **9.** to flame or light up suddenly. **10.** to give out or reflect bright spots of light. **11.** to move or pass suddenly. **12.** to speak or act with sudden anger. ◇*v.t.* **13.** to give out (fire or light) in sudden flashes. **14.** to cause to flash. **15.** to send out like a flash. **16.** *Colloq.* to show off, esp. quickly. ◇*adj.* **17.** showy. **18.** quick or sudden: *a flash flood.* **19.** (formerly) of or related to thieves, etc. [ME *flasche(n)* from b. FLOW (or FLOOD) and WASH]

flashback /ˈflæʃbæk/, *n.* **1.** a part of a film, novel, etc., showing an event or scene which happened before the main action. **2.** a sudden remembering of something from the past.

flashbulb /ˈflæʃbʌlb/, *n.* a glass bulb filled with oxygen and a thin sheet of magnesium or aluminium, giving a momentary bright light when fired, used in photography.

flashcard /ˈflæʃkɑːd/, *n.* a card with a picture, letter, word, etc., on it, held up before people for short time, and used in teaching, psychological testing, etc.

flash flood, *n.* a sudden, destructive short-lived flood, esp. in a desert, usu. due to heavy rain in mountains or hills.

flashgun /ˈflæʃɡʌn/, *n.* a device which at the same moment sets off a flashbulb and works the camera shutter.

flashing /ˈflæʃɪŋ/, n. Bldg Trades. a piece of sheet metal, etc., used to keep out water, and to cover and protect certain joints or angles, such as where a roof meets a wall or chimney.

flashlight /ˈflæʃlaɪt/, n. a source of bright light as used in flash photography.

flashpoint /ˈflæʃpɔɪnt/, n. 1. the lowest temperature at which a vapor above a liquid can be set alight or exploded. 2. Colloq. a point or moment at which an explosion takes place or control is lost.

flashy /ˈflæʃi/, adj., flashier, flashiest. 1. flashing or bright, esp. for short time. 2. bright and showy.

flask /flask/, n. a bottle-shaped container, made of metal, glass, etc.: *a flask of oil; a brandy flask*. [OE *flasce, flaxe*]

flat[1] /flæt/, adj., flatter, flattest, adv., n. ◇adj. 1. even or smooth in surface. 2. level; horizontal: *a flat roof*. 3. lying at full length or spread out. 4. wholly on or against something: *a ladder flat against a wall*. 5. thrown down or on the ground, esp. of fallen trees or buildings. 6. (of the heel of a shoe) low and broad. 7. (of feet) having little or no arch. See **flatfoot**. 8. emptied of air: *a flat tyre*. 9. clear and positive; absolute: *a flat refusal*. 10. without variation: *a flat rate; a flat price*. 11. uninteresting or dull. 12. tasteless. 13. no longer bubbly: *flat lemonade*. 14. not glossy: *flat paint*. 15. (of a painting, etc.) lacking contrast, or shading. 16. Music. **a.** (of a note) lowered a semitone in pitch: *B flat*. **b.** below the correct pitch; too low (opposed to *sharp*). ◇adv. 17. in a flat position. 18. exactly: *I'll give you $20 flat*. 19. **fall flat**, to fail. 20. **flat out**, Colloq. **a.** fast or hard as possible. **b.** very busy. **c.** lying spread out. ◇n. 21. something flat. 22. a flat surface, side or part of anything: *the flat of a blade; the flat of the hand*. 23. flat or level ground. 24. a marsh or shallow. 25. Music. the ♭ sign, which when placed before a note lowers it one semitone. [ME, from Scand]

flat[2] /flæt/, n., v., flatted, flatting. ◇n. 1. a set of rooms for living in, usu. on one floor of a building (block of flats), and usu. rented. See **home unit**. ◇v.i. to live in a flat. [OE *flet* floor, house, hall]

flatette /flæt'et/, n. a small flat (**flat**[2]).

flatfish /ˈflætfɪʃ/, n., pl. -fishes, (esp. collectively) -fish. any of a group of fishes including the halibut, flounder, and sole, with a flat body. They swim on one side and (in the adult) have both eyes on the other side.

flatfoot /ˈflætfʊt/, n., pl. -feet. (a foot having) a condition in which the arch of the foot is flattened so that all of the sole rests on the ground.

flat-footed /flæt-ˈfʊtəd/, adj. 1. having flat feet. 2. Colloq. awkward; clumsy. 3. Colloq. unprepared; unable to react quickly.

flathead /ˈflæthed/, n. any of various long fishes living on the sea bottom which have flattened, ridged heads.

flatten /ˈflætn/, v.t., v.i. to make or become flat.

flatter /ˈflætə/, v.t. 1. to (try to) please (someone) by compliments or praise, esp. insincerely. 2. to describe, show, or picture (too) favorably. 3. to please (oneself) with a thought or belief: *He flattered himself that he might come first*. ◇v.i. 4. to use flattery. [? OF *flat(t)er* caress with the hand, smooth, flatter, of Frankish orig.]

flattery /ˈflætəri/, n., pl. -teries. 1. the act of flattering. 2. overdone, insincere praise. [ME, from OF: a flatterer]

flatulence /ˈflætjələns/, n. 1. bubbles of gas in the stomach, intestines, etc., causing burping and/or wind. 2. empty, showy, wordy, or insincere talk. Also, **flatulency**. [F, from L: a blowing] —**flatulent**, adj.

flatworm /ˈflætwɜm/, n. any of various worms with a soft, solid, usu. flattened body, including flukes and tapeworms.

Flaubert /floʊˈbɛə/, n. **Gustave** /ˌgystav/, 1821–1880, French novelist; noted for *Madame Bovary* (1857), *A Sentimental Education* (1869) and *The Temptation of St Anthony* (1874).

flaunt /flɔnt/, v.t., v.i. to show off boldly. [Scand]

flautist /ˈflɔtəst/, n. a flute player. [It: flute]

flavo-, a word part meaning 'yellow'. Also, before vowels, **flav-**. [combining form representing L *flāvus*]

flavor or **flavour** /ˈfleɪvə/, n. 1. a taste, esp. a characteristic taste of something or a noticeable element in the taste of a thing. 2. a substance used to add flavor. 3. the typical quality of a thing. ◇v.t. 4. to add flavor to. [ME, from OF, from L: emit an odor]

flavoring or **flavouring** /ˈfleɪvərɪŋ/, n. a substance used to give a particular taste to a food or drink: *artificial lemon flavoring*.

flaw /flɔ/, n. 1. a fault; defect. 2. a crack, break, scratch, etc. ◇v.t., v.i. 3. to make or become cracked or faulty. [ME, from Scand]

flax /flæks/, n. a slender, upright plant with narrow leaves and blue flowers, grown for its fibre (made into linen) and seeds (used for linseed oil). [OE *fleax*]

flaxen /ˈflæksən/, adj. 1. made of or like flax. 2. pale yellow.

flay /fleɪ/, v.t. 1. to strip off the skin or outer covering of. 2. to criticise or scold unmercifully. [OE *flēan*] —**flayer**, n.

flea /fli/, n. 1. any of many small, wingless, blood-sucking insects feeding on mammals and birds, and with strong back legs for jumping. 2. **flea in one's ear**, Colloq. a sharp scolding. [OE *flēah, flēa*]

flea-bitten /ˈfli-bɪtn/, adj. 1. bitten by fleas. 2. full of fleas. 3. Colloq. worn and dirty.

flea market, n. a market where usu. second-hand or cheap articles are sold.

fleck /flek/, n. 1. any spot or patch of color, light, etc. ◇v.t. 2. to mark with flecks; spot; dapple. [Scand]

fled /fled/, v. past tense and past participle of **flee**.

fledge /fledʒ/, v.t., **fledged, fledging**. 1. to bring up (a young bird) until it is able to fly. 2. to supply with feathers: *to fledge an arrow*. [OE *-fligge*, in *unfligge* unfledged]

fledgling /'fledʒlɪŋ/, n. 1. a young bird just fledged. 2. an inexperienced person. Also, **fledgeling**.

flee /fliː/, v., **fled, fleeing**. ◇v.i. 1. to run away (from danger, etc.). 2. to move fast; fly. ◇v.t. 3. to run away from; escape. [OE *flēon*]

fleece /fliːs/, n., v., **fleeced, fleecing**. ◇n. 1. the coat of wool that covers a sheep or similar animal. 2. the wool shorn from a sheep at one time. 3. a fabric with a soft, woolly pile. ◇v.t. 4. to shear fleece from (a sheep). 5. to strip of money or belongings; swindle. [OE *flēos*] — **fleecy**, adj. — **fleeciness**, n.

fleet[1] /fliːt/, n. 1. a. the largest organised unit of naval ships, esp. under the command of one officer. b. a whole navy. 2. a group of vessels, aircraft, or vehicles in a single transport company. [OE *flēot* ship, craft, from *flēotan* float]

fleet[2] /fliːt/, adj. fast; swift: *fleet of foot*. [OE *flēotan* float] — **fleetness**, n.

fleeting /'fliːtɪŋ/, adj. passing quickly; transient; transitory.

Fleet Street, n. the British print media. [from *Fleet Street*, London, the traditional centre of British newspaper offices]

Flem, Flemish.

Fleming[1] /'flemɪŋ/, n. 1. a native of Flanders. 2. a Flemish-speaking Belgian. Cf. **Walloon**.

Fleming[2] /'flemɪŋ/, n. **Sir Alexander**, 1881–1955, Scottish bacteriologist; discoverer of penicillin, 1929; shared Nobel prize for medicine (1945) with Florey and Chain.

Flemington /'flemɪŋtən/, n. an Australian racecourse in the suburb of Flemington, Melbourne, Victoria; location of the running of the Melbourne Cup.

Flemish /'flemɪʃ/, adj. 1. relating to Flanders, its people, or their language. 2. relating to a school of painting developed in Flanders and northern France in the 15th century, characterised by cool, clear colors, and accurate proportions and perspective.

flesh /fleʃ/, n. 1. the soft substance of an animal body, consisting of muscle and fat. 2. such substance of animals as an article of food; meat. 3. the body, esp. as opposed to the spirit or soul. 4. man's physical or animal nature. 5. all mankind or all living creatures. 6. one's family. 7. the soft pulpy part of a fruit, vegetable, etc. 8. the skin, esp. with respect to color. 9. **in the flesh**, **a.** alive. **b.** in person. 10. **pound of flesh**, a person's right or due, taken without mercy and with a total disregard for others. [OE *flǣsc*]

fleshpots /'fleʃpɒts/, n.pl. places in which luxury or sensual pleasures are provided.

flesh wound, n. a slight wound, which does not reach beyond the flesh.

fleshy /'fleʃi/, adj., **fleshier, fleshiest**. 1. having much flesh; plump; fat. 2. consisting of or looking like flesh.

fleur-de-lis /ˌflɜː-də-ˈliː/, n., pl. **fleurs-de-lis** /ˌflɜː-də-ˈliːz/. a design like three petals of an iris tied by a band, once part of the coat-of-arms of the French royal family. [F: lily flower]

flew /fluː/, v. past tense of **fly**[1].

flex /fleks/, v.i., v.t. 1. to bend (something, as a part of the body). ◇n. 2. a small, flexible, insulated electric wire, esp. for supplying power to appliances in the home. [L] — **flexure**, n.

flexible /'fleksəbəl/, adj. 1. easily bent. 2. able to be changed or made to fit; adaptable. 3. willing to yield. [L *flexibilis*] — **flexibility**, n. — **flexibly**, adv.

flexitime /'fleksitaɪm/, n. an arrangement of ordinary hours of work in which employees may choose their starting, stopping and meal-break times but keep the same total number of hours worked.

flexor /'fleksə/, n. a muscle which serves to flex or bend part of the body (opposed to *extensor*). [NL. See FLEX, -OR[2]]

flibbertigibbet /'flɪbətidʒɪbət/, n. a talkative or unreliable person, usu. a young girl.

flick /flɪk/, n. 1. (the sound of) a sudden light blow or stroke, as with a whip or finger. 2. (pl.) Colloq. **a.** a cinema film. **b.** the cinema. ◇v.t. 3. to strike lightly, with a whip, finger, etc.: *The rider flicked the horse with his whip*. 4. to remove with such a stroke: *He flicked the dust from his coat*. [ME *flykke*; apparently imitative]

flicker /'flɪkə/, v.i. 1. to burn unsteadily. 2. to move quickly to and fro; vibrate. ◇n. 3. an unsteady flame or light. 4. (usu. pl.) → **trafficator**. 5. a flickering movement. 6. a thing passing quickly: *a flicker of hope*. [OE *flicorian* flutter]

flier /'flaɪə/, n. 1. something that flies, or moves with great speed. 2. a person who flies aeroplanes. Also, **flyer**.

flight[1] /flaɪt/, n. 1. the act, manner, or power of flying. 2. the distance or course covered by a flying object. 3. a number of beings or things flying through the air together: *a flight of swallows*. 4. a journey by air, esp. by aeroplane. 5. a trip on an airline, set for a certain time. 6. a reaching above ordinary limits: *a flight of fancy*. 7. a series of steps or stairs between two levels. [OE *flyht*]

flight[2] /flaɪt/, n. 1. the act of fleeing (running away). 2. **put to flight**, to force to flee; rout. 3. **take (to) flight**, to flee. [ME]

flightless /'flaɪtləs/, adj. unable to fly.

flight recorder, n. a box containing recording equipment which collects information about an aircraft's flight, used esp. to find the cause of a crash.

flighty /'flaɪti/, adj., **-tier, -tiest**. 1. often changing one's mind; frivolous. 2. with unreliable or changeable feelings; flirtatious. [FLIGHT[1] + -Y[1]] — **flightiness**, n.

flimsy /'flɪmzi/, adj., **-sier, -siest**, n., pl. **-sies**. ◇adj. 1. without material strength or

flimsy solidity: *a flimsy structure*. **2.** weak; inadequate; not carefully thought out: *a flimsy excuse or argument*. ◇*n*. **3.** a thin kind of paper, esp. for use in copying. [FILM (by metathesis) + -sy, adj. suffix] —**flimsily**, *adv*. —**flimsiness**, *n*.

flinch /flɪntʃ/, *v.i.* **1.** to draw back from what is dangerous, difficult, or unpleasant. **2.** to pull away under pain; wince. [? nasalised var. of d. *flitch* flit, shift (one's) position] —**flinchingly**, *adv*.

Flinders /'flɪndəz/, *n*. **Matthew**, 1774–1814, English-born naval navigator and explorer in Australia; with George Bass, the first to circumnavigate Van Diemen's Land and the Australian continent.

Flinders grass, *n*. any of various native annuals which can resist dry weather, are a valued food for livestock, and are plentiful in inland Australia.

Flinders Island, *n*. an island in Bass Strait, the largest of the Furneaux Group. 2072 km^2. [named after Matthew FLINDERS]

Flinders Ranges, *n.pl.* mountain ranges in south-eastern SA extending over 400 km from Port Pirie and Peterborough to the areas between Lake Torrens and Lake Frome. Highest peak, St Marys Peak, 1165 m.

fling /flɪŋ/, *v.*, **flung**, **flinging**, *n*. ◇*v.t.* **1.** to throw, cast, or hurl, often with force or impatience. **2.** to put suddenly or violently: *The police will fling them into gaol*. **3.** to throw aside or off. ◇*v.i.* **4.** to move with haste or violence; rush: *She would fling out of the room whenever annoyed*. ◇*n*. **5.** a time of completely pleasing oneself: *She had her fling when she was young*. **6.** an attack upon or attempt at something, as in passing: *I will have one last fling at that exam*. **7.** a lively Scottish dance characterised by flinging movements of the legs and arms (commonly called **Highland fling**). [ME]

flint /flɪnt/, *n*. **1.** a hard kind of stone, being a form of silica. **2.** a piece of this, esp. as used for striking fire. **3.** something very hard, like or as if like flint. [OE] —**flinty**, *adj*.

flintlock /'flɪntlɒk/, *n*. (formerly) a gun mechanism in which a piece of flint striking against steel produced sparks which ignited the powder.

flip /flɪp/, *v.*, **flipped**, **flipping**, *n*. ◇*v.t.* **1.** to toss or put in motion with a snap of a finger and thumb; flick. **2.** to move (something) with a jerk or jerks. ◇*v.i.* **3.** to strike quickly at something. **4.** to move with a jerk or jerks. **5. flip one's lid**, *Colloq.* to become angry. ◇*n*. **6.** a quick tap, strike, or movement. **7.** a somersault. [probably imitative]

flippant /'flɪpənt/, *adj*. marked by shallow or disrespectful levity (lack of proper seriousness). [orig. obscure] —**flippancy**, *n*.

flipper /'flɪpə/, *n*. **1.** the broad, flat limb of a seal, whale, etc., adapted for swimming. **2.** a rubber device like an animal's flipper, used as aid in swimming.

flip side, *n*. *Colloq.* the second side of a gramophone record, usu. carrying a less popular song.

flirt /flɜt/, *v.i.* **1.** to play at romantic love; coquet. **2.** to play or toy (with an idea, etc.). **3.** to dart about. ◇*n*. **4.** someone who plays at romantic love. [imitative] —**flirtation**, *n*. —**flirtatious**, *adj*.

flit /flɪt/, *v.*, **flitted**, **flitting**, *n*. ◇*v.i.* **1.** to move lightly and swiftly. **2.** to flutter, as a bird. **3.** *Colloq.* to change one's home, esp. quickly and secretly. ◇*n*. **4.** a light, swift movement; flutter. **5.** *Colloq.* a removal, esp. a secret one: *a moonlight flit*. [ME, from Scand]

flitch /flɪtʃ/, *n*. the side of a pig, salted and cured. [OE *flicce*]

float /floʊt/, *v.i.* **1.** to rest or move gently on the surface of a liquid. **2.** to rest or move as if in a liquid or gas: *The idea floated through my mind*. **3.** to move or drift about free from attachment. ◇*v.t.* **4.** to cause to float. **5.** to set going (a company, etc.). **6.** to sell (stocks, bonds, etc.) on the market. **7.** *Econ.* to allow the exchange value (of a country's money) to find its own level in a foreign exchange market. ◇*n*. **8.** something that floats as **a.** the hollow ball used to control the liquid level in a tank, cistern, etc. **b.** the hollow, boatlike part under an aeroplane allowing it to float on water. **c.** the cork on a fishing line. **d.** the air-filled organ supporting an animal in the water. **9.** a platform on wheels, bearing a display, and drawn in a procession. **10.** Also, **horse float**. a van or trailer for transporting horses. **11.** a quantity of money used by shopkeepers, etc. to provide change. [OE *flotian*]

floatation /floʊ'teɪʃən/, *n*. →**flotation**.

floater /'floʊtə/, *n*. **1.** someone or something which floats. **2.** a meat pie served in pea soup. **3.** *Mining.* a loose piece of ore found at the surface and sometimes indicating better ore at depth. [FLOAT + -ER^1]

floating /'floʊtɪŋ/, *adj*. **1.** able to float. **2.** not fixed or settled in a definite place: *a floating population*. **3.** *Finance.* **a.** (of money) in use, or continually turned over. **b.** made up of money due within a short time: *a floating debt*.

floating assets, *n.pl.* assets which are continually changing, e.g. cash, bills of exchange, etc.

floating currency, *n*. a country's money whose value is influenced by changes in the value of the money of other countries.

floating dock, *n*. a floating structure which may be lowered in the water to admit a ship and then raised to leave the ship dry for repairs, etc.

floating rib, *n*. *Anat.* one of the two lowest pairs of ribs in humans, which are attached neither to the breastbone nor to the other ribs.

flocculant /'flɒkjələnt/, *n*. a substance added to solutions to produce woolly-looking masses of particles.

flocculent /'flɒkjələnt/, *adj*. like tuft(s) of wool; fluffy. —**flocculence**, *n*.

flock^1 /flɒk/, *n*. **1.** a number of animals of one kind keeping, feeding, or kept together, now esp. of sheep or goats, or of birds. **2.** the members of a church. **3.** a crowd of people.

flock ◇*v.i.* **4.** to gather or go in a flock, company, or crowd. [OE *floc*]

flock² /flɒk/, *n.* **1.** a small bunch of wool, hair, etc. **2.** (*pl. or sing.*) wool ends, pieces of cloth, etc., used for stuffing furniture, bedding, etc. **3.** (*sing. or pl.*) finely powdered wool, cloth, etc., used to give a velvet-like finish to wallpaper. [ME, from OF, from L: flock of wool]

floe /floʊ/, *n.* (a small piece of) a field of floating ice formed on the surface of the sea, etc. [? Norw *flo*]

flog /flɒg/, *v.t.*, **flogged, flogging. 1.** to beat hard with a whip, stick, etc.; whip. **2.** *Colloq.* to sell or try to sell. **3.** to steal. ◇*v.* **4. flog a dead horse,** to make useless efforts. [? b. FLAY and *jog*, var. of JAG¹, *v.*, prick, slash]

flood /flʌd/, *n.* **1.** a great flowing or overflowing of water, esp. over land not usu. beneath water. **2.** any great outpouring or stream: *a flood of words; a flood of light.* **3.** the flowing in of the tide (opposed to ebb). ◇*v.t.* **4.** to cover with a flood. **5.** to oversupply: *They flooded us with gifts.* ◇*v.i.* **6.** to flow or pour in, or as if in, a flood: *The water flooded into the house.* **7.** to rise in a flood; overflow: *The river flooded.* [OE *flōd*]

floodbank /'flʌdbæŋk/, *n.* → levee¹ (defs 1, 2).

floodgate /'flʌdgeɪt/, *n.* **1.** a gate designed to control the flow of water. **2.** anything serving to control a flow or passage.

flood irrigation, *n.* a method of irrigation (watering land) in which **a.** water is run on a paddock to the depth of a few centimetres to supply enough moisture for growth of the crop. **b.** water is made to overflow a river embankment so as to flood nearby areas.

floodlight /'flʌdlaɪt/, *n.*, *v.*, **-lighted** or **-lit, -lighting.** ◇*n.* **1.** an artificial light which gives a relatively even light over a given area. **2.** a lamp producing such a light. ◇*v.t.* **3.** to provide light with a floodlight.

flood plain, *n.* a nearly flat plain along the course of a stream that is flooded at high water.

flood tide, *n.* the rising tide.

floor /flɔ/, *n.* **1.** that part of a room, etc. which forms its lower surface, and upon which one walks. **2.** a storey (level) of a building. **3.** a level supporting structure in any structure: *the floor of a bridge.* **4.** any more or less flat area or surface. **5.** *Parl.* the part of a legislative chamber, etc., where members sit, and from which they speak. **6.** the right of one member to speak: *The member for Wentworth has the floor.* **7.** the base or lower limit: *a price or wage floor.* ◇*v.t.* **8.** to cover or provide with a floor. **9.** to knock down. **10.** *Colloq.* to beat or defeat. **11.** *Colloq.* to completely confuse or puzzle: *That problem will floor him.* [OE *flōr*]

floorboard /'flɔbɔd/, *n.* a plank in a timber floor.

floor show, *n.* an entertainment given in a nightclub, etc., usu. with singing, dancing, or comic acts.

flop /flɒp/, *v.*, **flopped, flopping.** *Colloq.* ◇*v.i.* **1.** to fall down suddenly, esp. with a noise. **2.** to fall flat on the surface of water. **3.** to yield or break down suddenly; fail. ◇*v.t.* **4.** to drop, throw, or flap (something) noisily or heavily. ◇*n.* **5.** the act or sound of flopping. **6.** a failure. [var. of FLAP] —**floppy,** *adj.* —**floppily,** *adv.*

floppy disk /flɒpi 'dɪsk/, *n. Computers.* a magnetically coated circular plate used for storing information.

flora /'flɔrə/, *n.*, *pl.* **floras, florae** /'flɔri/. plants of a particular area or period, listed by species. [NL, from L *Flora* goddess of flowers]

floral /'flɔrəl, 'flɒrəl/, *adj.* relating to or consisting of flowers. [L: flower]

Florence /'flɒrəns/, *n.* a city in central Italy, in Tuscany, on the river Arno; capital of the former grand duchy of Tuscany. Pop. 428 443 (1986 est.). Italian, **Firenze.**

florescence /flə'rɛsəns/, *n.* the act, state, or period of flowering; bloom. [L: beginning to flower] —**florescent,** *adj.*

floret /'flɒrət/, *n.* **1.** a small flower. **2.** the flower of grasses together with its enclosing bracts. **3.** one of the groups of flowers making the head of a compound flower as in the daisy.

Florey /'flɔri/, *n.* **Howard Walter** (*Baron of Adelaide and Marston*), 1898–1968, Australian scientist; shared the Nobel prize for physiology and medicine as co-discoverer of penicillin in 1945.

florid /'flɒrəd/, *adj.* **1.** (of the face, cheeks) highly colored; ruddy. **2.** flowery; over-ornate: *florid music.* [L: flowery] —**floridity,** *n.*

Florida /'flɒrədə/, *n.* a state in the southeastern US between the Atlantic and the Gulf of Mexico. Pop. 11 675 000 (1986 est.); 151 670 km². *Cap.:* Tallahassee. *Abbrev.:* Fla

florin /'flɒrən/, *n.* (formerly) a silver coin worth two shillings. [ME, from F, from It *fiorino* a Florentine coin stamped with a lily, from L: flower]

florist /'flɒrəst/, *n.* a seller of flowers, etc.

-florous, an adjectival suffix meaning 'flowered'. [L -*flōrus* flowered]

floss /flɒs/, *n.* **1.** a cottony fibre yielded by silk-cotton trees. **2.** silk threads with little or no twist, used in weaving or in embroidery. **3.** any silky threadlike matter, as the silk of corn. **4.** Also, **dental floss.** a soft, waxed thread used for cleaning between the teeth. Also, (for defs 1-3), **floss silk.** [Scand] —**flossy,** *adj.*

flotation /floʊ'teɪʃən/, *n.* **1.** the act or state of floating. **2.** the floating of a business, loan, etc., esp. by selling shares. Also, **floatation.** [var. of floataation]

flotilla /flə'tɪlə/, *n.* **1.** a number of small naval vessels. **2.** a small fleet. [Sp: little fleet, from F, from OE *flota*]

flotsam and jetsam, /,flɒtsəm ən 'dʒɛtsəm/ *n.* **1.** the wreckage of a ship and its cargo found either floating upon the sea or washed ashore. **2.** odds and ends.

flounce¹ /flaʊns/, v., **flounced, flouncing**, n. ◇v.i. **1.** to go with an impatient or angry fling of the body (oft. fol. by *away, off, out*, etc.): *She would flounce out of the room in a rage.* ◇n. **2.** a flouncing movement. [Scand]

flounce² /flaʊns/, n., v., **flounced, flouncing**. ◇n. **1.** a strip of material, gathered and attached usu. at the base of a skirt. ◇v.t. **2.** to edge with a flounce. [OF: a wrinkle, fold, from Gmc] —**flouncing**, n.

flounder¹ /'flaʊndə/, v.i. **1.** to struggle with stumbling movements (oft. fol. by *along, on, through*, etc.). **2.** to struggle helplessly in embarrassment or confusion. ◇n. **3.** the action of floundering. [? b. FLOUNCE¹ and FOUNDER²]

flounder² /'flaʊndə/, n., pl. **-der**. any of many species of flatfishes, esp. as caught for food. [ME, from AF, from Scand]

flour /'flaʊə/, n. **1.** the fine, powdery substance obtained from grinding and bolting (sifting) wheat or other grain. **2.** any fine, soft powder. [ME; special use of FLOWER] —**floury**, adj.

flourish /'flʌrɪʃ/, v.i. **1.** to be in a strong, healthy state; thrive; prosper: *During this period art flourished.* **2.** to be at the height of fame or excellence. ◇v.t. **3.** to wave showily (a sword, a stick, the limbs, etc.) about in the air. ◇n. **4.** waving, as of a sword, a stick, or the like. **5.** anything used for display, as a decoration in writing or an elaborate passage in music. **6.** a trumpet call or fanfare. [ME, from OF, from L: bloom] —**flourishing**, adj.

flout /flaʊt/, v.t. to treat without respect; mock; scoff at. [ME *floute(n)*, var. of FLUTE, v.] —**flouter**, n. —**floutingly**, adv.

flow /floʊ/, v.i. **1.** to move along in or as in a stream. **2.** to stream or pour forth. **3.** to proceed continuously and smoothly, like a stream, as thought, speech, etc. **4.** to fall or hang loosely: *flowing hair.* **5.** to overflow with something: *a land flowing with milk and honey.* **6.** to rise and advance, as the tide (opposed to *ebb*). ◇n. **7.** the act, rate or amount of flowing. **8.** any continuous movement, as of thought, speech, trade, etc., like that of a stream of water. **9.** something that flows; stream. **10.** an outpouring of something, as in a stream: *a flow of blood.* **11.** the rise of the tide; flood (opposed to *ebb*). [OE *flōwan*]

flow chart, n. a diagram showing the step-by-step operation of a system. Also, **flow diagram, flow sheet**.

flower /'flaʊə/, n. **1.** the colored and decorative part of a plant. **2.** *Bot.* the sexual reproductive structure of an angiosperm (a plant whose seeds are enclosed in an ovary). **3.** a plant grown for the beauty of its flower. **4.** the state of bloom: *plants in flower.* **5.** the finest or choicest part or example. **6.** (*pl.*) *Chem.* a substance in the form of fine powder, esp. as obtained by sublimation: *flowers of sulfur.* ◇v.i. **7.** (of a plant) to produce flowers. **8.** to reach the stage of full development. [ME, from OF, from L] —**flowering**, adj.

flowerbed /'flaʊəbɛd/, n. a section of ground, esp. in a garden, where flowering plants are grown.

flowered /'flaʊəd/, adj. **1.** having flowers. **2.** decorated with (a pattern of) flowers.

flower girl, n. a very young girl attending a bride.

flowery /'flaʊəri/, adj., **-rier, -riest**. **1.** covered with flowers, or floral designs. **2.** containing highly ornamental language.

flown /floʊn/, v. past participle of **fly¹**.

flow-on /'floʊ-ɒn/, n. the spreading of wage and cost increases from one section of the workforce or community to another or others.

fl oz, *Symbol*. fluid ounce.

flu /flu/, n. *Colloq*. → **influenza**.

fluctuate /'flʌktʃueɪt/, v.i., **-ated, -ating**. **1.** (of opinion, temperature, prices, etc.) to change continually, from one course, position, condition, amount, etc., to another. **2.** to move in waves or like waves. [L: undulated] —**fluctuant**, adj. —**fluctuation**, n.

flue /flu/, n. **1.** the smoke passage in a chimney. **2.** any passage for air, gases, or the like. [OE *flēwsa* a flowing]

fluent /'fluənt/, adj. **1.** flowing smoothly and easily: *He speaks fluent French.* **2.** able to speak or write readily: *a fluent speaker.* **3.** easy; graceful: *fluent motion; fluent curves.* [L: flowing] —**fluency**, n.

fluff /flʌf/, n. **1.** light, soft particles, as from cotton or wool. **2.** a mass of this. **3.** *Colloq*. an error in performance, etc. ◇v.t. **4.** to shake or puff out (feathers, hair, etc.) into a fluffy mass. **5.** *Colloq*. to fail to perform properly: *to fluff the lines of a play.* [? b. *flue* fluff and PUFF] —**fluffy**, adj.

fluid /'fluəd/, n. **1.** a substance which is capable of flowing and offers little resistance to changes of shape; a liquid or a gas. ◇adj. **2.** capable of flowing; liquid or gaseous. **3.** changing readily; shifting; not fixed or stable. [L: flow] —**fluidity**, n.

fluid ounce, n. a unit of volume in the imperial system, equal to $\frac{1}{20}$ of a pint (28.413 062 5 x 10^{-3} litres) or, in the US, $\frac{1}{16}$ of a pint (29.573 529 562 5 x) 10^{-3} litres.

fluid pressure, n. the pressure exerted by a fluid, equal in all directions around a point and acting in a perpendicular direction to any surface.

fluke¹ /fluk/, n. **1.** a flat triangular piece at the end of each arm of an anchor, which catches in the ground. **2.** a barb, or the barbed head, of a harpoon, etc. **3.** either half of the triangular tail of a whale. [? special use of FLUKE³]

fluke² /fluk/, n., v., **fluked, fluking**. ◇n. **1.** any accidental advantage. **2.** an accidentally successful stroke in sport. ◇v.t. **3.** *Colloq*. to hit, make, or gain by a fluke. [orig. unknown]

fluke³ /fluk/, n. **1.** a type of flounder. **2.** a parasitic flatworm. [OE *flōc*]

fluky /'fluki/, adj., **flukier, flukiest**. **1.** *Colloq*. obtained by chance rather than skill.

fluky

2. (of a wind) uncertain. Also, **flukey**. —**flukiness**, *n*.

flung /flʌŋ/, *v*. past tense and past participle of **fling**.

flunk /flʌŋk/, *Colloq*. ◇*v.i*. 1. to fail, as a student in an examination. 2. to give up; back out (fol. by *out*). ◇*v.t*. 3. to fail (in an examination, etc.). [? akin to FLINCH, FUNK]

flunkey /'flʌŋki/, *n*., *pl*. **-keys**. 1. a male servant in livery (uniform). 2. someone who tries to win favor with another in a crawling, servile way; toady. [? alteration of *flanker*]

fluor-[1], a word part indicating the presence of fluorine. [combining form of FLUORINE]

fluor-[2], a word part indicating fluorescence. [combining form of FLUORESCENCE]

fluoresce /fluə'res, flə-/, *v.i*., **-resced**, **-rescing**. to show fluorescence.

fluorescence /fluə'resəns, flə-/, *n*. 1. a property of certain substances of giving out light when exposed to radiation or a stream of high energy particles, as electrons. 2. The light or luminosity so produced. —**fluorescent**, *adj*.

fluorescent tube, /fluə,resənt 'tjub/ *n*. an electric tube in which light is produced by the passage of electricity through a metallic gas enclosed in a tube or bulb.

fluoric /'fluərɪk, 'flu-/, *adj*., *Mineral*. relating to or obtained from fluorspar. [F *fluorique*, from *fluor* fluid acid, from L: a flowing]

fluoridation /fluərə'deɪʃən, 'flu-/, *n*. the addition of fluoride compounds to toothpaste, public water supplies, etc., to help in the prevention of tooth decay. [FLUORID(E) + -ATION] —**fluoridate**, *v*.

fluoride /'fluəraɪd, 'flu-/, *n*. 1. See **-ide**. 2. an organic compound with one or more hydrogen atoms substituted by fluorine atoms. ◇*adj*. 3. of or relating to a substance containing fluoride, as toothpaste.

fluorinate /'fluərəneɪt, 'flu-/, *v.t*., **-nated**, **-nating**. to treat or combine with fluorine. —**fluorination**, *n*.

fluorine /'fluərin, 'flu-/, *n*. a non-metallic element, a pale yellow corrosive gas, occurring combined, esp. in fluorspar, cryolite, phosphate rock, and other minerals. *Symbol*: F; *at. no*.: 9; *at. wt*: 18.9984.

fluorine dating, *n*. a method of determining the age of objects of plant or animal origin by means of their content of fluorine absorbed from surrounding ground water.

fluoroscope /'fluərəskoup/, *n*. a tube or box, fitted with a screen coated with a fluorescent substance, used for viewing objects exposed to X-rays, etc. [FLUOR-[2] + -O- + -SCOPE]

fluorspar /'fluəspɑ/, *n*. a common mineral, calcium fluoride, CaF_2, occurring in colorless, green, blue, purple, and yellow crystals, usu. in cubes, and the main source of fluorine. Also, **fluor**.

flurry /'flʌri/, *n*., *pl*. **-ries**, *v*., **-ried**, **-rying**. ◇*n*. 1. a sudden gust of wind. 2. sudden excitement or confusion; nervous hurry. ◇*v.t*. 3. to put (a person) into a flurry; fluster. [b. FLUTTER and HURRY]

flush[1] /flʌʃ/, *n*. 1. a blush; rosy glow. 2. a rushing, as of water. 3. a rush of emotion; elation: *the first flush of success*. 4. a glowing freshness or energy: *the flush of youth*. 5. a wave of heat experienced in fever, menopause, etc. ◇*v.t*. 6. to flood with water, esp. for cleaning purposes. ◇*v.i*. 7. to blush; redden. [from FLUSH[3]] —**flusher**, *n*.

flush[2] /flʌʃ/, *adj*. 1. even or level, as with a surface; in one plane. 2. well-supplied, as with money; affluent. 3. quite full; full to overflowing. ◇*adv*. 4. so as to be flush or even. 5. squarely; full on: *I hit him flush on the face*. ◇*n*. 6. fresh growth, as of shoots and leaves. [special use of FLUSH[1]]

flush[3] /flʌʃ/, *v.t*. 1. to cause (others) to reveal (themselves) (oft. fol. by *out*): *This should flush out our hidden supporters*. 2. to make (a hunted bird, animal or person) leave a hiding place. [ME *flussh*, orig. uncert.]

flush[4] /flʌʃ/, *n*. a hand or set of cards all of one suit. [L: FLUX]

fluster /'flʌstə/, *v.t*., *v.i*. 1. to make or become confused or nervous. ◇*n*. 2. confusion; nervous excitement. [compare Icel *flaustr* hurry, bustle]

flute /flut/, *n*., *v*., **fluted**, **fluting**. ◇*n*. 1. a musical wind instrument consisting of a tube with a series of fingerholes or keys in which the air is blown across a hole at the end or side of the tube. 2. *Archit. etc*. a groove, as along the length of a pillar. ◇*v.i*. 3. to produce flutelike sounds. 4. to play a flute. ◇*v.t*. 5. to utter in flutelike tones. 6. to form lengthwise grooves in. [ME, from OF, from Pr, from L: blown] —**fluted**, *adj*.

fluting /'flutɪŋ/, *n*. a series of flutes, grooves or furrows on a pillar, etc.

flutter /'flʌtə/, *v.i*. 1. to flap or wave lightly in the air: *The flags were fluttering*. 2. (of birds, etc.) to flap the wings, or fly with flapping movements. 3. to move with quick, uneven movements. 4. (of the heart, etc.) to beat fast and unevenly. 5. to tremble; be agitated. 6. *Swimming*. (of the feet) to kick up and down in turn, as in the crawl and backstroke. ◇*v.t*. 7. to cause to flutter; vibrate; agitate. ◇*n*. 8. a fluttering movement. 9. a state of nervous excitement or confusion. 10. *Colloq*. a small bet. [OE *floterian* float]

fluvial /'fluviəl/, *adj*. of, relating to, or produced by a river. [L: river]

fluvioglacial /,fluviou'gleɪʃəl/, *adj*. relating to streams flowing from glaciers or to deposits made by such streams.

flux /flʌks/, *n*. 1. a flowing or flow. 2. the flowing in of the tide. 3. a continuous movement or change: *to be in a state of flux*. 4. *Phys*. the rate of flow of a liquid, heat, etc. [ME, from L: a flowing]

fly[1] /flaɪ/, *v*., **flew**, **flown**, **flying**, *n*., *pl*. **flies**. ◇*v.i*. 1. to move through the air on wings as a bird or aircraft. 2. to be carried through the air by the wind or any other force. 3. to float or wave in the air: *The flag was flying*

in the breeze. **4.** to move or pass quickly. **5.** → **flee.** ◊*v.t.* **6.** to cause to fly: *to fly a model aeroplane.* **7.** to operate (an aircraft or spacecraft). **8.** to raise up (a flag). **9.** to travel over by flying. **10.** to transport by flying. **11.** to avoid; flee from. ◊*v.* **12.** Some special uses are:
fly in the face of, to refuse to obey or take notice of.
fly off the handle, *Colloq.* to lose one's temper, esp. unexpectedly.
fly a kite, *Colloq.* to test out reactions to an idea in advance.
fly at, to attack.
let fly, 1. to throw. **2.** to allow to come out freely, esp. in verbal attack: *He let fly his anger.* **3.** to make an attack, esp. verbally.
◊*n.* **13.** a narrow strip of material sewn along one edge of a garment, to help hide buttons or other fasteners, esp. that at the opening of a pair of trousers. **14.** a piece of material forming the door or outer roof of a tent. **15.** the act of flying. **16.** the length of a flag from the pole to the outer end. **17.** (*pl.*) *Theat.* the space and equipment above the stage. **18.** *Colloq.* an attempt: *Give it a fly.* [OE *flēogan*]

fly[2] /flaɪ/, *n., pl.* **flies. 1.** any of the group of two-winged insects, such as the common housefly. **2.** any of a number of other winged insects, such as the firefly. **3.** *Fishing.* a fishhook dressed to look like an insect. **4. fly in the ointment,** a slight fault that greatly lessens the value or pleasure of something. **5. be no flies on (someone),** *Colloq.* to be not easily tricked; be wary. [OE *flēoge, flȳge*]

Fly /flaɪ/, *n.* a river in western central NG, flowing south-east to the Gulf of Papua. PNG's longest river. About 1126 km.

flyblown /ˈflaɪbloʊn/, *adj.* **1.** (of meat) covered with the eggs or young larvae (maggots) of a blowfly. **2.** spoilt; corrupt.

flycatcher /ˈflaɪkætʃə/, *n.* any of numerous small, insect-eating birds, such as the Australian Jacky winter.

flyer /ˈflaɪə/, *n.* → **flier.**

flying /ˈflaɪɪŋ/, *adj.* **1.** that flies: *a flying insect.* **2.** floating, waving in the air: *flying banners; flying hair.* **3.** moving quickly. **4.** hasty: *a flying visit.* ◊*n.* **5.** the act of moving through the air on wings; flight.

flying boat, *n.* an aircraft with the underside shaped like the hull of a boat to enable it to take off and land on water.

flying buttress, *n.* a buttress which supports a wall by an arch that carries the thrust of the wall.

Flying Doctor Service, *n.* → **Royal Flying Doctor Service.**

Flying Dutchman /ˌflaɪɪŋ ˈdʌtʃmən/, *n.* a legendary phantom Dutch ship supposed to be seen at sea, esp. near the Cape of Good Hope.

flying fish, *n.* any of certain fishes with winglike pectoral fins which help them to glide for some distance through the air after leaping from the water.

flying fox, *n.* **1.** any of various large bats of Australia, tropical Asia and Africa, which have a foxlike head and feed on fruit. **2.** a cable-operated machine for transport over water or rough land.

flying phalanger, *n.* → **a glider** (def. 3). Also, **gliding possum.**

flying saucer, *n.* any of various disc-shaped objects reported to have been seen flying at high speeds and thought by some to come from outer space.

flying squirrel, *n.* a squirrel-like animal of the eastern US, with folds of skin connecting the front and back legs, enabling it to take long gliding leaps.

Flynn /flɪn/, *n.* **John,** 1880–1951, Australian clergyman and missionary; founder of the Royal Flying Doctor Service.

flystrike /ˈflaɪstraɪk/, *n.* → **blowfly strike.**

flytrap /ˈflaɪtræp/, *n.* any of various plants which entrap insects, esp. Venus's flytrap.

flyweight /ˈflaɪweɪt/, *n.* (in amateur boxing) a boxer who weighs between 48 and 51 kg.

flywheel /ˈflaɪwil/, *n.* **1.** a heavy wheel which equalises the speed of machinery with which it is connected. **2.** a wheel used to carry the piston over dead centre.

fm, 1. *Symbol.* fathom. **2.** *Abbrev.* from.

Fm, *Chem. Symbol.* fermium.

FM /ɛf ˈɛm/, *Abbrev.* **1.** frequency modulation. **2.** field marshal.

FO, *Abbrev.* **1.** field officer. **2.** flying officer.

foal /foʊl/, *n.* **1.** a young horse, donkey, etc., of either sex, not yet past its first birthday. ◊*v.i., v.t.* **2.** to bring forth (a foal). [OE *fola*]

foam /foʊm/, *n.* **1.** a collection of very small bubbles formed on the surface of a liquid by movement, fermentation, etc. **2.** foam-like perspiration formed on the skin of an animal after physical effort. **3.** a chemical substance sprayed from a fire-extinguisher to form a layer of small still bubbles which put out flames. **4.** a light material, either soft or stiff, produced by introducing gas bubbles into a substance such as plastic or resin. ◊*v.i.* **5.** to form or give out foam; froth. ◊*v.* **6. foam at the mouth,** to be filled with some emotion, esp. rage. [OE *fām*]

fob[1] /fɒb/, *n.* **1.** Also, **fob pocket.** a pocket just below the waistline in men's trousers or waistcoat to hold a watch, etc. **2.** a short chain or ribbon tied to a watch and worn hanging from such a pocket. [orig. unknown]

fob[2] /fɒb/, *v.t.*, **fobbed, fobbing.** *in the phrase,* **fob off 1.** to get rid of (goods) by tricking someone: *to fob off a stolen watch on a person.* **2.** to put off (a person) with tricks, lies, etc: *Don't try to fob me off with promises.*

focal length /ˈfoʊkəl lɛŋθ/, *n.* (of a mirror or lens) distance from the optical centre to the focal point.

focal point /ˈfoʊkəl pɔɪnt/, *n.* **1.** Also, **principal focus.** the focus (def. 2) for a beam of light rays parallel to the principal axis of a lens or mirror. **2.** *Colloq.* the main point of interest, attraction, activity, etc.

Foch /fɒʃ/, *n.* **Ferdinand**, 1851–1929, French marshal and commander-in-chief of the Allied forces in France during World War I.

focus /'foʊkəs/, *n., pl.* **-ci** /-saɪ, -kaɪ/, **-cuses**, *v.,* **-cused**, **-cusing**, or **-cussed**, **-cussing**. ◇*n.* **1.** *Phys.* a point at which rays of light, heat, or other radiation, meet after refraction or reflection. **2.** *Light.* **a.** a point which rays appear to come from or at which they would meet if they could be kept going in the same direction (**virtual focus**). **b.** the focal length of a lens. **c.** the condition of an image when it is sharp and clear. **d.** the position of a viewed object, or state of an optical device, necessary to produce a clear image: *in focus; out of focus.* **3.** →**focal point** (def. 2). **4.** *Geom.* one of the points from which the distances to any point of a given curve are in a linear relation. **5.** *Geol.* the point where an earthquake starts. **6.** *Med.* the main centre from which a disease develops or in which it localises. ◇*v.t.* **7.** to bring to a focus or into focus: *to focus a camera.* **8.** to concentrate: *to focus one's attention.* ◇*v.i.* **9.** to become focused. [L: hearth, fireplace]

fodder /'fɒdə/, *n.* food for cattle, horses, etc., esp. dried food, as hay, straw, etc. [OE *fodder, fōdor*]

foe /foʊ/, *n.* **1.** an enemy. **2.** an opponent in a game, etc. [OE (ge)fā(h) enemy]

foetus or **fetus** /'fiːtəs/, *n.* the young of an animal in the uterus or egg, esp. in its later stages. [L: a bringing forth, offspring, young] –**foetal**, *adj.*

fog /fɒg/, *n., v.,* **fogged, fogging.** ◇*n.* **1.** a cloudlike mass of tiny particles of water in the air near the earth's surface; thick mist. **2.** any darkened state of the atmosphere, or the substance which causes it. **3.** *Chem.* a colloidal system consisting of liquid particles spread through a gas. **4.** a state of mental confusion: *a fog of doubt.* **5.** *Photog.* a darkening of the whole or parts of a developed plate or print caused by the action of outside light. ◇*v.t., v.i.* **6.** to surround or become surrounded by fog; be or become blurry. [backformation from obs. *foggy* marshy, thick, murky] –**foggy**, *adj.*

foghorn /'fɒghɔːn/, *n.* **1.** *Naut.* a horn for sounding warning signals to ships, etc., in foggy weather. **2.** *Colloq.* a deep, loud voice.

fogy /'foʊgi/, *n., pl.* **-gies.** an old-fashioned person who does not like change. Also, **fogey.**

foible /'fɔɪbəl/, *n.* a slight strangeness in a person's character. [F: feeble]

foil[1] /fɔɪl/, *v.t.* to prevent from being successful; thwart: *She foiled him in his attempt to run away; We foiled his plans.* [ME *foile(n)*, from OF: trample]

foil[2] /fɔɪl/, *n.* **1.** a metallic substance formed into very thin sheets by rolling and hammering: *gold foil; aluminium foil.* **2.** anything that sets off the qualities of another thing by contrast. [ME *foile*, from OF, from L: leaf]

foil[3] /fɔɪl/, *n.* a light, thin sword with a button at the point, for use in fencing. [orig. uncert.]

foist /fɔɪst/, *v.t.* **1.** to sell or pass off (something, usu. of low quality) by trickery: *He foisted damaged goods onto the customer.* **2.** to bring or put secretly or dishonestly: *She foisted stolen goods into the room.* [probably from D: to take in hand]

Fokker /'fɒkə/, *n.* **Anthony Herman Gerard**, 1890–1939, Dutch aeroplane designer and builder.

fold[1] /foʊld/, *v.t.* **1.** to bend (cloth, paper, etc.) over upon itself. **2.** to close by bending and laying parts together (oft. fol. by *up*): *to fold up a map.* **3.** to cross (the arms, hands, legs, etc.). **4.** to bend or wind (fol. by *about, round,* etc.): *She folded her arms about his neck.* **5.** to enclose; wrap: *She folded the present in paper.* **6.** to hold or embrace: *He folded her in his arms.* **7.** *Cookery.* to mix (*in*), by gently turning one part over another with a spoon, etc. ◇*v.i.* **8.** to be folded or be able to be folded: *The doors fold back.* **9.** (of a business, etc.) to fail and be closed (sometimes fol. by *up*). ◇*n.* **10.** a part that is folded; pleat; layer: *fold of cloth.* **11.** a hollow part or crease made by folding: *to carry something in the fold of a dress.* **12.** a hollow place in hilly ground. **13.** *Geol.* a part of a rock bed which is folded or bent (as an **anticline** or **syncline**), or which connects two horizontal rock beds of different levels (as a **monocline**). [OE *faldan*]

fold[2] /foʊld/, *n.* **1.** an enclosure for animals, esp. sheep. **2.** a flock of sheep. ◇*v.t.* **3.** to contain (sheep, etc.) in a fold. [OE *fald, falod*]

-fold, a suffix joined to numerals and other words or stems of quantity to indicate multiplication by or division into a certain number, as in *twofold, manifold.* [OE *-fald*]

folder /'foʊldə/, *n.* an outer cover, usu. a folded sheet of light cardboard, for papers.

Foley /'foʊli/, *n.* **Larry** (*Laurence Foley*), 1849–1917, Australian boxer, one of the originators of gloved boxing in Australia.

foliage /'foʊliɪdʒ/, *n.* **1.** the leaves of a plant, collectively. **2.** leaves in general. Also, **foliature.** [F, from L: leaf] –**foliaged**, *adj.*

foliate /'foʊliət, -eɪt/, *adj.;* /'foʊlieɪt/, *v.,* **-ated, -ating.** ◇*adj.* **1.** having or covered with leaves. **2.** leaf-like. ◇*v.i.* **3.** to put forth leaves. [L: leafy]

foliation /foʊli'eɪʃən/, *n.* **1.** the act of putting forth leaves. **2.** the state of being in leaf. **3.** *Bot.* the arrangement of leaves within the bud. **4.** leaves; foliage. **5.** ornamentation with leaves. **6.** (of rocks) a pattern resulting from the separation of different minerals into parallel layers by metamorphic processes. **7.** the formation of metal into thin sheets.

Folies-Bergère /fɒli-beə'ʒeə/, *n.* a theatre in Paris, opened 1869, featuring spectacular musical revues.

folio /'foʊlioʊ/, *n., pl.* **-lios. 1.** a sheet of paper folded once to make two leaves (four pages) of a book. **2.** a volume having pages of the largest size. **3.** a leaf of a book, etc., numbered only on the front side. **4.** *Printing.* the page number of a book. **5.** *Bookkeeping.* a page

folio   397   **food processor**

of an account book or a double page with the same serial number. [L: leaf]

folk /fouk/, n., pl. **folk, folks**, adj. ◇n. **1.** people in general, esp. the common people of a country. **2.** (oft. pl.) the people of a particular class or group: *poor folks; country folk*. **3.** (pl.) Colloq. the people of one's own family. ◇adj. **4.** of or originating among the common people. [OE *folc*]

folk dance, n. (a piece of music for) a dance which originated among, and has been passed on through, the common people of a country. — **folk dancing**, n.

folklore /'fouklɔ/, n. the traditional beliefs, stories, customs, etc., of a people.

folk-rock /fouk-'rɒk/, n. folk music influenced by rock.

folk song, n. a song, usu. of a simple character, originating and handed down among the common people. — **folk singer**, n.

follicle /'fɒlɪkəl/, n. **1.** Bot. a dry one-celled seed fruit consisting of a single carpel, that splits along only one side to let out its seed, such as the fruit of the columbine. **2.** Anat. a small cavity, sac, or gland in the body. [L: little bellows, bag] — **follicular**, adj.

follow /'fɒloʊ/, v.t. **1.** to come after in natural order, etc.; succeed: *Age follows youth*. **2.** to go, come, or move behind in the same direction: *Go on ahead and I'll follow you*. **3.** to accept as a guide, authority or example: *I'll follow your advice; He follows the teachings of Christianity*. **4.** to move forward along (a path, etc.). **5.** to come after as a result: *It follows from this that he must be innocent*. **6.** to go after or along with (a person, etc.): *She follows her friend everywhere*. **7.** to chase; pursue: *Follow that car*. **8.** to take up as a job, etc.: *He decided to follow medicine*. **9.** to watch the movements, development, or course of: *He follows the news carefully*. **10.** to understand (an argument, etc.): *Do you follow this lesson?* ◇v.i. **11.** to come next after something else in natural order, etc. **12.** to happen after something else as a result. **13.** to go or come after a person or thing in movement: *Go on ahead and I'll follow*. ◇v. **14. follow out**, to carry out to the end; execute. **15. follow through**, to carry out completely an action, stroke in a ball game, etc. **16. follow up**, **a.** to examine closely; investigate. **b.** to take further action, etc., after a pause, esp. to increase the effect. [OE *folgian*]

follower /'fɒloʊə/, n. **1.** someone who follows another, esp. in regard to his ideas or beliefs; disciple. **2.** a person who copies or follows an example: *a follower of fashion*. **3.** a servant; attendant. **4.** a supporter, esp. of a particular team or sport. **5.** a part of a machine that receives movement from, or follows the movement of, another part.

following /'fɒloʊɪŋ/, n. **1.** a group of followers, supporters, etc.: *That politician has a large following*. **2. the following**, the things, lines, pages, etc., that come immediately after: *Please remember the following*. ◇adj. **3.** that follows: *a following wind*. **4.** that comes next in order or time: *the following day*. **5.** that is now to be mentioned, etc.: *the following points*.

folly /'fɒli/, n., pl. **-lies. 1.** the state or quality of being foolish. **2.** a foolish action, practice, idea, etc. **3.** (pl.) a theatrical revue. [ME *folie*, from OF: mad]

foment /fə'mɛnt/, v.t. **1.** to cause or help the growth or development of (discord, rebellion, etc.). **2.** to put warm or medicated liquid, cloths dipped in such liquid, etc., on to (the body) to lessen pain, etc. [LL, from L: warm application]

fond /fɒnd/, adj. **1.** liking; taking pleasure in (fol. by of): *fond of children; fond of drink*. **2.** loving; affectionate: *a fond look*. **3.** foolishly loving; doting: *a fond parent*. **4.** (of hopes, etc.) believed in without reason. **5.** Archaic. foolishly trusting. [ME *fonned* be foolish] — **fondness**, n.

Fonda family /'fɒndə/, n. a family of US film actors. **1. Henry**, 1905–82, stage and film actor; father of Jane and Peter. **2. Jane**, born 1937, film actor; Academy Awards 1977, 1978. **3. Peter**, born 1939, actor and film director.

fondant /'fɒndənt/, n. a sweet or icing made of a thick, creamy sugar paste. [F: melt]

fondle /'fɒndl/, v.t., **-dled, -dling.** to stroke or touch fondly; caress.

fondue /'fɒndju/, n. **1.** a dish of melted cheese and white wine, heated over a small burner at the table, into which pieces of bread are dipped before being eaten. **2.** any similar dish of oil or stock (def. 11) in which pieces of fish, meat, vegetable or fruit are individually cooked at the table before being eaten. [F: melt]

font¹ /fɒnt/, n. **1.** a large bowl, usu. of stone, in a church to hold the water used in baptism. **2.** a bowl for holy water. **3.** Archaic. →**fount¹**. [OE, from L: baptismal font, spring, fountain]

font² /fɒnt/, n. a complete set of printing type of one style and size. Also, **fount**. [F: melt, cast]

fontanelle /fɒntə'nɛl/, n. one of the spaces, closed by a membrane, between the bones of the skull of a baby. [F: little fountain]

food /fud/, n. **1.** anything that is eaten by a human or animal or taken in by a plant, and used for growth and nourishment. **2.** more or less solid nourishment (as opposed to *drink*). **3.** a particular kind of nourishment: *a breakfast food*. **4.** anything serving as nourishment for ideas, etc: *food for thought*. [OE *fōda*]

Food and Agriculture Organisation, n. the United Nations agency that administers development programs for increase in food production, etc., in underdeveloped countries. *Abbrev.:* FAO

food chain, n. a series of organisms in which the smallest is eaten by a larger one, which in turn is eaten by a still larger one, etc.

food poisoning, n. an illness caused by eating contaminated food or naturally poisonous substances, usu. marked by vomiting and diarrhoea.

food processor, n. an electric kitchen appliance used to shred, slice, juice, mash, etc.

foodstuff /'fudstʌf/, *n.* a substance or material suitable for food.

fool /ful/, *n.* **1.** someone who lacks sense; silly or stupid person. **2.** a clown, formerly kept by a person of rank for amusement; jester. **3.** someone who is made to appear a fool: *to make a fool of someone.* ◇*v.t.* **4.** to make a fool of; trick; deceive. ◇*v.i.* **5.** to act like a fool; joke; play. **6.** to waste time; trifle: *Don't fool around with minor details.* **7.** to play foolishly: *to fool with a loaded gun.* ◇*v.* **8. fool away**, to waste; squander: *to fool away time; to fool away money.* [ME *fol*, from OF, from LL: empty-headed fellow, from L: bellows]

foolery /'fuləri/, *n., pl.* **-eries.** foolish action or behavior.

foolhardy /'fulhadi/, *adj.*, **-dier, -diest.** bold without judgment; foolishly adventurous. **—foolhardiness**, *n.*

foolish /'fulɪʃ/, *adj.* **1.** silly; without sense: *a foolish person.* **2.** resulting from or showing silliness; unwise: *a foolish action; foolish speech.* **—foolishness**, *n.*

foolproof /'fulpruf/, *adj. Colloq.* with no possibility of mistake or misuse: *a foolproof machine; a foolproof method.*

foolscap /'fulzkæp/, *n.* a paper size. See Appendix. [so called from its former watermark, the outline of a fool's cap]

fool's gold, *n.* iron pyrites, sometimes mistaken for gold.

foot /fut/, *n., pl.* **feet**, *v.* ◇*n.* **1.** (in vertebrates) the end part of the leg, below the ankle joint, on which the body stands and moves. **2.** (in invertebrates) any part of the body similar in position or use. **3.** the unit of length in the imperial system based on the length of the human foot. It is divided into 12 inches and is equal to 0.3048 m. **4.** any thing or part similar to a foot in use. **5.** a part of anything at the end, or bottom, or opposite the top or head: *a foot of a hill; the foot of a page.* **6.** a group of syllables making up a metrical unit of a verse. **7.** Some special uses are:
put one's foot in one's mouth or **in it,** *Colloq.* to say or do something embarrassing.
fall on one's feet, to be lucky.
feet of clay, a fault or weakness in what would otherwise have been perfection.
have one foot in the grave, to be near death.
keep one's feet on the ground, to keep a sensible and practical outlook.
put one's best foot forward, **1.** to do one's very best. **2.** to walk as fast as possible.
put one's foot down, to be very firm. ◇*v.t.* **8.** *Colloq.* to pay or settle (a bill, etc.). [OE *fōt*]

foot-and-mouth disease /fut-ən-'mauθ dəziz/, *n.* an infectious virus disease of cattle and similar animals, marked by blisters about the hoofs and mouth.

football /'futbɔl/, *n.* **1.** any game in which the kicking of a ball has a large part, such as Australian Rules, Rugby Union, Rugby League, Soccer, etc. **2.** the ball used in such games. **—footballer**, *n.*

football pools, *n.pl.* organised betting on the results of football matches.

foothill /'futhɪl/, *n.* a hill at the base of a mountain or mountain range.

foothold /'futhould/, *n.* a place where one may stand or tread with safety in climbing, etc.

footie /'futi/, *n. Colloq.* → **football.** Also, **footy.**

footing /'futɪŋ/, *n.* **1.** a firm position; foothold. **2.** a foundation on which anything is established. **3.** a place or support for the feet. **4.** a firm placing of the feet. **5.** the condition of a relationship: *He is on a friendly footing with her.*

footlights /'futlaɪts/, *n. pl. Theat.* a row of lights at the front of a stage, nearly on a level with the feet of the performers.

footloose /'futlus/, *adj.* free to go or travel about without any responsibilities, etc.

footman /'futmən/, *n., pl.* **-men.** a male servant who attends the door, carriage, table, etc.

footnote /'futnout/, *n.* **1.** a note or explanation at the bottom of a page, referring to a particular part of what is written on the page. **2.** an added note, of less importance than the main statement, etc.

footpath /'futpaθ/, *n.* a path (usu. paved) at the side of a road or street for people to walk on.

Footscray /'futskreɪ/, *n.* an inner western industrial suburb of Melbourne, Victoria. Pop. 47 330 (1986).

footsore /'futsɔ/, *adj.* having sore feet, from much walking, etc.

footstep /'futstep/, *n.* **1.** a step of the foot, or the sound produced by it. **2.** the distance covered by the foot in stepping; pace. **3.** Also, **footprint.** a mark on the ground, made by a foot. **4. follow in someone's footsteps,** to copy someone or follow someone in a job, etc.

footwork /'futwɜk/, *n.* the manner of using the feet, as in sport, dancing.

fop /fɒp/, *n.* a man who is too concerned about his manners and appearance. [orig. uncert.]

for /fɔ; *weak forms* /fə, f/, *prep.* **1.** with the purpose of: *to go for a walk.* **2.** intended to be used by or in connection with: *a book for children; a box for gloves.* **3.** in order to obtain: *a law suit for damages.* **4.** with a tendency towards: *to long for a thing; to have an eye for beauty.* **5.** in return for: *Thank you for your efforts.* **6.** suitable for: *a subject for argument.* **7.** during: *for a long time.* **8.** in support of: *to stand for honest government.* **9.** in place of: *a substitute for butter.* **10.** in the interest of: *to act for a client.* **11.** in honor of: *to give a dinner for a person.* **12.** as punishment or reward for: *fined for stealing; kissed for being good.* **13.** with the purpose of reaching: *to start for Perth.* **14.** (indicating to whom or what something is intended): *a present for you; for the advantage of everybody.* **15.** in order to save: *to run for one's life.* **16.** (indicating who or what is concerned): *an engagement for this evening.* **17.**

such as results in: *his reason for going*. **18.** as having an effect on: *bad for one's health*. **19.** taking into account: *tall for his age*. **20.** in the character of, or as being: *to know a thing for a fact*. **21.** because of: *to shout for joy; famed for its beauty*. **22.** in spite of: *For all his rudeness, I still like him*. **23.** to the extent or amount of: *to walk for a mile*. **24.** (sometimes used with a noun or pronoun followed by an infinitive, to mean the same as a clause with *that* and the auxiliary *should*, etc.): *It is time for him to go*, meaning *It is time that he should go*. ◇*conj*. **25.** because; since: *She laughed, for she suddenly felt happy*. [OE]

for-, a prefix meaning 'away', 'off', or giving a negative force, as in *forswear*, *forbid*. [OE]

forage /'fɒrɪdʒ/, *n., v.*, **-raged, -raging.** ◇*n*. **1.** food for horses and cattle; fodder. **2.** the act of searching for food or provisions of any kind. ◇*v.i.* **3.** to wander in search of food or provisions. [ME, from OF: fodder, from Gmc] —**forager,** *n*.

foramen magnum /fə,reɪmən 'mægnəm/, *n*. the great hole at the base of the skull forming the passage to the spinal canal. [L: great hole]

foraminifer /fɒrə'mɪnəfə/, *n*. any of a group of small, mostly marine rhizopods commonly having a shell with many small holes. [L: hole]

forasmuch /fɒrəz'mʌtʃ/, *conj*. in view of the fact that; since (fol. by *as*).

foray /'fɒreɪ, 'fɒ-/, *n*. **1.** a sudden attack for the purpose of taking goods or provisions; raid. ◇*v.i.* **2.** to make a foray. [ME]

forbade /fə'bæd, -'beɪd/, *v*. past tense of **forbid.** Also, **forbad** /fə'bæd/.

forbear[1] /fɔ'bεə/, *v.*, **-bore, -borne, -bearing.** ◇*v.t.* **1.** to keep oneself back from; refrain from: *I will forbear punishing you*. ◇*v.i.* **2.** to hold back; refrain. **3.** to be patient. [OE *forberan*] —**forbearance,** *n*.

forbear[2] /'fɔbεə/, *n*. →**forebear.**

Forbes /fɔbz/, *n*. **George William,** 1869–1947, NZ politician; prime minister 1930–35.

forbid /fə'bɪd/, *v.t.*, **-bade** or **-bad, -bidden** or **-bid, -bidding. 1.** to command (a person, etc.) not to do, have, use, etc., something: *I forbid you to go*. **2.** to make a rule against (something); prohibit: *We forbid smoking here*. **3.** to prevent; make impossible: *The train strike forbids his departure*. [OE *forbēodan*]

Forbidden City /fə,bɪdn 'sɪti/, *n*. **the,** a walled part of Beijing, China, which encloses a group of palaces, shrines and halls used by former Chinese emperors.

forbidding /fə'bɪdɪŋ/, *adj*. **1.** causing dislike or fear: *a forbidding personality*. **2.** looking dangerous or threatening: *forbidding cliffs; forbidding clouds*.

forbore /fɔ'bɔ/, *v*. past tense of **forbear**[1].

force /fɔs/, *n., v.*, **forced, forcing.** ◇*n*. **1.** strength; intensity of effect: *the force of a blow; the force of an argument; the force of circumstances*. **2.** power, as of a ruler or nation; might. **3.** strength or power used upon a thing or person; violence: *to use force in order to do something; to use force on a person*. **4.** *Agric*. the ability of a dog to control sheep, etc. **5.** mental or moral strength; power of effective action. **6.** (*oft. pl.*) the army, navy and air force of a country. **7.** any body of people combined for joint action: *the police force*. **8.** *Phys*. **a.** an influence which produces or tends to produce motion or change of motion. **b.** the strength of this influence. **9.** any strong influence: *The changes in the law were brought about by social forces*. **10.** the binding power of an agreement, etc. **11. in force, a.** in operation, effect, etc.: *a law now in force*. **b.** in full strength: *Her friends came to see her in force*. ◇*v.t.* **12.** to make (oneself or someone) do something; compel: *She forced him to confess*. **13.** to drive by force; overcome the resistance of. **14.** to bring about or effect by force or as a necessary result: *to force a passage; to force a confession*. **15.** to put or impose (something) by force on or upon a person. **16.** to enter or take by force; overpower. **17.** to break open (a door, lock, etc.). **18.** Also, **force-ripen.** to cause (plants, fruits, etc.) to grow or ripen at an increased rate by artificial methods. **19.** *Agric*. to keep (sheep, etc.) moving through a race or yard, usu. using a dog. [ME, from F, from VL, from L: strong]

forced /fɔst/, *adj*. **1.** enforced; compulsory: *forced labor*. **2.** strained or unnatural: *a forced smile*. **3.** caused by an emergency: *the forced landing of an aeroplane*.

forceful /'fɔsfəl/, *adj*. full of force; powerful; effective.

forceps /'fɔsəps/, *n., pl.* **-ceps, -cipes** /-səpiz/. **1.** an instrument, such as pincers or tongs, for seizing and holding objects, used esp. in surgery and the delivery of babies. **2.** *Zool*. an organ looking like a forceps. [L]

forcible /'fɔsəbəl/, *adj*. **1.** brought about by force. **2.** having force; producing a powerful effect. **3.** (of reasoning) convincing.

ford /fɔd/, *n*. **1.** a shallow place where a river or other body of water may be crossed by walking. ◇*v.t.* **2.** to cross (a river, etc.) by a ford. [OE]

Ford /fɔd/, *n*. **1. Ford Madox** /fɔd 'mædəks/ (*Ford Madox Hueffer*), 1873–1939, English author. **2. Gerald,** born 1913, US Republican politician; 38th president of the US 1974–77. **3. Henry,** 1863–1947, US motor manufacturer.

Forde /fɔd/, *n*. **Francis Michael,** 1890–1983, Australian Labor politician; prime minister 6–13 July, 1945.

fore /fɔ/, *adj*. **1.** placed at or towards the front. **2.** first in place, time, order, etc.; forward; earlier. ◇*adv*. **3.** *Naut*. at or towards the bow (front). ◇*n*. **4.** the front of anything. **5. to the fore, a.** to or at the front. **b.** ready at hand. ◇*prep. and conj*. **6.** *Obs*. before.

fore-, a prefix form of **before** meaning 'front', (*forehead*), 'ahead of time' (*forecast*), 'superior' (*foreman*), etc. [ME and OE *for(e)*]

forearm[1] /'fɔram/, *n*. the part of the arm between the elbow and the wrist.

forearm / fɔr'am /, *v.t.* take up weapons in advance; prepare.

forebear / 'fɔbeə /, *n.* (*usu. pl.*) → **ancestor**. Also, **forbear**. [ME (Scot)]

forebode / fɔ'boud /, *v.t.*, **-boded, -boding. 1.** to be an omen or sign of; prophesy: *clouds that forebode a storm.* **2.** to have a feeling that warns of (evil). —**foreboding,** *n., adj.*

forecast / 'fɔkast /, *v.*, **-cast** or **-casted, -casting,** *n.* ◇*v.t.* **1.** to give an opinion about (a future event); predict. **2.** to be an early warning of; foreshadow. ◇*n.* **3.** a prediction, esp. about the weather. —**forecaster,** *n.*

forecastle / 'fouksəl /, *n.* a short raised deck in the front of a ship. Also, **fo'c'sle, forecastle head.**

foreclose / fɔ'klouz /, *v.*, **-closed, -closing.** ◇*v.t.* **1.** *Law.* to take away from someone the right to redeem (a property, pledge, etc.). **2.** to shut out; exclude. **3.** to prevent (someone) from doing something. **4.** to close, settle, or answer beforehand. ◇*v.i.* **5.** to foreclose a mortgage or pledge. [ME, from OF, from L] —**foreclosure,** *n.* —**foreclosable,** *adj.*

forefather / 'fɔfaðə /, *n.* → **ancestor**.

forefinger / 'fɔfiŋgə /, *n.* the first finger, next to the thumb; the index finger.

forefoot / 'fɔfut /, *n., pl.* **-feet** /-fit/. *Zool.* one of the front feet of a four-legged animal, or of an insect, etc.

forego / fɔ'gou /, *v.t., v.i.,* **-went, -gone, -going.** to go before. [OE *foregān* go before] —**foregoing,** *adj.* —**foregone,** *adj.*

foreground / 'fɔgraund /, *n.* (in a painting, photo, etc.) the part in or at the front (opposed to *background*).

forehand / 'fɔhænd /, *adj.* **1.** made to or from the right side of the body (when the player is right-handed). **2.** (of a payment, etc.) given or made in advance. ◇*n.* **3.** a position in front or above; advantage. **4.** *Tennis, etc.* a stroke made from the right side of the body with the palm of the hand facing the front (when the player is right-handed).

forehead / 'fɔrəd /, *n.* **1.** the part of the face above the eyes; brow. **2.** the fore or front part of anything. [OE *forhēafod*]

foreign / 'fɔrən /, *adj.* **1.** relating to, like, or coming from another country or nation. **2.** relating to dealings with other countries. **3.** outside one's own country, society, etc. **4.** *Law.* outside the legal power of the state; alien. **5.** not belonging: *a foreign substance in the eye; foreign to our discussion.* **6.** strange; unfamiliar. [ME, from OF, from L: out of doors, outside]

foreign affairs, *n.pl.* the activities of a nation arising from its relationship and dealings with other nations.

foreigner / 'fɔrənə /, *n.* a person not born in, or legally belonging to, a given country; alien.

foreign exchange, *n.* **1.** the buying and selling of the money of other countries. **2.** the money of other countries.

foreign legion, *n.* (esp. in the French army) a military body in the service of a state, including foreign soldiers who freely join.

forejudge / fɔ'dʒʌdʒ /, *v.t.,* **-judged, -judging.** to judge beforehand; prejudge.

foreknow / fɔ'nou /, *v.t.,* **-knew, -known, -knowing.** to know beforehand. —**foreknowledge,** *n.*

foreleg / 'fɔleg /, *n.* one of the front legs of a four-legged animal, or of an insect, etc.

forelimb / 'fɔlɪm /, *n.* a front limb of an animal.

forelock / 'fɔlɒk /, *n.* the lock of hair that grows from the front of the head.

foreman / 'fɔmən /, *n., pl.* **-men. 1.** a person in charge of a group of workers. **2.** the person who speaks for the rest of a jury.

forensic / fə'rensɪk, -zɪk /, *adj.* **1.** relating to or used in courts of law or public argument. **2.** suited to argumentation; argumentative. [L: of the forum] —**forensically,** *adv.*

forepaw / 'fɔpɔ /, *n.* either of the front feet of an animal that has paws.

forerunner / 'fɔrʌnə /, *n.* **1.** a person or thing that comes before another. **2.** a sign or warning of what may happen; portent.

foresee / fɔ'si /, *v.t., v.i.,* **-saw, -seen, -seeing.** to see beforehand. [OE *foresēon*] —**foreseer,** *n.*

foreshadow / fɔ'ʃædou /, *v.t.* to show beforehand; prefigure. —**foreshadower,** *n.*

foreshore / 'fɔʃɔ /, *n.* **1.** the part of the shore between the ordinary high-water mark and low-water mark. **2.** the ground between the water's edge and the land used for crops or building.

foresight / 'fɔsaɪt /, *n.* **1.** care for the future. **2.** the act or power of looking to the future. **3.** a view into the future.

foreskin / 'fɔskɪn /, *n.* → **prepuce**.

forest / 'fɔrəst /, *n.* **1.** a large area of land covered with trees. **2.** the trees alone: *to cut down a forest.* **3.** a thick cluster of many things. ◇*v.t.* **4.** to cover with trees. [ME, from OF, from L: outside]

forestall / fɔ'stɔl /, *v.t.* **1.** to prevent by action in advance. **2.** to deal with, meet, or recognise in advance of the natural or proper time. **3.** to buy up (goods) in advance, in order to increase the price. [OE *foresteall* intervention (to defeat justice), waylaying] —**forestaller,** *n.*

forester / 'fɔrəstə /, *n.* **1.** someone trained to care for forests. **2.** an officer having charge of a forest. **3.** See **kangaroo**.

forestry / 'fɔrəstri /, *n.* **1.** the science of planting and taking care of forests. **2.** the act of establishing and managing forests.

foretaste / 'fɔteɪst /, *n.;* / fɔ'teɪst /, *v.,* **-tasted, -tasting.** ◇*n.* **1.** a taste beforehand; anticipation. ◇*v.t.* **2.** to taste beforehand; enjoy by anticipation.

foretell / fɔ'tel /, *v.,* **-told, -telling.** ◇*v.t.* **1.** to tell of beforehand; predict. ◇*v.i.* **2.** to give a prediction. —**foreteller,** *n.*

forethought /'fɔθɔt/, *n.* **1.** careful planning in advance. **2.** a thinking of something beforehand; anticipation.

forever /fər'evə/, *adv.* **1.** without ever ending; eternally. **2.** continually; incessantly: *He's forever complaining.*

forewarn /fɔ'wɔn/, *v.t.* to warn beforehand.

foreword /'fɔwəd/, *n.* a short introduction at the front of a book; preface.

forfeit /'fɔfət/, *n.* **1.** a fine; penalty. **2.** the act of forfeiting. **3.** something lost because of crime, carelessness, neglect, etc. ◇*v.t.* **4.** to lose, or become liable to lose (something) because of a crime, fault, etc. ◇*adj.* **5.** lost in this way. [ME, from OF] —**forfeiter,** *n.* —**forfeiture,** *n.*

forgave /fə'geɪv/, *v.* past tense of **forgive.**

forge[1] /fɔdʒ/, *n., v.,* **forged, forging.** ◇*n.* **1.** the special fireplace or furnace in which metal is heated before shaping. **2.** → **smithy.** ◇*v.t.* **3.** to form by heating and hammering. **4.** to form or make in any way. **5.** to invent (a lie, etc.). **6.** to copy (a signature, etc.) in order to deceive. ◇*v.i.* **7.** to commit forgery. **8.** to work at a forge. [ME, from OF, from L: workshop] —**forger,** *n.*

forge[2] /fɔdʒ/, *v.i.,* **forged, forging.** to move forward with (great) effort or force (usu. fol. by *ahead*). [orig. uncert.]

forgery /'fɔdʒəri/, *n., pl.* **-geries. 1.** the making of a copy of a thing in order to deceive, as a coin, a work of art, a written work, etc. **2.** something, as a coin, a work of art, a writing, etc., produced by forgery. **3.** the act of making or producing falsely.

forget /fə'get/, *v.,* **-got** or (*Archaic*) **-gat; -gotten -got; -getting. 1.** to cease or fail to remember: **a.** a fact: *I forget his name.* **b.** to do: *I forgot to clean my teeth.* **c.** to take: *to forget the keys.* **d.** to mention: *I forgot my third point in the essay.* **e.** to use, put, make, etc.: *to forget a full stop.* **f.** to fail to do on purpose; disregard. ◇*v.i.* **3.** to cease or fail to think of something. ◇*v.* **4. forget it,** to drop the subject. **5. forget oneself, a.** to say or do something improper. **b.** to become absent-minded. **c.** to stop thinking of one's own feelings. [OE *forg(i)etan*] —**forgettable,** *adj.* —**forgetful,** *adj.*

forget-me-not /fə'gɛt-mi-nɒt/, *n.* a small plant with a light blue flower, regarded as a symbol of continuing love.

forgive /fə'gɪv/, *v.,* **-gave, -given, -giving.** ◇*v.t.* **1.** to give a free pardon for (an offence, debt, etc.); pardon. **2.** to give up all claims to (a debt, etc.). **3.** to give a free pardon to (a person). **4.** to cease to have feelings against (someone): *to forgive my enemies.* ◇*v.i.* **5.** to pardon an offence or an offender. [OE *forgiefan*] —**forgiveness,** *n.*

forgo /fɔ'goʊ/, *v.t.,* **-went, -gone, -going.** to do without; give up; renounce. [OE]

forgot /fə'gɒt/, *v.* past tense and past participle of **forget.**

forgotten /fə'gɒtn/, *v.* past participle of **forget.**

fork /fɔk/, *n.* **1.** an instrument having two or more prongs, for holding, lifting, etc., used for handling food or as a tool for farming or gardening. **2.** something like this in form. **3.** → **tuning fork. 4.** the place or part at which a thing, esp. a river or a road, divides into branches. **5.** each of the branches into which a thing divides. ◇*v.t.* **6.** to hold, raise, dig, etc., with a fork. **7.** *Colloq.* to hand over; pay (fol. by *over* or *out*). ◇*v.i.* **8.** to divide into branches. [OE *forca,* from L]

forked /fɔkt/, *adj.* **1.** having a fork or forking branches. **2.** zigzag, as lightning.

fork-lift /'fɔk-lɪft/, *n.* an electric truck with two power-operated arms for lifting and carrying goods.

forlorn /fə'lɔn/, *adj.* **1.** left alone or without something; abandoned; deserted (sometimes fol. by *of*): *forlorn of friends.* **2.** unhappy or miserable, in feeling, condition, or appearance. **3.** hopeless; desperate. [OE *forlēosan* lose, destroy]

form /fɔm/, *n.* **1.** the outer shape or appearance considered apart from color or material; configuration. **2.** the shape of a thing or person. **3.** a body, esp. that of a human being. **4.** something that gives shape; mould. **5.** a particular structural condition or character of a thing: *water in the form of ice.* **6.** *Lit, Music.* the manner or style of arranging parts for a pleasing result. **7.** *Art.* the organisation and relationship of lines, colors, shapes, etc., so as to create a coherent image. **8.** proper shape; good order. **9.** *Philos.* the structure, pattern, or nature of anything. **10.** a set or customary order or method of doing something or of behaving: *It is not good form to eat from your knife.* **11.** a set order of words, as for use in a religious ceremony or in a legal document. **12.** a document with blank spaces to be filled in: *a tax form.* **13.** the manner or method of performing something. **14.** (of health, fitness) condition, esp. good condition. **15.** *Gram.* any word, part of a word, or group of words arranged in a construction, which whenever used keeps the one basic meaning. **16.** a single division of a school containing students of about the same age. **17.** a long seat; bench. **18. a matter of form,** a simply routine activity. **19. bad form,** behavior that ignores social customs. **20. good form,** behavior that follows social customs. ◇*v.t.* **21.** to build or frame. **22.** to make or produce. **23.** to be the substance of; make up; constitute. **24.** to place in order; arrange; organise. **25.** to frame (ideas, opinions, etc.) in the mind. **26.** to develop (habits, friendships, etc.). **27.** to give shape to. **28.** to shape by discipline or instruction. ◇*v.i.* **29.** to take form. **30.** to be formed or produced. **31.** to take a particular form or arrangement. [ME, from OF, from L: form, figure, model, mould, sort]

-form, a suffix meaning 'having the form of', as in *cruciform, uniform.* [L *-formis*]

formal /'fɔməl/, *adj.* **1.** being in accordance with custom; conventional. **2.** marked by form or ceremony: *a formal occasion.* **3.** (of a person) excessively ceremonious. **4.** being a matter of form only; perfunctory. **5.** following official method: *a formal vote; a formal complaint.* **6.** *Educ.* gained in a recognised place of learning: *a formal education.* **7.** relating to the form or shape of a thing, rather than the content or meaning. ◇*n.* **8.** a dance or ball at which evening dress is to be worn.

formaldehyde /fɔ'mældəhaɪd/, *n.* a gas, HCHO, used in solution, as a disinfectant and preservative, and in the manufacture of resins and plastics. Also, **formaldehyd**. [FORM(IC ACID) + ALDEHYDE]

formalin /'fɔmələn/, *n.* a solution of formaldehyde used to sterilise non-boilable material, in the treatment of warts, and as a preservative for biological specimens.

formality /fɔ'mælɪti/, *n., pl.* **-ties. 1.** the quality of being formal; obedience to rules and customs; conventionality. **2.** too great an attention to rules; stiffness. **3.** an official or formal act; ceremony. **4.** something done only to obey outward form or custom.

format /'fɔmæt/, *n., v.,* **-matted, -matting.** ◇*n.* **1.** the general outward appearance of a book, newspaper, or magazine, etc., such as the typeface, binding, quality of paper, margins, etc. **2.** the plan or style of something: *the format of a television series.* **3.** *Photog.* the size and shape of a negative or print. **4.** *Computers.* an orderly arrangement of data elements to form a larger body of information as a file, etc. ◇*v.t.* **5.** to organise (a book, data, etc.) into a particular format. [F, from L: formed (in a certain way)]

formation /fɔ'meɪʃən/, *n.* **1.** the act or process of forming. **2.** the structure or arrangement. **3.** *Mil.* a particular arrangement of troops. **4.** a group of two or more aircraft flying as a unit according to a fixed plan. **5.** a team of gymnasts, etc., performing according to a routine. **6.** something formed. **7.** *Geol.* (a process resulting in) a series of beds of rock of one main mineral type, produced in a single period of deposition. **8.** *Biol.* a community of plants spreading over a very large natural area, the nature of which is determined by climate, e.g. rain forest, etc.

formative /'fɔmətɪv/, *adj.* **1.** giving form or shape; moulding. **2.** relating to development: *the formative period of a nation.* **3.** *Biol.* able to develop new cells or tissue by cell division and differentiation. ◇*n.* **4.** *Gram.* an affix (word part), esp. one which changes the part of speech of the base word, such as *-ness,* in *loudness, hardness,* etc.

former /'fɔmə/, *adj.* **1.** coming before in time; earlier; prior. **2.** past, long past, or ancient. **3.** coming before in order; being the first of two. See **latter. 4.** having held a particular office in the past: *a former president.* [OE *forma* first + -ER⁴]

formerly /'fɔməli/, *adv.* in time past; of old.

formica /fɔ'maɪkə/, *n. Bldg Trades.* a plastic usu. used in sheets as a heat-resistant covering for furniture, walls, etc. [Trademark]

formic acid /'fɔmɪk/, *n.* a colorless liquid, HCOOH, an acid once obtained from insects; methanoic acid. [L]

formidable /'fɔmədəbəl, fɔ'mɪdəbəl/, *adj.* **1.** to be feared or dreaded. **2.** of alarming strength, size, difficulty, etc. [F, from L: causing fear] —**formidably,** *adv.*

formula /'fɔmjələ/, *n., pl.* **-las, -lae** /-li/. **1.** a set form of words, as for stating something with authority, or for giving the correct method to be followed. **2.** *Maths.* a rule or principle often expressed in algebraic symbols. **3.** a fixed and successful method of doing something: *a formula for happiness.* **4.** *Chem.* an expression of the constituents of a compound by symbols and figures, as an **empirical formula,** or a **structural formula,** etc. **5.** a recipe or prescription. **6.** an official grouping of racing cars according to type, engine size, etc., for particular races. [L]

formulate /'fɔmjəleɪt/, *v.t.,* **-lated, -lating. 1.** to express in exact form; state clearly. **2.** to express in a formula. —**formulation,** *n.* —**formulator,** *n.*

formwork /'fɔmwɜk/, *n. Bldg Trades.* the temporary and shaped structure into which concrete is poured.

formyl /'fɔməl/, *n.* the radical, HCO—, derived from formic acid. [FORM(IC ACID) + -YL]

fornicate /'fɔnəkeɪt/, *v.i.,* **-cated, -cating.** to commit fornication. [L: brothel, arch, vault]

fornication /fɔnə'keɪʃən/, *n.* **1.** voluntary sexual intercourse between unmarried people. **2.** *Bible.* adultery.

Forrest /'fɒrəst/, *n.* **1. Alexander,** 1849–1901, Australian explorer and stock and station agent, responsible for the discovery of much valuable land between the De Grey River, WA, and Port Darwin. **2. Sir John,** 1847–1918, (*1st Baron Forrest of Bunbury*), brother of Alexander, Australian explorer and politician; premier of WA, 1890–1901.

forsake /fə'seɪk/, *v.t.,* **-sook, -saken, -saking. 1.** to leave; desert; abandon: *forsake one's friends.* **2.** to give up (a habit, way of life, etc.); renounce. [OE *forsacan* deny, give up] —**forsaken,** *adj.*

Forster¹ /'fɔstə/, *n.* **E(dward) M(organ),** English novelist and member of the Bloomsbury Group; wrote *A Passage to India* (1924).

Forster² /'fɔstə/, *n.* a town on the north coast of NSW; holiday resort. Pop. (with Tuncurry) 11 239 (1986).

forswear /fɔ'sweə/, *v.t.,* **-swore, -sworn, -swearing. 1.** to give up; renounce upon oath. **2.** to declare untrue, upon oath. **3. forswear oneself,** tell a lie while under oath; perjure oneself. [OE *forswerian*]

fort /fɔt/, *n.* **1.** any armed place built to keep enemies out and to house soldiers; fortification; fortress. **2. hold the fort,** to keep everything operating as usual. [F, from L: strong]

Fort Denison /fɔt 'dɛnəsən/, *n.* a small island in Sydney Harbor, NSW; used as a prison in the early colony; fort built 1857.

forte¹ /'fɔteɪ/, *n.* a strong point, as of a person; anything which one does particularly well: *Music is her forte.* [F]

forte² /'fɔteɪ/, *adv.* (a musical direction) loudly (opposed to *piano*). *Abbrev.*: f. [It, from L: strong]

forth /fɔθ/, *adv.* **1.** forwards; onwards or outwards in place or space. **2.** onwards in time or in order: *from that day forth*. **3.** out, as from hiding or inaction; into view. **4.** away; abroad. **5. and so forth**, and so on; et cetera. [ME and OE]

forthcoming /'fɔθkʌmɪŋ/, *adj.* **1.** about to appear; coming in time. **2.** ready when needed or expected. ◊*n.* **3.** a coming forth; appearance.

forthright /'fɔθraɪt/, *adj.* **1.** going straight to the point; outspoken. **2.** travelling in a straight course; direct; straightforward. ◊*adv.* **3.** straight or directly forward.

forthwith /fɔθ'wɪθ, -'wɪð/, *adv.* **1.** at once; without delay; immediately. **2.** as soon as can reasonably be expected.

fortieth /'fɔtiəθ/, *adj.* **1.** next after the 39th; 40th. **2.** being one of forty equal parts.

fortification /fɔtəfə'keɪʃən/, *n.* **1.** the act of strengthening. **2.** something which protects. **3.** (*oft. pl.*) a military work built to strengthen a position, e.g. a fort, wall, etc.

fortify /'fɔtəfaɪ/, *v.*, **-fied, -fying.** ◊*v.t.* **1.** to strengthen against attack; protect with fortifications. **2.** to make (something) strong, or resistant to strain, wear, etc. **3.** to strengthen (someone) mentally, emotionally, physically, etc. **4.** to enrich (food) by adding vitamins, etc. **5.** to add alcohol to (wines, etc.) to stop fermentation or to increase the strength. [ME, from F, from LL: make]

fortissimo /fɔ'tɪsɪmoʊ/, *adv.* (a musical direction) very loudly. *Abbrev.*: ff. [It, superlative of *forte*. See FORTE²]

fortitude /'fɔtətjud/, *n.* patient courage in times of sickness, hardship, etc.; moral strength. [L]

Fort Knox /fɔt 'nɒks/, *n.* a militarily controlled area in northern Kentucky; site of the storage place of the US gold reserves since 1936.

fortnight /'fɔtnaɪt/, *n.* the space of 14 nights and days; two weeks. [OE *fēowertēne niht* fourteen nights] — **fortnightly**, *adj., adv.*

fortress /'fɔtrəs/, *n.* **1.** a fort or group of forts, often including a town. **2.** any place of security: *My God is my fortress*. [ME, from OF: strong]

fortuitous /fɔ'tjuətəs/, *adj.* happening by chance or by good luck; accidental. [L: casual]

fortunate /'fɔtʃənət/, *adj.* **1.** having good fortune; lucky. **2.** bringing or promising good fortune; auspicious. [ME, from L: made prosperous or happy]

fortune /'fɔtʃən/, *n., v.*, **-tuned, -tuning.** ◊*n.* **1.** position in life as determined by wealth: *to make one's fortune*. **2.** amount of wealth. **3.** great wealth. **4.** chance; luck. **5.** (*oft. pl.*) anything which happens to someone as his fate or lot in life or in any particular action. **6.** lot; destiny. **7. tell someone's fortune**, to tell of coming events in a person's life. [ME, from F, from L: chance, luck, fortune]

fortune-teller /'fɔtʃən-telə/, *n.* someone who claims an ability to tell people what will happen in the future. — **fortune-telling**, *adj., n.*

forty /'fɔti/, *n., pl.* **-ties**, *adj.* ◊*n.* **1.** a cardinal number, ten times four (10 × 4). **2.** a symbol for this number, as 40 or XL or XXXX. **3.** (*pl.*) the numbers from 40 to 49 of a series, esp. years of a person's age, or the years of a century. **4. roaring forties**, *Geog.* those parts of the oceans in the southern hemisphere between latitudes 40° and 60° where northwesterly winds blow throughout the year. ◊*adj.* **5.** amounting to forty in number. [OE *fēowertig*]

forty-five /fɔti-'faɪv/, *n.* a gramophone record which turns 45 times a minute when being played.

forum /'fɔrəm/, *n., pl.* **forums, fora** /'fɔrə/. **1.** *Anc. Hist.* the marketplace or public square of an ancient Roman city, the centre of legal and other business. **2.** (something like) a court: *the forum of public opinion*. **3.** a meeting for the discussion of questions of public interest. [L]

forward /'fɔwəd; for def. 10 also /'fɔrəd/, *adj.* **1.** directed towards a point in advance, moving ahead; onward: *a forward step*. **2.** at the front: *the forward section of the plane*. **3.** well-advanced. **4.** ready, or eager; prompt. **5.** bold; presumptuous. **6.** of or relating to the future: *forward buying*. **7.** (of people or opinions) extreme; radical; progressive. ◊*n.* **8.** *Soccer, Hockey, etc.* a player placed in front of other members of his team. **9. a.** *Aust Rules.* one of six players who make up the forward line, the main attacking force of the team. **b.** *R Union.* one of the eight players in a team who form the scrum and act as a pack in rushing the ball forward and getting it to the three-quarters. **c.** *R League.* one of the six players with similar functions. ◊*adv.* **10.** towards the front of a ship or aeroplane. **11.** → **forwards**. ◊*v.t.* **12.** to send forward; transmit, esp. to a new address: *to forward a letter*. **13.** to advance or help onwards; hasten. [ME and OE *for(e)ward*]

forward line, *n. Soccer, Hockey, etc.* the attacking players of a team.

forwards /'fɔwədz/, *adv.* **1.** towards or at a place, point, or time in advance; onwards; ahead: *to move forwards*. **2.** towards the front. **3.** into view or consideration: *They pushed their views forwards*. Also, (esp. in figurative senses), **forward**.

forwent /fɔ'wɛnt/, *v.* past tense of *forgo*.

fossa /'fɒsə/, *n., pl.* **fossae** /'fɒsi/. *Anat.* a cavity, or depression in a bone, etc. [L: ditch, trench]

fossick /'fɒsɪk/, *v.i.* **1. a.** to search in a small way for mineral deposits, usu. over ground formerly worked by others. **b.** to search for small things: *to fossick through a drawer for scissors*. ◊*v.t.* **2.** to dig, hunt, (fol. by *out*). [Cornish d.]

fossil /ˈfɒsəl/, n. **1.** any remains, impression, or trace of an animal or plant of a former geological age, e.g. a skeleton or a footprint. **2.** *Colloq.* an old-fashioned person or thing. ◇*adj.* **3.** of the nature of a fossil: *fossil insects*. **4.** taken from below the earth's surface: *fossil salt*. [L: dug up] —**fossil-like,** *adj.*

fossil fuel, *n.* the remains of organisms (or their products) embedded in the earth, with high carbon and/or hydrogen contents, which are used as fuels; esp. coal, oil and natural gas.

fossorial /fɒˈsɔːriəl/, *adj.* **1.** digging or burrowing. **2.** *Zool.* suited for digging, as the hands, feet. [L: digger]

foster /ˈfɒstə/, *v.t.* **1.** to encourage the growth of: *to foster foreign trade.* **2.** to bring up; rear a child in a family not his by birth or adoption. **3.** to care for; cherish. **4.** to place (a child) in a foster home. ◇*adj.* **5.** of or relating to fostering: *a foster home*. [ME; OE *fōster* nourishment] —**fosterer,** *n.*

fought /fɔːt/, *v.* past tense and past participle of **fight**.

foul /faʊl/, *adj.* **1.** very unpleasant to the senses; loathsome: *a foul smell; a foul taste*. **2.** characterised by offensive matter; polluted: *foul air*. **3.** very dirty or muddy. **4.** blocked with foreign matter: *a foul drain*. **5.** (of weather) stormy. **6.** (in a moral sense) very unpleasant, as a crime, language; vile. **7.** against the rules of society, sport, etc.; unfair. **8.** caught; jammed: *a foul rope*. **9.** ugly or disagreeable. ◇*adv.* **10.** in a foul manner; unfairly. **11. fall foul of,** to have or be in trouble with. ◇*n.* **12.** a collision (as of boats, people). **13.** a breaking of the rules of a sport or game. ◇*v.t.* **14.** to make foul; defile. **15.** to block (a chimney or the bore of a gun). **16.** to collide with. **17.** to cause (a rope, etc.) to become caught. **18.** to dishonor; disgrace. ◇*v.i.* **19.** to become foul. **20.** *Naut.* to come into collision. **21.** to become entangled or clogged: *the anchor fouled*. ◇*v.* **22. foul up,** *Colloq.* to mess up; spoil; confuse. [OE *fūl*]

found¹ /faʊnd/, *v.* past tense and past participle of **find**. [OE *funde*]

found² /faʊnd/, *v.t.* **1.** to set up or establish (a business, etc.). **2.** (usu. in p.p.) **a.** to lay the lowest part of (a structure) on a firm base: *a house founded upon a rock*. **b.** to base; ground: *a story founded on fact*. [ME, from OF, from L: lay the bottom of]

foundation /faʊnˈdeɪʃən/, *n.* **1.** the basis of anything. **2.** the natural or prepared base on which some structure rests. **3.** *Bldg Trades.* the lowest part of a building, wall, etc., usu. of masonry, and partly or totally below the surface of the ground. **4.** the act of founding, setting up, establishing, etc. **5.** (a donation for the support of) an institution. ◇*adj.* **6.** of or relating to someone associated with the beginning: *a foundation member*.

Foundation Day, *n.* an annual holiday celebrated on the first Monday in June in WA to commemorate the state's foundation.

founder¹ /ˈfaʊndə/, *n.* someone who begins or establishes something.

founder² /ˈfaʊndə/, *v.i.* **1.** (of a ship) to fill with water and sink. **2.** (of buildings, etc.) to fall or sink down. **3.** to fail completely. **4.** to trip, break down, or go lame. [ME, from OF, from L: bottom]

foundling /ˈfaʊndlɪŋ/, *n.* a baby found abandoned; a child without a parent or guardian. [ME]

foundry /ˈfaʊndri/, *n., pl.* **-dries.** a place producing castings, in which molten metal is poured into moulds. [F]

fount¹ /faʊnt/, *n.* **1.** *Poetic.* a spring of water; fountain. **2.** origin; source. [short for FOUNTAIN]

fount² /fɒnt/, *n.* → **font²**. [F]

fountain /ˈfaʊntɪn/, *n.* **1.** a spring or source of water. **2.** the origin of anything. **3.** a jet or stream of water made to spout or rise from a structure, as to give water for drinking, or to serve for ornament. **4.** an (artistic) structure for sending up such a jet of water. **5.** a container for a liquid to be supplied gradually as in a fountain pen. [late ME, from OF, of or from a spring]

fountain pen, *n.* a pen with a holder for supplying ink to the point of the nib.

four /fɔː/, *n.* **1.** a cardinal number, three plus one (3 + 1). **2.** a symbol of this number, 4 or IV or IIII. **3.** a set of this many persons or things. **4.** *Rowing.* a crew of four rowers. **5.** *Cricket.* a hit scoring four runs, when the ball is hit to the boundary, but first touches the ground. **6. on all fours,** on the hands and feet (or knees). ◇*adj.* **7.** amounting to four in number. [OE *fēower*]

four-dimensional /fɔːdəˈmɛnʃənəl, -daɪ-/, *adj.* having or needing four dimensions, esp. the three spatial dimensions of length, breadth, and depth and the fourth dimension of time.

Four Horsemen of the Apocalypse, *n.pl.* four riders symbolising pestilence, war, famine, and death.

Fourier /ˌfʊəriˈeɪ/, *n.* **Jean Baptiste Joseph** /ʒɒ baˌtist ʒuːˈzɛf/, 1768–1830, French mathematician and physicist.

Fourier analysis /ˈfʊəriə əˈnæləsəs/, *n.* *Phys.* the breaking down of any periodic function such as a complex sound or electromagnetic wave-form into the sum of a number of sine and cosine functions. [named after Jean Baptiste Joseph FOURIER]

four-letter word, *n.* any short word considered offensive because of reference to sex or excrement.

fourscore /ˈfɔːskɔː/, *adj.* four times twenty; eighty.

four-stroke /ˈfɔːstroʊk/, *adj.* relating to an internal-combustion engine cycle in which one piston stroke out of every four is a power stroke.

fourteen /fɔːˈtiːn/, *n.* **1.** a cardinal number, ten plus four (10 + 4). **2.** a symbol for this number, as 14 or XIV or XIIII. ◇*adj.* **3.** amounting to fourteen in number. [OE *fēowertēne*] —**fourteenth,** *adj., n.*

fourth /fɔːθ/, *adj.* **1.** next after the third. **2.** being one of four equal parts. ◇*n.* **3.** a fourth

fourth

part, esp. of one ($\frac{1}{4}$). **4.** the fourth member of a series. **5.** *Music.* a note on the fourth degree from a given note (counted as the first). [OE *fēo(we)rtha*]

fourth dimension, *n.* the dimension of time. —**fourth-dimensional,** *adj.*

fourth estate, *n.* the public press, the newspapers or journalists collectively.

four-wheel drive, *n.* **1.** a mechanism which connects all four wheels of a motor vehicle to the source of power. **2.** a vehicle which has such a mechanism. *Abbrev.:* 4WD

fowl /faʊl/, *n., pl.* **fowls,** (*esp. collectively*) **fowl,** *v.* ◇*n.* **1.** a domestic hen or cock. **2.** a similar bird such as the turkey or duck. **3.** the flesh of a domestic fowl. **4.** any bird (now chiefly in combination): *waterfowl; wildfowl*. ◇*v.i.* **5.** to hunt or take wildfowl. [ME *foule*, OE *fugel*]

fox /fɒks/, *n.* **1.** a wild member of the dog family, commonly red in color, with a pointed muzzle, upright ears, and a long, bushy tail. **2.** the fur of this animal. **3.** a cunning or crafty person. ◇*v.t.* **4.** *Colloq.* to deceive or trick. **5.** to cause (papers, etc.) to discolor with reddish brown spots of mildew. **6.** *Colloq.* to fetch (often said to a dog as a command): *Fox it!* ◇*v.i.* **7.** to act cleverly in order to deceive. [OE]

Fox Glacier, *n.* a glacier in South Island, NZ, rising in the Southern Alps and flowing down their western slopes; descends to semi-tropical forests.

foxglove /'fɒksglʌv/, *n.* a European plant with drooping, tubular, purple or white flowers, and leaves that are used for medicine. See **digitalis**. [OE *foxes glōfa*]

foxhole /'fɒkshoʊl/, *n.* **1.** a fox's lair. **2.** a small pit, usu. for one or two men, used for cover in a battle area.

fox-hunting /'fɒks-hʌntɪŋ/, *n.* a sport in which people on horses follow a fox that is being pursued by a hound or hounds. —**fox-hunter,** *n.*

foxtrot /'fɒkstrɒt/, *n., v.*, **-trotted, -trotting.** ◇*n.* **1.** (the music for) a ballroom dance, in quadruple time, marked by various combinations of short, quick steps. ◇*v.i.* **2.** to dance a foxtrot.

foxy /'fɒksi/, *adj.*, **foxier, foxiest. 1.** foxlike; cunning or crafty: *a man with a foxy face*. **2.** discolored. **3.** fox-colored; yellowish or reddish brown.

foyer /'fɔɪjə/, *n.* an entrance hall to a theatre or hotel. [F: hearth, fireside (orig. a room to which theatre audiences went for warmth between the acts), from L: hearth]

fp, *Abbrev.* forte piano.

f.p., *Abbrev.* freezing point.

f.p.s. /ˌɛf piː 'ɛs/, *Abbrev.* **1.** foot-pound-second (system). **2.** feet per second.

Fr, *1. Abbrev.* Father. ◇*Symbol.* **2.** *Chem.* francium.

fracas /'fræka, -kəs/, *n.* a noisy disturbance or fight; uproar. [F, from It: smash, from L]

fragrance

fraction /'frækʃən/, *n.* **1.** *Maths.* **a.** one or more parts of a unit or whole number; the ratio between any two numbers. **b.** a ratio of algebraic quantities similar to the arithmetical vulgar fraction. **2.** a small part, piece or amount: *a fraction of the population; Open the door a fraction*. **3.** the act of breaking. **4.** *Chem.* a part of a chemical mixture, esp. when it has been separated out. [ME, from L: break]

fractional /'frækʃənəl/, *adj.* **1.** relating to fractions; comprising a part or the parts of a unit; constituting a fraction: *fractional numbers*. **2.** so small as to be meaningless. **3.** *Chem.* of or indicating a process, as distillation, etc., by which the substances of a mixture are separated using differences in properties, as boiling point, solubility, etc.

fractional distillation, *n.* a process in which the components of a liquid mixture, as crude petroleum, are separated by distilling the mixture at different temperatures and condensing the components separately.

fractionate /'frækʃəneɪt/, *v.t.*, **-nated, -nating. 1.** to separate (a mixture) into its constituents as by distillation, etc. **2.** to obtain by such a process. —**fractionation,** *n.*

fractious /'frækʃəs/, *adj.* **1.** cross; peevish: *a fractious child*. **2.** difficult to control: *a fractious horse*. [FRACT(ION) (in obs. sense of discord) + -OUS]

fracture /'fræktʃə/, *n., v.*, **-tured, -turing.** ◇*n.* **1.** a breaking or break, esp. of a bone (called *simple* when the bone does not come through the skin, and *compound* when it does). **2.** the act or manner of breaking. **3.** the characteristic appearance of a broken surface, as of a mineral. ◇*v.t., v.i.* **4.** to break or crack (a bone, etc.). [F, from L: breach] —**fractural,** *adj.*

fracture filling, *n. Geol.* material found in cracks in fissured rock; it is commonly of siliceous or carbonate composition and may have traces of ore minerals in it.

fracture zone, *n. Geol.* an area of a rock mass in which the fabric (def. 4) of the rock is disturbed by earth movement.

fragile /'frædʒaɪl/, *adj.* easily broken or damaged; delicate; brittle; frail. [L] —**fragility,** *n.*

fragment /'frægmənt/, *n.* **1.** a part broken off or detached: *scattered fragments of rock*. **2.** a part that is unfinished or incomplete: *fragments of a letter*. **3.** an odd piece, bit, or scrap. [L] —**fragmented,** *adj.*

fragmentary /'frægmәntri, -təri/, *adj.* composed of fragments; broken; disconnected; incomplete: *fragmentary evidence; fragmentary remains*.

fragmentation /ˌfrægmən'teɪʃən/, *n.* **1.** the act or process of fragmenting. **2.** breakdown; disintegration: *fragmentation of society*. **3.** fragments from an exploded bomb or hand grenade.

fragrance /'freɪgrəns/, *n.* sweet smell or scent; fragrant quality or odor. Also, **fragrancy**.

fragrant /ˈfreɪgrənt/, *adj.* **1.** having a sweet smell; sweet-scented. **2.** delightful; pleasant: *fragrant memories*. [L: smelling sweet]

frail /freɪl/, *adj.* **1.** weak; not robust; having delicate health. **2.** easily broken or destroyed; fragile: *frail cup; a frail excuse*. **3.** morally weak; not strong against temptation. [ME, from OF, from L: fragile]

frailty /ˈfreɪlti/, *n., pl.* **-ties. 1.** the quality or state of being frail. **2.** a moral weakness or a fault coming from it: *human frailty*.

frame /freɪm/, *n., v.*, **framed, framing.** ◇*n.* **1.** an enclosing border or case: *a picture frame; a door frame; a frame of trees round a house*. **2.** anything composed of parts fitted and joined together; a structure. **3.** the sustaining parts of such a structure: *the frame of a pair of spectacles; a house with a wooden frame*. **4.** body structure; build: *a heavy frame*. **5.** any of various machines operating on or within a framework. **6.** a machine or part of a machine used in textile production. **7.** the rigid part of a bicycle. **8.** a particular state, as of the mind: *an unhappy frame of mind*. **9.** form or structure in general; system; order. **10.** *Ship building.* one of the transverse structural members of a ship's hull, extending from the gunwale to the bilge or to the keel. **11.** a structure placed in a beehive on which bees build a honeycomb. **12.** *Colloq.* (in baseball) an inning. **13.** one of the successive small pictures on a strip of film. **14.** *Colloq.* (of livestock) a very thin animal. **15.** *Colloq.* → **frame-up**. ◇*v.t.* **16.** (of a boat, plan, poem, excuse, etc.) to form or make, put together; shape. **17.** to conceive or imagine, as ideas, plans. **18.** to shape or to prearrange falsely, as a plot, a race, etc. **19.** *Colloq.* to make someone appear guilty by a plot; incriminate. **20.** (of a picture) to provide with or put into a frame. **21.** to surround or act as a setting: *Ivy framed the window; Curly hair framed her face.* [OE: avail, profit] –**framer**, *n*.

frame of reference, *n.* **1.** a set or system of facts, ideas, etc., to which a thing relates and which gives the background information which allows it to be discussed or judged; context. **2.** a set of standards which determines and sanctions people's behavior and attitudes. **3.** *Phys.* a set of coordinates or reference axes for defining the position of a point or body.

frame-up /ˈfreɪm-ʌp/, *n. Colloq.* a scheme or plan to make someone else appear to be guilty of a crime. Also, **frame**.

framework /ˈfreɪmwɜk/, *n.* **1.** a structure composed of parts fitted and joined together; system. **2.** a structure designed to support or enclose something; frame or skeleton: *the steel framework of a ship*.

franc /fræŋk/, *n.* **1.** the monetary unit of France, Belgium, Switzerland, and various other countries. **2.** a former silver coin of France. [ME, from OF *franc*, so called from the ML legend *Francorum rex* king of the Franks (or French), on the first coin)]

France /fræns, frɑns/, *n.* a republic in western Europe, with coasts on the English Channel, the Atlantic Ocean and the Mediterranean Sea; first became a republic in 1793 after the French Revolution; the present Fifth Republic dates from 1958. Pop. 55 632 000 (1986 est.); 547 026 km². *Language:* French. *Currency:* franc. *Cap.:* Paris.

franchise /ˈfræntʃaɪz/, *n.* **1.** the rights of a citizen, esp. the right to vote; suffrage. **2.** any special right or privilege given by a government. **3.** permission given by a manufacturer to a distributor or retailer to sell his products. [ME, from OF: free]

Francis /ˈfrænsəs, ˈfrɑnsəs/, *n.* **Saint** (*Francis of Assisi*), 1181?–1226, Italian friar; founded Franciscan order. –**Franciscan**, *adj., n.*

francium /ˈfrænsiəm/, *n.* a radioactive element of the alkali metal group. *Symbol:* Fr; *at. no.:* 87; *at. wt:* 223.

Franco /ˈfræŋkoʊ/, *n.* **Francisco**, 1892–1975, Spanish military leader and dictator; head of state 1939–75.

Franco-, a word part meaning 'French' or 'France'. [combining form representing ML *Francus* a Frank, a Frenchman]

francophone /ˈfræŋkəfoʊn/, *adj.* French-speaking.

Franco-Prussian War /fræŋkoʊ-ˌprʌʃən ˈwɔ/, *n.* a war (1870–71) between France and Prussia, resulting in the ceding of Alsace and eastern Lorraine to Prussia.

frangipani /frændʒəˈpæni/, *n., pl.* **-nis.** **1.** a shrub or tree with thick, fleshy branches, cultivated for its strongly scented yellow and white, occasionally pink, flowers. **2.** a perfume prepared from, or imitating this scent. Also, **frangipanni**. [F, after the Marquis *Frangipani* of Rome, who invented a perfume for scenting gloves in the 16th C]

frank /fræŋk/, *adj.* **1.** open or unreserved in speech; candid; sincere. **2.** undisguised; downright: *frank mutiny*. ◇*n.* **3.** a signature or mark on a letter, parcel, etc., esp. showing postage has been, or is not required to be, paid. ◇*v.t.* **4.** to mark (a letter, parcel etc.) with a frank. [ME, from OF, from LL: free]

Frankenstein /ˈfræŋkənstaɪn/, *n.* **1.** the hero of Mary Shelley's novel, *Frankenstein*, a student who created a monster he could not control and brought about his own ruin. **2.** *Colloq.* a monstrous creature, esp. one which destroys its creator.

frankfurt /ˈfræŋkfət/, *n.* a reddish variety of sausage made of beef or pork, commonly cooked by steaming or boiling. Also, **frankfurter, frank.** [from FRANKFURT]

Frankfurt /ˈfræŋkfət/, *n.* a city in central Germany, in southern Hesse, on the river Main. Pop. 592 411 (1987 est.). Also, **Frankfurt am Main**.

frankincense /ˈfræŋkənsɛns/, *n.* an aromatic gum resin from certain Asiatic and African trees, used mainly for burning as incense. [ME, from OF: pure incense]

Frankland, *n.* a river in the north-west of Tasmania, rising west of Savage River and flowing north-west to meet the Arthur.

franklin /'fræŋklən/, n. (in the late Middle Ages) a landowner of free but not noble birth. [ME, from ML: free]

Franklin, n. **1. Benjamin**, 1706-90, American statesman, diplomat, author, scientist, and inventor. **2. (Stella Maria Sarah) Miles** ('*Brent of Bin Bin*'), 1879-1954, Australian novelist; author of *My Brilliant Career* (1901).

Frankston /'fræŋkstən/, n. a southern suburb of Melbourne, Vic, on Port Phillip Bay; a former coastal resort. Pop. 83 819 (1986).

frantic /'fræntɪk/, adj. **1.** wild with excitement, passion, fear, pain, etc.; frenzied; having or relating to frenzy. **2.** *Archaic.* insane or mad. [ME, from OF, from L: delirious, from Gk] —**frantically**, adv.

Franz Ferdinand /'frants 'fɜdənənd/, n. 1863-1914, Austrian archduke; his assassination precipitated the outbreak of World War I.

Franz Josef Glacier /frants 'dʒoʊsəf/, n. a glacier in South Island, NZ, rising in the Southern Alps and flowing from snowfields down the western slopes; descends to semi-tropical forests.

Fraser /'freɪzə/, n. **1. Dawn**, born 1937, Australian champion swimmer; the only swimmer to win gold medals in three successive Olympic Games (1956, 1960, 1964); became independent NSW MLA in 1988. **2. (John) Malcolm**, born 1930, Australian Liberal politician; prime minister 1975-83. **3. Peter**, 1884-1951, NZ Labour politician; prime minister 1940-49.

Fraser Island, n. an island off the south-east coast of Qld; the largest sand island in the world; subject of mining controversy between conservationists and the federal government in the 1970s. 159 000 ha. Also, **Great Sandy Island**. [named after Capt James *Fraser*, of the *Stirling Castle* murdered here in 1836]

fraternal /frə'tɜnəl/, adj. **1.** of or suitable to a brother or brothers; brotherly. **2.** of or being a society of men associated in brotherly union, as for mutual aid or benefit: *a fraternal society*. [L: brotherly + -AL¹] —**fraternally**, adv.

fraternal twin, n. one of twins produced from two different eggs, each fertilised by a different sperm. Also, **dizygotic twin**.

fraternise or **fraternize** /'frætənaɪz/, v.i., **-nised**, **-nising**. **1.** to associate in a brotherly or friendly way. **2.** to associate intimately with citizens of an enemy or conquered country. —**fraternisation**, n.

fraternity /frə'tɜnəti/, n., pl. **-ties**. **1.** a body of people associated as by ties of brotherhood. **2.** any body or class of people with common purposes, interest, etc: *the medical fraternity*. **3.** an organisation of laymen for pious or charitable purposes. **4.** brotherhood: *liberty, equality, and fraternity*. **5.** *US.* a student society organised for social and other purposes, and designated by two or more letters of the Greek alphabet. [ME, from OF, from L: brotherhood]

fraud /frɔd/, n. **1.** deceit, trickery, sharp practice, or an instance of it: *election frauds*. **2.** someone who makes deceitful pretences; impostor. **3.** *Law.* an advantage gained by unfair means; a false representation of fact made knowingly, or without belief in its truth, or recklessly, not knowing whether it is true or false. [ME, from OF, from L: cheating, deceit]

fraudulent /'frɔdʒələnt/, adj. **1.** (of people) given to or using fraud; cheating; dishonest. **2.** (of actions, methods, gains, etc.) marked by or coming from fraud. [ME, from L: cheating] —**fraudulence**, n.

fraught /frɔt/, adj. **1.** involving; attended (with); full (of): *an undertaking fraught with danger*; *a heart fraught with grief*. **2.** *Archaic or Poetic.* filled or laden (with): *ships fraught with precious wares*. **3.** *Colloq.* upset; anxious; tense. [ME, from MD or MLG: freight money]

fray¹ /freɪ/, n. **1.** a noisy fight or quarrel; brawl; skirmish. **2.** *Archaic.* fright. [aphetic var. of AFFRAY]

fray² /freɪ/, v.t. **1.** to wear (cloth, rope, etc.) to loose threads or fibres at the edge or end; cause to unravel. **2.** to wear by rubbing (sometimes fol. by *through*). **3.** to strain (a person's temper); exasperate; upset. ◇v.i. **4.** (of cloth, temper, etc.) to become worn through, or unravelled. [F, from L: rub]

frazzle /'fræzəl/, v., **-zled**, **-zling**, n. ◇v.i., v.t. **1.** to fray; wear to threads or shreds. **2.** to weary; tire out. ◇n. **3.** condition of being completely worn out or burnt: *worn to a frazzle*; *burnt to a frazzle*. [b. FRAY² and *fazzle*, ME *faselin* unravel]

freak /frik/, n. **1.** a sudden and apparently causeless happening; caprice: *By some freak he got out of gaol*. **2.** something abnormal or very unusual; monstrosity. **3.** a person or animal shown as an example of natural deformity. **4.** a person who has or adopts unconventional forms of behavior. **5.** *Colloq.* person who is enthusiastic about a particular thing: *a Jesus freak*; *a drug freak*. ◇adj. **6.** unusual; odd; irregular: *a freak wave*. ◇v.i. **7.** Also, **freak out**. *Colloq.* **a.** to have an extreme reaction, either good or bad, to something, esp. a drug-induced experience. **b.** to panic or get very angry. ◇v.t. **8.** to terrify, as an experience produced by hallucinogenic drugs. [? akin to OE *frician* dance] —**freakish**, **freaky**, adj.

freckle /'frekəl/, n., v., **-led**, **-ling**. ◇n. **1.** a small brownish spot in the skin, esp. on the face, neck, or arms. **2.** any small spot or discoloration. ◇v.t. **3.** to cover with freckles or produce freckles on. ◇v.i. **4.** to become freckled. [b. obs. *frecken* freckle (from Scand) and SPECKLE, n.] —**freckled**, adj.

Frederick the Great /'fredrɪk/, n. (*Frederick II*), 1712-86, king of Prussia 1740-86.

free /fri/, adj., **freer**, **freest**, adv., v., **freed**, **freeing**, n. ◇adj. **1.** (of people, choice, action, etc.) not confined; able to move or act at will; unrestricted. **2.** belonging to such people, etc.: *free movement*; *free entry*. **3.** having, marked

free   **freemasonry**

by, or existing under civil liberty as opposed to arbitrary or tyrannical government: *a free country; free speech*. **4.** not under foreign rule. **5.** at liberty, permitted, or able at will (to do something): *free to choose*. **6.** not subject to special regulation or restrictions: *free trade*. **7.** not keeping exactly to every word; not literal: *a free translation*. **8.** not subject to rules, set forms, etc.: *the free song of a bird; free verse*. **9.** (of a corridor, etc.) open, not blocked. **10.** available; unoccupied; not in use: *The music room is now free.* **11.** not being bound by some tie or burden (fol. by *from* or *of*): *free from matrimonial ties; free of taxes*. **12.** being safe or having immunity (fol. by *from* or *of*): *free from criticism; I'm free of you at last!* **13.** uncombined chemically: *free oxygen*. **14.** available or open to all: *a free port; a free market*. **15.** easy, firm, or unhindered in movement: *a free step*. **16.** loose, not held fast: *Tie the free end of the rope round your waist*. **17.** not joined to or in contact with something else: *a free surface*. **18.** acting without self-restraint or reserve: *too free with the tongue*. **19.** frank and open; unconstrained, unceremonious, or familiar: *a free manner*. **20.** morally unrestrained; loose; licentious. **21.** ready in giving; liberal: *to be free with one's advice*. **22.** provided without a charge or payment: *free milk*. **23. free and easy,** informal; casual. **24. make free with,** to treat or use too familiarly; take liberties with. ◇*adv*. **25.** in a free manner; freely. **26.** without cost or charge: *You can have it free.* ◇*v.t.* **27.** make free; set at liberty; release from bondage, imprisonment, or restraint. **28.** to free from obligation or deliver (fol. by *from*): *to free someone from prison*. **29.** to relieve or rid (usu. fol. by *of*): *I can free you of that debt.* **30.** to disengage (fol. by *from* or *of*): *He freed himself from the net.* ◇*n.* **31.** *Colloq.* →**free kick**. **32. for free,** *Colloq.* for nothing; gratis. [OE *frēo*, orig., dear, favored]

free association, *n.* **1.** the first association called forth by each of a series of stimulus words. **2.** a train of thought brought out in response to a single word.

freeborn /ˈfriːbɔn/, *adj.* **1.** born free, rather than in slavery, bondage, or vassalage. **2.** relating or suitable to people so born.

freedom /ˈfriːdəm/, *n.* **1.** the power to act or speak at will without fear of government oppression; civil liberty. **2.** political or national independence. **3.** a privilege enjoyed by a city or corporation. **4.** personal liberty, as opposed to bondage or slavery. **5.** the state of being unconfined: *to escape into freedom*. **6.** exemption from outside control, interference, regulation, etc.: *the freedom to do it in his own way*. **7.** an absence of or release from ties, obligations, etc. **8.** an exemption from something unpleasant or burdensome (fol. by *from*): *freedom from fear*. **9.** ease of movement or action. **10.** frankness of manner or speech. **11. a.** absence of ceremony or reserve; familiarity; impertinence: *freedom of behavior*. **b.** an instance of such behavior; a liberty; an impertinence. **12.** the right of enjoying all the privileges or rights of citizenship, membership, etc.: *freedom of the city*. [OE *frēodōm*]

free enterprise, *n.* the belief in or practice of a minimum amount of government control of private business and industry.

free fall, *n.* **1.** the motion of any object caused only by gravity. **2.** the part of a parachute descent before the parachute opens.

free-form /ˈfriːfɔm/, *adj.* having an asymmetrical shape or outline, usu. flowing, free of formal or traditional lines.

Free French /friː ˈfrɛntʃ/, *n.* (in World War II) those French who, under the leadership of General Charles de Gaulle, continued to resist the Nazis after the capitulation of France in 1940. Also, **Fighting French.**

free hand, *n.* the unrestricted freedom or authority (to do something).

freehand /ˈfriːhænd/, *adj.* done by the hand without guiding instruments, measurements, or other aids: *a freehand drawing*.

freehold /ˈfriːhoʊld/, *n.* **1. a.** ownership or tenure of property for an unlimited time and without any conditions. **b.** an estate held by such tenure. See **leasehold.** ◇*adj.* **2.** of or relating to such tenure, or to property in such tenure.

free kick, *n.* (in football) a kick awarded to a team after a mark or after an infringement by the opposing side.

freelance /ˈfriːlæns/, *n., v.,* **-lanced, -lancing,** *adj., adv.* ◇*n.* **1.** a journalist, commercial artist, editor, etc., who does not work on a regular salaried basis for any one employer. **2.** a mercenary soldier or military adventurer of the Middle Ages, often of knightly rank, who offered his services to any state, party, or cause. ◇*v.i.* **3.** to act or work as a freelance. ◇*adj.* **4.** of or relating to a freelance. ◇*adv.* **5.** in the manner of a freelance. —**freelancer,** *n.*

freeload /ˈfriːloʊd/, *v.i.* to manage to take food, benefits, etc., without paying or contributing; cadge. —**freeloader,** *n.*

free love, *n.* the belief in or practice of free choice in sexual relations, without the restraint of legal marriage or of any continuing obligations.

freeman /ˈfriːmæn/, *n., pl.* **-men. 1.** a person who is not a slave; someone not in bondage. **2.** someone who enjoys or is entitled to citizenship, franchise, or other special privilege.

Freemason /ˈfriːmeɪsən/, *n.* **1.** Also, **Mason.** a member of a widespread secret order (**Free and Accepted Masons**), having for its object mutual help and the fostering of brotherly love among its members. **2.** (*l.c.*) *Hist.* **a.** one of a class of skilled stoneworkers of the Middle Ages, possessed of secret signs and passwords. **b.** a member of a society composed of such workers, with honorary members (known as *accepted masons*) who were not connected with the building trades.

freemasonry /ˈfriːmeɪsənri/, *n.* **1.** a secret or tacit brotherhood; an instinctive sympathy. **2.** (*cap.*) the principles, practices, and institutions of Freemasons.

free-range /'fri:reɪndʒ/, *adj.* (of chickens or eggs) kept or produced in natural non-intensive conditions.

free selection, *n.* (formerly) land chosen, esp. for farming use, and taken up by lease or licence under various land acts, or after crown auction, as opposed to land granted by the Crown or taken by squatting.

free selector, *n.* a farmer who took up land under free selection.

freesia /'fri:ʒə/, *n.* a plant native to southern Africa, cultivated for its fragrant white, yellow, or sometimes other colored, tubular flowers. [NL; named after EM *Fries*, 1794–1878, Swedish botanist]

free speech, *n.* the right to voice one's opinions in public.

freestanding /'fri:stændɪŋ/, *adj.* free of attachment or support; standing independently: *a freestanding house.*

freestyle /'fri:staɪl/, *n.* **1.** *Swimming.* a race in which the competitors may use any stroke they choose, usu. the crawl. **2. a.** the style of swimming used in such a race. **b.** → **crawl** (def. 6). **3.** *Wrestling.* a style of wrestling in which almost every kind of hold is permitted; all-in wrestling. ◊*adj.* **4.** of or relating to freestyle.

free trade, *n.* **1.** trade between countries, free from governmental restrictions or duties. **2.** international trade free from protective tariffs, etc., and subject only to such tariffs as are needed for revenue. **3.** the system, principles, or maintenance of such trade. **4.** *Archaic.* smuggling.

free verse, *n.* poetry without fixed metrical forms and rhyme, in extreme instances consisting of little more than prose in lines of irregular length.

free vote, *n.* in a house of parliament, a vote on a motion in which members are free to vote according to their own judgment without being bound by any party policy or decision; conscience vote.

freeway /'fri:weɪ/, *n.* a road designed for high speed traffic. Also, **expressway**.

freewheel /'fri:wi:l/, *n.* **1.** a form of rear bicycle wheel which has a device freeing it from the driving mechanism as when the pedals are stopped in coasting. ◊*v.i.* **2.** to coast, with the wheels disengaged from the driving mechanism. **3.** *Colloq.* to act independently, particularly in personal or social matters.

free will, *n.* **1.** free choice; voluntary decision. **2.** the doctrine that the conduct of human beings expresses personal choice and is not simply determined by physical or divine forces.

freeze /fri:z/, *v.*, **froze, frozen, freezing**, *n.* ◊*v.i.* **1.** (of a liquid) to become hardened into ice or into a solid body by loss of heat. **2.** (of solid matter containing moisture) to become hard or rigid because of loss of heat. **3.** (of pipes, etc.) to become blocked with ice. **4.** to become fixed to something by or as if by the action of frost. **5.** to be of the degree of cold at which water freezes: *The weather is freezing.* **6.** to have the sensation of extreme cold. **7.** to die of frost or cold. **8.** to be chilled with fear, etc. **9. freeze over**, to become coated with ice. **10.** to stop moving suddenly as through fear, shock, etc. ◊*v.t.* **11.** to harden (something) into ice; congeal. **12.** to harden or stiffen by cold. **13.** to form ice on the surface of (a river or pond). **14.** to block or close (pipes) with ice (oft. fol. by *up*). **15.** to preserve (food) by placing it in a freezer, etc. **16.** to make (someone) motionless as through fear, shock, etc. **17.** to exclude, or compel to withdraw, from society, business, etc., as by chilling behavior, severe competition, etc. (fol. by *out*). **18.** *Finance.* to make (funds, etc.) unavailable: *Bank loans are frozen in economic depressions.* **19.** to fix (wages, prices, etc.) at a specific level. **20.** to remove sensation from, as with a local anaesthetic. ◊*n.* **21.** the act of freezing or state of being frozen. **22.** *Weather.* a period of very low temperatures, below 0° C. **23.** a frost. **24.** action by a government to fix wages, prices, etc. [OE *frēosan*]

freezer /'fri:zə/, *n.* (a compartment of) a refrigerator held at or below 0° C.

freezing point, *n.* the temperature at which a liquid freezes: *The freezing point of water is 0° C.*

freight /freɪt/, *n.* **1.** cargo or lading carried for pay by land, water, or air. **2.** the transporting of goods by rail, ship, etc. **3.** the charge made for transporting goods. ◊*v.t.* **4.** to load or lade with goods or merchandise for transport. **5.** to transport as freight: *Send by freight.* [ME, from MD or MLG: freight money]

freighter /'freɪtə/, *n.* **1.** a ship or aircraft that carries merchandise. **2.** someone who receives and forwards freight, esp. by chartering and loading ships.

Fremantle /'fri:mæntəl, frə'mæntəl/, *n.* a city and seaport within the metropolitan area of Perth, WA. Pop. 22 709 (1986). [named after Sir Charles Howe *Fremantle*]

French[1] /frentʃ/, *n.* **Leonard William**, born 1928, Australian artist, noted for his abstract portrayal of religious themes.

French[2] /frentʃ/, *adj.* **1.** of or relating to France, its people or their language. ◊*n.* **2.** *Colloq.* (*joc.*) mild swear words: *Pardon my French.* [OE *Franca* a Frank]

French bean, *n.* a small twining or bushy annual herb, cultivated for its slender green edible pods and seeds. Also, **kidney bean, haricot bean.**

French cricket, *n.* a game played with a ball and a cricket bat, in which the bat is held in front of the legs and the person batting can only be dismissed if the ball hits their legs or they are caught.

French dressing, *n.* (*oft l.c.*) a salad dressing prepared from oil, vinegar, salt, spices, etc.

French fries, *n.pl.* (*oft. l.c.*) thin strips of potato, fried.

French horn, *n.* a mellow-toned brass wind instrument derived from the hunting horn and consisting of a long, coiled tube ending in a flaring bell.

French Indochina, *n.* the former French colonial federation of Cochin-China, the protectorates of Annam, Cambodia, Tonkin, and Laos, and the leased territory of Kwangchowan. Ultimately it consisted of the three independent states of Vietnam, Cambodia, and Laos, Kwangchowan having reverted to the Chinese. See **Indochina**.

French letter, *n.* (*oft. l.c.*) *Colloq.* → **condom**.

French polish, *n.* (*oft. l.c.*) a solution of shellac in methylated spirits with or without some coloring material, and used as a high-quality furniture finish.

French Polynesia, *n.* a French overseas territory in the South Pacific, including the Society Islands, Marquesas Islands, and other widely scattered island groups. Pop. 143 000 (1979); 3999 km². *Cap.*: Papeete. Formerly, **French Oceania**.

French Revolution, *n.* the movement that, beginning in 1789, overthrew the absolute monarchy of the Bourbons and the system of class privilege, and ended in the seizure of power by Napoleon in 1799.

French seam, *n.* a seam in which the edges of the cloth are sewn first on the right side, then on the wrong, so as to be completely enclosed.

frenetic /frə'netɪk/, *adj.* frantic; frenzied. Also, **phrenetic**. [var. of PHRENETIC] —**frenetically**, *adv.*

frenzied /'frenzɪd/, *adj.* wildly excited or enthusiastic; frantic; mad. Also, **phrensied**.

frenzy /'frenzi/, *n.*, *pl.* **-zies**. **1.** violent agitation of mind; wild excitement or enthusiasm.
2. the violent excitement of a paroxysm of mania; mental derangement; delirium. [ME, from OF, from LL, from Gk]

freon /'friɒn/, *n.* any of various derivatives of ethane which are chemically unreactive; used in refrigerants, aerosols, etc. [Trademark]

freq., *Abbrev.* **1.** frequent. **2.** frequentative. **3.** frequently.

frequency /'frikwənsi/, *n.*, *pl.* **-cies**. **1.** Also, **frequence**. the state or fact of being frequent; frequent occurrence: *The frequency of road accidents in Australia is worrying.* **2.** rate of recurrence: *The frequency of road accidents is rising.* **3.** *Phys.* the number of regular cycles, oscillations, or vibrations of a wave motion or oscillation in unit time; the derived SI unit of frequency is the hertz. **4.** *Maths.* the number of times an event occurs. **5.** *Statistics.* the number of items occurring in a given category. See **relative frequency**. [L]

frequency band, *n.* (esp. in radio) a continuous set of frequencies between two nominated frequencies.

frequency distribution, *n.* the set of frequencies associated with the different categories, intervals, or values to which items in a statistical group belong.

frequency modulation, *n.* a broadcasting system, relatively free from static, in which the frequency of the transmitted wave is modulated or varied in accordance with the amplitude and pitch of the signal (opposed to *amplitude modulation*). *Abbrev.*: FM

frequent /'frikwənt/, *adj.*; /frə'kwɛnt/, *v.*, ◇*adj.* **1.** happening or occurring at short intervals: *to make frequent trips to a place.* **2.** habitual or regular: *a frequent guest.* ◇*v.t.* **3.** to visit often; go often to; be often in. [L: crowded] —**frequenter**, *n.*

frequentative /frə'kwɛntətɪv/, *adj.* (of a derived verb, or of an aspect of verb inflection) expressing repetition of the action denoted by the underlying verb.

fresco /'frɛskoʊ/, *n.*, *pl.* **-coes, -cos,** *v.*, **-coed, -coing.** ◇*n.* **1.** the art of painting on fresh lime plaster, as on a wall or ceiling, so that the pigments are absorbed (**true fresco**), or, less properly, on dried plaster, (**dry fresco**). **2.** a picture or design so painted. ◇*v.t.* **3.** to paint in fresco. [It: cool, from Gmc]

fresh /frɛʃ/, *adj.* **1.** newly made or obtained, etc.: *fresh footprints.* **2.** newly arrived: *fresh from school.* **3.** additional or further: *fresh supplies.* **4.** not salt: *fresh water.* **5.** (of meat, etc.) in good natural condition; unspoiled. **6.** not canned, frozen or preserved: *fresh food.* **7.** not tired; brisk; vigorous. **8.** not faded or worn. **9.** looking youthful and healthy. **10.** pure, cool, or refreshing, as air. **11.** inexperienced: *fresh to the job.* **12.** forward or presumptuous; cheeky. ◇*n.* **13.** the fresh part or time. **14.** →**freshet**. [OE *fersc*]

freshen /'frɛʃən/, *v.t.* **1.** to make fresh; refresh, revive, or renew. **2.** to remove saltiness from. ◇*v.i.* **3.** to become or grow fresh. **4.** to make oneself fresh, as by washing, etc. (usu. fol. by *up*). —**freshener**, *n.*

fresher /'frɛʃə/, *n.* **1.** a first-year student at a university or college. **2.** a novice. Also, **freshman**.

freshet /'frɛʃət/, *n.* **1.** a flood, or sudden rise in the level of a stream, due to heavy rains, etc. **2.** a freshwater stream flowing into the sea.

freshwater /'frɛʃwɔtə/, *adj.* of or living in water that is fresh, or not salt (opposed to *saltwater* or *marine*).

fret¹ /frɛt/, *v.*, **fretted, fretting.** ◇*v.t.,v.i.* **1.** to annoy or be annoyed; worry: *Don't fret (yourself) about that mistake.* **2.** to wear away or corrode; consume or be consumed. **3.** to stir up; move in agitation. ◇*n.* **4.** an annoyed state of mind; vexation: *to get in a fret.* [OE *fretan*]

fret² /frɛt/, *n.*, *v.*, **fretted, fretting.** ◇*n.* **1.** an interlaced, angular design; fretwork. **2.** an angular design of bands within a border. ◇*v.t.* **3.** to ornament with a fret or fretwork. [ME *frette*, of uncert. orig.]

fret³ /frɛt/, *n.* a ridge of wood or metal set across the fingerboard of a lute, guitar, etc., which helps the fingers to stop the strings at the right place for each semitone difference in pitch. [orig. uncert.]

fretful /'fretfəl/, *adj.* tending to fret; irritable; peevish.

fretwork /'fretwɜk/, *n.* **1.** ornamental work consisting of interlacing perforated parts. **2.** any pattern of dark and light, as sunlight and shadow.

Freud /frɔɪd/, *n.* **Sigmund**, 1856–1939, Austrian physician and founder of modern psychoanalysis.

Freudian /'frɔɪdiən/, *adj.* **1.** of or relating to Sigmund Freud, or to his doctrines, esp. in respect to the causes and treatment of neurotic and psychopathic states, the interpretation of dreams, etc. ◇*n.* **2.** a follower of the doctrines of Freud. **–Freudianism,** *n.*

Freudian slip, *n.* a mistake made in speaking which is taken to reveal the speaker's true or subconscious thoughts.

Freycinet /'freɪsənei/, *n.* **Louis-Claude de Saulces de** /,luiˈkloud də ˈsouls də/, 1779–1842, French naval navigator, explorer and cartographer; explored Australian waters in 1802–03, 1817 and 1818.

Fri, *Abbrev.* Friday.

friable /'fraɪəbəl/, *adj.* easily crumbled; crumbly: *friable rock.* [L] **–friability, friableness,** *n.*

friar /'fraɪə/, *n. Relig.* a brother or member of a Christian religious order, esp. the mendicant orders of Franciscans (**Grey Friars**), Dominicans (**Black Friars**), Carmelites (**White Friars**), and Augustinians (**Austin Friars**). [ME, from OF, from L: brother]

friar-bird /'fraɪə-bɜd/, *n.* a kind of honeyeating bird found in Australia and nearby areas, with a head partly naked like a friar, as the noisy friar-bird.

Friar Tuck, *n.* the jolly friar of Robin Hood's band.

fricassee /frɪkəˈsi, 'frɪkəsi/, *n., v.* /ˈfrɪəsi/, **-seed, -seeing.** ◇*n.* **1.** meat, esp. chicken or veal, stewed, and served in a white sauce made of its own stock. ◇*v.t.* **2.** to prepare as a fricassee. [F: to sauté and serve with sauce, from Pr, from L: fry]

fricative /'frɪkətɪv/, *adj.* **1.** (of consonants) marked by a noise produced by air being forced through an opening, as in *f, v, s,* etc. ◇*n.* **2.** a fricative consonant. [NL, from L: rub] **–frication,** *n.*

friction /'frɪkʃən/, *n.* **1.** the rubbing of the surface of one thing against that of another. **2.** *Mech., Phys.* resistance to the relative motion (sliding or rolling) of surfaces of bodies touching one another. **3.** a clashing or conflict, as of opinions, etc. [L: a rubbing] **–frictional,** *adj.*

Friday /'fraɪdeɪ, -di/, *n.* the sixth day of the week, following Thursday. [OE *Frīgedæg* Freo's day (OE goddess identified with Venus)]

fridge /frɪdʒ/, *n. Colloq.* **→refrigerator.**

friend /frɛnd/, *n.* **1.** a person, usu. not related, whom one knows and likes well. **2.** a well-wisher, patron, or supporter: *Bail was paid by a unknown friend.* **3.** someone on good terms with another person; someone not hostile: *We are friends today.* **4.** a member of the same nation, party, etc. [OE *frēond, frēogan* love] **–friendship,** *n.*

Friend /frɛnd/, *n.* **Donald Stuart Leslie**, 1914–89, Australian artist.

friendly /'frɛndli/, *adj.*, **-lier, -liest. 1.** like a friend; showing friendship; kind; welcoming: *a friendly greeting.* **2.** tending to approve, help, or support: *The authorities are friendly to my plan.* **3.** *Sport.* of a match which does not entail points in a competition. [OE *frēondlīc*]

friendly society, *n.* an association to which members pay regular sums, and which supports them and their families in sickness, old age, etc.

Friesian /'friʒən/, *n.* (one of) a breed of dairy cattle, usu. black and white in coloring and common in Australia.

frieze /friz/, *n.* **1.** a horizontal band between the architrave and the cornice, often ornamented with sculpture. **2.** any similar decorative band or feature, as on a wall or wallpaper. [F, from ML: embroidery, from L: Phrygian (work)]

frig /frɪdʒ/, *n. Colloq.* **→refrigerator.**

frigate /'frɪɡət/, *n.* a general-purpose warship of about 2700 tonnes, used as an escort vessel. [F, from It]

frigatebird /'frɪɡətbɜd/, *n.* a kind of large, greedy, tropical seabird with huge wings, forked tail and small legs and feet, noted for its powers of flight.

fright /fraɪt/, *n.* **1.** a sudden and extreme fear; a sudden terror. **2.** a person or thing of shocking, ugly, or silly appearance: *He looked a fright.* ◇*v.t.* **3.** *Poetic.* to frighten. [OE *fryhto*]

frighten /'fraɪtn/, *v.t.* **1.** to throw into a fright; terrify; scare. **2.** to drive (fol. by *away, off,* etc.) by scaring. **–frightener,** *n.*

frightful /'fraɪtfəl/, *adj.* **1.** such as to cause fright; dreadful, terrible, or alarming. **2.** horrible, shocking, or revolting. **3.** extremely bad: *frightful homework.* **4.** unpleasant; disagreeable: *We had a frightful time.* **5.** *Colloq.* very great.

frigid /'frɪdʒəd/, *adj.* **1.** very cold in temperature: *a frigid climate.* **2.** without warmth of feeling. **3.** stiff or formal: *a frigid manner.* **4.** sexually unresponsive. [L] **–frigidity, frigidness,** *n.*

Frigid Zone, *n. Geog.* either of the two regions between the poles and the polar circles.

frill /frɪl/, *n.* **1.** a trimming consisting of a strip of material or lace, gathered at one edge and left loose at the other; ruffle. **2.** something looking like a frill, e.g. the skin around the neck of some lizards. **3.** *Colloq.* an affectation of manner, style, etc. **4.** something useless or unnecessary. ◇*v.t.* **5.** to trim or ornament with a frill or frills. [? Flemish: frill (of a collar)]

frill-necked lizard, *n.* **1.** Also, **bicycle lizard.** a kind of lizard of northern Australia, that lives in trees and eats insects and small mammals, with a large, ruff-like, erectable frill behind the head. **2.** often, but incorrectly, the

frill-necked lizard, bearded lizard, which has a smaller frill. Also, **frilled lizard, frilled dragon, bearded dragon**.

fringe /frɪndʒ/, *n., v.,* **fringed, fringing,** *adj.* ◇*n.* **1.** an ornamental border of cords or threads, loose or tied in bunches, as on a rug. **2.** anything like this: *a fringe of trees about a field.* **3.** hair falling over the forehead. **4.** a border; margin; outer part or extremity: *the fringes of society; the fringe of town.* ◇*v.t.* **5.** to give a fringe to. **6.** to serve as a fringe for: *Trees fringe the field.* ◇*adj.* **7.** extra; on the side: *fringe benefits.* **8.** not socially acceptable. [ME, from OF, from LL: border, fringe]

fringe benefit, *n.* a reward received in addition to wages, as a pension, travel allowance, etc.

frippery /'frɪpəri/, *n., pl.* **-ries. 1.** cheap, useless or overdone ornamentation in clothes. **2.** empty show; ostentation. **3.** trifles; frivolity. [OF: rag]

frisk /frɪsk/, *v.i.* **1.** to dance, leap, skip; gambol; frolic. ◇*v.t.* **2.** *Colloq.* to search (a person) for hidden weapons, etc., by feeling his clothing. **3.** *Colloq.* to steal something from (someone) in this way. ◇*n.* **4.** a leap, skip; caper. [OF, from Gmc] — **frisker,** *n.*

frisky /'frɪski/, *adj.,* **friskier, friskiest.** lively; frolicsome; playful.

frit /frɪt/, *n., v.,* **fritted, fritting.** ◇*n.* **1. a.** fused or partially fused material used as a basis for glazes or enamels. **b.** the composition from which artificial soft porcelain is made. ◇*v.t.* **2.** to fuse (materials) in making a frit. [F, from It, from L: roast, fry]

fritter[1] /'frɪtə/, *v.t.* to waste little by little; squander (usu. fol. by *away*): *to fritter away one's money.* [earlier *fitter,* from *fit* part]

fritter[2] /'frɪtə/, *n.* a small cake of batter, sometimes containing fruit or some other ingredient, fried in deep fat or sautéed in a frying pan. [ME, from OF: fry]

fritz /frɪts/, *n.* **1.** *in the phrase,* **on the fritz,** *Colloq.* broken; not in working order. **2.** Also, **pork fritz.** a large, bland, pre-cooked sausage eaten cold; devon.

frivolous /'frɪvələs/, *adj.* **1.** of little or no weight, worth, or importance: *a frivolous objection.* **2.** lacking seriousness or sense: *frivolous behavior; a frivolous person.* [L: silly, trifling, paltry] — **frivolity,** *n.*

frizz /frɪz/, *v.,* **frizzed, frizzing,** *n., pl.* **frizzes.** ◇*v.t., v.i.* **1.** to form into small, tight curls or little tufts. ◇*n.* **2.** the condition of being frizzed. **3.** frizzed hair. [backformation from FRIZZLE]

frizzle /'frɪzəl/, *v.,* **-zled, -zling,** *n.* → **frizz.** [orig. obscure] — **frizzly,** *adj.*

fro /froʊ/, *adv. in the phrase* **to and fro, 1.** back and forwards. **2.** here and there. [ME, from Scand]

frock /frɒk/, *n.* **1.** a woman's or girl's dress. **2.** a loose outer garment worn by peasants and workmen; smock. **3.** a coarse outer garment with large sleeves, worn by monks. ◇*v.t.* **4.** to ordain as a priest. [ME, from OF, of Gmc orig.]

frog[1] /frɒg/, ◇*n.* **1.** any of various tailless amphibians, esp. those which live in water, and have web feet and long back legs for jumping. **2. a frog in the throat,** slight hoarseness. [OE *frogga*]

frog[2] /frɒg/, *n.* **1.** an ornamental fastening for a coat, etc., consisting of a button and loop. **2.** an apparatus at the join of railway tracks (or wires for electric trams, etc.) to allow the wheels to cross to the correct track. [? Pg, from L: flock]

frogman /'frɒgmən/, *n., pl.* **-men.** a man equipped for swimming underwater, esp. with a wetsuit, flippers, air cylinder(s), etc.

frogmarch /'frɒgmɑtʃ/, *v.t.* to force a person to walk by applying a half-nelson (wrestling hold) or taking him by the scruff of the neck and the trousers belt, and forcing him forward.

frogmouth /'frɒgmaʊθ/, *n.* any of various birds with wide bills, and soft wings, flying silently at night, in Australia and parts of Asia, e.g. the **tawny frogmouth.**

frolic /'frɒlɪk/, *n., v.,* **-icked, -icking.** ◇*n.* **1.** merry play; fun. **2.** a playful trick or prank. ◇*v.i.* **3.** to play merrily. [D: joyful] — **frolicsome,** *adj.*

from /frɒm; *weak form* frəm/, *prep.* a word marking a starting point, and used to express **1.** distance or separation in space, time, order, etc.: *a train running west from Sydney; from that time onwards; to wander from the path; to stop oneself from laughing.* **2.** difference or distinction: *to tell black from white; What is 5 from 10?* **3.** source or origin: *I got the idea from John; sketches drawn from nature.* **4.** means or agency: *I can tell from your face that you are worried.* **5.** cause or reason: *to die from starvation.* [OE *fram,* prep., from, as adv., forwards, forth]

frond /frɒnd/, *n.* **1.** a finely divided leaf, often large, esp. of ferns and some palms. **2.** a leaf-like body of a plant such as seaweed or lichen not divided into stem and leaves. [L: leafy branch]

front /frʌnt/, *n.* **1.** a part or surface facing forward or most often seen. **2.** any side or face. **3.** a place or position directly before anything. **4.** *Mil.* **a.** the first line or part of army, etc. **b.** the place where active operations are carried on. **5.** land facing a road, river, seashore, etc. **6.** a cover for activity, esp. illegal: *That restaurant is a front for a gambling club.* **7.** outward behavior or appearance. **8.** a group or movement with a particular aim, usu. political: *the feminist front.* **9.** something joined on or worn at front: *a shirt front.* **10.** *Weather.* a surface where two air-masses with different temperatures, meet. **11. up front,** in advance. ◇*adj.* **12.** of or relating to the front. **13.** placed in or at front. **14.** *Linguistics.* pronounced with the tongue forward in the mouth. The vowels of 'beet' and 'bat' are front vowels. ◇*v.t.* **15.** to face. **16.** to serve as a front to. ◇*v.i.* **17.** to face (towards, on to, etc.) **18.** Also, **front up.** *Colloq.* to arrive, turn up. [ME, from L: forehead, front]

frontage /'frʌntɪdʒ/, *n.* **1.** the front of a building or piece of land. **2.** the land meeting

frontage 	a river, street, etc. **3.** the space between a building and the front, etc.

frontal /'frʌntl/, *adj.* **1.** of, in, or at the front: *a frontal attack*. **2.** *Anat.* of or relating to the forehead. [LL, from L: front]

frontbencher /'frʌntbentʃə, frʌnt'bentʃə/, *n.* a member of parliament who is a government minister or opposition spokesperson.

frontier /frʌn'tɪə, 'frʌntɪə/, *n.* **1.** the part of a country where it meets another country; border. **2.** (oft. *pl.*) a new or undeveloped area of knowledge, etc.: *frontiers of medicine*. [ME *frountere*, from OF]

frost /frɒst/, *n.* **1.** the atmospheric temperature below freezing point. **2. a.** a covering of tiny ice particles, formed from the air at night on cold surfaces when the dewpoint is below freezing point (**white frost** or **hoarfrost**). **b.** a cold so intense as to blacken plants, without a white frost (**black frost**). **3.** the act or process of freezing. **4.** crushed glass of paper thickness, used for decoration. **5.** a coolness between people; unfriendliness. ◇*v.t.* **6.** to cover with frost. **7.** to give a frost-like surface to (glass, etc.). **8.** to ice (a cake, etc.) ◇*v.i.* **9.** to freeze or become covered with frost (oft. fol. by *up* or *over*). [OE *frost*] — **frosted**, *adj.*

Frost /frɒst/, *n.* **1. John**, 1784-1877, English Chartist, transported to Tasmania in 1840, as a political prisoner; on his return to England he publicised the horrors of convict life. **2. Robert Lee**, 1874-1963, US poet.

frostbite /'frɒstbaɪt/, *n., v.,* **-bit, -bitten, -biting.** ◇*n.* **1.** damage to body tissue by extreme cold. ◇*v.t.* **2.** to hurt by extreme cold. — **frostbitten**, *adj.*

frosting /'frɒstɪŋ/, *n.* **1.** a fluffy cake icing made of sugar, eggwhites, etc. **2.** a frostlike surface on metal, glass, etc.

frosty /'frɒsti/, *adj.,* **-tier, -tiest. 1.** very cold; freezing: *frosty weather.* **2.** made of, covered with, or like frost. **3.** unfriendly or cold in manner. — **frostily**, *adv.*

froth /frɒθ/, *n.* **1.** a mass of bubbles; foam. **2.** something unimportant or short-lived, esp. talk or ideas. ◇*v.t., v.i.* **3.** to (cause to) give out froth. [ME *frothe*]

frown /fraʊn/, *v.i.* **1.** to wrinkle the forehead as in anger or in deep thought. **2.** to look disapprovingly (fol. by *on* or *upon*): *to frown upon a plan.* ◇*n.* **3.** a frowning look or expression. [ME *froune(n)*, from OF: surly expression; of Celtic orig.]

frowzy /'fraʊzi/, *adj.,* **-zier, -ziest.** dirty and untidy. Also, **frowsy, frouzy.** [akin to FROWSTY]

froze /froʊz/, *v.* past tense of **freeze**.

frozen /'froʊzən/, *v.* **1.** past participle of **freeze.** ◇*adj.* **2.** made solid by cold. **3.** covered with ice. **4.** hurt or killed by cold. **5.** (of food) kept below 0°C for preservation. **6.** unfeeling or cold in manner. **7.** made unusable or not available: *a frozen bank account.* **8.** stopped, fixed or unmoving. [pp. of FREEZE]

fructify /'frʌktəfaɪ, frʊk-/, *v.t., v.i.* **-fied, -fying.** to (cause to) bear fruit or be productive. [ME *fructifie(n)*, from F, from L: bear fruit] — **fructification**, *n.*

fructose /'frʊktoʊz, -toʊs, 'frʌk-/, *n.* a white, crystalline, and very sweet sugar found in honey and fruit, $C_6H_{12}O_6$; fruit sugar. [L: fruit + -OSE²]

frugal /'frugəl/, *adj.* **1.** economical in using or in spending; sparing. **2.** costing little; scanty; meagre. [L: economical] — **frugality**, *n.*

fruit /frut/, *n.* **1.** *Bot.* the developed ovary of a seed plant with its contents and related parts. **2.** the eatable fleshy part of a plant developed from a flower, e.g. the banana, orange. **3.** any product of vegetable growth useful to people or animals. **4.** a product or result. ◇*v.t., v.i.* **5.** to (cause to) bear fruit. [ME, from OF, from L: enjoyment, proceeds, fruit]

fruit-bat /'frut-bæt/, *n.* any of various fruit-eating bats, including flying foxes.

fruit-fly /'frut-flaɪ/, *n.* any of various small two-winged flies, which lay their eggs in developing fruit and are serious pests. **2.** → **drosophila**.

fruitful /'frutfəl/, *adj.* **1.** bearing much fruit. **2.** productive; profitable: *fruitful inquiry.*

fruition /fru'ɪʃən/, *n.* **1.** the reaching of a goal or production of results: *the fruition of his labors.* **2.** the bearing of fruit. [ME, from LL: enjoyment]

fruity /'fruti/, *adj.,* **-tier, -tiest. 1.** like fruit in taste or smell. **2.** rich or mellow in tone: *a fruity voice.* **3.** *Colloq.* sexually suggestive; salacious.

frump /frʌmp/, *n.* an untidy, unfashionably dressed woman. [orig. unknown] — **frumpish, frumpy,** *adj.*

frustrate /frʌs'treɪt/, *v.t.* **-trated, -trating. 1.** to make (plans, efforts, etc.) have no effect; defeat; nullify. **2.** to prevent (someone) from doing something they set out to do; thwart. [L: having disappointed or deceived] — **frustration**, *n.*

frustrated /'frʌstreɪtəd/, *adj.* **1.** upset or annoyed by being prevented from achieving one's aims. **2.** sexually unsatisfied.

fry¹ /fraɪ/, *v.,* **fried, frying,** *n., pl.* **fries.** ◇*v.t., v.i.* **1.** to cook in fat or oil, usu. over direct heat. ◇*n.* **2.** a dish of something fried. [ME *frye(n)*, from F, from L] — **fryer** or **frier**, *n.*

fry² /fraɪ/, *n., pl.* **fry. 1.** young fish. **2.** offspring. **3. small fry, a.** unimportant people. **b.** young children. [ME]

Fry /fraɪ/, *n.* **1. Christopher**, born 1907, English dramatist, best known for his verse dramas. **2. Elizabeth**, 1780-1845, English Quaker and prison reformer.

ft, *Symbol.* foot or feet.

fuchsia /'fjuʃə/, *n.* a (small) shrub grown for its showy hanging flowers, usu. pink, red, or purple. [NL, named after Leonhard *Fuchs*, 1501-66, German botanist]

fuddle /'fʌdl/, *v.t.,* **-dled, -dling. 1.** to make drunk. **2.** to confuse; muddle. ◇*n.* **3.** a drunk or confused condition.

fudge¹ /fʌdʒ/, *n.* a soft sweet made of sugar, butter, and milk, usu. flavored with vanilla or chocolate. [orig. uncert.]

fudge² /fʌdʒ/, *n., v.t.,* **fudged, fudging.** to make, do, or present in a clumsy, dishonest, or approximate way: *to fudge the results.* [Brit d.]

fuel /'fjuəl, fjul/, *n., v.,* **-elled, -elling.** ◇*n.* **1.** any substance burned to provide power or heat, e.g. coal, wood, oil, petrol. **2.** petrol. **3.** a fissile material used in a nuclear reactor to produce energy. **4.** anything that feeds or encourages strong feeling, etc. **5.** food, esp. as used to produce energy. ◇*v.t.* **6.** to supply with fuel. ◇*v.i.* **7.** to get fuel (oft. fol. by *up*). [ME, from OF, from L: hearth, fireplace]

fuel cell, *n.* a cell (def. 6) in which a chemical reaction is used directly to produce electricity.

fuel-injection /'fjuəl-ɪndʒɛkʃən/, *n.* a method of spraying liquid fuel directly into the cylinders of an internal-combustion engine instead of using a carburettor. —**fuel-injector,** *n.*

fug /fʌɡ/, *n.* stale or smoky air in a closed room.

Fugard /'fugad/, *n.* Athol, born 1932, South African dramatist and theatre director, concerned esp. with the position of South Africa's black population under apartheid.

-fuge, a word part indicating 'flight' or 'driving away', as in *refuge, centrifuge.* [combining form representing L *-fugia,* from *fugāre* put to flight]

fugitive /'fjudʒətɪv, -ɪv/, *n.* **1.** a person who is running away: *a fugitive from justice.* ◇*adj.* **2.** having run away: *a fugitive slave.* **3.** passing quickly; fleeting. [L: fleeing]

fugue /fjug/, *n. Music.* a composition based on one or more themes which are announced by several voices or parts in turn and developed contrapuntally. See **counterpoint.** [F, from It, from L: flight] —**fugal,** *adj.*

Führer /'fjurə/, *n.* **der** /deə/, Adolf Hitler. Also, **Fuehrer.** [G: leader]

Fuji /'fudʒi/, *n.* an extinct volcano in central Japan, on Honshu island; the highest mountain in Japan, renowned for its beautiful symmetry. 3778 m. Also, **Fujiyama** /fudʒi'jamə/ or **Fujisan** /fudʒi'sæn/.

Fukuoka /fuku'ouka/, *n.* a city in southwestern Japan, on Kyushu island. Pop. 1 175 707 (1986 est.). Also, **Hu'uoka.**

-ful, a suffix meaning: **1.** full of or marked by: *shameful, beautiful, careful, thoughtful.* **2.** tending to or able to: *wakeful, harmful.* **3.** as much as will fill: *spoonful, handful.* [OE *-full,* *-ful, full*]

Fulbright /'fʊlbraɪt/, *n.* a grant awarded to US citizens for research or study abroad, or to citizens of other countries for research or study in the US. Also, **Fulbright scholarship.**

fulcrum /'fʊlkrəm/, *n., pl.* **-crums, -cra** /-krə/. a support or point on which a lever turns in moving something. [L: bedpost]

fulfil /fʊl'fɪl/, *v.t.,* **-filled, -filling. 1.** to carry out (something promised, requested, etc.). **2.** to do (something ordered or required). **3.** to satisfy (needs, people, etc.). **4.** to bring to an end or complete. **5. fulfil oneself,** to realise one's full potential; find one's place in life. [OE *fullfyllan*] —**fulfilled,** *adj.*

fulfilment /fʊl'fɪlmənt/, *n.* **1.** a carrying out; performance; completion. **2.** (a feeling of) satisfaction, esp. from finding a purpose or meaning for one's life.

full /fʊl/, *adj.* **1.** filled; containing all that can be held: *a full cup.* **2.** complete; whole; maximum: *a full supply; full pay.* **3.** (of garments, etc.) wide or loose. **4.** filled or rounded out in form. **5.** rich in sound, taste, etc. **6.** wholly or properly so, not secondarily or partially: *a full brother; a full professor.* **7.** having eaten plenty. **8.** *Colloq.* drunk. **9. full of,** very interested in or involved with. **10. full of oneself,** self-centred; vain. **11. full up,** having eaten enough. ◇*adv.* **12.** completely. **13.** exactly or directly: *The blow struck her full in the face.* **14.** *Archaic.* very: *full well.* ◇*n.* **15. in full, a.** to or for the full amount. **b.** not shortened or reduced. **16. on the full,** (of a ball) in flight before bouncing. **17. to the full,** in full measure; to the utmost extent. [OE *full, ful*] —**fully,** *adv.*

full-back /'fʊl-bæk, 'fʊl,bæk/, *n. Sport.* (in football, hockey, etc.) a defender in a team.

Full Bench, *n.* a sitting of a court or commission for an important matter, with all the judges of the court, etc., or several of them representing all.

full blood /'fʊl-blʌd/, *n.* **1.** a person of unmixed race. **2.** a purebred animal, esp. a horse.

full-blooded /'fʊl-blʌdəd/, *adj.* **1.** of unmixed race or breed. **2.** strong and active. **3.** rich and full.

full bore, *adv.* **1.** with maximum effort; with the greatest possible effort, speed or results. ◇*n.* **2.** the maximum production (of oil or gas from a drill hole).

full dress, *n.* **1.** a uniform worn on ceremonial or formal occasions. **2.** formal evening clothes. —**full-dress,** *adj.*

fuller's earth /fʊləz 'ɜθ/, *n.* an absorbent clay, used as a grease-remover, a filter, dusting powder, and paint extender.

full moon, *n.* → **moon** (def. 2c).

full point, *n.* → **full stop.**

full stop, *n.* a point or character (.) used to mark the end of a complete declarative sentence, indicate abbreviation, etc. Also, **full point.**

full toss, *n. Cricket.* a ball bowled which travels the whole way to the batsman without touching the ground. Also, **full pitch.**

fully-fledged /'fʊli-flɛdʒd/, *adj.* **1.** able to fly. **2.** fully developed, trained, or qualified. **3.** of full rank or standing.

fulmar /'fʊlmə/, *n.* any of certain oceanic birds of the petrel family, found in polar regions. [? lit., foul gull (with allusion to its stench), from Scand]

fulminate /'fʌlməneɪt, 'fʌl-/, *v.i., v.t.*, **-nated, -nating. 1.** to explode with a loud noise. **2.** to shout out disapprovingly or angrily (oft. fol. by *against*). [L: struck by lightning] —**fulmination**, *n.* —**fulminator**, *n.* —**fulminatory**, *adj.*

fulsome /'fʊlsəm/, *adj.* **1.** overdone or insincere: *fulsome praise*. **2.** disgusting, sickening. [ME *fulsum*]

fumarole /'fjuːmərəʊl/, *n.* a hole in or near a volcano, out of which hot vapor comes. [F, from LL: little smoke chamber, from L]

fumble /'fʌmbəl/, *v.*, **-bled, -bling.** ◇*v.i.* **1.** to feel about clumsily: *He fumbled for his shoes in the dark; He just fumbles about all day wasting time.* ◇*v.t.* **2.** to handle clumsily: *to fumble a ball.* ◇*n.* **3.** the act of fumbling. [LG] —**fumbling**, *adj., n.*

fume /fjuːm/, *n., v.*, **fumed, fuming.** ◇*n.* **1.** (*oft. pl.*) gas, smoke, or vapor. ◇*v.t.* **2.** to treat with fumes; fumigate. ◇*v.i.* **3.** to give out fumes. **4.** to show irritation or anger. [ME, from OF, from L: smoke, steam, fume] —**fuming**, *adj.*

fumigant /'fjuːməgənt/, *n.* any chemical, e.g. hydrogen cyanide or ethylene oxide, which is used in fumigation.

fumigate /'fjuːməgeɪt/, *v.t.*, **-gated, -gating.** to treat with smoke or fumes, to disinfect or kill pests. [L: smoked] —**fumigation**, *n.* —**fumigator**, *n.*

fun /fʌn/, *n.* **1.** joking; playfulness. **2.** enjoyment or pleasure. **3. for** or **in fun**, playfully; not seriously. **4. like fun**, *Colloq.* not at all. **5. make fun of, poke fun at,** to laugh at; ridicule. [? d. var. of obs. *fon, v.*, befool]

function /'fʌŋkʃən/, *n.* **1.** the normal or intended action, activity, or role of a person, thing, or organisation. **2.** ceremonious public or social occasion. **3.** *Maths.* a mathematical quantity whose value depends upon values of other quantities, called variables of the function. ◇*v.i.* **4.** to act or work (as); perform a function. [L: performance]

functional /'fʌŋkʃənəl/, *adj.* **1.** of or relating to function(s). **2.** designed to perform some function rather than for decoration: *a functional building.* **3.** useful; efficient. **4.** operating (correctly).

functionalism /'fʌŋkʃənəlɪzəm/, *n.* (in art, craft, and architecture), the placing of importance on designing things according to their function rather than for appearance.

functionary /'fʌŋkʃənri, -ʃənəri/, *n., pl.* **-ries.** → **official.**

fund /fʌnd/, *n.* **1.** a stock of money. **2.** a store or stock of something: *a fund of knowledge.* **3.** (*pl.*) ready money. ◇*v.t.* **4.** to put into a fund. **5.** to change (a short-term debt or debts) into a long-term debt or loan-bearing interest, represented by bonds. **6.** to provide a fund or funds for. [L: bottom]

fundamental /fʌndə'mɛntl/, *adj.* **1.** acting as, or being part of a foundation or basis; basic: *fundamental principles.* **2.** of or affecting the foundation or basis: *a fundamental change.* **3.** primary; essential. ◇*n.* **4.** a primary principle, rule, law, etc., which acts as the basis of a system. **5.** → **fundamental frequency.** [NL, from L: foundation]

fundamental constant, *n.* the value of one of certain basic physical quantities, such as the charge and mass of an electron, the masses of a proton and a neutron, the velocity of light, gravitational constant, etc., upon which numerical values of all physical features and events depend.

fundamental frequency, *n.* the component of lowest frequency in a complex sound.

fundamentalism /fʌndə'mɛntəlɪzəm/, *n. Relig.* **1.** a movement in American Protestantism which claims the literal truth of the Bible in every detail. **2.** any movement which stresses the literal application of the text, as the Koran, Bible, etc. —**fundamentalist**, *n., adj.*

fundamental unit, *n.* one of the units (esp. of mass, length, and time) taken as a basis for system of units.

funeral /'fjuːnrəl, 'fjuːnərəl/, *n.* **1.** the ceremonies connected with the burial or cremation and paying of respect to a dead person; obsequies. **2.** a funeral procession. [ME, from ML, from L: funeral, death] —**funerary**, *adj.*

funeral parlor *or* **funeral parlour**, *n.* an undertaker's place of business.

funereal /fjuː'nɪəriəl/, *adj.* **1.** of or relating to a funeral. **2.** sad; gloomy; dismal. [L: of a funeral + -AL¹]

funfair /'fʌnfɛə/, *n.* → **fair¹** (def. 1).

fungi /'fʌŋgi/, *n.* plural of **fungus.**

fungicide /'fʌŋgəsaɪd/, *n.* a substance, usu. spray or dust, used to kill fungi. [*fungi-* (combining form of FUNGUS) + -CIDE] —**fungicidal**, *adj.*

fungoid /'fʌŋgɔɪd/, *adj.* like a fungus.

fungous /'fʌŋgəs/, *adj.* **1.** of, relating to, or caused by fungi. **2.** like a fungus. [ME, from L: sponge, mushroom, fungus]

fungus /'fʌŋgəs/, *n., pl.* **fungi** /'fʌŋgi/, **funguses**, *adj.* ◇*n.* **1.** any of a group of plants including mushrooms, moulds, mildews, yeasts, etc., without chlorophyll, leaves and real stems or roots, which live on organic matter, dead or living. **2.** *Med.* a spongy unhealthy growth. ◇*adj.* **3.** → **fungous.** [L: mushroom, fungus]

funicular railway /fə'nɪkjələ/, *n.* a short railway system operating up steep slopes, in which cars or trains on cables move up and down at the same time, balancing each other's weight. Also, **funicular.** [L *funiculus* little rope + -AR¹]

funk¹ /fʌŋk/, *Colloq.* ◇*n.* **1.** fear or a condition of terror: *He was in a funk about his exams.* **2.** a coward. ◇*v.t.* **3.** to be afraid of. **4.** to fear and try to avoid. ◇*v.i.* **5.** to be in a funk. [? Flemish]

funk² /fʌŋk/, *n.* an up-tempo style of soul music, influenced by jazz, with much syncopation.

funky /'fʌŋki/, *adj.* **1.** exciting, satisfying or pleasurable. **2.** of or relating to funk music.

funnel /ˈfʌnəl/, *n., v.,* **-nelled, -nelling.** ◇*n.* **1.** a tube with a wide cone-shaped mouth and narrow neck, used for pouring powder, liquid, etc., through a small opening, as into bottles, etc. **2.** a chimney, esp. of a ship or steam-engine. **3.** a tube or shaft, such as for ventilation. ◇*v.t., v.i.* **4.** to move, pour, or converge through or as if through a funnel [ME *fonel*, from OF, from L]

funnel-web /ˈfʌnəl-web/, *n.* a large, black, poisonous spider of eastern Australia which builds a funnel-shaped web.

funny /ˈfʌni/, *adj.,* **-nier, -niest. 1.** causing laughter; amusing; comical. **2.** strange; odd; curious. [FUN, *n.* + -Y¹]

funny bone, *n.* a part of the elbow which, if hit, causes a peculiar tingling sensation in the arm.

fur /fɜ/, *n., v.,* **furred, furring.** ◇*n.* **1.** the skin of certain animals covered with fine, soft, thick, hairy coating. **2.** treated fur, used for garments, etc. **3.** a garment made of fur. **4.** any fur-like coating. ◇*v.t.* **5.** to coat with fur. [ME *furre*, from OF: line with fur, from Gmc] **– furry,** *adj.*

furbish /ˈfɜbɪʃ/, *v.t.* **1.** to mend or make new-looking (oft. fol. by *up*). **2.** to polish. [ME *furbish(en)*, from OF: polish, clean, from Gmc] **– furbisher,** *n.*

furious /ˈfjʊəriəs/, *adj.* **1.** full of fury, violent feeling, or anger. **2.** violent: *a furious storm.* **3.** fast, strong, active, etc.: *furious activity.* [ME, from L: raging]

furl /fɜl/, *v.t., v.i.* to roll up (a flag, etc.) tightly. [OF: to bind firm, from L]

furlong /ˈfɜlɒŋ/, *n.* a unit of distance in the imperial system, equal to 220 yards or 201.168 m. [OE *furlang*, from *furh* furrow + *lang* long]

furlough /ˈfɜloʊ/, *n.* leave of absence from duty, esp. for soldiers. [var. of *furloff*, from D: leave]

furnace /ˈfɜnəs/, *n.* **1.** a structure or apparatus for producing heat, for heating buildings, smelting ores, producing steam, etc. **2.** a very hot place. [ME *furneise*, from OF, from L: oven]

Furneaux Group /ˈfɜnoʊ grup/, *n.* a group of islands in Bass Strait, off the northeastern coast of Tasmania; muttonbirding. [named after Tobias *Furneaux* 1735–81, English naval officer who, in 1773 explored and charted much of the eastern and southern coasts of Van Dieman's Land]

furnish /ˈfɜnɪʃ/, *v.t.* **1.** to provide or supply. **2.** to fit up (house, room, etc.) with necessary equipment, esp. furniture, curtains, etc. [ME *furnisshe(n)*, from OF: accomplish, furnish, from Gmc] **– furnisher,** *n.*

furnishings /ˈfɜnɪʃɪŋz/, *n.pl.* equipment, furniture, carpets, etc., for a building or room.

furniture /ˈfɜnətʃə/, *n.* **1.** movable articles, e.g. tables, chairs, beds, desks, cupboards, etc., for use or ornament in house, office, etc. **2.** fittings or necessary equipment: *street furniture.* [F: furnish]

furore /ˈfjʊrɔ/, *n.* **1.** a general outburst of enthusiasm or excited disorder. **2.** anger or madness. [L: a raging]

furphy /ˈfɜfi/, *n., pl.* **-phies.** a rumor. [from John *Furphy*, manufacturer in Vic of water and sanitation carts, which during World War I were centres of gossip]

Furphy /ˈfɜfi/, *n.* Joseph ('*Tom Collins*'), 1843–1912, Australian writer and poet; author of *Such is Life* (1903).

furrier /ˈfʌriə/, *n.* a dealer in or maker of furs and fur garments.

furrow /ˈfʌroʊ/, *n.* **1.** a groove or small ditch made in the ground, esp. by a plough. **2.** any groove or wrinkle. ◇*v.t.* **3.** to make furrow(s) in: *Worry furrowed his brow.* [OE *furh*]

further /ˈfɜðə/, *compar. adv. and adj.,* *superl.* **furthest,** *v.* ◇*adv.* **1.** at or to a greater distance. **2.** to a greater degree. **3.** in addition. ◇*adj.* **4.** more distant; farther. **5.** longer. **6.** more. ◇*v.t.* **7.** to encourage; promote; help: *to further a cause.* [OE *furthor*] **– furtherance,** *n.*

furtive /ˈfɜtɪv/, *adj.* **1.** secret; stealthy: *a furtive glance.* **2.** sly; shifty: *a furtive manner.* [L: stolen]

fury /ˈfjʊri/, *n., pl.* **-ries. 1.** violent feeling, esp. anger; rage. **2.** violence; fierceness. **3.** a fierce and violent person. **4.** (*cap.*) in Greek and Roman mythology, one of the three serpent-haired goddesses of vengeance. [ME, from L: rage, madness]

fuse¹ /fjuz/, *n., v.,* **fused, fusing.** ◇*n.* **1.** *Elect.* a piece of wire placed in an electrical circuit, which melts if too high a current passes through it, breaking the circuit and thus preventing further damage. **2.** a tube, ribbon, etc., filled or soaked with a burnable substance, for setting off an explosive. **3. blow a fuse, a.** to cause a fuse to melt. **b.** *Colloq.* to lose one's temper. ◇*v.i.* **4.** to blow a fuse. [It, from L: spindle]

fuse² /fjuz/, *v.,* **fused, fusing.** ◇*v.t., v.i.* **1.** to combine by melting together. **2.** to join or unite into one. [L *fūsus*, pp.: poured, melted, cast]

fuselage /ˈfjuzəlɑʒ, -lɪdʒ/, *n.* the body of an aircraft. [F: spindle-shaped, from L]

Fushun /fuˈʃʌn, ˈfju-/, *n.* a city in Liaoning province, north-eastern China. Pop. 1 077 300 (1986).

fusiform /ˈfjuzəfɔm/, *adj.* pointed at each end, like some roots; spindle-shaped. [L: spindle + -I- + -FORM]

fusilier /fjuzəˈlɪə/, *n.* (formerly) a soldier armed with a **fusil** (type of musket). [F: musket]

fusillade /fjuzəˈleɪd, -ˈlɑd/, **1.** a firing of weapons continuously or at the same time. **2.** a firing or outpouring of anything: *a fusillade of questions.* [F: shoot, musket]

fusion /ˈfjuʒən/, *n.* **1.** the act, process, or result of fusing. **2.** anything which is fused. **3.** *Phys.* → **nuclear fusion.** [L: a pouring out]

fusion energy, *n. Phys.* energy released from nuclear fusion reaction.

fuss /fʌs/, *n.* **1.** extra or useless activity or worry. **2.** noise, confusion, or argument. **3. make a fuss of,** to treat with special care and fondness. ◇*v.i.* **4.** to make a fuss. ◇*v.t.* **5.** to bother or disturb esp. with unimportant things: *Don't fuss me!* [orig. unknown]

fusspot /'fʌspɒt/, *n. Colloq.* a fussy person.

fussy /'fʌsi/, *adj.,* **-sier, -siest. 1.** busy or worrying over small matters. **2.** very ornamented or detailed.

fusty /'fʌsti/, *adj.,* **-tier, -tiest. 1.** stale-smelling; stuffy; mouldy. **2.** old-fashioned. [ME, from OF: wine cask, log, from L: cudgel] **–fustily,** *adv.* **–fustiness,** *n.*

futile /'fjutail/, *adj.* incapable of producing any result; ineffective. [L: untrustworthy, vain, lit., that easily pours out] **–futility,** *n.*

future /'fjutʃə/, *n.* **1.** a time that is going to be or come, after the present time: *Things will be better in the future.* **2.** what will exist or happen in future time: *to tell the future.* **3.** future condition: *His future looks bright.* ◇*adj.* **4.** coming in, or relating to the future. [ME, from L: be]

future perfect, *n. Gram.* a tense which usu. indicates an action or state which will have been completed at some future point in time. See Appendix.

futures contract, *n.* an agreement for the purchase or sale of commodities on a particular date in the future.

futures exchange, *n.* a place where futures contracts are traded. Also, **futures market.**

future shock, *n. Psychol.* a type of neurosis among people threatened by technological and social change.

future tense, *n. Gram.* a tense indicating an action or state which will take place in the future. See Appendix.

futurism /'fjutʃərɪzəm/, *n.* an artistic and literary movement, originating in Italy in 1909, which expressed the movement and speed of the machine age. **–futurist,** *n., adj.*

futuristic /fjutʃə'rɪstɪk/, *adj.* **1.** relating to futurism. **2.** (of a work of art) in a modern style; not traditional. **3.** (of design in clothes, furniture, etc.) looking towards the space age.

futurology /fjutʃə'rɒlədʒi/, *n.* the prediction of the future as a result of the systematic study of present-day politics, economics etc. **–futurologist,** *n.*

fuzz /fʌz/, *n.* **1.** (a mass or coating of) a loose, light, fibrous, or fluffy matter. **2.** *Colloq.* the police force or a policeman.

fuzzy /'fʌzi/, *adj.,* **-zier, -ziest. 1.** of, like, or covered with fuzz. **2.** unclear; blurred. **–fuzziness,** *n.*

f.v., *Abbrev.* on the back of the page. [L *folio verso*]

fwd, *Abbrev.* forward.

FX / ɛf 'ɛks/, *n.pl. Colloq.* (in films, radio, etc.) special effects, e.g. bombs exploding, snow falling, etc.

-fy, suffix meaning: **1.** to make; cause to be; render, as in *simplify, beautify.* **2.** to become; be made, as in *liquefy.* Also, **-ify.** [F, from L: do, make]

Fysh /fɪʃ/, *n.* **Sir (Wilmot) Hudson,** 1895–1974, Australian pioneer airman and author; founder of Qantas in 1920.

Gg

G, g, /n./ *pl.* **G's** or **Gs, g's** or **gs. 1.** the seventh letter of the English alphabet. **2.** the seventh in order of a series. **3.** *Music.* the fifth note in the scale of C major.

g, *Symbol.* **1.** gram. **2.** *Phys.* the gravitational acceleration at earth's surface. Standard g is 9.806 65 m/s^2.

g., *Abbrev.* **1.** gauge. **2.** gender. **3.** genitive.

G, /dʒi/ *for def. 1. Abbrev.* **1.** (of a film) for general exhibition. **2.** German. **3.** (specific) gravity. ◇*Symbol.* **4.** *Phys.* gravitational constant.

Ga, *Chem. Symbol.* gallium.

gab /gæb/, *v.*, **gabbed, gabbing,** *n. Colloq.* ◇*v.i.* **1.** to talk for the sake of talking; chatter. ◇*n.* **2.** purposeless talk; chatter. **3.** ready, smooth speech: *the gift of the gab.* [var. of GOB^2 mouth, from Gaelic or Irish]

gabardine /ˈgæbəˌdin, ˈgæbədin/, *n.* → **gaberdine.**

gabble /ˈgæbəl/, *v.*, **-bled, -bling,** *n.* ◇*v.i.* **1.** to talk rapidly so that the words cannot be understood; jabber. **2.** (of geese, etc.) to make noisy, high sounds; cackle. ◇*v.t.* **3.** to speak (words, etc.) rapidly and unclearly. ◇*n.* **4.** rapid talk which cannot be understood. [from GAB] **— gabbler,** *n.*

gabbro /ˈgæbroʊ/, *n., pl.* **-bros.** a coarse-grained rock formed by volcanic action. [It, from L: smooth, hairless] **— gabbroic,** *adj.* **— gabbroidal,** *adj.* **— gabbroitic,** *adj.*

gaberdine /ˈgæbəˌdin, ˈgæbədin/, *n.* **1.** a closely woven fabric of wool, cotton or spun rayon. **2.** a man's long, loose outer garment, worn in the Middle Ages. Also, **gabardine.** [Sp, from MHG: pilgrimage]

gable /ˈgeɪbəl/, *n.* the triangular wall enclosed by the two slopes of a roof and a line across the eaves. [ME, probably from Scand] **— gabled,** *adj.*

Gable /ˈgeɪbəl/, *n.* **Clark,** 1901-60, US film actor; appeared in *Gone with the Wind* (1939).

Gabo Island /ˌgeɪboʊ ˈaɪlənd/, *n.* an island off the easternmost tip of Vic, about 2.5 km long; lighthouse.

Gabon /gəˈbɒn/, *n.* a republic in western central Africa, on the Atlantic Ocean, bordered by Equatorial Guinea, Cameroon and Congo. Pop. 1 151 000 (1985 est.); 267 667 km^2. *Languages:* French, also Fang and Bantu dialects. *Currency:* franc. *Cap.:* Libreville. **— Gabonese,** *n., adj.*

Gabriel /ˈgeɪbriəl/, *n. Bible.* one of the archangels, appearing usually as a divine messenger. [See Daniel, 8:16, 9:21; Luke, 1:19, 26. Heb: the man of God]

gage

gad /gæd/, *v.i.*, **gadded, gadding.** to move with no particular purpose from place to place, often hoping to find pleasure (fol. by *about*). [backformation from obs. *gadling* companion, from OE *gædeling*]

gadabout /ˈgædəbaʊt/, *n. Colloq.* someone who gads about; a restless person, esp. one who leads an active social life.

Gaddafi /gəˈdafi/, *n.* **Moamar al** /ˈmoʊəmə æl/, born 1942, Libyan revolutionary army officer and politician; became head of state in 1969. Also, **Khaddafi.**

gadfly /ˈgædflaɪ/, *n., pl.* **-flies. 1.** any fly that stings home or farm animals. **2.** someone who, by criticism and actions, unsettles self-satisfied opinions or established interests. [from ME *gad* a mining tool]

gadget /ˈgædʒət/, *n.* a small device which performs a particular job. [orig. uncert.]

Gael^1 /geɪl/, *n.* a Scottish Celt or Highlander. [Scot Gaelic *Gaidheal,* O Irish *Gaidel*]

Gael^2, *Abbrev.* Gaelic.

Gaelic /ˈgeɪlɪk/, *adj., n.* (of or relating to) the Celtic peoples or language of ancient Ireland and their modern descendants in Ireland and Scotland. [Scot Gaelic *Gaidheal,* OIrish *Gaidel*]

gaff /gæf/, *n.* **1.** a strong hook with a handle, used for landing large fish. **2.** *Naut.* a thick pole supporting the upper edge of a sail that lies along the length of a boat. ◇*v.t.* **3.** to hook or land with a gaff. [ME, from OF: boathook, probably of Celtic orig.]

gaffe /gæf/, *n.* a social mistake. [F]

gag^1 /gæg/, *v.*, **gagged, gagging,** *n.* ◇*v.t.* **1.** to stop up the mouth of (someone) so as to prevent sound or speech. **2.** to use force or official power to prevent (someone) from using free speech, etc. **3.** (in parliament) to close (a debate) when some members still wish to speak. ◇*v.i.* **4.** to be unable to swallow, and to heave as though vomiting. ◇*n.* **5.** something pushed into or tied around the mouth to prevent speech. **6.** forceful discouragement of freedom of speech. **7.** a closing of parliamentary debate when some members still wish to speak. [probably imitative of the sound of choking] **— gagger, gagster,** *n.*

gag^2 /gæg/, *v.*, **gagged, gagging,** *n.* ◇*v.i.* **1.** to make jokes. ◇*n.* **2.** a joke. [orig. uncert.] **— gagger,** *n.*

gaga /ˈgagə/, *adj. Colloq.* **1.** with a mind weakened by old age. **2.** childishly foolish; mad. **3.** fond to the point of silliness: *He is gaga about his new car.* [F: senile]

Gagarin /gəˈgarɪn/, *n.* **Major Yuri Alekseyevitch** /ˌjuri ælɪksˈjeɪjəvɪtʃ/, 1934-68, Soviet cosmonaut; made first flight in space, in the spacecraft Vostok 1, on 12 April 1961.

gage^1 /geɪdʒ/, *n.* **1.** something, as a glove, thrown down to show a challenge to fight. **2.** something given to someone to keep until a promise or debt is met; security. [ME, from OF: pledge, security; of Gmc orig.]

gage^2 /geɪdʒ/, *n., v.t.,* **gaged, gaging.** → **gauge.**

gaggle /'gægəl/, *n.* **1.** a flock of geese. **2.** any disorganised and usu. noisy group. [imitative]

gaiety /'geɪəti/, *n., pl.* **-ties. 1.** the state of being gay or cheerful. **2.** (*oft. pl.*) a time of making merry: *the gaieties of the New Year season.* **3.** showiness; finery: *gaiety of dress.* [F: gay]

gaily /'geɪli/, *adv.* **1.** merrily. **2.** showily.

gain /geɪn/, *v.t.* **1.** to obtain (something desired); acquire. **2.** to win: *gain the prize.* **3.** to get as an increase, addition or profit. **4.** to reach by effort: *The ship may gain a good harbor further along the coast.* ◇*v.i.* **5.** to improve; advance. **6.** (in chasing someone) to get nearer (fol. by *on* or *upon*). **7.** to get further away (from those chasing). ◇*v.* **8. gain ground,** to make an advance or obtain an advantage. **9. gain time,** to delay. ◇*n.* **10.** profit; advantage. **11.** (*pl.*) profits; winnings. **12.** an increase or advance. **13.** the act of gaining; acquisition. **14.** *Electronics.* the ratio of the output voltage, power, etc. to the input. **15.** (of an amplifier) volume. [OF: to get possession of, from Gmc: to plunder]

gainful /'geɪnfəl/, *adj.* profitable; lucrative.

gainsay /geɪn'seɪ/, *v.t.,* **-said, -saying. 1.** to say (something) is not so; deny. **2.** to speak or act against. [*gain*- against + SAY]

Gainsborough /'geɪnzbərə, 'geɪnzbrə/, *n.* **Thomas,** 1727–88, English painter, esp. of portraits and landscapes.

Gair /gɛə/, *n.* **Vincent Clair,** 1902–80, Australian state and federal politician; premier of Qld, 1952–57; originally a member of the ALP, formed the Qld Labor Party in 1957 and merged this with the DLP in 1962.

Gairdner /'gɛədnə/, *n.* **Lake,** a large salt lake in southern central SA; about 160 km long and 48 km wide.

gait /geɪt/, *n.* **1.** a particular manner of walking. **2.** any of the characteristic movement patterns of a horse, e.g. the trot, canter, or gallop. [Scot and N Eng spelling of GATE in various senses, including those above]

gaiter /'geɪtə/, *n.* a cloth or leather covering for the ankle and instep, and sometimes also the lower leg. [F]

gal., *Abbrev.* gallon(s).

gala /'gɑːlə/, *adj.* **1.** showy; festive: *His visits were always gala occasions.* ◇*n.* **2.** a festive occasion. [F, from It: festal pomp, finery, from OF: joy, pleasure, from MD: riches]

galactic /gə'læktɪk/, *adj. Astron.* relating to a galaxy (a large system of stars) esp. the Milky Way. [Gk: milky]

galah /gə'lɑː/, *n.* **1.** a small Australian cockatoo, pale grey above and deep pink below. **2.** *Colloq.* a fool; simpleton. [Aboriginal]

Galahad /'gæləhæd/, *n.* **Sir,** the noblest and purest knight of the Round Table in the Arthurian legend.

Galápagos Islands /gə,læpəgəs 'aɪləndz/, *n.pl.* an archipelago on the equator in the Pacific, about 965 km west of and belonging to Ecuador; many unique species of animal life. Pop. 8000 (1986 est.); 7845 km². Spanish, **Archipiélago de Colón.**

galaxy /'gæləksi/, *n., pl.* **-axies. 1.** *Astron.* **a.** any large system of stars held together by gravitation and separated from any other similar system by great areas of space. **b.** (*cap.*) **the Galaxy,** also, **Milky Way,** our galaxy, containing several billion stars, with the solar system about three fifths of the galaxy's radius from its centre. Diameter: approx. 100 000 light years. **2.** a gathering of famous people. [ME, from ML, from Gk: milk]

Galbraith /'gælbreɪθ/, *n.* **John Kenneth,** born 1908, US economist and diplomat; his economic works include *The Affluent Society* (1958) and *The New Industrial State* (1967).

gale /geɪl/, *n.* **1.** a strong wind. **2.** a sudden burst of noise: *a gale of laughter.* [orig. uncert.]

galena /gə'liːnə/, *n.* a very common heavy (sp. gr. 7.6) mineral, lead sulfide, PbS; the main ore of lead. [L: lead ore]

Galicia /gə'lɪʃə/, *n.* **1.** a former crownland of Austria, included in southern Poland after World War I, and now partly in the USSR. About 78 000 km². **2.** a maritime region in north-western Spain; a former kingdom, later a province. 26 170 km².

Galilee /'gæləliː/, *n.* **1.** an ancient Roman province in what is now northern Israel. **2. Sea of.** Also, **Lake Tiberias.** a lake in north-eastern Israel through which the river Jordan flows. 165 km², 209 m below sea-level. –**Galilean,** *n. adj.*

Galileo /gælɪ'leɪoʊ/, *n.* (*Galileo Galilei*), 1564–1642, Italian physicist, astronomer and mathematician; built the first astronomical telescope (1609) and made observations supporting the Copernican model of the solar system.

gall¹ /gɔl/, *n.* **1.** → bile. **2.** something very bitter or severe. **3.** bitterness of spirit; rancor. **4.** boldness; effrontery. [OE *galla*]

gall² /gɔl/, *n.* **1.** a sore on the skin, esp. of a horse, caused by rubbing. ◇*v.t.* **2.** to make sore by rubbing. **3.** to annoy. [special use of GALL¹]

gall³ /gɔl/, *n.* any abnormal vegetable growth on plants, with various causes, such as insects, bacteria, chemicals, etc. [ME, from L: the oak apple, gallnut]

gallant /'gælənt, gə'lænt/, *adj.* **1.** brave and noble: *gallant young men.* **2.** noticeably polite and attentive to women. ◇*n. Archaic.* **3.** a brave and stylish man. **4.** a young man fond of women. [OF: splendid, magnificent, from *galer* to rejoice]

gallantry /'gæləntri/, *n., pl.* **-tries. 1.** noble courage. **2.** gallant or polite attention to women. **3.** a gallant action or speech.

gall bladder, *n.* a membranous sac attached to the liver which stores bile.

galleon /'gæliən, 'gæljən/, *n.* a type of large Spanish sailing vessel of former times. [Sp: large galley]

gallery

gallery /'gæləri/, *n., pl.* **-leries**. **1.** a long, narrow, covered walk, open at one or both sides. **2.** a raised passageway along the outside or inside of the wall of a building; balcony. **3.** a raised section of flooring coming from the inner walls of a church, theatre, etc., to provide seating room. **4.** (those sitting in) the highest of such sections in a theatre. **5. play to the gallery**, to seek approval by playing to popular taste rather than considered judgment. **6.** a room or building for showing works of art or practising shooting. **7.** any underground passage, as in mining, etc. [It, from ML: vestibule]

galley /'gæli/, *n., pl.* **-leys**. **1.** an early seagoing vessel propelled by oars or by oars and sails. **2.** the kitchen of a ship or aircraft. **3.** *Print.* **a.** a long, narrow tray for holding type which has been set. **b.** Also, **galley proof**. a test copy made before arrangement into pages. [ME, from ML, from LGk]

galley slave, *n.* **1.** a person forced as punishment to row in a galley. **2.** *Colloq.* an overworked person; drudge.

Gallic /'gælɪk/, *adj.* relating to the French or France. [L *Gallicus*, from *Gallus* a Gaul, one of the people of ancient France]

gallinaceous /gælə'neɪʃəs/, *adj.* belonging to the group which includes the domestic fowls, pheasants, quails, etc. Also, **gallinacean**. [L: relating to poultry]

Gallinas Point /ga,jinəs 'pɔɪnt/, *n.* a cape in north-eastern Colombia; northernmost point in South America. Spanish, **Punta Gallinas**.

galling /'gɔlɪŋ/, *adj.* very annoying; exasperating.

Gallipoli /gə'lɪpəli/, *n.* a peninsula in western Turkey separating the Aegean Sea and the Dardanelles; site of the costly but unsuccessful campaign by the Allies in World War I.

gallium /'gæliəm/, *n.* a rare, bluish white, easily fusible trivalent metallic element, used in high-temperature thermometers because of its high boiling point (1700°C) and low melting point (30°C). *Symbol:* Ga; *at. no.:* 31; *at. wt:* 69.72. [NL, said to be from L *gallus* cock, translation of F *coq*, from the name of the discoverer, Lecoq de Boisbaudran]

gallivant /'gæləvænt/, *v.i.* to go from place to place in a carefree way, seeking amusement. Also, **galavant**. [? humorous alteration of GALLANT]

Gallo-, a word part meaning 'French'. [L, combining form of *Gallus* a Gaul]

gallon /'gælən/, *n.* a unit in the imperial system, for measuring liquids and dry goods, equal to 4.546 09 litres; imperial gallon. [ME: perhaps of Celtic orig.]

gallop /'gæləp/, *v.i.* **1.** to ride a horse at full speed. **2.** to go fast, race, or hurry. ◇*v.t.* **3.** to cause (a horse, etc.) to gallop. ◇*n.* **4.** a fast gait of the horse in which at times all four feet are off the ground at once. **5.** a run or ride at this gait. [F, from OLG: run well]

Galloway /'gæləweɪ/, *n.* an area of south-western Scotland; the **Mull of Galloway** is the southernmost point of Scotland.

Gambier

gallows /'gæloʊz/, *n., pl.* **-lows, -lowses**. **1.** a wooden frame used to hang condemned persons. **2.** death by hanging. **3.** a device on which animals killed for meat are hung. [OE *galgan*, pl. of *g(e)alga* gallows]

gallstone /'gɔlstoʊn/, *n.* a stone formed in the bile ducts or gall bladder.

gallup poll /'gæləp poʊl/, *n.* the questioning of a representative cross-section of the population in order to work out public opinion. [after George Horace *Gallup*, 1901–84, American statistician]

galore /gə'lɔ/, *adv.* (used only after nouns) in plenty: *There was food galore.* [Irish *go leóir* to sufficiency]

galoshes /gə'lɒʃəz/, *n. pl.* a pair of overshoes of a waterproof substance. [ME, from L: Gallic sandal]

Galsworthy /'gɔlzwɜði/, *n.* **John**, 1867–1933, English novelist, dramatist, and short-story writer; author of *The Forsyte Saga* (1906–28).

galumph /gə'lʌmpf, -'lʌmf/, *v.i.* to jump about in high spirits, often awkwardly. [b. GALLOP + TRIUMPH; coined by Lewis Carroll]

Galvani /gæl'vani/, *n.* **Luigi** /lu'idʒi/, 1737–98, an Italian physiologist whose experiments led to the discovery that electricity may result from chemical action.

galvanic /gæl'vænɪk/, *adj.* **1.** relating to or produced by galvanism. **2.** affecting or affected as if by galvanism. [from Luigi GALVANI]

galvanise or **galvanize** /'gælvənaɪz/, *v.t.*, **-nised, -nising**. **1.** to stimulate by or as by a galvanic current. **2.** to surprise into sudden activity. **3.** to coat (iron or steel) with zinc to prevent rust. —**galvanisation**, *n.*

galvanised iron or **galvanized iron**, *n.* (sheets of roofing material made of) iron coated with zinc to prevent rust.

galvanism /'gælvənɪzəm/, *n.* electricity produced by chemical action.

galvano-, a combining form representing **galvanic, galvanism**, as in *galvanometer*.

galvanometer /gælvə'nɒmətə/, *n.* an instrument for finding an electric current and measuring its strength and direction.

Galway /'gɔlweɪ/, *n.* a county in the western Republic of Ireland, in Connacht. Pop. 178 180 (1986); 5940 km². Irish, **Gaillimh**.

Gama /'gamə/, *n.* **Vasco da** /'væskoʊ da/, c. 1469–1524, Portuguese navigator and discoverer of the sea route from Portugal around the continent of Africa to India.

Gambia /'gæmbiə/, *n.* **The**, a republic on the west coast of Africa, around the river Gambia, and surrounded by Senegal; a British colony before independence in 1965. Pop. 787 400 (1987 est.); 11 295 km². *Languages:* English, also Mandinka, Fula and Wolof. *Currency:* dalasi. *Cap.:* Banjul. —**Gambian**, *n., adj.*

Gambier /'gæmbiə/, *n.* **Mount**, an extinct volcano in south-eastern SA; within its crater lie four lakes, one of which is the popular Blue Lake. 190 m.

gambit /'gæmbət/, *n.* **1.** an opening in chess, in which the player seeks by giving up a pawn or other piece to obtain some advantage. **2.** any act or course of action designed to obtain some advantage. [F, from It: a tripping-up]

gamble /'gæmbəl/, *v.*, **-bled, -bling,** *n.* ◇*v.i.* **1.** to play at any game of chance in which one risks losing something, usu. money. **2.** to risk money, etc., on the result of something involving chance. **3.** to act on favorable hopes: *The prime minister will gamble on public acceptance of his record to date.* ◇*v.t.* **4.** to lose by betting (usu. fol. by *away*). **5.** to risk. ◇*n.* **6.** any matter or thing involving risk or uncertainty. [? OE *gamenian* to sport, play] **–gambler,** *n.* **–gambling,** *n.*

gambol /'gæmbəl/, *v.*, **-bolled, -bolling,** *n.* ◇*v.i.* **1.** to jump about, as in dancing or playing; frolic. ◇*n.* **2.** a jumping about; frolic. [F: leap, from It: a kick]

game[1] /geɪm/, *n., adj.,* **gamer, gamest,** *v.*, **gamed, gaming.** ◇*n.* **1.** an amusement or activity to pass time. **2.** the apparatus used in playing any of certain games: *a shop selling toys and games.* **3.** a competition for amusement involving chance, skill, strength, etc., according to set rules. **4.** a definite section of play in a particular game: *a rubber of three games in bridge.* **5.** the number of points required to win a game. **6.** a particular manner of playing a game. **7.** an activity carried on according to set rules as in a game: *the game of politics.* **8.** *Colloq.* a business or profession. **9.** a trick; strategy: *I see through your game.* **10.** wild animals, including fishes, hunted for sport or food. **11.** any object of attack; prey. ◇**12.** Some special uses are:
game, set and match, complete victory (fol. by *to*).
give the game away, 1. to give up. **2.** to reveal a secret.
have the game sewn up, to be in charge of the situation.
off one's game, not giving one's best performance.
play the game, to act fairly or justly, or according to the rules.
◇*adj.* **13.** relating to animals hunted or taken as game. **14.** with fighting spirit; plucky: *as game as Ned Kelly.* **15.** *Colloq.* willing to undertake something dangerous or difficult (oft. fol. by *for* or by an infinitive): *I'm game to go bushwalking.* ◇*v.i.* **16.** to play games of chance for stakes; gamble. [OE *gamen*]

game[2] /geɪm/, *adj. Colloq.* lame: *a game leg.* [orig. uncert.]

Game /geɪm/, *n.* **Sir Philip Woolcott,** 1876–1961, English soldier and civil administrator; governor of NSW, 1930–35; dismissed premier JT Lang and his cabinet in an unprecedented move, in 1932.

gamecock /'geɪmkɒk/, *n.* a cock bred and trained for fighting.

gamesmanship /'geɪmzmənʃɪp/, *n.* the art or practice of winning games or gaining advantages without actually cheating.

gamete /'gæmit, gə'mit/, *n.* either of the two germ cells which unite to form a new organism. [NL, from Gk *gametē* wife or *gametēs* husband] **–gametal, gametic,** *adj.*

gametogenesis /gæmətoʊ'dʒɛnəsəs/, *n.* the development of gametes.

gametophyte /gə'mitoʊfaɪt/, *n.* the sexual form of a plant in the alternation of generations (opposed to *sporophyte*).

gaming /'geɪmɪŋ/, *n.* gambling.

gamma /'gæmə/, *n.* **1.** the third letter (Γ, γ, = English G, g) of the Greek alphabet. **2.** the third of any series.

gamma globulin, *n.* one of the proteins carried by the blood, which acts as an antibody.

gamma rays, *n.pl.* rays similar to X-rays, but of higher frequency and shorter wavelength, forming part of the radiation of radioactive substances.

gammon /'gæmən/, *n.* **1.** ham which is smoked or cured. **2.** meat from the lower end of a side of bacon. [ME, from ONF: ham, from *gambe* hoof, leg, from LL]

gammy /'gæmi/, *adj. Colloq.* → **game**[2].

gamo-, a word part meaning 'sexual union'. [combining form representing Gk *gámos* marriage]

-gamous, an adjectival word part, matching the noun part **-gamy,** as in *polygamous.* [Gk *-gamos* marrying]

gamut /'gæmət/, *n.* the whole scale or range. [ML, contraction of *gamma ut,* from *gamma,* used to represent the first or lowest tone (G) in the medieval scale + *ut* (later *do*)]

-gamy, 1. a word part meaning 'marriage', as in *polygamy.* **2.** *Biol.* a word part meaning 'sexual union'. [Gk *-gamía,* from *-gamos* marrying, married]

gander /'gændə/, *n.* **1.** the male of the goose. **2.** *Colloq.* a look at something. [OE *gan(d)ra*]

Gandhi /'gandi, 'gændi/, *n.* **1. Indira** /ɪn'dɪ ɪərə, 'ɪndərə/, 1917–84, Indian political leader; prime minister 1966–77, 1980–84; daughter of Jawaharlal Nehru; assassinated. **2. Mohandas Karamchand** /,moʊhəndəs kərəm'tʃʌnd/ (*Mahatma Gandhi*), 1869–1948, Hindu religious and political leader and social reformer; advocate of passive resistance; leader of Indian self-government movement; assassinated **3. Rajiv** /'radʒɪv/, 1944–91, son of Indira; prime minister of India 1984–89; assassinated.

gang /gæŋ/, *n.* **1.** a band or group: *a gang of boys.* **2.** a group of persons working together; squad; shift: *a gang of laborers.* **3.** a group of persons, often violent or criminal, associated for a particular purpose: *a gang of thieves.* ◇*v.i.* **4.** *Colloq.* to form or act as a gang. ◇*v.* **5. gang up on,** to combine against. [OE *gongan, gangan*]

Ganges /'gændʒiz/, *n.* a river flowing from the Himalayas in northern India southeast through Bangladesh to the Bay of Bengal; sacred to the Hindus. About 2415 km.

gang-gang /'gæŋ-gæŋ/, *n.* a greyish cockatoo, of south-eastern Australia, the male of which has a red head and crest. [Aboriginal]

gangling /'gæŋlɪŋ/, *adj.* awkwardly tall and thin. Also, **gangly** /'gæŋli/. [akin to obs. *gangrel* gangling person, from GANG]

ganglion /'gæŋgliən/, *n., pl.* **-glia** /-gliə/, **-glions**. **1.** *Anat.* a group of nerve cells outside the brain and spinal cord. **2.** a centre of force, activity, etc. [LL: kind of swelling, from Gk: tumor under the skin, on or near a tendon]

Gang of Four, *n.* the leadership of the radical faction of the Chinese Communist Party, arrested in October 1976 after the death of Mao Zedong. It comprised Zhang Zhunjiao, Wong Hongwen, Yao Wenyouan and Jiang Qing.

gangplank /'gæŋplæŋk/, *n.* a movable, usu. wooden, board, used as a bridge in passing into and out of a ship, etc.

gangrene /'gæŋgrin/, *n.* the death and decay of tissue, when the blood supply is cut off. [L, from Gk: an eating sore] —**gangrenous**, *adj.*

gangster /'gæŋstə/, *n.* a member of a gang of criminals.

gangway /'gæŋweɪ/, *n.* **1.** a passageway, often on a ship. **2.** (an opening or removable section of a ship's rail for) a gangplank. **3.** an aisle in a theatre. ◇ *interj.* **4.** clear the way! [OE *gangweg*]

gannet /'gænət/, *n.* any of several large coastal birds which dive from great heights to catch fish. [ME and OE *ganet*]

gantry /'gæntri/, *n., pl.* **-tries**. **1.** a bridgelike framework, as one holding railway signals above the tracks, etc. **2.** a wheeled frame supporting something, as a rocket or a travelling crane. [d. *gawn* (contraction of GALLON) + *-tree* supporting frame]

Ganymede /'gænimid/, *n. Class Myth.* a Trojan youth carried off by Zeus, to be his lover and cupbearer.

gaol /dʒeɪl/, *n.* → **jail**. [ME *gay(h)ole*, *gaile*, from ONF, from L: cavity, enclosure, cage]

gaolbird /'dʒeɪlbɜd/, *n.* → **jailbird**.

gaolbreak /'dʒeɪlbreɪk/, *n.* → **jailbreak**.

gaoler /'dʒeɪlə/, *n.* → **jailer**.

Gaoxiong /kaʊʃiˈʊŋ/, *n.* a seaport in south-western Taiwan. Pop. 1 302 849 (1986 est.). Formerly, **Kaohsiung, Takao**.

gap /gæp/, *n.* **1.** a break or opening, as in a fence, etc.; breach. **2.** any interruption in space or time. **3.** a wide difference in ideas, natures, etc. **4.** a deep, sloping cut in a mountain range. [ME, from Scand]

gape /geɪp/, *v.*, **gaped, gaping**, *n.* ◇ *v.i.* **1.** to stare with open mouth, as in wonder. **2.** to open the mouth wide, either intentionally or not. **3.** to split or become open wide. ◇ *n.* **4.** a wide opening. **5.** the act of gaping. [ME *gapen*, from Scand]

garage /'gæraʒ, -rɑdʒ, gəˈraʒ, -ˈrɑdʒ/, *n., v.*, **-raged, -raging**. ◇ *n.* **1.** a building for sheltering motor vehicles. **2.** an establishment where motor vehicles are repaired, petrol is sold, etc. ◇ *v.t.* **3.** to put or keep in a garage. [F: put in shelter, from Pr: keep, heed, from Gmc]

garb /gɑb/, *n.* **1.** clothes, esp. of a special style or kind. **2.** covering or form. ◇ *v.t.* **3.** to dress; clothe. [F, from It: grace, from Gmc]

garbage /'gɑbɪdʒ/, *n.* **1.** household waste; rubbish. **2.** anything worthless, undesirable, or unnecessary.

garble /'gɑbəl/, *v.t.*, **-bled, -bling**. **1.** to choose unfair or misleading parts from (facts, statements, writings, etc.); corrupt. **2.** to make (something) unable to be understood. [It, from Ar: sift, ? from LL: little sieve] —**garbler**, *n.*

Garbo /'gɑboʊ/, *n.* **Greta** (*Greta Louisa Gustafsson*), 1905–90, Swedish film actress, retired in 1941.

garcon /gɑˈsɒn/, *n.* a waiter. Also, **garçon**. [F: boy, waiter]

garden /'gɑdn/, *n.* **1.** a section of ground given over to the cultivation of useful or ornamental plants. **2.** an area, usu. with plants, trees, etc., used as a place of rest or pleasure: *a botanical garden; a roof garden*. ◇ *adj.* **3.** produced in a garden. **4.** (in town planning) planned so as to have many gardenlike open spaces: *a garden city*. **5. lead up the garden path**, *Colloq.* to trick or lead away from the truth. ◇ *v.i.* **6.** to lay out or cultivate a garden. [ME, from ONF, of Gmc orig.]

gardener /'gɑdnə/, *n.* **1.** a person employed to take care of a garden. **2.** someone who gardens.

gardenia /gɑˈdɪnjə, -niə/, *n.* an evergreen tree or shrub native to China, South Africa, etc., including species cultivated for their sweet-smelling, waxlike white flowers. [NL; named after Dr Alexander *Garden*, 1730–91]

Gardiner /'gɑdnə/, *n.* **Frank** (*Francis Gardiner*), 1830–?, Australian bushranger.

Garfield /'gɑfild/, *n.* **James Abram**, 1831–81, twentieth president of the US (1881).

garfish /'gɑfɪʃ/, *n., pl.* **-fishes**, (*esp. collectively*) **-fish**. any of many fishes found in Australian seas and estuaries, having a slender body and the lower jaw produced as a needle-like point. [ME *garfysshe*, from *gar* (OE *gār* spear) + *fysshe* FISH]

gargle /'gɑgəl/, *v.*, **-gled, -gling**, *n.* ◇ *v.i., v.t.* **1.** to wash (the throat or mouth) with a liquid held in the throat and kept moving by air from the lungs. ◇ *n.* **2.** any liquid used for gargling. [F: throat]

gargoyle /'gɑgɔɪl/, *n.* a spout, often in the shape of an ugly head, through whose open mouth rainwater is carried away from a building. [ME, from OF: throat]

Garibaldi /gærəˈbɒldi/, *n.* **Giuseppe** /dʒəˈzepi/, 1807–82, Italian patriot and general. —**Garibaldian**, *adj., n.*

garish /'gɛərɪʃ, 'gɑr-/, *adj.* too bright, brassy, or showy in presentation, dress, etc. [ME: stare]

garland /'gɑlənd/, *n.* **1.** a string of flowers, leaves, etc. worn for ornament or as an honor.

garland **2.** a collection of short written pieces, usu. poems and ballads. ◊*v.t.* **3.** to crown with a garland; cover with garlands. [ME, from OF]

Garland /'galənd/, *n.* **Judy** (*Frances Gumm*), 1922-69, US singer and film star; films include *The Wizard of Oz* (1939).

garlic /'galık/, *n.* **1.** a hardy plant, whose strong-smelling bulb is used in cookery and sometimes as a medicine. ◊*adj.* **2.** containing garlic. [OE *gār* spear + *lēac* leek]

garment /'gamənt/, *n.* **1.** an article of clothing. **2.** an outer covering. [ME, from OF: equip]

garner /'ganə/, *v.t.* **1.** to collect or store in or as in a garner; hoard. ◊*n.* **2.** (formerly) a building to store grain. **3.** a store of anything. [ME, from L: granary]

Garner /'ganə/, **Helen**, born 1942, Australian novelist and journalist; author of *Monkey Grip* (1977).

garnet /'ganət/, *n.* **1.** any of a group of hard, silicate minerals of which a deep red variety is used as a gem. **2.** deep red, as of a garnet. [ME, from ML: garnet, also pomegranate, lit., having grains or seeds]

garnish /'ganıʃ/, *v.t.* **1.** to fit out with something that improves the appearance. **2.** to make (a dish) more pleasing to the eye and taste. ◊*n.* **3.** something used to garnish food, as parsley. [ME, from OF: prepare]

garnishee /ganə'ʃi/, *v.*, **-sheed,** **-sheeing,** *n.* ◊*v.t.* **1.** to hold back (part of an employee's income) to meet debt repayments. ◊*n.* **2.** a person ordered by a court to pay money due to a debtor direct to his creditors.

garret /'gærət/, *n.* → **attic** (def. 1). [ME, from OF: watchtower]

Garrett /'gærət/, *n.* **Peter**, born 1953, Australian rock singer and political activist.

Garrick /'gærık/, *n.* **David**, 1717-79, English actor and theatrical manager.

garrison /'gærəsən/, *n.* **1.** a body of soldiers positioned in a place strengthened against attack. **2.** the place where they are positioned. ◊*v.t.* **3.** to provide (a fort, post, town, etc.) with a garrison. **4.** to occupy (a fort, etc.). [ME, from OF: defence]

garrotte /gə'rɒt/, *n., v.,* **-rotted, -rotting.** ◊*n.* **1.** a method of killing, originally with an instrument causing strangulation, later by one breaking the neck. **2.** the instrument used. ◊*v.t.* **3.** to kill by the garrotte. **4.** to strangulate, esp. for the purpose of robbery. Also, **garotte, garrote.** [Sp: orig. a stick (formerly used in drawing a cord tight), from Pr: cudgel, stick for twisting a cord tight, from Celtic *garra* leg]

garrulous /'gærələs/, *adj.* **1.** given to much talking, esp. about unimportant things. **2.** (of speech) wordy. [L: talkative] – **garrulity,** *n.*

garter /'gatə/, *n.* an elasticised band worn around the leg to keep up stockings or long socks. [ME, from ONF *garet* the bend of the knee, from Celtic: leg]

garter stitch, *n.* **1.** a plain stitch in knitting. **2.** the pattern produced by this.

gas[1] /gæs/, *n., pl.* **gases,** *adj., v.,* **gassed, gassing.** ◊*n.* **1.** *Phys.* a substance consisting of atoms or molecules which move about freely so that it takes up the whole of the space in which it is contained. **2.** any such substance used as a fuel, esp. coal gas or natural gas. **3.** a mistlike mass of fine particles, used in warfare to poison or otherwise harm the enemy. **4.** *Colloq.* empty talk. ◊*adj.* **5.** coming from, produced by, or involving gas: *a gas stove.* **6.** *Colloq.* great, wonderful: *a gas idea.* ◊*v.t.* **7.** to affect, overcome, or asphyxiate with gas or fumes. ◊*v.i.* **8.** *Colloq.* to spend time in empty talk. [coined by JB van Helmont, 1577-1644, Flemish chemist; suggested by Gk *cháos* chaos]

gas[2] /gæs/, *n.* *Chiefly US* *Colloq.* → **petrol.** [shortened form of GASOLINE]

gasbag /'gæsbæg/, *n., v.,* **-bagged, -bagging.** *Colloq.* ◊*n.* **1.** a talkative person; windbag. ◊*v.i.* **2.** to talk too much and too easily; chatter.

gas chamber, *n.* a closed room in which animals or human beings are killed by means of a poisonous gas.

gas constant, *n.* the constant in the gas laws, equal to about 8.31 joules per kelvin mole. *Symbol:* R Also, **universal gas constant.**

Gascony /'gæskəni/, *n.* a former province in south-western France. French, **Gascogne.**

Gascoyne /'gæskɔın/, *n.* **1. the,** a region in north-western WA. **2.** a river in western central WA, rising near the Collier Range and flowing west into Shark Bay. About 820 km.

gaseous /'gæsiəs, 'geı-/, *adj.* like, of or relating to gas.

gaseous diffusion, *n.* the gradual intermixing of molecules of one substance by molecules of gas, due to random movement of molecules.

gash /gæʃ/, *n.* **1.** a long, deep cut, esp. in the flesh. ◊*v.t.* **2.** to make a long, deep cut in; slash. [ONF *garser* scarify]

gasket /'gæskət/, *n.* **1.** anything used as a packing or jointing material for making joints fluid-tight. **2.** a piece of metal, rubber, etc. for making a gastight joint, esp. between the cylinder block and the cylinder head of an internal-combustion engine. **3.** *Naut.* one of several bands or lines used to bind a rolled-up sail. **4. blow a gasket,** to lose one's temper. [orig. uncert.]

gas laws, *n.pl.* the laws, esp. Boyle's law and Charles's law, which relate the pressure, volume, and temperature of a gas. The combined ideal gas law states that for one mole of an ideal gas the product of pressure and volume is equal to the product of absolute temperature and a constant known as the **gas constant.**

gasmask /'gæsmask/, *n.* a device worn over the face to protect against poisonous gases, fumes, etc.

gasoline /'gæsəlin/, *n.* *Chiefly US.* → **petrol.** Also, **gasolene.** [GAS[1] + -OL[2] + -INE[2]]

gasometer /ˈgæsɒmətə, gə-/, n. 1. a large tank for storing gas, esp. at a gasworks. 2. laboratory apparatus for measuring or storing gas. [F]

gasp /gæsp, gɑsp/, n. 1. a sudden, short breath, as in an effort to breathe. 2. a short jerky utterance, esp. as a result of fear or surprise. ◇v.i. 3. to catch the breath, or struggle for breath, with open mouth. 4. to long with breathless eagerness; desire (fol. by *for* or *after*). ◇v.t. 5. to utter with gasps (oft. fol. by *out, forth, away*, etc.). [ME, from Scand; akin to OE *gipian* yawn, *gipung* open mouth]

gassy /ˈgæsi/, adj., **-sier, -siest. 1.** full of or containing gas. 2. like gas.

gastric /ˈgæstrɪk/, adj. relating to the stomach.

gastric juice, n. the digestive fluid produced by the glands of the stomach, containing pepsin and other enzymes.

gastric ulcer, n. a wearing away of the stomach's inner wall.

gastritis /gæsˈtraɪtəs/, n. inflammation of the stomach, esp. of its mucous membrane.

gastro-, a word part meaning 'stomach', as in *gastropod*. Also, **gastero-, gastr-**. [Gk, combining form of *gastēr*]

gastroenteritis /ˌgæstroʊɛntəˈraɪtəs/, n. inflammation of the stomach and intestines.

gastroenterology /ˌgæstroʊɛntəˈrɒlədʒi/, n. the study of the structure and diseases of the organs for breaking down food. —**gastroenterologist,** n.

gastrointestinal /ˌgæstroʊɪnˈtɛstənəl/, adj. of or relating to the stomach and intestines.

gastronome /ˈgæstrənoʊm/, n. a person who enjoys and knows about good food; gourmet. [F]

gastronomy /gæsˈtrɒnəmi/, n. the art or science of good eating. [F, from Gk] —**gastronomic, gastronomical,** adj.

gastropod /ˈgæstrəpɒd/, n. any of a class of molluscs including the snails, slugs and whelks, having a flattened muscular foot on which they move about. [See GASTRO-, -POD]

gate /geɪt/, n. 1. a movable frame, in a fence or wall, or across a passageway. 2. an opening for passage into an enclosed area. 3. any narrow means of entrance. 4. a device for controlling the passage of water, steam, etc. in a dam, pipe, etc.; valve. 5. the number of persons who pay for admission to a sporting event. 6. Also, **gate money.** the money taken for entrance to a sporting event. 7. *Motor Vehicles.* the H-shaped arrangement controlling the gearstick movement. 8. *Elect.* an electronic circuit which controls the passage of information signals. [OE *gatu* gates, pl. of *geat* opening in a wall] —**gateman,** n.

gateau /ˈgætoʊ/, n., pl. **-teaux** /-toʊz, -toʊ/. a cake with a sponge, biscuit or pastry base topped with fruit, jelly, cream, etc. Also, **gâteau.** [F]

gatecrash /ˈgeɪtkræʃ/, v.i., v.t. attend (a party) uninvited, or to attend (a public entertainment, etc.) without a ticket.

gatehouse /ˈgeɪthaʊs/, n. a house at or over a gate, lived in by the keeper, etc.

gate-leg table, n. a table having sides which fold down and are supported when up by legs which swing out. Also, **gate-legged table.**

gateway /ˈgeɪtweɪ/, n. 1. any way of entering or leaving a place. 2. a passage or entrance which is closed by a gate.

gather /ˈgæðə/, v.t. 1. to bring (people, animals, or things) together into one group. 2. to collect gradually. 3. to find out or understand: *I gather that he'll be leaving.* 4. to pick (flowers, fruit, etc.). 5. to bring (someone or something) close: *He gathered her into his arms; He gathered up the ball.* 6. to prepare (one's energies or oneself) for an effort, etc. (oft. fol. by *up*). 7. to draw up (cloth) on a thread into small folds. 8. to wrinkle (the brow). 9. to increase (speed, etc.) as a car, boat, etc. ◇v.i. 10. to come together; assemble: *to gather round a fire; to gather in crowds.* 11. to increase. 12. to swell and form pus, as a sore. ◇n. 13. (usu. pl.) a fold in gathered cloth, etc. [OE *gaderian*, from *geador* together]

GATT /gæt/, *Abbrev.* General Agreement on Tariffs and Trade.

gauche /ɡoʊʃ/, adj. awkward; clumsy; tactless: *Her apology was as gauche as a schoolgirl's.* [F] —**gaucherie,** n.

gaucho /ˈɡaʊtʃoʊ/, n., pl. **-chos** /-tʃoʊz/. a South American cowboy, of mixed Spanish and Indian descent. [Sp]

Gaudi /gaʊˈdi/, n. **Antonio,** 1852–1926, Spanish art nouveau architect.

gaudy /ˈɡɔdi/, adj., **-dier, -diest.** too bright and showy; flashy. [orig. attributive use of *gaudy* large bead of rosary, feast]

gauge /ɡeɪdʒ/, v., **gauged, gauging,** n. ◇v.t. 1. to judge; estimate; appraise: *to gauge someone's feelings.* 2. to measure: *to gauge the depth of a river; to gauge the size of a force.* ◇n. 3. a standard of measure. 4. a way of judging; criterion; test. 5. any instrument for measuring pressure, volume, or size, as a pressure gauge, micrometer gauge, etc. 6. the thickness of various (usu. thin) objects. 7. the distance between two railway rails. [ME, from ONF: measuring rod; of Celtic orig.]

Gauguin /ɡoʊˈgæ̃/, n. **Paul,** 1848–1903, French post-impressionist painter, much of whose art reflects his years in Tahiti.

Gaul /ɡɔl/, n. a former region including France, northern Italy, Belgium, Germany west of the Rhine and the southern Netherlands. [L *Gallia*] —**Gaulish,** adj.

Gaullist /ˈɡɔləst, ˈɡoʊ-/, n. 1. a supporter of de Gaulle's postwar policies. 2. a French person who, during World War II, supported de Gaulle in his opposition to the German occupation of France.

gaunt /ɡɔnt/, adj. very thin; haggard. [ME, from F: yellowish]

gauntlet[1] /ˈɡɔntlət/, n. 1. a metal glove worn in medieval times to protect the hand. 2. a glove with a long cuff for the wrist. 3. **take up/throw down the gauntlet,** to

gauntlet accept/give out a challenge, originally to a duel. [ME, from OF: little glove, from Gmc]

gauntlet² /'gɔntlət/, *n. in the phrase* **run the gauntlet**. **1.** to be forced to run between two rows of men who strike with weapons as one passes (a former common military punishment). **2.** to do something very dangerous. [Swed *gatlopp*, lit., lane run]

gauss /gaus/, *n. Elect.* the unit of magnetic induction in the c.g.s. system, equal to 0.1×10^{-3} teslas. [named after KF GAUSS]

Gauss /gaus/, *n.* **Karl Friedrich** /kal 'fridrɪk/, 1777-1855, German mathematician, developed number theory and applied mathematics.

Gautama /'gautəmə/, *n.* the Sanskrit form of the name adopted by Siddhartha, the founder of Buddhism, on becoming a monk. Also, **Gotama**.

gauze /gɔz/, *n.* **1.** any thin transparent cloth. **2.** some similar open material, as of wire. [F *gaze*, named after *Gaza*, an eastern Mediterranean seaport]

gave /geɪv/, *v.* past tense of **give**.

gavel /'gævəl/, *n.* a small hammer used by the person in charge of a meeting to signal for quiet. [orig. unknown]

gavotte /gə'vɒt/, *n.* **1.** an old French dance in fairly quick 4/4 time. **2.** a piece of music for, or in the rhythm of, this dance. [F, from Pr *gavoto* dance of the Gavots (Alpine mountaineers)]

Gawain /'gaweɪn/, *n. Arthurian Legend.* one of the knights of the Round Table, King Arthur's nephew.

gawk /gɔk/, *n.* **1.** an awkward, foolish person. ◇*v.i.* **2.** *Colloq.* to stare stupidly. Also, **gawp**. [OE *gagol* foolish + *-oc* -OCK]

gawky /'gɔki/, *adj.*, **-kier**, **-kiest**. awkward; ungainly; clumsy.

Gawler /'gɔlə/, *n.* a town in south-eastern SA, north of Adelaide; wine, wheat and fruit area. Pop. 11 354 (1986). [named after G *Gawler*, governor of SA 1838–41]

gay /geɪ/, *adj.*, **gayer**, **gayest**. **1.** having or showing a happy mood: *gay spirits; gay music; gay scenes.* **2.** bright or showy: *gay colors; gay flowers; gay ornaments.* **3.** too concerned with pleasure; licentious. **4.** *Colloq.* homosexual. [ME, from OF]

Gay-Lussac's law /ˌgeɪ-luːˌsæks 'lɔː/, *n.* a law which states that when gases combine, they do so in a simple ratio, by volume, to each other and to the gaseous product. [named after JL *Gay-Lussac*, 1778-1850, French chemist and physicist]

Gaza Strip /ˌgazə 'strɪp/, *n.* an area on the eastern Mediterranean coast, formerly in the Palestine mandate; administered by Israel since 1967.

gaze /geɪz/, *v.*, **gazed**, **gazing**, *n.* ◇*v.i.* **1.** to look steadily and for a long time. ◇*n.* **2.** a long steady look. [ME, from Scand]

gazebo /gə'zibou/, *n., pl.* **-bos**, **-boes**. a structure having a wide view, esp. a turret, pavilion, or summerhouse. [? pseudo-Latin coinage on GAZE, *v.*, after L *vidēbō* I shall see]

gazelle /gə'zɛl/, *n.* any of various small antelopes, noted for graceful movements and large bright eyes. [F, from Ar]

gazette /gə'zɛt/, *n., v.*, **-zetted**, **-zetting**. ◇*n.* **1.** a newspaper (now common only in newspaper titles). **2.** an official government magazine, containing lists of government appointments, etc. ◇*v.t.* **3.** to announce or list in a gazette. [F, from It, orig. a Venetian coin (the price of the gazette)]

gazetteer /ˌgæzə'tɪə/, *n.* a geographical dictionary. [F (obs.) *gazettier*]

gazump /gə'zʌmp/, *v.t.* **1.** to bypass (a buyer of real estate with whom a price has been agreed) by selling at a higher price to another. **2.** to force a buyer to accept a price higher than that previously agreed upon.

GB /dʒi 'bi/, *Abbrev.* Great Britain.

Gdańsk /gə'dænsk/, *n.* a seaport, formerly a member of the Hanseatic League, in northern Poland; shipbuilding. Pop. 464 600 (1983 est.). German, **Danzig**.

GDP /dʒi di 'pi/, *Abbrev.* Gross Domestic Product.

GDR /dʒi di 'a/, *Abbrev.* German Democratic Republic.

Ge, *Chem. Symbol.* germanium.

geanticline /dʒi'æntəklaɪn/, *n. Geol.* an anticline that extends over a large part of the earth's surface.

gear /gɪə/, *n.* **1.** *Mech.* a device for passing on or changing movement, as by toothed wheels. **2.** tools or apparatus, esp. as used for a particular operation. **3.** personal possessions; goods. **4.** *Colloq.* clothes. ◇*v.t.* **5.** to provide with or connect by gearing. **6.** to prepare or fit (someone or something) for a particular situation: *He gears his cooking to his family's tastes.* [ME, from Scand]

gearbox /'gɪəbɒks/, *n.* the case in which gears are enclosed, esp. in a motor vehicle.

gearing /'gɪərɪŋ/, *n.* the parts collectively by which movement is passed on in machinery, esp. a series of toothed wheels.

gear-ratio /'gɪə-reɪʃioʊ/, *n.* **1.** the ratio of the speed of the rod driving a system of gears to that of the gear system itself. **2.** the ratio of the number of engine revolutions to the number of revolutions of the rear wheel of a motor car.

gearstick /'gɪəstɪk/, *n.* the device for connecting gears for passing on power, esp. in a motor vehicle. Also, **gearlever**, **gearshift**.

gearwheel /'gɪəwil/, *n.* a wheel having teeth which connect with those of another wheel or part.

gecko /'gɛkoʊ/, *n., pl.* **-os**, **-oes**. a small, harmless lizard mostly active at night. [Malay *gēkoq*; imitative]

gee¹ /dʒi/, *interj., n.* (a word of command to horses, etc., directing them to go faster (fol. by *up*).)

gee² /dʒi/, *interj.* (a word expressing surprise or delight.) Also, **gee whiz.** [var. of JESUS]

geebung /'dʒibʌŋ/, *n.* (an Australian shrub or tree with) small, juicy, but tasteless fruit. [Aboriginal]

geek /gik/, *n. Colloq.* a look. Also, **geez, gig, gink.** [? Brit d. *geck* to toss the head]

Geelong /dʒə'lɒŋ/, *n.* a city and port in southern Victoria, about 30 km south-west of Melbourne. Pop. 125 833 (1986).

geese /gis/, *n.* plural of **goose.**

geezer /'gizə/, *n. Colloq.* an odd character. Also, **geeser.** [from GUISE]

Gehenna /gə'hɛnə/, *n. Bible.* (in the Old Testament) any place of extreme torment or suffering, esp. the valley of Hinnom, near Jerusalem. [See II Kings 23:10, Jer. 19:5. LL, from Gk, from Heb]

Geiger counter /'gaɪgə kaʊntə/, *n.* an instrument for counting ionising particles, used to measure the degree of radioactivity after the explosion of an atom bomb, and to study cosmic rays, etc. Also, **Geiger-Müller counter.** [named after Hans *Geiger*, 1882-1947, German physicist]

geisha /'geɪʃə/, *n., pl.* **-sha, -shas.** a Japanese girl, trained to amuse men with singing, dancing and conversation. [Jap]

gel /dʒɛl/, *n., v.,* **gelled, gelling.** ◇*n.* **1.** *Phys Chem.* a semi-solid colloidal dispersion of a solid with a liquid or gas, as jelly, etc. See **sol².** **2.** a jelly-like substance applied to the hair in order to keep it in a particular style. ◇*v.i.* **3.** to form or become a gel. [short for GELATINE]

gelatine /'dʒɛlətin, dʒɛlə'tin/, *n.* **1.** an almost tasteless organic substance, obtained by boiling bones, skin, etc., of animals in water, and used in forming jellies, glues, etc. **2.** any of various similar substances, as vegetable gelatine. [F, from It: jelly, from L: frozen, congealed]

gelatinous /dʒə'lætənəs/, *adj.* **1.** jellylike. **2.** relating to or consisting of gelatine.

gelato /dʒə'latoʊ/, *n.* an iced sweet made from cream, milk or water, with fruit or other flavoring, and whipped at a very low temperature. [It]

geld /gɛld/, *v.t.,* **gelded** or **gelt, gelding.** to castrate (esp. animals). [ME, from Scand]

gelding /'gɛldɪŋ/, *n.* a castrated animal, esp. a horse. [ME, from Scand]

Geldof /'gɛldɒf/, *n.* **Bob** (*Robert Frederick Xenon Geldof*), born 1951, Irish rock singer and humanitarian; in 1984 founded Band Aid, a charity to raise money for African famine victims by the sale of records, rock concerts, etc.

gelignite /'dʒɛlɪgnaɪt/, *n.* an explosive containing nitroglycerine, nitrocellulose, potassium nitrate and wood pulp, which is used for blasting.

Gellert /'gɛlət/, *n.* **Leon,** 1892-1977, Australian poet and journalist; noted for his World War I poetry.

gem /dʒɛm/, *n.* **1.** a stone used in jewellery, after cutting and polishing. **2.** something or someone likened to a gem because of beauty or worth: *This stamp is the gem of the collection.* [ME, from F, from L: bud, jewel]

gemfish /'dʒɛmfɪʃ/, *n.* a popular silver food fish, found off the coast of NSW and Vic.

Gemini /'dʒɛmənaɪ/, *n.* **1.** the Twins, a constellation and sign of the zodiac. **2.** *Astronautics.* any of a series of manned US spacecraft launched between the Mercury and Apollo projects. [L, pl. of *geminus* twin]

gemma /'dʒɛmə/, *n., pl.* **gemmae** /'dʒɛmi/. **1.** *Bot.* a cell or group of cells, or a leaf- or budlike body, which separates from the parent plant and forms a new plant, as in mosses, liverworts, etc. **2.** a bud, esp. a leaf bud. **3.** *Zool.* → **gemmule.** [L: bud, germ]

gemmation /dʒɛ'meɪʃən/, *n.* the process of reproduction by gemmae.

gemmule /'dʒɛmjul/, *n.* **1.** *Bot.* → **gemma.** **2.** *Zool.* a mass of cells not sexually produced that will develop into an animal. **3.** *Biol.* one of the living units thought by Darwin to exist and be the bearers of hereditary characteristics. [L: little bud]

gemstone /'dʒɛmstoʊn/, *n.* a precious stone; jewel.

gen /dʒɛn/, *n., v.,* **genned, genning.** *Colloq.* ◇*n.* **1.** all the necessary information about a subject. ◇*v.i.* **2.** to become informed (about) (fol. by *up*). [shortened form of *general information*]

-gen, a suffix meaning **1.** something produced, or growing, as in *antigen*. **2.** something that produces, as in *hydrogen, oxygen*. [F *-gène,* from Gk *-genēs* born, produced, from *gen-* bear, produce]

gen., *Abbrev.* **1.** gender. **2.** general. **3.** genitive. **4.** genus.

Gen, *Abbrev.* **1.** *Mil.* General. **2.** *Bible.* Genesis.

gendarme /ʒɒn'dam/, *n., pl.* **-darmes** /-'damz/. (in France and other European countries) a military policeman who in peacetime does ordinary police work. [F: men at arms]

gender /'dʒɛndə/, *n.* **1.** *Gram.* **a.** (in many languages) a set of classes, such as masculine, feminine and neuter, which together include all nouns. **b.** one class of such a set. **2. a.** the condition of being male or female. **b.** *Colloq.* sex. [ME, from L: race, kind, sort, gender]

gene /dʒin/, *n.* the unit of inheritance, associated with deoxyribonucleic acid, which is situated on the chromosome, and which determines and passes on hereditary characteristics. [Gk: breed, kind]

genealogy /dʒini'ælədʒi/, *n., pl.* **-gies.** **1.** an account of the ancestry of a person or family. **2.** the study of family descent. [ME, from LL, from Gk: tracing of descent] —**genealogical, genealogic,** *adj.* —**genealogist,** *n.*

genera /'dʒɛnərə/, *n.* plural of **genus.**

general /'dʒenrəl/, *adj.* **1.** relating to, including, or for all; not particular: *a general election.* **2.** common; widespread; prevalent: *The general practice at this school is to wear uniforms.* **3.** not limited to one class or field; miscellaneous: *the general public; general knowledge.* **4.** not limited to particular details; not specific: *general instructions.* **5.** having a high or chief rank (oft. follows noun): *a general officer; governor-general.* ◇*n.* **6.** *Mil.* **a.** an officer of the highest rank in the Army. See Appendix. **b.** a military commander: *Julius Caesar was a great general.* **7. in general, a.** relating to the whole class referred to. **b.** commonly; usually. [ME, from L: of or belonging to a (whole) race, kind]

General Agreement on Tariffs and Trade, *n.* an international trade agreement made in 1948 to safeguard tariffs against other forms of economic protection. *Abbrev.:* GATT

general anaesthetic *or* **general anesthetic,** *n.* a drug which anaesthetises the whole body and brings about loss of consciousness.

General Assembly *n.* one of the principal bodies within the United Nations, and the only one in which all members are represented.

General Australian, *n.* that pronunciation of Australian English adopted by the majority of Australians.

general election, *n.* a parliamentary election, in which all seats in the house are thrown open, as a federal or state election for the Lower House.

generalise *or* **generalize** /'dʒenrəlaɪz/, *v., -lised, -lising.* ◇*v.t.* **1.** to give a general (rather than specific or special) character to. **2.** to form (a general principle, etc.) from studying facts, etc. **3.** to bring into general use or knowledge. ◇*v.i.* **4.** to form general ideas or principles. **5.** to talk generally or vaguely. —**generalisation,** *n.*

generality /dʒenə'ræləti/, *n., pl.* **-ties. 1.** a general or vague statement: *to speak in generalities.* **2.** a general principle, rule or law. **3.** the greater part; majority: *the generality of people.* **4.** the state or quality of being general.

generally /'dʒenrəli/, *adv.* **1.** with respect to the larger part; commonly: *a claim generally recognised.* **2.** usually; ordinarily: *He generally arrives at noon.* **3.** not relating to particular persons or things: *generally speaking.*

general practitioner, *n.* a doctor who does not specialise in any particular branch of medicine but is responsible for the general health of a number of people in a district. *Abbrev.:* GP

generate /'dʒenəreɪt/, *v.t.,* **-rated, -rating. 1.** to bring into existence; give rise to; produce: *The sun generates heat; His behaviour generated hatred in her.* **2.** *Geom.* to trace out (a figure) by the movement of another figure. [L: begotten]

generation /dʒenə'reɪʃən/, *n.* **1.** the whole body of people born about the same time: *the new generation.* **2.** a period of years (commonly thirty) accepted as the average difference of age between one generation of a family and the next. **3.** a single stage in the natural descent of human beings, animals, or plants. **4.** the act or process of generating; reproduction. **5.** *Geom.* the production of a figure by the movement of another figure. [ME, from L]

generation gap, *n.* the difference in opinions and understanding between members of different generations.

generative /'dʒenərətɪv/, *adj.* **1.** relating to the production of offspring. **2.** capable of generation.

generator /'dʒenəreɪtə/, *n.* a machine which changes mechanical energy into electrical energy; dynamo. [L]

generic /dʒə'nerɪk/, *adj.* **1.** relating to a genus. **2.** referring to all the members of a genus or class. **3.** known by name of the product itself, not by particular brand name. Also, **generical.** [L *genus* kind + -IC]

generosity /dʒenə'rɒsəti/, *n., pl.* **-ties. 1.** the quality of being generous. **2.** a generous act. [L: nobility, excellence]

generous /'dʒenərəs, 'dʒenrəs/, *adj.* **1.** ready to give freely; unselfish. **2.** free from smallness or pettiness of mind or character. **3.** given freely: *a generous gift.* **4.** plentiful; abundant: *a generous portion.* **5.** (of soil) rich; fertile. [L: of noble birth]

genesis /'dʒenəsəs/, *n., pl.* **-ses** /-sɪz/. **1.** origin; production; creation. **2.** (*cap.*) the first book of the Old Testament, telling of the beginnings of the world and of man. [ME, from L, from Gk: origin, creation]

genetic /dʒə'netɪk/, *adj.* **1.** *Biol.* relating or according to genetics. **2.** relating to origin. Also, **genetical.** [Gk: generative]

genetic code, *n.* the code, based on the arrangement of the molecular elements of the chromosomes, by which hereditary characteristics are passed on.

genetic engineering, *n.* the alteration of the chromosome structure of cells of organisms in an attempt to control the characteristics of the organisms that are reproduced.

genetics /dʒə'netɪks/, *n.* the science of heredity, dealing with similarities and differences of related organisms. —**geneticist,** *n.*

Geneva /dʒə'nivə/, *n.* a city in south-western Switzerland, on Lake Geneva; seat of the League of Nations, 1920–46. Pop. 159 895 (1986 est.).

Geneva Convention, *n.* an international agreement establishing rules for the treatment during war of the sick, the wounded, and prisoners of war. [orig. formulated in 1864 at GENEVA]

Genevieve /'dʒenəviv/, *n.* **Saint,** AD c. 422–512, French nun, patron saint of Paris.

Genghis Khan /ˌgeŋgəs 'kan/, *n.* 1162–1227, Mongol conqueror of most of Asia and of eastern Europe to the river Dnieper. Also, **Jenghis Khan, Jenghiz Khan.**

genial /'dʒiniəl/, *adj.* **1.** sympathetically cheerful; cordial: *a genial personality; a genial host.* **2.** enlivening; supporting life; pleasantly warm, or mild. [L: festive, jovial, pleasant, lit.,

genial ... relating to generation or to marriage] —**geniality**, *n*.

genic /'dʒɛnɪk/, *adj*. of, relating to, or originating from a gene or genes.

genie /'dʒini/, *n*. a spirit of Arabian mythology. [F, from L *genius*. See GENIUS]

genital /'dʒɛnɪtl/, *adj*. relating to (the organs of) reproduction. [L]

genitals /'dʒɛnɪtlz/, *n.pl*. the reproductive organs, esp. the external sex organs. Also, **genitalia** /dʒɛnə'teɪliə/.

genitive case /'dʒɛnətɪv keɪs/, *n. Gram*. See case[1] and Appendix. [ME, from L: relating to generation]

genius /'dʒiniəs/, *n., pl*. **geniuses** *for defs 1-4, 7*, **genii** /'dʒiniaɪ/ *for defs 5, 6*. **1.** great natural ability for original ideas; highest level of mental ability. **2.** a person having such ability. **3.** natural ability: *He has a genius for fixing cars*. **4.** special character or spirit of a nation, period, language, etc. **5.** the spirit which attends and guards a place, etc. **6.** either of two opposed spirits, one good and the other evil, supposed to attend a person throughout his or her life. **7.** a person who strongly influences the life of another: *She is my evil genius*. [L: guardian spirit, any spiritual being, disposition, orig. a male generative or creative principle]

Genoa /'dʒɛnəwə/, *n*. Italy's most important seaport, situated in the north-western region of Liguria. Pop. 731 484 (1986 est.).

genocide /'dʒɛnəsaɪd/, *n*. the planned killing of a whole national or racial group. [Gk *géno(s)* race + -CIDE; coined by Dr Raphael Lemkin, 1944] —**genocidal**, *adj*.

genome /'dʒinoʊm/, *n*. the complete genetic material for any cell.

genotype /'dʒɛnətaɪp/, *n*. **1.** the basic hereditary structure of an organism. **2.** its breeding formula of genes. **3.** a group of organisms with a common heredity.

-genous, a suffix forming adjectives from nouns ending in -**gen** and -**geny**. [-GEN + -OUS]

genre /'ʒɒnrə/, *n*. **1.** kind; sort; genus. **2.** *Art*. paintings etc., which represent scenes from ordinary life (as opposed to landscapes, etc.). [F: kind]

gent /dʒɛnt/, *n. (oft. joc.)* a gentleman.

genteel /dʒɛn'til/, *adj*. **1.** belonging or suited to polite society. **2.** unnaturally polite or proper in manners and speech. [F]

gentian /'dʒɛnʃən/, *n*. a type of herb with blue, or sometimes white, yellow or red, flowers. [ME, from L; said to be named after *Gentius*, an Illyrian king]

gentile /'dʒɛntaɪl/, *adj., n*. (of or relating to) any person or people not Jewish, esp. Christians. [ME, from L: belonging to a people, national, LL: foreign]

gentility /dʒɛn'tɪləti/, *n., pl*. -**ties**. **1.** the quality or state of being genteel. **2.** birth into the upper classes.

gentle /'dʒɛntl/, *adj.*, -**tler**, -**tlest**. **1.** kindly; amiable: *gentle words*. **2.** not severe, rough, or violent: *a gentle wind; a gentle tap*. **3.** gradual: *a gentle slope*. **4.** of upper class birth or family. **5.** easily handled: *a gentle animal*. **6.** soft or low: *a gentle sound*. **7.** *Archaic*. polite; refined: *a gentle lady*. **8.** *Archaic*. noble; chivalrous: *a gentle knight*. [ME, from OF: of good family, noble, excellent, from L]

gentleman /'dʒɛntlmən/, *n., pl*. -**men**. **1.** (as a polite form of speech) any man. **2.** a man of high social position by birth, esp. one who does not work for a living. **3.** *Brit Hist*. a man above the rank of yeoman.

gentlemen's agreement, *n*. an agreement made binding by honor alone, not law.

gentlewoman /'dʒɛntlwumən/, *n., pl*. -**women**. **1.** a woman of upper-class family or breeding; lady. **2.** *Brit Hist*. a woman who attends upon a lady of rank.

gentry /'dʒɛntri/, *n*. **1.** people of high birth or social position. **2.** *Brit*. the land-owning class below the nobility. [ME, from *gent* noble + -RY]

genuflect /'dʒɛnjəflɛkt/, *v.i*. to bend the knee or knees, esp. as mark of respect or worship. [L *genū* knee + *flectere* bend]

genuine /'dʒɛnjuən/, *adj*. **1.** being truly such; real; authentic: *genuine regret; genuine worth*. **2.** sincere; free from pretence: *a genuine person*. [L: native, natural, authentic, genuine]

genus /'dʒinəs/, *n., pl*. **genera** /'dʒɛnərə/. **1.** a kind; sort; class. **2.** *Biol*. the main subdivision of a family or subfamily of animals or plants, usu. consisting of more than one species, basically very similar to one another and regarded as very closely related. [L: race, stock, kind, sort, gender]

-geny, a suffix meaning 'origin'. [Gk -*geneia*, from -*genēs* born, produced. See -GEN]

geo-, a word part meaning 'the earth', as in *geology, geocentric*. [Gk, combining form of *gē*]

geocentric /dʒioʊ'sɛntrɪk/, *adj*. **1.** *Astron*. viewed or measured from the centre of the earth. **2.** having or representing the earth as a centre: *a geocentric theory of the universe*.

geochemistry /dʒioʊ'kɛməstri/, *n*. the science dealing with chemical structure of and changes in the earth, esp. the crust. —**geochemist**, *n*.

geodesic /dʒioʊ'dɛsɪk, -'dɪsɪk/, *adj*. **1.** Also, **geodesical**. relating to the geometry of curved surfaces, in which geodesic lines replace the straight lines of plane geometry. ◇*n*. **2.** Also, **geodesic line**. the shortest line on a given surface and connecting two given points.

geodesic dome, *n*. a dome built from a latticework of polygons so that the pressure load is shared evenly throughout the structure, with the result that the larger the dome, the stronger it is.

geography /dʒi'ɒgrəfi/, *n., pl*. -**phies**. **1.** the study of the earth's surface and the interrelations of such features as climate, relief, soil, vegetation, population, land use, industries, or states. **2.** the natural features of an area. [L,

geography   429   **germ**

from Gk] —**geographer**, *n.* —**geographical**, *adj.*

geoid /'dʒiɔid/, *n.* **1.** an imaginary surface representing the average sea-level over the ocean and under the land masses. **2.** the geometrical figure formed by this surface, being an ellipsoid flattened at the poles. [Gk: earthlike]

geological time, /dʒiəˌlɒdʒɪkəl 'taɪm/ *n.* the time covering the development of the planet earth to the present; about 5000 million years.

geology /dʒi'ɒlədʒi/, *n., pl.* **-gies. 1.** the science which deals with the structure of the earth, esp. the rocks of which it is formed. **2.** the geological characteristics of a particular place. [NL. See GEO-, -LOGY] —**geologist**, *n.* —**geological**, *adj.*

geometric /dʒiə'mɛtrɪk/, *adj.* **1.** of or relating to geometry. **2.** similar to or using the lines or figures of geometry: *a geometric pattern.* Also, **geometrical**.

geometric progression, *n.* a series of terms in which each is different from the following by a constant ratio, as 1, 3, 9, 27, 81 and 243.

geometry /dʒi'ɒmətri/, *n.* **1.** the branch of mathematics which deals with the properties of figures in space. **2.** the shape of a surface or solid. [ME, from L, from Gk]

geomorphic /dʒiou'mɔfɪk/, *adj.* **1.** of or relating to the figure of the earth, or the forms of its surface. **2.** similar to the earth in form.

geomorphology /ˌdʒioumɔ'fɒlədʒi/, *n.* the study of the characteristics, origin, and development of land forms.

geophysics /dʒiou'fɪzɪks/, *n.* the physics of the earth, esp. the study by instruments of the parts of the earth which cannot be reached by people. —**geophysicist**, *n.*

Geordie /'dʒɔdi/, *n.* a person who works or lives near the river Tyne in north-eastern England. [diminutive of *George*, proper name]

George[1] /dʒɔdʒ/, *n.* **Saint**, died AD 303?, Christian martyr, patron saint of England; hero of a legend in which he killed a dragon.

George[2] /dʒɔdʒ/, *n.* **Lake**, a basin in NSW, between Goulburn and Canberra; noted for its tendency to periodically completely dry up.

George III, *n.* 1738–1820, king of England 1760–1820 (grandson of George II). His periodic insanity led to regency rule by his son from 1811.

George V, *n.* 1865–1936, king of England 1910–36 (son of Edward VII); changed the name of the royal house to Windsor.

George VI, *n.* 1895–1952, king of England 1936–52 (second son of George V); succeeded to the throne on the abdication of his brother, Edward VIII.

George Town, a town in northern Tas, near the mouth of the Tamar River; site of the first white settlement in northern Tas, 1804. Pop. 5315 (1986).

georgette /dʒɔ'dʒɛt/, *n.* thin silk or rayon crepe of dull finish. Also, **georgette crepe**.

Georgia /'dʒɔdʒə/, *n.* **1.** a republic in western Asia, bordering on the Black Sea; a constituent member of the Soviet Union 1922–91, known as the **Georgian Soviet Socialist Republic**; previously an independent kingdom for about 2000 years. Pop. 5 443 000 (1989 est.); 43 290 km^2. *Cap.:* Tbilisi. **2.** a state in the south-eastern US. Pop. 6 104 000 (1986 est.); 152 489 km^2. *Cap:* Atlanta. *Abbrev.:* Ga —**Georgian**, *n., adj.*

Georgian /'dʒɔdʒiən, -dʒən/, *adj.* relating to the four Georges, kings of England (1714–1830), or their period.

geosyncline /dʒiou'sɪŋklaɪn/, *n.* a part of the earth's crust that has sunk inwards, usu. long and containing great thicknesses of rocks. —**geosynclinal**, *adj.*

geotectonic /ˌdʒioutɛk'tɒnɪk/, *adj.* relating to the structure of the earth's crust or the arrangement and form of its elements.

geothermic /dʒiou'θɜmɪk/, *adj.* of or relating to the inner heat of the earth. Also, **geothermal** /dʒiou'θɜməl/.

geotropic /dʒiou'trɒpɪk/, *adj.* taking a particular direction in relation to the earth:
a. positively geotropic, directed downwards.
b. negatively geotropic, directed upwards.
c. transversely geotropic, directed horizontally.

geotropism /dʒi'ɒtrəpɪzəm/, *n.* the response of a plant or an animal to gravitation, as the direction of growth of plants. **Positive geotropism** is a movement towards the earth, **negative geotropism** a movement away.

ger., *Abbrev.* **1.** gerund. **2.** gerundive.

Ger, *Abbrev.* **1.** German. **2.** Germany.

Geraldton /'dʒɛrəltən/, *n.* a port on the western coast of WA, east of the Houtman Abrolhos; the state's second largest port; important fishing centre, port for gold and iron ore fields. Pop. 21 726 (1986). [named after a governor of WA, Charles Fitz*gerald*]

Geraldton waxflower, *n.* an evergreen shrub of western Australia, often cultivated elsewhere for its delicate, often pale pink flowers. Also, **Geraldton wax**.

geranium /dʒə'reɪniəm/, *n.* a common garden plant, some types of which are climbers, mostly having red, pink or purple flowers. See **pelargonium**. [L, from Gk: crane's-bill]

geriatric /dʒɛri'ætrɪk/, *adj.* **1.** of or relating to geriatrics or to old people. ◇*n.* **2.** an old person, esp. one who is ill. [Gk *gēras* old age + *iātrikós* of medicine]

geriatrics /dʒɛri'ætrɪks/, *n.* the branch of medicine dealing with old people. —**geriatrician, geriatrist**, *n.*

germ /dʒɜm/, *n.* **1.** a micro-organism, esp. when disease-producing; microbe. **2.** that from which anything originates, as an idea. **3.** that from which a living organism develops, as a bud, offshoot, seed or embryo in its early stages. **4.** *Biol.* the first stage in development or evolution, as a germ cell or ancestral form. [F]

german /ˈdʒɜmən/, *adj.* **1.** having the same father and mother (always placed after the noun): *a brother-german.* **2.** having a parent who is the brother or sister of one's father or mother: *a cousin-german.* [L: having the same father (and mother)]

German /ˈdʒɜmən/, *adj.* relating to Germany, its inhabitants, or their language.

germane /dʒɜˈmeɪn/, *adj.* closely related; pertinent: *a remark germane to the question.* [var. of GERMAN]

German East Africa, *n.* a former German territory in eastern Africa; now comprised of Tanzania, Rwanda, and Burundi.

Germanic /dʒɜˈmænɪk/, *adj.* of the Teutonic race, the peoples belonging to it, or the group of languages spoken by these peoples; Teutonic.

germanium /dʒɜˈmeɪniəm/, *n.* a rare metallic element, normally tetravalent, with a greyish white color. *Symbol:* Ge; *at. no.:* 32; *at. wt:* 72.59. [NL, from L *Germānia* country of the Germans]

German measles, *n.* an infectious disease marked by fever and rash, usu. not serious except in a pregnant woman, when it may cause her baby to be born deformed; rubella.

German New Guinea, *n.* former name of the Trust Territory of New Guinea, comprising the north-eastern section of the main island of New Guinea, the Bismarck Archipelago and adjacent islands; administered by Germany until World War I.

German shepherd, *n.* (oft. l.c.) a breed of large dog much used for police work, or as guide-dogs, etc.; Alsatian.

Germany /ˈdʒɜməni/, *n.* **1.** a country in central Europe, bounded by Czechoslovakia, Poland, Austria, Liechtenstein, Switzerland, France, Luxembourg, Belgium and the Netherlands; united under Prussian leadership in 1871; partitioned as **East Germany** and **West Germany** in the late 1940s during the Allied occupation after World War II; reunified in 1990. Pop. 78 000 000 (1990 est.); 357 041 km². *Language:* German. *Currency:* Deutschmark. *Cap.:* Berlin. Official name, **Federal Republic of Germany.** German, **Deutschland.**

germ cell, *n. Biol.* the sexual reproductive cell at any stage from the primordial cell to the mature gamete.

germinal /ˈdʒɜmənəl/, *adj.* **1.** relating to a germ or germs. **2.** of the nature of a germ or germ cell. **3.** in the earliest stage of development: *germinal ideas.*

germinate /ˈdʒɜməneɪt/, *v.,* -nated, -nating. ◇*v.i.* **1.** to begin to grow or develop. **2.** *Bot.* **a.** (of a seed, bulb, etc.) to develop into a plant. **b.** to sprout; put forth shoots. ◇*v.t.* **3.** to cause to develop; produce. [L] —**germination,** *n.* —**germinator,** *n.*

germ theory, *n. Biol.* the theory that living matter cannot be produced by evolution or development from non-living matter, but only from germs or seeds.

Geronimo /dʒəˈrɒnəmoʊ/, *n.* c. 1834–1909, Apache Indian chief, who led guerrilla raids against Mexican and US troops.

gerontology /dʒɛrənˈtɒlədʒi/, *n.* the study of old age. —**gerontologist,** *n.*

-gerous, a combining form meaning 'bearing' or 'producing'. [L *-ger* bearing + -OUS]

gerrymander /ˈdʒɛrimændə/, *n.* **1.** *Politics.* an arrangement of the political divisions of an electorate, etc., made so as to give one party an unfair advantage in elections. ◇*v.t.* **2.** *Politics.* to arrange (an electorate, etc.) in such a way. [(Gerry (governor of Massachusetts, US, whose party in 1812 redistributed the electoral boundaries of Massachusetts) + (SALA)MANDER (from a fancied resemblance to this animal of the gerrymandered map of Massachusetts)]

gerund /ˈdʒɛrənd/, *n. Gram.* a noun formed from a verb as *running* and *writing* in the sentences 'Running is good exercise' and 'Writing is easy'. [L *gerere* bear, conduct]

gerundive /dʒəˈrʌndɪv/, *n. Gram.* (sometimes) the English *-ing* form of a verb when it has a mixture of noun and adjective uses, as *being fixed* in the sentence 'I depend on the car being fixed'. [LL *gerundīvus,* from *gerundium* GERUND]

Gestalt /ɡəˈʃtælt/, *n., pl.* -stalten /-ˈʃtæltən/. (in psychology) an organised arrangement or pattern of experiences or acts: *The Gestalt of a melody is distinct from the separate notes.* [G: form]

Gestalt psychology, *n.* a school of psychology which believes that experiences and behavior are not based on the sum of individual reactions, etc., but on organised patterns which are considered whole units and called *Gestalten.*

Gestapo /ɡəˈstɑpoʊ/, *n.* the Secret State Police of Nazi Germany who acted brutally to suppress opposition to Hitler's regime. [G *Ge(heime) Sta(ats)po(lizei)*]

gestate /ˈdʒɛsteɪt/, *v.t.,* -tated, -tating. to carry in the uterus from conception to birth. [L: carried]

gestation /dʒɛsˈteɪʃən/, *n.* the act or period of gestating. [L *gestātiō* a carrying]

gesticulate /dʒɛsˈtɪkjəleɪt/, *v.,* -lated, -lating. ◇*v.i.* **1.** to make or use movements, esp. of the hands. ◇*v.t.* **2.** to express by gesticulating. [L: having made mimic gestures] —**gesticulation,** *n.* —**gesticulation,** *n.*

gesture /ˈdʒɛstʃə/, *n., v.,* -tured, -turing. ◇*n.* **1.** a movement of part of the body that expresses an idea or feeling: *a gesture of impatience.* **2.** any action intended for effect or as a formality: *a gesture of friendship.* ◇*v.i.* **3.** to make or use gestures. ◇*v.t.* **4.** to express by gestures. [ME, from L: bear, conduct]

get /ɡɛt/, *v.,* **got, getting.** ◇*v.t.* **1.** to obtain by any means: *to get a new dress; to get service.* **2.** to bring; fetch: *I will go and get it.* **3.** to receive or be given: *He got five years for theft.* **4.** to obtain by work; earn: *He gets $200 a week.* **5.** to hear or understand: *I didn't get the last word.* **6.** to suffer from (an illness, etc.): *Have you got a cold?* **7.** to reach (someone): *Can you get him on the phone?* **8.** to cause to be or do: *I must get my hair cut; I can't get the fire to burn.* **9.** *Colloq.* to be under a duty to; be obliged to: *You have got to go.* **10.** to prepare: *to get dinner.* **11.** to give birth to (now usu. of animals). **12.** *Colloq.* to hit: *The bullet got him in the leg.* **13.** *Colloq.* to repay for some wrongdoing: *I'll get you for that.* **14.** *Colloq.* to puzzle; baffle: *This question has got me.* **15.** to answer: *Who'll get the phone?* ◊*v.i.* **16.** to come to or arrive: *When did you get there?* **17.** to become; grow: *to get tired.* **18.** to succeed in coming or going (fol. by *away, in, into, out, over, through*, etc.). ◊*v.* **19.** Some special uses are:

get about, 1. to move about. **2.** (of news, etc.) to become known.
get across, to make understood.
get ahead, to be successful; make progress.
get at, 1. to reach; make contact with: *I can't get at it.* **2.** *Colloq.* to suggest; imply: *What's she getting at?* **3.** *Colloq.* to cause to be dishonest, by bribery, etc.
get away, 1. to escape. **2.** to go away, esp. on holiday: *We shall get away this evening.*
get away with, to avoid punishment or blame for.
get back, 1. to return. **2.** to receive as a profit. **3.** to take revenge on (fol. by *at*).
get by, to manage in spite of difficulties.
get down to, to attend to; concentrate on.
get off, 1. to escape punishment, etc. **2.** to start a journey; leave. **3.** to come down from (a horse, train, etc.).
get on, 1. to age. **2.** to go ahead; make progress. **3.** to agree or be friendly (with).
get on one's nerves, to annoy; irritate.
get out, 1. (of information) to become publicly known. **2.** to succeed in solving (a puzzle, etc.).
get over, 1. to overcome (a difficulty, etc.). **2.** to recover from (a shock, illness, etc.).
get round, 1. to get into favor with (someone). **2.** to overcome (difficulties, etc.).
get round to, to come at last to (doing something).
get through to, 1. to make a telephone connection with. **2.** *Colloq.* to make (someone) understand.
get under one's skin, to annoy; irritate.
get up, 1. to sit up or stand. **2.** to rise from bed. **3.** to increase in force or violence (of wind, sea, etc.). **4.** to dress finely. **5.** to prepare, arrange, or organise: *to get up a party.* **6.** to gain a knowledge of: *to get up a subject.* **7.** to take part in (bad behavior, etc.) (fol. by *to*). [ME *geten*, from Scand]

getaway /'getəweɪ/, *n. Colloq.* an escape.

Gethsemane /gɛθ'sɛməni/, *n.* a garden east of Jerusalem; the scene of Christ's agony and betrayal. [See Matthew 26:36, etc.]

Gettysburg /'gɛtɪzbɜg/, *n.* a small town in the US, in southern Pennsylvania, site of an important defeat of Confederate forces, 1863, during the American Civil War; national cemetery and military park.

Gettysburg Address, *n.* President Lincoln's address at the dedication of the national cemetery at Gettysburg, in 1863.

gewgaw /'gigɔ, 'gjugɔ/, *n.* **1.** a bit of showy or useless ornament or jewellery. ◊*adj.* **2.** showy, but without value.

geyser /'gizə, 'gaɪzə/, *n.* a hot spring which at times sends up jets of water and steam into the air. [Icel *Geysir*, i.e. gusher, name of a hot spring in Iceland, from *geysa* rush furiously, gush]

geyserite /'gizəraɪt, 'gaɪ-/, *n.* a variety of opaline silica found about openings of geysers and hot springs.

GG /dʒi 'dʒi/, *Abbrev.* Governor-General.

Ghan /gæn/, *n.* **1.** *Colloq.* one of the Afghan camel drivers who came to Australia between 1860 and the 1920s. **2. the**, the Central Australia railway service which runs from Adelaide, SA, through Port Pirie to Alice Springs, NT. [a contraction of *Afghan*, the railway having been named after the Afghan camel-drivers]

Ghana /'ganə/, *n.* a republic on the west coast of Africa, bordered by Côte d'Ivoire, Togo and Upper Volta. Pop. 13 482 000 (1987 est.); 238 537 km². *Languages*: English, also local Sudanic dialects, chiefly Akan. *Currency*: new cedi. *Cap.*: Accra. –**Ghanaian, Ghanian**, *n.*, *adj.*

ghastly /'gastli/, *adj.*, -**lier**, -**liest**, *adv.* ◊*adj.* **1.** frightful; dreadful; horrible: *a ghastly murder.* **2.** very pale: *a ghastly look.* **3.** *Colloq.* bad; unpleasant: *a ghastly failure.* ◊*adv.* **4.** *Archaic.* with a deathlike appearance: *ghastly pale.* [OE *gāstlic* spectral]

gherkin /'gɜkən/, *n.* a small, unripe fruit of some common varieties of cucumber, used in pickling. [var. of *gurchen* (from G)]

ghetto /'gɛtoʊ/, *n.*, *pl.* **ghettos, ghettoes.** the part of a city in which any minority or poor group lives. [It (Venetian), b. Heb *ghēt* separation and It *ge(t)to* foundry, the name of Jewish quarter in Venice in the 16th C]

Ghiberti /gɪ'bɛəti/, *n.* **Lorenzo** /ləˈrɛntsoʊ/, 1378?–1455, Florentine sculptor and painter; noted for the bronze Gates of Paradise, doors of the Baptistery at Florence.

ghost /goʊst/, *n.* **1.** the spirit of a dead person imagined as wandering among or haunting living people. **2.** only a shadow or trace: *ghost of a chance.* **3.** (*cap.*) a spiritual being: *Holy Ghost.* **4.** *TV.* an annoying secondary image. **5. give up the ghost**, **a.** to die. **b.** (of machinery) to break down completely. ◊*v.t.* **6.** to work as a ghost writer for (someone). [OE *gāst*]

ghost gum, *n.* an inland Australian species of eucalypt, with a smooth white trunk.

ghost town, *n.* a deserted or nearly deserted town, such as a formerly wealthy goldmining town.

ghost writer, *n.* someone who writes speeches, stories, etc., for another who takes the honor.

ghoul /gul/, *n.* **1.** an evil spirit of oriental legend imagined to feed on human bodies. **2.** someone who enjoys what others find revolting. [Ar. *ghūl*]

GHQ /dʒi eɪtʃ 'kju/, *Abbrev.* General Headquarters.

GI /dʒi 'aɪ/, *n. Colloq.* a soldier, usu. not an officer, in any of the US armed forces. [abbrev. orig. of *galvanised iron*, used in US Army bookkeeping entries of articles made of it; then, by association with *government issue*, of the full range of articles issued and, finally, of the soldiers themselves]

Giacometti /dʒakoʊ'meti/, *n.* **Alberto** /al'bɛatoʊ/, 1901–66, Swiss sculptor and painter.

giant /'dʒaɪənt/, *n.* **1.** an imaginary creature of human form but superhuman size, strength, etc. **2.** someone or something of unusually great size, importance, intelligence, etc.: *an intellectual giant.* ◇*adj.* **3.** gigantic; huge: *the giant cactus.* [ME, from OF, from L, from Gk]

giant kingfisher, *n.* → kookaburra (def. 1).

giant perch, *n.* a large, silvery-grey, valued food fish found in coastal rivers of tropical northern Australia and the Indo-Pacific; barramundi.

Giant's Causeway, *n.* a promontory composed of hexagonal basalt columns in northern county Antrim, Northern Ireland.

gibber[1] /'dʒɪbə/, *v.i.* **1.** to speak in a disjointed way; chatter. ◇*n.* **2.** gibbering speech. [? obs. *gib*, v., caterwaul, behave like a cat]

gibber[2] /'gɪbə/, *n.* a stone; boulder. [Aboriginal]

gibberellic acid /dʒɪbə,rɛlɪk 'æsəd/, *n.* a metabolic product of a type of fungus, which stimulates plant growth.

gibberish /'dʒɪbərɪʃ/, *n.* fast talk which does not make sense. [GIBBER[1] + -ISH[1]]

gibber plain, /'gɪbə pleɪn/ *n.* a flat piece of desert land in dry areas of Australia, with many large boulders.

gibbet /'dʒɪbət/, *n., v.,* **-beted, -beting.** ◇*n.* **1.** a gallows with an arm at the top, from which the bodies of criminals were hung in chains and left hanging after execution. ◇*v.t.* **2.** to hang on a gibbet (until dead). **3.** to hold up to public scorn. [ME, from OF: little staff]

gibbon /'gɪbən/, *n.* any of the small, slender, long-armed apes found in southern Asia. [F, apparently from a dialect of India]

Gibbon /'gɪbən/, *n.* **Edward**, 1737–94, English historian, author of *The History of the Decline and Fall of the Roman Empire* (1776–88).

gibbous /'gɪbəs/, *adj.* **1.** humpbacked. **2.** (of a heavenly body) viewed so as to appear convex on both sides, such as the moon when more than half-full but less than full. Also, **gibbose** /'gɪboʊs/. [L: humped]

Gibbs /gɪbz/, *n.* **(Cecilia) May**, 1877–1969, Australian writer and illustrator of children's books, born in England; author of *Gumnut Babies* (1916).

gibe /dʒaɪb/, *v.,* **gibed, gibing**, *n.* ◇*v.i.* **1.** to use mocking words; scoff. ◇*n.* **2.** a taunting or sarcastic remark. Also, **jibe**. [? from OF: handle roughly, shake]

giblet /'dʒɪblət/, *n.* (*usu. pl.*) the heart, liver, or gizzard from a fowl. [ME, from OF: dish of game]

Gibraltar /dʒə'brɒltə, dʒa'brɒltə/, *n.* **1.** a British territory including an important naval and air base situated on a narrow promontory near the southern tip of Spain. Pop. 29 166 (1987 est.); 6 km². **2. Rock of.** Ancient name, **Calpe.** a long, precipitous mountain nearly coextensive with Gibraltar; one of the Pillars of Hercules. 426 m high; 4 km long. **3. Strait of,** a strait between Europe and Africa at the Atlantic entrance to the Mediterranean. 13–38 km wide. —**Gibraltarian**, *adj., n.*

Gibson /'gɪbsən/, *n.* **Mel**, born 1956 in the US, Australian actor, star of the *Mad Max* films.

Gibson Desert, *n.* an area of high plain in eastern central WA bounded by the Hopkins and Macdonald lakes to the east and Lake Disappointment in the west. 1.74 million ha. [named after Alfred *Gibson* who died on Ernest Giles' 1874 expedition]

giddy /'gɪdi/, *adj.,* **-dier, -diest.** **1.** silly and light; impulsive; flighty: *a giddy mind.* **2.** affected with a whirling sensation; dizzy: *During the dance the girl became giddy.* **3.** causing dizziness: *a giddy climb.* [OE *gydig* mad, from *god*; orig. sense presumably god-possessed, in a state of divine frenzy]

Gideon /'gɪdiən/, *n. Bible.* Hebrew liberator and religious leader, conqueror of the Midianites and judge in Israel for forty years. [See Judges 6-8]

gidgee /'gɪdʒi/, *n.* **1.** a small Australian tree which gives off an unpleasant smell at the approach of rain; stinking wattle. **2.** a long spear made from gidgee wood. Also, **gidya** /'gɪdiə/, **gidyea** /'gɪdiə/. [Aboriginal]

Gielgud /'gilgʊd/, *n.* **1. Sir John**, born 1904, English actor and stage director. **2.** his niece, **Maina**, born 1945, English ballet dancer; became artistic director of the Australian Ballet in 1982.

gift /gɪft/, *n.* **1.** something given; a present. **2.** the act of giving. **3.** a special ability or talent: *He has the gift of song.* **4.** *Colloq.* anything very easily obtained or understood: *The exam question was a gift.* **5. look a gift-horse in the mouth**, to accept a gift ungratefully or critically. [ME, from Scand]

gifted /'gɪftəd/, *adj.* provided with natural gifts; talented: *a gifted artist.*

gift token, *n.* a voucher given as a present allowing someone to choose goods worth a certain amount, usu. from a particular shop. Also, **gift voucher.**

gig[1] /gɪg/, *n.* **1.** *Naut.* a long, fast-pulling boat used esp. for racing. **2.** a light, two-wheeled, one-horse carriage. [orig. uncert.]

gig[2] /gɪg/, *n. Colloq.* **1.** a concert performance of jazz or modern popular music. **2.** a job, esp. a booking for a musician to perform. [orig. unknown]

gig[3] /gɪg/, *n. Colloq.* → geek.

gigantic /dʒaɪ'gæntɪk/, *adj.* **1.** of, like, or suitable for a giant. **2.** very large; huge. [L: giant + -IC]

giggle /'gɪgəl/, v., **-gled, -gling.** ◇v.i.
1. to laugh in a silly way, as from high spirits or uncontrolled amusement; titter. ◇n. 2. a laugh of this type. [apparently backformation from obs. *giglet* giddy, laughing girl] **–giggler,** n.

gigolo /'ʒɪgəloʊ/, n., pl. **-los.** 1. a man supported by a woman, esp. a young man supported by an older woman, in return for companionship. 2. a male professional dancing partner. [F]

Gilbert /'gɪlbət/, n. 1. **John,** 1810?–45, Australian naturalist and explorer, born in England. 2. **John,** c. 1842–65, Australian bushranger, associated first with Frank Gardiner's and then Ben Hall's gang. 3. **Kevin,** 1933–93, Australian playwright, poet, and Aboriginal activist; wrote the play *The Cherry Pickers.* 4. **Sir William Schwenck** 1836–1911, English dramatist, humorist and poet; collaborator with Sullivan.

Gilbert & Ellice Islands /'ɛlas/, n.pl. former name of **Kiribati** and **Tuvalu.**

gild /gɪld/, v.t., **gilded** or **gilt, gilding.** 1. to coat with gold, gold leaf, or a gold-colored substance. 2. to make (something) look (deceptively) bright or pleasing. [OE *gyldan,* from GOLD]

Giles /dʒaɪlz/, n. **(William) Ernest (Powell),** 1835–97, Australian explorer, born in England; crossed the western half of Australia from Port Augusta, SA, to Perth, WA, in 1875, and then back again across the Gibson Desert in 1876.

gilgai /'gɪlgaɪ/, n. a soil formation often found throughout inland Australia, forming a wavy surface, probably caused by swelling and cracking of clays during wet and dry seasons. Also, **ghilgai.** [Aboriginal]

gill[1] /gɪl/, n. 1. the organ that fish and other sea creatures use for breathing. It may be found inside or outside the body and is usu. feathery in appearance. 2. one of the plates on the underside of the cap of a fungus such as the mushroom. 3. **white / green at the gills,** Colloq. white-faced through fear, tiredness, sickness, etc. [ME, from Scand]

gill[2] /dʒɪl, gɪl/, n. a unit of liqid measure in the imperial system, equal to ¼ pint, or about 142 ml. [ME, from OF: wine measure]

Gill /gɪl/, n. **Samuel Thomas,** 1818–80, Australian artist and lithographer, born in England; depicted life of the goldfields, bush and town.

Gilmore /'gɪlmɔ/, n. **Dame Mary Jean,** 1865–1962, Australian poet, author and journalist; campaigner for peace and social reform; wrote the verse collection *The Wild Swan* (1930).

gilt /gɪlt/, v. 1. a past tense and past participle of gild. ◇adj. 2. gilded; golden in color. ◇n. 3. the gold or other material applied in gilding.

gilt-edged /'gɪlt-ɛdʒd/, adj. 1. having the edges gilded: *gilt-edged paper.* 2. of the highest order or quality: *gilt-edged securities.*

gimcrack /'dʒɪmkræk/, n. a showy, useless trifle; gewgaw. [orig. uncert.]

gimlet /'gɪmlət/, n. 1. a small tool for making holes, with a pointed screw at one end and a handle at the other. 2. a tree found in western Australia, with a twisted, furrowed trunk. ◇adj. 3. deeply penetrating, or thought to be deeply penetrating: *gimlet eyes.* [ME, from OF: little wimble]

gimmick /'gɪmɪk/, n. Colloq. an odd choice of dress, manner, voice, etc., or an unusual action or trick, esp. one used to gain publicity. [? b. *gimmer* trick finger-ring and MAGIC]

gin[1] /dʒɪn/, n. an alcoholic drink obtained by distilling spirits again with juniper berries, orange peel, angelica root, etc. [D, *genever,* from OF, from L: juniper]

gin[2] /dʒɪn/, n., v., **ginned, ginning.** ◇n. 1. a machine for separating cotton from its seeds. 2. a trap; snare. ◇v.t. 3. to clear (cotton) of seeds with a gin. 4. to catch (animals, etc.) in a gin. [ME, from OF: engine]

gin[3] /dʒɪn/, n. a card game similar to rummy. Also, **gin rummy.** [? a pun: *gin = rum*]

gin[4] /dʒɪn/, n. (*oft. offensive*) an Aboriginal woman. [Aboriginal]

ginger /'dʒɪndʒə/, n. 1. a pungent, spicy plant, found esp. in South East Asia, whose root stem is used in cooking and medicine. 2. a reddish brown or tawny color. 3. Colloq. sharpness; animation. [OE, from L, from Gk: ginger, apparently from Prakrit]

ginger ale, n. a soft drink flavored with ginger, oft. used to mix with brandy, etc.

ginger beer, n. a soft drink made of water, sugar, yeast, etc., flavored with ginger.

gingerbread /'dʒɪndʒəbrɛd/, n. 1. a type of cake flavored with ginger and treacle or golden syrup. 2. something showy but cheap and without taste. [alteration of ME: preserved ginger, from ML]

ginger group, n. a group of members within an organisation who try to make the larger group more active, lively or modern.

gingerly /'dʒɪndʒəli/, adv. with great care or caution; warily.

gingham /'gɪŋəm/, n. cotton cloth, usu. striped or checked, woven from yarn that has already been dyed. [F, from Malay: striped]

gingivitis /dʒɪndʒə'vaɪtəs/, n. inflammation of the gums.

gink /gɪŋk/, n. Colloq. →**geek.**

ginseng /'dʒɪnsɛŋ/, n. 1. either of two plants, found in China, Korea, etc., or North America, yielding an aromatic root which is widely used in medicine by the Chinese. 2. the root itself. 3. a preparation made from it. [Chinese (Mandarin)]

Giorgione /dʒɔ'dʒoʊni/, n. (*Giorgione da Castelfranco, Giorgio Barbarelli*). 1478?–1511, Italian painter, esp. of landscapes with figures.

Giotto /'dʒɒtoʊ/, n. c. 1266–1337, Florentine painter and architect, introduced a narrative and naturalistic style to painting.

Gippsland /ˈgɪpslənd/, *n.* a fertile area of south-eastern Vic between the Great Dividing Range and the coast, stretching from the NSW border to the western shore of Westernport. 31 000 km². [named after Sir George *Gipps*, 1791–1847, governor of NSW 1838–46]

gipsy /ˈgɪpsi/, *n., pl.* **-sies. 1.** (*oft. cap.*) someone who belongs to a wandering Caucasian race of Hindu origin. **2.** someone who looks or lives like a gipsy. Also, **gypsy.** [backformation from *gipcyan*, var. of EGYPTIAN]

giraffe /dʒəˈrɑːf/, *n.* a cud-chewing animal of Africa with spots and a long neck, the tallest of existing four-legged animals. [F, from Ar, probably of African orig.]

gird /gɜːd/, *v.t.* **girt** or **girded, girding. 1.** to fasten with a belt or girdle. **2.** to surround; hem in. **3.** to prepare (oneself) for action (oft. fol. by *up*). **4.** to supply; endow. [OE *gyrdan*]

girder /ˈgɜːdə/, *n.* (in building) any main horizontal supporting beam, made of steel, reinforced concrete or wood. [GIRD + -ER¹]

girdle¹ /ˈgɜːdl/, *n., v.,* **-dled, -dling.** ◇*n.* **1.** a belt, cord, etc., worn about the waist. **2.** a light piece of underwear, usu. elastic, which supports the stomach and hips. **3.** any encircling band; compass; limit. ◇*v.t.* **4.** to encircle or enclose with a belt. [OE *gyrdel*]

girdle² /ˈgɜːdl/, *n.* → **griddle.**

girl /gɜːl/, *n.* **1.** a female child or young woman. **2.** a female servant. **3.** *Colloq.* a sweetheart; girlfriend. **4.** *Colloq.* woman. [ME *gurle, girle* child, young person, OE *gyrl-* in *gyrlgyden* virgin goddess]

girl Friday, *n. Colloq.* a female secretary and general assistant in an office.

girl guide, *n.* a member of an organisation of girls, called the Girl Guides, which aims at developing health, character, and practical skills.

girt /gɜːt/, *v.* past tense and past participle of **gird.**

girth /gɜːθ/, *n.* **1.** the measure around anything; circumference. **2.** a band passed under the stomach of a horse, etc., to keep a saddle or pack firmly on its back. [ME, from Scand]

gismo /ˈgɪzmoʊ/, *n. Colloq.* gadget. Also, **gizmo.**

gist /dʒɪst/, *n.* the substance of a matter; essential part: *the gist of an argument.* [OF: lie, rest, from L]

give /gɪv/, *v.,* **gave, given, giving.** ◇*v.t.* **1.** to deliver (something) freely; hand over: *to give someone a present.* **2.** to pay (someone) (a price) (for something): *I will give you $20 for this.* **3.** to grant (permission or opportunity) to; assign; award: *to give him a chance.* **4.** to show, present or offer: *I give you the Mayor; to give a concert.* **5.** to appoint or assign (something) (to someone) as a right, share, etc.: *to give a child a name; to give him the prize.* **6.** *Colloq.* to tell; offer as explanation: *Don't give me that.* **7.** to set aside; devote: *He gives great attention to detail.* **8.** to admit to (someone) the truth of (something): *I'll give you that.* **9.** to provide: *to give aid; to give evidence.* **10.** (usu. in passive) to provide as the basis of further calculation: *Given A and B, C follows.* **11.** to produce: *to give good results.* **12.** to make (a movement): *The car gave a lurch.* **13.** to send out or speak: *to give a cry; to give a command.* **14.** (usu. in passive) to cause: *I was given to understand that the concert was free.* **15.** to pass or impart (something) to (someone): *give advice; give someone a cold.* **16.** to deal with or administer: *give a child a smack; give a medicine.* **17.** to yield; surrender: *The army had to give ground before the enemy.* **18.** to act as host at: *to give a party.* ◇*v.i.* **19.** to make a gift or gifts. **20.** to draw back; relax: *You must learn to give a little.* **21.** to break up; fail. **22.** to be facing a particular direction: *The house gives on to the seafront.* ◇*v.* **23.** Some special uses are:
give away, 1. to give as a present. **2.** to ceremonially present (the bride) to the bridegroom at a wedding. **3.** to let (a secret) be known. **4.** to betray (a person).
give in, 1. to admit defeat. **2.** to hand in.
give off, to send out; emit (fumes, etc.).
give out, 1. to become worn out or used up. **2.** to send out; emit. **3.** to distribute; issue. **4.** *Cricket.* (of an umpire) to declare a batsman out.
give or take, with an allowance made on either side: *ten years, give or take.*
give over, 1. to transfer. **2.** to set aside for a specific purpose: *The evening was given over to dancing.* **3.** *Colloq.* to stop.
give rise to, to be the origin of; cause; result in.
give up, 1. to lose all hope. **2.** to abandon as hopeless. **3.** to stop doing; forsake: *give up a job.* **4.** to surrender. **5.** to devote entirely: *We gave up a week for the preparations.* **6.** to inform against.
◇*n.* **24.** the act or fact of yielding to pressure; elasticity: *Feel the give in this material.* [ME, from Scand] **–giver,** *n.*

given /ˈgɪvən/, *v.* **1.** past participle of **give. 2.** assigned as a basis of calculation, reasoning, etc.: *Given A and B, C follows.* ◇*adj.* **3.** stated, fixed, or made particular: *at a given time; a given size.* **4.** addicted or disposed (fol. by *to*): *given to drink.*

gizzard /ˈgɪzəd/, *n.* the second, grinding and muscular, stomach of birds. [ME, from OF, from L: cooked entrails of poultry]

glacé /ˈglæseɪ, ˈglɑː-/, *adj.* **1.** covered with sugar; candied: *glacé fruit.* **2.** smooth and shiny, as silk. [F: ice, from L]

glacial /ˈgleɪʃəl, ˈgleɪsiəl/, *adj.* **1.** having ice in large masses or glaciers. **2.** due to or connected with the action of ice or glaciers. **3.** cold as ice; icy. **4.** *Chem.* having an icelike form, as glacial acetic acid. [L: icy]

glacial epoch, *n.* **1.** the Pleistocene epoch, during which much of the Northern Hemisphere was covered by great ice sheets; ice age. **2.** any of the ice ages, e.g. Permian and late Pre-Cambrian in Australia.

glacier /ˈgleɪsɪə, ˈglæsɪə/, *n.* a large mass of ice formed from snow falling and building up over years, which moves slowly down a valley or outwards from its centre. [F: ice, from L]

glad /glæd/, *adj.*, **gladder, gladdest. 1.** delighted or pleased (fol. by *at*, etc., or an infinitive or clause): *to be glad at the news; glad to go; glad that she has come.* **2.** thankful; grateful (fol. by *of*): *I'd be glad of a little help.* **3.** (by looks or words, etc.) showing cheerfulness, joy, or pleasure. **4.** connected with or giving joy or pleasure: *a glad occasion; glad tidings.* [OE]

gladden /'glædn/, *v.t.* to make glad: *Her smile gladdens my heart.* **—gladdener,** *n.*

glade /gleɪd/, *n.* an open space in a forest. [akin to GLAD (in obs. sense 'bright')]

gladiator /'glædieɪtə/, *n. Rom Hist.* a man, often a slave, who fought another man or animal to entertain the public. [L]

gladiolus /glædi'oʊləs/, *n., pl.* **-lus,** *-li* /-laɪ/, **-luses.** a plant native mainly to South Africa, with upright leaves and spikes of colored flowers; sword lily. [L: little sword]

glad rags, *n.pl. Colloq.* best clothes worn for special occasions.

Gladstone[1] /'glædstən/, *n.* **William Ewart,** 1809–98, British statesman; prime minister 1868–74, 1880–85, 1886, 1892–94; introduced educational reform and the secret ballot.

Gladstone[2] /'glædstən/, *n.* a coastal city and port in central eastern Qld, south-east of Rockhampton. Pop. 22 033 (1986).

Gladstone bag, *n.* a light travelling bag hinged to open into two compartments. [named after William Ewart GLADSTONE]

glamor *or* **glamour** /'glæmə/, *n.* (appearance of) charm and beauty; fascination. [from GRAMMAR in obs. sense of 'occult learning', 'magic']

Glamorganshire /gləˈmɔgənʃɪə, -ʃə/, *n.* a former county of south-eastern Wales, now divided into West Glamorgan, Mid Glamorgan and South Glamorgan. Also, **Glamorgan.**

glance /glæns, glans/, *v.*, **glanced, glancing,** *n.* ◇*v.i.* **1.** to look quickly. **2.** to flash; gleam. **3.** to hit and go off at an angle: *The blow glanced off the man's chest.* **4.** to make a brief reference to, in passing: *We'll just glance at the history of the subject.* ◇*n.* **5.** the act of glancing. [ME: strike a glancing blow, from OF: slip]

gland /glænd/, *n. Anat.* an organ or tissue which makes and secretes a substance used elsewhere in the body (*secretion*), or eliminated from the body (*excretion*). [OF, from L: a little corn]

glandular /'glændʒələ/, *adj.* **1.** consisting of, containing, or bearing glands. **2.** of, relating to, or looking like a gland.

glandular fever, *n. Med.* an infectious disease marked by sudden fever, swelling of the lymph nodes, and an increase in the number of white blood cells with only one nucleus; infectious mononucleosis.

glans /glænz/, *n., pl.* **glandes** /'glændiz/. the head of the penis (**glans penis**) or of the clitoris (**glans clitoridis**). [L: acorn]

glare /glɛə/, *n., v.*, **glared, glaring.** ◇*n.* **1.** a strong, bright light; brilliant or dazzling light: *The glare of oncoming car lights; the glare of ice.* **2.** showy appearance; dazzle. **3.** a fierce look: *She gave him a glare for his bad manners.* ◇*v.i.* **4.** to shine with a strong, dazzling light. **5.** to be too brightly decorated. **6.** to be very bright in color. **7.** to be very noticeable. **8.** to give a (long) fierce look. [ME]

Glaser /'gleɪzə/, *n.* **Donald Arthur,** born 1926, US physicist; invented the bubble chamber which detects elementary atomic particles; Nobel prize 1960.

Glasgow /'glæzgoʊ/, *n.* a seaport in south-western Scotland, on the Clyde; university founded 1451; shipyards. Pop. 733 800 (1985 est.).

glass /glas/, *n.* **1.** a hard more or less transparent substance produced by the melting of silica and silicates. The type used for windows, bottles, etc., contains silica, soda, and lime. **2.** any substance similar to glass, e.g. fused borax, obsidian, etc. **3.** something made of glass, e.g. a mirror, barometer, etc. **4.** (*pl.*) an aid for poor eyesight, consisting usu. of two glass lenses set in a frame which rests on the nose and is held in place by pieces passing over the ears. **5.** household articles ornaments, etc. made of glass; glassware. **6.** a glass container for cold drinks. **7.** the quantity contained in a drinking glass. ◇*adj.* **8.** made of glass. **9.** fitted with panes of glass; glazed. ◇*v.t.* **10.** to fit with panes of glass; cover with or put in glass. [OE] **—glasslike,** *adj.*

glass-blowing /'glas-bloʊɪŋ/, *n.* the art or method of shaping glass into forms for use as glassware, ornaments, laboratory equipment, etc. by blowing by mouth or by mechanical means. **—glass-blower,** *n.*

glasshouse /'glashaʊs/, *n.* → **greenhouse.**

Glasshouse Mountains, *n.* a number of eroded volcanic pillars in south-eastern Qld, 66 km north of Brisbane. Highest peak, Beerwah, 556 m.

glassy /'glasi/, *adj.*, **glassier, glassiest. 1.** glasslike. **2.** (of the eyes) having a fixed, unintelligent stare.

Glastonbury /'glæstənbəri, -bri/, *n.* a town in Somerset in south-western England; prehistoric lake villages; allegedly the burial place of King Arthur. Pop. 6773 (1981).

glauberite /'glɔbəraɪt, 'glaʊ-/, *n.* a mineral, sulfate of calcium and sodium, $Na_2Ca(SO_4)_2$, usu. occurring with rock salt in salt deposits. [named after JR *Glauber*, 1604–68, German chemist]

glaucoma /glɔˈkoʊmə/, *n.* a disease of the eye, marked by increased pressure within the eyeball and loss of eyesight. [Gk: opacity of the crystalline lens] **—glaucomatous,** *adj.*

glaucous /'glɔkəs/, *adj.* **1.** light bluish green or greenish blue. **2.** *Bot.* covered with a whitish coating, as a plum. [L, from Gk: gleaming, silvery, grey, bluish green]

glaze /gleɪz/, *v.*, **glazed, glazing,** *n.* ◇*v.t.* **1.** to fit with glass; cover with or as if with glass. **2.** *Pottery.* **a.** to produce a vitreous waterproof surface (either shiny or matt) on (pots). **b.** to cover with a glaze, before firing.

glaze

3. *Cookery.* to cover (food) with a glaze (def. 9). **4.** *Painting.* to cover (a painted surface, etc.) with a thin coat of transparent color in order to change the tone slightly. ◇*v.i.* **5.** to become glazed or glassy: *His eyes glazed over as he remembered the past.* ◇*n.* **6.** a smooth shiny surface on certain materials. **7.** *Pottery.* (a substance used to produce) this surface on glazed pottery. **8.** *Painting.* a thin coat of transparent color, over a painted surface. **9.** *Cookery.* something used to coat food, as **a.** egg-white on pastry, or syrup on a cooked tart. **b.** stock cooked down to a thin paste, used on meats. [ME *glasen*]

glazier /'gleɪzɪə/, *n.* someone who fits windows, etc., with glass. [ME *glasier,* from *glas* GLASS + -IER]

glazing /'gleɪzɪŋ/, *n.* **1.** the act of fitting with glass; the business of a glazier. **2.** glass set, or to be set, in frames, etc. **3.** the act of putting on a glaze. **4.** the surface of anything glazed.

gleam /glim/, *n.* **1.** a flash or beam of light. **2.** dim light as of polished surfaces. **3.** a brief or slight show: *a gleam of interest; a gleam of hope.* **4. gleam in one's eye,** a look showing humor or unstated intentions. ◇*v.i.* **5.** to give out a gleam or gleams. **6.** to appear suddenly and clearly, like a flash of light. [OE]

glean /glin/, *v.t.* **1.** to gather slowly and with difficulty in bits: *to glean information.* **2.** to gather (grain, etc.) after the reapers have finished. [ME, from OF, from LL, of Celtic orig.]

glee /gli/, *n.* **1.** a feeling of joy; exultation. **2.** an unaccompanied song, for three or more voices. [OE]

glen /glen/, *n.* a small, narrow valley. [ME, from Gaelic]

Glenbawn Dam /glenbɔn 'dæm/, *n.* a dam in eastern NSW, on the Hunter River, 10 km north of Aberdeen.

Glencoe /glen'kou/, *n.* a narrow valley in western Scotland; site of the massacre of the Macdonald clan by the Campbells, 1692.

Gleneagles Agreement /glen'igəlz əgrimənt/, *n.* a Commonwealth agreement signed in 1977 at Gleneagles, Scotland, opposing sporting links with South Africa as a protest against apartheid.

Glenelg /glə'nelg/, a city in SA, part of the western suburbs of Adelaide, on Gulf St Vincent; site of temporary settlement by Colonel Light in 1837. Pop. 13 248 (1986).

Glen Innes /glen 'ɪnəs/, *n.* a town in north-eastern NSW, in the New England region. Pop. 5971 (1986).

glib /glɪb/, *adj.,* **glibber, glibbest.** speaking or spoken easily though often insincerely: *a glib speaker; a glib tongue; glib words.* [backformation from obs. *glibbery* slippery, from D]

glide /glaɪd/, *v.,* **glided, gliding,** *n.* ◇*v.i.* **1.** to move smoothly along, as if without effort, as a flying bird, a boat, a skater, etc. **2.** to go quietly or unnoticed; slip (fol. by *in, out,* etc.). **3.** *Aeron.* to move in the air, esp. at an easy angle downwards, by the action of gravity, air-currents, etc., without use of an engine. **4.** *Music.* to pass from note to note without a break; slur. ◇*v.t.* **5.** to cause to glide. ◇*n.* **6.** a gliding movement, as in dancing. **7.** *Linguistics.* →**semivowel.** [OE]

glider /'glaɪdə/, *n.* **1.** someone or something that glides. **2.** *Aeron.* a motorless aeroplane used in gliding. **3.** any of the tree-living marsupials of Australia and NG with a parachute-like membrane along the side of the body by means of which they can glide, and a long and bushy, rather than a prehensile (grasping), tail. Some examples are the mouse-sized **pygmy glider** of eastern Australia, the fluffy or **yellow-bellied glider** of north-eastern Australia, the small honey-eating **sugar glider** of eastern Australia and NG, and the large **greater glider.** Also, **flying phalanger, gliding possum.**

glimmer /'glɪmə/, *n.* **1.** a faint or unsteady light; gleam. **2.** a dim recognition; inkling. ◇*v.i.* **3.** to shine or appear faintly or unsteadily; flicker. [ME: gleam] —**glimmering,** *n.*

glimpse /glɪmps/, *n., v.,* **glimpsed, glimpsing.** ◇*n.* **1.** a quick sight or view. ◇*v.t.* **2.** to catch a glimpse of. [ME *glymsen*]

glint /glɪnt/, *n.* **1.** a gleam or flash. **2. glint in one's eyes,** →**gleam** (def. 4). ◇*v.i.* **3.** to gleam or flash. [ME, var. of obs. Scand]

glissando /glɪ'sændou/, *n., pl.* **-di** /-di/, *adj.* (a special effect) performed by sliding one finger quickly over the keys of a piano or the strings of a harp. [pseudo-It, from F: slide]

glisten /'glɪsən/, *v.i.* to shine with a sparkling (usu. reflected) light. [OE: glitter]

glitch /glɪtʃ/, *n. Colloq.* an extra electric current or signal, esp. one that interferes in some way with the working of a system.

glitter /'glɪtə/, *v.i.* **1.** to shine with a bright, sparkling light. **2.** to make a brilliant show. ◇*n.* **3.** glittering light or lustre; splendor. [ME, from Scand] —**glittery, glittering,** *adj.*

gloat /glout/, *v.i.* to look at or think about something or someone with intense (and usu. smug) satisfaction: *to gloat over another's misfortunes.* [? Scand: grin, smile scornfully]

glob /glɒb/, *n. Colloq.* a rounded lump of some soft substance: *a glob of cream.* [? b. GLOBE and BLOB]

global /'gloubəl/, *adj.* **1.** round; spherical. **2.** world-wide: *global war.* **3.** all-inclusive; comprehensive.

globe /gloub/, *n.* **1.** the earth (usu. prec. by *the*). **2.** any planet, etc. **3.** any sphere on which is shown a map of the earth (terrestrial globe) or of the heavens (celestial globe). **4.** a round body; sphere. **5.** anything more or less round, as a lampshade, etc. **6.** →**bulb** (def. 2). [F, from L: round body or mass, ball, globe]

globetrotter /'gloubtrɒtə/, *n. Colloq.* someone who travels widely.

globule /'glɒbjul/, *n.* a small globe, or round body, esp. a drop of liquid. [F, from L: little globe] —**globular,** *adj.*

glockenspiel /ˈglɒkənspil, -kənʃpil/, *n. Music.* an instrument made of steel bars set in a frame and hit with hammers. [G: bell + play]

gloom[1] /glum/, *n.* darkness; dimness. [OE: twilight]

gloom[2] /glum/, *n.* 1. a condition of (great) unhappiness; melancholy. 2. a depressed look or expression. ◇*v.i.* 3. to look unhappy; frown. [ME: frown]

gloomy[1] /ˈglumi/, *adj.*, **gloomier, gloomiest.** dark; deeply shaded. [GLOOM[1] + -Y[1]]

gloomy[2] /ˈglumi/, *adj.*, **gloomier, gloomiest.** 1. causing gloom; depressing: *a gloomy future.* 2. feeling unhappy; melancholy. [GLOOM[2] + -Y[1]]

glorify /ˈglɔrɪfaɪ/, *v.t.*, **-fied, -fying.** 1. to praise; extol. 2. to change into something more splendid or beautiful. 3. to honor (esp. God). [ME, from OF, from LL] —**glorification,** *n.*

glorious /ˈglɔriəs/, *adj.* 1. wonderful; delightful: *to have a glorious time.* 2. giving glory: *a glorious victory.* 3. full of glory; entitled to fame: *England is glorious in her poetry.* 4. bright and beautiful: *the glorious heavens.* [ME, from AF, from L: full of glory]

glory /ˈglɔri/, *n., pl.* **glories,** *v.*, **gloried, glorying.** ◇*n.* 1. praise and honor: *paths of glory.* 2. something that brings honor; an object of pride: *Her hair was her crowning glory.* 3. adoring praise or thanksgiving: *Give glory to God.* 4. beauty; magnificence: *the glory that was Rome.* 5. a state of contentment, as resulting from success and fame. 6. the beauty of heaven; heaven. ◇*v.i.* 7. to rejoice; exult (fol. by *in*). ◇*interj.* 8. (*cap.*) Also, **Glory be!** (a mild expression of surprise, elation, or exultation.) [ME, from OF, from L: glory, fame, vainglory, boasting]

glory box, *n.* a chest in which young women store clothes, linen, etc., in preparation for marriage; hope chest.

gloss[1] /glɒs/, *n.* 1. surface lustre: *gloss of satin.* 2. an attractive appearance or manner hiding the real nature. ◇*v.t.* 3. to put a gloss upon. 4. to give a false appearance to (oft. fol. by *over*). [Scand]

gloss[2] /glɒs/, *n.* 1. an explanation in a footnote of a technical or unusual expression in a text. 2. a glossary. 3. a cleverly misleading explanation. ◇*v.t.* 4. to put glosses on; annotate. 5. to cover up; explain away (oft. fol. by *over*): *to gloss over a mistake.* [L: (explanation of) hard word, from Gk: tongue]

glossary /ˈglɒsəri/, *n., pl.* **-ries.** a list of basic technical and difficult words in a subject or field, with definitions. [L: GLOSS[2]]

glosso-, a word part meaning 'tongue', or 'language', as in *glossolalia.*

glossolalia /ˌglɒsəˈleɪliə/, *n.* non-meaningful speech, often connected with a religious experience or schizophrenic disorders. [NL, from Gk: tongue + talk, babble]

glossopteris /gləˈsɒptərəs/, *n.* a type of extinct plant, the fossil remains of which are found widely in Permian rocks of the Southern Hemisphere.

glossy /ˈglɒsi/, *adj.*, **glossier, glossiest,** *n.* ◇*adj.* 1. having a gloss; shiny. ◇*n.* 2. a photograph printed on glossy paper. 3. a magazine printed on glossy paper. [GLOSS[1], *n.* + -Y[1]]

-glot, a suffix showing ability in language, as in *polyglot.* [Gk *glōtta* tongue]

glottis /ˈglɒtəs/, *n. Anat.* an opening at the upper part of the larynx, between the vocal cords. [NL, from Gk: the mouth of the windpipe] —**glottal,** *adj.*

Gloucestershire /ˈglɒstəʃɪə, -ʃə/, *n.* a county in south-western England. Pop. 517 100 (1986 est.); 3251 km[2]. *Administrative Centre:* Gloucester.

glove /glʌv/, *n., v.*, **gloved, gloving.** ◇*n.* 1. a covering for the hand, with a separate part for each finger and for the thumb. 2. a similar covering, but without divisions for the fingers, as a boxing glove or a mitten. ◇*v.t.* 3. to cover with or as if with a glove. 4. to serve as a glove for. [OE]

glove box, *n.* a small space in a motor car, set into the dashboard, for storing small objects, as gloves, maps, etc.

Glover /ˈglʌvə/, *n.* **John,** 1767–1849, Australian landscape painter, born in England.

glow /gloʊ/, *n.* 1. the light given out by an extremely hot substance; incandescence. 2. brightness of color. 3. a state of bodily heat. 4. warmth of feeling, etc.; ardor. ◇*v.i.* 5. to give out bright light and heat without flame. 6. to shine like something strongly heated. 7. to show a strong, bright color. 8. to be extremely hot. 9. to show strong feelings; show enthusiasm: *She was glowing with pride.* [OE]

glower /ˈgloʊə, ˈglaʊə/, *v.i.* 1. to look angrily; stare with sullen dislike. ◇*n.* 2. a glowering look; frown. [obs. *glow* stare, of uncert. orig.]

glow-worm /ˈgloʊ-wɜm/, *n.* a firefly, esp. the wingless female or the glowing larva.

gluco- /ˈglukoʊ-/, a prefix showing the presence of glucose in a substance.

glucose /ˈglukoʊz, -oʊs/, *n. Chem.* a sugar, $C_6H_{12}O_6$, the major energy source for most living cells. [F, from Gk: sweet + -OSE[2]]

glue /glu/, *n., v.*, **glued, gluing.** ◇*n.* 1. impure gelatine obtained by boiling skins, hoofs, and other animal substances in water, used to stick things together. 2. any of various preparations of this substance. 3. any adhesive substance made from resin, etc. ◇*v.t.* 4. to join or fasten with or as if with glue. [ME, from OF, from LL]

gluhwein /ˈgluwaɪn/, *n.* red wine heated with spices; mulled wine. [G: glow-wine]

glum /glʌm/, *adj.*, **glummer, glummest.** in low spirits; dejected; morose. [cf. LG: turbid, muddy]

glut /glʌt/, *v.*, **glutted, glutting,** *n.* ◇*v.t.* 1. to feed or fill totally; sate: *to glut the appetite.* 2. to overfeed or overfill. 3. **glut the market,** to give too large a supply of any article so that the price is unusually low. ◇*n.* 4. a full

glut 438 **go**

supply. **5.** an oversupply. [ME: glutton, from OF: greedy]

glutamine /'glutəmin/, *n.* an amino acid found in proteins, which is an important source of ammonia and nitrogen for the body. [GLUT(EN) + AMINE]

gluten /'glutn/, *n.* **1.** a tough, sticky substance left when the flour of wheat, etc. is washed to remove the starch. **2.** glue, or some gluey substance. [L: glue] —**glutenous**, *adj.*

glutinous /'glutənəs/, *adj.* like glue; gluey; sticky. [L: gluey, viscous]

glutton /'glʌtn/, *n.* **1.** someone who eats too much. **2.** someone who overdoes something. **3.** someone who will always do more of something unpleasant or difficult (fol. by *for*): *a glutton for punishment; a glutton for work.* [ME, from OF, from L] —**gluttonous**, *adj.* —**gluttony**, *n.*

glyceride /'glɪsəraɪd/, *n.* an ester obtained from the reaction of glycerol with a fatty acid. See **fat** (def. 8). [from GLYCER(INE) + -IDE]

glycerine /glɪsə'rin, 'glɪsərən/, *n. Chem.* → **glycerol**. Also, **glycerin** /'glɪsərən/. [F, from Gk: sweet + -INE²]

glycerol /'glɪsərɒl/, *n.* a colorless, odorless, sweet, liquid alcohol, $HOCH_2CHOCH_2OH$, obtained by the saponification of natural fats and oils, and used as a solvent, plasticiser, or sweetener. —**glyceric**, *adj.*

glyceryl trinitrate, /ˌglɪsərəl traɪ'naɪtreɪt/ *n.* → **nitroglycerine**.

glycogen /'glaɪkədʒən/, *n.* a white, tasteless, animal starch found in liver and muscles, which serves as a store of glucose. [Gk: sweet + -GEN] —**glycogenic**, *adj.*

glycol /'glaɪkɒl/, *n.* **1.** a colorless, sweet-tasting liquid, used as an antifreeze in motor cars. **2.** any of a group of alcohols containing two hydroxyl groups. [b. GLYC(ERINE) and (ALCOH)OL] —**glycolic**, *adj.*

glycolysis /glaɪ'kɒləsəs/, *n.* the breakdown of sugars and starch by enzymes, causing the release of energy and production of lactic or pyruvic acid in organisms.

GMT /dʒi em 'ti/, *Abbrev.* Greenwich Mean Time.

gnarled /nald/, *adj.* **1.** (of trees) full of or covered with knots. **2.** (of persons) having a rugged, weatherbeaten appearance. [var. of *knurled*, ridged]

gnash /næʃ/, *v.t.* to grind (the teeth) together, esp. in anger or pain. [Scand]

gnat /næt/, *n.* any of various small insects having a single pair of wings. [OE]

gnaw /nɔ/, *v.*, **gnawed**, **gnawed** or **gnawn**, **gnawing**. ◇*v.t.* **1.** to wear away or remove by continual biting. **2.** to make by gnawing. **3.** to eat away, as an acid does; corrode. ◇*v.i.* **4.** to chew at something. **5.** to eat away, as pain or worry (usu. fol. by *at*): *The problem gnawed at his mind.* [OE]

gnawing /'nɔ-ɪŋ, 'nɔrɪŋ/, *n.* **1.** the act of someone who or something which gnaws. **2.** a continual pain suggesting gnawing: *the gnawings of hunger.*

gneiss /naɪs/, *n.* a metamorphic rock with bands of different colors and composition, some rich in felspar and quartz, others rich in hornblende or mica. [G] —**gneissic**, *adj.*

gnome /noum/, *n.* **1.** (in fairy stories) one of a type of small beings supposed to live underground and to guard treasure, usu. thought of as shrivelled little old men. **2.** a small statue, thought to resemble a gnome, esp. as placed in a garden. [F, from NL]

gnomic /'noumɪk, 'nɒm-/, *adj.* **1.** like or containing short, wise, pithy expressions of a general truth. **2.** relating to someone noted for use of gnomic expressions. Also, **gnomical**. [Gk]

gnosis /'nousəs/, *n.* knowledge of spiritual things; mystical knowledge. [NL, from Gk: knowledge]

-gnosis, a suffix relating to recognition, esp. of a medical condition, as in *diagnosis*. [Gk: knowledge]

gnostic /'nɒstɪk/, *adj.* Also, **gnostical**. **1.** relating to knowledge. **2.** having knowledge, esp. knowledge of spiritual things. **3.** (*cap.*) related to or common to the Gnostics. ◇*n.* **4.** (*cap.*) a member of any of certain sects among, or religiously similar to, the early Christians, who claimed to have superior knowledge of spiritual things. [LL, from Gk: pertaining to knowledge] —**Gnosticism**, *n.*

GNP /dʒi en 'pi/, *Abbrev.* gross national product.

gnu /nu/, *n.*, *pl.* **gnus**, (*esp. collectively*) **gnu**. any of several African antelopes marked by an oxlike head, curved horns, and a long, flowing tail; wildebeest.

go /gou/, *v.*, **went**, **gone**, **going**, *n.*, *pl.* **goes**, *adj.* ◇*v.i.* **1.** to move or pass along; proceed. **2.** to move away or out; depart (opposed to *come* or *arrive*). **3.** to keep or be in motion; act, work, or run: *The motor won't go.* **4.** to become: *to go mad.* **5.** to continue to be in a particular condition: *to go hungry.* **6.** to be known: *to go by a name.* **7.** to reach or extend: *This road goes to the city.* **8.** (of time) to pass; elapse. **9.** to be sold: *The house went for a song.* **10.** *Colloq.* to compare; to be normally: *She's quite young as grandmothers go.* **11.** to turn out: *How did the game go?* **12.** to belong; have a place: *This book goes on the top shelf.* **13.** (of colors, etc.) to be suited; harmonise. **14.** to fit (into, round, etc.): *The little cup goes into the big one.* **15.** to be used up, finished or consumed: *The biscuits went quickly.* **16.** *Colloq.* to say: *And he goes "rack off!"* **17.** to fail; give way. **18.** to carry force: *What I say goes.* **19.** to be contained (fol. by *into*): *4 goes into 12.* **20.** to add up to a result: *the items which go to make up a total.* **21.** to be about to or intending to (used in the pres. part. fol. by an infinitive): *He is going to write.* **22.** to make a specified sound, effect, etc. when operated: *The gun went bang.* ◇*v.t.* **23.** to pass on: *He went his way.* ◇**24.** Some special uses are:
go all out, *Colloq.* to use the utmost energy.
go along with, to agree; accept.
go around, to be enough for all: *enough food to go around.*

go back on, *Colloq.* to fail to keep (a promise, etc.).
go by, 1. to pass: *I'll drop in as I go by.* **2.** to be guided by: *I'll go by what he suggested.*
go Dutch, to share the expenses of a night out.
go for, 1. to attack. **2.** to be attracted to: *I go for music in a big way.* **3.** to aim for: *He's going for the chairmanship.* **4.** to apply to: *That rule goes for all of us.*
go halves, (of two people) to share equally (*in*).
go in for, to make (something) a special interest: *I go in for jazz.*
go into, to study or examine thoroughly.
go off, 1. to explode. **2.** (of food, etc.) to become bad: *The meat's gone off.* **3.** to take place (in a particular manner): *The rehearsal went off well.* **4.** *Colloq.* to come to dislike: *I've gone off chocolate lately.* **5.** to go away: *He's gone off to Europe.*
go on, 1. to take place. **2.** to talk continually: *He went on all day about his trip.* **3.** nonsense! (an exclamation of disbelief). **4.** to use as evidence: *Going on the police records, he's guilty.* **5.** *Colloq.* to get near (an age or a time): *He's going on seventy; It's going on midnight.*
go out, 1. to come to a stop; end: *The lights went out.* **2.** to attend social events, etc. away from home. **3.** to be broadcast.
go over, 1. to read or reread. **2.** to repeat. **3.** to examine. **4.** to be received in a particular way: *My proposal went over very badly.* **5.** to change sides, etc.: *He's gone over to Labor.*
go through, 1. to undergo; endure: *go through great misery.* **2.** to continue (an activity) to its end: *I went through with your plan.* **3.** to examine in order. **4.** to be accepted.
let go, 1. to release. **2.** to express (one's feelings, etc.) esp. in attacking: *She really let go at him.*
let oneself go, 1. to stop caring for one's appearance. **2.** to become uninhibited.
◇*n*. **25.** the act of going: *the come and go of the seasons.* **26.** *Colloq.* energy: *to be full of go.* **27.** someone's turn to play or to try something: *It's Jane's go on the swing.* **28.** *Colloq.* something that goes well; a success: *to make a go of painting.* **29.** Some special uses are:
all the go, *Colloq.* in the current fashion.
from go to whoa, from beginning to end.
from the word go, from the very beginning.
have (give it) a go, *Colloq.* to make an attempt; try.
no go, *Colloq.* not possible.
on the go, *Colloq.* very active.
open go, a situation in which normal restraints do not apply: *It was open go at the bar that night.*
◇*adj.* **30.** ready, working properly: *All instruments are go.* [OE]

goad /goʊd/, *n.* **1.** (anything like) a stick with a pointed end that pricks or wounds, used for driving cattle, etc. ◇*v.t.* **2.** to tease (someone) or drive (animals) with or as if with a goad; provoke. [OE]

goal /ɡoʊl/, *n.* **1.** something that someone directs efforts towards; aim or end. **2.** *Sport.* an area, basket, cage, object or structure towards which players try to advance the ball. **3.** the act of throwing or kicking the ball through or over the goal. **4.** the score made by doing this. [ME: boundary, limit]

goalkeeper /'goʊlkipə/, *n.* (in soccer, hockey, etc.) the player whose duty it is to stop the ball from going through, into, or over the goal.

goanna /goʊ'ænə/, *n.* any of various large Australian monitor lizards, e.g. the common lace monitor which occurs throughout mainland Australia. [from IGUANA]

goat /goʊt/, *n.* **1.** any of various agile hollow-horned cud-chewing animals related to sheep, native to rocky and mountainous areas and domesticated throughout the world. **2.** *Colloq.* a fool: *to make a goat of oneself.* **3. get (on) one's goat,** *Colloq.* to annoy; enrage; infuriate. [OE]

goatee /goʊ'ti/, *n.* a man's beard cut to a point on the chin.

gob[1] /ɡɒb/, *n.* a mass or lump. [ME: lump, mass, from OF]

gob[2] /ɡɒb/, *Colloq.* ◇*n.* **1.** the mouth: *Shut your gob.* ◇*v.i.* **2.** to spit. [Gaelic or Irish. See GAB]

gobbet /'ɡɒbət/, *n.* a piece or hunk, esp. of raw flesh. [ME, from OF: little gob]

gobble[1] /'ɡɒbəl/, *v.*, **-bled, -bling.** ◇*v.t.* **1.** to swallow quickly in large pieces; gulp. **2.** *Colloq.* to seize greedily or eagerly. ◇*v.i.* **3.** to eat quickly. [from GOB[1]] — **gobbler**, *n.*

gobble[2] /'ɡɒbəl/, *v.i.*, **-bled, -bling.** to make the throaty cry of a turkey cock. [var. of GABBLE taken as imitative of the cry]

gobbledegook /'ɡɒbldi,ɡʊk, -,ɡuk/, *n.* *Colloq.* language marked by the use of too many words, roundabout expression, and jargon: *the gobbledegook of government reports.*

gobbler /'ɡɒblə/, *n.* a turkey cock.

go-between /'goʊ-bətwin/, *n.* someone who acts as an agent between people or parties.

Gobi /'goʊbi/, *n.* a desert in eastern Asia, mostly in Mongolia. About 1 295 000 km².

goblet /'ɡɒblət/, *n.* a drinking vessel with a foot and stem. [ME, from OF: little cup; of Celtic orig.]

goblin /'ɡɒblən/, *n.* an ugly trouble-making elf. [ME, from F, from MHG: goblin]

goby /'goʊbi/, *n., pl.* **-bies,** (*esp. collectively*) **-by.** a member of a family of sea and freshwater fishes, mostly small and having the pelvic fins united to form a suction disc that allows them to attach to rocks, as the **flathead goby,** of eastern Australia. [L, from Gk: kind of fish]

go-cart /'goʊ-kat/, *n.* **1.** a small, wheeled vehicle for children to ride in. **2.** → **go-kart.**

God /ɡɒd/, *n.* **1.** (in the Jewish, Christian, Muslim faiths, etc.) the Supreme Being, creator and ruler of the universe. **2.** the Supreme Being in relation to a particular quality: *the God of justice.* **3.** (*l.c.*) a being, esp. male, worshipped as ruling over some area of worldly affairs. **4.** (*l.c.*) an image of a deity; idol. **5.** (*l.c., pl.*) the highest level of seating in a theatre. **6. God's own country,** (*usu. ironic*) one's own country seen as perfect. ◇*interj.* **7.** (an exclamation used to express weariness, annoyance, disappointment, etc.) [OE god, G

Godard /ɡoˈda/, n. **Jean-Luc** /ʒɔ̃-ˈlyk/, born 1930, French film director.

godchild /ˈɡɒdtʃaɪld/, n., pl. **-children**. someone for whom a person (godparent) takes responsibility at baptism.

goddess /ˈɡɒdəs, ˈɡɒdɛs/, n. **1.** a female god or deity. **2.** an adored or very beautiful woman.

Goderich /ˈɡoʊdrɪtʃ/, n. **Frederick John Robinson, Viscount** (*1st Earl of Ripon*), 1782–1859, English statesman; prime minister 1827–28.

godforsaken /ˈɡɒdfəseɪkən/, adj. *Colloq.* desolate; remote.

Godiva /ɡəˈdaɪvə/, n. (*Lady Godiva*), wife of Leofric, Earl of Mercia (11th century). According to legend, she rode naked through the streets of Coventry to win relief for the people from a burdensome tax.

godly /ˈɡɒdli/, adj., **-lier, -liest**. conforming to God's laws; pious.

godparent /ˈɡɒdpɛərənt/, n. a man (**godfather**) or woman (**godmother**) who sponsors (answers for) a child at baptism.

godsend /ˈɡɒdsɛnd/, n. something unexpected but welcome and timely, as if sent by God. [earlier *God's send*, var. of *God's sond* or *sand*, OE *sand, sond* message, service]

godspeed /ɡɒdˈspid/, **1.** *interj.* God speed you. ◇*n.* **2.** a wish given to someone setting out on a journey or project.

Goebbels /ˈɡəbəlz/, n. **Paul Joseph** /paʊl ˈjoʊsɛf/, 1897–1945, German Nazi politician; minister of propaganda under Hitler 1933–45.

goer /ˈɡoʊə/, n. **1.** a person who attends regularly (usu. used in combination): *a cinemagoer*. **2.** *Colloq.* someone or something that moves fast. **3.** *Colloq.* any activity, undertaking, etc., which promises success.

Goering /ˈɡɜrɪŋ/, n. →**Göring**.

goes /ɡoʊz/, v. **1.** third person singular present of **go**. ◇*n.* **2.** plural of **go**.

Goethe /ˈɡɜtə/, n. **Johann Wolfgang von** /ˌjoʊhan ˈvɔlfɡaŋ fɒn/, 1749–1832, German writer of poetry, drama, novels and philosophy; best known for his lyrical poetry and his dramatic poem *Faust* (1808; 1832).

goethite /ˈɡoʊθaɪt, ˈɡɜtaɪt/, n. a very common mineral, found in crystals, more commonly in yellow or brown earthy masses, an ore of iron. Also, **göthite**. [named after JW von GOETHE. See -ITE¹]

goggle /ˈɡɒɡəl/, n., v., **-gled, -gling**. ◇*n.* **1.** (*pl.*) large glasses, often with special lenses, fitting close to the face, used to protect the eyes from wind, dust, heat, water, etc. ◇*v.i.* **2.** to stare with eyes wide open. **3.** to roll the eyes. [ME: look aside; orig. uncert.]

going /ˈɡoʊɪŋ/, n. **1.** a departure: *a safe going and return*. **2.** the condition of something, as the ground, as affecting progress: *The going was bad*. ◇*adj.* **3.** moving or working, as machinery. **4.** succeeding in business: *a going concern*. **5.** available: *What's going for tea tonight?* **6. going on**, nearly: *It is going on four o'clock*. **7. the going thing**, something of the moment considered fashionable.

going-over /ˌɡoʊɪŋˈoʊvə/, n., pl. **goings-over**. *Colloq.* **1.** a thorough examination. **2.** a severe beating.

goings-on /ˌɡoʊɪŋzˈɒn/, n.pl. *Colloq.* actions, conduct, or behavior, esp. if unacceptable.

goitre /ˈɡɔɪtə/, n. an enlargement of the thyroid gland, on the front and sides of the neck. [F, from L: throat]

go-kart /ˈɡoʊ-kart/, n. a small, light, low-powered vehicle used for racing. Also, **go-cart, kart**.

gold /ɡoʊld/, n. **1.** a precious yellow metal, non-rusting, and able to be moulded. *Symbol.*: Au; *at. no.*: 79; *at. wt*: 196.967. **2.** money; wealth. **3.** something compared to this metal in brightness, preciousness, etc.: *a heart of gold*. **4.** a bright metallic yellow color, sometimes shading towards brown. ◇*adj.* **5.** consisting of, or like gold. [ME and OE]

Gold Coast, n. a local government area on the south-eastern coast of Qld; one of Australia's principal tourist areas. Pop. 130 304 (1986).

golden /ˈɡoʊldən/, adj. **1.** of the color of gold; yellow: *golden hair*. **2.** made of gold: *golden keys*. **3.** like gold in value; excellent: *a golden chance*. **4.** gifted; likely to succeed. *golden girl*. **5.** relating to the fiftieth event of a series, as a wedding anniversary.

golden age, n. **1.** *Myth.* the first and best age of the world, when mankind lived in innocence and happiness. **2.** the most successful period in the history of a nation, literature, etc.: *golden age of drama; golden age of Greece*.

Golden Dragon, n. →**Gulden Draak**.

Golden Fleece, n. *Gk Legend.* the fleece of gold taken from the winged ram on which Phrixus was carried to Colchis, recovered from King Aeëtes by Jason and the Argonauts. See **Medea**.

Golden Gate, n. a strait in western California between San Francisco Bay and the Pacific; spanned by the **Golden Gate Bridge**, whose channel span of 1281 m is one of the longest single spans in the world.

golden handshake, n. *Colloq.* a gift sometimes given to workers when they leave, in recognition of their services, or given as compensation when they are dismissed.

golden mean, n. **1.** a happy medium between extremes; a moderate course of action. **2.** a mathematical proportion thought to be ideal, used in art and architecture. [translation of *aurea mediocritas* (Horace)]

Golden Mile, n. the name given to a gold reef in the East Coolgardie goldfield in WA; claimed to be the richest square mile in the world.

golden retriever, n. one of a breed of retriever dogs with a thick, wavy, golden coat.

golden rule, n. **1.** a rule of conduct that advises that people should treat each other in the same way they would wish to be treated. **2.** any very important rule, esp. of conduct.

golden syrup, *n.* a sweet gold-colored syrup used in cooking and as a sauce for desserts, etc.

Golden Temple, *n.* a Sikh shrine standing on an island in the centre of the sacred Pool of Immortality at Amritsar.

Golden Triangle, *n.* (in popular usage) a drug network area on the Burmese-Thai-Laotian border.

golden wattle, *n.* a broad-leafed Australian tree with groups of small round yellow flowers; floral emblem of the Commonwealth of Australia.

goldfield /'gouldfild/, *n.* a area in which gold is mined.

goldfinch /'gouldfɪntʃ/, *n.* a European songbird, with red face and wings marked with yellow, now common in Australia. [OE *goldfinc*]

goldfish /'gouldfɪʃ/, *n., pl.* **-fishes**, (*esp. collectively*) **-fish**. a small fish of the carp family, popular for aquariums and pools.

Golding /'gouldɪŋ/, *n.* **William (Gerald)**, born 1911, English novelist; best known for *Lord of the Flies* (1954); Nobel prize for literature 1983.

gold leaf, *n.* gold beaten into a very thin sheet, used for gilding, etc.

goldmine /'gouldmaɪn/, *n.* **1.** a mine yielding gold. **2.** a source of great wealth, advantage etc.: *a goldmine of information*. **–goldminer**, *n.* **–goldmining**, *n.*

Goldoni /goul'douni/, *n.* **Carlo**, 1707–93, Italian dramatist; his more than 250 plays marked a change to more realistic comedy from the commedia dell'arte.

gold plate, *n.* (tableware covered with) a plating of gold.

gold record, *n.* a gold-plated record made by a recording company and given to the artists, etc., when a certain number of copies of the record (in Australia, 20 000) have been sold.

gold reserve, *n.* the total collection of gold held by an authority, used for international payments, and to safeguard the value of a country's coins and paper money.

gold rush, *n.* the rapid movement of many people to an area where gold has been discovered.

Goldsbrough, Mort and Co /'goulzbrə/, *n.* an Australian wool company founded in 1881 by Richard Goldsbrough. Formerly, **R Goldsbrough and Co**, 1881–88.

Goldsmith /'gouldsmɪθ/, *n.* **Oliver**, 1728–74, Irish author of prose, drama, and poetry; works include the play *She Stoops to Conquer* (1773).

gold standard, *n.* a money system which bases the value of a country's money on gold of a fixed weight and fineness. See **managed currency**.

Goldstein /'gouldstin/, *n.* **Joseph Leonard**, born 1940, US physician; winner with Michael S Brown of the 1985 Nobel prize for physiology or medicine for work on cholesterol metabolism.

gold top, *n.* a mushroom, oft. with a yellowish cap, which when eaten can cause hallucinations. Also, **gold cap**.

Goldwyn /'gouldwən/, *n.* **Samuel** (*Samuel Goldfish*), 1882–1974, Hollywood film producer.

golf /gɒlf/, *n.* **1.** an outdoor game, in which a small ball is driven with special clubs into each of a number of holes in as few strokes as possible. ◊*v.i.* **2.** to play golf. [ME (Scot); orig. uncert.] **–golfer**, *n.*

golf ball, *n.* **1.** a small white ball with a hard rubber centre, used in playing golf. **2.** *Colloq.* a movable metal ball bearing the type in an electric typewriter.

Goliath /gə'laɪəθ/, *n.* **1.** a person of great strength or size; a giant. **2.** *Bible.* a gigantic Philistine champion who was slain by David with a stone from his sling. [See I Sam 17. From L (Vulgate), from Gk (Septuagint), representing Heb *Golyath*]

golliwog /'gɒliwɒg/, *n.* a soft, black-faced doll. Also, **gollywog**. [var. of *Golliwogg*, name of a doll coined c. 1910 by Florence and Bertha Upton, US writers for children]

Gomorrah /gə'mɒrə/, *n.* the ancient city destroyed (with Sodom) for the wickedness of its inhabitants. Also, **Gomorrha**. [See Genesis 18–19]

-gon, a suffix indicating geometrical figures having a certain number or kind of angles, as in *polygon*, *pentagon*. [Gk *-gōnos* (neut. *-gōnon*) -angled, -angular]

gonad /'gounæd/, *n.* the sex gland, male or female, in which the reproductive cells are produced. [NL, from Gk: offspring, seed]

gondola /'gɒndələ/, *n.* **1.** a long, narrow boat with a high peak at each end and often a small cabin near the middle, used on the canals in Venice, Italy. **2.** a basket beneath a balloon, for carrying passengers, etc. [It (Venetian), from Rom root *dond-* to rock]

gondolier /gɒndə'lɪə/, *n.* a person who rows or poles a gondola. [F, from It]

Gondwana /gɒnd'wanə/, *n.* an ancient continent including India, Australia, Antarctica, parts of Africa and South America in Palaeozoic and Mesozoic times. Also, **Gondwanaland**. [region in India, from Skt]

gone /gɒn/, *v.* **1.** past participle of **go**. ◊*adj.* **2.** lost; without hope. **3.** *Colloq.* in a state of excitement (as by the influence of drugs, music, etc.). **4. far gone**, *Colloq.* much advanced; deeply involved. **5. gone on**, *Colloq.* having strong feelings for: *He is gone on rock music*.

goner /'gɒnə/, *n. Colloq.* someone or something dead, lost, or past saving, etc.

gong /gɒŋ/, *n.* (something like) an oriental bronze disc, which, when struck with a soft-headed stick, etc., gives a loud ringing tone. [Malay]

-gonium /-'gouniəm/, a word part referring to reproductive cells. [NL, from Gk *-gonia*, combining form representing *goneía* generation]

gono-, a word part meaning 'sexual' or 'reproductive', as in *gonocyte*. [Gk, combining form of *gónos*, *gonē* seed, generation, etc.]

gonocyte /'gɒnoʊsaɪt/, *n. Biol.* a germ cell, esp. during the maturation phase; oocyte or spermatocyte.

gonorrhoea /gɒnə'riə/, *n.* a contagious disease of the sex organs. [Gk *gono-* GONO- + *rhoía* a flow] — **gonorrhoeal**, *adj.*

-gony, a word part meaning 'production', 'genesis', 'origination', as in *cosmogony*. [L *-gonia*, from Gk. See -GONIUM, -GENY]

goo /guː/, *n. Colloq.* sticky matter. [short for *burgoo*, an oatmeal gruel]

good /gʊd/, *adj.*, **better**, **best**, *n.*, *interj.*
◊*adj.* **1.** morally excellent; righteous; pious: *a good man.* **2.** satisfactory in quality, quantity, etc.; excellent: *good food.* **3.** right; proper: *If it seems good to you, then do it.* **4.** well-behaved: *a good child.* **5.** helpful; beneficial (oft. fol. by *for*): *This medicine is good for you.* **6.** (of food) fresh and nutritious. **7.** honorable; worthy: *a good name.* **8.** safe; reliable: *good brakes.* **9.** close; loyal: *a good friend.* **10.** beautiful; fine: *She has a good figure.* **11.** agreeable; pleasant: *Have a good time.* **12.** satisfactory for the purpose: *a good day for fishing.* **13.** sufficient; ample: *a good supply.* **14.** (of clothes) best; newest: *Save your good clothes for going out.* **15.** full: *a good three miles.* **16.** clever; skilful: *a good farmer.* **17.** (used in combination with times of day, as a greeting, farewell, etc.): *good afternoon; good night.* ◊**18.** Some special uses are:
as good as, almost; practically: *He's as good as finished.*
as good as gold, *Colloq.* well-behaved.
good for, **1.** legal; valid: *That ticket is good for a month.* **2.** giving (a person) a right to: *That is good for a beer or two.* **3.** (of a person) willing to provide: *He is always good for a meal.*
good grief, *Colloq.* (an expression of surprise, etc.).
◊*n.* **19.** profit; advantage: *It's for your own good; the greatest good of the greatest number.* **20.** (*sometimes cap.*) the force which governs correct and honorable action: *We believe good will triumph.* **21.** (*pl.*) possessions, esp. movable ones. **22.** (*pl.*) articles of trade, esp. those transported by land. ◊**23.** Some special uses are:
be up to no good, *Colloq.* to be doing wrong.
do good, **1.** to perform actions of kindness, charity, etc. **2.** to have a beneficial effect on: *It does me good to see you.*
for good, finally; for ever.
make good, **1.** to pay for: *I'll make good your losses.* **2.** to fulfil: *He made good his promise.* **3.** to be successful.
◊*interj.* **24.** (an expression of approval or satisfaction. **25. good on / for you,** *Colloq.* (an expression of approval, encouragement, etc.) [OE *gōd*; ? orig. meaning fitting, suitable, and akin to GATHER]

goodbye /gʊd'baɪ/, *interj.*, *n.*, *pl.* **-byes.**
◊*interj.* **1.** farewell (an expression commonly used at parting). ◊*n.* **2.** a farewell. (contraction of *God be with you (ye)*]

good faith, *n.* **1.** honesty or sincerity: *to act in good faith.* **2.** expectation of such qualities in others: *to take a job in good faith.*

Good Friday, *n.* the Friday before Easter, a holy day of the Christian Church, observed as the anniversary of the crucifixion of Jesus.

Good Hope, *n.* **Cape of** → **Cape of Good Hope.**

goodnight /gəd'naɪt/, *n.*; /'gʊdnaɪt/, *adj.*
◊*n.* **1.** a leave-taking; a farewell. ◊*adj.* **2.** of or relating to a parting, esp. final or at night: *a goodnight kiss.*

goodwill /gʊd'wɪl/, *n.* **1.** friendly feelings; benevolence: *I have nothing but goodwill towards him.* **2.** cheerful agreement; willingness: *He carried the heavy parcel with goodwill.* **3.** *Comm.* the value to a business of its name for good service, as opposed to the value of goods.

gooey /'guːi/, *adj.*, **gooier**, **gooiest.** *Colloq.* **1.** like goo; sticky. **2.** sentimental; soppy.

goof /guːf, gʊf/, *Colloq.* ◊*n.* **1.** a foolish person. ◊*v.i.* **2.** to slip up; blunder. **3. goof off**, to daydream; waste time. ◊*v.t.* **4.** to spoil (something); bungle (oft. fol. by *up*). [obs. *goff* dolt, from F] — **goofy**, *adj.*

goog /gʊg/, *n. Colloq.* **1.** an egg. **2. full as a goog**, **a.** very drunk. **b.** well-fed.

googly /'guːgli/, *n.* (in cricket) a ball which looks as if it will bounce in one direction but in fact goes the other way. [orig. unknown]

Goolagong /'guːləgɒŋ/, *n.* **Evonne Fay** → **Evonne Fay Cawley.**

goon /guːn/, *n. Colloq.* **1.** a stupid person. **2.** a hooligan or tough. **3. the Goons**, a group of comedians who presented a popular BBC radio comedy show between 1951 and 1960. The show featured Spike Milligan, Peter Sellers, Harry Secombe and (1951–52) Michael Bentine.

goose /guːs/, *n.*, *pl.* **geese.** **1.** a large web-footed bird with long neck, sometimes kept on farms for food. **2.** the female of this bird, as separate from male (or gander). **3.** the flesh of the goose. **4.** a silly or foolish person. **5. cook someone's goose**, *Colloq.* to ruin a person's hopes or plans. [OE *gōs* (pl. *gēs*)]

gooseberry /'gʊzbəri, -bri/, *n.*, *pl.* **-ries.** **1.** a small, acidic, round berry. **2.** the shrub the berry grows on. **3. play gooseberry**, to accompany people who might like to be alone.

goose pimples, *n.pl.* a rough condition of the skin looking like that of a plucked goose, caused by cold or fear. Also, **goose bumps, goose flesh.** — **goosepimply**, *adj.*

goosestep /'guːsstɛp/, *n.*, *v.*, **-stepped, -stepping.** ◊*n.* **1.** an unusual marching step in which the legs are swung high with straight, stiff knees. ◊*v.i.* **2.** to march in a goosestep.

gopher /'goʊfə/, *n.* any of various terrestrial rodents of western North America. [? F *gaufre* honeycomb]

Gorbachev /'gɒbətʃɒf, gəbə'tʃɒf/, *n.* **Mikhail Sergeyevich** /'mɪkaɪl sə'geɪəvɪtʃ/, born 1931, Soviet statesman; became general secretary of the Soviet Communist Party in 1985; Soviet president from 1988 to dissolution of the Union in 1991; 1990 Nobel Peace Prize.

Gorbals /'gɔbəlz/, *n.* **the**, an inner suburb of Glasgow, formerly noted for its slums.

Gordon[1] /'gɔdn/, *n.* **Adam Lindsay**, 1833–70, Australian poet and horseman, born in the Azores; author of the verse collection *Bush Ballads and Galloping Rhymes* (1870).

Gordon[2] /'gɔdn/, *n.* a river in western Tas, rising south-west of Lake King William and flowing westerly to Macquarie Harbor; dammed in the early 1970s to form the Gordon and Pedder reservoirs; Gordon hydro-electric power scheme. About 200 km.

gore[1] /gɔ/, *n.* blood from a wound, esp. when clotted. [OE *gor* dung, dirt]

gore[2] /gɔ/, *v.t.*, **gored**, **goring**. (of an animal) to pierce with the horns or tusks. [ME *goren*. Cf. GORE[3]]

gore[3] /gɔ/, *n.* a triangular piece of cloth, etc., sewn into a dress, a sail, etc., to give greater width or shape. [OE *gāra* corner from *gār* spear]

gorge /gɔdʒ/, *n.*, *v.*, **gorged**, **gorging**. ◇*n.* **1.** a narrow valley with steep, rocky walls, esp. one through which a stream runs. **2.** the contents of the stomach. **3.** the throat; gullet. ◇*v.t.* **4.** to stuff with food (mainly reflexive or passive): *He gorged himself*. [ME, from OF: throat, from LL b. L *gurges* stream, abyss and *gula* throat]

gorgeous /'gɔdʒəs/, *adj.* **1.** splendid in appearance or coloring; magnificent. **2.** *Colloq.* very good; enjoyable. [ME, from OF: fashionable, gay]

Gorgon /'gɔgən/, *n. Gk Legend.* any of three sisters whose heads were covered with snakes instead of hair, and whose glance turned the beholder to stone. —**Gorgonian**, *adj.*

gorilla /gə'rɪlə/, *n.* the largest member of the ape family, found in western equatorial Africa. [NL, from Gk; said to be of African orig.]

Göring /'gɜrɪŋ/, *n.* **Hermann Wilhelm** /,hɜmən 'vɪlhelm/, 1893–1946, German Nazi party leader; chief of the Gestapo, minister of aviation, field marshal, commander-in-chief of the Air Force and economic dictator of the Third Reich. Also, **Goering**.

Gorki[1] /'gɔki/, *n.* **Maxim** (*Aleksei Peshkov*), 1868–1936, Russian novelist, short-story writer, and dramatist; gained renown as a spokesman for the outcasts of society. Also, **Gorky**.

Gorki[2] /'gɔki/, *n.* a port and city of the central USSR, at the meeting of the Volga and Oka Rivers; birthplace of Maxim Gorki. Pop. 1 409 000 (1986 est.). Formerly, **Nizhni Novgorod**.

gormandise *or* **gormandize** /'gɔməndaɪz/, *v.i.*, *v.t.*, **-dised**, **-dising**. to eat in great quantity. [F: gluttony] —**gormandiser**, *n.*

gormless /'gɔmləs/, *adj. Colloq.* (of a person) dull; stupid. [dialect *gaum* attention, heed] —**gormlessness**, *n.*

Goroka /gə'roukə/, *n.* a town in the province of Eastern Highlands, PNG. Pop. 25 000 (1984).

gorse /gɔs/, *n. Bot.* a low, branching, spiny shrub with yellow flowers. [OE *gors(t)*] —**gorsy**, *adj.*

Gorton /'gɔtn/, *n.* **Sir John Grey**, born 1911, Australian Liberal politician; prime minister 1968–71.

gory /'gɔri/, *adj.*, **gorier**, **goriest**. **1.** covered or stained with gore; bloody. **2.** *Colloq.* distasteful; unpleasant: *He read the gory details of the accident.*

Gosford /'gɔsfəd/, *n.* a city on the central coast of NSW, at the northern end of Brisbane Water. Pop. (with Woy Woy) 109 278 (1986).

gosh /gɒʃ/, *interj.* (a cry of surprise). [a euphemistic var. of *God!*]

goshawk /'gɒʃɔk/, *n.* any of various powerful, short-winged hawks, formerly much used in falconry. [OE *gōshafoc* goosehawk]

gosling /'gɒzlɪŋ/, *n.* a young goose. [ME, from Scand]

go-slow /ˌgou-'slou/, *adj.*, *n. Colloq.* (relating to) the intentional action of workers in an industrial struggle of slowing down the rate of work.

gospel /'gɒspəl/, *n.* **1.** (*oft. cap.*) the teachings of Christ and the apostles, as found in the first four books of the New Testament. **2.** (*usu. cap.*) one of these books. **3.** something regarded as true and totally believed: *to take as gospel.* ◇*adj.* **4.** relating to the gospel. [OE *gōd* GOOD + *spell* tidings]

gospel music, *n.* music based on hymns, mainly using voices in full, rich harmony.

gossamer /'gɒsəmə/, *n.* **1.** a fine cobweb, seen on grass and bushes, or floating in the air in calm weather, esp. in autumn. **2.** any very delicate type of material. ◇*adj.* **3.** Also, **gossamery** /'gɒsəməri/. of or like gossamer. [ME *gos(e)-somer*. See GOOSE, SUMMER; possibly first used as name for late mild autumn (Indian summer) time when goose was a favorite dish, then transferred to the filmy matter also found in that season]

Gosse /gɒs/, *n.* **William Christie**, 1842–81, Australian surveyor and explorer, born in England; named Ayers Rock, 1873.

gossip /'gɒsəp/, *n.*, *v.*, **-siped** *or* **-sipped**, **-siping** *or* **-sipping**. ◇*n.* **1.** idle useless talk, esp. about the affairs of others; rumor. **2.** light, familiar talk or writing. **3.** someone who talks gossip. ◇*v.i.* **4.** to talk about the affairs of others. [OE *godsipp*, godparent] —**gossiper**, *n.* —**gossipy**, *adj.*

got /gɒt/, *v.* past tense and past participle of **get**.

Goth /gɒθ/, *n.* one of a Teutonic people who, in the third to fifth century AD, invaded and settled in parts of the Roman Empire. [ME *Gothe*, from LL]

Gotham /'goutəm/ *for def. 1*; /'gɒθəm, 'gou-/ *for def. 2*, *n.* **1.** an English village near Nottingham, proverbial for the foolishness of its inhabitants; the Wise Men of Gotham feigned stupidity to deter King John from living among them. **2.** the city of New York.

Gothic /'gɒθɪk/, *adj.* **1.** relating to a style of building found in western Europe from the 12th to 16th century, having pointed arches, a rib-like (vaulted) roof, etc. **2.** (esp. in literature) having horrible and frightening images: *a Gothic novel.* **3.** *Print.* (of a typeface) having elaborate pointed letters. [LL *Gothicus*]
–**Gothically**, *adv.*

Götterdämmerung /gɜtə'dɛmərʊŋ/, *n.* (in German mythology) the twilight of the gods; the final destruction of the world by the forces of evil.

gouache /gu'aʃ, -'æʃ/, *n.* **1.** (a method of painting with) opaque watercolor. **2.** a painting using gouache. [F, from It: puddle, spray of water, from L: water]

gouda /'gaʊdə, 'gu-/, *n.* a smooth, mild-tasting cheese, often made in a large wheel shape. [named after *Gouda*, Holland, where this cheese was orig. made]

gouge /gaʊdʒ/, *n., v.,* **gouged, gouging.** ◇*n.* **1.** a tool with a curved blade, used for making grooves in wood. **2.** a hole made by this tool. ◇*v.t.* **3.** to dig out with or as if with a gouge. [F, from LL]

goulash /'gulæʃ/, *n. Cookery.* a meat stew containing onions and paprika. [Hung]

Goulburn /'goʊlbən/, *n.* **1.** a city in south-eastern NSW, at the junction of the Wollondilly and Mulwaree rivers; important rail centre. Pop. 21 552 (1986). **2.** a river in northern central Victoria, rising on the northern slopes of the Great Dividing Range and flowing north-west to become a tributary of the Murray River. About 550 km. **3.** a river in central eastern NSW, rising in the Great Dividing Range and flowing east to join the Hunter River near Singleton. [named after Frederick *Goulburn*, 1788-1837, the first official Colonial Secretary of NSW 1821-24]

Gould /guld/, *n.* **1. Elizabeth**, 1804–41, English natural history artist in Australia 1838-40. **2. John**, 1804-81, husband of Elizabeth, English ornithologist in Australia 1838-40. **3. Shane**, born 1957, Australian champion swimmer, winner of three gold medals in the 1972 Olympic Games. **4. William Buelow**, 1801–53, Australian convict and artist, born in the UK, responsible for the paintings of a number of botanical specimens.

Gouldian finch /ˌguldɪən 'fɪntʃ/, *n.* a brightly-colored bird of tropical northern Australia. Also, **painted finch, purple-breasted finch.** [named after Elizabeth GOULD]

Gould Leagues, *n.pl.* organisations established in 1908 to promote the knowledge and protection of Australian wildlife; work in association with the state departments of education. [named after John GOULD]

gourd /guəd, gɔd/, *n.* **1.** the fruit of a particular climbing plant whose dried shell is used for bottles, bowls, etc. **2.** a gourd-shaped, small-necked bottle. [ME, from F, from L]

gourmand /gɔ'mɒnd, 'gɒmənd/, *n.* someone fond of good eating. Also, **gormand.** [ME, from F: gluttonous]

gourmet /'guəmeɪ, 'gɔ-/, *n.* someone with great knowledge of good food and its presentation. [F, from OF: wine merchant's man]

gout /gaʊt/, *n.* a disease of the joints of the hands and feet, causing pain and swelling. [ME, from OF, from L: a drop, ML: gout]

Gov, *Abbrev.* governor. Also, **gov.**

Gove Peninsula /goʊv pə'nɪnʃələ/, *n.* a peninsula on the north-eastern point of Arnhem Land, NT; site of an Aboriginal reserve and of bauxite mining and alumina production.

govern /'gʌvən/, *v.t.* **1.** to rule by right of authority.: *to govern a state.* **2.** to have a directing influence over; guide: *Anger governed his decision.* **3.** to hold in control: *to govern your temper.* **4.** to serve as a law for: *the principles governing a case.* **5.** *Gram.* to control (the case of a noun or the mood of a verb); for example, in 'They helped us', the verb *'helped'* is said to govern the objective case of the pronoun. ◇*v.i.* **6.** to have a controlling influence. [ME, from L, from Gk: steer, guide, govern]
–**governable**, *adj.*

governess /'gʌvənəs/, *n.* a woman who directs the education of children, usually in their own homes.

government /'gʌvənmənt/, *n.* **1.** the authoritative direction and control over communities, societies and states. **2.** the form or system of rule by which a state, community, etc., is governed: *coalition government.* **3.** (*sometimes treated as pl.*) the governing group of people in a state, community, etc.; the administration: *The government was defeated in the last election.* **4.** direction; control; rule: *the government of your conduct.* –**governmental**, *adj.*

governor /'gʌvənə, 'gʌvnə/, *n.* **1.** someone placed in control of an organisation, society, etc.: *governor of a bank.* **2. a.** the representative of the king or queen with powers given by law, in a British dependent territory: *Phillip was the first governor of Australia.* **b.** the main representative of the king or queen in a state of the Commonwealth of Australia. **3.** the executive head of a state in the US. **4.** *Mach.* a device for controlling a supply of fuel in an engine. [ME, from L: steersman, director]

Governor /'gʌvənə/, *n.* **Jimmy**, 1875–1901, Australian outlaw; the subject of Thomas Keneally's novel *The Chant of Jimmie Blacksmith* (1972).

governor-general /gʌvənə-'dʒɛnrəl/, *n., pl.* **governor-generals, governors-general.** the main representative of the king or queen in certain independent Commonwealth countries.

Govt, *Abbrev.* government. Also, **govt.**

gown /gaʊn/, *n.* **1.** a woman's dress, worn on formal occasions. **2.** a loose, flowing garment in various forms, worn to represent an office or profession: *a judge's gown.* ◇*v.t., v.i.* **3.** to dress in a gown. [ME, from LL; orig. uncert.]

Goya /'gɔɪə/, *n.* **Francisco de** (*Francisco José de Goya y Lucientes*), 1746–1828, Spanish painter and engraver; much of his work depicts cruelty of war, in particular, the invasion of Spain by Napoleon.

GP /dʒi 'pi/, *Abbrev.* general practitioner.

GPO /dʒi pi 'oʊ/, *Abbrev.* General Post Office.

GPS /dʒi pi 'ɛs/, *Abbrev.* Greater Public Schools.

gr., *Abbrev.* **1.** grade. **2.** grain; grains. **3.** gross.

Graafian follicle /ˌgrafiən 'fɒlikəl/, *n.* one of many small sacs within the ovary which, at ovulation, discharges an ovum. Also, **Graafian vesicle**. [named after R de Graaf, 1641–73, Dutch anatomist]

grab /græb/, *v.*, **grabbed, grabbing,** *n.* ◇*v.t.* **1.** to take hold of suddenly; snatch. **2.** to take illegal possession of: *to grab land*. **3.** *Colloq.* to affect: *How does that grab you?* ◇*n.* **4.** the act of grabbing. [MD and MLG *grabben*] —**grabber,** *n.*

Gracchi /'græki/, *n.pl* **the**, Gaius and Tiberius Gracchus.

Gracchus /'grækəs/, *n.* **1. Gaius Sempronius** /'gaɪəs sɛm'proʊniəs/, 153?–121 BC, Roman political reformer and orator. **2.** his brother, **Tiberius Sempronius** /taɪ-'bɪəriəs/, 163?–133 BC, Roman reformer and orator.

grace /greɪs/, *n., v.,* **graced, gracing**. ◇*n.* **1.** fineness or beauty of form, manner, movement, etc. **2.** a pleasing or attractive quality. **3.** favor or goodwill: *to find favor with God*. **4.** mercy; pardon: *His freedom was an act of grace*. **5.** (*pl.*) an affected manner resulting from pride or vanity: *to put on airs and graces*. **6.** *Theol.* **a.** the free, undeserved favor and love of God. **b.** a moral excellence (virtue) from God: *the Christian graces*. **7.** a short prayer before or after a meal. **8.** (*usu. cap.*) a title used in addressing a duke, duchess, or archbishop, and formerly also a sovereign (preceded by *your, his,* etc.). **9.** (*cap.*) *Class Myth.* one of three sister goddesses, controlling all beauty and charm in nature and humanity. **10. fall from grace, a.** *Theol.* to descend into sin. **b.** to lose favor, esp. with someone in authority. **11. have the grace to,** to be so kind as to (do something). **12. with (a) bad grace,** unwillingly; reluctantly. ◇*v.t.* **13.** to lend or add grace to; adorn. **14.** to favor or honor: *to grace an occasion with your presence*. [ME, from L: favor, gratitude, agreeableness]

Grace /greɪs/, *n.* **W(illiam) G(ilbert),** 1848–1915, English cricketer.

graceful /'greɪsfəl/, *adj.* characterised by grace of form, manner, movement, or speech; elegant.

grace-note /'greɪs-noʊt/, *n. Music.* a note which is not part of the harmony or melody, added as an embellishment.

gracious /'greɪʃəs/, *adj.* **1.** showing grace or favor; kind; courteous. **2.** showing politeness to someone felt to be of less importance. ◇*interj.* **3.** (an expression of surprise, etc.). [ME, from L: enjoying or showing favor]

grad., *Abbrev.* **1.** graduate. **2.** graduated.

gradation /grə'deɪʃən/, *n.* any change taking place through a series of stages, by degrees, or gradually. —**gradate,** *v.*

grade /greɪd/, *n., v.,* **graded, grading,** *adj.* ◇*n.* **1.** a degree in a scale, as of position, advancement, quality, value, etc. **2.** a class of people or things of the same position, quality, etc. **3.** a step or stage in a course or method. **4.** a division of a school in terms of pupils' age or ability. **5.** a number, letter, etc., representing the quality of a student's work. **6.** → **gradient** (def. 2). **7. make the grade,** to reach a desired standard. ◇*v.t.* **8.** to arrange in a series of grades; class; sort. **9.** to determine the grade of. **10.** to make level: *to grade a road*. ◇*adj.* **11.** *Sport.* played in grades: *grade cricket*. [F, from L *gradus* step, stage, degree]

-grade, a word part meaning 'walking', 'moving', 'going', as in *retrograde*. [combining form representing L *gradus* step, or *gradi, v.,* walk. See GRADE, GRADIENT]

grader /'greɪdə/, *n.* **1.** someone or something that grades. **2.** a motor-driven vehicle, with a blade for pushing earth, used for levelling roads.

gradient /'greɪdiənt/, *n.* **1.** the degree of slope or steepness in a road, railway, etc. **2.** a sloping surface; ramp. **3.** *Phys.* **a.** change in a variable quantity, as temperature or pressure, per unit distance. **b.** a curve showing this rate of change. ◇*adj.* **4.** rising or falling by regular degrees of slope. [L: walking, going]

gradual /'grædʒuəl/, *adj.* **1.** taking place, changing, moving, etc., by degrees or little by little. **2.** not steep: *a gradual slope*. [See GRADE]

graduate /'grædʒuət/, *n., adj.;* /'grædʒueɪt/, *v.,* **-ated, -ating**. ◇*n.* **1.** someone who has received a degree on completing a course of study, as at university or college. ◇*adj.* **2.** of or relating to graduates: *a graduate course*. ◇*v.i.* **3.** to receive a degree on completing a course of study. **4.** to pass by degrees; change gradually. ◇*v.t.* **5.** to divide into degrees or other divisions, as the scale of a thermometer. [ML: admit to an academic degree, from L *gradus* step, grade] —**graduator,** *n.*

graduation /grædʒu'eɪʃən/, *n.* **1.** the act or result of graduating. **2.** a ceremony in which university degrees are presented.

Graeco-, word part meaning 'Greek'. [L, combining form of *Graecus*]

Graeco-Roman /ˌgrikoʊ-'roʊmən, ˌgrɛ-/, *adj.* relating to Greek and Roman influences, as found in Roman sculpture. Also, **Greco-Roman.**

graffiti /grə'fiti/, *n.pl., sing.* **graffito** /grə'fitoʊ/. drawing or words written on walls. [It: a scratch, from Gk: mark, draw, write]

graft[1] /graft/, *n.* **1.** *Hort.* a shoot or part of a plant (the scion) placed in a groove or slit in another plant (the stock) so as to be fed by and united with it. **2.** *Surg.* a piece of living tissue cut from one part of a person and placed else-

graft where on their body or on another person's body. ◇*v.t.* **3.** to insert (a graft) into a plant or tree. **4.** to cause (a plant) to grow through grafting. **5.** *Surg.* to transplant (a part of living tissue) as a graft. ◇*v.i.* **6.** to become grafted. [ME, from OF: stylus, pencil, from LL, from Gk: stylus] −**grafter**, *n.* −**grafting**, *n.*

graft² /graft/, *n.* **1.** work, esp. hard work. **2.** the gaining of money unfairly, by the dishonest use of one's position: *graft and corruption.* ◇*v.i.* **3.** to work hard. **4.** to practise graft. [Brit d.]

Grafton /'graftən/, *n.* a city in the North Coast district of NSW, on the Clarence River; centre of the Clarence River district. Pop. 16 647 (1986).

Grahame /'greɪəm/, *n.* **Kenneth**, 1859−1932, Scottish author, esp. of children's stories; best-known work *The Wind in the Willows* (1908).

grail /greɪl/, *n.* the cup thought to be used by Jesus at the Last Supper; Holy Grail. [ME, from OF, from ML: plate, bowl]

grain /greɪn/, *n.* **1.** a small hard seed, esp. a seed of one of the cereal plants: wheat, rye, oats, etc. **2.** the plants themselves. **3.** any small, hard particle, as of sand, gold, pepper, etc. **4.** the smallest unit of weight in most imperial systems, originally set by the weight of a large grain of wheat. **5.** the smallest possible amount of anything: *a grain of truth.* **6. with a grain of salt**, without fully believing. **7.** the direction of the fibres in wood or cloth. **8.** *Gems.* a unit of weight for pearls equal to 50 mg or ¼ carat. **9.** the size of particles making up any substance: *sugar of fine grain.* **10.** granular texture or appearance: *a stone of coarse grain.* **11.** *Geol.* a direction of splitting in rock. **12.** natural character: *to go against the grain.* ◇*v.t.* **13.** to form into grain; granulate. [ME, from OF, from L: grain, seed] −**grainer**, *n.*

Grainger /'greɪndʒə/, *n.* **(George) Percy**, 1882−1961, Australian pianist and composer; noted for his musical innovations.

gram /græm/, *n.* a metric unit of mass, one thousandth of a kilogram. *Symbol:* g [F, from LL, from Gk: a small weight, orig. something drawn]

-gram¹, a word part meaning something drawn or written, as in *diagram, telegram.* [Gk *-gramma* something drawn or written, or *-grammon* relating to a stroke or line]

-gram², a word part meaning grams; or of relating to a gram, as in *kilogram.* [Gk *grámma* small weight]

gramineous /grə'mɪnɪəs/, *adj.* like grass. [L: relating to grass]

gramma /'græmə/, *n.* a type of pumpkin, the fruit of which has an orange flesh and skin.

grammar /'græmə/, *n.* **1.** (a description of) the parts of a language (sounds, words, formation and arrangement of words, etc.) regarded as a system or structure: *English grammar.* **2.** →**syntax**. **3.** speech or writing conforming to standard usage: *He knows his grammar.* **4.** a book containing a grammar. [ME, from OF, from L, from Gk: relating to letters or literature]

grammarian /grə'mɛərɪən/, *n.* a specialist in the study of grammar.

grammatical /grə'mætɪkəl/, *adj.* **1.** relating to grammar: *grammatical analysis.* **2.** conforming to standard usage: *grammatical speech.*

Grammy /'græmɪ/, *n. US.* one of the awards presented annually by the National Academy of Recording Arts and Sciences for excellence in various categories of recorded music.

gramophone /'græməfoʊn/, *n.* → **record-player**.

Grampians /'græmpɪənz/, *n.pl.* a series of three sandstone ranges in western Vic forming the western end of the Great Dividing Range. 145 km long. Highest peak, Mt William, 1168 m.

grampus /'græmpəs/, *n.* **1.** a mammal of the dolphin family, found in northern seas. **2.** any of various related marine mammals as the killer whale. [OF, from ML: fat fish]

gran /græn/, *n. Colloq.* a grandmother. Also, **granny**.

Granada /grə'nadə/, *n.* a city in southern Spain in Andalusia, once capital of the Moorish kingdom of Granada; site of the Alhambra palace (13th−14th centuries), a great Moorish monument. Pop. 256 528 (1986 est.).

granary /'grænərɪ/, *n., pl.* **-ries.** a storehouse for grain. [L]

grand /grænd/, *adj.* **1.** impressive in size, appearance or effect: *grand mountain scenery.* **2.** stately; majestic; dignified. **3.** splendid; magnificent: *a grand palace.* **4.** noble; fine: *a grand old man.* **5.** highest, or very high, in importance or official position: *a grand ruler.* **6.** main; principal; chief: *the grand staircase.* **7.** complete; comprehensive: *a grand total.* **8.** *Colloq.* first-rate; very good: *grand weather.* **9.** younger or older by one generation than the specified relationship (used in compounds), as in *grandfather, grandchild,* etc. ◇*n.* **10.** → **piano¹** (def. 2). **11.** *Colloq.* a thousand dollars. [ME, from L: large, full-grown, great, grand]

Grand Canal, *n.* **1.** a canal in eastern China, extending from Beijing south to Hangzhou; the longest canal in the world. About 1706 km. **2.** a large canal in Venice, Italy, forming the main thoroughfare.

Grand Canyon, *n.* a spectacular gorge in northern Arizona, US, carved by the Colorado River. 349 km long; 6−29 km wide; 1.6 km greatest depth.

grand duke, *n.* **1.** the ruler of an area (a grand duchy), next in importance to king. **2.** (formerly) the son or grandson of a Russian tsar. −**grand duchess**, *n. fem.*

grandeur /'grændʒə/, *n.* the state or quality of being grand; imposing greatness. [F]

grandfather clock, *n.* a clock with a pendulum, in a tall wooden case.

grand final, *n.* (in a sporting competition) the final game to decide the winner.

grandiloquent /græn'dıləkwənt/, *adj.* speaking in a grand or over-important style; bombastic.

grandiose /'grændiouz/, *adj.* **1.** grand; impressive. **2.** too grand or stately; pompous. [F, from It] —**grandiosity,** *n.*

Grand National, *n.* the annual steeplechase run at Aintree, Liverpool, UK, since 1839.

grand opera, *n.* a serious drama set to music, the words being sung throughout.

grandparent /'grændpɛərənt/, *n.* the parent of one's own parent.

grand piano, *n.* → **piano**[1] (def. 2).

grandstand /'grændstænd, 'grænd-/, *n.* **1.** the main stand for viewers (spectators) at a racecourse, sports field, etc. ◇*v.i.* **2.** to behave in an attention-seeking way, in order to impress. ◇*adj.* **3.** from a good point for viewing: *a grandstand view of the fight.*

grange /greɪndʒ/, *n. Brit.* **1.** a farm. **2.** (formerly) a farmhouse belonging to a feudal manor or a religious establishment, where crops were stored. [ME, from AF, from L: grain]

granite /'grænət/, *n.* a granular igneous rock composed mainly of felspar (orthoclase) and quartz, usu. with one or more other minerals, as mica, hornblende, etc., much used in building, and for monuments, etc. [It: grained, from L: grain]

granivorous /grə'nɪvərəs/, *adj.* feeding on grain and seeds.

granny flat /'græni flæt/, *n.* a self-contained area of a house, designed either for a relative such as a grandmother to live in, or to be rented.

granny knot, *n.* a square (reef) knot in which the second part is crossed the wrong way. [orig. a sailor's disapproving term for such a knot]

Granny Smith, *n.* a type of apple with green skin, suitable for eating raw or cooking. [from Maria Ann *Smith*, d. 1870, who first produced them at Eastwood, Sydney]

grant /grænt, grant/, *v.t.* **1.** to give or allow, esp. formally: *to grant permission; to grant a pension.* **2.** to agree to: *to grant a request.* **3.** to admit or accept: *I grant that point.* **4.** to give or transfer, esp. by formal legal document: *to grant property.* **5. take for granted,** to accept (something) without questioning or appreciating it. ◇*n.* **6.** something which is granted, e.g. a sum of money or piece of land. **7.** the act of granting. **8.** *Law.* a document which transfers property from one person to another. [ME, from AF: promise, authorise, confirm, approve, from L: trust, believe]

Grant /grænt, grant/, *n.* **1.** Cary (*Alexander Archibald Leach*), 1904–86, British-born Hollywood film actor; won Academy Award for contributions to American cinema 1970. **2.** Ulysses S(impson), 1822–85, Union general in the American Civil War and 18th president of the US, 1869–77.

granular /'grænjələ/, *adj.* **1.** of, like, or made of granules or grains. **2.** having a grainy structure or surface. —**granularity,** *n.*

granulate /'grænjəleɪt/, *v.,* **-lated, -lating.** ◇*v.t.* **1.** to form into granules or grains. ◇*v.i.* **2.** to become granular. [GRANUL(E) + -ATE[1]] —**granulator,** *n.* —**granulation,** *n.*

granule /'grænjul/, *n.* a little grain or particle. [L: little grain]

grape /greɪp/, *n.* **1.** a small, round, smooth-skinned greenish or purplish fruit which grows in bunches on vines, used for eating or making wine. **2.** any vine bearing grapes. **3. the grape,** *Colloq.* wine. **4.** a dull, dark purplish red. [ME, from OF: cluster of fruit or flowers; of Gmc orig.]

grapefruit /'greɪpfrut/, *n.* (a tree bearing) large, roundish, yellow-skinned eatable citrus fruit with sour, juicy flesh.

grapevine /'greɪpvaɪn/, *n.* **1.** a vine that bears grapes. **2.** *Colloq.* an informal way in which information is carried, esp. rumor: *I heard it on the grapevine.*

graph /græf, graf/, *n.* **1.** a diagram showing relationships between two or more things by dots, lines, curves, bars, etc. **2.** *Maths.* a curve showing a given function. ◇*v.t.* **3.** to draw a graph of. **4.** to draw (a curve) to show a given function. [short for *graphic formula*]

graph-, a form of **grapho-** before vowels.

-graph, a word part meaning: **1.** drawn or written, as in *autograph, monograph.* **2.** something that draws, writes, records, etc., as in *telegraph.* [Gk: (something) drawn or written, also one who draws or writes]

graphic /'græfɪk/, *adj.* **1.** life-like; vivid: *a graphic description of a scene.* **2.** relating to use of diagrams, graphs, etc. **3.** relating to writing. **4.** *Maths.* relating to use of diagrams instead of calculation to solve equations, etc. Also, **graphical.** [L, from Gk: drawing, writing] —**graphically,** *adv.*

graphic arts, *n.pl.* forms of art, e.g. design, drawing, painting, engraving, used to express ideas artistically. —**graphic artist,** *n.*

graphics /'græfɪks/, *n.* **1.** the art of drawing, esp. in mathematics, engineering, etc. **2.** the use of diagrams for calculation. **3.** the production of patterns and diagrams by computer. **4.** design combining diagrams or pictures with printing or writing. [GRAPH + -ICS]

graphite /'græfaɪt/, *n.* a soft blackish allotrope (form) of carbon with a metallic sheen and greasy feel, used in so-called lead pencils, and to reduce friction in machines, etc.; black lead. [G, from Gk: mark, draw, write + -ITE] —**graphitic,** *adj.*

grapho-, a word part meaning 'writing', as in *graphology.* Also, **graph-.** [Gk]

graphology /græ'fɒlədʒi/, *n.* the study of handwriting, esp. as regarded as an expression of a writer's character.

graph paper, *n.* paper with small squares on it for drawing graphs and diagrams.

-graphy, a word part meaning: **1.** a process or form of drawing, writing, etc., as in *photography, typography*. **2.** a descriptive science, as in *geography*. [Gk]

grapnel /'græpnəl/, *n.* **1.** a tool consisting of one or more claws for hooking and holding something; grapple. **2.** a small anchor with three or more hooks. Also, *Naut.*, **grappling iron**. [ME, from OF: little hook]

Grappelli /grə'peli/, *n.* **Stephane** /'stefən/, born 1908, French jazz violinist.

grapple /'græpəl/, *n., v.*, **-pled, -pling**. ◇*n.* **1.** a grapnel (def. 1). **2.** the act of seizing or gripping. **3.** a grip or close hold in fighting or wrestling. ◇*v.t.* **4.** to seize, hold, or fasten. **5.** to engage in a struggle with. ◇*v.i.* **6.** to hold or make fast to something as with a grapple. **7.** to use a grapple. **8.** to grip another, or each other, as in wrestling; clinch. **9.** to try to deal (fol. by *with*): *to grapple with a problem*. [OE: seize]

grasp /græsp, grasp/, *v.t.* **1.** to seize and hold, esp. with the fingers. **2.** to lay hold of with the mind; understand. ◇*v.i.* **3.** to seize something firmly or eagerly. ◇*n.* **4.** a grip of the hand. **5.** the power of seizing and holding; reach: *She has it within her grasp.* **6.** hold, possession, or control. **7.** understanding: *a subject beyond my grasp.* [ME]

grasping /'græspɪŋ, 'grasp-/, *adj.* greedy.

grass /gras/, *n.* **1.** any of various plants with jointed stems, long narrow leaves and flower spikelets, producing grains, including lawn grasses (such as couch), cereals (such as wheat or oats), bamboo, etc. **2.** plants on which animals graze or which are cut and dried as hay. **3.** grass-covered ground; lawn or pasture. **4.** *Colloq.* → **marijuana**. ◇*v.t.* **5.** to grow grass over. ◇*v.i.* **6.** *Colloq.* to inform (*on*). [OE] —**grassy**, *adj.*

grasshopper /'græshɒpə/, *n.* any of various plant-eating land insects with large back legs for jumping, many of which destroy crops, etc.

grassland /'græslænd/, *n.* **1.** *Geog.* an area where natural plant growth is mostly perennial grasses, with few trees. **2.** pasture.

grass parrot, *n.* any of various parrots, esp. the budgerigar, which feed on grass seeds.

grassroots /gras'ruts, 'grasruts/, *Colloq.* ◇*n.pl.* **1.** the basics. ◇*adj.* **2.** coming from ordinary people.

grasstree /'gras,tri/, *n.* **1.** any of several woody-stemmed Australian plants with a tuft of long grass-like leaves, bearing long dense flower spike; black boy; yakka; xanthorrhoea. **2.** any of various other plants with leaves somewhat like grass.

grate¹ /greɪt/, *n.* **1.** a frame of metal bars for holding fuel when burning. **2.** → **grating**. **3.** a fireplace. [ME, from It, from L: wickerwork, hurdle]

grate² /greɪt/, *v.*, **grated, grating**. ◇*v.t.* **1.** to rub together with a rough sound: *to grate the teeth*. **2.** to rub into small particles against a rough surface or surface with many sharp-edged openings: *to grate cheese*. ◇*v.i.* **3.** to irritate or annoy. **4.** to make a sound like rough scratching; scrape. [ME, from OF, of Gmc orig.]

grateful /'greɪtfəl/, *adj.* thankful; appreciative. [obs. *grate* pleasing, thankful, from L]

gratify /'grætəfaɪ/, *v.t.*, **-fied, -fying**. **1.** to give pleasure or satisfaction to (people). **2.** to satisfy; indulge; humor: *to gratify desire*. [F, from L: do a favor to, oblige, gratify] —**gratification**, *n.* —**gratifying**, *adj.*

grating /'greɪtɪŋ/, *n.* an open framework of parallel or crossing bars used as a cover or guard.

gratis /'grɑtəs/, *adv., adj.* for nothing; free of cost. [L]

gratitude /'grætətjud/, *n.* the feeling of being grateful or thankful. [L: pleasing, thankful]

gratuitous /grə'tjuətəs/, *adj.* **1.** freely given or obtained. **2.** without reason, cause, or excuse: *a gratuitous insult*. [L: free, spontaneous] —**gratuitousness**, *n.*

gratuity /grə'tjuəti/, *n., pl.* **-ties**. **1.** a gift, usu. of money, for service given; tip. **2.** something given without being owed or demanded.

grave¹ /greɪv/, *n.* **1.** a hole dug in the earth for burying a dead body. **2.** any place for burying a body; tomb or sepulchre. **3.** any place that receives what is dead, lost or past. **4.** death. **5. turn in one's grave**, (of a dead person) to be (thought to be) shocked by some modern event. [OE]

grave² /greɪv/, *adj.*, **graver, gravest**. **1.** solemn. **2.** important. **3.** serious; critical. [F, from L: heavy]

grave accent /grav 'æksənt/ *n.* the mark (`) used to show a form of vowel sound (as in French *père*), the full pronunciation of a syllable in poetry (as in *belovèd*), etc.

gravel /'grævəl/, *n.* **1.** small stones. **2.** a mixture of small stones and sand. [ME, from OF: little sandy shore; of Celtic orig.]

gravelly /'grævəli/, *adj.* **1.** consisting of, full of, or like gravel. **2.** (of the voice) rough.

graven /'greɪvən/, *adj.* carved; engraved. [from Archaic *grave*, from OE *grafan*]

graven image, *n.* → **idol**.

Graves /greɪvz/, *n.* **Robert (Ranke)**, 1895–1985, English novelist, poet and scholar; works include *Goodbye to All That* (1929) and *I, Claudius* (1934).

Gravettian /grə'vetiən/, *adj.* relating to or characteristic of an Upper Palaeolithic culture of Europe.

gravid /'grævəd/, *adj.* → **pregnant**. [L]

gravimetric /grævə'metrɪk/, *adj.* **1.** relating to measurement by weight. **2.** *Chem.* indicating a method of analysis of a substance by changing it to another known substance which can be isolated and weighed (opposed to *volumetric*).

gravitate /'grævəteɪt/, *v.i.*, **-tated, -tating**. **1.** to move or tend to move under the influence of gravity. **2.** to sink or fall. **3.** to tend to

gravitate 449 **Great Sandy Island**

move or be attracted (fol. by *to* or *towards*). [L: heavy] —**gravitative**, *adj.*

gravitation /græv'teɪʃən/, *n.* **1.** *Phys.* **a.** a force of attraction between all particles or bodies or acceleration of one towards the other. One example is the falling of objects to the earth. **b.** a falling or moving caused by gravitation. **2.** an attraction or tendency to move (towards). —**gravitational**, *adj.*

gravitational constant, *n.* the constant in Newton's law of gravitation, equal to 6.67×10^{-11} N.m^2/kg^2. *Symbol:* G

gravitational field, *n.* the space in which a body with finite mass has a noticeable force of attraction on another body of finite mass.

gravity /'grævəti/, *n., pl.* **-ties. 1.** gravitation, esp. the force of attraction by which earthly bodies tend to fall towards the centre of the earth. **2.** heaviness or weight: *centre of gravity; specific gravity.* **3.** solemnity; dignity; seriousness. **4.** seriousness; critical quality: *the gravity of his illness.* [L: heaviness]

gravure /grə'vjuə/, *n.* (the plate used in) a process of printing, such as photogravure.

gravy /'greɪvi/, *n., pl.* **-vies. 1.** the juices that drip from meat during cooking. **2.** a sauce made from this with flour, etc. [ME, from OF: kind of dressing]

Gray /greɪ/, *n.* **1. Robin Trevor**, born 1940, Australian state Liberal politician; premier of Tasmania 1982–89. **2. Thomas**, 1716–71, English poet; wrote *Elegy written in a Country Churchyard* (1751).

grayling /'greɪlɪŋ/, *n.* **1.** a small freshwater fish of south-eastern Australia with a narrow grey band along the sides and marked yellow fin. **2.** elsewhere, a type of freshwater fish related to trout.

graze[1] /greɪz/, *v.,* **grazed, grazing.** ◇*v.i.* **1.** to feed on growing grass, like cattle, sheep, etc. ◇*v.t.* **2.** to feed on (growing grass). **3.** to put cattle, sheep, etc., to feed on (grass, etc.). [OE: grass]

graze[2] /greɪz/, *v.,* **grazed, grazing,** *n.* ◇*v.t.* **1.** to touch or rub lightly in passing. **2.** to rub or scratch some skin from. ◇*v.i.* **3.** to lightly touch or rub. ◇*n.* **4.** a light touch or rub. **5.** a scratch; abrasion. [orig. uncert.]

grazier /'greɪziə/, *n.* the owner of a property on which sheep or cattle are grazed.

grease /gris/, *n.; v.* /griz, gris/, *v.,* **greased, greasing.** ◇*n.* **1.** melted animal fat. **2.** any fatty or oily substance. **3.** a substance used to reduce friction in machines, etc.; lubricant. ◇*v.t.* **4.** to put grease on; lubricate. [ME, from OF, from L: fat] —**greasy**, *adj.*

greasepaint /'grispeɪnt/, *n.* theatrical make-up.

great /greɪt/, *adj.* **1.** large in size. **2.** large in number. **3.** unusual in degree; extreme: *great pain.* **4.** notable or remarkable: *a great occasion.* **5.** famous. **6.** important. **7.** main; principal. **8.** in high official or social position. **9.** high, grand, or noble: *great thoughts.* **10.** *Colloq.* very good; fine. **11.** younger or older by one generation than the specified relationship (used in compounds), as in *great-aunt, great-grandchild,* etc. [OE] —**greatness**, *n.* —**greatly**, *adv.*

Great Artesian Basin, *n.* a large artesian water-bearing basin underlying one fifth of Australia's area, including about two-thirds of Qld's area; one of the world's largest: 1 735 300 km^2.

great-aunt /'greɪt-ant/, *n.* the aunt of one's father or mother.

Great Australian Bight, *n.* the widest inlet on the Australian coastline, stretching from Cape Pasley, WA to the southern tip of the Eyre Peninsula in SA.

Great Barrier Reef, *n.* the world's longest coral reef, extending from near PNG down the coast of Qld to Lady Elliot Island just below the Tropic of Capricorn. About 2000 km.

Great Bear, *n. Astron.* the most prominent constellation in the northern heavens, containing the seven stars that form the Plough. Also, **Ursa Major**.

Great Britain, *n.* an island in north-western Europe, separated from the mainland by the English Channel and the North Sea; has many offshore islands; together with Northern Ireland forms the UK; comprises England, Scotland and Wales. Pop. 56 763 500 (1986 est.); 229 983 km^2. Also, **Britain**. See **United Kingdom**.

great circle, *n.* a circle on a sphere formed by the plane passing through the centre of the sphere. The shortest distance between any two points on the sphere is along the great circle passing through them.

greatcoat /'greɪtkoʊt/, *n.* a heavy overcoat.

Great Dane, *n.* one of a breed of large, powerful, short-haired dogs.

Great Dividing Range, *n.* the eastern highlands of Australia, extending from Cape York Peninsula down the eastern coast to western Vic. Highest peak (Australia's highest mountain) Mt Kosciusko, 2228 m.

Great Dog, *n. Astron.* the constellation Canis Major.

Great Lake, *n.* Australia's largest freshwater lake on the Central Plateau of Tasmania less than 8 km from the Great Western Tiers. 24 km long and up to 8 km wide.

Great Lakes, *n.pl.* a series of five large lakes between the US and Canada, connected with the Atlantic by the St Lawrence: Lakes Erie, Huron, Michigan, Ontario and Superior.

great-nephew /'greɪt-nɛfju, -nɛvju/, *n.* the son of one's nephew or niece.

great-niece /'greɪt-nis/, *n.* the daughter of one's nephew or niece.

Great Plains, *n.* a semi-arid region east of the Rocky Mountains of the US and Canada.

Great Sandy Desert, *n.* a large, extremely arid desert area in northern inland WA south of the Kimberleys and north of the Tropic of Capricorn.

Great Sandy Island, *n.* → **Fraser Island**.

Great Schism, *n.* a period of controversy in the Roman Catholic church (1378–1417) during which there were two rival popes, one at Rome and one at Avignon.

Great Trek, *n. S African Hist.* a mass emigration of settlers of Dutch origin from the Cape of Good Hope to the north and east, about 1835–46.

great-uncle /ˈgreɪt-ʌŋkəl/, *n.* the uncle of one's father or mother.

Great Victoria Desert, *n.* a large desert area north of the Nullarbor plain extending from Lake Barlee, WA across north-western SA.

Great Wall of China, *n.* a system of walls constructed as a defence for China against the nomads of the regions that are now Mongolia and Manchuria; completed in the third century BC, but later repeatedly modified and rebuilt. About 2250 km long.

Great War, *n.* →World War I.

Great Western, *n.* a town in western Vic near Ararat; noted producer of wines and champagne.

great white heron, *n.* a large white egret of south-eastern Europe, tropical Africa, Asia, NZ and America.

grebe /griːb/, *n.* any of various waterbirds with lobed (not webbed) toes, little tail, and weak legs. [F, orig. uncert.]

Grecian /ˈgriːʃən/, *adj., n.* Greek.

Greco-, a form of **Graeco-**.

Greece /griːs/, *n.* a republic in south-eastern Europe, consisting of many islands and the south part of the Balkan peninsula between the Ionian and Aegean Seas; noted for its ancient civilisations. Pop. 10 010 000 (1987 est.); 131 957 km². *Language:* Greek. *Currency:* drachma. *Cap.:* Athens. Greek, **Ellás**.

greed /griːd/, *n.* great or unreasonable desire, esp. for food or wealth. [OE] –**greedy,** *adj.* –**greedily,** *adv.* –**greediness,** *n.*

Greek /griːk/, *adj.* **1.** relating to Greece, the Greeks, or their language. ◇*n.* **2.** a native or inhabitant of Greece. **3.** the language of the ancient Greeks and any of the languages which have developed from it.

Greek Orthodox Church /griːk/, *n.* → Orthodox Church.

green /griːn/, *adj.* **1.** of the color of growing leaves, between yellow and blue in the spectrum. **2.** covered with plants, grass, leaves, etc.; verdant: *green fields.* **3.** consisting of green vegetables: *a green salad.* **4.** full of life and vigor. **5.** not dried or cured; unseasoned. **6.** unripe. **7.** untrained; inexperienced. **8.** easily fooled; gullible. **9.** fresh or new. **10.** pale; sickly. **11.** not cooked, fired, set or otherwise fully processed. **12.** *Colloq.* jealous. **13.** concerned with or relating to the protection of the natural environment: *the green vote.* ◇*n.* **14.** a green color. **15.** grassy land; a plot of grassy ground: *the village green.* **16.** *Golf.* Also, **putting green.** the area of lawn at the end of the fairway, which surrounds the hole. **17.** *Bowls.* a level plot of smooth, green lawn used for playing bowls. **18.** (*pl.*) **a.** the leaves and stems of plants, e.g. lettuce, used for food. **b.** fresh leaves or branches of trees, shrubs, etc., used for decoration. ◇*v.i., v.t.* **19.** to become or make green. [OE]

green ban, *n.* the refusal by building workers to do work which would result in the destruction of anything of natural or historical importance.

Green Beret, *n.* an informal name for a commando in the British or US forces.

Greene /griːn/, *n.* **Graham,** 1904–91, English novelist; his works include *The Power and the Glory* (1940).

greenery /ˈgriːnəri/, *n., pl.* **-eries. 1.** green growth or vegetation; verdure. **2.** a place where green plants are grown or kept.

greenfly /ˈgriːnflaɪ/, *n.* any of certain greenish insects, esp. the green aphid.

greengage /ˈgriːngeɪdʒ/, *n.* one of several varieties of light green plums. [GREEN + *Gage,* named after Sir William *Gage,* who introduced it into England c. 1725]

greengrocer /ˈgriːngroʊsə/, *n.* **1.** a seller of fresh vegetables and fruit. **2.** Also, **green Monday.** a large, common bright green cicada, with slightly darker green markings on the head and thorax.

greenhorn /ˈgriːnhɔːn/, *n. Colloq.* an inexperienced person. [orig. applied to an ox with green or young horns]

greenhouse /ˈgriːnhaʊs/, *n.* a building, chiefly of glass, used for cultivation or protection of plants by trapping heat from the sun.

greenhouse effect, *n.* the increase in the temperature of the earth caused by its atmosphere acting as the glass of a greenhouse does, possibly to be increased as pollution adds more and more carbon dioxide to the atmosphere.

Greenland /ˈgriːnlənd/, *n.* the largest island in the world, lying north-east of North America; home rule approved by Denmark instituted in 1979. Pop. 54 000 (1987 est.). About 2 175 432 km² (over 1 812 860 km² ice-capped). –**Greenlander,** *n.*

green light, *n.* **1.** the green traffic light used as a signal to mean 'go'. **2.** *Colloq.* permission; authorisation.

green Monday, *n.* → **greengrocer** (def. 2).

Green Party, *n.* a left-wing German political party, whose program includes ecological issues, nuclear disarmaments, and the breaking down of large economic concerns into smaller units. German, **Die Grünen**.

Greenpeace /ˈgriːnpiːs/, *n.* an international organisation of conservation activists, formed in Canada in 1971.

green pepper, *n.* the mild-tasting immature fruit of the sweet pepper used as a vegetable.

greenstick fracture, *n.* a partial fracture of a bone of a young person or animal, in which only one side of a bone is broken.

greenstone /ˈgriːnstoʊn/, *n.* **1.** altered basic igneous rocks, colored by the presence of

chlorite, hornblende, etc. **2.** a hard, green nephrite gemstone, found in the South Island of NZ, used in Maori tools and ornaments.

Greenway /'grinweɪ/, n. **Francis Howard**, 1777–1837, Australian architect, born in England; emancipated by Governor Macquarie, he designed many early buildings, the best-known being St Matthew's church at Windsor, NSW.

Greenwich Mean Time /'grenɪtʃ/, n. the mean solar time of the meridian through Greenwich, south-east London, widely used throughout the world as the basis for calculating local time.

greet /grit/, v.t. **1.** to address with some form of welcome. **2.** to receive with demonstrations of feeling: *His speech was greeted with laughter.* **3.** to meet; appear to: *Music greets the ear.* [OE]

greeting /'gritɪŋ/, n. **1.** the act or words of someone who greets. **2.** (usu. pl.) a friendly message: *Send greetings.*

gregarious /grə'gɛəriəs/, adj. **1.** (of animals) living in groups. **2.** *Bot.* growing in open clusters. **3.** (of people) fond of company; sociable. [L]

Gregg /grɛg/, n. **Sir Norman McAlister**, 1892–1966, Australian ophthalmologist, discovered the possible effects of German measles in pregnant women in 1941.

Gregorian /grə'gɔriən/, adj. relating to any of the popes named Gregory.

Gregorian calendar, n. the calendar now in use in which the ordinary year consists of 365 days, and a leap year of 366 days. [introduced by Pope Gregory XIII in 1582]

Gregorian chant, n. → **plainsong**.

Gregory /'grɛgəri/, n. **1. Sir Augustus Charles**, 1819–1905, Australian explorer and surveyor, born in England; surveyor-general of Qld 1859–75. **2. Charles W**, 1878–1910, Australian cricketer; made Australian and world record score 318 runs in one day. **3. Francis Thomas**, 1821–88, brother of Augustus Charles, Australian surveyor and explorer, born in England.

Greiner /'graɪnə/, n. **Nicholas Frank**, born 1947, Australian state Liberal politician; premier of NSW 1988–92.

gremlin /'grɛmlən/, n. **1.** a playful invisible being, said by airmen in World War II to cause engine trouble, etc. **2.** any source of mischief. [orig. uncert.]

grenade /grə'neɪd/, n. a small bomb thrown by hand or fired from a rifle. [F, from Sp *granada* pomegranate, from *granado* having grains, from L]

grenadier /grɛnə'dɪə/, n. **1.** (formerly) a soldier in a special unit of men specially chosen for their height and strength. **2.** (formerly) a soldier who threw grenades. [F, from *grenade* GRENADE]

Grenville /'grɛnvəl/, n. **1. George**, 1712–70, British statesman; prime minister 1763–65. **2. William Wyndham** (*Baron Grenville*), 1759–1834, son of George, British statesman; prime minister 1806–07.

grevillea /grɛ'vɪliə/, n. any shrub or tree of a very large, mainly Australian genus many of which are attractive ornamentals, oft. with spiky bright colored flowers. [NL, from Charles F Greville, died 1809, Scottish botanist]

grew /gru/, v. past tense of **grow**.

grey /greɪ/, adj. **1.** of a color between white and black, having no definite hue; ash-colored. **2.** dark, overcast, dismal, gloomy: *The cloudy sky was grey.* **3.** relating to old age: *grey power.* ◇n. **4.** any achromatic color. **5.** grey material or clothing: *to dress in grey.* ◇v.i. **6.** to make or become grey. [OE *græg*]

Grey /greɪ/, n. **1. Charles, 2nd Earl**, 1764–1845, British statesman; prime minister 1830–34. **2. Lady Jane** (*Lady Jane Dudley*), 1537–54, descendant of Henry VII; executed as usurper of the Crown.

grey area, n. an issue which is not clear-cut; a subject which is vague or ill-defined.

greyhound /'greɪhaʊnd/, n. one of a breed of tall, slender dogs, known for their keen sight and speed. [ME *gre(i)hound*, apparently from Scand]

grey matter, n. **1.** nervous tissue, esp. of the brain and spinal cord, containing both fibres and nerve cells, and of a dark reddish-grey color. **2.** *Colloq.* brains or intellect.

grey nurse shark, n. a common shark of Australian waters growing to 160 kg with long, thin, ripping teeth.

grid /grɪd/, n. **1.** a grating of crossed bars; gridiron. **2.** a network of cables, pipes, etc., for the supply of electricity, gas, water, etc. **3.** a network of horizontal and vertical lines on a map, printer's layout, plan, etc. [backformation from GRIDIRON]

griddle /'grɪdl/, n., v., **-dled, -dling**. ◇n. **1.** a flat, heated surface on top of a stove for cooking. ◇v.t. **2.** to cook on a griddle. Also, **girdle**. [ME, from OF: gridiron]

gridiron /'grɪdaɪən/, n. **1.** a utensil consisting of parallel metal bars on which to grill meat, etc. **2.** any framework or network like a gridiron. **3.** a type of football played in US, similar to Rugby, with two teams of 11 players. [ME *gredirne*]

grief /grif/, n. **1.** keen mental suffering or distress through problem or loss; sorrow; regret. **2.** a cause or occasion of keen distress or sorrow. **3. come to grief**, to come to a bad end; turn out badly. [ME, from OF: *grieve*]

Grieg /grig/, n. **Edvard Hagerup**, 1843–1907, Norwegian composer of the nationalist school; best known for the incidental music for Ibsen's *Peer Gynt* (1874–75).

grievance /'grivəns/, n. **1.** a wrong, real or imagined, considered as grounds for complaint: *a popular grievance.* **2.** resentment against an unjust act: *to have a grievance against someone.*

grieve /griv/, v.i., v.t. **grieved, grieving**. to feel or cause to feel grief. [ME, from OF, from L: weigh down] **–griever**, n.

grievous

grievous /'grivəs/, *adj.* **1.** causing grief or sorrow: *grievous news.* **2.** very bad; flagrant; atrocious: *a grievous fault.* **3.** full of or expressing grief; sorrowful: *a grievous cry.* [ME, from OF]

griffin /'grɪfən/, *n. Myth.* a monster, usu. having the head and wings of an eagle and the body of a lion. [ME, from L, from Gk]

Griffin /'grɪfən/, *n.* **Walter Burley**, 1876–1937, Australian architect, born in US; designer of the original plan, later modified, for the city of Canberra.

Griffith /'grɪfəθ/, *n.* a town in central NSW, north-west of Leeton; wineries. Pop. 13 630 (1986). [named after A *Griffith* a former state minister of public works]

grill /grɪl/, *n.* **1.** → **griller**. **2.** a meal in which the meat component is grilled. ◇*v.t.* **3.** to cook under a griller. **4.** *Colloq.* to subject to severe cross-examination or questioning. [F *gril* gridiron, from L: wickerwork, hurdle]

grille /grɪl/, *n.* **1.** an openwork screen usu. of metal and often of ornamental design, as for a window, gate or the front of a motor car. **2.** a grating or screen in a ventilation system. [F: grating]

griller /'grɪlə/, *n.* a cooking device in which meat, etc., is cooked by exposure to direct radiant heat.

grim /grɪm/, *adj.*, **grimmer**, **grimmest**. **1.** severe; stern; unrelenting: *grim necessity.* **2.** of a threatening or unpleasant character; repellent: *a grim joke.* **3.** of a fierce or forbidding appearance: *a grim face.* **4.** fierce or cruel: *a grim warrior.* **5.** *Colloq.* disagreeable; unpleasant. [ME and OE]

grimace /'grɪməs, grə'meɪs/, *n., v.*, **-maced**, **-macing**. ◇*n.* **1.** a twisted, unnatural or ugly expression of the face. ◇*v.i.* **2.** to make grimaces. [F, from Sp: panic, fear, from Goth]

Grimaldi family /grə'mældi ˌfæməli/, *n.* a European ruling house which includes the royal family of Monaco.

Grimaldi man, *n.* a type of prehistoric man thought variously to resemble present-day African or Mediterranean peoples. [named after the Italian *Grimaldi* caves where skeletons of this type were found]

grime /graɪm/, *n.* dirt or foul matter, esp. on or in a surface. [apparently special use of OE *grīma* mask, to denote layer of dust, etc., that forms on the face and elsewhere] —**grimy**, *adj.*

grin /grɪn/, *v.*, **grinned**, **grinning**, *n.* ◇*v.i.* **1.** to smile broadly. **2.** to draw back the lips so as to show the teeth, as in pain, amusement, etc. **3. grin and bear it**, *Colloq.* to suffer without complaint. ◇*v.t.* **4.** to express by grinning. ◇*n.* **5.** the act of grinning; a broad smile. [OE *grennian*]

grind /graɪnd/, *v.*, **ground**, **grinding**, *n.* ◇*v.t.* **1.** to wear, smooth, or sharpen by friction; whet: *to grind a lens, axe, etc.* **2.** to reduce to fine particles as by pounding or crushing; pulverise. **3.** to oppress or torment. **4.** to rub harshly or grate together; grit: *to grind one's teeth.* **5.** to operate by turning a crank: *to grind a barrel organ.* **6.** to produce by grinding: *to grind flour.* ◇*v.i.* **7.** to perform the operation of reducing to fine particles. **8.** to be polished or sharpened by friction. ◇*n.* **9.** the act of grinding. **10.** a grinding sound. **11.** *Colloq.* laborious or unvarying work or study: *It was a real grind.* **12. daily grind**, the daily routine of work. [OE *grindan*] —**grinder**, *n.*

grindstone /'graɪndstoʊn/, *n.* **1.** a rotating solid stone wheel used for sharpening, shaping, etc. **2.** → **millstone**.

grip /grɪp/, *n., v.*, **gripped** or **gript**, **gripping**. ◇*n.* **1.** the act of grasping; a seizing and holding fast; firm grasp: *the grip of a vice.* **2.** the power of gripping. **3.** a hold or control. **4.** a bag. **5.** mental or intellectual hold; competence. **6.** any special method of clasping hands. **7.** a handle. **8. come / get to grips with**, to deal with, tackle (an enemy, a problem, etc.). ◇*v.t.* **9.** to grasp or seize firmly; hold fast. **10.** to take hold on; hold the interest of. [OE *gripe* grasp]

gripe /graɪp/, *v.*, **griped**, **griping**, *n.* ◇*v.i.* **1.** *Colloq.* to complain constantly; grumble. ◇*n.* **2.** *Colloq.* an objection; complaint. **3.** (*usu. pl.*) an intermittent spasmodic pain in the bowels. [OE *grīpan*]

grippe /grɪp/, *n.* → **influenza**. [F, from *gripper* sieze, b. with Russ *khrip* hoarseness]

grisly /'grɪzli/, *adj.*, **-lier**, **-liest**. frightening; grim; gruesome: *a grisly monster face.* [OE *grislic* horrible]

grist /grɪst/, *n.* **1.** corn to be ground. **2.** ground corn; meal produced from grinding. **3. it's all grist to the mill**, everything available can be used. [OE *grīst*, from *grindan* GRIND]

gristle /'grɪsəl/, *n.* → **cartilage**. [ME and OE]

grit /grɪt/, *n., v.*, **gritted**, **gritting**. ◇*n.* **1.** fine, stony, or hard particles such as are deposited like dust from the air, etc. **2.** *Geol.* a sandstone made of coarse angular grains and very tiny stones. **3.** firmness of character; unconquerable spirit; pluck. ◇*v.t.* **4.** to clamp or clench: *to grit the teeth.* ◇*v.i.* **5.** to give forth a grating sound, as of sand under the feet; grate. [OE *grēot*] —**gritty**, *adj.*

grizzle[1] /'grɪzəl/, *v.i., v.t.*, **-zled**, **-zling**. to become or make grey. [ME, from OF: grey] —**grizzled**, *adj.*

grizzle[2] /'grɪzəl/, *v.i.*, **-zled**, **-zling**. to whimper; whine.

grizzly bear, *n.* a large, fierce bear of western North America, varying in color from greyish to brownish.

groan /groʊn/, *n.* **1.** a low, sad sound expressing pain or grief. **2.** a loud murmur made as a sign of disapproval, etc. ◇*v.i.* **3.** to utter a deep sound expressive of grief or pain; moan. **4.** to make a sound similar to a groan; creak; resound loudly. **5.** to suffer (fol. by *beneath, under, with*). [OE *grānian*]

groats /groʊts/, *n.pl.* **1.** hulled grain, as oats. **2.** the parts of oat kernels used as food. [OE *grotan* coarse meal]

grocer /'grousə/, *n.* a shopkeeper who supplies food such as flour, sugar, coffee, etc., and often other household goods. [ME, from OF, from LL *grossus* gross]

grocery /'grousəri/, *n., pl.* **-ceries. 1.** a grocer's store or business. **2.** (*usu. pl.*) goods sold by grocers.

grog /grɒg/, *n.* **1.** *Colloq.* alcohol, particularly cheap alcohol. **2.** (formerly) an alcoholic mixture, esp. of rum and water. [from *grogram* the material of the cloak of Admiral Vernon ('Old Grog'), who in 1740 ordered water to be issued with sailors' pure spirits]

groggy /'grɒgi/, *adj.*, **-gier, -giest.** *Colloq.* **1.** staggering, as from tiredness or fighting. **2.** drunk.

groin /grɔɪn/, *n.* **1.** *Anat.* the fold or hollow on either side of the body where the thigh joins the abdomen. **2.** *Archit.* the curved line or edge formed by the intersection of two vaults. **3.** → **groyne.** [ME *grynde.* See OE *grynde* abyss]

Gromyko /grə'mikoʊ/, *n.* **Andrei Andreyevich** /ˌændreɪ ən'dreɪjəvɪtʃ/, 1909–89, Soviet statesman and diplomat, born in Byelorussia; foreign minister of the Soviet Union 1957–1985; president 1988–89.

groom /grum/, *n.* **1.** a person in charge of horses or a stable. **2.** → **bridegroom. 3.** an officer of a royal household. ◊*v.t.* **4.** to tend carefully as to person and dress; make neat or tidy. **5.** to tend (horses). **6.** to prepare for a special purpose: *to groom a political candidate.* [ME *grom(e)* boy, groom]

groomsman /'grumzmən/, *n., pl.* **-men.** a man who attends the bridegroom at a wedding.

Groote Eylandt /grut 'aɪlənd/, *n.* an island off Arnhem Land's east coast, in the Gulf of Carpentaria; an Aboriginal reserve.

groove /gruv/, *n., v.,* **grooved, grooving.** ◊*n.* **1.** a furrow or channel cut or formed by a tool, etc. **2.** a habit; routine: *to get into a groove.* **3.** the track of a gramophone record in which the needle or stylus moves. ◊*v.t.* **4.** to cut a groove in: furrow. [ME *grofe, groof* mining shaft, OE *grōf* ditch, sewer]

groovy /'gruvi/, *adj. Colloq.* exciting or satisfying.

grope /groʊp/, *v.i.,* **groped, groping. 1.** to feel about with the hands; feel one's way. **2.** to search blindly or uncertainly. [OE *grāpian,* from *grāp, n.,* grasp]

groper /'groʊpə/, *n., pl.* **-pers,** (*esp. collectively*) **-per.** any of several species of large Australian or NZ fish with an enormously wide mouth opening. [Pg *garupa*]

Gropius /'groʊpiəs/, *n.* **Walter,** 1883–1969, US architect and educator born in Germany; founder of the Bauhaus.

Grose /groʊs/, *n.* **Francis,** 1758–1814, English army officer and administrator; first commander of the NSW Corps; acting governor of NSW 1792–94.

gross /groʊs/, *adj., n., pl.* **grosses** for def. 6, **gross** for def. 7; *v.* ◊*adj.* **1.** whole, entire, or total, without anything taken out or off: *gross profits; gross weight.* **2.** glaringly bad; flagrant: *gross injustice.* **3.** coarse; vulgar; indelicate: *gross tastes.* **4.** large, big, or bulky. **5.** *Colloq.* objectionable; repulsive; disagreeable. ◊*n.* **6.** the main body, bulk or mass. **7.** a unit consisting of 12 dozen, or 144. ◊*v.t.* **8.** to make a gross profit of; earn a total of. [ME, from OF: large, from LL: thick]

gross domestic product, *n.* the total annual value of all legal goods and services produced in a country. *Abbrev.:* **GDP**

gross national product, *n.* the gross domestic product of a country, plus the total of net incomes from abroad. *Abbrev.:* **GNP**

grotesque /groʊ'tɛsk/, *adj.* **1.** fantastic in the shaping and combination of forms, as in ornamental work combining unlikely-looking human and animal figures with scrolls, foliage, etc. **2.** odd or unnatural in shape, appearance, or character; bizarre. [F, from It: grotesque decoration, such apparently as was found in ancient excavated dwellings), from *grotta.* See GROTTO]

grotto /'grɒtoʊ/, *n., pl.* **-toes, -tos. 1.** a cave or cavern. **2.** an artificial cave-like structure. [It *grotta,* from VL: crypt, from Gk: vault]

grotty /'grɒti/, *adj. Colloq.* **1.** dirty. **2.** useless. [alteration of GROTESQUE]

grouch /graʊtʃ/, *Colloq.* ◊*v.i.* **1.** to be sulky or bad-tempered; show discontent; complain. ◊*n.* **2.** a sulky or morose person or mood. [var. of obs. *grutch,* from OF *groucher* grumble]

ground[1] /graʊnd/, *n.* **1.** the earth's solid surface; firm or dry land. **2.** earth or soil: *stony ground.* **3.** land having a special character: *rising ground.* **4.** (*oft. pl.*) land occupied, or taken over, for a special use: *hospital grounds; school grounds.* **5.** (*oft. pl.*) the foundation or basis; motive; reason: *grounds for a statement.* **6.** subject for study or discussion: *The inquiry covered much ground.* **7.** the main surface or background in art, etc. **8.** (*pl.*) dregs or sediment: *coffee grounds.* **9.** → **earth** (def. 8). **10.** *Music.* → **ground bass.** ◊**11.** Some special uses are:

break new ground, to begin a fresh operation.
common ground, matters for agreement.
cut the ground from under someone's feet, to upset by anticipating a person's arguments, plans, etc.
gain ground, to advance; make progress.
have one's feet on the ground, to be sensible and level-headed.
hold or **stand one's ground,** to keep to one's position.
lose ground, to lose what has been gained; retreat; give way.
run to ground, to hunt down; track down.
◊*adj.* **12.** situated on, or at, or close to, the surface of the earth: *the ground floor.* **13.** relating to the ground. **14.** *Mil.* operating on land: *ground forces.* ◊*v.t.* **15.** to lay or set on the ground. **16.** to place on a foundation; found; fix firmly; settle or establish. **17.** to teach the basic principles to. **18.** *Elect.* to establish an earth for (a circuit, device, etc.). **19.** *Naut.* to run aground. **20.** to prevent (an aircraft or a

pilot) from flying. ◇v.i. **21.** to come to or strike the ground. [OE *grund*]

ground² /graυnd/, v. **1.** past tense and past participle of **grind**. ◇adj. **2.** reduced to fine particles or dust by grinding. **3.** having a surface roughened as by grinding: *ground glass*. **4.** minced, as of meat.

ground bass, n. *Music*. a short repeated bass line underneath changing melodies or rhythms.

grounding /'graυndɪŋ/, n. a basic knowledge of a subject: *a good grounding in maths*.

groundless /'graυndləs/, adj. without basis or reason: *groundless fears*.

groundmass /'graυndmæs/, n. the crystalline, granular, or glassy base or matrix of a porphyry, in which the larger crystals are enclosed.

groundsel /'graυnsəl/, n. a weed with small yellow flowers. [OE *gund* pus + *swelgan* swallow (from its use as a poultice)]

groundsheet /'graυndʃit/, n. a waterproof sheet spread on the ground to give protection against dampness.

groundsman /'graυndzmən/, n., pl. **-men**. someone responsible for the care and maintenance of a cricket ground, sports field, etc.

ground speed, n. the speed of an aircraft in relation to the ground. See **airspeed**.

ground state, n. the most stable energy state of a particle, nucleus, atom, or molecule.

ground swell, n. **1.** a broad, deep swell or rolling of the sea, due to a distant storm or gale. **2.** a strong movement of public opinion.

ground zero, n. the point on the earth directly below the point at which a nuclear weapon explodes. Also, **surface zero**.

group /grup/, n. **1.** a number of people or things gathered, or considered as being connected in some way. **2.** a number of businesses, etc., connected in organisation and finance. **3.** *Chem.* **a.** a number of atoms in a molecule connected or arranged together in a particular manner that keeps its identity but cannot exist independently; a radical: *the hydroxyl group, −OH*. **b.** a vertical column of the periodic table containing elements with similar properties. **4.** *Geol.* a division of stratified rocks consisting of two or more formations. **5.** a collection of musicians who play together: *pop group*; *rock group*. **6.** —**blood group**. **7.** a grouping of similar plants or animals but which are not related under a scientific classification. −v.t., v.i. **8.** to form into a group or groups. [F, from It, of Gmc orig.] −**grouping**, n.

group therapy, n. the treatment of a group of psychiatric patients in sessions where problems are shared and discussed.

grouse¹ /graυs/, n., pl. **grouse**. a fowl-like game bird of the Northern Hemisphere, with a plump body and protective (often brown) coloring. [orig. unknown]

grouse² /graυs/, v., **groused**, **grousing**, n. *Colloq.* ◇v.i. **1.** to grumble; complain. ◇n. **2.** a complaint. [orig. unknown]

grouse³ /graυs/, adj. *Colloq.* very good.

grout /graυt/, n. **1.** a thin, coarse mortar poured into the joints of tiles, brickwork, etc. ◇v.t. **2.** to fill up, form or finish the spaces between (stones, etc.) with grout. [OE *grūt*]

Grout /graυt/, n. *Wally* (Arthur Theodore Wallace Grout, 'The Grix'), 1927-68, Australian Test cricketer.

grove /groυv/, n. a small wood or group of trees. [OE *grāf*]

grovel /'grɒvəl/, v.i., **-elled**, **-elling**. **1.** to humble oneself with loss of self-respect. **2.** to lie or crawl with face downwards, esp. fearfully. [obs. *grufe* face down (from Scand)]

grow /groυ/, v., **grew**, **grown**, **growing**. ◇v.i. **1.** (of a living organism) to increase by natural development by absorbing food; increase in size or substance. **2.** to come to be, or issue as from a germ, stock, or source. **3.** to increase gradually; become greater. **4.** to come to be, or become, by degrees: *to grow old*. **5. grow up**, to increase in growth, become mature. ◇v.t. **6.** to cause to grow: *He grows corn*. **7.** to allow to grow: *to grow a beard*. **8.** to cover with a growth (*usu.* in the passive): *a field grown with corn*. ◇v. **9. grow on**, **a.** to gain an increasing influence, effect, etc. **b.** to win the admiration of by degrees. **10. grow out of**, **a.** to outgrow. **b.** to develop from. [OE *grōwan*]

grower /'groυə/, n. **1.** someone who grows anything. **2.** a plant that grows in a certain way: *a quick grower*.

growl /graυl/, v.i. **1.** to utter a deep sound of anger or hostility: *The dog growled*. **2.** to murmur or complain angrily; grumble. ◇n. **3.** the act or sound of growling. [ME *groule* rumble (said of the bowels)]

grown /groυn/, v. **1.** past participle of **grow**. ◇adj. **2.** arrived at full growth or maturity; adult: *a grown man*.

growth /groυθ/, n. **1.** the act, process, or manner of growing; development; gradual increase. **2.** a stage of development. **3.** something that grows or has grown: *a growth of weeds*. **4.** *Pathol.* a diseased mass of tissue, as a tumor.

growth hormone, n. a hormone produced by the pituitary gland which controls the growth of the body.

groyne /grɔɪn/, n. a small jetty built out into the sea or a river which helps prevent erosion of the beach or bank. Also, **groin**.

grub /grʌb/, n., v., **grubbed**, **grubbing**. ◇n. **1.** the bulky larva of certain insects, esp. beetles. **2.** *Colloq.* food. **3.** to dig up by the roots; uproot (oft. fol. by *up* or *out*). ◇v.i. **4.** to dig; search by or as by digging. **5.** to lead a hard-working life; drudge. [ME *grubbe(n)* dig]

grubber /'grʌbə/, n. **1.** —**mullygrubber**. **2.** Also, **grubber kick**. *Rugby Football.* a kick which sends the ball along the ground.

grubby /'grʌbi/, adj., **-bier**, **-biest**. **1.** dirty; slovenly. **2.** overrun with or affected by grubs or larvae. [GRUB, n. + -Y¹]

grudge /grʌdʒ/, *n., v.,* **grudged, grudging.** ◇*n.* **1.** a feeling of ill will or resentment as a result of a personal injury, insult, etc. ◇*v.t.* **2.** to give or permit unwillingly. **3.** to envy (another). [from OF: murmur, grumble]

gruel /'gruəl/, *n.* a light, usu. thin, cooked cereal made by boiling meal, esp. oatmeal, in water or milk. [ME, from OF: meal, from Gmc]

gruelling /'gruəlɪŋ/, *adj.* very tiring; exhausting; severe.

gruesome /'grusəm/, *adj.* so as to make one shudder; inspiring horror; revolting. [*grue, v.,* shudder + -SOME¹]

gruff /grʌf/, *adj.* **1.** low and harsh; hoarse: *a gruff voice.* **2.** rough; surly: *a gruff manner.* [D, from *ge-* prefix + *rof,* akin to OE *hrēof* rough]

grumble /'grʌmbəl/, *v.,* **-bled, -bling,** *n.* ◇*v.i.* **1.** to murmur in discontent; complain ill-humoredly. **2.** to speak low, indistinct sounds; growl. ◇*v.t.* **3.** to express or utter with murmuring or complaining; rumble. ◇*n.* **4.** an ill-humored complaining; murmur; growl. [OE *grymman* wail, mourn]

grummet /'grʌmət/, *n. Mach.* a ring or eyelet of metal, rubber, etc. [F: curb of bridle, from LL: throat]

grump /grʌmp/, *n.* → **grouch.**

grumpy /'grʌmpi/, *adj.,* **-pier, -piest.** bad-tempered; surly. [Brit d. *grump* grumble]

grunt /grʌnt/, *v.i.* **1.** to utter a deep guttural sound as of or like a pig. **2.** to grumble, as in discontent. ◇*v.t.* **3.** to express with a grunt. ◇*n.* **4.** the sound of grunting. **5.** → **grunter** (def. 3). [OE *grunian* grunt]

grunter /'grʌntə/, *n.* **1.** a pig. **2.** any animal or person that grunts. **3.** any of several Australian freshwater fish that make grunting noises as they breathe, e.g. **silver perch, spangled perch.**

gruyère /'grujə, gru'jeə/, *n.* a firm pale yellow type of Swiss cheese. [named after *Gruyère,* district in Switzerland]

gr. wt, *Abbrev.* gross weight.

Gs, *Symbol.* gauss.

G-string /'dʒiːstrɪŋ/, *n.* **1.** a loincloth. **2.** a similar covering, usu. decorated, worn by entertainers for striptease dancing, etc. [orig. uncert.]

Gt Br, *Abbrev.* Great Britain. Also, **Gt Brit**

Guadalcanal /gwadəlkə'næl/, *n.* the largest of the Solomon Islands in the southern Pacific; site of US victory over the Japanese, 1942–43; self-governing. Pop. 50 327 (1986); 6475 km².

Guadeloupe /gwadə'lup/, *n.* two islands separated by a narrow channel in the Leeward Islands of the West Indies; together with five dependencies they form a department of France. Pop. 334 000 (1985 est.); 1779 km². *Cap.:* Basse-Terre.

Guam /gwam/, *n.* an island in the northern Pacific, east of the Philippine Islands; US naval and air force base. Pop. 124 000 (1987); 534 km². *Cap.:* Agaña.

Guangzhou /'gwʌŋ'dʒoʊ/, *n.* a seaport in south-eastern China; the capital of Guangdong province. Pop. 3 221 600 (1984). Formerly, **Canton.**

guano /'gwanoʊ/, *n., pl.* **-nos.** droppings from seabirds. [Sp, from Quechua *huanu* dung]

guarantee /gærən'tiː/, *n., v.,* **-teed, -teeing.** ◇*n.* **1.** → **guaranty** (def. 1). **2.** a promise or assurance, (esp. given in writing) that a manufacturer will make good any defects under certain conditions. **3.** someone who gives a guarantee; guarantor. **4.** someone to whom a guarantee is made. **5.** → **guaranty** (def. 2). **6.** something that has the force or effect of a guaranty of *Wealth is no guarantee of happiness.* ◇*v.t.* **7.** to secure, as by giving or taking security. **8.** to accept responsibility: *to guarantee the carrying out of a contract.* **9.** to (promise to) compensate (fol. by *from, against,* or *in*): *to guarantee someone against loss.* **10.** to promise [apparently from GUARANTY]

guarantor /gærən'tɔː/, *n.* someone who makes or gives a guarantee or guaranty.

guaranty /'gærənti/, *n., pl.* **-ties,** *v.,* **-tied, -tying.** ◇*n.* **1.** a pledge, or promise accepting responsibility for someone else's debts, liabilities, obligations etc. **2.** anything which is taken or presented as security. **3.** the act of giving security. ◇*v.t.* **4.** to guarantee. [AF: warrant]

guard /gad/, *v.t.* **1.** to keep safe from harm; protect; watch over: *to guard the rights of children.* **2.** to keep from escaping: *to guard a prisoner.* **3.** to keep in control or check: *to guard the tongue.* **4.** to make safe: *This temporary railing will guard the open hole.* ◇*v.i.* **5.** to take precautions (fol. by *against*): *to guard against mistakes; to guard against illness.* ◇*n.* **6.** someone who guards, protects, or keeps watch. **7.** a restrictive watch, as over a prisoner: *to be kept under close guard.* **8.** a device designed for guarding against injury, loss, etc.: *a safety guard on a machine.* **9.** → **safeguard. 10.** *Basketball.* one of the defensive players in a team. **11.** an official in general charge of a railway train. **12. off/on (one's) guard,** unprepared/ready to meet a sudden attack. [ME *garde,* from F, of Gmc orig.]

guarded /'gadəd/, *adj.* **1.** cautious; careful: *to be guarded in one's speech.* **2.** protected or watched, as by a guard.

guardian /'gadiən/, *n.* **1.** someone who guards, protects, or preserves. **2.** *Law.* someone who is entrusted by law with the care of another person or property, esp. of a minor or of someone legally unable to look after his own affairs. ◇*adj.* **3.** guarding; protecting: *a guardian angel.* [ME, from AF] **–guardianship,** *n.*

Guatemala /gwʌtə'malə/, *n.* a republic in central America, on the Pacific Ocean, bordered by Mexico, Honduras, Belize and El Salvador. Pop. 8 434 800 (1987 est.); 108 889 km². *Language:* Spanish, also Indian dialects.

Guatemala

Currency: quetzal. *Cap.:* Guatemala City. —**Guatemalan**, *n., adj.*

guava /'gwavə/, *n.* a tropical American tree or shrub with a fruit used for making jam, jelly, etc. [Sp, from S Amer name]

gub /gʌb/, *n. Colloq. (offensive) (in Aboriginal use)* a white man. Also, **gubber**, **gubba**, **gubbah**. [Aboriginal: white demon]

gudgeon /'gʌdʒən/, *n.* **1.** any of various species of small sea and freshwater fish as the **snakehead gudgeon**, of northern Australia. **2.** someone who is easily misled or cheated. ◇*v.t.* **3.** to cheat; dupe. [ME, from OF, from L: GOBY]

guerilla /gə'rɪlə/, *n.* **1.** a member of a small, independent band of soldiers which worries the enemy by surprise raids, attacks on communication and supply lines, etc. ◇*adj.* **2.** relating to such fighters or their method of warfare. Also, **guerrilla**. [Sp, diminutive of *guerra* WAR]

Guernica /gɜ'nikə, 'gwɛənikə/, *n.* a town in northern Spain destroyed in 1937 by German bombers serving the nationalist forces in the Spanish Civil War; subject of a painting by Pablo Picasso. Pop. 15 149 (1970).

Guernsey /'gɜnzi/, *n., pl.* **-seys**. **1.** one of a breed of dairy cattle. **2.** (*l.c.*) a close-fitting knitted jumper, often worn by seamen, footballers, etc. [from the Isle of *Guernsey*, in the English Channel]

guess /gɛs/, *v.t.* **1.** to form an opinion of at random or from evidence admittedly uncertain: *to guess the age of a woman*. **2.** to estimate or conjecture correctly: *to guess a riddle*. **3.** to think, believe, or suppose: *I guess I can get there in time*. ◇*v.i.* **4.** to form an estimate or conjecture (oft. fol. by *at*): *to guess at the height of a building*. **5.** to estimate or conjecture correctly. ◇*n.* **6.** a notion, judgment, or conclusion gathered from mere probability or imperfect information; conjecture; surmise. **7.** the act of forming an opinion in this manner. [ME, probably from Scand]

guest /gɛst/, *n.* **1.** someone who is entertained at the house or table of another. **2.** a person, esp. an entertainer, who is invited to take part in a show, a club act, etc.: *special guest*; *surprise guest*. **3.** a person who pays for lodging, and sometimes food, at a hotel, etc. [ME, from Scand]

guesthouse /'gɛsthaʊs/, *n., pl.* **-houses** /-haʊzəz/. a house where paying guests can stay; boarding house.

Guevara /gə'varə/, *n.* **Che** /tʃeɪ/ (*Ernesto Guevara*), 1928–67, Latin-American guerilla leader, born in Argentina, who aided Castro in achieving revolution in Cuba (1959); held several posts in the new government till 1965; executed by Bolivian forces.

guff /gʌf/, *n. Colloq.* foolish talk; nonsense.

guffaw /gʌ'fɔ, gə-/, *n.* **1.** a loud, coarse burst of laughter. ◇*v.i.* **2.** to laugh loudly and noisily.

Guiana /gi'anə, gaɪ-/, *n.* a vast tropical region in north-eastern South America, bounded by the Orinoco, Río Negro, Amazon and the Atlantic. About 1 787 100 km².

guidance /'gaɪdns/, *n.* **1.** the act of guiding; leadership; direction. **2.** advice; instruction.

guide /gaɪd/, *v.*, **guided**, **guiding**, *n.* ◇*v.t.* **1.** to lead as to a place; show the way to. **2.** to direct the movement or course of: *to guide a horse*. **3.** to lead, direct or advise in any course or action. ◇*n.* **4.** someone who guides, esp. a person employed to guide travellers, tourists, mountaineers, etc. **5.** a book with information for travellers, tourists, etc. **6.** anything that guides, as a device for guiding forward movement in a machine. **7.** → **girl guide**. [ME, from OF, from Gmc]

guide-dog /'gaɪd-dɒg/, *n.* a dog specially trained to lead or guide a blind person.

guideline /'gaɪdlaɪn/, *n.* **1.** a line drawn as a guide for further writing, drawing, etc. **2.** (*usu. pl.*) a statement of government or business policy.

Guienne /gwi'jɛn/, *n.* a former province of south-western France; together with Gascony comprised the duchy of Aquitaine in the 12th century; one of the regions causing conflict between France and England over many years. Also, **Guyenne**.

guild /gɪld/, *n.* **1.** an organisation of people with common professional or cultural interests formed for their mutual aid and protection. **2.** *Mediev Hist.* a similar union most often formed in one trade or industry. [ME, from Scand]

guilder /'gɪldə/, *n.* a unit of currency in the Netherlands.

guile /gaɪl/, *n.* cunning; deceitfulness; treachery. [ME, from OF; of Gmc orig.] —**guileless**, *adj.*

Guillaux /gwiloʊ/, *n.* **Maurice**, French aviator in Australia; flew Australia's first official airmail from Melbourne to Sydney (1914).

guillotine /'gɪlətin/, *n.;* /gɪlə'tin/, *v.*, **-tined**, **-tining**. ◇*n.* **1.** an instrument for beheading persons by means of a heavy blade falling between two grooved posts. **2.** a device with a long blade for trimming paper. **3.** a time limit on a parliamentary debate. ◇*v.t.* **4.** *Parl.* to limit the time allowed for debate of (each section of a bill). **5.** to behead by the guillotine. [F; named after JI *Guillotin*, 1738–1814, French physician, who urged its use]

guilt /gɪlt/, *n.* **1.** the fact or state of having committed an offence or crime. **2.** a feeling of responsibility or sadness for some crime, wrong, etc.; remorse. [OE *gylt* offence]

guilty /'gɪlti/, *adj.*, **-tier**, **-tiest**. **1.** justly chargeable with guilt (oft. fol. by *of*): *guilty of murder*. **2.** marked by or involving guilt: *guilty intent*. **3.** showing a sense of guilt: *a guilty conscience*. [OE *gyltig*] —**guiltily**, *adv.* —**guiltiness**, *n.*

guinea /'gɪni/, *n.* **1.** (formerly) a British coin. **2.** until decimal currency, the sum of 21 shillings.

Guinea /'gɪni/, n. **1.** a republic on the west coast of Africa, bordered by Sierra Leone, Liberia, Senegal, Mali and Côte d'Ivoire; a part of French West Africa before independence in 1958. Pop. 6 380 000 (1987 est.); 245 857 km². *Languages:* French and eight national languages, chiefly Susu and Malinke. *Currency:* Syli. *Cap.:* Conakry. Official name, **Popular and Revolutionary Republic of Guinea.** Formerly, **French Guinea. 2.** (formerly) a coastal region in western Africa, extending from the river Gambia to the Gabon estuary. **–Guinean,** *n., adj.*

guineafowl /'gɪnifaʊl/, n. a fowl, originally from Africa, which has (usu.) dark grey feathers with small white spots.

guineapig /'gɪnipɪg/, n. **1.** a short-eared, short-tailed rodent, usu. white, black and brownish, much used in scientific experiments. **2.** a person used as the subject of an experiment. [GUINEA + PIG¹; reason for associating animal with Guinea unknown]

Guinevere /'gwɪnəvɪə/, n. *Arthurian Legend.* the wife of King Arthur, and mistress of Lancelot. Also, **Guinever** /'gwɪnəvə/.

Guinness /'gɪnəs/, n. **Sir Alec,** born 1914, British stage and film actor; won Academy Award for his performamce in *The Bridge on the River Kwai* (1957).

guise /gaɪz/, n. **1.** outside appearance in general: *an old principle in a new guise.* **2.** (false) outward show: *under the guise of friendship.* [ME, from OF, from Gmc]

guitar /gə'ta/, n. a musical stringed instrument with a long fretted neck and a flat, violin-like body. The strings, usu. six in number, are plucked with the fingers or a plectrum. [Sp, from Gk: cithara] **–guitarist,** *n.*

Gujarat /gudʒə'rat/, n. **1.** a region in western India, north of the Narbada River. **2.** a state in western India. Pop. 34 085 799 (1981); 186 837 km². *Cap.:* Gandhinagar. Also, **Gujerat. –Gujarati,** *adj., n.*

Gulag /'gulæg/, n. formerly, the central administrative department of the Soviet security service, which maintained prisons and labor camps. [Russ *G(lavnoye) U(pravleniye) Ispravitelno-Trudovykh) Lag(erei)* Main Administration for Corrective Labor Camps]

gulch /gʌltʃ/, n. *US.* a deep, narrow ravine, esp. one marking the course of a stream or torrent. [orig. uncert.]

Gulden Draak /ˌguldən 'drak/, n. a Dutch vessel which was wrecked on the south-western coast of WA on 28 April 1656. Also, **Golden Dragon.**

gulf /gʌlf/, n. **1.** a section of an ocean or sea partly bounded by land. **2.** a deep hollow; chasm. **3.** any wide separation: *The gulf between his parents widened.* [ME, from OF, from It, from Gk: bosom, gulf]

Gulf Country, n. a name commonly given to the coastal lowlands at the base of the Gulf of Carpentaria, Qld.

Gulf District, n. a district in southern PNG.

Gulf of Papua, n. a gulf forming the southern coastline of PNG.

Gulf States, *n.pl.* the oil-producing states around the Persian Gulf: Iran, Iraq, Kuwait, Saudi Arabia, Bahrain, Qatar, the United Arab Emirates, and Oman.

Gulf Stream, n. a warm ocean current of the North Atlantic, flowing from the Gulf of Mexico, then north-west along the south-eastern coast of the US, then east to the North Atlantic Drift.

Gulf St Vincent n. a large inlet in southeastern SA; Adelaide lies on its eastern shore while the western shore is formed by the Yorke Peninsula. [named by Matthew Flinders after Sir John Jervis, Earl *St Vincent,* 1735–1823, British naval leader]

Gulf War, n. **1.** a war between Iran and Iraq, 1980–90, which involved territorial disputes over the oil-rich provinces on their joint border. **2.** a war between Iraq and a coalition of forces led by the United States in January–February 1991, resulting from Iraq's invasion of Kuwait in August 1990; concluded when Iraq was forced to withdraw.

gull /gʌl/, n. any of many long-winged, webfooted, water birds usu. white with grey back and wings. [ME]

gullet /'gʌlət/, n. **1.** the oesophagus, or tube by which food and drink swallowed pass to the stomach. **2.** the throat or neck. [ME, from OF, from L: throat]

gullible /'gʌləbəl/, *adj.* easily deceived or cheated. **–gullibility,** *n.* **–gullibly,** *adv.*

gully /'gʌli/, *n., pl.* **-lies. 1.** a small valley or canyon cut by running water. **2.** a ditch or gutter. **3.** *Cricket.* (the player in) a fielding position between slips and point. [var. of GULLET]

gully trap, n. a water-sealed trap through which house drainage is connected to outside drains.

gulp /gʌlp/, *v.i.* **1.** to swallow quickly, usu. in astonishment, fear, etc. **2.** to gasp or choke as when drinking large quantities of liquids. ◇*v.t.* **3.** to swallow quickly, often in large amounts (usu. fol. by *down*). ◇*n.* **4.** the act of gulping. **5.** an amount swallowed at one time; mouthful. [ME *gulpe(n)*] **–gulper,** *n.*

Gulpilil /'gʌlpəlɪl/, n. **David,** born 1953, Australian actor and Aboriginal dancer.

gum¹ /gʌm/, n., v., **gummed, gumming.** ◇*n.* **1.** any of various sticky, shapeless substances which ooze from plants, hardening on exposure to the air, and soluble in, or forming a sticky mass with, water. **2.** any similar discharge, e.g. resin, etc. **3.** Also, **gum tree.** any tree or shrub of a mostly Australian genus of which some yield eucalyptus oil and some hardwood timber, and bear gumnuts as fruits; eucalypt. **4.** glue; mucilage. **5.** → **chewing gum.** ◇*v.t.* **6.** to cover or stick together with gum. **7.** to clog with or as if with gum (oft. fol. by *up*). ◇*v.i.* **8.** to become sticky; become clogged with a substance. [ME, from L, from Gk]

gum² /gʌm/, *n.* (*oft. pl.*) the firm, fleshy tissue around the bases of the teeth. [OE *gōma* palate, inside of the mouth]

gum arabic /gʌm 'ærəbɪk/, *n.* a gum obtained from the acacia, used in making ink, in medicine, etc.

Gumbo /'gʌmbou/, *n.* (*sometimes l.c.*) a French patois used by Creoles in the West Indies and Louisiana.

gumboil /'gʌmbɔɪl/, *n.* a small abscess on the gum.

gumboot /'gʌmbut/, *n.* a rubber boot, usu. reaching to the knee.

gummy¹ /'gʌmi/, *adj.*, **-mier**, **-miest**. 1. having the nature of gum; viscid. 2. covered with or clogged by gum or sticky matter.

gummy² /'gʌmi/, *adj.*, **-mier**, **-miest**, *n.*, *pl.* **-mies**. ◇*adj.* 1. showing the gums: *a gummy smile.* ◇*n.* 2. *Colloq.* an old toothless sheep.

gummy shark, *n.* a slender and harmless Australian shark.

gumnut /'gʌmnʌt/, *n.* the woody ripe capsule (def. 2a) of the eucalyptus.

gumption /'gʌmpʃən/, *n. Colloq.* 1. courage; resourcefulness. 2. practical commonsense. [orig. Scot]

gum tree, *n.* 1. → **gum¹** (def. 3). 2. any of various other gum-yielding trees.

gun /gʌn/, *n.*, *v.*, **gunned**, **gunning**, *adj.* ◇*n.* 1. a metallic tube, with its stock or carriage and attachments, from which heavy missiles are thrown by the force of an explosive; a piece of ordnance. 2. any portable firearm, e.g. rifle, revolver, etc. 3. any similar device for projecting something: *a cement gun.* 4. *Colloq.* a champion, esp. in shearing. 5. **jump the gun**, to begin very early; be overeager. 6. **stick to one's guns**, to maintain one's position in an argument, etc., against opposition. ◇*v.i.* 7. to shoot or hunt with a gun. ◇*v.t.* 8. to shoot with a gun (oft. fol. by *down*). ◇*adj.* 9. *Colloq.* relating to someone who is expert, esp. in shearing: *a gun shearer.* [ME *gunne*, *gonne*, apparently short for *Gunilda* (L), *gonnyld* (ME), name for engine of war, from Scand]

gunboat diplomacy /,gʌnbout də'ploʊməsi/, *n.* diplomacy or foreign affairs together with the use or threat of military force.

guncotton /'gʌnkɒtn/, *n.* a highly explosive cellulose nitrate.

gun dog, *n.* a dog trained to help hunters when they shoot game.

gung ho, *adj.* overly eager and enthusiastic. [pidgin English, from Mandarin Chinese *kung* work + *ho* together]

gunk /gʌŋk/, *n. Colloq.* 1. oversweet or unhealthy food. 2. rubbish.

gunman /'gʌnmən/, *n.*, *pl.* **-men**. a man armed with, or expert with, a gun, esp. one ready to use a gun unlawfully.

gunmetal /'gʌnmetl/, *n.* 1. any of various alloys or metallic substances with a dark grey or blackish color or finish, used for chains, belt buckles, etc. 2. a bluish dark grey.

Gunn /gʌn/, *n.* **Mrs Aeneas** (*Jeannie Gunn*), 1870–1961, Australian novelist; author of *We of the Never Never* (1908).

gunnel /'gʌnəl/, *n.* → **gunwale**.

gunner /'gʌnə/, *n. Mil.* a private in the Royal Australian Artillery. See Appendix.

gunnery /'gʌnəri/, *n.* the art and science of making and managing (large) guns.

gunny /'gʌni/, *n.*, *pl.* **-nies**. 1. a strong, coarse material made commonly from jute, used for sacking, etc. 2. Also, **gunnybag**, **gunnysack**, a bag or sack made of this material. [Hind: sack]

gunpowder /'gʌnpaʊdə/, *n.* an explosive mixture of saltpetre (potassium nitrate), sulfur, and charcoal, used esp. in gunnery.

Gunpowder Plot, *n.* an unsuccessful plot or supposed plot led by Guy Fawkes to kill James I, the Lords, and the Commons assembled in Parliament on 5 November 1605, by an explosion of gunpowder, in revenge for the laws against Roman Catholics.

gun-running /'gʌn-rʌnɪŋ/, *n.* the smuggling of guns, etc., into a country.

gunsmith /'gʌnsmɪθ/, *n.* someone who makes or repairs firearms.

gunwale /'gʌnəl/, *n.* 1. the upper edge of the side of a vessel or boat. 2. the uppermost planking of a ship, next below the bulwarks. Also, **gunnel**. [GUN + *wale* a plank; so called because guns were set upon it]

Gunwinggu /gʊn'wɪŋgu/, *n.* an Australian Aboriginal language used mainly at Oenpelli, NT.

gunyah /'gʌnjə/, *n.* an Aborigine's hut made of tree branches and bark; humpy; miamia; wurley. Also, **gunya**. [Aboriginal]

guppy /'gʌpi/, *n.*, *pl.* **-pies**. a small fish common in home aquariums.

gurgle /'gɜgəl/, *v.*, **-gled**, **-gling**, *n.* ◇*v.i.* 1. to flow in a broken, irregular, noisy, current: *Water gurgles from a bottle.* 2. to make a sound as of water doing this (often used of birds or human beings). ◇*n.* 3. the act or noise of gurgling. [? imitative]

Gurindji /gə'rɪndʒi/, *n.* 1. an Australian Aboriginal language of the Victoria River area near Wave Hill, NT. 2. the tribe which speaks this language; successfully claimed tribal land at Wattie Creek, 600 km south of Darwin.

Gurkha /'gɜkə/, *n.* 1. a member of a warlike Rajput people, Hindu in religion, living in Nepal. 2. a member of this people, serving as a soldier in the Indian or British army. Also, **Ghurkha**.

gurnard /'gɜnəd/, *n.*, *pl.* **-nards**, (*esp. collectively*) **-nard**. a sea fish having a spiny head with armored cheeks. [ME, from OF: *grunter*, from Pr: grunt, from L: grunt]

guru /'gʊru/, 'gʊru/, *n.* an influential teacher and spiritual guide. [Hindi]

gush /gʌʃ/, *v.i.* 1. to issue with force, as fluid escaping; flow suddenly and in large amounts. 2. *Colloq.* to express oneself emotionally. 3. to have a large flow of something, as

gush of blood, tears, etc. ◇*n.* **4.** a sudden and large discharge or outflow of fluid. **5.** gushing or effusive language. [ME *gusche*]

gusset /'gʌsət/, *n.* an angular piece of material inserted in a garment to strengthen, enlarge or give freedom of movement to some part of it. [ME, from OF: pod, husk]

gust /gʌst/, *n.* **1.** a sudden, strong blast or rush of wind, rain, fire, etc. **2.** an outburst of strong feeling. [Scand]

gusto /'gʌstoʊ/, *n.* hearty enjoyment, as in eating, drinking, action, etc.: *to tell a story with gusto.* [It, from L: taste, relish]

gut /gʌt/, *n., v.,* **gutted, gutting,** *adj.* ◇*n.* **1.** → **intestine** (def. 1). **2.** (*pl.*) the intestines; entrails. **3.** (*pl.*) *Colloq.* the stomach or abdomen. **4.** (*pl.*) *Colloq.* courage; endurance: *to have guts.* **5.** the tissue or fibre of the intestine: *sheep's gut.* **6.** the processed gut of an animal, used for violin strings, etc. **7.** (*pl.*) *Colloq.* essential parts or contents: *the guts of the motor.* ◇*v.t.* **8.** to take out the guts of; disembowel. **9.** to rob or plunder of contents. **10.** to destroy the inside of: *Fire gutted the building.* ◇*adj.* **11.** of or relating to feelings or intuition: *a gut response.* [OE *guttas*, pl., akin to *gēotan* pour]

Gutenberg /'gutənbɜg/, *n.* **Johannes** /joʊ'hanəs/ (*Johann Gensfleisch*), c. 1398–1468, German printer; inventor of printing by movable type.

Guthrie /'gʌθri/, *n.* **1. Samuel,** 1782–1848, US chemist and physicist; discovered chloroform (1831) and produced an early version of the percussion cap. **2. Woody** (*Woodrow Wilson Guthrie*), 1912–67, influential US folk singer, guitarist and composer.

gutless /'gʌtləs/, *adj.* **1.** cowardly. **2.** (of a car, etc.) lacking in power.

gutser /'gʌtsə/, *n. Colloq.* **1.** Also, **guts.** a person who eats too much. **2. come a gutser,** to fall over or fail.

gutsy /'gʌtsi/, *adj. Colloq.* **1.** full of courage; full of guts. **2.** strong, full-bodied: *a gutsy wine.* **3.** greedy; gluttonous.

gutta-percha /ˌgʌtə-'pɜtʃə/, *n.* the white milky juice of a Malaysian tree, used in the arts, medicine, and manufacturing.

gutter /'gʌtə/, *n.* **1.** a channel at the side (or in the middle) of a road or street, for carrying away surface water. **2.** any similar channel, for carrying off fluid. **3.** Also, **guttering,** a channel at the eaves or roof of a building, for carrying off rainwater. **4.** the lowest social conditions in the community: *the language of the gutter.* ◇*v.i.* **5.** to form gutters, as running water does. **6.** (of a lighted candle) to melt away quickly and irregularly. [ME, from OF, from L: a drop]

guttersnipe /'gʌtəsnaɪp/, *n.* a street urchin.

guttural /'gʌtərəl/, *adj.* **1.** relating to the throat. **2.** harsh; throaty. [NL, from L: throat]

guy[1] /gaɪ/, *n.* **1.** *Colloq.* a man or boy. **2.** *Colloq.* any person. **3.** *Brit.* an effigy (likeness) of Guy Fawkes, carried about and burnt on Guy Fawkes Day. [from *Guy* Fawkes, the leader of the GUNPOWDER PLOT]

guy[2] /gaɪ/, *n., v.,* **guyed, guying.** ◇*n.* **1.** a rope or appliance used to guide and steady something being pulled up or lowered, or to secure anything tending to shift its position. ◇*v.t.* **2.** to guide, steady, or hold firmly with a guy or guys. [ME, from OF: a guide]

Guyana /gi'anə/, *n.* a republic on the north coast of South America, bordered by Venezuela, Suriname and Brazil. Pop. 802 000 (1987); 214 969 km². *Languages:* English, also Hindi, Urdu, and American Indian dialects. *Currency:* Guyana dollar. *Cap.:* Georgetown. Official name, **Cooperative Republic of Guyana.** Formerly, **British Guiana.** –**Guyanese, Guyanan,** *n., adj.*

Guy Fawkes Day *n.* 5 November, the anniversary of the Gunpowder Plot, celebrated by fireworks, etc.

guzzle /'gʌzəl/, *v.t., v.i.,* **-zled, -zling.** to drink (or sometimes eat) frequently and greedily.

Gwydir /'gwaɪdə/, *n.* a river in northern NSW, rising north of the New England Range and flowing north-west to enter the Barwon River. About 670 km.

Gwyn /gwɪn/, *n.* **Nell** (*Eleanor Gwynne*), 1650–87, English comic actress, mistress of Charles II.

gybe /dʒaɪb/, *v.,* **gybed, gybing.** *n.* → **jibe**[1].

gym /dʒɪm/, *n.* **1.** → **gymnasium. 2.** → **gymnastics.**

Gymea lily /ˌgaɪmiə 'lɪli/, *n.* a plant of eastern Australia with a tall flower stem bearing a head of red flowers. Also, **giant lily.**

gymkhana /dʒɪm'kanə/, *n.* **1.** a horse-riding event with games and contests. **2.** a festival of gymnastics. [Hind: ball house, racquet-court]

gymnasium /dʒɪm'neɪziəm/, *n., pl.,* **-siums, -sia** /-ziə/. a building or room equipped for gymnastics and sport. [L, from Gk]

gymnast /'dʒɪmnæst, -nəst/, *n.* someone trained and skilled in gymnastics. [Gk: trainer of athletes]

gymnastic /dʒɪm'næstɪk/, *adj.* relating to exercises which develop flexibility, strength, and agility.

gymnastics /dʒɪm'næstɪks/, *n.* **1.** (*treated as pl.*) gymnastic exercises. **2.** (*treated as sing.*) the practice or art of gymnastic exercises.

gymnosperm /'dʒɪmnoʊˌspɜm/, *n.* a plant having its seeds exposed, not enclosed in an ovary (opposed to *angiosperm*). [NL, from Gk] –**gymnospermous,** *adj.*

Gympie /'gɪmpi/, *n.* a city in south-eastern Qld, about 40 km north-west of Tewantin; earlier famous goldmining town. Pop. 10 772 (1986).

gyn-, *Abbrev.* variant of **gyno-.**

gynaecology *or* **gynecology** /gaɪnə-ˈkɒlədʒi/, *n.* the branch of medical science which deals with diseases, etc., particular to women. —**gynaecologist**, *n.* —**gynaecological**, *adj.*

Gyngell /ˈgɪndʒəl/, *n.* **Bruce**, born 1929, Australian media administrator; first person to appear on Australian television (1956).

gyno-, a word part meaning 'woman', 'female', as in *gynoecium*. Also, **gyn-**. [Gk, combining form of *gynē* woman]

gynoecium /dʒaɪˈnisiəm/, *n.*, *pl.* **-cia** /-siə/. the pistil or seed-bearing part of a flower. Also, **gynaeceum**, **gynaecium**, **gynecium**. [NL, from *gyn-* GYN- + Gk *oikíon* house]

-gynous, an adjective combining form referring to the female sex, as in *androgynous*. [Gk *-gynos*, from *gynē* woman]

gyp /dʒɪp/, *v.*, **gypped**, **gypping**, *n. Colloq.* ◇*v.t.* **1.** to cheat; swindle. ◇*n.* **2.** a swindle. Also, **gip**. [orig. uncert.]

gypsum /ˈdʒɪpsəm/, *n.* a very common mineral, hydrated calcium sulfate, used esp. to make plaster of Paris. [L, from Gk: chalk, gypsum]

gypsy /ˈdʒɪpsi/, *n.*, *pl.* **-sies.** → **gipsy**.

gyrate /dʒaɪˈreɪt/, *v.i.*, **-rated**, **-rating**. to move in a circle or spiral, or round a fixed point; whirl. [L: wheeled round, turned] —**gyration**, *n.* —**gyratory**, *adj.*

gyre /dʒaɪə/, *n.* **1.** a ring or circle. **2.** a circular course or motion.

gyro-, a word part meaning: **1.** 'ring', 'circle'. **2.** 'spiral'. [Gk, combining form of *gŷros* ring, circle]

gyrocompass /ˈdʒaɪroʊˌkʌmpəs/, *n.* a compass using a gyroscope instead of a magnetised needle, the gyroscope being so mounted that its axis always points to the geographical north. Also, **gyroscopic compass**.

gyroscope /ˈdʒaɪrəskoʊp/, *n.* a rotating wheel inside a frame which lets its axis turn in any direction. When the wheel is spinning, it is able to maintain the same absolute direction in space. [F. See GYRO-, -SCOPE] —**gyroscopic**, *adj.*

Hh

H, h, *n., pl.* **H's** or **Hs, h's** or **hs. 1.** the eighth letter of the English alphabet. **2.** the eighth in a series.

h, *Phys. Symbol.* Planck's constant.

h., *Abbrev.* **1.** hard(ness). **2.** height. **3.** hour.

H, *Symbol.* **1.** (of pencils) hard. **2.** *Elect.* henry. **3.** hot. **4.** *Chem.* hydrogen. **5.** *Phys.* **a.** strength of magnetic field. **b.** enthalpy. **6.** heroin.

ha, *Abbrev.* hectare.

habeas corpus /ˌheɪbɪəs ˈkɔːpəs/, *n.* a written order to a person who holds another in custody, commanding him to produce the other person before the court, so that the legality of his imprisonment may be tested. [L: may you have the body (the first words of the writ)]

haberdasher /ˈhæbədæʃə/, *n.* someone who sells buttons, needles, ribbons, etc. [AF: kind of fabric] **—haberdashery,** *n.*

habit /ˈhæbət/, *n.* **1.** a constant tendency to act in a certain way. **2.** a particular practice or custom: *It is my habit to read before bed.* **3.** a behavior or need that is difficult to stop; addiction; compulsion: *Smoking has become a habit.* **4.** a customary practice or use: *to act from force of habit.* **5.** a condition: *a habit of mind.* **6.** a characteristic appearance or form of growth of an animal or plant: *a twisting habit.* **7.** *Chem.* the characteristic crystalline form of a mineral. **8.** the dress of a particular profession, religious order, etc.: *a monk's habit.* **9.** a woman's riding dress. [L: condition, appearance, dress]

habitable /ˈhæbɪtəbəl/, *adj.* able to be lived in.

habitat /ˈhæbətæt/, *n.* **1.** the type of place where a particular animal or plant naturally lives or grows, as warm seas, mountain tops, fresh waters, etc. **2.** a place of living; abode; habitation. [L: it inhabits]

habitation /ˌhæbəˈteɪʃən/, *n.* **1.** a place of living; dwelling. **2.** the act of inhabiting or living in.

habitual /həˈbɪtʃuəl/, *adj.* **1.** done by habit: *habitual courtesy.* **2.** being something by habit: *a habitual drunkard.* **3.** commonly used; usual: *She took her habitual place at the table.* [LL]

habituate /həˈbɪtʃueɪt/, *v.t.,* **-ated, -ating.** to make (someone or something) used (*to*); accustom. [LL: bring into a condition, from L: habit]

habitué /həˈbɪtʃueɪ/, *n.* someone who goes regularly to a place, as the theatre, etc. [F: habituate]

hacienda /ˌhæsiˈendə/, *n.* (the main house on) a landed estate or farm. [Sp: landed property, estate, from L: things to be done]

haema-

hack[1] /hæk/, *v.t.* **1.** to cut or chop with, or as if with, rough, heavy blows. **2.** to clear (a path) by cutting down undergrowth, etc. **3.** to purposely kick the shins of, as in Rugby football. ◇*v.i.* **4.** to make rough cuts. ◇*n.* **5.** a cut; gash; notch. **6.** a tool, e.g. an axe, hoe, pick, etc., for hacking. **7.** the act of hacking. **8.** a short, broken cough. [OE: hack to pieces]

hack[2] /hæk/, *n.* **1.** a riding horse kept for hire to the public, or used for ordinary riding. **2.** an old or worn-out horse. **3.** someone who does routine or poor quality literary or other work for a living; someone who does hackwork. **4.** Also, **hacker.** *Computers. Colloq.* a programming enthusiast who gains access to the system of a company, government, etc., and without permission uses or changes information. ◇*v.t.* **5.** *Colloq.* to put up with; endure. ◇*v.i.* **6.** to ride a horse on the road at an ordinary pace. ◇*adj.* **7.** hired; of a hired sort: *hack work.* **8.** unoriginal; hackneyed; trite. [short for HACKNEY]

hacker /ˈhækə/, *n.* → **hack**[2] (def. 4).

hackle /ˈhækəl/, *n.* **1.** the long neck feather or feathers of a rooster. **2.** the hair on a dog's neck. **3.** (*pl.*) a comb for flax or hemp. **4. with one's hackles up,** very angry; on the point of fighting. [ME *hakell*]

hackney /ˈhækni/, *n., pl.* **-neys. 1.** a horse for ordinary riding or driving. **2.** a carriage kept for hire. [ME *hakeney*; orig. uncert.]

hackneyed /ˈhæknid/, *adj.* made commonplace or trite; stale.

hacksaw /ˈhæksɔː/, *n.* a saw for cutting metal, consisting of a narrow, fine-toothed blade fixed in a frame.

hackwork /ˈhækwɜːk/, *n.* the routine side of creative or artistic work, thought of as mundane, esp. in the literary field.

had /hæd/; *weak forms,* /həd, əd, d/, *v.* **1.** past tense and past participle of **have. 2. have had,** to be extremely annoyed with: *I have had this government.* **3. have had it,** *Colloq.* **a.** to be extremely annoyed. **b.** to be extremely tired. **4. be had,** to be cheated or deceived.

haddock /ˈhædək/, *n., pl.* **-docks,** (*esp. collectively*) **-dock.** a food fish of the northern Atlantic, related to but smaller than the cod. [ME *haddoc*; orig. unknown]

hades /ˈheɪdiz/, *n.* **1.** (*also cap.*) hell. **2.** (*cap.*) *Gk Myth.* the gloomy underground place of the dead, ruled over by Pluto.

Hadlee /ˈhædli/, *n.* **Richard John,** born 1951, New Zealand cricketer; record test wicket-taker.

hadn't /ˈhædnt/, *v.* a short form of *had not.*

Hadrian /ˈheɪdriən/, *n.* AD 76–138, Roman emperor AD 117–138. Also, **Adrian.**

Hadrian's Wall /ˈheɪdriənz wɔːl/, *n.* a wall of defence for the Roman province of Britain, constructed by Hadrian between the Solway Firth and the mouth of the Tyne.

haem-, variant of **haemo-,** before vowels, as in *haemal.* See **haemat-.**

haema-, variant of **haemo-**

haemal /'himəl/, *adj.* of or relating to the blood or blood vessels.

haemat-, a prefix equivalent to **haemo-**, as in *haematic*. Also, **haemato-**.

haematic /hɪ'mætɪk/, *adj.* of or relating to blood. [Gk: of the blood]

haematite /'himətaɪt/, *n.* a very common mineral, iron oxide, Fe_2O_3, found in steel-grey to black crystals and in red earthy masses; the main ore of iron. Also, **hematite**. [L: haematite, from Gk: bloodlike]

haemato-, a prefix equivalent to **haemo-**, as in *haematogenous*.

haematology or **hematology** /himə'tɒlədʒi, hem-/, *n.* the study of the nature, function, and diseases of the blood. [HAEMATO- + -LOGY] —**haematologist**, *n.*

haematoma or **hematoma** /himə'toumə, hem-/, *n., pl.* **-mata** /-mətə/, **-mas**. a bruise or collection of blood in a tissue.

haematosis /himə'tousəs, hem-/, *n.* the formation of blood. [Gk: make into blood]

-haemia, variant of **-aemia**.

haemo-, a word part meaning 'blood' as in *haemoglobin*. Also, **haem-**. See **haema-, haemat-, haemato-**. [Gk]

haemodialysis /,himoudaɪ'æləsəs/, *n.* → **dialysis** (def. 2).

haemoglobin or **hemoglobin** /himə'gloubən/, *n.* a protein in blood which carries oxygen to the tissues. When combined with oxygen, it gives the bright red color to arterial blood, and when without oxygen, the blue-red of venous blood results.

haemophilia or **hemophilia** /himə'fɪliə/, *n.* a hereditary disease carried by females but showing itself in males, marked by a tendency to bleed heavily from any wound, however small, because one of the blood-clotting factors is absent. [NL, from Gk]

haemophiliac or **hemophiliac** /himə'fɪliæk/, *n.* a person or organism which has haemophilia.

haemorrhage or **hemorrhage** /'hemərɪdʒ/, *n., v.,* **-rrhaged, -rrhaging. 1.** a discharge. ◇*v.i.* **2.** to bleed severely. [L, from Gk: a violent bleeding] —**haemorrhagic**, *adj.*

haemorrhoid or **hemorrhoid** /'hemərɔɪd/, *n.* (*usu. pl.*) a painful swelling of a vein in the anus; pile. [L: piles, from Gk]

hafnium /'hæfniəm/, *n.* a metallic element with a valency of four, found in zirconium ores. Symbol: Hf; at. no.: 72: at. wt: 178.49. [*Hafn(ia)*, L name of Copenhagen + -IUM]

haft /'haft/, *n.* **1.** the handle, esp. of a knife, sword, dagger, etc. ◇*v.t.* **2.** to provide with a haft; set in a haft (*oft. in pp.*): *a hafted knife*. [ME; OE *hæft*]

hag /hæg/, *n.* **1.** an ugly, often cruel or evil, old woman. **2.** a witch. **3.** → **hagfish**. [OE: fury, witch] —**haggish**, *adj.*

Hagen /'hagən/, *n.* **Mount**, a mountain in the Western Highlands province of PNG. About 3999 m.

hagfish /'hægfɪʃ/, *n., pl.* **-fishes**, (*esp. collectively*) **-fish**. a type of eel-like fish with a circular mouth designed for sucking its victims. Also, **hag**.

haggard /'hægəd/, *adj.* tired-looking, as from long suffering, worry, ill-health, etc.; gaunt. [orig. uncert. ? F]

haggis /'hægəs/, *n.* a dish, orig. Scottish, made of the heart, liver, etc., of a sheep, etc., minced with suet and oatmeal, seasoned, and boiled in the stomach of the animal. [? OE: meat]

haggle /'hægəl/, *v.,* **-gled, -gling,** *n.* ◇*v.i.* **1.** to argue in a tiresome way about the price of something; bargain. **2.** to argue; wrangle; cavil. ◇*n.* **3.** a dispute or wrangle over terms. [from *hag*, cut hew, hack, from Scand]

hagio-, a word part meaning 'saint'. Also, **hagi-**. [Gk: sacred, holy]

hagiography /hægi'ɒgrəfi/, *n., pl.* **-phies. 1.** the lives of the saints as a form of literature. **2.** a life so written. Also, **hagiology.** —**hagiographer**, *n.*

Hague /heɪg/, *n.* **The**, a city in western Netherlands, near the North Sea; seat of the government, royal residence, and Permanent Court of International Justice. Pop. 443 961 (1986 est.). Dutch **Den Haag**, or **'s Gravenhage**.

Haig /heɪg/, *n.* **Douglas, 1st Earl,** 1861–1928, British field marshal; commander-in-chief of the British forces in France from 1915–18.

haiku /'haɪku/, *n.* a Japanese verse form, developed in the 16th century, usu. containing 17 syllables arranged in three lines of five, seven, and five syllables respectively.

hail[1] /heɪl/, *v.t.* **1.** to greet; salute; welcome. **2.** to greet or name as: *to hail Caesar as victor.* **3.** to approve with enthusiasm; acclaim. **4.** to attract attention by calling out to: *to hail a person; to hail a taxi.* ◇*v.* **5. hail from**, to come from or belong to (a place). ◇*n.* **6.** a shout or call to attract attention. **7. within hail**, within reach of the voice. ◇*interj.* **8.** *Poetic.* (an exclamation of greeting or salutation.) [ME: health, from Scand]

hail[2] /heɪl/, *n.* **1.** a (shower of) small balls or lumps of ice falling from the clouds. **2.** a shower of anything: *a hail of bullets.* ◇*v.i.* **3.** to pour down hail: *It is hailing.* **4.** to fall as if hail: *Bullets hailed down.* ◇*v.t.* **5.** to pour down as if, or like, hail: *It was hailing bullets.* [OE *hægl*]

Hail Mary, *n.* → **Ave Maria**.

hailstone /'heɪlstoun/, *n.* a ball or lump of hail. [ME, from HAIL[2] + STONE]

hailstorm /'heɪlstɔm/, *n.* a storm with hail; heavy fall of hail.

Haines /heɪnz/, *n.* **Janine**, born 1945, the first Australian Democrat in federal parliament; became party parliamentary leader in 1986.

Haiphong /haɪ'fɒŋ/, *n.* a seaport in North Vietnam, near the Gulf of Tonkin. Pop. 330 755 (1979).

hair /heə/, *n.* **1.** one of the many fine, usu. cylindrical, threadlike growths from the skin of people and animals. **2.** the mass of these which cover the human head or the body of an animal. **3.** a similar outgrowth from the body of insects or from the outer cells of plants. **4.** a very small amount, degree, etc.: *He lost the race by a hair.* ◇**5.** Some special uses are:
let one's hair down, to behave in a relaxed, or free manner.
make one's hair stand on end, to terrify.
split hairs, to make fine or unnecessary distinctions.
tear one's hair out, to show great emotion, as anger, anxiety, etc.
without turning a hair, showing no emotion. [ME *ha(i)re*, from OE]

hairdo /'heədu/, *n., pl.* **-dos.** the style in which someone's hair is arranged, cut, tinted, etc.

hairdresser /'heədresə/, *n.* someone who arranges or cuts hair, esp. women's hair.

hairline /'heəlaɪn/, *n.* **1.** a line formed where the hair begins at the forehead. **2.** a very thin line, as a pen or brush stroke.

hairline fracture, *n.* a break or fault in a bone, metal casting, etc., which shows itself as a very thin line on the surface.

hairpiece /'heəpis/, *n.* a full or partial wig.

hairpin /'heəpɪn/, *n.* a thin U-shaped piece of wire, shell, etc., used by women to fasten up the hair.

hairpin bend, *n.* a bend in a road which doubles back in a U-shape.

hair's-breadth /'heəz-bredθ, -breθ/, *n.* **1.** a very small space or distance. ◇*adj.* **2.** very narrow or close: *a hair's-breadth escape.* Also, **hairsbreadth, hairbreadth.**

hairspring /'heəsprɪŋ/, *n.* a fine, spiralled spring in a watch or clock for regulating the balance wheel.

hair-trigger /'heə-trɪgə/, *n.* a trigger that allows the firing mechanism of a firearm to be worked by very slight pressure.

hairy /'heəri/, *adj.*, **-rier, -riest. 1.** covered with hair; having much hair. **2.** consisting of or looking like hair. **3.** *Colloq.* difficult: *a hairy problem.* **4.** *Colloq.* frightening: *a hairy drive.*

Haiti /'heɪti, ha'iti/, *n.* a republic in the West Indies, occupying the western part of the island Hispaniola and some smaller islands, about 80 km from Cuba; under the authoritarian Duvalier regime 1957–86. Pop. 5 532 000 (1987 est.); 27 750 km². *Languages:* French and Haitian creole. *Currency:* gourde. *Cap.:* Port-au-Prince. —**Haitian,** *adj., n.*

hajji /'hædʒi/, *n., pl.,* **-jis.** a Muslim who has performed his pilgrimage to Mecca. [Turk, from Ar *hājjī* pilgrim]

haka /'hakə/, *n.* NZ a Maori ceremonial posture dance with singing. [Maori]

hake /heɪk/, *n.* any of several marine food fishes related to the cod.

hakea /'heɪkiə/, *n.* a type of Australian shrub or tree that has a hard woody fruit with winged seeds.

halberd /'hælbəd/, *n.* a long-handled weapon with a head combining an axe blade and a spear point, used esp. in the 15th and 16th centuries. Also, **halbert** /'hælbət/, **haubert** /'houbət/. [late ME, from MF, from MHG]

halcyon /'hælsiən/, *n.* **1.** *Myth.* a bird, usu. said to be the kingfisher, supposed to breed about the time of the winter solstice and then to have the power of calming winds and waves. ◇*adj.* **2.** calm, or peaceful; tranquil. **3.** carefree; joyous. [L, from Gk: kingfisher]

hale[1] /heɪl/, *adj.,* **haler, halest.** healthy; robust; vigorous. [OE *hāl*]

hale[2] /heɪl/, *v.t.,* **haled, haling.** to bring (someone) by force; drag: *to hale a man into court.* [ME, from OF: hale, haul, from Gmc]

half /haf/, *n., pl.* **halves** /havz/, *adj., adv.* ◇*n.* **1.** one of the two equal parts into which anything can be divided (½). **2.** *Sport.* either of the two periods of some games. **3.** one of a pair. **4. the half of it,** a more important part: *You don't know the half of it!* ◇*adj.* **5.** being one of two equal (or nearly equal) parts: *a half orange.* **6.** being equal to only about half of the full amount: *half speed.* **7.** partial or incomplete: *a half measure.* ◇*adv.* **8.** to the measure of half: *half full.* **9.** in part; partly: *half done; half built.* **10.** to some extent: *I half like it.* **11. by half,** by a great deal; by too much: *too clever by half.* [OE]

half-back /'haf-bæk/, *n.* **1.** *Rugby.* the player who puts the ball in the scrum, and tries to catch it as it comes out. **2.** *Aust Rules.* any of the three players on the line between the centre-line and the full-back line. **3.** *Soccer.* one of the three players in the next line behind the forward line. Also, **half.**

half-baked /'haf-beɪkt/, *adj.* **1.** not cooked enough. **2.** *Colloq.* **a.** not completed: *a half-baked plan.* **b.** lacking wisdom or experience.

half-blood /'haf-blʌd/, *n.* **1.** the relation between people who have only one of their parents in common. **2.** →**half-breed. 3.** an animal which has only one parent of pure blood.

half-breed /'haf-brid/, *n.* **1.** *Offensive.* →**half-caste. 2.** an animal bred from different breeds.

half-brother /'haf-brʌðə/, *n.* a brother related through one parent only.

half-caste /'haf-kast/, *n.* a person of mixed race.

half-cocked /haf-'kɒkt/, *adv. Colloq.* in the phrase **go off half-cocked,** to act prematurely. [from *half-cock,* the halfway, safety-locked position of the hammer of a firearm]

half-crown /'haf-kraʊn/, *n.* (formerly) a silver-nickel coin worth two shillings and sixpence. Also, **half-a-crown.**

half-forward /'haf-fɔwəd/, *n.* (in Aust Rules) any of the three players on the line between the centre-line and the full-forward line.

half-hearted /'haf-hatəd/, *adj.* having or showing little willingness or enthusiasm.

half-hitch /ˈhaf-hɪtʃ/, *n.* a knot made by passing the end of a rope round its standing part and bringing it up through the bight.

half-life /ˈhaf-laɪf/, *n.* the time taken for half of a sample of a radioactive substance to decay, i.e. for half of the atoms present to break up.

half-mast /haf-ˈmast/, *n.* **1.** a position roughly halfway below the top of a mast, flagpole, etc. **2. at half-mast**, (of a flag) half lowered to show respect for the dead, or as a distress signal. ◇*adv.* (of the way a flag is flown) at a halfway position.

half-measure /ˈhaf-mɛʒə/, *n.* an incomplete course of action; inadequate measure.

half-moon /haf-ˈmuːn/, *n.* **1.** →**moon** (def. 2b). **2.** something of the shape of a half-moon or crescent.

half note, *n. US Music.* →**minim** (def. 2).

halfpenny /ˈheɪpni/, *n., pl.* **halfpennies** /ˈheɪpniz/, *for def. 1;* **halfpence** /ˈheɪpəns/ *for def. 2; adj.* ◇*n.* **1.** (formerly) a bronze coin of half the value of a penny. **2.** the sum of half a penny. ◇*adj.* **3.** of the price or value of a halfpenny: *a halfpenny bun.* **4.** of very small value.

half-sister /ˈhaf-sɪstə/, *n.* a sister related through one parent only.

half-time /haf-ˈtaɪm/, *n.* a rest period or interval between the two halves of a game, match, etc.

halftone /ˈhaftoʊn/, *n.* **1.** *Painting, Photog., etc.* a value halfway between high light and deep shade. **2.** *Print.* a process of producing a gradual variation of dark and light by a system of very small dots.

half-truth /ˈhaf-truːθ/, *n.* an idea or statement only partly true, esp. one meant to mislead or deceive.

halfway /ˈhafweɪ/, *adv.;* /ˈhafweɪ/, *adj.* ◇*adv.* **1.** with half the distance covered: *to go halfway to a place.* **2.** to or at half the distance: *The rope reaches only halfway.* **3. meet halfway**, to compromise. ◇*adj.* **4.** midway, as between two places or points: *halfway mark.* **5.** incomplete; partial: *halfway measures.*

halfway house, *n.* **1.** (formerly) an inn situated halfway through one's journey. **2.** a house, usu. run by an organisation, in which former prisoners, drug addicts, etc., can live until able to organise their own affairs.

halfwit /ˈhafwɪt/, *n. (offensive)* someone who is considered stupid.

halibut /ˈhælɪbət/, *n., pl.* **-buts**, *(esp. collectively)* **-but. 1.** Also, **Queensland halibut.** a dusky brown fish, making fine eating found in tropical waters of Australia and elsewhere. **2.** either of two kinds of large flatfishes, of the North Atlantic and the North Pacific, widely used for food. [from OE: *hālig* holy + *butte* kind of fish; so called because eaten on holy days]

Halicarnassus /ˌhælɪkəˈnæsəs/, *n.* an ancient city of Caria, in south-western Asia Minor, site of the Mausoleum, one of the Seven Wonders of the World.

halitosis /hælɪˈtoʊsəs/, *n.* bad breath. [NL, from L: breath]

hall /hɔːl/, *n.* **1.** an entrance area or room of a house or building. **2.** a corridor or passageway. **3.** a large building or room for public use, as meetings, etc.: *a church hall; a town hall.* **4.** a large building for a residence, teaching, etc., in a university or college. **5.** the owner's house on a large landed estate. **6.** the main room in a medieval castle or the like, used for eating, sleeping, and entertaining. [OE]

Hall /hɔːl/, *n.* **1. Ben(jamin)**, 1837–65, Australian bushranger. **2. Sir John**, 1824–1907, NZ statesman; prime minister 1879–82. **3. Rodney**, born 1935, Australian poet and novelist; works include the novel *Just Relations* (1982).

hallelujah /hæləˈluːjə/, *interj.* **1.** Praise ye the Lord! ◇*n.* **2.** a cry of 'hallelujah!': *The crowd gave a loud hallelujah.* [Heb: praise ye Jehovah]

Halley's comet /ˈhæliz/, *n.* a comet which appears every 75 or 76 years, its last appearance being in 1986. [named after Edmund *Halley*, 1656–1742, British astronomer who first predicted its return]

hallmark /ˈhɔːlmɑːk/, *n.* **1.** an official mark or stamp indicating a standard of purity, used in marking gold and silver articles. **2.** any mark or special sign of genuineness, good quality, etc. **3.** any outstanding feature or characteristic. Also, **plate-mark.** [from Goldsmiths' *Hall*, London, the seat of the Goldsmiths' Company which tested and marked gold and silver articles]

hallo /həˈloʊ, haː-/, *interj., n., v.* →**hello.** Also, **halloa** /həˈloʊ/.

hallow /ˈhæloʊ/, *v.t.* **1.** to make holy; sanctify; consecrate. **2.** to honor as holy. [OE *hālgian*, from *hālig* HOLY]

Halloween /ˌhæloʊˈiːn, hæləˈwiːn/, *n.* the evening of 31 October, the eve of All Saints' Day. Also, **Hallowe'en.** [*hallow* saint + *een* eve]

hallucinate /həˈluːsəneɪt/, *v.,* **-nated, -nating.** ◇*v.t.* **1.** to give hallucinations to. ◇*v.i.* **2.** to experience hallucinations. [L: wander in mind, dream]

hallucination /həˌluːsəˈneɪʃən/, *n.* **1.** something seen, heard, etc., by the senses, which does not come from any source outside the mind. It can be produced by certain drugs, and when experienced often or for a long time indicates mental illness. See **delusion** (def. 2) and **illusion** (def. 4). **2.** a suffering from illusion or false notions. —**hallucinatory,** *adj.*

hallucinogen /həˈluːsənədʒən/, *n.* a drug or chemical able to produce hallucinations. [HALLUCIN(ATION) + -GEN] —**hallucinogenic,** *adj.*

halo /ˈheɪloʊ/, *n., pl.* **-loes, -los,** *v.,* **-loed, -loing.** ◇*n.* **1.** a light or radiance surrounding the head in a picture of a sacred person or being; nimbus; aureole. **2.** a glory around anything seen as very precious or wonderful: *the halo around Shakespeare's plays.* **3.** a circle of light, usu. white, seen round the sun or moon, caused

halo by the refraction of light in suspended ice crystals in the earth's atmosphere. See **corona** (def. 1). ◇*v.t.* **4.** to surround with a halo. [L: from Gk: disc, halo, threshing floor (on which the oxen trod out a circular path)]

halo-, a word part meaning 'salt', as in **halogen**. [Gk, combining form of *háls*]

halogen /'hæləʤən, 'hæl-/, *n.* the name of group of strongly electronegative elements, fluorine, chlorine, iodine, and bromine, etc., which have similar, graded properties.

Hals /hɑls/, *n.* **Frans** /frɑns/, 1580?–1666, Dutch painter of portraits and scenes from ordinary life.

halt[1] /hɔlt, hɒlt/, *v.i.* **1.** to stop for a while, as in marching, etc. ◇*v.t.* **2.** to cause to stop: *The police halted the stranger.* ◇*n.* **3.** a stop for a while; temporary stop. **4.** a stopping-place on a railway line, smaller than a station, where a train stops only for a short time. ◇*interj.* **5.** (a command to stop and stand still, esp. as to soldiers.) [G: *stoppage*]

halt[2] /hɔlt, hɒlt/, *v.i.* **1.** to stumble as in speech, reasoning, etc.; falter. **2.** to be in doubt; waver; hesitate. ◇*adj.* **3.** *Archaic.* unable to walk properly; lame; limping. ◇*n.* **4.** *Archaic.* lameness; a limp. [OE *h(e)alt*] –**halting**, *adj.*

halter /'hɔltə, 'hɒltə/, *n.* **1.** a rope or strap with a noose, for leading or fastening horses or cattle. **2.** a rope with a noose for hanging criminals. [OE *hælftre*]

halve /hɑv/, *v.t.*, **halved, halving. 1.** to divide in halves; share equally. **2.** to reduce to half: *to halve the volume of sound.* [ME *halven*, from HALF]

halves /hɑvz/, *n.* **1.** plural of **half. 2. by halves**, **a.** incompletely. **b.** half-heartedly. **3. go halves**, divide equally; share.

halyard /'hæljəd/, *n.* the rope or tackle used to raise or lower a sail, yard, flag, etc. Also, **halliard**. [ME: that which hales or hauls (from HALE[2] + -IER); influenced by YARD[1]]

ham /hæm/, *n., v.*, **hammed, hamming.** ◇*n.* **1.** the upper part of a pig's leg, from hip to hock; haunch. **2.** the meat of this part, esp. salted or smoked. **3.** the part of the leg behind the knee. **4.** (*oft. pl.*) the back of the thigh or of the thigh and the buttock together: *to sit on the hams.* **5.** *Colloq.* **a.** an actor who overacts. **b.** overacting. **6.** *Colloq.* an amateur: *a radio ham.* ◇*v.i.* **7.** *Colloq.* to act in an exaggerated or unnatural way; overact: *to ham it up.* [OE *hamm*]

Hamburg /'hæmbɜg/, *n.* a city and state in northern Germany, on the Elbe; the largest seaport in continental Europe, formerly a member of the Hanseatic League. Pop. 571 267 (1987 est.).

hamburger /'hæmbɜgə/, *n.* **1.** a flat round cake of minced beef, seasoned and fried. **2.** a bread roll containing a hamburger, onion, etc.

Hamersley Range /'hæməzli/, *n.* a plateau in north-western WA, south-east of the Fortescue River; iron ore deposits.

ham-fisted /'hæm-fɪstəd/, *adj.* clumsy. Also, **ham-handed**.

Hamilton[1] /'hæməltən/, *n.* **Sir Ian Standish Monteith**, 1853–1947, British general; led the disastrous Gallipoli expedition (1915).

Hamilton[2] /'hæməltən/, **1.** a city in NZ on central North Island. Pop. 96 700 (1985 est.). **2.** a city in the Western District, Vic, between Portland and Ararat. Pop. 9969 (1986).

hamlet /'hæmlət/, *n.* a very small village, or groups of houses. [ME *hamlet*, from OF, from Gmc: *land*]

hammer /'hæmə/, *n.* **1.** a tool with a heavy metal head set crosswise on a handle, used for beating metals, driving in nails, etc. **2.** any tool like a hammer. **3.** *Firearms.* that part of the lock which hits and explodes the percussion cap; cock. **4.** a padded lever that hits the strings of a piano. **5. come** or **go under the hammer**, to be sold by auction. ◇*v.t.* **6.** to beat or drive with or as with a hammer. **7.** to form with a hammer (oft. fol. by *out*), as a sheet of metal, etc. **8.** to fasten into place with a hammer. **9.** to put together or build with a hammer and nails: *to hammer a box together.* **10.** to hit with some force; pound: *to hammer the table.* **11.** to make or work out laboriously (oft. fol. by *out*): *to hammer out a plan.* **12.** to state forcefully; present (facts, etc.) aggressively: *to hammer home an idea.* **13.** to attack with questions; interrogate relentlessly: *The Minister was hammered by the Opposition at question time.* ◇*v.i.* **14.** to strike blows with or as if with a hammer. **15.** to work laboriously (oft. fol. by *away*): *to hammer away at an argument.* [OE *hamor*]

hammer and sickle, *n.* the emblem of communism, adopted in the USSR in 1923, the hammer and sickle being the tools of workers and peasants.

hammer and tongs, *adv. Colloq.* with great noise, vigor, or energy.

hammerhead /'hæməhɛd/, *n.* **1.** the head of a hammer. **2.** a shark with a head shaped like a double-headed hammer.

Hammerstein /'hæməstaɪn/, **Oscar** (*Oscar Hammerstein II*), 1895–1960, US lyricist and librettist.

Hammett /'hæmət/, *n.* (**Samuel**) **Dashiell** /'dæʃəl/, 1894–1961, US crime novelist and short-story writer; author of *The Maltese Falcon* (1930).

hammock /'hæmək/, *n.* a hanging bed or couch made of canvas, netting, etc. [Sp *hamaca*; of W Ind orig.]

Hammond /'hæmənd/, *n.* **Dame Joan Hood**, born 1912 in NZ, Australian soprano.

Hammurabi /hæmə'rɑbi/, *n.* fl. c. 2100 BC, king of Babylonia; famous code of laws made in his reign.

hamper[1] /'hæmpə/, *v.t.* **1.** to hold back; impede; hinder. ◇*n.* **2.** *Naut.* articles which, while necessary to a ship's equipment, are often in the way. [ME *hampren*, orig. uncert.]

hamper[2] /'hæmpə/, *n.* a large box or covered basket made from cane, wickerwork, etc., used for carrying food, as for a picnic. [ME *hampere*]

Hampshire /'hæmpʃə, -fə/, n. a county in southern England on the English Channel. *Administrative Centre:* Winchester. Pop. 1 527 700 (1986 est.); 4274 km². *Abbrev.:* Hants

hamster /'hæmstə/, n. a short-tailed, burrowing rodent, with large cheek pouches, living in parts of Europe and Asia. [G]

hamstring /'hæmstrɪŋ/, n., v., **-strung** or (*Rare*) **-stringed**; **-stringing**. ◇n. 1. (in humans) any of the tendons bounding the ham (def. 3). 2. (in quadrupeds) the great tendon at the back of the hock. ◇v.t. 3. to cut the hamstring or hamstrings of and thus cripple. 4. to make useless; cripple; thwart.

Han /hæn/, n. a Chinese dynasty, 206 BC–AD 220, with an interregnum, AD 9–25; noted for the revival of letters and the beginnings of Buddhism; its bureaucracy became a model for later dynasties.

Hancock /'hæŋkɒk/, n. **Tony**, 1924–68, British comedian.

hand /hænd/, n. 1. (in humans) a prehensile (able to grasp) part at the end of the arm, consisting of the palm and five fingers. 2. a similar part of the forelimb in any of the higher animals. 3. the end part of any limb when prehensile, as the hind foot of a monkey. 4. something like a hand in shape or function: *the hands of a clock*. 5. a worker; laborer: *a factory hand*. 6. someone who does a particular thing: *a book by several hands*. 7. the people of any company or number: *All hands on deck*. 8. (*oft. pl.*) possession or power; control; custody: *to have someone's fate in one's hands*. 9. help; cooperation: *a helping hand*. 10. side: *on every hand; on the other hand*. 11. a source, as of information or of supply: *at first hand*. 12. style of handwriting. 13. someone's signature. 14. skill; execution: *a painting that shows a master's hand*. 15. a person, with reference to action, ability, or skill: *a poor hand at writing letters*. 16. a promise of marriage. 17. a unit of measurement in the imperial system, used in giving the height of horses, etc., equal to four inches (approx. ten cm). 18. *Cards*. the cards dealt to or held by each player at one time. 19. bundle or bunch, as a cluster of bananas, or tobacco leaves tied together. 20. a burst of clapping for a performer: *to get a big hand*. ◇21. Some special uses are:

at hand, 1. within reach. 2. near in time. 3. ready for use.

at the hand(s) of, from the action or by the power of.

by hand, by the use of the hands rather than machine.

change hands, to pass from one owner to another.

come to hand, to be received; come within one's reach.

declare one's hand, to show what one is going to do.

free hand, freedom to act as desired.

give a hand, to help; assist.

hand over fist, easily or in large quantities.

hands down, totally; completely; easily.

hand to hand, (of fighting) at close quarters.

in hand, 1. under control. 2. in immediate possession: *cash in hand*. 3. in process: *Keep to the matter in hand*.

keep one's hand in, to keep in practice.

lay hands on, 1. to beat up; assault. 2. to place one's hands on the head of (a person) as part of a religious ceremony.

lay one's hands on, *Colloq*. to obtain.

off one's hands, out of one's responsible charge or care.

old hand, 1. an experienced person; veteran. 2. *Obs*. a former convict.

on or **upon one's hands**, under one's care, management, or responsibility.

out of hand, 1. beyond control: *to let one's temper get out of hand*. 2. at once; without delay.

out of one's hands, not one's responsibility; out of one's control.

play into the hand of, to put oneself unknowingly in the power of an enemy.

show of hands, a method of voting by counting the hands raised for or against a motion.

throw in one's hand, to give up; stop doing something; surrender.

turn one's hand to, to turn one's energies to; set to work at.

upper hand, a position of marked superiority; whip hand.

◇v.t. 22. to deliver or pass with the hand: *Hand me the jam please*. 23. to help or conduct with the hand. 24. *Naut*. to furl (a sail). 25. to pass on; transmit (fol. by *on*). ◇v. 26. Some special uses are:

hand down, 1. to deliver (the decision of a court). 2. to send or transmit from the higher to the lower, in space or time: *to hand down to posterity*.

hand in, to present for acceptance.

hand it to, to give due credit to.

hand out, to distribute.

hand over, 1. to deliver into another's keeping. 2. to give up control of.

◇adj. 27. of, belonging to or for the use of the hand: *hand cream; a hand basin*. 28. done or made by hand: *a hand signal*. 29. able to be carried in, or worn on, the hand: *a hand mirror*. 30. worked by hand: *hand shears*. [OE]

handbag /'hændbæg/, n. a small bag for carrying in the hand, to contain money and personal articles, etc.

handball /'hændbɔl/, n. 1. a game in which a small ball is batted against a wall with the (usu. gloved) hand. 2. a game like tennis in which the players hit the ball with their hands rather than with racquets. ◇v.i. 3. *Aust Rules*. to hold the ball in one hand and hit it away with the clenched fist of the other.

handbill /'hændbɪl/, n. a small printed bill (def. 3) or announcement, usu. for distribution by hand.

handbook /'hændbʊk/, n. a small book or treatise used for guidance; manual: *a handbook of car maintenance*.

handbrake /'hændbreɪk/, n. a brake worked by a hand lever.

handbreadth /'hændbredθ, -bretθ/, n. a unit of linear measure from six to ten cm. Also, **hand's-breadth**.

handclap /'hændklæp/, n. the striking of one palm against the other, usu. repeatedly to show appreciation.

handcuff /'hændkʌf/, n. 1. a ring-shaped fastening for the wrist, usu. one of a pair connected by a short chain or linked bar; shackle for the wrist. ◊v.t. 2. to put handcuffs on.

handed /'hændəd/, adj. 1. having a hand or hands. 2. of or relating to preference or necessity in the use of hands: *right-handed*, *one-handed*. 3. done by a specified number of hands: *a double-handed game*.

Handel /'hændl/, n. **George Frederick** (*Georg Friedrich Händel*). 1685–1759, British composer born in Germany, remembered for oratorios, esp. the *Messiah* (1741), and orchestral and chamber music.

handful /'hændful/, n., pl. **-fuls**. 1. as much or as many as the hand can hold or contain: *a handful of nuts*. 2. a small quantity or number: *a handful of men*. 3. *Colloq.* something or someone that is as much as one can manage: *That child is a handful*.

handicap /'hændikæp/, n., v., **-capped**, **-capping**. ◊n. 1. a race, etc., in which certain disadvantages or advantages of weight, distance, time, past records, etc., are placed upon competitors to make their chances of winning equal. 2. the disadvantage or advantage itself. 3. any disadvantage that makes success more difficult; encumbrance. 4. a physical disability. ◊v.t. 5. to be a handicap or disadvantage to: *His age handicaps him*. 6. to assign handicaps to (competitors). [orig. *hand i' cap* (with *i'* for *in* before a consonant), referring to the deposit of stakes or forfeits in a cap or hat] —**handicapper**, n.

handicapped /'hændikæpt/, adj. 1. disabled; crippled. 2. mentally retarded. 3. (of a player, competitor, etc.) having a handicap.

handicraft /'hændikra:ft/, n. 1. manual skill. 2. an art or occupation done by hand. [OE *handcræft*, modelled on HANDIWORK]

hand-in-glove /hænd-ɪn-'glʌv/, adv. in close working relationship (*with*).

handiwork /'hændiwɜk/, n. 1. Also, **handwork**. work done by the hands. 2. the work or action of a particular maker, craftsperson, etc. [OE *handgeweorc*]

handkerchief /'hæŋkətʃif/, n. a small usu. square piece of fabric, for wiping the face, nose, etc.

handle /'hændl/, n., v., **-dled**, **-dling**. ◊n. 1. the part of a thing which is intended to be held by the hand in using or moving it. 2. *Colloq.* something that may be taken advantage of in bringing about a result. 3. *Colloq.* a title in front of one's name. 4. *Colloq.* a person's name. ◊v.t. 5. to touch or feel with the hand. 6. to employ, or use: *He can handle his fists well in a fight*. 7. to manage, direct, or control: *The captain cannot handle his soldiers*. 8. to deal with (as a matter or subject). 9. to deal with or treat in a particular way: *You must handle old people with respect*. 10. to deal or trade in (goods, etc.). ◊v.i. 11. to respond to handling: *How does the car handle?* [OE *handlian* from *hand* HAND]

handlebar /'hændlba:/, n. (*usu. pl.*) the curved steering bar of a bicycle, etc.

handler /'hændlə/, n. 1. *Boxing.* a person who helps in the training of a fighter. 2. a person who trains and manages a dog, etc.

handmaid /'hændmeɪd/, n. a female servant or one who looks after the needs of another. Also, **handmaiden**.

hand-me-down /'hænd-mi-daʊn/, n. *Colloq.* an article of clothing handed down to someone else.

handout /'hændaʊt/, n. 1. a prepared written statement given out to inform. 2. a free sample given as for advertisement. 3. food, money or the like given to those in need. Also, **hand-out**.

hand-pick /hænd-'pɪk/, v.t. to choose carefully.

handpiece /'hændpis/, n. the part of a telephone or intercom held to the ear.

handrail /'hændreɪl/, n. a rail serving as a support or guard at the side of stairs, etc.

hand-reading /'hænd-ridɪŋ/, n. → palmistry.

handset /'hændset/, n., v., **-set**, **-setting**. ◊n. 1. a telephone part combining the receiver and mouthpiece in one unit, held by the hand. ◊v.t. 2. *Print.* to set (type) by hand.

handshake /'hænʃeɪk, 'hænd-/, n. a shaking of another's right hand as in greeting, agreement, etc.

handsome /'hænsəm/, adj., **-somer**, **-somest**. 1. of fine or admirable appearance; comely. 2. large in amount: *a handsome fortune*. 3. generous: *a handsome gift*. [ME orig., easy to handle]

handspring /'hændsprɪŋ/, n. a turning of the body in the air while being supported by the hands.

handstand /'hændstænd, 'hænd-/, n. a balancing upside down on one's hands.

hand tennis, n. → handball (def. 2).

hand-to-mouth /hænd-tə-'maʊθ/, adj. barely existing; precarious.

handwriting /'hænd,raɪtɪŋ/, n. 1. writing done with the hand. 2. a style of writing.

handy /'hændi/, adj., **-dier**, **-diest**. 1. close at hand. 2. ready or skilful with the hands; deft; dexterous. 3. easy to handle: *a handy ship*. 4. convenient or useful: *a handy tool*. —**handily**, adv. —**handiness**, n.

handyman /'hændimæn/, n. a man hired to do odd jobs.

hang /hæŋ/, v., **hung** or (*esp. for capital punishment and suicide*) **hanged**, **hanging**, n. ◊v.t. 1. to fasten a thing so that it is supported only from above; suspend. 2. to suspend so as to allow free movement as on a hinge. 3. to put (a person) to death by suspending from a rope around the neck. 4. to bend downwards: *I hang my head in shame*. 5. to furnish with something suspended: *She will hang the room*

with curtains. **6.** to attach (paper, etc.) to walls. **7.** *Art.* to show (a painter's work). **8.** (used in forcible expressions): *I'll be hanged if I do.* **9.** (of one juror) to keep (a jury) from bringing in a verdict. ◇*v.i.* **10.** to be suspended, sometimes swinging freely. **11.** to die by hanging. **12.** to be dependent: *The results hang on his skill.* **13.** to be doubtful or undecided; remain unfinished. **14.** to rest or float in the air. **15.** to remain in attention: *She would hang on his words.* ◇*v.* **16.** Some special uses are:
hang about or **around**, to spend time aimlessly.
hang (around) with (someone), to spend time in (someone's) company.
hang back, to be reluctant to proceed.
hang in, *Colloq.* to keep trying.
hang in the balance, to be in doubt.
hang on, 1. to attempt to preserve existing conditions. **2.** to stay: *Evil still hangs on in the city.* **3.** to wait: *Hang on! I'm not quite ready.*
hang out, 1. to lean through an opening. **2.** *Colloq.* to live at a particular place.
hang together, 1. to hold together. **2.** to be consistent: *His statements do not hang together.*
hang up, 1. to suspend on a hook or peg. **2.** to break off a telephone conversation by putting down the receiver.
◇*n.* **17.** the way in which a thing hangs: *the hang of the curtains.* **18.** *Colloq.* the manner of doing, using, etc., something: *to get the hang of it.* **19.** *Colloq.* meaning or force: *I have the hang of what you say.* **20.** the least degree of care, concern, etc.: *not to give a hang.* [OE *hangian*]

hangar /'hæŋə/, *n.* a shed or shelter, usu. for aircraft. [F, ? from Gmc]

hangdog /'hæŋdɒg/, *adj.* having a sorrowful, guilty or pitiful appearance.

hanger /'hæŋə/, *n.* a shaped support on which anything, such as clothing, is hung.

hanger-on /hæŋər-'ɒn/, *n., pl.* **hangers-on**. someone who holds onto a place or connection; a follower.

hang-glider /'hæŋ-glaɪdə/, *n.* **1.** a simple aircraft without a motor, which is carried by air currents and from which a person hangs. **2.** the person operating such a glider. **–hang-glide**, *v.* **–hang-gliding**, *n.*

hangi /'hʌŋi/, *n. NZ.* **1.** a Maori oven in which food is steamed over hot stones in the ground. **2.** food prepared in this manner. **3.** a feast at which such food is served. [Maori]

hanging /'hæŋɪŋ/, *n.* **1.** death by suspending on a rope, gallows, etc. **2.** (*oft. pl.*) something that hangs on the walls of a room. ◇*adj.* **3.** positioned at a height: *a hanging garden.*

Hanging Gardens of Babylon, *n.pl.* one of the Seven Wonders of the World, believed to be the ornamental gardens on the terraced ziggurats of ancient Babylon.

hangman /'hæŋmən/, *n., pl.* **-men**. someone who hangs persons condemned to death; public executioner.

hangover /'hæŋoʊvə/, *n. Colloq.* **1.** something left from a former state of affairs. **2.** the after-effects of drinking too much alcohol.

hang-up /'hæŋ-ʌp/, *n. Colloq.* something which causes unease in a person.

hank /hæŋk/, *n.* **1.** a coil, as of thread or yarn. **2.** a definite length of thread or yarn. [ME, from Scand]

hanker /'hæŋkə/, *v.i.* to have an unsatisfied longing (oft. fol. by *after*, *for*, or an infinitive). [? from D] **–hankering**, *n.*

hanky /'hæŋki/, *n. Colloq.* **→handkerchief**. Also, **hankie**.

hanky-panky /ˌhæŋki-'pæŋki/, *n. Colloq.* **1.** trickery. **2.** sexual play.

Hannan /'hænən/, *n.* **Paddy** (*Patrick Hannan*), 1843–1925, Australian prospector, born in Ireland; discovered the Kalgoorlie goldfield.

Hannibal /'hænəbəl/, *n.* 247–183? BC, Carthaginian general who crossed the Alps and invaded Italy.

Hanoi /hæ'nɔɪ/, *n.* the capital of Vietnam, in the northern part. Pop. 2 674 400 (1983).

Hanover[1] /'hænəvə/, *n.* **1.** the name of the English royal family from 1714 to 1901. **2.** the name of a princely house of Germany 1692–1815. **–Hanoverian**, *adj.*

Hanover[2] /'hænəvə/, *n.* a former province in northern Germany; now a district in Lower Saxony. 38 705 km^2.

Hanrahan /'hænrəhæn/, *n.* **Barbara**, 1939–91, Australian novelist; works include *The Frangipani Gardens* (1980).

Hansard /'hænsɑd/, *n.* the official printed reports of parliament. [so called after the *Hansard* family who printed the *Journals of the House of Commons* in England from 1774]

Hanseatic League /hænsiˌætɪk 'liɡ/, *n.* a medieval league of towns of northern Germany and adjacent countries for the promotion and protection of commerce.

hansom /'hænsəm/, *n.* a two-wheeled, covered vehicle drawn by one horse, for two passengers, the driver being on a raised seat behind. [named after JA *Hansom*, 1803–82, English patentee]

haphazard /hæp'hæzəd/, *adj.* **1.** dependent on chance: *a haphazard meeting.* ◇*adv.* **2.** by chance. [Archaic *hap* chance + HAZARD]

hapless /'hæpləs/, *adj.* unfortunate; unlucky.

haplo-, a word part meaning 'single', 'simple'. [Gk, combining form of *haplóos*]

haploid /'hæplɔɪd/, *adj.* Also, **haploidic**. **1.** single; simple. **2.** *Biol.* relating to a single set of chromosomes. ◇*n.* **3.** *Biol.* an organism or cell having only one complete set of chromosomes.

haplosis /hæp'loʊsəs/, *n.* the production of haploid chromosome groups during meiosis.

happen /'hæpən/, *v.i.* **1.** to come to pass; take place; occur. **2.** to come to pass without a clear reason or design; chance. **3.** to have the fortune or occasion (to do or be as indicated): *I happened to see him.* **4.** to come, to a person

happy /'hæpi/, *adj.*, **-pier, -piest. 1.** expressing pleasure, contentment, or gladness. **2.** delighted, or glad, as over a particular thing. **3.** fortunate or lucky: *a happy event.* **4.** (of actions, ideas, etc.) fitting or chosen well. **5. happy as Larry,** *Colloq.* very happy. **6. happy days!** *Colloq.* (*sometimes expecting the opposite*) Have a good time! [ME; from *hap,* chance]

happy-go-lucky /,hæpi-gou-'lʌki/, *adj.* trusting cheerfully to luck.

Happy Hunting Grounds, *n.pl.* (in North American Indian mythology) the world inhabited by souls after death; the afterlife.

Hapsburg /'hæpsbɜg/, *n.* a German princely family, prominent since the 11th century, members have been sovereigns of the Holy Roman Empire, Austria, Spain, etc. German, **Habsburg.** [shortening of *Habichtsburg* (hawk's castle), a castle in Switzerland]

harangue /hə'ræŋ/, *n., v.,* **-rangued, -ranguing. ◇***n.* **1.** a noisy, strongly-worded speech, often full of blame for those listening. ◇*v.t., v.i.* **2.** to address (someone) in, or give, a harangue. [F, from Gmc]

harass /'hærəs, hə'ræs/, *v.t.* **1.** to trouble by repeated attacks, etc., as in war; harry; raid. **2.** to disturb continually. [OF *harer* set a dog on] —**harassment,** *n.*

Harbin /ha'bɪn/, *n.* a city in north-eastern China, the capital of Heilongjiang province. Pop. 2 217 300 (1985 est.). Formerly, **Ha-erh-pin.**

harbinger /'habɪnə, -bɪndʒə/, *n.* **1.** someone who goes before and makes known the approach of another. **2.** that which tells of a future event; an omen. [ME, from OF: provide lodging for]

harbor *or* **harbour** /'habə/, *n.* **1.** a body of water along the shore deep enough for ships, providing protection from winds, waves, and currents. **2.** any place of shelter or refuge. ◇*v.t.* **3.** to give shelter or a place of hiding to. **4.** to hold in the mind: *After such an experience, she will harbor distrust for a time.* [OE *hereberg* lodgings, quarters, from *here* army + (*ge*)*beorg* refuge]

harborage *or* **harbourage** /'habərɪdʒ/, *n.* **1.** a shelter for ships, as in a harbor. **2.** shelter or lodging.

hard /had/, *adj.* **1.** solid and firm to the touch; not soft. **2.** firmly formed; tight: *a hard knot.* **3.** difficult to do, deal with or explain. **4.** needing or done with great energy or persistence: *hard work.* **5.** doing work this way: *a hard worker.* **6.** violent; severe: *a hard rain.* **7.** rough; harsh: *hard treatment; a hard master.* **8.** unpleasant; bad: *hard luck.* **9.** causing pain, poverty, etc.; austere: *hard times.* **10.** unfeeling; callous: *a hard heart.* **11.** unable to be explained away: *hard facts.* **12.** unfriendly; not easily moved: *hard feelings.* **13.** unpleasant to the eye, ear, etc. **14.** severe in terms: *a hard bargain.* **15.** not influenced by softer feelings; shrewd: *a hard head.* **16. a.** alcoholic: *hard drink.* **b.** dangerously addictive: *hard drugs.* **17.** (of water) containing mineral salts which interfere with the action of the soap. **18. do (it) the hard way,** to choose a needlessly difficult way of doing (something). **19. hard cash,** actual banknotes and coin, rather than cheques, etc. **20. hard cheese/cheddar/luck,** *Colloq.* bad luck. **21. hard up,** *Colloq.* urgently in need of something, esp. money. ◇*adv.* **22.** with a great output of energy: *to work hard.* **23.** earnestly or carefully: *Look hard at this photograph.* **24.** severely; badly; gallingly: *It goes hard.* **25.** so as to be solid or firm: *frozen hard.* **26.** closely, fully, or to the extreme limit: *Turn hard left.* **27. hard by,** close or nearby. **28. hard put (to it),** in great difficulties. [OE *heard*]

hard and fast, *adj.* **1.** strongly binding: *hard and fast rules.* ◇*adv.* **2.** firmly and securely.

hardback /'hadbæk/, *n.* a book bound in stiff covers.

hard-bitten /'had-bɪtn/, *adj.* (of a person) tough; not easily broken; stubborn.

hardboard /'hadbɔd/, *n.* material made from wood fibres pressed into sheets.

hard case, *n.* **1.** a person who lacks gentleness and distrusts softness or sincerity in others. **2.** a cleverly funny person. **3.** someone who cannot be changed for the better. **4.** a person suffering from drug addiction, esp. to alcohol. —**hard-case,** *adj.*

hard core, *n.* the unyielding members forming the central strength of a group.

hard-core /'had-kɔ/, *adj.* **1.** of or belonging to the hard core: *a hard-core Communist.* **2.** of or relating to a continuing social condition: *hard-core unemployment.* **3.** with explicit details of sex: *hard-core pornography.* **4.** physically addictive: *hard-core drugs.*

hard court, *n.* a tennis court with a surface of sand, asphalt, etc. —**hard-court,** *adj.*

harden /'hadn/, *v.t.* **1.** to make hard or harder. **2.** to make unyielding; make unfeeling or pitiless. **3.** to strengthen with respect to any part of character; toughen. **4.** to make (something) able to last. ◇*v.i.* **5.** to become hard or harder. **6.** to become unfeeling or pitiless. **7.** to become strengthened in character or determination. [HARD + -EN[1]]

hard-hat /'had-hæt/, *adj.* of or relating to an area, job, etc., in which a safety helmet must be worn.

hard-hearted /'had-hatəd/, *adj.* unfeeling; merciless; pitiless.

hard-hit /'had-'hɪt/, *adj.* severely affected: *hard-hit by the floods.*

hardihood /'hadihud/, *n.* hardy spirit or character; boldness or daring.

hardiness /'hadinəs/, *n.* **1.** strength and health; ability to bear anything; toughness. **2.** hardihood; fearlessness.

Harding /'hadɪŋ/, *n.* **Warren Gamaliel** /gə'meɪliəl/, 1865–1923, 29th president of the US, 1921–23.

hard labor *or* **hard labour,** *n.* work forced on criminals as a punishment, oft. as part of a court ruling.

hardline /'hadlaɪn/, *adj.* not turning from a set idea, policy, etc.: *a hardline attitude to drugs.*

hardly /'hadli/, *adv.* **1.** almost not at all; barely. **2.** probably not: *He will hardly come now.* **3.** with difficulty. **4.** severely.

hardness /'hadnəs/, *n.* **1.** that quality in impure water which is given by the presence of dissolved salts. **2.** *Mineral.* the ability of a substance to scratch another or be scratched by another. See **Mohs scale**.

hardnose /'hadnoʊz/, *n.* **1.** → **recidivist**. **2.** a person unwilling to give in.

hard-pressed /had'prest/, *adj.* under pressure; harassed (oft. fol. by *by*): *He was hard-pressed by lack of time.*

hard rock, *n.* rock music which emphasises a strong simple rhythm and an energetic style, and usu. greatly amplified.

hard sell, *n.* a method of advertising or selling which is direct, forceful, and demanding. — **hard-sell**, *adj.*

hardship /'hadʃɪp/, *n.* **1.** a condition that bears hard upon one; great trial, oppression, or need. **2.** something hard to bear.

hardtop /'hadtɒp/, *n.* a car, esp. a sports car, which does not have a movable top.

hardware /'hadweə/, *n.* **1.** building materials, tools, etc. **2.** the mechanical equipment necessary for carrying out an activity, opposed to the theory making it possible. **3.** the physical components of a computer system, as the circuitry, magnetic tape units, etc. (opposed to *software*).

hardwood /'hadwʊd/, *n.* a (tree yielding) hard, dense timber as the eucalyptus, oak, cherry, etc.

hardy /'hadi/, *adj.*, **-dier, -diest. 1.** able to stand up to tiredness, hardship, etc. **2.** (of plants) able to withstand the cold of winter in the open air. **3.** bold or daring. [ME, from OF: hardened, from Gmc]

Hardy /'hadi/, *n.* **1. Frank** (*Francis Joseph Hardy*), born 1917, Australian radical political writer and lecturer; works include the novel *Power Without Glory* (1950). **2. Thomas**, 1840–1928, English novelist and poet; novels are mainly set in Dorset and include *Far from the Madding Crowd* (1874).

hare /heə/, *n., pl.* **hares**, (*esp. collectively*) **hare**, *v.*, **hared, haring.** ◇*n.* **1.** a rabbit-like mammal with long ears, a divided upper lip and lengthened back limbs for leaping. ◇*v.i.* **2.** to run fast. [OE *hara*]

harebrained /'heəbreɪnd/, *adj.* without sense or reason; reckless.

Hare Krishna /hari 'krɪʃnə/, *n. Colloq.* a member of a Hindu sect which emphasises love of Krishna, a Hindu god. [from the chant *Hare Krishna* Lord Krishna]

harelip /'heəlɪp/, *n.* a lip, usu. the upper one, which at birth has a vertical gap in it, similar to the divided lip of a hare.

harem /'heərəm, ha'rim/, *n.* **1.** that part of an oriental palace or house in which the women live. **2.** the women in an oriental household, mother, sisters, wives, mistresses, servants, etc. [Ar: forbidden]

hare-wallaby /'heə-wɒləbi/, *n.* any of various small wallabies similar to hares in their speed and jumping ability, e.g. the **wurrup**, of central Australia, with an orange ring around the eye and orange hair behind the legs, and the **munning**, of WA, with bands of black and white across the back.

Hargrave /'hagreɪv/, *n.* **Lawrence**, 1850–1915, Australian aeronautical pioneer, born in England; his experiments with models and kites contributed to development of aeroplanes.

Hargraves /'hagreɪvz/, *n.* **Edward Hammond**, 1816–91, Australian gold discoverer, born in England; found gold at Ophir in NSW in 1851, using experience gained on the Californian goldfields.

Hargreaves /'hagriːvz/, *n.* **James**, died 1778, English inventor (of the spinning jenny).

haricot /'hærəkoʊ/, *n.* → **French bean**. [F]

hark /hak/, *v.i.* **1.** (*used mainly as a command*) to listen; hearken. ◇*v.* **2. hark back**, to return to a previous point or subject. [ME *herk(i)en*]

Harlem /'haləm/, *n.* the chief black section of New York City, in the north-eastern part of Manhattan.

Harlequin /'haləkwən/, *n.* a droll character in comedy (orig. the early Italian) and pantomime, usu. masked, dressed in particolored spangled tights, and bearing a wooden sword or magic wand. [F; OF *Harlequin, Herlequin*, from ME *Herle King* King Herla (mythical figure); modern meaning from It *arlecchino*, from F *Harlequin*]

harlot /'halət/, *n.* **1.** (*insulting*) a woman who shares her sexual favors among many. **2.** → **prostitute**. [ME, from OF: rogue, knave; orig. uncert.]

harm /ham/, *n.* **1.** damage; hurt. **2.** moral damage; evil; wrong. ◇*v.t.* **3.** to do harm to; injure; damage; hurt. [OE *hearm*]

harmonic /ha'mɒnɪk/, *adj.* **1.** relating to harmony, as opposed to melody and rhythm. **2.** marked by harmony; consonant. **3.** *Phys.* a whole-number multiple of given frequency. 256, 512, and 768 cycles per second are first, second, and third harmonics of 256 cycles per second. [L, from Gk: skilled in music]

harmonica /ha'mɒnɪkə/, *n.* a musical instrument having a set of small metallic reeds played by blowing; a mouth organ.

harmonic minor, *n.* the minor musical scale from which chords are formed.

harmonics /ha'mɒnɪks/, *n.* **1.** the science of musical sounds. **2.** (*treated as pl.*) those notes sounded by the vibrations of fractional parts ($\frac{1}{2}$, $\frac{1}{3}$, etc.) of the string producing the fundamental note.

harmonious /ha'moʊniəs/, *adj.* **1.** marked by agreement in feeling or action. **2.** agreeable to the ear; tuneful; melodious.

harmonise *or* **harmonize** /'haːmənaɪz/, *v.*, **-nised**, **-nising**. ◇*v.t.* **1.** to bring into agreement. **2.** *Music.* to join with a harmony that sounds pleasing to the ears. ◇*v.i.* **3.** to be in agreement in action, sense, or feeling. **4.** to sing in harmony.

harmonium /haːˈmoʊniəm/, *n.* a reed organ, esp. one in which the air is forced outwards through the reeds. [F, from L *harmonia* HARMONY]

harmony /'haːməni/, *n.*, *pl.* **-nies**. **1.** agreement; accord. **2.** a consistent, orderly, or pleasing arrangement of parts; congruity. **3. a.** a combination of notes at the one time, as opposed to melody and rhythm. **b.** the science of the structure, relations, and practical combination of chords. [ME, from L, from Gk: a joining, concord, music]

harness /'haːnəs/, *n.* **1.** the combination of straps, bands, and other parts forming the working gear of a horse. **2.** a similar combination worn by persons for safety. **3. in harness, a.** side by side; together. **b.** working; at one's job. ◇*v.t.* **4.** to put a harness on (a horse, etc.). **5.** to bring under conditions for working: *It is possible to harness water power.* [ME, from OF, ? from OHG]

Harold II, *n.* c. 1022–1066, king of England in 1066 (successor of Edward the Confessor and son of Earl Godwin); defeated by William the Conqueror in the Battle of Hastings.

harp /haːp/, *n.* **1.** a musical instrument consisting of a triangular frame and strings which are plucked with the fingers. ◇*v.i.* **2.** to continue to speak or write (fol. by *on* or *upon*) in an annoying way. [OE *hearpe*]

harpoon /haːˈpuːn/, *n.* **1.** a spearlike weapon attached to a rope, and thrown or shot to catch large fish. ◇*v.t.* **2.** to strike, catch, or kill with or as with a harpoon. [D, from F: grapple, of Gmc orig.]

harpsichord /'haːpsəkɔːd/, *n.* a keyboard instrument, historically before the piano, in common use from the 16th to the 18th century, and used again in the 20th. [F, *harpe* harp + *chorde* string (see CHORD¹)]

Harpur /'haːpə/, *n.* **Charles**, 1813–68, Australian writer; oft. considered Australia's first noteworthy poet.

harpy /'haːpi/, *n.* **1.** a greedy, snatching person. **2.** an unattractive, bad-tempered, old woman. **3.** (*cap.*) Gk *Myth.* a rapacious and filthy monster with a woman's head and a bird's body. [LGk: lit., snatcher]

harridan /'hærədən/, *n.* a bad-tempered violent woman.

harrier¹ /'hæriə/, *n.* any of various hawks which fly back and forth over pasturelands searching for the small birds and mammals on which they feed. [HARRY, *v.*, + -ER¹]

harrier² /'hæriə/, *n.* **1.** a breed of small hounds used in hunting hare. **2.** a cross-country runner. [special use of HARRIER¹, by association with HARE]

Harris /'hærəs/, *n.* **1. Alexander** ('*An Emigrant Mechanic*'), 1805–74, English-born writer in Australia, 1825–40; author of *The Emigrant Family: Or, the Story of an Australian Settler* (1849) **2. Max(well Henry)**, born 1921, Australian journalist, editor and poet; one of the founding editors of *Angry Penguins*. **3. Rolf**, born 1930, Australian entertainer, composer and musician.

Harrison /'hærəsən/, *n.* **1. Benjamin**, 1833–1901, 23rd president of the US 1889–93; grandson of William Henry Harrison. **2. George**, born 1943, British pop singer, guitarist and composer; lead guitarist for the Beatles. **3. James**, c. 1815–93, Australian journalist and inventor of refrigerating machinery, born in Scotland. **4. William Henry**, 1773–1841, US general; ninth president of the US in 1841.

harrow /'hæroʊ/, *n.* **1.** a wheel-less frame set with teeth, etc., drawn over ploughed land to level it, break dirt up, etc. ◇*v.t.* **2.** to draw a harrow over (land, etc.). [ME *haru*, *harwe*]

harrowing /'hæroʊɪŋ/, *adj.* keenly and painfully disturbing: *a harrowing experience.*

harry /'hæri/, *v.t.*, **-ried**, **-rying**. **1.** to worry; torment. **2.** to completely ruin, as in war; devastate. [OE *her(g)ian* ravage (from *here* army)]

harsh /haːʃ/, *adj.* **1.** ungentle and unpleasant in action or effect. **2.** rough to the touch or to any of the senses. [ME *harsk*]

hart /haːt/, *n.*, *pl.* **harts**, (*esp. collectively*) **hart**. a male of the deer, commonly the red deer. [OE *heort*]

Hart /haːt/, *n.* **1. William Ewart**, 1885–1943, Australian pioneer aviator.

hartebeest /'haːtəbiːst/, *n.* a large red antelope of southern Africa. [Afrikaans: hart beast]

Hartigan /'haːtəgən/, *n.* **Patrick Joseph** ('*John O'Brien*'), 1878–1952, Australian author and priest; wrote the verse collection *Around the Boree Log and Other Verses* (1921).

Hartnett /'haːtnət/, *n.* **Sir Laurence John**, 1898–1986, Australian engineer and company director, born in England; creator of the first mass-produced all-Australian car, the Holden.

Hartog /'haːtog/, *n.* **Dirck** /dɔk/, Dutch sea captain; the first European to land on the western coast of Australia, 1616.

harum-scarum /ˌheərəmˈskeərəm/, *adj.* **1.** not thinking about the results; rash. ◇*adv.* **2.** wildly; rashly. [? var. of *hare 'em scare 'em* (with obs. *hare* harry, scare)]

Harvard /'haːvəd/, *n.* the university founded by John Harvard in 1636, in the US, at Cambridge, Massachusetts.

harvest /'haːvəst/, *n.* **1.** (the season of) the gathering of crops. **2.** a crop or yield, as of grain. **3.** a supply of anything gathered and stored up: *a harvest of nuts.* **4.** the result of any process. ◇*v.t.* **5.** to gather (a crop). **6.** to gather the crop from: *He will harvest the fields.* ◇*v.i.* **7.** to gather a crop; reap. [OE *hærfest*]

harvester /'haːvəstə/, *n.* a type of machine for harvesting field crops.

harvest moon, *n.* the moon at and about the period of fullness which is nearest to the autumnal equinox.

Harvey /ˈhɑːvi/, n. **William**, 1578-1657, English physician, discoverer of the circulation of the blood.

has /hæz/, weak forms /həz, əz/, v. third person singular present indicative of *have*.

has-been /ˈhæz-bin/, n. Colloq. a person or thing that is no longer effective, successful, popular, etc.

hash¹ /hæʃ/, n. **1.** a dish of chopped, cooked meat, reheated in a highly flavored sauce. **2.** a mess. **3.** any preparation of old material worked over. **4. make a hash of**, to spoil or make a mess of something. [F *hache* axe]

hash² /hæʃ/, n. Colloq. →hashish.

hashish /ˈhæʃiʃ, ˈhæʃiːʃ/, n. the purified resin from the flowering tops, leaves, etc., of Indian hemp, smoked, chewed, etc. as a drug. [Ar]

hasn't /ˈhæzənt/, v. a short form of *has not*.

hasp /hæsp, hɑsp/, n. a fastening for a door, lid, etc., esp. one passing over a hook and fastened by a pin or a padlock. [OE *hæsp*, *hæpse*]

hassle /ˈhæsəl/, n., v., -led, -ling. ◇n. **1.** a quarrel; squabble. **2.** a struggle: *Today was a real hassle*. ◇v.t. **3.** to worry; harass: *Don't hassle me*.

hassock /ˈhæsək/, n. **1.** a thick, firm cushion used for kneeling. **2.** a thick clump of grass. [OE *hassuc* coarse grass]

haste /heɪst/, n. **1.** energetic speed in motion or action, often as a result of something urgent. **2.** thoughtless speed: *Haste makes waste*. **3. in haste**, with speed, quickly. **4. make haste**, to force oneself to do something quickly. [ME, from OF, from Gmc]

hasten /ˈheɪsən/, v.i. **1.** to move or act with haste; hurry. ◇v.t. **2.** to cause to hasten; accelerate.

Hastings /ˈheɪstɪŋz/, n. **1.** a seaport in south-eastern England; William the Conqueror defeated the Anglo-Saxons near here in the **Battle of Hastings**, 1066; one of the Cinque Ports. Pop. 74 803 (1981). **2.** a town in NZ, in the eastern part of the North Island. Pop. (with Napier) 112 700 (1984).

hasty /ˈheɪsti/, adj., **hastier, hastiest**. **1.** moving or done with haste. **2.** too quick in movement or action; rash: *a hasty reply*. **3.** done with or marked by thoughtless or angry haste: *hasty words*. **4.** easily excited to anger; quick-tempered; irascible. [ME, from OF]

hat /hæt/, n. **1.** a shaped covering for the head, usu. worn outdoors. ◇**2.** Some special uses are:
  at the drop of a hat, without thinking or pausing.
  eat one's hat, Colloq. to be very surprised if a certain event happens.
  old hat, Colloq. (of ideas, etc.) old-fashioned.
  talk through one's hat, Colloq. to speak without knowledge of the true facts.
  under one's hat, Colloq. secret: *Keep this information under your hat*.

hatch¹ /hætʃ/, v.t. **1.** to bring forth (young) from the egg. **2.** to make up; devise; concoct: *They have hatched a plan*. ◇v.i. **3.** to emerge from the egg. ◇n. **4.** the act of hatching. **5.** that which is hatched, as a family of chickens. [ME *hacche*]

hatch² /hætʃ/, n. **1.** a cover for an opening in a ship's deck, a floor, a roof, etc. **2.** the opening itself. **3.** (oft. pl.) →**hatchway**. **4.** an opening in the wall between a kitchen and dining room, through which food is served. **5. down the hatch**, Colloq. drink up! [OE *hæcc* grating, hatch]

hatch³ /hætʃ/, v.t. to mark with lines, esp. closely set parallel lines. [F *hacher* chop, hash, hatch]

hatchback /ˈhætʃbæk/, n. a car fitted with a top-opening door at the back which includes the rear-vision window.

hatchery /ˈhætʃəri/, n., pl. **-eries**. a place for hatching the eggs of hens, fish, etc.

hatchet /ˈhætʃət/, n. **1.** a small, short-handled axe for use with one hand; tomahawk. **2. bury the hatchet**, to make peace. [ME, from F: little axe, from Gmc]

hatchet man, n. **1.** a man employed to perform unpleasant tasks. **2.** a hired killer.

hatchway /ˈhætʃweɪ/, n. **1.** an opening (covered by a hatch) in a ship's deck, for passage to parts below, esp. the hold; hatch. **2.** the opening of any small door, as in a floor, etc.

hate /heɪt/, v., **hated, hating**, n., adj. ◇v.t. **1.** to regard with a strong dislike; detest. **2.** to dislike; be unwilling: *I hate to do it*. ◇v.i. **3.** to feel hatred. ◇n. **4.** hatred; strong dislike. **5.** the object of hatred. ◇adj. **6.** given over to expressing dislike: *a hate session*. [OE *hatian*]

hateful /ˈheɪtfəl/, adj. deserving or causing hate; detestable; odious.

Hathaway /ˈhæθəweɪ/, n. **Anne**, 1557-1623, the wife of William Shakespeare.

hatred /ˈheɪtrəd/, n. the feeling of someone who hates; detestation. [ME]

Hatshepsut /hætˈʃɛpsʊt/, n. c. 1512-c.1482 BC, Egyptian queen of the 18th dynasty, the only woman pharaoh.

hatstand /ˈhætstænd/, n. a tall stand with spreading arms or pegs on which hats, coats, etc., are hung.

hatter /ˈhætə/, n. **1.** a maker or seller of hats. **2. mad as a hatter**, very different from normal; crazy.

hat-trick /ˈhæt-trɪk/, n. **1.** Cricket. the act by one bowler of bowling out three batsmen with three balls, one after the other. **2.** any similar feat in other sports with a set of three items.

haughty /ˈhɔːti/, adj., **-tier, -tiest**. proudly disregarding the claims of others; arrogant; supercilious. [F: high]

haul /hɔːl/, v.t. **1.** to pull or draw with force. **2. haul over the coals**, Colloq. to blame; scold. **3. haul up**, Colloq. **a.** to bring up, as before someone higher in rank for a scolding. **b.** to change the course of (a ship), esp. so as to sail closer to the wind. ◇v.i. **4.** to pull. **5. haul off**, Naut. to change the course

haul of a ship so as to get farther off from an object. ◇*n.* **6.** the act of hauling; a strong pull. **7.** the distance over which anything is hauled. **8.** *Fishing.* the quantity of fish taken at one draught of the net. **9.** *Colloq.* the taking of anything, or that which is taken. [ME *hale(n)*, from Gmc]

haulage /'hɔlɪdʒ/, *n.* **1.** transport, esp. heavy road transport. **2.** the charge for hauling, as on a railway.

haulier /'hɔliə/, *n.* a person or company engaged in haulage (def. 1).

haunch /hɔntʃ/, *n.* **1.** the fleshy part of the body about the hip. **2.** the back part of an animal; hindquarter. [ME *hanche*, from Gmc]

haunt /hɔnt/, *v.t.* **1.** to reappear frequently to after death. **2.** to push in upon continually: *memories that haunt one*. **3.** to worry: *His guilt haunted him*. **4.** to visit frequently. **5.** to be often with. ◇*n.* **6.** (*oft. pl.*) a place visited often: *I will return to my old haunts*. [ME *haunten*, from Gmc]

haunted /'hɔntəd/, *adj.* **1.** visited by ghosts: *a haunted house*. **2.** worried by something: *haunted by fear*.

haunting /'hɔntɪŋ/, *adj.* **1.** (of music) as though calling up memories; fascinating. **2.** (of a memory, etc.) continually coming back to one.

haute cuisine /out kwə'zin/, *n.* cooking of a high standard. [F]

Havana /hə'vænə/, *n.* a seaport in and the capital of Cuba, on the north-western coast. Pop. 2 014 806 (1986 est.). Spanish, **Habana**.

have /hæv/, *v.*, *present tense sing.* **I have**; **you have**; **he, she, it has**; *pl.* **we, you, they have**; *past tense and past participle* **had**; *present participle* **having**; *old forms* **thou hast**; **he hath**. ◇*v.t.* **1.** to own; possess; to hold for use: *to have a house*; *to have a car*. **2.** to be made of or to contain: *This box only has 11 eggs*. **3.** to hold or possess in some other relationship: *He has two brothers*; *to have a partner*. **4.** to possess as a characteristic, part, or feature: *I have a bad temper*; *The book has an index*. **5.** to get, receive, or take: *I had no news for six months*. **6.** to be required or forced (fol. by an infinitive): *I have to stop now*. **7.** to experience: *to have a pleasant time*. **8.** to hold (a social occasion, etc.): *to have a party*. **9.** to eat or drink: *She had a meal*. **10.** to hold in mind, etc.: *to have doubts*. **11.** to cause or require: *Have it ready at 5 pm*. **12.** to put or keep in a particular place: *Let's have the desk in the corner*. **13.** to engage in: *to have a talk*. **14.** to be scheduled for: *I have two meetings tomorrow*. **15.** to show in action: *to have mercy*. **16.** to allow: *I will not have it*. **17.** to buy, accept or take: *I'll have this one, thanks*. **18.** to invite or expect visitors, etc.: *We have friends coming for tea*. **19.** to state or maintain: *Rumor has it so*. **20.** to know or understand, esp. for use: *to have Greek*. **21.** to give birth to. ◇*v.* **22.** Some special uses are:
have done, to finish (oft. fol. by *with*).
have had it, *Colloq.* **1.** to die, be defeated, etc. **2.** to become no longer popular or useful.
have had (someone/something), *Colloq.* to be annoyed with: *I've had this job*.
have it out, to have an (honest) argument or discussion.
have on, **1.** to be wearing. **2.** to have arranged: *What do you have on tomorrow?*
have someone on, *Colloq.* **1.** to tease or deceive someone. **2.** to fight or compete with someone.
have to do with, **1.** to have dealings with: *She will have nothing to do with him*. **2.** to concern: *That has nothing to do with you*.
◇*v.* **23.** a word used as an auxiliary verb with **a.** the past participle of another verb, to form the perfect tenses: *We have seen him*. **b.** the past participle of the verb **be** and the present participle of another verb, to form the perfect continuous tenses: *We have been swimming*. ◇*n. Colloq.* **24.** a trick: *It was a bit of a have*. **25. the haves and the have-nots**, *Colloq.* the rich and the poor. [ME *have(n)*, OE *habban*]

haven /'heɪvən/, *n.* **1.** a harbor or port. **2.** any place of shelter and safety. [OE *hæfen*]

haven't /'hævənt/, *v.* a short form of *have not*.

haversack /'hævəsæk/, *n.* any bag carried on the back or shoulders, used by soldiers, bushwalkers, etc. [F *havresac*, from LG: oat sack]

havoc /'hævək/, *n.* **1.** great damage; devastation. **2. play havoc with**, to destroy or totally confuse. [ME, from AF, var. of OF *havot*, used esp. in phrase *crier havot* cry havoc, give the call for pillaging; probably from Gmc]

Hawaiian Islands /həwaɪən 'aɪləndz/, *n.pl.* a group of islands in the northern Pacific, 3363 km south-west of San Francisco, a US state. Pop. 1 062 000 (1986 est.); 16 705 km². *Cap.:* Honolulu. Also, **Hawaii**. Formerly, **Territory of Hawaii**, **Sandwich Islands**.

Hawaiki /'hawaiki/, *n.* the legendary Polynesian ancestral homeland of the NZ Maori. [Maori]

Haw-Haw /'hɔ-hɔ/, *n.* **Lord**. → **William Joyce**.

hawk[1] /hɔk/, *n.* **1.** any of several birds of prey which are active by day, e.g. the falcons, buzzards, kites, harriers, etc. **2.** any of certain other birds, e.g. the nighthawk. **3.** a politician or political adviser who favors an aggressive foreign policy (opposed to *dove*). ◇*v.i.* **4.** to hunt with hawks trained to pursue game. [OE *hafoc*] —**hawkish**, *adj.*

hawk[2] /hɔk/, *v.t.*, *v.i.* to offer for sale by shouting in a street or from door to door; peddle. [MLG *hoker*]

Hawke /hɔk/, *n.* **Robert James Lee**, born 1929, Australian federal Labor politician and former president of the ACTU; prime minister 1983–91.

hawker /'hɔkə/, *n.* someone who travels from place to place selling goods. [apparently from MLG]

Hawker /'hɔkə/, *n.* **Harry George**, 1889–1921, Australian pioneer aviator.

Hawkesbury /'hɔksbri/, *n.* a river in eastern NSW, rising in the Great Dividing Range and flowing north-east then south-east

Hawkesbury to enter the sea north of Sydney; part of the Nepean-Warragamba river system. About 480 km.

hawse /hɔz/, n. the part of a ship's bow with holes for cables to pass through. [ME *halse*, probably from Scand]

hawser /'hɔzə/, n. a small cable or large rope used in mooring, towing, etc. [ME, from OF: raise, from L: high]

hawthorn /'hɔθɔn/, n. a small thorny tree grown in hedges, with white or pink blossoms and bright fruit. [OE *haguthorn*]

hay /heɪ/, n. **1.** grass cut and dried for use as animal feed. **hit the hay**, to go to bed. **3. make hay while the sun shines**, to make the most of an opportunity. [ME; OE *hēg, hieg*]

Hayden /'heɪdn/, n. **Bill** (*William George Hayden*), born 1933, Australian federal Labor politician; Leader of the Opposition 1978–83; Minister for Foreign Affairs 1983–88; became governor-general of Australia in 1989.

Haydn /'haɪdn/, n. (**Franz**) **Joseph** /frants 'jousef/, 1732–1809, Austrian composer, especially known for his oratorios, symphonies and chamber music.

Hayes /heɪz/, n. **William Henry** ('*Bully*'), 1829–77, US-born adventurer and swindler in Australia and NZ.

hay fever, n. an allergy affecting the mucous membranes of the eyes, nose and throat, caused by pollen, usu. in spring and summer.

haystack /'heɪstæk/, n. a stack of hay with a cone-shaped or ridged top, built up in the open air for storage. Also, **hayrick**.

haywire /'heɪwaɪə/, n. **1.** wire used to bind hay. ◇*adj.* **2.** out of order. **3.** out of control; crazy: *to go haywire*.

hazard /'hæzəd/, n. **1.** a risk; exposure to danger or harm. **2.** the cause of such a risk; a possible source of harm, injury, difficulty, etc.: *The motor car has become a major hazard in modern life*. **3.** chance; uncertainty. ◇*v.t.* **4.** to be so bold as to offer (a statement, guess, etc.). **5.** to risk; venture. [ME, from OF, from Ar *az-zahr* the die] — **hazardous**, *adj.*

haze /heɪz/, n. **1.** particles of vapor, dust, etc., near the surface of the earth, causing an appearance of thin mist. **2.** uncertainty or vagueness of the mind, feelings, etc. [orig. obscure] — **hazy**, *adj.*

hazel /'heɪzəl/, n. **1.** (the wood of) a small tree of Europe or America which bears edible nuts. **2.** a light greenish brown color. ◇*adj.* **3.** light greenish brown. [OE *hæs(e)l*]

hazelnut /'heɪzəlnʌt/, n. the nut of the hazel.

Hazlitt /'hæzlət/, n. **William**, 1778–1830, English critic and essayist.

Hazzard /'hæzəd/, n. **Shirley**, born 1931, Australian novelist and short-story writer; author of the novel *The Transit of Venus* (1980).

HB /eɪtʃ 'bi/, *adj.* **1.** (of pencils) hard and black. ◇*n.* **2.** such a pencil.

H-bomb /'eɪtʃ-bɒm/, n. hydrogen bomb.

h. & c., *Abbrev.* hot and cold (water).

HCF /eɪtʃ si 'ef/, n. — **highest common factor**. Also, **h.c.f.** [abbrev.]

hdqrs, *Abbrev.* headquarters.

he /hi/; *weak form* /i/, *pron., poss.* **his**, *obj.* **him**, *pl.* **they**; *n., pl.* **hes**. **1.** the male being in question or last mentioned. **2.** anyone; that person: *He who hesitates is lost.* ◇*n.* **3.** any male person or animal (correlative to *she*). ◇*adj.* **4.** male or masculine, esp. of animals: *a he-goat*. [OE *hē* (gen. *his*, dat *him*, acc. *hine*)]

He, *Chem. Symbol.* helium.

HE, *Abbrev.* **1.** His Eminence. **2.** His Excellency. **3.** (*sometimes l.c.*) high explosive.

head /hɛd/, n. **1.** the upper part of the human body, joined to the trunk by the neck. **2.** the similar part of an animal's body. **3.** the head as the place of thought, memory, understanding, etc.: *to have a head for mathematics*. **4.** the position of leadership; greatest authority. **5.** someone who has authority over others; a leader or chief. **6.** the top, or upper end of anything: *the head of a page*. **7.** the front part of anything; a projecting part: *the head of a procession*. **8.** a person (with reference to the mind, character, etc.): *wise heads*. **9.** a person or animal as one of a number (with pl. **head**): *ten head of cattle; to charge so much a head*. **10.** a measurement to show the difference in height between two people, or the distance between two horses in a race: *taller by a head; to win by a head*. **11.** a climax or crisis; conclusion: *to bring matters to a head*. **12.** a rounded part of a plant, usu. at the top of the stem: *a head of lettuce*. **13.** the part of a cereal plant, as wheat, barley, etc., containing the fruit, grains and/or kernels. **14.** the striking part of a tool, weapon, etc. (opposed to the gripping part), as of a golf club etc. **15.** the fully developed part of an abscess, boil, etc. **16. a.** a projecting point of a coast, esp. when high, e.g. a cape, headland, or promontory. **b.** (*pl.*) the entrance to a natural harbor. **17.** the side of a coin bearing a head or other figure (opposed to *tail*). **18.** the source of a river or stream. **19.** the front part of a ship, etc. **20.** a ship's toilet. **21.** the stretched membrane covering the end of a drum, etc. **22.** the height of the free surface of a liquid above a given level. **23.** *Mach.* a device on turning and boring machines, esp. lathes, holding cutting tools to the work. **24.** the pressure of a confined body of steam, etc., per unit of area. **25.** the height of a column of fluid required for a certain pressure. **26.** the part or parts of a tape-recorder which record, reproduce, or wipe off electromagnetic signals on the tape. **27.** Some special uses are: **come to a head**, to reach a crisis.

go to one's head, **1.** to make one confused or dizzy. **2.** to make one conceited.

head and shoulders (above), by far superior to.

lose one's head, to panic, esp. in an emergency.

make head or tail of, to understand; work out.

off the top of one's head, without preparation; impromptu.

over one's head, **1.** passing over one (unfairly) to a higher authority. **2.** beyond one's understanding.

head   475   **heady**

turn someone's head, to make someone vain. ◇*adj.* **28.** situated at the top or front: *the head division of a parade.* **29.** being in the position of leadership. **30.** coming from in front: *a headwind.* ◇*v.t.* **31.** to go at the head of or in front of; lead; precede: *to head a list.* **32.** to be the head or chief of. **33.** to turn the head or front of in a particular direction: *to head the boat for the shore.* **34.** to provide with a head or heading: *This chapter is headed 'History'.* ◇*v.i.* **35.** to move forwards towards a point; go in a certain direction (oft. fol. by *for*). ◇*v.* **36. head off**, to intercept (something) and force (it) to change course. [OE *hēafod*]

-head[1], a suffix meaning state, condition, character, etc., as in *godhead*, and other words, now mostly archaic or obsolete, many being superseded by forms in **-hood**. [ME *-hede, -hed,* from *hede* rank, condition, character]

-head[2], a suffix indicating a person typified by a particular thing, as *acidhead*.

headache /'hedeɪk/, *n.* **1.** a pain in the head. **2.** *Colloq.* a troublesome or worrying problem.

headcount /'hedkaʊnt/, *n.* a count of the number of people in a group.

headdress /'heddrɛs/, *n.* a covering or decoration for the head.

-headed, a suffix meaning: **1.** having a particular kind of head: *long-headed, wrong-headed.* **2.** having a particular number of heads: *two-headed.*

header /'hedə/, *n.* **1.** a form of reaping machine which cuts off and gathers only the head of the grain. **2.** *Bldg Trades.* a brick laid with its length across the thickness of a wall, so that only the square section shows in the finished wall. **3.** *Colloq.* a dive headfirst, as into water.

headfirst /hed'fɜst/, *adv.* **1.** with the head in front or bent forwards; headlong. **2.** too quickly; rashly; precipitately. Also, **headforemost** /hed'fɔməʊst/.

head-hunting /'hed-hʌntɪŋ/, *n.* **1.** (among certain primitive tribes) the practice of hunting and attacking people to obtain human heads as trophies or for use in religious ceremonies. **2.** *Colloq.* the getting rid of political enemies. —**head-hunter,** *n.*

heading /'hedɪŋ/, *n.* **1.** a title or caption of a page, chapter, etc. **2.** a section of a subject of discourse; a topic. **3.** a horizontal tunnel in the earth, for working a mine, for drainage, etc.; drift.

headlamp /'hedlæmp/, *n.* →**headlight.**

headland /'hedlənd, -lænd/, *n.* a promontory (high piece of land) extending into a sea or lake.

headlight /'hedlaɪt/, *n.* a light equipped with a reflector, on the front of any vehicle.

headline /'hedlaɪn/, *n.* **1.** a display line (usu. in bold print) over an article, etc., as in a newspaper. **2.** (*pl.*) important news: *Drought is in the headlines again.*

headlong /'hedlɒŋ/, *adv.* **1.** headfirst: *to plunge headlong.* **2.** rashly; without thought. **3.** with great speed; precipitately. ◇*adj.* **4.** done or going with the head foremost. **5.** marked by haste; precipitate. **6.** rash; impetuous. [ME *hed* HEAD + *long,* adv. suffix]

headmaster /'hedmɑstə, hɛd'mɑstə/, *n.* the male principal of a school.

headmistress /'hedmɪstrəs, hɛd'mɪstrəs/, *n.* the female principal of a school.

head-on /hed-'ɒn/, *adv.*; /'hed-ɒn/, *adj.*; ◇*adv.* **1.** with the head or front striking or opposed to something: *The cars came to a halt head-on.* ◇*adj.* **2.** of or relating to what has met head-on: *a head-on collision.* **3.** of or relating to a direct confrontation: *a head-on argument.*

headphone /'hedfoʊn/, *n.* (*oft. pl.*) a device consisting of one or two earphones with attachments for holding them over the ears.

headquarters /'hedkwɔtəz, hɛd'kwɔtəz/, *n.pl. or sing.* **1.** any centre from which official orders are sent out: *police headquarters.* **2.** any centre of operations: *(election) campaign headquarters.* **3.** the offices of a military commander; the place from where a commander usu. sends out orders. **4.** a military unit consisting of the commander, his staff, and other assistants. **5.** the building occupied by a headquarters.

headset /'hedsɛt/, *n.* →**headphone.**

headshrinker /'hedʃrɪŋkə/, *n.* **1.** a head-hunter who shrinks and preserves the heads of his victims. **2.** Also, **shrink.** *Colloq.* a psychiatrist.

headsman /'hedzmən/, *n., pl.* **-men.** someone who cuts off the heads of condemned prisoners; public executioner.

headspring /'hedsprɪŋ/, *n.* **1.** the source of a stream. **2.** the source of anything.

headstand /'hedstænd/, *n.* the position of the body in which it is balanced vertically, with the head and hands on the ground.

head start, *n.* an advantage at the start of a race, competition, etc.

headstone /'hedstoʊn/, *n.* a stone set at the head of a grave.

headstream /'hedstrim/, *n.* a stream that forms the source of a river.

headstrong /'hedstrɒŋ/, *adj.* **1.** determined to have one's own way; wilful. **2.** coming from wilfulness: *a headstrong course.*

headwaters /'hedwɔtəz/, *n. pl.* the upper branches of a river.

headway /'hedweɪ/, *n.* **1.** a moving forwards or ahead; advance. **2.** progress in general. **3.** rate of progress.

headwind /'hedwɪnd/, *n.* a wind that blows directly against the course of a ship.

headword /'hedwɜd/, *n.* **1.** a word heading or beginning a chapter, paragraph, etc. **2.** a word or expression beginning an entry in a dictionary, etc., which the rest of the entry explains and describes.

heady /'hedi/, *adj.*, **-ier, -iest. 1.** thoughtlessly hasty. **2.** exciting; intoxicating.

heal /hil/, *v.t.* **1.** to make whole or sound; restore to health. **2.** to make better anything evil or upsetting; amend: *to heal a quarrel*. **3.** to make clean; cleanse; purify. ◇*v.i.* **4.** to bring about a cure. **5.** to become whole or sound; get well (oft. fol. by *up* or *over*): *The wound is healing nicely*. [OE *hǣlan*, from *hāl* hale, WHOLE] **–healer,** *n.* **–healing,** *n., adj.*

health /helθ/, *n.* **1.** freedom from disease or sickness. **2.** a general state of well-being of the body, mind, society, etc. **3.** a polite wish for a person's health, happiness, etc., esp. as a toast. [OE *hǣlth*, from *hāl* hale, whole]

health food, *n.* food that is noted for its health-giving properties or freedom from additives.

health inspector, *n.* an officer appointed to look over working and living conditions, buildings, etc., in an area, to make sure that they are in keeping with health regulations.

healthy /'helθi/, *adj.,* **-thier, -thiest. 1.** having health: *a healthy body; a healthy mind*. **2.** relating to health: *a healthy appearance*. **3.** leading to health; healthful: *healthy games*.

heap /hip/, *n.* **1.** a group of things, lying one on another; pile: *a heap of stones*. **2.** *Colloq.* a great quantity or number; multitude: *He has made a heap of money*. **3.** *Colloq.* something very old and broken down, esp. a motor car. ◇*v.t.* **4.** to gather, put, or cast in a heap; pile (oft. fol. by *up, on, together,* etc.). **5.** to collect; accumulate; amass (oft. fol. by *up*): *to heap up riches*. **6.** to give in great quantity: *to heap blessings upon someone*. **7.** to load or supply abundantly with something: *to heap a person with favors*. ◇*v.i.* **8.** to form into a heap: *Sand heaped up round the pole*. [OE *hēap* heap, multitude, troop]

hear /hɪə/, *v.,* **heard** /hɜd/, **hearing.** ◇*v.t.* **1.** to perceive by the ear. **2.** to listen to: *to refuse to hear a person*. **3.** to learn by the ear or by being told; be informed of: *to hear news*. **4.** to be among the audience at or of: *to hear an opera*. **5.** (of a king, teacher, judge, etc.) to listen to formally or officially. **6.** to listen to favorably. ◇*v.i.* **7.** to have perception of sound by the ear; have the sense of hearing. **8.** to listen or take notice (in command, 'hear! hear!', used to show approval of a speaker's words). **9.** to receive information by the ear, by letter, etc.: *to hear from a friend*. **10.** to listen with favor or agreement: *He would not hear of it*. ◇ *v.* **11. hear things,** to imagine noises; hallucinate. **12. hear out,** to listen to (someone or something) until the end. [OE *hēran*]

Heard and McDonald Islands /hɜd ən mək'dɒnəld/, *n.pl.* an Australian Antarctic territory in the Southern Ocean, about 4023 km south-west of Fremantle.

hearing /'hɪərɪŋ/, *n.* **1.** the sense or faculty by which sound is perceived. **2.** the act of perceiving sound. **3.** an opportunity to be heard: *to grant a hearing*. **4.** *Law.* the presentation of a matter before a court of law. **5.** earshot: *out of hearing*.

hearing aid, *n.* a small amplifier, worn behind the ear, to improve one's hearing.

hearken /'hakən/, *v.t., v.i. Archaic.* to listen or attend (to). Also, **harken.** [OE *he(o)rcnian*; akin to HARK]

hearsay /'hɪəseɪ/, *n.* gossip; rumor.

hearse /hɜs/, *n.* a special car for carrying a dead person to the place of burial. [ME, from OF: harrow, frame]

heart /hat/, *n.* **1.** the hollow muscular organ which, by rhythmic contraction and dilation, keeps the blood in circulation throughout the body. **2.** this organ considered as the centre of life, vital powers, thought, emotion, etc.: *to die of a broken heart*. **3.** emotions and affections (oft. opposed to the *head*): *to win someone's heart*. **4.** feeling; sensibility; capacity for sympathy: *to have no heart*. **5.** spirit; courage; enthusiasm: *to take heart*. **6.** the innermost or middle part of anything: *the heart of a lettuce*. **7.** the most important part; core: *the very heart of the matter*. **8.** the breast; bosom: *to clasp a person to one's heart*. **9.** a person, esp. in expressions of praise or affection: *dear heart*. **10.** a figure thought to look like a heart, with rounded sides meeting in a point at the bottom and curving inwards to a cusp at the top (♥). **11.** *Cards.* **a.** a card marked with heart-shaped figures in red. **b.** (*pl.*) the suit of such cards. **12.** (of land, crops) good condition. ◇**13.** Some special uses are:

after one's own heart, appealing to one's taste or affection.

at heart, in one's thoughts: *At heart she thought he was a bore*.

be all heart, (*usu. ironic*) to be full of consideration and kindness.

break the heart of, to crush with sorrow or disappointment.

by heart, from memory.

close to one's heart, deeply affecting one's interests and affections.

cry one's heart out, to cry bitterly or violently.

eat one's heart out, to grieve, brood or fret, esp. with envy.

from (the bottom of) one's heart, sincerely.

have a change of heart, to go back on a decision or opinion.

have a heart, to be reasonable; show mercy.

have at heart, to be very interested in: *He has your best interest at heart*.

have one's heart in one's mouth, to be very frightened.

heart and soul, completely; wholly: *He loves her heart and soul*.

heart of hearts, the depth of one's feelings: *He knew in his heart of hearts that he was wrong*.

lose one's heart, to fall in love.

not to have the heart, to be too kind or sensitive of another's feelings (to do or say something): *She didn't have the heart to tell him to leave*.

set one's heart at rest, to stop one worrying; ease one's anxieties.

take heart, to find new courage or strength.

take to heart, 1. to think seriously about. **2.** to be deeply affected by; grieve over.

to one's heart's content, as much as one wishes.

wear one's heart upon one's sleeve, to show openly one's feelings, intentions, etc.

heart 477 **heave**

with all one's heart, with all willingness; heartily. [OE *heorte*]

heartache /'hateɪk/, n. sorrow; mental anguish.

heart attack, n. **1.** a sudden stopping of the blood supply to the heart muscles; myocardial infarction. **2.** →**coronary thrombosis**.

heartbeat /'hatbit/, n. a pulsation of the heart, including one complete systole and diastole.

heartbreak /'hatbreɪk/, n. crushing sorrow or grief. —**heartbreaking**, adj.

heartbroken /'hatbroʊkən/, adj. crushed with sorrow or grief.

heartburn /'hatbən/, n. a burning sensation in the abdomen or chest.

hearten /'hatn/, v.t. to give courage to; cheer.

heartfelt /'hatfɛlt/, adj. deeply or sincerely felt; earnest: *heartfelt joy; heartfelt words*.

hearth /haθ/, n. **1.** that part of the floor of a room on which the fire is made or above which is a stove, fireplace, furnace, etc. **2.** the fireside; home. **3.** *Metall.* the lower part of a blast furnace, etc., in which the molten metal collects and from which it is tapped out. [OE *he(o)rth*]

hearthstone /'haθstoʊn/, n. **1.** the stone forming a hearth. **2.** the fireside; home.

heartless /'hatləs/, adj. unfeeling; cruel: *heartless words*.

heart-rending /'hat-rɛndɪŋ/, adj. causing sharp mental pain.

heartstrings /'hatstrɪŋz/, n.pl. the deepest feelings; strongest affections: *to pull at one's heartstrings*.

heart-throb /'hat-θrɒb/, n. someone to whom one is very attracted, sexually or romantically.

heart-to-heart /'hat-tə-hat/, adj.; / hat-tə-'hat/, n. ◇adj. **1.** frank; sincere. ◇n. **2.** a frank and sincere conversation, usu. between two people.

heart transplant, n. an operation in which the heart of one person is transplanted into the body of another.

heart-warming /'hat-wɔmɪŋ/, adj. emotionally moving in a way which brings out a pleased and approving response.

hearty /'hati/, adj., -tier, -tiest, n., pl. -ties. ◇adj. **1.** warm-hearted; affectionate; cordial; friendly: *a hearty welcome*. **2.** heartfelt; genuine; sincere: *hearty approval*. **3.** enthusiastic; vigorous: *a hearty laugh*. **4.** physically vigorous; strong and well: *hale and hearty*. **5.** large or satisfying: *a hearty meal*. **6.** enjoying or needing abundant food: *a hearty appetite*. **7.** (of soil) fertile. ◇n. **8.** *Colloq.* a brave or good fellow. **9.** a sailor. —**heartily**, adv. —**heartiness**, n.

heat /hit/, n. **1.** the quality or condition of being hot; hot temperature: *Feel the heat of the bath water before you get in*. **2.** a sensation of hotness or warmth; heated bodily condition. **3.** *Phys.* a form of energy which raises the temperature of the body to which it is added. It is equal to the total kinetic energy of the motion of the atoms or molecules in the body. **4.** *Phys.* the amount of heat (def. 3) given out or absorbed per unit amount of substance in a process such as combustion, freezing, vaporisation, etc.: *the latent heat of vaporisation*. **5.** hot season or weather: *summer heat*. **6.** warmth or intensity of feeling: *the heat of an argument*. **7.** the height of intensity of any action: *the heat of the moment*. **8.** *Colloq.* pressure of police, prison, etc.: *Lie low while the heat's on*. **9.** a single course in or division of a race, etc. **10.** *Zool.* **a.** sexual excitement in animals, esp. females. **b.** the period or duration of such excitement. **11. on heat**, (of female animals) in a state of sexual excitement occurring at oestrus. **12. put the heat on**, *Colloq.* to put pressure on. ◇v.t., v.i. **13.** to make or become hot or warm. **14.** to excite or become excited in mind or feeling. [OE *hǣtu*]

heat capacity, n. the amount of heat (in joules) needed to raise the temperature of a substance one kelvin; thermal capacity.

heat content, n. *Phys.* →**enthalpy**.

heated /'hitəd/, adj. **1.** warmed; having the temperature raised. **2.** angry; inflamed; vehement.

heater /'hitə/, n. an apparatus for heating, as a furnace or stove.

heath /hiθ/, n. **1.** an area of open, uncultivated land covered by low, usu. small-leaved, shrubs. **2.** any of various low evergreen shrubs common on wasteland, as the common heather of England and Scotland with small pinkish purple flowers. **3.** any of certain Australian plants looking like heaths. [OE *hǣth*]

Heath /hiθ/, n. **Sir Edward (Richard George)**, born 1916, British politician, leader of the Conservative Party 1965–75; prime minister 1970–74.

heathen /'hiðən/, n., pl. -thens, -then, adj. ◇n. **1.** an unconverted individual of a people which does not recognise the God of the Bible; one who is neither Christian, Jewish, nor Muslim; pagan. **2.** an irreligious person. ◇adj. **3.** pagan; relating to the heathen. **4.** irreligious or unenlightened. [OE *hǣthen*; commonly explained as meaning orig. heath-dweller]

heather /'hɛðə/, n. any of various heaths, esp. **Scotch heather**. See **heath** (def. 2). [b. HEATH and obs. *hadder* heather (orig. uncert.)] —**heathery**, adj.

heat sink, n. anything designed to conduct heat away and allow its harmless dissipation, as a metal plate attached to a transistor which is producing heat, the special layers in the skin of supersonic aircraft, etc.

heatwave /'hitweɪv/, n. **1.** an air mass of high temperature, covering a wide area and moving fairly slowly. **2.** a prolonged period of very hot weather.

heave /hiv/, v., **heaved** or (*Chiefly Naut.*) **hove**, **heaving**, n. ◇v.t. **1.** to raise or lift with effort or force; hoist. **2.** to lift and throw, often with effort or force: *to heave an anchor over-*

heave board. **3.** *Naut.* to haul, draw, or pull with a rope. **4.** *Colloq.* to throw: *Heave it over here, will you?* **5.** to utter slowly and with effort: *to heave a sigh.* **6.** to cause to rise or swell. **7.** *Geol.* to cause a horizontal displacement in (a stratum, vein, etc.). See **heave** (def. 18). ◇*v.i.* **8.** (of the sea, one's chest, etc.) to rise and fall. **9.** to breathe with effort; pant. **10.** to vomit; retch. **11.** to rise as if thrust up, as a hill; swell or bulge. **12.** *Naut.* to haul or pull, as at a rope. ◇*v.* **13. heave in sight,** to rise into view from below the horizon, as a ship. **14. heave to,** *Naut.* to stop: *We hove to in the next bay.* ◇*interj.* **15. heave ho!,** (an exclamation used when heaving the anchor up, etc.) ◇*n.* **16.** the act of heaving. **17.** (of the sea) the force of the swell. **18.** *Geol.* **a.** a horizontal part of the displacement from a fault. **b.** a displacement of the floor of a mine. [OE *hebban*]

heave-ho /ˈhiv-hou, hiv-ˈhou/, *n.* dismissal, esp. from a job.

heaven /ˈhevən/, *n.* **1.** the place where God and the angels live; place or state of existence of the blessed after earthly life. **2.** (*cap.*, *oft. pl.*) the celestial powers; God. **3.** a euphemistic term for God in various emphatic expressions: *for heaven's sake.* **4.** (*chiefly pl.*) sky; firmament. **5. a.** a place or state of supreme bliss: *a heaven on earth.* **b.** *Colloq.* something very pleasing: *This drink is just heaven.* **6. heavens!,** (an exclamation to express surprise.) **7. move heaven and earth,** to do all that is possible. **8.** See **seventh heaven.** [OE *hefen, heofon*]

heavenly /ˈhevənli/, *adj.* **1.** blissful; beautiful: *a heavenly spot.* **2.** of or in the sky or space: *the heavenly bodies.* **3.** of, belonging to, or coming from the heaven of God, the angels, etc: *heavenly judgment.* **4.** divine; celestial: *heavenly peace.*

heavily /ˈhevəli/, *adv.* **1.** with great weight or burden: *a heavily loaded cart.* **2.** in an oppressive manner: *Cares weigh heavily upon him.* **3.** severely; intensely: *to suffer heavily.* **4.** to a large amount; densely; thickly: *heavily wooded.* **5.** with effort; laboriously; sluggishly: *He walked heavily across the room.* —**heaviness**, *n.*

heavy /ˈhevi/, *adj.*, **-ier, -iest,** *n.*, *pl.* **-vies,** *v.*, **-vied, -vying,** *adv.* ◇*adj.* **1.** of great weight; hard to lift or carry: *a heavy load.* **2.** of great amount, force, intensity, etc.: *a heavy vote.* **3.** bearing hard upon; harsh; oppressive: *heavy taxes.* **4.** having much weight in proportion to bulk; being of high specific gravity: *a heavy metal.* **5.** broad, thick, or coarse; not delicate: *heavy lines.* **6.** more than the usual weight: *a heavy cargo.* **7.** concerned with the manufacture of heavy goods: *heavy industry.* **8.** *Mil.* **a.** heavily armed or equipped. **b.** of the larger sizes: *heavy weapons.* **9.** serious; grave: *a heavy offence.* **10.** hard to deal with; trying; difficult: *a heavy task.* **11.** being such in an unusual degree: *a heavy smoker.* **12.** weighted or laden: *air heavy with moisture.* **13.** depressed with trouble or sorrow; showing sorrow: *a heavy heart.* **14.** overcast or cloudy: *heavy sky.* **15.** clumsy; slow in movement or action: *heavy hand; a heavy walk.* **16.** without interest; ponderous; dull: *a heavy style.* **17.** loud and deep: *a heavy sound.* **18.** dense in substance; insufficiently raised or leavened: *heavy bread.* **19.** not easily digested: *heavy food.* **20.** (of music, literature, etc.) intellectual or deep. **21.** important; serious: *a heavy emotion.* **22.** pregnant: *heavy with child.* **23.** *Theat.* serious; sober; sombre: *a heavy part.* **24.** *Colloq.* using force or pressure; coercive; threatening: *The cops were really heavy.* **25.** *Chem.* referring to an isotope of greater atomic weight: *heavy hydrogen.* ◇*n.* **26.** *Colloq.* someone important in any particular area: *The heavies were all up on the stage.* **27.** *Colloq.* a detective. ◇*v.t.* **28.** to put pressure on; confront. ◇*adv.* **29.** heavily. [OE *hefig,* from *hefe weight*] —**heaviness,** *n.*

heavy-duty /ˈhevi-djuti/, *adj.* **1.** strong; sturdy; durable. **2.** having a high import or export tax rate.

heavy-handed /ˈhevi-hændəd/, *adj.* **1.** oppressive; harsh. **2.** clumsy. **3.** using more than necessary of a certain ingredient, etc.

heavy-hearted /ˈhevi-hatəd/, *adj.* sorrowful; melancholy; dejected.

heavy-laden /ˈhevi-leɪdn/, *adj.* **1.** loaded with a heavy burden. **2.** very weary or troubled.

heavyweight /ˈheviweɪt/, *n.* **1.** someone of more than average weight. **2.** a boxer in the heaviest group; amateur fighter of over 81 kg in weight. **3.** *Colloq.* a person of considerable power, influence, or forcefulness in any field: *She's a literary heavyweight.*

Hebraic /həˈbreɪk, hi-/, *adj.* Hebrew. [LL, from Gk]

Hebrew /ˈhibru/, *n.* **1.** a member of that branch of the Semitic race descended from the line of Abraham; Israelite; Jew. ◇*adj.* **2.** of or relating to the Hebrews or their language. [ME, from L, from Gk, from Aram, from Heb: one from beyond]

Hebrides /ˈhɛbrədiz/, *n.pl.* a group of islands off the western coast of and belonging to Scotland; divided into the **Outer Hebrides** (Lewis, Harris, etc.) and **Inner Hebrides** (Skye, Mull, etc.). Pop. 31 766 (1981); about 7511 km². Also, **Western Islands.** —**Hebridean,** *adj.*

Hecate /ˈhɛkəti/, *n. Gk Myth.* a goddess of the underworld. Also, **Hekate.** [L from Gk]

heck /hɛk/, *n., interj.* (euphemism for 'hell'): *What the heck; Get the heck out of here.*

heckle /ˈhɛkəl/, *v.t.,* **-led, -ling.** to torment or harass (esp. a public speaker) with questions and gibes; badger. [ME *hechele*] —**heckler,** *n.*

hectare /ˈhɛktɛə/, *n.* a surface measure, the common unit of land measure in the metric system, equal to 100 ares, or 10 000 square metres (approx. 2.47 acres). *Symbol:* ha [F. See HECTO-, ARE²]

hectic /ˈhɛktɪk/, *adj.* **1.** marked by great excitement, passion, activity, confusion, haste: *a hectic meeting; a hectic day.* **2.** relating to feverish symptoms, as flushing, hot skin, etc. [LL, from Gk: habitual, hectic]

hecto- /'hɛktə-/, a prefix indicating 10² of a given unit, as in *hectogram*. Also, *before vowels*, **hect-**. Symbol: h [F, from Gk *hekatón* hundred]

hector /'hɛktə/, n. **1.** a blustering, domineering fellow; swashbuckler; bully. **2.** (*cap*.) *Gk Myth*. the eldest son of Priam; a prominent warrior in the Trojan wars, killed by Achilles. ◇*v.t., v.i.* **3.** to treat or act with insolence and bullying.

Hecuba /'hɛkjubə/, n. *Gk Legend*. the wife of Priam, mother of Hector, Paris, Cassandra and Helenus; she was later turned into a fiery-eyed dog.

he'd /hid/, short form of **1.** he had. **2.** he would.

hedge /hɛdʒ/, n., v., **hedged, hedging**. ◇*n*. **1.** a row of bushes or small trees planted close together, esp. when forming a fence or boundary. **2.** any barrier or boundary: *a hedge against misfortune*. **3.** an investment, money policy, etc., designed to offset losses caused by inflation, etc. ◇*v.t.* **4.** to enclose with or separate by a hedge (oft. fol. by *in, off, about*, etc.): *to hedge off a garden*. **5.** to surround so as to prevent escape or free movement; hem in; obstruct (oft. fol. by *in, about*): *to be hedged by difficulties*; *hedged in by enemies*. **6.** to protect (a bet, etc.) by taking some offsetting risk. ◇*v.i.* **7.** to avoid taking an open or decisive course; be evasive: *Stop hedging and say what you will do*. [OE]

hedgehog /'hɛdʒhɒg/, n. a spiny, nocturnal, insect-eating mammal of Europe, Africa and Asia.

hedgerow /'hɛdʒrou/, n. a row of bushes or trees forming a hedge.

hedonism /'hidənɪzəm, 'hɛ-/, n. **1.** the teaching that pleasure or happiness is the highest good. **2.** devotion to pleasure. —**hedonist**, n., adj. —**hedonistic**, adj.

-hedron, a combining form indicating geometrical solid figures having a certain number of faces, as in *polyhedron*. [Gk]

heed /hid/, v.t., v.i. **1.** to give attention (to); (have) regard; notice. ◇*n*. **2.** careful attention; notice; observation (usu. with *give* or *take*). [OE *hēdan*]

heedless /'hidləs/, adj. careless; thoughtless.

heehaw /'hihɔ/, n. **1.** the braying sound made by a donkey. **2.** rude laughter. ◇*v.i.* **3.** to bray. [imitative]

heel¹ /hil/, n. **1.** (in humans) the back part of the foot, below and behind the ankle. **2.** a corresponding part in animals. **3.** the part of a stocking, shoe, etc., covering the heel. **4.** the back part of the sole of a shoe. **5.** the part of the palm of a hand or glove nearest the wrist. **6.** something like the human heel in position, shape, etc.: *a heel of bread*. **7.** the last part of anything: *the heel of a session*. **8.** *Bot*. the older basal part of a shoot removed from a plant which usu. produces roots easily when planted. **9.** *Colloq*. a contemptible person; cad. ◇**10.** Some special uses are: **cool/kick one's heels**, *Colloq*. to be kept waiting, esp. deliberately. **dig one's heels in**, to be obstinate, stubborn like a mule. **down at heel**, **1.** having the shoe heels worn down. **2.** shabby or uncared for in appearance. **3.** reduced to poverty. **kick up one's heels**, to enjoy oneself. **on the heels of**, closely following. **show a clean pair of heels**, to run away from and escape. **take to one's heels**, to run off or away. **to heel**, **1.** (of a dog) following someone with the nose close to their left heel. **2.** under control. ◇*v.t.* **11.** to put heels on (shoes). **12.** to kick or move with the heel. **13.** to follow at the heels of. ◇*v.i.* **14.** to follow at one's heels. [OE *hēl(a)*, apparently from *hōh* HOCK¹]

heel² /hil/, v.i. **1.** (of a ship, etc.) to lean to one side; cant; tilt. ◇*v.t.* **2.** to cause to lean or cant. ◇*n*. **3.** a heeling movement; cant. [OE *h(i)eldan* bend, incline]

heeler /'hilə/, n. **1.** *Colloq*. a dog which follows at one's heels. **2.** (of a cattle or sheep dog) one which rounds up stock by following and nipping their heels.

heft /hɛft/, v.t. **1.** to try the weight of by lifting. **2.** to heave or lift. ◇*n*. **3.** *Archaic*. weight; heaviness. [from HEAVE]

hefty /'hɛfti/, adj., **-tier, -tiest**. *Colloq*. **1.** heavy; weighty. **2.** big and strong; powerful; muscular.

Hegel /'heɪgəl/, n. Georg Wilhelm Friedrich /geɪ,ɔg ,vɪlhɛlm 'fridrɪx/, 1770–1831, German idealist philosopher. —**Hegelian**, adj. —**Hegelianism**, n.

Hegelian dialectic /həˌgeɪliən daɪə'lɛktɪk/, n. a pattern or mechanism of development by inner conflict, the scheme of which is *thesis*, *antithesis* and *synthesis* (i.e., an original tendency, its opposing tendency, and their unification in a new movement). [named after GWF HEGEL]

hegemony /'hɛgəməni, 'hɛdʒ-, hə'gɛməni/, n., pl. **-nies**. **1.** the leadership or dominance of one state over others. **2.** leadership; predominance. [Gk] —**hegemonic**, adj.

Hegira /'hɛdʒərə/, n. **1.** the flight of Mohammed from persecutions in Mecca to his successes in Medina. (The date of Mohammed's flight, AD 622, is the starting point in the Muslim calender). **2.** the Muslim era itself. Also, **Hejira**. [ML, from Ar *hijra* departure, migration]

Heidelberg /'haɪdlbɜg/, n. **1.** a city in West Germany in northern Baden-Württemberg; university, founded 1385. Pop. 136 227 (1987 est.). **2.** a city in Vic and suburb of Melbourne; site location of the 1956 Olympic Village. Pop. 61 917 (1986).

Heidelberg man, n. the primitive human, *Homo erectus*, as reconstructed from the Heidelberg jaw found in 1907 near Heidelberg, West Germany.

heifer /'hɛfə/, n. a cow that has not produced a calf and is under three years of age. [OE]

height /haɪt/, *n.* **1.** the distance from bottom to top: *The height of the tree is 20 metres.* **2.** extent upwards; altitude; stature; distance upwards; elevation: *height above sea level.* **3.** a high place or level; hill or mountain. **4.** the highest part; top; apex. **5.** the highest or central point; utmost degree: *the height of the season.* [OE. See HIGH, -TH[1]]

heighten /ˈhaɪtn/, *v.t.* **1.** to make higher. **2.** to make more intense: *to heighten the effect of a play by dramatic lighting.* ◇*v.i.* **3.** to become higher. **4.** to increase; augment.

heinous /ˈheɪnəs, ˈhiː-/, *adj.* hateful; odious; gravely reprehensible: *a heinous offence.* [ME, from OF: hatred; of Gmc orig.]

Heinze /ˈhaɪnz/, *n.* **Sir Bernard Thomas**, 1894–1982, Australian musician, conductor and teacher.

heir /ɛə/, *n.* **1.** *Law.* someone who inherits the property or title of a dead person. **2.** someone to whom something falls or is due: *the heir to the throne.* **3.** a person, society, etc., considered as continuing a tradition, policy, or the like established earlier. [ME, from OF, from L]

heir apparent, *n.*, *pl.* **heirs apparent**. an heir whose right cannot be lost as long as he survives the ancestor.

heiress /ˈɛərɛs, -əs/, *n.* **1.** a female heir. **2.** a woman inheriting or expected to inherit great wealth.

heirloom /ˈɛəluːm/, *n.* **1.** any family possession handed down from generation to generation. **2.** *Law.* (formerly) a personal chattel (def.1) that descends to the heir according to the terms of a will. [HEIR + LOOM[1], orig. tool or implement]

heir presumptive /prəˈzʌmptɪv/, *n.* an heir whose expectation may be defeated by the birth of a nearer heir.

heist /haɪst/, *v.t.* **1.** to rob; steal. ◇*n.* **2.** a robbery; burglary. Also, **hoist**.

hekto-, a variant of **hecto-**.

held /hɛld/, *v.* past tense and past participle of **hold**.

Hele /ˈhiːl/, *n.* **Sir Ivor Henry Thomas**, born 1912, Australian oil painter and draughtsman; official war artist World War II; winner of the Archibald Prize 1951, 1953, 1954, 1955, 1957.

Helen /ˈhɛlən/, *n.* *Gk Legend.* the beautiful daughter of Zeus and Leda, and the wife of Menelaus of Sparta. Her abduction by Paris caused the Trojan war.

heli-, a variant of **helio-**, before vowels, as in *helianthus.*

heliacal /həˈlaɪəkəl/, *adj.* relating to or occurring near the sun, as of the risings and settings of stars. Also, **heliac** /ˈhiːliæk/. [Gk: of the sun]

helical /ˈhɛlɪkəl/, *adj.* relating to or having the form of a helix.

helicoid /ˈhɛlɪkɔɪd/, *adj.* coiled or curving like a helix; spiral. [Gk: of spiral form] — **helicoidal**, *adj.*

helicopter /ˈhɛlɪkɒptə, ˈhɛlə-/, *n.* a wingless aircraft kept in the air by a large horizontal propeller turning on a vertical axis. [F. See HELIX + Gk *pterón* wing]

helio-, a word part meaning 'sun', as in *heliograph.* Also, **heli-**. [Gk, combining form of *hēlios*]

heliograph /ˈhiːliəgræf, -graf/, *n.* **1.** a device for signalling by means of a movable mirror which flashes beams of light to a distant point. **2.** an apparatus for photographing the sun. ◇*v.t., v.i.* **3.** to communicate by heliograph. — **heliographer**, *n.* — **heliographic**, *adj.* — **heliography**, *n.*

Helios /ˈhiːliɒs/, *n.* *Gk Myth.* the sun-god, represented as driving a chariot across the sky. [Gk: the sun, the sun-god]

heliotrope /ˈhiːliətroʊp, ˈhiːliə-, ˈhɛljə-, ˈhɪljə-/, *n.* **1.** *Bot.* any plant that turns towards the sun. **2.** a European garden plant with small, fragrant purple flowers. [F, from L, from Gk: sundial, plant which turns its leaves to the sun]

heliotropic /hiːliəˈtrɒpɪk/, *adj.* growing towards the light. — **heliotropism**, *n.*

helipad /ˈhɛlɪpæd/, *n.* a touching-down place for helicopters.

heliport /ˈhɛlɪpɔːt/, *n.* a landing place for helicopters, often the roof of a building, with facilities for passenger handling.

helium /ˈhiːliəm/, *n.* an inert gaseous element present in the sun's atmosphere, in certain radioactive minerals (as pitchblende), etc. *Symbol*: He; *at. no.*: 2; *at. wt*: 4.0026. [Gk *hēlios* sun]

helix /ˈhiːlɪks, ˈhɛl-/, *n.*, *pl.* **helices** /ˈhɛləsiːz, ˈhiːl-/, **helixes**. **1.** a spiral. **2.** *Geom.* a curve assumed by a straight line drawn on a plane when that plane is wrapped round a cylindrical surface of any kind, esp. a right circular cylinder, as the curve of a screw thread. **3.** *Anat.* a curved fold forming most of the rim of the external ear. [L, from Gk: anything of spiral shape]

hell /hɛl/, *n.* **1.** a place or state of punishment of the wicked after death; place of evil and condemned spirits. **2.** any place or state of torment or misery: *a hell on earth.* **3.** the powers of evil. **4.** anything that causes torment; any severe or frightful experience, mental or physical. **5.** the place of the dead; Hades. ◇**6.** Some special uses are:

for the hell of it, for no particular reason; for its own sake.
hell for leather, at top speed; recklessly fast.
hell of a, **1.** extremely difficult or unpleasant. **2.** notable; remarkable. Also, **helluva**.
hell's bells, (a mild curse).
hell's teeth, (an exclamation of great surprise, anger, etc.)
hell to pay, serious consequences.
like hell, **1.** very much (used as general intensive). **2.** not at all; definitely not.
merry hell, **1.** chaos; turmoil; pandemonium. **2.** a severe reaction; severe pain.
raise hell, to cause very great trouble.
◇*interj.* **7.** (an exclamation of annoyance, disgust, etc.). [OE *hel(l)*]

he'll /hɪl/, a short form of **1.** he will. **2.** he shall.

Hellas /'hɛlæs/, n. ancient and modern Greek name of **Greece**.

hell-bent /hɛl'bɛnt/, adj. stubbornly or recklessly determined.

hellcat /'hɛlkæt/, n. **1.** an evil-tempered, unmanageable woman. **2.** a hag or witch.

Hellene /'hɛlin/, n. a Greek. [Gk]

Hellenic /hɛ'lɛnɪk, hə-, 'hɛlənɪk/, adj. **1.** relating to the modern Greeks. **2.** relating to the ancient Greeks, or their language, culture, etc., before the time of Alexander the Great (contrasted with *Hellenistic*).

Hellenistic /hɛlə'nɪstɪk/, adj. **1.** like or following Greek usage. **2.** relating to the Greeks or their language, culture, etc., after the time of Alexander the Great when Greek characteristics were changed by foreign elements.

Hellespont /'hɛləspɒnt/, n. the ancient name of the **Dardanelles**. [Gk]

hellfire /hɛl'faɪə, 'hɛlfaɪə/, n. (punishment in) the fire of hell.

hellhole /'hɛlhoʊl/, n. *Colloq.* a highly unpleasant place.

hellhound /'hɛlhaʊnd/, n. **1.** a devil; demon; fiend. **2.** a very evil man. [OE *hellehund* hell's hound]

Hellman /'hɛlmən/, n. **Lillian**, 1905–84, US playwright and civil rights activist.

hello /hʌ'loʊ, hə-/, interj., n., pl. **-los**, v., **-loed**, **-loing**. ◇*interj.* **1.** (an exclamation to attract attention, answer a telephone, or express greeting.) **2.** (an exclamation of surprise, etc.) ◇*n.* **3.** the call 'hello'. ◇*v.i.* **4.** to call 'hello'. Also, **hallo**, **hullo**. [var. of HALLO]

hell's angel, n. (orig.) a member of a group of lawless, usu. leather-jacketed, motor-cyclists known for their disturbance of civil order in the US, esp. California, later applied to similar people elsewhere.

helm /hɛlm/, n. **1.** a tiller or wheel by which the rudder of a ship is controlled. **2.** an entire steering apparatus. **3.** a moving of the helm: *Give her full helm.* **4.** a place or post of control: *the helm of affairs.* [OE *helma*]

helmet /'hɛlmət/, n. **1.** a defensive covering for the head **a.** worn for protection by construction workers, firefighters, divers, etc. **b.** made of wire mesh to protect the heads and faces of fencers, etc. **2.** anything looking like a helmet in form or position. [ME, from OF: from Gmc]

helminth /'hɛlmɪnθ/, n. a worm, esp. a parasitic worm. [Gk *hélmins*]

helminthic /hɛl'mɪnθɪk/, adj. **1.** relating to worms. **2.** used to get rid of intestinal worms. Also, **helminthous**.

helmsman /'hɛlmzmən/, n., pl. **-men**. a man at the helm who steers a ship.

helot /'hɛlət/, n. a slave; serf; bondman. [name of the serfs in Sparta, ancient city in S Greece, who were owned by the state and under allotment to landowners] —**helotry**, n.

help /hɛlp/, v., **helped** or (*old form*) **holp**; **helped** or (*old form*) **holpen**; **helping**; n., *interj.* ◇*v.t.* **1.** to do something with (a person) so that it is done more easily; aid; assist: *to help a man in his work.* **2.** to give strength or means to; contribute aid; assist in doing: *medicines that help digestion.* **3.** to relieve (someone) in need, sickness, pain, or distress. **4.** to avoid; refrain from (with *can* or *cannot*): *He can't help doing it.* **5.** to be of use; remedy: *Nothing will help the position now.* **6.** to contribute an improvement to: *The use of a little make-up would help her appearance.* **7.** to serve food to at table (fol. by *to*): *help her to salad.* ◇*v.i.* **8.** to give aid; be of service or advantage: *Every little helps.* ◇*v.* **9. help oneself (to)**, to take at will. **10. help out**, to come to one's aid in or as in a crisis or difficulty. ◇*n.* **11.** the act of helping; aid or assistance; relief or succor. **12.** someone or something that helps. **13.** a domestic servant or farm laborer. **14.** a means of remedying, stopping, or preventing: *The thing is done, and there is no help for it now.* ◇*interj.* **15.** (a call for assistance.) **16. so help me**, (an exclamation giving a pledge of the speaker's truthfulness). [OE *helpan*] —**helper**, n. —**helpful**, adj.

helping /'hɛlpɪŋ/, n. **1.** the act of someone or something that helps. **2.** a serving of food; portion. ◇*adj.* **3.** giving assistance, support, etc.: *a helping hand.*

helpless /'hɛlpləs/, adj. **1.** unable to look after oneself; weak or dependent: *a helpless invalid.* **2.** without help, aid, or succor: *helpless victims of the earthquake.* **3.** incapable; inefficient; shiftless.

Helpmann /'hɛlpmən/, n. **Sir Robert Murray**, 1909–86, Australian dancer, choreographer, actor and director; co-artistic director of the Australian Ballet 1965–74, and sole artistic director 1975–76.

helpmate /'hɛlpmeɪt/, n. **1.** a companion and helper. **2.** a wife or husband.

helpmeet /'hɛlpmit/, n. *Archaic.* helpmate.

Helsinki /hɛl'sɪŋki/, n. a seaport in and the capital of Finland, on the southern coast. Pop. 487 749 (1987 est.). Swedish, **Helsingfors**.

Helsinki Agreement, n. an agreement on human rights between eastern and western European nations, signed at Helsinki in 1975.

helter-skelter /hɛltə-'skɛltə/, adv. in headlong, disorderly haste: *to run helter-skelter.* [imitative]

Helvetian /hɛl'viʃən/, adj. Swiss. [L]

hem[1] /hɛm/, v., **hemmed**, **hemming**, n. ◇*v.t.* **1.** to enclose or confine (fol. by *in*, *round*, or *about*): *hemmed in by enemies.* **2.** to fold back and sew down the edge of (cloth, a garment, etc.). ◇*n.* **3.** a border made by folding back the edge of cloth and sewing it down. [OE *hem*]

hem[2] /hɛm/, interj., v., **hemmed**, **hemming**. ◇*interj.* **1.** (an utterance sounding like a slight clearing of the throat, used to attract attention, express doubt, etc.). ◇*v.i.* **2.** to utter the sound 'hem'. ◇*v.* **3. hem and haw**, to avoid giving a direct answer. [imitative]

hem-, *Chiefly US.* variant of **haem-**.

he-man /'hi:mæn/, *n. Colloq.* a tough or very masculine man.

hemi-, a prefix meaning 'half', as in *hemisphere.* See **semi-**. [Gk]

hemicycle /'hɛmɪsaɪkl/, *n.* **1.** a semicircle. **2.** a semicircular structure. [F, from L, from Gk] — **hemicyclic**, *adj.*

Hemingway /'hɛmɪŋweɪ/, *n.* **Ernest,** 1898–1961, US novelist and short-story writer; Nobel prize for literature 1954.

hemisphere /'hɛməsfɪə/, *n.* **1.** half of the earth or sky. **2.** a map or projection of either of these. **3.** half of a sphere. **4.** *Anat.* either half of the cerebrum. [L, from Gk] — **hemispherical,** *adj.*

hemlock /'hɛmlɒk/, *n.* **1.** a poisonous herb with spotted stems, finely divided leaves, and small white flowers, used medicinally as a powerful sedative drug. **2.** a poisonous drink made from this herb. [OE *hemlic, hym(e)lic (e),* ? from *hymele* hop plant + *-k* suffix (see -OCK). Note that both hemlock and hops have a sedative effect]

hemp /hɛmp/, *n.* **1.** a tall herb, native to Asia, but cultivated in many parts of the world, and yielding hashish, cannabis, etc. **2.** the strong fibre of this plant used for making coarse cloth, ropes, etc. [OE *henep, hænep*] — **hempen,** *adj.*

hemstitch /'hɛmstɪtʃ/, *v.t.* **1.** to sew along a line from which threads have been drawn out, stitching the crossthreads into a series of little groups. ◇*n.* **2.** the stitch used for this.

hen /hɛn/, *n.* **1.** the female of the domestic fowl. **2.** the female of any bird. [OE *hen(n)* (from OE *hana* cock)]

hen-and-chicken fern /hɛn-ən-'tʃɪkən fɜn/, *n.* a fern of eastern Australia, so called because new shoots grow on the parent fern.

hence /hɛns/, *adv.* **1.** for this reason; therefore: *This meat is of the best quality and hence more expensive.* **2.** from this time; from that time: *a month hence.* **3.** *Archaic.* away from here: *Go hence.* [ME *hen(ne)s*]

henchman /'hɛntʃmən/, *n., pl.* **-men.** a faithful attendant or follower, esp. one who obeys a leader without regard for principle or honesty. [ME *henchemanne, henxtman,* probably orig. meaning groom, and apparently from OE *hengest* stallion + *mann* man]

hendeca-, a word part meaning 'eleven'. [Gk *héndeka*]

henge /hɛndʒ/, *n.* a type of ritual monument consisting of upright stones in a circle, usu. surrounded by a ditch. [backformation from STONEHENGE]

henna /'hɛnə/, *n.* **1.** a shrub or small tree of Asia and the Middle East. **2.** a reddish orange dye made from the leaves of this plant. **3.** a reddish or orange-brown color. [Ar]

henpeck /'hɛnpɛk/, *v.t.* (of a wife) to order about or find fault with (her husband). — **henpecked,** *adj.*

henry /'hɛnri/, *n., pl.* **-rys.** *Elect.* the derived SI unit of inductance, equivalent to the inductance of a circuit in which an electromotive force of one volt is produced by a current in the circuit which varies at the rate of one ampere per second. *Symbol:* H [named after Joseph *Henry,* 1797–1878, US physicist]

Henry IV, *n.* (*Bolingbroke*), 1367–1413, king of England 1399–1413 (successor of Richard II, son of John of Gaunt, and first king of the house of Lancaster).

Henry V, *n.* (*of Monmouth*), 1387–1422, king of England 1413–22 (son of Henry IV); defeated the French at Agincourt (1415), occupied Normandy (1419), recognised as heir to Charles VI of France.

Henry VIII, *n.* 1491–1547, king of England 1509–47, and of Ireland 1541–47 (son of Henry VII); his reign popularly remembered for his six marriages.

Henry's law, *n.* the principle that the mass of a gas dissolved by a given volume of liquid at constant temperature is directly proportional to the pressure of the gas. [named after William *Henry,* 1774–1836, English chemist]

Henty /'hɛnti/, *n.* **Edward,** 1810–78, grazier, born in England; the first European to settle permanently in Vic.

he-oak /'hi:oʊk/, *n.* any of various types of casuarina tree.

hepatic /hə'pætɪk/, *adj.* **1.** relating to or acting on the liver. **2.** liver-colored; dark reddish brown. [L, from Gk: of the liver]

hepatitis /hɛpə'taɪtəs/, *n.* a serious viral disease marked by inflammation or enlargement of the liver. See **serum hepatitis.** [NL, from Gk]

Hepburn /'hɛpbɜn/, *n.* **1. Audrey** (*Edda Hepburn van Heemstra*), 1929–93, US film actor, born in Belgium; films include *My Fair Lady* (1964). **2. Katharine,** born 1909, US film actor; won Academy Awards for several films including *Guess Who's Coming to Dinner* (1967).

hepta-, a prefix meaning 'seven'. Also, before vowels, **hept-**. [Gk, combining form of *heptá*]

heptagon /'hɛptəgɒn, -gən/, *n.* a plane figure with seven angles and seven sides. [Gk: seven-cornered] — **heptagonal,** *adj.*

heptahedron /hɛptə'hidrən/, *n., pl.* **-drons, -dra** /-drə/. a solid figure with seven faces. — **heptahedral,** *adj.*

Heptateuch /'hɛptətjuk/, *n.* the first seven books of the Old Testament. [LL *Heptateuchos,* from Gk: seven-volume (work)]

Hepworth /'hɛpwəθ/, *n.* **Dame Barbara,** 1903–75, English abstract sculptor.

her /hɜ/; *weak forms* /hə, ə/, *pron.* **1.** objective form of *she.* ◇*adj.* **2.** possessive form of *she,* used before a noun (See **hers**). [OE *hire*]

Hera /'hɪərə/, *n. Gk Myth.* a goddess, wife and sister of Zeus and queen of heaven. Also, **Here.** [L from Gk]

Heraclitus /hɛrə'klaɪtəs/, *n.* (*'the Weeping Philosopher'*) c.535–c.475 BC, Greek philosopher.

herald /ˈherəld/, *n.* **1.** someone, oft. an official, who carries messages or makes announcements. **2.** a person or thing that tells of the approach of somebody or something; harbinger: *A cloudy sky is the herald of rain.* **3.** an officer who arranged medieval tournaments, etc., later employed to keep records of the use of coats of arms. ◇*v.t.* **4.** to tell of the approach of. [ML *heraldus* (of Gmc orig.)]

heraldic /həˈrældɪk/, *adj.* of or relating to heralds or heraldry.

heraldry /ˈherəldri/, *n., pl.* **-dries. 1.** the science of tracing and recording coats of arms, family histories, etc. **2.** coats of arms collectively; armorial bearings.

herb /hɜb/, *n.* **1.** a flowering plant whose stem above ground does not become woody but decays after the yearly growing season. **2.** such a plant when used for its medicinal properties, taste, smell, etc. [ME, from F, from L: grass, herb] —**herbal**, *adj.*

herbaceous /hɜˈbeɪʃəs/, *adj.* **1.** Also, **herbal.** of, relating to, or of the nature of a herb. **2.** (of plants or plant parts) not woody. **3.** (of flowers, etc.) having the outward color, etc. of an ordinary leaf.

herbage /ˈhɜbɪdʒ/, *n.* **1.** herbaceous plants in general. **2.** the leaves and stems of herbaceous plants. **3.** plants fed on by animals. [ME, from F: grass]

herbalist /ˈhɜbələst/, *n.* someone who collects or deals in herbs, esp. medicinal herbs.

Herbert /ˈhɜbət/, *n.* **(Alfred Francis) Xavier** /ˈzɛrviə/, 1901–84, Australian novelist; author of *Poor Fellow My Country* (1975).

herbicide /ˈhɜbəsaɪd/, *n.* a chemical or biological substance which kills plants or slows down their growth.

herbivore /ˈhɜbəvɔ/, *n.* an animal that feeds on plants. —**herbivorous**, *adj.*

Herculaneum /hɜkjəˈleɪniəm/, *n.* a buried city at the foot of Mt Vesuvius, in south-western Italy; destroyed together with Pompeii by an eruption, AD 79.

herculean /hɜkjəˈliən, hɜˈkjuliən/, *adj.* **1.** needing great strength; very hard to perform: *a herculean task.* **2.** having great strength, courage, or size. [from HERCULES; L, from Gk]

Hercules /ˈhɜkjəliz/, *n. Class Myth.* a hero of great strength and courage who performed 12 extraordinary tasks. Also, **Alcides.** Greek, **Heracles, Herakles.** [L, from Gk, lit., having the glory of Hera]

herd /hɜd/, *n.* **1.** a number of animals, esp. cattle, kept, feeding, or travelling together; flock. **2.** a large group of people. ◇*v.i.* **3.** to unite or move about in a herd. ◇*v.t.* **4.** to form into a herd. **5.** to drive or lead a herd. [OE *heord*] —**herdsman**, *n.*

here /hɪə/, *adv.* **1.** in this place (opposed to *there*): *Put it here.* **2.** to or towards this place: *Come here.* **3.** at this point: *Here the speaker paused.* **4.** (oft. used in calling for attention, pointing out some person or thing present, answering a rollcall, etc.) **5. here and now,** immediately. **6. here and there,** in or to various places. **7. neither here nor there,** not important or to the point; irrelevant. ◇*n.* **8.** this place. **9. here and now, a.** the immediate present. **b.** this world; this life. [OE *hēr*]

hereafter /hɪərˈaftə/, *adv.* **1.** after this in time or order. **2.** in the life after death. ◇*n.* **3.** a future life after death. **4.** future time. [OE]

hereby /hɪəbaɪ/, *adv.* by means of this; as a result of this.

hereditary /həˈrɛdətri/, *adj.* **1.** passing, or able to be passed, naturally from parents to offspring: *a hereditary disease.* **2.** relating to inheritance or heredity: *hereditary descent.* **3.** passed on by one's ancestors; traditional: *a hereditary enemy.* **4.** *Law.* **a.** passed on, or able to be passed on by inheritance: *hereditary ownership; hereditary title.* **b.** holding a title, etc., by inheritance: *a hereditary owner.* [L: of an inheritance]

heredity /həˈrɛdəti/, *n., pl.* **-ties. 1.** the passing on of characteristics from parents to offspring. **2.** the characteristics so passed on. [L: heirship, inheritance]

Hereford /ˈhɛrəfəd/, *n.* a highly productive breed of beef cattle, with red body, white face, and other white markings. [named after HEREFORDSHIRE]

Herefordshire /ˈhɛrəfədʃɪə, -ʃə/, *n.* a former county in western England, now part of Hereford and Worcester county.

herein /hɪərˈɪn/, *adv.* in or into this place, piece of writing, etc. [OE]

hereof /hɪərˈɒv/, *adv.* **1.** of this. **2.** concerning this.

heresy /ˈhɛrəsi/, *n., pl.* **-sies. 1.** a belief or teaching opposed to those accepted or established by a church or religious system. **2.** the holding of such belief. **3.** any belief or opinion opposed to that which is generally accepted. [ME, from L, from Gk: a taking, choice]

heretic /ˈhɛrətɪk/, *n.* a person who believes in a heresy. [ME, from LL, from Gk: able to choose] —**heretical**, *adj.*

hereto /hɪəˈtu/, *adv.* to this place, thing, piece of writing, agreement, etc.: *attached hereto.*

heretofore /hɪətuˈfɔ/, *adv.* before this time.

hereupon /hɪərəˈpɒn/, *adv.* following immediately upon this.

Hereward /ˈhɛrəwəd/, *n.* (**'the Wake'**), Anglo-Saxon defender of the Isle of Ely and Fens against William the Conqueror, 1070–71; an English folk hero.

herewith /hɪəˈwɪθ/, *adv.* **1.** together with this. **2.** by means of this.

heritable /ˈhɛrətəbəl/, *adj.* **1.** able to be inherited. **2.** able to inherit. [ME, from OF] —**heritability**, *n.*

heritage /ˈhɛrətɪdʒ/, *n.* **1.** something which comes or belongs to one by reason of birth; something inherited. **2.** the culture, traditions and national assets preserved from one generation to another. **3.** something deserved because of one's way of behavior, etc.: *the heritage of the righteous*. **4.** *Law.* property which has been or may be inherited by legal descent. [ME, from OF: inherit, from LL]

Herman /'hɜmən/, *n.* **Sali** /'sali/, 1898-1993, Australian artist born in Switzerland; particularly known for Sydney urban scenes.

Hermannsburg /'hɜmənzbɜg/, *n.* a mission station in central Australia, on the Finke River in southern central NT; established by the Lutheran church in 1877. Pop. 506 (1986).

hermaphrodite /hɜ'mæfrədaɪt/, *n.* **1.** a person, animal or flower having both male and female sexual organs. ◇*adj.* **2.** *Bot.* → **monoclinous**. [ME, from L, from Gk *hermaphróditos*. As proper name, son of Hermes and Aphrodite (Greek deities), who became united in body with the nymph Salmacis while bathing in her fountain] —**hermaphroditic,** *adj.* —**hermaphroditism,** *n.*

hermeneutic /hɜmə'njutɪk/, *adj.* aiming to explain or interpret. Also, **hermeneutical**. [Gk: of interpreting] —**hermeneutist,** *n.*

Hermes /'hɜmiz/, *n.* *Gk Myth.* a deity, herald and messenger of the gods, and god of roads, commerce, invention, cunning, and theft.

hermetic /hɜ'mɛtɪk/, *adj.* **1.** made airtight. **2.** relating to the practice of magic, etc. Also, **hermetical**. [ML *hermēticus*, from *Hermes* Trismegistus, said to have invented a seal to make vessels airtight] —**hermetically,** *adv.*

hermit /'hɜmət/, *n.* **1.** someone who lives alone in a faraway place for religious reasons. **2.** any person living alone and having few social relations. **3.** *Zool.* an animal which lives mainly alone. [ME, from LL, from Gk: a hermit, lit., of the desert] —**hermitic, hermitical,** *adj.*

hermitage /'hɜmətɪdʒ/, *n.* **1.** a place where a hermit lives. **2.** any place where a person lives away from others.

Hermitage /'hɜmətɪdʒ/, *n.* **the,** an art museum in Leningrad, built by Catherine the Great as a palace.

hermit crab, *n.* any of a group of crustaceans which protect their soft parts by living in the empty shells of certain molluscs.

hernia /'hɜniə/, *n., pl.* **-nias.** the pushing out of an organ or tissue through an opening in surrounding tissues, esp. in the area of the abdomen; a rupture. [ME, from L]

hero /'hɪəroʊ/, *n., pl.* **-roes. 1.** a man of great courage, admired for his noble deeds. **2.** a man who is greatly admired for any quality. **3.** the main male character in a story, play, etc. **4.** (in ancient mythology) a being of godlike strength and ability, sometimes honored as a god. [ME *heroës*, pl., from L, from Gk]

Hero and Leander /liˈændə/, *n.* *Gk Legend.* two lovers in a Greek poem. Leander drowned while swimming the Hellespont to visit Hero, who upon finding his body, hurled herself to the rocks beside it.

Herod Antipas /ˌhɛrəd 'æntɪpæs/, *n.* died after AD 39, ruler of Galilee AD 4–39; executed John the Baptist and presided at the trial of Jesus.

Herodotus /hɛ'rɒdətəs/, *n.* 484?–425? BC, Greek historian; wrote the first western historical work, dealing with the wars between the Greeks and Persians (490–479 BC).

heroic /hə'roʊɪk/, *adj.* Also, **heroical. 1.** like a hero; daring; noble: *a heroic explorer.* **2.** dealing with heroes: *heroic poetry.* **3.** like heroic poetry in language or style; grand; exalted. ◇*n.* **4.** (*usu. pl.*) → **heroic verse. 5.** (*pl.*) language or behavior that is unusually grand. —**heroically,** *adv.*

heroic age, *n.* a period said to be marked by heroic activity, as that of ancient Greece or Rome. See **age** (def. 10).

heroic couplet, *n.* a pair of rhyming iambic lines of five metrical feet, used originally in heroic verse.

heroic verse, *n.* a form of verse used in heroic poetry, such as, in classical poetry, the hexameter, and in English, the iambic pentameter.

heroin /'hɛroʊən/, *n.* a dangerous, addictive drug, made from morphine. [Trademark (effect of drug is to make one feel like a 'hero'); G, from Gk]

heroine /'hɛroʊən/, *n.* **1.** a female hero. **2.** the main female character in a story, play, etc. [L, from Gk: hero]

heroism /'hɛroʊɪzəm/, *n.* the qualities or actions of a hero or heroine.

heron /'hɛrən/, *n.* any of a group of long-legged, long-necked, long-billed wading birds including the true herons, bitterns, egrets, etc. [ME, from OF, from Gmc]

Herophilus /hɪəˈrɒfələs/, *n.* died 280? BC, Greek physician; the first western anatomist, he distinguished nerves from blood vessels and sensory from motor nerves.

hero-worship /'hɪəroʊ-wɜʃɪp/, *n., v.,* **-shipped, -shipping.** ◇*n.* **1.** the worship of heroes who have become honored as gods, as in ancient times. **2.** great admiration for another person. ◇*v.t.* **3.** to feel great admiration for. —**hero-worshipper,** *n.*

herpes /'hɜpiz/, *n.* an infection of the skin or mucous membrane marked by groups of blisters which break and spread. [L, from Gk: lit., a creeping] —**herpetic,** *adj.*

herpes simplex, *n.* **1.** → **cold sore. 2.** a similar form of herpes found on the genitals.

herpes zoster, *n.* → **shingles.**

herpetology /hɜpə'tɒlədʒi/, *n.* the branch of zoology that deals with reptiles and amphibians. [Gk: reptile] —**herpetological,** *adj.*

herring /'hɛrɪŋ/, *n., pl.* **-rings,** (*esp. collectively*) **-ring.** a marine fish found in great numbers in the North Sea and the North Atlantic, important as a food fish. [OE *hǣring*]

herringbone /'hɛrɪŋboʊn/, *n.* **1.** a pattern of joining rows of parallel lines so arranged that any two rows have the form of a V or an upside down V; used in needlework, bricklaying, etc. **2.** a sewing stitch similar to cross-stitch.

hers /hɜz/, *pron.* 1. (a form of the possessive *her*, used without a noun following): *The fault was hers.* 2. the person(s) or thing(s) belonging to her: *herself and hers.*

herself /hə'sɛlf/, *pron.* 1. the reflexive form of *her*: *She cut herself.* 2. the emphatic form of *her* or *she*: *She used it for herself; She herself did it.* 3. her proper or normal self: *She is herself again.*

Hershey /'hɜʃi/, *n.* **Alfred Day**, born 1908, US biologist; discovered that DNA was the genetic material of life; 1969 Nobel prize for physiology or medicine with Delbrück and Luria.

Hertfordshire /'hatfədʃɪə, -ʃə/, *n.* a county in south-eastern England. Pop. 985 700 (1986 est.); 1637 km². *Administrative Centre:* Hertford. Also, **Herts.**

hertz /hɜts/, *n.* the derived SI unit of frequency, defined as the frequency of a periodic phenomenon (regularly repeating event) of which the periodic time is one second; one cycle per second. *Symbol:* Hz [named after HR *Hertz*, 1857–94, German physicist]

Hervey Bay /'havi/, *n.* a bay with a town of the same name on its southern shore in south-eastern Qld. Pop. 14 410 (1986). [named by James COOK in 1770 after Capt Augustus John *Hervey*, 2nd Earl of Bristol]

he's /hiz/, the short form of *he is* or *he has*.

hesitant /'hɛzətənt/, *adj.* hesitating; undecided. **– hesitancy, hesitance,** *n.*

hesitate /'hɛzəteɪt/, *v.i.* **-tated, -tating.** 1. to hold back because of being doubtful or undecided: *He hesitated to join the army; Her mother hesitated about letting her go out.* 2. to stop for a short time; pause. 3. to lack readiness in speech; stammer. [L: stuck fast] **– hesitation,** *n.* **– hesitative,** *adj.*

hessian /'hɛʃən/, *n.* a strong cloth made from jute, used for sacks, carpet backing, etc.

Hess's law /'hɛsəz lɔ/, *n.* a law which states that if a chemical reaction happens in stages, the sum of the heat produced in each stage is equal to the total heat produced when the reaction happens directly. [named after GH *Hess*, 1806–50, Russian chemist]

hetero-, a word part meaning 'other' or 'different', as in *heterogeneous*. Also, before vowels, **heter-**. [Gk, combining form of *héteros*]

heterodox /'hɛtərədɒks, 'hɛtrə-/, *adj.* not in accordance with established or accepted teachings or opinions, esp. in religion; unorthodox. [Gk: of another opinion] **– heterodoxy,** *n.*

heterogamous /hɛtə'rɒgəməs/, *adj.* 1. *Biol.* having unlike gametes, or reproducing by the union of such gametes (opposed to *isogamous*). 2. *Bot.* having flowers of two sexually different kinds (opposed to *homogamous*). **– heterogamy,** *n.*

heterogeneous /hɛtərou'dʒiniəs/, *adj.* 1. different in kind; unlike. 2. made of parts of different kinds; having widely unlike elements. [ML, from Gk: of different kinds] **– heterogeneity,** *n.*

heteromorphic /hɛtərou'mɔfɪk/, *adj.* 1. *Biol.* dissimilar in shape, structure, or size. 2. *Insects.* having completely different forms at various stages. Also, **heteromorphous.** **– heteromorphism, heteromorphy,** *n.*

heterosexual /hɛtərou'sɛkʃuəl/, *adj.* 1. *Biol.* relating to the other sex or to both sexes. 2. marked by or relating to sexual feeling for a person (or people) of the opposite sex. ◇*n.* 3. a heterosexual person. **– heterosexuality,** *n.*

heterotrophic /hɛtərou'trɒfɪk/, *adj.* (of an organism) needing an outside supply of organic material as food (opposed to *autotrophic*).

heterozygote /hɛtərou'zaɪgout/, *n. Biol.* a hybrid containing genes for two unlike characteristics; an organism which will not breed true to type. **– heterozygous,** *adj.*

het up /hɛt 'ʌp/, *adj. Colloq.* anxious; worried. [alteration of *heated-up*]

heuristic /hju'rɪstɪk/, *adj.* 1. helping to find out; furthering investigation. 2. (of a teaching method) encouraging students to discover for themselves. [Gk *heurís(kein)* find out] **– heurism,** *n.*

hew /hju/, *v.t.*, **hewed, hewed** or **hewn, hewing.** 1. to cut with an axe, sword, etc., chop. 2. to make or shape with cutting blows: *to hew a passage.* [OE *hēawan*]

Hewett /'hjuət/, *n.* **Dorothy Coade**, born 1923, Australian playwright, poet and writer.

Hewson /'hjusən/, *n.* **John Robert**, born 1946, Australian federal Liberal politician; became Leader of the Opposition in 1990.

hex /hɛks/, *n.* 1. an evil spell or charm. 2. a powerful evil influence over someone or something. ◇*v.t.* 3. to wish or bring misfortune on, as if by an evil spell. [G *Hexe* witch. See HAG]

hexa-, a prefix meaning 'six', as in *hexagon*. Also, before vowels **hex-**. [Gk, combining form of *héx*]

hexachlorophene /hɛksə'klɔrəfin/, *n.* an antiseptic substance, oft. used in soaps and creams for the skin. Also, **hexachlorophane.**

hexadecimal /hɛksə'dɛsəməl/, *adj.* relating to a number system used in computing having 16 as its base.

hexagon /'hɛksəgɒn, -gən/, *n.* a plane figure with six angles and six sides. **– hexagonal,** *adj.*

hexagram /'hɛksəgræm/, *n.* 1. a six-pointed starlike figure formed of two equal-sided triangles placed across each other with their sides parallel and their centres at the same point. 2. *Geom.* a figure of six lines.

hexahedron /hɛksə'hidrən/, *n., pl.* **-drons, -dra** /-drə/. a solid figure with six faces. **– hexahedral,** *adj.*

hexameter /hɛk'sæmətə/, *n.* a line of verse with six metrical feet, used in Greek and Latin epic and other poetry. [L, from Gk]

hexane /'hɛksein/, *n.* any of the five isomeric saturated hydrocarbons (alkanes), C_6H_{14}, obtained from petroleum. [Gk *héx* six (with reference to the atoms of carbon) + -ANE]

hexapod /ˈheksəpɒd/, *n.* **1.** an insect. ◇*adj.* **2.** having six feet. [Gk: six-footed] —**hexapodous**, *adj.*

hey /heɪ/, *interj.* (an exclamation used to call attention, give encouragement, etc.) Also, **heigh**, **ha**.

heyday /ˈheɪdeɪ/, *n.* the stage or period of highest success or fullest strength. [alteration of *high day*]

Heyerdahl /ˈheɪjədal/, *n.* Thor /tɔ/, born 1914, Norwegian anthropologist; leader of the Kon-Tiki expedition, which demonstrated that the Polynesians could have migrated from South America.

Heysen /ˈhaɪsən/, *n.* **Sir (Wilhelm Ernst) Hans (Franz)**, 1877–1968, Australian painter of watercolour landscapes, born in Germany.

h.f., (*sometimes cap.*) *Elect. Abbrev.* high frequency.

Hf, *Chem. Symbol.* hafnium.

Hg, *Chem. Symbol.* mercury. [L *hydrargyrus*, from Gk]

hi /haɪ/, *interj.* (an exclamation, esp. of greeting.)

hiatus /haɪˈeɪtəs/, *n.*, *pl.* **-tuses**, **-tus**. a break, with a part missing; interruption: *a hiatus in a text; a hiatus in a discussion.* [L: gap] —**hiatal**, *adj.*

hiatus hernia, *n.* the pushing out of part of the stomach through an opening in the oesophagus.

Hiawatha /haɪəˈwɒθə/, *n.* a Mohawk Indian leader of the 16th century who founded a league which ended much feuding among Iroquois tribes.

Hibberd /ˈhɪbəd/, *n.* **Jack** (*John Charles Hibberd*), born 1940, Australian playwright; wrote *Dimboola* (1974).

hibernal /haɪˈbɜnəl/, *adj.* of or relating to winter; wintry. [LL: winter]

hibernate /ˈhaɪbəneɪt/, *v.i.* **-nated**, **-nating**. **1.** to spend the winter in a sleep-like condition, as certain animals do. **2.** to keep away from social activity. [L: wintered] —**hibernation**, *n.*

Hibernian /haɪˈbɜniən/, *adj.* Irish. [L *Hibernia* Ireland + -AN]

hibiscus /haɪˈbɪskəs/, *n.* a kind of herb, shrub or tree with broad, showy, short-lived flowers. [L, from Gk: mallow]

hiccup /ˈhɪkəp/, *n.* **1.** a quick taking in of breath suddenly checked by the closure of the upper part of the throat, producing a characteristic sound. ◇*v.i.* **2.** to make the sound of a hiccup. Also, **hiccough** /ˈhɪkʌp/. [imitative]

hick /hɪk/, *n. Colloq.* a country person, thought of as being simple and unstylish. [familiar form of *Richard*, man's name]

hickory /ˈhɪkəri/, *n.*, *pl.* **-ries**. any of a group of North American trees, certain of which, as the pecan, bear sweet nuts (hickory nuts), and others, as the shagbark, also yield valuable hard wood. [Amer Ind]

Hicks /hɪks/, *n.* **Point**, a promontory on the eastern coast of Vic, comprising four smaller points projecting seaward. [named after Zachary *Hickes*, James COOK's first lieutenant, first to see land in that region]

hid /hɪd/, *v.* past tense and past participle of **hide**[1].

hidden /ˈhɪdn/, *v.* past participle of **hide**[1].

hide[1] /haɪd/, *v.*, **hid**, **hidden** or **hid**, **hiding**, *n.* ◇*v.t.* **1.** to prevent from being seen or discovered; conceal: *She hides her money under her bed; The clouds hide the sun.* ◇*v.i.* **2.** to hide oneself; be concealed. ◇*n.* **3.** a covered place to hide in while shooting or watching wildlife. [OE *hȳdan*]

hide[2] /haɪd/, *n.* **1.** the skin of an animal, raw or dressed. **2.** *Colloq.* the human skin. **3.** *Colloq.* daring rudeness: *He's got a hide!* **4. neither hide nor hair**, not a sign; no clue. [OE *hȳd*]

hideaway /ˈhaɪdəweɪ/, *n. Colloq.* a place for hiding; refuge.

hidebound /ˈhaɪdbaʊnd/, *adj.* narrow and unchanging in opinion. [HIDE[2] + BOUND[1]]

hideous /ˈhɪdiəs/, *adj.* **1.** very ugly: *a hideous monster.* **2.** shocking to the moral sense: *a hideous crime.* [ME, from AF: horror, fear]

hide-out /ˈhaɪd-aʊt/, *n.* a hiding place for those who are being chased, esp. by the law.

hiding[1] /ˈhaɪdɪŋ/, *n.* the act of hiding or state of being hidden: *to remain in hiding.* [HIDE[1] + -ING[1]]

hiding[2] /ˈhaɪdɪŋ/, *n.* **1.** a beating. **2.** a defeat.

hidy-hole /ˈhaɪdi-hoʊl/, *n.* a hiding place. Also, **hidey hole**.

hierarchy /ˈhaɪəraki/, *n.*, *pl.* **-chies**. **1.** any system of people or things organised in grades, etc. **2.** *Science.* a series of groupings of graded rank. The terms *phylum*, *class*, *order*, *family*, *genus*, and *species* make up a hierarchy in zoology. **3.** a body of church rulers arranged in graded ranks. —**hierarchical**, *adj.*

hieratic /haɪəˈrætɪk/, *adj.* **1.** relating to priests or the priesthood. **2.** relating to a form of writing based on shortened hieroglyphics, used by ancient Egyptian priests. **3.** relating to certain styles in art whose types or methods are fixed by religious tradition. Also, **hieratical**. [L, from Gk: priestly, sacerdotal]

hieroglyphic /haɪərəˈglɪfɪk/, *n.* **1.** Also, **hieroglyph**. a picture or symbol used in a writing system, particularly that of the ancient Egyptians, to represent a word or sound. **2.** (*usu. pl.*) writing using such pictures. **3.** (*pl.*) writing that is difficult to read. ◇*adj.* **4.** Also, **hieroglyphical**. relating to or written in hieroglyphics. [LL, from Gk]

hi-fi /ˈhaɪ-faɪ/, *adj.* **1.** → **high-fidelity**. ◇*n.* **2.** a high-fidelity record-player, etc.

high /haɪ/, *adj.* **1.** having a great extent upwards; lofty; tall. **2.** having a particular extent upwards: *two metres high*. **3.** situated above the ground or some base; elevated. **4.** lying or being above the general or normal level: *high ground; a river high after rain.* **5.** above the common degree or measure; strong; intense:

high   487   **High Mass**

a high speed; a high temperature; a high price. **6.** based on a judgment of great amount, value, or excellence: *a high estimate; a high opinion.* **7.** important in rank, position, opinion of others, etc.: *a high official.* **8.** sharp in sound; shrill. **9.** going to or coming from a high place: *a high jump; a high dive.* **10.** chief; principal; main: *the high altar of a church.* **11.** very serious; of great consequence: *high treason.* **12.** (of a period of time) at its fullest point of development: *the high Renaissance.* **13.** advanced to the greatest fullness: *high tide.* **14.** merry; elated: *high spirits.* **15.** *Colloq.* under the influence of alcohol or drugs: *He's high on dope.* **16.** based on costly habits; luxurious: *high living.* **17.** *Biol.* having a relatively complex structure: *the higher mammals.* **18.** *Phonet.* pronounced with the tongue relatively close to the roof of the mouth: *high vowels.* **19.** (of meat, esp. game) slightly bad or tainted. **20. high and mighty,** proud; haughty: *a high and mighty manner.* ◇*adv.* **21.** at or to a high point, place, level, rank, amount, price, or degree. **22. high and dry,** *Colloq.* left without help; stranded; deserted. **23. high and low,** everywhere. ◇*n.* **24.** that which is high; a high level: *Prices reached a new high.* **25.** *Meteorol.* a pressure system marked by relatively high pressure at its centre; an anticyclone. **26. on a high,** in a state of pleasant sensations oft. brought about by drugs. **27. on high, a.** at or to a height; above. **b.** in heaven. [OE *hēah*]

highborn /'haɪbɔn/, *adj.* of high rank by birth.

highbred /'haɪbrɛd/, *adj.* **1.** of a good breed. **2.** showing good breeding: *highbred manners.*

highbrow /'haɪbraʊ/, *Colloq. n.* a person who has or thinks he or she has good taste in artistic or intellectual matters. ◇*adj.* **1.** approved of by highbrows: *a highbrow play.*

High Church, *n.* a party in the Anglican church which places importance on church authority, ceremony, etc. (opposed to *Low Church*). –**High-Church,** *adj.* –**High Churchman,** *n.*

high-class /'haɪ-klɑs/, *adj.* of superior quality.

high commissioner, *n.* the chief representative of a country belonging to the Commonwealth of Nations, posted in another member country.

High Court of Australia, *n.* a federal court established under the Constitution with jurisdiction over constitutional matters and jurisdiction to hear appeals from the Supreme Courts of the states.

highest common factor, *n.* the greatest number which is a factor (def. 2) of all the numbers in a certain group of numbers. For example, 8 is the highest common factor of 24 and 32. Also, **HCF, h.c.f.**

high explosive, *n.* a class of explosive, such as TNT, in which the reaction is almost immediate, used in shells and bombs.

highfalutin /haɪfə'lutn/, *adj. Colloq.* sounding or looking more important than it really is; pompous; pretentious: *highfalutin words.* Also, **highfaluting.**

high-fidelity /haɪ-fə'dɛləti/, *adj.* (of an amplifier, radio receiver, etc.) reproducing the full range of the original sounds almost exactly. Also, **hi-fi.**

high-flier /haɪ-'flaɪə/, *n.* **1.** someone who has high aims, etc. **2.** *Stock Exchange.* a share which unexpectedly rises quickly in price. Also, **high-flyer.**

high-flown /'haɪ-floʊn/, *adj.* **1.** having high aims, etc. **2.** showing too great a sense of importance; pretentious: *high-flown ideas; high-flown language.*

high frequency, *n.* **1.** a radio frequency between 3 and 30 megacycles per second. *Abbrev.:* h.f. ◇*adj.* **2.** of a sound which is high in pitch. –**high-frequency,** *adj.*

High German /haɪ 'dʒɜmən/, *n.* any form of the German language of central and southern Germany, Switzerland, and Austria, including Old High German and Middle High German.

high-grade /'haɪ-greɪd/, *adj.* **1.** of good or superior quality. **2.** (of ore) with a relatively high yield of the metal for which it is mined.

high-handed /'haɪ-hændəd/, *adj.* using power without consideration; overbearing; arbitrary: *a high-handed manner.* –**high-handedness,** *n.*

high jinks /'haɪ dʒɪŋks/, *n.pl. Colloq.* lively merrymaking.

high jump, *n.* **1.** *Athletics.* an event in which the winner is the one who jumps over the highest bar. **2. for the high jump,** *Colloq.* about to face an unpleasant punishment, etc.

highland /'haɪlənd/, *n.* **1.** an area of high ground; a plateau. **2.** (*pl.*) a mountainous or hilly area. –**highlander,** *n.*

Highland fling, *n.* a lively Scottish country dance, a form of the reel.

Highlands /'haɪləndz/, *n.pl.* **1.** a mountainous region of Scotland north of the Lowlands; highest point, Ben Nevis 1343 m.

highlight /'haɪlaɪt/, *v.t.* **1.** to make noticeable or prominent; emphasise. **2.** (in photography, painting, etc.) to show up (the areas of greatest brightness) with paint or by exposing lighter areas. **3.** to dye (part of hair) with a light color. ◇*n.* **4.** a noticeable or striking part: *the highlight of his talk.* **5.** *Art.* the point of strongest light in a picture or form.

highly /'haɪli/, *adv.* **1.** in or to a high degree: *highly amusing.* **2.** with high favor or praise: *to speak highly of a person.* **3.** at or to a high price: *You'll pay highly for your wickedness.*

highly strung, *adj.* tense and nervous. Also, **high-strung.**

highly-wrought /'haɪli-rɔt/, *adj.* **1.** made with much skill; ornate. **2.** highly upset or agitated. Also, **high-wrought.**

High Mass, *n.* a sung mass celebrated with full rituals, usu. including use of incense, etc.

high-minded /ˈhaɪ-maɪndəd/, *adj.* **1.** having or showing high principles or feelings. **2.** proud; arrogant. —**high-mindedness**, *n.*

highness /ˈhaɪnəs/, *n.* **1.** the state of being high. **2.** (*cap.*) a title of honor given to members of a royal family with *His, Her, Your*, etc.

high-pitched /ˈhaɪ-pɪtʃt/, *adj.* **1.** *Music.* played or sung at a high pitch. **2.** (of a discussion, argument, etc.) marked by strong feeling; intense. **3.** (of a roof) very steep.

high-powered /ˈhaɪ-paʊəd/, *adj.* forceful; energetic; vigorous: *a high-powered sales campaign.*

high-pressure /ˈhaɪ-prɛʃə/, *adj.* **1.** having or using pressure above the normal: *high-pressure steam.* **2.** forceful; persistent: *high-pressure salesmanship.*

high priest, *n.* **1.** a chief priest. **2.** a person in a position of power or influence, or a specialist in a particular field. **3.** *Judaism.* the highest-ranking priest who alone may enter the holy of holies.

high relief, *n.* → **alto-rilievo**.

high-rise /ˈhaɪ-raɪz/, *adj.* (of a building) having many storeys.

high school, *n.* → **secondary school**. —**high-schooler**, *n.*

high seas, *n.pl.* the open waters of any sea or ocean.

high-speed /ˈhaɪ-spid/, *adj.* **1.** operating, or able to operate at a high speed. **2.** *Photog.* (of film) useable with little light and short exposures. **3.** (of steel) especially hard and able to keep its hardness even at red heat, so that it can be used for lathe tools.

high-spirited /ˈhaɪ-spɪrətəd/, *adj.* having a high, proud, or bold spirit.

high-tech /ˈhaɪ-tɛk/, *adj.* ultra-modern, esp. using materials or styles associated with high technology.

high technology, *n.* the most modern and sophisticated machines and processes, esp. electronic.

high-tension /ˈhaɪ-tɛnʃən/, *adj.* (of a device, circuit, etc.) operating, or capable of operating, under a relatively high voltage, usu. 1000 volts or more.

high time, *n.* **1.** the right time, just before it is too late: *It's high time that was done.* **2.** *Colloq.* an enjoyable and gay time.

high treason, *n.* treason against king, queen or state.

highway /ˈhaɪweɪ/, *n.* **1.** a main road, esp. one between towns. **2.** any public passage, either a road or waterway.

highwayman /ˈhaɪweɪmən/, *n., pl.* **-men.** (formerly) a robber on a highway, esp. one on horseback.

hijack /ˈhaɪdʒæk/, *v.t.* **1.** to steal (something that is transporting or being transported): *He hijacked the lorry and its goods.* **2.** to seize by force or threat of force (a vehicle, esp. a passenger-carrying vehicle): *They hijacked the airliner.* [? from HIGH(WAYMAN) + *jack* hunt by night with the aid of a jacklight] —**hijacker**, *n.*

hike /haɪk/, *v.*, **hiked, hiking**, *n.* ◇*v.i.* **1.** to walk a long distance, esp. through the country, for pleasure. ◇*v.t.* **2.** to increase (a fare, price, etc.) (fol. by *up*). ◇*n.* **3.** a long walk, esp. in the country. **4.** an increase in wages, fares, prices, etc. [? akin to HITCH] —**hiker**, *n.*

hilarious /həˈlɛəriəs/, *adj.* **1.** noisily gay and cheerful. **2.** very funny, causing great amusement. —**hilariousness, hilarity**, *n.*

Hildegard of Bingen /ˈhɪldəgad əv ˈbɪŋən/, *n.* 1098–1179, distinguished German abbess, visionary, naturalist, playwright, poetess and composer.

hill /hɪl/, *n.* **1.** a naturally raised part of the earth's surface, smaller than a mountain. **2.** a heap or pile made by humans or animals: *an anthill.* **3. as old as the hills**, *Colloq.* very old. **4. take to the hills**, to run away and hide. **5. over the hill**, past the peak of physical or other condition. [OE *hyll*]

Hill /hɪl/, *n.* **Ernestine**, 1899–1972, Australian writer; author of the novel *My Love Must Wait* (1941).

Hillary /ˈhɪləri/, *n.* **Sir Edmund Percival**, born 1919, NZ explorer and mountaineer; climbed Mt Everest in 1953.

hillbilly /ˈhɪlbɪli/, *n., pl.* **-lies.** *Orig US.* someone living in the backwoods or mountains; rustic; yokel. [HILL + *Billy*, pet var. of *William*, man's name]

Hill End, *n.* a former goldrush town in eastern central NSW, north of Bathurst.

hillock /ˈhɪlək/, *n.* a little hill. —**hillocky**, *adj.*

hilly /ˈhɪli/, *adj.*, **hillier, hilliest. 1.** having many hills: *hilly country.* **2.** elevated; steep. —**hilliness**, *n.*

hilt /hɪlt/, *n.* **1.** the handle of a weapon or tool, esp. a sword or dagger. **2. to the hilt**, fully; completely: *armed to the hilt.* [OE *hilt, hilte*]

hilum /ˈhaɪləm/, *n., pl.* **-la** /-lə/. *Bot.* a mark on a seed made by the separation from its stalk. [L: little thing, trifle]

him /hɪm/, *pron.* the objective case of *he*. [OE. See HE]

Himalayas /hɪməˈleɪəz/, *n.pl.* **the**, a lofty mountain system extending about 2400 km along the border between India and the Xizang Autonomous Region (Tibet). Highest peak (in the world), Mt Everest, 8848 m. Also, **the Himalaya, Himalaya Mountains**. [Skt: lit. snow-dwelling] —**Himalayan**, *adj.*

Himmler /ˈhɪmlə/, *n.* **Heinrich** /ˈhaɪnrɪk/, 1900–45, Nazi leader in Germany; chief of police and head of the Gestapo and the SS from 1936.

himself /hɪmˈsɛlf/, *pron.* **1.** the reflexive form of *him*: *He cut himself.* **2.** an emphatic form of *him* or *he* used: **a.** as object: *He used it for himself.* **b.** in apposition to a subject or

hind[1] /hamd/, *adj.*, **hinder**, **hindmost** or **hindermost**. placed behind or at the back; posterior: *the hind legs of an animal*. [? short for BEHIND, but compare OE *hindan*, adv., from behind]

hind[2] /hamd/, *n.* the female of the (red) deer. [OE]

Hindemith /'hɪndəmɪt/, *n.* **Paul** /paʊl/, 1895-1963, German composer.

Hindenburg /'hɪndənbɜːg/, *n.* **Paul von** /paʊl fon/, (*Paul von Beneckendorff und von Hindenburg*), 1847-1934, German field marshal; second president of Germany 1925-34.

Hindenburg line, *n.* a line of elaborate fortification established by the German army in World War I, near the French-Belgian border, from Lille south-east to Metz.

hinder /'hɪndə/, *v.t.* **1.** to check; interrupt; retard: *to be hindered by storms*. **2.** to prevent from acting or taking place; stop: *to hinder a man from committing a crime*. [OE *hindrian* behind, back]

Hindi /'hɪndi/, *n.* **1.** one of the modern Indic languages of northern India, usu. divided into Eastern and Western Hindi. **2.** a literary language derived from Hindustani, used by Hindus. [Hind, from *Hind* India]

Hindmarsh /'haɪndmɑːʃ/, *n.* **Sir John**, 1785-1860, English naval officer and colonial governor; governor of SA 1836-38.

hindquarter /'haɪndkwɔːtə/, *n.* the rear part esp. of a four-legged animal.

hindrance /'hɪndrəns/, *n.* **1.** a stopping, impeding, or preventing. **2.** a means or cause of hindering.

hindsight /'haɪndsaɪt/, *n.* the understanding of what was needed to be done in an event, after it has happened: *Hindsight is easier than foresight*.

Hindu /'hɪndu, hɪn'du/, *n.* **1.** someone who follows Hinduism, esp. a native of India. ◊*adj.* **2.** of or relating to Hindus or Hinduism. Also, **Hindoo**. [Hind, Pers, from *Hind* India]

Hinduism /'hɪnduɪzəm/, *n.* the main religion of India, with a complex body of religious, social, cultural, and philosophical beliefs, and a strict system of castes (social ranks).

Hindu Kush /hɪndu 'kʊʃ/, *n.* a lofty mountain system largely in north-eastern Afghanistan, extending west from the Himalayas. Highest peak, Tirach Mir, 7748 m. Also, **Hindu Kush Mountains**.

Hindustan /hɪndu'stɑːn/, *n.* the Persian name of India, esp. the part north of the Deccan.

Hindustani /hɪndu'stɑːni/, *n.* **1.** a standard language or lingua franca of northern India based on a dialect of Western Hindi spoken around Delhi. ◊*adj.* **2.** of or relating to Hindustan, its people, or their languages. Also, **Hindoostani**. [Hind, Pers, from HINDUSTAN]

hinge /hɪndʒ/, *n.*, *v.*, **hinged**, **hinging**. ◊*n.* **1.** a movable joint or device on which a door, gate, shutter, lid, etc., turns or moves. **2.** that on which something turns or depends; principle; central rule. ◊*v.i.* **3.** to depend or turn on, or as if on, a hinge: *Everything hinges on his decision*. ◊*v.t.* **4.** to supply with or attach by hinge(s). [OE *hencg*] **– hinged**, *adj.*

Hinkler /'hɪŋklə/, *n.* **Bert** (*Herbert John Louis Hinkler*), 1892-1933, Australian pioneer aviator.

hint /hɪnt/, *n.* **1.** an indirect or hidden suggestion; an intimation. **2.** a brief, helpful suggestion; piece of advice. ◊*v.i.*, *v.t.* **3.** to make an indirect suggestion or allusion (usu. fol. by *at*): *He hinted at his latest idea*; *She hinted she'd like to stay for coffee*. [Brit obs. *hent*, v., seize] **– hinter**, *n.*

hinterland /'hɪntəlænd/, *n.* **1.** the inland area supplying goods to a port. **2.** the land lying behind a coastal district. [G: hinder land, land behind]

hip[1] /hɪp/, *n.* **1.** the projecting part of each side of the body formed by the side of the pelvis and the upper part of the femur, with the flesh covering them; haunch. **2.** the joint of the hip. **3.** *Archit.* the angle formed by the meeting of two sloping sides or ends of a roof. [OE *hype*]

hip[2] /hɪp/, *n.* the ripe fruit of a (wild) rose. Also, **rosehip**. [OE: hip, brier]

hipbath /'hɪpbɑːθ/, *n.* a bath in which someone can sit, but not lie down.

hippie /'hɪpi/, *n.* someone who rejects traditional society to live according to ideas of universal love or union with nature. Also, **hippy**.

Hippocrates /hɪ'pɒkrətiz/, *n.* 460?-357 BC, Greek physician, known as the father of medicine. **– Hippocratic**, *adj.*

Hippocratic oath /hɪpə,krætɪk 'oʊθ/, *n.* the oath stating the (ethical) duties of doctors, sometimes taken by medical graduates. [named after HIPPOCRATES]

hippodrome /'hɪpədroʊm/, *n.* **1.** an arena for horseriding events, etc. **2.** (in ancient Greece and Rome) a course or circus for horse and chariot races. **3.** a variety theatre; music hall. [L from Gk]

Hippolyte /hɪ'pɒləti/, *n.* *Gk Legend.* a queen of the Amazons, married to Theseus. Also, **Hippolyta**.

hippopotamus /hɪpə'pɒtəməs/, *n.*, *pl.* **-muses**, **-mi** /-maɪ/. a large plant-eating mammal with a thick hairless body, short legs and large head, found in and near the rivers and lakes of Africa. [L, from LGk: the horse of the river]

hip roof, *n.* a roof with sloping ends and sides.

hipsters /'hɪpstəz/, *n.pl.* trousers hanging from the hips rather than the waist.

hire /haɪə/, *v.*, **hired**, **hiring**, *n.* ◊*v.t.* **1.** to engage the services of (someone) for payment: *to hire a cook*. **2.** to engage the temporary use of (something) for payment: *to hire a car*. ◊*n.* **3.** a price (to be) paid, for the temporary use of goods or labor. **4.** the act of hiring. [OE *hȳr*]

hireling /ˈhaɪəlɪŋ/, *n., adj.* (*usu.* offensive) (someone) working only for payment; mercenary.

hire-purchase /haɪə-ˈpɜːtʃəs/, *n.* a system whereby a seller leases goods to a purchaser at a rental which provides for payment of the full price in instalments, the seller retaining ownership until the final instalment is paid.

Hirohito /hɪroʊˈhitoʊ/, *n.* 1901-89, emperor of Japan 1926-89.

Hiroshima /hɪroʊˈʃimə, -ˈrɒʃəmə/, *n.* a seaport in south-western Japan, on Honshu Island; the first military use of the atomic bomb, 6 August 1945. Pop. 343 968 (1940); 171 902 (1946); 1 005 176 (1986 est.).

hirsute /ˈhɜːsjut/, *adj.* **1.** hairy. **2.** *Bot, Zool.* covered with long, stiff hairs. [L: rough, hairy] **—hirsuteness**, *n.*

his /hɪz/; *weak form* /ɪz/, *pron.* **1.** the possessive case of *he*: *This book is his.* **2.** the person(s) or thing(s) belonging to him: *himself and his.* **3. of his,** belonging to or associated with him: *a friend of his.* ◊*adj.* **4.** belonging to, relating to, or owned by him; made, done, experienced, etc., by him: *his house.* [OE. See HE]

Hispanic /hɪsˈpænɪk/, *adj.* **1.** Spanish or Portuguese. **2.** Latin American. [from L *Hispania* the Spanish peninsula (with Portugal)]

hiss /hɪs/, *v.i.* **1.** to make a sharp sound like that of the letter *s* prolonged, as a goose or snake does. **2.** to express disapproval or hatred by making this sound. ◊*v.t.* **3.** to show disapproval of by hissing. **4.** to utter with a hiss. ◊*n.* **5.** a hissing sound, esp. in disapproval. [OE *hyscan* jeer at, rail]

histamine /ˈhɪstəmɪn/, *n.* an amine released in damaged tissues and causing inflammation (an allergic symptom). [HIST(IDINE) + AMINE] **—histaminic**, *adj.*

histidine /ˈhɪstədɪn/, *n.* an amino acid occurring in proteins, and changed in most cells into histamine. [HIST(O)- + -ID(E) + -INE²]

histo-, a word part meaning 'tissue', as in *histology*. Also, before vowels, **hist-**. [Gk: web, tissue]

histogram /ˈhɪstəɡræm/, *n. Stats.* a graph of a frequency distribution in which a vertical column shows the frequency or number of units for each equal division marked on the horizontal axis.

histology /hɪsˈtɒlədʒi/, *n.* the science dealing with organic tissues and their structure. **—histological, histologic**, *adj.* **—histologist**, *n.*

histolysis /hɪsˈtɒləsəs/, *n.* the breaking up or dissolution of organic tissues.

historian /hɪsˈtɔriən/, *n.* **1.** a writer of history. **2.** an expert in history.

historic /hɪsˈtɒrɪk/, *adj.* **1.** well-known or important in history: *historic scenes.* **2.** likely to go down in history: *the historic opening of the new stadium.* Also, **historical**.

historical /hɪsˈtɒrɪkəl/, *adj.* **1.** relating to or dealing with history or past events. **2.** relating to history as opposed to legend or fiction: *the historical King Arthur.* [L, from Gk]

historical materialism, *n.* the part of Marxist theory which maintains that ideas and institutions develop upon an economic base, that they are changed by class struggles, and that each ruling class produces another class which will destroy it, the final stage being a classless society.

historical method, *n.* the development of general principles by the study of historical facts.

historical present, *n.* the present tense of a verb when it is used in a narrative to indicate past events: *I walk in yesterday and what do I find?*

historicity /hɪstəˈrɪsəti/, *n.* historical authenticity.

historiography /hɪstɔriˈɒɡrəfi/, *n.* **1.** the writing of history, esp. as based on the critical examination of primary sources. **2.** the study of the method and development of historical writing. **—historiographer**, *n.*

history /ˈhɪstri, ˈhɪstəri/, *n., pl.* **-ries. 1.** the branch of knowledge dealing with past events. **2.** the record of past events, esp. in connection with the human race. **3.** the written story of the past events of a particular people, country, period, person, etc. **4.** an unusual past: *a ship with a history.* **5.** a drama representing historical events. **6. be history,** to be dead, ruined or broken beyond repair. **7. make history,** to achieve lasting fame. [ME, from L, from Gk: a learning or knowing by inquiry]

histrionic /hɪstriˈɒnɪk/, *adj.* **1.** relating to actors or acting. **2.** artificial; theatrical: *histrionic tears.* Also, **histrionical**. [LL]

histrionics /hɪstriˈɒnɪks/, *n.pl.* **1.** artificial or melodramatic behavior or outburst. **2.** acting; theatricals.

hit /hɪt/, *v.,* **hit, hitting,** *n., adj.* ◊*v.t.* **1.** to give or deal a blow or stroke; bring forcibly into collision. **2.** to come against with an impact or collision, as a missile, falling body, etc.: *The ball hit her head.* **3.** to reach with a missile, weapon, blow, etc.: *I hit the target with my arrow.* **4.** to drive or propel by a stroke: *to hit a ball with a club.* **5.** to have a marked effect on; affect severely: *Her death hit him hard.* **6.** *Colloq.* to reach or achieve: *Our savings hit $300; The story hit the headlines on Tuesday.* **7.** to come or light upon; meet; find: *to hit the right road.* **8.** to arrive at: *to hit town.* **9.** to demand or obtain money from: *The building company hit me for $1000.* ◊*v.i.* **10.** to strike; deal a blow or blows. ◊**11.** Some special uses are:
hit home, to have the desired effect on someone.
hit it off, *Colloq.* to get on well together; agree.
hit off, to make a beginning.
hit on/upon, find by chance.
hit the nail on the head, to state or sum up exactly.
hit the road/trail, to leave; depart: *time to hit the road.*
hit the roof, *Colloq.* to show extreme anger.

hit up, *Tennis, Squash, etc.* to warm up before a game by hitting the ball back and forth across the net, etc. ◇*n.* **12.** an impact or collision, as of one thing against another. **13.** a stroke that reaches an object; blow. **14.** *Colloq.* a shot of any drug; fix. **15. to be a hit**, to be a success. ◇*adj.* **16.** successful; popular: *a hit song*. [OE, from Scand]

hit-and-run /ˌhɪt-n-ˈrʌn/, *adj.* **1.** of or relating to a driver, who after being involved in an accident, leaves without stopping to give help or take any responsibility. **2.** of or relating to such an accident.

hitch /hɪtʃ/, *v.t.* **1.** to make fast, esp. temporarily, by a hook, rope, etc.; tether. **2.** to harness (an animal) to a vehicle (oft. fol. by *up*). **3.** to tug or jerk (usu. fol. by *up*): *to hitch one's trousers up*. **4.** *Colloq.* to obtain or seek to obtain (a ride) from a passing vehicle: *We hitched a ride to school*. ◇*v.i.* **5.** *Colloq.* → **hitchhike**. ◇*n.* **6.** *Naut.*, *etc.* a kind of knot. **7.** a halt; obstruction: *a hitch in the proceedings*. **8.** a hitching movement; a jerk or tug. **9.** *Colloq.* a ride from a passing vehicle. [ME *hytche(n)*; orig. uncert.] –**hitcher**, *n.*

Hitchcock /ˈhɪtʃkɒk/, *n.* **Alfred Joseph**, 1899–1980, English film director, in the US after 1939; films include suspense thrillers *Vertigo* (1958) and *Psycho* (1960).

hitchhike /ˈhɪtʃhaɪk/, *v.i.*, **-hiked**, **-hiking**. *Colloq.* to travel by obtaining rides in passing vehicles. –**hitchhiker**, *n.*

hither /ˈhɪðə/, *adv.* **1.** to or towards this place; here: *to come hither*. **2. hither and thither**, this way and that; in various directions. ◇*adj.* **3.** on or towards this side; nearer: *the hither side of the hill*. [OE *hider*]

hitherto /hɪðəˈtu/, *adv.* up to this time; until now: *a fact hitherto unknown*.

Hitler /ˈhɪtlə/, *n.* **Adolf** ('der Führer') 1889–1945, Nazi dictator of Germany, born in Austria; chancellor 1933–45; dictator 1934–45.

hit man, *n. Colloq.* a hired assassin.

hit parade, *n.* a selection of the most popular songs on the radio.

hive /haɪv/, *n.*, *v.*, **hived**, **hiving**. ◇*n.* **1.** an artificial shelter for honeybees; beehive. **2.** the bees living in such a hive. **3.** something like a beehive. **4.** a place full of busy people: *a hive of industry*. ◇*v.i.*, *v.t.* **5.** to enter, or cause (bees) to enter, a hive. ◇*v.* **6. hive off**, to break away from a group. [OE *hyf*]

hives /haɪvz/, *n.* any of various skin diseases which cause a rash. [orig. Scot]

HM, *Abbrev.* Her (or His) Majesty.

HMAS /ˌeɪtʃ em ˌeɪ es/, *Abbrev.* Her (or His) Majesty's Australian Ship.

HMS /ˌeɪtʃ em es/, *Abbrev.* Her (or His) Majesty's Service/Ship.

ho /hoʊ/, *interj.* **1.** (an exclamation of surprise, gladness, derision, etc.) **2.** (a call to attract attention, sometimes used after a word indicating a destination): *Westward ho!* [ME]

Ho, *Chem. Symbol.* holmium.

hoard /hɔd/, *n.* **1.** a gathering of something for preservation or future use: *a hoard of gold*. ◇*v.t.*,*v.i.* **2.** to gather (money, food, etc.) for preservation or future use, esp. in a secret place. [OE] –**hoarder**, *n.*

hoarding /ˈhɔdɪŋ/, *n.* **1.** a temporary fence around a building site. **2.** a large board on which advertisements or notices are displayed. [obs. *hoard*, n., apparently from ME: hurdle]

hoarfrost /ˈhɔfrɒst/, *n.* → **frost** (def. 2).

hoarse /hɔs/, *adj.*, **hoarser**, **hoarsest**. having a weak and breathy tone of voice; husky. [ME *hoors*, apparently from Scand] –**hoarseness**, *n.*

hoary /ˈhɔri/, *adj.*, **hoarier**, **hoariest**. **1.** grey or white, esp. with age. **2.** very old; venerable. –**hoariness**, *n.*

hoax /hoʊks/, *n.* **1.** a funny or mischievous deception, esp. a practical joke. ◇*v.t.* **2.** to deceive by a hoax. [contraction of HOCUS(-POCUS)] –**hoaxer**, *n.*

hob /hɒb/, *n.* **1.** a shelf around a fireplace, for kettles, saucepans, etc. **2.** the flat cooking top of a (fuel) stove. [var. of obs. *hub* hob (in a fireplace)]

Hobart /ˈhoʊbat/, *n.* the capital of Tas, on the Derwent River; seaport. Pop. 168 359 (1981).

hobble /ˈhɒbəl/, *v.*, **-bled**, **-bling**, *n.* ◇*v.i.* **1.** to walk lamely; limp. **2.** to go unsteadily and irregularly: *hobbling verse*. ◇*v.t.* **3.** to cause to limp. **4.** to tie loosely together the legs of (a horse, etc.) so as to prevent free motion. ◇*n.* **5.** an uneven, halting walk; limp. **6.** a rope, strap, etc., used to hobble an animal. [ME: protuberance, uneven ground] –**hobbler**, *n.* –**hobbling**, *adj.*

hobby /ˈhɒbi/, *n.*, *pl.* **-bies**. **1.** a spare-time activity, pastime, etc., followed for pleasure or relaxation. **2.** → **hobbyhorse** (def. 1). [ME *hoby*, *hobyn*, probably for *Robin*, or *Robert*, common name for horse]

hobby farm, *n.* a farm kept for interest's sake, usu. not the owner's main source of income. –**hobby farmer**, *n.*

hobbyhorse /ˈhɒbihɔs/, *n.* **1.** a stick with a horse's head, or a rocking horse, ridden by children. **2.** a favorite topic; obsessive idea.

hobgoblin /ˈhɒbɡɒblən/, *n.* **1.** a mischievous goblin. **2.** anything causing superstitious fear; bogy.

hobnail /ˈhɒbneɪl/, *n.* a large-headed nail for protecting the soles of heavy boots. [HOB + NAIL] –**hobnailed**, *adj.*

hobnob /ˈhɒbnɒb/, *v.i.*, **-nobbed**, **-nobbing**. to associate (*with*) on very friendly terms: *He hobnobbed with the boss to try to get a promotion*. [earlier *hab* or *nab* alternately, lit., have or have not]

hobo /ˈhoʊboʊ/, *n.*, *pl.* **-bos**, **-boes**. **1.** a tramp or vagrant. **2.** a travelling worker. [rhyming formation, ? based on *beau* fop, used as a (sarcastic) word of greeting, e.g. in *hey*, *bo!*] –**hoboism**, *n.*

Hobson's choice /ˌhɒbsənz ˈtʃɔɪs/, *n.* the choice of taking either the thing offered or

Hobson's choice nothing; the absence of real choice. [after Thomas *Hobson*, 1544-1631, of Cambridge, who hired out horses, and obliged each customer to take the horse nearest the stable door or none at all]

Ho Chi Minh /ˌhou ˌtʃi 'mɪn/, *n.* 1892-1969, Vietnamese statesman; president of North Vietnam 1945-69.

Ho Chi Minh City, *n.* a port in southern Vietnam on the Saigon River. Pop. 2 441 185 (1979). Formerly (until 1976), **Saigon**.

hock[1] /hɒk/, *n.* the joint in the hind leg of the horse, and other animals, corresponding to the ankle in humans but raised from the ground and protruding backwards when bent. [OE *hōh* hock, heel]

hock[2] /hɒk/, *n.* 1. a dry white wine, made from grapes grown along the Rhine river. 2. any similar wine made elsewhere. [Rhine wine produced near Hochheim, Germany]

hock[3] /hɒk/, *Colloq.* ◇*v.t.* 1. → **pawn**[1]. 2. to sell (esp. illegally). ◇*n.* 3. **in hock**, pawned. [D: *hovel*, prison, debt]

hockey /'hɒki/, *n.* a team game in which sticks with curved ends are used to drive a ball into a goal. [*hock* stick with hook at one end, var. of HOOK]

Hockney /'hɒkni/, *n.* **David**, born 1937, English painter.

hocus-pocus /ˌhoukəs-'poukəs/, *n.* 1. a formula used in conjuring or performing magic. 2. skilful use of the hands to confuse an audience. 3. trickery. 4. unnecessary elaboration to cover a deception or to make a basically simple thing appear more mysterious. [orig. jugglers' jargon, simulating Latin]

hod /hɒd/, *n.* 1. a long narrow container for carrying bricks, etc., fixed on a pole and carried on the shoulder. 2. → **coalscuttle**. [MD *hodde* basket]

Hoddle /'hɒdl/, *n.* **Robert**, 1794-1881, Australian surveyor, born in England; designer of the plan for the city of Melbourne, 1837.

Hodgkin /'hɒdʒkən/, *n.* **Alan Lloyd**, born 1914, English physiologist; Nobel prize (1963) for work on nerve impulses.

hoe /hou/, *n., v.,* **hoed, hoeing.** ◇*n.* 1. a long-handled tool with a thin, flat blade used to break up the soil. ◇*v.t., v.i.* 2. to dig, scrape, weed, cultivate, etc., with a hoe. ◇*v.* 3. **hoe in**, *Colloq.* to begin doing something (often eating) energetically. 4. **hoe into**, *Colloq.* **a.** to eat (food) heartily. **b.** to attack (a person) strongly, usu. with words. **c.** to take up (a job) with energy. [ME, from OF, from Gmc]

Hoffmann /'hɒfman/, *n.* **Ernst Theodor Wilhelm** /ˌɛənst ˌteɪəˈdɔ 'vɪlhɛlm/, 1776-1822, German writer, musician, painter, and jurist; famous for his fantastic tales.

hog /hɒg/, *n., v.,* **hogged, hogging.** ◇*n.* 1. a pig, esp. a male whose testicles have been removed. 2. *Colloq.* a selfish, greedy, or filthy person. 3. **go the whole hog**, *Colloq.* to do completely and thoroughly. ◇*v.t.* 4. *Colloq.* to take more than one's share of. [OE *hogg*]

Hogan /'hougən/, *n.* **Paul** ('*Hoges*'), born 1940, Australian comic actor.

Hogarth /'hougaθ/, *n.* **William**, 1697-1764, English painter and engraver, noted for his moral and satirical works. —**Hogarthian**, *adj.*

hogget /'hɒgət/, *n.* (the meat of) a young sheep, from ten months to the cutting of its first two adult teeth.

hogmanay /ˌhɒgmə'neɪ, 'hɒgmənei/, *n. Scot* (*oft. cap.*) New Year's Eve. [OF *aguillanneuf* New Year's Eve; orig. unknown]

hogshead /'hɒgzhɛd/, *n.* 1. a measure of volume in the imperial system, equal to 52 gallons (approx. 236.4 litres). 2. a container (esp. of beer or cider) of approximately this volume. [ME *hoggeshed*, lit., hog's head; unexplained]

hogwash /'hɒgwɒʃ/, *n.* meaningless talk.

hoi polloi, *n.* the common people (sometimes preceded by *the*). [Gk: the many]

hoist /hɔɪst/, *v.t.* 1. to raise or lift, esp. by some mechanical device. 2. *Colloq.* to steal, esp. from a shop. 3. *Colloq.* to throw. ◇*n.* 4. an apparatus for hoisting, e.g. a lift or a clothes hoist. 5. the act of hoisting. [later form of d. *hoise*]

Hokkaido /hɒ'kaɪdou/, *n.* a large island in northern Japan. Pop. 5 678 000 (1986 est.); 78 485 km². *Cap.:* Sapporo. Formerly, **Yezo**.

Hokonui /houkə'nui/, *adj.* relating to a geological period in NZ which corresponds with the Triassic and Jurassic periods.

hokum /'houkəm/, *n. US Colloq.* 1. nonsense. 2. elements of low comedy or farce in a play, etc. [b. HOCUS-POCUS and BUNKUM]

Holbein /'hɒlbaɪn/, *n.* 1. **Hans** ('*the Elder*'), c. 1460-1524, German painter. 2. his son, **Hans** ('*the Younger*'), 1497?-1543, German painter, important portraitist of the European Renaissance; court painter to Henry VIII.

hold[1] /hould/, *v.,* **held;** *held* or (*old forms*) **holden; holding;** *n.* ◇*v.t.* 1. to have or keep in the hand; grasp. 2. to set aside; retain. 3. to bear or support with the hand, arms, etc., or by any means. 4. to keep in a particular state, relation, etc.: *We could hold the enemy in check.* 5. to keep (a person) from going free; detain: *They held him for three days.* 6. to bind: *I will hold him to his promise.* 7. to engage in; carry on; pursue: *They will hold a meeting.* 8. to have the ownership or use of; occupy: *He will hold office.* 9. to contain: *This bottle holds two litres.* 10. to think or believe: *to hold a belief.* 11. to regard or consider: *She holds him responsible; I hold that dear.* 12. *Law.* (of a court) to decide. ◇*v.i.* 13. to stay in a particular state, relation, etc.: *Please hold still.* 14. to remain fast; cling: *The anchor holds.* 15. to keep a grasp on something. 16. to keep one's firm or loyal position. 17. to be in force: *The rule does not hold.* 18. to stop (usu. as a command). ◇**19.** Some special uses are:
hold down, to continue to hold (a position, job, etc.), esp. in spite of difficulties.
hold forth, to speak long and loudly about something.

hold good, to be true.
hold in, to check; restrain.
hold it, to stop; wait.
hold off, 1. to keep apart or at a distance. 2. to keep from doing something.
hold on, 1. to keep a firm hold on something. 2. to continue; persist. 3. *Colloq.* to stop or wait (mainly as a command).
hold one's own, to keep one's position or condition despite difficulties.
hold one's tongue / peace, to keep silent.
hold out, 1. to offer or present. 2. to stretch forth. 3. to last: *I hope the bread holds out till Monday.* 4. to refuse to yield or submit.
hold over, to keep for future action; postpone.
hold to, to keep to, or abide by: *I'm holding to my resolution.*
hold up, 1. to display. 2. to delay. 3. to stop by force in order to rob.
hold water, 1. to not let water run through. 2. to prove sound or true: *Mr Black's claims will not hold water.*
hold with, to agree with; approve of: *I don't hold with the new policy.*
◇*n.* 20. the act or way of holding firmly by a grasp of the hand or by some other physical means; grasp; grip: *take hold*; *a wrestling hold.* 21. something to hold a thing by, e.g. a handle. 22. a controlling force: *to have a hold on someone.* 23. *Archaic.* a place strengthened against attack. [OE h(e)aldan] **– holder,** *n.*

hold² /hoʊld/, *n. Naut.* the inside of a ship below the deck, esp. part used for storage. [var. of HOLE]

Holden /ˈhoʊldən/, *n.* **Sir Edward Wheewall**, 1885–1947, Australian company director; one of the founders of Holden's Motor Body Builders in 1917, later known as General Motors-Holden's Ltd.

holdfast /ˈhoʊldfɑːst/, *n.* 1. something used to hold a thing in place. 2. *Bot.* a sucker-like organ attaching a plant to something.

Holdfast Bay, *n.* the site of the first settlement in SA, in that area which is now known as Glenelg.

holding /ˈhoʊldɪŋ/, *n.* (oft. pl.) property owned, esp. stocks and shares or land.

holding company, *n.* a company able to control or earn income from other companies either by controlling their boards of directors, or by owning shares in those companies.

hold-up /ˈhoʊld-ʌp/, *n. Colloq.* 1. the forcible stopping and robbing of a person, bank, etc. 2. a delay; stoppage.

hole /hoʊl/, *n., v.,* **holed, holing.** ◇*n.* 1. an opening through anything. 2. a hollow place in a solid body. 3. a home dug in the ground by an animal; burrow. 4. a small, shabby or dirty house, town, etc.: *This place is a hole!* 5. *Colloq.* an awkward or embarrassing situation: *He found himself in a hole.* 6. *Colloq.* a fault or flaw: *They will pick holes in our plan.* 7. *Golf.* **a.** a small cavity or cup in the ground into which the ball is to be hit. **b.** any of the sections of a course, each with a tee, fairway and green: *They're on the 17th hole.* ◇*v.t.* 8. to make a hole or holes in. 9. to put or drive into a hole. ◇*v.* 10. **hole up**, **a.** (of an animal) to go into a hole for the winter. **b.** to hide (often from the police). [OE *hol* hole, cave, den] **– holey,** *adj.*

hole in the heart, *n.* a condition, often present at birth, in which one heart chamber has an abnormal opening in its wall.

holey dollar, *n.* (formerly) a silver dollar from which the centre had been removed, making two separate coins. See **dump²**. Also, **holy dollar**.

holiday /ˈhɒlədeɪ/, *n.* 1. a day on which ordinary business is stopped, often in memory of some event, person, religious feast, etc. 2. (oft. pl.) a break from work oft. involving a trip away from home; vacation. ◇*adj.* 3. relating to or suited to a holiday: *a holiday frame of mind.* ◇*v.i.* 4. to take a holiday: *She will holiday on the Gold Coast.* [OE *hāligdæg* holy day]

holiness /ˈhoʊlinəs/, *n.* 1. the state or character of being holy; sanctity. 2. (cap.) a title of the pope, and formerly also of other high church officials, etc. (preceded by *his* or *your*).

Holinshed /ˈhɒlɪnʃɛd/, *n.* **Raphael**, died c. 1580, history writer; his *Chronicles of England, Scotlande, and Irelande* (1577) are the source for several of Shakespeare's plays.

holland /ˈhɒlənd/, *n.* a type of coarse linen fabric, used for clothes, window blinds, etc.

Holland¹ /ˈhɒlənd/, *n.* **Sir Sidney George**, 1893–1961, NZ National Party politician; prime minister 1949–57.

Holland² /ˈhɒlənd/, *n.* → the **Netherlands**.

holler /ˈhɒlə/, *v.i., v.t.* 1. to cry aloud or shout (something). ◇*n.* 2. a loud cry of pain, surprise, to attract attention, etc. [F *holà* stop]

hollow /ˈhɒloʊ/, *adj.* 1. having a hole or space within; not solid; empty. 2. having a depression or dip: *a hollow surface.* 3. (of the cheeks or eyes) sunken. 4. (of sound) dull; muffled; not resonant. 5. without real worth, false or insincere; vain: *a hollow victory*; *hollow praise.* 6. hungry. ◇*n.* 7. an empty space within anything; a hole or depression. 8. valley: *the hollow of a hill.* ◇*v.t., v.i.* 9. to make or become hollow. ◇*adv.* 10. *Colloq.* completely: *He was beaten hollow.* [OE *holh* hollow (place)]

holly /ˈhɒli/, *n., pl.* **-lies.** 1. a European tree or shrub with shiny, sharp-edged leaves and small, whitish flowers followed by bright red berries. 2. the leaves and berries of this plant, oft. used for decoration at Christmas time. [OE *holegn*]

Holly /ˈhɒli/, *n.* **Buddy** (*Charles Harden Holley*), 1936–59, US pop singer, guitarist and composer; influential songwriter.

hollyhock /ˈhɒlihɒk/, *n.* a commonly grown tall plant with showy flowers of various colors. [ME]

Hollywood /ˈhɒliwʊd/, *n.* the northwestern part of Los Angeles, California; centre of the US film industry.

Holmes /hoʊmz/, *n.* **Sherlock**, a fictional detective in many mystery stories by Sir Arthur Conan Doyle.

Holmes à Court /'houmz ə kɔːt/, n. **Robert** (*Michael Robert Hamilton Holmes à Court*), 1937-90, Australian financier.

holmium /'hɒlmiəm/, n. a rare-earth element. *Symbol:* Ho; *at. no.:* 67; *at. wt:* 164.93. [NL; named after STOCKHOLM]

holo-, a word part meaning 'whole' or 'entire', as in *holocaust*. [Gk, combining form of *hólos*]

holocaust /'hɒləkɒst, -kɔːst/, n. **1.** great or total destruction of life, esp. by fire. **2.** (*cap.*) **the Holocaust**, the mass murder of Jews by the Nazis. [Gk *holókauston* a burnt offering]

Holocene /'hɒləsin/, adj. *Geol.* of or relating to the Recent period. [HOLO- + -CENE]

hologram /'hɒləgræm/, n. a negative produced by holography.

holograph /'hɒləgræf/, adj. **1.** Also, **holographic** /hɒlə'græfɪk/. wholly written by the person in whose name it appears: *a holograph letter*. ◇n. **2.** a holograph book or document. [LL, from Gk]

holography /hɒ'lɒgrəfi/, n. a form of photography in which no lens is used and in which a photographic plate records the interference pattern between two parts of a laser beam. The result is a plate which when exposed to bright light seems to reproduce a three-dimensional image. – **holographic**, adj.

Holst /hɒlst/, n. **Gustav Theodore** 1874-1934, English composer of operas, orchestral and chamber music; wrote *The Planets* (1917).

Holstein /'houlstaɪn/, n. a district in northern West Germany at the base of the peninsula of Jutland; a former duchy. See **Schleswig-Holstein**.

holster /'houlstə/, n. a leather case for a gun, attached to a belt or saddle. [Swed]

Holt /hɒlt/, n. **Harold Edward**, 1908-67, Australian Liberal politician; prime minister 1966-67.

Holtermann /'hɒltəmən/, n. **Bernhardt Otto**, 1838-85, Australian goldminer, born in Germany; largest specimen of reef gold then known in the world discovered on his claim in 1872.

holus-bolus /ˌhoulǝs-'boulǝs/, adv. *Colloq.* all at once or all together.

holy /'houli/, adj., **-lier, -liest**, n., pl. **-lies**. ◇adj. **1.** specially recognised as set aside to a god; consecrated: *a holy day*. **2.** given over to the service of God, the Church, or religion: *a holy man*. **3.** of religious character, purity, etc.: *a holy love*. **4.** deserving deep respect: *a holy shrine*. ◇n. **5.** a holy place or thing. [OE *hālig, hǣleg*]

Holy Alliance, n. a league formed by the principal sovereigns of Europe (without the pope and the rulers of Britain and Turkey) in 1815 after the fall of Napoleon, with the professed object of Christian brotherhood, but the practical object of repressing revolution.

Holy City, n. a city regarded as particularly sacred by followers of a religion, as Jerusalem by Jews and Christians.

Holy Communion, n. **1.** → **communion** (def. 3b). **2.** *Relig.* a ceremony in which bread and wine are shared in commemoration of the Lord's Supper. See **Eucharist, mass**[2].

Holy Ghost, n. → **Holy Spirit**.

Holy Grail, n. (in medieval legend) a cup or chalice used by Jesus at the Last Supper, and in which Joseph of Arimathaea received the last drops of Jesus' blood at the cross; subsequently sought by many knights.

Holyoake /'hɒliouk/, n. **Sir Keith Jacka**, 1904-83, NZ National Party politician; prime minister 1957 and 1960-72; governor-general 1977-80.

holy of holies, n. **1.** a place of special sacredness. **2.** the inner chamber of a Jewish temple.

holy orders, n. **1.** the rank or position of an ordained Christian minister. **2.** the major ranks of the Christian ministry.

Holy Roman Empire, n. the empire in western and central Europe which began with the coronation of Otto the Great, king of Germany, as Roman emperor in 962, and ended with the renunciation of the Roman imperial title by Francis II in 1806, regarded as the continuation of the Western Empire with the pope as spiritual head. It is sometimes regarded as originating with Charlemagne, who was crowned Roman emperor in 800.

Holy See, n. the diocese, court or office of the pope.

Holy Spirit, n. the third person of the Trinity.

Holy Writ, n. the Scriptures.

homage /'hɒmɪdʒ/, n. **1.** respect given. **2.** a formal declaration by which a feudal tenant promised faith and service to his lord. [ME, from OF, from LL *homo* vassal, L man]

homburg /'hɒmbɜːg/, n. a hat with a soft top dented from front to back and a narrow brim.

home /houm/, n., adj., adv., v., **homed, homing**. ◇n. **1.** a house or other shelter that is the fixed place where a person, etc. lives. **2.** a place which has special meaning for someone, often a birthplace. **3.** (*oft. cap.*) a place of care for the homeless, sick, etc.: *old people's home*. **4.** a place to which someone or something is native. **5.** (in games) the goal; base. **6. a home away from home**, a place having the comforts of home. **7. at home**, **a.** in a situation familiar to one; comfortable. **b.** ready to receive social visits. **c.** familiar with; accustomed to (fol. by *with*). **d.** (of a football team, etc.) in one's own town or grounds. ◇adj. **8.** of, relating to, or connected with one's home, town, centre of operations, or country; domestic. **9.** that strikes to the mark aimed at; to the point: *a home truth*. **10. home and hosed**, finished successfully. ◇adv. **11.** to, towards, or at home. **12.** to the mark or point aimed at: *That statement will strike home*. **13.** *Naut.* as far as possible. **14. bring home to**, to cause (someone) to realise (something) fully: *His mother's sadness brought his misdeeds home to him*. ◇v.i. **15.** (of birds and animals) to return home from a distance. ◇v.t. **16.** to direct (something with a homing device) towards an airport, target, etc. ◇v. **17. home in on**, to find or be directed to (something) by or as if by radar. [OE *hām* home, dwelling]

home-brew /houm-'bru:/, *n.*, a home-brewed drink, esp. beer.

home economics, *n.* the art and science of making a home comfortable, including the purchase and preparation of food, the selection and making of clothing, the choice of furnishings, etc. Also, **home science**.

homeland /'houmlænd/, *n.* someone's native land.

homely /'houmli/, *adj.*, **-lier, -liest. 1.** proper or suited to the home or to ordinary life; plain; unpretentious: *a homely food.* **2.** not good-looking; plain: *a homely face.* [ME] –**homeliness**, *n.*

homeo-, variant of **homoeo-**.

homeostasis /houmiou'steisəs/, *n.* the continuing of fairly constant conditions within a body, by the coordinated working of various parts. Also, **homoeostasis**. –**homeostatic**, *adj.*

Homer /'houmə/, *n.* c. ninth century BC, Greek epic poet, reputed author of the *Iliad* and *Odyssey*.

Homeric /hou'merɪk/, *adj.* **1.** of, relating to, or suggestive of Homer, ninth century BC poet, or his poetry. **2.** heroic, epic, or on a large scale: *Homeric laughter.*

home rule, *n.* self-government in internal affairs by those living in a dependent country.

home science, *n.* → home economics.

homesick /'houmsɪk/, *adj.* longing for home.

homespun /'houmspʌn/, *adj.* **1.** (made of cloth) spun at home. **2.** plain; unpolished; simple. ◇n. **3.** cloth made at home, or of homespun yarn.

homestead /'houmsted/, *n.* the main home on a sheep or cattle station or large farm.

home stretch, *n.* **1.** the straight part of a racetrack leading to the finish line, after the last turn. Also, **home straight. 2.** *Colloq.* the last stages of any undertaking.

home truth, *n.* a disagreeable statement of fact that hurts the feelings.

home unit, *n.* **1.** one of a number of separate living quarters in the same building, each owned under separate title. **2.** a block of such units. Also, **unit**.

homeward /'houmwəd/, *adj., adv.* (directed) towards home.

homewards /'houmwədz/, *adv.* towards home.

homework /'houmwɜk/, *n.* **1.** the part of a lesson or lessons prepared outside school hours. **2. do one's homework**, *Colloq.* to do work beforehand for a meeting, etc.

homicide /'hɒməsaɪd/, *n.* **1.** the killing, lawful or unlawful, of one human being by another. **2.** a murderer. [ME, from OF, from L] –**homicidal**, *adj.*

homily /'hɒməli/, *n., pl.* **-lies. 1.** a religious talk addressed to people; a sermon. **2.** words aimed to advise or give direction. [ML, from Gk: discourse] –**homiletic**, *adj.*

homing device, *n.* the apparatus in a guided missile, aeroplane, etc., which aims it towards its objective.

homing pigeon, *n.* a pigeon trained to fly home from a distance.

hominid /'hɒmənɪd/, *n.* a member of the family including man and his manlike ancestors. Also, **hominoid**.

hominoid /'hɒmənɔɪd/, *adj.* **1.** manlike. **2.** of or relating to the category which includes man and the anthropoid apes. ◇n. **3.** a man-like creature.

homo-, a combining form meaning 'the same' (opposed to *hetero-*), as in *homocentric*. [Gk, combining form of *homós* same]

homocentric /houmou'sentrɪk/, *adj.* having or relating to the same centre; concentric.

homoeo-, a word part meaning 'similar' or 'like', as in *homoeopathy*. Also, **homeo-, homoio-**. [Gk *homoio-*, combining form of *hómoios* like]

homoeopathy or **homeopathy** /houmi-'ɒpəθi/, *n.* a method of treating disease with small amounts of drugs, which produce in a healthy person symptoms similar to those of the disease. –**homoeopathic**, *adj.* –**homoeopathist**, *n.*

homoeothermic /houmiou'θɜmɪk/, *adj.* keeping nearly the same body temperature despite changes in surrounding temperatures; warm-blooded. Also, **homothermous**.

Homo erectus /ˌhoumou ə'rektəs/, *n.* a genus, no longer living, of apelike humans; Pithecanthropus.

homogamous /hɒ'mɒgəməs/, *adj.* having flowers which do not differ sexually (opposed to *heterogamous*). [Gk *homógamos* married to the same wife]

homogeneous /houmə'dʒiniəs, hɒmə-/, *adj.* **1.** made up of parts all of the same kind. **2.** of the same kind or nature; basically alike. **3.** *Chem.* (of a mixture or solution) evenly mixed throughout. [Gk: of the same kind] –**homogeneity**, *n.*

homogenise or **homogenize** /hə'mɒdʒənaɪz/, *v.t.* **-nised, -nising. 1.** to make (something) homogeneous. **2.** to treat (milk) so that the fat globules become evenly dispersed. ◇v.i. **3.** to become homogeneous. –**homogenisation**, *n.* –**homogeniser**, *n.*

homogenous /hə'mɒdʒənəs/, *adj.* **1.** similar in structure because from the same origin. **2.** → homogeneous.

homograph /'hɒməgræf/, *n.* a word of the same written form as another, but of different origin and meaning, as *fair*[1] and *fair*[2]. –**homographic**, *adj.*

homologous /hə'mɒləgəs/, *adj.* **1.** having the same or a similar relation or relative position. **2.** *Biol.* corresponding in type of

homologous structure and in origin, but not necessarily in use: *The wing of a bird and the foreleg of a horse are homologous.* **3.** *Chem.* of the same chemical type or series, but differing by a fixed increase in certain constituents: *the alkanes are a homologous series.* [Gk: agreeing, of one mind]

homologous chromosomes, *n.pl.* pairs of similar chromosomes, one from the mother and one from the father, which pair during cell division.

homology /hə'mɒlədʒi/, *n., pl.* **-gies. 1.** the state of being homologous. **2.** *Biol.* a basic similarity of structure due to a common origin. [Gk: agreement, assent, conformity]

homolysis /hɒ'mɒləsəs/, *n.* the splitting of a molecule into two neutral atoms.

homomorphism /hoʊmoʊ'mɔfɪzəm/, *n.* **1.** *Biol.* similarity in form but not in type of structure or origin. **2.** *Zool.* similarity between the young and the adult. Also, **homomorphy.** — **homomorphic, homomorphous,** *adj.*

homonym /'hɒmənɪm/, *n.* **1.** a word like another in sound and sometimes in spelling, but different in meaning, as *meat* and *meet.* **2.** → **homophone. 3.** → **homograph.** [L: having the same name, from Gk]

homophone /'hɒməfoʊn, 'hoʊmə-/, *n.* **1.** a word pronounced the same as another, regardless of spelling as *heir* and *air.* **2.** (in writing) an element which represents the same spoken unit as another, as (usu.) English *ks* and *x.* — **homophonic,** *adj.*

Homo sapiens /ˌhoʊmoʊ 'sæpiɛnz, -iənz/, *n.* the single surviving species of the genus *Homo;* modern human beings. [NL, from L *homo* man + *sapiens* intelligent, wise]

homosexual /hoʊmoʊ'sɛkʃuəl, hoʊmə-/, *adj.* **1.** relating to or showing homosexuality. ◇*n.* **2.** a homosexual person, esp. a male.

homosexuality /ˌhoʊmoʊsɛkʃu'ælətɪ, ˌhoʊmə-/, *n.* sexual feeling for a person of the same sex as oneself.

homozygote /hoʊmoʊ'zaɪgoʊt, hoʊmə-/, *n.* an organism with identical pairs of genes with respect to any given pair of hereditary characters, and therefore breeding true for those characteristics. — **homozygous,** *adj.*

homunculus /hɒ'mʌŋkjələs/, *n., pl.* **-li** /-laɪ/. a small human; dwarf. [L: little man]

hon., *Abbrev.* honorary.

Hon, *Abbrev.* Honourable.

Honduras /hɒn'djʊərəs/, *n.* a republic in Central America, on the Caribbean Sea, bordered by Guatemala, El Salvador and Nicaragua. Pop. 4 657 000 (1987 est.); 112 088 km². *Languages:* Spanish, also English. *Currency:* lempira. *Cap.:* Tegucigalpa. — **Honduran,** *n., adj.*

hone /hoʊn/, *n., v.,* **honed, honing.** ◇*n.* **1.** a fine dense stone, esp. one for sharpening razors. ◇*v.t.* **2.** to sharpen on or as if on a hone. **3.** to cut back; trim. [OE *hān*-stone, rock]

Honecker /'hoʊnəkə/, *n.* **Erich** /'ɛrɪk/, born 1912, East German statesman; elected head of state of East Germany in 1976.

honest /'ɒnəst/, *adj.* **1.** honorable in principles, intentions, and actions; upright. **2.** showing honor and fairness. **3.** got or acquired fairly: *honest money.* **4.** truthful; candid. **5. make an honest woman of,** *Colloq.* to marry. [ME, from L *honestus* honorable, worthy, virtuous]

honestly /'ɒnəstli/, *adv.* **1.** with honesty. ◇*interj.* **2.** (an exclamation used to emphasise the honesty of one's intentions, statements, etc.). **3.** (an expression of annoyance).

honesty /'ɒnəsti/, *n.* **1.** the quality of being honest. **2.** truthfulness or sincerity. **3.** a plant bearing purple flowers and disc-shaped seed pods with a satiny membrane.

honey /'hʌni/, *n.* **1.** a sweet, sticky fluid produced by bees from the nectar collected from flowers. **2.** something sweet, delicious, or delightful. **3.** *Colloq.* a person or thing which draws admiration: *That machine is a honey.* **4.** sweet one; darling. ◇*adj.* **5.** of or like honey; sweet; dear. [OE *hunig*]

honeybee /'hʌnibi/, *n.* a bee that collects and stores honey.

honeycomb /'hʌnikoʊm/, *n.* **1.** a structure of wax containing rows of six-sided cells, made by bees for keeping honey, pollen and bee eggs. **2.** anything having this structure. ◇*adj.* **3.** like honeycomb in structure or appearance. ◇*v.t.* **4.** to make like a honeycomb; pierce with many holes. [OE *hunigcamb*]

honeydew /'hʌnidju/, *n.* **1.** a sweet material which passes out from the leaves of certain plants in hot weather. **2.** sugary material produced by aphids, etc.

honeydew melon, *n.* a sweet-flavored, green-fleshed melon with a smooth, white skin.

honeyeater /'hʌniˌitə/, *n.* any of many, mainly Australasian birds with a beak and tongue able to get nectar from flowers.

honeymoon /'hʌnimun/, *n.* **1.** a holiday spent by a husband and wife after their wedding. **2.** any period of happy relationship. ◇*v.i.* **3.** to spend one's honeymoon (usu. fol. by *in* or *at*). [traditionally referred to an equation between the changes of love and the phases of the moon]

honeysuckle /'hʌnisʌkəl/, *n.* **1.** a type of climbing shrub grown for its sweet-smelling white, yellow, or red tube-shaped flowers. **2.** → **banksia.** [OE *hunisūce* honeysuck + *-el*]

hongi /'hɒŋi/, *n. NZ.* a Maori greeting, characterised by touching or rubbing noses. [Maori]

Hong Kong /hɒŋ 'kɒŋ/, *n.* Also, **Hongkong.** a British crown colony in south-eastern China, comprising the island of Hong Kong (83 km²) and the adjacent mainland; due to revert to China in 1997. Pop. 5 602 000 (1987 est.); 1031 km². *Cap.:* Victoria.

Honiara /hɒni'arə/, *n.* the capital of the Solomon Islands in the southern Pacific, on Guadalcanal Island. Pop. 30 499 (1986 est.).

honk /hɒŋk/, *n.* **1.** the cry of the wild goose. **2.** any similar sound, as a motor-car horn. ◇*v.i.* **3.** to make a honk. [imitative]

honky-tonk /ˈhɒŋkɪ-tɒŋk/, *adj., n. Music.* (of or relating to) a style of ragtime pianoplaying. [orig. uncert.]

Honolulu /hɒnəˈluːluː/, *n.* a seaport in the Hawaiian Islands, on the island of Oahu; capital of Hawaii. Pop. 372 330 (1986 est.).

honor *or* **honour** /ˈɒnə/, *n.* **1.** high public respect; fame; glory: *a roll of honor.* **2.** good name or reputation, for worthy or proper behavior: *Her honor is at stake!* **3.** a source of credit or pride: *to be an honor to one's family.* **4.** a show of respect: *to be received with honor.* **5.** special favor; privilege: *I have the honor of your company.* **6.** (*usu. pl.*) high rank, or distinction: *political honors.* **7.** a title of respect, esp. of certain judges (preceded by *His, Your,* etc.). **8.** honest and moral character or principles: *a man of honor.* **9.** (*pl.*) (in universities) an academic standard gained in a degree examination, higher than that needed for a pass degree. **10. do honor to, a.** to show respect to. **b.** to be a credit to. **11. do the honors,** to act as host. **12. on one's honor,** accepting personal responsibility for one's actions or the truthfulness of one's words. ◇*v.t.* **13.** to hold in high respect; revere. **14.** to treat with honor. **15.** to place honor upon. **16.** to keep or fulfil: *to honor a promise.* **17.** to show a polite regard for: *to honor an invitation.* **18.** to accept and pay (a cheque, etc.) when due. [ME, from OF, from L: repute]

honorable *or* **honourable** /ˈɒnərəbəl/, *adj.* **1.** in accordance with principles of honor; upright: *an honorable man.* **2.** of high office or nobility, illustrious; distinguished. **3.** (*cap.*) a title given to certain high officials: *the honorable member.*

honorarium /ɒnəˈrɛərɪəm/, *n., pl.* **-rariums, -raria** /-ˈrɛərɪə/. a payment given in recognition of professional services on which no price is set. [L: honorary]

honorary /ˈɒnərəri/, *adj.* **1.** given for honor only: *an honorary title.* **2.** holding a title or position given for honor only: *an honorary president.* **3.** (of a position, job, etc.) unpaid: *the honorary secretary of the committee.* **4.** given, made, or serving as a sign of honor: *an honorary gift.* ◇*n.* **5.** a specialist working in a public hospital. [L: relating to honor]

honorific /ɒnəˈrɪfɪk/, *adj.* **1.** doing or giving honor. ◇*n.* **2.** (in certain languages, as Chinese and Japanese) a class of forms used to show respect, esp. in conversation. **3.** a title of respect, as *Doctor, Professor, Rt Hon.* [L]

Hons, *Abbrev.* Honors.

Honshu /ˈhɒnʃuː/, *n.* the chief island of Japan. Pop. 106 200 000 (1988); 230 124 km². Also, **Hondo.**

hood /hʊd/, *n.* **1.** a soft covering for the head and neck, sometimes joined to a garment. **2.** something looking like this, as a hood-shaped petal, etc. **3.** a piece of hood-shaped material, worn with an academic gown, the color and material of the lining depending on the degree held and the university by which the degree was given. **4.** the folding roof of a convertible car. **5.** *Colloq.* a criminal. [OE *hōd*] **—hooded,** *adj.*

-hood, a suffix forming abstract nouns of state, condition, character, nature, etc., or a body of persons of a particular character or class: *childhood, likelihood, priesthood, sisterhood.* [OE *hād* condition, state, etc.]

Hood[1] /hʊd/, *n.* **1. Thomas,** 1799–1845, English poet and humorist. **2. Robin.** → **Robin Hood.**

hoodlum /ˈhʊdləm/, *n.* **1.** a person breaking the law; ruffian. **2.** a wild, noisy, or rough child or young person. [orig. uncert.]

hoodwink /ˈhʊdwɪŋk/, *v.t.* **1.** to deceive; humbug. **2.** to cover or hide. **—hoodwinker,** *n.*

hoof /hʊf/, *n., pl.* **hoofs, hooves,** *v.* ◇*n.* **1.** the horny covering protecting or covering the foot in certain animals, as the ox, horse, etc. **2.** the entire foot of a horse, donkey, etc. **3.** a hoofed animal; one of a group (herd). **4.** *Colloq.* (*joc.*) the human foot. **5. on the hoof,** (of sheep, cattle, etc.) alive. ◇*v.i.* **6. hoof it,** *Colloq.* to walk. [OE *hōf*] **—hoofed,** *adj.*

hook /hʊk/, *n.* **1.** a curved or angular piece of metal, etc., for catching, pulling, or supporting something. **2.** something that catches; a trap. **3.** something curved or bent like a hook, e.g. a sharp bend in a road, a curved spit of land, etc. **4.** *Cricket, Golf, etc.* the manner of hitting the ball so that it curves. **5.** *Boxing.* a curving blow made with the arm bent: *a right hook.* **6.** *Music.* the line joined to the stem of a quaver, semiquaver, etc. **7. by hook or by crook,** by any means, fair or unfair. **8. hook, line, and sinker,** completely. **9. off the hook, a.** out of trouble. **b.** (of a telephone) with the receiver lifted. **10. put the hooks into,** *Colloq.* to borrow from. ◇*v.t.* **11.** to seize, fasten, or catch hold of and draw in with or as if with a hook. **12.** to make hook-shaped; crook. **13.** *Boxing.* to strike with a hook. **14.** *Cricket, Golf.* to hit (the ball) with a hook. ◇*v.i.* **15.** to become fastened by or as if by a hook; join on. **16.** to curve or bend like a hook. **17.** *Cricket, Golf.* (of the player) to make a hooking stroke. [OE *hōc*]

hookah /ˈhʊkə/, *n.* a pipe with a long tube by which the smoke of tobacco, etc., is drawn through a container of water and cooled. Also, **hooka.** [Ar: box, vase, pipe for smoking]

hook and eye, a fastening arrangement used on clothes, etc., consisting of a hook on one part, which catches on to a bar or loop on the other part.

hooked /hʊkt/, *adj.* **1.** bent like a hook; hook-shaped. **2.** made with or having a hook. **3.** caught, as a fish. **4.** *Colloq.* addicted; obsessed (usu. fol. by *on*). **5.** *Colloq.* married.

hooker /ˈhʊkə/, *n.* **1.** *Rugby.* the central forward in the front row of the scrum, whose job it is to pull back the ball with his foot. **2.** *Colloq.* a prostitute. [HOOK + -ER[1]]

hook-up /ˈhʊk-ʌp/, *n.* **1.** a combination; connection. **2.** *Radio, TV.* a link-up of different stations for a special broadcast.

hookworm /ˈhʊkwɜːm/, *n.* any of certain bloodsucking worms, living in the intestine of man and other animals.

hooky

hooky /'hʊki/, *n. Colloq.* absence from school without permission: *to play hooky*. Also, **hookey**.

hooligan /'hulɪɡən/, *Colloq.* ◇*n.* **1.** a young street rough; hoodlum. ◇*adj.* **2.** of or like hooligans. [var. of *Houlihan*, Irish surname which came to be associated with rowdies] – **hooliganism**, *n.*

hoop /hup/, *n.* **1.** a circular band or ring of metal, wood, or other stiff material. **2.** such a band to hold together the staves of a cask, barrel, etc. **3.** a large ring of wood or plastic for children's games. **4.** something like a hoop. **5.** one of the iron arches used in croquet. **6.** a circular band of stiff material used to expand a woman's skirt. **7.** a large ring, with paper stretched over it through which circus animals, etc., jump. **8. go through the hoop**, to go through a bad time. **9. jump through hoops**, to obey without question. **10. put through (the) hoops**, to force into a series of often unreasonable tests. ◇*v.t.* **11.** to bind or fasten a hoop. [late OE *hōp*] – **hooped**, *adj.*

hoopla /'huplə/, *n.* a game in which hoops are thrown in an attempt to encircle objects offered as prizes.

hoop pine, *n.* a valuable softwood timber tree of northern Australia and New Guinea.

hooray /həˈreɪ, ˈhureɪ/, *interj.* **1.** (a cry of joy, approval, or the like). ◇*v.i.* **2.** to shout 'hooray'. Also, **hoorah**, **hurray**.

hooroo /'huru/, *interj. Colloq.* goodbye. Also, **hooray**, **ooray**, **ooroo**.

hoot /hut/, *v.i.* **1.** to cry out or shout, esp. in disapproval. **2.** (of an owl) to utter its cry. **3.** to make a similar sound. **4.** to blow a horn or factory hooter; honk. **5.** to laugh. ◇*v.t.* **6.** to attack with shouts of disapproval. **7.** to drive (*out, away, off*, etc.) by hooting. **8.** to express in hoots. ◇*n.* **9.** the cry of an owl. **10.** any similar sound. **11.** a cry or shout, esp. of disapproval. **12.** *Colloq.* a thing of no value: *I don't give a hoot*. **13.** an amusing or funny thing. [ME *huten*]

hooter /'hutə/, *n.* **1.** someone who hoots. **2.** a siren as used in factories, schools, etc. **3.** a horn on a motor vehicle. **4.** *Colloq.* the nose.

hoover /'huvə/, *n.* **1.** → **vacuum cleaner**. ◇*v.t.* **2.** to clean with a hoover. [Trademark]

Hoover /'huvə/, *n.* **Herbert Clark**, 1874–1964, 31st president of the US 1929–33.

hooves /huvz/, *n.* a plural of **hoof**.

hop¹ /hɒp/, *v.*, **hopped**, **hopping**, *n.* ◇*v.i.* **1.** to jump; move by jumping with all feet off the ground. **2.** to spring or jump on one foot. **3.** to make a flight or trip. **4.** to limp. ◇*v.t.* **5.** *Colloq.* to jump off (something raised), or over (a fence, etc.) **6.** *Colloq.* to get into or out of a car, train, etc. (fol. by *in*, *on* or *off*). ◇*v.* **7. hop it**, *Colloq.* to go away (usu. as a command). **8. hop into**, *Colloq.* **a.** to set about (something) energetically: *He hopped into the job at once*. **b.** to put (clothes) on quickly: *He hopped into his coat*. **9. hop up and down**, *Colloq.* to express anger. **10. hop to**, to come

hopping-mouse

or act quickly (oft. as command): *hop to it*. ◇*n.* **11.** the act of hopping. **12.** a jump on one foot. **13.** *Colloq.* the flight of an aeroplane. **14.** *Colloq.* a dance. **15. on the hop**, **a.** unprepared: *caught on the hop*. **b.** busy, moving. [OE *hoppian*]

hop² /hɒp/, *n.* **1.** a climbing plant, which has female flowers in cone-like forms, and bunches of small male flowers. **2.** (*pl.*) the dried ripe cones of the female flowers of the hop plant, used in beer making, medicine, etc. **3.** (*pl.*) → **beer**. [ME *hoppe*, from MD]

hope /houp/, *n.*, *v.*, **hoped**, **hoping**. ◇*n.* **1.** the expectation of something desired. **2.** one occasion of such expectation or desire: *a hope of success*. **3.** a ground for expecting something: *There is no hope of his recovery*. **4.** a person or thing that expectations are centred in: *the hope of the family*. **5. some hope!** (an expression of hopelessness, resignation, or disbelief). ◇*v.t.* **6.** to look forward to with desire. **7.** to trust in the truth of a matter (with a clause): *I hope that you are satisfied*. ◇*v.i.* **8.** to have an expectation of something desired: *We continue to hope*. **9. hope against hope**, to continue to hope, although the occasion points against such hope. [OE *hopa*]

Hope /houp/, *n.* **1. A**(lec) **D**(erwent), born 1907, Australian poet and critic, noted for his classical style; author of the poetry collection *The Wandering Islands* (1955). **2. Bob** (*Leslie Townes Hope*), born 1903 in Britain, US comedian.

hopeful /'houpfəl/, *adj.* **1.** expressing hope: *hopeful words*. **2.** promising advantage or success: *a hopeful outlook*. ◇*n.* **3.** a promising young person. – **hopefulness**, *n.*

hopefully /'houpfəli/, *adv.* **1.** in a hopeful way. **2.** *Colloq.* it is hoped: *Hopefully the drought will soon end*.

hopeless /'houpləs/, *adj.* **1.** giving no hope; desperate: *a hopeless case*. **2.** without hope; despairing: *hopeless grief*. **3.** not able to be fixed or solved: *a hopeless problem*. **4.** not able to learn, perform, act, etc.; incompetent: *a hopeless singer*. – **hopelessness**, *n.*

Hopeless /'houpləs/, *n.* **Mount**, a small rise in north-eastern SA, near Lake Eyre; a landmark for explorers. [named by EJ EYRE in 1840 due to a decision to leave such a desolate region]

Hopkins /'hɒpkɪnz/, *n.* **1. Gerard Manley**, 1844–89, English poet and Jesuit priest; devised sprung rhythm in his poetry. **2. Livingston**, 1846–1927, Australian cartoonist, watercolorist, and etcher, born in the US; worked with the Sydney *Bulletin* using the pseudonym of 'Hop'.

hoplite /'hɒplaɪt/, *n.* a heavily armed foot soldier of ancient Greece. [Gk]

hopper /'hɒpə/, *n.* **1.** someone or something that hops. **2.** any one of various jumping insects, as grasshoppers, cheese maggots, etc. **3.** a funnel-shaped container in which materials are stored for a short time and later released through the bottom.

hopping-mouse /'hɒpɪŋ-maʊs/, *n.* any of various native rodents, which hop rapidly like

hopping-mouse   499   **horrid**

a kangaroo, are active by night, and dig burrows, living mostly in central and western Australia, e.g. the brown **dargawarra** or **spinifex hopping-mouse**, the fawn-colored **oorarrie**, and the **wilkintie**.

hopsack /'hɒpsæk/, *n.* **1.** a coarse, jute material for making sacks. **2.** a fabric with a coarse surface, used to make clothing. Also, **hopsacking**.

hopscotch /'hɒpskɒtʃ/, *n.* a children's game in which the player hops from one square to another of a diagram drawn on the ground, without touching a line. [HOP¹ + *scotch* to cut, score]

Horace /'hɒrəs/, *n.* (*Quintus Horatius Flaccus*), 65–8 BC, Roman lyric poet and satirist.

Horatius /hə'reɪʃɪəs/, *n. Rom Legend.* a hero celebrated for his defence of the bridge over the Tiber against the Etruscans.

horde /hɔd/, *n., v.*, **horded, hording.** ◇*n.* **1.** (*oft. insulting*) a great company; multitude. **2.** a nomadic group esp. of Mongols. **3.** a moving pack of animals, insects, etc. ◇*v.i.* **4.** to gather in a horde. [Pol, from Turkic: camp]

horehound /'hɔhaʊnd/, *n.* a herb containing a bitter juice which is used in medicine. [OE *hārhūne*, from *hār* grey + *hūne* horehound]

horizon /hə'raɪzən/, *n.* **1.** the line or circle where the earth and sky appear to meet (**apparent** or **visible horizon**). **2.** the limit or range of understanding, knowledge, or the like. **3.** *Geol.* a plane in rock strata with particular features, esp. fossil species. **4.** one of the series of distinctive layers found in a vertical cross-section of any well-developed soil. [L, from Gk: bounding circle, horizon]

horizontal /hɒrə'zɒntl/, *adj.* **1.** at right-angles to the upright (vertical). **2.** lying down. **3.** near, on, or parallel to the horizon. **4.** measured or contained in a plane parallel to the horizon: *a horizontal distance*. ◇*n.* **5.** a horizontal line, plane, position, etc.

hormone /'hɔmoʊn/, *n.* **1.** any of various substances formed in the endocrine glands, which activate certain other organs when carried to them in body fluids. **2.** an artificial substance having the same effect. [Gk: setting in motion] — **hormonal,** *adj.*

Hormuz /'hɔmuz/, *n.* **Strait of,** a strait between Iran and Oman, connecting the Persian Gulf and the Gulf of Oman. Also, **Ormuz.**

horn /hɔn/, *n.* **1.** a hard, often curved and pointed, hollow growth (usu. one of a pair) on the head of certain mammals, as cattle, sheep, etc. (**true horn**). **2.** each of the pair of solid, usu. branched bony growths, (antlers) on the head of a deer, which usu. drop off each year. **3.** an outgrowth from the head of an animal looking like a horn, as a feeler, tentacle, crest, etc. **4.** the substance of which true horns are made. **5.** any similar substance, as that of hoofs, nails, etc. **6.** something formed from or looking like the hollow horn of an animal: *a drinking horn.* **7.** *Music.* a wind instrument, originally formed from the hollow horn of an animal but now usu. made of brass or other metal, e.g. French horn. **8.** *Colloq.* the trumpet or saxophone. **9.** an instrument for sounding a warning signal: *a motor horn.* **10.** *Elect.* → **tweeter. 11.** anything having the outward shape of a horn, e.g. the pommel of a saddle, the pointed end of a crescent moon, etc. **12. draw/pull one's horns in, a.** to save; cut down on one's activities. **b.** to withdraw; retreat. ◇*v.t.* **13.** to wound with the horns; gore. ◇*v.i.* **14. horn in,** *Colloq.* to push oneself forward on others: *Can I horn in on your conversation?* ◇*adj.* **15.** made of horn. [OE *horn*] — **horned,** *adj.*

Horn /hɔn/, *n.* **the** → **Cape Horn.**

hornbill /'hɔnbɪl/, *n.* any of several large tropical birds, characterised by a very large bill with a horny growth on the top.

hornblende /'hɔnblɛnd/, *n.* any of the common dark-colored aluminous types of amphibole mineral. [G]

Horne /hɔn/, *n.* **Donald Richmond,** born 1921, Australian writer, academic, editor and arts administrator; author of *The Lucky Country* (1964).

hornet /'hɔnət/, *n.* **1.** a large, strong, wasp having a very severe sting. **2. mad as a hornet,** *Colloq.* very angry. [OE *hyrnet(u)*]

hornet's nest, *n.* a great deal of trouble; hostility.

hornpipe /'hɔnpaɪp/, *n.* **1.** an English folk clarinet with an ox horn to hide the reed and another one to form the bell. **2.** a lively dance (originally to hornpipe music) popular among sailors. **3.** a piece of music for or in the style of such a dance.

horn-rimmed /'hɔn-rɪmd/, *adj.* (of spectacles) with frames made of horn, tortoiseshell, or a plastic looking like horn.

horny /'hɔni/, *adj.*, **-nier, -niest. 1.** horn-like through hardening; callous: *horny hands.* **2.** consisting of a horn or a hornlike substance. **3.** having a horn, horns or hornlike structures. **4.** *Colloq.* sexually excited; randy. — **horniness,** *n.*

horology /hə'rɒlədʒi/, *n.* the art or science of making timepieces or of measuring time. — **horologist,** *n.*

horoscope /'hɒrəskoʊp/, *n.* **1.** the art or practice of foretelling future events by looking at the stars and planets. **2.** a diagram of the heavens used for this purpose. **3.** a forecast of the future made by this method. [OE, from L, from Gk: sign in the ascendant at time of birth]

horrendous /hɒ'rɛndəs, hə-/, *adj.* dreadful; horrible. [L: bristle, shudder]

horrible /'hɒrəbəl/, *adj.* **1.** causing or tending to cause horror; dreadful: *a horrible sight.* **2.** very unpleasant; deplorable: *horrible conditions.* [ME, from OF, from L: terrible, fearful] — **horribly,** *adv.*

horrid /'hɒrəd/, *adj.* **1.** such as to cause horror; dreadful. **2.** *Colloq.* very unpleasant: *horrid weather.* [L: bristling, rough]

horrific /hɒˈrɪfɪk, hə-/, *adj.* causing horror. [L]

horrify /ˈhɒrɪfaɪ/, *v.t.*, **-fied, -fying.** to cause to feel horror; shock greatly. [L: cause horror]

Horrocks /ˈhɒrəks/, *n.* **John Ainsworth**, 1818–46, Australian pioneer explorer and pastoralist, born in England; first person to use camels for exploration.

horror /ˈhɒrə/, *n.* **1.** great fear or disgust: *to draw back in horror.* **2.** anything that creates such a feeling: *the horrors of war.* **3.** *Colloq.* something considered ugly or bad: *That hat is a horror.* **4.** a strong or painful dislike: *a horror of violence.* **5.** (*pl.*) *Colloq.* **a.** a great feeling of fear: *Heights give me the horrors.* **b.** → **delirium tremens.** [L]

hors d'oeuvre /ɔː ˈdɜːv/, *n.* a small piece of food served before a meal; appetiser; canapé. [F: aside from (the main body of the) work]

horse /hɔːs/, *n., pl.* **horses**, (*esp. collectively*) **horse**, *v.*, **horsed, horsing.** ◇*n.* **1.** a large, solid-hoofed, four-legged animal used for riding or pulling or carrying loads. **2.** a male horse, fully-grown and past its fourth birthday. **3.** any animal of the horse family which includes the ass, zebra, etc. **4.** something on which a person rides, sits, or exercises as if on a horse's back: *a rocking horse.* **5.** a leather-covered block, used for jumping and other gymnastic exercises. **6.** a frame, block, etc., with legs on which something is placed or supported. **7.** *Colloq.* → **heroin.** ◇**8.** Some special uses are: **a dark horse**, a person of unknown ability. **eat like a horse**, to have a big appetite. **from the horse's mouth**, from a reliable source.
hold one's horses, to hold back.
horse of another colour, a different thing altogether.
look a gift-horse in the mouth, to criticise a gift; accept a gift ungratefully.
get on one's high horse, to become offended, esp. because of possible hurt to one's pride. ◇*v.t.* **9.** to set (someone) on horseback. ◇*v.i.* **10. horse about/around**, to act or play roughly. [OE *hors*]

horse chestnut, *n.* **1.** a tree having large leaves, groups of white, red, or yellow flowers and shiny brown nutlike seeds. **2.** the seed itself.

horseflesh /ˈhɔːsfleʃ/, *n.* **1.** the flesh of a horse. **2.** horses collectively, esp. for riding, racing, etc.

horsefly /ˈhɔːsflaɪ/, *n., pl.* **-flies.** → **march fly.**

horse latitudes, *n. pl.* belts of northern and southern latitudes lying between the area of westerly winds and the area of the trade winds.

horse mackerel, *n.* any of several fish having a curving body and sharply spined fins, found in Australian waters and the Pacific coast of the US.

horseplay /ˈhɔːspleɪ/, *n.* rough noisy play.

horsepower /ˈhɔːspaʊə/, *n.* a unit of measurement of power, or rate of doing work, in the imperial system, equal to 745.7 watts.

horserace /ˈhɔːsreɪs/, *n.* a race between horses with riders (jockeys). **—horseracing,** *n.*

horseradish /ˈhɔːsrædɪʃ/, *n.* **1.** a plant, grown for its strongly flavored root. **2.** its root, used as a sauce and in medicine.

horse sense, *n. Colloq.* **1.** practical, common sense. **2.** the ability to judge horseflesh, to ride well, etc.

horseshoe /ˈhɔːsʃuː/, *n.* **1.** a U-shaped iron plate nailed to a horse's hoof to protect it. **2.** something shaped like a horseshoe. **3.** a sign of good luck. ◇*adj.* **4.** with the shape of a horseshoe.

horseshoe crab, *n.* any of various crabs with a shell shaped rather like a horseshoe; king crab.

Horsham /ˈhɔːʃəm/, *n.* a city in central western Vic, on the Wimmera River; commercial centre for much of the Wimmera district. Pop. 12 174 (1986).

horsy /ˈhɔːsi/, *adj.*, **-sier, -siest. 1.** relating to, like, or of the nature of a horse: *horsy talk.* **2.** dealing with or interested in horses, horseracing, etc. **—horsiness,** *n.*

hortatory /ˈhɔːteɪtəri, ˈhɔːtətri/, *adj.* encouraging; urging to some course of behavior or action: *a hortatory speech.* Also, **hortative,** /ˈhɔːtətɪv/. [LL: encouraging]

horticulture /ˈhɔːtəkʌltʃə/, *n.* **1.** the growing of fruit, vegetables, and flowers, etc. for sale to the public. **2.** the science or art of growing fruit, vegetables, flowers or ornamental plants. [*horti-* (combining form of L *hortus* garden) + CULTURE] **—horticultural,** *adj.* **—horticulturist, horticulturalist,** *n.*

Horus /ˈhɔːrəs/, *n. Egyptian Myth.* a god of the sky, the son of Osiris and Isis, usu. shown with a falcon's head. [Gk *Hōros* from Egyptian, lit. hawk]

hosanna /hoʊˈzænə/, *interj.* **1.** (an exclamation, orig. a request to God to be saved, used in praise of God or Christ). ◇*n.* **2.** a cry of 'hosanna'. **3.** a shout of praise or love. [LL, from Gk, from Heb: save, pray!]

hose /hoʊz/, *n., pl.* **hose**, (*Archaic*) **hosen**, *v.*, **hosed, hosing.** ◇*n.* **1.** clothing for the foot and lower part of the leg; stockings. **2.** a covering for the legs and thighs, as tights, formerly worn by men. **3.** a tube, able to be bent, for carrying water, etc.: *a garden hose.* ◇*v.t.* **4.** to water, wash, or wet by means of a hose. [OE]

hosiery /ˈhoʊzəri/, *n.* **1.** hose or stockings of any kind. **2.** the business of someone who sells stockings, etc.

hosp., *Abbrev.* hospital.

hospice /ˈhɒspəs/, *n.* **1.** a house of shelter or rest for pilgrims, strangers, etc., esp. one kept by a religious order. **2.** a hospital for dying patients. [F, from L: hospitality]

hospitable /hɒsˈpɪtəbəl/, *adj.* **1.** giving a generous welcome to guests or strangers: *a hospitable city.* **2.** showing acceptance; open (fol. by *to*): *hospitable to new ideas.* [F (obs.), from L: receive as a guest]

hospital /ˈhɒspɪtl/, n. **1.** an establishment in which sick or injured people are given medical or surgical treatment. **2.** a similar establishment for the care of animals. [ME, from OF, from LL: inn, from L: pertaining to guests, hospitable]

hospitality /hɒspəˈtælətɪ/, n., pl. **-ties.** the act of treating guests or strangers with generosity and kindness.

host¹ /hoʊst/, n. **1.** someone who receives guests in his or her own home or elsewhere: *the host at a party*. **2.** the landlord of an inn. **3.** an animal or plant from which a parasite gains food. ◇v.t. **4.** to act as a host (def. 1). **5.** to compere (a television show, etc.). [ME, from OF, from L: host, guest, stranger]

host² /hoʊst/, n. a great number of persons or things: *a host of details*. [ME, from OF, from ML: army, from L: stranger, enemy]

hostage /ˈhɒstɪdʒ/, n. a person given or held in the hope of forcing certain actions to take place, as the payment of money (ransom), etc. [ME, from OF: guest, from L]

hostel /ˈhɒstəl, hɒsˈtɛl/, n. **1.** an establishment where people can live and eat at rather low cost, such as one for students, nurses, etc. **2.** → **youth hostel.** [ME, from OF: guest] —**hostelling,** n.

hostess /ˈhoʊstɛs/, n. **1.** a woman who receives guests; female host. **2.** → **air hostess. 3.** a paid dancing partner.

hostile /ˈhɒstaɪl/, adj. **1.** opposed in feeling, action, or character; unfriendly; antagonistic: *a hostile crowd*. **2.** of or characteristic of an enemy: *hostile ground*. [late ME, from L: enemy]

hostility /hɒsˈtɪlətɪ/, n., pl. **-ties. 1.** unfriendliness; enmity; antagonism. **2.** an unfriendly act. **3.** (pl.) acts of warfare.

hot /hɒt/, adj., **hotter, hottest,** adv. ◇adj. **1.** having or giving heat; having a high temperature: *a hot stove*. **2.** having and sensing a feeling of great bodily heat. **3.** (of food, etc.) having an effect as of burning on the tongue, skin, etc.: *a hot curry*. **4.** having or showing strong feeling; ardent; excited: *hot temper*. **5.** violent, angry, or forceful: *the hottest battle*. **6.** strong or fresh, as a scent or trail. **7.** new; fresh: *hot off the press*. **8.** close: *to be hot on someone's heels*. **9.** (of colors) mainly red. **10.** *Games*. close to the object or answer: *You're getting hot*. **11.** popular: *the hot favorite (horse)*. **12.** (of motor cars) tuned for high speeds: *a hot rod*. **13.** *Colloq*. recently stolen: *hot goods*. **14.** radioactive, esp. to a harmful degree. ◇**15.** Some special uses are:
hot and bothered, upset; flustered.
hot under the collar, angry; annoyed.
in hot water, *Colloq*. in trouble.
not so/too hot, *Colloq*. **1.** not very good. **2.** unwell.
sell/go like hot cakes, to sell or be removed quickly.
◇adv. **16.** in a hot manner. [OE *hāt*]

hot air, n. *Colloq*. empty, exaggerated talk or writing.

hotbed /ˈhɒtbɛd/, a place of rapid growth, esp. of something bad: *a hotbed of crime*.

hot-blooded /ˈhɒt-blʌdəd/, adj. adventurous; excitable; impetuous.

hotchpotch /ˈhɒtʃpɒtʃ/, n. **1.** an unordered mixture; jumble. **2.** a thick soup made from meat and vegetables. Also, **hodgepodge.** [rhyming var. of *hotchpot*, from OF; stew]

hot cross bun, n. a bun with a cross on it, eaten chiefly on Good Friday.

hot dog, n. a hot frankfurter or sausage, esp. as served in a split bread roll with mustard or sauce.

hotel /hoʊˈtɛl/, n. a building providing shelter and food for guests; public house. [F: hostel]

hotelier /hoʊˈtɛlɪə/, n. someone who manages a hotel or hotels.

hotfoot /ˈhɒtfʊt/, v.i. **1.** Also, **hotfoot it.** to move with great speed. ◇adv. **2.** with great speed.

Hotham /ˈhɒθəm/, n. **Sir Charles,** 1806-55, English colonial administrator; governor of Vic 1855.

hothead /ˈhɒthɛd/, n. someone who is easily angered.

hot-headed /ˈhɒt-hɛdəd/, adj. hot or fiery in spirit or temper; rash. —**hot-headedness,** n.

hothouse /ˈhɒthaʊs/, n. **1.** a heated greenhouse for the growth of tender plants. ◇adj. **2.** of or relating to a delicate plant grown in a hothouse. **3.** *Colloq*. delicate; over-protected.

hot money, n. *Colloq*. money in a money market which is likely to be withdrawn quickly following small changes in market conditions.

hotplate /ˈhɒtpleɪt/, n. an electrically heated metal plate or ring, usu. on top of an electric stove.

hotpot /ˈhɒtpɒt/, n. meat cooked with potatoes, etc., in a covered pot.

hot rod, n. *Colloq*. an (old) car whose engine has been altered for increased speed.

hot seat, n. **1.** the electric chair. **2.** *Colloq*. a position in which there are difficulties or dangers.

hot-shot /ˈhɒt-ʃɒt/, adj. **1.** having great abilities. ◇n. **2.** one who has great abilities, and often likes to make them known.

hot spot, n. **1.** an unpleasantly hot place. **2.** *Geol*. a place of high heat near the earth's surface. **3.** a place where dangerous political tensions exist, which may develop into revolution, war, etc. **4.** a nightclub, or the like.

Hottentot /ˈhɒtəntɒt/, n. a member of an African people of yellowish brown color and low stature, sometimes said to be of mixed Bushman and Bantu origin. [D (Afrikaans); imitative of the language]

hot-water bottle, n. a flat oblong container, usu. of rubber, which is filled with hot water and used to warm parts of the body, or a bed.

Houdini /huːˈdiːnɪ/, n. **Harry** (*Erich Weiss*), 1874-1926, US magician and escape artist.

hound /haʊnd/, *n.* **1.** a dog of any various breeds used in hunting. **2.** any dog. **3.** *Colloq.* a mean, worthless fellow. **4. ride to hounds,** to foxhunt. ◊*v.t.* **5.** to hunt or track with hounds, or as a hound does; pursue. **6.** to worry continually. [OE *hund*]

hound's-tooth /'haʊndz-tuθ/, *adj.* **1.** printed, decorated, or woven with a pattern of broken checks. ◊*n.* **2.** a pattern of contrasting jagged checks.

hour /aʊə/, *n.* **1.** a space of time equal to one 24th part of a mean solar day; 60 minutes. **2.** a limited period of time. **3.** a particular time: *his hour of victory*. **4.** the present time: *the man of the hour.* **5.** the time shown by a timepiece: *What is the hour?* **6.** (*pl.*) time spent in work, study, etc.: *office hours.* **7.** (*pl.*) the usual time of going to bed and getting up: *to keep late hours.* **8.** the distance normally covered in an hour's travelling. **9.** *Astron.* a unit of measure representing 15 degrees, or the 24th part of a great circle. **10. one's hour, a.** the time to die. **b.** a very important moment. **11. the small hours,** the hours just after midnight. [ME, from OF, from L: time, season, hour, from Gk]

hourglass /'aʊəglas/, *n.* **1.** an instrument for measuring time, consisting of two bulbs of glass joined by a narrow passage through which a quantity of sand (or mercury) runs in just an hour. ◊*adj.* **2.** having a narrow waist.

houri /'hʊəri, 'hʊri/, *n., pl.* **-ris.** any beautiful woman, esp. of eastern origin. [F, from Pers, from Ar: having black eyes like a gazelle]

hourly /'aʊəli/, *adj.* **1.** of, relating to, happening, or done each hour. **2.** frequent; continual. ◊*adv.* **3.** every hour. **4.** frequently.

house /haʊs/, *n., pl.* **houses** /'haʊzəz/, /haʊz/, *v.,* **housed, housing**; /haʊs/, *adj.* ◊*n.* **1.** a building for human living. **2.** a place of rest, etc., as of an animal. **3.** a household. **4.** a building for any purpose: *a house of worship.* **5.** (an audience in) a theatre. **6.** an inn. **7.** a family seen as consisting of ancestors and descendants: *the house of Windsor.* **8.** the building in which a legislative group meets. **9.** the group itself: *the House of Representatives.* **10.** a business establishment: *the house of Dior.* **11.** a special group in a school, containing children of all ages and classes. **12.** (the members of) a boarding-house forming part of a school. **13.** any of the 12 divisions of the zodiac. ◊**14.** Some special uses are:
the little house, *Colloq.* an outside toilet.
keep house, to look after a home.
keep open house, to be very welcoming to guests.
like a house on fire, very well; with great speed.
bring down the house, to be very well received.
on the house, free, as a gift from the management.
the house, *Colloq.* the main home on a sheep or cattle station.
◊*v.t.* **15.** to provide with a house. **16.** to give shelter to; lodge. **17.** to put in a safe place. ◊*v.i.* **18.** to take shelter; dwell. ◊*adj.* **19.** of or relating to a house. [OE *hūs*] **—houseless,** *adj.*

house arrest, *n.* enclosed in one's own house (by an authority): *He's being held under house arrest.*

houseboat /'haʊsboʊt/, *n.* a boat fitted up for use as a floating home but not suited to rough water.

housebreaker /'haʊsbreɪkə/, *n.* someone who breaks into and enters a house to rob it. **—housebreaking,** *n.*

housebroken /'haʊsbroʊkən/, *adj.* able to act in a manner suited to being indoors.

housecoat /'haʊskoʊt/, *n.* a dresslike garment of one piece, worn about the house.

housefly /'haʊsflaɪ/, *n., pl.* **-flies.** a common two-winged insect, found in nearly all parts of the world, which feeds on rubbish, food, etc., and spreads disease.

house guest, *n.* a guest who is living at one's home for a short period of time.

household /'haʊshoʊld/, *n.* **1.** all the people of a house; a family, including servants, etc. ◊*adj.* **2.** of or relating to a household; domestic: *household furniture.* **3.** used for looking after and keeping a house: *household polish.* **4.** of or relating to the royal household: *the household guard.* **5.** very common.

householder /'haʊshoʊldə/, *n.* **1.** someone who owns or lives in a house. **2.** the head of a family.

household word, *n.* a well-known phrase or word.

housekeeper /'haʊskipə/, *n.* someone in charge of the cleaning, cooking, etc. for a household, esp. when paid as an employee.

houselights /'haʊslaɪts/, *n.pl.* the lights of a theatre, cinema, etc., which are lowered during a performance.

housemaid /'haʊsmeɪd/, *n.* a female servant employed in general work in a household.

House of Assembly, *n.* the lower house in the SA and Tas parliaments.

House of Commons, *n.* the elective house of the British parliament.

House of Lords, *n.* the non-elective house of the parliament of Great Britain and Northern Ireland; the highest court of appeal.

House of Representatives, *n.* **1.** the lower legislative branch of the federal parliament of Australia, elected on a population basis and having approx. twice as many members as the Senate. **2.** a similar body elsewhere, as Mexico, Japan, etc.

houseproud /'haʊspraʊd/, *adj.* overly careful about the appearance of one's house.

Houses of Parliament, *n. Brit.* **1.** the upper and lower chambers of the British legislature. **2.** the building in which they meet.

house-train /'haʊs-treɪn/, *v.t.* to train (an animal) so that it can be kept indoors.

house-warming /'haʊs-wɔmɪŋ/, *n.* a party given to celebrate moving into a new house.

housewife /ˈhaʊswaɪf/, n., pl. **-wives** /-waɪvz/. 1. a woman, esp. a married one, who is in charge of a household. 2. a small case for needles, thread, etc. —**housewifely**, adj.

house wine, n. bulk wine served by a club or restaurant, often bearing the establishment's label.

housie-housie /ˈhaʊzi-haʊzi/, n. a gambling game in which players put markers on a card of numbered squares according to the numbers drawn and announced by a caller. Also, **housey-housey**, **housie**.

housing /ˈhaʊzɪŋ/, n. 1. something serving as a shelter, covering, or similar; a shelter; lodging. 2. houses collectively. 3. the supplying of houses for the community: *the housing of immigrants*. 4. the covering or framework which protects or supports part of a machine such as a bearing, pump or wheel: *the housing of an engine*.

Housman /ˈhaʊsmən/, n. **A(lfred) E(dward)**, 1859–1936, English poet and classical scholar; works include *A Shropshire Lad* (1896).

Houston /ˈhjustən/, n. a city in the US, in south-eastern Texas; a port on a ship canal, about 80 km from the Gulf of Mexico. Pop. 1 728 910 (1986 est.).

Houtman Abrolhos /ˈhaʊtmən əˈbrɒlɒs/, n.pl. three groups of islands and coral reefs in the Indian Ocean west of Geraldton, WA. [named in 1619 after Frederik de *Houtman* a Dutch sea captain]

hove /hoʊv/, v. past tense and past participle of **heave**.

hovea /ˈhoʊviə/, n. an Australian plant with clusters of small purple pea-shaped flowers.

hovel /ˈhɒvəl/, n. 1. a small, mean-looking house or hut. 2. an open shed, as for sheltering cattle, tools, etc. [ME *hovel*, *hovyl*; orig. uncert.]

Hovell /ˈhɒvəl/, n. **William Hilton**, 1786–1875, Australian explorer, born in England; accompanied Hamilton Hume on an overland expedition to Port Phillip 1824.

hover /ˈhɒvə/, v.i. 1. to hang suspended in the air: *a hovering bird*. 2. to linger near by: *to hover around a sick child*. 3. to remain in an uncertain state; waver: *hovering between life and death*. ◇n. 4. the act or state of hovering. [ME *hoveren*; orig. uncert.] —**hoverer**, n. —**hoveringly**, adv.

hovercraft /ˈhɒvəkrɑːft/, n. a vehicle able to travel over the ground or water on a cushion of air.

how /haʊ/, adv. 1. in what way or manner; by what means: *How did it happen?* 2. to what extent, degree, etc.: *How much?* 3. by what unit: *How do you sell these apples — by the kilogram?* 4. in what state or condition: *How are you?* 5. for what reason; why. 6. to what effect or with what meaning: *How do you mean?* 7. what? 8. (used to add intensity): *How well I remember*. 9. **and how**, *Colloq.* very much indeed; certainly. ◇conj. 10. concerning the condition or state in which: *She wondered how she appeared to a stranger*. 11. concerning the extent or degree to which: *I don't mind how long you take*. [OE *hū*]

Howard /ˈhaʊəd/, n. 1. **Catherine**, c. 1520–42, fifth wife of Henry VIII; beheaded. 2. **John Winston**, born 1939, Australian federal Liberal politician; Leader of the Opposition 1985–89.

howbeit /haʊˈbiət/, adv. nevertheless. [ME *how be hit* however it may be]

howdah /ˈhaʊdə/, n. a seat, usu. with railing and canopy, placed on the back of an elephant. [Hind, from Ar]

Howe /haʊ/, n. **Jack** (*John Robert Howe*), 1855–1922, Australian champion shearer.

Howe family /haʊ/, n. a family of Australian pioneer printers and publishers including 1. **George**, 1769–1821, first editor and printer in Australia, born on St Christopher Island; issued the first book printed in Australia *New South Wales General Standing Orders* (1802), and the first newspaper, the *Sydney Gazette and New South Wales Advertiser* (1803). 2. **Robert**, 1795–1829, son of George, born in London; published the first periodical in Australia, the *Australian Magazine* (1821), and the first hymn book, *An Abridgement of the Wesleyan Hymns* (1821).

however /haʊˈevə/, conj. 1. nevertheless; yet; in spite of that. ◇adv. 2. to whatever extent or degree; no matter how (far, much, etc.): *However hard he tries, he'll never win*. 3. in whatever condition, state, or manner: *Go there however you like*. 4. Also, **how ever**. (interrogatively) how in any circumstances: *How ever did you manage?* [ME]

howl /haʊl/, v.i. 1. to utter a loud, long, sad cry, as that of a dog or wolf. 2. to make a similar cry in distress, pain, rage, etc.; wail. 3. to make a sound like an animal howling: *The wind is howling*. ◇v.t. 4. to utter as a howl. 5. to drive or force by howls: *They howled him out of town*. 6. **howl down**, to prevent (someone) from speaking by talking loudly: *They wouldn't listen to his excuse, but just howled him down*. ◇n. 7. the cry of a dog, wolf, etc. 8. a cry or wail, as of pain or rage. 9. a sound like wailing: *the howl of the wind*. [ME; imitative]

howler /ˈhaʊlə/, n. *Colloq.* an especially glaring and stupid mistake.

howling /ˈhaʊlɪŋ/, adj. *Colloq.* enormous; very great: *His play was a howling success*.

howsoever /haʊsoʊˈevə/, adv. 1. to whatever extent or degree. 2. in whatever manner.

hoy /hɔɪ/, interj. 1. (an exclamation to attract attention.) ◇n. 2. **give a hoy**, to call out; attract attention. [ME]

hoyden /ˈhɔɪdən/, n. a rude or ill-bred girl; tomboy. [orig. uncert.]

HP /eɪtʃˈpi/, *Abbrev.* 1. hire purchase. 2. Also, **h.p.** horsepower.

HQ /eɪtʃˈkju/, *Abbrev.* headquarters. Also, **h.q.**

hr, *Abbrev.* hour.

HR, *Abbrev.* House of Representatives.

HRH, /eɪtʃ ɑr 'eɪtʃ/ *Abbrev.* His, or Her, Royal Highness.

HSC /eɪtʃ es 'si/, *Abbrev.* Higher School Certificate.

ht, *Abbrev.* height.

Huang He /hwʌŋ 'heɪ/, *n.* a river flowing from western China into an inlet of Huang Hai. About 4345 km. Formerly, **Hwang Ho** or **Huang Ho**. English, **Yellow River**.

hub /hʌb/, *n.* **1.** the central part of a wheel into which the spokes are inserted. **2.** the part in a central position around which all else revolves: *the hub of the universe.*

hubble-bubble /'hʌbəl-bʌbəl/, *n.* → **hookah**.

hubbub /'hʌbʌb/, *n.* a loud, confused noise, as of many voices; tumult.

hubris /'hjubrəs/, *n.* an inflated sense of self, leading to one's downfall. Also, **hybris**. [Gk] **— hubristic,** *adj.*

huckster /'hʌkstə/, *n.* a seller of small articles; a hawker. Also, **hucksterer**. [ME]

huddle /'hʌdl/, *v.,* **-dled, -dling,** *n.* ◇*v.t.* **1.** to heap or crowd together. **2.** to draw (oneself) closely together; nestle (oft. fol. by *up*). **3.** to do hastily and carelessly (oft. fol. by *up, over,* or *together*). ◇*v.i.* **4.** to gather or crowd together in a confused mass. ◇*n.* **5.** a confused heap, mass, or crowd; a jumble. **6.** confusion or disorder. **7.** *Colloq.* a meeting held in secret. [orig. uncert.] **— huddler,** *n.*

Hudson /'hʌdsən/, *n.* **Henry**, died 1611?, English navigator and explorer in North America.

Hudson Bay, *n.* a large inland sea in northern Canada. About 1368 km long; about 966 km wide; about 1 036 000 km^2.

hue /hju/, *n.* **1.** that property of color by which various parts of the spectrum can be told apart, such as red, blue, etc. **2.** a variety of a color; a tint: *pale hue.* **3.** a color: *all the hues of the rainbow.* [OE *hīw* form, appearance, color] **— hued,** *adj.*

hue and cry, *n.* any public outcry or alarm against or over something.

huff /hʌf/, *n.* **1.** a sudden surge of anger; fit of resentment: *to leave in a huff.* ◇*v.i.* **2.** to puff or blow. [imitative] **— huffish,** *adj.* **— huffy,** *adj.*

hug /hʌg/, *v.,* **hugged, hugging,** *n.* ◇*v.t.* **1.** to clasp tightly in the arms, esp. with fondness; embrace. **2.** to hold firmly or fondly to: *to hug an opinion.* **3.** to keep close to, as in sailing, horseracing or going along: *to hug the shore; to hug the rails.* ◇*n.* **4.** a tight clasp with the arms; a warm embrace. [? ON: *console*]

huge /hjudʒ/, *adj.,* **huger, hugest. 1.** very large in quantity, amount, or extent: *a huge mountain.* **2.** large in scope, character, etc. [ME; orig. uncert.] **— hugeness,** *n.*

Hughes /hjuz/, *n.* **1. Thomas**, 1822–96, English novelist; author of *Tom Brown's Schooldays* (1857). **2. William Morris** ('Billy', 'the Little Digger'), 1862–1952, Australian federal politician; prime minister, representing Labor, 1915–16, the National Labor Party 1916–17, and the Nationalists 1917–23.

Hugo /'hjugoʊ/, *n.* **Victor Marie**, 1802–85, French poet, novelist, and dramatist; leading exponent of romanticism; wrote *Les Misérables* (1862).

Huguenot /'hjugənoʊ/, *n.* a French Protestant, esp. of the 16th and 17th centuries.

hui /'hui/, *n. NZ.* a Maori community gathering. [Maori]

hula-hula /hulə-'hulə/, *n.* a type of Hawaiian dance, with complicated arm movements, which tells a story in mime. Also, **hula**. [Hawaiian]

hulk /hʌlk/, *n.* **1.** the body of an old ship. **2.** a vessel specially built to serve as a storehouse, prison, etc., which is not used for sea service. **3.** a large or unwieldy person or mass of anything. **4.** a burnt-out or stripped vehicle, building, or similar. [OE *hulc,* probably from ML, from Gk: trading vessel]

hulking /'hʌlkɪŋ/, *adj.* bulky; heavy and clumsy. Also, **hulky**.

hull[1] /hʌl/, *n.* **1.** the husk, shell, or outer covering of a seed or fruit. **2.** the calyx (ring of leaves) of certain fruits, as the strawberry and raspberry. **3.** any covering or envelope. ◇*v.t.* **4.** to remove the hull of. [ME; OE *hulu* husk, pod] **— huller,** *n.*

hull[2] /hʌl/, *n.* **1.** the frame or body of a ship, not including masts, yards, sails, and rigging. **2.** *Aeron.* the boatlike fuselage (body) of a flying boat on which the plane lands or takes off. [orig. uncert.]

hullabaloo /hʌləbə'lu/, *n.* a loud noise or disturbance; an uproar.

hullo /'hʌloʊ, hə'loʊ/, *interj., n., v.i.* → **hello**.

hum /hʌm/, *v.,* **hummed, humming,** *n., interj.* ◇*v.i.* **1.** to make a low, continuous, droning sound. **2.** to give forth an indistinct sound of mingled voices or noises. **3.** to make an indistinct sound in hesitation, embarrassment, dissatisfaction, etc. **4.** to sing with closed lips and without words. **5.** *Colloq.* to be busy and active: *The shop hummed all day.* ◇*v.t.* **6.** to sound or sing by humming. **7.** to bring, put, etc., by humming: *to hum a child to sleep.* ◇*n.* **8.** the act of humming, an indistinct murmur. ◇*interj.* **9.** (an inarticulate sound uttered in hesitation, dissatisfaction, etc.) [ME; imitative] **— hummer,** *n.* **— humming,** *adj.*

human /'hjumən/, *adj.* **1.** of, relating to, or characteristic of mankind: *human nature; the human race.* **2.** having the weaknesses and faults of ordinary people: *human error.* ◇*n.* **3.** a human being. [L: *of a man*]

human being, *n.* a member of the human race, *Homo sapiens*.

humane /hju'meɪn/, *adj.* **1.** characterised by tenderness and compassion for the suffering or distressed: *humane feelings.* **2.** (of branches of learning or literature) tending to refine; civilising: *humane studies.* [var. of HUMAN]

humanism /'hjumənɪzm/, n. 1. any system of thought or values based on human effort or achievements rather than religion. 2. devotion to or study of the humanities. 3. (*sometimes cap.*) the studies, principles or culture of the Humanists (def. 4).

humanist /'hjumənəst/, n. 1. a student of human nature or affairs. 2. someone devoted to or familiar with the humanities. 3. a classical scholar. 4. (*sometimes cap.*) one of the scholars of the Renaissance who studied and gained an understanding of the cultures of ancient Rome and Greece. 5. (*sometimes cap.*) someone who favors the thought and practice of humanism (def. 1). —**humanistic**, adj.

humanitarian /hjumænə'teəriən/, adj. 1. having regard to the interests of all mankind; philanthropic. 2. relating to moral or religious principles. ◇n. 3. someone who professes moral or religious attitudes to humanity. —**humanitarianism**, n.

humanity /hju'mænəti/, n., pl. **-ties**. 1. the human race; mankind. 2. the condition or quality of being human; human nature. 3. the quality of being humane; kindness; benevolence. 4. **humanities**, **a.** the study of Latin and Greek classics. **b.** the study of literature, philosophy, art, etc., as distinct from social and physical sciences. [ME, from F, from L]

humanly /'hjumənli/, adv. 1. in a human manner; by human means. 2. according to human knowledge or ability. 3. from a human point of view.

human nature, n. 1. the quality basic to all people because of their common humanity. 2. the make-up or conduct of human beings that makes them different from other animals.

humanoid /'hjumənɔɪd/, adj. 1. like a human. ◇n. 2. (in science fiction) a robot made in human form.

humble /'hʌmbəl/, adj., **-bler, -blest,** v., **-bled, -bling.** ◇adj. 1. low in position, grade, or importance, etc.; lowly: *humble origin*. 2. modest; meek; without pride. 3. courteously respectful: *in my humble opinion*. 4. low in height, level, etc. ◇v.t. 5. to lower in condition, importance, or dignity; abase. 6. to make meek: *to humble one's heart*. [ME, from OF, from L: low, humble]

humble pie, n. 1. *Obs.* pie made of the innards of deer, etc. 2. **eat humble pie**, to be forced to apologise humbly; be humiliated. [ME *umbles* innards]

Humboldt Current /'hʌmboult kʌrənt/, n. a cold ocean current of the southern Pacific, flowing north along the coasts of Chile and Peru. Also, **Peru Current**.

humbug /'hʌmbʌg/, n., v., **-bugged, -bugging.** n. 1. *Colloq.* the quality of falseness or deception. 2. *Colloq.* someone who misleads others by deceit; cheat; impostor. 3. a type of hard, peppermint sweet. ◇v.t. 4. to deceive by humbug; delude. ◇v.i. 5. to practise humbug. [orig. unknown] —**humbugger**, n.

humdinger /'hʌmdɪŋə/, n. *Colloq.* someone or something quite remarkable.

humdrum /'hʌmdrʌm/, adj. 1. lacking variety; dull: *a humdrum existence*. ◇n. 2. a dull person, talk or routine. [varied reduplication of HUM]

Hume /hjum/, n. **Hamilton**, 1797–1873, Australian explorer. See **Hovell**.

Hume Highway, n. a highway connecting Sydney and Melbourne, an inland route. Over 900 km. [named after Hamilton HUME who pioneered the route in 1824 with William HOVELL]

humerus /'hjumərəs/, n., pl. **-meri** /-məraɪ/. 1. (in humans) the single long bone in the arm which goes from the shoulder to the elbow. 2. a similar bone in the forelimbs of other animals or in the wings of birds. [L: shoulder] —**humeral**, adj.

humid /'hjuməd/, adj. moist or damp, with liquid or vapor: *humid air*. [L: moist]

humidifier /hju'mɪdəfaɪə/, n. a device for regulating air moisture content and temperature in an air-conditioned room or building.

humidity /hju'mɪdəti/, n. 1. a damp, moist condition. 2. *Meteorol.* a condition of the atmosphere concerned with the amount of water-vapor in the atmosphere.

humiliate /hju'mɪlieɪt/, v.t., **-ated, -ating**. to lower the pride or self-respect of; mortify. [LL: humbled] —**humiliation**, n.

humility /hju'mɪləti/, n., pl. **-ties**. the quality of having a modest sense of one's own importance. [ME, from F, from L]

hummingbird /'hʌmɪŋbɜd/, n. a very small American bird with narrow wings (whose rapid movement produces a hum), slender bill, and usu. colorful feathers.

hummock /'hʌmək/, n. a small hill rising above the general level of a marshy area. —**hummocky**, adj.

humor or **humour** /'hjumə/, n. 1. the quality of being funny: *the humor of a situation*. 2. the ability to know or express what is amusing or funny: *a sense of humor*. 3. speech or writing showing humor. 4. sudden, odd behavior; whim; caprice. 5. *Physiol. Obs.* one of the four chief bodily fluids, blood, choler, phlegm, and melancholy (black bile) regarded as being responsible for a person's physical and mental constitution. 6. *Biol.* any animal or plant fluid, whether natural or diseased, such as the blood or lymph. 7. **out of humor,** displeased or dissatisfied; cross. ◇v.t. 8. to act according to the humor of; indulge: *to humor a child*. [ME, from AF, from L: moisture, liquid] —**humorless**, adj.

humorist /'hjumərəst/, n. someone who has or uses humor, particularly a writer, artist, etc.

humorous /'hjumərəs/, adj. 1. characterised by humor; amusing; funny: *the humorous side of things*. 2. having or showing humor; droll; facetious: *a humorous person*. 3. *Obs.* relating to the bodily humors.

hump /hʌmp/, n. 1. a rounded swelling on the back, as a curvature of the spine in humans or that normally present in certain humped

hump animals such as the camel and bison. **2.** a low, rounded rise of ground; hummock. **3. the hump,** *Colloq.* fit of bad humor: *to get the hump.* **4. over the hump,** over the worst part or period of a difficult, dangerous, etc., time. ◇*v.t.* **5.** to carry: *to hump the bluey.* [backformation from *humpbacked*] –**humped,** *adj.* –**humpy,** *adj.*

humpback /'hʌmpbæk/, *n.* a person with a humplike back. –**humpbacked,** *adj.*

Humphries /'hʌmfriz/, *n.* (**John**) **Barry,** born 1934, Australian actor and writer of satirical drama; best known for his character Dame Edna Everage.

humpy /'hʌmpi/, *n.* **1.** a temporary bush shelter used by Aborigines; gunyah. **2.** any rough dwelling; bush hut. [Aboriginal]

humus /'hjuməs/, *n.* the dark organic material in soils, produced by the decomposition of vegetable or animal matter, necessary to fertility and favorable moisture supply. [L: earth, ground]

Hun /hʌn/, *n.* **1.** a member of a warlike Asian people who devastated Europe in the fourth and fifth centuries. **2.** *Colloq.* a German soldier, unit, aircraft, or the like in World Wars I and II. **3.** *Colloq.* any German. [sing. of *Huns,* OE *Hūnas;* from native name]

hunch /hʌntʃ/, *v.t.* **1.** to thrust out or up in a hump: *to hunch one's back.* ◇*v.i.* **2.** to walk, sit, or stand in a bent position (usu. fol. by *up*). ◇*n.* **3.** *Colloq.* a feeling or suspicion. [apparently backformation from *hunchbacked*]

hunchback /'hʌntʃbæk/, *n.* → **humpback.** –**hunchbacked,** *adj.*

hundred /'hʌndrəd/, *n., pl.* **-dreds,** (*as after a numeral*) **-dred. 1.** a cardinal number, 10 times 10. **2.** a symbol for this number, as 100 or C. **3.** a set of a hundred persons or things. ◇*adj.* **4.** amounting to one hundred in number. [OE *hundred*]

hundredfold /'hʌndrədfoʊld/, *adj.* **1.** having one hundred parts or members. **2.** one hundred times as great or as much. ◇*adv.* **3.** in hundredfold measure.

hundreds and thousands, *n.pl.* very small, brightly colored sugary balls, used in decorating cakes, sweets etc.

hundredth /'hʌndrədθ/, *adj.* **1.** the next number after the 99th. **2.** being one of one hundred equal parts. ◇*n.* **3.** one hundredth part, esp. of one ($\frac{1}{100}$). **4.** the hundredth member of a series.

hundredweight /'hʌndrədweɪt/, *n., pl.* **-weights,** (*as after a numeral*) **-weight.** A unit of weight in the imperial system, equal to 112 lb. (approx. 50.8 kg) and, in the US, to 100 lb. (approx. 45.36 kg). *Symbol:* cwt

Hundred Years War, *n.* the series of wars between France and England from 1338 to 1453.

hung /hʌŋ/, *v.* past tense and past participle of **hang.**

Hung, *Abbrev.* **1.** Hungarian. **2.** Hungary.

Hungary /'hʌŋɡəri/, *n.* a republic in central Europe, bordered by Slovakia, Ukraine, Romania, Yugoslavia, Croatia, and Austria; part of the Austro-Hungarian Empire before its dissolution in 1918; a socialist republic 1949–89; parliamentary democracy from 1990. Pop. 10 608 000 (1987 est.); 93 036 km². *Language:* Hungarian. *Currency:* forint. *Cap.:* Budapest. Hungarian, **Magyarország.** –**Hungarian,** *adj.*

hunger /'hʌŋɡə/, *n.* **1.** a painful sensation or state of exhaustion caused by the need of or desire for food: *to collapse from hunger.* **2.** a strong or eager desire: *hunger for praise.* ◇*v.i.* **3.** to feel hunger; be hungry. **4.** to have a strong desire. [ME, OE *hungor*]

hunger strike, *n.* a consistent refusal to eat, as a protest against imprisonment, restraint, etc.

hungry /'hʌŋɡri/, *adj.,* **-grier, -griest. 1.** craving food; having a keen appetite. **2.** showing characteristics of hunger or meanness: *a lean and hungry look.* **3.** strongly or eagerly desirous: *She was hungry for learning.* **4.** marked by scarcity of food: *a hungry country.* [ME; OE *hungrig*]

hunk /hʌŋk/, *n.* a large piece or lump; a chunk: *It was a big hunk of cake.*

hunt /hʌnt/, *v.t.* **1.** to chase (game or other wild animals) with the purpose of catching or killing. **2.** to search (an area) for game. **3.** to chase with force, hostility, etc.: *He was hunted from the village.* **4.** to search for; seek; so as to obtain or find. ◇*v.i.* **5.** to take part in the chase. **6.** to make a search (oft. fol. by *for* or *after*). **7. hunt down,** to pursue with intent to kill or capture. ◇*n.* **8.** the act of hunting game or other wild animals; the chase. **9.** a group of people who meet together to hunt. **10.** a district in which hunts take place. **11.** a search; pursuit. [OE *huntian*] –**hunting,** *n.*

Hunt /hʌnt/, *n.* **1.** (**William**) **Holman,** 1827–1910, English Pre-Raphaelite painter. **2. (James Henry) Leigh,** 1784–1859, English essayist and poet.

Hunter¹ /'hʌntə/, *n.* **John,** 1737–1821, Scottish-born naval officer, governor of NSW 1795–1800.

Hunter² /'hʌntə/, *n.* a coastal river system in central eastern NSW, rising in the Mt Royal Range and flowing south to the estuary at Newcastle. [named after Governor John HUNTER]

Hunter Valley, *n.* a region on the central coast of NSW, encompassing several major cities including Maitland and Newcastle; noted for its vineyards.

hunting /'hʌntɪŋ/, *n.* any periodic variation in the speed of an engine, or in the position of the needle of a measuring instrument.

huntress /'hʌntrəs/, *n.* a woman who hunts.

huntsman /'hʌntsmən/, *n., pl.* **-men. 1.** the man in charge of the hounds during a hunt. **2.** someone who hunts game, etc.

huntsman spider, *n* any of numerous species of medium to large spiders with flattened, brown or grey, hairy bodies. See **tarantula.**

Huon pine /ˌhjuɒn 'paɪn/, *n.* a large coniferous (cone-bearing) timber tree found in Tas. [named after the river *Huon* in Tas]

hurdle /'hɜdl/, *n., v.,* **-dled, -dling.** ◇*n.*
1. a movable rectangular frame of interlaced twigs, crossed bars, or similar, used as a temporary fence over which horses or runners must leap in a race. **2. the hurdles,** a race in which such barriers are leapt. **3.** a difficult problem to be overcome; obstacle. ◇*v.t., v.i.* **4.** to leap over (a hurdle, etc.) as in a race. [OE *hyrdel*]
—**hurdler,** *n.*

hurdy-gurdy /'hɜdi-gɜdi/, *n., pl.* **-dies.**
1. a barrel organ or similar instrument played by turning a handle. **2. on the hurdy-gurdy,** *Colloq.* involved in a mindless and seemingly never-ending round of activities. [apparently imitative]

hurl /hɜl/, *v.t.* **1.** to drive or throw with great force. **2.** to state with strong feelings. [ME]

Hurley /'hɜli/, *n.* **James Francis,** 1885–1962, Australian photographer and film-maker.

hurly-burly /'hɜli-bɜli/, *n., pl.* **-burlies,** *adj.* ◇*n.* **1.** violent emotion; commotion; tumult. ◇*adj.* **2.** full of commotion; tumultuous. [modified form of *hurling and burling*]

hurray /hə'reɪ/, *interj., v.i., n.* → **hooray.** Also, **hurrah.**

hurricane /'hʌrəkən, -ɪkən/, *n.* **1.** a violent, tropical, cyclonic storm. **2.** a storm of the most intense severity. **3.** anything suggesting a violent storm. **4.** → **hurricane lamp.** [Sp, from Carib]

hurricane lamp, *n.* **1.** a kerosene lamp, the flame of which is protected by a glass chimney or other similar device. **2.** a candlestick with a chimney.

hurried /'hʌrid/, *adj.* **1.** driven or made to hurry, as a person. **2.** characterised by or done with hurry; hasty.

hurry /'hʌri/, *v.,* **-ried, -rying,** *n., pl.* **-ries.** ◇*v.i.* **1.** to move, proceed, or act with haste, often undue haste. ◇*v.t.* **2.** to drive or move (someone or something) with speed, often with confused haste. **3.** to hasten; urge forwards (oft. fol. by *up*). **4.** to force with undue haste to thoughtless action: *to be hurried into a decision.* ◇*n.* **5.** the need or desire for haste: *to be in a hurry to begin.* **6.** a hurried movement or action; haste. [orig. obscure; ? imitative]

hurt /hɜt/, *v.,* **hurt, hurting,** *n.* ◇*v.t.* **1.** to cause bodily pain to or in: *The wound still hurts him.* **2.** to harm or damage (a material object, etc.) by rough use, or otherwise: *to hurt furniture.* **3.** to harm or cause mental pain to; grieve: *to hurt someone's feelings; to hurt someone's reputation.* ◇*v.i.* **4.** to cause pain (bodily or mental): *My finger still hurts.* **5.** to cause injury, damage, or harm. ◇*n.* **6.** a blow; bodily injury. **7.** damage or harm. **8.** wounded feelings. [ME, probably from OF: strike against]

hurtle /'hɜtl/, *v.,* **-tled, -tling,** *n.* ◇*v.i.* **1.** to rush violently and noisily: *The hail hurtled down in the storm.* **2.** to resound, as in rapid motion. ◇*v.t.* **3.** to drive violently; fling; dash. **4.** to dash against; collide with. [ME; frequentative of HURT]

husband /'hʌzbənd/, *n.* **1.** the man of a married couple (correlative of *wife*). ◇*v.t.* **2.** to manage, esp. with careful economy: *to husband one's resources.* [OE *hūsbōnda,* from *hūs* house + *bōnda* householder]

husbandman /'hʌzbəndmən/, *n., pl.* **-men.** *Archaic.* a farmer.

husbandry /'hʌzbəndri/, *n.* **1.** the business of a farmer; agriculture; farming. **2.** careful or thrifty management; frugality; thrift.

hush /hʌʃ/, *interj.* **1.** (a command to be silent or quiet.) ◇*v.i.* **2.** to become or be silent or quiet. ◇*v.t.* **3.** to make silent; silence. **4.** to keep secret. **5.** to calm: *to hush someone's fears.* ◇*n.* **6.** silence or quiet, esp. after noise. ◇*adj.* **7.** *Archaic.* silent; quiet.

hush-hush /'hʌʃ-hʌʃ/, *adj. Colloq.* highly secret and private.

hush money, *n.* a payment of money used to keep someone silent about something.

husk /hʌsk/, *n.* **1.** the dry external covering of certain fruits or seeds, esp. of an ear of corn. **2.** the outer part of anything, esp. when dry or worthless. ◇*v.t.* **3.** to remove the husk from.
—**husker,** *n.*

husky[1] /'hʌski/, *adj.,* **-kier, -kiest. 1.** *Colloq.* burly; big and strong. **2.** having a semi-whispered vocal tone; somewhat hoarse. **3.** abounding in husks. **4.** like husks. [HUSK, *n.* + -Y[1]] —**huskiness,** *n.*

husky[2] /'hʌski/, *n., pl.* **-kies.** (*also cap.*) an Eskimo dog. [? a shortened var. of ESKIMO]

hussar /hə'zɑ/, *n.* (orig.) one of a body of light Hungarian cavalry formed during the 15th century. [Hung]

Hussein[1] /hu'seɪn, -'saɪn/, *n.* born 1935, became king of Jordan in 1952.

Hussein[2] /hu'seɪn/, *n.* **Saddam** /sə'dæm/, (*at-Tikriti*), born 1937, Iraqi political leader; became president in 1979; led Iraq to war with Iran 1980–90; in 1990 annexed Kuwait which led to the Gulf War of 1991.

hussy /'hʌsi, 'hʌzi/, *n., pl.* **-sies. 1.** an ill-behaved girl. **2.** a rude woman. [familiar var. of HOUSEWIFE]

hustings /'hʌstɪŋz/, *n.pl.* electioneering platform or proceedings. [ME, from Scand]

hustle /'hʌsəl/, *v.,* **-tled, -tling,** *n.* ◇*v.i.* **1.** to work quickly with great energy. **2.** to push or force one's way. ◇*v.t.* **3.** to force roughly or hurriedly: *They hustled him out of the city.* **4.** to shake or push roughly. **5.** to urge to greater efforts; hurry along. ◇*n.* **6.** energetic activity, as in work. **7.** impolite shoving, pushing, etc. —**hustler,** *n.*

hut /hʌt/, *n.* **1.** a simple, small house, as a beach hut, bushwalker's hut. **2.** (in snow country) a large building for accommodating skiers. **3.** a house for employees on a sheep or cattle station. [F, from G]

hutch /hʌtʃ/, *n.* a pen or coop for confining small animals: *a rabbit hutch.* [ME, from OF, from ML: chest]

hutkeeper /'hʌtkipə/, *n.* (formerly) **1.** a cook, caretaker, etc., of a hut used by a convict gang. **2.** an assigned man or stockman's offsider fulfilling such a function.

Hutton /'hʌtn/, *n.* **Sir Edward Thomas Henry**, 1848–1923, English army officer in Australia 1893–97, 1902–04; responsible for forming a single army out of the various state forces and for the organisation of land defence in Australia.

Hutt River Province /hʌt/, *n.* a 75 km² area of land in WA, which was declared independent by its owner, Leonard George Casley, in 1970. Neither the WA nor the Australian government recognises the province.

Huxley family /'hʌksli/, *n.* a prominent English family including **1. Thomas Henry**, 1825–95, biologist, anthropologist and philosopher in Australia 1847–50; supported the theories of Charles Darwin. **2. Aldous Leonard** /'ɔldəs ˌlenəd/, 1894–1964, son of Thomas, novelist and essayist, best known for his novel *Brave New World* (1932).

Hu Yaobang /hu jaʊ'bʌŋ/, *n.* 1915–89, Chinese statesman; general secretary of the Communist party 1980–87.

Huygens /'haɪgənz/, *n.* **Christian**, 1629–95, Dutch mathematician, physicist, and astronomer; inventor of the pendulum clock (1657). Also, **Huyghens**.

hyacinth /'haɪəsənθ/, *n.* **1.** a type of bulbous plant widely cultivated for its spikes of fragrant, white or colored, bell-shaped flowers. **2.** reddish-orange zircon. [L, from Gk: kind of flower, also a gem]

hyalo-, a word part meaning 'glass', before vowels, **hyal-**. [Gk, combining form of *hýalos*]

hybrid /'haɪbrɪd, -brəd/, *n., adj.* **1.** (offspring) having parents of different races, breeds, varieties, etc. **2.** (anything) derived from many sources, or composed of different elements: *a hybrid computer*. [L: offspring of a tame sow and wild boar, a mongrel] –**hybridism**, *n.*

Hyderabad /'haɪdərəbæd, 'haɪdrə-/, *n.* **1.** a former state in southern India; now a part of Andhra Pradesh. **2.** a city in India, the capital of Andhra Pradesh, in the western part. Pop. 2 150 000 (1981).

hydr-¹, variant of **hydro-¹**, before vowels, as in *hydrangea*.

hydr-², variant of **hydro-²**, before vowels, as in *hydrazine*.

hydra /'haɪdrə/, *n., pl.* **-dras, -drae** /-dri/. **1.** (*sometimes cap.*) any persistent evil arising from many sources or difficult to overcome. **2.** *Zool.* a type of freshwater polyp. [a monstrous serpent of Greek mythology, slain by Hercules, represented as having nine heads, each of which was replaced by two after being cut off, unless the wound was cauterised; L, from Gk: water-serpent]

hydrangea /haɪ'dreɪndʒə/, *n.* a variety of shrub which has large showy white, pink, green or blue flower clusters. [NL]

hydrant /'haɪdrənt/, *n.* an outlet, from a water main usu. in the street, for drawing water; often used for fighting fires.

hydrate /'haɪdreɪt/, *n., v.,* **-drated, -drating.** ◇*n.* **1.** any of a class of compounds containing chemically combined water, esp. salts containing water of crystallisation. ◇*v.t.* **2.** to combine chemically with water. –**hydration**, *n.* –**hydrator**, *n.* –**hydrated**, *adj.*

hydraulic /haɪ'drɒlɪk/, *adj.* **1.** operated by or employing water or other liquid. **2.** relating to water or other liquid, or to hydraulics. [L, from Gk: pertaining to the water organ, an ancient musical instrument]

hydraulic brake, *n.* a type of brake operated by fluid pressures in cylinders and connecting tubular lines.

hydraulics /haɪ'drɒlɪks/, *n.* the science dealing with the laws governing water or other liquids in motion and their applications in engineering. [pl. of HYDRAULIC]

hydrazine /'haɪdrəzin, -zaɪn/, *n.* a compound, N_2H_4, which is a weak base in solution and forms many salts resembling ammonium salts, used as a reducing agent and as a jet-propulsion fuel.

hydric /'haɪdrɪk/, *adj.* **1.** containing hydrogen. **2.** relating to an environment containing or needing a lot of moisture. See **mesic, xeric**.

hydride /'haɪdraɪd/, *n.* See **-ide**.

hydro /'haɪdroʊ/, *adj.* →**hydro-electric**.

hydro-¹, a word part meaning 'water', as in *hydrogen*. Also, **hydr-**. [Gk, combining form of *hýdōr* water]

hydro-², *Chem.* a word part often indicating combination of hydrogen with a negative element or radical as in *hydrochloric acid*. Also, **hydr-**. [combining form of HYDROGEN]

hydrocarbon /haɪdroʊ'kabən/, *n.* any of a class of organic compounds containing only hydrogen and carbon, such as methane, CH_4, ethylene, C_2H_4, acetylene, C_2H_2 (aliphatic hydrocarbons), and benzene, C_6H_6 (an aromatic hydrocarbon).

hydrocephalus /haɪdroʊ'sefələs/, *n.* an accumulation of serous fluid within the cranium, esp. in infancy, often causing great enlargement of the skull, and compression of the brain. Also, **hydrocephaly** /haɪdroʊ'sefəli/. [NL, from Gk: water in the head] –**hydrocephalic, hydrocephalous**, *adj.*

hydrochloric acid, *n.* a colorless, poisonous fuming liquid formed by the solution of hydrogen chloride in water, used extensively in chemical and industrial processes; the commercial form is muriatic acid.

hydrodynamic /ˌhaɪdroʊdaɪ'næmɪk/, *adj.* relating to forces in, or motions of, fluids.

hydrodynamics /ˌhaɪdroʊdaɪ'næmɪks/, *n.* the science of the mechanics of fluids, generally liquids.

hydro-electric /ˌhaɪdroʊ-ə'lektrɪk/, *adj.* relating to the generation and distribution of electric energy from the energy of falling water or other hydraulic source. –**hydro-electricity**, *n.*

hydrofoil /'haɪdrəfɔɪl/, *n.* **1.** one of two or more ski-like members which support the hull

hydrofoil   509   **hylo-**

of a boat above the surface of the water when a certain speed has been reached. **2.** a boat equipped with hydrofoils.

hydrogen /ˈhaɪdrədʒən/, *n.* a colorless, odorless, flammable gas, which combines chemically with oxygen to form water; the lightest of the elements. *Symbol:* H; *at. no.:* 1; *at. wt:* 1.00797. [F]

hydrogenate /haɪˈdrɒdʒəneɪt/, *v.t.*, **-nated, -nating.** to combine or treat with hydrogen: *to hydrogenate vegetable oil to fat.* — **hydrogenation,** *n.*

hydrogen bomb, *n.* a bomb whose potency is based on the release of nuclear energy resulting from the fusion of hydrogen isotopes in the formation of helium.

hydrogen bond, *n.* an important electrostatic chemical bond occurring between covalently bonded hydrogen atoms and strongly electronegative atoms such as oxygen, nitrogen, etc., as in ice, graphite, DNA, etc.

hydrogen chloride, *n.* a colorless, poisonous gas, HCl, obtained by burning hydrogen in chlorine, etc.

hydrogen ion, *n.* ionised hydrogen of the form H_2.

hydrogen ion concentration, *n.* the number of moles of hydrogen ion in a litre of solution; a measure of the acidity or alkalinity of a solution. See **pH.**

hydrogen peroxide /pəˈrɒksaɪd/, *n.* a colorless, unstable, oily liquid, H_2O_2, the aqueous solution of which is used as an antiseptic and a bleaching agent.

hydrogen sulfide, *n.* a colorless, flammable, cumulatively poisonous gas, H_2S, smelling like rotten eggs; sulfuretted hydrogen.

hydrokinetic /ˌhaɪdroʊkaɪˈnetɪk, -kə-/, *adj.* **1.** relating to the motion of fluids. **2.** relating to hydrokinetics. Also, **hydrokinetical.**

hydrology /haɪˈdrɒlədʒi/, *n.* the science dealing with water on the land, or under the earth's surface, its properties, laws, geographical distribution, etc. — **hydrologic, hydrological,** *adj.* — **hydrologist,** *n.*

hydrolysis /haɪˈdrɒləsəs/, *n., pl.* **-ses** /-siz/. chemical decomposition by which a compound is changed into other compounds by taking up the elements of water, as salts of weak acids, etc.

hydrometallurgy /ˌhaɪdroʊˈmetəlɜːdʒi/, *n.* the practice of removing metals from ores by leaching with solutions such as mercury, cyanides, acids, brines, etc. — **hydrometallurgical,** *adj.*

hydrometer /haɪˈdrɒmətə/, *n.* a sealed cylinder with a weighted bulb and graduated stem for determining the specific gravity of liquids by reading the level of the liquid. — **hydrometric, hydrometrical,** *adj.* — **hydrometry,** *n.*

hydronium /haɪˈdroʊniəm/, *adj.* (of a hydrogen ion) hydrated with a water molecule. Also, **hydroxonium.**

hydropathy /haɪˈdrɒpəθi/, *n.* the treatment of disease by the use of water. — **hydropathic,** *adj.*

hydrophobic /ˌhaɪdrəˈfoʊbɪk/, *adj. Chem.* having little or no attraction for water.

hydrophone /ˈhaɪdrəfoʊn/, *n.* **1.** an instrument employing the principles of the microphone, used to detect the flow of water through a pipe. **2.** a device for finding sources of sound under water, as for detecting submarines by the noise of their engines, etc.

hydrophyte /ˈhaɪdrəfaɪt/, *n.* a plant growing in water or very moist ground. — **hydrophytic,** *adj.*

hydroplane /ˈhaɪdrəpleɪn/, *n., v.,* **-planed, -planing.** ◇*n.* **1.** → **seaplane. 2.** a light, high-powered boat, usu. with one or more steps in the bottom, designed to plane along the surface of the water at very high speeds. ◇*v.i.* **3.** to skim over water in the manner of a hydroplane.

hydroponics /haɪdrəˈpɒnɪks/, *n.* the cultivation of plants by placing the roots in solutions rather than in soil. — **hydroponic,** *adj.*

hydrosol /ˈhaɪdrəsɒl/, *n.* a colloidal suspension in water.

hydrosphere /ˈhaɪdrəsfɪə/, *n.* all the water on the earth's surface.

hydrothermal /haɪdroʊˈθɜːməl/, *adj.* relating to the action of hot, aqueous solutions or gases within or on the surface of the earth.

hydrotropic /haɪdrəˈtrɒpɪk/, *adj.* relating to the growth of plants in response to water.

hydrous /ˈhaɪdrəs/, *adj.* **1.** containing water. **2.** *Chem.* containing water, as in hydrates or in hydroxides.

hydroxide /haɪˈdrɒksaɪd/, *n.* compound containing the hydroxyl (−OH⁻) group.

hydroxonium /haɪdrɒkˈsoʊniəm/, *n.* → **hydronium.**

hydroxyl /haɪˈdrɒksəl/, *n.* the univalent negatively-charged radical, −OH⁻, containing hydrogen and oxygen.

hydrozoan /haɪdrəˈzoʊən/, *adj.* **1.** relating to a class of solitary or colonial coelenterates. ◇*n.* **2.** a member of this class.

hyena /haɪˈinə/, *n.* a nocturnal, flesh-eating, dog-like mammal, feeding chiefly on carrion. [L, from Gk: hog]

hyeto-, a word part meaning 'rain'. [combining form of Gk *hyetós*]

hygiene /ˈhaɪdʒin/, *n.* the science which deals with the preservation of health. Also, **hygienics** /haɪˈdʒinɪks/. [F, from Gk: healthful, sanitary]

hygienic /haɪˈdʒinɪk/, *adj.* **1.** sanitary; clean. **2.** relating to hygiene.

hygro-, a word part meaning 'wet', 'moist'. Also, before vowels, **hygr-.** [Gk, combining form of *hygrós*]

hygrometry /haɪˈgrɒmətri/, *n.* the branch of physics that studies humidity.

hygroscopic /haɪgrəˈskɒpɪk/, *adj.* absorbing or attracting moisture from the air.

hylo-, a word part meaning 'wood', 'matter'. [Gk, combining form of *hýlē*]

hymen /'haɪmən/, *n.* **1.** the membrane that usu. partly covers the opening of the vagina until it is broken, often at first sexual intercourse. **2.** (*cap.*) *Gk Myth.* the god of marriage, represented as a young man bearing a bridal torch. [Gk: thin skin, membrane]

hymn /hɪm/, *n.* a song or ode in praise or honor of God. [LL, from Gk]

hymnal /'hɪmnəl/, *n.* **1.** Also, **hymnbook**. a book of hymns for use in divine worship. ◇*adj.* **2.** of or relating to hymns.

hyp-, variant of **hypo-**, before most vowels, as in *hypaesthesia*.

hyp., *Abbrev.* **1.** hypotenuse. **2.** hypothesis. **3.** hypothetical.

hype[1] /haɪp/, *n., v.,* **hyped, hyping.** *Orig. US.* ◇*n.* **1.** a fraud; racket; swindle. ◇*v.t.* **2.** to bluff or con, as by false publicity. [orig. unknown]

hype[2] /haɪp/, *n., v.,* **hyped, hyping.** *Colloq.* ◇*n.* **1.** a hypodermic needle. ◇*v.t.* **2.** to increase the power, speed, etc. of a car engine, etc. (usu. fol. by *up*): *He hyped up his Holden.* **3.** to persuade, exhort to greater achievement, as of a coach convincing a team that success can be theirs. [shortened form of HYPODERMIC]

hyper /'haɪpə/, *adj. Colloq.* nervous; on edge; over-stimulated.

hyper-, a prefix meaning 'over', and usu. implying excess or exaggeration. [Gk, representing *hypér*, prep., over, above, beyond, as adv. overmuch, beyond measure]

hyperactive /haɪpər'æktɪv/, *adj.* overactive.

hyperbola /haɪ'pɜːbələ/, *n., pl.* **-las**. a plane curve formed by the intersection of a cone by a plane having an angle to the base greater than that of the side of the cone to the base. [NL, from Gk: a throwing beyond] — **hyperbolic**, *adj.*

hyperbole /haɪ'pɜːbəli/, *n.* an obvious overstatement made for effect and not intended to be taken literally. [L, from Gk: a throwing beyond, excess, hyperbole, also a hyperbola] — **hyperbolic**, *adj.* — **hyperbolism**, *n.* — **hyperbolise**, *v.*

hypersensitive /haɪpə'sɛnsətɪv/, *adj.* **1.** excessively sensitive. **2.** *Pathol.* allergic to a substance to which a normal individual does not react. — **hypersensitivity**, *n.*

hypertension /haɪpə'tɛnʃən/, *n.* the elevation of the blood pressure, esp. the diastolic pressure, the chief sign of arterial disease. — **hypertensive**, *adj.*

hyperventilation /ˌhaɪpəvɛntə'leɪʃən/, *n.* the excessive exposure of the lungs to oxygen resulting in a rapid loss of carbon dioxide from the blood; abnormally increased respiration. — **hyperventilate**, *v.i.*

hypha /'haɪfə/, *n., pl.,* **-phae** /fiː/ (in fungi) one of the threadlike elements of the mycelium. [NL, from Gk web] — **hyphal**, *adj.*

hyphen /'haɪfən/, *n.* **1.** a short stroke (-) used to connect parts of a compound word or parts of a word divided for any purpose. ◇*v.t.* **2.** to hyphenate. [LL, from Gk: name of sign]

hyphenate /'haɪfəneɪt/, *v.t.,* **-nated, -nating,** to write with or join by a hyphen. — **hyphenation**, *n.* — **hyphenated**, *adj.*

hypno-, a word part meaning 'sleep' or 'hypnosis', as in *hypnology*. Also, before vowels (usu.), **hypn-**. [Gk, combining form of *hýpnos* sleep]

hypnosis /hɪp'noʊsəs/, *n. pl.* **-ses** /-siːz/. **1.** *Psychol.* a trance-like mental state brought about in a cooperative subject by suggestion. **2.** → **hypnotism**. [NL, from Gk: put to sleep] — **hypnotic**, *adj., n.*

hypnotherapy /hɪpnoʊ'θɛrəpi/, *n.* the treatment of disease by means of hypnosis. — **hypnotherapeutic**, *adj.*

hypnotise *or* **hypnotize** /'hɪpnətaɪz/, *v.t.,* **-tised, -tising.** to put in the hypnotic state. — **hypnotisable**, *adj.* — **hypnotisation**, *n.* — **hypnotiser**, *n.*

hypnotism /'hɪpnətɪzəm/, *n.* the science or act of inducing hypnosis. — **hypnotist**, *n.*

hypo /'haɪpoʊ/, *n. Colloq.* a hypodermic needle or injection. [short for HYPODERMIC]

hypo-, a prefix meaning 'under', either in place or in degree ('less', 'less than'). [Gk, representing *hypó*, prep. and adv., under]

hypochondria /haɪpə'kɒndrɪə/, *n. Psychol.* a condition characterised by depressed spirits and fancies of ill health. [LL: pl., the abdomen, — thought to be the seat of melancholy] — **hypochondriac**, *adj., n.*

hypocrisy /hɪ'pɒkrəsi/, *n., pl.* **-sies.** the act of pretending to have a character or beliefs, principles, etc., that one does not possess. [ME, from OF, from LL, from Gk: acting of a part, pretence]

hypocrite /'hɪpəkrɪt/, *n.* a person given to hypocrisy; someone who pretends virtue or piety. [ME, from OF, from LL, from Gk: actor, pretender, hypocrite] — **hypocritical**, *adj.* — **hypocritically**, *adv.*

hypodermic /haɪpə'dɜːmɪk/, *adj.* **1.** relating to the introduction of liquid medicine under the skin: *a hypodermic needle.* **2.** of the parts under the skin, as tissue. ◇*n.* **3.** a hypodermic injection or syringe. — **hypodermically**, *adv.*

hypodermic syringe, *n.* a small syringe having a detachable hollow needle used to inject solutions under the skin.

hypogene /'haɪpədʒiːn/, *adj.* formed beneath the earth's surface, as granite (opposed to *epigene*).

hypostasis /haɪ'pɒstəsəs/, *n., pl.* **-ses.** *Philos.* **1.** that which stands under and supports; foundation. **2.** an underlying or essential part of anything. [LL, from Gk: substance, nature, essence, also sediment] — **hypostatic**, *adj.*

hypotenuse /haɪ'pɒtənjuːz/, *n.* the side of a right-angled triangle opposite the right angle. [LL, from Gk: subtending]

hypothalamus /haɪpəˈθæləməs/, *n.* the part of the middle brain concerned with emotional expression and bodily responses.

hypothermia /haɪpəˈθɜmiə/, *n.* **1.** a subnormal body temperature. **2.** the artificial reduction of body temperature to slow metabolic processes, usu. to make heart surgery possible. – **hypothermal**, *adj.*

hypothesis /haɪˈpɒθəsəs/, *n., pl.* **-ses** /-siz/. **1.** a proposition, idea, theory or other statement adopted as a starting point for discussion, investigation, study, etc. **2.** a statement accepted as basic in an argument. **3.** a guess; assumption. [NL, from Gk: supposition, basis]

hypothesise /haɪˈpɒθəsaɪz/, *v.*, **-sised, -sising.** ◇*v.i.* **1.** to form a hypothesis. ◇*v.t.* **2.** to assume by hypothesis.

hypothetical /haɪpəˈθɛtɪkəl/, *adj.* **1.** assumed by hypothesis; supposed: *a hypothetical case.* **2.** relating to, involving, or of the nature of hypothesis: *hypothetical reasoning.*

hypothyroidism /haɪpəˈθaɪrɔɪdɪzəm/, *n.* abnormally diminished activity of the thyroid gland.

hyssop /ˈhɪsəp/, *n.* an aromatic herb with blue flowers. [L, from Gk: kind of plant]

hyster-, a variant of **hystero-**, before vowels; as in *hysterectomy*.

hysterectomy /hɪstəˈrɛktəmi/, *n., pl.* **-mies.** the removal of the uterus.

hysteresis /hɪstəˈrisəs/, *n.* (in the elastic or magnetic behavior of materials) the delay shown by material in reacting to a stress applied. [NL, from Gk: deficiency] – **hysteretic**, *adj.*

hysteria /hɪsˈtɪəriə/, *n.* **1.** senseless emotionalism; emotional frenzy. **2.** a mental disorder characterised by violent emotional outbreaks, affecting sensory and motor functions. – **hysteric**, *n.* – **hysterical**, *adj.*

hystero-, a word part meaning 'uterus'. Also, **hyster-**. [Gk, combining form of *hystéra*]

Hz, *Phys. Symbol.* hertz.

Ii

I, i, *n., pl.* **I's** or **Is**, **i's** or **is**. **1.** the ninth letter of the English alphabet. **2.** the ninth in any series. **3.** the Roman numeral for one. See **Roman numerals**.

-i-, an ending for the first part of many compounds, often used in English as a connective, as in *Frenchify*.

i., *Abbrev.* intransitive.

I[1] /aɪ/, *pron., poss.* **my** or **mine**, *obj.* **me**; *pl. nom.* **we**, *poss.* **ours** or **our**, *obj.* **us**; *n., pl.* **I's**. ◇*pron.* **1.** the subject form of the singular pronoun of the first person, used by a speaker of himself or herself. ◇*n.* **2.** the pronoun *I* used as a noun: *The 'I' in this novel is John.* **3.** *Philos.* the ego. [OE *ic, ih*]

I[2], *Chem. Symbol.* iodine.

-ia, a suffix of nouns, used in medicine (disease: *malaria*), in geography (countries: *Romania*), in botany (genera: *Wisteria*), in Latinising plurals (*Reptilia, bacteria*), etc. [L or Gk]

-ial, a variant of **-al**[1], as in *judicial, imperial*. [L *-iālis, -iāle*, adj. suffix]

iamb /ˈaɪæmb, ˈaɪæm/, *n.* a metrical foot of two syllables, a short one followed by a long one, or an unaccented by an accented (˘ ¯). In *Come live with me and be my love*, there are four iambs. [L: an iambic verse or poem] **–iambic**, *adj.*

-ian, a variant of **-an**, as in *amphibian, Grecian*. [L *-iānus*]

Iberia /aɪˈbɪərɪə/, *n.* a peninsula in southwestern Europe, comprising Spain and Portugal. Also **Iberian Peninsula**.

Iberian /aɪˈbɪərɪən/, *adj.* **1.** relating to Iberia or its inhabitants. ◇*n.* **2.** one of the ancient inhabitants from whom the Basques are supposed to be descended.

ibid. /ˈɪbɪd/, *Abbrev.* ibidem.

ibidem /ˈɪbədəm, ɪˈbaɪdəm/, *adv.* (used in citations, bibliographies, etc.) in the same book, chapter, page, etc. [L]

ibis /ˈaɪbəs/, *n.* a type of wading bird of warm areas, related to herons and storks, and having a long, thin, down-curved beak. [L, from Gk; of Egyptian orig.]

-ible, a variant of **-able**, occurring in words taken from the Latin, as in *credible, horrible*, or based on the Latin type as *reducible*. [ME, from OF, from L *-ibilis*]

Ibsen /ˈɪbsən/, *n.* **Henrik** /ˈhɛnrɪk/, 1828–1906, Norwegian dramatist and poet; famous for his social plays, such as *A Doll's House* (1879), and his later, symbolic plays, such as *Hedda Gabler* (1890).

i/c, *Abbrev.* in charge.

-ic, **1.** a suffix added to nouns or other stems to form adjectives meaning 'relating or belonging to', as in *poetic, metallic, Homeric*. **2.** *Chem.* a suffix showing that an element is present in a compound at a high valency, e.g. sulfuric acid. [Gk *-ikos*]

-ical, a compound suffix forming adjectives from nouns (*rhetorical*), providing synonyms to words ending in *-ic* (*poetical*), and providing an adjective with additional meanings to those in the *-ic* form (*economical*). [-IC + -AL[1]]

Icarus /ˈɪkərəs, ˈaɪkə-/, *n. Gk Legend.* the son of Daedalus; with his father escaped from Crete using wings made of wax and feathers, but flew so high that the sun melted his wings and he drowned in the Aegean.

ICBM /ˌaɪ si bi ˈɛm/, *Abbrev.* intercontinental ballistic missile.

ice /aɪs/, *n., v.,* **iced, icing,** *adj.* ◇*n.* **1.** the solid form of water, produced by freezing. **2.** the frozen surface of a body of water. **3.** any substance like this, e.g. dry ice. **4.** a frozen dessert made of sweetened water and fruit juice. **5.** formality; reserve: *A few jokes will break the ice.* **6. cut no ice**, *Colloq.* to make no mark; produce no effect (oft. fol. by *with*). **7. on ice**, waiting or in readiness: *He keeps the plan on ice for some time*. **8. on thin ice**, in a risky situation. ◇*v.t.* **9.** to change into ice; freeze. **10.** to cool or refrigerate with ice. **11.** to cover (cakes, etc.) with icing. ◇*v.i.* **12.** to freeze (oft. fol. by *up*). ◇*adj.* **13.** of or with ice. [OE *īs*]

-ice, a suffix used in many nouns to show state or quality, as in *service, justice*. [ME, from OF, from L *-itius, -itia, -itium*]

ice age, *n.* (sometimes caps) →**glacial epoch**.

iceberg /ˈaɪsbɜg/, *n.* **1.** a large floating mass of ice, broken off from a glacier. **2.** *Colloq.* a person who swims regularly in winter. [half Anglicisation, half adoption of D: ice mountain]

icebound /ˈaɪsbaʊnd/, *adj.* **1.** held fast by ice; frozen in. **2.** shut off by ice: *an icebound harbor*.

icebox /ˈaɪsbɒks/, *n.* **1.** a box or chest to hold ice for keeping food, etc., cool. **2.** a section in a refrigerator for keeping ice.

icebreaker /ˈaɪsbreɪkə/, *n.* **1.** a strong ship for breaking channels through ice. **2.** *Colloq.* anything which encourages people to feel comfortable with each other.

icecap /ˈaɪskæp/, *n.* a cap of ice over an area (sometimes huge), sloping in all directions from the centre.

ice-cream /ˈaɪs-krim/, *n.* a frozen food made of cream or milk, sweetened and flavored.

ice hockey, *n.* a game like hockey, played on an ice-rink by two teams of six players each.

Iceland /ˈaɪslənd, -lænd/, *n.* an island republic in the North Atlantic Ocean near the Arctic Circle; under Danish rule before independence in 1944. Pop. 245 000 (1987 est.); 103 000 km². *Language:* Icelandic. *Currency:* krona. *Cap.:* Reykjavík. **–Icelandic**, *adj.*

icepack /'aɪspæk/, *n.* **1.** a large area of floating ice. **2.** a bag filled with crushed ice for cooling parts of the body.

icepick /'aɪspɪk/, *n.* a pick or other tool for breaking ice.

ice point, *n.* the melting point of ice.

ice skate, *n.* (*usu. pl.*) (a shoe fitted with) a thin metal runner for moving along on ice. —**ice-skate**, *v.i.*

I Ching /i 'tʃɪŋ/, *n.* an ancient Chinese book of wisdom and divination; a source of Confucian and Taoist philosophy.

ichthyo-, a word part meaning 'fish', as in *ichthyology*. Also, before vowels, **ichthy-**. [Gk, combining form of *ichthýs*]

ichthyology /ɪkθi'ɒlədʒi/, *n.* the branch of zoology that deals with fishes. —**ichthyologic, ichthyological**, *adj.* —**ichthyologist**, *n.*

-ician, a suffix applied to a person skilled in a field, as in *tactician*. [-IC + -IAN]

icicle /'aɪsɪkəl/, *n.* a hanging, tapering mass of ice formed by the freezing of dripping water. [OE *īsgicel*]

icing /'aɪsɪŋ/, *n.* **1.** a mixture of sugar and water, or sometimes egg whites, for covering cakes, etc. **2.** → **frosting**.

icon /'aɪkɒn/, *n.* **1.** a picture, image, or other representation. **2.** *Relig.* a representation in painting, enamel, etc., of Christ, a saint, etc., looked on as sacred. Also, **eikon, ikon**. [L, from Gk: likeness, image] —**iconic**, *adj.*

icono-, a word part meaning 'likeness' or 'image'. [Gk, combining form of *eikṓn*]

iconoclast /aɪ'kɒnəklæst/, *n.* **1.** a breaker or destroyer of images, esp. religious ones. **2.** someone who attacks established beliefs. [LL, from LGk] —**iconoclastic**, *adj.* —**iconoclasm**, *n.*

-ics, a suffix of nouns indicating the body of matters, facts, knowledge, principles, etc., relating to a subject, and thus naming the science or art, as in ethics, physics, politics, tactics. [pl. of -IC]

icy /'aɪsi/, *adj.*, **icier, iciest. 1.** made of, covered with, or like ice. **2.** cold. **3.** without warmth of feeling; frigid: *an icy stare.* [OE *īsig*] —**iciness**, *n.*

id /ɪd/, *n.* (in Freudian theory) the part of the personality which is part of the unconscious and which is the source of instinctive energy. [special use of L: it]

-id[1], a suffix of nouns and adjectives indicating members of a zoological family, as in *cichlid*, or of some other group or division, as in *arachnid*. [NL *-idae*, in zoological family names, from Gk]

-id[2], a noun ending, as in *pyramid*. [Gk]

id., *Abbrev.* idem.

I'd /aɪd/, contraction of *I would* or *I had*.

ID /aɪ 'di/, *n. Abbrev.* identification.

-idae, a suffix forming the names of families in zoology, as in *Canidae*. [NL, from Gk]

Idaho /'aɪdəhoʊ/, *n.* a state in the north-western US. Pop. 1 003 000 (1986 est.); 216 413 km². *Cap.:* Boise. *Abbrev.:* Ida, Id —**Idahoan**, *n., adj.*

-ide, *Chem.* a suffix showing that a compound is made up of two elements only, the one with the suffix being negatively charged, as in *sodium chloride*. [abstracted from OXIDE]

idea /aɪ'dɪə/, *n.* **1.** a mental picture. **2.** a thought; notion: *What an idea!* **3.** an impression: *a general idea of what it's like.* **4.** an opinion, view, or belief: *Your idea about the plan is wrong.* **5.** a feeling: *I have an idea he'll be late again.* **6.** a plan of action; intention: *the idea of becoming an engineer.* **7.** *Philos.* **a.** a concept developed by the mind. **b.** a conception of what is desirable, or what ought to be; ideal. **8.** *Obs.* a likeness. [L, from Gk: see]

ideal /aɪ'dɪəl/, *n.* **1.** an idea of something at its most perfect. **2.** a standard of excellence: *to set high ideals.* **3.** a perfect example; something to be copied. **4.** an ultimate object or goal: *My ideal is to finish in six weeks.* **5.** something which exists only in idea: *an ideal of goodness.* ◇*adj.* **6.** perfect and seen as a standard: *ideal beauty; ideal behavior.* **7.** seen as the best or most suitable: *That's the ideal car for us.* **8.** existing only in idea; imaginary. [LL, from L: idea]

ideal gas, *n. Phys.* a theoretical idea of a gas as consisting of perfectly elastic molecules between which no forces of attraction exist.

idealise *or* **idealize** /aɪ'dɪəlaɪz/, *v.t.*, **-lised, -lising. 1.** to make (something) ideal; represent (something) in an ideal form. **2.** to make (something) out to be better than it is. —**idealisation**, *n.*

idealism /aɪ'dɪəlɪzəm/, *n.* **1.** the following of, or attachment to, ideals of behavior, etc.: *Only a man of his idealism could work with the poor like that.* **2.** the tendency to represent things as they ought to be rather than as they are. **3.** imaginative treatment of subjects in art or literature (opposed to *realism*). **4.** *Philos.* a theory which holds that the only thing that really exists is the mind and thought. —**idealist**, *n.*

ideally /aɪ'dɪəli/, *adv.* **1.** according to an ideal; perfectly: *Ideally, we should be able to trust other people.* **2.** in idea, thought, or imagination.

idem /'ɪdem, 'aɪdem/, *pron., adj.* the same. [L]

identical /aɪ'dentɪkəl/, *adj.* **1.** agreeing exactly. **2.** exactly similar: *The children had identical clothes.* **3.** being the same one: *That's the identical car I saw yesterday.*

identical twins, *n. pl.* twins which develop from one fertilised ovum.

identification /aɪ,dentəfə'keɪʃən/, *n.* **1.** the act or result of identifying: *His identification by the police put an end to his freedom.* **2.** something that identifies one, as a driver's licence, passport, etc.: *They wouldn't let me in without identification.*

identify /aɪ'dentəfaɪ/, *v.*, **-fied, -fying.** ◇*v.t.* **1.** to recognise, or establish as being a particular person or thing. **2.** to make, see, or treat as the same. **3.** to associate in feeling,

identify interest, action, etc. (fol. by *with*): *I will always identify him with horseracing.* **4.** *Biol.* to determine to what group (a given specimen) belongs. **5.** *Psychol.* to make (oneself) one in feeling with another person by putting oneself in his or her place. **6.** to serve to identify: *Her red hair will identify her.* ◇*v.i.* **7.** to make oneself one in feeling with another or others; empathise. —**identifiable**, *adj.*

identikit /ɑɪˈdentɪkɪt/, *n.* **1.** pictures of typical parts of faces which can be put together to make a likeness of someone being sought by police. **2.** a picture so made up. [Trademark]

identity /ɑɪˈdentəti/, *n., pl.* **-ties**, *adj.* ◇*n.* **1.** the condition or fact of being or remaining the same one: *The group kept its identity under different leaders.* **2.** the condition of being oneself or itself, and not another: *He doubted his own identity.* **3.** *Colloq.* an odd, interesting or famous person; a character: *a local identity.* **4.** sameness, likeness or association: *The two groups showed identity of function.* **5.** *Maths.* an equation which is true for all values of its variables. ◇*adj.* **6.** serving to identify: *identity card.* [LL, apparently from L: repeatedly the same]

ideo-, a word part meaning 'idea', as in ideology. [Gk, combining form of *idéa* idea]

ideology /ˌɑɪdɪˈɒlədʒi/, *n., pl.* **-gies**. **1.** a body of doctrine, myth, and symbols of a social or political movement or group: *Marxist ideology.* **2.** *Philos.* the science of ideas. —**ideological**, *adj.* —**ideologist**, *n.*

ides /ɑɪdz/, *n.pl.* (in the ancient Roman calendar) the 15th day of March, May, July, or October, and the 13th day of the other months. [F, from L]

idio-, a word part meaning 'peculiar' or 'proper to one', as in *idiosyncrasy.* [Gk, combining form of *ídios* own, private, peculiar]

idiocy /ˈɪdiəsi/, *n., pl.* **-cies**. **1.** an extreme degree of mental deficiency. **2.** an (example of) very foolish action or behavior. [? Gk: uncouthness, defenceless condition]

idiolect /ˈɪdioʊlekt/, *n.* an individual's personal variety of a language. [IDIO- + Gk: to speak]

idiom /ˈɪdiəm/, *n.* **1.** a form of expression peculiar to a language, esp. one having a meaning other than its literal one, such as *It's raining cats and dogs.* **2.** a variety or form of a language. **3.** the peculiar character of a language. **4.** distinct style or character, as in music, art, etc.: *the idiom of Bach.* [LL, from Gk: a peculiarity]

idiomatic /ˌɪdiəˈmætɪk/, *adj.* **1.** peculiar to or typical of a language. **2.** showing the typical ways of expression of a speaker, group, dialect, etc. Also, **idiomatical**. [Gk]

idiosyncrasy /ˌɪdioʊˈsɪŋkrəsi/, *n., pl.* **-sies**. any tendency, characteristic, manner of expression, etc., unique to an individual. [Gk] —**idiosyncratic**, *adj.*

idiot /ˈɪdiət/, *n.* **1.** a person who is extremely mentally deficient. **2.** a very foolish or stupid person. [ME, from L, from Gk: a private, non-professional, or ignorant person] —**idiotic**, *adj.*

-idium, a diminutive suffix used in zoological, biological, botanical, anatomical, and chemical terms.

idle /ˈɑɪdl/, *adj.*, **idler, idlest**, *v.*, **idled, idling**. ◇*adj.* **1.** unemployed, or doing nothing: *idle workmen.* **2.** unoccupied, as time: *idle hours.* **3.** not in use: *idle machinery.* **4.** habitually doing nothing or avoiding work: *idle fellow.* **5.** worthless, meaningless or vain: *idle talk; idle pleasures.* **6.** unfounded: *idle fears.* **7.** futile or ineffective: *idle threats.* **8. the idle rich**, people rich enough not to have to work. ◇*v.i.* **9.** to spend time doing nothing or in worthless activities. **10.** to move idly; loiter; saunter. **11.** (of an engine) to operate with the transmission disengaged at minimum speed. ◇*v.t.* **12.** to waste: *to idle the hours away.* [ME and OE *idel*] —**idleness**, *n.* —**idly**, *adv.*

idler /ˈɑɪdlə/, *n.* someone who wastes time.

idol /ˈɑɪdl/, *n.* **1.** a statue, etc., worshipped as a god. **2.** *Bible.* a false god, as of a heathen people. **3.** any person or thing blindly adored or revered. [ME, from OF, from L, from Gk: image, phantom, idol]

idolatry /ɑɪˈdɒlətri/, *n., pl.* **-tries**. **1.** worship of idols. **2.** blind adoration, reverence, or devotion. [ME, from OF, from LL, from Gk] —**idolatrous**, *adj.* —**idolater**, *n.*

idolise *or* **idolize** /ˈɑɪdəlɑɪz/, *v.t.* **-lised, -lising**. to regard with blind adoration or devotion. —**idolisation**, *n.*

Idriess /ˈɪdrəs/, *n.* **Ion Llewellyn**, 1889–1979, Australian novelist; author of *Lasseter's Last Ride* (1931).

idyll /ˈɑɪdəl, ˈɪdəl/, *n.* **1.** a poem or piece of prose consisting of a 'little picture', usu. describing pleasant country scenes or any charmingly simple episode. **2.** a simple descriptive or narrative piece in verse or prose. **3.** an episode or scene of pastoral charm. **4.** a piece of music of a pastoral or sentimental character. [L, from Gk diminutive: form]

idyllic /ɑɪˈdɪlɪk, ɪˈdɪlɪk/, *adj.* **1.** suggesting or suitable for an idyll; charmingly simple or poetic: *an idyllic scene on the river.* **2.** of, relating to, or of the nature of an idyll. —**idyllically**, *adv.*

-ie, noun suffix, the same as -y[2], used colloquially: **1.** as an endearment, or affectionately, esp. with and among children: *doggie*, dog; *littlie*, child. **2.** as a common abbreviation: *budgie*, budgerigar; *conchie*, conscientious, or a conscientious objector; *mossie*, mosquito; *postie*, postman. **3.** to form nouns: *greenie*, conservationist; *stubbie*, small, squat beer bottle.

i.e., *Abbrev.* that is. [L *id est*]

-ier, a variant of **-eer**, as in *brigadier*. [F, from L]

-ies, a word part representing the plural formation of nouns and third person singular of verbs for words ending in -y, -ie, and sometimes -ey. See -s[2], -s[3] and -es.

if /ɪf/, *conj.* **1.** in case that; supposing that; on condition that: *I'll come if you want me to.* **2.** even though: *If you did say it, I didn't hear you.* **3.** whether: *I don't know if I can do it.* **4. if only**, (used to introduce a phrase

if 515 **ill-fated**

expressing a wish, esp. one that probably cannot be fulfilled): *If only I had known!* ◇*n.* **5.** a condition; a supposition: *ifs and buts.* **6.** *Colloq.* something doubtful: *At this stage the plan is a big if.* [ME; OE *gif*]

-ify, a variant of **-fy**, used when the stem ends in a consonant or consonant sound, as in *solidify* or *intensify.* [-I- + -FY]

igloo /ˈɪglu/, *n., pl.* **-loos.** a dome-shaped Eskimo hut, built of blocks of hard snow. [Eskimo: house]

Ignatius of Loyola /ɪɡˌneɪʃəs əv lɔɪˈoʊlə/, *n.* **Saint** (*Iñigo López de Recalde*), 1491–1556, Spanish soldier and priest; founder of the Jesuit order.

igneous /ˈɪɡniəs/, *adj.* relating to or of the nature of fire. [L: of fire]

igneous rock, *n.* rock formed from magma which has cooled and solidified either at the earth's surface (volcanic rock) or deep within the earth's crust (plutonic rock).

ignite /ɪɡˈnaɪt/, *v.*, **-nited, -niting.** ◇*v.t.* **1.** to set on fire; kindle. ◇*v.i.* **2.** to take fire; begin to burn. [L] **–ignitable, ignitible,** *adj.* **–ignitability, ignitibility,** *n.*

ignition /ɪɡˈnɪʃən/, *n.* **1.** the act or result of igniting. **2.** (in an internal-combustion engine) the process which ignites the fuel in the cylinder.

ignition coil, *n.* an induction coil used in an internal-combustion engine for converting the battery voltage to the high tension required by the sparking plugs.

ignoble /ɪɡˈnoʊbəl/, *adj.* **1.** of low character, aims, etc.; mean; base. **2.** of low grade or quality; inferior. **3.** not of noble birth. [L: unknown, of low birth]

ignominy /ˈɪɡnəməni/, *n., pl.* **-minies.** **1.** disgrace; dishonor; public contempt. **2.** low quality or behavior; a cause of disgrace. [L: disgrace, dishonor] **–ignominious,** *adj.*

ignoramus /ɪɡnəˈreɪməs/, *n., pl.* **-muses.** someone who knows little or nothing. [L: we do not know, we disregard]

ignorant /ˈɪɡnərənt/, *adj.* **1.** knowing little or nothing; unlearned. **2.** lacking a particular knowledge: *ignorant of mathematics.* **3.** uninformed; unaware. **4.** due to or showing lack of knowledge: *an ignorant statement.* **5.** *Colloq.* ignorant of polite ways, etc.; ill-mannered; boorish. [ME, from L: not knowing] **–ignorance,** *n.*

ignore /ɪɡˈnɔː/, *v.t.*, **-nored, -noring.** to take no notice of: *ignore his remarks.* [L: not to know; disregard]

iguana /ɪˈɡwɑːnə/, *n.* a type of large lizard of tropical America, oft. with spiny outgrowths on the head and back. [Sp, from Amer Ind]

ikebana /ɪkiˈbɑːnə/, *n.* the art of Japanese flower arrangement.

ikon /ˈaɪkɒn/, *n.* → **icon.**

il-¹, a variant of **in-²**, before *l.*

il-², a variant of **in-³**, before *l*, as in *illogical.*

-il, a variant of **-ile**, as in *civil.*

-ile, adjective suffix expressing capability, aptitude, etc., as in *agile, ductile, fragile, tensile, volatile.* Also, **-il.** [L *-ilis*]

Ile de France /il də ˈfrɒ̃s/, *n.* a region and former province in northern France, including Paris and the region around it. Pop. 10 250 800 (1986 est.).

ileum /ˈɪliəm/, *n. Anat.* the third and lowest division of the small intestine, continuous with the jejunum and ending at the caecum. [NL, from LL: groin, flank]

Iliad /ˈɪliæd/, *n.* a Greek epic poem describing the siege of Troy, ascribed to Homer. [L *Ilias*, from Gk, from *Ilion* Ilium, Troy] **–Iliadic,** *adj.*

-ility, a compound suffix making abstract nouns from adjectives by replacing the adj. suffixes: -il(e), -le, as in *civility, sterility, ability.* [F, from L *-ilitas*]

ilk /ɪlk/, *adj.* **1.** same. ◇*n.* **2.** family, class, or kind: *he and all his ilk.* [OE *elc, ylc,* EACH]

ill /ɪl/, *adj.*, **worse, worst,** *n., adv.* ◇*adj.* **1.** sick or unwell. **2.** evil, wicked, or bad: *ill repute.* **3.** offensive or faulty: *ill manners.* **4.** unfriendly or hostile: *ill feeling.* **5.** unfavorable; adverse: *ill luck.* ◇*n.* **6.** evil. **7.** harm; injury. **8.** a disease; ailment. **9.** trouble; misfortune. ◇*adv.* **10.** wickedly. **11.** unsatisfactorily or poorly. **12.** in an unfriendly or hostile manner: *ill disposed.* **13.** unfavorably or unfortunately. **14.** with displeasure or offence: *to take it ill.* **15.** with trouble, difficulty, or inconvenience: *Buying a new car is an expense we can ill afford.* [ME, from Scand]

I'll /aɪl/, short form of *I will* or *I shall.*

ill-advised /ˈɪl-ədˈvaɪzd/, *adj.* acting or done without proper consideration; imprudent.

ill-assorted /ˈɪl-əsɔːtəd/, *adj.* badly matched.

Illawarra /ɪləˈwɒrə/, *n.* a district on the south coast of NSW, between northern Greater Wollongong and the Shoalhaven River.

Illawarra flame-tree, *n.* → **flame-tree.**

Illawarra shorthorn, *n.* → **Australian Illawarra Shorthorn.**

ill-bred /ˈɪl-brɛd/, *adj.* rude; unmannerly: *ill-bred children.* **–ill-breeding,** *n.*

ill-defined /ˈɪl-dəfaɪnd/, *adj.* unclear; blurred.

illegal /ɪˈliːɡəl/, *adj.* not legal; unauthorised. [ML, from L] **–illegality,** *n.*

illegible /ɪˈlɛdʒəbəl/, *adj.* impossible or hard to read; indecipherable: *This letter is completely illegible.* **–illegibility,** *n.*

illegitimate /ɪləˈdʒɪtəmət/, *adj.* **1.** against the law: *an illegitimate act.* **2.** born outside marriage: *an illegitimate child.* **3.** not allowed; irregular; not in good usage: *an illegitimate use of words.* **4.** an illegitimate person; bastard. **5.** (formerly) a free settler (as opposed to a *legitimate*). **–illegitimacy,** *n.*

ill-fated /ˈɪl-feɪtəd/, *adj.* **1.** sure to come to an unhappy end: *an ill-fated expedition.* **2.** bringing bad fortune; unlucky.

ill-founded /ˈɪlˈfaʊndəd/, *adj.* illogical or not based on facts: *an ill-founded argument.*

ill-gotten /ˈɪlˈgɒtn/, *adj.* gained in unlawful ways: *ill-gotten gains.*

ill health, *n.* bad health. Also, **ill-health.**

ill humor *or* **ill humour**, *n.* bad temper or mood. —**ill-humored**, *adj.*

illiberal /ɪˈlɪbərəl, -ˈlɪbrəl/, *adj.* **1.** narrow-minded; bigoted. **2.** without culture; unscholarly; vulgar. **3.** *Rare.* ungenerous; miserly. [L: mean, sordid] —**illiberality**, *n.*

illicit /ɪˈlɪsɪt/, *adj.* unlawful; unlicensed. [L: forbidden]

Illinois[1] /ɪləˈnɔɪ/, *n., pl.* **-nois** /-nɔɪ, -nɔɪz/ **1.** (*pl.*) a confederacy of North American Indians of Algonquian stock, formerly occupying Illinois and adjoining regions westward. **2.** An Indian of this confederacy.

Illinois[2] /ɪləˈnɔɪ/, *n.* a state in the central US; a part of the Midwest. Pop. 11 553 000 (1986 est.); 146 076 km². *Cap.:* Springfield. *Abbrev.:* Ill [F, from Illinois Indian] —**Illinoisan**, *n., adj.*

illiterate /ɪˈlɪtərət, ɪˈlɪtrət/, *adj.* **1.** unable to read and write: *an illiterate tribe.* **2.** lacking education. **3.** showing lack of culture. ◇ *n.* **4.** an illiterate person. [L: unlettered] —**illiteracy, illiterateness**, *n.*

ill-mannered /ˈɪlˈmænəd/, *adj.* rude; impolite.

ill-natured /ˈɪlˈneɪtʃəd/, *adj.* **1.** having or showing an unkindly or unpleasant nature. **2.** cross; peevish.

illness /ˈɪlnəs/, *n.* **1.** a state of bad health; sickness. **2.** an attack of sickness; disease.

illogical /ɪˈlɒdʒɪkəl/, *adj.* not according to the rules of logic; unreasonable. —**illogicality**, *n.*

ill-treat /ɪlˈtriːt/, *v.t.* to treat badly; maltreat. —**ill-treatment**, *n.*

illuminate /ɪˈluːməneɪt/, *v.,* **-nated, -nating.** ◇ *v.t.* **1.** to supply with light; light up: *to illuminate a building.* **2.** to decorate with lights. **3.** to throw light on (a subject), make clear or lucid. **4.** to enlighten (someone), as with knowledge. **5.** to decorate (a letter, page, manuscript, etc.) with color, gold, etc. ◇ *v.i.* **6.** to display lights, as in celebration. [L.]

illumination /ɪˌluːməˈneɪʃən/, *n.* **1.** an act or result of illuminating. **2.** a decoration consisting of lights. **3.** the intellectual or spiritual enlightenment. **4.** the amount of light falling on a unit area of surface per second; the derived SI unit of illumination is the lux (lumen per square metre). **5.** a supply of light. **6.** decoration, as of a letter, page, or manuscript, with a painted design in color, gold, etc.

illumine /ɪˈluːmən/, *v.t., v.i.,* **-mined, -mining.** to make or become illuminated. [ME, from F, from L: light up] —**illuminable**, *adj.*

illus., *Abbrev.* **1.** illustrated. **2.** illustration.

ill-use /ɪlˈjuːz/, *v.t.,* **-used, -using.** to treat badly, unjustly, or cruelly. —**ill use**, *n.*

illusion /ɪˈluːʒən/, *n.* **1.** something that deceives by giving a false impression; something unreal. **2.** the act of deceiving; deception; delusion; mockery (def. 4). **3.** (the condition of being under) a false impression or belief. **4.** *Psychol.* normal false perception of some object or situation (e.g. optical illusions). See **delusion** (def. 2), **hallucination**. [ME, from L: mocking, illusion] —**illusionary**, *adj.*

illusive /ɪˈluːsɪv/, *adj.* → **illusory.** —**illusiveness**, *n.*

illusory /ɪˈluːzəri/, *adj.* **1.** deceptive. **2.** unreal. —**illusorily**, *adv.* —**illusoriness**, *n.*

illustrate /ˈɪləstreɪt/, *v.t.,* **-strated, -strating. 1.** to make clear by examples; exemplify: *His story illustrated his theory.* **2.** to provide (a book, etc.) with pictures, for decoration or to make the text clearer. [L: illuminated]

illustrated /ˈɪləstreɪtəd/, *adj.* having pictures.

illustration /ɪləˈstreɪʃən/, *n.* **1.** a picture in a book, etc. **2.** a comparison or example meant to explain or make clear. **3.** the act of making clear; explanation; elucidation.

illustrative /ˈɪləstreɪtɪv, ɪˈlʌstrətɪv/, *adj.* serving to illustrate.

illustrator /ˈɪləstreɪtə/, *n.* **1.** an artist who makes illustrations. **2.** someone or something that illustrates.

illustrious /ɪˈlʌstriəs/, *adj.* **1.** famous; highly distinguished; renowned. **2.** (of deeds, etc.) glorious. **3.** *Archaic.* bright; luminous. [L: lit up; bright]

illuviation /ɪˌluːviˈeɪʃən/, *n. Geog.* deposition at a lower level of material removed by eluviation from a higher level.

ill will, *n.* hostile or unfriendly feeling: *I bear you no ill will.*

ILO /ˌaɪ el ˈoʊ/, *n.* → **International Labour Organisation.**

im-[1], a variant of **in-**[2] used before *b, m,* and *p,* as in *imbue, immerse.*

im-[2], a variant of **in-**[3] used before *b, m,* and *p,* as in *immoral, imparity, imperishable.*

im-[3], a variant of **in-**[1], before *b, m,* and *p,* as in *imbed, impearl.*

I'm /aɪm/, contraction of *I am.*

image /ˈɪmɪdʒ/, *n., v.,* **-aged, -aging.** ◇ *n.* **1.** a likeness of a person, animal, or thing. **2.** the optical counterpart or appearance of an object, produced by a mirror, lens, etc. **3.** a mental picture; idea; conception. **4.** the impression a public figure or group works to create for the public. **5.** form; appearance. **6.** Also, **spitting image.** a counterpart or copy: *The child is the image of its mother.* **7.** a symbol or emblem. **8.** a type or embodiment. **9.** a description of something in speech or writing. **10.** *Rhet.* a figure of speech, esp. a metaphor or a simile. ◇ *v.t.* **11.** to picture or represent in the mind; imagine; conceive. **12.** to make an image of. [ME, from F, from L: copy, image]

imagery /ˈɪmɪdʒri, -dʒəri/, *n., pl.* **-ries. 1.** the formation of images, figures, or likenesses

imagery of things, or such images collectively: *dream imagery*. **2.** metaphors, similes, etc., collectively.

imaginary /ɪˈmædʒənəri, -ənri/, *adj.* existing only in the imagination or fancy; not real; fancied: *an imaginary illness*.

imaginary number, *n.* the square root of a negative number, thus √−1 is an imaginary number, indicated by i; $i^2 = -1$.

imagination /ɪˌmædʒəˈneɪʃən/, *n.* **1.** the act or faculty of forming mental images of what is not actually present to the senses: *The imagination of such things is dangerous; She has a powerful imagination.* **2.** the mind, as forming such images: *It's all in her imagination.* **3.** the power of reproducing images stored in the memory under the suggestion of associated images (**reproductive imagination**), or of recombining former experiences in the creation of new images different from any known by experience (**productive** or **creative imagination**). **4.** the faculty of producing ideal creations consistent with reality, as in literature (distinguished from *fancy*). [ME, from L]

imaginative /ɪˈmædʒənətɪv/, *adj.* **1.** marked by or showing the use of imagination: *an imaginative tale.* **2.** relating to or concerned with imagination: *the imaginative faculty.* **3.** able to imagine: *a highly imaginative person.* **4.** fanciful.

imagine /ɪˈmædʒɪn/, *v.*, **-ined, -ining**. ◇*v.t.* **1.** to form a mental image of (something not actually present to the senses): *to imagine a pleasant scene.* **2.** to think, believe, or suppose: *She imagined that she saw it.* **3.** to guess: *I cannot imagine what you mean.* ◇*v.i.* **4.** to form mental images of things not present to the senses; use the imagination. **5.** to suppose; think; conjecture. [ME, from F, from L: picture to oneself, fancy] − **imaginable,** *adj.*

imago /ɪˈmeɪɡoʊ/, *n., pl.* **imagos, imagines** /ɪˈmeɪdʒəniːz/. an adult insect. [NL, special use of L: image]

imam /ɪˈmɑːm/, *n.* the prayer-leader of a mosque. [Ar: leader, guide]

imbalance /ɪmˈbæləns/, *n.* lack of balance; unevenness.

imbecile /ˈɪmbəsɪl, -saɪl/, *n.* **1.** a person mentally deficient, but less so than an idiot (def. 1). **2.** *Colloq.* a stupid person; fool. ◇*adj.* **3.** mentally weak. **4.** silly; absurd. [F, from L: weak, feeble] − **imbecility,** *n.*

imbibe /ɪmˈbaɪb/, *v.t., v.i.,* **-bibed, -bibing**. to drink, absorb, or take in (liquid, an idea, etc.). [ME, from L: drink in] − **imbibition,** *n.*

imbroglio /ɪmˈbroʊliəʊ/, *n., pl.* **-os**. a confusing or difficult situation. [It: confusion]

imbue /ɪmˈbjuː/, *v.t.,* **-bued, -buing**. **1.** to soak or fill, as with feelings, opinions, etc. **2.** to soak with moisture, fill with color, etc. [L]

imit., *Abbrev.* **1.** imitation. **2.** imitative.

imitate /ˈɪmɪteɪt/, *v.t.,* **-tated, -tating**. **1.** to use as a model. **2.** to copy, as a style, etc.; mimic. **3.** to make a copy of; reproduce closely. **4.** to have or take the appearance of; simulate. [L: having copied] − **imitative,** *adj.* − **imitable,** *adj.*

imitation /ˌɪmɪˈteɪʃən/, *n.* **1.** the result or product of imitating: *The statue was a good imitation of the original.* **2.** an act of imitating: *imitation of his behavior.* **3.** *Biol.* the close likeness of an organism to some other organism or to objects in its environment. **4.** a false copy; counterfeit. **5.** mimicry. ◇*adj.* **6.** made to look like something real or superior: *imitation pearls.* [L]

immaculate /ɪˈmækjʊlət, -kjə-/, *adj.* **1.** free from spot or stain; spotlessly clean. **2.** free from moral blemish or impurity; pure; undefiled. **3.** free from fault or flaw; free from errors, as a text. [late ME, from L: unspotted] − **immaculacy, immaculateness,** *n.*

Immaculate Conception, *n.* the Catholic doctrine that the Virgin Mary was without the stain of original sin.

immanent /ˈɪmənənt/, *adj.* **1.** remaining within; inherent. **2.** (of a mental act) taking place within the mind and having no effect outside it. **3.** (of God) present in everything. [LL: remaining in] − **immanence, immanency,** *n.*

Immanuel /ɪˈmænjʊəl/, *n.* a name to be given to Christ as the son of a virgin. Also, **Emmanuel.** [See Matthew 1:23, Isaiah 7:14. Heb: God with us]

immaterial /ˌɪməˈtɪəriəl/, *adj.* **1.** unimportant: *It's immaterial to me whether you come or not.* **2.** not material; spiritual. [ML, from LL, from F]

immature /ˌɪməˈtjʊə, -tjɔː/, *adj.* not mature, ripe, developed, or perfected. [L: unripe] − **immaturity, immatureness,** *n.*

immeasurable /ɪˈmeʒərəbəl/, *adj.* not able to be measured; limitless.

immediate /ɪˈmiːdiət/, *adj.* **1.** happening or done without delay; instant: *an immediate reply.* **2.** relating to the present time or moment: *our immediate plans.* **3.** with no time coming between; next in order: *the immediate future.* **4.** with no object or space coming between; nearest or next: *in the immediate vicinity.* **5.** with no medium or agent coming between; direct: *an immediate cause.* [ML: not mediate] − **immediacy,** *n.*

immediately /ɪˈmiːdiətli/, *adv.* **1.** at once; without delay; instantly. **2.** closely or directly: *involved immediately in our plans.* **3.** close by: *immediately in the vicinity.* ◇*conj.* **4.** as soon as: *I'll come immediately I've finished.*

immemorial /ˌɪməˈmɔːriəl/, *adj.* reaching back beyond memory, record, or knowledge: *from time immemorial.* [ML, from L]

immense /ɪˈmens/, *adj.* **1.** very great; vast; huge. **2.** immeasurable; boundless. **3.** *Colloq.* very good. [L: boundless, unmeasured] − **immensity,** *n.*

immerse /ɪˈmɜːs/, *v.t.,* **-mersed, -mersing**. **1.** to plunge into or place under a liquid; sink; submerge. **2.** to baptise by putting under water. **3.** to involve deeply; absorb (*usu.* in passive): *He was immersed in thought; immersed in work.* [L: dipped]

immersion /ɪˈmɜːʃən, -ʒən/, *n.* **1.** the act or result of immersing. **2.** baptism by plunging

immersion

the whole person into water. **3.** the condition of being deeply involved; absorption. **4.** *Astron.* the disappearance of a heavenly body as it passes either behind or into the shadow of another.

immigrant /'ɪmǝgrǝnt/, *n.* **1.** someone or something that immigrates. **2.** someone who comes to live in a new country. ◇*adj.* **3.** immigrating: *an immigrant bird.*

immigrate /'ɪmǝgreɪt/, *v.i.,* **-grated, -grating. 1.** to pass or come into a new place of living. **2.** to come to live in a new country. [L] **—immigration,** *n.*

imminent /'ɪmǝnǝnt/, *adj.* likely to happen at any moment; impending: *War is imminent.* [L: projecting over] **—imminence,** *n.*

immobile /ɪ'moʊbǝl/, *adj.* **1.** not able to be moved. **2.** not moving; motionless. [L] **—immobility,** *n.* **—immobilise,** *v.t.*

immoderate /ɪ'mɒdǝrǝt, -drǝt/, *adj.* **1.** too great; excessive; extreme. **2.** without restraint; intemperate. [L: without measure] **—immoderateness, immoderation,** *n.*

immodest /ɪ'mɒdǝst/, *adj.* **1.** indecent; shameless: *immodest behavior; immodest dress.* **2.** bold; forward; impudent. **—immodesty,** *n.*

immolate /'ɪmǝleɪt/, *v.t.,* **-lated, -lating.** to (kill as a) sacrifice. [L: sacrificed, orig., sprinkled with sacrificial meal] **—immolator,** *n.* **—immolation,** *n.*

immoral /ɪ'mɒrǝl/, *adj.* wrong according to the moral law or to accepted patterns of behavior. **—immorality,** *n.*

immortal /ɪ'mɔtl/, *adj.* **1.** undying: *immortal spirit.* **2.** celebrated in undying memory; imperishable: *immortal fame; immortal name; immortal songs.* **3.** lasting, perpetual, or constant: *an immortal memory.* ◇*n.* **4.** someone of lasting fame, as Shakespeare, Bach, etc. **5.** (*usu. pl.*) one of the gods of Greek and Roman mythology. [ME from L: undying] **—immortality,** *n.*

immortalise or **immortalize** /ɪ'mɔtǝlaɪz/, *v.t.,* **-lised, -lising. 1.** to make immortal. **2.** to give unending fame to; perpetuate. **—immortalisation,** *n.*

immovable /ɪ'muvǝbǝl/, *adj.* **1.** not able to be moved; fixed: *an immovable rock.* **2.** not moving; motionless: *a kangaroo immovable on a rock.* **3.** not able to be changed: *an immovable regulation.* **4.** lacking or not showing feeling; stiff: *an immovable heart.* **5.** firm; steadfast; unyielding: *He's immovable in his decision.* ◇*n.pl.* **6.** *Law.* lands, with the trees, buildings, etc., on them. Also, **immoveable.** **—immovability, immovableness,** *n.*

immune /ǝ'mjun, ɪ-/, *adj.* **1.** protected from a disease, danger, harm, etc. **2.** free; not subject to; exempt. [ME, from L: exempt] **—immunity,** *n.*

immunise or **immunize** /'ɪmjunaɪz, -jǝ-/, *v.t.,* **-nised, -nising.** to make immune, esp. by inoculation. **—immunisation,** *n.*

immunology /ɪmju'nɒlǝdʒi/, *n.* the branch of medical science which deals with immunity from disease and the production of

518

impassive

such immunity. **—immunologic, immunological,** *adj.* **—immunologist,** *n.*

immure /ɪ'mjuǝ/, *v.t.,* **-mured, -muring. 1.** to enclose within walls. **2.** to shut in; confine; imprison. [ML, from L] **—immurement,** *n.*

immutable /ɪ'mjutǝbǝl/, *adj.* changeless; unalterable. **—immutability, immutableness,** *n.*

imp /ɪmp/, *n.* **1.** a little devil or demon; evil spirit. **2.** a mischievous child. [ME and OE *impe* a shoot, a graft]

imp., *Abbrev.* **1.** imperative. **2.** imperfect. **3.** imperial.

Imp, *Abbrev.* **1.** Emperor. [L *Imperator*] **2.** Empress. [L *Imperatrix*]

impact /'ɪmpækt/ *n.;* /ɪm'pækt/ *v.* ◇*n.* **1.** the striking of one body against another. **2.** an effect; an impinging: *the impact of light on the eye.* **3.** forcible contact: *The impact of the accident threw him on to the road.* **4.** influence, as of a new idea, etc.: *The impact of new sales techniques on the market.* **5. make an impact on,** to impress. ◇*v.t.* **6.** to drive or press closely or firmly into something; pack in. ◇*v.i.* **7.** *Colloq.* to collide. [L: to strike against] **—impaction,** *n.*

impacted /ɪm'pæktǝd/, *adj.* **1.** wedged in, or tightly packed. **2.** *Dentistry.* (of a tooth) firmly embedded in the jawbone and not able to grow out.

impair /ɪm'pɛǝ/, *v.t., v.i.* to make or become worse; lessen in value, excellence, etc. [ME, from OF, from L] **—impairment,** *n.*

impale /ɪm'peɪl/, *v.t.,* **-paled, -paling. 1.** to fix upon or pierce through with a sharpened stake, etc. **2.** to punish or torture (a person) by doing this to the body. **3.** to make helpless as if pierced through. Also, **empale.** [ML, from L] **—impalement,** *n.*

impalpable /ɪm'pælpǝbǝl/, *adj.* **1.** not able to be felt by touch; intangible. **2.** not able to be understood: *impalpable distinctions.* **3.** (of powder) so fine that when rubbed between the fingers no grit is felt.

impart /ɪm'pat/, *v.t.* **1.** to tell or make known: *to impart a secret.* **2.** to give; bestow; communicate: *to impart satisfaction; to impart wisdom.* **3.** to give out a part or share of. [ME, from L: share] **—imparter,** *n.*

impartial /ɪm'paʃǝl/, *adj.* fair; unbiased; just. **—impartiality, impartialness,** *n.*

impassable /ɪm'pasǝbǝl/, *adj.* that cannot be passed over, through, or along: *muddy, impassable roads.* **—impassability,** *n.*

impasse /'ɪmpas/, *n.* **1.** a position from which there is no escape. **2.** a road or way that has no outlet. [F]

impassioned /ɪm'pæʃǝnd/, *adj.* filled with passion; passionate; ardent: *The student made an impassioned speech against war.*

impassive /ɪm'pæsɪv/, *adj.* **1.** without emotion; apathetic; unmoved. **2.** calm; serene. **—impassiveness, impassivity,** *n.*

impasto /ɪmˈpæstoʊ/, *n.* **1.** (in painting) the laying on of colors thickly. **2.** color laid on in this way. [It]

impatient /ɪmˈpeɪʃənt/, *adj.* **1.** not patient; not bearing pain, opposition, etc., calmly. **2.** showing lack of patience: *an impatient answer.* **3.** restless in desire or expectation; eagerly wanting (to do something). [ME, from L: not bearing or enduring] —**impatience,** *n.*

impeach /ɪmˈpiːtʃ/, *v.t.* **1.** to question the credibility of: *to impeach a witness.* **2.** to bring a charge against a person relating to treason or some other serious criminal offence. [ME, from OF: hinder, from LL: catch, entangle, from L: fetter] —**impeachable,** *adj.* —**impeachment,** *n.*

impeccable /ɪmˈpɛkəbəl/, *adj.* **1.** faultless: *impeccable manners.* **2.** not liable to sin; free from the possibility of doing wrong. [LL] —**impeccability,** *n.*

impecunious /ˌɪmpəˈkjuːniəs/, *adj.* having no money; penniless; poor. —**impecuniousness, impecuniosity,** *n.*

impedance /ɪmˈpiːdəns/, *n.* **1.** the resistance in an electric circuit to an alternating current, measured in ohms. *Symbol:* Z **2.** obstruction; resistance.

impede /ɪmˈpiːd/, *v.t.* **-peded, -peding.** to slow down in movement or progress by means of obstacles; obstruct; hinder. [L: entangle, hamper (orig., as to the feet)]

impediment /ɪmˈpɛdəmənt/, *n.* **1.** some physical defect, esp. a speech disorder: *an impediment in speech.* **2.** an obstruction; hindrance; obstacle. [ME, from L: hindrance] —**impedimental,** *n.*

impel /ɪmˈpɛl/, *v.t.* **-pelled, -pelling. 1.** to drive or urge forward; press on; compel. **2.** to drive, or cause to move, onwards; propel. [L]

impend /ɪmˈpɛnd/, *v.i.* **1.** to be near at hand; imminent. **2.** to hang; overhang (fol. by *over*). [L: hang over] —**impending,** *adj.*

impenetrable /ɪmˈpɛnətrəbəl/, *adj.* **1.** not penetrable; not able to be penetrated, pierced, or entered. **2.** not open to ideas, influences, etc. **3.** not able to be understood; unfathomable: *an impenetrable mystery.* **4.** *Phys.* unable to share the same space with any other body. —**impenetrableness, impenetrability,** *n.*

imperative /ɪmˈpɛrətɪv/, *adj.* **1.** not to be avoided; necessary: *an imperative duty.* **2.** like or expressing a command; commanding. **3.** *Gram.* relating to the verb mood used in commands, requests, etc. ◇*n.* **4.** a command. **5.** *Gram.* **a.** the imperative mood. **b.** a verb in this mood, as *Listen! Go! Run!* etc. [L]

imperator /ˌɪmpəˈrɑːtɔː, -ˈreɪtə/, *n.* **1.** an all-powerful ruler. **2.** a title of the Roman emperors. **3.** the title given to a Roman general who had succeeded in battle. [L. See EMPEROR]

imperceptible /ˌɪmpəˈsɛptəbəl/, *adj.* very slight, gradual; not easily perceived: *imperceptible changes in height.* —**imperceptibility, imperceptibleness,** *n.*

imperfect /ɪmˈpɜːfəkt/, *adj.* **1.** marked by defects; faulty. **2.** not perfect; lacking completeness: *imperfect hearing.* ◇*n.* **3.** →**imperfect tense.** [L: unfinished] —**imperfection,** *n.*

imperfect tense, *n. Gram.* the tense which indicates action going on but not completed, esp. in the past. For example, in the sentence *He was building the wall when it happened,* the verb *was building* is in the imperfect tense. See Appendix.

imperial /ɪmˈpɪəriəl/, *adj.* **1.** of or relating to an empire, emperor or empress. **2.** typical of the power of a ruling state over those countries, etc., under its control. **3.** having the power of an emperor or ruler. **4.** having a commanding or domineering quality, manner, or appearance; imperious. **5.** very fine or grand; magnificent. **6.** (of weights and measures) of the system legally established in Britain. **7.** (*oft. cap.*) of or relating to the British Empire. ◇*n.* **8.** a small, pointed beard growing beneath the lower lip. [ME, from L: of the empire or emperor]

imperialism /ɪmˈpɪəriəlɪzəm/, *n.* **1.** the policy of widening the rule or power of an empire or nation over foreign countries, or of holding colonies and dependencies. **2.** imperial government or system of government. —**imperialist,** *n., adj.* —**imperialistic,** *adj.*

imperil /ɪmˈpɛrəl/, *v.t.* **-rilled, -rilling.** to put in a position where something may cause harm; endanger.

imperious /ɪmˈpɪəriəs/, *adj.* **1.** ruling over in a severe, domineering manner; overbearing; dictatorial: *an imperious tyrant; imperious temper.* **2.** urgent; imperative: *imperious need.* [L: commanding]

impermanent /ɪmˈpɜːmənənt/, *adj.* not lasting or permanent. —**impermanence, impermanency,** *n.*

impermeable /ɪmˈpɜːmiəbəl/, *adj.* not allowing passage of another substance, esp. a fluid, through pores, etc.; not permeable. —**impermeability, impermeableness,** *n.*

impersonal /ɪmˈpɜːsənəl/, *adj.* **1.** without personal reference; not personal: *an impersonal remark.* **2.** having no personality: *an impersonal god.* **3.** *Gram.* (relating to a verb) having only third person singular forms, such as *it is raining.* —**impersonality,** *n.* —**impersonalise,** *v.t.*

impersonate /ɪmˈpɜːsəneɪt/, *v.t.* **-nated, -nating. 1.** to take the character of; pretend to be. **2.** to represent in personal or bodily form; personify; typify. **3.** to act (a part), esp. on the stage. —**impersonator,** *n.*

impertinence /ɪmˈpɜːtənəns/, *n.* **1.** rudeness; insolence; presumption. **2.** something foolish enough to be funny or not important; triviality; absurdity. **3.** something rude or impertinent. —**impertinent,** *adj.*

imperturbable /ˌɪmpəˈtɜːbəbəl/, *adj.* not able to be easily shaken or excited; calm: *imperturbable state of mind.* —**imperturbability,** *n.*

impervious /ɪmˈpɜːviəs/, *adj.* **1.** not allowing passage, esp. of substances that flow;

impervious — impose

impermeable: *impervious to water*. **2.** not moved or affected by (fol. by *to*): *impervious to reason*. Also, **imperviable**.

impetigo /ˌɪmpəˈtaɪgoʊ/, *n.* a contagious skin disease, esp. of children. [L: attack]

impetuous /ɪmˈpɛtʃuəs/, *adj.* **1.** acting with or noted for sudden or hasty energy: *an impetuous person*. **2.** moving with great force; violent: *the impetuous winds*. [ME, from L: an attack] — **impetuosity**, *n.*

impetus /ˈɪmpətəs/, *n.*, *pl.* **-tuses**. **1.** a moving force; impulse; stimulus: *a fresh impetus*. **2.** a force that starts a body moving or tends to keep it moving and resisting changes in its motion; energy of motion. [L: onset]

impf., *Abbrev.* imperfect.

impiety /ɪmˈpaɪəti/, *n.*, *pl.* **-ties**. **1.** lack of reverence for God; lack of piety; ungodliness. **2.** an act, practice, etc., which shows lack of reverence for God.

impinge /ɪmˈpɪndʒ/, *v.i.*, **-pinged**, **-pinging**. **1.** to strike or knock; collide (fol. by *on*, *upon*, or *against*): *Rays of light impinge on the eye*. **2.** to go beyond the proper limits; trespass; infringe. [L: drive in or at, strike against]

impious /ˈɪmpiəs, ɪmˈpaɪəs/, *adj.* **1.** lacking deep respect and love for God; ungodly; irreverent. **2.** not respectful and loving towards parents; undutiful. [L]

impish /ˈɪmpɪʃ/, *adj.* of or like an imp; mischievous.

implacable /ɪmˈplækəbəl/, *adj.* not able to be appeased or calmed; not placable; inexorable: *an implacable enemy*. — **implacability**, **implacableness**, *n.*

implant /ɪmˈplænt, -ˈplɑnt/, *v.*; /ˈɪmplænt, -plɑnt/, *n.* ◇*v.t.* **1.** to teach or instil (an idea, principle, etc.) so as to fix it firmly in the mind: *implant sound principles*. **2.** to plant in something; infix: *implant living tissue*. **3.** to plant: *implant the seeds*. ◇*n.* **4.** *Med.* tissue implanted into the body from another body or part of the same body. [IM-¹ + PLANT, *v.*] — **implantation**, *n.*

implausible /ɪmˈplɔzəbəl/, *adj.* not plausible, seeming not to be true or believable. — **implausibility**, *n.*

implement /ˈɪmpləmənt/, *n.*; /ˈɪmpləmɛnt/, *v.*, ◇*n.* **1.** an instrument, tool, or utensil used for a special purpose: *farm implements*; *kitchen implements*. ◇*v.t.* **2.** to put (a plan, etc.) into effect. [ME, from LL: a filling up (hence, probably, a thing that completes a want), from L] — **implementation**, *n.*

implicate /ˈɪmplɪkeɪt/, *v.t.*, **-cated**, **-cating**. **1.** to involve as being concerned in a matter, affair, condition, etc.: *to be implicated in a crime*. **2.** to suggest as a necessary condition; imply. [L: entangled, involved]

implication /ˌɪmplɪˈkeɪʃən/, *n.* **1.** something implied or suggested as naturally to be understood without being actually stated. **2.** the state of being involved in some matter: *implication in a crime*.

implicit /ɪmˈplɪsɪt/, *adj.* **1.** (of belief, obedience, etc.) unquestioning; absolute: *She has implicit faith in God*. **2.** suggested, rather than actually stated: *implicit agreement*. **3.** contained in effect, although not in name or fact; inherent (fol. by *in*). [L: entangled, involved]

implied /ɪmˈplaɪd/, *adj.* included, pointed out or suggested without being actually stated or expressed; understood: *an implied rebuke*.

implode /ɪmˈploʊd/, *v.i.*, **-ploded**, **-ploding**. to burst inwards (opposed to *explode*). [IM-¹ + -*plode*, modelled on EXPLODE] — **implosion**, *n.*

implore /ɪmˈplɔr/, *v.t.*, **-plored**, **-ploring**. **1.** to call upon (a person) in an urgent or humble manner, for help, mercy, etc.; beseech; entreat: *They implored him to go*. **2.** to make an urgent, humble request for (help, mercy, pardon, etc.): *implore forgiveness*. [L: invoke with tears]

imply /ɪmˈplaɪ/, *v.t.*, **-plied**, **-plying**. **1.** to include as a necessary condition: *Speech implies a speaker*. **2.** (of words) to mean or signify. **3.** to suggest (something) without expressly stating it. [ME, from OF, from L: enfold, entangle, involve]

impolite /ˌɪmpəˈlaɪt/, *adj.* not polite or well-mannered; uncivil; rude.

impolitic /ɪmˈpɒlətɪk/, *adj.* not wise; inexpedient; injudicious: *an impolitic comment*.

import /ɪmˈpɔt, ˈɪmpɔt/, *v.*; /ˈɪmpɔt/, *n.* ◇*v.t.* **1.** to bring in from a foreign country, as goods, etc., for sale, use, processing, or to sell again to another country. **2.** to make known or express, as a meaning with words, actions, etc. ◇*n.* **3.** something that is brought in from abroad; an imported commodity or article. **4.** the act of importing or bringing in, as of goods from abroad. **5.** meaning; implication; purport. **6.** importance; consequence. [ME, from L: bring in, bring about] — **importable**, *adj.* — **importer**, *n.* — **importation**, *n.*

importance /ɪmˈpɔtns/, *n.* **1.** the quality or fact of being important. **2.** important position or standing; personal or social consequence. **3.** important manner.

important /ɪmˈpɔtnt/, *adj.* **1.** having great meaning or effect: *an important event*. **2.** mattering much (fol. by *to*): *details important to a fair decision*. **3.** having more than usual claim to consideration or notice: *an important example*. **4.** prominent; leading: *an important part*; *an important citizen*. **5.** having great influence or power, such as a person, social position, family, etc. [F, from ML: be of consequence, L: bring in, cause]

importunate /ɪmˈpɔtʃənət/, *adj.* **1.** urgent or persistent in demands or questions. **2.** troublesome.

importune /ɪmˈpɔtʃun, ˌɪmpɔˈtjun/, *v.t.*, **-tuned**, **-tuning**. to trouble or annoy with persistent, urgent demands. [ME, from MF, from L: unfit, inconvenient, troublesome] — **importunity**, *n.*

impose /ɪmˈpoʊz/, *v.*, **-posed**, **-posing**. ◇*v.t.* **1.** to lay on or set as something to be paid, put up with, obeyed, fulfilled, etc.: *to impose taxes*. **2.** to push or force (oneself, one's

impose company, etc.) upon others. **3.** to pass off dishonestly or deceptively. ◇*v.i.* **4.** to make a mark on the mind. **5.** to push or force oneself or one's needs: *to impose upon someone's kindness.* [F]

imposing /ɪmˈpoʊzɪŋ/, *adj.* making an impression on the mind, as by great size, stately appearance, etc.

imposition /ˌɪmpəˈzɪʃən/, *n.* **1.** the laying on of something as a burden, duty, etc. **2.** something placed on someone, as a burden; unusual or extraordinarily difficult requirement or task. **3.** an imposing upon a person as by taking advantage of their good nature, or something that has the effect of doing this. **4.** the ceremonial laying on of hands, as in confirmation.

impossible /ɪmˈpɒsəbəl/, *adj.* **1.** not possible; that cannot be, exist, or happen. **2.** not able to be done or effected: *It is impossible for my son to carry me.* **3.** not able to be true. **4.** not to be done, put up with, etc.: *an impossible situation.* **5.** hopelessly unsuitable; objectionable: *an impossible person.* [ME, from L] –**impossibility**, *n.*

impostor /ɪmˈpɒstə/, *n.* someone who uses tricks to deceive others, esp. by assuming a false name or character. [L: impose]

imposture /ɪmˈpɒstʃə/, *n.* the action or practice of tricking and deceiving others. [L: impose]

impotent /ˈɪmpətənt/, *adj.* **1.** lacking power or ability (to do something). **2.** without force or effectiveness. **3.** lacking bodily strength and command, as an aged person or a cripple. **4.** (of a male) completely lacking in sexual power. See **frigid**. –**impotence**, *n.*

impound /ɪmˈpaʊnd/, *v.t.* **1.** to shut up in a pound, as a stray animal. **2.** to confine within an enclosure or within limits: *The soldiers impounded the prisoners.* **3.** to seize or take; confiscate, esp. by law, as a document for evidence.

impoverish /ɪmˈpɒvərɪʃ, -vrɪʃ/, *v.t.* **1.** to cause to become poor: *The country was impoverished by war.* **2.** to make poor in quality, etc.; exhaust the strength or richness of: *to impoverish the soil.* [ME, from OF]

impracticable /ɪmˈpræktɪkəbəl/, *adj.* **1.** not able to be put into practice with the available means: *an impracticable plan.* **2.** not meant for practical use or purposes, as an instrument, material, etc. –**impracticability, impracticableness**, *n.*

impractical /ɪmˈpræktɪkəl/, *adj.* not practical. –**impracticality, impracticalness**, *n.*

imprecate /ˈɪmprəkeɪt/, *v.*, -**cated**, -**cating**. ◇*v.t.* **1.** to call down or invoke (esp. evil or curses) upon a person, etc. ◇*v.i.* **2.** to curse; swear. [L: invoke] –**imprecation**, *n.* –**imprecator**, *n.* –**imprecatory**, *adj.*

imprecise /ˌɪmprəˈsaɪs/, *adj.* not carefully and clearly stated; ill-defined. –**imprecision**, *n.*

impregnable /ɪmˈpregnəbəl/, *adj.* **1.** strong enough to resist attack; not to be taken by force: *an impregnable fort.* **2.** not to be overcome or overthrown: *an impregnable argument.* [ME, from F] –**impregnability**, *n.*

impregnate /ˈɪmpregneɪt/, *v.t.*, -**nated**, -**nating**. **1.** to make pregnant; get with child or young. **2.** to fertilise. **3.** to saturate. [LL: made pregnant] –**impregnation**, *n.* –**impregnator**, *n.*

impresario /ˌɪmprəˈsɑriou/, *n., pl.* -**os**. **1.** the organiser or manager of an opera, ballet, theatre company or orchestra. **2.** a personal manager, teacher, or trainer of concert artists. [It]

impress /ɪmˈpres/, *v.*, -**pressed** or (*Archaic*) -**prest**, -**pressing**; /ˈɪmpres/, *n.* ◇*v.t.* **1.** to affect deeply or strongly in mind or feelings, esp. favorably. **2.** to produce a favorable reaction in: *Her manners impressed us.* **3.** to fix firmly in the mind, as ideas, facts, etc. **4.** to produce (a mark, figure, etc.) by pressure; stamp; imprint. ◇*n.* **5.** a mark made by or as by pressure; stamp; imprint. [ME, from L: pressed upon] –**impresser**, *n.*

impression /ɪmˈpreʃən/, *n.* **1.** a strong effect produced on the mind, feelings, etc. **2.** the first effect upon the mind in outward or inward sensation. **3.** an idea, belief, etc., that is often unclear. **4.** a mark, indentation, figure, etc., produced by pressure. **5.** *Print, etc.* **a.** the process or result of printing from type, plates, etc. **b.** a printed copy from type, a plate, etc. **6.** a mould taken in plastic materials, plaster of Paris, etc. **7.** imitation, esp. for entertainment, of the habits of some person or type. [ME, from L]

impressionable /ɪmˈpreʃənəbəl, -ˈpreʃnəbəl/, *adj.* **1.** easily influenced; susceptible. **2.** able to be influenced.

impressionism /ɪmˈpreʃənɪzəm/, *n.* a style of painting, music, etc., concerned with exploring the mood, feelings or changing impressions of or induced by a subject. –**impressionist**, *n., adj.*

impressive /ɪmˈpresɪv/, *adj.* such as to impress the mind: *an impressive speech.*

imprimatur /ˌɪmprəˈmɑtə, -ˈmeɪtə/, *n.* **1.** official permission to print or publish a book, etc. **2.** licence; sanction; approval. [NL: let it be printed]

imprint /ˈɪmprɪnt/, *n.*; /ɪmˈprɪnt/, *v.* ◇*n.* **1.** a mark made by pressure. **2.** any impressed effect. **3.** information printed at the foot or back of the titlepage of a book giving the name of the publisher, etc. ◇*v.t.* **4.** to impress (a quality, character, or distinguishing mark). **5.** to fix firmly on the mind, etc. ◇*v.i.* **6.** to learn to identify, by voice, smell, etc. (fol. by *on*): *Ducklings imprint on the mother's voice.* [ME, from OF, from L: impress, imprint]

imprison /ɪmˈprɪzən/, *v.t.* **1.** to put into a prison. **2.** to shut up as if in a prison. –**imprisonment**, *n.*

improbable /ɪmˈprɒbəbəl/, *adj.* unlikely to be true or to happen.

impromptu /ɪmˈprɒmptju/, *adj.* **1.** made or done without preparation: *an impromptu talk.* **2.** suddenly or quickly prepared, made, etc.: *an impromptu dinner.* ◇*adv.* **3.** without

impromptu preparation: *a speech made impromptu.* ◇*n.* **4.** something impromptu, as a speech, musical composition, etc. [F, from L: in readiness]

improper /ɪm'prɒpə/, *adj.* **1.** not proper; not really belonging, or right: *an improper use for a thing.* **2.** not in accordance with correct behavior, manners, etc.: *improper language.* **3.** unsuitable: *improper tools.*

improper fraction, *n.* a fraction having the number above the line (numerator) greater than number below the line (denominator).

impropriety /ɪmprə'praɪətɪ/, *n., pl.* **-ties.** the quality of being improper or incorrect, in action, behavior, etc.

improve /ɪm'pruːv/, *v.*, **-proved, -proving.** ◇*v.t.* **1.** to bring into a better condition: *to improve one's health.* **2.** make good use of: *to improve an opportunity.* ◇*v.i.* **3.** to increase in value, excellence, etc.: *The situation is improving.* **4.** to make improvements (fol. by *on* or *upon*): *to improve on one's earlier work.* [AF, from OF] —**improvable,** *adj.*

improved pasture, *n.* **1.** an improved type of plant, grown on farmland as food for animals. **2.** an area of land on which such a crop is grown.

improvement /ɪm'pruːvmənt/, *n.* **1.** a change or addition whereby a thing is improved. **2.** a bringing into a more valuable or desirable condition, as of land; a making or becoming better; a betterment.

improvident /ɪm'prɒvədənt/, *adj.* **1.** careless; thoughtless. **2.** failing to provide for future needs. —**improvidence,** *n.*

improvise *or* **improvize** /'ɪmprəvaɪz/, *v.*, **-vised, -vising.** ◇*v.t.* **1.** to prepare or provide quickly, using the materials at hand. **2.** to compose (poetry, music, etc.) at a moment's notice. ◇*v.i.* **3.** to create, prepare, etc. at a moment's notice: *He improvised a way of fixing the tap.* [F, from It, from L: unforeseen, unexpected] —**improviser,** *n.* —**improvisation,** *n.*

imprudent /ɪm'pruːdənt/, *adj.* not wise; rash. [L] —**imprudence,** *n.*

impudent /'ɪmpjudənt, -pjə-/, *adj.* marked by a shameless boldness; insolent: *impudent behavior.* [L: shameless] —**impudence,** *n.*

impugn /ɪm'pjuːn/, *v.t.* to attack by words or arguments; challenge as false. [ME, from OF, from L: attack] —**impugnable,** *adj.*

impulse /'ɪmpʌls/, *n.* **1.** the influence of a particular feeling, mental state, etc.: *to act under the impulse of pity.* **2.** a sudden desire to act, as without thought: *He ran on impulse.* **3.** (the effect of) an action or force driving (someone) onwards: *The impulse to win kept him going.* **4.** *Physiol.* a stimulus carried by the nerves or muscles. **5.** *Elect.* a single, usu. sudden, flow of current in one direction. [L: a push against]

impulsive /ɪm'pʌlsɪv/, *adj.* given to acting on sudden thoughts or desires: *an impulsive child.* **2.** having the power or effect of urging or driving onward: *impulsive forces.*

impunity /ɪm'pjuːnətɪ/, *n.* freedom from punishment or harm resulting from one's action: *I can speak with impunity.* [L: omission of punishment]

impure /ɪm'pjuə/, *adj.* **1.** not pure; mixed with other matter: *impure water.* **2.** changed by something added, as color. **3.** (of art, architecture, etc.) showing a mixture of styles. **4.** (of things, animals, etc.) unclean, esp. in relation to religious beliefs. **5.** not morally pure; unchaste: *impure language.* [L: not pure] —**impurity,** *n.*

impute /ɪm'pjuːt/, *v.t.*, **-puted, -puting.** **1.** to attribute (something unpleasant) to a person: *I impute to him the disaster which followed.* **2.** to consider (something) as coming from a cause or source: *We impute her happiness to her new job.* [ME, from L: bring into the reckoning] —**imputation,** *n.* —**imputable,** *adj.* —**imputative,** *adj.*

Imran Khan /ˌɪmrɑːn 'kɑːn/, *n.* born 1952, Pakistani cricketer; noted as an all-rounder and Test Captain.

in /ɪn/, *prep.* a particle expressing: **1.** containment within space, limits, surroundings, etc.: *in the city; in politics.* **2.** containment within, or found during, or at the end of, a period or limit of time: *in ancient times; return in ten minutes.* **3.** condition, relation, manner, etc.: *in darkness; in sickness; in crossing the street; in French.* **4.** object or purpose: *in honor of the event.* **5.** movement or direction from without to a point within (now usu. *into*), or a change from one condition to another: *to put in operation; break in two.* **6.** pregnant with: *The cow's in calf again.* **7.** Some special uses are:

be in it, to be part of an action.
in it, of advantage: *What's in it for me?*
in that, for the reason that.
nothing in it, (in a competition) no difference in performance, etc.

◇*adv.* **8.** in or into some place, position, state, etc. **9.** on the inside, or within. **10.** in one's house or office. **11.** in power. **12.** owning, or living in. **13.** having the turn to play, in a game. **14. count in,** to include in a future plan. **15.** in favor; on friendly terms: *He's in with the director.* **16.** in fashion: *High heels are in this year.* **17.** in season: *Oranges are in now.* ◇**18.** Some special uses are:

in for, 1. about to undergo (esp. something unpleasant). **2.** entered for. **3.** sharing in.
in for it, about to be punished.
in on, having a share in or a part of, esp. something secret: *He's in on the plot; in on the secret.*
well in with, on good terms with.

◇*n.* **19.** (*pl.*) those who are in, as the political party in power. **20. ins and outs, a.** windings and turnings. **b.** fine details. [ME and OE]

in-¹, a prefix representing English *in*, as in *income, inland,* and also used to form verbs, as in *intrust, inweave,* etc. [ME and OE]

in-², a prefix of Latin origin meaning primarily 'in', used also to form verbs with the same force as **in-¹**, as in *incarcerate.* Also, **il-¹, im-¹, ir-²**. See **em-¹, en-¹**. [L, representing *in*, prep.]

in-³, a prefix of Latin origin similar to English *un-*, having a negative force, freely used to create word forms in English, esp. adjectives, and nouns, as in *inattention, inexpensive, inorganic.* Also, **il-², im-², ir-²**. [L]

-in[1], a noun suffix used in chemical and mineralogical names mainly for certain neutral compounds, as *albumin*, and for other pharmaceutical substances, as *penicillin* and *aspirin*. [NL]

-in[2], the second part of a compound, indicating a communal session of the activity named, as *sit-in, sleep-in, slim-in, teach-in*.

in., *Abbrev.* inch; inches.

In, *Chem. Symbol.* indium.

inability /ɪnəˈbɪləti/, *n.* lack of ability, power, skill, etc.

in absentia /ɪn æbˈsentiə, -ʃə/, *adv.* in or during (one's) absence. [L]

inaccessible /ɪnəkˈsesəbəl/, *adj.* not able to be reached; unapproachable.

inaccuracy /ɪnˈækjʊrəsi/, *n., pl.* **-cies.** 1. the quality of being incorrect. 2. something which is incorrect. —**inaccurate**, *adj.*

inactive /ɪnˈæktɪv/, *adj.* 1. not active; inert. 2. lazy; indolent; passive. —**inactivity, inactiveness**, *n.*

inadequate /ɪnˈædəkwət/, *adj.* 1. not adequate. 2. (of a person) lacking the abilities or qualities thought to be necessary.

inadvertent /ɪnədˈvɜtnt/, *adj.* 1. not paying attention; heedless. 2. unintentional: *an inadvertent insult*. —**inadvertence**, *n.*

inalienable /ɪnˈeɪliənəbəl/, *adj.* not able to be given to another: *inalienable rights*.

inane /ɪnˈeɪn/, *adj.* 1. lacking sense or ideas; silly: *inane questions*. 2. empty; void. [L: empty, vain] —**inanity**, *n.*

inanimate /ɪnˈænəmət/, *adj.* 1. not living; lifeless. 2. spiritless; dull.

inappreciable /ɪnəˈpriʃəbəl/, *adj.* very slight or gradual, as not to be noticed; insignificant: *an inappreciable difference*.

inappropriate /ɪnəˈproʊpriət/, *adj.* not appropriate or fitting.

inapt /ɪnˈæpt/, *adj.* 1. not suited or fitted. 2. without ability. —**inaptitude**, *n.*

inarticulate /ɪnaˈtɪkjələt/, *adj.* 1. (of speech) not clear or understandable: *inarticulate sounds*. 2. unable to use clear speech: *inarticulate with anger*. [LL: not distinct]

inasmuch as /ɪnəzˈmʌtʃ əz/, *conj.* 1. in view of the fact that; seeing that; since. 2. in so far as; to such a degree as.

inattentive /ɪnəˈtentɪv/, *adj.* not paying attention (*to*).

inaugural /ɪnˈɔgjərəl/, *adj.* 1. of or relating to a formal beginning of something: *an inaugural flight*. ◇*n.* 2. an address, as by a president, at the beginning of a term of office. [F, from L: INAUGURATE]

inaugurate /ɪnˈɔgjəreɪt/, *v.t.*, **-rated, -rating.** 1. to make a formal beginning of; initiate; commence; begin. 2. to introduce into office, etc., with formal ceremonies; install. [L: consecrated or installed with augural ceremonies] —**inauguration**, *n.* —**inaugurator**, *n.*

inauspicious /ɪnɔˈspɪʃəs/, *adj.* unfavorable; showing a bad omen.

inborn /ˈɪnbɔn/, *adj.* given by nature; innate: *an inborn clumsiness*.

inbred /ˈɪnbrɛd/, *adj.* 1. developed within; innate; native. 2. resulting from or involved in breeding with close relatives.

inbreeding /ˈɪnbridɪŋ/, *n.* production of offspring resulting from the mating of related individuals such as cousins, brother-sister, or self-fertilising plants. —**inbreed**, *v.*

Inca /ˈɪŋkə/, *n.* one of the dominant groups of South American Indians who occupied Peru prior to the Spanish conquest. [Sp, Pg, from Quechua] —**Incan**, *n., adj.*

incalculable /ɪnˈkælkjʊləbəl, -kjə-/, *adj.* 1. not able to be calculated; beyond calculation. 2. not able to be forecast.

in camera /ɪn ˈkæmərə/, *adv.* 1. (of a case) heard by a judge in his private room or in court with the public kept out. 2. in private; in secret: *The meeting was held in camera*. [L: in the chamber]

incandescence /ɪnkænˈdesəns/, *n.* 1. the state of a body caused by near white heat, when it may be used as a source of artificial light. 2. artificial light from a body which has been raised to a high temperature.

incandescent /ɪnkænˈdesənt/, *adj.* 1. (of light, etc.) produced by heat. 2. glowing or white with heat. 3. very bright; brilliant. [L: growing hot] —**incandesce**, *v.*

incantation /ɪnkænˈteɪʃən/, *n.* 1. the chanting of words thought to have magical power. 2. spell; charm. [ME, from LL: enchantment]

incapable /ɪnˈkeɪpəbəl/, *adj.* 1. not able. 2. not having the ability or power for a certain act (fol. by *of*). 3. without ordinary ability; incompetent: *incapable workers*. [LL]

incapacitate /ɪnkəˈpæsəteɪt/, *v.t.*, **-tated, -tating.** to make unable or unfit; disqualify. —**incapacitation**, *n.*

incapacity /ɪnkəˈpæsəti/, *n., pl.* **-ties.** lack of ability; incapability. [ML]

incarcerate /ɪnˈkasəreɪt/, *v.t.*, **-rated, -rating.** 1. to imprison; confine. 2. to enclose; constrict closely. [ML, from L] —**incarceration**, *n.*

incarnate /ɪnˈkanət, -neɪt/, *adj.*; /ˈɪnkaneɪt/, *v.*, **-nated, -nating.** ◇*adj.* 1. having a bodily, esp. a human, form; personified: *a devil incarnate; goodness incarnate*. ◇*v.t.* 2. to put into a clear form, as an idea. 3. to be the form or type of. [ME, from LL: made flesh] —**incarnation**, *n.*

incendiary /ɪnˈsendʒəri/, *adj., n., pl.* **-aries.** ◇*adj.* 1. used or meant for setting property on fire: *incendiary bombs*. 2. of or relating to the criminal setting on fire of property. 3. likely to cause trouble, discontent, etc.; inflammatory: *incendiary speeches*. ◇*n.* 4. someone who unlawfully sets fire to buildings; arsonist. 5. *Mil.* a shell, bomb, etc., containing phosphorus or similar material producing great heat. 6. one who stirs up trouble, discontent, etc.; an agitator. [L: causing fire]

incense[1] /'ɪnsens/, *n.* **1.** gum or other substance producing a sweet smell when burnt. **2.** perfume or smoke arising from such a substance when burnt. [LL: incense]

incense[2] /ɪn'sens/, *v.t.*, **-censed, -censing.** to make angry; enrage. [ME, from L: set on fire, kindled]

incentive /ɪn'sentɪv/, *n.* **1.** something that influences (someone) to act. ◊*adj.* **2.** influencing, as to action; stimulating; provocative. **3.** of or relating to extra money, etc., given to workers, to encourage them to greater effort.

inception /ɪn'sepʃən/, *n.* a beginning; start.

incessant /ɪn'sesənt/, *adj.* continuing without stopping: *an incessant noise.* [LL: unceasing]

incest /'ɪnsest/, *n.* (the crime of) sexual intercourse between closely related people. [ME, from L: unchaste]

incestuous /ɪn'sestʃuəs/, *adj.* **1.** guilty of incest. **2.** relating to incest. **3.** (of people) spending all their time with a particular group, institution, etc., to the exclusion of outside influence.

inch /ɪntʃ/, *n.* **1.** the unit of length in the imperial system, $\frac{1}{12}$ foot or 25.4×10^{-3} m (25.4 mm). **2.** a very small amount of anything. **3. by inches, a.** by a small amount: *He escaped death by inches.* **b.** Also, **inch by inch.** very gradually. **4. every inch,** in every way: *every inch a king.* **5. within an inch of,** almost; very near: *She came within an inch of being killed.* ◊*v.t., v.i.* **6.** to move by inches, or a small amount at a time. [ME; OE *ynce*, from L: twelfth part, inch, ounce]

inchoate /'ɪnkoʊeɪt/, *adj.* **1.** just begun; incipient. **2.** not fully formed; rudimentary. **3.** lacking organisation; unformed. [L: begun]

incidence /'ɪnsədəns/, *n.* **1.** the extent of a thing or the range within which it happens: *the incidence of disease.* **2.** the falling, or direction or manner of falling, of a ray of light, etc., on a surface.

incident /'ɪnsədənt/, *n.* **1.** an event; occurrence. **2.** a particular event, or action, as in a story or play. **3.** something unimportant that happens in connection with something else. **4.** an event, perhaps arising from political unrest, which may lead to war, etc. ◊*adj.* **5.** →**incidental** (defs 1 and 2). [ME, from L: befalling]

incidental /ɪnsə'dentl/, *adj.* **1.** happening or likely to happen, as something unimportant at the same time as something of greater importance takes place. **2.** likely to happen or naturally happening (fol. by *to*). **3.** coming as a small addition to the regular or main amount: *incidental costs.* ◊*n.* **4.** something incidental, as an event. **5.** (*pl.*) minor costs. —**incidentally,** *adv.*

incinerate /ɪn'sɪnəreɪt/, *v.*, **-rated, -rating.** ◊*v.t.* **1.** to reduce to ashes; cremate. ◊*v.i.* **2.** to burn to ashes. [ML, from L]

incinerator /ɪn'sɪnəreɪtə/, *n.* an apparatus for burning; a furnace.

incipient /ɪn'sɪpiənt/, *adj.* beginning to exist or appear; in an initial stage. [L] —**incipience,** *n.*

incise /ɪn'saɪz/, *v.t.*, **-cised, -cising.** to cut into; cut marks, etc., upon. [F, from L: cut into] —**incised,** *adj.*

incision /ɪn'sɪʒən/, *n.* **1.** a cut; gash; notch. **2.** a cutting into, esp. for medical purposes. **3.** sharpness; keenness esp. of wit, etc. [ME, from L]

incisive /ɪn'saɪsɪv/, *adj.* **1.** sharp; penetrating; biting: *an incisive tone of voice.* **2.** clear; keen; acute: *incisive thoughts.* **3.** used for cutting: *the incisive teeth.* —**incisiveness,** *n.*

incisor /ɪn'saɪzə/, *n.* a tooth in the front part of the jaw, used for cutting. [NL]

incite /ɪn'saɪt/, *v.t.*, **-cited, -citing.** to urge on; stimulate or prompt to action. [late ME, from L: set in motion] —**incitement,** *n.*

incivility /ɪnsə'vɪləti/, *n., pl.* **-ties.** the act, quality or fact of being rude.

inclement /ɪn'klemənt/, *adj.* (of the weather, etc.) stormy; severe. [L: harsh] —**inclemency,** *n.*

inclination /ɪnklə'neɪʃən/, *n.* **1.** a tendency; preference (esp. of the mind or will): *much against his inclination.* **2.** something to which one has a tendency. **3.** the act or result of inclining. **4.** a change or amount of change from a normal, esp. horizontal or vertical, direction or position. **5.** a sloped surface. **6.** *Maths.* the difference in direction of two lines or two planes as measured by the angle between them. [late ME, from L: a leaning] —**inclinational,** *adj.*

incline /ɪn'klaɪn/, *v.*, **-clined, -clining;** /'ɪnklaɪn, ɪn'klaɪn/, *n.* ◊*v.i.* **1.** to have a mental tendency; be disposed. **2.** to move from the vertical or horizontal; slant. **3.** to tend, in a physical sense: *The leaves incline to a blue color.* **4.** to tend in course or character. **5.** to lean; bend. ◊*v.t.* **6.** to influence (a person) in mind, habit, etc. (fol. by *to*). **7.** to bow (the head, etc.). **8.** to cause to lean or bend. **9.** to turn towards: *incline one's ear.* ◊*n.* **10.** an inclined surface; a slope. [L: incline]

inclinometer /ɪnklə'nɒmətə/, *n.* **1.** *Aeron.* an instrument for measuring the angle an aircraft makes with the horizontal. **2.** an instrument for measuring the slope or dip of the earth's magnetic force using a magnetic needle.

include /ɪn'klud/, *v.t.*, **-cluded, -cluding.** **1.** to contain, embrace, or comprise. **2.** to place in a group, class, etc. **3.** to contain as a smaller element within something larger. [ME, from L: shut in]

inclusion /ɪn'kluʒən/, *n.* **1.** the act of including. **2.** the condition of being included. **3.** *Biol.* a body found in the cytoplasm, as a granule, etc. **4.** *Mineral.* a solid body or body of gas or liquid enclosed within the mass of a mineral. **5.** *Geol.* **a.** a piece of another substance enclosed in a crystal. **b.** a piece of older rock enclosed in an igneous rock. [L]

inclusive /ɪn'klusɪv/, *adj.* **1.** being included for consideration; taking into account:

from six to ten inclusive. **2.** including a great deal, or everything concerned; comprehensive.

incognito /ɪnˈkɒɡˈnitoʊ/, *adj., adv., n., pl.* **-tos, -ti** /-ti/. ◇*adj., adv.* **1.** hiding one's name, appearance, etc., esp. to avoid recognition. ◇*n.* **2.** false character or disguise used to hide one's real identity. [It, from L: unknown]

incoherent /ɪnkoʊˈhɪərənt/, *adj.* **1.** without proper order; disjointed; rambling: *an incoherent sentence.* **2.** marked by unordered thought or language: *incoherent with rage.* **3.** loose; not attached: *incoherent dust.*

income /ˈɪnkʌm, ˈɪŋ-/, *n.* **1.** the returns from one's work, property, business, etc.; revenue; receipts. **2.** something that comes in.

income tax, *n.* a yearly government tax on personal incomes.

incommensurable /ɪnkəˈmɛnʃərəbəl/, *adj.* **1.** having no common measure or standard of comparison. **2.** *Maths.* (of two or more quantities) **a.** having no common measure. **b.** referring to two numbers that are not both integral multiples of the same number.

incommensurate /ɪnkəˈmɛnʃərət/, *adj.* not equal in measure; disproportionate; inadequate: *income incommensurate to our wants.*

incommode /ɪnkəˈmoʊd/, *v.t.* **-moded, -moding.** to discomfort; to inconvenience; to bother. [L]

incommunicable /ɪnkəˈmjuːnɪkəbəl/, *adj.* not able to be passed on or told to others.

incommunicado /ˌɪnkəmjuːnəˈkɑːdoʊ/, *adj.* (esp. of a prisoner) not allowed any communication with others. [Sp: COMMUNICATE]

incommunicative /ɪnkəˈmjuːnɪkətɪv/, *adj.* not expressing one's thoughts to others; reserved.

incomparable /ɪnˈkɒmpərəbəl, -prəbəl/, *adj.* not able to be compared with; unequalled: *incomparable beauty.*

incompatible /ɪnkəmˈpætəbəl/, *adj.* **1.** not able to exist together in peace. **2.** opposed in character; discordant. **3.** not able to exist together or be joined. **4.** *Logic.* (of two or more propositions) that cannot be true at the same time. **5.** *Biol.* of or relating to the inability of cells or tissue from one individual to combine with those of another as in transplantation, grafting or blood transfusions.

incompetent /ɪnˈkɒmpətənt/, *adj.* **1.** lacking the necessary skill or ability: *an incompetent worker.* ◇*n.* **2.** an incompetent person. [LL: insufficient] **-incompetence,** *n.*

incomplete /ɪnkəmˈpliːt/, *adj.* not complete; lacking some part. [ME, from LL]

incomprehensible /ˌɪnkɒmprəˈhɛnsəbəl/, *adj.* not understandable; unintelligible. **-incomprehensibility,** *n.*

incomprehension /ˌɪnkɒmprəˈhɛnʃən/, *n.* failure to understand; lack of comprehension.

inconceivable /ɪnkənˈsiːvəbəl/, *adj.* unimaginable; unthinkable; incredible.

inconclusive /ɪnkənˈkluːsɪv/, *adj.* **1.** not such as to settle a question: *inconclusive evidence.* **2.** without final results: *inconclusive experiments.*

incongruous /ɪnˈkɒŋɡruəs/, *adj.* **1.** out of keeping or place; inappropriate; absurd: *an incongruous effect.* **2.** not agreeing in character; lacking harmony of parts: *incongruous mixtures.* [L] **-incongruent,** *adj.* **-incongruity,** *n.*

inconsequent /ɪnˈkɒnsəkwənt/, *adj.* **1.** marked by lack of order or pattern in thought, speech, or action. **2.** not following as a conclusion: *an inconsequent solution.* **3.** not to the point; irrelevant: *an inconsequent remark.* **4.** not in keeping with the general character or design: *inconsequent ornamentation.* [L: without connection] **-inconsequence,** *n.*

inconsequential /ˌɪnkɒnsəˈkwɛnʃəl/, *adj.* **1.** of no importance; trivial. **2.** lacking order; illogical; irrelevant.

inconsiderate /ɪnkənˈsɪdərət, -drət/, *adj.* **1.** without proper regard for the rights or feelings of others: *It was inconsiderate of him to forget.* **2.** thoughtless.

inconsistent /ɪnkənˈsɪstənt/, *adj.* **1.** lacking order between the different parts or elements; self-contradictory: *inconsistent behavior.* **2.** lacking agreement, as one thing with another; at variance. **3.** acting not in accordance with stated principles. **-inconsistency,** *n.*

inconsolable /ɪnkənˈsoʊləbəl/, *adj.* not able to be comforted: *inconsolable grief.*

inconspicuous /ɪnkənˈspɪkjuəs/, *adj.* not noticeable or prominent.

inconstant /ɪnˈkɒnstənt/, *adj.* changeable; fickle; variable: *inconstant winds.* **-inconstancy,** *n.*

incontestable /ɪnkənˈtɛstəbəl/, *adj.* not to be questioned or argued; incontrovertible: *incontestable proof.*

incontinent /ɪnˈkɒntənənt/, *adj.* **1.** not holding or held in; unceasing or unrestrained: *an incontinent flow of talk.* **2.** lacking in control, esp. over sexual needs. **3.** *Pathol.* not able to hold natural discharges esp. of urine. [ME, from L: not holding back] **-incontinence, incontinency,** *n.*

incontrovertible /ˌɪnkɒntrəˈvɜːtəbəl/, *adj.* not able to be argued against; indisputable. **-incontrovertibility,** *n.*

inconvenience /ɪnkənˈviːniəns/, *n., v.,* **-ienced, -iencing.** ◇*n.* **1.** the quality or condition of being inconvenient. **2.** something that causes discomfort, trouble, etc. ◇*v.t.* **3.** to put to inconvenience; incommode.

inconvenient /ɪnkənˈviːniənt/, *adj.* awkward; inopportune; disadvantageous or troublesome: *an inconvenient time for a visit.* [ME, from L: not agreeing]

incorporate /ɪnˈkɔːpəreɪt/, *v.,* **-rated, -rating;** /ɪnˈkɔːpərət, -prət/, *adj.* ◇*v.t.* **1.** to create or form a legal association. **2.** to form into a society or organisation. **3.** to introduce into or include in, as a part within a whole. **4.** to form or combine into one body as ingredients. **5.** to collect in a body; organise. ◇*v.i.* **6.** to unite or combine so as to form one body.

incorporate

◇*adj.* **7.** formed, as a company. [ME, from LL: embodied]

incorporated /ɪnˈkɔːpəreɪtəd/, *adj.* **1.** formed as a company. **2.** combined in one body; made part of. —**incorporation**, *n.*

incorrect /ɪnkəˈrɛkt/, *adj.* **1.** not correct as to fact: *an incorrect statement.* **2.** improper: *incorrect behavior.* **3.** not correct in form or manner: *an incorrect copy.*

incorrigible /ɪnˈkɒrədʒəbəl/, *adj.* **1.** bad beyond correction or improvement: *an incorrigible liar.* **2.** uncontrollable; wilful: *an incorrigible child.* **3.** firmly fixed; not easily changed: *an incorrigible habit.* ◇*n.* **4.** someone who is incorrigible.

incorrupt /ɪnkəˈrʌpt/, *adj.* **1.** honest or pure; morally upright. **2.** not influenced by a gift of money (bribe). Also, **incorrupted.** —**incorruptible**, *adj.*

increase /ɪnˈkriːs/, *v.*, **-creased, -creasing.** /ˈɪnkriːs/, *n.* ◇*v.t.* **1.** to make greater; augment; add to. **2.** to make more in number. ◇*v.i.* **3.** to become greater or more in number: *Sales increased.* ◇*n.* **4.** growth in amount or numbers: *the increase of crime.* **5.** the act or process of increasing. **6.** the amount by which something is increased. **7.** product; profit; interest. [ME, from AF, from L]

incredible /ɪnˈkrɛdəbəl/, *adj.* **1.** seeming too extraordinary to be possible: *an incredible act of courage.* **2.** not believable. —**incredibility**, *n.*

incredulity /ɪnkrəˈdjuːləti/, *n.* refusal or inability to believe.

incredulous /ɪnˈkrɛdʒələs/, *adj.* **1.** not willing to believe; sceptical. **2.** showing lack of belief: *an incredulous smile.*

increment /ˈɪnkrəmənt, ˈɪŋ-/, *n.* **1.** something added or gained. **2.** profit. **3.** the act or process of increasing; growth. **4.** an increase in salary as payment for increases in skill or experience. **5.** *Maths.* **a.** the difference between two values of a variable. **b.** the increase of a function due to this. [ME, from L: an increase] —**incremental**, *adj.*

incriminate /ɪnˈkrɪməneɪt/, *v.t.*, **-nated, -nating. 1.** to charge with a crime or fault. **2.** to involve in crime or wrongdoing, or appear to do so: *Her evidence at the trial incriminated him.* [ML: accused of a crime] —**incriminatory**, *adj.*

incubate /ˈɪnkjubeɪt, ˈɪŋ-/, *v.*, **-bated, -bating.** ◇*v.t.* **1.** to sit upon (eggs) for the purpose of hatching. **2.** to hatch (eggs), as by sitting upon them or by artificial heat. **3.** to keep (bacterial mixtures, etc.) at the best temperature for growth. **4.** to keep at even temperature, as babies born too early (prematurely). ◇*v.i.* **5.** to sit upon eggs. **6.** to grow; take shape. [L: hatched, sat on] —**incubation**, *n.*

incubator /ˈɪnkjubeɪtə, ˈɪŋ-/, *n.* **1.** an apparatus for hatching eggs artificially, consisting of a case heated by a lamp or the like. **2.** a boxlike apparatus in which prematurely born babies are kept at a suitable temperature. **3.** an apparatus in which bacteria, etc., are grown at a suitable temperature. [L]

incubus /ˈɪnkjubəs, ˈɪŋ-/, *n.*, *pl.* **-bi** /-baɪ/, **-buses. 1.** an imaginary demon or evil spirit believed to have sexual relations with sleeping women. **2.** something that weighs upon one like a nightmare. **3.** a nightmare. [ME, from LL: nightmare, ML: a demon, from L: lie on]

inculcate /ˈɪnkʌlkeɪt/, *v.t.*, **-cated, -cating.** to place in the mind by repeated statement; instil (usu. fol. by *upon* or *in*). [L: stamped in, impressed upon]

incumbent /ɪnˈkʌmbənt/, *adj.* **1.** resting on one; obligatory: *a duty incumbent upon me.* **2.** lying, leaning, or pressing on something: *incumbent posture.* ◇*n.* **3.** the holder of an office. [ME, from L: leaning upon]

incumbrance /ɪnˈkʌmbrəns/, *n.* → **encumbrance.**

incur /ɪnˈkɜː/, *v.t.*, **-curred, -curring. 1.** to run or fall into (some consequence, usu. undesirable or harmful). **2.** to bring upon oneself: *to incur his anger.* [ME, from L: run into, or against] —**incurrable**, *adj.*

incurable /ɪnˈkjurəbəl/, *adj.* **1.** not curable. ◇*n.* **2.** person with an incurable disease or condition.

incursion /ɪnˈkɜːʒən/, *n.* a sudden, uninvited entrance into a place, etc.; invasion; attack: *an incursion into enemy territory; an incursion on my privacy.* [ME, from L: onset]

Ind, *Abbrev.* **1.** India. **2.** Indian. **3.** Indies.

indebted /ɪnˈdɛtəd/, *adj.* **1.** owing money. **2.** being under a debt of gratefulness for favors, help, etc., received.

indecent /ɪnˈdiːsənt/, *adj.* **1.** offending against what is recognised as proper or in good taste; vulgar: *indecent language.* **2.** morally offensive; obscene: *indecent conduct.*

indecent assault, *n.* a form of sexual assault, but without grievous bodily harm or rape.

indecipherable /ɪndəˈsaɪfrəbəl/, *adj.* not able to be deciphered.

indecision /ɪndəˈsɪʒən/, *n.* inability to decide.

indecisive /ɪndəˈsaɪsɪv, -ˈsɪzɪv/, *adj.* **1.** not leading to a clear decision or result: *a severe but indecisive battle.* **2.** marked by indecision; irresolute: *an indecisive person.*

indeclinable /ɪndəˈklaɪnəbəl/, *adj.* not declined, esp. of a word belonging to a group most of whose members are declined, as the Latin *decem* (ten).

indecorous /ɪnˈdɛkərəs/, *adj.* not proper or in good taste; unseemly. [L] —**indecorum, indecorousness**, *n.*

indeed /ɪnˈdiːd/, *adv.* **1.** in fact, in reality; truly. ◇*interj.* **2.** (expression of surprise, disbelief, etc.)

indefatigable /ɪndəˈfætɪgəbəl/, *adj.* not able to be tired out: *an indefatigable worker.* [L]

indefeasible /ɪndə'fizəbəl/, *adj. Law.* not able to be done away with, forfeited or made void.

indefensible /ɪndə'fensəbəl/, *adj.* 1. not able to be excused or justified: *an indefensible remark.* 2. not able to be defended by force of arms: *an indefensible coastline.*

indefinable /ɪndə'faɪnəbəl/, *adj.* not able to be described or defined.

indefinite /ɪn'defənət/, *adj.* 1. without fixed limit: *an indefinite number.* 2. not clear in meaning, etc.; vague. 3. *Gram.* not limiting or making particular, as the indefinite pronoun *some.*

indefinite article, *n.* the article (*a* or *an*) which means 'single but not particular'.

indehiscent /ɪndə'hɪsənt/, *adj. Bot.* not splitting open to release seeds.

indelible /ɪn'deləbəl/, *adj.* 1. not able to be wiped out or obliterated: *an indelible memory.* 2. making indelible marks: *an indelible pencil.* [L: that cannot be destroyed]

indelicate /ɪn'delɪkət/, *adj.* offensive to a sense of what is proper or modest; unrefined. –**indelicacy**, *n.*

indemnify /ɪn'demnəfaɪ/, *v.t.*, **-fied, -fying.** 1. to pay (someone) back for damage, loss, costs, etc. 2. to protect against possible loss, damage, etc.; insure.

indemnity /ɪn'demnəti/, *n., pl.* **-ties.** 1. protection or security (e.g. through insurance) against damage or loss. 2. payment for damage or loss. 3. legal exemption from penalties brought about by one's actions, oft. given to public officers, etc. [late ME, from L: unharmed]

indent /ɪn'dent/ *v.;* /'ɪndent/ *n.* ◇*v.t.* 1. to make deep hollows or notches in: *The sea indents the coast.* 2. to set in or back from the margin: *to indent the first line of a paragraph.* 3. to make an order for goods, etc., upon (someone, a company, etc.). 4. to order (goods, etc.). ◇*v.i.* 5. to make out an order, etc., in two copies. ◇*n.* 6. an official order for goods. 7. Also, **indentation**. a toothlike hollow or notch. 8. Also, **indentation, indention**. the setting of a line back from the margin. 9. → **indenture**. [ME, from OF: tooth]

indenture /ɪn'dentʃə/, *n., v.,* **-tured, -turing.** ◇*n.* 1. a written agreement between two or more parties. 2. an agreement by which a person, such as an apprentice, is bound to work for another. 3. a formal agreement between a group of bondholders and the debtor concerning the debt. ◇*v.t.* 4. to bind (an apprentice, etc.) by indenture. [ME, from OF: indentation]

Independence Day /ɪndə'pendəns deɪ/, *n. US.* 4 July, a holiday commemorating the adoption of the Declaration of Independence on 4 July 1776.

independent /ɪndə'pendənt/, *adj.* 1. not influenced by opinions, actions, etc. of others: *an independent thinker; independent research.* 2. not under another's control or authority; autonomous: *an independent nation.* 3. not depending on someone or something else for existence, operation, help, support, etc. 4. refusing to accept others' help or support. 5. showing a spirit of independence; self-confident. 6. (of a school) non-government. 7. *Maths.* (of a quantity or variable) having a value which does not depend on the value of another quantity or variable. ◇*n.* 8. an independent person or thing. 9. *Politics.* someone who does not belong to any organised party and therefore votes freely. –**independence**, *n.*

independent clause, *n.* → **main clause.**

in-depth /'ɪn-depθ/, *adj.* thorough: *an in-depth discussion.*

indescribable /ɪndə'skraɪbəbəl/, *adj.* too extreme to be described: *indescribable beauty; indescribable wickedness.*

indestructible /ɪndə'strʌktəbəl/, *adj.* not able to be destroyed.

indeterminable /ɪndə'tɜmənəbəl/, *adj.* 1. not able to be determined or ascertained. 2. not able to be decided or settled.

indeterminate /ɪndə'tɜmənət/, *adj.* 1. not fixed; indefinite; uncertain; vague. 2. not settled or decided. 3. *Maths.* (of a quantity) having no fixed value. 4. *Engineering.* (of a framework, etc.) such that its forces cannot be determined by simple vector analysis.

index /'ɪndeks/, *n., pl.* **-dexes, -dices** /-dəsiz/, *v.* ◇*n.* 1. an alphabetical list of names, places, or subjects in a book, showing their page number, etc. 2. something used or serving to point out; a sign; indication: *a true index of his character.* 3. a pointer or indicator in a scientific instrument. 4. a piece of wood, metal, or the like, serving as a pointer or indicator. 5. *Science.* a number or formula indicating some property, ratio, etc., of a thing: *refractive index.* 6. *Alg.* a. an exponent. b. the integer n in a radical $\sqrt[n]{}$ – defining the nth root: $\sqrt[3]{7}$ is a radical having index 3. 7. (*cap.*) a list of books which Catholics were forbidden by the Church to read without special permission, or which were not to be read unless shortened or corrected. 8. *Obs.* a preface. ◇*v.t.* 9. to provide (a book, etc.) with an index. 10. to enter (a word, etc.) in an index. 11. to change (wages, taxes, etc.) regularly in accordance with changes in prices of goods, etc. [ME, from L: index, forefinger, sign]

indexation /ɪndek'seɪʃən/, *n.* the adjustment of one variable in the light of changes in another variable. See **wage indexation**.

index finger, *n.* → **forefinger**.

index number, *n.* a number showing change in amount or size of prices, wages, employment, etc., relative to the amount or size at a particular point, usu. taken to be 100.

India /'ɪndiə/, *n.* a federal republic in southern Asia, forming a subcontinent south of the Himalaya mountains, with the Arabian Sea to the west and the Bay of Bengal to the east; a British colony before independence in 1947 when divided into India and Pakistan on a broad religious basis (Hindu and Muslim respectively); a republic since 1950. Pop. 783 044 000 (1987 est.); 3 287 263 km².

India | 528 | indirect tax

Languages: Hindi and English, also many regional languages. *Currency:* rupee. *Cap.:* New Delhi. Hindi, **Bharat**.

Indian /ˈɪndiən/, *n.* **1.** (a member of) any of the races of people native to India or the East Indies. **2.** (a member of) any of the races of people native to America. ◇*adj.* **3.** relating to India or the East Indies.

Indiana /ɪndiˈænə/, *n.* a state in the central US; a part of the Midwest. Pop. 5 504 000 (1986 est.); 93 994 km^2. *Cap.:* Indianapolis. *Abbrev.:* Ind —**Indianian**, *adj.*, *n.*

Indian corn, *n.* →**maize**.

Indian file, *n.* →**single file**.

Indian hemp, *n.* a tall herb, native to Asia but cultivated in many parts of the world and yielding hashish, cannabis, etc.

Indian ink, *n.* ink made with a black coloring substance mixed with glue.

Indian Mutiny, *n.* a revolt of native Indian regiments in British India, 1857–59, resulting in the transfer of the administration of India from the East India Company to the Crown.

Indian Ocean, *n.* an ocean south of Asia, east of Africa and west of Australia. About 73 426 500 km^2.

Indian Pacific, *n.* **the,** a railway service established in 1970, operating between Sydney and Perth.

Indian summer, *n.* **1.** a period of summer weather coming after the end of the summer season. **2.** a happy and peaceful time experienced in old age.

indiarubber /ɪndiəˈrʌbə/, *n.* **1.** a highly elastic substance obtained from the milky juice of numerous tropical plants, used in art and manufacture, as for rubbing out pencil marks, etc.; rubber. ◇*adj.* **2.** of, made of, or relating to indiarubber. Also, **india rubber**.

indic., *Abbrev.* indicative. Also, **ind.**

indicate /ˈɪndəkeɪt, -dɪkeɪt/, *v.t.*, **-cated, -cating. 1.** to be a sign of; imply: *His slowness indicates unwillingness.* **2.** to point out or point to; direct attention to: *to indicate a place on a map.* **3.** to show, or make known: *A thermometer indicates temperature.* **4.** to state or express, esp. briefly: *He indicated his intentions.* [L] —**indication**, *n.*

indicative /ɪnˈdɪkətɪv/, *adj.* **1.** giving an indication; showing (fol. by *of*): *Shiny hair is indicative of good health.* **2.** *Gram.* relating to the mood of the verb used in statements of actuality, questions, etc., as opposed to statements of possibility, wish, etc. In the sentence *John plays football,* the verb *plays* is in the indicative mood. ◇*n.* **3.** *Gram.* the indicative mood. [late ME, from L]

indicator /ˈɪndəkeɪtə, ˈɪndɪ-/, *n.* **1.** a pointing or directing device, such as a pointer on an instrument or a flashing light on a motor car. **2.** an apparatus for recording variations of pressure or vacuum in a cylinder of an engine. **3.** *Chem.* a substance used to show (as by a strong change in color) the point at which a certain reaction is completed.

indices /ˈɪndəsiz/, *n.* a plural of **index**.

indict /ɪnˈdaɪt/, *v.t.* to charge with an offence or crime; accuse. [ME, from AF: accuse, indict]

Indies /ˈɪndiz/, *n.pl.* **the 1.** a region in and near southern and South-East Asia; India, Indochina and the East Indies. **2.** →**East Indies. 3.** →**West Indies**.

indifferent /ɪnˈdɪfrənt/, *adj.* **1.** without interest or concern; not caring. **2.** having neither favorable nor unfavorable feelings towards some thing or person. **3.** neither good nor bad in character or quality: *an indifferent specimen.* **4.** not very good: *an indifferent play; indifferent health.* **5.** unimportant; immaterial. **6.** neutral in chemical, electrical, or magnetic quality. **7.** *Biol.* not differentiated or specialised, as cells or tissues. [ME, from L]

indigenous /ɪnˈdɪdʒənəs/, *adj.* originating in and typical of a particular area or country; native (usu. fol. by *to*): *plants indigenous to Australia; an indigenous population.* [L: native] —**indigenousness**, *n.* —**indigene**, *n.*

indigent /ˈɪndədʒənt/, *adj.* needy; poor. [ME, from L] —**indigence**, *n.*

indigestible /ɪndəˈdʒɛstəbəl, ɪndaɪ-/, *adj.* not able to be digested; not easily digested.

indigestion /ɪndəˈdʒɛstʃən, ɪndaɪ-/, *n.* difficulty in digesting food, or pain caused by this; dyspepsia. —**indigestive**, *adj.*

indignant /ɪnˈdɪgnənt/, *adj.* feeling or showing indignation. [L]

indignation /ɪndɪgˈneɪʃən/, *n.* strong displeasure at something thought to be unworthy, unjust, or wrong.

indignity /ɪnˈdɪgnəti/, *n., pl.* **-ties**. treatment causing loss of respect or dignity; humiliation. [L: unworthiness]

indigo /ˈɪndɪgoʊ/, *n., pl.* **-gos,** *adj.* ◇*n.* **1.** a blue dye obtained from various plants. **2.** any of various plants which yield this dye. **3.** Also, **indigo blue.** a deep violet blue. ◇*adj.* **4.** of the color indigo. [Sp or Pg, from L: indigo] —**indigoid**, *adj.*

indirect /ɪndəˈrɛkt, ɪndaɪˈrɛkt/, *adj.* **1.** not direct in space; not following a straight line: *They took an indirect course across the park.* **2.** coming or resulting otherwise than directly or immediately: *an indirect effect.* **3.** not direct in action; not straightforward: *indirect methods.* **4.** not direct in bearing, use, force, etc.: *indirect evidence.* **5.** *Gram.* not consisting exactly of the words originally used, as in *He said he was hungry* instead of the direct *He said, 'I am hungry'*.

indirect object, *n.* (in English and some other languages) the object with reference to which, for whom, etc., the action of a verb is performed, for example *the boy* in *He gave the boy a book* or *He gave a book to the boy.* See **direct object**.

indirect speech, *n.* → **reported speech.**

indirect tax, *n.* tax paid by people who pass the cost on to others, as sales tax which is put on goods before they reach the buyer and is finally paid as part of the market price.

indiscreet /ɪndəsˈkrit/, *adj.* not discreet, not wise or carefully judged: *indiscreet praise*.

indiscretion /ɪndəsˈkrɛʃən/, *n.* **1.** lack of discretion; imprudence. **2.** an indiscreet act or speech.

indiscriminate /ɪndəsˈkrɪmənət/, *adj.* making no choices or distinction; random: *indiscriminate in his friendships; indiscriminate killing.* —**indiscrimination**, *n.*

indispensable /ɪndəsˈpɛnsəbəl/, *adj.* **1.** not dispensable; absolutely necessary: *an indispensable employee.* **2.** not able to be disregarded: *an indispensable duty.* —**indispensability, indispensableness**, *n.*

indisposed /ɪndəsˈpoʊzd/, *adj.* **1.** sick or ill, esp. slightly: *indisposed with a cold.* **2.** unwilling; disinclined. —**indisposition**, *n.*

indisputable /ɪndəsˈpjutəbəl/, *adj.* not disputable; not open to question. —**indisputability, indisputableness**, *n.*

indissoluble /ɪndəˈsɒljubəl/, *adj.* not able to be dissolved, undone, or destroyed. —**indissolubility**, *n.*

indistinct /ɪndəsˈtɪŋkt/, *adj.* **1.** not distinct; not clearly defined. **2.** not clear to the eye, ear, or mind. [L]

indistinguishable /ɪndəsˈtɪŋwɪʃəbəl/, *adj.* not distinguishable.

indium, *n.* a rare, metallic element, soft, white and malleable. *Symbol:* In; *at. no.:* 49; *at. wt:* 114.82.

individual /ɪndəˈvɪdʒuəl/, *adj.* **1.** single; particular; separate: *the individual members of a club.* **2.** relating to or characteristic of a single person or thing: *individual tastes; an individual style.* **3.** intended for one person only: *individual servings; He needs individual attention.* ⋄*n.* **4.** a single human being or thing. **5.** *Colloq.* a person: *a strange individual.* **6.** *Biol.* **a.** a single or simple organism able to exist independently. **b.** a member of a compound organism or colony. [ME, from L: indivisible]

individualism /ɪndəˈvɪdʒuəlɪzəm/, *n.* **1.** a social theory supporting the freedom, rights, or independent action of the individual person. **2.** the principle or habit of independent thought or action; individuality. **3.** the putting of private or individual concerns above common or collective interests; egoism. **4.** *Philos.* **a.** a theory that nothing exists but the individual self; pure egoism. **b.** the doctrine that nothing is real but individual things. **c.** the principle that all actions are performed for the advantage of the individual. —**individualist**, *n.* —**individualistic**, *adj.*

individuality /ˌɪndəvɪdʒuˈælətɪ/, *n., pl.* **-ties. 1.** the particular character, or sum of qualities, which marks one person or thing off from others: *a person of marked individuality.* **2.** the state or quality of being individual; existence as a separate individual.

individually /ɪndəˈvɪdʒuəlɪ/, *adv.* **1.** in an individual manner. **2.** separately; one at a time: *I will speak to you all individually.*

indivisible /ɪndəˈvɪzəbəl/, *adj.* not able to be divided. —**indivisibility**, *n.*

Indochina /ɪndoʊˈtʃaɪnə/, *n.* **1.** a peninsula in South-East Asia between the Bay of Bengal and the South China Sea, comprising Vietnam, Cambodia, Laos, Thailand, Malaysia and Burma. Also, **Farther India. 2.** → **French Indochina.**

indoctrinate /ɪnˈdɒktrənɛt/, *v.t.*, **-nated, -nating. 1.** to instruct (someone) in a belief, doctrine, etc. **2.** to do this so thoroughly that the belief, etc., is accepted without question. **3.** to teach. [L: teaching] —**indoctrination**, *n.*

Indo-European /ˌɪndoʊ-jurəˈpiən/, *n.* **1.** a major family of languages that includes most of the languages of Europe (now spread to other parts of the world), many of those of Asia, and a few scattered others. **2.** the prehistoric parent language of this family. **3.** a member of any of the peoples speaking an Indo-European language. -*adj.* **4.** of or relating to Indo-European.

indolent /ˈɪndələnt/, *adj.* tending to avoid work; lazy. [LL: not suffering] —**indolence**, *n.*

indomitable /ɪnˈdɒmətəbəl/, *adj.* not able to be defeated or overcome: *an indomitable person; indomitable courage.* [L: tame]

Indonesia /ɪndəˈniʒə/, *n.* a republic in south-east Asia, consisting of a group of about 3000 islands lying between the Malay peninsula and New Guinea, principally Java, Sumatra, Kalimantan (part of Borneo), Sulawesi (Celebes), Irian Jaya (West New Guinea), the Moluccas, Bali, and Timor; a Netherlands colony, except for the Portuguese colony of East Timor, before independence in 1945; a republic since 1950. Pop. 172 245 000 (1987 est.); 1 919 443 km^2. *Languages:* Bahasa Indonesia, also many local languages, mainly Javanese. *Currency:* rupiah. *Cap.:* Jakarta. Formerly, **Dutch East Indies.** —**Indonesian**, *n., adj.*

indoor /ˈɪndɔ/, *adj.* happening, used, living, etc., inside a house or building: *indoor games; indoor plant.*

indoors /ɪnˈdɔz/, *adv.* in or into a house or building.

Indra /ˈɪndrə/, *n. Hinduism.* the greatest of the Vedic gods, the god of rain and thunder.

indubitable /ɪnˈdjubɪtəbəl/, *adj.* not able to be doubted; certain.

induce /ɪnˈdjus/, *v.t.*, **-duced, -ducing. 1.** to lead or move by persuasion or influence to some action, state of mind, etc.: *I will induce him to go.* **2.** to produce or cause: *This drug induces sleep.* **3.** *Phys.* to produce (an electric current, etc.) by induction. **4.** to cause (labor of childbirth) to begin, by giving a drug, etc. [ME, from L: lead in, bring in, persuade] —**inducement**, *n.*

induct /ɪnˈdʌkt/, *v.t.* to lead or bring in; install, esp. formally, in a place, office, etc. [ME, from L]

inductance /ɪnˈdʌktəns/, *n.* **1.** that property of a circuit which allows electromagnetic induction to take place, either because of induction (def. 1) or because of a change in its current. The derived SI unit is the henry.

inductance 530 **ineffectual**

2. a piece of equipment providing inductance in a circuit, etc.; inductor.

induction /ɪnˈdʌkʃən/, n. **1.** *Elect.* **a.** the process by which a body with electrical or magnetic properties produces such properties in a nearby body without touching it directly. **b.** the tendency of electric currents to resist change. **2.** *Elect.* the process by which an electrical conductor may be charged. **3.** *Philos.* **a.** the logical process of discovering general explanations for a whole class of facts by reasoning from a set of particular facts known from evidence based on experience. **b.** the conclusion thus reached. **4.** the act of inducing (defs 3 and 4). **5.** the act of inducting. [ME, from L]

induction coil, n. a device consisting of two coils sharing a common soft iron core. When the inner coil is excited by rapidly interrupted or variable current, high voltage is produced in the outer coil.

inductive /ɪnˈdʌktɪv/, adj. **1.** relating to or using electrical or magnetic induction: *an inductive machine*. **2.** relating to or based on logical induction: *inductive reasoning*.

inductor /ɪnˈdʌktə/, n. **1.** a device whose main purpose is to introduce inductance into an electric circuit. **2.** one who inducts, as into office.

indulge /ɪnˈdʌldʒ/, v., **-dulged, -dulging.** ◇v.t. **1.** to yield to or satisfy (desires, feelings, etc.). **2.** to yield to the wishes of (oneself or another): *You indulge that child too much*; *I'll indulge myself with a chocolate*. ◇v.i. **3.** to indulge oneself; yield to one's own will or wish (oft. fol. by *in*): *to indulge in apple pie*. **4.** *Colloq.* to drink too much alcohol. [L: be kind, yield, grant]

indulgence /ɪnˈdʌldʒəns/, n. **1.** the act or practice of indulging or satisfying a desire: *Too much indulgence in eating is not good for you.* **2.** the act of indulging the wishes or behavior of others: *She showed indulgence towards her children*. **3.** something indulged in. **4.** *Rom Cath Ch.* the giving of freedom from punishment still due to sin after it has been forgiven. Also, **indulgency.** – **indulgent**, adj.

industrial /ɪnˈdʌstriəl/, adj. **1.** relating to, of the nature of, or resulting from industry: *the industrial arts*. **2.** having highly developed industries: *an industrial nation*. **3.** working in an industry or industries: *industrial employees*. **4.** relating to the workers in industries: *industrial training*. **5.** used in industry: *industrial diamonds*.

industrial action, n. organised action, such as a strike or go-slow, taken by a group of workers, to gain better pay, conditions, etc., or an objective thought to be in the general public good.

industrial arts, n.pl. skills and techniques required in industry, as technical drawing, metalwork, etc.

industrial estate, n. an area of land specially put aside for the building of factories, etc.

industrialise or **industrialize** /ɪnˈdʌstriəlaɪz/, v.t., **-lised, -lising.** to introduce industry into (an area or country) on a large scale. – **industrialisation**, n.

industrialism /ɪnˈdʌstriəlɪzəm/, n. the economic organisation of society built largely on industry rather than farming, craftsmanship, or trade.

industrialist /ɪnˈdʌstriəlɪst/, n. someone who manages or owns an industrial business.

industrial relations, n.pl. **1.** the management or study of the relations between employers and employees. **2.** the relationship between employers and employees.

industrial revolution, n. **1.** the social, economic and physical changes that happen in a country when mechanised industry is introduced on a wide scale. **2.** (*oft. caps*) the period in history when such a development took place in England in the late 18th and early 19th centuries.

Industrial Workers of the World, n. an organisation founded in Chicago, US, in 1905 and in Australia in 1907, to promote a single union for all workers; declared illegal in 1917. *Abbrev.*: IWW Also, **Wobblies.**

industrious /ɪnˈdʌstriəs/, adj. hardworking; diligent. [L: diligent]

industry /ˈɪndəstri/, n., pl. **-tries. 1.** a particular branch of manufacture: *the steel industry*. **2.** any large-scale business activity: *the tourist industry*. **3.** manufacture as a whole: *the growth of industry in underdeveloped countries*. **4.** ownership and management of companies, factories, etc.: *disagreement between labor and industry*. **5.** hard or steady work: *He lacks industry*. [ME, from L: diligence]

-ine¹, adjective suffix meaning 'of or relating to', 'of the nature of', 'made of', 'like', as in *crystalline, equine, marine*. [L *-inus*]

-ine², **1.** a noun suffix indicating some action, art, place, etc., as in *discipline, doctrine, medicine, latrine*. **2.** a noun suffix with various meanings, as in *famine, routine, vaseline*. **3.** a noun suffix used particularly in chemical terms, as *bromine, chlorine*, and esp. names of basic substances, as *amine, aniline, caffeine, quinine*. See **-in¹**. [F, from L *-ina*]

inebriate /ɪnˈibrieɪt/, v., **-ated, -ating;** /ɪnˈibriət/, adj., n. ◇v.t. **1.** to make drunk; intoxicate. **2.** to excite mentally or emotionally; exhilarate. ◇adj. **3.** Also, **inebriated.** drunk; intoxicated. ◇n. **4.** an inebriated person; drunkard. [L] – **inebriation**, n.

inedible /ɪnˈɛdəbəl/, adj. unfit to be eaten. – **inedibility**, n.

ineffable /ɪnˈɛfəbəl/, adj. **1.** not able to be spoken or expressed, because of extreme emotion, etc.: *ineffable joy*. **2.** too holy to be spoken. [ME, from L] – **ineffability, ineffableness**, n.

ineffective /ɪnəˈfɛktɪv/, adj. not effective.

ineffectual /ɪnəˈfɛktʃuəl/, adj. **1.** without satisfactory effect: *an ineffectual remedy*; *an ineffectual effort*. **2.** powerless: *an ineffectual person*.

inefficient — infanta

inefficient /ɪnəˈfɪʃənt/, *adj.* not able to do something or perform in a capable, quick way. —**inefficiency**, *n.*

inelegant /ɪnˈɛləɡənt/, *adj.* not elegant or refined; vulgar. —**inelegance, inelegancy**, *n.*

ineligible /ɪnˈɛlɪdʒəbəl/, *adj.* not eligible; not fit or qualified to be chosen. —**ineligibility**, *n.*

ineluctable /ɪnəˈlʌktəbəl/, *adj.* not able to be escaped from: *an ineluctable destiny*. [L] —**ineluctability**, *n.*

inept /ɪnˈɛpt/, *adj.* 1. not fit or suitable; inappropriate: *an inept choice*. 2. awkward or inefficient: *an inept attempt at a catch*. 3. foolish; absurd: *an inept remark*. [L] —**ineptness**, *n.*

ineptitude /ɪnˈɛptɪtjud/, *n.* 1. the quality of being inept. 2. an inept act or remark.

inequality /ɪnəˈkwɒlətɪ/, *n., pl.* **-ties.** 1. the condition of being unequal: *inequality of treatment; the inequality between rich and poor*. 2. unevenness; lack of smoothness. 3. *Maths.* an expression of two unequal quantities connected by the sign > or < as, $a > b$, *'a* is greater than b'; $a < b$, *'a* is less than b'. [late ME, from ML: unevenness]

inequitable /ɪnˈɛkwətəbəl/, *adj.* not equitable; unfair. —**inequity**, *n.*

ineradicable /ɪnəˈrædəkəbəl/, *adj.* not eradicable; not able to be completely done away with or removed.

inert /ɪnˈɜt/, *adj.* 1. having no power of action, movement, or resistance: *inert matter*. 2. without active properties: *an inert drug*. 3. inactive; slow: *an inert person*. [L: unskilled, idle] —**inertness**, *n.*

inert gas, *n.* any of the chemically inactive gases (helium, neon, argon, krypton, xenon or radon); rare gas; noble gas.

inertia /ɪnˈɜʃə/, *n.* 1. inert condition; inactivity; sluggishness. 2. *Phys.* **a.** the tendency of matter to continue in a state of rest or to move uniformly in straight line. **b.** a similar or comparable property of a force: *electric inertia*. [L: lack of skill, inactivity]

inescapable /ɪnəsˈkeɪpəbəl/, *adj.* not able to be escaped or ignored.

inessential /ɪnəˈsɛnʃəl/, *adj.* not essential; not necessary.

inestimable /ɪnˈɛstəməbəl/, *adj.* too great to be measured or estimated. [ME, from F, from L]

inevitable /ɪnˈɛvətəbəl/, *adj.* not able to be avoided, or escaped; certain or necessary: *an inevitable ending*. [ME, from L] —**inevitability, inevitableness**, *n.*

inexact /ɪnəɡˈzækt, ˌɪnɛɡ-/, *adj.* not exact. —**inexactitude, inexactness**, *n.*

inexcusable /ɪnəkˈskjuzəbəl, ɪnɛk-/, *adj.* not excusable; not able to be explained away or justified. —**inexcusability**, *n.*

inexhaustible /ɪnəɡˈzɔstəbəl, ɪnɛɡ-/, *adj.* 1. not able to be used up: *an inexhaustible supply*. 2. unfailing; tireless. —**inexhaustibility, inexhaustibleness**, *n.*

inexorable /ɪnˈɛksərəbəl, ɪnˈɛɡz-/, *adj.* 1. not able to be changed; unyielding: *inexorable facts*. 2. not to be persuaded, or influenced by prayers or begging. [L] —**inexorability, inexorableness**, *n.*

inexpedient /ɪnəkˈspidɪənt, ɪnɛk-/, *adj.* not expedient; not suitable, or advisable. —**inexpedience, inexpediency**, *n.*

inexpensive /ɪnəkˈspɛnsɪv, ɪnɛk-/, *adj.* not expensive; costing little.

inexperience /ɪnəkˈspɪərɪəns, ɪnɛk-/, *n.* lack of experience, or of knowledge or skill gained from experience. —**inexperienced**, *adj.*

inexpert /ɪnˈɛkspɜt/, *adj.* not expert; unskilled. —**inexpertness**, *n.*

inexplicable /ɪnəkˈsplɪkəbəl, ɪnɛk-/, *adj.* not able to be explained. [late ME, from L: that cannot be unfolded] —**inexplicability, inexplicableness**, *n.*

inexplicit /ɪnəkˈsplɪsət, ɪnɛk-/, *adj.* not explicit or clear. [L] —**inexplicitness**, *n.*

inexpressible /ɪnəkˈsprɛsəbəl, ɪnɛk-/, *adj.* not able to be expressed or represented in words: *inexpressible grief*. —**inexpressibility, inexpressibleness**, *n.*

in extremis /ɪn ɛkˈstrimɪs/, *adv.* near death. [L: in the extremes]

inextricable /ɪnɛksˈtrɪkəbəl, ɪnˈɛks-/, *adj.* 1. from which one cannot remove or extricate oneself: *an inextricable maze; an inextricable relationship*. 2. not able to be undone, freed, etc: *an inextricable knot*. 3. not able to be put in order or solved: *inextricable confusion*. [late ME, from L] —**inextricability, inextricableness**, *n.*

infallible /ɪnˈfæləbəl/, *adj.* 1. not able to make a mistake or be wrong: *an infallible judge; an infallible statement*. 2. completely trustworthy or sure: *an infallible rule*. 3. unfailing in operation; certain: *an infallible remedy*. 4. *Rom Cath Ch.* not able to be wrong in stating matters of faith or morals. [late ME, from ML] —**infallibility, infallibleness**, *n.*

infamous /ˈɪnfəməs/, *adj.* 1. of ill fame; having a very bad reputation: *an infamous city*. 2. deserving or causing shame or bad repute: *infamous conduct*. [ME, from L]

infamy /ˈɪnfəmɪ/, *n., pl.* **-mies.** 1. ill fame; public dishonor. 2. infamous character or conduct. 3. an infamous act or happening. [late ME, from L]

infancy /ˈɪnfənsɪ/, *n., pl.* **-cies.** 1. the state or period of being an infant; early childhood. 2. a similar period in the existence of anything: *the infancy of a nation*. [L: inability to speak]

infant /ˈɪnfənt/, *n.* 1. a child during the earliest period of its life; a baby. 2. *Law.* a person who is not of full age, esp. one who is not yet 18 years of age. 3. anything in the first stage of existence. ◇*adj.* 4. of or relating to infants or infancy: *infant years*. 5. being in infancy: *an infant child; an infant industry*. [L: young child, properly adj., not speaking]

infanta /ɪnˈfæntə/, *n.* a daughter of the king of Spain or Portugal.

infante /ɪnˈfænti/, *n.* a son of the king of Spain or Portugal.

infanticide /ɪnˈfæntəsaɪd/, *n.* 1. the killing of an infant. 2. the practice of killing newborn children. 3. someone who kills an infant. [LL]

infantile /ˈɪnfəntaɪl/, *adj.* 1. characteristic of or like an infant; childish: *infantile behavior*. 2. of or relating to infants: *infantile disease*. Also, **infantine**. [LL]

infantile paralysis, *n.* → **poliomyelitis**.

infantry /ˈɪnfəntri/, *n.* soldiers or military units that fight on foot, with hand weapons. [F, from It: youth, foot soldier. See INFANT]

infatuated /ɪnˈfætʃueɪtɪd/, *adj.* made foolish by love; blindly in love (oft. fol. by *with*).

infect /ɪnˈfɛkt/, *v.t.* 1. to cause (a person, organ, wound, etc.) to be affected by disease-producing germs; contaminate. 2. to affect with something that changes quality, character, or condition, esp. unfavorably: *to infect the air with poison gas*. 3. to fill with some feeling, belief, opinion, etc.: *to infect someone with greed; to infect someone with high spirits*. [ME, from L: put in, dyed, imbued, infected]

infection /ɪnˈfɛkʃən/, *n.* 1. an infecting with germs of disease. 2. something that infects. 3. state of being infected. 4. infectious disease. 5. an infecting with a feeling, idea, etc.

infectious /ɪnˈfɛkʃəs/, *adj.* 1. passed on by infection: *infectious disease*. 2. causing infection. 3. tending to spread from one to another: *Laughter is infectious*. Also, **infective**.

infelicity /ˌɪnfəˈlɪsəti/, *n., pl.* **-ties.** 1. the state of being unhappy. 2. a misfortune. 3. unsuitability of action, expression, etc. 4. (*oft. pl.*) something unsuitable or inapt, such as a remark, action or point of style. —**infelicitous**, *adj.*

infer /ɪnˈfɜ/, *v.t.,* **-ferred, -ferring.** 1. to come to (an opinion or judgment) by reasoning from known facts or evidence. 2. *Colloq.* to suggest as a conclusion; imply. [L: bring in or on, infer]

inference /ˈɪnfərəns/, *n.* 1. the act or process of inferring. 2. the result of inferring; conclusion. 3. *Colloq.* a suggestion; implication. —**inferential**, *adj.*

inferior /ɪnˈfɪəriə/, *adj.* 1. lower in position, rank, or degree (fol. by *to*). 2. of comparatively low importance, value or quality: *an inferior brand; an inferior worker*. 3. lower in place or position (now chiefly in scientific or technical use). ◇*n.* 4. someone inferior to another or others. [ME, from L] —**inferiority**, *n.*

inferiority complex, *n. Psychiat.* a disorder arising from strong feelings of inferiority, and resulting in either extreme shyness or aggressiveness.

infernal /ɪnˈfɜnəl/, *adj.* 1. of or relating to hell: *the infernal regions*. 2. devilish; fiendish; hellish: *an infernal plot*. 3. *Colloq.* hateful: *an infernal nuisance*. [ME, from LL: of the lower regions]

inferno /ɪnˈfɜnoʊ/, *n., pl.* **-nos.** 1. hell. 2. any hell-like place esp. one with heat or fire: *The house became a blazing inferno*. [It: hell, from L: underground]

infertile /ɪnˈfɜtaɪl/, *adj.* not fertile; unproductive: *infertile soil*. —**infertility**, *n.*

infest /ɪnˈfɛst/, *v.t.* to be numerous in, in a harmful or troublesome manner: *Rats infested the house*. [late ME, from L: assail, molest] —**infestation**, *n.*

infidel /ˈɪnfədel/, *n.* 1. one who does not accept a particular religious faith. ◇*adj.* 2. without religious faith. 3. not accepting a particular faith; heathen. 4. of or relating to unbelievers. [late ME, from L: unfaithful, LL unbelieving]

infidelity /ˌɪnfəˈdɛləti/, *n., pl.* **-ties.** 1. unfaithfulness, esp. within a sexual relationship. 2. an act of unfaithfulness. 3. lack of religious faith.

infighting /ˈɪnfaɪtɪŋ/, *n.* 1. *Boxing.* fighting at close range. 2. a struggle for power among members of the same organisation. —**infighter**, *n.*

infiltrate /ˈɪnfɪltreɪt/, *v.t.,* **-trated, -trating.** 1. to pass into or through by filtering. 2. to pass into or join (an organisation) etc., without attracting attention, for the purpose of influencing or controlling it: *The troops infiltrated the enemy lines; The spies infiltrated the government department*. —**infiltrator**, *n.* —**infiltration**, *n.*

infinite /ˈɪnfənət/, *adj.* 1. immeasurably great: *a truth of infinite importance; infinite number*. 2. without limits, absolute: *the infinite wisdom of God*. 3. endless; inexhaustible. 4. *Maths.* not finite. ◇*n.* 5. something which is infinite. 6. **the Infinite** or **the Infinite Being**, God. 7. boundless regions of space. [ME, from L]

infinitesimal /ˌɪnfɪnəˈtɛzməl, -ˈtɛsəməl/, *adj.* 1. immeasurably small. 2. *Maths.* relating to infinitesimals. ◇*n.* 3. an infinitesimal quantity. 4. *Maths.* a variable having zero as a limit.

infinitive /ɪnˈfɪnətɪv/, *Gram.* ◇*n.* 1. (in English) the simple form of the verb (*come, take, eat*) used after auxiliary verbs (I didn't *eat*), or this simple verb coming after *to* (I wanted *to come*). 2. (in many languages) a simple form of the verb which does not have a subject (*I, he,* etc.) or number (singular or plural), as in Latin *esse* to be, *fuisse* to have been. ◇*adj.* 3. of or relating to the infinitive or its meaning. [late ME, from L: unlimited, indefinite]

infinity /ɪnˈfɪnəti/, *n., pl.* **-ties.** 1. the state of being infinite: *the infinity of the universe*. 2. infinite space, time, or quantity. 3. an indefinitely great amount, number or extent. 4. *Maths.* the concept of increasing without bound. [ME, from L]

infirm /ɪnˈfɜm/, *adj.* 1. weak in body or health. 2. not firm in purpose, etc; irresolute. 3. not solid, or strong: *an infirm support*. 4. (of an argument, etc.) without a strong base; unsound. [ME, from L] —**infirmity**, *n.*

infirmary /ɪnˈfɜməri/, *n., pl.* **-ries.** a place for the care of the weak, sick, or injured; hospital. [L: infirm]

infix /ˈɪnfɪks/, *v.;* /ˈɪnfɪks/, *n.* ◇*v.t.* **1.** to fix, fasten, or drive in. **2.** to fix in the mind or memory; implant. ◇*n. Gram.* **3.** a word part inserted in the body of a word. See **prefix, suffix.** [L: fastened in] — **infixion,** *n.*

in flagrante delicto /ɪn fləˌɡrænti dəˈlɪktoʊ/, *adv.* in the very act of committing the offence: *He was caught in flagrante delicto.* [L]

inflame /ɪnˈfleɪm/, *v.t.,* **-flamed, -flaming. 1.** to set aflame or afire. **2.** to light or redden with or as with flames: *The setting sun inflames the sky.* **3.** to arouse to a high degree of passion or feeling. **4.** to cause to redden through anger, rage, or some other emotion. **5.** to bring up redness in: *Crying had inflamed her eyes.* **6.** to raise (the blood, bodily tissue, etc.) to feverish heat. [ME, from OF, from L: set on fire] — **inflamer,** *n.* — **inflamingly,** *adv.*

inflammable /ɪnˈflæməbəl/, *adj.* → **flammable.** — **inflammability, inflammableness,** *n.* — **inflammably,** *adv.*

inflammation /ˌɪnfləˈmeɪʃən/, *n.* **1.** the act of inflaming. **2.** the state of being inflamed. **3.** *Pathol.* the reaction of the body to harmful causes, commonly marked by heat, redness, swelling, pain, etc.

inflammatory /ɪnˈflæmətəri, -tri/, *adj.* **1.** tending to inflame; kindling passion, anger, etc.: *inflammatory speeches.* **2.** *Pathol.* relating to or accompanied by inflammation. — **inflammatorily,** *adv.*

inflate /ɪnˈfleɪt/, *v.,* **-flated, -flating.** ◇*v.t.* **1.** to stretch; swell or puff out; dilate; distend. **2.** to swell with gas: *to inflate a balloon.* **3.** to puff up with pride, satisfaction, etc.: *Winning the race inflated his ego.* **4.** to expand (currency, prices, etc.) too much; raise above the previous or proper amount or value. ◇*v.i.* **5.** to cause inflation. **6.** to become inflated. [L: puffed up] — **inflatable,** *adj.* — **inflator,** *n.*

inflated /ɪnˈfleɪtəd/, *adj.* **1.** swollen with air or gas; distended. **2.** puffed up, as with pride. **3.** overdone or boastful, as language; turgid; bombastic. **4.** resulting from inflation: *inflated values of land.*

inflation /ɪnˈfleɪʃən/, *n.* **1.** an excessive increase of the currency of a country, esp. by the issuing of paper money that is not backed by gold reserves. **2.** a substantial rise of prices caused by excessive levels of demand or spending, and/or rising costs of production. **3.** the act of inflating. **4.** the state of being inflated. — **inflationary,** *adj.*

inflect /ɪnˈflɛkt/, *v.t.* **1.** to bend; turn from a direct line or course. **2.** to modulate (the voice). **3.** *Gram.* to apply inflection to (a word). ◇*v.i.* **4.** *Gram.* to be marked by inflection. [ME, from L: bend]

inflection /ɪnˈflɛkʃən/, *n.* **1.** change in pitch or tone of voice; modulation. **2.** *Gram.* **a.** the putting of an ending on to the stem (basic part) of a word to make the word do a different job in a sentence. **b.** the set of forms of a single word changed in this way. **c.** the affix added to the stem to produce this change. For example: the *-s* in *dogs* and *-ed* in *played* are inflections. **3.** *Maths.* a change of curvature from convex to concave or vice versa. Also, **inflexion.** — **inflectional,** *adj.* — **inflectionally,** *adv.*

inflexible /ɪnˈflɛksəbəl/, *adj.* **1.** not able to bend; rigid. **2.** unyielding in temper or purpose: *inflexible under threat.* **3.** not able to change. [ME, from L] — **inflexibility, inflexibleness,** *n.*

inflict /ɪnˈflɪkt/, *v.t.* to impose as something that must be borne: *to inflict punishment.* [L: struck against] — **inflictor,** *n.*

infliction /ɪnˈflɪkʃən/, *n.* **1.** the act of inflicting. **2.** something inflicted, as punishment, suffering, etc.

inflorescence /ˌɪnfləˈrɛsəns/, *n.* **1.** a flowering. **2.** *Bot.* the arrangement of flowers on the axis; the flower cluster. [LL: coming into flower] — **inflorescent,** *adj.*

inflow /ˈɪnfloʊ/, *n.* that which flows in; influx.

influence /ˈɪnfluəns/, *n., v.,* **-enced, -encing.** ◇*n.* **1.** force or power exerted (knowingly or unknowingly) by someone or something on another, and producing change in behavior, opinion, etc. **2.** a thing or person that exerts such action or power. ◇*v.t.* **3.** to exercise influence on; modify; affect, or sway. [ME, from ML: lit., a flowing in, from L] — **influencer,** *n.*

influent /ˈɪnfluənt/, *adj.* **1.** flowing in. ◇*n.* **2.** → **tributary.** [ME, from L: flowing in]

influential /ˌɪnfluˈɛnʃəl/, *adj.* having or exerting influence, esp. great influence. [ML: INFLUENCE + -AL¹]

influenza /ˌɪnfluˈɛnzə/, *n. Pathol.* a contagious epidemic disease marked by exhaustion, and blocked nose and throat, caused by a virus. [It: influx of disease, epidemic, influenza. See INFLUENCE]

influx /ˈɪnflʌks/, *n.* **1.** the act of flowing in; an inflow. **2.** the place at which one stream flows into another or into the sea. **3.** the arrival of people or things in large numbers or great quantity. [L: flow in]

inform /ɪnˈfɔm/, *v.t.* **1.** to give knowledge of a fact or circumstance to: *I informed him of my arrival.* ◇*v.i.* **2.** to give information, esp. to furnish incriminating evidence to a prosecuting officer. [L]

informal /ɪnˈfɔməl/, *adj.* **1.** not according to usual forms; irregular: *informal proceedings.* **2.** without ceremony: *an informal visit.* **3.** loose in structure, as speech; colloquial. **4.** (of a vote) invalid. ◇*adv.* **5. vote informal,** to mark a ballot-paper incorrectly so that the vote will not be counted. — **informality,** *n.*

informant /ɪnˈfɔmənt/, *n.* someone who informs or gives information.

information /ˌɪnfəˈmeɪʃən/, *n.* **1.** knowledge given or received concerning some fact or circumstance; news. **2.** knowledge on various

information

subjects, however obtained. **3.** (in communication theory) a quantitative measure of the contents of a message. [L]

informative /ɪnˈfɔːmətɪv/, *adj.* affording information; instructive: *an informative book.* Also, **informatory** /ɪnˈfɔːmətəri, -tri/.

informed /ɪnˈfɔːmd/, *adj.* knowledgeable, aware of facts as a basis for opinion: *informed readers will judge the matter fairly.*

informer /ɪnˈfɔːmə/, *n.* someone who gives incriminating evidence to a prosecuting officer.

infra-, a prefix meaning 'below' or 'beneath', as in *infra-axillary* (below the axilla). [L]

infraction /ɪnˈfrækʃən/, *n.* a breaking; breach; violation; infringement: *an infraction of a treaty; an infraction of a law.*

infra-red /ˈɪnfrə-red/, *adj.*; /ɪnfrəˈred/ *n.*, (of or related to) part of the invisible electromagnetic spectrum next to the red end of the visible spectrum and of longer wavelength than red light.

infrastructure /ˈɪnfrəstrʌktʃə/, *n.* the basic framework or underlying foundation (as of an organisation or a system).

infrequent /ɪnˈfriːkwənt/, *adj.* happening at long intervals or not often: *infrequent visits.* — **infrequency**, *n.*

infringe /ɪnˈfrɪndʒ/, *v.,* **-fringed, -fringing.** ◇*v.t.* **1.** to break, as a rule; violate or transgress. ◇*v.i.* **2.** to move in, encroach or trespass (fol. by *on* or *upon*): *Don't infringe on his privacy.* [L: break off] — **infringement,** *n.*

infuriate /ɪnˈfjʊərieɪt/, *v.t.,* **-ated, -ating. 1.** to make furious; enrage. **2.** to annoy intensely. [ML: enraged] — **infuriatingly,** *adv.* — **infuriation,** *n.*

infuse /ɪnˈfjuːz/, *v.t.,* **-fused, -fusing. 1.** to introduce as by pouring; cause to penetrate; instil (fol. by *into*). **2.** to inspire (with); imbue: *infused with energy.* **3.** to soak or steep (a plant, etc.) in hot water to draw out its flavor, value, as tea, herbs, etc. [ME, from L: poured in or on] — **infuser,** *n.* — **infusive,** *adj.*

infusion /ɪnˈfjuːʒən/, *n.* **1.** the act of infusing. **2.** a liquid extract obtained from a substance by steeping or soaking it in hot water.

-ing[1], a suffix forming a noun from a verb, as in *the art of building, a new building, cotton wadding;* also forming nouns from words other than verbs, as in *offing, shirting.* [ME *-ing,* OE *-ing, -ung*]

-ing[2], a suffix forming the present participle of verbs, such participles often being used as adjectives, as in *warring factions.* See **-ing**[1]. [ME *-ing, -inge*]

Ingamells /ˈɪŋɡəmelz/, *n.* **Rex** (*Reginald Charles Ingamells*), 1913–55, Australian poet; founder of the Jindyworobak movement, 1938.

ingenious /ɪnˈdʒiːniəs/, *adj.* **1.** (of things, actions, etc.) showing cleverness of invention or construction: *an ingenious machine.* **2.** clever at working out ways of doing and making things; inventive: *an ingenious mechanic.* [ME, from L: of good natural talents]

ingenue /ˈɒʒəˈnuː, -ˈnjuː/, *n.* **1.** the part of an ingenuous girl, esp. as represented on the

inhalation

stage. **2.** an actress who plays such a part. [F, from L]

ingenuity /ɪndʒəˈnjuːəti/, *n., pl.* **-ties. 1.** the quality of being ingenious; inventive talent. **2.** skilfulness of contrivance or design, as of things, actions, etc. [L: frankness, See INGENUOUS]

ingenuous /ɪnˈdʒenjuəs/, *adj.* open, straightforward, sometimes easily deceived; artless; innocent. [L: native, innate, freeborn, noble, frank]

ingest /ɪnˈdʒest/, *v.t. Physiol.* to put or take (food, etc.) into the body. [L: carried, or poured in] — **ingestion,** *n.*

Ingham /ˈɪŋəm/, *n.* a town in north-eastern Qld, on the Herbert River; sugar cane. Pop. 5202 (1986).

ingot /ˈɪŋɡət/, *n.* a block cast from melted metal poured into a mould (**ingot mould**), and stored for further use. [ME: mould for metal]

ingrained /ˈɪŋɡreɪnd/, *adj.* **1.** fixed firmly as into cracks: *ingrained dirt.* **2.** deep-rooted: *ingrained habits.*

ingrate /ˈɪŋɡreɪt/, *n.* an ungrateful person. [ME, from L: unpleasing, not grateful]

ingratiate /ɪnˈɡreɪʃieɪt/, *v.t.,* **-ated, -ating.** to act in a way that will make others pleased with (oneself): *He ingratiated himself with his boss.* [L] — **ingratiatingly,** *adv.* — **ingratiation,** *n.*

ingratitude /ɪnˈɡrætɪtjuːd/, *n.* the state of being ungrateful.

ingredient /ɪnˈɡriːdiənt/, *n.* any part in a whole or mixture: *the ingredients of a cake.* [late ME, from L: entering]

Ingres /ˈæɡrə/, *n.* **Jean Auguste Dominique** /ʒɒ̃ oʊˌɡyst dɒmiˈniːk/, 1780–1867, French neoclassicist painter; influenced by Byzantine art.

ingress /ˈɪŋɡres/, *n.* **1.** the act or right of going in. **2.** a means or place of going in; entrance.

in-group /ˈɪn-ɡruːp/, *n.* a group giving favorable treatment and acceptance to its own members and no-one else.

ingrown /ˈɪnɡroʊn/, *adj.* **1.** having grown into the flesh: *an ingrown toenail.* **2.** grown within or inwards.

inguinal /ˈɪŋɡwənəl/, *adj.* of, relating to, or placed in the groin. [L]

inhabit /ɪnˈhæbət/, *v.t.* to live or dwell in (a place), as persons or animals. [L] — **inhabitable,** *adj.* — **inhabitability,** *n.* — **inhabitation,** *n.*

inhabitant /ɪnˈhæbətənt/, *n.* a person or animal that inhabits a place; permanent resident. Also, *Obs.,* **inhabiter.** [late ME, from L: dwelling in]

inhalant /ɪnˈheɪlənt/, *adj.* **1.** serving for inhalation. ◇*n.* **2.** an apparatus or medicine used for inhaling.

inhalation /ɪnhəˈleɪʃən/, *n.* **1.** the act of inhaling. **2.** a medicinal preparation to be inhaled.

inhale

inhale /ɪnˈheɪl/, v., **-haled, -haling.** ◇v.t. **1.** to breathe in; draw in by, or as by, breathing: *to inhale air.* ◇v.i. **2.** to draw into the lungs, esp. smoke of cigarettes, cigars, etc.: *Do you inhale?* [L]

inharmonic /ɪnhɑːˈmɒnɪk/, adj. not harmonic.

inharmonious /ɪnhɑːˈmoʊniəs/, adj. not harmonious; discordant. [IN.[3] + HARMONIOUS]

inhere /ɪnˈhɪər/, v.i., **-hered, -hering.** to exist permanently and inseparably (in), as a quality, element, etc.; to be inherent. [L: stick in or to]

inherent /ɪnˈhɛrənt, ɪnˈhɪərənt/, adj. existing in something as a permanent and inseparable part or quality. [L: sticking in or to]

inherit /ɪnˈhɛrət/, v.t. **1.** to take or receive (property, a right, a title, etc.) as the heir of the former owner. **2.** to possess as a hereditary characteristic: *She inherited her mother's blue eyes.* ◇v.i. **3.** to take or receive property, etc., as being heir to it. [ME, from OF, from L: inherit] **–inheritable,** adj.

inheritance /ɪnˈhɛrətəns/, n. **1.** property passing at the owner's death to the heir. **2.** a hereditary characteristic or characteristics. **3.** anything received from ancestors as if by succession: *an inheritance of family pride.* **4.** portion, peculiar possession, or heritage: *the inheritance of the saints.* **5.** the act or fact of inheriting: *to receive property by inheritance.*

inhibit /ɪnˈhɪbət/, v.t. **1.** to check or hinder (an action, impulse, etc.). **2.** to prohibit; forbid. **3.** *Chem.* to decrease the rate of or stop a chemical reaction. [late ME, from L: held back, restrained] **–inhibiter, inhibitor,** n.

inhibition /ɪnəˈbɪʃən, ɪnhɪ-/, n. **1.** the act of inhibiting. **2.** the state of being inhibited. **3.** *Psychol.* the blocking of any psychological process by another psychological process.

inhospitable /ɪnhɒsˈpɪtəbəl/, adj. **1.** (of persons, actions, etc.) not welcoming guests or strangers. **2.** (of a region, climate, etc.) not offering shelter, favorable conditions, etc. **–inhospitableness,** n. **–inhospitably,** adv. **–inhospitality,** n.

inhuman /ɪnˈhjuːmən/, adj. **1.** lacking natural human feeling or sympathy for others; brutal. **2.** not human. [late ME, from L]

inhumane /ɪnhjuːˈmeɪn/, adj. not humane; lacking humanity or kindness.

inhumanity /ɪnhjuːˈmænəti/, n., pl. **-ties.** **1.** the state or quality of being inhuman or inhumane; cruelty: *man's inhumanity to man.* **2.** an inhuman or inhumane act.

inimical /ɪˈnɪmɪkəl/, adj. unfriendly or hostile, to people or things: *a climate inimical to health.* [LL, from L: unfriendly, an enemy] **–inimicality,** n.

inimitable /ɪˈnɪmɪtəbəl/, adj. not able to be imitated, unique. **–inimitability, inimitableness,** n.

535

injustice

iniquity /ɪˈnɪkwəti/, n., pl. **-ties.** wickedness. [ME, from L: injustice] **–iniquitous,** adj.

init., *Abbrev.* initial.

initial /ɪˈnɪʃəl/, adj., n., v., **-ialled, -ialling.** ◇adj. **1.** of or relating to the beginning; incipient: *the initial step in a process.* ◇n. **2.** an initial letter, as of a word. **3.** the first letter of a proper name. **4.** a letter of extra size, oft. decorated, used at the beginning of a chapter or other division of a book, etc. ◇v.t. **5.** to mark or sign with an initial or initials, esp. as an indication of responsibility for or approval of contents. [L: of the beginning]

initiate /ɪˈnɪʃieɪt/, v., **-ated, -ating.** /ɪˈnɪʃiət, -eɪt/, adj., n. ◇v.t. **1.** to begin, set going, or originate. **2.** to introduce into the knowledge of some art or subject. **3.** to admit with formal rites into secret knowledge, a society, etc. ◇adj. **4.** admitted into a society, etc., or into the knowledge of a subject. ◇n. **5.** someone who has been initiated. [L: begun, initiated] **–initiator,** n.

initiation /ɪnɪʃiˈeɪʃən/, n. **1.** formal admission into a society, etc. **2.** a ceremony of admission. **3.** the starting of a chain reaction in fissile material, as in an atomic bomb.

initiative /ɪˈnɪʃiətɪv/, n. **1.** an introductory act or step; leading action: *to take the initiative.* **2.** readiness and ability to initiate action; enterprise: *to lack initiative.*

inject /ɪnˈdʒɛkt/, v.t. **1.** *Med.* to force a fluid, by means of a syringe and needle, into (a person, a part of the body, etc.). **2.** to introduce (something new or different) into a thing: *to inject comedy into a situation.* [L: thrown or put in]

injection /ɪnˈdʒɛkʃən/, n. **1.** the act of injecting. **2.** that which is injected. **3.** a liquid injected into the body, esp. for medicinal purposes.

in-joke /ˈɪn-dʒoʊk/, n. a joke understood only by those knowing the situation which has produced it.

injudicious /ɪndʒuːˈdɪʃəs/, adj. showing lack of judgment; unwise.

injunction /ɪnˈdʒʌŋkʃən/, n. **1.** *Law.* an order by a judge or court requiring a person or persons not to do or (more commonly) not to do a particular thing. **2.** a command, order or direction. [LL: command]

injure /ˈɪndʒə/, v.t., **-jured, -juring.** **1.** to do or cause harm of any kind to; damage; hurt; impair. **2.** to do wrong or injustice to. [back-formation from INJURY, n.] **–injured,** adj.

injurious /ɪnˈdʒʊəriəs/, adj. **1.** harmful or hurtful. **2.** (of something said or done) offensive. [late ME, from L: wrongful]

injury /ˈɪndʒəri/, n., pl. **-ries.** **1.** harm of any kind done or received. **2.** a wrong or injustice done or suffered. **3.** *Law.* the infringement of another's legal right. [ME, from L: wrong, harm, insult]

injustice /ɪnˈdʒʌstəs/, n. **1.** the quality or fact of being unjust. **2.** an unjust action or situation. [ME, from F, from L]

ink /ɪŋk/, *n.* **1.** a fluid used for writing or printing. **2.** a dark, protective fluid given out by the cuttlefish, etc. ◇*v.t.* **3.** to mark, stain, or cover with ink. [ME, from OF, from LL, from Gk: kind of ink]

inkling /'ɪŋklɪŋ/, *n.* **1.** a slight suggestion; hint. **2.** an uncertain idea; notion. [ME: to hint at]

inkwell /'ɪŋkwel/, *n.* a container for ink, esp. one set into the surface of a desk.

inlaid /'ɪnleɪd/, *adj.* **1.** set in the surface of a thing: *an inlaid pattern in wood.* **2.** made with something set in the surface: *an inlaid table.*

inland /'ɪnlænd/, *adj.* **1.** relating to or situated in the inner part of a country or area: *inland cities.* **2.** carried on within a country; domestic: *inland trade.* ◇*adv.* **3.** in or towards the inner part of a country. ◇*n.* **4.** the inner part of a country, away from the border. [ME and OE] —**inlander,** *n.*

in-law /'ɪn-lɔ/, *n.* a relative by marriage.

inlay /ɪn'leɪ/, *v.,* **-laid, -laying;** /'ɪnleɪ/, *n.* ◇*v.t.* **1.** to ornament (an object) with thin layers of fine materials set in its surface. **2.** to fix (layers of fine materials) in a surface of an object. ◇*n.* **3.** work or decoration made by inlaying. **4.** a layer of fine material set in something else. **5.** *Dentistry.* a filling of metal, etc., which is fitted and fastened into a tooth as a solid mass.

inlet /'ɪnlɛt/, *n.* **1.** a stretch of water, usu. long and narrow, reaching into land from the shore line, or a narrow passage between islands. **2.** a place of admission; an entrance.

in loco parentis /ɪn loukou pə'rɛntəs/, *adv.* in the place of a parent. [L]

inmate /'ɪnmeɪt/, *n.* one of those having to stay in a hospital, prison, etc.

in memoriam /ɪn mə'mɔriəm/, *adv.* in memory (of). [L]

inmost /'ɪnmoʊst/, *adj.* **1.** situated furthest within. **2.** closest to one: *his inmost thoughts.* [OE *innemest*]

inn /ɪn/, *n.* a small hotel that provides beds, food, alcohol, etc., for travellers. [OE *inn* house]

Innamincka /ɪnə'mɪŋkə/, *n.* a small township in north-eastern SA, on Cooper Creek; Philip Parker King, the lone survivor of the Burke and Wills expedition, was found near here. [Aboriginal *Yidniminkani* you go into the hole there]

innards /'ɪnədz/, *n.pl.* the inward parts of the body; entrails; viscera.

innate /ɪn'eɪt/, *adj.* **1.** inborn; existing as or if existing in one from birth; *innate shyness.* **2.** basic to the character of something. **3.** arising naturally from the mind, rather than learned from experience: *innate ideas.* [late ME, from L: inborn] —**innateness,** *n.*

inner /'ɪnə/, *adj.* **1.** situated further within; interior: *an inner door.* **2.** more private or secret: *the inner circle of his friends.* **3.** mental or spiritual: *the inner life.* **4.** not obvious; esoteric: *an inner meaning.* ◇*n.* **5.** (the shot striking) the ring nearest the bull's-eye of a target. [OE *inne* within]

innermost /'ɪnəmoʊst/, *adj.* furthest inwards; inmost. [ME, from INNER + -MOST]

inner tube, *n.* a rubber tube which fits inside the outer cover of a pneumatic (air-filled) tyre.

innervate /'ɪnəvɛt/, *v.t.,* **-vated, -vating. 1.** to supply nervous energy to. **2.** to supply nerves to (a body, organ, etc.). [IN.[2] + NERVE + -ATE[1]] —**innervation,** *n.*

innings /'ɪnɪŋz/, *n.pl.* (treated as sing.) **1.** *Cricket.* **a.** the turn of any one member of the batting team to bat. **b.** that division of a match in which all the members of a team have their turn at batting, until all are out or the team declares. **2.** any opportunity for some activity; a turn.

Innisfail /'ɪnəsfeɪl/, *n.* a coastal town in north-eastern Qld, at the junction of the North Johnstone and South Johnstone Rivers. Pop. 8113 (1986).

innkeeper /'ɪnkipə/, *n.* someone who looks after an inn.

innocent /'ɪnəsənt/, *adj.* **1.** free from any wrong; pure. **2.** not brought about by an evil intention: *an innocent mistake.* **3.** free from any quality that can cause harm; harmless: *innocent fun.* **4.** having or showing the simplicity of an unworldly person. ◇*n.* **5.** an innocent person. **6.** a young child. **7.** a person without cunning or deceit. **8.** a fool. [ME, from L: harmless] —**innocence,** *n.*

Innocent /'ɪnəsənt/, *n.* the name adopted by 13 popes, notably **Innocent II** (*Gregorio Papareschi*), died 1143, pope 1130-43.

innocuous /ɪn'ɒkjuəs/, *adj.* not harmful; harmless. [L]

innovate /'ɪnəveɪt/, *v.i.,* **-vated, -vating.** to bring in something new (fol. by *on* or *in*). [L: renewed, altered] —**innovative, innovatory,** *adj.* —**innovator,** *n.* —**innovation,** *n.*

innuendo /ɪnju'ɛndoʊ/, *n., pl.* **-dos, -does. 1.** an indirect suggestion about a person or thing, esp. of an unpleasant nature. **2.** *Law.* (in a defamation action) the explanation or making clear of the words said to be defamatory. [L: intimation]

innumerable /ɪ'njumərəbəl, ɪ'njumrəbəl/, *adj.* **1.** very many. **2.** not able to be counted.

innumerate /ɪ'njumərət/, *adj.* **1.** not knowing the basic principles of mathematics. **2.** showing little or no skill in mathematics.

inoculate /ɪ'nɒkjəleɪt/, *v.t.,* **-lated, -lating. 1.** to implant (a disease) in a body by the introduction of germs or a virus, to produce a mild form of the disease and thus give immunity. **2.** to treat (a person or animal) thus. [late ME, from L: grafted; implanted] —**inoculative,** *adj.* —**inoculator,** *n.* —**inoculation,** *n.*

inoffensive /ɪnə'fɛnsɪv/, *adj.* **1.** doing no harm; harmless; unoffending. **2.** not being a cause of offence.

inoperable /ɪn'ɒpərəbəl, -'ɒprə-/, *adj.* **1.** not able to be used or operated upon. **2.** not admitting of a surgical operation without risk.

inoperative /ɪnˈɒpərətɪv, -ˈɒprə-/, *adj.* 1. not in operation. 2. without effect: *inoperative treatment.*

inopportune /ɪnˈɒpətjuːn/, *adj.* (of a time, event, etc.) not suitable; inappropriate: *an inopportune visit.* —**inopportuneness, inopportunity,** *n.*

inordinate /ɪnˈɔːdənət/, *adj.* not within proper limits; excessive: *inordinate demands.* [ME, from L: disordered]

inorganic /ɪnɔːˈɡænɪk/, *adj.* 1. not having the basic form which living bodies all have. 2. *Chem.* having to do with compounds not containing carbon, excepting cyanides and carbonates. See **organic** (def. 1). —**inorganically,** *adv.*

in-patient /ˈɪn-peɪʃənt/, *n.* a patient who lives in, while being treated in a hospital.

input /ˈɪnpʊt/, *n.* something that is put in, as the current fed into an electrical circuit, etc.

inquest /ˈɪnkwɛst/, *n.* 1. a legal or judicial inquiry, esp. before a jury. 2. one made by a coroner, esp. one inquiring into unexplained deaths. 3. the body of people holding such an inquiry, esp. a coroner's jury. [ME, from OF, from L: (a thing) inquired into]

inquietude /ɪnˈkwaɪətjuːd/, *n.* 1. restlessness; uneasiness. 2. (*pl.*) disquieting thoughts.

inquire /ɪnˈkwaɪə/, *v.i.* -quired, -quiring. to search or examine into the particulars of (fol. by *into*). Also, **enquire.** [L] —**inquirer,** *n.*

inquiring /ɪnˈkwaɪərɪŋ/, *adj.* questioning; curious: *an inquiring look.*

inquiry /ɪnˈkwaɪəri/, *n., pl.* -ries. 1. a search or investigation into a matter. 2. the act of inquiring; interrogation. Also, **enquiry.**

inquisition /ɪnkwəˈzɪʃən/, *n.* 1. an investigation or inquiry, as one conducted by judicial or non-judicial officers. 2. (*cap.*) *Rom Cath Ch.* a special court for the defence of Catholic teaching and the judgment of heresy. [ME, from L: a searching into] —**inquisitorial,** *adj.*

inquisitive /ɪnˈkwɪzətɪv/, *adj.* 1. overly curious; prying. 2. inquiring; eager for knowledge.

inquisitor /ɪnˈkwɪzətə/, *n.* 1. someone who inquires or investigates. 2. a member of the Inquisition. —**inquisitorial,** *adj.*

inroad /ˈɪnroʊd/, *n.* 1. (*usu. pl.*) forcible entry which reduces the area, amount, etc., of something: *inroads on our savings.* 2. an attack on land, etc., held by an enemy.

insalubrious /ɪnsəˈluːbriəs/, *adj.* unfavorable to health. —**insalubrity,** *n.*

insane /ɪnˈseɪn/, *adj.* 1. not of sound mind; mentally unbalanced. 2. set apart for the care of insane people. 3. totally senseless: *an insane attempt.* 4. *Colloq.* amazing. —**insanity,** *n.*

insanitary /ɪnˈsænətəri, -tri/, *adj.* unclean and likely to carry infection.

insatiable /ɪnˈseɪʃəbəl/, *adj.* not able to be satisfied: *insatiable desire.* —**insatiably,** *adv.*

inscribe /ɪnˈskraɪb/, *v.t.,* -scribed, -scribing. 1. to write or cut (words, characters, etc.). 2. to mark (a surface) with words, etc., in a way which is long-lasting. 3. to address or dedicate (a book, photograph, etc.) informally, esp. by a handwritten note. 4. to enter (a name) on an official list. 5. *Geom.* to draw (one figure) within another figure so that the inner lies in the boundary of the outer at as many points as possible. [L: write in or upon] —**inscriber,** *n.*

inscription /ɪnˈskrɪpʃən/, *n.* 1. something inscribed, as a historical or other record cut, painted or written on stone or other hard surface. 2. a short, more or less informal dedication, as of a book or a work of art. 3. a note inscribed in a book, usu. signed. [ME, from L] —**inscriptional, inscriptive,** *adj.*

Inscription /ɪnˈskrɪpʃən/, *n. Cape,* a cape on the north-west coast of WA; former site of pewter plates inscribed by the explorers Dirck Hartog, 1616 and Willem de Vlamingh, 1697.

inscrutable /ɪnˈskruːtəbəl/, *adj.* 1. not able to be searched or looked at closely. 2. not easily understood; mysterious; enigmatic. [late ME, from LL] —**inscrutability, inscrutableness,** *n.* —**inscrutably,** *adv.*

insect /ˈɪnsɛkt/, *n.* 1. *Zool.* a class of small, air-breathing arthropod animals with bodies clearly divided into three parts, head, thorax, and abdomen, and with three pairs of legs, and usu. two pairs of wings. 2. any small animal such as a spider, tick, or centipede, which seems to be similar to a true insect (def. 1). [L: cut in or up (so-called from the segmented form)]

insecticide /ɪnˈsɛktəsaɪd/, *n.* a substance or preparation used for killing insects. [L] —**insecticidal,** *adj.*

insectivore /ɪnˈsɛktəvɔː/, *n.* an animal or plant which eats insects. [NL, from L] —**insectivorous,** *adj.*

insecure /ɪnsəˈkjʊə/, *adj.* 1. open to danger; unsafe. 2. not firm or safe: *insecure foundations.* 3. not free from fear, doubt, etc. —**insecurity,** *n.*

inseminate /ɪnˈsɛmənɛɪt/, *v.t.,* -nated, -nating. 1. to place or introduce seed into. 2. to introduce semen into (a female) to cause fertilisation; impregnate. [L: sown, planted in] —**insemination,** *n.*

insensate /ɪnˈsɛnseɪt, -sət/, *adj.* 1. not having sensation: *insensate stone.* 2. without feeling; unfeeling. 3. without sense, understanding, or judgment.

insensible /ɪnˈsɛnsəbəl/, *adj.* 1. incapable of feeling or sensing. 2. unconscious, unaware, or unappreciative: *We are not insensible of your kindness.* 3. not able to be noticed by the senses: *insensible changes.* 4. unresponsive or lacking in feeling. —**insensibly,** *adv.* —**insensibility,** *n.*

insensitive /ɪnˈsɛnsətɪv/, *adj.* 1. not sensitive: *an insensitive skin.* 2. not affected by influences: *insensitive to light.* 3. having a lack of feeling: *an insensitive nature.* —**insensitivity,** *n.*

inseparable /ɪnˈsɛpərəbəl, -prə-/, *adj.* unable to be separated or parted: *inseparable companions.*

insert /ɪnˈsɜːt/, v.; /ˈɪnsɜːt/, n. ◇v.t. **1.** to put or set in: *Could a child insert the key in the lock?* **2.** to introduce into the body of something: *an advertisement inserted in the paper.* ◇n. **3.** something (to be) inserted. **4.** an extra leaf included when the book is bound. [L: put in]

insertion /ɪnˈsɜːʃən/, n. **1.** the act of inserting: *each insertion of an advertisement.* **2.** something inserted: *an insertion into a book; a lace insertion in material.*

in-service /ˈɪn-sɜːvəs/, adj. of or relating to training provided by employers, in connection with a person's current work.

inset /ˈɪnset/, n.; /ɪnˈset/, v. **-set, -setting**. ◇n. **1.** something put or set into or inside something else. ◇v.t. **2.** to set in; insert.

inside /ɪnˈsaɪd/, prep., adv.; /ˈɪnsaɪd/, n., adj. ◇prep. **1.** on the inner side of; within. **2.** before the passing of: *inside an hour.* ◇adv. **3.** in or into the inner part. **4.** indoors: *He is working inside.* **5.** by nature; fundamentally: *Inside, he's very kind.* **6.** *Colloq.* to or in prison. ◇n. **7.** the inner part, side or surface. **8.** (*oft. pl.*) *Colloq.* the inner parts of the body, esp. the stomach and intestines. **9.** the part of a curved track or course nearer to the centre of the curves; the inside lane: *a horse coming up fast on the inside.* **10.** an inner group of persons having private knowledge about a circumstance or case. **11. inside out**, **a.** with the inner side turned to face outwards. **b.** thoroughly; completely: *He knows his job inside out.* ◇adj. **12.** being on or in the inside. **13.** acting, done, or originating within a place: *The robbery was an inside job.* **14.** coming from the inner circle of those concerned in a case: *inside information.* **15.** being nearer to the centre and therefore shorter: *the inside lane of a track.*

insidious /ɪnˈsɪdiəs/, adj. **1.** intended to trap or deceive: *an insidious plot.* **2.** secretly deceitful: *an insidious enemy.* **3.** operating unnoticed but with serious effect: *an insidious disease.* [L: cunning, artful]

insight /ˈɪnsaɪt/, n. **1.** an understanding gained or given of something. **2.** ability to see into inner character or underlying truth: *a man of great insight.*

insignia /ɪnˈsɪɡniə/, n.pl. badges or special marks of office or honor. [L: mark, badge]

insignificant /ˌɪnsɪɡˈnɪfɪkənt/, adj. **1.** (of matters, details, etc.) unimportant or too small to matter. **2.** (of a person, people) of no influence or not worth consideration. **–insignificance**, n.

insincere /ˌɪnsɪnˈsɪə, -sɪn-/, adj. not sincere; not honest in expressing feeling. **–insincerity**, n.

insinuate /ɪnˈsɪnjuert/, v.t., **-ated, -ating**. **1.** to suggest or hint slyly. **2.** to bring indirectly and cleverly into the mind: *to insinuate doubt.* **3.** to bring into a position by indirect or artful methods: *He can insinuate himself into the boss's favor.* [L: brought in by windings or turnings] **–insinuation**, n.

insipid /ɪnˈsɪpəd/, adj. **1.** without noticeable, interesting, or attractive qualities. **2.** (of food and drink) without enough taste to be pleasing. [LL: tasteless]

insist /ɪnˈsɪst/, v.i. **1.** to be firm, on some matter of desire, demand, intention, etc. **2.** to declare with special emphasis. **3.** to continue to speak, act with earnestness or emphasis (fol. by *on* or *upon*): *I insist on one point in this argument.* [L: insist, stand or press upon] **–insistence, insistency**, n.

insistent /ɪnˈsɪstənt/, adj. **1.** insisting; persistent. **2.** forcing attention or notice: *an insistent tone.*

insobriety /ˌɪnsəˈbraɪəti/, n. lack of sobriety.

in so far, conj. to such an extent (usu. fol. by *as*).

insolent /ˈɪnsələnt/, adj. boldly rude or disrespectful; insulting: *an insolent reply.* [ME, from L: unaccustomed, unusual, excessive, arrogant] **–insolently**, adv. **insolence**, n.

insoluble /ɪnˈsɒljubəl/, adj. **1.** not able to be dissolved: *insoluble salts.* **2.** that cannot be worked out: *an insoluble problem.* [ME, from L] **–insolubility**, n.

insolvent /ɪnˈsɒlvənt/, adj. **1.** not able to pay one's debts. ◇n. **2.** someone who is insolvent. **–insolvency**, n.

insomnia /ɪnˈsɒmniə/, n. inability to sleep, esp. over a very long time; sleeplessness. [L] **–insomniac**, n., adj.

in so much, conj. **1.** to such an extent or degree (*that*); so (*that*). **2.** → **inasmuch as**.

insouciant /ɪnˈsuːsiənt, -sjənt/, adj. without anxiety; carefree. [F, from L] **–insouciance**, n.

inspect /ɪnˈspekt/, v.t. **1.** to look carefully at or over. **2.** to view or examine formally or officially: *The general will inspect the soldiers.* [L] **–inspection**, n.

inspector /ɪnˈspektə/, n. **1.** someone who inspects, as an inspector of taxes. **2.** a police officer ranking above sergeant and below chief inspector. [L] **–inspectorship**, n.

inspiration /ˌɪnspəˈreɪʃən/, n. **1.** an inspiring action or influence, person or thing, as a divine influence brought to bear on a person. **2.** something inspired, as a thought. **3.** the drawing of air into the lungs; inhalation. **4.** the act of inspiring. **5.** the state of being inspired. **–inspirational**, adj.

inspire /ɪnˈspaɪə/, v., **-spired, -spiring**. ◇v.t. **1.** to impart an enlivening, quickening, or exalting influence to: *His courage inspired his followers.* **2.** to produce or awaken (a feeling, thought, etc.): *She inspires confidence in others.* **3.** to affect with a particular feeling, thought, etc.: *inspire a person with distrust.* **4.** (of an influence, feeling, etc.) to move to action: *inspired by a belief in a better future.* **5.** to guide or communicate by a divine influence. **6.** to give rise to: *What inspired the quarrel?* **7.** to take (air, gases, etc.) into the lungs in breathing; inhale. ◇v.i. **8.** to give inspiration. **9.** to inhale. [ME, from L: breathe into] **–inspiringly**, adv.

instability /ɪnstə'bɪləti/, n. lack of continuing firmness in position.

install /ɪn'stɔl/, v.t. 1. to place in position for service or use. 2. to establish in any office, position, or place. 3. to establish in an office, etc., with special formalities. [ML. See IN-[2], STALL[1]] —**installer**, n. —**installation**, n.

instalment /ɪn'stɔlmənt/, n. 1. any of several parts into which a debt is divided for payment at fixed times. 2. a single part of several parts appearing or issued one after the other: *a serial in six instalments*.

instance /'ɪnstəns/, n., v., **-stanced, -stancing**. ◇n. 1. a case or example of anything: *a new instance of cruelty*. 2. a stage in a process: *in the first instance*. 3. **at the instance of**, at the suggestion of. 4. **for instance**, for example. ◇v.t. 5. to give as an instance or example. [ME, from AF, from L: presence, urgency]

instant /'ɪnstənt/, n. 1. a very short space of time; a moment: *not an instant too soon*. 2. the point of time now present, or present with regard to some action or event. ◇adj. 3. following without any interval of time; immediate: *instant relief*. 4. present; current: *the 10th instant* (the tenth day of the present month). 5. pressing or urgent: *instant need*. 6. (of a foodstuff) processed for simple preparation: *instant coffee*. [late ME, from L: standing upon, insisting, being at hand]

instantaneous /ɪnstən'teɪniəs/, adj. occurring, done, or completed in an instant.

instead /ɪn'stɛd/, adv. 1. in the place (*of*); in lieu (*of*): *Come by plane instead of by train*. 2. in one's (its, their, etc.) place: *She sent the boy instead*. [orig. two words, *in stead* in place]

instep /'ɪnstɛp/, n. 1. the arched upper surface of the human foot between the toes and the ankle. 2. the part of a shoe, etc., over the instep.

instigate /'ɪnstəgeɪt/, v.t., **-gated, -gating**. 1. to encourage (someone) to some (usu. unacceptable) action. 2. to bring about by urging; foment: *Your presence is sure to instigate a quarrel*. [L] —**instigator**, n. —**instigation**, n.

instil /ɪn'stɪl/, v.t., **-stilled, -stilling**. 1. to inject slowly or by degrees into the mind or feelings; insinuate: *Manners must be instilled in childhood*. 2. to put in drop by drop. [L: pour in by drops] —**instiller**, n. —**instillation**, n.

instinct /'ɪnstɪŋkt/, n. 1. a pattern of activity and response present at birth. 2. any natural tendency. 3. a natural skill for something: *an instinct for art*. [late ME, from L: instigation, impulse] —**instinctive**, adj.

institute /'ɪnstətjut/, v., **-tuted, -tuting**, n. ◇v.t. 1. to set up or establish: *institute a government*. 2. to set going; initiate: *institute a new course*. 3. to bring into use or practice: *institute laws*. 4. to establish in an office or position. ◇n. 5. a society or organisation for carrying on literary, scientific or educational work. 6. the building occupied by such a society. 7. *Educ.* **a.** an institution, usu. attended after high school level, which teaches technical subjects. **b.** a unit in a university for advanced instruction and research. 8. an established principle, law, custom, or organisation. [ME: set up, established, from L] —**institutor**, n.

institution /ɪnstə'tjuʃən/, n. 1. an organisation for the advancement of a particular purpose, usu. educational, charitable, etc. 2. a building used for such work, as a college, school, hospital, etc. 3. a concern engaged in some activity, as an insurance company. 4. any established law, custom, etc., in a particular culture, such as slavery. 5. the act of setting up; establishment: *the institution of laws*. —**institutional**, adj.

institutionalise or **institutionalize** /ɪnstə'tjuʃənəlaɪz/, v.t., **-lised, -lising**. 1. to make institutional. 2. to put (a person) into an institution. 3. to make (a person) dependent on an institution. —**institutionalisation**, n.

instruct /ɪn'strʌkt/, v.t. 1. to direct or command. 2. to furnish with knowledge; teach; train; educate. 3. to furnish with information; inform. 4. *Law.* **a.** (of a solicitor) to request a barrister to present a particular case in court and to furnish that barrister with the information and material necessary to do so. **b.** (of a judge) to outline what is relevant to a case, for the guidance of (the jury). [late ME, from L: built, prepared, furnished, instructed] —**instruction**, n. —**instructive**, adj. —**instructor**, n.

instrument /'ɪnstrəmənt/, n. 1. a mechanical device; tool: *a doctor's instruments*. 2. something made to produce musical sounds: *a stringed instrument*. 3. a thing with or by which something is done; a means: *an instrument of government*. 4. a formal legal document, as a contract, deed or will. 5. one who is used by another. 6. a device for measuring the present value of a quantity under observation. 7. an electrical device which gives information about the state of some part of an aircraft, car, etc. [ME, from L]

instrumental /ɪnstrə'mɛntl/, adj. 1. serving as a means. 2. of or relating to an instrument. 3. performed on or written for a musical instrument. 4. *Gram.* (in some inflected languages) of a case which indicates the means (person or thing) by or with which an action is done. [ME, from ML] —**instrumentality**, n.

instrumentalist /ɪnstrə'mɛntəlɪst/, n. a person who performs on a musical instrument.

instrumentation /ɪnstrəmən'teɪʃən/, n. 1. the arranging of music for instruments, esp. for an orchestra; orchestration. 2. the use of, or work done by, instruments.

instrument panel, n. a panel on the dashboard of a car or above aircraft controls, etc., which contains measuring instruments. Also, **instrument board**.

insubordinate /ɪnsə'bɔdənət/, adj. not obeying authority; disobedient: *insubordinate crew*. —**insubordination**, n.

insubstantial /ɪnsəb'stænʃəl/, adj. 1. not great in amount; slight. 2. without reality; unreal: *the insubstantial stuff of dreams*.

insufferable /ɪnˈsʌfərəbəl, -frəbəl/, *adj.* unbearable; intolerable: *insufferable rudeness.*

insufficiency /ɪnsəˈfɪʃənsi/, *n.* lacking in amount, force, or fitness; inadequateness. Also, **insufficience**. —**insufficient**, *adj.*

insular /ˈɪnsjʊlə, ˈɪnsjʊlə/, *adj.* 1. of or related to an island or islands. 2. narrow-minded. [LL: of an island] —**insularity**, *n.*

insulate /ˈɪnsjʊleɪt/, *v.t.*, **-lated, -lating.** 1. to cover or surround (an electric wire, etc.) with non-conducting material. 2. *Phys, etc.* to prevent or reduce the amount of electricity, heat, or sound passing to or from (something). 3. to place apart; segregate. 4. to put an insulating material in the roof of (a house) to keep in warmth in winter and keep out heat in summer. [L: made into an island] —**insulator**, *n.*

insulation /ɪnsjʊˈleɪʃən/, *n.* 1. material used for insulating. 2. the act or result of insulating.

insulin /ˈɪnsjʊlən, -sjələn, -sələn/, *n.* a hormone which allows the transport of glucose across cell membranes, and decreases the blood sugar level. A lack of insulin produces diabetes. [Trademark; L: island (with reference to the islands of the pancreas)]

insult /*n.* ˈɪnsʌlt; *v.* ɪnˈsʌlt/, ◊*v.t.* 1. to treat with offensive rudeness; affront. ◊*n.* 2. a cheeky or offensively rude action or speech; affront. 3. **add insult to injury,** to make a wrong worse than it was. [L: leap on or at, insult] —**insulting**, *adj.*

insuperable /ɪnˈsuːpərəbəl, -prəbəl, -sju-/, *adj.* not able to be passed over, overcome, or beaten: *an insuperable barrier.*

insurance /ɪnˈʃɔːrəns, -ˈʃʊə-/, *n.* 1. the act, system, or business of insuring property, life, the person, etc., against loss or harm. 2. the amount for which anything is insured.

insure /ɪnˈʃɔː, -ˈʃʊə/, *v.*, **-sured, -suring.** ◊*v.t.* 1. to guarantee against risk of loss or harm. 2. to obtain indemnity (protection) for in case of loss, damage, or death. ◊*v.i.* 3. to issue or take out an insurance policy. [var. of ENSURE] —**insured**, *n.* —**insurer**, *n.*

insurgent /ɪnˈsɜːdʒənt/, *n.* 1. someone who rises in forcible opposition to lawful authority. ◊*adj.* 2. rising in opposition; rebellious. [L: rising on or up] —**insurgence, insurgency**, *n.*

insurmountable /ɪnsəˈmaʊntəbəl/, *adj.* not able to be beaten, passed over, or overcome: *an insurmountable problem.*

insurrection /ɪnsəˈrɛkʃən/, *n.* the act of rising with weapons or open resistance against established authority. [late ME, from L: rise up]

intact /ɪnˈtækt/, *adj.* remaining unharmed, unchanged, sound, or whole; unimpaired. [late ME, from L]

intake /ˈɪnteɪk/, *n.* 1. a point at which a fluid is taken into a channel, pipe, etc. 2. the act of taking in. 3. (the quantity of) that which is taken in.

intangible /ɪnˈtændʒəbəl/, *adj.* 1. not able to be sensed by touching, as non-material things. 2. not definite or clear to the mind: *intangible arguments.* 3. existing only in connection with something else, as the goodwill of a business. ◊*n.* 4. something intangible.

integer /ˈɪntədʒə/, *n.* 1. **a.** any of the numbers 0, 1, -1, 2, -2, etc., used for counting, including zero and negative numbers. **b.** a whole number as opposed to a fraction, or a mixed number. 2. a complete thing. [L: untouched, whole, entire]

integral /ˈɪntəɡrəl/, *adj.* 1. belonging as a part of the whole: *the integral parts of the human body.* 2. necessary to the completeness of the whole. 3. made up of parts which together form a whole. 4. *Maths.* relating to or being an integer (a whole number); not fractional. ◊*n.* 5. an integral whole. 6. *Maths.* the result of the operation inverse to differentiation (see **integration**, def. 4); an expression from which a given function, equation, or system of equations is derived by differentiation. [LL]

integral calculus, *n.* →**calculus** (def. 1).

integrate /ˈɪntəɡreɪt/, *v.t.*, **-grated, -grating.** 1. to bring together (parts) into a whole. 2. to make up or complete as a whole, as parts do. 3. to show the total amount or value of. 4. *Maths.* to find the integral of. [L: made whole] —**integrated**, *adj.* —**integration**, *n.*

integrated circuit, *n.* an arrangement of interconnected circuit elements integrated with or deposited on a single semiconductor base. Also, **IC**

integrity /ɪnˈtɛɡrəti/, *n.* 1. honesty; uprightness. 2. the condition of being whole: *to preserve the integrity of the country.* 3. perfect condition: *the integrity of the text.* [late ME, from L]

integument /ɪnˈtɛɡjʊmənt/, *n.* 1. a skin, shell, etc. 2. a covering. [L]

intellect /ˈɪntəlɛkt/, *n.* 1. the power of the mind by which one knows, understands, or reasons. 2. mental ability, esp. of a high order. 3. a particular mind or minds, esp. of a high order. 4. the person or persons possessing such intellect. [ME, from L: a discerning, perceiving]

intellectual /ɪntəˈlɛktʃuəl/, *adj.* 1. of interest to the mind: *intellectual books.* 2. of or relating to the mind: *intellectual powers.* 3. directed towards things that need to use the mind: *intellectual tastes.* 4. showing mental ability, esp. to a high degree: *an intellectual writer.* ◊*n.* 5. an intellectual person. [ME, from L] —**intellectually**, *adv.* —**intellectuality**, *n.*

intelligence /ɪnˈtɛlədʒəns/, *n.* 1. the ability to understand, learn, and to control behavior in any new event. 2. good mental ability. 3. (*oft. cap.*) an intelligent being, esp. not in bodily form. 4. knowledge of an event, circumstance, etc., received or given; news; information. 5. the gathering or giving of information, esp. in military affairs. 6. a group of people working to obtain such information; secret service. 7. the ability which a computerised machine obtains from programs built into it to recognise certain conditions and perform varying tasks without the need of an operator.

intelligence quotient, n. →IQ.

intelligent /ɪnˈtelədʒənt/, adj. 1. having a good understanding or mental ability: *intelligent pupils*. 2. showing quickness of understanding: *an intelligent answer*. 3. of or relating to a computerised piece of machinery which is programmed to recognise certain sets of conditions and to carry out varying tasks without the need of an operator. [L]

intelligentsia /ɪnˌteləˈdʒentsiə/, n.pl. intellectuals viewed as a social class. [Russ, from L *intelligentia* intelligence]

intelligible /ɪnˈtelɪdʒəbəl/, adj. able to be understood; comprehensible. [ME, from L]

intemperate /ɪnˈtempərət, -prət/, adj. 1. given to or characterised by drinking too much. 2. not controlled (as in passion, appetite etc.); unrestrained. 3. extreme in temperature, as climate, etc. — **intemperance**, n.

intend /ɪnˈtend/, v.t. 1. to have in mind as something to be done or brought about: *He intends to join*. 2. to design for a particular purpose, use, etc.: *a book intended for study*. 3. to design; to express or indicate. ◇v.i. 4. to have a purpose or design: *He may intend otherwise*. [ME, from L: extend, intend]

intended /ɪnˈtendəd/, adj. 1. designed or meant: *to produce the intended effect*. 2. expected; prospective: *an intended buyer*. ◇n. 3. *Colloq*. an intended husband or wife.

intense /ɪnˈtens/, adj. 1. existing or happening in a high degree: *intense heat*. 2. strong, eager, as sensations, or emotions: *intense joy*. 3. of an extreme kind; very great, etc.: *an intense wind*. 4. *Photog*. a. strong: *intense light*. b. → **dense** (def. 3). 5. strenuous; earnest, as activity, thought, etc.: *an intense game*. 6. having or showing great strength of feeling, as a person, the face, language, etc. [ME, from L: stretched tight, intense]

intensifier /ɪnˈtensəfaɪə/, n. *Gram*. a word or word part which increases the effect of the meaning of the word or phrase but has by itself little meaning, e.g. *very*.

intensify /ɪnˈtensəfaɪ/, v.t., v.i., **-fied**, **-fying**. to make or become intense or more intense. — **intensification**, n.

intension /ɪnˈtenʃən/, n. 1. an increase in degree; intensification. 2. high degree; intensity. 3. *Logic*. the total of the elements contained in a concept or suggested by a term. See **extension** (def. 7). [L]

intensity /ɪnˈtensəti/, n., pl. **-ties**. 1. the quality or condition of being intense. 2. great energy, strength, etc., as of activity, thought, or feeling. 3. high degree, as of cold. 4. the degree or extent to which something is intense, as a voice tone, or a color range. 5. *Photog*. a. strength, as of light. b. → **density** (def. 3). 6. *Phys*. a. the strength of an electric current in amperes. b. the strength of an electrical or magnetic field. c. the size or strength of force, per unit of area, volume, etc.

intensive /ɪnˈtensɪv/, adj. 1. of, relating to, or marked by intensity: *intensive fire from machine guns*. 2. *Econ*. of methods aimed to increase effectiveness, as, in agriculture, the use of fertilisers, etc., to improve the quality and quantity of crops (opposed to *extensive*). 3. *Gram*. showing increased force. For example: *certainly*, *completely* are intensive adverbs. ◇n. 4. something that intensifies. 5. *Gram*. → **intensifier**. [ML]

intent[1] /ɪnˈtent/, n. 1. an intending, as to carry out some act: *criminal intent*. 2. something that is intended; purpose; aim; etc.: *My intent was to buy*. 3. *Law*. the state of a person's mind which directs their actions towards a particular object. 4. **to all intents and purposes**, a. for all practical purposes; practically. b. for all the ends and purposes in view. 5. the end or object intended. [ME, from OF, from L]

intent[2] /ɪnˈtent/, adj. 1. firmly fixed or directed (upon something): *an intent look*. 2. having the eyes or thoughts firmly fixed on something: *intent on one's job*. 3. serious in purpose: *an intent person*. [L: stretched, intent]

intention /ɪnˈtenʃən/, n. 1. the act of deciding upon some action or result; a purpose or design. 2. the end or object intended. 3. (pl.) *Colloq*. purposes with respect to marriage. 4. *Logic*. the mental act of firstly directing attention to something. 5. meaning. [L]

intentional /ɪnˈtenʃənəl/, adj. 1. done with intention or on purpose: *an intentional insult*. 2. *Metaphys*. a. relating to an appearance, phenomenon, or representation in the mind; phenomenal; representational. b. relating to the ability of mind to direct thought to objects of all sorts.

inter /ɪnˈtɜ/, v.t., **-terred**, **-terring**. to place (a dead body, etc.) in a grave or tomb. [ME, from OF]

inter-, a prefix meaning 'between', 'among', 'together', as in *intercellular*, *intercity*, *intermarry*. [L, combining form of *inter*, adv. and prep., between, among, during]

inter., *Abbrev*. intermediate.

interact /ɪntərˈækt/, v.i. to act on each other. — **interaction**, n.

inter alia /ɪntər ˈeɪliə/, adv. among other things. [L]

intercede /ɪntəˈsid/, v.i., **-ceded**, **-ceding**. to act on behalf of someone in trouble: *to intercede with the governor for a thief*. [L: intervene] — **interceder**, n.

intercept /ɪntəˈsept/, v.; /ˈɪntəsept/, n. ◇v.t. 1. to take or seize on the way from one place to another: *to intercept a letter*. 2. to stop the natural course of (light, water, etc.). 3. to take possession of (a ball, etc.) passed or thrown to an opponent. 4. to prevent or cut off the operation or effect of: *to intercept the view*. 5. *Chiefly Maths*. to mark off or include, as between two points or lines. ◇n. 6. an act of intercepting. 7. the taking possession of the ball from one's opposition. 8. *Maths*. an intercepted part of a line. [L] — **interceptor**, n. — **interception**, n.

intercession /ɪntəˈseʃən/, 1. an acting on behalf of someone in difficulty or trouble. 2. *Church*. a prayerful request to God on behalf of another or others. [L]

intercessor /ɪntə'sesə, 'ɪntəsesə/, *n.* someone who intercedes.

interchange /ɪntə'tʃeɪndʒ/, *v.*, **-changed, -changing**; /'ɪntətʃeɪndʒ/, *n.* ◇*v.t.* **1.** to put each of (two things) in the place of the other; transpose. **2.** to give and receive (things) one to another; exchange: *They interchanged gifts.* **3.** to cause to follow one after the other: *to interchange cares with pleasures.* ◇*v.i.* **4.** to happen by turns; alternate. **5.** to change places, as two persons or things. ◇*n.* **6.** the act of interchanging. **7.** a changing of places, as between two persons or things. [INTER- + CHANGE] —**interchangeable,** *adj.*

intercom /'ɪntəkɒm/, *n. Colloq.* — **intercommunication system.**

intercommunication system, *n.* an audio system for sending spoken messages within a place, as an office, school, ship, etc.

intercontinental /,ɪntəkɒntə'nentl/, *adj.* **1.** between continents. **2.** travelling, or able to travel, between continents: *intercontinental flights; intercontinental ballistic missile.*

intercostal /ɪntə'kɒstəl/, *adj. Anat.* **1.** relating to muscles, parts, or intervals between the ribs. **2.** found between the ribs. [NL]

intercourse /'ɪntəkɔs/, *n.* **1.** dealings or exchange between individuals. **2.** interchange of thoughts, feelings, etc. **3.** → **sexual intercourse.**

interdependent /ɪntədə'pendənt/, *adj.* dependent on each other. —**interdependence,** **interdependency,** *n.*

interdict /'ɪntədɪkt, -daɪt/, *n.*; /ɪntə'dɪkt, -'daɪt/, *v.*, ◇*n.* **1.** *Civil Law.* any ruling of a court or an official which forbids an act. ◇*v.t.* **2.** to forbid; prohibit. [L]

interdisciplinary /ɪntə'dɪsəplənəri, -nri/, *adj.* of or relating to education courses, committees, etc., in which two or more areas of learning (disciplines) work together.

interest /'ɪntrəst, -tərəst/, *n.* **1.** the feeling of one whose attention is particularly held by something: *to have great interest in a subject.* **2.** a particular feeling of this kind: *a person of varied sporting interests.* **3.** the power of exciting such feeling: *questions of great interest.* **4.** importance: *a matter of great interest.* **5.** a business, cause, etc., in which a number of persons are interested. **6.** a share in or the right of ownership of property, business, etc. **7.** a number or group of persons, having a common interest: *the banking interest.* **8.** advantage; self-interest: *to have one's own interest in mind.* **9.** *Comm.* **a.** payment, or a sum paid, for the use of money borrowed (the principal). **b.** the rate per cent per unit of time represented by such payment. ◇*v.t.* **10.** to hold or excite the attention of: *The story interested me.* **11.** to concern (a person, etc.) in something; involve: *Every citizen is interested in this law.* **12.** to cause to take a personal concern or share: *to interest a person in an event.* [late ME, from L]

interested /'ɪntrəstəd/, *adj.* **1.** having an interest in something; concerned: *Those interested should come now.* **2.** having a share; participating; having money involved: *one interested in the profits.* **3.** having the attention held: *an interested onlooker.* **4.** influenced by personal or selfish reasons: *an interested buyer.*

interesting /'ɪntrəstɪŋ/, *adj.* **1.** creating a feeling of interest: *an interesting face.* **2.** exciting and holding the attention: *an interesting book.*

interface /'ɪntəfeɪs/, *n.*; /ɪntə'feɪs/, *v.*, **-faced, -facing.** ◇*n.* **1.** a surface regarded as the common boundary to two bodies or spaces. **2.** a point or area at which any two systems act on each other. ◇*v.t.* **3.** to cause (two systems) to act on each other. **4.** to place an interfacing into.

interfacing /'ɪntəfeɪsɪŋ/, *n.* cloth placed between outer material and facing to give firmness.

interfere /ɪntə'fɪə/, *v.i.*, **-fered, -fering.** **1.** to be in opposition; clash: *The claims of one nation may interfere with those of another.* **2.** to take a part in the affairs of others; intervene; meddle: *to interfere in someone's argument.* **3.** (of things) to strike against each other. **4.** *Phys.* to cause interference. **5.** to molest sexually (fol. by *with*). [OF: strike each other]

interference /ɪntə'fɪərəns/, *n.* **1.** the act or fact of interfering. **2.** *Phys.* the action of waves (of light, sound, etc.) which strengthen or cancel each other when they meet. **3.** *Radio.* **a.** the jumbling of radio signals by receiving signals other than the desired ones. **b.** the signals so produced.

interfuse /ɪntə'fjuz/, *v.*, **-fused, -fusing.** ◇*v.t.* **1.** to pour (something) between or through. **2.** to combine with something; intersperse. **3.** to mix or join, one with another. ◇*v.i.* **4.** to become mixed or joined, one with another. [L] —**interfusion,** *n.*

intergalactic /ɪntəgə'læktɪk/, *adj.* existing or happening between galaxies.

interglacial /ɪntə'gleɪʃəl, -'gleɪsɪəl/, *adj.* occurring or formed between times of glacial action.

interim /'ɪntərəm/, *n.* **1.** the time coming between; an intervening time: *in the interim.* **2.** an arrangement for a short period of time. ◇*adj.* **3.** belonging to an intervening period of time: *an interim report.* **4.** existing for a short time; temporary: *an interim order.* [L: in the meantime]

interior /ɪn'tɪəriə/, *adj.* **1.** being within; internal: *the interior parts of a house.* **2.** existing inside and at a distance from the coast or border; inland: *the interior parts of a country.* **3.** inside a country, etc.; domestic: *the interior trade.* **4.** inner, private, or secret: *an interior meeting.* **5.** mental or spiritual. **6.** *Geom.* (of an angle) inner, as an angle formed between two parallel lines when cut by a third line, or an angle formed by two adjacent sides of a closed polygon. ◇*n.* **7.** the internal part; the inside. **8.** *Art.* **a.** the inside part of a building, considered as a whole from the point of view of artistic design, etc., or a single room or apartment so considered. **b.** a painting of the inside of a building, room, etc. **9.** the inland parts of a country, etc. **10.** the domestic affairs of a country as separate from its foreign affairs: *the Department of the Interior.* **11.** the inner nature of anything. [L: inner]

interior decorator, *n.* a person whose work is planning the decoration, furnishings, etc., of homes, rooms, or offices.

interj., *Abbrev.* interjection.

interject /ɪntəˈdʒɛkt/, *v.t.* **1.** to throw in quickly between other things; to interpolate: *interject a careless remark.* **2.** to interrupt a conversation or speech; heckle. [L] —**interjection,** *n.* —**interjector,** *n.*

interlace /ɪntəˈleɪs/, *v.,* **-laced, -lacing.** ◇*v.i.* **1.** to cross one another as if woven together; intertwine: *interlacing branches.* ◇*v.t.* **2.** to place (threads, branches, etc.) so as to intercross one another. **3.** to connect; blend. **4.** to scatter through; intermingle.

interline /ɪntəˈlaɪn/, *v.t.,* **-lined, -lining.** to write or place (words, etc.) between the lines of writing or print. [late ME, from ML]

interlining /ˈɪntəlaɪnɪŋ/, *n.* **1.** an inner lining placed between the ordinary lining and the outer material of a garment. **2.** material used for this purpose.

interlock /ɪntəˈlɒk/, *v.;* /ˈɪntəlɒk/, *n.* ◇*v.i.* **1.** to connect with each other: *The pieces of a jigsaw interlock.* **2.** to fit into each other, as parts of machinery. ◇*v.t.* **3.** to lock one with another. **4.** to fit the parts of (something) together so that all must move together. ◇*n.* **5.** *Textiles.* a smooth knitted fabric, esp. one made of cotton thread. —**interlocker,** *n.*

interlope /ˈɪntəloʊp/, *v.i.,* **-loped, -loping.** **1.** to force into some area or field of trade without proper permission. **2.** to force oneself into the affairs of others. [INTER- + LOPE, *v.*] —**interloper,** *n.*

interlude /ˈɪntəlud/, *n.* **1.** a period, space, etc. **2.** a short performance (music, drama, etc.) as between the acts of a play. **3.** a period of inactivity; lull. [ME, from ML]

intermarry /ɪntəˈmæri/, *v.i.,* **-ried, -rying.** **1.** to become connected by marriage, as two families, tribes, etc. **2.** to marry within the limits of the family or of near relationship. —**intermarriage,** *n.*

intermediary /ɪntəˈmidiəri, -dʒəri/, *adj., n., pl.* **-aries.** ◇*adj.* **1.** being between; intermediate. **2.** acting between persons, parties, etc.: *an intermediary power.* ◇*n.* **3.** a person or agency acting between two people, things, etc.; go-between.

intermediate /ɪntəˈmidiət, -dʒət/, *adj.* **1.** being, placed, or acting between two points, stages, things, persons, etc. **2.** *Geol.* (of igneous rocks) having between 52 and 65 per cent silica. ◇*n.* **3.** *Chem.* a substance formed during a chemical process before the final product is obtained. [ML, from L: between]

interment /ɪnˈtɜmənt/, *n.* burial.

intermesh /ɪntəˈmɛʃ/, *v.i.* to fit well together.

intermezzo /ɪntəˈmɛtsoʊ/, *n., pl.* **-zos, -zi** /-tsi/. a short dramatic or musical piece of light character, introduced between the acts of a long musical work, drama or opera. [It, from L: between]

interminable /ɪnˈtɜmənəbəl/, *adj.* **1.** unending: *interminable talk.* **2.** endless; having no limits: *interminable sufferings.* [ME, from LL]

intermission /ɪntəˈmɪʃən/, *n.* a short period of time; an interval, esp. in the cinema. [L]

intermittent /ɪntəˈmɪtənt/, *adj.* **1.** stopping for a time: *His studies were intermittent.* **2.** stopping and starting; recurring: *intermittent rain.*

intern¹ /ɪnˈtɜn/, *v.t.* to force to live within certain limits without the freedom to leave them, as prisoners of war, etc. [F, from L: internal] —**internment,** *n.*

intern² /ˈɪntɜn/, *n.* a doctor, working as a full-time member of a hospital, usu. a recent graduate of a university. [F, from L: internal]

internal /ɪnˈtɜnəl/, *adj.* **1.** relating to or existing on the inside of something; interior: *internal organs.* **2.** to be taken inwardly: *internal medicines.* **3.** existing or found within the limits of something. **4.** relating to or happening within a country; domestic: *internal affairs.* **5.** of the mind or soul; mental or spiritual; subjective. [ML, from L: inward]

internal-combustion engine, *n.* an engine of one or more working cylinders in which the process of burning of fuel and air (combustion) takes place within the cylinder.

internalise or **internalize** /ɪnˈtɜnəlaɪz/, *v.t.,* **-lised, -lising.** **1.** to keep from the expression (of emotion). **2.** to establish (information, values, etc.) within oneself.

international /ɪntəˈnæʃnəl/, *adj.* **1.** between or among nations: *an international sports event.* **2.** of or relating to different nations or their citizens: *a matter of international concern.* **3.** concerning the relations between nations: *international law.*

International /ɪntəˈnæʃnəl/, *n.* **1.** a socialist association (in full, **International Workingmen's Association**) intended to unite the working classes of all countries, formed in 1864, and dissolved in 1876 (**First International**). **2.** an international socialist association formed in 1889, uniting socialist groups or political parties of various countries (**Second International**). **3.** a communist association formed in Moscow in 1919 (dissolved, 1943), uniting communist groups of various countries and advocating revolution (**Third** or **Communist International**). **4.** the socialist association formed in 1923 by the uniting of the Second International and the Vienna Internationale (**Labour and Socialist International**). **5.** a loose federation of small ultraradical groups formed in 1936, hostile to the Soviet Union (sometimes called the **Fourth** or **Trotskyist International**).

International Date Line, *n.* → date line (def. 2).

Internationale /ɪntənæʃəˈnal/, *n.* **1.** → **International. 2.** a revolutionary song, first sung in France in 1871 and since popular as a song of workers and Communists.

internationalism /ɪntəˈnæʃnəlɪzəm/, *n.* **1.** the principle of nations working together for their common good. **2.** international character, relations, or control.

International Labour Organisation, *n.* an organisation formed in 1919, devoted to standardising international labor practices and including representatives of government, management, and labor. Also, **ILO**.

international nautical mile, *n.* See **mile** (def. 2).

International Phonetic Alphabet, *n.* an alphabet designed to provide a clear and universally understood system of letters and other signs for writing the speech sounds of all languages. *Abbrev.*: IPA

International System of Units, *n.* an internationally recognised system of metric units, now used as the basis of Australia's metric system, in which the seven base units are the metre, kilogram, second, ampere, kelvin, mole and candela. *Abbrev.*: SI Also, **Système International d'Unités**. See **metric system**.

internecine /ɪntəˈnisəm/, *adj.* marked by much killing; destructive on all sides. [L: slaughter]

internee /ˌɪntəˈni/, *n.* someone held as a prisoner of war, or as a citizen of an enemy country in time of war.

interpersonal /ɪntəˈpɜsənəl/, *adj.* of or concerning relations between people.

interplay /ˈɪntəpleɪ/, *n.*; /ɪntəˈpleɪ/, *v.* ◇*n.* **1.** the effect of actions on each other: *the interplay of emotions*. ◇*v.i.* **2.** to exercise an influence on each other.

Interpol /ˈɪntəpɒl/, *n.* an association of over one hundred national police forces, whose main duty is to fight international crime. [*Inter*(*national Criminal*) *Pol*(*ice Organisation*)]

interpolate /ɪnˈtɜpəleɪt/, *v.t.*, **-lated**, **-lating**. **1.** to change (a message, etc.) by the placement of new matter, esp. secretly or without authorisation. **2.** to place or introduce (something additional) between other things or parts; interject; interpose. [L: furbished, altered, falsified] —**interpolation**, *n.* —**interpolator**, *n.*

interpose /ɪntəˈpoʊz/, *v.*, **-posed**, **-posing**. ◇*v.t.* **1.** to place between; cause to intervene: *to interpose oneself between two fighters*. **2.** to put (something which blocks) between, or in the way. **3.** to put in (a remark, etc.) in the midst of a conversation, etc. ◇*v.i.* **4.** to come between other things. **5.** to step in between opposing parties; mediate. **6.** to make a remark by way of interruption. [F. See INTER-, POSE] —**interposal**, *n.* —**interposition**, *n.*

interpret /ɪnˈtɜprət/, *v.t.* **1.** to give the meaning of; explain: *to interpret dreams*. **2.** to understand in a particular way; construe: *to interpret an action as being friendly*. **3.** to bring out the meaning of (a dramatic work, music, etc.) by performance. **4.** to translate. ◇*v.i.* **5.** to translate what is said in a foreign language. **6.** to give an explanation. [ME, from L: explain] —**interpretable**, *adj.*

interpretation /ɪnˌtɜprəˈteɪʃən/, *n.* **1.** the act of interpreting; elucidation: *the interpretation of nature*. **2.** an explanation given: *to put a wrong interpretation on a message*. **3.** a way of interpreting. **4.** the performing of a dramatic part, music, etc., so as to bring out the meaning, or to give one's particular idea of it. **5.** translation. [ME, from L] —**interpretative**, *adj.* —**interpretational**, *adj.*

interpreter /ɪnˈtɜprətə/, *n.* **1.** someone who explains or interprets. **2.** *Computers*. a program which causes a computer to obey instructions in some code different from the basic code of the computer.

interracial /ɪntəˈreɪʃəl/, *adj.* **1.** existing between races, or members of different races. **2.** of or for persons of different races: *interracial camps for children*.

interregnum /ɪntəˈregnəm/, *n.*, *pl.* **-nums**, **-na** /nə/. **1.** a period of time between the close of a king or queen's rule and the beginning of the next. **2.** any period during which a state has no ruler or only a short-term governing body. **3.** any pause or interruption in continuity. [L] —**interregnal**, *adj.*

interrelate /ɪntərəˈleɪt/, *v.t.*, **-lated**, **-lating**. to bring into a shared relation. —**interrelated**, *adj.* —**interrelation**, *n.*

interrogate /ɪnˈterəgeɪt/, *v.*, **-gated**, **-gating**. ◇*v.t.* **1.** to ask a series of questions of (a person), esp. in a close or formal way; question. ◇*v.i.* **2.** to ask questions. [late ME, from L] —**interrogation**, *n.* —**interrogator**, *n.*

interrogation mark, *n.* → **question mark**.

interrogative /ɪntəˈrɒgətɪv/, *adj.* **1.** relating to or pointing to a question. **2.** *Gram.* (of an element or construction) forming a question: *an interrogative pronoun*; *an interrogative sentence*. ◇*n.* **3.** *Gram.* an interrogative word, element, or construction, as 'who?' and 'what?'

interrupt /ɪntəˈrʌpt/, *v.*; /ˈɪntərʌpt/, *n.* ◇*v.t.* **1.** to make a break in (an otherwise continuous course, process, condition, etc.). **2.** to break off or cause to cease, as in the midst or course: *He interrupted his work to answer the phone*. **3.** to stop (a person) in the midst of doing or saying something. ◇*v.i.* **4.** to cause a break; interrupt action or speech: *Please don't interrupt*. ◇*n.* **5.** *Computers*. a command causing the computer to change from one program, usu. the background, to another, usu. to perform a shorter task, after which it returns to where it left off. [ME, from L: broken apart] —**interruptive**, *adj.* —**interrupter**, *n.* —**interruption**, *n.*

Interscan /ˈɪntəskæn/, *n.* a microwave landing system for aircraft, developed in Australia by the CSIRO.

intersect /ɪntəˈsekt/, *v.t.* **1.** to cut or divide by passing through or lying across: *One road intersects another*. ◇*v.i.* **2.** to cross, as lines. **3.** *Geom.* to have one or more points in common: *intersecting lines*. [L: cut off]

intersection /ɪntəˈsekʃən, ˈɪntəsekʃən/, *n.* **1.** the act, fact, or place of intersecting. **2.** a place where two or more roads meet.

intersperse /ɪntəˈspɜːs/, *v.t.*, **-spersed, -spersing. 1.** to scatter here and there among other things: *to intersperse flowers among shrubs.* **2.** to vary with something scattered or introduced here and there: *His speech was interspersed with pauses.* [L: strewn] —**interspersion**, *n.*

interstate /ˈɪntəsteɪt/, *adj.*; /ɪntəˈsteɪt/, *adv.* ◊*adj.* **1.** between states: *interstate trade.* ◊*adv.* **2.** for a short time in a state (def. 7) where one does not live: *travelling interstate.* **3.** from another state: *He gets his machinery interstate.* See **intrastate**.

interstice /ɪnˈtɜːstəs/, *n., pl.* **-tices** /-təsɪz/. a small or narrow space between things or parts; chink; crevice. [L: space between] —**interstitial**, *adj.*

intertwine /ɪntəˈtwaɪn/, *v.*, **-twined, -twining.** ◊*v.i.* **1.** to twist together. ◊*v.t.* **2.** to interweave with one another. —**intertwinement**, *n.* —**intertwiningly**, *adv.*

interurban /ˈɪntərɜːbən/, *adj.* between cities or towns.

interval /ˈɪntəvəl/, *n.* **1.** a period of time coming between two events: *an interval of fifty years.* **2.** a period of stopping; a pause: *intervals between attacks.* **3.** a break, as between acts of a play in a theatre. **4.** a space intervening between things, points, etc.: *an interval of three metres between each row.* **5. at intervals**, at particular times or places with gaps in between. **6.** *Music.* the difference in pitch between two notes as, **a. harmonic interval**, an interval between two notes sounded at the same time. **b. melodic interval**, an interval between two notes sounded one after the other. [ME, from L]

intervene /ɪntəˈviːn/, *v.i.*, **-vened, -vening. 1.** to come between in action; intercede: *to intervene in a dispute.* **2.** to come or be between, as in place, time, or a series. **3.** (of things) to happen without plan so as to change a result: *War intervened in my studies.* [L: come between] —**intervener**, *n.*

intervention /ɪntəˈvɛnʃən/, *n.* **1.** the act or fact of intervening. **2.** the unwelcome entry of one country in the affairs of another. —**interventional**, *adj.*

interview /ˈɪntəvjuː/, *n.* **1.** a meeting of people face to face, esp. for formal meetings in business, radio, television, etc. **2.** the conversation of a writer or reporter with a person from whom material for a news or feature story, etc., is wanted. **3.** the report of such conversation. ◊*v.t.* **4.** to have an interview with. [F: see (each other)] —**interviewer**, *n.* —**interviewee**, *n.*

interweave /ɪntəˈwiːv/, *v.*, **-wove** or **-weaved; -woven** or **-wove** or **-weaved; -weaving.** ◊*v.t.* **1.** to weave together, one with another, as threads, branches, etc. **2.** to combine as if by weaving: *to interweave truth with lies.* ◊*v.i.* **3.** to become woven together. —**interweavement**, *n.* —**interweaver**, *n.*

intestate /ɪnˈtɛsteɪt, -tət/, *adj.* **1.** (of a person) dying without having made a will. **2.** (of things) not placed by will. ◊*n.* **3.** one who dies intestate. [ME, from L: having made no will] —**intestacy**, *n.*

intestine /ɪnˈtɛstən/, *n.* **1.** *Anat.* (*oft. pl.*) the lower part of the alimentary canal, going from the stomach to the anus. **2.** *Anat.* a particular section of this area: the **small intestine** containing the duodenum, jejunum, and ileum; the **large intestine** containing the caecum, colon, and rectum. [L: entrails] —**intestinal**, *adj.*

intimacy /ˈɪntəməsi/, *n., pl.* **-cies. 1.** close, personal friendship. **2.** sexual intercourse.

intimate[1] /ˈɪntəmət/, *adj.* **1.** associated in close personal relations: *an intimate friend.* **2.** involving personally close association: *an intimate group.* **3.** private; closely personal: *one's intimate affairs.* **4.** having sexual relations. **5.** aimed at establishing a feeling of friendliness (as in a restaurant, etc). **6.** detailed; deep: *an intimate knowledge of a subject.* **7.** close union: *an intimate mixture.* **8.** inmost; deep within. **9.** relating to the inmost nature; intrinsic: *the intimate structure of an organism.* ◊*n.* **10.** an intimate friend. [in form from LL: put or pressed into, but with sense of inmost]

intimate[2] /ˈɪntəmeɪt/, *v.t.*, **-mated, -mating. 1.** to make known indirectly; hint; suggest. **2.** to make known, esp. formally; announce. [LL: put or pressed into, announced] —**intimation**, *n.*

intimidate /ɪnˈtɪmədeɪt/, *v.t.*, **-dated, -dating. 1.** to make frightened; overawe. **2.** to force into or stop from some action by using fear: *to intimidate a voter.* [ML: made afraid. See TIMID] —**intimidation**, *n.* —**intimidator**, *n.*

into /ˈɪntuː/; *before consonants* /ˈɪntə/, *prep.* **1.** in to; in and to; to; a word expressing **a.** movement or direction toward the inner part: *to run into the room.* **b.** involvement or placement within: *He is well into the book.* **c.** change to new relations, conditions, etc.: *He turned into a frog.* **2.** *Maths.* being the divisor of: *2 into 10 equals 5.* **3.** *Colloq.* having an enthusiasm for: *I am into health foods.* [ME *in to*]

intolerable /ɪnˈtɒlərəbəl/, *adj.* **1.** not able to be suffered; unendurable: *intolerable pain.* **2.** not to be allowed: *intolerable waste of money.* —**intolerably**, *adv.*

intolerant /ɪnˈtɒlərənt/, *adj.* **1.** not allowing opinions (esp. religious) different from one's own; bigoted: *an intolerant speaker.* **2.** not able or not wishing to make allowance for others (fol. by *of*): *intolerant of smokers.* —**intolerance**, *n.*

intonation /ɪntəˈneɪʃən/, *n.* **1.** the pattern of pitch changes in speech. **2.** the manner of producing musical notes, particularly the relation in pitch of notes to their key or harmony.

intone /ɪnˈtoʊn/, *v.*, **-toned, -toning.** ◊*v.i.* **1.** to speak with a particular tone. **2.** to give variety of tone to; vocalise. **3.** to speak on one pitch level; to speak in a monotone. ◊*v.i.* **4.** to speak or recite in a singing voice, esp. on one level. **5.** *Music.* to produce a note, or a particular series of notes, like a scale, esp. with the voice; sing or chant. [late ME, from ML]

in toto /ɪn 'toʊtoʊ/, *adv.* in all; in the whole; wholly. [L]

intoxicant /ɪn'tɒksəkənt/, *adj.* **1.** intoxicating. ◊*n.* **2.** something that intoxicates, as liquor or certain drugs.

intoxicate /ɪn'tɒksɪkeɪt/, *v.*, **-cated, -cating.** ◊*v.t.* **1.** to affect (someone) with loss of control over physical and mental powers; make drunk. **2.** to excite mentally beyond self-control or reason. ◊*v.i.* **3.** to cause or produce drunkenness or excitement: *intoxicating drink; intoxicating news.* [ME, from ML: poisoned. See TOXIC] **–intoxicating,** *adj.* **–intoxicative,** *adj.*

intoxication /ɪn,tɒksə'keɪʃən/, *n.* **1.** drunkenness; inebriation. **2.** *Pathol.* poisoning. **3.** the act of intoxicating. **4.** a feeling of great excitement; exhilaration.

intra-, a prefix meaning 'within', freely used to form English, and esp. scientific words, sometimes opposed to *extra-*. See **intro-**. [L: within]

intractable /ɪn'træktəbəl/, *adj.* hard to deal with; unmanageable; stubborn. **–intractability, intractableness,** *n.* **–intractably,** *adv.*

intrans., *Abbrev.* intransitive.

intransigent /ɪn'trænsədʒənt/, *adj.* **1.** (esp. in politics) keeping firmly to one's own ideas or position; uncompromising; irreconcilable. ◊*n.* **2.** someone who is firm or immovable in this way. [F, from Sp] **–intransigence, intransigency,** *n.*

intransitive /ɪn'trænsətɪv/, *adj.* **1.** having the quality of an intransitive verb. ◊*n.* **2.** intransitive verb.

intransitive verb, *n.* a verb that needs no direct object to complete its sense in a particular context, e.g. *come, sit, lie,* etc.

intrastate /'ɪntrəsteɪt/, *adj.* within a state: *intrastate trade.*

intra-uterine device /ɪntrə-'jutəraɪn, də,vaɪs/, *n.* → IUD

intravenous /ɪntrə'vinəs/, *adj.* **1.** within a vein or the veins. **2.** indicating or relating to an injection into a vein.

in-tray /'ɪn-treɪ/, *n.* a tray for incoming letters, etc., awaiting attention.

intrazonal soil /ɪntrə'zoʊnəl ,sɔɪl/, *n.* one of a group of mature soils which have been more affected by some local factor or relief or rock type than by climate and vegetation.

intrepid /ɪn'trɛpəd/, *adj.* fearless; dauntless: *intrepid courage.* [L: not alarmed] **–intrepidity,** *n.*

intricate /'ɪntrəkət/, *adj.* **1.** puzzlingly detailed or fine; entangled or involved: *a maze of intricate paths; intricate pattern of lace.* **2.** hard to understand; confusingly complicated: *an intricate machine.* [late ME, from L: entangled] **–intricateness, intricacy,** *n.*

intrigue /ɪn'trig/, *v.*, **-trigued, -triguing;** /ɪn'trig, 'ɪntrig/, *n.* ◊*v.t.* **1.** to excite the curiosity or interest of by puzzling or unusual qualities: *This book intrigues me.* ◊*v.i.* **2.** to carry on underhand scheming; plot craftily. **3.** to carry on a secret love affair. ◊*n.* **4.** the use of underhand scheming to get something: *political intrigue.* **5.** an example of this. **6.** a secret love affair. **7.** a series of complications forming the plot of a play. [F, from It from L: entangle, perplex] **–intriguer,** *n.* **–intriguingly,** *adv.*

intrinsic /ɪn'trɪnzɪk, -sɪk/, *adj.* belonging to a thing by its very nature: *intrinsic merit.* [ML: inward] **–intrinsically,** *adv.*

intro-, a prefix meaning 'inwardly', 'within', occasionally used to form English words. See **intra-**. [L: inwardly, within]

intro., *Abbrev.* **1.** introduction. **2.** introductory. Also, **introd.**

introduce /ɪntrə'djus/, *v.t.*, **-duced, -ducing.** **1.** to bring into notice, knowledge, use, etc.: *to introduce a fashion.* **2.** to bring forward for consideration, as a bill in parliament, etc. **3.** to present or bring forward with material that explains or prepares for the main part: *to introduce a book with a long preface.* **4.** to bring (someone) to the knowledge or experience of something (fol. by *to*): *to introduce a person to chess.* **5.** to lead, bring, or put into a place, surroundings, etc.: *to introduce a figure into a design; to introduce a subject of conversation.* **6.** to bring (a person) to meet another; present: *He introduced his sister to us.* [late ME, from L: lead in] **–introducer,** *n.* **–introducible,** *adj.*

introduction /ɪntrə'dʌkʃən/, *n.* **1.** the act of introducing. **2.** the formal presentation of one person to another or others. **3.** something introduced. **4.** the first part (of a book, piece of music, etc.) explaining or leading up to the main part. **5.** a book, etc., that sets out basic information: *an introduction to botany.* [ME, from L] **–introductory,** *adj.*

introspection /ɪntrə'spɛkʃən/, *n.* examination of one's mental states or feelings.

introvert /'ɪntrəvɜt/, *n., adj.*; /ɪntrə'vɜt/, *v.* ◊*n.* **1.** *Psychol.* someone concerned mainly with their own thoughts or mental states. See **extrovert.** ◊*adj.* **2.** (of behavior, etc.) turned inwards upon the self. ◊*v.t.* **3.** to turn inwards. **4.** to turn (the mind, etc.) inwards or upon the self. [L]

intrude /ɪn'trud/, *v.*, **-truded, -truding.** ◊*v.t.* **1.** to push or bring in without reason, permission, or welcome. **2.** to push or force in. ◊*v.i.* **3.** to push oneself in; come uninvited: *to intrude upon his privacy.* [L: thrust in] **–intruder,** *n.* **–intrudingly,** *adv.*

intrusive /ɪn'trusɪv, -zɪv/, *adj.* **1.** intruding. **2.** of or marked by intrusion. **3.** *Geol.* **a.** (of rocks) having been forced, while molten or plastic, into fissures or other openings or between layers of other rocks. **b.** indicating or relating to plutonic rocks. **–intrusiveness, intrusion,** *n.*

intuition /ɪntju'ɪʃən/, *n.* **1.** the direct perception of truths, facts, etc., independently of any reasoning process. **2.** a truth or fact perceived in this way. [ML, from L: look at, consider] **–intuitional,** *adj.* **–intuitive,** *adj.*

intumescence /ɪntʃu'mesəns/, n. 1. a swelling up. 2. swollen state. 3. swollen mass. —**intumescent**, adj.

inundate /'ɪnʌndeɪt/, v.t., -dated, -dating. to overspread with or as with a flood; flood; deluge; overwhelm: *to inundate surrounding country; to be inundated with work*. [L: overflowed] —**inundation**, n. —**inundator**, n.

inure /ən'juə, ɪn-/, v., inured, inuring. ◇v.t. 1. to toughen or harden by exercise; accustom; habituate (fol. by *to*): *to inure a person to danger; to inure someone to hard work*. ◇v.i. 2. *Law*. to come into use; take or have effect. Also, **enure**. [late ME] —**inurement**, n.

inv., *Abbrev*. invoice.

invade /ɪn'veɪd/, v., -vaded, -vading. ◇v.t. 1. to enter as or like an enemy: *Caesar invaded Britain; Locusts invaded the fields*. 2. to enter or penetrate: *The poison invaded his system; Cooking smells invaded the bedroom*. 3. to intrude upon; violate: *to invade privacy; to invade rights*. ◇v.i. 4. to make an invasion. [late ME, from L: go into, attack] —**invader**, n.

invalid[1] /'ɪnvəlɪd, -lɪd/, n. 1. a weak or sick person. 2. a serviceman disabled for active service. ◇adj. 3. weak or sick: *his invalid sister*. 4. of or for invalids: *invalid food*. ◇v.t., v.i. 5. to make or become an invalid: *invalided for life*. 6. to retire (a serviceman) from active service, because of illness or injury (oft. fol. by *out*). [L: infirm, not strong] —**invalidism**, n.

invalid[2] /ɪn'vælɪd/, adj. lacking strength, truth or sense: *invalid arguments*. 2. without legal force, or void, as a contract. [IN-[3] + VALID] —**invalidity**, n.

invalidate /ɪn'vælɪdeɪt/, v.t., -dated, -dating. 1. to make invalid. 2. to take legal force or efficacy from. —**invalidation**, n. —**invalidator**, n.

invaluable /ɪn'væljəbəl/, adj. of value too great to be measured; priceless. —**invaluableness**, n. —**invaluably**, adv.

invariable /ɪn'vɛəriəbəl/, adj. 1. always the same; not variable or varying. —**invariability**, n. 2. an invariable quantity; a constant. —**invariability**, **invariableness**, n. —**invariably**, adv.

invasion /ɪn'veɪʒən/, n. 1. the act of invading or entering as an enemy. 2. the coming of anything troublesome or harmful, as disease. 3. infringement by intrusion: *invasion of privacy*. [LL: an attack] —**invasive**, adj.

invective /ɪn'vɛktɪv/, n. 1. a strong verbal attack involving blame; denunciation; vituperation. ◇adj. 2. abusive; denunciatory; vituperative. [ME, from LL: abusive]

inveigh /ɪn'veɪ/, v.i. to attack strongly in words; rail: *to inveigh against democracy*. [ME, from L: carry or bear into, assail]

inveigle /ɪn'veɪgəl/, v.t., -gled, -gling. to persuade by enticements; beguile (fol. by *into*, sometimes *from*, *away*, etc.): *to inveigle a person into playing bridge*. [late ME, from F: blind, delude] —**inveiglement**, n. —**inveigler**, n.

invent /ɪn'vɛnt/, v.t. 1. to make or think up (something new); devise: *to invent a machine*. 2. to create with the imagination: *to invent a story*. 3. to make up something false; fabricate: *to invent excuses*. ◇v.i. 4. to make or think up something new: *He has been inventing for years*. [late ME, from L: discovered, found out] —**inventor**, n.

invention /ɪn'vɛnʃən/, n. 1. the act of inventing or creating. 2. anything invented or devised. 3. (the use of) imaginative or creative power in literature or art. 4. the power or faculty of inventing, devising, or originating. 5. something made up falsely; fabrication. 6. *Music*. a short piece, contrapuntal in nature, generally based on one subject. [ME, from L]

inventive /ɪn'vɛntɪv/, adj. 1. good at inventing: *an inventive mind*. 2. relating to or showing invention. —**inventiveness**, n.

inventory /'ɪnvəntri, ɪn'vɛntəri/, n., pl. -tories, v., -toried, -torying. ◇n. 1. a detailed list of articles, goods, etc., kept by merchants, etc. 2. (the items in) a complete listing of work, materials, goods, etc., in a business. 3. the value of a stock of goods. ◇v.t. 4. to make an inventory of; enter in an inventory. [late ME, from ML: list] —**inventorial**, adj. —**inventorially**, adv.

Inverell /ɪnvə'rɛl/, n. a town in northeastern NSW, on the Macintyre River; mineral resources. Pop. 9693 (1986).

Inverness /ɪnvə'nɛs/, n. a former county in north-western Scotland, now part of Highland region. Also, **Inverness-shire**.

inverse /ɪn'vɜs, 'ɪnvɜs/, ◇adj. 1. turned in the opposite position or direction, or turned upside down: *inverse order*. 2. opposite to in nature or effect: *Subtraction is the inverse operation to addition*. ◇n. 3. direct opposite or upside down state. [L: turned about]

inverse function, n. a mathematical function which replaces another function when the dependent and independent variables of the first function are interchanged, as $\log x$ is the inverse function, of e^x.

inversion /ɪn'vɜʒən/, n. 1. the act of inverting or the state of being inverted. 2. anything inverted. 3. any change from the normal word order of a language, esp. for literary effect, as 'Came the dawn', instead of 'The dawn came'. 4. *Music*. **a**. process, or result, of rearranging the notes of an interval or chord so that the original bass becomes an upper voice. **b**. (in counterpoint) the placement of the upper voice part below the lower, and vice versa. [L] —**inversive**, adj.

invert /ɪn'vɜt, v.; 'ɪnvɜt/, adj. ◇v.t. 1. to turn upside down, inside out, or inwards. 2. to turn in the opposite position, direction, or order. 3. to turn or change to the opposite or contrary: *to invert a process*. ◇v.i. 4. to turn inside out, or to the opposite, etc. ◇adj. 5. *Chem*. inverted. [L: turn about, upset] —**invertible**, adj.

invertebrate /ɪn'vɜtəbrət, -breɪt/, adj. 1. *Zool*. without a backbone. 2. of or relating to animals without backbones. ◇n. 3. an invertebrate animal. 4. someone of weak character; a spineless person. —**invertebracy**, **invertebrateness**, n.

inverted comma, *n.* → **quotation mark**.

inverted snob, *n.* someone who, for questionable motives, avoids or shows contempt for people of high social standing while declaring loyalty to the poor and lowly. —**inverted snobbery**, *n.*

invest /ɪnˈvest/, *v.t.* **1.** to put money into something offering profitable returns, e.g. shares. **2.** to spend: *to invest in gold; to invest time and effort.* **3.** to clothe with or as with a garment: *Spring invests the trees with leaves.* **4.** to endow; endue: *to invest a friend with every virtue.* **5.** to settle or vest (a power, right, etc.) in a person. **6.** to clothe in or with the insignia of office. **7.** to put or install in an office or position; furnish with power, authority, rank, etc. ◇*v.i.* **8.** to invest money; make an investment. [late ME, from L: clothe] —**investor**, *n.*

investigate /ɪnˈvestɪɡeɪt/, *v.t., v.i.*, **-gated, -gating.** to search or inquire into (something); to examine (something): *to investigate a murder; They began to investigate yesterday.* [L: tracked, traced out] —**investigator**, *n.* —**investigation**, *n.* —**investigative, investigatory**, *adj.*

Investigator /ɪnˈvestɪɡeɪtə/, *n.* the vessel which Matthew Flinders used to survey the south coast of Australia 1801–02.

investiture /ɪnˈvestɪtʃə/, *n.* **1.** the formal, ceremonious giving of certain rights or powers, or installing into office. **2.** an official government ceremony for receiving of public honors and awards. [ME, from ML]

investment /ɪnˈvestmənt/, *n.* **1.** the investing of money in order to make a profit. **2.** a particular example or way of investing: *Their investments are all in gold.* **3.** something in which money is invested, as housing, minerals, etc. **4.** the spending of anything for some purpose: *The investment of time in that program is huge.* **5.** the act of investing or the state of being invested, as with a garment or quality. **6.** *Biol.* any covering or outer layer.

inveterate /ɪnˈvetərət/, *adj.* **1.** confirmed in a habit, practice, feeling, etc.: *an inveterate gambler.* **2.** firmly established over a long time; chronic. [ME, from L: rendered old] —**inveterately**, *adv.* —**inveterateness**, *n.*

invidious /ɪnˈvɪdiəs/, *adj.* **1.** attracting hatred or envy: *an invidious honor.* **2.** meant to excite ill will or resentment or give offence: *invidious remarks; invidious comparisons.* [L: envious] —**invidiousness**, *n.*

invigorate /ɪnˈvɪɡəreɪt/, *v.t.*, **-rated, -rating.** to fill with life and energy: *to invigorate the body.*

invincible /ɪnˈvɪnsəbəl/, *adj.* **1.** that cannot be overcome; unconquerable: *an invincible force; invincible ignorance.* **2.** that cannot be passed over; insuperable; insurmountable: *invincible difficulties.* [ME, from L] —**invincibility, invincibleness**, *n.* —**invincibly**, *adv.*

inviolable /ɪnˈvaɪələbəl/, *adj.* **1.** that must not be broken or violated; sacred: *an inviolable sanctuary; inviolable rights.* **2.** that cannot be injured; indestructible. —**inviolability, inviolableness**, *n.* —**inviolably**, *adv.*

inviolate /ɪnˈvaɪələt, -leɪt/, *adj.* free from attack, injury, disturbance, etc.: *inviolate peace; inviolate laws.* —**inviolacy, inviolateness**, *n.*

invisible /ɪnˈvɪzəbəl/, *adj.* **1.** not able to be seen by the eye: *invisible spirits.* **2.** withdrawn from or out of sight: *The dog lay invisible under the bushes.* **3.** unable to be grasped by the mind; unreal: *invisible differences.* **4.** hidden from public knowledge. ◇*n.* **5.** an invisible thing or being. **6. the invisible, a.** the unseen or spiritual world. **b.** (*cap.*) God. —**invisibility, invisibleness**, *n.* —**invisibly**, *adv.*

invitation /ɪnvəˈteɪʃən/, *n.* **1.** the act of inviting: *The way you drive is an invitation to death.* **2.** the written or spoken form with which someone is invited. **3.** attraction; allurement. ◇*adj.* **4.** only for invited people or teams: *an invitation golf match.* [L]

invite /ɪnˈvaɪt/, *v.t.* **-vited, -viting. 1.** to ask in a polite or friendly way to some place or activity: *to invite friends to dinner.* **2.** to ask for politely or formally: *to invite donations.* **3.** to act so as to bring on or make probable: *to invite danger.* **4.** to give occasion for: *The complexity of Donne's poetry invites study.* **5.** to attract; entice, allure, or tempt. [L] —**inviter**, *n.*

inviting /ɪnˈvaɪtɪŋ/, *adj.* especially attractive; alluring; tempting: *an inviting offer.*

in vitro /ɪn ˈvɪtroʊ/, *adv., adj.* in an artificial environment, as a test tube. [NL: lit., in glass]

in-vitro fertilisation *or* **in-vitro fertilization**, *n.* → **IVF**

invocation /ɪnvəˈkeɪʃən/, *n.* **1.** the act of calling upon a god, etc., for help, protection, inspiration, etc. **2.** the form of words used for this, esp. as part of a public religious service. **3.** a calling upon a spirit by incantation, or the incantation or magical formula used. —**invocatory**, *adj.*

invoice /ˈɪnvɔɪs/, *n., v.*, **-voiced, -voicing.** ◇*n.* **1.** an itemised list of goods, with prices, delivered or sent to a buyer. ◇*v.t.* **2.** to present an invoice to (a buyer, etc.). **3.** to make an invoice of. **4.** to enter in an invoice. [from F: sending, thing sent. See ENVOY]

invoke /ɪnˈvoʊk/, *v.t.* **-voked, -voking. 1.** to call for with earnest desire: *to invoke God's mercy.* **2.** to appeal to, as for confirmation: *to invoke the constitution.* **3.** to put into effect: *to invoke the power of a law.* **4.** to call forth or upon (a spirit) by incantation; conjure. [late ME, from L] —**invoker**, *n.*

involuntary /ɪnˈvɒləntri/, *adj.* **1.** done without one's own will: *an involuntary listener.* **2.** unintentional: *an involuntary mistake.* **3.** *Physiol.* acting independently of, or done or occurring without, conscious control: *involuntary muscles.* —**involuntarily**, *adv.*

involute /ˈɪnvəlut/, *adj.* **1.** involved; intricate. **2.** *Bot.* (of a leaf) rolled inwards from the edge. **3.** *Zool.* (of shells) having the whorls closely wound. [L: rolled up]

involution /ɪnvəˈluʃən/, *n.* **1.** the act or result of involving. **2.** something complicated or involved. **3.** *Bot., etc.* **a.** a rolling up or

involution   549   **Iowa**

folding in on itself. **b.** a part formed in this way. **4.** *Biol.* retrograde development; degeneration. **5.** *Physiol.* bodily changes involving a lessening of activity, esp. of the sex organs, in late middle age. [LL: a rolling up] —**involutional**, *adj.*

involve /ɪnˈvɒlv/, *v.t.*, **-volved**, **-volving**. **1.** to include as a necessary circumstance, condition, etc.; imply; entail: *Her work involves a knowledge of horses.* **2.** to affect: *The change of times will involve you.* **3.** to include: *This program involves more people.* **4.** to bring into difficulties (fol. by *with*): *a plot to involve one government with another.* **5.** to associate esp. with a crime, etc.; implicate. **6.** to be very interested in or occupied with: *She is deeply involved in music.* **7.** to associate closely (fol. by *with*): *Their work is involved with the blind.* **8.** to roll up on itself; wind spirally; coil; wreathe. [ME, from L: roll in or on, enwrap, involve] —**involver**, *n.* —**involvement**, *n.*

involved /ɪnˈvɒlvd/, *adj.* **1.** difficult; complicated; intricate: *Her statistical procedures were very involved.* **2.** deeply concerned: *He is a caring and involved social worker.* **3.** (often placed after its noun) implicated (in a crime): *One of the soldiers involved shot himself.* **4.** closely associated, esp. sexually (fol. by *with*): *She had been involved with Harry years before.*

invulnerable /ɪnˈvʌlnrəbəl/, *adj.* **1.** unable to be wounded, hurt, or damaged. **2.** proof against attack: *invulnerable arguments.* —**invulnerability**, *n.*

inward /ˈɪnwəd/, *adj.* **1.** going or directed towards the inside or interior: *an inward glance.* **2.** situated within; inner; interior; internal: *an inward room.* **3.** essential; intrinsic; inherent: *the inward nature of a thing.* **4.** mental; spiritual: *inward peace.* ◇*adv.* **5.** inwards. ◇*n.* **6.** an inward or internal part; the inside. [OE *in(ne)weard*]

inwardness /ˈɪnwədnəs/, *n.* **1.** the state of being inward or internal. **2.** depth of thought or feeling; earnestness. **3.** the direction of the mind towards one's spiritual nature. **4.** the inward or intrinsic character of a thing. **5.** inward meaning.

inwards /ˈɪnwədz/, *adv.* **1.** towards the inside or interior, as of a place, a space, or a body. **2.** into the mind or spirit: *to direct the mind inwards.* **3.** in the mind or spirit, or mentally or spiritually; inwardly. Also, **inward**. [INWARD + adv. genitive *-s*]

Io, *Chem. Symbol.* ionium.

iod-, variant of **iodo-**, usu. before vowels, as in *iodic*.

iodine /ˈaɪədin, ˈaɪədaɪn/, *n.* a non-metallic element occurring as a greyish black crystalline solid, which becomes a dense violet vapor when heated, used as an antiseptic. The radioactive isotope, iodine-131, is used in the diagnosis and treatment of disorders of the thyroid gland. *Symbol*: I; *at. no.*: 53; *at. wt*: 126.9044. Also, **iodin** /ˈaɪədən/. [F, from Gk: properly, rust-colored, but taken to mean violet-like]

iodise *or* **iodize** /ˈaɪədaɪz/, *v.t.*, **-dised**, **-dising**. *Chem.* to treat or combine with iodine.

iodo-, word part meaning 'iodine', as in *iodometry*. Also, **iod-**. [combining form representing NL *iōdum*]

ion /ˈaɪən/, *n.* an electrically charged atom, radical, or molecule, formed by the loss or gain of one or more electrons, as Na$^+$ Cl$^-$, Ca^{++}, S$^=$. See **cation**, **anion**, and **valency**. [Gk: go] —**ionic**, *adj.*

-ion, a noun suffix indicating action or process, state or condition, or sometimes things or people, as in *allusion*, *communion*, *flexion*, *fusion*, *legion*, *opinion*, *suspicion*, *union*. Also, **-tion** and **-ation**. See **-cion**, **-xion**. [L *-io*, suffix forming nouns, esp. from verbs]

Iona /aɪˈoʊnə/, *n.* a small island in the Hebrides, off the western coast of Scotland; centre of early Celtic Christianity.

Ionia /aɪˈoʊniə/, *n.* an ancient region on the western coast of Asia Minor and adjacent islands; colonised by the ancient Greeks.

Ionian Sea /aɪˌoʊniən ˈsiː/, *n.* an arm of the Mediterranean between southern Italy, eastern Sicily, and Greece.

Ionic /aɪˈɒnɪk/, *adj. Archit.* indicating or relating to one of the three Greek pillars, noted for its slender proportions and the scrolls on the capitals. [L from Gk]

ionic bond, *n. Chem.* →**electrovalent bond**.

ionisation chamber *or* **ionization chamber** /aɪənaɪˈzeɪʃən tʃeɪmbə/, *n.* a device for measuring the strength of ionising radiation, consisting of a gas-filled container in which are two electrodes with a potential difference between them. The radiation ionises the gas, and the current flowing between the electrodes is a measure of its strength.

ionisation potential *or* **ionization potential**, *n.* the energy needed to remove an electron from an atom.

ionise *or* **ionize** /ˈaɪənaɪz/, *v.*, **-nised**, **-nising**. ◇*v.t.* **1.** to separate or change into ions. **2.** to produce ions in. ◇*v.i.* **3.** to become changed into ions, as by dissolving. —**ionisation**, *n.* —**ioniser**, *n.*

ionising radiation *or* **ionizing radiation**, *n.* any radiation which causes ionisation in the matter through which it passes.

ionosphere /aɪˈɒnəsfɪə/, *n.* a succession of ionised layers that constitute the outer regions of the earth's atmosphere beyond the stratosphere, considered as beginning with the Heaviside layer at about 100 kilometres and stretching upwards several hundred kilometres.

iota /aɪˈoʊtə/, *n.* **1.** the ninth letter (I, ι, = English I, i) of the Greek alphabet (the smallest letter). **2.** very small quantity; tittle; jot.

IOU /aɪ oʊ ˈjuː/, *n.* a written acknowledgment of a debt. [from the pronunciation of 'I owe you']

-ious, an ending consisting of the suffix **-ous** with a preceding original or euphonic vowel **i**. See **-eous**.

Iowa /ˈaɪəwə/, *n.* **1.** a state in the central US; a part of the Midwest. Pop. 2 851 000

(1986 est.); 145 765 km². *Cap.*: Des Moines. *Abbrev.*: Ia **–Iowan,** *adj., n.*

IPA /ˌaɪ piː ˈeɪ/, *Abbrev.* International Phonetic Alphabet.

Ipswich /ˈɪpswɪtʃ/, *n.* a town in south-eastern Qld; commercial and industrial centre. Pop. 71 861 (1986).

IQ /ˌaɪ ˈkjuː/, *n.* the relation of a person's mental age to actual (chronological) age. A child with a mental age of 12 years and an actual age of 10 years has an intelligence rating of 1.2 (usu. expressed as 120). Also, **intelligence quotient.** [abbrev.]

ir-¹, variant of **in-²**, before *r*, as in *irradiate*.

ir-², variant of **in-³**, before *r*, as in *irreducible*.

Ir, *Chem. Symbol.* iridium.

IRA /ˌaɪ ɑːr ˈeɪ/, *n.* a secret Irish nationalist organisation, formed to promote guerrilla activities against the British and later against Northern Ireland. Also, **Irish Republican Army.**

Iran /ɪˈræn, -ˈrɑːn/, *n.* a republic in south-western Asia, on the Persian Gulf; a monarchy until 1979 when Shah Mohammed Reza Pahlavi was deposed; continuing border disputes with Iraq. Pop. 49 930 000 (1987 est.); 1 648 000 km². *Language:* Persian (Farsi), also Turkic, Kurdish and other minority languages. *Currency:* rial. *Cap.*: Teheran. Official name, **Islamic Republic of Iran.** Formerly, **Persia.** **–Iranian,** *n., adj.*

Iraq /ɪˈrɑːk/, *n.* a republic in south-western Asia, almost land-locked but with a narrow outlet to the Persian Gulf; a part of the Ottoman Empire before World War I. Pop. 16 476 000 (1987 est.); 438 317 km². *Languages:* Arabic, also Kurdish. *Currency:* dinar. *Cap.*: Baghdad. **–Iraqi,** *n., adj.*

irascible /ɪˈræsəbəl/, *adj.* **1.** easily made angry: *an irascible old man.* **2.** marked by, excited by, or coming from anger: *an irascible nature.* [L] **–irascibility, irascibleness,** *n.* **–irascibly,** *adv.*

irate /aɪˈreɪt/, *adj.* angry; enraged. [L]

ire /aɪə/, *n.* anger; wrath. [ME, from OF, from L] **–ireful,** *adj.*

Ireland¹ /ˈaɪələnd/, *n.* **David,** born 1927, Australian novelist; author of *The Glass Canoe* (1976).

Ireland² /ˈaɪələnd/, *n.* **1.** an island off north-western Europe, part of the British Isles; a British dependency from the 16th century until 1801 when united with Great Britain; divided into the Irish Free State and Northern Ireland in 1921. **2.** Also, **Irish Republic, Southern Ireland.** Formerly (1921–37), **Irish Free State.** a republic occupying most of the island of Ireland; achieved independence with dominion states under the British crown in 1921; a republic since 1949. Pop. 3 560 000 (1987 est.); 70 283 km². *Languages:* English and Irish. *Currency:* Irish pound. *Cap.*: Dublin. Official name, **Republic of Ireland.** Irish, **Éire.** **3.** See **Northern Ireland.**

Irene /aɪˈriːni/, *n. Gk Myth.* the daughter of Themis by Zeus; the goddess of peace; Roman counterpart, Pax.

Irian Jaya /ˌɪriən ˈdʒajə/, *n.* an Indonesian province, comprising the western part of the island of New Guinea. Pop. 1 363 500 (1986 est.); 421 981 km². *Cap.*: Jayapura. Formerly, **Netherlands New Guinea, Dutch New Guinea, Irian Barat.** English, **West Irian.**

iridescent /ɪrəˈdɛsənt/, *adj.* showing a play of lustrous, changing rainbow colors. [L: rainbow] **–iridescence,** *n.*

iridium /aɪˈrɪdiəm, əˈrɪdiəm/, *n.* a precious metallic element resembling platinum, used in platinum alloys and for the points of gold pens. *Symbol:* Ir; *at. wt:* 192.2; *at. no.* 77; *sp. gr.:* 22.4 at 20°C. [NL, from L *īris* rainbow; named from its iridescence in solution]

iris /ˈaɪrəs/, *n., pl.* **irises, irides** /ˈaɪrədiːz/. **1.** *Anat.* the round colored part of the eye surrounding the opening or pupil. **2.** a type of perennial plant with handsome flowers and sword-shaped leaves; fleur-de-lis. **3.** (*cap.*) *Gk Myth.* a messenger of the gods, regarded as the goddess of the rainbow. [ME, from L, from Gk]

Irish /ˈaɪrɪʃ/, *adj., n., pl.* **Irish.** ◇*adj.* **1.** of or typical of Ireland or its people. ◇*n.* **2.** the people of Ireland and their descendants elsewhere. **3.** the Celtic language of Ireland in its historical (Old Irish, Middle Irish) or modern form. **4. get one's Irish up,** *Colloq.* to become angry. [ME, from OE *Īras*, pl., people of Ireland]

Irish Exiles /ˌaɪrɪʃ ˈɛgzaɪlz/, *n.pl.* three separate groups of political prisoners transported from Ireland to Australia; the first after the Irish insurrection of 1798; the second, members of the Young Ireland movement, in 1848 and the third, a group of Fenian prisoners in 1867.

Irish Republican Army, *n.* → **IRA**

Irish setter, *n.* See **setter.**

irk /ɜːk/, *v.t.* to weary, annoy, or trouble: *It irked him to wait.* [ME, from Scand; see **WORK**]

irksome /ˈɜːksəm/, *adj.* causing weariness, disgust, or annoyance: *irksome restrictions.*

iron /ˈaɪən/, *n.* **1.** *Chem.* **a.** a ductile, malleable, silver-white metallic element, much used in forms containing carbon (see **pig-iron, cast iron, steel,** and **wrought iron**) for making tools, machinery, etc. Symbol: Fe (L *ferrum*); *at. no.*: 26; *at. wt*: 55.847. **b.** the same element found in food, used in forming blood. **2.** something hard, strong, rigid, unyielding, etc.: *hearts of iron.* **3.** a tool, weapon, etc., made of iron. **4.** a tool used heated for pressing cloth, etc. **5.** any iron-headed golf club used on the fairway. **6.** a branding iron. **7.** → **harpoon.** **8.** (*pl.*) **a.** an iron shackle or fetter: *body irons; leg irons.* **b.** iron supports to correct leg malformations, etc. **9.** → **stirrup.** **10. strike while the iron is hot,** to act quickly while the opportunity is still available. ◇*adj.* **11.** made of iron. **12.** strong; extremely robust or hardy: *iron constitution.* **13.** strong; rigid; unyielding:

an iron will. **14.** cruel; harsh or stern. ◇*v.t.* **15.** to press (clothes) with a heated iron. **16.** to chain up with irons; shackle; fetter. ◇*v.i.* **17.** to press clothes, etc., with a heated iron. ◇*v.* **18. iron out, a.** to press (clothes, etc.) **b.** to smooth and remove (problems and difficulties, etc.). **c.** *Colloq.* to flatten; knock down. [OE *iren, isen, isern*]

Iron Age, *n*. **1.** *Archaeol.* the time following the Stone and Bronze Ages, when early man lived and made tools of iron. **2.** (*l.c.*) See **age** (def. 10).

ironbark /'aɪənbak/, *n*. a gum tree with a typical dark deeply fissured bark.

Iron Chancellor, *n*. the → **Bismarck**.

Iron Cross, *n*. a German Order founded in 1813, medals of which are awarded for outstanding bravery.

Iron Curtain, *n*. the name formerly given to the ideological division between countries under Soviet government or influence, and the rest of the world; physically formed by the frontiers between the former West Germany, Austria, and Italy on the one side, and the former East Germany, Czechoslovakia, Hungary and Yugoslavia on the other.

Iron Gate, *n*. a gorge cut by the Danube through the Carpathian Mountains, between Yugoslavia and south-western Romania. 3 km long. Also, **Iron Gates**.

iron gum, *n*. one of several types of gum tree which have particularly strong wood.

iron hand, *n*. severe control; strictness. –**iron-handed**, *adj*.

ironic /aɪ'rɒnɪk/, *adj*. **1.** of, relating to, or marked by irony: *an ironic compliment*. **2.** using, or given to irony: *an ironic speaker*. Also, **ironical** /aɪ'rɒnɪkəl/. [L, from Gk: dissembling, feigning ignorance] –**ironically**, *adv*. –**ironicalness**, *n*.

ironing /'aɪənɪŋ/, *n*. **1.** the act or process of pressing clothes, etc., with a heated iron. **2.** clothes, etc., that have been ironed, or are to be ironed: *to fold up the ironing*.

Iron Knob, *n*. a town in southern SA, west of Whyalla; site of rich iron ore deposits.

iron lace, *n*. cast-iron ornamentation often of an intricate kind associated particularly with 19th century terrace houses.

iron lung, *n*. a chamber in which alternate pulsations of high and low pressure can be used to force normal lung movements, used esp. in some cases of poliomyelitis.

ironmonger /'aɪənmʌŋgə/, *n*. someone who sells metal goods, tools, etc.

irons /'aɪənz/, *n.pl.* **1.** fetters and chains: *Clap him in irons!* **2. irons in the fire**, separate interests, projects, etc.: *I have many irons in the fire*.

ironstone /'aɪənstoʊn/, *n*. **1.** any ore of iron (commonly a carbonate of iron) with clayey or siliceous impurities. **2.** *Geol.* sandstone containing 20 to 30 per cent of iron oxide, usu. limonite. **3.** hard white stoneware pottery.

ironware /'aɪənwɛə/, *n*. articles of iron, as pots, kettles, tools, etc.; hardware.

ironwood /'aɪənwʊd/, *n*. any of various trees with hard heavy wood.

irony /'aɪrəni/, *n., pl.* **-nies. 1.** a figure of speech or literary device in which the apparent meaning is the opposite of that intended, and is made clear by the context or tone. **2.** something said with irony. **3.** pretended ignorance in a discussion (**Socratic irony**). **4.** the effect or implication of a speech or situation in a play, etc., understood by the audience but not by the characters (**dramatic irony**). **5.** the outcome of events opposite to what was, or might have been, expected. [L, from Gk: dissimulation, understatement]

irradiate /ɪ'reɪdieɪt/, *v.,* **-ated, -ating**; /ɪ'reɪdiət, -eɪt/, *adj.* ◇*v.t.* **1.** to throw (intellectual or spiritual) light on; illuminate; enlighten. **2.** to brighten as if with light. **3.** to radiate (light, etc.). **4.** to heat with radiant energy. **5.** to cure or treat by exposure to radiation, as of ultraviolet light. **6.** to expose to radiation. ◇*v.i.* **7.** to send out rays; shine. **8.** to become radiant. ◇*adj.* **9.** bright; full of light. [L: illumined] –**irradiation**, *n*. –**irradiative**, *adj*. –**irradiator**, *n*.

irrational /ɪ'ræʃənəl/, *adj*. **1.** without the power of reason: *irrational animals*. **2.** lacking sound judgment; absurd. **3.** not in accordance with reason; illogical: *irrational fear*. **4.** *Maths.* **a.** (of numbers) not expressible as a ratio of two integers. **b.** (of functions) not expressible as a ratio of two polynomials. ◇*n.* **5.** an irrational number or quantity. [late ME, from L] –**irrationality, irrationalism**, *n*.

Irrawaddy /ɪrə'wɒdi/, *n*. a river flowing south through Burma to the Bay of Bengal. About 2012 km.

irreconcilable /ɪ'rɛkənsaɪləbəl/, *adj*. that cannot be made to agree; incompatible: *two irreconcilable statements*. –**irreconcilability, irreconcilableness**, *n*. –**irreconcilably**, *adv*.

irrecoverable /ɪrə'kʌvərəbəl, -'kʌvrə-/, *adj*. that cannot be got back or made better: *irrecoverable debt; irrecoverable sorrow.* –**irrecoverableness**, *n*. –**irrecoverably**, *adv*.

irredeemable /ɪrə'dimǝbǝl/, *adj*. **1.** not able to be bought back or paid off. **2.** (of certain paper money) not able to be turned into coin. **3.** not able to be reformed. **4.** hopeless; irreparable.

irreducible /ɪrə'djusəbəl/, *adj*. **1.** not able to be reduced or diminished: *the irreducible minimum*. **2.** not able to be brought into a different condition or form. –**irreducibility, irreducibleness**, *n*. –**irreducibly**, *adv*.

irrefutable /ɪ'rɛfjətəbəl, ɪrə'fjutəbəl/, *adj*. not able to be disproved; incontrovertible: *irrefutable logic*. –**irrefutability**, *n*. –**irrefutably**, *adv*.

irregardless /ɪrə'gɑdləs/, *adj*. *Colloq.* regardless; notwithstanding.

irregular /ɪ'rɛgjələ/, *adj*. **1.** without evenness or symmetry: *an irregular pattern*. **2.** not according to any fixed principle, method, or rate; variable: *irregular intervals*. **3.** not

irregular

according to rules or accepted principles: *irregular behavior*. **4.** *Gram.* not inflected in the usual way: *The verbs 'keep' and 'see' are irregular in their inflection*. ◇*n.* **5.** someone or something that is irregular [ML. See IR-², REGULAR] — **irregularity**, *n.*

irrelevant /ɪˈrɛləvənt/, *adj.* **1.** not on the subject or to the point; not applicable or pertinent: *irrelevant remarks*. **2.** *Law.* (of evidence) having no value as proof upon any issue in the case. — **irrelevance, irrelevancy**, *n.*

irreligious /ɪrəˈlɪdʒəs/, *adj.* **1.** not religious. **2.** showing disregard for or hostility to religion; impious; ungodly. [LL] — **irreligion**, *n.*

irreparable /ɪˈrɛpərəbəl, ɪˈrɛprəbəl/, *adj.* not able to be made good or rectified: *irreparable loss*. — **irreparability, irreparableness**, *n.* — **irreparably**, *adv.*

irreplaceable /ɪrəˈpleɪsəbəl/, *adj.* not able to be replaced: *an irreplaceable souvenir*.

irrepressible /ɪrəˈprɛsəbəl/, *adj.* not able to be put down or repressed. — **irrepressibility, irrepressibleness**, *n.* — **irrepressibly**, *adv.*

irreproachable /ɪrəˈproʊtʃəbəl/, *adj.* free from blame. — **irreproachability, irreproachableness**, *n.* — **irreproachably**, *adv.*

irresistible /ɪrəˈzɪstəbəl/, *adj.* not able to be resisted or withstood; tempting: *an irresistible impulse; irresistable food*. — **irresistibility**, *n.* — **irresistibly**, *adv.*

irresolute /ɪˈrɛzəlut/, *adj.* weak of purpose; doubtful or undecided; wavering.

irrespective /ɪrəˈspɛktɪv/, *adj.* without regard to; independent (fol. by *of*): *irrespective of all rights*.

irresponsible /ɪrəˈspɒnsəbəl/, *adj.* **1.** not trustworthy or careful; not answerable or accountable: *an irresponsible ruler*. **2.** lacking the ability to be trustworthy or accountable: *mentally irresponsible*. ◇*n.* **3.** an irresponsible person. — **irresponsibility, irresponsibleness**, *n.* — **irresponsibly**, *adv.*

irretraceable /ɪrəˈtreɪsəbəl/, *adj.* not able to be gone back on: *an irretraceable step*.

irretrievable /ɪrəˈtrivəbəl/, *adj.* not able to be got back. — **irretrievability**, *n.* — **irretrievably**, *adv.*

irreverence /ɪˈrɛvrəns, ɪˈrɛvərəns/, *n.* lack of reverence or respect. — **irreverent**, *adj.*

irreversible /ɪrəˈvɜːsəbəl/, *adj.* not reversible; not able to be changed or undone: *an irreversible decision*. — **irreversibility**, *n.*

irrevocable /ɪˈrɛvəkəbəl/, *adj.* not to be revoked or recalled: *an irrevocable decree*. — **irrevocability, irrevocableness**, *n.*

irrigate /ˈɪrəɡeɪt/, *v.t.*, **-gated, -gating**. **1.** to supply (land) with water by means of canals, etc., and thus increase its productivity. **2.** *Med.* to supply (a wound, etc.) with a continual flow of some liquid. [L] — **irrigation**, *n.* — **irrigator**, *n.* — **irrigable**, *adj.*

irritable /ˈɪrətəbəl/, *adj.* **1.** easily irritated. **2.** *Physiol, Biol.* showing ability to be excited to a characteristic action by a stimulus, such as heat, etc. [L] — **irritability, irritableness**, *n.*

irritant /ˈɪrətənt/, *adj.* **1.** irritating. ◇*n.* **2.** anything that irritates. [L] — **irritancy**, *n.*

irritate /ˈɪrəteɪt/, *v.t.* **1.** to excite to impatience or anger. **2.** *Physiol, Biol.* to excite (a living system) to some characteristic action. **3.** to make (a part of the body, wound, etc.) sensitive or sore. [L] — **irritation**, *n.* — **irritative, irritating**, *adj.*

irrupt /ɪˈrʌpt/, *v.i.* to burst suddenly (into). — **irruption**, *n.* — **irruptive**, *adj.*

Irving /ˈɜːvɪŋ/, *n.* **Washington**, 1783–1859, US essayist, story writer, and historian.

is /ɪz/; *weak forms* /z, s/, *v.* third person singular present indicative of **be**. [OE *is*. See BE]

Is, *Abbrev.* **1.** *Bible*. Also, **Isa** Isaiah. **2.** Also, **is.** Island. **3.** Isle.

Isaac /ˈaɪzək/, *n.* a Hebrew patriarch, son of Abraham and Sarah, and father of Jacob. [See Genesis 17:19]

Isaacs /ˈaɪzəks/, *n.* **Sir Isaac Alfred**, 1855–1948, Australian jurist; governor-general of Australia 1931–36.

Isabella I /ɪzəˈbɛlə/, *n.* ('the Catholic'), 1451–1504, joint ruler, 1474–1504, of Castile and León, with her husband Ferdinand V, and patron of Columbus. Spanish, **Isabel** /isaˈbɛl/.

Isaiah /aɪˈzaɪə/, *n.* **1.** a major Hebrew prophet of the eighth century BC. **2.** a long book of the Old Testament; the first book of the major prophets. [ult. from Heb: *Yesha'yāh*, lit., Jehovah's salvation']

-isation, a noun suffix, combination of **-ise** with **-ation**.

ISBN /ˌaɪ ɛs biː ˈɛn/, *Abbrev.* International Standard Book Number.

Iscariot /əsˈkæriət/, *n.* the surname of Judas, the betrayer of Jesus. [See Mark 3:19, 14:10-11. Gk: from Heb: man of *Kerioth* (a place in Palestine)]

-ise¹ *or* **-ize**, a suffix of verbs having the following senses: **a.** intransitively, of following some line of action, practice, etc., as in *apologise, economise*, or of becoming (as indicated), as *crystallise*. **b.** transitively, of acting towards or upon, treating in a particular way, as in *baptise, colonise*, or of making (as indicated), as in *civilise, legalise*. See **-ism** and **-ist**. [from (often directly) Gk *-izein*]

-ise², a noun suffix meaning quality, condition, or use, as in *merchandise, franchise*.

-ish¹, **1.** a suffix used to form adjectives from nouns, with the sense of: **a.** 'belonging to' (a people, country, etc.), as in *British, Danish*. **b.** 'having the nature of', 'like', as in *babyish, mulish*. **c.** 'liking', 'tending to', as in *bookish, freakish*. **2.** a suffix used to form adjectives from other adjectives, with the sense of 'somewhat', 'rather', as in *oldish, reddish*. [ME; OE *-isc*]

-ish², a suffix forming simple verbs as in *finish*. [F *-iss-*, extended stem of verbs in *-ir*, from L]

Isherwood /ˈɪʃəwʊd/, n. **Christopher**, 1904–86, English novelist and dramatist; author of the novel *Goodbye to Berlin* (1939).

Isis /ˈaɪsəs/, n. an Egyptian fertility goddess, sister and wife of Osiris, usu. distinguished by the sun disc and cow's horns on her head. [L, from Gk, from Egyptian *Ese*]

Islam /ˈɪzlæm, -lam/, n. **1.** the religion of the Muslims, based on the teachings of Mohammed as set down in the Koran, the main principle being complete worship of an only god, Allah. **2.** all Muslim believers, their civilisation, and their lands. [Ar: submission (to the will of God)] – **Islamic**, adj. – **Islamism**, n. – **Islamite**, n.

Islamabad /ɪzˈlaməbad, ɪzˈlæməbæd/, n. the capital of Pakistan in the north on the Potwar Plateau. Pop. 359 000 (1983).

island /ˈaɪlənd/, n. **1.** an area of land completely surrounded by water, and not large enough to be called a continent. **2.** something like an island in that it is alone, or isolated or cut off: *traffic island*. [OE *īland*, *īgland*] – **island-like**, adj.

islander /ˈaɪləndə/, n. a person who is native to or lives on an island.

isle /aɪl/, n. a small island. [ME, from OF, from L]

-ism, a suffix of nouns meaning action or practice, state or condition, principles, beliefs, a usage or characteristic, etc., as in *baptism*, *barbarism*, *criticism*, *Darwinism*, *realism*. See -**ist** and -**ise**[1]. [from (often directly) Gk -*ismos*, -*isma*, noun suffix. See -ISE[1]]

isn't /ˈɪzənt/, v. the short form of *is not*.

iso-, **1.** a prefix meaning 'equal'. **2.** *Chem.* a prefix added to the name of a compound to show it is an isomer with a branched chain. Also, **is-**. [Gk: equal]

isobar /ˈaɪsəba/, n. **1.** *Meteorol, etc.* a line drawn on a weather map, etc., connecting all points having the same barometric pressure. **2.** *Phys, Chem.* one of two or more elements of different atomic number, but the same atomic weight. [Gk: of equal weight]

isobaric /aɪsəˈbærɪk/, adj. **1.** having or showing equal barometric pressure. **2.** of or relating to isobars.

isobath /ˈaɪsəbæθ/, n. a line drawn on a map of the oceans, connecting all points having the same depth. – **isobathic**, adj.

isoclinal /aɪsoʊˈklaɪnəl/, adj. **1.** sloping or dipping at an equal angle in the same direction. **2.** relating to a line on the earth's surface connecting points of equal dip or slope of the earth's magnetic field. Also, **isoclinic** /aɪsoʊˈklɪnɪk/. [Gk: equally balanced]

isocline /ˈaɪsəklaɪn/, n. a fold of rock strata in which the parts on each side dip in the same direction. [Gk: equally balanced]

isogamous /aɪˈsɒgəməs/, adj. having two similar gametes, or reproducing by the union of such gametes (opposed to *heterogamous*). – **isogamy**, n.

isolate /ˈaɪsəleɪt/, v.t., -**lated**, -**lating**. **1.** to set or place apart, so as to be alone. **2.** *Med.* to keep (an infected person) apart from non-infected ones. **3.** *Chem.* to obtain (a substance) in a pure state. **4.** to track down or find out: *They isolated the fault*. [backformation from *isolated*] – **isolation**, n. – **isolator**, n. – **isolable**, adj.

isolationism /aɪsəˈleɪʃənɪzəm/, n. the policy of keeping a nation separate from others by not taking part in international affairs. – **isolationist**, n.

isomer /ˈaɪsəmə/, n. **1.** *Chem.* a compound which is isomeric with one or more other compounds. **2.** *Phys.* a nuclide which is isomeric with one or more other nuclides.

isomeric /aɪsoʊˈmɛrɪk/, adj. *Chem.* (of compounds) made of the same kinds and numbers of atoms but differing in the arrangement of the atoms and, therefore, in one or more properties. [Gk: having equal parts] – **isomerism**, n.

isometric /aɪsəˈmɛtrɪk/, adj. Also, **isometrical**. **1.** relating to or having equality of measure. **2.** relating to isometrics. ◇ n. **3.** (*pl.*) a system of exercises in which muscles are tensed against each other or against a fixed object. [Gk: of equal measure] – **isometrically**, adv.

isomorphic /aɪsəˈmɔfɪk/, adj. *Biol.* being of the same or like form; different in ancestry, but alike in appearance.

isomorphous /aɪsəˈmɔfəs/, adj. (of a substance) having similar crystal structure, and usu. similar chemical composition, to another substance.

isosceles /aɪˈsɒsəliz/, adj. (of a triangle) having two sides equal. [LL, from Gk: with equal legs]

isoseismic /aɪsoʊˈsaɪzmɪk/, adj. relating to equal intensity of earthquake shock. Also, **isoseismal**.

isostasy /aɪˈsɒstəsi/, n. *Geol.* the theoretical condition of the earth's crust in which the forces tending to raise balance those tending to lower. [ISO- + Gk: a standing] – **isostatic**, adj.

isotherm /ˈaɪsəθɜm/, n. **1.** *Geog.* a line (on a map) connecting points on the earth's surface having the same (mean) temperature. **2.** *Phys, Chem.* → **isothermal line**. [ISO- + Gk: heat]

isothermal /aɪsəˈθɜməl/, adj. **1.** *Phys, Chem.* of or at the same temperature: *isothermal expansion of a gas*. **2.** *Meteorol.* of or relating to an isotherm. ◇ n. **3.** → **isotherm**.

isothermal line, n. a line or graph showing relations of variables under conditions of uniform temperature.

isotone /ˈaɪsətoʊn/, n. one of two or more atoms whose nuclei contain the same number of neutrons although they have different atomic numbers.

isotope /ˈaɪsətoʊp/, n. any of two or more forms of a chemical element, having the same number of protons in the nucleus and, hence, the same atomic number, but having different numbers of neutrons in the nucleus and, hence, different atomic weights. Isotopes of an element

isotope   554   **-ite**

have almost identical properties. [ISO- + Gk: place] **–isotopic,** *adj.*

isotopic number /ˌaɪzəˌtɒpɪk ˈnʌmbə/, *n.* the difference between the number of neutrons and the number of protons in an isotope; neutron excess.

isotropic /ˌaɪsəˈtrɒpɪk/, *adj. Phys.* having one or more properties that are the same in all directions. [ISO- + Gk: turn, way] **–isotropy,** *n.*

Israel /ˈɪzreɪl/, *n.* **1.** a republic in south-western Asia, on the eastern shore of the Mediterranean Sea; formerly Palestine, an Arab-inhabited part of the Ottoman Empire before World War I; a British mandate 1920–48 during which time settled by Jewish immigrants; established as a Jewish state in 1948 since when border disputes with Arab neighbors. Pop. 4 449 100 (1987 est.); 20 700 km^2 (not including area occupied in 1967 Six-Day War). *Languages:* Hebrew, also Arabic. *Currency:* shekel. *Cap.:* Jerusalem **2.** the ancient kingdom of the twelve Hebrew tribes, on the south-western shore of the Mediterranean. **3.** the kingdom of the ten northern Hebrew tribes, in the northern part of this area. **4.** the people traditionally descended from Jacob, the father of the twelve Hebrew patriarchs; the Hebrew or Jewish people.

Israeli /ɪzˈreɪli/, *n., pl.* **-lis,** *adj.* ◇*n.* **1.** a native or inhabitant of Israel. ◇*adj.* **2.** of Israel.

Israelite /ˈɪzrəlaɪt/, *n.* **1.** a Hebrew; Jew. **2.** *Old Testament.* one of God's chosen people. ◇*adj.* **3.** relating to Israel; Jewish.

issue /ˈɪʃu, ˈɪʃju, ˈɪsju/, *n., v.,* **issued, issuing.** ◇*n.* **1.** an act of sending out; delivery; emission. **2.** something which is sent or issued. **3.** the quantity issued at one time: *the latest issue of a magazine.* **4.** a point of disagreement or discussion: *He raised a new issue during the argument; They were discussing political issues.* **5.** the most important point in a disagreement or discussion: *the real issue.* **6.** the final result, effect or outcome: *the issue of a contest.* **7.** a giving out of food, clothing, equipment, etc., to one or more soldiers, or to a military unit. **8.** offspring: *to die without issue.* **9.** a going, coming, passing, or flowing out: *free issue and entry.* **10.** that which comes out, such as a stream, blood from a wound, etc. **11. at issue,** in disagreement: *a point at issue.* **12. join issue,** to join in disagreement. **13. take issue,** to disagree. ◇*v.t.* **14.** to put out; deliver for use, sale, etc. **15.** to publish. **16.** to give out (food, clothing, etc.) to one or more soldiers or to a military unit. **17.** to send out; discharge; emit. ◇*v.i.* **18.** to go, pass, come, or flow out; emerge: *to issue forth to battle.* **19.** to be published. **20.** to result (oft. fol. by *from*). **21.** to end (oft. fol. by *in*). [ME, from OF, from L: go out]

-ist, a suffix of nouns, meaning someone who does, practises, or is concerned with something, or holds certain principles, beliefs, etc., as in *dramatist, machinist, realist, socialist.* See **-ism** and **-ise**[1]. [from (often directly) Gk *-istēs* noun suffix. See ISE[1], -ISM]

Istanbul /ˈɪstænˌbʊl/, *n.* a city in European Turkey, on the Bosporus. Pop. 5 475 982 (1985). Formerly, **Constantinople.** Ancient, **Byzantium.** [Turk alter. of MGk *eis tēn pólin* in (to) the city]

isthmus /ˈɪsməs/, *n., pl.* **-muses.** a narrow piece of land with water on both sides, connecting two larger masses of land. [L, from Gk: narrow passage, neck, isthmus]

-istic, a suffix of adjectives (and in the plural of nouns from adjectives) formed from nouns ending in *-ist*, and relating to such nouns, or to nouns in *-ism*, as in *idealistic, socialistic,* etc. In nouns it has usu. a plural form, as in *linguistics.* [-IST + -IC]

it /ɪt/; *weak form* /ət/, *pron., poss.* **its** or (*Obs.*) **it,** *obj.* **it,** *pl.* **they.** a personal pronoun of the third person neuter gender, which is used: **1.** in place of a neuter noun or a noun representing something possessing sex when sex is not made known or considered: *The baby lost its rattle.* **2.** to refer to some matter expressed or understood, or not made definite: *How is it going?* **3.** to refer to the subject of inquiry or attention, in sentences asking or stating what or who this is: *Who is it? It is the postman.* **4.** as the grammatical subject of a clause of which the real subject is a phrase or clause, generally following: *it is hard to believe that.* **5.** in impersonal constructions: *It is raining.* **6.** without definite force after an intransitive verb: *to foot it* (go on foot). **7. with it, a.** fashionable. **b.** well-informed. [ME and OE *hit*]

italic /ɪˈtælɪk/, *adj.* **1.** relating to a style of printing types in which the letters usu. slope to the right (thus, *italic*), used for emphasis, etc. ◇*n.* **2.** (*oft. pl.*) italic type. [L]

Italy /ˈɪtəli/, *n.* a republic in southern Europe, consisting of a peninsula extending into the Mediterranean Sea, and a number of islands, principally Sicily and Sardinia; unified as a kingdom in 1870; a republic since 1946. Pop. 57 256 000 (1987 est.); 301 278 km^2. *Language:* Italian. *Currency:* lira. *Cap.:* Rome. Italian, **Italia. –Italian,** *adj., n.*

Itar-Tass /ˈaɪtɑ tæs/, *n.* a Russian news-gathering agency, covering also the other member states of the CIS; the successor of the Soviet agency, **Tass.** [Russ.: I(nformation) T(elegraphic) A(gency of) R(ussia) T(ele-graphic) A(gency of the) S(overeign) S(tates)]

itch /ɪtʃ/, *v.i.* **1.** to have an irritation of the skin which causes a desire to scratch. **2.** to have a desire to do or to get something: *to itch after fame.* **3. an itching palm,** greed for money. ◇*n.* **4.** the sensation of itching. **5. the itch,** an infectious disease of the skin; scabies. **6.** a restless desire or longing: *an itch for travel.* [OE *gicc(e)an*] **–itchy,** *adj.* **–itchiness,** *n.*

-ite[1], a suffix of nouns meaning esp. **1.** people connected with a place, tribe, leader, belief, system, etc., as in *Israelite, laborite.* **2.** minerals and fossils, as in *ammonite, anthracite.* **3.** explosives, as in *cordite, dynamite.* **4.** chemical compounds, esp. salts of acids whose names end in *-ous*, as in *phosphite, sulfite.* **5.** commercial products, as in *vulcanite*. [from (often directly) Gk *-itēs* (fem. *-itis*), noun and adj. suffix]

-ite², a suffix forming adjectives and nouns from adjectives, and some verbs, as in *opposite, requisite, erudite*, etc. [L *-itus, -ītus,* pp. ending]

item /'aɪtəm/, *n.* **1.** a separate article or particular: *fifty items on the list.* **2.** a separate piece of information in a newspaper, etc. [ME, from L: (adv.) just so, likewise]

itemise *or* **itemize** /'aɪtəmaɪz/, *v.t.,* **-mised, -mising.** to state by items; give the particulars of: *to itemise an account.* —**itemisation,** *n.*

iterate /'ɪtəreɪt/, *v.t.,* **-rated, -rating.** to say or do (something) again or repeatedly. [L] —**iteration,** *n.* —**iterative,** *adj.*

itinerant /aɪ'tɪnərənt/, *adj.* **1.** travelling from place to place, esp. in the course of business or duty. ◇*n.* **2.** someone who travels from place to place. [LL] —**itinerancy,** *n.*

itinerary /aɪ'tɪnərɪ/, *n., pl.* **-ries. 1.** a line of travel; route. **2.** an account or record of a journey. **3.** a plan of travel.

-ition, a noun suffix, as in *expedition, competition,* etc., being *-tion* after a vowel, or, in other words, **-ite¹** + **-ion.** [L *-itio, -ītio*]

-itious, a suffix of adjectives connected with nouns in *-ition,* as *expeditious,* etc. [L *-icius, -īcius*]

-itis, a noun suffix used in medical terms meaning inflammation of some part or organ, as in *bronchitis, gastritis.* [Gk. See -ITE¹]

-itive, a suffix of adjectives and nouns of adjectival origin, as in *definitive, fugitive.* [L *-itivus, -ītivus*]

it'll /'ɪtl/, *v.* short form of *it will* or *it shall.*

-itol, a suffix used in names of alcohols containing more than one hydroxyl group. [-ITE¹ + -OL¹]

its /ɪts/, *adj., pron.* possessive form of *it.* [poss. case of IT, formerly written *it's*]

it's /ɪts/, short form of *it is.*

itself /ɪt'sɛlf/, *pron.* **1.** the reflexive form of *it: The cat licked itself.* **2.** an emphatic form of *it: The job itself is interesting.* **3.** in its normal state: *My dog is itself again.*

-ity, a suffix forming nouns of condition, characteristics, etc., as in *jollity, civility.* [ME, from F, from L *-itāt-,* stem of *-itas*]

IUD /aɪ ju 'di/, *n.* a contraceptive device, usu. made of metal or plastic, inserted into the uterus. Also, **intra-uterine device, IUCD** [abbrev.]

-ium, a suffix of Latin origin, used esp. to form names of metallic elements.

Ivan IV, *n.* (*'the Terrible'*), 1530–84, grand duke of Muscovy 1533–47, and first tsar of Russia, 1547–84.

-ive, a suffix of adjectives and nouns of adjectival origin, expressing tendency, use, connection, etc., as in *active, destructive, detective, passive.* See **-ative.** [L *-īvus*]

I've /aɪv/, *v.* short form of *I have.*

IVF /aɪ vi 'ɛf/, *n.* the fertilisation of an egg, esp. a human ovum, by a sperm in a test tube, the resulting embryo to be implanted in a uterus. Also, **in-vitro fertilisation.** [abbrev.]

ivory /'aɪvəri, 'aɪvri/, *n., pl.* **-ries,** *adj.* ◇*n.* **1.** a hard white substance, a variety of dentine, forming the main part of tusks of the elephant, walrus, etc., used for carved ornaments, piano keys, etc. **2.** a tusk, as of an elephant. **3.** any substance like ivory. **4.** *Colloq.* a tooth, or the teeth. **5.** an article made of ivory. **6.** a creamy white color. ◇*adj.* **7.** consisting or made of ivory. **8.** of the color ivory. [ME, from OF, from L: made of ivory]

Ivory Coast /,aɪvəri 'koʊst/, *n.* the, → **Côte d'Ivoire.**

ivory tower, *n.* a place away from reality and worldly acts and ideas.

ivy /'aɪvi/, *n., pl.* **ivies. 1.** a climbing vine, with smooth, shiny, evergreen leaves, widely grown as an ornamental. **2.** any of various similar climbing or trailing plants. [ME; OE *ifig*]

Ivy League, *n. US.* a group of highly regarded universities and colleges, esp. Yale, Harvard, Princeton, Columbia, Dartmouth, Cornell, Pennsylvania, and Brown, with high social and scholastic reputations.

-ization → **-isation.**

-ize, variant of **-ise¹.**

Jj

J, j, *n., pl.* **J's** or **Js**, **j's** or **js.** the tenth letter of the English alphabet.

J, *Abbrev.* **1.** Journal. **2.** Judge. **3.** Justice. ◇*Symbol.* **4.** *Phys.* joule.

jab /dʒæb/, *v.*, **jabbed, jabbing,** *n.* ◇*v.i., v.t.* **1.** to push or poke (somebody or something) sharply with something sharp or pointed. ◇*n.* **2.** a quick push or poke with something sharp or pointed. [var. (orig. Scot) of JOB²]

jabber /ˈdʒæbə/, *v.i., v.t.* **1.** to speak (words) quickly, unclearly, or foolishly; chatter. ◇*n.* **2.** rapid or foolish talk; gibberish. [apparently imitative]

Jabiluka /dʒæbəˈlukə/, *n.* a uranium mining deposit in the Alligator Rivers region, NT.

jabiru /ˈdʒæbəru/, *n.* a type of stork, the only one found in Australia, white with a green-black head, neck and tail, found along the north and east coast. [SAmer Ind]

jacana /dʒəˈkanə/, *n.* any of various birds, such as the lotus bird of northern and eastern Australia, which have very long toes and a long, sharp hind claw for running on floating vegetation. [Pg, from SAmer Ind]

jacaranda /dʒækəˈrændə/, *n.* a type of tall tropical American tree, grown in many warm countries for its pale purplish-blue flowers. [SAmer Ind]

jack /dʒæk/, *n.* **1.** a man. **2.** (*cap. or l.c.*) a sailor. **3.** any of various mechanical devices, esp. for raising heavy weights short distances. **4.** any of the four playing cards with a picture of a knave. **5. a.** a knucklebone or plastic copy, a set of which is used in a children's game where they are thrown into the air and caught on the back of the hand. **b.** (*pl.*) the game itself. **6.** a small bowl used as a mark for players to aim at, in the game of bowls. **7.** a small flag used by a ship as a signal, or to show nationality. **8.** *Elect.* a connecting device to which the wires of a circuit may be joined and which is arranged to receive a plug. **9.** any of several sea fishes, as trevally, horse mackerel, etc. **10. every man jack,** everyone without exception. ◇*v.t.* **11.** to lift or move with a jack or other device for raising (usu. fol. by *up*). **12.** *Colloq.* to raise (prices, wages, etc.) (usu. fol. by *up*). ◇*v.* **13. jack up,** *Colloq.* to refuse to do something. ◇*adj.* **14. jack of,** tired of. [orig. proper name *Jack*, earlier *Jacken*]

jackal /ˈdʒækəl/, *n.* **1.** any of several races of wild dog of Asia and Africa, which hunt in packs at night. **2.** someone who does another person's hard or uninteresting work. [Turk, from Pers]

jackass /ˈdʒækæs/, *n.* **1.** a male donkey. **2.** a very stupid or foolish person. **3.** a kookaburra. **4.** the grey butcher bird.

Jacobean

jack boot, *n.* a large leather boot reaching up to the knee, orig. one serving as armor, now often associated with the exercise of unjust force or power.

jackdaw /ˈdʒækdɔ/, *n.* a shiny black European bird of the crow family. [JACK + ME *jackdaw*]

jackeroo /dʒækəˈru/, *n.* **1.** someone learning to work on a sheep or cattle station. ◇*v.i.* **2.** to work as a trainee on such a station. Also, **jackaroo.** [b. *Jack* Christian name + (KANGA)ROO]

jacket /ˈdʒækət/, *n.* **1.** a short coat, in various forms, worn by both men and women. **2.** Also, **dust jacket, dustcover.** a removable (usu. paper) cover for protecting the binding of a book. **3.** the skin of a potato. **4.** the outer covering of a boiler, pipe, tank, etc. **5.** the natural coat of certain animals. [ME, from OF]

Jackey Jackey /ˈdʒæki ˌdʒæki/, *n.* an Aboriginal guide; the sole survivor of EB Kennedy's expedition to Cape York Peninsula in 1848. Tribal name, **Galmahra.**

jackhammer /ˈdʒækhæmə/, *n.* a hand-held hammer drill operated by compressed air, used for drilling rocks.

jack-in-the-box /ˈdʒæk-ɪn-ðə-bɒks/, *n.* **1.** Also, **jack-in-a-box.** a toy consisting of a figure, enclosed in a box, which springs out when the lid is unfastened. **2.** a seashore tree, widespread from Asia to northern Australia and the western Pacific.

jackknife /ˈdʒæknaɪf/, *n., pl.* **-knives,** *v.,* **-knifed, -knifing.** ◇*n.* **1.** a large knife with a blade that folds into the handle. **2.** a dive during which the body bends so that the hands touch the toes. ◇*v.i.* **3.** to bend or fold up, like a jackknife. **4.** (of a semi-trailer) to go out of control in such a way that the trailer swings round at a sharp angle.

jack-of-all-trades /ˌdʒæk-əv-ˈɔl-treɪdz/, *n.* someone who can do any work but has no one special skill.

jackpot /ˈdʒækpɒt/, *n.* **1.** the chief prize to be won on a poker machine, or in a lottery, game, competition, etc. **2. hit the jackpot,** to win the chief prize on a poker machine etc.; be very lucky or successful.

Jackson /ˈdʒæksən/, *n.* **1. Andrew,** 1767–1845, US general, seventh president of the US, 1829–37. **2. Glenda,** born 1936, English actor of stage and film. **3. Michael,** born 1958, US pop singer and songwriter. **4. Thomas Jonathan** ('Stonewall *Jackson*'), 1824–63, Confederate general in the American Civil War.

Jacob /ˈdʒeɪkəb/, *n. Bible.* a son of Isaac, the younger twin brother of Esau, and father of the 12 patriarchs. [LL, from Gk *Iákōbos* Jacob, James, from Heb, explained as one who takes by the heel, a supplanter. See Genesis 25:24–35, 27:36]

Jacobean /dʒækəˈbiən/, *adj.* **1.** of or relating to the period of James I of England: *Jacobean drama.* **2.** of or relating to a style of architecture and furnishings which was popular in England in the early 17th century and showed Italian influence. ◇*n.* **3.** a person of the Jacobean period. [NL, from LL *Jacōbus* James + -AN]

Jacobite /'dʒækəbaɪt/, *n.* a supporter of James II of England after his overthrow (1688), or of his descendants. [from LL *Jacōbus* James (see JACOB)]

Jacobite Rebellion, *n. English Hist.* the rebellion led by Charles Edward Stuart, the Young Pretender, in which a number of Highland Clans achieved an initial victory over the English but were later defeated in 1746 at Culloden.

Jacob's ladder *n. Bible.* a ladder leading up to heaven which Jacob saw in his dream. [See Genesis 28:12]

jade /dʒeɪd/, *n.* **1.** either of two minerals, jadeite or nephrite, sometimes green, highly valued as an ornamental stone for carvings, jewellery, etc. **2.** Also, **jade green.** a green color, varying from bluish-green to yellowish-green. [F, from Sp, from L]

jaded /'dʒeɪdəd/, *adj.* **1.** worn out with tiredness. **2.** worn out by too much satisfaction: *a jaded appetite.*

jaffle /'dʒæfəl/, *n.* a pie made from two pieces of bread with a savory or sweet filling, cooked in a special double-sided mould.

jag¹ /dʒæg/, *n., v.,* **jagged, jagging.** ◇*n.* **1.** part of an edge or surface that sticks out sharply; projection. ◇*v.t.* **2.** to cut along the edge so as to form sharp, tooth-like points in. [ME ? imitative]

jag² /dʒæg/, *n. Colloq.* any single activity kept on without stopping, often for too long: *a drinking jag; a fishing jag.* [US d. *jag* a load carried on the back; thus as much drink as a person can carry]

jagged /'dʒægəd/, *adj.* having sharp tooth-like points along the edge or surface. Also, **jaggy.** – **jaggedness**, *n.*

Jagger /'dʒægə/, *n.* **Mick**, born 1943, English lead singer of the rock group the Rolling Stones.

jaguar /'dʒægjuə/, *n.* a large, fierce, spotted cat of tropical America.

jail *or* **gaol** /dʒeɪl/, *n.* **1.** prison. ◇*v.t.* **2.** to take into or hold in prison; imprison. [ME, from OF: prison, cage, from L: cavity, enclosure, cage. See GAOL]

jailbird *or* **gaolbird** /'dʒeɪlbɜd/, *n.* someone who is or has been kept in prison.

jailbreak *or* **gaolbreak** /'dʒeɪlbreɪk/, *n.* escape from prison by means of force.

jailer *or* **gaoler** /'dʒeɪlə/, *n.* someone in charge of a prison; warder.

Jaipur /dʒaɪ'puə/, *n.* a former state in northern India, now part of Rajasthan.

Jakarta /dʒə'katə/, *n.* a seaport in and the capital of Indonesia, on the north-western coast of Java. Pop. 7 829 000 (1986 est.). Former spelling, **Djakarta**. Formerly, **Batavia**.

jake /dʒeɪk/, *adj. Colloq.* all right.

jalopy /dʒə'lɒpi/, *n., pl.* **-lopies.** *Colloq.* an old motor car.

jam¹ /dʒæm/, *v.,* **jammed, jamming**, *n.* ◇*v.t.* **1.** to press or push violently between bodies or surfaces, into a limited space, or against some object. **2.** to fill or block up by crowding: *Crowds jammed the doorways.* **3.** to cause to become caught or displaced, so that it cannot work: *I have jammed the wheel of this machine.* **4.** *Radio.* to interrupt (signals, etc.) by sending out others of about the same frequency. **5.** to apply (brakes) forcibly (fol. by *on*). ◇*v.i.* **6.** to become fixed or stuck fast. **7.** to press or push violently into a limited space or against one another. **8.** (of a machine, etc.) to become unworkable as through the sticking or displacement of a part. **9.** *Music.* to take part in a jam (def. 13). ◇*n.* **10.** the act of jamming. **11.** the state of being jammed. **12.** a mass of things or people jammed together: *a traffic jam.* **13.** Also, **jam session.** a meeting of musicians for the performance of improvised jazz, usu. for their own enjoyment. **14.** *Colloq.* a difficult or awkward situation. [apparently imitative. Compare CHAMP¹]

jam² /dʒæm/, *n.* a food made of whole fruit boiled with sugar and preserved. [? same as JAM¹] –**jammy**, *adj.*

Jamaica /dʒə'meɪkə/, *n.* a parliamentary state in the West Indies, the third largest island in the Caribbean Sea; a British colony before independence in 1962. Pop. 2 365 000 (1987 est.); 10 991 km². *Language:* English, also a local patois. *Currency:* Jamaican dollar. *Cap.:* Kingston. –**Jamaican**, *n., adj.*

jamb /dʒæm/, *n.* the side piece of a doorway, window, or other opening. Also, **jambe**. [ME, from F: leg, jamb, from LL: hoof]

jamboree /dʒæmbə'ri/, *n.* **1.** a large gathering of boy scouts, usu. national or international. **2.** *Colloq.* any noisy merrymaking. [apparently b. JABBER and F *soirée*, with *-m-* from JAM¹ crowd]

James¹ /dʒeɪmz/, *n.* **1.** an apostle, brother of the apostle John. [See Matthew 4:21]

James² /dʒeɪmz/, *n.* **Henry**, 1843–1916, US novelist in England.

James I, *n.* 1566–1625, king of England 1603–25; as **James VI**, king of Scotland 1567–1625.

James II, *n.* 1633–1701, king of England 1685–88; as **James VII**, king of Scotland 1685–88.

James VI, *n.* title of James I in his position as king of Scotland.

James VII, *n.* title of James II in his position as King of Scotland.

Jamestown /'dʒeɪmztaʊn/, *n.* a ruined village in eastern Virginia; the first permanent English settlement in North America, 1607.

Jančaek /'janətʃɛk/, *n.* **Leoš** /'lɛʊʃ/, 1854–1928, Czech composer influenced by folk music; known for operas including *Jenufa* (1904).

jangle /'dʒæŋgəl/, *v.,* **-gled, -gling**, *n.* ◇*v.i.* **1.** to make a hard, metallic sound: *The keys jangled.* ◇*v.t.* **2.** to cause to make a hard, metallic sound: *He jangled the keys.* **3.** to cause

jangle to become upset or tense: *The argument jangled my nerves.* ◇*n.* **4.** a hard metallic sound. [ME, from OF: chatter, tattle; ? of Gmc orig.]

janitor /'dʒænətə/, *n.* a doorkeeper or porter. [L: doorkeeper. See JANUS] —**janitorial**, *adj.*

Jansz /dʒæns/, *n.* **Willem**, born 1570, Dutch sea-captain and explorer; leader of the first European expedition known to have landed in Australia, near the Wenlock River in Qld. Also, **Janssen**.

January /'dʒænjuəri/, *n., pl.* **-ries.** the first month of the year, containing 31 days. [L: the month of JANUS]

Janus /'dʒeɪnəs/, *n.* a Roman god, regarded as presiding over doors and gates and over beginnings and endings, commonly represented with two faces looking in opposite directions. [L]

Japan /dʒə'pæn/, *n.* a monarchy in eastern Asia, consisting of an archipelago of more than 3000 islands, chiefly Hokkaido, Honshu, Shikoku and Kyushu; in 1946 a democratic constitution, abolishing the doctrine of the Emperor's divinity, was introduced. Pop. 122 100 000 (1987 est.); 377 784 km². *Language:* Japanese. *Currency:* yen. *Cap.:* Tokyo. —**Japanese**, *n., adj.*

jape /dʒeɪp/, *n.* a joke; jest. [ME; orig. uncert.]

japonica /dʒə'pɒnɪkə/, *n.* any of several garden shrubs with white, pink or red flowers. [NL, fem. of *Japonicus* of Japan]

jar¹ /dʒa/, *n.* **1.** an earthen or glass container with a wide opening, usu. cylindrical. **2.** *Colloq.* a glass of beer. [F, from Pr or Sp, from Ar: earthen vessel]

jar² /dʒa/, *v.*, **jarred, jarring**, *n.* ◇*v.i.* **1.** to produce a harsh, unpleasant sound; grate. **2.** to have an upsetting effect upon the nerves, feelings, etc. **3.** to shake or rattle. **4.** to disagree; conflict; clash: *These ideas jar with my beliefs.* ◇*v.t.* **5.** to cause to make a hard, unpleasant sound. **6.** to cause to shake or rattle. **7.** to have an upsetting effect upon (the feelings, nerves, etc.) (oft. fol. by *on*). ◇*n.* **8.** a harsh, unpleasant sound. **9.** a shaking movement, caused by a blow, etc. **10.** an upsetting effect upon the mind or feelings due to some shock. **11.** disagreement; conflict, as of opinions, colors, etc. [cf. OE *cearcian* creak]

Jardine family /dʒa'din/, *n.* an important Australian pioneering family, including **1. Frank** (*Francis Lascelles Jardine*), 1841–1919, explorer in northern Qld; long association with the now deserted Somerset settlement off Cape York. **2. Alexander William**, 1843–1920, brother of Frank, explorer with him in northern Qld, and engineer.

jargon /'dʒagən/, *n.* **1.** the language used specially by people in the same job, etc.: *medical jargon.* **2.** (*oft. offensive*) any talk or writing which one does not understand. **3.** meaningless talk or writing; gibberish. [ME from OF; orig. uncert.]

jarrah /'dʒærə/, *n.* a large tree of western Australia with long-lasting dark red wood. [Aboriginal]

Jaruzelski /jærə'zelski/, *n.* **Wojciech Witold** /,vɔɪtʃek 'vɪtolt/, born 1923, Polish general; became premier of Poland in 1981.

Jas, *Bible. Abbrev.* James.

jasmine /'dʒæzmən/, *n.* any of several types of shrub or climbing plant with sweet-smelling flowers. [F, from Ar, from Pers]

Jason /'dʒeɪsən/, *n. Gk Legend.* the leader of the expedition of the Argonauts in search for the Golden Fleece.

jasper /'dʒæspə/, *n.* an opaque, oft. highly colored, variety of quartz, commonly used in ornamental carvings. [ME, from OF, from L, from Gk; of Eastern orig.]

jaspilite /'dʒæspəlaɪt/, *n. Geol.* a formation consisting of alternating layers of jasper and iron oxide.

jaundice /'dʒɔndəs/, *n., v.*, **-diced, -dicing.** ◇*n.* **1.** *Med.* a diseased condition of the body due to increased bile in the blood, marked by yellowness of the skin, whites of the eyes, etc., and by tiredness. **2.** a state of feeling in which ideas or judgment are influenced by bitterness, jealousy, etc. ◇*v.t.* **3.** to cause to have jaundice. **4.** to influence (ideas, judgment, etc.) with feelings of bitterness, jealousy, etc: *Her envy jaundiced her view of his achievements.* [ME, from OF, from L: greenish yellow]

jaunt /dʒɔnt/, *v.i.* **1.** to make a short journey, esp. for pleasure. ◇*n.* **2.** such a journey. [? nasalised var. of *jot* jog, jolt]

jaunty /'dʒɔnti/, *adj.*, **-tier, -tiest. 1.** showing gaiety in manner or movement: *He walked with a jaunty step.* **2.** (of clothing, etc.) trim and fashionable. [earlier *janty*, from F *gentil*] —**jauntiness**, *n.*

Java /'dʒavə/, *n.* an island in Indonesia, lying south of Borneo and Sumatra. Pop. (with Madura) 96 892 900 (1983 est.); 126 703 km². Indonesian, **Jawa**. —**Javanese**, *n., adj.*

Java man *n.* →**Pithecanthropus**. Also, **Trinil man**.

javelin /'dʒævələn/, *n.* a spear to be thrown by hand, esp. one thrown for distance in athletics. [F *javeline*; probably from Celtic]

jaw /dʒɔ/, *n.* **1.** one of the two bones or structures (upper and lower) which form the framework of the mouth. **2.** *Dentistry.* either of these containing all its teeth and covered by the soft tissues. **3.** anything likened to these: *the jaws of death; jaws of a valley.* **4.** one of two or more parts of a machine, etc., which crush or hold something: *the jaws of a vice.* **5.** *Colloq.* continual talk, esp. of moralising nature. ◇*v.t.* **6.** *Colloq.* to talk disapprovingly to; admonish. [ME, from OF: cheek, jaw]

jay /dʒeɪ/, *n.* **1.** any of a number of Australian birds such as certain currawongs and cuckoo-shrikes. **2.** any of several birds of Europe and America, all of them gaily colored and noisy. **3.** *Colloq.* a simple-minded or foolish person. [ME, from OF]

Jaya /'dʒaɪə/, *n*. **Mount**, a mountain in eastern Indonesia, in West Irian in the Surdirman Range; highest mountain on the island of New Guinea. 5029 m. Formerly, **Mount Carstensz, Sukarno Peak**.

Jayapura /dʒaɪə'pʊərə/, *n*. a port in north-eastern Indonesia, capital of Irian Jaya. Pop. 151 308 (1980). Formerly, **Sukarnapura, Kotabaru, Hollandia**.

jaywalk /'dʒeɪwɔːk/, *v.i. Colloq*. to cross a street carelessly, not taking notice of a pedestrian crossing, traffic lights, etc. [JAY (see def. 3) + WALK] —**jaywalker**, *n*. —**jaywalking**, *n*.

jazz /dʒæz/, *n*. **1**. a type of popular music of American Negro origin, marked by frequent improvisation and syncopated rhythms. **2. all that jazz**, *Colloq*. all that sort of thing. ◇*adj*. **3**. of the nature of or relating to jazz. ◇*v.t.* **4**. *Colloq*. to put energy or liveliness into (oft. fol. by *up*). [orig. obscure; said to have been long used by Negroes of the southern US, esp. those of Louisiana]

jazzy /'dʒæzi/, *adj*., **-zier, -ziest. 1.** *Colloq*. relating to or suggestive of jazz music; wildly active or lively. **2.** having very bright colors.

jealous /'dʒɛləs/, *adj*. **1**. feeling bitterness at the success, possessions, etc., of another person or towards the person himself: *I am jealous of him; I am jealous of his achievements*. **2.** marked by or arising from such a feeling: *He made jealous plans*. **3.** inclined to or troubled by fears of a rival: *a jealous husband*. **4.** watchful in keeping or guarding something: *The cat was jealous of her kittens*. **5.** (in biblical use) demanding complete faithfulness: *a jealous God*. [ME, from OF, from L, from Gk: ZEAL] —**jealousy, jealousness**, *n*.

jeans /dʒinz/, *n.pl*. trousers of usu. hard-wearing material, as denim or corduroy. [probably from F *Gênes* Genoa]

jeep /dʒip/, *n*. a small motor vehicle for driving in rough conditions, used esp. for military purposes. [? special use of *jeep*, name of fabulous animal in comic strip 'Popeye', or alteration of *GP* (for General Purpose Vehicle)]

jeer /dʒɪə/, *v.i.* **1**. to make fun of something or someone rudely; speak mockingly. ◇*v.t.* **2**. to make fun of; scoff at. **3**. to drive (*out, off*, etc.) by jeers. ◇*n.* **4**. a jeering remark. [? OE *cēir* clamor]

Jefferson /'dʒɛfəsən/, *n*. **Thomas**, 1743–1826, US writer, and third president of the US, 1801–09. —**Jeffersonian** *adj., n*.

Jehovah /dʒə'hoʊvə/, *n*. **1**. a name of God in the Old Testament. **2**. (in modern Christian use) God.

Jehovah's Witness, *n*. a member of a sect of Christians who believe that the establishment of God's rule on earth is near, that war is unlawful, and that the power of the state must be opposed when it goes against religious principles.

jejune /dʒə'dʒun/, *adj*. **1**. lacking in substance; simple and immature. **2**. unsatisfying to the mind; dull; boring. [L: fasting, empty, dry, poor] —**jejuneness, jejunity**, *n*.

jejunum /dʒə'dʒunəm/, *n*. the middle part of the small intestine. [L: empty]

Jekyll-and-Hyde /dʒɛkəl-ən-'haɪd/, *adj*. (of a person) having both very good and very bad qualities. [named after *Dr Jekyll and Mr Hyde* (1886), a novel by RL STEVENSON]

jelly /'dʒɛli/, *n., pl*. **-lies**, *v.,* **-lied, -lying**. ◇*n.* **1**. food with a soft, elastic consistency due to the use of gelatine, etc., such as fruit juice boiled down with sugar. **2**. anything of the consistency of jelly. ◇*v.t.* **3**. to bring to the consistency of jelly. [ME, from OF, from L: frozen]

jelly blubber, *n*. →**jellyfish**.

jellyfish /'dʒɛlifɪʃ/, *n., pl*. **-fishes**, (*esp. collectively*) **-fish**. any of various marine invertebrates of a soft, jelly-like structure, esp. one with an umbrella-shaped body and long tentacles; a medusa.

jemmy /'dʒɛmi/, *n., pl*. **-mies**, *v.,* **-mied, -mying**. ◇*n.* **1**. a short crowbar. ◇*v.t.* **2**. to force open (a door, etc.) with a jemmy. [apparently a form of *James*]

Jenner /'dʒɛnə/, *n*. **Edward**, 1749–1823, English physician, discoverer of smallpox vaccine.

Jenolan Caves /dʒə,noʊlən 'keɪvz/, *n.pl*. a limestone cave system on the western side of the Great Dividing Range in south-eastern NSW, extending unbroken for 20 km; the system is the longest explored in Australia. [from *Genowlan*, the Aboriginal name for a mountain in the area]

jeopardise or **jeopardize** /'dʒɛpədaɪz/, *v.t.,* **-dised, -dising**. to put in jeopardy; risk.

jeopardy /'dʒɛpədi/, *n*. the danger or risk of loss or harm: *His life was in jeopardy*. [ME, from OF *jeu parti*, lit., divided game, even game or chance]

Jer, *Bible. Abbrev*. Jeremiah.

Jerba /'dʒɜbə/, *n*. an island off the coast of Tunisia; the lotus-eaters' island of Greek mythology. Pop. 70 217 (1975); 513 km². Also, **Djerba**.

jerboa /dʒɜ'boʊə/, *n*. **1**. Also, **jerboa pouched mouse, jerboa kangaroo**. either of two small meat-eating marsupial mice, the **wuhl-wuhl** or **pitchi-pitchi**, of central deserts, and the **kultarr**, of central Australia, each mistakenly believed to hop like a kangaroo instead of using all four limbs. See **marsupial mouse**. **2.** a jumping rodent of North Africa and Asia, with long legs and tail. [NL, from ML, from Ar: flesh of the loins (from the highly developed thighs)]

Jeremiah /dʒɛrə'maɪə/, *n*. **1**. c. 650–585 BC, a major Hebrew prophet. **2**. a book of the Old Testament.

Jericho /'dʒɛrɪkoʊ/, *n*. an ancient city of Palestine, north of the Dead Sea.

jerk[1] /dʒɜk/, *n*. **1**. a quick, sudden push, pull, throw, or other movement. **2.** *Colloq*. a stupid or annoying person. ◇*v.t.* **3**. to push, pull, twist or throw with a quick, sudden movement. **4**. to speak (words) with sudden stops and starts (usu. fol. by *out*). ◇*v.i.* **5**. to make quick, sudden movements. [apparently imitative] —**jerky**, *adj.* —**jerkiness**, *n.*

jerk² /dʒɜk/, *v.t.* to preserve (meat) by cutting in small long pieces and drying in the sun. [Amer Sp: jerked meat, from Quechua]

jerkin /'dʒɜkən/, *n.* a short, close-fitting, sleeveless coat.

jerry-build /'dʒeri-bɪld/, *v.t.*, **-built**, **-building**. to build cheaply and poorly. —**jerry-built**, *adj.*

jerry can, *n.* an oblong can for carrying liquids, esp. petrol.

jersey /'dʒɜzi/, *n.* 1. (*cap.*) a breed of dairy cattle whose milk contains a large amount of butterfat. 2. a close-fitting, long-sleeved, knitted outer garment for the upper part of the body; jumper² (def. 1). 3. a machine-knitted cloth of wool, silk or artificial fibre, used for garments, etc. [from the island of *Jersey*, in the English Channel]

Jerusalem /dʒə'rusələm/, *n.* an ancient holy city in the Judaean Hills 55 km from the Mediterranean Sea; place of pilgrimage for Jews, Christians, and Muslims; capital of Israel since 1950. Pop. 431 800 (1983).

Jerusalem artichoke, *n.* a type of sunflower, with edible underground stems. [*Jerusalem*, alteration (by popular etymology) of It *girasole* sunflower]

Jervis Bay /dʒɜvəs 'beɪ/, *n.* an inlet of the Pacific Ocean on the south coast of NSW; the southern headland of the bay is part of the ACT; holiday resort, naval training college. See **Australian Defence Force Academy**. [named after Admiral Sir John *Jervis*]

jest /dʒest/, *n.* 1. a joke. 2. joking or fun: *He spoke half in jest, half in earnest.* 3. something or someone joked about. ◇*v.i.* 4. to speak in a playful or joking way. [var. of *gest*, from L: perform]

jester /'dʒestə/, *n.* 1. someone who jests. 2. a professional fool or clown kept by a prince or noble, esp. during the Middle Ages.

Jesuit /'dʒezjuət/, *n.* a member of a male religious order, the Society of Jesus, founded at the time of the Reformation to defend and promote Roman Catholicism. [named after the Society of *Jesus* founded by Ignatius Loyola in 1534]

Jesus /'dʒizəs/, *n.* See **Christ** (def. 2). Also, **Jesus Christ**. [ME and OE, from LL, from Gk, from Heb: Jehovah is salvation]

jet¹ /dʒet/, *n.*, *v.*, **jetted**, **jetting**. ◇*n.* 1. a stream of liquid or gas flowing from a small opening, such as a spout. 2. the opening used: *a gas jet.* 3. → **jet plane**. ◇*v.i.* 4. to rush out in a stream; spout. 5. to travel by jet plane. [F]

jet² /dʒet/, *n.* 1. a hard black coal, used when polished for making jewellery, buttons, etc. 2. Also, **jet black**. a deep, shiny black color. [ME, from OF, from L, from Gk, from *Gágai*, town in Lycia, Asia Minor]

jet lag, *n.* bodily discomfort caused by the change in normal patterns of eating and sleeping during a long plane journey.

jet plane, *n.* an aeroplane operated by jet propulsion.

jet propulsion, *n.* a method of producing a driving force upon an air or water craft through the action of a high-velocity jet, usu. of heated gases, sent out towards the rear. Also, **reaction propulsion**. —**jet-propelled**, *adj.*

jettison /'dʒetəsən, -zən/, *n.* 1. the act of throwing cargo, etc., overboard to lighten a ship or aircraft. ◇*v.t.* 2. to throw (cargo, etc.) overboard, esp. to lighten a ship or aircraft. 3. to throw off (something unwanted). [AF, var. of OF: throw]

jetty /'dʒeti/, *n.*, *pl.* **-ties**. a wharf or pier. [ME, from OF: throw]

Jew /dʒu/, *n.* 1. a person descended from the Hebrews; Israelite. 2. a person whose religion is Judaism. 3. a member of the ancient tribe or nation of Judah. 4. another word for **Israeli**. [ME, from OF, from L, from Gk, from Heb: Judah] —**Jewess**, *n. fem.*

jewel /'dʒuəl/, *n.*, *v.*, **-elled**, **-elling**. ◇*n.* 1. a cut and polished precious stone; gem. 2. an article for personal ornament, usu. set with precious stones. 3. a thing or person of great worth. 4. a precious stone used as a bearing in a watch or delicate instrument. ◇*v.t.* 5. to set or ornament with jewels. [ME, from AF, from L: jest, sport]

jewellery /'dʒuəlri/, *n.* jewels; articles made of gold, silver, precious stones, etc., for personal ornament.

jewfish /'dʒufɪʃ/, *n.*, *pl.* **-fishes**, (*esp. collectively*) **-fish**. any of several types of large, marine, Australian fishes valued as food and for sport, such as the mulloway.

Jewish /'dʒuɪʃ/, *adj.* 1. of, relating to, or characteristic of the Jews; Hebrew. ◇*n.* 2. Yiddish. —**Jewishness**, *n.*

Jewry /'dʒuri/, *n.*, *pl.* **-ries**. the Jewish people collectively. [ME, from AF]

jew's-harp /'dʒuz-hap/, *n.* a small musical instrument having a circular metal frame with a metal tongue which is plucked while the frame is held between the teeth. [apparently jocular in orig., as it is not a harp and has no connection with the Jews]

Jezebel /'dʒezəbel/, *n.* the wife of Ahab, king of Israel, notorious for her shameless conduct. [See I Kings 16:31, 21:25; II Kings 9:30-37]

Jhabvala /dʒab'valə/, *n.* **Ruth Prawer** /'prawə/, born 1927, British writer, born in Germany; noted for novels about the British in India, such as *Heat and Dust* (1975).

Jiang Jie-shi /dʒiˈaŋ dʒieˈʃi/, *n.* 1887-1975, president of China 1928-31, 1943-49; political leader in Taiwan 1950-75. Formerly, **Chiang Kai-shek**.

Jiang Qing /dʒiˈaŋ 'tʃɪŋ/, *n.* born 1913, Chinese Communist actress and politician; widow of Mao Zedong; a leading member of the Gang of Four. Formerly, **Chiang Ch'ing**.

jib¹ /dʒɪb/, *n.* 1. a triangular sail set in front of the forward mast. 2. any of certain similar

jib 561 **Job**

sails set beyond the jib proper, as a **flying jib**. [? akin to GIBBET]

jib² /dʒɪb/, *v.i., v.t.,* **jibbed, jibbing**. →**jibe¹**.

jib³ /dʒɪb/, *v.,* **jibbed, jibbing**. ◇*v.i.* **1.** (of an animal, etc.) to move restlessly sideways or backwards instead of forwards; baulk. **2.** to hold back at doing something. ◇*v.* **3. jib at**, show unwillingness. [orig. uncert.]

jibe¹ /dʒaɪb/, *v.,* **jibed, jibing**, *n.* ◇*v.i.* **1.** to shift from one side to the other when running before the wind, as a sail. **2.** to alter the course so that the sail moves in this manner. ◇*v.t.* **3.** to cause (a sail, etc.) to jibe. ◇*n.* **4.** the act of jibing. Also, **gybe**. [D]

jibe² /dʒaɪb/, *v.t., v.i.,* **jibed, jibing**. →**gibe**. –**jiber**, *n.*

jiffy /ˈdʒɪfi/, *n., pl.* **-fies**. *Colloq.* a very short time. Also, **jiff**. [orig. unknown]

jig¹ /dʒɪɡ/, *n., v.,* **jigged, jigging**. ◇*n.* **1.** a device for holding the work in a machine tool. ◇*v.t.* **2.** to treat, cut, or produce by using a jig. [var. of GAUGE]

jig² /dʒɪɡ/, *n., v.,* **jigged, jigging**. ◇*n.* **1.** (music for) a fast, lively, irregular dance for one or more people, usu. in triple time. ◇*v.t., v.i.* **2.** to dance, play or sing (a jig, etc.). **3.** to move with a jerky action. [apparently var. of JOG, v.]

jigger /ˈdʒɪɡə/, *n.* **1.** any of various mechanical devices, many of which have a jerky movement. **2.** *Billiards.* a long-handled support for a cue. **3.** a measure for alcohol. [JIG¹ + -ER¹]

jiggle /ˈdʒɪɡəl/, *v.,* **-gled, -gling**, *n.* ◇*v.t., v.i.* **1.** to move up and down with short, quick jerks. ◇*n.* **2.** a jiggling movement. [frequentative of JIG²]

jigsaw /ˈdʒɪɡsɔ/, *n.* **1.** a narrow saw mounted vertically in a frame, used for cutting curves, etc. **2.** Also, **jigsaw puzzle**. small, irregularly shaped pieces of wood or cardboard, which, when correctly fitted together, form a picture.

jihad /dʒəˈhæd/, *n.* a holy war fought by Muslims against unbelievers. Also, **jehad**. [Ar: effort, strife]

jillaroo /dʒɪləˈru/, *n.* a female worker on a sheep or cattle station. [modelled on JACKEROO]

jilt /dʒɪlt/, *v.t.* to cast off (a lover or sweetheart) after a close friendship or engagement. [orig. uncert.] –**jilter**, *n.*

Jinan /ˈdʒɪnæn/, *n.* a city in north-eastern China; the capital of Shandong province. Pop. 1 110 500 (1985 est.). Formerly, **Tsinan, Chinan**.

Jindyworobak /dʒɪndiˈwɒrəbæk/, *n.* a literary movement founded in Australia in 1938 by Rex Ingamells with the intention that Australian culture should be based on the Australian environment. [Aboriginal *Jindyworobak* to join or annex]

Jingdezhen /ˈdʒɪŋdədʒən/, *n.* a city in south-eastern China, in north-eastern Jiangxi province; porcelain industry established sixth century AD. Pop. 294 700 (1985 est.). Formerly, **Kingtechen, Chingtechen, Fou-liang, Fowliang**.

jingle /ˈdʒɪŋɡəl/, *v.,* **-gled, -gling**, *n.* ◇*v.i.* **1.** to make clinking or tinkling sounds, as coins, keys, etc. **2.** to move with such sounds. **3.** to sound in a manner like this, as verse or any pattern of words: *a jingling ballad.* ◇*v.t.* **4.** to cause to jingle. ◇*n.* **5.** a ringing or tinkling sound, as of small bells. **6.** a musical pattern of like sounds, as in rhyme; jingling verse. **7.** a simple, bright rhyme often set to music, used esp. for advertising. [ME; apparently imitative]

jingoism /ˈdʒɪŋɡoʊɪzəm/, *n.* strong, extreme love for one's country. [*jingo* (used in chauvinist song advocating belligerent British policy against Russia in 1878) + -ISM] –**jingoist**, *n., adj.* –**jingoistic**, *adj.*

jinx /dʒɪŋks/, *Colloq.* ◇*n.* **1.** someone or something supposed to bring bad luck. ◇*v.t.* **2.** to bring bad luck to someone; hex. [var. of *jynx*, from L, from Gk: bird (woodpecker) used in witchcraft, hence, a spell]

jitter /ˈdʒɪtə/, *Colloq.* ◇*n.* **1.** (*pl.*) nervousness; nerves (usu. prec. by *the*). **2.** *Elect.* rapid changes in a signal caused by an uneven voltage. ◇*v.i.* **3.** to behave nervously. [var. of *chitter* shiver]

jittery /ˈdʒɪtəri/, *adj.* nervous; jumpy.

jive /dʒaɪv/, *n., v.,* **jived, jiving**. ◇*n.* **1.** a lively dance performed to music with a strong beat. ◇*v.i.* **2.** to dance to rhythmic music. [orig. uncert.]

Jn, *Bible. Abbrev.* John.

jnr, *Abbrev.* junior.

Joan of Arc /ˌdʒoʊn əv ˈɑk/, *n.* ('Maid of Orléans'), 1412–31, French heroine who aroused the spirit of nationalism in France against the English and was burnt by them as a witch; made a saint in 1920. French, **Jeanne d'Arc**.

job¹ /dʒɒb/, *n., v.,* **jobbed, jobbing**, *adj.* ◇*n.* **1.** a piece of work done for money. **2.** the unit or material being worked upon. **3.** anything one has to do; task. **4.** a position of employment. **5.** *Colloq.* an affair; matter: *to make the best of a bad job.* **6.** *Colloq.* robbery, or any criminal deed. **7. a good job**, *Colloq.* a lucky state of affairs. **8. just the job**, *Colloq.* exactly what is needed. **9. the devil's own job**, a very difficult experience. ◇*v.i.* **10.** to work at jobs, or odd pieces of work. ◇*v.t.* **11.** to buy in large quantities and sell to dealers in small lots. **12.** to let out (work) in separate parts, as among different contractors or workmen. ◇*adj.* **13.** of or for a particular job. **14.** bought or sold together: *a job lot*. [orig. uncert.]

job² /dʒɒb/, *v.t., v.i.,* **jobbed, jobbing**. *Colloq.* to hit; punch: *Shut up or I'll job you.* [ME ? imitative. Compare JAB]

Job /dʒoʊb/, *n.* **1.** the innocent hero of an Old Testament book who showed great piety in the face of much undeserved suffering. **2.** the book itself. [Heb]

jobber /'dʒɒbə/, *n.* **1.** a wholesale merchant, esp. one selling to retailers. **2.** a pieceworker.

job lot, *n.* **1.** any large lot of goods for sale. **2.** a mixed quantity of goods.

Jocasta /dʒoʊ'kæstə/, *n. Gk Legend.* the wife of Laius (king of Thebes), and the mother, and later the wife, of Oedipus.

jockey /'dʒɒki/, *n., pl.* **-eys**, *v.*, **-eyed**, **-eying**. ◇*n.* **1.** someone who professionally rides horses in races. ◇*v.t.* **2.** to ride (a horse) as a jockey. **3.** to bring, put, etc., by skilful handling. **4.** to trick or cheat. ◇*v.* **5. jockey for**, to attempt to gain (a good position, a job, etc.). [diminutive of *Jock*, Scot var. of *Jack*]

jockstrap /'dʒɒkstræp/, *n. Colloq.* a support for the genitals; usu. of elastic cotton webbing, and worn by male athletes, dancers, etc. [obs. Brit colloq. *jock* penis]

jocose /dʒə'koʊs/, *adj.* characterised by joking; jesting; humorous. [L] **—jocoseness**, *n.* **—jocosity**, *n.*

jocular /'dʒɒkjələ/, *adj.* given to, characterised by, or suited to joking; waggish; facetious. [L] **—jocularity**, *n.*

jocund /'dʒɒkənd/, *adj.* cheerful; merry. [ME, from LL: pleasant] **—jocundity**, *n.*

Jodhpur /'dʒɒd'pʊə/, *n.* **1.** Also, **Marwar**. a former state in north-western India, now in Rajasthan. **2.** a town in India, in western central Rajasthan. Pop. 506 345 (1981).

jodhpurs /'dʒɒdpəz/, *n.pl.* riding pants reaching to the ankle, and fitting closely from the knee down. [named after JODHPUR]

joey /'dʒoʊi/, *n., pl.* **-eys**. **1.** any young animal, esp. a kangaroo. **2.** *NZ.* an opossum. **3.** a young child. [Aboriginal]

jog /dʒɒg/, *v.*, **jogged**, **jogging**, *n.* ◇*v.t.* **1.** to move or shake with a push or jerk. **2.** to give a slight push to, as to gain attention; nudge. **3.** to stir up (the memory) by a reminder. ◇*v.i.* **4.** to move with a jolt or jerk. **5.** to run at a jogtrot. **6.** to go in a steady fashion (fol. by *on* or *along*). ◇*n.* **7.** a shake; nudge. **8.** a slow, steady walk, trot, etc. **9.** the act of jogging. [b. *jot* jolt and *shog* shake (both now Brit d.)] **—jogger**, *n.*

Jogjakarta /dʒɒgdʒə'katə/, *n.* → **Yogyakarta**.

jogtrot /'dʒɒgtrɒt/, *n.* a slow, regular, bouncing pace or trot, as of a horse.

Johannesburg /dʒoʊ'hænəsbɜg/, *n.* a city in the Republic of South Africa, in southern Transvaal; goldmines. Pop. 1 609 408 (1986). Also, **Jo'burg**.

john¹ /dʒɒn/, *n. Colloq.* (*oft. cap.*) a policeman. [rhyming slang, *John* Hop, COP]

john² /dʒɒn/, *n. Colloq.* a toilet.

John /dʒɒn/, *n.* **1.** an apostle, brother of the apostle James. **2.** *New Testament.* the fourth Gospel. **3.** the name of 23 popes.

John Birch Society /bɜtʃ/, *n.* an extreme right-wing organisation founded in 1958 with the object of combating alleged communist activities in the US. [named after *John Birch*, Baptist missionary and US army intelligence officer, died 1945]

John Bull, *n.* **1.** the English people. **2.** the typical Englishman. [character created in 1712 by John Arbuthnot]

John Dory *n.* a thin, deep-bodied, high quality food fish of Australian waters. [*John* + DORY]

johnnycake /'dʒɒnikeɪk/, *n.* a small flat cake of wheatmeal or flour, cooked on both sides in a campfire. [orig. obscure. The first element may be from obs. *jonakin, jonikin* (apparently of Indian origin), a form of thin griddlecake]

John of Gaunt *n.* (*Duke of Lancaster*), 1340–99, English soldier and statesman; fourth son of Edward III and founder of the royal house of Lancaster (his son became Henry IV).

John Paul II, *n.* (*Karol Wojtyla*), born 1920 in Poland, elected pope in 1978, the first non-Italian pope since 1522.

Johnson /'dʒɒnsən/, *n.* **1. Amy**, 1904–41, English air pilot; several record flights including one to Australia (1930). **2. Andrew**, 1808–75, US Democrat politician; 17th president of the US 1865–69. **3. Lyndon Baines** ('*LBJ*'), 1908–73, US Democrat politician; 36th president of the US 1963–69.

Johnston /'dʒɒnstən/, *n.* **George Henry**, 1912–70, Australian journalist and novelist; author of *My Brother Jack* (1964).

John the Baptist, *n. New Testament.* forerunner of Jesus; baptised followers in the Jordan; beheaded by Herod. [See Matthew 3]

join /dʒɔɪn/, *v.t.* **1.** to bring or put together (sometimes fol. by *up*). **2.** to come into contact, or union with: *The stream joins the river.* **3.** to bring together in relation, action, etc.: *to join forces.* **4.** to become a member of (a society, party, army, etc.). **5.** to come into the company of: *I'll join you later.* **6.** to meet in (battle, etc.). **7.** *Geom.* to draw a curve or straight line between. ◇*v.i.* **8.** to come into or be in contact or connection. **9.** to become united, associated, or combined (fol. by *with*). **10.** to take part with others (oft. fol. by *in*). **11. join up**, to enlist in one of the armed forces. ◇*n.* **12.** a place or line of joining; a seam. **13.** *Geom.* an interval between two points on a line. [ME, from OF, from L: join, yoke]

joiner /'dʒɔɪnə/, *n.* **1.** someone who or something that joins. **2.** a craftsman who works in wood already cut and shaped, esp. one who fits skirting boards, built-in cupboards, etc. in a house.

joint /dʒɔɪnt/, *n.* **1.** the place in which two things, or parts of one thing, are joined. **2.** (in an animal body) **a.** movable place or part where two bones, etc. join. **b.** the hingelike or other arrangement of such a part. **3.** *Biol.* **a.** a part, esp. of an animal or plant body, connected with another part by an articulation, node, or the like. **b.** a part between two articulations, nodes, or the like. **4.** one of the pieces into which a carcass is divided by a butcher. **5.** *Geol.* a split or parting which sharply breaks the even physical appearance of a rock mass. **6.** *Colloq.* a house, office, etc., regarded as in some

joint sense one's own: *Come round to my joint*. **7.** a low-class bar, restaurant, etc.; dive. **8.** *Colloq.* a marijuana cigarette. **9. out of joint, a.** out of position; dislocated. **b.** out of order. ◇*adj.* **10.** shared by two or more: *a joint account*. **11.** joined as in relation, interest, or action: *joint owners*. **12.** held, done, etc., by two or more in common: *a joint effort*. **13.** *Parl.* of or relating to both houses. ◇*v.t.* **14.** to unite by a joint. **15.** to form or provide with a joint. **16.** to divide (meat, etc.) at a joint. [ME, from OF, from L]

jointly /ˈdʒɔɪntli/, *adv.* together; in common.

joint sitting, *n. Govt.* both the houses of parliament sitting together, to resolve a deadlock after a double dissolution.

joist /dʒɔɪst/, *n.* any of the parallel lengths of timber, steel, etc., used for supporting floors, ceilings, etc. [ME, from OF, from L: lie]

joke /dʒouk/, *n., v.,* **joked, joking.** ◇*n.* **1.** something said or done to excite laughter or amusement. **2.** an amusing or laughable fact or event. **3.** a thing or person laughed at rather than taken seriously. **4.** a matter for joking about: *The loss was no joke*. **5. the joke is on (someone)**, *Colloq.* (said of a person who has become the object of laughter usu. after a change of fortune). ◇*v.i.* **6.** to speak or act in a playful or merry way. [L: jest, sport]

joker /ˈdʒoukə/, *n.* **1.** someone who jokes. **2.** an extra playing card in a pack, used in some games, often counting as the highest card. **3.** *Colloq.* a person; bloke.

jollity /ˈdʒɒləti/, *n., pl.* **-ties. 1.** a happy state, or action. **2.** (*pl.*) happy occasions.

jolly /ˈdʒɒli/, *adj.,* **-lier, -liest,** *v.,* **-lied, -lying,** *adv.* **1.** in good spirits, gay: *In a moment he was as jolly as ever*. **2.** cheerfully agreeable or inviting. **3.** *Colloq.* amusing; pleasant. ◇*v.t.* **4.** *Colloq.* to talk or act agreeably to (someone) in order to keep them in good humor (oft. fol. by *along*); cajole; flatter. ◇*adv.* **5.** *Colloq.* very; extremely: *jolly well*. [ME, from OF] **—jolliness,** *n.*

Jolson /ˈdʒɒlsən/, *n.* **Al** (*Asa Yoelson*), 1886-1950, US singer, known esp. for his film roles; star of the first major sound picture *The Jazz Singer* (1927).

jolt /dʒoult/, *v.t.* **1.** to bump or shake as by a sudden rough push. ◇*v.i.* **2.** to move in an irregular or bumpy manner. ◇*n.* **3.** a jolting shock or movement. [b. Brit d. *jot* jolt and obs. *joll* knock about] **—jolty,** *adj.*

Jon, *Bible. Abbrev.* Jonah.

jonah /ˈdʒounə/, *n.* **1.** a person regarded as bringing bad luck. **2.** (*cap.*) *Bible.* a Hebrew prophet who was thrown overboard from his ship to calm a tempest; swallowed by a large fish and lived in its belly three days. **3.** *Bible.* a book of the Old Testament.

jonathan /ˈdʒɒnəθən/, *n.* a variety of red apple that ripens in early autumn.

Jones /dʒounz/, *n.* **1. Casey** /ˈkeɪsi/ (*John Luther Jones*), 1864?—1900, US train driver whose heroic death in a train crash inspired popular songs about him. **2. Inigo** /ˈɪnɪgou/, 1573-1652, English architect; established the Palladian style in England. See Andrea **Palladio.**

jonquil /ˈdʒɒŋkwɪl/, *n.* a type of narcissus with long, narrow leaves and sweet-smelling yellow or white flowers. [F, from Sp, from L: a rush]

Jordan /ˈdʒɔdn/, *n.* **1.** a kingdom in southwestern Asia, bordered by Israel, Syria, Iraq and Saudi Arabia; a British mandate from 1922 to independence in 1946; part of its territories occupied by Israel in the 1967 war. Pop. 2 853 000 (1987 est.); 97 740 km². *Language:* Arabic. *Currency;* dinar. *Cap.:* Amman. Official name, **Hashemite Kingdom of Jordan.** Formerly, **Trans-Jordan. 2.** a river flowing from southern Lebanon through the Sea of Galilee south then to the Dead Sea. About 320 km.

Jorgensen /ˈdʒɔgənsən/, *n.* **Jorgen,** 1780-1841, Australian mariner, convict, explorer and author, born in Denmark; helped establish Hobart Town and the settlement at Newcastle.

Josh, *Bible. Abbrev.* Joshua.

Joshua /ˈdʒɒʃuə/, *n. Bible.* **1.** the successor of Moses as leader of the Israelites. Exodus 17:9-14. **2.** a book of the Old Testament. [Heb]

joss house /ˈdʒɒs haus/, *n.* a Chinese temple.

jostle /ˈdʒɒsəl/, *v.,* **-tled, -tling,** *n.* ◇*v.t.* **1.** to strike or push roughly or rudely. **2.** to force by or as if by pushing: *He jostled me out of the way*. ◇*v.i.* **3.** to come together (fol. by *with*) or strike or push (fol. by *against*) as in passing or in a crowd. **4.** to struggle as with rough pushing, etc., for room, advantage etc. ◇*n.* **5.** a bump, shock, or push. Also, **justle.** [ME]

jot /dʒɒt/, *n., v.,* **jotted, jotting.** ◇*n.* **1.** the least part of something; a little bit: *I don't care a jot*. ◇*v.t.* **2.** to write down briefly (usu. fol. by *down*). [L: IOTA]

jotter /ˈdʒɒtə/, *n.* **1.** someone who jots things down. **2.** a small notebook.

jotting /ˈdʒɒtɪŋ/, *n.* **1.** the act of someone who jots. **2.** a brief note.

joule /dʒul/, *n.* the derived SI unit of work or energy, equal to the work done when a force of one newton moves its point of application one metre in the direction of the force, or the work done per second by a current of one ampere flowing through the resistance of one ohm. *Symbol:* J [named after JP *Joule,* 1818-89, British physicist]

Joule's law *n.* **1.** the principle that the internal energy of a given mass of gas is independent of its volume or pressure and depends only on its temperature. **2.** the principle that heat produced by an electric current is equal to the product of the resistance of the circuit through which it is passing, the square of the current, and the time for which it flows.

journal /ˈdʒɜnəl/, *n.* **1.** a daily record, as of experiences, or thoughts; diary. **2.** a record of the daily business of a public or governing body. **3.** a newspaper. **4.** any magazine, esp. one published by a learned society. **5.** *Bookkeeping.* **a.** a daybook. **b.** (in double entry) a book in which all transactions are entered (from the daybook). **6.** *Mech.* the part of a shaft or axle in actual contact with a bearing. [ME, from OF, from LL: DIURNAL]

journalese /dʒɜːnəˈliːz/, *n.* a hackneyed style of newspaper writing.

journalism /ˈdʒɜːnəlɪzəm/, *n.* **1.** the work of writing for, editing, and running newspapers and magazines. **2.** newspapers collectively. —**journalist**, *n.* —**journalistic**, *adj.*

journey /ˈdʒɜːni/, *n., pl.* **-neys**, *v.,* **-neyed, -neying.** ◇*n.* **1.** the course of travel from one place to another, esp. by land. **2.** the distance travelled, or suitable for travelling, in a given time: *a day's journey.* ◇*v.i.* **3.** to travel. [ME, from OF, from L: of the day, daily]

journeyman /ˈdʒɜːnimən/, *n., pl.* **-men.** someone who has served their apprenticeship at a trade or handicraft, and who works at it for another. [obs. *journey* a day's work + MAN]

joust /dʒaʊst/, *n.* **1.** a fight between two armored knights on horseback using lances. ◇*v.i.* **2.** to fight in a joust. [ME, from OF, from L: near] —**jouster**, *n.*

Jove /dʒəʊv/, *n.* **1.** *Rom Myth.* the greatest of the gods; Jupiter. ◇*interj.* **2. by Jove,** (a cry of surprise, an exclamation, etc.)

jovial /ˈdʒəʊviəl/, *adj.* characterised by a joyous humor or a spirit of good fellowship. [L: of Jupiter (in astrology the planet is regarded as exerting a happy influence)] —**joviality**, *n.*

jowl[1] /dʒaʊl/, *n.* **1.** a jaw, esp. the underjaw. **2.** the cheek. [OE *ceafl* jaw]

jowl[2] /dʒaʊl/, *n.* a fold of flesh hanging from the jaw or throat. See **dewlap, wattle** (def. 3). [ME, apparently from OE *ceole* throat]

joy /dʒɔɪ/, *n.* **1.** the emotion of great pleasure arising from present or expected good. **2.** a source or cause of gladness or delight. **3.** outward rejoicing. **4. not to have any joy,** to be unsuccessful (oft. fol. by *of*). ◇*v.i.* **5.** to feel joy; be glad. [ME, from OF, from L pl.: joy, gladness] —**joyful, joyous**, *adj.*

Joyce /dʒɔɪs/, *n.* **1. James (Augustine Aloysius)**, 1882–1941, Irish novelist, short-story writer and poet; developed the techniques of stream of consciousness and the coining of word blends; author of *Ulysses* (1922) and *Finnegans Wake* (1939). **2. William** ('*Lord Haw-Haw*'), 1906–46, British traitor, executed for his Nazi propaganda radio broadcasts.

Joye /dʒɔɪ/, *n. Col* (**Colin Frederick Jacobsen**), born 1938, Australian rock singer and musician, lead singer of the Joy Boys.

joy-ride /ˈdʒɔɪraɪd/, *n. Colloq.* a pleasure ride, as in a motor car, esp. when the car is driven wildly or stolen. —**joy-rider**, *n.* —**joy-riding**, *n., adj.*

joystick /ˈdʒɔɪstɪk/, *n.* **1.** the control stick of an aeroplane. **2.** a device with a lever resembling the joystick of an aeroplane, used to change the position of the cursor, etc., on a computer screen. [from jocular comparison with a penis]

JP /dʒeɪ ˈpiː/, *n.* → **Justice of the Peace.** [abbrev.]

Jr, *Abbrev.* Junior. Also, **jr.**

Juan Carlos I /hwan ˈkalɒs/, *n.* born 1938, king of Spain since 1975; first king of the restored monarchy after Franco's death.

jube /dʒuːb/, *n.* a fruit-flavored, chewy lolly made with gelatine. Also, **jujube.**

jubilant /ˈdʒuːbələnt/, *adj.* **1.** rejoicing; exultant. **2.** expressing or exciting joy. [L] —**jubilance, jubilancy,** *n.*

jubilate /ˈdʒuːbəleɪt/, *v.i.,* **-lated, -lating. 1.** to show or feel great joy; rejoice. **2.** to celebrate a jubilee or joyful occasion. [L *jūbilātus,* pp. of *jūbilāre* shout for joy] —**jubilatory,** *adj.* —**jubilation,** *n.*

jubilee /ˈdʒuːbəli/, *n.* **1.** a celebration of any of certain anniversaries, as the 25th (**silver jubilee**), 50th (**golden jubilee**), or 60th or 75th (**diamond jubilee**). **2.** the completion of the 50th year of any continuous course or period. **3.** any season or occasion of rejoicing. [ME, from F, from LL, from Gk, from Heb: ram, ram's horn (used as a trumpet); see Leviticus 25: 9)]

Jud, *Bible. Abbrev.* Judges.

Judaism /ˈdʒuːdeɪˌɪzəm/, *n.* the religion of the Jews, basing its authority on the writings of the Old Testament and the teaching of the rabbis.

judas /ˈdʒuːdəs/, *n.* **1.** someone disloyal enough to act against a friend; traitor. **2.** (*cap.*) *Bible.* Judas Iscariot, the disciple who betrayed Jesus. [See Mark 3:19]

Judea /dʒuːˈdiːə/, *n.* the southern part of Palestine under the Romans. Also, **Judaea.** —**Judean, Judaean,** *adj., n.*

Judg, *Bible. Abbrev.* Judges.

judge /dʒʌdʒ/, *n., v.,* **judged, judging.** ◇*n.* **1.** a public officer having the power to hear and decide cases in a court of law. **2.** a person appointed to decide in any competition or contest. **3.** someone having the knowledge to pass judgment: *a judge of horses.* ◇*v.t.* **4.** to try (a person or a case) as a judge does. **5.** to form a judgment or opinion of or upon. **6.** to decide lawfully or authoritatively. ◇*v.i.* **7.** to act as a judge. **8.** to form an opinion. [ME, from OF, from L]

Judges /ˈdʒʌdʒəz/, *n.* a book in the Old Testament.

judgment *or* **judgement** /ˈdʒʌdʒmənt/, *n.* **1.** the act of judging. **2.** *Law.* a decision about a case in court. **3.** the ability to judge wisely; discretion. **4.** the forming of an opinion, idea or conclusion. **5.** the opinion formed. **6.** a misfortune seen as coming from God, as for sin. **7.** (*oft. cap.*) the final trial of all mankind, both the living and the dead, at the end of the world (oft., **Last Judgment**).

judicature /ˈdʒuːdəkətʃə/, *n.* **1.** the carrying out of justice, as by judges or courts. **2.**

the office, position, or authority of a judge. **3.** the area of power of a judge or court. **4.** a body of judges. [ML: judged]

judicial /dʒu'dɪʃəl/, *adj.* **1.** relating to judgment in courts of justice or to the carrying out of justice: *a judicial inquiry*. **2.** relating to courts of law or to judges: *judicial functions*. **3.** likely to make or give judgments; critical. **4.** relating to judgment in a fight or contest. [ME, from L: of a court of justice]

judiciary /dʒu'dɪʃəri/, *adj., n., pl.* **-aries.** ◇*adj.* **1.** relating to judgment in courts of justice; judicial. ◇*n.* **2.** a system of courts of justice in a country. **3.** judges collectively.

judicious /dʒu'dɪʃəs/, *adj.* discreet; prudent; well-advised: *a judicious choice*. [F, from L: judgment]

judo /'dʒudoʊ/, *n. Sport.* a style of self-defence, a form of jujitsu, that emphasises the sporting element. [Jap: lit., soft way]

jug /dʒʌg/, *n., v.,* **jugged, jugging.** ◇*n.* **1.** a vessel in various forms for holding liquids, commonly having a handle, often a lip, and sometimes a lid. **2.** *Colloq.* prison. **3.** music performed on jugs, washboards, etc. ◇*v.t.* **4.** to stew or boil (meat) in a jug or jar. **5.** *Colloq.* to imprison. [? special use of *Jug*, var. of *Joan* or *Joanna*]

juggernaut /'dʒʌgənɔt/, *n.* **1.** anything in which a person blindly places their faith, or to which they are cruelly sacrificed. **2.** any large, destructive force, esp. a vehicle. [from an idol of India, annually drawn on an enormous vehicle under whose wheels devotees are said to have thrown themselves to be crushed; Hind, from Skt: lord of the world]

juggle /'dʒʌgəl/, *v.,* **-gled, -gling,** *n.* ◇*v.t.* **1.** to keep (several objects, as balls, etc.) in continuous movement in the air at the same time by tossing and catching. **2.** to alter by trickery: *to juggle accounts*. ◇*v.i.* **3.** to perform acts of skill, such as tossing up and keeping in continuous movement a number of balls, etc. **4.** to use trickery. ◇*n.* **5.** the act of juggling; a trick. [ME, from OF, from L: jest] —**juggler,** *n.* —**jugglery,** *n.*

jugular /'dʒʌgjulə/, *adj.* **1.** *Anat.* **a.** of or relating to the throat or neck. **b.** of or relating to any of certain large veins of the neck. **2.** (of a fish) having the pelvic fins at the throat, before the pectoral fins. [NL, from L: collarbone, throat]

juice /dʒus/, *n.* **1.** the liquid part of a plant or animal substance. **2.** any natural fluid coming from an animal body. **3.** liquid, as from a fruit. **4.** strength; essence. **5.** *Colloq.* **a.** electric power. **b.** petrol, oil, etc., used to run an engine. **6.** *Colloq.* any alcoholic drink. [ME, from OF, from L: broth]

juicy /'dʒusi/, *adj.,* **-cier, -ciest. 1.** full of juice; succulent. **2.** interesting; colorful; spicy. —**juiciness,** *n.*

jujitsu /dʒu'dʒɪtsu/, *n. Sport.* a Japanese method of defending oneself without weapons, using the strength and weight of the opponent to overcome him or her. Also, **jiujitsu, jiujutsu, jujutsu.** [Jap: soft (or pliant) art]

jukebox /'dʒukbɒks/, *n.* a coin-operated record-player permitting choice of the record to be played.

Julian /'dʒuliən/, *adj.* of or relating to Julius Caesar.

Julian calendar, *n.* the calendar established by Julius Caesar in 46 BC which fixed the length of the year at 365 days, with 366 days in every fourth year (leap year), and months similar to today's. See **Gregorian calendar**.

Julius /'dʒuliəs/, *n.* **Sir George Alfred,** 1873–1946, Australian engineer, born in England; inventor of the automatic totaliser, in 1907, used on racecourses throughout the world.

Julius Caesar *n.* → **Caesar** (def. 1).

July /dʒə'laɪ/, *n., pl.* **-lies.** the seventh month of the year, containing 31 days. [OE *Julius*, from L; named after *Julius* CAESAR, who was born in this month]

jumble /'dʒʌmbəl/, *v.,* **-bled, -bling,** *n.* ◇*v.t.* **1.** to mix in a confused mass. **2.** to confuse mentally. ◇*v.i.* **3.** to be mixed up. ◇*n.* **4.** confused mixture; a medley. **5.** a state of confusion or disorder. [? b. JOIN and TUMBLE] —**jumbler,** *n.*

jumbo /'dʒʌmboʊ/, *n., pl.* **-bos,** *adj. Colloq.* ◇*n.* **1.** an elephant. **2.** any very large intercontinental jet plane, esp. the Boeing 747. **3.** anything bigger than usual. ◇*adj.* **4.** very large: *a jumbo sale*. [named after *Jumbo*, an elephant at the London Zoo, subsequently sold to Phineas T Barnum]

jumbuck /'dʒʌmbʌk/, *n. Colloq.* a sheep. [Aboriginal corruption of *jump up*]

jump /dʒʌmp/, *v.i.* **1.** to spring clear of the ground or other support by a sudden muscular effort; leap. **2.** to move quickly: *She jumped into a taxi*. **3.** to rise suddenly: *He jumped from his chair*. **4.** to move suddenly, as from surprise or shock; start: *The loud noise made him jump*. **5.** to rise suddenly in amount, price, etc. **6.** to pass too quickly: *to jump to a conclusion*. **7.** to move or change suddenly, or aimlessly: *She jumped from one topic of conversation to another*. **8.** (of a typewriter) to leave out letters, etc., because of a fault. **9.** *Colloq.* (of a tooth, etc.) to hurt; throb. ◇*v.t.* **10.** to leap or spring over. **11.** to cause to jump or leap. **12.** to skip or pass over; bypass. **13.** to leave secretly from or avoid. **14.** to seize (a mining claim, etc.) on the ground of some error in the holder's title. **15.** to advance too far on another's rights. **16.** (of a train) to spring off or leave (the track). ◇*v.* **17.** Some special uses are:

jump at, accept eagerly: *He jumped at the chance of a new job*.

jump on/upon, to scold; reprimand.

jump the gun, *Colloq.* to obtain an unfair advantage.

jump the queue, to obtain something out of one's proper turn.

jump to it, *Colloq.* to hurry.

◇*n.* **18.** a leap. **19.** a space or obstacle cleared in a leap. **20.** a descent by parachute from an aircraft. **21.** a sudden rise in amount, price, etc. **22.** a sudden (usu. unexpected) change

jump

from one point or thing to another. **23.** *Sport.* any of several athletic games which include a leap or jump. **24.** a sudden start, as from nervous excitement. **25. one jump ahead,** in a position of advantage. [apparently imitative]

jumper[1] /'dʒʌmpə/, *n.* **1.** someone or something that jumps. **2.** *Elect.* Also, **jumper lead.** a short length of wire used to make a (temporary) connection, esp. between a flat car battery and a charged one. [JUMP, v. + -ER[1]]

jumper[2] /'dʒʌmpə/, *n.* **1.** an outer garment, usu. of wool, for the upper part of the body; pullover, sweater. **2.** a loose, outer jacket, worn esp. by sailors. [F: jacket]

jump-start /'dʒʌmp-stat/, *v.t.* **1.** → **clutch-start** (def. 1). **2.** to start (a car etc.) by connecting its battery by means of jumper leads to the battery of another car.

jumpy /'dʒʌmpi/, *adj.*, **jumpier, jumpiest. 1.** characterised by or inclined to sudden, involuntary starts, esp. from nervousness, fear, etc. **2.** moving in jumps or starts. **— jumpiness,** *n.*

Jun, *Abbrev.* **1.** June. **2.** junior.

junction /'dʒʌŋkʃən/, *n.* **1.** the act of joining; combination. **2.** the state of being joined; union. **3.** a place where roads or railway lines meet or cross. **4.** *Elect.* (in a transistor, etc.) a point or surface where two materials having different electrical properties connect. **5.** a cable linking two telephone exchanges. [L: a joining]

juncture /'dʒʌŋktʃə/, *n.* **1.** a point of time, esp. one of importance. **2.** a very important state of affairs; a crisis. **3.** the line or point at which two bodies are joined. **4.** the act or state of being joined; junction. **5.** something by which two things are joined. [ME, from L: joining, joint]

June /dʒun/, *n.* the sixth month of the year, containing thirty days. [ME; OE *Iuni,* from L]

Jung /juŋ/, *n.* **Carl Gustav** /kal 'gustaf/, 1875–1961, Swiss psychiatrist and psychologist; developed concepts of the psychological types of extroversion and introversion. **— Jungian,** *adj., n.*

jungle /'dʒʌŋgəl/, *n.* **1.** wild land covered with dense plant growth. **2.** a tropical rainforest with very thick undergrowth. **3.** anything confusing, or in disorder. **4.** any place or situation characterised by a struggle for existence, competition, etc. [Hind, from Skt: dry, desert]

junior /'dʒunjə/, *adj.* **1.** younger, often shortened to *Jr* or *Jun* after a family name. **2.** of something made for young people: *a junior textbook.* **3.** of lower rank or standing. ◇*n.* **4.** a person who is younger than another. **5.** any child, esp. a male. **6.** someone who is of more recent entrance into, or of lower standing in, an office, class, etc. **7.** *Law.* a barrister who has not been appointed a Queen's Counsel. [L: young]

juniper /'dʒunəpə/, *n.* an evergreen shrub or tree whose cones form purple berries used in making gin and in medicine. [ME, from L. See GIN[1]]

jury

junk[1] /dʒʌŋk/, *n.* **1.** any old or unwanted material, as metal, paper, etc. **2.** *Colloq.* anything that is regarded as worthless; trash. **3.** *Colloq.* any narcotic drug. ◇*v.t.* **4.** to throw aside as junk. [orig. uncert.]

junk[2] /dʒʌŋk/, *n.* a flat-bottomed ship used in Chinese and other waters. [Pg *junco,* from Malay *jong, ajong,* apparently from Javanese *jong*]

junket /'dʒʌŋkət/, *n.* **1.** a sweet custard-like food; curds and whey. **2.** a feast; picnic. **3.** a trip, as by an official body or an individual politician, paid for by the public. ◇*v.i.* **4.** to feast; go on a pleasure trip. **5.** to go on a junket (def. 3). [ME, from L]

junkie /'dʒʌŋki/, *n. Colloq.* a drug addict. Also, **junky.**

Juno /'dʒunou/, *n. Rom Myth.* a goddess, the wife of Jupiter, presiding over marriage and women; Greek counterpart, Hera.

junta /'dʒʌntə/, *n.* a small ruling group in a country, either elected or self-chosen, esp. one which has come to power after a revolution. [Sp, from L: joined]

Jupiter /'dʒupətə/, *n.* **1.** *Rom Myth.* the god of the heavens; his presence was believed to be indicated by atmospheric phenomena, such as thunder; Jove; Greek counterpart, Zeus. **2.** the largest planet, fifth in order from the sun. It has 12 satellites. [L, var. of *Jūppiter,* contraction of *Jovis pater* father Jove]

Jurassic /dʒu'ræsɪk/, *adj. Geol.* **1.** relating to a period of the Mesozoic era, following the Triassic and coming before the Cretaceous. ◇*n.* **2.** the Jurassic period. [F]

juridical /dʒu'rɪdɪkəl/, *adj.* **1.** of or relating to the carrying out of justice. **2.** legal. Also, **juridic.** [L: relating to justice]

jurisdiction /dʒurəs'dɪkʃən/, *n.* **1.** the right or power to bring justice into operation, by hearing and deciding disputes. **2.** power; authority. **3.** the range or area of legal or other authority. [ME, from L: administration of the law, authority] **— jurisdictional,** *adj.*

jurisprudence /dʒurəs'prudns/, *n.* **1.** the science or philosophy of law. **2.** a body or system of laws. [L: the science of the law] **— jurisprudential,** *adj.*

jurist /'dʒurəst, 'dʒuə-/, *n.* an expert in the law. [ML, from L: right, law] **— juristic,** *adj.*

juror /'dʒuərə, 'dʒurə/, *n.* **1.** a member of any jury. **2.** one of the group from which a jury is chosen. [ME, from AF, from L: swearer]

jury[1] /'dʒuəri, 'dʒuri/, *n., pl.* **-ries. 1.** a group of people chosen from the general public and sworn to decide on the facts in a trial on the basis of the evidence presented in court. **2.** a body of people chosen to judge prizes, etc., as in a competition. [ME, from AF, from L: swear]

jury[2] /'dʒuəri, 'dʒuri/, *adj. Naut.* temporary; makeshift. [first found in *jury mast,* probably from OF, from L: help]

jussive /'dʒʌsɪv/, *adj. Gram.* expressing a mild command. The jussive mood is used in the Semitic languages. [L: commanded]

just /dʒʌst/, *adj.* **1.** fair, honest: *to be just in one's business.* **2.** in accordance with true principles; even-handed: *a just award.* **3.** rightful; lawful: *a just claim.* **4.** true; correct: *a just answer.* **5.** given rightly, or deserved, as a punishment, reward, etc. **6.** in accordance with standards; proper, or right. ◇*adv.* **7.** but a moment before: *They have just gone.* **8.** exactly; precisely: *That is just the point.* **9.** by a small amount; barely: *It just missed the mark.* **10.** only; merely: *He is just an ordinary man.* **11.** *Colloq.* actually; truly: *The weather is just glorious.* [ME, from L: righteous]

justice /'dʒʌstəs/, *n.* **1.** the quality of being just; righteousness. **2.** rightfulness or lawfulness, as of a claim or title. **3.** a moral principle determining just conduct. **4.** just conduct, dealing, or treatment. **5.** the giving of what is deserved, as by punishment or reward. **6.** the keeping or carrying out of law, as by legal or other means: *a court of justice.* **7.** judgment of persons or causes by legal process: *to carry out justice in a community.* **8.** a judge or magistrate. **9.** (*cap.*) the title of the judges in the state Supreme courts and in the federal courts. **10. do justice to, a.** to give what is due to (a person or thing, etc.). **b.** to show (oneself) in favorable terms. **c.** to show full approval of (something) by action. [ME, from OF, from L]

justice of the peace, *n.* a person legally appointed as a justice within a certain district to keep the peace and to carry out certain duties. Also, **JP**

justifiable /'dʒʌstəfaɪəbəl/, *adj.* able to be shown to be just or right; defensible.
—**justifiability, justifiableness**, *n.*

justify /'dʒʌstəfaɪ/, *v.t.*, **-fied, -fying. 1.** to show (an act, claim, etc.) to be just or right. **2.** to defend as blameless, just, or right. **3.** to declare guiltless; absolve; acquit. **4.** to adjust the spacing between words to make lines of print fit exactly a certain line length or space. [ME, from OF, from LL: act justly towards]
—**justification**, *n.*

Justinian I /dʒʌs'tɪniən/, *n.* ('the Great', *Flavius Anicius Justinianus*) AD 483–565, Byzantine emperor AD 527–565, whose leading jurists formulated a code of laws called the **Justinian Code**.

jut /dʒʌt/, *v.*, **jutted, jutting.** *n.* ◇*v.i.* **1.** to reach beyond the main body or line; project; protrude (oft. fol. by *out*). ◇*n.* **2.** something that juts out. [var. of JET[1], v.]

jute /dʒut/, *n.* **1.** a strong fibre used for making fabrics, cord, etc. **2.** a coarse cloth woven from jute fibres; gunny. [Bengali, from Skt: braid of hair]

Jute /dʒut/, *n.* a member of a continental Germanic tribe which invaded Britain in the fifth century and settled in Kent. [ML *Iutī*]

Jutland /'dʒʌtlənd/, *n.* a peninsula comprising the continental portion of Denmark; 29 554 km². Danish, **Jylland**.

juvenile /'dʒuvənaɪl/, *adj.* **1.** of, relating to, or suitable for young people: *juvenile behavior; juvenile books; a juvenile court.* **2.** young. **3.** like the behavior or thoughts of a young person; frivolous. ◇*n.* **4.** a young person; a youth. [L: of youth] —**juvenileness**, *n.*

juxta-, a word part meaning 'near', 'close to', 'beside'. [combining form representing L *juxtā*, prep. and adv.]

juxtapose /dʒʌkstə'pouz, 'dʒʌkstəpouz/, *v.t.*, **-posed, -posing.** to place close together or side by side. —**juxtaposition**, *n.*

Kk

K, k, *n.*, *pl.* **K's** or **Ks**, **k's** or **ks**. the 11th letter of the English alphabet.

k, *Symbol.* **1.** kilo-. **2.** Boltzmann's constant.

K, *Symbol.* **1.** *Chem.* potassium. [L *kalium*] **2.** *Phys.* kelvin. **3.** equilibrium constant. ◇*Abbrev.* **4.** *Music.* Köchel (used in numbering works of Mozart. **5.** *Bible.* Kings. **6.** *Computers.* 2^{10} words, bytes or bits.

kA, *Symbol.* kiloamperes.

Ka, *Chem.* the equilibrium constant of an acid and water mixture containing ions and un-ionised molecules.

Kaaba /'kɑbə/, *n.* a small cube-shaped building in the Great Mosque at Mecca, containing a sacred stone; the most sacred shrine of the Muslims. Also, **Caaba**.

Kabul /kə'bʊl, 'kabul/, *n.* the capital of Afghanistan, in the north-eastern part. Pop. 1 179 341 (1984 est.).

kadaicha man /kə'daɪtʃə mæn/, *n.* (among tribal Aborigines) the man given the power to avenge a wrong felt by a tribal member, by pointing the bone at the wrongdoer. [Aboriginal] Also, **kadaitja man**, **kurdaitcha man**.

kadaicha shoes, *n.pl.* (in certain central Australian Aboriginal tribes) shoes made of human hair, string and emu feathers, matted with human blood, worn by the kadaicha man so that his footsteps may not be traced. Also, **kadaitja shoes**, **kurdaitcha shoes**.

Kaffir /'kæfə/, *n.* (*oft. offensive*) a South African negro. [Ar: unbeliever]

Kafka /'kæfkə/, *n.* **Franz** /frants/, 1883–1924, Jewish Czech novelist and short-story writer, writing in German; wrote the novels *The Trial* (1925) and *The Castle* (1926).

kainite /'kaɪnaɪt, 'keɪ-/, *n.* a mineral double salt of magnesium sulfate and potassium chloride, $MgSO_4·KCl·3H_2O$; a source of potassium salts.

Kaiser /'kaɪzə/, *n.* **1.** a German emperor. **2.** an Austrian emperor. **3.** *Hist.* a ruler of the Holy Roman Empire. [G, from Scand, from L *Caesar*]

kaleidoscope /kə'laɪdəskoup/, *n.* a tube with pieces of colored glass or paper in one end, showing different mirrored symmetrical patterns when turned around. [Gk]

Kalgoorlie /kæl'guəli/, *n.* a town in southern central WA; gold and nickel mining. Pop. (with Boulder) 22 232 (1986).

kalsomine /'kælsəmaɪn/, *n.* a white or tinted wash (paint) for walls, ceilings, etc.

Kameraigal /'kæmәraɪgəl/, *n.* an Australian Aboriginal language formerly spoken in the Sydney region. Also, **Cammeraygal**.

Kanpur

Kamikaze /kæmə'kazi/, *n.* **1.** a member of a Japanese air force corps in World War II whose mission was to crash their aircraft, loaded with explosives, into an enemy target. ◇*adj.* **2.** of or relating to a Kamikaze. **3.** (*l.c.*) *Colloq.* (*joc.*) dangerous; suicidal: *his Kamikaze driving*. [Jap: divine wind]

Kamilaroi /'kæmɪlərɔɪ/, *n.* an Australian Aboriginal language of the central north-west of NSW.

kampong /'kæmpɒŋ, kæm'pɒŋ/, *n.* a village in Malaysia or Indonesia. [Malay]

Kampuchea /kæmpə'tʃɪə/, *n.* a republic in south-east Asia, on the Gulf of Thailand; part of French Indochina before independence in 1953; a republic since 1970. Pop. 7 688 000 (1987 est.); 181 035 km². *Language:* Khmer, also French. *Currency:* riel. *Cap.:* Phnom-Penh. Also, **Cambodia**.

Kanak /kə'næk, kə'nak/, *n.* a member of the Melanesian population of New Caledonia.

kanaka /kə'nækə/, *n.* **1.** a Pacific islander, formerly one kidnapped and brought to Australia as a laborer. **2.** (*cap.*) a native Hawaiian. [Hawaiian: lit., man]

Kandinski /kæn'dɪnski/, *n.* **Vasili** /va'sili/, 1866–1944, Russian painter and author; widely considered the originator of abstract art.

kangaroo /kæŋgə'ru/, *n.* **1.** a large herbivorous (plant-eating) marsupial (pouched mammal) of Australia, with powerful hind legs for leaping, a sturdy tail for support and balance, a small head, and very short forelimbs. The recognised types of great kangaroo are: **a.** the **great grey** or **forester**, of eastern Australia and Tas, up to about 2 m tall, with woolly fur. **b.** the **western grey** or **western forester**, of west and southern Australia, up to about 1.8 m tall. **c.** the **wallaroo** or **euro**, of rocky areas of mainland Australia, up to about 1.2 m tall, stocky, with coarse hair. **d.** the **antelope kangaroo**, of northern Qld to WA, up to about 1.7 m tall. **e.** the **red** or **plains kangaroo**, widespread in inland Australia, up to about 2 m tall, with a slender body. **2.** See **tree-kangaroo**. **3.** See **rat-kangaroo**. [Aboriginal]

kangaroo bar, *n.* a heavy metal bar in front of the radiator of a motor vehicle which protects the vehicle if it strikes kangaroos or stock. Also, **bull bar**.

kangaroo court, *n. Colloq.* a court set up without proper authority and held in mock or informal manner, by prisoners in a gaol, or by trade unionists in judging workers who do not follow union decisions.

kangaroo grass, *n.* a tall grass widespread in forest and grassland in Australia and providing useful animal feed.

Kangaroo Island, *n.* a large island off the coast of SA, about 145 km long and 55 km wide; timber production.

kangaroo-paw /kæŋgə'ru-pɔ/, *n.* a western Australian plant with flowers looking like the paw of a kangaroo, esp. the red and green kangaroo-paw, the floral emblem of WA.

Kanpur /kan'pʊə/, *n.* a city in northern India, on the Ganges. Pop. 1 481 789 (city),

1 639 064 (urban agglomeration) (1981). Also, **Cawnpore.**

Kansas /'kænzəs/, n. a state in the central US. Pop. 2 461 000 (1986 est.); 213 095 km². *Cap.*: Topeka. *Abbrev.*: Kans, Kan **—Kansan,** *n., adj.*

Kant /kænt/, n. **Immanuel** /i'mænjuəl/, 1724–1804, German idealist philosopher. **—Kantian,** *adj., n.*

Kantianism /'kæntiənɪzəm/, n. *Philos.* the doctrine of Immanuel Kant that every physical appearance is only a sensation induced in the observer's brain, and has no relevance to the real nature of the thing.

kaolin /'keɪəlɪn/, n. **1.** a rock composed mostly of clay minerals of the kaolinite group. **2.** a fine white clay used in the manufacture of porcelain and used medically as an absorbent; china clay. [F, from Chinese *Kao-ling* high hill, name of a mountain in China which yielded the first kaolin sent to Europe]

kapai /'kæpaɪ/, *interj.* NZ *Colloq.* **1.** (an exclamation of pleasure, approval, etc.) ◊*adj.* **2.** good; agreeable. [Maori]

Kapital /kapi'tal/, n. **das** /das/, a book (1867) by Karl Marx, which analyses political economy as the division of classes; the theoretical basis of modern communism.

kapok /'keɪpɒk/, n. a cotton-like substance from the seeds of trees in south-east Asia, Africa and tropical America, used for stuffing pillows, etc. [Malay]

kaput /kæ'pʊt, kə-/, *adj. Colloq.* ruined or not working. [G]

Karachi /kə'rɑtʃi/, n. a seaport in and the former capital of Pakistan, in the southern part, near the Indus delta. Pop. 5 208 132 (1981).

karate /kə'rɑti/, n. a method of defensive fighting in which hands, elbows, feet, and knees are the only weapons used. See **judo**. [Jap: lit., empty hand]

Karitane /'kærətani/, *adj.* of or relating to a nurse or hospital for the care of mothers and newborn children. [from *Karitane*, a town in NZ near the home of Sir Frederic Truby King, founder of the Plunket Society which advocated certain methods of child care and child welfare.

Karloff /'kɑlɒf/, n. **Boris** (*William Pratt*), 1887–1969, English film actor, best known for his roles in horror films, esp. as the monster in *Frankenstein* (1931).

karma /'kɑmə/, n. **1.** *Hinduism, Buddhism, etc.* the justice by which a person has a status in life according to his actions in his last life. **2.** fate; destiny. [Skt: deed, action]

Karnak /'kɑnæk/, n. a village in Upper Egypt, on the Nile; the northern part of the ruins of ancient Thebes.

Karpov /'kɑpɒf/, n. **Anatoly** /ana'tɔlija/, born 1931, world champion Russian chess player until his defeat in 1985.

karrabul /'kærəbʊl/, n. See **nail-tailed wallaby.**

Karratha /kə'rɑθə/, n. a town in western WA, west of Roebourne; centre for mining projects carried out in the Pilbara region. Pop. 9533 (1986).

karri /'kæri/, *n., pl.* **-ris.** a fast growing western Australian gum tree, valuable for its hard, durable timber. [Aboriginal]

karst /kɑst/, n. *Geog.* a barren region of limestone or dolomite and marked by underground drainage systems, sinkholes, gorges, etc. [named after the *Karst* region in NW Yugoslavia]

karyo-, a word part meaning 'nucleus of a cell'. [Gk: nut, kernel]

karyokinesis /ˌkæriəʊkə'nisəs, -kaɪ-/, n. → **mitosis.** [KARYO- + Gk: *kínēsis* movement] **—karyokinetic,** *adj.*

karyoplasm /'kæriəʊplæzəm/, n. *Biol.* the substance of the nucleus of a cell. **—karyoplasmic,** *adj.*

karyotin /kæri'əʊtən/, n. *Biol.* → **chromatin.**

karyotype /'kæriətaɪp/, n. the appearance (size, shape, and number) of the chromosomes in a cell.

kashmir /kæʃ'mɪə/, n. → **cashmere.**

Kashmir /'kæʃmɪə/, n. a mountainous area in south-western Asia, in 1972 partitioned as **Jammu and Kashmir,** under Indian control, 139 000 km², and **Azad Kashmir,** under the control of Pakistan, 83 800 km². A northern area has been controlled by China since 1962. *Cap.*: Srinagar (summer), Jammu (winter) (Jammu and Kashmir); Muzaffarabad (Azad Kashmir). Also **Cashmere.**

Kasparov /'kæspərɒf/, n. **Garry**, born 1963, Russian chess player; 1985 defeated Karpov to become the youngest ever world champion.

kata-, variant of **cata-.** Also, **kat-, kath-.**

katabatic /ˌkætə'bætɪk/, *adj.* (of winds and air currents) blowing downhill, as during the night when air in the upper slopes is cooled by radiation and so becomes more dense.

Kata Tjuta /kɑtə'dʒʊtə/, n. a group of monoliths in the south-western NT, near Uluru. Highest point, 1069 m. Also, **Katatjuta.** Formerly, **the Olgas.** [Aborig.]

Katherine /'kæθərən/, n. a town in northern central NT, on the Katherine River. Pop. 5691 (1986).

Katmandu /kætmæn'du/, n. the capital of Nepal, in the southern part. Pop. 235 160 (1981).

Katoomba /kə'tumbə/, n. a tourist resort in the Blue Mountains; an administrative and commercial centre. Pop. (with Wentworth Falls) 15 627 (1986).

Kaunda /kɑ'ʊndə/, n. **Kenneth David**, born 1924, Zambian statesman; leader of independence movement and first president of Zambia 1964–91.

kauri /'kaʊri/, *n., pl.* **-ris.** a tall conebearing tree of NZ, yielding valuable timber and a resin. Also, **kauri pine.** [Maori]

Kavel /'kavəl/, n. **August Ludwig Christian**, 1798–1860, Australian Lutheran minister,

Kavel born in Germany; emigrated with his congregation and founded the first German settlements in Australia.

Kawasaki /kawəˈsaki/, n. a seaport in central Japan, on Honshu island, near Tokyo. 1 106 148 (1986 est.).

kayak /ˈkaɪæk/, n. **1.** a light Eskimo hunting canoe, made watertight by a cover round the waist of the person sitting in it. **2.** any light canoe. Also, **kaiak**. [Eskimo]

Kaye /keɪ/, n. **Danny** (*David Daniel Kaminski*), 1913–87, US film actor and comedian.

Kazakhstan /kaˈzakstan/, n. a republic in Asia between the Caspian Sea and China; a member of the CIS; a constituent republic of the Soviet Union 1922–91, known as the **Kazakh Soviet Socialist Republic**. Pop. 16 536 000 (1989 est.); 2 734 781 km². *Language*: Kazakh. *Cap*.: Alma-Ata. Also, **Kazakstan**, n., adj.

Kb, *Symbol*. the equilibrium constant of a base and water mixture containing ions and un-ionised molecules.

KBE /keɪ bi ˈi/, *Abbrev*. Knight (Commander of the Order) of the British Empire.

kc, *Symbol*. kilocycle; kilocycles.

KC /keɪ ˈsi/, *Abbrev*. **1.** King's Counsel. **2.** Knight Commander.

Keating /ˈkitɪŋ/, n. **Paul John**, born 1944; Australian federal Labor politician; treasurer 1983–91; became prime minister in 1991.

Keaton /ˈkitn/, n. **1. Buster** (*Joseph Francis Keaton*), 1895–1966, US comic actor and director; star of many silent films. **2. Diane** (*Diane Hall*), born 1946, US film actress; won Academy Award for her performance in *Annie Hall* (1977).

Keats /kits/, n. **John**, 1795–1821, English romantic poet.

kebab /kəˈbæb/, n. → **shish kebab**. Also, **kabob, cabob, kabab, kebob**. [Ar]

Kedah /ˈkɛdə/, n. a state in Malaysia, on the south-western Malay Peninsula. Pop. 1 263 155 (1985 est.); 9479 km². *Cap*.: Alor Star.

keel /kil/, n. **1.** a long piece of timber or iron stretching the length of a ship at the bottom, that holds the whole framework together. **2. on an even keel**, in a steady or balanced state or manner. ◇v. **3. keel over**, **a.** (of a ship) to turn or roll on to the keel. **b.** *Colloq*. to collapse suddenly. [ME, from Scand]

Keeling Islands Also, **Cocos (Keeling) Islands**. /ˈkilɪŋ aɪləndz/, n. → **Cocos Islands**.

keen¹ /kin/, adj. **1.** sharp; cutting easily: *a keen blade*. **2.** strong and clear, as in eyesight, hearing, mind etc. **3.** (of prices) kept cheap by competition with others. **4.** intense, as feeling, desire, etc. **5.** ardent; eager (oft. fol. by *about, for*, etc., or an infinitive). **6.** having a fondness or devotion (for) (fol. by *on*). [OE *cēne*] **–keenness**, n.

keen² /kin/, n. **1.** a wailing lament for the dead. ◇v.i. **2.** to wail in lamentation for the dead. [Irish: lament] **–keener**, n.

keep /kip/, v., **kept, keeping**, n. ◇v.t. **1.** to continue in one's action or conduct: *to keep watch; to keep step; to keep silence*. **2.** to cause to continue in some place or state: *to keep a light burning*. **3.** to make (something) stay in condition or order, as by care and labor: *to keep a house clean*. **4.** to prevent from coming or going; detain: *to keep someone prisoner*. **5.** to have habitually in stock or for sale: *Do you keep shoelaces in this shop?* **6.** to have in one's service or for one's use or enjoyment: *to keep a car*. **7.** to associate with: *to keep bad company*. **8.** to withhold from the knowledge of others: *to keep a secret*. **9.** to not use; reserve: *Let's keep the cake until tomorrow*. **10.** to restrain: *For heaven's sake keep him from laughing*. **11.** to record (business transactions, etc.) regularly: *to keep records; to keep a diary*. **12.** to follow; fulfil; observe; obey: *to keep one's word; to keep the law*. **13.** to follow traditional customs at (festival or season): *to keep Christmas*. **14.** to carry on (an establishment, business, etc.); manage: *to keep house*. **15.** to guard, protect. **16.** to support (a person, etc.). **17.** to take care of; tend: *to keep sheep*. **18.** to save, hold, or retain in possession: *I found it and I'm going to keep it*. ◇v.i. **19.** to continue in an action, course, position, state, etc.: *Please keep in touch*. **20.** to stay in a particular state: *to keep cool*. **21.** to stay in a place: *to keep indoors*. **22.** to continue without spoiling: *The milk will keep in the fridge*. **23.** to stay (fol. by *away, back, off, out*, etc.): *Please keep off the grass*. **24.** to stop oneself from doing something: *Try to keep from smiling*. ◇v. **25.** Some special uses are:
keep at, **1.** to continue; persist in: *Try to keep at your homework*. **2.** to bully; nag.
keep down, **1.** to prevent from rising. **2.** to continue in: *to keep down a job*. **3.** to consume (food) without vomiting it.
keep on, to continue; persist.
keep time, **1.** to record time, as a watch or clock does. **2.** to beat, mark, or observe the rhythmic accents of music, etc.
keep to, **1.** to follow, adhere to (an agreement, plan, facts, etc.). **2.** to confine oneself to: *to keep to one's bed*.
keep track of (tabs on), to keep account of.
keep up, to hold an equal rate of speed, activity, or progress, as with another. ◇n. **26.** subsistence; board and lodging: *to work for one's keep*. **27.** the central tower of a medieval castle. **28. for keeps**, *Colloq*. **a.** for keeping as one's own permanently: *It's yours for keeps*. **b.** altogether; permanently: *We have broken up for keeps*. [OE *cēpan*, observe, heed, regard, await, take]

keeper /ˈkipə/, n. **1.** someone who keeps, guards, or watches. **2.** the person in charge of something valuable, as an attendant in a museum, zoo, etc. **3.** something that keeps, or serves to guard, hold in place, retain, etc.

keeping /ˈkipɪŋ/, n. **1.** proper conformity or fitness in things or elements associated together: *His deeds are not in keeping with his words*. **2.** care; observance; custody: *to take into one's keeping*.

Keepit Dam /ˈkipət dæm/, n. a dam on the Namoi River, NSW, used for stock and domestic purposes, irrigation and hydroelectricity.

Keesing /'kiːsɪŋ/, *n.* **Nancy**, 1923–93, Australian writer; works include *John Lang and 'The Forger's Wife'* (1979).

keg /keg/, *n.* **1.** (in the imperial system) a barrel or container, usu. holding nine gallons (40.9 litres) or 18 gallons (81.8 litres). **2.** a barrel of beer. [late ME, from Scand]

Keilor /'kiːlə/, *n.* a city within the metropolitan area of Melbourne, Vic. Pop. 93 327 (1986).

Keller /'kelə/, *n.* **Helen (Adams)**, 1880–1968, US author, blind and deaf from early childhood, who learned to speak, read and write; noted for her work with handicapped people.

Kelly /'keli/, *n.* a family of bushrangers who have achieved legendary status in Australia, esp. **Ned** (*Edward Kelly*), 1855–80, leader of the Kelly Gang.

Kelly Gang, *n.* an Australian gang of bushrangers operating in Victoria in the 1870s, comprising Ned Kelly, Dan Kelly, Stephen Hart and Joseph Byrne; praised by many of their contemporaries, the Kelly Gang has achieved legendary fame throughout Australia.

kelp /kelp/, *n.* any of the large brown seaweeds. [ME ult. orig. unknown]

kelpie /'kelpi/, *n.* one of a breed of Australian sheepdogs developed from imported Scottish collies. [probably from the name of an early specimen of the breed]

kelvin /'kelvən/, *n.* the base SI unit of thermodynamic temperature, equal to the fraction 1/273.16 of the temperature of the triple point of water. As a unit of temperature interval, one kelvin is equivalent to one degree Celsius. See **Celsius, absolute zero.** Symbol: K [named after Lord *Kelvin*, 1824–1907, British physicist and mathematician]

Kelvin scale, *n.* a scale of temperature (**Kelvin temperature**), based on thermodynamic principles, in which zero is equivalent to −273.16°C or −459.69°F.

Kembla /'kɛmblə/, *n.* **Mount**, a mountain in south-eastern NSW, west of Port Kembla; coal-mining; site of Australia's worst mining disaster, in which 95 men died (1902). 534 m.

Kemp /kemp/, *n.* **Roger**, 1908–87, Australian artist; noted symbolic expressionist.

Kempsey /'kempsi/, *n.* a town and shire on the north coast of NSW, on the Macleay River. Pop. 9335 (1986).

ken /ken/, *n., v.,* **kenned** or **kent, kenning.** ◇*n.* **1.** range of sight or vision. **2.** knowledge; mental perception. ◇*v.t.* **3.** *Scot.* to have acquaintance with. [OE *cennan*]

Kendall /'kendəl/, *n.* **Thomas Henry**, 1839–82, Australian poet; works include the collections *Leaves from Australian Forests* (1869) and *Songs from the Mountains* (1880).

Keneally /kə'niːli/, *n.* **Thomas Michael**, born 1935, Australian novelist; works include *The Chant of Jimmie Blacksmith* (1972) and *Schindler's Ark* (1982); awarded the Booker Prize 1982.

Kennedy /'kɛnədi/, **Edmund Besley Court**, 1818–48, Australian explorer, born in Guernsey.

Kennedy family, *n.* a family prominent in US social and political life, including **1. Joseph Patrick**, 1888–1969, US diplomat and father of John, Robert and Edward. **2. John Fitzgerald**, 1917–63, Democratic politician; 35th president of the US 1961–63; involved US forces in the Bay of Pigs invasion of Cuba 1961; assassinated. **3. Robert Francis**, 1925–68, Democratic senator and attorney-general; assassinated during campaign for presidential nomination. **4. Edward Moore**, born 1932, Democratic senator; contender for the presidency, 1980.

kennel /'kɛnəl/, *n., v.,* **-nelled, -nelling.** ◇*n.* **1.** a house for a dog or dogs. **2.** (*usu. pl., treated as sing.*) an establishment where dogs are bred or boarded. ◇*v.t.* **3.** to put into or keep in a kennel. [ME, from AF, from VL, from L: dog]

Kenny /'keni/, *n.* **Elizabeth**, 1886–1952, Australian nurse; noted for her unorthodox treatment of poliomyelitis.

Kent /kent/, *n.* a county in south-eastern England. Pop. 1 500 900 (1986 est.); 3950 km². *Administrative Centre:* Maidstone.

kentia palm /'kentiə pam/, *n.* a palm, native to Lord Howe Island but widely grown as an ornamental.

Kentucky /kɛn'tʌki/, *n.* a state in the eastern central US. Pop. 3 728 000 (1986 est.); 104 623 km². *Cap.:* Frankfort. *Abbrev.:* Ky, Ken —**Kentuckian**, *n., adj.*

Kenya /'kɛnjə/, *n.* a republic in eastern Africa, on the Indian Ocean, bordered by Somalia, Ethiopia, Sudan, Uganda and Tanzania; a British protectorate and colony before independence in 1963. Pop. 22 020 000 (1987 est.); 580 367 km². *Languages:* Swahili, also English, Kikuyu and Luo. *Currency:* Kenya shilling. *Cap.:* Nairobi. —**Kenyan**, *n., adj.*

Kepler /'kɛplə/, *n.* **Johann** /'jouhan/, 1571–1630, German astronomer and mathematician; his laws of planetary motion form the basis of modern astronomy. —**Keplerian**, *adj.*

kept /kept/, *v.* past tense and past participle of **keep.**

keratin /'kɛrətən/, *n.* an animal protein found in horn, feathers, hair and hoofs. Also, **ceratin.** [Gk: horn] —**keratinous**, *adj.*

keratoid /'kɛrətɔɪd/, *adj.* looking like a horn; horny. [Gk]

kerb /kɜb/, *n.* **1.** a line of joined stones or concrete at the edge of a street, wall, etc. ◇*v.t.* **2.** to furnish with, or protect by a kerb. [var. spelling of CURB]

kerchief /'kɜtʃəf, kə'tʃif/, *n.* **1.** a cloth worn as a head covering, esp. by women. **2.** a cloth worn or carried on the person. [ME, from OF]

Kerenski /kə'rɛnski/, *n.* **Aleksandr Feodorovich** /əlɪk'sandə fi'ɔdərəvɪtʃ/, 1881–1970,

Russian liberal revolutionary leader; prime minister, 1917; overthrown by the Bolsheviks. Also, **Kerensky.**

Kermadec Islands /'kɜmədɛk aɪləndz/, *n.pl.* a group of islands lying about 1000 km north-east of NZ; a NZ possession. 34 km².

kernel /'kɜnəl/, *n.* **1.** the softer, usu. edible, part in the shell of a nut or the stone of a fruit. **2.** a grain, as of wheat. **3.** the central part of anything; nucleus; core. [OE *cyrnel*, diminutive of *corn* seed, grain]

kero /'kɛroʊ/, *n. Colloq.* → **kerosene.**

kerosene /'kɛrəsin, 'kɛrəsin/, *n.* a mixture of liquid hydrocarbons, obtained in the distillation of petroleum, with boiling points in the range 150°–300°C, used for lamps, engines, heaters. Also, **kerosine.** [Gk: wax]

Kerouac /'kɛruæk/, *n.* **Jack** (*Jean-Louis Lefris de Kérouac*), 1922–69, US novelist, born in Canada.

Kerr /kɜ/, *n.* **Sir John Robert**, 1914–91, Australian lawyer and governor-general 1974–77. See **The Dismissal.**

Kerr effect, *n.* the rotation of the plane of polarisation of light when it is passed through certain liquids or solids to which potential difference is applied.

Kerr Hundredweight, *n.* the first reported large gold nugget in Australia found about 80 km north of Bathurst, NSW, in July 1851; contained 39 564 grams of gold.

Kerry /'kɛri/, *n.* a county in the south-western Republic of Ireland in Munster province. Pop. 123 922 (1986); 4701 km². Irish, **Ciarraí.** *County Town:* Tralee.

kestrel /'kɛstrəl/, *n.* a common small falcon, of the northern parts of the Eastern Hemisphere, noted for hovering in the air with its head to the wind. [var. of earlier *castrel*]

ketch /kɛtʃ/, *n.* a vessel with a large mainmast and a smaller mast in front. [earlier *catch*, apparently from CATCH]

ketchup /'kɛtʃəp/, *n.* a sauce or condiment for meat, fish, etc.: *tomato ketchup.* [apparently from Chinese (Amoy d.): brine of pickled fish]

ketone /'kitoʊn/, *n.* any of a class of organic compounds, containing the carbonyl group, –CO, attached to two organic radicals, e.g. acetone, CH_3COCH_3. [G]

kettle /'kɛtl/, *n.* a portable container with a lid, a spout, and a handle, in which to boil water. [ME, from Scand, from L diminutive: bowl, pot]

kettledrum /'kɛtldrʌm/, *n.* a drum consisting of a hollow half sphere of brass or copper with a skin stretched over it, which can be accurately tuned.

keV /kɛɪ i 'vi/, *Phys. Symbol.* kilo-electron volt(s).

kewpie /'kjupi/, *n.* a small, very plump doll, usu. made of plaster or celluloid. [Trademark]

key /ki/, *n., pl.* **keys,** *v.,* **keyed, keying.** ◇*n.* **1.** an instrument for fastening or opening a lock by moving its bolt. **2.** a means of understanding, solving, etc.: *the key to a problem.* **3.** a book, etc., containing the solutions to problems given elsewhere as exercises. **4.** the system or pattern used to decode a cryptogram, etc. **5.** an explanation of abbreviations, symbols, etc., used in a dictionary, map, etc. **6.** an instrument for grasping and turning a bolt, nut, etc., as for winding a clockwork mechanism. **7.** one of a set of levers or parts pressed in operating a telegraph, typewriter, etc. **8.** *Music.* **a.** the part of the lever mechanism of a piano, organ, or woodwind instrument, which a finger operates. **b.** the keynote or tonic of a scale. **c.** the relationship between all notes in a given unit of music to a single note or a tonic; tonality. **d.** the principal tonality of a composition: *a symphony in the key of C minor.* **9.** tone or pitch, as of voice: *to speak in a high key.* **10.** the arrangement of light and dark areas in a painting. ◇*adj.* **11.** chief; major; fundamental; indispensable: *the key industries of a nation.* ◇*v.t.* **12.** to bring to a particular degree of intensity of feeling, excitement, energy, etc. (oft. fol. by *up*) (oft. in passive): *He was very keyed up before the grand final.* **13.** to adjust (one's speech, actions, etc.) in order meet the needs of the situation: *The teacher keyed the lesson to a year 8 level.* **14.** *Music.* to regulate the key or pitch of. **15.** to lock with, or as if with, a key. **16.** *Bldg Trades.* to prepare (a surface) by roughening, etc., to receive paint. [OE *cǣg*]

keyboard /'kibɔd/, *n.* **1.** the row or set of keys on a piano, typewriter, etc. ◇*v.t.* **2.** to enter (data) by means of a keyboard. –**keyboarder,** *n.*

Keynes /keɪnz/, *n.* **John Maynard, 1st Baron**, 1883–1946, English economist and writer, instrumental in the foundation of the International Monetary Fund and the World Bank.

Keynesian /'kinziən/, *adj.* **1.** relating to the economic theories, policies, etc., of JM Keynes and followers, esp. the policy of keeping high employment and of controlling inflation by capital and public investment and by varying taxation and interest rates. ◇*n.* **2.** someone who supports the theories, policies, etc., of Keynes. [from John Maynard KEYNES]

key signature, *n.* (in musical notation) the group of sharps or flats placed after the clef to show the tonality or key of the music following.

keystone /'kistoʊn/, *n.* **1.** the wedge-shaped piece at the top of an arch, regarded as holding the other pieces in place. **2.** something on which associated things depend.

kg, *Symbol.* kilogram; kilograms.

KG /keɪ 'dʒi/, *Abbrev.* Knight of the Garter.

KGB /keɪ dʒi 'bi/, *n.* formerly, the secret police of the Soviet Union. [Russ lit., Committee of State Security]

Khachaturian /kætʃə'tʊəriən/, *n.* **Aram Ilyich** /'arəm ɪl'jitʃ/, 1903–78, Russian composer, born in Georgia.

khaki /ka'ki, 'kaki/, *n., pl.* **-kis,** *adj.* ◇*n.* **1.** a dull yellowish greenish brown color. **2.** a stout uniform cloth of this color, worn esp. by soldiers. ◊*adj.* **3.** of the color of khaki. **4.** made of khaki. [Hind: dusty]

khan /kɑn/, *n.* **1.** the supreme ruler of the Tartar tribes, as well as emperor of China, during the Middle Ages, being a descendant of Genghis Khan. **2.** a title of respect in Iran, Afghanistan, Pakistan, etc. [ME from Turk: lord, prince]

Khartoum /kɑˈtum/, *n.* the capital of Sudan, in the western part, at the junction of the White and Blue Nile rivers; besieged, 1895; retaken by the British, 1898. Pop. 476 218 (1983). Also, **Khartum**.

Khmer Republic /kmɛə, kmɜ rəˈpʌblɪk/, *n.* a republic in south-east Asia, formerly the kingdom of Cambodia.

Khmer Rouge, *n.* the Cambodian Communist party which emerged as a significant rebel force during the 1960s and seized power in 1970.

Khomeini /hoʊˈmeɪni/, *n.* **Ayatollah Ruhollah** /aɪəˈtɒlə ruˈhɒlə/ (*Ruhollah Hendi*), 1901–89, spiritual leader of Iran's Shiite Muslims and became unofficial leader of Iran in 1979.

Khrushchev /krusˈtʃɒf/, *n.* **Nikita Sergeyevich** /nɪˈkitə sɪəˈɡeɪjəvɪtʃ/, 1894–1971, Soviet statesman, born in Russia; first secretary of the Soviet Communist Party 1953–64; premier of the Soviet Union 1958–64.

Khyber Pass /ˈkaɪbə pɑs/, the chief mountain pass between Pakistan and Afghanistan, west of Peshawar; route of Persian, Greek, Tatar, Mogul and Afghan invasions of India. 53 km long; 2080 m high. Also, **Khaibar Pass**.

kHz, *Symbol.* kilohertz.

Kiama /kaɪˈæmə/, *n.* a town on the south coast of NSW; famous for its ocean blowhole. Pop. 9184 (1986). [Aboriginal]

Kiandra /kaɪˈændrə/, *n.* a former goldmining town in south-eastern NSW; claimed to be the site of the second oldest ski club in the world.

kia-ora /kɪəˈɔrə/, *interj.* NZ. good luck. [Maori]

kibble /ˈkɪbəl/, *v.,* **-bled, -bling,** *adj.* ◊*v.t.* **1.** to grind into small particles. ◊*adj.* **2.** of or relating to wheat, grain, etc., which has been kibbled.

kibbutz /kɪˈbʊts/, *n., pl.* **kibbutzim** /kɪˈbʊtsɪm, kɪbʊtˈsim/. (in Israel) an agricultural settlement run on socialist principles, worked by a group of people. [Modern Heb: gathering]

kick /kɪk/, *v.t.* **1.** to hit or strike with the foot. **2.** to drive, force, make, etc. by or as if by kicking: *I kicked him down the stairs.* **3.** *Football.* to score (a goal) by kicking a ball through or over the goal. **4.** *Colloq.* to get rid of (a bad habit). ◊*v.i.* **5.** to strike out with the foot. **6.** *Colloq.* to resist, object, or complain. **7.** (of a gun when fired) to spring back; recoil. **8. kick off, a.** *Aust Rules, Rugby, Soccer.* to kick the ball into play to start or restart a game. **b.** to start. **9. kick on,** to continue. **10. kick the bucket,** *Colloq.* to die. **11. kick upstairs,** *Colloq.* to promote someone to a position with status but no real power. ◊*n.* **12.** the act of kicking; a blow or thrust with the foot. **13.** *Football.* **a.** a kicked ball: *His first kick hit the cross-bar.* **b.** the distance covered by a kicked ball: *a long kick for touch.* **14.** a recoil, esp. of a gun. **15.** *Colloq.* any act, sensation, etc., that gives pleasure or satisfaction: *to get a kick out of music.* **16. a kick in the pants,** a sharp criticism given to make someone work harder, etc. **17. a kick in the teeth,** a severe set-back. **18. for kicks,** *Colloq.* for the excitement. [ME] – **kickable,** *adj.* – **kicker,** *n.*

kick-off /ˈkɪk-ɒf/, *n.* **1.** *Sport.* the first kick that starts the play in a football game. **2.** *Colloq.* the beginning or first stage of something.

kid¹ /kɪd/, *n., v.,* **kidded, kidding,** *adj.* ◊*n.* **1.** a young goat. **2.** Also, **kidskin.** soft leather made from skin of a young goat. **3.** *Colloq.* a child or young person. ◊*v.i.* **4.** (of a goat) to give birth to young. ◊*adj.* **5.** young; younger than: *my kid brother.* [ME, apparently from Scand]

kid² /kɪd/, *v.t., v.i.,* **kidded, kidding.** *Colloq.* to tease; banter; joke (with); deceive. [? special use of KID¹ (def. 3)]

kid gloves, *n.pl.* **1.** gloves made of kid. **2. handle with kid gloves,** to handle very gently or tactfully.

Kidman /ˈkɪdmən/, *n.* **Sir Sidney** ('*The Cattle King*'), 1857–1935, Australian pastoralist; his land-holdings comprised one tract from the Channel Country, through western NSW to Vic and another through central Australia to northern SA.

kidnap /ˈkɪdnæp/, *v.t.,* **-napped, -napping.** to steal or take away (a child or other person); abduct; carry off (a person) against his will by unlawful force or by fraud, often with a demand for ransom. [KID¹ (def. 3) + obs. *nap,* v., seize] – **kidnapper,** *n.*

kidney /ˈkɪdni/, *n., pl.* **-neys. 1.** either of a pair of bean-shaped glandular organs, in humans and other animals about 10 cm in length, in the back part of the abdominal cavity, which get rid of waste from the blood. **2.** the meat of an animal's kidney used as a food. [ME]

kidney bean, *n.* **1.** → **French bean. 2.** the dried seed of the French bean, esp. if dark in color.

kidney machine, *n.* a machine for carrying out the function of the kidneys, used by a person who has defective kidneys.

Kidston /ˈkɪdstən/, *n.* a goldmining centre in central eastern Qld, west of Townsville; Australia's largest goldmine 1985–86.

Kiev /ˈkiɛf/, *n.* the capital city of Ukraine, on the river Dnieper. Pop. 2 495 000 (1986 est.). Russian, **Kijev.**

kikuyu /kaɪˈkuju/, *n.* **1.** a tough grass, introduced from Africa, used for lawns and pasture. **2.** (*cap.*) a Negroid people of eastern Africa, living chiefly on the high foothills of Mt Kenya.

Kildare /kɪl'dɛə/, *n.* a county in eastern Republic of Ireland, in Leinster. Pop. 116 015 (1986); 1694 km². Irish, **Cill Dara.** *County Town:* Naas.

Kilimanjaro /kɪləmən'dʒaroʊ/, *n.* a volcanic mountain in northern Tanzania; highest peak in Africa. 5889 m.

Kilkenny /kɪl'kɛni/, *n.* a county in the south-eastern Republic of Ireland, in Leinster. Pop. 73 094 (1986); 2062 km². Irish, **Cill Chainnigh.**

kill /kɪl/, *v.t.* **1.** to take life from (any living thing); cause the death of; slay. **2.** to destroy; to do away with; extinguish: *to kill hope.* **3.** to spoil the effect of: *He killed her joke by giving away the punch line.* **4.** to pass (the time) while waiting for something to come, happen, or the like: *He read a book to kill time until the bus came.* **5.** to overcome completely or with irresistible effect: *Her sense of humor kills me.* **6.** to defeat or veto (a legislative bill, etc.). ◇*v.i.* **7.** to cause or inflict death. **8.** to commit murder. **9.** to have an irresistible effect: *dressed to kill.* ◇*v.* **10. kill off**, to destroy completely and often indiscriminately. **11. kill two birds with one stone**, to achieve two (or more) objectives by one action. ◇*n.* **12.** the act of killing (game, etc.). **13.** an animal or animals killed. [ME, apparently from OE *-colla* (in *morgen-colla* morning slaughter)] **– killer,** *n.*

Killarney /kɪ'lɑni/, *n.* a town in the south-western Republic of Ireland, in Kerry; tourist resort. Pop. 7693 (1981).

killer whale, *n.* a swift, predatory, toothed whale, *Orcinus orca*, of worldwide distribution; grampus.

killjoy /'kɪldʒɔɪ/, *n.* a person or thing that spoils the joy or enjoyment of others.

kiln /kɪln/, *n.* **1.** an oven or furnace for burning, baking, or drying something, esp. one for baking bricks or pottery. ◇*v.t.* **2.** to burn, bake, or treat in a kiln. [OE *cyl(e)n*, from L: kitchen]

kilo /'kiloʊ/, *n. Colloq.* → **kilogram**.

kilo- /'kɪlə-/, a prefix denoting 10³ of a given unit, as in *kilogram*. *Symbol:* k [F, representing Gk *chílioi* thousand]

kilogram /'kɪləgræm/, *n.* **1.** a unit of mass equal to 1000 grams. **2.** *Phys.* the SI unit of mass, internationally agreed to equal the mass of a metal cylinder kept at Sèvres, France. *Symbol:* kg [F *kilogramme*. See KILO-, -GRAM²]

kilogram-force /kɪləgræm-'fɔs/, *n.* a non-SI unit of force, equal to 9.806 65 newtons. *Symbol:* kgf

kilohertz /'kɪləhɜts/, *n.* a unit of frequency equal to 1000 hertz; used to express radio frequency. *Symbol:* kHz

kilojoule /'kɪlədʒul/, *n.* 1000 joules; the unit used to express the fuel or energy value of food; the quantity of a food capable of producing such a unit of energy. *Symbol:* kJ [KILO- + JOULE]

kilometre /'kɪləmitə, kə'lɒmətə/, *n.* a unit of length, the common measure of distances, equal to 1000 metres. *Symbol:* km. [F *kilomètre*. See KILO-, -METRE] **– kilometric, kilometrical,** *adj.*

kiloton /'kɪlətʌn/, *n.* **1.** 1000 tons. **2.** an explosive force equal to that of 1000 tons of TNT.

kilowatt /'kɪləwɒt/, *n.* 1000 watts. *Symbol:* kW [KILO- + WATT]

kilowatt hour /kɪləwɒt 'aʊə/, *n.* a unit of energy of equal value to that transferred or spent in one hour by one kilowatt of power, 3.6 x 10⁶ joules. *Symbol:* kW h

kilt /kɪlt/, *n.* any short, pleated skirt, esp. one worn by men in the Scottish Highlands. [ME, probably from Scand]

kilter /'kɪltə/, *n. in the phrase* **out of kilter**, not in working order; out of order: *The engine was out of kilter.*

Kimberley Region /'kɪmbəli ridʒən/, *n.* a large region in the north-western corner of Australia, bounded on the south by 19° S latitude (north of the Great Sandy Desert), on the east by the NT border and on the north and west by coastline; sparsely-settled area. Also, **the Kimberleys.**

kimono /'kɪmənoʊ, kə'moʊnoʊ/, *n., pl.* **-nos. 1.** a wide-sleeved robe characteristic of Japanese costume, tied at the waist with a (wide) sash. **2.** a woman's loose dressing-gown. [Jap]

kin /kɪn/, *n.* **1.** someone's relatives as a group; kindred. ◇*adj.* **2.** of kin; related; akin. [ME; OE *cynn* from Gmc root equivalent to L *gen-*, Gk *gen-*, Skt *jan-* beget, produce]

-kin, a diminutive suffix, attached to nouns to signify a small object of the kind mentioned, as in *lambkin, catkin.* [ME]

kina /'kinə/, *n.* the larger unit of currency in PNG. [Papuan]

Kinabalu /kɪnəbə'lu/, *n.* a mountain in Malaysia, in northern Borneo in central Sabah; highest peak in Borneo. 4125 m.

kind¹ /kaɪnd/, *adj.* **1.** of a good or well-wishing nature or disposition, as a person; benevolent. **2.** having, showing, or proceeding from benevolence: *kind words.* **3.** well-meant; cordial: *kind regards.* [OE *gecynd* nature. See KIND²] **– kindness,** *n.*

kind² /kaɪnd/, *n.* **1.** a class or group of individuals of the same nature or character, esp. a natural group of animals or plants. **2.** nature or character as determining likeness or difference between things: *things differing in degree rather than in kind.* **3.** a person or thing as being of a particular character or class: *He is a strange kind of hero.* **4.** something not quite exact: *The vines formed a kind of roof.* **5.** *Archaic.* nature or character: *after one's kind.* **6. in kind, a.** in something of the same kind; in the same way: *to retaliate in kind.* **b.** in goods or natural produce, instead of money. [OE *gecynd*]

kindergarten /'kɪndəgatn/, *n.* a school for very young children, using games, music, toys, etc. to develop their minds, bodies and relationships with others. [G: lit., children's garden, coined by Friedrich Froebel, 1782–1852, German educational reformer]

kindle /'kɪndəl/, v., **-dled, -dling.** ◇v.t. **1.** to set (a fire, flame, etc.) burning or blazing. **2.** to set fire to, or ignite (fuel or any combustible matter). **3.** to excite; stir up or set going; animate, rouse, or inflame. **4.** to light up, illuminate, or make bright. ◇v.i. **5.** (of fuel, a fire or flame) to begin to burn. **6.** to become excited, inflamed; become ardent. **7.** to become lit up, bright, or glowing, as the sky at dawn or the eyes with enthusiasm. [ME, probably from Scand] **–kindler,** n.

kindling /'kɪndlɪŋ/, n. material, esp. sticks of wood, for starting a fire.

kindly /'kaɪndli/, adj., **-lier, -liest,** adv. ◇adj. **1.** having, showing, or coming from a kind nature or spirit; kind-hearted; good-natured; sympathetic. **2.** pleasant; genial; benign. **3.** favorable, as soil for crops. ◇adv. **4.** in a kind manner. **5.** heartily; cordially: *We thank you kindly.* **6.** with liking; favorably: *to take kindly to an idea.* **7.** obligingly; please: *Kindly go away.* [OE *gecyndelic* natural]

kindred /'kɪndrəd/, n. **1.** a body of people related to one another, or a family, tribe, or race. **2.** one's relatives as a group; kinsfolk; kin. ◇adj. **3.** associated by origin, nature, qualities, etc.: *kindred languages.* **4.** related by birth or descent, or having kinship: *kindred tribes.* [ME. See KIN, -RED]

kine /kaɪn/, n.pl. *Archaic.* plural of **cow.**

kinematics /kaɪnə'mætɪks, kɪn-/, n. **1.** the branch of mechanics which studies motion without considering mass or force (**applied kinematics**). **2.** the theory of mechanical contrivance for converting one kind of motion into another (**applied kinematics**). [Gk: motion] **–kinematic, kinematical,** adj.

kinetic /kə'nɛtɪk, kaɪ-/, adj. **1.** relating to motion. **2.** caused by motion. [Gk]

kinetic energy, n. energy which a body has because it is moving, or which a system has because its parts are moving.

kinetics /kə'nɛtɪks, kaɪ-/, n. the branch of mechanics which deals with the action of forces in producing or changing the motion of masses.

king /kɪŋ/, n. **1.** a man who has chief authority over a country and people, usu. for life and by hereditary right; monarch; sovereign. **2.** (*cap.*) a title of God or Christ: *King of Heaven.* **3.** a person or thing outstanding in its class: *The lion is the king of beasts.* **4.** a playing card bearing the formalised picture of a king. **5.** the chief piece in a game of chess, moving one square at a time in any direction. **6.** a man who has grown wealthy and powerful from a specified industry: *a cattle king.* ◇adj. **7.** the largest: *king size; king prawn.* [ME; OE *cyng, cyning*] **–kingly,** adj.

King /kɪŋ/, n. **1. Billie Jean** (née *Billie Jean Moffit*), born 1943, US tennis player; Wimbledon champion 1966–68, 1972–73, 1975; US Open Champion 1967, 1971–72, 1974. **2. John,** 1841–72, Australian explorer, born in Ireland; a member, and the only survivor, of Burke and Wills's expedition (1860–61). **3. Martin Luther,** 1929–68, US Baptist minister and civil rights leader; assassinated. **4. Philip Gidley,** 1758–1808, English naval officer and colonial administrator; governor of NSW 1800–1806. **5. Phillip Parker,** 1791–1856, son of Philip Gidley, Australian naval officer and coastal explorer.

Kingaroy /'kɪŋə'rɔɪ/, n. a town and shire in south-eastern Qld north of Toowoomba; Australia's largest peanut-producing area. Pop. 6362 (1986). [Aboriginal *kinjerroy* red ant]

King Billy /kɪŋ 'bɪli/, n. the name given to an Aborigine, presumed to be the leader of a local tribe near Ballarat, Vic, at the time of the 1850s gold rushes.

kingdom /'kɪŋdəm/, n. **1.** a state or government having a king or queen as its head. **2.** anything thought of as making up a region or sphere of independent action or control: *the kingdom of the mind.* **3.** a region or section of nature, esp. one of the three great divisions of natural objects: *the animal, vegetable, and mineral kingdoms.* **4.** the spiritual authority of God; state of spiritual awareness. [ME; OE *cyningdōm*]

kingfish /'kɪŋfɪʃ/, n., pl. **-fishes,** (esp. collectively) **-fish. 1.** any of various fishes noted for size or some other quality. **2.** the Spanish mackerel.

kingfisher /'kɪŋfɪʃə/, n. a type of fish- or insect-eating bird found in most parts of the world, with thick beak and small feet, and often brilliantly colored.

King George Sound, n. a large inlet on the south-western coast of WA; on its western shore stands the port of Albany. [named after GEORGE III]

King Island, n. an island in Bass Strait north-west of Tas. About 64 km long and 26 km wide. [named after Governor PG KING]

kingpin /'kɪŋpɪn/, n. **1.** the pin by which a stub axle is united by means of a joint to an axle beam or steering head in a motor car. **2.** *Colloq.* the most important person in a company, etc.

king prawn, n. a large, edible prawn of eastern Australian waters, brownish in color with a blue tail; red when cooked.

Kings /kɪŋz/, n. pl. certain books of the Bible which contain the history of the reigns of the kings of Israel and Judah (usu. the 11th and 12th books of the Old Testament, called I Kings and II Kings).

Kingsford Smith /kɪŋzfəd 'smɪθ/, n. Sir **Charles** ('*Smithy*'), 1897–1935, Australian pioneer airman; in 1928 with Charles Ulm he made the first flight over the Pacific, in 1929 he made the first east-west crossing of the Atlantic and the first aerial circumnavigation of the world.

Kingsley /'kɪŋzli/, n. **1. Charles,** 1819–75, English clergyman, novelist, and poet; wrote the children's book *The Water Babies* (1863). **2.** his brother, **Henry,** 1830–76, English novelist; wrote two novels with Australian settings, *The Recollections of Geoffry Hamlyn* (1859) and *The Hillyars and the Burtons* (1865).

Kingston /'kɪŋstən/, **1.** a town in Tas, near Hobart; resort. Pop. 10 932 (1986). **2.** a township in and the capital of Norfolk Island; convict ruins.

King William pine, *n.* a valuable softwood tree, used for building, found in damp forests in Tas. Also, **King Billy pine.**

kink /kɪŋk/, *n.* **1.** a twist, as in a thread, rope, or hair, caused by its doubling or bending upon itself. **2.** a mental twist; an odd idea; a whim. **3.** a turning away from normal, esp. normal sexual, behavior. ◇*v.i.*, *v.t.* **4.** to form or cause to form a twist or twists, as a rope. [D: twirl]

kinky /ˈkɪŋki/, *adj.*, **-kier, -kiest. 1.** full of twists. **2.** *Colloq.* interesting in a peculiar way. **3.** *Colloq.* having unusual tastes; perverted. **4.** *Colloq.* odd; mad. **– kinkiness,** *n.*

Kinnock /ˈkɪnək/, *n.* **Neil,** born 1942, British politician; leader of the Labour Party 1983–92.

Kinross /kɪnˈrɒs/, *n.* a former county of eastern central Scotland, now part of Tayside and central regions. Also, **Kinross-shire.**

kinsfolk /ˈkɪnzfoʊk/, *n.pl.* relatives or kindred. Also, **kinfolks, kinfolk.**

kinship /ˈkɪnʃɪp/, *n.* **1.** the state or fact of being in family relationship. **2.** relationship by nature, qualities, etc.; affinity.

kinsman /ˈkɪnzmən/, *n.*, *pl.* **-men. 1.** a male blood relative. **2.** (sometimes) a relative by marriage. **– kinswoman,** *n. fem.*

kiosk /ˈkiɒsk/, *n.* **1.** a small, light structure for the sale of newspapers, cigarettes, sandwiches and drinks, etc. **2.** *Brit.* a telephone box. [Turk: pavilion]

kip /kɪp/, *n.* *Chiefly Brit. Colloq.* sleep. [orig. uncert.]

Kipling /ˈkɪplɪŋ/, *n.* **(Joseph) Rudyard** /ˈrʌdjəd/, 1865–1936, English novelist and poet, born in India; especially known for his 'Jungle Books' for children.

kipper[1] /ˈkɪpə/, *n.* **1.** a method of curing fish by splitting, salting, drying, and smoking. **2.** a fish prepared in this way, esp. a herring or salmon. ◇*v.t.* **3.** to cure (herring, salmon, etc.). [? OE *cypera* spawning salmon]

kipper[2] /ˈkɪpə/, *n.* an Aboriginal youth who has completed the initiation rite. [Aboriginal]

Kirby /ˈkɜbi/, *n.* **Michael Donald,** born 1939, Australian judge, became president of the Court of Appeal in the Supreme Court of NSW in 1984.

Kirchhoff's laws /ˈkɜkɒfs lɔz/, *n.pl.* *Physics.* two laws relating to electrical circuits which state: **1.** that in any network of wires the algebraic sum of the currents which meet at a point is zero. **2.** that the algebraic sum of the electromotive forces in any closed circuit is equal to the algebraic sum of the products of the resistances of each portion of the circuit and the currents flowing through them. [named after GR *Kirchhoff*, 1824–87, German physicist]

Kirghizia /kɜˈgɪziə/, *n.* a republic in central Asia bordered by Kazakhstan, Uzbekistan, Tadzhikistan and China; a member of the CIS; a constituent republic of the Soviet Union 1936–91, known as the **Kirghiz Soviet Socialist Republic.** Pop. 4 291 000 (1989 est.); about 201 502 km². *Language:* Kirghiz. *Cap.:* Frunze. Also, **Kirgizia. – Kirghiz,** *n.*, *adj.*

Kiribati /ˈkɪrɪbæs/, *n.* a republic consisting of a group of islands in the western Pacific; part of the British Colony of Gilbert and Ellice Islands until 1975; fully independent since 1979. Pop. 66 000 (1987 est.); 712 km². *Languages:* I-Kiribati (Gilbertese) and English. *Currency:* Australian dollar. *Cap.:* Bairiki. Formerly, **Gilbert Islands.**

kirk /kɜk/, *n. Scot.* a church. [ME, from Scand]

Kirkpatrick /kɜkˈpætrɪk/, *n.* **John Simpson** (*The Man with the Donkey*), 1892–1915, English-born Australian soldier during World War I, renowned for his heroism in carrying the wounded from the Gallipoli battle field.

kismet /ˈkɪzmət, ˈkɪs-/, *n.* fate; destiny. [Turk, from Pers, from Ar: divide]

kiss /kɪs/, *v.t.*, *v.i.* **1.** to touch or press (someone or something) with the lips, in a sign of greeting, affection, etc. **2.** to touch gently or lightly. ◇*n.* **3.** the act of kissing. **4.** a slight touch. [OE *cyssan* from *coss* a kiss] **– kissable,** *adj.*

Kissinger /ˈkɪsɪndʒə/, *n.* **Henry,** born 1923, German-born US academic and diplomat; Secretary of State 1973–76; shared Nobel Peace Prize 1972.

kit /kɪt/, *n.*, *v.*, **kitted, kitting.** ◇*n.* **1.** a set or collection of tools, supplies, etc., for a special purpose: *a first-aid kit.* **2.** a set or collection of parts to be put together: *a model aircraft kit.* **3.** a case containing tools, parts, etc. **4.** *Chiefly Mil.* a set of clothing or personal articles for a special purpose: *The soldiers were issued with a complete kit.* **5. the (whole) kit and caboodle,** *Colloq.* the whole thing. ◇*v.t.* **6.** *Mil.* to provide with a kit. [ME, apparently from MD: kind of tub]

Kitakyushu /kitaˈkjuʃu/, *n.* a port and industrial centre in Japan, in northern Kyushu; formed in 1963 by the joining of Wakamatsu, Yawata, Tobata, Moji, and Kokura. Pop. 1 045 000 (1987).

kitbag /ˈkɪtbæg/, *n.* a long canvas bag in which soldiers, etc., carry their personal belongings.

kitchen /ˈkɪtʃən/, *n.* a room or place set aside for the preparing and cooking of food. [OE *cycene*, from L]

Kitchener /ˈkɪtʃənə/, *n.* **Horatio Herbert** (*Earl Kitchener of Khartoum and of Broome*), 1850–1916, British field marshal and statesman.

kite /kaɪt/, *n.* **1.** a light frame covered with some thin material, to be flown in the wind at the end of a long string. **2.** a type of medium-sized hawk with long wings and tail. **3.** *Maths.* a plane figure with four sides, having two pairs of adjacent equal sides, so that the figure looks like a diamond with one end longer than the other. [OE *cÿta*]

kith /kɪθ/, *n.* in the phrase **kith and kin,** friends and relatives. [OE *cÿth, cÿththu* knowledge, acquaintance, native land]

kitsch /kɪtʃ/, *adj., n.* (relating to) showy, self-important, and worthless art, literature, etc. [G]

kitten /'kɪtn/, *n.* **1.** a young cat. **2.** a playful or lively girl. ◇*v.i.* **3.** (of cats) to give birth. [ME, from d. OF]

kitty /'kɪti/, *n., pl.* **-ties. 1.** a collection, usu. of small amounts of money, used for a special purpose by a group of people. **2.** *Cards.* a pool (def. 5) into which each player places a stake. [from *kitcot*, var. of *kidcot* prison, from KID¹ (in sense of slave or criminal) + COT²]

kiwi /'kiwi/, *n.* **1.** a flightless bird of NZ, with vestigial wings, thick legs and a long, thin bill. **2.** (*cap.*) *Colloq.* any person from NZ. [Maori]

Kiwi fruit, *n.* → **Chinese gooseberry.**

KKK, *Abbrev.* Ku Klux Klan.

kL, *Symbol.* kilolitre.

klaxon /'klæksən/, *n.* a type of warning horn with an unpleasant sound, originally used in motor vehicles. [Trademark]

Klee /kleɪ/, *n.* **Paul,** 1879–1940, Swiss painter; founding member of the expressionist group *der Blaue Reiter.*

kleptomania /kleptəˈmeɪniə/, *n.* an irresistible desire to steal, without regard to personal needs. [NL, from Gk] **–kleptomaniac,** *n.*

Klippel /'klɪpəl/, *n.* **Robert,** born 1920, Australian contemporary sculptor, noted for his metal junk sculpture.

km, *Symbol.* kilometre(s).

km/s, *Symbol.* kilometres per second.

km/h, *Symbol.* kilometres per hour.

knack /næk/, *n.* the ability or power of doing something easily and with special skill, etc.; aptitude. [ME]

knacker /'nækə/, *n.* **1.** someone who buys old or useless horses to kill for pet meat, etc. **2.** someone who buys old houses, ships, etc., to break them up and sell the materials. [Scand] **–knackery,** *n.*

knapsack /'næpsæk/, *n.* a leather or canvas case for clothes, etc., carried on the back. [LG]

knave /neɪv/, *n.* **1.** an unprincipled or dishonest man or boy. **2.** *Cards.* a playing card bearing the picture of a prince, in most games counting as next below the queen in its suit; jack. **3.** *Archaic.* a male servant or man of humble position. [ME; OE *cnafa*] **–knavish,** *adj.*

knead /niːd/, *v.t.* **1.** to work (dough, etc.) into a uniform mixture by pressing, folding and stretching. **2.** to handle or massage (the body, etc.) by similar movements. [OE *cnedan*] **–kneader,** *n.*

knee /niː/, *n., v.,* **kneed, kneeing.** ◇*n.* **1.** the joint or area in humans between the thigh and the lower part of the leg. **2.** a similar joint or area of other animals with backbones, as in the leg of a bird, the hind limb of a horse, etc. **3.** the part of a garment covering the knee. **4.** something that looks like a knee joint, esp. when bent. **5. bring someone to his knees,** to force someone to give in. ◇*v.t.* **6.** to hit or touch with the knee. [OE *cnēo(w)*]

kneecap /'niːkæp/, *n.* the flat, movable bone at the front of the knee; patella.

kneel /niːl/, *v.i.,* **knelt** or **kneeled, kneeling.** to fall or rest on the knee(s). [OE *cnēow* KNEE] **–kneeler,** *n.*

knell /nel/, *n.* **1.** the sound made by a bell rung slowly for a death or a funeral. **2.** any sound telling of the death of a person or the end, failure, etc., of something. ◇*v.i.* **3.** to give out a sad, threatening, or warning sound, esp. a funeral bell. ◇*v.t.* **4.** to tell or call by, or as by, a bell. [OE *cnyllan* strike, ring (a bell)]

Knesset /'knesət/, *n.* the parliament of Israel. [Heb: lit., gathering]

knew /njuː/, *v.* past tense of **know.**

knickerbockers /'nɪkəbɒkəz/, *n.pl.* **1.** loosely fitting, short trousers gathered in at the knee. **2.** a similar garment worn as fancy underpants. [from *Knickerbocker,* a descendant of the Dutch settlers of New York]

knick-knack /'nɪk-næk/, *n.* a small ornament, trifle or gimcrack. Also, **nick-nack.**

knife /naɪf/, *n., pl.* **knives** /naɪvz/, *v.,* **knifed, knifing.** ◇*n.* **1.** a cutting instrument consisting mainly of a thin blade (usu. of steel and with a sharp edge) joined to a handle. **2.** any blade for cutting, as in a tool or machine. **3. get one's knife into,** to desire to hurt someone. **4. put the knife into,** to destroy a person, or their good name with evil intention. ◇*v.t.* **5.** to apply a knife to; cut, wound, etc., with a knife. **6.** to endeavor to defeat in a secret or underhand way. [OE *cnīf*]

knife edge, *n.* **1.** the edge of a knife. **2.** anything very sharp. **3.** a position of dubious safety.

knight /naɪt/, *n.* **1.** *Medieval Hist.* **a.** a soldier on horseback, serving under someone of higher rank in the feudal system. **b.** a man, usu. of noble birth, who, after a time in service as page and squire, was raised to honorable military rank and bound to chivalrous conduct. **2.** a man upon whom a certain honor, like that of the medieval knight, and with it the title *Sir,* is given by a ruler for life, because of personal worth or for service to the country. **3.** *Chess.* a piece shaped like a horse's head. **4.** a member of any order or association of men bearing the name of *Knights.* ◇*v.t.* **5.** to give (a man) the title of knight. [OE *cniht* boy, manservant] **–knightly,** *adj.* **–knighthood,** *n.*

knight-errant /naɪt-ˈerənt/, *n., pl.* **knights-errant.** a medieval knight who travelled in search of adventures, to show military skill, etc. **–knight-errantry,** *n.*

Knights of the Round Table, *n. pl.* (*Arthurian Legend*) an order of knights of the court of King Arthur.

knit /nɪt/, *v.,* **knitted** or **knit, knitting.** ◇*v.t.* **1.** to make (a garment, etc.) by crossing together loops of yarn either by hand using long straight needles or by machine. **2.** to join

knit (parts, members, etc.) closely and firmly together. **3.** to contract into folds or wrinkles: *to knit your brow.* ◇*v.i.* **4.** to grow or become closely and firmly joined together, as broken bones do. [OE *cnyttan* tie] **– knitter**, *n.*

knitting needle, *n.* a straight, slender rod of steel, plastic, etc., with one or both ends tapered, used in knitting.

knob /nɒb/, *n.* **1.** a part sticking out, usu. rounded, forming the handle of a door, drawer, etc. **2.** a rounded lump on the surface or at the end of something, e.g. a knot on a tree trunk, a rounded hill, etc. [ME] **– knobby**, **knobbly**, *adj.*

knock /nɒk/, *v.i.* **1.** to strike a sounding blow with the hand, fist, or anything hard, esp. on a door, window, etc., as in asking for entry, calling attention, giving a signal, etc. **2.** (of an engine) to make a metallic noise as a result of a fault. **3.** to crash or bump: *The branch knocked against the roof.* ◇*v.t.* **4.** to give a sounding or forcible blow to; hit; strike; beat: *The carpenter knocked the nail in.* **5.** to drive, force, or make by a blow or blows: *to knock a man senseless.* **6.** to strike (a thing) against something else. **7.** *Colloq.* to find fault with; criticise: *She always knocks my ideas.* **8.** to subtract or deduct (fol. by *off*): *to knock $200 off the price.* ◇**9.** Some special uses are:
knock back, 1. *Colloq.* to eat or drink up, esp. rapidly: *He knocked back two pies.* **2.** *Colloq.* to refuse: *The council knocked back the plans for our garage.* **3.** to set back; impede.
knock down, 1. to strike to the ground with a blow. **2.** (in auctions) to show the sale of (the thing bid for) by a blow with a hammer. **3.** to reduce the price of.
knock it off, *Colloq.* stop it (usu. used as a command, to put an end to an argument, fight, etc.).
knock off, *Colloq.* **1.** to stop an activity, esp. work. **2.** to steal. **3.** to kill.
knock on, *Rugby* to knock (the ball) forwards in catching it, and so break the rules.
knock out, 1. to defeat (an opponent) in a boxing match by striking him down with a blow after which he does not rise within a certain time. **2.** to cause (someone) to lose consciousness. **3.** to destroy; damage severely.
knock together, to put together quickly or roughly.
knock up, 1. to wake (someone) up; arouse. **2.** to put together (something) hastily or roughly. **3.** *Sport.* to score runs, tries, etc. **4.** *Tennis.* to practise, esp. before a game begins. **5.** to wear out; exhaust. **6.** *Colloq.* to make pregnant.
◇*n.* **10.** the act or sound of knocking. **11.** a rap, esp. at a door. **12.** a blow; thump. **13.** the noise resulting from the faulty working of some part of an engine. [OE *cnocian*]

knockabout /'nɒkəbaut/, *n.* **1.** *Colloq.* a station hand; odd-job man. ◇*adj.* **2.** rough; boisterous: *a knockabout comedy.*

knock-back /'nɒk-bæk/, *n. Colloq.* a refusal; rejection.

knockdown /'nɒkdaun/, *adj.* **1.** such as to knock something down; overwhelming; irresistible: *a knockdown blow.* **2.** put together in separate parts, so as to be readily knocked down or taken apart, e.g. a boat, a piece of furniture, etc. **3. knockdown price**, the set price of an article at an auction, below which it cannot be knocked down.

knocker /'nɒkə/, *n.* **1.** a hinged knob, bar, etc., on a door, for use in knocking. **2. on the knocker**, *Colloq.* at the right time, punctual: *He was there on the knocker.*

knock-knee /'nɒk-ni/, *n.* **1.** an inward curving of the legs, causing the knees to knock together in walking. **2.** (*pl.*) such knees. **– knock-kneed**, *adj.*

knockout /'nɒkaut/, *n.* **1.** the act of knocking out. **2.** a knockout blow. **3.** *Colloq.* a person or thing of overpowering success or attractiveness. ◇*adj.* **4.** that knocks out.

knoll /nɒl/, *n.* a small, rounded hill; hillock. [OE *cnol*]

Knossos /'nɒsəs, 'knɒ-/, *n.* a ruined city in Crete; capital of the ancient Minoan civilisation, site of the palace of Minos. Also, **Cnossus**.

knot /nɒt/, *n., v.*, **knotted, knotting.** ◇*n.* **1.** a crossing over and through of a cord, rope, etc., drawn tight into a lump or knob, used for fastening two cords, etc., together or to something else. **2.** a band of silk or similar material tied in a knot, as an ornament. **3.** a small group of people or things. **4.** the hard, cross-grained mass of wood at the place where a branch joins the trunk of a tree. **5.** a part of this mass showing in a piece of wood used for building. **6.** a unit of speed, used in sea and air travel and the study of weather patterns, equal to one international nautical mile per hour or 0.514 444 44 m/s (approx. 1.85 km/h). **7. at a rate of knots**, very fast. **8.** a tie; bond. ◇*v.t.* **9.** to tie in a knot or knots; form knots in. **10.** to make safe by a knot. ◇*v.i.* **11.** to become tied in a knot or knots. **12.** to form knots or joints. [OE *cnotta*]

knothole /'nɒthoul/, *n.* a hole in a board of wood formed by the falling out of a knot.

knotty /'nɒti/, *adj.*, **-tier, -tiest. 1.** marked by knots; full of knots. **2.** hard or difficult to understand: *a knotty problem.* **– knottiness**, *n.*

know /nou/, *v.*, **knew, known, knowing,** *n.* ◇*v.t.* **1.** to see or understand as fact or truth, or with clearness and certainty: *I know that he is my son.* **2.** to have fixed in the mind or memory: *to know a poem by heart.* **3.** to be familiar with or aware of, to have met or come across before (a thing, place, person, etc.), usu. by sight, experience, or report: *I know that story.* **4.** to understand from experience: *to know how to make something.* **5.** to be able to see the differences of (one) from another: *to know good from bad.* ◇*v.i.* **6.** to have knowledge, or clear and certain understanding, as of fact or truth. **7.** to be familiar or aware, as of some fact, position, or happening; have information, as about something. ◇*n.* **8. in the know**, having inside knowledge. [OE (ge)cnāwan] **– knowable**, *adj.*

know-all /'nou-ɔl/, *n. Colloq.* someone who claims to know everything, or everything about a particular subject.

know-how /'nouhau/, *n.* knowledge of how to do something; skill for a particular thing.

knowing /'nouɪŋ/, *adj.* **1.** sharp; shrewd; astute; often suggesting a secret understanding of matters: *He gave me a knowing look.* **2.** having knowledge or information; intelligent; wise. **3.** conscious; intentional; deliberate.

knowledge /'nɒlɪdʒ/, *n.* **1.** familiarity with facts, truths, or principles, as gained from study, examination, research, experience or report. **2.** the body of truths or facts built up by mankind in the course of time. **3.** the fact or state of knowing. **4.** something that is known, or may be known. **5.** the sum of what is known. **6.** *Law or Archaic.* sexual intercourse: *carnal knowledge.* **7. to one's knowledge, a.** according to what one knows for certain. **b.** (with a negative) so far as one knows: *I never saw him, to my knowledge.* [ME]

knowledgeable /'nɒlədʒəbəl/, *adj.* possessing knowledge or understanding; intelligent.

known /noun, 'nouən/, *v.* past participle of **know**.

known quantity, *n.* a quantity whose value is given, in algebra, etc., frequently represented by a letter from the first part of the alphabet, as *a*, *b*, or *c*.

Knox[1] /nɒks/, *n.* **John**, 1505?–72, leader of the Protestant Reformation in Scotland, preacher, statesman, and historian.

Knox[2] /nɒks/, *n.* a city in Vic, in the outer eastern suburbs of Melbourne; mixed industry. Pop. 104 207 (1986).

knuckle /'nʌkəl/, *n., v.,* **-led, -ling.** ◇*n.* **1.** a joint of a finger, esp. one of the joints where the fingers meet the rest of the hand. ◇*v.i.* **2.** to apply oneself vigorously or earnestly, as to a task (fol. by *down*): *to knuckle down to work.* **3.** to yield or submit (oft. fol. by *down* or *under*). ◇*v.t.* **4.** to attack, with fists or knuckledusters. [ME]

knuckle-duster /'nʌkəl-dʌstə/, *n.* a piece of metal fitted across the knuckles, used as a weapon.

KO /keɪ 'ou/, *n. Abbrev.* → **knockout** (def. 2). Also, **k.o.**

koala /kou'alə/, *n.* a slow-moving, tailless, grey, furry marsupial, which lives in trees and is native to Australia, about 75 cm long. Also, **koala bear**. [Aboriginal]

Kobe /'koubi/, *n.* a seaport in Japan, on southern Honshu island. Pop. 1 422 922 (1986 est.).

koel /'kouəl/, *n.* a type of cuckoo, of north and eastern Australian coastal areas and islands to the north, shiny blue-black (male) with a long tail and a 'cooee' call; cooee bird; black cuckoo. [Hind, from Skt]

Kohl /koul, kɔl/, *n.* **Helmut**, born 1930, German statesman; became chancellor of West Germany in 1982 and chancellor of the reunited Germany in 1990.

Kokoda Trail /kə'koudə treɪl/, *n.* a trail in PNG between Port Moresby and the village of Kokoda, about 240 km long; the Australian and Papuan soldiers in World War II successfully prevented a Japanese invasion along the trail in 1942.

komodo dragon /kə,moudou 'drægən/, *n.* a giant monitor (lizard) of the island of Komodo in Indonesia; up to 3.5m long.

Kongfuzi /'kʊŋfudzi/, *n.* 551–479 BC, Chinese philosopher and teacher of principles of conduct. He stressed treating others as one would wish to be treated, loyalty, intelligence, and the fullest development of the individual in the five chief relationships of life: ruler and subject, father and son, elder and younger brother, husband and wife, friend and friend. Also, **Kongzi**. Formerly, **Kung-fu-tse**. English, **Confucius**.

Kon-Tiki /kɒn-'tiki/, *n.* a raft of green balsa wood on which an expedition led by Thor Heyerdahl in 1947 floated from Peru to the Marquesas. [named after *Kon-Tiki*, a member of a Peruvian race who, according to legend, floated from Peru to Polynesia]

kookaburra /'kʊkəbʌrə/, *n.* either of two Australian kingfishers famous for their rough voices and a call that is like human laughter: **a.** Also, **laughing kookaburra**. the large, dark brown and white **common kookaburra**, native to eastern Australia and introduced into western Australia and Tas; giant kingfisher, laughing jackass. **b.** a slightly smaller bird with a paler head, the **blue-winged kookaburra**, of tropical northern Australia and NG; barking jackass; howling jackass. [Aboriginal]

Koonalda Cave /ku'nældə keɪv/, *n.* a cave in south-western SA, below the Nullarbor Plain; prehistoric human markings dating back some 20 000 years.

Kooning /'kounɪŋ/, *n.* **Wilhelm de** /'wɪlhɛlm də/, born 1904, US abstract expressionist painter born in Holland.

Koori /'kʊəri/, *n.* **1.** an Aborigine. ◇*adj.* **2.** Aboriginal. Also, **Koorie**. [Aboriginal]

koradji /kɒ'radʒi/, *n.* → **medicine man**. [Aboriginal]

Koran /kɔ'ran, kə-/, *n.* the holy book of Islam, believed by Muslims to contain things made known in Arabic by Allah directly to Mohammed. [Ar: reading, recitation] –**Koranic**, *adj.*

Korea /kə'riə/, *n.* a former country in north-eastern Asia, occupying the Korean peninsula between the Sea of Japan and the Yellow Sea; a monarchy before annexation by Japan in 1910; divided into two occupied zones after World War II with Soviet forces in the North and US forces in the South; these became **North Korea** and **South Korea**. Korean, **Chosŏn**, Japanese, **Chosen**. –**Korean**, *adj., n.*

Korean War /kə'riən wɔ/, *n.* a war, 1950–53, fought between North Korea supported by Communist China, and South Korea supported by the UN.

korowai /'kɒrouwaɪ/, *n. NZ.* a cloak or mantle worn by Maoris and made of woven scraped flax with black fringing.

Kosciusko /kɒzi'ɒskou/, *n.* **Mount**, the highest mountain in Australia, in the Snowy Mountains in south-eastern NSW. 2228 m. [named by explorer PE STRZELECKI after T *Kosciusko*, Polish patriot and general]

kosher /'kouʃə, 'kɒʃə/, *adj.* **1.** (of meat, etc.) lawful, prepared or cleaned according to the Jewish law. **2.** (of shops, houses, etc.) selling or using kosher food. **3.** *Colloq.* proper or correct. [Heb: fit, proper, lawful]

Kosygin /kə'sigən/, *n.* **Aleksei Nikolayevich** /əlɪk'sjeɪ nɪkə'lajəvɪtʃ/, 1904–80, Soviet statesman, born in Russia; prime minister of the Soviet Union 1964–80.

kowari /kə'wari/, *n.* See **marsupial mouse**.

Kowloon /kau'lun/, *n.* a peninsula in south-eastern China, opposite Hong Kong island; a part of Hong Kong. 7.8 km². Chinese, **Jiulong**.

Kow Swamp /'kau swɒmp/, *n.* an important archaeological site in northern central Vic; site of pre-modern Aboriginal remains.

kowtow /kau'tau/, *v.i.* **1.** to knock the forehead on the ground while kneeling, as an act of respect, worship, apology, etc. **2.** to act in a slavelike manner. ◇*n.* **3.** the act of kowtowing. Also, **kotow**. [Chinese (Mandarin): knock-head]

Kr, *Chem. Symbol.* krypton.

Krakatoa /kræka'toua/, *n.* a small volcanic island in Indonesia between Java and Sumatra; site of the most violent volcanic eruption in recorded history, 1883. Also, **Krakatau** /'krækətau/.

kremlin /'kremlən/, *n.* **1.** a heavily armed place in a Russian town or city; citadel. **2.** (*cap.*) such a place in the city of Moscow, including within its walls the chief office of the Soviet government. [Russ: citadel]

kris /kris/, *n.* a short sword or heavy knife with a wavy blade, used by the Malays. [Malay]

Krishna /'krɪʃnə/, *n.* **1.** the most popular Hindu god, as an incarnation of Vishnu. **2.** a river in southern India, flowing from the Western Ghats east to the Bay of Bengal. About 1290 km. Also, **Kistna**. [Skt: black]

Krupp family /krʌp/, *n.* a German family of steel and armament manufacturers, based in Essen, including **1. Friedrich**, 1787–1826, considered to have founded the family business. **2. Alfred** ('*Cannon King*'), 1812–87, son of Friedrich, inventor and metallurgist, famous for his siege guns used in Franco-Prussian war. **3. Gustav Krupp von Bohlen und Halbach**, 1870–1950, son-in-law of Friedrich Alfred; under his management the steel works provided the foundation for German rearmament during World War II; indicted as a war criminal at Nuremberg trials.

krypton /'krɪptɒn/, *n.* an inert gaseous element. *Symbol:* Kr; *at. no.:* 36; *at. wt:* 83·80. [NL, from Gk: hidden. See CRYPT]

K2 /keɪ 'tu/, *n.* a mountain in India, in northern Kashmir in the Karakoram range; second highest mountain in the world. 8610 m. Also, **Dapsang, Godwin Austen**.

Kuala Lumpur /kwalə 'lumpuə, -pə/, *n.* the capital of Malaysia, in the south-western Malay Peninsula; former capital of Selangor (1880–1974), of the British colony of the Federated Malay States (1896), of independent Malaya (1957); designated a federal Territory since 1974. Pop. 1 103 200 (1987 est.).

Kublai Khan /kublə 'kan/, *n.* 1216?–94, Mongol emperor 1259–94, founder of the Yüan dynasty in China; grandson of Genghis Khan.

kudos /'kjudɒs/, *n.* glory; renown. [Gk]

Ku Klux Klan /ku klʌks 'klæn/, **1.** a secret organisation in the southern US, active for several years after the Civil War, which aimed to fight Negro emancipation and Northern supremacy. **2.** a secret organisation (**Knights of the Ku Klux Klan**) inspired by the former, founded in 1915 and active in the southern and other parts of the US, admitting to membership none but native-born, white, gentile, Protestant Americans. Also, **Ku Klux**. *Abbrev.:* KKK [? from Gk *kýklos* circle + modification of CLAN]

kultarr /'kʊltɑ/, *n.* See **jerboa** (def. 1).

kumquat /'kʌmkwɒt/, *n.* **1.** a small, round, or oblong citrus fruit with a sweet skin and acid pulp, used chiefly for jams. **2.** a small tree bearing such a fruit. Also, **cumquat**. [Chinese: gold orange]

kung-fu /kʊŋ-'fu, kʌŋ-'fu/, *n.* karate in the form developed in China.

Kunming /kʊn'mɪŋ/, *n.* a city in the capital of Yunnan province, south-western China; eastern terminus of the Burma Road. Pop. 950 000 (1985 est.).

Kurd /kɜd/, *n.* a member of a pastoral and warlike people speaking an Iranian language and dwelling chiefly in Kurdistan, in south-western Asia.

Kurnell /kə'nel/, *n.* an area near the southern head of Botany Bay, NSW; the site of the first landing of James Cook in Australia.

Kurosawa /kuərə'sawə/, *n.* **Akira** /a'kirə/, born 1910, Japanese film director.

kurrajong /'kʌrədʒɒŋ/, *n.* a flowering tree with thick, leathery pods and shining leaves, wide-spread in eastern Australia where it is valued as food for animals. Also, **currajong**. [Aboriginal]

Kurri Kurri /'kʌri kʌri/, *n.* a town in the City of Greater Cessnock, NSW; residential centre for local mine employees. Pop. (with Weston) 13 411 (1986).

Kuttabul /'kʌtəbʊl/, *n.* a Royal Australian Navy depot ship that was sunk on 2 June 1942 by a Japanese midget submarine at Garden Island, Sydney, NSW; 19 lives were lost.

Kuwait /ku'weɪt/, *n.* a monarchy (emirate) in south-western Asia, on the north-western coast of the Persian Gulf; a British protectorate before independence in 1961; invasion by Iraq

in 1990 led to the Gulf War of 1991 when US-led forces expelled Iraqi army. Pop. 1 688 400 (1983); 17 818 km². *Language:* Arabic, also English. *Currency:* dinar. *Cap.:* Kuwait.
—**Kuwaiti**, *n., adj.*

kW, *Abbrev.* kilowatt.

kwashiorkor /kwæʃiˈɔkə/, *n.* a disease, chiefly of children, associated with a diet lacking in protein. [native name in Ghana]

kWh, *Symbol.* kilowatt hour.

Kwinana /kwəˈnanə/, *n.* a town, shire and port in south-western WA, south of Perth; important industrial area. Pop. 11 798 (1986).

kylie /ˈkaɪli/, *n.* a boomerang having one side flat and the other curved. Also, **kiley**. [Aboriginal]

Kyrie eleison /ˌkɪərieɪ əˈleɪsɒn, -sən/, *n.* 'Lord, have mercy', a petition used: **a.** in various offices of the Eastern and Roman churches. **b.** as a response in Anglican services. [Gk *Kýrie eléēson*]

Kyoto /kiˈoutoʊ/, *n.* a city in central Japan, in southern central Honshu; the capital of Japan, 784–1868. Pop. 1 480 355 (1986 est.). Also, **Kioto**.

Ll

L, l, *n., pl.* **L's** or **Ls, l's** or **ls.** 1. the 12th letter of the English alphabet. 2. something having a shape like that of the letter L.

l, *Symbol.* litre.

l., *Abbrev.* 1. law. 2. left. 3. length. 4. (*pl.* **ll.**) line(s).

L, *Abbrev.* 1. Lake. 2. Latin. 3. latitude. 4. law. 5. length. 6. litre. 7. left. ◇*Symbol.* 8. the Roman numeral for 50. See **Roman numerals.** 9. learner (driver).

la /lɑ/, *n. Music.* See **solfège** and **solfa.**

La, *Chem. Symbol.* lanthanum.

LA /ˈel ˈeɪ/, *Abbrev.* 1. Legislative Assembly. 2. Los Angeles.

lab /læb/, *n. Colloq.* laboratory.

label /ˈleɪbəl/, *n., v.,* **-belled, -belling.** ◇*n.* 1. a slip of paper, etc., for fixing onto something to show its nature, ownership, where it is going, etc. 2. a short word or phrase of description for a person, group, movement, etc. 3. *Colloq.* a trade name, esp. of a gramophone record company. ◇*v.t.* 4. to mark with or describe by or on a label: *The bottle was labelled poison.* 5. to describe; classify: *They labelled him as a troublemaker.* 6. *Phys.* to replace (a stable atom) in a compound by a radioactive isotope of that atom so that its path through a mechanical or biological system can be traced. [ME, from OF, ? from Gmc]

labellum /ləˈbɛləm/, *n., pl.* **-bella.** *Bot.* a petal, or part of a corolla, esp. on an orchid, different in color, etc., from the others. [L: little lip]

labial /ˈleɪbiəl/, *adj.* 1. relating to or like a labium. 2. of or relating to lips. 3. *Phonet.* needing or using lip movement, as *p, v, m, w,* or a rounded vowel. [ML, from L: lip]

labiate /ˈleɪbiət, ˈleɪbiˌeɪt/, *adj.* lipped; having parts which are shaped or arranged like lips.

labiodental /ˌleɪbioʊˈdɛntl/, *adj. Phonet.* with the lower lip close to the upper front teeth, as in *f* or *v.*

labium /ˈleɪbiəm/, *n., pl.* **-bia** /-biə/. 1. a lip or lip-like part. 2. *Anat.* one of the four 'lips' guarding the opening of the vulva. [L: lip]

labor or **labour** /ˈleɪbə/, *n.* 1. physical work done usu. for money. 2. those employed in such work considered as a class, esp. as organised in trade unions and political parties. 3. work, esp. of a hard or tiring kind. 4. a work or job done or to be done: *the 12 labors of Hercules.* 5. the pains and efforts of childbirth. ◇*v.i.* 6. to perform labor; use one's powers of body or mind; work; toil. 7. to be burdened or troubled: *You are laboring under a misunderstanding.* 8. (of a ship) to roll or pitch (def. 12) heavily. ◇*v.t.* 9. to work hard and long at; elaborate: *Don't labor the point.* [ME, from OF, from L: toil, distress]

laboratory /ləˈbɒrətri/, *n., pl.* **-ries.** a building or room fitted with apparatus for carrying out scientific research, experiments, tests, etc., or for making chemicals, medicines, etc. [ML: workshop]

Labor Day or **Labour Day,** *n.* in many countries, a public holiday in honor of labor; celebrated in all states of Australia, on different dates; it commemorates the 19th-century trade union campaign for shorter working hours. Also, **Eight-Hour Day.**

labored or **laboured** /ˈleɪbəd/, *adj.* 1. made or done with great care, pains and detail. 2. not easy or natural: *His breathing became labored.*

laborer or **labourer** /ˈleɪbərə/, *n.* 1. someone employed in work which needs bodily effort rather than skill or training. 2. someone who works hard.

labor force or **labour force,** *n.* the portion of a community available for work, esp. as employees.

labor-intensive or **labour-intensive** /ˈleɪbər-ɪnˌtɛnsɪv/, *adj. Econ.* of or relating to an industry which, while not needing a very large capital investment in machinery, etc., needs a relatively large labor force (opposed to *capital-intensive*).

laborious /ləˈbɔriəs/, *adj.* 1. needing a lot of work or effort: *a laborious job.* 2. taking pains or wanting to do work well. [ME, from L]

labor party or **labour party,** *n.* 1. a political party that represents the interests of working people. 2. (*caps*) such a party in various countries, such as the UK. (For Australia, see **Labor Party.**)

Labor Party, *n.* one of the main political parties in Australia, generally representing the interests of trade unions and working people. Also, **Australian Labor Party.**

labrador /ˈlæbrədɔ/, *n.* (one of) a breed of large dog with black or golden coat of short hair. Also, **labrador retriever.** [named after *Labrador,* a peninsula in north-eastern N America, where the breed originated]

laburnum /ləˈbɜnəm/, *n.* a small tree, mainly European, tree with seed pods and yellow hanging flowers, similar to those of wisteria. [L]

labyrinth /ˈlæbərɪnθ/, *n.* 1. a confusing and complicated network of passages in which it is difficult to find one's way or to reach the exit; maze. 2. a complicated or twisting arrangement of streets, ideas, etc. 3. (*cap.*) *Gk Myth.* the Cretan maze inhabited by the Minotaur. [L *labyrinthus,* from Gk *labýrinthos*] — **labyrinthine,** *adj.*

lace /leɪs/, *n., v.,* **laced, lacing.** ◇*n.* 1. a netlike ornamental material made of threads by hand or machine. 2. a cord or string for

lace holding or drawing together, as when passed through holes in opposite edges: *shoe laces.* ◇*v.t.* **3.** to fasten or draw together with a lace: *to lace school shoes.* **4.** to pass (a cord, etc.) through holes: *to lace ribbon through a blouse.* **5.** to twist or weave together; intertwine. **6.** to add spirits to (coffee or other drinks). [ME, from OF: noose, string, from L: noose, snare] **—lacy,** *adj.*

lacebark /'leɪsbɑk/, *n.* a tree of eastern Australian brush forests, with pink, bell-shaped flowers. Also, **lacewood.**

lace monitor, *n.* a large, common, tree-climbing goanna of Australia.

lacerate /'læsəreɪt/, *v.t.*, **-rated, -rating.** to tear roughly; mangle. [L] **—lacerated,** *adj.* **—laceration,** *n.*

lacewing /'leɪswɪŋ/, *n.* any of various insects with delicate lace-like wings, whose larvae live mainly on aphids.

Lachlan /'lɒklən/, *n.* a river in southern NSW, rising south-west of Goulburn and flowing north-west, west and south-west to its junction with the Murrumbidgee River west of Hay. About 1500 km.

lachrymal /'lækrəməl/, *adj.* of, relating to, or producing tears. [ML, from L: tear]

lachrymose /'lækrəmoʊs/, *adj.* **1.** given to shedding tears; tearful. **2.** tending to cause tears; mournful. [L: tear]

lack /læk/, *n.* **1.** an incompleteness or absence of something needed, wanted or usual. **2.** something lacking or wanting: *Skilled labor was the chief lack.* ◇*v.t.* **3.** to have less than enough of or be without: *She lacks strength.* ◇*v.i.* **4.** (of something needed or desired) to be absent. [ME, from MLG or MD: deficiency]

lackadaisical /lækə'deɪzɪkəl/, *adj.* weak in spirit or interest; listless. [*lackadaisy,* var. of *lackaday* + -ICAL]

lackey /'læki/, *n., pl.* **-eys,** *v.,* **-eyed, -eying.** ◇*n.* **1.** a male servant in uniform who attends the door, waits at table, etc. **2.** a follower who attempts to win favor by unquestioning obedience. ◇*v.t.* **3.** to attend (someone) as a lackey does. [F, from Sp: foot soldier]

laconic /lə'kɒnɪk/, *adj.* using few words; concise. Also, **laconical.** [L, from Gk: Laconian (of Sparta, whose inhabitants were noted for brief, pithy speech)]

lacquer /'lækə/, *n.* **1.** a protective coating of a resin dissolved in a volatile solvent. **2.** any of various resinous varnishes giving a highly polished surface on wood, etc. ◇*v.t.* **3.** to coat with or as if with lacquer. [F, from Ar, from Pers]

lacrosse /lə'krɒs/, *n.* a game played by two teams of ten players each, who try to send a ball through a goal using long-handled racquets. [F *la crosse* the crook (the racquet used in the game)]

lact-, a word part meaning 'milk'. Also, **lacto-.** [L *lacti-,* combining form of *lac*]

lactate /læk'teɪt/, *v.i.,* **-tated, -tating.** to produce milk. **—lactation,** *n.*

lacteal /'læktɪəl/, *adj.* relating to, consisting of, or like milk; milky. [L: milky]

lactic /'læktɪk/, *adj.* relating to or obtained from milk.

lactic acid, *n. Chem.* an acid found **a.** in sour milk. **b.** in muscle tissue after exercise.

lacto-, a variant of **lact-,** before consonants.

lactobacillus /ˌlæktoʊbə'sɪləs/, *n., pl.* **-cilli** /-'sɪlaɪ/. any of a group of bacteria which produce large amounts of lactic acid in the fermentation of carbohydrates, esp. in milk.

lactose /'læktoʊz, -oʊs/, *n.* a crystalline disaccharide (sugar), $C_{12}H_{22}O_{11}$, present in milk; milk sugar.

lacuna /lə'kjunə, -'ku-/, *n., pl.* **-nae** /-ni/, **-nas.** **1.** a space, as in plant or animal tissue. **2.** a gap where something is missing, as in something written. [L: gap]

lad /læd/, *n.* **1.** a boy or young man. **2.** *Colloq.* (in familiar use) any male. Also, **laddie.** [OE *Ladda* (nickname), of obscure orig.]

ladder /'lædə/, *n.* **1.** a structure of wood, metal, or rope, with two sidepieces joined by bars, allowing a person to climb up or down. **2.** a line in a stocking, etc., where stitches have come undone. **3.** a means of rising, as to greatness: *ladder of success.* **4.** a ranking in order: *low on the social ladder.* ◇*v.t.* **5.** to cause a ladder in (a stocking). ◇*v.i.* **6.** (of a stocking) to develop a ladder. [OE]

lade /leɪd/, *v.t.,* **laded, laden** or **laded, lading. 1.** to load, esp. with too much burden (*usu. in passive*): *He was laden with responsibilities.* **2.** to fill plentifully (*usu. in passive*): *trees laden with fruit.* [OE: load, draw (water)]

lading /'leɪdɪŋ/, *n.* load; freight; cargo: *a bill of lading.*

ladle /'leɪdl/, *n., v.,* **-dled, -dling.** ◇*n.* **1.** a long-handled tool with a cup-shaped bowl for carrying liquids, as from pot to plate. ◇*v.t.* **2.** to dip or carry with or as if with a ladle. [OE: LADE]

lady /'leɪdi/, *n., pl.* **-dies,** *adj.* ◇*n.* **1.** a woman of good family or social position, or of good breeding, refinement, etc. **2.** a polite term for any woman. **3.** (*cap.*) **a.** a less formal substitute for the title and rank of various positions held by British women. **b.** a prefix to a title of honor or respect: *Lady Mayoress.* **4.** *Rom Cath Ch.* (*cap.*) the Virgin Mary (usu., **Our Lady**). ◇*adj.* **5.** female. [OE: ? orig. meaning loaf-kneader]

ladybird /'leɪdibəd/, *n.* a small oval beetle with an orange back spotted with black. Also, **lady beetle.** [LADY (Virgin Mary) + BIRD; i.e., (our) Lady's bird]

Lady Day, *n.* **1.** the feast of the Annunciation, 25 March. **2.** one of various days celebrated in honor of the Virgin Mary.

lady-in-waiting /ˌleɪdi-ɪn-'weɪtɪŋ/, *n., pl.* **ladies-in-waiting.** a lady in attendance upon a queen or princess.

lady-killer /'leɪdi-kɪlə/, *n. Colloq.* a man supposed to be dangerously fascinating to women.

Ladysmith /ˈleɪdɪsmɪθ/, *n.* a city in the eastern part of the Republic of South Africa, in Natal; beseiged by Boers 1899–1900.

Lae /leɪ/, *n.* a town in the province of Morobe, PNG, on the eastern coast of the island of New Guinea. Pop. 75 800 (1986 est.).

Laertes /leɪˈɜːtiz/, *n. Gk Legend.* the father of Odysseus.

Lafayette /lafɛɪˈet, lafaˈjet/, *n.* **Marie Joseph Paul Yves Roch Gilbert du Motier** /maˌri ʒouˌzef pɒl iv rɒk ʒilˌbeə dy mɒtiˈe/, **Marquis de**, 1757–1834, French soldier, statesman, and liberal leader, who served on the side of the colonists in the War of American Independence and took a leading part in the French revolutions of 1789 and 1830.

La Fontaine /la fɒˈteɪn/, *n.* **Jean de** /ʒɒ̃ də/, 1621–95, French poet and writer of fables.

Laforgue /laˈfɔg/, *n.* **Jules** /ʒyl/, 1860–87, French symbolist poet whose use of free verse influenced the development of 20th century poetry.

lag[1] /læg/, *v.*, **lagged**, **lagging**, *n.* ◇*v.i.* **1.** to move slowly; fall behind (oft. fol. by *behind*). **2.** to decrease; wane: *His interest in the project is lagging.* ◇*n.* **3.** a falling behind; retardation. **4.** *Mech.* the amount of falling behind of some movement. [Scand]

lag[2] /læg/, *n.* a convict, esp. one continually breaking the law: *an old lag.* [orig. unknown]

lag[3] /læg/, *v.t.* **lagged**, **lagging**. to cover (pipes) with insulation to stop heat loss. –**lagging**, *n.*

lager /ˈlagə/, *n.* a German type of beer, stored for up to several months. [G]

lagerphone /ˈlagəfoʊn/, *n.* a homemade musical percussion instrument, made of beer bottle tops loosely nailed to a broom handle.

laggard /ˈlægəd/, *adj.* **1.** backward; slow; lagging. ◇*n.* **2.** someone who moves slowly; lingerer.

lagoon /ləˈgun/, *n.* **1.** an area of shallow water separated from the sea by low banks. **2.** any small, pondlike body of water, often joining a larger body of water. **3.** a stretch of open water, sometimes seasonal, smaller than a lake. [It, Sp, from L: pool, pond]

Lagos /ˈleɪgɒs/, *n.* a seaport in and the capital of Nigeria, in the south-western part on the Bight of Benin. Pop. 1 097 000 (1986 est.).

lah /la/, *n. Music.* See **solfa**.

Lahore /ləˈhɔ/, *n.* a city in Pakistan in the north-eastern part; the capital of Punjab province. Pop. 2 952 689 (1981).

laid /leɪd/, *v.* past tense and past participle of **lay**[1].

laid-back /ˈleɪd-bæk/, *adj.* relaxed; nonchalant; at ease. Also, **laidback**.

Laing /læŋ, leɪŋ/, *n.* **R(onald) D(avid)**, 1927–89, Scottish psychiatrist noted for his views on schizophrenia which challenged the medical model of mental illness.

lair[1] /leə/, *n.* the den or resting place of a wild beast. [OE]

lair[2] /leə/, *n. Colloq.* **1.** a flashily dressed young man of bold and sometimes rude behavior. **2. lair it up**, to behave in a bold and rude manner. –**lairy**, *adj.*

laissez faire /ˌleɪseɪ ˈfeə/ *n.* **1.** the theory which holds that government should enter as little as possible in the direction of economic affairs. **2.** the idea of leaving people to conduct their own affairs. Also, **laisser faire**. [F: lit., allow to act] –**laissez-faire**, *adj.*

laity /ˈleɪəti/, *n.* **1.** laypeople, as different from the clergy. **2.** people outside any profession as different from those within it. [LAY[3] + -TY[2]]

lake[1] /leɪk/, *n.* a large area of water (fresh or salt) surrounded by land. [OE: stream, pool, pond]

lake[2] /leɪk/, *n.* a red pigment prepared from cochineal. [F, from Pers]

Lake District, *n.* a picturesque mountainous region abounding in lakes, in north-western England. Also, **Lakeland**.

Lake Mungo /leɪk ˈmʌŋgoʊ/, *n.* a dry lakebed, part of Willandra Lakes; important archaeological site.

Lake Poets, *n.pl.* the poets Wordsworth, Coleridge, and Southey; so named from their residence in the Lake District.

Lalor /ˈleɪlə/, *n.* **Peter**, 1827–89, Australian politician, born in Ireland; leader of the Eureka rebellion, 1854.

lam /læm/, *v.t.*, **lammed**, **lamming**. *Colloq.* to beat; strike. [Scand]

lama /ˈlamə/, *n.* a priest or monk of the form of Buddhism found in Tibet, Mongolia, etc. [Tibetan: is silent]

La Mama /la ˈmamə/, *n.* a 'cafe' theatre established in Melbourne in 1965; prominent in the 1970s as an impetus for 'new wave' Australian theatre.

Lamarckism /ləˈmakɪzəm/, *n.* the theory that characteristics developed in an individual through habit, use, disuse, etc., may be passed on to offspring. [named after Jean Baptiste de *Lamarck*, 1744–1829, French biologist who first systematically propounded the theory]

Lamartine /lamaˈtin/, *n.* **Alphonse Marie Louis de** /alˌfɒs maˌri ˈlui də/, 1790–1869, French poet, historian, and statesman.

lamb /læm/, *n.* **1.** (the meat of) a young sheep. **2.** someone who is young, gentle, soft-natured, etc. **3. the Lamb (of God)**, Christ. **4.** someone who is easily cheated. ◇*v.i.* **5.** to give birth to a lamb. [OE]

Lamb /læm/, *n.* **Charles** ('*Elia*'), 1775–1834, British essayist and critic.

lambaste /læmˈbeɪst/, *v.t.*, **-basted**, **-basting**. to beat or scold severely.

Lambe /læm/, *n.* **David**, 1803–43, Australian architect, born in England; Tasmania's first Colonial Architect.

lambent /ˈlæmbənt/, *adj.* **1.** running or moving lightly over a surface: *lambent tongues of flame.* **2.** playing lightly and cleverly over a subject: *lambent wit.* **3.** softly bright: *a*

lambent *steady, lambent light.* [L: licking] **–lambency,** *n.*

Lambert /'læmbət/, *n.* **George Washington Thomas**, 1873–1930, Australian painter and sculptor, born in Russia.

Lambing Flat Riots /'læmɪŋ/, *n.* the name given to violent anti-Chinese demonstrations during 1860–61 on the Lambing Flat goldfields near the present-day site of Young, NSW.

lambkin /'læmkən/, *n.* **1.** a little lamb. **2.** any young and tender creature. [ME]

lamb's fry, *n.* lamb's liver, when used for food.

lame /leɪm/, *adj.*, **lamer**, **lamest**, *v.*, **lamed, laming.** ◇*adj.* **1.** having a physical disability, esp. in the foot or leg. **2.** poor in quality or quantity; insufficient: *a lame excuse.* ◇*v.t.* **3.** to make lame. [OE] **–lameness**, *n.*

lamé /'lameɪ/, *n.* an ornamental fabric in which metallic threads are woven with silk, wool, etc. [F: laminated, from OF: gold or silver thread or wire]

lamella /lə'melə/, *n., pl.* **-mellae** /-'meli/, **-mellas.** a thin plate, scale, membrane, or layer, as of bone, tissue, cell walls, etc. [L] **–lammellar**, *adj.*

lament /lə'ment/, *v.t.* **1.** to feel or express sorrow for: *lament his absence; lament his stupidity.* ◇*v.i.* **2.** to feel, show, or express grief or sorrow (oft. fol. by *over*). ◇*n.* **3.** a formal expression of sorrow, esp. in verse or song. [L: wail, weep] **–lamentable**, *adj.* **–lamentation**, *n.* **–lamented**, *adj.*

lamina /'læmənə/, *n., pl.* **-nae** /-ni/, **-nas.** a thin plate, scale, or layer. [L: thin plate, leaf, layer] **–laminar**, *adj.*

laminate /'læmənət/, *v.*, **-nated, -nating,** /'læməneɪt, -nət/, *adj.* ◇*v.t.* **1.** to separate, split, beat or roll into thin layers. **2.** to make by placing layer upon layer. **3.** to cover with laminae (layers). ◇*adj.* **4.** made of, or having, a lamina or laminae. [LAMIN(A) + -ATE¹] **–lamination**, *n.*

lamington /'læmɪŋtən/, *n.* a cube of sponge cake covered with chocolate icing and dried coconut. [apparently named after Baron *Lamington*, 1860–1940, governor of Qld, 1895–1901]

Lamington Plateau, *n.* a part of the McPherson Range in south-eastern Qld, 19 425 ha. [See LAMINGTON]

lamp /læmp/, *n.* **1.** a device for using a light-supplying source, as gas or electricity. **2.** a vessel for containing a flammable liquid, as oil, which is burnt at a wick as a means of lighting. **3.** anything giving intellectual or spiritual light. [ME, from OF, from L, from Gk: torch, light, lamp]

lampoon /læm'pun/, *n.* **1.** a strong satire attacking a person, government, etc., in either prose or verse. ◇*v.t.* **2.** to attack in a lampoon. [F] **–lampooner, lampoonist**, *n.*

lamprey /'læmpri/, *n., pl.* **-preys.** a type of eel-like fish, some species of which attach themselves to fish and suck their blood. [ME, from OF, from LL]

Lancashire /'læŋkəʃɪə, -ʃə/, *n.* a county in north-western England; formerly included Furness and the cities of Manchester and Liverpool. Pop. 1 380 700 (1986 est.); 3043 km². *Administrative Centre:* Preston. *Abbrev.:* Lancs

Lancaster /'læŋkæstə/, *n.* **1.** an English royal house which reigned 1399–1461, descended from John of Gaunt (Duke of Lancaster), and including Henry IV, Henry V, and Henry VII. See **Wars of the Roses.** **2. GB** (*Edith Joan Lyttleton*), 1874–1945, Australian novelist and short-story writer. **– Lancastrian**, *n., adj.*

lance /læns, lans/, *n., v.*, **lanced, lancing.** ◇*n.* **1.** a long, spearlike weapon with a metal head, used by soldiers on horseback in charging. **2.** a soldier armed with this weapon. **3.** any sharp instrument like a lance, as a spear for killing a whale. **4. →lancet.** ◇*v.t.* **5.** to open with, or as if with, a lancet: *She will lance the boil.* **6.** to pierce with a lance. [ME, from F, from L]

Lancelot /'lansəlɒt/, *n. Arthurian Legend.* the greatest of Arthur's knights, and the lover of Queen Guinevere.

lancet /'lansət, 'lans-/, *n.* **1.** a small surgical instrument, usu. sharp-pointed and two-edged. **2.** *Archit.* a narrow arch or window with a pointed top. [ME, from OF: LANCE]

land /lænd/, *n.* **1.** the solid substance of the earth's surface not covered by water. **2.** the ground, esp. with reference to quality, character, or use: *forest land.* **3.** *Econ.* natural resources as a factor of production. **4.** a part of the earth's surface marked off by natural or political boundaries; country; region. ◇*v.t.* **5.** to bring to or put on land or shore: *to land passengers or goods from a ship.* **6.** to bring into, or cause to arrive in, any place, position, or condition. **7.** *Colloq.* to gain or obtain: *to land a job.* **8.** to bring (a fish) to land, or into a boat, etc. **9.** to give (someone) a task which they may be unwilling to perform (fol. by *with*): *The headmaster landed him with the job of tidying up.* ◇*v.i.* **10.** to come to land or shore: *The boat lands at Devonport.* **11.** to go or come ashore from a ship or boat. **12.** to come to rest upon the ground (or elsewhere), as from a plane, etc. **13.** to come to rest or arrive in any place, position, or condition. **14. land on one's feet,** to be successful in a situation which might have gone badly. [OE]

landed /'lændəd/, *adj.* **1.** owning land: *landed gentry.* **2.** consisting of land: *landed estate.*

landfall /'lændfɔl/, *n.* **1.** an approach to or sighting of land. **2.** land sighted or reached.

landform /'lændfɔm/, *n.* any of the many features which make up the surface of the earth, e.g. plain, mountain, valley, etc.

landing /'lændɪŋ/, *n.* **1.** the act of someone or something which lands. **2.** a place where people or goods are landed, as from a ship. **3.** *Archit.* the floor at the head or foot of a flight of stairs.

landlady /'lændleɪdi/, *n., pl.* **-dies. 1.** a woman who owns and leases (rents out) land, buildings, etc. **2.** a woman who owns or runs an inn or boarding house.

landlocked /'lændlɒkt/, *adj.* **1.** shut in more or less completely by land. **2.** (of some fish) living in waters shut off from the sea.

landlord /'lændlɔd/, *n.* **1.** a man who owns and leases (rents out) land, buildings, etc., to another. **2.** a man who owns or runs an inn, boarding house, etc.

landlubber /'lændlʌbə/, *n.* an inexperienced seaman.

landmark /'lændmak/, *n.* **1.** an easily seen object on land that serves as a guide, esp. to ships at sea. **2.** an event or part that stands out: *The Eureka rebellion was a landmark in our history.* **3.** something used to mark the outer limits of a piece of land.

landmass /'lændmæs/, *n.* a large body of land surrounded by water, e.g. a continent.

landmine /'lændmaɪn/, *n.* → **mine**² (def. 6).

land rights, *n.pl.* the rights of those first living in a country to possess land, esp. sacred tribal grounds.

Landsat /'lændsæt/, *n.* a series of US scientific satellites carrying remote sensing systems which transmit information about the earth's surface, including the location of mineral deposits, population densities, crop production estimates, etc.

landscape /'lændskeɪp/, *n., v.,* **-scaped, -scaping.** ◇*n.* **1.** a view of country scenery from a single point of view. **2.** a painting of natural scenery. ◇*v.t.* **3.** to design and create a new appearance for (a piece of land). [earlier *landskap*, from D]

landslide /'lændslaɪd/, *n.* **1.** the sliding down of a mass of soil, rock, etc., on a steep slope. **2.** any overwhelming victory, esp. an election in which one person or party receives by far the most votes.

Landsteiner /'lændstaɪnə/, *n.* **Karl,** 1868–1943, US physician, born in Austria; discovered the four major blood groups, A, B, AB and O.

Landy /'lændi/, *n.* **John,** born 1930, Australian runner; second in the world to break the four-minute mile.

lane /leɪn/, *n.* **1.** a narrow way or passage between fences, walls, or houses. **2.** a strip of road marked out for a single line of vehicles. **3.** a fixed course followed by ocean-going ships, or by aircraft. **4.** (in racing) each of the spaces between the marked lines which indicate the courses of the competitors. **5.** the narrow alley on which the ball is bowled in tenpin bowling. [OE]

Lane /leɪn/, *n.* **1. Frederick Claude Vivian** ('*Freddy*'), 1880–1969, Australian champion swimmer; the first Australian to win a gold medal in swimming (1900) and the first man to swim 100 yards in one minute. **2. William,** 1861–1917, Australian radical political and union activist, born in England; author of *The Workingman's Paradise* (1892); established 'New Australia' in Paraguay in 1893.

Lang /læŋ/, *n.* **1. John Dunmore,** 1799–1878, Australian Presbyterian clergyman and political and social activist, born in Scotland. **2. John Thomas** (*Jack*, '*the Big Fella*'), 1876–1975, Australian Labor politician; premier of NSW 1925–27 and 1930–32, when he was dismissed by the governor, Sir Philip Game.

Lange /'lɒŋi/, *n.* **David Russell,** born 1942, NZ Labour politician; prime minister 1984–89.

Langland /'læŋlənd/, *n.* **William,** c. 1330–c.1400, English poet; author of *Piers Plowman.* Also, **Langley.**

Langtry /'læŋtri/, *n.* **Lillie** (*Emilie Charlotte Le Breton,* '*the Jersey Lily*'), 1852–1929, English actress and mistress of Edward VII.

language /'læŋgwɪdʒ, 'læŋwɪdʒ/, *n.* **1.** communication by voice in which the arrangement of sounds produced by a speaker has meaning for a listener. **2.** any set or system of chosen symbols allowing people to communicate with those others who are familiar with the system. **3.** any basis of communication and understanding. **4.** a form or manner of expression: *in his own language.* [ME, from OF: tongue, from L]

langue d'oc /lɒŋgə 'dɒk/, *n.* the Romance language of medieval southern France.

Languedoc /lɒgdɒk/, *n.* **1.** a former province in southern France. *Cap.*: Toulouse. **2.** the language of medieval southern France.

langue d'oïl /lɒŋgə dɒ'il/, *n.* the language of medieval northern France.

languid /'læŋgwəd/, *adj.* **1.** drooping from weakness or tiredness; faint. **2.** lacking in spirit or interest; indifferent. **3.** slow and graceful in movement. [L]

languish /'læŋgwɪʃ/, *v.i.* **1.** to become or be weak or without spirit. **2.** to lose activity and strength. **3.** to suffer under any unfavorable conditions: *They could languish in gaol for years.* **4.** to be weakened by desire or longing for. [ME, from F, from L]

languor /'læŋgə/, *n.* **1.** physical weakness or faintness. **2.** lack of energy; indolence. **3.** emotional softness or tenderness. **4.** lack of spirit. **5.** a comforting or heavy stillness. [L] **– languorous,** *adj.*

lank /læŋk/, *adj.* **1.** thinly built; lean. **2.** (of plants, etc.) too long and thin. **3.** (of hair) straight and lifeless. [OE]

lanolin /'lænələn/, *n.* a fatty substance from wool used in ointments. Also, **lanoline** /'lænəlin/. [L: wool]

lantana /læn'tanə/, *n.* any of several originally tropical plants, including one with yellow or orange flowers which has become a troublesome weed in temperate and tropical areas. [NL]

lantern /'læntən/, *n.* a semi-transparent case for enclosing a light and protecting it from

lantern 587 **lariat**

the wind, rain, etc. [ME, from F, from L, from Gk: a light torch]

lanthanide /'lænθənaɪd/, n. any of the closely related metallic elements with atomic numbers 57–71. Also, **lanthanon**.

lanthanum /'lænθənəm/, n. a rare-earth, trivalent, metallic element, similar to aluminium. *Symbol:* La; *at. no.:* 57; *at. wt:* 138.91. [NL, from Gk: escape notice]

lanyard /'lænjəd/, n. 1. *Naut.* a short rope to hold something, esp. to hold and tighten rigging. 2. a colored cord worn around the shoulder of military (or some other) uniforms. [ME]

Lanzhou /lan'dʒoʊ/, n. a city in northern China on the Huang River; capital of Gansu province. Pop 1 144 500 (1985 est.). Formerly, **Lanchow**.

Laocoön /leɪˈɒkoʊɪn/, n. *Gk Legend.* a priest of Apollo at Troy who warned the Trojans against the Trojan Horse and, with his two sons, was killed by serpents sent by Athena or Apollo.

Laos /laʊs/, n. a republic in south-east Asia, bordered by China, Vietnam, Cambodia, Thailand and Burma. Pop. 3 757 000 (1987 est.); 236 800 km². *Languages:* Lao, also French and tribal languages, such as Meo. *Currency:* new kip. *Cap.:* Vientiane. Official name, **Lao People's Democratic Republic**. —**Laotian**, *adj., n.*

lap[1] /læp/, n. 1. the front part of the body from the waist to the knees, but only when one is in a sitting position. 2. this part of the body, seen as a place where a child, animal, etc. may be held or nursed. 3. that in which anything rests or is cared for or taken charge of. 4. a part of a garment which folds over another. 5. **in the lap of luxury**, in a wealthy position. [OE *læppa*]

lap[2] /læp/, v., **lapped, lapping**, n. ◇v.t. 1. to lay (something) partly over something underneath. 2. to lie partly over (something underneath); overlap. 3. to get a lap or more ahead of (a competitor) in racing. 4. to cut or polish (a gem, etc.) with a lap (def. 9). ◇v.i. 5. to fold or wind round something. 6. to lie upon and reach beyond a thing. ◇n. 7. the act of lapping or of overlapping. 8. a single round or circuit of the course in racing. 9. a rotating wheel with a polishing powder on its surface, used for gems, cutlery, etc. See **lapidary**.

lap[3] /læp/, v., **lapped, lapping**, n. ◇v.t., v.i. 1. (of water) to wash against or beat upon (something) with a gentle splashing. 2. to take up (liquid) with the tongue. ◇v. 3. **lap up**, **a.** to drink (liquid) as a cat does. **b.** to accept eagerly: *He lapped up all the attention.* ◇n. 4. (the sound of) the lapping of water against something. [OE *lapian*]

lapel /ləˈpɛl/, n. the part of a collar folded back over the chest. [little LAP[1]] —**lapelled**, *adj.*

La Pérouse /la pəˈruːz/, n. Jean François de Galaup /ʒɒ̃ frɑ̃,swa də gaˈloʊ/, Comte de, 1741–88, French-born explorer and navigator in Australia.

lapidary /'læpədəri/, n., pl. **-ries**, adj. ◇n. 1. a person who cuts and polishes precious stones. 2. an expert on precious stones. ◇adj. 3. relating to the cutting of stones. [ME, from L: of stones or stone]

lapis lazuli, /,læpəs 'læzjuli, -laɪ/ n. 1. a deep blue stone used mainly for ornamental purposes. 2. the color of sky blue; azure. [ML, from L]

Lapland /'læplənd/, n. a region inhabited by Lapps in northern Norway, northern Sweden, northern Finland, and the Kola peninsula of north-western Russia.

lap-lap /'læp-læp/, n. a cloth around the waist or loins worn in PNG and the South Pacific.

lapse /læps/, n., v., **lapsed, lapsing**. ◇n. 1. a slip or small mistake: *a lapse of memory.* 2. a failure through some fault or bad management: *a lapse of justice.* 3. a passing away, esp. of time: *a lapse of three years.* 4. a slipping or sinking, often to a lower degree or moral condition: *a lapse into drunkenness.* 5. a falling into disuse. ◇v.i. 6. to pass slowly, silently, or by degrees. 7. *Law.* (of an estate, right, etc.) to fall away, or pass on (to someone else) owing to certain conditions not being met. 8. to fall or sink to a lower grade or condition. 9. to fall into disuse. 10. to make a slip or error. 11. (of time) to pass away. [late ME, from L: a fall, slip]

laptop /'læptɒp/, adj. (of a computer) portable and small enough to be operated while held on one's knees. See **desktop**.

Larakia /lærəˈkiə/, n. the Australian Aboriginal language formerly spoken in the Darwin region. Also, **Larrakeah**.

larceny /'lasəni/, n., pl. **-nies**. *Law.* the wrongful taking and carrying away of the personal goods of another. [ME, from L: robbery] —**larcenous**, *adj.*

lard /lad/, n. 1. pig fat melted down for use in cooking. ◇v.t. 2. to prepare or enrich (lean meat, etc.) with pork or bacon. 3. to add to (speech, talk, etc.) for improvement or ornamentation. [ME, from OF, from L: fat of pork]

larder /'ladə/, n. a room or place where food is kept; pantry. [ME, from OF: LARD]

large /ladʒ/, adj., **larger, largest**, n. ◇adj. 1. being of more than common size, amount, or number. 2. of great range: *large powers.* 3. on a great scale: *a large producer.* ◇n. 4. **at large**, **a.** in a free state: *The murderer is at large.* **b.** as a whole; in general: *the country at large.* [ME, from OF, from L: abundant]

largely /'ladʒli/, adv. 1. to a great extent; in great part. 2. in great quantity; much.

largess /laˈdʒɛs/, n. 1. gifts or a gift (as of money) generously bestowed. 2. *Archaic.* generosity. Also, **largesse**. [ME, from OF: LARGE]

largo /'lagoʊ/, adv. (musical direction) in a slow and solemn manner. [It, from L: large]

lariat /'læriət/, n. US. →**lasso**. [Sp: the rope]

lark[1] /lak/, *n.* any of a family of small birds, mostly of the Old World, noted for their singing in flight. [OE]

lark[2] /lak/, *n. Colloq.* **1.** something done for fun; a prank. ◊*v.i.* **2.** to have fun. Also, **skylark**. [orig. uncert.]

Larousse /la'rus/, *n.* **Pierre Athanase** /piɛə ata'naz/, 1817-75, French grammarian, lexicographer, and encyclopedist.

larrikin /'lærəkən/, *n. Colloq.* **1.** (formerly) a rough and sometimes violent young man. **2.** a young person who gets up to tricks. [? Brit (Warwickshire and Worcestershire) d.: mischievous youth] —**larrikinism**, *n.*

larva /'lavə/, *n., pl.* **-vae** /-vi/. the young of any insect which goes through metamorphosis (changes in body structure) before becoming adult. [NL, special use of L: ghost, skeleton, mask] —**larval**, *adj.*

Larwood /'lawud/, *n.* **Harold**, born 1904, English cricketer, noted for his fast bowling.

laryngeal /lærən'dʒiəl/, *adj.* of or relating to the larynx. Also, **laryngal** /lə'ɹɪŋɡəl/. [NL]

laryngitis /lærən'dʒaitəs/, *n.* an inflammation of the larynx oft. causing temporary loss of the voice. [NL]

laryngo-, combining form of **larynx**. Also, before vowels, **laryng-**.

larynx /'lærɪŋks/, *n., pl.* **larynges** /lə'rɪndʒiz/, **larynxes**. **1.** *Anat.* the hollow space at the upper end of the human trachea (windpipe) containing the vocal cords. **2.** a similar structure in other animals. [NL, from Gk]

Lascaux cave /'laskoʊ keɪv/, *n.* a cave in the Dordogne region of central France, containing Palaeolithic wall paintings esp. of animals, dating from about 17 000 years ago.

lascivious /lə'sɪviəs/, *adj.* **1.** full of strong and often uncontrolled sexual appetite. **2.** encouraging (someone) to strong sexual desire. [LL, from L: wantonness] —**lasciviousness**, *n.*

laser /'leɪzə/, *n.* a device for producing a strong, sharply defined, single-color beam of radiation with waves in phase. [*l*(ight) *a*(mplification) *b*y *s*(timulated) *e*(mission) *o*f *r*(adiation)]

lash[1] /læʃ/, *n.* **1.** a piece of cord forming the striking part of a whip. **2.** a swift stroke or blow, with a whip, etc. **3.** a swift sweeping movement; switch: *a lash of an animal's tail.* **4.** a violent beating, esp. of waves, rain, etc., against something. **5.** an eyelash. ◊*v.t.* **6.** to strike or drive, usu. with a whip. **7.** to beat violently or sharply against. **8.** to fling or switch suddenly and swiftly: *The cow lashed its tail.* ◊*v.i.* **9.** to strike strongly at, as with a weapon, etc. (oft. fol. by *out*). **10.** to burst into violent action or speech (fol. by *out*). [ME]

lash[2] /læʃ/, *v.t.* to bind or fasten with a rope, cord, or the like. [special use of LASH[1]]

lashing[1] /'læʃɪŋ/, *n.* **1.** a whipping. **2.** a severe scolding. **3.** (*pl.*) *Colloq.* large quantities (usu. fol. by *of*). [LASH[1] + -ING[1]]

lashing[2] /'læʃɪŋ/, *n.* **1.** a binding or fastening with a rope or the like. **2.** the rope, etc. used. [LASH[2] + -ING[1]]

lass /læs/, *n.* a girl or young woman. Also, **lassie**. [ME]

Lasseter's Reef /'læsətəz/, *n.* an alleged reef of gold claimed by Harry Bell Lasseter (1880-1931?) to exist somewhere in the vicinity of the Petermann and MacDonnell Ranges in the western NT; the claim has generated numerous expeditions.

lassitude /'læsətjud/, *n.* weariness of body or mind; languor. [L: weariness]

lasso /læ'su/, *n., pl.* **-sos**, **-soes**, *v.,* **-soed**, **-soing**. ◊*n.* **1.** a long rope with a running noose at one end, used for catching horses, cattle, etc. ◊*v.t.* **2.** to catch with a lasso. [Sp, from L: noose, snare]

last[1] /last/, *adj.* **1.** occurring or coming latest, or after all others, as in time, order, or place. **2.** latest; most recent: *last week.* **3.** being the only remaining: *Pat's last dollar.* **4.** final: *in his last hours.* **5.** deciding: *the last word in an argument.* **6.** utmost; extreme. **7.** coming after all others in importance or suitability. **8. on one's last legs**, about to collapse. ◊*adv.* **9.** after all others: *I went last.* **10.** on the most recent occasion: *I last saw her at the dance.* **11.** in the end; finally. ◊*n.* **12.** anything which is last. **13.** the end or conclusion. **14. at (long) last**, after much time has passed; eventually. **15. see the last of**, to see for the final time; say goodbye to. [OE super. of *lær* late] —**lastly**, *adv.*

last[2] /last/, *v.i.* **1.** to go on, or continue in progress, existence or life; endure. **2.** to be enough (fol. by *for*): *This money will last for three weeks.* **3.** to continue in force, strength, effectiveness, etc.: *Would he last in a race?* [OE: follow, perform, continue] —**lasting**, *adj.*

last[3] /last/, *n.* a model of the human foot on which boots or shoes are made or fixed. [OE: sole of foot, track)]

last-ditch /'last-dɪtʃ/, *adj.* made in or as a final and desperate effort.

Last Judgment, *n.* the final trial of all mankind, both the living and the dead, at the end of the world.

last post, *n.* a signal on a bugle used to give notice to retire for the night, or at military funerals.

last sacraments, *n.pl. Rom Cath Ch.* the sacraments of penance, viaticum and extreme unction given to a dying person. Also, **last rites**.

Last Supper, *n.* the supper of Jesus and the apostles on the eve of the Crucifixion.

Las Vegas /læs 'veɪɡəs/, *n.* a city in south-eastern Nevada, famous for its gambling casinos. Pop. 193 240 (1986 est.).

latch /lætʃ/, *n.* **1.** a device for holding a door, etc., closed, made of a bar which falls or slides into a hole, catch, etc. ◊*v.t.* **2.** to close or fasten (a door, etc.) with a latch. ◊*v.* **3. latch on to**, *Colloq.* **a.** to fasten (oneself) to. **b.** to understand; comprehend. [OE: take hold of, catch, take]

latchkey /ˈlætʃki/, *n.* a key for drawing back a latch, esp. on an outer door.

latchkey child, *n.* a child whose parents are absent from home before or after school hours and who is unattended for that time and usu. must look after himself or herself.

late /leɪt/, *adj.*, **later** or **latter**, **latest** or **last**, *adv.*, **later**, **latest**. ◇*adj.* **1.** occurring, coming, or being after the usual or proper time: *a late dinner; a late crop.* **2.** continued until after the usual time or hour; protracted: *a late session.* **3.** far advanced in time: *a late hour.* **4.** belonging to the time just before the present: *the latest fashions.* **5.** having recently died: *the late king.* **6.** belonging to an advanced stage in the history or development of something: *late Latin.* **7. of late**, recently. ◇*adv.* **8.** after the usual or proper time, or after delay: *They came late.* **9.** until after the usual time or hour: *He works late.* **10.** at or to an advanced time, period, or stage. **11.** recently but not now. [OE *læt* slow, late] —**lateness**, *n.*

lately /ˈleɪtli/, *adv.* recently; of late; not long since.

latent /ˈleɪtnt/, *adj.* **1.** hidden; concealed; present, but not visible or apparent: *latent ability.* **2.** *Pathol.* (of an infectious agent) dormant. **3.** *Psychol.* below the surface, but able to achieve expression. **4.** *Bot.* (of buds) dormant or undeveloped. [L: lying hid] —**latency**, *n.*

latent heat, *n.* **1.** (of fusion) the heat required to effect the change of state from solid to liquid. **2.** (of vaporisation) the heat required to effect the change of state from liquid to gas.

lateral /ˈlætərəl, ˈlætrəl/, *adj.* **1.** of or relating to the side; sideways: *a lateral view; a lateral branch; a lateral road.* ◇*n.* **2.** a lateral part or extension, as a branch. [L: side]

lateral thinking, *n.* a way of thinking by making associations with other apparently unrelated areas, rather than by following one logical train of thought.

laterite /ˈlætəraɪt/, *n.* *Geog.* a reddish iron-bearing soil formed in tropical regions by the decomposition of the underlying rock. [L: brick]

latest /ˈleɪtəst/, *adj.* (*superlative of* **late**). **1.** after all others. **2.** most up to date; current. ◇*n.* **3. at the latest**, not any later than (a particular time).

latex /ˈleɪtɛks/, *n.*, *pl.* **latices** /ˈlætəsiz/, **latexes** /ˈleɪtɛksəz/. *Bot.* a milky liquid in certain plants, esp. those giving indiarubber. [L: liquid]

lath /laθ/, *n.*, *pl.* **laths** /laðz, laθs/. *n.* one of several thin, narrow strips of wood used to form a groundwork for supporting slates or tiles on a roof or for plastering, etc. [ME]

lathe /leɪð/, *n.* a machine which shapes a piece of wood, metal, etc., by holding and turning it against a cutting tool. [ME, from Scand]

lather /ˈlæðə/, *n.* **1.** foam or froth made from soap and water. **2.** foam or froth formed by heavy sweating. ◇*v.t.*, *v.i.* **3.** to form or cover with, or become covered with lather. [OE] —**lathery**, *adj.*

Latin /ˈlætn/, *n.* **1.** the language used in ancient Rome, which later became an official language used throughout Europe for literature, law, religion, etc. See **vernacular**. **2.** a member of any Latin race. ◇*adj.* **3.** indicating or relating to those peoples (the Italians, French, Spanish, Portuguese, Romanians, etc.) using languages derived from Latin (def. 1). [OE, from L]

Latin America, *n.* the part of the American continents south of the US, in which Romance languages are officially spoken. —**Latin-American**, *adj.*

Latin Quarter, *n.* the quarter of Paris on the south side of the Seine, frequented for centuries by students and artists. [F *Quartier Latin*]

latitude /ˈlætətjud/, *n.* **1.** *Geog.* **a.** the angular distance north or south from the equator of a point on the earth's surface, measured on the meridian of the point. **b.** a place marked by such a latitude. **2.** freedom from narrow restrictions: *After leaving school he had more latitude in dress.* **3.** *Astron.* Also, **celestial latitude.** the angular distance of a heavenly body from the ecliptic. [ME, from L: breadth] —**latitudinal**, *adj.*

La Trappe /la ˈtrap/, *n.* an abbey in Normandy, France, at which the Trappist order was founded.

latrine /ləˈtrin/, *n.* a toilet, esp. in an army camp, etc. [F, from L]

La Trobe /lə ˈtroʊb/, *n.* **Charles Joseph**, 1801–75, Australian administrator, born in London; lieutenant-governor of Vic 1851–54.

Latrobe Valley /ləˌtroʊb ˈvæli/, *n.* a valley in Gippsland, Vic, which runs east-west along the **Latrobe River** from Moe to Sale; important industrial area, coal-mining, power-generating plants, gas and oil treatment plant, etc. [named after LA TROBE]

latter /ˈlætə/, *adj.* **1.** the second mentioned of two (opposed to *former*): *I prefer the latter idea to the former.* **2.** further on in time; later: *in these latter days of human progress.* **3.** nearer to the end: *the latter years of his life.* [OE]

latter-day /ˈlætə-deɪ/, *adj.* **1.** of a day or period further on; modern: *latter-day problems.* **2.** of the last days of the world.

lattice /ˈlætəs/, *n.* **1.** a structure of crossed wooden or metal strips with open spaces between, used as a screen, support for plants, etc. **2.** Also, **crystal lattice**, **space lattice**. a regular network of fixed points about which molecules, atoms, or ions vibrate in a crystal structure. [ME, from OF, from Gmc]

Latvia /ˈlætviə/, *n.* a republic in northern Europe on the Baltic Sea; a constituent republic of the Soviet Union 1949–91, known as the **Latvian Soviet Socialist Republic**. Pop. 2 680 000 (1989 est.); 65 773 km². *Language:* Latvian. *Cap.:* Riga. —**Latvian**, *n., adj.*

laud /lɔd/, *v.t.* to praise; extol. ◇*n.* **2.** music or a song in praise or honor of anyone. [ME, from L: praises] —**laudable**, *adj.* —**laudation**, *n.* —**laudatory**, *adj.*

laudanum

laudanum /'lɔdnəm/, *n.* opium in alcohol, formerly used to lessen pain. [ML var. of *ladanum*; used by Paracelsus (1493-1541) to name a medicine based on opium]

laugh /laf/, *v.i.* **1.** to express amusement, joy, contempt, etc., by an explosive, inarticulate sound of the voice, and by certain expressions of the face. **2.** to make a cry or sound like human laughter, as kookaburras, hyenas, etc. ◇*v.t.* **3.** to drive, put, bring, etc., by or with laughter: *They laughed him out of the room.* **4.** to say with laughter: *'No', she laughed.* ◇*v.* **5. laugh off**, to dismiss (a situation, criticism, etc.) by treating lightly or with ridicule. ◇*n.* **6.** the act or sound of laughing. **7.** (*oft. ironic*) a cause for laughter: *That's a laugh.* [OE]

laughable /'lafəbəl/, *adj.* funny; amusing; ridiculous.

laughing gas, *n.* nitrous oxide, N_2O, which when breathed in sometimes causes exhilaration or laughter, sometimes used as an anaesthetic in dentistry, etc.

laughing jackass, *n.* → kookaburra.

laughing-stock /'lafɪŋ-stɒk/, *n.* someone or something that is laughed at or ridiculed.

laughter /'laftə/, *n.* **1.** the action or sound of laughing. **2.** a feeling of the emotion expressed by laughing: *inward laughter*. [ME; OE *hleahtor*]

Launceston /'lɒnsɛstən/, *n.* a city in northern Tas, on the junction of the North and South Esk Rivers and Tamar River. Pop. 61 492 (1986). [named in honor of the Cornish town in which Governor King was born]

launch[1] /lɔntʃ/, *n.* **1.** a heavy, open, or half-decked boat. **2.** the largest boat carried by a warship. [Sp, Pg]

launch[2] /lɔntʃ/, *v.t.* **1.** to set (a boat, newly built ship) afloat; lower or slide into the water. **2.** to get going: *to launch a scheme; to launch a book.* **3.** to send forth; throw or hurl: *to launch a spear; to launch a plane from an aircraft carrier.* ◇*v.i.* **4.** to burst out or plunge boldly (into action, speech, etc.). **5.** to start out or forth; push out or put forth on the water. ◇*n.* **6.** the act of launching a boat, glider, etc. [ME, from ONF: LANCE]

launching pad, *n.* a base from which a rocket is launched. Also, **launch pad**.

launder /'lɔndə/, *v.t.* **1.** to wash and iron (clothes, etc.). **2.** *Colloq.* to make (money from crime) appear legal. ◇*v.i.* **3.** to do or wash laundry. **4.** to undergo washing and ironing: *This shirt launders beautifully.* [ME: one who washes, from OF, from L: wash]

laundromat /'lɔndrəmæt/, *n.* *Orig. US.* a public laundry with coin-operated washing machines, dryers, etc. Also, **laundrette** /lɔn'drɛt/. [Trademark]

laundry /'lɔndri/, *n.*, *pl.* -**dries**. **1.** clothes, etc., to be washed or that have been washed. **2.** a room in a house set aside for the washing of clothes. **3.** a business where laundry is done commercially. **4.** the act of laundering.

law

laureate /'lɔriət/, *adj.* **1.** crowned or adorned with laurel as a mark of honor. **2.** specially recognised or distinguished: *poet laureate.* [ME, from L]

laurel /'lɒrəl/, *n.* **1.** a small evergreen tree of Europe with aromatic leaves used in cookery; sweet bay. **2.** (a wreath of) leaves of this tree as a sign of victory or distinction. **3. rest on one's laurels**, to be satisfied with one's present achievements (and not look for further challenge). [ME, from F, from OF, from L: laurel]

Laurel and Hardy /ˌlɒrəl ən 'hadi/, *n.pl.* a team of US comic film actors, **Stan Laurel** (*Arthur Stanley Jefferson*), 1890-1965, the thin one, and **Oliver Hardy**, 1892-1957, the fat one.

lava /'lavə/, *n.* **1.** molten or fluid rock (magma), which comes out of a volcano. **2.** the igneous rock formed when this solidifies. [It (Neapolitan): stream]

Laval /la'val/, *n.* **Pierre** /pi'ɛə/, 1883-1945, French politician; premier of France 1931-32, 1935-36; premier of Vichy France 1942-44; convicted of treason and executed.

lavatory /'lævətri/, *n.*, *pl.* -**ries**. (a room with) a water-closet or urinal; toilet. [ME, from LL]

lave /leɪv/, *v.t.*, *v.i.*, **laved**, **laving**. *Poetic.* to wash or bathe. [OE: pour water on, wash]

lavender /'lævəndə/, *n.* **1.** a pale, bluish purple color. **2.** a small Old World shrub with spikes of pleasant-smelling pale purple flowers, giving an oil (**oil of lavender**) used in medicine and perfumery, or dried to be put in amongst clothes or sheets. ◇*adj.* **3.** pale bluish-purple. [ME, from AF, from ML]

Laver /'leɪvə/, *n.* **Rod**(*ney George*), born 1938, Australian tennis player; in 1962 completed the 'grand slam' of international tennis by winning the Australian, Wimbledon, French and US championships.

lavish /'lævɪʃ/, *adj.* **1.** using or giving plentifully or generously (oft. fol. by *of*): *lavish of time.* **2.** plentiful; abundant; profuse: *lavish gifts; lavish spending.* ◇*v.t.* **3.** to give plentifully or generously: *to lavish favors.* [ME: profusion, from OF: deluge]

Lavoisier /la'vwaziei/, *n.* **Antoine Laurent** /ˌtwan lɔ'rɒ̃/, 1743-94, French chemist whose concepts form the basis of modern chemistry; discovered that oxygen was involved in combustion, respiration and rusting.

law /lɔ/, *n.* **1.** (one of) a set of rules made by a government or ruling body: *A new law was passed by Parliament; Law is one of the foundations of society.* **2.** the controlling influence of such rules; the ordered condition of society brought about by their observance: *to keep law and order.* **3.** the people or bodies that help to keep these rules, e.g. the police: *to bring down the law on someone.* **4.** a system or collection of such rules: *English law; civil law.* **5.** the branch of knowledge concerned with these rules; jurisprudence: *to study law.* **6.** a particular area of such rules: *commercial law.* **7.** law as an occupation: *to practise law.* **8.** legal

law 591 **lay**

action; litigation. **9.** any (set of) rules or principles of proper conduct. **10. a.** *Philos, Sci.* a statement of the relation between events which is always the same under the same conditions: *law of gravity.* **b.** a mathematical rule. **11.** a commandment or revelation from God. **12. the Law,** the Mosaic Law (often opposed to *the Gospel*). **13.** the five books of Moses (the Pentateuch) containing this system and forming the first of the three Jewish divisions of the Old Testament; Torah. **14. be a law unto oneself,** to do what one wishes, without respect for rules. **15. lay down the law,** to give an order or opinion with unnecessary or unpleasant force. [OE, from Scand]

Law /lɔ/, *n.* **1. Andrew Bonar,** 1858–1923, British politician born in Canada, prime minister of Great Britain 1922–23.

lawful /'lɔfəl/, *adj.* **1.** allowed or recognised by law; according to law: *lawful marriage.* **2.** entitled by law: *lawful king.*

Lawler /'lɔlə/, *n.* **Ray(mond Evenor),** born 1921, Australian playwright; wrote *The Summer of the Seventeenth Doll* (1955).

lawless /'lɔləs/, *adj.* **1.** regardless of or against the law: *lawless violence.* **2.** uncontrolled by law; unbridled: *lawless passions.*

Law Lords, *n.pl.* those members of the House of Lords who take part in its judicial proceedings.

lawn[1] /lɔn/, *n.* a stretch of grass-covered land, esp. one closely mowed, as near a house, etc. [OF: wooded ground; of Celtic orig.]

lawn[2] /lɔn/, *n.* a thin or sheer linen or cotton fabric, either plain or printed. [ME; probably named after *Laon*, a town in N France, where much linen was made]

lawn bowls, *n.* a game in which the players roll weighted balls along a very smooth lawn in an effort to make them stop as near as possible to a target ball called the jack.

law of diminishing returns, *n.* the principle that the returns on total output decrease as labor and capital are expanded beyond a certain point.

law of supply and demand, *n.* the principle that the price of goods and services is determined by the forces of supply and demand, so that, for example, all other things being equal, an increase in demand causes the price to rise, while an increase in supply causes the price to fall.

Lawrence /'lɒrəns/, *n.* **T(homas) E(dward)** ('*Lawrence of Arabia*'; after 1927, *Thomas Edward Shaw*), 1888–1935, British soldier, archaeologist, and writer. **–Lawrentian,** *adj.*

lawrencium /lɒ'rɛnsiəm, lɔ-/, *n.* a transuranic element produced synthetically. *Symbol:* Lr; *at. no.:* 103. [named after Ernest O *Lawrence,* 1901–58, US physicist, inventor of cyclotron]

Lawson, *n.* **1. Henry,** 1867–1922, Australian writer of verse and prose; noted for his depiction of Australian bush life; works include the short-story collection *While the Billy Boils* (1896). **2. William,** 1774–1850, Australian explorer and official, born in England; member of the NSW Corps and participant in the Blaxland, Wentworth and Lawson expedition that crossed the Blue Mountains, 1813.

lawsuit /'lɔsut/, *n.* the prosecution of a claim in a law court.

lawyer /'lɔjə/, *n.* a person who is qualified to practise law, esp. a barrister or solicitor.

lax /læks/, *adj.* **1.** loose; careless or negligent: *lax morals.* **2.** vague: *lax views on a subject.* **3.** loose or slack: *a lax cord; lax bowels.* [ME, from L: loose, slack] **–laxness,** *n.* **–laxity,** *n.*

laxative /'læksətɪv/, *n. Med.* **1.** a medicine or substance for relieving constipation. ◇*adj.* **2.** having the effect of a laxative; mildly purgative. [L: loosening]

lay[1] /leɪ/, *v.,* **laid, laying,** *n.* ◇*v.t.* **1.** to put or place in a position of rest or stillness: *to lay a book on a desk.* **2.** to bring down: *to lay a person low.* **3.** to get rid of; allay; appease: *to lay fears; to lay ghosts.* **4.** to put to or apply: *to lay a hand on a child.* **5.** to bring forth (an egg). **6.** to place as a bet: *I'll lay you ten to one.* **7.** to put away for future use (fol. by *by*): *to lay money by.* **8.** to present or bring to someone's notice: *He laid his case before the commission.* **9.** *Law.* to make or bring forward; prefer (def. 2): *to lay charges.* **10.** to attribute; ascribe; impute: *to lay the blame on someone.* **11.** to place as a burden, duty, penalty, etc.: *to lay an embargo on shipments of oil.* **12.** to place or arrange in the proper position: *to lay bricks; to lay carpet.* **13.** to set (a table). **14.** to put on or spread over a surface: *to lay rugs on the floor.* **15.** to invent, arrange or set: *to lay plans; to lay a trap.* **16.** *Colloq.* to have sexual intercourse with. ◇*v.i.* **17.** to lay eggs: *The chooks are laying badly at the moment.* **18.** to deal blows (fol. by *on, at, about, into,* etc.). ◇**19.** Some special uses are:
lay hands on, 1. to find or get: *I can't lay my hands on that file.* **2.** to grab or get hold of.
lay hold of or **on,** to seize; grasp.
lay in, to build up a store of: *to lay in supplies.*
lay it on, to exaggerate.
lay off, 1. to dismiss (a workman), esp. temporarily. **2.** *Colloq.* to stop (work, etc.). **3.** *Colloq.* (usu. as command) to stop annoying (someone).
lay on, to provide: *to lay on a fine dinner.*
lay on hands, to place the hands on someone's head in giving spiritual power, holy orders, etc.
lay oneself open, to expose oneself (to criticism, etc.).
lay out, 1. to arrange or spread out in order. **2.** to stretch out and prepare (a body) for burial. **3.** *Colloq.* to spend (money, one's energy). **4.** to knock unconscious.
lay up, 1. to store for future use. **2.** to cause to stay in bed or indoors.
lay waste, to devastate.
◇*n.* **20.** the way or position in which something is laid or lies. [OE: LIE[2]]

lay[2] /leɪ/, *v.* past tense of **lie**[2].

lay[3] /leɪ/, *adj.* **1.** of or relating to or done by the people or laity, as distinguished from the clergy: *a lay preacher.* **2. lay brother/sister,** a man or woman belonging to a religious order and under vows, but doing mainly manual work. **3.** not belonging to a particular profession, esp. to the law or medicine. [ME, from OF, from LL]

lay[4] /leɪ/, *n.* a song: *the lays of Ancient Rome*. [ME, from OF, ? from Gmc]

lay-by /'leɪ-baɪ/, *n.* **1.** a system of buying an article by paying a deposit and making regular payments before the article is collected: *to put a dress on lay-by*. **2.** something bought in this way. ◇*v.t.* **3.** to put (something) on lay-by.

layer /'leɪə/, *n.* **1.** a thickness of some substance laid on or spread over a surface; stratum. **2. a.** a plant stem fastened to the soil so that it can grow roots and become a separate plant. **b.** a plant grown in this way. ◇*v.t.* **3.** to make a layer of. **4.** to grow by making layers. [ME, from LAY[1] + -ER[1]]

layette /leɪ'et/, *n.* a complete outfit of clothes, etc., for a newborn baby. [F: box, drawer]

layman /'leɪmən/, *n., pl.* **-men.** an ordinary person who is not a member of the clergy or some profession. [LAY[3] + MAN]

layout /'leɪaʊt/, *n.* an arrangement or plan, esp. of a page of a book, newspaper, etc.

Lazarus /'læzərəs/, *n. Bible.* **1.** the beggar in the parable of Lazarus and the rich man (Luke 16:19–31). **2.** the brother of Mary and Martha, and friend of Jesus who raised him from the dead. (John 11:1–44; 12:1–18).

laze /leɪz/, *v.*, **lazed, lazing.** ◇*v.i.* **1.** to be lazy; idle or lounge lazily. ◇*v.t.* **2.** to pass (time) lazily (fol. by *away*). ◇*n.* **3.** the act of lazing.

lazy /'leɪzi/, *adj.*, **-zier, -ziest. 1.** disliking work or effort; idle. **2.** slow-moving; sluggish: *a lazy stream.* **3.** peaceful: *a lazy afternoon.* [orig. uncert.] —**lazily**, *adv.* —**laziness**, *n.*

lb., *pl.* **lbs, lb.** *Symbol.* pound (weight). [L *libra*, the ancient Roman pound (weight)]

l.b.w. /ˌel bi 'dʌbəlju/, *n.* (in cricket) → **leg before wicket.** [abbrev.]

l.c. /ˌel 'si/, *Abbrev.* (in printing) lower case.

LC /ˌel 'si/, *Abbrev.* Legislative Council.

l.c.d. /ˌel si 'di/, *Abbrev.* lowest common denominator.

l.c.f. /ˌel si 'ef/, *Abbrev.* lowest common factor.

l.c.m. /ˌel si 'em/, *Abbrev.* least or lowest common multiple. Also, **LCM.**

LCP /ˌel si 'pi/, *Abbrev.* Liberal-Country Party (coalition).

lea /li/, *n. Archaic.* an area of grassland; meadow. [OE]

leach /litʃ/, *v.t.* **1.** to cause (water, soluble matter, etc.) to filter down through something. **2.** to remove soluble matter from (ashes, soil, etc.) by filtering: *Heavy rain leaches the soil.* [var. of OE *leccan* moisten, wet]

lead[1] /lid/, *v.*, **led, leading,** *n., adj.* ◇*v.t.* **1.** to go before or with to show the way: *She led him to the house.* **2.** to move along while holding and guiding: *to lead a horse by a rope.* **3.** to guide in direction, action, opinion, etc.; influence: *too easily led.* **4.** to bring (water, wire, etc.) in a particular course. **5.** to serve to bring (someone) to a place: *The next road will lead you to the town.* **6.** to command or direct (an army, discussion, etc.). **7.** to go at the head of (a procession, list, etc.). **8.** to act as leader of (an orchestra, etc.). **9.** to go through or pass: *to lead a happy life.* ◇*v.i.* **10.** to act as a guide; show the way. **11.** to be led, or accept being led: *The horse leads easily if you talk to it.* **12.** to give passage to a place: *The road leads to the hills.* **13.** to go first; be in advance: *The white horse is leading.* **14.** to have the directing or main part. **15.** to start; take the initiative (oft. fol. by *off*): *to lead off with a song.* ◇*v.* **16. lead (someone) on,** to make (someone) continue in a foolish belief or action; lure. **17. lead up to,** to prepare gradually for. ◇*n.* **18.** the first or foremost position: *in the lead.* **19.** the amount or distance ahead: *The grey has a lead of five metres.* **20.** the leading or directing position; initiative: *to take the lead.* **21.** a strap for holding a dog, etc.; leash. **22.** a clue. **23.** *Theat.* (the actor playing) the main part in a play. **24.** *Elect.* flex. **25.** *Engineering.* the interval by which a periodic signal precedes another signal of the same phase. ◇*adj.* **26.** solo or dominating, as in a musical structure: *lead singer; lead guitar.* **27.** acting as leader: *lead mare.* [OE]

lead[2] /led/, *n.* **1.** *Chem.* a heavy, soft, malleable bluish-grey metal, used for piping, roofing, etc., and in paint, petrol, etc. Symbol: Pb; *at. no.:* 82; *at. wt:* 207.19. **2.** something made of this metal, esp. **a.** a plummet for measuring the depth of water. **b.** *Print.* a strip of lead inserted to increase the space between lines. **3.** bullets; shot. **4. a.** graphite. **b.** a small stick of this used in pencils. **5. swing the lead,** to be idle when there is work to be done; malinger. ◇*v.t.* **6.** to cover, line, weight, treat, etc. with lead. ◇*adj.* **7.** containing or made of lead. [OE]

leaden /'ledn/, *adj.* **1.** consisting or made of lead. **2.** very heavy and hard to move: *leaden eyes; leaden limbs.* **3.** oppressive; burdensome: *leaden fear.* **4.** slow; sluggish: *leaden pace.* **5.** dull, spiritless or gloomy: *leaden thoughts.* **6.** dull grey: *leaden skies.*

leader /'lidə/, *n.* **1.** someone or something that leads. **2.** *Music.* **a.** the main violinist, cornet-player, or singer in an orchestra, band, or chorus, to whom solos are usu. given. **b.** → **concertmaster.** **3.** → **editorial.** —**leadership**, *n.*

leading[1] /'lidɪŋ/, *n.* **1.** the act of someone or something that leads; guidance, direction. ◇*adj.* **2.** directing; guiding. **3.** most important; chief; principal. [LEAD[1] + -ING[1]]

leading[2] /'ledɪŋ/, *n.* a covering or framing of lead. [LEAD[2] + -ING[1]]

leading light /ˌlidɪŋ 'laɪt/, *n. Colloq.* a person who is outstanding in a particular area.

leading note /ˌlidɪŋ 'nout/, *n. Music.* the seventh note of a diatonic scale.

leading question /ˌlidɪŋ 'kwestʃən/, *n.* a question worded so as to suggest the desired answer.

leadlight window /ˌledlaɪt ˈwɪndoʊ/, n. a window made from small pieces of (colored) glass set in a lead frame.

lead line /ˈled laɪn/, n. *Naut.* a line used in measuring the depth of water. See **plumbline**.

leaf /liːf/, n., pl. **leaves** /liːvz/, v. ◇n. **1.** one of the wide, flat, usu. green, organs growing from the stem of a plant. **2.** a page of a book, with both sides included. **3.** a thin sheet of metal, etc.: *gold leaf*. **4.** an extra part of a table top used to increase its size. **5. take a leaf out of someone's book**, to follow someone's example. **6. turn over a new leaf**, to begin new and better behavior or action. ◇v.i. **7.** to put forth leaves. ◇v. **8. leaf through**, to turn the pages of quickly. [OE] —**leafy**, adj.

leaflet /ˈliːflət/, n. **1.** one of the separate divisions of a compound leaf. **2.** a small or young leaf. **3.** a small flat or folded sheet of printed information.

leaf spring, n. *Mach.* a long, narrow, multiple spring made of several layers of spring metal bracketed together.

league[1] /liːɡ/, n., v., **leagued, leaguing**, adj. ◇n. **1.** an agreement or association made between people, nations, etc., out of common interest or for mutual help or service; covenant; compact. **2.** a group of people, nations, etc. in such an association; confederacy. **3.** an association of sporting clubs which arranges matches between teams of similar standard. **4.** (*cap.*) → **Rugby League**. **5. in league**, acting with or having an agreement; allied (oft. fol. by *with*). ◇v.t., v.i. **6.** to unite or join in a league; combine. ◇adj. **7.** of or belonging to a league. **8.** (*cap.*) of or relating to Rugby League. [ME, from OF, from It, from L: bind]

league[2] /liːɡ/, n. a former unit of distance, of about 5 km. [ME, from LL]

League of Nations, n. the organisation of the nations of the world to promote world peace and cooperation which was created by the Treaty of Versailles (1919) and dissolved, April 1946, by the action of its 21st assembly.

Leahy /ˈleɪi/, n. **Michael James**, 1901–79, and his brother **Dan**, 1912–91, Australian gold prospectors, cattle pioneers and explorers in the island of New Guinea.

leak /liːk/, n. **1.** an unintended hole or crack which lets water, gas, etc., in or out. **2.** (any way or means of) unintended entrance or escape. **3.** the act of leaking or draining; leakage. **4.** (a seemingly) accidental giving out of confidential information. ◇v.i. **5.** to let water, gas, etc., in or out by an unintended hole or crack: *The roof is leaking.* **6.** to pass in or out in this way: *gas leaking from a pipe.* **7.** to become known in spite of efforts at secrecy (fol. by *out*): *The truth will leak out.* ◇v.t. **8.** to let (water, money, etc.) flow in or out. **9.** to let or give out (confidential information), esp. to the media. [ME, from Scand] —**leaky**, adj.

leakage /ˈliːkɪdʒ/, n. **1.** the act of leaking; a leak. **2.** (an amount of) something which leaks in or out.

Leakey family /ˈliːki/, n. a family of British anthropologists whose discoveries of hominid fossils in eastern Africa have contributed greatly to the study of human evolution. **1. Louis Seymour Bazett**, 1903–72, esp. noted for the discovery of the remains of Australopithecus (1.75 million years) and Homo erectus (1 million years) at Olduvai Gorge, Kenya. **2. Mary**, born 1913, his wife and co-worker; findings of Homo fossils more than 3.75 million years old. **3. Richard**, born 1944, their son and co-worker; found important fossil deposits in Ethiopia and Kenya.

lean[1] /liːn/, v., **leant** or **leaned, leaning**, n. ◇v.i. **1.** to bend from an upright position; incline. **2.** to be drawn to; tend or incline towards: *to lean towards socialism.* **3.** to rest against or on something for support: *to lean against a wall.* **4.** to depend or rely: *to lean on empty promises.* ◇v.t. **5.** to bend; incline: *He leant his head forward.* **6.** to cause to lean or rest (fol. by *against, on, upon,* etc.): *lean your arm against the railing.* ◇v. **7. lean on**, to put pressure on; intimidate. **8. lean over backwards**, See **backwards** (def. 7). ◇n. **9.** a slope; slant; inclination: *The lean on that building is dangerous.* [OE *hleonian*]

lean[2] /liːn/, adj. **1.** (of people or animals) thin; with little flesh. **2.** (of meat) with little or no fat. **3.** poor, empty, or scarce: *lean diet; lean years.* ◇n. **4.** the lean part of anything. [OE *hlǣne*]

leangle /ˈliːæŋɡəl/, n. a heavy Aboriginal weapon; club. [Aboriginal]

leaning /ˈliːnɪŋ/, n. a tendency; inclination: *strong literary leanings.*

lean-to /ˈliːn-tuː/, n., pl. **-tos**. a shelter made of wood, galvanised iron, etc., propped against a building or wall.

leap /liːp/, v., **leapt** or **leaped, leaping**, n. ◇v.i. **1.** to jump or move quickly: *to leap over a ditch; to leap aside.* **2.** to come too quickly: *to leap to conclusions.* ◇v.t. **3.** to jump over: *to leap a wall.* **4.** to pass over as if by a leap: *to leap difficulties.* ◇v. **5. leap at**, to accept eagerly: *to leap at the chance.* ◇n. **6.** a jump, spring, or bound. **7.** the space cleared in a leap. **8.** a sharp change, esp. a rise: *leap in prices.* **9. leap forward**, a sudden forward development. **10. by leaps and bounds**, very quickly. **11. leap in the dark**, action taken without knowing the outcome. [OE: leap, run]

leapfrog /ˈliːpfrɒɡ/, n., v., **-frogged, -frogging**. ◇n. **1.** a game in which one player leaps over the bent back of another. ◇v.t., v.i. **2.** to jump over (a person or thing) in, or as if in, leapfrog.

leapt /lɛpt/, v. a past tense and past participle of **leap**.

leap year, n. a year of 366 days every fourth year, with the extra day on 29 February.

Lear /ˈlɪə/, n. **Edward**, 1812–88, English humorist and painter; best known for his limericks and nonsense poems.

learn /lɜːn/, v., **learnt** or **learned** /lɜːnd/, **learning**. ◇v.t. **1.** to come to have knowledge of or skill in by study, instruction, or experience: *to learn French; to learn that roads are dangerous.* **2.** to memorise: *learn your*

learn

spelling. **3.** to come to know; find out; ascertain: *to learn the truth.* **4.** to come to have (a habit, etc.): *to learn cleanliness.* **5.** *(in nonstandard usage)* to teach (someone) a lesson: *I'll learn you.* ◇*v.i.* **6.** to get knowledge or skill: *to learn quickly.* **7.** to find out; get news (fol. by *of*): *to learn of an accident.* [OE *leornian*] —**learner,** *n.*

learned /'lɜnəd/, *adj.* **1.** with much knowledge from study; scholarly: *a learned judge.* **2.** of or showing learning: *a learned book.*

learning /'lɜnɪŋ/, *n.* **1.** knowledge gained by study: *a person of great learning.* **2.** the act or process of getting knowledge or skill.

lease /lis/, *n., v.,* **leased, leasing.** ◇*n.* **1.** a contract giving possession and use of land or buildings, for a definite period, in return for regular payments. **2.** the period of time for which it is made: *a lease of six months.* **3. a new lease of life,** renewed energy or strength. ◇*v.t.* **4.** to give the temporary possession or use of (land or buildings) to another; let. **5.** to take or hold by a lease. [ME, from AF, from OF, from L: loosen]

leasehold /'lishoʊld/, *n.* **1.** land or buildings held under a lease. See **freehold.** ◇*adj.* **2.** held by lease. —**leaseholder,** *n.*

leash /liʃ/, *n.* **1.** a strap for holding a dog. ◇*v.t.* **2.** to hold in or as if in a leash. [ME, from OF, from L: loose, lax]

least /list/, *adj.* **1.** smallest; slightest: *the least distance.* ◇*n.* **2.** the smallest amount, quantity, degree, etc. **3. at least, a.** at the smallest or lowest estimate: *at least 5 cm long.* **b.** at any rate; in any case. **4. in the least,** in the smallest degree: *'Do you mind?' 'Not in the least.'* ◇*adv.* **5.** to the smallest extent, amount, or degree: *He was the least prepared.* [OE *lǣst*, superl. of *lǣs(sa)* LESS]

leather /'lɛðə/, *n.* **1.** the skin of animals prepared for use by tanning. ◇*v.t.* **2.** to cover or furnish with leather. [OE *lether* (in compounds)] —**leathery,** *adj.*

leatherjacket /'lɛðədʒækət/, *n.* **1.** a type of fish which has a hard skin which can be removed in one piece like a jacket. **2.** a mixture of flour and water, cooked on red-hot coals.

leatherwood /'lɛðəwʊd/, *n.* a type of Australian or US tree with tough bark.

leave[1] /liv/, *v.,* **left, leaving.** ◇*v.t.* **1.** to go away from: *to leave the house.* **2.** to let stay or be as stated: *to leave a door unlocked; leave your coat off.* **3.** to stop doing; desist from (fol. by *off*). **4.** to let (someone) remain without interference: *leave him alone; leave her be.* **5.** to let (something) remain for action or decision: *leave it until tomorrow.* **6.** to omit; exclude (fol. by *out*): *He left his sister out of the game.* **7.** to allow to remain in the same place, condition, etc.: *leave them here; leave them as they are.* **8.** to have remaining behind: *The wound left a scar; He leaves a widow; 2 from 4 leaves 2.* **9.** to give for use after one's death or departure; bequeath. ◇*v.i.* **10.** to go away; depart: *We leave for Tasmania tomorrow.* [OE *lǣfan*]

leave[2] /liv/, *n.* **1.** permission to do something. **2.** permission to be absent: *to be on leave.* **3.** the time this permission lasts: *thirty days' leave.* **4.** farewell: *to take leave of someone.* [OE *lēaf*]

leaven /'lɛvən/, *n.* **1.** a mass of fermenting dough kept for producing fermentation in a new batch of dough. **2.** any substance which produces fermentation, as yeast. **3.** something which works in another thing to produce change. ◇*v.t.* **4.** to produce bubbles of gas in (a dough or batter). **5.** to spread through so as to change. [ME, from OF, from L: that which raises] —**leavening,** *n.*

leaves /livz/, *n.* plural of **leaf.**

Lebanon /'lɛbənɒn/, *n.* a republic in western Asia, on the Mediterranean Sea, bordered by Syria and Israel; presence of Palestinian guerrilla groups has caused military reprisals by Israel and civil war between these and right-wing Christian groups. Pop. 2 762 000 (1987 est.); 10 452 km^2. *Languages:* Arabic, also French, Kurdish and Armenian. *Currency:* Lebanese pound. Also, **the Lebanon.** —**Lebanese,** *adj.*

lecher /'lɛtʃə/, *n.* a man who continually looks for sexual experiences. [ME, from OF: gourmand, sensualist] —**lecherous,** *adj.* —**lechery,** *n.*

lecithin /'lɛsəθən/, *n.* a naturally occurring lipid containing nitrogen and phosphorus. [Gk: egg yolk]

Le Châtelier's principle /lə ʃə'tɛljəz prɪnsəpəl/, *n.* the principle which states that if a system is in equilibrium a change in one of the conditions will shift the equilibrium so that the system tends to return to its original condition. [named after HL *Le Châtelier*, 1850–1936, French chemist]

Le Corbusier /lə kɔbyzi'eɪ/, *n.* (*Charles Edouard Jeanneret*), 1887–1965, Swiss architect in France whose modular designs greatly influenced modern architecture.

lectern /'lɛktən/, *n.* a reading desk, esp. in a church. [ME *lettrun*, from OF, from ML, from L: read]

lecture /'lɛktʃə/, *n., v.,* **-tured, -turing.** ◇*n.* **1.** a prepared speech before an audience, esp. to teach or inform: *a lecture on Picasso.* **2.** a long and solemn scolding. ◇*v.i.* **3.** to read a prepared speech for teaching or information: *to lecture on Picasso.* ◇*v.t.* **4.** to read such a speech to (an audience): *to lecture students on Picasso.* **5.** to scold at length. [ME, from LL, from L: read] —**lecturer,** *n.*

led /lɛd/, *v.* past tense and past participle of **lead**[1].

ledge /lɛdʒ/, *n.* any narrow, horizontal part sticking out from an upright surface: *a window ledge; a ledge of rock.* [OE *lecg* (exact meaning not clear), from *lecgan* LAY[1]]

ledger /'lɛdʒə/, *n. Bookkeeping.* an account book of final entry, containing all the accounts. [ME]

Le Duc Tho /leɪ dʊk 'toʊ/, *n.* 1911–90, Vietnamese politician who negotiated the ceasefire between North Vietnam and the US (1973); refused Nobel Peace prize 1973.

lee /liː/, *n.* **1.** → **shelter** (def. 1). **2.** the side or part that is sheltered or turned away from the wind. [OE *hlēo* shelter]

leech /liːtʃ/, *n.* **1.** a bloodsucking worm formerly much used by doctors for bloodletting. **2.** a person who clings to another so that he can gain or profit; parasite. **3.** *Archaic.* a doctor (def. 1); physician. ◇*v.t.* **4.** to apply leeches to in order to bleed. [OE *lǣce*]

Leeds /liːdz/, *n.* a city in northern England, in West Yorkshire; centre of clothing manufacture. Pop. 710 100 (1985).

leek /liːk/, *n.* a plant of the lily family, similar to the onion but having a cylindrical bulb, and used in cookery. [OE *lēac*]

Lee Kuan Yew /liː kwan 'juː/, *n.* born 1923, Singapore politian; co-founder of the Socialist People's Action Party; prime minister 1959–90.

leer /lɪə/, *n.* **1.** a sidelong look, esp. an unpleasantly suggestive one. ◇*v.i.* **2.** to look with a leer. [special use of obs. *leer* cheek, OE *hlēor*]

lees /liːz/, *n.pl.* dregs, esp. of wine.

Leeton /'liːtn/, *n.* a town and shire in southern NSW, south-east of Griffith; headquarters of the Murrumbidgee Irrigation Area and of the Rice Marketing Board for NSW. Pop. 6421 (1986).

Leeuwin /'luːən/, *n.* **Cape,** a cape forming part of the south-western coast of WA.

leeward /'liːwəd/, *Naut.* /'luːəd/, *adj., adv.* of, in or toward the direction towards which the wind blows (opposed to *windward*).

leeway /'liːweɪ/, *n.* **1.** the amount of leeward movement of a ship or aeroplane which is being blown off course. **2.** *Colloq.* extra space, time, money, etc.

left[1] /lɛft/, *adj.* **1.** belonging or relating to the side of a person or thing which is turned towards the west when the person or thing is facing north (opposed to *right*). **2.** belonging or relating to the political left (see def. 4). ◇*n.* **3.** the left side. **4.** (*oft. cap.*) a party or group holding socialist or radical political ideas. **5.** a blow with the left hand, as in boxing. [ME; special use of d. OE *left* (OE *lyft*) weak, infirm]

left[2] /lɛft/, *v.* **1.** past tense and past participle of **leave**[1]. ◇*adj.* **2.** remaining.

Left Bank, *n.* a district of Paris, on the southern bank of the Seine, famous for its bohemian atmosphere which attracts artists, students, etc.

left-handed /'lɛft-hændəd/, *adj.* **1.** using the left hand more than the right. **2.** for use by or performed by the left hand. **3.** insincere or ambiguous: *a left-handed compliment.* **4.** awkward; clumsy.

leftist /'lɛftɪst/, *n.* **1.** a member of a socialist or radical party or a person in agreement with their ideas. ◇*adj.* **2.** having socialist or radical political ideas. [LEFT[1] (def. 4) + -IST]

leftward /'lɛftwəd/, *adj.* **1.** on or towards the left. ◇*adv.* **2.** Also, **leftwards.** towards or on the left.

left wing, *n.* the members of a socialist or radical political party or section of a party. —**left-wing,** *adj.* —**left-winger,** *n.*

leg /lɛg/, *n., v.*, **legged, legging.** ◇*n.* **1.** one of the limbs or bodily parts which support and move the human or animal body. **2.** something similiar to a leg in use, position, or appearance, such as one of the supports of a piece of furniture. **3.** the part of a garment which covers the leg. **4.** a section of a journey, race, competition, etc. **5.** *Cricket.* that half of the field which is behind the batter as he or she stands ready to receive the bowling (opposed to *off*). **6. a leg up,** support given to help in climbing. **7. have not a leg to stand on,** to have no good reason or excuse. **8. pull (someone's) leg,** to make fun of or tease (someone). ◇*v.* **9. leg it,** *Colloq.* to walk or run. [ME, from Scand]

legacy /'lɛgəsi/, *n., pl.* **-cies. 1.** *Law.* a gift of property or money made by will; a bequest. **2.** anything handed down by an ancestor, etc. **3.** a result: *This is a legacy of the war in Vietnam.* **4.** (*cap.*) an Australian organisation formed in 1923 to care for the families of those who had died during World War I and which extended in later years to the families of all deceased ex-servicemen. [ME, from OF: legateship, from L: LEGATE]

legal /'liːgəl/, *adj.* **1.** appointed, established, or authorised by law: *This is the legal fare.* **2.** of or relating to law: *the legal profession.* **3.** permitted by law: *Such acts are not legal.* [L: relating to law] —**legality,** *n.*

legalise *or* **legalize** /'liːgəlaɪz/, *v.t.*, **-lised, -lising.** to make legal. —**legalisation,** *n.*

legal tender, *n.* money which may be lawfully offered in payment of debts and which may not be refused.

legate /'lɛgət/, *n.* **1.** →**envoy. 2.** an official representative of the pope in a foreign country. **3.** *Rom Hist.* an assistant to a general in the army or to the governor of a province. [ME, from L: deputy]

legatee /lɛgə'tiː/, *n.* someone to whom a legacy is given.

legation /lə'geɪʃən/, *n.* (the house and offices of) a diplomatic minister and his staff when the minister is not of the rank of an ambassador. [late ME, from L: embassy]

legato /lə'gatoʊ/, *adv.* (usu. a musical direction) in a smooth, even style, without breaks. [It, from L: hind]

leg before wicket, *n. Cricket.* the act of stopping with the leg or some other part of the body a ball which would otherwise have hit the wicket, for which a batsman may be declared out. Also, **l.b.w.**

legend /'lɛdʒənd/, *n.* **1.** a story handed down by tradition from earlier times and popularly accepted as being based on historical fact. **2.** something written on a coin, coat of arms, or under a picture, etc. **3.** notes that explain a table, map, drawing etc. **4.** a famous or admirable person about whom legend-like stories are told. [ME, from OF, from ML: things to be read]

legendary /'lɛdʒəndəri, -dri/, *adj.* **1.** relating to or described in a legend or legends. **2.** worthy to be described in legend.

Léger /leɪ'ʒɛr/, *n.* **Fernand** /fɛə'nɒ̃/, 1881–1955, French cubist artist.

legerdemain /lɛdʒədə'meɪn/, *n.* **1.** → **sleight** (def. 2). **2.** trickery; deception. [ME, from F *léger de main* light(ness) of hand]

leghorn /'lɛghɔn/, *for def. 1;* /lɛ'gɔn/, *for def. 2, n.* **1.** (a hat made of) a fine, smooth, plaited straw. **2.** a Mediterranean breed of the domestic fowl.

legible /'lɛdʒəbəl/, *adj.* able to be read, esp. easily. [ME, from L: read] **– legibility,** *n.*

legion /'lidʒən/, *n.* **1.** *Rom Hist.* a unit of foot soldiers, numbering from 3000 to 6000 men, usu. combined with a cavalry division. **2.** any large body of armed men. **3.** any great number, whether of people or things. [ME, from OF, from L] **– legionary,** *adj., n.*

legionnaire /lidʒə'nɛə/, *n.* a member of a legion, esp. the French Foreign Legion. [F]

Legion of Honour, *n.* a French order of distinction, instituted in 1802 by Napoleon, membership being granted for meritorious civil or military services.

legislate /'lɛdʒəsleɪt/, *v.i.,* -lated, -lating. to make laws. **– legislator,** *n.* **– legislative,** *adj.*

legislation /lɛdʒəs'leɪʃən/, *n.* **1.** the act of making laws. **2.** a law or a body of laws made. [L: the proposing of a law]

Legislative Assembly /'lɛdʒəslətɪv ə'sɛmbli/, *n.* **1.** the lower chamber of certain bicameral parliaments. **2.** the lower house of the parliaments of NSW, Vic and WA. **3.** the only house in the Qld parliament.

Legislative Council, *n.* **1.** the upper chamber of certain bicameral parliaments. **2.** the upper house of the parliaments of all Australian states except Qld.

legislature /'lɛdʒəsleɪtʃə, -lətʃə/, *n.* the law-making body of a country or state.

legitimate /lə'dʒɪtəmət/, *adj.;* /lə'dʒɪtəmeɪt/, *v.,* -mated, -mating; /lə'dʒɪtəmət/, *n.* ◇*adj.* **1.** in accordance with the law, or any established rules. **2.** in accordance with the laws of reasoning; logical: *a legitimate conclusion.* **3.** reasonable; justifiable: *a legitimate demand.* **4.** born of parents legally married. **5.** ruling by the principle of hereditary right: *a legitimate sovereign.* **6.** *Theat.* relating to plays or acting with a serious and literary purpose. ◇*v.t.* **7.** to make or declare lawful. **8.** to show or declare to be just or proper. ◇*n.* **9.** (formerly) a convict. [late ME, from L: lawful] **– legitimacy,** *n.*

leg side, *n. Cricket.* → **leg** (def. 5).

legume /'lɛgjum/, *n.* **1.** any of a family of flowering plants which have pods as fruits, esp. those used for feed, food, or a soil-improving crop. **2.** any table vegetable of this family, such as peas, beans, etc. [F, from L: something gathered (or picked)] **– leguminous,** *adj.*

Le Havre /lə 'havrə/, *n.* a seaport in northern France, on the English Channel, at the mouth of the Seine. Pop. 198 700 (1982).

lei /leɪ/, *n., pl.* **leis.** (in the Hawaiian Islands) a circular arrangement of flowers, leaves, etc., for the neck or head. [Hawaiian]

Leichhardt /'laɪkhɑt/, *n.* **(Friedrich Wilhelm) Ludwig** /'ludvɪg/, 1813–48?, Australian explorer and naturalist, born in Prussia; carried out explorations in 1844, 1846 and the last in 1848, the fate of the members of this expedition not being known.

leilira /laɪ'lɪərə/, *n.* a multipurpose stone knife with a resin hand grip or a resin-hafted wooden handle. [Aboriginal]

leisure /'lɛʒə/, *n.* **1.** time that is free from work or duty; ease: *a life of leisure.* **2. at leisure, a.** with free time. **b.** without haste. **3. at one's leisure,** when one has leisure. [ME, from OF, from L: be permitted]

leisurely /'lɛʒəli/, *adj.* without haste; unhurried: *a leisurely manner;* a leisurely walk.

leitmotiv /'laɪtmouˌtif/, *n.* **1.** (in a music drama) a musical phrase or theme that represents throughout the work a particular person, idea, etc. **2.** the main theme of a work of literature, etc. Also, **leitmotif.** [G: leading motive]

Le Mans /lə 'mɒ̃, lə 'mɒnz/, *n.* an international 24-hour motor race held every June at Le Mans, France.

lemming /'lɛmɪŋ/, *n.* a small, mouselike animal of far northern areas, as Norway, Sweden, and elsewhere, noted for its mass migrations in times of population increases. [Norw]

lemon /'lɛmən/, *n.* **1.** (a tree bearing) a yellowish acid citrus fruit. **2.** a clear, light yellow color. **3.** *Colloq.* something disappointing or unpleasant. ◇*adj.* **4.** made or flavored with lemons. **5.** of a lemon color. [ME, from OF, from Ar, Pers]

lemonade /lɛmə'neɪd/, *n.* a carbonated soft drink made of lemons, sugar, etc. [F: lemon]

lemur /'limə/, *n.* any of various small mammals, related to the monkeys, that live in trees, are mainly active at night, usu. have a fox-like face and woolly fur, and are found chiefly in Madagascar. [NL, from L: ghosts, spectres; so called because of nocturnal habits]

lend /lɛnd/, *v.,* **lent, lending.** ◇*v.t.* **1.** to give the temporary use of (money, etc.), usu. charging interest. **2.** to give the use of (something) with the understanding that it shall be returned. **3.** to give; impart: *Distance lends enchantment to the view.* **4.** to provide in order to help: *I will lend my support to the cause.* ◇*v.* **5. lend oneself/itself,** to be suitable for something: *This room lends itself to study.* **6. lend a hand,** to help. [OE *lǣnan,* from *lǣn* loan] **– lender,** *n.*

length /lɛŋθ/, *n.* **1.** the measure of anything from end to end: *the length of a river.* **2.** the extent from beginning to end of a series, account, book, etc. **3.** extent in time; duration:

length   597   **Lesbos**

the length of a battle. **4.** a piece of a certain length: *a length of rope*. **5.** the longest side or part of something. **6.** the quality or fact of being long: *a journey remarkable for its length*. **7.** the measure from end to end of a horse, boat, etc., as a unit of distance in racing. **8.** *Cricket.* the distance travelled by the ball before it pitches on to the wicket, after delivery by the bowler. **9. at length, a.** to or in the full extent. **b.** after a time; finally. **10. go to any length(s)**, to do whatever is necessary, no matter how difficult, dangerous, etc. [ME and OE, from *lang* LONG¹]

lengthen /ˈlɛŋθən/, *v.t., v.i.* to make or become greater in length.

lengthways /ˈlɛŋθweɪz/, *adv.* in the direction of the length. Also, **lengthwise**.

lengthy /ˈlɛŋθi/, *adj.*, **-thier, -thiest**. having or being of great length, esp. speeches, writings, etc. —**lengthiness**, *n.*

lenient /ˈliniənt/, *adj.* not severe in treatment, spirit, or tendency; mild: *a lenient punishment*. [L: softening] —**leniency, lenience**, *n.*

Lenin /ˈlɛnən/, *n.* **Vladimir Ilich** (*Vladimir Ilich Ulyanov*), 1870–1924, Russian revolutionary leader and writer; chief leader of the 1917 Revolution, and head of the Soviet government 1917–1924.

Leningrad /ˈlɛnəngræd/, *n.* former name of **St Petersburg** (1924–91).

lenitive /ˈlɛnətɪv/, *adj.* reducing pain, etc.; soothing: *a lenitive medicine*.

lenity /ˈlɛnəti/, *n., pl.* **-ties. 1.** the quality or fact of being mild or gentle. **2.** a lenient act. [L]

Lennon /ˈlɛnən/, *n.* **John Winston**, 1940–80, British pop singer, composer and musician; a founding member of the Beatles.

Lennox /ˈlɛnəks/, *n.* **David**, 1788–1873, Australian pioneer bridge-builder and surveyor, born in Scotland.

lens /lɛnz/, *n., pl.* **lenses. 1.** a piece of transparent substance, usu. glass, having two opposite surfaces, either one or both curved, used for bringing together or spreading light rays, as in magnifying, or in correcting faults of eyesight. **2.** a combination of such pieces. **3.** *Anat.* the part of the eye that focuses light rays on the retina; crystalline lens. **4.** *Geol.* a body of ore or rock thick in the middle and thin at the edges, similar to a lens. [L: a lentil (which is shaped like a biconvex lens)]

lent /lɛnt/, *v.* past tense and past participle of **lend**.

Lent /lɛnt/, *n.* **1.** a yearly season of fasting and penitence in preparation for Easter, beginning on Ash Wednesday and including the next forty weekdays before Easter, observed by some Christian Churches. **2.** Also, **lent term**. the first term of the year at some universities. [OE *len(c)ten* spring, Lent] —**Lenten**, *adj.*

lentil /ˈlɛntəl/, *n.* a plant with flattened seeds which are used as a food, similar to peas and beans. [ME, from F, from L: a lentil]

lento /ˈlɛntoʊ/, *adv.* **1.** (a musical direction) slowly. ◇*adj.* **2.** slow. [It, from L]

Lenz's law /ˈlɛnzəz lɔ/, *n.* the law which states that when an electric circuit and a magnetic field move relative to each other, the current induced in the circuit will have a magnetic field opposing the motion. [named after H *Lenz*, 1804–65, German physicist]

Leo /ˈlioʊ/, *n.* a constellation and sign of the zodiac, represented by a lion. [L. See LION]

Leo X, *n.* (*Giovanni de' Medici*), 1475–1521, Italian ecclesiastic and patron of Renaissance art; pope 1513–21; excommunicated Luther (1521).

Leonardo da Vinci /liəˈnadoʊ da ˈvɪntʃi/, *n.* 1452–1519, Italian painter, sculptor, architect, musician, engineer, mathematician, and scientist; painted the *Mona Lisa* c. 1503–05. —**Leonardesque**, *adj.*

leonine /ˈliənaɪn/, *adj.* of, relating to, or like the lion. [ME, from L]

Leonov /ˈlɛɪnɒf/, *n.* **Aleksei** /aˈlɛksɛɪ/, born 1934, Russian cosmonaut; the first man to walk in space (1965).

leopard /ˈlɛpəd/, *n.* **1.** a large, fierce, spotted Asiatic or African animal, of the cat family, usu. yellowish brown, with black markings. **2.** any of various related animals, e.g. the jaguar (**American leopard**), and the cheetah (**hunting leopard**). [ME, from OF, from LL, from LGk] —**leopardess**, *n. fem.*

leopard seal, *n.* → **sea leopard**.

leotard /ˈliətad/, *n.* a close-fitting one-piece garment, worn by dancers, etc. [named after Jules *Léotard*, 19th C French acrobat]

leper /ˈlɛpə/, *n.* a person suffering from leprosy. [ME, from OF, from L, from Gk: scaly]

lepidopterous /lɛpəˈdɒptərəs/, *adj.* belonging to or relating to an order of insects consisting of the butterflies and moths.

leprechaun /ˈlɛprəkɒn/, *n.* (in Irish folklore) a fairy or sprite, shaped like a little man. [from Irish *lupracān* a little sprite]

leprosy /ˈlɛprəsi/, *n.* an infectious disease variously marked by sores and scabs, loss of fingers and toes, loss of feeling in certain nerve areas, etc. [LL. See LEPER]

lepton /ˈlɛptɒn/, *n. Phys.* any of a group of elementary particles which includes electrons and neutrinos.

leptospermum /lɛptoʊˈspɜməm/, *n.* a type of shrub or small tree, in Australia often called **tea-tree**.

lesbian /ˈlɛzbiən/, *n.* a homosexual female. [from LESBOS (Lesvos), birthplace of Sappho, a homosexual poetess of the 6th C BC] —**lesbianism**, *n.*

Lesbos /ˈlɛzbɒs/, *n.* a Greek island in the north-eastern Aegean, near the Turkish coast. Pop. 104 620 (1981); 2165 km². Formerly, **Mytilene**. Modern Greek, **Lesvos**.

lese-majesty

lese-majesty /liz-'mædʒəsti/, n. a crime or offence against the ruling power in a state; treason. [F, from L: injured sovereignty]

lesion /'liʒən/, n. a wound; injury. [late ME, from L: an injury]

Leslie /'lezli/, n. **Patrick**, 1815-81, Australian pastoralist and agriculturalist; pioneer of the Darling Downs, Qld.

Lesotho /lɪ'sutu, lə'soutou/, n. a kingdom in southern Africa, entirely surrounded by the Republic of South Africa; a British protectorate before independence in 1966. Pop.: 1 628 000 (1987 est.); 30 355 km². Language: Sesotho and English. Currency: loti. Cap.: Maseru. Formerly, **Basutoland**.

less /les/, adv. **1.** to a smaller extent, amount, or degree: *less exact*. ◇adj. **2.** smaller in size, amount, degree, etc.: *less energy*. **3.** lower in rank or importance: *no less a person than the manager*. ◇n. **4.** a smaller amount or quantity. ◇prep. **5.** subtracting; minus: *a year less two days*. [OE lǣs(sa)]

-less, a suffix of adjectives **1.** meaning 'without', as in *childless, legless*. **2.** indicating that something cannot be done, as in *countless*. [OE *-lēas*, representing *lēas*, adj., free from, without]

lessee /le'si/, n. someone to whom the lease of a property is given.

lessen /'lesən/, v.i., v.t. to become or make less.

lesser /'lesə/, adj. being smaller in size, amount, importance, etc., than another: *a lesser evil*. [late ME, from LESS + -ER⁴]

lesson /'lesən/, n. **1.** a length of time during which a pupil or class is taught one subject. **2.** part of a book or other material given to a pupil to be learned or studied. **3.** a piece of practical wisdom or knowledge learned: *This experience taught me a lesson*. **4.** something from which one can learn, such as a warning example: *This experience was a lesson to me*. **5.** part of the Bible, etc., read during a religious service. [ME, from OF, from L: a reading]

lessor /le'sɔ, 'lesɔ/, n. someone who gives a lease of a property.

lest /lest/, conj. **1.** for fear that: *He did not move lest he fall*. **2.** (after words expressing fear, danger, etc.) that: *There was danger lest they might be discovered*. [OE]

let¹ /let/, v., **let, letting**, n. ◇v.t. **1.** to allow or permit. **2.** to allow to pass, go, or come. **3.** to rent or hire out (land, buildings, rooms, equipment, etc.) (sometimes fol. by *out*). **4.** to give (a contract for work): *He lets work to carpenters*. **5.** to cause or make: *I'll let you know the news*. **6.** (as an auxiliary in a suggestion, order, etc.): *let me see; let us go*. ◇v. **7.** Some special uses are:
let alone/let be, to stop bothering, arguing with, etc.
let down, to lower.
let (someone) down, to disappoint (someone); fail.
let go, Colloq. **1.** to express anger, or other emotion, freely. **2.** to stop holding onto someone or something.
let off, 1. to excuse from (punishment, work, etc.). **2.** to explode (a firework, etc.).
let off steam, to express one's anger, etc., in a free and harmless manner.
let on, Colloq. to tell, esp. a secret.
let out, 1. to tell (a secret, etc.). **2.** to make (a garment, etc.) larger. **3.** to give out: *He let out a laugh*. **4.** to free.
◇n. **8.** a letting of a property; lease. [OE *lǣtan*]

let² /let/, n., v., **letted** or **let, letting**. ◇n. **1.** Archaic. something that prevents; an obstruction: *without let or hindrance*. **2.** Tennis, etc. interference with the course of the ball or the action of a player on account of which the point must be played again. ◇v.t. **3.** Archaic. to stand in the way of; hinder. [OE: slow; tardy]

-let, a suffix, used mostly to mean 'small' as in *booklet, rivulet*. [OF, from L]

letdown /'letdaʊn/, n. a disappointment.

lethal /'liθəl/, adj. of, relating to, or causing death. [L]

lethargy /'leθədʒi/, n., pl. **-gies. 1.** a state of sleepy dullness; inactivity; apathy. **2.** Med. a disorder marked by great sleepiness. [LL, from Gk: drowsiness] —**lethargic**, adj.

Lethe /'liθi/, n. Gk Myth. a river in Hades, whose water caused those who drank it to forget the past.

letter /'letə/, n. **1.** a message in writing or printing addressed to a person or group. **2.** one of the marks or signs used in writing and printing to represent speech sounds. **3.** actual wording, as opposed to general meaning: *You must follow these orders to the letter; the letter of the law*. **4.** (pl.) literature in general, or the writing of literature: *a man of letters*. ◇v.t. **5.** to mark or write with letters. [ME, from L *littera* alphabetic character, pl. *litterae* epistle, writings]

lettered /'letəd/, adj. educated or learned, esp. in literature.

letterhead /'letəhed/, n. a printed heading on writing paper, giving the name and address of a company, person, etc.

letter of credit, n. an order from a bank, allowing a person named to draw money up to a particular amount from that or connected banks.

letterpress /'letəpres/, n. **1.** a method of printing from raised blocks of type. **2.** printed matter in a book, etc., as opposed to pictures, etc.

lettuce /'letəs/, n. a plant with large green leaves which are much used for salad. [ME, from OF, from L]

let-up /'let-ʌp/, n. Colloq. a pause or slowing down of activity.

leucine /'lusin/, n. an essential amino acid in proteins.

leuco-, a word part meaning 'white'. Also, before vowels, **leuc-**. [Gk *leuko-*, combining form of *leukós*]

leucocyte /'lukəsaɪt/, n. one of the white or colorless cells of the blood, concerned in the

leucocyte destruction of disease-producing bacteria, etc.; white blood cell.

leukaemia or **leukemia** /lu'kimiə/, n. a disease, usu. causing death, marked by overproduction of white blood cells. Also, **leucaemia**. [NL, from Gk: white]

Levant /lə'vænt/, n. the lands bordering the eastern shore of the Mediterranean and the Aegean, esp. Syria, Lebanon, and Israel. [F, properly ppr. of (se) lever rise (with reference to the rising sun). —**Levantine**, adj., n.

levee[1] /'levi/, n. 1. a raised bank of silt built up naturally by a river during flooding. 2. a man-made bank built to prevent overflowing of a river. 3. Agric. one of the small continuous banks of raised ground surrounding fields that are to be irrigated. [F: raise. See LEVER]

levee[2] /'levi, 'leveɪ/, n. 1. Hist. an occasion for the receiving of visitors held early in the morning by a king, queen, etc. 2. any formal reception of guests. [F: a rising. See LEVER]

level /'levəl/, adj., n., v., -elled, -elling, adv. ◇adj. 1. having no part higher than another; having an even surface. 2. not sloping; horizontal. 3. equal: *Their abilities are level.* 4. mentally well-balanced; sensible: *a level head.* 5. **one's level best**, Colloq. one's very best. ◇n. 6. an instrument used for determining whether a surface is horizontal. 7. a horizontal line or plane with respect to height: *The water level is rising.* 8. level position or condition. 9. level surface. 10. a position or rank, high or low: *You are acting on the level of a child; The talks were held at government level.* 11. **find one's level**, to find the most suitable place for oneself, esp. with regard to the people around. 12. **on the level**, sincere; honest. ◇v.t. 13. to make (a surface) level or even: *to level ground before building.* 14. to raise or lower to a particular level, or position. 15. to bring (something) to the level of the ground: *The explosion levelled the building.* 16. to bring (two or more things) to an equality of rank, condition, etc. 17. to aim (a weapon, criticism, etc.) at a target. 18. to turn (a look, etc.) in a particular direction. ◇v.i. 19. to arrive at a common or stable level (oft. fol. by out): *Food prices levelled last year.* ◇adv. 20. in a level, direct or even way. [ME, from OF, from L: a balance, level] —**leveller**, n.

level crossing, n. the place where a road and railway cross at the same level.

level-headed /'levəl-hedəd/, adj. being practical and calm, with good judgment.

lever /'livə/, n. 1. a bar turning about a fixed point or axis, which lifts a weight at one end when force is applied to the other. 2. any of various devices operating on this principle, such as a crowbar. ◇v.t. 3. to move with a lever. [ME, from OF: raise, from L: lighten, lift, raise]

leverage /'livərɪdʒ/, n. 1. the action of a lever. 2. the mechanical power gained by using a lever. 3. power; means of influence: *His position gives him a lot of leverage.*

leveret /'levərət/, n. a young hare. [ME, from OF, from L: hare]

leviathan /lə'vaɪəθən/, n. 1. any very large sea animal, such as the whale. 2. any very large thing, esp. a ship. [ME, from LL, from Heb: ? the coiling up (of a snake)]

Lévi-Strauss /ˌleɪvi-'straʊs/, n. Claude, born 1908, French social anthropologist.

Levit, Bible. Abbrev. Leviticus.

levitate /'levɪteɪt/, v.t., v.i., -tated, -tating. to (cause to) rise or float in the air, esp. by means of some supposedly supernatural power. [LEVIT(Y) + -ATE[1]; modelled on GRAVITATE] —**levitation**, n.

Leviticus /lə'vɪtəkəs/, n. the third book of the Old Testament, containing laws relating to the priests and Levites and to the forms of Jewish ceremonial observance.

levity /'levəti/, n. lack of proper seriousness of mind, character, or behavior: *She accused him of levity in his attitude to the problem.* [L]

levy /'levi/, n., pl. **-ies**, v., **-ied**, **-ying**. ◇n. 1. the raising or collecting of money, soldiers, etc., by legal power or force. 2. something which is raised thus, such as a tax or a group of soldiers. ◇v.t. 3. to place (a tax): *to levy a duty on imported wines.* 4. to start, or make (war). [ME, from F: raise. See LEVER]

lewd /lud, ljud/, adj. marked by, or exciting, indecent sexual desire: *a lewd look; a lewd song.* [ME: ignorant, from OE: of the people] —**lewdness**, n.

Lewers /'luəz/, n. 1. **Gerald Francis**, 1905-62, Australian sculptor; noted woodcarver. 2. **Margo** (Margo Plate), 1908-78, Australian painter, interior decorator, potter and fabric designer.

Lewis /'luəs/, n. 1. **C(live) S(taples)**, 1898-1963, English novelist and essayist. 2. **Essington**, 1881-1961, Australian company executive and mining engineer; chief general manager of BHP 1938-50. 3. **Sinclair**, 1885-1951, US novelist, dramatist, and journalist; author of *Babbitt* (1922).

lexical /'leksɪkəl/, adj. 1. relating to words or to a vocabulary, such as that of a writer or a language. 2. relating to or of the nature of a lexicon. [LEXIC(ON) + -AL[1]]

lexicography /ˌleksə'kɒgrəfi/, n. the writing or compiling of dictionaries. —**lexicographic**, **lexicographical**, adj. —**lexicographer**, n.

lexicon /'leksəkən/, n. 1. a dictionary, esp. of Greek, Latin, or Hebrew. 2. a list of words belonging to a particular subject, language, etc. [ML (much used in Latin titles of dictionaries), from Gk: of or for words]

l.f., Radio. Abbrev. low frequency.

Lhasa /'lasə/, n. the capital of the Xizang AR in the south-eastern part; sacred city of Tibetan Buddhism; until 1904 known as the Forbidden City. Pop. 343 200 (1982). About 3658 m. Also, **Lassa**.

Li, Chem. Symbol. lithium.

liability /ˌlaɪə'bɪləti/, n., pl. **-ties**. 1. (pl.) debts (opposed to *assets*). 2. something or someone that is a disadvantage: *A sick employee*

liability *is a liability.* **3.** the state or fact of being liable: *liability to error; liability to disease.*

liable /'laɪəbəl/, *adj.* **1.** open or subject to something possible or likely, esp. something undesirable: *liable to injury.* **2.** likely: *Problems are liable to appear.* **3.** having a legal responsibility: *liable for costs.* [late ME, from F: bind]

liaise /li'eɪz/, *v.i.*, **-aised, -aising.** to communicate and act together (usu. fol. by *with*). [from LIAISON]

liaison /li'eɪzɒn/, *n.* **1.** *Mil.*, *etc.* a communication between units, in order to ensure connected action. **2.** a similar connection or relation between non-military groups, etc. **3.** a sexual relationship outside marriage. [F, from L: a binding]

liana /li'ɑnə/, *n.* a climbing tropical plant. Also, **liane** /li'ɑn/. [F, from L]

liar /'laɪə/, *n.* someone who tells lies.

libation /laɪ'beɪʃən/, *n.* the pouring out of wine or other liquid in honor of a god. [ME, from L]

libel /'laɪbəl/, *n.*, *v.*, **-belled, -belling.** ◇*n.* **1.** *Law.* **a.** damage to a person's name or reputation by written or printed matter. **b.** the crime or tort of publishing such matter. **2.** anything that deliberately or damagingly misrepresents. ◇*v.t.* **3.** to publish a libel against. **4.** to misrepresent damagingly. [ME, from L: book] **—libellous,** *adj.*

liberal /'lɪbrəl, 'lɪbərəl/, *adj.* **1.** favorable to development and change in social, religious or political affairs. **2.** (*cap.*) of or relating to the Liberal political party. **3.** favorable to the principle of leaving the individual as free as possible in finding self-expression or self-fulfilment. **4.** broad-minded; tolerant. **5.** generous: *a liberal giver; a liberal gift.* **6.** not strict: *a liberal interpretation of a rule.* ◇*n.* **7.** a person with liberal ideas, esp. in religion or politics. **8.** (*oft. cap.*) a member of the Liberal political party. [ME, from L: relating to a free man]

liberal arts, *n. pl.* →**art** (def. 4). [anglicisation of L: arts of free men]

liberalism /'lɪbrəlɪzəm, -bərəl-/, *n.* **1.** liberal principles, in religion or politics, etc. **2.** (*sometimes cap.*) principles and practices of a Liberal political party.

liberality /lɪbə'ræləti/, *n.*, *pl.* **-ties. 1.** the quality of being liberal in giving; generosity. **2.** breadth of mind, tolerance.

Liberal Party, *n.* **1.** one of the main political parties in Australia, generally representing the interests of private business and opposed to socialism and the Labor Party; formed with its present organisation and name by Robert Menzies in 1945. Formerly, **Fusion Liberal Party, Nationalist Party, United Australia Party. 2.** a political party in Great Britain, a fusion of Whigs and Radicals, formed in the 1830s, and one of the dominant political parties until after World War I; in March 1988 merged with the Social Democratic Party to form the Social and Liberal Democrats. **3.** any of certain political parties elsewhere.

liberate /'lɪbəreɪt/, *v.t.*, **-rated, -rating. 1.** to set free (a prisoner, occupied land, etc.). **2.** to free from old-fashioned social standards. [L] **—liberator,** *n.* **—liberation,** *n.*

Liberia /laɪ'bɪəriə/, *n.* a republic on the west coast of Africa, bordered by Sierra Leone, Guinea and Côte d'Ivoire; established in 1822 as a home for freed Afro-American slaves; a republic since 1847. Pop. 2 356 000 (1987 est.); 97 754 km². *Language:* English and tribal languages, of the Mande, Kru and Atlantic groups. *Currency:* Liberian dollar. *Cap.:* Monrovia. **—Liberian** *n.*, *adj.*

libertarian /lɪbə'tɛəriən/, *n.* someone who believes in freedom of thought, behavior, etc. [LIBERT(Y) + -ARIAN] **—libertarianism,** *n.*

libertine /'lɪbətin/, *n.* someone who does not exercise self-control, esp. in moral or sexual matters; a licentious person. [ME, from L: freedman] **—libertinism, libertinage,** *n.*

liberty /'lɪbəti/, *n.*, *pl.* **-ties. 1.** freedom from harsh or oppressive government. **2.** freedom from foreign rule; independence. **3.** freedom from limitations on the power or right of doing, thinking, speaking, etc., according to choice. **4.** freedom from imprisonment, etc. **5.** disrespectful freedom in action or speech, or an example of it: *to take a liberty.* **6. at liberty, a.** free from imprisonment, etc. **b.** not busy. **c.** free or permitted to do a particular thing: *You are at liberty to go home.* [ME, from OF, from L]

Liberty Plains, *n.* an 18th century name for a district in south-western Sydney, NSW; the first free settlers to arrive in NSW were granted land there in 1792.

libidinous /lə'bɪdənəs/, *adj.* full of sexual desire; lustful. [ME, from L]

libido /lə'bidoʊ/, *n.* **1.** *Psychol.* all of the instinctive energies and desires which come from the id. **2.** the sexual urge. [L: pleasure, longing] **—libidinal,** *adj.*

Libra /'librə, 'lɪbrə/, *n.* constellation and sign of the zodiac, represented by a balance. [L: pound, balance, level]

librarian /laɪ'brɛəriən/, *n.* **1.** a person trained in organising and managing a library. **2.** a person in charge of a library. **—librarianship,** *n.*

library /'laɪbri, -brəri/, *n.*, *pl.* **-ries. 1.** a room or building containing books and other material for reading, study, or reference. **2.** such a place from which the public may borrow books, etc. **3.** a collection of books, etc. **4.** a collection of films, records, music, etc. [ME, from L: place to keep books]

libretto /lə'brɛtoʊ/, *n.*, *pl.* **-tos, -ti** /-ti/. the text or words of an opera or other long musical work. [It, from L] **—librettist,** *n.*

Libya /'lɪbjə/, *n.* a republic in northern Africa, on the Mediterranean Sea, bordered by Tunisia, Algeria, Niger, Chad, Egypt and Sudan. Pop. 4 132 000 (1987 est.); 1 775 500 km². *Language:* Arabic, also English and Italian. *Currency:* dinar. *Cap.:* Tripoli. Official name, **Socialist People's Libyan Arab Jamahiriya. —Libyan,** *adj.*, *n.*

lice /laɪs/, *n.* plural of **louse**.

licence /'laɪsəns/, *n.* **1.** formal permission to do something, as to carry on some business, sell alcoholic drinks, etc. **2.** such permission in written form; a certificate or permit. **3.** freedom from strict rules of action, speech, writing style, etc.: *poetic licence*. **4.** uncontrolled freedom of behavior. [ME, from OF, from L]

license /'laɪsəns/, *v.t.*, **-censed, -censing.** to give formal permission to.

licensee /laɪsən'siː/, *n.* someone to whom a licence is given, esp. to sell alcoholic drinks.

licentiate /laɪ'sɛnʃiət/, *n.* someone who has received a licence from a university, etc., to practise a particular art or profession.

licentious /laɪ'sɛnʃəs/, *adj.* uncontrolled in sexual behavior. [ML]

lichen /'laɪkən/, *n.* (any one of) a group of moss-like plants that grow in greenish, grey, yellow, brown, or blackish patches or bushlike forms on rocks, trees, etc. [L, from Gk] –**lichenous,** *adj.*

licit /'lɪsət/, *adj.* permitted; lawful. [late ME, from L]

lick /lɪk/, *v.t.* **1.** to pass the tongue over the surface of. **2.** to change the condition of by strokes of the tongue: *to lick the plate clean*. **3.** to pass or play lightly over, as flames do. **4.** *Colloq.* to defeat. ◊*v.* **5. lick into shape,** to bring to a state of completion or perfection. **6. lick one's wounds,** to go away and recover after a defeat. ◊*n.* **7.** a stroke of the tongue over something. **8.** *Colloq.* great speed. [OE *liccian*]

licking /'lɪkɪŋ/, *n. Colloq.* **1.** a beating. **2.** a defeat.

licorice /'lɪkərɪʃ, 'lɪkrɪʃ, -rəs/, *n.* → **liquorice**.

lid /lɪd/, *n.* **1.** a movable piece, whether separate or joined on, for closing the opening of a container, etc. **2.** an eyelid. **3. put the lid on,** to put an end to. [OE *hlid*] –**lidded,** *adj.*

Liddell /lɪ'dɛl/, *n.* a town in central eastern NSW, near Muswellbrook, in the Hunter Valley; site of a thermal power station, one of the largest in Australia.

Lidice /'lɪdɪtʃi, 'lɪdəsi/, *n.* a village in Bohemia in the Czech Republic which was destroyed and its male inhabitants murdered by the Nazis in 1942 as a reprisal for the assassination of a high-ranking Nazi official; now a national monument.

lie[1] /laɪ/, *n., v.,* **lied, lying.** ◊*n.* **1.** a false statement made in order to deceive; an untruth. **2.** something that gives a false effect. **3. give the lie (to), a.** to charge with telling a lie. **b.** to show to be false; belie. ◊*v.i.* **4.** to speak falsely intending to deceive. **5.** to give a false effect. [OE *lēogan*]

lie[2] /laɪ/, *v.,* **lay, lain, lying,** *n.* ◊*v.i.* **1.** to be in a horizontal and flat position, as on a bed or the ground; recline. **2.** to take such a position (fol. by *down*): *to lie down on the ground*. **3.** to be buried (in a particular spot): *Here lies John Brown*. **4.** to rest in a horizontal position: *A book is lying on the table*. **5.** to be or remain in a position or state: *to lie in ambush*. **6.** to rest, press, or weigh (fol. by *on* or *upon*): *These things lie upon my mind*. **7.** to be found, occur, or be (where specified): *The fault lies here*. **8.** to be placed or situated: *land lying along the coast*. **9.** to consist or be grounded (fol. by *in*): *The real remedy lies in education*. **10.** to be in or have a specified direction: *The trail from here lies to the west*. ◊*v.* **11.** Some special uses are: **as far as in me lies,** to the best of my ability. **let sleeping dogs lie,** to avoid any disturbance, or a controversial topic or action.

lie in, 1. to be confined in childbed. **2.** to stay late in bed.

lie in state, (of a corpse) to be honorably displayed, as in a church, etc.

lie low, to be in hiding.

lie off, (of a ship) to stand some distance away from the shore.

lie to, *Naut.* (of a ship) to lie comparatively stationary, usu. with the head as near the wind as possible.

lie with, 1. to be the responsibility of: *It lies with you to resolve the problem*. **2.** to have sexual intercourse with.

take lying down, to submit without resistance or protest.

◊*n.* **12.** the manner of lying; the relative position or direction in which something lies: *lie of the land*. **13.** *Golf.* the ground position of the golf ball. [OE *licgan*]

Liechtenstein /'lɪktənstaɪn/, *n.* a principality in central Europe on the Upper Rhine, between Austria and Switzerland; an independent state since 1719. Pop. 27 490 (1987 est.); 160 km². *Language:* German (Alemanni). *Currency:* Swiss franc. *Cap.:* Vaduz.

lieder /'liːdə/, *n.pl.* (oft. treated as a sing. collective noun) German songs, esp. of the Romantic composers. [G, plural of *lied* song]

lief /liːf/, *adv.* **1.** Also, **lieve.** gladly; willingly. ◊*adj. Archaic.* **2.** willing. **3.** beloved; dear. [OE *lēof*]

liege /liːdʒ, liːʒ/, *n.* **1.** a lord entitled to loyalty and service. **2.** Also, **liegeman.** a person owing loyalty and service to a ruler, etc.; vassal. ◊*adj.* **3.** loyal; faithful. [ME, from OF: liege, free, exempt, from LL: free man, of Gmc orig.]

lieu /luː, ljuː/, *n. in the phrase* **in lieu of,** instead of. [ME, from F, from L: place]

lieutenant /lɛf'tɛnənt/; *US.* /luː'tɛnənt/, *n. Mil.* See Appendix. [ME, from F *lieutenant*, lit. holding a place, from L]

life /laɪf/, *n., pl.* **lives. 1.** the condition which separates animals and plants from inorganic objects and dead organisms. It is marked by continual activity, growth, metabolism, reproduction and the ability to change according to the surroundings. These qualities arise from the relationships of energy with protoplasm. **2.** the animate existence of an individual: *to risk one's life*. **3.** a similar state or existence thought of as belonging to the soul: *eternal life*. **4.** condition of existence as a human being: *Life wasn't meant to be easy*. **5.**

period of existence from birth to death: *In later life she became more placid.* **6. a.** period of existence, activity, or effectiveness of something non-living, as a machine: *a machine with a life of ten years.* **b.** *Phys.* Also, **lifetime**. the average period between the appearance and disappearance of a particle. **7.** a living being: *Several lives were lost.* **8.** living things as a group, whether animals or plants: *insect life.* **9.** the course or manner of existence: *married life.* **10.** a biography: *a life of Galileo.* **11.** liveliness; vivacity; animation: *a speech full of life.* **12.** existence in the world of business, society, etc.: *My life is ruined!* **13.** someone who makes something lively: *She was the life of the party.* **14.** a prison sentence covering the rest of the convicted person's natural life. ◇**15.** Some special uses are:
(a matter of) life and death, an emergency; a matter of huge importance.
come to life, to show liveliness or vigor.
for dear life, urgently; desperately.
from (the) life, (of a drawing, painting, etc.) drawn from a living model.
[OE *līf*]

life assurance, *n.* → **life insurance.**

lifebelt /ˈlaɪfbɛlt/, *n.* a ring of material that cannot sink, for keeping a person afloat in the water.

lifeblood /ˈlaɪfblʌd/, *n.* **1.** blood needed for life. **2.** something which gives life to or supports anything. Also, **life's blood.**

lifeboat /ˈlaɪfbəʊt/, *n.* **1.** a boat kept on shore, esp. built for rescuing people from ships in distress along the coast. **2.** a boat carried on a large ship for use in case of shipwreck.

lifebuoy /ˈlaɪfbɔɪ/, *n.* a buoyant (floating) ring that can be thrown to someone who needs help to stay afloat.

life cycle, *n. Biol.* the course of development from the fertilisation of the egg to the production of a new generation of germ cells, i.e. from the beginning of the life of one individual of a species to the stage of its sexual maturity.

lifeguard /ˈlaɪfgɑːd/, *n.* **1.** → **lifesaver** (def. 1). **2.** one of a bodyguard of soldiers.

Life Guards, *n.pl.* a cavalry regiment of the British Household Brigade, distinguished by their scarlet uniform jackets and white helmet plumes.

life insurance, *n.* insurance which pays money to the person insured when they reach a certain age, or when the person insured dies to someone they have named. Also, **life assurance.**

life jacket, *n.* a sleeveless jacket filled with air for keeping a person afloat in water. Also, **life vest.**

lifeless /ˈlaɪfləs/, *adj.* **1.** not ever having life; inanimate: *lifeless matter.* **2.** having no living things: *a lifeless planet.* **3.** deprived of life; dead: *lifeless bodies.* **4.** lacking liveliness or spirit: *lifeless performance.*

lifelike /ˈlaɪflaɪk/, *adj.* **1.** looking like a real person: *a lifelike portrait.* **2.** creating an impression of real life: *a lifelike novel.*

lifeline /ˈlaɪflaɪn/, *n.* **1.** a line or rope for saving life, e.g. one attached to a lifeboat. **2.** a route over which supplies can be sent to an area otherwise cut off. **3.** anything supplying emergency help, communication, counselling, etc.

lifelong /ˈlaɪflɒŋ/, *adj.* lasting or continuing throughout life: *lifelong friend; lifelong regret.*

lifesaver /ˈlaɪfseɪvə/, *n.* **1.** someone who gives up time, without being paid, to make sure that people on beaches swim in safe places, and to rescue them if necessary. **2.** someone or something that comforts or helps another: *That bank loan was a lifesaver.*

life sciences, *n.pl.* the sciences concerned with living things, e.g. biology, botany, etc.

life-size /ˈlaɪf-saɪz/, *adj.* of the size of the (living) original: *life-size statue.* Also, **life-sized.**

lifestyle /ˈlaɪfstaɪl/, *n.* the way of life chosen by a person or group.

life support system, *n.* all the equipment which makes human life possible in a situation in which people would normally die, as for astronauts, burn-damaged patients, etc.

lifetime /ˈlaɪftaɪm/, *n.* **1.** the time that one's life continues: *Peace in our lifetime.* **2.** → **life** (def. 6b). **3.** lasting a lifetime.

lift /lɪft/, *v.t.* **1.** to move or bring (something) upwards from the ground or other support to some higher position; hoist. **2.** to raise or direct upwards: *to lift the hand; to lift the eyes.* **3.** to raise in rank, condition, estimation, etc.; elevate or exalt. **4.** to make louder: *to lift the voice.* **5.** to bring to an end: *to lift a ban.* **6.** *Colloq.* **a.** to copy; plagiarise. **b.** to steal. ◇*v.i.* **7.** to go up; give to upward pressure: *The lid won't lift.* **8.** (of clouds, fog, etc.) to rise and gradually disappear. ◇*n.* **9.** the act of lifting, raising, or rising: *the lift of a hand.* **10.** the distance anything is raised. **11.** a lifting or raising force. **12.** a moving platform or cage for bringing goods, people, etc., from one level to another in a building. **13.** any device or apparatus for lifting. **14.** a free ride in a vehicle. **15.** a raising of spirits or feelings; encouragement. **16.** an upward force of air acting on an aeroplane wing, etc. [ME, from Scand]

lift-off /ˈlɪft-ɒf/, *n.* Also, **blast-off.** the start of a rocket's flight from its launching pad.

ligament /ˈlɪgəmənt/, *n., pl.* **ligaments, ligamenta** /lɪgəˈmɛntə/. *Anat.* a band of tissue, usu. white and fibrous, for connecting bones, holding organs in place, etc. [ME, from L: a tie, band]

ligand /ˈlɪgənd, ˈlaɪ-/, *n.* a molecule, atom or ion bonded to the central metal atom or ion in a coordination compound.

ligature /ˈlɪgətʃə/, *n.* **1.** the act of binding or tying up. **2.** anything that serves for binding or tying up, e.g. a band, bandage, or cord. **3.** *Print, Writing.* a stroke, bar or character which combines two letters. **4.** *Music.* → **slur** (def. 6). **5.** *Med.* a thread or wire for tying blood vessels, etc. [ME, from L: bind]

light¹ /laɪt/, *n., adj., v.,* **lit** or **lighted**, **lighting**. ◇*n.* **1.** something which makes things able to be seen, or gives illumination. **2.** *Phys.* **a.** electromagnetic radiation to which the eyes and brain react, ranging in wavelength from about 4×10^7 to 7.7×10^7 metres and travelling at a speed of 2.9979×10^8 metres per second. **b.** the sensation produced by it on the organs of sight. **c.** a similar form of radiation which cannot be seen, e.g. ultraviolet or infra-red rays. **3.** something which gives light, e.g. the sun, a lamp, etc. **4.** the light given by a particular thing; radiance; illumination: *the light of a candle.* **5.** the light from the sun; daylight. **6.** dawn. **7.** the way in which a thing appears or is seen: *This shows him in a good light.* **8.** a gleam or sparkle, as in the eyes. **9.** a thing which gives fire, e.g. a spark, flame, match, etc.: *Could you give me a light?* **10.** the condition of being clearly seen, shown up, or revealed to public notice or knowledge: *To come to light.* **11.** new knowledge or information: *to throw light on a mystery.* **12.** a person who is a shining example; luminary. **13.** → **traffic light.** ◇**14.** Some special uses are:
bring to light, to discover; reveal.
in a good/bad light, under favorable/unfavorable circumstances.
in the light of, taking into account; considering.
see the light, 1. to come into existence. **2.** (of a book, etc.) to be made public, or published. **3.** to realise the truth of something. **4.** to be converted, esp. to Christianity.
◇*adj.* **15.** having light or illumination, rather than dark: *the lightest room in the house.* **16.** pale, or not deep or dark in color. ◇*v.t.* **17.** to set burning (a candle, lamp, pipe for smoking, etc.); kindle (a fire); ignite (fuel, a match, etc.). **18.** to switch on (an electric light). **19.** to give light to; illuminate. **20.** to cause (the face, etc.) to brighten or become animated (oft. fol. by *up*): *A smile lit up her face.* ◇*v.i.* **21.** to take fire or become kindled. **22.** to become bright as with light or color: *The sky lights up at sunset.* **23.** (of the face, etc.) to brighten with liveliness or joy (oft. fol. by *up*). [OE *lēoht*]

light² /laɪt/, *adj.* **1.** of little weight; not heavy: *a light load.* **2.** of little weight in proportion to bulk; of low specific gravity: *a light metal.* **3.** of less than the usual or average weight: *light clothing.* **4.** of small amount, force, intensity, etc.: *a light rain; a light sleep.* **5.** not heavy or serious: *light reading; light music.* **6.** of little importance; trivial: *The loss was light.* **7.** easily digested: *a light meal.* **8.** nimble or agile: *light on one's feet.* **9.** free from sorrow or care: *a light heart.* **10.** cheerful; gay: *a light laugh.* **11.** dizzy; slightly delirious: *light-headed.* **12. make light of,** to treat as of little importance. ◇*adv.* **13.** lightly. **14.** *Colloq.* with little or no luggage: *to travel light.* [OE *lēoht*]

light³ /laɪt/, *v.i.,* **lighted** or **lit**, **lighting**. **1.** to get down from a horse or a vehicle; alight. **2.** to come to rest on a spot or thing; land: *The butterfly lit on a flower.* **3.** to come by chance, happen, or hit (fol. by *on* or *upon*): *to light on a clue.* **4.** (of a stroke, weapon, vengeance, choice, etc.) to fall on a place or person. [OE: alight, orig. make light, relieve of a weight]

Light /laɪt/, *n.* **William,** 1786–1839, Australian naval captain and surveyor-general, born in Malaya; founder of Adelaide.

light barrier, *n.* the speed of light as the maximum speed at which anything can go.

lighten¹ /ˈlaɪtn/, *v.i.* **1.** to become lighter or less dark; brighten. **2.** to shine, gleam, or be bright. **3.** to flash like lightning. **4.** (of the face, eyes, etc.) to brighten or light up. ◇*v.t.* **5.** to illuminate. **6.** to brighten (the eyes, features, etc.). **7.** to make lighter; make less dark. [ME]

lighten² /ˈlaɪtn/, *v.t., v.i.* **1.** to make or become less in weight. **2.** to make or become less hard to bear. **3.** to make or become more cheerful or glad. [ME]

light-fingered /ˈlaɪt-fɪŋgəd/, *adj.* having clever fingers, esp. in picking pockets.

light-headed /ˈlaɪt-hedəd/, *adj.* **1.** having a frivolous or changeable nature: *light-headed young people.* **2.** dizzy, drunk, or delirious.

light-hearted /ˈlaɪt-hatəd/, *adj.* carefree; cheerful.

lighthouse /ˈlaɪthaʊs/, *n.* a tower or other structure showing a light or lights to guide ships.

lighting /ˈlaɪtɪŋ/, *n.* **1.** the act of setting something burning or shining. **2.** (in theatre, films) the arrangement and effect of lights. **3.** the way light falls upon a face, object, etc., esp. in a picture.

lightly /ˈlaɪtli/, *adv.* **1.** with little weight, force, etc.: *to press lightly on a bell.* **2.** to only a small amount or degree: *It was snowing lightly.* **3.** easily, quickly or nimbly: *to jump lightly out of the way.* **4.** cheerfully: *to take the news lightly.* **5.** without proper consideration or reason (often with a negative): *I do not lightly refuse him.* **6.** without interest; indifferently: *to think lightly of one's achievements.*

light meter, *n.* (in photography) an instrument which measures the amount of light and shows the proper exposure for a given scene. Also, **exposure meter**.

lightning /ˈlaɪtnɪŋ/, *n.* a sudden flash of light in the sky, caused by the discharge of atmospheric electricity.

lightning conductor, *n.* a strip of metal, usu. copper, attached to any tall structure to carry any electrical charge from lightning down to the earth, to prevent damage to the building. Also, **lightning rod**.

Lightning Ridge, *n.* an opal-mining settlement in north-western NSW; popular tourist area. Pop. 1292 (1986).

lightweight /ˈlaɪtweɪt/, *adj.* **1.** light in weight. **2.** unimportant, not serious; trivial. ◇*n.* **3.** one of less than average weight. **4.** *Colloq.* a person of little mental force or of slight influence or importance. **5.** a boxer who weighs between 57 and 60 kg (in amateur ranks).

light-year /ˈlaɪt-jɪə/, *n.* the distance travelled by light in one year (9.46×10^{12}

light-year   604   **limbo**

kilometres), used as a unit in measuring distances between stars.

ligneous /ˈlɪgnɪəs/, *adj.* of the nature of, or like, wood; woody. [L: wooden]

lignite /ˈlɪgnaɪt/, *n.* imperfectly formed coal, usu. dark brown, and often having a distinct woody texture; brown coal; wood coal. See **coal**. [F, from L: wood] — **lignitic**, *adj.*

ligno-, a word part meaning 'wood'. [combining form representing L. *lignum*]

like¹ /laɪk/, *prep., adj., adv., n.* ◇*prep.* **1.** in the same way as; similarly to; in a manner usual to: *They lived like kings.* **2.** typical or characteristic of: *an act of kindness just like him.* **3.** having similarity to; resembling: *He is like his father.* **4.** for example; as; such as: *The basic needs of life, like food and drink.* **5.** showing a probability of: *It looks like being a fine day.* **6.** (introducing an emphatic comparison): *like hell; like anything.* ◇*adj.* **7.** of the same form, appearance, kind, character, amount, etc.: *of a like mind.* **8.** similar; corresponding; analogous: *drawing, painting, and like arts.* **9.** bearing resemblance: *a like portrait.* ◇*adv.* **10.** *Colloq.* (in non-standard use) as if: *He acted like he was afraid.* ◇*n.* **11.** something of a similar nature (preceded by *the*): *oranges, lemons, and the like.* **12.** a similar person or thing; counterpart; match; equal: *No one has seen his like in a long time.* [OE: of the same body, or form]

like² /laɪk/, *v.*, **liked**, **liking**, *n.* ◇*v.t.* **1.** to take pleasure in; find pleasant or agreeable to one's taste: *I like eating.* **2.** to regard with favor, or have a kindly or friendly feeling for (a person, etc.): *I like you.* ◇*v.i.* **3.** to wish or feel inclined: *Come whenever you like.* ◇*n.* **4.** (*usu. pl.*) a favorable feeling; preference: *likes and dislikes.* [OE] — **likeable**, *adj.*

-like, a suffix of adjectives, meaning 'typical of', 'having the character or form of', as in *childlike, lifelike, horselike*, sometimes hyphenated.

likelihood /ˈlaɪklihʊd/, *n.* chance; probability.

likely /ˈlaɪkli/, *adj.*, **-lier, -liest**, *adv.* ◇*adj.* **1.** probably or apparently going (to do, be, etc.): *likely to happen.* **2.** seeming like truth, fact, or certainty; credible; probable: *a likely account of what happened.* **3.** seeming suitable: *a likely spot to build on.* ◇*adv.* **4.** probably. [ME, from Scand]

like-minded /ˈlaɪkmaɪndəd/, *adj.* having a similar opinion or interest.

liken /ˈlaɪkən/, *v.t.* to represent as similar or like; compare.

likeness /ˈlaɪknəs/, *n.* **1.** a representation, picture, or image, esp. a portrait. **2.** the appearance of something; semblance: *to assume the likeness of a swan.* **3.** the condition or fact of being like.

likewise /ˈlaɪkwaɪz/, *adv.* **1.** also; too; moreover. **2.** in the same or similar manner. [abbrev. of *in like wise*]

liking /ˈlaɪkɪŋ/, *n.* **1.** a feeling that something is pleasant; a preference: *a liking for sport.* **2.** pleasure or taste: *much to his liking.* **3.** the condition or feeling of one who likes. [OE: *lícung*]

lilac /ˈlaɪlək/, *n.* **1.** a shrub found in temperate climates with large clusters of fragrant purple or white flowers. **2.** a pale reddish purple. ◇*adj.* having the color of lilac. [F, from Ar, from Pers: bluish]

Lillee /ˈlɪli/, *n.* **Dennis Keith**, born 1949, Australian cricketer; fast bowler and record Test wicket-taker.

Lilliputian /lɪləˈpjuʃən/, *adj.* **1.** tiny; diminutive. ◇*n.* **2.** a tiny person. [from *Lilliput*, an imaginary island inhabited by tiny people, in *Gulliver's Travels* (1726) by Jonathan Swift]

lilly pilly /ˈlɪli ˌpɪli/, *n.* a tree with purplish white fruits, common along streams and in rainforests of eastern Australia. [orig. uncert.]

lilt /lɪlt/, *n.* **1.** rhythmic swing or flow. **2.** a lilting song or tune. ◇*v.i., v.t.* **3.** to sing or play in a light, tripping, or rhythmic manner. [ME]

lily /ˈlɪli/, *n., pl.* **-ies**, *adj.* ◇*n.* **1.** a plant with a scaly bulb and showy, funnel-shaped or bell-shaped flowers of various colors. **2.** →**fleur-de-lis**. ◇*adj.* **3.** delicate, fair or white as a lily. **4.** pure; unspoiled. [OE, from L]

lily-livered /ˈlɪli-lɪvəd/, *adj.* weak; cowardly.

lily-of-the-valley /lɪli-əv-ðə-ˈvæli/, *n., pl.* **lilies-of-the-valley.** a stemless herb with a raceme of drooping, bell-shaped, fragrant white flowers.

Lima /ˈlimə/, *n.* the capital and largest city of Peru, in the western part, near the Pacific coast. Pop. 5 875 900 (1987 est.).

lima bean /ˈlaɪmə ˌbin/, *n.* a kind of bean with a broad, flat seed much used for food.

limb¹ /lɪm/, *n.* **1.** a part or member of an animal body, different from the head and trunk, as a leg, arm, or wing. **2.** a large or main branch of a tree. **3.** a part or member sticking out: *the four limbs of a cross.* **4. out on a limb**, in an exposed position; cut off from others. [OE *lim*]

limb² /lɪm/, *n.* **1.** the edge of the disc of the sun, moon, or planet. **2.** the graduated edge of a quadrant or similar instrument. **3.** *Bot.* the expanded portion of a petal, sepal, or leaf. [L: border]

limber¹ /ˈlɪmbə/, *adj.* **1.** bending easily; flexible; pliant. **2.** marked by ease in bending the body; supple; lithe. ◇*v.i.* **3.** to make oneself limber (fol. by *up*).

limber² /ˈlɪmbə/, *n.* a detachable forepart of a guncarriage, consisting of two wheels, an axle, a pole, etc. [ME, ? from F]

limbo¹ /ˈlɪmboʊ/, *n., pl.* **-bos.** **1.** (*oft. cap.*) a supposed place on the edge of hell or heaven, where unbaptised babies go after death (**limbo of infants**), or where people who died before the coming of Christ went to await His coming (**limbo of the fathers** or **patriarchs**). **2.** a place where people or things are regarded as being put when cast aside, forgotten, past, or out of date. [ME, from ML *in limbo* on the border (of hell)]

limbo² /ˈlɪmboʊ/, *n.* a type of dance where each dancer in turn bends backwards in order to pass underneath a horizontal bar which is gradually lowered. [WInd native name]

lime¹ /laɪm/, *n., v.,* **limed, liming.** ◊*n.* **1.** the oxide of calcium, CaO, a white caustic (burning) solid (**quicklime** or **unslaked lime**) prepared by heating limestone, etc., used in making mortar and cement. When treated with water it produces calcium hydroxide, Ca(OH)₂, or **slaked lime**. **2.** any calcium compound for improving crops on soils without enough lime. ◊*v.t.* **3.** to treat (soil, etc.) with lime or compounds of calcium. [OE *lim*]

lime² /laɪm/, *n.* **1.** a small, greenish yellow, acid fruit of a tropical citrus tree related to the lemon. ◊*adj.* **2.** of the greenish yellow color of the lime. [F, from Sp]

limelight /ˈlaɪmlaɪt/, *n.* **1.** (formerly) a strong light, made by heating a cylinder of lime in a flame of mixed gases, directed upon the stage to light up particular persons or objects. **2.** the position in the public interest; notoriety. **3. steal the limelight,** to make oneself the centre of attention.

limerick /ˈlɪmərɪk/, *n.* a type of humorous verse of five lines. [named after LIMERICK; orig., a song with refrain, 'Will you come up to Limerick?']

Limerick /ˈlɪmərɪk/, *n.* a county in southwestern Republic of Ireland, in Munster. Pop. 164 204 (1986); 2685 km².

limestone /ˈlaɪmstoʊn/, *n.* a rock consisting wholly or chiefly of calcium carbonate, originating mainly from the calcareous remains of shells and other organisms, and when heated yielding quicklime.

limey /ˈlaɪmi/, *n., pl.* **-meys,** *adj. Colloq.* ◊*n.* **1.** a British sailor or ship. **2.** an Englishman. ◊*adj.* **3.** British. [from the prescribed use of lime juice against scurvy in British ships in the 18th C]

limit /ˈlɪmət/, *n.* **1.** the end or furthest point of something: *the limit of vision.* **2.** a boundary or bound, as of a country, district, etc. **3.** *Maths.* **a.** (of a function at a point) a number such that the value of the function can be made arbitrarily close to this number by restricting its argument to be sufficiently near the point. **b.** (of a sequence to infinity) a number such that the elements of the sequence eventually approach its value. **4. the (dizzy) limit,** someone or something that annoys beyond endurance. ◊*v.t.* **5.** keep within fixed limits (fol. by *to*): *to limit answers to 25 words.* **6.** to confine or keep within limits: *to limit expenditures.* [ME, from OF, from L: boundary]

limitation /lɪməˈteɪʃən/, *n.* **1.** something which limits; a limit or bound; a limited condition or circumstance; restriction. **2.** a limiting condition: *He should know his limitations.* **3.** the act of limiting. **4.** the condition of being limited.

limited /ˈlɪmətəd/, *adj.* **1.** kept within limits; restricted or narrow: *a limited space.* **2.** having only certain governing powers set down in a constitution: *a limited monarchy.* **3.** having to pay only some debts or liabilities.

limited company, *n.* a company whose shareholders, if the company goes bankrupt and has to close down, are liable to pay for the company's debts only to the limit of the value of their own shares. Also, **limited-liability company.**

limited liability, *n.* the having to pay only some of the debts of a trading company or limited partnership.

limn /lɪm/, *v.t.* to represent in drawing or painting. [ME, from OF, from L: light]

limonite /ˈlaɪmənaɪt/, *n.* an important iron ore, varying in color from dark brown to yellow. [Gk: meadow] — **limonitic,** *adj.*

limousine /ˈlɪməzin, lɪməˈzin/, *n.* any large, comfortable car, esp. one driven by a chauffeur or paid driver. [F: cloak, from *Limousin,* a former province in central France]

limp¹ /lɪmp/, *v.i.* **1.** to walk with difficulty, with a jerky or labored movement, when one leg or foot is sore or lame. **2.** to move along in a jerky or hesitating manner: *His verse limps.* ◊*n.* **3.** a jerky movement; lame gait. [ME]

limp² /lɪmp/, *adj.* **1.** lacking stiffness or firmness, as of substance, structure, bodily frame: *a limp body.* **2.** tired; lacking vitality. **3.** (of character) without proper firmness, force, energy, etc.

limpet /ˈlɪmpət/, *n.* **1.** *Zool.* a marine creature with a cone-shaped shell, that sticks very firmly to rocks. **2.** someone who refuses to be moved from a position or office. [OE, from LL: limpet, LAMPREY]

limpid /ˈlɪmpəd/, *adj.* **1.** (of water, air, crystal, etc.) clear, transparent. **2.** clear, explaining the meaning well; lucid: *a limpid style of writing.* [L]

Limpopo /lɪmˈpoʊpoʊ/, *n.* a river rising in southern Transvaal, Republic of South Africa, flowing north, then east, forming the border of the Republic with Zimbabwe, then south through Mozambique to the Indian Ocean. About 1600 km. Also, **Crocodile River.**

linchpin /ˈlɪntʃpɪn/, *n.* **1.** a pin put through the end of an axle to keep the wheel on. **2.** the main point of a plan, argument, etc.; key point. **3.** the main or key person or event, in a play, etc. Also, **lynchpin.** [OE]

Lincoln /ˈlɪŋkən/, *n.* **Abraham,** 1809–65, 16th president of the US, 1861–65, remembered esp. for saving the Union in the American Civil War and for abolishing slavery; assassinated by John Wilkes Booth.

Lincolnshire /ˈlɪŋkənʃɪə, -ʃə/, *n.* a county in eastern England. Pop. 567 200 (1986 est.); 6897 km². *Administrative Centre:* Lincoln. *Abbrev.:* Lincs. Also, **Lincoln.**

linctus /ˈlɪŋktəs/, *n.* a soothing medicine for the throat and chest. [L: lick]

Lindbergh /ˈlɪndbɜg, ˈlɪnbɜg/, *n.* **Charles Augustus,** 1902–97, US aviator who made the first non-stop solo transatlantic flight in 1927.

Lindeman Group /ˌlɪndəmən ˈgrup/, *n.pl.* a group of islands off the eastern coast of Qld, between the Whitsunday Group and Cumberland Islands.

Lindrum /'lɪndrəm/, *n.* **1. Walter Albert**, 1898–1960, billiard player; world champion 1932–50. **2. Horace**, 1912–74, nephew of Walter, billiard and snooker player; world professional snooker champion 1952.

Lindsay /'lɪmzi/, *n.* **1.** an Australian family of artists and writers. **2. Percival Charles**, 1870–1952, illustrator and landscape painter. **3.** his brother, **Sir Lionel Arthur**, 1874–1961, etcher, printmaker, art critic, painter, and cartoonist. **4.** their brother, **Norman Alfred William**, 1879–1969, influential artist and writer; author of the children's book *The Magic Pudding* (1918). **5.** their sister, **Ruby**, 1885–1919, book and magazine illustrator. **6.** their brother, **Sir (Ernest) Daryl**, 1889–1976, painter; noted for his landscapes. **7. Lady Joan**, 1896–1984, wife of Sir Daryl, artist and novelist; author of *Picnic at Hanging Rock* (1967). **8. Jack**, 1900–90, son of Norman, radical writer, historian, translator and critic.

line[1] /laɪn/, *n., v.,* **lined, lining.** ◇*n.* **1.** a mark or stroke, having length but usu. very little breadth, made with a pen, pencil, tool, etc., on a surface, as a way of showing, or symbol of, the idea of direction. **2.** something like a line, e.g. a band of color, a seam, a furrow, etc.: *lines of stratification in rock.* **3.** a wrinkle on the face, etc. **4.** something arranged along a (straight) line; a row or series: *a line of trees; a line of people.* **5.** a row of written or printed letters, words, etc.: *a page of thirty lines.* **6.** *Poetry.* → **verse** (def. 2). **7.** (*pl.*) the spoken words of a drama, etc., or of an actor's part: *The hero forgot his lines.* **8.** a story told as an excuse or trick: *He gave me the old line about working late.* **9.** a short written message; a letter: *Please drop me a line.* **10.** a sign of difference; boundary; limit: *to draw a line between right and wrong; I draw the line at rudeness.* **11.** a course of action, thought, procedure, etc.: *the Communist Party line.* **12.** a course of direction; route: *the line of march.* **13.** a continuous series of persons or animals in order through time, esp. in family descent: *a line of great kings.* **14.** (*pl.*) an appearance of structure: *a ship of fine lines.* **15.** (*pl.*) a plan of building, action, or procedure: *two books written on the same lines.* **16.** a kind of activity or business: *What line is your father in?* **17.** any transport company or system: *He owns a line of oil tankers.* **18.** a strip of railway track, a railway, or a railway system: *railway line; the eastern suburbs line.* **19.** *Art.* a mark from a crayon, pencil, brush, etc., in a work of graphic art, which shows direction and marks the edges of forms, used either singly, or with other lines to make shading. **20.** *Maths.* a continuous stretch of length, straight or curved, without breadth or thickness; the trace of a moving point. **21.** the circle of the earth's globe or the corresponding one (thought of) in the sky: *the equinoctial line.* **22.** a supply of goods to be sold of the same general class: *What lines do you carry in this shop?* **23.** *Music.* one of the parts, usu. melodic, of a composition for many instruments or voices: *Soprano line; violin line.* **24.** the line of arrangement of an army or of the ships of a fleet as drawn up ready for battle. **25.** a thread, string, or the like, for fishing or other uses. **26.** a cord or rope in various uses on a ship. **27.** a wire or cable for a telephone or telegraph. **28.** a telephonic channel to a particular person or department: *The line is busy.* **29.** *Sport.* a mark showing the boundaries or divisions of a field or court. ◇**30.** Some special uses are:
bring into line, to cause or persuade to agree or conform.
come / fall into line, to agree; conform.
get one's lines crossed, to misunderstand.
in line, **1.** agreeing with others; conforming. **2.** well-placed; with a good chance: *in line for promotion.*
lay it on the line, to state the case openly and honestly.
out of line, not according to standard practice, agreement, etc.; deviant.
read between the lines, to find (in something spoken or written) more meaning than the words seem to express.
the line, the equator.
toe the line, to obey; conform.
◇*v.i.* **31.** to take a position in a line; range or queue (oft. fol. by *up*). ◇*v.t.* **32.** to bring into a line, or into agreement with others (oft. fol. by *up*). **33.** to cover or mask with lines (oft. in passive): *Wrinkles lined his face; His face was lined with wrinkles.* **34.** to form a line along: *People lined the streets.* ◇*v.* **35. line up**, to get hold of; make available: *We must line up a chairman for the conference.* [ME, partly from OF, from VL, from L: thread; line]

line[2] /laɪn/, *v.t.,* **lined, lining. 1.** to cover or fit on the inner side with something: *to line a drawer with paper; to line a coat with silk.* **2.** to cover: *The walls were lined with bookcases.* **3.** to fill: *He lined his pockets with money.* [OE, from L]

lineage /'lɪniɪdʒ/, *n.* descent from a line of ancestors; ancestry.

lineal /'lɪniəl/, *adj.* **1.** (of a descendant, ancestor, etc.) being in the direct line (def. 13). **2.** of or passed on by lineal descent. **3.** linear. [ME, from L: LINE[1]]

lineament /'lɪniəmənt/, *n.* a feature or detail of a face, body, or figure; outline or contour of a face, etc. [ME, from L]

linear /'lɪniə/, *adj.* **1.** stretched in a line: *a linear series.* **2.** relating to length, measurement in one dimension only: *linear measure.* **3.** of or relating to a line or lines: *linear perspective.* **4.** of or relating to a work of art with strong outlines and edges of forms, or marked by having lines (rather than masses or areas): *a linear painting; a linear design.* **5.** looking like a line; narrow: *linear nebulae; a linear leaf.* **6.** *Maths.* of a line that can be shown on a graph and described by such an equation as $x + y = 3$. [L: LINE[1]]

Linear A, *n.* an undeciphered system of writing found in inscriptions on tablets, pottery, etc., found at Minoan sites on Crete.

Linear B, *n.* an ancient system of writing, found in inscriptions in Crete and southern Greece, and generally accepted as being an early form of Greek.

linear equation, *n.* an equation, all of whose variables are in the first degree.

linen /'lɪnən/, n. 1. cloth woven from flax thread. 2. clothes, tea towels, etc., made of linen, cotton, etc. ◇adj. 3. made of linen. [OE *linnen*]

line of force, n. a line in a field of force (esp. magnetic or electrical). The direction of a line at any point is the same as the direction of force in the field at that point.

line printer, n. a machine which prints the output of a computer one line at a time.

liner[1] /'laɪnə/, n. 1. a large ship or aeroplane for carrying passengers. 2. Also, **eyeliner**. cosmetic used to make the eyes more noticeable.

liner[2] /'laɪnə/, n. something used as a lining: *nappy liner*.

linesman /'laɪnzmən/, n., pl. **-men**. 1. *Sport*. an official on the edge of a playing field who helps the referee or umpire to decide whether the ball is still in play. 2. someone who puts up or repairs telephone, electric power, or other overhead wires. 3. a member of a surf-lifesaving team who handles the line taken out to a swimmer. Also, **lineman**.

line spectrum, n. an emission or absorption spectrum consisting of a number of sharply defined lines, as produced by an element in the atomic state. Each line corresponds to a particular wavelength.

line-up /'laɪn-ʌp/, n. 1. (the members of) a particular order or grouping of people or things, for action, inspection, etc., as in a sporting team, a music band, etc. 2. a sequence of programs or events: *Tonight's TV line-up is a knockout*. Also, **lineup**.

ling /lɪŋ/, n., pl. **lings**, (*esp. collectively*) **ling**. a common fish, reddish-brown in color with a small barbel on the chin, found around the southern coast of Australia; beardie. [ME]

-ling[1], a noun suffix meaning 1. something inferior and detestable: *hireling; underling*. 2. something small or unimportant: *duckling*. [ME and OE]

-ling[2], an adverbial suffix expressing direction, position, state, etc., as in *darkling, sideling*. [ME and OE]

linger /'lɪŋgə/, v.i. 1. to stay on in a place longer than is usual or expected, as if not wanting to leave it. 2. to stay with something, as if interested or enjoying it: *He lingered over his book; to linger over a cup of coffee*. 3. to be slow in action; delay; dawdle. [OE: delay]

lingerie /'lɒnʒəreɪ/, n. underwear, nightwear, etc., worn by women. [F, from L: flax]

lingo /'lɪŋgoʊ/, n., pl. **-goes**. *Colloq.* language. [Lingua Franca, from L]

lingua franca /lɪŋgwə 'fræŋkə/, n. any language used between people who do not share a native or first language, such as a pidgin language, or an accepted set of symbols and signs.

lingual /'lɪŋgwəl/, adj. 1. of or relating to the tongue. 2. relating to languages. [ML, from L: tongue, language]

linguist /'lɪŋgwəst/, n. 1. a person who is skilled in foreign languages; polyglot. 2. a person who studies linguistics. [L: language]

linguistics /lɪŋ'gwɪstɪks/, n. the science of language, including phonetics, phonemics, morphology, and syntax.

Lini /'lini/, n. **Father Walter Hadye**, born 1942, Vanuatuan politician; first prime minister of the republic of Vanuatu 1980–91.

liniment /'lɪnəmənt/, n. a liquid preparation, usu. oily, for rubbing or putting on the skin, in the treatment of sprains, bruises, etc. [ME, from LL]

lining /'laɪnɪŋ/, n. something which covers the inside surface of something else. [ME]

link /lɪŋk/, n. 1. one of the rings or separate pieces of which a chain is made up. 2. anything used for connecting one part or thing with another; a bond or tie. 3. *Mach*. a rigid movable piece or rod connected with other parts by means of pivots or the like, for the purpose of transmitting motion. ◇v.t. 4. to join by or as by a link or links. ◇v.i. 5. to join; unite. 6. **link up**, to join or get in touch; communicate (fol. by *with*). [ME, from Scand]

linkage /'lɪŋkɪdʒ/, n. 1. the act of linking. 2. the condition or manner of being linked. 3. a system of links.

Linnaeus /lɪ'niəs, lɪ'neɪəs/, n. **Carolus** /'kærələs/ (*Carl von Linné*), 1707–78, Swedish botanist who established the binomial system of scientific nomenclature based mainly on the number or characteristics of the stamens and pistils.

linnet /'lɪnət/, n. a small song bird, found mainly in Europe. [ME, from OF *lin* flax (because the bird feeds on flax seeds)]

linocut /'laɪnoʊkʌt/, n. 1. a design or image cut into a block of linoleum, for making prints. 2. a print made from such a cut.

linoleum /laɪ'noʊliəm/, n. a floor-covering made by coating a coarse cloth with linseed oil, powdered cork, and rosin, and adding pigments. Also, **lino** /'laɪnoʊ/. [L]

linotype /'laɪnətaɪp/, n. 1. a composing machine worked by a keyboard which makes solid lines of type from molten metal for printing newspapers, etc. 2. the type produced by such a machine. [Trademark; orig. phrase '*line o' type*' line of type]

linseed /'lɪnsid/, n. the seed of the flax plant. [OE *līn* flax + *sǣd* seed]

lint /lɪnt/, n. 1. a soft material for dressing wounds, etc., made from specially treated linen cloth. 2. bits of thread or fluff. [? OE *linwyrt*, from *līn* flax + *wyrt* WORT]

lintel /'lɪntl/, n. a horizontal piece of wood or stone to support the bricks, etc., above an opening such as a window or a door. Also, **lintol**. [ME, from OF, from VL: boundary]

lion /'laɪən/, n. 1. a large, honey-colored member of the cat family, living in Africa and southern Asia, the male of which usu. has a mane. 2. a man of great strength, courage, etc. 3. a well-known or important person many people want to meet: *a literary lion*. 4. **the lion's share**, the largest share or portion of anything. [ME, from OF, from L, from Gk]

lioness /'laɪənɛs/, n. female lion.

lion-hearted /'laɪən-hatəd/, *adj.* courageous; brave.

lionise *or* **lionize** /'laɪənaɪz/, *v.t.*, **-nised, -nising.** to treat (a person) as well-known or famous. See **lion** (def. 3). —**lionisation**, *n.*

lip /lɪp/, *n.* **1.** either of the two fleshy parts or folds forming the edges of the mouth and important for speech. **2.** (*pl.*) these parts as the organs of speech. **3.** a lip-like part or structure. **4.** *Zool.* → **labium. 5.** any edge or rim. **6. bite one's lip,** to try hard (and succeed) in not showing feelings, esp. anger or annoyance. **7. give (someone) lip,** to talk, esp. to someone in a higher position, in a cheeky or insolent manner. **8. keep a stiff upper lip,** to face trouble or pain without showing one's feelings. [OE]

lip-, variant of **lipo-,** before vowels.

lipase /'lɪpeɪz, 'laɪ-/, *n.* an enzyme produced by the liver, pancreas, etc., which changes oils or fats into fatty acids and glycerol.

lipid /'lɪpɪd, 'laɪ-/, *n.* any of a group of organic compounds, the best known being the fats and oils, also including waxes, steroids, etc. See **fat** (def. 8).

Lipmann /'lɪpmən/, *n.* **Fritz Albert,** 1899–1986, German-American biochemist; with Krebs, shared the Nobel prize for physiology or medicine (1953) for his discovery of coenzyme A and its role in metabolism.

lipo-, *Chem.* a word part meaning 'fat'. Also, **lip-.** [Gk, *lípos* fat]

lipoid /'lɪpɔɪd, 'laɪpɔɪd/, *adj.* fatty; like fat.

lip-read /'lɪp-rid/, *v.i.,* **-read** /-red/, **-reading.** to understand spoken words by watching the movement of a speaker's lips.

lip-service /'lɪp-sɜvəs/, *n.* the saying of something without meaning it; insincere profession of devotion or goodwill.

lipstick /'lɪpstɪk/, *n.* a hard paste in a stick shape for coloring the lips.

liquefied petroleum gas, *n.* a mixture of hydrocarbon gases, e.g. butane and propane, liquefied and stored under pressure for use as a gas fuel. Also, **bottled gas.** *Abbrev.:* LPG

liquefy /'lɪkwəfaɪ/, *v.t., v.i.* **-fied, -fying.** to make or become liquid. [late ME, from L: make liquid] —**liquefier,** *n.*

liqueur /lə'kjuə, lə'kɜ/, *n.* any of a class of alcoholic liquors, usu. strong, sweet, and highly flavored. [F]

liquid /'lɪkwəd/, *adj.* **1.** composed of molecules which move freely among themselves but do not tend to separate like those of gases; neither gaseous nor solid. **2.** of or relating to liquids: *liquid measure.* **3.** flowing like water; fluid. **4.** clear, transparent, or bright: *liquid eyes.* **5.** sounding smoothly or agreeably: *He spoke in liquid tones.* **6.** in cash or easily changed into cash: *liquid assets.* **7. go liquid,** to change assets (goods or property possessed) for cash. ◇*n.* **8.** a liquid substance. [ME, from L]

liquidambar /ˌlɪkwəd'æmbə/, *n.* a large American tree with star-shaped leaves and, in warm regions, giving out a sweet-smelling liquid used in medicine. [NL]

liquid assets, *n.pl. Econ.* **1.** that part of a trading bank's assets which consist of its notes and coins, its cash with the Reserve Bank of Australia and its Commonwealth Treasury bills. **2.** a company's cash and assets that can be easily realised (changed into cash).

liquidate /'lɪkwədeɪt/, *v.,* **-dated, -dating.** ◇*v.t.* **1.** to get rid of (a debt etc.); settle or pay: *to liquidate a claim.* **2.** to change into cash. **3.** to get rid of, esp. by killing or other violent means. **4.** to break up or do away with; abolish. ◇*v.i.* **5.** (of a company) to pay off debts or accounts and finish up; wind up; go into liquidation. [ML, from L] —**liquidation,** *n.*

liquidator /'lɪkwədeɪtə/, *n.* a person appointed to carry out the winding up of a company and the settling of the debts.

liquidity /lə'kwɪdəti/, *n.* **1.** a liquid state or quality. **2.** condition of having assets either in cash or readily convertible into cash.

liquid oxygen, *n.* oxygen in its liquid state; a pale blue liquid which boils at $-182.9°$ C; used as an oxidant in rockets.

liquor /'lɪkə/, *n.* **1.** strong alcoholic drink distilled from wine (brandy) or grain (whisky, etc.). **2.** a solution of a substance, esp. a concentrated one used in an industrial process. [L: liquid (state), liquid]

liquorice /'lɪkərɪs, 'lɪkrɪʃ, -rəs/, *n.* **1.** a leguminous plant of Europe and Asia. **2.** the sweet-tasting dried root of this plant, or an extract made from it, used in medicine, confectionery, etc. [ME, from AF, from LL, from Gk]

Lisbon /'lɪzbən/, *n.* a seaport in and the capital of Portugal, on the Tagus estuary. Pop. 827 867 (1985 est.). Portuguese, **Lisboa** /liʒ'bouə/.

lisle /laɪl/, *n.* **1.** a type of strong cotton thread, used esp., formerly, to make stockings. ◇*adj.* **2.** made of lisle thread. [named after *Lisle* (now Lille), town in N France where it was first made]

Lismore /'lɪzmɔ/, *n.* a city in the north coast region of NSW, on the north arm of the Richmond River; NSW's major dairying area. Pop. 24 896 (1986). [named after the Island of *Lismore* near the west coast of Scotland]

lisp /lɪsp/, *n.* **1.** a speech defect consisting in pronouncing *s* and *z* like the *th* sounds of *thin.* **2.** the act, habit, or sound of lisping. ◇*v.t., v.i.* **3.** to pronounce or speak with a lisp. [OE *wlisp* lisping]

lissom /'lɪsəm/, *adj.* **1.** lithe, esp. of body; limber or supple. **2.** active or agile. [var. of *lithesome*]

list¹ /lɪst/, *n.* **1.** a series of items, as names, etc., set down one after the other. ◇*v.t.* **2.** to set down together in a list; make a list of. **3.** to enter in a list with others.

list² /lɪst/, *n.* **1.** (of a ship) a lean to one side. ◇*v.i., v.t.* **2.** (to cause to) lean to one side: *The ship listed to starboard.* [orig. obscure]

listen /ˈlɪsən/, *v.i.* **1.** to give attention with the ear: *to listen to music; to listen for footsteps.* **2.** to give heed; take advice. ◇*v.* **3. listen in, a.** to eavesdrop. **b.** to listen to a radio program. [OE *hlysnan*]

Lister /ˈlɪstə/, *n.* **Joseph, 1st Baron**, 1827–1912, English surgeon; the first to use antiseptics in surgery.

listing /ˈlɪstɪŋ/, *n.* an entry in a list, as in a catalogue, telephone directory, etc.

listless /ˈlɪstləs/, *adj.* (feeling) without energy or interest in anything: *She was listless after he went; a listless mood.* [late ME]

lists /lɪsts/, *n.pl.* **1.** (a fence enclosing) the field of battle at a tournament or joust. **2.** any place or scene of fighting. **3. enter the lists**, to take part in a struggle or debate. [ME *liste* boundary, limit]

Liszt /lɪst/, *n.* **Franz**, 1811–86, Hungarian Romantic composer and virtuoso pianist.

lit /lɪt/, *v.* past tense and past participle of **light**[1] and **light**[3].

lit., *Abbrev.* **1.** litre. **2.** literal. **3.** literally. **4.** literary. **5.** literature.

litany /ˈlɪtəni/, *n., pl.* **-nies. 1.** a form of prayer consisting of a series of invocations followed by responses. **2.** a long and boring account: *The Opposition recited a litany of the Government's mistakes.* [LL, from Gk: litany, an entreating]

-lite, a word part used in names of minerals or fossils as in *chrysolite*. See **-lith**. [F, from Gk: stone]

literacy /ˈlɪtərəsi/, *n.* the ability to read and write.

literal /ˈlɪtrəl, ˈlɪtərəl/, *adj.* **1.** following the exact words of the original: *a literal translation.* **2.** (of people) tending to understand words too strictly or unimaginatively; matter-of-fact; prosaic: *a literal mind.* **3.** being the natural, basic, or strict meaning of a word; not figurative or metaphorical. **4.** true to fact; not exaggerated: *a literal statement of conditions.* **5.** of or relating to the letters of the alphabet: *a literal mistake.* [ME, from LL: LETTER]

literalism /ˈlɪtrəlɪzəm, ˈlɪtərəlɪzəm/, *n.* **1.** a keeping to the exact letter or the literal sense, as in translation or interpretation. **2.** an exact representation or portrayal, without idealisation, in art or literature. **—literalist,** *n., adj.* **—literalistic,** *adj.*

literary /ˈlɪtərəri, ˈlɪtrəri/, *adj.* **1.** of or relating to books and writings, esp. those classed as literature: *literary history; literary critic.* **2.** of the formal language of literature: *A literary style avoids colloquialisms.* **3.** engaged in writing or in writing about books, etc., as a profession: *a literary man.* **4.** bookish; pedantic: *a literary manner.*

literate /ˈlɪtərət/, *adj.* **1.** able to read and write. **2.** educated. **3.** literary (def. 2): *a highly literate style.* ◇*n.* **4.** someone who can read and write. [ME, from L *lettered*]

literature /ˈlɪtrətʃə, ˈlɪtərətʃə/, *n.* **1.** writings in which expression and form, together with ideas of lasting and universal interest, are important features, as poetry, drama, history, biography, essays, etc. **2.** all the writings of a particular language, period, people, etc.: *the literature of Australia; Russian medieval literature.* **3.** writings dealing with a particular subject: *the literature on sailing ships.* **4.** the profession of a writer or author. **5.** *Colloq.* printed matter of any kind, as circulars or advertising matter. [ME, from L, from L: learning]

lith-, a combining form meaning 'stone'. Also, **litho-**. [Gk, combining form of *líthos*]

-lith, a noun ending meaning 'stone', as in *megalith*, sometimes occurring in words, as *batholith*, that are variants of forms in *-lite*. See **-lite**. [see LITH-]

lithe /laɪð/, *adj.* bending easily; pliant; limber; supple. Also, **lithesome** /ˈlaɪðsəm/. See **lissom**. [OE *līthe*]

Lithgow /ˈlɪθgoʊ/, *n.* a city in NSW west of the Blue Mountains; mining and manufacturing area. Pop. 12 369 (1986). [named after William *Lithgow*, auditor-general of NSW]

Lithgow pottery, *n.* **1.** an Australian pottery works, established at Lithgow, NSW, in 1880. **2.** the pottery made there.

lithic /ˈlɪθɪk/, *adj.* relating to or consisting of stone. [Gk: of stones]

-lithic, a suffix with the same meaning as **lithic**, used esp. in archaeology, as in *palaeolithic*.

lithium /ˈlɪθiəm/, *n.* a soft silver-white metallic element (the lightest metal). *Symbol:* Li; *at. no.:* 3; *at. wt:* 6·939. [NL, from Gk: stone; so named because found in minerals]

litho-, a variant of **lith-**, before consonants, as in *lithography*.

litho., *Abbrev.* **1.** lithograph. **2.** lithography.

lithography /lɪˈθɒgrəfi/, *n.* the art or process of printing a picture, writing, etc., from a flat surface of aluminium, zinc or stone, with some greasy or oily substance. **—lithograph,** *n.* **—lithographer,** *n.* **—lithographic,** *adj.*

lithosphere /ˈlɪθəsfɪə/, *n. Geol.* the crust of the earth.

Lithuania /lɪθjuˈeɪniə/, *n.* a republic in northern Europe on the Baltic Sea; a constituent republic of the Soviet Union 1940–91, known as the **Lithuanian Soviet Socialist Republic**. Pop. 3 690 000 (1989 est.); 62 419 km². *Language:* Lithuanian. *Cap.:* Vilnius. Lithuanian, **Lietuva. —Lithuanian,** *n., adj.*

litigant /ˈlɪtəgənt/, *n., adj.* (someone) concerned in a lawsuit. [L]

litigate /ˈlɪtəgeɪt/, *v.*, **-gated, -gating.** ◇*v.t.* **1.** to make (something) the subject of a lawsuit; to contest at law. **2.** to dispute (a point, etc). ◇*v.i.* **3.** to carry on a lawsuit. [L] **—litigable,** *adj.* **—litigator,** *n.*

litigation /lɪtəˈgeɪʃən/, *n.* **1.** the process of litigating. **2.** → **lawsuit**.

litmus /ˈlɪtməs/, *n.* a blue coloring matter obtained from certain lichens. In alkaline solution litmus turns blue, in acid solution red. Strips of paper soaked in a solution of litmus are used for this test. [ME, from Scand]

litre /ˈlitə/, *n.* a unit of capacity in the metric system, equal to 10^{-3} m³. *Symbol:* L, 1 [F, from LL, from Gk: pound]

-litre, a word part meaning litres; of or relating to litres, as in *centilitre*.

litter /ˈlitə/, *n.* **1.** things scattered about; scattered rubbish. **2.** an untidy condition. **3.** a number of baby animals born at one time. **4.** → stretcher. **5.** a small carriage without wheels, carried between shafts by men or horses. **6.** *Agric.* **a.** a bed or layer of various materials, esp. of straw and dung in an animal shed. **b.** straw, hay, etc., used as a protection for plants. **7.** a mass of dead leaves and twigs scattered on the ground in a forest: *leaf litter.* ◇*v.t.* **8.** to scatter things over (a place): *to litter the bush with bottles.* **9.** to scatter (things) in disorder: *to litter bottles round the bush.* **10.** to be scattered about (a place) in disorder (oft. fol. by *up*): *Bottles are littering (up) the bush.* **11.** to provide straw, etc. for animals or plants. ◇*v.i.* **12.** to give birth to a litter. [ME, from AF, from L]

litterbug /ˈlitəbʌg/, *n.* someone who drops rubbish, esp. in public places.

little /ˈlitl/, *adj.*, **less** or **lesser**, **least**; or **littler**, **littlest**; *adv.*, **less**, **least**; *n.* ◇*adj.* **1.** small in size, number, or amount: *a little child; little hope.* **2.** short; brief: *a little while.* **3.** enough to have an effect; appreciable: *having a little trouble; to lose a little sleep.* **4.** being such on a small scale: *little farmers.* **5.** weak: *a little voice.* **6.** unimportant; trivial: *little worries.* **7.** narrow or mean: *a little mind.* **8.** endearingly small: *Bless your little heart!* **9.** amusingly small: *I understand his little ways.* ◇*adv.* **10.** not at all (before a verb): *He little knows what awaits him.* **11.** not much: *a mind little changed by circumstances.* **12.** not often: *I see my mother very little.* ◇*n.* **13.** a small amount, quantity, or degree: *little to worry about.* **14.** short distance: *Please step back a little.* **15.** short time: *Stay here a little.* **16. little by little,** by degrees; gradually. **17. make little of, a.** to treat as unimportant; disparage. **b.** to understand only partly: *I can make little of your writing.* **18. not a little,** a very great deal; considerable. [ME and OE *lytel*]

Little Bighorn /ˌlitl ˈbigho:n/, *n.* a river in western central US; scene of the battle (1876) in which the Sioux and Cheyenne Indians, led by Sitting Bull and Crazy Horse, defeated and killed General Custer and his troops.

Little Desert, *n.* an area in western Vic, extending from the SA border to Dimboola; semi-arid and sandy. [named by early pioneers to describe the unsuitability of its soil for agriculture]

Little Digger, *n.* → William Morris Hughes.

Little John *n.* the largest and strongest member of Robin Hood's band.

liturgy /ˈlitədʒi/, *n., pl.* **-gies. 1.** a form of public worship; ritual: *Greek Orthodox liturgy.* **2.** a particular arrangement of services: *the Easter liturgy.* [ML, from Gk: public duty, public worship] —**liturgical,** *adj.* —**liturgist,** *n.*

live¹ /liv/, *v.*, **lived** /livd/, **living.** ◇*v.i.* **1.** to have life, as an animal or plant; be alive. **2.** to remain alive: *to live long.* **3.** to remain: *looks which lived in my memory.* **4.** to keep life going: *to live on $50 a week; to live on rice.* **5.** to dwell; reside: *to live in a cottage.* **6.** to pass life (as specified): *They lived happily ever after.* **7.** to direct or regulate one's life: *to live by the golden rule.* **8.** to experience or enjoy life to the full. ◇*v.t.* **9.** to pass: *to live a life of ease.* **10.** to carry out or show in one's life: *to live an honest life.* ◇*v.* **11.** Some special uses are: **live and learn,** to learn through experience. **live down,** to live so as to cause (something bad or shameful) to be forgotten: *to live down a mistake.* **live it up,** *Colloq.* to indulge in pleasure and luxuries; go on a spree. **live with,** *Colloq.* to live together with, as a husband or wife or lover. **live with oneself,** to live according to one's conscience; keep one's self-respect. [OE *lifian, libban*]

live² /laiv/, *adj.* **1.** living or alive: *live animals.* **2.** full of energy, activity or brilliance. **3.** *Colloq.* of interest at the moment: *a live issue.* **4.** still burning: *live coals.* **5.** flowing freely: *live water.* **6.** loaded or unexploded: *live cartridge.* **7.** charged with electricity: *live wire.* **8.** (of a radio or television program) broadcast or televised at the moment it is being presented at the studio. **9.** relating to an actual public performance in a theatre, etc., opposed to a filmed or recorded performance. **10. live weight,** the weight of an animal while living. ◇*adv.* **11.** (of a radio or television program) not taped; broadcast at the time of its happening: *This race is brought to you live from the Olympic swimming pool.* [var. of ALIVE]

livelihood /ˈlaivlihud/, *n.* a means of supporting life: *to gain a livelihood from writing.* [OE: life-support]

lively /ˈlaivli/, *adj.*, **-lier, -liest. 1.** energetic; vigorous; animated: *a lively discussion.* **2.** spirited; vivacious; gay: *a lively tune.* **3.** eventful or exciting: *a lively time.* **4.** vivid or keen: *a lively color; a lively imagination.* [OE *liflic*]

liven /ˈlaivən/, *v.t., v.i.* to make or become more lively (oft. fol. by *up*).

liver¹ /ˈlivə/, *n.* **1.** the organ that produces bile and performs various metabolic functions; formerly supposed to be the seat of love, desire, courage, etc. **2.** this organ in animals, eaten as food. See **lamb's fry.** ◇*adj.* **3.** reddish-brown. [OE *lifer*]

liver² /ˈlivə/, *n.* someone who leads a certain kind of life: *an evil liver.* [LIVE¹ + -ER¹]

liver fluke *n.* a parasitic flatworm which lives in sheep's livers.

liverish /ˈlivəriʃ/, *adj.* **1.** feeling sick; bilious. **2.** cross; cranky; peevish. Also, **livery.**

Liverpool /ˈlivəpul/, *n.* **1.** a city and seaport in north-western England, on the Mersey estuary; administrative centre of Merseyside. Pop. 510 700 (1982). **2.** a city in NSW, forming part of the Sydney metropolitan area. Pop. 93 215 (1986). **3.** a river in the NT,

Liverpool in Arnhem Land, flowing into the Arafura Sea. About 145 km.

Liverpudlian /livə'pʌdliən/, n. 1. a native or inhabitant of Liverpool. ◇adj. 2. relating to Liverpool or to Liverpudlian.

liverwort /'livəwɜːt/, n. a kind of primitive, moss-like plant that grows in damp places.

liverwurst /'livəwɜːst/, n. a sausage made with a large percentage of liver.

livery /'livəri/, n., pl. **-ries**. 1. the distinctive clothes worn by servants, or formerly by a lord's retainers. 2. the distinctive clothes worn by an official, a member of a company or guild, etc. 3. typical dress, garb, or outward appearance: *the green livery of summer.* 4. the feeding or stabling of horses for pay. [ME, from AF, from L: liberate]

lives /laɪvz/, n. plural of **life**.

livestock /'laɪvstɒk/, n. horses, cattle, sheep, etc. on a farm or station.

livewire /'laɪvwaɪə/, n. an energetic, alert person.

livid /'lɪvɪd/, adj. 1. (of the face, nails, etc.) discoloured by bruising; black-and-blue. 2. dull or dark greyish blue. 3. angry; enraged. [L]

living /'lɪvɪŋ/, adj. 1. alive. 2. in existence or use: *living languages.* 3. active; strong: *a living faith.* 4. in its natural state and place: *to cut into the living rock.* 5. lifelike: *the living image.* 6. of or relating to living beings: *within living memory.* 7. absolute; entire (used as an intensifier): *to scare the living daylights out of someone.* ◇n. 8. the act or condition of someone or something that lives: *Living is very expensive these days.* 9. the manner of life: *holy living.* 10. livelihood: *to earn one's living.* 11. **the living**, (*collectively*) those alive at any given time.

Livingstone /'lɪvɪŋstən/, n. **David**, 1813–73, Scottish missionary and explorer in Africa.

Livy /'lɪvi/, n. (*Titus Livius*), 59 BC–AD 17, Roman historian.

Li Xiannian /li ʃɛn'jɛn/, n. 1905–92, Chinese communist statesman; president 1983–89.

lixivium /lɪk'sɪviəm/, n., pl. **lixiviums, lixivia** /lɪk'sɪviə/. a solution, containing alkaline salts, obtained by leaching wood ashes with water; lye. [L: made into lye]

lizard /'lɪzəd/, n. 1. a reptile with long thin body, short legs and usu. long tail, ranging in size from small skinks to the large goanna. 2. leather made from the skin of lizards, used for making shoes, etc. [ME, from OF, from L]

Lizard Island, n. an island off the Qld coast in the northern part of the Great Barrier Reef, north of Cooktown.

Lk, *Abbrev. Bible.* Luke.

ll., *Abbrev.* lines.

'll, short form of *will* or *shall*.

llama /'lɑːmə/, n. 1. a South American ruminant related to the camel, with a long upright neck, and kept for its woolly hair and for carrying loads. 2. the fleece of the llama. [Sp, from SAmer Ind]

Llanfairpwllgwyngyll /hlan,vaɪəpʊl-'gwʊŋɪl/, n., a village in north-western Wales, in Anglesey; in unabbreviated form, **Llanfairpwllgwyngyllgogerychwyrndrobwllllantysiliogogogoch**, famous as the longest place name in Great Britain. Also, **Llanfairpwll** or **Llanfair PG**.

Lloyd /lɔɪd/, n. **Clive Hubert**, born 1944, West Indian cricketer; a noted batsman and former Test captain.

Lloyd George /lɔɪd 'dʒɔːdʒ/, n. **David** (*1st Earl of Dwyfor*), 1863–1945, British statesman who introduced various social reforms; prime minister 1916–22.

Lloyd's /lɔɪdz/, n. an association of English insurance underwriters, founded in 1688, orig. to arrange marine insurance, but now issuing policies on nearly all types of insurance. [named after Edward *Lloyd*, 1688–1726, who opened a coffee-house where the original insurers met]

load /loʊd/, n. 1. something carried on a cart, etc.; burden. 2. the quantity carried, taken as a unit of measure or weight. 3. anything carried or held up from the ground: *the load of fruit on a tree.* 4. something that weighs down or oppresses: *a load on my mind.* 5. the amount of work required of a person, machine, organisation, etc.; workload. 6. (*pl.*) *Colloq.* a lot of: *loads of people.* 7. *Elect.* the power delivered by a generator, motor, power station, or transformer (oft. fol. by *on*). 8. *Elect, Phys.* resistance or impedance connected to a network containing a source(s) of electromotive force. 9. *Mech.* the external resistance overcome by an engine, dynamo, etc., under a given condition, measured by the power required. 10. **get a load of**, *Colloq.* **a.** to look at; observe. **b.** to listen; to hear. ◇v.t. 11. to put a load on or in: *to load a cart.* 12. to take on as a load: *to load coal.* 13. to supply plentifully or generously with something: *to load a person with gifts.* 14. to give emotional or other bias to. 15. to weigh down, burden, or oppress. 16. to weight (dice) unevenly to make them fall with a particular face upwards. 17. to charge (a gun, etc.) with bullets or supply (a camera) with film. ◇v.i. 18. to put on or take on a load: *The ship is loading tomorrow.* 19. to get into a bus, etc.: *The football fans loaded into special buses.* [ME]

loaded /'loʊdəd/, adj. 1. carrying a load: *a loaded ship.* 2. charged: *a loaded gun.* 3. (of a question, statement, etc.) unfair; weighted so as to produce a prejudicial effect. 4. (of dice) dishonestly weighted. 5. *Colloq.* very rich. 6. *Colloq.* drunk or under drugs.

loading /'loʊdɪŋ/, n. 1. a load or the act of loading. 2. an extra payment to employees in recognition of some aspect of their work, as shift work, special conditions, etc., or as a holiday bonus. 3. an extra premium for something seen as a risk by an insurance company.

loaf[1] /loʊf/, n., pl. **loaves** /loʊvz/. 1. a quantity of bread or cake baked in a mass of particular form. 2. a shaped or moulded mass

loaf of food, as of sugar, chopped meat, etc.: *a veal loaf*. [OE: loaf, bread]

loaf² /louf/, *v.i.* **1.** to go or sit about lazily and without purpose. **2.** to pass the time in doing nothing. ◇*v.t.* **3.** to pass away (time etc.) in doing nothing: *to loaf one's life away*. ◇*n.* **4.** restful and free time. **5.** an easy job. [? G: tramp, vagabond] —**loafer**, *n.*

loam /loum/, *n.* loose soil made up of clay and sand, esp. a kind containing organic matter and of great fertility. [OE *lām*]

loan /loun/, *n.* **1.** the act of lending; the giving of something to be used by someone for a short time: *the loan of a book*. **2.** something given to someone on condition of being returned, esp. a sum of money lent at interest. ◇*v.t.* **3.** to lend. **4.** to lend (money) at interest. ◇*v.i.* **5.** to make a loan or loans. [OE, apparently from Scand]

loath /louθ/, *adj.* **1.** unwilling; reluctant. **2. nothing loath**, very willingly. Also, **loth**. [OE: hostile, hateful]

loathe /louð/, *v.t.*, **loathed, loathing**. **1.** to feel hatred, distaste, or strong opposition for. **2.** to feel physical disgust for (food, etc.). [OE: be hateful] —**loathsome**, *adj.*

loaves /louvz/, *n.* plural of **loaf¹**.

lob /lɒb/, *n.*, *v.*, **lobbed, lobbing**. ◇*n.* **1.** *Tennis*. a ball hit high into the opponent's court. ◇*v.t.* **2.** *Tennis*. to send (a ball) high into the air. **3.** to throw in a careless or untidy fashion. ◇*v.i.* **4.** *Tennis*. to lob a ball. ◇*v.* **5. lob in**, *Colloq*. to arrive without warning. [ME: a fish; later, country bumpkin; as v., move clumsily]

lobate /'loubeɪt/, *adj.* having a lobe or, lobes. [NL, from LL: LOBE]

lobby /'lɒbi/, *n.*, *pl.* **-bies**, *v.*, **-bied, -bying**. ◇*n.* **1.** a passage way, or entrance hall, as in a public building, often serving as a waiting room. **2.** a group of people who attempt to get popular and political support for some particular cause, originally those who oft. visited rooms or entrance halls of parliaments. **3.** a particular interest, cause, etc., supported by a group of people. ◇*v.i.* **4.** to oft. visit the entrance hall of a legislative chamber to influence the members. **5.** to request the votes of members of a law-making body. ◇*v.t.* **6.** to influence (lawmakers), or urge or obtain the passage of (a bill), by trying to enlist political support. [ML: covered walk; of Gmc origin] —**lobbyist**, *n.*

lobe /loub/, *n.* **1.** a roundish part which stands out, as of an organ, a leaf, etc. **2.** *Anat.* the soft, hanging, lower part of the outer ear. [F, from LL, from Gk] —**lobed**, *adj.*

Lobethal /'loubəθəl/, *n.* a town in southeastern SA in the Mount Lofty Ranges; contains the Onkaparinga woollen mill; settled by German Lutherans in 1841. Pop. 1580 (1986). Formerly (1914–36), **Tweedvale**. [from Luther's translation of the Bible (2 Chronicles 20:26): valley of praise]

lobotomy /lə'bɒtəmi/, *n.* the cutting into or across a lobe of the brain to alter the way the brain works, esp. in the treatment of mental disorders.

lobster /'lɒbstə/, *n.* **1.** Also, **spiny lobster**. a type of large, edible, stalk-eyed, crustacean with ten legs and a hard skeleton or shell on the outside of its body, having a long tail, and lengthened whip-like feelers, found in Australian and NZ waters and widely scattered elsewhere; crayfish. **2.** a similar type of crustacean of the northern Atlantic, but having the first pair of legs changed into large, sharply-tipped claws. [L *locusta* influenced by OE *loppestre*, from *loppe* spider (both creatures having many projecting parts)]

local /'loukəl/, *adj.* **1.** relating to or marked by place, or position in space. **2.** typical of, or limited to a particular place (or places): *a local custom*. **3.** relating to a town or a small area rather than the whole state or country. **4.** relating to or affecting particular part (or parts), as of a system or object: *a local disease*. **5.** (of anaesthesia or an anaesthetic) acting on only a section of the body, without causing loss of consciousness. ◇*n.* **6.** a local train, bus, etc. **7.** a suburban newspaper. **8.** the closest or preferred hotel in the neighborhood of one's home or place of work. **9.** an inhabitant of a particular place. **10.** a local anaesthetic. See def. 5. [ME, from LL, from L: place]

locale /lou'kɑːl/, *n.* a place or locality, esp. with direction of attention to events or conditions connected with it. [F]

Local Court, *n.* **1.** (in NSW, WA and Tas) a magistrate's court. **2.** (in the NT) a court with jurisdiction equivalent to that of a District or County Court in the states.

local government, *n.* the management of the affairs of some particular area smaller than that of a state, such as a shire, municipality, town, etc., by officers elected by the residents and ratepayers of that area.

localise or **localize** /'loukəlaɪz/, *v.t.*, **-lised, -lising**. to fix in, give, make over or limit to, a particular place or area.

locality /lou'kæləti/, *n.*, *pl.* **-ties**. **1.** a place, spot, or area. **2.** the place in which a thing is or happens.

locate /lou'keɪt/, *v.*, **-cated, -cating**. ◇*v.t.* **1.** to discover the place of: *to locate a leak in a pipe*. **2.** to set, fix, or establish in a place, position, or locality; settle: *to locate the headquarters in Norfolk Island*; *The offices are located in High St.* **3.** to show the place or location of: *The map locates the mine here*. [L: placed]

location /lou'keɪʃən/, *n.* **1.** a house or place of business: *a good location for a doctor*. **2.** a place or position: *a house in a fine location*. **3.** a piece of land in a particular place and with limits: *a mining location*. **4.** *Films*. a place, outside the studio, providing suitable surroundings for photographing plays, events, etc. **5.** the act of settling in a certain position or place.

loc. cit., *adv.* in the place or passage already mentioned. [L *locō citātō*]

loch /lɒk/, *n.* *Scot.* **1.** a lake. **2.** Also, **sea loch**. an arm of the sea, esp. when partly landlocked. [Gaelic]

Loch Ness monster /nes/, *n.* a monster supposed to inhabit Loch Ness in northern Scotland.

loci /'lɒki, 'louki/, *n.* plural of **locus**.

lock[1] /lɒk/, *n.* **1.** a device for fastening a door, gate, lid, drawer, etc., in position when closed, consisting of a bolt or system of bolts driven forwards and withdrawn by a mechanism operated by a key, dial, etc. **2.** a device to keep a wheel from turning around. **3.** the device in a gun by means of which it can be kept from firing. **4.** an enclosed part of a canal, river, etc., with gates at each end, for raising or lowering vessels from one level to another. **5.** a type of hold in wrestling, esp. any hold in which an arm or leg of one wrestler is held about the body of the opponent. **6.** the radius of turning in the steering machinery of a vehicle. **7.** *Rugby Football.* Also, **lock forward.** the forward who packs down in the third row of the scrum with his head between the two second rowers. **8. lock, stock, and barrel,** altogether; completely. ◊*v.t.* **9.** to fasten or make safe (a door, building, etc.) by the operation of a lock. **10.** to shut in a place fastened by a lock or locks, as for safety or to keep in check: *to lock a prisoner in a cell; Lock the dog up when I go out.* **11.** to keep out by or as if by a lock: *We will lock the gate-crashers out.* **12.** to make fast or immovable by or as by a lock: *to lock a wheel.* **13.** to fasten or fix firmly, as by joining parts together. **14.** to join firmly by connecting or twisting together: *to lock arms.* ◊*v.i.* **15.** to become locked: *This door locks with a key.* **16.** to become fastened, fixed, or interlocked. [OE: fastening]

lock[2] /lɒk/, *n.* **1.** a twist or length of hair. **2.** (*pl.*) the hair of the head. **3.** a tuft or small amount of cotton, flax, etc. **4.** (*usu. pl.*) a second cut or small amount of wool from the lower parts of the legs and edges of the fleece. [OE: lock of hair]

Locke /lɒk/, *n.* **John,** 1632–1704, English philosopher and political theorist.

locker /'lɒkə/, *n.* a chest, drawer, cupboard, etc., that may be locked, esp. one for personal use: *I put my lunch in my locker at school.*

locket /'lɒkət/, *n.* a small case for a small picture, a lock of hair, etc., usu. worn on a chain hung round the neck. [ME, from F: latch, catch, from OF: little lock, from Gmc]

lockjaw /'lɒkdʒɔ/, *n.* → **tetanus.**

locksmith /'lɒksmɪθ/, *n.* someone who makes or mends locks.

lockup /'lɒkʌp/, *n.* **1.** a prison, esp. a local prison to which offenders are taken before their first court hearing. **2.** a garage or other storage space, usu. rented, able to be locked up.

Lockyer /'lɒkjə/, *n.* **Edmund,** 1784–1860, Australian explorer, born in England; founder of Albany, WA, and explorer of the Brisbane River, Qld.

locomotion /loukə'mouʃən/, *n.* the act or power of moving from place to place. [L: place + MOTION]

locomotive /loukə'moutɪv/, *n.* **1.** an engine which drives itself forward, running on a railway track, designed to pull railway carriages or trucks. **2.** any vehicle able to drive itself from place to place. ◊*adj.* **3.** moving or travelling by means of its own machinery or powers. **4.** having to do with movement from place to place. [L: place + MOTIVE]

locum /'loukəm/, *n.* a temporary stand-in for a doctor, lawyer, etc. Also, **locum tenens** /loukəm 'tenənz/. [ML: one holding the office (of another)]

locus /'lɒkəs, 'loukəs/, *n., pl.* **loci** /'lɒki, 'louki/. **1.** a place; a locality. **2.** *Maths.* a curve or other figure considered as produced by a point, line, or surface, which moves or is placed according to a fixed law. [L: place]

locust /'loukəst/, *n.* **1.** any of the grasshoppers with short feelers, including the species which migrate in large numbers and destroy plants over wide areas. **2.** *Colloq.* → **cicada.** [ME, from L]

locution /lə'kjuʃən/, *n.* **1.** a particular form of expression; a phrase or expression. **2.** style of speech or verbal expression; phraseology. [ME, from L]

Loddon /'lɒdn/, *n.* a river in western central Vic which rises in the Great Dividing Range, flows north-west and then north to meet an anabranch and then the Murray itself at Swan Hill. 320 km.

lode /loud/, *n.* **1.** a veinlike deposit, usu. yielding metal. **2.** any body of ore set off from the rock formations next to it. [OE: way, course, carrying]

lodestar /'loudsta/, *n.* **1.** a star that shows the way. **2.** something that serves as a guide or on which the attention is fixed. Also, **loadstar.** [ME *loode sterre*]

lodestone /'loudstoun/, *n.* (a magnet made of) a variety of the mineral magnetite which possesses magnetic polarity and attracts iron. [LOAD + STONE]

lodge /lɒdʒ/, *n., v.*, **lodged, lodging.** ◊*n.* **1.** a small, slight, or rough shelter or place to live, made of branches, poles, skins, earth, rough boards, etc.; cabin or hut. **2.** a building used for temporary, usu. holiday, housing: *fishing lodge; ski lodge.* **3.** a small house as in a park or on an estate, lived in by a caretaker, gardener, etc. **4.** the meeting place of a branch of a secret society. **5.** a cave or shelter of an animal or animals, esp. of beavers. ◊*v.i.* **6.** to have a shelter or quarters, esp. temporarily, as in a place or house. **7.** to be fixed or implanted, or be caught in a place or position. ◊*v.t.* **8.** to provide with a shelter or rooms, esp. temporarily. **9.** to provide with a room or rooms in one's house for payment, or have as a lodger. **10.** to put (something) in a certain place for safety, storage or keeping. **11.** to put or send into a particular place: *to lodge a bullet in someone's heart.* **12.** to lay (information, a complaint, etc.) before a court, etc. [ME, from OF: hut, orig. leafy shelter, from Gmc] —**lodgment,** *n.*

lodger /'lɒdʒə/, *n.* someone who lives in hired quarters in another's house. See **boarder.**

lodging /'lɒdʒɪŋ/, *n.* **1.** a place to live in a house, esp. in rooms for hire: *to provide board and lodging*. **2.** a place to stay, esp. temporarily. **3.** (*pl.*) a room (or rooms) hired in another's house.

loess /'loʊəs/, *n.* a loamy deposit formed by the wind, usu. yellowish and calcareous.

loft /lɒft/, *n.* **1.** the space between the underside of a roof and the ceiling of the room beneath it. **2.** the upper level in a church, hall, etc., thought of and made for a special purpose: *a choir loft*. **3.** *Golf.* to slope the face of (a club). **4.** *Golf, Cricket, etc.* to hit (a ball) into the air or over an obstacle. **5.** to clear (an obstacle) in this way. [OE, from Scand]

lofty /'lɒftɪ/, *adj.*, **-tier, -tiest. 1.** reaching high in the air; of imposing height: *lofty mountains*. **2.** high above others in rank, dignity, or character. **3.** (of writings, etc.) noble in style or feeling. **4.** proud; haughty.

log /lɒg/, *n., v.,* **logged, logging.** ◇*n.* **1.** a rounded, uncut part or length of the trunk or a large limb from a tree. **2.** something heavy or inert. **3.** *Naut.* **a.** a device for determining the speed and distance covered by a ship. **b.** the official (daily) record which a ship's master is commanded by law to keep, of particulars of a ship's voyage, as weather, crew, cargo, etc. **4.** Also, **flightlog.** a listing of the course, weather patterns and other related information concerning an air journey. **5.** the record of the operation of a machine. **6.** a written request or listing: *the trade union's log of claims*. ◇*v.t.* **7.** to cut (trees) into logs. **8.** to cut down trees (on land). **9.** to enter (information) in a ship's or aeroplane's log. **10.** to submit (a claim). [ME]

Logan[1] /'loʊgən/, *n.* **1. Patrick,** c. 1791–1830, Scottish soldier and explorer in Australia 1825–30.

Logan[2] /'loʊgən/, *n.* a city in Qld, on the Logan River; residential area of Brisbane. Pop. 117 191 (1986).

loganberry /'loʊgənberɪ, -brɪ/, *n., pl.* **-ries.** (a large, dark red, acid fruit of) a plant with long jointed, woody stems lying flat on the ground. [named after JH *Logan*, 1841–1928, of California, US, by whom first grown]

logarithm /'lɒgərɪðəm/, *n.* the exponent of that power to which a fixed number (called the *base*) must be raised in order to produce a given number: *From* $2^3 = 8$, *it can be seen that 3 is the logarithm of 8 to the base 2.* [NL, from Gk *lógos* proportion + *arithmós* number]

logbook /'lɒgbʊk/, *n.* → **log** (defs 3b, 4).

logger /'lɒgə/, *n.* a person who cuts trees into suitable lengths after the trees have been cut down.

loggerhead /'lɒgəhɛd/, *n.* **1.** a ball or bulb of iron with a long handle, used, after being heated, to melt tar, heat liquids, etc. **2. at loggerheads,** supporting opposing points of view. [*loggerheaded*, var. of obs. *log-headed* stupid]

loggia /'loʊdʒɪə, 'lɒdʒɪə/, *n.* **1.** a covered way open to the air on at least one side. **2.** a space within the body of a building but open to the air on one side, serving as an open-air room or as an entrance area outside the main door. [It]

logging /'lɒgɪŋ/, *n.* the process, work, or business of cutting down trees and getting out logs from the forest for use in building.

logic /'lɒdʒɪk/, *n.* **1.** the science which carefully examines the principles governing correct or reliable reasoning. **2.** reasoning or arguing, or an instance of it. **3.** a system or principles of reasoning related to any branch of knowledge or study. **4.** reasons or sound sense, as in things said or actions. **5.** persuading force: *the irresistible logic of facts*. [ME, from ML, from Gk: pertaining to reason] **— logician,** *n.*

logical /'lɒdʒɪkəl/, *adj.* **1.** according to the principles of the science of reasoning: *a logical reason*. **2.** reasoning in accordance with the principles of logic: *a logical mind*. **3.** reasonable; reasonably to be expected: *War was the logical consequence of such threats*. **4.** having to do with or relating to logic. **— logicality, logicalness,** *n.*

Logie /'loʊgɪ/, *n.* a statuette awarded annually by the Australian television industries to outstanding television practitioners. [after John *Logie* BAIRD, inventor of television, and coined by Graham KENNEDY when in 1958 he received the first award]

logistics /lə'dʒɪstɪks/, *n.* the branch of military science concerned with the mathematics of transportation and supply, and the movement of troops. [F: lodging]

logo-, a word part indicating 'speech'. [Gk, combining form of *lógos* word, speech]

-logy, 1. a combining form naming sciences or bodies of knowledge, as in *theology, zoology*. **2.** an ending of many nouns directing attention to writing, collections, as in *trilogy, anthology*. [Gk *-logia,* from *log-* speak, *lógos* discourse]

loin /lɔɪn/, *n.* **1.** (*usu. pl.*) the part or parts of the body of man or of a four-footed animal on either side of the spine, between the ribs and hipbone. **2.** a standard cut of lamb, veal, or pork from the upper part between ribs and hip including the lower eight ribs. **3. gird up one's loins,** to make ready or prepare oneself for action of some kind. [ME, from OF, from L]

loincloth /'lɔɪnklɒθ/, *n.* a piece of cloth worn about the loins or hips.

Loire /lwa/, *n.* a river flowing from southern France into the Atlantic; the longest river in France, its valley is noted for chateaus and wine production. About 1010 km.

loiter /'lɔɪtə/, *v.i.* **1.** to stay longer than usual with nothing to do, or stay aimlessly in or about a place. **2.** to move or go in a slow or unwilling manner: *to loiter along*. **3.** to waste or take a long time over work, etc. ◇*v.t.* **4.** to pass (time, etc.) in an aimless manner or doing nothing: *He loitered away the day listening to the radio.* [? ME: lurk] **— loiterer,** *n.*

loll /lɒl/, *v.i.* **1.** to lean or lean back in a carefree or lazy manner; lounge: *to loll on a sofa*. **2.** to hang loosely or sink down. ◇*v.t.* **3.** to allow to hang or sink down. [ME *lolle*]

Lollard /ˈlɒlad/, n. an English or Scottish follower of the religious teaching of John Wyclif from the 14th to the 16th century. [ME, from MD, *lollaerd* mumbler, from *lollen* mumble, hum]

lollipop /ˈlɒlipɒp/, n. a kind of boiled sweet, oft. fixed to the end of a stick.

lollop /ˈlɒləp/, v.i. to move with jumping, awkward springs. [extension of LOLL, in this sense perhaps influenced by GALLOP]

lolly /ˈlɒli/, n. 1. any sweet, esp. a boiled one. 2. *Colloq.* the head. 3. *Colloq.* money. 4. **do one's lolly**, *Colloq.* to lose one's temper.

Lombardy /ˈlɒmbədi/, n. a region in northern Italy bordering on the Alps; former kingdom. Pop. 8 881 683 (1986 est.); 23 802 km^2. Cap.: Milan. Italian, **Lombardia**.

Lomond /ˈloʊmənd/, n. 1. **Ben → Ben Lomond**. 2. **Loch**, a lake in south-western Scotland, north of Glasgow; Scotland's largest lake. 85 km^2.

London[1] /ˈlʌndən/, n. 1. a metropolis in south-eastern England, on the Thames; capital of the UK. 2. **City of**, an administrative division in the central part of London: the old city and ancient nucleus of the metropolis. Pop. 5100 (1985 est.); 2.6 km^2. 3. **Greater**, a metropolitan county formed in 1965 from the City and the former London and Middlesex counties, and parts of Essex, Kent, Surrey, and Hertfordshire. Pop. 6 767 500 (1985 est.); 1610 km^2.

London[2] /ˈlʌndən/, n. **Jack**, 1876–1916, US short-story writer, novelist and adventurer.

Londonderry /ˈlʌndənderi/, n. former name of **Derry**.

London Missionary Society, n. an Anglican and Nonconformist missionary group formed in 1795 whose early activities resulted in the establishment of Congregational churches in Australia.

lone /loʊn/, adj. 1. being alone; unaccompanied; solitary: *a lone traveller*. 2. standing apart, or away from anything else: *a lone house*. 3. *Poetic.* lonely. [var. of ALONE]

lonely /ˈloʊnli/, adj., **-lier**, **-liest**. 1. alone; solitary; without company. 2. lacking sympathetic or friendly companionship or relationships: *a lonely exile*. 3. far away from men or from places where humans live or go: *a lonely desert*. 4. standing apart; isolated: *a lonely tower*. 5. affected with, marked by, or causing a depressed feeling of being alone; lonesome: *a lonely heart*. – **loneliness**, n.

loner /ˈloʊnə/, n. someone who dislikes company.

lonesome /ˈloʊnsəm/, adj. lonely in feeling; depressed by a sense of being alone: *to feel lonesome*.

long[1] /lɒŋ/, adj., **longer** /ˈlɒŋɡə/, **longest** /ˈlɒŋɡəst/, n., adv. ◇adj. 1. having considerable or great distance from end to end; not short: *a long distance*. 2. lasting a considerable or great amount of time: *a long visit*. 3. having many articles; of more than average number: *a long list*. 4. having considerable or great distance from beginning to end, as a series, account, book, etc.; not brief. 5. having a stated distance in space, duration, etc.: *ten metres long*. 6. beyond the normal distance in space, duration, quantity, etc.: *a long match*. 7. going a great distance in space or time: *a long memory*. 8. not likely: *a long chance*. 9. concentrated; intense: *taking a long look at his faults*. 10. **in the long run**, after a long course of experience; in the final result. ◇n. 11. something that is long. 12. **before long**, in the near future; soon. 13. **the long and the short of**, the central part; substance of; gist. ◇adv. 14. for or through a great distance of space or, esp., time: *a reform long advocated*. 15. for or throughout a stated amount, esp. of time: *How long did he stay?* 16. gone, busy with, delaying, etc., a long or a stated amount of time: *Don't be long*. 17. (for emphasis, after nouns marking a period of time) throughout the whole length: *all summer long*. 18. at a point of time far distant from the time mentioned: *long before*. 19. **so** (or **as**) **long as**, provided that. 20. **so long**, *Colloq.* goodbye. [OE] – **longish**, adj.

long[2] /lɒŋ/, v.i. to have an unceasing or very strong desire, esp. for something not immediately possible or available (if ever). [OE *langian* seem long, arouse desire in]

Long /lɒŋ/, n. 1. **Crawford Williamson**, 1815–78, US surgeon; pioneered the use of ether as an anaesthetic. 2. **Sydney**, 1871–1955, Australian painter and etcher.

long division, n. a process for dividing one number by a second, in which the first step consists of obtaining the first number of the result and the partial remainder by repeated tests. At each step the next number of the result and the partial remainder are obtained.

long-drawn /ˈlɒŋ-drɔn/, adj. drawn out; prolonged: *a long-drawn narrative*.

longevity /lɒnˈdʒɛvəti/, n. 1. length or duration of life. 2. long life; great duration of life.

Longfellow /ˈlɒŋfeloʊ/, n. **Henry Wadsworth**, 1807–82, US poet, best known for narrative poems such as *The Song of Hiawatha*. (1855).

longhand /ˈlɒŋhænd/, n. writing of the ordinary kind, in which the words are written out in full (opposed to **shorthand**).

longing /ˈlɒŋɪŋ/, n. 1. a longstanding or deep desire. ◇adj. 2. having or showing such desire: *a longing look*.

Long Island, n. an island in south-eastern New York; the boroughs of Brooklyn and Queens of New York City are situated at its western end; La Guardia and John F Kennedy airports. 190 km long; 19–32 km wide; 4356 km^2.

longitude /ˈlɒŋɡətjud/, n. *Geog.* the angular distance east or west on the earth's surface, measured along the equator by the angle contained between the meridian of a particular place and some prime meridian, as that of Greenwich, or by the similar difference in time. [ME, from L: length]

longitudinal /lɒngə'tjudənəl/, *adj.* **1.** relating to length: *longitudinal distance.* **2.** going onwards in the direction of the length of a thing; running lengthways.

longitudinal wave, *n. Physics.* a wave in which the vibration or oscillation is in the direction of propagation, as a sound wave.

long johns, *n.pl. Colloq.* a pair of long warm underpants.

long jump, *n.* an event in athletics in which the aim is to jump the greatest distance.

Long March, *n.* a march of about 10 000 km undertaken in 1934–35 by about 100 000 Chinese Communists, led by Mao Zedong, after they were forced to leave Jiangxi in south-eastern China; about 8000 finally reached Shaanxi in north-western China.

Long Parliament, *n. English Hist.* the parliament summoned by Charles I that assembled on 3 November 1640, was expelled by Cromwell in 1653, reconvened in 1659, and was dissolved in 1660.

long-playing /'lɒŋ-pleɪɪŋ/, *adj.* (of a gramophone record) being made to revolve at 33⅓ r.p.m. *Abbrev.:* LP

long-sighted /'lɒŋ-saɪtɪd/, *adj.* **1.** able to see distant objects better than those near at hand. **2.** having great foresight; foreseeing remote results.

longstanding /'lɒŋstændɪŋ/, *adj.* existing or happening for a long time: *a longstanding feud.*

long-suffering /'lɒŋ-sʌfərɪŋ/, *adj.* **1.** patiently putting up with being hurt and angered. ◇*n.* **2.** long and patient bearing of being hurt or made angry.

long-term /'lɒŋ-tɜm/, *adj.* going on over a lengthy period of time.

long wave, *n.* a wave of the same nature as light with a wavelength of over one kilometre, as a radio wave; an electromagnetic wave. –**long-wave**, *adj.*

longwinded /'lɒŋwɪndəd/, *adj.* **1.** using too many words in speech or writing. **2.** writing or talking far too long and without stopping.

Lonsdale /'lɒnzdeɪl/, *n.* **William**, 1799–1864, Australian army officer and administrator, born in England; appointed first police magistrate and commandant of the settlement at Port Phillip in 1836.

loo /lu/, *n. Colloq.* a toilet. [var. of LAVATORY]

loofah /'lufə/, *n.* **1.** a tropical, climbing herb. **2.** the fibrous network of its fruit, used as a bath sponge. [Ar]

look /lʊk/, *v.i.* **1.** to fix the eyes upon something or in some direction in order to see. **2.** to direct one's eyes in a particular way: *to look questioningly at a person.* **3.** to use the sight in trying to find, examining, watching, etc.: *to look through the papers.* **4.** to tend, as in bearing or importance: *Conditions look towards war.* **5.** to appear or seem (as specified) to the eye: *to look pale.* **6.** to seem to the mind: *The case looks promising.* **7.** to direct the mind or attention: *to look at the facts.* **8.** to have an outlook or afford a view: *The window looks upon the street.* **9.** to face or front: *The house looks east.* ◇*v.t.* **10.** to try to find; seek (fol. by *up, out,* etc.): *to look a name up in a directory.* **11.** to express or suggest by looks: *She looked all sympathy.* **12.** to view or examine carefully (fol by *over*): *She looked over the new flat.* **13.** to direct a look towards: *She looked him full in the face.* **14.** to have the appearance fitting for: *to look one's age; to look an idiot.* **15.** to visit or get in touch with (fol by *up*): *to look up an old school-friend.* ◇*v.* **16.** Some special uses are:
it looks like it, it seems likely.
look after, to take care of: *to look after a child.*
look down on, to have disrespect for; regard with disdain.
look down one's nose, to regard with barely hidden disrespect.
look for, **1.** to try to find (a person or thing). **2.** to expect; anticipate.
look forward to, to expect with pleasure.
look in, to come or go in for a short visit.
look into, to examine; investigate.
look like, to seem likely to; appear probable: *The horse looks like winning.*
look lively or **sharp**, to make haste; be alert.
look on, to be a mere spectator.
look out, **1.** to look forwards, as from a window. **2.** to be on guard. **3.** to take watchful care: *to look out for oneself.*
look to, **1.** to give attention to. **2.** to direct the hopes to (someone) for something desired. **3.** to look forward hopefully to.
look up, *Colloq.* to rise in amount or value; improve: *Things are looking up.*
look up to, to regard with admiration.
◇*n.* **17.** the act of looking: *a look of enquiry.* **18.** a search or examination using the eyes. **19.** the way of looking or appearing to the eye or mind; aspect: *the look of an honest man.* **20.** (*pl.*) general appearance: *to like the looks of a place; good looks.* [OE *lōcian*]

looking glass, *n.* a mirror.

lookout /'lʊkaʊt/, *n.* **1.** a watch kept for something that may come or happen. **2.** a person or group placed or employed to keep such a watch. **3.** a station or place from which a watch is kept. **4.** a view; prospect; outlook. **5.** a place on a high point, esp. a mountain, from which one can admire the view. **6.** *Colloq.* the proper object of one's watchful care or concern: *That's his lookout.*

loom[1] /lum/, *n.* a machine or apparatus for weaving yarn or thread into a fabric. [OE: tool, implement]

loom[2] /lum/, *v.i.* to appear unclearly, or come into view in an unclear, enlarged and frightening form. [cf. d. Swed *loma* move slowly]

loon /lun/, *n.* any of several large, short-tailed web-footed, fish-eating diving birds of the Northern Hemisphere, e.g. the common loon or great northern diver, of the Old and New Worlds.

loony /'luni/, *adj.*, **loonier**, **looniest**, *n.*, *pl.* **loonies**. *Colloq.* ◇*adj.* **1.** crazy; lunatic. **2.** very or senselessly foolish. ◇*n.* **3.** →

loony

lunatic. Also, **looney, luny**. [var. of *luny*, familiar shortening of LUNATIC]

loop /lup/, *n.* **1.** a folding or doubling of a part of a cord, lace, ribbon, etc., upon itself, so as to leave an opening between the parts. **2.** anything shaped more or less like a loop, as a line drawn on paper, a part of a letter, a part of a path, a line of movement, etc. **3.** a curved piece or a ring of metal, wood, etc., used for the putting in of something, or as a handle, or otherwise. **4.** *Aeron.* an exercise carried out in such a manner that the aeroplane performs a closed curve in a vertical plane. **5.** *Phys.* the part of vibrating string, column of air, etc., between two nodes next to each other; antinode. **6.** *Med.* an intra-uterine contraceptive device, formerly made in metal, now in plastic. **7.** *Elect.* a closed electric or magnetic circuit. ◇*v.t.* **8.** to form into a loop or loops. **9.** to make a loop or loops in. **10.** to enfold or encircle in or with something arranged in a loop. **11.** to fasten by forming into a loop, or by means of something formed into a loop. **12.** to fly (an aeroplane) in a loop or series of loops. ◇*v.i.* **13.** to make or form a loop or loops. ◇*v.* **14. loop the loop**, *Aeron.* to perform a loop (def. 4). [ME *loupe*]

loophole /'luphoul/, *n.* **1.** a small or narrow opening in a wall, for admitting light and air, or particularly, in a stronghold, for the discharge of weapons. **2.** an opening. **3.** an outlet, as for means of escape or avoidance.

loose /lus/, *adj.*, **looser, loosest**, *n.*, *adv.*, *v.*, **loosed, loosing**. ◇*adj.* **1.** free from cords, ropes, or binding: *to get one's hand loose.* **2.** free or freed from fastening or binding: *a loose end.* **3.** uncombined, as a chemical element. **4.** not bound together, as papers or flowers. **5.** not put in a packet or other container: *loose mushrooms.* **6.** not set apart for a particular purpose: *loose funds.* **7.** unrestrained: *a loose tongue.* **8.** (of the bowels) lax or open. **9.** free from moral check, or careless in principle or behavior. **10.** not firm or stiff: *a loose tooth; a loose rein.* **11.** (of garments) not fitting closely. **12.** having spaces between the parts, or open: *a loose weave.* **13.** (of earth, soil, etc.) not sticking together: *loose sand.* **14.** not complete, exact, or careful: *loose thinking.* **15.** free from controlling conditions or factors: *The Commonwealth of Nations is a loose association of sovereign states.* **16. at a loose end**, **a.** in an unsettled or disorderly condition. **b.** having nothing to do; unoccupied. ◇*n.* **17. on the loose**, free from check or control. ◇*adv.* **18.** in a loose manner; loosely. **19.** so as to become free, independent, etc.: *He cut loose from his family.* ◇*v.t.* **20.** to let loose, or free from check or control. **21.** to free from (force, duty, punishment, etc.). **22.** to shoot, or let fly. **23.** to make less tight; slacken or relax. ◇*v.i.* **24.** to let go a hold. [ME, from Scand]

loose-leaf /'lus-lif/, *adj.* (of a book, etc.) having separate leaves that may be put in or removed without tearing.

loosen /'lusən/, *v.t., v.i.* to make or become loose or looser.

loot /lut/, *n.* **1.** anything dishonestly and cruelly taken for oneself: *a burglar's loot; loot taken in war.* **2.** *Colloq.* money. ◇*v.t., v.i.* **3.** to plunder or rob (a city, house, etc.), esp. in war. [Hind]

lop /lɒp/, *v.t.*, **lopped, lopping. 1.** to cut off the branches, twigs, etc., of (a tree or other plant). **2.** to cut off (branches, twigs, etc.) from a tree or other plant. **3.** to cut off (head, limbs) from a person or animal. [ME: small branch, etymologically identical with obs. *lop* spider, both objects being marked by many projecting parts]

lope /loup/, *v.*, **loped, loping**, *n.* ◇*v.i.* **1.** to move or run with leaping steps, as a four-footed animal, or with a long, easy step, as a person. ◇*n.* **2.** the act or movement of loping. **3.** a long, easy step. [ME, var. of obs. *loup* leap, from Scand]

lopsided /'lɒpsaɪdəd/, *adj.* **1.** sloping or leaning to one side. **2.** heavier, larger, or more developed on one side than on the other; asymmetrical.

loquacious /lə'kweɪʃəs/, *adj.* **1.** talking or tending to talk a lot or freely; talkative. **2.** marked by or showing a tendency to talk too much: *a loquacious mood.* – **loquacity, loquaciousness**, *n.*

loquat /'loukwɒt, -kwət/, *n.* a small, evergreen tree native to China and Japan, but grown elsewhere for ornament and for its yellow plum-like fruit. [Cantonese: rush orange]

lord /lɔd/, *n.* **1.** someone who has power over others; master; chief; ruler. **2.** a feudal ruler, esp. of a manor. **3.** a titled nobleman, or person of high rank. **4.** (*cap.*) the title given to a mayor, bishop, earl, etc.: *Lord Mayor; my Lord bishop.* **5.** (*cap.*) God. **6.** (*cap.*) Jesus Christ. ◇*v.i.* **7.** to behave in a lordly manner; domineer: *to lord it over someone.* [OE *hláf* LOAF[1] + *weard* keeper]

Lord /lɔd/, *n.* **Simeon** /'sɪmiən/, 1771–1840, Australian merchant and manufacturer, born in England; came to the colonies as a convict.

Lord Chamberlain, *n.* the chief officer in the British royal household, responsible for arrangements at state occasions, in charge of many royal staff and formerly licenser of plays and public theatres.

Lord Haw-Haw /lɔd 'hɔ-hɔ/, *n.* → William **Joyce**.

Lord Howe Island, *n.* an island off the northern coast of NSW; tourist resort. 15 km[2].

lordly /'lɔdli/, *adj.*, **-lier, -liest. 1.** grand, or making a splendid appearance or show. **2.** rudely overbearing: *lordly contempt.*

lord mayor, *n.* (in some cities, e.g. Sydney, Melbourne, etc.) → **mayor**.

Lords /lɔdz/, *n.* **the**, → **House of Lords**.

Lord's /lɔdz/, *n.* a cricket ground at St John's Wood, in northern London; headquarters of the Marylebone Cricket Club (MCC).

Lord's Supper, *n.* **the**, **1.** the Last Supper of Jesus and His disciples. **2.** the sacrament in memory of this; communion; mass.

lore /lɔ/, *n.* **1.** the body of knowledge, esp. of a traditional, story-telling, or popular type, on a particular subject: *the lore of herbs.* **2.** learning or knowledge. [OE *lār*]

Lorelei /'lɔrəlaɪ/, *n. German Legend.* a siren who, by her singing, caused sailors to wreck their boats on her rock in the Rhine; created by Clemens Brentano in a poem in 1800. [G]

Lorenz /'lɔrents/, *n.* Konrad Zacharias, 1903–89, Austrian zoologist; shared Nobel prize for physiology or medicine (1973) with Tinbergen and von Frisch, for work in ethology; author of *On Aggression* (1963).

lorgnette /lɔ'njet/, *n.* a pair of eyeglasses mounted on a long handle. [F: look sidelong at, eye, from OF: squinting]

lorikeet /'lɔrəkit, lɔrə'kit/, *n.* a type of small, brightly-colored parrot found mainly in Australasia having a brush-like tongue specialised for feeding on nectar. [LORY + (PARA)KEET]

Lorraine /lɔ'reɪn/, *n.* **1.** a medieval kingdom in western Europe along the Moselle, Meuse, and Rhine Rivers. **2.** German, **Lothringen.** See **Alsace-Lorraine.**

lorry /'lɔri/, *n.* → **truck**[1] (def. 1).

lory /'lɔri/, *n., pl.* **-ries.** any of various lorikeets and parrots of the Malay Archipelago, Australasia, etc. [Malay]

Los Angeles /lɒs 'ændʒələs, -liz/, *n.* a seaport in the US, in south-western California. Pop. 3 259 300 (1986 est.); with suburbs, 9 600 000 (1979); 1171 km².

lose /luz/, *v.*, **lost, losing.** ◇*v.t.* **1.** to come to be without, by some chance, and not know the whereabouts of: *to lose a ring.* **2.** to suffer the loss or deprivation of: *to lose one's life.* **3.** to have taken away by death: *to lose a child.* **4.** to fail to keep control of: *to lose balance.* **5.** to cease to have: *to lose all fear.* **6.** to bring to destruction or ruin (now chiefly in the passive): *Ship and crew were lost.* **7.** to have slip from sight, hearing, attention, etc.: *to lose a face in a crowd.* **8.** to become separated from and without knowledge of (the way, etc.). **9.** to leave far behind in a chase, race, etc. **10.** to use to no purpose, or waste: *to lose time in waiting.* **11.** to fail to have, get, catch, etc.; miss: *to lose an opportunity.* **12.** to fail to win (a prize, stake, etc.). **13.** to be defeated in (a game, lawsuit, battle, etc.). **14.** to cause the loss of: *The delay lost the battle for them.* **15.** to let (oneself) go out of the right way; become bewildered: *to be lost in a wood.* **16.** to absorb or take up completely in something to the shutting out of knowledge or consciousness of all else (usu. used reflexively or in the passive): *to be lost in thought.* ◇*v.i.* **17. lose face,** to lose worth or dignity by having a mistake or foolish action made public. **18. lose out,** *Colloq.* to be defeated or bettered: *I lost out to my rival.* **19. lose out on,** *Colloq.* to fail to carry through (a goal, etc.): *I lost out on that deal.* [OE *leōsan*] **–loser,** *n.*

loss /lɒs/, *n.* **1.** damage or disadvantage from failure to keep, have, or get: *to bear the loss of a robbery.* **2.** that which is lost. **3.** the amount or number lost. **4.** a coming to be without something that one has had: *loss of friends.* **5.** bereavement. **6.** the accidental losing of something dropped, misplaced, etc.: *to discover the loss of a document.* **7.** a losing by defeat, or by failure to win: *the loss of a bet.* **8.** a failure to make good use of something, as time; waste. **9.** a failure to preserve or keep: *loss of speed.* **10.** destruction or ruin. **11. at a loss, a.** in a state of uncertainty or confusion. **b.** in a state of self consciousness for lack of something: *to be at a loss for words.* **12. a dead loss, a.** a complete failure. **b.** a completely useless person or thing. [OE: destruction]

lost /lɒst/, *adj.* **1.** no longer possessed or kept: *lost friends.* **2.** no longer to be found: *lost articles.* **3.** confused as to place, direction, etc. **4.** (of time, etc.) wasted. **5.** not achieved or won: *a lost prize.* **6.** attended with defeat: *a lost battle.* **7.** destroyed or ruined. **8. lost to, a.** no longer belonging to. **b.** no longer open to: *The opportunity was lost to him.* **c.** unfeeling to: *to be lost to all sense of duty.* ◇*v.* **9.** past tense of **lose.**

lot /lɒt/, *n.* **1.** one of a set of objects drawn from a box, hat, etc., to decide a question or choice by chance. **2.** the drawing of such objects as a method of deciding something: *to choose a person by lot.* **3.** the decision or choice so made. **4.** one's share or part given by lot. **5.** the part in life given to someone by fate or providence; fortune; destiny. **6.** a separate part or piece of land; plot: *a parking lot.* **7.** a separate part or parcel of anything, as of things bought. **8.** a number of things or people collectively. **9.** *Colloq.* a person of a particular sort: *He's a bad lot.* **10.** a great many or a great deal: *a lot of books.* **11. the lot,** the whole amount or quantity. **12. throw in one's lot with,** to give one's whole support to. ◇*adv.* **13. a lot,** to a great degree; much: *That is a lot better.* [OE *hlot*]

Lot /lɒt/, *n. Bible.* the nephew of Abraham. His wife was changed into a pillar of salt for looking back during their flight from Sodom. [See Genesis 13:1-12, 19. Heb]

Lothians /'loʊðiənz/, *n.pl.* **The,** three former counties in Scotland: East Lothian, Midlothian, West Lothian.

lotion /'loʊʃən/, *n.* a liquid containing medicines or oils, etc., to be used on the skin. [ME, from L: a washing]

lots /lɒts/, *n.pl. Colloq.* a large quantity or number: *lots of money; lots of people.*

lottery /'lɒtəri, 'lɒtri/, *n., pl.* **-teries. 1.** a method of raising money, esp. for government, charity, etc. by the sale of a large number of numbered tickets, and the drawing of prize-winning numbers by lot. **2.** any affair of chance. [It: lot, from F, from Gmc]

lotto /'lɒtoʊ/, *n.* **1.** → **housie-housie. 2.** any similar game in which items have to be matched. [It]

lotus /'loʊtəs/, *n.* **1.** a plant mentioned in Greek legend as yielding a fruit which produced a state of dreamy and contented forgetfulness in those who ate it. **2.** any of several water-lilies or similar plants, e.g. the sacred lotus of India, whose seeds are used for food, or the white-flowered Egyptian lotus, common in the Nile river. **3.** a picture of such a plant, common in Egyptian and Hindu ornamental art. [L, from Gk]

lotus bird, *n.* the Australian jacana.

loud /laʊd/, *adj.* **1.** striking strongly upon the organs of hearing, as sound, noise, the voice, etc.; strongly audible. **2.** making, giving out, or speaking with strong and easily heard sounds: *loud knocking.* **3.** full of sound or noise. **4.** noisy or crying out loudly. **5.** definite or firm: *to be loud in praising someone.* **6.** (of colors, clothes, etc.) offensively or overly showy; garish. **7.** (of manners, people, etc.) very coarse; vulgar. [OE *hlūd*]

loudhailer /laʊd'heɪlə/, *n.* a megaphone with a built-in amplifier.

loudspeaker /laʊd'spikə, 'laʊdspikə/, *n.* a device by which speech, music, etc., can be made easily heard throughout a room, hall, etc.

Louis¹ /'luəs/, *n.* Joe (*Joseph Louis Barrow*), 1914–81, US world heavyweight champion boxer.

Louis² /'lui, lu'i/, *n.* the name of 18 kings of France.

Louis XIV, *n.* ('*the Sun King*'), 1638–1715, king of France 1643–1715; absolute monarch; son of Louis XIII.

Louis XVI, *n.* 1754–93, king of France from 1774; grandson of Louis XV; deposed in 1792, guillotined, with his wife Marie Antoinette, in 1793.

Louis XVIII, *n.* 1755–1824, king of France 1814–24; younger brother of Louis XVI; forced to flee when Napoleon returned to power during the Hundred Days.

Louisiana /luizi'ænə/, *n.* a state in the southern US. Pop. 4 501 000 (1986 est.); 125 672 km². *Cap.*: Baton Rouge. *Abbrev.*: La —**Louisianan, Louisianian,** *adj., n.*

Louisiana Purchase, *n.* **The,** a huge territory which the US purchased from France in 1803, extending from the Mississippi to the Rocky Mountains and from the Gulf of Mexico to Canada.

Louis Philippe /,lui fi'lip/, *n.* 1773–1850, king of France 1830–48.

lounge /laʊndʒ/, *v.*, **lounged, lounging,** *n.* ◇*v.i.* **1.** to pass time lazily and with nothing to do. **2.** to lie back lazily; loll. **3.** to move or go (*about, along, off,* etc.) in an unhurried, lazy manner: *lounge about in the sun.* ◇*n.* **4.** Also, **lounge room.** a room in a private house for relaxation and entertainment. **5.** a large room in a hotel, etc., used by guests for relaxation purposes. **6.** (in a cinema) the most comfortable seats which also cost the most. **7.** → **couch¹** (def. 1). [? obs. *lungis* laggard, from OF: one who is long (i.e. slow)]

Lourdes /lʊədz/, *n.* a town in southwestern France; famous shrine and centre of pilgrimage. Pop. 17 619 (1982).

louse /laʊs/, *n., pl.* **lice** /laɪs/ or (def. 2) **louses;** *v.,* **loused, lousing.** ◇*n.* **1.** any of various small, wingless, blood-sucking insects living in the hair or skin of man and other mammals. **2.** *Colloq.* someone who deserves to be despised. ◇*v.t.* **3.** *Colloq.* to spoil (fol. by *up*). [OE *lūs* (pl. *lȳs*)]

lousy /'laʊzi/, *adj.,* **lousier, lousiest. 1.** infested with lice. **2.** *Colloq.* mean or hateful. **3.** *Colloq.* of little value; trifling: *a lousy $2.* **4.** *Colloq.* unwell.

lout /laʊt/, *n.* **1.** *Colloq.* a rough, uncivilised and sometimes violent young man. **2.** an awkward, stupid person; boor. [perhaps from obs. *lout* stoop, bow low]

louvre /'luvə/, *n.* (one of) an arrangement of overlapping, sloping wooden or glass boards covering a window, allowing in air and light but not rain. [ME, from OF; orig. uncert.]

Louvre /'luvrə/, *n.* a royal palace (begun 1541) in Paris, largely occupied since 1793 by a famous museum and art gallery.

love /lʌv/, *n., v.,* **loved, loving.** ◇*n.* **1.** strong affection for another person. **2.** sexual desire, or its gratification. **3.** an object of love; sweetheart. **4.** a feeling of warm personal attachment, as for a friend, parent, child, etc. **5.** a strong liking for anything: *love of books.* **6.** *Tennis, etc.* nothing; no score. **7. for the love of,** for the sake of. **8. in love,** feeling deep passion (oft. fol. by *with*). **9. make love,** to have sexual intercourse. ◇*v.t.* **10.** to feel love for. [OE *lufu*]

lovelorn /'lʌvlɔn/, *adj.* sorrowing from unhappiness in love.

lovely /'lʌvli/, *adj.,* **-lier, -liest. 1.** charmingly beautiful. **2.** having a beauty that appeals to the heart as well as to the eye, as a person, a face, etc. **3.** *Colloq.* delightful, or highly pleasing: *We had a lovely time.* [OE: amiable] —**loveliness,** *n.*

lover /'lʌvə/, *n.* **1.** a person who is in love with another. **2.** a sexual partner, esp. someone having a love affair. **3.** a person who has a strong liking for something: *a lover of music; a lover of nature.*

loving /'lʌvɪŋ/, *adj.* feeling or showing love; affectionate; fond: *loving glances.*

low¹ /loʊ/, *adj.* **1.** being or happening not far above the ground, floor, or base: *a low shelf.* **2.** (of a heavenly body) not far above the horizon. **3.** lying or being below the general level: *low ground.* **4.** relating to areas near the sea-level or sea as opposed to highland or inland areas. **5.** (of a bow) deep. **6.** (of a garment) cut so as to leave neck and shoulders exposed. **7.** not high or tall: *low walls.* **8.** rising only slightly from a surface. **9.** (of a river, etc.) of less than average height or depth. **10.** reduced to the least height, depth, or the like: *low tide.* **11.** lacking in strength; feeble; weak. **12.** small in amount, degree, force, etc.: *a low number.* **13.** indicated by a small number: *low latitude* (one near the equator). **14.** having no great amount, value, or excellence: *a low opinion of something.* **15.** unhappy: *low spirits.* **16.** of lesser rank or quality: *low birth.* **17.** (of thought or expression) lacking in worth. **18.** hidden; unnoticeable: *lie low.* **19.** mean or nasty: *a low trick.* **20.** coarse or rude: *low company.* **21.**

low¹ *Biol.* having a relatively simple structure. **22.** *Music.* (of sounds) produced by relatively slow vibrations, and therefore low in pitch. **23.** not loud: *a low whisper.* **24.** (of a vowel) with the tongue held fairly low in the mouth. ◇*adv.* **25.** in or to a low position, point, degree, etc. **26.** near the ground, floor, or base; not aloft. **27.** at or to a low pitch. **28.** in a low tone; softly; quietly. ◇*n.* **29.** that which is low; a low level. **30.** *Weather.* a pressure system with relatively low pressure at the centre. **31.** a point of least value, amount, etc.; nadir: *Prices reached an all-time low.* [ME, from Scand]

low² /loʊ/, *v.i.* **1.** to make the sound typical of cattle. ◇*n.* **2.** the act or the sound of lowing. [OE *hlōwan*]

Low /loʊ/, *n.* **Sir David**, 1891-1963, British political cartoonist, born in NZ.

lowboy /'loʊbɔɪ/, *n.* a piece of furniture for holding clothes, similar to but lower than a wardrobe.

lowbrow /'loʊbraʊ/, *n. Colloq.* a person uninterested in higher forms of music, art, etc.

Low Church, *n.* the part of the Anglican Church which holds evangelical views (opposed to *High Church*). —**Low-Church**, *adj.*

Low Countries, *n.* the lowland region near the North Sea, forming the lower basin of the Rhine, Meuse, and Scheldt Rivers, divided in the Middle Ages into numerous small states; corresponding to modern Netherlands, Belgium, and Luxembourg.

low-down /'loʊ-daʊn/, *adj.* low; dishonorable; mean.

lowdown /'loʊdaʊn/, *n. Colloq.* the actual facts or truth on some subject.

Lowell /'loʊəl/, *n.* **Robert**, 1917-77, US poet.

lower /'loʊə/, *adj.* **1.** comparative of **low¹**. **2.** (*oft. cap.*) *Geol.* indicating an earlier division of a period, system, etc.: *the lower Palaeozoic.* ◇*v.t.* **3.** to reduce in amount, price, degree, force, etc. **4.** to make (the voice, etc.) less loud. **5.** to bring down in rank or estimation; humble; degrade. **6.** to let down or make lower. **7.** *Music.* to make lower in pitch; flatten. ◇*v.i.* **8.** to become lower or less. **9.** to descend; sink.

Lower /'loʊə/, *n.* **Lennie** (*Leonard Waldemere Lower*), 1903-47, Australian writer; his satiric humor is evident in the novel *Here's Luck* (1930).

lower case, *n.* a small letter type (opposed to *capital*). *Abbrev.:* l.c. [from the arrangement of cases of type in a printery (small letters in lower case, capitals in upper case)] —**lower-case**, *adj.*

lower house, *n.* the law-making body in a parliament of two houses (upper and lower), usu. larger and more directly representative of the people. Also, **lower chamber**.

Lower Hutt /loʊə 'hʌt/, *n.* a town in NZ, in the southern part of the North Island. Pop. 62 900 (1985 est.).

lowering /'laʊərɪŋ/, *adj.* **1.** (of the sky, clouds, etc.) dark and threatening. **2.** (of the face, etc.) frowning. [ME]

lowest common denominator, *n.* → **common denominator**.

low frequency, *n.* a radio frequency in the range 30 to 300 kilohertz. —**low-frequency**, *adj.*

Low German, *n.* the Germanic speech of northern Germany and the Low Countries; Plattdeutsch.

low-key /'loʊ-ki/, *adj.* **1.** done in a quiet way; restrained. **2.** (of a person) not given to displays of feeling; quiet; unobtrusive.

lowland /'loʊlənd/, *n.* land which is low with respect to a neighboring country. —**lowlander**, *n.*

Low Latin, *n.* any form of non-classical Latin, as Late Latin, Vulgar Latin, or Medieval Latin.

lowly /'loʊli/, *adj.*, **-lier, -liest**, *adv.* ◇*adj.* **1.** humble in station, condition, or nature. **2.** low in growth or position. **3.** humble in spirit; meek. ◇*adv.* **4.** in a low position, manner, or degree. **5.** in a lowly manner; humbly.

low-pressure /'loʊ-prɛʃə/, *adj.* having a low or below-normal pressure (as of steam, etc.).

low relief, *n.* → **bas-relief**.

lowry /'laʊri/, *n.* → **rosella**. [var. of LORY]

low-voltage /'loʊ-voʊltɪdʒ/, *adj.* indicating an electric system with an operating voltage under 250 volts.

loyal /'lɔɪəl/, *adj.* **1.** faithful where such honor is due, as to a king or queen, country, state, friend, etc. **2.** faithful to one's promises, responsibilities or undertakings. [F, from L: legal] —**loyalty**, *n.*

Loyalist /'lɔɪəlɪst/, *n.* **1.** a Protestant in Ulster, Northern Ireland, who supports British rule.

Loyola /lɔɪ'oʊlə/, *n.* **Ignatius** /ɪg'neɪʃəs/, (*Iñigo López de Recalde*), 1491-1556, Spanish soldier, priest, and saint, founder of the Jesuit order.

lozenge /'lɒzəndʒ/, *n.* a small, originally diamond-shaped sweet, often medicated. [ME, from OF, apparently from Pr: stone slab]

LP /ɛl 'pi/, *adj.* **1.** → **long-playing**. ◇*n.* **2.** such a record. [L(ONG)-P(LAYING)]

LPG /ɛl pi 'dʒi/, *n.* a mixture of hydrocarbon gases, e.g. butane and propane, liquefied and stored under pressure for use as a gas fuel. Also, **bottled gas**, **liquefied petroleum gas**. [abbrev.]

L-plate /'ɛl-pleɪt/, *n.* the letter L, shown front and back on a car, motor cycle, etc., being driven by someone who is learning to drive. [L learner + PLATE]

Lr, *Chem. Symbol.* lawrencium.

l.s.d. /ɛl ɛs 'di/, *n.* **1.** pounds, shillings, and pence. **2.** *Colloq.* money. [L *librae, solidi, denarii* (Roman coinage)]

LSD /ɛl ɛs 'di/, *n.* lysergic acid diethylamide, a drug which produces heightened perception as well as temporary hallucinations and sometimes a schizophrenia-like state.

Lt, *Abbrev.* Lieutenant.

Ltd, *Abbrev.* limited. See **limited company**.

Lu, *Chem. Symbol.* lutetium.

Luanda /lu'ændə/, *n.* a seaport in and the capital of Angola. Pop. 1 134 000 (1982). Also, **Loanda, São Paulo de Loanda**.

lubber /'lʌbə/, *n.* **1.** a big, awkward, stupid person. **2.** (among sailors) an awkward or unskilled seaman; landlubber. [ME]

lubra /'lubrə/, *n.* (*sometimes offensive*) an Aboriginal woman. [Aboriginal]

lubricate /'lubrəkeɪt/, *v.t.,* -cated, -cating. **1.** to apply some oily, greasy, or other substance to, so that moving parts will work more easily. **2.** to make slippery or smooth. [L: made slippery] —**lubricant**, *n.* —**lubrication**, *n.* —**lubricative**,

lubricity /lu'brɪsɪti/, *n., pl.,* -ties. **1.** slipperiness or oily smoothness. **2.** lewdness.

Lucas Heights, *n.* the research establishment of the Australian Nuclear Science and Technology Organisation, south-east of Sydney, NSW, erected in 1955.

lucerne /'lusən/, *n.* a plant with bluish purple flowers used as feed for animals; alfalfa. [F, from Pr, from L: light]

lucid /'lusəd/, *adj.* **1.** shining or bright. **2.** clear or transparent. **3.** easily understood: *a lucid explanation.* **4.** with clear understanding; rational: *in one of his more lucid moments.* [L]

Lucifer /'lusəfə/, *n.* **1.** the leader of an uprising of angels, who fell from heaven; Satan. **2.** the planet Venus when appearing as the morning star. [L: the morning star]

luck /lʌk/, *n.* **1.** something which happens to a person, either good or bad, as if by chance. **2.** good fortune; advantage or success considered as the result of chance: *She wished him luck.* ◇**3.** Some special uses are:

bad luck! (an exclamation of sympathy to someone in trouble).

down on one's luck, in poor or unfortunate circumstances.

good luck! (an exclamation passing on the good wishes of the speaker).

half your luck! (an expression indicating jealousy of someone else's good luck).

here's luck! (an expression of goodwill, esp. as a toast).

no such luck, (*usu. ironic*) unfortunately not.

push one's luck, to try to stretch one's luck too far.

[ME, from LG or D]

Lucknow /'lʌknaʊ/, *n.* a city in India, the capital of Uttar Pradesh, in the southern central part; the British were besieged here for several months (1857–58) during the Mutiny. Pop. 895 721 (1981).

lucky /'lʌki/, *adj.,* -ier, -iest. **1.** having good luck; fortunate. **2.** happening fortunately: *a lucky accident.* **3.** bringing or predicting good luck, or supposed to do so: *a lucky penny.*

lucrative /'lukrətɪv/, *adj.* profitable; remunerative: *a lucrative business.* [ME, from L]

lucre /'lukə/, *n.* gain or money as the object of mean and selfish desire. [ME, from L: gain]

Lucretia /lu'kriʃə/, *n. Rom Myth.* a Roman woman who committed suicide after being raped by Sextus; the subject of Shakespeare's *Rape of Lucrece.*

Lucretius /lu'kriʃəs/, *n.* (*Titus Lucretius Carus*), c.99–c.55 BC, Roman poet and philosopher. —**Lucretian**, *adj.*

Luddite /'lʌdaɪt/, *n.* a member of any of various bands of workmen in England (1811–16) organised to destroy manufacturing machinery, believing that its use diminished employment. [named after Ned *Ludd,* fl. 1779, a Leicestershire workman] —**Luddism**, *n.*

luderick /'ludərɪk/, *n.* a popular Australian estuarine and rock fish; nigger; black bream. [Aboriginal]

ludicrous /'ludəkrəs/, *adj.* so stupid as to cause laughter; ridiculous. [L: sportive]

ludo /'ludoʊ/, *n.* a children's game played on a board with counters and dice.

luff /lʌf/, *v.i.* to bring the head of a ship closer to or directly into the wind, with sails shaking. [ME, apparently from OF: a contrivance for altering a ship's course, of Gmc orig.]

Luftwaffe /'lʊftvafə/, *n. German.* the German Air Force.

lug[1] /lʌg/, *v.,* lugged, lugging, *n.* ◇*v.t., v.i.* **1.** to pull along or carry with effort. ◇*n.* **2.** a forcible pull. [ME, from Scand]

lug[2] /lʌg/, *n.* **1.** *Colloq.* an ear. **2.** a piece sticking out by which anything is held or supported.

luggage /'lʌgɪdʒ/, *n.* trunks, suitcases, etc., used in travelling; baggage. [LUG[1] + -AGE]

lugger /'lʌgə/, *n.* a small ship with lugsails, often used in island trading, fishing, etc. [from LUGSAIL]

Lugosi /lə'goʊsi/, *n.* **Bela** (*Béla Lugosi Blasko*), 1888–1956, Hungarian-born US actor, chiefly remembered in horror films such as *Dracula* (1931).

lugsail /'lʌgsəl/, *n.* a four-sided sail supported on a bar which hangs sloping from the mast. [*lug* pole (now d.) + SAIL]

lugubrious /lə'gubriəs/, *adj.* mournful; gloomy; dismal. [L: mournful]

Luke /luk/, *n. Bible.* **1.** the Evangelist; an early Christian disciple, probably a gentile, a physician, and companion of St Paul. **2.** the third Gospel, in the New Testament. [L, from Gk *Loukâs*]

lukewarm /'lukwɔm/, *adj.* **1.** moderately warm; tepid. **2.** having or showing little eagerness; indifferent: *a lukewarm response.* [ME *lukewarme,* from *luke* tepid (from OE) + *warme* WARM]

lull /lʌl/, *v.t.* **1.** to put to sleep or rest by singing, rocking, etc. **2.** to calm or quiet. **3.** to lead into a false sense of security. ◇*v.i.* **4.** to become lulled, quieted, or stilled. ◇*n.*

lull

5. a short time of quiet or stillness: *a lull in a storm*. [ME *lulle*]

lullaby /'lʌləbaɪ/, *n., pl.* **-bies,** *v.,* **-bied, -bying.** ◇*n.* **1.** a song sung to lull a baby to sleep. ◇*v.t.* **2.** to lull, esp. with a lullaby. [ME interj. *lulla!* (from LULL) + *-by* (from BYE-BYE)]

lumbago /lʌm'beɪgoʊ/, *n.* rheumatic pain in the muscles of the small of the back. [LL, from L: loin]

lumbar /'lʌmbə/, *adj.* of or relating to the lower part of the back. [NL, from L: loin]

lumber /'lʌmbə/, *n.* **1.** timber sawn or split into boards, etc. **2.** various useless articles that are stored away. ◇*v.i.* **3.** to cut timber and prepare it for market. ◇*v.t.* **4.** to heap together in disorder. **5.** to fill up with various useless articles; encumber. **6.** *Colloq.* to leave (somebody) with (some disagreeable job, etc.). [orig. uncert.]

lumberjack /'lʌmbədʒæk/, *n. Chiefly US, Canada. n.* someone who fells and removes trees.

lumen /'lumən/, *n., pl.,* **-mens, -mina.** the derived SI unit of luminous flux, equal to the light emitted in a unit solid angle of one steradian by a point source with intensity of one candela. *Symbol:* lm. [L: light, window]

luminance /'lumənəns/, *n.* the measure (in candelas per square metre) of brightness of a point on surface which is radiating or reflecting light. *Symbol:* L

luminary /'lumənəri, -mɛnri/, *n., pl.* **-naries. 1.** a heavenly body, as the sun or moon. **2.** a body or thing that gives light. **3.** a person whose learning, etc., enlightens others. **4.** a famous person; celebrity. [ME, from ML: a light, lamp, heavenly body]

luminescence /lumə'nɛsəns/, *n.* light given out from a substance, but not as a result of a process which involves the production of heat (opposed to *incandescence*). It includes phosphorescence, fluorescence, etc. **– luminescent,** *adj.*

luminous /'lumənəs/, *adj.* **1.** radiating or reflecting light; bright. **2.** well-lighted. **3.** enlightening, as a writer or his writings. **4.** easily understood; clear. [ME, from L] **– luminosity,** *n.*

luminous efficiency, *n.* **1.** (of a light source) the ratio of light given out to energy input, esp. when expressed as lumens per watt for electric lamps. **2.** (of a radiation) the ratio of luminous flux to radiant flux.

luminous flux, *n.* the rate of transmission of luminous energy (light), measured in lumens.

luminous intensity, *n.* (of a point source of light) the luminous flux given out per unit solid angle, measured in candela.

lump /lʌmp/, *n.* **1.** a piece or mass of solid matter of no particular shape. **2.** a swelling: *a lump on the head*. **3.** a collection or mass. **4.** *Colloq.* a stupid, awkward person. **5. have a lump in the throat,** *Colloq.* to feel as though about to cry. ◇*adj.* **6.** in the form of a lump or lumps: *lump sugar*. **7.** including a number of items taken together: *a lump sum*. ◇*v.t.* **8.** to unite or deal with in one collection or mass: *We can lump all the rubbish together*. ◇*v.i.* **9.** to move heavily. [ME *lumpe*] **– lumpy,** *adj.*

Luna /'lunə/, *n.* **1.** the moon, personified by the Romans as a goddess. **2.** *Alchemy.* silver. **3.** Also, **Lunik.** a series of lunar space probes developed by the Soviet Union, of which Luna 9 made the first soft moon landing in 1966. [L: moon]

lunacy /'lunəsi/, *n., pl.* **-cies. 1.** any form of insanity (unsoundness of mind). **2.** foolishness: *Her decision to leave was total lunacy*. [LUN(ATIC) + -ACY]

lunar /'lunə/, *adj.* **1.** of, relating to, or like the moon: *the lunar orbit*. **2.** measured by the moon's revolutions: *a lunar month*. **3.** resembling the moon; round or crescent-shaped. [L: of the moon, crescent]

lunatic /'lunətɪk/, *n.* **1.** an insane person; one whose mind is unsound. ◇*adj.* **2.** mad; insane. [ME, from LL: mad, from L: moon]

lunatic asylum, *n.* a psychiatric hospital.

lunch /lʌntʃ/, *n.* **1.** a meal taken at midday or shortly after; luncheon. ◇*v.i.* **2.** to eat lunch. [short for LUNCHEON]

luncheon /'lʌntʃən/, *n.* → **lunch.** [b. LUMP and *d. nuncheon* (ME *nonshench,* from *non* noon + *shench* (OE *scenc*) a drink)]

lunette /lu'nɛt/, *n.* any of various objects or spaces with the shape of a half-moon or half-circle. [F: little moon]

lung /lʌŋ/, *n.* **1.** either of the two saclike breathing organs in the thorax of man and the higher vertebrates. **2.** a similar organ in certain invertebrates. [OE *lungen*]

lunge /lʌndʒ/, *n., v.,* **lunged, lunging.** ◇*n.* **1.** a sudden forceful movement forwards, as with a sword in fencing. ◇*v.i.* **2.** to make a lunge. [F: lengthen, extend, from L]

lungfish /'lʌŋfɪʃ/, *n., pl.* **-fishes,** (*esp. collectively*) **-fish.** a type of tropical freshwater fish with lung-like structures as well as gills.

luni-, a word part meaning 'moon'. [combining form representing L *lūna*]

lupin /'lupən/, *n.* a European plant with edible seeds, or an American plant with a wide range of flower colors. [ME, from L]

lurch[1] /lɜtʃ/, *n.* **1.** a sudden leaning or roll to one side. **2.** an unsteady staggering movement. ◇*v.i.* **3.** to make a lurch; stagger. [orig. uncert.; first in nautical use]

lurch[2] /lɜtʃ/, *n.* the position of someone in a helpless situation: *He will leave her in the lurch*. [F: discomfited]

lure /luə, 'ljuə/, *n., v.,* **lured, luring.** ◇*n.* **1.** anything that attracts. **2.** a device used to attract fish. ◇*v.t.* **3.** to attract; entice; allure. [ME, from OF, from Gmc]

lurex /'lurɛks, 'luə-/, *n.* (a fabric made from) a yarn which includes metallic thread. [Trademark]

lurid /'lurəd/, *adj.* **1.** lit up or shining with an unnatural (esp. red) glare. **2.** sensational:

lurid *tales.* **3.** terrible in fierceness and wildness: *lurid crimes.* [L: pale yellow, wan]

lurk /lɜk/, *v.i.* **1.** to remain or be in or about a place secretly. **2.** to move with secrecy; slink; steal. ◇*n.* **3.** a convenient, often underhand, method of performing a task, earning a living, etc. **4.** a job. [ME]

luscious /'lʌʃəs/, *adj.* **1.** highly pleasing to the taste or smell. **2.** sweet to the senses or the mind. **3.** very attractive. [late ME; ? var. of DELICIOUS]

lush /lʌʃ/, *adj.* **1.** (of plants and vegetation) tender and juicy; succulent; luxuriant. **2.** with strong-growing vegetation. **3.** *Colloq.* having luxury and comfort. **4.** sexually attractive. [ME, from OF: loose, slack]

lust /lʌst/, *n.* **1.** passionate desire (fol. by *for* or *of*): *lust for power.* **2.** sexual desire, esp when uncontrolled. ◇*v.i.* **3.** to have a strong desire, esp. sexual desire (oft. fol. by *for* or *after*). [OE] —**lustful**, *adj.*

lustre /'lʌstə/, *n.* **1.** the condition or quality of shining by reflecting light: *the lustre of satin.* **2.** radiant brightness; radiance. **3.** radiance of beauty, glory, etc.: *achievements that add lustre to her name.* **4.** the shiny, metallic surface of some pottery or porcelain. **5.** *Mineral.* the nature of the surface of a mineral with respect to its reflecting qualities. This is one of the properties by which minerals are defined. [F, from It: to shine, from L: illuminate] —**lustrous**, *adj.*

lusty /'lʌsti/, *adj.*, **-tier, -tiest. 1.** full of or having healthy fitness. **2.** (of a meal, etc.) hearty or large and enjoyable. [ME] —**lustily**, *adv.* —**lustiness**, *n.*

lute /lut/, a stringed musical instrument formerly much used, usu. pear-shaped and having a long, fretted neck. [ME, from OF, from Pr, from Ar] —**lutenist**, *n.*

lutetium /lu'tiʃəm/, *n.* a lanthanide, trivalent, metallic element. *Symbol:* Lu; *at. no.:* 71; *at. wt:* 174.97. Also, **lutecium.** [NL, from L *Lutetia* Paris]

Luther /'luθə/, *n.* Martin, 1483–1546, German leader of the Protestant Reformation; theological writer, and translator of the Bible.

Lutheran /'luθərən/, *adj.* **1.** of or relating to Luther, following his doctrines, or belonging to one of the Protestant churches which bears his name. ◇*n.* **2.** a follower of Luther, or of his doctrines; a member of the Lutheran Church. [from Martin LUTHER] —**Lutheranism**, *n.*

Lutine bell /,lutin 'bɛl/, *n.* the ship's bell of the vessel 'Lutine'; now kept at Lloyd's and always rung before an important announcement, as of the loss of a vessel.

Lutyens /'lʌtʃənz/, *n.* Sir Edwin, 1869–1944, English architect; planned New Delhi, India.

lux /lʌks/, *n., pl.* **lux.** the derived SI unit of illumination, defined as one lumen per square metre. *Symbol:* lx [L: light]

Luxembourg /'lʌksəmbɜg/, *n.* **1.** a grand duchy in western Europe, south-east of Belgium, between France and Germany. Pop. 365 500 (1982); 2586 km². *Languages:* French and German. *Currency:* (Belgian) franc. *Cap.:* Luxemburg. **2.** the capital of Luxembourg (def. 1), an industrial city in the southern central part. Pop. 86 200 (1986 est.).

Luxemburg /'lʌksəmbɜg/, *n.* Rosa, 1871–1919, German socialist theorist and political leader; assassinated after leading, with Karl Liebknecht, an unsuccessful Communist revolution in 1919.

Luxor /'lʌksɔ/, *n.* a town in Upper Egypt, on the Nile; ruins of ancient Thebes. Pop. 147 900 (1986 est.).

luxuriant /lʌg'ʒuriənt/, *adj.* **1.** (of plants, etc.) plentiful or strong in growth. **2.** (of soil, etc.) producing in plenty. **3.** richly plentiful. [L: growing rank] —**luxuriance**, *n.*

luxuriate /lʌg'ʒurieɪt/, *v.i.*, **-ated, -ating. 1.** to treat oneself totally to luxury; revel. **2.** to take great delight: *to luxuriate in success.* [L: indulged to excess]

luxury /'lʌkʃəri/, *n., pl.* **-ries**, *adj.* ◇*n.* **1.** anything contributing to extremely comfortable living, usu. not a necessary thing. **2.** any form or means of enjoyment. **3.** the enjoyment of costly food, clothing, comforts, etc. ◇*adj.* **4.** relating to luxury. [ME: lust, from L] —**luxurious**, *adj.*

Luzon /lu'zɒn/, *n.* the chief island of the Philippines in the northern part of the group. Pop. 20 300 000 (1975); 104 688 km². *Cap.:* Manila.

lx, *Phys. Symbol.* lux.

-ly, **1.** the normal adverbial suffix, added to almost any descriptive adjective, and meaning 'in a .... way', as in *gladly, gradually.* **2.** the adverbial suffix applied to units of time, meaning 'per', as in *hourly.* **3.** an adjective suffix meaning 'like', as in *saintly, manly.* [ME *-li, -ly, lich(e),* OE *-līc*]

Lycaon /laɪ'keɪɒn/, *n. Gk Myth.* an Arcadian king who tested the divinity of the disguised Zeus by offering him a plate of human flesh. As punishment, Zeus turned him into a wolf.

Lycett /'laɪsət/, *n.* Joseph, 1774?–?, Australian landscape painter and convict, born in England.

lychee /laɪ'tʃi/, *n.* the fruit of a Chinese tree, with a thin shell covering a sweet jelly-like pulp. [Chinese]

Lycurgus /laɪ'kɜgəs/, *n.* fl. ninth century BC, political reformer of Sparta, reputed founder of Spartan constitution and educational system.

Lydia /'lɪdiə/, *n.* an ancient kingdom in western Asia Minor; under Croesus, a wealthy empire including most of Asia Minor.

lye /laɪ/, *n.* a solution resulting from leaching, percolation, or the like. [OE]

lying[1] /'laɪɪŋ/, *n.* **1.** the telling of lies; untruthfulness. ◇*adj.* **2.** untruthful; false: *a lying report.*

lying[2] /'laɪɪŋ/, *v.* present participle of **lie.**

lying-in /laɪŋ-'ɪn/, *n.* **1.** the time of confinement to give birth. ◇*adj.* **2.** relating to childbirth: *a lying-in hospital*.

lymph /lɪmf/, *n.* a clear, yellowish, slightly alkaline fluid coming from the tissues of the body by way of a system of capillaries and vessels, through the lymph glands, and then passing into the blood. [L: water]

lymph-, a combining form of **lymph**, as in *lymphatic*.

lymphatic /lɪm'fætɪk/, *adj.* **1.** relating to, containing, or carrying lymph: *a lymphatic system*. **2.** slow or without energy in thought and action (once thought to be caused by too much lymph in the system). [NL: relating to lymph]

lymph gland, *n.* any of the glandlike bodies, e.g. tonsils, in the lymphatic system, where antibodies and white blood cells (**lymphocytes**) are produced, and where bacteria are destroyed. Also, **lymph node, lymphatic gland**.

lynch /lɪntʃ/, *v.t.* to put (someone) to death (by hanging, burning, etc.) by group action without authority or process of law. [named after Captain William *Lynch*, 1742-1820, of Virginia, US, who introduced the practice] —**lynching**, *n.*

lynx /lɪŋks/, *n., pl.* **lynxes**, (*esp. collectively*) **lynx**. any of various wildcats having long limbs and a short tail, and usu. with tufted ears. [ME, from L, from Gk]

lyo-, a word part meaning 'dispersion', 'solution', 'dissolved'. [combining form representing Gk *lýein* dissolve]

Lyons[1] /'laɪənz/, *n.* **1. Dame Enid Muriel**, 1897-1981, Australian politician; one of the first two women members of the House of Representatives **2.** her husband, **Joseph Aloysius**, 1879-1939, Australian politician; prime minister 1932-39.

lyre /'laɪə/, *n.* a stringed musical instrument of ancient Greece. [ME, from OF, from L, from Gk]

lyrebird /'laɪəbəd/, *n.* either of two ground-dwelling birds of south-eastern Australia, noted for their ability to copy other sounds, and the attractive mating displays of the males.

lyric /'lɪrɪk/, *adj.* Also, **lyrical** (for defs 1-5). **1.** (of poetry) having the form and musical quality of a song. **2.** relating to or writing such poetry: *a lyric poet*. **3.** of or enjoying a heartfelt expression of feeling. **4.** relating to or using singing. **5.** (of a voice) light in volume and tone. ◇*n.* **6.** a lyric poem. **7.** (*oft. pl.*) the words of a song. [L, from Gk: of a lyre] —**lyricism**, *n.* —**lyricist**, *n.*

-lyse, a word part making verbs of processes represented by nouns in *-lysis*, as in *catalyse*. [from -LYSIS, influenced by -ISE[1]]

lysergic acid /laɪ,sɜdʒɪk 'æsəd/, *n.* **1.** a crystalline tetracyclic acid which can be produced from ergot. **2.** *Colloq.* → **LSD**.

lysine /'laɪsin/, *n.* an essential amino acid in proteins. [Gk *lýsis* a loosing + -INE[2]]

-lysis, a word part meaning 'breaking down', 'decomposition', as in *analysis, electrolysis*. [Gk]

lyso-, a word part meaning 'decomposition'. Also, **lys-**. [Gk]

-lyte, a word part indicating something put through a certain process (indicated by a noun ending in *-lysis*), as in *electrolyte*. [Gk *-lytos* that may be or is loosed]

-lytic, an ending of adjectives corresponding to nouns in *-lysis*, as in *analytic*. [Gk]

Mm

M, m, *n., pl.* **M's** or **Ms**, **m's** or **ms**. **1.** the 13th letter of the English alphabet. **2.** the Roman numeral for 1000.

m, *Symbol.* **1.** metre. **2.** milli-.

m., *Abbrev.* **1.** male. **2.** married. **3.** masculine. **4.** noon. [L *meridies*] **5.** mile. **6.** million. **7.** minute. **8.** month.

M, *Abbrev.* **1.** (of a film) for mature audiences. **2.** Majesty. **3.** medieval. **4.** meridian. **5.** moon. [L *meridies*] **6.** Monday. **7.** (*pl.* **MM**) Monsieur. ◇*Symbol.* **8.** mega-.

mA, *Symbol.* milliampere.

ma'am /mæm, mam/; *if unstressed* /məm/, *n.* madam.

Maatsuyker Group /mat'saɪkə, -'sukə grup/, *n.pl.* a group of islands off the south coast of Tas, south-east of the South-West Cape; location of Australia's southernmost lighthouse.

Mab /mæb/, *n.* (in the folklore of England and Ireland) a fairy queen supposed to create dreams.

Mabuiag /'mɒbwiʌg/, *n.* an Australian Aboriginal language used in the Torres Strait Islands.

macabre /mə'kabə, -brə/, *adj.* horrible; grim; ghastly. [ME, from F, ? from Ar: graveyard]

macadam /mə'kædəm/, *n.* **1.** a road made by laying and rolling layers of broken stones. **2.** the broken stone used for this. [named after JL *McAdam*, 1756–1836, Scottish inventor]

macadamia nut, /mækə'deɪmiə nʌt/, *n.* **1.** a hard-shelled, edible nut. **2.** a tree, native to eastern Australia, which bears this nut.

Macao /mə'kaʊ/, *n.* a Portuguese overseas territory in southern China, on a peninsula of Macao and two small adjacent islands at the mouth of the Zhujiangkou; 15 km^2.

macaque /mə'kak/, *n.* a type of Asian monkey with pouched cheeks, a dog-like muzzle and usu. short tail. [F, from Pg *macaco*, from Fiot, a Congolese language]

macaroni /mækə'roʊni/, *n.* Italian pasta, prepared from wheat flour, in the form of dried, hollow tubes. [It, from LGk: food of broth and pearl barley, orig. happiness]

MacArthur /mə'kaθə/, *n.* **Douglas,** 1880–1964, US general; supreme commander of Allied forces in the Pacific during World War II and of UN forces in Korea (1950–51).

Macarthur /mə'kaθə/, *n.* **1. John,** 1767–1834, pastoralist and soldier, born in England; prominent in the early development of the colony of NSW, particularly in the sheep-breeding industry. **2.** his wife, **Elizabeth,** 1767?–1850, pastoralist, born in England.

Macassar /mə'kæsə/, *n.* → **Ujung Pandang.**

macerate

McAuley /mə'kɔli/, *n.* **James Phillip,** 1917–76, Australian lyric poet and critic; founding editor of *Quadrant* in 1956.

macaw /mə'kɔ/, *n.* a type of large, long-tailed tropical American parrot, with colorful feathers and harsh voice. [Pg *macao;* of Brazilian orig.]

Macbeth /mək'bɛθ, mæk-/, *n.* died 1057, king of Scotland 1040–57.

McBride /mək'braɪd/, *n.* **William Griffith,** born 1927, Australian gynaecologist and medical researcher; discovered that thalidomide taken during pregnancy causes birth defects.

McCarthyism /mə'kaθi,ɪzəm/, *n.* **1.** an unfounded public accusation of disloyalty, esp. of pro-Communist activity. **2.** unfairness in methods of inquiry. **3.** a continuous search for disloyalty, esp. in government offices. [named after JR *McCarthy*, 1909–57, US politician]

McCartney /mə'katni/, *n.* **(James) Paul,** born 1942, British pop singer, composer and musician; founding member of the Beatles.

McCormick /mə'kɔmɪk/, *n.* **Cyrus Hall,** 1809–84, US inventor of the mechanical reaper.

McCrae /mə'kreɪ/, *n.* **Hugh Raymond,** 1876–1958, Australian poet, writer and illustrator.

McCubbin /mə'kʌbən/, *n.* **Frederick,** 1855–1917, Australian artist; noted for his portrayal of Australian bush scenes.

MacDonald /mək'dɒnəld/, *n.* **(James) Ramsay.** 1866–1937, British statesman and leader of the Labour Party; prime minister in 1924 and 1929–35.

McDonald /mək'dɒnəld/, *n.* **Garry,** born 1948, Australian actor and comedian.

McDonald Island, *n.* → **Heard and McDonald Islands.**

MacDonnell /mək'dɒnəl/, *n.* **Sir Richard Graves,** 1814–81, English administrator in Australia; governor of SA 1855–62, greatly encouraged the agricultural and pastoral industries, predicting a good future for wine in the colony.

mace /meɪs/, *n.* **1.** *Hist.* a clublike weapon of war often with a spiked metal head. **2.** a staff carried before or by certain officials as a symbol of office. [ME, from OF]

Macedonia /mæsə'doʊniə/, *n.* **1.** an ancient country in the Balkan Peninsula, north of ancient Greece. **2.** a republic in south-eastern Europe; a constituent republic of Yugoslavia until secession in 1991–92. Pop. 2 111 000 (1989 est.); 25 713 km^2. *Cap.:* Skopje. **3.** a region in southern Europe, including this republic and parts of Greece and Bulgaria. —**Macedonian,** *n., adj.*

McEnroe /'mækənroʊ/, *n.* **John,** born 1959, US tennis player; a US Open and Wimbledon champion.

macerate /'mæsəreɪt/, *v.*, **-rated, -rating.** ◇*v.t.* **1.** to soften, or separate the parts of (a substance) by soaking in liquid. **2.** to cause to grow thin. ◇*v.i.* **3.** to become thin; waste away. [L] —**maceration**, *n.*

McEwen /məˈkjuən/, *n.* **Sir John,** 1900–80, Australian Country Party politician; prime minister, 1967–68.

McGill /məˈgɪl/, *n.* **Linda,** born 1945, Australian swimmer; Commonwealth gold medalist 1962 and the first Australian to swim the English Channel 1965.

mach /mæk/, *n.* See **mach number**.

machete /məˈʃɛti/, *n.* a large, heavy knife used esp. in Latin-American countries as both a tool and a weapon. [Sp, from L: slaughter]

Machiavelli /mækiəˈveli/, *n.* **Niccoló di Bernardo,** 1469–1527, Italian statesman and writer on government; author of the political treatise *The Prince* (1513).

Machiavellian /mækiəˈveliən/, *adj.* **1.** being or acting according to Machiavelli's political ideas, by supporting the use of trickery and deceit. **2.** with secretive and dishonest cunning; wily; astute. [from Niccolò di Bernardo MACHIAVELLI]

machinate /ˈmæʃəneɪt, ˈmækəneɪt/, *v.i.,* **-nated, -nating.** to plan or scheme, esp. with evil purpose. [L] —**machinator**, *n.* —**machination**, *n.*

machine /məˈʃin/, *n., v.,* **-chined, -chining.** ◇*n.* **1.** an apparatus used to perform work, consisting of parts having separate jobs but working together. **2.** something operated by a machine, e.g. a car, bicycle or aeroplane. **3.** *Mech.* **a.** a device which changes force or motion. **b. simple machines,** the six (sometimes more) basic mechanisms, i.e., the lever, wheel and axle, pulley, screw, wedge, inclined plane. **4.** any large working system: *the Labor Party machine.* **5.** the group of people managing a political party or other organisation. ◇*v.t.* **6.** to make, prepare, or finish with a machine. [F, from L, from Gk]

machine-gun /məˈʃin-gʌn/, *n., v.,* **-gunned, -gunning.** ◇*n.* **1.** a small weapon, able to deliver a rapid and continuous fire of bullets. ◇*v.t.* **2.** to shoot at, using a machine-gun.

machinery /məˈʃinəri/, *n., pl.* **-ries. 1.** machines or machinery apparatus. **2.** parts of a machine, as a whole: *the machinery of a watch.* **3.** any system by which action is continued: *the machinery of government.*

machismo /məˈtʃɪzmoʊ, məˈkɪzmoʊ/, *n.* strong and aggressive masculine display.

mach number /ˈmæk nʌmbə/, *n.* a number indicating the ratio between the airspeed of an object and the speed of sound at a given altitude, etc. [named after Ernst *Mach*, 1838–1916, Austrian physicist]

macho /ˈmætʃoʊ, ˈmækoʊ/, *n.* **1.** a man who displays machismo. ◇*adj.* **2.** displaying supposedly male qualities. [Mex Sp]

-machy, a combining form meaning combat, as in *logomachy.* [Gk *-machia,* from *-machos* fighting]

Macintyre /ˈmækəntaɪə/, *n.* a river in north-eastern NSW, rising on the western slopes of the New England Range and flowing north then west to join the Weir River and become the Barwon.

Mackay /məˈkaɪ, məˈkeɪ/, *n.* a coastal city in north-eastern Qld, south-east of Proserpine; major sugar producer. Pop. 38 603 (1986).

McKay /məˈkaɪ/, *n.* **1. (James) Fred(erick),** born 1907, Australian minister and pioneer of the flying doctor service. **2. Hugh Victor,** 1865–1926, Australian inventor and businessman; produced the Sunshine Harvester.

McKell /məˈkɛl/, *n.* **Sir William John,** 1891–1985, Australian Labor politician; premier of NSW, 1941–47 and governor-general of Australia 1947–53.

Mackellar /məˈkɛlə/, *n.* **(Isobel Marion) Dorothea,** 1885–1968, Australian poet; author of 'My Country' (1908).

Mackenzie /məˈkɛnzi/, *n.* **Kenneth Ivo** ('*Seaforth*'), 1913–55, Australian poet and novelist; works include the collection of poetry *Our Earth* (1937) and the novel *The Young Desire It* (1937).

mackerel /ˈmækərəl/, *n.* **1.** a common iridescent greenish fish widely distributed in waters of Australia, NZ and various parts of the Pacific. **2.** a plentiful food fish of the North Atlantic. [ME, from OF; orig. unknown]

McKern /məˈkɜn/, *n.* **Leo** (*Reginald McKern*), born 1920, Australian-born actor and director in England; noted for the television series *Rumpole of the Bailey*.

Mackerras family /məˈkɛrəs/, *n.* an Australian family of brothers, noted for their contribution to education and the arts, including **1. Sir (Alan) Charles,** born 1925 in the US, Australian conductor. **2. Colin Patrick,** born 1939, academic and writer in Asian studies. **3. Malcolm Hugh,** born 1939, political analyst and lecturer.

McKie /məˈki/, *n.* **Ronald,** born 1909, Australian journalist and novelist; wrote *The Mango Tree* (1974).

MacKillop /məˈkɪləp/, *n.* **Mary Helen (Mother Mary of the Cross),** 1842–1909, Australian nun and teacher; co-founder of the Sisters of St Joseph of the Sacred Heart; her impending sainthood, which will make her Australia's first saint, was announced in 1973.

McKinlay /məˈkɪnli/, *n.* **John,** 1819–72, Australian explorer, born in Scotland; leader of the party that searched for Burke and Wills in 1861.

McKinley[1] /məˈkɪnli/, *n.* **William,** 1843–1901, 25th president of US, 1897–1901.

McKinley[2] /məˈkɪnli/, *n.* **Mount,** a mountain in central Alaska; highest peak of North America. 6187 m.

mackintosh /ˈmækəntɒʃ/, *n.* (the fabric for) a waterproof raincoat. Also, **macintosh.** [named after Charles *Macintosh*, 1766–1843, the inventor]

Mackintosh /'mækəntɒʃ/, n. **Charles Rennie**, 1868–1928, Scottish architect; one of the pioneers of modern architecture.

MacLaine /mə'kleɪn/, n. **Shirley**, born 1934, US film actress; noted for such films as *Irma La Douce* (1963) and *Terms of Endearment* (1984).

McLaren /mə'klærən/, n. **Jack**, 1887–1954, Australian writer; author of *My Crowded Solitude* (1926), recounting his experiences travelling in New Guinea.

Macleod /mə'klaʊd/, n. **John James Rickard**, 1876–1935, Scottish physiologist; shared the 1923 Nobel prize for medicine for the discovery of insulin.

McLuhan /mə'kluən/, n. **(Herbert) Marshall**, 1911–80, Canadian writer and teacher; writer of *The Medium is the Message* (1967).

McMahon /mək'man/, n. **Sir William**, 1908–88, Australian Liberal politician; prime minister, 1971–72.

Macmillan /mək'mɪlən/, n. **(Maurice) Harold (1st Earl of Stockton)**, 1894–1986, British statesman; Conservative prime minister 1957–63.

McMillan /mək'mɪlən/, n. **Angus**, 1810–65, Australian explorer and cattle trader, born in Scotland; responsible for pioneering Gippsland.

McMurdo Sound /mək,mɜdoʊ 'saʊnd/, n. an inlet of the Ross Sea, in Antarctica, north of Victoria Land.

Macquarie /mə'kwɒri/, n. **1. Elizabeth Henrietta** (*née* Campbell) 1778–1835, Scottish wife of Lachlan; her given and maiden names feature in many Australian geographical landmarks. **2. Lachlan**, 1762–1824, Scottish soldier and governor of NSW 1810–24; his term of office was notable for his encouragement of public works programs, further inland exploration and creation of new towns as well as for humanitarian policies towards convicts.

Macquarie Harbour, n. an inlet on the western coast of Tas; penal settlement 1822–34. 32 km long. [named after Governor MACQUARIE]

macramé /mə'krami/, n. a type of lace or ornamental work made by knotting thread or cord in patterns.

macro-, a prefix meaning 'long', 'large', 'great', 'excessive', used esp. in scientific words (contrasting with *micro-*), as in *macrocosm*, *macropod*. Also, before vowels, **macr-**. [Gk *makro-*, combining form of *makrós*]

macrobiotic /,mækroʊbaɪ'ɒtɪk/, adj. (of foods) tending to make life longer.

macrocosm /'mækrəkɒzəm/, n. the great world, or universe (opposed to *microcosm*). [F, from ML]

macro-economics /,mækroʊ-ekə'nɒmɪks, -ɪks-/, n. the study of an economic system as a whole, as opposed to micro-economics. [MACRO- + ECONOMICS]

macron /'mækrɒn/, n. a short horizontal line used over a vowel to indicate that it is a 'long' sound, as in *fāte*. [Gk: long]

macropod /'mækrəpɒd/, adj. **1.** of or related to a family of plant-eating marsupials including the kangaroos, wallabies, rat-kangaroos and tree-kangaroos, having short forelimbs, long hind limbs for hopping, and long, muscular tails. ◇n. **2.** a macropod marsupial. Also, **macropodid**. [MACRO- + -POD]

macroscopic /mækrə'skɒpɪk/, adj. **1.** visible to the naked eye (opposed to *microscopic*). **2.** concerned with large units or issues; comprehensive.

macrostructure /'mækroʊstrʌktʃə/, n. *Metall*. the general crystalline structure of metals and alloys as seen on an etched surface by the naked eye.

macrozamia /mækroʊ'zeɪmiə/, n. a group of Australian plants with stiff, palm-like leaves and nut-like fruit.

mad /mæd/, adj., **madder**, **maddest**. **1.** disordered in mind; insane. **2.** *Colloq.* angry: *He is mad at me.* **3.** (of wind, etc.) wild and violent. **4.** (of animals) **a.** abnormally angry: *a mad bull.* **b.** affected with rabies; rabid: *a mad dog.* **5.** wildly excited; frantic: *mad haste.* **6.** senseless; foolish: *a mad scheme.* **7.** *Colloq.* wild with eagerness or desire; infatuated: *He is mad about her.* **8.** *Colloq.* wildly gay or merry: *They had a mad time at the party.* **9. like mad**, **a.** in the manner of somebody mad. **b.** with great haste, etc. [OE]

Madagascar /mædə'gæskə/, n. a republic consisting of one large island and several small ones in the western Indian Ocean, about 500 km from the African coast; a French colony before independence in 1960. Pop. 10 605 000 (1987 est.); 587 041 km². *Languages*: Malagasy and French, also local dialects such as Hova. *Currency*: franc. *Cap.*: Antananarivo. Official name, **Democratic Republic of Madagascar**. Formerly, **Malagasy Republic**. —**Madagascan**, n., adj.

madam /'mædəm/, n., pl. **madams** /'mædəmz/, **mesdames** /meɪ'dæm, -'dam/. **1.** a polite term of address used orig. to a woman of rank, but now to any woman. **2.** the woman in charge of a brothel. [ME, from OF, orig. *ma dame* my lady]

Madame /mə'dam, 'mædəm/, n., pl. **mesdames** /meɪ'dæm, -'dam/. the French title of respect and form of address for a married woman (equivalent to *Mrs*). *Abbrev.*: Mme, pl. Mmes [F. See MADAM]

Madang /mə'dæŋ/, n. **1.** a province in northern PNG. Pop. 245 700 (1986 est.); 29 000 km². *Administrative Centre*: Madang. **2.** a coastal town in the province of Madang, PNG. Pop. 24 000 (1986 est.).

madcap /'mædkæp/, adj. **1.** very lively; wildly impulsive: *a madcap girl*. ◇n. **2.** a madcap person, esp. a girl.

madden /'mædn/, v.t., v.i. to make or become mad or angry.

madding /'mædɪŋ/, adj. **1.** mad; acting as if mad: *the madding crowd*. **2.** making mad.

made /meɪd/, v. **1.** past tense and past participle of **make**. ◇adj. **2.** produced by making, preparing, etc.: *a made dish*. **3.**

made 628 **Maginot line**

certain of success or fortune: *a made man*; *You've got it made.*

madeira /məˈdɪərə/, *n.* a rich, strong, white wine like sherry. [from *Madeira*, an island off the coast of Africa, where it was orig. made]

mademoiselle /ˌmædəmwəˈzɛl, ˌmæmwəˈzɛl, mæmˈzɛl/, *n., pl.* **mesdemoiselles** /ˌmeɪdəmwəˈzɛl/. (*cap.*) the French title of respect and term of address for a girl or unmarried woman (equivalent to *Miss*). *Abbrev.*: Mlle, *pl.* Mlles [F: my damsel]

Madhya Pradesh /ˈmʌdjə prɑːˈdɛʃ/, *n.* a state in central India. Pop. 52 178 844 (1981); 443 410 km². *Cap.*: Bhopal.

Madison /ˈmædəsən/, *n.* **James,** 1751–1836, fourth president of the US, 1809–17.

Madison Avenue, *n.* a street in New York City on which are concentrated the offices of many advertising and public relations firms and which has, therefore, become a symbol of their attitudes, methods, etc.

Madonna /məˈdɒnə/, *n.* (a picture or statue representing) the Virgin Mary. [It: my lady]

Madras /məˈdræs, -drɑːs/, *n.* a seaport in and the capital of the southern Indian state of Tamil Nadu, on the Bay of Bengal. Pop. 3 276 622 (1981).

Madrid /məˈdrɪd/, *n.* the capital of Spain, in the central part; lies at an elevation of 640 m, the highest capital in Europe. Pop. 3 053 101 (1986 est.).

madrigal /ˈmædrɪɡəl/, *n.* **1.** a short lyric poem which can be set to music, esp. a love poem (popular in 16th century and later in Italy, France, England, etc.). **2.** a part-song without instrumental accompaniment, usu. for five or six voices. [It, from ML: simple, naive, from L: womb]

maelstrom /ˈmeɪlstrəm/, *n.* **1.** a large whirlpool. **2.** a state of great confusion or agitation; turbulence. [from *Maelstrom*, famous whirlpool off the coast of Norway; early mod. D]

maestro /ˈmaɪstroʊ/, *n., pl.* **-tri** /-triː/. **1.** a master of any art, esp. a great or famous musical composer, teacher, or conductor. **2.** (*cap.*) a title of respect for such a person. [It: master]

Mae West /meɪ ˈwɛst/, *n.* an inflatable lifejacket. [named after *Mae West*, 1892–1980, US actress]

Mafeking /ˈmæfəkɪŋ/, *n.* a South African town in the north-east of Cape Province; until 1965, administrative headquarters of the British Protectorate of Bechuanaland; Boer siege, 1899. Pop. 6500 (1971).

Mafia /ˈmɑːfɪə, ˈmæfɪə/, *n.* **1.** (in Sicily) a 19th-century secret society acting in a popular spirit of hostility to legal restraint and to the law, often manifesting itself in criminal acts. **2.** a criminal secret society of Sicilians or other Italians, at home or in foreign countries. Also, **Maffia.** [It (Sicilian): boldness, bravery, from L: Matthew]

mafic /ˈmæfɪk/, *adj.* (of some igneous rocks and the minerals in them) made up mainly of the magnesium rock-forming silicates. See **felsic.**

magazine /ˌmæɡəˈziːn/, *n.* **1.** a paper-covered publication containing various stories, articles, advertisements, etc., appearing at regular intervals. **2.** a program on radio or television, usu. documentary, on a variety of subjects. **3.** a place for keeping explosives in a fort or warship. **4.** a military storehouse. **5.** *Guns.* a container for cartridges, which is attached to some types of automatic weapons and replaced when empty. **6.** *Photog.* a light-proof enclosure containing film. ◊*adj.* **7.** of or relating to a magazine. [F, from It: storehouse, from Ar]

Magdalenian /ˌmæɡdəˈlɪniən/, *adj.* denoting the Upper Palaeolithic period or culture characterised by the highest level of industry and art reached by Cro-Magnon man. [Latinised form of (La) *Madeleine*, France, where implements and art of this period were found]

Magellan /məˈdʒɛlən/, *n.* **Ferdinand,** c. 1480–1521, Portuguese navigator, discoverer of the Strait of Magellan and the Philippine Islands.

Magellanic clouds /ˈmædʒəlænɪk klaʊdz/, *n.pl.* two cloud-like patches of very distant stars to one side of the Milky Way in the southern sky. [named after Ferdinand MAGELLAN]

maggot /ˈmæɡət/, *n.* **1.** the larvae of flies and other insects, that live on rotting food etc. **2.** an odd fancy; whim. [ME; orig. uncert.] –**maggoty,** *adj.*

Magi /ˈmeɪdʒaɪ/, *n.pl., sing.* **-gus** /-ɡəs/. (*also l.c.*) the three wise men who came from the east to Jerusalem to worship the child Jesus. [see MAGUS] –**Magian,** *adj.* –**Magianism,** *n.*

magic /ˈmædʒɪk/, *n.* **1.** (the exercise of) the art of producing effects or controlling events by supernatural powers or by command of occult forces in nature. **2.** the effects produced. **3.** a magical act. **4.** any extraordinary influence or attraction: *the magic in a great name.* **5.** a theatrical performance of tricks; legerdemain; conjuring. ◊*adj.* Also, **magical. 6.** done by magic: *magic spells.* **7.** mysteriously attractive: *magic beauty.* **8.** of, relating to, or due to magic: *magic rites.* [ME, from LL, from L, from Gk] –**magically,** *adv.*

magician /məˈdʒɪʃən/, *n.* **1.** someone skilled in magic arts. **2.** a juggler; conjurer. [ME, from OF, from L]

magic number, *n.* any one of the numbers 2, 8, 20, 28, 50, 82, or 126; atomic nuclei containing these numbers of neutrons or protons are very stable.

magic square, *n.* a square pattern of integers such that the sums of the numbers in each row, column, and diagonal are all equal.

Maginot line /ˌmæʒɪnoʊ ˈlaɪn/, *n.* a zone of French fortifications erected along the French-German border in the years preceding

Maginot line

World War II. [named after André *Maginot*, 1877–1932, French minister of war]

magisterial /mædʒəˈstɔːriəl/, *adj.* **1.** full of authority; masterly: *a magisterial pronouncement.* **2.** of (the rank of) or suitable to a magistrate or his office. [ML, from L: MASTER]

magistrate /ˈmædʒəstreɪt, -trət/, *n.* an official, sometimes a justice of the peace, who sits as a judge in the magistrate's court. [ME, from L: the office of a chief]

Magistrate's Court, *n.* **1.** a court used to try less serious criminal offences or to hear certain civil matters, presided over by a magistrate. **2.** (*caps*) (in Vic and Qld) the title of such a court. See **Court of Petty Sessions, Court of Summary Jurisdiction, Local Court.**

magma /ˈmægmə/, *n. Geol.* the very hot molten rock under the solid crust of the earth, and from which igneous rocks are formed. [L, from Gk: a salve] – **magmatic**, *adj.*

Magna Carta /ˌmægnə ˈkɑːtə/, *n.* the 'great charter' of English liberties, forced from King John by the English barons at Runnymede, 15 June 1215. [ML: great charter]

magnanimous /mæɡˈnænəməs/, *adj.* **1.** generous in forgiving. **2.** high-minded; noble. [L: great-souled] – **magnanimity**, *n.*

magnate /ˈmægneɪt, ˈmægnət/, *n.* someone with influence, power and wealth, esp. in a field of business: *a mining magnate.* [late ME, from LL, from L: great]

magnesia /mægˈniːʃə, -ˈniːʒə, -ˈniːziə/, *n.* a magnesium oxide, MgO, a white substance used as a medicine for indigestion and constipation. Also, **magnesium oxide.** [ME, from ML (in alchemy), from Gk: (the) Magnesian (stone); i.e. stone from Magnesia in Thessaly]

magnesite /ˈmægnəsaɪt/, *n.* a mineral, magnesium carbonate, $MgCO_3$, usu. occurring in white masses.

magnesium /mæɡˈniːziəm/, *n.* a light, ductile, silver-white metal used in lightweight alloys. *Symbol*: Mg; *at. no.*: 12; *at. wt*: 24.312. [NL, from MAGNESIA]

magnet /ˈmægnət/, *n.* **1.** a piece of iron or steel which has the property of attracting certain substances, esp. iron; any piece of metal with ferromagnetic properties. **2.** → **lodestone. 3.** any thing or person that attracts: *She was the magnet of all eyes in the room.* [late ME, from L: lodestone, magnet, from Gk: (stone) of Magnesia (in Thessaly), lodestone]

magnetic /mæɡˈnɛtɪk/, *adj.* **1.** of or relating to a magnet or magnetism: *a magnetic field.* **2.** having the properties of a magnet. **3.** relating to the earth's magnetism: *the magnetic equator.* **4.** strongly attractive: *a magnetic personality.* – **magnetically**, *adv.*

magnetic compass, *n.* an instrument consisting of a magnetic needle which swings in the direction of the earth's magnetic poles.

magnetic field, *n.* the area of force around a magnet or a wire or coil carrying electric current which shows itself as a force on magnetic objects within that space.

magnetic flux, *n.* the total size of a magnetic field. The derived SI unit of magnetic flux is the weber.

magnetic flux density, *n.* the density of a magnetic field, i.e. the magnetic flux per unit area at right angles to the force; magnetic induction. The derived SI unit of magnetic flux density is the tesla.

magnetic induction, *n.* **1.** the induction of magnetism in a body by an external magnetic field. **2.** → **magnetic flux density.**

magnetic north, *n.* the direction in which the needle of a compass points, differing in most places from true north.

magnetic pole, *n.* **1.** a pole of a magnet. **2.** either of the two points on the earth's surface where the compass needle stands vertical, one in the Arctic, the other in the Antarctic.

magnetic storm, *n.* a sudden disturbance in the earth's magnetic field associated with sunspot activity.

magnetic tape, *n.* a plastic tape coated with a ferromagnetic powder, esp. iron oxide, used to record sound and video signals and to store computer information.

magnetise or **magnetize** /ˈmægnətaɪz/, *v.t.*, **-tised, -tising. 1.** to communicate magnetic properties to. **2.** to have an attracting or forceful influence upon. – **magnetisation**, *n.* – **magnetiser**, *n.*

magnetism /ˈmægnətɪzəm/, *n.* **1.** typical qualities of magnets. **2.** something which produces magnetic effects. **3.** the branch of science dealing with magnetic effects. **4.** an attracting power or charm.

magnetite /ˈmægnətaɪt/, *n.* common black iron oxide, Fe_3O_4, that is strongly attracted by a magnet and is an important iron ore.

magneto /mæɡˈniːtoʊ/, *n., pl.* **-tos.** a small electric generator, the poles of which are permanent magnets, used esp. for producing sparks in a car engine. [short for MAGNETO-ELECTRIC (machine)]

magneto-, a combining form of **magnet** or **magnetic.**

magni-, **1.** a word part meaning 'large', 'great', as in *magnify.* **2.** *Zool.* a word part indicating length. [L, combining form of *magnus* great]

magnification /ˌmægnəfəˈkeɪʃən/, *n.* **1.** the act or result of magnifying. **2.** the power to magnify.

magnificent /mæɡˈnɪfəsənt/, *adj.* **1.** splendid in appearance: *a magnificent cathedral.* **2.** very fine; superb: *a magnificent opportunity.* **3.** noble; sublime: *a magnificent poem.* **4.** great in deeds (now only as a title): *Lorenzo the magnificent.* [OF, from L] – **magnificence**, *n.*

magnify /ˈmægnəfaɪ/, *v.*, **-fied, -fying.** ◊*v.t.* **1.** (of a lens) to increase the apparent size of. **2.** to make greater in size; enlarge. **3.** to cause to seem greater or more important. **4.** *Archaic.* to praise; extol. ◊*v.i.* **5.** (of a lens) to increase the apparent size of an object. [ME, from L: make much of] – **magnifier**, *n.*

magnitude /'mægnətʃud/, *n.* **1.** size; extent: *the magnitude of an angle; the magnitude of the loss.* **2.** greatness or importance: *affairs of magnitude.* **3.** *Astron.* the degree of brightness of a star: *Sirius is a star of the first magnitude.* [ME, from L: greatness]

magnolia /mæg'nouliə/, *n.* a large shrub or small tree with large, showy, perfumed flowers in white, purple, etc. [NL; named from P *Magnol*, 1638-1715, French botanist]

magnum /'mægnəm/, *n., pl.* **-nums.** *n.* a wine bottle holding about 2.25 litres. [L: great]

magpie /'mægpaɪ/, *n.* **1.** Also, **Australian magpie.** a common black and white bird with a solid body, strong legs and large pointed bill, found throughout Australia and NG. **2.** an unrelated European bird, black and white and blue, with a long tail. **3.** someone who talks too much; chatterbox. **4.** Also, **bowerbird.** someone who collects useless objects. [from *Mag*, familiar var. of *Margaret*, woman's name + *pie* (see PIED)]

magpie goose, *n.* a large black and white goose found in freshwater areas of northern Australia and nearby islands.

magpie lark, *n.* a common Australian black and white bird which builds its mud nest high in a tree; mudlark; peewee; peewit.

Magritte /ma'grit/, *n.* **René** /rə'neɪ/, 1898-1967, Belgian surrealist painter.

magus /'meɪgəs/, *n., pl.* **-gi** /-dʒaɪ/. *n.* an ancient astrologer or magician. [ME, from L, from Gk, from OPers]

maharaja /mahə'radʒə/, *n.* the title of certain great ruling princes in India. Also, **maharajah.** [Skt: great rajah]

maharani /mahə'rani/, *n.* the wife of a maharaja. [Hind: great queen]

maharishi /mahə'rɪʃi/, *n.* a Hindu teacher; mystic. [Hind]

Mahathir bin Mohamad /ma,hatɪə bɪn mə'hamәd/, *n.* **Datuk Seri**, born 1925, Malaysian politician; became prime minister in 1981.

mahatma /mə'hatmə, -'hætmə/, *n.* (*oft. cap.*) (the title of) a wise and holy leader: *Mahatma Gandhi.* [Skt: great-souled]

mah-jong /'ma-dʒɒŋ/, *n.* a game of Chinese origin, usu. for four persons, with 136 (or sometimes 144) domino-like pieces or tiles, counters, and dice. [Chinese (Mandarin): sparrow (lit., hemp-bird), pictured on the first tiles of one of the suits]

Mahler /'malə/, *n.* **Gustav** /'gustaf/, 1860-1911, Austrian composer and conductor; composed the symphonic song cycle *Das Lied von der Erde* (1908).

mahogany /mə'hɒgəni/, *n., pl.* **-nies**, *adj.* ◇*n.* **1.** (the wood of) a type of tropical American tree giving a hard, reddish brown wood highly valued for making furniture. **2.** (the wood of) any of various Australian related or similar trees, e.g. swamp mahogany. **3.** a reddish brown color. ◇*adj.* **4.** relating to or made of mahogany. [? WInd]

maid /meɪd/, *n.* **1.** a girl; young unmarried woman. **2.** an older unmarried woman; spinster (usu. in the expression *old maid*). **3.** a female servant. [var. of MAIDEN]

maiden /'meɪdn/, *n.* **1.** a girl; young unmarried woman; virgin. ◇*adj.* **2.** of, for or relating to a girl or unmarried woman. **3.** unmarried: *a maiden lady.* **4.** made, tried, appearing, etc., for the first time: *maiden voyage; a maiden speech.* **5.** (of a knight, soldier, racehorse or weapon) untested; untried. [OE]

maidenhair /'meɪdnhɛə/, *n.* a type of fern with fine, glossy black stalks and delicate, fan-shaped fronds.

maidenhead /'meɪdnhɛd/, *n.* **1.** virginity. **2.** → **hymen.**

maiden name, *n.* a woman's surname before marriage.

maiden over, *n.* (in cricket) an over in which no runs are made.

Maid Marian /meɪd 'mɛəriən/, *n.* **1.** (orig.) Queen of the May, one of the characters in the old morris dance. **2.** Robin Hood's sweetheart.

mail[1] /meɪl/, *n.* **1.** letters, parcels, etc., arriving or sent by post. **2.** a system of sending of letters, etc., by post: *The mail is usually reliable.* **3.** a train, boat or aircraft by which mail is carried: *The mail is due in at 5 o'clock.* ◇*adj.* **4.** of or relating to mail: *a mailbag.* ◇*v.t.* **5.** to send by mail. [ME: bag, from OF, from Gmc]

mail[2] /meɪl/, *n.* **1.** flexible armor made of small interlinked rings. ◇*v.t.* **2.** to clothe or arm with mail. [ME, from F, from L: spot, mesh of a net]

mailbox /'meɪlbɒks/, *n.* **1.** a box for posting letters. **2.** a box at the front gate or front door of a house for receiving mail.

Mailer /'meɪlə/, *n.* **Norman**, born 1923, US author, essayist and journalist; wrote *The Armies of the Night* (1968).

maillot /meɪ'jou/, *n.* **1.** → **tights. 2.** a tight-fitting one-piece swimming costume. [F: swaddling clothes]

mail order, *n.* **1.** an order for goods, etc., received and sent by post. **2.** a system of buying where orders, payment and goods go by mail. – **mail-order**, *adj.*

maim /meɪm/, *v.t.* **1.** to harm (somebody) in a limb so that it becomes useless; mutilate; cripple. **2.** to damage; make defective; incapacitate. [var. of MAYHEM] – **maimed**, *adj.*

main /meɪn/, *adj.* **1.** most important or biggest; chief; principal: *the main office.* **2.** utmost; sheer: *by main force.* ◇*n.* **3.** the principal pipe in a system distributing water, gas, etc. **4.** the principal wire or cable distributing electricity. **5.** strength (only in the expression *with might and main*). **6.** *Poetic.* the ocean. **7. in the main,** for the most part. [OE: strength, power]

main clause, *n.* (in a complex sentence) the clause which can stand on its own as a sentence; independent clause; principal clause. For example, in 'I was out when he came in', the italicised part is a main clause.

Maine /meɪn/, *n.* a state in the northeastern US, on the Atlantic coast. Pop. 1 174 000 (1986 est.); 86 027 km². *Cap.:* Augusta. *Abbrev.:* Me

mainland /'meɪnlænd, -lənd/, *n.* **1.** the biggest land mass in an area, distinguished from nearby islands. **2. the mainland,** *Tas.* continental Australia. —**mainlander,** *n.*

mainline /'meɪnlaɪn/, *v.i., v.t.,* **-lined, -lining.** *Colloq.* to inject (a narcotic drug) directly into the vein.

mainstay /'meɪnsteɪ/, *n.* **1.** *Naut.* a rope supporting the mainmast from in front. **2.** chief support: *His interest is the mainstay of the group.*

mainstream /'meɪnstrim/, *n.* the chief tendency or trend: *in the mainstream of fashion.*

maintain /meɪn'teɪn, mən-/, *v.t.* **1.** to keep in existence; keep up; preserve: *to maintain good relations with NZ; to maintain life in the Antarctic.* **2.** to keep in good condition, operation, etc.: *to maintain order; to maintain roads.* **3.** to keep; hold on to; retain: *to maintain the lead in a race.* **4.** to keep or hold against attack: *to maintain one's ground.* **5.** to hold; declare; assert: *I maintain that it is right.* **6.** to provide with a living: *He maintained his parents in their old age.* [ME, from F, from L: hold in the hand]

maintenance /'meɪntənəns/, *n.* **1.** the act of maintaining or condition of being maintained. **2.** a means of support; livelihood. **3.** *Law.* money paid for the support of a spouse or children after divorce.

Maitland /'meɪtlənd/, *n.* a city in eastern NSW, on the flood plain of the Hunter River; stockyards, textile manufacturing and coalmining. Pop. 43 247 (1986).

maize /meɪz/, *n.* **1.** a tall cultivated grain plant bearing yellow grain in large cobs or spikes; Indian corn. **2.** its grain. **3.** a pale yellow color. [Sp, from Taino, a WInd language]

majesty /'mædʒəsti/, *n., pl.* **-ties. 1.** great dignity; loftiness; grandeur: *The majesty of Beethoven's ninth symphony.* **2.** supreme greatness or authority; sovereignty: *the majesty of God.* **3.** (*usu. cap.*) a title used when speaking of or to a king or queen (prec. by *his, her, your,* etc.). [ME, from F, from L: greatness, grandeur] —**majestic,** *adj.* —**majestically,** *adv.*

major /'meɪdʒə/, *n.* **1.** *Mil.* a rank in the army. See Appendix. **2.** a person of full legal age (opposed to *minor*). **3.** the main field of study chosen by a student: *a BA with a major in philosophy.* ◇*adj.* **4.** greater in size, amount, importance, etc.: *the major part of the town; a major question.* **5.** *Music.* **a.** (of an interval) being between the tonic and the second, third, sixth, or seventh degrees of a major scale: *the major scale; the major third, sixth, etc.* **b.** (of a chord) having a major third between the root (def. 8) and the note next above it. ◇*v.i.* **6.** to follow a main course of study (fol. by *in*): *to major in philosophy.* [ME, from L: greater, larger, superior]

Major /'meɪdʒə/, *n.* **John,** born 1943, English politician; became British Conservative Party leader and prime minister in 1990.

Majorca /mə'jɔkə/, *n.* a Spanish island in the western Mediterranean; the largest of the Balearic Islands. Pop. 460 030 (1970); 3639 km². *Cap.:* Palma. Spanish, **Mallorca.**

majority /mə'dʒɒrəti/, *n., pl.* **-ties. 1.** the greater part or number: *the majority of mankind.* **2.** the number of votes, seats, etc., by which a candidate or government wins an election: *a majority of 200 votes.* **3.** the party with the majority (def. 2). **4.** a state or time of being of full legal age: *to reach one's majority.* [F, from ML, from L: MAJOR]

Major Mitchell, *n.* a handsome white and pink cockatoo found in dry regions of Australia; Leadbeater's cockatoo.

major scale, *n. Music.* a scale with a major third between the tonic and the third tone.

major third, *n. Music.* an interval of two whole tones, e.g. from C to E.

make /meɪk/, *v.,* **made, making,** *n.* ◇*v.t.* **1.** to bring into existence by shaping material, combining parts, etc.; devise: *to make a bookcase; to make a dress.* **2.** to cause: *to make trouble.* **3.** to cause to be or become; render: *to make an old man young; to make him sick.* **4.** to appoint; constitute: *to make someone a judge.* **5.** to prepare for use: *to make a bed; to make a fire.* **6.** to cause or compel (to do something): *to make a horse go.* **7.** to produce, earn, or win for oneself: *to make a fortune; to make a friend.* **8.** to compose; create: *to make a poem; to make a play.* **9.** to fix; establish; enact: *to make laws.* **10.** to become by development; prove to be: *He will make a good lawyer.* **11.** to judge or understand: *What do you make of it?* **12.** to estimate; reckon: *I make the distance ten metres.* **13.** (of material or parts) to compose; form; add up to: *2 and 2 make 4; Two bags make a kilo of flour.* **14.** to serve for or as: *This book makes good reading.* **15.** to be sufficient to constitute; be essential to: *It takes hard work to make a good team.* **16.** to put forth; deliver: *to make a speech.* **17.** to travel (a distance) or reach (a speed): *to make 100 km an hour.* **18.** to arrive at, esp. safely or in time: *to make a port; to make the first throw.* **19.** to achieve a position in or on: *to make the honors list.* **20.** *Sport, Games.* to earn as a score. ◇*v.i.* **21.** to cause oneself or something to be in a certain condition: *to make sure; to make ready.* **22.** to show oneself in action or behavior: *to make merry.* **23.** to start off going or doing: *to make for home; They made to go.* ◇ **24.** Some special uses are:

make a face, to grimace.

make as if or **as though,** to act as if; pretend.

make away with, 1. to get rid of. **2.** to kill or destroy. **3.** to steal or abduct.

make believe, to pretend.

make do, to manage with the means available, however small or inadequate.

make eyes, to flirt (fol. by *at*).

make for, to travel towards or try to reach.

make good, 1. to achieve (a goal). **2.** to become a success.

make it, 1. to achieve one's object. **2.** to have

sexual intercourse (usu. fol. by *with*). **3.** to arrive successfully: *I didn't think I'd make it!*
make like, *Colloq.* **1.** to copy. **2.** to pretend.
make love, to have sexual intercourse.
make off, to run away.
make off with, to steal.
make out, 1. to write out a bill, cheque, form, etc. **2.** to see and understand; decipher: *I can't make out your handwriting.* **3.** to present as; impute to be: *He made me out a liar.* **4.** *Colloq.* to manage: *to make out on $50 a week.*
make tracks, *Colloq.* to depart.
make up, 1. (of parts) to form. **2.** to put together; construct; compile. **3.** to invent; concoct: *to make up a story.* **4.** to compensate for; make good. **5.** to complete. **6.** to prepare; put in order: *to make up a bed.* **7.** to bring to a decision: *He made up his mind.* **8.** Also, **make it up.** to become reconciled after a quarrel. **9.** to put cosmetics on the face. **10.** to put on cosmetics, wigs, etc., for the stage.
make up to, *Colloq.* to try to be friendly with; fawn on.
◇*n.* **25.** a style or manner of being made; build: *material of an uneven make.* **26.** a type or brand: *our own make.* **27. on the make,** *Colloq.* **a.** seeking gain or one's own advantage. **b.** looking for a sexual partner. [OE *macian*]

makeshift /'meɪkʃɪft/, *n.* **1.** a substitute; temporary expedient. ◇*adj.* **2.** serving as a makeshift.

make-up /'meɪk-ʌp/, *n.* **1.** (the putting on of) cosmetics. **2.** the costume, face-paint, wigs, etc., worn on the stage. **3.** the manner of being made up or put together; composition. **4.** bodily or mental constitution: *his emotional make-up.* **5.** *Print.* the arrangement of type, pictures, etc., into columns or pages.

making /'meɪkɪŋ/, *n.* **1.** the act or process of being made. **2.** a means or cause of success: *to be the making of someone.* **3.** (oft. *pl.*) the possibility of being; potential: *She has the makings of a fine singer.* **4. in the making,** being made; not yet finished. **5. the makings,** *Colloq.* tobacco and paper used to roll a cigarette by hand.

mako /'meɪkoʊ/, *n.* Also, **blue pointer.** a very fast, vigorous shark of Indo-Pacific waters, with a blue back and pointed snout, highly valued as a game fish.

mal-, a prefix meaning 'bad', 'wrongful', 'ill', as in *maladjustment, malpractice.* [F, from L]

Malacca /məˈlækə/, *n.* **Strait of,** a strait between Sumatra and the Malay Peninsula. 56-297 km wide.

malachite /ˈmæləkaɪt/, *n.* an ore of copper, green copper carbonate, used for ornamental articles. [F, from Gk]

maladjustment /ˌmæləˈdʒʌstmənt/, *n.* **1.** a being out of right order or position. **2.** *Psychol.* a failure to relate successfully to people or surroundings, often a sign of mental disturbance. —**maladjusted,** *adj.*

malady /ˈmælədi/, *n., pl.* **-dies. 1.** an illness or disease. **2.** any form of disorder: *social maladies.* [ME, from OF: sick, from LL: ill-conditioned]

Malagasy /ˌmæləˈgæsi/, *n., adj.* ◇*n.* **1. Malagasy Republic.** See **Madagascar.** ◇*adj.* **2.** of or relating to Madagascar (formerly the Malagasy Republic).

malaise /mæˈleɪz/, *n.* a vague feeling of bodily weakness or mental discomfort. [F]

malapropism /ˈmæləprɒpˌɪzəm/, *n.* **1.** the act or habit of misusing similar-sounding words, as in *He ran the whole gambit of emotions,* instead of *He ran the whole gamut of emotions.* **2.** a word so misused. [from Mrs *Malaprop,* a character noted for her misapplication of words, in *The Rivals* (1775) by RB Sheridan, 1751-1816, Irish dramatist]

malaria /məˈlɛəriə/, *n.* an infectious disease marked by chills, fever and sweating; it is caused by a parasite carried by mosquitos. [It, contraction of *mala aria* bad air] —**malarial, malarian, malarious,** *adj.*

Malawi /məˈlawi/, *n.* a republic in southern central Africa, bordered by Zambia, Mozambique, and Tanzania. Pop. 7 499 000 (1987 est.); 118 484 km^2. *Languages:* English and Chichewa. *Currency:* kwacha. *Cap.:* Lilongive. Formerly, **Nyasaland.**

Malay /məˈleɪ/, *adj.* of or relating to Malaya.

Malaya /məˈleɪə/, *n.* **States of,** that part of Malaysia in the southern Malay Peninsula, constituting West Malaysia; consisting of the former Federated Malay States, the former Unfederated Malay States, and the former Straits Settlements of Penang and Malacca (now Melaka). Pop. 15 557 000 (1985 est.); 131 590 km^2.

Malay Peninsula /məˈleɪ/, *n.* a peninsula in south-east Asia, consisting of the States of Malaya and the southern part of Thailand. Also, **Malaya.**

Malaysia /məˈleɪʒə/, *n.* a federal monarchy in south-east Asia, consisting of 13 states of which 11 are on the Malay peninsula and two, Sabah and Sarawak, on the island of Borneo (Kalimantan); established in 1963 by the union of the Federation of Malaya (a former British protectorate) with Singapore, Sarawak and Sabah (former British colonies); Singapore seceded in 1965. Pop. 16 538 000 (1987 est.); 329 750 km^2. *Languages:* Malay, also English, Tamil and Iban. *Currency:* ringgit or Malaysian dollar. *Cap.:* Kuala Lumpur. —**Malaysian,** *adj., n.*

malcontent /ˈmælkəntɛnt/, *adj.* **1.** discontented; dissatisfied. ◇*n.* **2.** a malcontent person; grumbler; complainer. [OF. See MAL-, CONTENT^2]

male /meɪl/, *adj.* **1.** (of people, animals and plants) belonging to the sex which sends sperm to the female egg in the creation of new life. **2.** relating to or typical of this sex; masculine. **3.** composed of males: *a male choir.* ◇*n.* **4.** a man or boy. **5.** any animal of the male sex. **6.** *Bot.* a plant which has stamens. [ME, from OF, from L]

male chauvinist, *n.* **1.** a man who regards women as being by nature unreasonable, weak-willed, unpractical, not interested in ideas, etc.,

male chauvinist and who shows this in his behavior. **2. male chauvinist pig,** (*offensive*) an extreme male chauvinist. ◇*adj.* **3.** showing discriminatory or stereotyped ideas about women. —**male chauvinism,** *n.*

malediction /ˌmæləˈdɪkʃən/, *n.* (the saying of) a curse. [late ME, from L: abuse] —**maledictory,** *adj.*

malefactor /ˈmæləfæktə/, *n.* **1.** a criminal. **2.** someone who does evil. [late ME, from L] —**malefactress,** *n. fem.* —**malefaction,** *n.*

malevolent /məˈlevələnt/, *adj.* wishing evil or harm to others; showing ill will: *a malevolent look.* [L: wishing ill] —**malevolence,** *n.*

malformation /ˌmælfɔːˈmeɪʃən, -fə-/, *n.* faulty formation or structure, esp. in a living body: *a malformation of the bones.* —**malformed,** *adj.*

malfunction /mælˈfʌŋkʃən/, *v.i.* **1.** to fail to function properly. ◇*n.* **2.** failure to function properly. [MAL- + FUNCTION]

Mali /ˈmɑli/, *n.* a republic in western Africa, bordered by Algeria, Mauritania, Senegal, Guinea, Côte d'Ivoire, Upper Volta and Niger; part of French West Africa before independence in 1960. Pop. 7 919 893 (1986); 1 204 350 km². *Languages:* French and local languages including Berber and Arabic. *Currency:* franc. *Cap.:* Bamako. Formerly, **French Sudan.**

malice /ˈmæləs/, *n.* the desire to hurt or harm another person. [ME, from OF, from L: badness, spite]

malicious /məˈlɪʃəs/, *adj.* **1.** showing malice; malignant; malevolent. **2.** *Law.* done with deliberate intent to harm: *malicious arrest*; *malicious damage.*

malign /məˈlaɪn/, *v.t.* **1.** to speak ill of; slander. ◇*adj.* **2.** evil in effect; pernicious; baleful. **3.** having or showing an evil turn of mind; malevolent. [ME, from OF, from L: ill-disposed]

malignant /məˈlɪgnənt/, *adj.* **1.** causing suffering or distress; malicious. **2.** very dangerous; harmful in influence or effect. **3.** *Pathol.* deadly; tending to produce death, as a disease, tumor, etc. [LL: injuring maliciously] —**malignance, malignancy,** *n.*

malinger /məˈlɪŋgə/, *v.i.* to pretend to be sick or injured, esp. to avoid duty, work, etc. [F: sickly, ailing]

Malinowski /ˌmæləˈnɒfski/, *n.* **Bronislaw Kasper** /ˌbrɒnɪslav ˈkæspə/, 1884–1942, Polish anthropologist in the US; worked in New Guinea and Melanesia.

mall /mɔl, mæl/, *n.* **1.** a shaded public walk. **2.** a shopping complex. [ME, from OF, from L: hammer; by association an alley where the game *pall-mall* was played (using a mallet)]

mallard /ˈmælad/, *n., pl.* **-lards,** (*esp. collectively*) **-lard. 1.** a common wild duck, from which domestic ducks are descended. **2.** a male of this species. [ME, from OF, probably from Gmc proper name *Madalhart*, given to the duck in a beast epic]

malleable /ˈmæliəbəl/, *adj.* **1.** able to be shaped by hammering or rolling. **2.** easily changed or influenced. [ME, from OF, from L: beat with a hammer] —**malleability,** *n.*

mallee /ˈmæli/, *n.* **1.** any of various Australian types of gum tree which have several thin stems rising from a large underground root stock. **2. the mallee, a.** an area of scrub where the main type of tree is a mallee. **b.** any remote, isolated or unsettled area. [Aboriginal]

mallee fowl, *n.* a greyish-brown, spotted, Australian bird which builds its nest in mounds, found in dry inland scrub areas. Also, **mallee bird, mallee hen.**

Mallee Region, *n.* a region in north-western Vic; bounded by the Murray and Wimmera rivers. 44 000 km². Also, **the Mallee.**

mallee snake, *n.* → **common brown snake.**

mallet /ˈmælət/, *n.* **1.** a hammer-like tool with a wooden or plastic head used for driving tools with wooden handles, so that these do not split. **2.** a wooden tool used to hit balls in croquet or polo. **3.** a type of western Australian gum tree. [ME, from OF]

malnutrition /ˌmælnjuˈtrɪʃən/, *n.* **1.** the lack of properly nourishing food. **2.** a condition of poor health, often close to starvation, resulting from this.

malodor *or* **malodour** /mælˈoʊdə/, *n.* a bad smell; stench. —**malodorous,** *adj.*

Malouf /məˈluf/, *n.* **David,** born 1934, Australian novelist, poet and short-story writer; author of *Harland's Half-Acre* (1984).

malpractice /mælˈpræktəs/, *n.* improper or criminal action by a professional person, as a doctor, accountant, etc.

malt /mɔlt, mɒlt/, *n.* **1.** germinated grain (usu. barley), used in brewing and distilling. **2.** a liquor produced from malt by fermentation, as beer or ale. **3.** malt extract. ◇*v.t., v.i.* **4.** to turn (grain) into malt. [OE] —**malty,** *adj.*

Malta /ˈmɔltə, ˈmɒltə/, *n.* a republic consisting of a group of islands in the central Mediterranean Sea; a British colony before independence in 1964. Pop. 345 000 (1987 est.); 316 km². *Languages:* Maltese and English, also Italian. *Currency:* Maltese lira. *Cap.:* Valletta. —**Maltese,** *adj., n.*

Malthusian /mælˈθjuziən/, *adj.* of or relating to the theory that population tends to increase faster than resources, and should be checked by social and moral restraints. [from TR *Malthus*, 1766–1834, English political economist]

maltose /ˈmɔltoʊz, -toʊs, ˈmɒl-/, *n.* a white crystalline disaccharide (sugar), $C_{12}H_{22}O_{11}$, containing two glucose units. Also, **malt sugar.** [MALT + -OSE²]

maltreat /mælˈtrit/, *v.t.* to treat roughly or cruelly; abuse. [F]

maluka /məˈlukə/, *n.* **1.** the boss. **2.** (*cap.*) a form of address to one's superior. [Aboriginal]

mama /məˈmɑ/, *n.* mother; mamma.

mamilla /mæˈmɪlə/, *n., pl.* **-millae** /-ˈmɪli/. any nipple-like outgrowth. [L: little MAMMA²] **—mamillary,** *adj.*

mamma¹ /ˈmʌmə, məˈmɑ/, *n.* (*esp.* in *children's speech*) mother. [reduplication of a syllable common in natural infantile utterance]

mamma² /ˈmæmən/, *n., pl.* **mammae** /ˈmæmi/. *n.* the organ in female mammals which forms milk; breast or udder. [OE, from L: breast, pap] **—mammary,** *adj.*

mammal /ˈmæməl/, *n.* a member of the Mammalia, a class of vertebrates whose young feed upon milk from the mother's mamma. Most species (except cetaceans) are more or less hairy, all have a diaphragm, and all (except the monotremes) are viviparous (live-bearing). [LL: of the breast] **—mammalian,** *adj., n.*

mammon /ˈmæmən/, *n.* **1.** *Bible.* riches or material wealth. **2.** (*cap.*) riches seen as an evil spirit or god. [LL, from Gk, from Aram: riches]

mammoth /ˈmæməθ/, *n.* **1.** a very large hairy elephant with long curved tusks, that no longer exists. ◇*adj.* **2.** huge; gigantic: *a mammoth enterprise.* [Russ]

Mammoth Cave, *n.* a limestone cave in south-western WA, so named due to its vast size.

man /mæn/, *n., pl.* **men,** *v.,* **manned, manning.** ◇*n.* **1.** *Anthrop.* an individual of the Homo genus and of the mammal class, at the highest level of animal development, mainly characterised by his mental powers. **2.** the human being separate from other beings, animals, or things; the human race; mankind: *the civilisations of man.* **3.** human being; person. **4.** (an adult) male human being, as distinguished from woman. **5.** a husband: *man and wife.* **6.** a male person in a lower position: *the officers and men of the army.* **7.** a strong, brave, honorable person: *Stand up and be a man.* **8.** a male servant; valet. **9.** one of the pieces used in playing certain games, as chess or draughts. **10.** *Hist.* a vassal; liegeman. **11. man and boy,** from childhood. **12. the man on the land,** the farmer. **13. the man in the street,** the average man. **14. to a man,** all; to the last man. ◇*v.t.* **15.** to provide with personnel: *to man a ship; to man a garrison.* **16.** to take one's place for service: *to man a gun; to man a post.* [OE]

mana /ˈmɑnə/, *n.* **1.** *Anthrop.* an impersonal, supernatural force which may be concentrated in objects or people. **2.** power; prestige; authority; influence. [Maori or ? Polynesian]

manacle /ˈmænəkəl/, *n.* (*usu. pl.*) **1.** a pair of iron rings linked by a chain, used on prisoners; handcuffs. **2.** any restraint. [ME, from OF: handcuff, from L: hand]

manage /ˈmænɪdʒ/, *v.,* **-aged, -aging.** ◇*v.t.* **1.** to bring about; succeed in accomplishing: *He managed to see the governor.* **2.** to take charge or care of: *to manage a business.* **3.** to handle or control: *to manage a horse; to manage a child.* **4.** to be able to use properly: *Can you manage that knife?* ◇*v.i.* **5.** to be able to make do: *Can you manage on $50 a week?* [It: handle, train (horses), from L: hand] **—manageable,** *adj.* **—manageability, manageableness,** *n.*

managed currency, *n.* a form of money management where the buying power of a nation's currency is altered by the authorities to influence business activity and prices (contrasted with *gold standard*). See **gold standard.**

management /ˈmænɪdʒmənt/, *n.* **1.** handling, direction, or control. **2.** skill in managing; executive ability: *Good management can prevent strikes.* **3.** the person or people running a business, etc.: *This shop is under new management.* **4.** such people taken as a whole: *fights between labor and management.*

manager /ˈmænədʒə/, *n.* **1.** someone who manages: *She is a good manager of her household.* **2.** someone in charge of a business, sporting team, or client, etc. **—managership,** *n.*

manageress /mænədʒəˈrɛs, ˈmænədʒərəs/, *n.* a female manager.

managerial /mænəˈdʒɪəriəl/, *adj.* relating to management or a manager: *managerial expenses.*

mañana /mænˈjɑnə, mən-/, *n., adv.* tomorrow; the indefinite future. [Sp]

manchester /ˈmæntʃəstə/, *n.* **1.** sheets, towels, etc., as sold in shops. **2.** (*cap.*) a city in England, in Lancashire; connected to the Mersey estuary by a ship canal (57 km long); textile industry. Pop. 448 604 (1981).

Manchuria /mænˈtʃʊəriə/, *n.* a region in north-eastern China, formerly comprising nine provinces of that country; ancestral home of the Manchus. 1 069 670 km². **—Manchurian,** *adj., n.*

-mancy, a word part meaning 'divination', as in *necromancy.* [ME, from OF, from LL from Gk: divination]

mandala /mænˈdɑlə/, *n.* a mystic symbol of the universe, in the form of a circle enclosing a square; used chiefly by Hindus and Buddhists as an aid to meditation. [Skt: circle]

Mandalay /ˈmændəˌleɪ/, *n.* a city in central Burma, on the river Irrawaddy; the former capital of Upper Burma. Pop. 532 895 (1983).

mandarin /ˈmændərən, mændəˈrɪn/, *n.* **1.** (formerly) a member of any of the nine ranks of public officials in the Chinese Empire. **2.** an official or bureaucrat, esp. one who makes himself elite or unavailable. **3.** (*cap.*) the standard Chinese language. **4.** Also, **mandarine.** (a tree producing) a small, sweet type of orange; tangerine. [Chinese pidgin E, from Pg, from Skt: thought, counsel]

mandatary /ˈmændətəri/, *n., pl.* **-ries.** a person or nation holding a mandate. Also, **mandatory.** [L: mandate]

mandate /ˈmændeɪt/, *n., v.,* **-dated, -dating.** *n.* **1.** (formerly) a commission given

mandate

by the League of Nations to administer a territory. **2.** a mandated territory. **3.** a command; order. **4.** *Politics.* an instruction or permission from the electorate for a certain policy: *The Government has no mandate for higher taxes.* ◇*v.t.* **5.** to give (a territory, etc.) to the charge of a particular nation under a mandate. [L: commit, enjoin, command] —**mandator**, *n.*

mandatory /'mændətri, -təri/, *adj., n., pl.* **-ries.** ◇*adj.* **1.** relating to, of the nature of, or containing a mandate. **2.** obligatory. **3.** *Law.* allowing no choice. **4.** (of a nation) having received a mandate. ◇*n.* **5.** a person or nation holding a mandate. Also, **mandatary.**

Mandela /mæn'deɪlə, -'delə/, *n.* **Nelson (Rolihlahla)**, born 1918, South African political activist; national organiser of the African National Congress, imprisoned on a charge of treason 1962–90.

mandible /'mændəbəl/, *n.* **1.** a bone of the lower jaw. **2.** (in birds) **a.** the lower part of the beak. **b.** (*pl.*) the upper and lower parts of the beak. **3.** (in insects, etc.) one of the pair of biting mouth parts. [LL: jaw] —**mandibular**, *adj.* —**mandibulate**, *adj.*

mandolin /mændə'lɪn/, *n.* a stringed musical instrument with a small pear-shaped wooden body and a fretted neck. Also, **mandoline.** [F, from It]

mandrake /'mændreɪk/, *n.* a narcotic European herb with a root often thought to look like a human body.

mandrax /'mændræks/, *n.* a sedative drug. [Trademark]

mandrill /'mændrəl/, *n.* a large, ferocious-looking baboon of western Africa, the male of which has blue and red markings on the face.

Mandurah /'mændʒərə/, *n.* a coastal town and shire in south-western WA, south of Perth; tourism. Pop. 18 016 (1987).

mane /meɪn/, *n.* **1.** the long hair growing on the neck of some animals, as the horse, lion, etc. **2.** a long, bushy, often uncared for head of hair. [OE *manu*]

Manet /ma'neɪ/, *n.* **Edouard** /eɪ'dwa/, 1832–83, French painter whose style strongly influenced the impressionists.

manganese /mæŋgə'niz/, *n.* a hard, brittle, greyish white metallic element used in alloys with steel and other metals to give them toughness. Symbol: Mn; at. no.: 25; at. wt: 54.938. [F, from It, from ML: magnesia]

manganite /'mæŋgənaɪt/, *n.* a grey to black mineral, hydrous manganese oxide, MnO(OH), a minor ore of manganese. [MANGAN(ESE) + -ITE¹]

mange /meɪndʒ/, *n.* a skin disease caused by parasitic mites affecting animals and sometimes man, marked by loss of hair and scabby eruptions. [ME, from OF: itch, from L: chew]

manger /'meɪndʒə/, *n.* a box or trough from which horses or cattle eat. [ME, from OF, from L: chew]

mangle¹ /'mæŋgəl/, *v.t.,* **-gled, -gling. 1.** to cut, slash, or crush so as to disfigure: *a corpse mangled in battle.* **2.** to spoil; mar: *to mangle a text by poor typesetting.* [ME, from AF, ? frequentative of OF: maim] —**mangler**, *n.*

mangle² /'mæŋgəl/, *n., v.,* **-gled, -gling.** ◇*n.* **1.** a machine for smoothing, or pressing water, etc., out of cloth by means of rollers; wringer. ◇*v.t.* **2.** to smooth with a mangle. [D]

mango /'mæŋgoʊ/, *n., pl.* **-goes, -gos.** a large, yellow tropical fruit. [Pg, from Malay, from Tamil]

mangrove /'mæŋgroʊv, 'mæn-/, *n.* a type of tree with aerial roots found in subtropical and tropical countries on salt or brackish mudflats. [Sp]

mangy /'meɪndʒi/, *adj.,* **-gier, -giest. 1.** having, caused by, or like mange. **2.** mean; contemptible. **3.** dirty or unhealthy-looking; squalid; shabby. —**mangily**, *adv.* —**manginess**, *n.*

manhandle /'mænhændl/, *v.t.,* **-dled, -dling. 1.** to handle roughly. **2.** to move by force of men, without machines.

Manhattan /mæn'hætn/, *n.* an island at the northern end of New York Bay, bounded by the Hudson, Harlem and East Rivers; one of the five boroughs of New York City. 57 km².

manhole /'mænhoʊl/, *n.* a covered hole, as an entrance to a sewer, drain, steam boiler, etc.

manhood /'mænhʊd/, *n.* **1.** the condition or qualities of being a man or adult male person. **2.** men collectively. **3.** the state of being human. **4.** the human male sex organs or sexual powers.

man-hour /'mæn-aʊə/, *n.* an hour of work by one person, used as an industrial time unit.

mania /'meɪniə/, *n.* **1.** great excitement or enthusiasm; craze. **2.** *Psychol.* a violent or excitable form of madness. [ME, from L, from Gk: madness]

-mania, combining form of **mania** (as in *megalomania*), extended to mean exaggerated desire or love for, as *balletomania*.

maniac /'meɪniæk/, *n., adj.* (someone who is) violently mad; raving with madness. —**maniacal**, *adj.*

manic /'mænɪk/, *adj.* **1.** relating to mania. **2.** *Colloq.* relating to manic-depression. [Gk: insane]

manic-depressive /ˌmænɪk-də'prɛsɪv/, *n., adj.* (someone) having a mental disorder marked by alternating periods of excitement and depression. —**manic-depression**, *n.*

manicure /'mænəkjʊə/, *n., v.,* **-cured, -curing.** ◇*n.* **1.** the care of the hands and fingernails. ◇*v.t.* **2.** to care for (the hands and fingernails). [F, from L: hand care] —**manicurist**, *n.*

manifest /'mænəfəst, -fɛst/, *adj.* **1.** plain; apparent; obvious; evident: *a manifest error; Dislike was manifest on his face.* ◇*v.t.* **2.** to show plainly: *His dislike manifested itself in rudeness.* ◇*n.* **3.** a list of cargo carried by land, sea or air. **4.** → **manifesto.** [ME, from L: palpable, evident]

manifestation /mænəfes'teɪʃən/, *n.* **1.** the act of manifesting or state of being manifested. **2.** something which shows plainly: *His rudeness was the manifestation of his dislike.* **3.** *Spiritualism.* the appearance of a spirit.

manifesto /mænə'festoʊ/, *n., pl.* **-tos** or **-toes.** a public declaration by a government, or group of any kind, setting out its ideas, or reasons for acting. [It: manifest, n.]

manifold /'mænəfoʊld/, *adj.* **1.** of many and various kinds: *manifold duties.* **2.** in many or various ways. ◇*n.* **3.** something having many different parts or features. **4.** a copy; facsimile. **5.** a pipe or chamber with several inlets or outlets. **6.** very fine typing paper. ◇*v.t.* **7.** to make copies of, as with carbon paper. [OE *manigfeald*]

manikin /'mænɪkɪn, -ɪkən/, *n.* **1.** a little man; dwarf; pygmy. **2.** a mannequin. **3.** a model of the human body for teaching anatomy, showing how operations are done, etc. Also, **manakin, mannikin.** [D: little man]

manila /mə'nɪlə/, *n.* **1.** fibrous material from a Philippine tree used for making paper, rope, etc. **2.** (*cap.*) a seaport in and the capital of the Republic of the Philippines, on southern Luzon island. See **Quezon City.** Pop. 1 728 441 (1984 est.).

manipulate /mə'nɪpjəleɪt/, *v.t.,* **-lated, -lating. 1.** to handle, manage, or use, esp. with skill. **2.** to manage, influence or change cleverly and unfairly for one's own advantage: *to manipulate people; to manipulate prices.* **3.** to treat by handling: *to manipulate the spine.* [F, from L: handful] —**manipulative, manipulatory,** *adj.* —**manipulation,** *n.* —**manipulator,** *n.*

mankind /mæn'kaɪnd/ *for def. 1;* /'mænkaɪnd/ *for def. 2, n.* **1.** the human race; human beings collectively. **2.** men, as distinguished from women.

manly /'mænli/, *adj.,* **-lier, -liest.** having qualities seen as proper to a man, as bravery, honorableness, etc.

Manly /'mænli/, *n.* a suburb of Sydney, near North Head at the entrance to Port Jackson; tourism. [named by A PHILLIP because of the 'manly' attributes of the Aborigines]

Mann /man/, *n.* **1. Leonard,** 1895–1981, Australian novelist and poet; known esp. for his World War I novel *Flesh in Armour* (1932). **2. Thomas** /'toʊmas/, 1875–1955, German novelist, in the US after 1938; Nobel prize for literature 1929; works include the novella *Death in Venice* (1912) and the novel *Doctor Faustus* (1947).

manna /'mænə/, *n.* **1.** food sent from heaven to the ancient Jews in the desert. **2.** spiritual food or anything that comforts or sustains. **3.** a substance produced by insects living on many Australian gum trees, once used by Aborigines as food. **4. manna from heaven,** a welcome surprise. [OE, from LL, from Gk, from Heb]

mannequin /'mænəkən, -kwən/, *n.* **1.** a model of the human figure used by dressmakers, etc. **2.** → **model** (def. 5). [F, from D: little man]

manner /'mænə/, *n.* **1.** a way of doing or happening: *Hold the pencil in this manner.* **2.** a typical way of doing: *houses built in the Mexican manner.* **3.** (*pl.*) the customs and ways of living of a people, class or period: *Victorian manners; comedy of manners.* **4.** (*pl.*) ways of behaving, esp. according to polite standards: *Have you no manners?* **5.** a way of behaving towards others: *He has an awkward manner.* **6.** kind; sort: *all manner of things.* **7.** typical style in art, literature, etc.: *verses in the manner of Spenser.* **8. to the manner born,** (as if) accustomed or destined by birth (to a high position, etc.). [ME, from AF: orig., way of handling, from L: of or for the hand]

mannered /'mænəd/, *adj.* **1.** having (certain) manners: *ill-mannered.* **2.** having mannerisms; affected: *mannered prose.*

mannerism /'mænərɪzəm/, *n.* **1.** the continual use of certain effects of style in writing, for show rather than meaning. **2.** a habitual and particular way of behaving. **3.** (*usu. cap.*) the style of late 16th century European art, mainly in Italy. —**mannerist,** *n.* —**manneristic,** *adj.*

Manning /'mænɪŋ/, *n.* a coastal river of northern NSW, rising in the Mt Royal Range and flowing east, entering the Pacific Ocean north-east of Taree. About 225 km.

Mannix /'mænɪks/, *n.* **Daniel,** 1864–1963, Australian Roman Catholic prelate, born in Ireland; archbishop of Melbourne 1917–63.

manoeuvre /mə'nuvə/, *n., v.,* **-vred, -vring.** ◇*n.* **1.** the planned and regulated movement of soldiers, warships, etc. **2.** (*pl.*) a series of tactical military exercises. **3.** a clever or skilful move: *By that manoeuvre we have stopped them competing with us.* ◇*v.t., v.i.* **4.** to move (soldiers, etc.) in a tactical manner. **5.** to manipulate or move with skill: *to manoeuvre (a car) out of a tight parking spot.* [F: manipulation, from LL: work by hand] —**manoeuvrable,** *adj.* —**manoeuvrability,** *n.*

man-of-war /mæn-əv-'wɔ/, *n., pl.* **men-of-war. 1.** a warship. **2.** See **Portuguese man-of-war.** Also, **man-o'-war.**

manometer /mə'nɒmətə/, *n.* an instrument for determining the pressure of gases, vapours, or liquids. [F *manomètre,* from Gk *mānó(s)* thin, rare + F *-mètre* METER]

manor /'mænə/, *n.* **1.** a landed estate, originally of a feudal lord who let land out to farmers in return for crops and services. **2.** the house of a lord. [ME, from OF: dwell, from L: remain] —**manorial,** *adj.*

manpower /'mænpaʊə/, *n.* **1.** the power supplied by the physical effort of a man or men. **2.** a unit of power, commonly taken as $\frac{1}{10}$ horsepower. **3.** rate of work as measured by this unit.

manse /mæns/, *n.* **1.** the house and land of a clergyman, usu. of the Presbyterian or Uniting Church. **2.** (orig.) the house of a landholder, with the land attached. [ME, from ML: dwelling, from L: remain]

Mansfield /'mænsfild/, *n.* **1. George Allen**, 1834-1908, Australian architect; designed many public buildings in NSW. **2. Katherine** (*Kathleen Beauchamp, Mrs John Middleton Murry*), 1888-1923, English short-story writer, born in NZ.

-manship, a noun suffix indicating skill or knowledge in an activity, as *gamesmanship, one-upmanship, craftsmanship*.

mansion /'mænʃən/, *n.* a large or grand house. [ME, from OF, from L]

manslaughter /'mænslɔtə/, *n.* **1.** the killing of a human being by another human being; homicide. **2.** *Law.* the killing of a human being unlawfully but without malice (hurtful intention).

manta ray, /'mæntə reɪ/ *n.* a large harmless flat fish with gills on its undersurface and side flaps of up to six metres across. Also, **manta**.

mantelpiece /'mæntlpis/, *n.* a shelf above a fireplace, or ornamental surrounding structure. Also, **mantle**.

mantilla /mæn'tɪlə/, *n.* **1.** a silk or lace headscarf arranged over a high comb and falling over the back and shoulders, worn in Spain, Mexico, etc. **2.** short mantle or light cloak. [Sp]

mantis /'mæntəs/, *n., pl.* **-tises, -tes** /-tiz/. a flesh-eating insect with long neck and large eyes, noted for its way of holding its forelegs doubled up as if in prayer. Also, **praying mantis**. [NL, from Gk: prophet, kind of insect]

mantissa /mæn'tɪsə/, *n.* the decimal part of a logarithm. See **characteristic** (def. 3). [L: an addition]

mantle /'mæntl/, *n., v.,* **-tled, -tling.** ◇*n.* **1.** Also, **mantua**. a loose cloak. **2.** something that covers, surrounds, or hides. **3.** a network hood for a gas jet, which becomes incandescent when lit. **4.** the back and wing feathers of a bird. **5.** the outer surrounding masonry of a blast furnace over the hearth. **6.** *Geol.* the layer of the earth between the crust and the core, consisting of solid rock. **7.** → **mantelpiece**. ◇*v.t.* **8.** to cover or be covered with or as with a mantle: *Snow mantled the peaks.* [OE *mæntel*, from L: cloak]

mantra /'mæntrə/, *n.* a word, phrase or verse repeated as a sacred formula in Hinduism and Mahayana Buddhism as an aid to meditation. Also, **mantram**. [Skt: speech, hymn] – **mantric**, *adj.*

manual /'mænjuəl/, *adj.* **1.** of or done by the hand: *manual work*. **2.** using human energy, power, etc.: *a manual drill.* ◇*n.* **3.** a book giving information or instructions; handbook. **4.** *Music.* a keyboard of an organ played with the hands. **5.** a car whose gears are changed by hand. [L: of the hand]

manufacture /mænjə'fæktʃə, 'mænjəfæktʃə/, *n., v.,* **-tured, -turing.** ◇*n.* **1.** the making of goods by hand or machinery, esp. on a large scale. **2.** the making of anything. ◇*v.t.* **3.** to make or produce by hand or machinery, esp. on a large scale. **4.** to make up; concoct: *to manufacture arguments.* **5.** to produce in a mechanical way. [F, from L] – **manufacturer**, *n.* – **manufacturing**, *n.*

Manukau /'manəkaʊ/, *n.* a city in the northern part of the North Island, NZ. Pop. 177 248 (1986).

manure /mə'njuə/, *n., v.,* **-nured, -nuring.** ◇*n.* **1.** fertiliser, esp. animal excrement. ◇*v.t.* **2.** to treat (land) with fertiliser; put manure on. [ME, from AF: work by hand, from OF]

Manus /'mænəs/, *n.* a province of PNG, comprising a number of islands in the Bismarck Archipelago. Pop. 29 900 (1986 est.); 2100 km^2. *Administrative Centre:* Lorengau.

manuscript /'mænjəskrɪpt/, *n.* **1.** a book, document, letter, musical score, etc., written by hand. **2.** an author's copy of his work, written by hand or typed, used as the basis for typesetting. **3.** writing, as distinguished from print. ◇*adj.* **4.** written by hand or typed, not printed. [ML: handwritten]

Manx cat, /mæŋks/ *n.* a tailless variety of the domestic cat. [from the Isle of Man]

many /'mɛni/, *adj.,* **more, most,** *n.* ◇*adj.* **1.** forming a large number: *many people.* **2.** relatively numerous (after *as, so, too,* or *how*): *Six may be too many.* **3.** being one of a large number (fol. by *a* or *an*): *many a day.* ◇*n.* **4.** a great or considerable number (oft. fol. by a noun with *of* expressed or understood): *a great many of the people.* **5.** (as a collective plural) many people or things. **6. a good** (**great**) **many,** a large number. [OE *manig*]

Mao /maʊ/, *adj.* of the plain, practical style of clothing common in China since the 1949 revolution: *a Mao suit; a Mao cap.* [named after MAO ZEDONG.

Maoism /'maʊɪzəm/, *n.* the principles of Communism as explained by Mao Zedong. [named after MAO ZEDONG] – **Maoist**, *n.*

Maori /'maʊri/, *n., pl.* **-ris, -ri,** *adj.* ◇*n.* **1.** a member of the brown-skinned Polynesian people of NZ. ◇*adj.* **2.** of or relating to the Maoris or their language. [Maori: lit., of the usual kind (as opposed to foreigners)]

Maoriland /'maʊrilænd/, *n.* New Zealand.

Maoritanga /'maʊritʌŋə/, *n.* the qualities inherent in being a Maori, relating to heritage, culture, etc. [Maori]

Mao Zedong /maʊ zi'dʊŋ/, *n.* 1893-1976, Chinese statesman; founded the Chinese Communist Party (1921); established a soviet republic in south-eastern China (1931-34); founded the People's Republic of China 1949 and was chairman of this until 1959. He was party chairman until his death; he instigated the Cultural Revolution. Formerly, **Mao Tse-tung**.

map /mæp/, *n., v.,* **mapped, mapping.** ◇*n.* **1.** a drawing or other representation of a part or the whole of the earth's surface, or of the stars, moon, etc. **2.** a plan or diagram: *I'll draw you a map of how to get there.* **3. off the map**, out of existence; into oblivion: *Whole cities were wiped off the map.* **4. put on the**

map, to make widely known; make famous. ◇*v.t.* **5.** to represent in or as in a map; delineate. **6.** to plan or sketch (oft. fol. by *out*): *to map out a new career*. [ML: map, from L: napkin]

maple /'meɪpəl/, *n.* a tree of the northern parts of the earth, with many-pointed leaves, valued for shade and ornament and for its wood; from the sap of some maples **maple syrup** and **maple sugar** are obtained. [OE *mapel-* in *mapeltrēow* maple tree]

map projection, *n.* → **projection** (def. 4).

Maquis /ma'kiː/, *n., pl.* **Maquis**. (*sometimes l.c.*) a member of one of the French underground groups resisting the Germans in World War II. [F, special use of *maquis, makis* wild, bushy land (Corsican d.)]

mar /mɑ/, *v.t.*, **marred, marring.** to spoil; damage; impair. [OE *merran* hinder, waste]

Mar, *Abbrev.* March.

marabou /'mærəbuː/, *n.* **1.** a type of large stork found in Africa and Indonesia. **2.** a material made of marabou down. Also, **marabout.** [F]

maraca /mə'rækə/, *n. Music.* a gourd filled with pebbles, seeds, etc., shaken rhythmically in Latin-American bands.

Maralinga /mærə'lɪŋɡə/, *n.* the site of British atomic weapon testing in 1956-57, located north of the Nullarbor Plain, SA; now contaminated by plutonium. [Aboriginal: thunder]

Maranoa /mærə'noʊə/, *n.* a river in southeastern Qld, rising near the Carnarvon Range and flowing south to join the Balonne River. 530 km.

Marat /ma'rɑ/, *n.* **Jean Paul** /ʒɔ̃ pɒl/, 1743-93, French revolutionary and political writer of the French revolution; assassinated by Charlotte Corday.

marathon /'mærəθɒn, -θən/, *n.* **1.** a foot race of 26 miles 385 yards, or 42 195 metres. **2.** any long-distance or endurance contest: *a dance marathon*. [from *Marathon*, a plain in Attica, NE of Athens, from which, following the defeat of the Persians there in 490 BC, a runner took the news to Athens, about forty kilometres away]

maraud /mə'rɔd/, *v.i., v.t.* to search for things to steal, destroy, etc; raid. [F: rogue, vagabond] **—marauder,** *n.* **—marauding,** *adj.*

marble /'mɑbəl/, *n., adj., v.,* **-bled, -bling.** ◇*n.* **1.** a hard limestone, able to be polished and much used in sculpture and architecture. **2.** a work of art carved in marble. **3.** something like marble in hardness, coldness, smoothness, etc. **4.** *Games.* **a.** a little ball of stone, glass, etc., used in a children's game. **b.** (*pl.* used as *sing.*) the game itself, the aim of which is to win all one's opponent's marbles, by hitting them out of a circle, etc. ◇*adj.* **5.** consisting of marble. **6.** like marble, as being hard, cold, unfeeling, etc. **7.** of marbled pattern or color. ◇*v.t.* **8.** to color or pattern like marble. [ME, from OF, from L]

Marc /mak/, *n.* **Franz** /frænts/, 1880-1916, German expressionist painter; known for his animal studies.

marcasite /'mɑkəsaɪt/, *n.* a common mineral of the same composition as pyrite, but differing in crystal system. [ML, from Ar, from Aram]

Marceau /ma'soʊ/, *n.* **Marcel** /ma'sɛl/, born 1923, French actor and performer of mime and pantomime.

march[1] /matʃ/, *v.i.* **1.** (of soldiers) to walk with regular and measured steps. **2.** to walk in a stately manner. **3.** to advance. ◇*v.t.* **4.** to cause to march. ◇*n.* **5.** the act or course of marching. **6.** the distance covered in a single course of marching. **7.** forward movement: *the march of time*. **8.** a piece of music suited to marching. **9. steal a march,** to gain an advantage secretly (usu. fol. by *on* or *upon*). [F: go, earlier trample, from L: hammer] **—marcher,** *n.*

march[2] /matʃ/, *n.* a piece of land along a border of a country; frontier. [ME, from OF, from Gmc]

March /matʃ/, *n.* the third month of the year, containing 31 days. [ME, from AF, from L *Martius*, lit., month of Mars]

march fly, *n.* a fly which sucks the blood of mammals and gives a painful bite; horsefly.

marchioness /maʃə'nɛs/, *n.* the wife or widow of a marquis. [ML]

Marconi /ma'koʊni/, *n.* **Guglielmo** /ɡu'ljɛlmoʊ/, 1874-1937, Italian inventor of the first successful wireless telegraph.

Marco Polo /ˌmakoʊ 'poʊloʊ/, *n.* → Marco **Polo.**

Marcos /'makɒs/, *n.* **Ferdinand Edrilan,** 1917-89, Filippino politician; president of the Philippines 1965-86.

Marcus Aurelius /makəs ɔ'reɪliəs/, *n.* (*Marcus Aurelius Antoninus*) AD 121-180, emperor of Rome AD 161-180; Stoic philosopher and writer.

Marcuse /ma'kjuːs/, *n.* **Herbert,** 1898-1979, US sociologist and political philosopher, born in Germany. **—Marcusian,** *adj. n.*

Mardi gras /'mɑdi gra/, *n.* **1.** Shrove Tuesday; the last day before Lent which is celebrated with special carnival festivities. **2.** (*also l.c.*) a festive carnival on any date. [F: meat-eating Tuesday]

mare /mɛə/, *n.* a female horse, fully grown and past its fourth birthday. [OE *mere, myre* fem. of *mearh* horse]

Mareeba /mə'ribə/, *n.* a town in northern Qld, on the Barron River; tobacco farming. Pop. 6614 (1986).

mare's-nest /'mɛəz-nɛst/, *n.* something imagined to be an extraordinary discovery but proving not to be real; delusion; hoax.

margarine /madʒə'rin, mag-, 'madʒərən/, *n.* a butter-like product made from vegetable or animal oils, etc. [F, from Gk: white of pearl]

margin /'madʒən/, *n.* **1.** an edge; border. **2.** the space beside the writing on a page. **3.** a limit, or a condition, etc., beyond which something ceases to exist or be possible: *the margin of understanding.* **4.** an amount allowed beyond what is actually necessary: *a margin of error.* **5.** *Finance.* an amount of money (security), left with a broker to provide against loss in business dealings. **6.** *Comm.* the difference between the cost of a product and the amount for which it is sold. **7.** *Econ.* the point at which the return barely covers the cost of production, and below which production is unprofitable. **8.** that part of a wage, added to the basic wage, offered because of the employee's particular skills. **9.** an allowance made as a safety precaution: *a margin of safety.* [ME, from L: border, edge]

marginal /'madʒənəl/, *adj.* **1.** relating to a margin. **2.** situated on the edge or border. **3.** written in the margin of a page: *a marginal note.* **4.** barely enough; slight. **5.** *Econ.* **a.** supplying goods at a rate just covering the cost of production. **b.** of or relating to goods produced and marketed at margin: *marginal profits.* **6.** of or relating to an electoral division in which the outcome of voting is likely to result in victory only by a small amount. **7.** of or relating to the rate at which the margin (def. 8) is paid. [L: margin]

marguerite /magəˈrit/, *n.* a flower of the daisy family. [F: daisy, pearl, from L: pearl]

Marianne /mariˈan/, *n.* a female figure symbol of the French republic after the Revolution (1789).

Marie Antoinette /ˌmari ɒntwəˈnɛt/, *n.* 1755–93, queen of France 1774–93; wife of Louis XVI and daughter of Maria Theresa; unpopular with the French people and executed in the French Revolution.

marigold /'mærɪgoʊld/, *n.* any of the various chiefly golden-flowered plants with strong-scented leaves. [ME, from MARY (the Virgin) + GOLD]

marijuana /mærəˈwanə/, *n.* **1.** the Indian hemp plant. **2.** its dried leaves and flowers, used in cigarettes and food as a drug. Also, **marihuana.** See **cannabis.** [Amer Sp]

marimba /məˈrɪmbə/, *n.* a musical instrument, formed of strips of wood of various sizes struck by hammers or sticks. [EAfrican lang.]

marina /məˈrinə/, *n.* a boat basin (def. 4) with a dock and other services for small craft. [It and Sp: of the sea]

marinade /mærəˈneɪd/, *n.;* /'mærəneɪd/, *v.,* **-naded, -nading.** ◇*n.* **1.** a liquid, e.g. wine mixed with oil and seasonings, in which meat, etc., may be soaked before cooking. **2.** a liquid, e.g. brandy, in which fruits, etc., may be soaked before serving. ◇*v.t.* **3.** → **marinate.** [F: pickle in brine]

marinate /'mærəneɪt/, *v.t.,* **-nated, -nating.** to let (food) stand in a liquid before cooking or serving in order to give flavor; marinade. [F]

marine /məˈrin/, *adj.* **1.** living in, produced by or relating to the sea. **2.** relating to shipping; nautical; naval; maritime. **3.** serving on shipboard, as soldiers. ◇*n.* **4.** seagoing vessels collectively. **5.** one of a class of naval troops serving both on ship and on land. [ME, from L: of the sea]

mariner /'mærənə/, *n.* **1.** a seaman; sailor. **2.** (*cap.*) any of a number of US space probes which provided information on the planets Mercury, Venus and Mars between 1962 and 1973. [ME, from F]

Marion du Fresne /mariˌɒ̃ dju ˈfreɪn/, *n.* **Nicholas,** died 1772, French explorer in Australian and NZ waters.

marionette /mærɪəˈnɛt/, *n.* a puppet moved by strings fixed to its jointed limbs. [F, from *Marion,* diminutive of *Marie* Mary]

Marist /'marəst, 'mærəst/, *n.* a member of the 'Society of Mary', founded in 1816 for missionary and educational work in the name of the Virgin Mary.

marital /'mærətəl/, *adj.* of or relating to marriage. [L]

maritime /'mærətaɪm/, *adj.* **1.** connected with the sea in relation to shipping, etc.: *maritime law.* **2.** of or relating to the sea. **3.** living near the sea. [L: of the sea]

Maritime Strike, *n.* a strike in 1890 in Australia and NZ, which began with the maritime industry and spread to other industries; important in establishing the ALP and the system of conciliation and arbitration.

marjoram /'madʒərəm/, *n.* a plant of the mint family used in cookery. [ME, from OF, from L]

mark[1] /mak/, *n.* **1.** a visible trace or impression upon anything, as a line, cut, stain, etc.: *a birthmark.* **2.** a badge, brand, or other visible sign. **3.** a sign used in writing or printing: *a punctuation mark.* **4.** a sign, usu. a cross, made by a person unable to write his signature. **5.** a device, sign, label, etc., used to show ownership, origin, quality, etc. **6.** a sign; token; indication. **7.** a symbol used in judging behavior, ability, knowledge, etc., as of pupils in a school. **8.** something used to show position, e.g. a bookmark. **9.** a recognised or required standard: *to be below the mark.* **10.** importance; repute; distinction: *a man of mark.* **11.** a special characteristic. **12.** (*usu. cap.*) a sign for a model of a weapon, motor vehicle, etc., generally used together with a number: *the Mark-4 weapon-carrier.* **13.** a target; goal. **14.** *Athletics.* the starting point in a contest. **15.** *Bowls.* See **jack** (def. 6). **16.** *Rugby.* the place from or behind which a free kick is taken. **17.** *Aust Rules.* the action of catching the ball on the full, after it has travelled not less than nine metres directly from the kick of another player. **18. make one's mark,** to become famous or successful. **19. overstep the mark,** to break the rules. **20. wide of the mark,** incorrect; irrelevant. ◇*v.t.* **21.** to be a special feature of: *The day was marked by rain.* **22.** to put a mark or marks on. **23.** to join or fix to (something) figures or signs showing price, quality, brand name, etc. **24.** to judge and record the quality or correctness of (schoolwork, etc.). **25.** to show or form by marks (oft. fol. by *out*). **26.**

to single out; destine (oft. fol. by *out*). **27.** to record (score, list, etc.). **28.** to give attention to; observe. **29.** *Sport.* to watch and keep close to (an opponent) with the intention of gaining advantage. ◇*v.i.* **30.** to take notice; consider. **31. mark down,** to reduce the price of. **32. mark off,** to separate, as by a line or limit. **33. mark up, a.** to mark with numbers or signs. **b.** to increase the price of. [OE *mearc* boundary, landmark]

mark² /mak/, *n.* **1.** a former silver coin of Germany, until 1924 the monetary unit. **2.** → **deutschmark.** [OE *m(e)arc*]

Mark /mak/, *n. Bible.* **1.** one of the 12 apostles, traditionally considered the author of the second Gospel. **2.** the second Gospel, in the New Testament. [L: *Marcus*]

marked /makt/, *adj.* **1.** strikingly noticeable; conspicuous: *with marked success.* **2.** *Linguistics.* (of a phonetic or syntactic unit) abnormal. **3.** watched, so as to find fault or lay blame: *a marked man.* **4.** having a mark or marks.

marker /'makə/, *n.* **1.** someone who marks (examinations, scores, etc.). **2.** something used as a mark, e.g. a bookmark, etc.

market /'makət/, *n.* **1.** a meeting of people for selling and buying. **2.** an open space or a covered building where such meetings are held. **3.** store for the sale of food. **4.** trade or traffic, esp. as regards a particular commodity. **5.** (the field of business of) a body of persons trading in a particular commodity: *the cotton market.* **6.** demand for a commodity: *a good market for leather.* **7.** an area where anything is or may be sold: *the foreign market.* **8.** present price or value: *a rising market.* **9. in the market for,** ready to buy. **10. on the market,** for sale; available. **11. play the market,** to buy and sell on the stock exchange. ◇*v.i.* **12.** to deal (buy or sell) in a market. ◇*v.t.* **13.** to carry or send to market for sale. **14.** to sell. [ME and late OE, from L: trading, traffic, market] – **marketable,** *adj.*

market economy, *n.* an economic structure in which the movement of resources is achieved by the interacting decisions of persons supplying and demanding those resources rather than by the decisions of a government, etc.

marketeer /makə'tɪə/, *n.* someone active in or supporting a particular market: *black marketeer.*

market garden, *n.* a garden or small area where vegetables and fruit are grown for sale. – **market gardener,** *n.*

marksman /'maksmən/, *n., pl.* -**men.** one skilled in shooting at a mark. – **marksmanship,** *n.* – **markswoman,** *n. fem.*

marl¹ /mal/, *n.* **1.** a soil consisting of clay and calcium carbonate, used esp. as a fertiliser. **2.** impure limestones. ◇*v.t.* **3.** to fertilise with marl. [ME, from OF, from L]

marl² /mal/, *n.* See **bandicoot.** [Aboriginal]

Marlborough Province /,malbərə, -brə, ,mɔl- 'prɒvəns/, *n.* a province in the north-eastern part of the South Island, NZ. About 10 930 km².

Marley /'mali/, *n.* **Bob** (*Robert Nesta Marley*), 1945–80, Jamaican singer and composer; leading exponent of reggae music, with his band, the Wailers.

marlin /'malən/, *n.* a type of large, powerful, game-fish having the upper jaw lengthened into a rounded spear, for a **striped marlin,** found seasonally in coastal waters off eastern Australia.

marlinespike /'malənspaɪk/, *n.* a pointed metal tool used for separating the strands of rope in splicing, etc. [D: tie, cord]

marlock /'malɒk/, *n.* a type of medium-height gum tree, with thick, narrow leaves and horn-shaped buds, found in south-western Australia.

Marlowe /'maloʊ/, *n.* **Christopher** 1564–93, English dramatist and poet; his plays include *Doctor Faustus* (1604) and *Edward II* (c. 1592).

marmalade /'maməleɪd/, *n.* a jelly-like jam containing small pieces of fruit (usu. citrus). [ME, from F, from Pg: quince, from L, from Gk: honey apple]

marmoreal /ma'mɔrɪəl/, *adj.* of or like marble. Also, **marmorean.** [L]

marmoset /'maməset/, *n.* a small, squirrel-like South and Central American monkey with soft fur and a long non-grasping tail. [ME, from OF: grotesque little figure]

marmot /'mamət/, *n.* a bushy-tailed, thickset rodent. [F, from L: mouse of the mountains]

Maroochydore /mə'rutʃɪdɔ/, *n.* a holiday resort in south-eastern Qld, at the mouth of the Maroochy River. Pop. (with Mooloolaba) 20 635 (1986). [Aboriginal: *marutchi-dora* water where the black swan lives]

maroon¹ /mə'run, mə'run/, *n.* **1.** a dark brownish red. **2.** a firework exploding with a loud noise, esp. one used as a warning signal. ◇*adj.* **3.** of a dark brownish red color. [F, from It: chestnut]

maroon² /mə'run/, *v.t.* **1.** to put ashore and leave on a deserted island or coast as punishment. **2.** to place apart as if on a deserted island. [F]

marquee /ma'ki/, *n.* a large tent used for entertainment, etc. [assumed sing. of MARQUISE taken as pl.]

marquis /'makwəs, ma'ki/, *n.* a nobleman ranking below a duke and above an earl or count. Also, **marquess.** [OF]

marquise /ma'kiz/, *n.* **1.** the wife of a marquis. **2.** *Gems.* a common shape for a cut diamond, the pointed oval. [F, fem. of MARQUIS]

Marrakech /'mærəkɛʃ/, *n.* a city in western Morocco, former capital at various times. Pop. 439 728 (1982). Also, **Marrakesh.**

marram grass /'mærəm gras/, *n.* a tough grass with creeping stems and stiff leaves, common in coastal sand-dunes.

marri /'mæri/, *n.* a gum tree, native to WA which is widely grown for its colored flowers.

marriage /'mærɪdʒ/, *n.* **1.** the legal union of a man with a woman for life; wedlock. **2.** the legal or religious ceremony of marriage. **3.** any close union: *a marriage of ideas.* [ME, from OF] – **marriageable**, *adj.*

marriage celebrant, *n.* a person authorised to perform a marriage, esp. in a civil service.

marron /'mærɒn/, *n.* a large freshwater crayfish of WA. [Aboriginal]

marrow /'mæroʊ/, *n.* **1.** the soft, fatty vascular tissue in the cavities of bones. **2.** the inmost or necessary part. **3.** strength; vitality. **4.** a large vegetable with skin color ranging from white to yellow or green, widely used as food; vegetable marrow. [OE *mearg*]

marrowbone /'mæroʊboʊn/, *n.* a bone containing marrow that can be eaten.

marry /'mæri/, *v.*, **-ried, -rying.** ◊*v.t.* **1.** to take in marriage. **2.** to unite as husband and wife. **3.** to give in marriage. **4.** to unite closely. ◊*v.i.* **5.** to take a husband or wife; wed. [ME, from F, from L: wed]

Mars /maz/, *n.* **1.** *Rom Myth.* the god of war; Greek counterpart, Ares. **2.** *Astron.* the planet next outside the earth, fourth in order from the sun.

Marsden /'mazdən/, *n.* **Samuel,** 1764–1838, Australian clergyman, magistrate and grazier, born in England; a noted opponent of Governor Macquarie.

Marseilles /ma'seɪ/, *n.* a seaport in southeastern France, the capital of Bouches-du-Rhône department. Pop. 1 110 511 (1982). French, **Marseille.**

marsh /maʃ/, *n.* an area of low, wet land; swamp. [OE *mere* pool + *-isc* -ISH¹] – **marshy**, *adj.* – **marshland**, *n.*

Marsh /maʃ/, *n.* **Rodney,** born 1947, Australian cricketer, noted wicketkeeper.

marshal /'maʃəl/, *n., v.,* **-shalled, -shalling.** ◊*n.* **1.** an officer of the highest rank in the armed forces. See Appendix. **2.** the title of various officials having certain police duties. **3.** a high officer of a royal household. **4.** a person who arranges or runs ceremonies, races, etc. ◊*v.t.* **5.** to arrange in proper order. **6.** to organise for battle, etc. **7.** to lead. [ME, from OF, from VL: groom, from Gmc] – **marshalcy, marshalship**, *n.* – **marshaller**, *n.*

Marshall /'maʃəl/, *n.* **Alan,** 1902–84, Australian novelist and short-story writer; well-known for his autobiographical trilogy, including *I Can Jump Puddles* (1955).

Marshall Plan, *n.* a plan for aiding the economic recovery of European countries after World War II, originated by George C Marshall, US secretary of state, in 1947. Later called **European Recovery Program.** Also, **Marshall Aid.**

marsh gas, *n.* a gas made by the decomposition of organic matter, consisting largely of methane.

marshmallow /'maʃmæloʊ, -mɛl-/, *n.* a soft sticky sweet made from gelatine, sugar and flavoring. [OE *merscmealwe*]

marsupial /ma'supiəl, -'sjup-/, *n.* **1.** an order of Australian and South and Central American mammals whose young are carried and fed (usu. in a pouch) on the mother's abdomen for some months after birth. Marsupials bear live young, but do not have a placenta. ◊*adj.* **2.** of or relating to marsupials. [L. See MARSUPIUM]

marsupial cat, *n.* → **native cat.**

marsupial mole, *n.* a small, Australian burrowing marsupial found in dry areas.

marsupial mouse, *n.* any of various small Australian marsupials looking rather like mice or rats, e.g. the **dunnart,** with soft fur, insect-eating, and found throughout Australia, the **antechinus,** with bristly fur, found in various, usu. woodland, parts of Australia, the **mulgara,** a meat-eating, burrowing animal of dry inland Australia, and the **kowari,** with a brushy tail, of central Australia, and thought to be related to the native cat. See **jerboa** (def. 1).

marsupium /ma'supiəm, -sjup-/, *n., pl.* **-pia** /-piə/. **1.** the pouch or fold of skin on the abdomen of a female marsupial which provides food and shelter for the developing young. **2.** a structure in certain other animals for enclosing eggs or young. [L: pouch, from Gk]

mart /mat/, *n.* **1.** a market; trading centre. **2.** a shop. [D]

marten /'matn/, *n., pl.* **-tens,** (*esp. collectively*) **-ten.** a small furry mammal of northern US and Canada. [ME, from OF, from Gmc]

Martens /'matənz/, *n.* **Conrad,** 1801–78, Australian landscape painter, born in London; topographer on the *Beagle* with Charles Darwin.

Martha /'maθə/, *n. Bible.* the sister of Lazarus, whose house in Bethany Jesus often visited. [See Luke 10:38–42; John 11:1–44]

martial /'maʃəl/, *adj.* **1.** warlike; brave. **2.** connected with the army and navy. **3.** relating to war: *martial music.* **4.** characteristic of a warrior: *a martial stride.* [ME, from L: of Mars]

martial arts, *n.pl.* the several forms of unarmed self-defence originating in China, Korea and Japan, as judo, kung-fu, etc.

martial law, *n.* law placed upon an area by military forces when the civil authority has broken down.

Martian /'maʃən/, *n.* a supposed inhabitant of the planet Mars.

martin /'matn/, *n.* any of various small, insect-eating birds, related to the swallow. [late ME, from *Martin* man's name]

martinet /matə'nɛt/, *n.* someone who strongly enforces rules. [from General *Martinet,* French drillmaster of the reign of Louis XIV]

martini /ma'tini/, *n.* a cocktail, mostly of gin, with vermouth. [from *Martini* and Rossi, Italian winemakers]

martyr /'matə/, *n.* **1.** someone who is put to death or suffers greatly for a belief, principle, or cause. **2.** someone undergoing severe or continuous suffering. **3.** someone who goes to

martyr

great trouble for others, in order to feel self-righteous and to receive pity. ◇v.t. **4.** to put to death as a martyr. **5.** to make a martyr of. **6.** to torment or torture. [OE *martyr*, from L, from Gk: witness] —**martyrdom**, *n.*

marvel /'mavəl/, *n., v.*, **-velled, -velling.** ◇n. **1.** a wonderful thing. ◇v.t. **2.** to wonder at (usu. fol. by a clause as object). ◇v.i. **3.** to be filled with wonder. [ME, from F, from L: wonderful things]

Marvell /maval/, *n.* **Andrew,** 1621-78, English poet, satirist and parliamentarian.

marvellous /'mavələs/, *adj.* **1.** wonderful; surprising; extraordinary. **2.** excellent; superb. **3.** unbelievable.

Marx /maks/, *n.* **Karl** 1818-83, German founder of Marxism; produced much of the theory of modern socialism and communism with Friedrich Engels; outlined in *The Communist Manifesto* (1848). *Das Kapital* (1867; 1885; 1895) contains his theory of class struggle and the economics of capitalism. —**Marxian**, *adj.*

Marx Brothers, *n.* **the,** US family of vaudeville and film comedians including **Harpo Marx** (*Arthur*) 1893-1964, **Zeppo Marx** (*Herbert*) 1901-79, **Groucho Marx** (*Julius*) 1895-1977, and **Chico Marx** (*Leonard*) 1891-1961. Their films include *Animal Crackers* (1930) and *Duck Soup* (1933).

Marxism /'maksızəm/, *n.* the system of thought developed by Karl Marx, esp. the doctrine that the state throughout history has been a device for the exploitation of the masses by a dominant class, that class struggle has been the main agency of historical change, and that the capitalist state contained from the first the 'seeds of its own decay' and will inevitably, after a transitional period known as 'the dictatorship of the proletariat', be followed by a socialist order and a classless society. [named after Karl MARX] —**Marxist**, *n., adj.*

Mary /'meəri/, *n.* the mother of Jesus, often called the **Virgin Mary** or **Saint Mary.** [ME *Marie*, OE *Maria*, from L, from Gk, from Heb *Miryām*]

Mary I, *n.* ('Bloody Mary'), 1516-58, queen of England 1553-58, and wife of Philip II of Spain; the epithet '*Bloody*' arose from the executions of Protestants during her reign which saw the restoration of Roman Catholicism in England. Also, **Mary Tudor.**

Maryborough /'merəbərə/, *n.* a city in south-eastern Qld, south of Bundaberg; major industrial area. Pop. 20 177 (1986).

Mary Kathleen /,meəri 'kæθlin/, *n.* a district in north-western Qld, near Mount Isa; former mining township and location of the largest known deposit of uranium in Australia.

Maryland /'meərilænd, 'merələnd/, *n.* a state in the eastern US, on the Atlantic coast. Pop. 4 463 000 (1986 est.); 27 392 km². *Cap.:* Annapolis. *Abbrev.:* Md

Mary Magdalene /,meəri 'mægdəlin/, *n.* Mary of Magdala, mentioned in Luke 8:2, and traditionally identified with the repentant woman in Luke 7:37-50.

Mason-Dixon line

Mary Stuart /,meəri 'stjuət/, *n.* 1542-87, queen of Scotland 1542-67; beheaded for plotting to assassinate her cousin, Queen Elizabeth of England. Also, **Mary, Queen of Scots.**

marzipan /'mazəpæn/, *n.* a paste-like sweet made of almonds. [G]

Masai /'mæsaɪ, ma'saɪ/, *n., pl.* **-sais,** (*esp. collectively*) **-sai. 1.** a member of an African people inhabiting the grasslands of Kenya and Tanzania. ◇*adj.* **2.** of or relating to this people or their language.

masc., *Abbrev.* masculine.

mascara /mæs'karə/, *n.* a substance used to color the eyelashes. [Sp: a mask]

mascot /'mæskɒt/, *n.* a person, animal, or thing supposed to bring good luck. [F, from Pr: witch; of Gmc orig.]

masculine /'mæskjələn/, *adj.* **1.** having manlike qualities; manly: *a masculine voice.* **2.** relating to or characteristic of a man: *masculine clothes.* **3.** *Gram.* of or relating to the gender to which males, and things classified by convention as masculine, belong. **4.** (of rhyming words) having the final syllable stressed as in *defend, pretend.* **5.** (of a woman) mannish. ◇*n.* **6.** *Gram.* the masculine gender. **7.** a noun or another element marking that gender. [ME, from L *masculinus* male] —**masculinity**, *n.*

Masefield /'meɪsfild/, *n.* **John,** 1878-1967, English poet, dramatist, and novelist; poet laureate from 1930 until his death.

mash /mæʃ/, *n.* **1.** a soft mass. **2.** a soft condition. **3.** a mixture of boiled grain, bran, etc., fed warm to horses and cattle. ◇*v.t.* **4.** to crush. **5.** to reduce to a soft mass, as by heating or pressure. **6.** to mix (crushed malt, etc.) with hot water. [OE *māsc-* (in compounds)]

mask /mask/, *n.* **1.** a covering for the face, esp. one worn to change the appearance. **2.** anything that hides or alters; disguise; pretence. **3.** a likeness of a face, as one moulded in plaster after death. **4.** a likeness of a face or head, often ugly, used as an ornament. **5.** a covering of wire, gauze, tinted glass, cloth, etc., to protect the face, as from dust, smoke, glare, etc. **6.** → **gasmask. 7.** any of various devices, used by skin-divers to protect the face. ◇*v.t.* **8.** to hide; disguise. **9.** to cover with a mask. ◇*v.i.* **10.** to put on a mask; disguise oneself. [F, from It, from LL]

masochism /'mæsəkızəm/, *n.* **1.** a condition in which sexual satisfaction depends on suffering. **2.** a condition in which one looks for and sometimes takes pleasure from suffering. [named after Leopold von Sacher *Masoch*, 1836-95, Austrian novelist, who described it] —**masochist**, *n.* —**masochistic**, *adj.*

mason /'meɪsən/, *n.* **1.** one who builds or works with stone. **2.** (*oft. cap.*) → **Freemason.** [ME, from OF, from LL: beat; of Gmc orig.] —**masonry**, *n.*

Mason-Dixon line /meɪsən-'dɪksən/, *n.* the boundary between Pennsylvania and Maryland, partly surveyed by Charles Mason and Jeremiah Dixon between 1763 and 1767, popularly considered before the abolition of slavery as a line of demarcation between the free and slave states. Also, **Mason and Dixon's line**.

masonic /mə'sɒnɪk/, *adj.* (*oft. cap.*) relating to or characteristic of Freemasons or Freemasonry.

masonite /'meɪsənaɪt/, *n.* a type of woodfibre material, pressed in sheets. [Trademark]

masonry /'meɪsənri/, *n., pl.* **-ries. 1.** the art or work of a mason. **2.** (*oft. cap.*) → **freemasonry**.

masquerade /mæskə'reɪd, mɑs-/, *n., v.*, **-raded, -rading.** ◇*n.* **1.** a gathering of persons wearing masks and often fantastic costumes, for dancing, etc. **2.** a false outward show; disguise. ◇*v.i.* **3.** to go about with a false character. **4.** to change oneself, as with a mask. **5.** to take part in a masquerade. [F, from It: mask] – **masquerader**, *n.*

mass[1] /mæs/, *n.* **1.** a body of matter, usu. of indefinite shape and size: *a mass of snow*. **2.** a grouping of separate particles, parts, or objects regarded as forming one body: *a mass of sand*. **3.** a large group, number, or quantity: *a mass of errors*. **4.** an area, as of color, light, or shade in a painting. **5.** the main body; bulk: *the great mass of Australian products*. **6.** size; bulk. **7.** *Phys.* that property of a body, sometimes described as the amount of matter in it, equal to the weight of the body (gravitational mass) or to the force acting on it divided by its acceleration (inertial mass). **8. the masses,** the great body of the common people. ◇*v.i.* **9.** to come together in or form a mass: *the clouds are massing in the west*. ◇*v.t.* **10.** to gather into a mass; assemble: *to mass troops*. [ME, from L *massa* mass, lump]

mass[2] /mæs/, *n.* **1.** *Relig.* the celebration of the Eucharist. See **high mass. 2.** a musical setting of certain parts of this service. Also, **Mass**. [OE *mæsse*, from L]

Massachusetts /mæsə'tʃusəts/, *n.* a state in the north-eastern US, on the Atlantic coast. 5 832 000 (1986 est.); 21 384 km². *Cap.*: Boston. *Abbrev.*: Mass

massacre /'mæsəkə/, *n., v.*, **-cred, -cring.** ◇*n.* **1.** the unnecessary and merciless killing of a (large) number of people. ◇*v.t.* **2.** to kill unnecessarily or in a massacre. [F, from OF: to butcher]

massage /'mæsɑʒ, 'mæsɑdʒ/, *n., v.*, **-saged, -saging.** ◇*n.* **1.** the act or art of treating the body by rubbing, pressing, or the like, to improve health. ◇*v.t.* **2.** to treat by massage. [F: knead] – **massager, massagist,** *n.*, – **massageuse,** *n. fem.*

mass defect, *n.* the difference between the mass of a nucleus and the total mass of its protons and neutrons, being equal to the amount of energy needed to split the nucleus into its parts.

mass-energy equation, *n.* a formula derived from the theory that mass and energy are connected and equivalent. It states that the energy of a high-speed particle is equal to its mass times the square of the velocity of light (E = mc²).

masseur /mæ'sɜ/, *n.* a man who practises massage. [F] – **masseuse,** *n. fem.*

Massey /'mæsi/, *n.* **William Ferguson,** 1856–1925, NZ politician; born in Ireland; prime minister 1912–25.

massif /'mæsɪf/, *n.* a compact part of a mountain range, containing one or more summits. [F: massive]

Massif Central /,masif sõ'tral/, *n.* a plateau region in southern central France. About 93 230 km². Highest peak, Puy de Sancy, 1886 m.

massive /'mæsɪv/, *adj.* **1.** consisting of or forming a large mass. **2.** large, in size or amount. **3.** solid; substantial; great. **4.** *Mineral.* without outward crystal form. **5.** *Geol.* → **homogeneous**. [ME, from F] – **massiveness,** *n.*

mass media, *n.* the means of communication, as radio, television, newspapers, magazines, etc., that reach large numbers of people. Also, **the media.**

mass-produce /mæs-prə'djus/, *v.t.*, **-duced, -ducing.** to manufacture in large quantities by machine processes. – **mass-production,** *n.*

mass spectrometer, *n.* an apparatus for separating atoms or molecules of different masses by using the fact that ions of such substances are deflected in a magnetic field by an amount which depends on the mass. Also, **mass spectroscope.**

mast /mɑst/, *n.* **1.** a tall pole rising from the deck of a boat, supporting the sails, etc. **2.** any upright pole, as a support for an aerial, etc. [OE *mæst*] – **mastlike,** *adj.*

mast-, variant of **masto-,** before vowels, as in *mastectomy*.

mastectomy /mæs'tɛktəmi/, *n., pl.* **-mies.** the operation of removing the breast. [MAST- + -ECTOMY]

master /'mɑstə/, *n.* **1.** someone who has control over or use of something: *a master of several languages*. **2.** an employer of workmen or servants. **3.** Also, **master mariner.** the commander of a merchantman. **4.** the male head of a household. **5.** the owner of a slave, horse, dog, etc. **6.** a male teacher. **7.** a person whose teachings one accepts or follows. **8.** a winner; victor. **9.** a workman qualified to teach apprentices and to carry on his trade alone: *master builder*. **10.** a person highly skilled in something, as a job, art, or science. **11.** (someone holding) a title given to a bridge or chess player who has won or been placed high in official international contests. **12.** *Educ.* someone who has a master's degree. **13.** a boy or young man (used mainly as a term of address). **14.** a title given to the head of a college at certain universities. **15.** the head teacher in a particular subject department in a secondary school: *the history master*. **16.** the original tape of a recording. **17. master and servant,** *Law.* the relationship which exists when the master or employer has the right to tell the servant or

master 644 **materialism**

employee what to do, and to control how he does it; a master is liable for a tort (non-criminal offence) committed by his employee in the course of his employment. ◇*adj.* **18.** being master. **19.** chief; principal: *the master bedroom.* **20.** directing; controlling. **21.** dominating; predominant. **22.** being a master qualified to carry on a trade. **23.** being a master of some job, skill, art, etc. ◇*v.t.* **24.** to control; conquer. **25.** to rule as a master. **26.** to make oneself master of; to become an expert in. [OE *magister*, from L] **—masterful,** *adj.* **—masterly,** *adj.*

mastermind /'mɑstəmaɪnd/, *v.t.* **1.** to plan and direct activities skilfully. ◇*n.* **2.** someone who creates or organises a particular project, scheme, etc.

master of ceremonies, *n.* someone who directs the entertainment at a party, dinner, etc.

masterpiece /'mɑstəpis/, *n.* **1.** one's most excellent production: *the masterpiece of a painter.* **2.** any production of masterly skill or excellence.

mastery /'mɑstəri/, *n., pl.* **-ries. 1.** command, control, as of a subject. **2.** victory. **3.** expert skill or knowledge.

masthead /'mɑsthed/, *n.* **1.** the top of the mast of a ship. **2.** a statement printed at the top of the front page of a newspaper, etc., giving the name, owner, etc.

mastic /'mæstɪk/, *n.* **1.** the resin from a small evergreen tree, used in making varnish. **2.** *Bldg Trades.* a preparation used for sealing joints, window frames, etc. [ME, from OF, from L, from Gk]

masticate /'mæstəkeɪt/, *v.t., v.i.,* **-cated, -cating.** to chew. [LL: chewed] **—mastication,** *n.*

mastiff /'mæstɪf/, *n.* one of a breed of large, powerful, short-haired dogs having an apricot, fawn, or brindled coat. [ME, from OF]

mastitis /mæs'taɪtəs/, *n.* **1.** *Pathol.* inflammation of the breast. **2.** *Vet Sci.* inflammation of the udder of cows.

masto-, a word part meaning breast, mastoid. Also, **mast-.** [Gk, combining form of *mastó* breast]

mastoid /'mæstɔɪd/, *adj.* **1.** resembling a breast or nipple. **2.** of the nipple-like process of the temporal bone behind the ear. ◇*n. Anat.* **3.** mastoid process. [Gk: like the breast]

masturbate /'mæstəbeɪt/, *v.i.,* **-bated, -bating.** to engage in masturbation. **—masturbator,** *n.*

masturbation /mæstə'beɪʃən/, *n.* stimulation by rubbing the genitals resulting in orgasm; onanism (def. 2). [L]

mat /mæt/, *n., v.,* **matted, matting.** ◇*n.* **1.** a piece of fabric of rushes, straw, etc., used to cover a floor. **2.** a small piece of material, set under a dish of food, lamp, etc. **3.** a thick floor covering, as of padded canvas, for wrestling, etc. **4.** a thick and tangled mass. **5. put on the mat,** to scold. ◇*v.t.* **6.** to

scold. ◇*v.i.* **7.** to become entangled. [OE *meatt(e)*, from LL]

matador /'mætədɔ/, *n.* the bullfighter who kills the bull in a bullfight. [Sp, from L: slayer]

Mata Hari /mætə 'hɑri/, *n.* (*Gertrud Margareta Zelle*), 1876–1917, Dutch dancer in France; executed as a spy by the French.

match¹ /mætʃ/, *n.* **1.** a short, thin piece of wood, etc., tipped with a chemical substance which produces fire when rubbed on a rough surface. **2.** a cord, or the like, which burns at an even rate, used to fire cannon, etc. [ME, from OF]

match² /mætʃ/, *n.* **1.** a person or thing that equals or looks like another in some way. **2.** a person or thing that is an exact copy of another; pair. **3.** someone able to handle another as an equal. **4.** a contest; game. **5.** a person suitable as a partner in marriage. **6.** a marriage arrangement. ◇*v.t.* **7.** to equal, or be equal to. **8.** to be the match of. **9.** to make similar to; adapt. **10.** to fit together. **11.** to produce an equal to: *I will match your offer.* **12.** to place in opposition. **13.** to provide with a competitor of equal power. **14.** to prove a match for. **15.** to unite in marriage. ◇*v.i.* **16.** to be equal. **17.** to be similar in size, shape, etc. [OE *gemæcca* mate, fellow] **—matchable,** *adj.* **—matcher,** *n.*

matchmaker /'mætʃmeɪkə/, *n.* someone who matches partners in marriage. **—matchmaking,** *n., adj.*

matchwood /'mætʃwʊd/, *n.* **1.** wood suitable for matches. **2.** tiny pieces; splinters.

mate /meɪt/, *n., v.,* **mated, mating.** ◇*n.* **1.** one of any pair. **2.** a husband or wife. **3.** one of a pair of mated animals. **4.** *Colloq.* **a.** a friend; comrade. **b.** (a form of address): *How are you going, mate?* **5.** an officer of a merchant ship who ranks below the captain. **6.** an assistant to a tradesman. **7. be mates with,** to be good friends with. ◇*v.t., v.i.* **8.** to join or associate as a mate or as mates. **9.** to marry. **10.** to pair, as animals. [ME, from MLG, var. of *gemate*]

material /mə'tɪəriəl/, *n.* **1.** the substance of which a thing is made. **2.** anything serving as raw matter for working upon. **3.** a person showing likely ability in a skill or job. **4.** information, ideas, for future use. **5.** cloth; fabric. **6.** (*pl.*) articles needed for making or doing something: *writing materials.* ◇*adj.* **7.** physical; corporeal. **8.** relating to or concerned with matter: *material force.* **9.** over-concerned with material things or interests. **10.** relating to the physical rather than the spiritual or intellectual. **11.** of importance. **12.** necessary; pertinent (fol. by *to*). [ME, from LL: matter]

materialise or **materialize** /mə'tɪəriəlaɪz/, *v.,* **-lised, -lising.** ◇*v.t.* **1.** to give material form to. **2.** to take on material qualities. ◇*v.i.* **3.** to assume bodily form. **4.** to appear. **—materialisation,** *n.*

materialism /mə'tɪəriəlɪzəm/, *n.* **1.** *Philos.* the theory which places all things in the universe in a material framework. **2.** concern for material rather than spiritual objects, needs, etc. **—materialist,** *n.*

materially /mə'tɪərɪəlɪ/, *adv.* **1.** to an important degree; considerably. **2.** with reference to matter; physically.

maternal /mə'tɜnəl/, *adj.* **1.** of or relating to, having the qualities of, or being a mother. **2.** coming from a mother. **3.** related through a mother: *his maternal aunt.* [ME, from L: of a mother]

maternity /mə'tɜnətɪ/, *adj., n.* (belonging to or characteristic of) motherhood.

mateship /'meɪtʃɪp/, *n.* **1.** the quality or state of being a friend. **2.** a form of conduct among men stressing equality and friendship.

matey /'meɪtɪ/, *Colloq.* ◇*adj.* **1.** friendly. ◇*n.* **2.** (a form of address) comrade; chum.

math., *Abbrev.* mathematical.

mathematical /mæθə'mætɪkəl/, *adj.* **1.** of, relating to, or of the nature of mathematics. **2.** used in the operations of mathematics. **3.** having the exactness of mathematics. Also, **mathematic**.

mathematics /mæθə'mætɪks/, *n.* the science dealing with the measurement, properties, and relations of quantities, including arithmetic, geometry, algebra, etc. [pl. of *mathematic*, from L, from Gk: pertaining to science] —**mathematician**, *n.*

maths /mæθs/, *n.* →**mathematics**.

Mathura /mʌ'θuərə/, *n.* a city in India, in western Uttar Pradesh: Hindu shrine and holy city; reputed birthplace of Krishna. Pop. 147 493 (1978). Formerly, **Muttra**.

matilda /mə'tɪldə/, *n. Colloq.* a swag. [see WALTZ[2]]

matinee /'mætəneɪ/, *n.* an entertainment held in the daytime, usu. in the afternoon. Also, **matinée**. [F. See MATINS]

matins /'mætn/, *n.* **1.** *Church.* **a.** the first of seven canonical hours, or the service for it, properly beginning at midnight, sometimes at daybreak. **b.** the order for public morning prayer in the Anglican Church. [ME, from OF *matin* morning, from L]

Matisse /ma'tis/, *n.* **Henri** /ɒ̃'ri/, 1869–1954 French painter and sculptor; with fellow painters formed the Fauve group.

matri-, a word part meaning 'mother'. [L, combining form of *māter*]

matriarch /'meɪtrɪak, 'mæt-/, *n.* **1.** a woman holding a position of leadership in a family or tribe. **2.** a woman who dominates any group or field of activity. —**matriarchal**, **matriarchic**, *adj.*

matriarchy /'meɪtrɪakɪ, 'mæt-/, *n., pl.* **-chies.** a form of social organisation, in which the mother is the head of the family, and descent is reckoned through the female line.

matrices /'meɪtrəsiz/, *n.* plural form of **matrix**.

matriculate /mə'trɪkjəleɪt/, *v.,* **-lated, -lating.** ◇*v.i.* **1.** to be admitted to membership, esp. of a university or the like. **2.** to pass matriculation (def. 2). ◇*v.t.* **3.** to enrol. [LL: public register, roll] —**matriculant**, *n.* —**matriculator**, *n.*

matriculation /mətrɪkjə'leɪʃən/, *n.* **1.** the process of being admitted to certain universities, or tertiary institutions. **2.** a secondary school examination which must be passed before admission to a tertiary institution.

matrilineal /mætrə'lɪnɪəl/, *adj.* of, relating to, or founded on the recognition of kinship and descent through the female line. Also, **matrilinear.** —**matriline**, *n.*

matrimony /'mætrəmənɪ/, *n., pl.* **-nies.** the rite, ceremony, or sacrament of marriage. [ME, from L: marriage] —**matrimonial**, *adj.*

matrix /'meɪtrɪks/, *n., pl.* **matrices** /'meɪtrəsiz/, **matrixes**. **1.** that which gives origin or form to a thing. **2.** *Biol.* the intercellular substance of a tissue. **3.** the rock in which a crystallised mineral is embedded. **4.** *Print.* a mould for casting. **5.** a positive or negative copy of an original disc recording, used in reproducing other copies. **6.** in a punching machine, a perforated block upon which the object to be punched is rested. **7.** *Maths, Computers.* a rectangular array of numbers. **8.** *Computers.* a rectangular array of logical elements acting as a selection system. **9.** *Geol.* the material of smaller grainsize in a sedimentary rock containing material of two separate grainsizes. [L: breeding animal, LL: womb, source]

matron /'meɪtrən/, *n.* **1.** a married woman, esp. one of middle age and sedate character. **2.** a woman in charge of domestic arrangements in a school, hospital, prison, etc. **3.** the former name of a **director of nursing**. [ME, from OF, from L: married woman] —**matronage**, *n.* —**matronal**, *adj.*

matt /mæt/, *adj.* **1.** not shiny; dull in surface. ◇*n.* **2.** a dull surface, without shine. **3.** a tool, as a punch, for producing such a surface. ◇*v.t.* **4.** to finish with a matt surface. Also, **mat**. [F, *mat* dead]

Matt, *Bible. Abbrev.* Matthew.

matted /'mætəd/, *adj.* **1.** having a thick growth or a tangled mass. **2.** formed of or covered with mats or matting.

matter /'mætə/, *n.* **1.** the substance of which physical objects are made. **2.** physical substance in general (solid, liquid, or gaseous). **3.** whatever occupies space. **4.** a particular kind of substance: *coloring matter.* **5.** a substance from a living body, esp. pus. **6.** ideas or arguments in a book, etc., as separate from the form. **7.** a thing, affair, or business: *a matter of life and death.* **8.** an amount; limit: *a matter of ten kilometres.* **9.** something of importance: *It is no matter.* **10.** the trouble; difficulty (prec. by *the*): *There is nothing the matter.* **11.** a reason; cause. **12.** *Print.* **a.** a copy. **b.** the type set up. **13. as a matter of fact**, actually. **14. for that matter**, as far as that is concerned. **15. matter of course**, a logical and certain outcome of events. ◇*v.i.* **16.** to be of importance: *It matters little.* [ME, from OF, from L: stuff, material]

Matterhorn /'mætəhɔn/, *n.* a peak in the Pennine Alps on the Swiss-Italian border. 4504 m. French, **Mont Cervin**.

matter-of-fact /ˌmætər-əv-'fækt/, *adj.* not imaginative; commonplace.

Matthew /'mæθju/, *n. Bible.* **1.** a customs collector at Capernaum summoned to be one of the twelve apostles. **2.** the first Gospel in the New Testament. [See Matthew 9:9–13. F: *Mathieu*, from LL: *Matthaeus*, from Gk: *Matthaîos*, from Heb: *Mattīthyāh*]

matting /'mætɪŋ/, *n.* **1.** a coarse fabric such as grass or straw, used for covering floors, etc. **2.** material for mats.

mattock /'mætək/, *n.* a tool for loosening the soil, shaped like a pickaxe, but having one end broad instead of pointed. [OE *mattuc*]

mattress /'mætrəs/, *n.* a case filled with soft material, as cotton, etc., and often with springs, used as or on a bed. [ME, from OF, from It, from Ar: *mat*, cushion]

maturate /'mætʃəreɪt, -tjʊ-/, *v.i.*, **-rated, -rating. 1.** → **suppurate. 2.** → **mature.** [L: ripened] —**maturative,** *adj.* —**maturation,** *n.*

mature /mə'tjuə/, *adj., v.,* **-tured, -turing.** ◊*adj.* **1.** complete in natural growth or development. **2.** ripe, as fruit. **3.** relating to full mental and emotional development; sensible and reasonable. **4.** *Comm.* having reached the limit of its time, i.e. become due or payable. ◊*v.t., v.i.* **5.** to make or become mature. **6.** to bring or come to full development. [ME, from L: ripe; timely, early] —**maturity,** *n.*

maudlin /'mɔdlən/, *adj.* tearfully or weakly emotional or sentimental. [from *Maudlin,* var. of *Magdalen* (Mary Magdalene), often represented in art as weeping] —**maudlinness,** *n.*

Maugham /mɔm, 'mɔəm/, *n.* **(William) Somerset,** 1874–1965, English novelist, dramatist, and short-story writer; his novel *Of Human Bondage* (1915) is in part a fictionalisation of his own youth.

maul /mɔl/, *n.* **1.** a heavy hammer. **2.** *Rugby Football.* a loose scrum around the ball carrier. ◊*v.t.* **3.** to handle roughly and possibly injure. [var. of MALL] —**mauler,** *n.*

Mau Mau /'maʊ maʊ/, *n.* a political movement among the Kikuyu of Kenya, founded in 1952, aimed by terrorist activities at driving out European settlers.

Mauritius /mə'rɪʃəs/, *n.* a republic, consisting of the island of Mauritius and several other islands, in the Indian Ocean, east of Madagascar; settled mainly from East Africa and India. Pop. 1 040 000 (1987); 2040 km². Languages: English, also French and Creole. Currency: rupee. Cap.: Port Louis. —**Mauritian,** *n., adj.*

mausoleum /ˌmɔsə'liəm, mɔz-/, *n., pl.* **-leums, -lea** /-'liə/. **1.** a stately and magnificent tomb. **2.** *Colloq.* a large unwelcoming building. **3.** (*cap.*) the magnificent tomb of Mausolus (King of Caria) erected at Halicarnassus in Asia Minor in 350 BC. See **Seven Wonders of the World.** [L, from Gk] —**mausolean,** *adj.*

mauve /moʊv/, *n.* **1.** a pale bluish purple. ◊*adj.* **2.** of a mauve color. [F, from L]

maverick /'mævərɪk/, *n.* **1.** an animal found without an owner's brand. **2.** a loner; dissenter. [probably named after Samuel *Maverick,* 1803–70, a Texas (US) cattle-raiser who neglected to brand his cattle]

maw /mɔ/, *n.* the mouth, throat, etc., as involved in eating. [OE *maga*]

mawkish /'mɔkɪʃ/, *adj.* characterised by feelings expressed in a foolish, over-emotional way. [*mawk* maggot (from Scand)]

Mawson[1] /'mɔsən/, *n.* **Sir Douglas,** 1882–1958, Australian explorer, geologist and scientist, born in England; led the Australian Antarctic expedition of 1911–12, and two further cruises to Antarctica between 1929 and 1931.

Mawson[2] /'mɔsən/, *n.* an Australian research station in Antarctica, established in 1954; first permanent Australian base in Antarctica. [named after Sir Douglas MAWSON]

max., *Abbrev.* maximum.

maxi /'mæksi/, *adj., n.* (of or relating to) a full-length dress, skirt, etc., for day wear.

maxilla /mæk'sɪlə/, *n., pl.* **maxillae** /mæk'sɪli/. **1.** the jaw or jawbone, esp. the upper. **2.** one of the paired appendages immediately behind the mandibles of arthropods. [L: jaw] —**maxillary,** *adj.*

maxim /'mæksəm/, *n.* **1.** a short expression, of a general truth, esp. as to conduct. **2.** a principle of conduct. [ME, from OF, from L *maxima (prōpositiō),* lit., greatest (proposition)]

maxima /'mæksəmə/, *n.* a plural form of **maximum.**

maximise or **maximize** /'mæksəmaɪz/, *v.t.,* **-mised, -mising.** to increase to the greatest possible amount or degree. —**maximisation,** *n.*

maximum /'mæksəməm/, *n., pl.* **-ma** /-mə/, **-mums,** *adj.* ◊*n.* **1.** the greatest quantity or amount possible or allowable, etc. (opposed to *minimum*). **2.** *Maths.* a value of a function at a certain point which is greater than any other near that point. ◊*adj.* **3.** greatest possible; highest. **4.** relating to a maximum. [L: the greatest] —**maximal,** *adj.*

may[1] /meɪ/, *auxiliary verb, pres. sing.* and *pl.* **may;** *past sing.* and *pl.* **might;** *old forms* thou **mayest** or **mayst;** with no imperative, infinitive or participle forms. it is used to express: **a.** possibility, opportunity, or permission: *You may enter.* **b.** wish; prayer: *may you live long.* **c.** condition, purpose, result, etc.: *He eats so he may stay healthy.* [OE *mæg,* 1st and 3rd pers. sing. pres. ind. of *magan*]

may[2] /meɪ/, *n.* → **hawthorn.** [from MAY[1]]

May[1] /meɪ/, *n.* **Phil(ip) William,** 1864–1903, English artist and cartoonist in Australia.

May[2] /meɪ/, *n.* the fifth month of the year, containing 31 days. [ME; OE *Maius,* from L]

Maya[1] /'maɪə, 'majə, -jə/, *n.* the Hindu goddess of illusion.

Maya² /ˈmaɪə, ˈmeɪə/, n., pl. **-ya, -yas.** a member of an aboriginal people of Yucatán which had attained a relatively high civilisation in pre-European America. **—Mayan,** n., adj.

maybe /ˈmeɪbi, meɪˈbi/, adv. perhaps. [short for *it may be*]

Mayday /ˈmeɪdeɪ/, n. an international radio telephonic signal for help, used by ships or aircraft. [F; alteration of *m'aider* help me]

May Day, n. the first day of May, long celebrated with various festivities, as the crowning of the May queen, dancing round the maypole, etc., and, in recent years, often marked by labor rallies.

Mayflower /ˈmeɪflaʊə/, n. the ship in which the Pilgrim Fathers sailed from Plymouth to Massachusetts in 1620.

mayhem /ˈmeɪhem/, **1.** any uproar or fight. Also, **maihem. 2. be mayhem,** *Colloq.* to be in a state of disorder or confusion. [ME, from OF: injury]

Mayo /ˈmeɪoʊ/, n. a county in north-western Republic of Ireland, in Connacht province. Pop. 115 016 (1986); 5397 km². *County town:* Castlebar. Irish, **Maigh Eo.**

mayonnaise /meɪəˈneɪz/, n. a thick dressing used for salads or vegetables. [F, from *Mahon*, a port of the Balearic Islands]

mayor /meə/, n. the elected leader in a local government body, usu. of a city or town. [ME *maire*, from F, from L *mājor* greater] **—mayoralty,** n.

mayoress /ˈmeərəs, -rəs, meəˈres/, n. the wife of a mayor.

maypole /ˈmeɪpoʊl/, n. a high pole, decorated with flowers or ribbons, used for dancing.

maze /meɪz/, n. **1.** a confusing network of connecting paths or passages, esp. of hedges in a park, etc.; labyrinth. **2.** a state of confusion. **3.** a winding movement, as in dancing. [ME; var. of AMAZE]

mazurka /məˈzɜːkə/, n. (the music for) a lively Polish dance in triple time. [Pol, from *Mazur* of Mazoria (district in Poland)]

Mazzini /maˈtsiːni/, n. **Giuseppe** /dʒəˈzepi/, 1805–72, Italian political theorist and revolutionary, who agitated for Italian unification and independence.

mb, *Abbrev.* millibar.

MBE /ˌem biː ˈiː/, *Abbrev.* Member of the Order of the British Empire.

Mc-, variant of **Mac-;** entries beginning **Mc-** are sorted alphabetically with those beginning **Mac-.**

MC /ˌem ˈsiː/, n. **1.** → **master of ceremonies.** ◇*Abbrev.* **2.** Military Cross.

Md, *Chem. Symbol.* mendelevium.

me¹ /miː/, *pers. pron.* objective case of the pronoun *I*. [ME *mē*, OE *me*, dat. sing.]

me² /miː/, n. *Music.* Also, **mi.** See **solfa.**

mead /miːd/, n. an alcoholic drink made from honey and water.

Mead /miːd/, n. **Margaret,** 1901–78, US anthropologist; writings include *Coming of Age in Samoa* (1928).

meadow /ˈmedoʊ/, n. **1.** *Brit.* a piece of grassland, used for growing hay or as pasture for animals. **2.** *US.* a low, level grassed area, as along a river. [ME *medwe*, OE *mædw-*] **—meadowy,** adj.

meagre /ˈmiːgə/, adj. **1.** lacking in quantity or quality. **2.** lean, or thin. [ME, from OF, from L: lean]

meal¹ /miːl/, n. **1.** one of the regular times for food, as breakfast, lunch, or dinner. **2.** the food served or eaten. [OE *mæl* measure, fixed time, occasion, meal]

meal² /miːl/, n. **1.** the edible part of any grain (except wheat), ground into a coarse powder. **2.** any powdery substance, as of nuts or seeds, like meal. [OE *melu*] **—mealy,** adj.

Meale /miːl/, n. **Richard Graham,** born 1932, Australian composer, noted for his opera *Voss* (1982).

mealy bug, n. a plant-sucking insect having a body covered with powdery wax.

mealy-mouthed /ˈmiːli-maʊðd/, adj. avoiding the use of plain terms, as from shyness or insincerity.

mean¹ /miːn/, v., **meant, meaning.** ◇*v.t.* **1.** to propose, intend; to do, say, etc.: *I mean to talk to him.* **2.** to intend for a particular purpose, end, etc.: *They were meant for each other.* **3.** (of words, things, etc.) to signify. ◇*v.i.* **4.** to have intentions: *He means well.* [OE *mænan*]

mean² /miːn/, adj. **1.** poor in grade, quality or character: *He is no mean performer.* **2.** low in station, rank, etc. **3.** of little importance. **4.** unimpressive; shabby: *a mean abode.* **5.** small-minded; ignoble: *mean motives.* **6.** unwilling to give; miserly: *He is mean about money.* **7.** *Colloq.* small; ashamed: *I feel mean not having helped.* **8.** *Colloq.* troublesome; vicious, as a horse. **9.** (of someone in a competitive activity) skilful; accomplished: *He's a mean bowler.* **10.** *Colloq.* powerful: *a big, mean motor.* [OE *gemǣne*]

mean³ /miːn/, n. **1.** (usu. pl. but used as sing.) an agency, method, etc., used to reach an end: *a means of transport.* **2.** (*pl.*) funds, esp. of money: *to live beyond one's means.* **3.** that which is halfway between two end points. **4.** *Maths.* a quantity having a value intermediate between the values of other quantities; an average, esp. the arithmetic mean. ◇**5.** Some special uses are:
by all means, 1. at any cost. **2.** (in emphasis) certainly: *Go, by all means.*
by any means, in any way.
by means of, by the use of.
by no means, in no way; not at all.
◇*adj.* **6.** having a middle position. **7.** intermediate in kind, quality, degree, time, etc. [ME, from OF, from LL: in the middle]

meander /miˈændə/, *v.i.* **1.** to go by a winding course. **2.** to wander. ◇*n.* **3.** a wandering path or course, esp. of a river. [L, from

meander

Gk: a winding, orig. the name of a winding river (now Mendere) in W Asia Minor]

mean deviation, *n.* the average of the absolute values of a set of deviations from an accepted norm in a statistical distribution.

meaning /'minɪŋ/, *n.* **1.** something which is intended to be, or actually is, said or shown; significance. ◇*adj.* **2.** intending: *He is very well-meaning.* **3.** expressive: *a meaning look.* —**meaningful**, *adj.*

mean solar day, *n.* See **day** (def. 3).

mean solar time, *n.* →**mean time**.

means test, *n.* **1.** an inquiry into the income and resources of a person, to determine his or her right to gain a pension, allowance, etc. ◇*v.t.* **2.** to make such an inquiry into (a person's income, etc.). Also, **means-test**.

meant /mɛnt/, *v.* past tense and past participle of **mean**[1].

mean time, *n.* the time at a given place on earth based on a day of 24 hours. Also, **mean solar time**.

meantime /'mintaɪm/, *n.* **1.** the time between events: *in the meantime.* ◇*adv.* **2.** meanwhile.

meanwhile /'minwaɪl, min'waɪl/, *adv.* during the interval; at the same time.

measles /'mizəlz/, *n.* **1.** an infectious disease occurring mostly in children, characterised by fever and the appearance of small red spots. **2.** any of certain other similar diseases, as rubella (**German measles**). [ME, from G: spot]

measure /'mɛʒə/, *n., v.,* **-ured, -uring.** ◇*n.* **1.** the act or process of judging the size, quantity, etc., of something. **2.** the size, quantity, etc., so judged. **3.** an instrument for measuring. **4.** a unit or standard of measurement. **5.** system of measurement. **6.** a quantity; degree; proportion. **7.** a limit: *to know no measure.* **8.** a law. **9.** an action intended as a means to an end: *to take measures to prevent theft.* **10.** a rhythmical movement, as in poetry or music. **11.** a metrical unit. **12.** (*pl.*) *Geol.* beds; strata. **13. for good measure**, as an extra precaution. **14. get someone's measure**, *Colloq.* to gain advantage over someone. **15. get the measure of someone**, to gain equality with someone. ◇*v.t.* **16.** to decide the size, quantity, etc., of. **17.** to mark or lay off or out, by measure (oft. fol. by *off* or *out*). **18.** to judge the amount, value, etc., of, by comparison with some standard. **19.** to serve as the measure of. **20.** to alter; adjust. **21.** to bring into competition. **22. measure up to**, to be suitable for. ◇*v.i.* **23.** to take measurements. **24.** to be of a certain measure. [ME, from OF, from L] —**measurer**, *n.*

measured /'mɛʒəd/, *adj.* **1.** decided or given by measure. **2.** regular; uniform, as in movement. **3.** slow; deliberate: *measured speech.* **4.** in the form of metre or verse; metrical.

measurement /'mɛʒəmənt/, *n.* **1.** the act of measuring. **2.** the extent, size, etc., decided by measuring. **3.** a system of measuring.

meat /mit/, *n.* **1.** the flesh of animals as used for food. **2.** *Archaic.* food in general: *meat and drink.* **3.** the edible part of a fruit, nut, etc. **4.** the main substance of something, as an argument. [ME and OE *mete*]

Mecca /'mɛkə/, *n.* **1.** a place regarded as a centre of interest or activity and visited by many people. **2.** (*also l.c.*) any situation in which people consider they would be happy. **3.** city in Western Saudi Arabia; birthplace of Mohammed and spiritual centre of Islam to which Moslem pilgrims journey. Pop. 366 801 (1974).

mechanic /mə'kænɪk/, *n.* a skilled worker with tools or machines. [ME, from L, from Gk: of machines]

mechanical /mə'kænɪkəl/, *adj.* **1.** having to do with machinery or tools. **2.** of the nature of or produced by such means. **3.** acting or performed without originality, spirit, etc.; automatic. **4.** belonging or relating to the subject matter of mechanics. **5.** reducing the spiritual to the material; materialistic. **6.** relating to material objects or physical conditions: *prevented by mechanical difficulties.*

mechanics /mə'kænɪks/, *n.* **1.** the branch of knowledge concerned with machinery. **2.** the science dealing with the action of forces on bodies and with movement.

mechanise *or* **mechanize** /'mɛkənaɪz/, *v.t.,* **-nised, -nising. 1.** to operate or perform by machinery. **2.** to introduce machinery into (an industry, etc.). **3.** *Mil.* to equip with tanks, etc. —**mechanisation**, *n.*

mechanism /'mɛkənɪzəm/, *n.* **1.** a piece of machinery. **2.** the machinery, or other physical means, by which something is performed. **3.** the structure, or arrangement of parts of a machine or of anything similar. **4.** such parts collectively. **5.** *Philos, Biol.* a natural process seen as being machine-like. [NL, from Gk] —**mechanistic**, *adj.*

medal /'mɛdl/, *n.* a flat piece of metal, round or in the shape of a star, cross, etc., with writing or a design, made in memory of a person, action, or event, or given as a reward for bravery, excellence, etc. [F, from It, from L: metal] —**medallic**, *adj.*

medallion /mə'dæljən/, *n.* **1.** a large medal. **2.** something shaped like a medallion, as part of a design on buildings or furniture. [F, from It: large medal]

Medan /'meɪdan/, *n.* a city in Indonesia, in north-eastern Sumatra. Pop. 1 966 000 (1983).

Medawar /'mɛdəwə/, *n.* **Sir Peter Brian,** 1915–87, English zoologist; Nobel prize (with Sir Macfarlane Burnet) for work on immunology.

meddle /'mɛdl/, *v.i.,* **-dled, -dling.** to busy oneself unnecessarily with something that does not concern one; interfere. [ME, from OF, from L: mix] —**meddler**, *n.*

Medea /mə'diə/, *n. Gk Legend.* a sorceress, daughter of the king of Colchis, and wife of Jason, whom she assisted in obtaining the Golden Fleece.

media /'midiə/, *n.* **1.** a plural of **medium**. **2.** → **mass media**.

Media /'midiə/, *n.* an ancient country in western Asia, south of the Caspian Sea, corresponding generally to north-western Iran. *Cap.*: Ecbatana.

mediaeval /medi'ivəl/, *adj.* → **medieval**. —**mediaevalism**, *n.* —**mediaevalist**, *n.*

medial /'midiəl/, *adj.* **1.** situated in or relating to the middle. **2.** of an average. **3.** ordinary. [LL, from L: middle]

median /'midiən/, *adj.* **1.** indicating or relating to a plane dividing something into two equal parts, esp. one dividing an animal into right and left halves. **2.** situated in or relating to the middle; medial. ◇*n.* **3.** the middle number in a given series of numbers. **4.** a line through a vertex of a triangle dividing the opposite side into two equal parts. [L: in the middle]

mediant /'midiənt/, *n.* the third degree of a scale.

mediate /'midieɪt/, *v.*, **-ated, -ating**. ◇*v.t.* **1.** to bring about (an agreement, peace, etc.) by acting between disagreeing parties. **2.** to settle (disagreements, etc.) in this way. ◇*v.i.* **3.** to act between disagreeing parties to bring about an agreement, etc. [ME, from LL: divided, situated in the middle] —**mediator**, *n.* —**mediation**, *n.* —**mediatory, mediative**, *adj.*

medic /'medɪk/, *n. Chiefly US Colloq.* a doctor or medical student. Also, **medico**.

medical /'medɪkəl/, *adj.* **1.** of or relating to the science or practice of medicine. **2.** that helps in curing; medicinal: *medical properties.* ◇*n.* **3.** a medical examination. [LL, from L: of healing]

Medicare /'medɪkeə/, *n.* a national health insurance program for all Australians introduced in 1983, financed by a tax levy.

medicate /'medəkeɪt/, *v.t.*, **-cated, -cating**. to treat with medicine. [L: cured] —**medicative**, *adj.*

medication /medə'keɪʃən/, *n.* **1.** the act of treating with medicine. **2.** a substance that cures or heals; medicine.

Medici /mə'ditʃi/, *n.* **Catherine de'** 1519–89, member of an Italian family of the city of Florence, rich and powerful in the 15th and 16th centuries; she became queen of Henry II of France, and mother of Francis II, Charles IX, and Henry III.

medicine /'medəsən, 'medsən/, *n.* **1.** any substance used in treating disease. **2.** the art or science of studying, treating or preventing disease. **3.** the art or science of treating disease with drugs or healing substances (as opposed to *surgery*). **4.** the medical profession. **5.** any unpleasant treatment or experience, esp. one supposed finally to have a good effect. [ME, from L] —**medicinal**, *adj.*

medicine man, *n.* (among primitive peoples) a man supposed to possess mysterious or supernatural powers.

medieval /medi'ivəl/, *adj.* of or relating to, characteristic of, or in the style of the Middle Ages. See **Middle Ages**. Also, **mediaeval**. [NL *medi(um) aev(um)* middle age + -AL¹]

Medieval Greek, *n.* the Greek language of the Middle Ages, usu. dated AD 700–1500. Also, **Middle Greek**.

Medieval Latin, *n.* the Latin language of the literature of the Middle Ages, usu. dated AD 700–1500, including many Latinised words from other languages.

Medina /me'dinə/, *n.* a town in western Saudi Arabia, where Mohammed was first accepted as the supreme Prophet from Allah, and where his tomb is situated. Pop. 290 000 (1980 est.). Arabic, **Al-Madinah**.

mediocre /midi'oukə, 'midioukə/, *adj.* neither good nor bad; ordinary: *a person of mediocre abilities.* [F, from L: in a middle state] —**mediocrity**, *n.*

meditate /'medəteɪt/, *v.*, **-tated, -tating**. ◇*v.t.* **1.** to consider in the mind as something to be done or effected; intend or plan: *He meditated robbery; I meditated whether to go home.* ◇*v.i.* **2.** to think deeply; reflect (sometimes fol. by *on* or *upon*). [L] —**meditator**, *n.* —**meditation**, *n.* —**meditative**, *adj.*

Mediterranean race /medətə'reɪniən reɪs/, *n.* a Caucasian race division inhabiting the area bordering the Mediterranean Sea.

Mediterranean Sea, *n.* the sea between Africa, Europe, and Asia. About 2 965 321 km²; greatest known depth, 4400 m.

medium /'midiəm/, *n., pl.* **-dia** /-diə/, **-diums**, *adj.* ◇*n.* **1.** a middle state or condition; mean. **2.** something in between in nature or degree; something intermediate. **3.** a substance, such as air, etc., through which a force acts or an effect is produced. **4.** the natural surroundings of an organism. **5.** any surrounding things, conditions, or influences; environment. **6.** a means; agent: *Newspapers are used as an advertising medium.* **7.** *Biol.* a substance in which specimens are shown or preserved. **8.** *Bacteriol.* a substance in or upon which microorganisms are grown for study. **9.** *Painting.* the material or method used by an artist. **10.** a person serving or thought to serve as a means of communication between living people and the spirits of the dead. ◇*adj.* **11.** middling in degree, quality, etc.: *a man of medium size.* [L: middle, intermediate]

medium frequency, *n.* a radio frequency of between 30 and 300 kilohertz. *Abbrev.:* m.f.

medium wave, *n.* an electromagnetic wave with a wavelength of 200–1000 metres. —**medium-wave**, *adj.*

medley /'medli/, *n., pl.* **-leys**, *adj.* ◇*n.* **1.** a mixture, esp. of different kinds of things; jumble. **2.** a piece of music combining passages from various works. **3.** *Swimming.* a race in which a competitor swims different strokes, in a particular order. ◇*adj.* **4.** mixed; mingled. [ME, from OF: a mixing]

medulla /mə'dʌlə/, *n., pl.* **-dullae** /-'dʌli/. *Bot.* → **pith** (def. 2). [L: marrow, pith]

medusa /məˈdjusə/, *n., pl.* **-sas, -sae** /-si/. → **jellyfish**. —**medusoid**, *adj.*

Medusa /məˈdjusə/, *n., pl.* **-sas**. *Gk Legend.* that one of the three Gorgons who was slain by Perseus and whose head was afterwards carried on the shield of Athena.

meek /mik/, *adj.* humbly patient, esp. in response to bad treatment, etc.; submissive. [ME *make, meoc,* from Scand]

meerschaum /ˈmɪəʃəm/, *n.* (a tobacco pipe made of) a white, claylike, mineral substance. [G: sea foam]

meet[1] /mit/, *v.,* **met, meeting,** *n.* ◇*v.t.* **1.** to come into connection or contact with. **2.** to come before or to (the eye, ear, etc.). **3.** to come face to face with or into the presence of; encounter. **4.** to go to the place of arrival of: *to meet guests at the door.* **5.** to come into the company of (a person, etc.) for dealings, talks, etc. **6.** to be introduced to; make the acquaintance of: *to meet the governor.* **7.** to face directly or without avoidance: *He met her gaze.* **8.** to oppose: *to meet an attack with a counterattack.* **9.** to deal effectively with (an objection, difficulty, etc.). **10.** to satisfy (needs, responsibilities, demands, expectations, etc.). **11.** to experience: *to meet hostility.* ◇*v.i.* **12.** to come face to face, or into company: *We met in the street.* **13.** to come together for action, talk, etc.; assemble: *The society will meet every week.* **14.** to become personally known to someone. **15.** to come into connection or join: *The railway lines meet here.* ◇*v.* **16. meet (someone) halfway,** to reach an agreed compromise. **17. meet with, a.** to come across; encounter. **b.** to experience; receive (praise, blame, etc.). ◇*n.* **18.** a meeting, esp. for a sporting event. **19.** the people at such a meeting. [OE *mētan, gemētan,* from *mōt, gemōt* meeting. See MOOT]

meet[2] /mit/, *adj. Archaic.* suitable; fitting; proper. [ME *mete*]

meeting /ˈmitɪŋ/, *n.* **1.** a coming face to face. **2.** a coming together; assembly. **3.** a series of races or other sporting events. **4.** an assembly for religious worship. **5.** a coming into or being in connection; junction or union.

mega- /ˈmɛgə-/, a prefix meaning **1.** 10^6 of a given unit, as in *megaton*. Symbol: M **2.** 'great', 'huge', as in *megalith*. Also, before vowels, **meg-**. [Gk, combining form of *mégas*]

megahertz /ˈmɛgəhɜts/, *n.* a unit of radio-frequency equal to 1×10^6 hertz. *Symbol:* MHz

megalith /ˈmɛgəlɪθ/, *n.* a stone of great size, esp. in ancient constructions or prehistoric monumental remains. —**megalithic**, *adj.*

megalo-, a word part meaning bigness or exaggeration. [Gk, combining form of *mégas* great]

megalomania /mɛgələˈmeɪniə/, *n.* a mental disorder marked by false belief in one's own greatness, wealth, power, etc. [NL. See MEGALO-, -MANIA] —**megalomaniac**, *n.*

megalopolis /mɛgəˈlɒpələs/, *n.* a huge urban region, often consisting of towns and suburbs which have merged into one gigantic area.

megaphone /ˈmɛgəfoʊn/, *n.* an instrument for increasing the volume of sound, or for directing it, usu. funnel-shaped and held in the hand. —**megaphonic**, *adj.*

megapode /ˈmɛgəpoʊd/, *n.* any of a family of large-footed birds, of South East Asia, Australasia and Polynesia, which construct a mound of earth or plant matter either for use in display, or as an incubator for their eggs; mound bird; mound builder.

megaspore /ˈmɛgəspɔ/, *n.* the larger of the two kinds of spores produced by some ferns.

megaton /ˈmɛgətʌn/, *n.* **1.** one million tons. **2.** the explosive force equal to that of one million tons of TNT.

Meillon /ˈmɛljən/, *n.* **John,** 1934–89, Australian actor and former child performer.

Mein Kampf /maɪn ˈkæmf/, *n.* the autobiography of Adolf Hitler, setting forth his political philosophy and his plan for the German conquest of Europe; first published 1925. [G: my struggle]

meiosis /maɪˈoʊsəs/, *n.* the development process of gametes, consisting of two cell divisions, in the course of which the chromosomes are duplicated only once so that the diploid chromosome number becomes reduced to the haploid. [Gk: a lessening] —**meiotic**, *adj.*

Meir /meɪˈɪə, mɑ-/, *n.* **Golda** /ˈɡoʊldə/ (**Golda Mabovitch**), 1898–1978, Israeli politician; prime minister 1969–74.

Meistersinger /ˈmaɪstəsɪŋə/, *n., pl.* **-singer**. a member of one of the guilds, chiefly of workingmen, established during the 14th, 15th, and 16th centuries in the principal cities of Germany, for the cultivation of poetry and music. Also, **mastersinger**.

Mekong /miˈkɒŋ/, *n.* a river flowing from western China south-east along most of the boundary between Thailand and Laos to the South China Sea. 4184 km. Chinese, **Lantsang**.

melaleuca /mɛləˈlukə/, *n.* a type of tree or shrub mainly found in Australia, usu. on river banks or in swamps; paperbark; tea-tree. [NL, from Gk *méla(s)* black + *leukós* white, with reference to the black trunk and white branches]

melancholia /mɛlənˈkoʊliə/, *n.* a mental disease marked by feelings of great sadness, depression and fear for the future. [LL. See MELANCHOLY] —**melancholiac**, *n.*

melancholy /ˈmɛlənkɒli/, *n., pl.* **-cholies,** *adj.* ◇*n.* **1.** a feeling of sadness, esp. when happening often or lasting a long time; depression. **2.** quiet thoughtfulness; pensiveness. ◇*adj.* **3.** suffering from, marked by, or showing melancholy: *a melancholy mood.* **4.** causing melancholy: *a melancholy occasion.* **5.** quietly thoughtful; pensive. [ME, from LL, from Gk: black bile] —**melancholic**, *adj.*

Melanesia /mɛləˈniʒə/, *n.* one of the three principal divisions of Oceania, comprising the island groups in the South Pacific, north-east of Australia. [Gk *méla(s)* black + Gk *nêsos* island + *-ia*; so named from black appearance of the islands seen from the sea] —**Melanesian**, *n., adj.*

melange /ˈmeɪlɒnʒ/, *n.* a mixture; medley. Also, **mélange**. [F: mix]

melanin /ˈmelənən/, *n.* the dark pigment in the body of man and certain animals, found in the hair, skin, etc.

melano-, word part meaning 'black'. Also, **melan-**. [Gk, combining form of *méla(s)* black]

melanoma /meləˈnoumə/, *n.* a malignant tumor formed from cells containing dark pigments, esp. in skin. [NL. See MELANO-, -OMA]

Melba /ˈmelbə/, *n.* **Dame Nellie** (*Helen Porter Mitchell*), 1861–1931, Australian soprano.

Melbourne[1] /ˈmelbən/, *n.* the capital city of Vic, on the banks of the Yarra River and at the head of Port Phillip Bay; Australia's second largest city. Pop. 2 645 484 (1986). [named by Governor BOURKE in 1837 in honor of Lord *Melbourne*, British prime minister]

Melbourne[2] /ˈmelbən/, *n.* **HMAS**, a Royal Australian Navy aircraft carrier; collided with the HMAS *Voyager* off Jervis Bay in 1964 with a loss of 82 lives, and collided with the *Frank E Evans*, a US destroyer, in the South China Sea in 1969, when 74 lives were lost.

Melbourne Cup, *n.* a horse-race held annually in Melbourne on the first Tuesday in November, first run in 1861. Official name, **Fosters Melbourne Cup**.

Meldrum /ˈmeldrəm/, *n.* (**Duncan**) **Max**, 1875–1955, Australian artist, born in Scotland; considered art as 'the science of optical analysis'.

melee /ˈmeleɪ, -ˈliː/, *n.* **1.** a confused general hand-to-hand fight. **2.** a noisy or confused situation. [F]

meliorate /ˈmiːliəreɪt/, *v.i.*, *v.t.*, **-rated**, **-rating**. to make or become better; ameliorate; improve. [LL] —**melioration**, *n.* —**meliorative**, *adj.* —**meliorator**, *n.*

mellifluous /məˈlɪfluəs/, *adj.* **1.** sweetly or smoothly flowing: *mellifluous voices.* **2.** flowing with or sweetened with honey. Also, **mellifluent**. [ME, from LL: flowing with honey] —**mellifluence**, *n.*

mellow /ˈmeloʊ/, *adj.* **1.** soft and sweet from ripeness, as fruit. **2.** fully developed in flavor, as wines. **3.** softened, made kindly or genial by age or experience: *a mellow old man.* **4.** soft and rich, as sound, tones, color, light, etc. **5.** soft or moist, as soil. ⬥*v.t.*, *v.i.* **6.** to make or become mellow. [OE *meru* tender, soft]

melodic /məˈlɒdɪk/, *adj.* **1.** → **melodious**. **2.** relating to melody as distinguished from harmony and rhythm.

melodious /məˈloʊdiəs/, *adj.* **1.** of the nature of or marked by melody; tuneful. **2.** producing melody.

melodrama /ˈmelədrɑːmə/, *n.* **1.** a play, etc., in which action and emotions are exaggerated beyond what is realistic. **2.** any situation or behavior marked by exaggerated emotions. [F, from It: musical drama, from Gk: music drama]

melodramatic /melədrəˈmætɪk/, *adj.* **1.** of or like melodrama; sentimental and exaggerated. ⬥*n.* **2.** (*pl.*) melodramatic behavior.

melody /ˈmelədi/, *n.*, *pl.* **-dies**. **1.** musical sounds in an agreeable order or arrangement. **2.** *Music.* **a.** the arrangement or order of single notes in musical compositions, as opposed to harmony and rhythm; tune. **b.** the main part in a harmonic composition; air. [ME, from OF, from LL, from Gk: singing, choral song] —**melodist**, *n.*

melon /ˈmelən/, *n.* a type of large, juicy fruit, usu. roundish in shape and having a rind. [ME, from OF, from LL, from Gk: apple-like gourd]

Melos /ˈmiːlɒs/, *n.* an island of the Cyclades group, in the Aegean, south of Greece; statue of **Venus de Milo** found here, 1920. Pop. 8613 (1971); 158 km². Also, **Milo, Milos**.

melt /melt/, *v.*, **melted, melted** or **molten, melting**, *n.* ⬥*v.t.*, *v.i.* **1.** to (cause to) be reduced to liquid by heat, as ice, snow, butter, metal, etc. **2.** (not in scientific use) to (cause to) become liquid; dissolve. **3.** to (cause to) pass away or fade gradually (oft. fol. by *away*). **4.** to (cause to) pass, change, or become mixed gradually (oft. fol. by *into*). **5.** to (cause to) become softened in feeling: *His heart melted with love; Pity melted her heart.* ⬥*n.* **6.** the act or process of melting. **7.** a substance which is melted. [OE *meltan*, *v.i.*— *m(i)eltan*, *v.t.*] —**melter**, *n.*

melting point, *n.* the equilibrium temperature of the solid and liquid phases of a substance at a particular pressure (usu. at standard pressure, 101.325 kilopascals).

melting pot, *n.* any situation in which there is a mixture of different elements or ideas, such as a society of people of various races.

Melton /ˈmeltn/, *n.* a town and shire in southern Vic, west of Melbourne. Pop. 24 394 (1986).

Melville[1] /ˈmelvəl/, *n.* **1. Captain** (*Francis McCallum*), 1822–57, Australian bushranger and former convict; leader of the Mt Macedon bushrangers. **2. Herman**, 1819–91, US novelist; writer of *Moby Dick* (1851) and *Billy Budd* (written 1891, published 1924).

Melville[2] /ˈmelvəl/, *n.* **Cape**, a promontory in northern Qld, on the east coast of Cape York Peninsula; about 300 people killed there in 1899 when cyclones destroyed a pearling fleet.

Melville Island, *n.* an island off the north coast of the NT, north of Darwin; unsuccessful attempt in 1824 to establish a convict settlement at Fort Dundas; fishing and pearling. Pop. 695 (1986); about 5801 km².

member /ˈmembə/, *n.* **1.** each of the people forming a society, party, parliament, or other body. **2.** a part of any structural whole, such as a limb of the body. [ME, from OF, from L: limb, part]

membrane /ˈmembreɪn/, *n.* **1.** a thin sheet of animal or vegetable tissue, serving to line an organ, connect parts, etc. **2.** *Chem.* a thin sheet of material, natural or synthetic, which allows substances in solution to pass through it. [L:

membrane

membrane the skin that covers the several members of the body, parchment] —**membranous**, *adj.*

memento /mə'mentoʊ/, *n., pl.* **-tos, -toes.** something that serves as a reminder of what is past or gone. [L: remember]

memo /'mɛmoʊ, 'mi-/, *n., pl.* **memos.** → **memorandum.**

memoir /'mɛmwɑ/, *n.* 1. (*pl.*) records of facts or events in connection with a particular subject, historical period, etc., based on the personal experience of the writer. 2. (*pl.*) → **autobiography.** 3. → **biography.** [F]

memorabilia /mɛmərə'bɪliə/, *n.pl., sing.* **-rabile** /-'ræbəli/. 1. matters or events worth being remembered. 2. things collected for the sake of memory. [L]

memorable /'mɛmrəbəl, -ərəbəl/, *adj.* worth remembering; notable: *a memorable speech.* [L]

memorandum /mɛmə'rændəm/, *n., pl.* **-dums, -da** /-də/. 1. a note made of something to be remembered. 2. a short record or written statement of something. 3. a note, as one sent from one member of a firm to another, regarding business matters. 4. a written statement which includes the main terms of a shipment of unsold goods and allows their return within a particular time. [L]

memorandum of association, *n.* a document essential for the registration of a company, containing the company name, details of how it is financed and the extent of its members' liability. The memorandum and articles of association form the company's constitution. See **articles of association.**

memorial /mə'mɔriəl/, *n.* 1. something intended to remind people of a person, event, etc., such as a monument. ◇*adj.* 2. serving to remind people of a person or thing; commemorative: *memorial services.* [ME, from L: of memory]

memorise *or* **memorize** /'mɛməraɪz/, *v.t.,* **-rised, -rising.** to put into the memory, or learn by heart: *He finally memorised the poem.*

memory /'mɛməri/, *n., pl.* **-ries.** 1. the mental ability of recording, retaining or recalling facts, experiences, etc. 2. this ability as possessed by a particular person: *He has a good memory.* 3. the length of time over which memory extends: *a time within the memory of living people.* 4. something remembered; a recollection: *his earliest memories.* 5. the total of what is remembered by a person: *to draw from memory.* 6. something remembered about a person or thing, esp. after death; reputation. 7. remembrance; commemoration: *a monument in memory of Captain Cook.* 8. Computers. the part of a digital computer in which data and instructions are held until they are needed. [ME, from L]

Memphis /'mɛmfəs/, *n.* a ruined city in Upper Egypt, on the Nile, south of Cairo; the ancient capital of Egypt.

mem-sahib /ˈmɛm-sa-ɪb, -saːhɪb/, *n.* (in India formerly) a native term of address to a European lady. [Hind]

men /mɛn/, *n.* plural of **man.**

menace /'mɛnəs/, *n., v.,* **-aced, -acing.** ◇*n.* 1. something that threatens to cause evil, harm, etc. 2. *Colloq.* → **nuisance.** ◇*v.t.* 3. to threaten. [ME, from OF, from L: a threat]

menagerie /mə'nædʒəri/, *n.* (a place containing) a collection of wild or strange animals, esp. for show. [F: management of a household]

menarche /'mɛnak/, *n.* the onset of menstruation in a young woman. See **menopause.** [NL, from Gk: beginning of a month]

mend /mɛnd/, *v.t.* 1. to make whole or sound by repairing: *to mend clothes; to mend a car.* 2. to set right; make better; improve: *You should mend your ways.* ◇*v.i.* 3. to heal or recover: *The wound is mending.* 4. (of conditions) to improve. ◇*n.* 5. a mended place. 6. **on the mend,** improving, in health or in general state of affairs. [var. of AMEND] —**mendable,** *adj.* —**mender,** *n.*

mendacious /mɛn'deɪʃəs/, *adj.* 1. false or untrue: *a mendacious report.* 2. lying or untruthful: *a mendacious person.* —**mendacity,** *n.*

mendelevium /mɛndə'liviəm/, *n.* a synthetic, radioactive element. *Symbol:* Md; *at. no.:* 101; *at. wt:* 258; *half-life:* 1.5 hrs. [named after Dmitri *Mendelyeev,* 1834–1907, Russian chemist, + *-*IUM]

Mendel's laws /'mɛndəlz lɔz/, *n.pl.* the basic principles of heredity, stating: **a.** that the pairs of hereditary units carried by each somatic cell separate completely during meiosis. **b.** that the separation of each pair happens independently of that of any other pair. —**Mendelian,** *adj.* —**Mendelism,** *n.*

Mendelssohn /'mɛndlsən/, *n.* **Felix** (*Jacob Ludwig Felix Mendelssohn-Bartholdy*) 1809–47, German composer of overtures, symphonies, an oratorio, *Elijah* (1846), piano works and songs.

mendicant /'mɛndəkənt/, *adj.* 1. begging, or living on charitable gifts. ◇*n.* 2. beggar. 3. mendicant friar. [L: begging]

Mendonça /mɛn'dɒnsə/, *n.* **Cristovão de** /'krɪstovaʊ deɪ/, leader of a Portuguese fleet of three ships thought to have sailed down the east coast of Australia, 1521–22; map of the coast later known as the Dauphin Map.

Menelaus /mɛnə'leɪəs/, *n. Gk Legend.* a king of Sparta, brother of Agamemnon and husband of Helen; one of the leaders of the Greek forces in the war against Troy.

menhir /'mɛnhɪə/, *n.* an upright monumental stone from prehistoric times, standing either alone or with others. [Breton *men hir* long stone]

menial /'miniəl/, *adj.* 1. relating to or suitable for servants: *menial work.* 2. → **servile.** ◇*n.* 3. a servant. [ME, from AF, from L: household]

Menindee Lakes /mənɪndi 'leɪks/, *n.pl.* a series of lakes and dams in western NSW; source of water supply for local irrigation and for Broken Hill.

meninges /mə'nɪndʒiz/, *n.pl., sing.* **meninx** /'mɪnɪŋks/. the three membranes

meninges that surround the brain and spinal cord. [NL, from Gk: membrane, esp. of the brain] —**meningeal**, *adj.*

meningitis /ˌmenən'dʒaɪtəs/, *n.* an inflammation of the meninges. [NL, from Gk] —**meningitic**, *adj.*

meniscus /mə'nɪskəs/, *n.*, *pl.* **-nisci** /-'nɪsaɪ/. 1. a body in the shape of a quarter moon; crescent. 2. the curved upper surface of a column of liquid. [NL, from Gk: crescent, little moon] —**meniscoid**, *adj.*

meno-, a word part meaning 'month'. [Gk, combining form of *mē*]

menopause /'menəpɔz/, *n.* the period of irregular menstrual cycles happening before the final stopping of menstruation, usu. between ages of 45 and 55. [MENO- + PAUSE] —**menopausic**, **menopausal**, *adj.*

menorah /mə'nɔrə/, *n.* a candelabrum with seven candles used in Jewish religious services.

menses /'mensiz/, *n.pl.* the flow of blood and mucus from the uterus, usu. happening monthly. [L, pl. of *mensis* month]

Menshevik /'menʃəvɪk/, *n., pl.* **-viki** /-vɪ'ki/, **-viks**. (formerly) a member of the less extreme socialist party in Russia opposing the Bolsheviks. [Russ: one of smaller (group), from *menshe* less]

menstruate /'menstrueɪt/, *v.i.*, **-ated**, **-ating**. to have a flow of menses. —**menstruation**, *n.*

mensuration /ˌmenʃə'reɪʃən/, *n.* 1. the branch of mathematics which deals with the determination of length, area, and volume. 2. the act or art of measuring. [LL] —**mensural**, *adj.* —**mensurative**, *adj.*

-ment, a suffix of nouns, meaning an action or state resulting (*development*, *refreshment*), a product (*fragment*), or means (*ornament*). [F, from L *-mentum*, suffix forming nouns, usu. from verbs]

mental /'mentl/, *adj.* 1. of, for, or relating to the mind. 2. performed by or existing in the mind: *mental arithmetic*. 3. for or relating to those with disordered minds: *a mental asylum*. 4. *Colloq.* foolish or mad. [ME, from LL]

mentality /men'tælətɪ/, *n., pl.* **-ties**. 1. mental ability; intellect: *a person of average mentality*. 2. way of thinking; frame of mind: *of a vulgar mentality*.

menthol /'menθɒl/, *n.* a colorless, crystalline alcohol, $C_{10}H_{20}O$, present in peppermint oil, used in perfume, cigarettes, and sweets, and for colds because of its cooling effect on mucous membranes. [G, from L: mint] —**mentholated**, *adj.*

mention /'menʃən/, *v.t.* 1. to speak or write briefly; refer to incidentally. 2. to put forward the name of, as for an honor; cite. ◇*v.* 3. **not to mention**, in addition to. ◇*n.* 4. a mentioning; reference. 5. recognition, as deserving an honor, etc. [L: a calling to mind, mention] —**mentioner**, *n.*

mentor /'mentɔ/, *n.* a wise and trusted adviser. [from *Mentor*, friend of Odysseus and guardian of his household when he went to Troy]

menu /'menju, 'mɪnju/, *n.* 1. a list of the dishes served at a meal or in a restaurant. 2. the dishes served. [F: detailed list, orig. adj., small, from L: minute]

Menuhin /'menjuən/, *n.* **Yehudi** /jə'hudi/, born 1916, US violinist, living in England since 1959.

Menzies /'menzɪz/, *n.* **Sir Robert Gordon**, 1894–1978, Australian federal Liberal politician; prime minister 1939–41 and 1949–66.

meow /mi'aʊ/, *v.i.* → **miaow**.

mephistophelian /ˌmefɪstə'filiən/, *adj.* full of evil; cunning. [from *Mephistopheles*, one of the seven chief devils of medieval demonology; represented in Goethe's *Faust* as a crafty, scoffing fiend]

mercantile /'mɜkəntaɪl/, *adj.* of or relating to trade; commercial. [F, from It, from L: trading]

Mercator's projection /mɜˌkeɪtəz prə'dʒekʃən/, *n.* a map projection with parallels and meridians forming a rectangular grid, used particularly for navigation, although the scale varies and shapes of large areas are distorted. [named after Gerhardus *Mercator*, 1512–94, Flemish cartographer, geographer and mathematician]

mercenary /'mɜsənri, -sənəri/, *adj., n., pl.* **-naries**. ◇*adj.* 1. working or acting only for payment. 2. relating to soldiers hired to serve in a foreign army. ◇*n.* 3. a mercenary soldier. [L: hired for pay]

mercer /'mɜsə/, *n.* a dealer in textile cloths, esp. silks, etc. [ME, from OF: goods, wares, from L]

mercerise or **mercerize** /'mɜsəraɪz/, *v.t.*, **-rised**, **-rising**. to treat (cotton thread or cloth) with caustic alkali, to increase strength, lustre, and suitability for dyeing. [from J *Mercer*, English calico printer, the patentee (1850) of the process]

merchandise /'mɜtʃəndaɪs/, *n.;* /'mɜtʃəndaɪz/, *v.*, **-dised**, **-dising**. ◇*n.* 1. goods; commodities. 2. all the goods kept by a store. ◇*v.i., v.t.* 3. to sell (goods). [ME, from OF: merchant] —**merchandiser**, *n.*

merchant /'mɜtʃənt/, *n.* 1. someone who buys and sells goods for profit. 2. *Colloq.* a person noted for a particular kind of behavior: *panic merchant; standover merchant*. ◇*adj.* 3. relating to trade or commerce: *a merchant ship*. 4. relating to the merchant navy. [ME, from OF, from L: trade]

merchant bank, *n.* a private banking firm, the main business of which is accepting foreign bills of exchange, underwriting new issues of securities, etc. —**merchant banker**, *n.* —**merchant banking**, *n.*

merchantman /'mɜtʃəntmən/, *n., pl.* **-men**. a trading ship.

merchant navy /n./ **1.** the trading ships of a nation. **2.** the people working on these ships. Also, **mercantile marine, merchant marine.**

Mercia /ˈmɜːsiə/, n. an early English kingdom in central Britain.

merciful /ˈmɜːsəfəl/, adj. exercising, or having mercy; compassionate.

merciless /ˈmɜːsələs/, adj. without mercy; pitiless.

Mercouri /mɜːˈkuri/, n. **Melina** /məˈlinə/, born 1923, Greek actress and politician.

mercurial /mɜːˈkjuriəl/, adj. **1.** relating to, consisting of, containing, or caused by the metal mercury. **2.** light and changeable of mind, mood, etc. **3.** emotionally unreliable; fickle.

mercury /ˈmɜːkjəri/, n., pl. **-ries.** **1.** *Chem.* a heavy, silver-white, liquid metallic element; quicksilver. *Symbol:* Hg (for **hydrargyrum**); at. no.: 80; at. wt: 200.59. **2.** (*cap.*) a Roman deity, messenger of the gods, and god of commerce, dexterity, and eloquence; Greek counterpart, Hermes. **3.** a messenger, or carrier of news (sometimes used as name of a newspaper, etc.). **4.** (*cap.*) *Astron.* the planet nearest the sun having a mean distance from the sun of about 57 900 000 km, and a period of revolution of 87.969 days. Its diameter is 4844 km. [ME, from L *Mercurius*] —**mercuric,** *adj.*

mercy /ˈmɜːsi/, n., pl. **-cies.** **1.** kindness shown by not punishing or hurting an offender, enemy, etc.; clemency. **2.** tendency to show mercy: *an enemy wholly without mercy.* **3.** an act of mercy. **4. at the mercy of (someone),** in someone's power; defenceless. [ME, from OF: favor, thanks, from L: pay, ML: mercy]

mercy killing, n. → **euthanasia.**

mere /mɪə/, adj., superl. **merest.** being nothing more nor better than what is stated: *You are a mere child.* [ME, from L: pure, unmixed, mere]

Meredith /ˈmɛrədəθ/, n. **George,** 1828–1909, English novelist and poet; best known for his novel *The Egoist* (1879). **2. Louisa Anne,** 1812–95, Australian writer and naturalist, born in England.

merely /ˈmɪəli/, adv. only as stated, and nothing more; simply: *I merely do what I'm told.*

meretricious /mɛrəˈtrɪʃəs/, adj. **1.** falsely or showily attractive; tawdry. **2.** insincere. [L: of prostitutes]

merge /mɜːdʒ/, v.i., v.t., **merged, merging. 1.** to unite or combine. **2.** to (cause to) be swallowed up or absorbed or lose separateness by combination (oft. fol. by *in* or *into*). [L: dip, plunge, sink]

merger /ˈmɜːdʒə/, n. **1.** the combination of two or more companies by the making over of all the properties to one of them. **2.** any combination of two or more businesses into one.

meridian /məˈrɪdiən/, n. **1.** *Geog.* **a.** a great circle of the earth passing through the poles and any given point on the earth's surface and cutting the equator at right angles. **b.** the half of such a circle included between the poles. **2.** an imaginary line on the earth's surface which coincides with the horizontal component of the earth's magnetic field. **3.** the point or period of greatest development, power, etc.; zenith. [L: of midday, of the south] —**meridional,** *adj.*

Mérimée /meɪriˈmeɪ/, n. **Prosper** /prɒsˈpeə/, 1803–70, French short-story writer, novelist, and essayist; his novel *Carmen* (1845) was the basis of Bizet's opera.

meringue /məˈræŋ/, n. a mixture of sugar and beaten eggwhites formed into small cakes and baked, or spread over a dish, etc. [F, ? from G: cake of Mehringen]

merino /məˈrinoʊ/, n., pl. **-nos.** **1.** (*cap.*) one of a variety of sheep, originating in Spain, valued for its fine wool. **2.** wool from such sheep. **3.** a knitted cloth made of wool or wool and cotton. **4. pure merino,** (formerly) a free settler (opposed to *legitimate*). [Sp, from L (*ariēs*) *mājōrīnus* (male sheep) of the larger sort]

meristem /ˈmɛrɪstɛm/, n. cells which grow and divide to form the tissue of a plant; embryonic tissue. [Gk: divided] —**meristematic,** *adj.*

merit /ˈmɛrət/, n. **1.** excellence; worth. **2.** something that deserves reward or praise; a commendable quality, act, etc.: *the merits of a book; the merits of a performance.* **3.** (*pl.*) the basic right and wrong of a matter: *the merits of a case.* **4.** something that is deserved, whether good or bad. **5.** (*sometimes pl.*) the state or fact of deserving: *to treat a person according to his merits.* ◇*v.t.* **6.** to be worthy of; deserve. [ME, from F, from L: deserved, earned]

meritocracy /mɛrəˈtɒkrəsi/, n. **1.** people collectively who have reached high positions by reason of real or supposed ability or merit (contrasted with *aristocracy*, etc.). **2.** government by such people.

meritorious /mɛrəˈtɔːriəs/, adj. deserving of reward or praise; possessing merit. [ME, from ML: meritorious, L: serving to earn money]

Merlin /ˈmɜːlən/, n. *Arthurian Legend.* a venerable magician and counsellor to King Arthur. [Welsh: unexplained, from *Myrddin*]

mermaid /ˈmɜːmeɪd/, n. an imaginary female sea creature with the head and body of a woman and the tail of a fish. [ME, from *mere* lake, from L + MAID]

Merriman /ˈmɛrɪmən/, n. **Sir Walter Thomas,** 1882–1972, Australian pastoralist; his Merino studs made a substantial contribution to the quality of the national wool clip.

merrin /ˈmɛrən/, n. → **nail-tailed wallaby.**

merry /ˈmɛri/, adj., **-rier, -riest. 1.** full of cheer, joy, or gaiety; festive. **2.** *Archaic.* pleasant or delightful: *merry England.* **3.** *Colloq.* slightly drunk. **4. make merry,** to be bright and happy or have fun. [OE *myr(i)ge* pleasant, delightful] —**merriness,** n. —**merriment,** n.

merry-go-round /ˈmɛri-goʊ-ˌraʊnd/, n. **1.** a machine consisting of a round platform which turns around in a circle and is fitted with wooden horses, etc., on which people ride for amusement. **2.** any rapid round of events, social activities, etc.

Mersey /'mɜzi/, *n.* **1.** a river in north-western England, forming the border of Lancashire and Cheshire, flowing from Derbyshire west to the Irish Sea. 113 km. **2.** a river in northern Tas, rising in the central plateau and flowing north, east then north, entering Bass Strait at Devonport; hydro-electric power stations. About 160 km.

mesa /'meɪsə/, *n.* a land form with a relatively flat top and surrounded wholly or in part with steep rock walls, common in dry parts of the south-western US but also found in areas of inland Australia. [Sp, from L: table]

mésalliance /me'zæliəns/, *n.* a marriage with a person of lower social rank. [F]

mescal /mes'kæl/, *n.* a type of cactus, of the southern US and northern Mexico, whose button-like tops (**mescal buttons**) are dried and used as a stimulant, esp. by the American Indians. [Sp, from S Amer Ind]

mescaline /'meskəlin, -lən/, *n.* a white water-soluble crystalline powder, $C_{11}H_{17}NO_3$, obtained from mescal buttons, used to produce hallucinations. Also, **mescalin**.

mesh /meʃ/, *n.* **1.** one of the open spaces of a net, etc. **2.** (*pl.*) the threads of a net. **3.** (*pl.*) any means of catching or holding fast: *caught in the meshes of the law.* **4.** a network or net. **5.** a knitted, woven, or knotted cloth, with open spaces between the threads. **6.** a netlike structure of links or wires. **7.** *Mech.* the locking together or engagement of gear teeth. ◇*v.t., v.i.* **8.** to catch or become caught in or as in a net. **9.** to (cause to) interlock. [see OE *mǣx* and *mǣscre* net]

mesmerise or **mesmerize** /'mezməraɪz/, *v.t.*, **-rised**, **-rising**. **1.** to hypnotise. **2.** to hold all the attention of; fascinate. —**mesmerism**, **mesmerisation**, *n.* —**mesmeriser**, *n.*

meso-, a word part meaning 'middle', chiefly in scientific terms. Also, **mes-**. [Gk, combining form of *mésos* middle]

mesoderm /'mesoʊdəm, 'mɪz-/, *n.* the middle germ layer of an animal embryo. —**mesodermal**, **mesodermic**, *adj.*

Mesolithic /mesoʊ'lɪθɪk, miz-/, *adj.* (*sometimes l.c.*) of, relating to, or characteristic of a period between the Palaeolithic and Neolithic periods of the Stone Age.

meson /'mizɒn/, *n.* any of a group of elementary particles, all of which have rest masses between that of the electron and the proton. Also, **mesotron**.

mesophyll /'mesoʊfɪl, 'mɪz-/, *n.* the cell tissue which forms the inside parts of a leaf, usu. containing chlorophyll.

Mesopotamia /mesəpə'teɪmiə/, *n.* an ancient country in Asia between the rivers Tigris and Euphrates. —**Mesopotamian**, *adj., n.*

mesosphere /'mesoʊsfɪə, 'mɪz-/, *n.* **1.** the layer of atmosphere between the ionosphere and the exosphere (400 to 950 km). **2.** the layer of atmosphere above the stratosphere (30 to 80 km). —**mesospheric**, *adj.*

Mesozoic /mesə'zoʊɪk, mɪz-/, *Geol.* ◇*adj.* **1.** relating to the geological era of rocks between the Palaeozoic and Cainozoic; era of reptiles. ◇*n.* **2.** the era of rocks including the Triassic, Jurassic, and Cretaceous periods or systems.

mess /mes/, *n.* **1.** a dirty or untidy condition: *His room was in a mess.* **2.** a difficult or confused situation: *His life was in a mess.* **3.** a dirty or untidy thing or mass of things: *a mess of papers.* **4.** the place where a group of people, esp. in the army, regularly eat together. **5.** such a group. **6.** a meal so eaten. **7.** *Navy.* the living area of the crew. **8.** a soft or unattractive preparation of food. **9.** *Colloq.* a person whose life is in a confused state. ◇*v.t.* **10.** to make dirty or untidy (oft. fol. by *up*). **11.** to make (affairs, etc.) confused (oft. fol. by *up*). ◇*v.i.* **12.** to eat in company, as a member of a mess. **13.** to make a mess. ◇*v.* **14. mess around** or **about**, *Colloq.* **a.** to busy oneself in an untidy or confused way. **b.** to waste time. **c.** to play the fool. [ME, from OF: lit., put (on the table), from L: sent, put]

message /'mesɪdʒ/, *n.* **1.** information, advice, direction, etc., sent through a messenger or by other means. **2.** the moral or meaning of a book, film, painting, etc. **3.** a job to be done such as shopping; errand. **4. get the message**, *Colloq.* to understand. [ME, from OF: envoy, from L: sent]

message stick, *n.* a carved stick or block of wood used among some primitive peoples when sending messages.

Messalina /mesə'laɪnə/, *n.* **Valeria** /və'lɪəriə/, died AD 48, third wife of the Roman emperor Claudius, notorious for her immorality.

Messel /'mesəl/, *n.* **Harry**, born 1922 in Canada, Australian physicist.

messenger /'mesəndʒə/, *n.* someone who carries a message or goes on an errand, esp. as a matter of duty or official business. [ME, from OF: MESSAGE]

Messenger /'mesəndʒə/, *n.* **Herbert Henry** ('*Dally*'), 1883–1959, Australian rugby league footballer.

messenger RNA, *n.* the RNA containing the information for the synthesis of particular proteins.

Messenia /me'siniə/, *n.* the south-western area of the Peloponnesus in southern Greece.

Messiah /mə'saɪə/, *n.* **1.** the title given to an expected deliverer of the Jewish people. **2.** the title given to Jesus as the deliverer of the Jewish people. **3.** any expected deliverer. [var. of L *Messias* (Vulgate), from Gk form of Heb: anointed] —**Messianic**, *adj.*

messmate /'mesmeɪt/, *n.* any of a number of Australian gum trees, found esp. on the tablelands of NSW.

Messrs, *Abbrev.* messieurs (used as if a plural of *Mr*).

met /met/, *v.* past tense and past participle of **meet**.

meta-, a prefix meaning 'among', 'together with', 'after', 'behind', and often indicating change, found chiefly in scientific words. [Gk, representing *metá*, prep., with, after]

metabolise or **metabolize** /mə'tæbəlaɪz/, v.t., **-lised, -lising.** to subject to metabolism; change by metabolism.

metabolism /mə'tæbəlɪzəm/, n. the sum of the processes or chemical changes in an organism or a single cell by which food is built up (*anabolism*) into living protoplasm and by which protoplasm is broken down (*catabolism*) into simpler compounds with the exchange of energy. [META- + Gk *bolē* change + -ISM] —**metabolic**, adj.

metacarpus /metə'kapəs/, n. the structure of the five bones between the wrist and the fingers. —**metacarpal**, adj.

metal /'metl/, n., v., **-alled, -alling.** ◇n. **1.** any of a group of elements, e.g. gold, silver, copper, tin, etc., which are shiny in appearance, malleable, ductile, generally electropositive, and are good conductors of electricity. **2.** a mixture composed wholly or partly of these substances; alloy. **3.** See **mettle**. **4.** Also, **road metal.** broken stone used for stability and drainage on railway tracks or for surfacing roads or mixing with cement to make concrete; blue metal. ◇v.t. **5.** to supply or cover with metal. [ME, from OF, from L: mine, mineral, metal, from Gk: mine]

metallic /mə'tælɪk/, adj. **1.** of, relating to, or consisting of metal. **2.** like metal: *metallic lustre*; *metallic sounds*. **3.** *Chem.* **a.** (of a metal element) being in the free or uncombined state: *metallic iron*. **b.** containing or yielding metal.

metalloid /'metəlɔɪd/, n. *Chem.* **1.** a nonmetal. **2.** an element which is both metallic and non-metallic, e.g. arsenic, silicon, or bismuth.

metallurgy /'metələdʒi, mə'tælədʒi/, n. the science of separating metals from their ores, making alloys, or working metals to desired shapes or qualities. [NL, from Gk: mineworker] —**metallurgic, metallurgical**, adj. —**metallurgist**, n.

metalwork /'metlwək/, n. **1.** the art or craft of making metal objects. **2.** shaped metal objects.

metamorphic /metə'mɔfɪk/, adj. **1.** relating to or marked by change of form, or metamorphosis. **2.** *Geol.* (of rocks) showing changes in structure made by heat or pressure, as marble does. See **rock**[1] (def. 2a).

metamorphism /metə'mɔfɪzəm/, n. **1.** → metamorphosis. **2.** *Geol.* a change in the structure or composition of a rock, due to natural forces such as pressure and heat, esp. when the rock becomes harder and more completely crystalline.

metamorphosis /metə'mɔfəsəs/, n., pl. **-ses** /-siz/. **1.** a change of form, structure, substance or character; transformation. **2.** the form resulting from any such change. **3.** a change of form during the growth of an animal by which it is adapted temporarily to a special environment or way of living usu. different from that of the stage before: *the metamorphosis of tadpoles into frogs*. [L, from Gk: transformation]

metaphase /'metəfeɪz/, n. *Biol.* the middle stage in mitotic cell division, in which the chromosomes in the equatorial plane of the cell split.

metaphor /'metəfə, -fɔ/, n. **1.** a figure of speech in which a word or phrase is used to describe something in a way that does not fit it in reality, as a method of suggesting likeness, e.g. *A mighty fortress is our God*; *Your bad moods are a cloud in my life*. **2. mixed metaphor,** a figure of speech in which two or more metaphors are used, producing a mixture of ideas that don't fit together, e.g. *The king put the ship of state on its feet*. [L: from Gk: a transfer] —**metaphorical, metaphoric,** adj.

metaphysical /metə'fɪzɪkəl/, adj. **1.** relating to or of the nature of metaphysics. **2.** *Philos.* concerned with subjects beyond the measurable physical world, such as the meaning of life, how the world began, what truth is, etc. **3.** relating esp. to that group of early 17th century English poets of whom John Donne was the chief, whose style is highly intellectual, philosophical, clever and witty.

metaphysics /metə'fɪzɪks/, n. the branch of philosophy which deals with first principles, including the sciences of being (*ontology*) and of the origin and structure of the universe (*cosmology*). It is always closely connected with a theory of knowledge (*epistemology*). [ML: from MGk: the (works) after the physics; with reference to the arrangement of Aristotle's writings] —**metaphysician,** n.

metasomatism /metə'soʊmətɪzəm/, n. *Geol.* **1.** the replacement of minerals or rocks by others of different chemical composition as a result of hot, dissolved material entering from external sources. **2.** → **replacement** (def. 3). [Gk]

metastasis /mə'tæstəsəs/, n., pl. **-ses** /-siz/. *Med.* the movement of cancerous cells to other parts of the body via the circulation, lymphatics, or membranous surfaces. [LL, from Gk: removal]

metatarsus /metə'tasəs/, n., pl. **-si** /-sɪ/. the structure of the five bones between the ankle and the toes. [NL. See META-, TARSUS] —**metatarsal,** adj.

metathesis /mə'tæθəsəs/, n. the exchange of position of letters, syllables, or sounds in a word. [LL, from Gk: transposition] —**metathetic,** adj.

metazoan /metə'zoʊən/, adj. **1.** belonging or relating to the phylum which includes all the animals above the protozoans, i.e., those organisms which are composed of many cells. ◇n. **2.** any member of this phylum. [NL, from Gk *meta-* META- + *zōion* animal] —**metazoic,** adj.

Metcalf /'metkaf/, n. Donald, born 1929, Australian scientist, active in cancer research.

mete /mit/, v.t., **meted, meting.** to distribute or give out, usu. by measure; allot (usu. fol. by *out*): *to mete out punishment*. [ME; OE *metan*]

meteor /'mitiə, -ɔ/, n. a passing fiery streak in the sky produced by a meteoroid going through the earth's atmosphere. [late ME, from NL, from Gk: raised, high in air]

meteoric /miti'ɒrɪk/, *adj.* **1.** relating to or like a meteor. **2.** consisting of meteors: *a meteoric shower.* **3.** flashing like a meteor; brilliant only for a time: *a meteoric career.* **4.** swift or rapid: *a meteoric rise to power.*

meteorite /'mitiərait/, *n.* a mass of stone or metal that has reached the earth from outer space; a fallen meteoroid. — **meteoritic,** *adj.*

meteoroid /'mitiərɔid/, *n.* any of the small bodies, often remnants of comets, travelling through space, which, when meeting the earth's atmosphere, are heated to the point where they light up, thus becoming meteors.

meteorology /mitiə'rɒlədʒi/, *n.* the science dealing with the earth's atmosphere, esp. as relating to weather. [Gk. See METEOR, -LOGY] — **meteorologist,** *n.* — **meteorological,** *adj.*

meter /'mitə/, *n.* **1.** an instrument that measures, esp. one that automatically measures and records the quantity of gas, water, electricity, etc., passing through it. ◇*v.t.* **2.** to measure by means of a meter. [ME; from METE + -ER[1]]

-meter[1], a word part used in the names of instruments for measuring quantity, extent, degree, etc., as in *altimeter, barometer.* [NL, from Gk]

-meter[2], (in words taken from Greek or Latin) a word part meaning having (a certain number of) metrical feet in verse, as in *pentameter, trimeter.* [See METRE[2]]

methadone /'mɛθədoʊn/, *n.* a synthetic substitute for morphine, used in the treatment of morphine addiction.

methane /'miθeɪn/, *n.* a colorless, odorless, flammable gas, CH_4, the main constituent of marsh gas and firedamp of coal mines, the first member of the alkane series of hydrocarbons. [METH(YL) + -ANE]

methane series, *n.* → **alkane series.**

methanoic acid /mɛθə'noʊɪk/, *n.* → **formic acid.**

methanol /'mɛθənɒl/, *n.* → **methyl alcohol.**

methedrine /'mɛθədrin, -aɪn/, *n.* a powerful drug stimulating the central nervous system; methyl amphetamine. [Trademark]

metho /'mɛθoʊ/, *n. Colloq.* → **methylated spirits.**

method /'mɛθəd/, *n.* **1.** a way of going about something, esp. an orderly or systematic way: *a method of instruction.* **2.** a way of doing something, esp. in accordance with a definite plan: *Please use the proper method in this geometry problem.* **3.** order or system: *to work with method.* **4. method in one's madness,** reason or sense underneath one's apparent stupidity. **5.** (*usu. cap.*) Also, **Stanislavsky Method.** a way of acting in which the actor first explores the inner motivation of the character to be portrayed, so that the actor's reactions are spontaneous rather than intellectual. [L: mode of procedure, method, from Gk: a following after, method]

methodical /mə'θɒdɪkəl/, *adj.* done or acting in a careful, ordered way; systematic: *That scientist achieved great results from methodical study.*

Methodist /'mɛθədəst/, *n.* a member of one of the Christian denominations which grew out of the revival of religion led by John Wesley. — **Methodism,** *n.*

methodology /mɛθə'dɒlədʒi/, *n., pl.* **-gies.** the science of method, esp. a branch of logic dealing with the logical principles underlying the organisation of the various special sciences, and the conduct of scientific enquiry.

methuselah /mə'θuzələ/, *n.* **1.** a very old person. **2.** (*cap.*) a biblical patriarch before the Flood who according to tradition lived 969 years. [See Genesis 5:27. From Heb *M'thushelah*]

methyl /'mɛθəl/, *n.* a univalent hydrocarbon radical, CH_3-, derived from methane. [F]

methyl alcohol, *n.* a colorless, flammable, poisonous alcohol, CH_3OH, used as a fuel, solvent, etc.; methanol.

methylate /'mɛθəleɪt/, *v.t.*, **-lated, -lating.** to replace a hydrogen atom with methyl. — **methylation,** *n.*

methylated spirits /ˌmɛθəleɪtəd 'spɪrəts/, *n.* an ethyl alcohol with 5–10 per cent of methyl alcohol, used as a fuel, solvent, cleaner, etc.

methylene /'mɛθəlin/, *n.* a bivalent hydrocarbon radical, CH_2-, derived from methane. [F, from Gk]

meticulous /mə'tɪkjələs/, *adj.* careful about small details: *He was meticulous about his personal appearance.* [L: fearful]

metier /'mɛtieɪ/, *n.* a trade; profession; line of work or activity. Also, **métier.** [F, from L: MINISTRY]

metonymy /mə'tɒnəmi/, *n.* a figure of speech in which something is replaced by another word closely associated with it, e.g.: *The kettle is boiling.* [LL, from Gk: a change of name] — **metonymic,** *adj.*

metre[1] /'mitə/, *n.* a base SI unit of measurement of the length equal to 1.094 yards. *Symbol:* m [F, from Gk: measure]

metre[2] /'mitə/, *n.* the arrangement of words in poetry into lines or verses with certain rhythmic patterns; poetic measure. [ME, from F, from L]

-metre, a word part meaning metres; of or relating to a metre, as in *kilometre.* [See METRE[1]]

metre-kilogram-second system, *n.* a system of units used in science, based on the metre, kilogram, and second as the fundamental units of length, mass, and time. *Abbrev.:* m.k.s. (system), MKS (system). See **SI unit.**

metric /'mɛtrɪk/, *adj.* relating to the metre or to the system of measures and weights originally based upon it. [F]

metrical /ˈmɛtrɪkəl/, *adj.* **1.** relating to metre or poetic measure. **2.** written in metre or verse.

metricate /ˈmɛtrəkeɪt/, *v.t.*, **-cated, -cating.** to convert to metric units.

metrication /ˌmɛtrəˈkeɪʃən/, *n.* the process of conversion from British or imperial units to the metric system.

metric system, *n.* the decimal system of measurement. The modern metric system, known as the International System of Units (SI), comprises seven *base units*, the metre (m), kilogram (kg), second (s), ampere (A), kelvin (k), mole (mol), and candela (cd), two *supplementary units*, the radian (rad) and the steradian (sr), and *derived units*.

metric ton, *n.* → **tonne**.

metro /ˈmɛtroʊ/, *n.* an underground railway system in certain cities, esp. Paris. [F]

metronome /ˈmɛtrənoʊm/, *n.* a device for marking time, esp. for music. [Gk: measure] – **metronomic**, *adj.*

metropolis /məˈtrɒpələs/, *n., pl.* **-lises** /-ləsiz/. **1.** a large city (not necessarily the capital) in a country, state, or region. **2.** the mother city or parent state of an ancient Greek (or other) colony. [LL, from Gk: a mother state or city]

metropolitan /ˌmɛtrəˈpɒlətən/, *adj.* of, relating to, or characteristic of a metropolis or chief city, or of the people who live in it.

-metry, a word part meaning the process of measuring, abstract for *-meter*, as in *anthropometry, chronometry*. [Gk: measuring]

Metternich /ˈmɛtənɪk/, *n.* **Prince Klemens Wenzel Nepomuk Lothar von** /ˈkleɪmɛns ˌvɛntsəl ˌneɪpoʊmʊk ˈloʊtə fɒn/, 1773–1859, Austrian statesman; foreign minister 1809–48, chancellor 1821–48.

mettle /ˈmɛtl/, *n.* **1.** the particular character or temper of a person or animal: *to try a man's mettle*. **2.** energy, vigor; spirit; courage. **3. on one's mettle**, eager to do one's best. [var. of METAL]

mettlesome /ˈmɛtlsəm/, *adj.* spirited; courageous. Also, **mettled** /ˈmɛtld/.

MeV, *Phys. Symbol.* million electron-volts. Also, **Mev**

mew /mju/, *n.* **1.** the sound a cat makes. ◇*v.i.* **2.** to make this sound. [imitative]

mews /mjuz/, *n.pl. usu. construed as sing.* **1.** a set of stables or garages, around a yard, court, or alley, usu. including living quarters. **2.** a street, yard, or court lined by buildings originally used as stables and servants' quarters. [orig. pl. of *mew* cage for hawks]

Mex, *Abbrev.* **1.** Mexico. **2.** Mexican.

Mexico /ˈmɛksɪkoʊ/, *n.* **1.** a federal republic in Central America, on the Pacific Ocean and the Gulf of Mexico, bordered by the US, Belize and Guatemala; a Spanish colony before independence in 1821; ceded about one half of its territory to the US in the 1830s and 1840s, including Texas, New Mexico and California. Pop. 81 323 000 (1987 est.); 1 958 201 km^2. *Language*: Spanish. *Currency*: peso. *Cap.*: Mexico City. Official name, **United Mexican States**. Spanish, **Méjico**. **2. Gulf of,** an arm of the Atlantic Ocean between the US, Mexico and Cuba, linked to it by the Florida Strait. – **Mexican**, *n., adj.*

Mexico City, *n.* the capital of Mexico, in the central part. Pop. 8 831 079 (1980 est.). About 2255 m above sea level. Spanish, **Ciudad de México**.

mezzanine /ˈmɛzənin, mɛzəˈnin/, *n.* a low storey or floor in a building between two other storeys of greater height. [F, from It, from L: median]

mezzo /ˈmɛtsoʊ/, *adj.* middle; medium; half. [It, from L: middle]

mezzosoprano /ˌmɛtsoʊsəˈprɑnoʊ/, *n., pl.* **-nos, -ni** /-ni/. (a person having) a voice or voice part halfway in the range between soprano and contralto. [It]

m.f., *Abbrev.* medium-frequency.

MF, *Abbrev.* Middle French.

MFN, *Abbrev.* most favored nation.

Mg, *Chem. Symbol.* magnesium.

MGB /ˌɛm dʒi ˈbi/, *n.* the Soviet secret police from 1946–53. [Russ *M(inisterstvo) G(osudarstvennoi) B(ezopasnosti)*, literally, Ministry of State Security]

MGk, *Abbrev.* Medieval Greek.

mgr, *Abbrev.* manager.

MHA /ˌɛm eɪtʃ ˈeɪ/, *Abbrev.* Member of the House of Assembly.

MHG, *Abbrev.* Middle High German.

MHR /ˌɛm eɪtʃ ˈɑ/, *Abbrev.* Member of the House of Representatives.

mi /mi/, *n. Music.* See **solfège, solfa**.

MIA /ˌɛm aɪ ˈeɪ/, *n.* Murrumbidgee Irrigation Area. [abbrev.]

Miami /maɪˈæmi/, *n.* a town in the US, in south-eastern Florida; winter seaside resort. Pop. 373 940 (1986 est.).

mia-mia /ˈmaɪə-maɪə, ˈmiə-miə/, *n.* a bush shelter used by Aborigines; gunyah; humpy; wurley. [Aboriginal]

miaow /miˈaʊ, mjaʊ/, *n.* **1.** the sound a cat makes. ◇*v.i.* **2.** to make such a sound. Also, **meow, miaou, miaul** /miˈaʊl/. [imitative]

miasma /miˈæzmə/, *n., pl.* **-mata** /-mətə/, **-mas.** poisonous vapors or germs infecting the atmosphere. [NL, from Gk: pollution] – **miasmal, miasmatic, miasmatical, miasmic,** *adj.*

mica /ˈmaɪkə/, *n.* any member of a group of minerals, hydrous disilicates of aluminium with other bases, chiefly potassium, magnesium, iron, and lithium, that separate easily (by cleavage) into thin, tough, often transparent sheets. [NL, special use of L: crumb, grain, little bit] – **micaceous**, *adj.*

mice /maɪs/, *n.* plural of **mouse**.

Michael /ˈmaɪkəl/, *n. Bible.* a militant archangel. [See Daniel 10:13]

Michaelmas /'mɪkəlməs/, n. a festival celebrated on 29 September in honor of the archangel Michael. Also, **Michaelmas Day**. [OE (Sanct) Michaeles masse St Michael's mass]

Michelangelo /maɪkəl'ændʒəloʊ/, n. (Michelagniolo di Ludovico Buonarroti), 1475–1564, Italian sculptor, painter, architect, and poet; outstanding figure of the Renaissance. Famous sculptures include David (1501–04) and Moses (c. 1515), which was commissioned for the tomb of Julius II. His paintings include the ceiling of the Sistine Chapel, depicting the biblical history of man, and also in the Sistine, The Last Judgment (1533–41). His architecture is represented in the dome of St Peter's, Rome.

Michigan /'mɪʃəgən/, n. **1.** a state in the northern central US. Pop. 9 014 000 (1986 est.); 150 767 km². Cap.: Lansing. Abbrev.: Mich **2. Lake**, a lake between Wisconsin and Michigan; one of the five Great Lakes. About 58 012 km².

Mick /mɪk/, n. Colloq. **1.** a Roman Catholic (esp. of Irish extraction). **2.** Irishman.

micra /'maɪkrə/, n. a plural of **micron**.

micro- /'maɪkroʊ-/, **1.** a prefix meaning **a.** 'very small', as in micro-organism, microcosm. **b.** 'enlarging' or 'amplifying', as in microphone, microscope. Also, before vowels, **micr-**. **2.** a prefix meaning 10⁻⁶ of a given unit, as in microvolt. Symbol: μ [Gk combining form of mikrós small]

microbe /'maɪkroʊb/, n. a micro-organism, usu. a bacterium, esp. one causing disease; germ. [F, from Gk: small life] –**microbial, microbic,** adj.

microbiology /ˌmaɪkroʊbaɪ'ɒlədʒi/, n. the science and study of microscopic and submicroscopic organisms. –**microbiological,** adj. –**microbiologist,** n.

microcline /'maɪkroʊˌklaɪn/, n. a mineral of the felspar group, potassium aluminium silicate, $KAlSi_3O_8$, with the same composition as orthoclase but a different crystal system, used in making porcelain.

micrococcus /maɪkroʊ'kɒkəs/, n., pl. **-cocci** /-'kɒksaɪ/. any member of the genus Micrococcus, comprising globular or oval bacterial organisms, of which certain species cause disease, and others produce fermentation, coloration, etc. [NL. See MICRO-, COCCUS]

microcosm /'maɪkrəkɒzəm/, n. **1.** a little world (opposed to macrocosm). **2.** anything regarded as a world in miniature. [F, from LL, from LGk: little world] –**microcosmic, microcosmical,** adj.

micro-economics /ˌmaɪkroʊ-ekə'nɒmɪks/, n. the study of the economic system in terms of its different sectors (opposed to macroeconomics). [MICRO- + ECONOMICS]

microfiche /'maɪkroʊfiʃ/, n. a microfilmed transparency about the size and shape of a filing card which may have on it many pages of print. [F]

microfilm /'maɪkroʊfɪlm/, n. **1.** a narrow film, esp. of motion-picture type, on which very small images are made. ◇v.t. **2.** to record on microfilm.

micrometer /maɪ'krɒmətə/, n. a device for measuring very small distances, angles, etc., used with a telescope or microscope. –**micrometry,** n.

Micronesia /maɪkrə'niʒə/, n. one of the three groups into which the Pacific islands are divided, the other two being Melanesia and Polynesia; includes Guam, Kiribati, Marshall, Mariana and Caroline island groups and Nauru island. –**Micronesian,** n., adj.

micro-organism /maɪkroʊ-'ɔgənɪzəm/, n. a microscopic (animal or vegetable) organism.

microphone /'maɪkrəfoʊn/, n. an instrument which is able to transform the air-pressure waves of sound into changes in electric currents or voltages. Adjectives such as capacitor, crystal, velocity, etc., describe the method of developing the electric quantity. –**microphonic,** adj.

microprocessor /maɪkroʊ'proʊsesə/, n. a small computer, based on a single chip (def. 6) as the central processing unit.

microscope /'maɪkrəskoʊp/, n. an optical instrument with magnifying lens(es) for examining objects too small to be seen, or to be seen clearly and in detail, by the naked eye. [MICRO- + Gk: view]

microscopic /maɪkrə'skɒpɪk/, adj. **1.** so small as to be invisible or unclear without the use of the microscope. **2.** very small; tiny. **3.** of or relating to the microscope or its use. –**microscopically,** adv.

microwave /'maɪkrəweɪv/, n. an electromagnetic wave of very high frequency, with a wavelength range from 50 cm to 1 mm.

microwave oven, n. an oven which cooks with unusual speed, by passing microwaves through food and generating heat inside it.

mid¹ /mɪd/, adj. central; at or near the middle point: in the mid nineties of the last century. [ME; OE midd]

mid² /mɪd/, prep. →amid. Also, **'mid**.

mid-, combining form of 'middle'.

midair /mɪ'deə/, n. **1.** any raised position above the ground. **2.** a position or state where things are not decided or finished.

Midas /'maɪdəs/, n. Gk Legend. a king of Phrygia, who was given by Dionysus the power of turning into gold whatever he touched.

midday /'mɪdeɪ/, n. **1.** the middle of the day; noon. ◇adj. **2.** of or relating to the middle part of the day. [ME; OE middæg]

midden /'mɪdn/, n. **1.** a dunghill or refuse heap. **2.** a mound consisting of shells of edible molluscs and other refuse, marking the site of prehistoric human habitation. [ME, from Scand]

middle /'mɪdl/, adj. **1.** being the same distance from both ends: the middle point of a line. **2.** being neither of any two opposites, but between them; halfway; intermediate; medium: middle size; middle distance. **3.** (cap.) (in various studies, e.g. history of a language, geology, history) being of the period of time that comes between other periods that are called Old and New, Upper and Lower, etc.: Middle English;

middle

Middle Kingdom. ◇*n.* **4.** the point, part, etc., which is the same distance from both ends of something. **5.** the waist, or middle part of the human body. **6. middle of the road**, not too much one way or the other; mediocre. [ME and OE *middel*]

Middle Ages, *n.pl.* the time in European history between classical antiquity and the Italian Renaissance (from the late fifth century to about AD 1350); sometimes restricted to the later part of this period (after 1100); sometimes extended to 1450 or 1500.

middle C, *n. Music.* the note indicated by the first leger line above the bass stave and the first below the treble stave, being neither a high nor a low note.

middle class, *n.* a social grouping of people who are neither very rich, nor come from a long established and well-off family, nor very poor, but work at a job that pays them well enough to live comfortably, e.g. business people, doctors, lawyers, teachers, public servants, etc. **a.** *Brit.* the class which, in the social structure, is between the aristocracy and the working class. **b.** a class of business people or merchants which became common in Europe towards the end of the Middle Ages, marking the change to modern economy. **–middle-class**, *adj.*

Middle Dutch, *n.* the Dutch language from about 1100 to about 1500.

middle ear, *n.* the section of the ear recessed into the temporal bone, lying between the inner ear and the eardrum and containing the three small bones which join them; tympanum.

Middle East, *n.* the lands from the eastern shores of the Mediterranean and Aegean to India. **–Middle Eastern**, *adj.*

Middle English, *n.* the English language of the period approximately 1100–1450.

Middle French, *n.* the French language of the period approximately 1400–1600.

Middle High German, *n.* the High German language from approximately 1100–1450.

Middle Kingdom, *n.* Also, **Middle Empire**. the second great period in the history of the ancient Egyptian kingdom, about 2200 BC to 1690 BC, comprising dynasties XI–XIV. See **Old Kingdom, New Kingdom**.

Middle Low German, *n.* Low German of the period approximately 1100–1500.

middleman /ˈmɪdlmæn/, *n., pl.* **-men. 1.** a person who makes a profit by buying from producers and selling to retailers or consumers. Also, **middle man. 2.** someone who acts as an intermediary between others.

middle-of-the-road /ˌmɪdl-əv-ðə-ˈroʊd/, *adj.* between extremes; moderate.

Middle Palaeolithic /ˌmɪdl pæliəˈlɪθɪk/, *n.* the period between the Lower and the Upper Palaeolithic, usu. equated with the Mousterian. ◇*adj.* **1.** of or pertaining to this period.

Middlesex /ˈmɪdlseks/, *n.* a former county in south-eastern England, now an area administered by various inner and outer London boroughs. *Abbrev.*: Middx

Middleton /ˈmɪdltən/, *n.* **Thomas**, c. 1570–1627, English dramatist, author (with Rowley) of *The Changeling*.

middleweight /ˈmɪdlweɪt/, *n.* **1.** a boxer weighing between 71 and 75 kg (in the amateur ranks) or between 69.853 and 72.574 kg (in the professional ranks). **2.** a professional wrestler weighing between 76.204 and 78.925 kg.

middling /ˈmɪdlɪŋ/, *adj.* **1.** medium in size, quality, grade, rank, etc.; moderately large, good, etc. **2.** *Colloq.* in fairly good health. **3.** *Colloq.* second-rate; mediocre.

middy /ˈmɪdi/, *n.pl.* **-dies.** a medium size glass, mainly used for serving beer.

midge /mɪdʒ/, *n.* **1.** a type of two-winged insect, some of which bite. See **gnat. 2.** *Colloq.* a small person. [OE *mycg*]

midget /ˈmɪdʒət/, *n.* a very small person or thing. [MIDGE + -ET]

midi /ˈmɪdi/, *adj., n.* (relating to) a dress, skirt, or coat, with the hemline down to the middle of the calves.

Midlands /ˈmɪdləndz/, *n.pl.* the central part of England; the midland counties, including Warwickshire, Northamptonshire, Leicestershire, Nottinghamshire, Derbyshire, Staffordshire, the West Midlands and the eastern part of Hereford and Worcester.

midnight /ˈmɪdnaɪt/, *n.* **1.** the middle of the night; 12 o'clock at night. ◇*adj.* **2.** of or relating to midnight. **3.** like midnight, as in darkness: *midnight blue*. **4. burn the midnight oil**, to study or work far into the night.

midnight sun, *n.* the sun visible at midnight in midsummer in arctic and antarctic regions.

mid-off /mɪd-ˈɒf/, *n.* (in cricket) a fielding position on the off side, near the bowler.

mid-on /mɪd-ˈɒn/, *n.* (in cricket) a fielding position on the on side near the bowler.

midriff /ˈmɪdrɪf/, *n.* **1.** the diaphragm (in the human body). **2.** the middle part of the body, between chest and waist. [OE *midd* mid + *hrif* belly]

midshipman /ˈmɪdʃɪpmən/, *n., pl.* **-men.** a probationary rank held by naval cadets to see whether they can qualify as officers.

midst /mɪdst/, *n.* **1.** the position of anything surrounded by other things or parts, or coming in the middle of a period of time, course of action, etc. **2.** the middle point, part, or stage. **3. in our (your, their) midst**, among us (you, them). [ME *middes* middle]

Midway Islands /ˌmɪdweɪ ˈaɪləndz/, *n.pl.* several islets in the northern Pacific, about 1931 km north-west of Hawaii; the Japanese were defeated in a naval battle, June 1942. Pop. 2200 (1970); 5 km².

mid wicket, *n.* (in cricket) an on-side fielding position between square leg and mid-on.

midwife /ˈmɪdwaɪf/, *n., pl.* **-wives** /-waɪvz/. a person trained to help women in childbirth. [ME, from *mid* with, + WIFE] **–midwifery**, *n.*

mien /min/, *n.* the way a person has of showing character, feeling, etc.: *a man of noble mien*. [influenced by F, from Breton: beak]

Mies van der Rohe /'mis væn də 'rouə/, *n.* **Ludwig** /'lυdvɪg/, 1886-1969, US architect, born in Germany; pioneer of modern architecture of a functional, pure geometrical style.

MI5 /em aɪ 'faɪv/, *n.* Military Intelligence, section five; formerly an official and now a popular name for the counter-intelligence agency of the British government.

might[1] /maɪt/, *v.* **1.** past tense of **may**. **2.** an auxiliary verb showing possibility: *He might be lost.* [OE]

might[2] /maɪt/, *n.* **1.** the power to do or accomplish; ability. **2.** effective power or force of any kind. **3.** superior power: *the doctrine that might makes right.* **4. with might and main,** with the greatest strength, vigor, force, or effort. [OE]

mighty /'maɪti/, *adj.,* **-tier, -tiest. 1.** having, showing or marked by might or power: *mighty rulers.* **2.** of great size; huge: *a mighty oak.*

migraine /'maɪgreɪn, 'miːgreɪn/, *n.* a very bad headache often on one side of the head only and usu. associated with nausea. [F]

migrant /'maɪgrənt/, *n.* **1.** someone who leaves his own country to go to live in another; immigrant; emigrant. **2.** an animal or bird which migrates. ◇*adj.* **3.** of or relating to migration or migrants. [L]

migrate /maɪ'greɪt/, *v.i.,* **-grated, -grating. 1.** (of certain animals, esp. birds) to spend a part of each year, or of a lifetime, in one place, then to travel to another to escape a harsh winter, or to breed. **2.** (of people) to go to live in another country. [L] **– migrator,** *n.* **– migratory,** *adj.*

migration /maɪ'greɪʃən/, *n.* **1.** the action of migrating. **2.** a number or body of persons or animals migrating together. **3.** *Chem.* movement or change of place of atoms within a molecule. [L]

mikado /mə'kadoʊ/, *n., pl.* **-dos.** (*oft. cap.*) (formerly) a title of the Emperor of Japan. [Jap: exalted gate]

Miklouho-Maclay /ˌmɪkləhoʊ-mə.ˈkleɪ/, *n.* **Baron Nicolai Nicolaievitch** /'nɪkəlaɪ nɪkə.laɪəvɪtʃ/ 1846–88, Russian explorer and scientist; responsible for the setting up of a marine laboratory in Sydney.

mil /mɪl/, *Abbrev. n.* **1.** a millilitre (0.001 of a litre), or cubic centimetre. **2.** a unit of length equal to 0.001 of an inch, used in measuring the diameter of wires. [short for L: thousandth]

Milan /mə'læn/, *n.* a city in Italy, in west central Lombardy; famous cathedral. Pop. 1 507 877 (1986 est.). Italian, **Milano.** **– Milanese,** *n., adj.*

mild /maɪld/, *adj.* **1.** gentle in feeling or behavior towards others. **2.** (of manners, speech, etc.) showing such gentleness. **3.** (of air, weather, etc.) not cold, severe, or extreme. **4.** not sharp, pungent, or strong: *a mild flavor.* **5.** gentle or moderate in degree, character or intensity: *mild regret; mild pain.* [OE]

mildew /'mɪldjuː/, *n.* **1.** a plant disease caused by a fungus usu. marked by a whitish coating or a change in color on the surface. **2.** any of these fungi. **3.** a similar coating or change in color, due to fungi, on fabrics, paper, leather, wood, etc., when exposed to moisture, esp. in damp weather. ◇*v.i.* **4.** to become covered with mildew. [OE: honeydew]

Mildura /mɪl'djʊərə/, *n.* a city in northern Vic on the Murray River; the centre of the Mallee wheat and grazing region. Pop. 20 512 (1986).

mile /maɪl/, *n.* **1.** a unit of measurement of length in the imperial system, equal to 5280 feet (1609.34 m). **2. nautical, international nautical** or **sea mile,** unit of measurement of length used in marine or aeronautical navigation, equal to 1852 m. **3.** (*oft. pl.*) a large distance or quantity: *miles of paperwork.* [OE, from L: a thousand]

mileage /'maɪlɪdʒ/, *n.* **1.** the total length or distance stated in miles. **2.** a travelling allowance estimated at a certain rate per mile. **3.** the number of miles travelled by a motor vehicle on a particular amount of fuel. **4. get mileage out of,** *Colloq.* to gain use or advantage from.

Miles Franklin Award /maɪlz 'fræŋklən/, *n.* an annual literary award for an Australian novel. [from the estate of *Miles Franklin,* Australian novelist]

milestone /'maɪlstoʊn/, *n.* **1.** Also, **mile post.** a stone set up to mark the distance to or from a town or city esp. along a highway. **2.** an event marking an important point in someone's life or career.

Milgate /'mɪlgeɪt/, *n.* **Rodney,** born 1934, Australian painter and playwright.

milieu /mi'ljɜ/, *n.* the total surrounding area, state or atmosphere in which someone lives or operates; environment: *the social milieu; the cultural milieu.* [F, from L]

militant /'mɪlətənt/, *adj.* **1.** wanting to fight, esp. for a cause; aggressive: *a militant reformer.* ◇*n.* **2.** a militant person. [ME, from L: serving as a soldier] **– militancy,** *n.*

militarism /'mɪlətərɪzəm/, *n.* **1.** a state of thinking and acting in a military way. **2.** the principle of keeping large armies, navies, etc., ready for war. **3.** the tendency to regard military efficiency as more important than any other area of government. **– militarist,** *n.* **– militaristic,** *adj.*

military /'mɪlətri, -təri/, *adj.* **1.** of or relating to the armed forces. ◇*n.* **2.** soldiers generally; the armed forces: *the military.* [L]

militate /'mɪləteɪt/, *v.i.,* **-tated, -tating.** to influence or work (*against* or *in favor of*).

militia /mə'lɪʃə/, *n.* **1.** a body of men enrolled for military service, called out at set times for drill and exercise but for actual service only in emergencies. **2.** a body of citizen soldiers (as distinguished from professional soldiers). [L: military service, soldiery]

miljee /ˈmɪldʒi/, *n.* a small acacia tree widely distributed in inland Australia.

milk /mɪlk/, *n.* **1.** an opaque white liquid produced by female mammals to feed their young. The milk of the cow and some other animals is used for food or for making cheese, butter, etc. **2.** any liquid like this, e.g. the liquid in a coconut. **3. cry over spilt milk,** to be upset over something which cannot be changed. ◇*v.t.* **4.** to press or draw milk by hand or machine from the udder of (a cow or other animal). **5.** to draw venom from (a spider, snake, etc.). **6.** to draw (the sap) from certain plants, e.g. rubber tree. **7.** to draw (something) out as if by milking; extract: *to milk someone of money*; *to milk a car (of petrol).* ◇*v.i.* **8.** (of a cow etc.) to yield milk. [OE] —**milker,** *n.*

milk bar, *n.* a shop where drinks, esp. milk shakes, ice cream, sandwiches, etc., are sold.

milk of magnesia /mægˈniʃə, -ˈniʒə, -ˈniziə/, *n.* a suspension of magnesium hydroxide, Mg(OH)$_2$, used medicinally as an antacid or laxative for stomach and bowel upsets.

milksop /ˈmɪlksɒp/, *n.* **1.** a dish of bread, etc., soaked in milk, given to children and invalids. **2.** a weak, cowardly or effeminate man or youth. —**milksopism,** *n.*

milk tooth, *n.* one of the temporary or first teeth of a mammal which are replaced by the permanent teeth. Also, **baby tooth.**

milky /ˈmɪlki/, *adj.,* **-kier, -kiest. 1.** like milk in color or consistency. **2.** of a chalky white.

Milky Way, *n.* the faintly luminous band stretching across the heavens, composed of uncountable stars too faint to be seen without a telescope. This band is the further side of the spiral galaxy to which our solar system belongs; the galaxy. [translation of L *via lactea*]

mill /mɪl/, *n.* **1.** a building or establishment with machinery for various manufacturing operations, esp. the spinning or weaving of cotton or wool, or grinding of grain into flour. **2.** a machine for grinding, crushing, or extracting liquid from any solid substance: *a coffee mill; a cider mill.* **3. go through the mill,** to undergo a difficult experience. **4. run of the mill,** commonplace; conventional. ◇*v.t.* **5.** to grind, work, treat, or shape in or with a mill. **6.** to finish the edge of (a coin, knob etc.) with a series of fine notches or slanting grooves. ◇*v.i.* **7.** (of a herd of cattle or a crowd of people) to move confusedly within an area (oft. fol. by *about*). [OE, from L: millstone, mill]

Mill /mɪl/, *n.* **John Stuart,** 1806–73, English philosopher and economist; main works include *Utilitarianism* (1861), *On Liberty* (1859), *A System of Logic* (1843), *Principles of Political Economy* (1848).

Millais /ˈmɪleɪ/, *n.* **Sir John Everett,** 1829–96, English painter; founder of the Pre-Raphaelite Brotherhood.

millennium /məˈlɛniəm/, *n., pl.* **-niums, -nia** /-niə/. **1.** a period of a thousand years. **2.** the period of 'a thousand years' (phrase variously interpreted) during which some believe that Christ is to reign on earth, according to the prophetic statement in Rev 20:1–7. **3.** a period of general goodness and happiness, esp. in the future. [NL, from L *mille* thousand + *-ennium*] —**millennial,** *adj.*

miller /ˈmɪlə/, *n.* someone who keeps or operates a mill, esp. a flour mill. [ME]

Miller /ˈmɪlə/, *n.* **1. Arthur,** born 1915, US playwright; best-known plays include *Death of a Salesman* (1949) and *The Crucible* (1953). **2. Godfrey Clive,** 1893–1964, Australian painter and art teacher, born in New Zealand. **3. Henry Valentine,** 1891–1980, US novelist; wrote *Tropic of Cancer* (1934). **4. Keith Ross,** born 1919, Australian cricketer; played in 55 tests 1946–56.

millet /ˈmɪlət/, *n.* a cereal grass cultivated widely in Asia and in southern Europe for its small seed or grain (used as a food for man and fowls). [ME, from F, from L]

Millet /ˈmɪleɪ, mɪˈleɪ/, *n.* **Jean François** /ʒɒ frɒˈswa/, 1814–75, French painter noted for his depiction of rustic scenes.

Millett /ˈmɪlət/, *n.* **Kate,** born 1934, US author and feminist; her works include *Sexual Politics* (1970) and *Flying* (1974).

milli- /ˈmɪli-/, a prefix denoting 10^{-3} of a given unit, as in *milligram*. Symbol: m [L, combining form of *mille* a thousand]

milliard /ˈmɪliad, ˈmɪljad/, *n.* a thousand millions. [F, from L: thousand]

millibar /ˈmɪliba/, *n.* a widely used unit of atmospheric pressure, equal to 0.001 bar or 100 pascals.

Milligan /ˈmɪləgən/, *n.* **Spike** (*Terence Alan Milligan*), born 1919 in India, British comedian and writer; one of the Goons.

milligram /ˈmɪligræm/, *n.* a unit of mass equal to 0.001 gram. Symbol: mg

millilitre /ˈmɪlilitə/, *n.* a unit of capacity equal to 0.001 litre. Symbol: ml

millimetre /ˈmɪlimitə/, *n.* a unit of length equal to 0.001 metre. Symbol: mm

millimetre of mercury, *n.* a non-SI unit of measurement of pressure, approx. equal to 133.3 pascals. Symbol: mmHg

milliner /ˈmɪlənə/, *n.* someone who makes or sells hats for women. [var. of obs. *Milaner* an inhabitant of Milan, a dealer in articles from Milan] —**millinery,** *n.*

milling /ˈmɪlɪŋ/, *n.* **1.** the act or process of grinding, treating or shaping in a mill. **2.** the process of producing smooth or shaped surfaces. **3.** the process of finishing the edge of a coin, etc., with fine notches or transverse grooves.

million /ˈmɪljən/, *n.* **1.** a cardinal number, one thousand times one thousand, or 10^6. **2.** (of pounds, dollars, etc.) the amount of a thousand thousand units of money. **3.** a very great number. **4. one in a million,** someone or something of great worth. ◇*adj.* **5.** amounting to one million in numbers. [ME, from OF, from It, from L] —**millionth,** *adj.*

millionaire /ˈmɪljəˈnɛə/, *n.* **1.** a person who owns a million or millions (of pounds, dollars, etc.). **2.** a very rich person. [F: MILLION]

millipede /ˈmɪləpɪd/, *n.* a creature with a long body made up of many parts or segments, most of which have two pairs of legs. Also, **millepede**. [L: wood louse]

millpond /ˈmɪlpɒnd/, *n.* **1.** a pond for supplying water to drive a millwheel. **2.** an area of very calm water.

millstone /ˈmɪlstoʊn/, *n.* **1.** either of a pair of large circular stones between which grain or other substance is ground, as in a mill. **2.** something that grinds or crushes. **3.** a heavy burden, esp. in the phrase *a millstone around one's neck* (in allusion to Matt 18:6).

millwheel /ˈmɪlwiːl/, *n.* a wheel, esp. a waterwheel, to drive a mill.

Milne /mɪln/, *n.* **A(lan) A(lexander)**, 1882–1956, English writer of plays, books for children, and novels; best-known works include verse in *When We Were Very Young* (1924) and *Now We Are Six* (1927) and the story *Winnie-The-Pooh* (1926).

Milne Bay /mɪln/, *n.* a province of PNG, comprising the easternmost part of the mainland and a number of islands. Pop. 150 600 (1986 est.); 14 000 km². *Administrative Centre*: Alotau.

milt /mɪlt/, *n.* **1.** the secretion of the male generative organs of fishes. **2.** the organs themselves. ◊*v.t.* **3.** to extract the eggs or sperm from (a fish) for artificial spawning. [OE]

Milton /ˈmɪltn/, *n.* **John**, 1608–74, English poet. His major works are the epics *Paradise Lost* (1667; 1674), *Paradise Regained* (1671) and the tragedy *Samson Agonistes* (1671). —**Miltonic**, *adj.*

mime /maɪm/, *n., v.*, **mimed, miming.** ◊*n.* **1.** the art of acting out a character, scene, feelings, etc., by bodily gestures and movements and facial expressions, but without speaking. **2.** a play or entertainment in which the performers express themselves by such acting. **3.** an actor in a mime, esp. a clown or comedian. **4.** (a player in) an ancient Greek or Roman kind of farce which depended for effect largely upon silly actions and gestures. ◊*v.t.* **5.** → **mimic**. ◊*v.i.* **6.** to play a part by mimicry, esp. without words. [L, from Gk] —**mimer**, *n.*

mimetic /məˈmɛtɪk/, *adj.* characterised by, showing, or like mimicry.

mimic /ˈmɪmɪk/, *v.*, **-icked, -icking,** *n.* ◊*v.t.* **1.** to copy in action, speech, etc., often playfully or hurtfully; imitate. **2.** (of things) to take on the appearance, behavior of; simulate. ◊*n.* **3.** someone able to imitate the characteristic voice or movements of others. **4.** someone or something which imitates; an imitator or imitation. [L, from Gk: belonging to mimes]

mimicry /ˈmɪmɪkri/, *n., pl.* **-ries. 1.** the act, practice, or art of mimicking. **2.** *Zool.* Also, **mimesis** /ˈmɪmɪsɪs/, the close external resemblance, as if from imitation of an animal to some different animal or to surrounding objects, esp. as serving for protection or concealment. **3.** an instance, performance, or result of mimicking.

mimosa /məˈmoʊsə/, *n.* **1.** a large group of plants native to tropical or warm regions, including trees, shrubs, etc., having small flowers with round heads or cylindrical spikes. **2.** *Obs.* → **wattle**. [NL, from L: MIME; apparently so named from seeming mimicry of animal life in closing its leaves when touched]

Min, *Abbrev.* **1.** Minister. **2.** Ministry.

minaret /mɪnəˈrɛt, ˈmɪnərɛt/, *n.* a tall tower attached to a Muslim mosque (place of worship), from which the muezzin calls the people to prayer. [Sp, from Ar: lighthouse]

mince /ˈmɪns/, *v.*, **minced, mincing,** *n.* ◊*v.t.* **1.** to cut or chop into very small pieces. **2.** to divide (land, a subject, etc.) into small parts. **3.** to soften (one's words, etc.) to a milder form. ◊*v.i.* **4.** to speak, walk, or move with a show of daintiness. ◊*n.* **5.** minced meat. [ME, from OF: make small, from L: small] —**mincer**, *n.*

mincemeat /ˈmɪnsmit/, *n.* **1.** a mixture composed of minced apples, suet, candied peel, etc., with raisins, currants, etc., for filling a pie (mince pie). **2. make mincemeat of,** *Colloq.* **a.** to attack and do harm to. **b.** to make a successful attack on with words; berate.

mincing /ˈmɪnsɪŋ/, *adj.* (of behavior, speech, a person, etc.) elegant in an affected way.

mind /maɪnd/, *n.* **1.** that which thinks, feels, and wills, uses perception, judgment, memory, etc. **2.** the intellect or understanding, as opposed to feeling and willing; intelligence. **3.** a person considered in relation to intellectual power: *the greatest minds of the time.* **4.** sound mental condition: *You could lose your mind worrying too much.* **5.** way of thinking and feeling: *many men, many minds.* **6.** opinion or feelings: *I can read your mind.* **7.** inclination or desire. **8.** a conscious or intelligent being: *the idea of a mind controlling the universe.* **9.** memory: *Keep this date in mind.* **10. a piece of one's mind,** a scolding. **11. make up one's mind,** to come to a decision. **12. out of one's mind,** severely disturbed or upset. **13. presence of mind,** ability to act quickly and effectively when faced with danger or difficulty. ◊*v.t.* **14.** to pay attention to (a person, advice, instructions, etc.). **15.** to apply oneself or attend to: *Mind your own business!* **16.** to look after; tend. **17.** to be careful about: *Mind what you say.* **18.** to care about or feel concern at. **19.** (*in negative expressions and questions*) to feel inconvenienced by; object to: *You don't mind my departure?* **20.** *Archaic.* to remember or remind. ◊*v.i.* **21.** (*mainly as a command*) to take notice, observe, or understand: *Mind you, I think he's wrong.* **22.** to be careful. **23.** (*oft. in negative expressions and questions*) to care, feel concern, or object: *Mind if I go?* [OE: memory, thought]

Mindanao /mɪndəˈnaʊ/, *n.* the second largest island of the Philippines, in the southern part of the group. Pop. 10 894 000 (1978); 94 623 km².

mindful /ˈmaɪndfəl/, *adj.* careful; aware (usu. fol. by *of*).

mine[1] /maɪn/, *pron.* **1.** possessive form of *I*, used after the verb 'to be' or without a noun following: *That book is mine; a friend of mine.* **2.** the person(s) or thing(s) belonging to me: *me and mine.* ◇*adj.* **3.** *Archaic.* my (used before a vowel or *h*, or after a noun): *mine eyes; lady mine.* [OE]

mine[2] /maɪn/, *n., v.*, **mined, mining.** ◇*n.* **1.** an excavation made in the earth to remove ores, precious stones, coal, etc. **2.** a deposit of such minerals, either under the ground or at its surface. **3.** a store of anything: *This book is a mine of information.* **4.** an underground passage dug to reach under an enemy's position, usu. for placing explosives. **5.** a device containing a large charge of explosive in a watertight casing placed in the sea for the purpose of blowing up an enemy vessel. **6.** a similar device used on land; landmine. ◇*v.i.* **7.** to dig in the earth for the purpose of removing ores, coal, etc. **8.** to remove ores, etc., from mines. **9.** to dig or lay mines, as in military operations. ◇*v.t.* **10.** to dig in (earth, etc.) to obtain ores, coal, etc. **11.** to remove (ores, coal, etc.) from a mine. **12.** to make underground passages in or under; burrow. **13.** to dig or lay military mines under. [ME, from OF, of Celtic orig.]

minefield /ˈmaɪnfiːld/, *n.* an area on land or water where mines have been laid.

miner[1] /ˈmaɪnə/, *n.* a person who works in a mine.

miner[2] /ˈmaɪnə/, *n.* a type of bird with a yellow beak and yellow or yellow-brown legs, which lives in colonies, e.g. **the noisy miner** or **bellbird**.

mineral /ˈmɪnərəl, ˈmɪnrəl/, *n.* **1.** a substance obtained by mining; ore. **2.** any of a class of substances occurring in nature, usu. inorganic substances of definite chemical composition and definite crystal structure and also natural products of organic origin, as coal, etc. **3.** a substance neither animal nor vegetable. ◇*adj.* **4.** of the nature of or containing minerals. **5.** neither animal nor vegetable; inorganic: *the mineral kingdom.* [ME, from ML: of a mine, from OF: MINE²]

mineralogy /mɪnəˈrælədʒi, -ˈrɒl-/, *n.* the science of minerals. —**mineralogical**, *adj.* —**mineralogist**, *n.*

mineral water, *n.* water containing dissolved mineral salts or gases.

miner's right, *n.* an official licence to mine, as for gold.

Minerva /məˈnɜːvə/, *n. Rom Myth.* the goddess of wisdom, the arts, and war; Greek counterpart, Athena.

minestrone /mɪnəˈstrouni/, *n.* a soup containing vegetables, herbs, pasta, etc., in chicken or meat stock. [It: soup, from L: serve, wait upon]

minesweeper /ˈmaɪnswiːpə/, *n.* a ship used for searching a body of water to remove enemy mines.

Ming /mɪŋ/, *n.* **1.** the dynasty which ruled China from 1368 to 1644, under which art flourished and there were important revisions of Confucian philosophy. ◇*adj.* **2.** indicating objects, esp. a type of porcelain, produced during the Ming dynasty.

mingle /ˈmɪŋgəl/, *v.*, **-gled, -gling.** ◇*v.i.* **1.** to become mixed or united. **2.** to take part with others; participate. ◇*v.t.* **3.** to mix or combine; blend. **4.** to unite or join: *Joy mingled with pain.* [OE *mengan*] —**mingler**, *n.*

mingy /ˈmɪndʒi/, *adj. Colloq.* mean; miserly. [b. M(EAN²) + (ST)INGY]

mini /ˈmɪni/, *Colloq.* ◇*n.* **1.** → miniskirt. ◇*adj.* **2.** small; miniature.

mini-, a word part meaning 'small' or 'miniature', as in *miniskirt*. [abbrev. of MINIATURE]

miniature /ˈmɪnətʃə/, *n.* **1.** a representation of anything on a very small scale. **2.** a very small painting, esp. a portrait. ◇*adj.* **3.** on a very small scale; reduced. [It, from L]

minibus /ˈmɪnibʌs/, *n.* a motor vehicle for carrying between five and ten passengers.

minim /ˈmɪnəm/, *n.* **1.** the smallest unit of liquid measure in the imperial system, equal to $59.193\,880 \times 10^{-6}$ litres. **2.** *Music.* a note, equal in time value to one half of a semibreve. **3.** something very small or insignificant. [ME, from L: least, smallest]

minimise *or* **minimize** /ˈmɪnəmaɪz/, *v.t.*, **-mised, -mising.** **1.** to reduce to the smallest possible amount. **2.** to represent at the lowest possible estimate; to belittle. —**minimisation**, *n.* —**minimiser**, *n.*

minimum /ˈmɪnəməm/, *n., pl.* **-mums, -ma** /-mə/, *adj.* ◇*n.* **1.** the least quantity or amount possible, allowable, etc. **2.** the lowest amount, value, or degree reached or recorded (opposed to *maximum*). **3.** *Maths.* the value of a function at a certain point which is less than or equal to the value at nearby points. ◇*adj.* **4.** that is a minimum. **5.** least possible. **6.** lowest. [L] —**minimal**, *adj.*

minimum wage, *n.* the lowest wage legally payable to any adult employee covered by a particular award or agreement.

mining /ˈmaɪnɪŋ/, *n.* the action, process, or industry of removing ores, etc., from mines.

minion /ˈmɪnjən/, *n.* (*oft. offensive*) a favorite, esp. someone who behaves slavishly to keep the favor of his master. [F]

miniskirt /ˈmɪniskɜːt/, *n.* a very short skirt. Also, **mini**.

minister /ˈmɪnəstə/, *n.* **1.** someone authorised to conduct religious worship, esp. of the Protestant churches. **2.** (*oft. cap.*) a person appointed by the sovereign or leader of a government to be head of an administrative department: *the minister of Education.* **3.** a diplomatic representative sent by one government to another. **4.** a person acting as the agent or instrument of another. ◇*v.i.* **5.** to give service, care, or aid. [L: servant] —**ministerial**, *adj.*

ministration /mɪnəsˈtreɪʃən/, *n.* (an example of) the ministering of care, aid, religious service, etc. —**ministrative,** *adj.*

ministry /ˈmɪnɪstri/, *n., pl.* **-tries.** 1. the service, work, or profession of a minister of religion. 2. the body of ministers of religion; the clergy. 3. the service, work, department, or headquarters of a minister of state. 4. ministers of state taken as a group. 5. the act of ministering; ministration; service. [ME, from L: office, service]

mink /mɪŋk/, *n., pl.* **minks,** (*esp. collectively*) **mink.** 1. a weasel-like animal, esp. that of North America. 2. the valuable fur of this animal. [Scand]

min min /ˈmɪn mɪn/, *n.* a will-o'-the-wisp, said to be seen in outback areas. [Aboriginal]

Minneapolis /mɪniˈæpələs/, *n.* a city in the US, in south-eastern Minnesota, on the Mississippi. Pop. 356 840 (1986 est.).

Minnesota /mɪnəˈsoʊtə/, *n.* a state in the north central US. Pop. 4 214 000 (1986 est.); 217 719 km². *Cap.:* St Paul. *Abbrev.:* Minn —**Minnesotan,** *n., adj.*

minnow /ˈmɪnoʊ/, *n., pl.* **-nows,** (*esp. collectively*) **-now.** a small European fish. [OE]

Minoan /məˈnoʊən/, *adj.* of or relating to the ancient advanced civilisation of Crete, dating (approximately) from 3000 to 1100 BC. [MINO(S) + -*an*]

minor /ˈmaɪnə/, *adj.* 1. lesser, as in size, amount, or importance, or being the lesser of two: *a minor share; minor faults.* 2. under legal age. 3. of or relating to the minority. 4. *Music.* **a.** (of an interval) smaller by a semitone than the corresponding major interval. **b.** (of a chord) having a minor third (interval of three semitones) between the root and the note next above it. ◇*n.* 5. a person under legal age. 6. *Music.* a minor interval, chord, scale, etc. [L: less, inferior, younger]

minority /maɪˈnɒrəti, mə-/, *n., pl.* **-ties,** *adj.* ◇*n.* 1. the smaller part or number. 2. a smaller party or group opposed to a majority, as in voting or other action. 3. a group having in common national, religious, or other ties different from those of the majority of those living in a country. 4. the state or period of being a minor or under legal age. ◇*adj.* 5. of or relating to a minority.

Minos /ˈmaɪnɒs/, *n. Gk Myth.* son of Zeus, and king and lawgiver of Crete; after death, a judge in the lower world.

Minotaur /ˈmɪnətɔː/, *n. Gk Myth.* a mythical monster, with the head of a bull and body of a man, confined in the Cretan labyrinth and fed with human flesh. It was killed by Theseus, with the help of Ariadne. [L *Minōtaurus,* from Gk MINO(S) + *taûros* bull]

Minsk /mɪnsk/, *n.* the capital city of Belarus; became capital of the CIS in 1991. Pop. 1 510 000 (1986 est.).

minstrel /ˈmɪnstrəl/, *n.* 1. a medieval musician who sang or recited poetry to the accompaniment of instruments. 2. *Poetry.* any musician, singer, or poet. 3. one of a group of comedians, usu. white men made up as Negroes, presenting songs, jokes, etc. [ME, from OF: servant, from LL]

mint¹ /mɪnt/, *n.* 1. any of several herbs whose fresh-smelling leaves are used in cooking, including peppermint, spearmint, etc. 2. a sweet flavored with peppermint. ◇*adj.* 3. flavored with or containing mint: *mint sauce.* [OE, from L, from Gk]

mint² /mɪnt/, *n.* 1. a place where money is made by public authority. 2. a great amount, esp. of money. ◇*adj.* 3. in new condition as when first issued: *in mint condition.* ◇*v.t.* 4. to coin (money). 5. to make as if by coining: *to mint words.* [OE: coin, from L: money] —**minter,** *n.*

minuet /mɪnjuˈet/, *n.* 1. a slow stately dance of French origin. 2. a piece of music for such a dance or in its rhythm. [F: very small (with reference to the small steps taken in the dance)]

minus /ˈmaɪnəs/, *prep.* 1. decreased by: *10 minus 6.* 2. lacking or without: *a party minus a leader.* ◇*adj.* 3. involving or indicating subtraction: *the minus sign.* 4. negative: *a minus quantity.* ◇*n.* 5. **— minus sign.** 6. a minus quantity. [L]

minuscule /ˈmɪnəskjuːl/, *adj.* 1. (of letters) small, not capital. 2. very small; tiny. [L: rather small] —**minuscular,** *adj.*

minus sign, *n.* the symbol (−) indicating subtraction.

minute¹ /ˈmɪnət/, *n., v.,* **-uted, -uting,** *adj.* ◇*n.* 1. the sixtieth part of an hour; sixty seconds. 2. any short space of time: *Wait a minute.* 3. a point of time, an instant, or moment: *Come here this minute!* 4. (*pl.*) the official record of the proceedings at a meeting. 5. *Geom. etc.* the sixtieth part of a degree, or sixty seconds (often represented by the sign '), as 12° 10' (12 degrees and 10 minutes). 6. **up to the minute,** very modern; latest; most up to date. ◇*v.t.* 7. to record (something) in a memorandum or in the minutes of a meeting. ◇*adj.* 8. prepared in a very short time: *a minute steak.* [ME, from OF, from ML: small part or division, from L]

minute² /maɪˈnjuːt/, *adj.,* **-nuter, -nutest.** 1. extremely small, as in size, amount, or degree. 2. of very small scope or individual importance: *minute details.* 3. attentive to or concerned with very small details or particulars: *a minute report.* [ME, from L: made small]

minutia /maɪˈnjuːʃə, -tiə/, *n., pl.* **-tiae** /-ʃii, -tiː/. (*usu. pl.*) a small or unimportant detail. [L: smallness]

minx /mɪŋks/, *n.* a cheeky or flirtatious girl. [? from *minikins* little person]

Miocene /ˈmaɪəsiːn/, *adj.* 1. relating to a series of the Tertiary period. ◇*n.* 2. a division of the Tertiary after Oligocene and before Pliocene.

miracle /ˈmɪrəkəl/, *n.* 1. an effect in the physical world which is not explained by human or natural powers and is therefore said to be due to supernatural forces. 2. a wonder-

miracle   666   **misfit**

ful thing; marvel. **3.** a wonderful example of some quality: *a miracle of grace*. [ME, from OF, from L]

miracle play, *n.* a medieval form of theatre dealing with biblical stories or saints' lives.

miraculous /məˈrækjələs/, *adj.* **1.** of the nature of a miracle; marvellous. **2.** performed by or as if by a supernatural power. [ML, from L]

mirage /məˈrɑʒ/, *n.* **1.** an illusion in which a person sees distant objects as much closer than they really are, or sees objects which do not exist at all. **2.** something unreal. [F: look at (oneself) in a mirror, see reflected, from VL]

mire /ˈmaɪə/, *n., v.*, **mired, miring.** ◇*n.* **1.** a piece of wet, swampy ground. **2.** deep mud. ◇*v.t.* **3.** to cause to stick fast in mire. **4.** to soil with mire. [ME, from Scand] —**miry**, *adj.*

mirrnyong /ˈmɜnjɒŋ/, *n.* a pile of shells, ashes, etc., in a place once used for cooking by the Aborigines. [Aboriginal]

mirror /ˈmɪrə/, *n.* **1.** a surface, now usu. glass with a metallic backing, which reflects images. **2.** such a surface set into an ornamental frame. **3.** any reflecting surface, as that of calm water. **4.** something that gives a true picture of something else. ◇*v.t.* **5.** to reflect, esp. in a mirror. [ME, from OF, from ML: wonder at, admire]

mirror image, *n.* an image of an object as viewed in a mirror so that the right side appears to be the left and vice versa.

mirth /mɜθ/, *n.* **1.** joyous gaiety; rejoicing. **2.** humorous amusement, as at something ridiculous. [OE *myr(g)th*, *myrigth*, from *myrige* MERRY] —**mirthful**, *adj.*

mis-[1], a prefix applied to various parts of speech, meaning 'ill', 'mistaken', 'wrong', or simply stating the negative, as in *misprint*, *mistrust*. [OE *mis(s)-*]

mis-[2], variant of *miso-*, before some vowels, as in *misanthrope*.

misadventure /mɪsədˈvɛntʃə/, *n.* **1.** (a piece of) ill fortune. **2.** *Law.* an accident, as where a person, without intending to harm, kills another.

misanthrope /ˈmɪzənθroʊp/, *n.* a hater of mankind. Also, **misanthropist** /mɪˈzænθrəpɪst/. [Gk: hating mankind] —**misanthropic**, *adj.* —**misanthropy**, *n.*

misapprehension /ˌmɪsæprəˈhɛnʃən/, *n.* misunderstanding.

misappropriate /mɪsəˈproʊprieɪt/, *v.t.*, **-ated, -ating. 1.** to put to a wrong use. **2.** to use wrongfully or dishonestly for oneself (as money, etc.). —**misappropriation**, *n.*

miscarriage /mɪsˈkærɪdʒ, ˈmɪskærɪdʒ/, *n.* **1.** failure to obtain the right or desired result: *a miscarriage of justice*. **2.** failure of a letter, etc., to reach where it is sent. **3.** the expelling by a uterus of an unborn organism before it can live.

miscarry /mɪsˈkæri/, *v.i.*, **-ried, -rying. 1.** to be unsuccessful. **2.** (of a letter) to go astray. **3.** to have a miscarriage.

miscegenation /ˌmɪsɛdʒəˈneɪʃən, mɪsɛdʒəˈneɪʃən/, *n.* interbreeding between different races, esp. between black and white. [L]

miscellaneous /mɪsəˈleɪniəs/, *adj.* **1.** consisting of members or elements of different kinds. **2.** of mixed character. [L: mixed]

miscellany /məˈsɛləni/, *n., pl.* **-nies. 1.** a miscellaneous collection of pieces by several writers, dealing with various topics. **2.** (*oft. pl.*) a miscellaneous collection of articles or entries, as in a book.

mischance /mɪsˈtʃæns, -ˈtʃɑns/, *n.* ill luck; misfortune. [ME, from OF]

mischief /ˈmɪstʃəf/, *n.* **1.** conduct meant to tease or cause annoyance. **2.** a tendency to tease: *full of mischief*. **3.** harm or trouble, esp. when due to some person or cause. [ME, from OF: succeed ill]

mischievous /ˈmɪstʃəvəs/, *adj.* **1.** fond of mischief, as children. **2.** (of speeches, looks, etc.) knowingly teasing. **3.** (of people, actions, etc.) annoying in either a hurtful or playful way.

miscible /ˈmɪsəbəl/, *adj.* able to be mixed. [L: mix] —**miscibility**, *n.*

misconceive /mɪskənˈsiv/, *v.t., v.i.*, **-ceived, -ceiving.** to misunderstand. —**misconceiver**, *n.* —**misconception**, *n.*

misconduct /mɪsˈkɒndʌkt/, *n.* **1.** behavior that is not proper. **2.** unlawful conduct by an official in regard to his office.

miscreant /ˈmɪskriənt/, *adj.* **1.** evil; villainous. ◇*n.* **2.** a criminally evil person; villain. [ME, from OF]

misdeed /mɪsˈdid/, *n.* a wicked action.

misdemeanor or **misdemeanour** /mɪsdəˈminə/, *n.* **1.** a case of bad behavior; misdeed. **2.** *Law.* any criminal offence, esp. (before 1967) not considered as a felony or treason.

miser /ˈmaɪzə/, *n.* **1.** a person who lives in very poor surroundings in order to save and store money. **2.** a mean, greedy person. [L: wretched, unhappy, sick, bad] —**miserly**, *adj.*

miserable /ˈmɪzrəbəl, -zərəbəl/, *adj.* **1.** totally unhappy, uneasy, or uncomfortable. **2.** completely poor; needy. **3.** of completely unattractive character or quality; contemptible. **4.** causing unhappiness: *a miserable existence*. **5.** worthy of pity; deplorable: *a miserable failure*. [L: pitiable]

misère /mɪˈzɛə/, *n. Cards.* **1.** a hand which contains no winning cards. **2.** a bid made by a player who has such a hand, declaring that they will take no tricks. [F: misery]

misery /ˈmɪzəri/, *n., pl.* **-ries. 1.** great unhappiness of mind. **2.** a cause of such unhappiness, as poor conditions, etc. **3. put out of misery, a.** to put right a worrying situation for someone. **b.** to kill or make unconscious a person or animal so as to end pain.

misfire /ˌmɪsˈfaɪə/, *v.i.* **1.** (of a gun, etc.) to fail to fire. **2.** to fail to have the intended result.

misfit /mɪsˈfɪt/, *v.*, **-fitted, -fitting**; /ˈmɪsfɪt/, *n.* ◇*v.t., v.i.* **1.** to fit badly. ◇*n.* **2.** a bad fit, as an ill-fitting garment, etc. **3.**

misfit someone who cannot fit into a particular set of social surroundings.

misfit river, *n. Geog.* a small river or stream which finds a course within the course cut earlier by a larger river.

misfortune /mɪsˈfɔtʃən/, *n.* **1.** bad fortune; ill luck. **2.** an instance of this.

misgiving /mɪsˈgɪvɪŋ/, *n.* a feeling of doubt, distrust, or worry.

mishap /ˈmɪshæp/, *n.* an unfortunate accident.

mishmash /ˈmɪʃmæʃ/, *n.* a disordered mass of things thrown together; jumble.

Mishnah /ˈmɪʃnə/, *n., pl.* **Mishnayoth** /mɪʃnəˈjoʊθ/. the collection of oral laws made by Judah ha-Nasi (AD c. 135–c. 220), which forms the basis of the Talmud. Also, **Mishna**. [Heb.: repetition, study]

mislay /mɪsˈleɪ/, *v.t.,* **-laid, -laying. 1.** to put in a place afterwards forgotten. **2.** to lay or place wrongly; misplace. —**mislayer,** *n.*

mislead /mɪsˈlid/, *v.t.,* **-led, -leading. 1.** to lead or guide wrongly. **2.** to lead into error of conduct, thought, or judgment. —**misleader,** *n.* —**misleading,** *adj.*

misnomer /mɪsˈnoʊmə/, *n.* **1.** a name or designation used wrongly. **2.** a mistake in naming a person or thing. [ME, from OF]

miso-, a word part referring to 'hate'. [Gk, combining form of *misein* to hate]

misogamy /məˈsɒgəmi/, *n.* hatred of marriage. —**misogamist,** *n.*

misogyny /məˈsɒdʒəni/, *n.* hatred of women. [Gk] —**misogynist,** *n.* —**misogynous,** *adj.*

misplace /mɪsˈpleɪs, ˈmɪspleɪs/, *v.t.,* **-placed, -placing. 1.** to put in a wrong place. **2.** to place improperly, unsuitably, or unwisely. —**misplacement,** *n.*

misprint /ˈmɪsprɪnt/, *n.;* /mɪsˈprɪnt/, *v.,* ◇*n.* **1.** a mistake in printing. ◇*v.t.* **2.** to print incorrectly.

misrepresent /mɪsrɛprəˈzɛnt/, *v.t.* to represent incorrectly, improperly, or falsely.

miss[1] /mɪs/, *v.t.* **1.** to fail to hit, light upon, meet, catch, receive, obtain, attain, accomplish, see, hear, etc. **2.** to fail to perform, attend to, be present at, etc.: *He might miss the appointment.* **3.** to notice the absence or loss of, often with regret. **4.** to escape or avoid: *She just missed being caught.* **5.** to fail to understand: *It is easy to miss the point of the lecture.* ◇*v.i.* **6.** to fail to hit, light upon, receive, etc. something. **7.** to be unsuccessful. **8.** *Colloq.* (of an internal combustion engine) to fail to fire in one or more cylinders. **9. miss out,** to fail to be present, as at a function, or to fail to receive, esp. something desired (oft. fol. by *on*). **10. miss the boat** or **bus,** *Colloq.* to be too late, fail to take an opportunity. **11. not (never) miss a trick,** *Colloq.* (oft. offensive) never to fail to use an opportunity, etc. ◇*n.* **12.** a failure to hit, meet, obtain or achieve something. **13.** *Colloq.* an avoidance: *Give it a miss.* [OE]

miss[2] /mɪs/, *n., pl.* **misses. 1.** (*cap.*) the normal title of respect for an unmarried woman, placed before the name. **2.** (without the name) a term of address to any woman, esp. someone in a position of authority. **3.** a young unmarried woman; girl.

missal /ˈmɪsəl/, *n. Rom Cath Ch.* the book containing the prayers and rites for celebrating mass for a complete year. [ME, from ML, from LL: MASS[2]]

misshapen /mɪsˈʃeɪpən/, *adj.* badly shaped; deformed.

missile /ˈmɪsaɪl/, *n.* **1.** an object or weapon able to be thrown, hurled, or shot. **2.** Also, **guided missile.** a flying bomb whose flight can be controlled. [L: something which can be thrown]

missing /ˈmɪsɪŋ/, *adj.* lacking; absent; not found.

missing link, *n.* **1.** an animal supposed to supply the connecting link between the anthropoid apes and man. **2.** something lacking for the completion of a series of any kind.

mission /ˈmɪʃən/, *n.* **1.** a body of people sent to a foreign country to carry out discussions, establish relations, etc. **2.** the business of an agent, envoy, etc. **3.** *Mil.* an operation on land, sea, or in the air, carried out against an enemy. **4.** a body of persons sent into or living in a foreign land for religious work among the people. **5.** missionary duty or work. **6.** a duty someone sets for him or herself. [L: a sending]

missionary /ˈmɪʃənri/, *n., pl.* **-ries,** *adj.* ◇*n.* **1.** a person sent out, usu. to a foreign country, to preach and teach their religious faith. ◇*adj.* **2.** relating to or connected with religious missions. **3.** engaged in such a mission, or devoted to work connected with missions.

missis /ˈmɪsəs, -səz/, *n. Colloq.* →**missus.**

Mississippi /mɪsəˈsɪpi/, *n.* **1.** a state in the southern US. Pop. 2 625 000 (1986 est.); 123 584 km². *Cap.:* Jackson. *Abbrev.:* Miss **2.** a river flowing from northern Minnesota south to the Gulf of Mexico; the principal river of the US, 3975 km; from the headwaters of the Missouri to the Gulf of Mexico, 6418 km.

missive /ˈmɪsɪv/, *n.* **1.** a written message; letter. ◇*adj.* **2.** sent, esp. from an official place. [ME, from ML, from L: sent]

Missouri /məˈzʊəri/, *n.* **1.** a state in the central US. Pop. 5 006 000 (1986 est.); 180 455 km². *Cap.:* Jefferson City. *Abbrev.:* Mo **2.** a river flowing from south-western Montana into the Mississippi north of St Louis, Missouri. 4382 km.

missus /ˈmɪsəs, -səz/, *n. Colloq.* **1.** a man's wife. **2.** the mistress of a house. **3.** *Colloq.* (in address, without the name) madam. Also, **missis.** [spoken form of MRS]

mist /mɪst/, *n.* **1.** a cloud-like collection of water vapor hanging in the atmosphere at or near the earth's surface. **2.** *Meteorol.* (by international agreement) a very thin fog in which the horizontal visibility is greater than one

mist kilometre. **3.** something which looks like or blurs vision like a mist. **4.** a hazy appearance before the eyes, as due to tears, etc. **5.** a suspension of a liquid in a gas. ◇*v.t., v.i.* **6.** to make or become misty. [OE]

mistake /məˈsteɪk/, *n., v.,* **-took, -taken, -taking.** ◇*n.* **1.** an error in action, opinion or judgment. **2.** something understood wrongly. ◇*v.t.* **3.** to take or regard as something or somebody else: *It is possible to mistake margarine for butter.* **4.** to understand wrongly; misunderstand; misjudge. ◇*v.i.* **5.** to be in error. [ME, from Scand] —**mistakeable**, *adj.*

mistaken /mɪsˈteɪkən/, *adj.* **1.** wrongly understood or done. **2.** wrong; erroneous. **3.** having made a mistake.

mister /ˈmɪstə/, *n.* **1.** (*cap.*) the normal title of respect for a man, placed before the name (usu. written *Mr*). **2.** *Colloq.* (in address, without the name) sir. **3.** (a title used in addressing a surgeon as opposed to *doctor*). [var. of MASTER]

mistletoe /ˈmɪsəltoʊ/, *n.* a group of plants which grow parasitically on other plants, much used in Christmas decorations. [OE]

mistletoe bird, *n.* a small common Australian bird which feeds on berries including mistletoe.

mistook /mɪsˈtʊk/, *v.* past tense of **mistake.**

mistral /ˈmɪstrəl/, *n.* a cold, dry, northerly wind common in southern France and neighboring areas. [F: master wind, from Pr: important, from L: master]

mistress /ˈmɪstrəs/, *n.* **1.** a woman who has authority or control as over a house, servants, etc. **2.** a female owner, as of horse, dog, etc. **3.** a female head teacher in a particular subject department in a secondary school. **4.** a woman who has a continuing sexual relationship with one man outside marriage. **5.** *Archaic or Poetic.* sweetheart. **6.** *Archaic.* a term of address for a woman. See **Mrs** and **miss.** [ME, from OF, fem. of *maistre* MASTER]

mistrial /mɪsˈtraɪəl/, *n. Law.* a trial without legal effect because of some fundamental error in the proceedings.

mistrust /mɪsˈtrʌst/, *n.* **1.** lack of trust; distrust. ◇*v.t.* **2.** to regard with mistrust; distrust. ◇*v.i.* **3.** to be distrustful.

misty /ˈmɪsti/, *adj.,* **-tier, -tiest. 1.** covered or clouded by mist. **2.** of the nature of or consisting of mist. **3.** appearing as if seen through mist: *misty outlines.* **4.** obscure; vague. [OE]

misunderstand /ˌmɪsʌndəˈstænd, mɪsˌʌn-/, *v.i., v.t.,* **-stood, -standing.** to understand incorrectly (words, actions or a person).

misunderstood /ˌmɪsʌndəˈstʊd, mɪsˌʌn-/, *adj.* **1.** understood incorrectly. **2.** not appreciated.

misuse /mɪsˈjus/, *n.;* /mɪsˈjuz/, *v.,* **-used, -using.** ◇*n.* **1.** wrong or improper use; misapplication. ◇*v.t.* **2.** to use wrongly or improperly; misapply. **3.** to ill-use; maltreat. —**misusage**, *n.*

mitochondrion

Mitchell[1] /ˈmɪtʃəl/, *n.* **1. David Scott,** 1836–1907, Australian lawyer whose collection of Australiana formed the basis of the Mitchell Library, Sydney. **2. Helen Porter** → Dame Nellie **Melba. 3. Dame Roma Flinders,** born 1913, Australian lawyer; first Australian woman QC (1962), first woman judge of the Supreme Court 1965–83; became governor of SA in 1991, the first woman governor in Australia. **4. Sir Thomas Livingstone,** 1792–1855, Australian surveyor and explorer, born in Scotland; led four expeditions through NSW and Vic.

Mitchell[2] /ˈmɪtʃəl/, a river in northern Qld, rising in the Great Dividing Range near Atherton Tableland and flowing north-west to the Gulf of Carpentaria. 560 km.

Mitchell grass, *n.* a drought-resistant native pasture grass, plentiful in western Qld and NSW.

mite[1] /maɪt/, *n.* any of various small arachnids, many being parasitic on plants and animals, others living in cheese, flour, etc. [OE]

mite[2] /maɪt/, *n.* **1.** a very small sum of money. **2.** a very small object, creature or child. ◇*adv.* **3.** to a limited degree; somewhat (preceded by *a*): *a mite stupid.* [ME, from MD]

Mitford family /ˈmɪtfəd/, *n.* a family of English aristocratic background, which included five daughters noted for their literary, social or political activity. **1. Nancy,** 1904–73, comic novelist and social commentator; her works include *Love in a Cold Climate* (1949) and *Noblesse Oblige* (1956). **2. Diana,** born 1910, a society belle of the 1920s and one of those who inspired the early novels of Evelyn Waugh; married **Sir Oswald Mosley. 3. Unity,** 1914–48, close friend of Hitler and outspoken admirer of Nazism. **4. Jessica,** born 1917, became a communist during the Spanish Civil War; critic of American culture as in *The American Way of Death* (1963). **5. Deborah,** born 1920, by marriage Duchess of Devonshire and mistress of Chatsworth, England's stateliest home.

Mithraism /ˈmɪθreɪˌɪzəm/, *n.* an ancient Persian religion worshipping Mithras, seen as a source of some Christian moral teaching. Also, **Mithraicism** /mɪθˈreɪəsɪzəm/.

Mithras /ˈmɪθræs/, *n.* in Persian mythology, the god of light and truth and later of the sun. Also, **Mithra.** [L, from Gk, from OPers *Mithra*]

mitigate /ˈmɪtəgeɪt/, *v.,* **-gated, -gating.** ◇*v.t.* **1.** to lessen in force (grief, pain, etc.). **2.** to moderate the severity of (anything worrying). ◇*v.i.* **3.** to become milder. [ME, from ML] —**mitigatory**, *adj.* —**mitigator**, *n.* —**mitigation**, *n.*

mitochondrion /maɪtoʊˈkɒndrɪən/, *n., pl.* **-ia** /-ɪə/. one of the tiny granules, present in living cells, regarded as responsible for respiration and energy production. [Gk *mítos* thread + *chóndrion* granule] —**mitochondrial**, *adj.*

mitosis /məˈtoʊsəs, maɪ-/, n. an asexual method of cell division in which the chromosomes in the cell nucleus double and then separate to form two identical cells. [NL. from Gk *mitos* a thread + *-osis* -OSIS] —**mitotic**, *adj.*

mitre /ˈmaɪtə/, n., v., **-tred, -tring.** ◇n. **1.** the tall, ornamented headdress of a bishop as symbol of his official position. **2.** the joining surface or bevel on either of the pieces joined in a mitre-joint. ◇v.t. **3.** to join with or shape with a mitre-joint. [ME, from L, from Gk: belt, headband, headdress]

mitre-joint /ˈmaɪtə-dʒɔɪnt/, n. a joint formed when two pieces of identical cross-section are joined at the ends, and where the joined ends are bevelled at equal angles.

mitt /mɪt/, n. **1.** a type of glove extending only to, or slightly over, the fingers. **2.** *Baseball.* a type of glove having the side next to the palm of the hand protected by a large, thick pad. **3.** a mitten. **4.** *Colloq.* a hand. [var. of MITTEN]

mitten /ˈmɪtn/, n. **1.** a type of hand-covering, enclosing the four fingers together and the thumb separately. **2.** a mitt (def. 1). [ME, from OF, from Gallo-Rom: half (glove), from L: middle]

Mitterrand /mitɛˈrɔ̃/, n. **François Maurice Marie** /frɔ̃ˌswa mɔˌris maˈri/, born 1916, French politician; French Socialist leader since 1971; became president of France in 1981.

mix /mɪks/, v., **mixed** or **mixt, mixing,** n. ◇v.t. **1.** to put together (substances or things) into one mass. **2.** to combine, unite, or join: *to mix business and pleasure.* **3.** to put in as an added element or ingredient: *mix eggs into the flour.* **4.** to form by combining ingredients: *She will mix a cake.* **5.** to confuse completely (fol. by *up*). **6.** to put together (the separate tracks of a recording). ◇v.i. **7.** to become mixed: *Oil and water will not mix.* **8.** to associate, as in company. **9. mix up in,** to involve in. **10. mix with,** to associate socially with. ◇n. **11.** a mixture, as a prepared blend of ingredients to which it is necessary to add only liquid. [F, from L: mixed]

mixed farming, n. farming which involves more than one type of activity, often growing crops and raising livestock.

mixed marriage, n. a marriage between persons of different religions or races.

mixed metaphor, n. See **metaphor** (def. 2).

mixed number, n. a number consisting of a whole number and a fraction, as $4\frac{1}{2}$.

mixer /ˈmɪksə/, n. **1.** *Colloq.* a person, with reference to their ability to get on with people: *a good mixer.* **2.** a kitchen utensil or electrical appliance used for beating. **3.** an electrical system, as in a broadcasting studio, providing for the mixing, etc., of sounds from various sources.

mixture /ˈmɪkstʃə/, n. **1.** the product of mixing. **2.** any combination of differing elements, kinds, qualities, etc. **3.** *Chem, Phys.* two or more substances not chemically united, and which are mixed in no fixed proportion to each other. **4.** the state of being mixed. [L]

mix-up /ˈmɪks-ʌp/, n. a confused state of things; muddle; tangle.

mizzenmast /ˈmɪzənmast, -məst/, n. **1.** the mast closest to the stern (back) of a three-masted ship or the third on a ship with more than three masts. **2.** the second and shorter of the two masts of a small sailing vessel. Also, **mizenmast.**

Mk, *Abbrev. Bible.* Mark.

m.k.s. /ɛm keɪ ˈɛs/, *Abbrev.* metre-kilogram-second system. Also, **MKS**

MLA /ɛm ɛl ˈeɪ/, *Abbrev.* Member of the Legislative Assembly.

MLC /ɛm ɛl ˈsi/, *Abbrev.* Member of the Legislative Council.

Mlle, *Abbrev. pl.* **Mlles.** Mademoiselle.

Mme, *Abbrev. pl.* **Mmes.** Madame.

mmHg, *Abbrev.* millimetre(s) of mercury.

Mn, *Chem. Symbol.* manganese.

mnemonic /nəˈmɒnɪk/, *adj.* **1.** helping, or intended to help, the memory. ◇n. **2.** a verse or the like intended to help the memory. [Gk: of memory]

Mo[1], *Chem. Symbol.* molybdenum.

Mo[2] /moʊ/, n. → Roy **Rene.**

moa /ˈmoʊə/, n. any of the extinct, flightless birds of NZ similar to an ostrich. [Maori]

moan /moʊn/, n. **1.** a long, low, sound made from or as if from physical or mental suffering. **2.** any similar sound: *the moan of the wind.* **3.** *Archaic and now Colloq.* complaint. ◇v.i. **4.** to utter moans, as of pain or grief. **5.** (of the wind, sea, trees, etc.) to make any sound suggestive of such moans. **6.** to state in complaint. ◇v.t. **7.** to lament or bemoan: *to moan one's fate.* [OE: complain of, lament] —**moaner,** n.

moat /moʊt/, n. **1.** a deep, wide trench surrounding a town or castle, etc., usu. filled with water. ◇v.t. **2.** to surround with a moat. [ME: moat, (earlier) mound, from OF: mound, eminence; probably from Celtic or Gmc]

mob /mɒb/, n., adj., v., **mobbed, mobbing.** ◇n. **1. a.** a large number, esp. of people, sometimes disorderly and destructive. **b.** a group of people, as friends, not necessarily large: *We'll invite the mob over for tea.* **2.** a collection of animals: *a mob of sheep.* **3.** the common mass of people. ◇adj. **4.** of, relating to, typical of, or suitable for a mob: *mob violence.* ◇v.t. **5.** to crowd around in great and noisy numbers: *The fans will mob the pop star at the concert.* **6.** to surround and attack with violence: *The peasants mobbed the coach, destroying it.* [short for L *mōbile vulgus* the movable (i.e. excitable) common people]

mobile /ˈmoʊbaɪl/, *adj.* **1.** moving readily; movable. **2.** (of facial expression) changing easily. **3.** (of the mind) responding quickly; versatile. ◇n. **4.** an arrangement of delicately balanced movable parts (of metal, wood etc.), usu. hanging. [L: movable] —**mobility,** n.

mobilise *or* **mobilize** /ˈmoʊbəlaɪz/, *v.*, **-lised, -lising.** ◇*v.t.* **1.** to put (armed forces) into readiness for duty, esp. in war. **2.** to make ready, as for a particular job: *They must mobilise their energies.* **3.** to put into use. ◇*v.i.* **4.** to be organised, etc., for war. [F] **—mobilisation,** *n.*

mobility /moʊˈbɪləti, mə-/, *n. Sociol.* the movement of people in a population, as from place to place, or job to job, or social class to social class.

möbius strip /ˈmɜːbiəs/, *n.* a continuous one-sided surface, as formed by half-twisting a strip, as of paper, and joining the ends. [named after August Ferdinand *Möbius*, 1790–1868, German mathematician]

moccasin /ˈmɒkəsən/, *n.* a shoe made completely of soft leather. [NAmer Ind]

Mocha /ˈmoʊkə, ˈmɒkə/, *n.* a seaport in south-western Yemen; formerly important for the export of Arabian coffee. Pop. 5000 (1972). Also, **Mokha.**

mock /mɒk/, *v.t.* **1.** to make fun of; ridicule. **2.** to imitate; mimic. **3.** to defy. **4.** to deceive, or disappoint. ◇*v.i.* **5.** to use ridicule; scoff; jeer (oft. fol. by *at*). **6. mock up,** to build, esp. quickly, as a mock-up. ◇*adj.* **7.** being a copy or imitation, or having merely the likeness of something: *a mock battle.* [ME, from OF; orig. uncert.] **—mocker,** *n.*

mockery /ˈmɒkəri/, *n., pl.* **-ries. 1.** an action or speech that unkindly laughs at something of a serious nature. **2.** a subject or occasion of unkind laughter at something. **3.** a copy, esp. of a ridiculous or unsatisfactory kind. **4.** something pretended that aims to belittle or show no respect; mocking pretence. **5.** something absurdly or offensively inadequate or unfitting.

mockingbird /ˈmɒkɪŋbɜːd/, *n.* any of various birds known for their ability to copy other bird sounds.

mock-up /ˈmɒk-ʌp/, *n.* a model, built to scale, (of a machine, book, etc.) used for testing or teaching.

modal /ˈmoʊdl/, *adj.* **1.** of or relating to mode, manner, or form. **2.** *Music.* **mode¹** (def. 3). **3.** *Gram.* showing or relating to mood. [ML, from L: MODE¹] **—modality,** *n.*

mode¹ /moʊd/, *n.* **1.** a method; way. **2.** the natural manner of existence or action of anything. **3.** *Music.* the arrangement of the diatonic tones of an octave. **4.** *Geol.* the actual mineral composition of a rock, given in percentages by weight. [ME, from L: due measure; manner]

mode² /moʊd/, *n.* **1.** customary or normal usage in manners, dress, etc. **2.** the style or fashion of the moment. [F, from L: MODE¹]

model /ˈmɒdl/, *n., adj., v.,* **-elled, -elling.** ◇*n.* **1.** a standard or example for copying or comparison. **2.** a representation, usu. on a small scale: *a model of an aircraft.* **3.** an image in clay, wax, etc. **4.** a person, who poses for a painter, photographer, etc. **5.** someone employed to wear and show new clothes to customers; mannequin. **6.** a form or style. ◇*adj.* **7.** serving as a model. **8.** worthy to serve as a model; exemplary. ◇*v.t.* **9.** to form or plan according to a model. **10.** to make a model of. **11.** to form in clay, wax, etc. **12.** to show, esp. by wearing. ◇*v.i.* **13.** to make models. **14.** to produce designs in clay, wax, etc. **15.** to be employed as a model. [F, from It, from L: MODE¹] **—modeller, modelling,** *n.*

moderate /ˈmɒdrət, -əret/, *adj., n.;* /ˈmɒdəreɪt/, *v.,* **-rated, -rating.** ◇*adj.* **1.** keeping within proper bounds; not extreme: *a moderate request.* **2.** of medium quantity, power, etc.: *a moderate income.* **3.** fair; mediocre: *moderate ability.* ◇*n.* **4.** someone who is moderate in opinion or action. ◇*v.t., v.i.* **5.** to make or become less extreme, severe, etc. **6.** to hold the place of authority, as at a public meeting; preside (over). [ME, from L] **—moderation,** *n.*

moderator /ˈmɒdəreɪtə/, *n.* **1.** someone or something that moderates. **2.** an officer holding the highest authority, as over a public meeting, a religious body in the Uniting Church, etc. **3.** *Phys.* a substance, such as graphite or heavy water, used in nuclear reactors to slow down fast neutrons produced by fission to speeds more suitable for causing further fission. **4.** → **chairperson. 5.** *NSW.* an exam for students at year 10, the purpose of which is to establish relative standards between schools.

modern /ˈmɒdn/, *adj.* **1.** of or relating to present and recent time. **2.** characteristic of present and recent time. **3.** of or relating to various styles of jazz, since the 1940s. ◇*n.* **4.** a person of modern times. **5.** someone whose views and tastes are modern. [LL, from L: just now] **—modernity,** *n.*

Modern English, *n.* the English language since c. 1475.

Modern French, *n.* the French language since c. 1600.

Modern Greek, *n.* the Greek language since c. 1500.

modern history, *n.* **1.** history since the Renaissance. **2.** history since the French Revolution (1789).

modest /ˈmɒdəst/, *adj.* **1.** having or showing a moderate view of one's abilities. **2.** not showy or extravagant: *a modest house.* **3.** moderate. **4.** having or showing regard for proper behavior, speech, dress, etc.; decent. [L: keeping due measure] **—modesty,** *n.*

modicum /ˈmɒdəkəm/, *n.* a small quantity. [ME, from L]

modification /ˌmɒdəfəˈkeɪʃən/, *n.* **1.** the act of partly changing something. **2.** the state of being partly changed. **3.** a variety. **4.** *Biol.* a change in a living organism gained from its own activity or environment and not passed to its descendants. **5.** a limitation; qualification.

Modified Australian /ˌmɒdəfaɪd ɒˈstreɪljən/, *n.* that pronunciation of Australian English which seeks to imitate British upper

Modified Australian   **Moldova**

class speech, usu. considered affected and unacceptable.

modifier /ˈmɒdəfaɪə/, *n.* **1.** someone or something that partly changes something. **2.** *Gram.* a word, phrase, or sentence part which limits the sense of another word, phrase, or part: *Adjectives are modifiers.*

modify /ˈmɒdəfaɪ/, *v.*, **-fied, -fying.** ◇*v.t.* **1.** to change somewhat the form or qualities of. **2.** *Gram.* (of a word, phrase, etc.) to limit or add detail to the meaning of another word, as an adverb does to a verb. For example, in *He ran slowly, slowly* modifies *ran.* **3.** to reduce in degree. ◇*v.i.* **4.** to change; to become changed. [ME, from L: set limits to] – **modifiable**, *adj.* – **modificatory**, *adj.*

Modigliani /moudiˈljani/, *n.* **Amedeo** /ameɪˈdiou/, 1884–1920, Italian painter and sculptor; noted for the elongated proportions of his portraits.

Modred /ˈmoudrəd/, *n. Arthurian Legend.* the nephew and treacherous killer of Arthur. Also, **Mordred.**

modular /ˈmɒdʒələ/, *adj.* **1.** of or relating to a module. **2.** composed of standardised units for easy building or arrangement: *a modular home.*

modulate /ˈmɒdʒəleɪt/, *v.t.*, **-lated, -lating. 1.** to tone down; to regulate or adjust to a certain measure. **2.** to change (the voice) fittingly in speech. **3.** *Music.* **a.** to tune to a certain pitch or key. **b.** to change the volume of (tone). **4.** *Radio.* to cause the amplitude, frequency, etc. of (the carrier wave) to change in accordance with the soundwaves or other signals. [L: having measured] – **modulation**, **modulator**, *n.*

module /ˈmɒdʒul/, *n.* **1.** a standard or unit for measuring. **2.** a structural part used as a basic unit for do-it-yourself furniture. **3.** a self-contained unit within a course of study. **4.** *Archit.* the size of some part, taken as a unit of measure. **5.** *Electronics.* a small, standard unit which can be used in the making of a piece of equipment. **6.** *Astronautics.* a section of a space vehicle able to function as a separate unit: *command module.* [L: a small measure]

modulus /ˈmɒdʒələs/, *n., pl.* **-li** /-laɪ/. **1.** *Maths.* **a.** (of a number, esp. a complex number) magnitude or absolute value. **b.** See **congruent** (def. 3). **2.** *Phys.* → **coefficient** (def. 3). [L: a small measure]

mogo /ˈmougou/, *n.* an Aboriginal stone hatchet. [Aboriginal]

mogul /ˈmougəl/, *n.* **1.** an important person. **2.** (*cap.*) a Mongol or Mongolian. ◇*adj.* **3.** (*cap.*) of or relating to the Moguls or their empire. [from one of the Mongol conquerors of India who ruled from 1526 to 1857; from Ar and Pers *Mughul* Mongol]

mohair /ˈmouhɛə/, *n.* **1.** the coat of an Angora goat. **2.** fabric made from this hair. [obs. *mo(cayare)* mohair (from Ar) + HAIR]

Moham, *Abbrev.* Mohammedan.

Mohammed /mouˈhæməd/, *n.* AD 570?–632, Arab prophet, founder of Islam. His teaching started in Mecca in 610 but he was forced to flee to Medina in 622. He eventually succeeded in establishing the principles of Islam over all Arabia. Also, **Mahomet, Mahound.**

Mohammedan /məˈhæmədən/, *adj.* **1.** of or relating to Mohammed, or his religious system; Islamic; Muslim. Also, **Muhammadan, Muhammedan.**

Mohawk /ˈmouhɔk/, *n. pl.* **-hawks,** (*esp. collectively*) **-hawk. a.** a member of a tribe of North American Indians, the most easterly of the Iroquois Five Nations, formerly resident along the Mohawk river, New York. [NAmer Ind (Narragansett): they eat animate things (hence, man-eaters)]

Mohican /ˈmouəkən, mouˈhikən/, *n., pl.* **-cans,** (*esp. collectively*) **-can.** a member of a tribe or confederacy of North American Indians of Algonquian speech, centralised formerly in the upper Hudson Valley. [Algonquian: wolf]

Mohorovicic discontinuity /məˈhɔrə-ˌvɪtʃɪk dɪskɒntəˈnjuəti/, *n.* the dividing line between the earth's crust and mantle where a sudden change occurs in the velocity of earthquake waves. Also, **moho.**

Mohs scale /ˈmouz skeɪl/, *n.* a scale for measuring the hardness of a mineral by determining its ability to withstand scratching by other minerals of known hardness. [after F Mohs, 1773–1839, German mineralogist]

moiety /ˈmɔɪəti/, *n., pl.* **-ties. 1.** a half. **2.** an undetermined part. **3.** *Anthrop.* one of two units into which a tribe is divided on the basis of descent through one parent only. [ME, from OF, from LL: half, L: the middle]

moist /mɔɪst/, *adj.* **1.** slightly wet; damp; humid. **2.** (of the eyes) tearful. [ME, from OF: moist, mouldy] – **moisten**, *v.*

moisture /ˈmɔɪstʃə/, *n.* water or other liquid making anything moist.

moke /mouk/, *n. Colloq.* **1.** donkey. **2.** a horse of poor quality.

mol, *Symbol.* mole[4].

molal /ˈmoulal/, *adj.* **1.** relating to or containing a mole[4]. **2.** relating to a solution containing one mole[4] of solute per 1000 grams of solvent. – **molality**, *n.*

molar[1] /ˈmoulə/, *n.* **1.** a tooth adapted for grinding. ◇*adj.* **2.** suited to grinding, as teeth. **3.** relating to such teeth. [L: grinder]

molar[2] /ˈmoulə/, *adj.* **1.** *Phys.* relating to a body of matter as a whole, and contrasted with molecular and atomic. **2.** *Chem.* relating to a solution containing one mole[4] of solute per litre of solution. [L: mass + -AR[1]]

molarity /məˈlærəti/, *n.* the number of moles[4] of solute per litre of solution.

molasses /məˈlæsəz/, *n.* the syrup taken from raw sugar. [Pg, from LL: honey]

Moldova /mɒlˈdouvə/, *n.* **1.** a republic in south-eastern Europe between Ukraine and Romania; a member of the CIS; a constituent republic of the Soviet Union 1940–91, known as the **Moldavian Soviet Socialist Republic.** Pop. 4 338 000 (1989 est.); 33 670 km[2]. *Language:* Romanian. *Cap.:* Kishinev. **2.** a historic region comprising this republic and part of north-eastern Romania. Also, **Moldavia.** – **Moldovan**, *n., adj.*

mole¹ /moul/, n. a small spot, usu. dark, on human skin. [OE]

mole² /moul/, n. 1. a small insect-eating mammal, living mainly underground. 2. a person who has a job in the government of the enemy in order to act as a spy. [ME]

mole³ /moul/, n. 1. a huge structure, esp. of stone, set up in the water, for a breakwater or a pier. 2. a harbor protected by such a structure. [L: mass, dam]

mole⁴ /moul/, n. *Chem.* the amount of a substance whose weight, in grams, is equal to the molecular weight of the substance, e.g. one mole of carbon-12 weighs 12 grams; grammolecule. *Symbol:* mol [G, from *Molekül* MOLECULE]

molecular /məˈlɛkjələ/, adj. relating to, caused by or consisting of molecules.

molecular formula, n. a formula of a chemical compound showing the number and type of atoms present in each molecule.

molecular weight, n. the average weight of a molecule of an element or compound measured in units based on one twelfth of the weight of an atom of carbon-12.

molecule /ˈmɒlɪkjuːl/, n. 1. *Chem, Phys.* the smallest unit of an element or compound that can exist independently showing the properties of that element or compound, consisting of more than one atom chemically bonded to another, e.g. hydrogen (H$_2$), sodium chloride (NaCl). 2. any very small particle. [L: mass]

molest /məˈlɛst/, v.t. to bother or annoy so as to cause harm. [ME, from L] —**molestation**, n.

Molière /ˈmɒliɛə/, n. (*Jean Baptiste Poquelin*), 1622–73, French comic dramatist; works include *Le Misanthrope* (1666) and *Le Malade Imaginaire* (1673).

Molina /mouˈliːnə/, n. **Tirso de** /ˈtɪəsou deɪ/, (*Gabriel Téllez*), ?1571–1648, Spanish dramatist, created the character of Don Juan.

moll /mɒl/, n. *Colloq.* 1. the girlfriend of a gangster, thief, etc. 2. → **tart²** (def. 2). 3. → **prostitute**. 4. the girlfriend of a surfie, bikie, etc. [short for *Molly*]

mollify /ˈmɒləfaɪ/, v.t., -**fied**, -**fying**. 1. to soften in feeling or temper. 2. to lessen, as anger. [ME, from L: soften] —**mollifyingly**, adv.

mollusc /ˈmɒləsk/, n. any of several animals without backbones, usu. having a hard shell and a soft body, as the snail, octopus, etc. [NL, from L: soft (applied to a thin-shelled nut)] —**molluscan**, adj., n.

mollycoddle /ˈmɒlɪkɒdl/, v.t., -**dled**, -**dling**. to treat tenderly; pamper. [*Molly* (var. of MARY) + CODDLE]

Molnar /ˈmɒlnə/, n. **George**, born 1910 in Hungary, Australian cartoonist and architect.

moloch /ˈmoulɒk/, n. 1. (*cap.*) Also, **Molech**. anything seen as demanding terrible sacrifice: *the Moloch of war*. 2. a spiny Australian lizard. 3. → **mountain devil**. 4. (*cap.*) Also, **Molech**. a Semitic deity whose worship was marked by the sacrifice of children offered by their own parents. [L, from Gk, from Heb *Mōlek*, orig. *melek* king]

Molonglo /məˈlɒŋglou/, n. a river in south-eastern NSW, rising near Captains Flat and flowing north-north-west to join the Murrumbidgee River within the ACT and form Lake Burley Griffin. About 100 km.

Molotov cocktail /mɒlətɒv ˈkɒkteɪl/, n. a fire-producing bomb consisting of a bottle filled with petrol etc. and sealed with a rag which is lit before the bottle is thrown. [named after Viacheslav Mikhailovich *Molotov*, 1890–1986, Soviet statesman]

molten /ˈmoultn/, v. 1. past participle of **melt**. ◇adj. 2. made liquid by heat. 3. produced by melting and casting.

Moluccas /məˈlʌkəz/, n.pl. a group of islands in Indonesia between Celebes and PNG. Pop. 1 659 100 (1986 est.); about 77 700 km². *Cap.:* Amboina. Formerly, **Spice Islands**. Indonesian, **Maluku**.

Molvig /ˈmɒlvɪg/, n. **Jon**, 1923–70, Australian landscape and portrait painter; winner of the Archibald Prize in 1966.

mol. wt, *Abbrev.* molecular weight.

molybdenum /məˈlɪbdənəm/, n. a silverwhite high-melting metalloid, alloyed with iron in making hard, high-speed cutting tools. *Symbol:* Mo; *at. no.:* 42; *at. wt:* 95.94. [NL, from L, from Gk]

moment /ˈmoumənt/, n. 1. a short space of time; an instant. 2. the present or other particular time. 3. importance; consequence: *of great moment*. 4. *Statistics.* the average of a given power of the values of a set of variates. 5. *Phys.* a measure of the tendency to cause rotation around a point or axis, equal to the product of the force and its perpendicular distance from the point or axis. [ME, from L: movement, moment of time, etc.]

momentarily /ˈmoumǝntrəli/; *Chiefly US*, /moumǝnˈtɛrəli/, adv. 1. for a moment: *to stop momentarily*. 2. every moment: *danger momentarily increasing*. 3. at any moment: *momentarily likely*.

momentary /ˈmoumǝntri/, adj. 1. lasting only a moment. 2. occurring at any moment. 3. happening at every moment.

moment of inertia, n. a measure of the resistance of a body to rotation, depending on the axis of spin and distribution of weight. *Symbol:* I

momentous /mouˈmɛntǝs, mǝ-/, adj. of great importance.

momentum /məˈmɛntəm/, n., pl. **ta** /-tǝ/. 1. a measure of the movement in a body which is equal to its mass multiplied by the speed at which it moves. 2. force, as of a moving body. [L]

mon-, variant of **mono-**, before vowels.

Mon, *Abbrev.* Monday.

Monaco /məˈnakou/, n. a principality in south-western Europe, on the Mediterranean,

Monaco

Monaco within the south-eastern part of France. Pop. 27 063 (1982); 1.8 km². *Languages:* French, also Italian and English. *Currency:* franc. *Cap.:* Monaco-Ville. —**Monacan**, *n., adj.*

monad /'mɒunæd/, *n.* **1.** *Philos.* an entity, viewed as the ultimate unit of being. **2.** *Chem.* an element having the valency of one. [LL, from Gk: unit]

Monaghan /'mɒnəhən/, *n.* a county in north-eastern Republic of Ireland. Pop. 52 332 (1986); 1290 km². *County town:* Monaghan. Irish, **Muineachán.**

Mona Lisa /ˌmɒunə 'lizə/, *n.* a famous portrait by Leonardo da Vinci of a young woman with an enigmatic smile. Also, **La Gioconda.**

monarch /'mɒnək, -ak/, *n.* **1.** a hereditary ruler, as a king, queen, etc. **2.** the only and all-powerful ruler of a state. **3.** someone or something that holds the position of greatest power or importance. [ME, from L, from Gk: ruling alone] —**monarchal,** *adj.*

monarchy /'mɒnəki/, *n., pl.* **-chies.** a government or state in which the supreme power is held in fact or in name by a monarch (known as an **absolute** or **despotic monarchy** when the monarch's authority is not limited by laws or a constitution, and as a **limited** or **constitutional monarchy** when the monarch's authority is limited). [ME, from LL, from Gk]

Monaro /mə'nɛərou/, *n.* a district in south-eastern NSW, between the border of Vic and Queanbeyan; Merino wool.

Monash /'mɒnæʃ/, *n.* **Sir John**, 1865–1931, Australian civil engineer and army commander.

monastery /'mɒnəstri, -təri/, *n., pl.* **-teries.** the home of a group of monks, living apart from the world under religious orders. [ME, from LL, from LGk: solitary dwelling]

monastic /mə'næstɪk/, *adj.* Also, **monastical. 1.** of or relating to monasteries. **2.** of, relating to, or characteristic of monks, or the like: *monastic vows of poverty.* [ML, from LGk: living in solitude] —**monasticism,** *n.*

monatomic /mɒnə'tɒmɪk/, *adj. Chem.* having one atom in the molecule.

Monday /'mʌndeɪ, -di/, *n.* the second day of the week, following Sunday. [OE: moon's day]

Mondriaan /'mɔndrian/, *n.* **Piet**, 1872–1944, Dutch painter; exponent of abstract and geometric art.

Monet /mɒ'neɪ/, *n.* **Claude** /kloud/, 1840–1926, French painter; leading figure in the impressionist movement.

monetary /'mʌnətri, -təri/, *adj.* of or relating to money, or money matters. [L: relating to the mint]

money /'mʌni/, *n., pl.* **-eys, -ies. 1.** gold, silver, or other metal given by public authority as a standard of exchange and a measure of value. **2.** coin in present use. **3.** coins, banknotes, tokens, etc. generally accepted in payment. **4.** property in terms of its money value. **5.** an amount of money. **6.** wealth viewed in terms of money. [ME, from OF, from L: mint, money]

moneychanger /'mʌniˌtʃeɪndʒə/, *n.* a person whose business it is to change money at a fixed or official rate.

money-grubber /'mʌniˌgrʌbə/, *n. Colloq.* a greedy person only interested in making money. —**money-grubbing,** *adj.*

moneylender /'mʌniˌlɛndə/, *n.* a person whose business it is to lend money at interest.

money market, *n. Finance.* a market in which large amounts of money are borrowed and lent for short periods of time.

money order, *n.* an order for the payment of money, as one issued by a post office and payable in cash on demand. See **postal order.**

mongan /'mɒŋgən/, *n.* See **ringtail possum.** [Aboriginal]

Monge /mõʒ/, *n.* **Gaspard** /gas'pa/, (*Comte de Péluse*), 1746–1818, French mathematician; founder of descriptive geometry, which represents three-dimensional solids on a two-dimensional plane.

monger /'mʌŋgə/, *n.* (*usu. in compounds*) **1.** a dealer in some goods: *a fishmonger.* **2.** someone who is concerned with unpleasant or unimportant information. [OE, from L: trader] —**mongering,** *n., adj.*

Mongol /'mɒŋgəl/, *n.* **1.** one of an Asian people now living chiefly in Mongolia. **2.** someone having Mongoloid characteristics. —**Mongolian,** *adj.*

Mongol Empire, *n.* an empire that, under Genghis Khan in the 13th century, encompassed the larger part of Asia and extended to the river Dnieper in eastern Europe.

Mongolia /mɒŋ'goulɪə/, *n.* **1.** a republic in central Asia, between Russia and China; a Chinese province before independence in 1911; a socialist republic since 1924. Pop. 1 987 000 (1987 est.); 1 565 000 km². *Languages:* Khalkha Mongolian, also Kazakh. *Currency:* tugrik. *Cap.:* Ulan Bator. Official name, **Mongolian People's Republic.** Formerly, **Outer Mongolia. 2.** a vast area in central Asia, in the 13th century the kingdom of Genghis Khan.

mongolism /'mɒŋgəlɪzəm/, *n.* →**Down syndrome.**

Mongoloid /'mɒŋgəlɔɪd/, *adj.* **1.** relating to the race of people marked by yellowish skin, slanting eyes and straight black hair, including the Mongols, Chinese, Japanese, Thais, Burmese, etc. See **Negroid** and **Caucasian. 2.** (*oft. l.c.*) *Pathol.* of, relating to, or characteristic of Down syndrome. ◇*n.* **3.** (*oft. l.c.*) *Pathol.* someone with Down syndrome. **4.** someone belonging to the Mongoloid race.

mongoose /'mɒŋgus/, *n., pl.* **-gooses.** a ferret-like flesh-eating mammal, used for killing rats, etc. [Marathi (a language of W India)]

mongrel /'mʌŋgrəl/, *n.* **1.** any plant or animal (esp. a dog) resulting from the crossing of different breeds or varieties. **2.** any cross between different things. ◇*adj.* **3.** of or like a mongrel. **4.** of little value. [obs. *mong* mixture (OE *gemang*) + -REL]

monism /'mɒnɪzəm/, n. Philos. the theory that there is one basic substance or principle, as mind (*idealism*) or matter (*materialism*), or something that is neither mind nor matter but the ground of both. See **pluralism** (def. 1). [NL, from Gk: single] —**monist**, n. —**monistic**, adj.

monitor /'mɒnətə/, n. **1.** someone who keeps order, esp. in school. **2.** (in schools) a pupil responsible for a particular task, as putting fresh chalk at the blackboard each morning. **3.** something that serves to remind or give warning. **4.** a device used to check or record the operation of a machine or system. **5.** a large lizard found in Africa, South-East Asia and Australia, and supposed to warn of the presence of crocodiles. **6. a.** *TV.* a screen used to check the quality of the signal being sent. **b.** *Computers.* a VDU. ◇*v.t.* **7.** to check, look at, or record, the operation of (a machine, etc.), without interfering with the operation. **8.** to keep careful watch over. [L]

monk /mʌŋk/, n. a member of a religious order who has withdrawn from the world, often living under vows of poverty, chastity, and obedience. [OE, from LL, from LGk: solitary]

monkey /'mʌŋki/, n., pl. **-keys**, v., **-keyed**, **-keying**. ◇n. **1.** a long-tailed member of the mammalian order Primates, living in trees. **2.** a person likened to such an animal, as an annoyingly playful child. **3. make a monkey of**, to make a fool of. **4. monkey business**, trickery. ◇*v.i.* **5.** *Colloq.* to play; fool (oft. fol. by *about with* or *with*). [apparently from LG]

monkey-wrench /'mʌŋki-rentʃ/, n. a spanner or wrench with a moveable jaw, for turning nuts of different sizes, etc.

mono-, a word part: **1.** meaning 'alone', 'single', 'one'. **2.** meaning 'having a thickness of one molecule'. **3.** used in chemistry to apply to compounds containing one atom of a particular element. Also, **mon-**. [Gk, combining form of *mónos* alone]

monobasic /mɒnoʊ'beɪsɪk/, adj. **1.** *Chem.* (of an acid) containing one replaceable hydrogen atom. **2.** *Biol.* (of genera) established on the basis of a single species or genus.

monocarp /'mɒnoʊkɑːp/, n. a plant that dies after having produced fruit once only. —**monocarpic**, adj.

monochromatic /mɒnəkroʊ'mætɪk/, adj. of, producing, or relating to one color or one wavelength.

monochrome /'mɒnəkroʊm/, n. **1.** a painting or drawing in different shades of a single color. **2.** the art or method of making these. **3.** a black and white photograph. [Gk: of one color] —**monochromic, monochromical**, adj. —**monochromist**, n.

monocle /'mɒnəkəl/, n. an eyeglass for one eye. [F, from LL: one-eyed] —**monocled**, adj.

monoclinal /mɒnoʊ'klaɪnəl/, adj. dipping in one direction, as a strata of rocks.

monoclinous /mɒnoʊ'klaɪnəs, 'mɒnəklaɪnəs/, adj. (of a plant type, etc.) having both the stamens and pistils in the same flower.

monocotyledon /ˌmɒnoʊkɒtə'liːdən/, n. a plant with only one cotyledon (seed leaf).

monody /'mɒnədi/, n., pl. **-dies**. **1.** a Greek poem sung by a single voice, as in a tragedy; lament. **2.** *Music.* a style of composition written mainly for one part or melody. See **polyphonic**. [LL, from Gk: a solo, lament] —**monodist**, n.

monoecious /mɒ'niːʃəs/, adj. **1.** *Biol.* having both male and female organs in the same individual; hermaphroditic. **2.** *Bot.* (of a plant species, etc.) having the stamens and the pistils in separate flowers on the same plant. Also, **monecious**. [MON- + Gk *oikíon* house + -OUS]

monogamy /mə'nɒgəmi/, n. **1.** marriage of one woman with one man. **2.** *Zool.* the habit of having only one mate. —**monogamist**, n. —**monogamous**, adj.

monogram /'mɒnəgræm/, n. a design made up of one or more letters, often one's initials. [LL, from LGk: single-lettered character] —**monogrammatic**, adj.

monograph /'mɒnəgræf, -grɑːf/, n. a book or writing on a particular subject. —**monographic**, adj. —**monographer**, n.

monolith /'mɒnəlɪθ/, n. **1.** a single block or piece of stone of great size. **2.** → **obelisk**. **3.** something like a large block of stone, esp. in having a huge, uniform quality or character. [LL, from Gk: made of one stone] —**monolithic**, adj.

monologue /'mɒnəlɒg/, n. **1.** a long talk by a single speaker. **2.** a poem, dramatic piece, etc., in which a single person speaks alone. **3.** a form of dramatic entertainment by a single speaker. [F, from Gk: speaking alone]

monomer /'mɒnəmə/, n. *Chem.* a molecule of low molecular weight capable of reacting with identical or different monomers to form a polymer. —**monomeric**, adj.

monomial /mɒ'noʊmiəl/, adj. **1.** *Alg.* consisting of one term only. **2.** *Biol.* relating to a name which consists of a single word or term. ◇n. **3.** *Alg.* a monomial expression or quantity.

mononuclear /mɒnoʊ'njuːkliə/, n. a cell having only one nucleus. Also, **mononucleate** /mɒnoʊ'njuːkliət/.

monophonic /mɒnə'fɒnɪk/, adj. of or indicating a system of sound reproduction through only one loudspeaker (opposed to *stereophonic*).

monoplane /'mɒnəpleɪn/, n. an aeroplane with only one pair of wings.

monoploid /'mɒnoʊplɔɪd/, adj. having or being a chromosome number which is the haploid number.

monopolise or **monopolize** /mə'nɒpəlaɪz/, v.t., **-lised**, **-lising**. **1.** to get, have, or exercise complete control of (a market, article, etc.). **2.** to obtain complete possession of. —**monopolisation**, n.

monopoly /məˈnɒpəli/, *n., pl.* **-lies.** **1.** the total control of an article or service in a particular market. **2.** the exclusive right to carry on such a trade or service, given by a government, etc. **3.** the total ownership or control of something. **4.** an article, service, etc., over which there is total control. **5.** a company or the like having such control. [L, from Gk: a right of exclusive sale]

monorail /ˈmɒnoʊreɪl/, *n.* a railway with carriages running on a single (usu. overhead) rail.

monosaccharide /mɒnoʊˈsækəraɪd, -rəd/, *n.* a simple sugar, such as glucose, fructose, etc., found in nature or obtained by the breakdown of polysaccharides (sugars).

monosodium glutamate /mɒnəˌsoʊdiəm ˈglutəmeɪt/, *n.* a sodium salt used in cooking to make the natural flavor of a dish stronger; chinese salt.

monosyllable /ˈmɒnəsɪləbəl/, *n.* a word of one syllable, as *yes*. — **monosyllabic,** *adj.*

monotone /ˈmɒnətoʊn/, *n.* **1.** a series of speech sounds in a single unvaried tone. **2.** a single tone without variation in pitch. **3.** the saying or singing of words in such a tone. [NL, from LGk: of one tone]

monotonic /mɒnəˈtɒnɪk/, *adj. Maths.* (of a function) steadily increasing or steadily decreasing.

monotonous /məˈnɒtənəs/, *adj.* **1.** unvarying in any way: *a monotonous voice.* **2.** like a sound continuing on one note. **3.** limited to a narrow pitch range.

monotony /məˈnɒtəni/, *n.* **1.** lack of variety. **2.** the sameness of sound, tone or pitch. [LGk]

monotreme /ˈmɒnətrim/, *n.* the egg-laying mammals, platypus and echidna, found only in the region of Australia. [MONO- + Gk: hole] — **monotrematous,** *adj.*

monotricha /mɒˈnɒtrɪkə/, *n. pl.* bacteria having the organs of movement at one pole. [MONO- + Gk: hair] — **monotrichous,** *adj.*

monovalent /mɒnoʊˈveɪlənt/, *adj.* **1.** *Chem.* having a valency of one; univalent. **2.** *Bacteriol.* (of a tissue, etc.) able to resist a specific disease organism because of the presence of the proper antibodies or antigens. — **monovalence,** *n.*

monoxide /məˈnɒksaɪd/, *n.* an oxide with one oxygen atom to the molecule, e.g. *carbon monoxide.*

monozygotic /ˌmɒnoʊzaɪˈɡɒtɪk/, *adj.* (of twins, etc.) produced from a single zygote (fertilised egg cell).

Monroe /mənˈroʊ, ˈmʌnroʊ/, *n.* **1. James,** 1758–1831, the fifth president of the US, 1817–25. **2. Marilyn** (*Norma Jean Baker*), 1926–62, US film actress; films include *Bus Stop* (1956) and *Some Like it Hot* (1959).

Monrovia /mɒnˈroʊviə/, *n.* a seaport in and the capital of Liberia on the Atlantic. Founded in 1821 when US slaves were freed on the site. Pop. 425 000 (1984 est.).

monseigneur /mōseɪˈnjɜ/, *n., pl.* **messeigneurs** /meɪsenˈjɜ/. **1.** a French title of honor given to special people such as princes, bishops, etc. **2.** a person having this title. [F: my lord]

monsoon /mɒnˈsun/, *n.* the seasonal wind of the Indian Ocean and Indonesia, blowing in the Southern Hemisphere from the south-east in winter and north-west in summer. [D, from Pg, from Ar: season, seasonal wind, monsoon] — **monsoonal,** *adj.*

monster /ˈmɒnstə/, *n.* **1.** an imaginary animal of part animal and part human form, such as a centaur, griffin, etc. **2.** an animal or a plant of abnormal form or structure. **3.** a person who excites horror. **4.** any animal or thing of huge size. ◇ *adj.* **5.** huge; monstrous. [ME, from OF, from L: omen, prodigy]

monstera deliciosa /mɒnˌstɪərə dəˈlisiˈoʊsə/, *n.* **1.** a tropical plant having large, cut-edged leaves and fruit able to be eaten. **2.** the long, cone-shaped fruit of this plant; fruit salad plant.

monstrous /ˈmɒnstrəs/, *adj.* **1.** huge; great: *a monstrous sum.* **2.** frightful; very ugly. **3.** shocking; revolting: *a monstrous proposal.* **4.** differing greatly from the natural form or type. **5.** having the nature or appearance of a monster. [ME, from LL: strange] — **monstrosity,** *n.*

montage /mɒnˈtɑʒ/, *n.* **1.** the art or method of arranging different (parts of) pictures in one composition. **2.** a technique of film editing in which several shots are partially superimposed to form a single image. [F: mounting, putting together]

Mont Blanc /mō ˈblō/, *n.* → Mont **Blanc.**

Monte Carlo /ˌmɒnti ˈkaloʊ/, *n.* a town in Monaco principality, south-eastern France; gambling; resort. Pop. 9948 (1968).

Montessori /mɒntəˈsɔri/, *n.* **Maria,** 1870–1952, Italian educational reformer; devised the Montessori method of teaching children.

Monteverdi /mɒntəˈveədi/, *n.* **Claudio** /ˈklaudioʊ/, 1567–1643, Italian composer of early baroque music, including madrigals, operas, ballet music, songs, masses and vespers.

Montezuma II /mɒntəˈzjumə/, *n.* c. 1477–1520, last Aztec emperor of Mexico, 1503–20; killed by Spanish conquistador, Cortés.

Montfort /ˈmɒntfət/, *n.* **Simon de** (*Earl of Leicester*), c. 1208–65, English soldier and statesman; led the baronial revolt against Henry III; ruled England 1264–65.

Montgolfier /mōgɒlfiˈeɪ/, *n.* **Joseph Michel** /ʒouˌzɛf miˈʃɛl/, 1740–1810, and his brother **Jacques Étienne** /ʒak ɛtiˈɛn/, 1745–99, French inventors of the first practical hot-air balloon.

Montgomery /məntˈgɒməri/, *n.* **Bernard Law** (*1st Viscount Montgomery of Alamein*), 1887–1976, British field marshal who played a major role in the Allied defeat of Germany in World War II.

month /mʌnθ/, *n.* **1.** any of the 12 parts into which the calendar year is divided **(calendar month)**. **2.** the time from any day of one calendar month to the same day of the next. **3.** a period usu. of four weeks or of thirty days. [OE]

Montmartre /mōˈmatrə/, *n.* a hilly section in the northern part of Paris; artists' centre; famous cafes.

Montparnasse /mōpaˈnas/, *n.* a district in the southern part of Paris; noted for its artists and writers.

Montreal /mɒntriˈɔl/, *n.* a seaport in Canada, in southern Quebec, on an island in the St Lawrence. Pop. 2 921 357 (1986).

Mont-Saint-Michel /mō-sæ-miˈʃel/, *n.* a rocky islet near the coast in north-western France, in an inlet of the Gulf of St Malo; famous abbey and fortress.

Monty Python /mɒnti ˈpaɪθən/, *n.* a British comedy team comprising John Cleese, Graham Chapman, Terry Jones, Eric Idle, Michael Palin, and Terry Gilliam; made the television series *Monty Python's Flying Circus*, and films including *And Now For Something Completely Different* (1971) and *Monty Python and the Holy Grail* (1975).

monument /ˈmɒnjəmənt/, *n.* **1.** something made in memory of a person, event, etc., as a statue, etc. **2.** any building, etc., from a past age, seen as of historical or archaeological importance. **3.** any work, writing, etc., by which to remember a person after death. **4.** any long-lasting or important example of something. [ME, from L]

monumental /mɒnjəˈmentl/, *adj.* **1.** like a monument; huge. **2.** (of a work of art) **a.** great, in size or idea. **b.** noble in thought and deed. **c.** of lasting importance.

-mony, a noun suffix meaning result or condition. [L *-mōnia*, *-mōnium*]

mooch /mutʃ/, *v.i. Colloq.* to walk around in an aimless and unhappy way. Also, **mouch**. [ME]

mood[1] /mud/, *n.* **1.** a frame of mind or feeling at a particular time. **2.** (*pl.*) fits of uncertainty; gloominess. [OE: mind, spirit, mood]

mood[2] /mud/, *n. Gram.* a set of verb forms which explain the action expressed by a verb in terms of **a.** certainty (indicative mood): *He will go.* **b.** wish or desire (subjunctive mood): *He may go.* **c.** command (imperative mood): *Go!* [special use of MOOD[1], influenced by MODE[1]]

moody /ˈmudi/, *adj.*, **-dier**, **-diest**. **1.** coming from or given to ill-tempered or unhappy moods. **2.** having varied moods; temperamental.

Moomba Festival /ˌmumbə ˈfestəvəl/, *n.* a festival held annually in Melbourne, Vic; includes a variety of cultural and sporting activities, the majority of which take place alongside or on the Yarra River.

moon /mun/, *n.* **1.** the body which circles the earth monthly at a distance of 384 403 km. **2.** this heavenly body in different stages of the lunar month. **a. new moon**, (the time of) the moon when in conjunction (def. 5) with the sun and therefore invisible, or the moon soon afterwards when seen as a thin crescent. **b. half-moon**, (the time of) the moon when half its disc is lit by the sun as seen from earth, occurring at either quarter. **c. full moon**, (the time of) the moon when the whole is lit by the sun as seen from earth, occurring when in opposition to the sun. **3.** any planetary satellite. **4.** something shaped like a moon. **5. once in a blue moon**, very rarely; seldom. ◇*v.i.* **6.** *Colloq.* to wander about or look dreamily (oft. fol. by *about*). [OE]

Moonie oilfield /ˌmuni ˈɔɪlfild/, *n.* Australia's first commercial oil field, in southern Qld, discovered in 1961.

moonlight /ˈmunlaɪt/, *n.* **1.** the light of the moon. ◇*adj.* **2.** relating to moonlight. **3.** lit by moonlight. **4.** happening by moonlight. ◇*v.i. Colloq.* **5.** to work at a second job, often at night.

Moonlite /ˈmunlaɪt/, *n.* **Captain** (*Andrew George Scott*), 1842–80, Australian bushranger, born in Ireland.

moonshine /ˈmunʃaɪn/, *n.* **1.** the light of the moon. **2.** *US Colloq.* smuggled or illegally distilled liquor.

moonstone /ˈmunstoʊn/, *n.* a pearly-white variety of felspar used as a gem.

moor[1] /mɔ/, *n.* an area of open, damp, wasteland, often overgrown with small shrubs, common in high latitudes and altitudes where drainage is poor; heath (def. 1). [OE]

moor[2] /mɔ/, *v.t.* **1.** to tie up (a ship, etc.) as by cables and anchors or by lines. **2.** to tie, or fix firmly. ◇*v.i.* **3.** to moor a ship, etc. [OE] – **mooring(s)**, *n.*

Moor /mɔ/, *n.* a Muslim of the mixed Berber and Arab people inhabiting north-west Africa, who invaded and conquered Spain in the eighth century. [ME, from OF, from L, from Gk *Maûros*] – **Moorish**, *adj.*

Moorabbin /məˈræbən/, *n.* a city in the Melbourne metropolitan area. Pop. 95 291 (1986).

Moore /mɔ, mʊə/, *n.* **1. Henry**, 1898–1986, English abstract sculptor; his work is primarily simple massive forms. **2. Tom Inglis** (*Thomas Inglis Moore*), 1901–79, Australian writer and critic; one of the pioneer teachers of Australian literature.

Moorehead /ˈmɔhed/, *n.* **Alan McCrae**, 1910–83, Australian-born writer and war correspondent living in London and India; author of *Gallipoli* (1956).

moorhen /ˈmɔhen/, *n.* Also, **dusky moorhen**. a brownish black water bird with a red frontal shield.

Moorhouse /ˈmɔhaʊs/, *n.* **Frank**, born 1938, Australian short-story writer; wrote the collection *The Americans, Baby* (1972).

moose /mus/, *n., pl.* **moose**. a large animal of the deer family, the male of which has large branching antlers. [NAmer Ind]

moot /mut/, *adj.* **1.** doubtful; debatable. ◇*v.t.* **2.** to bring forward (any point, subject, etc.) for discussion. ◇*n.* **3.** *Hist.* an Early English gathering of people, exercising political and legal powers. [OE: meeting, assembly] — **mooter**, *n.*

mop /mɒp/, *n., v.*, **mopped, mopping**. ◇*n.* **1.** a bundle of coarse fibre or cloth, etc., fastened at the end of a stick or handle, used for washing floors or dishes. **2.** a thick mass, as of hair. ◇*v.t.* **3.** to rub, clean, or remove with a mop. **4. mop up**, to clean up. [ME]

mope /moʊp/, *v.i.*, **moped, moping**. to be sunk in a lifeless, unhappy mood. [var. of obs. *mop* make a wry face]

mopoke /ˈmoʊpoʊk/, *n.* **1.** an Australian and NZ owl, esp. the **boobook**, having a call sounding like the word 'mopoke'. **2.** *Colloq.* a slow or stupid person. Also, **morepork** /ˈmɔpɔk/. [imitative]

moraine /məˈreɪn/, *n.* a ridge, or irregular mass of rocks, gravel, sand and clay, carried in or on a glacier. [F] — **morainal, morainic**, *adj.*

moral /ˈmɒrəl/, *adj.* **1.** relating to or concerned with right conduct or the distinction between right or wrong: *moral considerations*. **2.** able to act according to the rules of right conduct. **3.** sexually virtuous; chaste. **4.** of, relating to, or producing an effect upon the mind, feelings, or on results generally: *moral support*. **5.** having definite possibilities: *a moral certainty*. ◇*n.* **6.** the moral teaching or practical lesson contained in a fable, tale, etc. **7.** *Colloq.* a certainty: *It's a moral to win*. **8.** (*pl.*) principles or habits with respect to right or wrong conduct; ethics. **9.** (*pl.*) behavior or habits in sexual matters. [ME, from L: relating to manners, customs] — **moralist**, *n.*

morale /məˈrɑl/, *n.* moral or mental condition with respect to cheerfulness, confidence, etc.: *the morale of soldiers*. [F]

moralise *or* **moralize** /ˈmɒrəlaɪz/, *v.*, **-lised, -lising**. ◇*v.i.* **1.** to make moral judgments. ◇*v.t.* **2.** to explain in a moral sense. — **moralistic**, *adj.*

morality /məˈræləti/, *n., pl.* **-ties**. **1.** in accordance with the rules of right conduct. **2.** sexual virtue; chastity. **3.** moral quality or character. **4.** a system of morals; ethics. **5.** moral teaching.

morality play, *n.* a form of drama popular from the 14th to the 16th centuries, strongly emphasising good and evil.

moral support, *n.* a person or thing that provides comfort and encouragement.

Morant /məˈrænt/, *n.* Harry Harbord ('*Breaker*'), 1865–1902, Australian soldier and balladist, born in England; court-martialled and executed during the Boer War.

morass /məˈræs/, *n.* **1.** an area of low, soft, wet ground; marsh. **2.** muddy ground. [D, from OF, of Gmc orig.]

moratorium /mɒrəˈtɔriəm/, *n., pl.* **-toria** /-ˈtɔriə/, **-toriums**. **1.** a general suspension of some type of legal obligation. **2.** a period of such a suspension. **3.** a stopping of activity for a while, as in making political decisions, for the purpose of deferring a decision on a particular course of action. [NL, from L: delay]

moray /ˈmɔreɪ/, *n., pl.* **-rays**. *n.* a type of eel found among rocks and weeds in northern Australia and in the Mediterranean where it is valued as a food.

morbid /ˈmɔbəd/, *adj.* **1.** suggesting an unhealthy mental state. **2.** affected by, coming from, or characteristic of disease. [L: sickly] — **morbidity**, *n.*

mordant /ˈmɔdnt/, *adj.* **1.** biting, hurtful, as humor, a speaker, etc. **2.** having the property of fixing colors, as in dyeing. ◇*n.* **3.** a substance used in dyeing to fix the coloring matter. **4.** an acid, etc. used in etching to eat (def. 2) out the lines, etc. [ME, from OF, from L: bite]

more /mɔ/, *adj., superl.* **most**, *n., adv.* ◇*adj.* **1.** in greater quantity, measure, degree, or number. **2.** additional, further: *Do not lose any more time.* ◇*n.* **3.** an additional quantity or number. **4.** a greater quantity or degree. ◇*adv.* **5.** in or to a greater degree: *more slowly.* **6.** in addition; again. **7. more or less**, to a certain degree. [OE]

More /mɔ/, *n.* **Sir Thomas**, 1478–1535, English statesman and author; lord chancellor to Henry VIII; his opposition to Henry's claim to be supreme head of the Church of England led to his execution; canonised in 1935.

Moree /ˈmɔri/, *n.* a town in north-eastern NSW, on the Gwydir River; hot artesian-bore baths and nearby a major satellite telecommunications station. Pop. 10 215 (1986).

moreover /mɔrˈoʊvə/, *adv.* beyond what has been said; further; besides.

mores /ˈmɔreɪz/, *n.pl.* unquestioned customs and moral views of a group. [L: customs]

Moresby /ˈmɔzbi/, *n.* **John**, 1830–1922, English-born naval officer and explorer; in Australia 1871–74 policing the recruitment of Kanaka labor; explored areas of New Guinea.

Moreton Bay /ˈmɔtn beɪ/, *n.* a large bay in southern Qld into which the Brisbane River flows; three large islands, Stradbroke, Moreton and Bribie, lie to the east and north. [named after James Douglas, Earl of *Morton*, (misspelt 'Moreton') 1702–68, President of the Royal Society 1764]

Moreton Bay fig, *n.* a huge spreading tree, native to the east coast of Australia, which bears small, purplish fruit.

Morgan /ˈmɔgən/, *n.* **Daniel** ('*Mad Morgan*'), 1830–65, notorious Australian bushranger.

morganatic /mɔgəˈnætɪk/, *adj.* relating to a form of marriage in which a man of high rank takes a wife of lower rank with the ruling that neither she nor her children shall have any claim to his rank or property. [ML (*mātrimōnium ad*) *morganāticam* (marriage with) morning gift (in lieu of a share in the husband's possessions)]

Morgan le Fay /ˈmɔgən lə ˈfeɪ/, *n. Celtic and Arthurian Legend.* the fairy sister of King Arthur. Also, **Morgain le Fay, Morgana.**

morgue /mɔg/, *n.* **1.** a place where the bodies of persons found dead are kept for identification. **2.** *Journal Colloq.* the reference library of clippings, books, etc., kept by a newspaper, etc. [F; orig. name of building in Paris so used]

moribund /ˈmɒrəbʌnd/, *adj.* **1.** in a dying state. **2.** almost at an end. [L] —**moribundity,** *n.*

Moriori /mɒriˈɒri/, *n.* **1.** a Polynesian culture in NZ and the Chatham Islands, earlier than Maori culture; the culture of the moa hunters. **2.** the language of the Moriori.

Mormon /ˈmɔmən/, *n.* **1.** member of a religious body founded in the US in 1830 by Joseph Smith and calling itself 'The Church of Jesus Christ of Latter-day Saints'. **2. The Book of,** a sacred book of the Mormon Church, supposed to be an abridgment by a prophet (**Mormon**) of a record of certain ancient peoples in America, written on golden plates and discovered and translated (1827–30) by Joseph Smith. ◇*adj.* **3.** of or relating to the Mormons or their religious system. —**Mormonism,** *n.*

morn /mɔn/, *n. Poetic.* morning. [OE: morning]

mornay /ˈmɔneɪ/, *adj.* covered with a thick white sauce containing cheese. [orig. uncert.]

morning /ˈmɔnɪŋ/, *n.* **1.** the beginning of day; dawn. **2.** the first part of the day, from dawn, or from midnight, to noon. ◇*adj.* **3.** of or relating to morning. [ME]

morning dress, *n.* formal daytime dress, consisting for men of morning coat, grey striped trousers, a light-colored top-hat, etc.

morning glory, *n., pl.* **-ries.** a climbing plant with funnel-shaped flowers of various colors.

morning sickness, *n.* a feeling of sickness coming often in the morning, and suffered in the first months of pregnancy.

morning star, *n.* a bright planet, seen in the east before sunrise.

Mornington Island /ˌmɔnɪŋtən ˈaɪlənd/, *n.* an island in the Gulf of Carpentaria, the largest of the Wellesley Islands. About 60 km long, and on average 20 km wide.

Mornington Peninsula, *n.* a peninsula in southern Vic, extending from the Melbourne suburb of Frankston towards Bass Strait; the site of the first attempt at settlement in Vic; holiday resorts.

Morobe /ˈmɒrəbi/, *n.* a province of PNG, in the north-east. Pop. 357 100 (1986 est.); 34 500 km². *Administrative Centre:* Lae.

Morocco /məˈrɒkoʊ/, *n.* a kingdom in north-western Africa on the Atlantic Ocean and Mediterranean Sea; Pop. 23 119 000 (1987 est.); 458 730 km². *Languages:* Arabic, also Berber, Spanish and French. *Currency:* dirham. *Cap.:* Rabat. French, **Maroc.** —**Moroccan,** *n., adj.*

moron /ˈmɔrɒn/, *n.* **1.** a person of abnormally low intelligence. **2.** *Colloq.* a stupid person. [Gk: dull, foolish] —**moronic,** *adj.*

morose /məˈroʊs/, *adj.* gloomily or nastily ill-humored as a person, mood, etc. [L: fretful]

morph-, variant of **morpho-** before vowels.

-morph, a word part meaning 'form'. [Gk *morphē* form]

morpheme /ˈmɔfim/, *n. Linguistics.* the smallest unit of meaning in a language: either a word, as *girl, world,* or part of a word, as *-ish* or *-ly* in *girlish* and *worldly.* [MORPH(O)- + *-eme,* as in *phoneme*] —**morphemic,** *adj.*

Morphett /ˈmɔfət/, *n.* **Sir John,** 1809–92, Australian pioneer and politician, born in England; assisted William Light in laying out Adelaide; helped found the *South Australian* newspaper.

Morpheus /ˈmɔfiəs/, *n. Gk Myth.* a minor deity, son of the god of sleep; the god of dreams. [ME from L from Gk *morphē* form, in allusion to the forms seen in dreams]

-morphic, a word part used as an adjective ending, similar to **-morph,** as in *anthropomorphic.* [Gk: form + -IC]

morphine /ˈmɔfin/, *n.* a bitter, crystalline alkaloid, extracted from opium and used in medicine to relieve pain and induce sleep. Also, **morphia** /ˈmɔfiə/. [F, from G. See MORPHEUS)]

morpho-, a word part similar to **-morph.**

morphology /mɔˈfɒlədʒi/, *n.* **1.** the study of form, structure, and the like. **2.** that branch of biology which deals with the form and structure of animals and plants. **3.** that branch of linguistics concerned with the patterns of word formation in a particular language. **4.** the study of the physical form of lands, areas, or towns. —**morphological,** *adj.*

-morphous, a word part used as an adjective ending, similar to **-morph,** as in *amorphous.* [Gk *-morphos,* from *morphē* form]

Morris /ˈmɒrəs/, *n.* **William,** 1834–96, English poet, artist, and socialist writer; founder of the Arts and Crafts Movement.

morrow /ˈmɒroʊ/, *n. Archaic.* **1.** morning. **2.** the day after this. [OE: morning]

Morse /mɔs/, *n.* **1. Helen,** born in London, 1946, Australian stage, television and film actor. **2. Samuel Finley Breeze,** 1791–1872, US inventor of a telegraph system and morse code.

morse code, *n.* a coded system for signalling and conveying information in which each letter is represented by short or long sounds (dots and dashes).

morsel /ˈmɔsəl/, *n.* **1.** a bite, or small piece of food, etc. **2.** a small piece, quantity, or amount of anything; scrap. [ME, from OF: a small bite, from L: bite]

Mort /mɔt/, *n.* **Thomas Sutcliffe,** 1816–78, Australian merchant, born in England; pioneer in use of freezing for meat export.

mortal /ˈmɔtl/, *adj.* **1.** subject to death: *mortal man.* **2.** human: *this mortal life.* **3.**

mortal

belonging to this world. **4.** relating to death: *mortal throes*. **5.** (of a sin) serious enough to cause spiritual death (opposed to *venial*). **6.** causing death; fatal: *a mortal wound*. **7.** to the death: *mortal combat*. **8.** deadly: *mortal enemy*. **9.** dreadful: *in mortal fear*. **10.** *Colloq.* very great; extreme: *in a mortal hurry*. **11.** *Colloq.* possible: *of no mortal use*. ◇*n.* **12.** a human being. [ME, from L: subject to death]

mortality /mɔ'tæləti/, *n.*, *pl.* **-ties. 1.** the condition of being mortal. **2.** humanity. **3.** relative frequency of death or death rate: *Child mortality was high*. **4.** death or destruction on a large scale.

mortar[1] /'mɔtə/, *n.* **1.** a bowl-shaped vessel of hard material, in which drugs, etc., are ground to powder with a pestle. **2.** a short cannon for throwing shells at high angles. **3.** some similar device, as for throwing fireworks or a lifeline. [OE, from L: vessel in which substances are pounded, or one in which MORTAR[2] is made]

mortar[2] /'mɔtə/, *n.* **1.** a mixture, of lime, cement, etc., sand, and water, used for binding bricks, etc., together. ◇*v.t.* **2.** to fix with mortar. [ME, from F, from L]

mortarboard /'mɔtəbɔd/, *n.* **1.** a board used by bricklayers to hold mortar. **2.** a type of square-shaped cap worn by university students, teachers, etc.; trencher.

Morte d'Arthur /mɔt 'dɑθə/, *n.* a compilation and translation of French Arthurian romances made by Sir Thomas Malory and printed by Caxton in 1485.

mortgage /'mɔgɪdʒ/, *n.* **1.** *Law.* a charge placed on property and payable by the borrower as a security for the repayment of money lent. **2.** → **pledge**. ◇*v.t.* **3.** to place a property under a mortgage. [ME, from OF *mort* dead + *gage* pledge]

mortgagee /mɔgə'dʒi/, *n.* someone to whom property is mortgaged.

mortgagor /'mɔgədʒə, mɔgə'dʒɔ/, *n.* someone who mortgages property. Also, **mortgager**.

mortice /'mɔtəs/, *n.*, *v.*, **-ticed, -ticing.** ◇*n.* **1.** a deep rectangular hole in one piece of wood, etc., into which is fitted another piece of wood, so as to form a joint (**mortice and tenon joint**). ◇*v.t.* **2.** to join by a mortice. **3.** to cut a mortice in. [ME, from OF, ? from Ar: made fast]

mortification /mɔtəfə'keɪʃən/, *n.* **1.** shame, as by some wound to pride; humiliation. **2.** the cause of such mortification. **3.** *Theol.* the practice of self-denial by harsh discipline to overcome desire for sin and to strengthen the will.

mortify /'mɔtəfaɪ/, *v.*, **-fied, -fying.** ◇*v.t.* **1.** to shame, as by a severe wound to the pride. **2.** *Theol.* to bring (the body, passions, etc.) into control by self-denial and strict discipline. ◇*v.i.* **3.** to practise mortification. [ME, from OF, from LL: kill, destroy]

mortuary /'mɔtʃəri/, *n.*, *pl.* **-ries**, *adj.* ◇*n.* **1.** a place for the safe-keeping of the dead, until burial, etc. ◇*adj.* **2.** relating to or connected with death. [ME, from L: belonging to the dead]

Morwell /'mɔwəl/, *n.* a town and shire in south-eastern Vic, in the centre of the Latrobe Valley; large deposits of brown coal. Pop. 16 387 (1986).

morwong /'mɔwɒŋ/, *n.* a salt-water fish of southern Australia and NZ used as food.

mosaic /moʊ'zeɪɪk, mə'zeɪɪk/, *n.* **1.** a picture or pattern made of small pieces of colored stone, glass, etc. **2.** the process of producing it. **3.** something like a mosaic in form. **4.** *Plant Pathol.* a symptom of various virus diseases, a patchy variation of color. **5.** *Genetics.* an organism, usu. animal, composed of a mixture of genetically separate tissues; chimera. ◇*adj.* **6.** relating to or like a mosaic. [ME, from ML: of the Muses, artistic] —**mosaicist**, *n.*

Moscow /'mɒskoʊ/, *n.* the capital of Russia in the central part of European Russia. Pop. 8 527 000 (1986 est.). Russian, **Moskva**.

Moselle /moʊ'zɛl/, *n.* **1.** German, **Mosel**. a river flowing from the Vosges mountains in north-eastern France into the Rhine in western Germany. 515 km. **2.** (*l.c.*) a light white wine orig. grown in the Rhine Valley.

Moses[1] /'moʊzəz/, *n.* the liberator of the Hebrews from Egypt, their leader throughout the years in the desert and, according to tradition, Israel's first lawgiver. [See Exodus 2, Deuteronomy 34. L from Gk from Heb *Mōsheh*]

Moses[2] /'moʊzəz/, *n.* **1. Anna Mary Robertson** ('*Grandma*'), 1860–1961, US primitive painter. **2. Sir Charles Joseph Alfred**, 1900–88, Australian broadcasting executive, born in England; general manager of the ABC 1935–65.

Mosley /'moʊzli/, *n.* **Sir Oswald Ernald**, 1896–1980, British politician; founder of the British Union of Fascists (1932).

mosque /mɒsk/, *n.* a Muslim place of worship. [F, from It, from Ar: prostrate oneself, worship]

mosquito /məs'kitoʊ/, *n.*, *pl.* **-toes, -tos**. a flying insect, the female of which sucks animal blood and, in so doing, passes on certain diseases, as malaria and yellow fever. [Sp, from L: a fly]

moss /mɒs/, *n.* small leafy-stemmed plants growing in clusters on moist ground, tree trunks, rocks, etc. [OE: bog]

most /moʊst/, *adj.*, *superl.* of **more**, *n.*, *adv.* ◇*adj.* **1.** in the greatest quantity, amount, degree, or number. **2.** in the majority of instances: *Most exercises are good*. **3.** greatest, as in size or range: *the most part*. ◇*n.* **4.** the greatest quantity, amount, or degree; the utmost. **5.** the greatest number. **6.** the majority of persons (*construed as pl.*). ◇*adv.* **7.** in or to the greatest range or degree (in this sense much used before adjectives and adverbs). [OE]

-most, a use of *most* as a suffix, as in *utmost*, *foremost*. [ME]

most favored nation or **most favoured nation**, *n.* a country with which trade is carried on under conditions which are no less favorable than those relating to trade with any other country. *Abbrev.*: MFN

mostly /'moustli/, *adv.* **1.** for the most part. **2.** chiefly.

mote /mout/, *n.* a particle, esp. of dust. [OE: speck]

motel /mou'tel/, *n.* a roadside hotel providing lodging for travellers in self-contained, serviced units, with parking for their vehicles.

motet /mou'tet/, *n. Music.* church music, usu. for two or more voices. [ME, from OF]

moth /mɒθ/, *n., pl.* **moths.** a flying insect similar to the butterfly, but having feathery antennae and nocturnal (night) habits. [OE]

mothball /'mɒθbɔl/, *n.* **1.** a small ball of naphthalene or the like, stored with clothes, etc., to kill moths. **2. in mothballs**, no longer in use. ◇*v.t.* **3.** to put out of use.

mother /'mʌðə/, *n.* **1.** a female parent. **2.** (*oft. cap.*) one's own mother. **3.** *Colloq.* a mother-in-law, step-mother, or adoptive mother. **4.** a familiar term for an old woman. **5.** the head of a female religious community. **6.** a woman looked upon as a mother, or exercising control like that of a mother. **7.** the qualities characteristic of a mother: *The mother in her prompted her to comfort the lost child.* ◇*adj.* **8.** that is a mother: *a mother bird.* **9.** relating to or characteristic of a mother: *mother love.* **10.** coming from one's mother: *Her mother tongue is Italian.* **11.** having a relation like that of a mother: *a mother church.* ◇*v.t.* **12.** to be the mother of. **13.** to take as one's own. **14.** to care for as a mother does. [OE]

Mother Goose, *n.* the legendary author of many folk nursery jingles. [from F *Contes de ma mère l'Oye* 'Mother Goose's Tales', a collection of stories by C Perrault]

motherhood /'mʌðəhud/, *n.* the state of being a mother.

mother-in-law /'mʌðər-ən-lɔ/, *n., pl.* **mothers-in-law.** the mother of one's husband or wife.

motherland /'mʌðəlænd/, *n.* **1.** the country in which someone was born. **2.** the country where someone's family originally lived: *Greece is the motherland of many Australians.*

mother-of-pearl /mʌðər-ɒv-'pɜl/, *n.* the hard, shiny, colorful lining of certain shells, as of the pearl oyster; nacre.

motif /mou'tif, 'moutæf/, *n.* **1.** a repeated subject or idea in a literary, artistic or musical work, or in the works of a writer, etc.: *the motif of madness in King Lear; the scarab motif in Egyptian art.* **2.** a repeated figure in a design, as of wallpaper. **3.** a main idea or feature: *Light and dark is a leading motif in Rembrandt's painting.* [F]

motile /'moutaɪl/, *adj. Biol.* moving, or able to move, by itself: *motile cells; motile spores.* [L: moved] —**motility**, *n.*

motion /'mouʃən/, *n.* **1.** the process or power of moving: *Animals have the power of motion, unlike plants.* **2.** a movement: *a slight motion of the air.* **3.** the manner of moving the body; gait: *to walk with a swaying motion.* **4.** a bodily movement; gesture: *He made a motion for her to go out.* **5.** an idea or plan of action formally put to an assembly for consideration: *to move a motion in Parliament.* **6.** → **faeces. 7. in motion**, moving: *The train was already in motion when they got on.* ◇*v.t., v.i.* **8.** to direct by a gesture of the hand or head: *He motioned to her to come.* [ME, from L: a moving]

motion picture, *n.* → **film** (def. 4).

motivate /'moutəveɪt/, *v.t.*, **-vated**, **-vating.** to provide with a strong reason for doing something.

motivation /moutə'veɪʃən/, *n.* a set of motives for action; a providing of motives; inducement. —**motivational**, *adj.*

motive /'moutɪv/, *n.* **1.** a strong reason or need that drives someone to do something: *His motive was hatred.* **2.** → **motif** (def. 1). ◇*adj.* **3.** of or causing motion. [ML: a moving cause, from L: moved]

motley /'mɒtli/, *adj., n., pl.* **-leys.** ◇*adj.* **1.** made up of different parts; diverse; heterogeneous: *a motley crowd.* **2.** of different colors combined. ◇*n.* **3.** the traditional fool's garment in various colors. [ME]

motor /'moutə/, *n.* **1.** a fairly small and powerful engine, esp. an internal-combustion engine in a car, boat, etc. **2.** (now rare) a self-powered vehicle, as a car. **3.** someone or something that imparts motion, esp. a contrivance (as a steam engine) which receives and modifies energy from some natural source in order to utilise it in driving machinery, etc. ◇*adj.* **4.** causing or imparting motion: *motor energy.* **5.** relating to, used for or operated by a motor: *motor oil; motor cycle.* **6.** *Physiol.* to do with movement: *The fall has damaged some of her motor nerves.* ◇*v.i.* **7.** (now rare) to travel by car; drive. [L: one who moves]

motorbike /'moutəbaɪk/, *n.* → **motorcycle.**

motor car, *n.* a passenger vehicle driven by its own power, usu. by an internal-combustion or diesel engine, and used for road travel.

motorcycle /'moutəsaɪkəl/, *n.* a large heavy bicycle driven by its own power, and able to carry one or two people. —**motorcyclist**, *n.*

motorist /'moutərəst/, *n.* someone who owns and drives a car.

mottle /'mɒtl/, *v.t.*, **-tled**, **-tling.** to make variously colored with spots or blotches. [from MOTLEY] —**mottled**, *adj.*

motto /'mɒtou/, *n., pl.* **-toes, -tos.** a short saying taken as a guiding principle, often written on a badge, coat-of-arms, etc.: *'Be prepared' is the motto of the Scouts.* [It]

Motu /'moutu/, *n.* the language of an aboriginal people of southern Papua.

mould¹ /mould/, *n.* **1.** a hollow form used to shape melted or soft material: *Pottery is some-*

mould *times made in a mould.* **2.** a frame, etc., on which something is made. **3.** a shape or form: *made in his father's mould.* ◇*v.t.* **4.** to work into a required shape or form; shape: *to mould a figure in clay; to mould someone's character.* **5.** *Foundry.* to form a mould of or from, in order to make a casting. [ME, from OF, from L: module] —**moulder**, *n.*

mould[2] /moʊld/, *n.* a growth of very small fungi forming on organic matter, and usu. causing decay. [ME]

mould[3] /moʊld/, *n.* **1.** crumbly sweet soil resulting from or rich in decayed organic matter: *leaf mould.* **2.** *Poetic.* the ground or earth. [OE]

moulder /'moʊldə/, *v.t., v.i.* to turn or cause to turn to dust by natural decay; crumble; waste away. [obs. *mold* crumble away]

moulding /'moʊldɪŋ/, *n.* **1.** the act or process of decaying or crumbling away. **2.** something moulded. **3.** *Archit, etc.* **a.** (a decorative shape given to) a strip of wood used on walls, furniture, etc. **b.** a decorative shape or design in plaster, esp. on a ceiling.

mouldy /'moʊldi/, *adj.,* **-dier, -diest. 1.** overgrown or covered with mould. See **mould**[2]. **2.** stale from decay or age; musty: *a mouldy smell.*

moult /moʊlt/, *v.t., v.i.* **1.** (of birds, insects, reptiles, etc.) to lose or throw off (old feathers, skin, etc.). ◇*n.* **2.** the act or process of moulting. [OE, from L: change] —**moulter**, *n.*

mound /maʊnd/, *n.* **1.** a heap of earth, stones, etc., esp. one made long ago and formed over a grave. **2.** a natural rise in the ground; hillock; knoll. **3.** a heap or mass of anything: *mound of hay; a mound of work.* ◇*v.t.* **4.** to form into a mound; heap up. [OE: hand, protection]

mount[1] /maʊnt/, *v.t.* **1.** to go up; ascend: *to mount the stairs.* **2.** to get up on (a platform, a horse, etc.) **3.** to set on horseback (*usu. pass.*): *They were mounted on two handsome bays.* **4.** to raise or put (guns, etc.) into position for use. **5.** (of a ship or ship) to have (guns) in position for use. **6.** to go or put on (guard), as a sentry. **7.** (of a male animal) to climb up on (a female) for copulation. **8.** to fix on or in a setting: *to mount a photograph; to mount a jewel.* **9.** to put on (a play, exhibition, etc.). **10.** to prepare (a dead animal or skeleton) as a specimen. **11. a.** to prepare (a slide) for a microscope. **b.** to prepare (a specimen, etc.) by placing it on a slide. ◇*v.i.* **12.** to rise or go to a higher position, etc.; ascend. **13.** to rise in amount (oft. fol. by *up*): *Costs are steadily mounting.* **14.** to get up on a platform, horse, etc. ◇*n.* **15.** a horse for riding. **16.** a backing or setting: *The print looks fine with a grey mount.* **17.** *Microscopy.* a prepared slide. [ME, from OF, from L: mountain]

mount[2] /maʊnt/, *n.* a mountain or hill (now mainly poetic, except in names, as *Mount Wellington*). [OE, from L]

mountain /'maʊntən/, *n.* **1.** a natural raised part of the earth's surface, higher than a hill. **2.** something like this in size or shape: *a mountain of ice.* **3.** a huge amount: *I have mountains of reading to do for this essay.* **4. make a mountain out of a molehill,** to make something more important than it really is, esp. of a complaint. ◇*adj.* **5.** of or living on mountains: *mountain air; mountain plants.* [ME, from OF: mountain, from L] —**mountainous**, *adj.*

mountain ash, *n.* a name used to refer to some Australian gum trees.

mountain devil, *n.* **1.** Also, **moloch.** a spiny, grotesque-looking lizard found in lowland and mountain regions of southern, central and western Australia. **2.** a woody shrub of sandstone areas of NSW.

mountaineer /maʊntə'nɪə/, *n.* **1.** someone who climbs mountains. ◇*v.i.* **2.** to climb mountains. —**mountaineering**, *n.*

mountain lion, *n.* → **puma.**

mountain range, *n.* a series of connected mountain ridges with more or less parallel lines of mountains, closely related in origin, etc.

Mountbatten of Burma /maʊnt'bætn əv 'bɜmə/, *n.* **Louis, 1st Earl,** 1900–79, British admiral; viceroy of India 1947; governor-general of India 1947–48; died as a result of a bomb explosion for which the Provisional wing of the IRA claimed responsibility.

Mount Charlotte /maʊnt 'ʃalət/, *n.* a gold mine in Kalgoorlie, WA; the only remaining underground mine there.

Mount Gambier /maʊnt 'gæmbɪə/, *n.* **1.** a city in the far south-east of SA at the foot of the mountain bearing the same name. Pop. 20 813 (1986). **2.** → **Gambier.** [named after the British admiral, James *Gambier*]

Mount Isa /maʊnt 'aɪzə/, *n.* a city in north-western Qld, at the northern end of the Selwyn Range; silver, lead, zinc, and copper mining; Australia's major copper centre in the 1970s. Pop. 23 348 (1986).

Mount Lyell /maʊnt 'laɪəl/, *n.* a mining area in central western Tas, just north of Queenstown; early gold and silver mining; now copper extracted with silver and gold as by-products; lunar landscape due to early smelting methods which killed vegetation.

Mount Mulligan /maʊnt 'mʌləgən/, *n.* a former coalmining town and mountain in northern Qld, west of Cairns; scene of Qld's worst mining disaster in 1921 in which 75 men died. [named after JV *Mulligan*, explorer and prospector, who visited the area in 1874]

Mount Stromlo Observatory /'strɒmloʊ/, *n.* an astronomical observatory established in Canberra in 1923; the largest of its kind in Australia. Formerly, the **Commonwealth Solar Observatory.**

mourn /mɔn/, *v.t., v.i.* **1.** to feel or express sorrow (over something lost or gone): *to mourn the loss of freedom.* **2.** to grieve or express grief (for the dead); lament. [OE] —**mourner**, *n.*

mournful /'mɔnfəl/, *adj.* **1.** showing sorrow or grief; sorrowful; sad. **2.** gloomy; sombre; dreary; dismal: *mournful shadows.*

mourning /'mɔnɪŋ/, n. **1.** the act of someone who mourns; sorrowing; lamentation. **2.** clothes, esp. black worn as a sign of grief for someone's death. **3. in mourning,** a time of mourning following the death of a relative, etc. ◇adj. **4.** of, relating to, or used in mourning.

mouse /maʊs/, n., pl. **mice** /maɪs/; /maʊz/, v., **moused, mousing.** ◇n. **1.** a small rodent that lives in the bush or infests houses. **2.** Colloq. someone who is very quiet and shy, esp. a girl or woman. **3.** a handheld device used to position the cursor on a VDU. ◇v.i. **4.** to hunt for or catch mice. [OE mūs (pl. mȳs)]

mouse spider, n. a strong, lively ground-tunnelling spider of Australia. The female is blackish-brown but the male has a red head.

moussaka /mʊˈsɑːkə/, n. a Balkan and Middle Eastern dish with layers of minced lamb, tomatoes and aubergines topped with a thick white sauce and baked. [Ar, from Turk]

mousse /mus/, n. any of various preparations of whipped cream, beaten eggs, gelatine, etc., with something added to give a sweet or savory taste: *chocolate mousse; fish mousse*. [F: froth]

moustache /məˈstɑːʃ/, n. hair growing on the upper lip of men. [F, from It, from Gk: upper lip, moustache]

Mousterian /muˈstɪəriən/, adj. **1.** relating to Palaeolithic human relics having the workmanship, finish, and character of the flint scrapers found in south-western France. ◇n. **2.** the general culture of this period of the Palaeolithic, c. 70 000 BC to 32 000 BC. [from *Le Moustier*, a cave in SW France, containing flint implements of this period]

mousy /'maʊsi/, adj., **-sier, -siest. 1.** like a mouse in colour, smell, etc. **2.** grey-brown or colourless; drab. **3.** quiet and shy. Also, **mousey.**

mouth /maʊθ/, n., pl. **mouths** /maʊðz/; /maʊð/, v. ◇n. **1.** the opening in the face through which a person or animal takes in food or makes sounds. **2.** a person or animal as needing food: *two more mouths to feed*. **3.** the opening of a cave, pot, etc. **4.** the place where a river flows into the sea. **5. by word of mouth,** by the spoken word, not in writing; orally. **6. down in the mouth,** unhappy; depressed. **7. shoot one's mouth off,** Colloq. to talk angrily or indiscreetly. ◇v.t. **8.** to utter in a pompous or empty way: *politicians mouthing promises*. **9.** to form words without sound. **10.** to press, rub, or mumble with the mouth or lips. ◇v.i. **11.** to speak pompously or emptily. [OE]

mouthful /'maʊθfʊl/, n., pl. **-fuls. 1.** an amount (of food, water, etc.) taken into the mouth at one time. **2.** a small amount: *a mere mouthful*. **3.** a large amount: *You've said a mouthful*.

mouth organ, n. → harmonica.

mouthpiece /'maʊθpis/, n. **1.** a part of a musical instrument, telephone, etc., held in or to the mouth. **2.** a part of a horse's bridle held in the mouth. **3.** Sport. a guard for the teeth. **4.** someone or something that speaks for or represents another; spokesperson.

mouth-to-mouth /maʊθ-tə-'maʊθ/, adj. indicating a method of artificial respiration in which air is breathed rhythmically into the mouth of the patient.

movable /'muvəbəl/, adj. **1.** able to be moved. **2.** changing from one date to another in different years: *Easter is a movable feast*. ◇n. **3.** a piece of furniture not fixed in place. **4.** (usu. pl.) Law. a piece of personal property not attached to land. Also, **moveable.** —**movability,** n.

move /muv/, v., **moved, moving,** n. ◇v.i. **1.** to change position. **2.** to go from one place to another: *We're moving to Sydney next year*. **3.** to advance or make progress: *Business is moving at last*. **4.** to have a regular motion: *That part moves up and down when you press the button*. **5.** (of the bowels) to operate. **6.** to be active in a particular area: *to move in society*. **7.** to take action; make a move: *If you move now it won't be too late*. **8.** to make a formal request, etc.: *to move for a new trial*. ◇v.t. **9.** to change the place or position of: *to move the piano to another room*. **10.** to set or keep going: *to move the traffic along*. **11.** to stir or prompt to some action: *What moved you to do this?* **12.** to cause (the bowels) to operate. **13.** to affect with emotion; touch: *The letter moved him*. **14.** to put formally to a court or assembly: *to move a motion*. ◇v. **15. move heaven and earth,** to do the most one can. **16. move in,** to come to live in a new house. **17. move out,** to leave a house. ◇n. **18.** the act of moving; a movement. **19.** a change of living place: *This is our fifth move in three years*. **20.** an action towards an end; step: *a move in the right direction*. **21.** Games, etc. the right or turn to move. **22. get a move on,** Colloq. hurry up. **23. on the move,** moving. [ME, from AF, from L]

movement /'muvmənt/, n. **1.** the act, process or result of moving. **2.** a particular manner of moving: *the graceful movements of a dancer*. **3.** (chiefly pl.) (a set of) actions or activities: *Can you trace your movements of the past week?* **4.** Mil. a change of position of soldiers or ships. **5.** the rapid progress of events; momentum. **6.** the movement of events in a story, play, etc. **7.** the suggestion of action in a painting, etc. **8.** a group or a number of groups of people working for a particular cause or purpose: *the conservation movement*. **9.** the course or tendency of affairs in a particular field; trend: *the movement towards shorter working hours*. **10.** an emptying (of the bowels). **11.** the mechanism of a clock. **12.** Music. **a.** the main division or section of a sonata, symphony, etc. **b.** time; tempo; motion; rhythm.

movie /'muvi/, n. **1.** → film (def. 4a). **2. the movies,** → film (def. 4b).

moving /'muvɪŋ/, adj. **1.** able or designed to move. **2.** in movement. **3.** having a strong effect on one's feelings, esp. of pity.

mow /moʊ/, v., **mowed, mown** or **mowed, mowing.** ◇v.t. **1.** to cut down (grass, grain, etc.) with a scythe or machine. **2.** to kill in great numbers, as men in battle (fol. by *down*).

◇*v.i.* **3.** to cut down grass, grain, etc. [OE] —**mower**, *n*. —**mowing**, *n*.

Mozambique /ˌmoʊzæm'biːk/, *n*. Also, **Moçambique**. a republic on the east coast of Africa, bordered by Tanzania, Malawi, Zambia, Zimbabwe, South Africa and Swaziland; a Portuguese colony and overseas province before independence in 1975. Pop. 14 516 200 (1987 est.); 799 380 km². *Languages:* Portuguese, also African languages. *Currency:* metical. *Cap.:* Maputo. Official name, **People's Republic of Mozambique**. Formerly, **Portuguese East Africa**.

Mozart /'moʊtsɑːt/, *n*. **Wolfgang Amadeus** /ˌvɒlfgæŋ amə'deɪəs/, 1756–91, Austrian composer; a prolific musician throughout his short life; his works include operas, as *The Marriage of Figaro* (1786), *Don Giovanni* (1787) and *The Magic Flute* (1791), orchestral music including symphonies and concertos, chamber music, sonatas, songs, and masses.

mozzarella /mɒtsə'relə/, *n*. a soft, white, Italian cheese. [It: a slice]

MP / em 'piː/, *Abbrev.* **1.** Member of Parliament. **2.** Military Police.

mph, *Abbrev.* miles per hour.

mps, *Abbrev.* miles per second.

Mr /'mɪstə/, *n.*, *pl.* **Messrs** /'mesəz/. mister; the title put before a man's name or position: *Mr Lawson*; *Mr Prime Minister*.

Mrs /'mɪsəz/, *n*. mistress; the title put before the name of a married woman: *Mrs Jones*. [var. of MISTRESS. See MISSUS]

Mrs Macquarie's Chair /mə'kwɒriz/, *n*. a seat hewn in rock in the Domain on the southern shore of Port Jackson, Sydney, NSW; originally made for Elizabeth Macquarie.

Ms /məz/, *n*. the title put before the name of a woman, used to avoid indicating whether she is married or not: *Ms Smith*. [var. of MISTRESS]

MS, *Abbrev.* **1.** pl. **MSS**. manuscript. **2.** Multiple Sclerosis.

Mt, *Abbrev.* **1.** pl. **Mts**. mount: *Mt Kosciusko*. **2.** Also, **mt**. mountain. **3.** *Bible*. Matthew.

mtg, *Abbrev.* **1.** meeting. **2.** mortgage.

Mubarak /mu'bærɛk/, *n*. **Muhammad Hosni** /məˌhæməd 'hɒzni/, born 1929, Egyptian statesman; became president in 1981.

much /mʌtʃ/, *adj.*, **more**, **most**, *n.*, *adv.* ◇*adj.* **1.** in great quantity, amount, measure, or degree: *much work*. ◇*n.* **2.** a great quantity or amount: *Much of this is true*. **3.** a great, important, or notable thing or matter: *The house is not much to look at*. **4. to make much of, a.** to treat as of great importance. **b.** to treat (a person) with attention or fondness. **5. as much,** the same; precisely that: *as much as to say*. **6. much of a muchness,** (of two or more things) very similar; with little to choose between them. ◇*adv.* **7.** greatly: *much pleased*. **8.** nearly or about; approximately: *This is much the same as the others*. [OE]

mucilage /'mjuːsəlɪdʒ/, *n*. **1.** a type of thin glue for sticking things together. **2.** a gummy substance found in plants. [ME, from F, from LL: a musty juice] —**mucilaginous**, *adj*.

muck /mʌk/, *n*. **1.** farmyard dung; manure. **2.** dirt; filth. **3.** *Colloq.* something of no value; rubbish. **4. make a muck of,** *Colloq.* to spoil; impair; disrupt. ◇*v.t.* **5.** to manure. **6.** to make dirty; soil. **7.** to remove muck from (oft. fol. by *out*). **8.** *Colloq.* to spoil; make a mess of (fol. by *up*). **9. muck about or around,** *Colloq.* to fool about; idle; potter. **10. muck in,** *Colloq.* to share, esp. a place to live. **11. muck up,** *Colloq.* to misbehave. [ME, from Scand] —**mucky**, *adj*.

muckrake /'mʌkreɪk/, *v.i.*, **-raked**, **-raking**. *Colloq.* to look for and publicise corruption by important officials, politicians, etc. [MUCK + RAKE¹] —**muckraker**, *n*. —**muckraking**, *n*.

muck-up /'mʌk-ʌp/, *n*. *Colloq.* **1.** a muddle; fiasco. **2.** (*in children's speech*) someone who misbehaves, esp. in school.

mucous /'mjuːkəs/, *adj.* **1.** of or like mucus. **2.** containing or producing mucus: *the mucous membrane*. [L: slimy] —**mucosity**, *n*.

mucous membrane, *n*. the thin membrane or skin that lines the body cavities and produces mucus.

mucus /'mjuːkəs/, *n*. a thick, slimy liquid produced by the mucous membranes. [L]

mud /mʌd/, *n*. **1.** wet, soft, almost liquid earth; mire. **2.** *Colloq.* → mortar². **3. one's name is mud,** *Colloq.* one is in disgrace. **4. throw (sling) mud at,** *Colloq.* to speak ill of; abuse; vilify. [ME]

mud crab, *n*. a large crab of the mangrove regions of NSW and Qld. Also, **muddie**.

muddle /'mʌdl/, *v.*, **-dled**, **-dling**, *n*. ◇*v.t.* **1.** to mix up or jumble together in a confused way. **2.** to make confused in mind, or unable to think clearly. **3.** to make confused or stupid with alcohol; befuddle. ◇*v.* **4. muddle through,** to succeed or arrive at something in spite of confusion or lack of planning. ◇*n.* **5.** a confused state of mind: *He always gets in a muddle when he has to buy tickets*. **6.** a confused state of affairs; mess. [MUD + -*le*] —**muddler**, *n*.

muddy /'mʌdi/, *adj.*, **-dier**, **-diest**, *v.*, **-died**, **-dying**. ◇*adj.* **1.** covered with mud. **2.** (of water) containing mud; turbid. **3.** (of color) not clear or pure. **4.** (of the complexion) dull. **5.** not clear in mind. **6.** (of thought, expression, literary style, etc.) obscure or vague. ◇*v.t.* **7.** to make muddy. **8.** to make turbid. **9.** to make confused or obscure. ◇*v.i.* **10.** to become muddy or turbid.

mudflat /'mʌdflæt/, *n*. an area of muddy ground covered by water at high tide.

mudflow /'mʌdfloʊ/, *n*. **1. a.** a mixture of water and volcanic matter flowing from a volcano. **b.** a body of rock formed from this. **2.** a flow of mud from a mud volcano. **3.** a fluid mass of soil, which becomes unstable as a result of heavy rain or melting snow.

Mudgee /'mʌdʒi/, *n*. a town and shire in central eastern NSW north-north-west of

Mudgee

Orange; grape-growing, fine wool and merino studs. Pop. 6576 (1986).

mudguard /'mʌdgad/, n. a guard or shield shaped to fit over the wheels of a car or bicycle to prevent splashing of water, mud, etc.

Mudie /'mudi/, n. Ian, 1911-76, Australian poet.

mudlark /'mʌdlak/, n. 1. → **magpie lark**. 2. Also, **mudrunner**. *Horseracing.* a horse that performs very well on wet tracks. 3. *Brit Colloq.* → **guttersnipe**.

mudskipper /'mʌdskɪpə/, n. a type of tropical Australian fish with bulging eyes and stiffened pectoral fins which allow it to skip over mudflats and climb over rocks and mangrove roots. Also, **mudhopper**.

mudslinging /'mʌd-slɪŋə/, n. personal accusations used as a tactic in political debate, etc. **– mudslinger**, n.

Mueller /'mjulə/, n. **Baron Sir Ferdinand Jakob Heinrich von**, 1825-96, Australian botanist and explorer, born in Germany; his discoveries added much to the knowledge of botany of Vic; initiated the building of the National Herbarium in Melbourne.

muesli /'mjuzli/, n. a breakfast cereal of a mixture of oats, wheatgerm, chopped fruit, nuts, etc. [Swiss G]

muezzin /mu'ɛzən/, n. a Muslim crier who, from a minaret or other part of a mosque, calls the faithful to prayer. [Ar]

muff /mʌf/, n. 1. a woollen or fur wrap for the hands. ◊v.t., v.i. 2. *Colloq.* to perform clumsily; bungle. [D, from F]

muffin /'mʌfən/, n. a thick, flat yeast cake, grilled and topped with butter.

muffle /'mʌfəl/, v., **-fled**, **-fling**. ◊v.t. 1. to wrap in a cloak, shawl, scarf, etc., esp. about the face and neck (oft. fol. by *up*). 2. to wrap with something to deaden or prevent sound: *to muffle drums*. 3. to deaden (sound) by wrappings or other means. ◊v.i. 4. to wrap oneself (*up*) as in garments or other wrappings. ◊n. 5. an oven or arched chamber in a furnace or kiln, used for heating substances without direct contact with the fire. [ME, from OF]

muffler /'mʌflə/, n. 1. a heavy neck scarf used for warmth. 2. a device that reduces noise on a machine, esp. on a car engine.

mufti /'mʌfti/, n., pl. **-tis**. 1. civilian dress as opposed to military or other uniform, or as worn by someone who usu. wears a uniform. 2. a Muslim legal adviser in religious law. [Ar: lit., someone who delivers a judgment]

mufti day, n. a day at school on which pupils are permitted to wear casual clothes instead of school uniform, usu. as a fund-raising exercise.

mug /mʌg/, n., v., **mugged**, **mugging**, adj. ◊n. 1. a large drinking cup, usu. used without a saucer. 2. the quantity it holds. 3. *Colloq.* the face. 4. *Brit Colloq.* the mouth. 5. *Colloq.* a fool; person who is easily duped. ◊v.t. 6. *Colloq.* to attack and rob. ◊adj. 7. *Colloq.* stupid. [ME, from Scand] **– mugger**, n.

Mugabe /mu'gabi/, n. **Robert**, born 1925, Zimbabwean politician; became prime minister of Zimbabwe in 1980.

mugga /'mʌgə/, n. a pink-flowering iron-bark, a striking tree with dark, fissured bark, native to eastern Australia.

muggins /'mʌgənz/, n. *Colloq.* a fool, oft. used comically by speakers to refer to themselves: *And who has to finish the job? Muggins!* [? orig. surname *Muggins*]

muggy /'mʌgi/, adj., **-gier**, **-giest**. (of the atmosphere, weather, etc.) damp and close; humid and oppressive. [d. *mug* mist, from Scand]

mug shot, n. a photograph, usu. of the head only, taken for police records.

Muhammad Ali /muhæməd a'li/, n. (*Cassius Marcellus Clay*) born 1942, US boxer; first won title of world heavyweight champion in 1964.

Muhammadan /mə'hæmədən/, adj., n. → **Mohammedan**. Also, **Muhammedan**.

mulatto /mju'lætoʊ, mə-/, n., pl. **-tos** or **-toes**, adj. ◊n. 1. a child of white and Negro parents. ◊adj. 2. of a light brown color (similar to the skin of a mulatto). [Sp and Pg, from L: a mule; so called from the hybrid origin]

mulberry /'mʌlbəri, -bri/, n., pl. **-ries**. 1. (a tree bearing) dark purple fruit like a long blackberry, and leaves used as food for silk worms. 2. a dark, reddish purple color. [OE, from L]

mulch /mʌltʃ/, n. 1. straw, leaves, loose earth, etc., spread on the ground to protect the roots of newly planted trees, crops, etc. ◊v.t. 2. to cover with mulch. [ME: soft, OE: mellow]

Muldoon /mʌl'dun/, n. **Sir Robert David**, 1921-92, NZ National Party politician; prime minister 1975-84.

mule /mjul/, n. 1. the offspring of a male donkey and a female horse. 2. *Colloq.* a stupid or stubborn person. [ME, from OF, from L]

muleteer /mjulə'tɪə/, n. 1. a driver of mules. 2. *Colloq.* → **half-caste**. [F]

mulga /'mʌlgə/, n. 1. (the wood of) several species of wattle, esp. the type found in drier parts of Australia. 2. the bush; back country. 3. an Aborigine's shield. 4. **up (in) the mulga**, in the bush. ◊adj. 5. of or relating to trees, grass, etc., which grows typically in the bush. [Aboriginal]

mulgara /mʌl'garə/, n. See **marsupial mouse**. [Aboriginal]

mulga snake, n. a large, brown, fierce and dangerous snake found in Australia generally and often confused with the common brown snake.

mulga wire, n. *Colloq.* → **bush telegraph**.

mulish /'mjulɪʃ/, adj. stubborn; obstinate; intractable.

mull[1] /mʌl/, v.t. to think about; ponder (fol. by *over*). [? orig. Brit d.: muddle, crumble, from MD]

mull² /mʌl/, *v.t.* (of wine, ale) to heat, sweeten, and spice for drinking: *mulled cider*. [orig. uncert.]

mullah /'mʌlə, 'mʊlə/, *n.* (in Muslim countries) the title of respect for someone who is learned in, teaches, or explains the sacred law. Also, **mulla**. [Turk, Pers, and Hind, from Ar: patron, lord]

Müller /'mylə/, *n.* **Paul Hermann**, 1899-1965, Swiss chemist; synthesised DDT (1939) and discovered its toxic effect on insects; Nobel prize 1948.

mullet /'mʌlət/, *n., pl.* **-lets**, (*esp. collectively*) **-let.** any of various sea and freshwater fish with round, silver-grey bodies, as the sea mullet found widely in Australian waters. [ME, from OF, from L: red mullet]

mulligatawny /mʌləgə'tɔni/, *n.* a soup flavored with curry. [Ind: pepper water]

Mulliken /'mʌləkən/, *n.* **Robert Sanderson**, 1896-1986, US physicist and chemist who researched the nature of chemical bonds and molecular structure; Nobel prize for chemistry 1966.

mullion /'mʌliən, 'mʌljən/, *n.* **1.** an upright piece of stone or wood dividing parts of a window, wood panel, etc. ◇*v.t.* **2.** to form into divisions by the use of mullions. [OF; orig. uncert.]

mullock /'mʌlək/, *n.* **1.** rubbish from mining. **2.** anything valueless. **3. poke mullock at,** to make fun of; ridicule. ◇*v.i.* **4.** *Colloq.* to work in a careless way. [Brit d. *mull* rubbish + -OCK]

mulloway /'mʌləweɪ/, *n.* a large Australian sea fish important as game and food; jewfish. [orig. uncert.]

mullygrubber /'mʌlɪɡrʌbə/, *n. Cricket, etc.* a ball delivered in such a way that it does not bounce when it hits the ground. Also, **grubber**.

multi-, a word part meaning 'many'. [L, combining form of *multus* much, many]

multicellular /mʌltɪ'seljələ/, *adj.* made up of several or many cells.

multicultural /mʌltɪ'kʌltʃərəl/, *adj.* of or relating to a society which has within it several large groups of people of different cultures and races.

multifaceted /mʌltɪ'fæsətəd/, *adj.* **1.** (of a gem) having many facets or cut surfaces. **2.** having many parts to be considered.

multifarious /mʌltə'fɛəriəs/, *adj.* having many different parts or kinds. [L: manifold]

multigrade /'mʌltɪɡreɪd/, *adj.* indicating a motor oil with a stable viscosity level over a wide range of temperatures.

multilateral /mʌltɪ'lætərəl, -'lætrəl/, *adj.* **1.** having many sides; many-sided. **2.** *Govt.* indicating an agreement or arrangement between three or more nations; multipartite.

multimillionaire /mʌltɪmɪljə'nɛə/, *n.* a rich person who has several million dollars.

multinational /mʌltɪ'næʃənəl/, *adj.* of, relating to, or spreading across many nations: *a multinational corporation*; *a multinational company*.

multiparous /mʌl'tɪpərəs/, *adj.* producing many young at one birth. [NL]

multipartite /mʌltɪ'patait/, *adj.* **1.** divided into many parts; having many divisions. **2.** *Govt.* → **multilateral** (def. 2). [L: much-divided]

multiple /'mʌltəpəl/, *adj.* **1.** consisting of or having many parts, elements, relations, etc.; manifold. ◇*n.* **2.** *Maths.* a number which can be divided by a smaller number an exact number of times: *12 is a multiple of 2*. [F, from LL: manifold]

multiple sclerosis, *n.* a disease of the central nervous system which may affect many different bodily functions, esp. gait, sight and coordination, as well as memory, mental functions and personality. *Abbrev.:* MS

multiplex /'mʌltɪpleks/, *adj.* manifold; multiple. [L: manifold]

multiplicate /'mʌltəpləkeɪt/, *adj.* multiple; manifold. [ME, from L: multiplied]

multiplication /mʌltəplə'keɪʃən/, *n.* **1.** the act of multiplying or state of being multiplied. **2.** *Arith.* the process of finding the number (*the product*) resulting from the addition of a given number (*the multiplicand*) to itself as many times as there are units in another given number (*the multiplier*); 4 x 3 means that 4 is added to 4 three times. *Symbol:* × **3.** *Maths.* any generalisation of this operation applicable to numbers other than integers, such as fractions, irrationals, vectors, etc. **4.** *Physics.* the process by which additional neutrons are produced by a chain reaction in a nuclear reactor. – **multiplicational,** *adj.* – **multiplicative,** *adj.*

multiplication table, *n.* a list in which the product of any two numbers of a set (usu. of the integers 1 to 12) is given.

multiplicity /mʌltə'plɪsəti/, *n., pl.* **-ties.** **1.** a great number or variety. **2.** the state of being many. [LL]

multiplier /'mʌltəplaɪə/, *n. Maths.* the number by which another number is to be multiplied.

multiply /'mʌltəplaɪ/, *v.,* **-plied, -plying.** ◇*v.t.* **1.** to make many; increase the number, quantity, etc., of. **2.** *Maths.* to find the product of by multiplication. ◇*v.i.* **3.** to grow in number, quantity, etc.; increase. **4.** *Maths.* to perform the process of multiplication. **5.** to increase in number by natural generation. [ME, from OF, from L]

multitude /'mʌltətjud/, *n.* **1.** a great number; host: *a multitude of friends*. **2.** a great number of people gathered together; crowd; throng. **3. the multitude,** the common people. **4.** the state of being many. [ME, from L] – **multitudinous,** *adj.*

mum¹ /mʌm/, *adj.* **1.** silent; not saying a word: *to keep mum*. ◇*interj.* **2.** Say nothing! Be silent! ◇*n.* **3.** silence: *Mum's the word*. [ME; imitative]

mum² /mʌm/, *v.i.*, **mummed, mumming.** to act as a mummer. Also, **mumm.** [v. use of MUM¹]

mum³ /mʌm/, *n. Colloq.* mother.

mumble /'mʌmbəl/, *v.*, **-bled, -bling,** *n.* ◇*v.t., v.i.* **1.** to utter or speak unclearly, as with partly closed lips; mutter low, indistinct words. ◇*n.* **2.** a low, confused utterance or sound. [ME: make inarticulate sounds] **–mumbler,** *n.*

mumbo jumbo /ˌmʌmbou 'dʒʌmbou/, *n.* **1.** meaningless words or ritual. **2.** speech or writing that is meaningless, often supposed to be high-sounding and important; gibberish. [from the name of a god formerly worshipped by certain W African tribes]

mummer /'mʌmə/, *n.* (formerly) one of a group of actors wearing masks or special costumes who went round houses in England at Christmas, etc., performing short plays of an old and traditional kind. [ME, from OF: MUM²] **–mummery,** *n.*

mummify /'mʌməfaɪ/, *v.*, **-fied, -fying.** ◇*v.t.* **1.** to make (a dead body) into a mummy. **2.** to make like a mummy. ◇*v.i.* **3.** to dry or shrivel up. **–mummification,** *n.*

mummy¹ /'mʌmi/, *n., pl.* **-mies,** *v.*, **-mied, -mying.** ◇*n.* **1.** the dead body of a person or animal preserved by special treatment in ancient Egypt, etc., or by some natural means. ◇*v.t.* **2.** to make into or like a mummy; mummify. [ME, from ML, from Ar, from Pers: asphalt]

mummy² /'mʌmi/, *n. Colloq.* mother.

mumps /mʌmps/, *n.pl.*, treated as sing. an infectious viral disease marked by inflammatory swelling of glands in the neck and elsewhere. [orig. meaning 'grimace'; imitative]

munch /mʌntʃ/, *v.t., v.i.* to chew steadily or strongly, often making a noise. [ME: eat, chew; orig. unknown] **–muncher,** *n.*

Munch /mʊŋk/, *n.* **Edvard** /'ɛdvad/, 1863–1944, Norwegian artist; key figure in the development of modern expressionism.

Münchhausen /'mynʃhaʊzən/, *n.* **1. Karl Friedrich Hieronymus** /kal ˌfridrɪk hiɛˈroʊnəməs/, **Baron** von 1720–97, German soldier and teller of unbelievable tales. ◇*adj.* **2.** *Psychol.* of or relating to a syndrome in which a patient pretends to be ill in order to be admitted to a hospital. English, **Munchausen.**

mundane /'mʌndeɪn, mʌn'deɪn/, *adj.* **1.** of or relating to the world, universe, or earth, esp. as contrasted with heaven; worldly; earthly: *mundane affairs.* **2.** ordinary; boring; pedestrian. [L: the world]

Mundey /'mʌndi/, *n.* **Jack,** born 1932, Australian trade union leader, environmentalist and alderman; noted for instigation of 'green bans'.

mung bean /'mʌŋ bin/, *n.* a small greygreen bean grown in Asia as a food crop and for bean sprouts.

Munich /'mjunɪk/, *n.* a city in Germany, the capital of Bavaria, in the south-eastern part. Pop. 1 274 716 (1987 est.). German, **München.**

Munich Pact, *n.* the pact signed by Germany, Great Britain, France and Italy on 29 September 1938, by which the Sudetenland was ceded to Germany. Also, **Munich Agreement.**

municipal /mju'nɪsəpəl, mjun'sɪpəl/, *adj.* of or relating to a municipality: *municipal library.* [L]

municipality /mjunəsə'pæləti/, *n., pl.* **-ties.** **1.** an area of land marked out for the purposes of local government. **2.** the people in such an area, seen as a community. **3.** the governing body of such an area.

munition /mju'nɪʃən/, *n.* **1.** (usu. pl.) materials used in war, esp. weapons and ammunition. ◇*v.t.* **2.** to provide with munitions. [L: fortification]

munning /'mʌnɪŋ/, *n.* See **hare-wallaby.** [orig. uncert.]

muntries /'mʌntriz/, *n.* a flat-growing shrub found in dry sandy areas of SA and in western Vic.

mural /'mjurəl/, *n., adj.* (a painting, etc.) done or fixed on a wall. [F, from L]

Murchison /'mɜtʃəsən/, *n.* a river in the central west of WA, with headwater tributaries in the Robinson Ranges; the river flows southwesterly to empty into Gantheaume Bay. About 700km.

murder /'mɜdə/, *n.* **1.** *Law.* the unlawful intentional killing of another person. **2. scream (yell) (cry) blue murder,** *Colloq.* to make a noisy outburst; complain vociferously. **3.** *Colloq.* a very difficult or unpleasant task: *Gardening in the heat is murder.* ◇*v.t.* **4.** *Law.* to kill (another person) intentionally. **5.** to kill inhumanly or cruelly. **6.** to spoil: *If you speak like that you will murder the play.* ◇*v.i.* **7.** to commit murder. [OE] **–murderer,** *n.* **–murderess,** *n. fem.* **–murderous,** *adj.*

Murdoch /'mɜdɒk/, *n.* **1. Dame (Jean) Iris,** born 1919, British novelist born in Ireland; her novels reflect her philosophical interests; works include *Under the Net* (1954) and *The Bell* (1958). **2. Sir Keith Arthur,** 1885–1952, newspaper magnate. **3. (Keith) Rupert,** born 1931, publisher, holding controlling interests in a variety of Australian and overseas forms of media, publishing and printing; became a US citizen in 1985.

murex /'mjurɛks/, *n., pl.* **murices** /'mjurəsiz/, **murexes.** **1.** a shellfish giving the famous purple dye of the ancient world. **2.** a shell used as a trumpet, as in representations of Tritons in art. **3.** a purplish red color. [L: the purple fish]

muriatic acid /mjuriˌætɪk 'æsəd/, *n.* the commercial name for hydrochloric acid.

murk /mɜk/, *n.* darkness; gloom. Also, **mirk.** [OE] **–murky,** *adj.*

Murmansk /mɜ'mænsk/, *n.* a seaport (ice-free) and railway terminus in the north-western USSR in Europe, on the Murman Coast. Pop. 426 000 (1976 est.).

murmur /'mɜmə/, *n.* **1.** any low, continuous sound, as of a creek, the wind, trees,

murmur | 687 | **mushroom**

voices, etc. **2.** a mumbled or private complaint, one not made openly. **3.** *Med.* an abnormal sound from the heart. ◇*v.i.* **4.** to make a low or continuous sound. **5.** to speak softly or unclearly: *He murmured to himself all the time they were speaking.* **6.** to complain in private, not openly. ◇*v.t.* **7.** to say softly or unclearly: *He murmured the words into her ear.* [ME, from L] —**murmuring**, *adj.* —**murmurous**, *adj.*

murrain /'mʌreɪn/, *n.* a disease of cattle, e.g. anthrax, foot-and-mouth disease, etc. [ME, from F: plague, from L: die]

Murray[1] /'mʌri/, **1. Sir James Augustus Henry**, 1837–1915, Scottish lexicographer and linguist; one of the original editors (1879–1915) of what became the *Oxford English Dictionary*. **2. Sir John Hubert Plunkett**, 1861–1940, Australian administrator in New Guinea; became the first Lieutenant-Governor in 1908 when New Guinea was renamed Papua and possession given to Australia. **3. Les**, born 1938, Australian poet, editor and literary critic; author of *The Vernacular Republic: Poems 1961–1981* (1982).

Murray[2] /'mʌri/, *n.* a river forming the border between NSW and Vic; rising in the Great Dividing Range and flowing westerly into SA where it then flows south to enter Lake Alexandrina. About 2600 km.

Murray Bridge, *n.* a town in south-eastern SA, east of Adelaide; one of the largest dairy factories in Australia. Pop. 11 893 (1986).

Murray cod, *n.* a large Australian freshwater fish found mainly in the Murray-Darling river system.

Murray Grey, *n.* a breed of grey beef cattle developed in Vic, produced by mating a very light roan Shorthorn cow with an Aberdeen Angus bull.

murri /'mʊri/, *n.* an Aborigine. [Aboriginal]

Murrumbidgee /mʌrəm'bɪdʒi/, *n.* a river in south-eastern NSW, rising in the Great Dividing Range near Kiandra and flowing generally west to become a tributary of the Murray River; the second largest river in the state. About 2170 km. [Aboriginal: big water]

Murrumbidgee Irrigation Area, *n.* an irrigation area in central south-western NSW, centred on the Murrumbidgee River; project began in 1906. About 510 000 ha. Also, **MIA**

Murrumbidgee whaler, *n.* a swagman going round the Australian inland rivers, living by begging and fishing. [from MURRUMBIDGEE] —**Murrumbidgee whaling**, *n.*

Mururoa Atoll /murə,rouə 'ætɒl/, *n.* a coral atoll in the Tuamotu Archipelago; scene of French nuclear tests since 1966.

Murwillumbah /mə'wɪləmbə/, *n.* a town in north-eastern NSW, on the Tweed River. Pop. 7678 (1986). [Aboriginal]

Mus, *Abbrev.* **1.** museum. **2.** music. **3.** musical. **4.** musician.

muscat /'mʌskət/, *n.* **1.** (*cap.*) a grape with strong sweet smell and taste. **2.** a sweet wine made from this grape. [F, from Pr, from LL: musk]

muscatel /mʌskə'tel/, *n.* the muscat grape, esp. in the dried form as a raisin. [ME, from OF, from Pr]

muscle /'mʌsəl/, *n., v.,* **-cled**, **-cling**. ◇*n.* **1.** a bundle of fibres in the animal body which can contract and relax to cause movement. **2.** muscular strength; brawn. **3.** power used with force: *political muscle.* ◇*v.i.* **4.** *Colloq.* to make or push one's way by force. ◇*v.* **5. muscle in (on)**, *Colloq.* to force one's way in(to), in order to obtain a share of something. [F, from L: lit., little mouse (from the appearance of certain muscles)] —**muscly**, *adj.*

muscle bound, *adj.* having muscles enlarged and inelastic from too much exercise.

muscle fibre, *n.* any of the long contractible cells which make up the muscles.

Muscovite /'mʌskəvaɪt/, *n.* **1.** a native or inhabitant of Moscow. ◇*adj.* **2.** an archaic word for **Russian**.

Muscovy /'mʌskəvi/, *n.* (in Russian history) a principality having as its capital the ancient city of Moscow.

Muscovy duck, *n.* a large, crested, domesticated duck; when wild it is glossy black with a large white patch on each wing.

muscular /'mʌskjələ/, *adj.* **1.** of or relating to muscle or the muscles. **2.** having well-developed muscles; brawny. —**muscularity**, *n.*

musculature /'mʌskjələtʃə/, *n.* the muscular system of the body or of its parts. [F, from L]

muse[1] /mjuz/, *v.t., v.i.,* **mused**, **musing**. to think deeply (on something), often in a dreamy state; meditate. [ME, from OF: ponder, loiter] —**muser**, *n.*

muse[2] /mjuz/, *n.* **1.** (*also cap.*) *Class Myth.* one of nine sister goddesses of ancient Greece who were in charge of literature, drama, dancing, art and science, and who inspired poets, etc. **2.** the poet's inspiration. Also, **Muse**. [ME, from OF, from L *Mūsa*, from Gk *Moûsa*]

museum /mju'ziəm/, *n.* a building where objects of scientific, artistic, and historical interest are kept, shown and studied. [L, from Gk: seat of the Muses, place of study, library]

mush[1] /mʌʃ/, *n.* **1.** a thick, soft mass, esp. corn meal boiled in water or milk. **2.** anything unpleasantly lacking in firmness, force, dignity, etc. **3.** *Colloq.* maudlin sentimentality in books, films, etc. [b. (obs.) *moose* thick vegetable porridge and MASH, n.] —**mushy**, *adj.*

mush[2] /mʌʃ/, *v.t.* **1.** to go or travel on foot, esp. over the snow with a dog team. ◇*interj.* **2.** (an order to start or speed up a dog team.) ◇*n.* **3.** a journey by mushing. [? from F: advance]

mushroom /'mʌʃrum/, *n.* **1.** a fleshy fungus, some kinds of which can be eaten, usu. having an umbrella shape. See **toadstool**. **2.**

mushroom   688   **muster**

something like a mushroom in shape or speed of growth, esp. the cloud produced by a nuclear bomb explosion. ◊*adj.* **3.** of, related to, or made of mushrooms. **4.** like a mushroom in shape or in quick growth. ◊*v.i.* **5.** to pick mushrooms for eating. **6.** to spread or grow quickly. [late ME, from F, from LL]

music /'mjuzɪk/, *n.* **1.** (the art of organising) sounds in significant forms to express ideas and emotions through the elements of melody, harmony, rhythm, etc. **2.** musical works taken together: *the music of Bach; 19th-century music.* **3.** music as written or printed: *I'll see if I can get the music for that sonata.* **4.** any sweet or pleasing sound: *the music of the birds; the music of the waves.* **5. face the music**, to face the unpleasant results of one's actions. [ME, from L, from Gk *mousikē (téchnē)* orig., any art over which the Muses presided]

musical /'mjuzɪkəl/, *adj.* **1.** of, related to, or producing music: *a musical instrument.* **2.** of the nature of or like music; melodious; harmonious: *a musical voice.* **3.** fond of or skilled in music: *She is very musical.* **4.** set to or accompanied by music: *a musical comedy.* —**musicality**, *n.*

musical chairs, *n.pl.* (*treated as sing.*) a children's game in which the players walk to music around a number of chairs (one less than the number of players) and try to find a seat when the music stops.

music hall, *n.* a theatre or hall for variety entertainment.

musician /mju'zɪʃən/, *n.* **1.** someone who makes music a profession, esp. as a performer on an instrument. **2.** someone skilled in playing a musical instrument.

musicology /mjuzə'kɒlədʒi/, *n.* the scholarly or scientific study of music. —**musicological**, *adj.* —**musicologist**, *n.*

music sticks, *n.pl.* a musical instrument consisting of wooden sticks which are struck together, esp. as used in Aboriginal music. Also, **songsticks**.

musing /'mjuzɪŋ/, *adj.* **1.** absorbed in thought; meditative; contemplative. ◊*n.* **2.** meditation; contemplation.

musk /mʌsk/, *n.* **1.** a strong-smelling substance produced by the male musk deer, and used in perfumery. **2.** a synthetic imitation of this. **3.** a smell of musk, or some similar smell. [ME, from LL, from LGk, from Pers] —**musky**, *adj.*

musk deer, *n.* a small, hornless, deer-like animal of central Asia.

musk duck, *n.* **1.** a southern Australian duck, the male of which sends out a smell of musk. **2.** → **Muscovy duck**.

musket /'mʌskɪt/, *n.* a hand-gun for foot soldiers, from which the modern rifle developed. [F, from It]

musketeer /mʌskə'tɪə/, *n.* a soldier armed with a musket.

musketry /'mʌskətri/, *n.* **1.** *Mil.* instruction in the art of using firearms. **2.** *Archaic.* muskets collectively or soldiers armed with them.

muskrat /'mʌskræt/, *n., pl.* **-rats**, (*esp. collectively*) **-rat**. **1.** a large North American water rodent with a musky smell. **2.** its thick, light brown fur.

Muslim /'muzləm, 'mʌz-/, *adj., n., pl.* **-lims, -lim**. ◊*adj.* **1.** of or related to the religion, law, or civilisation of Islam. ◊*n.* **2.** a follower of Islam. Also, **Moslem**. [Ar: one who accepts *Islam*, lit., submission]

muslin /'mʌzlən/, *n.* a fine, light cotton material. [F, from It: muslin, from *Mussolo* Mosul, city in Iraq]

Musquito /məs'kitou/, *n.* ('King Musquito', 'The Black Napoleon'), died 1825, Australian convict and tracker; formed a gang known as the 'Tame Mob' in Tas and was later executed for murder.

mussel /'mʌsəl/, *n.* a sea or freshwater shellfish that can be eaten and has a black double shell. [MLG]

Mussolini /musə'lini/, *n.* **Benito** (*Il Duce*), 1883–1945, Italian Fascist leader and prime minister of Italy 1922–43; forced to resign after the Allied invasion of Sicily; eventually shot by Italian partisans.

must¹ /mʌst, məs/; *weak forms* /məst, məs/, *aux. v.* **1.** to be bound by some obligation: *I must keep my word.* **2.** to be forced to by necessity: *Man must eat to live.* **3.** may reasonably be supposed to: *It must be nearly 50 km away.* **4.** to be certain to: *Man must die.* **5.** to have to; ought to; should: *I must go soon.* **6.** *Archaic.* (sometimes used without *go, get,* or some similar verb easily understood): *We must away.* ◊*n. Colloq.* **7.** anything seen as necessary: *This law is a must.* [OE]

must² /mʌst/, *n.* new wine; unfermented grape juice. [OE, from L: fresh wine]

mustang /'mʌstæŋ/, *n.* a small wild horse of the American plains, descended from Spanish stock. [Sp: wild]

mustard /'mʌstəd/, *n.* **1.** (a hot seasoning made from seeds of) a plant with yellow flowers and thin pods. **2. keen as mustard**, very keen or eager. ◊*adj.* **3.** brownish-yellow in color. [ME, from OF: powdered mustard seed and must]

mustard gas, *n.* a gas used in chemical warfare, producing burns, blindness, and death.

muster /'mʌstə/, *v.t.* **1.** to gather (soldiers, sailors, workers, etc.) into a group. **2.** to round up (sheep, etc.). **3.** to gather or get together (oft. fol. by *up*): *He mustered all his courage.* ◊*v.i.* **4.** (of soldiers) to come together into a group. **5.** to round up sheep, etc. ◊*n.* **6.** a gathering or coming together into a group. **7.** a rounding up of sheep, etc. **8.** Also, **muster roll**. (formerly) a list of men enrolled in a military or naval unit. **9. pass muster**, to measure up to certain standards. [ME, from OF, from L: show] —**musterer**, *n.* —**mustering**, *n.*

musty /ˈmʌsti/, *adj.*, **-tier, -tiest. 1.** having a smell or taste that suggests mould, as old buildings, long-closed rooms, food, etc. **2.** made stale by time: *musty laws*.

Muswellbrook /ˈmʌsəlbrʊk/, *n.* a town and shire in the upper Hunter Valley, NSW; coalmining and grape-growing. Formerly, **Muscle Brook**. Pop. 9988 (1986).

mutant /ˈmjutnt/, *adj.* **1.** undergoing or resulting from mutation. ◇*n.* **2.** a new type of organism produced as the result of mutation. [L: changing]

mutate /mjuˈteɪt/, *v.*, **-tated, -tating.** ◇*v.t.* **1.** to change; alter. ◇*v.i.* **2.** to change into something else; undergo mutation. –**mutative,** *adj.*

mutation /mjuˈteɪʃən/, *n.* **1.** the act or process of changing. **2.** a change in form, qualities, or nature. **3.** *Biol.* **a.** the sudden appearance of a new hereditary characteristic in an animal or plant, caused by a change in a gene or chromosome. **b.** (a type of) plant or animal resulting from this; mutant. **4.** *Phonet.* → **umlaut.** [ME, from L]

mute /mjut/, *adj.*, *n.*, *v.*, **muted, muting.** ◇*adj.* **1.** not speaking; silent. **2.** unspoken; done or made by gesture: *a mute question*. **3.** not able to speak; dumb. **4.** *Gram.* (of letters) silent; not pronounced. ◇*n.* **5.** someone who cannot speak. **6.** something put in or on a musical instrument to deaden its sound. ◇*v.t.* **7.** to deaden the sound of (a musical instrument, etc.). **8.** to soften; reduce in volume. [L: silent; dumb]

mutilate /ˈmjutəleɪt/, *v.t.*, **-lated, -lating. 1.** to cut parts off (a living or dead body) so as to damage or disfigure it. **2.** → **castrate. 3.** to injure or spoil by removing or damaging parts: *The article was mutilated by poor editing*. [L: cut off, maimed] –**mutilation,** *n.* –**mutilator,** *n.*

mutineer /mjutəˈnɪə/, *n.* someone who revolts or mutinies. [F, from OF: rebellion, from L: move]

mutiny /ˈmjutəni/, *n.*, *pl.* **-nies,** *v.*, **-nied, -nying.** ◇*n.* **1.** a revolt or rebellion against people in charge, esp. by soldiers or sailors against their officers. ◇*v.i.* **2.** to commit the offence of mutiny; revolt against constituted authority. –**mutinous,** *adj.*

mutt /mʌt/, *n. Colloq.* **1.** a dog, esp. a mongrel. **2.** a stupid person; simpleton. [orig. uncert.; ? shortened from *muttonhead*]

mutter /ˈmʌtə/, *v.i.* **1.** to speak unclearly or in a low tone, often in talking to oneself or in making complaints, threats, etc.; murmur; grumble. **2.** to make a low, rumbling sound: *The waves muttered all night in his ears*. ◇*v.t.* **3.** to utter unclearly or in a low tone. ◇*n.* **4.** a muttering. [ME: speak, OE: speak in public] –**mutterer,** *n.*

mutton /ˈmʌtn/, *n.* the flesh of sheep, used as food, usu. older flesh than lamb or hogget. [ME, from OF; of Celtic orig.] –**muttony,** *adj.*

mutton-bird /ˈmʌtn-bɜd/, *n.* **1.** any of various types of petrel, including the short-tailed shearwater of the Pacific Ocean, which in summer nests in Tas, SA, Vic, and the islands of Bass Strait. **2.** *Colloq.* Also, **mutton-bird eater.** an inhabitant of northern Tas. Also, **muttonbird.**

mutton-chops /ˈmʌtn-tʃɒps, ˌmʌtnˈtʃɒps/, *n.pl.* side-whiskers narrow at the top, and broad and trimmed short at the bottom. Also, **mutton-chop whiskers.**

mutual /ˈmjutʃuəl/, *adj.* **1.** owned, felt or done by each of two or more towards the other or others; reciprocal: *mutual aid*. **2.** having the same relation each towards the other or others: *mutual enemy*. **3.** of or belonging to each of two or more; common: *a mutual friend*. [ME, from L: reciprocal] –**mutuality,** *n.*

mutual fund, *n.* an investment trust which pools the money of a large number of investors and invests on their behalf.

mutual insurance, *n.* insurance in which the insured become members of a company (**mutual company**) and share its profits.

mutualism /ˈmjutʃuəlɪzəm/, *n.* **1.** the achieving of individual and collective well-being through mutual dependence. **2.** *Biol.* → **symbiosis.**

muu-muu /ˈmu-mu/, *n.* a long, loose dress, usu. brightly colored. [Hawaiian]

muzak /ˈmjuzæk/, *n.* recorded background music played continuously in places of work, hotels, etc., or over the telephone, and meant to make people feel happy and at ease. [Trademark]

Muzorewa /muzəˈreɪwə/, *n.* **Abel Tendekayi,** born 1925, Zimbabwean bishop and politician; Zimbabwe's first prime minister 1979–80.

muzzle /ˈmʌzəl/, *n.*, *v.*, **-zled, -zling.** ◇*n.* **1.** the front end of the barrel of a gun. **2.** the jaws, mouth and nose of an animal. **3.** a small cage, of wire or straps, fastened over an animal's mouth to stop it biting, eating, etc. ◇*v.t.* **4.** to put a muzzle on (an animal or its mouth). **5.** to stop (someone) speaking or expressing an opinion by any means; gag. [ME, from OF: little muzzle]

Mv, *Chem. Symbol.* (formerly) mendelevium.

MVO, *Abbrev.* Member (fourth or fifth class) of the Royal Victorian Order.

Mx, *Symbol.* maxwell.

my /maɪ/; *weak forms* /mi, mə/, *pron.* **1.** possessive form of *I* and *me*, used before a noun: *my house*. ◇*interj.* **2.** *Colloq.* (an exclamation of surprise): *Oh my!* [OE *mīn*. See MINE¹]

my-, a word part meaning 'muscle'. Also, **myo-.** [Gk, combining form of *mȳs*]

myalgia /maɪˈældʒə/, *n.* pain in the muscles; muscular rheumatism.

myall¹ /ˈmaɪɔl/, *n.* **1.** any of several wattle trees. **2.** a hard fine-grained wood of such a tree used for carving. [Aboriginal]

myall² /ˈmaɪɔl/, *n.* **1.** an Aboriginal living in a traditional tribal way, outside European civili-

myall sation. **2.** anything wild or uncivilised. ◇*adj.* **3.** wild or uncivilised. [Aboriginal]

Myall Creek massacre, *n.* the massacre of 28 Aboriginal men, women and children by station hands at Myall Creek, near Inverell, NSW in 1838; seven of the station hands were convicted of murder and subsequently hanged.

myall snake, *n.* a small snake of southern and inland Australia, not considered dangerous; saltbush snake.

Myanmar /'mɪənmɑ/, *n.* → **Burma.**

myc-, a word part meaning 'fungus'. Also, **myco-.** [combining form representing Gk *mýkēs*]

mycelium /maɪ'sɪliəm/, *n., pl.* **-lia** /-lɪə/. the main body part of a fungus when made up of thread-like parts. [NL, from Gk] **—myceloid,** *adj.*

Mycenae /maɪ'siːni/, *n.* an ancient city in southern Greece, in Argolis; notable ruins.

Mycenaean /maɪsə'niːən/, *adj.* **1.** of or relating to the ancient southern Greek city of Mycenae. **2.** indicating or relating to the Aegean civilisation of Mycenae (c. 1600 BC to c. 1100 BC).

myco-, variant of **myc-,** before consonants, *mycobacterium.*

mycology /maɪ'kɒlədʒi/, *n.* the branch of botany that deals with fungi. **—mycologist,** *n.*

Myer /'maɪə/, *n.* Sidney Baevski, 1878–1934, Australian retail trader and philanthropist, born in Russia; founder of Myers Pty Ltd (1917) and benefactor of the Sidney Myer Trust, established for charitable purposes.

myna /'maɪnə/, *n.* a noisy, half-tame chocolate-brown bird with a black head, and yellow beak and legs, introduced from Asia and now common around large cities and canegrowing areas in eastern Australia. Also, **Indian myna.** [Hind: a starling]

myo-, variant of **my-,** before consonants.

myocardium /maɪoʊ'kɑdiəm/, *n.* the muscular substance of the heart. **—myocardial,** *adj.*

myogenic /maɪoʊ'dʒɛnɪk/, *adj.* of or relating to muscle: *myogenic pain.*

myopia /maɪ'oʊpiə/, *n.* short- or nearsightedness (opposed to *hypermetropia*). [NL, from Gk: short-sighted] **—myopic,** *adj.*

myriad /'mɪriəd/, *n.* **1.** (*oft. pl.*) a very great number: *a myriad of stars.* ◇*adj.* **2.** of an indefinitely great number; innumerable: *myriad stars.* **3.** having very many aspects, etc.: *the myriad mind of Shakespeare.* **4.** ten thousand. [Gk: ten thousand]

myriapod /'mɪriəpɒd/, *adj.* (a creature) with very many jointed legs, as the centipede. Also, **myriapodous** /mɪri'æpədəs/. [NL, from Gk *mȳriá(s)* MYRIAD + *poús* foot]

myrmeco-, a word part meaning 'ant'. [Gk, combining form of *mýrmēx*]

myrnonger /'mɜnɒŋgə/, *n.* an Aborigine. [var. MYRRNONG]

Myron /'maɪrən/, *n.* fl. c. 450 BC, Greek sculptor; famous for his *Discobolus,* a statue of an athlete hurling a discus.

myrrh /mɜ/, *n.* a bitter-smelling resin used in incense, perfume, etc. [OE, from L, from Gk]

myrrnong /'mɜnɒŋ/, *n.* Also, **blackfellow's yam.** a plant with a yellow flower and a root used as food by Australian Aborigines. [Aboriginal]

myrtaceous /mɜ'teɪʃəs/, *adj.* **1.** belonging to the myrtle family of plants, which includes the myrtle, the guava, the gum trees, etc. **2.** of, relating to, or looking like the myrtle. [LL: of myrtle]

myrtle /'mɜtl/, *n.* **1.** a shrub of southern Europe with evergreen leaves, sweet-smelling white flowers and berries, used as an emblem of love. **2.** any of certain other plants, as **Tasmanian myrtle.** [ME, from OF, from L, from Gk]

myself /maɪ'sɛlf, mə'sɛlf/, *pron.* **1.** reflexive form of *me*: *I cut myself.* **2.** emphatic form of *me* or *I,* used: **a.** as object: *I used it for myself.* **b.** in apposition to a subject or object: *I myself did it.* **3.** one's proper or normal self; one's normal state of mind (used after *be, become,* or *come to*): *I am myself again.*

Mysore /maɪ'sɔ/, *n.* a city in southern India, in the southern part of Karnataka state. Pop. 441 754 (1981).

mysterious /məs'tɪəriəs/, *adj.* **1.** full of or attended by mystery: *a mysterious stranger.* **2.** puzzling; inexplicable. **3.** suggesting a mystery: *a mysterious smile.*

mystery /'mɪstri, -təri/, *n., pl.* **-ries. 1.** anything that is kept secret or remains unexplained or unknown; puzzle: *the mysteries of nature; It's a mystery how I came to lose that money.* **2.** anything that makes people curious: *the mystery of the scream in the night.* **3.** the condition or character of being unexplained; obscurity: *conversations wrapped in mystery.* **4.** the truth unknowable except by divine revelation: *the mystery of the Trinity.* **5.** (*pl.*) ancient religions which admitted people by secret ceremonies whose meaning was known only to those specially introduced to them. **6.** (*pl.*) secret ceremonies: *the mysteries of freemasonry.* [ME, from L, from Gk]

mystery play, *n.* a medieval religious play originating in the liturgy and usu. dealing with the life, death and resurrection of Christ.

mystic /'mɪstɪk/, *adj.* **1.** spiritually meaningful or symbolic, as the dove used to symbolise the Holy Ghost. **2.** of or relating to mysteries (defs 5 and 6): *mystic rites.* **3.** occult: *a mystic formula.* ◇*n.* **4.** someone who reaches, or tries to reach, a state of union with God and a knowledge of spiritual truths through prayer and contemplation. [ME, from L, from Gk: mystic, secret] **—mystical,** *adj.*

mysticism /'mɪstəsɪzəm/, *n.* the beliefs or practice of mystics (def. 4).

mystify /'mɪstəfaɪ/, *v.t.,* **-fied, -fying. 1.** to make (someone) wonder; bewilder: *His* *disappearance completely mystifies me.* **2.** to involve (a subject, etc.) in mystery or obscurity. [F] —**mystification**, *n.*

mystique /mɪs'tik/, *n.* an air of mystery or mysterious power surrounding some person, object, belief, etc. [F]

myth /mɪθ/, *n.* **1.** an ancient and traditional story, usu. about a god or hero, or an event before history began, which may try to explain natural phenomena, customs, etc.: *myths about the Norse gods; myths about the origin of fire.* **2.** stories or matter of this kind: *in the realm of myth.* **3.** any invented story. **4.** an imaginary thing or person. [NL, from LL, from Gk: Word, speech, tale, legend, myth] —**mythical**, **mythic**, *adj.*

mythology /mə'θɒlədʒi/, *n., pl.* **-gies.** **1.** the body of myths of a particular people or person: *Greek mythology; the mythology surrounding Hitler.* **2.** myths collectively. **3.** the science of myths. [ME, from LL, from Gk: legend] —**mythological**, *adj.* —**mythologist**, *n.*

myxomatosis /mɪksəmə'tousəs/, *n.* a highly infectious viral disease of rabbits, introduced into Britain and Australia to reduce the rabbit population.

Nn

N, n, /n./, pl. **N's** or **Ns**, **n's** or **ns**. **1.** the fourteenth letter of the English alphabet. **2.** *Maths. Symbol*. an indefinite constant whole number, as in an equation.

n-, *Chem*. normal (indicating an unbranched aliphatic carbon chain): *an n-butyl ester*. See **iso-** (def. 2).

n., *Abbrev*. **1.** born. [L *nātus*] **2.** neuter. **3.** noon. **4.** noun.

N, *Symbol* **1.** *Chem*. nitrogen. **2.** *Chem*. normal (strength solution). **3.** *Phys*. newton. ◇*Abbrev*. **4.** north(ern). **5.** navy. **6.** Norse.

n.a., *Abbrev*. **1.** not applicable. **2.** not available. Also, **n/a**.

Na, *Chem. Symbol*. sodium. [L *natrium*]

nab /næb/, *v.t.*, **nabbed, nabbing**. *Colloq*. to catch or seize, esp. suddenly. [orig. uncert.]

Nabarlek /ˈnabələk/, *n*. a uranium field in northern central NT.

Nabokov /ˈnæbəkɒf/, *n*. **Vladimir Vladimirovich** /vlaˌdimɪə vlaˈdimɪrəvɪtʃ/, 1899–1977, US writer and poet, born in Russia; author of *Lolita* (1955).

nacre /ˈneɪkə/, *n*. → **mother-of-pearl**. [F, from ML, ? from Pers (Kurdish): pearl oyster] – **nacreous**, *adj*.

Nader /ˈneɪdə/, *n*. **Ralph**, born 1934, US lawyer and advocate of consumer rights and protection.

nadir /ˈneɪdɪə/, *n*. **1.** the point of the celestial sphere directly beneath any place or observer and opposite to the zenith. **2.** the lowest point of anything, such as of misfortune. [ME, from Ar: corresponding, opposite (i.e., to the Zenith)]

nag[1] /næg/, *v.*, **nagged, nagging**. ◇*v.i.* **1.** to keep on finding fault, complaining, or making demands (oft. fol. by *at*). **2.** to be the cause of continual pain or discomfort, as a headache, feeling of guilt, etc. (oft. fol. by *at*). ◇*v.t.* **3.** to annoy (someone) by nagging. [Scand] – **nagger**, *n*.

nag[2] /næg/, *n*. **1.** a small horse, or pony, esp. for riding. **2.** *Colloq*. a horse, esp. an old or worn-out one. [ME *nagge*]

Nagasaki /næɡəˈsaki/, *n*. a seaport in south-western Japan, on Kyushu island; the second military use of the atomic bomb, 9 August 1945. Pop. 252 630 (1940); 174 141 (1946); 448 554 (1986 est.).

Nagoya /naˈɡɔɪjə/, *n*. a city in central Japan, on Honshu island. Pop. 2 130 632 (1986 est.).

Nagpur /naɡˈpʊə/, *n*. a city in India, in north-eastern Maharashtra; former capital of the Central Provinces and Berar (later Madhya Pradesh). Pop. 1 219 461 (1981).

---

nail /neɪl/, *n*. **1.** a thin piece of metal, usu. with one end pointed and the other enlarged, for driving into or through wood, etc., to hold separate pieces together. **2.** a thin, horny plate, growing on the upper side of the end of a finger or toe. **3. hit the nail on the head**, to say or do exactly the right thing. **4. on the nail**, *Colloq*. at once or on the spot. ◇*v.t.* **5.** to fasten with a nail or nails: *to nail the cover on a box*. **6.** to shut within something by driving nails in: *to nail goods up in a box*. **7.** to keep firmly in one place or position: *Fear nailed him to the spot*. **8.** *Colloq*. to catch or seize. **9.** *Colloq*. to catch (a person) in some difficulty, a lie, etc. [OE *nægl*]

nail-tailed wallaby /ˌneɪl-teɪld ˈwɒləbi/, *n*. any of three types of wallaby, the **karrabul**, of northern Australia, the **merrin**, of NSW and southern Qld, or the **wurrung**, of south-central Australia, characterised by a horny, nail-like tip at the end of a long, thin tail and a white stripe on the cheek, hip, and shoulder.

Naipaul /ˈnaɪpɔl/, *n*. **V(idiadhar) S(urajprasad)**, born 1932, Trinidadian writer, esp. of novels concerned with social conditions in the Caribbean and other parts of the world.

Nairobi /naɪˈroʊbi/, *n*. the capital of Kenya, in the southern part. Pop. 1 162 200 (1985).

naive /naɪˈiv, na-/, *adj*. having or showing simplicity of nature; unsophisticated. Also, **naif**, **naïve**. [F, from L: native, natural] – **naivety**, *n*.

Nakasone /ˌnakəˈsoʊneɪ/, *n*. **Yasuhito** /jasəˈhɪəroʊ/, 1918–87, Japanese statesman; prime minister 1982–87.

naked /ˈneɪkəd/, *adj*. **1.** without clothing or covering; nude: *a naked person*. **2.** bare of any covering, vegetation, leaves, etc.: *naked fields*; *naked trees*. **3.** without the usual covering: *a naked sword*; *a naked wall*. **4.** (of the eye, sight, etc.) without the help of glasses, microscope or other instrument. **5.** simple; unadorned: *the naked truth*; *a naked outline of facts*. **6.** open to view: *a naked vein of ore*. **7.** *Bot*. (of seeds) not enclosed in an ovary. **8.** *Zool*. having no covering of hair, feathers, shell, etc. [OE *nacod*]

Namaliu /ˈnæməlju/, *n*. **Rabbie** /ˈræbi/, born 1947, PNG politician; prime minister 1988–92.

Namatjira /næmətˈdʒɪərə/, *n*. **Albert**, 1902–59, Australian artist; noted for his watercolor landscapes of central Australia.

Nambour /ˈnæmbɔ/, *n*. a town in south-eastern Qld, near Maroochydore; major industry is sugar cane growing. Pop. 9579 (1986). [Aboriginal: red-flowering tea-tree]

namby-pamby /ˈnæmbiˌpæmbi/, *adj*., *n., pl*. **-bies**. ◇*adj*. **1.** weakly simple; insipid. ◇*n*. **2.** a namby-pamby person. [orig. a nickname, *Namby Pamby*, for Ambrose Philips, d. 1749, English poet; first used by Henry Carey in 1726 as title of poem ridiculing Philips' verses]

name /neɪm/, *n., v.*, **named, naming**. ◇*n.* **1.** a word or a combination of words by

name

which a person, place, or thing, class, or any object of thought, is known. **2.** title only, as opposed to fact: *king in name only.* **3.** any word, used descriptively; an epithet: *to call him bad names.* **4.** a general opinion about qualities of a person, place, etc.; reputation: *a bad name; a good name.* **5.** good reputation; fame: *They made a name for themselves.* **6.** a famous person. **7. in the name of, a.** with appeal to: *In the name of mercy, stop screaming!* **b.** by the authority of: *Open in the name of the law!* **c.** on behalf of: *to vote in the name of others.* **8. to one's name,** belonging to one: *not a cent to my name.* ◊*v.t.* **9.** to give a name to: *to name a baby.* **10.** to mention by name: *three people were named in the report.* **11.** to appoint to or nominate for some duty or office: *I have named you for the position.* **12.** to make definite mention of; specify: *to name a price.* **13.** to tell the name of: *Name the capital of France.* [OE *nama*]

name-dropper /'neɪm-drɒpə/, *n.* someone who mentions the names of famous people as though they were personal friends, in order to seem important. — **namedropping**, *n.*

namely /'neɪmli/, *adv.* that is to say: *two cities, namely, Sydney and Melbourne.*

namesake /'neɪmseɪk/, *n.* someone having, or given, the same name as another. [alteration of *name's sake*]

Namibia /nə'mɪbiə/, *n.* a republic in southwestern Africa on the Atlantic coast, bordered by the Republic of South Africa, Botswana and Angola; a centre of opposition to the South African apartheid system; a UN territory before independence in 1990. Pop. 1 198 100 (1987 est.); 824 292 km². *Languages:* Afrikaans and English, *Currency:* rand. *Cap.:* Windhoek. Formerly, **German South-west Africa.** Also, **South-West Africa.** —**Namibian**, *n., adj.*

namma hole /'næmə houl/, *n.* a hole in the ground forming a natural reservoir. Also, **gnamma hole.** [Aboriginal]

Namoi /'næmɔɪ/, *n.* a river in north-eastern NSW, rising south-east of Tamworth and flowing north-west to join the Barwon River at Walgett. 847 km.

Nanjing /næn'dʒɪŋ/, *n.* a port in eastern China on the Chang (Yangtze) River; the capital of Jiangsu province. Pop. 2 207 500 (1984). Formerly, **Nanking.**

nankeen /næn'kin/, *n.* **1.** a firm, longlasting, yellow or buff cotton cloth, orig. from China. **2.** a yellow or buff color. [named after *Nankin* NANJING]

nankeen kestrel, *n.* a small falcon, reddish brown above and white below, found in Australia, Tas and NG; windhover; sparrowhawk.

nanny /'næni/, *n., pl.* **-ies. 1.** a children's nurse. **2.** *Colloq.* grandmother. [alteration of female Christian name *Ann*]

nannygai /'nænɪɡaɪ/, *n.* a fish of fine flavor, found around the southern half of the Australian coast. [Aboriginal]

nanny-goat /'næni-ɡoʊt/, *n.* a female goat.

nano- /'nænoʊ-/, a prefix meaning **1.** 10^{-9} of a given unit, as in *nanometre. Symbol:* n **2.** very small in size. [combining form of L *nānus* dwarf; from Gk]

Nansen passport /ˌnænsən 'pæspɔt/, *n.* a passport issued by the League of Nations after World War I to people without nationality. [named after F *Nansen* 1861–1930, Norwegian explorer and League of Nations' high commissioner for refugees]

Naomi /neɪ'oʊmi/, *n. Bible.* the mother-in-law of Ruth. [Heb; see Ruth 1:2, etc.]

nap¹ /næp/, *v.,* **napped, napping,** *n.* ◊*v.i.* **1.** to have a short sleep. **2.** to be off one's guard: *I caught him napping.* ◊*n.* **3.** a short sleep. [OE *hnappian*]

nap² /næp/, *n.* **1.** the short ends of fibres on the surface of cloth drawn up by brushing, etc. **2.** any soft, hairy coating, as on plants. [OE *-hnoppe* (in *wullhnoppa* tuft of wool)]

napalm /'neɪpam, 'næpam/, *n.* a highly flammable mixture of fatty acids and petrol forming a sticky gel used in flame throwers and fire bombs. [NA(PHTHA) + *palm(itate)* salt from palm oil]

nape /neɪp/, *n.* the back (of the neck). [ME]

napery /'neɪpəri/, *n.* household linen, esp. for the table. [ME, from OF: tablecloth]

naphtha /'næfθə/, *n.* a petrol product used as a solvent, fuel, etc. [L, from Gk]

naphthalene /'næfθəlin/, *n.* a white crystalline cyclic hydrocarbon, $C_{10}H_8$, used in making dyes, as a moth repellent, etc. Also, **naphthaline, naphthalin.** [NAPHTH(A) + AL(COHOL) + -ENE]

Napier¹ /'neɪpiə/, *n.* **John,** 1550–1617, Scottish mathematician and inventor of logarithms; influential in introduction of decimal notation. Also, **Neper.**

Napier² /'neɪpiə/, *n.* a city on the south-eastern coast of the North Island of NZ; port, airport. Pop. 50 500 (1985).

napkin /'næpkən/, *n.* **1.** → **serviette. 2.** → **nappy.** [ME: little tablecloth, from F, from L: cloth]

Naples /'neɪpəlz/, *n.* a seaport in south-western Italy, the capital of Campania region. Pop. 1 208 545 (1984). Italian, **Napoli.**

Napoleon I /nə'poʊliən/, *n.* (*Napoleon Bonaparte*), 1769–1821, French general; came to power in the coup of 1799; crowned himself Emperor of France in 1804; greatly extended the French Empire; defeat at the Battle of Waterloo marked the end of his reign. French, **Napoléon.**

Napoleon III, *n.* (*Louis Napoleon Bonaparte*), 1808–73, president of France 1848–52; emperor of France 1852–70; deposed following Franco-Prussian War (son of Louis Bonaparte, nephew of Napoleon I).

Napoleonic Wars /nəpoʊli,ɒnɪk 'wɔz/, *n.pl.* a series of wars, 1805–1815, waged by France under Napoleon I against England, Prussia, Austria, and Russia, sometimes individually and sometimes as allies.

nappe /næp/, *n.* a large overturned anticlinical fold of rock layer, oft. pushed away from its roots by earth movements.

nappy /'næpi/, *n., pl.* **-pies.** a piece of cloth or some disposable material, fastened round a baby's legs and waist to absorb and contain its excrement. [alteration of NAPKIN]

narcissism /'nasəsɪzəm/, *n.* great admiration for oneself or one's own qualities; self-love. [G. See NARCISSUS def. 2] —**narcissistic**, *adj.*

narcissus /na'sɪsəs/, *n., pl.* **-cissuses, -cissi** /-'sɪsaɪ/. **1.** any of a group of bulbous plants bearing flowers with a cup-shaped corona, such as the wild daffodil. **2.** (*cap.*) *Gk Myth.* (*cap.*) a beautiful youth who fell in love with his own reflection in water, pined away, and was changed into the narcissus plant. [L, from Gk: plant named from its narcotic properties]

narcosis /na'kousəs/, *n.* a state of sleep, drowsiness, or unconsciousness, esp. produced by a drug. [NL, from Gk: a benumbing]

narcotic /na'kɒtɪk/, *n.* **1.** any of class of addictive substances, e.g. morphine, that relieve pain, cause sleepiness, etc. ◇*adj.* **2.** relating to, of the nature of, or producing narcosis. **3.** relating to narcotics or their use. [Gk: making stiff or numb]

nark /nak/, *Colloq.* ◇*n.* **1.** an informer or spy, esp. for the police. **2.** a person who continually complains and spoils the pleasure of others. ◇*v.t.* **3.** to annoy by complaining, etc. ◇*v.i.* **4.** to act as an informer. [Gipsy: nose]

Narrabri /'nærəbraɪ/, *n.* a town and shire in north-eastern NSW, on an anabranch of the Namoi River; large oilseed mill. Pop. 7246 (1986).

narrate /nə'reɪt/, *v.i., v.t.,* **-rated, -rating.** to relate or tell the story of (events, experiences, etc.) in speech or writing. [L] —**narrator**, *n.* —**narration**, *n.*

narrative /'nærətɪv/, *n.* **1.** a story of events, experiences, etc. **2.** the act or art of narrating. ◇*adj.* **3.** using the form of a narrative: *a narrative poem.* **4.** of or relating to narration: *narrative skill.*

Narrogin /'nærədʒən/, *n.* a town in south-western WA, north-west of Wagin. Pop. 4266 (1986). [Aboriginal: place of water]

narrow /'nærou/, *adj.* **1.** not broad or wide: *a narrow room.* **2.** limited in size, range, or amount: *narrow circumstances; narrow resources.* **3.** lacking breadth of view or sympathy: *a narrow person; a narrow mind.* **4.** only just succeeding: *a narrow escape.* **5.** careful; minute: *a narrow search.* ◇*v.i., v.t.* **6.** to become or make narrower in width, range, outlook, etc. **7.** a narrow part, place or thing. **8.** (*pl.*) the narrow part of a strait, river, ocean current, etc. [OE *nearu*]

NASA /'næsə/, *n. US.* a civilian agency coordinating US aeronautical and space activities. Also, **National Aeronautics and Space Administration.** [abbrev.]

nasal /'neɪzəl/, *adj.* **1.** of or relating to the nose. **2.** *Linguistics.* with the voice coming through the nose, either partly (as in French nasal vowels) or wholly (as in *m, n,* or the *ng* of *song*). ◇*n.* **3.** *Linguistics.* a nasal speech sound. [L: nose] —**nasality,** *n.*

nasalise or **nasalize** /'neɪzəlaɪz/, *v.i., v.t.,* **-lised, -lising.** to pronounce (a sound) nasally by allowing some of the voice to come through the nose. —**nasalisation,** *n.*

nascent /'næsənt/, *adj.* beginning to exist or develop: *the nascent republic.* [L: being born] —**nascence, nascency,** *n.*

Nash /næʃ/, *n.* **1. John,** 1752–1835, English town-planner and architect; designed Regent's Park in London. **2. (Frederic) Ogden,** 1902–71, US humorous poet. **3. Sir Walter,** 1882–1968, English-born politician in NZ; leader of Labour Party 1950–63, prime minister 1957–60.

Nashville /'næʃvəl/, *n.* a city in the US, the capital of Tennessee, in the central part; centre of country and western music. Pop. 473 670 (1986 est.).

Nasser /'næsə, 'na-/, *n.* **Gamal Abdel** /gamal 'æbdel/ 1918–70, Egyptian military leader; president of Egypt 1956–70; member of group that dethroned Farouk in 1952.

nasturtium /nə'stɜʃəm/, *n.* a garden plant, much cultivated for its showy flowers of yellow, red, or other colors. [L: a type of cress]

nasty /'nasti/, *adj.,* **-tier, -tiest. 1.** unpleasant; disgusting: *a nasty mess; nasty weather.* **2.** offensive: *a nasty taste; a nasty smell; a nasty habit.* **3.** spiteful; vicious: *a nasty dog; a nasty mind.* **4.** painful; dangerous: *a nasty cut.* [ME, orig. uncert.]

-nasty, a suffix indicating irregularity of cellular growth because of some pressure. [Gk *nastós* squeezed together + -Y³]

natal /'neɪtl/, *adj.* of or relating to one's birth. [ME, from L]

Natal /nə'tæl/, *n.* a province in eastern South Africa. Pop 2 145 018 (1985); 91 385 km². *Cap.:* Pietermaritzburg.

Nathan /'neɪθən/, *n.* **Isaac,** 1790–1864, English-born musician in Australia; composed operas, operettas and a large collection of Australian and Aboriginal melodies.

Nathanael /nə'θænjəl/, *n.* (in the New Testament) one of the apostles; a Galilean sometimes identified with Bartholomew.

nation /'neɪʃən/, *n.* **1.** a people of one ethnic family speaking one native language. **2.** an aggregation of unified people or peoples having a national language and government in common: *Australia today is one nation.* [ME, from L: birth]

national /'næʃnəl, 'næʃənəl/, *adj.* **1.** of or relating to a nation as an organised whole: *national affairs.* **2.** peculiar or common to the whole people of a nation: *national customs.* ◇*n.* **3.** a citizen of a particular nation.

National Aboriginal Conference, *n.* an elected body representing Aboriginal interests,

National Aboriginal Conference 695   natural history

set up by the Australian federal government in 1975 to replace the existing National Aboriginal Consultative Committee.

National Aeronautics and Space Administration, *n.* →NASA

National Civic Council, *n.* an Australian right-wing movement with a Roman Catholic base, formed in 1957 to fight communist influences.

National Country Party, *n.* the former name of the **National Party.** *Abbrev.*: NCP

National Estate, *n.* **the,** a collective term referring to those sites in Australia, either natural or man-made, which have particular historic, scientific or social significance, and which are substantially protected by parliamentary act.

nationalism /'næʃnəlɪzəm/, *n.* **1.** love of one's own nation; patriotism. **2.** desire for national advancement or independence. **3.** the policy of placing the interests of a nation above the interests of other nations or the common interests of all nations. **–nationalist,** *n.* **–nationalistic,** *adj.*

Nationalist Party, *n.* the former name of the Liberal Party in Australia; formed in 1917 under the leadership of William Morris Hughes; replaced by the United Australia Party in 1931 and then the Liberal Party in 1944.

nationality /næʃə'nælətɪ, næʃ'næl-/, *n., pl.* **-ties. 1.** the condition of being a member of a particular nation: *This form requires you to state your nationality.* **2.** the condition of belonging to a particular nation, or to one or more of its members: *the nationality of a ship.* **3.** a nation or people. **4.** national quality or character.

national park, *n.* → **park** (def. 2).

National Party, *n.* **1.** The Australian political party which, since early this century, under various names, has represented rural interests; first won federal parliamentary seats in WA in 1918. Formerly, **National Country Party, Country Party.** *Abbrev.*: NP **2.** a NZ political party formed by non-labor groups in 1936.

national service, *n.* (in many countries) compulsory service in the armed forces for a particular period.

National Trust of Australia, *n.* an institution whose function is to acquire and conserve lands and buildings of special historic, aesthetic or other interest.

nation-state /'neɪʃən-steɪt/, *n.* an independent state populated by the people of one nation only.

native /'neɪtɪv/, *adj.* **1.** belonging to the place or surroundings in which one was born or a thing came into being: *his native land.* **2.** belonging to a person or thing by birth or nature; inborn (oft. fol. by *to*). **3.** born, growing or produced in a particular place; indigenous (oft. fol. by *to*): *native people; native plants; native pottery.* **4.** of, relating to, or characteristic of natives: *native customs; native government.* **5.** belonging or relating to someone by reason of birthplace or nationality: *her native language; native rights.* **6.** remaining in a natural state; unadorned: *native beauty.* **7.** found in nature rather than artificial, as a mineral substance. ◇*n.* **8.** a person originally living in a place or country, esp. as distinguished from strangers, foreigners, colonisers, etc.: *the natives of Chile.* **9.** someone born in a particular place or country: *a native of Muswellbrook.* **10.** an animal or plant native to a particular area. [L: native, innate, natural]

native bear, *n.* → **koala.**

native cat, *n.* any of four cat-sized marsupials that hunt other animals for food and have thin white-spotted bodies and very pointed noses, namely, the **quoll,** of eastern Australia, the **chuditch** or **western native cat,** the **satanellus** of northern Australia, and the **tiger cat,** of eastern Australia; marsupial cat; dasyure.

native companion, *n.* → **brolga.**

native oak, *n.* → **casuarina.**

nativity /nə'tɪvətɪ/, *n., pl.* **-ties.** *n.* **1.** birth. **2.** (*cap.*) the birth of Christ. **3.** (*cap.*) the church celebration of the birth of Christ; Christmas. [ME, from LL]

NATO /'neɪtoʊ/, *n.* a military alliance established in 1949 linking a group of European countries with the US and Canada. Also, **North Atlantic Treaty Organisation.** [abbrev.]

natter /'nætə/, *v.i. Colloq.* **1.** to talk rapidly and informally; chatter. ◇*n.* **2.** an informal, friendly conversation; a chat.

natty /'nætɪ/, *adj.*, **-tier, -tiest.** neatly smart in dress or appearance; trim: *a natty white uniform.* [? akin to NEAT]

natural /'nætʃərəl, 'nætʃrəl/, *adj.* **1.** existing in, formed or established by nature; not artificial: *a natural bridge; natural resources.* **2.** of or relating to nature: *natural science.* **3.** in a state of nature; uncultivated or wild. **4.** of, relating to, or based on nature; inborn; innate: *natural ability; a manner natural to an aristocrat.* **5.** free from pretence or affectation: *a natural manner.* **6.** in accordance with the nature of things; normal: *It was natural that he should hit back; a natural outcome.* **7.** based upon the inborn moral feeling of mankind: *natural justice.* **8.** in accordance with the ordinary course of nature; not unusual, exceptional or irregular: *a natural death.* **9.** by birth only, and not legally recognised; illegitimate: *a natural child.* **10.** true to nature; life-like. **11.** being such by nature; born such: *a natural fool.* **12.** *Maths.* of or relating to a sine, tangent, etc., which is expressed as the actual value, not the logarithm. ◇*n.* **13.** *Colloq.* a thing or person that is by nature satisfactory or successful. **14.** *Music.* **a.** a white key on the piano, etc. **b.** the sign ♮, placed before a note, stopping the effect of a previous sharp or flat. [ME, from L: by birth, in accordance with nature]

natural gas, *n.* a combustible gas formed naturally in the earth, usu. consisting of methane with hydrogen, etc., used as a fuel, etc.

natural history, *n.* **1.** the science or study dealing with all objects in nature. **2.** the sum of knowledge connected with such objects.

naturalise *or* **naturalize** /'nætʃrəlaɪz/, v., -lised, -lising. ◇v.t. **1.** to give (a foreign person) the rights and privileges of citizenship. **2.** to introduce (animals or plants) into an area and cause to grow or live as if native. **3.** to introduce (foreign practices, words, etc.) into a country or into general use: *to naturalise a French phrase.* **4.** to accustom to a place or to new surroundings. ◇v.i. **5.** to become naturalised, or as if native. —**naturalisation**, *n.*

naturalism /'nætʃrəlɪzəm/, *n.* **1.** (in literature) **a.** a theory of writing which states that life, actions, surroundings, etc., can and should be represented in realistic detail. **b.** any writing which does this. **2.** (in the arts) **a.** a method of presenting nature in a detailed and lifelike form. **b.** a style of painting marked by realistic representation of nature. **3.** *Philos.* a view of the world which takes account only of natural elements and forces, not the supernatural or spiritual.

naturalist /'nætʃrəlɪst/, *n.* **1.** someone who studies natural history, esp. a zoologist or botanist. **2.** a supporter of naturalism. —**naturalistic**, *adj.*

Naturaliste /'nætʃrəlɪst/, *n.* **Cape**, a promontory in south-western WA on the southern point of Geographe Bay. [named by Nicholas Baudin after his ship Le *Naturaliste*]

natural logarithm, *n.* a logarithm using the number 2.71828182... as a base. *Symbol:* log$_e$ or h

natural number, *n.* any of the positive numbers 1, 2, 3, etc.

natural science, *n.* the science or knowledge dealing with objects in nature, as distinguished from mental or moral science, etc.

natural selection, *n.* a process of evolution in which those with characteristics best adapted to their surroundings survive in the struggle for existence, thus passing on their characteristics to the next generation.

nature /'neɪtʃə/, *n.* **1.** the basic or fundamental qualities belonging to a person or thing; native or inherent character: *the nature of atomic energy.* **2.** inborn tendencies directing conduct: *a man with a good nature.* **3.** kind, or sort: *These books are of the same nature.* **4.** the physical world, esp. as surrounding human beings and existing independently of their activities. **5.** the total of the forces at work throughout the universe. **6.** reality, without any effect of art: *true to nature.* **7.** the basic powers, physical drives, feelings, etc., of person or animal. **8.** a wild, uncultivated state. **9. of / in the nature of,** basically the same as: *This remark is in the nature of advice.* [ME, from L: birth, natural character]

nature strip, *n.* **1.** → **verge**¹ (def. 3a). **2.** a narrow piece of land between two lanes of traffic where grass, shrubs, etc., are planted.

naturopathy /ˌnætʃə'rɒpəθi/, *n.* a method of treating illness using natural foods, herbs, exercise, sunlight, etc. —**naturopath** /'nætʃərəˌpæθ/, *n.*

naught /nɔt/, *n.* **1.** *Archaic or Poetic.* nothing. **2.** destruction, ruin, or complete failure: *to bring to naught; to come to naught.* **3. set at naught,** to regard or treat as of no importance. [OE *nā* NO¹ + *wiht* thing]

naughty /'nɔti/, *adj.*, **-tier**, **-tiest**. **1.** badly behaved; mischievous: *a naughty child.* **2.** improper; obscene: *a naughty word.*

Nauru /nɑ'ru/, *n.* an island republic in the central Pacific Ocean, about 40 km south of the equator. Pop. 8100 (1987 est.); 21 km². *Languages:* Nauruan, also English. *Currency:* Australian dollar. Formerly, **Pleasant Island**. —**Nauruan**, *n., adj.*

nausea /'nɔziə, 'nɔsiə/, *n.* **1.** sickness in the stomach; a feeling of wanting to vomit. **2.** great disgust. [L, from Gk] —**nauseous**, *adj.*

nauseate /'nɔziˌeɪt, 'nɔsi-/, *v.t., v.i.,* **-ated**, **-ating.** to (cause to) feel nausea. [L: having been seasick] —**nauseation**, *n.*

nautical /'nɔtɪkəl/, *adj.* of or relating to seamen, ships, or navigation. [L, from Gk: relating to ships or sailors]

nautical mile, *n.* See **mile**.

nautilus /'nɔtələs/, *n., pl.* **-luses**, **-li** /-laɪ/. any of various molluscs having tentacles joined to the head and a spiral shell divided into many inside sections with pearly walls. [L, from Gk: sailor]

Navaho /'nævəhoʊ, 'nɑv-/, *n., pl.* **-hos**, **-hoes.** one of a North American Indian people found in New Mexico and Arizona, and now constituting the largest tribal group in the US.

naval /'neɪvəl/, *adj.* of or relating to a navy: *a naval battle; naval affairs.*

Navarre /nə'vɑ/, *n.* a former kingdom in south-western France and northern Spain established by the Basques in the eighth century. Spanish, **Navarra** /nɑ'bɑrɑ/.

nave /neɪv/, *n.* the middle part, lengthwise, of a church, usu. having the aisles on either side and reaching from the entrance to the chancel. [ML]

navel /'neɪvəl/, *n.* a small round hollow in the middle of the abdomen where the umbilical cord was joined. [OE *nafela*]

navel orange, *n.* a type of orange having at the top a navel-like formation containing a small secondary fruit.

navigate /'nævəgeɪt/, *v.i., v.t.,* **-gated**, **-gating. 1.** to travel (across the sea, a river, etc.) in a ship, or (through the air) in an aircraft. **2.** to direct or manage (a ship, aircraft, etc.) on its course. [L] —**navigator**, *n.* —**navigation**, *n.* —**navigable**, *adj.*

Navratilova /ˌnævrætɪ'loʊvə/, *n.* **Martina**, born 1956, Czech-born US tennis player; Wimbledon champion 1978, 1979, 1982–87, 1990.

navvy /'nævi/, *n., pl.* **-vies.** a worker employed in making roads, railways, etc.

navy /'neɪvi/, *n., pl.* **-vies. 1.** the whole body of warships belonging to a country or ruler. **2.** such a body of warships together with their officers and men, equipment, etc. **3.** Also, **navy blue.** a dark blue color, as of a naval uniform. [ME from OF, from L: ship]

nay /neɪ/, *adv.* **1.** no (used in dissent, denial, or denial). **2.** not only but also: *many good, nay, noble qualities.* ◇*n.* **3.** a refusal or denial. **4.** a negative vote or voter, as in Parliament. [ME, from Scand]

Nazarene /'næzərin/, *n.* **1.** a native or inhabitant of the town of Nazareth, as Jesus Christ (**the Nazarene**). **2.** a Christian (so called by the Jews, Muslims, etc.) [from NAZARETH]

Nazareth /'næzərəθ/, *n.* a town in northern Israel; the childhood home of Jesus. Pop. 36 700 (1975).

Nazi /'natsi/, *n., pl.* **-zis. 1.** a member of the National Socialist German Workers' party, which was founded in 1919 and in 1933, under Adolf Hitler, obtained political control of Germany; it consequently established a dictatorship on the principles of control over all cultural, economic, and political activities of the people, belief in the supremacy of Hitler as Führer, anti-Semitism, and the establishment of Germany as a dominant world power. **2.** (*oft. l.c.*) someone who supports the fascist ideas characteristic of this party, esp. racist nationalism. [G, short for *Nazi(onalsozialist)* National Socialist] —**Nazism,** *n.*

Nb, *Chem. Symbol.* niobium.

NB /ɛn 'bi/, *Abbrev.* nota bene (note well). Also, **n.b.**

NCO /ɛn si 'oʊ/, *n. Abbrev.* non-commissioned officer.

NCP /ɛn si 'pi/, *Abbrev.* National Country Party.

Nd, *Chem. Symbol.* neodymium.

Ne, *Chem. Symbol.* neon.

NE *Abbrev.* north-east(ern). See Appendix.

Neanderthal man /ni'ændəθəl ˌmæn/, *n.* the species of primeval man widespread in Europe in the Palaeolithic period. [so called because earliest evidence was discovered at *Neanderthal*, a valley near Düsseldorf, West Germany]

neap /nip/, *n.* one of the tides, midway between spring tides, which have the least height. Also, **neap tide.** [OE *nēpflōd* neap flood]

Neapolitan /niə'pɒlətən/, *adj.* of or relating to Naples.

near /nɪə/, *adv.* **1.** close; at, within, or to a short distance: *to stand near.* **2.** close in time: *Christmas is coming near.* **3. near at hand,** close by. ◇*adj.* **4.** being close by; not distant, in place or time: *the near hill; the near future.* **5.** less distant: *the near side.* **6.** close in relationship or friendship: *our nearest relation; those near to us.* **7.** almost correct; *a near answer.* **8.** close to one's interests or feelings: *matters near to us.* **9.** only just successful: *a near escape.* **10.** (in riding or driving) on the left (opposed to *off*): *the near wheel; the near hind leg.* ◇*prep.* **11.** at, within, or to a short distance from: *countries near the equator.* **12.** close upon in time: *near the beginning of the year.* **13.** close upon (a condition, etc.): *work near completion.* **14.** close to (doing something): *This act came near spoiling his chances.* ◇*v.i.,*

v.t. **15.** to come close (to); approach. [OE *nēar,* compar. of *nēah* NIGH]

nearby /'nɪəbaɪ/, *adj.*; /nɪə'baɪ/, *adv.* near; not far off.

Near East, *n.* an indefinite geographical term, usu. meaning the Balkan States, Egypt, and the countries of south-western Asia.

nearly /'nɪəli/, *adv.* **1.** almost: *nearly dead with cold.* **2.** closely: *an answer nearly resembling mine; people nearly related to each other.*

near miss, *n.* **1.** a narrow escape from an accident, etc. **2.** *Colloq.* anything which only just fails to be successful.

neat /nit/, *adj.* **1.** in a pleasingly orderly condition; tidy: *a neat room.* **2.** tidy in appearance, habits, etc.: *a neat person.* **3.** of a simple, pleasing appearance: *a neat cottage.* **4.** clever in character or performance: *a neat plan.* **5.** (of alcoholic drinks) without any other drink added; undiluted. [F: clean, from L: bright, fine, neat]

Nebraska /nə'bræskə/, *n.* a state in the central US. Pop. 1 598 000 (1986 est.); 200 466 km². *Cap.:* Lincoln. *Abbrev.:* Nebr *or* Neb —**Nebraskan,** *n., adj.*

Nebuchadnezzar /ˌnɛbjəkəd'nɛzə/, *n.* a king of Babylonia, 604?–561? BC and conqueror of Jerusalem. Also, **Nebuchadrezzar.** [See II Kings 24–25]

nebula /'nɛbjələ/, *n., pl.* **-lae** /-li/, **-las.** *Astron.* a cloudlike patch in the sky, usu. consisting of a galaxy of stars. [L: mist, vapor, cloud] —**nebular,** *adj.*

nebulous /'nɛbjələs/, *adj.* **1.** unclear, vague or confused: *a nebulous memory.* **2.** cloudy or cloudlike. **3.** of or characteristic of a nebula. [ME, from L]

necessarily /ˈnɛsəˌsɛrəli/, *adv.* **1.** by or of necessity: *You may not necessarily agree.* **2.** as a necessary result: *A rainy day is not necessarily cold.*

necessary /'nɛsəsɛri, 'nɛsəsri/, *adj., n., pl.* **-saries.** ◇*adj.* **1.** unable to be done without or dispensed with: *Regular meals are necessary for health; Buy only the necessary things.* **2.** that must happen or exist; inevitable: *War was a necessary result of the arms race.* **3.** (*usu. pl.*) something necessary. [ME, from L: unavoidable, indispensable]

necessitate /nə'sɛsəteɪt/, *v.t.,* **-tated, -tating.** to make necessary: *The breakdown of the motor necessitated a halt.*

necessity /nə'sɛsəti/, *n., pl.* **-ties. 1.** something necessary or indispensable: *the necessities of life.* **2.** the fact of being necessary or indispensable. **3.** an urgent need or requirement for something: *a necessity for a decision.* **4.** the state or fact of being necessary or inevitable. **5.** the state or fact of being in difficulty or need; poverty. [ME, from L: exigency]

neck /nɛk/, *n.* **1.** the part of the body of an animal or human which connects the head to the rest. **2.** a standard cut of meat, esp. lamb, from this area, used mainly for chops, stews, etc. **3.** the part of a garment covering or going around the neck. **4.** any narrow, connecting,

neck

necklike part, such as the thin part of a bottle, violin, etc. **5.** (*usu. pl.*). the cuttings of wool which are removed from the back of a fleece during wool rolling. **6.** a narrow piece of land, such as an isthmus. **7.** → **strait** (def. 1). **8. neck and neck**, completely even in a race, etc. **9. neck of the woods**, a particular area or place: *We don't often see you in this neck of the woods*. **10. stick one's neck out**, to act, speak, etc., so as to leave oneself open to criticism, risk, etc. ◇*v.i.* **11.** *Colloq.* to kiss, etc., during love play. [OE *hnecca*]

neckerchief /ˈnɛkətʃɪf/, *n.* a cloth worn round the neck by women or men.

necklace /ˈnɛkləs/, *n.* an ornament of precious stones, beads, etc., worn esp. by women round the neck. Also, **necklet**.

necktie /ˈnɛktaɪ/, *n.* → **tie** (def. 11).

necr-, a word part meaning 'dead', 'corpse', 'death'. Also, before consonants, **necro-**. [Gk *nekr-*, *nekro-*, combining forms of *nekrós* person, corpse]

necromancy /ˈnɛkrəˌmænsi/, *n.* **1.** magic in general. **2.** the foretelling of the future through supposed communication with the dead. [L, from Gk] —**necromancer**, *n.*

necrophilia /nɛkrəˈfɪliə/, *n.* an abnormal attraction, often sexual, to dead bodies. Also, **necrophilism** /nəˈkrɒfəlɪzəm/. —**necrophiliac**, *n., adj.*

necropolis /nəˈkrɒpələs/, *n., pl.* **-lises**. a burial ground; cemetery. [NL, from Gk: city of the dead]

necrosis /nəˈkroʊsəs/, *n.* **1.** *Med.* the death of a piece of tissue or an organ. **2.** *Bot.* a diseased condition in plants resulting from the death of tissue. [NL, from Gk: a killing]

nectar /ˈnɛktə/, *n.* **1.** *Bot.* a sweet liquid in a plant which attracts the insects or birds that pollinate the flower, and which is made into honey by bees. **2.** the drink of the gods of classical mythology. **3.** any delicious drink. [L, from Gk] —**nectareous**, *adj.*

nectarine /ˈnɛktərən, nɛktəˈrin/, *n.* a type of peach, the skin of which has no down. [NECTAR + -INE[1]]

nee /neɪ/, *adj.* born (placed after the name of a married woman to introduce her maiden name). Also, **née** /neɪ/. [F]

need /nid/, *n.* **1.** something necessary or wanted; requirement: *to meet the needs of the occasion*. **2.** an urgent want of something necessary: *He has no need of your kindness*; *the need for leadership*. **3.** a necessity arising from a particular situation: *There is no need to worry*. **4.** a situation or time of difficulty or want: *a friend in need*. ◇*v.t.* **5.** to have need of; require: *to need money*. **6.** to be under a necessity (fol. by infinitive, sometimes without *to*): *He need not go*; *She needs to see her friend*. ◇*v.i.* **7.** to be in need or want. [OE *nēd*]

needful /ˈnidfəl/, *adj.* necessary: *needful supplies*.

needle /ˈnidl/, *n., v.,* **-dled, -dling**. ◇*n.* **1.** a small, thin, pointed instrument, now usu. of steel, with a hole for thread, used in sewing.

negative

2. a thin, rod-like instrument for use in knitting, or one hooked at the end for use in crocheting, etc. **3.** *Med.* **a.** a thin, pointed, steel instrument used in sewing tissues, etc., during surgical operations. **b.** a hypodermic needle. **4.** any of various objects suggesting a needle in shape, such as a sharp-pointed mass of rock. **5.** the magnetic pointer in a compass which indicates the direction of north. **6.** a pointed instrument used in engraving, etc. **7.** *Bot.* a needle-shaped leaf of a pine tree, etc. **8.** *Zool.* a thin, sharp spike. ◇*v.t.* **9.** to sew or pierce with a needle. **10.** to urge to action by making sharp remarks; goad. **11.** to make fun of (someone); tease. [d. OE *nēdl*]

needle point, *n.* embroidery on canvas done so as to cover the area completely with even stitches causing it to look like tapestry.

needless /ˈnidləs/, *adj.* not needed; unnecessary: *a needless waste of food*.

needlework /ˈnidlwɜk/, *n.* the act or product of working with a needle in sewing, embroidery, etc.

needy /ˈnidi/, *adj.,* **-dier, -diest**. in need or want; very poor: *a needy family*.

ne'er-do-well /ˈnɛə-du-wɛl/, *adj.* **1.** worthless. ◇*n.* **2.** a worthless person.

nefarious /nəˈfɛəriəs/, *adj.* very wicked; iniquitous: *nefarious practices*. [L: impious]

Nefertiti /nɛfəˈtiti/, *n.* Egyptian queen, wife of Akhenaten. Also, **Nofretete**.

negate /nəˈgeɪt/, *v.t.,* **-gated, -gating**. **1.** to remove the effect of; nullify: *to negate a ruling*. **2.** to prove untrue; deny: *to negate a belief*. [L] —**negatory**, *adj.*

negation /nəˈgeɪʃən/, *n.* **1.** the act or fact of negating. **2.** the absence or opposite of something actual or positive.

negative /ˈnɛgətɪv/, *adj., n., v.,* **-tived, -tiving**. ◇*adj.* **1.** expressing or containing a refusal or denial: *a negative statement*; *a negative answer*. **2.** marked by the absence of positive qualities: *a negative character*. **3.** *Maths, Phys.* **a.** involving or indicating subtraction; minus. **b.** opposite to positive. **4.** *Med.* failing to show a positive result in a test for a particular disease caused by bacteria or viruses. **5.** *Photog.* indicating an image in which the relation of light and shade are reversed. **6.** *Elect.* relating to the kind of electricity developed on resin, etc., when rubbed with flannel, or that present at the pole from which electrons leave an electric generator or battery; having an excess of electrons. **7.** relating to the south-seeking pole of a magnet. **8.** **a.** *Chem.* (of a radical) having more electrons than the neutral atom or molecule and so being negatively charged. **b.** *Chem.* → **electronegative**. ◇*n.* **9.** a negative statement, word, opinion, etc. **10.** the side of a question which opposes the positive side. **11.** *Maths.* a negative quantity or symbol. **12.** *Photog.* a negative image on film, plate, etc., used chiefly for printing positive pictures. **13.** *Elect.* the negative plate or element in a voltaic cell. ◇*v.t.* **14.** to negate. **15.** to disprove. **16.** to refuse consent to; veto. [ME, from L: denying] —**negativity**, *n.*

negative ion, *n.* → **anion.**

Negev /nə'gev/, *n.* a desert area in southern Israel on the Gulf of Aqaba. 12 170 km². Also, **Negeb.**

neglect /nə'glekt/, *v.t.* **1.** to pay no attention to; disregard: *He neglected her entreaties.* **2.** to fail to care for or treat properly: *They neglected their children.* **3.** to fail to (do something) through carelessness, etc.: *He neglected to count the money.* ◇*n.* **4.** the act or fact of neglecting. **5.** the fact or state of being neglected. [L: unheeded] —**neglectful,** *adj.*

negligee /'negləʒeɪ/, *n.* a woman's dressing-gown, esp. one of very light material. [F: neglected]

negligence /'neglədʒəns/, *n.* **1.** the state or fact of neglecting: *They showed negligence towards their family.* **2.** *Law.* failure to take that degree of care which the law requires for the protection of the interests of other people. —**negligent,** *adj.*

negligible /'neglədʒəbəl/, *adj.* able to be neglected or disregarded; very little. —**negligibility,** *n.*

negotiable /nə'goʊʃəbəl/, *adj.* **1.** able to be negotiated. **2.** (of bills, etc.) able to be transferred in title by delivery. —**negotiability,** *n.*

negotiate /nə'goʊʃieɪt/, *v.,* **-ated, -ating.** ◇*v.i.* **1.** to deal with another or others in the preparation of some kind of agreement, such as an international treaty or business arrangement. ◇*v.t.* **2.** to arrange for or bring about by talking and settlement of terms: *to negotiate a loan.* **3.** to clear or pass through or around: *The car negotiated the twisting mountain road.* **4.** to transfer (a bill of exchange, etc.) by endorsement or delivery. **5.** to sell or transfer: *to negotiate securities.* [L] —**negotiator,** *n.* —**negotiation,** *n.*

Negro /'niːgroʊ/, *n., pl.* **-groes,** *adj.* ◇*n.* **1.** a member of a negroid race. **2.** a person having some negroid ancestry. ◇*adj.* **3.** → **Negroid.** Also, **negro.** [Sp and Pg: a black person, Negro, from L: black] —**Negress,** *n. fem.*

Negroid /'niːgrɔɪd/, *adj.* **1.** of, indicating, or relating to one of the three main races of mankind, marked by brown-black skin colouring, a broad and flat nose, full lips, etc., and including the dark-skinned people of Africa and their descendants elsewhere. See **Caucasian, Mongoloid.** ◇*n.* **2.** a person of a Negroid race.

Nehru /'neɪruː/, *n.* **Jawaharlal** /dʒəwəhə'lɑːl/, 1889–1964, Indian nationalist political leader; first prime minister of the republic of India 1947–64; policies included international non-alignment.

neigh /neɪ/, *n.* **1.** the sound a horse makes; whinny. ◇*v.i.* **2.** to make such a sound; to whinny. [OE *hnǣgan*]

neighbor or **neighbour** /'neɪbə/, *n.* **1.** someone who lives near another, esp. in the house next door or in the same street. **2.** a person or thing that is near another. **3.** a fellow human being anywhere: *Love thy neighbor.* [OE *nēah* nigh + *gebūr* dweller, countryman] —**neighborly,** *adj.*

neighborhood or **neighbourhood** /'neɪbəhʊd/, *n.* **1.** the region near or round about some place or thing; vicinity. **2.** a part of a town or city, oft. marked by some quality: *a fashionable neighborhood.* **3.** a number of persons living near one another or in a particular place: *The whole neighborhood was there.*

neighboring or **neighbouring** /'neɪbərɪŋ/, *adj.* living or placed near.

Neilson /'nɛlsən/, *n.* **John Shaw,** 1872–1942, Australian poet; works include 'The Orange Tree' (1923).

neither /'naɪðə, 'niːðə/, *adj.* **1.** not either; not one or other: *Neither statement is true.* ◇*pron.* **2.** not either; not the one or the other: *Neither of the statements is true.* ◇*conj.* **3.** not either (connected by *nor*): *Neither you nor I know the answer.* [ME *neither* (from *ne* NOT + EITHER)]

Nelson[1] /'nɛlsən/, *n.* **Viscount Horatio,** 1758–1805, British admiral, renowned as a tactician; famous victories over Napoleon I, esp. Trafalgar (1805), at which he was killed.

Nelson[2] /'nɛlsən/, *n.* a city on the central northern coast of the South Island of NZ; apple and pear growing, dairy and beef industries. Pop. 81 160 (1986).

Nelson Bay, *n.* a town and resort in NSW on the south-eastern shore of Port Stephens. Pop. 9376 (1986).

nemat-, a word part referring to threadlike things, esp. to *nematodes.* Also, before consonants, **nemato-.** [Gk, combining form of *nēma* thread]

nematode /'nɛmətoʊd/, *n.* one of a class of parasitic or free-living, smooth, elongated worms.

nemesis /'nɛməsəs/, *n., pl.* **-ses** /-siːz/. fate, esp. one that punishes. [named after *Nemesis,* who, in classical mythology, was the goddess of retribution or vengeance; L, from Gk]

neo-, a word part meaing 'new', 'recent', used in combination, as in *Neo-Gothic.* [Gk, combining form of *néos*]

neodymium /nioʊ'dɪmiəm/, *n.* a rare-earth, metallic, trivalent element occurring with cerium and other rare-earth metals, and having rose- to violet-colored salts. *Symbol:* Nd; *at. wt:* 144.24; *at. no.:* 60; *sp. gr.:* 6.9 at 20°C.

Neogene /'niːədʒiːn/, *n.* the later of the two periods into which the Cainozoic era is divided in an international classification, comprising the Miocene, Pliocene, Pleistocene and Recent epochs.

Neolithic /niːə'lɪθɪk/, *n.* the later Stone Age, marked by well-finished polished tools of flint and other stone.

neologism /ni'ɒlədʒɪzəm/, *n.* **1.** a new word or phrase. **2.** the introduction or use of new words, or new meanings of words. [F]

neon /'niːɒn/, *n.* an inert gaseous element chiefly used in lamps. *Symbol:* Ne; *at. no.:* 10; *at. wt:* 20.183. [NL, from Gk: new]

neon lamp, *n.* an electric discharge lamp consisting of a glass tube containing neon gas which gives a red glow when a voltage is applied across the electrodes. Also, **neon light.**

neophyte /'nioufaɪt/, *n.* **1.** a person being trained in the first steps of religious worship. **2.** a beginner in anything. [LL, from Gk: newly planted] **–neophytic,** *adj.*

neoplasm /'nɪouplæzəm/, *n.* the new growth of different or abnormal tissue; tumor. **–neoplastic,** *adj.*

Neozoic /niou'zouɪk/, *adj.* of or relating to the geological era lasting from the end of the Mesozoic to the present time.

Nepal /nə'pɔl/, *n.* a kingdom in southern Asia, in the Himalaya mountains, between India and China. Pop. 17 567 000 (1987 est.); 145 391 km². *Languages:* Nepali; also other Indo-Aryan and Tibeto-Burman languages. *Currency:* rupee. *Cap.:* Kathmandu.

Nepean /nə'piən/, *n.* a river in eastern NSW, rising near Wollongong and flowing north to the Hawkesbury, retaining its name up until the meeting with the Grose River; important source of Sydney's water supply. 145 km.

nephew /'nɛfju, 'nɛvju/, *n.* a son of one's brother or sister, or of one's husband's or wife's brother or sister. [ME, from OF, from L: grandson, nephew]

nepho-, a word part meaning 'cloud'. [Gk, combining form of *néphos* cloud]

nephr-, a variant of **nephro-**, before vowels.

nephrite /'nɛfraɪt/, *n.* a mineral varying from whitish to dark green in color. See **jade** (def. 1). [G]

nephritis, *n.* inflammation of the kidneys. **–nephritic,** *adj.*

nephro-, a word part referring to the kidneys. Also, **nephr-**. [Gk, combining form of *nephrós* kidney]

nepotism /'nɛpətɪzəm/, *n.* the practice of giving a job or position to a relative or friend rather than to a person with better qualifications. [F, from It, from L: descendant]

Neptune /'nɛptjun/, *n.* **1.** *Rom Myth.* the god of the sea; Greek counterpart, Poseidon. **2.** the sea or ocean. **3.** *Astron.* the eighth planet in order from the sun; two satellites, Triton and Nereid.

neptunium /nɛp'tjuniəm/, *n.* a radioactive synthetic element, which decays rapidly to U-235. *Symbol:* Np; *at. no.:* 93; *at. wt:* 237.

Nereid /'nɪəriəd/, *n., pl.* **Nereides** /nə'riədiz/. **1.** (*sometimes l.c.*) *Gk Myth.* any one of the fifty daughters of the ancient sea-god Nereus. **2.** the smaller of the two satellites of Neptune. See **Triton.**

Nero /'nɪərou/, *n.* (*Nero Claudius Caesar Drusus Germanicus, Lucius Domitius Ahenobarbus*), AD 37–68, Roman emperor AD 54–68, notorious for his cruelty and corruption.

nerve /nɜv/, *n., v.,* **nerved, nerving.** ◇*n.* **1.** one or more bundles of fibres, forming part of a system which carries the impulses of feeling, motion, etc., between the brain or spinal cord and other parts of the body. **2.** energy, firmness or courage esp. in difficult circumstances: *a position requiring nerve.* **3.** (*pl.*) nervousness: *a fit of nerves.* **4.** *Colloq.* overconfidence in a sometimes rude way: *He had the nerve to ask me for payment.* **5. get on one's nerves,** to irritate. ◇*v.t.* **6.** to give strength, vigor, or courage to. [ME, from L]

nerve centre, *n.* (of a large company, movement, or organisation) the centre from which plans, policies, and movements are directed.

nerve gas, *n.* a paralysing, oft. fatal gas, used during war.

nerve impulse, *n.* a wave of electrical and chemical activity passing along nerve fibres and acting as a stimulus to muscle, gland, or other nerve cells.

nerve-racking /'nɜv-rækɪŋ/, *adj.* causing great worry or fear.

Nervi /'nɛəvi/, *n.* **Pier Luigi** /pjɛə lu'idʒi/, 1891–1979, Italian architect.

nervous /'nɜvəs/, *adj.* **1.** of or relating to the nerves: *central nervous system.* **2.** very excited or uneasy, esp. while waiting for something to happen; not confident; frightened. [ME, from L: sinewy]

nervous breakdown, *n.* the loss (usu. temporary) of a person's ability to cope with the responsibilities and activities of everyday life.

nervous system, *n.* **1.** the system of nerves and nerve centres in an animal. **2.** a particular part of this system: **a. central** or **cerebrospinal nervous system**, the brain and spinal cord. **b. peripheral nervous system,** the system of nerves and ganglia derived from the central system, comprising the cranial nerves, the spinal nerves, the various sense organs, etc. **c. autonomic nervous system,** the system of nerves and ganglia which supply the walls of the vascular system and the various viscera and glands.

nervy /'nɜvi/, *adj.,* **-vier, -viest.** **1.** nervous (def. 2). **2.** becoming easily excited or angry; irritable.

-ness, a suffix used to form, from adjectives and participles, nouns meaning quality or state: *darkness, goodness, kindness, obligingness, preparedness.* [OE *-nes(s)*]

Ness /nɛs/, *n.* **1. Loch,** a lake in northwestern Scotland. About 35 km long and 1.5 km wide. **2.** See **Loch Ness monster.**

nest /nɛst/, *n.* **1.** a structure made or a place used by a bird for hatching its eggs and bringing up its young. **2.** a place used by insects, fishes, turtles, rabbits, etc., for putting their eggs or young in. **3.** a number of birds or animals living in such a place. **4.** a comfortable place to live or to go to sometimes; a snug retreat. **5.** a group of things of the same type or form but of different sizes, that fit within each other: *a nest of tables, trays, etc.* **6.** a place where something bad goes on: *a robbers' nest.* ◇*v.t.* **7.** to settle or place in a nest. ◇*v.i.* **8.** to build or have a nest: *The swallows nested under the eaves.* **9.** to search for nests: *to go nesting.* [ME and OE]

nestle /'nesəl/, *v.i.*, **-tled, -tling**. to lie close, like a bird in a nest; snuggle or cuddle. [OE *nestlian*]

nestling /'neslɪŋ/, *n.* a young bird in the nest.

Nestor /'nestə/, *n. Gk Legend.* the oldest and wisest of the Greeks in the Trojan War.

net[1] /net/, *n., v.,* **netted, netting**, *adj.* ◇*n.* **1.** a lacelike fabric with a uniform mesh made by knotting or weaving threads together; netting. **2.** such a fabric made from fine threads for people to wear, or to keep off mosquitoes, flies, etc. **3.** such a fabric made from strong cord or rope with bigger spaces, for catching fish, birds, or other animals. **4.** anything used to catch or snare. **5.** → **network**. **6.** a piece of netting used in various sports. esp. tennis, netball, soccer, etc. ◇*v.t.* **7.** to cover, screen, or enclose with a net or netting. **8.** to catch or snare with, or as with, a net: *to net fish*. ◇*adj.* **9.** made in the form of or like a net. [OE *net(t)*]

net[2] /net/, *adj., n., v.,* **netted, netting**. ◇*adj.* **1.** remaining after charges, debts, tax, etc., have been paid: *net earnings; net income (opposed to gross)*. **2.** sold at net prices. **3.** (of weight) relating to contents only, and not including packaging. **4.** final, after gains and losses have been allowed at; conclusive: *the net result*. ◇*n.* **5.** net income, profits, or the like. See **gross** (def. 1). ◇*v.t.* **6.** to gain or produce as clear profit. Also, **nett**. See **gross** (def. 1). [F: clean, clear. See NEAT]

netball /'netbɔl/, *n.* game similar to basketball played by two teams of seven players, usu. women.

nether /'neðə/, *adj.* **1.** lying, or thought of as lying, beneath the earth's surface; infernal: *the nether world*. **2.** lower or under: *his nether lip*. [ME; OE *neothera*]

Netherlands /'neðələndz/, *n.* **the. 1.** a kingdom in north-western Europe on the North Sea, bordered by Germany and Belgium. Pop. 14 615 000 (1987 est.); 33 939 km². *Language*: Dutch. *Currency*: guilder. *Cap.*: Amsterdam, with the seat of government at the Hague. Dutch, **Nederland**. —**Netherlander**, *n.*

nett /net/, *adj., n., v.t.* → **net**[2].

netting /'netɪŋ/, *n.* a type of fabric made of net: *fish netting; mosquito netting*.

nettle /'netl/, *n., v.,* **-tled, -tling**. ◇*n.* **1.** a widely distributed plant armed with stinging hairs. **2. grasp the nettle**, *Colloq.* to approach an unpleasant task with courage and determination. ◇*v.t.* **3.** to make (someone) angry; irritate, provoke, or vex. [ME; OE *netele*]

network /'netwɜk/, *n.* **1.** any netlike combination of lines, passages, filaments, etc.: *railway network*. **2.** netting or net. **3.** a group of connected radio or television stations, sometimes commonly owned, and from which the same programs may be broadcast.

neur-, variant of **neuro-**, before vowels.

neural /'njurəl/, *adj.* of or relating to a nerve or the nervous system.

neuralgia /nju'rældʒə/, *n.* a sharp and paroxysmal pain along a nerve. [NL. See NEUR-, -ALGIA] —**neuralgic**, *adj.*

neuritis /nju'raɪtəs/, *n.* inflammation of or continuous pain in a nerve. [NL. See NEUR-, -ITIS] —**neuritic**, *adj.*

neuro-, a word part meaning 'tendon', 'nerve'. Also, **neur-**. [Gk, combining form of *neûron*]

neurology /nju'rɒlədʒi/, *n.* the science of the nerves or the nervous system, esp. its diseases. —**neurological**, *adj.* —**neurologist**, *n.*

neurone /'njuroun/, *n.* any of the cells which make up the nervous tissue; nerve cell. See **dendrite** (def. 2), **axon**. Also, **neuron** /'njurɒn/. [Gk: nerve] —**neuronic**, *adj.*

neurosis /nju'rousəs/, *n., pl.* **-ses** /-siz/. an emotional disorder in which someone suffers feelings of anxiety, obsessional thoughts, compulsive acts, and physical complaints without any real evidence of disease.

neurotic /nju'rɒtɪk/, *adj.* **1.** having a neurosis. **2.** relating to the nerves or to nervous disease. ◇*n.* **3.** a person affected with neurosis.

neuter /'njutə/, *adj.* **1.** *Gram.* of or relating to the gender which is neither masculine nor feminine, referring to objects and abstractions, of no sex, and to animals of unknown sex. **2.** sexless, apparently sexless, or of indeterminate sex, as a hermaphrodite or castrated person. **3.** *Zool.* of the workers among bees and ants having imperfectly developed sexual organs. **4.** *Bot.* having neither stamens nor pistils; asexual. ◇*n.* **5.** *Gram.* the neuter gender. **6.** an animal or person made sterile by castration. **7.** a neuter insect. ◇*v.t.* **8.** to castrate. [L: neither]

neutral /'njutrəl/, *adj.* **1.** (of a person or state) not taking part in a quarrel or war between others. **2.** of no particular kind, color, characteristics, etc.; indefinite. **3.** grey; without hue; achromatic. **4.** *Linguistics*. relating to the vowel schwa (ə). **5.** *Biol.* neuter. **6.** *Chem.* **a.** neither acid nor alkaline; having a pH of 7: *a neutral solution*. **b.** of or relating to an atom, molecule, group, etc., which is neither positively or negatively charged (as opposed to an ion). **7.** *Elect.* neither positive nor negative; not electrified; not magnetised. ◇*n.* **8.** a person or a state that remains neutral in a war or quarrel. **9.** a citizen of a neutral nation. **10.** *Mech.* the position of the gears in a vehicle where they are not engaged. [ME, from L]

neutralise or **neutralize** /'njutrəlaɪz/, *v.t.,* **-lised, -lising**. **1.** to make neutral. **2.** to make ineffective; counteract. **3.** to declare a country neutral; invest with neutrality. **4.** *Chem.* to make chemically neutral, as by adding acid to alkali. —**neutralisation**, *n.* —**neutraliser**, *n.*

neutrality /nju'træləti/, *n.* **1.** the state of being neutral. **2.** the attitude or status of a nation which does not take part in a war between other nations: *the continuous neutrality of Switzerland*.

neutrino /nju'triːnoʊ/, *n.*, *pl.* **-nos.** an elementary particle with zero electric charge and zero rest mass.

neutron /'njuːtrɒn/, *n.* a neutral elementary particle with the same mass as a proton, which is in all atomic nuclei except normal hydrogen. [NEUTR(AL) neither positive nor negative + *-on* (after ELECTRON, PROTON)]

neutron bomb, *n.* a nuclear weapon which releases a shower of neutrons but little blast, thus killing people but causing little damage to property. Also, **clean bomb.**

Nevada /nə'vaːdə/, *n.* a state in the western US. Pop. 963 000 (1986 est.); 286 297 km². *Cap.:* Carson City. *Abbrev.:* Nev

never /'nevə/, *adv.* **1.** not ever; at no time. **2.** not at all; absolutely not; not even. **3.** to no extent or degree. [OE *næfre*]

never-never /nevə-nevə/, *Colloq.* ◊*n.* **1.** (*sometimes cap.*) desert country where hardly anybody lives; a remote and isolated region. ◊*adj.* **2.** imaginary: *never-never land.*

nevertheless /nevəðə'les/, *adv.* a strong form of *but*; however; nonetheless; notwithstanding.

new /njuː/, *adj.* **1.** recently arrived or made, or having only lately come or been brought into being: *a new book; new Australians.* **2.** of a kind now existing or appearing for the first time; novel: *They have made a new bomb.* **3.** having only lately or only now come into knowledge: *a new chemical element.* **4.** unfamiliar, strange or unaccustomed (fol. by *to*): *ideas new to us; I'm new to this work.* **5.** having only lately come to a position, job, etc.: *a new minister.* **6.** coming or occurring afresh; further; additional: *new gains.* **7.** fresh or unused: *a new sheet.* **8.** different and better, physically or morally: *The operation made a new man of him.* **9.** other than the former or the old: *a new era.* [ME and OE *newe*]

New Australia, *n.* a settlement established by William Lane in Paraguay in 1893 as an attempt to achieve an ideal state of socialism; the community collapsed in 1915.

New Australian, *n. Colloq.* an immigrant, esp. a person whose native language is not English; migrant.

New Britain, *n.* an island in the southern Pacific, north-east of New Guinea; the largest island in the Bismarck Archipelago; part of PNG. Pop. 142 241 (1980); about 38 000 km².

New Caledonia, *n.* **1.** an island in the southern Pacific, about 1300 km east of Australia. 16 120 km². **2.** an overseas territory of France comprising this island and other smaller islands; formerly a penal colony. Pop. 152 000 (1987); 18 734 km². *Cap.:* Nouméa. French, **Nouvelle-Calédonie.**

Newcastle[1] /'njuːkasəl/, *n.* **Thomas Pelham Holles** /peləm 'hɒləs/, **1st Duke of,** 1693–1768, British statesman; Whig prime minister 1754–56, 1757–62.

Newcastle[2] /'njuːkasəl, -kæsəl/, *n.* **1.** a city in NSW situated north of Sydney at the mouth of the Hunter River; coal mining, site of BHP Ltd's first steel works in 1915. Pop. 255 787 (1986). **2.** Also, **Newcastle upon Tyne.** a seaport in north-eastern England, on the river Tyne; shipbuilding. Pop. 281 000 (1982).

new chum, *n.* **1.** someone inexperienced in some field; novice: *a new chum on the job.* **2.** (*formerly*) **a.** a newly transported convict. **b.** a newly arrived British immigrant.

Newcombe /'njuːkəm/, *n.* **John David,** born 1944, Australian tennis player; a Wimbledon singles and doubles champion.

Newcomen /'njuːkʌmən/, *n.* **Thomas,** 1663–1729, English blacksmith; inventor of an early steam-engine (1712).

newcomer /'njuːkʌmə/, *n.* someone who has newly come; a new arrival.

New Deal, *n.* the program of the US Democratic party under President Franklin D Roosevelt that sought to bring economic relief to the US after the Depression of the 1930s. –**New Dealer,** *n.*

New Delhi, *n.* See **Delhi.**

New England, *n.* **1.** an area in northern NSW; a series of plateaus and highlands bounded in the south by the Great Dividing Range and in the north by the NSW–Qld border; agriculture, grazing, orchard and vegetable growing. **2.** six states in the north-eastern US: Connecticut, Maine, Massachusetts, Rhode Island, Vermont, New Hampshire and Maine. –**New Englander,** *n.*

newfangled /'njuːfæŋgəld/, *adj.* (*disapproving*) new-fashioned; of a new kind: *newfangled ideas.* [ME, from OE]

New Forest, *n.* a region of forest and heath in England, in southern Hampshire. 375 km².

Newfoundland /njuː'faʊndlənd, 'njuːfəndlənd/, *n.* **1.** a large island in the eastern part of Canada, separated from the mainland by the Strait of Belle Isle. 110 681 km². **2.** (*l.c.*) one of a breed of very large, shaggy dogs, orig. from this island, noted for being intelligent, easily trained and good at swimming.

New Guard, *n.* a private organisation formed in Sydney, NSW, in 1931, established along military lines, with the aims of serving the throne and suppressing signs of communism.

New Guinea /njuː 'gɪni/, *n.* **1.** a large island north of Australia; divided into the Indonesian province of Irian Jaya in the west and Papua New Guinea in the east. Pop. 4 770 500 (1986 est.); about 800 000 km². **2. Trust Territory of,** a former territory under the trusteeship of Australia, including north-eastern New Guinea, the Bismarck Archipelago, Bougainville, and other islands.

New Hampshire, *n.* a state in the north-eastern US. Pop. 1 027 000 (1986 est.); 24 097 km². *Cap.:* Concord. *Abbrev.:* NH

New Hebrides, *n.* former name of **Vanuatu.**

New Holland, *n.* (*formerly*) the name given to Australia by the Dutch explorers of the 17th century. [L *Nova Hollandia*]

New Ireland, *n.* an island in the southern Pacific, in the Bismarck Archipelago, north-east of New Guinea; part of PNG. Pop. (with adjacent islands) 77 200 (1986 est.); about 9850 km².

New Italy, *n.* the name given to a settlement established in the 1880s on the Richmond River near Lismore in northern NSW; the inhabitants were Italian survivors of the scheme to form a colony in New Ireland.

New Jersey, *n.* a state in the eastern US, on the Atlantic coast. Pop. 7 620 000 (1986 est.); 20 295 km². *Cap.:* Trenton. *Abbrev.:* NJ — **New Jerseyite,** *n.*

New Kingdom, *n.* the third great period in the history of the ancient Egyptian kingdom, 1580–1085 BC, comprising dynasties XVIII–XX. Also, **Middle Empire.** See **Old Kingdom, Middle Kingdom.**

New Latin, *n.* the Latin which became current (notably in scientific literature) after the Renaissance (approx. 1500). Also, **Neo-Latin.**

Newman[1] /'njumən/, *n.* **Paul,** born 1925, US film actor and director.

Newman[2] /'njumən/, *n.* **Mount,** a mountain in the Pilbara region of central WA; rich in iron ore deposits. 1128m.

New Mexico, *n.* a state in the south-western US. Pop. 1 479 000 (1986 est.); 315 115 km². *Cap.:* Santa Fe. *Abbrev.:* N Mex, NM — **New Mexican,** *n.,* *adj.*

new moon, *n.* → **moon** (def. 2a).

New Norcia /nju 'nɔsiə/, *n.* a missionary settlement on the Moore River, WA, established in 1846 by Benedictine monks.

New Norfolk, *n.* a town in southern Tas, on the Derwent River; formerly a convict settlement. Pop. 9832 (1986).

New Orleans /nju 'ɔliənz, ɔ'linz/, *n.* a port in the US, in south-eastern Louisiana, on the Mississippi; founded as French colony in 1718; sold to the US in 1803. Pop. 554 500 (1986 est.).

new penny, *n.* → **penny** (def. 2).

news /njuz/, *n.pl. (treated as sing.)* **1.** a report of any recent event, situation, etc. **2.** a report of events published in a newspaper, journal, radio, television, or any other medium. **3.** information, events, etc., considered as suitable for reporting: *It's very interesting, but it's not news.* **4.** information not known before: *That's news to me.* **5.** newsprint or newspaper. **6. bad news,** *Colloq.* someone (or something) from whom nothing good is to be expected: *Ideas like that are really bad news.* [ME *news*, pl. of ME, OE *newe* that which is new, n. use of *newe*, adj.]

news agency, *n.* an organisation which collects news and supplies it to newspapers, television and radio stations, etc.

newsagency /'njuzeɪdʒənsi/, *n.* a shop which sells principally newspapers, magazines, stationery, and books. — **newsagent,** *n.*

newscast /'njuzkast/, *n., v.,* **-cast, -casting.** ◇*n.* **1.** a radio or television broadcast of news reports. ◇*v.i.* **2.** to broadcast a news bulletin. — **newscaster,** *n.*

newsletter /'njuzletə/, *n.* a small publication, often printed by photocopy, duplicator, etc., esp. one circulating among people who share the same interests.

newsman /'njuzmæn/, *n.* **1.** someone who sells or distributes newspapers, periodicals, etc. **2.** a reporter on a newspaper.

New South Wales, *n.* a State in eastern Australia. Pop. 5 401 881 (1986); 801 431 km². *Cap.:* Sydney. *Abbrev.:* NSW

New South Wales Corps, *n.* a military unit raised in England for service in NSW; first detachment arrived 1790; became known as the 'Rum Corps'.

newspaper /'njuzpeɪpə/, *n.* **1.** a printed publication issued at regular times, usu. daily or weekly, and commonly containing news, comment, features, and advertisements. **2.** an organisation publishing a newspaper. **3.** a single copy or issue of a newspaper.

newspeak /'njuspik/, *n.* the language of politicians and government officials, considered to be deliberately misleading or unclear.

newsprint /'njuzprɪnt/, *n.* the paper used or made to print newspapers on.

newsreel /'njuzril/, *n.* a short film showing current news events.

New Stone Age, *n.* the neolithic era.

newt /njut/, *n.* a small, semi-aquatic salamander of Europe, North America, and northern Asia. [ME]

New Test, *Abbrev.* New Testament.

New Testament, *n.* those books in the Bible which were produced by the early Christian Church, and were added to the Jewish scriptures (Old Testament).

newton /'njutn/, *n.* the derived SI unit of force; the force needed to give an acceleration of one metre per second per second to a mass of one kilogram. *Symbol:* N [named after Sir Isaac NEWTON]

Newton /'njutn/, *n.* **Sir Isaac,** 1642–1727, English scientist, mathematician, and philosopher; formulator of the law of gravity.

Newton's law of gravitation, *n.* a law stating that any two bodies attract each other with a force proportional to the product of their masses and inversely proportional to the square of the distance between them. [See NEWTON]

Newton's laws, *n.pl.* three classical laws of motion: **1.** all bodies continue in a state of rest or uniform motion unless they are acted upon by an external force. **2.** the rate of change of momentum of a body is proportional to force applied to it. **3.** to every action there is an equal and opposite reaction. [See NEWTON]

new wave, *n.* **1.** a movement or trend breaking with traditional ideas in art, literature, politics, etc. **2.** a form of rock music of the 1970s in the style of punk rock, but marked by greater imaginativeness and performance skills.

New World, *n.* **The,** the Western Hemisphere; the American continents.

new year, *n.* **1.** the year coming or newly begun. **2.** *(caps)* the first day or days of a year. **3.** *(caps)* New Year's Day.

New Year's Day, *n.* the first day of the year; 1 January.

New Year's Eve, *n.* the night of 31 December, usu. observed with merrymaking.

New York, *n.* **1.** Also, **New York State**. a state in the north-eastern US. Pop. 17 772 000 (1986 est.); 127 169 km². *Cap.:* Albany. *Abbrev.:* NY **2.** Also, **New York City**. a seaport in the US, in south-eastern New York at the mouth of the Hudson; the largest city in the US, comprising the boroughs of Manhattan, Queens, Brooklyn, the Bronx, and Richmond. Pop. 7 262 700 (1986). —**New Yorker**, *n.*

New Zealand *n.* a parliamentary state in the South Pacific, comprising two major islands (North Island and South Island) and various minor islands; an independent member of the Commonwealth. Pop. 3 341 000 (1987 est.); 269 057 km². *Languages:* English, and Maori. *Currency:* NZ dollar. *Cap.:* Wellington. *Abbrev.:* NZ [D *Nieuw Zeeland* New Zeeland, the name given by Abel Tasman in 1642] —**New Zealander**, *n.*

next /nekst/, *adj.* (*superl. of* **nigh**), *adv.* ◇*adj.* **1.** immediately following in time, order, importance, etc.: *the next day*. **2.** nearest in place or position: *the next room*. **3.** nearest in relationship or kinship. ◇*adv.* **4.** in the nearest place, time, importance, etc: *You're next in the queue*. **5.** on the first subsequent occasion: *when next we meet*. [OE *nēxt*]

next of kin, *n.* a person's nearest relative or relatives.

nexus /'neksəs/, *n., pl.* **nexus**. **1.** a tie or link; means of connection. **2.** a connected series. [L]

NG /en 'dʒi/, *Abbrev.* New Guinea.

Ni, *Chem. Symbol.* nickel.

Niagara Falls /naɪ,ægrə, -,ægərə 'fɔlz/, *n.pl.* the falls of the river Niagara: the **Horseshoe Falls** in Ontario, Canada (48m high, 792m wide), separated by Goat Island from the **American Falls** in New York State, US (51 m high, 427 m wide).

nib /nɪb/, *n.* **1.** the point of a pen, esp. a small, tapering metallic device with a split tip for drawing up ink and for writing. **2.** (of a bird) a bill or beak. **3.** the point of anything. [OE *nybba* point (in a place name)]

nibble /'nɪbəl/, *v.,* -**bled,** -**bling,** *n.* ◇*v.i., v.t.* **1.** to bite off small bits from (something). **2.** to bite slightly or gently. ◇*n.* **3.** a small piece; morsel: *Each nibble was eaten*. **4.** the act or an instance of nibbling. [late ME] —**nibbler**, *n.*

Nicaragua /nɪkə'rægjuə/, *n.* a republic in the Central American isthmus between the Pacific Ocean and the Caribbean Sea, bordered by Honduras and Costa Rica. Pop. 3 502 000 (1987 est.); 127 662 km². *Language:* Spanish. *Currency:* córdoba. *Cap.:* Managua. —**Nicaraguan**, *n., adj.*

nice /naɪs/, *adj.,* **nicer, nicest**. **1.** pleasing; agreeable; delightful: *a nice visit*. **2.** kind; amiably pleasant: *They are always nice to strangers*. **3.** marked by or requiring great accuracy, precision, skill, or delicacy: *a nice analysis*. **4.** suitable or proper: *not a nice song*. **5.** carefully neat as to dress, habits, etc. [ME, from OF: simple, from L: not knowing]

Nicene Creed /,naɪsin 'krid/, *n.* a formal statement of the chief principles of Christian belief. [from *Nicaea*, ancient city in NW Asia Minor where Creed formulated in AD 325]

nicety /'naɪsəti/, *n., pl.* -**ties**. **1.** a delicate or fine point: *niceties of manners; niceties of protocol*. **2. to a nicety**, in great detail; with precision. [ME, from OF: NICE]

niche /nɪtʃ/, *n.* **1.** a part set back into a wall, etc., usu. ornamented, round in section and arched, for a statue or other decorative object. **2.** a place or position suitable and comfortable for a person or thing: *I have found my niche in society*. **3.** *Ecol.* the position or function of an organism in a community of plants and animals. [F: to make a nest, from Gallo-Rom, from L: nest]

Nicholas /'nɪkələs/, *n.* **1. Saint**, fl. fourth century, bishop in Asia Minor, patron saint of Russia, protector of children. **2.** →**Santa Claus**.

Nicholas II, *n.* 1868–1918, last tsar of Russia 1894–1917; executed in exile by revolutionaries, 1918.

Nicholls /'nɪkəlz/, *n.* **1. Pastor Sir Douglas Ralph**, 1906–88, Australian Aboriginal spokesman and administrator; governor of SA 1976–77. **2. William Henry**, 1885–1951, Australian botanist; noted for his study of orchids.

Nichols /'nɪkəlz/, *n.* **George Roberts**, 1809–57, Australian lawyer and politician; first native-born Australian admitted as a solicitor in NSW.

Nicholson /'nɪkəlsən/, *n.* **1. Sir Charles**, 1808–1903, English-born Australian collector of antiquities; donated his collection of classical and Egyptian antiquities to the University of Sydney in 1860. **2. Jack**, born 1937, US film actor; films include *One Flew Over the Cuckoo's Nest* (Academy Award 1976).

Nicias /'nɪsiəs/, *n.* died 414 BC, Athenian aristocratic statesman and general; secured peace with Sparta (421 BC), marking the end of the first part of the Peloponnesian War.

nick /nɪk/, *n.* **1.** a small cut; notch; groove. **2. in good nick**, in good physical condition. **3. in the nick of time**, at the last possible moment: *She was rescued in the nick of time*. ◇*v.t.* **4.** to make a nick or nicks in; notch. **5.** *Colloq.* to steal. ◇*v.* **6. nick off**, *Colloq.* to leave; disappear. [late ME]

nickel /'nɪkəl/, *n., v.,* -**elled,** -**elling**. ◇*n.* **1.** *Chem.* a hard, silvery white, easily worked metallic element, similar to iron and cobalt, and much used in making alloys, etc. Symbol: Ni; *at. no.:* 28; *at. wt:* 58.71. **2.** *US.* A coin composed of or containing nickel, now a five-cent piece. ◇*v.t.* **3.** to cover or coat with nickel. [Swed]

nickel silver, *n.* a silver-white alloy containing copper (52-80%), zinc (10-35%) and nickel (5-35%), used for making utensils, drawing instruments, etc.

nickname /ˈnɪkneɪm/, *n., v.,* **-named, -naming.** ◇*n.* **1.** a name added to or put in place of the proper name of a person, place, etc. **2.** a short form of a proper name, as *Jim* for *James*. ◇*v.t.* **3.** to give a nickname to, or call by a particular nickname. [ME]

Nicolle /nɪˈkɒl/, *n.* **Eugene Dominique** /juˈdʒin dɒməˈnik/, 1823–1909, Australian inventor, born in France; invented ice-making machinery.

nicotine /ˈnɪkəˌtin, ˈnɪkətɪn/, *n.* a poisonous alkaloid, the active substance in tobacco. Also, **nicotin** /ˈnɪkətən/. [F, from Jacques *Nicot*, 1530–1600, who introduced tobacco into France in 1560] **—nicotinic,** *adj.*

nictitating membrane /ˌnɪktəteɪtɪŋ ˈmɛmbreɪn/, *n.* the thin membrane, or inner third eyelid, present in many animals, and able to be drawn across the eyeball, as for protection.

NIDA /ˈnaɪdə/, *n.* National Institute of Dramatic Art, an Australian government assisted body, established in 1958.

niece /nis/, *n.* a daughter of one's brother or sister, or of one's husband's or wife's brother or sister. [ME, from OF]

Nietzsche /ˈnitʃə/, *n.* **Friedrich Wilhelm,** 1844–1900, German philosopher; his philosophy was a forerunner of existentialism.

nifty /ˈnɪfti/, *adj.,* **-tier, -tiest.** *Colloq.* smart or clever; stylish; fine: *a nifty little car*. [orig. theatrical slang]

Nigeria /naɪˈdʒɪəriə/, *n.* a federal republic in west Africa on the Gulf of Guinea, bordered by Benin, Niger, Chad and Cameroon; Eastern Region seceded as independent Republic of Biafra in 1967 but surrendered at end of civil war (1970). Pop. 100 595 700 (1987 est.); 923 768 km². Languages: English, also Hansa, Yoruba and Ibo. Currency: naira. *Cap.*: Lagos. **—Nigerian,** *n., adj.*

niggard /ˈnɪɡəd/, *n.* someone who is very unwilling to spend money or give things; a mean, stingy person. [ME] **—niggardly,** *adj., adv.*

nigger /ˈnɪɡə/, *n.* (offensive) **1.** a Negro. **2.** a member of any dark-skinned race. [from F, from Sp: NEGRO]

niggerhead /ˈnɪɡəhɛd/, *n.* **1.** a hard black stone common in coal measures. **2.** a type of native grass with tufted seedheads, often blackish in color, resistant to dry weather.

niggle /ˈnɪɡəl/, *v.,* **-gled, -gling.** ◇*v.i.* **1.** to make constant small criticisms or demands: *to niggle at someone*. ◇*v.t.* **2.** to irritate; annoy. [Scand] **—niggler,** *n.*

niggling /ˈnɪɡlɪŋ/, *adj.* **1.** worrying; persistent; nagging: *a niggling thought*. **2.** too concerned with small details; petty. Also, **niggly.**

nigh /naɪ/, *Archaic*. ◇*adv.* **1.** near in space, time, or relation: *The time of judgment is nigh*. **2.** nearly or almost: *It is nigh on 12 o'clock*. ◇*prep.* **3.** near. [ME *nigh(e), neye,* OE *nēah, nēh*]

night /naɪt/, *n.* **1.** the time of darkness between sunset and sunrise. **2.** nightfall: *Night comes quickly*. **3.** a state or time of obscurity, ignorance, misfortune, etc. [ME; OE *niht, neaht*]

night blindness, *n.* a condition of the eyes in which sight is normal in the day or in a strong light, but is poor or completely gone at night or in a dim light.

nightcap /ˈnaɪtkæp/, *n.* **1.** (formerly) a cap for the head, worn in bed. **2.** *Colloq.* a drink, usu. alcoholic, taken before going to bed.

nightclub /ˈnaɪtklʌb/, *n.* a place of entertainment, open until late, offering food, drink, cabaret, dancing, etc.

nighthawk /ˈnaɪthɔk/, *n.* →**nightjar.**

nightingale /ˈnaɪtɪŋɡeɪl/, *n.* a small migratory bird of the thrush family known for the singing of the male, esp. at night during the breeding season. [OE *nihtegale* lit., night singer (cf. OE *galan* sing)]

Nightingale /ˈnaɪtɪŋɡeɪl/, *n.* **Florence,** 1820–1910, English nurse; reformer of hospital nursing.

nightjar /ˈnaɪtdʒa/, *n.* a type of nocturnal insect-eating bird, esp. the **spotted nightjar,** found throughout Australia.

nightly /ˈnaɪtli/, *adj.* **1.** coming, happening, appearing, or active at night: *nightly revels*. **2.** coming or happening each night: *nightly prayers*. **3.** of, relating to, or typical of night. ◇*adv.* **4.** at or by night. **5.** on every night: *For one week only, performances will be given nightly.*

nightmare /ˈnaɪtmɛə/, *n.* **1.** a very bad dream, causing fear and distress. **2.** a very upsetting or frightening experience. [ME (*mare* evil spirit)] **—nightmarish,** *adj.*

nightsoil /ˈnaɪtsɔɪl/, *n.* human excreta carted away regularly and buried.

night watch, *n.* **1.** a watch or guard kept during the night. **2.** (*usu. pl.*) a period or division of the night in which the watch is kept.

nightwatchman /naɪtˈwɒtʃmən/, *n., pl.* **-men** /-mən/. **1.** a man employed to guard property, etc., at night. **2.** *Cricket Colloq.* a low order batsman, who is sent in to bat late in the afternoon.

nihilism /ˈnaɪəlɪzəm, ˈni-/, *n.* **1.** the total lack of belief in religion or moral principles and duties, or in established laws and institutions. **2.** *Philos.* **a.** the belief that there is no objective basis of truth. **b.** an extreme form of scepticism, saying that nothing really exists. **3.** (*sometimes cap.*) the principles of a Russian revolutionary group in the latter half of the 19th century. [L] **—nihilist,** *n.* **—nihilistic,** *adj.*

Nike /ˈnaɪki/, *n. Gk Myth.* **1.** the goddess of victory, represented as a winged maiden; Roman counterpart, Victoria. **2.** the goddess Athena as the giver of victory.

nil /nɪl/, *n.* nothing. [L]

Niland /ˈnaɪlənd/, *n.* **D'Arcy Francis,** 1917–67, Australian writer and journalist; wrote the novel *The Shiralee* (1955).

Nile /naɪl/, *n.* **1.** a river in eastern Africa, flowing north from Lake Victoria to the Mediterranean. 5589 km (from the headwaters of the river Kagera, about 6450 km). **2. Blue,** a tributary of the Nile, flowing from Lake Tana in Ethiopia into the Nile at Khartoum. **3. White,** a part of the Nile above Khartoum.

nimble /ˈnɪmbəl/, *adj.*, **-bler, -blest. 1.** quick, light and easy in movement; agile; active; rapid: *nimble feet.* **2.** quick in understanding, planning, etc.: *nimble wits; a nimble mind.* [ME]

nimbus /ˈnɪmbəs/, *n., pl.* **-bi** /-baɪ/, **-buses. 1.** a cloud or light of some kind surrounding a person or thing; aura. **2.** *Art.* a usu. round area representing a light around the head of a divine or sacred person or a king; halo. **3.** a rain cloud (usu. used as a word-part: *cumulo-nimbus, nimbo-stratus*). [L: rainstorm, thunder-cloud]

Niña /ˈninə, ˈninjə/, *n.* one of the three ships Columbus commanded on his first voyage to the New World (1492).

nine /naɪn/, *n.* **1.** a cardinal number, eight plus one. **2.** a symbol for this number, as 9 or IX. **3.** a set of nine persons or things: *a nine.* **4. dressed (up) to the nines,** *Colloq.* smartly dressed or overdressed. ◊*adj.* **5.** amounting to nine in number. [ME; OE *nigen*]

ninepins /ˈnaɪnpɪnz/, *n.pl.* (construed as *sing.*) a game played with nine wooden pins at which a ball is bowled to knock them down; skittles.

nineteen /naɪnˈtin, ˈnaɪntin/, *n.* **1.** a cardinal number, ten plus nine. **2.** a symbol for this number, as 19 or XIX. **3. talk nineteen to the dozen,** to talk very quickly or excitedly. ◊*adj.* **4.** amounting to 19 in number. [ME] **–nineteenth,** *adj., n.*

Nineteen Counties, *n.pl.* the name given to the districts of settlement in NSW in 1829.

ninety /ˈnaɪnti/, *n., pl.* **-ties,** *adj.* ◊*n.* **1.** a cardinal number, ten times nine. **2.** a symbol for this number, as 90 or XC. **3.** (*pl.*) the numbers from 90 to 99 of a series, esp. with reference to the years of a person's age, or the years of a century, esp. the 19th: *The nineties were a fascinating time.* ◊*adj.* **4.** amounting to ninety in number. [OE *nigontig*] **–ninetieth,** *adj., n.*

Nineveh /ˈnɪnəvə/, *n.* the ancient capital of Assyria; its ruins are opposite Mosul, on the river Tigris, in northern Iraq.

ninny /ˈnɪni/, *n., pl.* **-nies.** a fool; a simpleton.

ninth /naɪnθ/, *adj.* **1.** next after the eighth. **2.** being one of nine equal parts. ◊*n.* **3.** a ninth part, esp. of one ($\frac{1}{9}$). **4.** the ninth member of a series. **5.** *Music.* a note distant from another note by an interval of an octave and a second.

niobium /naɪˈoʊbiəm/, *n.* a steel-grey metallic element like tantalum. *Symbol:* Nb; *at. no.:* 41; *at. wt:* 92.906. Formerly, **columbium.** [NL; named after *Niobe*, in Greek mythology daughter of Tantalus, because found with tantalum. See -IUM] **–niobic,** *adj.* **–niobous,** *adj.*

nip /nɪp/, *v.*, **nipped, nipping,** *n.* ◊*v.t.* **1.** to press sharply between two surfaces or points; pinch or bite. **2.** to take off by pinching, biting, or snipping (usu. fol. by *off*). **3.** to check in growth or development: *to nip a plot in the bud.* **4.** to affect sharply or painfully, as cold does. ◊*n.* **5.** the act of nipping; a pinch. **6.** (of cold or frosty air) a biting quality. **7.** a biting taste or tang, as in cheese. **8.** a small bit or quantity of anything. [ME]

nipper /ˈnɪpə/, *n.* **1.** someone or something which nips. **2.** (*usu. pl.*) a tool for nipping, as pincers or forceps: *tile nippers.* **3.** one of the large claws of a crab, lobster etc. **4.** *Colloq.* a small boy or younger brother.

nipple /ˈnɪpəl/, *n.* **1.** a part of the breast, where, in the female, the milk ducts discharge; teat. **2.** something resembling it, such as the mouthpiece of a baby's bottle or the small valve on a grease gun through which oil is discharged. [orig. uncert.]

Nippon /ˈnɪpɒn/, *n.* → **Japan.** [short for *Nippon-koku*, lit., land of the origin of the sun]

nippy /ˈnɪpi/, *adj.*, **-pier, -piest. 1.** that nips; sharp; biting. **2.** (of the weather) bitingly cold. **3.** *Colloq.* active; nimble.

nirvana /nɜˈvanə, nɪə-/, *n.* **1.** (*oft. cap.*) (in Buddhism) a state, arrived at through much practice, of being completely peaceful and calm in the body, mind and spirit. **2.** freedom from pain, worry, and the outside world. [Skt: a blowing out (as of a light)]

nisi /ˈnaɪsaɪ/, *conj.* **1.** unless. ◊*adj.* **2.** *Law.* (of a court order, decree, etc.) depending on certain conditions; not coming into effect unless someone fails to prove that it should be cancelled before a certain time: *a decree nisi.* [L]

Nissen hut /ˈnɪsən hʌt/, *n.* a long, steel prefabricated shelter esp. used by soldiers. [named after Colonel PN *Nissen*, 1871–1930, British mining engineer, the inventor]

nit /nɪt/, *n.* **1.** the egg of a parasitic insect attached to a hair, or a fibre of clothing; particularly the egg of a louse. **2.** the insect while young. **3.** *Colloq.* a foolish or stupid person. [OE *hnitu*]

nitpick /ˈnɪtpɪk/, *v.i.* to be too critical, concerned with small details that are not really importan*. [NIT + PICK¹] **–nitpicker,** *n.* **–nitpicking,** *n., adj.*

nitr-, variant of **nitro-,** before vowels.

nitrate /ˈnaɪtreɪt/, *n., v.*, **-trated, -trating.** ◊*n.* **1.** *Chem.* See **-ate².** **2.** fertiliser consisting of potassium nitrate or sodium nitrate. ◊*v.t.* **3.** to treat with nitric acid or a nitrate. **4.** to convert into a nitrate. [NITRE + -ATE²]

nitration /naɪˈtreɪʃən/, *n.* nitrification.

nitre /ˈnaɪtə/, *n.* **1.** white potassium nitrate, KNO_3, used in making gunpowder, etc.; saltpetre. **2.** sodium nitrate, $NaNO_3$; Chile saltpetre. [ME, from L, from Gk: natron, native sodium carbonate]

nitric /ˈnaɪtrɪk/, *adj.* **1.** *Chem.* containing nitrogen, usu. in the pentavalent state. **2.** of or pertaining to nitre. [F]

nitric acid, *n.* a corrosive liquid, HNO_3, with powerful oxidising properties.

nitrify /'naɪtrəfaɪ/, *v.t.*, **-fied, -fying. 1.** to change (organic compounds of nitrogen) to nitrites or nitrates, esp. by bacterial action. **2.** to fertilise (soil, etc.) with nitrates. [F] – **nitrification**, *n.*

nitrile /'naɪtrəl, -traɪl/, *n.* any of a class of organic compounds with the general formula RCN. Also, **nitril** /'naɪtrəl/. [NITR(OGEN) + -ILE]

nitrite /'naɪtraɪt/, *n.* See **-ite**[1].

nitro-, 1. a word part meaning the group NO_2. **2.** a wrong name for the nitrate group NO_3, as in *nitrocellulose*. Also, **nitr-**. [Gk, combining form of *nítron* native sodium carbonate]

nitrobacteria /ˌnaɪtroʊbækˈtɪəriə/, *n.pl.* bacteria of the soil, concerned with nitrification. Also, **nitric bacteria**.

nitrogen /'naɪtrədʒən/, *n.* a colorless, odorless, gaseous element which forms most of the atmosphere and is present (combined) in animal and vegetable tissues, chiefly in proteins. It is used in compounds as fertiliser, explosives, and dyes. *Symbol:* N; *at. no.:* 7; *at. wt:* 14.0067. [F] – **nitrogenous**, *adj.*

nitrogen cycle, *n.* the continuous interaction of nitrogen and nitrogen compounds in nature between the atmosphere, the soil, and the various organisms to which nitrogen is essential.

nitrogen dioxide, *n.* a dark brown poisonous gas, NO_2, used as a nitrating and oxidising agent.

nitrogen fixation, *n.* **1.** any process of combining free nitrogen from the air with other elements, either by chemical means or by bacterial action, used esp. in the preparation of fertilisers, industrial products, etc. **2.** this process as performed by bacteria (**nitrogen fixers**) found in nodules of leguminous plants, such as peas, which make the resulting nitrogenous compounds available to their host plants. – **nitrogen-fixing**, *adj.*

nitrogenous /naɪˈtrɒdʒənəs/, *adj.* containing nitrogen.

nitroglycerine /naɪtroʊˈɡlɪsərɪn/, *n.* a colorless, highly explosive oil, the main chemical of dynamite and certain rocket powders. Also, **nitroglycerin** /naɪtroʊˈɡlɪsərən/.

nitro group /'naɪtroʊ ɡrup/, *n.* the univalent radical $-NO_2$.

nitrous /'naɪtrəs/, *adj.* containing nitrogen in its lower valency states, as nitrous oxide, N_2O, called laughing gas, used as an anaesthetic. [L: full of natron. See NITRE]

nitty-gritty /ˈnɪti-ˌɡrɪti/, *n. Colloq.* the centre of a matter: *Let's get down to the nitty-gritty.* [orig. uncert.]

nitwit /'nɪtwɪt/, *n.* a slow-thinking or foolish person.

Niue /'njueɪ/, *n.* an island in the South Pacific between Tonga and the Cook Islands; a self-governing territory of New Zealand. Pop. 3000 (1985 est.); about 260 km². Also, **Savage Island**. – **Niuan**, *n., adj.*

Niu Gini /nju 'ɡɪni/, *n.* → **New Guinea**.

Niven /'nɪvən/, *n.* **David**, 1909–83, British film actor; films include *Separate Tables* (1958) for which he won an Academy Award.

nix /nɪks/, *Colloq.* ◇*n.* **1.** nothing. ◇*adv.* **2.** no. [G: nothing]

Nixon /'nɪksən/, *n.* **Richard Milhous**, born 1913, 37th president of the US 1969–74; during his term the US recognised the government of the People's Republic of China and withdrew from the Vietnam War; following Watergate, he became the first US president to resign from office.

Njord /njɔd/, *n. Scand. Myth.* the father of Frey and Freya; the dispenser of riches. Also, **Njorth** /njɔθ/.

Nkomo /əŋˈkoʊmoʊ/, *n.* **Joshua**, born 1917, Zimbabwean politician; leader, with Robert Mugabe of the Patriotic Front (1976–80); government minister (1980–82).

NNE, *Abbrev.* north-north-east. See Appendix.

NNW, *Abbrev.* north-north-west. See Appendix.

no[1] /noʊ/, *adv., n., pl.* **noes**. ◇*adv.* **1.** a word used: **a.** to express denial, disagreement, or refusal, as in reply (opposed to *yes*). **b.** to add force to an earlier negative, or to change or limit an earlier statement: *We will not give in, no, never!*; *I have seen her twice, no three times.* **3.** not in any degree; not at all (used with a comparative): *He is no better.* **4.** not: *whether or no.* ◇*n.* **5.** an act of speaking of the word 'no'. **6.** a disagreement or refusal. **7.** a negative vote or voter. [ME; OE *nā*]

no[2] /noʊ/, *adj.* **1.** not any: *no money.* **2.** very far from being a; not at all a: *He is no genius.* [var. of NONE]

No[1], *Abbrev.* **1.** number. ◇*Symbol.* **2.** *Chem.* nobelium.

No[2] /noʊ/, *n.* a type of highly stylised Japanese classical drama, first developed in the 15th century, employing music, dancing, a chorus, symbolic scenery, and elaborate costumes and masks. Also, **Noh, Nō**. [Jap: lit., ability]

nob /nɒb/, *n. Colloq.* a member of an exclusive social group. [orig. uncert.]

no-ball /noʊ-ˈbɔl/, *n. Cricket.* a ball bowled in a way not allowed by the rules and automatically giving the batsman a score of one run.

nobble /'nɒbəl/, *v.t.,* **-bled, -bling.** *Colloq.* **1.** to disable (a horse), esp. by drugging it. **2.** to win (a person, etc.) over by underhand means. **3.** to cheat people out of money; swindle. **4.** to catch or seize. [backformation from *nobbler*, var. of HOBBLER (*an 'obbler* being taken as *a nobbler*)]

nobelium /noʊˈbiliəm/, *n.* a synthetic, radioactive element. *Symbol:* No; *at. no.:* 102; *at. wt:* 225. [*Nobel* Institute, where first identified + -IUM]

Nobel prize, *n.* one of a number of prizes awarded annually for achievement during the preceding year in physics, chemistry, medicine, literature, and the promotion of peace; prize for economics added in 1969. [awarded from the bequest of Alfred *Nobel*, 1833–96, Swedish chemist, inventor and philanthropist]

nobility /nou'biləti/, *n., pl.* **-ties. 1.** the noble class of a country. **2.** noble birth or rank. **3.** the state or quality of being noble. **4.** high moral excellence. **5.** greatness; grandeur. [ME, from OF, from L]

noble /'noubəl/, *adj.*, **nobler, noblest,** *n.* ◇*adj.* **1.** noted by birth, rank, or title. **2.** belonging to or making up a class (the nobility) possessing a social or political importance passed down from parents to children, in a country or state. **3.** of a high moral character: *a noble thought.* **4.** of an admirably high quality; superior. **5.** forceful in appearance; stately: *a noble monument.* **6.** *Chem.* inert; chemically inactive. **7.** (of some metals, as gold and platinum) not able to be corroded in air or water, and very valuable and scarce. ◇*n.* **8.** a person of noble birth or rank; nobleman. [ME, from OF, from L: well-known, high-born] **–nobly,** *adv.*

noble gas, *n. Chem.* → **rare gas.**

nobleman /'noubəlmən/, *n., pl.* **-men.** a man of noble birth or rank; noble. **–noblewoman,** *n. fem.*

nobody /'noubɒdi, -bədi/, *pron., n., pl.* **-bodies.** ◇*pron.* **1.** no person. ◇*n.* **2.** a person of no importance, esp. socially.

no-claim bonus /nou-'kleim ,bounəs/, *n. Insurance.* a reduction in premium payments offered to policy holders who have made no claim for some time.

nocti-, a word part meaning 'night'. Also (before a vowel), **noct-.** [L, combining form of *nox*]

nocturnal /nɒk'tɜnəl/, *adj.* **1.** of or relating to the night. **2.** done, happening, or coming by night. **3.** (of many animals) active by night. **4.** (of some flowers) opening by night and closing by day. [late ME, from L: of or in the night]

nocturne /'nɒktɜn/, *n. Music.* **1.** a piece for the night or evening. **2.** an instrumental piece of music of a dreamy or thoughtful character. [F, from LL: of the night]

nod /nɒd/, *v.*, **nodded, nodding,** *n.* ◇*v.i.* **1.** to make a slight, quick downwards movement of the head, esp. in agreement, greeting, command, etc. **2.** to let the head fall forwards with a sudden movement when sleepy. **3.** to grow careless, inattentive, or dull. **4.** (of trees, flowers, etc.) to bend down with a swinging movement. ◇*v.t.* **5.** to bend down (the head) in a short, quick movement. **6.** to express or show by such a movement of the head: *to nod agreement.* ◇*v.* **7. nod off,** *Colloq.* to go to sleep. ◇*n.* **8.** a short, quick bending down of the head, esp. in agreement, greeting, command, or sleepiness. **9.** a bending or swinging movement of anything. **10. get the nod,** *Colloq.* to gain approval or permission. **11. give the nod to,** *Colloq.* to allow; permit. [ME; orig. obscure]

noddy /'nɒdi/, *n., pl.* **-dies. 1.** any of several rather dark, white-capped terns often found in warm coastal and offshore areas, usu. so fearless of man as to seem stupid. **2.** a fool; simpleton. [? n. use of *noddy*, *adj.*, silly; orig. uncert.]

node /noud/, *n.* **1.** a knot, lump, or knob. **2.** a difficulty; complication. **3.** a centring point of component parts. **4.** *Bot.* **a.** a joint in a stem. **b.** a part of a stem which normally bears a leaf. **5.** *Phys.* a point, line, or region in a vibrating medium at which there is no displacement as in standing waves. [L: knot] **–nodose,** *adj.* **–nodal,** *adj.*

nodule /'nɒdʒul/, *n.* **1.** a small knot, or part sticking out. **2.** a small rounded mass or lump. **3.** *Bot.* → **tubercle.** [L: node] **–nodular,** *adj.* **–nodulous,** *adj.*

Noel /nou'ɛl/, *n.* **1.** Christmas. **2.** (*l.c.*) a Christmas song or carol. [F, from L: birthday]

noggin /'nɒgən/, *n.* **1.** a small cup or mug. **2.** *Colloq.* the head. **3.** → **nogging.**

nogging /'nɒgɪŋ/, *n.* the short lengths of wood placed horizontally between upright studs in a timber frame wall. Also, **noggin.**

no-hoper /nou-'houpə/, *n. Colloq.* **1.** someone who shows no ability: *He is a real no-hoper at tennis.* **2.** a social misfit.

noise /nɔɪz/, *n., v.*, **noised, noising.** ◇*n.* **1.** a sound, esp. of a loud, unpleasant, or confused kind: *deafening noise.* **2.** a sound of any kind. **3.** loud shouting or outcry; clamor. **4.** *Elect.* interference which degrades the useful information in a signal. **5.** *Archaic.* a rumor. ◇*v.t.* **6.** to spread (a report, rumor, etc.). [ME, from OF, from L: seasickness]

noisome /'nɔɪsəm/, *adj.* **1.** offensive or sickening, often as to smell. **2.** harmful to health; injurious; noxious. [ME]

noisy /'nɔɪzi/, *adj.*, **noisier, noisiest. 1.** making a lot of noise: *a noisy crowd.* **2.** full of noise: *a noisy street.* **–noisily,** *adv.* **–noisiness,** *n.*

noisy miner, *n.* a miner of eastern Australia marked by its brown wings with grey-white feathers and noted for harsh-sounding cries; soldier bird.

Nolan /'noulən/, *n.* **Sir Sidney Robert,** 1917–92, Australian artist; noted for his paintings of the Australian outback.

Nolde /'nɒldə/, *n.* **Emil,** 1867–1956, German expressionist painter.

nom., *Abbrev.* nominative.

nomad /'noumæd/, *n.* **1.** someone of a race or tribe without a fixed place to live, but moving about according to the state of the land for grazing, the food supply, etc. **2.** any wanderer. [L, from Gk: roaming (like cattle)] **–nomadic,** *adj.* **–nomadism,** *n.*

no-man's-land /'nou-mænz-lænd/, *n.* **1.** an area not possessed by any power, e.g. the area between opposing armies. **2.** any place which is to be avoided as dangerous. **3.** a condition or period of insecurity resulting from the loss or disturbance of culture or identity.

nom de plume /'nɒm də plum/, *n.* → **pen-name.** [coined in E from F words; lit., pen name]

nomenclature /nəˈmenklətʃə, ˈnoumənkleɪtʃə/, n. 1. a set or system of names or terms, esp. those used in a particular science or art. 2. the names or terms forming a set or system. [L]

nominal /ˈnɒmənəl/, adj. 1. being so in name only; so-called: *nominal peace*. 2. (of a price, consideration, etc.) named only as a matter of form, being small in comparison with the actual value. 3. of, relating to, or consisting in a name or names. 4. *Gram.* **a.** of, relating to, or producing a noun or nouns. **b.** used as or like a noun. [ME, from L: pertaining to names]

nominate /ˈnɒməneɪt/, v.t., **-nated, -nating.** 1. to put forward as a proper person for appointment or election to an office. 2. to appoint for a duty or office. 3. to enter (a horse, etc.) in a race. [L: named] —**nomination,** n. —**nominator,** n.

nominative /ˈnɒmənətɪv, ˈnɒmnə-/, adj. 1. put forward usu. for election etc.; appointed by nomination. ◇n. 2. *Gram.* →**nominative case.** [L: serving to name]

nominative case, n. *Gram.* See **case**[1] and Appendix.

nominee /nɒməˈni/, n. 1. someone put forward usu. to fill an office or stand for election. 2. a person appointed by another to act in their place.

-nomy, a word part meaning 'distribution', 'arrangement', 'management', or having reference to laws or government, as in *astronomy, economy, taxonomy*. [Gk *-nomía*, from *nómos* custom, law. See -IA]

non-, a prefix indicating 1. the fact of not being a member of a particular class or group: *a non-Jew; a non-metal*. 2. objective negation or opposition: *non-porous, non-recurrent*. 3. failure to fulfil a claim: *a non-event; a non-hero*. 4. the absence of activity or performance in the area named: *non-arrival, non-publication*. [representing L *nōn* not; not a L prefix]

nonaggression /nɒnəˈɡreʃən/, n. the planned avoidance of any offensive action, esp. where hostility exists.

nonagon /ˈnɒnəɡɒn, -ɡən/, n. a polygon having nine angles and nine sides. [L: ninth] —**nonagonal,** adj.

nonce /nɒns/, n. 1. the one or particular occasion or purpose. 2. **for the nonce,** for this one occasion only; for the time being. [ME]

nonchalant /ˈnɒnʃələnt/, adj. coolly unconcerned; indifferent; casual. [F] —**nonchalance,** n.

non-combatant /nɒn-ˈkɒmbətənt/, n. 1. someone who is not a fighter; a civilian in time of war. 2. someone connected with but not fighting in a military or naval force, e.g. a doctor, priest, etc.

non-commissioned /ˈnɒn-kəmɪʃənd/, adj. not commissioned (applied esp. to military employees such as sergeants and corporals, ranking below warrant officer).

non-committal /ˈnɒn-kəmɪtl/, adj. not binding oneself to a particular view, course, etc.: *a non-committal answer*.

non compos /nɒn ˈkɒmpəs/, adj. *Colloq.* 1. in an unclear or confused state of mind. 2. not of sound mind; mentally incapable. [short for L *non compos mentis*]

non-conductor /nɒn-kənˈdʌktə/, n. a substance which does not readily conduct or pass along heat, sound, electricity, etc.; an insulator. —**non-conducting,** adj.

nonconformist /nɒnkənˈfɔːməst/, n. 1. someone who refuses to conform, esp. to an established Church such as the Church of England. 2. someone who does not follow the accepted social standards of behavior, etc. —**nonconformity, nonconformance,** n.

nondescript /ˈnɒndəskrɪpt/, adj. 1. of no recognised, definite, or particular type or kind: *a nondescript garment*. ◇n. 2. a person or a thing of no particular type or kind. [NON- + L: described]

none /nʌn/, pron. 1. no one; not one: *There is none to help*. 2. not any: *That is none of your business*. 3. no part; nothing. 4. (*treated as pl.*) no, or not any, people or things: *None were suitable*. ◇adv. 5. in no way; not at all: *The supply is none too great*. [OE *nān*]

nonentity /nɒnˈentəti/, n., pl. **-ties.** 1. a person or thing of no importance. 2. something which does not exist, or exists only in the imagination. 3. non-existence. [NON- + ENTITY]

nonetheless /nʌnðəˈles/, adv. however; nevertheless. Also, **none the less.**

non-fiction /nɒn-ˈfɪkʃən/, n. 1. a class of writing comprising works dealing with facts and historical events, rather than imaginative narration. ◇adj. 2. Also, **non-fictional.** relating or referring to writing of this class.

nonflammable /nɒnˈflæməbəl/, adj. not easily set alight; slow-burning; not flammable.

nong /nɒŋ/, n. *Colloq.* a fool; idiot. [orig. uncert.]

non-intervention /ˌnɒn-ɪntəˈvenʃən/, n. a failure or refusal to come between two or more parties esp. to prevent a bad outcome.

no-nonsense /ˈnoʊ-nɒnsəns/, adj. *Colloq.* 1. practical. 2. strict. 3. not showy; modest.

nonpareil /ˈnɒnpərel, -reɪl/, adj. 1. having no equal; peerless. ◇n. 2. a person or thing having no equal; something unique. [late ME, from F]

nonplus /nɒnˈplʌs/, v., **-plussed, -plussing,** n. ◇v.t. 1. to puzzle completely. ◇n. 2. a state of complete puzzlement. [L: not more, no further]

non-productive /nɒn-prəˈdʌktɪv/, adj. 1. not producing goods directly, such as employees in charge of other employees, inspectors, etc. 2. producing nothing; unhelpful.

non-proliferation /ˌnɒn-prəlɪfəˈreɪʃən/, n. the attempt to prevent any increase in the world supply of nuclear weapons.

non-representational /ˌnɒn-reprəzənˈteɪʃənəl/, adj. not looking like any object in physical nature: *a non-representational painting*.

non-sectarian /nɒn-sekˈtɛəriən/, adj. not associated with any one religious group.

nonsense /ˈnɒnsəns/, *n.* **1.** ideas or words which make no sense or are foolish. **2.** a senseless or foolish action or behavior, etc.: *to stand no nonsense from a person.* **3.** silliness; absurdity. – **nonsensical**, *adj.*

non sequitur /nɒn ˈsɛkwɪtə/, *n.* a conclusion which does not come or derive logically from earlier statements. [L: it does not follow]

non-U /nɒnˈju/, *adj. Colloq.* not accepted by or typical of the upper class. [NON- + U(*pper class*)]

non-violence /nɒn-ˈvaɪələns/, *n.* **1.** the principle of avoiding the use of violence on all occasions. **2.** the practice of this principle. – **non-violent**, *adj.*

noodle /ˈnudl/, *n.* a type of pasta, cut into long, narrow, flat strips and served in soups or, with a sauce, as a main dish. [G]

nook /nʊk/, *n.* **1.** a corner, esp. in a room. **2.** any small, private or hidden place. [ME]

noolbenger /ˈnʊlbɛŋə/, *n.* See **possum**.

noon /nun/, *n.* **1.** midday; the middle of the day, when the sun is directly overhead. **2.** 12 o'clock in the daytime. **3.** the highest, brightest, or finest point or part. Also, **noontide**. [OE *nōn*, from L: ninth hour]

no-one /ˈnoʊ-wʌn/, *pron.* nobody. Also, **no one**.

Noosa Heads /ˌnusə ˈhɛdz/, *n.* a tourist resort in coastal eastern Qld, north of Tewantin. Pop (with Tewantin) 11 296 (1986).

noose /nus/, *n., v.,* **noosed, noosing.** ◊*n.* **1.** a loop with a running knot, which tightens as the rope is pulled: *a hangman's noose.* **2.** a tie; snare. ◊*v.t.* **3.** to catch or hold by or as if by a noose. [probably from OF, from L: knot]

nope /noʊp/, *adv. Colloq.* an emphatic form of **no**[1].

nor /nɔ/, *conj.* a negative conjunction used: **1.** together with *neither*: *He could neither read nor write.* **2.** to continue the force of a negative, such as *not, no, never*, etc., from a preceding clause: *I never saw him again, nor did I regret it.* **3.** after a positive clause, in the sense of *and...not*: *Our daughter passed brilliantly, nor could we have wished for more.* [OE *nōther*]

nor[1] /nɔ/, *n., adj., adv. Chiefly Naut.* north.

Nor, *Abbrev.* North.

Nordic /ˈnɔdɪk/, *adj.* belonging or relating to a Caucasian type, with tall build, fair hair, blue eyes, and long head, seen most clearly in Scandinavians. [F from *nord* north, from Gmc]

Norfolk /ˈnɔfək/, *n.* a county in eastern England. Pop. 727 800 (1986 est.); 5320 km². *Administrative Centre:* Norwich.

Norfolk Island, *n.* an external territory of Australia situated east-north-east of Sydney, NSW; former penal settlement. About 8 km long and 5 km wide. Pop. 1977 (1986).

Norfolk Plains, *n.* an early name for a district south of Launceston, Tas; settled by people from Norfolk Island in 1813.

norm /nɔm/, *n.* **1.** a standard, model, or pattern. **2.** an average or mean. **3.** *Educ.* **a.** a marked standard of average performance of people of a given age, background, etc. **b.** a standard of average performance by a person. [L: carpenter's square, rule, pattern]

normal /ˈnɔməl/, *adj.* **1.** keeping to the standard or the common type; regular, usual, natural, or not abnormal: *the normal procedure.* **2.** serving to fix a standard. **3. a.** just about average in respect to intelligence, personality, emotional balance, etc. **b.** without any mental irregularities; sane. **4.** *Maths.* (of a line, etc.) being at right angles; perpendicular. **5.** *Chem.* **a.** (of a solution) containing one equivalent weight of the chemical in question in one litre of solution. **b.** relating to an aliphatic hydrocarbon having a straight unbranched carbon chain, each carbon atom of which is joined to no more than two other carbon atoms. See **n-**. **c.** relating to a normal element. **6.** *Biol, Med, etc.* **a.** free from any infection. **b.** happening naturally. ◊*n.* **7.** the standard or type. **8.** the normal form or state; the average or mean. **9.** *Maths.* a perpendicular line or plane, esp. one perpendicular to a tangent line of a curve, or a tangent plane of a surface, at the point of contact. [L: made according to a carpenter's square or rule] – **normalcy**, *n.* – **normality**, *n.* – **normalisation**, *n.*

normal curve, *n. Stats.* a bell-shaped curve giving the normal distribution of probability associated with the different values of a variable which is spread randomly through a population.

normal distribution, *n. Stats.* a form of distribution in which the highest frequency is at the mean score, or in which the mean, median and mode are equal. Also, **Gaussian distribution**.

normalise or **normalize** /ˈnɔməlaɪz/, *v.,* **-lised, -lising.** ◊*v.t.* **1.** to make normal. ◊*v.* **2. normalise relations**, to re-establish normal diplomatic relations with a country. – **normalisation**, *n.*

normally /ˈnɔməli/, *adv.* as a rule; regularly; according to rule, general custom, etc.

Norman[1] /ˈnɔmən/, *n.* **1.** a member of that branch of the Northmen or Scandinavians who in the tenth century conquered Normandy. **2.** one of the mixed Scandinavian and French race later inhabiting this region, which conquered England in 1066. **3.** *Archit.* relating to or naming a variety of the Romanesque style. [ME, backformation from OF *Normans*, *pl.* of *Normant* Northman]

Norman[2] /ˈnɔmən/, *n.* a river in northern Qld rising in the Gregory Range and flowing in a north-westerly direction into the Gulf of Carpentaria. 420 km.

Norman Conquest, *n.* the conquest of England by the Normans, under William the Conqueror, in 1066.

Normandy /ˈnɔməndi/, *n.* an area in northern France on the English Channel; invaded and settled by Northmen in the tenth century; it became a duchy and later a province; its capital was Rouen. Allied invasion World War II began 6 June 1944. French, **Normandie**.

normative /ˈnɔmətɪv/, *adj.* concerning or establishing a norm, esp. one regarded as the standard of correctness in speech and writing.

Norse /nɔs/, *adj.* belonging or relating to (ancient) Norway or Scandinavia. [probably from D]

north /nɔθ/, *n.* **1.** a cardinal point of the compass to the right of a person facing the setting sun or the west. See Appendix. **2.** the direction in which this point lies. **3.** → **magnetic north. 4.** (*l.c. or cap.*) an area in this direction. ◇*adj.* **5.** lying towards or placed in the north. **6.** directed or moving forwards towards the north. **7.** (of a wind, etc.) coming from the north. **8.** (*cap.*) marking the northern part of an area, nation, country, etc.: *north Atlantic.* ◇*adv.* **9.** towards or in the north. **10.** from the north. Also, *esp. Naut*, **nor'**. [ME and OE]

North /nɔθ/, *n.* **Frederick (2nd Earl of Guilford)**, 1732–92, British statesman; prime minister 1770–82.

Northam /ˈnɔðəm/, *n.* a town and shire in south-eastern WA, north-east of Perth; an important rail centre. Pop. 6377 (1986).

North America, *n.* the northernmost continent of the Western Hemisphere, extending from Central America to the Arctic Ocean. Highest point, Mt McKinley, Alaska, 6187 m; lowest, Death Valley, California, 84 m below sea-level. 24 400 000 km². **– North American**, *n.*, *adj.*

North Atlantic Drift, *n.* a continuation of the Gulf Stream, flowing north-east across the Atlantic Ocean towards the British Isles.

North Atlantic Treaty Organisation, *n.* →NATO

North Carolina, *n.* a state in the south-eastern US, on the Atlantic coast. Pop. 6 331 000 (1986 est.); 14 794 km². *Cap.*: Raleigh. *Abbrev.*: NC **– North Carolinian**, *n.*, *adj.*

Northcote /ˈnɔθkɒt/, *n.* a city and municipality within Melbourne, Vic; its southern boundary is the site of the making of the treaty between John Batman and the Aborigines. Pop. 48 552 (1988).

Northcott /ˈnɔθkɒt/, *n.* **Sir John**, 1890–1966, Australian soldier and governor of NSW 1946–57; the first Australian to hold this office.

North Dakota *n.* a state in the northern central US. Pop. 679 000 (1986 est.); 183 022 km². *Cap.*: Bismarck. *Abbrev.*: N Dak **– North Dakotan**, *n.*, *adj.*

north-east /nɔθˈist/, *n.*, /ˈnɔθ-ist/. ◇*n.* **1.** the point or direction midway between north and east. See Appendix. ◇*adj.* **2.** (of a wind) coming from the north-east. Also, *esp. Naut*, **nor'-east. – north-eastern**, *adj.*

north-easter /nɔθˈistə/, *n.* a wind from the north-east. Also, *esp. Naut*, **nor'-easter.**

northerly /ˈnɔðəli/, *adj.* **1.** moving, directed, or placed towards the north. **2.** (of a wind) coming or placed from the north. ◇*adv.* **3.** towards the north. **4.** from the north. **– northerliness**, *n.*

northern /ˈnɔðən/, *adj.* **1.** in, towards, or (of a wind) from the north. **2.** of or relating to the north. [ME and OE *northerne*]

Northern /ˈnɔðən/, *n.* a province in eastern PNG. Pop. 90 300 (1986 est.); 22 800 km². *Administrative Centre:* Popondetta. Also, **Oro.**

northerner /ˈnɔðənə/, *n.* a person who lives or was born in a northern country or area.

Northern Hemisphere, *n.* the half of the earth between the North Pole and the equator.

Northern Ireland, *n.* a country in north-western Europe, part of the UK; a division of the island of Ireland in the north-eastern part; separated from the rest of Ireland which became autonomous in 1922; limited self-government with a separate parliament but since 1974 directly under UK rule because of violent conflict between Catholic and Protestant populations. Pop. 1 567 000 (1986 est.); 14 120 km². *Cap.*: Belfast. See **United Kingdom**.

northern lights, *n.pl.* → **aurora borealis.**

Northern Territory, *n.* a self-governing territory occupying the central part of the northern half of Australia. Pop. 154 848 (1986); 1 346 200 km². *Administrative Capital:* Darwin. *Abbrev.*: NT

North Island, *n.* one of the two main islands of NZ, separated from the South Island by Cook Strait. About 114 700 km².

North Korea, *n.* a republic in north-eastern Asia, occupying the northern part of the Korean peninsula, bordered by China and South Korea. Pop. 21 390 000 (1987 est.); 120 538 km². *Language:* Korean. *Currency:* won. *Cap.*: Pyongyang. Official name, **Democratic People's Republic of Korea**. See **Korea**. **– North Korean**, *n.*, *adj.*

North Pole, *n.* **1.** that end of the earth's axis of rotation marking the northernmost point on the earth. **2.** *Astron.* the zenith of the earth's north pole.

North Sea, *n.* an arm of the Atlantic between the east coast of Great Britain and the European mainland. About 520 600 km²; greatest depth, 609 m.

Northumberland /nɔˈθʌmbələnd/, *n.* **1.** a county in north-eastern England. Pop. 301 100 (1986 est.); 5229 km². *Administrative Centre:* Newcastle upon Tyne. *Abbrev.*: Northld, Northumb **2. Cape**, a promontory in the south-eastern corner of SA, the state's most southerly point.

Northumbria /nɔˈθʌmbriə/, *n.* an early English kingdom extending from the Humber north to the Firth of Forth.

North Vietnam, *n.* a region in northern Vietnam; between 1954 and 1976 a communist republic. 164 060 km².

northward /ˈnɔθwəd/, *adj.* **1.** moving, bearing, facing, or placed towards the north. ◇*n.* **2.** the northward part, direction, or point. ◇*adv.* **3.** Also, **northwards**, towards the north.

north-west /nɔθˈwɛst/, *n.*; /ˈnɔθ-wɛst/, *adj.* ◇*n.* **1.** the point or direction midway between north and west. See Appendix. ◇**2.**

(of a wind) coming from the north-west. Also, *esp. Naut,* **nor'-west.** – **north-western,** *adj.*

North West Cape, *n.* the northernmost point of a cape enclosing Exmouth Gulf in north-western WA; site of the US Naval Communications Station.

north-wester /nɔθ-'westə/, *n.* a wind from the north-west. Also, *esp. Naut,* **nor'-wester.**

North-West Passage, *n.* a ship route along the arctic coast of Canada and Alaska, joining the Atlantic and Pacific oceans.

North West Shelf, *n.* the name commonly given to a part of the continental shelf off Australia's north-western coast; location of a natural gas field.

Norton /'nɔtn/, *n.* **John,** 1862–1916, English-born Australian journalist and politician; editor and sole proprietor of the newspaper *Truth* in 1890; member NSW Legislative Assembly 1898.

Norway /'nɔweɪ/, *n.* a kingdom in north-western Europe, in the western part of the Scandinavian peninsula, bordered by Sweden, Finland and Russia; gained independence from Sweden in 1905. Pop. 4 180 000 (1987 est.); 323 895 km². *Language:* Norwegian. *Currency:* krone. *Cap.:* Oslo. Norwegian, **Norge.**

nos-, a variant of **noso-,** before vowels.

Nos, *Abbrev.* numbers. Also, **nos.**

nose /noʊz/, *n., v.,* **nosed, nosing.** ◇*n.* **1.** the part of the face or head which contains the nostrils, providing passage for air in breathing, etc. **2.** this part as the organ of smell: *The aroma of coffee greeted his nose.* **3.** the sense of smell: *a dog with a good nose.* **4.** an ability of understanding or finding out: *a nose for news.* **5.** the quality of prying or interfering: *Keep your nose out of it.* **6.** something regarded as looking like the nose, e.g. the prow of a ship, the front end of an aircraft. **7.** (of wines) → **bouquet** (def. 2). **8.** the length of the nose of a horse or other animal as a measure in racing. ◇**9.** Some special uses are:

by a nose, *Colloq.* by a very small amount.
lead by the nose, to exercise complete control over.

on the nose, *Colloq.* **1.** smelly, esp. because decayed. **2.** unpleasant; distasteful.
pay through the nose, to pay too high a price.
turn one's nose up, to be ungrateful or contemptuous.
under one's nose, in an obvious place.
◇*v.t.* **10.** to sense by or as if by the nose. **11.** to bring the nose close to; sniff: *to nose a glass of wine.* **12.** to move or push forward. **13.** to touch or rub with the nose; nuzzle. ◇*v.i.* **14.** to smell; sniff. **15.** to look for as if by smelling (fol. by *after, for,* etc.); pry (fol. by *about, into,* etc.): *The dog nosed for a lost bone; He is nosing into my papers.* **16.** to move or push forwards. **17.** to meddle or pry. [ME; OE *nosu*]

nosebag /'noʊzbæɡ/, *n.* a bag for feeding horses, placed before the mouth with bands around the head.

nosedive /'noʊzdaɪv/, *n., v.,* **-dived, -diving.** ◇*n.* **1.** a drop of an aeroplane with the front part of the craft straight downwards. **2.** any sudden drop. ◇*v.i.* **3.** to go into a nosedive.

nosegay /'noʊzɡeɪ/, *n.* a bunch of flowers, or herbs; bouquet; posy. [ME; lit., a *gay* (obs., something pretty) for the NOSE (i.e., to smell)]

nosey /'noʊzi/, *adj.,* **-sier, -siest.** → **nosy.**

noso-, a word part meaning 'disease'. Also, **nos-.** [Gk, combining form of *nósos*]

nostalgia /nɒs'tældʒə/, *n.* a longing and desire for home, family and friends, or for the past. [NL, from Gk: a return to home] –**nostalgic,** *adj.* –**nostalgically,** *adv.*

Nostradamus /ˌnɒstrə'dɑməs, -'deɪməs/, *n.* (*Michel de Notredame*) 1503–66, French astrologer and physician. –**Nostradamic,** *adj.*

nostril /'nɒstrəl/, *n.* one of the outside openings of the nose. [OE *nosterl*]

nostrum /'nɒstrəm/, *n.* **1.** a medicine falsely claiming power to cure. **2.** a medicine made by the person who suggests its use or sells it. **3.** a pet plan or invention for doing something. [L: our, ours (cf. def. 3)]

nosy /'noʊzi/, *adj.,* **-sier, -siest.** *Colloq.* overly interested in the affairs of others; prying; inquisitive. Also, **nosey.** –**nosily,** *adv.* –**nosiness,** *n.*

nosy parker, *n.* someone who continually looks into the affairs of others; meddler; stickybeak.

not /nɒt/, *adv.* (a word expressing negation, denial or refusal): *not far; You must not do that.* [ME]

nota bene /ˌnoʊtə 'beneɪ/, note well. *Abbrev.:* NB [L]

notable /'noʊtəbəl/, *adj.* **1.** worthy of note or notice: *a notable success.* **2.** noticeable, important, or famous. ◇*n.* **3.** a notable person. [ME, from L] –**notability,** *n.* –**notably,** *adv.*

notary /'noʊtəri/, *n., pl.* **-ries.** an official, usu. a solicitor, given the power to certify contracts, recognise deeds, etc. Also, **notary public.** [ME, from L: shorthand writer, clerk, secretary] –**notarial,** *adj.*

notation /noʊ'teɪʃən/, *n.* **1.** a system of graphic symbols for a specialised use, other than ordinary writing: *Musical notation uses lines to represent pitch and other symbols to represent time or rhythm.* **2.** the process of noting or setting down by means of a special system of signs. **3.** the act of noting, marking, or setting down in writing. **4.** a note or record. [L: a marking]

notch /nɒtʃ/, *n.* **1.** an angular cut, mark, or hollow in a narrow object or surface or an edge. **2.** a cut made in a stick or other object for record, usu. in keeping a score. **3.** *Geog.* an area cut away by the action of waves on the base of a cliff. **4.** *Colloq.* a step or degree. ◇*v.t.* **5.** to cut or make a notch or notches in. **6.** to record by a notch or notches. **7.** to score, usu. in a game (fol. by *up*): *He notched up three more deals before Saturday.* [AF]

note /noʊt/, *n., v.,* **noted, noting.** ◇*n.* **1.** a short record of something set down to help the memory. **2.** (*pl.*) a record of a speech, lecture, etc., or of one's own thoughts on something. **3.** an explanation, opinion, or mention of other sources, added by an editor or author to a passage in a book. **4.** a short written or printed statement giving particulars or information. **5.** a short informal letter. **6.** a formal diplomatic or official message or information in writing. **7.** a paper recognising money owed and promising payment; promissory note. **8.** high rank; distinction: *a man of note*. **9.** importance; consequence: *no other thing of note this year*. **10.** notice; heed: *Take careful note of this rule*. **11.** a characteristic feature. **12.** a sound (of musical quality) produced by a singer, instrument, bird, etc. **13.** *Music.* a sign or character used to represent a sound, where its position shows its pitch, and its form shows its length. **14.** a signal, hint, suggestion, etc.: *a note of warning*; *a note of unhappiness in her voice*. ◊*v.t.* **15.** to mark down, usu. in writing. **16.** to make particular mention of in a writing. **17.** to give attention or heed to. **18.** to take notice of; perceive. [ME, from L: a mark]

noted /ˈnoʊtəd/, *adj.* **1.** famous; celebrated. **2.** specially looked at or noticed.

nothing /ˈnʌθɪŋ/, *n.* **1.** no thing; not anything; naught: *Say nothing*. **2.** no part, share, or mark (fol. by *of*): *The place shows nothing of its former beauty*. **3.** something that is nonexistent. **4.** something or somebody of no importance. **5.** an action, matter, thing, or remark of little importance. **6.** something that is without quantity or size. ◊**7.** Some special uses are:
for nothing, free of charge.
make nothing of, 1. to be unable to understand. **2.** to cope easily with; treat lightly.
next to nothing, very little.
nothing doing, *Colloq.* no; definitely not.
nothing for it, no other course of action is open. ◊*adv.* **8.** in no respect or degree; not at all: *It was nothing like what we expected*. [orig. two words. See NO¹, THING]

notice /ˈnoʊtɪs/, *n., v.,* **-ticed, -ticing.** ◊*n.* **1.** information or intelligence: *to give notice of a thing*. **2.** a suggestion or warning. **3.** a note, sign, etc. carrying information or warning. **4.** an act of making known the end, at a given time, of an agreement, usu. for renting or employment, given by one of the parties to the agreement. **5.** the act of watching, understanding, attending or regarding: *worthy of notice*. **6.** interested or favorable attention. **7.** a short written mention or account, esp. of a newly published book; a review. ◊*v.t.* **8.** to pay attention to or take notice of. **9.** to perceive: *Did you notice her hat?* **10.** to treat with attention, politeness, or favor. **11.** to recognise having met someone before. **12.** to mention or direct someone's attention to; point out, usu. a person. [late ME, from OF, from L: a being known, fame, knowledge] —**noticer,** *n.*

noticeable /ˈnoʊtɪsəbəl/, *adj.* able to be noticed readily. —**noticeably,** *adv.*

notification /ˌnoʊtəfəˈkeɪʃən/, *n.* **1.** the act of making known, or giving notice. **2.** a formal informing. **3.** a notice.

notify /ˈnoʊtəfaɪ/, *v.t.,* **-fied, -fying. 1.** to give notice to, or inform, of something. **2.** to make known; give information of: *The sale was notified in the newspapers*. [ME, from OF, from L: make known] —**notifiable,** *adj.* —**notification,** *adj.* —**notifier,** *n.*

notion /ˈnoʊʃən/, *n.* **1.** a general, unclear or imperfect idea of something: *notions of beauty*. **2.** an opinion, view, or belief. **3.** a fanciful or foolish idea; whim. [L: a becoming acquainted, conception, notion]

notional /ˈnoʊʃənəl/, *adj.* **1.** having to do with or expressing a belief or idea. **2.** of the nature of a belief. **3.** beginning in and reasoned in the mind without basis in the real world. **4.** not real; imaginary; ideal.

not negotiable, *adj.* of or relating to a cheque which is crossed and has the words 'not negotiable' written on it, commonly held to mean that the cheque can be paid only into the account, the name of which appears on the cheque.

Notogaea /ˌnoʊtəˈdʒiə/, *n.* a biogeographical area of the earth's land area including Australia, NZ, part of SE Asia, and the islands of the Pacific. Formerly, Central and South America were also included. [NL, from Gk]

notoriety /ˌnoʊtəˈraɪəti/, *n., pl.* **-ties. 1.** the condition of being notorious or widely known. **2.** a widely known or well-known person.

notorious /nəˈtɔriəs/, *adj.* **1.** widely but unfavorably known: *a notorious gambler*. **2.** publicly or generally known: *notorious crimes*. [ML, from L: known]

Notre Dame /ˌnɒtrə ˈdam/, *n.* a famous early Gothic cathedral in Paris (started 1163).

Nottinghamshire /ˈnɒtɪŋəmʃɪə, -ʃə/, *n.* a county in central England. Pop. 1 006 400 (1986 est.); 2225 km². Administrative Centre: Nottingham. *Abbrev.:* Notts

notwithstanding /ˌnɒtwɪθˈstændɪŋ/, *prep.* **1.** without being withstood or prevented by; in spite of. ◊*adv.* **2.** nevertheless; yet (used after the statement it changes). ◊*conj.* **3.** in spite of the fact that; although. [ME]

nougat /ˈnugɑ/, *n.* a hard, pastelike sweet, usu. white or pink, containing almonds or other nuts. [F, from Pr, from LL: nut]

nought /nɔt/, *n.* the sign in mathematics which stands for zero (0). [OE *nōht*]

Nouméa /nuˈmiə/, *n.* the capital of New Caledonia, on the south-western coast. Pop. 60 112 (1983).

noun /naʊn/, *n.* **1.** (in most languages) one of the main form classes, or 'parts of speech', made up of words marking person, places, things, and such other words as show similar grammatical behavior, as English *friend, city, desk, whiteness, virtue*. **2.** any such word. ◊*adj.* **3.** Also, **nounal.** relating to or resembling a noun. [ME, from AF, from L: name]

nourish /ˈnʌrɪʃ/, *v.t.* **1.** to keep alive with food, etc.; supply with what is necessary for maintaining life. **2.** to encourage or further

nourish growth. [ME, from OF, from L: suckle, feed, maintain] —**nourishing**, *adj.* —**nourishment**, *n.*

nous /naʊs/, *n. Colloq.* common sense. [Gk: mind, intellect]

nouveau riche /nuvoʊ 'riʃ/, *n., pl.* **nouveaux riches** /nuvoʊ 'riʃ/. someone who has recently become rich. [F]

Nov, *Abbrev.* November.

Nova Scotia /ˌnoʊvə 'skoʊʃə/, *n.* a peninsula and province in south-eastern Canada; once a part of the French province of Acadia. Pop. 873 119 (1986); 55 490 km². *Cap.*: Halifax. —**Nova Scotian**, *n., adj.*

novel[1] /'nɒvəl/, *n.* **1.** a piece of fictitious writing which tells a story and is quite long, usu. having a plot that is developed by the actions, thoughts, speech, etc., of the characters. **2.** (formerly) a short story. [It, from L: new kind of story] —**novelist**, *n.*

novel[2] /'nɒvəl/, *adj.* of a new kind, or different from anything seen or known before: *a novel idea.* [ME, from L: new]

novelette /nɒvə'lɛt/, *n.* a short novel, esp. one that is commonplace and plays on the emotions.

novella /nɒ'vɛlə/, *n., pl.* **-le** /-li/. a short novel, more detailed than a short story. [It]

novelty /'nɒvəlti/, *n., pl.* **-ties. 1.** unusual character, newness, or strangeness. **2.** a new thing, experience, or undertaking. **3.** a new or novel article of trade; a variety of goods differing from the usual kinds. **4.** a decorative and usu. worthless article. ◇*adj.* **5.** of or relating to a new game, article, etc: *a novelty toy.* [ME, from OF, from LL: newness]

November /noʊ'vɛmbə, nə-/, *n.* the 11th month of the year, containing 30 days. [ME and OE and L: the ninth month of the early Roman year]

Novgorod /'nɒvgərɒd/, *n.* a city in north-western Russia on the Volkhov River; a former capital of Russia. Pop. 215 000 (1984).

novice /'nɒvəs/, *n.* **1.** someone who is new to the conditions, work, etc., in which he or she is placed; a tyro: *a novice in politics.* **2.** someone who has been received into a religious order or church for a period of testing before taking vows. [ME, from OF, from L: new]

novitiate /noʊ'vɪʃiət, -ieɪt/, *n.* **1.** the state or period of being a newcomer to a religious order or church. **2.** the quarters taken up by religious newcomers during the period of testing. **3.** the state or period of being a beginner in anything. **4.** a novice. Also, **noviciate**. [ML, from L: new]

Novocastrian /noʊvə'kæstriən/, *n.* one who was born in Newcastle, NSW, or who has come to regard it as their home town.

now /naʊ/, *adv.* **1.** at the present time or moment: *He is here now.* **2.** (more pronounced) immediately or at once: *now or never.* **3.** at this point in time in some period under consideration: *The case now passes to the jury.* **4.** at the time or moment only just past: *I saw him just now in the street.* **5.** in these present times; nowadays. **6.** in the present or existing conditions; as matters stand. **7.** (often used as the first word before some statement, question, etc.): *Now, what does he mean?* **8.** (to strengthen a command, request, etc.): *Come now, stop that!* **9. now and again** or **now and then**, occasionally. **10. now that,** inasmuch as. ◇*conj.* **11.** now that; since, or seeing that. ◇*n.* **12.** the present time or moment: *the here and now.* ◇*interj.* **13. now, now!** (an expression used to scold or calm someone.) [ME; OE *nū*]

nowadays /'naʊədeɪz/, *adv.* **1.** at the present day; in these times. ◇*n.* **2.** the present. [ME]

nowhere /'noʊwɛə/, *adv.* **1.** in, at, or to no place; not anywhere. ◇*n.* **2.** a state of seeming non-existence; a place unknown: *He disappeared into nowhere.* **3.** a state of not being known. **4. get nowhere,** to achieve nothing. [ME; OE *nāhwær*]

Nowra[1] /'naʊrə/, *n.* **Louis,** born 1950, Australian playwright and novelist.

Nowra[2] /'naʊrə/, *n.* a town in the South Coast region of NSW, on the Shoalhaven River. Pop. (with Bomaderry) 19 553 (1986). [Aboriginal]

noxious /'nɒkʃəs/, *adj.* **1.** harmful or hurtful to health or bodily well-being: *noxious vapors.* **2.** morally harmful; pernicious. **3.** (of an animal, insect, plant, etc.) declared harmful by law for removal or destruction. [L: hurtful] —**noxiousness**, *n.*

nozzle /'nɒzəl/, *n.* a spout, at the end of a pipe, etc., for pushing out liquids or gases in a stream or spray, usu. of a hose or rocket. [NOSE + *-le,* diminutive suffix]

Np, *Chem. Symbol.* neptunium.

NRC /ɛn a 'si/, *Abbrev.* (of a film) not recommended for children.

NSW /ɛn ɛs 'dʌbəlju/, *Abbrev.* New South Wales.

-n't, a combining form of *not,* as in *didn't, won't, can't.*

NT, *Abbrev.* **1.** New Testament. **2.** Northern Territory.

nth[1], *Abbrev.* north.

nth[2] /ɛnθ/, *adj.* **1.** standing as a sign for the last in an unlimited series of decreasing or increasing values, amounts, etc. **2. the nth degree** or **power, a.** a high (sometimes, any) degree or power. **b.** the farthest point.

nthn, *Abbrev.* northern.

NTP /ɛn ti 'pi/, *n.* normal temperature and pressure; a temperature of 0° C and a pressure of 101 325 pascals. Also, **STP**

nt wt, *Abbrev.* net weight.

nuance /'njuɒns, nju'ans/, *n.* a shade of color, expression, meaning, feeling, etc. [F]

nub /nʌb/, *n.* a knob or lump. Also, **nubble.** [var. of KNOB]

nubile /'njubaɪl/, *adj.* (of a girl or young woman) marriageable, esp. as to age or bodily development. [L] —**nubility,** *n.*

nuclear /'njuːkliə/, *adj.* **1.** of, relating to, or forming a nucleus. **2.** relating to or powered by atomic energy: *nuclear war; nuclear submarine.* **3.** armed with nuclear weapons: *a nuclear power.*

nuclear bomb, *n.* → **atomic bomb.**

nuclear energy, *n.* → **atomic energy.**

nuclear family, *n.* **1.** the family as a unit of social organisation, made up of only parents and children, where the children are the responsibility of the parents alone. **2.** the standardised idea of this unit, typically seen as husband, wife, and two children.

nuclear fission, *n.* a nuclear reaction where an atomic nucleus of an element of high atomic number, e.g. uranium, breaks down into two or more nuclei, part of its mass being changed into energy.

nuclear fusion, *n.* the coming together of two light atomic nuclei, e.g. deuterium, to form a single nucleus together with a release of energy.

nuclear power, *n.* **1.** → **atomic power.** **2.** a country which uses nuclear energy or nuclear weapons.

nuclear reaction, *n.* any reaction which involves a change in the structure or energy state of the nuclei of the interacting atoms.

nuclear reactor, *n.* the apparatus in which a selfsustaining chain reaction is maintained and controlled for the production of nuclear energy, material, or radioactive isotopes.

nucleic acid, *n.* a polynucleotide chain, present in all living cells and viruses. The two main types are ribonucleic acid and deoxyribonucleic acid.

nucleon /'njuːklɒn/, *n.* any constituent (proton or neutron) of atomic nuclei.

nucleotide /'njuːkliətaɪd/, *n.* an important constituent of ATP and the nucleic acids, made of a nitrogenous base, sugar and phosphate.

nucleus /'njuːkliəs/, *n., pl.* **-clei** /-kliaɪ/, **-cleuses. 1.** a central part or thing about which other parts or things are grouped. **2.** anything making up a central part, foundation, or beginning. **3.** *Biol.* a mass (usu. rounded) of protoplasm, encased in a delicate membrane, present inside nearly all living cells and forming a necessary element in their growth, metabolism and reproduction. **4.** *Anat.* a mass of grey matter in the brain and spinal cord in which incoming nerve fibres form connections with outgoing fibres. **5.** *Phys.* the central core of an atom, made of protons and neutrons, with a net positive charge equal to the number of protons. [L: nut, kernel, fruit stone]

nude /njuːd/, *adj.* **1.** unclothed, as a person, the body, etc.; naked. **2.** without the usual coverings, furnishings, etc.; bare. ◊*n.* **3. in the nude,** undressed. **4.** a nude figure, esp. as represented in art. [L: bare] —**nudeness, nudity,** *n.*

nudge /nʌdʒ/, *v.,* **nudged, nudging,** *n.* ◊*v.t.* **1.** to push or shake slightly, esp. with the elbow, usu. in calling attention or giving a piece of advice or with secret meaning. ◊*n.* **2.** a slight push or shake. [orig. obscure]

nudism /'njuːdɪzəm/, *n.* the practice of going without clothes as a means of healthful living. —**nudist,** *n.*

Nuffield awards /,nʌfiːld ə'wɔːdz/, *n.pl.* awards provided by the Nuffield Foundation since 1948 enabling travel and study opportunities to suitably qualified Australians, including research graduates and farmers.

nugget /'nʌgət/, *n.* **1.** a lump of something. **2.** a lump of native gold. [apparently from Brit d. *nug* lump, block]

nuisance /'njuːsəns/, *n.* **1.** a highly unpleasant or annoying thing or person. **2.** something offensive or annoying to a person or to all the people in a certain area to the disadvantage of their legal rights. [ME, from OF: harm, from L]

null /nʌl/, *adj.* **1.** of no effect, importance, or worth. **2.** being none, lacking, or nonexistent. **3. null and void,** having no legal force or effect. **4.** zero. [L: none]

nulla-nulla /'nʌlə-nʌlə/, *n.* an Aboriginal club or heavy weapon. Also, **nulla.** [Aboriginal]

Nullarbor Plain /,nʌləbɔː 'pleɪn/, *n.* a plain lying behind the Great Australian Bight, stretching from the WA–SA border 300 km to the west and 250 km to the east, at its widest 400 km. [L: no tree]

nulli-, a word part meaning 'none'. [L, combining form of *nullus*]

nullify /'nʌləfaɪ/, *v.t.,* **-fied, -fying. 1.** to make ineffective, not successful, or of no importance. **2.** to make or declare legally empty or inoperative: *to nullify a contract.* [LL: make null, dispose] —**nullification,** *n.*

null set, *n.* a mathematical set having no elements; empty set.

Num, *Bible. Abbrev.* Numbers.

numb /nʌm/, *adj.* **1.** deprived of or lacking in the power of sensation and movement: *fingers numb with cold.* **2.** of the nature of a lack of sensation and movement: *a numb sensation.* ◊*v.t.* **3.** to make numb. [OE *numen,* pp. of *niman* take] —**numbness,** *n.*

numbat /'nʌmbæt/, *n.* a small, reddish-brown marsupial which feeds on insects, with a long bushy tail, a pointed snout, and black and white stripes across the back, found in certain areas of south-western Australia; banded anteater. [Aboriginal]

number /'nʌmbə/, *n.* **1.** the sum, total or count of a collection of units or any generalisation of this idea. **2.** → **integer. 3.** → **numeral. 4.** → **arithmetic. 5.** the particular number given to anything in order to fix its place in a series: *a house number.* **6.** a word or symbol, or a combination of words or symbols, used in counting or to stand for a total. **7.** one of a series of things marked by numbers. **8.** a single part of a book put out in parts. **9.** a single issue of a magazine put out at regular intervals. **10.** any of a collection of poems or songs. **11.** a single part of a (theatrical) program. **12.** a quantity (large or small) of people: *What number do we have coming tonight?* **13.** a certain (usu. large) collection, company, or

number

quantity. **14.** (*pl.*) considerable collections or quantities. **15.** (*pl.*) strength in numbers, esp. in a political party, organisation, etc. **16.** quantity as made up of units. **17.** *Gram.* (in many languages) a part of the inflection of nouns, verbs, and related word classes, usu. expressing the number of people or objects referred to, often as simply termed either *singular* or *plural*. **18. do a number,** to perform a particular piece, or routine. **19. without number,** of which the number is unknown or too great to be counted: *stars without number.* ◇*v.t.* **20.** to find out the number of. **21.** to mark with or make clear by number(s). **22.** to count over or mention one by one. **23.** to fix or limit the number of. **24.** to include in a number: *I number him among my friends.* **25.** to live or have lived (so many years). **26.** to have in number: *That collection numbers twenty paintings.* **27.** to amount to in number: *a crew numbering fifty men.* ◇*v.i.* **28.** to be numbered or included: *He numbers among my friends.* [ME, from OF, from L] —**numberer,** *n.*

numberless /'nʌmbələs/, *adj.* **1.** countless; myriad; innumerable. **2.** without a number or numbers.

numberplate /'nʌmbəpleɪt/, *n.* a plate, carried by motor vehicles, bearing a registration number. Also, **registration plate.**

Numbers /'nʌmbəz/, *n.* the fourth book of the Old Testament (so called because it relates the numbering of the Israelites after the exodus from Egypt).

numbfish /'nʌmfɪʃ/, *n.*, *pl.* **-fishes,** (*esp. collectively*) **-fish.** an electric ray (fish), so called from its power of making numb its prey by means of electric shocks.

numbskull /'nʌmskʌl/, *n. Colloq.* a dull, slow-thinking person; dunce. [NUMB + SKULL]

numeracy /'njumərəsi/, *n.* basic skill in mathematics.

numeral /'njumərəl/, *n.* **1.** a word or words expressing a number: *cardinal numerals.* **2.** a letter or figure, or a group of letters or figures, being a sign of a number: *the Roman numerals.* ◇*adj.* **3.** of or relating to number; consisting of numbers. **4.** expressing or being a sign of numbers. [LL, from L: number]

numerate /'njumereɪt/, *v.*, **-rated, -rating;** /'njumərət/, *adj.* ◇*v.t.* **1.** to number; count; enumerate. **2.** to read (an expression in numbers). ◇*adj.* **3.** having some knowledge of or practice in mathematics. [L] —**numeracy,** *n.* —**numeration,** *n.*

numerator /'njumereɪtə/, *n. Maths.* that term (usu. written above the line) of a fraction which shows how many parts of a unit are taken. [LL: a counter]

numerical /nju'merɪkəl/, *adj.* **1.** of or relating to number; of the nature of number. **2.** being a sign of a number: *numerical symbols.* **3.** bearing, or pointed out by, a number. **4.** expressed by a number or figure, or by figures, and not by a letter or letters. **5.** *Maths.* being a mark of value or size without regard to sign: *The numerical value of* −10 *is greater than that of* −5. Also, **numeric.**

nurse shark

numerology /njumə'rɒlədʒi/, *n.* the study of numbers (esp. one's birth year, etc.), supposedly to determine their influence on one's life and future. [L: number] —**numerological,** *adj.*

numerous /'njumərəs/, *adj.* **1.** very many; forming a great number. **2.** consisting of or including a great number of units or individual people. [L]

numismatics /njuməz'mætɪks/, *n.* the science of coins and medals. —**numismatist,** *n.*

nun /nʌn/, *n.* a woman who has given herself up to a religious life under solemn promises to live in a state of obedience, chastity and poverty. [ME and OE *nunne,* from LL]

Nunawading /nʌnə'wɒdɪŋ/, *n.* a city in the outer eastern metropolitan area of Melbourne, Vic. Pop. 93 327 (1986).

nunnery /'nʌnəri/, *n.*, *pl.* **-neries.** a religious house for nuns; convent.

nuptial /'nʌpʃəl/, *adj.* **1.** of or relating to marriage or the marriage ceremony: *nuptial vows.* ◇*n.* **2.** (*usu. pl.*) marriage; wedding. [L: relating to marriage]

Nuremberg /'njuərəmbəɡ/, *n.* a city in Germany, in northern central Bavaria; war crimes trials of Nazis, 1945–46. Pop. 467 392 (1987 est.). German, **Nürnberg.**

Nureyev /nu'reɪjef/, *n.* **Rudolf Hametovich,** 1938–93, Soviet-born ballet dancer; defected to the West in 1961.

Nurmi /'nɜmi/, *n.* **Paavo Johannes** (*'The Flying Finn'*), 1897–1973, Finnish runner; winner of nine gold and three silver Olympic medals during the 1920s.

nurse /nɜs/, *n., v.,* **nursed, nursing.** ◇*n.* **1.** a person (woman or man) who has the care of the sick or infirm. **2.** a woman who has the general care of a child or children. **3.** a woman employed to breastfeed a young child; wet nurse. ◇*v.t.* **4.** to tend in sickness or infirmity. **5.** to seek to cure (a cold, etc.) by taking care of oneself. **6.** to look after carefully so as to aid growth, development, etc.; foster; cherish (a feeling, etc.). **7.** to treat or handle with care in order to further one's own interests. **8.** to bring up, train, or care for. **9.** to hold or handle, esp. fondly or tenderly. **10.** to hold while travelling: *You can nurse this box.* **11.** to breastfeed (a young child). **12.** to feed and tend when a child is very young. ◇*v.i.* **13.** to act as nurse; tend the sick or infirm. **14.** to breastfeed a child. **15.** (of a child) to take the breast. [ME, from OF, from LL: nurse] —**nurser,** *n.*

nursery /'nɜsri/, *n., pl.* **-eries. 1.** a room or place set apart for young children. **2.** a school for very young children. **3.** any place in which something is born, fed, and looked after. **4.** a place where young trees or other plants are raised for sale.

nursery rhyme, *n.* a short, simple poem or song for children.

nurse shark, *n.* a type of shark widely distributed, having a groove on each side of the head.

nursing home, /ˈnɜsɪŋ hoʊm/, *n.* a nursing residence equipped for the care of patients who have long term or terminal diseases, or who are handicapped in some way.

nurture /ˈnɜtʃə/, *v.,* -tured, -turing, *n. adj.* ◊*v.t.* **1.** to feed, nourish, or support during the stages of growth, esp. children or young; rear. **2.** to bring up; train; educate. ◊*n.* **3.** upbringing or training. **4.** education; breeding. **5.** nourishment or food. [ME, from OF, from L]

nut /nʌt/, *n., v.,* nutted, nutting. ◊*n.* **1.** a dry fruit consisting of a kernel or meat enclosed in a woody or leathery shell, which can usually be eaten. **2.** the kernel itself. **3.** *Bot.* a hard, one-seeded fruit that does not open when it becomes ripe, e.g. the chestnut or the acorn. **4.** any of various devices or parts supposed in some way to look like a nut. **5.** a small lump of coal. **6.** *Colloq.* the head. **7.** *Colloq.* an enthusiast: *He's quite a nut about trains.* **8.** *Colloq.* a foolish or odd person. **9.** *Colloq.* an insane person. **10.** a block (usu. of metal) with a thread, used to screw on the end of a bolt, etc. **11. hard nut to crack, a.** a difficult question, undertaking, or problem. **b.** a person who is difficult to convince, understand, or know. ◊*v.i.* **12.** to look for or gather nuts. ◊*v.* **13. nut out,** to think out; solve (a problem, a plan of action, etc.). ◊*adj.* **14.** made of or being a sign of the wood of any nut-bearing tree, e.g. walnut, hickory. [OE *hnutu*]

nutcracker /ˈnʌtkrækə/, *n.* (*oft. pl.*) an instrument for cracking nuts.

nutmeg /ˈnʌtmeɡ/, *n.* the hard, sweetly-smelling seed of the fruit of a South East Asian tree, used for flavoring food, etc. [ME]

nutrient /ˈnjutriənt/, *adj.* **1.** containing or carrying nutriment, as solutions or the vessels of the body. **2.** supplying with food; giving nutriment. ◊*n.* **3.** a substance that provides food and energy. [L: nourishing]

nutriment /ˈnjutrəmənt/, *n.* **1.** any matter that, taken into a living organism, serves to support it in its existence, helping growth, replacing loss, and providing energy. **2.** something that provides food; nourishment. [L]

nutrition /njuˈtrɪʃən/, *n.* **1.** the act or process of feeding or of being fed. **2.** food; nutriment. **3.** the process by which the food material taken into an organism is changed into living tissue, etc. **– nutritional, nutritious,** *adj.* **– nutritionist,** *n.*

nuts /nʌts/, *Colloq.* ◊*interj.* **1.** (an expression of defiance, disgust, etc.) ◊*adj.* **2.** crazy; insane. **3.** very strongly attracted (fol. by *on* or *over*): *I'm nuts over her.*

nutshell /ˈnʌtʃɛl/, *n.* **1.** the shell of a nut. **2. in a nutshell,** in very short form; in a few words: *Just tell me the story in a nutshell.*

nutty /ˈnʌti/, *adj.,* -tier, -tiest. **1.** containing nuts. **2.** nutlike, esp. in taste. **3. nutty as a fruitcake,** *Colloq.* completely mad.

nuzzle /ˈnʌzəl/, *v.,* -zled, -zling. ◊*v.i.* **1.** to push the nose forward (fol. by *against, in, up,* etc.): *The pup nuzzled up close to the sick child.* **2.** to cuddle up with someone. ◊*v.t.* **3.** to touch or rub with the nose. **4.** to push the nose against or into: *The pup nuzzled me.* [ME]

NW, *Abbrev.* **1.** north-west. **2.** north-western. See Appendix.

Nyerere /nɪəˈrɛəri/, *n.* **Julius Kambarage** /ˌdʒuliəs kæmbəˈraɡi/, born 1922, African statesman, president of Tanzania 1964–85.

nylon /ˈnaɪlɒn/, *n.* **1.** an artificial material able to be shaped when very hot into fibres, sheets, etc., of great strength, and elasticity, used for yarn (esp. for stockings and socks), for bristles (esp. for brushes), etc. **2.** (*pl.*) stockings made of nylon. [Trademark]

nymph /nɪmf/, *n.* **1.** a mythical being, thought of as a beautiful young woman living in the sea, woods, mountains, fields, etc. **2.** a beautiful or graceful young woman. **3.** *Chiefly Poetic.* a pure young woman. **4.** *Entomol.* **a.** Also, **nympha.** the young of an insect without metamorphosis. **b.** → **pupa.** [ME, from OF, from L, from Gk: nymph, pupa] **– nymphal, nymphean,** *adj.*

nymphomania /nɪmfəˈmeɪniə/, *n.* uncontrollable sexual desire in women. [NL, from Gk] **– nymphomaniac,** *adj., n.*

NZ /ɛn ˈzɛd/, *Abbrev.* New Zealand.

Oo

O, o, *n.*, *pl.* **O's** or **Os**; **o's, os,** or **oes**. **1.** the 15th letter of the English alphabet. **2.** something resembling the letter O in shape. **3.** zero; nought (0).

o' /ə/, *prep.* a shortened form of *of*, as in: *o'clock; will-o'-the-wisp*.

o-, a variant of **ob-**, before *m*, as in *omission*.

-o-, an ending for the first part of many compounds, often used in English as a connective, as in *speedometer*.

-o, a suffix used: **1.** in colloquial abbreviations, as *arvo*, afternoon; *combo*, combination, etc. **2.** to refer to a person **a.** in a particular occupation, as *bottle-o*, bottle collector; *garbo*, garbage collector, etc. **b.** of particular habits, as *weirdo*, one whose behavior is very odd; *wino*, a wine addict. **3.** in colloquial responses showing agreement, as *goodo, righto*.

O[1], *Abbrev.* **1.** *Elect.* ohm. **2.** old. ◊*Symbol*. **3.** *Chem.* oxygen.

O[2] /oʊ/, *interj.* **1.** (a word used before a name in address, esp., as in solemn or poetic language, to show earnestness): *Praise the Lord, O Jerusalem.* **2.** (an expression of surprise, pain, longing, gladness, etc.).

O' /oʊ/, a prefix meaning 'descendant', in Irish family names: *O'Brien, O'Connor*. [representing Irish ō descendant]

oaf /oʊf/, *n.* an awkward or stupid person. [OE ælf elf]

Oahu /oʊˈɑhu/, *n.* the third largest and most important of the Hawaiian Islands. Pop. 740 600 (1979); 1525 km². *Main town:* Honolulu.

oak /oʊk/, *n.* **1.** a tree with hard, durable wood, bearing the acorn as fruit. ◊*adj.* **2.** Also, **oaken**. (of furniture, etc.) made of oak. [OE āc]

OAM /oʊ eɪ ˈem/, *Abbrev.* Medal of the Order of Australia.

oar /ɔ/, *n.* **1.** an instrument for propelling a boat, sometimes used also for steering, consisting of a long wooden pole with a blade at one end. **2. put one's oar in**, to interfere; meddle. **3. rest on one's oars**, to take things easily. [OE ār]

oasis /oʊˈeɪsəs/, *n., pl.* **oases** /-siz/. a fertile place in a desert. [L, from Gk, ? from Egypt]

oat /oʊt/, *n.* **1.** (*usu. pl.*) a cereal grass, cultivated for its edible seed. **2.** (*pl.*) the seeds, used esp. for oatmeal, and to feed horses. **3. sow (one's) wild oats**, to throw oneself into the wild activities of youth, esp. in sexual matters. [OE āte]

oath /oʊθ/, *n., pl.* **oaths** /oʊðz/. **1.** a solemn appeal to God, to prove the truth of a statement or the binding character of a promise. **2.** use of the name of God or anything sacred in an improper or blasphemous way. **3.** any profane expression; curse. **4. on (under) oath**, *Law.* having sworn to tell the truth. [OE āth]

oatmeal /ˈoʊtmil/, *n.* a meal made from oats and used in porridge, etc.

ob-, a prefix meaning 'towards', 'to', 'on', 'over', 'against'. Also, **o-, oc-, of-, op-**. [L: towards, to, about, before, on, over, against]

obdurate /ˈɒbdʒərət/, *adj.* **1.** hardened against persuasion; hard-hearted. **2.** refusing to change one's ways: *an obdurate sinner.* [ME, from L: hardened] —**obduracy, obdurateness,** *n.*

OBE /oʊ bi ˈi/, *Abbrev.* **1.** Officer (of the Order) of the British Empire. **2.** Order of the British Empire.

obedience /əˈbidiəns/, *n.* the condition or act of obeying or being willing to obey. —**obedient**, *adj.*

obeisance /oʊˈbeɪsns/, *n.* **1.** a movement of the body expressing deep respect; a bow or curtsy. **2.** obedience or respect, as due to a superior. [ME, from OF: obedience] —**obeisant**, *adj.*

obelisk /ˈɒbələsk/, *n.* **1.** a four-sided tapering pillar of stone, with a pyramidal top. **2.** something like this, as the dagger (†) used in printing as a reference mark. [L, from Gk: pointed pillar]

Oberammergau /oʊbəˈræməgaʊ/, *n.* a village in Germany, south-west of Munich; famous for the passion play performed every ten years.

obese /oʊˈbis/, *adj.* (of a person, animal, etc.) too fat; corpulent. [L] —**obesity**, *n.*

obey /oʊˈbeɪ/, *v.t.* **1.** to fulfil or act according to the commands of: *Obey your parents.* **2.** to fulfil (a command, etc.). **3.** to act true to (some guiding principle, impulse, etc.). ◊*v.i.* **4.** to be obedient. [ME, from OF, from L]

obituary /əˈbɪtʃəri/, *n., pl.* **-aries**, *adj.* ◊*n.* **1.** a notice of a person's death usu. with a short biographical sketch, as in a newspaper. ◊*adj.* **2.** relating to or recording a death: *an obituary notice.* [NL, from L: death]

obj., *Abbrev.* **1.** object. **2.** objection. **3.** objective.

object /ˈɒbdʒɛkt/, *n.;* /əbˈdʒɛkt/, *v.*, ◊*n.* **1.** something that may be seen or touched. **2.** a thing or person to which attention or action is directed: *an object of study.* **3.** the result towards which effort is directed: *the object of our visit.* **4.** a person treated in terms of meeting a particular need in others: *a love object; sex object.* **5.** *Gram.* a noun or something standing for it which represents the goal of an action (after a verb) or the ending point of a relation (after a preposition). **6.** *Philos.* something towards which thinking is directed. **7. no object**, *Colloq.* not a problem: *Money is no object.* ◊*v.i.* **8.** to offer a reason or argument in opposition. **9.** to express or feel disapproval. [ME, from L: thrown before, presented, exposed, opposed, reproached with] —**objector**, *n.*

objection /əb'dʒekʃən/, *n.* **1.** something brought forward or said in disagreement or disapproval. **2.** a cause or grounds for objecting. **3.** a feeling of disapproval or dislike.

objectionable /əb'dʒekʃənəbəl/, *adj.* able to be objected to; unpleasant; offensive: *an objectionable smell; an objectionable person.*

objective /əb'dʒektɪv/, *n.* **1.** something aimed at; a goal. ◇*adj.* **2.** belonging to the object of thought rather than to the thinking subject (opposed to *subjective*). **3.** free from personal feelings or bias; unbiased. **4.** (of a person, book, etc.) intent upon or dealing with things outside the mind rather than thoughts or feelings. [ML] —**objectivity**, *n.*

objective case, *n. Gram.* See **case**[1] and Appendix.

objet d'art /ɒbʒɛ 'da, ɒbjeɪ/, *n., pl.* **objets d'art** /ɒbʒɛ 'da, ɒbjeɪ/. an article of artistic worth. [F]

oblation /oʊ'bleɪʃən, ɒ-/, an offering, now esp. to God. [ME, from L]

obligate /'ɒbləgeɪt/, *v.t.,* **-gated, -gating.** to bind morally or legally: *She is obligated to care for the building.* [ME, from L]

obligation /ɒblə'geɪʃən/, *n.* **1.** a binding requirement to act in a particular way; duty. **2.** the binding power or force of a promise, law, duty, agreement, etc. **3.** *Law.* a legal relationship between two people in which one person's right is the other person's duty. **4.** a debt, esp. a debt of gratitude owed for a benefit, favor, etc. —**obligatory**, *adj.*

oblige /ə'blaɪdʒ/, *v.,* **obliged, obliging.** ◇*v.t.* **1.** to require or force, as by law, command, conscience, or necessity. **2.** to place under a debt of gratitude for some benefit, favor, or service. **3.** to favor or provide (fol. by *with*): *He obliged us with a song.* ◇*v.i.* **4.** to do something as a favor: *He'll do anything to oblige.* [ME, from OF, from L: bind or tie around]

obliging /ə'blaɪdʒɪŋ/, *adj.* (of a person) willing to do favors or services: *The clerk was most obliging.*

oblique /ə'blik/, *adj.* **1.** neither parallel nor at 90° to a given line or surface; slanting; sloping. **2.** not straight or direct. **3.** *Gram.* indicating any case of a noun except nominative and vocative, or except these two and accusative. [ME, from L] —**obliquity**, *n.*

obliterate /ə'blɪtəreɪt/, *v.t.,* **-rated, -rating. 1.** to do away with; destroy. **2.** to blot out or make (writing, marks, etc.) unreadable; cancel; efface. [L: erased]

oblivion /ə'blɪviən/, *n.* **1.** the condition of being forgotten. **2.** the forgetting, or forgetfulness, of something: *five minutes of oblivion.* [ME, from L]

oblivious /ə'blɪviəs/, *adj.* **1.** forgetful; without remembrance: *oblivious of my former failure.* **2.** unmindful; unconscious (fol. by *of* or *to*): *She was oblivious of his love.* [ME, from L]

oblong /'ɒblɒŋ/, *adj.* **1.** in the form of a rectangle; of greater length than breadth. ◇*n.* **2.** an oblong figure. [ME, from L: rather long, oblong]

obloquy /'ɒbləkwi/, *n., pl.* **-quies. 1.** shame resulting from public blame. **2.** blame or insulting language aimed at a person, etc., esp. by numbers of people. [ME, from LL: contradiction]

obnoxious /əb'nɒkʃəs, ɒb-/, *adj.* objectionable; offensive; odious. [L: exposed to harm]

oboe /'oʊboʊ/, *n.* a woodwind instrument with a double reed. [It, from F] —**oboist**, *n.*

Obote /oʊ'boʊteɪ/, *n.* (**Apollo**) **Milton,** born 1924, Ugandan statesman; prime minister 1962–66; president 1966–71 and 1980–85.

O'Brien /oʊ'braɪən/, *n.* **Edna,** born 1932, Irish writer of novels, plays and short stories, esp. concerning the situation of women; works include *The Country Girls* (1960).

obscene /əb'sin, ɒb-/, *adj.* **1.** offensive to modesty or decency; indecent; lewd. **2.** disgusting; repulsive; abominable. [L: of evil omen, offensive, disgusting] —**obscenity**, *n.*

obscure /əb'skjʊə, -'skjʊə/, *adj.,* **-scurer, -scurest,** *v.,* **-scured, -scuring.** ◇*adj.* **1.** (of meaning) not clear or plain; uncertain. **2.** little seen or noticed: *the obscure beginnings of a great movement.* **3.** not readily or easily seen. **4.** dark, as from lack of light; murky; dim. ◇*v.t.* **5.** to make obscure, dark, dim, etc. [ME, from L: dark, dim, unknown, ignoble] —**obscurity**, *n.*

obsequies /'ɒbsəkwiz/, *n.pl.* funeral ceremonies. [ME, from ML: funeral rites]

obsequious /əb'sikwiəs, ɒb-/, *adj.* being over-eager to serve or please. [ME, from L]

observance /əb'zɜvəns/, *n.* **1.** the action of obeying or following: *observance of laws.* **2.** a keeping or celebration by proper procedure, ceremonies, etc. **3.** observation.

observant /əb'zɜvənt/, *adj.* **1.** observing or regarding attentively; watchful. **2.** quick to notice; alert. [ME, from L]

observation /ɒbzə'veɪʃən/, *n.* **1.** the act of noticing or watching. **2.** the habit of observing or noticing. **3.** notice: *You cannot escape observation.* **4.** the act of noting something, for some scientific or other special purpose. **5.** information received this way. **6.** a remark or comment.

observatory /əb'zɜvətri/, *n., pl.* **-tories. 1.** an institution or building used for observing various natural phenomena, usu. equipped with a powerful telescope. **2.** a place giving a wide-ranging view.

observe /əb'zɜv/, *v.,* **-served, -serving.** ◇*v.t.* **1.** to see, notice, or regard with attention. **2.** to watch, view, or note for some scientific, official, or other special purpose: *The scientist will observe the eclipse.* **3.** to remark; comment. **4.** to obey or follow: *People must observe the law.* **5.** to show regard for by some activity, ceremonies, etc.: *The people will observe a new holiday.* ◇*v.i.* **6.** to notice. **7.** to act as an observer. **8.** to remark or comment (usu. fol. by *on* or *upon*). [ME, from L: watch, comply with, observe]

obsess /əb'sɛs, ɒb-/, *v.t.* to trouble, or take over the thoughts, feelings, etc., of; haunt: *He is obsessed by a fear of cancer*. [L: besieged, beset] —**obsessive**, *adj.*

obsession /əb'sɛʃən/, *n.* a persistent idea, feeling, etc., which controls a person's behavior.

obsidian /ɒb'sɪdiən/, *n.* volcanic glass, usu. of a dark color. [L: relating to *Obsius*, reputed discoverer of a similar mineral]

obsolescent /ɒbsə'lɛsənt/, *adj.* **1.** (of a word, etc.) passing out of use. **2.** (of machinery, weapons, etc.) going out of date. **3.** *Biol.* (of organs, markings, etc.) gradually disappearing or imperfectly developed. [L] —**obsolescence**, *n.*

obsolete /'ɒbsəlit/, *adj.* **1.** fallen into disuse, or no longer in use: *an obsolete word*. **2.** out of date: *an obsolete battleship*. **3.** *Biol.* imperfectly developed in comparison with the corresponding character in other individuals, as of the opposite sex or of a related species. [L]

obstacle /'ɒbstəkəl/, *n.* something that stands in the way: *The log was an obstacle on the road; His bad manners were an obstacle to success.* [ME, from OF, from L]

obstetrics /ɒb'stɛtrɪks, əb-/, *n.* the branch of medicine concerned with caring for and treating women in, before and after childbirth; midwifery. —**obstetrician**, *n.* —**obstetric**, *adj.*

obstinate /'ɒbstənət/, *adj.* **1.** firmly and often stupidly keeping to one's purpose, opinion, etc. **2.** carried out without stopping: *obstinate resistance.* **3.** not easily controlled: *the obstinate growth of weeds.* [ME, from L: determined] —**obstinacy**, *n.*

obstreperous /əb'strɛpərəs, ɒb-/, *adj.* resisting control in a noisy manner; unruly. [L: clamorous]

obstruct /əb'strʌkt/, *v.t.* **1.** to block or close up (a way, road, channel, etc.). **2.** to make difficult or oppose the passage, progress, course, etc., of. **3.** to come in the way of or shut out (a view, etch.). [L] —**obstructive**, *adj.* —**obstructiveness**, *n.*

obstruction /əb'strʌkʃən/, *n.* **1.** something that obstructs: *obstructions to shipping.* **2.** the act of obstructing. **3.** *Football, Hockey, etc.* a foul or infringement whereby a player puts his or her body between an opponent and the ball so as to form an obstacle.

obtain /əb'teɪn/, *v.t.* **1.** to come into possession of; get or acquire; procure, as by effort or request. ◇*v.i.* **2.** to hold good or be valid: *the morals that obtained in Rome.* [ME, from OF, from L: take hold of, get, prevail, continue]

obtrude /əb'trud/, *v.*, **-truded, -truding.** ◇*v.t.* **1.** to push forward or upon, esp. without right or invitation: *He would obtrude his opinions upon others.* **2.** to push out. ◇*v.i.* **3.** to push oneself or itself forward, esp. too much; intrude. [L: thrust upon or into] —**obtrusive**, *adj.*

obtuse /əb'tjus, ɒb-/, *adj.* **1.** (of an angle) being between 90° and 180°. **2.** not sharply shaped or pointed. **3.** insensitive or dull in awareness or feeling; stupid. [L: dulled]

obverse /'ɒbvɜs/, *n.* **1.** the side of a coin, medal, etc., which bears the head or main design (opposed to *reverse*). **2.** the front or main face of anything. **3.** a counterpart (something that is very like or goes with another). ◇*adj.* **4.** turned towards or facing one. **5.** corresponding to something else as a counterpart. [L: turned towards or against]

obviate /'ɒbvieɪt/, *v.t.*, **-ated, -ating.** to meet and get rid of or prevent (difficulties, objections, etc.) by effective measures: *This will obviate the necessity of beginning again.* [LL: met, opposed, prevented] —**obviation**, *n.*

obvious /'ɒbviəs/, *adj.* easily recognised or understood: *an obvious advantage.* [L: in the way, meeting]

oc-, a variant of **ob-** before *c*, as in *Occident.*

O'Casey /oʊ'keɪsi/, *n.* **Sean** /ʃɒn/, 1884-1964, Irish dramatist, many of whose plays depict the life of Ireland's poor.

occasion /ə'keɪʒən/, *n.* **1.** a particular time, esp. as marked by certain happenings. **2.** a special or important time, event, ceremony, etc. **3.** a convenient or favorable time; opportunity. **4.** the ground, reason, or cause of some action or result. **5. on occasion,** now and then; occasionally. **6. rise to the occasion,** to show oneself equal to a task. ◇*v.t.* **7.** to give cause for; bring about: *Her exam results occasion a celebration.* [ME, from L: opportunity, fit time]

occasional /ə'keɪʒənəl/, *adj.* **1.** happening or appearing now and then: *an occasional visitor.* **2.** intended for use whenever needed: *an occasional table.* **3.** for a special occasion, ceremony, etc.: *occasional verses.*

Occident /'ɒksədənt/, *n.* **1.** countries in Europe and America (contrasted with the *Orient*). **2.** (*also l.c.*) the Western Hemisphere; the west. [ME, from L *occidens* the west, sunset; properly ppr., going down] —**Occidental**, *adj.*

occiput /'ɒksɪpʊt/, *n.*, *pl.* **occipita** /ɒk'sɪpətə/. the back part of the head or skull. [ME, from L] —**occipital**, *adj.*

occlude /ə'klud/, *v.t.*, **-cluded, -cluding. 1.** to close, shut, or stop up (a passage, etc.). **2.** to shut in, out, or off. **3.** *Chem.* (of some solids) to absorb and hold gases or liquids, in tiny pores on their surfaces. [L: shut up, close up] —**occlusion**, *n.*

occult /'ɒkʌlt, ə'kʌlt/, *adj.* **1.** beyond the bounds of ordinary knowledge; mysterious. **2.** not disclosed; secret. **3.** relating to certain so-called sciences, as magic, astrology, etc., which claim knowledge or use of secret or mysterious means. ◇*n.* **4.** occult studies or sciences. **5.** the supernatural. [L: covered concealed] —**occultism**, *n.*

occupant /'ɒkjəpənt/, *n.* someone who lives or is established in a house, estate, office, etc. [L] —**occupancy**, *n.*

occupation /ɒkjə'peɪʃən/, *n.* **1.** someone's usual employment, business, etc. **2.** possession, as of a place. **3.** the act of occupying. **4.** the condition of being occupied. **5.** a period during which a country is under foreign military control. [ME, from L: seizing, employment] —**occupational**, *adj.*

occupy /'ɒkjəpaɪ/, *v.t.*, **-pied, -pying. 1.** to take up (space, time, etc.). **2.** to busy or employ (the mind, attention, etc., or the person): *The thought of the job would always occupy her mind.* **3.** to seize possession of (land, etc.). **4.** to hold (a position, office, etc.). **5.** to be living in (a place) as its tenant. [ME, from OF, from L: take possession of, take up, employ]

occur /ə'kɜ/, *v.i.*, **-curred, -curring. 1.** to come to pass, take place, or happen. **2.** to be met with or found; appear: *Gum trees occur in many parts of Australia.* **3.** to suggest itself in thought (usu. fol. by *to*): *A strange idea has occurred to me.* [L: run against, go up to, meet, befall] —**occurrence**, *n.*

ocean /'oʊʃən/, *n.* **1.** a large body of salt water which covers almost ¾ of the earth's surface. **2.** any of the geographical divisions of this body (Atlantic, Pacific, Indian, Arctic, and Antarctic). [L, from Gk: the ocean, orig. the great stream supposed to encompass the earth] —**oceanic**, *adj.*

Oceania /oʊʃi'aniə, oʊsi-/, *n.* the islands of the central and southern Pacific, including Micronesia, Melanesia, and Polynesia; sometimes also, Australasia and the Malay Archipelago. —**Oceanian**, *adj., n.*

Ocean Island, *n.* former name of **Banaba**.

oceanography /oʊʃən'ɒgrəfi/, *n.* a branch of physical geography dealing with the ocean. —**oceanographer**, *n.* —**oceanographic**, *adj.*

ocelot /'ɒsəlɒt/, *n.* a spotted, leopard-like cat of North and South America. [F, from Nahuatl: field tiger]

ochre /'oʊkə/, *n.* **1.** a class of natural earths, ranging in color from pale yellow to orange and red, and used as pigments. **2.** the color of ochre. [ME, from OF, from L, from Gk: yellow ochre] —**ochreous**, *adj.*

-ock, a noun suffix used to make descriptive names, as in *ruddock* (lit., the red one) or to indicate smallness, as in *hillock*, etc. [OE *-oc, -uc*]

ocker /'ɒkə/, *n. Colloq.* **1.** the uncultivated Australian working man considered as a type. **2.** an insensitive, narrow-minded Australian who considers his ideas and values the only possible ones. **3.** an Australian male displaying qualities considered to be typically Australian, as good humor, helpfulness, and ability to overcome difficulties. ◇*adj.* **4.** distinctively Australian: *an ocker sense of humor.* Also, **okker**. [var. of *Oscar*, esp. the character in the television program by Ron Frazer]

o'clock /ə'klɒk/, *adv.* of or by the clock (used in stating or enquiring the hour of the day): *It is now one o'clock.*

O'Connor /oʊ'kɒnə/, *n.* **Charles Yelverton**, 1843–1902, Australian engineer, born in Ireland; constructed a pipeline carrying water from the Darling Range to Coolgardie.

oct-, a variant of **octa-** or **octo-** before a vowel.

Oct, *Abbrev.* October.

octa-, a word part meaning 'eight'. Also, **oct-, octo-**. [Gk, combining form of *októ*]

octad /'ɒktæd/, *n.* **1.** a group or series of eight. **2.** *Chem.* an element, etc., having a valency of eight. [LL *octas*, from Gk *oktás*]

octagon /'ɒktəgɒn, -gən/, *n.* a closed figure having eight angles and eight sides. [Gk: octangular. See OCTA-, -GON] —**octagonal**, *adj.*

octahedron /ɒktə'hidrən/, *n., pl.* **-drons, -dra** /-drə/. a solid figure having eight faces. [Gk *oktáedron*. See OCTA-, -HEDRON] —**octahedral**, *adj.*

octane /'ɒkteɪn/, *n.* a hydrocarbon of the alkane series, C_8H_{18}, having 18 isomeric forms, some of which are obtained from petroleum. [OCT- + -ANE]

octave /'ɒktɪv/, *n.* **1.** *Music.* **a.** a note on the eighth degree from a given note (counted as the first). **b.** the interval between such notes. **2.** a series or group of eight. **3.** → **octet**. [ME, from L: eighth] —**octaval**, *adj.*

octavo /ɒk'tavoʊ, -'teɪv-/, *n.* **1.** a book size made with sheets folded to form eight leaves or sixteen pages. *Abbrev.*: 8vo *or* 8°. **2.** a paper size. See Appendix. [short for NL phrase: in an eighth (of a sheet)]

octet /ɒk'tɛt/, *n.* **1.** (a musical composition for) a group of eight singers or instruments. **2.** Also, **octave**. a group of eight lines of verse, esp. at the beginning of a sonnet. **3.** *Chem.* a stable group of eight electrons which form a shell (def. 7) around an atomic nucleus. **4.** any group of eight. Also, **octette**.

octo-, a variant of **octa-**.

October /ɒk'toʊbə/, *n.* the tenth month of the year, containing 31 days. [ME and OE, from L: eighth month of the early Roman year]

Octobrist /ɒk'toʊbrəst/, *n.* a member of a Russian political party, so called because it based its policy on Tsar Nicholas II's manifesto of October 1905. [trans. of Russ *oktyabrist*]

octogenarian /ˌɒktoʊdʒə'nɛəriən/, *adj.* **1.** of the age of eighty years. **2.** between eighty and ninety years old. ◇*n.* **3.** an octogenarian person. [L: containing eighty]

octopus /'ɒktəpəs, -pʊs/, *n., pl.* **-puses, -pi** /-paɪ/. a sea animal with a soft, oval body and eight arms with suckers, which lives mostly on the sea bottom. [NL, from Gk: eight-footed]

octopus strap, *n.* a stretchable rope with hooks on either end used for fastening luggage to roof-racks, etc.

ocular /'ɒkjələ/, *adj.* **1.** of, relating to, or like the eye: *ocular movements.* **2.** performed or received by the eye or eyesight. ◇*n.* **3.** the eyepiece of a viewing instrument, as a microscope. [LL: of the eyes]

O/D *Abbrev.* **1.** on demand. **2.** overdraft. **3.** overdrawn.

odd /ɒd/, *adj.* **1.** differing in character from what is ordinary or usual. **2.** (of people, manners, etc.) considered different; peculiar or strange. **3.** out-of-the-way: *in odd parts of the globe.* **4.** (of a number) leaving a remainder of one when divided by two (as opposed to *even*). **5.** additional to a whole mentioned in round numbers: *She owed him fifty-odd dollars.* **6.** additional to what is taken into account: *ten dollars and a few odd cents.* **7.** being part of a pair, set, or series of which the rest is lacking: *an odd glove.* **8.** (of a pair) not matching: *He was wearing odd shoes.* **9.** left over after the rest have been consumed, used up, divided into pairs, etc. **10.** occasional or casual: *odd jobs.* **11.** not forming part of any particular group, set, or class: *odd bits of information.* **12. odd man out,** one left over when the rest have been arranged in pairs, or in a convenient group or groups. [ME, from Scand]

oddball /ˈɒdbɔːl/, *n., adj. Colloq.* (someone who is) unusual or peculiar. Also, **odd bod.**

oddity /ˈɒdəti/, *n., pl.* **-ties. 1.** an odd characteristic or peculiarity. **2.** an odd person or thing.

oddment /ˈɒdmənt/, *n.* **1.** an odd article, bit, left-over, etc. **2.** an article belonging to a broken or incomplete set.

odds /ɒdz/, *n.* (*usu.* treated as *pl.*) **1.** an equalising allowance given to a weaker side in a competition. **2.** the amount by which the bet of one party is more than that of the other. **3.** the balance of probability in favor of something happening or being the case. **4.** the advantage on the side of one of two competing parties. ◇**5.** Some special uses are:
at odds, in disagreement.
make no odds, to be of no importance.
odds and ends, odd bits; scraps; remnants; fragments.
over the odds, too much.

odds-on /ˈɒdz-ɒn/, *adj.* (of a chance) more likely to win, succeed, etc.

ode /oʊd/, *n.* a lyric poem typically of varied or irregular metrical form and expressing noble feeling. [F, from LL, from Gk: song]

-ode[1], a suffix of nouns indicating something having some similarity to what is indicated by the first part of the word, as in *phyllode.* [Gk]

-ode[2], a noun suffix meaning 'way', as in *anode, electrode.* [Gk: way]

Oder /ˈoʊdə/, *n.* a river flowing from the Oder Mountains in the north-eastern Czech Republic through south-western Poland and along the border between Germany and Poland and into the Baltic. About 880 km. Czech and Polish, **Odra.**

Odessa /oʊˈdɛsə/, *n.* a seaport in Ukraine, on the Black Sea; the principal export centre of Ukrainian grain. 1 132 000 (1986 est.).

Odin /ˈoʊdən/, *n. Scand Myth.* the chief deity, being the god of wisdom, culture, war, and the dead. Also, **Othin.** [Icel *Odhinn,* c. E *Woden,* G *Wotan*]

odious /ˈoʊdiəs/, *adj.* **1.** deserving of or exciting hatred. **2.** highly offensive; disgusting. [ME, from L: hateful]

odium /ˈoʊdiəm/, *n.* **1.** hatred; dislike. **2.** the shame attaching to something hated. [L: hatred]

odonto-, a word part meaning 'tooth'. Also, **odont-.** [Gk, combining form of *odoús*]

odontology /ɒdɒnˈtɒlədʒi/, *n.* **1.** the study of the teeth and their surrounding tissues, and their diseases. **2.** → **dentistry.** – **odontological,** *adj.*

odor or **odour** /ˈoʊdə/, *n.* **1.** the property of a substance which affects the sense of smell. **2.** an agreeable scent; fragrance. **3.** a bad smell. [ME, from OF, from L] – **odorous,** *adj.*

odoriferous /oʊdəˈrɪfərəs/, *adj.* yielding an odor, esp. a sweet-smelling one. [ME, from L: bringing odors]

O'Dowd /oʊˈdaʊd/, *n.* **Bernard Patrick,** 1866–1953, Australian radical activist; poet and author of the poem *The Bush* (1912).

Odysseus /əˈdɪsiəs/, *n. Gk Legend.* the son of Laertes, husband of Penelope, and father of Telemachus; wisest and most cunning of the Greek leaders at Troy who devised the strategy of the Wooden Horse; his journey home involved him in many adventures, including the blinding of the Cyclops. Latin, **Ulysses.**

odyssey /ˈɒdəsi/, *n.* **1.** any long series of wanderings. **2.** (*cap.*) Homer's epic poem describing the ten years' wandering of Odysseus in returning to Ithaca after the Trojan War. [Gk *Odýsseia* from *Odysseús* ODYSSEUS] – **Odyssean,** *adj.*

OECD /oʊ i si ˈdi/, *n.* Organisation for Economic Cooperation and Development; founded in 1961, replacing the OEEC, to coordinate economic and social policies; 24 member nations. [abbrev.]

oedema /əˈdimə/, *n., pl.* **-mata** /-mətə/. the leaking of fluid into tissue spaces and body cavities. Also, **edema.** [NL, from Gk: a swelling] – **oedematous, oedematose,** *adj.*

Oedipus /ˈidəpəs/, *n. Gk Legend.* a son of Laius and Jocasta. Reared by the king of Corinth, he unwittingly slew his father and later solved the riddle of the Sphinx, for which he was made King of Thebes and thus unknowingly, husband of his mother. When the nature of these deeds was learnt, Jocasta hanged herself, and Oedipus tore out his eyes.

Oedipus complex, *n.* the unconscious desire of a child for a sexual relationship with the parent of the opposite sex, usu. used of a boy's desire for his mother. [orig. with ref. to the Greek legend of OEDIPUS]

o'er /ɔː/, *prep., adv. Poetic.* over.

oesophagus /əˈsɒfəgəs/, *n., pl.* **-gi** /-gaɪ/. the tube connecting the back of the mouth with the stomach; gullet. Also, **esophagus.** [NL, from Gk] – **oesophageal,** *adj.*

oestrogen /ˈistrədʒən, ˈɛs-/, *n.* any one of a group of female sex hormones secreted by the

oestrogen ovaries and responsible for secondary female characteristics. Also, **estrogen**.

oestrous cycle /'ɪstrəs ˌsaɪkəl/, n. a cycle of physiological changes in sexual and other organs in female mammals.

oestrus /'ɪstrəs, 'es-/, n. the oestrous cycle in female mammals. Also, **oestrum** /'ɪstrəm, 'es-/. [L, from Gk: gadfly, sting, frenzy] – **oestrous**, adj.

of /ɒv/; weak form /əv/, prep. a particle indicating: **1.** distance or direction from, separation, deprivation, riddance, etc.: *within a metre of.* **2.** origin or source: *of good family; the plays of Shakespeare.* **3.** cause, occasion, or reason: *He will die of hunger.* **4.** material, substance, or contents: *a packet of sugar; a suit of wool.* **5.** a relation of identity: *the city of Sydney.* **6.** belonging or possession, connection, or association: *the queen of England; the property of all.* **7.** inclusion in a number, class, or whole: *one of us.* **8.** objective relation: *the ringing of bells.* **9.** reference or respect: *talk of peace.* **10.** qualities: *a man of tact.* **11.** time: *of an evening.* **12.** attaching a quality to: *It was good of you to come.* **13.** *Chiefly Archaic.* the person by whom something is done: *beloved of all.* [ME and OE]

of-, a variant of **ob-**, before *f*, as in *offend*.

O'Farrell /oʊˈfærəl/, n. **Henry James**, 1833–68, Australian Fenian supporter, born in Ireland; made an assassination attempt on visiting Alfred, Duke of Edinburgh, in Sydney in 1868.

off /ɒf/, adv. **1.** away from a position occupied, or from connection, or attachment: *take off one's hat; The handle has come off.* **2.** to or at a distance from, or away from, a place: *He ran off.* **3.** differing from, esp. from what is normal or regular. **4.** less: *ten per cent off on all cash purchases.* **5.** away; distant (in future time): *Summer is only a week off.* **6.** out of operation; disconnected. **7.** away from normal employment: *We have four days off at Easter.* **8.** so as to finish or complete; completely: *We kill off rats.* **9. be off**, to depart; leave. **10. off and on**, Also, **on and off**. occasionally. ◇prep. **11.** away from: *He fell off a horse.* **12.** differing from (something normal or usual): *off his balance.* **13.** not up to the usual standard of: *off his game.* **14.** away or disengaged from (duty, work, etc.). **15.** *Colloq.* avoiding (some food, activity, etc.): *He is off gambling.* **16.** distant from: *a waterhole a fair way off the track.* **17.** *Colloq.* from, indicating source: *I bought it off him.* ◇adj. **18.** no longer in effect or operation: *The agreement is off.* **19.** away from work: *His off hours are spent shopping.* **20.** not so good as usual: *an off year for apples.* **21.** off-color; unwell: *I am a bit off today.* **22.** (of food) unfit for eating. **23.** *Cricket.* See **off side**. **24.** (of items in a menu) not available. ◇interj. **25.** (a command to go away.) [ME and OE of of, off]

offal /'ɒfəl/, n. **1.** the parts of a butchered animal which are not eaten, as the intestines, etc. **2.** the brains, liver, tripe, etc. of an animal, used as food. **3.** anything worthless; rubbish. [ME]

off-beat /'ɒf-bit/, adj. **1.** unusual; unconventional. **2.** (in jazz, etc.) having a strong accent on the second and fourth beat of a four-beat bar. ◇n. **3.** *Music.* an unaccented beat of a bar.

off-color *or* **off-colour** /'ɒf-kʌlə/; (*esp. after a verb*) /ɒf-'kʌlə/, adj. **1.** Also, **off**. *Colloq.* unwell. **2.** of doubtful taste: *an off-color story.*

offcourse /'ɒfkɔs/, adj. of or relating to what is, or takes place, away from a racecourse, usu. betting.

off-cut /'ɒf-kʌt/, n. a small length of timber or other material, left over after special orders have been prepared.

Offenbach /'ɒfənbɑk/, n. **Jacques** /ʒak/, 1819–80, French composer; known for operettas including *The Tales of Hoffmann* (1881).

offence /əˈfens/, n. **1.** a wrong; a sin. **2.** any crime. **3.** something that offends: *an offence to his sense of right.* **4.** the feeling of displeasure caused. **5.** an act of attacking: *weapons of offence.* **6.** the people, side, etc., attacking. [ME, from L]

offend /əˈfend/, v.t. **1.** to cause displeasure in the mind or feelings. **2.** to affect (the sense, taste, etc.) disagreeably. ◇v.i. **3.** to give offence or cause displeasure. **4.** to commit a sin, crime, or fault. [ME, from OF, from L: strike against, displease] – **offender**, n.

offensive /əˈfensɪv/, adj. **1.** causing offence or displeasure; irritating; highly annoying. **2.** disagreeable to the sense: *an offensive odor.* **3.** unacceptable to one's sense of what is right or proper; insulting. **4.** (of a word) **a.** used purposely in order to insult the hearer. **b.** not acceptable in polite conversation. **5.** relating to offence or attack: *offensive movements.* ◇n. **6.** a position or attitude of offence or attack: *The army took the offensive.* **7.** a military attack or any similar action: *the big Soviet offensive.*

offer /'ɒfə/, v.t. **1.** to present for acceptance or consideration. **2.** to show intention or willingness (to do something). **3.** to present solemnly as an act of worship, as to God, etc. **4.** to attempt to do or make: *They will offer battle; Do not offer resistance.* **5.** to present for sale. **6.** to bid as a price: *He will offer $50 for the radio.* ◇v.i. **7.** to present itself; occur: *whenever an occasion offered.* ◇n. **8.** an act of offering or what is offered. **9.** a proposal of marriage. **10.** a proposal to give or accept something as a price for something else; a bid: *an offer of $180,000 for a house.* [OE offrian, from L]

offering /'ɒfərɪŋ/, n. something offered, often in worship, as to God or the church.

offertory /'ɒfətəri, -tri/, n., pl. **-ries**. **1.** the offering of the bread and wine to God in a Holy Communion service. **2. a.** the music during which the offering of the people is received at a church service. **b.** the offerings themselves. [ME, from LL]

offhand /ɒfˈhænd/, adv.; /'ɒfhænd/, adj. ◇adv. **1.** without previous thought or prepa-

offhand ration; extempore: *He decided offhand.* ◇*adj.* Also, **offhanded. 2.** done or made offhand. **3.** informal or casual, sometimes to the point of rudeness: *an offhand manner.*

office /ˈɒfəs/, *n.* **1.** a room or place for the carrying-out of business, etc. **2.** a place in which the clerical work of a business is done. **3.** a place where tickets, etc., are sold, information given, etc. **4.** a building or a set of rooms given to the business of a government organisation: *the post office.* **5.** a position of duty, trust, or authority, esp. in the government or in some company, society, etc. **6.** a duty of a person or agency: *the office of adviser.* **7.** something (good, or occasionally, bad) done for another: *It was through your good offices that I got the job.* **8.** *Chiefly Brit.* a department of government: *the Foreign Office.* [ME, from OF, from L: service, duty, ceremony]

officer /ˈɒfəsə/, *n.* **1.** someone who holds a position of rank or authority in an army, navy, airforce, or any similar organisation. **2.** a policeman. **3.** the master or captain of a ship not part of the navy. **4.** a person appointed or elected to some position of responsibility and authority in the public service, or in some society, etc. [ME, from OF, from ML, from L: office]

official /əˈfɪʃəl/, *n.* **1.** someone who holds an office or is charged with some duty. ◇*adj.* **2.** of or relating to an office or position of duty, trust, or authority: *official powers.* **3.** approved or given with the authority of a particular organisation: *an official report.* **4.** appointed or given authority to act in a special capacity: *an official representative.* **5.** formal or ceremonious: *an official dinner.* [LL, from L: office] —**officialdom**, *n.*

officiate /əˈfɪʃieɪt/, *v.i.*, **-ated, -ating. 1.** to perform the duties of any office or position. **2.** to perform the office of a priest or minister. [ML, from L: office] —**officiation**, *n.*

officious /əˈfɪʃəs/, *adj.* **1.** forward in forcing one's services upon others: *an officious employee.* **2.** marked by or coming from such forwardness: *officious behavior.* [L: obliging, dutiful]

offing /ˈɒfɪŋ/, *n.* **1.** *Naut.* a position at a distance from the shore. **2. in the offing, a.** not very far away. **b.** ready to happen, appear, etc.

off-limits /ˈɒf-ˌlɪməts/, *adj.* out of bounds.

off-load /ˈɒf-ˌloʊd/, *v.t.* **1.** to unload (goods, etc.). **2.** to get rid of. ◇*v.i.* **3.** to unload.

off-peak /ˈɒf-ˌpiːk/, *adj.* of or relating to a period of time of less activity than the period of highest demand.

off-putting /ˈɒf-ˌpʊtɪŋ/, *adj. Colloq.* discouraging; disconcerting.

off-season /ˈɒf-ˌsiːzən/, *n.* a time of reduced activity for business or the manufacturing industry: *Some workers may lose their jobs in the off-season.*

offset /ˈɒfset, ɒfˈset/, *v.*, **-set, -setting**; /ˈɒfset/, *n., adj.* ◇*v.t.* **1.** to balance as by something else; counterbalance: *The gains offset the losses.* ◇*n.* **2.** something that offsets or compensates. **3.** any offshoot; branch. **4.** *Print.* an impression from an inked design, etc. on a lithographic stone or metal plate, made on another surface, and then transferred to paper. ◇*adj.* **5.** of, or relating to an offset.

offshoot /ˈɒfʃuːt/, *n.* **1.** a shoot from a main stem, as of a plant. **2.** a branch, or a descendant, of a family or race. **3.** anything seen as coming from a main stock.

offshore /ɒfˈʃɔː/, *adv.;* /ˈɒfʃɔː, ɒfˈʃɔː/, *adj.* ◇*adv.* **1.** off or away from the shore. ◇*adj.* **2.** moving or being away from the shore: *an offshore wind.*

off side, *n.* (in cricket) that half of the field towards which the batsman's feet point as he or she stands ready to receive the bowling (opposed to *leg side*). Also, **off.**

offside /ɒfˈsaɪd, ˈɒfsaɪd/, *adj.* **1.** *Soccer, Rugby, Hockey, etc.* illegally between the ball and the opposing team's goal line and outside one's own team's half of the field when the ball is in play. **2.** opposed; uncooperative: *I don't want him offside.*

offsider /ɒfˈsaɪdə/, *n.* a partner; friend; assistant.

offspring /ˈɒfsprɪŋ/, *n.* **1.** the children or young of a particular parent. **2.** a descendant. **3.** the product, result, or effect of something. [ME and OE *ofspring*]

oft /ɒft/, *adv. Chiefly Poetic.* often. [OE *oft*]

often /ˈɒfən, ˈɒftən/, *adv.* **1.** many times; frequently. **2.** in many cases. [ME]

ogee /ˈoʊdʒiː/, *n.* a double curve (like the letter S) formed by the union of a concave and a convex line.

ogle /ˈoʊɡəl/, *v.*, **ogled, ogling.** ◇*v.t.* **1.** to eye with sexual interest. **2.** to eye; look at. ◇*v.i.* **3.** to cast glances showing sexual interest. [apparently from D: to eye]

O'Grady /oʊˈɡreɪdi/, *n.* **John Patrick,** 1907–81, Australian writer; works include the novel *They're a Weird Mob* (1957), written under the pseudonym of Nino Culotta.

ogre /ˈoʊɡə/, *n.* **1.** a monster, of fairy tales and legends, supposed to live on human flesh. **2.** a person likened to such a monster. [F]

oh /oʊ/, *interj.* (an expression showing surprise, pain, disapproval, etc., or for attracting attention.)

Ohio /oʊˈhaɪoʊ/, *n.* **1.** a state in the north-eastern central US; a part of the Midwest. Pop. 10 752 000 (1986 est.); 106 765 km^2. *Cap.*: Columbus. **2.** a river in the US, formed by the confluence of the Allegheny and Monongahela Rivers at Pittsburgh, Pennsylvania, flowing south-west to the Mississippi in southern Illinois. 1579 km. —**Ohioan**, *n., adj.*

ohm /oʊm/, *n.* the derived SI unit of resistance; the resistance of a conductor in which one volt produces a current of one ampere. Symbol: Ω [named after GS *Ohm*, 1787–1854, German physicist]

OHMS, *Abbrev.* On Her (or His) Majesty's Service.

Ohm's law, *n.* a law which states that in any electric circuit the current flowing is proportional to the voltage and inversely proportional to the resistance. [named after GS *Ohm*. See OHM]

o.h.v., *Abbrev.* overhead valve.

-oic, a noun suffix indicating the presence of carboxyl groups (COOH−) in a compound, as in *ethanoic acid, propanoic acid,* etc.

-oid, a suffix used to form adjectives meaning 'like' or 'resembling', and nouns meaning 'something resembling' what is meant by the first part of the word as in *alkaloid, anthropoid, cuboid.* [Gk: having the form of, like]

-oidea, a suffix used in naming zoological classes or entomological superfamilies. [NL]

oil /ɔɪl/, *n.* **1.** any of a class of liquid substances, chemically similar to fats, which are obtained from animal or vegetable sources, and used for cooking, perfumes, etc. **2.** → **petroleum** (def. 1). **3.** some substance having an oily nature. **4.** *Painting.* **a.** an oil color. **b.** an oil painting. **5. burn the midnight oil,** to stay up late at night to study, work, etc. **6. the good (dinkum) oil,** correct (and usu. profitable) information. **7. pour oil on troubled waters,** to calm. ◇*v.t.* **8.** to smear, or supply with oil. **9.** to give information to (fol. by *up*). **10.** to bribe. ◇*adj.* **11.** from, relating to, or like oil. **12.** concerned with the production or use of oil. [ME, from OF, from L: (olive) oil]

oilcloth /ˈɔɪlklɒθ/, *n.* cotton cloth made waterproof with oil and pigment.

oil rig, *n.* →**rig** (def. 7).

oilskin /ˈɔɪlskɪn/, *n.* **1.** cotton cloth made waterproof by treatment with oil and used for rainwear, etc. **2.** (*oft. pl.*) clothing made of it.

oily /ˈɔɪli/, *adj.,* **oilier, oiliest. 1.** of, relating to or like oil. **2.** containing oil. **3.** covered with oil. **4.** smooth, as in manner or speech; unctuous.

ointment /ˈɔɪntmənt/, *n.* a soft, greasy preparation, often medicated, for applying to the skin; unguent. [ME, from OF]

okay /oʊˈkeɪ/, *Colloq. adj.* **1.** all right; correct. ◇*adv.* **2.** well; correctly. ◇*v.t.* **3.** to put an 'okay' on (a request, etc.); approve; accept. ◇*n.* **4.** approval, agreement or acceptance. Also, **ok, OK.** [from the 'OK Club', formed in 1840 with the initials of 'Old Kinderhook' (Kinderhook, New York State, being birthplace of the then US President.)]

O'Keefe /oʊˈkif/, *n.* **Johnny** (*John Michael O'Keefe*), 1935–78, Australian rock'n'roll singer; one of the most influential figures in Australian pop music.

Okinawa /oʊkəˈnawə/, *n.* the largest of the Ryukyu Islands, in the northern Pacific, southwest of Japan. Pop. 1 190 000 (1986); 1409 km².

Oklahoma /oʊkləˈhoʊmə/, *n.* a state of the southern central US. Pop. 3 305 000 (1986 est.); 181 090 km². *Cap.:* Oklahoma City. *Abbrev.:* Okla —**Oklahoman,** *n., adj.*

okra /ˈɒkrə, ˈoʊk-/, *n.* a tall plant grown for its soft pods, used in soups, etc. [a W African language]

-ol[1], a noun suffix used in the names of chemical products, etc., representing 'alcohol', as in *glycerol, phenol.* [short for ALCOHOL or PHENOL]

-ol[2], a variant of **-ole.**

-olatry, a word part meaning 'worship of', as in *demonolatry.* [Gk: service, worship]

old /oʊld/, *adj.,* **older, oldest** or **elder, eldest,** *n.* ◇*adj.* **1.** far advanced in years or life. **2.** of or relating to a long life. **3.** having the appearance or characteristics of advanced age: *prematurely old.* **4.** having reached a given age: *a man thirty years old.* **5.** having existed for a long time, or made long ago: *old wine.* **6.** long known or in use: *the same old excuse.* **7.** former, past, or ancient, as time, days, etc.: *old kingdom.* **8.** no longer modern or recent: *He exchanged his old car for a new one.* **9.** having been so formerly: *the old boys of a school.* **10.** worn; decayed; dilapidated. **11.** (*cap.*) (in the history of a language) of or belonging to the earliest stage of development: *Old English.* **12.** of long experience: *an old hand at the game.* **13.** *Colloq.* (showing friendly feeling): *good old Henry.* ◇*n.* **14.** an old or former time. **15.** old people collectively: *the old.* **16.** (used in combination) a person or animal of a given age or age-group: *a class of five-year-olds.* [ME; OE *ald, eald*]

Old Bailey, *n.* the main criminal court of London.

olden /ˈoʊldən/, *adj.* of old; ancient: *olden days.*

Old English, *n.* the English of periods before 1100; Anglo-Saxon.

Old French, *n.* the French language of periods before 1400.

Old Glory, *n.* the US flag.

old guard, *n.* **1.** the members of any group, country, etc., who are given to keeping existing conditions; ultra-conservatives. **2.** the members of a former generation, or the supporters of a former order, who survive to see their way of life or their cause become unpopular. [translation of F *Vieille Garde,* Napoleon's imperial guard]

Old Kingdom, *n.* the period in the history of ancient Egypt comprising the third to sixth dynasties, from 2700 to 2200 BC.

old maid, *n.* **1.** a woman, esp. not young, who has remained unmarried; spinster. **2.** *Colloq.* a person with the supposed characteristics of an old maid.

Old Nick, *n.* the devil; Satan. [contraction of *Nicholas*]

Old Norse, *n.* the language of Scandinavia and Iceland up to the 15th century.

Old Stone Age, *n.* the Palaeolithic period.

Old Testament, *n.* the collection of biblical books comprising the Hebrew Scriptures of 'the old covenant', and being the first of the two main divisions of the Christian bible.

Olduvai Gorge /ˌɒldjuvaɪ 'gɔdʒ/, n. a gorge in Tanzania in which is located a site containing fossils providing evidence of Palaeolithic cultures.

old-world /'ould-wəld/, adj. of or relating to the ancient world or to a former period of history.

Old World, n. **the**, that part of the world that was known before the discovery of the Americas, comprising Europe, Asia, Africa, and sometimes including Australia.

-ole, a noun suffix meaning 'oil'. [representing L *oleum*]

oleaginous /ouli'ædʒənəs/, adj. **1.** having the nature or qualities of oil. **2.** containing or producing oil. [L: of the olive]

oleander /ouli'ændə, ɒli-/, n. a poisonous evergreen shrub with rose-colored or white flowers. [ML]

olearia /ɒli'ɛəriə/, n. a large shrub or tree of Australia, NG and NZ, with daisy-like, usu. white, flowers.

olefine /'oulǝfǝn, -fin/, n. →**alkene**. Also, **olefin** /'oulǝfǝn/. [F: oil-forming] — **olefinic**, adj.

oleic acid /ouˌliɪk 'æsəd/, n. an oily liquid, an unsaturated fatty acid, present in fats and oils as the glyceride ester. See **fatty acid**.

oleo-, a word part meaning 'oil'. [L, combining form of *oleum*]

olfaction /ɒl'fækʃən/, n. **1.** the act of smelling. **2.** the sense of smell. [obs. *olfact* to smell] — **olfactory**, adj.

Olgas /'ɒlgəz/, n.pl. **the**, → **Kata Tjuta**.

oligarchy /'ɒləgaki/, n., pl. **-chies. 1.** a form of government in which the power rests with a few people or a clique. **2.** a state so governed. **3.** the ruling few collectively. [Gk] — **oligarch**, n. — **oligarchic**, adj.

oligo-, a word part meaning 'few', 'little'. Also, before a vowel, **olig-**. [Gk: small, (pl.) few]

oligotrophic /ɒləgou'trɒfɪk, -'troufɪk/, adj. (of rivers or lakes) deficient in plant nutrients. [OLIGO- + TROPHIC]

Oligocene /ɒ'lɪgousin/, n., adj. Geol. (relating to) a division of the Tertiary that follows the Eocene and comes before the Miocene. [Gk]

Oliphant /'ɒləfənt/, n. **Sir Mark** (*Marcus Laurence Elwin Oliphant*), born 1901, Australian physicist and administrator; governor of SA 1971–76.

olive /'ɒləv, -lɪv/, n. **1.** a fruit-bearing evergreen tree, of Mediterranean and other warm regions. **2.** a small, oval fruit, valuable for eating and as a source of oil. **3.** the olive, or a branch of olive, seen as a symbol of peace. **4.** a shade of brownish or yellowish green. ◇adj. **5.** of, relating to, or made of olives. **6.** of the color olive. [ME, from OF, from L]

Olives /'ɒləvz/, n. **Mount of**, a small ridge east of Jerusalem; site of Bethany and Gethsemane in the New Testament. Highest point, 834 m. Also, **Olivet**.

Olivier /ɒ'lɪviə/, n. **Lord Laurence Kerr** (*Baron Olivier of Brighton*), 1907–89, English actor, producer and director; widely considered the leading actor of the twentieth century.

olivine /ɒlə'vin, 'ɒləvin/, n. *Mineral.* a very common mineral, magnesium iron silicate, often found in olive green to grey-green masses as an important part of basic igneous rocks. [L: olive]

Olsen /'oulsən/, n. **John**, born 1928, Australian artist; work includes the mural *Five Bells* in the Sydney Opera House.

Olympia /ə'lɪmpiə/, n. a plain in ancient Elis, Greece, where the Olympic games were held.

Olympian /ə'lɪmpiən/, adj. **1.** of or relating to the gods of ancient Greece, who lived on Mt Olympus. **2.** grand; superior. ◇n. **3.** someone who has competed in the Olympic games.

Olympic /ə'lɪmpɪk/, adj. **1.** relating to the Olympic games. **2.** of a standard suitable for the Olympic games. ◇n. **3. the Olympics**, → **Olympic games**.

Olympic games, n. pl. **1.** the greatest of the games or festivals of ancient Greece, held every four years in the plain of Olympia in Elis, in honor of Zeus. **2.** Also, **the Olympics**. a modern revival of these games consisting of international competitions in running, jumping, swimming, shooting, etc., held every four years since 1896, each time in a different country.

Olympus /ə'lɪmpəs/, n. **Mount**, Greek, **Ólimbus**, a mountain in north-eastern Greece, on the boundary between Thessaly and Macedonia; supposed home of the gods of ancient Greece. 2966 m.

OM /ou 'ɛm/, *Abbrev.* Order of Merit.

-oma, pl. **-omas, -omata**. a suffix of nouns indicating a tumor, as in *carcinoma, sarcoma*. [Gk]

O'Malley /ou'mæli/, n. **King**, c. 1858–1953, Australian federal politician, probably born in Canada; instrumental in the foundation of the Commonwealth Bank and in securing land for the Federal capital.

Omar Khayyám /ˌoumə kaɪ'æm/, n. died 1123?, Persian poet and mathematician, some of whose poems (*The Rubaiyat*) were translated by the English poet Edward FitzGerald.

omasum /ou'meɪsəm/, n., pl. **sa** /-sə/. the third stomach of a cud-chewing animal, as a cow, sheep, goat, etc. [NL, from L: bullock's tripe]

ombudsman /'ɒmbədzmən/, n. an official appointed by a parliament, city council, etc., to look into public complaints against the government or its agencies. [Swed: commissioner]

omega /'oumǝgǝ, ou'migǝ, -'meɪ-/, n. **1.** the last letter (Ω, ω = English long O, o) of the Greek alphabet. **2.** the last of any series; the end. [Gk: lit., great *o*]

Omega /oʊ'migə/, *n.* a maritime navigation system, which can also be used by aircraft, with eight base stations in the world including one at Darriman in Gippsland, Vic.

omelette /'ɒmlət/, *n.* a dish consisting of eggs beaten and fried, often served folded round vegetables, etc. [F: thin plate]

omen /'oʊmən/, *n.* **1.** anything happening or understood to be a sign of future good or evil. **2.** something that foreshadows a future event; presage. [L]

ominous /'ɒmənəs/, *adj.* telling of approaching evil; threatening. [L: portentous]

omission /oʊ'mɪʃən, ə-/, *n.* **1.** the act or fact of failing to include something. **2.** something not included. [ME, from LL]

omit /oʊ'mɪt, ə-/, *v.t.*, **omitted, omitting. 1.** to leave out. **2.** to fail to do, make, use, send, etc.: *to omit a greeting.* [ME, from L: let go, neglect, omit]

omni-, a word part meaning 'all', used in combination as in *omniactive* (all-active, active everywhere). [L, combining form of *omnis*]

omnibus /'ɒmnɪbəs, -bəs/, *n., pl.* **-buses. 1.** → **bus. 2.** a volume of reprinted works by a single author or works related in interest or nature. [L: lit., for all (dat. pl. of *omnis*)]

omnipotent /ɒm'nɪpətənt/, *adj.* **1.** almighty, or limitless in power, as God. **2.** having unlimited or very great authority. [ME, from L: almighty] **—omnipotence,** *n.*

omnipresent /ɒmnə'prezənt/, *adj.* present everywhere at the same time: *the omnipresent God.* [ML] **—omnipresence,** *n.*

omniscient /ɒm'nɪsiənt, ɒm'nɪʃənt/, *adj.* knowing all things. [OMNI- + L *sciens*, ppr., knowing] **—omniscience,** *n.*

omnivorous /ɒm'nɪvərəs/, *adj.* **1.** eating all kinds of foods without regard to quality, etc. **2.** eating both animal and plant foods. **3.** taking in everything, as with the mind. [L] **—omnivore,** *n.*

Omsk /ɒmsk/, *n.* a city in the western USSR in Asia, on the river Irtysh. Pop. 1 122 000 (1986 est.).

on /ɒn/, *prep.* a particle expressing: **1.** position above and in contact with a supporting surface: *on the table.* **2.** contact with any surface: *the picture on the wall.* **3.** closeness: *a house on the coast.* **4.** situation, place, etc.: *a scar on the face.* **5.** support, dependence, manner of movement: *on foot.* **6.** state, condition, course, etc.: *on the way.* **7.** ground; basis: *on good authority.* **8.** risk; liability: *on pain of death.* **9.** time or occasion: *on Sunday.* **10.** reference to something else: *on the left.* **11.** direction or end of motion *to march on Parliament House.* **12.** object of action, thought, desire, etc.: *to gaze on a scene.* **13.** membership: *on the committee.* **14.** agency or means: *to speak on the telephone.* **15.** manner: *on the cheap.* **16.** subject; reference: *views on public matters.* **17.** responsibility for cost: *Drinks are on the house.* **18.** direction of attention or emotion: *Don't go crook on me.* ◇*adv.* **19.** on oneself or itself: *to put one's coat on.* **20.** fast; tight: *to hold on.* **21.** towards: *to look on.* **22.** forwards, onwards or along: *further on.* **23.** continuously: *to work on.* **24.** into or in active operation: *to turn the gas on.* ◇**25.** Some special uses are:

on and off, not regularly.

get on to, 1. to follow up. **2.** (of a person) to contact.

on and on, at great length.

go on at, *Colloq.* to scold.

have oneself on, *Colloq.* to think oneself better than one really is.

◇*adj.* **26.** operating or in use: *The heating is on.* **27.** occurring; taking place: *Is there anything on tomorrow?* **28.** *Cricket.* → **leg side. 29. be on about,** be concerned about; to complain. **30. be on at,** to nag. **31. not on,** *Colloq.* not a possibility. ◇*n.* **32.** *Cricket.* the on side. [OE *on, an* on, in, to]

onanism /'oʊnənɪzəm/, *n.* **1.** (in sexual intercourse) withdrawal before orgasm takes place. **2.** → **masturbation.** [from Onan, son of Judah (Gen 38:9). See -ISM]

once /wʌns/, *adv.* **1.** at one time in the past; formerly. **2.** a single time: *once a day.* **3.** even a single time; ever: *if the facts once become known.* **4.** by a single degree: *a cousin once removed.* **5. once and for all,** finally and decisively. **6. once in a while,** occasionally. **7. once upon a time,** long ago. ◇*conj.* **8.** if ever. **9.** whenever. ◇*n.* **10.** a single occasion: *Once is enough.* **11. all at once, a.** suddenly. **b.** immediately. **c.** at the same time: *Three things happened all at once.* [OE ānes]

oncourse /'ɒnkɔs/, *adj.*; /ɒn'kɔs/, *adv.* ◇*adj.* **1.** of or relating to facilities or activities on a racecourse: *oncourse betting.* ◇*adv.* **2.** on a racecourse.

one /wʌn/, *adj.* **1.** being a single unit or individual, rather than two or more: *one apple.* **2.** being a person, thing, etc., of the kind indicated: *one member of the party.* **3.** some (day, etc., in the future): *You will see him one day.* **4.** single through union or agreement: *of one mind.* **5.** a certain (oft. used in naming a person otherwise unknown or undescribed): *One John Smith was chosen.* **6.** a particular (day, time, etc. in the past): *one evening last week.* **7.** a special person or thing: *the one man we can trust.* ◇*n.* **8.** the first and lowest whole number. **9.** a single person or thing: *to come one at a time.* **10.** an unusual person: *He's a one.* ◇**11.** Some special uses are:

at one, in a state of unity or agreement: *hearts at one.*

get it in one, *Colloq.* to hit on the correct answer, etc., at one's first attempt.

one and all,

one by one, singly and in succession.

◇*pron.* **12.** a person or thing of a given number or kind: *one of the poets.* **13.** (*in certain pronoun combinations*) a person unless definitely specified otherwise: *every one.* **14.** (*with a defining clause or other qualifying words*) a person, or special being or agency: *the evil one.* **15.** anyone: *as good as one would hope.* **16.** a person like oneself: *What would one do in the situation?* **17.** a person or thing of the kind just mentioned: *The paintings are fine ones.* [OE]

-one, a noun suffix used in the names of chemical derivatives, esp. ketones. [GK]

one-eyed /'wʌn-aɪd/; (*esp. after verbs*) /wʌn-'aɪd/, *adj.* **1.** having only one eye. **2.** having a strong preference in favor of someone or something.

O'Neill /ou'nil/, *n.* **Eugene Gladstone**, 1888-1953, US dramatist; author of the epic drama *Long Day's Journey into Night* (1941); Nobel prize for literature, 1936.

one-off /'wʌn-ɒf/, *n., adj.* (something which is) individual; unique.

onerous /'ounərəs/, *adj.* hard to bear; oppressive. [ME, from L]

oneself /wʌn'self/, *pron.* a person's self (often used for emphasis or reflexively): *One hurts oneself by such methods.*

one-sided /wʌn-saɪdəd/, *adj.* **1.** considering only one side of a matter or question; partial, unjust, or unfair: *a one-sided judgment.* **2.** unbalanced; unequal: *a one-sided fight.* **3.** existing or happening on one side only. **4.** having but one side.

one-upmanship /wʌn-'ʌpmənʃɪp/, *n.* the art or practice of gaining an advantage over others, by using power, position, etc.

onion /'ʌnjən/, *n.* **1.** a widely grown plant, having a strong-smelling bulb that is popular as food. **2.** *Colloq.* the head. **3. know one's onions**, *Colloq.* to know one's job completely. **4. off one's onion**, *Colloq.* mad. [ME, from OF, from L: large pearl, onion]

onion grass, *n.* **1.** an introduced weed of lawns and pastures having underground corms. **2.** → **onion weed**.

onion weed, *n.* a slender plant with small white flowers, which seeds as well as reproduces from bulbs, and which infests lawns.

only /'ounli/, *adv.* **1.** without others or anything further; alone: *Only he remained.* **2.** no more than; merely: *If you would only go away.* **3.** as recently as: *He was here only a moment ago.* **4.** solely; exclusively: *I work here only.* **5. only too**, very; extremely: *She was only too pleased to come.* ◊*adj.* **6.** single; sole: *an only son.* **7.** single in an quality etc. ◊*conj.* **8.** but; except: *I would have gone, only you objected.* [OE *ānlīc*]

onomatopoeia /ˌɒnəmætə'piə/, *n.* the formation of a name or word by imitating the sound associated with the thing referred to, as in *mopoke* and *buzz*. [LL, from Gk: the making of words] —**onomatopoeic**, *adj.*

onrush /'ɒnrʌʃ/, *n.* a strong forward rush, flow, etc.

onset /'ɒnset/, *n.* **1.** an attack: *a violent onset.* **2.** a beginning; start.

on side, *n. Cricket.* → **leg** (def. 5).

onside /ɒn'saɪd/, *adj.* **1.** not offside. **2.** in agreement.

onslaught /'ɒnslɔt/, *n.* a violent attack or assault.

Ontario /ɒn'tɛəriou/, *n.* **1.** a province in southern Canada, bordering on the Great Lakes. Pop. 9 113 515 (1986 est.); 1 068 587 km². *Cap.*: Toronto. **2. Lake**, the smallest of the Great Lakes, between New York and Ontario. About 300 km long; about 12 130 km². —**Ontarian**, *n., adj.*

onto /'ɒntu/, *prep.* to a place or position on; upon; on.

ontogeny /ɒn'tɒdʒəni/, *n.* the development of an individual organism (as contrasted with *phylogeny*).

ontology /ɒn'tɒlədʒi/, *n.* **1.** the science of being, as such. **2.** *Phil.* the branch of metaphysics that studies the nature of being. [NL, from Gk] —**ontological**, *adj.*

onus /'ounəs/, *n.* a responsibility; burden. [L: load, burden]

onward /'ɒnwəd/, *adj.* **1.** directed or moving forwards. ◊*adv.* **2.** onwards. [ME. See ON, -WARD]

onwards /'ɒnwədz/, *adv.* **1.** towards a point ahead or in front; forwards. **2.** at a position or point in front.

onyx /'ɒnɪks/, *n. Mineral.* a type of quartz consisting of straight bands which differ in color. [ME, from L, from Gk: nail, claw, veined gem]

oo-, a word part meaning 'egg'. [Gk, combining form of *ōión*]

oocyte /'ouəsaɪt/, *n. Biol.* the female germ cell in the maturation stage. Also, **ovocyte**.

Oodgeroo Noonuccal /ˌudʒəru nu'nʌkəl/, *n.* born 1920, Australian poet and Aboriginal activist. Formerly, **Kath Walker**.

oogamy /ou'ɒgəmi/, *n. Biol.* the union during the process of sexual reproduction, of the rather large female gamete (sex cell) with the small male gamete.

oogenesis /ouə'dʒenəsəs/, *n. Biol.* the origin and development of the ovum.

oogonium /ouə'gouniəm/, *n., pl.* **-nia** /-niə/, **-niums**. **1.** *Biol.* one of the female germ cells at the multiplication stage, before the maturation stage. **2.** *Bot.* a one-celled female reproductive organ in certain plants. [NL]

Ooldea /'uldiə/, *n.* a small settlement and railway siding in south-western SA; important meeting place for Aboriginal tribes before settlement by Europeans. [Aboriginal: meeting place at the water]

oolite /'ouəlaɪt/, *n.* **1.** a small, rounded mass of mineral matter, formed in shallow water under special conditions. **2.** a limestone composed of such masses, in some places altered to ironstone by replacement with iron oxide. [F] —**oolitic**, *adj.*

oomph /umf/, *n. Colloq.* **1.** energy; vitality. **2.** sex appeal.

oophyte /'ouəfaɪt/, *n.* the plant which produces the gametes (sex cells), in flowerless plants as mosses and ferns.

oorarrie /u'rari/, *n.* See **hopping mouse**.

Oort /ɔt/, *n.* **Jan Hendrik** /jɒn 'hendrɪk/, born 1900, Dutch astronomer; discovered the spiral structure of the Milky Way.

ooze[1] /uz/, *v.*, **oozed**, **oozing**, *n.* ◊*v.i.* **1.** (of moisture, air, etc.) to pass slowly, as through small openings. **2.** (of a substance) to give out moisture, etc. **3.** (of information, charm, etc.)

ooze to pass (*out*, etc.) slowly or unnoticeably. ◇*v.t.* **4.** to give out (moisture, charm, etc.). ◇*n.* **5.** something that oozes. [OE *wōs* juice, moisture]

ooze² /uz/, *n.* **1.** a chalky mud covering parts of the ocean bottom. **2.** soft mud, or slime. **3.** a marsh; bog. [OE *wāse* mud]

op-, a variant of **ob-**, before *p*, as in *oppose*.

op., *Abbrev.* **1.** operation. **2.** opus.

OP /ou 'pi/, *adj.* out of print.

opacity /ou'pæsəti/, *n., pl.* **-ties**. **1.** the condition or quality of not allowing light to shine through; opaqueness. **2.** uncertainty of meaning; lack of clarity. **3.** mental dullness. [L: shade]

opal /'oupəl/, *n.* a mineral, a form of silica found in many varieties and colors and valued as gem. [L, from Gk] —**opaline**, *adj.*

opaque /ou'peɪk/, *adj.* **1.** not allowing light to pass through. **2.** not able to give off radiation, sound, heat, etc. **3.** not shining or bright. **4.** hard to understand, as an argument or reason. **5.** unintelligent. [ME, from L: shady, darkened]

op art /ɒp 'at/, *n.* a style of abstract art which uses visual effects to give a sensation of movement.

op. cit. /ɒp 'sɪt/, *Abbrev.* in the work cited, or mentioned. [L *opere citātō*]

OPEC /'oupɛk/, *n.* Organisation of Petroleum Exporting Countries; formed in 1960 to coordinate members' policies regarding petroleum, in order to safeguard their interests. [abbrev.]

open /'oupən/, *adj.* **1.** (of a door) not shut. **2.** (of a house, box, etc.) not closed, covered, or shut up. **3.** (of a space) not enclosed. **4.** able to be entered, used, shared, etc., by all: *an open competition*. **5.** (of shops, etc.) ready to do business: *open to the public*. **6.** (of a court hearing, etc.) able to be attended by members of the public. **7.** available (oft. fol. by *to*): *The course is open to all students*. **8.** unfilled, as a position. **9.** without limitations as to hunting or fishing: *open season*. **10.** (of a question) undecided. **11.** having no cover, roof, etc. **12.** bare; exposed. **13.** (of speech, looks, etc.) not hiding anything; frank: *an open face*. **14.** generous; liberal. **15.** *Music.* (of a string) not stopped by a finger. **16.** *Phonet.* pronounced with a relatively large opening above the tongue: '*Cot*' *has a more open vowel than* '*caught*'. ◇*v.t.* **17.** to move (a door, gate, etc.) from a closed position so as to allow passage. **18.** to make (a house, box, etc.) open (oft. fol. by *up*). **19.** to make available, as for use. **20.** to clear (a passage, etc.) of obstructions. **21.** to uncover, lay bare. **22.** to make public; reveal. **23.** to make ready to receive knowledge, etc. **24.** to expand, extend. **25.** to establish for the use of the public: *to open an office*. **26.** to begin, start: *to open a talk*. **27.** to cut or break into. **28.** to make an opening in. ◇*v.i.* **29.** to become open. **30.** to allow movement (*into*, *to*, etc.): *The door opened into a garden*. **31.** (of a shop, etc.) to open its doors to the public. **32.** (of a school) to begin a term. **33.** (of a play) to begin a season or tour. **34.** to come apart, or burst open. **35.** to become uncovered or revealed. **36.** to open a book, etc.: *Open at page 32*. **37.** to begin, start. ◇*v.* **38. open up, a.** to make ready for use, as new land. **b.** to begin firing. ◇*n.* **39.** an open or clear space. **40.** the open air, water, etc. **41.** a situation where nothing is hidden. **42.** an opening. **43.** a sporting competition in which both amateurs and professionals may take part. [ME and OE]

open-and-shut /'oupən-ən-ʃʌt/, *adj.* easily decided; obvious.

open book, *n.* **1.** a person whose feelings or thoughts are not easily hidden. **2.** anything which can be easily understood.

open chain, *n.* the linking of atoms in an organic molecule in a chain not a ring.

open cut, *n. Mining.* a shallow, open pit allowing mining of near surface rock layers.

open government, *n. Govt.* a system whereby the public has the legal right to obtain official information or documents unless otherwise stated by law, and whereby public servants are not prevented from giving official information except for reasons of national security.

opening /'oupnɪŋ, 'oupənɪŋ/, *n.* **1.** a making or becoming open. **2.** a space or place, not in use. **3.** a gap; hole. **4.** the act of beginning. **5.** the first part of anything. **6.** a vacancy. **7.** an opportunity. **8.** an official beginning. **9.** the first performance of a theatrical production, etc.

opening address, *n. Law.* the statement of the case made by counsel to the court before any evidence is presented.

openly /'oupənli/, *adv.* **1.** in an obvious way. **2.** in an honest way.

open-minded /'oupən-maɪndəd/, *adj.* having or showing a mind open to new arguments or ideas.

open-range /'oupən-reɪndʒ/, *adj. Agric.* of or relating to the pasturing of cattle, etc., on unfenced land, with, as a result, no control over types and quantities of feed.

open verdict, *n.* the finding at the end of an inquest that there is insufficient evidence to reach a definite conclusion as to the immediate cause of death, or as to whether any criminal act was involved.

opera /'ɒprə, 'ɒpərə/, *n.* **1.** a long dramatic composition in which music is an essential factor, consisting of recitatives, arias, choruses, etc., with orchestral accompaniment, scenery, acting, and sometimes dancing; a musical drama. **2.** the form of musical and dramatic art represented by such compositions. [It, from L: service, work, a work] —**operatic**, *adj.*

operable /'ɒpərəbəl, 'ɒprə-/, *adj.* **1.** able to be put into practice. **2.** admitting of a surgical operation.

operate /'ɒpəreɪt/, *v.*, **-rated, -rating**. ◇*v.i.* **1.** to work or run, as a machine does. **2.** to work or use a machine, apparatus, etc. **3.** to use force or influence (oft. fol. by *on* or *upon*). **4.** to perform some process of work or treatment. **5.** *Surg.* to perform an operation on a patient with instruments, so as to remedy deformity, injury, or disease. **6.** *Mil, Navy.* to

operate give orders and carry out military acts, opposed to staff work. **7.** to carry on buying and selling in shares, etc. ◇*v.t.* **8.** to manage (a machine, etc.) at work: *to operate a switchboard*. **9.** to keep (a machine, factory, etc.) working. **10.** to bring about, as by action. [L: having done work, having had effect]

operating /'ɒpəreɪtɪŋ/, *adj.* used for or in surgical operations: *an operating theatre*; *an operating table*.

operation /ɒpə'reɪʃən/, *n.* **1.** the act, process, or manner of operating. **2.** the condition of being in use or working order: *a rule no longer in operation*. **3.** the power of operating. **4.** a course of productive or industrial activity: *building operations*. **5.** a particular course or process: *mental operations*. **6.** a business transaction, esp. one on a large scale: *operations in oil*. **7.** *Surg.* a procedure of operating on the body of a patient. **8.** *Maths.* a process such as addition. **9.** a military campaign.

operational /ɒpə'reɪʃənəl/, *adj.* **1.** of or relating to an operation or operations. **2.** ready for use. **3.** *Mil.* of, relating to, or involved in military operations.

operative /'ɒpərətɪv, 'ɒprə-/, *n.* **1.** a worker, esp. someone skilled in productive or industrial work; artisan. ◇*adj.* **2.** operating, or exerting force or influence. **3.** having force, or being in operation: *laws operative in a community*. **4.** serving the purpose; effective. **5.** concerned with, or relating to work.

operator /'ɒpəreɪtə/, *n.* **1.** a worker; someone employed or skilled in operating a machine, apparatus, etc.: *a wireless operator*. **2.** someone who conducts some working or industrial establishment or system: *the operators of a mine*. **3.** someone who deals in shares, etc., esp. speculatively or on a large scale. **4.** *Colloq.* someone who successfully handles people or situations for self-gain: *He's a smooth operator*.

operculum /ə'pɜkjələm/, *n., pl.* **-la** /-lə/, **-lums**. **1.** *Bot., Zool., etc.* a part or organ serving as a lid or cover. **2.** *Zool.* **a.** the gill cover of fishes and amphibians. **b.** (in many gastropods) a horny plate closing the opening of the shell. [L: a cover, lid]

operetta /ɒpə'retə/, *n.* a short opera, usu. of a light character. [It, diminutive of *opera* OPERA]

ophthalmic /ɒf'θælmɪk/, *adj.* of or relating to the eye.

ophthalmo-, a word part meaning 'eye'. [Gk, combining form of *ophthalmós*]

ophthalmology /ɒfθæl'mɒlədʒi/, *n.* the science dealing with the structure, functions, and diseases of the eye. **–ophthalmologist**, *n.*

-opia, a word part of nouns, meaning a condition of sight or of the organs of sight, as in *myopia*. [Gk: eye]

opiate /'oʊpiət, -eɪt/, *n.* **1.** a medicine containing opium, and having the ability to produce sleep; narcotic. **2.** anything that causes dullness or inaction, or that calms the feelings. ◇*adj.* **3.** mixed with opium. **4.** producing sleep; soporific. [ML from L: OPIUM]

opine /oʊ'paɪn/, *v.t., v.i.,* **opined, opining.** to think; hold or express an opinion. [L: think, deem]

opinion /ə'pɪnjən/, *n.* **1.** a judgment or belief not held firmly enough to produce certainty. **2.** a personal view: *public opinion*. **3.** *Law.* formal non-binding advice on the legal position of some matter, as given by counsel or by a court. [ME, from OF, from L suppo-sition]

opinionated /ə'pɪnjəneɪtəd/, *adj.* having high regard for one's own opinions; conceitedly dogmatic.

opium /'oʊpiəm/, *n.* the thick juice of the opium poppy, containing morphine and other alkaloids, of great value in medicine to relieve pain, produce sleep, etc. [ME, from L, from Gk: juice]

opium poppy, *n.* a poppy, from South East Asia, with white or red flowers which are a source of opium.

opossum /ə'pɒsəm/, *n.* **1.** *NZ.* the brush-tailed possum, introduced from Australia. **2.** a marsupial, about the size of a large cat, common in the southern US, which pretends to be dead when caught. [Algonquian]

Oppenheimer /'ɒpənhaɪmə/, *n.* **J(ulius) Robert,** 1904–67, US nuclear physicist; directed the design and building of the first atom bomb (1943–45); opposed the development of the hydrogen bomb.

opponent /ə'poʊnənt/, *n.* someone who is on the opposite side in a contest, argument, etc.; adversary. [L: opposing] **–opponency**, *n.*

opportune /'ɒpətjun/, *adj.* **1.** favorable; appropriate. **2.** happening or coming at a good time; timely. [ME, from L]

opportunism /ɒpə'tjunɪzəm, 'ɒpətjunɪzəm/, *n.* the practice, as in politics, of changing actions, etc., to suit the occasion (often without thought of principles). **–opportunist**, *n., adj.*

opportunity /ɒpə'tjunəti/, *n., pl.* **-ties.** a suitable or favorable time or occasion.

opportunity shop, *n.* a shop run by a church, charity, etc., for the sale of second-hand goods, esp. clothes.

oppose /ə'poʊz/, *v.,* **-posed, -posing.** ◇*v.t.* **1.** to act in opposition to; resist; combat. **2.** to stand in the way of; hinder. **3.** to use or to take as being opposite: *words opposed in meaning*. ◇*v.i.* **4.** to be or act in opposition. [ME, from OF]

opposite /'ɒpəsɪt/, *adj.* **1.** placed or lying against or facing something else: *They were seated at opposite ends of a room*. **2.** completely different, as in nature, qualities, result, etc. ◇*n.* **3.** someone or something that is opposite or contrary: *My opinion is the opposite of his*. **4.** → **antonym.** ◇*prep.* **5.** facing: *She sat opposite me*. **6.** in a position creating a unity with some other position: *She played opposite a famous actor*. ◇*adv.* **7.** on opposite sides. [ME, from L: put before or against, opposed]

opposition /ɒpə'zɪʃən/, *n.* **1.** the action of opposing. **2.** opposing feelings; antagonism.

opposite   731   **Orange Free State**

3. an opposing group or body. **4.** (*usu. cap.*) the major political party opposed to the party in power. **5.** the condition or position of being placed opposite. **6.** *Astron.* the situation of two heavenly bodies when they differ by 180°. [L]

oppress /əˈpres/, *v.t.* **1.** to lie heavily upon (the mind, a person, etc.), as a care, sorrow, etc. **2.** to subject to a cruel exercise of authority or power. [ME, from L: press against, subdue] **– oppressor**, *n.* **– oppression**, *n.*

oppressive /əˈpresɪv/, *adj.* **1.** unjustly cruel, as a dictator, taxes, etc.; tyrannical. **2.** causing discomfort because uncomfortably great, etc.: *oppressive heat.* **3.** upsetting, as sorrows.

-opsis, a word part indicating apparent likeness. [Gk: appearance, sight]

opt /ɒpt/, *v.i.* **1.** to make a choice; choose. ◇*v.* **2. opt out**, to decide not to join in. [F, from L: choose, wish]

optic /ˈɒptɪk/, *adj.* **1.** relating to the eye as the organ of sight, or sight as a function of the brain. **2.** optical. ◇*n.* **3.** (*usu. pl.*) the eye. [ML, from Gk: of sight]

optical /ˈɒptɪkəl/, *adj.* **1.** acting by means of sight or light, as instruments. **2.** made to help the sight. **3.** relating to sight; visual: *an optical illusion.*

optician /ɒpˈtɪʃən/, *n.* **1.** someone who makes glasses for remedying defects of vision, in accordance with a prescription. **2.** a maker or seller of optical glasses and instruments. [F, from ML: OPTICS]

optics /ˈɒptɪks/, *n.* the branch of physical science that deals with the properties and nature of light and vision. [pl. of OPTIC. See -ICS]

optimism /ˈɒptəmɪzəm/, *n.* **1.** the inclination or tendency to hope for the best. **2.** the belief that good finally overcomes evil in the world. **3.** the doctrine that the existing world is the best of all possible worlds. **4.** the belief that goodness spreads through all reality. [NL, from L: best] **– optimist**, *n.* **– optimistic**, *adj.*

optimum /ˈɒptəməm/, *n., pl.* **-ma** /-mə/, **-mums**, *adj.* ◇*n.* **1.** the best point, degree, amount, etc., for the purpose. ◇*adj.* **2.** best; most favorable. [L: best]

option /ˈɒpʃən/, *n.* **1.** the power or freedom to choose. **2.** something which may be or is chosen. **3.** the act of choosing. **4.** the right, as by an agreement, to buy a property within a certain time. [L: choice] **– optional**, *adj.*

optometry /ɒpˈtɒmətri/, *n.* the practice or art of testing the eyes by means of suitable instruments or appliances, for defects of vision, in order to supply suitable glasses. **– optometrist**, *n.*

opulent /ˈɒpjələnt/, *adj.* **1.** wealthy or rich, as persons or places. **2.** richly supplied; abundant or plentiful: *opulent sunshine.* [L: rich, wealthy] **– opulence**, *n.*

opus /ˈoʊpəs/, *n., pl.* **opera** /ˈɒpərə/. **1.** a work or composition (esp. musical). **2.** one of the musical compositions of a composer as numbered according to order of publication. *Abbrev.:* op. [L: work, labor, a work]

or[1] /ɔ/, *conj.* a particle used **1.** to connect words, phrases, or clauses representing alternatives: *to be or not to be.* **2.** often in paired relationship: *either . . . or; or . . . or; whether . . . or.* [ME]

or[2] /ɔ/, *n.* the color gold or yellow. [ME, from F, from L: gold]

-or[1], a suffix of nouns meaning a state or condition, a quality or property, etc., as in *error, terror, colo(u)r, hono(u)r.* [ME, from AF, from L]

-or[2], a suffix of nouns indicating someone or something that performs an action, or has some particular role or office, as in *actor, creditor, elevator.* In some cases it is used in place of **-er**[1], as in *sailor, survivor, vendor.* [L; in some cases replacing ME *-our*]

oracle /ˈɒrəkəl/, *n.* **1.** (esp. in ancient Greece) a saying, often hard to understand, given by a priest or priestess as the response of a god to a question. **2.** the source of such a reply: *the oracle of Apollo at Delphi.* **3.** a divine communication or revelation. **4.** the holy of holies in the Jewish temple. See I Kings, 6:16, 19-23. **5.** any person or thing serving as a means for contact with godlike forces. **6.** any statement made or received as being unquestionably correct. **7.** a person who makes such statements. [ME, from OF, from L] **– oracular**, *adj.*

oral /ˈɔrəl/, *adj.* **1.** spoken. **2.** employing speech, as teachers or methods of teaching. **3.** of or relating to the mouth. **4.** done or taken by the mouth: *an oral dose of medicine.* **5.** *Zool.* relating to that surface of polyps and sea animals which contains the mouth and tentacles. **6.** *Phonet.* spoken with none of the voice sounding through the nose; *b* and *v* are oral consonants, and the normal English vowels are oral. ◇*n.* **7.** an oral examination. [L: mouth]

Orana /əˈrænə/, *n.* a region in NSW, comprising most of the central third of the state's northern half. Formerly, until 1972, **North-Western Region.** [Aboriginal: welcome]

orange /ˈɒrɪndʒ/, *n.* **1.** a round, reddish yellow citrus fruit. **2.** the white-flowered evergreen tree bearing such fruit. **3.** a reddish yellow color. ◇*adj.* **4.** of or relating to the orange. **5.** made with or having the flavor of oranges. **6.** reddish yellow. [ME, from OF, from Ar, from Pers, from Skt]

Orange[1] /ˈɒrɪndʒ/, *n.* a European princely family, originating in the French principality of Orange, ruling in England from 1688 to 1694, and in the Netherlands since 1815. Also, **Orange-Nassau.**

Orange[2] /ˈɒrɪndʒ/, *a* city in eastern central NSW, north-west of Bathurst; apple-growing area. Pop. 28 935 (1986).

orange blossom, *n.* the flower of the orange, much worn by brides.

Orange Free State, *n.* a province in the central Republic of South Africa; a Boer republic, 1854-1900; a British colony (**Orange**

River Colony), 1900–10. Pop. 1 776 903 (1985); 128 586 km². *Cap.*: Bloemfontein.

Orangeman /ˈɒrɪndʒmən/, *n., pl.* **-men.** **1.** a member of a secret society formed in the north of Ireland in 1795, having for its object the maintenance of the Protestant religion and political ascendancy. **2.** a Northern Ireland protestant.

orang-outang /əˈræŋ-ətæŋ/, *n.* a large, long-armed, tree-climbing ape, found in parts of Indonesia. Also, **orang, orang-utan** /əˈræŋ-ətæŋ/. [Malay: man of the woods]

oration /ɒˈreɪʃən/, *n.* **1.** a formal speech, esp. one given on a special occasion. **2.** a speech noted for its elevated style, diction, or delivery. [ME, from L: speech, discourse, prayer]

orator /ˈɒrətə/, *n.* someone who delivers an oration; a public speaker, esp. one of much skill. [L: speaker, supplicant]

oratorio /ɒrəˈtɔriou/, *n., pl.* **-rios.** *Music.* a long dramatic composition, usu. based upon a religious theme, for solo voices, chorus, and orchestra. [It, from LL]

oratory /ˈɒrətri/, *n.* **1.** grand and powerful speaking. **2.** the art of public speaking. —**oratorical**, *adj.*

orb /ɔb/, *n.* **1.** *Chiefly Poetic.* any of the heavenly bodies: *the orb of day* (the sun). **2.** a sphere or globe. **3.** *Chiefly Poetic.* the eyeball or eye. **4.** a globe bearing a cross, as a sign of royalty. ◇*v.t.* **5.** to form into a circle or sphere. ◇*v.i.* **6.** to move in an orbit. [L: circle, disc, orb]

orbit /ˈɔbət/, *n.* **1.** the curved path followed by a planet, satellite, etc., about a body, as the earth or sun. **2.** a person's scope of activity. **3.** *Anat.* the eye socket. **4.** *Zool.* the part surrounding the eye of a bird or insect. **5.** an orb or sphere. **6.** *Chem.* the path of an electron around the nucleus of an atom. ◇*v.t., v.i.* **7.** to (cause to) move or travel in an orbital path. [L: wheel track, course, circuit] —**orbital**, *adj.*

orb-weaver /ˈɔb-wivə/, *n.* a spider which weaves an orb-shaped web each night, to catch night-flying insects.

orchard /ˈɔtʃəd/, *n.* (an enclosed area of) cultivated fruit trees. [OE *orceard*] —**orchardist**, *n.*

orchestra /ˈɔkəstrə/, *n.* a group of players of musical instruments, usu. performing classical or semi-classical music: *string orchestra*; *symphony orchestra*. See **brass** (def. 3), **string** (def. 7), **percussion** (def. 4), **woodwind.** [L, from Gk: the space on which the chorus in Ancient Greek theatre danced] —**orchestral**, *adj.*

orchestrate /ˈɔkəstreɪt/, *v.t.*, **-trated, -trating. 1.** to compose or arrange (music) to enable it to be performed by an orchestra. **2.** to put together in a well planned way: *to orchestrate a conference.* —**orchestration**, *n.*

orchid /ˈɔkəd/, *n.* a plant growing in temperate and tropical areas, either on the ground or on trees, usu. with long leaves from a central mass of fibrous roots and/or bulbs, and with unusual and beautiful flowers. The group includes the cymbidium, dendrobium, and others. [NL]

Orcus /ˈɔkəs/, *n. Rom Myth.* **1.** the world of the dead; Greek name, Hades. **2.** the god of the underworld also known as Pluto.

Ord /ɔd/, *n.* a river in the East Kimberley district of northern WA, dammed in 1970–72 as part of the **Ord River Irrigation Scheme**. [named after Sir Harry *Ord*, governor of WA 1878–80]

ordain /ɔˈdeɪn/, *v.t.* **1.** to appoint to church office (a minister, deacon, etc.), after a course of training; confer holy orders upon. **2.** to order; decree; enact. **3.** (of God, fate, etc.) to determine some future events: *Fate ordains when we should die.* [ME, from OF: from L: order, arrange, appoint]

ordeal /ɔˈdil, ˈɔdil/, *n.* **1.** any severe test or trial; a trying experience. **2.** an ancient form of trial in which accused people were subjected to danger from fire, water or poison and from which, if innocent, they would be protected by divine power. [OE *ordēl*]

order /ˈɔdə/, *n.* **1.** a command given by someone with the right or power to do so; an injunction. **2.** the way in which people or things are placed, one after (or under) another; succession; sequence. **3.** a condition in which everything is in its proper place; methodical arrangement. **4.** a proper, satisfactory or working condition or state: *My watch is out of order.* **5.** any class, kind, or sort, of persons or things, seen to be different from others in nature or character: *talents of a high order.* **6.** *Biol.* a major division of a class (def. 8) grouped according to shared characteristics. **7.** *Hist.* a rank or class of persons in the community: *Serfs belonged to the lowest social order.* **8.** a body of persons of the same profession, occupation, or interests or living under the same religious, moral or social rules: *the clerical order*; *the Franciscan order.* **9.** any of the degrees or grades of ordained people in a Christian Church, e.g. bishop, priest, etc. **10.** (*usu. pl.*) the rank of an ordained Christian minister: *to take holy orders.* **11.** *Hist.* a society of knights, of combined military and monastic character, as in the Middle Ages, e.g. the Knights Templar, etc. **12.** a condition of society in which most people obey the laws; absence of revolt, unruliness, etc.: *The police keep law and order.* **13.** the usual way of doing things in society or in social groups, meetings, etc. **14. a.** a request to make or supply something (usu. for money): *shoes made to order.* **b.** the goods purchased. **c.** a written request to pay money or deliver goods. **15.** *Maths.* degree, as in algebra. ◇**16.** Some special uses are:
a tall order, *Colloq.* a difficult task.
call to order, to establish order at a meeting.
in order, 1. in a proper state; correctly arranged. **2.** suitable; appropriate.
in order that, so that: *I gave him a list in order that he would remember everything.*
in order to, as a means to: *I ran in order to catch the bus.*
on order, ordered but not yet received.

out of order, 1. not functioning properly; broken. **2.** not in accordance with recognised parliamentary or debating rules. ◇*v.t.* **17.** to give an order or command to (someone): *to order someone to go*. **18.** to direct to be made or supplied; to give an order for: *We ordered two steaks; The doctor ordered medicine for the patient*. **19.** to arrange in a good or suitable order. ◇*v.i.* **20.** to give orders: *to order rather than obey*. **21.** to order food, etc. [ME, from OF, from L: row, rank, regular arrangement]

orderly /'ɔdəli/, *adj., n., pl.* **-lies.** ◇*adj.* **1.** arranged in an approved order, or tidy manner. **2.** systematic; disciplined: *an orderly mind*. **3.** willing to obey rules or laws: *an orderly citizen*. ◇*n.* **4.** someone, esp. a soldier or hospital employee, who performs general duties. **—orderliness,** *n.*

ordinal /'ɔdənəl/, *n.* a number or numeral which describes a place in a series or the order in which things occur, e.g. first, second, third. Also **ordinal number**. See **cardinal number**. [ME, from L: order]

ordinance /'ɔdənəns/, *n.* an authoritative rule, law or regulation. [ME, from OF: to order, from L]

ordinary /'ɔdənəri, 'ɔdənri/, *adj., n., pl.* **-ries.** ◇*adj.* **1.** of the usual or common kind. **2.** somewhat inferior. **3.** customary; normal: *for all ordinary purposes*. ◇*n.* **4.** something regular, customary or usual. **5. out of the ordinary**, unusual. [ME, from L: of the usual order] **—ordinariness,** *n.* **—ordinarily,** *adv.*

ordinary share, *n. Comm.* a share (def. 2) which ranks for dividends after preference shares and before deferred shares.

ordination /ɔdə'neɪʃən/, *n.* **1.** *Church.* the ceremony of ordaining. **2.** the fact of having been ordained. [ME, from L: an ordering]

ordnance /'ɔdnəns/, *n.* military weapons of all kinds with their equipment, supplies, etc. [var. of ORDINANCE]

Ordovician /ɔdou'vɪʃən/, *adj., n.* (relating to) the period or system following the Cambrian and before the Silurian. [L *Ordovicēs,* pl., an ancient British tribe in N Wales]

ordure /'ɔdʒuə/, *n.* filth; dung; excrement. [ME, from OF: filthy, from L: horrid]

ore /ɔ/, *n.* **1.** a metal-bearing mineral or rock, esp. when valuable enough to be mined. **2.** a mineral, etc., as a source of some non-metallic substance such as sulfur. [OE *ār* brass]

oregano /ɒrə'ganoʊ/, *n.* spicy plant of the mint family, used in cookery.

Oregon /'ɒrəgən/, *n.* a state in the northwestern US, on the Pacific coast. Pop. 2 698 000 (1986 est.); 251 489 km². *Cap.:* Salem. *Abbrev.:* Oreg, Ore **—Oregonian,** *n., adj.*

Oregon Trail, *n.* a route for westward pioneers in the US, starting in Missouri and reaching Oregon, much used in the mid-19th century. About 3200 km long.

organ /'ɔgən/, *n.* **1.** a musical instrument **(pipe organ)** with one or more keyboards and consisting of one or more sets of pipes sounded by means of compressed air. **2.** a musical instrument **(electronic** or **electric organ)** resembling a pipe organ and having pipes but worked by electric currents. **3.** (in an animal or a plant) a part which performs a special function, e.g. the heart. **4.** an instrument or means of performing some function. **5.** a means of expressing thoughts, opinions, etc., e.g. a newspaper: *'Warcry' is an organ of the Salvation Army.* [ME, from L, from Gk: instrument, tool, bodily organ, musical instrument]

organdie /'ɔgəndi/, *n., pl.* **-dies.** a fine, thin, crisp cotton material. [F]

organic /ɔ'gænɪk/, *adj.* **1.** relating to a class of chemical compounds consisting of all compounds of carbon except for its oxides, sulfides, and metal carbonates. **2.** typical of, relating to or coming from living organisms: *organic remains found in rocks; organic fertiliser.* **3.** relating to the organ(s) of an animal or plant. **4.** marked by the systematic arrangement of parts; organised. **5.** of or relating to the constitution or structure of a thing. **6.** relating to the cultivation of fruit and vegetables without using chemical fertilisers or pesticides. [L, from Gk] **—organically,** *adv.*

organic chemistry, *n.* that branch of chemistry dealing with organic compounds of carbon.

organisation or **organization** /ɔgənaɪ'zeɪʃən/, *n.* **1.** the act of organising. **2.** the condition or manner of being organised. **3.** something which is organised. **4.** any organised whole. **5.** a body of people organised for some purpose. **6.** the people or structure involved in running a business, club, political party, etc.

Organisation for Economic Cooperation and Development, *n.* →OECD

Organisation of Petroleum Exporting Countries, *n.* →OPEC

organise or **organize** /'ɔgənaɪz/, *v.,* **-nised, -nising.** ◇*v.t.* **1.** to form into a group esp. for united action: *to organise a party; to organise a club.* **2.** to bring together in an orderly way: *to organise facts.* **3.** to arrange: *I have organised a holiday for us.* **4.** to build a trade union among: *to organise workers.* ◇*v.i.* **5.** to combine in an organised company, party, etc.: *Workers organised into trade unions in the 19th century.* [ME, from ML, from L: organ]

organism /'ɔgənɪzəm/, *n.* **1.** *Biol.* an individual composed of mutually dependent parts which work together to develop and support life. **2.** any form of animal or plant life: *microscopic organisms.* **3.** anything that can be compared with a living being because of its complex structure.

organist /'ɔgənəst/, *n.* someone who plays an organ.

organo-, a word part meaning 'organ' or 'organic'. [Gk, combining form of *órganon*]

organza /ɔ'gænzə/, *n.* a material made from a mixture of silk or nylon with cotton, similar to organdie but less fine.

orgasm /'ɔgæzəm/, n. a complex series of pleasurable responses of the genital organs and skin at the climax of a sexual act. [NL, from Gk: swell, be excited]

orgy /'ɔdʒi/, n., pl. **-gies**. 1. wild or drunken feasting (often marked by immoral behavior). 2. any activity marked by wild, uncontrolled behavior: *an orgy of killing*. 3. (pl.) secret ceremonies connected with the worship of some ancient Greek and Roman gods accompanied by wild dancing and singing, drinking, etc. [L, from Gk] — **orgiastic**, adj.

oriel /'ɔriəl/, n. a type of bay window, esp. in an upper storey. [ME, from OF: porch, passage, gallery, from L: gilded]

orient /'ɔriənt, -o-/, n., adj.; /'ɔrient, -o-/, v. ◇n. 1. **the Orient**, the East; the countries to the east (and south-east) of the Mediterranean esp. the countries of eastern Asia. ◇adj. 2. *Poetic.* eastern or oriental. ◇v.t., v.i. 3. → **orientate**. [ME, from L: the east, sunrise (n. use of ppr., rising)] — **Oriental**, adj., n.

orientate /'ɔrientert, 'ɔri-/, v.t., v.i., **-tated, -tating**. to find or adjust in relation to new surroundings or ideas. Also, **orient**.

orientation /,ɔrien'teɪʃən, ,ɔriən-/, n. 1. the act or process of orientating. 2. the condition of being orientated. 3. *Psychol.* the ability to locate oneself in one's environment with reference to time, place, and people.

orienteering /ɔriən'tɪərɪŋ/, n. a sport in which competitors race on foot, skis, bicycle, etc., over a course consisting of a number of checkpoints which must be found with maps or compasses.

orifice /'ɔrəfəs/, n. the mouth or opening of a hole. [F, from L]

orig., *Abbrev.* 1. origin. 2. original. 3. originally.

origami /ɔrə'gami/, n. the art of folding paper into the shapes of flowers, birds, etc. [Jap]

origin /'ɔrədʒən/, n. 1. a starting point, source or beginning: *the origin of a stream; the origin of a plan*. 2. birth; parentage; extraction: *Scottish origin*. 3. *Maths.* the point of intersection of two or more axes in a system of Cartesian or polar coordinates; the point from which a measurement is taken. [L: beginning, source, rise]

original /ə'rɪdʒənəl/, adj. 1. first; earliest: *The original binding of the book is very old.* 2. new; fresh; novel: *an original way of advertising*. 3. doing or done by oneself independently; not derived from another: *original thinking; original research.* 4. being that from which a copy, translation, etc., is made: *The original letter is in the National Library.* ◇n. 5. the primary form or type. 6. an original work, writing, etc., as opposed to a copy. 7. something represented by a picture, description, etc. 8. someone who thinks or acts for himself or herself. 9. someone who behaves in unusual or odd ways; eccentric. — **originality**, n.

originally /ə'rɪdʒənəli/, adv. 1. in the first state or condition; by origin: *The letter wasn't sealed originally.* 2. at first: *originally they were going to come*. 3. in an original, novel, or very individual manner: *She writes very originally.*

original sin, n. *Theol.* a tendency to evil, the result of Adam's sin, handed down to all people as part of their nature.

originate /ə'rɪdʒəneɪt/, v.t., v.i., **-nated, -nating**. to (cause to) begin: *The ancient Greeks originated the Olympic Games; The Olympic Games originated in ancient Greece.*

Orinoco /ɒrə'noukou/, n. a large river in northern South America, flowing from southern Venezuela into the Atlantic. About 2575 km.

oriole /'ɔriouːl/, n. any of a number of insect and fruit-eating birds found throughout the world, e.g. the **yellow oriole**, of northern Australasia. [ML, var. of L: golden]

Orkney Islands /,ɔkni 'aɪləndz/, n. pl. an island group off the north-eastern tip of Scotland. Pop. 19 400 (1986 est.); 974 km². *Administrative Centre:* Kirkwall.

Orléans /ɔ'liənz, ɔleɪ'ɔleɪ'ɔ̃/, n. a city in northern France, on the river Loire; siege raised by Joan of Arc, 1428. Pop. 105 589 (1982).

ornament /'ɔnəmənt/, n.; /'ɔnəment/, v. ◇n. 1. something added for beauty rather than to be useful: *architectural ornaments.* 2. an object meant to be beautiful rather than useful: *china ornaments.* 3. a person who adds importance, honor, etc., to surroundings, society, etc.: *an ornament to his profession.* 4. outward show: *The white chairs outside their house are just for ornament.* 5. *Music.* a note or group of notes not part of the melody, as a trill. ◇v.t. 6. to furnish with ornaments. 7. to be an ornament to. [L: equipment, ornament] — **ornamental**, adj. — **ornamentation**, n.

ornate /ɔ'neɪt/, adj. covered with ornaments or very showy or fine: *ornate handwriting; ornate buildings.* [ME, from L: adorned]

ornitho-, a word part meaning 'bird'. Also, **ornith-**. [Gk, combining form of *órnis* wing]

ornithology /ɔnə'θɒlədʒi/, n. that branch of zoology that deals with birds. — **ornithologist**, n.

ornithorhynchus /ɔnəθə'rɪŋkəs/, n. → **platypus**. [NL, from Gk]

oro-, a word part meaning 'mountain', *orogenesis*. [Gk, combining form of *óros*]

orographic rainfall /,ɒrəgræfɪk 'reɪnfɔl/, n.pl. rainfall formed by the passage of air over mountains.

orotund /'ɒroutʌnd/, adj. 1. (of the voice or utterance) marked by strength, fullness, richness, and clearness. 2. (of a style of speaking) too rich; pompous or bombastic. [L: with round mouth]

orphan /'ɔfən/, n. 1. a child with no parents. ◇adj. 2. of or for orphans: *an orphan institution.* 3. having no parents. ◇v.t. 4. to cause to become an orphan: *The accident orphaned the children.* [late ME, from LL, from Gk: without parents, bereaved]

orphanage /'ɔfənɪdʒ/, n. a place where orphans live.

Orpheus /'ɔfiəs/, *n. Gk Myth.* a Thracian poet and musician who followed his dead wife Eurydice to Hades but, as he lead her out, he was unable to keep his promise to Pluto not to look back, and lost her for ever. — **Orphean**, **Orphic**, *adj.*

Orpington /'ɔpɪŋtən/, *n.* one of a breed of large white-skinned chickens. [from *Orpington*, town in England]

orris /'ɒrəs/, *n.* a type of iris with a sweet-smelling root. Also, **orrice**. [unexplained var. of IRIS]

Ortega Saavedra /ɔ'teɪgə sa'veɪdrə/, *n.* **Daniel**, Nicaraguan politician; became president in 1985.

Orth, *Abbrev.* Orthodox.

ortho-, a word part meaning 'straight', 'upright', 'correct', used in combination. [Gk: straight, correct]

orthocentre /'ɔθoʊsentə/, *n.* the point of intersection of the altitudes of a triangle.

orthoclase /'ɔθoʊklæs, 'ɔθəkleɪz/, *n.* a very common mineral of the felspar group, potassium aluminium silicate, $KAlSi_3O_8$, occurring as an important part of many igneous rocks; used in the manufacture of porcelain. [Gk]

orthodontics /ɔθə'dɒntɪks/, *n.* that branch of dentistry concerned with the correction of irregularities of the teeth or jaw. Also, **orthodontia**. [NL, from Gk] — **orthodontic**, *adj.* — **orthodontist**, *n.*

orthodox /'ɔθədɒks/, *adj.* **1.** according to accepted religious opinion or teaching. See **heterodox**. **2.** (*cap.*) of or relating to the Greek Orthodox Church or to Orthodox Judaism. **3.** (of ideas, manners, dress, etc.) accepted or approved; conventional. [LL, from Gk: right in opinion]

Orthodox Church, *n.* the Christian Church of the countries which once made up the Eastern Roman Empire, and of countries evangelised from it, as Russia; the Church(es) in agreement with the Greek patriarchal see (**see**[2]) of Constantinople.

orthodoxy /'ɔθədɒksi/, *n., pl.* **-doxies. 1.** accepted belief or practice. **2.** orthodox character: *His orthodoxy is beyond question.*

orthogonal /ɔ'θɒgənəl/, *adj.* **1.** *Maths.* relating to or involving right angles or perpendicular lines: *an orthogonal projection.* **2.** *Crystall.* referable to a rectangular set of axes. [obs. *orthogon(ium)* (from LL, from Gk: right-angled)] — **orthogonally**, *adv.*

orthography /ɔ'θɒgrəfi/, *n., pl.* **-phies. 1.** the art or manner of writing words with the proper letters; spelling. **2.** the study of spelling. **3.** an orthogonal projection, or an elevation drawn by means of it. [ME, from L, from Gk: correct writing]

orthopaedics *or* **orthopedics** /ɔθə'pidɪks/, *n.* (that branch of medicine that deals with) the correction or cure of deformities and diseases of the spine, bones, etc. Also, **orthopaedy** /'ɔθəpidi/. [Gk] — **orthopaedic**, *adj.* — **orthopaedist**, *n.*

orthoptics /ɔ'θɒptɪks/, *n.* that branch of medicine dealing with the correction of disorders of vision by exercises.

Orwell /'ɔwel, -wəl/, *n.* **George** (*Eric Arthur Blair*), 1903–1950, English novelist and essayist; author of satirical novels *Animal Farm* (1945) and *1984* (1949). — **Orwellian**, *adj.*

-ory[1], an adjective suffix meaning 'having the function or effect of', as in *compulsory, contributory, declaratory, illusory.* [L]

-ory[2], a noun suffix indicating a place or an instrument or thing for some purpose, as in *directory, dormitory, purgatory.* [L]

os /ɒs/, *n., pl.* **ossa** /'ɒsə/. a bone. [L]

o/s *Abbrev.* **1.** out of stock. **2.** (in banking) outstanding.

Os, *Chem. Symbol.* osmium.

Osaka /oʊ'sakə/, *n.* a seaport in southern Japan, on Honshu island. Pop. 2 643 213 (1986 est.).

Osborne /'ɒzbən/, *n.* **John James**, born 1929, English dramatist; his play, *Look Back in Anger* (1956), introduced to drama the 'angry young man'.

Osburn /'ɒzbən/, *n.* **Lucy**, 1835–91, Australian nurse, born in England; introduced Florence Nightingale's principles of nursing to NSW.

Oscar /'ɒskə/, *n.* one of a group of statuettes awarded annually by the American Academy of Motion Picture Arts for outstanding achievement by a film actor, director, etc. [? from a remark made by an official on first seeing the statuette that it reminded him of his Uncle Oscar]

oscillate /'ɒsəleɪt/, *v.i.,* **-lated, -lating.** to swing or move to and fro, as or like a pendulum; fluctuate. [L *oscillātus*, pp., swung] — **oscillator**, *n.*

oscillation /ɒsə'leɪʃən/, *n.* **1.** (the act of) swinging to and fro; fluctuation. **2.** a single swing, or movement in one direction, of an oscillating body, etc. **3.** *Phys.* a repetitive to and fro motion of an object; regular variation in value, etc., as in alternating current, etc.

oscilloscope /ə'sɪləskoʊp/, *n.* a device which shows varying voltage or current flow as waves, etc., on a fluorescent screen.

osculate /'ɒskjəleɪt/, *v.t., v.i.,* **-lated, -lating. 1.** to kiss (someone). **2.** to bring or come into close contact or union. [L: kissed] — **osculatory**, *adj.* — **osculation**, *n.*

-ose[1], an adjective suffix meaning 'full of', 'abounding in', 'given to', 'like', as in *jocose, otiose, verbose.* [L]

-ose[2], a noun ending used to form chemical terms, esp. the names of sugars and other carbohydrates, as *fructose, lactose,* and (rarely) of protein derivatives. [abstracted from GLUCOSE]

O'Shane /oʊ'ʃeɪn/, *n.* **Pat**(*ricia June*), born 1941, Australian lawyer; head of NSW Department of Aboriginal Affairs 1981–86; first Aboriginal magistrate, appointed in 1986.

osier /ˈouʒə/, n. (a twig from) a willow, used for wickerwork. [ME, from F]

Osiris /ouˈsaɪrɪs/, n. one of the principal Egyptian gods, brother and husband of Isis, usu. represented as a mummy wearing the crown of Upper Egypt.

-osis, pl. **-oses**. a noun suffix indicating action, process, state, condition, etc., as in *metamorphosis*, and in many pathological terms, as *tuberculosis*. [Gk]

-osity, a noun suffix equivalent to -ose¹ (or -ous) plus -ity.

Oslo /ˈɒzlou/, n. a seaport in and the capital of Norway, in the south-eastern part at the head of **Oslo Fiord**, an inlet (about 120 km long) of the Skagerrak. Pop. 451 484 (1987 est.). Formerly, Christiania.

osmium /ˈɒzmiəm/, n. a hard, heavy, metallic element used for electric-light filaments, etc., having the greatest density of any known material. Symbol: Os; at. no.: 76; at. wt: 190.2. [NL, from Gk: smell, odor; named from the penetrating smell of one of its oxides]

osmosis /ɒzˈmousəs/, n. the tendency of a liquid to pass through a semipermeable membrane into a solution where its concentration is lower. [NL, from Gk: a thrusting]

osprey /ˈɒspri, ˈɒspreɪ/, n., pl. **-preys**. a large hawk which feeds on fish. [ME, from F, b. with L]

ossify /ˈɒsəfaɪ/, v., **-fied, -fying**. ◇v.t. 1. to turn into, or harden like, bone. 2. to make (attitudes, opinions, etc.) rigid or unbending. ◇v.i. 3. to become bone, or hard like bone. 4. to become rigid or unbending in attitudes, opinions, etc. [L] —**ossification**, n.

ostensible /ɒsˈtensəbəl/, adj. outward; pretended; professed: *The ostensible reason for her lateness was that she missed the train.* [F, from L, displayed]

ostentation /ˌɒstenˈteɪʃən/, n. a showing of knowledge, possessions, etc., to make people think highly of one. Also, **ostentatiousness**. [ME, from L] —**ostentatious**, adj.

osteo-, a word part meaning 'bone'. Also, before vowels, **oste-**. [Gk, combining form of *ostéon*]

osteoarthritis /ˌɒstiouəˈθraɪtəs/, n. a degenerative type of chronic arthritis.

osteomyelitis /ˌɒstioumaɪəˈlaɪtəs/, n. *Med.* an inflammation of the bone marrow, which causes the discharge of pus.

osteopathy /ˌɒstiˈɒpəθi/, n. a theory of disease and a method of treatment that supposes that most diseases are due to deformation of some part of the body and can be cured by some kind of manipulation. —**osteopath**, n. —**osteopathic**, adj.

ostler /ˈɒslə/, n. someone who takes care of horses, esp. at an inn. Also, **hostler**.

ostracise or **ostracize** /ˈɒstrəsaɪz/, v.t., **-cised, -cising**. 1. to agree to have nothing to do with (a person); to single (someone) out for exclusion from society, or banishment. 2. (in ancient Greece) to banish (a citizen) for a time by popular vote. [Gk: potsherd, orig. a piece of earthenware used as a token in a ballot] —**ostracism**, n.

ostrich /ˈɒstrɪtʃ/, n. a large bird that runs fast but cannot fly, the largest of existing birds, native to Africa and Arabia. [ME, from OF, from LL, from Gk] —**ostrich-like**, adj.

Oswald /ˈɒzwəld/, n. **Lee Harvey**, 1939–63, the US man charged with the assassination of President JF Kennedy, on 22 November 1963.

ot-, a variant of **oto-** before vowels.

other /ˈʌðə/, adj. 1. additional or further: *He and one other person were there.* 2. different from the one or ones spoken of: *in some other city.* 3. different in nature or kind: *I would not have him other than he is.* 4. being the remaining one or ones: *the other hand; the other people.* 5. former: *men of other days.* 6. **every other**, every alternate: *a meeting every other week.* 7. **the other day (night**, etc.), recently, esp. in the last few days. 8. **the other half**, *Colloq.* the rich or the poor (but esp. the poor): *See how the other half lives.* 9. **the other side**, a. *Spiritualism.* a place where the spirits of dead people live. b. *NZ Colloq.* Australia. ◇*pron.* 10. the other one: *Each praises the other.* 11. another person or thing. 12. some person or thing else: *some day or other.* ◇*adv.* 13. otherwise. [ME; OE ōther]

otherwise /ˈʌðəwaɪz/, adv. 1. under other circumstances: *I might otherwise have come.* 2. in another manner; differently: *Try to see it otherwise.* 3. in other respects: *an otherwise happy life.* ◇adj. 4. other or different; of another nature or kind. [OE (on) ōthre wīsan in other manner]

otherworldly /ʌðəˈwɜːldli/, adj. 1. of, relating to, or directed towards, another world, esp. the world of imagination, or the world after death. 2. impractical; neglectful.

otic /ˈoutɪk, ˈɒtɪk/, adj. of or relating to the ear; auricular. [Gk]

-otic, an adjective suffix meaning: 1. 'suffering from', as in *neurotic.* 2. 'producing', as in *hypnotic.* 3. 'resembling', as in *quixotic.* [Gk]

otiose /ˈoutious/, adj. unnecessary; superfluous. [L *ōtiōsus*] —**otiosity**, n.

otitis /ouˈtaɪtəs/, n. inflammation of the ear.

oto-, a word part meaning 'ear'. [Gk, combining form of *oûs*]

otology /ouˈtɒlədʒi/, n. the science of the ear and its diseases.

Ottawa /ˈɒtəwə/, n. 1. the capital of Canada, in south-eastern Ontario. Pop. (with Hull) 819 263 (1986 est.). 2. a river in south-eastern Canada, flowing generally south-east along the boundary between Ontario and Quebec into the St Lawrence at Montreal. 1102 km. 3. (pl.) a tribe of Algonquian Indians of Canada, forced into the Lake Superior and Lake Michigan regions by the Iroquois confederacy. [Canadian F *Otana, Otawa*, from d. Ojibwa (Cree, Ottawa, Chippewa) *adaawe* to trade]

otter /ˈɒtə/, n., pl. **-ters**, (esp. collectively) **-ter**. a furry, meat-eating water mammal with

otter webbed feet and a long tail slightly flattened to act as a rudder. [OE *oter, ot(o)r*]

ottoman /ˈɒtəmən/, *n., pl.,* **-mans. 1.** a low, cushioned seat without back or arms. **2.** a low chest with padded top.

Ottoman /ˈɒtəmən/, *adj.* Turkish. Also, **Othman.** [F, from Ar, from *Othman* Osman I, founder of the OTTOMAN EMPIRE]

Ottoman Empire, *n.* a former Turkish empire, founded about 1300 by Osman, which held sway over large dominions in Asia, Africa, and Europe for more than six centuries until its collapse after World War I. *Cap.:* Constantinople. Also, **Turkish Empire.**

ouch /aʊtʃ/, *interj.* (an exclamation expressing sudden pain).

ought[1] /ɔt/, *v. aux.* **1.** was (were) or am (is, are) bound in duty or moral obligation: *Every citizen ought to help.* **2.** should according to necessity, justice, fitness, probability, etc. (usu. fol. by an infinitive: *He ought to be punished; He ought to be there by 2 o'clock.* [OE *āhte*, past of *āgan* OWE]

ought[2] /ɔt/, *n., adv.* zero; nothing. (var. of NOUGHT, a nought being taken as *an ought*]

ouija /ˈwidʒə, -dʒi/, *n.* a board used in seances to receive messages from dead people. Also, **ouija board.** [F *oui* yes + G *ja* yes]

ounce /aʊns/, *n.* **1.** a unit of weight in the imperial system, equal to $\frac{1}{16}$ lb. avoirdupois or 28.35×10^{-3} kg. **2.** → **fluid ounce. 3.** any small quantity. [ME, from OF, from L: twelfth part, inch, ounce]

our /aʊə/, *pron.* or *adj.* the possessive form corresponding to *we* and *us*, used before a noun: *We have sold our house.* See **ours.** [OE *ūre*]

-our → **-or**[1].

ours /aʊəz/, *pron.* **1.** a form of *our* used after a verb, or without a noun following: *Those books are ours.* **2. of ours**, belonging to us: *a friend of ours.*

ourself /aʊəˈsɛlf/, *pron.* a form corresponding to *ourselves*, used of a single person, esp. (like *we* for *I*) in the royal or formal style.

ourselves /aʊəˈsɛlvz/, *pron. pl.* **1.** a reflexive form of *us*: *We hurt ourselves.* **2.** an emphatic form of *us* or *we* used: **a.** as object: *We used it for ourselves.* **b.** in apposition to a subject or object: *We ourselves did it.*

-ous, 1. an adjective suffix meaning 'full of', 'abounding in', 'given to', 'characterised by', 'having', 'of the nature of', 'like', etc.: *glorious, joyous, mucous, nervous, sonorous, wondrous.* **2.** *Chem.* a suffix used to indicate the lower of two possible valencies, compared to the suffix *-ic*, as sulfurous acid, H_2SO_3, compared to sulfuric acid, H_2SO_4. Also, **-eous, -ious.** [ME, from OF, from L]

oust /aʊst/, *v.t.* to push out or expel from a place or position occupied. [AF, from L: to be in the way, protect against] —**ouster**, *n.*

out /aʊt/, *adv.* **1.** forth or away from a place, position, state, etc.: *out of the room; out of order; to hire out; to vote out.* **2.** away from one's home: *to set out on a journey.* **3.** into the open: *to go out for a walk.* **4.** to the end; so as to finish; completely: *dry out; empty out; tired out; fight it out.* **5.** no longer burning or giving light; extinguished: *The lamp went out.* **6.** not in fashion: *That style has gone out.* **7.** into sight, notice or knowledge: *The stars came out; The book came out in May; He has been found out.* **8.** beyond a point or surface: *to stretch out; stick out.* **9.** into existence or activity: *Fever broke out.* **10.** away from existence: *The sound faded out; to paint out; to blot out.* **11.** from a source (with *of*): *made out of scraps.* **12.** into some arrangement: *to sort out; to fit out.* **13.** so as to take away from (with *of*): *to cheat out of money.* **14.** to a state of lack (with *of*): *to run out of coal.* **15.** from among many: *to pick out.* **16.** from a centre: *to spread out.* **17.** aloud: *to call out.* **18.** on strike: *The miners are coming out.* **19. go all out**, to spend the greatest possible energy or use every possible means to do something. **20. out and away**, by far: *He is out and away the best at it.* **21. out-and-out**, complete; absolute. **22. out here**, **a.** in Australia. **b.** in a town or place thought of as being far from the main centre. ◇*adj.* **23.** torn or worn into holes: *His trousers were out at the knees.* **24.** incorrect or inaccurate: *He is out in his calculations.* **25.** not burning or giving light: *The fire is out.* **26.** lacking; without: *We are out of eggs.* **27.** unconscious; senseless: *The boxer was out for five minutes.* **28.** finished; ended: *before the month is out.* **29.** *Tennis*, etc. beyond the boundary lines. **30.** *Cricket*, etc. removed from play. **31. out to it**, *Colloq.* **a.** unconscious. **b.** asleep. ◇*prep.* **32.** forth from: *out the door; out the window.* **33.** outside and towards: *out the back; out the front.* ◇*interj.* **34.** go away! ◇*n.* **35.** the various parts (of some intricate thing): *the ins and outs of politics.* **36.** a means of escape: *He always left himself an out.* ◇*v.i.* **37.** to become known: *Murder will out.* [ME; OE *ūt*]

out-, the use of **out**, *adv., prep.,* or *adj.,* as a prefix, occurring in various senses in compounds, as in *outcast, outcome, outside*, and used also to form many transitive verbs indicating a going beyond or surpassing, as in *outbid, outdo, outlast, outstay,* and many other words in which the meaning is easily seen.

outback /ˈaʊtbæk/, *n.* **1.** (*sometimes cap.*) the most remote parts of the inland or back country (def. 5). ◇*adj.* **2.** of, related to, or located in the outback. ◇*adv.* **3.** in or to the outback: *to live outback.*

outboard /ˈaʊtbɔd/, *adj., adv.* on the outside, or away from the centre, of a boat, aircraft, etc.

outbreak /ˈaʊtbreɪk/, *n.* a sudden occurrence: *outbreak of war; outbreak of sickness.*

outbuilding /ˈaʊtbɪldɪŋ/, *n.* a building set apart from a main building.

outburst /ˈaʊtbɜst/, *n.* **1.** a bursting forth. **2.** a sudden and violent pouring out: *an outburst of tears; an outburst of anger.*

outcast /ˈaʊtkast/, *n.* **1.** someone who is not accepted by home or society. **2.** a homeless wanderer; vagabond. ◇*adj.* **3.** cast out from home or society. **4.** rejected or discarded.

outcome /'autkʌm/, n. something that results from something; a consequence.

outcrop /'autkrɒp/, n.; /aut'krɒp/, v., **-cropped, -cropping.** ◊n. **1.** a part that shows above or beyond: *an outcrop of rock*. **2.** a sudden or unexpected occurrence; outbreak: *an outcrop of labor unrest*. ◊v.i. **3.** to show above or beyond another layer.

outcry /'autkraɪ/, n., pl. **-cries. 1.** a loud noise; clamor. **2.** a strong cry of protest or indignation.

outdate /aut'deɪt/, v.t., **-dated, -dating.** to make out-of-date or old-fashioned. — **outdated**, adj.

outdo /aut'du/, v.t., **-did, -done, -doing.** to surpass in doing or performance; surpass.

outdoor /'autdɔ/, adj. **1.** being or used out of doors. **2.** fond of activities done in the open air: *an outdoor type*.

outdoors /aut'dɔz/, adv. **1.** outside a house; in the open air. ◊n. **2.** the world outside houses; open air. **3. the great outdoors,** the natural environment, esp. wild areas.

outer /'autə/, adj. **1.** farther out; external; of or relating to the outside. ◊n. **2.** that part of a sportsground which is without shelter. **3. on the outer,** *Colloq.* shut out from the group; mildly ostracised. [compar. of OUT]

outfall /'autfɔl/, n. the outlet or place where a river, drain, sewer, etc., flows out.

outfield /'autfild/, n. **1.** *Cricket.* that part of the field farthest from the batsman. **2.** *Baseball.* (the players in) that part of the field beyond the diamond. **3.** outlying land or region.

outfit /'autfɪt/, n., v., **-fitted, -fitting.** ◊n. **1.** the equipment for some activity: *a skier's outfit; an explorer's outfit*. **2.** a set of articles for any purpose: *a model aircraft outfit*. **3.** a set of clothes, esp. women's, worn together. **4. a.** a group of people working together: *military outfit*. **b.** *Colloq.* a shop or business with its equipment. ◊v.t. **5.** to provide with an outfit; fit out; equip.

outflank /aut'flæŋk/, v.t. **1.** to go beyond the flank of (an opposing army, etc.); outmanoeuvre by a flanking movement. **2.** to get the better of (an opponent, etc.).

outfox /aut'fɒks/, v.t. to get an advantage over; outwit.

outgoing /'autgouɪŋ/, adj. **1.** going out; departing: *outgoing trains; the outgoing manager*. **2.** interested in and responsive to others: *an outgoing personality*. ◊n. **3.** (usu. pl.) an amount of money spent; outlay; expenses.

outgrow /aut'grou/, v., **-grew, -grown, -growing.** ◊v.t. **1.** to grow too large for. **2.** to grow faster than. **3.** to leave behind: *to outgrow a bad reputation*. ◊v.i. **4.** to grow out; protrude.

outgrowth /'autgrouθ/, n. **1.** a natural development, product, or result. **2.** an extra result. **3.** a growing out or forth. **4.** something that grows out; offshoot; excrescence.

outhouse /'authaus/, n. **1.** an outbuilding. **2.** an outside toilet.

outing /'autɪŋ/, n. a pleasure trip; excursion.

outlandish /aut'lændɪʃ/, adj. **1.** very strange in appearance; fantastic; freakish; bizarre. **2.** out-of-the-way; remote.

outlast /aut'last/, v.t. to last longer than.

outlaw /'autlɔ/, n. **1.** a criminal, esp. formerly, one who is cut off from the protection of the law. **2.** a wild or untameable animal. ◊v.t. **3.** to cut off from the protection of the law. **4.** to forbid with the strong agreement of society. [OE *ūtlage*] — **outlawry**, n.

outlay /'autleɪ/, n.; /aut'leɪ/, v., **-laid, -laying.** ◊n. **1.** the spending of money, energy, etc. **2.** the amount spent. ◊v.t. **3.** to spend.

outlet /'autlet, -lət/, n. **1.** an opening or passage by which anything is let out; vent; exit. **2.** *Comm.* **a.** a market for goods. **b.** a shop, etc., selling a wholesaler's or manufacturer's goods. **3.** a means of expression: *outlet for emotion*.

outline /'autlaɪn/, n., v., **-lined, -lining.** ◊n. **1.** a line, drawn or imagined, which traces round the shape of an object; the contour. **2.** a drawing with such lines only. **3.** a general account giving only the main points. **4.** (pl.) the main points or necessary parts of a subject. ◊v.t. **5.** to draw the outline of, or draw in outline. **6.** to give the main points of (a subject, etc.).

outlive /aut'lɪv/, v.t., **-lived, -living. 1.** to live longer than. **2.** to live through: *The ship outlived the storm*.

outlook /'autluk/, n. **1.** the view from a place; prospect. **2.** a mental point of view. **3.** what is likely for the future: *political outlook*.

outlying /'autlaɪɪŋ/, adj. far from the centre or main body; remote.

outmoded /aut'moudəd/, adj. out of style or no longer used.

out-of-date /'aut-əv-deɪt/, adj. no longer in style or use. Also (*esp. after a verb*), **out of date.**

out-of-doors /'aut-əv-dɔz, aut-əv-'dɔz/, adj.; /aut-əv-'dɔz/, adv., n. ◊adj. **1.** Also, **out-of-door;** (*esp. after a verb*) **out of doors,** outdoor. ◊adv., n. **2.** → **outdoors.**

out-of-pocket /'aut-əv-pɒkət/, adj. of or relating to what has been spent in cash: *out-of-pocket expenses*. Also (*esp. after a verb*), **out of pocket.**

out-of-the-way /'aut-əv-ðə-weɪ/, adj. **1.** far from the places where people live or go; remote; secluded. **2.** unusual. Also (*esp. after a verb*), **out of the way.**

outpatient /'autpeɪʃənt/, n. a person who receives treatment at a hospital but does not live there while having it.

outpost /'autpoust/, n. **1.** (a group of soldiers at) a place away from the main body of an army. **2.** any faraway settlement: *an outpost of civilisation*.

outpouring /'autpɔrɪŋ/, n. a flowing out: *an outpouring of emotion*.

output /ˈaʊtpʊt/, *n.* **1.** the act of producing or the amount produced: *a huge output of energy.* **2.** a product or yield, as of a mine. **3.** *Computers.* the information obtained from a computer on completion of an operation.

outrage /ˈaʊtreɪdʒ/, *n., v.,* **-raged, -raging.** ◇*n.* **1.** a very wrong act that goes beyond all accepted limits of behavior, esp. one of great cruelty or violence. **2.** a feeling of very strong anger. ◇*v.t.* **3.** to subject to great violence or humiliation. **4.** to affect with a sense of offended right or decency; shock. **5.** to rape (a woman). [ME, from OF: push beyond bounds] —**outrageous**, *adj.*

outrider /ˈaʊtraɪdə/, *n.* **1.** an attendant riding before or beside a carriage. **2.** a motorcyclist riding ahead of a car to guard it or clear a passage for it.

outrigger /ˈaʊtrɪɡə/, *n.* **1.** (a canoe with) floats attached to the side of the hull by long poles. **2.** (a racing shell with) a bracket extending outwards to support a rowlock.

outright /ˈaʊtraɪt/, *adj.* **1.** complete; total: *an outright loss.* **2.** downright; unqualified: *an outright refusal.* ◇*adv.* **3.** completely; entirely. **4.** openly. **5.** at once.

outset /ˈaʊtsɛt/, *n.* the beginning or start.

outside /ˈaʊtsaɪd/, *n., adj.*; /aʊtˈsaɪd/ *adv., prep.* ◇*n.* **1.** the outer side, surface, or part; exterior: *The outside of the house has been painted.* **2.** the outer aspect or appearance: *On the outside he's always so calm.* **3.** the space outside or beyond an enclosure, boundary, etc. **4. at the outside,** *Colloq.* at the limit: *not more than ten at the outside.* ◇*adj.* **5.** being, acting, done, or originating beyond an enclosure, boundary, etc.: *outside noises.* **6.** situated on or relating to the outside; exterior; external: *outside walls.* **7.** not belonging to or connected with an institution, society, etc.: *outside influences.* **8.** extremely unlikely: *an outside chance.* ◇*adv.* **9.** on or to the outside: *It is cold outside tonight.* ◇*prep.* **10.** on or towards the outside of: *It is dark outside the house.* **11.** *Colloq.* except for (usu. fol. by *of*).

outsider /aʊtˈsaɪdə/, *n.* **1.** someone not belonging to a particular group, set, party, etc. **2.** a racehorse, etc., not included among the favorites.

outsize /ˈaʊtsaɪz/, *n.* **1.** an unusual or irregular size. **2.** a garment of such a size, esp. when larger. ◇*adj.* **3.** Also, **outsized.** unusually or abnormally large; larger than average: *outsize dresses.*

outskirts /ˈaʊtskɜts/, *n.pl.* the outer areas (of a town, etc.).

outspoken /ˈaʊtspoʊkən/, *adj.* **1.** expressed openly or frankly: *outspoken criticism.* **2.** free or open in speech: *outspoken people.*

outstanding /aʊtˈstændɪŋ/, *adj.* **1.** striking; prominent; conspicuous. **2.** unpaid; unsettled: *outstanding debts.* **3.** standing out; projecting.

outstretch /aʊtˈstrɛtʃ/, *v.t.* **1.** to stretch forth; extend. **2.** to stretch beyond (a limit, etc.). **3.** to stretch out; expand.

outstrip /aʊtˈstrɪp/, *v.t.,* **-stripped, -stripping. 1.** to outdo; surpass; excel. **2.** to pass in running or swift travel; leave behind.

outward /ˈaʊtwəd/, *adj.* **1.** of or relating to what is seen or apparent, as opposed to the underlying nature; superficial: *Only her outward looks were calm*; *the outward man.* **2.** relating to the outside; outer. **3.** directed towards the outside: *outward gaze.* ◇*adv.* **4.** Also, **outwards.** towards the outside; out. **5.** away from port: *outward bound.* [ME; OE *ūtweard*]

Outward Bound, *n.* a program originated by Dr Kurt Hahn in Britain in 1941 to encourage young people to attain greater self-knowledge and self-determination by means of challenging outdoor experiences; founded in Australia in 1958.

outweigh /aʊtˈweɪ/, *v.t.* **1.** to be more valuable, important, etc. than: *The advantages of the plan outweighed its faults.* **2.** to weigh more than.

outwit /aʊtˈwɪt/, *v.t.,* **-witted, -witting.** to get the better of by cleverness.

ova /ˈoʊvə/, *n.* plural of **ovum.**

oval /ˈoʊvəl/, *adj.* **1.** egg-shaped. **2.** ellipsoidal or elliptical. ◇*n.* **3.** any oval thing: *to cut out an oval from paper.* **4.** a flat area, of whatever shape, for sporting activities. [NL, from L: egg]

ovary /ˈoʊvəri/, *n., pl.* **-ries. 1.** *Anat., Zool.* the female reproductive gland which produces the ova, or eggs, and female hormones. **2.** *Bot.* the enlarged lower part of the pistil, that contains the ovules. [NL, from L: egg] —**ovarian**, *adj.*

ovate /ˈoʊveɪt/, *adj.* **1.** egg-shaped. **2.** *Bot.* having a shape like the longitudinal section of an egg, as a leaf. [L: egg-shaped]

ovation /oʊˈveɪʃən/, *n.* enthusiastic applause. [L: rejoicing]

oven /ˈʌvən/, *n.* an enclosed space or vessel for baking food or for heating or drying. [ME; OE *ofen*]

ovenproof /ˈʌvənpruːf/, *adj.* not damaged by use in a hot oven.

Ovens /ˈʌvənz/, *n.* a river in north-eastern Vic, rising near Mt Hotham and flowing in a north-westerly direction into the Murray River near Corowa. 200 km.

ovenware /ˈʌvənwɛə/, *n.* heat-resistant dishes in which food can be baked in an oven.

over /ˈoʊvə/, *prep.* **1.** above in place or position; higher up than: *a roof over our heads.* **2.** above and to the other side of: *to leap over a wall.* **3.** above in power, so as to control. **4.** on or upon: *Put a cloth over it to keep the flies off.* **5.** on or on top of: *She hit him over the head.* **6.** here and there on or in; around: *at various places over the country.* **7.** through all parts of: *to look over some papers.* **8.** across: *to go over a bridge*; *lands over the sea.* **9.** throughout: *over a great distance.* **10.** more than: *over a kilometre.* **11.** rather than: *to choose this over that.* **12.** during: *over a long time*; *to stop work over the holidays.* **13.** about: *to quarrel over it.* **14.** by means of: *over the phone*; *over the radio.* **15. to be all over,** *Colloq.* to show

great or too great affection and attention towards. **16. over and above**, besides; in addition to. **17. over the fence**, unreasonable; unfair. ◇*adv.* **18.** over the top or edge of something: *to climb over.* **19.** so as to cover the surface: *to paint a thing over.* **20.** through: *Read it over; Think it over.* **21.** at some distance in a direction pointed out: *over by the hill.* **22.** to the other side: *to sail over.* **23.** across: *When are you coming over to see us?; I'll give it over to you.* **24.** down or upside down: *to knock over; to turn over.* **25.** in repetition: *twenty times over.* **26.** remaining: *to pay the full sum and something over.* **27.** beyond a period of time: *to stay over till Monday.* ◇**28.** Some special uses are:
all over, **1.** everywhere. **2.** thoroughly; entirely. **3.** done with; finished. **4.** typical of: *That's him all over.*
all over with, done with; finished.
over again, once more.
over against, **1.** opposite to; in front of. **2.** as contrasted with: *to set truth over against falsehood.*
over and over (again), repeatedly.
◇*adj.* **29.** at an end; done; past: *when the war was over.* ◇*n.* **30.** Cricket. **a.** the number of balls (eight in Australia and NZ, six elsewhere) delivered between successive changes of bowlers. **b.** the part of the game played between such changes. [ME, OE *ofer*]

over-, the use of **over**, *prep., adv.,* or *adj.,* as a prefix, occurring in various senses in compounds, as in *overboard, overcoat, overhang, overlap, overlord, overrun, overthrow,* and esp. used, with the sense of 'over the limit', 'to excess', 'too much', 'too', to form verbs, adjectives, adverbs, and nouns, as *overact, overcapitalise, overcrowd, overfull, overmuch, oversupply, overweight,* and many others, mostly self-explanatory. A hyphen, usually not used with old or well-established formations, is often used in new coinages, or in other compounds where it is desirable to show up the parts, as in *over-age.*

overall /ˈouvərɔl/, *adj., n.;* /ouvərˈɔl/, *adv.* ◇*adj.* **1.** from one extreme limit of a thing to another: *the overall length of a bridge.* **2.** with everything included: *an overall estimate.* ◇*n.* Also, **overalls. 3. a.** a boilersuit. **b.** loose trousers of strong material, usu. with a bib and shoulder straps, worn by workmen and young children. ◇*adv.* **4.** covering or including everything; altogether: *the position viewed overall.*

overarm /ˈouvəram/, *adj.* **1.** performed with the arm raised above the shoulder, as bowling. **2.** of or relating to a style of swimming similar to the crawl (def. 6). ◇*adv.* **3.** in an overarm manner: *to swim overarm.*

overawe /ouvərˈɔ/, *v.t., -awed, -awing.* to frighten by filling with great wonder; intimidate.

overbalance /ouvəˈbæləns/, *v.t., v.i., -anced, -ancing.* to (cause to) lose balance or to fall or turn over.

overbear /ouvəˈbɛə/, *v., -bore, -borne, -bearing.* ◇*v.t.* **1.** to push over or down by weight or force; overcome. **2.** to force (wishes, objections, etc.) aside. **3.** to force (someone) to agree with one. ◇*v.i.* **4.** to produce fruit or children so much that health is damaged. –**overbearing**, *adj.*

overbid /ouvəˈbɪd/, *v., -bid, -bidden* or *-bid, -bidding;* /ˈouvəbɪd/, *n.* ◇*v.t., v.i.* **1.** to bid more than the value of (a thing). **2.** to bid more than someone else. ◇*n.* **3.** higher bid.

overboard /ˈouvəbɔd/, *adv.* over the side of a ship, etc., esp. into or in the water: *to fall overboard.*

overbridge /ˈouvəbrɪdʒ/, *n.* a bridge for taking cars over a railway line, or pedestrians over a main road.

overcast /ˈouvəkast/, *adj.* **1.** (of the sky) overspread with clouds. **2.** dark; gloomy.

overcharge /ouvəˈtʃadʒ/, *v., -charged, -charging;* /ˈouvətʃadʒ/, *n.* ◇*v.t., v.i.* **1.** to charge (someone) too high a price. ◇*n.* **2.** a charge which is more than a fair price.

overcoat /ˈouvəkout/, *n.* a coat worn over ordinary clothing in cold weather; greatcoat.

overcome /ouvəˈkʌm/, *v., -came, -come, -coming.* ◇*v.t.* **1.** to get the better of in a struggle; conquer; defeat. **2.** to win against (opposition, difficulties, etc.) or not give in to (temptation, etc.). **3.** (of liquor, drugs, emotion, etc.) to make (a person) weak, helpless, or unconscious; overpower. ◇*v.i.* **4.** to gain the victory; conquer. [ME, OE *ofercuman*]

overdo /ouvəˈdu/, *v.t., -did, -done, -doing.* **1.** to do too much of: *to overdo exercise.* **2.** to carry beyond the proper limit. **3.** to overact (a part); exaggerate. **4.** to cook too much. –**overdone**, *adj.*

overdose /ˈouvədous/, *n.;* /ouvəˈdous/, *v., -dosed, -dosing.* ◇*n.* **1.** a dose of a drug that is enough to make sick or kill. ◇*v.i.* **2.** to take an overdose.

overdraft /ˈouvədraft/, *n.* **1.** (an amount of) money drawn out of the bank that is more than one has in one's account. **2.** a loan given by the bank.

overdraw /ouvəˈdrɔ/, *v., -drew, -drawn, -drawing.* ◇*v.t.* **1.** to take more money out of an account than there is in it. **2.** to exaggerate (*usu. in pass.*): *His story was wildly overdrawn.* ◇*v.i.* **3.** to overdraw an account.

overdress /ouvəˈdrɛs/, *v.t., v.i.* to dress better or more formally than is necessary.

overdrive /ouvəˈdraɪv/, *v., -drove, -driven, -driving;* /ˈouvədraɪv/, *n.* ◇*v.t.* **1.** to overwork; push or carry to excess. **2.** to drive too hard. ◇*n.* **3.** *Mech.* an extra gear that allows a car to drive at high speeds with the smallest possible use of petrol.

overdue /ˈouvədju/, *adj.* late; long awaited.

overestimate /ouvərˈɛstəmeɪt/, *v., -mated, -mating;* /ouvərˈɛstəmət/, *v.t.* **1.** to have too high an opinion of (a person, etc.). ◇*n.* **2.** an estimate that is too high. –**overestimation**, *n.*

overflow /ouvəˈflou/, *v., -flowed, -flown, -flowing;* /ˈouvəflou/, *n.* ◇*v.i.* **1.** (of a river,

overflow water in a glass, etc.) to flow or run over (banks, etc.). **2.** to pass from one place to another because the first is too full: *The crowd overflowed into the street.* **3.** to be filled or supplied plentifully (fol. by *with*): *a heart overflowing with gratitude.* ◇*v.t.* **4.** to flow over; flood; inundate. **5.** to flow over or beyond (the brim, banks, borders, etc.). ◇*n.* **6.** an overflowing or flooding: *the yearly overflow of the Nile.* **7.** something that flows or runs over: *to carry off the overflow from a fountain.* **8.** an outlet for overflowing liquid. **9.** an area of land covered by water in time of floods. **10.** too much of anything; excess.

overgrown /ouvəˈgroun/, *adj.* (of a garden, etc.) covered by plants esp. by weeds, usu. because of neglect.

overhang /ouvəˈhæŋ/, *v.*, **-hung, -hanging**; /ˈouvəhæŋ/, *n.* ◇*v.t.* **1.** to hang over: *A tree overhung the cliff.* **2.** to be spread over: *A dark sky overhangs the earth.* **3.** to threaten: *the sadness which overhung him.* ◇*v.i.* **4.** to hang over; project or jut out over something below. ◇*n.* **5.** an overhanging; projection: *an overhang of two metres.*

overhaul /ouvəˈhɔl/, *v.*; /ˈouvəhɔl/, *n.* ◇*v.t.* **1.** to examine for repair. **2.** to make any necessary repairs to; restore to proper condition. **3.** to gain upon; overtake. ◇*n.* **4.** a thorough examination.

overhead /ouvəˈhɛd/, *adv.*; /ˈouvəhɛd/, *adj.*, *n.* ◇*adv.* **1.** straight up in the air or sky: *The aircraft was right overhead when the bomb fell.* ◇*adj.* **2.** placed, working, or passing overhead: *overhead wires.* ◇*n.* **3.** (*pl.*) the general cost of running a business.

overhear /ouvəˈhɪə/, *v.t.*, **-heard, -hearing.** to hear (speech, etc., or a speaker) without the speaker's intention or knowledge.
– **overhearer,** *n.*

overjoyed /ouvəˈdʒɔɪd/, *adj.* made very joyful; overcome with joy.

overkill /ˈouvəkɪl/, *n.* the use of more material or energy than is necessary to achieve an aim.

overland /ˈouvəlænd/, *adv.* **1.** over or across the land. **2.** by land: *We are going overland from Sydney to Darwin.* ◇*adj.* **3.** going on or done by land: *the overland route.* ◇*v.t.*, *v.i.* **4.** to drive (sheep, etc.) overland for long distances.

overlander /ˈouvəlændə/, *n.* a drover bringing stock overland, esp. through remote areas, as from the NT to Adelaide.

Overland Telegraph Line, *n.* the first overhead telegraphic line in Australia which connects Darwin, NT, to Adelaide, SA; completed in 1872 and spans 2900 km.

overlap /ouvəˈlæp/, *v.*, **-lapped, -lapping**; /ˈouvəlæp/, *n.* ◇*v.t.*, *v.i.* **1.** to stretch over and cover a part of (something else): *Branches are overlapping the house; Tiles are laid so that they overlap.* **2.** to coincide in part with; correspond partly with: *Your job overlaps (with) mine.* ◇*n.* **3.** an overlapping. **4.** the amount of overlapping: *an overlap of two centimetres.* **5.** an overlapping part or place.

overlay¹ /ouvəˈleɪ/, *v.*, **-laid, -laying**; /ˈouvəleɪ/, *n.* ◇*v.t.* **1.** to lay or place (one thing) over or upon another. **2.** to cover with a decorative layer: *wood richly overlaid with gold.* ◇*n.* **3.** something laid over something else; a covering. **4.** decorative layer: *an overlay of gold.* [ME]

overlay² /ouvəˈleɪ/, *v.* past tense of **overlie.**

overleaf /ouvəˈlif/, *adv.* on the other side of the page: *continued overleaf.*

overlie /ouvəˈlaɪ/, *v.t.*, **-lay, -lain, -lying.** **1.** to lie over or upon, as a covering, stratum, etc. **2.** to smother (a baby) by lying upon it, as in sleep.

overlook /ouvəˈlʊk/, *v.t.* **1.** to fail to notice: *to overlook a misspelt word.* **2.** to disregard; ignore: *I will overlook your lateness this time.* **3.** to look over, as from a higher position: *to overlook the crowd.* **4.** to give a view down over: *a hill overlooking the sea.*

overly /ˈouvəli/, *adv.* overmuch; excessively; too: *a voyage not overly dangerous.*

overnight /ouvəˈnaɪt/, *adv.*; /ˈouvənaɪt/, *adj.*, *n.* ◇*adv.* **1.** during the night: *to stay overnight.* **2.** on the evening before: *Preparations were made overnight.* **3.** suddenly; very quickly: *New towns sprang up overnight.* ◇*adj.* **4.** done, happening, or continuing during the night: *an overnight stop.* **5.** staying for one night: *overnight guests.* **6.** designed to be used one night or very few nights: *overnight bag.* **7.** happening suddenly or rapidly: *an overnight success.* ◇*n.* **8.** an overnight stopover during a plane journey, etc.

overpass /ˈouvəpas/, *n.* a bridge designed to take traffic on one road over a cross road.

overpower /ouvəˈpaʊə/, *v.t.* **1.** to overcome; overwhelm; affect or impress excessively. **2.** to overcome by greater force: *to overpower a maniac.* **3.** to overcome the bodily or mental powers of: *overpowered with wine.*
– **overpowering,** *adj.*

overreach /ouvəˈritʃ/, *v.t.* to defeat (oneself) by doing too much or being too clever.

overriding /ˈouvəraɪdɪŋ/, *adj.* more important than any other.

overrule /ouvəˈrul/, *v.t.*, **-ruled, -ruling.** **1.** to rule against or disallow the arguments of (a person). **2.** to rule or decide against (a plea, argument, etc.); disallow.

overrun /ouvəˈrʌn/, *v.*, **-ran, -run, -running**; /ˈouvərʌn/, *n.* ◇*v.t.* **1.** to spread over quickly and occupy (a country): *In 1940 German armies overran the Low Countries.* **2.** to take possession of (an enemy position, etc.). **3.** (of vermin, etc.) to swarm over in great numbers. **4.** (of weeds, etc.) to spread or grow rapidly over. ◇*v.i.* **5.** to extend beyond the proper or desired limit. ◇*n.* **6.** an amount overrunning or carried over; excess. [OE *oferyrnan*]

overseas /ouvəˈsiz/, *adv.*; /ˈouvəsiz/, *adj.* ◇*adv.* **1.** over, across, or beyond the sea; abroad. ◇*adj.* **2.** of or relating to passage over the sea: *overseas travel.* **3.** situated beyond the sea: *overseas countries.* **4.** foreign: *overseas military service.*

oversee /ˈouvəˈsiː/, *v.t.*, **-saw, -seen, -seeing. 1.** to direct (work or workers); supervise; manage. **2.** to see or watch without being seen. [OE *ofersēon*]

overseer /ˈouvəsiə, -siːə/, *n.* **1.** a supervisor. **2.** a farm manager. **3.** (formerly) the supervisor of a convict gang. [ME]

overshadow /ouvəˈʃædou/, *v.t.* **1.** to be more important, active, or noticeable than: *She always overshadowed him at parties.* **2.** to cast a shadow over. **3.** to make dark or gloomy. **4.** to shelter or protect. [OE *ofersceadwian*]

overshoot /ouvəˈʃuːt/, *v.t.*, **-shot, -shooting. 1.** to shoot or go beyond (a point, limit, etc.): *to overshoot the mark*. **2.** (of an aircraft) to go further than the stopping point when landing. **3.** to go further in anything than is intended or proper, or to go too far. [ME]

oversight /ˈouvəsait/, *n.* **1.** a failure to notice or take into account. **2.** something left out or not done by mistake. **3.** watchful care; supervision. [ME]

overstate /ouvəˈsteit/, *v.t.*, **-stated, -stating.** to state too strongly; exaggerate in statement: *to overstate a case.* **— overstatement,** *n.*

overstay /ouvəˈstei/, *v.t.* to stay beyond the time of: *He overstayed his welcome.*

overstep /ouvəˈstɛp/, *v.t.*, **-stepped, -stepping.** to go beyond: *to overstep the limit.*

overstock /ouvəˈstɒk/, *v.*; /ˈouvəstɒk/, *n.* ◇*v.t.* **1.** to keep more than enough of (in a shop, etc.). **2.** to keep more cattle, etc., on a piece of land than the land can feed. ◇*n.* **3.** a supply beyond what is needed.

oversubscribed /ˈouvəsəbskraibd/, *adj.* (of shares, issues, theatre tickets, etc.) having applications to buy exceeding the number available.

overt /ˈouvət/, *adj.* open to view or knowledge; not concealed or secret: *overt hostility; overt behavior.* [ME, from OF: open, from L] **— overtly,** *adv.*

overtake /ouvəˈteik/, *v.*, **-took, -taken, -taking.** ◇*v.t.* **1.** to catch up with: *The police overtook the speeding car.* **2.** to come up with or pass in anything. **3.** to come upon suddenly or unexpectedly (said esp. of night, storm, death, etc.). **4.** to pass (another car). ◇*v.i.* **5.** to pass another car: *No overtaking on the bridge.* [ME]

overtax /ouvəˈtæks/, *v.t.* **1.** to tax too heavily. **2.** to make too great demands on: *I had overtaxed my strength.*

overthrow /ouvəˈθrou/, *v.*, **-threw, -thrown, -throwing**; /ˈouvəθrou/, *n.* ◇*v.t.* **1.** to put down from a position of power; depose; overcome, defeat, or vanquish. **2.** to put an end to by force: *to overthrow the government.* **3.** to throw (something) too far: *to overthrow the ball so it goes past the line.* ◇*n.* **4.** an act of overthrowing: *the overthrow of the government.* **5.** *Cricket.* **a.** a ball returned by a fielder which is not caught at the wicket. **b.** a run scored as a result of this.

overtime /ˈouvətaim/, *n.* **1.** time worked before or after regular working hours; extra time. **2.** the pay for such time. ◇*adj.* **3.** of or relating to overtime: *overtime pay.*

overtone /ˈouvətoun/, *n.* (*usu. pl.*) an extra meaning; additional implication; nuance: *There were overtones of resentment in his voice.*

overture /ˈouvətʃuə/, *n.* **1.** an introductory offer or proposal: *peace overtures.* **2.** *Music.* **a.** an orchestral piece introducing an opera, oratorio, etc. **b.** an independent piece of similar character. [ME, from OF, from L: opening]

overturn /ouvəˈtɜːn/, *v.t.* **1.** to put an end to by force; overthrow. **2.** to turn over on its side, face, or back; upset. **3.** to turn (a decision, judgment, etc.) the other way; reverse: *The ruling was overturned in the High Court.* ◇*v.i.* **4.** to turn over; be upset; capsize. [ME]

overview /ˈouvəvjuː/, *n.* a general view that takes everything into account.

overweening /ˈouvəwiːnɪŋ/, *adj.* **1.** imagining too much of oneself; conceited; arrogant; self-opinionated. **2.** exaggerated; excessive: *overweening pride.* [OVER + *ween*, from OE *wēnan* think, have an opinion]

overweight /ˈouvəweit/, *n.* **1.** extra weight; excess of weight. **2.** too great a weight: *overweight is a cause of disease.* ◇*adj.* **3.** weighing more than is normal or proper: *She came back from the holiday very overweight.*

overwhelm /ouvəˈwelm/, *v.t.* **1.** to come upon so as to crush or bury: *Feelings overwhelmed him.* **2.** to overcome by force; vanquish; defeat. [ME] **— overwhelming,** *adj.*

overwork /ouvəˈwɜːk/, *v.*, **-worked** or **-wrought, -working**; /ˈouvəwɜːk/, *n.* ◇*v.t.* **1.** (*often used before a verb*) to cause to work too hard or too long; weary or exhaust with work: *She has overworked herself this term.* **2.** to use too much (*usu. as pp.*): *The word 'literally' is overworked and is losing its meaning.* ◇*v.i.* **3.** to work too hard; work to excess. ◇*n.* **4.** work that is beyond one's strength or ability. [OE *oferwyrcan*]

overwrought /ouvəˈrɔːt/, *adj.* **1.** worked up; excessively excited. **2.** very worried; having highly strained nerves.

ovi-, a word part meaning 'egg', as in *oviparous*. [L, combining form of *ōvum*]

Ovid /ˈɒvəd/, *n.* (*Publius Ovidius Naso*) 43 BC–AD 17?, Roman poet. **— Ovidian,** *adj.*

ovine /ˈouvain/, *adj.* relating to or of the nature of, or like sheep. [LL, from L: sheep]

oviparous /ouˈvɪpərəs/, *adj.* producing ova or eggs which are matured or hatched after being sent out from the body, as birds, most reptiles and fishes, etc. [L: egg-laying] **— oviparity,** *n.*

ovipositor /ouviˈpɒzətə/, *n.* (in certain insects) an organ at the end of the abdomen, by which eggs are laid.

ovocyte /ˈouvəsait/, *n.* → **oocyte.**

ovoid /ˈouvɔid/, *adj.* **1.** having the solid form of an egg. **2.** → **ovate** (def. 2). ◇*n.* **3.** an ovoid body. [L: egg]

ovoviviparous /ˌouvouvəˈvɪpərəs/, *adj.* producing eggs which are hatched within the body, so that the young are born alive but without placental attachment, as certain reptiles, fishes, etc.

ovulate /ˈɒvjəleɪt/, *v.i.*, **-lated, -lating.** to shed eggs from an ovary or ovarian follicle. —**ovulation,** *n.*

ovule /ˈɒvjuːl/, *n.* **1.** *Biol.* a small egg. **2.** *Bot.* an unfertilised seed. [NL: little egg]

ovum /ˈouvəm/, *n., pl.* **ova** /ˈouvə/. *Biol.* **a.** an egg, in a broad biological sense. **b.** the female reproductive cell, which after fertilisation is able to develop into a new individual; gamete. [L: egg]

owe /ou/, *v.t.*, **owed, owing. 1.** to admit or recognise as the cause of; be indebted or beholden for (usu. fol. by *to*): *He owes his good fortune to his friend's advice.* **2.** to have to pay or repay, or to give (oft. fol. by *to* or a simple dative): *I owe him $20 for the tickets; I owe him a good turn; to owe thanks.* [OE *āgan*]

Owen /ˈouən/, *n.* **1. Robert,** 1771–1858, British industrialist and social reformer. **2. Wilfred,** 1893–1918, English poet.

Owens /ˈouənz/, *n.* **Jesse** (*John Cleveland*), 1913–80, US track athlete; winner of four gold medals at the 1936 Olympic Games.

Owen Stanley Range /ˌouən ˈstænli/, *n.* a mountain range in south-eastern PNG. Highest peak, Mt Victoria, 4073 m. [named after Captain Owen STANLEY who charted the NG coast 1845–50]

owing /ˈouɪŋ/, *adj.* **1.** unpaid or due: *to pay what is owing.* **2. owing to, a.** because of; on account of: *owing to the train strike I have to drive into the city.* **b.** to be seen as the cause of; attributable to: *His good fortune is said to be mostly owing to his friend's help.* See **due** (def. 3).

owl /aul/, *n.* **1.** a bird with a broad head and large eyes, which feeds, usu. at night, on mice, small birds and reptiles, etc. **2.** a person who tends to be active at night. **3.** a person of owl-like solemnity or appearance. **4.** a wise person. [OE *ūle*]

owlet-nightjar /ˌaulət-ˈnaɪtdʒə/, *n.* a small nocturnal, insect-eating bird with brown and grey feathers, large eyes and a wide beak, found all over Australia and in NG.

own /oun/, *adj.* **1.** belonging or relating to oneself or itself (usu. used after a possessive to strengthen the idea of ownership, interest, or relation given by the possessive): *his own money.* **2. be one's own master,** to be independent. ◇*n.* **3.** something belonging to one: *It is his own.* ◇**4.** Some special uses are: **come into one's own, 1.** to receive an inheritance. **2.** to reach a situation where one's qualities or skills become respected or able to be used.
get one's own back, to have revenge.
of one's own, belonging to oneself.
on one's own, *Colloq.* alone or without help. [ME *owen;* OE *āgen,* orig. pp. of *āgan* have, possess. See OWE] ◇*v.t.* **5.** to have or hold as belonging to one; possess. **6.** to admit, acknowledge: *to own a fault; to own himself a failure.* **7.** to acknowledge as one's own: *I own him as my father.* ◇*v.i.* **8.** to confess (oft. fol. by *up*): *Will the boy who has done this please own up!* [OE *agnian*] —**owner,** *n.* —**ownership,** *n.*

ox /ɒks/, *n., pl.* **oxen. 1.** →**bullock** (def. 1). **2.** a related animal (of either sex) such as the buffalo or bison. [OE *oxa*]

oxa-, *Chem.* a prefix meaning 'oxygen when it replaces carbon'.

oxalate /ˈɒksəleɪt/, *n.* See **-ate**².

oxalic acid /ɒkˌsælɪk ˈæsəd/, *n.* a white, crystalline, dibasic acid, (COOH)$_2$·2H$_2$O, first discovered in the juice of a species of oxalis, used in textile and dye making, in bleaching, etc.

oxalis /ˈɒksələs/, *n.* a clover-like weed as the yellow wood sorrel and yellow-flowered oxalis. [L, from Gk: sorrel]

Oxbridge /ˈɒksbrɪdʒ/, *n.* Oxford and Cambridge considered together, esp. as typifying traditional educational standards.

oxen /ˈɒksən/, *n.* plural of **ox.**

Oxford /ˈɒksfəd/, *n.* a city in southern England; famous university (founded in the 12th century); headquarters of the Royalists during the Civil War; administrative centre of Oxfordshire. Pop. 119 909 (1981).

oxidate /ˈɒksədeɪt/, *v.t., v.i.*, **-dated, -dating.** to oxidise. —**oxidation,** *n.* —**oxidative,** *adj.*

oxidation number, /kəˈdeɪʃən nʌmbə/ *n.* the number of electrons which must be added or subtracted to make an ion neutral. In FeCl$_3$, the ferric ion needs three more electrons, so its oxidation number is 3.

oxide /ˈɒksaɪd/, *n.* a compound, usu. containing two elements only, one of which is oxygen, as *mercuric oxide.* [F, from *ox(ygène)* oxygen + *(ac)ide* acid]

oxidise or **oxidize** /ˈɒksədaɪz/, *v.*, **-dised, -dising.** ◇*v.t.* **1.** to change (an element) into its oxide; to combine with oxygen. **2.** to cover with a coating of oxide, or rust. **3.** to take away hydrogen from (a substance). **4.** to increase the valency of (an element) by removing electrons. **5.** (of a wine) to combine with oxygen, damaging color, smell and taste. ◇*v.i.* **6.** to become oxidised. —**oxidisable,** *adj.* —**oxidisation,** *n.* —**oxidiser,** *n.*

oxidising agent, *n.* any substance which brings about an oxidation process.

Oxley /ˈɒksli/, *n.* **John Joseph William Molesworth,** 1785–1828, English-born Australian pioneer, surveyor and explorer.

Oxon /ˈɒkˈsɒn/, *Abbrev.* **1.** Oxford. [L *Oxonia*] **2.** of Oxford. [L *Oxoniensis*] **3.** Oxfordshire.

oxy-, combining form of **oxygen,** sometimes used as an equivalent of *hydroxy-*.

oxyacetylene /ˌɒksiəˈsɛtələn/, *adj.* of or relating to a mixture of oxygen and acetylene.

oxygen /ˈɒksədʒən/, *n.* a colorless, odorless gaseous element, making up about one fifth of

oxygen the volume of the atmosphere and present in a combined state throughout nature. It is the supporter of combustion in air. Weight of 1 litre at 0° C and 760 mm pressure: 1.4290 grams. *Symbol:* O; *at. wt:* 15.9994; *at. no.:* 8. [F: acid-producer]

oxygenate /ɒkˈsɪdʒəneɪt/, *v.t.*, **-nated, -nating.** to treat or combine, esp. to enrich, with oxygen. Also, **oxygenise.** — **oxygenation,** *n.*

oxymoron /ɒksɪˈmɔrɒn/, *n., pl.* **-mora** /-ˈmɔrə/. a figure of speech using a contradiction, as in *cruel kindness* or *to make haste slowly*. [NL, from Gk: pointedly foolish]

o.y.o., *Abbrev.* own-your-own. Also, **OYO**

oyster /ˈɔɪstə/, *n.* **1.** a shellfish with a double shell of irregular shape, found on the sea bottom or sticking to rocks, and widely grown as food. **2.** *Colloq.* a person who does not say much. **3.** something from which one may get advantage: *The world is my oyster.* **4.** a greyish-white color. [ME, from OF, from L, from Gk]

oystercatcher /ˈɔɪstəkætʃə/, *n.* a black or black-and-white bird with a long red beak, living on beaches and estuaries around Australia, and elsewhere in the world, esp. the **sooty oystercatcher,** with red eyes and bill, with a loud call, found around Australian seashores.

oz, *Abbrev.* **1.** ounce. **2.** Also, **ozs** extra ounces.

Oz /ɒz/, *adj., n. Colloq.* Australia. Also, **oz.**

ozone /ˈoʊzoʊn/, *n.* **1.** *Chem.* a form of oxygen, O₃, with three atoms to the molecule, with a peculiar chlorine-like smell, produced when an electric spark is passed through air, as after a thunderstorm. It is a powerful oxidising agent, used for bleaching, sterilising water, etc. **2.** *Colloq.* pure, fresh air: *Come down to the beach and breathe the ozone.* [F, from Gk *ózein* smell + *-one* -ONE]

ozone layer, *n.* a region in the outer part of the stratosphere at a height of about 30 kilometres, where much of the atmospheric ozone (O₃) occurs. Also, **ozonosphere.**

Pp

P, p, *n., pl.* **P's** or **Ps, p's** or **ps. 1.** the 16th letter of the English alphabet. **2. mind one's p's and q's,** to be careful to be polite.

p /piː/, *Abbrev.* penny or pence.

p., *Abbrev.* **1.** page. **2.** part. **3.** past. **4.** per. **5.** *Music.* softly. [It *piano*] **6.** population.

P, *Symbol.* **1.** *Chem.* phosphorus. **2.** pressure. **3.** (of a driver's licence) provisional.

pa /pɑː/, *n. Colloq.* father.

p.a., *Abbrev.* per annum (yearly).

Pa, *Chem. Symbol.* protactinium.

PA /piː 'eɪ/, *Abbrev.* **1.** public-address system. **2.** power of attorney.

pabulum /'pæbjələm/, *n.* food, esp. for the mind. [L: food, fodder]

pace /peɪs/, *n., v.,* **paced, pacing.** ◇*n.* **1.** rate, or movement in general: *a pace of 10 kilometres an hour.* **2.** the rate or style of doing anything: *They live at a tremendous pace.* **3.** a single step: *She took three paces across the room.* **4.** the distance covered in a step: *Stand six paces inside the gates.* **5.** a manner of stepping; gait. **6.** the step of a horse, etc., in which the feet on the same side are lifted and put down together. **7. put through one's paces,** to cause to perform or show ability. ◇*v.t.* **8.** to set the pace for: *This racehorse always paces the favorite.* **9.** to go across with paces or steps: *He paced the floor anxiously.* **10.** to measure by paces. **11.** to train to a certain pace: *to pace a horse.* ◇*v.i.* **12.** to walk with regular paces, either fast or slow, esp. when nervous, bored, etc.: *The job applicant paced up and down the hall.* **13.** (of horses) to go at a pace (def. 6), esp. in racing. [ME, from OF, from L: a pace, a step, lit., a stretch (of the leg)]

pacemaker /'peɪsmeɪkə/, *n.* **1.** a person, thing or group that sets the pace, in racing, lifestyle, etc. **2.** *Med.* an instrument placed beneath the skin to control the rate of the heartbeat.

pacer /'peɪsə/, *n.* **1.** → **pacemaker. 2.** a horse trained to pace, or whose natural step is a pace (def. 6).

pachyderm /'pækɪdɜːm/, *n.* any of the large, thick-skinned, hoofed mammals, such as the elephant, hippopotamus, and rhinoceros. [F, from Gk: thick-skinned] — **pachydermatous, pachydermic,** *adj.*

pacific /pə'sɪfɪk/, *adj.* **1.** tending to make peace; conciliatory: *a pacific statement.* **2.** liking peace; peaceable: *a pacific personality.* **3.** peaceful: *pacific state of affairs.* [L: peacemaking]

Pacific Ocean, *n.* the world's largest ocean; lies between the American continents and Asia and Australia; divided by the equator into the North Pacific and South Pacific. About 179.7 million km^2; greatest known depth about 11 000 m.

pacifism /'pæsəfɪzəm/, *n.* **1.** opposition to war or violence of any kind. **2.** the principle or policy that all differences between nations may be settled without war and that permanent international peace may thus be established. [PACIF(IC) + -ISM] — **pacifist,** *n.*

pacify /'pæsəfaɪ/, *v.t.,* **-fied, -fying.** to bring into a state of peace; calm: *to pacify an angry man.* [late ME, from L: make peace] — **pacifiable,** *adj.*

pack^1 /pæk/, *n.* **1.** a parcel or packet of anything wrapped or tied up. **2.** a load carried on the back by a person or animal. **3.** the method, materials, etc., used in making a pack or parcel: *a vacuum pack.* **4.** a company of people (esp. criminals): *a pack of thieves.* **5.** a group or unit of cubs (def. 4) or brownies. **6.** *Rugby.* **a.** the forwards of a team collectively, esp. acting together in rushing the ball forward or as a scrum. **b.** the forwards of two opposing teams in a scrum. **7.** a group of certain animals of the same kind: *a pack of wolves.* **8.** a group of things, usu. not material objects: *a pack of lies.* **9.** a complete set, esp. of 52 playing cards. **10.** *Med.* **a.** cloths wrapped around the body for healing or soothing purposes. **b.** material put into a wound or natural opening of the body to prevent bleeding, etc. **11.** a paste put on the face, etc., to improve the condition or appearance of the skin. **12. go to the pack,** to become worse in condition, performance, etc.; degenerate. ◇*v.t.* **13.** to make into a pack or parcel. **14.** to bring or make (animals, ice, etc.) into a group or closely formed mass. **15.** to fill (a container) with articles: *to pack a suitcase.* **16.** to arrange (articles) in a container: *to pack clothes into a suitcase.* **17.** to press together within; cram: *The crowd packed the hall.* **18.** to cover or envelop with something pressed closely around: *to pack a wound with ice.* **19.** to send away hurriedly (usu. fol. by *off, away,* etc.): *I packed him off to school.* **20.** to put a load upon (a horse, etc.) **21.** *Colloq.* to be able to perform (forceful blows): *He packs a mighty punch.* ◇*v.i.* **22.** to pack goods, etc., to make them ready for carrying, storing, etc. (oft. fol. by *up*). **23.** to crowd together: *Everyone packed into the room.* **24.** to become a tightly formed mass: *Wet snow packs readily.* **25.** to collect into a pack: *The dogs began to pack.* **26.** to leave hastily (fol. by *off, away,* etc.). **27.** *Rugby.* to form a scrum (oft. fol. by *down*). ◇*v.* **28. pack the game / it in,** to give up; stop doing something. [ME, from Flem, D or LG]

pack^2 /pæk/, *v.t.* to collect, arrange, or manipulate (cards, people, etc.) so as to serve one's own purposes: *to pack a jury.* [? var. of PACT]

package /'pækɪdʒ/, *n., v.,* **-aged, -aging.** ◇*n.* **1.** a parcel; bundle. **2.** something in which articles are packed, as a box, crate, etc. **3.** the act of packing goods, etc. **4.** a group of things considered as a single unit. ◇*v.t.* **5.** to put into wrappings or a container. **6.** to combine as a single unit.

Packer family /'pækə/, *n.* an Australian family notable in the areas of media and sport, including **1. Sir (Douglas) Frank Hewson**, 1906-74, media proprietor; began publication of the *Australian Women's Weekly* in 1933; chairman of Australian Consolidated Press and television stations in NSW and Melbourne. **2.** his son, **Kerry Francis Bullmore**, born 1937, media proprietor; chairman of Consolidated Press Holdings Ltd 1974-87; established an Australian World Series Cricket team in 1977.

packet /'pækət/, *n.* **1.** a small pack or package of anything: *a packet of biscuits.* **2.** a paper or cardboard container used to hold the articles in such a package: *Don't throw away the packet.* **3.** a ship that carries mail, passengers, and goods regularly on a fixed route. **4.** *Colloq.* a large sum of money. [diminutive of PACK¹]

pack-ice /'pæk-aɪs/, *n.* an area of large blocks of floating ice driven together over a long period by winds, currents, etc., found in polar seas.

packing /'pækɪŋ/, *n.* **1.** the act or work of someone or something that packs. **2.** any material used for packing or making watertight, etc., such as a fibrous substance closing a joint.

pact /pækt/, *n.* an agreement; compact. [ME, from L: agreed]

pad¹ /pæd/, *n., v.,* **padded, padding.** ◇*n.* **1.** a mass of some soft material, used to give comfort, protection, or shape. **2.** a guard for the leg, containing soft material and stiffeners, worn by certain players in cricket, hockey, etc. **3.** Also, **writing pad.** a number of sheets of paper held together at one edge. **4.** a soft block of absorbent material for inking a rubber stamp. **5.** the soft, fleshy underside of the feet of some animals, as dogs, foxes. **6.** the large floating leaf of the waterlily. **7.** → **launching pad**. **8.** *Colloq.* a place where someone lives, esp. a single room. ◇*v.t.* **9.** to furnish, protect, or fill out with a pad or padding. **10.** to fill out (writing or speech) with unnecessary words or matter (sometimes fol. by *out*). [special uses of obs. *pad* bundle to lie on, ? b. PACK¹ and BED]

pad² /pæd/, *n., v.,* **padded, padding.** ◇*n.* **1.** a soft, dull sound, as of a footstep on the ground. ◇*v.t.* **2.** to travel along (a path, etc.) on foot. ◇*v.i.* **3.** to travel on foot: *I've been padding around the world.* **4.** to walk with soft footsteps: *I'm padding around trying not to wake anyone.* [D or LG; orig. beggars' and thieves' slang]

padding /'pædɪŋ/, *n.* **1.** soft material used to pad. **2.** unnecessary matter used to fill out a speech, etc.

paddle¹ /'pædl/, *n., v.,* **-dled, -dling.** ◇*n.* **1.** a short oar held in the hands (not in the rowlock) and used esp. for moving a canoe through the water. **2.** one of the broad blades of a paddlewheel or waterwheel. **3.** a shutter that lets waters into or out of a lock, reservoir, etc. **4.** the flipper or limb of a penguin, turtle, whale, etc. **5.** the act of paddling. ◇*v.t., v.i.* **6.** to propel (a canoe, etc.) with a paddle. [orig. obscure] — **paddler**, *n.*

paddle² /'pædl/, *v.i.,* **-dled, -dling. 1.** to walk or play with bare feet in shallow water, etc. **2.** to let the fingers, feet, etc., play in water. [orig. uncert.]

paddle-steamer /'pædl-stimə/, *n.* a boat driven by paddlewheels which are turned by a steam engine. Also, **paddleboat.**

paddlewheel /'pædlwil/, *n.* a wheel with floats or paddles on its edge, for driving a boat over the water.

paddock /'pædək/, *n.* **1.** a large fenced area of land, usu. used for grazing stock. **2.** *Brit.* a small field, esp. for pasture, near a stable or house. **3.** Also, **saddling paddock**. *Horseracing.* the area in which horses are saddled before a race and to which the winners are brought back for the presentation of prizes. **4.** *Motor Racing.* the area near the pits, in which cars are prepared for a race. **5.** *NZ.* a football field. ◇*v.t.* **6.** to enclose (animals) in a paddock. [var. of *parrock*, OE *pearroc* enclosure (orig. fence)]

paddy¹ /'pædi/, *n.* **1.** rice as a crop, uncut or gathered. **2.** Also, **paddy field**. wet, often flooded, land on which rice is grown. [Malay]

paddy² /'pædi/, *n. Colloq.* a fit of anger; rage. [from *Paddy* an Irishman (the Irish being seen as quick-tempered)]

paddymelon /'pædiˌmɛlən/, *n.* either of two southern African plants, now widespread in Australia: **1.** a trailing herb, with small melon-like fruit, harmful to farm animals. **2.** a vine, producing a fruit sometimes used for making jam. [? PADDY¹ (def. 3) + MELON]

paddy-wagon /'pædi-wægən/, *n.* a police van for carrying prisoners.

paddywhack /'pædiwæk/, *n. Colloq.* a spanking.

pademelon /'pædɪmɛlən/, *n.* See **wallaby**. [alteration (by association with *melon*) of an Aboriginal word]

padlock /'pædlɒk/, *n.* **1.** a removable lock having a turning or sliding curved clasp which passes through a staple, ring, etc., and is then fastened. ◇*v.t.* **2.** to fasten with a padlock. [late ME]

padre /'padreɪ/, *n.* **1.** father (used esp. with regard to a priest). **2.** a military or naval chaplain. [Sp, Pg, It, from L: father]

paean /'piən/, *n.* a song of praise, joy, or triumph. Also, **pean.** [L, from Gk *Paiān*, Homer's name for the physician of the gods, later Apollo]

paed- or **ped-**, a word part meaning 'child'. Also, **paedi-, paedo-**. [Gk]

paediatrics or **pediatrics** /pidi'ætrɪks/, *n.* the study and treatment of the diseases of children. [Gk] — **paediatric**, *adj.* — **paediatrician**, *n.*

pagan /'peɪgən/, *n.* **1.** one of a people or group believing in some religion other than Christianity (used with regard to the ancient Romans, Greeks, etc., and sometimes the Jews). **2.** someone who is not a Christian, a Jew, or a Muslim. **3.** an irreligious person;

heathen. ◇*adj.* **4.** of, relating to, or typical of pagans. [ME, from L: civilian; so called (by the Christians) because not a soldier of Christ] —**paganism,** *n.*

page[1] /peɪdʒ/, *n.* **1.** one side of a sheet of paper of a book, letter, etc. **2.** the whole sheet of paper of a book, etc.: *Write on both sides of the page.* **3.** an event or period: *a glorious page in history.* [F, from L]

page[2] /peɪdʒ/, *n., v.,* **paged, paging.** ◇*n.* **1.** a boy servant or attendant. **2.** a young man in attendance on a person of rank. **3.** a young male attendant, usu. in uniform, in a hotel, etc.; pageboy. ◇*v.t.* **4.** to try to find (a person) by calling out their name, or using a public-address system or a pager, as in a hotel, hospital, business office, etc. [ME, from OF, from It, from Gk: boy, servant]

Page /peɪdʒ/, *n.* **Sir Earle Christmas Grafton,** 1880–1961, Australian Country Party politician; prime minister for 19 days in 1939.

pageant /'pædʒənt/, *n.* **1.** a colorful public show, illustrating an historical event or other subject, often including a procession of people in costume. **2.** any showy display. [ME; orig. obscure] —**pageantry,** *n.*

pageboy /'peɪdʒbɔɪ/, *n.* **1.** →**page**[2] (def. 3). **2.** a young boy who acts as an attendant at weddings or social occasions. **3.** A woman's hairstyle in which the hair falls straight and is rolled under at the bottom.

pager /'peɪdʒə/, *n.* a small device which may be carried in the pocket, etc., and which receives signal signals, used as a means of contacting or giving information to the person carrying it.

pagoda /pə'goʊdə/, *n.* (in India, Burma, China, etc.) a sacred building, usu. more or less pyramidal in shape or forming a tower of many storeys. [Pg; orig. uncert.]

Pago Pago /ˌpæŋoʊ 'pæŋoʊ, peɪgoʊ 'peɪgoʊ/, *n.* the chief harbor and town of American Samoa, on Tutuila island; naval station. Pop. 3075 (1980). Also, **Pagopago.**

paid /peɪd/, *v.* past tense and past participle of **pay**[1].

pail /peɪl/, *n.* →**bucket.** [OE *pægel* wine vessel]

pain /peɪn/, *n.* **1.** bodily or mental suffering or discomfort (opposed to *pleasure*). **2.** a feeling of hurt in a particular part of the body. **3.** (*pl.*) very careful efforts: *Great pains have been taken.* **4. on pain of,** at the risk of receiving the punishment of: *He was told that he could return only on pain of death.* **5.** Also, **pain in the neck.** *Colloq.* an annoying or unpleasant person or thing. ◇*v.i., v.t.* **6.** to cause pain or suffering to (someone). [ME, from OF, from L: penalty, pain, from Gk: fine]

Paine /peɪn/, *n.* **Thomas,** 1737–1809, American writer on government and religion, born in England.

painful /'peɪnfəl/, *adj.* **1.** affected with or causing pain: *painful sunburn; painful legs.* **2.** difficult and slow: *painful efforts.*

painstaking /'peɪnzteɪkɪŋ/, *adj.* extremely careful: *painstaking work.*

paint /peɪnt/, *n.* **1.** a substance consisting of solid coloring matter mixed with a liquid, and used to coat a surface. **2.** the dried surface coloring. **3.** the solid coloring matter alone; pigment. **4.** *Colloq.* a cosmetic substance used to color the face. ◇*v.t.* **5.** to represent (an object, person, etc.) with paint. **6.** to make (a picture, etc.) with paint. **7.** to represent or describe in words, as if painting a picture: *His words painted a scene of destruction; He's not as bad as he's painted.* **8.** to coat (something) with paint. **9.** to put on like paint: *She painted lotion onto the wound.* ◇*v.i.* **10.** to coat something with paint. **11.** to paint a picture, etc. ◇*v.* **12. paint the town red,** *Colloq.* to have a wild party. [ME, from OF, from L: paint, adorn]

painter[1] /'peɪntə/, *n.* **1.** an artist who paints pictures. **2.** someone whose work is painting the surfaces of buildings, fences, etc. [ME, from AF, from L]

painter[2] /'peɪntə/, *n.* a rope for fastening a boat to a ship, wharf, etc. [? var. of Brit d. *panter* noose, from OF: rope to hang things on]

painting /'peɪntɪŋ/, *n.* **1.** a picture or pattern done in paints. **2.** the act, art, or work of someone who paints.

pair /peə/, *n., pl.* **pairs, pair,** *v.* ◇*n.* **1.** two things of the same kind, matched for use together: *a pair of gloves.* **2.** a combination of two parts joined together: *a pair of scissors.* **3.** two people, animals, etc., regarded as being connected in some way: *a pair of fools; a happy, married pair.* **4. a.** two members on opposite sides in a house of parliament, etc., who arrange together not to vote on a particular occasion, in order to permit absence, etc. **b.** the arrangement thus made. **5.** *Cards.* two cards of the same number or rank, without regard to suit or color: *a pair of tens.* **6.** *Rowing.* a racing boat having two rowers, with one oar each. ◇*v.t.* **7.** to arrange in pairs. **8.** to cause to be joined sexually; cause to mate or couple. ◇*v.i.* **9.** to separate into pairs (oft. fol. by *off*). **10.** to form a pair or pairs. [ME, from OF, from L: equal]

paisley /'peɪzli/, *n., pl.* **-leys. 1.** a soft woollen cloth woven with a colorful and very detailed pattern. **2.** any pattern similar to that woven on paisley. [named after *Paisley,* town in Scotland]

Paisley /'peɪzli/, *n.* **Ian Richard Kyle,** born 1926, Northern Ireland politician and leading spokesman for the militant Protestant faction.

pakeha /'pakəha, 'pakiha/, *n.* NZ. a European; white man. [Maori]

Pakistan /ˌpakə'stan, ˌpækə-/, *n.* a republic in southern Asia, bordered by India, Afghanistan, Iran and China; part of the British Indian Empire before independence in 1947 when Pakistan was created as a separate Islamic state; a republic since 1956; orig. in two parts, East and West Pakistan, separated by Indian territory; East Pakistan seceded as Bangladesh in 1971. Pop. 89 729 000 (1983); 803 943 km². *Languages:* Urdu, also Punjabi, Sindhi, Pushtu and English. *Currency:* rupee. *Cap.:* Islamabad. Official name, **Islamic Republic of Pakistan.** —**Pakistani,** *n., adj.*

pal /pæl/, *n., v.*, **palled, palling.** *Colloq.* ◇*n.* **1.** a friend; comrade. ◇*v.i.* **2.** to become friendly (oft. fol. by *up*): *He soon palled up with her.* [Gipsy: brother] —**pally,** *adj.*

palace /'pæləs/, *n.* **1.** the official home of a king, queen, bishop, or other person of very high rank. **2.** a very large, stately house. **3.** a large building for shows or other entertainment. [ME, from OF, from L: palace]

paladin /'pælədən/, *n.* a knightly or heroic champion in medieval times. [F, from It, from L: belonging to the palace; first applied to the 12 peers or knightly champions of CHARLEMAGNE]

palaeo-, a prefix meaning 'old', 'ancient'. Also, before most vowels, **palae-**. [Gk]

Palaeocene /'pæliəsin, 'pei-/, *adj., n.* (of or relating to) a division of the Tertiary period or system that comes before Eocene.

Palaeolithic /ˌpæliə'lɪθɪk, ˌpei-/, *adj., n.* (of or relating to) the earliest part of the Stone Age, marked by the making of chipped stone tools. Also, **palaeolithic.**

Palaeolithic man, *n.* any of the primitive species of man (Java, Neanderthal, etc.) living in the Palaeolithic period.

palaeontology /ˌpæliɒn'tɒlədʒi, ˌpei-/, *n.* the science of the forms of life existing in former geological periods, as represented by fossil animals and plants. [F] —**palaeontologist,** *n.*

Palaeozoic /ˌpæliou'zouɪk, ˌpei-/, *adj., n.* (relating to) the oldest geological era or rocks, consisting of divisions from Cambrian to Permian. [Gk]

palatable /'pælətəbəl/, *adj.* **1.** agreeable to the taste: *palatable food.* **2.** agreeable to the mind or feelings: *palatable reading matter.* —**palatability,** *n.*

palatal /'pælətl/, *adj.* **1.** *Anat.* of or relating to the palate. **2.** *Linguistics.* pronounced with the tongue held close to the hard palate, e.g. the *y* of *yield* is a palatal consonant. [PALAT(E) + -AL¹]

palate /'pælət/, *n.* **1.** the roof of the mouth, consisting of bone (**hard palate**) in front and of a fleshy structure (**soft palate**) at the back. **2.** the sense of taste. **3.** mental taste or liking. [ME, from L]

palatial /pə'leɪʃəl/, *adj.* relating to, or like a palace: *a palatial house.* [L: PALACE]

palatine /'pælətaɪn/, *adj.* **1.** possessing royal privileges: *a count palatine.* **2.** of or relating to a count palatine. **3.** (in late Roman and Byzantine times) a court official. [ME, from L: belonging to the palace, imperial (as n., a palace officer)] —**palatinate,** *n.*

Palatine Hill, *n.* one of the seven hills on which Rome was built.

palaver /pə'lavə/, *n.* **1.** (*now rare*) long talks between travellers or traders and native peoples; parley. **2.** idle, useless or foolish talk. **3.** any unnecessarily long business; bother: *The palaver of writing out new instructions.* ◇*v.i.* **4.** to talk for a long time to little purpose. [Pg, from L: PARABLE]

pale¹ /peɪl/, *adj.*, **paler, palest,** *v.*, **paled, paling.** ◇*adj.* **1.** of a whitish appearance; without much color: *a pale face.* **2.** of a low degree of color: *pale yellow.* **3.** lacking in brightness; dim: *the pale moon.* **4.** faint; feeble: *a pale attempt.* ◇*v.i.* **5.** to become pale. **6.** to seem less in importance, strength, etc. (fol. by *before, beside,* etc.): *Her happiness paled before that of her friend.* [ME, from OF, from L: pallid]

pale² /peɪl/, *n.* **1.** a long, pointed piece of wood, such as part of a fence; stake; picket. **2.** a fence made of pales. **3.** limits or bounds: *outside the pale of the Church.* **4. beyond the pale,** outside the limits of what is socially or morally acceptable. [ME, from F, from L: stake]

paleface /'peɪlfeɪs/, *n.* a white person (expression said to have been used by the Amer Indians).

Palestine /'pæləstaɪn/, *n.* **1.** Also, **Holy Land.** Biblical name, **Canaan.** an ancient country in south-western Asia, on the eastern coast of the Mediterranean. **2.** a former British mandate comprising part of this country, now divided between the state of Israel and part of the state of Jordan. —**Palestinian,** *adj.*

Palestine Liberation Organisation, *n.* → PLO

palette /'pælət/, *n.* **1.** a thin board, usu. oval or oblong, with a thumb hole at one end, used by painters to lay and mix colors on. **2.** the range of colors used by a particular artist. Also, **pallet.** [F: palette, flat-bladed implement, from L: spade, shovel]

palindrome /'pælɪndroum/, *n.* a word, sentence, etc., reading the same backwards as forwards, as *Madam, I'm Adam.* [Gk *palíndromos* running back]

paling /'peɪlɪŋ/, *n.* **1.** a fence of pales. **2.** a pale, as in a fence. [ME]

palisade /ˌpælə'seɪd/, *n.* **1.** a fence of pales set firmly in the ground for enclosure or defence. **2.** one of the pales pointed at the top, set firmly in the ground in a close row with others, for defence. [F: furnish with a paling, from L: PALE²]

pall¹ /pɔl/, *n.* **1.** a cloth for spreading over a coffin, etc. **2.** something that covers with darkness or low spirits: *A pall of smoke hung over the city.* [ME; OE *pæll*, from L: cloak, covering]

pall² /pɔl/, *v.i.* **1.** to have a tiring or boring effect (fol. by *on* or *upon*): *Her constant talking began to pall on me.* **2.** to become uninteresting: *Stamp collecting has palled as a hobby.* [ME]

Palladio /pə'ladiou/, *n.* **Andrea,** 1508–80, Italian architect who used ideas in ancient Roman architecture, esp. of symmetry and harmonic proportions, and developed these in a distinctive way, to such an extent that a style of architecture is named after him. —**Palladian,** *adj.*

palladium /pə'leɪdiəm/, *n.* a rare metallic element like platinum, silver-white, ductile and malleable, harder than platinum. Symbol: Pd;

palladium

at. no.: 46; *at. wt*: 106.4. [NL; named (1803) after the asteroid *Pallas*, then recently discovered]

Pallas /'pæləs/, *n.* **1.** a name of Athena (often **Pallas Athene** /ə'θiːniː/). **2.** *Astron.* one of the asteroids; revolves around the sun in a period of 462 years. [L, from Gk] —**Palladian**, *adj.*

pallbearer /'pɔːlbɛərə/, *n.* one of the people who carry or attend the coffin at a funeral.

pallet[1] /'pælət/, *n.* **1.** a bed or mattress of straw. **2.** a small or poor bed. [ME, from OF, from L: chaff]

pallet[2] /'pælət/, *n.* **1.** a tool consisting of a flat blade with a handle, used for shaping by potters, etc. **2.** a movable platform on which goods are placed for storage or moving, esp. goods lifted by a fork-lift truck. **3.** →**palette**. [F: PALETTE]

palliate /'pælieɪt/, *v.t.*, -**ated**, -**ating**. **1.** to cause (an offence, etc.) to appear less serious; excuse. **2.** to lessen the severity of (a disease, etc.). [L: covered with a cloak] —**palliation**, *n.* —**palliative**, *adj.*, *n.*

pallid /'pæləd/, *adj.* pale; lacking in color. [L]

pallor /'pælə/, *n.* unnatural paleness, such as that caused by fear, ill health, or death. [L]

palm[1] /pam/, *n.* **1.** that part of the inner surface of the hand which reaches from the wrist to the bases of the fingers. **2.** a similar part of the forefoot of an animal. **3.** the part of a glove covering the palm. **4.** a linear measure based on either the breadth of the hand (7 to 10 cm) or its length (18 to 25 cm). **5. cross / grease / oil someone's palm,** to bribe someone. ◇*v.t.* **6.** to conceal (a card, coin, etc.) in the hand in the course of a game, the performance of a trick, etc. ◇*v.* **7. palm off,** to get (something) accepted by trickery (fol. by *on* or *upon*): *He tried to palm off the broken watch on me.* [L: palm, hand, blade of an oar] —**palmar**, *adj.*

palm[2] /pam/, *n.* **1.** one of a group of plants, most of which are tall unbranched trees with a crown of large pinnate or fan-shaped leaves. **2.** the leaf or branch of a palm tree, esp. as formerly used as a sign of victory. [ME and OE, from L: palm tree; etymologically identical with PALM[1]]

palmate /'pælmeɪt, -mət/, *adj.* **1.** (of a leaf, antler, etc.) shaped like an open palm, or like a hand with the fingers stretched out. **2.** *Zool.* webfooted. Also, **palmated**. [L] —**palmation**, *n.*

Palmer[1] /'pamə/, *n.* **Vance** (*Edward Vivian Palmer*), 1885–1959, Australian writer, literary critic, and editor; author of *The Passage* (1930); a central figure in the development of Australia's literary identity.

Palmer[2] /'pamə/, *n.* a former goldfield near Cooktown in northern Queensland.

Palmerston[1] /'paməstən/, *n.* **Henry John Temple, 3rd Viscount,** 1784–1865, British statesman; prime minister 1855–58 and 1859–65.

pamphlet

Palmerston[2] /'paməstən/, *n.* the former name of **Darwin**.

Palmerston North, *n.* a city on southern North Island, NZ. Pop. 62 700 (1985 est.).

palmistry /'paməstri/, *n.* the art or practice of telling a person's fortune or character by the length and pattern of the lines of the palm of the hand. [ME] —**palmist**, *n.*

Palm Sunday, *n.* the Sunday before Easter, celebrated in memory of Christ's triumphal entry into Jerusalem.

Palm Valley, *n.* an area in the south-western NT on a tributary of the Finke River, south of Hermannsburg. [named for the luxuriant vegetation of the valley, including the palm *Livistona mariae*]

palmy /'pami/, *adj.*, -**mier**, -**miest**. having good fortune; flourishing: *palmy days.*

palomino /pælə'miːnoʊ/, *n., pl.* -**nos**. a tan or cream-colored horse with a white mane and tail. Also, **palamino**. [Sp]

palpable /'pælpəbəl/, *adj.* **1.** able to be easily seen, heard, understood, etc.; obvious: *a palpable lie.* **2.** able to be touched or felt: *a palpable lump in the stomach.* [ME, from L: touch] —**palpability**, *n.*

palpate /'pælpeɪt/, *v.t.*, -**pated**, -**pating**. to examine by the sense of touch, esp. in medicine. [L: touched, stroked] —**palpation**, *n.*

palpitate /'pælpəteɪt/, *v.i.*, -**tated**, -**tating**. **1.** (of the heart, etc.) to beat unnaturally fast, from effort, emotion, disease, etc. **2.** to shake slightly; tremble: *He palpitated with fear.* [L: moved quickly] —**palpitant**, *adj.* —**palpitation**, *n.*

palsy /'pɔlzi/, *n., pl.* -**sies**. →**paralysis**. [ME, from OF, from L: PARALYSIS] —**palsied**, *adj.*

paltry /'pɔltri/, *adj.*, -**trier**, -**triest**. **1.** small; trifling: *a paltry sum of money.* **2.** worthless: *paltry rags; a paltry coward.* [apparently from d. *palt* rubbish]

Pamirs /pə'mɪəz/, *n.pl.* **the,** a lofty plateau in central Asia, where the Hindu Kush, Tien Shan, and Himalayan mountain systems converge. Highest peaks about 7620 m. Also, **Pamir**.

pampas /'pæmpəz, -əs/, *n.pl.* the great grassy plains lying in the rain shadow of the Andes, and south of the forested lowlands of the Amazon basin. [Sp, from Quechua] —**pampean**, *adj.*

pamper /'pæmpə/, *v.t.* **1.** to satisfy the wants of (a person, etc.) too much; indulge: *to pamper an appetite.* **2.** to spoil (a person, etc.) by being over indulgent: *to pamper a child.* [ME]

pamphlet /'pæmflət/, *n.* **1.** Also, **brochure**. a small book, usu. with paper covers and stitched or stapled, containing information about a place, advertisements, etc. **2.** a single sheet of paper containing political advice, advertisements, etc., that is handed out in the street, put in letterboxes, etc. **3.** a short piece of writing, usu. in unbound form, on some

pamphlet

subject of current interest: *a political pamphlet*. [ME] —**pamphleteer**, *n.*

pan[1] /pæn/, *n., v.*, **panned, panning.** ◇*n.* **1.** a dish, usu. broad, shallow and open, and made of metal, used for cooking and other household purposes: *a frying pan; bed pan.* **2.** any dishlike container or part, such as the scales of a balance. **3.** a vessel in which gold or other heavy, valuable metals are separated from gravel, etc., by shaking with water. **4.** a slight dip in the ground, such as a natural one containing water, etc., or an artificial one for drying up salt water to make salt. ◇*v.t.* **5.** to wash (gravel, sand, etc.) in a pan, to separate the gold or other heavy valuable metal. **6.** to separate (gold, etc.) by such washing. **7.** *Colloq.* to criticise severely: *The critics panned the new play.* ◇*v.i.* **8.** to wash gravel, etc., in a pan, looking for gold. [ME and OE *panne*]

pan[2] /pæn/, *v.i., v.t.*, **panned, panning.** *Films, TV, etc.* to operate (a camera) so that it moves continuously in order to film a wide area, or to keep a moving person or object in view. [shortened form of PANORAMA]

pan-, a word part or prefix meaning 'all', esp. in terms meaning the union or association together, of all the branches of a race, people, church, etc., as in *pan-Celtic, pan-Christian.* [Gk]

Pan /pæn/, *n. Gk Myth.* the god of forests, pastures, flocks, and shepherds, represented with the head, chest, and arms of a man, and the legs and sometimes the horns and ears of a goat. —**Pandean, Panic,** *adj.*

panacea /pænə'siə/, *n.* a cure for all diseases, problems, etc. [L, from Gk] —**panacean,** *adj.*

panache /pə'næʃ, -'nɑʃ/, *n.* a grand, stylish manner; flamboyance. [F, from It, from L: feather]

Panama /'pænəmə/, *n.* **1.** a republic in Central America, at the southern end of the Isthmus of Panama. Pop. 2 274 400 (1987 est.). 77 082 km[2]. *Language:* Spanish. *Currency:* balboa. *Cap:* Panama City. **2. Isthmus of,** Formerly, **Isthmus of Darien.** an isthmus separating North and South America. Least width, 50 km. —**Panamanian,** *n., adj.*

Panama Canal, *n.* a canal extending southeast from the Atlantic to the Pacific across the Isthmus of Panama; 64 km long.

Panama hat, *n. (sometimes l.c.)* a fine plaited hat made of the young leaves of a South American palmlike plant.

pancake /'pænkeɪk/, *n., v.*, **-caked, -caking.** ◇*n.* **1.** a thin, flat cake made from a batter of eggs, flour, sugar, and milk, cooked in a frying pan. **2.** make-up packed hard into stick or cake form. ◇*v.i.* **3.** (of an aeroplane, etc.) to drop flat to the ground after levelling off a few feet above it.

pancreas /'pæŋkrɪəs/, *n.* a gland lying near the stomach, producing the hormone insulin, and important digestive enzymes. [NL, from Gk: sweetbread] —**pancreatic,** *adj.*

panda /'pændə/, *n.* either of two mammals closely related to the bear and mainly feeding on plants: **a.** the cat-sized **lesser panda**, of the Himalayas, which has reddish brown fur. **b.** the bearlike **giant panda**, of central China, which is boldly marked in black and white. [F, perhaps from Nepalese]

pandemonium /pændə'moʊnɪəm/, *n.* **1.** (*oft. cap.*) the place where all the demons live; hell. **2.** (a place of) wildly noisy or lawless confusion. [from *Pandaemonium*, Milton's name for the capital of hell]

pander /'pændə/, *n.* **1.** a go-between in affairs of love; procurer. ◇*v.i.* **2.** to act as a pander. **3.** to go too far in satisfying (fol. by *to*): *to pander to a child's demands.* [var. of *pandar*, generalised use of ME *Pandare* Pandarus, who (in works by Chaucer, Shakespeare and others) acted as procurer of Cressida for Troilus]

pandit /'pʌndɪt/, *n.* (in India) a learned man (used as a title of respect). See **pundit**. [Hind, from Skt: learned]

Pandora /pæn'dɔrə/, *n. Class Myth.* the first mortal woman, on whom all the gods and goddesses bestowed gifts; sent by Zeus to bring misery to mankind as punishment because Prometheus had stolen fire from heaven. [L from Gk: lit., all-gifted]

Pandora's box, *n.* anything that produces many troubles, esp. something expected at first to give blessings. [in classical mythology, a box or jar given by Zeus to PANDORA, which contained all human ills]

pane /peɪn/, *n.* a single plate of glass, esp. when in a frame and forming part of a window. [ME, from OF, from L: a cloth, rag]

panegyric /pænə'dʒɪrɪk/, *n.* a speech or writing in praise of a person or thing; eulogy. [L, from Gk: festival oration] —**panegyrical,** *adj.* —**panegyrist,** *n.*

panel /'pænəl/, *n., v.*, **-elled, -elling.** ◇*n.* **1.** a division of a ceiling, door, etc., or of any surface sunk below or raised above the general level, or enclosed by a frame. **2.** a thin, flat piece of wood, etc. **3.** a broad piece of the same or another material set in or on a woman's dress, etc. for ornament. **4.** *Elect.* a division of a switchboard containing a set of related cords, jacks, relays, etc. **5.** the section of a machine on which controls, dials, etc., are fixed: *the instrument panel of a car.* **6.** *Law.* a list of people called for service in a jury. **7.** any list or group of people, as one gathered to answer questions, discuss matters, judge a competition, etc. ◇*v.t.* **8.** to arrange in, or provide or ornament with, a panel or panels. [ME, from OF: piece (of anything), from L: rag]

panel beater, *n.* someone who beats sheet metal into shapes for the bodywork of motor vehicles, etc.

panellist /'pænəlɪst/, *n.* a member of a small group organised for public discussion, etc., as on television.

pang /pæŋ/, *n.* a sudden, short, sharp feeling of mental or bodily pain: *a pang of remorse; a pang of hunger.* [orig. uncert.]

Pangu Pati /pæŋ'gu pati/, *n.* a Papua New Guinea urban-based political party.

panic /'pænɪk/, *n., adj., v.,* **-icked, -icking.** ◇*n.* **1.** a sudden terror, with or without clear cause. ◇*adj.* **2.** (of fear, terror, etc.) suddenly destroying self-control and causing hasty, unreasoned action. ◇*v.t., v.i.* **3.** to (cause to) feel panic. [F, from L, from Gk: relating to or caused by Pan] – **panicky**, *adj.* – **panic-stricken, panic-struck**, *adj.*

panicle /'pænɪkəl/, *n. Bot.* **1.** a compound raceme. **2.** any loose, branching flower cluster. [L: tuft on plants] – **panicled, paniculate**, *adj.*

Pankhurst family /'pæŋkhəst/, *n.* a family of English female suffragists, including **Emmeline**, 1857–1928, founder of the Women's Social and Political Union (1903) to agitate for voting rights for women.

pannier /'pæniə/, *n.* a basket, for carrying provisions, etc., usu. carried on a person's back or on each side of the back of a bicycle or animal. [ME, from OF, from L: basket for bread]

pannikin /'pænɪkən/, *n.* **1.** a small pan or metal cup. ◇*adj.* **2.** relating to someone who acts importantly when in reality they are not: *a pannikin boss; a pannikin snob.*

panoply /'pænəpli/, *n., pl.* **-plies. 1.** a complete suit of armor. **2.** a complete covering or show of something. [Gk: complete suit of armor] – **panoplied**, *adj.*

panorama /pænə'rɑmə/, *n.* **1.** an uninterrupted view over a wide area. **2.** a long pictorial representation of a scene, often shown a part at a time and made to pass continuously before the viewers. **3.** a continuously passing or changing scene: *the panorama of city life.* **4.** a thorough coverage, as of a subject. [Gk] – **panoramic**, *adj.*

panpipe /'pænpaɪp/, *n.* a simple wind instrument consisting of a series of pipes of gradually increasing length, the notes being produced by blowing across the upper ends. Also, **Pan's pipes.**

pansy /'pænzi/, *n., pl.* **-sies. 1.** a type of garden plant with white, yellow, or purple velvety flowers. **2.** *Colloq.* an effeminate man; homosexual. [F: pansy, lit., thought]

pant /pænt/, *v.i.* **1.** to breathe hard and quickly because of effort, emotion, etc. **2.** to give out steam, etc., in loud puffs. **3.** to desire greatly: *He panted for revenge.* **4.** to move up and down violently or rapidly; throb: *His heart was panting.* ◇*v.t.* **5.** to speak (words) breathlessly. ◇*n.* **6.** a short, quick, difficult effort of breathing; a gasp. **7.** an up and down movement of the chest, etc; throb. [ME, probably (with ref. to the feeling of oppression in nightmare) from L: phantasm, idea, FANTASY] – **pantingly**, *adv.*

pantaloons /pæntə'lunz, 'pæntəlunz/, *n.pl. Obs.* men's trousers. [F, from It]

pantechnicon /pæn'tɛknɪkən/, *n.* a large van for moving furniture. [Gk; orig. the name of a bazaar in 19th C London, which became a furniture warehouse]

pantheism /'pænθiɪzəm/, *n.* the belief in which God is identified with the material universe or the forces of nature and therefore is thought to be impersonal. See **theism**. [Gk] – **pantheist**, *n.* – **pantheistic**, *adj.*

pantheon /pæn'θiən/, *n.* **1.** a public building containing tombs or memorials of the famous dead of a nation. **2.** all the gods believed in by a particular people considered collectively. **3.** (*cap.*) a domed circular temple at Rome, erected AD 120–24 by Hadrian using an older porch built by Agrippa 27 BC, and used as a Christian church since 609. [ME, from L, from Gk: of all gods]

panther /'pænθə/, *n., pl.* **-thers**, (*esp. collectively*) **-ther. 1.** a leopard, esp. in its black form. **2.** *US.* a cougar or puma. [L, from Gk]

panties /'pæntiz/, *n.pl.* underpants worn by women and girls.

pantihose /'pæntihoʊz/, *n.* women's tights, usu. made out of stocking material. Also, **pantyhose.**

pantograph /'pæntəgræf, -grɑf/, *n. Elect.* a current collector, fitted to the roof of a train, etc., sprung so as to keep contact with an overhead wire.

pantomime /'pæntəmaɪm/, *n.* **1.** a form of theatre common during the Christmas season, based loosely on one of several fairytales, and including stock character types. **2.** → **mime** (def. 2). **3.** action without speech to give a message, etc. [L, from Gk: all-imitating] – **pantomimic**, *adj.*

pantry /'pæntri/, *n., pl.* **-tries.** a room or cupboard in which food, etc., or tableware are kept. [ME, AF, from OF: servant in charge of bread, from L: bread]

pants /pænts/, *n.pl.* **1.** trousers. **2.** women's underpants. [familiar abbrev. of PANTALOONS]

panzer /'pænzə/, *adj.* **1.** armored: *a panzer division.* ◇*n.* **2.** a tank. [G]

pap¹ /pæp/, *n.* **1.** soft food for babies or sick people, such as bread soaked in water or milk. **2.** books, ideas, talk, etc., considered as demanding only a low standard of intelligence or attention. [ME]

pap² /pæp/, *n. Archaic.* a teat or nipple. [ME]

papa /pə'pɑ/, *n.* father. [F, from L]

papacy /'peɪpəsi/, *n., pl.* **-cies. 1.** the office, dignity, or position of the pope. **2.** the system of church government in which the pope is the supreme head. **3.** the time during which a pope is in office. [ME, from ML: pope, father]

papal /'peɪpəl/, *adj.* of or relating to the pope or the papacy. [ME, from ML: pope]

Papal States, *n.pl.* a large district in central Italy ruled as a temporal domain by the popes from 755 until the final unification of Italy in 1870; partially annexed by Italy, 1860. Also, **States of the Church.**

Papandreou /pæpən'dreɪu/, *n.* **Andreas**, born 1919, Greek socialist politician; became prime minister in 1981.

Papanicolaou smear /pæpə'nɪkəlaʊ smɪə/, n. →**Pap smear**. [from George *Papanicolaou*, 1883–1962, US scientist, who devised this test]

papaya /pə'paɪə/, n. →**pawpaw**.

paper /'peɪpə/, n. **1.** a substance made from straw, wood, or other fibrous material, usu. in thin sheets, for writing or printing on, wrapping things in, etc. **2.** a piece, sheet, or leaf of this. **3.** one or more sheets of this bearing writing or printing; document. **4.** →**wallpaper**. **5.** paper money. **6.** (pl.) documents establishing identity, nationality, etc., of a person, ship, etc.: *ship's papers*. **7.** a set of examination questions, or of written answers to them. **8.** an essay or article on a particular subject. **9.** a newspaper. **10. on paper, a.** in written form. **b.** in the planning stage. **c.** in theory rather than practice: *It seems all right on paper, but will it work?* ◇v.t. **11.** to decorate (a wall, room, etc.) with wallpaper. **12.** to line with paper: *to paper a shelf*. ◇adj. **13.** made or consisting of paper. **14.** like paper; thin; flimsy. **15.** existing on paper only and not in reality: *paper profits*. [ME and OE, from L: paper, PAPYRUS] – **papery**, adj.

paperback /'peɪpəbæk/, n. a book bound in a soft paper cover, usu. cheaper than a hardback book.

paperbark /'peɪpəbɑk/, n. (a tree bearing) a form of bark, consisting of many thin layers of papery material, some parts of which peel off.

paperboy /'peɪpəbɔɪ/, n. a boy employed to deliver or sell newspapers, etc.

paperclip /'peɪpəklɪp/, n. a small piece of wire bent into a form suitable for holding together papers, etc.

papergirl /'peɪpəgɜl/, n. a girl employed to deliver or sell newspapers, etc.

paper tiger, n. someone or something that is strong or powerful in appearance but not in reality.

paperweight /'peɪpəweɪt/, n. a small, heavy object laid on papers to keep them from moving.

papier-mâché /peɪpə-'mæʃeɪ/, n. a substance made of paper pulp, sometimes mixed with glue and other materials, or of layers of paper glued and pressed together, and used when moist to form models, boxes, etc., and which become hard and strong when dry. [F: chewed paper]

papilla /pə'pɪlə/, n., pl. **-pillae** /-'pɪli/. any small nipple-like structure on the body, such as a hair root. [L: nipple] – **papillary**, adj. – **papillose**, adj.

papism /'peɪpɪzəm/, n. (usu. offensive) the faith, practice, membership, and government of the Roman Catholic Church. – **papist**, n. – **papistry**, n.

papoose /pə'pus/, n. **1.** a North American Indian baby or young child. **2.** Colloq. any baby. Also, **pappoose**. [Algonquian (Amer Indian)]

paprika /'pæprɪkə, pə'prikə/, n. the dried fruit of a cultivated form of red capsicum ground as a spice, milder than ordinary red pepper. [Hung]

Pap smear, n. a medical test in which a smear (def. 6), from the cervix or vagina, is used to detect cancer; cervical smear. [abbreviated form of PAPANICOLAOU SMEAR]

Papua /'pap,uə/, n. **1. Territory of,** a former Australian territory in south-eastern New Guinea, including the adjacent islands; now part of Papua New Guinea. **2. Gulf of,** a large gulf of the Coral Sea, on the south-eastern coast of New Guinea. [Malay: lit., frizzled]

Papua New Guinea, n. a parliamentary state in the south-west Pacific, comprising the eastern half of the island of New Guinea and various island groups; a territory of Australia 1949–75, now an independent member of the Commonwealth. Pop. 3 500 000 (1987 est.); 475 369 km^2. *Languages:* Pidgin English, Motu, various native dialects. *Currency:* kina. *Cap.:* Port Moresby. – **Papua New Guinean**, n., adj.

papyrus /pə'paɪrəs/, n., pl. **-pyri** /-'paɪraɪ/. **1.** a tall water plant, of the Nile valley, Egypt, and elsewhere. **2.** material for writing on, prepared from thin pieces of this plant laid together, wet, pressed, and dried, used by the ancient Egyptians, Greeks, and Romans. **3.** an ancient document written on this material. [ME, from L, from Gk: the plant papyrus, something made from papyrus]

par /pa/, n. **1.** a level of equality in value or position: *The gains and losses are on a par.* **2.** an average or normal amount, degree, quality, condition, etc.: *below par; above par.* **3.** *Comm.* **a.** the legally established value of the unit of money of one country in terms of that of another using the same metal as a standard of value (**mint par of exchange**). **b.** the state of the shares of any business, loan, etc., when they may be bought at the original price (called **issue par**) or at their face value (called **nominal par**). Such shares are said to be at par. **4.** *Golf.* the number of strokes allowed to a hole or course as a standard for a good player. [L: equal]

para-[1], a prefix meaning 'beside', 'near', 'beyond', 'aside', and sometimes indicating change or modification, chiefly in scientific words. Also, before vowels, **par-**. [Gk, combining form of *pará*, prep.]

para-[2], a prefix of a few words meaning 'guard against', as in *parachute*. [F, from It, from L: prepare]

para., *Abbrev.* paragraph.

parable /'pærəbəl/, n. a short story, meant to teach some truth or moral lesson, often by using the apparent meaning of the characters or events to represent a deeper moral truth. [ME, from LL: comparison, parable, proverb, word, from Gk: a placing beside, comparison]

parabola /pə'ræbələ/, n. *Geom.* a plane curve formed by the intersection of a cone with a plane parallel to its side. [NL, from Gk] – **parabolic**, adj. – **paraboloid**, adj., n.

paracetamol /ˈpærəˈsitəmɒl/, n. a pain-killing drug.

parachute /ˈpærəʃut/, n., v., **-chuted, -chuting.** ◊n. 1. a cloth apparatus used in descending safely through air, esp. from an aircraft, being umbrella-like in form and made effective by the resistance of the air, which opens it during the descent so as to reduce the rate of the fall. ◊v.t. 2. to land (troops, equipment, etc.) by parachute. ◊v.i. 3. to descend by parachute. [F, from *para-* PARA.[2] + *chute* a fall. See CHUTE] —**parachutist**, n.

paraclete /ˈpærəklit/, n. 1. someone called in to help; an advocate or comforter. 2. (*cap.*) the Holy Spirit. [LL, from Gk]

parade /pəˈreɪd/, n., v., **-raded, -rading.** ◊n. 1. a show, display: *to make a parade of one's emotions.* 2. a gathering of troops, scouts, etc. for inspection or display. 3. a body of people marching in the street to celebrate some public event; procession: *a parade of bands and floats.* 4. a walk for pleasure or display; promenade. ◊v.t. 5. to show something off: *to parade opinions.* 6. to show by making someone or something walk or move along: *to parade cattle.* ◊v.i. 7. to march or go with display. 8. to walk in a public place to show oneself. [F, from Sp, from L: prepare]

paradigm /ˈpærədaɪm/, n. 1. *Gram.* the set of all forms containing a particular part or element, esp. the set of all inflected forms of a single root, stem, or theme, e.g. *boy, boys, boy's, boys'* makes up the paradigm of the noun *boy*. 2. a pattern; example. [late ME, from LL, from Gk: pattern] —**paradigmatic, paradigmatical**, adj.

paradise /ˈpærədaɪs/, n. 1. →**heaven.** 2. a place of great beauty or delight. 3. the greatest happiness, joy. [ME, from LL, from Gk: park, from OPers: enclosure]

paradox /ˈpærədɒks/, n. 1. a fact which seems to show two opposite ideas at the same time, but which needs both ideas to make a truth: *It is a paradox that he is both very sensitive and very cruel.* 2. any person or thing seeming to show contradictions. [L, from Gk: contrary to received opinion, incredible] —**paradoxical**, adj.

paraffin /ˈpærəfən/, n. 1. *Chem.* See **alkane series.** 2. →**paraffin oil.** 3. *Brit.* →**kerosene.** [G, from L]

paraffin oil, n. a mixture of hydrocarbons obtained from petroleum used as a laxative. Also, **liquid paraffin.**

paraffin wax, n. a white translucent solid with a melting point of 50°–60°C, consisting of the higher members of the alkane series; used for candles, waxed papers, polishes, etc.

paragon /ˈpærəgən/, n. a model or pattern of excellence, or of a particular excellence: *a paragon of virtue.* [MF, from It: touchstone, comparison, paragon]

paragraph /ˈpærəgræf, -graf/, n. 1. a part of written or printed matter dealing with a particular subject or point, beginning on a new line. 2. a small part or article in a newspaper. ◊v.t. 3. to divide into paragraphs. [LL, from Gk: line or mark in the margin]

Paraguay /ˈpærəgwaɪ, -gweɪ/, n. a republic in central South America, bordered by Brazil, Argentina and Bolivia; a Spanish colony before independence in 1811. Pop. 3 897 000 (1987 est.); 406 752 km². *Languages:* Spanish and Guaraní. *Currency:* quaraní. *Cap.:* Asunción. —**Paraguayan**, n., adj.

parakeet /ˈpærəkit/, n. a kind of small parrot usu. with a long, pointed tail, e.g. the budgerigar. Also, **paraquet, paroquet, parrakeet, parroket, parroquet.** [It: parson]

parallax /ˈpærəlæks/, n. the change in position of objects that seems to happen when the person looking changes position. [Gk: change] —**parallactic**, adj.

parallel /ˈpærəlɛl/, adj., n., v., **-leled, -leling** or **-lelled, -lelling.** ◊adj. 1. having the same direction, course, or tendency; corresponding; similar; analogous: *parallel forces.* 2. *Geom.* **a.** (of straight lines) lying in the same plane but never meeting however far extended. **b.** (of planes) having common perpendiculars. **c.** (of a single line, plane, etc.) equidistant from another or others, at all corresponding points (fol. by *to* or *with*). 3. *Music.* (of two voice parts) going along so that the interval between them remains the same. 4. *Computers, etc.* meaning or relating to a system in which several activities are carried on at the same time. ◊n. 5. anything parallel. 6. *Geog.* a circle on the earth's surface formed by the intersection of a plane parallel to the plane of the equator, bearing east and west and shown in degrees of latitude north or south of the equator along the arc of any meridian. 7. something the same; correspondence; analogy: *His musical ability is without parallel.* 8. *Elect.* a connection of two or more circuits in which all ends having the same instantaneous polarity are electrically connected together and all ends having the opposite polarity are similarly connected. The element circuits are said to be **in parallel** (opposed to *in series*). ◊v.t. 9. to make parallel in any way. [L, from Gk: beside one another]

parallelogram /pærəˈlɛləgræm/, n. a quadrilateral the opposite sides of which are parallel. [Gk: bounded by parallel lines]

paralyse /ˈpærəlaɪz/, v.t., **-lysed, -lysing.** 1. to stop (some of the muscles of the body) working, so that the affected part cannot move by itself. 2. to stop all activity in (something): *to paralyse trade.*

paralysis /pəˈræləsəs/, n., pl. **-ses** /-siz/. 1. the loss of power of a voluntary muscular contraction. 2. a more or less complete crippling, as of powers or activities: *a paralysis of trade.* [L, from Gk: palsy]

paralytic /pærəˈlɪtɪk/, n. 1. someone who is paralysed. ◊adj. 2. affected with paralysis. 3. *Colloq.* very drunk.

paramedical /pærəˈmɛdɪkəl/, adj. related to and helping the medical profession, as an ambulance man, etc.

parameter /pəˈræmətə/, n. 1. any variable quality or characteristic of something: *The*

parameterₛ *of voice quality include breathiness and nasality.* **2.** *Maths.* one of the independent variables in a set of parametric equations. **3.** *Maths.* a variable which may be kept constant while the effect of other variables is investigated. —**parametric**, *adj.*

parametric equation /ˌpærəˌmetrɪk iˈkweɪzən/, *n.* one of two or more mathematical equations in which the coordinates of points on a curve or surface are given in terms of one or more variables (parameters, def. 2) of that curve or surface.

paramount /ˈpærəmaʊnt/, *adj.* above others in rank, authority or importance. [AF: above, from L] —**paramountcy**, *n.*

paramour /ˈpærəmɔ/, *n.* an illicit lover, esp. of a married person. [ME, from OF, orig. phrase *par amour* by love, by way of (sexual) love, from L]

paranoia /pærəˈnɔɪə/, *n. Psychol.* a condition in which the patient suffers from delusions such as that of persecution or of being a very great person. [NL, from Gk: derangement] —**paranoiac**, *n., adj.* —**paranoid**, *adj.*

parapet /ˈpærəpət/, *n.* **1. a.** a wall, or bank of earth or stone, behind which soldiers can shoot at an enemy. **b.** a wall raised above the main wall or rampart of a permanent fortification. **2.** any protective wall or barrier at the edge of a balcony, roof, bridge, etc. [It, from L] —**parapeted**, *adj.*

paraphernalia /pærəfəˈneɪliə/, *n.pl.* (sometimes treated as sing.) **1.** goods, equipment, baggage belonging to someone, oft. thought of as a nuisance. **2.** any mixed collection of articles. [ML, from LL, from Gk: bride's belongings other than dowry]

paraphrase /ˈpærəfreɪz/, *n., v.*, **-phrased, -phrasing.** ◇*n.* **1.** a saying or writing of a text or passage in another way, esp. to make it shorter, simpler and clearer. **2.** the act or process of paraphrasing. ◇*v.t., v.i.* **3.** to make a paraphrase of. [F, from L, from Gk] —**paraphrastic**, *adj.*

paraplegia /pærəˈplidʒə/, *n.* paralysis of the lower part of the body. [NL, from Gk: paralysis one side] —**paraplegic**, *adj., n.*

parasite /ˈpærəsaɪt/, *n.* **1.** an animal or plant which lives on or in an organism of another species (the host), from the body of which it obtains food. **2.** someone who lives on others, or another, without doing anything in return. [L, from Gk: one who eats at the table of another] —**parasitic**, *adj.* —**parasitism**, *n.*

parasol /ˈpærəsɒl/, *n.* a woman's small or lightweight sun umbrella; sunshade. [F, from It, from L]

paratrooper /ˈpærətrupə/, *n.* a soldier who reaches battle, esp. behind enemy lines, by landing from an aeroplane by parachute. [PARA(CHUTE) + TROOPER]

par avion /par ˈævjɒn/, *adv.* by aeroplane (as a label for letters, etc. to be sent airmail). [F]

parboil /ˈpɑbɔɪl/, *v.t.* to boil until only half cooked; precook. [ME, from OF, from LL]

parcel /ˈpasəl/, *n., v.*, **-celled, -celling.** ◇*n.* **1.** a thing or things wrapped or packaged together; package or bundle. **2.** a separate or distinct part of anything: *a parcel of land.* ◇*v.t.* **3.** to divide into or distribute in parcels or portions (usu. fol. by *out*). **4.** to make into a parcel, or put up in parcels, as goods (oft.fol. by *up*): *to parcel up groceries.* [ME, from OF, L: particle]

parch /pɑtʃ/, *v.t.* **1.** to make very dry: *parched by desert winds.* ◇*v.i.* **2.** to become parched; undergo drying by heat. [ME; orig. uncert.]

parchment /ˈpatʃmənt/, *n.* **1.** the skin of sheep, goats, etc., prepared for use as a writing material, etc. **2.** a manuscript or document on such material. **3.** a paper looking like this material. [ME, from OF, b. LL: parchment and L: Parthian (leather)]

pardon /ˈpadn/, *n.* **1.** forgiveness or favorable attitude: *I beg your pardon.* **2.** *Law.* **a.** a giving of pardon for a crime. **b.** the document or warrant by which such pardon is declared. ◇*v.t.* **3.** to withhold the penalty for (an offence): *He will pardon your crimes.* **4.** to excuse (an action or person); to make courteous allowance for: *Pardon me, madam.* ◇*interj.* **5.** (a conventional form of apology): *Pardon, what did you say?* [ME, from OF, from LL: grant]

pardoner /ˈpadənə/, *n.* **1.** someone who pardons. **2.** *Hist.* a church official who grants indulgences (def. 4).

pare /peə/, *v.t.*, **pared, paring.** **1.** to cut off or remove the outer layer of; peel: *to pare apples.* **2.** to cut down on anything; make less: *to pare down one's expenses.* [ME, from OF: prepare, trim, from L]

parenchyma /pəˈrɛŋkɪmə/, *n. Bot.* the fundamental (soft) cellular tissue of plants, as in the softer parts of leaves, the pulp of fruits, the pith of stems, etc. [NL, from Gk: lit, something poured in beside] —**parenchymatous**, *adj.*

parent /ˈpeərənt/, *n.* **1.** a father or a mother. **2.** an author or source. ◇*adj.* **3.** resembling a parent in a relationship: *parent figure; parent company; parent tree.* [ME, from L] —**parenthood**, *n.* —**parentage**, *n.*

parental /pəˈrɛntl/, *adj.* relating to or having the quality of a parent: *parental feelings.*

parenthesis /pəˈrɛnθəsəs/, *n., pl.* **-ses** /-siz/. **1.** a descriptive, qualifying or explanatory word, phrase, clause, or sentence which interrupts the sentence construction without otherwise changing it, shown in writing by commas, brackets, or dashes, e.g.: *William Smith — you know him well — will be here soon.* **2.** one of the upright brackets ( ) used to mark off such a construction. **3.** a gap; interval. [ML, from Gk: a putting in beside] —**parenthetic**, *adj.* —**parenthesise**, *v.t.*

Parents and Citizens Associations, *n.pl.* Australian non-political organisations formed by parents of children attending government schools and other citizens with the purpose of fostering local interest and support for the school.

Parer /ˈpærə/, n. **1. Damien,** 1912–44, Australian photographer, noted for his work during World War II. **2. Raymond John Paul,** 1894–1967, Australian aviator and pioneer of aviation in PNG.

par excellence /par ˈɛksələns/, adv. above all others; pre-eminently. [F]

parfait /paˈfeɪ/, n. a dessert, served in a tall glass, made from layers of ice-cream, fruit, jelly, syrup, nuts, etc. [F: lit., perfect]

pariah /pəˈraɪə/, n. **1.** any person or animal generally despised; outcast. **2.** (cap.) a member of a low caste in southern India. [Tamil: lit., drummer (from a hereditary duty of the caste)]

parietal /pəˈraɪətl/, adj. **1.** Anat. referring to the side of the skull, or to any wall or wall-like structure. **2.** Bot. relating to or arising from a wall, usu. applied to ovules when they proceed from or are borne on the walls or sides of the ovary. [LL, from L: wall]

Paris[1] /ˈpærəs/, n. Gk Legend. a Trojan youth, son of King Priam and Hecuba. His abduction of Helen led to the Trojan War.

Paris[2] /ˈpærəs/, n. **1.** the capital of France, in the northern part, on the Seine. Pop. 2 165 892 (city), 8 706 963 (metropolitan) (1982). **2.** a department comprising this city. [L *Lutetia Parīsiōrum*, LL *Parīsiī*, orig. name of the Gallic tribe living there] — **Parisian,** n., adj.

Paris Commune, n. a socialist government of Paris from 18 March to 27 May, 1871; suppressed by the National Assembly in a battle in which 33 000 people were killed.

parish /ˈpærɪʃ/, n. **1.** an ecclesiastical district having its own church and clergyman. **2.** a local church with its field of activity. **3.** Brit. a civil district or administrative division. **4.** the people of a parish (church or civil). [ME, from OF, from LL, from Gk]

parishioner /pəˈrɪʃənə/, n. someone who is a member of a parish. [earlier *parishion*, from OF]

parity /ˈpærəti/, n. **1.** equality in amount, status, or character. **2.** similarity; correspondence; analogy. [LL, from L: equal]

park /pak/, n. **1.** an area of land within a town, with sporting and other facilities set aside for public use: *Hyde Park*. **2.** an area of land set apart by a city or a nation, to be kept in its natural state for the benefit of the public: *Kosciusko National Park*. **3.** an enclosed area of land for wild animals: *a lion park*. ◇v.t. **4.** to put or leave (a car, etc.) for a time in a particular place, as at the side of the road. **5.** to assemble (artillery, etc.) in compact arrangement. ◇v.i. **6.** to park a car, bicycle, etc. [ME, from OF; of Gmc orig.]

Park /pak/, n. **Ruth,** born 1923? in NZ, Australian writer; author of *The Harp in the South* (1948).

parka /ˈpakə/, n. **1.** a strong waterproof jacket with a hood, orig. for use in polar regions, now commonly used for any outdoor activity. **2.** a fur coat, cut like a shirt, worn in northeastern Asia and Alaska. [Aleut, a language spoken by the Aleutian Indians of the Alaskan Peninsula]

Park Avenue, n. a street in New York City, which, because of its large, expensive flats, has come to represent luxury, the height of fashion, etc.

Parkes /paks/, n. **Sir Henry,** 1815–96, Australian politician, born in England; contributed much to Australian federation.

Parkes Radio Telescope, n. a powerful radio telescope, with a subsidiary telescope, north of Parkes in western NSW, opened in 1961.

parking meter, n. a clockwork mechanism activated by a coin which checks the amount of time a car has been parked in a particular place.

Parkinson /ˈpakɪnsən/, n. **Sydney,** c. 1745–71, Scottish artist; employed on James Cook's 1770 voyage as natural history draughtsman.

Parkinson's disease, n. a form of paralysis marked by uncontrollable shaking, stiff muscles and weak movement; shaking palsy. Also, **Parkinsonism.** [named after James *Parkinson*, 1755–1824, English physician who first described it]

parlance /ˈpaləns/, n. a way of speaking, or language; idiom; vocabulary: *legal parlance*. [AF, from L]

parley /ˈpali/, n., pl. **-leys,** v., **-leyed, -leying.** ◇n. **1.** a talk, discussion, or conference, esp. between opposing forces. ◇v.i. **2.** to hold a parley. [F: speech]

parliament /ˈpaləmənt/, n. **1.** (usu. cap.) **a.** the national assembly of elected representatives, consisting of an upper and lower house, which, with the Sovereign, makes the laws of the nation. **b.** a similar assembly in each state of Australia. **2.** the legislature of Great Britain, historically the assembly of the three estates, now consisting of the House of Commons, which exercises effective power, the House of Lords, and the Sovereign. **3.** a similar assembly in other countries. [ME, from OF] — **parliamentary,** adj.

parliamentarian /paləmənˈtɛəriən/, n. **1.** a Member of Parliament. **2.** someone skilled in parliamentary procedure or debate. **3.** someone who supports a parliamentary system.

parliamentary privilege /palə,mentri ˈprɪvəlɪdʒ/, n. the special rights enjoyed by parliament and its members which allow members to say things freely in parliament that they could be prosecuted for outside, and which generally protect them from criticism.

parlor or **parlour** /ˈpalə/, n. **1.** a room where visitors are received and entertained. **2.** a semi-private room in a hotel, club, etc. for relaxation, entertainment, etc.; a lounge. **3.** a room fitted up for receiving business patrons or customers: *a beauty parlor; a funeral parlor*. [ME, from AF]

parlormaid or **parlourmaid** /ˈpaləmeɪd/, n. a female servant who waits at table, etc.

Parlt, Abbrev. Parliament.

Parnassus /pɑˈnæsəs/, *n*. **Mount**, a mountain in central Greece, in ancient Phocis; sacred to Apollo and the Muses, and symbolic of poetic inspiration and achievement. Modern, **Liakoura**. 2459 m.

Parnell /pɑˈnɛl/, *n*. **Charles Stewart**, 1846–91, Irish political leader, who turned the dream of Irish Home Rule into an attainable goal.

parochial /pəˈroukiəl/, *adj*. **1.** of or relating to a parish or parishes. **2.** confined to or interested only in one's own parish, or some particular narrow place or field of activity. [ME, from LL, from LL] —**parochialism**, *n*.

parody /ˈpærədi/, *n., pl*. **-dies**, *v*., **-died, -dying**. ◇*n*. **1.** a humorous or satirical imitation of a serious piece of literature, writing or music. **2.** a badly done imitation; travesty. ◇*v.t*. **3.** to imitate (a composition, author, etc.) in such a way as to ridicule. [L, from Gk: burlesque poem] —**parodist**, *n*.

parole /pəˈroul/, *n., v*., **-roled, -roling**. ◇*n*. **1.** the freeing, temporary or permanent, of a person from prison, on the condition that they will behave well, before the end of their sentence (def. 2b). **2.** a word of honor given or pledged. ◇*v.t*. **3.** to put on parole. [F: word, from L]

Paroo /ˈpɑru/, *n*. a river which rises in south-western Qld and then flows southerly to north-western NSW; in wet times it flows to join the Darling near Wilcannia. 530 km.

paroo dog, *n*. a rattle which is shaken to frighten sheep into movement. [from PAROO]

-parous, an adjective ending meaning 'bringing forth', 'bearing', 'producing', as in *oviparous, viviparous*. [L: bring forth]

paroxysm /ˈpærəksɪzəm/, *n*. a sudden fit of violent action or emotion: *paroxysms of rage; paroxysms of coughing*. [ML, from Gk: irritation] —**paroxysmal**, *adj*.

parquet /ˈpɑkeɪ, ˈpɑki/, *adj., n*. (made of) short pieces of wood inlaid so as to form a pattern: *a parquet floor*. [F: part of a park, flooring] —**parquetry**, *n*.

Parramatta /pærəˈmætə/, *n*. a city in NSW in Sydney's metropolitan west; Australia's second settlement. Pop. 130 783 (1986). [Aboriginal: head of the river *or* the place where eels lie down]

parricide /ˈpærəsaɪd/, *n*. (the act of) someone who kills either of their parents or anyone else like a parent. [F, from L, apparently from *pater* father] —**parricidal**, *adj*.

parrot /ˈpærət/, *n*. **1.** any of numerous hook-billed, fleshy-tongued, often brightly colored birds such as the cockatoo, lory, macaw, parakeet, etc., esp. those valued as cagebirds because they can be taught to talk. **2.** a person who unintelligently repeats the words or imitates the actions of another. ◇*v.t*. **3.** to repeat or imitate like a parrot. [F, diminutive of *Pierre* Peter]

parrotfish /ˈpærətfɪʃ/, *n*. a brightly colored fish living in Australian coastal waters.

parry /ˈpæri/, *v*., **-ried, -rying**, *n., pl*. **-ries**. ◇*v.t*. **1.** (in fencing, etc.) to stop or knock aside (a blow, weapon, etc.). **2.** to turn aside or avoid (something): *to parry a question*. ◇*n*. **3.** an act of parrying. [probably from F, from It: ward off, protect, from L: make ready, prepare]

parse /pɑz/, *v.t*., **parsed, parsing**. to describe (a word or series of words) grammatically, telling the part of speech, inflectional form, function in the sentence, etc. [L: part, as in part of speech]

Parsee /pɑˈsi/, *n*. one of a Zoroastrian sect in India, descendants of the Persians who settled in India in the eighth century to escape Muslim persecution. Also, **Parsi**. [Pers and Hind: *Pārsī* a Persian]

parsimony /ˈpɑsəməni/, *n*. very great meanness in spending money; niggardliness. [ME, from L: lit., sparingness] —**parsimonious**, *adj*.

parsley /ˈpɑsli/, *n*. a nutritious garden herb with sweet-scented leaves which are used to garnish or season food, or as a salad vegetable. [ME, b. OF and OE]

parsnip /ˈpɑsnɪp/, *n*. a plant with a large whitish root, grown as a vegetable. [ME, from OF, from L]

parson /ˈpɑsən/, *n*. a clergyman or minister. [ME, from ML: parson, from L: person. See PERSON]

parsonage /ˈpɑsənɪdʒ/, *n*. the place provided by a church for a parson to live in.

Parsons /ˈpɑsənz/, *n*. **Sir Charles Algernon**, 1854–1931, English engineer who developed the steam turbine.

part /pɑt/, *n*. **1.** a division of a whole; a piece, portion, fragment, fraction, or section; constituent. **2.** each of a number of more or less equal divisions making up a whole: *a third part*. **3.** (*usu. pl*.) a place; region: *foreign parts*. **4.** a piece for replacing a worn-out section of a tool, machine, etc.: *spare parts*. **5.** *Music*. a separate line of music performed by voice or instrument in a work written for several voices or instruments: *the soprano part*. **6.** an interest or activity in something; participation: *to take a part in something*. **7.** someone's share in some action; a duty, function, or office: *Nature didn't do her part*. **8.** a character acted in a play or in real life; role. **9.** the words or lines given to an actor to be learned. **10.** (*usu. pl*.) a personal or mental quality or ability: *a man of parts*. **11. for my** (**his**, etc.) **part**, so far as concerns me (him, etc.). **12. part and parcel**, an essential part. **13. play a part**, **a.** to act like a particular character; pretend. **b.** to make oneself useful or active in something. **14. take someone's part**, to support or defend. ◇*v.t*. **15.** to divide (a thing) into parts; break; cleave. **16.** to make or keep divided (two or more things or people, or someone or something from another); draw or hold apart; separate: *to part lovers; to part hair; to part curtains*. ◇*v.i*. **17.** to be or become divided into parts; break or cleave. **18.** (of people or things) to go apart from each other or one another (sometimes fol.

by *from*): *We'll part no more.* ◇*v.* **19. part with,** to give up; relinquish: *I parted with my gold.* ◇*adj.* **20.** in part; partial: *part man, part beast.* ◇*adv.* **21.** in part; partly: *part cooked; part made.* [ME, OE, from L: piece, portion]

part., *Abbrev.* participle.

partake /paˈteɪk/, *v.*, **-took, -taken, -taking.** ◇*v.i.* **1.** to act in something with other people; participate (fol. by *in*). **2.** to receive, take, or have a share (fol. by *of*). ◇*v.t.* **3.** to take or have a part in; share. [backformation from *partaking, partaker*, translation of L] **—partaker,** *n.*

partheno-, a word part meaning 'virgin', 'without fertilisation', as in *parthenogenesis*. [combining form of Gk *parthénos* virgin]

parthenogenesis /paθənouˈdʒɛnəsəs/, *n.* a type of reproduction marked by the development of an egg without fertilisation. **—parthenogenetic,** *adj.*

Parthenon /ˈpaθənɒn, -nən/, *n.* the temple of Athena on the Acropolis of Athens, completed (structurally) about 438 BC, regarded as the finest example of Doric temple architecture. [L from Gk, from *parthénos* virgin (*Athene Parthénos* Athene the Virgin)]

partial /ˈpaʃəl/, *adj.* **1.** relating to a part. **2.** being in part only; not total or general; incomplete: *partial blindness.* **3.** *Bot.* secondary or subordinate: *a partial umbel.* **4.** supporting a person, group, party, etc. in a quarrel or argument; biased. **5.** liking (something) very much (fol. by *to*): *I'm partial to chocolate.* [ME, from L: PART] **—partiality,** *n.*

partial pressure, *n.* a pressure that one gas in a mixture of gases would have if it were there alone occupying the same volume as the whole mixture, at the same temperature.

participate /paˈtɪsəpeɪt/, *v.i.*, **-pated, -pating.** to have a part in something or do something with other people (fol. by *in*): *to participate in a business deal.* [L] **—participant,** *n., adj.* **—participation,** *n.*

participle /ˈpatəsɪpəl/, *n.* a word formed from a verb, used **a.** as an adjective, e.g., *burning* in *a burning candle* or *devoted* in *his devoted friend.* **b.** in compound verbs, e.g., *burning* in *The candle has been burning* or *devoted* in *She has devoted herself to her career.* **c.** See **gerund.** [ME, from OF, from L: a sharing] **—participial,** *adj.*

particle /ˈpatɪkəl/, *n.* **1.** a small portion, piece, or amount; a very small bit: *a particle of dust.* **2.** *Phys.* an elementary particle. **3.** *Gram.* a small word such as an article, preposition, or conjunction. [ME, from L: PART]

particular /paˈtɪkjələ/, *adj.* **1.** relating to some one person, thing, group, class, occasion, etc., rather than to others or all; special, not general: *someone's particular interests.* **2.** individual, or single, or considered separately: *each particular item.* **3.** different from others or from the ordinary; marked; unusual. **4.** more than usual; special: *to take particular pains; a particular friend of mine.* **5.** giving attention to details: *to be particular about one's food.* ◇*n.* **6.** (of an item in a list) an individual or distinct part: *to record particulars.* **7.** a point or detail: *a report complete in every particular.* **8. in particular,** particularly; especially: *one book in particular.* [L: of a part, partial] **—particularism,** *n.* **—particularity,** *n.*

particularly /paˈtɪkjəlɒli/, *adv.* **1.** in a particular or exceptional degree; especially: *He read it with particularly great interest.* **2.** in a particular manner; specially; individually. **3.** in detail; minutely.

parting /ˈpatɪŋ/, *n.* **1.** a dividing or separating. **2.** a separating (from someone); leave-taking; departure: *a sad parting.* **3. parting of the ways,** a leave-taking, esp. a final one. ◇*adj.* **4.** given, taken, done, etc., when going away: *a parting shot; a parting glance.* **5.** dividing; separating.

partisan /ˈpatəzən, patəˈzæn/, *n.* **1.** a supporter of a person, party, or cause; adherent. **2.** *Mil.* a member of a party of light or irregular troops, esp. when resisting an invader or conqueror; guerilla. [F, from It, from L]

partition /paˈtɪʃən/, *n.* **1.** division (of one thing) into shares. **2.** separation of two or more things. **3.** something that separates, e.g. a wall or barrier. **4.** the date or period of the division of a country or state into two or more new countries, or states: *before partition.* ◇*v.t.* **5.** to divide into parts. **6.** to divide or separate by a partition. [ME, from L]

partly /ˈpatli/, *adv.* in part; in some measure; not wholly.

partner /ˈpatnə/, *n.* **1.** a person who shares or takes part in something; an associate. **2.** *Law.* someone who starts or joins a business with other people, usu. sharing its risks and profits. **3.** See **silent partner. 4.** a husband or a wife. **5.** someone's companion in a dance. ◇*v.t.* **6.** to associate as a partner or partners. **7.** to be, or act as, the partner of. [ME]

part of speech, *n.* any of the major form classes of a language, which make up the whole vocabulary, e.g., in Latin, a word is either a *noun, verb, pronoun, adjective, adverb, preposition, conjunction,* or *interjection.*

partridge /ˈpatrɪdʒ/, *n., pl.* **-tridges,** (*esp. collectively*) **-tridge.** a bird often hunted and eaten, esp. the **common partridge** of Europe. [ME, from OF, from L, from Gk]

part-song /ˈpat-sɒŋ/, *n.* a song with parts for several voices, esp. one meant to be sung without instrumental accompaniment. **—part-singing,** *n.*

part-time /ˈpat-taɪm, pat-ˈtaɪm/, *adj.*; /pat-ˈtaɪm/, *adv.* ◇*adj.* **1.** of, relating to, or occupying less than all normal working hours: *part-time work.* ◇*adv.* **2.** during less than all normal working hours: *I work part-time.*

parturition /patʃəˈrɪʃən/, *n.* the act of bringing forth young; childbirth. [L]

party /ˈpati/, *n., pl.* **-ties,** *adj.* ◇*n.* **1.** a group of people gathered together: *We met a party of travellers on the road.* **2.** a social gathering of invited guests at a private house or elsewhere: *to give a party.* **3.** (*oft. cap.*) a group of people with the same ideas and purpose, opposed to others, esp. in politics, etc.: *the Australian Labor Party.* **4.** *Law.* a person immediately concerned in some transaction or legal proceeding. **5.** the person under consideration (in a legal document). **6.** a person in general: *A certain party has arrived.* **7. come to the party**, to help, esp. with money; fall in with one's plans. ◇*adj.* **8.** of or relating to a party or faction: *party issues.* **9.** of or for a social gathering: *a party dress.* [ME, from OF: PART]

party line, *n.* **1.** a telephone line shared by two or more subscribers. **2.** the boundary line between adjoining houses or properties. **3.** the policies and practices of a group, stated with the authority of the group leaders: *the Communist party line.*

party politics, *n.* politics practised for the good of a particular party rather than for the good of the whole country.

pascal /'pæskəl, pæs'kal/, *n.* the SI unit of pressure, equal to one newton per square metre. Symbol: Pa [named after Blaise PASCAL]

Pascal /pas'kal/, *n.* **Blaise** /bleɪz/, 1623–62, French philosopher, mathematician, and physicist, whose most famous work is the *Pensées* (1670).

paschal /'pæskəl/, *adj.* **1.** relating to the Passover. **2.** relating to Easter. [ME, from LL]

paspalum /pæs'peɪləm/, *n.* a type of grass native to southern America but now one of the most widespread grasses in the higher-rainfall areas of Australia.

pass /pas/, *v.*, **passed** or (*Rare*) **past**, **passed** or **past**, **passing**, *n.* ◇*v.t.* **1.** to go by or move past (something); leave behind: *We have passed the right place.* **2.** to go by without acting upon or noticing; leave unmentioned. **3.** to not make payment of (a dividend, etc.). **4.** to go or get through (a channel, barrier, etc.). **5.** to do successfully (an examination, etc.). **6.** to get through (an obstacle, experience, ordeal). **7.** to go beyond (a point, degree, stage, etc.); transcend; exceed; surpass. **8.** to cause to go or move onwards: *to pass a rope through a hole.* **9.** to live during; spend: *to pass time.* **10.** to cause to be accepted or received: *I'll pass that idea.* **11.** to send, transfer, or transmit; deliver: *Pass the butter please.* **12.** to pronounce; utter: *to pass remarks.* **13.** to cause or allow to go through a test, etc: *to pass a student.* **14.** to send out of the body; discharge: *to pass urine.* **15.** to approve; sanction: *to pass a bill.* **16.** to express or pronounce: *to pass an opinion.* **17.** *Football, Hockey, etc.* to send (the ball, etc.) to another player. **18.** to overtake. ◇*v.i.* **19.** to go or move onwards; proceed. **20.** to go on or slip away; elapse: *Time passes.* **21.** to come to an end, as a thing in time: *Sorrow passes after a while.* **22.** to go on or take place; happen; occur: *to learn what has passed.* **23.** to go by or move past: *The procession is passing.* **24.** to be accepted or received (fol. by *for* or *as*): *material that passed for silk.* **25.** to be carried or transferred. **26.** to go backwards and forwards between two people: *Sharp words passed between them.* **27.** to move through or across: *to pass from a solid to a liquid state; to pass over a stream.* **28.** to go or get through something: *to pass with honors.* **29.** to go unnoticed; be unimportant: *Let that pass, it's not needed.* **30.** to be approved by vote: *That bill passed.* **31.** to throw a ball from one to another. ◇ **32.** Some special uses are:
bring to pass, to cause to happen.
come to pass, to happen.
pass away, to die.
pass off, to cause to be accepted or received in a false character: *He passed himself off as my servant.*
pass on, **1.** to die. **2.** to move to another place.
pass out, **1.** *Colloq.* to faint. **2.** to complete the course, as at an academy.
pass over, to disregard.
pass the buck, to avoid responsibility by passing it to another.
pass up, *Colloq.* to refuse; reject: *to pass up an opportunity.*
◇*n.* **33.** a narrow route through a low part in a mountain range. **34.** (a piece of paper showing) permission or licence to pass, go, come, or enter: *a bus pass; a military pass.* **35.** a free ticket. **36.** the passing of an examination, etc., esp. without honors: *He got only a pass.* **37.** the sending of a ball, etc., from one player to another in ball games. **38.** *Cards.* an act of not bidding or raising another bid. **39.** a stage in experience or procedure; a particular stage or state of affairs: *Things have come to a pretty pass.* **40. make a pass**, to make a sign or gesture showing sexual desire to another person (usu. fol. by *at*). [ME]

pass., *Abbrev.* **1.** passenger. **2.** passive.

passable /'pasəbəl/, *adj.* **1.** able to be passed. **2.** able to be gone through or over: *a passable stream; a passable road.* **3.** fair, or moderate; tolerable: *a passable knowledge of history.* [ME, from F: PASS]

passably /'pasəbli/, *adv.* fairly; moderately.

passage /'pæsɪdʒ/, *n., v.*, **-saged**, **-saging**. ◇*n.* **1.** a part of a writing or speech; a paragraph, verse, etc.: *a passage of Scripture.* **2.** *Music.* **a.** a scale- or arpeggio-like series of notes introduced as an ornament; a run, roulade, or flourish. **b.** a phrase or other division of a piece. **3.** the act of passing: *the passage of time; the passage of events.* **4.** permission to pass: *to refuse passage through a territory.* **5.** a means of passing; a way, route, avenue, channel, corridor, etc. **6.** movement from one place or state to another; transit: *a rough passage.* ◇*v.i.* **7.** to make a passage; cross; pass; voyage. [ME, from OF: PASS]

passbook /'pasbʊk/, *n.* a small book recording a customer's deposits and withdrawals in a bank or building society.

passé /pa'seɪ/, *adj.* out-of-date. [F]

passed /past/, *adj.* **1.** having passed or been passed. **2.** having passed an examination or test. **3. passed in**, relating to goods, land, etc., which, at auction, do not reach the reserve price and are withdrawn from sale.

passenger /'pæsəndʒə/, *n.* someone who travels on a vehicle: *the passengers of a ship.* [ME, from OF]

passer-by /pasə-'baɪ/, *n., pl.* **passers-by.** someone who goes past.

passerine /'pæsəraɪn/, *adj.* **1.** belonging or relating to the Passeriformes, an order of perching birds, including the finches, thrushes, warblers, swallows, crows, larks, etc. ◇*n.* **2.** any bird of this order. [L *passerīnus* of a sparrow]

passing /'pasɪŋ/, *adj.* **1.** going by; elapsing: *a passing parade; passing time.* **2.** not staying; fleeting or transitory: *a passing cold.* **3.** done quickly and briefly; cursory: *to make only a passing mention.* ◇*n.* **4.** the act of someone that passes or causes something to pass. **5. in passing,** while passing, going on, or proceeding.

passion /'pæʃən/, *n.* **1.** any strong feeling or emotion, such as hope, fear, joy, grief, anger, love, desire, etc. **2.** strong, emotional, sexual love. **3.** a person who is the object of such a feeling: *She was his passion.* **4.** a strong or extravagant fondness, enthusiasm, or desire for anything: *a passion for music.* **5.** (*oft. cap.*) the sufferings of Christ from the Last Supper to his death on the Cross. [ME, from OF, from L: suffering]

passionate /'pæʃənət/, *adj.* showing passion: *a passionate advocate of socialism; passionate language; passionate grief.* [late ME, from ML]

passionfruit /'pæʃənfrut/, *n.* a small, purplish fruit, the seeds and pulp of which can be eaten.

passive /'pæsɪv, -səv/, *adj.* **1.** not doing, being inactive, letting things happen to (someone); inert; quiescent: *a passive character; passive resistance.* **2.** suffering action, acted upon, or being the object of action (opposed to *active*). **3.** *Gram.* See **passive voice. 4.** *Electronics.* (of an electronic component, or a complete circuit) not able to amplify or switch a signal, as a resistor or capacitor (opposed to an active circuit component, as a transistor or valve). **5.** (of a metal) having a protective oxide film on the surface making it unable to be attacked. ◇*n.* **6.** → **passive voice.** [ME, from L: capable of feeling] — **passivity,** *n.*

passive resistance, *n.* the expression of disapproval of authority or of specific laws by various non-violent acts.

passive voice, *n.* a type of verb form which indicates that the subject of the verb is having the action done to it, rather than doing the action themselves, e.g. *was punished* in *He was punished for breaking the rules* or *have been stung* in *I have been stung by a bee.* See **active voice.**

Passover /'pasouvə/, *n.* an annual feast (def. 1) of the Jews, commemorating the delivery of the ancient Hebrews from slavery in Egypt to the Promised Land in Palestine. [orig. verbal phrase *pass over*]

passport /'paspɔt/, *n.* **1.** an official document identifying the person named in it and giving permission to visit foreign countries. **2.** anything that gives admission or acceptance: *a passport to fame.* [F *passeport,* from *passe(r)* PASS + *port* PORT¹]

password /'paswəd/, *n.* a secret word, made known only to certain people to identify them and allow them to go to otherwise forbidden areas.

past /past/, *v. Rare.* **1.** past participle and occasional past tense of **pass.** ◇*adj.* **2.** gone by in time: *past feelings.* **3.** belonging to, or having existed or occurred in time before this: *past ages.* **4.** gone by just before the present time; just passed: *the past year.* ◇*n.* **5.** the time gone by: *far back in the past.* **6.** the events of that time: *to forget the past.* **7.** a past history, life, career, etc.: *a glorious past.* **8.** a past career which is kept concealed: *a woman with a past.* **9.** → **past tense.** ◇*adv.* **10.** so as to pass by or beyond; by: *The troops marched past.* ◇*prep.* **11.** beyond in time; after: *past noon.* **12.** beyond in position; farther on than: *the house past the church.* **13.** beyond the reach, scope, influence, or power of: *past belief.* [see PASS, *v.*]

pasta /'pæstə, 'pas-/, *n.* a preparation made from a dough or paste of wheat flour, salt, water, and sometimes egg, such as spaghetti, macaroni, etc. [It, from LL: dough, PASTE]

paste /peɪst/, *n., v.,* **pasted, pasting.** ◇*n.* **1.** a mixture of flour and water, used for sticking paper. **2.** any material or preparation in a soft mass: *a toothpaste.* **3.** dough, esp. when prepared with shortening, for making pastry. **4.** a sweet confection-like dough: *almond paste.* **5.** food reduced to a smooth, soft mass, for spreading on bread or for seasoning. **6.** a mixture of clay, water, etc., for making earthenware, porcelain, etc. ◇*v.t.* **7.** to fasten or stick with paste. **8.** *Colloq.* to beat or scold someone. [ME, from OF, from LL, from Gk: barley porridge]

pasteboard /'peɪstbɔd/, *n.* **1.** a stiff, firm board, made from layers of paper pasted together, or layers of paper pulp pressed together, used for book covers. ◇*adj.* **2.** made of pasteboard. **3.** not of real quality; flimsy; sham.

pastel /'pæstl/, *n.* **1.** a soft, subdued shade of color. **2.** (a crayon made with) a kind of dried paste, made of pigments ground with chalk and mixed with gum water. **3.** the art of drawing with such crayons. **4.** a drawing so made. ◇*adj.* **5.** having a soft, subdued shade. **6.** drawn with pastels. [F, from Pr, from LL: PASTE]

Pasternak /'pæstənæk/, *n.* **Boris Leonidovich** /bɒ'ris lɪə'nidəvɪtʃ/, 1890–1960, Russian poet, novelist, and translator; best known for his novel *Doctor Zhivago* (1958).

Pasteur /pas't3/, *n.* **Louis** /'lui/, 1822–1895, French chemist and bacteriologist; considered to be the founder of microbiology.

pasteurise or **pasteurize** /'pastʃəraɪz/, *v.t.,* **-rised, -rising.** to expose (milk, etc.) to a high temperature, usu. about 60°C, in order to destroy certain micro-organisms and prevent or arrest fermentation. [named after Louis PASTEUR. See -ISE¹] — **pasteurisation,** *n.*

pastiche /pæs'tiʃ/, n. any work of art, literature, or music consisting of motifs borrowed from one or more masters or works of art. [F, from It *pasticcio*]

pastime /'pɑstaɪm/, n. something to do which makes time pass pleasantly; amusement, or sport: *to play cards for a pastime*. [late ME]

past master, n. 1. someone who has filled the office of master in a guild, lodge, etc. 2. someone who has great experience in any profession, art, etc.

pastor /'pɑstə/, n. someone who has spiritual care of a number of people; minister; clergyman. [L: shepherd] —**pastorate**, n.

pastoral /'pɑstərəl, -trəl/, adj. 1. relating to shepherds, or country life. 2. (of land) used for pasture. 3. having the simplicity or charm of such country: *pastoral scenery*. 4. (of a work of art, music, literature) describing the life of shepherds or of the country. [ME, from L: relating to a shepherd]

pastorale /pɑstə'rɑl/, n. a composition written in imitation of the music of shepherds. [It, from L]

pastoralist /'pɑstərəlɪst/, n. someone who grows cereal crops in addition to raising livestock, usu. on a large property.

past participle, n. a participle with past or perfect meaning; perfect participle, e.g. *fallen, sung, defeated*.

pastry /'peɪstri/, n., pl. **-tries**. 1. a mixture of flour, water and fat, cooked as a crust for pies, etc. 2. foods made with pastry, such as pies, tarts, etc. [PAST(E) + -RY]

past tense, n. a verb form which refers to events that have already happened. See Appendix.

pasture /'pɑstʃə/, n., v., **-tured, -turing**. ◇n. 1. ground covered with grass, etc., used or suitable for the grazing of cattle, etc.; grassland. ◇v.t. 2. to feed (cattle, etc.) by putting them to graze on pasture. ◇v.i. 3. (of cattle, etc.) to graze upon pasture. [ME, from OF, from LL: lit., feeding, grazing] —**pasturable**, adj.

pasty[1] /'peɪsti/, adj. of or like paste in consistency, color, etc.; whitish or sick-looking: *a pasty complexion*. [PASTE, n. + -Y[1]]

pasty[2] /'pæsti, 'pɑsti/, n., pl. **pasties**. a type of pie in which a circular piece of pastry is folded around a filling of vegetables, meat, etc., and baked. Also, **Cornish pasty**. [ME, from OF]

pat[1] /pæt/, v., **patted, patting**, n. ◇v.t. 1. to strike lightly with the palm of the hand, foot, or an implement. 2. to tap or stroke gently with the palm or fingers as an expression of affection, approval, etc. ◇v.i. 3. to strike lightly or gently. 4. to walk or run with lightly sounding footsteps. ◇v. 5. **pat (someone) on the back**, *Colloq*. to congratulate or encourage with praise. ◇n. 6. a light stroke or blow with something flat. 7. a small mass of something shaped by patting: *a butter pat*. [ME; akin to PUTT]

pat[2] /pæt/, adj. 1. exactly to the point or purpose; apt. ◇adv. 2. exactly or perfectly; aptly. 3. **off pat**, exactly or perfectly. [apparently akin to PAT[1]]

pat., *Abbrev*. 1. patent. 2. patented.

Patagonia /pætə'gouniə/, n. an arid, tableland region in the extreme southern part of South America, extending from the Andes to the Atlantic; mostly in southern Argentina, partly in southern Chile. —**Patagonian**, n., adj.

patch /pætʃ/, n. 1. a piece of material used to mend a hole or break, or strengthen a weak place: *a patch on a sail*. 2. a piece of material used to cover or protect a wound, an injured part, etc.: *a patch over the eye*. 3. a small piece of anything, as land, road, etc. 4. **hit a bad patch**, to suffer a lot of bad luck, esp. financial. 5. **not a patch on**, *Colloq*. not comparable to; not nearly as good as. ◇v.t. 6. to mend or strengthen with a patch or patches. 7. to repair or restore, esp. in a hasty or makeshift way (usu. fol. by *up*). 8. to settle; smooth over: *They patched up their quarrel*. [ME, orig. uncert.]

patchwork /'pætʃwɜk/, n. 1. work made of pieces of cloth or leather of various colors or shapes sewn together, used esp. for covering quilts, cushions, etc. 2. something made up of various pieces or parts put together: *a patchwork of verses*.

patchy /'pætʃi/, adj., **-ier, -iest**. 1. marked by or like patches. 2. of unequal quality; irregular; not uniform.

pate /peɪt/, n. 1. the head. 2. the crown or top of the head: *a man with a bald pate*. [ME]

pâté /'pæteɪ, 'pɑ-/, n. a paste or spread made of finely minced liver, meat, fish, etc., and served as an hors d'oeuvre. [F]

patella /pə'telə/, n., pl. **-tellae** /-'teli/. *Anat*. the kneecap. [L: small pan, kneepan] —**patellar**, adj. —**patellate**, adj.

patent /'peɪtnt/, n. 1. a government grant to an inventor, giving the right to make, use and sell an invention without competition. 2. an invention, process, etc., which has been patented. ◇adj. 3. (of a product, invention, etc.) specially protected by a patent: *a patent door*. 4. open to view or knowledge; manifest; evident; plain. 5. lying open, or not shut in. 6. *Chiefly Bot*. expanded or spreading. ◇v.t. 7. to take out a patent on; obtain the exclusive rights to (an invention) by a patent. [ME, from L: lying open] —**patentable**, adj.

patent leather, n. 1. leather lacquered to produce a hard, glossy, smooth finish. 2. any imitation of this. —**patent-leather**, adj.

patent medicine, n. a medicine distributed by a company which has a patent on its manufacture.

paterfamilias /peɪtəfə'mɪliæs, pɑ-/, n., pl. **patresfamilias** /peɪtreɪzfə'mɪliəs, pɑ-/. the male head of a family. [L]

paternal /pə'tɜnəl/, adj. 1. having the quality of a father; fatherly: *paternal affection*. 2. of or having to do with a father: *paternal possessions*. 3. related on the father's side: *my paternal uncle*. [L: fatherly]

paternalism /pə'tɜːnəlɪzəm/, n. the principle or practice where a government or any person in authority manages the affairs of a country or community by looking after them as a father should (oft. disapproving, because it implies that the people are children). —**paternalistic**, adj. —**paternalistically**, adv.

paternity /pə'tɜːnəti/, n. 1. derivation from a father. 2. the state of being a father; fatherhood. [ME, from L: fatherly]

Paterson /'pætəsən/, n. **A(ndrew) B(arton)** ('Banjo'), 1864–1941, Australian poet and balladist of the bush; author of *The Man from Snowy River and Other Verses* (1895) and the poem 'Waltzing Matilda' (1895).

Paterson's curse, n. a biennial plant from the Mediterranean area, but widely growing in settled parts of Australia, having blue-purple flowers; salvation Jane.

path /pɑːθ/, n. 1. a way beaten or trodden by the feet of men or beasts. 2. a walkway in a garden or through grounds. 3. any way, route or course. 4. a way of doing something; direction: *the right path in life*. [ME; OE *pæth*]

-path, a suffix used to form nouns indicating: **a.** a person suffering from a particular disease, as in *neuropath*. **b.** a person who treats disease by methods other than those of established western medicine, as in *naturopath, osteopath*. [backformation from -PATHY]

path., Abbrev. 1. pathological. 2. pathology.

pathetic /pə'θetɪk/, adj. 1. arousing feelings, esp. pity or sadness; full of pathos. 2. *Colloq.* miserably inadequate: *Her vegetables made a pathetic display at the annual produce fair.* [LL, from Gk: sensitive]

-pathic, a word part forming adjectives from nouns ending in *-pathy*, as *psychopathic*. [see -PATHY, -IC]

patho-, a word part meaning 'suffering', 'disease', 'feeling', as in *pathology*. [Gk, combining form of *páthos*]

pathogen /'pæθədʒən/, n. a disease-producing organism. Also, **pathogene** /'pæθədʒiːn/. —**pathogenic**, adj.

pathogenesis /pæθə'dʒenəsəs/, n. the production and development of disease. Also, **pathogeny** /pə'θɒdʒəni/. —**pathogenetic**, adj.

pathology /pə'θɒlədʒi/, n., pl. **-gies**. 1. the science of the origin, nature, and course of diseases. 2. the conditions and processes of a disease. —**pathologist**, n. —**pathological**, adj.

pathos /'peɪθɒs/, n. the quality or power, in speech, literature, music, etc., of arousing a feeling of pity or sympathetic sadness. [Gk: suffering, disease, feeling]

-pathy, a noun ending meaning 'suffering', 'feeling', as in *anthropopathy, antipathy, sympathy*, and 'disease' as in *neuropathy, psychopathy*, and used in names for ways of treating disease, as in *homoeopathy, osteopathy*. [Gk]

patience /'peɪʃəns/, n. 1. calm endurance, without complaint. 2. calmness in waiting: *Have patience a little longer.* 3. a quiet and controlled keeping on with something; perseverance: *to labor with patience.* 4. a card game, usu. played by one person alone. [L]

patient /'peɪʃənt/, n. 1. someone who is under medical or surgical treatment. 2. someone or something that undergoes action (opposed to *agent*). ◊*adj*. 3. quietly persevering; diligent: *patient workers*. 4. letting things happen to one calmly and without complaining. 5. waiting with calmness: *Be patient.* [L: suffering, enduring]

patina /'pætɪnə, pə'tiːnə/, n. 1. a film, usu. green, caused by oxidisation on the surface of old bronze, and thought highly of as ornamental. 2. a similar film or coloring on some other substance. 3. a shiny quality on a surface, made by being used or rubbed for a long time. [It, from L: dish, through meaning tarnish (on metal dish)]

patio /'pætioʊ, 'peɪtioʊ/, n., pl. **-tios**. an area, usu. paved, in or next to a house, used for outdoor living. [Sp]

patisserie /pə'tɪsəri/, n. a shop selling pastries and fancy cakes. [F]

patois /'pætwɑː/, n., pl. **patois** /'pætwɑːz/. any form of speech used by people in isolated country areas. [F, from OF: handle clumsily]

Paton /'peɪtn/, n. **Alan Stewart**, 1903–88, South African novelist, noted for his novel *Cry the Beloved Country* (1948), which is concerned with racial conflict in his homeland.

pat. pend., Abbrev. patent pending.

patri-, a word part meaning 'father'. [LL, combining form of *pater*]

patrial /'peɪtriəl/, adj. of or relating to one's fatherland. [ML, from L]

patriarch /'peɪtriɑːk, 'pæt-/, n. 1. one of the people in the Bible thought of as fathers of the human race, from Adam to Abraham. 2. one of the three great founders or progenitors of the Israelites, Abraham, Isaac, or Jacob, or one of Jacob's 12 sons. 3. one of the elders or high ranking members of a church or community. 4. an old man to whom respect is due. 5. the male head of a family or tribal line. [ME, from LL, from Gk: head of a family] —**patriarchal**, adj.

patriarchy /'peɪtriɑːki, 'pæt-/, n., pl. **-archies**. a form of social organisation in which the father is head of the family, and in which descent is reckoned in the male line, the children belonging to the father's clan.

patrician /pə'trɪʃən/, adj., n. 1. (relating to) a member of the original senatorial aristocracy in ancient Rome. 2. (of, belonging to or with the quality of) any noble or aristocrat. [ME, from L: of the rank of the senators, patricians]

patricide /'pætrəsaɪd/, n. (the act of) someone who kills his or her father. Also, **parricide**. [PATRI- + -CIDE] —**patricidal**, adj.

patrilineal /pætrə'lɪniəl/, adj. of descent or title traced through the male line. [L *pater* father + E *lineal*]

patrimony /'pætrəməni/, *n., pl.* **-nies.** property inherited from one's father or ancestors. [L: paternal estate] —**patrimonial**, *adj.*

patriot /'peɪtriət, 'pæt-/, *n.* a person who loves his or her country. [LL, from Gk: fellow countryman] —**patriotic**, *adj.* —**patriotism**, *n.*

patrol /pə'troʊl/, *v.*, **-trolled, -trolling**, *n.* ◊*v.t., v.i.* **1.** to go regularly around (a place) to make sure there is no trouble. ◊*n.* **2.** a person or a body of people who patrol. **3.** the act of patrolling. [F: patrol] —**patroller**, *n.*

patron /'peɪtrən/, *n.* **1.** someone who supports a shop, hotel, etc. by spending money there. **2.** a protector or supporter of a person, cause, institution, art, or enterprise: *the club's patron.* **3.** *Rom Hist.* someone who protected and helped another (the client) in return for certain benefits, often the ex-master of a freed slave. [ME, from OF, from L: patron] —**patroness**, *n. fem.*

patronage /'pætrənɪdʒ/, *n.* **1.** the financial support given to a shop, hotel, etc., by customers. **2.** the position, encouragement, or support of a patron. **3.** the control of appointments to the public service or of other political favors. **4.** the offices or other favors so controlled. **5.** condescending favor: *an air of patronage.*

patronise *or* **patronize** /'pætrənaɪz/, *v.t.*, **-nised, -nising. 1.** to be a customer to a shop, restaurant, etc. **2.** to treat (someone) kindly, but as an inferior; to be condescending. **3.** to act as patron towards; support.

patron saint, *n.* a saint regarded as the special guardian of a person, trade, place, etc.

patronymic /pætrə'nɪmɪk/, *n.* a name derived from the name of a father or ancestor: *Williamson* (son of William) or *Macdonald* (son of Donald). [LL, from Gk: pertaining to one's father's name]

patter[1] /'pætə/, *v.i.* **1.** to strike or move with a succession of slight tapping sounds. ◊*n.* **2.** a pattering sound: *the light patter of the rain.* [frequentative of PAT[1]]

patter[2] /'pætə/, *n.* **1.** the slick and fast speech used by a salesperson to praise what he or she wants to sell, a magician while performing tricks, or comedian or other entertainer. **2.** rapid speech; mere chatter; gabble. **3.** the jargon of any class, group, etc.; cant. ◊*v.i.* **4.** to talk fast, esp. with little regard to content; chatter. [var. of *pater* in *Pater noster* Our Father]

pattern /'pætn/, *n.* **1.** a decorative repeated design: *a wallpaper pattern.* **2.** any repeated design or marking, natural or man-made: *patterns of frost on the window.* **3.** style or type in general: *patterns of economic growth.* **4.** a model or guide for something to be made: *a paper pattern for a dress.* **5.** *Metall.* a model or form, usu. of wood or metal, used in a foundry to make a mould. ◊*v.t.* **6.** to model: *He patterns himself on his father.* **7.** to cover or mark with a pattern. [ME, from ML: model, example, from L: patron]

Patton /'pætn/, *n.* **George Smith**, 1885–1945, US general in Europe during World War II.

patty /'pæti/, *n., pl.* **-ies. 1.** a little pie; a pasty: *oyster patties.* **2.** a savory mixture formed into a ball or shape and cooked on a griddle or deep-fried. [F]

paucity /'pɔsəti/, *n.* smallness of quantity; fewness; scantiness: *paucity of material.* [ME, from L]

Paul /pɔl/ *n.* **1. Saint**, died c. 67, the great Christian missionary, apostle to the gentiles, author of several epistles in the New Testament. **2.** the name of six popes. [L: *Paulus*: replacing ME *Poul* (from OF) and OE *Paulus* (from L)]

Pauling /'pɔlɪŋ/, *n.* **Linus Carl**, born 1901, US chemist; won the Nobel prize for chemistry in 1954 and the Nobel Peace prize in 1962.

paunch /pɔntʃ/, *n.* **1.** the belly or abdomen. **2.** a large, prominent belly. [ME, from ONF, from L] —**paunchy**, *adj.*

pauper /'pɔpə/, *n.* a very poor person, sometimes supported by a community. [L: poor (man)] —**pauperism**, *n.*

pause /pɔz/, *n., v.,* **paused, pausing.** ◊*n.* **1.** a stop or rest for a short time, esp. in speech or action; delay; hesitation. **2.** a break or rest in speaking or reading, depending on sense, grammatical relations, punctuation etc. **3.** *Poetry* → **caesura. 4.** *Music.* the symbol ⌣ or ⌢ placed under or over a note or rest to indicate that it is to be prolonged. **5. give pause**, to cause to hesitate. ◊*v.i.* **6.** to make a pause; stop; wait; hesitate. **7.** to dwell or linger (fol. by *upon*). [late ME, from L, from Gk: cessation] —**pausal**, *adj.*

pave /peɪv/, *v.t.,* **paved, paving. 1.** to cover or lay (a road, walk, etc.) with stones, bricks, tiles, wood, concrete, etc., to make a firm, level surface. **2.** to prepare (the way) for. [ME, from OF, from Rom, for L: beat down]

pavement /'peɪvmənt/, *n.* a paved walk or footway at the side of a street or road. [ME, from OF: a floor beaten down]

pavilion /pə'vɪljən/, *n.* **1.** a light, open structure for shelter, pleasure, etc., in a park. **2.** a projecting part at the front or side of a building. **3.** a large tent on posts. [ME, from OF, from L: tent, orig. butterfly]

paving /'peɪvɪŋ/, *n.* **1.** the act or technique of paving. **2.** a paved area. **3.** material for paving. ◊*adj.* **4.** relating to paving: *paving stone.*

Pavlov /'pævlɒv/, *n.* **Ivan Petrovich** /ˌɪvan pɪ'trɒvɪtʃ/, 1849–1936, Russian physiologist and physician, best known for his discovery of the conditioned reflex; Nobel prize for medicine 1904.

pavlova /pæv'loʊvə/, *n.* a dessert made of a large soft-centred meringue, usu. roughly circular and having a top filled with whipped cream and often topped with fruit, esp. passionfruit. [named after Anna *Pavlova*, 1885–1931, Russian ballerina]

paw /pɔ:/, *n.* **1.** the foot of an animal with nails or claws. **2.** the foot of any animal. **3.** *Colloq.* (*joc.*) the human hand. ◇*v.t., v.i.* **4.** to strike or scrape with the paws or feet. **5.** *Colloq.* to handle clumsily, rudely, or too familiarly. [ME, from OF, of Gmc orig.]

pawn[1] /pɔn/, *v.t.* **1.** to deposit as security for a debt, while retaining ownership: *to pawn a watch for $30.* **2.** to pledge or stake: *I pawn my honor.* ◇*n.* **3.** the state of being deposited or held as security: *jewels in pawn.* **4.** the act of pawning. [late ME, from OF]

pawn[2] /pɔn/, *n.* **1.** *Chess.* one of the 16 pieces of lowest value, usu. moving one square straight ahead, but capturing diagonally. **2.** an unimportant person used as the tool of another: *He was only a pawn in the game.* [ME, from AF, var. of OF, from LL: foot soldier]

pawnbroker /'pɔnbroukə/, *n.* someone who lends money at interest in return for goods deposited. If the goods are not bought back within a certain time they can be sold. **–pawnbroking,** *n.*

pawpaw /'pɔpɔ/, *n.* a large, yellow, melon-like fruit originally from tropical America and much prized for its delicious taste and digestive qualities. Also, **papaya**. [Sp of Carib orig.]

Pax /pæks/, *n. Rom Myth.* the goddess of peace; Greek counterpart, Irene.

pay /peɪ/, *v.,* **paid, paying,** *n.* ◇*v.t.* **1.** to get rid of (a debt, obligation, etc.) by giving or doing something. **2.** to give (money, etc.) in return for goods or services, or as compensation for harm done. **3.** to bring a worthwhile return to; be profitable to: *It pays me to be honest.* **4.** to yield as a return: *The stock pays 4 per cent.* **5.** to give or render: *to pay attention to; to pay someone a visit.* ◇*v.i.* **6.** to give money, etc., due: *Have you paid yet?* **7.** to bring a worthwhile return: *Honesty pays.* **8.** to suffer, or be punished for something; make amends: *I'll make you pay for that mistake.* ◇*v.* **9.** Some special uses are:
pay off, 1. to discharge a debt in full. **2.** to discharge from one's employ and pay any wages, etc., due. **3.** to yield profit: *That gamble paid off.*
pay out, to punish in revenge.
pay up, 1. to pay upon demand: *Pay up or else!* **2.** to pay fully or promptly: *The loan is all paid up now.*
put paid to, put an end to; prevent.
◇*n.* **10.** wages, salary; stipend. [ME, from F, from L: pacify] **–payable,** *adj.* **–payment,** *n.*

pay-as-you-earn tax, *n.* a system of collection of income tax where the employer takes the amount from the employee's wage before he or she receives it. Also, **PAYE tax.**

payload /'peɪloud/, *n.* **1.** the income-producing part of a cargo. **2.** *Mil.* the warhead, its container and activating devices in a missile.

payola /peɪ'oulə/, *n. US.* a bribe, esp. for the promotion of a commercial product through the abuse of one's position or influence.

payroll /'peɪroul/, *n.* **1.** a roll or list of people to be paid wages, with the amounts due. **2.** the money or salaries paid out.

payroll tax, *n.* a tax levied by a government on employers, based on the salaries and wages paid out.

Pb, *Chem. Symbol.* lead. [L *plumbum*]

p.c., *Abbrev.* per cent.

P & C /pi ən 'si/, *Abbrev.* Parents and Citizens Association.

PC, *Abbrev.* **1.** Privy Council. **2.** Privy Councillor.

pd, *Abbrev.* paid.

p/d, *Abbrev.* postdated.

p.d., *Abbrev.* potential difference.

Pd, *Chem. Symbol.* palladium.

PE, *Abbrev.* Physical Education.

pea /pi/, *n., pl.* **peas,** (*Archaic*) **pease. 1.** the round, highly nutritious seed of a hardy plant grown widely, or the plant itself. **2.** related plants, or their seed: *chickpea.* **3.** something as small as a pea. [backformation from *pease* (orig. sing., but later taken as pl.)] **–pealike,** *adj.*

peace /pis/, *n.* **1.** freedom from war, fighting or quarrelling. **2.** an agreement between contending sides to stop further fighting. **3.** freedom from civil upset; public order and security. **4.** freedom from mental disturbance: *peace of mind.* **5.** quiet; stillness; silence; tranquillity; calm. **6. hold one's peace,** to remain quiet; to keep silent. **7. keep the peace,** not to create a disturbance, esp. civil. **8. make one's peace,** to settle a quarrel and become friendly again with someone. [ME, from OF, from L: peace] **–peaceable,** *adj.* **–peaceful,** *adj.*

peace-pipe /'pis-paɪp/, *n.* the pipe smoked by the North American Indians as a sign of peace.

peach /pitʃ/, *n.* **1.** (a tree bearing) round, juicy fruit enclosing a single stone, of many varieties, and widely cultivated in temperate climates. **2.** the color of a peach, a light pinkish yellow. **3.** *Colloq.* a person or thing esp. admired or liked. ◇*adj.* **4.** of the color peach. **5.** flavored or cooked with peaches. [ME, from OF] **–peachy,** *adj.*

peacock /'pikɒk/, *n., pl.* **-cocks,** (esp. collectively) **-cock. 1.** the male of the **peafowl,** a pheasant native to India but now widely domesticated, known for the spectacular eye-like patterning of its richly colored tail feathers. **2.** a vain person. ◇*v.i.* **3.** to walk proudly like a peacock; make a boastful display. [ME, from L]

Peacock /'pikɒk/, *n.* **Andrew Sharp,** born 1939, Australian Liberal politician.

peak[1] /pik/, *n.* **1.** the pointed top of a mountain. **2.** a mountain with a pointed top. **3.** the pointed top of anything. **4.** the highest or greatest point: *the peak of his career.* **5.** *Elect, Mech, etc.* the maximum value of a quantity during a specified time: *a voltage peak.* **6.** a projecting point: *the peak of a man's beard; the peak of a cap.* ◇*v.i.* **7.** to project in a peak. **8.** to reach a highest point. [b. PIKE[2] (or PICK[2]) and BEAK[1]] **–peaked,** *adj.*

peak² /piːk/, *v.i.* to become weak, thin, and sickly. [orig. uncert.] – **peaky**, *adj.* – **peaked**, *adj.*

peak hour, *n.* the time at which city traffic is thickest. Also, **peak period, rush hour.** – **peak-hour,** *adj.*

peal /piːl/, *n.* **1.** a loud, long, drawn-out sound of bells. **2.** any other loud, prolonged sound: *peal of cannon; a peal of thunder.* **3.** a set of bells tuned to one another. ◇*v.i.* **4.** to sound forth in a peal; resound: *to peal with laughter.* [ME]

peanut /ˈpiːnʌt/, *n.* **1.** Also, **groundnut.** the fruit (pod) or the edible seed of a leguminous plant native to Brazil, the pod of which is forced underground in growing, where it ripens. **2.** (*pl.*) *Colloq.* any small amount, esp. of money. ◇*adj.* **3.** of or relating to the peanut or peanuts. **4.** made with or from peanuts.

pear /pɛə/, *n.* the edible fruit, typically rounded but elongated and growing smaller towards the stem, of a widely cultivated tree. [OE *pere*, from LL]

pearl /pɜːl/, *n.* **1.** a hard, smooth, usu. white, shiny, round mass found in oysters and other molluscs, grown as a protective coating around a piece of grit, etc. inside the shell. **2.** an artificial substance that looks like a pearl. **3.** nacre, or mother-of-pearl. **4.** something precious or special; the finest example of anything. **5.** a very pale grey color, almost white. ◇*v.i.* **6.** to look for pearls. ◇*adj.* **7.** of the color or lustre of pearl; nacreous. **8.** relating to, or made with pearls or mother-of-pearl. [ME, from OF, from ML *perla*] – **pearly**, *adj.*

Pearl Harbor, *n.* a harbor near Honolulu, on the island of Oahu in the Hawaiian Islands; surprise attack by Japan on the US naval base there 7 December 1941.

Pearl River, *n.* → Zhujiang.

peasant /ˈpɛzənt/, *n.* **1.** one of a class of people of so-called inferior social rank, living and working on the land but usu. not owning land; rustic. **2.** *Colloq.* a person who does not appreciate the finer things of life; a gross, insensitive person; a boor. ◇*adj.* **3.** having to do with peasants, their crafts, traditions, etc. [late ME, from AF, from LL, from L: district] – **peasantry**, *n.*

Peasants' Revolt, *n.* an insurrection led by Wat Tyler in England in 1381 in protest against an attempt by landlords to revert to old servile tenures.

peashooter /ˈpiːʃuːtə/, *n.* a tube through which dried peas are blown, usu. by children.

pea soup, *n.* **1.** a thick soup made from split peas. **2.** Also, **pea souper.** *Colloq.* a thick, dirty fog.

peat /piːt/, *n.* **1.** soil of partially decomposed plants, in marshy or damp regions, drained and cultivated, cut out and dried for use as fuel. **2.** this substance as fuel. [ME; orig. uncert.] – **peaty**, *adj.*

pebble /ˈpɛbəl/, *n.* a small, rounded stone, esp. one worn by the action of water.

pecan /ˈpiːkæn, pɪˈkæn/, *n.* a hickory tree orig. from the lower Mississippi valley, southern US, and grown for its oval, smooth-shelled nut with a sweet, oily, edible kernel. [Algonquian: hard-shelled nut]

peccadillo /pɛkəˈdɪloʊ/, *n., pl.* **-loes, -los.** a small sin or offence; a trifling fault. [Sp, from L: a sin]

peck¹ /pɛk/, *n.* **1.** a dry measure in the imperial system, equal to 8 quarts or 9.09×10^{-3} m³; the fourth part of a bushel. **2.** a container for measuring this quantity. **3.** a considerable quantity: *a peck of trouble.* [ME; orig. unknown]

peck² /pɛk/, *v.t.* **1.** to strike or make dents with the beak, as a bird does, or with some pointed instrument, esp. with quick, repeated movements. **2.** to take (food, etc.) bit by bit: *The chicken pecked the grain.* **3.** to kiss in a hasty dabbing manner. ◇*v.i.* **4.** to make strokes with the beak or a pointed instrument. **5.** to pick or nibble at food. **6.** to nag (fol. by *at*): *Stop pecking at me!* ◇*n.* **7.** a pecking stroke. **8.** a hasty kiss: *a peck on the cheek.* [ME; ? var. of PICK¹]

pecking order, *n.* **1.** the natural order of importance seen in a flock of poultry or in any birds that live in flocks. **2.** any order of importance or precedence.

pectin /ˈpɛktɪn/, *n.* any of various polysaccharides in ripe fruits, which dissolve in sugared boiling water, forming a gel upon cooling, used in jam-making. [*pect(ic)* + -IN¹] – **pectic**, *adj.*

pectoral /ˈpɛktərəl/, *adj.* **1.** relating to the breast or chest; thoracic: *the pectoral muscle.* **2.** worn on the breast or chest: *the pectoral cross of a bishop.* [late ME, from L: relating to the breast]

pectoral fin, *n.* (in fishes) either of a pair of fins situated behind the head, one on each side, and corresponding to the forelimbs of higher vertebrates.

peculate /ˈpɛkjəleɪt/, *v.i., v.t.,* **-lated, -lating.** to take for one's own use (money or goods entrusted to one's care); embezzle. [L: having embezzled] – **peculation**, *n.* – **peculator**, *n.*

peculiar /pəˈkjuːliə, -ljə/, *adj.* **1.** strange, odd, or queer: *a peculiar old man.* **2.** uncommon; unusual: *a peculiar hobby.* **3.** belonging to a certain person or group, opposed to others (fol. by *to*): *an expression peculiar to Australia.* [late ME, from L: relating to one's own] – **peculiarity**, *n.*

pecuniary /pəˈkjuːniəri, -nəri/, *adj.* **1.** consisting of or given or taken in money: *pecuniary penalties.* **2.** relating to money: *pecuniary affairs.* [L: relating to money]

ped-¹, → **paed-.**

ped-², variant of **pedi-.**

-ped, a word part meaning 'foot', used to form adjectives and nouns, as *biped, quadruped.* See **-pod.** [L, combining form of *pēs* foot]

ped., *Abbrev.* **1.** pedal. **2.** pedestal.

pedagogue /'pɛdəgɒg/, *n.* **1.** a teacher of children; schoolteacher. **2.** someone who is pedantic, dogmatic, and formal. [ME, from OF, from L, from Gk: a teacher of boys] – **pedagogic**, *adj.* – **pedagogy**, *n.*

pedal /'pɛdl/, *n., v.,* **-alled, -alling,** *adj.* ◇*n.* **1.** a lever worked by the foot, in musical instruments, e.g. organ, piano, harp, and in a sewing machine, bicycle, motor car, etc. ◇*v.t.* **2.** to work or use the pedals of: *to pedal a bicycle.* ◇*v.i.* **3.** to operate the pedals. ◇*adj.* **4.** relating to a pedal or pedals. **5.** consisting of pedals: *a pedal keyboard.* [F, from It, from L: (something) relating to the foot]

pedalfer /pə'dælfə/, *n.* a type of soil lacking in lime but containing accumulations of aluminium and iron components. [Gk + L]

pedant /'pɛdnt/, *n.* someone who puts too much importance on small details of learning, or who possesses mere book-learning without practical wisdom. [It: teacher, pedant] – **pedantic,** *adj.* – **pedantry,** *n.*

Pedder /'pɛdə/, *n.* **Lake,** orig. a small glacial lake in south-western Tas; in 1972 the damming of the Serpentine River caused the flooding of the lake and the formation of Pedder Reservoir, a water storage for the Gordon hydro-electric power scheme.

peddle /'pɛdl/, *v.,* **-dled, -dling.** ◇*v.t.* **1.** to carry (goods) about for sale; hawk. **2.** to deal out in small quantities. ◇*v.i.* **3.** to travel about selling small wares. **4.** to occupy oneself with small unimportant things; trifle. [apparently a backformation from PEDLAR, and in part confused with PIDDLE]

-pede, a word part meaning 'foot', as in *centipede.* [F, from L, a combining form of *pēs* foot]

pederasty /'pɛdəræsti/, *n.* homosexual relations, esp. those between a male adult and a boy. – **pederast,** *n.* – **pederastic,** *adj.*

pedestal /'pɛdəstl/, *n.* **1.** a support or base for a column, statue, vase, etc. **2.** a supporting structure or piece; base. **3. set on a pedestal,** to think someone wonderful in an unreal way: *He set her on a pedestal until he discovered her true nature.* [F, from It]

pedestrian /pə'dɛstriən/, *n.* **1.** someone who goes or travels on foot; walker. ◇*adj.* **2.** going or performed on foot; walking. **3.** relating to walking. **4.** dull; commonplace; prosaic. [L: on foot]

pedestrian crossing, *n.* a marked section of roadway where motorists have to stop to allow pedestrians to cross. See **zebra crossing.**

pedi-, a word part meaning 'foot', as in *pedicure.* Also, **ped-**[2]. [L, combining form of *pēs*]

pedicel /'pɛdəsɛl/, *n. Bot.* a small stalk. [NL, diminutive of: PEDICLE]

pedicle /'pɛdɪkəl/, *n.* a small stalk or stalklike support; pedicel or peduncle. [L: foot]

pedicure /'pɛdəkjuə/, *n.* professional care or treatment of the feet. [F, from L]

pedigree /'pɛdəgri/, *n.* **1.** a line of ancestors or line of descent, esp. when recorded, of men or animals; lineage: *a dog of good pedigree.* **2.** a genealogical table: *a family pedigree.* **3.** derivation from a source: *the pedigree of a word.* [ME, apparently from OF: lit., foot of a crane, said to refer to a mark having three branching lines, used in old genealogical tables]

pediment /'pɛdəmənt/, *n. Archit.* a low triangular gable crowned with a projecting cornice, in the Greek, Roman, or Renaissance style, esp. over a portico or porch or at the ends of a gable-roofed building. [? from L, a prop of a vine] – **pedimental,** *adj.*

pedlar /'pɛdlə/, *n.* someone who peddles. Also, **pedler.** [ME] – **pedlary,** *n.*

peduncle /pə'dʌŋkəl/, *n.* **1.** *Bot.* **a.** a flower stalk, supporting either a cluster or a solitary flower. **b.** a stalk bearing the fructification in fungi, etc. **2.** *Zool.* a stalk or stem; stalklike part or structure. [NL, diminutive of L: foot] – **peduncled, peduncular, pedunculate,** *adj.*

pee /pi/, *v.,* **peed, peeing,** *n. Colloq.* ◇*v.i.* **1.** to urinate. ◇*n.* **2.** an act of urination.

peek /pik/, *v.i.* **1.** to peep; peer. ◇*n.* **2.** a peeking look or glance. [ME]

peel /pil/, *v.t.* **1.** to strip off the skin, rind, bark, etc. ◇*v.i.* **2.** (of skin, etc.) to come off. ◇*v.* **3. keep (one's) eye(s) peeled,** *Colloq.* to keep a close watch. ◇*n.* **4.** the skin or rind of a fruit, etc. [ME] – **peeler,** *n.* – **peeling,** *n.*

Peel /pil/, *n.* **Sir Robert,** 1788–1850, British statesman; prime minister 1834–35 and 1841–46; responsible for the reorganisation of the London police force.

peen /pin/, *n.* the sharp, spherical, or otherwise modified end of the head of a hammer, opposite to the face. Also, **pein.** [earlier *pen*; orig. uncert.]

peep[1] /pip/, *v.i.* **1.** to look through a small opening, or from a hiding place. **2.** to look slyly, pryingly, or furtively. **3.** to come partially into view; begin to appear: *The sun is peeping over the horizon.* ◇*n.* **4.** a peeping look or glance. [? assimilated var. of PEEK]

peep[2] /pip/, *v.i.* **1.** to utter the shrill little cry of a young bird, mouse, etc.; cheep; squeak. **2.** to speak in a thin, weak voice. ◇*n.* **3.** a peeping cry or sound. [ME]

peeping Tom, *n.* someone, usu. male, who looks secretly and slyly at (usu.) women for sexual pleasure; voyeur. [allusion to the man who peeped at Lady Godiva riding naked through Coventry]

peepshow /'pipʃoʊ/, *n.* pictures or objects in a box, etc., viewed through a small opening.

peer[1] /pɪə/, *n.* **1.** a person of the same social rank or standing; an equal before the law. **2.** an equal in any respect. **3.** a nobleman. [ME, from OF from L: equal] – **peeress,** *n. fem.*

peer[2] /pɪə/, *v.i.* **1.** to look closely in order to see clearly. **2.** to peep out or appear slightly. [late ME; orig. uncert.]

peerage /'pɪərɪdʒ/, *n.* a group of peers of a country.

peer group, *n.* a group of people of about the same age, social background or class.

peerless /ˈpɪələs/, *adj.* having no peer or equal; matchless.

peeve /piv/, *v.*, **peeved, peeving**, *n. Colloq.* ◇*v.t.* **1.** to make (someone) annoyed. ◇*n.* **2.** an annoyance: *my pet peeve*. [backformation from PEEVISH]

peevish /ˈpivɪʃ/, *adj.* cross; easily annoyed; irritable. [ME *pevysh*; orig. unknown]

peewee /ˈpiwi/, *n.* →**magpie lark**.

peewit /ˈpiwɪt/, *n.* →**magpie lark**.

peg /pɛg/, *n., v.*, **pegged, pegging**. ◇*n.* **1.** a pin of wood or other material driven or fitted into something, as to fasten parts together, to hang things on, to fasten a rope on, to stop a hole, or to mark a point in the ground. **2.** a reason: *a peg to hang a grievance on*. **3.** *Colloq.* a degree: *to come down a peg*. **4.** a pin of wood or metal to which one end of a string of a violin, etc., is fastened, and which may be turned to change the tension of the string, in order to tune the instrument. **5. off the peg**, (of a garment) ready-made. **6. take down a peg**, to humble. **7. square peg in a round hole**, *Colloq.* a misfit. ◇*v.t.* **8.** to drive a peg into. **9.** to fasten with, or as if with, pegs. **10.** to mark with pegs (oft. fol. by *out*). **11.** to keep (prices, wages, etc.) at a set level. ◇*v.i.* **12.** to work steadily (fol. by *away, along, on*, etc.). ◇*v.* **13. peg out**, to mark out a gold claim. [ME]

Pegasus /ˈpɛgəsəs/, *n. Class Myth.* a winged horse, sprung from the blood of the slain Medusa, who with a stroke of his hoof caused the spring Hippocrene to open up on Mt Helicon, from which came the modern association with the Muses and poetry. See **Bellerophon**.

peg leg, *n.* an artificial leg, usu. one of wood.

pejorative /pəˈdʒɒrətɪv/, *adj.* (of a word, comment, etc.) showing disapproval; deprecatory. [L: having been made worse]

Peking /piˈkɪŋ/, *n.* former name of Beijing.

Pekingese /pikəˈniz/, *n.* a small, long-haired dog orig. from China. Also, **Pekinese**.

Peking man, *n.* a type of early ape-like man, known from remains found near Peking (Beijing), China.

pekoe /ˈpikoʊ/, *n.* a high-quality kind of black tea from Ceylon, India, and Java. [Chinese (Amoy d.): white down]

pelargonium /pɛləˈgoʊniəm/, *n.* a type of plant, the cultivated species of which are usu. called geranium. [NL, from Gk: stork]

pelf /pɛlf/, *n.* (*offensive*) money or riches. [ME, from OF: spoil; orig. uncert.]

Pelham /ˈpɛləm/, *n.* **Henry**, 1695?–1754, British statesman; prime minister 1743–54.

pelican /ˈpɛlɪkən/, *n.* a type of large, web-footed seabird, having a large fish-catching bill with a pouch beneath. [ME and OE, from LL, from Gk]

pellagra /pəˈleɪgrə, pəˈlægrə/, *n.* a disease caused by vitamin deficiency, marked by skin rashes, nervous disorders, and diarrhoea. [It: skin] —**pellagrous**, *adj.*

pellet /ˈpɛlət/, *n.* **1.** a small rounded piece, esp. of food or medicine. **2.** one of the small non-explosive bullets fired from a shotgun. [ME, from OF, from L: ball]

Pelletier /pɛlɛtiˈeɪ/, *n.* **Pierre Joseph** /piˌɛə ʒoʊˈzɛf/, 1788–1842, French chemist and pharmacist who first isolated chlorophyll and discovered chemical substances such as strychnine and quinine.

pell-mell /pɛlˈmɛl/, *adv.* **1.** in a confused mass or crowd. **2.** in disorderly, headlong haste. Also, **pellmell**. [F]

pellucid /pəˈlusəd/, *adj.* **1.** allowing the passage of light; translucent. **2.** clear, like water. [L: transparent]

pelmet /ˈpɛlmət/, *n.* an ornamental covering (of board or material) hiding a curtain rail.

Peloponnesian War /pɛləpəˌnizən ˈwɔ/, *n.* a war between Athens and Sparta from 431 to 404 BC which resulted in the transfer of dominance in Greece from Athens to Sparta.

Peloponnesus /pɛləpəˈnisəs/, *n.* the southern peninsula of Greece; the seat of the early Mycenaean civilisation and of the powerful city-states of Sparta, Argos, etc. Pop. 1 012 528 (1981); 21 642 km². Greek, **Pelopónnisos** /pɛləˈpouniːsɒs/. Also, **Peloponnese, Peloponnesos** or **Morea**. —**Peloponnesian**, *adj., n.*

Pelsaert /ˈpɛlsɑt/, *n.* **François** or **Francisco**, c. 1590–1630, Belgium-born Dutch East India Company official; commander of the *Batavia* which was wrecked off the WA coast, and supposed to have slept one night on the mainland while seeking assistance; recorded the existence of wallabies in Australia.

pelt¹ /pɛlt/, *v.t.* **1.** to attack with repeated blows or with missiles. **2.** to throw (things). ◇*v.i.* **3.** (of rain) to fall very heavily. **4.** to throw missiles. **5.** to hurry: *He pelted down the hill*. ◇*n.* **6. full pelt**, with the greatest energy or speed. [orig. uncert.; ? akin to PELLET]

pelt² /pɛlt/, *n.* the skin of an animal with or without the hair. [ME, orig. uncert., ultimately from L *pellis*]

pelvis /ˈpɛlvəs/, *n., pl.* **-ves** /-viz/. a basin-like cavity in the lower part of the trunk of humans and many other vertebrates. [L: basin] —**pelvic**, *adj.*

pen¹ /pɛn/, *n., v.*, **penned, penning**. ◇*n.* **1.** any instrument for writing with ink, e.g. a biro, nib, fountain pen or quill. **2.** the pen as a symbol of writing or authorship: *The pen is mightier than the sword*. ◇*v.t.* **3.** to write with a pen. [ME, from OF, from LL: pen, from L: feather]

pen² /pɛn/, *n., v.*, **penned** or **pent, penning**. ◇*n.* **1.** an enclosure for domestic animals or livestock. **2.** any place of confinement. ◇*v.t.* **3.** to put in or as if in a pen. [OE *penn*; orig. uncert.]

Pen, *Abbrev.* peninsula.

penal /'pinəl/, *adj.* **1.** of or relating to punishment of crimes: *penal laws; a penal settlement.* **2.** subject to punishment: *a penal offence.* [ME, from L: relating to punishment]

penal code, *n.* all the laws dealing with crimes and punishment.

penal colony, *n. Hist.* a colony established to receive convicts and built in part through convict labor.

penalise *or* **penalize** /'pinəlaɪz/, *v.t.*, **-lised, -lising. 1.** to punish or disadvantage (someone). **2.** to declare (an action) to be punishable by law.

penal settlement, *n. Aust Hist.* a place of punishment for convicts, usu. in an isolated area remote from free settlements, e.g. Port Arthur in Tas.

penalty /'penəlti/, *n., pl.* **-ties. 1.** a punishment for breaking a law or rule. **2.** a loss or forfeiture which someone brings upon himself by non-fulfilment of an obligation. **3.** the consequence of a wrongful or foolish action. **4.** *Sport.* **a.** a free shot, kick, etc. allowed to one team or player, because the other has broken a rule. **b.** *Golf.* a stroke added to a player's score after a ball lands out of bounds, in water, etc. [PENAL + -TY²]

penalty rate, *n.* a rate of pay determined by an award, higher than the usual rate, for working outside normal hours.

penance /'penəns/, *n.* **1.** punishment undergone as a sign of being sorry for sin. **2.** *Rom Cath Ch.* such punishment ordered by a church authority after confession, and followed by forgiveness of the sin. [ME, from OF, from L]

Penang /pə'næŋ/, *n.* → **Pinang**.

pence /pɛns/, *n.* pl. plural of **penny**, usu. used in compounds: *fourpence*.

penchant /'penʃənt/, *n.* a taste or liking for something. [F, from L: hang]

pencil /'pensəl/, *n., v.,* **-cilled, -cilling.** ◇*n.* **1.** a thin, pointed tube of wood, etc., with a core of graphite, chalk, etc., used for drawing or writing. **2.** a slender, pointed piece of some marking substance. ◇*v.t.* **3.** to use a pencil on. [ME, from OF, from VL var. of L: brush]

pendant /'pendənt/, *n.* **1.** a hanging ornament, such as on a necklace or earring. **2.** a chandelier. ◇*adj.* **3.** hanging. **4.** overhanging. Also, **pendent.** [ME, from OF: hang, from L]

pending /'pendɪŋ/, *prep.* **1.** while awaiting; until: *pending his return.* **2.** in the period before the decision or finish of; during: *pending the official talks.* ◇*adj.* **3.** remaining undecided; awaiting decision. [PEND(ENT) + -ING²]

pendulous /'pendʒələs/, *adj.* **1.** hanging loosely. **2.** swinging freely. [L: hanging, swinging]

pendulum /'pendʒələm/, *n.* **1.** something hung from a fixed point and moving backwards and forwards (by the action of gravity and acquired kinetic energy). **2.** such a device used for controlling the movement of clockwork. [NL, properly neut. of L: hanging, swinging]

pene-, a prefix meaning almost, as in *peneplain.* Also, *before a vowel,* **pen-,** as in *peninsula.* [L]

Penelope /pə'nɛləpi/, *n. Gk Myth.* the wife of Odysseus who, during her husband's long absence, remained faithful to him in spite of numerous suitors.

peneplain /'pinəplein, pinə'plein/, *n.* an area reduced almost to a plain by erosion. Also, **peneplane.** [L]

penetrate /'penətreɪt/, *v.,* **-trated, -trating.** ◇*v.t.* **1.** to go into or through with a sharp instrument. **2.** to enter the interior of. **3.** to enter and spread through; permeate. **4.** to affect deeply. **5.** to understand. ◇*v.i.* **6.** to enter, reach, or pass through, as if by piercing. [L] —**penetrable**, *adj.* —**penetrating**, *adj.* —**penetration**, *n.*

penfriend /'penfrɛnd/, *n.* a person, esp. one in another country, with whom a friendship is kept going through letter-writing.

penguin /'pengwən, 'pengwən/, *n.* any of various flightless birds living in or near the water in the Southern Hemisphere, with webbed feet, and wings reduced to flippers, as the **Adelie penguin**, sometimes found on the southern coast of Australia.

penicillin /penə'sɪlən/, *n.* a powerful antibacterial substance produced by certain moulds. [L *pēnicillus* small brush + -IN¹]

peninsula /pə'nɪnsələ/, *n.* a piece of land almost surrounded by water, esp. one connected with the mainland by only a narrow neck. [L] —**peninsular**, *adj.*

penis /'pinəs/, *n., pl.* **-nes** /-niz/, **-nises** /-nəsəz/. the male organ of sexual union and urination. [L: orig., tail] —**penile** *adj.*

penitent /'penətənt/, *adj.* **1.** sorry for wrong-doing or fault and willing to put things right; repentant; contrite. ◇*n.* **2.** a penitent person. [L: repenting] —**penitence**, *n.* —**penitential**, *adj.*

penitentiary /penə'tɛnʃəri/, *n., pl.* **-ries,** *adj.* ◇*n.* **1.** a place for imprisonment and punishment taking the form of correction and training designed to change behavior. ◇*adj.* **2.** of or relating to punishment as a sign of being sorry for wrongdoing; penitential. [ME, from ML, from L: penitence]

penknife /'pennaɪf/, *n., pl.* **-knives** /-naɪvz/. a small pocket-knife, originally for making and mending quill pens.

Penn /pɛn/, *n.* **William,** 1644–1718, English Quaker who founded the colony of Pennsylvania.

pen-name /'pɛn-neɪm/, *n.* a name taken to write under; author's pseudonym; nom de plume.

pennant /'penənt/, *n.* **1.** Also, **pendant, pennon.** a long triangular flag, widest next to the mast, and going almost to a point, carried on naval or other vessels or used in signalling, etc. **2.** any flag serving as a sign, usu. of success in a sporting event, esp. a running race, etc. [var. of PENDANT]

Penney /'peni/, *n.* Sir William George, born 1909, English atomic scientist.

penniless /'penələs/, *adj.* without a penny; destitute of money.

Pennines /'penaɪnz/, *n.pl.* a range of low mountains in England extending from the Trent north to the Cheviots. Highest point, Crossfell, 893 m. Also, **Pennine Chain**.

Pennsylvania /pensəl'veɪnɪə/, *n.* a state in the eastern US. Pop. 11 889 000 (1986 est.); 117 412 km². *Cap.:* Harrisburg. *Abbrev.:* Pa, Penn, or Penna —**Pennsylvanian**, *n., adj.*

penny /'peni/, *n., pl.* **pennies**, (*esp. collectively*) **pence**. **1.** (formerly) a bronze or copper coin, of Britain and some other countries, equal to $\frac{1}{12}$ of a shilling or $\frac{1}{240}$ of a pound. *Abbrev.:* d **2.** a bronze coin of the UK equal to a 100th part of a pound; new penny. *Abbrev.:* p **3.** a bronze coin of Canada and the US, the 100th part of a dollar; a cent. **4.** the least possible sum of money: *I haven't got a penny.* **5. a bad penny**, a bad or undesirable person or thing. **6. the penny drops**, the explanation or remark is understood. **7. a pretty penny**, a considerable amount of money. **8. spend a penny**, to go to the toilet. [OE *penig, pening, pending*]

penny dreadful, *n.* a piece of cheap, popular, sensational literature.

penny-farthing /peni-'faðɪŋ/, *n.* a high bicycle of an early type with one large wheel in front and one small wheel behind.

penny pincher, *n.* a mean, small-minded person. —**penny-pinching**, *adj.*

pennyweight /'peniweɪt/, *n.* a unit of mass in the imperial system, equal to $\frac{1}{20}$ of an ounce. *Symbol:* dwt

penology /pi'nɒlədʒi/, *n.* the science of the punishment of crime and management of prisons. [PEN(AL) + -O- + -LOGY] —**penological**, *adj.* —**penologist**, *n.*

pen-pusher /'pen-pʊʃə/, *n. Colloq.* someone who works with a pen, esp. a clerk in an unimportant and uninteresting job.

Penrith /'penrɪθ/, *n.* a city in Sydney, NSW, in the western metropolitan area. Pop. 135 342 (1986).

pension /'penʃən/; /'pɒsɪ̃/ *for def. 3, n.* **1.** a fixed regular payment made in consideration of past services, injury or loss, old age, poverty, etc. **2.** an allowance or annuity. **3.** (in Europe) a boarding house, small hotel, or school. ◇*v.t.* **4.** to give a pension to. **5.** to cause to leave an office, job or active life on a pension (fol. by *off*). [L: payment] —**pensionable**, *adj.* —**pensionary**, *adj., n.* —**pensioner**, *n.*

pensive /'pensɪv/, *adj.* **1.** deeply, seriously, or sadly thoughtful. **2.** expressing thoughtfulness or sadness. [F: think]

pent /pent/, *v.* **1.** past tense and past participle of **pen**². ◇*adj.* **2.** shut in. **3.** limited.

pent-, a word part meaning five. Also, before consonants, **penta-**. [Gk, combining forms of *pénte*]

pentacle /'pentəkəl/, *n.* a figure, usu. a five-pointed star. Also, **pentagram, pentangle**. [probably from F, or from ML]

pentagon /'pentəgən, -gən/, *n.* **1.** a closed plane figure having five angles and five sides. **2.** (*cap.*) **a.** the five-sided building in Arlington, Virginia, containing most US Defence Department offices. **b.** the US Defence Department. [L, from Gk] —**pentagonal**, *adj.*

pentameter /pen'tæmətə/, *n.* one line of a poem made up of five metrical feet. [L, from Gk]

Pentateuch /'pentətjuk/, *n.* the first five books of the Old Testament, considered as a group. [L, from Gk: consisting of five books] —**Pentateuchal**, *adj.*

pentathlon /pen'tæθlən/, *n.* a competition of five different track and field events, won by the competitor having the highest total score. [Gk]

pentatonic scale /pentə,tɒnɪk 'skeɪl/, *n. Music.* a scale having only five tones, esp. the one corresponding to the black keys of the piano.

Pentecost /'pentəkɒst/, *n.* a Christian festival reminding people of the descent of the Holy Spirit upon the apostles on the day of the Jewish festival.

Pentecostal /pentə'kɒstl/, *adj.* of or relating to any of various modern Christian groups that stress the power of the Holy Spirit in the believer.

penthouse /'penthaʊs/, *n., pl.* **-houses** /-haʊzəz/. **1.** a separate flat on a roof. **2.** a sloping roof, or a shed with a sloping roof coming out from a wall or the side of a building, usu. to shelter a door. [ME, apparently from OF, from L: hang to or on, append]

pent-up /'pent-ʌp/, *adj.* shut-in; confined; restrained: *pent-up rage.*

penult /pə'nʌlt/, *n.* the last syllable but one in a word. Also, **penultima** /pə'nʌltəmə/. [L: last but one]

penultimate /pə'nʌltəmət/, *adj.* next to the last.

penumbra /pə'nʌmbrə/, *n., pl.* **-brae** /-bri/, **-bras**. a partial or imperfect shadow outside the complete shadow (umbra) of a body, usu. a planet, where the light from the source of illumination is only partly cut off. [NL, from L] —**penumbral**, *adj.*

penury /'penjəri/, *n.* **1.** great poverty; destitution. **2.** lack of food, etc.; dearth; insufficiency. [ME, from L: want, scarcity] —**penurious**, *adj.*

peon¹ /'piən/, *n.* (in Spanish America, etc.) a day worker, usu. doing unskilled farm work. [Sp, from L: foot soldier]

peon² /pjun, 'pɪən/, *n. India.* **1.** a foot soldier. **2.** a messenger or attendant. [Pg and F: foot soldier, pedestrian, day laborer] —**peonage**, *n.*

peony /'piəni/, *n., pl.* **-nies**. a type of garden plant or shrub with large showy pink, red or yellow flowers. [L, from Gk, from *Paiōn*

peony

the physician of the gods (because the plant was used in medicine)]

people /'pipəl/, n., pl. **-ple, -ples** for def. 1, v., **-pled, -pling.** ◇n. **1.** the whole body of members making up a community, tribe, race, or nation. **2.** the members of any particular group, company, or number: *the people of a parish*. **3.** people in relation to a ruler, leader, etc.: *the king and his people*. **4.** one's family or relatives: *to visit one's people*. **5.** the members of any group or number to which one belongs. **6.** the body of those citizens of a state able to vote: *representatives chosen by the people*. **7.** the common people or general population: *a man of the people*. **8.** people in general, whether men or women: *People may say what they please*. **9.** human beings marked off as different from animals. ◇v.t. **10.** to supply with people; populate. [ME, from AF, from L: people]

pep /pep/, n., v., **pepped, pepping.** ◇n. *Colloq.* **1.** spirit or life; vigor; energy; animation: *I need a cold shower to give me pep in the morning*. ◇v.t. **2.** to give spirit or energy to (fol. by *up*): *Pep up my drink with some more lemonade*. [short for PEPPER] **—peppy,** adj.

pepper /'pepə/, n. **1.** a seasoning, biting to the taste, used to give extra flavor to food and obtained from the dried berries of a tropical climbing plant; black pepper; white pepper. **2.** cayenne (**red pepper**), prepared from types of capsicum. **3.** any species of capsicum, or its fruit (green or red, hot or sweet), as the capsicum or common pepper of the garden. ◇v.t. **4.** to season with or as with pepper. **5.** to sprinkle like pepper. **6.** to shower with shot or flying objects, etc. [OE *piper*, from L, from Gk: pepper; of Eastern orig.]

peppercorn /'pepəkɔn/, n. a berry of the black pepper plant often dried and used in pickling. [OE *piporcorn*]

peppermint /'pepəmɪnt/, n. **1.** a herb grown for its biting, strongly smelling oil. **2.** any of several types of gum tree with oils rich in peppermint and characteristic bark. **3.** a sweet flavored with peppermint.

peppertree /'pepə,tri/, n. any of several evergreen trees, mostly native to South America and grown in subtropical areas as ornamentals because of their evergreen leaves and bright red fruits.

peppery /'pepəri/, adj. **1.** being like pepper; full of pepper; pungent. **2.** of or relating to pepper. **3.** sharp or stinging, as speech. **4.** irritable, esp. of people or their temper. **—pepperiness,** n.

pep pill, n. a pill or tablet that consists of a stimulant drug, as amphetamine.

Peppin /'pepən/, n. **George Hall**, 1800–72, Australian sheepbreeder, born in England; founder of the Wanganella breed.

pepsin /'pepsən/, n. an enzyme produced by the stomach that breaks down protein. Also, **pepsine.** [Gk]

pep talk, n. an energetic talk to a person or group calculated to excite action or support for a cause, increase determination to succeed, etc.

perception

peptic /'peptɪk/, adj. **1.** relating to or concerned in digestion; digestive. **2.** helping digestion. **3.** of pepsin. **4.** associated with the action of digestive substances: *a peptic ulcer*. [L: able to digest]

peptic ulcer, n. an ulcer of the mucous membrane of the stomach or duodenum, caused by the overactivity of gastric juices.

peptide /'peptaɪd/, n. a compound containing two or more amino acids in which the carboxyl group of one is linked to the amino group of the other. [PEPT(IC) + -IDE]

Pepys /pips/, n. **Samuel**, 1633–1703, English government official and diarist; his famous diary gives eyewitness accounts of the Plague and the Great Fire of London. **—Pepysian,** adj.

per /pɜ/; weak form /pə/, prep. through; by; for each: *per annum* (by the year), *per diem* (by the day), *per yard* (for each yard), etc. [L. See PER.]

per-, a prefix meaning 'through', 'thoroughly', 'utterly', 'very', as in *pervert, pervade, perfect*. [L (in some words from OF or F), representing *per*, prep., through, by]

perambulate /pə'ræmbjəleɪt/, v., **-lated, -lating.** ◇v.t. **1.** to walk through, about, or over; travel through; traverse. **2.** to go across and examine or check in detail. ◇v.i. **3.** to walk or travel about; stroll. [L] **—perambulation,** n. **—perambulatory,** adj.

perambulator /pə'ræmbjəleɪtə/, n. → **pram.**

per capita, adv. by each single person. [L]

perceive /pə'siv/, v.t., **-ceived, -ceiving.** **1.** to gain knowledge of through one of the senses; discover by seeing, hearing, etc. **2.** to understand with the mind; apprehend. [ME, from OF, from L: seize, receive, understand] **—perceivable,** adj.

per cent, adv. **1.** by the hundred; for or in every hundred (used in expressing proportions, rates of interest, etc.): *to get 3 per cent. interest*. ◇n. **2.** a proportion; percentage. **3.** a quantity of goods which bears a mentioned rate of interest. Symbol: % Also, **percent.** [orig. *per cent.*, abbrev. of L *per centum* by the hundred]

percentage /pə'sentɪdʒ/, n. **1.** a rate or proportion per hundred. **2.** an allowance, duty, rate of interest, etc. on one hundred. **3.** a proportion in general. **4.** *Colloq.* gain; advantage.

percentile /pə'sentaɪl/, n. *Stat.* one of the values of a variable which divides the distribution of the variable into one hundred groups having equal frequencies. Thus, there are one hundred percentiles, each having the same number of people, things, etc., but a varying range of scores. [PER CENT + -ile]

perceptible /pə'septəbəl/, adj. able to be perceived; appreciable: *quite a perceptible time*.

perception /pə'sepʃən/, n. **1.** the action or ability of gaining knowledge through the senses; cognition. **2.** an immediate or instinctive recognition. **3.** the result or product of perceiving. [late ME, from L: a receiving, hence apprehension] **—perceptual,** n.

perceptive /pə'septɪv/, *adj.* **1.** having the power or ability of gaining knowledge through the senses. **2.** of or relating to perception. **3.** having quick understanding or insight. −**perceptiveness**, *n.*

Perceval /'pɜːsəvəl/, *n.* **Spencer**, 1762-1812, British statesman; prime minister 1809-12.

perch[1] /pɜːtʃ/, *n.* **1.** a pole or rod usu. fixed between two supports to serve as a roost for birds. **2.** any thing or place serving for a bird, or for anything else, to alight or rest upon. **3.** a position or station high above the ground. **4.** a measurement in the imperial system of length equal to 5.0292 m. ◇*v.i.* **5.** (of a bird) to land or rest upon a perch. **6.** to settle or rest in some high position, as if on a perch. ◇*v.t.* **7.** to set or place (something) on, or as if on, a perch: *I perched the vase on the highest shelf.* [ME, from OF, from L: pole, measuring rod]

perch[2] /pɜːtʃ/, *n., pl.* **perches**, (*esp. collectively*) **perch**. *n.* **1.** any of a number of types of Australian food and sport fishes, mainly freshwater but some living in the sea, such as the **red perch**, which is a pink color, with a dark patch on each side. **2.** → **giant perch**. **3.** a spiny freshwater fish which has been introduced into some rivers of south-eastern Australia, from Europe and the US. [ME, from OF, from L, from Gk: perch]

perchance /pə'tʃæns, -'tʃɑːns/, *adv. Poetic or Archaic.* **1.** maybe; possibly. **2.** by chance. [ME, from AF: by chance]

percipient /pə'sɪpiənt/, *adj.* **1.** gaining knowledge through the senses. **2.** having this knowledge or understanding. ◇*n.* **3.** someone or something that understands with the aid of the senses. [L: perceiving] −**percipience**, **percipiency**, *n.*

Percival /'pɜːsəvəl/, *n. Arthurian Legend.* a knight of King Arthur's court who sought the Holy Grail. Also, **Perceval**, **Percivale**.

percolate /'pɜːkəleɪt/, *v.*, **-lated**, **-lating**. ◇*v.t.* **1.** to cause (a liquid) to pass through something porous (with tiny openings); filter. **2.** (of a liquid) to filter through; permeate. **3.** to make (coffee) in a percolator. ◇*v.i.* **4.** to pass through a porous substance; filter; ooze. **5.** to become known gradually: *The news percolated through to our office.* [L: strained through] −**percolation**, *n.*

percolator /'pɜːkəleɪtə/, *n.* **1.** a type of coffeepot in which boiling water is forced up a hollow stem, filters through ground coffee, and returns to the pot below. **2.** something that percolates.

percussion /pə'kʌʃən/, *n.* **1.** the striking of one body against another with some force; impact. **2.** the striking of musical instruments to produce notes. **3.** a sharp light blow, esp. one for setting off a cap formerly used to discharge firearms. **4.** *Music.* the group of instruments in an orchestra which are played by striking. −**percussive**, *adj.*

percussion instrument, *n.* a musical instrument, e.g. a drum, cymbal, piano, etc., which is struck to produce a sound, as distinct from a bowed or blown instrument. −**percussionist**, *n.*

Percy /'pɜːsi/, *n.* **Sir Henry** ('*Hotspur*'), 1364-1403, English military leader, killed near Shrewsbury in a rebellion he led against Henry IV of England.

perdition /pə'dɪʃən/, *n.* **1.** the condition of final spiritual ruin or damnation. **2.** hell. [ME, from L: act of destroying]

peregrinate /'perəgrəneɪt/, *v.*, **-nated**, **-nating**. ◇*v.i.* **1.** to travel or journey. ◇*v.t.* **2.** to travel over; traverse. [L: having travelled]

peremptory /pə'remptri, -tɔːri/, *adj.* leaving no chance for denial or refusal; imperative: *a peremptory command.* [L: destructive, decisive] −**peremptoriness**, *n.*

perennial /pə'rɛniəl/, *adj.* **1.** lasting for a long time; enduring. **2.** *Bot.* having a life cycle lasting more than two years. **3.** (of a stream, etc.) lasting or continuing throughout the year. **4.** everlasting; continuing; recurrent; perpetual. ◇*n.* **5.** a perennial plant. **6.** something continuing or recurrent. [L: lasting through the year]

perentie /pə'rɛnti/, *n.* the largest Australian lizard, dark in color with large pale yellow spots; found in dry areas of northern and central Australia. [Aboriginal]

Peres /pə'rɛz/, *n.* **Shimon** /ʃə'moʊn/, born 1923 in Poland, Israeli politician; prime minister 1984-86.

perfect /'pɜːfəkt/, *adj., n.;* /pə'fɛkt/, *v.* ◇*adj.* **1.** having all the necessary parts, characteristics, etc.; complete. **2.** without blemish or defect; faultless: *perfect skin; perfect beauty.* **3.** completely suited for a particular purpose or occasion. **4.** completely matching a type; exact: *a perfect circle.* **5.** correct in every detail: *a perfect copy.* **6.** pure or unmixed: *perfect yellow.* **7.** complete; unqualified; absolute: *a perfect mastery; a perfect stranger.* **8.** *Music.* relating to the consonances produced by unison, octave, fifth and fourth intervals. ◇*n.* **9.** *Gram.* → **perfect tense**. ◇*v.t.* **10.** to bring to completion; complete, or finish. **11.** to make perfect or faultless; bring to perfection. **12.** to bring nearer to perfection; improve. [L: performed, completed]

perfectible /pə'fɛktəbəl/, *adj.* able to become, or be made, perfect.

perfection /pə'fɛkʃən/, *n.* **1.** the state or quality of being perfect. **2.** the highest degree of skill or excellence, usu. in some art. **3.** the act or fact of perfecting: *The perfection of musical skill takes a lifetime.*

perfectionist /pə'fɛkʃənəst/, *n.* **1.** someone who adheres to some doctrine concerning perfection. **2.** someone who demands nothing less than perfection in any area of activity, behavior, etc. −**perfectionism**, *n.*

perfect tense, *n. Gram.* the tense marking an action or state which is completed. See Appendix.

perfidy /'pɜːfədi/, *n., pl.* **-dies**. the carefully considered breaking of faith or trust; faithlessness; treachery. [L: faithlessness] −**perfidious**, *adj.*

perforate /'pɔfəreɪt/, v.t., **-rated, -rating.** 1. to make a hole or holes in (something) by punching, piercing, etc. 2. to pierce through or to the inside of; penetrate. [L: having been pierced through] —**perforation**, n. —**perforated**, adj.

perforce /pəˈfɔːs/, adv. of necessity. [ME, from OF: by force]

perform /pəˈfɔːm/, v.t. 1. to carry out; execute; do: *to perform miracles*. 2. to go through in proper form: *to perform a ceremony*. 3. to fulfil: *He performed his duty*. 4. to act (a play, a part, etc.), as on the stage. 5. to play or sing (music), esp. before an audience. ◇v.i. 6. to fulfil a command, promise, or undertaking. 7. to carry out or do something. 8. to act in a play. 9. to perform music. 10. to display anger. [ME, from AF] —**performer**, n.

performance /pəˈfɔːməns/, n. 1. a musical, dramatic or other amusement: *What performances are there on in town?* 2. the performing of ceremonies, or of music, or of a play, part, etc.: *His performance of Hamlet was brilliant*. 3. the carrying out or doing of work, acts, or deeds. 4. the way in which something, esp. a machine, car, etc., reacts under certain conditions or fulfils the purpose for which it was intended.

perfume /'pɔfjuːm/, n.; /pəˈfjuːm/, v., **-fumed, -fuming.** ◇n. 1. a substance, extract, or preparation designed to give out an agreeable smell. 2. the smell, scent, odor itself. ◇v.t. 3. (of substances, flowers, etc.) to give a sweet or pleasant smell to: *The flowers perfumed the room*. 4. to put perfume in (something): *to perfume notepaper*. [F: to scent] —**perfumery**, n.

perfunctory /pəˈfʌŋktəri/, adj. 1. done only as an uninteresting duty; mechanical; indifferent, careless, or superficial: *perfunctory courtesy*. 2. acting only out of duty; formal; official. [LL, from L: performed]

pergola /'pɜːɡələ, pəˈɡoʊlə/, n. a shelter formed of trellises supported on posts, over which vines or other plants are grown. [It, from L: shed, vine arbor]

perhaps /pəˈhæps, præps/, adv. maybe; possibly. [ME]

peri-, a prefix meaning 'around', 'about', 'beyond'. [Gk, prefix and prep.]

perianth /ˈpɛriænθ/, n. Bot. the calyx and corolla considered together, esp. where they are similar. [short for *perianthium*, from NL]

pericardium /pɛriˈkɑːdiəm/, n., pl. **-dia** /-diə/. the membranous baglike structure enclosing the heart. [NL, from Gk]

pericarp /'pɛrikɑːp/, n. Bot. the walls of a ripened ovary or fruit; seed capsule; seed vessel. [NL, from Gk: pod, husk] —**pericarpial**, adj.

Pericles /'pɛrəkliːz/, n. c. 490–429 BC, Athenian political leader who initiated the great building program responsible for the Parthenon.

pericline /'pɛriklaɪn/, n. Geol. a dome-shaped structure in which strata dip away from a central point. [Gk *periklinēs* sloping on all sides]

perigee /'pɛrədʒiː/, n. the point in an orbit round the earth that is nearest to the earth (opposed to *apogee*). [F, from NL, from Gk: close around the earth] —**perigeal, perigean**, adj.

Périgord /peɪriˈɡɔː/, n. a former province in south-western France.

perihelion /pɛriˈhiːliən/, n., pl. **-lia** /-liə/. the point of the orbit of a planet, comet, or artificial satellite which is nearest the sun (opposed to *aphelion*). [NL, from Gk]

peril /'pɛrəl/, n., v., **-rilled, -rilling.** ◇n. 1. danger; risk; jeopardy. ◇v.t. 2. to put in danger; imperil. [ME, from F, from L] —**perilous**, adj.

perimeter /pəˈrɪmətə/, n. 1. the circumference or outer boundary of a figure or area. 2. the length of such a boundary. [L, from Gk] —**perimetric, perimetrical**, adj. —**perimetry**, n.

perineum /pɛrəˈniəm/, n., pl. **-nea** /-ˈniə/. *Anat.* the area between the front of the anus and the vulva or the scrotum. [NL, from Gk]

period /'pɪəriəd/, n. 1. a part of time, history, life, etc., characterised by certain events or conditions. 2. any stated divison or part of time. 3. *Educ.* a particular length of time in a school timetable set aside for a single subject. 4. *Geol.* the main division of a geological era, represented in the earth's crust by systems of rocks laid down during it. It is divided into epochs. 5. *Phys.* the time of one complete cycle of a motion. 6. *Astron.* the time in which a planet or satellite revolves about its controlling body. 7. *Chem.* the group of elements forming a horizontal row in the periodic table. 8. the point of completion or end of a round of time or course of action. 9. → **menstruation**. 10. → **full stop**. 11. a complete sentence, esp. one worked out with great care. ◇adj. 12. relating to, marking, characteristic of, copying, or representing (the fashions of) a particular period of history: *period costumes*. [ME, from L, from Gk: a going around, cycle, period]

periodic /pɪəriˈɒdɪk/, adj. 1. marked by periods or rounds that come back again and again. 2. happening or appearing at regular intervals. 3. ceasing and then beginning again, etc. 4. *Phys.* recurring after equal intervals of time. 5. of or relating to a period, esp. of the revolution of a heavenly body. [L, from Gk]

periodical /pɪəriˈɒdɪkəl/, n. 1. a magazine, journal, etc., brought out at regular intervals. ◇adj. 2. brought out at regular intervals. 3. of or relating to such magazines, etc. 4. → **periodic**.

periodic table, n. *Chem.* a table in which the chemical elements are arranged in order of their atomic numbers and in rows and columns so that elements with similar chemical properties are in the same column.

peripatetic /ˌpɛrɪpəˈtɛtɪk/, adj. 1. walking or travelling about; itinerant. ◇n. 2. someone who walks or travels about. [orig. with ref. to the philosophy of or the followers of Aristotle, 384–322 BC, who taught while walking in the

Lyceum of ancient Athens; ME, from L, from Gk: walking about]

peripheral /pə'rɪfərəl/, *adj.* **1.** relating to, placed in, or making up the outside of a body, etc. **2.** of little importance; not essential; superficial.

periphery /pə'rɪfəri/, *n., pl.* **-ries. 1.** the outside boundary of any surface or area. **2.** the outside surface, or outside, of a body. [LL, from Gk]

periphrasis /pə'rɪfrəsəs/, *n., pl.* **-ses** /-siz/. **1.** a roundabout way of speaking; circumlocution. **2.** a roundabout expression. Also, **periphrase** /'perɪfreɪz/. [L, from Gk] –**periphrastic**, *adj.*

periscope /'perəskoup/, *n.* an instrument consisting basically of a tube with an arrangement of prisms or mirrors by which a view at the surface of water, etc., may be seen from below or behind. [Gk: look around] –**periscopic**, *adj.*

perish /'perɪʃ/, *v.i.* **1.** to die, through violence, lack of food, etc.: *to perish in battle.* **2.** to pass away; decay and disappear. **3.** to rot: *Rubber perishes.* **4.** to suffer destruction: *Whole cities perish in an earthquake.* **5.** to suffer spiritual death. **6.** to suffer greatly from cold, hunger, etc. [ME, from OF, from L: pass away, perish]

perishable /'perɪʃəbəl/, *adj.* **1.** likely to pass away; subject to decay or destruction. ◇*n.* **2.** (*usu. pl.*) a perishable thing, esp. food.

peristaltic /perə'stæltɪk/, *adj.* marking or relating to the waves, tightening and then opening, of a tubular muscle system or cylindrical structure, esp. the wavelike circular contractions of the alimentary canal. [Gk: compressing] –**peristalsis**, *n.*

peritoneum /perətə'niəm/, *n., pl.* **-nea** /-'niə/. the membrane lining the abdominal cavity. Also, **peritonaeum**. [LL, from Gk: stretched over] –**peritoneal**, *adj.*

peritonitis /ˌperətə'naɪtəs/, *n. Med.* a painful swelling of the peritoneum. [NL, from Gk: stretched round or over]

periwinkle[1] /'perɪwɪŋkəl/, *n.* **1.** any of various salt-water sea-snails, esp. used for food; gastropods. **2.** the shell of any of various other small creatures with shells made up of a single piece. [OE *pinewincle*]

periwinkle[2] /'perɪwɪŋkəl/, *n.* any plant of several related families with pink or blue flowers. [OE *perwince*, from L]

perjure /'pɜdʒə/, *v.t.*, **-jured**, **-juring.** to make (oneself) guilty of swearing falsely, or of intentionally making a false statement under oath. [late ME, from L] –**perjurer**, *n.*

perjury /'pɜdʒəri/, *n., pl.* **-ries.** the intentional making of a false statement in court, before a court of justice. [ME, from AF, from L]

perk[1] /pɜk/, *v.t., v.i.* to make or become lively, strong or active, esp. after sadness or sickness (fol. by *up*). [ME]

perk[2] /pɜk/, *n.* → **perquisite** (def. 2).

perky /'pɜki/, *adj.*, **-kier, -kiest.** easy and active; brisk; pert.

perm /pɜm/, *n.* **1.** → **permanent wave.** ◇*v.t.* **2.** to give (the hair) a permanent wave.

permafrost /'pɜməfrɒst/, *n.* ground that is always frozen.

permanent /'pɜmənənt/, *adj.* lasting or intended to last for a very long time; remaining unchanged; not temporary; enduring; abiding. [ME, from L: remaining throughout] –**permanence, permanency**, *n.*

permanent-press /'pɜmənənt-prɛs/, *adj.* of or relating to a garment which is treated so that it does not lose its creases in washing or wearing.

permanent wave, *n.* a wave set into the hair by a special chemical method and remaining for a number of months.

permanent way, *n.* the parts, such as rails, sleepers, etc. which make up the main running track of a railway.

permanganate /pə'mæŋɡənət, -nət/, *n.* a powerful oxidising agent as in potassium permanganate. See **-ate**[2].

permeability /ˌpɜmiə'bɪləti/, *n.* **1.** the property or state of being permeable. **2.** *Phys.* **a.** the ratio of flux density in a material to the magnetising force producing it (**absolute magnetic permeability**). **b.** the ratio of flux density produced in a material to that which would be produced in a vacuum by the same magnetising force (**relative magnetic permeability**).

permeable /'pɜmiəbəl/, *adj.* able to be passed through, usu. by liquids. [L]

permeate /'pɜmieɪt/, *v.*, **-ated, -ating.** ◇*v.t.* **1.** to pass through the substance or mass of. **2.** to enter through the pores, etc., of. **3.** to spread through; pervade; saturate. ◇*v.i.* **4.** to enter and spread; become diffused. [L: passed through] –**permeation**, *n.*

Permian /'pɜmiən/, *adj., n.* (relating to) the period or system following the Carboniferous and before the Triassic, characterised by prominence of salt deposits and, in the Southern Hemisphere, by extensive glaciers. [named after *Perm*, a town in European Russia (where such strata occur) + -IAN]

permissible /pə'mɪsəbəl/, *adj.* → **allowable.** –**permissibility**, *n.*

permission /pə'mɪʃən/, *n.* **1.** the act of permitting; a formal or express allowance or consent. **2.** the freedom given to do something. [ME, from L]

permissive /pə'mɪsɪv/, *adj.* **1.** giving permission. **2.** sexually and morally easy-going: *We are living in a permissive society.* –**permissiveness**, *n.*

permit /pə'mɪt/, *v.*, **-mitted, -mitting;** /'pɜmɪt/, *n.* ◇*v.t.* **1.** to allow (a person, etc.) to do something: *Permit me to explain.* **2.** to let (something) be done or happen: *The law permits the sale of such drugs.* **3.** to agree to. **4.** to give the chance for: *Vents permit the escape of gases from the laboratory.* ◇*v.i.* **5.** to give

permit permission; allow freedom to do something. **6.** to afford the chance or possibility: *Write when time permits.* **7.** to allow or admit (fol. by *of*): *statements that permit of no denial.* ◇*n.* **8.** a written order giving leave to do something. **9.** an official certificate of permission; licence. **10.** permission. [late ME, from L: to let go through]

permittivity /pəmɪˈtɪvəti/, *n.* **1. absolute permittivity,** the ratio of electric displacement to electric field strength in a dielectric medium. **2. relative permittivity,** the ratio of the absolute permittivity of a medium to the absolute permittivity of a vacuum; dielectric constant.

permutation /pɜmjəˈteɪʃən/, *n.* **1.** *Maths.* **a.** the act of changing the order of elements arranged in a particular order (as, *abc* into *acb*, *bac*, etc.), or of arranging a number of elements in groups made up of equal numbers of the elements in different orders (as, *a* and *b* in *ab* and *ba*). **b.** any of the resulting arrangements or groups. **2.** the act of making different in some way; alteration.

pernicious /pəˈnɪʃəs/, *adj.* **1.** highly hurtful; ruinous: *pernicious teachings.* **2.** deadly; fatal. **3.** evil or wicked. [L]

pernickety /pəˈnɪkəti/, *adj. Colloq.* **1.** hard to please; fastidious; fussy. **2.** needing particular care. [orig. Scot.]

Péron /ˈpɛrɒn/, *n.* **François,** 1775–1810, French-born naturalist in Australia; sailed with Nicholas Baudin on an exploration which touched on a number of places in Australia 1800–04.

Perón /pɛˈroʊn/, *n.* **Eva** /ˈɛɪvə/, *(Maria Eva Duarte de Perón)* *('Evita'),* 1919–1952, Argentine radio and film actress; active in politics, welfare and reform.

peroration /pɛrəˈreɪʃən/, *n.* the closing part of a speech in which the speaker repeats and stresses the main points. [late ME, from L]

peroxide /pəˈrɒksaɪd/, *n., adj., v.,* **-ided, -iding.** ◇*n.* **1.** *Chem.* **a.** an oxide derived from hydrogen peroxide which contains the -O-O- group. **b.** hydrogen peroxide, H_2O_2. ◇*adj.* **2.** (of the hair) bleached by peroxide (def. 1b): *She's a peroxide blonde.* ◇*v.t.* **3.** to use peroxide (def. 1b) on (the hair) as a bleach.

perpendicular /pɜpənˈdɪkjələ/, *adj.* **1.** upright; vertical. **2.** *Geom.* meeting a given line or surface at right angles. **3.** (*cap.*) *Archit.* marking or relating to a style of architecture, the last stage of English Gothic, marked by the vertical lines of its tracery. ◇*n.* **4.** a line or plane at right angles to another line. **5.** an instrument for showing the upright line from any point. **6.** an upright position. [L] —**perpendicularity,** *n.*

perpetrate /ˈpɜpətreɪt/, *v.t.,* **-trated, -trating.** to do, carry out, or commit (a crime, etc.). [L] —**perpetration,** *n.* —**perpetrator,** *n.*

perpetual /pəˈpɛtʃuəl/, *adj.* **1.** continuing or lasting forever or without fixed limit: *perpetual snows.* **2.** continuing or continued without a break or interruption: *a perpetual stream of visitors.* [ME, from L] —**perpetuality,** *n.*

perpetual motion, *n.* the movement of a theoretical machine that would continue to operate for ever without loss of energy and without receiving any energy from outside.

perpetuate /pəˈpɛtʃueɪt/, *v.t.,* **-ated, -ating.** to make able to last for a very long time; preserve from oblivion. [L] —**perpetuation, perpetuance,** *n.* —**perpetuator,** *n.*

perpetuity /pɜpəˈtjuəti/, *n., pl.* **-ties.** **1.** endless or long life or existence without fixed limit. **2.** something that is lasting. **3.** an annuity paid for life. **4. in perpetuity,** forever. [ME, from F, from L]

perplex /pəˈplɛks/, *v.t.* **1.** to cause to be puzzled over what is not understood or certain; bewilder; confuse mentally. **2.** to make (a matter, question, etc.) difficult or confused. **3.** to hold back with difficulties, confusion, or uncertainty. [ME, from L: involved] —**perplexity,** *n.* —**perplexing,** *adj.* —**perplexed,** *adj.*

perquisite /ˈpɜkwəzət/, *n.* **1.** an extra fee or profit that normally comes over and above fixed income, salary, or wages. **2.** Also, **perk. a.** anything usually supposed to be allowed or left to an employee or servant as a natural advantage of the position held. **b.** any extra payment, bonus, etc., coming with a particular post which an employee receives in addition to normal wages. **3.** something regarded as due by right. [late ME, from ML: sought for]

per se /pɜ ˈseɪ/, *adv.* by or in itself; intrinsically. [L]

persecute /ˈpɜsəkjut/, *v.t.,* **-cuted, -cuting.** **1.** to constantly treat (someone) unjustly or harshly; harass persistently. **2.** to harm or punish for sticking to principles or religious faith. **3.** to annoy by continual attentions, demands, etc. [backformation from *persecution,* conformed to L: having pursued] —**persecution,** *n.* —**persecutor,** *n.* —**persecutory,** *adj.*

Persephone /pəˈsɛfəni/, *n. Gk Myth.* daughter of Zeus and Demeter, kidnapped by Pluto (or Hades) to be his wife and queen of the lower world, but allowed to return every year. Also, *Latin,* **Proserpina.**

Persepolis /pəˈsɛpələs/, *n.* an ancient capital of Persia; its imposing ruins are in southern Iran, about 48 km north-east of Shiraz.

Perseus /ˈpɜsiəs/, *n. Gk Myth.* a hero, the son of Zeus and Danaë, who slew the gorgon Medusa, and afterwards saved Andromeda from a sea-monster.

persevere /pɜsəˈvɪə/, *v.i.,* **-vered, -vering.** to continue in anything undertaken; maintain a purpose in spite of difficulty or obstacles. [ME, from F, from L: continue steadfastly] —**perseverance,** *n.*

Persia /ˈpɜʒə/, *n.* **1.** an ancient empire situated in western and south-western Asia; at its peak it extended from Egypt and the Aegean to India; conquered by Alexander the Great,

334–331 BC. **2.** former official name (until 1935) of **Iran**. —**Persian**, *n., adj.*

Persian cat /ˌpɜːʒən 'kæt/, *n.* a variety of domestic cat with long, silky hair and bushy tail, probably originating in Persia.

Persian Gulf, *n.* an arm of the Arabian Sea, extending north-west between Arabia and Iran. About 966 km.

persiflage /'pɜːsəflɑːʒ/, *n.* **1.** light, bantering talk. **2.** a light style of treating a subject. [F: banter lightly]

persimmon /'pɜːsəmən, pə'sɪmən/, *n.* any of various trees of North America, with refreshing, plumlike fruit becoming sweet and able to be eaten when thoroughly ripe, and those of Japan and China, with soft, rich red or orange fruits. [Algonquian: (artificially) dried fruit]

persist /pə'sɪst/, *v.i.* **1.** to continue steadily or firmly in some state, purpose, course of action, etc., esp. in spite of opposition, etc. **2.** to last; endure. **3.** to be demanding in a statement or question. [L: to continue steadfastly] —**persistence**, *n.*

persistent /pə'sɪstənt/, *adj.* **1.** continuing, esp. in spite of opposition, etc.; persevering. **2.** lasting; enduring. **3.** continued; constantly repeated. —**persistence**, *n.*

person /'pɜːsən/, *n.* **1.** a human being, whether man, woman, or child: *the only person in sight.* **2.** a human being as different from an animal or thing. **3.** the actual self or individual personality of a human being. **4.** the living body of a human being, often including the clothes worn. **5.** the body in its outward aspect. **6.** *Gram.* (in some languages) a type of verb form and of pronoun grouping, showing differences between the speaker (**first person**), the one spoken to (**second person**), and anyone or anything else spoken of (**third person**), e.g.: *I* and *we* (first person), *you* (second person), and *he, she, it* and *they* (third person). The verb form is in the same person as the pronoun, as in *I swim* or *He swims.* **7.** **in person**, in one's own bodily presence: *to apply for a job in person.* [ME, from OF, from L: actor's mask, character acted, personage, being]

-person, a noun suffix used to avoid the mention or implication of sex, as in *chairman, salesman*; hence *chairperson, salesperson.*

persona /pɜː'sonə/, *n., pl.* **-nae** /-niː/. **1.** a person. **2.** (in the psychology of CG Jung) the outer or public personality, which is presented to the world and does not represent the inner personality. [L: mask]

personable /'pɜːsənəbəl/, *adj.* of pleasing personal appearance; comely; presentable.

personage /'pɜːsənɪdʒ/, *n.* **1.** a person of note or importance. **2.** any person. **3.** a character in a play, story, etc. [late ME, from OF]

personal /'pɜːsənəl/, *adj.* **1.** of or relating to a particular person; individual; private: *a personal matter.* **2.** relating to, directed to, or aimed at, a particular person: *a personal favor.* **3.** directed to a particular person in a belittling or offensive sense or manner: *personal remarks.* **4.** done, affected, held, etc., in person: *personal service.* **5.** relating to or characteristic of a person or self-conscious being. **6.** of the nature of an individual, reasoning being: *a personal God.* **7.** relating to the physical person or body: *personal cleanliness.* **8.** *Law.* marking or relating to property made up of movable goods, money, etc. (as distinct from *real*). **9. be personal**, to make belittling or insulting remarks about a person rather than talking about the actual question. **10. get personal**, to touch on secret or private matters. [ME, from L]

personal identification number, *n.* → **PIN**

personalise *or* **personalize** /'pɜːsənəlaɪz/, *v.t.*, **-lised**, **-lising**. **1.** to make personal. **2.** to mark (something) to show the name or initials of the owner.

personality /pɜːsə'næləti/, *n., pl.* **-ties**. **1.** a clearly marked or notable personal character: *a man with personality.* **2.** a person as a being formed of a grouping together of qualities. **3.** *Psychol.* (an organised pattern of) all the mental, emotional, social, etc., characteristics of a particular person. **4.** the quality of being a person; existence as a self-conscious being; personal identity. **5.** a well-known or outstanding person; celebrity.

personally /'pɜːsənəli/, *adv.* **1.** as regards onself: *Personally I don't care to go.* **2.** as an individual person: *He hates me personally.* **3.** in person. **4.** as if meant for one's own person: *Don't take his bluntness personally.*

personal pronoun, *n.* any one of the pronouns which indicate grammatical person (*I, we, thou, you, he, she, it, they*).

persona non grata /pɜːˌsoʊnə nɒn 'grɑːtə/, *n.* an unacceptable or unwelcome person. [L]

personate /'pɜːsəneɪt/, *v.t.*, **-nated**, **-nating**. **1.** to act or present (a character in a play, etc.). **2.** to take on the character or appearance of; pass oneself off as, esp. to deceive; impersonate. [LL] —**personation**, *n.* —**personative**, *adj.* —**personator**, *n.*

personification /pɜːˌsɒnəfə'keɪʃən/, *n.* **1.** the giving of personal nature or character to non-living objects or abstract notions, esp. as a rhetorical device, as in: *The book was begging to be opened.* **2.** *Art, etc.* the representation of a thing or abstraction in the form of a person. **3.** a person or thing representing a quality or the like; embodiment: *Hamlet is the personification of unhappiness.* **4.** an imaginary person or creature thought to represent a thing or abstraction: *A man with horns and a tail is the popular personification of the Devil.*

personify /pə'sɒnəfaɪ/, *v.t.*, **-fied**, **-fying**. **1.** to give a personal nature or character to (a non-living object or an idea), esp. in speech or writing. **2.** to represent (a thing or idea) in the form of a person, usu. in art. **3.** to express (a quality, idea, etc.) in a real person or thing. **4.** to be an example or expression of; typify. **5.** → **personate**. [PERSON + -(I)FY] —**personifier**, *n.*

personnel /ˌpɜsəˈnel/, n. the group of people employed in any work or service. [F, n. use of adj.]

perspective /pəˈspektɪv/, n. 1. the art of showing the three-dimensional quality of a scene, building, etc., on a flat surface. 2. the relation of parts to one another and to the whole, in a mental view or outlook. 3. a scene, esp. one stretching into the distance; vista. 4. the appearance of objects in relation to position, distance, etc. 5. **in perspective, a.** according to the laws of perspective. **b.** in true proportion. ◇adj. 6. of or relating to the art of perspective, or represented according to its laws. [ME, from ML: science of optics, from L: see through]

perspex /ˈpɜspeks/, n. a clear plastic resin, which is soft and easily moved when heated, used instead of glass in certain cases, as in framing pictures, etc. [Trademark]

perspicacious /ˌpɜspəˈkeɪʃəs/, adj. having keen mental powers of understanding and recognition; discerning. [*perspicaci(ty)* + -OUS] —**perspicacity**, n.

perspicuous /pəˈspɪkjuəs/, adj. 1. clear in expression or statement; lucid. 2. → **perspicacious.** [late ME, from L] —**perspicuousness**, n. —**perspicuity**, n.

perspiration /ˌpɜspəˈreɪʃən/, n. 1. the act or process of perspiring. 2. something that is perspired; sweat.

perspire /pəˈspaɪə/, v., **-spired, -spiring.** ◇v.i. 1. to get rid of a watery substance through the pores of the skin; sweat. ◇v.t. 2. to give out through the pores; exude. [L: breathe through] —**perspiration**, adj.

persuade /pəˈsweɪd/, v.t., **-suaded, -suading.** 1. to urge (a person, etc.), by advice, reasons, influence, etc., to do something: *We could not persuade him to wait.* 2. to cause to believe; convince. [L] —**persuasive**, adj. —**persuadable, persuasible**, adj. —**persuader**, n.

persuasion /pəˈsweɪʒən/, n. 1. the act of persuading or trying to persuade. 2. the power of persuading; persuasive force. 3. a belief; conviction. 4. (people having) a form or system of belief, esp. religious belief. 5. *Colloq.* a kind or sort: *of the heathen persuasion.* [ME, from L] —**persuasive**, adj.

pert /pɜt/, adj. 1. bold; forward; impertinent; impudent; saucy. 2. lively; sprightly; in good health. [ME, from OF]

pertain /pəˈteɪn/, v.i. 1. to have reference or relation; relate: *documents pertaining to the case.* 2. to belong or be joined to as a part, addition, possession, property, etc. (fol. by *to*). 3. to belong properly or fittingly; be appropriate. [ME, from OF, from L: extend, reach, relate]

Perth /pɜθ/, n. a city in, and the capital of, WA, in the south-western part, on the Swan River. Pop. 895 710 (1986).

pertinacious /ˌpɜtəˈneɪʃəs/, adj. 1. holding fast to a purpose, course of action, or opinion. 2. continued and often repeated: *pertinacious efforts.* [L] —**pertinacity**, n.

pertinent /ˈpɜtənənt/, adj. relating to the matter in hand; relevant; apposite: *pertinent details.* [ME, from L] —**pertinence, pertinency**, n.

perturb /pəˈtɜb/, v.t. 1. to disturb or disquiet greatly in mind; agitate. 2. to disturb greatly; throw into disorder or confusion; derange. [ME, from L *perturbāre*] —**perturbable**, adj. —**perturbation**, n.

Peru /pəˈru/, n. a republic in western South America on the Pacific Ocean, bordered by Ecuador, Colombia, Brazil, Bolivia and Chile; a Spanish colony before independence in 1826. Pop. 20 727 000 (1987 est.); 1 285 216 km². *Languages:* Spanish and Quechua. *Currency:* sol. *Cap.:* Lima. —**Peruvian**, n., adj.

peruse /pəˈruz/, v.t., **-rused, -rusing.** 1. to read through, esp. with thoroughness or care. 2. to read or study. [late ME] —**perusal**, n.

perv /pɜv/, *Colloq.* ◇n. 1. → **pervert.** ◇v.i. 2. to look at with sexual desire or longing (fol. by *on*). Also, **perve.**

pervade /pəˈveɪd/, v.t., **-vaded, -vading.** 1. to spread its presence, activities, influence, etc., throughout: *Spring pervaded the air.* 2. to go, pass, or spread through. [L] —**pervasion**, n. —**pervasive**, adj.

perverse /pəˈvɜs/, adj. 1. determined or likely to go against what is expected or desired; contrary. 2. marked by or coming from such a determination: *a perverse mood.* 3. wayward; cantankerous. 4. turned away from what is right, good, or proper; wicked. [ME, from L: turned the wrong way, awry] —**perverseness, perversity**, n. —**perversive**, adj.

perversion /pəˈvɜʒən/, n. 1. the act of perverting. 2. the state of being perverted. 3. a perverted form of something. 4. *Psychol.* an abnormal condition of the sexual impulses (**sexual perversion**). 5. *Pathol.* a change to what is unnatural or abnormal: *a perversion of function.*

pervert /pəˈvɜt/, v.; /ˈpɜvɜt/, n. ◇v.t. 1. to turn or lead away from the right course, either in moral or mental matters, judgments, etc. 2. to bring over to a religious belief regarded as false or wrong. 3. to turn to an improper use. 4. to change or twist out of shape; distort. 5. to bring to a less excellent state; vitiate or debase. 6. to affect with a perversion. ◇n. 7. *Psychol, Pathol.* someone affected with perversion. 8. someone who has been perverted. [ME, from L] —**perverter**, n. —**perverted**, adj.

pervious /ˈpɜviəs/, adj. 1. admitting a passage or entrance; permeable: *pervious soil.* 2. open to reason, feeling, etc. [L]

peseta /pəˈsetə, -ˈseɪ-/, n. the basic unit of currency in Spain.

peso /ˈpeɪsoʊ/, n. the basic unit of currency in Mexico, Cuba, and the Philippines. [Sp: weight, from L *pensum*, weight]

pessary /ˈpesəri/, n., pl. **-ries.** *Med.* 1. a device worn in the vagina to treat displacement of the uterus or stop conception from taking

pessary place. 2. a vaginal tablet placed so as to kill infection or prevent conception. [ME, from L, from Gk: orig., oval stone used in a game]

pessimism /'pesɪmɪzəm, 'pez-/, n. 1. the tendency of someone to take the worst possible view. 2. the belief that the existing world is the worst of all possible worlds, or that all things naturally tend to evil. 3. the belief that the evil and pain in the world are not made up for by the good and happiness. [L] —**pessimist**, n. —**pessimistic**, adj.

pest /pest/, n. 1. a harmful, destructive, or troublesome thing or person; nuisance. 2. a deadly disease spreading from person to person; pestilence, esp. the bubonic plague. 3. an organism harmful to crops, etc. [L: plague, disease]

pester /'pestə/, v.t. to trouble continually with unimportant annoyances, etc.; torment. [? OF: hobble (a horse)]

pesticide /'pestəsaɪd/, n. a chemical substance for destroying pests (def. 3), such as mosquitoes, flies, etc.

pestiferous /pes'tɪfərəs/, adj. 1. carrying or producing disease. 2. dangerous in any way. [L: plague-bringing]

pestilence /'pestələns/, n. 1. a deadly disease spread from person to person. 2. something that produces or tends to produce such a disease. 3. → **bubonic plague**. —**pestilential**, adj.

pestilent /'pestələnt/, adj. 1. (of a disease) infectious. 2. destructive to life; deadly; poisonous. 3. hurtful to peace, morals, etc. 4. troublesome or annoying. 5. dangerous or harmful. [ME, from L]

pestle /'pesəl/, n. an instrument for breaking up and grinding substances in a mortar (a bowl-shaped vessel made of hard material). [ME, from OF, from L: pounded]

pet¹ /pet/, n., adj., v., **petted, petting**. ◇n. 1. any animal living with humans that is cared for with warmth and liking. 2. a person treated as especially dear; a favorite. 3. a thing treated as particularly dear. ◇adj. 4. treated as a pet, as an animal. 5. treated as especially dear, and favored, as a child or other person. 6. favorite: *a pet theory*. 7. most important; principal: *pet aversion*. 8. showing affection: *a pet name*. ◇v.t. 9. to treat as a pet; fondle; indulge. 10. to pat or stroke fondly, or kiss, hold or touch someone. [? backformation from *pet lamb* hand reared lamb, itself ? shortened var. of *petty lamb* little lamb, where *petty* marks affection]

pet² /pet/, n., v., **petted, petting**. ◇n. 1. a fit of crossness; peevishness: *to be in a pet*. ◇v.i. 2. to be cross; sulk; be peevish. [apparently backformation from *pettish/petulant*]

Pétain /per'tæ/, n. **Henri Philippe** /ˌɒnri fi'lip/, 1856–1951, French general and politician; head of state for the Vichy government 1940–44; convicted of treason 1945.

petal /'petl/, n. one of the floral leaves of a flower, usu. delicate to touch and of some color other than green. [NL: petal, from Gk: leaf] —**petalled**, adj.

petard /pə'tɑd/, n. 1. a large weapon formerly used to explode or blow in a door or gate, form a break in a wall, etc. 2. a kind of firework. [F: break wind, explode, from L: break wind]

peter /'pitə/, v.i. to gradually become smaller or weaker and then disappear or cease (fol. by *out*). [orig. unknown]

Peter /'pitə/, n. Also, **Simon Peter** or **Saint Peter**. died AD 67?, one of the twelve apostles, a fisherman on the sea of Galilee; reputed author of two New Testament epistles bearing his name. 2. either of the two Epistles of Peter.

Peter I, n. ('*the Great*') 1672–1725, tsar of Russia 1682–1725.

Peterloo massacre /ˌpitəlu 'mæsəkə/, n. an incident at St Peter's Fields near Manchester, England, in 1819, when the crowd at a meeting calling for political and economic reform was charged by soldiers, and people were killed and injured. [*Peterloo*: (St) Peter('s Fields) + (WATER)LOO]

Peter Pan /pitə 'pæn/, n. the boy who didn't want to grow up, hero of the play *Peter Pan* (1904) by JM Barrie.

pethidine /'peθədin, -dən/, n. a painkilling drug, chemically similar to morphine.

petiole /'petioul/, n. *Bot.* a slender stalk by which a leaf is joined to the stem; a leafstalk. [F, from L: little foot, stem, stalk] —**petiolar**, adj.

petite /pə'tit/, adj. (of women) little; of small size; tiny. [F]

petite bourgeoisie /ˌpeti bʊəwa'zi/, n. the section of the middle class having least wealth, standing, etc., esp. shopkeepers, clerks, etc.

petition /pə'tɪʃən/, n. 1. a formally drawn-up request addressed to a person or a body of people in power, desiring some favor, right, mercy, or other benefit. 2. a request made for something desired, esp. a respectful or humble request, usu. to someone or those in power: *a petition for aid*. 3. something that is sought by request, etc. 4. *Law*. an application for an order of a court or for some action relating to the law. 5. a prayer, usu. to God.; supplication. ◇v.t. 6. to beg, usu. for something desired; supplicate; entreat. 7. to address a formal petition to (a ruler, a law-making body, etc.). 8. to ask by petition for (something) (fol. by *that*). ◇v.i. 9. to present a petition. 10. to address a formal petition. [ME, from L] —**petitionary**, adj. —**petitioner**, n.

petit mal /peti 'mæl/, n. a mild epilepsy in which the sufferer may lose consciousness or normal use of the body for up to thirty seconds. [F: little illness]

petit point /peti 'pɔɪnt/, n. a small diagonal stitch in embroidery worked over a single-thread canvas. [F: small point]

Petra /'petrə/, n. an ancient city in south-western Jordan; unusual ruined buildings, carved out of stratified rock of various colors.

petrel /'petrəl/, n. 1. a type of sea-bird, e.g. the mutton-bird. 2. → **storm-petrel**. [F]

Petri dish /'pitri dɪʃ/, n. a shallow, round, glass dish, used esp. for growing bacteria, etc. [named after JR *Petri*, died 1921, German biologist]

Petrie /'pitri/, n. **Sir Flinders**, 1853-1942, English Egyptologist and archaeologist.

petrify /'petrəfaɪ/, v., **-fied, -fying**. ◇v.t. **1.** to change into stone or a stony substance. **2.** to stiffen, or deaden; make inert; benumb; make rigid. **3.** to make stupid or deaden with great surprise, fear, or other strong emotion. ◇v.i. **4.** to become petrified. [F, from L: rock, stone, from Gk] **–petrifaction, n.**

petro-, a word part meaning 'stone' or 'rock'. [Gk, combining form of *pétra* rock, *pétros* stone]

petrogenesis /petrou'dʒɛnəsəs/, n. the mode of formation of rocks, esp. of igneous rocks.

Petrograd /'petrou,græd/, n. former name of St Petersburg (1914-24).

petrol /'petrəl/, n. a mixture of rapidly evaporating liquid hydrocarbons, used as a solvent and widely as a fuel in internal-combustion engines; gasoline. [F, from ML: PETROLEUM]

petroleum /pə'trouliəm/, n. **1.** Also, **rock-oil**. an oily, usu. dark-colored liquid (a mixture of various hydrocarbons), occurring naturally in various parts of the world, and commonly obtained by drilling. It is used (in its natural state or after certain treatment) as a fuel, or separated by distillation into petrol, paraffin products, etc. **2.** → **petrol**. [ML: rock oil] **–petrolic, adj.**

petroleum jelly, n. a soft or semi-solid oily substance obtained from petroleum, used as a basis for ointments, etc.

petrology /pə'trɒlədʒi/, n., pl. **-gies**. the scientific study of rocks, including their origin, structure, changes, etc. **–petrologist, n.**

Petrov Case /'petrɒf keɪs/, n. a controversy resulting from the defection of two Soviet Embassy officials in Canberra, Vladimir and Evdokia Petrov, in 1954; this led to a Royal Commission into Soviet espionage in Australia and to domestic political repercussions.

petticoat /'petikout/, n. **1.** an underskirt worn by women and girls; slip. ◇adj. **2.** female or feminine. [ME; see PETTY, COAT]

pettifog /'petifɒg/, v.i., **-fogged, -fogging**. **1.** to argue over small and unimportant details. **2.** to carry on an unimportant or deceitful law business. [backformation from *pettifogger*, from PETTY + *fogger* (of obscure orig.)] **–pettifogger, n. –pettifoggery, n.**

petty /'peti/, adj., **-tier, -tiest**. **1.** of small importance; trifling; trivial: *petty grievances*. **2.** of lesser or secondary importance, worth, etc. **3.** having or showing narrow ideas, interests, etc.: *petty minds*. **4.** mean or ungenerous in small or unimportant things: *a petty revenge*. [ME, from OF] **–pettily, adv. –pettiness, n.**

Petty /'peti/, n. **Bruce Leslie**, born 1929, Australian cartoonist and caricaturist.

petty cash, n. a small store of money set aside to meet additional expenses, esp. for office supplies.

petulant /'petʃələnt/, adj. moved to or showing sudden, impatient annoyance, esp. over some unimportant thing or event, etc.: *a petulant toss of the head*. [L: forward, pert, wanton] **–petulance, n.**

petunia /pə'tjunjə/, n. a type of plant native to tropical America but grown elsewhere, bearing funnel-shaped flowers of various colors. [NL, from Guarani: tobacco]

pew /pju/, n. **1.** (in a church) one of a group of fixed benchlike seats (with backs). **2.** *Colloq.* any chair; any place to sit down: *Take a pew*. [ME, from OF: balcony, from L: elevated place, balcony]

pewter /'pjutə/, n. **1.** any of various alloys in which tin is the chief part, originally one of tin and lead. **2.** a vessel or utensil made of such an alloy. ◇adj. **3.** consisting or made of pewter: *a pewter mug*. [ME, from OF; orig. uncert.] **–pewterer, n.**

p.f., *Music*. *Abbrev*. **1.** pianoforte (piano). **2.** soft followed by loud; 'piano' followed by 'forte'. [It]

pH /pi 'eɪtʃ/, n. a measure of acidity or alkalinity, as of soil, water, etc., on a scale, running from 1 (extreme acidity) to 14 (extreme alkalinity), equal to the negative logarithm of the concentration of the hydrogen ion in gram atoms per litre. So a pH of 5 indicates a concentration of 10^{-5} gram atoms of hydrogen ions in one litre.

phaeton /'feɪtən/, n. **1.** a light four-wheeled carriage, usu. having two seats facing forward. **2.** (*cap.*) *Class. Myth.* the son of Helios, the sun-god. For one day he was allowed to drive his father's chariot, but drove too near earth, and had not Zeus killed him with a thunderbolt, would have set the world on fire. [F, from L, from Gk: lit., shining]

-phage, a word part meaning 'eating', 'devouring'. [F, from L, from Gk *-phagos*]

phago-, a word part corresponding to *-phage*. [Gk]

-phagous, a word part used as an adjective ending meaning 'eating', 'feeding on', 'devouring'. [L, from Gk]

-phagy, a word part used as a noun ending meaning 'eating', 'devouring', esp. as a practice or habit. [Gk]

phalanger /fə'lændʒə/, n. any of many tree-living marsupials of Australia, most having tails which can wrap around branches, and including brush-tailed possums and cuscuses. [NL, from Gk: bone of finger or toe; with reference to the webbed digits of the hind feet]

phalanx /'fælæŋks/, n., pl. **phalanxes** /'fælæŋksəz/, **phalanges** /fə'lændʒiz/. **1.** (in ancient Greece) a body of heavily armed foot soldiers in close formation with shields joined and long spears overlapping. **2.** a closely grouped body of people, animals, or things. **3.** a number of people, etc., united for a common purpose. [L, from Gk]

phallus /'fæləs/, n., pl. **phalluses, phalli** /'fælaɪ/. an image of the erect male penis, standing for the reproductive power of nature

phallus in some religious systems. [L, from Gk] – **phallic**, *adj.*

-phane, a word part indicating apparent likeness to some particular substance. [Gk]

phantasm /'fæntæzəm/, *n.* **1.** a ghostly appearance; apparition. **2.** a creation of the imagination or fancy. **3.** a seeming likeness of something. **4.** a mental image or representation of a real object. [LL, from Gk] – **phantasmal**, *adj.*

phantasmagoria /fæn,tæzmə'gɔriə/, *n.* **1.** a changing series of phantasms, or unreal happenings, as in a dream or as produced by the imagination. **2.** a changing scene made up of many parts. **3.** a series of changing scenes, as where figures change in size, melt away, pass into each other, etc. [NL, from Gk] – **phantasmagorial, phantasmagoric, phantasmagorical**, *adj.*

phantom /'fæntəm/, *n.* **1.** an image appearing in a dream or formed in the mind. **2.** a ghostly appearance. **3.** a thing or person that is little more than an appearance or show. **4.** an appearance without material substance. ◇*adj.* **5.** of the nature of a phantom; unreal; illusive; spectral. [ME, from OF, from LL PHANTASM]

-phany, a noun ending meaning 'appearance', 'manifestation', as of a god or a supernatural being, as in *epiphany*. [Gk]

Pharaoh /'fɛəroʊ/, *n.* the title of the ancient Egyptian kings. [OE *Pharao*, from L, from Gk, from Heb, from Egyptian: great house] – **Pharaonic**, *adj.*

pharisee /'færəsi/, *n.* **1.** a person who strictly observes the outer forms and ceremonies of religion without following its spirit. **2.** (*cap.*) one of an ancient Jewish sect which observed strictly the traditions and the written law, seeking its interpretation, its members attempting self-perfection for the coming of the Messiah. [ME and OE *farisē*, from L: from Gk, from Aram: separated] – **pharisaism**, *n.* – **pharisaic**, *adj.*

Phar Lap /'fɑ læp/, *n.* an Australian racehorse, born in NZ; won the Melbourne Cup in 1930 in spite of a heavy handicap.

pharmaceutical /famə'sjutɪkəl/, *adj.* relating to pharmacy. Also, **pharmaceutic**. [L, from Gk]

pharmaceutics /famə'sjutɪks/, *n.* → pharmacy (def. 1). [orig. pl. of *pharmaceutic*]

pharmacist /'faməsəst/, *n.* a professional person who prepares and dispenses drugs and medicines.

pharmacology /famə'kɒlədʒi/, *n.* the science of drugs, their properties, uses, and effects. [NL, from Gk] – **pharmacological**, *adj.* – **pharmacologist**, *n.*

pharmacopoeia /faməkə'piə/, *n.* a book containing a list of medicinal drugs with their preparation, properties, uses, etc. [NL, from Gk: art of preparing drugs] – **pharmacopoeial**, *adj.*

pharmacy /'faməsi/, *n., pl.* **-cies.** **1.** Also **pharmaceutics.** the practice of preparing and dispensing medicinal drugs. **2.** a chemist's shop. [LL, from Gk: the practice of a druggist]

Pharos /'fɛərɒs/, *n.* **1.** a small peninsula in northern Egypt at Alexandria; in ancient times it was an island on which a lighthouse was built. **2.** this lighthouse, one of the Seven Wonders of the World.

pharyngo-, a word part meaning 'pharynx'. [Gk: throat]

pharynx /'færɪŋks/, *n., pl.* **pharynges** /fə'rɪndʒiz/, **pharynxes.** the tube, with its surrounding membrane and muscles, which connects the mouth and nose passages with the oesophagus. [NL, from Gk: throat] – **pharyngeal**, *adj.*

phase /feɪz/, *n., v.,* **phased, phasing.** ◇*n.* **1.** any of the appearances in which a thing of varying states shows itself to the eye or mind. **2.** a stage of change or development. **3.** the particular appearance presented by the moon or a planet, etc., at a given time. **4.** *Biol.* an aspect of or stage in meiosis or mitosis. **5.** *Zool.* any of the stages of development of certain animals which take on a different color according to the breeding condition. **6.** *Chem, Phys.* a physically separate, homogeneous part of a mixed system: *the solid, liquid, and gaseous phases of a substance.* **7.** *Phys, Elect.* a particular stage or point of advancement of a wave cycle. **8. out of phase**, not working or happening together. ◇*v.t.* **9.** to plan or arrange in phases. **10.** to introduce (into a system or the like) in stages. ◇*v.* **11. phase in**, to introduce gradually and fit into a system or the like. **12. phase out**, to take out gradually from a system. [backformation from *phases*, pl. of Gk *phasis*] – **phaser**, *n.*

phase shift, *n.* **1.** a change of phase in a wave form. **2.** that part of one cycle of a wave form by which the wave form has been delayed.

phase velocity, *n. Phys.* (of a wave) the velocity of the wavefronts.

-phasia, a word part referring to disordered speech, as in *aphasia*. Also, **-phasy**. [Gk: speak]

pheasant /'fɛzənt/, *n., pl.* **pheasants**, (*esp. collectively*) **pheasant.** any of various large, long-tailed, usu. attractively-colored birds originally native to Asia, and raised for eating or for their ornamental value in Australia. [ME, from AF, var. of OF, from Pr, from L, from Gk: Phasian (bird)]

phen-, a word part used in chemical terms to indicate derivation from benzene, sometimes used with particular reference to phenol. Also, before consonants, **pheno-**. [Gk: shining; with reference orig. to products from the manufacture of illuminating gas]

phenobarbitone /fɛnə'babətoʊn/, *n.* a barbiturate in the form of a white, odorless powder which causes sleepiness. Also, **phenobarbital** /fɛnə'babətl/.

phenol /'finɒl/, *n.* carbolic acid, C_6H_5OH, or any similar derivative of benzene used as a disinfectant, antiseptic, and in organic synthesis. [PHEN- + -OL[1]] – **phenolic**, *adj.*

phenolphthalein /ˌfinəl'θælin, ˌfinəl'fθælin, -θeɪl-, -iən/, n. a white crystalline compound, used as an indicator in acid-base titration.

phenomena /fə'nɒmənə/, n. plural of **phenomenon**.

phenomenal /fə'nɒmənəl/, adj. **1.** out of or above the bounds of the ordinary. **2.** of or relating to a phenomenon or phenomena.

phenomenalism /fə'nɒmənəlɪzəm/, n. Philos. **1.** the manner of thinking that considers things as phenomena only. See **positivism**. **2.** the philosophical theory that phenomena are the only objects of knowledge, or the only realities.

phenomenon /fə'nɒmənən/, n., pl. **-na** /-nə/. **1.** a fact or happening observed or observable: *the phenomena of nature*. **2.** something that seems beyond the ordinary to the observer; a remarkable thing or person. **3.** Philos. an appearance or immediate object of awareness in experience. [LL, from Gk: (that which is) appearing]

phenotype /'finoutaɪp/, n. the observable hereditary characters arising from the interaction of the genotype and its environment. [PHENO(MENON) + TYPE]

phenyl /'fɛnəl, 'finəl/, n. a univalent radical, C_6H_5, from benzene. [F]

pheromone /'fɛrəmoun/, n. any of a large group of compounds produced by animals, esp. insects, in response to sex, food, etc., and used as a chemical means of communication. [Gk]

phew /fju/, interj. (an exclamation of impatience, tiredness, surprise, relief, etc.).

phial /'faɪəl/, n. a small vessel usu. of glass, for liquids. [ME, from OF, from LL, from Gk: saucer-like drinking vessel]

Phidias /'fidiəs/, n. c. 500–c. 432 BC, Greek sculptor; sculpted the *Athena Parthenos* of the Parthenon and the great statue of Zeus at Olympia, one of the Seven Wonders of the World.

phil-, a word part meaning 'loving', as in *philanthropy*. Also, **philo-**. [Gk, combining form of *phílos* loving, dear]

-phil, a word part meaning 'loving', 'friendly', or 'lover', 'friend', serving to form adjectives and nouns, as *Anglophil*, *bibliophil*. Also, **-phile**. [L, from Gk: dear, beloved, occurring in proper names]

Philadelphia /filə'dɛlfiə/, n. a city in the US, in south-eastern Pennsylvania, on the Delaware River. Pop. 1 640 102 (1985).

philander /fə'lændə/, v.i. (of a man) to carry on flirtations. [Gk: man-loving (person), later used in fiction as proper name, given to a lover] —**philanderer**, n.

philanthropy /fə'lænθrəpi/, n., pl. **-pies**. **1.** love of mankind, esp. as shown in deeds of practical giving. **2.** an action or work based on philanthropy. [LL, from Gk] —**philanthropist**, n. —**philanthropic**, adj.

philately /fə'lætəli/, n. the collecting and study of postage stamps, stamped envelopes, postmarks, postcards, covers and similar material. [F] —**philatelic, philatelical**, adj. —**philatelist**, n.

-phile, a variant of **-phil**.

philharmonic /ˌfilhɑ'mɒnɪk, ˌfiləmɒnɪk/, adj. fond of music; music-loving, used esp. in the name of certain musical societies and their concerts. [F]

-philia, a word part used as a noun ending meaning 'fondness', 'strong desire' or 'attraction'. [NL, from Gk: loving]

Philip /'filəp/, n. **1.** one of the twelve apostles. **2.** Prince (*Duke of Edinburgh*), born 1921, husband of Queen Elizabeth II of England.

Philip II, n. 382–336 BC, king of Macedonia 359–336 (father of Alexander the Great).

philippic /fə'lɪpɪk/, n. any speech of bitter attack. [from the speeches of Demosthenes, 384–322 BC, Athenian orator, attacking *Philip*, King of Macedon; L, from Gk: relating to Philip]

Philippines /'filəpinz/, n. **the**, a republic in the western Pacific Ocean, consisting of an archipelago of which the main islands are Luzon and Mindanao; a Spanish colony before being ceded to the US after the Spanish-American War (1898); an independent republic since 1946. Pop. 53 357 000 (1987 est.). 300 000 km². *Languages*: Pilipino and English, also Cebuano, Ilocano and other local languages. *Currency*: peso. *Cap.*: Manila.

philistine /'filəstam/, n. **1.** someone looked down upon as lacking in and insensitive to culture, etc., or contentedly ordinary in ideas and tastes. ◇adj. **2.** lacking in culture; commonplace. [named after a native or inhabitant of *Philistia*, an ancient country on the east coast of the Mediterranean; ME, from LL, from LGk, from Heb] —**philistinism**, n.

Phillip /'filəp/, n. Arthur, 1738–1814, British naval officer; captain general of the First Fleet and founder of a settlement in NSW; first governor of the new colony 1788–92.

Phillip Island, n. an island lying across the entrance to Westernport in southern Vic; tourist resort. 100 km². [named after Arthur PHILLIP]

philo-, a variant of **phil-**, before consonants, as in *philosopher*.

philodendron /ˌfilə'dɛndrən/, n. a tropical American climbing plant usu. with smooth, shiny, evergreen leaves, often used as an ornamental house plant. [NL]

philology /fə'lɒlədʒi/, n. **1.** the study of written records. **2.** linguistics. [ME, from L, from Gk: love of learning and literature] —**philologist**, n. —**philologic**, adj.

Philomela /filou'milə/, n. Gk Legend. the daughter of a king of Athens; turned into a nightingale after her brother-in-law raped her and cut out her tongue.

philosopher /fə'lɒsəfə/, n. **1.** someone who is well read in philosophy. **2.** a person whose life, actions, judgments, etc., are determined by the light of philosophy or reason. **3.** a person who is calm and reasoned, esp. in

philosopher difficult times. [ME, from AF, from L, Gk: lover of wisdom]

philosopher's stone, *n.* an imaginary substance once believed able to change other metals into gold or silver.

philosophical /filə'sɒfikəl/, *adj.* **1.** of or relating to philosophy: *philosophical studies*. **2.** versed in or occupied with philosophy, as people. **3.** proper to or befitting a philosopher. **4.** rationally or sensibly calm in trying circumstances: *a philosophical acceptance of necessity*. **5.** (formerly) of or relating to natural philosophy or physical science. Also, **philosophic**.

philosophise *or* **philosophize** /fə'lɒsəfaɪz/, *v.i.* **-phised, -phising.** to reason, theorise or moralise. – **philosophiser**, *n.*

philosophy /fə'lɒsəfi/, *n., pl.* **-phies. 1.** the study or science of the truths or principles underlying all knowledge and being, including natural, moral and metaphysical philosophy. **2.** any system of philosophical principles: *the philosophy of Spinoza*. **3.** the study or science of the principles of a particular branch or subject of knowledge: *the philosophy of history*. **4.** a system of principles for guidance in practical affairs. [ME, from L, from Gk: lit., love of wisdom]

-philous, a word part used as an adjective ending meaning 'loving'. [L, from Gk]

Philp /'fɪlp/, *n.* **Sir Robert**, 1851–1922, Australian shipping agent and politician, born in Scotland; premier of Qld 1899–1903. See **Burns, Philp and Co Ltd**.

philtre /'fɪltə/, *n.* a potion, drug, or the like, supposed to bring about love. [F, from L, from Gk: love charm]

phlebo-, a word part meaning 'vein'. Also, before a vowel, **phleb-**. [Gk: vein]

phlegm /flɛm/, *n.* **1.** *Physiol.* the thick mucus produced in the breathing passages and discharged by coughing, etc., esp. during a cold, etc. **2.** (formerly) that one of the four humors supposed to cause a general lack of energy or interest. [ME, from OF, from LL, from Gk: flame, clammy humor]

phlegmatic /flɛg'mætɪk/, *adj.* **1.** not easily excited to action or feeling; sluggish or apathetic. **2.** cool or self-possessed. [LL, from Gk]

phloem /'floʊəm/, *n.* (in plants) that part of the cell tissue which carries food within the plant. [G, from Gk]

phlox /flɒks/, *n.* a plant from North America grown for its showy flowers of various colors. [L, from Gk: kind of plant, orig., flame]

Phnom Penh /ˌpnɒm 'pɛn/, *n.* a city in south-east Asia, the capital of Cambodia. Pop. 600 000 (1983). Also, **Pnom Penh**. Khmer, **Phnum Pénh**.

-phobe, a word part used as a noun ending meaning 'one who fears or dreads' and often suggesting hatred, as in *Anglophobe*. [F, from L: fearing, from Gk]

phobia /'foʊbiə/, *n.* any fear or dread which controls a person's mind. [independent use of -PHOBIA] – **phobic**, *adj.*

-phobia, a word part used as a noun ending meaning 'fear' or 'dread' often with the added sense of hatred, as in *hydrophobia*. [L, from Gk]

Phoenicia /fə'nɪʃə/, *n.* an ancient maritime country on the east coast of the Mediterranean. – **Phoenician**, *n., adj.*

phoenix /'finɪks/, *n.* a mythical bird of great beauty, said to have burned itself on a funeral pile, and to have risen afresh from its ashes to live again. Also, **Phoenix**. [ME and OE *fēnix*, from ML, from Gk]

phon-, a word part meaning 'voice', 'sound'. Also, **phono-**. [Gk, combining form of *phōnē*]

phone /foʊn/, *n. Colloq.* → **telephone**. [short for TELEPHONE]

-phone, a word part meaning 'sound', esp. used in names of instruments, as in *xylophone, megaphone, telephone*. [combining form representing Gk *phōnē*]

phoneme /'foʊnim/, *n.* the smallest distinctive group or class of speech sounds in a language. The phonemes of a language contrast with one another; e.g., in English, *pip* differs from *nip, tip*, etc., by contrast of a phoneme (p) with other phonemes. [Gk: a sound] – **phonemic**, *adj.* – **phonemics**, *n.*

phonetic /fə'nɛtɪk/, *adj.* **1.** of or relating to speech sounds and their production. **2.** agreeing with or corresponding to pronunciation: *phonetic transcription*. Also, **phonetical**. [NL, from Gk]

phonetics /fə'nɛtɪks/, *n.* **1.** the science of speech sounds and their production. **2.** the phonetic system, or the body of phonetic facts, of a particular language. – **phonetician**, *n.*

phoney /'foʊni/, *adj.*, **-nier, -niest**, *n., pl.* **-nies** *or* **-neys**. *Colloq.* ⋄*adj.* **1.** (of a person or thing) false; fraudulent. ⋄*n.* **2.** a person or thing whose appearance, claims, etc., are false or insincere; fake. Also, **phony**. [Irish]

phonics /'fɒnɪks/, *n.* a method of teaching reading, pronunciation, and spelling based upon the phonetic interpretation of ordinary spelling.

phono-, a variant of **phon-**, before consonants, as in *phonogram*.

phonogram /'foʊnəgræm/, *n.* a telegram phoned to a person. – **phonogramic**, *adj.*

phonograph /'foʊnəgræf, -graf/, *n. Now only US.* → **record-player**.

phonology /fə'nɒlədʒi/, *n.* **1.** phonetics or phonemics, or both together. **2.** the body of phonetic and phonemic facts of a language. – **phonologic, phonological**, *adj.*

phony /'foʊni/, *adj.*, **-nier, -niest**, *n., pl.* **-nies**. → **phoney**.

-phony, a word part used in abstract nouns related to **-phone**, as in *telephony*. [Gk]

phooey /'fui/, *Colloq. interj.* an exclamation indicating disbelief, dismissal, etc. [var. of PHEW]

-phore, a word part used as a noun ending meaning 'thing or part bearing (something)', as in *ommatophore*. [NL, from Gk: bearing]

-phorous, a word part used as an adjective ending meaning 'bearing', 'having'. [NL, from Gk: bearing]

phosph-, a variant of **phospho-**, before vowels, as in *phosphate*.

phosphate /'fɒsfeɪt/, *n.* **1.** *Chem.* See **-ate**[2]. **2.** *Agric.* a fertiliser containing compounds of phosphorus. [F] **— phosphatic**, *adj.*

phospho-, a word part representing phosphorus. Also, **phosph-**.

phosphor /'fɒsfə/, *n.* a substance which is able to store energy from ultra-violet or other ionising radiations, and release it later as light; any substance which has luminescence. [See PHOSPHORUS]

phosphoresce /fɒsfə'rɛs/, *v.i.*, **-resced, -rescing.** to give out light with little or no heat, as phosphorus. [PHOSPHOR(US) + -ESCE]

phosphorescence /fɒsfə'rɛsəns/, *n.* the property and appearance of being luminous at temperatures below white heat, as from slow oxidation, in the case of phosphorus, or after exposure to light or other radiation. **— phosphorescent**, *adj.*

phosphoric /fɒs'fɒrɪk/, *adj.* containing phosphorus, esp. in its pentavalent state.

phosphoric acid, *n.* any of three acids, but usu. that with the formula H_3PO_4.

phosphorite /'fɒsfəraɪt/, *n.* a massive form of the mineral apatite, which is the main source of phosphate for fertilisers.

phosphorous /'fɒsfərəs, -frəs/, *adj.* containing phosphorus with a valence of 3.

phosphorus /'fɒsfərəs/, *n., pl.* **-ri** /-raɪ/. *Chem.* a solid non-metallic element in three allotropic forms: white or yellow (poisonous, flammable, and phosphorescent); red (less reactive and less poisonous); black (electrically conducting, insoluble in most solvents). Compounds of phosphorus are found in all plants and animals and are used in matches, fertilisers, etc. *Symbol:* P; *at. no.:* 15; *at. wt:* 30.9738. [NL, special use of L: the morning star, from Gk: light-bringer]

photic /'foutɪk/, *adj.* **1.** of or relating to light. **2.** relating to the production of light by organisms, or their excitation by means of light.

photo /'foutou/, *n., pl.* **-tos.** → **photograph**.

photo-, **1.** a word part meaning 'light' (sometimes used to represent 'photographic' or 'photograph'). **2.** a word part meaning liberated by light or other radiation, as *photoelectron*. [Gk, combining form of *phôs* light]

photocopy /'foutoukɒpi/, *n., pl.* **-copies**, *v.*, **-copied, -copying.** *— n.* **1.** a photographic reproduction of written or printed material. *— v.t.* **2.** to make a photocopy of. **— photocopier**, *n.*

photoelectric /ˌfoutouə'lɛktrɪk/, *adj.* relating to the electrical effects produced by light. Also, **photoelectrical**.

photoelectric cell, *n.* a device used for the detection and measuring of light.

photoelectron /ˌfoutouə'lɛktrɒn/, *n.* an electron liberated from a substance due to the effect of light radiation.

photoengraving /ˌfoutouən'greɪvɪŋ/, *n.* the process of reproducing photographs on printing plates.

photo finish, *n.* a close race in which the decision is made from a photograph at the finishing line.

photogenic /foutə'dʒɛnɪk, -'dʒɪnɪk/, *adj. Photog.* being a good subject for photography, esp. said of a person.

photograph /'foutəgræf, -graf/, *n.* **1.** a picture produced by photography. *◇v.t.* **2.** to take a photograph of. *◇v.i.* **3.** to appear in a certain way in a photograph: *Do you photograph well?*

photographic /foutə'græfɪk/, *adj.* **1.** of or relating to photography. **2.** (of memory, description, etc.) very realistic and detailed: *a photographic memory.*

photography /fə'tɒgrəfi/, *n.* the process or art of producing images of objects on sensitised surfaces by the chemical action of light or of other forms of radiant energy, as X-rays, etc. **— photographer**, *n.*

photogravure /foutəgrə'vjuə/, *n.* any of various processes, based on photography, by which a figured engraving is formed on a metal plate, from which ink reproductions are made. [F]

photolithograph /foutou'lɪθəgræf, -graf/, *n.* **1.** a lithograph printed from a stone, etc., upon which a picture or design has been formed by photography. *◇v.t.* **2.** to make a photolithograph of. **— photolithography**, *n.*

photolysis /fou'tɒləsəs/, *n.* the breakdown of materials under the influence of light. [NL, from Gk] **— photolytic**, *adj.*

photon /'foutɒn/, *n.* a quantum of light energy, which is proportional to the frequency of the radiation. [PHOTO-; modelled on ELECTRON, PROTON]

photosphere /'foutousfɪə/, *n. Astron.* the luminous envelope of gas surrounding the sun. **— photospheric**, *adj.*

photostat /'foutəstæt/, *n.* **1.** a special camera for making exact copies of maps, drawings, pages of books, etc., which photographs directly as a positive on sensitised paper. **2.** a copy or photograph made with such a camera. *◇v.t., v.i.* **3.** to make a photostat copy or copies (of). *◇adj.* **4.** Also, **photostatic**. relating to such a camera or copy. [Trademark]

photosynthesis /foutou'sɪnθəsəs/, *n.* the synthesis of carbohydrates by plants from carbon dioxide and water in the presence of light and chlorophyll (the catalyst). [NL. See PHOTO-, SYNTHESIS] **— photosynthetic**, *adj.*

phototaxis /foutou'tæksəs/, *n.* the movement of an organism towards or away from light. Also, **phototaxy**. [NL. See PHOTO-, -TAXIS]

phototropic /foʊtoʊˈtrɒpɪk/, *adj.* **1.** taking a particular direction under the influence of light. **2.** growing towards or away from the light. **—phototropism**, *n.*

photovoltaic /ˌfoʊtoʊvɒlˈteɪk/, *adj.* providing a source of electric current under the influence of light or similar radiation.

phrasal verb /ˈfreɪzəl ˈvɜːb/, *n.* a verb phrase consisting of a verb and a particle which together have meaning as a unit; in *How much did he put in?*, the words *put* and *in* together make a phrasal verb with the sense of *contribute*.

phrase /freɪz/, *n., v.,* **phrased, phrasing.** ◇*n.* **1.** *Gram.* **a.** group of two or more words arranged in a grammatical construction. **b.** such a group without a finite verb and acting as a unit within a clause. **2.** a way of speaking. **3.** an expression, sometimes having special interest or importance. **4.** a short remark. **5.** *Music.* a group of notes forming a recognisable pattern. ◇*v.t.* **6.** to express or word in a particular way. [backformation from *phrases*, pl. of LL *phrasis*, from Gk: speech, phraseology, expression] **—phrasal,** *adj.*

phraseology /ˌfreɪziˈɒlədʒi/, *n.* **1.** the manner or style of verbal expression; characteristic language: *the phraseology of lawyers.* **2.** phrases or expressions: *medical phraseology.* [NL, from Gk] **—phraseological,** *adj.*

phratry /ˈfreɪtri/, *n., pl.* **-tries.** a grouping of clans or other social units within a tribe. [Gk *phratría*]

phrenetic /frəˈnɛtɪk/, *adj.* → **frenetic.** [ME, from OF, from L, from LGk]

phrenology /frəˈnɒlədʒi/, *n.* the theory that one's mental powers are shown by the shape of the skull. [Gk] **—phrenologist,** *n.*

phylactery /fəˈlæktəri/, *n., pl.* **-teries.** either of two small leather cases containing slips written with certain texts from the Scripture, worn by Jews during prayer to remind them to keep the law. [LL, from Gk: outpost, safeguard, amulet]

-phyll, a word part used as a noun ending meaning 'leaf', as in *chlorophyll*. Also, **-phyl.** [Gk]

phyllo-, a word part meaning 'leaf'. Also, before vowels, **phyll-.** [Gk, combining form of *phýllon*]

phyllode /ˈfɪloʊd/, *n.* a larger petiole resembling and having the function of, a leaf. [F, from NL, from Gk: leaf-like]

-phyllous, a word part used as an adjective ending meaning 'having leaves', 'leaved', or suggesting some connection with a leaf. [Gk: pertaining to a leaf]

phylo-, a word part meaning 'tribe'. [Gk]

phylogeny /faɪˈlɒdʒəni/, *n., pl.* **-nies.** the development or evolution of a kind of animal or plant; racial history. Also, **phylogenesis** /ˌfaɪloʊˈdʒɛnəsəs/. **—phylogenetic, phylogenic,** *adj.*

phylum /ˈfaɪləm/, *n., pl.* **-la** /-lə/. *Biol.* the primary division of the animal or vegetable kingdom, as the arthropods, molluscs, spermatophytes. [NL, from Gk: race, tribe]

-phyre, a word part used to form names of porphyritic rocks, as in *granophyre*. [Gk: porphyry]

phys. ed., *Abbrev.* physical education.

physic /ˈfɪzɪk/, *n.* **1.** a medicine, esp. one which causes the bowels to empty. **2.** *Archaic.* the medical profession. [ME, from ML, from Gk: science of nature]

physical /ˈfɪzəkəl, ˈfɪzɪkəl/, *adj.* **1.** relating to the body; bodily: *physical exercise.* **2.** of or relating to material nature; material. **3.** indicating or relating to the properties of matter and energy other than those that are chemical or peculiar to living matter; relating to physics. [ME, from ML: PHYSIC]

physical chemistry, *n.* that branch of chemistry which deals with the relations between the physical and chemical properties of substances.

physical education, *n.* instruction given in exercises, sports, etc., for the development and health of the body.

physical geography, *n.* that part of geography concerned with natural features of the earth's surface, as land forms, drainage features, climates, ocean currents, soils, vegetation, and animal life.

physical science, *n.* the study of natural laws and processes other than those dealing with living matter, as in physics, chemistry, etc. See **natural science.**

physician /fəˈzɪʃən/, *n.* **1.** a person legally qualified to practise medicine. **2.** a person working in general medicine (diagnosis, treatment with drugs, etc.) as opposed to surgery. **3.** someone skilled in the art of healing. [ME, from OF, from ML: PHYSIC]

physicist /ˈfɪzəsəst/, *n.* a person trained in physics and its methods.

physics /ˈfɪzɪks/, *n.* the science dealing with natural laws and properties of matter and energy, other than those limited to living matter and chemical changes. [pl. of PHYSIC]

physio-, a word part representing **physical, physics.** [Gk: nature]

physiognomy /ˌfɪziˈɒnəmi/, *n., pl.* **-mies.** **1.** the facial features, esp. as considered as a guide to character. **2.** the art of determining personal characteristics from the facial features or body form. **3.** the general or characteristic appearance of anything. [Gk: the judging of one's nature] **—physiognomic, physiognomical,** *adj.* **—physiognomist,** *n.*

physiology /ˌfɪziˈɒlədʒi/, *n.* the science dealing with the working of living organisms or their parts. [L, from Gk] **—physiologist,** *n.* **—physiological,** *adj.*

physiotherapy /ˌfɪzioʊˈθɛrəpi/, *n.* the treatment of disease or bodily weaknesses by physical means, such as massage, exercise, etc. **—physiotherapist,** *n.*

physique /fəˈziːk/, *n.* **1.** human bodily structure or type: *a good muscular physique.* **2.** *Geog.* the structure or type of a given area. [F, from L, from Gk]

-phyte, a word part used as a noun ending meaning 'a growth', 'plant', as in *epiphyte*. [combining form representing Gk *phytón*]

phyto-, a word part meaning 'plant'. Also, before vowels, **phyt-**. [Gk: plant]

phytophthora /faɪˈtɒfθərə/, *n.* **1.** a group of destructive parasitic fungi which attack the roots of plants and trees. **2.** the disease caused by such a fungus. [NL, from Gk: destructive]

pi /paɪ/, *n., pl.* **pis**. **1.** the 16th letter (Π, π) of the Greek alphabet. **2.** *Maths.* (the letter π, used as the symbol for) the ratio (3.141 592 +) of the circumference of a circle to its diameter. [Gk]

Piaf /piˈaf/, *n.* Edith /ˈidəθ/ (*Edith Giovanna Gassion*), 1914–63, French singer.

pianissimo /piəˈnɪsəmoʊ/, *adv.* (a musical direction) very softly. *Abbrev.* pp. [It, from L]

piano[1] /piˈænoʊ, piˈanoʊ/, *n.* **1.** a musical instrument in which hammers, operated from a keyboard, strike upon metal strings. **2. grand piano,** a piano with a harp-shaped body supported horizontally. **3. upright piano,** a piano with a rectangular body placed vertically. [It, short for *pianoforte* or *fortepiano* PIANOFORTE] **–pianist,** *n.*

piano[2] /piˈanoʊ/, *adv.* (a musical direction) softly. *Abbrev.* p. [It, from L: PLAIN]

piano accordion, *n.* an accordion having a piano-like keyboard for the right hand.

pianoforte /piænoʊˈfɔːteɪ, pianoʊ-/, *n.* → **piano**[1]. [It]

pianola /piəˈnoʊlə/, *n.* → **player piano**. [Trademark]

piano roll, *n.* a roll of paper prepared for use on a player piano.

piazza /piˈætsə, -a-/, *n., pl.* **piazzas**. **1.** an open square or public place in a city or town. **2.** an arcade or covered walk, as around a public square or in front of a building. [It, from L, from Gk: broad street]

pica /ˈpaɪkə/, *n.* **1.** (in printing) a size of type, about 12 point. **2.** the height of this type size (4.22 mm). [AL: book of rules for church services]

picador /ˈpɪkədɔː/, *n.* one of the horsemen who goad a bullfight by annoying and enraging the bull by pricking it with lances. [Sp: prick, pierce]

Picardy /ˈpɪkədi/, *n.* a region in northern France, comprising the departments of Somme, Oise, and Aisne; formerly a province. Pop. 1 774 000 (1986 est.); 19 635 km². *Cap.*: Amiens. French, **Picardie**.

picaresque /pɪkəˈrɛsk/, *adj.* of or relating to the not-too-wicked and usu. playful misdeeds of adventure-seeking wanderers. [F, from Sp: rogue, from F: native of Picardy]

Picasso /pəˈkæsoʊ, -ˈkasoʊ/, *n.* Pablo /ˈpæbloʊ/, 1881–1973, Spanish painter and sculptor, a resident of France, who, with Braque and others, developed cubism; during the 1930s he made increasing use of surrealism and symbolic archetypes.

picayune /pɪkeɪˈjun/, *n., adj. Colloq.* (a person or thing) of little value or worth. [from *picayune*, a Spanish coin, formerly used in some southern states of the US, from F, from Pr, from L: money]

piccaninny /ˈpɪkənɪni/, *n., pl.* **-nies**. **1.** a Negro or colored child. **2.** an Aboriginal child. [Negro pidgin E: child, from Pg: very little]

piccolo /ˈpɪkəloʊ/, *n., pl.* **-los**. a small flute, sounding an octave higher than the ordinary flute. [It: small]

pick[1] /pɪk/, *v.t.* **1.** to choose carefully. **2.** to choose (one's way or steps), as over rough ground, etc. **3.** to seek and find occasion for: *He will pick a quarrel*. **4.** to steal the contents of (a person's pocket, purse, etc.). **5.** to open (a lock) with wire, etc. **6.** to pierce, dig into, or break up (something) with a pointed instrument. **7.** to form (a hole, etc.) by such action. **8.** to clear (a thing) of something by using a pointed instrument, fingers, etc.: *She would pick her teeth after every meal*. **9.** to pluck or gather: *They can pick flowers*. **10.** (of birds or other animals) to take up (small bits of food) with the beak or teeth. **11.** to separate, pull apart, or pull to pieces (fibres, etc.). **12.** *Music.* to pull sharply (the strings of an instrument). ◇*v.i.* **13.** to strike with or use a pointed instrument or the like on something. **14.** to eat with small bites. **15.** to make a careful selection. **16.** to thieve. ◇*v.* **17.** Some special uses are:
pick and choose, to choose with great care, esp. fussily.
pick at, *Colloq.* **1.** to find fault with, in a mean way. **2.** to eat very little of: *The child picked at her food*.
pick holes in, to find fault with.
pick off, to single out and shoot.
pick on, *Colloq.* **1.** to annoy; tease. **2.** to choose (a person) for blame or for some work, often out of a feeling of dislike.
pick out, 1. to choose. **2.** to see (a thing) separately from surrounding things. **3.** to make out (sense or meaning) **4.** to take out by picking.
pick (someone's) brains, to find out as much as one can, from someone else's knowledge of a subject.
pick to pieces, to criticise, esp. in unimportant detail.
pick up, 1. to take up. **2.** to recover or regain (health, courage, etc.). **3.** to learn without special teaching. **4.** to get (something) or come to know (someone) by chance. **5.** to take (a person or thing) into a car, ship, etc. **6.** to bring into the range of observation, etc.: *Can you pick up NZ on your radio?* **7.** to gain, esp. in speed. **8.** *Colloq.* to improve. **9.** *Colloq.* to arrest.

◇*n.* **18.** a choice or selection. **19.** the choicest or most desirable part, example, or examples. **20.** the quantity of a crop picked at a particular time. **21.** → **plectrum**. [ME] **–picker,** *n.*

pick[2] /pɪk/, *n.* **1.** a hand tool consisting of an iron bar, pointed at one or both ends, fixed to a wooden handle, and used for breaking up soil, rock, etc. **2.** any pointed or other tool or instrument for picking. [OE *pīc*]

pickaxe /ˈpɪkæks/, n. a pick, esp. a mattock. [PICK² + AXE]

picker /ˈpɪkə/, n. 1. a person who gathers fruit, vegetables, etc. 2. Also, **picker-up**. person who gathers the fleece from the floor and puts it on the sorting table. [PICK¹, v. + -ER¹]

picket /ˈpɪkət/, n. 1. a pointed stick or post put into the ground to form a fence, to fasten something to, etc. 2. a body of people placed by a trade union outside a factory, etc., to prevent workers from entering during a strike. 3. *Mil.* a small body of soldiers stationed out from a force to warn against an enemy's approach. ◇*v.t.* 4. to enclose, fence, or make secure with pickets. 5. to fasten to a picket. 6. to place pickets at, as during a strike. 7. *Mil.* to guard, (a camp, etc.) with pickets. [F: pointed stake, military picket] —**picketer**, n.

picking /ˈpɪkɪŋ/, n. 1. the amount of something picked. 2. (*pl.*) things or scraps remaining and worth picking up or making use of. 3. (*pl.*) things obtained by means not strictly honest. [PICK¹ + -ING¹]

pickle /ˈpɪkəl/, n., v., **-led, -ling**. ◇n. 1. (*oft. pl.*) vegetables, as cucumbers, onions, cauliflowers, etc., preserved in vinegar, salt, etc., and eaten *usu.* with meats. 2. a liquid prepared with salt or vinegar for the preservation of fish, meat, vegetables, etc., or for the hardening of wood, leather, etc. 3. *Metall.* an acid or other chemical solution in which metal objects are dipped to remove oxide scale, etc. 4. *Colloq.* a problem situation. ◇*v.t.* 5. to preserve in pickle. 6. to clean or treat (objects) in a chemical pickle. [ME, from MD or MLG]

pickpocket /ˈpɪkpɒkət/, n. someone who steals from the pockets, handbags, etc., of people in public places.

pick-up /ˈpɪk-ʌp/, n. 1. *Colloq.* someone met informally, esp. in the hope of sexual adventure. 2. Also, **pick-up truck**. a small, open-bodied delivery truck. 3. *Radio*. **a**. the process of receiving soundwaves in a transmitting set in order to change them into electrical waves. **b**. a receiving or recording device; microphone. 4. Also, **cartridge**. a device which gives off electric or acoustic signals in accordance with the variations on a gramophone record. 5. a stop made to collect a passenger, parcel, load, etc., as by a taxi, bus, etc. 6. the passenger or item so collected.

picnic /ˈpɪknɪk/, n., v., **-nicked, -nicking**. ◇n. 1. an outing in which people carry food with them and share a meal in the open air. 2. the meal eaten on such an outing. 3. *Colloq.* an enjoyable experience or time. 4. *Colloq.* an easy thing to do. ◇*v.i.* 5. to hold, or take part in, a picnic. [F; orig. unknown]

picnic races, *n.pl.* horseraces held in the country, *usu.* for non-professionals.

Pict /pɪkt/, n. one of a race of people of disputed origin who formerly inhabited parts of Northern Britain, and in the ninth century became united with the Scots. [ME from L: painted]

pictograph /ˈpɪktəgræf, -grɑːf/, n. a pictorial sign or symbol. [L: painted, represented pictorially] —**pictographic**, *adj*. —**pictography**, n.

pictorial /pɪkˈtɔːriəl/, *adj*. 1. relating to, expressed in, or of the nature of, a picture or pictures: *pictorial writing*. 2. consisting of or containing pictures: *a pictorial history*. ◇n. 3. a newspaper or magazine made up mainly of pictures or photographs. [LL, from L: painter]

picture /ˈpɪktʃə/, n., v., **-tured, -turing**. ◇n. 1. a representation or image made upon a surface, *usu.* flat. 2. any image able to be seen: *the pictures made by reflections in water*. 3. mental image; idea. 4. the words describing something: *Gibbon's picture of ancient Rome*. 5. a very beautiful object or model: *She looks a picture in her new dress*; *She's a picture of health*. 6. how things are or look in a particular situation; set of circumstances; scene: *the employment picture*. 7. → **film** (def. 4b). 8. **the pictures**, (a film shown in) a cinema. 9. **get the picture, be in the picture**, to understand the situation. 10. **put in the picture**, to inform. ◇*v.t.* 11. to form a mental image of: *He couldn't picture himself doing such a thing*. 12. to describe in an imaginary way: *He pictured a greatly improved life for them*. [MF, from L]

picturesque /ˌpɪktʃəˈrɛsk/, *adj*. 1. looking like a picture; charming or quaint. 2. (of written or spoken language) strongly descriptive; vivid or graphic. [PICTURE + -ESQUE] —**picturesqueness**, n.

picture theatre, n. a cinema.

picture tube, n. → **cathode-ray tube**.

piddle /ˈpɪdl/, *v.i.*, **-dled, -dling**. *Colloq.* → **urinate**.

piddling /ˈpɪdlɪŋ/, *adj*. unimportant; trifling; petty. Also, **piddly**.

pidgin /ˈpɪdʒən/, n. a language used by people who have different first languages, which mixes words, grammar, etc., from all those languages. Also, **pigeon**. [? Chinese pronunciation of BUSINESS]

pie /paɪ/, n. 1. a baked dish with a filling (of meat, fish, fruit, etc.) enclosed in or covered by pastry, etc. 2. **have a finger in every pie**, to have an interest in or play a part in many affairs. 3. **pie in the sky**, false or imaginary hope for future good. [ME; orig. uncert.]

piebald /ˈpaɪbɔːld/, *adj*. 1. having patches of black and white or of other colors. ◇n. 2. a piebald animal, esp. a horse. [*pie* (see PIED) + BALD]

piece /piːs/, n., v., **pieced, piecing**. ◇n. 1. a limited bit or quantity of something: *a piece of land*; *a piece of cloth*. 2. a bit of something that forms a mass or body: *a piece of cake*. 3. one of the parts into which something is broken; fragment: *to tear a letter into pieces*. 4. a part of a working whole, as in a machine: *To mend it you have to take it to pieces*. 5. an individual article of a set: *a dinner service of 36 pieces*; *chess pieces*. 6. (*pl.*) wool from the skirtings. 7. the amount of work forming a single job: *piece work*. 8. an individual artistic, literary, dramatic, or musical work. 9. an individual thing of a class or kind: *a piece of furniture*. 10. an example of something; instance; specimen: *a*

fine piece of workmanship. **11.** (*offensive*) a woman: *She's a nice little piece.* **12.** a coin: *a five-cent piece.* ◊ **13.** Some special uses are:
a piece of cake, *Colloq.* something that is very easy to achieve.
a piece of one's mind, outspoken criticism or scolding.
go to pieces, to lose emotional or physical control of oneself.
nasty piece of work, a very unpleasant or malicious person.
of a piece, of the same kind; consistent.
say one's piece, to express an opinion; speak one's mind.
take a piece out of, to scold severely.
◊*v.t.* **14.** to mend (something broken); reassemble (usu. fol. by *together*). **15.** to fit together, as pieces or parts: *to piece ideas together.* **16.** to complete, enlarge, or stretch out by making additions (usu. fol. by *out*). **17.** to add as a piece or part (fol. by *into, onto*): *to piece new palings into a fence.* See **part.** [ME *pece*, from OF, from Rom *pettia* broken piece, piece of land, of Celtic orig.]

pièce de résistance / pi,ɛs də rə'zıstɑ̃s /, *n.* the most important or exciting thing in a series, esp. a dish in a meal. [F]

piecemeal /'pismil/, *adv.* **1.** piece by piece; gradually. ◊*adj.* **2.** done piece by piece; fragmentary. [ME]

piece-picker /'pis-pɪkə/, *n.* a woolshed hand who takes skirtings from the roller and sorts them into varieties defined by the classer.

piecework /'piswɜk/, *n.* work done and paid for by the piece (def. 7). —**pieceworker,** *n.*

pied /paɪd/, *adj.* having patches of two or more colors. [*pie* magpie (with reference to its black-and-white feathers)]

Piedmont /'pidmont, 'pjɛidmɒnt/, *n.* a region in north-western Italy. Pop. 4 394 312 (1986 est.); 29 358 km². *Cap.*: Turin. Italian, **Piemonte.** [It from *Piemonte*, lit., foothill (region)]

Pied Piper / paɪd 'paɪpə /, *n.* the hero of a German legend, popularised in 1842 by Robert Browning.

pier /pɪə/, *n.* **1.** a structure built out into the water as a landing place for ships or as a pleasure ground; breakwater; jetty. **2.** one of the supports of a span of a bridge. [ME, from ML]

pierce /pɪəs/, *v.t.,* **pierced, piercing. 1.** to go or run into or through (something); puncture; penetrate: *The needle pierced his fingers; The beam of light pierced the darkness.* **2.** to make a hole or opening in; perforate: *to pierce ears.* **3.** (of the eye or mind) to see into or through. **4.** to affect sharply with some sensation or emotion, as of cold, pain, grief, etc. **5.** to sound sharply through (the air, etc.). [ME, from OF, from L: pierced] —**piercer,** *n.* —**piercingly,** *adv.*

Pierce /pɪəs/, *n.* **Franklin,** 1804–69, 14th president of the US 1853–57.

Pierrot /pɪə'roʊ/, *n.* a male character in French pantomime, having a whitened face and wearing a loose white fancy costume. [F, from *Pierre,* man's name]

Piers Plowman / pɪəz 'plaʊmən /, *n.* (*The Vision concerning Piers Plowman*) an alliterative poem, written in three main versions (1360–99) by William Langland.

piety /'paɪəti/, *n., pl.* **-ties. 1.** reverence for God, or regard for religious duties. **2.** dutiful respect for parents or others. [ME, from L: duty]

piezoelectricity / paɪˌizoʊəlɛk'trɪsəti /, *n.* electricity produced by pressure, as in a crystal subjected to compression along a certain axis. [*piezo-* (combining form representing Gk: press, squeeze) + ELECTRICITY] —**piezoelectric,** *adj.* —**piezoelectrically,** *adv.*

piffle /'pɪfəl/, *n., v.,* **-fled, -fling.** ◊*n. Colloq.* **1.** nonsense; idle talk. ◊*v.i.* **2.** to talk nonsense. —**piffling,** *adj.*

pig /pɪg/, *n.,* ◊*n.* **1.** a domesticated mammal with a flat snout, curly tail, and bristly skin, that eats anything; a sow, hog, or boar; swine. See **hog.** **2.** the flesh of the pig as food; pork. **3.** *Colloq.* a greedy, dirty or selfish person. **4.** *Colloq.* (*offensive*) a policeman. **5.** *Metall.* an oblong casting of metal, esp. from a blast furnace; ingot. **6. a pig in a poke,** something bought without being examined. **7. make a pig of oneself,** to eat or drink too much. [OE *picg*]

pigeon¹ /'pɪdʒən/, *n.* a common bird, easily tamed, having a plump body, short legs and small head, often a pest in cities. [ME, from OF, from LL: pigeon]

pigeon² /'pɪdʒən/, *n.* **1.** → **pidgin. 2.** *Colloq.* responsibility; concern: *That's his pigeon.*

pigeonhole /'pɪdʒənhoʊl/, *n., v.,* **-holed, -holing.** ◊*n.* **1.** one of a set of small compartments in a desk, cupboard, etc., used for papers, etc. ◊*v.t.* **2.** to put away for future use or notice. **3.** to give a definite place to in some orderly system. **4.** to put aside and do nothing about.

pigeon-toed /'pɪdʒən-toʊd/, *adj.* with the toes or feet turned inwards.

pigface /'pɪgfeɪs/, *n.* a succulent creeping plant with large showy daisy-like purple, pink or white flowers and succulent fruit.

piggery /'pɪgəri/, *n., pl.* **-geries.** the place where pigs are kept.

piggyback /'pɪgibæk/, *n., adv.* (a ride) on the back or shoulders.

piggy bank, *n.* a children's moneybox, usu. shaped like a pig.

pig-headed /'pɪg-hɛdəd/, *adj.* stupidly obstinate.

pig-iron /'pɪg-aɪən/, *n.* **1.** iron produced in a blast furnace, poured into special moulds in preparation for making wrought iron, cast iron, or steel. **2.** iron in the unrefined state, before making into steel, alloys, etc.

piglet /'pɪglət/, *n.* a young pig. Also, **pigling.**

pigment /'pɪgmənt/, *n.* **1.** (coloring matter used to make) paint. **2.** *Biol.* a substance

pigment causing coloring in plant or animal cells or tissues. [ME, from L] —**pigmentation** *n.* —**pigmentary, pigmental,** *adj.*

pigmy /ˈpɪgmɪ/, *n., pl.* **-mies**, *adj.* → **pygmy.**

Pigs /pɪgz/, *n.* **Bay of,** a bay on the southwest coast of western central Cuba; attempted invasion by US-backed forces 1961.

pigskin /ˈpɪgskɪn/, *adj., n.* (made of) leather from the skin of a pig.

pigstick /ˈpɪgstɪk/, *v.i.* to hunt wild pigs with a spear, on foot or on horseback. —**pigsticking, pigsticker,** *n.*

pigsty /ˈpɪgstaɪ/, *n., pl.* **-sties.** a pen with shelter for pigs.

pigtail /ˈpɪgteɪl/, *n.* a plait or braid of hair.

pikau /ˈpikaʊ/, *NZ.* ◇*n.* **1.** a swag. ◇*v.t.* **2.** to carry on the back. [Maori]

pike[1] /paɪk/, *n., pl.* **pikes,** (*esp. collectively*) **pike.** a large, thin, long-nosed, fierce freshwater fish of the Northern Hemisphere. [ME, short for *pikefish,* so called from its pointed snout]

pike[2] /paɪk/, *n., v.,* **piked, piking.** ◇*n.* **1.** *Hist.* a weapon with a long shaft and small metal head, used by foot soldiers. ◇*v.t.* **2.** to wound, or kill with a pike. [F]

pike[3] /paɪk/, *v.i.,* **piked, piking.** *Colloq.* **1.** to let down; abandon (fol. by *on*): *Don't pike on me.* **2. pike out,** to go back on an arrangement; shirk; opt out (fol. by *on*): *He piked out on the deal.* —**piker,** *n.*

pikelet /ˈpaɪklət/, *n.* a small thick, pancake, cooked in a frying pan; drop scone; Scotch pancake.

pilaf /ˈpɪlæf/, *n.* a rice dish of Central Asian origin consisting of rice, pre-cooked or raw, fried in butter or other fat with stock, meats, vegetables, nuts, etc. Also, **pilaff, pilau, pilaw.** [Pers]

pilaster /pəˈlæstə/, *n.* a square pillar, with capital and base, built out from a wall. [F, from It, from L: pillar]

Pilate /ˈpaɪlət/, *n.* **Pontius** /ˈpɒnʃəs/, Roman procurator of Judea, AD 26–36?; ordered the crucifixion of Christ.

Pilbara /ˈpɪlbrə/, *n.* a large area in the north-west of WA, enclosed by the De Grey River system in the north and the Ashburton River system in the south. 443 915 km^2.

pilchard /ˈpɪltʃəd/, *n.* a small fish found in great numbers in shoals around the southern half of the Australian coast; sardine. [earlier *pilcher,* etym. uncert.]

pile[1] /paɪl/, *n., v.,* **piled, piling.** ◇*n.* **1.** an orderly heap: *a pile of boxes.* **2.** *Colloq.* a large number, quantity, or amount: *a pile of things to do; a pile of money.* **3.** *Phys.* a latticework of uranium and various moderating substances used to make plutonium in the production of atomic energy, including a means of controlling the nuclear chain reaction; atomic pile; nuclear reactor. ◇*v.t.* **4.** to lay or put in a pile (oft. fol. by *up* or *on*): *to pile up papers; to pile up sand.* **5.** to accumulate (fol. by *up*): *to pile up wealth.* **6.** to cover or load with a pile or piles: *to pile a truck with stones.* ◇*v.i.* **7.** to become heaped up; accumulate (fol. by *up*): *Evidence piled up; money piles up.* **8.** *Colloq.* to get somewhere in a disorderly crowd (fol. by *in, into, out,* etc.): *We all piled into the car.* **9.** to gather or rise in a pile: *Snow piled (up) against the door* **10.** *Colloq.* (of a car, driver, etc.) to crash (fol. by *up*). ◇*v.* **11. pile on the agony, pile it on,** *Colloq.* to overdo words, emotion, etc.; exaggerate. [ME, from OF, from L: pillar, pier, mole]

pile[2] /paɪl/, *n.* long heavy beam driven vertically into the ground or the bed of a river, etc., to support a structure, e.g. a bridge. [ME and OE *pīl* shaft, stake, from L: javelin]

pile[3] /paɪl/, *n.* the raised surface on cloth or carpet, made of upright cut or looped yarns. [ME, from L: hair] —**pileous,** *adj.*

pile[4] /paɪl/, *n.* (*usu. pl.*) → **haemorrhoid.** [ME]

pile-up /ˈpaɪl-ʌp/, *n. Colloq.* a traffic accident where several cars, etc., crash into each other.

pilfer /ˈpɪlfə/, *v.t.* **1.** to steal (a small amount or object). *v.i.* **2.** to practise petty theft. [apparently from AF or OF: pillage, rob] —**pilferer,** *n.* —**pilferage,** *n.*

pilgrim /ˈpɪlgrəm/, *n.* **1.** someone who makes a long journey to a holy or respected place as an act of devotion. **2.** *Poetic.* a traveller or wanderer. [ME, from AF (unrecorded), from ML: pilgrim, L: foreigner]

pilgrimage /ˈpɪlgrəmɪdʒ/, *n.* **1.** a journey made by a pilgrim. **2.** any long journey. [ME, from AF]

Pilgrim Fathers, *n.pl. US Hist.* the English Puritan separatists who founded the colony of Plymouth, Massachusetts, in 1620.

Pilgrim's Progress *n.* an allegory (1678) by John Bunyan.

piling /ˈpaɪlɪŋ/, *n.* **1.** piles collectively. See **pile**^{2}. **2.** a structure made of piles. [PILE^2 + -ING^1]

pill /pɪl/, *n.* **1.** a small, round solid containing medicine, to be swallowed whole; tablet. **2.** something unpleasant that has to be accepted or put up with: *a bitter pill to swallow.* **3.** *Colloq.* an unpleasant or uninteresting person: *I'm not going out with that little pill!* **4. sugar the pill,** to make bearable some unpleasant experience. **5. the pill,** *Colloq.* oral contraceptive. [late ME, probably from MD or MLG, from L: ball]

pillage /ˈpɪlɪdʒ/, *v.* **-laged, -laging,** *n.* ◇*v.t.,v.i.* **1.** to rob (someone) with open violence, as in war; plunder. ◇*n.* **2.** the act of plundering, esp. in war. [ME, from OF: rob, plunder] —**pillager,** *n.*

pillar /ˈpɪlə/, *n.* **1.** a long, thin upright structure supporting part of a building, or standing alone as a monument; column. **2.** anything used as or looking like this. **3.** a person who is a chief supporter of a state, institution, etc.: *a pillar of society.* **4. from pillar to post,** from one difficult situation to another. [ME, from OF, from L: pillar, PILE^1]

Pillars of Hercules, *n.pl.* the two promontories on opposite sides of the eastern end of the Strait of Gibraltar; the Rock of Gibraltar in Europe, and the Jebel Musa in Africa, supposed to have been raised by Hercules. [trans. of L *Columnae Herculis*, Gk *Hērakleíou stēlaí*]

pillbox /ˈpɪlbɒks/, *n.* **1.** a small box, usu. shallow and often round, for holding pills. **2.** a small hat of similar shape. **3.** a small, low structure of reinforced concrete enclosing machine-guns.

pillion /ˈpɪljən/, *n.* **1.** a pad or cushion attached behind a saddle. **2.** an extra saddle behind the driver's seat on a motorcycle. ◇*adj.* **3.** riding on a pillion: *a pillion passenger.* ◇*adv.* **4.** on a pillion: *to ride pillion.* [apparently from Gaelic: cushion, from L: skin, pelt]

pillory /ˈpɪləri/, *n., pl.* **-ries,** *v.,* **-ried, -rying.** ◇*n.* **1.** a wooden framework with holes for the head and hands, in which an offender was locked, and made to suffer public scorn. ◇*v.t.* **2.** to set in the pillory. **3.** to heap public scorn or abuse on. [ME, from OF, from Pr, ? from ML: court (lit., mirror) to the glory of God]

pillow /ˈpɪloʊ/, *n.* **1.** a bag filled with feathers, plastic foam, or other soft material, used as a support for the head during sleep. **2.** anything used to support the head; a headrest. ◇*v.t.* **3.** to rest on or as on a pillow: *He pillowed his head on his arm.* [OE *pyle, pylu* from L]

pilot /ˈpaɪlət/, *n.* **1.** a person who guides or steers ships into or out of a harbor or through difficult waters. **2.** *Aeron.* the person who controls an aeroplane. **3.** a guide or leader. ◇*v.t.* **4.** to guide or steer. **5.** to guide or lead, as through unknown places, difficult affairs, etc. **6.** to act as pilot on, in or over. ◇*adj.* **7.** experimental: *a pilot study; a pilot film.* **8.** of or relating to pilots. **9.** acting as a guide. [F, from It, from MGk: rudder] —**pilotage,** *n.*

pilot light, *n.* **1.** a small flame kept burning continuously, used for relighting a gas burner. **2.** a light on an electrical control, serving to show that the current is on.

pilsener /ˈpɪlsənə/, *n.* a light pale beer or lager. Also, **pilsner.** [G, adj. from *Pilsen,* a city in Czechoslovakia where orig. made]

Piltdown man /ˈpɪltdaʊn mæn/, *n.* a supposedly very early form of human, *Eoanthropus,* whose existence was deduced from bone fragments found at Piltdown, Sussex, England, in 1912; these were shown in 1953 to have been assembled as a hoax.

pimento /pəˈmentoʊ/, *n., pl.* **-tos.** the dried fruits of a West Indian tree, used as a spice; allspice. [Sp: pepper, allspice, from LL: plant juice, pigment]

pimp /pɪmp/, *n.* **1.** someone who finds customers for a prostitute or brothel; procurer. **2.** someone who gives information about criminals to the police. ◇*v.i.* **3.** to procure; solicit. **4.** to inform (on).

pimpernel /ˈpɪmpənel/, *n.* a common small plant, as the scarlet pimpernel, with red, purplish or white flowers that close with bad weather. [ME, from OF, from L: consisting of peppercorns]

pimple /ˈpɪmpl/, *n.* a small, usu. inflammatory swelling or raising of the skin; papule or pustule. [ME] —**pimply,** *adj.*

pin /pɪn/, *n., v.,* **pinned, pinning.** ◇*n.* **1.** a small, thin, piece of wood, metal, etc., used to fasten or hold things together; bolt; peg. **2.** a short, thin pointed piece of wire with a head at one end, for fastening cloth or paper. **3.** a safety pin. **4.** a badge or brooch. **5.** the part of the key which enters the lock. **6.** anything working or looking more or less like a pin, as a rolling pin, hairpin, ninepin, etc. **7.** a very small thing or amount; trifle: *not worth a pin.* ◇*v.t.* **8.** to fasten or attach with or as if with a pin or pins. **9.** to hold (a person, etc.) fast in a spot or position: *The branch pinned him down.* **10.** to obtain agreement to a course of action, promise, etc.: *See if you can pin him down about coming on Friday.* [ME; OE *pinn* peg]

PIN /pɪn/, *n.* a sequence of numbers and/or letters used as part of an identification procedure in electronic banking, as with an automatic teller machine. Also, **personal identification number, PIN number.** [abbrev.]

pinafore /ˈpɪnəfɔː/, *n.* **1.** a loose dress worn over clothing to protect it. **2.** a sleeveless dress with a low neck, worn with a jumper particularly in winter. Also, **pinny.** [PIN, v., + A¹ + FORE¹]

Pinang /pəˈnæŋ/, *n.* **1.** an island in South-East Asia, off the western coast of the Malay Peninsula. **2.** a state including this island and parts of the adjacent mainland; part of Malaysia. Pop. 1 047 282 (1985 est.); 1036 km². Also, **Penang.**

pinball /ˈpɪnbɔːl/, *n.* a game played on a pinball machine, with a sloping board marked with holes and pins which catch or contact a ball driven by a spring; the score is electrically recorded.

pince-nez /ˈpæns-neɪ, ˈpɪns-neɪ/, *n.* a pair of spectacles kept in place by a spring which pinches the nose. [F: pinch nose]

pincers /ˈpɪnsəz/, *n.pl. or sing.* **1.** a gripping tool with two pivoted limbs forming a pair of jaws and a pair of handles (often called a **pair of pincers**). **2.** *Zool.* a grasping organ or pair of organs looking like this: *a crab's pincers.* [ME, from OF: PINCH]

pinch /pɪntʃ/, *v.t.* **1.** to press between finger and thumb, the jaws of a tool, or any two opposed surfaces. **2.** to squeeze painfully: *My shoe is pinching me.* **3.** to cramp; restrict (usu. *in passive*): *to be pinched for space.* **4.** to make (the face) thin and drawn (usu. *in passive*): *to be pinched with pain; to be pinched with cold.* **5.** to reduce or narrow (usu. *in passive*): *to be pinched for money.* **6.** to put a pinch or small quantity of into something: *to pinch snuff.* **7.** *Colloq.* to steal. **8.** *Colloq.* (of the police) to take hold of; arrest; nab. ◇*v.i.* **9.** to press or be pressed painfully: *My shoe pinches.* **10.** to cause sharp discomfort or distress: *when hunger pinches.* **11.** to spend as little money as possible: *pinch and scrape.* ◇*n.* **12.** the act of pinching; nip; squeeze. **13.** a very small

pinch quantity of anything: *pinch of salt*. **14.** sharp or painful stress: *the pinch of hunger*. **15.** a situation or time of special stress; emergency: *Any help is useful in a pinch.* **16. pinch of salt.** See **grain** (def. 6). **17. at a pinch,** if necessary; in an emergency or crisis. [ME, from OF, from LL] **—pincher,** *n.*

pinchbeck /'pɪntʃbɛk/, *n.* **1.** an alloy of copper and zinc, used in imitation of gold. **2.** something that pretends to be something else. ◇*adj.* **3.** made of pinchbeck. **4.** sham; spurious. [named after the inventor, Christopher Pinchbeck (died 1732), a London clockmaker]

Pinchgut /'pɪntʃgʌt/, *n.* → **Fort Denison.**

pindan scrub /ˌpɪndæn 'skrʌb/, *n.* thin, scrubby vegetation, growing in arid country. [Aboriginal]

Pindar /'pɪndə/, *n.* 518–438 BC, Greek lyric poet, who was a religious conservative and showed the gods as powerful, righteous forces. **—Pindaric,** *adj.*

pine[1] /paɪn/, *n.* an evergreen cone-bearing tree with long needle-shaped leaves; many types are good sources of timber, and also of turpentine, tar, pitch, etc. [ME; OE *pīn*, from L] **—piny,** *adj.*

pine[2] /paɪn/, *v.i.*, **pined, pining. 1.** to suffer with longing, or long painfully (fol. by *for* or *after*). **2.** to fail gradually in health from grief, etc.; languish (fol. by *away*). [ME; OE *pīnian* to torture, from L: punishment]

pineal gland /'pɪnɪəl glænd/, *n.* a gland in the midbrain of vertebrates, which secretes the hormone melatonin. Also, **pineal body.**

pineapple /'paɪnæpəl/, *n.* a large fleshy tropical fruit (looking rather like a pine cone) with a crown of leaves on top.

pine cone, *n.* the cone (def. 3) of a pine[1].

Pine Gap, *n.* a joint US-Australian defence space research facility near Alice Springs in the NT, operated by the CIA.

pin-feather /'pɪn-fɛðə/, *n.* an undeveloped feather of a bird.

ping /pɪŋ/, *v.i.* **1.** to produce a sharp, ringing, high-pitched sound like that of a bullet striking an object, or of a small bell. **2.** *Motor Vehicles.* → **knock** (def. 2). ◇*n.* **3.** a pinging sound. [imitative] **—pinger,** *n.*

ping-pong /'pɪŋ-pɒŋ/, *n.* → **table tennis.** [PING, n., on model of *ding-dong*, etc.]

pinion[1] /'pɪnjən/, *n. Mach.* **1.** a small cogwheel engaging with a larger cogwheel or with a rack. **2.** an arbor or spindle with teeth which engage with a cogwheel. [F: pinion, from OF: battlement, from L: pinnacle]

pinion[2] /'pɪnjən/, *n.* **1.** the long end joint of a bird's wing carrying the primary feathers. **2.** a bird's wing. **3.** a feather. ◇*v.t.* **4.** to cut off the pinion of (a wing) or bind (the wings), as in order to stop a bird flying. **5.** to restrain (a person) by tying the arms or hands. [ME, from OF: feather, from L]

pink[1] /pɪŋk/, *n.* **1.** a pale red color. **2.** a garden plant with pink flowers, related to the carnation. **3.** the highest degree: *in the pink* *of health.* ◇*adj.* **4.** of the color pink. **5.** having left-wing political opinions. [orig. uncert.]

pink[2] /pɪŋk/, *v.t.* **1.** to pierce or stab. **2.** to cut a notched pattern on the edge of (a piece of material). **3.** to cut small holes in (cloth, leather, etc.). **4.** *Agric.* to shear so closely that the skin of the sheep is exposed. [ME *pynke(n)* make points (marks) or holes (with a sharp instrument)]

pink elephant, *n.* an imaginary thing seen by someone who is drunk; a hallucination. See **delirium tremens.**

pinkie /'pɪŋki/, *n.* the little finger or toe.

pinking shears, *n.pl.* scissors with notched blades, used for giving a scalloped or notched edge to material to stop it fraying.

pinna /'pɪnə/, *n., pl.* **pinnae** /'pɪni/, **pinnas. 1.** *Bot.* one of the leaflets of a pinnate leaf. **2.** *Zool.* **a.** a feather, wing, or winglike part. **b.** a fin or flipper. **3.** *Physiol.* the auricle of the ear. [L: feather (pl. wing), fin] **—pinnal,** *adj.*

pinnace /'pɪnəs/, *n.* a boat carried on a ship, used for going ashore, etc. [F, from It or from Sp, from L: pine tree]

pinnacle /'pɪnəkəl/, *n.* **1.** a tall thin mountain top or rock formation. **2.** the highest point of anything: *the pinnacle of fame.* **3.** *Archit.* an upright pointed part on top of a building, usu. conical in shape; turret; spire. [ME, from OF, from LL: pinnacle]

pinnate /'pɪneɪt, -ət/, *adj.* **1.** looking like a feather. **2.** having parts arranged on each side of a common axis. **3.** *Bot.* (of a leaf) with leaflets arranged on each side of a stalk. Also, **pinnated.** [L: feathered, pinnate] **—pinnately,** *adv.* **—pinnation,** *n.*

pinpoint /'pɪnpɔɪnt/, *n.* **1.** the point of a pin. **2.** something very small: *a pinpoint of light.* ◇*v.t.* **3.** to describe or point out the position of something exactly.

pinprick /'pɪnprɪk/, *n.* **1.** any small puncture made by or as by a pin. **2.** any small annoyance. **—pinpricking,** *n.* **—pin-prick,** *v.*

pins and needles, *n.pl.* a tingling in the limbs with the return of feeling after numbness.

pinstripe /'pɪnstraɪp/, *n. Textiles.* (a pattern with) a very narrow stripe.

pint /paɪnt/, *n.* a liquid measure of capacity in the imperial system equal to ⅛ gallon, or 0.568 litres or, in the US, to 0.104 gallon, or 0.473 litres. [ME, from F, from MD: plug]

Pinta /'pɪntə/, *n.* one of the three ships under Columbus on his voyage to America.

Pinter /'pɪntə/, *n.* **Harold,** born 1930, English playwright and actor; wrote *The Caretaker* (1960).

Pintubi /'pɪntəbi/, *n.* an Australian Aboriginal language spoken in the region near the western border of the NT.

pintuck /'pɪntʌk/, *n.* **1.** a very narrow fold or tuck on a garment, esp. for ornament. ◇*v.t.* **2.** to make such a fold in a garment.

pin-up /'pɪn-ʌp/, *n. Colloq.* a picture of an attractive man or woman pinned up on a wall, etc., to be admired.

pioneer /paɪə'nɪə/, *n.* **1.** someone who first enters or settles a region. **2.** someone who is the first in any field of activity: *pioneers in cancer research*. **3.** *Ecol.* a plant or animal which successfully invades and becomes established in a bare area. **4.** (*cap.*) a series of unmanned US spacecraft with lunar, solar, interplanetary and planetary missions. ◇*v.i.* **5.** to act as a pioneer: *Last century they were pioneering in Central Australia*. ◇*v.t.* **6.** to be a pioneer in: *to pioneer the western plains; to pioneer the development of a new process*. [F: pioneer, from OF: foot soldier]

pious /'paɪəs/, *adj.* **1.** having or showing religious devotion or dutiful respect. **2.** showing pretended or mistaken religious feeling; hypocritical; sanctimonious. **3.** belonging to religion; sacred not secular: *pious literature*. **4.** heartfelt; earnest. [L]

pip[1] /pɪp/, *n.* **1.** one of the spots on dice, playing cards, or dominoes. **2.** each of the small segments into which the surface of a pineapple is divided. **3.** *Mil. Colloq.* a badge of rank worn on the shoulders of certain commissioned officers. [earlier *peep*; orig. unknown]

pip[2] /pɪp/, *n.* **1.** a contagious disease of birds, esp. poultry, marked by thick mucus in the mouth and throat. **2.** (*joc.*) any minor sickness in a person. **3. give (someone) the pip**, *Colloq.* to annoy; irritate, esp. without intention: *His stupidity gives me the pip*. [ME, apparently from MD, from VL, for L: phlegm, pip]

pip[3] /pɪp/, *n.* the seed of a fruit, esp. an apple or orange. [short for PIPPIN]

pip[4] /pɪp/, *v.t.*, **pipped, pipping.** *Colloq.* to beat narrowly in a race: *The favorite was pipped at the post*.

pip[5] /pɪp/, *n.* **1.** a short high-pitched sound made by a radio receiver, echo-sounder, etc. **2.** the signal on the screen of a radar set.

pipe /paɪp/, *n., v.*, **piped, piping.** ◇*n.* **1.** a hollow cylinder for carrying water, gas, etc., over a distance; tube. **2.** anything of a similar tubular or cylindrical shape, as an organ in an animal body. **3.** a tube of wood, clay, etc. with a small bowl at one end, used for smoking tobacco. **4. a.** a musical wind instrument consisting of a single tube, as a flute, clarinet, or oboe. **b.** one of the wooden or metal tubes from which the sounds of an organ are produced. **c.** (*usu. pl.*) a set of flutes, as pan-pipes. **d.** (*pl.*) → **bagpipes. 5.** *Naut.* a boatswain's whistle. **6.** a vertical mass of rock, found in southern Africa, in which diamonds are found. **7.** *Bot.* the hollow stem of a plant. **8.** a large wine cask holding 477 litres. ◇*v.i.* **9.** to play on a pipe. **10.** *Naut.* to announce orders, etc., by a boatswain's pipe. **11.** to speak with a high squeaky voice. **12.** *Mining.* to cut forming a cylindrical hole. **13.** to form cylindrical or conical holes during moulding, as in casting steel ingots. ◇*v.t.* **14.** to convey by means of pipes: *to pipe gas from SA to NSW*. **15.** to play (music) on a pipe. **16.** to announce, order, etc., by sounding the boatswain's pipe: *to pipe the captain aboard*. **17.** to bring, lead, etc., by playing on a pipe. **18.** to trim or finish (a garment, etc.) with piping. ◇*v.* **19. pipe down,** *Colloq.* to become or keep quiet. **20. pipe up,** *Colloq.* to begin to talk, esp. unexpectedly. [ME and OE *pīpe*, from L: chirp] – **piper,** *n.*

pipedream /'paɪpdriːm/, *n.* an impossible hope or fancy.

pipeline /'paɪplaɪn/, *n.* **1.** a series of pipes joined together to form a conduit for carrying water, gas, etc., over long distances. **2. in the pipeline,** on the way; in preparation.

pipe organ, *n.* an organ with pipes, as distinct from a reed organ. See **organ** (def. 1).

pipette /pɪ'pet/, *n.* a thin glass tube for measuring and carrying liquids in small quantities. Also, **pipet.** [F: pipe]

pipi /'piːpiː/, *n.* a burrowing shellfish that can be eaten. [Maori]

piping /'paɪpɪŋ/, *n.* **1.** pipes collectively. **2.** material formed into a pipe or pipes: *We bought three metres of piping*. **3.** the act of someone or something that pipes. **4.** the sound of pipes. **5.** a high squeaky sound. **6.** a tubular band of material, sometimes with a cord inside, for trimming clothes, cushions, etc. ◇*adj.* **7.** high and squeaky: *a piping voice*. **8. piping hot,** very hot.

pipit /'pɪpət/, *n.* a small brown bird found all over Australia, looking a little like a lark. [imitative of its note]

pippin /'pɪpən/, *n.* **1.** a type of apple. **2.** *Bot.* a seed. [ME, from OF: fruit seed, pip; orig. uncert.]

pippy /'pɪpiː/, *n.* → **pipi.**

pipsqueak /'pɪpskwiːk/, *n. Colloq.* a small or unimportant person or thing.

piquant /'piːkənt/, *adj.* **1.** pleasantly sharp in taste; pungent; biting; tart. **2.** pleasantly sharp, interesting, attractive or stimulating. [F: pricking, pungent] – **piquancy,** *n.* – **piquantly,** *adv.*

pique /piːk/, *v.*, **piqued, piquing,** *n.* ◇*v.t.* **1.** to annoy by hurting one's pride or vanity (*oft. in passive*): *to be piqued at a refusal*. **2.** to excite or affect with interest, curiosity, etc. ◇*n.* **3.** anger, resentment, or ill feeling over some slight offence or from hurt pride. [F: prick, sting]

piranha /pə'rɑːnə/, *n.* a small, fierce freshwater fish of South America. [Pg]

pirate /'paɪrət/, *n., v.*, **-rated, -rating.** ◇*n.* **1.** someone who robs or does illegal violence at sea. **2.** a pirate ship. **3.** someone who takes and uses the work or idea of someone else without permission. **4.** Also, **pirate radio.** a radio station broadcasting on an unauthorised wavelength, and often operating outside territorial waters or in a foreign country to avoid payment of copyright fees, etc. ◇*v.t.* **5.** to take and use (someone else's work or idea) without permission. ◇*v.i.* **6.** to commit or practise piracy. [ME, from L, from Gk] – **piracy,** *n.* – **piratical,** *adj.* – **piratically,** *adv.*

pirouette /pɪruˈet/, *n., v.,* **-etted, -etting.** ◇*n.* **1.** a whirling about on one foot or on the points of the toes, as in dancing. ◇*v.i.* **2.** to perform a pirouette; whirl on the toes. [F: top, whirligig, whirl]

pirri point /ˈpɪri pɔɪnt/, *n.* an early Aboriginal tool consisting of a pointed stone trimmed to a useful shape on one side.

Pisa /ˈpizə/, *n.* a city in north-western Italy, on the river Arno; famous for the Leaning Tower. Pop. 104 477 (1986 est.).

Pisano /piˈsanoʊ/, *n.* **1. Giovanni** /dʒəˈvani/, c. 1245– c. 1320, Italian sculptor and architect, influenced by French Gothic sculpture. **2.** his father, **Niccola** /ˈnikəla/, c. 1220–78, Italian sculptor and architect in the classical style.

piscatorial /pɪskəˈtɔriəl/, *adj.* of or relating to fishermen or fishing. Also, **piscatory** /ˈpɪskətəri, -tri/. [L]

Pisces /ˈpaɪsiz/, *n.* **1.** the Fishes, a constellation and sign of the Zodiac. **2.** *Zool.* the class of vertebrates that includes most fish. [L, pl. of *piscis* fish]

pisci-, a word part meaning 'fish'. [L, combining form of *piscis*]

piscine /ˈpɪsin/, *adj.* of or relating to fish. [L: fish]

piss /pɪs/, *v.i. Colloq.* **1.** to urinate. **2. piss off,** (*offensive*) to go away. [OF, from Rom: of echoic orig.] —**pissy,** *adj.*

Pissarro /piˈsaroʊ/, *n.* **Camille** /kəˈmil/, 1830?–1903, French impressionist painter.

pistachio /pɪsˈtɑʃioʊ/, *n., pl.* **-chios.** the nut of the fruit of a small tree of southern Europe and Asia Minor, used for flavoring. Also, **pistache** /pɪsˈtæʃ/. [It, from L, from Gk]

pistil /ˈpɪstl/, *n. Bot.* **1.** the female sex organ of a flower, consisting of ovary, style and stigma. **2.** =**gynoecium.** [NL: pistil, from L: pestle] —**pistillate,** *adj.*

pistol /ˈpɪstl/, *n.* a short gun intended to be held and fired with one hand. [F: pistol, from G, from Czech]

piston /ˈpɪstən/, *n.* a movable disc or cylinder fitting closely within a tube or hollow cylinder, and able to be driven alternately forwards and backwards in the tube by pressure, as in an internal-combustion engine; its motion is sent to other parts of a machine by a connecting rod (**piston rod**). [F, from It: pound, from L: pounded]

pit¹ /pɪt/, *n., v.,* **pitted, pitting.** ◇*n.* **1.** a hole or cavity in the ground. **2.** such a hole used as a trap. **3.** *Mining.* **a.** a hole made in digging for some mineral. **b.** the shaft of a coalmine. **c.** the mine itself. **4.** hell. **5.** any hollow or depression in a surface, as of scars in a face. **6.** a natural hollow or depression in the body: *the pit of the stomach.* **7.** an enclosure for animal fights. **8.** (in a theatre) **a.** the space where the orchestra sits in front of and under the stage. **b.** the part of the ground floor behind the stalls. **9.** the area beside a motor-racing track in which cars are repaired, or refuelled, during a race. **10. the pits,** *Colloq.* the most unpleasant (place, circumstance, condition, etc.). ◇*v.t.* **11.** to mark with pits or hollows: *Smallpox had pitted his face.* **12.** to set in active opposition: *He had to pit his strength against his enemy's.* ◇*v.i.* **13.** to become marked with pits or hollows. [ME and OE *pytt*, from L: well, pit, shaft] —**pitted,** *adj.*

pit² /pɪt/, *n., v.,* **pitted, pitting.** ◇*n.* **1.** the stone of a fruit, as of a cherry, peach, or plum. ◇*v.t.* **2.** to take out the stone from (a fruit, etc.). [D: kernel]

pitapat /ˈpɪtəpæt/, *adv.* **1.** with a quick series of beats or taps. ◇*n.* **2.** the movement or the sound of something going pitapat. [imitative]

Pitcairn Island /ˌpɪtkɛən ˈaɪlənd/, *n.* a small British island in the south Pacific, southeast of Tuamotu Archipelago; settled by mutineers of the *Bounty* in 1790. Pop. 68 (1987); 5 km². —**Pitcairnese,** *n., adj.*

pitch¹ /pɪtʃ/, *v.t.* **1.** to set up (a tent, camp, etc.). **2.** to put, set, or plant (cricket stumps, etc.) in a fixed place. **3.** to aim or set at a certain point, degree, level, etc.: *He pitched his hopes too high.* **4.** *Music.* to set the key of (a tune, etc.). **5.** to throw; toss. **6.** *Baseball.* to throw (the ball) to the batter. **7.** *Archit.* to build a roof with a certain slope. ◇*v.i.* **8.** to fall forward. **9.** to roll suddenly to one side; lurch. **10.** to throw; toss. **11.** to slope downwards. **12.** to dip with alternate fall and rise of bow and stern, as a ship, etc. ◇*v.* **13. pitch a tale,** to tell a story (esp. untrue). **14. pitch in,** *Colloq.* **a.** to join in. **b.** to begin strongly. **15. pitch into,** **a.** to attack (in words or action). **b.** to begin to do (something). ◇*n.* **16.** relative point, position, or degree. **17.** height: *pitch of an arch.* **18.** *Acoustics, Music.* the strongest audible frequency of a sound from a musical instrument, etc., by which it is compared with other sounds in highness or lowness. **19.** the act or manner of pitching. **20.** a throw, toss. **21.** the pitching movement of a ship, etc. **22.** degree of slope. **23. a.** *Sport.* the whole area of play, for cricket, football, etc. **b.** *Cricket.* the area between the wickets. **24.** a sales talk. **25.** a given plan of action. **26.** *Mech.* the distance between the corresponding surfaces of adjacent teeth of a gearwheel, etc. [ME]

pitch² /pɪtʃ/, *n.* **1.** a dark sticky substance used for making paths, etc., derived from coal tar. **2.** any of certain bitumens. **3.** any of various resins. [OE *pic,* from L]

pitch-black /ˈpɪtʃ-blæk/, *adj.* very black or dark.

pitchblende /ˈpɪtʃblɛnd/, *n.* the main ore of uranium and radium. [G]

pitcher¹ /ˈpɪtʃə/, *n.* a container, usu. with a handle and lip, for holding and pouring liquids. [ME, from OF]

pitcher² /ˈpɪtʃə/, *n. Baseball.* the player who throws the ball to the batter. [PITCH¹, *v.* + -ER¹]

pitchfork /ˈpɪtʃfɔk/, *n.* **1.** a fork for lifting and throwing hay, etc. ◇*v.t.* **2.** to throw with or as with a pitchfork.

pitchi /'pɪtʃi/, n. a large, shallow, wooden vessel used by Aboriginal women as a container for food or water and sometimes for carrying babies. [Aboriginal]

pitchi-pitchi /ˌpɪtʃi-'pɪtʃi/, n. See **jerboa** (def. 1). [Aboriginal]

pitchpipe /'pɪtʃpaɪp/, n. a small pipe, sounded to give the pitch for singing, tuning an instrument, etc.

piteous /'pɪtiəs/, adj. arousing or deserving pity. [*pite* PITY + -OUS] **–piteously**, adv.

pitfall /'pɪtfɔl/, n. 1. a hidden pit prepared as a trap for animals or people to fall into. 2. any trap or danger for the unprepared.

pith /pɪθ/, n. 1. any soft, spongy tissue or substance. 2. *Bot.* the central cylinder of parenchymatous tissue in the stems of dicotyledonous plants. 3. any of various similar inner parts of substances, as the centre of a log, a feather, etc. 4. the important part; essence. ◊v.t. 5. to destroy the spinal cord or brain of. [ME; OE *pitha* pith]

pithead /'pɪthɛd/, n. the top of a mine shaft.

Pithecanthropus /ˌpɪθɪ'kænθrəpəs/, n., pl. **-pi** /-paɪ/. a genus of apelike human beings, no longer living, now classified under the genus Homo; first known fossils of this species, Java man, discovered 1891-93. [NL, from Gk]

pith helmet, n. a sun-hat made of the dried pith of an Indian tree, and formerly worn by Europeans in tropical countries; topee.

pithy /'pɪθi/, adj., **-ier, -iest.** 1. full of strength, substance, or meaning; terse: *a pithy saying*. 2. of, like, or filled with pith.

pitiable /'pɪtiəbəl/, adj. 1. deserving to be pitied; lamentable. 2. worthless; contemptible.

pitiful /'pɪtəfəl/, adj. 1. causing or deserving pity. 2. causing contempt by smallness, poor quality, etc.: *pitiful attempts*. **–pitifully,** adv. **–pitifulness,** n.

pitiless /'pɪtələs/, adj. feeling or showing no pity; merciless.

Pitjantjatjara /pɪtʃəntʃə'tʃærə/, n. an Australian Aboriginal language of the desert area, near Ernabella, SA, still widely used. Also, **Pitjantjara** /pɪtʃən'dʒærə/.

Pitman /'pɪtmən/, n. **Sir Isaac**, 1813-97, English inventor of a system of shorthand.

Pitt /pɪt/, n. **William** ('*the Younger*'), 1759-1806, British statesman; prime minister 1783-1801 and 1804-06.

pittance /'pɪtns/, n. 1. a small sum of money for living costs. 2. any small part or amount. [ME, from OF]

pitter-patter /'pɪtə-pætə/, n. a fast procession of light beats or taps, as of rain.

pittosporum /pə'tɒspərəm/, n. a tree or shrub, found in Asia, Africa and the Australian region, often having white bell-shaped flowers and orange fruit.

pituitary /pə'tjuətri, -təri/, n., pl. **-taries.** *Med.* a small, oval, endocrine gland at the base of the brain which produces several hormones. Also, **pituitary gland.** [L: pertaining to, or secreting phlegm]

pituri /'pɪtʃəri/, n. an Australian shrub, the leaves and twigs of which are used by Aborigines as a drug. [Aboriginal]

pity /'pɪti/, n., pl. **pities,** v., **pitied, pitying.** ◊n. 1. kindly sorrow felt for the suffering or misfortune of another. 2. a cause for pity or sorrow. ◊v.t. 3. to be sorry for. [ME, from OF, from L: piety]

Pius XII /'paɪəs/, n. (*Eugenio Pacelli*), 1876-1958, Italian ecclesiastic; pope 1939-58; he kept silent concerning the extermination of Jews during World War II, wishing to preserve Vatican neutrality; the last absolute monarch of the Holy See.

pivot /'pɪvət/, n. 1. a pin or shaft on the end of which something rests and turns. 2. a thing or person on which something turns or depends. 3. *Rugby Union.* a half-back. ◊v.i. 4. to turn on or as on a pivot. ◊v.t. 5. to join by, or provide with a pivot. [F; orig. uncert.] **–pivotal,** adj.

pixie /'pɪksi/, n., pl. **pixies.** a fairy; sprite. Also, **pixy.** [orig. uncert.]

pizza /'pitsə, 'pɪtsə/, n. an Italian dish made from yeast dough covered with tomato, cheese, olives, etc.

pizzazz /pə'zæz/, n. *Orig. US.* spirit; panache; verve.

pizzicato /pɪtsə'katoʊ/, *Music* ◊adj. 1. played by plucking the strings with the finger instead of using the bow, as on a violin. ◊n. 2. a note or passage so played. [It: pick, twang (a stringed instrument)]

pizzle /'pɪzəl/, n. an animal's penis, esp. of a ram or bull.

pkt, *Abbrev.* packet.

pl., *Abbrev.* plural.

Pl, *Abbrev.* Place (in street names, etc.)

placard /'plækəd/, n. 1. a written or printed notice to be posted in a public place; a poster. ◊v.t. 2. to post placards on or in. 3. to give notice of by means of placards. [F, from D: flat board]

placate /plə'keɪt/, v.t., **-cated, -cating.** to make calm, peaceful; appease. [L] **–placatory,** adj.

place /pleɪs/, n., v., **placed, placing.** ◊n. 1. a particular part of space, of known or unknown area. 2. space in general (chiefly in connection with *time*). 3. a space or spot, used for a given purpose: *a place of worship*. 4. any part or spot in a body or surface: *a warm place by the fire*. 5. a particular passage in a book, etc. 6. a space or seat for a person, as in a train, etc. 7. the space or position normally or just filled by a person or thing: *I lost my place in the queue*. 8. position; situation: *if I were in your place*. 9. a proper or appropriate position: *not a hair out of place*. 10. a short street, a court, etc.: *Martin Place*. 11. a job, post, or office. 12. a function or duty. 13. position or standing in the social scale. 14. an area, esp.

place

one with a given name, as a town, etc. **15.** an open space, or square, as in a city. **16.** a house or building. **17.** stead or lieu: *Use water in place of milk.* **18.** a step or point in order of proceeding: *in the first place.* **19.** *Maths.* the position of a figure in a series, esp. in decimal notation: *In 6.35, the 5 is in the second decimal place.* **20.** *Drama.* one of the three unities. See **unity** (def. 6). **21.** *Sport.* the position of second or third (and sometimes also of first) in a race. ◇**22.** Some special uses are:
go places, *Colloq.* to be successful in one's work.
know one's place, to recognise one's (low) social rank and behave accordingly.
out of place, 1. not in the proper position. **2.** unsuitable.
put in one's place, to reduce someone's overhigh opinion of themselves.
take place, to happen.
◇*v.t.* **23.** to put in a particular place; set. **24.** to put in a suitable position, order or place. **25.** to fix (confidence, hope, etc.) in a person or thing. **26.** to find a job, situation, etc., for (a person). **27.** to give a certain position or rank to. **28.** to direct or aim with skill. **29.** to give a position to (a horse, etc.) usu. among the first three, at the finish of a race, etc.: *The horse was placed second.* **30.** to identify (someone) by remembering the place and circumstances where one has known or seen them before. [OE, from L: street, from Gk]
– **placement**, *n.*

placebo /pləˈsiːboʊ/, *n.*, *pl.* **-bos, -boes.** *Med.* a medicine which apparently performs no physical function but may help the patient mentally. [ME, from L: I shall be pleasing, acceptable]

placenta /pləˈsɛntə/, *n.*, *pl.* **-tas, -tae** /-tiː/. **1.** *Zool., Anat.* the organ formed in the lining of the mammalian uterus to provide food for the developing baby and to remove its waste products. **2.** *Bot.* **a.** that part of the ovary of flowering plants which bears the ovules. **b.** (in ferns, etc.) the tissue giving rise to sporangia. [NL: something having a flat circular form, from L: a cake, from Gk: flat cake]
– **placental**, *adj.*

placer /ˈpleɪsə/, *n. Mining.* a superficial gravel or similar deposit containing particles of gold, etc. See **lode**. [Amer Sp: sandbank]

placid /ˈplæsəd/, *adj.* pleasantly calm or peaceful; tranquil. [L *placidus*] – **placidity**, **placidness**, *n.*

plagiarise *or* **plagiarize** /ˈpleɪdʒəraɪz/, *v.i., *-rised, -rising.** (in art, literature, etc.) to take ideas, passages, etc., or their manner of expression and pass them off as one's own. – **plagiarism**, *n.* – **plagiarist**, *n.*

plagioclimax /ˌpleɪdʒioʊˈklaɪmæks/, *n.* → **disclimax**.

plague /pleɪɡ/, *n., v.,* **plagued, plaguing.** ◇*n.* **1.** a disease affecting large numbers of people at the same time, and causing many deaths. **2.** any cause of trouble or annoyance. **3.** a huge number of any pest: *a locust plague.* ◇*v.t.* **4.** to trouble in any manner; torment. [ME, from LL, from L: blow, wound]

Planck's constant

plaice /pleɪs/, *n., pl.* **plaice.** a European flatfish, important as food. [ME, from OF, from LL: flatfish, from Gk: flat]

plaid /plæd/, *n.* **1.** any cloth woven of different colored threads in a cross-barred pattern, esp. that worn about the shoulders of Scottish Highlanders. **2.** a pattern of this kind. ◇*adj.* **3.** having a plaid pattern. [Gaelic: blanket, plaid]

plain /pleɪn/, *adj.* **1.** clear to the eye or ear. **2.** clear to the mind; evident, obvious. **3.** easily understood: *plain talk.* **4.** total; downright: *plain silliness.* **5.** direct; candid. **6.** without special rank, importance, etc.: *plain people.* **7.** not beautiful. **8.** ordinary; simple; unadorned. **9.** (of paper) unruled. **10.** (of food) not rich, or difficult to prepare. **11.** flat; level: *plain country.* **12.** (of knitting) made of plain stitches. ◇*adv.* **13.** simply; absolutely. **14.** clearly; intelligibly. ◇*n.* **15.** a large, flat area of land. **16.** the simplest stitch in knitting. [ME, from OF, from L: flat, level, plane]

plain-clothes /ˈpleɪn-kloʊðz/, *adj.* wearing ordinary clothes rather than a uniform, as a policeman.

plain flour, *n.* white wheat flour that does not contain a raising agent.

plain sailing, *n.* **1.** sailing on a course free from difficulty. **2.** an easy, trouble-free course of action. Also, **plane sailing.**

plainsong /ˈpleɪnsɒŋ/, *n. Music.* one-part liturgical music used in the Christian Church from the earliest times; Gregorian chant. Also, **plainchant.** [ML]

plain-spoken /ˈpleɪn-spoʊkən/, *adj.* direct; candid.

plains turkey, *n.* → **bustard** (def. 1).

plaint /pleɪnt/, *n.* **1.** → **complaint. 2.** *Law.* a statement of complaint made to a court for the purpose of asking redress. [ME, from OF, from L: lamentation]

plaintiff /ˈpleɪntəf/, *n. Law.* someone who brings an action in a civil case. [ME, from OF]

plaintive /ˈpleɪntɪv/, *adj.* expressing sorrow or an unhappy state of mind; mournful. [ME, from OF]

plait /plæt/, *n.* **1.** a weaving together, as of strands of hair; a braid. ◇*v.t.* **2.** to weave strands together (of hair, threads, etc.). [ME, from OF, from L: folded]

plan /plæn/, *n., v.,* **planned, planning.** ◇*n.* **1.** a scheme or set of ideas for acting. **2.** a design or pattern of arrangement. **3.** a drawing made to scale to represent the top view or a horizontal cut of a building or machine, town, etc. ◇*v.t.* **4.** to form or arrange a plan for (any work or action). **5.** to draw or make a plan of (a building, etc.). ◇*v.i.* **6.** to make plans. [F, from L]

Planck's constant /ˌplæŋks ˈkɒnstənt/, *n. Phys.* a universal constant of action (approx. 6.626×10^{-34} joule seconds; *Symbol:* h) expressing the proportion of energy of any form of wavelike radiation to its frequency. [named after M *Planck*, 1858–1947, German physicist]

plane /pleɪn/, n. 1. a flat or level surface. 2. *Maths.* a surface such that the straight line joining any two separate points in it lies completely within it. 3. a level of character, existence, development, etc.: *a high moral plane*. 4. an aeroplane or hydroplane. ◇*adj.* 5. flat or level, as a surface. 6. of plane figures: *plane geometry*. [L: level ground]

plane² /pleɪn/, n., v., **planed, planing**. ◇n. 1. a tool used for removing, smoothing, or finishing the surface of wood, etc. ◇v.t. 2. to smooth as with a plane. 3. to remove as with a plane (fol. by *away* or *off*). ◇v.i. 4. to work with a plane. [ME, from F, from LL]

plane angle, n. an angle between two crossing lines.

plane figure, n. a figure whose parts all lie in one plane.

plane geometry, n. the geometry of figures whose parts all lie in one plane.

planet /'plænət/, n. *Astron.* a solid body moving around the sun or other star, and visible only by reflected light. Around the sun there are nine major planets (Mercury, Venus, Earth, Mars, Jupiter, Saturn, Uranus, Neptune, and Pluto). [ME, from LL, from Gk: lit.: wanderer]

planetarium /plænə'tɛəriəm/, n., pl. **-tariums, -taria** /-'tɛəriə/. 1. an apparatus or model representing the planetary system. 2. (a building or room containing) a device which projects a representation of the heavens upon a domed ceiling. [NL: planetary]

planetary /'plænətəri, -tri/, adj. 1. of, relating to, or like a planet or the planets. 2. *Mech.* naming or relating to a form of transmission (consisting of an epicyclic train of gears) for varying the speed in motor vehicles. [L]

plank /plæŋk/, n. 1. a long, thick, flat piece of timber. 2. something to stand on or to cling to for support. 3. **to walk the plank**, to be forced to walk to one's death by stepping off a plank extending from a ship's side over the water. ◇v.t. 4. to lay or cover with planks. [ME, from ONF, from L]

plankton /'plæŋktən/, n. small animal and plant organisms that float in the water, esp. at or near the surface. [G, from Gk (neut.): wandering]

planner /'plænə/, n. someone who plans, or something, e.g. a diary, to help one plan.

plant /plænt, plant/, n. 1. any member of the vegetable group of living organisms. 2. a herb or other small vegetable growth, in contrast to a tree or a shrub. 3. a seedling. 4. the machinery, tools, etc., and often the buildings, needed to carry on any industrial business. 5. *Colloq.* **a.** something or someone used to trap (criminals, etc.). **b.** a spy. ◇v.t. 6. to put (seeds, trees, etc.) in the ground for growth. 7. to fix (ideas, feelings, etc.) in someone's mind. 8. to put or set firmly in place. 9. *Colloq.* to deliver (a blow, etc.). 10. to locate; situate. 11. *Colloq.* to hide (stolen goods). 12. to place (evidence) so that its discovery will make an innocent person appear guilty. [ME and OE *plante,* from L: sprout, slip, graft]

Plantagenet /plæn'tædʒənət/, n. one of the line of English sovereigns from Henry II to Richard III. [F: lit., sprig of broom]

plantar /'plæntə/, adj. of or relating to the bottom of the foot: *plantar wart*. [L]

plantation /plæn'teɪʃən/, n. 1. a farm or estate, esp. in a tropical country, on which cotton, coffee, sugar, etc., is grown. 2. a group of planted trees. [late ME, from L: a planting]

planter /'plæntə, 'plɑntə/, n. 1. a machine for planting seeds in the ground. 2. the owner of a plantation.

plantigrade /'plæntəgreɪd/, adj. 1. walking on the whole sole of the foot, as man, bears, etc. ◇n. 2. a plantigrade animal. [NL, from L]

plant kingdom, n. the plants of the world collectively (as separate from *animal kingdom*). Also, **vegetable kingdom**.

plaque /plak, plæk/, n. 1. a thin, flat plate of metal, wood, etc., used to decorate a wall, etc. 2. a platelike brooch, esp. one worn as a badge. 3. a film on the teeth, containing bacteria. [F, from D *plak* flat board]

-plasia, a word part meaning 'biological cellular growth'. Also, **-plasy**. [NL, from Gk: a moulding]

-plasm, a word part used as a noun ending meaning 'something formed or moulded' in biological and other scientific terms, as in *protoplasm*. [combining form representing Gk *plásma*]

plasma /'plæzmə/, n. 1. *Anat.* the liquid part of blood or lymph, as separate from the red and white blood cells. 2. *Biol.* → protoplasm. 3. *Phys.* ionised gas which is highly conducting, although electrically neutral. Also, **plasm**. [LL, from Gk: something formed or moulded] —**plasmatic, plasmic**, *adj.*

plasmodium /plæz'moʊdiəm/, n., pl. **-dia** /-diə/. *Biol.* a mass or sheet of protoplasm formed by the union or contact of a number of bodies of single-celled organisms. [NL]

Plassey /'plæsi/, n. a village in north-eastern India, about 129 km north of Calcutta; Clive's victory over a Bengal army here (1757) led to the establishment of British power in India.

-plast, a word part used as a noun ending, meaning 'formed', 'moulded', esp. in biological and botanical terms, as in *protoplast*. [combining form representing Gk *plastós*]

plaster /'plɑstə/, n. 1. a thick mixture, as of lime, sand, water, and often hair, used for covering walls, ceilings, etc., where it hardens in drying. 2. calcined gypsum (**plaster of Paris**), a white powdery material which swells when mixed with water and sets rapidly, used for making moulds, etc. 3. a solid mixture for spreading upon cloth and placing on the body, esp. to keep a broken limb straight. 4. a small adhesive dressing for wounds. ◇v.t. 5. to cover (walls, etc.) with plaster. 6. to treat with

plaster plaster of Paris. **7.** to lay flat like a layer of plaster. **8.** to apply a plaster to (the body, etc.). **9.** to spread thickly: *To plaster a wall with posters*. [ME and OE, from VL and ML: plaster (both medical and builder's senses), from L, from Gk: salve]

plastic /'plæstɪk/, *adj.* **1.** concerned with or relating to moulding or modelling: *plastic arts*. **2.** able to be moulded or to receive form: *plastic substances*. **3.** Also, **anaplastic.** *Surg.* concerned with or relating to the fixing or changing of badly formed, injured, or lost parts: *plastic surgery*. **4.** able to be moulded; pliable: *the plastic mind of youth*. **5.** made of or containing plastic: *a plastic bag*. ◇*n.* **6.** any of a group of chemically-produced or natural materials which may be shaped when soft and then hardened, such as resins, polymers, etc. [L: that may be moulded, from Gk] – **plasticity,** *n.*

-plastic, a word part forming adjectives related to *-plast, -plasty,* as in *protoplastic*. [see PLASTIC]

plasticine /'plæstəsin/, *n.* plastic modelling clay, in various colors. [Trademark]

plastic paint, *n.* **1.** paint based on polyvinyl acetate, which can be thinned with water. **2.** *Colloq.* any paint which can be thinned with water.

plastic surgery, *n.* surgery which attempts to remodel badly formed or damaged parts of the body.

plastid /'plæstəd/, *n. Biol.* **1.** a structural unit consisting of a single cell. **2.** any of certain small specialised masses of protoplasm in certain cells. [G, from Gk]

-plasty, a word part used as a noun ending meaning 'formation', and found in the names of processes of plastic surgery, as *cranioplasty, dermatoplasty,* etc. [Gk]

-plasy, a variant of *-plasia*.

plate /pleɪt/, *n., v.,* **plated, plating.** ◇*n.* **1.** a shallow, usu. circular dish, from which food is eaten or served. **2.** a service of food for one person at the table. **3.** a complete course: *a cold plate*. **4.** a plate of sandwiches, cakes, etc., prepared and brought to a party, etc. **5.** dishes, knives, etc., made of or plated with gold or silver. **6.** a dish, used for collecting offerings in a church, etc. **7.** a thin, flat sheet of metal, etc. **8.** a flat, polished piece of metal on which something may be engraved. **9.** a sheet of metal for printing from, formed by stereotyping a page of type, or sheet of metal or plastic formed by moulding, etching, or photographic development. **10.** a printed impression from such a piece, or from some similar piece, as a woodcut. **11.** a full-page drawing forming part of a book. **12.** a light metal horseshoe. **13.** *Dentistry.* a piece of metal, vulcanite, or plastic substance, with artificial teeth or a wire attached. **14.** *Baseball.* the home base. **15.** → **plate glass. 16.** *Photog.* a chemically treated sheet of glass, metal, etc., on which to take a photograph. **17.** *Elect.* an electrode in an accumulator. **18.** *Geol.* one of a number of main areas of the earth's crust. **19. on a plate,** (of something offered) able to be taken without effort. ◇*v.t.* **20.** to coat (metal) with a thin film of gold, silver, etc. **21.** to cover with metal plates for protection, etc. [ME, from OF: flat piece, plate, probably from OF, from LL, from Gk: broad, flat]

plateau /'plætoʊ/, *n., pl.* **-eaus, -eaux** /-oʊz/. **1.** a large flat area of high elevation. **2.** any period of little or no progress, as in a person's learning, etc. [F, from OF: flat object]

plate glass, *n.* thick, polished glass formed by rolling the hot glass into a plate; used in large windows, mirrors, etc.

platelet /'pleɪtlət/, *n.* a very tiny disc found in large numbers in the blood, and important for blood clotting. [PLATE + -LET]

plate-mark /'pleɪt-mak/, *n.* → **hallmark.**

platform /'plætfɔm/, *n.* **1.** raised flooring, as in a hall, for use by public speakers, performers, etc. **2.** a raised area alongside the tracks of a railway station. **3.** the open entrance area at the end of a bus, etc. **4.** a flat elevated piece of ground. **5.** the body of principles which a political party uses to appeal to the public. **6.** a thick sole on a shoe. [F: flat form, plan, flat area, terrace]

Plath /plæθ/, *n.* **Sylvia,** 1932-63, US poet and novelist who spent her last years in England; became a cult figure after her suicide; wrote the novel *The Bell Jar* (1963).

plating /'pleɪtɪŋ/, *n.* **1.** a thin coating of gold, silver, etc. **2.** an outer layer of metal plates.

platino-, a combining form of **platinum.**

platinoid /'plætənɔɪd/, *adj.* **1.** like platinum. ◇*n.* **2.** any of the metals with which platinum is usu. associated. **3.** a mixture of copper, zinc, and nickel, to which small quantities of tungsten, aluminium, etc., have been added.

platinum /'plætənəm/, *n.* **1.** *Chem.* a heavy, greyish white, highly malleable and ductile metallic element, chemically rather inactive and fusible only at high temperatures, used esp. for making chemical and scientific apparatus and in jewellery. Symbol: Pt; *at. no.:* 78; *at. wt:* 195.09. **2.** a light metallic grey with very slight bluish tinge when compared with silver. [NL, from Sp: silver]

platitude /'plætətjud/, *n.* a flat, dull, or trite remark, esp. one spoken as if it were fresh and wise. [F: flat] – **platitudinous,** *adj.*

Plato /'pleɪtoʊ/, *n.* 427?-347 BC, Greek philosopher, who influenced the thought, religion and art of the Western World; his theory of ideas is explored in dialogues such as *Phaedo, Symposium* and *The Republic* in which Socrates is the central character.

Platonic /plə'tɒnɪk/, *adj.* **1.** (*l.c.*) purely spiritual; free from sensual desire: *Platonic love*. **2.** of or relating to Plato. – **Platonism,** *n.*

platoon /plə'tun/, *n.* **1.** a military sub-unit consisting of two or more sections. **2.** a company of people. [F: little ball, group, platoon]

platter /'plætə/, *n.* **1.** a large, shallow dish, commonly oval, for holding or serving meat,

platter   795   **pleasure**

etc. **2. on a platter,** (of something offered) able to be taken without effort. [ME, from AF, from OF: plate, dish]

platypus /ˈplætəpʊs/, n., pl. **-puses, -pi** /paɪ/. an egg-laying monotreme of Australia, living on land and water and having webbed feet and a bill like a duck's. [NL, from Gk: flat-footed]

plaudit /ˈplɔdət/, n. (usu. pl.) applause, approval, etc., as for an admired performance. [L]

plausible /ˈplɔzəbəl/, adj. having an appearance of truth or reason. [L] **—plausibility, plausibleness,** n. **—plausibly,** adv.

Plautus /ˈplɔtəs/, n. **Titus Maccius** /ˌtaɪtəs ˈmæksiəs/, c. 254– c. 184 BC, Roman comic dramatist, whose 21 surviving plays are based on Greek models, esp. those of Menander; influenced the development of comedy and Romantic drama in the West, as seen in the plays of Shakespeare, Ben Jonson and Molière.

play /pleɪ/, n. **1.** (a performance of) a dramatic composition; drama. **2.** (activity during) time free from work; leisure; recreation. **3.** fun; jest: *He said it in play.* **4.** the carrying on of a game. **5.** *Obs. (except in the expressions* **fair play,** *etc.)* action; conduct. **6.** elusive change, as of light or colors: *the play of light on the water.* **7.** freedom of movement, as of a part of a machine. **8.** freedom for action: *full play of the mind.* **9. in play,** *Sport.* (of a ball) in use and within bounds. ◇*v.t.* **10.** to act the part of (a person) in a dramatic performance: *to play Lady Macbeth.* **11.** to join in (a game, etc.). **12.** to oppose (another person or team, etc.) in a game: *We're playing Easts next week.* **13.** to move (an object) in a game: *to play a card.* **14.** to imitate in fun: *to play house.* **15.** to perform on (a musical instrument): *to play the flute.* **16.** to perform (music) on an instrument: *to play a tune on the flute.* **17.** to cause to move or change lightly or quickly: *to play colored lights on a fountain.* **18.** to operate: *to play a hose on a fire.* **19.** to allow (a hooked fish) to tire itself by pulling on the line. **20.** to bring to an end (fol. by *out*). ◇*v.i.* **21.** to exercise oneself in amusement or recreation. **22.** to do something only in sport, which is not to be taken seriously. **23.** to amuse oneself; trifle (fol. by *with*). **24.** to take part in a game. **25.** to act in a certain way: *to play fair.* **26.** to perform on stage, on an instrument, etc. **27.** (of an instrument or music) to sound in performance. **28.** to move freely, as a part of a machine. **29.** to move about lightly or quickly. **30.** to operate continuously: *It played on his nerves.* **31.** to work on (the feelings, etc., of another) for one's own purposes (fol. by *on* or *upon*): *She plays on his feeling of inferiority.* ◇*v.* **32.** Some special uses are:

play around, to make love without serious intentions.

play ball, to work in agreement with.

play down, to lessen the importance of.

play for time, to gain needed time by unnecessarily prolonging something.

play into the hands of, to act in such a way as to give an advantage to.

play off, a. to pit (two people, nations, etc.) against (each other) for one's own advantage. **b.** to play an extra game in order to settle (a tie).

play out, to play without attempting to score.

play the game, *Colloq.* to play in accordance with the rules.

play up to, to try to get into the favor of. [OE *plegan*]

playback /ˈpleɪbæk/, n. **1.** the reproduction of sound, music, etc., which has just been recorded. ◇*adj.* **2.** of or relating to a device used in reproducing such a recording.

playboy /ˈpleɪbɔɪ/, n. a wealthy, carefree man who spends most of his time at parties, nightclubs, etc.

player piano, n. a piano in which a mechanism turns a perforated paper roll, causing the piano keys to move in a particular order.

Playford /ˈpleɪfəd/, n. **Sir Thomas,** 1896–1981, Liberal Country League politician; premier of SA 1938–65 (a record term in Australia and the British Commonwealth).

playing card, n. **1.** one of the conventional set of 52 cards, used in playing various games of chance and skill. **2.** one of any set or pack of cards used in playing games.

play-off /ˈpleɪ-ɒf/, n. the playing off of a tie, as in sports.

playwright /ˈpleɪraɪt/, n. a writer of plays; dramatist. [PLAY + WRIGHT]

plaza /ˈplazə/, n. a public open space in a city or town. [Sp, from L]

plea /pli/, n. **1.** an appeal or request, esp. in defence or excuse. **2.** *Law.* a statement made by one party in answer to the accusation of the other party in a legal proceeding, e.g. a plea of not guilty in a criminal case. [ME, from OF, from ML: court, plea, from L: (thing which) seemed good, prescription, maxim]

plead /plid/, v., **pleaded** or **plead** /plɛd/, **pleading.** ◇*v.i.* **1.** to beg; make an appeal. **2.** to use arguments for or against something. **3.** *Law.* to make any plea in an action at law. ◇*v.t.* **4.** to claim in defence or excuse: *to plead ignorance.* **5.** *Law.* to present (a cause, etc.) by argument before a court. [ME, from OF: go to law, plead, from VL, from L: thing which pleases] **—pleading,** n.

pleasant /ˈplɛzənt/, adj. **1.** pleasing; agreeable; pleasurable. **2.** (of people, manners, etc.) agreeable socially. [ME, from OF PLEASE] **—pleasantly,** adv.

pleasantry /ˈplɛzəntri/, n., pl. **-tries. 1.** pleasant humor in conversation. **2.** a polite remark or action.

please /pliz/, v., **pleased, pleasing,** interj. ◇*v.t.* **1.** to act to the pleasure or satisfaction of (someone). ◇*v.i.* **2.** to like, wish, or choose: *Go where you please.* **3.** to be agreeable. ◇*interj.* **4.** if you are willing: *Please come here.* [ME, from OF, from L: please, seem good] **—pleasing,** adj.

pleasurable /ˈplɛʒərəbəl/, adj. giving pleasure; agreeable.

pleasure /ˈplɛʒə/, n., v., **-ured, -uring.** ◇*n.* **1.** a condition or feeling of being pleased.

pleasure 2. worldly or silly enjoyment: *the pursuit of pleasure*. 3. satisfaction to the senses. 4. a cause of enjoyment. 5. one's desire or choice: *What is your pleasure?* ◊*v.t.* 6. to give pleasure to; gratify. [ME, from OF PLEASE]

pleat /plit/, *n.* 1. a fold made in cloth and kept in place by pressing, stitching, etc. ◊*v.t.* 2. to fold or arrange in pleats. [var. of PLAIT]

plebeian /plə'biən/, *adj.* 1. belonging or relating to the common people, esp. in Ancient Rome. 2. common; vulgar. ◊*n.* 3. a plebeian person. [L: of the people]

plebiscite /'plɛbəsaɪt, -sət/, *n.* 1. a direct vote of the electors of a state in regard to some important public question; referendum. 2. a vote by which the people of a political unit decide upon self-government or union with another country. [L]

plectrum /'plɛktrəm/, *n., pl.* **-tra** /-trə/, **-trums**. a small piece of wood, metal, etc., for plucking the strings of a banjo, guitar, etc. [L, from Gk]

pledge /plɛdʒ/, *n., v.,* **pledged, pledging**. ◊*n.* 1. a solemn promise; vow. 2. a piece of personal property given as a security for the payment of a debt. 3. the condition of being given or held as security: *to put a thing in pledge*. 4. anything given or seen as a security of something. 5. a statement of support shown by drinking a person's health; toast. ◊*v.t.* 6. to bind by or as if by a pledge. 7. to promise solemnly to give, maintain, etc. 8. to give or leave as a pledge; pawn. 9. to vow, as one's honor, etc. 10. to give a pledge for. 11. to drink a pledge to. [ME, from OF, from ML, of Gmc orig.] — **pledger**, *n.*

-plegia, a word part used as a noun ending in medical terms meaning forms of paralysis, as in *paraplegia*. [Gk, combining form from *plēgē* blow, stroke]

Pleiades /'plaɪədiz/, *n.pl. Class Myth.* the seven daughters of Atlas and a nymph, pursued by Orion and transformed into the group of stars bearing their name (one star, missing, being the traditional **Lost Pleiad**).

Pleiocene /'plaɪoʊsin/, *adj., n.* → **Pliocene**.

Pleistocene /'plaɪstoʊsin/, *adj., n. Geol.* (relating to) the earlier division of the Quaternary period, following the Pliocene and before the Recent; ice age. [Gk]

plenary /'plinəri/, *adj.* 1. full; complete; entire. 2. attended by all qualified members, as a council. [late ME, from LL]

plenipotentiary /ˌplɛnəpə'tɛnʃəri/, *n., pl.* **-ries**, *adj.* ◊*n.* 1. (formerly) a person with full powers to negotiate on behalf of a state. ◊*adj.* 2. having full power or authority, as a diplomatic agent. 3. giving full power, as a commission. [ML, from LL]

plenitude /'plɛnətjud/, *n.* 1. fullness in quantity, measure, or degree; abundance. 2. the condition of being full. [L]

plentiful /'plɛntəfəl/, *adj.* 1. giving or existing in great amounts. 2. having a large supply of something.

plenty /'plɛnti/, *n.* 1. a full supply. 2. a great amount; abundance. 3. a time of full supply. ◊*adj.* 4. existing in great quantity or number (usu. after a verb): *This is plenty*. ◊*adv.* 5. *Colloq.* fully: *plenty good enough*. [ME, from OF, from L: fullness, abundance] — **plenteous**, *adj.*

Plenty /'plɛnti/, *n.* **Bay of**, a wide indentation of the Pacific Ocean on the north coast of North Island, New Zealand. About 153 km long.

plenum /'plinəm/, *n., pl.* **-nums, -na** /-nə/. 1. a container of air, or other gas, under greater than the surrounding pressure. 2. the whole of space regarded as being filled with matter. 3. a full assembly, as a joint legislative assembly. [L: full, filled, complete, abundant]

pleonasm /'pliənæzəm/, *n.* 1. the use of more words than are necessary to express an idea; redundancy. 2. a word or expression too many. [L, from Gk] — **pleonastic**, *adj.*

plethora /'plɛθərə/, *n.* overfullness; overabundance. [NL, from Gk: fullness]

pleura /'plurə/, *n., pl.* **pleurae** /'pluri/. a delicate membrane covering each lung in mammals and folded back as a lining of the corresponding side of the chest cavity. [NL, from Gk: rib, side] — **pleural**, *adj.*

pleurisy /'plurəsi/, *n.* painful swelling of the pleura. [ME, from OF, from LL, from Gk] — **pleuritic**, *adj.*

pliable /'plaɪəbəl/, *adj.* 1. easily bent; flexible. 2. easily influenced; yielding. [F: fold, bend] — **pliability**, *n.*

pliant /'plaɪənt/, *adj.* 1. bending readily; flexible; supple. 2. easily inclined or influenced; yielding; compliant. [ME, from OF: fold, bend]

pliers /'plaɪəz/, *n.pl.* small pincers with long jaws, for bending wire, holding small objects, etc.

plight[1] /plaɪt/, *n.* a condition, state, or situation (usu. bad). [ME, from AF, var. of OF: fold, manner of folding, condition]

plight[2] /plaɪt/, *v.t.* to give in promise; pledge (one's honor, etc.). [ME; OE *pliht* danger, risk]

plimsoll /'plɪmsəl/, *n. Brit.* → **sandshoe**. [probably from supposed resemblance between a PLIMSOLL LINE and the line of rubber binding the sole to the side of the shoe]

Plimsoll line, *n.* a line or mark required to be placed on the side of all British merchant vessels, showing the depth to which they may be legally loaded. Also, **Plimsoll mark**. [named after Samuel *Plimsoll*, 1824–98, politician and social reformer]

plinth /plɪnθ/, *n. Archit.* 1. the lower square part of the base of a column or pedestal. 2. a course of stones, as at the base of a wall. [L, from Gk: plinth, squared stone]

Pliny /'plɪni/, *n.* 1. ('the Elder', *Gaius Plinius Secundus*) AD 23–79, Roman naturalist, encyclopedist, and writer. 2. his nephew ('the

Pliny

Younger', Gaius Plinius Caecilius Secundus) AD 62?–113?, Roman writer, statesman, and orator.

Pliocene /'plaɪəʊsiːn/, adj., n. Geol. (relating to) the latest principal division of the Tertiary period, coming after the Miocene, and before the Pleistocene. Also, **Pleiocene**. [Gk]

PLO /piː ɛl 'əʊ/, n. an organisation formed in 1964 to represent Palestinian Arabs, with the aims of creating a state for them and removing the state of Israel. Also, **Palestine Liberation Organisation**. [abbrev.]

plod /plɒd/, v., **plodded, plodding**, n. ◇v.i. 1. to walk heavily; trudge. 2. to work onward in a dull way; drudge. ◇n. 3. a sound of or as of a heavy footstep. [? imitative] –**plodder**, n.

plonk[1] /plɒŋk/, v.t. 1. to place or drop heavily or suddenly (oft. fol. by *down*). ◇n. 2. the act or sound of plonking. ◇adv. 3. Colloq. exactly. Also, **plunk**. [imitative]

plonk[2] /plɒŋk/, n. Colloq. any alcoholic liquor, esp. cheap wine. [? var. of F (*vin*) *blanc* white (wine)]

plop /plɒp/, v., **plopped, plopping**, n. adv. ◇v.i. 1. to make a sound like that of a flat object striking water without a splash. 2. to fall heavily with such a sound. ◇n. 3. a plopping sound or fall. ◇adv. 4. with a plop. [imitative]

plosive /'pləʊsɪv, -zɪv/, adj., n. Linguistics. (relating to) a stop consonant that ends with an explosion of breath.

plot[1] /plɒt/, n., v., **plotted, plotting**. ◇n. 1. a secret plan or scheme to act for some purpose, usu. unlawful or evil. 2. the plan, scheme, or main story of a play, novel, poem, etc. ◇v.t. 3. to plan secretly (something harmful or evil). 4. to mark on a plan or map, as a ship's course, etc. 5. to make a plan or map of, as an area of land, a building, etc. 6. to determine and mark (points or a curve), as on graph paper. ◇v.i. 7. to form secret plots; conspire. [shortened form of OF *complot* crowd struggle, later concerted plan, orig. uncertain]

plot[2] /plɒt/, n. a small piece or area of ground. [ME and OE; orig. uncert.]

plough /plaʊ/, n. 1. an agricultural tool for cutting and turning over the soil. 2. any of various tools like this, as for cutting grooves or clearing snow. 3. (*cap.*) *Astron.* **the Plough**. Also, **Charles's Wain**. A group of seven stars in the constellation of the Great Bear. ◇v.t. 4. to turn up (the soil) with a plough. 5. to make (a furrow, etc.) with or as with a plough. ◇v.i. 6. to turn the soil with a plough. 7. to move through anything in the manner of a plough. 8. to work at something slowly and with determination (usu. fol. by *through*). ◇v. 9. **plough back**, to return (profits of a business) to that business. 10. **plough into**, to attack energetically. [ME; OE *plōh* ploughland]

ploughshare /'plaʊʃeə/, n. the blade of a plough which cuts the slice of earth.

plover /'plʌvə/, n. a small to medium-sized coastal bird, with a short, straight bill thickened at the end. [ME, from AF, from L: rain; the connection of the bird with rain being uncert.]

ploy /plɔɪ/, n. a scheme, as in conversation, to gain the advantage. [F *ployer*, from L *plicāre* fold]

pluck /plʌk/, v.t. 1. to pull off or out from the place of growth, as fruit, feathers, etc. 2. to pull with sudden force. 3. to sound (the strings of a musical instrument) by pulling at them with the fingers or a plectrum. ◇v.i. 4. to pull sharply; tug (*at*). ◇v. 5. **pluck up, a.** to pull up; uproot. **b.** to raise up (courage, spirit, etc.). ◇n. 6. the act of plucking; a pull or tug. 7. the heart, liver, and lungs, esp. of an animal used for food. 8. courage. [OE *pluccian*] –**plucker**, n. –**plucky**, adj.

plug /plʌg/, n., v., **plugged, plugging**. ◇n. 1. a piece of rubber or plastic for stopping the flow of water from a basin, etc. 2. a piece of wood or other material used to stop up a hole, to fill a gap, or to act as a wedge. 3. a device, usu. with three prongs, for linking an appliance to a power supply. 4. → **spark plug**. 5. *Geol.* → **volcanic plug**. 6. a cake of pressed tobacco. 7. *Colloq.* an advertisement, esp. freely given. ◇v.t. 8. to fill with or as with a plug. 9. *Colloq.* to mention (a song, product, etc.) favorably and often, as on radio, etc. 10. *Colloq.* to shoot. 11. to connect (an electrical device) with an outlet (fol. by *in*). ◇v.i. 12. *Colloq.* to work steadily or untiringly (usu. fol. by *on* or *away*). [MD: plug, peg]

plum[1] /plʌm/, n. 1. a deep-colored, smooth-skinned fruit, closely related to the cherry but with an oblong stone. 2. a tree bearing such a fruit. 3. a raisin, as in a cake or pudding. 4. a deep purple varying from bluish to reddish. ◇adj. 5. good or choice: *a plum job*. [ME; OE *plūme*, from Gk]

plum[2] /plʌm/, adj., adv. → **plumb**.

plumage /'pluːmɪdʒ/, n. the complete feathery covering of a bird. [late ME, from OF: feather]

plumb /plʌm/, n. 1. a small mass of lead or the like, used for various purposes. 2. the position of a plumbline when freely hung; the perpendicular. 3. **out of plumb, a.** not perpendicular. **b.** not working properly. ◇adj. 4. correct according to a plumbline. 5. *Colloq.* downright; absolute. ◇adv. 6. in a vertical direction. 7. exactly; precisely: *plumb in the middle*. 8. *Colloq.* completely; absolutely. ◇v.t. 9. to test by a plumbline. 10. to make vertical. 11. to measure (depth) by sounding. [ME, from OF, from L: lead]

plumber /'plʌmə/, n. someone who lays and repairs piping, fixtures, and appliances, in connection with the water supply, drainage systems, etc. [ME, from OF, from LL, from L: lead]

plumbing /'plʌmɪŋ/, n. 1. the system of pipes, etc., for carrying water, liquid wastes, etc., as in a building. 2. the work of a plumber.

plumbline /'plʌmlaɪn/, n. a string with a metal weight tied to one end, used to mark vertical lines, find the depth of water, etc.

plumbum /'plʌmbəm/, n. Chem. →**lead**². Symbol: Pb [L]

plume /plum/, n., v., **plumed, pluming.** ◇n. **1.** a feather, esp. a large, long, or showy one. **2.** any feathery part or formation. ◇v.t **3.** to cover with plumes. **4.** (of a bird) to tidy or preen (itself or its feathers). **5.** to pride (oneself). [OF, from L: feather]

plummet /'plʌmət/, v.i. **1.** to fall straight downwards. ◇n. **2.** →**plumbline**. [ME, from OF: lead]

plump¹ /plʌmp/, adj. **1.** well filled out or rounded in form. ◇v.i. **2.** to become plump (oft. fol. by *up* or *out*). ◇v.t **3** to make plump (fol. by *up* or *out*). [ME]

plump² /plʌmp/, v.i. **1.** to fall heavily or suddenly; drop; sink. **2.** to vote for or choose only one out of a number (fol. by *for*). ◇v.t. **3.** to drop or throw heavily or suddenly. [ME: probably imitative]

plunder /'plʌndə/, v.t. **1.** to rob by open force, as in war. ◇v.i. **2.** to take plunder. ◇n. **3.** the act of plundering; pillage. **4.** that which is taken in plundering; loot. [G]

plunge /plʌndʒ/, v., **plunged, plunging**, n. ◇v.t. **1.** to throw or thrust forcibly or suddenly into something; immerse: *to plunge a hand into water; to plunge a country into war*. ◇v.i. **2.** to throw oneself, or fall as if thrown, into water, a deep place, etc. **3.** to throw oneself forcefully into some condition, situation, etc. **4.** (of a cliff, a road, etc.) to descend quickly or steeply. **5.** (of a horse, ship, etc.) to fall violently forward. ◇n. **6.** the act of plunging. **7.** a leap or dive into water, etc. **8.** a headlong rush. **9.** a sudden, violent pitching movement. **10. take the plunge,** to start to do something. [ME, from OF, from L: lead]

plunk /plʌŋk/, v.t. **1.** to pluck (a stringed instrument); twang. ◇n., adv. **2.** →**plonk**¹. [imitative]

pluperfect tense /plu,pəfəkt 'tens/, n. Gram. See Appendix. [L: more than perfect]

plural /'plurəl/, adj. **1.** consisting of, containing, or relating to more than one. **2.** relating to or involving a number of people or things. ◇n. **3.** Gram. the plural number. [ME, from L]

pluralism /'plurəlɪzəm/, n. **1.** Philos. a theory or system that recognises more than one ultimate substance or principle. See **monism**, **dualism. 2.** a policy which supports a multi-cultural society. —**pluralist,** n. —**pluralistic,** adj.

plurality /plu'rælətɪ/, n., pl. **-ties. 1.** the condition or fact of being plural. **2.** more than half of the whole; the majority. **3.** a number greater than unity or one.

pluri-, a word part meaning 'several', 'many'. [L, combining form of *plūrēs*, pl.]

plus /plʌs/, prep. **1.** more by the addition of: *ten plus two*. ◇adj. **2.** involving or showing addition. **3.** positive: *a plus quantity*. **4.** Colloq. with something in addition: *He has energy plus*. **5.** Bot. indicating one of the two strains in fungi which must unite in the sexual process. ◇n. **6.** the plus sign (+). **7.** something additional. [L: more]

plush /plʌʃ/, n. **1.** a fabric of silk, cotton, wool, etc., having a longer pile than that of velvet. ◇adj. **2.** Also, **plushy.** (of a room, furniture, etc.) beautiful and costly. [F, from L: hair]

plus sign, n. the symbol (+) meaning addition or a positive quantity.

Plutarch /'plutak/, n. AD c. 46– c. 120, Greek biographer, best known for his *Parallel Lives* (c. 100) of Greek and Roman political and military leaders.

Pluto /'plutoʊ/, n. **1.** Gk Myth. Hades, the lord of the dead and the lower world. **2.** Astron. the ninth and outermost planet from the sun, discovered in 1930. [L, from Gk: *Ploútōn*] —**Plutonian,** adj.

plutocracy /plu'tɒkrəsɪ/, n., pl. **-cies. 1.** the rule or power of wealth. **2.** a government or state in which the wealthy class rules. [Gk] —**plutocrat,** n. —**plutocratic,** adj.

pluton /'plutɒn/, n. Geol. any body of igneous rock that became solid far below the earth's surface. [named after PLUTO] —**plutonic,** adj.

plutonium /plu'toʊnɪəm/, n. Chem. a radioactive element, with an important isotope, $^{239}_{94}$Pu, which is fissionable and can be produced in chain-reaction units from uranium-238; Symbol: Pu; *at. no.:* 94; *at. wt:* 244. [Gk]

pluvial /'pluvɪəl/, adj. **1.** rainy. **2.** Geol. due to rain. [L]

ply¹ /plaɪ/, v., **plied, plying.** ◇v.t. **1.** to use: *to ply the needle*. **2.** to carry on; practise: *to ply a trade*. **3.** to supply continuously: *to ply a person with drink*. **4.** to cross (a river, etc.), esp. regularly. ◇v.i. **5.** to travel regularly over a fixed course. **6.** to perform work busily: *To ply with the oars*. **7.** to direct the course, on water or otherwise. **8.** Naut. to make way windward by tacking. [ME, shortened form of ME *aplyen* apply]

ply² /plaɪ/, n., pl. **plies, plied, plying.** ◇n. **1.** a fold; a thickness. **2.** a strand of thread. **3.** bent; bias. ◇v.t. **4.** to bend, fold, or mould. [ME, from OF: fold, bend, from L: fold]

Plymouth /'plɪməθ/, n. a city and seaport in England, in south Devon; naval base. Pop. 242 560 (1981).

Plymouth Rock, n. a rock at Plymouth, Massachusetts, US, on which the Pilgrim Fathers are said to have landed in 1620.

plywood /'plaɪwʊd/, n. a material consisting of an odd number of thin sheets of wood glued together, used in building, etc.

p.m. /pi 'em/, *Abbrev.* **1.** after noon. [L *post meridiem*] **2.** post-mortem.

PM /pi 'em/, *Abbrev.* Prime Minster.

PMG /pi ɛm 'dʒi/, *Abbrev.* Postmaster General.

PMT /pi ɛm 'ti/, *Abbrev.* premenstrual tension.

pneumatic /nju'mætɪk/, adj. **1.** of or relating to air, or gases in general. **2.** operated

pneumatic	799	**poinsettia**

by air, or by pressure of air. [L, from Gk] **–pneumatically**, *adv.*

pneumo-, a word part referring to the lungs or breathing. [combining form representing Gk *pneúmōn* lung, or, less often, *pneûma* wind, air, breath]

pneumobacillus /ˌnjuːmoʊbəˈsɪləs/, *n., pl.* **-cilli** /-ˈsɪlaɪ/. a bacillus which causes certain diseases of the lungs, esp. pneumonia. [NL. See PNEUMO-, BACILLUS]

pneumonia /njuːˈmoʊnjə/, *n.* inflammation of the lungs. [NL, from Gk]

pneumonic /njuːˈmɒnɪk/, *adj.* **1.** of or relating to the lungs; pulmonary. **2.** relating to or suffering from pneumonia.

PNG /piː en ˈdʒiː/, *Abbrev.* Papua New Guinea.

Po, *Chem. Symbol.* polonium.

PO, *Abbrev.* **1.** petty officer. **2.** pilot officer. **3.** postal order. **4.** post office.

poach[1] /poʊtʃ/, *v.i.* to take game or fish illegally from another's land. [MF: thrust or put out (eyes), dig out with the fingers, probably from Gmc]

poach[2] /poʊtʃ/, *v.t.* to cook in liquid just below boiling point in a shallow pan. [F]

pock /pɒk/, *n.* **1.** a small swelling on the body containing pus, caused by a disease such as smallpox. **2.** a mark or spot left by or looking like such a swelling. [OE *poc*]

pocket /ˈpɒkət/, *n.* **1.** a small bag sewn into a garment, for carrying small articles. **2.** any container or hole similar to a pocket in form, such as a hollow in the earth, esp. one containing gold, etc. **3.** a small isolated area: *a pocket of resistance.* **4.** a small bag or net at the corner or side of a billiard table. **5.** *Aust Rules.* a side position. **6. in one's pocket**, under one's control. **7. line one's pockets**, to make money by dishonest means. **8. out of pocket**, without money or having made a loss. ◇*v.t.* **9.** to put (something) into one's pocket. **10.** to take possession of, often dishonestly. **11.** to hide or put away: *He pocketed his pride.* **12.** (in billiards) to drive (a ball) into a pocket. [ME, from AF, var. of F: bag]

pod /pɒd/, *n., v.,* **podded, podding.** ◇*n.* **1.** a long, two-sided seed case, as that of the pea or bean. ◇*v.i.* **2.** to produce pods. ◇*v.t.* **3.** to remove (peas, etc.) from a pod. [apparently backformation from *podder* peasecod-gatherer, from *pease* (See PEA) + *cod* bag pod]

-pod, a word part meaning 'footed', as in *cephalopod* (*pl.* **-poda**). [Gk: foot]

-poda, plural of **-pod**, as in *Cephalopoda*.

poddy /ˈpɒdi/, *adj.* (of a small animal, esp. a lamb or calf) requiring to be handfed. [? Brit. d. *poddy* fat]

podgy /ˈpɒdʒi/, *adj.,* **-ier, -iest.** short and fat; plump. Also, **pudgy.** **–podginess,** *n.*

podium /ˈpoʊdiəm/, *n., pl.* **-dia** /-diə/. **1.** a small platform for an orchestral conductor, public speaker, etc. **2.** *Archit.* a long continuous structure serving as a base of a wall, etc. [L: elevated place, balcony, from Gk: foot]

-podous, a word part used as an adjective ending, corresponding to *-pod*. [Gk: footed]

podsol /ˈpɒdsɒl/, *n.* an unproductive soil, found over large areas in northern North America and Eurasia and common in eastern Australia. Also, **podzol**. [Russ., adj.: resembling ashes] **–podsolic,** *adj.*

Poe /poʊ/, *n.* **Edgar Allan,** 1809–49, US poet, writer and critic; his story *The Murders in the Rue Morgue* (1841) is thought of as one of the first modern detective stories.

poem /ˈpoʊəm/, *n.* **1.** a piece of writing in verse form, esp. one marked by artistic construction and imaginative thought. **2.** a piece of writing which, though not in verse, is marked by beauty of language or thought: *a prose poem.* **3.** something having qualities that suggest or are similar to those of a poem. [L, from Gk: poem, something made]

Poeppel Corner /ˈpɜːpəl ˌkɔːnə/, *n.* the point where the boundaries of Qld, SA and NT meet, in the Simpson Desert. [named after Augustus *Poeppel,* government surveyor]

poesy /ˈpoʊəzi/, *n., pl.* **-sies**. *Archaic*. **1.** the work or art of writing poetry. **2.** poetry or verse in general. [ME, from OF, from L, from Gk: poetic composition, poetry, a making]

poet /ˈpoʊət/, *n.* **1.** someone who writes poetry. **2.** someone having the gift of poetic thought and imagination, together with the power of expression. [ME, from L, from Gk: poet, maker] **–poetess,** *n. fem.*

poetaster /poʊəˈtæstə/, *n.* a writer of poor quality poetry. [ML or NL]

poetic /poʊˈɛtɪk/, *adj.* **1.** possessing the qualities of poetry: *poetic descriptions of nature.* **2.** of or relating to a poet, poets, or poetry. **3.** (of a person) having the ability or feeling of a poet. **4.** suitable as a subject for poetry. Also, **poetical.** [L, from Gk]

poetic justice, *n.* the handing out of rewards and punishments to those who deserve them, as happens in literature rather than in real life.

poetic licence, *n.* freedom taken by a poet in not following the rules of language, logic, or fact, in order to produce a literary effect.

poet laureate, *n., pl.* **poets laureate**. (in Britain) an officer of the royal household, who writes poems for royal and national events.

poetry /ˈpoʊətri/, *n.* **1.** the art of writing or speaking in rhythmical verse in order to express beautiful, imaginative thoughts, etc. **2.** a written work in verse form. **3.** poetic qualities, spirit or feeling, however shown. **4.** something that suggests or is similar to poetry. [ME, from LL]

pogrom /ˈpɒɡrəm/, *n.* an organised mass killing, esp. of Jews. [Russ.: devastation, destruction]

poignant /ˈpɔɪnjənt, ˈpɔɪnənt/, *adj.* **1.** keenly affecting the feelings; deeply felt: *poignant sorrow; poignant suffering.* **2.** sharp to the taste or smell. [ME, from OF, from L: prick, pierce] **–poignancy,** *n.*

poinsettia /pɔɪnˈsɛtiə/, *n.* a plant, native to Mexico and Central America, with bright,

poinsettia

usu. scarlet, petal-like bracts. [NL, named after JR *Poinsett*, 1779–1851, US minister to Mexico, who discovered the plant there in 1828]

point /pɔint/, *n.* **1.** a sharp end, becoming gradually thinner, as that of a sword, pin, etc. **2.** the part of anything that sticks out and becomes gradually narrower, such as a cape of land. **3.** a pointed tool or instrument, such as an etching needle. **4.** a mark made with a sharp end of something; dot. **5.** a written or printed dot, such as a decimal point, full stop, etc. **6.** *Geom.* something that has position but not size or extension, such as the intersection of two lines. **7.** any definite position, as in a scale, course, journey, etc.: *boiling point; this point of time; at this point in our travels.* **8.** any of the 32 positions indicating direction, marked on a compass. **9.** the important or essential thing: *the point of the matter; the point of the story.* **10.** (*pl.*) suggestions: *points on how to get a job.* **11.** a single or separate article or detail; item: *points on a list.* **12.** (*pl.*) extremities, such as the ears, feet, etc., of an animal. **13.** the unit of count in the score of a game. **14.** *Cricket.* (the position of) the fielder who stands a short distance in front and to the offside of the batsman. **15.** *Aust Rules* — **behind** (def. 12). **16.** *Elect.* either of a pair of contacts that make or break the flow of current in a distributor. **17.** *Comm.* a unit of price movement in share dealings on the stock exchange. **18.** *Print.* a unit of measurement equal to 0.351×10^{-3} m. **19.** a unit of measurement of rainfall in the imperial system, equal to 0.254×10^{-3} m. **20.** (usu. *pl.*) *Railways.* a device for changing moving trains, etc., from one track to another, usu. consisting of a pair of movable rails. ◇**21.** Some special uses are:
at/on/upon the point of, close to: *on the point of death.*
make a point of, to consider as important; insist upon.
off the point, not relevant.
to the point, pertinent; relevant.
◇*v.t.* **22.** to direct (the finger, a weapon, the attention, etc.) at; to, or upon something. **23.** to show or direct attention to (something) by doing this (fol. by *out*). ◇*v.i.* **24.** to show or direct attention with the finger, etc.: *It's rude to point.* **25.** to direct the mind or thought in some direction: *Everything points to his guilt.* **26.** to aim. **27.** to face in or have a particular direction. **28.** *Naut.* to sail close to the wind. **29.** *Hunting.* (of a dog) to show the position of game by standing stiff and still, with the nose directed towards it. [ME, from OF]

point-blank /pɔint'blæŋk/, *adj.* **1.** aimed or fired straight at the mark at close range: *a point-blank shot.* **2.** straightforward; plain: *a point-blank statement.* ◇*adv.* **3.** with a direct aim at close range; straight. **4.** in a straightforward manner: *She refused point-blank.* [POINT, *v.* + BLANK (def. 17)]

Point Cook, *n.* a RAAF base and training school in southern Vic, near Melbourne on the western shore of Port Phillip Bay; first military flying course in 1914. See **Australian Defence Force Academy.**

poker

pointed /'pɔintəd/, *adj.* **1.** having a point or points; *a pointed arch; a pointed weapon.* **2.** having point or force; sharp: *pointed comment; pointed humor.* **3.** directed, or aimed, esp. at a person: *a pointed remark.*

pointer /'pɔintə/, *n.* **1.** a long, pointed stick used by teachers, etc., in indicating things on a map, blackboard, etc. **2.** the hand on a watch, machine, or instrument. **3.** a breed of short-haired hunting dog. **4.** a suggestion; piece of advice.

pointillism /'pwæntəlɪzəm, 'pɔintəlɪzəm/, *n.* a method of painting in which light is represented by putting many points or small dots of unmixed colors close together so that the colors appear mixed to the eye. [F: mark with points] —**pointillist,** *n.*

pointing /'pɔintɪŋ/, *n.* the treatment of mortar joints in brickwork or masonry, to make them waterproof, etc.

point of order, *n.* a question raised as to whether the proceedings of a meeting, etc., are according to the rules.

Point Puer /pɔint 'pjuə/, *n.* a headland in south-eastern Tas, adjacent to Port Arthur; formerly a juvenile penal settlement.

poise /pɔiz/, *n., v.,* **poised, poising.** ◇*n.* **1.** a state of balance, as from equality or equal spreading of weight. **2.** self-possession, confidence and grace of manner. ◇*v.t.* **3.** to balance evenly. **4.** to hold supported or raised in readiness: *to poise a spear.* ◇*v.i.* **5.** to be balanced. [late ME, from OF, from L: weigh] —**poised,** *adj.*

poison /'pɔizən/, *n.* **1.** any substance which causes death or illness. **2.** anything harmful to character, happiness, well-being, etc.: *Her remarks spread poison.* ◇*v.t.* **3.** to give poison to. **4.** to influence as poison does: *Jealousy poisoned her thoughts.* **5.** to put poison into or upon: *to poison food.* ◇*adj.* **6.** poisonous; causing poisoning: *a poison dart.* [ME, from OF: potion, draught, poison, from L] —**poisonous,** *adj.*

poison ivy, *n.* any of several North American shrubs, poisonous to the touch, with shiny leaves, green flowers, and whitish berries, esp. a climbing variety, growing on fences, rocks, trees, etc.

poke[1] /pouk/, *v.,* **poked, poking,** *n.* ◇*v.t.* **1.** to push against or into (something) with a finger, arm, stick, etc.; prod: *to poke a person in the ribs.* **2.** to make (a hole, one's way, etc.) by pushing. **3.** to push forward and show: *He poked his head round the door.* **4.** to force or drive (*away, in, out,* etc.) by pushing. ◇*v.i.* **5.** to make a pushing movement with a finger, stick, etc. **6.** to extend outwards; protrude (oft. fol. by *out*). **7.** to search (oft. fol. by *about* or *around*). ◇*v.* **8. poke fun at,** *Colloq.* to make appear foolish; ridicule. **9. poke one's nose into,** to interfere. ◇*n.* **10.** a push; thrust. [ME]

poke[2] /pouk/, *n. Obs.* a bag or sack. [ME]

poker[1] /'poukə/, a metal rod for stirring a fire. [POKE[1], *v.* + -ER[1]]

poker² /ˈpoukə/, *n.* a card game in which the players bet on the value of the cards in their hands.

poker machine, *n.* a coin-operated gambling machine. Also, **fruit machine, slot machine**.

poky /ˈpouki/, *adj.*, **-kier, -kiest.** small and lacking in space: *a poky room.* [POKE¹ + -Y¹]

Poland /ˈpoulənd/, *n.* a republic in eastern central Europe on the Baltic Sea, bordered by Germany, the Czech Republic, Slovakia, Ukraine, Belarus and Lithuania; independent since 1918; a socialist republic 1947-89; parliamentary democracy from 1989. Pop. 36 769 000 (1987 est.); 312 683 km². *Language:* Polish. *Currency:* zloty. *Cap.:* Warsaw. Polish, **Polska**.

polar /ˈpoulə/, *adj.* **1.** of or relating to a pole, as of the earth, a magnet, an electric cell, etc. **2.** opposite in character or action. **3.** *Chem.* having an uneven distribution of electric charge, within a molecule in water (H_2O) where the oxygen is slightly negatively charged and the hydrogen slightly positively charged. [ML, from L: POLE²]

polar axis, *n.* a line about which a body rotates, or about which a rotation is measured.

polar bear, *n.* a large white bear of the arctic area.

polar body, *n.* one of the tiny cells formed by the very unequal meiotic divisions of the ovum at or near the time of fertilisation.

polar circles, *n.pl.* the Arctic and Antarctic circles.

Polaris /pəˈlærəs/, *n.* a US intermediate range ballistic missile developed for firing from a submarine. [short for ML *stella polāris* polar star]

polarisation or **polarization** /poulərai-ˈzeɪʃən/, *n.* **1.** *Optics.* a condition, or the production of a condition, in which rays of light show different properties in different directions. **2.** *Chem.* the separation of a molecule into positive and negative ions.

polarise or **polarize** /ˈpoulərɑɪz/, *v.*, **-rised, -rising.** ◇*v.t.* **1.** to cause polarisation in. **2.** to give polarity to. ◇*v.i.* **3.** to gain polarity: *The meeting polarised into two opposing groups.* [POLAR + -ISE¹]

polarity /poʊˈlærəti/, *n.* **1.** *Phys.* **a.** (in magnets, batteries, etc.) the possession of positive or negative (or both) poles (**pole²**, def. 2). **b.** the tendency of a magnet, etc., to line up along the lines of force. **2.** the possession of two directly opposite ideas, principles or qualities.

polar lights, *n.pl.* the aurora borealis or the aurora australis.

polaroid /ˈpoulərɔɪd/, *n.* a material which polarises light, by allowing only light polarised in a particular direction to pass. [Trademark]

polaroid camera, *n.* a type of camera which takes instant, self-developing pictures. [Trademark]

pole¹ /poul/, *n.*, *v.*, **poled, poling.** ◇*n.* **1.** a long, usu. thin, piece of wood, metal, etc. **2.** a unit of length in the imperial system; a rod or square rod. **3. up the pole,** *Colloq.* **a.** in a difficult situation. **b.** slightly mad. ◇*v.i., v.t.* **4.** to propel (a boat, etc.) with a pole. [ME; OE *pāl*, from L: stake. See PALE²]

pole² /poul/, *n.* **1.** each of the extremities of the axis of the earth, or of any spherical body. **2.** *Phys.* each of the two areas of a magnet, electric battery, etc., at which opposite forces are concentrated. **3.** *Biol.* **a.** either end of an ideal axis in a nucleus, cell, or ovum. **b.** either end of a spindle-shaped figure formed in a cell during mitosis. **4. poles apart,** having completely opposite or widely different opinions, interests, etc. [ME, from L, from Gk: pivot, axis, pole]

Pole /poul/, *n.* a native or inhabitant of Poland. [G, sing. of *Polen*, from Pol *Poljane* Poles, lit., field-dwellers, from *pole* field]

poleaxe /ˈpoulæks/, *n., v.*, **-axed, -axing.** ◇*n.* **1.** a medieval weapon combining axe, hammer, and spike, used for fighting on foot. **2.** a similar axe, used in striking down animals. ◇*v.t.* **3.** to strike down with a poleaxe. [ME]

polecat /ˈpoulkæt/, *n.* **1.** a European mammal of the weasel family, with blackish brown fur, and which gives off an offensive smell. **2.** any of various North American skunks. [ME *polcat*; *pol-* of uncert. orig.]

polemic /pəˈlemɪk/, *n.* **1.** an argument about some opinion, teaching, etc. ◇*adj.* **2.** Also, **polemical.** of or relating to argument or disputation. [Gk: of or for war]

polemics /pəˈlemɪks/, *n.* the art or practice of argument or disputation, esp. in relation to beliefs or doctrines. **– polemicist,** *n.*

poler /ˈpoulə/, *n.* **1.** one of the two bullocks or horses nearest in the team to the wagon and harnessed to the pole; the polers do not take as much weight as the leaders, but are important in steering the wagon. **2.** *Colloq.* a lazy person; loafer.

Pole Star, *n. Astron.* a star of the second magnitude situated close to the north pole of the heavens, in the constellation Ursa Minor. Also **North Star, Polaris**.

police /pəˈlis/, *n., v.*, **-liced, -licing.** ◇*n.* **1.** an organised civil force for keeping order, preventing and investigating crime, and enforcing the laws. **2.** (*treated as pl.*) members of such a force. ◇*v.t.* **3.** to protect, control, or keep in order by police or as a police force does. [F: government, civil administration, police, from ML, var. of L: POLITY] **– policeman,** *n. masc.* **– policewoman,** *n. fem.*

police state, *n.* a country in which the police force is employed to discover and stop any opposition to the government in power.

policy¹ /ˈpɒləsi/, *n., pl.* **-cies. 1.** a definite course of action decided upon as necessary, correct, etc.: *a business policy; a nation's foreign policy.* **2.** practical wisdom; prudence: *It was good policy to agree.* [ME, from OF: government, civil administration, from L: POLITY]

policy² /ˈpɒləsi/, *n., pl.* **-cies.** a written contract of insurance. [F, from It, from ML, from Gk: a showing or setting forth]

poliomyelitis /ˌpouliouˈmaɪəˈlaɪtɪs/, *n.* an infectious viral disease, most common in young children, marked by inflammation of the nerve cells, mainly of the spinal cord, and resulting in muscular paralysis; infantile paralysis. Also, **polio**. [NL, from Gk: grey marrow]

-polis, a word part meaning 'city', as in *metropolis*. [Gk, combining form of *pólis*]

polish /ˈpɒlɪʃ/, *v.t.* **1.** to make smooth and shiny, esp. by rubbing: *to polish metal*. **2.** to make finished or refined: *He needs to polish his speech; to polish one's manners*. **3.** *Colloq.* to finish with quickly (fol. by *off*): *to polish off an opponent; to polish off a meal*. **4.** *Colloq.* to improve (fol. by *up*). ◊*v.i.* **5.** to become polished. ◊*n.* **6.** a substance used to give smoothness or shininess: *shoe polish*. **7.** the act of polishing. **8.** the smoothness and shininess of a surface. **9.** refinement; elegance. [ME, from F, from L] —**polished**, *adj.*

Polish /ˈpoʊlɪʃ/, *adj.* of or relating to Poland.

Politburo /ˈpɒlɪtbjʊəroʊ/, *n.* the chief policy-making and executive committee of a Communist party, such as that of the former Soviet Union. [Russ *Polit(icheskoe) Byuro* political bureau]

polite /pəˈlaɪt/, *adj.* **1.** showing good manners towards others, in behavior, speech, etc.; courteous. **2.** refined; cultured: *polite society*. [late ME, from L: polished] —**politeness**, *n.*

politic /ˈpɒlɪtɪk/, *adj.* **1.** wise in a practical way; prudent. **2.** political. See **body politic**. [ME, from L, from Gk: relating to citizens or to the state]

political /pəˈlɪtɪkəl/, *adj.* **1.** of, relating to, or dealing with politics: *a political writer*. **2.** having or trying to gain power in government or public affairs: *a political party*. **3.** of, relating to, or characteristic of political parties or government: *political measures*. **4.** *Colloq.* interested in politics: *He is not political*.

political asylum, *n.* →**asylum** (def. 3).

politician /pɒləˈtɪʃən/, *n.* a person who is active in party politics, esp. someone who holds a political office in government.

politicking /ˈpɒlətɪkɪŋ, pəˈlɪtəkɪŋ/, *n.* political activity, such as campaigns to gain publicity and win votes.

politics /ˈpɒlətɪks/, *n.* (*treated as sing. or pl.*) **1.** the science or art of government. **2.** political affairs, activities, or methods. **3.** political principles or opinions. **4.** the methods used to gain power or advancement within any organisation.

polity /ˈpɒləti/, *n., pl.* **-ties. 1.** a particular form or system of government (of a state, church, etc.). **2.** (the condition of being) a state or other organised community or body. [F, from L, from Gk: citizenship, government, form of government, commonwealth]

Polk /poʊk/, *n.* **James Knox**, 1795–1849, the 11th president of the US, 1845–49.

polka /ˈpɒlkə/, *n., v.,* **-kaed, -kaing.** ◊*n.* **1.** (the music for) a quick round dance of Bohemian origin, with music in duple time. ◊*v.i.* **2.** to dance the polka. [F and G, from Czech: half-step]

polka dot, *n.* **1.** a dot or round spot repeated to form a pattern on a cloth. **2.** a pattern of, or cloth with, such dots.

poll /poʊl/, *n.* **1.** the voting at an election. **2.** the number of votes placed. **3.** the numerical result of the voting. **4.** the counting or listing of people, as for purposes of taxing, voting, etc. **5.** (*usu. pl.*) the place where votes are taken. **6.** a gathering of public opinion on a subject, usu. by selective personal questioning. **7.** the back of the head. ◊*v.t.* **8.** to receive (votes) at the polls. **9.** to take the votes of. **10.** to place (a vote) at the polls. **11.** to cut off or cut short the hair, etc., of (a person, etc.) or the horns of (cattle). ◊*v.i.* **12.** to vote at the polls. ◊*adj.* **13.** (of cattle) bred to have no horns. [ME: head]

pollard /ˈpɒləd/, *n.* **1.** a tree cut back nearly to the trunk, so as to produce a thick mass of branches. **2.** an animal, such as an ox or sheep, without horns. **3.** a by-product of the milling of wheat, used esp. in poultry food. [apparently from POLL, *v.* + -ARD]

pollen /ˈpɒlən/, *n.* the fertilising cells of flowering plants, consisting of fine, powdery, yellowish grains, sometimes in masses. [L: fine flour, dust] —**polliniferous**, *adj.*

Pollen /ˈpɒlən/, *n.* **Daniel**, 1813–96, NZ politician, born in Ireland; prime minister of NZ 1876.

pollen count, *n.* a measure of the pollen in the air made as a guide to people allergic to it.

pollinate /ˈpɒlənɛɪt/, *v.t.,* **-nated, -nating.** to carry pollen for fertilisation from an anther to the stigma of (a flower). —**pollination**, *n.*

Pollock /ˈpɒlək/, *n.* **Jackson**, 1912–56, US abstract expressionist painter; abandoned conventional drawing for techniques of dripping and splashing paint on canvas.

pollute /pəˈlut/, *v.t.,* **-luted, -luting. 1.** to make unclean or impure. **2.** to spoil or foul, esp. with the by-products of industrial processes. **3.** to make morally impure; defile. **4.** to make ceremonially impure; desecrate. [L] —**pollutant**, *n.* —**pollution**, *n.* —**polluted**, *adj.*

Pollux /ˈpɒləks/, *n. Gk Myth.* See **Castor and Pollux**. Greek, **Polydeuces**. [L from Gk]

polo /ˈpoʊloʊ/, *n.* **1.** a game played on horseback by two teams with long-handled mallets and a wooden ball. **2.** any game similar to this, such as water polo. [Baltī (language of Kashmir)]

Polo /ˈpoʊloʊ/, *n.* **Marco**, c. 1254– c. 1324, Venetian traveller in Asia, esp. at the court of Kublai Khan.

polonium /pəˈloʊniəm/, *n.* a radioactive element formed in the decay of radium; radium F. *Symbol:* Po; *at. no.:* 84; *at. wt of most stable isotope:* 210. [ML: Poland (birthplace of Marie Curie, who discovered it in 1898)]

Pol Pot /pɒl ˈpɒt/, *n.* born 1925, Cambodian Communist politician; prime minister of Cambodia 1976, 1977–1979.

poltergeist /'pɒltəgaɪst/, n. a ghost or spirit which shows its presence by noises, knockings, movement of objects, etc. [G: lit., noise-ghost]

poltroon /pɒl'truːn/, n. a complete coward. [F *poltron* from It *poltro* lazy]

Polwarth /'pɒlwəθ/, n. a breed of sheep developed in Vic and used widely in the production of comeback ewes on mixed farms. [from *Polwarth*, a region in Vic]

poly-, a word part or prefix, meaning 'much', 'many', esp. in scientific or technical words. See **mono-**. [Gk, combining form of *polýs* much, many]

polyandry /pɒli'ændri/, n. the practice or condition of having more than one husband at one time. [Gk] – **polyandrous**, adj.

polyanthus /pɒli'ænθəs/, n. a type of primrose with brightly colored flowers. [NL, from Gk: having many flowers]

polychromatic /pɒlikrə'mætɪk/, adj. having many colors. Also, **polychrome**, **polychromic** /pɒli'kroʊmɪk/. – **polychromatism**, n.

Polyclitus /pɒli'klaɪtəs/, n. fl. c. 450– c. 420 BC, Greek sculptor, noted for his bronze and marble statues of athletes. Also, **Polycleitus**, **Polycletus**.

polyester /'pɒliestə/, n. a synthetic polymer in which the structural units are linked by ester groups.

polygamy /pə'lɪgəmi/, n. 1. the practice or condition of having more than one spouse, esp. wives, at one time. 2. *Zool.* the habit of mating with more than one of the opposite sex. – **polygamist**, n. – **polygamous**, adj.

polygenesis /pɒli'dʒɛnəsəs/, n. the descent of a species or race from more than one ancestral species. – **polygenetic**, **polygenic**, adj.

polyglot /'pɒliglɒt/, adj. 1. (of a person) knowing many or several languages. 2. (of a book) written in several languages. ◇n. 3. a polyglot person. 4. a book, esp. a Bible, containing the same text in several languages. [ML, from Gk: many-tongued]

polygon /'pɒlɪgən, -gɒn/, n. a figure, esp. a closed plane figure, having many (more than four) angles and sides. [L, from Gk: many-angled] – **polygonal**, adj.

polygyny /pə'lɪdʒəni/, n. the practice or condition of having more than one wife at one time. [Gk: having many wives + -Y³] – **polygynous**, adj.

polyhedron /pɒli'hidrən/, n., pl. **-drons**, **-dra** /-drə/. a solid figure having many faces. [Gk: having many bases] – **polyhedral**, adj.

polymer /'pɒləmə/, n. a compound of high molecular weight made by chemical combination of many molecules, often of the same compound (monomer). [Gk: of many parts] – **polymeric**, adj.

polymerise or **polymerize** /pə'lɪmərаɪz, 'pɒləmərаɪz/, v.t., v.i., **-rised**, **-rising**. to combine or cause to combine, so as to form a polymer. – **polymerisation**, n.

polymorphous /pɒli'mɔːfəs/, adj. having, taking on or passing through many or various forms, stages, etc. Also, **polymorphic**. – **polymorphism**, n.

Polynesia /pɒlə'niʒə/, n. one of the three principal divisions of Oceania, comprising those island groups in the Pacific lying east of Melanesia and Micronesia, and extending from the Hawaiian Islands south to NZ. It includes the Hawaiian Islands, Easter Island and the major island groups Samoa, Cook, Line, Tonga and French Polynesia. Water area: 39 000 000 km²; land area: 294 000 km². – **Polynesian**, n., adj.

polynomial /pɒli'noʊmiəl/, adj. 1. consisting of or marked by many or several names or terms. ◇n. 2. a polynomial name, term. 3. *Alg.* an expression consisting of a number of terms each of which has the form of a coefficient times a non-negative integral power of the variable, as $1 + 3x^2 + 4x^3$. [POLY- + *-nomial* as in BINOMIAL]

polyp /'pɒlɪp/, n. 1. *Zool.* **a.** type of coelenterate which has a base attached to a rock, etc., a tubelike body, and a free end with mouth and tentacles. **b.** an independent animal body forming part of a compound or colonial organism. 2. *Pathol.* a growth from a mucous surface, as of the nose. [F, from L, from Gk: octopus, also polyp (def. 2)] – **polypoid**, adj.

polyphonic /pɒlə'fɒnɪk/, adj. 1. consisting of many voices or sounds. 2. *Music.* having two or more voices or parts, each with an independent melody, but all harmonising; contrapuntal (opposed to *homophonic*). [Gk: having many tones]

polysaccharide /pɒli'sækərаɪd, -rəd/, n. a carbohydrate, as starch, cellulose, etc., containing more than three monosaccharide units per molecule, which can be broken down by acids or enzymes to monosaccharides.

polysaturated /pɒli'sætʃəreɪtəd/, adj. 1. of or relating to fats based wholly on saturated fatty acids such as stearic acid. 2. of or relating to foodstuffs, such as meat, rich in polysaturated fat, believed to be associated with cardiac disease.

polystyrene /pɒli'staɪriːn/, n. a clear, plastic polymer of styrene easily colored and moulded, used in the form of rigid white foam as an insulating material.

polysyllabic /ˌpɒlɪsə'læbɪk/, adj. 1. (of a word, etc.) consisting of many (more than three) syllables. 2. (of language, etc.) marked by such words. [ML, from Gk: of many syllables]

polythene /'pɒləθiːn/, n. a plastic polymer of ethylene used for containers, electrical insulation, packaging, etc. Also, **polyethylene**.

polyunsaturated /ˌpɒliʌn'sætʃəreɪtəd/, adj. *Chem.* 1. of or relating to a fat or oil based on fatty acids which have two or more double bonds per molecule, such as linoleic acid. 2. of or relating to food based on polyunsaturated oil or fat, as safflower oil, etc., or margarine.

polyurethane /pɒli'jʊərəθeɪn/, n. a polymer of urethane used in making rigid foam and rubber products for insulation, decoration, etc.

polyvalent /pɒliˈveɪlənt/, *adj. Chem.* having more than one valency.

polyvinyl acetate /pɒli,vaɪnəl ˈæsəteɪt/, *n.* →PVA

polyvinyl chloride, *n.* →PVC

pom /pɒm/, *n.* →pommy.

pomander /pəˈmændə/, *n.* (a container carrying) a mixture of sweet-smelling substances, formerly carried by a person for perfume or to guard against infection. [earlier *pomeamber*, from *pome* apple + AMBER]

pomegranate /ˈpɒməgrænət/, *n.* a round, many-seeded fruit with a tough rind (usu. red) whose seeds are covered by a pleasantly acid flesh. [ME, from OF, from L]

Pomeranian /pɒməˈreɪniən/, *n.* (one of) a breed of small dogs with long, thick, silky hair. [originating in *Pomerania*, a region of N central Europe, now largely in Poland]

Pomeroy /ˈpɒmərɔɪ/, *n.* **John**, 1872–1950, NZ inventor in Australia; responsible for the bullet effective against zeppelins used in World War I.

pommel /ˈpʌməl, ˈpɒməl/, *n., v.,* **-melled, -melling.** ◇*n.* Also, **pummel. 1.** a knob at the end of the handle of a sword, etc. **2.** the part which sticks out at the front and top of a saddle. ◇*v.t.* **3.** →**pummel.** [ME, from OF, from L: fruit]

pommy /ˈpɒmi/, *n., pl.* **-mies.** *Colloq.* an Englishman. [? abbrev. of *pomegranate*, rhyming slang for immigrant]

pomp /pɒmp/, *n.* a stately or splendid display; splendor; magnificence. [ME, from OF, from L, from Gk: orig., a sending]

Pompadour /ˈpɒmpədɔː/, *n.* **Marquise de** (*Jeanne Antoinette Poisson Le Normant D'Étoiles*), 1721–64, mistress of Louis XV of France; exerted a strong intellectual, cultural and political influence.

Pompeii /pɒmˈpeɪi/, *n.* an ancient city in south-western Italy at the foot of Mt Vesuvius; buried by an eruption, AD 79. —**Pompeian**, *n., adj.*

Pompey /ˈpɒmpi/, *n.* ('The Great', Gnaeus *Pompeius Magnus*), 106–48 BC, Roman general and statesman; a member of the first triumvirate.

pompom /ˈpɒmpɒm/, *n.* a tuft or ball of feathers, wool, etc., used in making hats, etc. [imitative]

pompous /ˈpɒmpəs/, *adj.* **1.** marked by a showy display of importance or rank: *a pompous bow.* **2.** (of language, style, etc.) showily important-sounding. **3.** marked by pomp, stately splendor, or magnificence. [ME, from LL] —**pomposity**, *n.*

ponce /pɒns/, *n. Colloq.* →**pimp.** [orig. uncert.] —**poncy**, *adj.*

poncho /ˈpɒntʃoʊ/, *n., pl.* **-chos.** a blanket-like cloak with a hole in the centre to put over the head. [SAmer Sp, from Araucanian: woollen fabric]

pond /pɒnd/, *n.* a body of water smaller than a lake, often made artificially. [ME, anomalous var. of POUND³]

ponder /ˈpɒndə/, *v.i., v.t.* to consider deeply or carefully; meditate (on). [ME, from OF, from L: ponder, weigh]

ponderous /ˈpɒndərəs, -drəs/, *adj.* **1.** of great weight; heavy; massive: *a ponderous mass of iron.* **2.** without lightness or ease; dull: *a ponderous discussion.* [ME]

pongo /ˈpɒŋgoʊ/, *n.* →**glider** (def. 3). [Aboriginal]

poniard /ˈpɒnjəd, -ad/, *n.* **1.** a dagger. ◇*v.t.* **2.** to stab with a poniard. [F, from L: fist]

pontiff /ˈpɒntɪf/, *n.* **1.** a high or chief priest. **2.** *Church.* a bishop, esp. used to describe the pope. —**pontifical**, *adj.*

pontificate /pɒnˈtɪfɪkət, *n.;* / pɒnˈtɪfɪkeɪt/, *v.,* **-cated, -cating.** ◇*n.* **1.** the office, or term of office, of a pontiff. ◇*v.i.* **2.** to speak in an important-sounding manner. **3.** to serve as a pontiff or bishop. [ML]

pontoon¹ /pɒnˈtuːn/, *n.* a boat, or some other floating structure, used as (one of the supports for) a temporary bridge or dock. [F, from L: bridge, pontoon, punt]

pontoon² /pɒnˈtuːn/, *n.* a gambling game, where the aim is to obtain cards whose total value is as near as possible to 21, without going over 21. [(? humorous) mispronunciation of F *vingt-et-un*: twenty-one]

pony /ˈpoʊni/, *n., pl.* **-nies. 1.** a horse of a small type, usu. not more than 13 or 14 hands high. **2.** a small glass for beer or spirits. [F, from L: young animal]

ponytail /ˈpoʊniteɪl/, *n.* a hairstyle in which the hair is tied at the back of the head and then hangs loose.

pooch /puːtʃ/, *n. Colloq.* a dog.

poodle /ˈpuːdl/, *n.* (one of) a breed of intelligent pet dogs, with thick, curly hair often trimmed to a special shape. [short for *poodle dog*, from G: splash-dog (because the poodle is a water-dog)]

poofter /ˈpʊftə/, *n. Colloq.* (*oft. offensive*) a male homosexual.

pool¹ /puːl/, *n.* **1.** a small body of standing water; pond. **2.** any small collection of liquid on a surface: *a pool of blood.* **3.** a still, deep place in a stream. **4.** a swimming pool. [ME and OE *pōl*]

pool² /puːl/, *n.* **1.** a group of competitors who agree to control the production, market, and price of some item for the advantage of all. **2.** a combination of interests, funds, etc., for common advantage. **3.** a group of people performing a service: *a typing pool.* **4.** the people involved. **5.** the sum of money that can be won in certain games. **6.** a billiards game where the object is to drive all the balls into the pockets with the cue ball. ◇*v.t.* **7.** to put (interests, money, etc.) into a common store, usu. for some undertaking. [F: hen; probably at first slang for BOOTY]

pools /puːlz/, *n.pl.* →**football pools.**

Poona /'puːnə/, n. a city in India, in western Maharashtra. Pop. 1 203 351 (1981). Also, **Pune**.

poop /puːp/, n. a deck or an enclosed space in the back part of a ship, above the main deck. [ME, from OF, from It, from L]

poor /pɔː/, adj. **1.** having little or no wealth, goods, or means of living. **2.** (of a country, institution, etc.) barely supplied with means of support. **3.** (of the circumstances, life, home, dress, etc.) marked by or showing a lack of money. **4.** lacking in something usu. considered desirable, as skill, ability, moral judgment, etc.: *a poor piece of work*. **5.** small or mean in amount or number: *a poor wage*. **6.** unfortunate or unlucky (used to express pity): *The poor mother was in despair.* ◇n. **7.** poor people as a group (usu. prec. by *the*). [ME, from OF, from L]

poorhouse /'pɔːhaʊs/, n. (formerly) a house lived in by very poor people, run at public expense.

poorly /'pɔːli/, adv. **1.** in a poor manner or way. ◇adj. (*used after a verb*) **2.** in poor health; somewhat ill.

pop[1] /pɒp/, v., **popped, popping**, n., adv. ◇v.i. **1.** to make a short, quick, explosive sound or report: *The cork will pop.* **2.** (of roasting corn, etc.) to burst open with such a sound. **3.** to come or go quickly, suddenly or unexpectedly (fol. by *in, into, out,* etc.). ◇v.t. **4.** to cause to make a sudden, explosive sound. **5.** to cause to burst open with such a sound, as a balloon, etc. **6.** to put quickly, suddenly or unexpectedly: *pop the books on the table.* **7.** *Colloq.* to fire (a gun, etc.). ◇v. **8. pop off**, *Colloq.* **a.** to depart, esp. quickly. **b.** to die, esp. suddenly. **9. pop the question**, *Colloq.* to propose marriage. ◇n. **10.** a short, quick, explosive sound. **11.** a shot with a firearm. **12.** *Colloq.* a single unit: *They cost five dollars a pop.* **13.** a carbonated drink, esp. a non-alcoholic one. ◇adv. **14.** with a pop. [ME; imitative]

pop[2] /pɒp/, adj., n. (relating to) music having great but often short-lived popularity, esp. among the young, and usu. marked by a continual rhythmic beat. [short for POPULAR]

pop[3] /pɒp/, n. *Colloq.* father, or grandfather.

pop., *Abbrev.* **1.** popular. **2.** population.

pop art, n. modern art which claims there is no difference between good and bad taste, and which draws images and materials from popular culture and industry, esp. mass production.

pope /poʊp/, n. (oft. cap.) the bishop of Rome as head of the Roman Catholic Church. [ME; OE *pāpa*, from ML: bishop, pope, orig. father, from Gk: father]

Pope /poʊp/, n. **Alexander**, 1688–1744, English poet of the Augustan period, who used satire to express social criticism, as in his mock epic poem *The Rape of the Lock* (1712–14).

popinjay /'pɒpəndʒeɪ/, n. **1.** a vain, chattering person. **2.** a woodpecker of Europe. [ME, from OF: parrot, from Sp, from Ar, from Pers]

poplar /'pɒplə/, n. a fast-growing tall tree yielding a useful, light, softwood. [ME, from OF]

poplin /'pɒplɪn/, n. a strong, finely ribbed cotton material, used for clothing. [F, from It: papal; so called from being made at the papal city of Avignon]

poppet /'pɒpət/, n. **1.** Also, **poppet valve**. a valve which in opening is lifted bodily from its seat instead of being hinged at one side. **2.** a term of affection for a girl or child. [earlier form of PUPPET]

poppy /'pɒpi/, n., pl. **-pies**. **1.** any of several plants with showy flowers of various colors. **2.** an extract, such as opium, from one of these. **3.** an orange-red color; scarlet. [ME; OE *popæg, papig*, from VL *papāvum*, for L *papāver*]

poppycock /'pɒpikɒk/, n. *Colloq.* nonsense; bosh. [Dutch d. *pappekak* soft dung]

populace /'pɒpjələs/, n. the common people of a population, as opposed to the higher classes. [F, from It: PEOPLE]

popular /'pɒpjələ/, adj. **1.** regarded with favor or approval by a particular set of people or the general public. **2.** of, relating to, or representing the people, or the common people: *popular discontent.* **3.** suited to or intended for the general mass of people: *popular lectures on science.* [L] **– popularity**, n.

populate /'pɒpjəleɪt/, v.t., **-lated, -lating**. **1.** (of a group) to live in; inhabit. **2.** to put people to live in: *The empire was going to populate its new lands with loyal subjects.* [ML: inhabited]

population /pɒpjə'leɪʃən/, n. **1.** (the total number of) people living in a country, town, or any area. **2.** the number of people belonging to a particular race or class in a place. **3.** *Stats.* the sum total of a defined group of events, objects, etc.

populous /'pɒpjələs/, adj. (of an area) full of people; well populated. [L]

porcelain /'pɔːsəlɪn, 'pɒsəlɪn/, n. **1.** a fine, glass-like material made of clay; china. **2.** a collection of objects made of this, as a tea-set, etc. [F, from It]

porch /pɔːtʃ/, n. **1.** a covered approach to a building or a doorway. **2.** → **portico**. [ME, from OF, from L: porch, portico]

porcupine /'pɔːkjəpaɪn/, n. a rodent covered with long, stiff spines. [ME, from OF: spine-pig]

porcupine fish, n. a spiny fish, poisonous to eat, found in Australian and NZ waters.

pore[1] /pɔː/, v.i., **pored, poring**. **1.** to think or consider carefully (fol. by *over, on,* or *upon*). **2.** to read or study with steady attention (fol. by *over*). [ME; orig. uncert.]

pore[2] /pɔː/, n. **1.** a very small opening or hole, as in the skin or a leaf, for perspiration, absorption, etc. **2.** a very small crevice in a rock, etc. [ME, from F, from L, from Gk: passage]

pork /pɔːk/, n. the flesh of pigs used as food. [ME, from OF, from L: hog, pig]

pornography /pə'nɒgrəfi/, *n.* obscene literature, art, or photography, meant to excite sexual desire. **Hard-core pornography** shows sexual activity openly, whereas **soft-core pornography** implies it. [Gk: writing of prostitutes] —**pornographic**, *adj.* —**pornographer**, *n.*

porous /'pɔrəs/, *adj.* full of pores through which water, air, etc., can pass. —**porosity**, **porousness**, *n.*

porphyrin /'pɔfərən/, *n.* any of a group of cyclic compounds, such as haemoglobin and chlorophyll, which, combined with iron or magnesium and a protein, are found in all cells.

porphyry /'pɔfəri/, *n., pl.* **-ries. 1.** any igneous rock containing large and easily seen crystals in a finegrained groundmass. **2.** a sweet variety of white wine. [ME, from AF, from ML, for L, from Gk: PURPLE] —**porphyritic**, *adj.*

porpoise /'pɔpəs/, *n., pl.* **-poises,** (*esp. collectively*) **-poise.** a sea mammal, 1.5 to 2.4 metres long, usu. blackish above and paler beneath, with a blunt, rounded snout. [ME, from OF, from LL: hogfish]

porridge /'pɒrɪdʒ/, *n.* a breakfast dish consisting of oatmeal, etc., with water, or milk. [var. of POTTAGE]

port[1] /pɔt/, *n.* **1.** a town or place where ships load or unload. **2.** a place along the coast where ships may take refuge from storms. [ME and OE, from L: harbor, haven]

port[2] /pɔt/, *Naut.* ◊*n.* **1.** the left-hand side of a ship or aircraft facing forward (opposed to *starboard*). ◊*adj.* **2.** on or relating to the port side. ◊*v.t.* **3.** to turn (a ship) to the port or left side. [orig. uncert.; perhaps because the larboard side was customarily next to the shore in port]

port[3] /pɔt/, *n.* a sweet, fortified wine, usu. dark red. [from *Oporto* (from Pg: the port), city in Portugal]

port[4] /pɔt/, *n.* **1.** *Naut.* a porthole. **2.** a steel door in the side of a ship for loading and unloading. **3.** *Mech.* an opening in the surface of a cylinder, for steam, air, water, etc. to pass through. **4.** a point on a computer for connection to other pieces of electrical equipment such as a printer. [ME and OE, from L: gate]

port[5] /pɔt/, *n.* **1.** a suitcase. **2.** *Qld.* a school bag, esp. one slung on the back; satchel.

portable /'pɔtəbəl/, *adj.* **1.** able to be transported. **2.** easily carried by hand. ◊*n.* **3.** something that is portable. [ME, from LL] —**portability**, *n.*

Port Adelaide /pɔt 'ædəleɪd/, *n.* the main port and harbor for SA, north-west of Adelaide; transport, industry and shipping centre. Pop. 35 407 (1981).

portal /'pɔtl/, *n.* door, gate, or entrance, esp. one of grand appearance, as in a palace. [ME, from ML, from L: gate]

Port Arthur *n.* an inlet and small town on the Tasman Peninsula in south-eastern Tas, south-east of Hobart; a notorious penal settlement 1830–77; now part of the National Estate.

Port Augusta /pɔt ə'gʌstə/, *n.* a city and port at the head of the Spencer Gulf in SA, north-north-west of Adelaide; railway centre. Pop. 15 291 (1986). [named after *Augusta* Young, wife of Sir HF YOUNG, governor of SA]

portcullis /pɔt'kʌləs/, *n.* a strong iron grating in the gateway of a castle, fort, etc., able to be raised or lowered so as to provide or prevent passage. [ME, from OF]

Port Darwin *n.* the harbor of Darwin, NT (which stands on its northern shore); extensively damaged in World War II in the first attack on Australian soil on 19 February 1942. [named after Charles DARWIN]

portend /pɔ'tend/, *v.t.* **1.** to indicate beforehand (often something undesirable), as an omen, etc. **2.** *Obs.* to signify. [ME, from L: point out, indicate, portend]

portent /'pɔtent/, *n.* **1.** an indication of something about to happen, esp. something of great effect. **2.** meaning: *a happening of evil portent.* [L: presaged] —**portentous**, *adj.*

porter[1] /'pɔtə/, *n.* a person employed to carry bags and other loads, as at a railway station, hotel, etc. [ME, from OF, from L: carry]

porter[2] /'pɔtə/, *n.* someone who has charge of a door or gate; doorkeeper; janitor. [ME, from AF, from L: gate]

Porter /'pɔtə/, *n.* **1.** Hal (*Harold Porter*), 1911–84, Australian novelist, short-story writer and playwright; his autobiography, *The Watcher on the Cast-Iron Balcony*, was published in 1963. **2. William Sidney** (*O Henry*), 1862–1910, US short-story writer, famous for his use of caricature and surprising endings.

Port Essington /pɔt 'esɪŋtən/, *n.* an inlet and natural harbor on the Cobourg Peninsula in the NT; site of abortive early settlement attempt.

portfolio /pɔt'foʊlioʊ/, *n., pl.* **-lios. 1.** a case for carrying loose papers, prints, etc. **2.** the office or post of a minister of state. **3.** a list of shares in businesses owned by a person or organisation. [It, from L]

Port Hedland /pɔt 'hedlənd/, *n.* a town, shire and seaport on the north-western coast of WA, south-west of Broome; iron-ore port. Pop. 13 069 (1986).

porthole /'pɔthoʊl/, *n.* an opening in the side of a ship, for admitting light and air.

portico /'pɔtəkoʊ/, *n., pl.* **-coes, -cos.** a structure consisting of a roof supported by pillars, forming the entrance to a temple, church, house, etc. [It, from L: porch, portico]

portion /'pɔʃən/, *n.* **1.** a part of any whole, whether actually separated from it or not. **2.** a part of a whole belonging to a person or group; share; allotment: *portion of an inheritance.* **3.** a quantity of food served for one person. **4.** → **dowry.** ◊*v.t.* **5.** to divide into or deal out in portions or shares (oft. fol. by *out*). [ME, from OF, from L: share, part]

Port Jackson *n.* the natural harbor forming the port of Sydney, NSW, comprising all the waters within an imaginary line joining North and South Heads, and including Sydney Harbor, Middle Harbor and North Harbor. 54 km^2.

Port Jackson fig, *n.* a large, shade-giving tree of coastal NSW, with a rust color on the lower surface of the leaves. [named after PORT JACKSON, NSW]

'Port Jackson Painter', *n.* a name given to the artist responsible for 250 unidentified drawings recording life at the first settlement at Port Jackson.

Port Jackson shark, *n.* a primitive mollusc-eating shark of eastern and southern Australian waters. [named after PORT JACKSON, NSW]

Port Kembla /pɔt 'kɛmblə/, *n.* a port and industrial centre on the south coast of NSW, south of Wollongong; now incorporated as part of the City of Wollongong. Pop. (with Wollongong) 208 651 (1981).

Portland[1] /'pɔtlənd/, *n.* **William Henry Cavendish Bentinck, 3rd Duke of,** 1738–1809, British statesman; prime minister 1783, 1807–09.

Portland[2] /'pɔtlənd/, *n.* **1.** a port on the southern coast of Vic, on Portland Bay. Pop. 10 934 (1986). **2.** a town in the central west of NSW; cement industry. Pop. 2002 (1986).

Portland cement, *n.* a type of hydraulic cement usu. made by burning a mixture of limestone and clay in a kiln. [named after the Isle of *Portland*, Dorset, England]

Port Lincoln, *n.* a city and harbor on the south-eastern coast of the Eyre Peninsula in SA. Pop. 11 552 (1986).

portly /'pɔtli/, *adj.,* **-lier, -liest.** large in person; stout; corpulent. [(DE)PORT(MENT) + -LY]

Port Macquarie, *n.* a town on the north coast of NSW, at the mouth of the Hastings River; popular tourist and fishing area. Pop. 22 884 (1986).

portmanteau /pɔt'mæntoʊ/, *n., pl.* **-teaus, -teaux.** a travelling case, esp. a leather one which opens into two halves. Also, **port.** [F: cloak-carrier]

portmanteau word, *n.* a word made by telescoping two other words, as *brunch* for *breakfast* and *lunch*. [from *Through the Looking Glass* by Lewis Carroll: 'You see, it's like a portmanteau . . . there are two meanings packed up in one word.']

Port Melbourne, *n.* a suburb of the Melbourne metropolitan area, on Port Phillip Bay, Vic. Pop. 8585 (1981).

Port Moresby /pɔt 'mɔzbi/, *n.* the capital and main seaport of PNG, on the south-eastern coast of the Gulf of Papua. Pop. 152 100 (1987 est.).

Port Phillip Bay, *n.* a large bay in southern Vic with Melbourne on its north shore.

Port Pirie /pɔt 'pɪəri/, *n.* a city and port in south-eastern SA, on the eastern shore of the Spencer Gulf; important railway centre. Pop. 13 960 (1986).

portrait /'pɔtrət, 'pɔtreɪt/, *n.* **1.** a likeness of a person, esp. of the face, usu. made from life. **2.** a verbal picture, usu. of a person. [F, from LL: portray, from L: bring forward] **–portraiture,** *n.*

portray /pɔ'treɪ/, *v.t.* **1.** to represent by a drawing, painting, or the like. **2.** to represent in acting, as on the stage. **3.** to describe in words. [ME, from OF, from LL: depict, from L: draw forth] **–portrayer,** *n.* **–portrayal,** *n.*

Portugal /'pɔtʃəgəl/, *n.* a republic in south-western Europe, on the Atlantic side of the Iberian Peninsula, and bordered by Spain; a republic since the overthrow of the monarchy in 1910. Pop. 10 312 000 (1987 est.). 92 072 km^2. *Language:* Portuguese. *Currency:* escudo. *Cap.:* Lisbon. **–Portuguese,** *n., adj.*

Portuguese man-of-war, /pɔtʃə‚gɪz mæn-əv-'wɔ/, *n.* **1.** → **bluebottle** (def. 1). **2.** → **jellyfish.**

pose /poʊz/, *v.,* **posed, posing.** ◊*v.i.* **1.** to act as a particular character, usu. with a view to the impression made on others. **2.** to pretend to be something or someone. **3.** (in modelling) to hold a position or attitude. ◊*v.t.* **4.** to place in a suitable position or attitude for a picture, etc.: *The photograher will pose the group.* **5.** to state or put forward for consideration: *The refugees pose a hard problem.* ◊*n.* **6.** a position held by the body. **7.** a position taken in thought or conduct. **8.** a pretence of being some character or having some quality or feeling which is generously false: *His generosity is a pose.* [ME, from OF, from LL: lay down]

Poseidon /pə'saɪdn/, *n. Gk Myth.* the god of the sea; Roman counterpart, Neptune.

poser /'poʊzə/, *n.* a question or problem that puzzles.

poseur /poʊ'zɜ/, *n.* a person who takes on a particular pose (def. 8) to impress others. [F: POSE]

posh /pɒʃ/, *adj. Colloq.* elegant; luxurious; smart; first-class. [? *p(ort) o(ut), s(tarboard) h(ome),* orig. with ref. to the better (i.e. cooler) accommodation on ships sailing from Britain to India, Aust, etc.]

position /pə'zɪʃən/, *n.* **1.** a place; location. **2.** proper place: *out of position.* **3.** condition, esp. in some particular state; situation: *He is in an awkward position.* **4.** rank or standing. **5.** high standing in society. **6.** a post of employment: *a position in a bank.* **7.** the manner of being placed or arranged. **8.** a way of viewing a matter; stand: *our position on this question.* ◊*v.t.* **9.** to put in a particular position; place. **10.** to determine the position of; locate. [ME, from L]

positive /'pɒzətɪv/, *adj.* **1.** actually laid down or expressed: *a positive declaration.* **2.** admitting of no question: *positive proof.* **3.** stated; express; emphatic. **4.** (of a person) sure in opinion or statement. **5.** overconfident. **6.** without relation to or comparison with other things; absolute (opposed to *relative* and *comparative*). **7.** *Colloq.* downright; out-and-out. **8.** possessing an actual force, being, existence, etc. **9.** *Philos.* based on matters of experience:

positive *philosophy.* See **positivism.** **10.** practical; not theoretical. **11.** marked by hopefulness: *a positive attitude.* **12.** consisting in or marked by the presence of definite or marked qualities (opposed to *negative*): *Light is positive, darkness negative.* **13.** proceeding in a direction assumed as that of increase, progress, or onward motion. **14.** *Elect.* relating to the kind of electricity developed on glass when rubbed with silk, or the kind of electricity present at that pole where electrons enter, or return to. **15.** *Chem.* (of a radical) having fewer electrons than the neutral atom or molecule and so being positively charged. **16.** *Chem.* → **electropositive. 17.** *Photog.* (of a print from a negative) showing the lights and shades as seen in the original. **18.** *Gram.* relating to the first degree of the comparison of adjectives and adverbs, as English *smooth* in contrast to *smoother* and *smoothest.* **19.** *Maths.* indicating a quantity greater than zero. **20.** *Biol.* moving towards the point of excitation: *a positive tropism.* **21.** (of blood, affected tissue, etc.) showing the presence of an organism which causes a disease. ◇*n.* **22.** something positive, as a quality, characteristic, quantity, etc. **23.** a positive quantity or symbol. **24.** *Photog.* a positive picture. **25.** *Gram.* (a form in) the positive degree. [L] −**positiveness,** *n.*

positivism /ˈpɒzɪtɪvɪzəm/, *n.* a philosophical system concerned with positive facts and phenomena, which discourages theorising about causes or origins. −**positivist,** *adj., n.* −**positivistic,** *adj.*

positron /ˈpɒzɪtrɒn/, *n.* an elementary particle with positive charge and mass equal to that of the electron; antiparticle of the electron. [POSIT(IVE) + (ELECT)RON]

poss., *Abbrev.* **1.** possession. **2.** possessive. **3.** possible.

posse /ˈpɒsi/, *n. Chiefly US.* a body of men called on by the sheriff to help preserve the peace. [ML: power, force, n. use of L inf., to be able, have power]

possess /pəˈzɛs/, *v.t.* **1.** to have belonging to oneself. **2.** to have, as a quality or the like: *to possess courage.* **3.** to keep control over (oneself, one's mind, etc.). **4.** (of a spirit, feeling or idea) to take over and control (a person). **5.** (of a man) to have sexual relations with. **6.** *Archaic.* to seize or take. [backformation from *possessor,* ME, from L] −**possessor,** *n.* −**possession,** *n.*

possessed /pəˈzɛst/, *adj.* **1.** moved by a strong feeling, madness, or some supernatural being; frenzied (oft. fol. by *by, of,* or *with*). **2.** self-possessed; calm; poised. **3. possessed of,** having; owning.

possession /pəˈzɛʃən/, *n.* **1.** the act of possessing or being possessed. **2.** ownership. **3.** *Law.* actual holding or occupancy, either with or without rights of ownership. **4.** a thing possessed. **5.** (*pl.*) property or wealth. **6.** control over oneself, one's mind, etc. **7.** control by a feeling, idea, etc. [ME, from L]

Possession Island, *n.* an island off the north-western tip of Cape York Peninsula, Qld,

in Endeavour Strait. [named by James COOK when he took possession of it in 1770]

possessive /pəˈzɛsɪv/, *adj.* **1.** of or relating to possession or ownership. **2.** seeking to control and influence, as though one's own, the behavior, etc., of others: *a possessive wife.*

possessive case, *n. Gram.* See **case**¹ and Appendix.

possible /ˈpɒsəbəl/, *adj.* **1.** that may or can be, exist, happen, be done, be used, etc.: *no possible cure.* **2.** that may be true or a fact, as something concerning which there is knowledge to the contrary: *It is possible that he went.* [ME, from L] −**possibility,** *n.*

possum /ˈpɒsəm/, *n.* **1.** any of many plant-eating, largely tree-living marsupials, from Australia, NG and neighboring islands, having both pairs of limbs well-developed for climbing and grasping, and a long, often prehensile tail, e.g. the **honey possum** or **noolbenger,** of south-western Australia, which is the size of a mouse and feeds on the nectar of banksia and bottlebrush trees, and the **striped possum,** of NG and northern Qld, with stripes from nose to tail, and with an extended fourth finger for digging grubs out of timber. See **brush-tailed possum, gliding possum, ringtail possum. 2.** *US.* → **opossum. 3. play possum,** *Orig. US. Colloq.* to pretend illness or death.

post¹ /poʊst/, *n.* **1.** a strong piece of timber, metal, or the like, set upright as a support, etc. **2.** *Horseracing.* a pole on a racecourse marking the starting or finishing points for races. ◇*v.t.* **3.** to fix (a notice, etc.) to a post, wall, etc. **4.** to bring to public attention with a notice: *We must post a reward.* **5.** to enter the name of in a published list. [ME and OE, from L]

post² /poʊst/, *n.* **1.** a position of duty, employment, or trust to which someone is appointed. **2.** the station or round of a soldier, or other person on duty. **3.** a military station with permanent buildings. **4.** *Mil.* either of two bugle calls (**first post** and **last post**) giving notice of the hour for retiring for the night. ◇*v.t.* **5.** to station at a post or place as a guard or for some other purpose. **6.** *Mil.* to transfer to another unit or command. [F, from It, from L: placed, put]

post³ /poʊst/, *n.* **1.** a single delivery of letters, packages, etc. **2.** the letters, packages, etc., themselves; mail. **3.** an established service for the carrying of letters, etc., esp. under government authority. **4.** → **post office.** ◇*v.t.* **5.** to place (a letter, etc.) in a post-box, post office, etc., for sending. **6.** *Bookkeeping.* **a.** to transfer (an entry or item) to the ledger. **b.** to make all the necessary entries in (the ledger, etc.). **7.** to supply with up-to-date information; inform: *Please keep me posted about any developments.* [F, from It: placed, put] −**postal,** *adj.*

post-, a prefix meaning 'behind', 'after', freely used as an English formative: *post-Elizabethan, postgraduate.* [L]

postage /ˈpoʊstɪdʒ/, *n.* a charge for the sending of a letter or other matter by post, usu. paid by means of a stamp.

postal order /ˈpoʊstəl ˌodə/, n. an order for the payment of money, bought from and generally cashed at a post office. Also, **postal note**. See **money order**.

postcard /ˈpoʊstkad/, n. a card of standard size, often having a photograph, picture, etc., on one side, on which a message may be written and sent by post.

post-chaise /ˌpoʊstˈʃeɪz/, n. a hired coach drawn by horses changed at each stage, used for rapid travelling in the 18th and early 19th centuries.

postcode /ˈpoʊstkoʊd/, n. a system of coded numbers added as part of the address on Australian mail which helps speed the delivery of mail throughout the country.

postdate /poʊstˈdeɪt/, v.t., **-dated**, **-dating**. 1. to date (a document, cheque, invoice, etc.) with a date later than the current date. 2. to follow in time.

poster /ˈpoʊstə/, n. 1. a large bill, often with photographs or illustrations, posted for advertisement or publicity. 2. Also, **newsposter**. a sheet of paper advertising the headlines of the day. [POST[1], v. + -ER[1]]

poste restante /ˌpoʊst rɒsˈtɒnt/, n. a department in a post office where letters may be kept until they are called for. [F: standing post]

posterior /pɒsˈtɪəriə/, adj. 1. being behind in position. 2. coming after in time; later; subsequent (sometimes fol. by *to*). 3. *Zool*. relating to the tail end of the body. ◇n. 4. the buttocks. [L: coming after]

posterity /pɒsˈtɛrəti/, n. the generations coming afterwards, collectively. [ME, from L]

postern /ˈpɒstən/, n. 1. a back door or gate. 2. any lesser or private entrance.

postgraduate /poʊstˈɡrædʒuət/, n. 1. someone studying at a university for a higher degree (one taken after a first degree). ◇adj. 2. of or relating to courses of study offered for a higher degree. Also, **post-graduate**.

posthaste /poʊstˈheɪst/, adv. with all possible speed. [POST[3] + HASTE]

posthumous /ˈpɒstjəməs/, adj. 1. (of books, music, medals, etc.) published or given after a person's death. 2. born after the death of the father. 3. arising, existing, or continuing after someone's death. [L: after death]

postilion /pɒsˈtɪljən/, n. someone who rides the left-hand horse of those drawing a carriage. Also, **postillion**. [F, from It: POST[3]]

post-mortem /ˌpoʊstˈmɔtəm/, adj.; /poʊstˈmɔtəm/, n. ◇adj. 1. after death. ◇n. 2. the examination of a dead body to determine the cause of death; autopsy. 3. the examination of the causes of failure of a plan, etc. 4. the summing-up of any event after it has ended. [L: after death]

post office, n. 1. a department of government responsible for a country's postal and telegraphic services. 2. a local office of this department for receiving, sorting and sending mail, selling postage stamps, providing telegraphic services, etc. —**post-office**, adj.

postpone /poʊstˈpoʊn, poʊsˈpoʊn/, v.t., **-poned**, **-poning**. to put off to a later time; defer: *He can postpone his departure an hour.* [L] —**postponement**, n.

postscript /ˈpoʊstskrɪpt/, n. 1. a paragraph, sentence, etc., added to a letter which has already been finished and signed. *Abbrev.*: PS. 2. any added part. [L: written after]

postulant /ˈpɒstjələnt/, n. a person who applies for something, esp. for admission into a religious order. [L: demanding] —**postulancy**, n.

postulate /ˈpɒstjəleɪt/, v., **-lated**, **-lating**; /ˈpɒstjələt/, n. ◇v.t. 1. to ask, demand, or claim. 2. to claim or take for granted the existence or truth of, esp. as a basis for reasoning. 3. *Geom*. to take as an axiom. ◇n. 4. something taken to be the case, without proof as a basis for reasoning, or as self-evident. [L: thing requested] —**postulation**, n.

posture /ˈpɒstʃə/, n., v., **-tured**, **-turing**. ◇n. 1. the position of the body and limbs as a whole: *a sitting posture*. 2. an unnatural attitude or position of the body. 3. mental or spiritual attitude. 4. a position, condition, or state, esp. of affairs. ◇v.t. 5. to place in a particular posture or attitude. ◇v.i. 6. to take on a particular posture, often for a special effect or for show. [F, from L] —**postural**, adj.

posy /ˈpoʊzi/, n., pl. **-sies**. a flower or small, neatly-arranged bunch of flowers. [var. of POESY]

pot /pɒt/, n., v., **potted**, **potting**. ◇n. 1. a container, usu. round and deep, used for home or other purposes. 2. such a vessel with its contents. 3. a vessel for trapping lobsters, etc. 4. *Colloq*. a large sum of money. 5. the sum of bets staked at one time, as in card games, esp. poker. 6. → **pot shot**. 7. a chamber-pot; potty. 8. (*pl.*) *Colloq*. a large quantity. 9. *Colloq*. → **marijuana**. 10. **go to pot**, to deteriorate. ◇v.t. 11. to put into a pot. 12. to cook or preserve (food) in a pot. 13. to plant in a pot of soil. 14. *Hunting*. **a.** to shoot (game birds) on the ground or water, or (game animals) at rest, instead of in flight or running. **b.** to shoot for food, not for sport. 15. *Colloq*. to capture or win. 16. *Billiards*. to pocket (a ball). [ME and OE *pott*]

potable /ˈpoʊtəbəl/, adj. fit or suitable for drinking. [LL, from L]

potage /pɒˈtaʒ/, n. soup. [F, from L: to drink]

potash /ˈpɒtæʃ/, n. 1. potassium carbonate, esp. the crude impure form obtained from wood ashes. 2. oxide of potassium, K_2O. 3. potassium: *carbonate of potash*. [earlier *pot-ashes*, pl., translation of early D]

potassium /pəˈtæsiəm/, n. a silvery white metallic element, which oxidises rapidly in air, and whose compounds are used esp. as fertiliser. *Symbol*: K; *at. no.*: 19; *at. wt*: 39.102. [NL] —**potassic**, adj.

potassium-argon dating, n. a method of dating minerals which is based on the rate of radioactive decay of potassium-40 to argon-40.

potassium nitrate, *n.* a crystalline compound, KNO₃, used in gunpowder, fireworks, fertilisers, preservatives, etc., also produced by nitrification in soil; saltpetre. See **-ate²**.

potato /pəˈteɪtoʊ/, *n., pl.* **-toes**. a type of root plant, high in starch, and used widely as a vegetable. [Sp: white potato, from Haitian]

potbelly /ˈpɒtbeli/, *n., pl.* **-lies**. a swollen belly. **—potbellied**, *adj.*

potch /pɒtʃ/, *n.* opal lacking the fine play of color which is seen in gem-quality opal; it is commonly the stone in which precious opal is found.

potent /ˈpoʊtnt/, *adj.* **1.** powerful; mighty. **2.** (of reasons, etc.) forceful. **3.** (of a drug) producing powerful physical or chemical effects. **4.** possessed of great power or authority. **5.** exercising great influence on a person. **6.** having sexual power. [L: powerful] **—potency**, *n.*

potentate /ˈpoʊtnteɪt/, *n.* someone who possesses great power; a sovereign, monarch, or ruler. [LL: potentate, from L: power, dominion]

potential /pəˈtɛnʃəl/, *adj.* **1.** possible as opposed to actual. **2.** able to be or become; latent. ◇*n.* **3.** *Phys.* → **potential energy**. **4.** possibility. **5.** Also, **electric potential**. a measure of the potential energy at a point of an electric charge relative to its potential energy at some other reference point, such as the earth (which is seen to have zero potential). [ME, from ML] **—potentiality**, *n.*

potential difference, *n.* the difference in potential between two points, defined as the work performed when unit positive charge is moved from one point to the other; voltage drop. *Abbrev.*: p.d.

potential energy, *n.* energy which is due to position rather than motion, as of a coiled spring or a raised weight (opposed to *kinetic energy*).

potentiometer /pətɛnʃiˈɒmətə/, *n. Elect.* an instrument for measuring electromotive force or difference in potential. [POTENTI(AL), *n.*, + -O- + -METER¹]

pothole /ˈpɒthoʊl/, *n.* **1.** a deep hole; pit. **2.** a more or less cylindrical hole formed in rock by the grinding action of pieces of rock, etc., in eddying (swirling) water.

potion /ˈpoʊʃən/, *n.* a drink, esp. one of a medicinal, poisonous, or magical kind. [L]

potluck /pɒtˈlʌk/, *n. Colloq.* whatever happens to be at hand without special preparation: *I'll take potluck*.

Potomac /pəˈtoʊmək/, *n.* a river in the US, flowing south-east from the Allegheny Mountains past Washington, DC, into Chesapeake Bay. 462 km long.

potoroo /poʊtəˈru/, *n.* See **rat-kangaroo**. [Aboriginal]

potpourri /pɒtˈpʊəri, poʊpəˈri/, *n., pl.* **-ris**. **1.** a mixture of dried petals of roses or other flowers with spices, etc., kept in a jar for the fragrance. **2.** any mixture of unrelated things. [F: rotten pot, translation of Sp]

potsherd /ˈpɒtʃɜd/, *n.* a broken piece of pottery. [POT + *sherd*, var. of SHARD]

pot shot, *n.* **1.** a shot fired with little regard to skill or from close range. **2.** a random or aimless shot. **3.** an attempt.

pottage /ˈpɒtɪdʒ/, *n.* **1.** a thick soup made of vegetables, with or without meat. **2. mess of pottage**, a small and almost worthless portion, reward, etc. [ME, from OF: pot]

potted /ˈpɒtəd/, *adj.* **1.** placed in a pot. **2.** preserved or cooked in a pot. **3.** *Colloq.* shortened, summarised, or condensed: *a potted version of the story*.

potter¹ /ˈpɒtə/, *n.* someone who makes earthen pots, bowls, etc. [ME; OE *pottere*]

potter² /ˈpɒtə/, *v.i.* **1.** to occupy oneself in an ineffective manner or with little energy, speed or purpose (fol. by *about*, *along*, etc.). **2.** to move or go slowly or aimlessly; loiter. [OE *potian* push, thrust]

Potter /ˈpɒtə/, *n.* **Beatrix**, 1866–1943, English writer and illustrator of children's stories, all with animals as characters.

pottery /ˈpɒtəri/, *n., pl.* **-teries**. **1.** dishes, pots, etc. made from clay or other earthy material and hardened by heat. **2.** a place where such are made. **3.** the art or business of a potter; ceramics. [late ME, from F: potter]

pottle /ˈpɒtl/, *n.* **1.** a former liquid measure equal to two quarts (approx. 2.25 litres). **2.** a pot or large drinking mug of this capacity. **3.** a small container or basket, as for fruit or the like. [ME, from OF: POT]

potty¹ /ˈpɒti/, *adj. Colloq.* foolish; crazy.

potty² /ˈpɒti/, *n. Colloq.* a chamber-pot, esp. one for a child. Also, **pottie**.

pouch /paʊtʃ/, *n.* **1.** a bag, sack, or similar container, esp. one for small articles. **2.** a small moneybag. **3.** something shaped or looking like a bag or pocket. **4.** *Zool.* a bag-like or pocket-like part, as the one beneath the bill of a pelican, or (esp.) the one in which the young of marsupials are carried. ◇*v.t.* **5.** to put into or enclose in a pouch, bag, or pocket; pocket. ◇*v.i.* **6.** to form a pouch or a cavity like a pouch. [ME, from ONF]

Poulenc /puˈlæk/, *n.* **Francis** /frɒˈsis/, 1899–1963, French composer, who was a member of the group of post-impressionist composers called *Les Six*.

poultice /ˈpoʊltəs/, *n., v.,* **-ticed, -ticing**. ◇*n.* **1.** a soft, moist mass of bread, meal, linseed, etc., applied to the body as a means of curing an ailment. ◇*v.t.* **2.** to apply a poultice to. [orig. *pultes*, L: thick pap]

poultry /ˈpoʊltri/, *n.* domestic fowls collectively, as chickens, turkeys, guineafowls, ducks, and geese. [ME, from OF: PULLET]

pounce /paʊns/, *v.,* **pounced, pouncing**, *n.* ◇*v.i.* **1.** to swoop down suddenly and lay hold, as a bird does on its prey. **2.** to spring, dash, or come suddenly. ◇*v.t.* **3.** to swoop down upon and seize suddenly, as a bird of prey does. ◇*n.* **4.** a claw or talon of a bird of prey. **5.** a sudden swoop, as on prey. [orig. uncert.]

pound¹ /paʊnd/, *v.t.* **1.** to strike repeatedly and with great force, as with a tool, the fist, heavy missiles, etc. **2.** to produce (sound) by striking or thumping, or with an effect of thumping (oft. fol. by *out*): *to pound out a tune on a piano*. **3.** to force (a way) by battering. **4.** to crush into particles or powder by beating with an instrument; pulverise. ◇*v.i.* **5.** to strike heavy blows repeatedly: *to pound on a door*. **6.** to beat or throb violently, as the heart or a drum. **7.** to go with heavy vigorous steps. [OE *pūnian*]

pound² /paʊnd/, *n.*, *pl.* **pounds**, (collectively) **pound**. **1.** either of two units in imperial measure, the **pound avoirdupois** (of 7000 grains, divided into 16 ounces, and equal to 0.453 592 37 kg) used for ordinary commodities, or the **pound troy** (of 5760 grains, divided into 12 ounces, equal to 0.373 241 721 6 kg) used for gold, silver, etc., and also serving as the basis of chemists' weight. **2.** the British unit of money (**pound sterling**) of the value of 100 new pence. **3.** a former unit of currency in Australia of the value of 240 pence. **4.** a note or coin of any of these units. [ME and OE *pund*, from L]

pound³ /paʊnd/, *n.* **1.** an enclosure maintained by public authorities for keeping stray or homeless animals. **2.** an enclosure for sheltering, keeping, confining, or trapping animals. **3.** an enclosure or trap for fish. ◇*v.t.* **4.** to shut up in or as in a pound; impound; imprison. [ME and OE *pund-*]

Pound /paʊnd/, *n.* **Ezra Loomis**, 1885–1972, US poet and critic, at the centre of the modern movement in British and American literature.

pour /pɔ/, *v.t.* **1.** to send (a liquid or fluid, or anything in loose particles) flowing or falling, as from a container or into, over, or on something. **2.** to send out or discharge, esp. continuously or rapidly. **3.** to send forth (words, etc.) as in a stream or flood (oft. fol. by *out* or *forth*). ◇*v.i.* **4.** to issue, move, or proceed in great quantity or number: *The crowd poured into the cricket ground*. **5.** to flow forth or along. **6.** to rain heavily. [ME; orig. uncert.]

Poussin /puˈsæ̃/, *n.* **Nicolas** /nikoˈla/, 1594–1655, French classical painter; known for his larger-than-life historical and religious works.

pout /paʊt/, *v.i.* **1.** to thrust out the lips, esp. in displeasure or sullenness. **2.** to look sullen. ◇*v.t.* **3.** to say with a pout. ◇*n.* **4.** a thrusting out of the lips, as in pouting. [ME]

pouter /ˈpaʊtə/, *n.* **1.** one who pouts. **2.** one of a breed of long-legged pigeons marked by the habit of puffing out the crop (def. 8).

poverty /ˈpɒvəti/, *n.* **1.** the condition of being poor. **2.** a shortage or lack of something stated: *poverty of ideas*. **3.** a shortage of desirable ingredients, qualities, etc.: *poverty of soil*. [ME, from OF, from L]

poverty line, *n.* the lowest income level at which it is possible to maintain an adequate standard of living.

POW /pi oʊ ˈdʌbəlju/, *Abbrev.* prisoner of war.

powder /ˈpaʊdə/, *n.* **1.** any dry substance made up of fine, loose particles, as produced by crushing or grinding; dust. **2.** such a substance used for some special purpose, as gunpowder, face powder, etc. ◇*v.t.* **3.** to reduce to powder; pulverise. **4.** to sprinkle or cover with, or as if with, powder. [ME, from OF, from L: dust] —**powdery**, *adj.*

Powell /paʊəl/, *n.* (**John**) **Enoch**, born 1912, British Conservative politician, opponent of non-white immigration into Britain.

power /ˈpaʊə/, *n.* **1.** the ability to do or act. **2.** (usu. *pl.*) a particular natural skill or ability of the body or mind. **3.** political or national strength: *the balance of power in Europe*. **4.** strength; might; force. **5.** possession of control over others; authority; ascendancy or influence: *the political party in power*; *a general's power over his army*. **6.** → **power of attorney**. **7.** someone or something that possesses or exercises authority or influence. **8.** (oft. *pl.*) a deity or divinity. **9.** *Colloq.* a large number or amount: *a power of good*. **10.** *Phys., Elect.* the time rate of transferring or transforming energy; work done, or energy transferred, per unit of time. **11.** *Mech.* energy or force available for application to work. **12.** *Maths.* the product obtained by multiplying a quantity by itself one or more times: *4 is the second, 8 the third, power of 2*. **13. the powers that be**, those in authority. ◇*v.t.* **14.** to supply or provide (a building, engine, etc.) with electricity or other means of power. [ME, from AF, from VL, for L]

powerful /ˈpaʊəfəl/, *adj.* **1.** having, using or producing great power, force or effect. **2.** physically strong. **3.** potent, as a drug. **4.** having great influence, as a speech, speaker, description, reason, etc. **5.** having great power, authority, or influence, as a nation; mighty. **6.** *Colloq.* great in number or amount: *a powerful lot of money*.

powerhouse /ˈpaʊəhaʊs/, *n.* → **power station**.

power of attorney, *n.* a written document given by one person or party to another authorising the latter to act for the former.

power point, *n.* a socket, connected to a power supply, usu. made of plastic and set in a wall, and into which the plug of an electrical appliance may be inserted.

power station, *n.* an industrial building in which electricity is generated.

power steering, *n.* a steering mechanism in a motor vehicle that provides mechanical or hydraulic aid in turning the wheels.

powwow /ˈpaʊwaʊ/, *n.* **1.** (among North American Indians) a ceremony, esp. with magic, feasting, and dancing, for the cure of disease, success in a hunt, etc. **2.** a council or conference of or with American Indians. **3.** *Colloq.* any conference or meeting. ◇*v.i.* **4.** to hold a powwow; confer. [Algonquian *pow wah* or *po-wah*]

pox /pɒks/, *n.* **1.** a disease marked by numerous pustules (pimple-like swellings) over the face and body, e.g. smallpox. **2.** → **syphilis.** [*pocks*, pl. of POCK]

pp., *Abbrev.* **1.** pages. **2.** *Music.* pianissimo.

p.p., *Abbrev.* past participle.

P-plate /'piː-pleɪt/, *n.* one of a pair of identification plates which by law must be displayed (at the front and rear) on any motor vehicle driven by a driver with a provisional licence.

p.p.m., *Chem. Abbrev.* parts per million.

PPS, *Abbrev.* second postscript. [L *post postscriptum*]

pr, *Abbrev.* **1.** pair(s). **2.** present. **3.** price. **4.** pronoun.

Pr, *Symbol.* **1.** *Chem.* praseodymium. ◇*Abbrev.* **2.** preferred (stock). **3.** Priest. **4.** Prince.

PR /piː 'aː/, *n.* →**public relations.** [abbrev.]

prac /præk/, *adj. Colloq.* practice: *prac teaching.*

practicable /'præktɪkəbəl/, *adj.* **1.** able to be put into practice or done, esp. sensibly or with the means one has; feasible: *a practicable idea; a practicable plan.* **2.** able or possible to be used or travelled over: *a practicable road.* [ML]

practical /'præktɪkəl/, *adj.* **1.** relating to practice or action: *practical mathematics.* **2.** consisting of, using, or resulting from practice or action: *a practical application of a rule.* **3.** relating to the ordinary business, or work of the world: *practical affairs.* **4.** adapted for actual use: *a practical method.* **5.** doing or experienced in actual practice or work: *a practical politician.* **6.** interested in or fitted for actual work: *a practical man.* **7.** mindful of the results, usefulness, possibilities, etc., of a certain action or method; sensible. **8.** matter-of-fact; prosaic. **9.** being so in effect; virtual: *a practical certainty.* **10.** of or relating to a practical (def. 11). ◇*n.* **11.** that part of a course of study which is meant to develop practical skills or to show the practical basis of a theory: *a Chemistry practical.* [PRACTIC(E) + -AL¹] —**practicality,** *n.*

practical joke, *n.* a trick played upon a person, often involving some physical action.

practically /'præktɪkli/, *adv.* **1.** in a practical manner. **2.** in effect; virtually. **3.** nearly; almost.

practice /'præktəs/, *n.* **1.** the usual manner of doing something: *normal business practice; normal law practice.* **2.** a habit or custom. **3.** repeated performance or methodical exercise for developing skills: *Practice makes perfect.* **4.** the action or process of doing something (opposed to *theory* or *speculation*). **5.** the exercise of a profession or occupation, esp. law or medicine. **6.** the business of a professional: *a doctor with a large practice.* **7.** dishonest dealing; trickery: *sharp practice.* **8. make a practice of,** to do (something) usually or by habit. ◇*adj.* **9.** of or relating to something which is done merely to develop skill, refresh one's memory, etc: *a practice shot.* [n. use of PRACTISE, *v.*]

practician /præk'tɪʃən/, *n.* someone who works at a profession or occupation; practitioner.

practise /'præktəs/, *v.,* **-tised, -tising.** ◇*v.t.* **1.** to carry out, follow, observe or use or do habitually or usually. **2.** to exercise or work in as a profession, art, or occupation: *to practise law.* **3.** to perform or do repeatedly in order to acquire skill or proficiency. ◇*v.i.* **4.** to act habitually; do something habitually or as a practice. **5.** to work in a profession, esp. law or medicine. **6.** to do something in order to improve one's skill: *to practise shooting.* [ME, from OF, *pra(c)tiser,* from LL: PRACTICAL]

practised /'præktəst/, *adj.* **1.** experienced; expert; proficient: *a practised speaker.* **2.** gained or made perfect through practice: *with practised ease.*

practitioner /præk'tɪʃənə/, *n.* someone working in the practice of a profession, etc. [modified form of PRACTICIAN]

prae-, a variant of **pre-.**

pragmatic /præg'mætɪk/, *adj.* **1.** treating historical events with special reference to their causes and results. **2.** *Philos.* of or relating to pragmatism. **3.** Also, **pragmatical.** concerned with practical outcomes or values. [L, from Gk: active, versed in state affairs; as n., a man of business or action] —**pragmatically,** *adv.*

pragmatism /'prægmətɪzəm/, *n.* **1.** character or conduct which places importance on practical values or attention to facts; practicality. **2.** *Philos.* a theory that difference of meaning depends on difference of practice and use. —**pragmatist,** *n., adj.*

Prague /praɡ/, *n.* the capital of the Czech Republic, in the central part, on the Vltava River; formerly the capital of Czechoslovakia. Pop. 1 193 513 (1986 est.). Czech, **Praha.** German, **Prag.**

prairie /'prɛəri/, *n.* a large, flat or slightly hilly, treeless area of grassland, esp. in the inland US and Canada. [F: field, from L: meadow]

praise /preɪz/, *n., v.,* **praised, praising.** ◇*n.* **1.** the act of expressing approval or admiration; commendation. **2.** the offering of grateful respect in words or song, as in worship. **3. sing (someone's) praises,** to praise (someone) very highly. ◇*v.t.* **4.** to express approval or admiration of; commend. **5.** to offer grateful respect to (God, etc.), esp. in words or song. [ME, from OF: value, prize, from L: price]

pram /præm/, *n.* a small, four-wheeled vehicle used for carrying a baby. [shortened form of PERAMBULATOR]

prance /præns, prans/, *v.,* **pranced, prancing,** *n.* ◇*v.i.* **1.** to spring, or move from the hind legs, as a horse. **2.** to move or go in a happy manner; swagger. **3.** to leap or dance. ◇*n.* **4.** the act of prancing. [ME, ? alliterative alteration of DANCE]

prandial /'prændiəl/, *adj.* of or relating to a meal, esp. dinner. [L: luncheon, meal]

prang /præŋ/, *Colloq.* ◇*v.t.* **1.** to crash (an aircraft, car, etc.); damage; destroy. ◇*v.i.* **2.** to have a crash. ◇*n.* **3.** a crash, as in a car.

prank /præŋk/, n. a playful trick with sometimes nasty intentions. [orig. uncert.]

praseodymium /ˌpreɪzɪouˈdɪmɪəm/, n. a rare-earth, trivalent, metallic element. *Symbol:* Pr; *at. no.:* 59; *at. wt:* 140.9.

prate /preɪt/, v., **prated, prating**, n. ◇v.i. **1.** to talk too much; chatter; babble. ◇v.t. **2.** to utter in empty or foolish talk. ◇n. **3.** empty or foolish talk. [late ME] **– prater**, n.

prattle /ˈprætl/, v., **-tled, -tling**, n. ◇v.i. **1.** to talk or chatter in a foolish way; babble. ◇v.t. **2.** to utter by chattering or babbling. ◇n. **3.** chatter; babble. [frequentative and diminutive of PRATE]

Pravda /ˈprɑvdə/, n. a Russian newspaper; formerly the official newspaper of the Soviet Communist party. [Russ: truth]

prawn /prɔn/, n. **1.** a ten-legged crustacean fished commercially and used as food. **2. come the raw prawn,** *Colloq.* to try to deceive; delude (fol. by *with*). ◇v.i. **3.** to catch prawns, as for food. [ME; orig. unknown]

praxis /ˈpræksəs/, n. **1.** practice, esp. as opposed to theory. **2.** habit; custom. **3.** a set of examples for practice. [ML, from Gk]

Praxiteles /prækˈsɪtəliz/, n. fl. c 350 BC, Greek sculptor; best-known surviving work is *Hermes and the Infant Dionysus*.

pray /preɪ/, v.t. **1.** to strongly urge (a person, etc.): *Tell me, I pray you*. **2.** to make a sincere request to (God, etc.). **3.** to offer (a prayer). ◇v.i. **4.** to make a strong plea as to a person. **5.** to make a sincere request to God, etc. **6.** to enter into spiritual union with God through prayer. [ME, from OF, from L: beg, pray]

prayer /preə/, n. **1.** a sincere and earnest petition to God, etc. **2.** the act or practice of praying to God, etc., as in thanks, praise or request. **3.** a form of words used in praying. **4.** something that is prayed for. [ME, from OF, from Rom: obtained by entreaty]

praying mantis, n. → mantis.

pre-, a prefix used to mean 'in advance of' (*prewar*), also 'early', 'beforehand' (*prepay*), and 'before', 'in front of' (*prefrontal*). [L]

preach /pritʃ/, v.t. **1.** to advise or teach (moral truth, right conduct, etc.) in speech or writing. **2.** to tell or make known by sermon (the gospel, etc.). ◇v.i. **3.** to deliver a sermon. **4.** to give heartfelt advice, as on religious subjects. [ME, from OF, from LL] **– preacher**, n. **– preaching**, n.

preamble /priˈæmbəl/, n. an introductory statement, esp. to a statute, deed, etc., giving the reasons and intentions of what is to follow. [ME, from F, from ML: walking before]

preamplifier /priˈæmpləfaɪə/, n. a device in the amplifier circuit of a radio or gramophone which increases the strength of a weak signal. Also, **preamp** /priˈæmp/, **preselector**.

prearrange /priəˈreɪndʒ/, v.t., **-ranged, -ranging**. to arrange beforehand.

Pre-Cambrian /ˌpriˈkæmbrɪən/, adj., n. (relating to) a geological period, age, or systems of rocks older than the Cambrian, characterised by almost complete lack of fossils.

precarious /prəˈkɛərɪəs/, adj. **1.** dependent on conditions beyond one's control; uncertain; insecure. **2.** dangerous; perilous; risky. [L: obtained by entreaty or by mere favor, hence uncertain, precarious]

precaution /prəˈkɔʃən/, n. a measure taken beforehand to prevent problems and to help obtain good results. [LL, from L: guard against] **– precautionary**, adj.

precede /priˈsid/, v., **-ceded, -ceding**. ◇v.t. **1.** to go before, as in place, order, rank, time, etc. **2.** to begin by something introductory; preface. ◇v.i. **3.** to go or come before. [ME, from L] **– preceding**, adj.

precedence /ˈprɛsədəns, priˈsidəns/, n. **1.** the act, right or fact of preceding. **2.** a coming before, in order, rank, time, etc.

precedent /ˈprɛsədənt, ˈpri-/, n. a past event or case which may serve as an example or reason for future action.

precept /ˈprisɛpt/, n. **1.** a direction given as a rule of action or conduct. **2.** an order as to moral conduct; a maxim. [ME, from L: instructed] **– preceptive**, adj.

preceptor /prəˈsɛptə/, n. an instructor; a teacher. [L]

precession /priˈsɛʃən/, n. **1.** the act or fact of preceding. **2.** *Mech.* the wobbling motion of a rotating body (as a spinning top, etc.) which makes the axis describe a cone. [ME, from LL, from L: gone before] **– precessional**, adj.

precinct /ˈprisɪŋkt/, n. **1.** a place or space of definite limits. **2.** (*oft. pl.*) an enclosing boundary or limit. **3.** (*pl.*) the areas immediately about any place; environs: *the precincts of a town*. [ME, from ML: girded about, surrounded]

precious /ˈprɛʃəs/, adj. **1.** of great price or value; valuable; costly: *precious metals*. **2.** of great moral or spiritual worth. **3.** dear; beloved. **4.** too delicate, refined, or nice. ◇n. **5.** precious one; darling. ◇adv. **6.** *Colloq.* extremely; very. [ME, from OF, from L: costly]

precipice /ˈprɛsəpəs/, n. **1.** a cliff with a vertical, nearly vertical, or overhanging face. **2.** a situation of great danger. [F, from L]

precipitant /prəˈsɪpətənt/, adj. **1.** falling or rushing headlong. **2.** hasty; rash. ◇n. **3.** *Chem.* anything that causes precipitation. [L: falling headlong] **– precipitancy**, n.

precipitate /prəˈsɪpəteɪt/, v., **-tated, -tating**; /prəˈsɪpətət/, adj., n. ◇v.t. **1.** to bring about quickly or suddenly: *to precipitate an argument*. **2.** *Chem.* to separate out (a dissolved substance) in solid form from a solution, as by means of a reagent. **3.** *Phys, Weather.* to change (moisture) from vapor into rain, dew, etc. **4.** to cast down headlong. ◇v.i. **5.** to separate from a solution as a precipitate. **6.** *Phys, Weather.* to be condensed as rain, dew, etc. ◇adj. **7.** headlong. **8.** moving with great haste. **9.** very sudden; abrupt. **10.** overhasty; rash. ◇n. **11.** *Chem.* a substance precipitated from a solution. **12.** *Phys, Weather.* moisture

precipitate condensed in the form of rain, dew, etc. [L: cast headlong] —**precipitateness**, *n*.

precipitation /prəsɪpə'teɪʃən/, *n*. 1. the act or fact of precipitating. 2. a casting down or falling headlong. 3. sudden haste. 4. unwise speed. 5. *Chem, Phys.* the precipitating of a substance from a solution. 6. *Weather*. **a.** falling products of condensation as rain, snow, hail. **b.** the amount of such within a given period.

precipitous /prə'sɪpətəs/, *adj*. 1. of the nature of a precipice. 2. very steep. 3. overhasty; rash. [PRECIPIT(ATE), *adj*., + -OUS]

precis /'preɪsɪ/, *n*., *pl*. -**cis**, *v*. ◇*n*. 1. a brief piece of writing containing the main points of a larger work; summary; abstract. ◇*v.t*. 2. to make a precis of. [F, N. use of adj., cut short, PRECISE]

precise /prə'saɪs/, *adj*. 1. exact; definite. 2. being just that, and neither more nor less: *the precise amount*. 3. being just that, and not some other: *the precise date*. 4. clear, distinct, as the voice. 5. exact in measuring, recording, etc., as an instrument. 6. very particular; puritanical. [L: cut short, brief]

precision /prə'sɪʒən/, *n*. 1. the quality or condition of being precise. 2. exactness; accuracy. 3. mechanical exactness. ◇*adj*. 4. of, relating to, or noted for exactness or accuracy.

preclude /prɪ'klud/, *v.t*., -**cluded**, -**cluding**. 1. to shut out; exclude; make impossible. 2. to prevent (a person, etc.) from doing something. [L: shut off, close] —**preclusion**, *n*.

precocious /prə'koʊʃəs/, *adj*. 1. forward in development (esp. mental), as a child. 2. relating to or showing early development. 3. *Bot*. flowering, fruiting, or ripening early. [*precoci(ty)* (from F: early maturity) + -OUS] —**precociousness, precocity**, *n*.

precognition /ˌprikɒg'nɪʃən/, *n*. knowledge of future events, esp. through extrasensory means. —**precognitive**, *adj*.

preconceive /prikən'siv/, *v.t*., -**ceived**, -**ceiving**. to form an idea of in advance. —**preconception**, *n*.

precondition /prikən'dɪʃən/, *n*. a preexisting condition; prerequisite.

precursor /ˌprɪ'kɜsə/, *n*. 1. someone or something that comes before; predecessor. 2. *Biochem.* a substance from which the next active substance is made by one or more enzymic reactions. [L] —**precursory, precursive**, *adj*.

predate /ˌprɪ'deɪt/, *v.t*., -**dated**, -**dating**. 1. to date before the actual time: *He predated the cheque by three days*. 2. to come before in date.

predatory /'prɛdətəri, -tri/, *adj*. 1. of, related to, or noted for robbing or plundering. 2. *Zool.* hunting other animals for food. [L]

predecessor /'pridəsɛsə/, *n*. 1. someone who comes before another in an office, position, etc. 2. anything replaced by something else. 3. an ancestor; forefather. [ME, from LL]

predestination /priˌdɛstə'neɪʃən/, *n*. 1. fate; destiny. 2. *Theol.* the action of God in determining beforehand whatever comes to pass.

predestine /pri'dɛstən/, *v.t*., -**tined**, -**tining**. to determine beforehand; predetermine.

predetermine /pridə'tɜmən/, *v.t*., -**mined**, -**mining**. to determine or decide beforehand. —**predetermination**, *n*.

predicament /prə'dɪkəmənt/, *n*. 1. an unpleasant, trying, or dangerous situation. 2. a particular state, condition, or situation. [ME, from LL, from L: proclaim]

predicate /'prɛdɪkeɪt/, *v*., -**cated**, -**cating**; /'prɛdɪkət/, *n*. ◇*v.t*. 1. to declare; proclaim. ◇*v.i*. 2. to make a declaration. ◇*n*. 3. *Gram*. (in many languages) the active verb in a sentence or clause together with all the words it governs and those which modify it, as *is here* in *Jack is here*. 4. *Logic.* something that is said of the subject in a proposition. [L: declared publicly, asserted, in LL preached] —**predicative**, *adj*.

predict /prə'dɪkt/, *v.t*. 1. to foretell; prophesy. ◇*v.i*. 2. to foretell the future. [L] —**predictor**, *n*. —**prediction**, *n*. —**predictable**, *adj*.

predilection /pridə'lɛkʃən/, *n*. a tendency of the mind in favor of something; preference. [PRE- + L: love, choice]

predispose /pridəs'poʊz/, *v.t*., -**posed**, -**posing**. ◇*v.t*. 1. to give a previous inclination or tendency to. 2. to make subject or liable: *He is predisposed to catching a cold*. —**predisposition**, *n*.

predominant /prə'dɒmənənt/, *adj*. 1. having power, authority, or influence over others. 2. prevailing. —**predominance**, *n*.

predominate /prə'dɒmənət/, *v*., -**nated**, -**nating**. ◇*v.i*. 1. to be the stronger or leading element. 2. to have controlling power (oft. fol. by *over*): *His will predominates over the meeting*. ◇*v.t*. 3. to control; dominate. [PRE- + L: ruled, dominated]

pre-eminent /pri-'ɛmənənt/, *adj*. superior to; surpassing others. [ME, from L: standing out, rising above] —**pre-eminence**, *n*.

pre-empt /pri-'ɛmpt/, *v.t*. 1. to occupy (land) in order to prove an established right to buy. 2. to get or gain beforehand. 3. to act before (someone else or someone else's action); anticipate. [*pre-emption* from PRE- + L *emptio* a buying] —**pre-emptory**, *adj*. —**pre-emption**, *n*.

preen /prin/, *v.t*. 1. to trim or arrange with the beak, as a bird does its feathers. 2. to prepare or dress (oneself) carefully. 3. to pride (oneself) on something well done, etc. [ME]

pref., *Abbrev*. 1. preface. 2. preference.

prefabricate /pri'fæbrəkeɪt/, *v.t*., -**cated**, -**cating**. 1. to make or build beforehand. 2. to make (houses, etc.) in standardised parts ready for quick construction. —**prefabricated**, *adj*.

preface /ˈprefəs/, *n., v.,* **-aced, -acing.** ◇*n.* **1.** a statement placed at the front of a book, explaining its purpose, etc. **2.** an introductory part, as of a speech. ◇*v.t.* **3.** to introduce by a preface. **4.** to serve as a preface to. [ME, from OF, from ML] **– prefatory,** *adj.*

prefect /ˈprifekt/, *n.* **1.** a person in a position of command, as, formerly, a chief magistrate in ancient Rome, or now, the chief administrative official of a department of France or Italy. **2.** (in many schools) one of a group of older pupils with responsibility for keeping order. [ME, from L: overseer, director, appointed as a superior]

prefer /prəˈfɜ/, *v.t.,* **-ferred, -ferring. 1.** to like better; choose above another. **2.** to put forward (a statement, charge, etc.) for consideration. **3.** to put forward or advance, as in rank or office. [ME, from L: bear before, set before, prefer] **– preferable,** *adj.*

preference /ˈprefərəns, ˈprefrəns/, *n.* **1.** the act or fact of preferring. **2.** something that is preferred. **3.** a practical advantage given to one over others. **4.** a right or claim before anyone else, as to payment of dividends, etc. **– preferential,** *adj.*

preference share, *n.* a share which ranks before ordinary shares in the right to be paid dividends.

preferential voting /prefəˌrenʃəl ˈvoutɪŋ/, *n. Govt.* a system of voting which allows voters to show their order of preference for candidates in the ballot.

preferment /prəˈfɜmənt/, *n.* advancement or promotion, as in rank.

prefigure /priˈfɪgə/, *v.t.,* **-ured, -uring. 1.** to represent beforehand by figure or type; foreshadow. **2.** to figure or represent to oneself beforehand. [late ME, from LL] **– prefigurative,** *adj.* **– prefiguration,** *n.*

prefix /ˈprifɪks/, *n.;* /priˈfɪks, ˈprifɪks/, *v.* ◇*n.* **1.** *Gram.* an affix which is put before a word, stem, or word part to add to or limit its meaning (as *un-* in *unkind*). ◇*v.t.* **2.** to fix or put before or in front. **3.** *Gram.* to add as a prefix. [ME, from L: fixed before]

pregnant /ˈpregnənt/, *adj.* **1.** being with child or young, as a woman or female mammal. **2.** filled; abounding (fol. by *with*): *words pregnant with meaning.* **3.** full of meaning: *a pregnant moment.* [ME, from L] **– pregnancy,** *n.*

prehensile /priˈhensaɪl/, *adj.* **1.** suited for seizing or grasping anything. **2.** fitted for grasping by folding round an object. [F, from L: seized]

prehistoric /ˌprihɪsˈtɒrɪk/, *adj.* of or belonging to a period before that of recorded history. Also, **prehistorical.**

prejudge /ˌpriˈdʒʌdʒ/, *v.t.,* **-judged, -judging.** to pass judgment on before having all the facts. **– prejudgment,** *n.*

prejudice /ˈpredʒədəs/, *n., v.,* **-diced, -dicing.** ◇*n.* **1.** an opinion (usu. unfavorable), formed beforehand or without knowledge, thought, or reason. **2.** disadvantage resulting from some judgment or action of another. **3.** the resulting injury or loss. **4. without prejudice,** *Law.* without dismissing, damaging, etc., a legal interest or demand. ◇*v.t.* **5.** to influence with a prejudice, favorable or unfavorable. **6.** to harm. [ME, from F, from L] **– prejudicial,** *adj.*

prelate /ˈprelət/, *n.* a clergyman of a high order, as an archbishop, bishop, etc. [ME, from ML: a civil or ecclesiastical dignitary]

preliminary /prəˈlɪmənəri/, *adj., n., pl.* **-naries.** ◇*adj.* **1.** coming before and leading up to the main matter or business; introductory. ◇*n.* **2.** an introductory step, measure, sporting contest, etc. [NL, from L: of a threshold]

prelude /ˈpreljud/, *n., v.,* **-uded, -uding.** ◇*n.* **1.** a preliminary to an action, event, condition, etc. **2.** *Music.* **a.** a rather short, independent instrumental composition. **b.** a piece which comes before a more important movement. ◇*v.t.* **3.** to serve as a prelude to. **4.** to introduce by a prelude. [F, from ML, from L: play beforehand]

premarital /ˌpriˈmærətl/, *adj.* before marriage.

premature /ˈpremətʃə, preməˈtjuə/, *adj.* **1.** coming into existence or occurring too soon. **2.** developed or ripe before the proper time. **3.** overhasty, as in action. [L]

premedication /ˌprimedəˈkeɪʃən/, *n.* the giving of drugs before an operation, to calm a patient.

premeditate /priˈmedəteɪt/, *v.t., v.i.,* **-tated, -tating.** to consider or plan beforehand. [L: meditated beforehand] **– premeditation,** *n.* **– premeditative,** *adj.*

premenstrual tension /priˌmenstruəl ˈtenʃən/, *n.* discomfort, both physical and emotional, experienced by some women in the week before menstruation.

premier /ˈpremiə/, *n.* **1.** the leader of a state government. **2.** (*pl.*) (in sport) the team which wins the season's competition. ◇*adj.* **3.** chief; leading. **4.** winning: *the premier team.* [F: first, from L: of the first rank]

premiere /ˈpremiˈeə/, *n., v.,* **premiered, premiering.** ◇*n.* **1.** a first public performance of a play, etc. ◇*v.t.* **2.** to present to the public for the first time. ◇*v.i.* **3.** (of a film, play, etc.) to have its first public showing. [F: lit., first (fem.)]

premise /ˈpreməs/, *n.* **1.** (*pl.*) a house or building with the grounds, etc., belonging to it. **2.** Also, **premiss.** a proposition (or one of several) from which a conclusion is drawn. **3.** a basis for reasoned argument. [ME, from ML: sent before]

premium /ˈprimiəm/, *n.* **1.** a prize to be won in a competition. **2.** a bonus, gift, or sum additional to price, wages, interest, etc. **3.** a bonus, prize, etc. as an added attraction to buy a product. **4.** an amount paid for a contract of insurance. **5.** a sum above the normally recognised value of a thing. **6. at a premium, a.** in high regard; in demand. **b.** at a high price. ◇*adj.* **7.** highly regarded, special. **8.** of highest quality; best. [L: profit]

premonition /prɛməˈnɪʃən, priː-/, n. 1. a warning feeling of something about to happen; forewarning. 2. → **presentiment**. [F (obs.), from LL] —**premonitory**, adj.

prenatal /ˌpriːˈneɪtl/, adj. → **antenatal**.

preoccupation /priɒkjəˈpeɪʃən/, n. 1. the state of being preoccupied. 2. anything to which one devotes oneself.

preoccupied /priˈɒkjəpaɪd/, adj. completely absorbed in thought; engrossed.

preordain /priːɔːˈdeɪn/, v.t. to ordain beforehand; destine.

prep /prɛp/, Colloq. ◇adj. 1. preparatory. ◇n. 2. a preparatory school. 3. → **preparation** (def. 2).

prep., Abbrev. 1. preparation. 2. preparatory. 3. preposition.

preparation /prɛpəˈreɪʃən/, n. 1. an action, measure, or arrangement by which a person prepares for something. 2. homework. 3. the act or fact of preparing. 4. something made ready, manufactured, or formed.

preparatory school /prəˈpærətri skuːl/, n. an independent primary school.

prepare /prəˈpɛə/, v., -pared, -paring. ◇v.t. 1. to make ready, or put in right condition, for something. 2. to get ready for eating, as a meal. 3. to manufacture, form, or create. ◇v.i. 4. to get ready. [L: make ready beforehand] —**preparedness**, n. —**preparatory**, adj.

preponderant /prəˈpɒndərənt, priː-, -drənt/, adj. greater in weight, force, influence, number, etc.; predominant. —**preponderate**, v. —**preponderance**, n.

preposition /prɛpəˈzɪʃən/, n. Gram. (in some languages) a part of speech, made up of words placed before nouns to show their relation to other words or their function in the sentence. *By, to, in, from* are prepositions in English. [ME, from L]

prepositive /priˈpɒzətɪv/, adj. put before; prefixed.

prepossess /priːpəˈzɛs/, v.t. 1. to possess or control mentally beforehand, as a prejudice does. 2. to prejudice or bias, esp. favorably. —**prepossession**, n.

prepossessing /priːpəˈzɛsɪŋ/, adj. able to impress, esp. favorably.

preposterous /prəˈpɒstərəs/, adj. directly opposite to nature, reason, or common sense; absurd. [L: with the hinder part foremost]

prepuce /ˈpriːpjuːs/, n. Anat. the fold of skin which covers the head of the penis or clitoris; foreskin. [ME, from F, from L]

prerequisite /priːˈrɛkwəzət/, adj. 1. needed beforehand. ◇n. 2. something prerequisite: *A knowledge of French was the only prerequisite for obtaining the job.*

prerogative /prəˈrɒgətɪv/, n. an exclusive or established right or privilege belonging to an office, position, or person. [ME, from L: voting first]

Pres, Abbrev. President.

presage /ˈprɛsɪdʒ/, n.; /ˈprɛsɪdʒ, prəˈseɪdʒ/, v., -saged, -saging. ◇n. 1. a feeling of something about to happen; presentiment. 2. something that foreshadows a future event; omen. 3. a forecast; prediction. ◇v.t., v.i. 4. to have a feeling that something is about to happen. 5. to forecast or make a forecast. [ME, from L] —**presager**, n.

Presb, Abbrev. Presbyterian.

presbyter /ˈprɛzbətə, ˈprɛspətə/, n. (in some churches) an office-bearer; elder. [LL, from Gk: older]

presbyterian /prɛzbəˈtɪəriən, prɛspə-/, adj. 1. relating to or based on the principle of church government by an elected group of elders from the congregation. 2. (cap.) indicating or relating to churches having this form of government. ◇n. 3. (cap.) a member of a Presbyterian church. [L: presbytery]

presbytery /ˈprɛzbətri, ˈprɛspə-/, n., pl. -teries. 1. a body of presbyters or elders. 2. (in some Christian denominations) **a**. one of the governing bodies, esp. of a district. **b**. the churches of such a district. 3. the part of a church in which the high altar is placed. 4. (now only in Roman Catholic use) a priest's house. [ME, from LL, from Gk]

preschool /ˈpriːskuːl/, adj. 1. of, relating to, or taught before compulsory school age. ◇n. 2. → **kindergarten**.

prescience /ˈprɛsiəns/, n. knowledge of things before they exist or happen; foreknowledge. [ME, from L: knowing before] —**prescient**, adj.

prescribe /prəˈskraɪb/, v., -scribed, -scribing. ◇v.t. 1. to lay down, in writing, etc., as a rule or a course to be followed; appoint. 2. Med. to order for use, as treatment. ◇v.i. 3. to lay down rules. 4. Med. to order treatment to be used. [L: write before, direct]

prescription /prəˈskrɪpʃən/, n. 1. Med. **a**. a direction (usu. written) by the doctor to the pharmacist for the preparation and use of a medicine. **b**. the medicine prescribed. 2. the act or result of prescribing. [ME, from L]

prescriptive /prəˈskrɪptɪv/, adj. giving directions or commands.

preselection /priːsəˈlɛkʃən/, n. Politics. the process within a party of choosing candidates to stand for election.

presence /ˈprɛzəns/, n. 1. the condition or fact of being present. 2. attendance or company. 3. close vicinity: *in the presence of friends.* 4. personal appearance or style, esp. of a grand, important kind: *a man of fine presence.* 5. a divine or spiritual being. [ME, from OF, from L]

present[1] /ˈprɛzənt/, adj. 1. being, existing, or happening at this time; now. 2. for the time being: *clothes for present use.* 3. in attendance (opposed to *absent*): *to be present at a wedding.* 4. being in a given place. 5. existing in a place, thing, combination, etc. ◇n. 6. the present time. 7. Gram. → **present tense**. [ME, from L: being before (one)]

present² /prəˈzent/, v.; /ˈprezənt/, n. ◇v.t.
1. to provide with a gift, etc., esp. by formal act. 2. to bring, offer, or give, often in a formal way: *to present a message.* 3. to provide (an opportunity, possibility, etc.). 4. to hand or send in, as a cheque. 5. to introduce (a person) to another. 6. to introduce to the public: *to present a new play.* 7. to come to show (oneself) before a person, etc. 8. to show; exhibit. 9. to bring before the mind. 10. to set forth in words. 11. to level or aim (a weapon). ◇n. 12. a gift. [ME, from OF, from L]

presentable /prəˈzentəbəl/, adj. 1. suitable as in appearance, dress, manners, etc. 2. fit to be seen.

present arms /ˌprezənt ˈamz/, n. a position in which a rifle is held in both hands vertically in front of the body, with the muzzle up and the trigger side of the gun forward.

presentation /prezənˈteɪʃən/, n. 1. the act or fact of presenting. 2. exhibition or representation, as of a play. 3. offering or delivering, as of a gift. 4. a gift.

presentiment /prəˈzentəmənt/, n. a feeling of something about to happen, esp. something evil; foreboding. [F (obs.), from L: perceive beforehand]

presently /ˈprezəntli/, adv. 1. in a little while; soon. 2. at this time, currently.

present participle, n. *Gram.* a participle with present meaning, as *growing* in 'a growing boy'.

present perfect, *Gram.* See Appendix.

present tense, n. *Gram.* a tense which indicates that the action or state is happening or exists at the moment of speaking. See Appendix.

preservative /prəˈzɜvətɪv/, n. 1. something that preserves. 2. a chemical substance used to preserve foods, etc., from decay. ◇adj. 3. tending to preserve.

preserve /prəˈzɜv/, v., **-served, -serving**, n. ◇v.t. 1. to keep alive or in existence. 2. to keep safe; save. 3. to keep up; maintain. 4. to keep possession of; retain. 5. to prepare (food etc.) so as to prevent decay. 6. to prepare (fruit, etc.) by cooking with sugar. ◇v.i. 7. to preserve fruit, etc. ◇n. 8. something that preserves. 9. something that is preserved. 10. (*usu. pl.*) fruit, etc., cooked with sugar. [ME, from L] —**preservation**, n. —**preservative**, adj.

preset /ˌpriˈset/, v., **-set, -setting**; /ˈpriset/, adj. ◇v.t. 1. to set in advance. ◇adj. 2. determined in advance to follow a certain course etc.

preside /prəˈzaɪd/, v.i., **-sided, -siding**. 1. to occupy the place of authority or control. 2. to exercise control. [L: sit before, guard, preside over]

president /ˈprezədənt/, n. 1. (*oft. cap.*) the highest official in a republic. 2. an officer chosen to exercise control over an organised body of people, as a council, society, etc. 3. *US.* the chief officer of a college or university, or chairman of a company, etc. [ME, from L: presiding; ruling] —**presidency**, n. —**presidential**, adj.

Presley /ˈprezli/, n. **Elvis Aaron**, 1935–77, US pop singer, guitarist, composer and film actor; one of the most influential rock'n'roll singers.

press¹ /pres/, v.t. 1. to act upon with weight or force. 2. to move by weight or force in a certain direction or position. 3. to squeeze. 4. to weigh heavily upon. 5. to make flat by subjecting to weight. 6. to hold closely; hug. 7. to iron (clothes, etc.). 8. to remove juice, etc., from by pressure. 9. to bother; harass. 10. to trouble, as by lack of something. 11. to urge; impel. 12. to urge onwards; hurry. 13. to urge (a person, etc.); beg. 14. to insist on. 15. to push forward. ◇v.i. 16. to use weight, force, or pressure. 17. to iron clothes, etc. 18. to bear heavily, as upon the mind. 19. to demand immediate attention. 20. to push forward. 21. to crowd; throng. ◇n. 22. newspapers, magazines, etc., or the group of people writing or presenting news. 23. comment in the newspapers, etc., on some matter of public interest, either approving (**good press**) or disapproving (**bad press**). 24. *Print.* → **printing press**. 25. an establishment for printing books, etc. 26. a type of machine for applying pressure. 27. a crowd. 28. pressure; urgency. 29. an upright case, etc. for holding clothes, books, etc. 30. **go to press**, to begin to be printed. [OE *press*, from ML]

press² /pres/, v.t. 1. to force into service, esp. naval or military. 2. to make use of in a manner different from that intended. [backformation from *prest*, take (men) for military service, from OF: furnish, lend, from L: perform, vouch for, excel]

press agency, n. → **news agency**.

press agent, n. a person employed to look after advertising and publicity of a theatre, performer, etc.

press conference, n. an interview of a famous person, public official, etc., by journalists.

press gallery, n. 1. a gallery kept apart for the press, esp. in a legislative chamber. 2. the group of reporters allowed to enter such a gallery.

pressing /ˈpresɪŋ/, adj. 1. urgent. ◇n. 2. an act or instance of someone or something that presses. 3. a run of gramophone records produced at one time.

press release, n. a piece of news prepared for and given to the press.

press secretary, n. someone who arranges the release of information to the press and public for a public figure, esp. a politician.

press-stud /ˈpres-stʌd/, n. a metal fastener, used esp. on clothing, in which two parts are pressed together.

press-up /ˈpres-ʌp/, n. → **push-up**.

pressure /ˈpreʃə/, n. 1. the application of force upon a body by another body in contact with it; compression. 2. *Phys.* the force per unit area exerted at a given point. The SI unit of pressure is the pascal. 3. the act or fact of

pressure pressing. 4. annoyance; harassment. 5. a condition of trouble or worry. 6. a driving force or influence. 7. urgency, as of business. [ME, from F (obs.), from L]

pressure cooker, /ˈpreʃə kukə/, n. a strong, closed vessel in which food may be cooked above the normal boiling point under pressure.

pressure gradient, n. Weather. the decrease in atmospheric pressure per unit of horizontal distance in the direction in which pressure decreases most quickly.

pressure group, n. a group, in politics, business, etc., which attempts to protect or advance its own interests.

pressure pack, n. a container from which a liquid is released as a gas, or under pressure of a gas; aerosol.

pressure point, n. any of the points in the body at which pressure applied with the fingers, a tourniquet, etc., will control bleeding from an artery at a point further away from the heart.

pressure suit, n. a garment designed to provide body pressure and air, for use in conditions of low pressure as in high-flying aircraft and spacecraft. Also, **pressurised suit**.

pressurise or **pressurize** /ˈpreʃəraɪz/, v.t., v.i., **-rised**, **-rising**. 1. to keep normal air pressure in (the cockpit or cabin of) an aeroplane designed to fly at high altitudes. 2. to compress (a gas or liquid) in order to create a pressure greater than normal.

prestige /presˈtiːʒ/, n. 1. reputation or influence arising from success, achievement, rank, etc. ◊adj. 2. typical of a person who has gained success, wealth, etc. [F: illusion, glamor, from L: illusion] —**prestigious**, adj.

presto /ˈprestoʊ/, adv. 1. quickly; rapidly. 2. Music. in quick tempo; to be played very fast. ◊adj. 3. quick. [It: quick, quickly, from LL: ready, L: at hand]

Preston[1] /ˈprestən/, n. Margaret Rose, 1875-1963, Australian painter.

Preston[2] /ˈprestən/, n. a city in southern Vic, in the Melbourne metropolitan area. Pop. 82 600 (1987 est.).

prestress /ˌpriːˈstres/, v.t. to produce an initial stress in (concrete), to cancel out stresses resulting from applied loads. —**prestressed**, adj.

presume /prəˈzjuːm/, v., **-sumed**, **-suming**. ◊v.t. 1. to take for granted; assume: *I presume you're tired*. 2. Law. to suppose as true in the absence of proof to the contrary. ◊v.i. 3. to take something for granted; suppose. 4. to act or proceed with inexcusable boldness. [ME, from L: take beforehand, venture]

presumption /prəˈzʌmpʃən/, n. 1. the act or fact of presuming. 2. supposition of something as true. 3. belief on reasonable grounds. 4. something that is presumed; an assumption. 5. a reason for presuming. 6. Law. an inference required or permitted by law as to the existence of one fact from proof of the existence of other facts. 7. inexcusable boldness. —**presumptive**, adj. —**presumptuous**, adj.

presuppose /ˌpriːsəˈpoʊz/, v.t. **-posed**, **-posing**. 1. to take for granted in advance. 2. (of a thing) to require as a prior condition: *An effect presupposes a cause*. —**presupposition**, n.

pretence /prəˈtens/, n. 1. a pretending; feigning. 2. a false show of something: *a pretence of friendship*. 3. a pretended reason or excuse; pretext. [ME, from AF, from ML: pretend]

pretend /prəˈtend/, v.t. 1. to put forward a false appearance of; feign. 2. to attempt falsely (to do something). 3. to claim falsely. ◊v.i. 4. to make believe. 5. to lay claim (fol. by *to*). [ME, from L: stretch forth, pretend]

pretender /prəˈtendə/, n. 1. someone who pretends. 2. someone who lays claim to a throne.

pretension /prəˈtenʃən/, n. 1. a laying claim to something. 2. a claim to something. 3. (oft. pl.) a claim made, esp. indirectly, to some quality, merit, etc.: *pretensions to good judgment*. 4. the act of pretending. 5. → allegation. 6. → pretext.

pretentious /prəˈtenʃəs/, adj. 1. full of pretension. 2. marked by supposed dignity or importance. 3. making an exaggerated outward show; ostentatious. [L: pretension]

preterite tense /ˈpretərət tens, ˈpretrət/, n. Gram. See Appendix. [ME, from L: gone by]

preternatural /ˌpriːtəˈnætʃərəl/, adj. 1. out of the ordinary course of nature; abnormal. 2. → supernatural.

pretext /ˈpriːtekst/, n. something that is put forward to hide a true purpose or object; an excuse. [L]

Pretoria /prəˈtɔːriə/, n. a city in the northeastern Republic of South Africa; the capital of Transvaal and seat of the executive government of the Republic of South Africa. Pop. 822 905 (1986).

pretty /ˈprɪti/, adj., **-tier**, **-tiest**, adv., v., **prettied**, **prettying**. ◊adj. 1. fair or attractive in a dainty way: *a pretty face*. 2. pleasant to look at or hear: *a pretty scene*; *a pretty tune*. 3. (ironic) dreadful: *a pretty mess*. 4. Colloq. fairly great: *a pretty sum*. 5. **pretty penny**, a great sum of money. ◊adv. 6. rather; moderately: *Her work was pretty good*. 7. very: *The wind blew pretty hard*. 8. **sitting pretty**, in a very satisfactory position. ◊v.t. 9. to make pretty: *She prettied herself up*. [OE *prættig* cunning, wily]

pretzel /ˈpretsəl/, n. a dry, crisp, salted biscuit, usu. in the form of a knot or stick. [G]

prevail /prəˈveɪl/, v.i. 1. to exist everywhere or generally: *Silence prevailed*. 2. to appear or happen as the more important feature or element; predominate. 3. to be superior in strength, power, etc. 4. to operate successfully. 5. to use persuasion successfully (fol. by *on*, *upon*, or *with*). [ME, from L: be more able]

prevalent /ˈprevələnt/, adj. widespread; in general use or acceptance. [L: prevailing] – **prevalence**, n.

prevaricate /prəˈværəkeɪt/, v.i., **-cated, -cating.** to act or speak evasively; to avoid telling the truth. [L: walked crookedly, deviated] – **prevarication**, n.

prevent /prəˈvent/, v.t. 1. to keep from happening; hinder. 2. to stop (a person, etc.), from doing something. [ME, from L: come before] – **preventable, preventible**, adj. – **prevention**, n.

preventive /prəˈventɪv/, n., adj. (a substance or measure) serving to prevent or stop something, esp. a disease. Also, **preventative**.

preview /ˈprivju/, n. 1. a view in advance, as of a film. ◇v.t. 2. to view in advance.

previous /ˈpriviəs/, adj. 1. coming or happening before something else; prior. 2. Colloq. done, happening, etc., before the proper time; premature. [L]

prey /preɪ/, n. 1. an animal hunted or seized for food, esp. by a flesh-eating animal. 2. a person or thing that falls victim to an enemy, disease, etc. 3. the action or habit of preying: *bird of prey*. ◇v.i. 4. to seek for and seize prey, as an animal does. 5. to profit by acting harmfully towards a victim (fol. by *on*). 6. to have a harmful or destructive influence. [ME, from OF, from L: booty, prey]

Priam /ˈpraɪəm/, n. *Gk Legend.* father of Hector and Paris and last king of Troy, at the capture of which he was slain.

Priapus /praɪˈeɪpəs/, n. *Gk and Rom Relig.* the personification as a god of the male procreative power, the deity of gardens and vineyards. [L, from Gk *Príāpos*] – **Priapean** /praɪəˈpiən/, adj.

price /praɪs/, n., v., **priced, pricing.** ◇n. 1. amount of money or its equivalent for which anything is bought, sold, or offered for sale. 2. amount offered for the capture of a person alive or dead. 3. something that must be given or done, in order to obtain a thing. 4. betting odds. 5. **at any price**, at any cost, no matter how great. 6. **beyond / without price**, unobtainable; priceless. ◇v.t. 7. to fix the price of. 8. *Colloq.* to ask the price of. [ME, from OF, from L: price, value, worth]

price control, n. *Econ.* the setting of maximum prices for certain goods and services by a government, as an economic policy.

price-cutting /ˈpraɪs-kʌtɪŋ/, n. the act of selling an article at a price under the usual or advertised price.

price index, n. *Econ.* a government study showing the general level of prices, e.g. the **consumer price index.**

priceless /ˈpraɪsləs/, adj. 1. having a value beyond all price; invaluable. 2. *Colloq.* delightfully amusing.

price war, n. a fiercely competitive price-cutting battle, usu. among those traders selling goods to the public.

pricey /ˈpraɪsi/, adj. *Colloq.* expensive.

Prichard /ˈprɪtʃəd/, n. **Katharine Susannah**, 1883–1969, Australian novelist, short-story writer, and poet, born in Fiji; wrote the novel *Coonardoo* (1929); a founding member of the Communist Party of Australia.

prick /prɪk/, n. 1. a small hole made by a needle, thorn, etc. 2. the act of pricking. 3. the feeling of being pricked. 4. *Colloq.* the penis. ◇v.t. 5. to pierce with a sharp point; puncture. 6. to affect with sharp pain, as from piercing. 7. to cause sharp mental pain to; sting, as with remorse or sorrow: *His conscience pricked him suddenly.* 8. to mark (a surface) with pricks or dots. 9. to cause to stand or point upwards: *The dog pricked its ears.* ◇v.i. 10. to perform the action of piercing something. 11. to have a feeling of being pricked. 12. to rise or point upwards, as ears of an animal. ◇v. 13. **prick up one's ears**, to listen, esp. to something of particular interest. [OE: puncture]

prickle /ˈprɪkəl/, n., v., **-led, -ling.** ◇n. 1. a sharp point. 2. a small, pointed outgrowth from the bark of a plant; thorn. ◇v.t. 3. to prick. 4. to cause a pricking feeling in. ◇v.i. 5. to tingle as if pricked. [OE]

prickly /ˈprɪkli/, adj., **-lier, -liest.** 1. full of prickles. 2. full of troublesome points. 3. easily angered.

prickly heat, n. a skin eruption accompanied by a prickling and itching sensation, due to an inflammation of the sweat glands.

prickly pear, n. 1. the pear-shaped, oft. prickly fruit of certain cactus plants native to North and South America. 2. the plants themselves, which were a serious problem in Australia until brought under control by the introduction of the cactoblastis moth.

pride /praɪd/, n., v., **prided, priding.** ◇n. 1. high (or too high) opinion of one's own dignity, importance, worth, etc. 2. the condition or feeling of being proud. 3. a noble sense of what is due to oneself or one's position or character; self-respect; self-esteem. 4. pleasure or satisfaction taken in something done or gained. 5. something of which a person is proud. 6. the best or most admired part of anything. 7. the most successful state or period: *in the pride of manhood.* 8. a company of lions. ◇v.t. 9. to be pleased with (oneself) because of some achievement, etc. (fol. by *on* or *upon*): *He prides himself on his sports record.* [ME; OE *pryde*]

pride of place, n. the highest or most important position.

priest /prist/, n. 1. someone whose duty it is to perform religious ceremonies, and esp. to make sacrificial offerings. 2. (in Christian use) a clergyman; minister. [OE *prēost*, from L] – **priestly**, adj.

priesthood /ˈpristhʊd/, n. 1. the condition or office of a priest. 2. priests collectively. [ME; OE *prēosthād*]

Priestley /ˈpristli/, 1. **J(ohn) B(oynton)**, 1894–1984, English novelist; many of his works show a concern for the nature of time. 2. **Joseph**, 1733–1804, English chemist, author, and clergyman; he discovered oxygen and several other gases.

prig /prɪg/, n. someone who is always concerned about duty, esp. in a self-righteous way. [? akin to PRINK]

prim /prɪm/, adj., **primmer, primmest.** adj. very proper, as a person, behavior, etc. [orig. obscure]

prim., Abbrev. 1. primary. 2. primate. 3. primitive.

primacy /ˈpraɪməsi/, n., pl. **-cies.** 1. the condition of being first in order, rank, importance, etc. 2. Church. the office, rank, or dignity of a primate. [ME, from ML, from L: PRIMATE]

prima donna /ˌprimə ˈdɒnə, ˌprɪmə/, n., pl. **prima donnas.** 1. the principal female singer of an operatic company. 2. Colloq. a temperamental, egotistical person who makes frequent outbursts of exaggerated feelings. [It: first lady]

prima facie /ˌpraɪmə ˈfeɪʃi/, adv. at first appearance. [L]

prima-facie evidence, n. Law. evidence that is enough to establish a fact, unless opposed.

primal /ˈpraɪməl/, adj. 1. first; original; primeval. 2. first of first importance; fundamental. [ML, from L: first]

primarily /ˈpraɪmrəli, ˈpraɪmərəli/, adv. 1. in the first place; chiefly. 2. at first; originally.

primary /ˈpraɪmərɪ, ˈpraɪmri/, adj., n., pl. **-ries.** ◇adj. 1. first or highest in rank or importance; chief; principal. 2. first in order in any series, order, etc. 3. making up, or belonging to, the first stage in any process. 4. original; not derived; basic. 5. immediate or direct; not involving intermediate agency. 6. relating to any of the set of flight feathers found on the end part of a bird's wing. 7. Elect. of or relating to the inducing circuit, coil, or current in an induction coil, etc. 8. Chem. involving, or obtained by replacement of one radical. ◇n. 9. the first in order, rank, or importance. 10. US. a meeting of the voters of a political party in an election district for choosing candidates for office, etc. 11. one of any set of primary colors. 12. a primary feather. [late ME, from L: of the first rank]

primary accent, n. → primary stress.

primary cell, n. a cell designed to produce electric current through an electrochemical reaction which is not easily reversible and so the cell, when discharged, cannot easily be recharged by an electric current.

primary color or **primary colour,** n. any of three colors (usu. said to be red, yellow and blue) regarded as basic, and which can produce all other colors by mixing.

primary consumer, n. a herbivore. See **secondary consumer, tertiary consumer.**

primary industry, n. any industry such as farming, forestry, mining, etc., which is involved in the growing, producing, extracting, etc., of natural resources.

primary producer, n. someone who works in a primary industry.

primary school, n. a school for full-time basic instruction of children from the age of six to about eleven years.

primary stress, n. the main or strongest accent of a word. Also, **primary accent.**

primate /ˈpraɪmət/ for def. 1; /ˈpraɪmeɪt/ for def. 2, n. 1. Church. the head bishop of a country; archbishop. 2. any mammal of the group that includes man, the apes, monkeys, lemurs, etc. [ME, from ML: chief bishop, LL: chief, head]

prime /praɪm/, adj., n., v., **primed, priming.** ◇adj. 1. first in importance, excellence, or value: prime time; prime beef. 2. first or highest in rank or authority; principal: the prime minister. 3. first in time; earliest; primitive. 4. original; fundamental: prime mover. 5. Maths. **a.** of a number which has itself and unity as its only factors. **b.** having no common divisor except unity: 2 is prime to 9. ◇n. 6. the period or condition of greatest vigor: prime of youth; prime of life. 7. Maths. → **prime number.** 8. Music. (in a scale) the tonic or keynote. ◇v.t. 9. to put gunpowder into (an old-fashioned gun). 10. to lay a train of gunpowder to (a charge, mine, etc.). 11. to pour water into (a pump) to prepare it for working. 12. to cover (a surface) with a preparatory coat of paint, etc. 13. to supply or prepare with information, words, etc., for use. [OE, from L: first]

prime cost, n. the expense of producing an article, in labor and materials, as different from the expense of advertising, etc.

prime meridian, n. a meridian from which longitude east and west is measured, usu. that of Greenwich, England.

prime minister, n. (oft. cap.) the leader of government in some political systems.

prime mover /praɪm ˈmuvə/, n. 1. Mech. **a.** the energy which moves a machine, as wind, electricity, etc. **b.** a machine which uses natural energy, as a waterwheel or steam-engine. 2. a powerful vehicle designed to pull a load, as in a semitrailer. 3. (in Aristotelian philosophy) something which is the first cause of all movement and does not itself move: Some philosophers think of God as the prime mover of the universe. 4. someone who is the main organiser of an undertaking.

prime number, n. a positive integer not exactly divisible by any integer except itself and unity: 5 is a prime number.

primer[1] /ˈprɪmə, ˈpraɪmə/, n. 1. a book for teaching children to read. 2. any small book of basic instruction. [ME, from ML]

primer[2] /ˈpraɪmə/, n. 1. a cap, cylinder, etc., containing an explosive, used for firing a charge of gunpowder. 2. a preparatory coat of paint, etc. [PRIME, v. + -ER[1]]

primeval /praɪˈmivəl/, adj. of or relating to the first age or ages, esp. of the world: primeval forms of life. Also, **primaeval.** [L: young + -AL[1]]

primipara /praɪˈmɪpərə/, n. 1. a woman who has given birth once. 2. a woman giving birth for the first time. [L]

primitive /ˈprɪmətɪv/, *adj.* **1.** being the first or earliest of the kind or in existence: *primitive forms of life*. **2.** typical of early ages or of an early state of human development: *primitive art; primitive peoples*. **3.** uncivilised; simple; crude. **4.** *Biol.* rudimentary; primordial. ◇*n*. **5.** a member of a primitive race or tribe. **6.** (a painting by) an artist who paints in a simple or naive style. [L: first of its kind; replacing ME *primitif*, from OF]

primogenitor /ˌpraɪmouˈdʒɛnətə/, *n.* **1.** a first parent or earliest ancestor. **2.** a forefather or ancestor. [ML, from L: at first + *genitor* male parent]

primogeniture /ˌpraɪmouˈdʒɛnətʃə/, *n.* **1.** the condition or fact of being the firstborn child in a family. **2.** *Law.* inheritance or succession by the eldest son. [ML, from L: firstborn]

primordial /praɪˈmɔːdɪəl/, *adj.* **1.** giving origin; elementary. **2.** *Biol.* primitive; initial; first. **3.** relating to, existing at or from the very beginning: *primordial matter*. [ME, from LL, from L: beginning]

primrose /ˈprɪmrouz/, *n.* **1.** a common perennial European plant, esp. that with pale yellow flowers. **2.** pale yellow. ◇*adj.* **3.** relating to the primrose. **4.** full of ease and pleasure: *the primrose path*. **5.** of a pale yellow. [ME, from ML: first rose]

primula /ˈprɪmjələ/, *n.* a type of plant (including the primrose) with flowers of many colors. [ML: kind of flower; short for *primula veris*, lit., first (flower) of spring]

primus /ˈpraɪməs/, *n.* a portable cooking stove burning butane or propane. [Trademark]

prin., *Abbrev.* principal.

prince /prɪns/, *n.* **1.** a son or near relative of a king or queen. **2.** a ruler of a small state, lower in rank than a king. **3.** someone or something that is important, or the best, in any class, group, etc.: *a merchant prince; a prince among poets*. [ME, from OF, from L: principal person]

princedom /ˈprɪnsdəm/, *n.* **1.** the position, rank, or dignity of a prince. **2.** a country ruled by a prince; principality.

princely /ˈprɪnsli/, *adj.*, **-lier, -liest. 1.** generous; liberal; lavish. **2.** magnificent. **3.** royal; noble.

Prince of Wales, *n.* a title conferred by the eldest son, or heir apparent, of the British sovereign.

princess /ˈprɪnsɛs/, *n.* **1.** a daughter or near relative of a king or queen. **2.** the wife of a prince. [ME, from F, fem. of *prince* PRINCE]

principal /ˈprɪnsəpəl/, *adj.* **1.** first or highest in rank, importance, value, etc.; chief; foremost. ◇*n.* **2.** the head of a school or college. **3.** someone who takes a leading part in a play, ballet, action, etc. **4.** something of chief importance. **5.** *Law.* **a.** a person authorising another (an agent) to represent him or her. **b.** a person directly responsible for a crime. See **accessory** (def. 2). **6.** someone who has a debt to pay back (opposed to an *endorser*). **7.** *Comm.* a sum of money on which interest is paid or profit gained. [ME, from L: first, chief]

principal axis, *n.* the straight line passing through both the centre of the surface of a lens or mirror and its centre of curvature.

principal clause, *n.* → **main clause**.

principal focus, *n.* → **focal point**.

principality /ˌprɪnsəˈpælətɪ/, *n., pl.* **-ties**. a small state ruled by a prince.

principal parts, *n.pl.* the main forms of a verb from which all the other forms can be worked out, as *sing, sang, sung; smoke, smoked*.

principle /ˈprɪnsəpəl/, *n.* **1.** a basic, primary, or general truth, on which other truths depend: *the principles of government*. **2.** a basic belief, teaching, or opinion: *the principles of the Stoics*. **3.** (*pl.*) guiding rules of right behavior. **4.** an inner guiding sense of the requirements of these: *a man of principle*. **5.** a rule used to determine action: *He acts on the principle that most people are stupid*. **6.** a rule or law in nature, shown in the working of a machine, system, etc.: *the principle of capillary attraction*. **7.** *Chem.* something that makes up a substance, esp. one giving to it some particular quality or effect. **8. in principle**, according to the rule generally followed. **9. on principle**, **a.** according to fixed rule, method, or practice. **b.** according to a personal rule for right behavior. [ME, from F, from L]

principled /ˈprɪnsəpəld/, *adj.* having guiding rules for right behavior: *high-principled*.

prink /prɪŋk/, *v.t.* **1.** to deck or dress for show. ◇*v.i.* **2.** to fuss over one's dress, esp. before a mirror.

print /prɪnt/, *v.t.* **1.** to produce (writing, a picture, etc.) by pressing an inked surface in the shape of letters, lines, a block, etc., on to paper. **2.** to cause (something written) to appear in print: *They are printing her poems*. **3.** to write separate letters rather than in handwriting: *Please print the answers clearly*. **4.** to mark (a surface, etc.) by pressing something into or on it. **5.** to make (a mark, etc.) by pressure: *Nervousness printed the marks of her fingernails on her palms*. **6.** to put into the mind or memory for a long time. **7.** *Photog.* to produce a positive picture from (a negative). **8.** *Computers.* to produce (a result, data, etc.) in written form on paper (oft. fol. by *out*). ◇*v.i.* **9.** to make letters, lines by printing: *We are printing all day tomorrow*. **10.** to give a mark on paper, etc., of a certain kind: *This typeface prints clearly*. **11.** to write in separate letters: *She is still printing at school because she hasn't learned running writing*. **12.** *Computers.* to produce results in an ordinary written form on paper (oft. fol. by *out*). ◇*n.* **13.** the condition of being printed as a book: *to appear in print*. **14. in print**, **a.** published. **b.** (of a book, etc.) still able to be bought from the publisher. **15. out of print**, (of a book, etc.) sold out by the publisher. **16.** printed lettering or matter: *large print; fine print*. **17. a.** a picture, design, etc., made by printing from an engraved block or plate, or through a screen. **b.** a printed photograph of a painting, etc.: *a Van Gogh print*. **18.** a mark made by the pressure of one

print

thing on another. **19.** a cloth with a design printed on it. **20.** *Photog.* a picture made from a negative. ◇*adj.* **21.** made of printed cloth, esp. cotton: *a print dress.* [ME, from OF: impression, print, from L: press] —**printable**, *adj.* —**printery**, *n.*

printed circuit, *n.* a circuit forming part of electronic equipment in which the wiring between parts, and some parts themselves, are printed on to an insulating board.

printer /'prɪntə/, *n.* a person or business engaged in the printing industry.

printing /'prɪntɪŋ/, *n.* **1.** the art, process, or business of producing books, newspapers, etc., by impression from movable types, plates, etc.; typography: *Printing is becoming very expensive.* **2.** the act of someone or something that prints. **3.** writing in separate or unjoined letters. See **cursive.**

printing press, *n.* a machine for printing on paper, etc., from type, plates, etc.

print media, *n.* newspapers and magazines (opposed to *electronic media*).

print-out /'prɪnt-aʊt/, *n.* results, data, etc., printed automatically by a computer in readable form.

prior¹ /'praɪə/, *adj.* **1.** earlier: *a prior agreement.* **2. prior to**, before; preceding. [L: former, earlier]

prior² /'praɪə/, *n.* **1.** an officer in an order or house of monks, sometimes next in rank below an abbot. **2.** the head of certain orders or houses of friars. [ME and OE, from ML: superior, head] —**priorate**, **priorship**, *n.*

prioress /'praɪərɛs/, *n.* a woman holding a position corresponding to that of a prior.

priority /praɪ'ɒrəti/, *n., pl.* **-ties. 1.** the condition of being earlier: *the priority of Aboriginal over white settlement in Australia.* **2.** the condition of being more important: *to get your priorities right.* **3.** the having of certain rights before another: *The main road has priority.*

priority-paid /praɪ,ɒrəti-'peɪd/, *adj.* of mail, the delivery of which is guaranteed within a stated time.

priory /'praɪəri/, *n., pl.* **-ries.** a religious house ruled by a prior or prioress, often dependent upon an abbey. [ME, from ML]

prise /praɪz/, *v.t.,* **prised, prising.** to raise, move, or force with or as with a lever. Also, *Chiefly US*, **pry.** [ME, from F: a taking hold, from L: seized]

prism /'prɪzəm/, *n.* **1.** a transparent object, usu. of glass and with triangular bases, used for *breaking* light down into the colors of the spectrum. **2.** *Geom.* a solid whose bases or ends are any equal and parallel polygons, and whose sides are parallelograms. **3.** a form of crystal consisting of faces which are parallel to the vertical axis and intersect the horizontal axes. [LL, from Gk: something sawed] —**prismatic**, *adj.*

prison /'prɪzən/, *n.* **1.** a public building where criminals and other people who have

private parts

broken the law are kept locked up. **2.** any place where people are kept against their will. **3.** the condition of being kept in prison: *Does prison help people to reform their lives?* [ME, from OF, from L: seizure, arrest]

prison-camp /'prɪzən-kæmp/, *n.* a camp for prisoners of war, political prisoners, etc.

prisoner /'prɪzənə, 'prɪznə/, *n.* **1.** someone who is kept in prison. **2.** someone who is caught or seized: *The robbers took him prisoner.*

prisoner of war, *n.* someone caught by an enemy in war. *Abbrev:* POW

prissy /'prɪsi/, *adj.,* **-sier, -siest.** *Colloq.* fussy; prim; affectedly nice. [b. PRIM and SISSY]

pristine /'prɪstin/, *adj.* **1.** of or relating to the earliest period or condition; original; primitive. **2.** having its original purity. [L: early]

privacy /'praɪvəsi, 'prɪvəsi/, *n., pl.* **-cies. 1.** the condition of being private; retirement; seclusion. **2.** secrecy. [PRIV(ATE) + -ACY]

private /'praɪvət/, *adj.* **1.** belonging to oneself or to someone in particular; being one's own: *private property.* **2.** relating to or affecting a particular person or people, and not others; individual; personal: *for your private satisfaction.* **3.** secret; confidential: *a private meeting.* **4.** not of an official or public character: *to retire to private life.* **5.** not open or available to people in general: *a private road.* **6.** without the presence of others; alone; secluded: *He's a private sort of person.* ◇*n.* **7.** *Mil.* a soldier of the lowest rank. See Appendix. **8. in private**, in secret; not publicly. [ME, from L: separate]

private bill, *n.* a parliamentary bill for the particular interest or benefit of some person or people.

private company, *n.* → **proprietary limited company.**

private enterprise, *n.* **1.** business activities not under state ownership or control. **2.** the principle of free enterprise or laissez-faire capitalism.

privateer /praɪvə'tɪə/, *n.* **1.** an armed ship, privately owned and manned, allowed by a government in wartime to fight enemy ships, esp. those carrying goods. **2.** a commander, or one of the crew, of such a ship. ◇*v.i.* **3.** to cruise as a privateer. [PRIVATE + -EER, modelled on VOLUNTEER]

private eye, *n. Colloq.* → **private investigator.**

private hotel, *n.* a hotel or boarding house that does not have a license to sell liquor.

private investigator, *n.* a detective not part of the police force, who hires out his or her services to the public. Also, **private eye.**

private means, *n.pl.* income which does not depend on money gained from working. Also, **independent means.**

private member's bill, *n.* a bill introduced by a backbench member of parliament or (rarely) by a minister acting as a member, rather than by the government.

private parts, *n.pl.* the outer sex organs; genitals. Also, **privy parts.**

private practice, *n.* **1.** a medical practice involving care for private, paying patients. **2.** self-employment.

private school, *n.* a school outside the state system of education, which is privately run and paid for, and which charges fees. Also, **independent school**.

private sector, *n.* that part of an economy which is owned and operated by individuals and privately owned companies (as opposed to the *public sector*).

privation /praɪˈveɪʃən/, *n.* lack or loss of the usual comforts or necessaries of life; hardship: *to lead a life of privation*. [ME, from L]

privatise or **privatize** /ˈpraɪvətaɪz/, *v.t.*, **-tised, -tising.** *n.* to transfer the ownership of (land, industries or organisations) from the state to the private sector.

privative /ˈprɪvətɪv/, *adj.* marked by the taking away of something, or lack of something. [L]

privet /ˈprɪvət/, *n.* a European evergreen shrub or small tree, of unusual hardiness, with small, strong-smelling white flowers, now considered a pest, because it overgrows areas of bush. [orig. uncert.]

privilege /ˈprɪvəlɪdʒ/, *n., v.,* **-leged, -leging.** ◇*n.* **1.** a special right or advantage enjoyed only by a certain person or people: *We had the privilege of meeting the great man.* **2.** a special right or protection given to people in authority or office; prerogative: *parliamentary privilege.* **3.** the principle or condition of enjoying special advantages: *The rich live a life of privilege.* **4.** any of the more important rights common to all citizens under a modern constitution: *Free speech is a privilege we try to preserve.* ◇*v.t.* **5.** to give a privilege to. **6.** to free; exempt (fol. by *from*). **7.** to allow (something otherwise forbidden) to happen or be done. [ME, from L: a law in favor of or against an individual] — **privileged**, *adj.*

privy /ˈprɪvi/, *adj., n., pl.* **privies.** ◇*adj.* **1.** sharing in the knowledge of something private or secret (usu. fol. by *to*): *Many people were privy to the plan.* **2.** private; assigned to private uses: *the privy purse.* **3.** *Archaic.* secret; concealed, hidden, or secluded. ◇*n.* **4.** an outhouse serving as a toilet. [ME, from OF, from L: separated, private] — **privily,** *n.*

Privy Council, *n.* (in Britain) a body of high-ranking people, who used to advise the king or queen on matters of state; membership now is mainly a mark of honor. — **Privy Councillor**, *n.*

prize¹ /praɪz/, *n.* **1.** a reward of victory in a race, competition, etc. **2.** that which is won in a lottery, raffle, etc. **3.** anything that someone tries hard to win, or anything greatly valued. ◇*adj.* **4.** having gained a prize; prize-winning. **5.** worthy of a prize; very valuable: *a prize bull.* **6.** remarkable: *a prize fool.* **7.** given or awarded as a prize: *a prize tour of NZ.* [ME, from OF: price, value, glory, from L]

prize² /praɪz/, *n.* something seized or captured in war, esp. an enemy ship with the goods it is carrying. [ME, from OF: seizing, capture, from L]

prize³ /praɪz/, *v.t.*, **prized, prizing.** to value highly. [ME, from OF: praise, from L]

prize fight, *n.* a fight between professional boxers for a money prize.

p.r.n., *Abbrev.* (used in prescriptions) as and when needed. [L *prō rē nātā*]

pro¹ /proʊ/, *adv., n., pl.* **pros.** ◇*adv.* **1.** in favor of (opposed to *con*). ◇*n.* **2.** someone who argues or votes in favor of something. **3.** an argument or vote in favor of something. [L: in favor of, for]

pro² /proʊ/, *n., pl.* **pros,** *adj. Colloq.* professional.

pro³ /proʊ/, *n., pl.* **pros.** *Colloq.* → **prostitute.**

pro-, **1.** a prefix indicating favor for some party, system, idea, etc., usu. without identity with the group, as *pro-British, pro-communist, pro-slavery,* having *anti-* as its opposite. **2.** a prefix of priority in space or time having esp. a meaning of advancing or projecting forwards or outwards, and also extended meanings, as *provision, prologue, proceed, produce, protract, pronoun, proconsul.* [L: for, in favor of]

probability /prɒbəˈbɪləti/, *n., pl.* **-ties.** **1.** the quality or fact of being probable. **2.** chance; likelihood: *There is a probability of his coming.* **3.** something that is probable or likely: *to see a thing as a probability.* **4.** *Stats.* a measure of the chances of an event happening, given by the ratio of the number of outcomes favoring the event to the total number of outcomes possible. **5. in all probability,** likely; very probably.

probability curve, *n. Stats.* **1.** a curve which describes the series of probabilities associated with the different values a variable may have. **2.** → **normal curve.**

probable /ˈprɒbəbəl/, *adj.* **1.** likely to happen or prove true. **2.** having more evidence for than against, but not proved true. **3.** giving ground for belief: *probable evidence.* [ME, from L]

probably /ˈprɒbəbli/, *adv.* most likely; in all likelihood.

probate /ˈproʊbeɪt/, *n.* **1.** *Law.* the official proving of a will as validly made according to the law. **2.** *Law.* an officially certified copy of a will so proved. ◇*adj.* **3.** of or relating to probate or a court of probate. [ME, from L: (a thing) proved]

probation /prəˈbeɪʃən/, *n.* **1.** (a period of) testing or trial of a person's behavior, character, qualifications, etc.: *He is on probation for holy orders.* **2.** *Law.* **a.** a method of dealing with offenders, esp. young people guilty of small crimes or first offences, by allowing them to go free as long as they keep the law, and are watched over by a person (**probation officer**) appointed for such duty. **b.** the condition of having been set free under these conditions. [ME, from L] — **probationer,** *n.*

probation system, *n. Aust Hist.* a system (which replaced the assignment system), under

probe /prəʊb/, v., **probed, probing,** n. ◇v.t., v.i. **1.** to examine or search thoroughly: *to probe a witness for evidence; to probe a wound.* ◇n. **2.** the act of probing. **3.** a thin surgical instrument for exploring the depth or direction of a wound, sinus, etc. **4.** *Aeron.* a spacecraft able to explore, examine and test conditions in space and radio back the results. [ML: test, in LL proof. See PROOF]

probity /ˈprəʊbəti/, n. honesty; uprightness; integrity. [L]

problem /ˈprɒbləm/, n. **1.** any question or matter involving doubt, uncertainty, or difficulty: *I have a problem trying to sell my house.* **2.** a question put forward for answering or discussing: *John can add up numbers, but he can't do problems.* ◇adj. **3.** difficult to deal with: *a problem child.* **4.** *Lit.* dealing with difficult social or moral choices: *a problem play.* [ME, from L, from Gk]

problematic /prɒbləˈmætɪk/, adj. of the nature of a problem; difficult or doubtful. **– problematically,** adv.

proboscis /prəˈbɒskəs, prəˈbəʊsɪs/, n., pl. **-boscises** /-ˈbɒskəsəz, -ˈbɒsəsəz/. **1.** an elephant's trunk. **2.** any long flexible nose, as of the tapir. **3.** *Insects.* **a.** a long, tubelike mouthpart used for feeding, as in flies and butterflies. **b.** any long or nose-like feeding organ. **4.** (*joc.*) the human nose. [L, from Gk]

procedure /prəˈsidʒə/, n. **1.** the act or manner of doing anything: *His usual procedure was to have a cup of coffee before doing his homework.* **2.** a particular course or way of action: *Moving house is not a simple procedure.* **3.** the way of doing business in law, parliament, etc. [F] **– procedural,** adj.

proceed /prəˈsid/, v.; /ˈprəʊsid/, n. ◇v.i. **1.** to move or go forward, esp. after stopping. **2.** to go on with any action or process: *They are proceeding with the work on the boat.* **3.** to go on (to or to do something): *to proceed to an apprenticeship after school.* **4.** *Law.* **a.** to begin and carry on a legal action. **b.** to take legal proceedings (fol. by *against*). **5.** to be carried on: *The boatbuilding is proceeding fast.* **6.** to go or come forth; issue. **7.** to arise, originate, or result. ◇n. **8.** (*usu.* pl.) money from a sale, etc. [ME, from L]

proceeding /prəˈsidɪŋ/, n. **1.** (a particular course of) action or behavior. **2.** the act of someone or something that proceeds. **3.** (pl.) the records of the activities of a society: *the proceedings of the Historical Society.* **4.** *Law.* (the starting or carrying on of) an action at law.

process /ˈprəʊsɛs/, n. **1.** a series of actions directed to some end: *the process of making butter.* **2.** a continuous action or series of changes: *the process of decay.* **3.** *Law.* **a.** the whole course of the proceedings in a legal action. **b.** a summons to appear before a court. **4.** *Biol.* a natural outgrowth; projection; appendage: *a process of a bone.* **5.** course or passing: *process of time.* **6. in (the) process of,** during the course of; in the middle of. ◇v.t. **7.** to treat, prepare or deal with in some particular way: *to process iron ore; to process cheques; to process film.* **8.** to turn (a foodstuff) into a marketable form by some special process: *to process cheese.* **9.** *Computers.* to manipulate (data) in order to abstract the required information. [ME, from F, from L: a going forward] **– processor,** n.

procession /prəˈsɛʃən/, n. **1.** an orderly line or group of people, cars, etc., moving along in a formal or ceremonious way, esp. in religious or civic ceremonies. **2.** the act of coming forth from a source. [early ME, from ML: a religious procession, in L a marching on]

processional /prəˈsɛʃənəl/, n. **1.** a hymn sung at an entry procession in church. **2.** a book containing hymns, litanies, etc., for use in religious processions.

process worker, n. a person engaged on a production line in a manufacturing process, who is not required to make adjustments to machinery or to use skills of fitting or adjustment.

proclaim /prəˈkleɪm/, v.t. **1.** to announce or declare publicly or in a tiresome way: *to proclaim one's opinions.* **2.** to announce or declare, publicly and officially: *to proclaim war; The Governor-General proclaimed the law.* **3.** (of things) to show or make known: *His speech proclaimed his ignorance.* [ME, from L]

proclamation /prɒkləˈmeɪʃən/, n. **1.** a public and official announcement. **2.** the act of proclaiming.

Proclamation Day, n. an annual holiday in SA, 28 December, commemorating the state's foundation.

proclivity /prəˈklɪvəti/, n., pl. **-ties.** a natural or habitual inclination or tendency; propensity; predisposition: *a proclivity to fault-finding.* [L: tendency, propensity]

procrastinate /prəʊˈkræstəneɪt/, v., **-nated, -nating.** ◇v.i. **1.** to delay: *to procrastinate until an opportunity is lost.* ◇v.t. **2.** to put off till another day or time; defer; delay. [L: put off till the morrow] **– procrastination,** n. **– procrastinator,** n.

procreate /ˈprəʊkrieɪt/, v.t., v.i., **-ated, -ating.** to bring (offspring) into being; beget or generate (offspring). [L] **– procreation,** n. **– procreator,** n.

procrustean /prəʊˈkrʌstiən/, adj. (*also cap.*) **1.** tending to make things fit some shape or standard at any cost. **2. procrustean bed,** a standard chosen or decided at random, to which strict agreement is forced. [from *Procrustes,* a brigand in Gk legend, who stretched or mutilated his victims to make them conform to the length of his bed]

proctor /ˈprɒktə/, n. **1.** (in certain universities) an official who, among other duties, has to make sure that students keep the rules. **2.** *Angl Ch.* a representative of the clergy in convocation. [contracted var. of *procurator* legal official] **– proctorial,** adj. **– proctorship,** n.

Proctor /ˈprɒktə/, n. **Thea** (*Althea Mary*), 1879–1966, Australian painter and teacher.

procumbent /proʊˈkʌmbənt/, *adj.* lying on the face; prone; prostrate. [L: falling forward]

procure /prəˈkjʊə/, *v.t.*, **-cured, -curing. 1.** to get, esp. by care, effort, or the use of special means: *to procure evidence*. **2.** to bring about, esp. by indirect or criminal means: *to procure a person's death*. **3.** to get (a woman) for another man's sexual gratification. [ME, from L: take care of, manage] — **procurable,** *adj.*

procurer /prəˈkjʊərə/, *n.* **1.** someone who procures (def. 3). **2.** → **pimp.** — **procuress,** *n. fem.*

prod /prɒd/, *v.*, **prodded, prodding,** *n.* ◇*v.t.* **1.** to poke or jab with something pointed: *to prod an animal with a stick*. **2.** to seek to wake to action as if by poking: *Will you prod Jim about handing that essay in?* ◇*n.* **3.** the act of prodding; poke; jab. **4.** a pointed instrument used to prod; goad.

prodigal /ˈprɒdɪɡəl/, *adj.* **1.** carelessly wasteful in spending; recklessly extravagant. **2.** very generous; lavish (fol. by *of*): *prodigal of smiles*. **3.** very plentiful; lavishly abundant; profuse. ◇*n.* **4.** someone who spends, or has spent, their money or property wastefully and carelessly; spendthrift. [ME, from L] — **prodigality,** *n.*

prodigious /prəˈdɪdʒəs/, *adj.* **1.** extraordinary in size, amount, extent, degree, force, etc.: *a prodigious noise*. **2.** wonderful or marvellous: *a prodigious feat*. [L]

prodigy /ˈprɒdɪdʒi/, *n., pl.* **-gies. 1.** a person, esp. a child, who has extraordinary gifts or powers: *a musical prodigy*. **2.** a wonderful example (fol. by *of*): *that prodigy of learning*. **3.** something wonderful; wonder. **4.** *Rare.* something extraordinary, regarded as of prophetic significance. [L: prophetic sign, omen]

produce /prəˈdjuːs/, *v.*, **-duced, -ducing;** /ˈprɒdjuːs/, *n.* ◇*v.t.* **1.** to bring into existence; give rise to; cause: *to produce steam*. **2.** to make by mental or physical work: *to produce a book; to produce a sculpture*. **3.** *Econ.* to make (something that can be bought or sold). **4.** to bring forth; bear; give birth to. **5.** to yield; provide, furnish, or supply: *a mine producing silver*. **6.** to bring forward; present: *When everyone had arrived, he produced his plan*. **7.** to bring (a play, film, etc.) before the public. **8.** *Geom.* to extend or prolong (a line). ◇*v.i.* **9.** to bring forth or yield offspring, products, etc. **10.** *Econ.* to create value; bring crops, goods, etc., into a state in which they will fetch a price. ◇*n.* **11.** something that is produced; yield; product. **12.** farm or natural products as a whole: *to take produce to market*. [L: lead or bring forward] — **producible,** *adj.*

producer /prəˈdjuːsə/, *n.* **1.** someone who produces. **2.** *Econ.* someone who creates value, or produces goods and services (opposed to *consumer*). **3.** the person who arranges the financing of a film production. **4.** the person who is responsible for a film, television, or radio production, or a music recording, who controls the performers, and who finally decides about artistic matters. See **director. 5.** *Theat.* the person responsible for the presentation of a play.

product /ˈprɒdʌkt/, *n.* **1.** something brought into existence by any action or work; effect or result. **2.** something produced by nature or by a natural process. **3.** *Chem.* a substance obtained from another substance through chemical change. **4.** *Maths.* the result obtained by multiplying two or more quantities together. [ME, from L *prōductum*, neut. pp., (thing) produced]

production /prəˈdʌkʃən/, *n.* **1.** the act of producing; creation; manufacture. **2.** something that is produced; product. **3.** *Econ.* the creation of value; producing of articles able to be bought and sold. **4.** the total amount produced: *Production from our farm is good this year*. **5.** the act of showing: *The production of the letter just at that moment created a sensation*. **6.** the staging of a play. [ME, from L]

productive /prəˈdʌktɪv/, *adj.* **1.** having the power of producing; generative; creative. **2.** producing easily or plentifully; fertile; prolific. **3.** *Econ.* producing or tending to produce goods and services that can be bought and sold. — **productivity, productiveness,** *n.*

productivity bargaining, /prɒdʌkˈtɪvəti ˌbɑːɡənɪŋ/, *n.* an agreement between employers and employees that certain changes in work practices, which will result in increased productivity, be made in exchange for higher wages.

proem /ˈproʊem/, *n.* an introduction; preface; preamble. [L, from Gk] — **proemial,** *adj.*

Prof, *Abbrev.* Professor.

profane /prəˈfeɪn/, *adj., v.,* **-faned, -faning.** ◇*adj.* **1.** marked by lack of respect for God or sacred things; irreligious, esp. speaking or spoken in open or implied contempt for sacred things. **2.** not sacred, or not given to sacred purposes; worldly; secular: *profane history*. **3.** common; vulgar; socially shocking: *profane language*. See **blasphemous.** ◇*v.t.* **4.** to misuse (anything that should be held in respect); defile; debase. **5.** to treat (anything holy) without respect. [ME, from F, from L: before (outside) the temple] — **profaneness, profanity,** *n.*

profess /prəˈfes/, *v.t.* **1.** to declare (a feeling, etc.), often insincerely; pretend to: *He professed great sorrow*. **2.** to declare openly; avow: *He professed his satisfaction; to profess faith in God*. **3.** to declare oneself skilled or expert in. **4.** to receive or admit into a religious order.

professed /prəˈfest/, *adj.* **1.** pretended; alleged. **2.** declared; avowed; acknowledged. **3.** claiming to be qualified; professional. **4.** having taken vows of, or been received into a religious order. [ME, from L: to declare, profess + -ED²]

profession /prəˈfeʃən/, *n.* **1.** an occupation requiring advanced knowledge in some area, esp. those of theology, law, and medicine. **2.** the people in a profession taken as a whole: *the medical profession*. **3.** a declaration, whether

profession

true or false; avowal: *professions of love.* **4.** the act of professing; declaration of belief in a faith: *the profession of Christianity.* **5.** a declaration made on entering a religious order. [ME, from L: public declaration]

professional /prəˈfeʃnəl, -ʃənəl/, *adj.* **1.** following an occupation to earn a living or make money by it: *a professional actor.* **2.** relating or suitable to, or engaged in a profession: *professional studies; a professional manner.* **3.** expert; competent: *The teachers at that school are very professional.* **4.** making a business of something not properly to be regarded as a business: *a professional politician.* **5.** done to earn a living or to make money: *professional football.* ◇*n.* **6.** someone belonging to one of the learned or skilled professions. **7.** someone who earns a living by an skill, sport, etc. (opposed to *amateur*). **8.** an expert in a game or sport, hired by a sports club to teach members. — **professionalism,** *n.*

professor /prəˈfesə/, *n.* **1.** a teacher of the highest rank, usu. holding a chair in a particular branch of learning, in a university or college. **2.** someone who professes his feelings, beliefs, etc. [ME, from L] — **professorial,** *adj.*

proffer /ˈprɒfə/, *v.t.* **1.** to put before a person for acceptance; offer. ◇*n.* **2.** the act of proffering. **3.** an offer. [ME, from OF]

proficient /prəˈfiʃənt/, *adj.* well advanced or expert in any skill or knowledge; skilled. [L: making progress] — **proficiency,** *n.*

profile /ˈproʊfaɪl/, *n., v.,* **-filed, -filing.** ◇*n.* **1.** an outline of the human face, esp. as seen from the side. **2.** a drawing, painting, etc., of the side view of the head. **3.** an outline of something seen against a background. **4.** *Archit., Engin.* a drawing of a section, esp. a vertical section, through something. **5.** a short and vivid sketch of the life and character of a person. **6. keep (maintain) a low profile,** *Colloq.* to act so as to be not easily noticed. ◇*v.t.* **7.** to draw or write a profile of. **8.** to be in the shape of a profile (*usu.* passive): *The oncoming figures were profiled against the sky.* [It: draw in outline, from L: PRO- + LL: thread]

profit /ˈprɒfət/, *n.* **1.** (*oft. pl.*) money made from the use of capital in any production or piece of business: **a. gross profit,** the whole sum made, less the immediate costs of production. **b. net profit,** the amount remaining after taking out all costs. **c.** the ratio of money made to the amount of capital spent. **2.** (*oft. pl.*) the money coming from rents, dividends, insurance, etc. **3.** any advantage; use; benefit: *You should have done it before. Doing it now won't be much profit to you.* ◇*v.i.* **4.** to gain advantage or use: *to profit from advice.* **5.** to make money: *to profit from business.* ◇*v.t.* **6.** to be of advantage or use to: *Study will profit you.* [ME, from OF, from L: progress, profit]

profitable /ˈprɒfətəbəl/, *adj.* **1.** bringing financial gain. **2.** helpful or useful.

profiteer /prɒfəˈtɪə/, *n.* **1.** someone who makes money in a greedy way, often by taking unfair advantage of people. ◇*v.i.* **2.** to act as a profiteer. — **profiteering,** *n.*

profit sharing, *n.* the sharing of profits, as between employer and employee, esp. in such a way that the employee receives, in addition to wages, a share in the profits of the business. — **profit-sharing,** *adj.*

profligate /ˈprɒflɪɡət/, *adj.* **1.** extremely and shamelessly immoral; thoroughly dissolute. **2.** carelessly wasteful; prodigal; extravagant. ◇*n.* **3.** a profligate person. [L: overthrown, ruined] — **profligacy,** *n.* — **profligateness,** *n.*

pro-forma /proʊ-ˈfɔːmə/, *adj.* done for the sake of an established form or procedure.

profound /prəˈfaʊnd/, *adj.* **1.** deep. **2.** having or showing great knowledge or deep understanding: *a profound thinker; a profound mind.* **3.** intense: *profound sleep.* **4.** going beyond the surface; not superficial or obvious: *profound insight.* **5.** of deep meaning; serious or abstruse: *a profound book.* ◇*n.* **6.** something that is profound: *a mind directed towards the profound.* [ME, from OF, from L] — **profoundness, profundity,** *n.*

profuse /prəˈfjuːs/, *adj.* **1.** spending or giving freely and plentifully; extravagant (oft. fol. by *in*). **2.** plentiful; abundant: *a profuse flow of blood; profuse apologies.* [ME, from L: poured forth] — **profuseness,** *n.* — **profusion,** *n.*

progenitor /prəˈdʒenətə/, *n.* **1.** a direct ancestor; forefather. **2.** an originator: *He is the progenitor of the plan.* [ME, from L]

progeny /ˈprɒdʒəni/, *n.* offspring; issue; descendants. [ME, from OF, from L]

progesterone /prəˈdʒestəroʊn/, *n.* a female steroid hormone which prepares the uterus for the fertilised ovum and helps to maintain pregnancy. [PRO- + GE(STATION) + STER(OL) + -ONE]

prognosis /prɒɡˈnoʊsəs/, *n., pl.* **-noses** /-ˈnoʊsiːz/. a doctor's opinion on the course a disease will take. [LL, from Gk: foreknowledge]

prognostic /prɒɡˈnɒstɪk/, *adj.* **1.** of or relating to prognosis. **2.** indicating something in the future. ◇*n.* **3.** a forecast or prediction. **4.** sign of something in the future; portent or omen. [L, from Gk]

prognosticate /prɒɡˈnɒstəkeɪt/, *v.t., v.i.,* **-cated, -cating.** to (make a) forecast; prophesy. — **prognostication,** *n.* — **prognosticator,** *n.*

program /ˈproʊɡræm/, *n., v.,* **-grammed, -gramming.** ◇*n.* **1.** a plan to be followed: *a program of study.* **2.** a list of things to be done; agenda: *a program for the day.* **3.** a list of pieces, performers, etc., in a concert or play. **4.** the contents of an entertainment: *There's a good program tonight.* **5.** *Radio, TV.* a particular item or production. **6.** *Computers.* a set of instructions in a computer language which will cause a computer to perform a desired operation. ◇*v.t.* **7.** *Computers.* to organise and arrange (data, etc.) relating to a problem so that it can be solved by a computer. ◇*v.i.* **8.** to plan a program: *If you program carefully you'll find you have time for everything.* Also,

programme. [LL, from Gk: public notice in writing] – **programmable, programable,** *adj.*

programmer /'prougræmə/, *n.* someone who prepares data, etc., for a computer.

progress /'prougres/, *n.;* /prə'gres/, *v.* ◇*n.* **1.** an advance step by step; improvement: *proper progress in studies.* **2.** advancement in general. **3.** growth or development. **4.** forward or onward movement: *We made good progress, doing thirty kilometres that day.* **5. in progress,** taking place; under way. ◇*v.i.* **6.** to advance; improve. **7.** to go forwards or onwards. [ME, from L: a going forward]

Progress /'prougres/, *n.* a series of USSR spacecraft, used to supply the Salyut manned space stations.

progression /prə'greʃən/, *n.* **1.** the act of progressing; forward or onward movement: *the progression of Europe towards war in the 1930s.* **2.** a passing from one member of a series to the next; succession; sequence. **3.** *Maths.* a sequence of numbers in which there is a constant relation between each number and its successor. See **arithmetic progression** and **geometric progression**. **4.** *Music.* the manner in which notes or chords follow one another.

progressive /prə'gresɪv/, *adj.* **1.** favoring or making change, improvement, or reform: *a progressive politician; a progressive school.* **2.** going forward or onwards; proceeding step by step: *progressive improvement in maths; a progressive disease.* ◇*n.* **3.** someone who favors (esp. political) progress or reform.

prohibit /prə'hɪbət/, *v.t.* **1.** to forbid by law or someone's order. **2.** to prevent; hinder: *His bad leg prohibits his running in the race.* [ME, from L: held back]

prohibition /prouə'bɪʃən/, *n.* **1.** the act of forbidding. **2.** a law or order that forbids (something). **3.** (*oft. cap.*) the forbidding by law of the making and sale of alcoholic drinks, esp. in the US between 1919 and 1933. – **prohibitionist,** *n.*

prohibitive /prə'hɪbətɪv/, *adj.* **1.** serving to forbid something. **2.** serving to prevent the use, purchase, etc., of something: *the prohibitive price of meat.* Also, **prohibitory.**

project /'proudʒekt, 'pro-/, *n.;* /prə'dʒekt/, *v.* ◇*n.* **1.** something that is thought of or planned; plan; scheme; undertaking. **2.** a special piece of work, usu. research, done by schoolchildren. ◇*v.t.* **3.** to throw. **4.** to set forth (a plan, future action); present. **5.** to make known (an idea, impression, etc.); communicate; convey. **6.** to throw upon a surface or into space: *to project a film; to project the voice.* **7.** to see (something in the mind) as real: *The child projected the monster from his imagination.* **8.** to cause to jut out or protrude: *to project the lips.* **9.** to represent (a solid object, esp. the earth) on a flat surface as a map. See **projection** (def. 4). **10.** to transform the points of (one figure) into those of another by any correspondence between points. ◇*v.i.* **11.** to jut out; protrude. **12.** to communicate or send an idea or impression. [ME, from L: (thing) thrown out] – **projective,** *adj.*

projectile /prə'dʒektaɪl/, *n.* **1.** *Mil.* an object fired from a gun. **2.** a thrown object; missile. ◇*adj.* **3.** (of a force) thrown forwards. **4.** (of movement) caused by hurling. **5.** (of a missile) able to be hurled forward: *A spear is a projectile weapon.* [NL: projecting]

projection /prə'dʒekʃən/, *n.* **1.** a part that sticks out. **2.** the condition or fact of sticking out. **3.** *Geom., etc.* the act, process, or result of projecting. **4.** Also, **map projection.** *Maps.* a representation of the earth's surface drawn over lines of latitude and longitude on a flat grid. **5.** *Photog.* **a.** the throwing of an image on to a screen. **b.** an image so formed. **6.** the act of seeing as real something that exists only in the mind. **7.** an image seen in this way: *The monster was a projection from his mind.* **8.** *Psychol.* a tendency to attribute to another person, or to the environment, what is actually within oneself. **9.** an act of planning. [L]

projectionist /prə'dʒekʃənəst/, *n.* someone who operates a film projector.

projector /prə'dʒektə/, *n.* a machine for throwing an image from a film or a slide on to a screen.

Prokofiev /prə'kɒfief/, *n.* **Sergei Sergeevich** /sɛə'geɪ sə'geɪjəvɪtʃ/, 1891–1953, Russian composer, whose musical style included both avant-garde and popular elements; noted for *Peter and the Wolf* (1936).

prolapse /'proulæps/, *n.;* /prə'læps/, *v.,* **-lapsed, -lapsing.** ◇*n.* **1.** Also, **prolapsus.** *Med.* a falling down of an organ or part, as the uterus, from its normal position. ◇*v.i.* **2.** to fall or slip down or out of place. [LL: a falling down]

proletarian /proulə'tɛəriən/, *adj.* **1.** relating or belonging to the proletariat. **2.** (in ancient Rome) belonging to the lowest or poorest class of people. ◇*n.* **3.** a member of the proletariat. Also, **proletary** and (*Colloq.*) **prole.** [L: a Roman citizen of the lowest class + -AN]

proletariat /proulə'tɛəriət/, *n.* **1.** the class in society that owns no large property, but has to work to live. **2.** the working class, or wage-earners in general. [F, from L: a Roman citizen of the lowest class + -*at* -ATE³]

proliferate /prə'lɪfəreɪt/, *v.i.,* **-rated, -rating.** to grow by multiplying. – **proliferation,** *n.*

prolific /prə'lɪfɪk/, *adj.* producing plentifully: *a prolific fruit tree; a prolific writer.* [ML, from L *prōli-* offspring + *-ficus* -FIC]

prolix /'prouliks/, *adj.* **1.** long and with too many words; wordy: *a prolix speech.* **2.** speaking or writing at great or boring length. [ME, from L: extended, long]

prologue /'proulɒg/, *n.* **1.** an introductory speech to a play, often in verse, usu. calling attention to the theme. **2.** an introduction to a book. **3.** any introductory thing. [ME, from L, from Gk]

prolong /prə'lɒŋ/, *v.t.* to make longer, in time or space: *to prolong a speech; to prolong a line.* [ME, from LL] – **prolongation,** *n.*

prom /prɒm/, *n.* **1.** → **prom concert**. **2.** *US Colloq.* a formal dance, esp. at a school or college. [short for PROMENADE]

prom concert, *n.* a concert at which some people sit on the floor or stand. [shortened form of *promenade concert*]

promenade /prɒmə'nɑːd/, *n., v.,* **-naded, -nading.** ◇*n.* **1.** an unhurried walk, esp. in a public place, for pleasure or show. **2.** an area suitable for such walking, esp. one along a seafront; esplanade. ◇*v.i.* **3.** to take a promenade. ◇*v.t.* **4.** to take or lead on or as on a promenade; parade. [F: lead out, take for a walk or airing]

Prometheus /prə'miːθiəs/, *n. Gk Myth.* a Titan fabled to have made men out of clay and to have stolen fire for them from Olympus. In punishment Zeus had him chained to a rock where a vulture daily gnawed his liver; eventually freed by Hercules. – **Promethean,** *adj.*

promethium /prə'miːθiəm/, *n.* a radioactive, rare-earth, metallic, trivalent element. Symbol: Pm; *at. no.:* 61; *at. wt:* 145.

prominence /'prɒmənəns/, *n.* **1.** Also, **prominency.** the condition of being prominent; conspicuousness. **2.** something that sticks up or out; a projection; protuberance: *The ground rose to a small prominence.*

prominent /'prɒmənənt/, *adj.* **1.** standing out so as to be easily seen; conspicuous. **2.** standing out beyond a surface or line; projecting. **3.** important; leading; well-known: *a prominent citizen.* [L: jutting out]

promiscuous /prə'mɪskjuəs/, *adj.* **1.** associating with several people or things, esp. partners in casual sexual relations; mixing indiscriminately. **2.** consisting of parts of different kinds brought together without order. [L] – **promiscuity, promiscuousness,** *n.*

promise /'prɒməs/, *n., v.,* **-ised, -ising.** ◇*n.* **1.** a declaration made to another person, that one will or will not do, give, etc., something in the future. **2.** a sign of future excellence or achievement: *a pianist who shows promise.* **3.** a hope or possibility: *The wind brought the promise of rain.* ◇*v.t.* **4.** to declare that one will or will not do something in the future (with an infinitive or clause): *to promise not to laugh; I promise that I'll come.* **5.** to make a promise of: *to promise help.* **6.** to give reason for expecting: *Tomorrow promises a lot of fun for everyone.* **7.** to engage to marry (*usu. in passive*): *John is promised to Mary.* **8.** to declare strongly: *I promise you I haven't got it.* ◇*v.i.* **9.** to give reason for expecting (oft. fol. by *well* or *fair*): *The weather promises well for tomorrow.* **10.** to make a promise: *Promise and I'll let you go.* [ME, from L] – **promiser;** *Law,* **promisor,** *n.*

Promised Land /ˌprɒməst 'lænd/, *n.* Canaan; the land promised by God to Abraham and his descendants. [See Genesis 12:7]

promising /'prɒməsɪŋ/, *adj.* likely to turn out well: *a promising young man.*

promissory note /'prɒməsəri ˌnoʊt/, *n.* a written promise to pay a stated sum of money to a particular person.

promontory /'prɒməntri/, *n., pl.* **-ries.** a high point of land or rock jutting out into the sea, etc.; headland. [ML]

promote /prə'moʊt/, *v.t.,* **-moted, -moting.** **1.** to advance in rank or position, etc.: *They promoted her to inspector.* **2.** to help the growth, development, progress, etc., of; foster: *Proper diet promotes health.* **3.** to help to arrange or organise: *to promote a match.* **4.** to bring to public notice; get publicity for: *to promote a new brand on television.* [ME, from L: moved forward, advanced]

promoter /prə'moʊtə/, *n.* someone who starts off or takes part in the organising of an undertaking.

prompt /prɒmpt/, *adj.* **1.** done at once or without delay; immediate: *a prompt reply.* **2.** quick to act as occasion demands: *prompt in paying debts.* **3.** ready and willing: *prompt to help.* ◇*v.t.* **4.** to move or spur to action: *Anxiety prompted her to speak.* **5.** to help (a person speaking) by suggesting something to be said. **6.** *Theat.* to remind (an actor or reciter) when to speak or what to say, from offstage. ◇*v.i.* **7.** *Theat.* to give offstage reminders. ◇*n.* **8.** an offstage reminder to an actor. [ME, from L: taken out, at hand] – **promptness, promptitude,** *n.*

prompter /'prɒmptə/, *n. Theat.* someone offstage who follows a play in performance from the script, so that they can remind actors when to speak or what to say.

promulgate /'prɒməlɡeɪt/, *v.t.,* **-gated, -gating.** **1.** to make known (a law or rule) by open declaration. **2.** to spread (a belief, teaching, etc.) widely among people. [L: made publicly known, published]

pron., *Abbrev.* **1.** pronoun. **2.** pronounced. **3.** pronunciation.

prone /proʊn/, *adj.* **1.** tending or inclined (to something); disposed; liable: *to be prone to anger.* **2.** lying face downwards. **3.** lying flat; prostrate. [ME, from L: turned or leaning forwards, inclined downwards]

prong /prɒŋ/, *n.* **1.** the thin, sharp-pointed part of a fork or an antler; tine. ◇*v.t.* **2.** to pierce or lift with a prong. [ME]

pronoun /'proʊnaʊn/, *n.* **1.** a part of speech made up of words which stand for nouns. **2.** any such word, as *I, you, he, this, who, what.* [F, from L] – **pronominal,** *adj.*

pronounce /prə'naʊns/, *v.,* **-nounced, -nouncing.** ◇*v.t.* **1.** to make the sound of (words, etc.): *to pronounce difficult words.* **2.** to sound (a word) in a particular way: *Australians pronounce 'controversy' in two ways.* **3.** to declare (a person or thing) to be something: *They pronounced him mad.* **4.** to say formally or solemnly: *to pronounce a judgment.* ◇*v.i.* **5.** to make the sound of words, etc.: *to pronounce clearly.* **6.** to make a statement or give an opinion (*usu. fol. by on*): *She is always pronouncing on how it should be done.* [ME,

from OF, from L: proclaim, announce, recite]
—**pronouncement**, n.

pronounced /prə'naʊnst/, adj. **1.** strongly marked: *a pronounced tendency*. **2.** decided; definite: *to have very pronounced views*.

pronto /'prontoʊ/, adv. Colloq. quickly; promptly. [Sp, from L. See PROMPT]

pronunciation /prənʌnsi'eɪʃən/, n. the act or result of making the sounds of speech. [ME, from L]

proof /pruːf/, n. **1.** something that shows that a thing is either true or false. **2.** a test; a trial: *to put a thing to the proof*. **3.** the effect of evidence in making the mind certain: *It was proof enough for her that he hadn't done it*. **4.** the condition of having been tested and approved. **5.** the relative strength of alcoholic liquors. **6.** *Photog.* a trial print from a negative. **7.** *Print.* a trial impression of composed type, taken to correct errors and make changes. ◇adj. **8.** strong enough to resist attack, danger, etc.: *proof against fire; proof against fear*. **9.** of standard strength, as alcoholic liquor. ◇v.t. **10.** to treat or coat (a material) in order to make it resistant to wear or damage. [ME, from OF, from L: prove]

-proof, a suffix meaning 'protected from', 'resistant to', etc., as in *waterproof*.

proofing /'pruːfɪŋ/, n. **1.** the act or process of making a thing resistant to wear, damage, etc. **2.** a chemical used to make materials waterproof.

proofread /'pruːfriːd/, v.t., v.i., -read /-red/, -reading. to read (printers' proofs, etc.) in order to find and mark mistakes to be corrected. —**proofreader**, n. —**proofreading**, n.

proof spirit, n. an alcoholic liquor, or a mixture of alcohol and water, containing 57.06 per cent alcohol by volume at a certain temperature.

prop[1] /prop/, v., **propped, propping**, n. ◇v.t. **1.** to support, or prevent from falling, with something that holds (a thing) up (oft. fol. by *up*): *to prop a roof; They propped her up with cushions*. **2.** to rest (a thing) against a support: *He propped the ladder against the wall*. **3.** to support or keep going: *to prop up a failing business*. ◇v.i. **4.** (of horses) to stop suddenly with all four legs stiff, jolting the rider. ◇n. **5.** a stick, pole, beam, or other support. **6.** a person or thing serving as a support. **7.** (*pl.*) *Colloq.* the legs. **8.** Also, **prop-forward**. *Rugby.* either of the two forwards outermost in the front row of the scrum. **9.** a sudden stop. [ME]

prop[2] /prop/, n. → **property** (def. 8).

prop., *Abbrev.* proprietor.

propaganda /propə'gændə/, n. **1.** the systematic spreading of a religion or doctrine. **2.** (the spreading of) ideas, arguments or facts used to persuade people to think well or badly about some person, cause, or movement: *Fascist propaganda; Marxist propaganda*. [It, from use of L *propāganda* in NL title, *Sacra Congregatio de Propaganda Fide*, a committee of cardinals established in 1622 by Pope Gregory XV for the propagation of the faith] —**propagandist**, n. —**propagandise**, v.

propagate /'propəgeɪt/, v., -**gated, -gating**. ◇v.t. **1.** to breed (plants, animals); cause to reproduce. **2.** (of a plant, animal) to breed; reproduce. **3.** to carry (characteristics, qualities) through offspring. **4.** to spread (ideas, etc.); disseminate. **5.** to carry, send, or help move through space or a medium: *to propagate sound*. ◇v.i. **6.** to breed. [L: propagated (orig. referring to plants by layers or slips)] —**propagator**, n. —**propagation**, n.

propane /'proʊpeɪn/, n. a gaseous hydrocarbon, C_3H_8, of the alkane series, found in petroleum. [*prop(ionic acid)* + -ANE]

propel /prə'pel/, v.t., -**pelled, -pelling**. **1.** to drive, or cause to move, forwards: *a boat propelled by oars*. **2.** to push or urge onwards. [L] —**propellent**, adj.

propellant /prə'pelənt/, n. **1.** a propelling agent. **2.** *Mil.* an explosive used in a gun to fire the bullet. **3.** *Aeron.* an explosive used to fire a rocket. **4.** a compressed gas used in an aerosol container to shoot out the liquid as a spray.

propeller /prə'pelə/, n. a device with a revolving hub and radiating blades, for driving a ship, plane, etc.

propene /'proʊpiːn/, n. → **propylene**.

propensity /prə'pensəti/, n., pl. -**ties**. a natural or habitual tendency or inclination: *a propensity to find fault*. Also, *Rare*, **propension**.

proper /'propə/, adj. **1.** suited to the purpose or circumstances; fit; suitable: *the proper time to plant*. **2.** doing or agreeing with what is thought to be good manners; correct; decorous. **3.** belonging or relating particularly to a person or thing: *Noise is proper to small children*. **4.** real; genuine: *Give me some proper facts this time and I'll believe you*. **5.** in the strict sense of the word (now usu. following the noun): *Shellfish do not belong to the fishes proper*. **6.** normal or regular: *That is not the proper way to do it*. **7.** *Colloq.* complete; thorough: *a proper thrashing*. **8.** *Rare.* excellent; fine: *You're a proper friend!* **9.** *Archaic.* belonging to oneself or itself; own. [ME, from OF, from L: one's own]

proper fraction, n. a fraction having the numerator less than the denominator.

proper noun, n. a noun that is the name of something, as a person, place, etc., and is used only of that particular person or thing: *Smith, Perth* in contrast to *person, city*. See **common noun**.

property /'propəti/, n., pl. -**ties**. **1.** something that one owns; the possession(s) of a particular owner. **2.** goods, lands, etc., owned: *a man of property*. **3.** a piece of land or building owned: *property near Bondi*. **4.** ownership: *the idea of private property*. **5.** Also, **country property**. a farm, station, orchard, etc. **6.** something used by or belonging to a person, a group of people, or the public: *The secret became common property*. **7.** a power or quality that something has naturally; an attribute: *the properties of oxygen*. **8.** Also, **prop.** *Theat.* a piece of furniture or decoration in a stage setting; any object handled or used by an actor in performance. [ME]

prophase /ˈproʊfeɪz/, *n.* the first stage of mitosis during which the chromosomes contract and become thicker and the nuclear membrane begins to disappear.

prophecy /ˈprɒfəsi/, *n., pl.* **-cies. 1.** a foretelling of what is to come; prediction. **2.** something said or revealed under the guidance of God; message of God. **3.** the action, function, or power of a prophet. [ME, from OF, from LL, from Gk]

prophesy /ˈprɒfəsaɪ/, *v.,* **-sied, -sying.** ◇*v.t.* **1.** to foretell; predict: *to prophesy a storm.* **2.** to declare (a message from God). ◇*v.i.* **3.** to say what will happen in the future. **4.** to speak as the mouthpiece of God. [v. use of and var. of PROPHECY] — **prophesier**, *n.*

prophet /ˈprɒfɪt/, *n.* **1.** someone who speaks as the mouthpiece of God. **2.** someone regarded as, or claiming to be, a great teacher or leader. **3.** someone who foretells the future or future events: *a weather prophet.* **4. the Prophet, a.** Mohammed, the founder of Islam. See **Koran. b.** Joseph Smith, founder of the Mormon Church. **5. the Prophets,** the books which form the second of the three Jewish divisions of the Old Testament. [ME, from L, from Gk: spokesman, interpreter, prophet] — **prophetess**, *n. fem.* — **prophetic**, *adj.*

prophylactic /ˌprɒfəˈlæktɪk/, *adj.* **1.** (of a drug) defending or protecting from disease. **2.** preventive; preservative; protective. ◇*n.* **3.** a prophylactic medicine or action. **4.** → **contraceptive.** [Gk]

prophylaxis /ˌprɒfəˈlæksəs/, *n.* (treatment for) the preventing of disease. [NL, from Gk]

propinquity /prəˈpɪŋkwəti/, *n.* **1.** nearness in place; proximity. **2.** nearness of relation; kinship. **3.** similarity. **4.** nearness in time. [ME, from L]

propitiate /prəˈpɪʃieɪt/, *v.t.,* **-ated, -ating.** to make favorably inclined; appease; conciliate. [L] — **propitiator**, *n.* — **propitiatory**, *adj.*

propitious /prəˈpɪʃəs/, *adj.* **1.** favorable: *propitious weather; propitious omens.* **2.** favorably inclined or disposed. [ME, from L]

Prop Ltd, *Abbrev.* proprietary limited.

proponent /prəˈpoʊnənt/, *n.* **1.** someone who puts forward a proposal. **2.** someone who supports a cause.

proportion /prəˈpɔːʃən/, *n.* **1.** comparative relation between things as to size, quantity, number, etc.; ratio: *a house tall in proportion to its width.* **2.** proper relation between things or parts; balance: *You must see things in proportion.* **3.** (*pl.*) dimensions: *a rock of gigantic proportions.* **4.** a part in relation to the whole: *a large proportion of the total.* **5.** *Maths.* the relation of four quantities such that the first divided by the second is equal to the third divided by the fourth; equality of ratios. ◇*v.t.* **6.** to put (the parts of) something into proper relationship: *to proportion a building.* [ME, from L]

proportional /prəˈpɔːʃənəl/, *adj.* **1.** having due proportion; corresponding. **2.** marked by or relating to proportion; relative. **3.** *Maths.* having the same or a constant ratio. — **proportionality**, *n.*

proportional representation, *n.* a system of electing representatives to a parliament in which there is a number of members representing each electorate. The number of successful candidates from each party is directly proportional to the percentage of the total vote won by the party.

proportionate /prəˈpɔːʃənət/, *adj.* in correct proportion; proportional.

proposal /prəˈpoʊzəl/, *n.* **1.** the act of proposing for acceptance, adoption, or performance. **2.** a plan or scheme offered. **3.** an offer, esp. of marriage.

propose /prəˈpoʊz/, *v.,* **-posed, -posing.** ◇*v.t.* **1.** to put forward (a matter, subject, case, etc.) to be considered, accepted, or acted on: *to propose a method; to propose a toast; to propose a question.* **2.** to put forward or suggest as something to be done: *He proposed that a messenger be sent.* **3.** to suggest (a person) for some position, office, membership, etc. **4.** to plan; design; intend: *I propose to teach Shakespeare this term.* ◇*v.i.* **5.** to suggest marriage: *John has proposed to Mary.* **6.** to form or hold a purpose or design. [ME, from F] — **proposer**, *n.*

proposition /ˌprɒpəˈzɪʃən/, *n.* **1.** the act of proposing, or a proposal of, something to be considered, accepted, or done. **2.** a plan or subject put forward for action or discussion. **3.** an offer of terms for a business deal. **4.** a thing or person considered as something to be dealt with or faced: *a tough proposition.* **5.** *Philos.* a statement in which something (a predicate) is affirmed or denied. **6.** a suggestion for sexual intercourse. ◇*v.t.* **7.** to propose a plan, deal, etc., to. **8.** to suggest sexual intercourse to. [ME, from L: a setting forth] — **propositional**, *adj.*

propound /prəˈpaʊnd/, *v.t.* to put forward for consideration, acceptance, or action. [ME, from L: set forth]

proprietary /prəˈpraɪətri/, *adj.* **1.** belonging to a proprietor or proprietors. **2.** being a proprietor or proprietors; holding property: *the proprietary class.* **3.** relating to property or ownership: *proprietary rights.* **4.** belonging or controlled as property: *proprietary company.* **5.** manufactured and sold only by the owner of the patent, formula, brand name, or trademark: *proprietary medicine.* [ME, from LL, from L: ownership]

proprietary limited company, *n.* a company with a limit of fifty shareholders, which cannot issue shares for public subscription and which is not listed on the stock exchange; shareholders enjoy limited liability on liquidation. Also, **proprietary company.**

proprietor /prəˈpraɪətə/, *n.* the owner of a business or property. [PROPRIET(Y) + -OR²]

propriety /prəˈpraɪəti/, *n., pl.* **-ties. 1.** a way of behaving accepted as good manners. **2.** rightness or suitability: *to question the propriety of something.* **3. the proprieties,** agreed standards or requirements of proper behavior. [ME, from L: peculiarity, ownership]

propulsion /prə'pʌlʃən/, n. 1. the act of propelling or driving forward or onward. 2. the condition of being so driven. [L: driven forward + -ION]

propyl /'proupəl/, n. a univalent radical, C_3H_7-, derived from propane. [*prop(ionic acid)* + -YL]

propylene /'proupəlin/, n. a colorless, unsaturated, gaseous hydrocarbon gas, C_3H_6. Also, **propene**.

pro rata /prou 'ratə/, adv. 1. in proportion; according to a certain rate. ◇adj. 2. proportionate. [ML: according to rate]

prorogue /prə'roug/, v.t., **-rogued**, **-roguing**. to discontinue meetings of (parliament, etc.) until the next session. [ME, from F, from L: prolong, protract, defer]

pros., *Abbrev.* prosody.

prosaic /prou'zeɪɪk, prə-/, adj. 1. commonplace or dull; matter-of-fact or unimaginative: *a prosaic mind*. 2. having the character or spirit of prose as opposed to poetry, as verse or writing. Also, **prosaical**. [ML, from L: prose] —**prosaically**, adv.

pros and cons /prouz ən 'konz/, n.pl. the arguments for and against something: *The committee had to consider all the pros and cons before making a decision*. [L: for and against]

proscenium /prə'siniəm/, n., pl. **-nia** /-niə/. 1. (in the modern theatre) the decorative arch or opening between the stage and the auditorium. 2. (in the ancient theatre) the stage. Also, **proscenium arch**. [L, from Gk *proskēnion*]

proscribe /prou'skraɪb/, v.t., **-scribed**, **-scribing**. 1. to denounce or forbid (a thing or practice). 2. (in ancient Rome) to put (a person) outside the protection of the law by putting his name on a public list. 3. to banish; exile. [L: write before, publish, proscribe] —**proscription**, n.

prose /prouz/, n. 1. the ordinary form of spoken or written language, without metrical structure (as distinguished from poetry or verse). 2. matter-of-fact or dull expression, talk, etc. [ME, from F, from L: straightforward (speech)]

prosecute /'prɒsəkjut/, v., **-cuted**, **-cuting**. ◇v.t. 1. *Law*. to institute and conduct criminal proceedings against (an accused). 2. to put into practice, carry on: *to prosecute an inquiry*. ◇v.i. 3. *Law*. to institute and conduct a criminal proceeding. [ME, from L: pursued, continued] —**prosecutor**, n.

prosecution /prɒsə'kjuʃən/, n. 1. *Law*. **a.** the institution and conduct of criminal proceedings against an accused. **b.** (in a criminal trial) the side prosecuting (as opposed to the *defence*). 2. the following through of a course of action.

proselyte /'prɒsəlaɪt/, n., v., **-lyted**, **-lyting**. ◇n. 1. someone who has changed from one opinion, religious belief, etc., to another; convert. ◇v.i., v.t. 2. → **proselytise**; [ME, from LL, from Gk: newcomer]

proselytise or **proselytize** /'prɒsələtaɪz/, v.i., v.t., **-tised**, **-tising**. to try to change another's opinion, religious belief, etc. to one's own. —**proselytism**, n.

prosody /'prɒsədi, 'prɒz-/, n. 1. the science or study of writing poetry. 2. a particular system of poetic writing: *Milton's prosody*. [late ME, from L, from Gk: tone or accent, modulation of voice, song sung to music] —**prosodic**, adj. —**prosodist**, n.

prospect /'prɒspɛkt/, n. 1. (*usu. pl.*) the apparent probability of advancement, success, profit, etc.: *good business prospects*. 2. a looking forward to, or hoping for something future or expected. 3. someone likely to meet expectations, such as a business customer, sportsman, etc. 4. a view or scene. 5. a mental view or survey of a subject, situation, etc. ◇v.i., v.t. 6. to search (an area) for gold, etc. [ME, from L: outlook, view]

prospective /prə'spɛktɪv/, adj. 1. of or in the future. 2. likely; expected; potential.

prospector /'prɒspɛktə/, n. a person who prospects for gold or other minerals.

prospectus /prə'spɛktəs/, n. 1. a statement which describes or advertises the issue of securities of a corporation, a new literary work, business, etc. 2. a pamphlet put out by a school, university, etc., giving details about its courses, etc. [L: outlook, view]

prosper /'prɒspə/, v.t., v.i. to (cause to be) successful or thrive. [late ME, from L: make prosperous] —**prosperity**, n.

prosperous /'prɒspərəs, -prəs/, adj. 1. having or marked by continued good fortune; flourishing; successful: *a prosperous business*. 2. wealthy: *a prosperous family*. 3. favorable or propitious. [ME, from L]

prostaglandin /prɒstə'glændən/, n. any of a large group of modified fatty acids, found in the body and affecting lipid metabolism and the muscular contractions of labor.

prostate gland /'prɒsteɪt ˌglænd/, n. a gland which surrounds the urethra of males at the base of the bladder.

prosthesis /prɒs'θisəs, prəs-/, n., pl. **-ses** /-siz/. the use of an artificial part to replace a damaged or missing part of the body. [LL, from Gk: a putting to, addition] —**prosthetic**, adj.

prosthetic group /prɒs'θɛtɪk ˌgrup/, n. a non-protein molecule combined with a protein, as the haem group in haemoglobin.

prostitute /'prɒstətjut/, n., v., **-tuted**, **-tuting**. ◇n. 1. a person, esp. a woman, who engages in sexual intercourse for payment. ◇v.t. 2. to make a prostitute of (oneself). 3. to put (one's abilities, etc.) to any unworthy use. [L: placed before, exposed publicly, prostituted] —**prostitution**, n.

prostrate /'prɒstreɪt/, v., **-trated**, **-trating**; /'prɒstreɪt/, adj. ◇v.t. 1. to throw (oneself) down in humility, worship, etc. 2. to throw (something or someone) down level with the ground. 3. to overcome, or make helpless or physically weak. ◇adj. 4. lying flat or at full length on the ground, often as sign of humility, worship, etc. 5. overcome, helpless, or physi-

prostrate

cally weak: *prostrate from grief; prostrate from the heat.* **6.** *Bot.* (of a plant or stem) lying flat on the ground. [ME, from L: spread out] —**prostration**, *n.*

Prot, *Abbrev.* Protestant.

protactinium /ˌproʊtækˈtɪniəm/, *n.* a radioactive, metallic element. *Symbol:* Pa; *at. no.:* 9; *at. wt:* 231. [PROT(O)- + ACTINIUM]

protagonist /prəˈtægənəst/, *n.* **1.** the leading character in a play, novel, etc. **2.** any leading character in the support of a movement, cause, etc. [Gk]

protea /ˈproʊtiə/, *n.* any of various southern African shrubs or trees with large showy flowers. [NL, from Gk; named after *Proteus,* a sea-god of classical mythology, who was able to assume different shapes at will]

protean /prəˈtiən, ˈproʊtiən/, *adj.* readily taking on different forms or characters. [from *Proteus* (see PROTEA) + -AN]

protect /prəˈtɛkt/, *v.t.* **1.** to defend or guard from injury, danger, annoyance, etc. **2.** *Econ.* to guard (a country's industry) from foreign competition by placing duties on imports. [L: covered over]

protection /prəˈtɛkʃən/, *n.* **1.** the act of protecting. **2.** the condition of being protected. **3.** something that protects. **4.** *Colloq.* money paid to criminals to stop their threatened violence. **5.** *Econ.* the system or theory of protecting home industries from foreign competition through duties placed on imports.

protectionism /prəˈtɛkʃənɪzəm/, *n.* the economic system or theory of protection. —**protectionist**, *n.*

protective /prəˈtɛktɪv/, *adj.* having the quality of, or designed for, protecting.

protective custody, *n.* the condition of being under police guard as a protection against threats, violence, etc.

protector /prəˈtɛktə/, *n.* **1.** someone or something that protects. **2.** *Hist.* a person in charge of a kingdom while the sovereign was unable to rule due to youth, absence, etc. —**protectress**, *n. fem.*

protectorate /prəˈtɛktərət, -trət/, *n.* **1.** a state or territory protected and partly controlled by a stronger state. **2.** the office or position of a protector. **3.** the government of a protector.

protégé /ˈproʊtəʒeɪ/, *n.* someone who is under the protection or friendly guidance of another. [F: protect, from L]

protein /ˈproʊtin/, *n. Biochem.* any of a group of organic compounds formed from amino acids, which are found in all cells and which include enzymes, plasma proteins, and structural proteins such as collagen. [G, from Gk: primary]

Proterozoic /ˌproʊtərəˈzoʊɪk, -rə-/, *adj., n.* (of or relating to) the era or rocks between Archaeozoic and Palaeozoic, thought to be marked by relative prominence of sedimentary rocks in a few of which fossils of early primitive organisms are found. Also, **Proterzoic.** [Gk]

prototype

protest /ˈproʊtɛst/, *n.;* /prəˈtɛst, proʊ-/, *v.* ◇*n.* **1.** an expression or declaration of objection or disapproval. ◇*v.i.* **2.** to express objection or disapproval. ◇*v.t.* **3.** to declare positively, often against opposition: *He protested that it was not true.* **4.** to make a formal declaration of the non-acceptance or non-payment of (a bill of exchange or note). [ME, from F, from L: declare publicly] —**pro estation**, *n.*

Protestant /ˈprɒtəstənt/, *n.* **1.** a member of any of those Christian groups which separated from the Church of Rome at the Reformation, or of any group descended from them. ◇*adj.* **2.** relating to Protestants or their religion. [L: protest; applied to the German princes who protested against the Diet of Speyer in 1529, which had denounced the Reformation] —**Protestantism**, *n.*

protestation /ˌprɒtəsˈteɪʃən, proʊ-/, *n.* **1.** a forceful declaration or affirmation. **2.** an expression of objection or disapproval; protest.

prothonotary /ˌproʊθəˈnoʊtəri, proʊˈθɒnətri/, *n., pl.* **-ries.** one of the main officials of a Supreme Court, who issues writs, etc. [ML, LL, from Gk] —**prothonotarial**, *adj.*

protium /ˈproʊtiəm/, *n.* an isotope of hydrogen. *Symbol:* H[1]; at. wt: 1.008.

proto-, a word part meaning **1.** first, earliest form of, as *prototype.* **2.** *Chem.* that one of a series of compounds which contains the minimum amount of an element. **3.** (*usu. cap.*) *Linguistics.* reconstructed earliest form of a language: *Proto-Germanic.* [Gk, combining form of *prôtos* first]

protocol /ˈproʊtəkɒl/, *n.* the rules of behavior and ceremony used on official occasions involving royalty, heads of state, diplomats, etc. [ML, from LGk: orig., a first leaf glued to the front of a manuscript containing notes as to contents]

proton /ˈproʊtɒn/, *n.* an elementary particle present in every atomic nucleus, the number of protons being different for each element. It has an electric charge equal in magnitude to that of the electron but of opposite sign, and a mass of 1.7×10^{-27} kg; hydrogen ion. [Gk: first]

protoplasm /ˈproʊtəplæzəm/, *n.* **1.** a complex, colorless, semiliquid substance regarded as the physical basis of all vegetable and animal life, having the power of movement, reproduction, etc. **2.** (formerly) cytoplasm. [G: from Gk] —**protoplasmic**, *adj.*

protoplast /ˈproʊtəplæst/, *n. Biol.* the protoplasm within a cell considered separately from the cell wall. [LL: the first man, from Gk: formed first] —**protoplastic**, *adj.*

prototrophic /ˌproʊtəˈtrɒfɪk/, *adj.* (of certain micro-organisms) having no particular nutritional requirements for growth. [Gk]

prototype /ˈproʊtətaɪp/, *n.* **1.** the original or model after which anything is formed. **2.** *Biol.* a primitive form regarded as the basis of a group; archetype. [NL, from Gk (neut.): original, primitive] —**prototypal, prototypic,** *adj.*

protozoan /prouta'zouan/, *adj.* **1.** Also, **protozoic.** belonging to or relating to the phylum including animals of one cell or of a colony of like cells. ◇*n.* **2.** any of these animals. [NL, from Gk]

protract /prə'trækt/, *v.t.* to draw out or lengthen in time; prolong. [L: drawn forth, drawn out] —**protraction**, *n.* —**protractive**, *adj.*

protractor /prə'træktə/, *n.* a flat semicircular instrument, graduated around the curved edge, used to measure or mark off angles.

protrude /prə'trud/, *v.t., v.i.,* **-truded, -truding.** to (cause to) project or stick out. [L] —**protrusion**, *n.* —**protrusive**, *adj.*

protuberant /prə'tjubərənt, -brənt/, *adj.* swelling or bulging out beyond the surrounding surface. [LL: swelling] —**protuberance**, *n.*

proud /praud/, *adj.* **1.** feeling pleasure or satisfaction over something thought of as honorable to oneself: *She was proud of her work; proud that her mother was there.* **2.** having or showing a high, esp. a too high, opinion of one's own worth, importance, etc. **3.** having or showing self-respect. **4.** highly honorable: *a proud achievement; a proud name.* **5.** (of things) grand or magnificent: *proud cities.* **6.** *Bldg Trades.* projecting beyond the surrounding surface or objects: *to stand proud.* ◇*adv.* **7. do (someone) proud, a.** to be a cause of pride to (someone). **b.** to entertain (someone) generously. [ME; late OE *prūd*, apparently from VL]

Proudhon /pru'dɒ̃/, *n.* **Pierre Joseph** /pjɛə ʒou'zef/, 1809–65, French socialist and writer; made the famous statement 'property is theft' in his pamphlet *What is Property?* (1840).

Proust /prust/, *n.* **Marcel** /ma'sɛl/, 1871–1922, French novelist, whose sevenvolume work *À la recherche du temps perdu* (1913–27) is concerned with the narrator's effort to recapture the past and preserve experience using the power of memory.

Prov, *Abbrev. Bible.* Proverbs.

prove /pruv/, *v.,* **proved, proved** or **proven, proving.** ◇*v.t.* **1.** to establish as true or genuine by evidence, argument, etc.: *to prove a theory; prove the worth of an object.* **2.** *Law.* to establish the validity of (a will, etc.). **3.** to put to the test; try out. **4.** to show (oneself) to have the character, ability, etc., expected of one. **5.** to determine the characteristics of by scientific tests: *to prove ore.* **6.** *Cookery.* to cause (dough) to rise before baking, by placing it in a warm place. ◇*v.i.* **7.** to turn out: *The report proved to be false.* [ME, from L: try, test, prove, approve]

provenance /'provənəns/, *n.* the place of origin, as of a work of art, etc. [F, from L: come forth]

Provence /prə'vɒ̃s/, *n.* a region in southeastern France, bordering on the Mediterranean; formerly a province; famous in the Middle Ages for poetry and chivalry.

provender /'provəndə/, *n.* **1.** dry food, such as hay, for livestock; fodder. **2.** food in general. [ME, from OF: prebend, provender, from LL]

proverb /'provəb/, *n.* **1.** a short, popular saying, that has been in use for a long time, expressing some familiar truth, as *A stitch in time saves nine.* **2.** a wise saying; precept. **3.** (*cap., pl.*) *Bible.* one of the books of the Old Testament, made up of sayings of wise men of Israel, including Solomon. [ME, from OF, from L]

proverbial /prə'vɜbiəl/, *adj.* **1.** relating to or characteristic of a proverb: *proverbial wisdom; proverbial sayings.* **2.** having become an object of common reference: *clean and fresh as the proverbial daisy.*

provide /prə'vaid/, *v.,* **-vided, -viding.** ◇*v.t.* **1.** to furnish or supply: *I will provide the food; I will provide you with food.* **2.** to give or yield: *Cows provide milk.* **3.** *Law.* to arrange for beforehand by a condition, etc. ◇*v.i.* **4.** to make arrangements for a future situation (usu. fol. by *for* or *against*). **5.** to supply means of support, etc. (oft. fol. by *for*). [ME, from L: foresee, look after, provide for] —**provider**, *n.*

provided /prə'vaidəd/, *conj.* on the condition or understanding (that): *I will consent, provided (that) all the others agree.* Also, **providing.**

providence /'provədəns/, *n.* **1.** the foreseeing care and protection given by God or by another force such as nature, fate, etc. to all creatures. **2.** (*cap.*) God. **3.** the careful and wise management of affairs, money, etc.

provident /'provədənt/, *adj.* **1.** careful in providing for the future. **2.** careful in the management of money, etc.; economical. [ME, from L: looking for, providing] —**providential**, *adj.*

province /'provəns/, *n.* **1.** an administrative division of a country. **2.** a territory, district, or region. **3.** the range or field of action of a person, business, branch of knowledge, etc. **4. the provinces,** the parts of a country outside the largest cities. [ME, from F, from L: province, official charge]

provincial /prə'vɪnʃəl/, *adj.* **1.** belonging to or characteristic of some particular province or provinces: *provincial customs.* **2.** having the manners characteristic of people living in a province or the provinces; narrow; unsophisticated. ◇*n.* **3.** someone who lives in or comes from the provinces. —**provincialism**, *n.*

provision /prə'vɪʒən/, *n.* **1.** a clause in a document, a law, etc., providing for a particular matter; stipulation; proviso. **2.** the providing or supplying of something, such as food or other necessities. **3.** an arrangement or preparation made beforehand. **4.** something provided. **5.** (*pl.*) supplies of food. ◇*v.t.* **6.** to supply with provisions. [ME, from L]

provisional /prə'vɪʒənəl/, *adj.* **1.** Also, **provisionary.** serving until permanently replaced; temporary; conditional: *a provisional agreement.* **2.** (*cap.*) relating to the faction of the Irish Republican Army and Sinn Fein that advocates the use of terrorist activity rather than peaceful, political methods.

provisional licence, *n.* a licence to drive a motor vehicle at a limited speed and with the use of P-plates, obtained after passing a driving test and usu. in force for one year.

provisional tax, *n.* tax paid in advance on income, other than salary and wages, to be gained in the next financial year.

proviso /prəˈvaɪzoʊ/, *n.*, *pl.* **-sos**, **-soes**. 1. a clause stating a condition in a legal document, etc. 2. a condition; stipulation. [late ME, from ML: it being provided that] **–provisory**, *adj.*

provocation /prɒvəˈkeɪʃən/, *n.* 1. the act of provoking. 2. something that provokes. [ME, from L: a calling forth]

provocative /prəˈvɒkətɪv/, *adj.* 1. tending or serving to provoke; exciting, irritating, or annoying. ◇*n.* 2. something provocative.

provoke /prəˈvoʊk/, *v.t.*, **-voked**, **-voking**. 1. to anger or annoy. 2. to stir up or arouse (action or feeling). 3. to excite (a person, etc.) to action. [ME, from L: call forth, challenge, provoke]

provost /ˈprɒvəst/, *n.* 1. *Church.* the head officer of a governing body of certain religious foundations. 2. the head of certain colleges, schools, etc. [ME; OE *profost*, from ML: one placed before, president]

prow /praʊ/, *n.* the front part of a ship or boat above the waterline; bow. [F, from d. It (Genoese), from L, from Gk]

prowess /ˈpraʊɪs, ˈpraʊɛs/, *n.* 1. bravery. 2. outstanding ability: *prowess at mathematics*. [ME, from OF: good, valiant, from L: be useful]

prowl /praʊl/, *v.i.* 1. to go about quietly, as if in search of prey, etc. ◇*n.* 2. the act of prowling. [ME; orig. uncert.]

prox., *Abbrev.* proximo. [L]

proximity /prɒkˈsɪmətɪ/, *n.* nearness in place, time, or relation. [late ME, from L]

proximo /ˈprɒksəmoʊ/, *adv.* in or of the next or coming month. *Abbrev.:* prox. See **ultimo**. [L: in the next month]

proxy /ˈprɒksɪ/, *n.*, *pl.* **proxies**. 1. the use of a person authorised to act for another: *to vote by proxy*. 2. a person so authorised; an agent. [ME]

prude /pruːd/, *n.* a person who is overly modest or proper. [F: a prude, as adj., prudish, from OF: worthy or respectable woman] **–prudish**, *adj.*

prudence /ˈpruːdns/, *n.* 1. careful practical wisdom; good judgment. 2. careful regard for one's own interests. 3. careful management; economy. **–prudent**, *adj.*

prune[1] /pruːn/, *n.* the purplish black dried fruit of any of several varieties of plum tree. [late ME, from F, from L: plum, from Gk: plum]

prune[2] /pruːn/, *v.t.*, **pruned**, **pruning**. 1. to cut undesired twigs, branches, or roots from; lop. 2. to remove (anything undesirable or unnecessary). [ME, from OF: prune (vines), from L]

prunus /ˈpruːnəs/, *n.* any shrub or tree of a group that includes the many varieties of plum, esp. garden varieties with dark purplish-red leaves.

prurient /ˈprʊərɪənt/, *adj.* 1. inclined to or causing sexual thoughts to an unusual degree. 2. itching. 3. *Bot.* causing itching. [L: itching] **–prurience, pruriency**, *n.*

Prussia /ˈprʌʃə/, *n.* a former state in northern Germany; as a former kingdom (with its capital at Berlin) it was the central state in the formation of the German Empire; dissolved March 1947. German, **Preussen**.

Prussian blue /prʌʃən ˈbluː/, *n.* (the color of) a dark blue, crystalline, iron compound used as a coloring substance in dyes, etc.

prussic acid /ˈprʌsɪk ˈæsəd/, *n.* a colorless, poisonous liquid, hydrogen cyanide dissolved in water, with a smell of bitter almonds. [*prussic*, from F: Prussia]

pry /praɪ/, *v.i.*, **pried**, **prying**. to look or search closely or curiously (oft. fol. by *into*). [ME; orig. uncert.]

prying /ˈpraɪɪŋ/, *adj.* curious or inquisitive to an undesirable degree.

Ps, *Abbrev. Bible.* Psalms.

PS, *Abbrev.* postscript.

psalm /sɑːm/, *n.* 1. a sacred song or hymn. 2. a poem of similar character. 3. (*cap.*, *pl.*) *Bible.* any of the 150 songs, hymns, and prayers which together form a book of the Old Testament (**Book of Psalms**). [OE ps(e)alm, sealm, from LL, from Gk: song sung to the harp, orig., a plucking, as of strings] **–psalmist**, *n.*

psalmody /ˈsɑːmədɪ, ˈsælmədɪ/, *n.*, *pl.* **-dies**. 1. an arrangement of psalms for singing. 2. psalms collectively. 3. the act or art of singing psalms. [ME, from LL, from Gk: singing to the harp]

Psalter /ˈsɔːltə/, *n.* (*sometimes l.c.*) a book containing psalms. [LL, from L: a psaltery, from Gk: a stringed instrument]

psaltery /ˈsɔːltərɪ/, *n.*, *pl.* **-teries**. an ancient musical instrument consisting of a flat sounding box with many strings which were plucked with the fingers or a plectrum. [L, from Gk: psaltery, later the Psalter]

pseudo /ˈsjuːdoʊ/, *adj.* 1. false; counterfeit; pretended. ◇*n.* 2. a person who pretends to be more knowledgeable, cultured, etc., than he or she is. [ME; independent use of PSEUDO-]

pseudo-, a word part meaning 'false', 'pretended'; in scientific use, indicating close or deceptive resemblance to the following element, used sometimes in chemical names of isomers. Also, before vowels, **pseud-**. [Gk: false]

pseudonym /ˈsjuːdənɪm/, *n.* a name taken by an author to hide his or her identity; penname. [Gk: false name] **–pseudonymity**, *n.*

pseudopodium /sjuːdoʊˈpoʊdɪəm/, *n.*, *pl.* **-dia** /-dɪə/. a temporary projection of the protoplasm of a protozoan, serving as an organ of movement, touch, etc. Also, **pseudopod** /ˈsjuːdoʊpɒd/. [NL, from Gk]

psoriasis /sə'raɪəsəs/, n. a common skin disease marked by scaly patches. [NL, from Gk]

psych /saɪk/, v.t. Colloq. to persuade by the use of psychological methods rather than openly by argument, esp. when leading oneself or others to perform better (oft. fol. by *up*): *The coach psyched them into winning.*

psych., Abbrev. **1.** psychological. **2.** psychology.

psyche /'saɪki/, n. **1.** the human soul, spirit, or mind. **2.** (*cap.*) *Gk Myth.* the soul, sometimes represented in art as a butterfly or a tiny winged being, and in the late classical era as a beautiful girl loved by Eros or Cupid. [L, from Gk: lit., breath]

psychedelic /saɪkə'delɪk/, adj. **1.** causing or relating to a mental state of enlarged consciousness, involving a sense of joy and increased awareness. **2.** relating to any of a group of drugs inducing such a state, esp. LSD. **3.** Colloq. having bright colors and an imaginative pattern. **4.** of or relating to music which is played very loud and accompanied by a lightshow. [Gk]

psychiatry /sə'kaɪətri, saɪ-/, n. the practice or science of treating mental diseases. [Gk] —**psychiatric, psychiatrical**, adj. —**psychiatrist**, n.

psychic /'saɪkɪk/, adj. Also, **psychical**. **1.** of or relating to the human soul or mind; mental (opposed to *physical*). **2.** *Psychol.* having extrasensory mental powers, such as clairvoyance, telepathy. **3.** done by, proceeding from or relating to non-physical forces. ◇n. **4.** a psychic person. [Gk: of the soul]

psycho /'saɪkoʊ/, n. Colloq. an insane person.

psycho-, a word part representing 'psyche' (as in *psychological*) and 'psychological' (as in *psychoanalysis*). Also, **psych-**. [Gk: breath, spirit, soul, mind]

psychoanalyse /saɪkoʊ'ænəlaɪz/, v.t., **-lysed, -lysing**. to treat by psychoanalysis.

psychoanalysis /ˌsaɪkoʊə'næləsəs/, n. a method of examining unconscious mental processes, and of treating neuroses, etc., based on a system of theories concerning the relation of conscious and unconscious psychological processes. —**psychoanalytic, psychoanalytical**, adj. —**psychoanalyst**, n.

psychogenic /saɪkoʊ'dʒenɪk/, adj. (of a disorder, etc.) of psychic or mental origin.

psychological warfare, n. the use of psychological methods, such as propaganda, to influence an enemy to accept a particular belief, stop wanting to resist, etc.

psychology /saɪ'kɒlədʒi/, n., pl. **-gies**. **1.** the science of the mind, or of mental states and processes; the science of human and animal behavior. **2.** the mental states and processes of a person or people, esp. as determining action: *the psychology of a soldier*. [NL, from Gk] —**psychologist**, n. —**psychological**, adj.

psychopathology /ˌsaɪkoʊpə'θɒlədʒi/, n. the science of diseases of the mind. —**psychopathological**, adj. —**psychopathologist**, n.

psychopathy /saɪ'kɒpəθi/, n. mental disease or disorder. —**psychopath**, n.

psychosis /saɪ'koʊsəs/, n., pl. **-ses** /-siz/. *Pathol.* any severe form of mental disorder or disease. [NL, from LGk] —**psychotic**, adj., n.

psychosomatic /ˌsaɪkoʊsə'mætɪk/, adj. relating to a physical disorder which is caused by, or influenced by, the emotional state of the patient.

psychotherapy /saɪkoʊ'θerəpi/, n. the science or art of treating mental disorders by psychological methods. —**psychotherapist**, n.

pt, Abbrev. **1.** point. **2.** pint. **3.** part.

p.t., Abbrev. **1.** past tense. **2.** part time.

Pt, Chem. Symbol. platinum.

PT, Abbrev. Physical Training.

pteridophyte /'terədoʊfaɪt/, n. any of a primary division of the vegetable kingdom consisting of plants which are without seeds and have vascular tissue, roots, stems and leaves. It includes ferns, horsetails, and club mosses. [NL, from Gk]

pterodactyl /terə'dæktl/, n. any member of an order of extinct flying reptiles, having a very long digit on the forelimb supporting a wing membrane. [NL, from Gk]

p.t.o. /pi ti 'oʊ/, Abbrev. please turn over. Also, **PTO**

Ptolemy /'tɒləmi/, n. (*Claudius Ptolemaeus*), fl. AD 127–151, Greek mathematician, astronomer, and geographer, at Alexandria; author of two influential texts *Geography* and the *Almagest*, in which he presented his system of astronomy. —**Ptolemaic**, adj.

ptomaine /tə'meɪn/, n. any of a class of basic nitrogenous substances, some very poisonous, produced during decay of animal or plant matter. Also, **ptomain**. [It, from Gk: dead body]

Pty, Abbrev. Proprietary.

pub /pʌb/, n. Colloq. a hotel. [short for *public house*]

puberty /'pjubəti/, n. the stage of sexual development at which a person is first capable of reproduction of offspring. [ME, from L]

pubes /'pjubiz/, n., pl. **-bes** /-biz/. **1.** the lower part of the abdomen. **2.** the hair appearing on this area at puberty. [L: pubic hair, groin] —**pubic**, adj.

pubescent /pju'besənt/, adj. **1.** arriving or arrived at puberty. **2.** *Bot, Zool.* covered with fine short hair or down. [L: reaching puberty, becoming hairy or downy] —**pubescence**, n.

public /'pʌblɪk/, adj. **1.** of, relating to, or affecting the people of a community, state, or nation as a whole: *public affairs*. **2.** done, provided, acting, etc., for the people as a whole: *a public official; a public library*. **3.** open to all the people: *a public meeting*. **4.** open to the view or knowledge of all: *The news became* *public.* **5.** known to the people generally: *a public figure.* **6. go public, a.** (of a proprietary limited company) to sell part or all of its capital to the public. **b.** (of a company) to seek listing on the stock exchange. ◇*n.* **7.** the people of a community, state, or nation as a whole. **8.** a particular section of the people: *the novel-reading public.* **9.** public view: *in public.* [L]

public-address system, *n.* an electronic system for amplifying sound in a public meeting place.

publican /ˈpʌblɪkən/, *n.* **1.** the owner or manager of a hotel. **2.** (in ancient Rome) a tax collector. [L]

publication /ˌpʌbləˈkeɪʃən/, *n.* **1.** the publishing of a book, magazine, etc. **2.** the condition or fact of being published. **3.** something which is published. [ME, from L]

public company, *n.* → **limited company.**

public convenience, *n.* a room, building, etc., having toilets, etc., for public use.

publicise *or* **publicize** /ˈpʌbləsaɪz/, *v.t.*, **-cised, -cising.** to bring to public notice; advertise.

publicity /pʌbˈlɪsɪti/, *n.* **1.** the means, process, or business of attracting public notice. **2.** any advertising matter, information, etc., intended to attract public notice.

public relations, *n.* the practice of working to present a favorable image of a company, government body, person, etc., to the public.

public school, *n.* **1.** → **state school.** **2.** (in some States and the UK) → **private school.**

public sector, *n.* that part of an economy which is owned and operated by governments and government authorities and enterprises (as opposed to the *private sector*).

public service, *n.* the departments and people responsible for administration of laws and government policy. **–public servant,** *n.*

public-spirited /ˌpʌblɪk-ˈspɪrətəd/, *adj.* having or showing an unselfish desire for the public good: *a public-spirited citizen; public-spirited action.*

public utility, *n.* an organisation performing a necessary public service, such as supplying gas, electricity or transport.

public works, *n.pl.* roads, dams, buildings, etc., constructed with government money for public use.

publish /ˈpʌblɪʃ/, *v.t.* **1.** to issue (a book, magazine, etc.) in printed copies for sale, etc., to the public. **2.** to issue to the public the works of (an author). **3.** to announce publicly; make generally known. ◇*v.i.* **4.** to have one's writing published: *Does he publish?* [ME, from F]

Puccini /puˈtʃini/, *n.* **Giacomo** /ˈdʒakoʊ-moʊ/, 1858–1924, Italian operatic composer.

puce /pjus/, *adj., n.* (of) a dark or purplish brown color. [F: lit., flea, from L]

puck /pʌk/, *n.* a flat rubber disc used in place of a ball in ice hockey. [var. of POKE¹]

pucker /ˈpʌkə/, *v.t., v.i.* **1.** to draw or gather into small folds or wrinkles. ◇*n.* **2.** a small fold; wrinkle. **3.** a puckered part of cloth, etc. [apparently a frequentative form connected with POKE² (bag)]

pudding /ˈpʊdɪŋ/, *n.* **1.** a soft, sweet or savory dish made in many forms, of flour (or rice, tapioca, etc.), milk and eggs, with fruit, meat, or other ingredients. **2.** a course in a meal following the main or meat course; dessert. **3.** a kind of sausage. [ME; orig. uncert.]

puddle /ˈpʌdl/, *n., v.,* **-dled, -dling.** ◇*n.* **1.** a small pool of liquid, esp. of dirty water left after rain. **2.** clay, or a similar material, which has been mixed with water for use as a watertight lining, etc. ◇*v.t.* **3.** to make (clay, etc.) into a puddle. [ME, apparently from OE *pudd* ditch]

puerile /ˈpjʊəraɪl/, *adj.* childish; foolish: *a piece of puerile writing.* [L] **–puerility,** *n.*

puerperal /pjuˈɜpərəl/, *adj.* of or relating to childbirth. [NL, from L: bringing forth children]

Puerto Rico /ˌpwɜtoʊ ˈrikoʊ/, *n.* a self-governing commonwealth associated with the US in the Caribbean Sea east of Hispaniola; comprises the island of Puerto Rico and many smaller islands. Pop. 3 300 000 (1987 est.); 8860 km². *Languages:* Spanish, English. *Currency:* US dollar. *Cap.:* San Juan. Formerly, **Porto Rico.** **–Puerto Rican,** *n., adj.*

puff /pʌf/, *n.* **1.** a short, quick sending out of wind, breath, air, vapor, etc. **2.** a single taking in and sending out of breath: *a puff of a cigarette.* **3.** the sound of a quick sending out of air, etc. **4.** a small quantity of vapor, smoke, etc., sent out at one time. **5.** a swelling; protuberance. **6.** a light pastry with a filling of cream, jam, etc. **7.** a mass of material gathered and held down at the edges but left full in the middle, as in a dress, etc. ◇*v.i.* **8.** to blow with puffs, as the wind. **9.** to give out a puff or puffs; breathe quickly after violent exercise, etc. **10.** to move with puffs. **11.** to take puffs at a cigarette, etc. **12.** to become swollen (usu. fol. by *up*). ◇*v.t.* **13.** to send out (air, vapor, etc.) in puffs. **14.** to drive or force along by puffing. **15.** to blow out with a puff (fol. by *out*): *to puff out a candle.* **16.** to smoke (a cigar, etc.). **17.** to swell or inflate, with air, pride, etc. **18.** to praise in exaggerated language. [ME, OE *pyff;* of imitative orig.] **–puffy,** *adj.* **–puffiness,** *n.*

puffball /ˈpʌfbɔl/, *n.* any of various fungi, marked by a ball-like fruit body which sends out a cloud of spores when broken.

puffed-up /ˈpʌft-ʌp/, *adj. Colloq.* self-important.

puffin /ˈpʌfən/, *n.* any of various seabirds of the auk family, with a peculiar bill, the most common type being found in large numbers on the coasts of the northern Atlantic, nesting in holes in the ground. [ME; orig. uncert.]

puff pastry, *n.* rich, flaky pastry used for pies, tarts, etc.

pug /pʌg/, *n.* a breed of dog, having a short, smooth coat of silver, fawn, or black, a deeply wrinkled face and a tightly curled tail. Also, **pugdog**. [orig. unknown]

Pugh /pjuː/, n. **Clifton Ernest**, 1924–90, Australian artist, noted for his bush paintings and portraits.

pugilist /ˈpjudʒəlɪst/, n. someone who fights with the fists; boxer. —**pugilism**, n. —**pugilistic**, adj. —**pugilistically**, adv.

pugnacious /pʌgˈneɪʃəs/, adj. given to fighting; aggressively quarrelsome. [L: combativeness] —**pugnacity**, n.

pug nose, n. a short nose turning sharply up at the tip. —**pug-nosed**, adj.

pukka /ˈpʌkə/, adj. Colloq. formal or proper in behavior, etc. Also, **pucka**. [Anglo-Indian: reliable, genuine, from Hind: cooked, ripe, mature]

pulchritude /ˈpʌlkrɪtjud, ˈpʊl-/, n. beauty. [ME, from L]

Pulitzer Prize, /ˈpʊlɪtsə ˈpraɪz/, n. one of a group of annual prizes in journalism, literature and music, [established by Joseph *Pulitzer*, 1847–1911, US journalist and publisher, born in Hungary]

pull /pʊl/, v.t. **1.** to draw, drag or haul towards or after oneself or itself: *to pull a heavy load up a hill.* **2.** to draw or tug at with force: *to pull a person's hair.* **3.** to draw apart or tear: *to pull something to pieces.* **4.** to draw out from a place of attachment, etc.: *to pull a tooth.* **5.** to cause to form (an expression of pain, discontent, etc.): *to pull a face.* **6.** to strain (a muscle, etc.) ◇v.i. **7.** to use a drawing, tugging, or hauling force (oft. fol. by *at*). **8.** to breathe in through a pipe, cigarette, etc. **9.** to be able to be pulled into a particular condition: *The juicer pulls apart for easy cleaning.* ◇ v. **10.** Some special uses are:
pull apart/to pieces, to examine in critical detail: *The teacher pulled his essay apart.*
pull in, **1.** (of a vehicle, driver, etc.) to move to the side of the road in order to stop. **2.** to arrive at a destination, stopping place, etc.: *The train pulled in to Central.* **3.** Colloq. to arrest (a person). **4.** to earn (as a wage or salary). **5.** to draw in or attract (a crowd, etc.).
pull off, Colloq. to succeed in gaining or performing something.
pull one's punches, **1.** Boxing. to give punches without full force. **2.** to limit the effect of an action, etc.; use restraint.
pull oneself together, to regain one's self-control.
pull one's weight, to take a full and fair share of work, responsibility, etc.
pull out, **1.** to leave; depart. **2.** Colloq. to withdraw from an agreement, undertaking, etc.
pull over, (of a vehicle, driver, etc.) to move towards the side of the road.
pull round/through, Colloq. to recover from an illness, misfortune, etc.
pull someone's leg, Colloq. to tease a person.
pull the rug from under someone's feet, Colloq. to place someone in a position of disadvantage.
pull up, **1.** (to cause to) stop. **2.** to correct or rebuke. **3.** to pull out of the ground; uproot. ◇n. **11.** an act of pulling or drawing. **12.** force used in pulling. **13.** a drawing of a liquid, cigarette smoke, etc., into the mouth. **14.** Colloq. a special influence or advantage. **15.** Colloq. the ability to attract or draw audiences, followers, etc. [OE *pullian* pull, pluck]

pullet /ˈpʊlət/, n. a hen less than one year old. [ME from OF: young hen, from LL: young animal, chicken]

pulley /ˈpʊli/, n., pl. **-leys**. **1.** a wheel with a grooved rim for carrying a line which is pulled at one end in order to raise a weight at the other end. **2.** a combination of such wheels in a block, or of such wheels or blocks in a tackle, to increase the power applied. **3.** a wheel driven by, or driving, a belt, etc., to give power. [ME, from OF, from a derivative of Gk: axle]

pullover /ˈpʊloʊvə/, n. → **jumper**[2].

pulmonary /ˈpʌlmənri, ˈpʊl-/, adj. of, relating to, or affecting the lungs. Also, **pulmonic**. [L: lung]

pulp /pʌlp/, n. **1.** the soft, juicy part of a fruit. **2.** the pith of the stem of a plant. **3.** the soft or fleshy part of an animal body. **4.** any soft, moist mass, such as that into which linen, wood, etc., are made in the production of paper. **5.** anything worthless, as a magazine containing sensational and lurid stories, articles, etc.; trash. ◇v.t., v.i. **6.** to reduce to, or become reduced to, pulp. [L] —**pulpy**, adj. —**pulpiness**, n.

pulpit /ˈpʊlpət/, n. a raised structure in a church, from which the priest or minister delivers a sermon, etc. [ME, from ML, from L: stage; platform]

pulpwood /ˈpʌlpwʊd/, n. spruce or other soft wood suitable for making paper.

pulsar /ˈpʌlsə/, n. one of a number of sources of pulsed radio signals detected within the galaxy but outside the solar system. [*puls*(ating *st*)*ar*]

pulsate /pʌlˈseɪt/, v.i., **-sated, -sating.** **1.** to beat rhythmically, as the heart; throb. **2.** to shake; vibrate; quiver. [L: pushed, struck, beaten] —**pulsation**, n. —**pulsator**, n.

pulse[1] /pʌls/, n., v., **pulsed, pulsing.** ◇n. **1.** the regular beating in the arteries caused by the contractions of the heart, esp. as felt in an artery at the wrist. **2.** a single beat or throb of the arteries or heart. **3.** any regular stroke, beat, or vibration. **4.** the underlying force of life, feeling, etc.: *the pulse of a nation.* **5.** a brief increase in the size of an electric current, voltage, etc. ◇v.i. **6.** to beat, throb or vibrate. [L: a pushing, beating, pulse]

pulse[2] /pʌls/, n. the seeds of certain plants, such as peas, beans, lentils, that can be eaten. [ME, from OF, from L: thick pap of meal, pulse, etc. See POULTICE]

pulverise *or* **pulverize** /ˈpʌlvəraɪz/, v., **-rised, -rising.** ◇v.t. **1.** to reduce to dust or powder, by pounding, grinding, etc. **2.** to destroy completely, demolish. ◇v.i. **3.** to become reduced to dust. [ME, from L: dust]

puma /ˈpjumə/, n. a large, tawny animal of the cat family, found in North and South

puma America; cougar; mountain lion. [Sp, from Quechua]

pumice /'pʌməs/, n. a porous or spongy form of volcanic glass, used, esp. when powdered, for rubbing, polishing, etc. Also, **pumice stone**. [ME, from OF, from L]

pummel /'pʌməl/, v.t., **-melled, -melling** or **-meled, -meling**. to beat with rapid blows with the fists, etc.

pump[1] /pʌmp/, n. **1.** an apparatus or machine for raising, driving, or forcing out liquids. ◇v.t. **2.** to raise, drive, etc., (a liquid) with a pump. **3.** to free from water, etc., by means of a pump (sometimes fol. by *out*). **4.** to fill with air by pumping (oft. fol. by *up*): *to pump up a tyre*. **5.** to move or operate by an up and down action like that on a pump handle. **6.** to drive, force, etc., as if from a pump: *Her enthusiasm pumped energy into the team*. **7.** to try to get information from by continual questioning, etc. ◇v.i. **8.** to raise or move water, etc., with a pump. **9.** to flow out in bursts, as if driven by a pump: *blood pumping from a wound*. **10.** to move up and down like a pump handle. [ME; orig. uncert.]

pump[2] /pʌmp/, n. a low, light shoe worn for dancing, etc. [orig. uncert.]

pumpernickel /'pʌmpənɪkəl/, n. a coarse, slightly sour bread made with wholemeal rye. [G]

pumpkin /'pʌmpkən/, n. the large, yellow-orange fruits of a group of climbing plants, eaten as a vegetable. [F: a melon, from L, from Gk]

pun /pʌn/, n., v., **punned, punning**. ◇n. **1.** the humorous use of words alike in sound but different in meaning; a play on words. ◇v.i. **2.** to make puns. [? short for obs. *pundigrion*, from It: fine point, quibble]

punch[1] /pʌntʃ/, n. **1.** a pushing blow, esp. with the fist. **2.** *Colloq.* a forceful effect. ◇v.t. **3.** to give a sharp blow to, esp. with the fist. [? var. of POUNCE]

punch[2] /pʌntʃ/, n. an apparatus for making holes in tickets, leather, etc., or for stamping a design on materials, forcing in nails, etc. [short for *puncheon* pointed tool]

punch[3] /pʌntʃ/, n. **1.** a drink consisting of wine or spirits mixed with water, fruit juice, etc. **2.** a beverage of two or more fruit juices, sugar and water, often carbonated. [? short for *puncheon* a cask; if so, a metonymic use]

Punch /pʌntʃ/, n. **1.** the chief character in the puppet show called 'Punch and Judy', a hook-nosed, ugly figure who behaves violently to his child, his wife (Judy), etc. **2. pleased as Punch**, delighted; highly pleased. [short for *Punchinello*, It, from L *pullus* young animal]

punch card, n. a card through which a pattern of holes is punched to represent information in a form which can be read by a computer. Also, **punched card**.

punch-drunk /'pʌntʃ-drʌŋk/, adj. **1.** having brain damage marked by unsteadiness of movement and caused by too many blows to the head. **2.** *Colloq.* unsteady in movement or dazed, as if suffering from this condition.

punch line, n. the last sentence, line, etc., of a joke, on which the whole joke depends.

punch-up /'pʌntʃ-ʌp/, n. *Colloq.* a fight.

punctilious /pʌŋk'tɪliəs/, adj. strict or exact in following the correct form of behavior, etc.

punctual /'pʌŋktʃuəl/, adj. **1.** strict about keeping to an appointed time; not late. **2.** made at an appointed or regular time: *punctual payment*. [ME, from ML, from L: a pricking, a point] **—punctuality,** n.

punctuate /'pʌŋktʃueɪt/, v.t., **-ated, -ating**. **1.** to mark with punctuation marks in order to make the meaning clear: *to punctuate a sentence*. **2.** to interrupt every so often: *They punctuated his speech with cheers*. **3.** to give point or emphasis to. [ML: pointed, from L: a point]

punctuation /pʌŋktʃu'eɪʃən/, n. the practice or system of putting commas, semicolons, colons, full stops, etc. (**punctuation marks**) into writing or printing in order to make the meaning clear.

puncture /'pʌŋktʃə/, n., v., **-tured, -turing**. ◇n. **1.** the act of making a mark on or a hole in something with a pointed instrument or object. **2.** a mark or hole so made. **3.** *Zool.* a small point-like depression. ◇v.t. **4.** to prick or make a hole in: *to puncture the skin with a pin; to puncture a tyre*. [L]

pundit /'pʌndət/, n. *Colloq.* someone who is knowledgeable on a subject; expert. [See PANDIT]

pungent /'pʌndʒənt/, adj. **1.** having a sharp, penetrating taste or smell; biting; acrid. **2.** (of speech or mind) caustic, biting, stimulating or sharply expressive: *pungent wit*. [L: pricking] **—pungency,** n.

Punic Wars /ˌpjunɪk 'wɔz/, n.pl. the three wars waged by Rome against Carthage, 264–241, 218–201, and 149–146 BC, resulting in the overthrow and annexation of Carthage to Rome.

punish /'pʌnɪʃ/, v.t. **1.** to make someone suffer because they have done wrong: *to punish a criminal*. **2.** to give a penalty for (an offence, fault, etc.): *to punish theft*. **3.** to handle severely or roughly: *The boxer really punished his opponent*. [ME, from OF, from L] **—punisher,** n. **—punishment,** n.

punitive /'pjunətɪv/, adj. used for, concerned with, or inflicting punishment: *punitive laws*. Also, **punitory** /'pjunətəri, -tri/.

Punjab /pʌn'dʒab, pʌn-/, n. **1.** a former province in north-western India; now divided between India and Pakistan. **2.** a state in north-western India. Pop. 16 788 915 (1981); 50 400 km². *Cap.*: Chandigarh.

punk /pʌŋk/, *Colloq.* ◇n. **1.** something or someone regarded as worthless, degraded or bad. **2.** a follower of punk rock and the style of dress and behavior that goes with it. **3.** → **punk rock**. ◇adj. **4.** worthless, degraded or of poor quality. **5.** relating to punk rock and the style of dress and behavior that goes with it. [orig. unknown]

punk rock, *n.* a type of rock music, usu. with a fast, energetic beat like early rock, which is associated with rebelliousness, great aggressiveness, violence and sexuality.

punnet /ˈpʌnət/, *n.* a small, shallow basket for small fruits, esp. strawberries. [diminutive of Brit d. *pun* POUND²]

punt¹ /pʌnt/, *n.* **1.** *Football.* a kick given to a dropped ball before it touches the ground. **2.** *Soccer.* a light, rising shot. [Brit d. *bunt, punt* push with force]

punt² /pʌnt/, *n.* **1.** a shallow, flat-bottomed, square-ended boat, usu. driven by pushing with a pole against the bottom of the river, etc. **2.** a ferry for carrying vehicles across rivers, etc. ◇*v.t.* **3.** to drive (a punt or other boat). **4.** to carry (a person) in a punt. [OE *punt*, from L: *punt*, PONTOON¹]

punt³ /pʌnt/, *v.i.* **1.** to gamble; wager; lay bets. ◇*n.* **2.** a wager; bet: *to take a punt*. [F, from Sp: point, from L] —**punter**, *n.*

puny /ˈpjuːni/, *adj.*, **-nier, -niest. 1.** small and weak. **2.** petty; insignificant: *puny efforts.*

pup /pʌp/, *n., v.,* **pupped, pupping.** ◇*n.* **1.** a young dog or other animal under one year; puppy. **2.** a foolish or vain boy or young man. ◇*v.i.* **3.** to give birth to pups. [shortened form of PUPPY]

pupa /ˈpjuːpə/, *n., pl.* **-pae** /-piː/. an insect in the non-feeding, usu. immobile, changing stage between the larva and sexually mature adult insect. [NL, from L: girl, doll, puppet] —**pupal**, *adj.*

pupate /pjuːˈpeɪt/, *v.i.*, **-pated, -pating.** to become a pupa. —**pupation**, *n.*

pupil¹ /ˈpjuːpəl/, *n.* someone who is being taught; a student. [ME, from OF, from L: orphan, ward]

pupil² /ˈpjuːpəl/, *n.* the expanding and contracting opening in the iris of the eye, through which light passes to the retina. [L: lit., little doll]

puppet /ˈpʌpət/, *n.* **1.** doll. **2.** an artificial figure of various kinds, moved by wires, hands, etc., usu. on a small stage; marionette. **3.** a person or group whose actions are controlled by another or others. ◇*adj.* **4.** controlled by external forces: *a puppet government.* [ME, apparently from MLG: doll, of Rom orig.] —**puppeteer**, *n.* —**puppetry**, *n.*

puppet state, *n.* a state whose government is more or less controlled by a more powerful state.

puppy /ˈpʌpi/, *n., pl.* **-pies. 1.** a young dog or other animal. **2.** a vain, or empty-headed young man. [F: doll, from LL]

puppy fat, *n.* fatness during adolescence.

Purcell /ˈpɜːsəl/, *n.* **Henry,** 1658?–95, English composer of a wide variety of choral, church and dramatic works.

purchase /ˈpɜːtʃəs/, *v.,* **-chased, -chasing,** *n.* ◇*v.t.* **1.** to get by the payment of money; buy. **2.** to win over by a bribe. **3.** to haul, draw, or raise, esp. by the aid of a mechanical power. ◇*n.* **4.** a buying. **5.** something which is purchased or bought. **6.** an effective hold or position for applying leverage. [ME, from AF: seek to obtain, procure]

purdah /ˈpɜːdə/, *n.* (in some Hindu and Muslim comunities). **1.** a screen hiding women from the sight of men or strangers. **2.** a system of keeping women in seclusion. [Urdu: curtain, from Pers]

pure /pjuə, pjɔː/, *adj.,* **purer, purest. 1.** free from outside matter, or from mixture with anything of a different, inferior, or spoiling kind: *pure gold; pure color.* **2.** (of literary style) straightforward; unaffected. **3.** abstract or theoretical (opposed to *applied*): *pure science.* **4.** clear and true: *a pure voice.* **5.** absolute; utter; sheer: *pure ignorance.* **6.** being that and nothing else; mere: *a pure accident.* **7.** clean; spotless; unsullied: *pure hands; a pure complexion.* **8.** inexperienced or uninterested in sexual matters; virginal. **9.** *Biol.* →**homozygous.** [ME, from OF, from L: clean, unmixed, plain, pure]

puree /ˈpjuəreɪ/, *n., v.,* **-reed, -reeing.** ◇*n.* **1.** vegetable or fruit cooked and put through a sieve, used for soups or other foods. ◇*v.t.* **2.** to make a puree of. Also, **purée.** [F: strain]

purgative /ˈpɜːɡətɪv/, *adj.* **1.** purging; cleansing; in particular, causing emptying of the bowels. ◇*n.* **2.** a purgative medicine or agent. [ME, from LL: cleansed]

purgatory /ˈpɜːɡətri/, *n., pl.* **-ries. 1.** (*also cap.*) (in the belief of Roman Catholics and others) a condition or place of temporary punishment after death, before going to heaven. **2.** any condition, situation, or place of temporary suffering. [ME, from LL: cleanse] —**purgatorial**, *adj.*

purge /pɜːdʒ/, *v.,* **purged, purging,** *n.* ◇*v.t.* **1.** to get rid of whatever is impure or undesirable; purify. **2.** to rid or clear: *to purge a party of undesirable members.* **3.** to get rid of by killing (an unwanted person): *to purge political opponents.* **4.** to clear (a person, etc.) of guilt. **5.** to clear away or wipe out legally (an offence, accusation, etc.) by making up for it. **6.** to clear or empty (the bowels, etc.). ◇*v.i.* **7.** to become cleansed or purified. ◇*n.* **8.** the act or process of purging. **9.** something that purges, as a purgative medicine or dose. **10.** the removing of political opponents, esp. by violence. **11.** the period when such a removing takes place: *He disappeared in Stalin's great purge of 1936–38.* [ME, from OF, from L: cleanse] —**purger**, *n.* —**purgation**, *n.*

purify /ˈpjuərəfaɪ/, *v.t.,* **-fied, -fying.** to make pure; free from evil; cleanse. [ME, from OF, from L] —**purification**, *n.* —**purifier**, *n.*

Purim /ˈpʊrɪm, pʊˈrɪm/, *n.* a Jewish festival, observed in February or March, in commemoration of the deliverance of the Jews from the massacre planned by Haman. [See Esther 9. Heb, pl. of *pūr*, said to mean lot]

purism /ˈpjuərɪzəm/, *n.* **1.** very careful keeping of or insistence on purity in language, style, etc. **2.** a theory and practice in art, originated in 1918, which reduces all natural appearances to a geometric simplicity typical of

purism machines. [PURE + -ISM] —**purist**, *n*. —**puristic**, *adj*.

puritan /ˈpjurətən/, *n*. **1.** someone who tries to be very pure or strict in moral and religious matters. **2.** (*cap.*) one of a class of Protestants who arose in the 16th century within the Church of England, demanding further reforms in doctrine and worship, and greater strictness in religious discipline, and during part of the 17th century constituting a powerful political party. ◇*adj.* **3.** relating to puritans. [LL: purity] —**puritanical**, *adj*. —**puritanism**, *n*.

purity /ˈpjurəti/, *n*. the condition or quality of being pure. [LL]

purl¹ /pɜl/, *v.i.* **1.** to flow with curling or rippling motions and murmuring sound, as a shallow stream does over stones. ◇*n.* **2.** the action or sound of purling. **3.** a circle or curl made by the motion of water; a ripple; eddy.

purl² /pɜl/, *v.t., v.i.* **1.** to knit with inversion of the stitch. **2.** to finish with loops or a looped edging. ◇*n.* **3.** a stitch used in hand knitting to make a rib effect. **4.** one of a series of small loops along the edge of lace braid. **5.** thread made of twisted gold or silver wire. Also, **pearl**. [orig. uncert.]

purloin /pɜˈlɔɪn/, *v.t.* **1.** to take dishonestly or steal. ◇*v.i.* **2.** to commit theft. [ME, from AF: put off, remove] —**purloiner**, *n*.

purple /ˈpɜpəl/, *n., adj., v.,* -**pled,** -**pling**. ◇*n.* **1.** any color having both red and blue, esp. a dark shade of such a color. **2.** cloth or clothing of this hue, esp. as formerly worn by persons of imperial, royal, or other high rank: *born to the purple.* ◇*adj.* **3.** of the color of purple. **4.** imperial or regal. **5.** brilliant or gorgeous. **6.** full of elaborate literary devices and pretentious effects: *a purple passage.* ◇*v.t., v.i.* **7.** to make or become purple. [OE (Northumbrian) *purpl(e)*, from L, from Gk: kind of shellfish yielding purple dye]

purport /ˈpɜpɔt, ˈpɜpɔt, -pət/, *v.;* /ˈpɜpɔt, -pət/, *n.* ◇*v.t.* **1.** to say or claim: *a document purporting to be official.* **2.** to bring to the mind as the meaning or thing meant; express; imply. ◇*n.* **3.** tenor, import, or meaning: *the purport of my words.* **4.** purpose or object. [late ME, from AF: convey]

purpose /ˈpɜpəs/, *n.* **1.** the object for which anything exists or is done, made, used, etc. **2.** an intended or desired result; end or aim. **3.** intention or determination: *a man of purpose.* **4.** a practical result, effect, or advantage: *to good purpose.* **5.** **on purpose**, by design; intentionally. [ME, from OF: PROPOSE] —**purposeful**, *adj*.

purr /pɜ/, *v.i.* **1.** to utter a low, continuous murmuring sound showing satisfaction, as a cat does. **2.** (of things) to make a sound like the purring of a cat. ◇*v.t.* **3.** to express by, or as if by, purring: *He purred his pleasure.* ◇*n.* **4.** the act or sound of purring. [imitative]

purse /pɜs/, *n., v.,* **pursed, pursing.** ◇*n.* **1.** a small bag, pouch, or case for carrying money. **2.** a purse with its contents: *Hand over your purse.* **3.** money, resources, or wealth: *the public purse.* **4.** any baglike receptacle. ◇*v.t.* **5.** to contract into folds or wrinkles; pucker: *to purse the lips.* [ME and OE *purs*, from LL: bag, from Gk: hide, leather]

purser /ˈpɜsə/, *n.* an officer, esp. on board a ship, who keeps accounts, etc.

purse strings, *n.pl.* **1.** the strings by which a purse is closed. **2. hold the purse strings**, to have the power to spend or withhold money.

pursuant /pəˈsjuənt/, *adj.* **1.** going along with or agreeing. **2.** pursuing. ◇*adv.* Also, **pursuantly. 3.** according (fol. by *to*): *to do something pursuant to an agreement.* **4.** in a manner agreeing with (fol. by *to*). —**pursuance**, *n*.

pursue /pəˈsju/, *v.,* -**sued,** -**suing**. ◇*v.t.* **1.** to follow in order to catch; chase. **2.** to follow close upon; go with; attend: *Bad luck pursued him.* **3.** to carry on: *to pursue a course of action; to pursue an idea; to pursue pleasure.* ◇*v.i.* **4.** to follow in pursuit. **5.** to continue. [ME, from AF, from L: follow, continue]

pursuit /pəˈsjut/, *n.* **1.** the act of pursuing: *in pursuit of the fox.* **2.** an effort to secure; quest: *the pursuit of happiness.* **3.** any occupation, pastime, or the like, regularly or usually pursued: *literary pursuits.* [ME, from AF: PURSUE]

purulent /ˈpjurələnt/, *adj.* full of, containing, forming, or discharging pus; suppurating: *a purulent sore.* [L] —**purulence**, **purulency**, *n*.

purvey /pəˈveɪ/, *v.t.* to provide or supply (esp. food or provisions). [ME, from AF, from L: foresee, provide for] —**purveyance**, *n*. —**purveyor**, *n*.

pus /pʌs/, *n.* a yellow-white substance found in abscesses, sores, etc., consisting of a liquid plasma in which leucocytes, etc., are suspended. [L] —**pussy**, *adj*.

push /pʊʃ/, *v.t.* **1.** to exert a force upon or against (a thing) in order to move it away. **2.** to move (*away, off,* etc.) by exerting force; shove; thrust; drive. **3.** to make by pushing obstacles aside: *to push one's way through the crowd.* **4.** to press or urge (a person, action, thing, etc.) towards some action or purpose. **5.** to peddle (narcotics). ◇*v.i.* **6.** to exert a thrusting force upon something: *Don't push.* **7.** to put forth strong or continuous efforts. ◇*v.* **8. push off**, **a.** to move away from the shore, etc., as the result of a push. **b.** *Colloq.* to leave; go away. **9. push on**, to continue; proceed. ◇*n.* **10.** an act of pushing; a shove or thrust. **11.** *Colloq.* drive or energy; enterprise: *He has a lot of push.* **12.** *Colloq.* a group or set of people who have a common interest or background: *the jazz push.* **13. the push**, *Colloq.* dismissal; rejection; the sack: *She gave him the push.* [ME, from OF, from L]

pushbike /ˈpʊʃbaɪk/, *n.* → **bicycle**.

push-button /ˈpʊʃ-bʌtn/, *n.* a device designed to close or open an electric circuit (to operate something) when a button or knob is depressed, and to return to a normal position when it is released. ◇*adj.* **2.** operated by push-buttons.

pushing /'pʊʃɪŋ/, *adv.* nearly; almost (a specified age, etc.): *pushing forty.*

Pushkin /'pʊʃkɪn/, *n.* **Aleksander Sergeevich** /əlɪk'sandə sə'geɪjəvɪtʃ/, 1799–1837, Russian poet, novelist and dramatist; noted esp. for *Eugene Onegin* (1823–31) and *Boris Godunuv* (1831).

pushover /'pʊʃoʊvə/, *n. Colloq.* **1.** anything done easily. **2.** an easily defeated person or team.

push-start /'pʊʃ-stat/, *v.t.* → **clutch-start** (def. 1).

push-up /'pʊʃ-ʌp/, *n.* an exercise in which one raises one's body from a lying down position upwards by pushing the floor with the hands, the feet remaining on the ground and the body and legs in a straight line. Also, **press-up.**

pushy /'pʊʃi/, *adj.* aggressive; presuming.

pusillanimous /pjusə'lænəməs/, *adj.* lacking strength of mind or courage; fainthearted; cowardly. [LL, from L] —**pusillanimity,** *n.*

puss /pʊs/, *n.* a cat. Also, **pussy.**

pussyfoot /'pʊsifʊt/, *v.i.* **1.** to move with a soft, stealthy tread like that of a cat. **2.** to act cautiously or timidly, as if afraid to commit oneself on a point at issue.

pussy willow, *n.* a small tree or shrub with silky catkins.

pustulant /'pʌstʃələnt/, *adj.* causing the formation of pustules. [LL]

pustule /'pʌstjul/, *n.* **1.** *Pathol.* a small swelling of the skin containing pus. **2.** any pimple-like or blister-like swelling. [ME, from L] —**pustular,** *adj.* —**pustulant,** *adj.*

put /pʊt/, *v.,* **put, putting,** *n.* ◇*v.t.* **1.** to move or place (anything) so as to get it into or out of some place or position: *to put a dish in a cupboard.* **2.** to bring into some relation, condition etc.: *to put everything in order; to put it in writing.* **3.** to place in the charge or power of a person, etc.: *to put oneself under a doctor's care.* **4.** to make someone go through or suffer something: *to put a person to death.* **5.** to set to a duty, task, action, etc.: *to put someone to work.* **6.** to judge or estimate: *He puts the distance at ten metres.* **7.** to wager; bet: *to put a bet on.* **8.** to set, give, or make: *to put an end to a practice.* **9.** to propose or submit for answer: *to put a question.* **10.** (in sport) to throw or cast, esp. with a forward motion of the hand when raised close to the shoulder: *to put the shot.* ◇*v.i.* **11.** to go, move, or proceed: *to put to sea.* ◇*v.* **12.** Some special uses are:
put about, 1. to spread (a rumor, etc.). **2.** to upset or inconvenience someone. **3.** *Naut.* to change direction on a course.
put across, to communicate; cause to be understood; explain effectively.
put aside, to save or store up. Also, **put away/by.**
put down, 1. to write down. **2.** to repress or suppress: *to put down a revolt.* **3.** to ascribe or attribute (usu. fol. by *to*): *I put my good health down to fresh air.* **4.** to destroy (an animal), esp. mercifully. **5.** to humiliate or scold.
put forward, to suggest or propose.
put in, 1. *Naut.* to enter a port or harbor. **2.** to apply (oft. fol. by *for*): *to put in for a job.* **3.** *Colloq.* to report (someone) for an offence.
put in the boot, *Colloq.* to attack savagely.
put across (someone), *Colloq.* to deceive or outwit.
put off, 1. to postpone. **2.** to distract (from): *to put someone off their work.* **3.** to disgust or cause to dislike: *The smell puts me off curry.*
put on, 1. to assume insincerely or falsely: *His sorrow is only put on.* **2.** to impose on. **3.** to cause to speak on the telephone: *She asked them to put on the manager.*
put one over, *Colloq.* to deceive; outwit; defraud.
put out, 1. to embarrass or annoy. **2.** to inconvenience.
put over, to communicate: *to put over an idea.*
put paid to, *Colloq.* to destroy finally: *Rain put paid to the picnic.*
put through, 1. to connect by telephone. **2.** to organise or carry into effect.
put up, 1. to erect. **2.** to provide (money, etc.). **3.** to have (someone) stay as a guest.
put upon, to impose on or take advantage of.
put up with, to endure; tolerate; bear.
◇*n.* **13.** a throw or cast, esp. one made with a forward motion of the hand when raised close to the shoulder, as in shot put. [ME]

putative /'pjutətɪv/, *adj.* commonly thought of as such; reputed; supposed. [late ME, from L: think]

putrefy /'pjutrəfaɪ/, *v.,* **-fied, -fying.** ◇*v.t.* **1.** to cause to rot or decay with an offensive smell. ◇*v.i.* **2.** to rot; become putrid. [ME, from OF, from L: rot] —**putrefaction,** *n.*

putrescent /pju'trɛsənt/, *adj.* becoming rotten; in process of putrefaction. [L: growing rotten]

putrid /'pjutrəd/, *adj.* **1.** (of animal or vegetable matter) in a state of foul decay or decomposition; rotten. **2.** having the smell of decaying flesh. **3.** thoroughly corrupt, disgusting, depraved, or bad. [L]

putt /pʌt/, *Golf.* ◇*v.t., v.i.* **1.** to strike (the ball) gently and carefully along the putting green towards the hole. ◇*n.* **2.** an act of putting. [var. of PUT]

putter /'pʌtə/, *n. Golf.* a club with a relatively short, stiff shaft and a wooden or iron head, used in putting. [PUTT + -ER¹]

putty /'pʌti/, *n., pl.* **-ties,** *v.,* **-tied, -tying.** ◇*n.* **1.** a kind of cement, soft like dough, made of whiting and linseed oil and used for fixing panes of glass in place, stopping up holes in woodwork, etc. **2.** any similar preparation. **3.** any person or thing easily moulded, influenced, etc.: *to be putty in someone's hands.* ◇*v.t.* **4.** to secure, cover, etc., with putty. [F: a potful]

put-upon /'pʊt-əpɒn/, *adj.* ill-used, or allowing others to demand things of one.

puzzle /'pʌzəl/, *n., v.,* **-zled, -zling.** ◇*n.* **1.** a toy or game designed to amuse by giving

puzzle   842   **pyroclastic**

difficulties to be solved by cleverness or patient effort. **2.** an obscure or uncertain matter, person or condition: *Your friend is a puzzle to me.* ◇*v.t.* **3.** to cause to feel uncertain; bewilder; perplex; confuse: *His behavior puzzles me.* **4.** to solve or unravel by careful study or effort: *to puzzle out the meaning of a sentence.* [orig. obscure] — **puzzlement,** *n.*

PVA /ˌpi vi 'eɪ/, *n. Chem.* a transparent resin, produced by the polymerisation of vinyl acetate, used as an adhesive, in paints and lacquers, etc. Also, **polyvinyl acetate.** [abbrev.]

PVC /ˌpi vi 'si/, *n. Chem.* a colorless water-resistant resin, produced by polymerisation of vinyl chloride, used in many products, including rainwear, garden hoses, gramophone records, and floor tiles. Also, **polyvinyl chloride.** [abbrev.]

p.w., *Abbrev.* per week.

pycnidium /pɪk'nɪdiəm/, *n., pl.* **-nidia** /-'nɪdiə/. a very small globe or flask-shaped asexual fungus fruit body. [NL]

pycno-, a word part meaning 'dense', 'close', 'thick', as in *pycnometer.* Also, **pykno-**; before vowels, **pych-.** [NL, combining form representing Gk *pyknós*]

pycnometer /pɪk'nɒmətə/, *n.* a flask holding a definite volume, used in determining relative density or specific gravity. Also, **pyknometer.** [PYCNO- + -METER¹]

pyelitis /paɪə'laɪtəs/, *n.* inflammation of the pelvis or outlet of the kidney. [NL, from Gk] — **pyelitic,** *adj.*

Pygmalion /pɪg'meɪliən/, *n. Gk Legend.* a sculptor and king of Cyprus, who fell in love with an ivory statue which he had made and which came to life in answer to his prayer. Compare **Galatea.**

pygmy /'pɪgmi/, *n., pl.* **-mies. 1.** a small or dwarfish person. **2.** anything very small of its kind. **3.** one of a people from equatorial Africa, mostly under 1.5 m in height. ◇*adj.* **4.** relating to small or dwarfish people. **5.** of very small size, capacity, power, etc. Also, **pigmy.** [ME, from L, from Gk: dwarfish]

pyjamas /pə'dʒaməz/, *n.* (*treated as pl.*) **1.** nightclothes consisting of loose trousers and jacket. **2.** loose trousers, usu. of silk or cotton, worn by both sexes in eastern countries. [Hind, from Pers: leg garment] — **pyjama,** *adj.*

pykno-, pycno-.

pylon /'paɪlɒn/, *n.* **1.** a steel tower or mast carrying electric, telephonic or other cables and lines. **2.** a tall structure at either side of a gate, bridge, or avenue, marking an entrance or approach. [Gk: gateway]

pyo-, word part meaning 'pus'. [Gk, combining form of *pýon*]

pyorrhoea /paɪə'riə/, *n.* a disease marked by the formation of pus at the root of the teeth. [NL] — **pyorrhoeal,** *adj.*

pyr-, a variant of **pyro-**, used occasionally before vowels or h, as in *pyran.*

pyramid /'pɪrəmɪd/, *n.* **1.** *Archit.* a massive structure built of stone, with square (or polygonal) base, and sloping sides meeting at an apex, such as those built by the ancient Egyptians as royal tombs or by the Mayas as platforms for their sanctuaries. **2.** anything of such form. **3.** a number of things heaped up or arranged in this form. **4.** *Geom.* a solid having the shape of a pyramid. **5.** *Econ.* a multi-company structure in which one company controls two or more companies, each of which may itself control a number of companies, and so on. [L *pyramis*, from Gk, of Egypt. orig.; replacing ME *pyramis*, from L] — **pyramidal,** *adj.*

Pyramus and Thisbe /ˌpɪrəməs ən 'θɪzbi/, *n.pl. Class Myth.* two young lovers of Babylon. Pyramus killed himself when he mistakenly thought Thisbe to be dead, and she committed suicide on discovering his body.

pyrazole /'pɪrəzɒl/, *n.* a colorless crystalline solid, $C_3H_4N_2$, the source of important dyestuffs.

pyre /'paɪə/, *n.* **1.** a pile or heap of wood or other burnable material. **2.** such a pile for burning a dead body. [L, from Gk]

pyrene /'paɪrin/, *n. Bot.* a fruit stone, esp. when there are several in a single fruit. [NL, from Gk: fruit stone]

Pyrenees /'pɪrəniz/, *n.pl.* a mountain range between Spain and France. Highest peak, Pic de Néthou, 3403 m.

pyrethrum /paɪ'riθrəm/, *n.* (an insecticide prepared from) a species of chrysanthemum.

pyrex /'paɪreks/, *n.* a heat-resistant glassware for baking, frying, etc. [Trademark]

pyridine /'paɪrədin/, *n.* a liquid organic base, C_5H_5N, with a pungent smell, found in coal tar, etc., the basis of many compounds, and used as a solvent and as an amine. [Gk] — **pyridic,** *adj.*

pyridoxine /ˌpaɪrə'dɒksin/, *n. Biochem.* a derivative of pyridine also known as vitamin B_6. [PYR- + -ID² + OX(YGEN) + -INE²]

pyrimidine /paɪ'rɪmədin/, *n.* **1.** a heterocyclic compound, $C_4H_4N_2$, containing two nitrogen atoms in the ring. **2.** any of a group of compounds containing this group. [alteration of PYRIDINE]

pyrite /'paɪraɪt/, *n.* a very common brass-yellow mineral, iron disulfide (FeS_2), with a metallic lustre, burnt to sulfur dioxide in the manufacture of sulfuric acid; fool's gold. Also, **pyrites, iron pyrites.** [L] — **pyritic, pyritical,** *adj.*

pyrites /paɪ'raɪtiz/, *n.* **1.** pyrite (sometimes called **iron pyrites**). **2.** → **marcasite. 3.** any of various other sulfides, as of copper, tin, etc. [L, from Gk: orig. adj., of or in fire]

pyro-, a word part used **1.** *Geol.* in the names of minerals, rocks, etc., indicating a quality produced by the action of fire. **2.** to mean 'of, relating to, or concerned with fire'. Also, before vowels, **pyr-.** [Gk, combining form of *pŷr* fire]

pyroclastic /paɪrou'klæstɪk/, *adj.* composed chiefly of volcanic fragments as agglomerate, tuff, and certain other rocks.

pyrogenic /paɪroʊˈdʒɛnɪk/, *adj.* **1.** producing heat or fever. **2.** (of igneous rocks) produced by fire.

pyromagnetic /ˌpaɪroʊmægˈnɛtɪk/, *adj.* **1.** relating to or depending upon the combined action of heat and magnetism. **2.** relating to magnetic properties as changing with the temperature.

pyromania /paɪrəˈmeɪniə/, *n.* a very great desire for setting things on fire. —**pyromaniac**, *n.* —**pyromaniacal**, *adj.*

pyrometer /paɪˈrɒmətə/, *n.* an apparatus for judging high temperatures which depends commonly on observation of color or measurement of electric current produced by heating of dissimilar metals. —**pyrometric**, *adj.*

pyrotechnics /paɪroʊˈtɛknɪks/, *n.* **1.** Also, **pyrotechny** /ˈpaɪroʊtɛkni/ the art of making and using fireworks. **2.** a brilliant or sensational display, of speaking, etc. —**pyrotechnic**, *adj.* —**pyrotechnist**, *n.*

pyroxene /ˈpaɪrɒksiːn/, *n.* a very common group of minerals of many varieties, silicates of magnesium, iron, calcium, and other elements, occurring in rocks, chiefly igneous. [F, from Gk] —**pyroxenic**, *adj.*

pyroxenite /paɪˈrɒksənaɪt/, *n.* a type of igneous rock composed largely of pyroxene of any kind.

Pyrrhic victory /ˈpɪrɪk ˈvɪktəri/, *n.* a victory gained at too great a cost. [from *Pyrrhus*, 319–272 BC, king of Epirus, who won such a victory over the Romans at Asculum in 279 BC]

pyrrhotite /ˈpɪrətaɪt/, *n.* a common mineral, iron sulfide (nearly FeS), occurring in crystalline and massive forms, of a bronze color and metallic lustre, and generally slightly magnetic. Also, **pyrrhotine** /ˈpɪrətaɪn/. [Gk: redness]

pyruvic acid /paɪˈruːvɪk/, *n.* an organic acid, $CH_3COCOOH$, important in many biochemical processes. [PYR(O)- + L *ūv(a)* grape + -IC]

Pythagoras /paɪˈθægərəs/, *n.* c. 582–c. 500 BC, Greek philosopher, mathematician, and religious reformer. —**Pythagorean**, *adj.*

Pythagoras's theorem, *n.* the geometrical theorem which states that, in a right-angled triangle, the square on the hypotenuse is equal to the sum of the squares on the other two sides. [see PYTHAGORAS]

Pythian games /ˈpɪθiən ɡeɪmz/, *n.pl.* one of the great national festivals of ancient Greece, held every four years at Delphi in honor of Apollo.

python /ˈpaɪθən/, *n.* **1.** any of various nonvenomous snakes, generally large and with vestiges of hind limbs, which kill by constriction. **2.** *Gk Myth.* (*cap.*) a huge servant or monster which guarded a chasm, fabled to have been slain by Apollo near Delphi. [L, from Gk]

pyx /pɪks/, *n.* **1.** *Rom Cath Ch.* **a.** the box or vessel in which the reserved Eucharist or communion elements are kept. **b.** a box for storing relics. **2.** a box or chest at a mint, in which specimen coins are deposited and reserved for trial by weight and assay. Also, **pix.** [ME, from L *pyxis*, from Gk: a box, orig., made of boxwood]

pyxidium /pɪkˈsɪdiəm/, *n., pl.* **pyxidia** /pɪkˈsɪdiə/. a seed vessel whose upper part opens like a lid to release the seeds inside. [NL, from GK: little box]

Qq

Q, q, *n., pl.* **Q's** or **Qs, q's** or **qs.** the 17th letter of the English alphabet.

q, *Symbol.* **1.** quintal. ◇*Abbrev.* **2.** quart. **3.** quarter. **4.** quarterly. **5.** quarto. **6.** queen. **7.** question.

Q, *Abbrev.* **1.** Queen. **2.** Queensland. **3.** Question. **4.** Quotient. **5.** quarto.

Qaddafi /gə'dɑfi/, *n.* **Moamar** /'mouəmɑ/ → **Gaddafi**.

Qantas /'kwɒntəs/, *n.* the Australian international airline, founded in 1920 as the Queensland and Northern Territory Aerial Services Ltd, with Sir Fergus McMartin as provisional chairman, PJ McGuinness and W Hudson Fysh as the pilots and WH Baird as the mechanic. [*Q*(ueensland) *a*(nd) *N*(orthern) *T*(erritory) *A*(erial) *S*(ervices)]

Qattara Depression /kə'tɑrə/, *n.* an arid basin in the Libyan Desert in north-western Egypt. 18 000 km². Lowest point 133 m below sea level.

QC /kju 'si/, *Abbrev.* Queen's Counsel.

QED /kju ɪ 'di/, which was to be shown or proved. [L *quod erat dēmonstrandum*]

Qing /tʃɪŋ/, *n.* the last imperial dynasty in China, 1644–1911, founded by the Manchus. Formerly, **Ch'ing**.

Qingdao /tʃɪŋ'daʊ/, *n.* a port in eastern China in eastern Shandong province. Pop. 1 470 000 (1985 est.). Formerly, **Tsingtao**.

Qld, *Abbrev.* Queensland.

QM, *Abbrev.* Quartermaster.

qq. v., *Abbrev.* which (words, etc.) see. [L *quae vidē*]

qr, *Abbrev.* quarter.

q.t. /kju 'ti/, *Colloq.* ◇*adj.* **1.** quiet. ◇*n.* **2. on the q.t.,** secretly.

qto, *Abbrev.* quarto.

qtr, *Abbrev.* **1.** quarter. **2.** quarterly.

qua /kweɪ, kwɑ/, *adv.* as; as being; in the character or capacity of. [L]

quack[1] /kwæk/, *v.i.* **1.** to utter the cry of a duck, or a sound like it. ◇*n.* **2.** the cry of a duck, or some similar sound. [imitative]

quack[2] /kwæk/, *n.* **1.** an ignorant or deceitful person who pretends to have medical or other skill; charlatan. ◇*adj.* **2.** relating to a quack: *a quack doctor; quack methods.* [D *quacksalver.* See QUACK[1], SALVE] —**quackery,** *n.*

quad[1] /kwɒd/, *n. Colloq.* a quadrangle, orig. of a college. [short for QUADRANGLE; orig. university slang]

quad[2] /kwɒd/, *n. Colloq.* → **quadruplet**.

quad[3] /kwɒd/, *n.* a paper size. See Appendix. [short for QUADRUPLE]

quadr-, a variant of **quadri-,** before vowels, as in *quadrangle*.

quadrangle /'kwɒdræŋgəl/, *n.* **1.** a plane figure having four angles and four sides; a quadrilateral. **2.** a quadrangular space or court wholly or nearly surrounded by buildings, as in a college, etc. **3.** a building or buildings about such a space or court. [ME, from LL: four-cornered (thing)] —**quadrangular,** *adj.*

quadrant /'kwɒdrənt/, *n.* **1.** a quarter of a circle; an arc of 90°. **2.** the area included between such an arc and two radii drawn one to each extremity. **3.** something shaped like a quarter of a circle, as a part of a machine. **4.** *Geom.* one of the four parts into which a plane is divided by two perpendicular lines. **5.** an instrument, usu. containing a graduated arc of 90°, used in astronomy, navigation, etc., for measuring altitudes. [ME, from L: fourth part] —**quadrantal,** *adj.*

quadraphonic /kwɒdrə'fɒnɪk/, *adj.* relating to four-channel sound reproduction. Also, **quadrophonic**.

quadrasonic /kwɒdrə'sɒnɪk/, *adj.* → **quadraphonic**. Also, **quadrisonic**.

quadrate /'kwɒdrət/, *adj.* **1.** square; rectangular. ◇*n.* **2.** a square, or something square or rectangular. [ME, from L: made square]

quadratic /kwɒd'rætɪk/, *adj.* **1.** square. **2.** *Alg.* involving the square and no higher power of the unknown quantity; the second degree: *a quadratic equation.* ◇*n.* **3.** *Alg.* a quadratic polynomial or equation.

quadrature /'kwɒdrətʃə/, *n.* **1.** the act of squaring. **2.** the act or process of finding a square equal in area to a given surface, esp. a surface bounded by a curve. [L]

quadri-, a word part meaning 'four'. Also, before vowels, **quadr-**. [L]

quadricentennial /kwɒdrəsɛn'tɛniəl/, *adj.* relating to, consisting of, or marking the end of, a period of 400 years.

quadriceps /'kwɒdrəsɛps/, *n.* the great muscle of the front of the thigh, which stretches the leg and is considered as having four heads or origins. [NL, from L]

quadrilateral /kwɒdrə'lætrəl, -'lætərəl/, *adj.* **1.** having four sides. ◇*n.* **2.** a plane figure having four sides and four angles. **3.** something of this form. [L: four-sided]

quadrille /kwə'drɪl/, *n.* **1.** a square dance for four couples. **2.** the music for such a dance. [F, from Sp: company, troop, from L]

quadrillion /kwɒ'drɪljən/, *n.* **1.** a million times a trillion, or 10^{24}. ◇*adj.* **2.** amounting to a quadrillion in number. [QUADR(I)- + (M)ILLION]

quadriplegia /kwɒdrə'plɪdʒə/, *n.* a condition in which the arms and legs are paralysed. [QUADRI- + (PARA)PLEGIA] —**quadriplegic,** *adj., n.*

quadrisonic /kwɒdrə'sɒnɪk/, *adj.* → **quadraphonic**.

quadruped /'kwɒdrəpɛd/, *adj.* **1.** four-footed. ◇*n.* **2.** an animal, esp. a mammal, with four feet. [L] **–quadrupedal,** *adj.*

quadruple /kwɒ'dru:pəl, 'kwɒdrəpəl/, *adj., n., v.,* **-pled, -pling.** ◇*adj.* **1.** fourfold; consisting of four parts: *a quadruple alliance.* **2.** four times as great. ◇*n.* **3.** a number, amount, etc., four times as great as another. ◇*v.t., v.i.* **4.** to make or become four times as great. [ME, from L]

quadruplet /kwɒ'dru:plət/, *n.* **1.** any group or combination of four. **2.** one of four children born at one birth. [QUADRUPLE + -ET]

quadruple time, *n. Music.* a rhythm of four beats to the bar with the accent on the first and third.

quaff /kwɒf/, *v.i., v.t.* **1.** to drink a beverage, esp. an alcoholic one, in large draughts, with hearty enjoyment. ◇*n.* **2.** the act of quaffing. [b. QUENCH and DRAUGHT]

quagmire /'kwɒgmaɪə, 'kwæg-/, *n.* **1.** a piece of water-soaked ground whose surface gives way under the foot; bog. **2.** a situation which is difficult to get out of. [*quag-* (? b. QUAKE and SAG) + MIRE]

quail[1] /kweɪl/, *n., pl.* **quails,** (*esp. collectively*) **quail.** a small ground-dwelling bird, heavy-bodied with a small head, short legs and rounded wings. [ME, from OF; of Gmc orig.]

quail[2] /kweɪl/, *v.i.* to lose heart or courage when faced with difficulty or danger; shrink with fear. [ME; orig. uncert.]

quaint /kweɪnt/, *adj.* strange or odd in an interesting, pleasing, or amusing way: *the quaint streets of an old English village.* [ME, from OF: clever, beautiful, from L: known]

quake /kweɪk/, *v.,* **quaked, quaking,** *n.* ◇*v.i.* **1.** (of people) to shake from cold, weakness, fear, anger, etc. **2.** (of things) to shake or tremble from shock, internal disturbance, or instability. ◇*n.* **3.** an earthquake. [ME; OE *cwacian* shake; tremble]

Quaker /'kweɪkə/, *n.* a member of the Society of Friends. [QUAKE, v., + -ER[1]; first used because George Fox, the founder, bade them 'tremble at the word of the Lord'] **–Quakerism,** *n.* **–Quakerish,** *adj.*

qualification /ˌkwɒlɪfəˈkeɪʃən/, *n.* **1.** a quality, achievement, etc., which fits a person for some job, position, etc. **2.** the act of qualifying. **3.** the state of being qualified. **4.** a modification, limitation, or restriction: *to assert a thing without any qualification.*

qualified /'kwɒlɪfaɪd/, *adj.* **1.** having qualities or accomplishments which fit a person for some job or position. **2.** modified, limited, or restricted in some way: *a qualified statement.*

qualify /'kwɒlɪfaɪ/, *v.,* **-fied, -fying.** ◇*v.t.* **1.** to fit with the proper or necessary qualities, skills, etc.; make competent. **2.** to attribute some quality or qualities to; characterise, call, or name. **3.** to modify in some way; limit; make less strong or positive: *to qualify a statement.* **4.** *Gram.* to modify or describe: *An adjective qualifies a noun.* ◇*v.i.* **5.** to make or show oneself fit or competent for something: *to qualify for a job.* **6.** to obtain authority, licence, power, etc. by fulfilling the necessary conditions. [ML] **–qualifier,** *n.*

qualitative /'kwɒlə,teɪtɪv, 'kwɒlətətɪv/, *adj.* relating to or concerned with quality or qualities.

qualitative analysis, *n.* chemical analysis of a substance to find out what it is made of.

quality /'kwɒləti/, *n., pl.* **-ties.** **1.** a distinguishing feature; a characteristic, property, or attribute. **2.** degree of excellence, fineness, etc., or grade of excellence: *food of poor quality; silk of the finest quality.* **3.** high grade; superiority; excellence: *goods of quality.* **4.** good or high social position, education, etc.: *a man of quality.* [ME, from L]

qualm /kwɑm/, *n.* **1.** an uneasy feeling that one may have done the wrong thing. **2.** a sudden sensation of faintness or illness, esp. of nausea. [OE *cwealm* torment, pain, plague]

quandary /'kwɒndri/, *n., pl.* **-ries.** a condition of not knowing what to do; dilemma. [orig. obscure]

quandong /'kwɒndɒŋ/, *n.* an Australian tree yielding a fruit which can be eaten raw or made into jams and jellies. [Aboriginal]

quantify /'kwɒntəfaɪ/, *v.t.,* **-fied, -fying.** to determine the quantity of; measure. [ML] **–quantification,** *n.* **–quantifiable,** *adj.*

quantitative /'kwɒntə,teɪtɪv, 'kwɒntətətɪv/, *adj.* **1.** that is or may be measured. **2.** of or relating to the describing or measuring of quantity.

quantitative analysis, *n.* chemical analysis of a substance to find out what the amounts and proportions of its constituents.

quantity /'kwɒntəti/, *n., pl.* **-ties.** **1.** an amount of anything. **2.** an amount or measure: *Mix the ingredients in the right quantities.* **3.** a considerable or great amount: *The mine has ore in quantity.* **4.** *Maths.* **a.** something to be treated according to a set of consistent rules. **b.** something having size, extent, amount, or the like. **c.** magnitude, size, volume, area, or length. [ME *quantite,* from L *quantitas*]

quantum /'kwɒntəm/, *n., pl.* **-ta.** **1.** a quantity or amount. **2.** *Phys.* **a.** one of the discrete quantities of energy of electromagnetic radiation or within atoms postulated by the quantum theory, equal to the product of Planck's constant (h) and the wave frequency. **b.** this amount of energy regarded as a unit. [L: how great, how much]

quantum mechanics, *n.* a method used to interpret atomic and subatomic systems based on quantum theory and wave mechanics. Also, **quantum theory.**

quantum theory, *n.* a theory that describes electromagnetic radiation in terms of quanta.

quarantine /'kwɒrəntin/, *n., v.,* **-tined, -tining.** ◇*n.* **1.** strict isolation to prevent the spread of disease. **2.** a period, originally forty days, of isolation required of ships, people, etc., when suspected of bringing some infectious disease to a port or place. **3.** a system of measures carried out by a public authority at ports, etc.,

quarantine for preventing the spread of disease. **4.** a place or station at which such measures are carried out, or where ships, people, etc., are kept in isolation. ◇*v.t.* **5.** to put in or subject to quarantine. [It, from L: forty]

quark /kwak/, *n.* any of three hypothetical particles which have been postulated as the basis of all other particles in the universe. [special use of *quark* in 'Three quarks for Muster Mark', from *Finnegan's Wake* by James JOYCE]

quarrel /'kworəl/, *n., v.,* -relled, -relling. ◇*n.* **1.** a disagreement usu. marking a break in friendly relations. **2.** a cause of complaint or angry feeling against a person, etc. ◇*v.i.* **3.** to disagree angrily or fall out. **4.** to argue angrily; wrangle. **5.** to raise a complaint, or find fault. [ME, from OF, from L: a complaint] —**quarreller**, *n.* —**quarrelsome**, *adj.*

quarry[1] /'kwori/, *n., pl.* -ries, *v.,* -ried, -rying. ◇*n.* **1.** a large pit, usu. open to the air, from which building stone, slate, or the like is obtained by cutting, blasting, etc. ◇*v.t.* **2.** to obtain (stone, etc.) from, or as from, a quarry. **3.** to make a quarry in. [ME, from ML: place where stone is squared, from L: to square]

quarry[2] /'kwori/, *n., pl.* -ries. **1.** an animal or bird hunted or chased. **2.** any object of a hunt or attack. [ME, from OF: skin, hide, from L]

quart /kwɔt/, *n.* a liquid measure in the imperial system, equal to ¼ gallon, or 1.136 litres. [ME, from F, from ML: fourth]

quarter /'kwɔtə/, *n.* **1.** one of the four equal or equivalent parts into which anything is or may be divided; ¼: *a quarter of an apple.* **2.** *US and Canada.* a quarter of a dollar (25 cents). **3.** a quarter of an hour (15 minutes). **4.** the moment marking this period. **5.** a quarter of a year. **6.** *Astron.* a quarter of the moon's monthly revolution around the earth. **7.** *Sport.* any one of the four periods that make up certain games, as Australian Rules, netball, etc. **8.** the area of any of the four main points of the compass. **9.** a region, district, or place. **10.** (*usu. pl.*) **a.** a living place; lodgings; residence. **b.** *Mil.* the buildings, houses, barracks, or rooms occupied by soldiers or their families. **11.** a part or member of a community, government, etc., which is not specified: *information from a high quarter.* **12.** mercy, esp. as shown to a beaten enemy in sparing his life and accepting his surrender. **13.** one of the four parts, each including a leg, of the body of a four-legged animal. **14.** *Naut.* the after part of a ship's side. ◇*v.t.* **15.** to divide into four equal or equivalent parts. **16.** to cut the body of (a person) into quarters, esp. in putting to death for treason or the like. **17.** to provide with lodgings in a particular place. **18.** to assign to a particular position for living purposes, action, etc., as on a ship. **19.** to cross (the ground) from left to right and right to left while advancing, as dogs in search of game. **20.** to place (different coats of arms) on the quarters of a shield. ◇*v.i.* **21.** to take up or be in quarters; lodge. ◇*adj.* **22.** being one of the four equal, or roughly equal, parts into which anything is or may be divided. [ME, from OF, from L: fourth part]

quaternary

quarterdeck /'kwɔtədɛk/, *n.* the upper deck between the mainmast and the stern of a ship.

quarter horse, *n.* a small horse with well developed hindquarters and chest, bred for speed over short distances, and used for roping and cutting out cattle.

quarterly /'kwɔtəli/, *adj., adv., n., pl.* -lies. ◇*adj., adv.* **1.** (happening, done, etc.) every three months. ◇*n.* **2.** a magazine or the like appearing every three months.

quartermaster /'kwɔtəmastə/, *n.* **1.** *Mil.* an officer in charge of quarters, food allowances, clothing, equipment, and transport. **2.** *Navy.* a seaman having charge of signals, steering apparatus, etc.

quarter note, *n. US Music.* → **crotchet** (def. 1).

quartet /kwɔ'tɛt/, *n.* **1.** any group of four persons or things, esp. singers or players. **2.** a musical composition for four voices or instruments. Also, **quartette**. [F, from It: fourth, from L]

quartile /'kwɔtaɪl/, *n. Stats.* one of the values of a variable which divides the distribution of the variable into four groups having equal frequencies. [ML, from L: fourth]

quarto /'kwɔtou/, *n., pl.* -tos. a paper size. See Appendix. [L]

quartz /kwɔts/, *n.* **1.** one of the commonest minerals, silicon dioxide SiO_2, having many varieties which differ in colour, lustre, etc., an important part of many rocks. ◇*adj.* **2.** → **quartz-crystal**. [G]

quartz crystal, *n.* a piece of piezoelectric quartz ground so as to vibrate at a particular frequency.

quartz-crystal /'kwɔts-krɪstəl/, *adj.* (of a watch, clock, etc.) having the function of the hairspring of a traditional clock performed by a quartz crystal, which gives great accuracy. Also, **quartz**.

quartzite /'kwɔtsaɪt/, *n.* a coarse-grained rock consisting basically of quartz in interlocking grains.

quasar /'kweɪza, -sa/, *n.* one of many extremely distant, very massive sources of high-energy, radio-frequency, electromagnetic radiation of unknown structure. [short for *quas(istell)ar (source)*]

quash[1] /kwɒʃ/, *v.t.* to put down completely; subdue. [ME, from OF, from L: shake]

quash[2] /kwɒʃ/, *v.t.* to make void or set aside (a law, decision, etc.). [ME, from OF, from L: shake]

quasi /'kwazi/, *adj.* **1.** resembling; as it were. ◇*adv.* **2.** seemingly, but not actually. [ME, from L]

quasi-, a prefix form of 'quasi', *adj.* and *adv.,* as in *quasi-official* meaning 'as though official'.

Quasimodo /kwazi'moudou/, a hunchbacked bellringer who is a character in Victor Hugo's novel *Notre-Dame de Paris* (1831).

quaternary /kwə'tɜnəri/, *adj., n., pl.* -ries. ◇*adj.* **1.** consisting of four. **2.** arranged in

quaternary   847   **questionable**

fours. **3.** (*cap.*) *Geol.* relating to the most recent geological period, being the last main division of the Cainozoic era, following the Tertiary. ◇*n.* **4.** a group of four. **5.** the number four. [ME, from L *quaternārius*]

quatrain /ˈkwɒtreɪn/, *n.* a stanza or poem of four lines of verse. [F]

quattrocento /ˌkwætroʊˈtʃentoʊ, kwɒt-/, *n.* the 15th century, used in reference to Italian art of that time. [It: 400, short for *mille quattrocento* 1400]

quaver /ˈkweɪvə/, *v.i.* **1.** to shake or tremble (now said usu. of the voice). **2.** to sound, speak, or sing in a shaking manner. ◇*v.t.* **3.** to express, say, or sing with a trembling voice. ◇*n.* **4.** a quavering shake or tone, esp. in the voice. **5.** *Music.* a note equal in length to half a crotchet. [ME; b. QUAKE and WAVER] **–quavery,** *adj.*

quay /kiː/, *n.* a landing place, built alongside water used by ships, for vessels unloading or loading cargo, etc. [OF]

Queanbeyan /ˈkwɪnbiən/, *n.* a city in NSW, just east of Canberra; agriculture; building industry. Pop. 21 850 (1986).

queasy /ˈkwiːzi/, *adj.*, **-sier**, **-siest**. **1.** (of the stomach, a person) given to feeling like vomiting. **2.** (of articles of food) tending to cause vomiting. **3.** (of feelings, etc.) uneasy or uncomfortable. **4.** too fussy or particular. [late ME; orig. obscure]

Quebec /kwəˈbek/, *n.* **1.** a province in eastern Canada. Pop. 6 540 276 (1986); 1 540 689 km². **2.** the capital of this province; a seaport on the St Lawrence; the capital of New France from 1663 to 1759, when it was taken by the English. Pop. 603 267 (1986).

queen /kwiːn/, *n.* **1.** the wife of a king. **2.** a female sovereign. **3.** a woman, or something personified as a woman, that is chief in any respect: *a beauty queen*. **4.** a playing card bearing the formalised picture of a queen, in most games counting as next below the king. **5.** *Chess.* the most powerful piece. **6.** the egg-laying female of ants, bees, wasps, or termites. **7.** *Colloq.* a male homosexual. ◇*v.i.* **8.** to behave in an overbearing manner (usu. fol. by indefinite *it*). **9.** **queen** (**it**) **up,** *Colloq.* (of a man) to put on female dress or manner. [ME; wife, queen] **–queenly,** *adj.*

Queen Anne, *adj.* relating to a style of architecture in England in the early 18th century combining classical and baroque elements.

queen dowager, *n.* the widow of a king.

queen mother, *n.* a queen dowager who is also mother of a ruling king or queen.

Queensberry rules, /ˈkwɪnzbəri rulz, -bri/ *n.pl.* the set of rules followed in modern boxing. [named after the 8th Marquess of *Queensberry*, 1844–1900, British sportsman]

Queen's Counsel, *n.* a member of the senior of the two grades of barrister. Compare **junior**. See also **silk**.

queen's English, *n.* standard southern British English, esp. as considered as correct usage. Also, **king's English**.

Queensland /ˈkwɪnzlənd, -lænd/, *n.* a state of Australia, in the north-east, separated from NSW in 1859. Pop. 2 587 315 (1986); 1 727 200 km². *Cap.:* Brisbane.

Queensland lungfish, *n.* a large, primitive, freshwater fish with a paddle-shaped tail and limblike fins, which usu. breathes through its gills but can also take air into a lung-like sac.

Queensland maple, *n.* an evergreen Australian tree with small flowers and a conelike fruit, and whose timber is valued for furniture.

Queensland nut, *n.* → **macadamia nut**.

queen's scout, *n.* a scout who has achieved the greatest degree of skill in scouting.

Queenstown /ˈkwɪnztaʊn/, *n.* a copper-mining town in western Tas, known for the barrenness of the hills surrounding it. Pop. 3593 (1986).

queer /kwɪə/, *adj.* **1.** strange from the normal point of view; singular or odd: *a queer idea*. **2.** *Colloq.* of questionable character; suspicious; shady. **3.** unwell; not normal: *I feel queer*. **4.** *Colloq.* mentally unbalanced. **5.** *Colloq.* homosexual. ◇*v.t.* **6.** *Colloq.* to spoil; jeopardise; ruin. ◇*n.* **7.** *Colloq.* a male homosexual. [G: oblique, cross, adverse]

quell /kwel/, *v.t.* **1.** to put an end to (disorder, mutiny, etc.); suppress; extinguish. **2.** to conquer; subdue. **3.** to quiet or calm (feelings, etc.). [OE: kill] **–queller,** *n.*

quench /kwentʃ/, *v.t.* **1.** to lessen (usu. thirst) by satisfying; allay. **2.** to put out (a fire, flames, etc.). **3.** to cool (hot steel, etc.) suddenly, by plunging into water. **4.** to overcome; stifle; subdue. [OE]

querulous /ˈkwerələs/, *adj.* complaining; peevish. [L]

query /ˈkwɪəri/, *n., pl.* **-ries**, *v.,* **-ried**, **-rying**. ◇*n.* **1.** a question; enquiry. **2.** doubt; uncertainty. ◇*v.t.* **3.** to ask or enquire about. **4.** to question (a statement, etc.) as doubtful or unable to be understood. **5.** to ask questions of. [L: ask]

quest /kwest/, *n.* **1.** a search made in order to find or obtain something: *a quest for gold*. ◇*v.i.* **2.** to search; seek (usu. fol. by *for* or *after*). [ME, from OF, from L: sought, asked] **–quester,** *n.*

question /ˈkwestʃən/, *n.* **1.** a sentence in which words, punctuation, etc., are put in such a way as to ask for or get information. **2.** a problem for discussion or under discussion. **3.** a matter or point of uncertainty or difficulty; a case (fol. by *of*): *It is a question of time*. **4.** the act of asking or enquiring; interrogation; a query. **5. beyond question,** without the need for argument. **6. call in** or **into question,** to demand something be explained or supported. **7. in question,** under consideration. **8. out of the question,** not to be considered; impossible. ◇*v.t.* **9.** to ask a question or questions of; interrogate. **10.** to make a question of; doubt. **11.** to challenge; dispute. ◇*v.i.* **12.** to ask a question or questions. [ME, from AF, from L] **–questioning,** *adj.*

questionable /ˈkwestʃənəbəl/, *adj.* **1.** of doubtful honesty, respectability, etc. **2.** open

questionable   848   **quince**

to question or argument; doubtful or uncertain: *Whether this is true is questionable.*

question mark, *n.* a mark indicating a question, as in English, the mark (?) placed after the question; interrogation mark.

questionnaire /kwestʃənˈeə, kes-/, *n.* a list of questions, usu. printed on a form, for obtaining information from people. [F]

question time, *n.* (in parliament) the period during which ministers reply to questions from members.

queue /kjuː/, *n., v.,* queued, queuing. ◇*n.* **1.** a file or line of people, vehicles, etc., waiting in turn to obtain something, move along a road, etc. **2.** a plait of hair worn hanging down behind. ◇*v.i.* **3.** to form in a line while waiting; line up (oft. fol. by *up*). [F, from L: tail]

Quezon City /ˈkeɪzɒn/, *n.* a city in the Philippines, on Luzon Island north-east of Manila; designated the national capital in 1948, but later replaced by Manila in 1976. Pop. 1 326 035 (1984 est.).

quibble /ˈkwɪbəl/, *n., v.,* -bled, -bling. ◇*n.* **1.** the use of language or argument about unrelated or unimportant detail to avoid the point being considered. ◇*v.i.* **2.** to avoid the real point by concentrating on less important things. [? from *quib* gibe, apparently var. of QUIP] —**quibbler,** *n.* —**quibbling,** *adj.*

quiche /kiːʃ/, *n.* a tart with a filling of eggs, milk and often cheese, originally from northeastern France. [F (Alsace d.), from G: cake]

quick /kwɪk/, *adj.* **1.** (of an action, process, etc.) done or happening with rapidity; prompt; immediate. **2.** that is over or completed within a short space of time. **3.** (of movement) swift or rapid. **4.** hasty; impatient: *a quick temper.* **5.** (of a person) acting, doing, understanding, etc., at once or immediately. ◇*n.* **6.** living people: *the quick and the dead.* **7.** the tender sensitive flesh of the living body, esp. that under the nails: *nails bitten down to the quick.* **8. cut to the quick,** to hurt deeply the feelings of. ◇*adv.* **9.** quickly. [OE: living] —**quickly,** *adv.*

quicken /ˈkwɪkən/, *v.t.* **1.** to make more rapid; accelerate; hasten: *She will quicken her pace.* **2.** to make quick or alive; restore life to. **3.** to give or restore strength or activity to: *Exciting travel stories can awaken any imagination.* ◇*v.i.* **4.** to become more active, sensitive, etc. **5.** to become alive; receive life. **6.** (of a child in the womb) to begin to make movements which can be felt by the mother. —**quickener,** *n.*

quicklime /ˈkwɪklaɪm/, *n.* unslaked lime. See **lime**[1].

quicksand /ˈkwɪksænd/, *n.* an area of soft or loose wet sand of considerable depth, yielding under weight and so dangerous to people, animals, etc., who may sink into it.

quicksilver /ˈkwɪksɪlvə/, *n.* **1.** the metallic element mercury. ◇*adj.* **2.** changing rapidly. [OE: living silver]

quick smart, *adv.* quickly; promptly.

quickstep /ˈkwɪkstep/, *n.* **1.** a rapid ballroom dance step. **2.** (formerly) a lively step used in marching.

quick-tempered /ˈkwɪk-tempəd/, *adj.* easily moved to anger.

quick-witted /ˈkwɪk-wɪtəd/, *adj.* able to think swiftly and effectively.

quid[1] /kwɪd/, *n.* a piece of something, esp. tobacco, for holding in the mouth and chewing. [OE: cud]

quid[2] /kwɪd/, *n., pl.* **quid, quids.** *Colloq.* **1.** (formerly) a pound in money, esp. £1 as a pound note. **2. a quick quid,** money earned with little effort, oft. by dishonest means. **3. not for quids,** never. **4. not the full quid,** mentally slow; dull. [orig. uncert.]

quiddity /ˈkwɪdəti/, *n., pl.* **-ties. 1.** that which makes a thing what it is; the essential nature. **2.** a small and unimportant point, as in argument. [ML, from L: what]

quid pro quo /kwɪd proʊ ˈkwoʊ/, *n.* **1.** one thing in return for another. **2.** *Law.* compensation, consideration. [L: something for something]

quiescent /kwiˈɛsənt/, *adj.* being at rest, quiet, or still. [L: keeping quiet] —**quiescence,** *n.*

quiet /ˈkwaɪət/, *n.* **1.** freedom from noise or other disturbance; tranquillity; rest; repose. **2.** peace; a peaceful condition of affairs. ◇*adj.* **3.** making no disturbance or trouble. **4.** free from unwanted or annoying activity; tranquil; peaceful: *a quiet life.* **5.** free from worrying feelings, etc. **6.** avoiding or free from busy activity: *a quiet evening at home.* **7.** still or moving gently: *quiet waters.* **8.** making no noise or sound, esp. no annoying sound: *quiet neighbors.* **9.** free, or comparatively free, from noise: *a quiet street.* **10.** holding back in speech, manner, etc.; saying little: *a quiet person.* **11.** (of speech, manner, etc.) said or done in a non-showy way; unobtrusive. **12. on the quiet,** *Colloq.* secretly. ◇*v.t., v.i.* **13.** to make or become quiet. [ME, from L: rest, repose] —**quietly,** *adv.* —**quietness,** *n.*

quieten /ˈkwaɪətn/, *v.t., v.i.* to make or become quiet.

quietus /kwaɪˈiːtəs/, *n.* **1.** a finishing stroke; anything that has the effect of ending or settling: *a quietus to a cruel story.* **2.** discharge or release from life. [ML: quit, from L: at rest]

quill /kwɪl/, *n.* **1.** one of the large feathers of the wing or tail of a bird. **2.** the hard, tubelike part of a feather of a bird, nearest the body. **3.** a feather, usu. of a goose, formed into a pen for writing. **4.** one of the hollow spines on an echidna. [ME]

quilt /kwɪlt/, *n.* **1.** a cover for a bed, made by stitching together, usu. in patterns or lines, two thicknesses of fabric filled with wool, down, etc. ◇*v.t.* **2.** to stitch together (two pieces of cloth with a soft filling), usu. in an ornamental pattern. [ME, from OF, from L: mattress, cushion] —**quilted,** *adj.*

quince /kwɪns/, *n.* the hard, yellowish, acid fruit of a small, hardy tree. [ME, from

quince

OF, from L, from Gk: quince, lit., (apple) of *Cydonia* (ancient city of Crete)]

quincunx /'kwɪn'kʌŋks/, *n.* an arrangement of five objects in a square or rectangle, one at each corner and one in the middle. —**quincuncial**, *adj.*

quinella /kwə'nelə/, *n.* a form of betting where bets are laid on the first and second place-getters in any order in the one race. [Amer Sp: a game of chance]

quinine /'kwɪnɪn, kwə'nin/, *n.* a bitter colorless alkaloid used in medicine as a stimulant and to treat malaria. [Sp (from Quechua: bark) + -INE²]

quinque-, a word part meaning 'five'. [L]

quinquereme /'kwɪŋkwərɪm/, *n.* an ancient ship having five banks of oars.

quinsy /'kwɪnzi/, *n., pl.* **-sies**. *Obs.* →**tonsillitis**. [ME, from ML, from LL, from Gk: sore throat]

quintal /'kwɪntl/, *n.* a unit of mass equal to 100 kg. Symbol: q [late ME, from ML, from Ar: weight of a hundred pounds, probably from L: hundred]

quintessence /kwɪn'tesəns/, *n.* **1.** the purest form of a substance. **2.** the most perfect example of something. [ME, from ML: fifth essence] —**quintessential**, *adj.*

quintet /kwɪn'tet/, *n.* **1.** any set or group of five persons or things, esp. singers or players. **2.** a musical composition for five voices or instruments. Also, **quintette**. [F, from It, from L: fifth]

quintuple /kwɪn'tʌpəl, kwɪn'tjupəl/, *adj., n., v.,* **-pled, -pling.** ◇*adj.* **1.** consisting of five parts. ◇*n.* **3.** a number, amount, etc., five times as great as another. ◇*v.t., v.i.* **4.** to make or become five times as great. [F]

quintuplet /kwɪn'tʌplət/, *n.* **1.** any group or combination of five. **2.** one of five children born at one birth.

quip /kwɪp/, *n., v.,* **quipped, quipping**. ◇*n.* **1.** a clever or witty saying. **2.** a sharp, cutting remark. ◇*v.i.* **3.** to utter quips. [L: indeed] —**quipster**, *n.*

quire /kwaɪə/, *n.* 24 sheets of paper of the same size. [ME]

Quirinal /'kwɪrənəl/, *n.* **1.** one of the Seven Hills of Rome on which the ancient city was built. **2.** the Italian civil authority or government (as distinguished from the Vatican). [L from *Quirīnus*, an early Roman god of war, identified with ROMULUS]

quirk /kwɜk/, *n.* **1.** a trick or peculiarity. **2.** a sudden twist, turn, or curve. [orig. obscure] —**quirky**, *adj.*

Quiros /'kwɪrɒs/, *n.* **Pedro Fernandez de**, 1565–1615, Spanish navigator, born in Portugal; made an unsuccessful attempt to find the Great South Land.

quisling /'kwɪzlɪŋ/, *n.* a person who is disloyal to his own country by helping an occupying enemy force. [from Vidkun *Quisling*, 1887–1945, pro-Nazi Norwegian leader]

quit /kwɪt/, *v.,* **quitted** or **quit, quitting,** *adj.* ◇*v.t.* **1.** to stop, cease, or discontinue. **2.** to depart from; leave. **3.** to give up; let go; relinquish. **4.** *Archaic.* to carry (oneself). ◇*v.i.* **5.** to cease from doing something; stop. **6.** to depart or leave. **7.** to give up one's job or position; resign. ◇*adj.* **8.** set free from responsibility, etc.; free, clear, or rid (usu. fol. by *of*). [ME, from OF, from ML: release, discharge, from LL: quiet]

quite /kwaɪt/, *adv.* **1.** completely, wholly, or entirely: *quite the opposite*. **2.** actually, really, or truly: *quite a sudden change*. **3.** to a partial or considerable degree: *quite pretty; quite a lot*. ◇*interj.* **4.** (an expression of agreement, etc.). [ME; adv. use of ME *quite*, adj., QUIT]

quitrent /'kwɪtrent/, *n.* rent paid instead of services which might otherwise have been required. Also, **quit-rent**. [QUIT, *adj.,* + RENT¹]

quits /kwɪts/, *adj.* **1.** on equal terms after paying back money due, returning blows received in a fight, etc. **2. call it quits**, *Colloq.* **a.** to leave an activity, esp. for a short while. **b.** to agree to end an argument, competition, etc. [See QUIT, *adj.,* -s of uncert. orig.]

quiver¹ /'kwɪvə/, *v.i., v.t.* **1.** to shake with a slight, rapid motion. ◇*n.* **2.** the act or condition of quivering; tremble; tremor. [ME] —**quivery**, *adj.*

quiver² /'kwɪvə/, *n.* a case for holding arrows. [ME, from OF *quivre*]

quixotic /kwɪk'sɒtɪk/, *adj.* given to unreal, sometimes dangerous ideas of bravery and love; visionary. [orig. with ref. to *Don Quixote*, the hero of a romance by Miguel de Cervantes, 1547–1616, Spanish novelist] —**quixotism**, *n.*

quiz /kwɪz/, *v.,* **quizzed, quizzing,** *n., pl.* **quizzes**. ◇*v.t.* **1.** to question closely. **2.** to examine or test (a student or class) informally by questions. ◇*n.* **3.** a general knowledge test, esp. as a show on radio, television, etc. **4.** an informal test of a student or class. [orig. uncert.]

quizzical /'kwɪzɪkəl/, *adj.* **1.** odd, queer, or comical. **2.** (of looks, etc.) knowing or teasing: *a quizzical smile*.

quod /kwɒd/, *n. Colloq.* prison. [orig. uncert.]

quoin /kɔɪn/, *n.* **1.** the outer solid angle of a wall or the like. **2.** one of the stones forming it. **3.** a wedge-shaped piece of wood, stone, etc. [var. of COIN]

quoit /kɔɪt/, *n.* **1.** Also, **deck quoit**. a flattish ring of iron or some other material thrown in play to encircle an upright peg. **2.** (*pl.,* treated as sing.) the game played this way. [ME *coyte*; orig. unknown]

quokka /'kwɒkə/, *n.* See **wallaby**. [Aboriginal]

quoll /kwɒl/, *n.* See **native cat**.

Quong Tart /kwɒŋ 'tat/, *n.* 1850–1903, Australian merchant and entrepreneur, born in China; active in promoting better relations between Europeans and Chinese in Australia.

quorum /ˈkwɔrəm/, n. the minimum number of members of a body required to be present to carry out business legally. [L: of whom; from a use of the word in commissions written in Latin]

quota /ˈkwoʊtə/, n. 1. a proportional share of a total which is due from, or belongs to, a particular district, area, person, etc. 2. the number of people of a particular group allowed to move to a country, join an institution, etc. 3. the maximum amount of something allowed to be produced in an orderly marketing system. [ML, short for L *quota pars* how great a part?]

quotation /kwoʊˈteɪʃən/, n. 1. a passage taken or repeated from a book, speech, etc. 2. the act or practice of quoting. 3. *Comm.* a statement of the present price of goods, shares, etc.

quotation mark, n. one of the marks used to indicate the beginning and end of a quotation, in English usu. consisting of an inverted comma (') at the beginning and an apostrophe (') at the end, or double marks at beginning and end (" ").

quote /kwoʊt/, v., **quoted, quoting**, n. ◇v.t. 1. to repeat (a passage, etc.) from a book, speech, etc. 2. to repeat words from (a book, author, etc.). 3. to bring forward or refer to. 4. *Comm.* to state (a price). ◇v.i. 5. to make a quotation or quotations, as from a book or author. ◇n. 6. a quotation. 7. → **quotation mark**. [ME, from ML: divide into chapters and verses, from L: how many] −**quotable**, *adj.*

quoth /kwoʊθ/, v.t. *Archaic.* said (used with nouns, and with first and third person pronouns, and always placed before the subject): *quoth he, 'Never more'.* [OE: say]

quotient /ˈkwoʊʃənt/, n. (in mathematics) the result of division; the number of times one quantity is contained in another. [ME, from L: how many times]

q.v. /kju 'vi/, (as an instruction denoting a cross-reference in a book, article, etc.) which see. [L *quod vide*]

Rr

R, r, *n., pl.* **R's** or **Rs, r's** or **rs.** 1. the 18th letter of the English alphabet. 2. See **three R's.**

r., *Abbrev.* 1. *Maths.* radius. 2. rare. 3. replacing. 4. right. 5. *Cricket, Baseball, etc.* runs. 6. *Maths.* ratio.

R /aː/ *for def. 1., Abbrev.* 1. (of a film) for restricted exhibition; not suitable for people under 18 years of age. 2. River. ◇*Symbol.* 3. *Phys, Chem.* gas constant. 4. *Chem.* radical. 5. *Phys.* roentgen. 6. *Elect.* resistance. 7. *Maths.* set of real numbers.

Ra, *Chem. Symbol.* radium.

Ra /rɑ/, *n.* the great sun-god of the Egyptians, the sovereign god of ancient Egypt, in art typically represented as a hawk-headed man bearing on his head the solar disc and the sacred royal asp. Also **Re.** [Egypt]

RAAF /a dʌbəl eɪ ˈef, ræf/, *Abbrev.* Royal Australian Air Force.

Rabaul /rəˈbaʊl/, *n.* a town in the province of East New Britain, PNG. Pop. 15 300 (1984).

rabbi /ˈræbaɪ/, *n., pl.* **-bis.** 1. the main religious official of a synagogue; spiritual leader of a Jewish community. 2. a Jewish scholar; someone who explains and teaches the Jewish law. [ME and OE, from L, from Heb: my master]

rabbit /ˈræbət/, *n., v.,* **-bited, -biting.** ◇*n.* 1. a small, long-eared, burrowing mammal of the hare family but smaller than the hare. 2. *Cricket.* a poor batsman. ◇*v.i.* 3. to hunt rabbits. 4. *Colloq.* to talk nonsense, usu. at length (fol. by *on*). [ME] **—rabbiter,** *n.*

rabbit-warren /ˈræbət-wɒrən/, *n.* → **warren.**

rabble /ˈræbəl/, *n.* 1. a disorderly crowd; mob. 2. (*offensive*) the lowest class of people (prec. by *the*). [ME]

rabblerouser /ˈræbəlraʊzə/, *n.* a troublemaker.

Rabelais /ˈræbəleɪ/, *n.* **François** /frɒˈswa/, c. 1490-1553, French satirist and humorist; author of *Gargantua and Pantagruel* (1534).

rabid /ˈræbəd/, *adj.* 1. extraordinarily unreasoning in opinion or practice: *a rabid isolationist.* 2. furious or raging; violently intense: *rabid hunger.* 3. affected with or relating to rabies; mad. [L: raving, mad]

rabies /ˈreɪbiz/, *n.* a fatal, infectious disease of the brain which occurs in all warm-blooded animals including man. It is caused by a particular virus which occurs in saliva and is transmitted by the bite of an animal (usu. a dog) which has the disease. [L: madness, rage]

Rachmaninoff

raccoon /rəˈkun/, *n.* any of several small flesh-eating animals found mainly in North America. They live in or among trees and have greyish fur, a sharp snout and a bushy ringed tail. Also, **racoon.** [NAmer Ind: he scratches with the hands]

race[1] /reɪs/, *n., v.,* **raced, racing.** ◇*n.* 1. a contest of speed, as in running, riding, driving, sailing, etc. 2. (*pl.*) a series of races, esp. horseraces or greyhound races run at a set time over a regular course. 3. any kind of competition: *the armaments race; the race for the presidency.* 4. *Geol.* a strong or rapid current of water, as in the sea or a river. 5. (the current of water in) an artificial channel, leading water to or from a place where its energy is used. 6. a narrow passageway for livestock, as one leading to a sheep dip. 7. *Mech.* a channel, groove, or the like, for a sliding or rolling part, as for ball-bearings. 8. **not in the race,** having no chance at all. ◇*v.i.* 9. to take part in a contest of speed; run a race. 10. to run, move, or go quickly. 11. (of an engine, wheel, etc.) to run or revolve with uncontrolled speed when the load is lessened while the driving power continues the same. ◇*v.t.* 12. to run a race with; try to beat in a contest of speed: *He raced me home.* 13. to cause to run in a race or races: *to race a horse.* ◇*v.* 14. **race off with,** *Colloq.* to steal. [ME, from Scand]

race[2] /reɪs/, *n.* 1. a group of people or a population connected by common descent, blood, or heredity. 2. a subdivision of a human stock (def. 6) with a combination of hereditary physical characteristics different from those of another race. 3. a group of tribes or peoples with the same language and culture. 4. *Zool.* variety; subspecies. 5. **the human race,** mankind; the human family. [F, from It: race, breed, lineage]

racecourse /ˈreɪskɔs/, *n.* a piece of ground on which horseraces are held for public entertainment.

racehorse /ˈreɪshɔs/, *n.* a horse bred or kept for racing.

raceme /rəˈsim, ˈreɪsim/, *n.* a cluster of flowers in which each flower is on a short stalk growing out from the main stem, as in the lily-of-the-valley. [L: cluster of grapes] **—racemiferous, racemose,** *adj.*

race relations, *n.pl.* the way in which two or more races of people, esp. living together in one country, behave towards each other.

race riot, *n.* an act of mob violence resulting from hatred between different races living in (an area of) one country.

racetrack /ˈreɪstræk/, *n.* 1. a track on which races, esp. motor races, are held. 2. → **racecourse.**

Rachel /ˈreɪtʃəl/, *n. Bible.* Jacob's favorite wife, and mother of Joseph and Benjamin. [See Genesis 29-35]

rachis /ˈreɪkəs/, *n., pl.* **rachises** /ˈreɪkəsiz/, **rachides** /ˈrækədiz, ˈreɪkə-/, *Zool.* the shaft of a feather. [NL, from Gk]

Rachmaninoff /rækˈmænənɒf/, *n.* **Sergei Vassilievich** /seəˈgjeɪ vaˈsiljəvɪtʃ/, 1873-1943,

Russian romantic composer and pianist. Also **Rachmaninov**.

racial /'reɪʃəl/, *adj.* **1.** relating to or typical of race or ancestry, or a race or races. **2.** relating to the relations between people of different races.

Racine /ræ'sin, ra'sin/, *n.* **Jean Baptiste** /ʒɒ̃ ba'tist/, 1639–99, French tragic dramatist; author of *Andromache* (1667).

racism /'reɪsɪzəm/, *n.* **1.** the belief that human races have special and different characteristics which determine their particular cultures, usu. involving the idea that one's own race is better than any other. **2.** offensive or even violent behavior to members of another race arising from such a belief. **3.** a policy or system of government and society based upon it. Also, **racialism**. —**racist**, *n., adj.*

rack[1] /ræk/, *n.* **1.** a framework of bars, wires, or pegs for holding things, hanging things on, etc.: *a shoe rack; a wine rack.* **2.** a spreading framework, fixed or movable, for carrying hay, straw, etc., in large loads. **3.** *Mech.* a bar with teeth on one of its sides, meant to mesh with the teeth of a pinion, etc. **4.** an apparatus formerly in use for torturing people by stretching the body. **5. on the rack**, in great pain, distress, or anxiety. ◇*v.t.* **6.** to cause great pain or unhappiness to; torment: *Fever racked her body.* **7.** to strain in mental effort: *to rack one's brains.* **8.** to strain by physical force or violence; shake violently. [ME, from MD or MLG]

rack[2] /ræk/, *n.* **1.** wreck; destruction. **2. rack and ruin**, disrepair or collapse, esp. owing to neglect; dilapidation. [var. of WRACK]

rack[3] /ræk/, *v.i. Colloq.* in the phrase **rack off**, to leave; go: *He racked off ages ago; Rack off, hairy legs!*

rack-and-pinion /ræk-ən-'pɪnjən/, *n.* a system for changing rotary to linear motion, which uses a pinion and a matching rack (def. 3).

racket[1] /'rækət/, *n.* **1.** a loud noise, esp. of a disturbing or confusing kind; din; uproar. **2.** *Colloq.* an organised, unlawful activity such as the taking of money by threat or violence from honest businesses: *the protection racket.* **3.** *Colloq.* a dishonest scheme, trick, etc. ◇*v.i.* **4.** to make a racket or noise. [? d. *rattick* RATTLE]

racket[2] /'rækət/, *n.* →**racquet**.

racketeer /rækə'tɪə/, *n.* someone engaged in a racket (def. 2).

rack of lamb, *n.* trimmed ribs or cutlets of lamb prepared for roasting in one piece.

rack-rent /'ræk-rɛnt/, *n.* an unreasonably high rent.

raconteur /rækɒn'tɜ/, *n.* a person skilled in telling stories about interesting and amusing events. [F]

racquet /'rækət/, *n.* **1.** a light bat having a network of cord, catgut or nylon, stretched in a more or less oval frame, used in tennis, etc. **2.** (*pl.* construed as *sing.*) a game of ball, played in a walled court, in which such racquets are used. Also, **racket, rackett**. [F]

racy /'reɪsi/, *adj.*, **-cier, -ciest. 1.** lively; vigorous; spirited. **2.** having an agreeably peculiar taste or flavor, as wine, fruits, etc. **3.** suggestive; risqué: *a racy story.* —**racily**, *adv.* —**raciness**, *n.*

rad[1], *Symbol.* radian.

rad[2] /ræd/, *n.* a non-SI unit of absorbed dose of ionising radiation equal to 0.01 joule per kilograms of material. See **radiation**. [short for RADIATION]

rad., *Abbrev.* radix.

radar /'reɪdɑ/, *n.* an apparatus to determine the presence and location of an object by measuring the time for the echo of a radio wave to return from it, and the direction from which it returns. [short for *ra(dio) d(etecting) a(nd) r(anging)*]

radar trap, *n.* a place beside a road where police have set up radar equipment to detect speeding motorists.

raddle /'rædl/, *n., v.,* **-dled, dling.** ◇*n.* **1.** a red variety of ochre. **2.** a colored mark, often red, placed upon a sheep so it will be recognised or to point out a badly shorn sheep. ◇*v.t.* **3.** to mark a sheep so that it will be recognised.

radial /'reɪdiəl/, *adj.* **1.** arranged like rays or radii. **2.** having spokes, bars, lines, etc., arranged like radii, as a machine. **3.** *Zool.* relating to structures that radiate from a central point, as the arms of a starfish. **4.** of, like, or relating to a radius or a ray. ◇*n.* **5.** → **radial-ply tyre.** [L: RADIUS]

radial-ply tyre, *n.* an air-filled tyre with flexible walls achieved by having the casing cords running radially and with additional thicknesses strengthening the tread only.

radian /'reɪdiən/, *n.* a supplementary SI unit of measurement of plane angle, being the angle between two radii of a circle which cut off on the circumference of an arc equal to the length of the radius. *Symbol:* rad

radiance /'reɪdiəns/, *n.* **1.** brightness or light which spreads out like rays: *the radiance of the tropical sun; Radiance lit her face.* **2.** → **radiation.** Also, **radiancy**.

radiant /'reɪdiənt/, *adj.* **1.** sending out rays of light; shining; bright: *the radiant sun; radiant colors.* **2.** bright with joy, hope, etc.: *radiant smiles.* **3.** *Phys.* sent out in rays, or by radiation. ◇*n.* **4.** a point or object from which rays come. [ME, from L: emitting rays]

radiant flux, *n.* the rate of transmission of radiant energy (such as heat), measured in watts.

radiata pine /reɪdi,atə 'paɪn/, *n.* a valuable softwood timber tree with a huge, broad dome and foliage of bright green needles, native to California but widely grown in Australia.

radiate /'reɪdieɪt/, *v.,* **-ated, -ating,** *adj.* ◇*v.i.* **1.** to spread or move like rays or radii from a centre. **2.** to send out rays, as of light or heat; irradiate. **3.** to come out or proceed in rays. ◇*v.t.* **4.** to send out in rays; disseminate as from a centre. **5.** (of persons) to show in large measure (good humor, generosity, etc.). ◇*adj.* **6.** radiating from a centre. **7.**

radiate 853 **radius**

represented with rays proceeding from it, as a head on a coin, in art, etc. [L]

radiation /reɪdi'eɪʃən/, *n.* **1.** *Phys.* the emission and spreading of particles (e.g. alpha or beta) or waves by a radioactive substance, or by a source of electromagnetic waves. **2.** the act or process of radiating. **3.** something which is radiated; a ray or rays. **4.** a radial arrangement of parts.

radiator /'reɪdieɪtə/, *n.* **1.** something which radiates. **2.** an apparatus for heating a room in which a cylindrical rod, heated red-hot electrically, radiates heat directly and sometimes via a reflector placed behind it. **3.** a type of heating device, as a series or coil of pipes through which steam or hot water passes. **4.** an apparatus made from thin-walled tubes and metal fins, used for cooling circulating water, as in the cooling system of a motor-car engine, etc. **5.** *Radio.* a type of aerial.

radical /'rædɪkəl/, *adj.* **1.** going to the root or origin; fundamental: *a radical change.* **2.** favoring extreme political, social or other reforms. **3.** forming the basis or foundation. **4.** existing as though a permanent part of the character of a thing or person: *radical defects of character.* **5.** *Maths.* relating to or forming a root. **6.** *Gram.* of or relating to a root (def. 7). ◊*n.* **7.** someone who holds or follows principles which are far from the ordinary; esp. left-wing political principles; an extremist. **8.** Also, **free radical.** *Chem.* a group (def. 3a) with at least one unpaired electron **9.** *Gram.* → **root**[1] (def. 7). [ME, from LL, from L: root]

radical sign, *n.* the symbol √ or √ (initially the first letter of *radix*) indicating extraction of a root of the following quantity: $\sqrt{a^2} = \pm a$, $\sqrt{a^3} \, b^3 = ab$.

radicle /'rædɪkəl/, *n.* **1.** (of plants) the primary root of an embryo (usu. seed). **2.** a tiny root. [L: little root]

radii, **radiai**, **-dii**/, *n.* plural of **radius**.

radio /'reɪdioʊ/, *n., pl.* **-dios**, *v.* **-dioed**, **-dioing**. ◊*n.* **1.** the sending of electrical signals through the air by electromagnetic waves to a receiving set; wireless telegraphy or telephony: *speeches broadcast by radio.* **2.** an apparatus for receiving radio broadcasts; wireless. **3.** a message sent by radio. ◊*v.t.* **4.** to transmit (a message, etc.) by radio. **5.** to send a message to (a person) by radio. ◊*v.i.* **6.** to transmit a message, etc., by radio. [short for *radiotelegraphic* (or *-telephonic*) *instrument, message,* or *transmission*]

radio-, a word part meaning **1.** radio. **2.** radial. **3.** radium, radioactive, or radiant energy. [orig. combining form of RADIUS]

radioactive /ˌreɪdioʊ'æktɪv/, *adj.* having, relating to, or caused by radioactivity.

radioactive age, *n.* the age of a mineral, fossil, etc., as estimated from its content of radioactive isotopes.

radioactive series, *n.* the series of isotopes of various elements through which a radioactive substance decays before it reaches a stable state.

radioactivity /ˌreɪdioʊæk'tɪvəti/, *n.* the property of spontaneous disintegration possessed by some elements due to changes in their atomic nuclei, along with the emission of alpha, or beta, and/or gamma radiation.

radioastronomy /ˌreɪdioʊə'strɒnəmi/, *n.* that branch of astronomy based on radiation of radio frequency (as different from light) received on earth.

radiocarbon dating, *n.* finding the age of objects of plant or animal origin from their content of radioactive carbon ($^{14}_{6}C$). Also, **carbon dating.**

radiofrequency /ˌreɪdioʊ'frikwənsi/, *n., pl.* **-cies.** any frequency of electromagnetic radiation within the radio band often used for broadcasting.

radiogram /'reɪdioʊˌgræm/, *n.* **1.** a combined radio and gramophone. **2.** a message sent by radiotelegraphy.

radiography /reɪdi'ɒgrəfi/, *n.* the production of pictures caused by the action of X-rays on a photographic plate, esp. as used in medicine; X-ray photography. —**radiographer**, *n.* —**radiographic**, *adj.*

radiology /reɪdi'ɒlədʒi/, *n.* **1.** the science dealing with X-rays or rays from radioactive substances, esp. for medical uses. **2.** the examining or photographing of organs, etc., with such rays. —**radiologist**, *n.* —**radiological**, *adj.*

radiometric dating, *n.* finding the age of a rock or mineral by measuring the ratios of certain radioactive isotopes contained in the specimen.

radiotelegraphy /ˌreɪdioʊtə'legrəfi/, *n.* telegraphy using radio waves without wires or cables.

radiotelephone /ˌreɪdioʊ'tɛləfoʊn/, *n.* a telephone in which the signal is sent by radio; wireless telephone. —**radiotelephonic**, *adj.* —**radiotelephony**, *n.*

radio telescope, *n.* a large parabolic reflector, used to pick up and focus radio signals coming from space. See **radioastronomy.**

radiotherapy /ˌreɪdioʊ'θerəpi/, *n.* the treatment of disease by X-rays or radioactive substances.

radio wave, *n.* an electromagnetic wave of radiofrequency.

radish /'rædɪʃ/, *n.* a hot-tasting white root with red skin, often eaten with salad. [OE, from L: root, radish]

radium /'reɪdiəm/, *n.* a naturally occurring radioactive metallic element with chemical properties resembling those of barium. *Symbol:* Ra; *at. no.:* 88; *at. wt. of most stable isotope:* 226. [NL, from L *radius* ray]

radius /'reɪdiəs/, *n., pl.* **-dii** /-diaɪ/, **-diuses. 1.** a straight line going from the centre of a circle or sphere to the circumference or surface. **2.** the length of such a line. **3.** any radial or radiating part. **4.** a circular area round some point: *every house within a radius of 50 kilometres.* **5.** *Anat.* one of the two bones of the forearm on the thumb side. **6.** *Zool.* a

radius — 854 — **raillery**

corresponding bone in the forelimb of other vertebrates. [L: staff, rod, spoke of a wheel, radius, ray or beam of light.

radius of curvature, *n.* the radius of that circle (called the osculating circle) whose arc best approximates a curve in the vicinity of a point on the curve.

radix /'reɪdɪks/, *n., pl.* **radices** /'reɪdəsiːz/, **radixes**. 1. *Maths.* a number taken as the base of a system of numbers, logarithms, etc. 2. *Bot.* a root. 3. *Gram.* → root¹ (def. 7). [L: root]

radon /'reɪdɒn/, *n.* a rare, inert, radioactive gaseous element produced in the disintegration of radium. *Symbol.*: Rn; *at. no.*: 86; *at. wt*: 222. [RAD(IUM) + -*on*, modelled on ARGON, NEON]

Raeburn /'reɪbən/, *n.* **Sir Henry**, 1756–1823, Scottish portrait painter.

RAF /ɑr eɪ 'ɛf, ræf/, *Abbrev.* Royal Air Force.

Rafferty /'ræfəti/, *n.* **Chips** (*John William Goffage*), 1909–71, Australian film actor and producer.

Rafferty's rules, *n.pl.* no rules at all, as of something organised in a slipshod way. Also, **Rafferty rules**. [Brit d. *rafferty* irregular; linked by association with the Irish surname *Rafferty*]

raffia /'ræfiə/, *n.* the fibre from the leafstalks of a palm of Madagascar, much used for tying plants, etc., and for making matting, baskets, hats, etc. [Malagasy]

raffish /'ræfɪʃ/, *adj.* 1. (of behavior, appearance) wild or free, and not very respectable; rakish. 2. vulgar, tawdry. [*raff* confused heap + -ISH¹]

raffle /'ræfəl/, *n., v.,* **-fled, -fling**. ◇*n.* 1. a lottery in which the prizes are usu. goods rather than money. ◇*v.t.* 2. to sell by a raffle (sometimes fol. by *off*): *to raffle (off) a watch*. [ME, from OF: kind of game at dice, net, plundering, from D: ravel]

Raffles /'ræfəlz/, *n.* **Sir Thomas Stamford**, 1781–1826, English colonial administrator; founded Singapore in 1819.

raft /rɑft/, *n.* 1. a floating platform for carrying people or goods on a river, etc. 2. a small inflatable rubber boat. [ME *rafte* beam, rafter, from Scand]

rafter /'rɑftə/, *n.* one of the sloping pieces of wood that form the framework of a roof. [OE *ræfterer*]

rag¹ /ræg/, *n.* 1. a worthless piece of cloth, esp. an old or torn one. 2. (*pl.*) ragged or tattered clothing. 3. a piece of cloth used for cleaning. 4. *Colloq.* a newspaper or magazine, esp. one thought to be of little value. 5. *Colloq.* a song or a piece of music in ragtime. 6. **glad rags**, *Colloq.* fine clothes. [ME *ragg(e)*, from Scand]

rag² /ræg/, *v.,* **ragged, ragging**, *n. Colloq.* ◇*v.t., v.i.* 1. to tease; torment. 2. to play rough jokes (on) or play about noisily. ◇*n.* 3. any disorderly or high-spirited behavior, esp. by a group of young people. [orig. uncert.]

ragamuffin /'rægəmʌfən/, *n.* a ragged, dirty person, esp. a child.

rag-and-bone man /ræg-ən-'boʊn mæn/, *n.* a dealer in old, unwanted clothing, furniture, etc. Also, **rag-and-bone merchant**.

ragbag /'rægbæg/, *n.* 1. a bag for scraps of material. 2. a very carelessly dressed person. 3. a confused mixture of anything.

rage /reɪdʒ/, *n., v.,* **raged, raging**. ◇*n.* 1. violent anger: *to fall into a rage*. 2. violence or intensity: *rage of wind; rage of thirst*. 3. *Colloq.* an exciting or entertaining event: *That party was a rage*. 4. **all the rage**, fashionable: *Long hair for men used to be all the rage.* ◇*v.i.* 5. to act or speak with fury; show or feel violent anger. 6. to move or happen with great violence: *The sea raged against the beach; the battle raged ten days*. 7. *Colloq.* to set about enjoying oneself: *Let's go raging*. [ME, from OF, from VL, from L *rabies* madness, rage]

ragged /'rægəd/, *adj.* 1. wearing old and torn clothes. 2. torn or worn to rags; tattered: *ragged clothing*. 3. uneven; jagged: *ragged stones*. 4. wild or uncared for: *a ragged garden*. 5. rough or faulty: *a ragged piece of work*. 6. rough or harsh: *a ragged voice*.

raglan /'ræglən/, *n.* 1. a loose overcoat whose sleeves are cut so as to continue up to the collar. ◇*adj.* 2. (of a garment or sleeve) made in such a manner. [named after Lord *Raglan*, 1788–1855, British field marshal]

ragout /'rægu/, *n.* a highly seasoned stew of meat and vegetables. Also, **ragoust, ragu**. [F: restore the appetite of]

ragtime /'rægtaɪm/, *n. Music.* a rhythm marked by frequent syncopation, such as is common in early American Negro piano music. [probably alteration of *ragged time*]

rag trade, *n. Colloq.* the clothing trade.

raid /reɪd/, *n.* 1. a sudden invasion by police: *a raid on a gambling house*. 2. *Mil.* a sudden attack on the enemy, esp. by air or by a small force. ◇*v.t., v.i.* 3. to attack; invade. [OE *rād* expedition, lit., riding]

rail¹ /reɪl/, *n.* 1. a horizontal bar of wood or metal used as a support or barrier. 2. a fence; railing, esp. (*pl.*) at a racecourse. 3. one of a pair of steel bars fixed to the ground along which trains run. 4. the railway, as a means of transport: *to travel by rail*. 5. **off the rails**, abnormal; insane; out of control. ◇*v.t.* 6. to furnish with a rail or rails. 7. to enclose with a fence or rail (usu. fol. by *in* or *off*). ◇*v.i.* 8. (of horses, etc. in a race) to run close to the rails. [ME, from OF, from L: rule, straight stick, bar]

rail² /reɪl/, *v.i.* to complain bitterly (oft. fol. by *at* or *against*): *to rail at fate*. [ME, from F: deride, from Pr: chatter, from L: shriek]

rail³ /reɪl/, *n.* a type of wading bird with short wings, strong legs and long toes, living in marshes around the world.

railing /'reɪlɪŋ/, *n.* 1. (oft. *pl.*) a barrier made of rails and supports, etc. 2. rails collectively: *The veranda railing needs painting.*

raillery /'reɪləri/, *n., pl.* **-ries**. good-humored teasing; banter. [F]

railroad /'reɪlroʊd/, n. 1. *US.* a railway. ◇v.t. 2. *Colloq.* to force or compel: *He was railroaded out of office.*

railway /'reɪlweɪ/, n. 1. a permanent road or way, laid with parallel metal rails, on which trains run. 2. such a track together with its trains, land and buildings. 3. the company of people owning or working it.

raiment /'reɪmənt/, n. *Archaic or Poetic.* clothing; apparel; attire. [ME]

rain /reɪn/, n. 1. water falling from the sky to the earth in drops condensed from vapor in the atmosphere. 2. a fall of rain: *The last rain we had was three months ago.* 3. (*pl.*) the seasonal rainfalls, or the rainy or wet season, in some regions, as India. 4. a large quantity of anything falling thickly: *a rain of blows.* 5. **right as rain**, perfectly all right. ◇v.i. 6. (of rain) to fall: *It rained all night.* 7. to fall like rain: *Tears rained from her eyes.* 8. (of the sky, clouds, etc.) to send down or let fall rain. ◇v.t. 9. to send down (rain, etc.): *It was raining huge drops.* 10. to give in great quantity: *to rain blows upon a person.* ◇v. 11. **rain cats and dogs**, to rain heavily. [OE *regn*]

rainbird /'reɪnbɜd/, n. a bird whose call is thought to be a sign of rain as, in Australia, the channel-billed cuckoo or the grey currawong.

rainbow /'reɪnboʊ/, n. 1. a bow or arc of colors appearing in the sky opposite the sun, due to the refraction and reflection of the sun's rays in drops of rain. 2. a similar bow in the spray of waterfalls, etc. 3. any array of many bright colors. 4. the spectrum. ◇adj. 5. multicolored. [OE *regnboga*]

rainbow lorikeet, n. an orange, green and blue parrot found in timbered areas from Cape York to southern Australia.

raincheck /'reɪntʃɛk/, n. *US.* 1. a ticket for use at a future time given to onlookers at a sports match stopped by rain. 2. **take a raincheck**, *Colloq.* to accept for the future something that is offered now (fol. by *on*).

raincoat /'reɪnkoʊt/, n. a waterproof coat, worn as a protection from rain.

rainfall /'reɪnfɔl/, n. the amount of water falling as rain, snow, etc., within a given time and area: *a rainfall of 1210 mm a year.*

rainforest /'reɪnfɒrəst/, n. thick forest found in tropical and temperate areas with high humidity and heavy rainfall all the year.

Rainier III /'reɪniə/, n. (*Rainier Louis Henri Maxence Bertrand de Grimaldi, Prince of Monaco*), born 1923, reigning prince of Monaco since 1949.

rain shadow, n. a drier area to the lee of a mountain range in the path of rain-bearing winds.

raise /reɪz/, v., **raised**, **raising**, n. ◇v.t. 1. to move to a higher position; lift up; elevate: *to raise one's hand.* 2. to cause to rise or stand up. 3. to build; erect: *to raise a monument.* 4. to cause to stick out; bring into relief: *to raise the skin in blisters.* 5. to cause to be; stir up: *to raise a revolt; to raise fears.* 6. to produce or rear: *to raise beans; to raise children.* 7. to bring up or put forward: *to raise a question; to raise an objection.* 8. to advance in rank: *to raise a person to Chief Justice.* 9. to collect: *to raise an army; to raise money.* 10. to make more intense, louder, etc. 11. to increase in amount: *to raise prices.* 12. *Maths.* to multiply (a number) by itself for a stated number of times: *100 is 10 raised to the power of 2.* 13. to contact by radio or telephone. ◇v.t. 14. **raise Cain** or **hell**, to make a disturbance. 15. **raise the roof**, *Colloq.* to cause a great noise, excitement, etc. ◇n. 16. (the amount of) a rise in wages. [ME, from Scand]

raisin /'reɪzən/, n. a dried sweet grape. [ME, from OF, from L: cluster of grapes]

raison d'être /ˌreɪzɒn 'dɛtrə/, n. reason for being. [F]

Raj /rɑdʒ/, n. **the**, the British rule in India before 1947.

rajah /'rɑdʒə, 'rɑdʒɑ/, n. (in India) (the title of) a king, prince or chief. Also, **raja**. [Hind]

Rajasthan /rɑdʒə'stɑn/, n. a state in northwestern India; formerly Rajputana and a group of small states. Pop. 34 261 862 (1981); 342 082 km^2. *Cap.:* Jaipur.

rake[1] /reɪk/, n., v., **raked**, **raking**. ◇n. 1. a long-handled tool with teeth for gathering together cut grass, etc., or for breaking and smoothing the surface of ground. ◇v.t. 2. to gather together or remove with a rake: *to rake dead leaves from a lawn.* 3. to clear, smooth, or prepare with a rake: *to rake a garden bed.* 4. to gather or collect a lot of (oft. fol. by *in*): *to rake in the money.* 5. to find, esp. with difficulty (oft. fol. by *up*): *Can't you rake up some evidence?* 6. to reveal (usu. fol. by *up*): *to rake up an old scandal.* 7. to search thoroughly through. 8. to sweep with gunfire: *The guns raked the town.* 9. to sweep with the eyes. ◇v.i. 10. to use a rake. [OE *raca*]

rake[2] /reɪk/, n. a dissolute, immoral man, esp. one in fashionable society. [short for *rakehell*, from RAKE[1] (def. 7) + HELL]

rake[3] /reɪk/, v., **raked**, **raking**, n. ◇v.i. 1. (of the mast, etc., of a ship, and of the floor of a stage) to slope. ◇n. 2. a slope. [orig. uncert.]

rakish[1] /'reɪkɪʃ/, adj. 1. smart; jaunty; dashing. 2. like a rake; dissolute.

rakish[2] /'reɪkɪʃ/, adj. (of ships) having a fast appearance.

Raleigh /'ræli, 'rɔli/, n. **Sir Walter**, 1552?–1618, English explorer and author, favorite of Queen Elizabeth I. Also, **Ralegh**.

rall., *Abbrev.* rallentando.

rallentando /rælən'tændoʊ/, adv. 1. (a musical direction) more and more slowly. ◇n. 2. a passage played in such a way. [It]

rally[1] /'ræli/, v., **-lied**, **-lying**, n., *pl.* **-lies**. ◇v.t. 1. to bring together or into order again: *to rally an army.* 2. to draw or call (people) together for common action. 3. to recover; revive: *He rallied his spirits.* ◇v.i. 4. to come together for common action. 5. to come together or into order again. 6. to recover a little or get fresh strength: *The stock market rallied today.* ◇n. 7. recovery from disorder or illness. 8. a public meeting for common

rally 856 **rangatira**

action: *a nuclear disarmament rally.* **9.** *Tennis, etc.* a long exchange of strokes. **10.** a car competition concerned with skill rather than speed. [F]

rally[2] /'ræli/, *v.t.*, **-lied, -lying.** to tease (someone) good-humoredly; banter. [F: RAIL[2]]

ram /ræm/, *n.*, *v.*, **rammed, ramming.** ◇*n.* **1.** an uncastrated male sheep. **2.** any of various devices for battering, crushing, driving, or forcing something: *battering ram.* ◇*v.t.* **3.** to drive or force by heavy blows. **4.** to strike with great force; dash violently against. **5.** to cram; stuff. [ME and OE]

ram-, a word part used to add force or emphasis, as in *ramshackle.* [see Icel *ram-* very, special use of *rammr* strong, akin to RAM]

RAM /ræm/, *n.* a computer memory which is so structured that each item can be accessed equally quickly. [R(*andom*)-A(*ccess*) M(*emory*)]

Rama /'ramə/, *n.* the name of three avatars (gods) of Vishnu and heroes of Hindu mythology: Balarama, Parashurama, and Ramachandra (esp. the last). [Skt]

Ramadan /ræmə'dan/, *n.* **1.** the ninth month of the Muslim year. **2.** the daily fast which is strictly ordered from dawn until sunset during this month. [Ar]

Ramayana /ra'maiənə/, *n.* one of the two great epics of India (the other being the Mahabharata). It is ascribed to the poet Valmiki, and was probably composed early in the Christian era. [Skt]

ramble /'ræmbəl/, *v.*, **-bled, -bling,** *n.* ◇*v.i.* **1.** to wander about in a leisurely manner. **2.** (of a stream or path) to have a wandering or twisting course. **3.** (of a house, etc.) to grow or be built in a haphazard way. **4.** to talk or write in an aimless way without a consistent train of thought. ◇*n.* **5.** a walk without a definite route, taken for pleasure. [? frequentative of ROAM] **-rambling,** *adj.*

rambler /'ræmblə/, *n.* **1.** someone or something that rambles. **2.** a climbing rose.

rami /'reimai/, *n.* plural of *ramus.*

ramification /ræməfə'keɪʃən/, *n.* **1.** the act or manner of ramifying. **2.** a branch: *the ramifications of a nerve.*

ramify /'ræməfai/, *v.t.*, *v.i.*, **-fied, -fying.** to divide or spread out into branches or branchlike parts. [F, from ML, from L]

ramjet /'ræmdʒet/, *n.* a jet-propulsion engine operated by the burning of fuel in a stream of air compressed by the forward speed of the aircraft.

ramose /'reimous, ræ'mous/, *adj.* **1.** having many branches. **2.** branching. [L]

ramp /ræmp/, *n.* **1.** a sloping surface or walkway connecting two different levels. **2.** → **cattlegrid.** ◇*v.i.* **3.** to rise or stand on the hind legs, as a four-legged animal. **4.** to act violently; rage; storm. [ME, from F: creep, crawl, climb]

rampage /'ræmpeidʒ/, *n.*; /ræm'peidʒ/, *v.*, **-paged, -paging.** ◇*n.* **1.** violent or furious behavior: *to go on the rampage.* ◇*v.i.* **2.** to rush, move, or act furiously or violently. [orig. Scot; apparently var. of *ramp-rage*] **-rampageous,** *adj.*

rampant /'ræmpənt/, *adj.* **1.** violent; raging; furious: *the rampant flood.* **2.** unchecked; in full sway: *the rampant growth of anarchy.* **3.** standing on the hind legs; ramping. **4.** *Heraldry.* (of a lion, bear, etc.) standing on its left hind leg with the foreclegs raised, the right higher than the left, and usu. with the head in profile. [ME, from OF: climb] **-rampancy,** *n.*

rampart /'ræmpat/, *n.* **1.** a mound of earth raised as a fortification, usu. with a stone or earth parapet built upon it. **2.** any defence. ◇*v.t.* **3.** to furnish with or as with a rampart. [F: fortify]

ramrod /'ræmrɒd/, *n.* **1.** a rod for pushing down the charge of a muzzle-loading gun. **2.** a cleaning rod for the barrel of a rifle, etc. **3. stiff as a ramrod,** (of a person) unbending; rigid.

Ramses /'ræmsiz/, *n.* the name of twelve kings of ancient Egypt. Also, **Rameses, Ramesses.**

ramshackle /'ræmʃækəl/, *adj.* loosely made or held together; rickety; shaky: *a ramshackle house.* [RAM- + *shackled,* shaken]

ran /ræn/, *v.* past tense of **run.**

RAN /ar eɪ 'ɛn/, *Abbrev.* Royal Australian Navy.

ranch /ræntʃ/, *n.* (esp. US) a farm for cattle, horses, etc., usu. with a large area of grazing land. [Sp *rancho,* mess, group of people who eat together] **-rancher,** *n.*

rancid /'rænsəd/, *adj.* having a stale, sour smell or taste: *rancid butter.* [L] **-rancidity,** *n.*

rancor or **rancour** /'ræŋkə/, *n.* continuing resentment or ill will. [ME, from OF, from LL: rank smell or taste, from L: to be rank] **-rancorous,** *adj.*

rand /rænd/, *n.*, *pl.* **rand.** the monetary unit of Southern Africa. *Abbrev.:* R [Afrikaans]

Randell /'ræn'del/, *n.* **William Richard,** 1824–1911, Australian paddle-steamer owner, born in England; first steam navigator of the Murray River.

random /'rændəm/, *adj.* **1.** going, made, happening, etc., without a definite aim, purpose, or reason. ◇*n.* **2. at random,** in a haphazard way. [ME, from OF: rushing movement, disorder]

random-access memory, *n.* → **RAM.**

random sampling, *n.* the drawing of a sample from a statistical population in which all members of the population have equal probabilities of being included in the sample.

randy /'rændi/, *adj.* **1.** *Colloq.* → **lecherous. 2.** sexually excited. [*rand* (var. of RANT) + -Y[1]]

rang /ræŋ/, *v.* past tense of **ring**[2].

rangatira /rʌŋəˈtɪərə, ræŋ-/, *n. NZ.* **1.** a Maori noble leader. **2.** *Colloq.* a chief, boss. [Maori]

range /reɪndʒ/, n., v., **ranged, ranging.** ◇n. **1.** limits within which there can be differences or variation: *range of prices*. **2.** limits within which something can be or work; scope: *within range of vision; an oboe has a different range from a flute*. **3.** the distance to which a bullet, rocket, etc., can travel. **4.** distance away: *at a range of 20 metres*. **5.** an area for shooting practice. **6.** the distance which a plane, ship, etc., can travel without refuelling. **7.** *Stats.* the difference between the smallest and largest varieties in a statistical distribution. **8.** a set or series: *We have a new range of goods in our shops*. **9.** Chiefly US. a wide open area of land. **10.** an area over which something is found, or occurs: *the range of a plant*. **11.** a chain of mountains. **12.** a cooking stove. ◇v.t. **13.** to set in order, esp. in a row or line; arrange. **14.** to place in a particular class; classify. **15.** to pass over or through (an area) in all directions: *The search party ranged the hills*. ◇v.i. **16.** to vary within certain limits: *prices ranging from $5 to $10*. **17.** to run or go in a certain direction; extend: *a boundary ranging east and west*. **18.** to wander; rove; roam: *The talk ranged over many subjects; to range through the bush*. **19.** to be found over an area: *a plant which ranges from Qld to NSW*. [ME, from OF: arrange in line]

rangefinder /'reɪndʒfaɪndə/, n. an instrument for telling the range or distance of an object, as in sighting a gun or focussing a camera.

ranger /'reɪndʒə/, n. **1.** a wanderer. **2.** a person employed to look after a nature reserve, park, etc. **3.** (*cap.*) a member of the senior division of the Girl Guides. **4.** (*cap.*) a series consisting of nine US spacecraft launched between 1961 and 1965; lunar probes designed to provide photographs of the moon's surface.

Ranger uranium mine, n. a mine in the NT, south-east of Darwin, near Mt Brockman; uranium discovered in 1969; government permission to mine and export given in 1977.

Rangoon /ræŋ'guːn/, n. a seaport in and the capital of Burma, in the southern part. Pop. 2 458 712 (1983).

rani /'rɑːni, rɑː'niː/, n., pl. **-nis.** (in India and elsewhere) **1.** the wife of a rajah. **2.** a reigning queen or princess.

rank¹ /ræŋk/, n. **1.** a class in the social scale or in any graded body: *people of every rank and station*. **2.** an official grade or position: *the rank of colonel*. **3.** high position in society; status: *pride of rank*. **4.** relative position or standing: *a writer of the highest rank*. **5.** a row, line, or series, esp. of soldiers standing side by side. **6.** (*pl.*) the main body of ordinary soldiers, workers, etc.: *to rise from the ranks*. **7. pull (one's) rank (on),** to resort to the use of a position of authority to compel action or behavior. ◇v.t. **8.** to arrange in a row or series. **9.** to arrange; classify. **10.** to put in a particular position, class, etc. ◇v.i. **11.** to have a place in a particular rank or class: *to rank third*. [OF *renc, reng,* of Gmc orig.]

rank² /ræŋk/, adj. **1.** growing too tall or coarse: *rank grass*. **2.** smelling or tasting strongly and offensively: *a rank cigar*. **3.** utter; unmistakable: *a rank outsider; rank treachery*. **4.** very coarse or indecent. [OE *ranc* proud, bold]

rank and file, n. the body of an army, union, etc., apart from the officers or leaders.

rankle /'ræŋkəl/, v.i., **-kled, -kling.** (of unpleasant feelings, experiences, etc.) to produce or continue to produce in the mind irritation or resentment; fester. [ME, from OF, from ML: ulcer, from L: little serpent, DRAGON]

ransack /'rænsæk/, v.t. **1.** to search thoroughly through (a house, drawer, etc.). **2.** to search (a place) for plunder; pillage. [ME, from Scand]

ransom /'rænsəm/, n. **1.** the buying back of a prisoner, kidnapped person, captured goods, etc., for a price. **2.** the price paid or demanded. **3. hold to ransom, a.** to keep (someone) prisoner until bought back at a price. **b.** to try to force (someone) to give in to one's demands. ◇v.t. **4.** to buy back from captivity. [ME, from OF, from L: REDEMPTION]

rant /rænt/, v.i. to speak in a loud, violent, or exaggerated way: *He always rants when playing Hamlet; rant and rave*. [MD *ranten* rave] **–ranter,** n. **–ranting,** adj.

ranunculus /rə'nʌŋkjələs/, n., pl. **-luses, -li** /-laɪ/. any of a large group of herb plants with leaves mostly divided, and flowers, usu. yellow, with five petals; buttercup. [L: little frog]

rap¹ /ræp/, v., **rapped, rapping,** n. ◇v.t. **1.** to strike, esp. with a quick, smart, or light blow. **2.** to say sharply or quickly (usu. fol. by *out*): *to rap out an oath*. ◇v.i. **3.** to knock smartly or lightly: *to rap on a door*. ◇v. **4. rap over** or **on the knuckles,** *Colloq.* to scold sharply; reprimand. ◇n. **5.** (the sound of) a quick, smart, or light blow. **6.** *Colloq.* blame: *to take the rap*. [ME]

rap² /ræp/, n. the smallest bit: *I don't care a rap.* [short for Irish-Gaelic *ropaire,* a counterfeit coin used in Ireland in the 18th C for a halfpenny]

rapacious /rə'peɪʃəs/, adj. greedy in a violent and unpleasant way; predatory; extortionate. [L: greediness] **–rapacity,** n.

rape¹ /reɪp/, n., v., **raped, raping.** ◇n. **1.** the crime of having sexual intercourse with a woman against her will. **2.** the act of having sexual intercourse with anyone against his or her will. **3.** any assault or act of aggression: *the rape of land.* ◇v.t. **4.** to commit the crime or act of rape on. [ME, from L: seize, carry off] **–rapist,** n.

rape² /reɪp/, n. a plant giving rapeseed oil, whose leaves are used to feed animals. Also, **rapeseed.** [ME, from L: turnip]

Raphael /'ræfeɪəl/, n. (*Raffaello Santi* or *Sanzio*), 1483–1520, Italian painter and architect; considered one of the greatest painters of the High Renaissance; works include the *Alba Madonna* and the *Transfiguration* (unfinished 1520).

rapid /'ræpəd/, *adj.* **1.** fast; quick; speedy: *rapid growth; a rapid worker.* ◇*n.* **2.** (*usu. pl.*) a part of a river where the current runs very quickly, esp. over a steep slope. [L] – **rapidity**, *n.*

rapid-fire /'ræpəd-faɪə/, *adj.* in quick succession: *rapid-fire questions.*

rapier /'reɪpɪə/, *n.* a sword with a long, thin, pointed blade, used only for thrusting. [F]

rapine /ræ'pin/, *n.* a violent seizing and carrying off of the property of others; plunder. [ME, from L]

rapport /ræ'pɔ/, *n.* close connection and sympathy between people or people and things. [F: bring back, refer]

rapprochement /rə'prɒʃmənt/, *n.* (of enemies) a coming to a friendly understanding. [F: bring near]

rapt /ræpt/, *adj.* **1.** giving the whole mind; deeply absorbed: *rapt in thought.* **2.** carried away with emotion; enraptured: *rapt with joy.* **3.** showing or coming from rapture: *a rapt smile.* [ME, from L: seized, transported]

raptorial /ræp'tɔrɪəl/, *adj.* **1.** preying upon other animals; predatory. **2.** formed for seizing prey, as the beak or claws of a bird. [NL]

rapture /'ræptʃə/, *n.* **1.** overpowering joy or delight; ecstasy. **2.** (*oft. pl.*) expression of such delight: *In raptures over a movie star.* – **rapturous**, *adj.*

rare[1] /rɛə/, *adj.*, **rarer, rarest. 1.** unusual; uncommon: *rare occasions; rare smiles; rare diseases.* **2.** thin; of low density or pressure: *rare mountain air.* **3.** unusual in excellence or greatness; remarkable: *rare tact; a rare find; sympathetic to a rare degree.* [ME, from L: thin, not dense]

rare[2] /rɛə/, *adj.*, **rarer, rarest.** (of meat) not well cooked; underdone. [OE *hrēr* lightly boiled (said of eggs)]

rare-earth elements, *n.pl.* a group of closely related metallic elements of atomic number 57 to 71 inclusive, with properties similar to aluminium; the lanthanides.

rarefaction /rɛərə'fækʃən/, *n.* **1.** the act or process of rarefying. **2.** the state of being rarefied. **3.** *Phys.* a region of reduced pressure in a medium through which a longitudinal wave (e.g. sound wave) travels.

rarefy /'rɛərəfaɪ/, *v.*, **-fied, -fying.** ◇*v.t.* **1.** to make rare, more rare, or less dense. **2.** to refine. ◇*v.i.* **3.** to become rare or less dense; become thinned. [L] – **rarefactive**, *adj.*

rare gas, *n.* → **inert gas.**

rarely /'rɛəli/, *adv.* not often; seldom: *He is rarely late.*

raring /'rɛərɪŋ/, *adj.* very eager: *He was raring to go.* [from d. *rare,* var. of REAR[2]]

rarity /'rɛərəti/, *n., pl.* **-ties. 1.** something interesting and uncommon: *The bird is a great rarity these days in NSW.* **2.** rare state or quality. **3.** thinness, as of air or a gas.

Rarotonga /rɛərə'tɒŋgə, -'tɒŋə/, *n.* one of the Cook Islands, in the South Pacific. 67 km².

RAS /ar eɪ 'ɛs/, *Abbrev.* Royal Agricultural Society.

rascal /'raskəl/, *n.* **1.** *Rare.* a dishonest person; knave. **2.** (*affectionate*) a child or young animal; scamp: *you little rascal.* [ME, from OF: rabble, from L: scratch] – **rascally**, *adj.*

rase /reɪz/, *v.t.*, **rased, rasing.** → **raze.**

rash[1] /ræʃ/, *adj.* foolish and hasty: *a rash promise; a rash person.* [ME] – **rashness**, *n.*

rash[2] /ræʃ/, *n.* **1.** (a breaking out of) red spots or patches, or itchiness, on the skin. **2.** a sudden large number: *a rash of complaints.* [F, from L: scratch]

rasher /'ræʃə/, *n.* a thin slice of bacon. [orig. uncert.]

Rasmussen /'rasmusən/, *n.* **Knud Johan Victor** /knud jɒ,han 'vɪktɔ/, 1879–1933, Danish arctic explorer; first to cross the Northwest Passage by dogsled 1921–24.

rasp /rasp, ræsp/, *v.t.* **1.** to scrape with a rough tool; abrade: *to rasp wood with a file.* **2.** to scrape or rub roughly: *The cat's tongue rasped my hand.* **3.** to grate upon or irritate (the nerves, feelings, etc.). **4.** to say with a grating sound. ◇*v.i.* **5.** to scrape or grate: *to rasp away at wood; rasp away at emotions.* **6.** to make a grating sound: *The door hinges rasped as he came in; 'No!' he rasped.* ◇*n.* **7.** the act of rasping or a rasping sound. **8.** a coarse file, with separate pointlike teeth. [ME, from OF: scrape, grate, from Gmc] – **rasping**, *adj.*

Rasp /rasp/, *n.* **Charles,** 1846–1907, Australian miner, born in Germany; discoverer of silver at Broken Hill, NSW, in 1883 and one of the original shareholders in BHP.

raspberry[1] /'razbəri, -bri/, *n., pl.* **-ries. 1.** the fruit of a kind of bramble, soft, juicy, and usu. red, similar in appearance to the blackberry. **2.** a dark reddish purple color. [*rasp*(*is*) raspberry (orig. uncert.) + BERRY]

raspberry[2] /'razbəri, -bri/, *n., pl.* **-ries.** *Colloq.* a rude sound expressing contempt made with the tongue and lips. [rhyming slang, *raspberry fart* fart]

Rasputin /ræs'pjutɪn/, *n.* **Grigori Efimovich** /grɪ,gɔrjə jɪ'fimɒvɪtʃ/, 1871–1916, Siberian peasant who posed as a monk and exerted great and malign influence over Tsar Nicholas II; assassinated by a group of noblemen.

Rastafarianism /rastə'fɛərɪənɪzəm/, *n.* a Jamaican cult, the members of which believe in black supremacy and the back-to-Africa movement. [after *Ras Tafari*, the name of HAILE SELASSIE before he was crowned emperor of Ethiopia in 1930; regarded by followers of the cult as a god] – **Rastafarian**, *n., adj.*

rat /ræt/, *n., v.*, **ratted, ratting.** ◇*n.* **1.** a long-tailed rodent similar to but larger than the mouse. **2.** any of various similar animals. **3.** → **desert rat. 4.** *Colloq.* someone who deserts a friend in time of need or trouble. **5.** *Colloq.* a wretched and contemptible person. **6. smell a rat,** *Colloq.* to be suspicious. ◇*interj.* **7.** (*pl.*) *Colloq.* (an exclamation of annoyance, disbelief,

rat denial, or disappointment). ◊v.i. **8.** *Colloq.* to desert one's friends, etc., in time of need or trouble (fol. by *on*): *a man who would rat on his friends.* **9.** *Colloq.* to inform (on); betray. **10.** *Colloq.* to go back on a statement, agreement, etc. (fol. by *on*). **11.** to hunt or catch rats. [OE *rat*]

ratatouille /rætə'tui/, *n.* a type of vegetable stew. [F]

ratbag /'rætbæg/, *n. Colloq.* **1.** a contemptible person; rogue. **2.** a person of odd ideas or behavior; eccentric.

ratchet /'rætʃət/, *n.* (a mechanism having) a toothed bar and wheel which engages with a pawl. [F: ratchet, bobbin, from It: distaff, from Gmc]

ratchet wheel, *n.* a toothed wheel on which a pawl catches, stopping the wheel going backwards.

rate[1] /reɪt/, *n., v.*, **rated, rating.** ◊*n.* **1.** a certain quantity or amount of one thing measured in relation to a unit of another: *at the rate of 60 kilometres an hour.* **2.** a charge or payment (per unit of quantity): *a rate of 10 cents in the dollar; rate of interest.* **3.** degree of speed: *to work at a steady rate.* **4.** (*usu. pl.*) a local property tax used for the upkeep of local services. **5.** degree or amount of excellence (usu. used in combination to form adjectives, as in *first-rate, second-rate*). **6. at any rate, a.** under any circumstances; in any case; at all events. **b.** at least; anyway. **7. at this rate,** if things go on in this way. ◊*v.t.* **8.** to consider as; set a certain value on: *a film rated R; He was rated one of the rich men of the city.* **9.** to value (property, etc.) for purposes of taxation, etc. **10.** to deserve: *That rates better treatment than you're giving it.* ◊*v.i.* **11.** to have value, standing, etc.: *She rates highly among scientists.* **12.** to have a position in a certain class: *That rates as the best jazz I've ever heard.* [ME, from ML: fixed amount or portion, rate, from L: fixed by calculation, determined]

rate[2] /reɪt/, *v.t., v.i.*, **rated, rating.** to scold severely. [ME]

ratepayer /'reɪtpeɪə/, *n.* someone who pays rates on property, esp. a householder.

rather /'raðə/; *def. 9 sometimes* /ra'ðɜ/, *adv.* **1.** somewhat; quite; to a certain extent: *rather good.* **2.** (with verbs) in some degree: *I rather thought you'd like it.* **3.** more properly; with better reason: *The opposite is rather to be supposed.* **4.** sooner or more willingly: *to die rather than yield; I would rather go today.* **5.** in preference (fol. by *than*): *I would like the blue wool rather than the yellow.* **6.** instead of (fol. by *than*): *He is a hindrance rather than a help.* **7.** on the contrary: *That useless cat won't hunt. Rather, he just watches the mice.* **8. would / had rather,** would prefer: *I had rather you didn't go; I would rather not do it.* ◊*interj.* **9.** *Chiefly Brit.* Yes, certainly: *Is it worth going to? Rather!* [OE *hrathor*, compar. of *hrathe* quickly]

ratify /'rætəfaɪ/, *v.t.*, **-fied, -fying.** to confirm; approve; sanction: *to ratify an agreement.* [ME, from OF, from L] — **ratifier**, *n.* — **ratification**, *n.*

rating /'reɪtɪŋ/, *n.* **1.** a classification of any kind. **2.** *Brit Navy.* a sailor who is not an officer. **3.** a person's or firm's credit standing. **4.** a measure of success based on audience size: *the rating of a television program.* **5.** an amount fixed as a municipal rate.

ratio /'reɪʃioʊ/, *n., pl.* **-tios. 1.** *Maths.* the relation between two similar magnitudes in respect to the number of times the first contains the second: *the ratio of 5 to 2, which may be written 5:2, or $\frac{5}{2}$.* **2.** proportional relation; quotient of two numbers. **3.** *Econ.* the relative value of gold and silver in a bimetallic currency system, fixed by the government of a country. [L: reckoning, relation, reason]

ration /'ræʃən/, *n.* **1.** a fixed allowance of food or other goods, esp. as enforced in wartime. **2.** (*usu. pl.*) a fixed allowance of food, clothing, etc., supplied to a soldier, sailor, shearer, etc. ◊*v.t.* **3.** to share out as rations: *We will need to ration the coffee. It's too expensive!* **4.** to put on, or keep to, rations or limited amounts. **5.** to supply with food, etc.: *to ration an army.* [F, from ML: allowance of provisions, L: account] — **rationing**, *n.*

rational /'ræʃnəl, 'ræʃənəl/, *adj.* **1.** reasonable; sensible: *a rational decision.* **2.** in possession of one's reason; sane: *The patient appeared perfectly rational.* **3.** having the power of reason: *Man is a rational animal.* **4.** of or based on reason: *the rational faculty; a rational explanation.* **5.** *Maths.* expressible as the quotient of two integers. [L] — **rationality**, *n.*

rationale /ræʃə'nɑl/, *n.* **1.** a statement of reasons or principles. **2.** rational basis; fundamental reasons for the existence of something. [L]

rationalise *or* **rationalize** /'ræʃnəlaɪz/, *v.*, **-lised, -lising.** ◊*v.t.* **1.** *Psychol.* to invent a rational, acceptable explanation for behavior which has its origin in the unconscious; to justify unconscious behavior. **2.** to make economical or efficient; organise. **3.** to make rational or in agreement with reason. **4.** *Maths.* to remove radicals from part of an expression without altering its value. **5.** to reorganise (a business, etc.) to make it more efficient and economical. ◊*v.i.* **6.** to use reason; think in a rational way. **7.** to reorganise a business, etc. **8.** to justify one's behavior by apparently sensible explanations, to deceive oneself or others. — **rationalisation**, *n.*

rationalism /'ræʃnəlɪzəm/, *n.* the principle or habit of accepting reason as the highest authority in matters of opinion, beliefs, or behavior. — **rationalistic**, *adj.*

rational number, *n.* one of the set of numbers which can be expressed as the quotient of two integers, when the denomination is not zero.

rat-kangaroo /ˌræt-kæŋɡə'ru/, *n.* a group of cat-sized or smaller kangaroos including **1.** the **bettong**, with a prehensile (grasping) tail, used to carry nesting material, e.g. the **boodie** or **tungoo**, a species of bettong which is active by night and lives in burrows. **2.** the **potoroo**, usu. with a pointed head like a bandicoot, living in low thick scrub and grassland. **3.** other

rat-kangaroo types, e.g. the **musk rat-kangaroo**, of northeastern Qld rainforests, and the large **rufous rat-kangaroo**, of eastern Australia, with greyred fur.

rat-race /'ræt-reɪs/, n. **1.** a fiercely competitive struggle for success, esp. in careers. **2.** the fast pace of city life.

Rats of Tobruk /təˈbruk/, n.pl. the name given to the Allied troops, including an Australian garrison and British and Polish units, which defended Tobruk, Libya, for seven months against the Italians and Germans in World War II.

rattan /rəˈtæn/, n. **1.** a kind of climbing palm. **2.** the tough stems of such palms, used for wickerwork, canes, etc. **3.** a stick or switch of this material. [Malay]

Rattigan /'rætəgən/, n. **Terence Mervyn**, 1911–77, English dramatist; works include *The Winslow Boy* (1946).

rattle /'rætl/, v., **-tled, -tling**. ◇v.i. **1.** to make a series of short sharp sounds: *The windows rattled in their frames.* **2.** to be filled with such sounds: *The hall was rattling with excitement.* **3.** to move or go, esp. quickly, with such sounds: *The old car rattled off up the street.* **4.** to talk quickly; chatter. ◇v.t. **5.** to cause to rattle: *He rattled the doorknob violently.* **6.** to say or perform in a quick or meaningless way: *to rattle off a speech.* **7.** *Colloq.* to confuse (a person); disconcert. ◇n. **8.** a series of short, sharp sounds, from hard things knocking against each other. **9.** something designed to make such sounds, as a child's toy or the wooden clacker used by football fans. **10.** a rattling sound in the throat of a dying person. [ME] —**rattly**, adj.

rattlesnake /'rætlsneɪk/, n. a poisonous American snake with horny rings at the end of the tail, which produce a rattling or whirring sound when shaken. Also, **rattler**.

rattletrap /'rætltræp/, n. **1.** a shaky, rattling old car, etc. **2.** *Colloq.* someone who talks too much; garrulous person. **3.** *Colloq.* the mouth.

ratty /'ræti/, adj., **-tier, -tiest**. **1.** full of rats. **2.** of or typical of a rat. **3.** wretched; shabby. **4.** annoyed; irritable. **5.** *Colloq.* slightly odd or mad.

raucous /'rɔkəs/, adj. harsh-sounding: *a raucous voice.* [L] —**raucousness, raucity**, n.

raunchy /'rɔntʃi/, adj. **1.** *US Colloq.* (usu. of a man) randy; lusty. **2.** exciting sexual desire; bawdy.

ravage /'rævɪdʒ/, n., v., **-aged, -aging**. ◇n. **1.** ruinous damage; havoc; devastation: *the ravages of war.* ◇v.t. **2.** to damage badly: *Sorrow ravaged her face.* [F] —**ravager**, n.

rave /reɪv/, v., **raved, raving**, n., adj. ◇v.i. **1.** to talk wildly, as in sickness. **2.** (of wind, water, storms, etc.) to make a wild or furious sound; rage. **3.** *Colloq.* to talk or write excitedly. ◇n. **4.** the act of raving. **5.** overdone praise. ◇adj. **6.** praising eagerly: *a rave review.* [ME, probably from OF: wander, be delirious]

ravel /'rævəl/, v., **-elled, -elling**, n. ◇v.t., v.i. **1.** to tangle or become entangled. **2.** to separate or become separated thread by thread. ◇n. **3.** a tangle; complication. [MD: entangle]

Ravel /rəˈvɛl, ra-/, n. **Maurice** /mɒˈriːs/, 1875–1937, French composer; works include *Boléro* (1928).

raven /'reɪvən/, n. **1.** either of two large, shiny black birds with loud harsh calls, the **Australian raven**, or the **little raven**. **2.** any of a number of similar birds of the crow family found elsewhere in the world. ◇adj. **3.** shiny black: *raven hair.* [OE]

Ravenna /rəˈvɛnə/, n. a city in northeastern Italy; the capital of Italy under the Byzantine Empire; tomb of Dante. Pop. 137 453 (1984).

ravenous /'rævənəs/, adj. **1.** extremely hungry. **2.** greedy. **3.** Also, **ravening**. fierce and dangerous because of hunger: *ravenous wolves.* [ME, from OF] —**ravenousness**, n.

ravine /rəˈviːn/, n. a long, deep, narrow valley, esp. one worn by water.

raving /'reɪvɪŋ/, adj. **1.** mad; delirious; frenzied. **2.** *Colloq.* extraordinary or remarkable: *a raving beauty.* ◇n. **3.** wild, meaningless talk.

ravioli /ˌræviˈoʊli/, n.pl. small envelopes of pasta containing minced meat, cooked and served in a tomato sauce. [It, from L: turnip, beet]

ravish /'rævɪʃ/, v.t. **1.** to fill with strong emotion, esp. joy. **2.** to seize and carry off by force. **3.** to rape (a woman). [ME, from OF, from L: seize, carry off] —**ravishment**, n.

ravishing /'rævɪʃɪŋ/, adj. enchanting; entrancing.

raw /rɔ/, adj. **1.** uncooked: *raw meat.* **2.** untreated; unrefined: *the raw edge of a piece of wood; raw material.* **3.** unnaturally or painfully exposed: *raw flesh; a raw wound.* **4.** crude or brutal: *raw passions.* **5.** ignorant or inexperienced: *a raw recruit.* **6.** *Colloq.* harsh or unfair: *a raw deal.* **7.** damp and cold: *raw weather.* **8.** undiluted: *raw spirits.* **9. the raw, a.** a crude, uncultured state: *The play was about life in the raw.* **b.** *Colloq.* naked; nude: *She sunbakes in the raw.* **c.** a sensitive place, etc.: *Her remark touched him on the raw.*

Rawalpindi /ˌrɔlˈpɪndi/, n. a city in Pakistan, in western Punjab; provisional capital of Pakistan 1959–67. Pop. 794 843 (1981).

rawhide /'rɔhaɪd/, n. **1.** the untanned skin of cattle. **2.** a rope or whip made of this.

rawlplug /'rɔlplʌg/, n. a plug of wood fibre or plastic, pushed into a hole in a wall to receive a screw. [Trademark]

raw material, n. material before it is processed in manufacturing.

raw score, n. the original mark given by an examiner to an individual test paper (opposed to the *scaled score*).

raw silk, n. silk as reeled from the cocoons.

ray¹ /reɪ/, n. **1.** a narrow beam of light. **2.** a slight showing of anything: *a ray of hope.* **3.**

Phys. **a.** any of the lines or streams in which light or particles appear to flow, often from a luminous object. **b.** the straight line perpendicular to the wavefront of radiant energy. **4.** *Maths.* one of a system of straight lines coming from a point. **5.** any of a system of parts radially arranged. **6.** *Zool.* **a.** one of the branches or arms of a starfish or other radiate animal. **b.** one of the jointed supports of the soft fins of fishes. **7.** *Astron.* one of the many long bright streaks radiating from the large craters of the moon. [ME, from OF, from L]

ray² /reɪ/, *n.* a fish related to the sharks, with a flat body fitted for life on the sea bottom, and having the gill openings on the lower surface. [ME, from F, from L]

ray³ /reɪ/, *n. Music.* Also, **re**. See **solfa**.

Raymond Terrace /ˌreɪmənd 'terəs/, *n.* a town and former river port on the Hunter River in eastern NSW. Pop. 8793 (1986).

rayon /'reɪɒn/, *n.* a textile made from cellulose; artificial silk. [F: ray, from OF]

raze /reɪz/, *v.t.*, **razed**, **razing**. to tear down or level to the ground; demolish. Also, **rase**. [ME, from F, from VL, from L: scraped]

razoo /rɑ'zuː/, *n. Colloq.* in the phrase **not have a brass razoo**, to have no money at all. [orig. uncert.]

razor /'reɪzə/, *n.* **1.** a sharp-edged instrument used esp. for shaving hair from the skin. **2.** a small electrical machine used for the same purpose. ◇*v.t.* **3.** to shave. [ME, from OF: scrape, shave, RAZE]

razorback /'reɪzəbæk/, *n.* **1.** a sharp ridge of land. **2.** a bullock, cow, etc., in poor condition.

razzamatazz /'ræzmətæz/, *n. Colloq.* **1.** noisy and showy activity. **2.** any traditional style of jazz. Also, **razzmatazz**.

razzle-dazzle /'ræzəl-dæzəl/, *n. Colloq.* noisy and showy activity; razzmatazz.

Rb, *Chem. Symbol.* rubidium.

RC /ɑ 'siː/, *Abbrev.* **1.** Red Cross. **2.** Roman Catholic.

rd, *Abbrev.* **1.** road. **2.** rod(s).

r.d., *Phys. Abbrev.* relative density.

Rd, *Abbrev.* Road.

RDF /ɑ di 'ɛf/, *Abbrev.* radio direction-finder.

re¹ /reɪ, riː/, *n. Music.* See **solfège** and **solfa**. [See GAMUT]

re² /riː, reɪ/, *prep.* in the case of; with reference to. [L]

re-, **1.** a prefix indicating repetition, as in *reprint, rebirth*. **2.** a prefix indicating withdrawal or backward movement, often figurative like 'back', applied often to stems not used as words, as in *revert, retract*. [L]

're, *v.* a shortened form of *are* as in: **we're, you're, they're.**

Re, *Chem. Symbol.* rhenium.

reach /riːtʃ/, *v.t.* **1.** to get to, or get as far as, in moving, going, travelling, etc.: *The boat reached the shore; This letter reached me.* **2.** to succeed in touching or taking: *to reach a book on a high shelf.* **3.** to stretch or hold out; extend: *to reach out a hand.* **4.** to get in touch with: *I can't reach him by telephone; You can't reach people who live in a dream.* ◇*v.i.* **5.** to get or come to a particular place, person, condition, etc. (oft. fol. by to): *Will the lamp cord reach (to the wall)?* **6.** to stretch: *He reached out for her; His power reaches throughout the land.* **7.** to stretch or amount; extend: *The coat reaches to the knee.* **8.** to move to take something: *to reach for a gun.* ◇*n.* **9.** the act of reaching: *to make a reach for a gun.* **10.** the distance of reaching: *within reach of his voice.* **11.** range of action, power, etc. **12.** the length of one's arm: *He has a long reach.* **13.** a continuous stretch of something: *a reach of woodland.* **14.** the level part of a canal between locks. **15.** the part of a river between bends. [OE *ræcan*]

re-act, *v.t.* to act or perform again; re-enact.

react /ri'ækt/, *v.i.* **1.** (of two things, esp. chemical substances) to act upon each other. **2.** to respond to a stimulus or situation (oft. fol. by *to*): *He reacted by braking suddenly.*

reactance /ri'æktəns/, *n.* that part of the impedance of an alternating-current circuit which is due to inductance and capacitance. [REACT + -ANCE]

reactant /ri'æktənt/, *n.* a substance which takes part in a chemical reaction.

reaction /ri'ækʃən/, *n.* **1.** a movement, tendency or action in an opposite direction. **2.** an action in response to a stimulus, influence, or some other event. **3.** a political tendency or movement back to former policies and against change: *Conservatism is often a reaction to socialism or radicalism.* **4.** *Chem.* the chemical action of substances upon each other; chemical change. **5.** → **nuclear reaction**. **6.** *Phys.* See **Newton's laws**.

reactionary /ri'ækʃənəri, -ʃənri/, *n., adj., pl.* **-aries**. (a person) favoring political reaction; a conservative. Also, **reactionist**.

reaction engine, *n.* an engine that develops thrust by reaction to the throwing out of a substance from it, esp. an engine that throws out a stream of gases from burning fuel, as a rocket or jet engine. Also, **reaction motor**.

reactivate /ri'æktɪveɪt/, *v.t.*, **-vated, -vating.** to make something active again.

reactive /ri'æktɪv/, *adj.* **1.** tending to react or marked by reaction. **2.** *Chem.* chemically active.

reactor /ri'æktə/, *n.* **1.** a substance or person undergoing a reaction. **2.** *Phys.* → **nuclear reactor**.

read¹ /riːd/, *v.*, **read** /rɛd/, **reading** /'riːdɪŋ/, *n.* ◇*v.t.* **1.** to look at and understand: *to read a book; to read a sign.* **2.** to say aloud (something written, etc.). **3.** to know enough of (a language) to be able to understand things written in it: *to be able to read French.* **4.** to understand (signs, characters, etc.) by

read   862   **reality**

touch: *to read Braille*. **5.** to (try to) understand: *to read a person's character; to read a person's thoughts; to read the sky; to read dreams.* **6.** to understand or take (something seen) in a particular way; interpret: *He read her look as a sign of annoyance.* **7.** to introduce (something not expressed or directly shown) into what is experienced: *He read annoyance into her look.* **8.** (of an instrument) to indicate a figure, etc.: *The thermometer reads 40 degrees.* **9.** (of a computer) to take (information) from punch cards. **10.** to study: *to read law.* ◇*v.i.* **11.** to look at writing, etc., and understand it. **12.** to say aloud, written or printed words that one is looking at: *to read to a person.* **13.** to get knowledge by reading: *to read widely in literature.* **14.** to have a certain wording: *The later copy reads differently.* **15.** to be able to be understood (as stated): *a rule that reads two different ways.* **16.** (of a computer) to take in information. ◇*v.* **17. read between the lines,** to see the truth, beyond appearances. **18. you wouldn't read about it!** (an exclamation of surprise, usu. not serious). ◇*n.* **19.** the act of reading: *I just lay in bed and had a good read.* [OE *rǣdan* counsel, consider, read]

read² /red/, *adj.* having knowledge gained by reading: *a widely read person.* [properly pp. of READ¹]

Read /rid/, *n.* **Richard,** c. 1765–?, Australian convict artist, born in England; painter of portraits, including several of Governor Macquarie.

readable /'ridəbəl/, *adj.* **1.** easy or interesting to read. **2.** able to be read; legible. —**readability, readableness,** *n.*

reader /'ridə/, *n.* **1.** someone who reads. **2.** a book of instruction and practice in reading. **3.** someone employed to read and report on manuscripts, etc., sent in for publication. **4.** someone who reads or recites before an audience. **5.** a university teacher ranking next below a professor. **6.** a proofreader. —**readership,** *n.*

readily /'rɛdəli/, *adv.* **1.** quickly; easily; promptly. **2.** willingly; in a ready manner.

readiness /'rɛdinəs/, *n.* **1.** the condition of being ready. **2.** quickness; promptness; ease; facility: *readiness to take offence.* **3.** willingness: *readiness to help others.*

reading /'ridɪŋ/, *n.* **1.** the action or practice of someone who reads. **2.** ability to read: *Good reading comes with practice.* **3.** the way a part in a play, etc., is performed by a particular person. **4.** knowledge through books: *a man of wide reading.* **5.** matter read or for reading: *a novel that makes good reading; Today's reading is from St John.* **6.** a particular understanding of something: *What is your reading of the situation?* **7.** a figure given by an instrument, as a thermometer. **8.** *Parl Proc.* the formal presentation of a bill. ◇*adj.* **9.** relating to, or used for, reading: *reading skill; reading glasses.* **10.** given to reading: *the reading public.*

ready /'rɛdi/, *adj.*, **readier, readiest,** *v.*, **readied, readying,** *n.* ◇*adj.* **1.** completely prepared or in the right condition for immediate action or use: *soldiers ready for battle; Dinner is ready; Are you ready to go out?* **2.** willing: *ready to forgive.* **3.** quick: *He's very ready to understand; a ready answer; a man of ready wit.* **4.** eager or likely; apt: *too ready to criticise others.* **5.** likely at any moment (to do something): *a tree ready to fall.* **6.** immediately available for use: *ready money.* ◇*v.t.* **7.** to prepare. ◇*n.* **8.** the condition or position of being ready: *to bring a rifle to the ready.* [OE *rǣde* ready]

reafforest /riə'fɒrəst/, *v.t.* to replant with forest trees. Also, **reforest.** —**reafforestation,** *n.*

Reagan /'reɪgən/, *n.* **Ronald Wilson,** born 1911, US Republican politician; 40th president of the US, 1981–89; former movie actor; governor of California 1966–74.

reagent /ri'eɪdʒənt/, *n.* a substance which, because of the reactions it causes, is used in chemical analysis.

real /rɪl/, *adj.* **1.** true (rather than merely appearing to be true): *the real reason for an act.* **2.** being or happening as a fact; actual (rather than imaginary): *a story taken from real life.* **3.** genuine; not counterfeit, artificial, or imitation: *a real antique; a real diamond.* **4.** sincere; not pretended; unfeigned: *real sympathy.* **5.** *Law.* indicating or relating to property that cannot be moved, as lands and buildings (opposed to *personal*). **6.** *Maths.* → **real number.** ◇*adv.* **7.** *Colloq.* very; really: *real good.* [ME, from LL, from L: thing; matter]

real estate, *n.* land and whatever is on or in it, as minerals, trees, buildings, fences, etc. Also, **real property.**

real image, *n. Optics.* an image formed by the actual convergence of rays, as the image produced by a camera (opposed to *virtual image*).

realisation *or* **realization** /rɪəlaɪ'zeɪʃən/, *n.* **1.** the making or being made real of something imagined, planned, etc.: *the realisation of a dream.* **2.** knowledge and awareness: *the realisation of his guilt.* **3.** the act or result of realising or the state of being realised.

realise *or* **realize** /'rɪəlaɪz/, *v.*, **-lised, -lising.** ◇*v.t.* **1.** to come to understand clearly: *He realised for the first time that he was alone.* **2.** to make real, or give reality to (a hope, fear, plan, etc.) (oft. in passive): *His worst fears were realised when the business collapsed.* **3.** to turn into cash: *to realise assets.* —**realisable,** *adj.*

realism /'rɪəlɪzəm/, *n.* **1.** the tendency to face facts and deal with things as they really are, rather than as they exist in some ideal world. **2.** the taking of a practical view in human problems rather than one based on principles of right and wrong. **3.** the treatment of subjects in literature or art with faithfulness to nature or to real life (opposed to *idealism*): *Hogarth is a master of realism.* —**realist,** *n.* —**realistic,** *adj.*

reality /ri'æləti/, *n., pl.* **-ties. 1.** the state or fact of being real: *the reality of death.* **2.** likeness to what is real: *His fears did have a certain reality.* **3.** a real thing or fact: *The accident was a reality, not a dream.* **4.** *Philos.* something that

reality exists independently of ideas about it. **5. in reality,** really; actually; in fact or truth.

really /'rɪəli/, *adv.* **1.** in reality; actually: *to see things as they really are.* **2.** truly; genuinely: *a really honest man.* **3.** indeed: *Really, this is too much.* **4.** extremely: *Really hot.*

realm /relm/, *n.* **1.** a kingdom: *the realm of England.* **2.** a region in which anything rules or is dominant: *the realm of dreams.* **3.** a field; sphere; province: *the realm of physics.* [ME, from OF: regal, from L]

real number, *n.* **1.** one of the set of numbers which include all rational and irrational numbers. **2.** → **decimal number**.

real-time /'ril-taɪm/, *adj.*; /ril-'taɪm/, *n.* ◇*adj.* **1.** of or relating to an analytical or computing device which processes information and outputs results at the same rate at which the original information is presented. ◇*n.* **2.** a method using real-time processing: *This machine processes in real-time.*

realtor /'rɪəltə, -tɔ-/, *n.* → **estate agent**.

realty /'rɪəlti/, *n.* → **real estate**.

real wages, *n.pl.* the wages paid for work done, expressed in terms of buying power (opposed to *money wages*, the actual amount of money paid out for work done).

ream /rim/, *n.* **1.** Also, **printer's ream.** a standard quantity of paper equal to 20 quires or 500 sheets (formerly 480 sheets). **2.** (*pl.*) *Colloq.* a large quantity. [ME, from OF, through Sp, from Ar: bundle or bale]

reamer /'rimə/, *n.* a rotating finishing tool with spiral or straight fluted cutting edges for finishing a hole to size and shape.

reap /rip/, *v.t.* **1.** to cut (grain, etc.) with a sickle, machine, etc., for harvest. **2.** to gather or take (a crop, harvest, etc.). **3.** to get as a return, payment, or result: *to reap large profits.* ◇*v.i.* **4.** to reap grain, etc. [OE]

reaper /'ripə/, *n.* **1.** a machine for cutting standing grain. **2.** someone who reaps. **3. the grim reaper,** Death personified.

rear[1] /rɪə/, *n.* **1.** the back of anything. **2.** a space or position behind anything. **3.** the behind; buttocks. **4.** the last portion of an army, fleet, etc. ◇*adj.* **5.** situated at or relating to the rear. [var. of ARREAR, n.]

rear[2] /rɪə/, *v.t.* **1.** to care for and support until fully grown: *to rear a child.* **2.** to raise by building; erect. **3.** to lift, raise, or hold up; elevate. ◇*v.i.* **4.** to rise on the hind legs, as a horse. **5.** (of persons) to start up in angry excitement, etc. (commonly fol. by *up*). [OE *rǣran* RAISE]

rearguard /'rɪəgɑd/, *n.* part of an army or military force separated from the main body to guard the rear from surprise attack, esp. in a retreat.

reason /'rizən/, *n.* **1.** a ground or cause, as for a belief, action, fact, event, etc.: *the reason for declaring war.* **2.** a statement in defence or explanation of belief or action. **3.** mental powers concerned with drawing conclusions. **4.** sound judgment; good sense. **5.** the normal Powers of the mind; sanity. **6. by reason of,** on account of; because of. **7. in or within reason,** within the limits of what may be expected; moderate. **8. it stands to reason,** it is obvious or reasonable. ◇*v.i.* **9.** to think or argue in a logical manner. **10.** to draw conclusions from facts or premises. ◇*v.t.* **11.** to think out (a problem, etc.) logically (oft. fol. by *out*). **12.** to conclude or judge (fol. by *that*). **13.** to bring, persuade, etc., by reason. [ME, from OF, from L: reckoning, account]

reasonable /'rizənəbəl/, *adj.* **1.** (of a person) having reason. **2.** agreeable to reason or sound judgment: *a reasonable choice.* **3.** not past the limit of reason; not excessive: *reasonable terms.* **4.** moderate or fair, as in price.

reasoning /'rizənɪŋ, 'rizənɪŋ/, *n.* **1.** the act or process of someone who reasons. **2.** the process of drawing conclusions from facts or theoretical statements. **3.** the reasons, arguments, proofs, etc., resulting from this process.

reassure /riə'ʃɔ/, *v.t.,* **-sured, -suring. 1.** to restore (a person, etc.) to confidence. **2.** to reinsure. **– reassurance,** *n.*

rebate[1] /'ribeɪt/, *n., v.,* **-bated, -bating.** ◇*n.* **1.** the return of part of an original amount paid for some service or commodity. ◇*v.t.* **2.** to allow as a discount. **3.** to take away (a certain amount), as from a total. [ME, from OF: beat or put down]

rebate[2] /'ribeɪt/, *n.* a cut or groove made on the edge or surface of a board, etc., to receive the end or edge of another similarly shaped board, etc. [ME, probably from OF *rabat* a beating down, or *rabot* a joiner's plane]

Rebecca /rə'bekə/, *n. Bible.* the wife of Isaac, and mother of Esau and Jacob. Also, **Rebekah.** [See Genesis 24–27]

rebel /'rebəl/, *n., adj.*; /rə'bel/, *v.,* **-belled, -belling.** ◇*n.* **1.** someone who resists, or rises in arms against, the established government. **2.** someone or something that resists any authority or control. ◇*adj.* **3.** fighting authority; rebellious. **4.** of or relating to rebels. ◇*v.i.* **5.** to rise in arms or active resistance against the government. **6.** to resist any authority. [ME, from OF, from L: wage war again (as conquered people)]

rebellion /rə'beljən/, *n.* **1.** open, organised, and armed resistance to the government or ruler. **2.** resistance against any authority or control. **3.** refusal to obey established customs, culture, etc. [ME, from L]

rebellious /rə'beljəs/, *adj.* **1.** disobeying lawful authority; insubordinate. **2.** relating to or like rebels or rebellion. **3.** (of things) resisting treatment; refractory. [ME]

rebound /rə'baʊnd/, *v.*; /'ribaʊnd, rə'baʊnd/, *n.* ◇*v.i.* **1.** to spring back from the force of impact. ◇*n.* **2.** the act of rebounding; recoil. **3. on the rebound, a.** in the act of bouncing back. **b.** during a period of reaction, as after an unhappy love affair: *She married him on the rebound.* [ME, from OF]

rebuff /rə'bʌf/, *n.* **1.** a sudden check, as to one making advances. **2.** a strong refusal of an offer, etc.; snub. **3.** a check to action or

rebuff progress. ◇*v.t.* **4.** to give a rebuff to; check; repel. [F, from It]

rebuke /rə'bjuk/, *v.*, **-buked, -buking**, *n.* ◇*v.t.* **1.** to scold; reprove. ◇*n.* **2.** a scolding; reprimand. [ME, from OF: beat back]

rebut /rə'bʌt/, *v.t.*, **-butted, -butting**. to oppose or prove false by proof or argument. [ME, from AF] —**rebuttal**, *n.*

rec., *Abbrev.* **1.** receipt. **2.** recipe. **3.** record.

recalcitrant /rə'kælsətrənt/, *adj.* **1.** resisting authority or control. ◇*n.* **2.** a recalcitrant person. [L: kicking back] —**recalcitrance**, *n.*

recall /rə'kɔl/, *v.*; /'rikɔl/, *n.* ◇*v.t.* **1.** to remember. **2.** to bring back in thought or attention. **3.** to take back or withdraw. **4.** to remove (a public official) from office. ◇*n.* **5.** the act of recalling. **6.** memory; recollection.

recant /rə'kænt/, *v.t.* **1.** to withdraw or disown (a statement, etc.), esp. formally; retract. ◇*v.i.* **2.** to disown an opinion, etc., esp. formally. [L] —**recantation**, *n.*

recapitulate /rikə'pɪtʃəleɪt/, *v.*, **-lated, -lating**. ◇*v.t.* **1.** to summarise, as at the end of a speech. **2.** *Zool.* (of a young animal) to repeat (ancestral evolutionary stages) during its development. ◇*v.i.* **3.** to sum up statements or matters. [LL]

recapitulation /ˌrikəpɪtʃə'leɪʃən/, *n.* **1.** the act of recapitulating. **2.** the state or fact of being recapitulated. **3.** a review or summary, as at the end of a speech. **4.** *Zool.* the repetition of ancestral evolutionary stages in the development of an individual. **5.** *Music.* (in a sonata-form movement) a restatement of the original musical theme or themes.

recd, *Abbrev.* received. Also, **rec'd**.

recede /rə'sid/, *v.i.*, **-ceded, -ceding**. **1.** to move back to a more distant point. **2.** to become more distant. **3.** to slope backwards: *a receding chin*. [ME, from L: go back]

receipt /rə'sit/, *n.* **1.** a written acknowledgment of having received money, goods, etc. **2.** (*pl.*) the amount or quantity received. **3.** the act or result of receiving. ◇*v.t.* **4.** to acknowledge in writing the payment of (a bill). [ME, from AF, from L: received]

receive /rə'siv/, *v.*, **-ceived, -ceiving**. ◇*v.t.* **1.** to take into one's hand or one's possession (something offered or delivered). **2.** to have (something) granted, etc.: *to receive an honorary degree*. **3.** to get or learn: *to receive news*. **4.** to take into the mind. **5.** to experience: *to receive attention*. **6.** to suffer or undergo: *to receive a broken arm*. **7.** to be at home to (visitors). **8.** to admit (a person) to a place. **9.** to admit to a condition, membership, etc.: *to receive someone into the Church*. **10.** to accept as authoritative, true, or approved: *a principle universally received*. ◇*v.i.* **11.** to receive something. **12.** *Radio.* to convert incoming electromagnetic waves into the original signal, as soundwaves or light on a television screen. [ME, from ONF, from L: take back, take to one's self, receive]

Received Standard English, *n.* the dialect of English which has won general acceptance in England and certain other places as 'correct'; the speech of the southern middle classes, the BBC, and the universities, historically deriving chiefly from the south-east Midland dialect of Middle English.

receiver /rə'sivə/, *n.* **1.** someone or something that receives. **2. a.** a device which receives electrical signals, waves, etc., and changes them to sounds or pictures, as a radio or television receiving set. **b.** the part of a telephone held to the ear. **3.** *Law.* a person appointed, usu. by a court, to take charge of a business or property of others, pending a law suit. **4.** *Comm.* someone appointed to receive money due. **5.** someone who knowingly receives stolen goods. **6.** a device for receiving or holding something. **7.** *Tennis.* the player who receives the ball from the server.

receivership /rə'sivəʃɪp/, *n.* **1.** *Law.* the condition of being in the hands of a receiver. **2.** the position or function of being a receiver in charge of managing the property of others.

recent /'risənt/, *adj.* **1.** lately happening, done, made, etc. **2.** not long past, as a period. **3.** (*oft. cap.*) *Geol.* relating to the later division of the Quaternary period, following the Pleistocene, and regarded as the present geological division. [L]

receptacle /rə'septəkəl/, *n.* that which receives or holds something; a container. [ME, from L]

reception /rə'sepʃən/, *n.* **1.** the act or result of receiving. **2.** an occasion when people are formally received. **3.** an office, desk, etc., where callers are received. **4.** *Radio.* the quality gained in receiving under given conditions. [ME, from L]

receptionist /rə'sepʃənəst/, *n.* a person employed to receive and direct callers, as in an office.

receptive /rə'septɪv/, *adj.* **1.** having the quality of receiving or taking in. **2.** able or quick to receive ideas, suggestions, etc.: *a receptive mind*.

receptor /rə'septə/, *n.* one of or a group of the end organs of sensory or afferent neurons, specialised to be sensitive to stimulating agents. [L: a receiver]

recess /rə'ses, 'rises/, *n.*; /rə'ses/, *v.* ◇*n.* **1.** a part or space that is set back, as an alcove in a room. **2.** (*usu. pl.*) a quiet, hidden inner area or part. **3.** a stopping for a time, from work, or some activity. ◇*v.t.* **4.** to place or set in a recess. **5.** to form as or like a recess. [L: a going back]

recession /rə'seʃən/, *n.* **1.** the act of moving back or withdrawing: *recession of the tide*. **2.** a part going or set back, as a wall, etc. **3.** a procession at the end of a church service. **4.** a period of bad economic circumstances, usu. less severe than a depression.

recessional /rə'seʃənəl/, *adj.* **1.** of or relating to a recession of the clergy and choir after a church service. **2.** of or relating to a recess, as of a law-making body.

recessive /rə'sesɪv/, *adj.* **1.** tending to move back; receding. **2.** *Biol.* relating to or

recessive 865 **recoil**

showing a recessive. ◇n. **3.** *Biol.* a hereditary character resulting from a gene which has less biochemical activity than another dominant gene, and hence is kept inactive when paired with it: *Blue eye color is a recessive, whereas brown is a dominant.*

Receveur /rəsə'vɜ/, *n.* **Louis**, ?–1788, a French friar and scientist on *L'Astrolabe* on the expedition to the Pacific commanded by La Pérouse; died at Botany Bay.

recherché /rə'ʃɛəfeɪ/, *adj.* **1.** found or chosen with care. **2.** elegant; over-refined. [F]

Recherche /rə'ʃɔʃ/, *n.* **Archipelago of the,** a group of more than 100 scattered islands off the southern coast of WA extending from south of Esperance 200 km to the east. [named after *La Recherche*, a ship of a 1792 French expedition]

recidivism /rə'sɪdəvɪzəm/, *n.* repeated or habitual relapse into crime. [L: relapsing] – **recidivist**, *n.* – **recidivistic**, *adj.*

recipe /'rɛsəpi/, *n.* any formula, esp. one for preparing a dish in cookery. [ME, from L: take, as used at the head of prescriptions]

recipient /rə'sɪpiənt/, *n.* someone or something that receives; receiver. [L: receiving]

reciprocal /rə'sɪprəkəl/, *adj.* **1.** given, felt, etc., by each towards each; mutual: *reciprocal love.* **2.** given, performed, felt, etc., in return: *reciprocal aid.* ◇n. **3.** something that is reciprocal to something else; a counterpart. **4.** *Maths.* the number by which a given quantity is multiplied to produce one. [L: returning, reciprocal]

reciprocate /rə'sɪprəkeɪt/, *v.*, **-cated**, **-cating.** ◇v.t. **1.** to give, feel, etc., in return. **2.** to give and receive reciprocally; interchange: *to reciprocate favors.* **3.** to cause to move alternately backwards and forwards. ◇v.i. **4.** to make return, as for something given. **5.** to make an interchange. **6.** to move alternately backwards and forwards. [L] – **reciprocative**, *adj.* – **reciprocation**, *n.*

reciprocity /rɛsə'prɒsəti/, *n.* **1.** reciprocal state or relation. **2.** exchange from one to another; reciprocation. **3.** in commercial dealings between countries, a policy of mutual exchange and the granting of advantages or privileges.

recital /rə'saɪtl/, *n.* **1.** a musical entertainment given usu. by a single performer. **2.** the act of reciting. **3.** a detailed statement. **4.** an account, story, etc.

recitation /rɛsə'teɪʃən/, *n.* **1.** the act of reciting. **2.** a saying or repeating in public of something from memory, (as poetry, etc.). **3.** → **elocution.** [L]

recitative /rɛsətə'tiv/, *adj.* **1.** of the nature of or resembling a recitation. ◇n. **2.** a style of vocal music in opera in which the words are sung in the rhythm of natural speech. **3.** a passage or piece in this style. [It: recite]

recite /rə'saɪt/, *v.*, **-cited**, **-citing.** ◇v.t. **1.** to repeat the words of (a poem, etc.), as from memory, esp. in a formal manner. **2.** to give an account of: *to recite one's adventures.* ◇v.i. **3.** to recite something from memory. [ME, from L: read aloud, repeat]

reckless /'rɛkləs/, *adj.* totally careless of the results of action. [OE *recēleas* careless]

reckon /'rɛkən/, *v.t.* **1.** to count or calculate as to number or amount. **2.** to consider (as stated): *to be reckoned a beauty.* **3.** *Colloq.* to think or suppose. ◇v.i. **4.** to count. **5.** to settle accounts, as with a person. **6.** to count, depend, or rely (*on*), as in expectation. **7.** to think; suppose. [OE (*ge*)*recenian*]

reckoning /'rɛkənɪŋ/, *n.* **1.** a count or calculation. **2.** the settlement of accounts, as between parties. **3.** a statement of an amount due; bill. **4.** an accounting, as for things received or done: *a day of reckoning.* **5.** → **dead reckoning.**

reclaim /rə'kleɪm/, *v.t.* **1.** to bring (waste or marshy land) into a condition for cultivation, etc. **2.** to recover (substances) in a pure or usable form from waste matter, etc. **3.** to bring back to more socially, morally, or religiously acceptable principles, ideas, etc. ◇n. **4.** recovery; reclamation: *beyond reclaim.* [ME, from OF, from L: cry out against] – **reclamation**, *n.*

reclassify /ˌri'klæsəfaɪ/, *v.t.*, **-fied**, **-fying.** **1.** to put into a new or another division or category. **2.** to classify again; reassess. – **reclassification**, *n.*

recline /rə'klaɪn, ri-/, *v.*, **-clined**, **-clining.** ◇v.i. **1.** to lean or lie back. ◇v.t. **2.** to cause to lean back on something. [ME, from L]

recluse /rə'klus/, *n.* a person who has little or no contact with society. [ME, from OF, from LL: shut up] – **reclusive**, *adj.* – **reclusion**, *n.*

recognisance or **recognizance** /rə'kɒgnəzəns/, *n.* **1.** the act of recognising; recognition. **2.** *Law.* a bond entered into before a court or a magistrate, binding a person to do a particular act. [ME, from OF]

recognise or **recognize** /'rɛkəgnaɪz/, *v.t.*, **-nised**, **-nising.** **1.** to know again: *I scarcely recognised him.* **2.** to identify from knowledge of appearance or character. **3.** to understand as existing or true; realise: *to be the first to recognise a fact.* **4.** to admit formally as existing: *One government recognises another.* **5.** to admit or treat as correct: *to recognise a claim.* **6.** to show acquaintance with (a person, etc.) as by a salute. **7.** to show approval of (kindness, merit, etc.) as by some reward. [*recogn*(*ition*) + -ISE[1]] – **recognisable**, *adj.*

recognition /rɛkəg'nɪʃən/, *n.* **1.** the act of recognising. **2.** the state of being recognised. **3.** an understanding of something as existing or true; realisation. [ME, from L]

recoil /rə'kɔɪl/ *for defs 1–3*; /rə'kɔɪl, 'rikɔɪl/ *for def.* 4., *v.i.* **1.** to draw back, as in fear or horror. **2.** to spring or fly back, as a result of force of impact or of a discharge, as a gun. **3.** to spring or come back; react (fol. by *on* or *upon*). ◇n. **4.** the act of recoiling. [ME, from OF, from L *re*- RE- + *cūlus* the buttocks]

recollect /rekə'lekt/, *v.t., v.i.* to recall to mind, by an act or effort of memory; remember. [L: collected again] **—recollection,** *n.*

recommend /rekə'mend/, *v.t.* **1.** to present as favorable or worthy: *to recommend a book.* **2.** to urge as advisable: *I recommend caution.* **3.** to advise to do something: *to recommend someone to wait.* **4.** to make acceptable or pleasing: *a plan that has little to recommend it.* [ME, from ML, from L: commend again] **—recommendation,** *n.*

recompense /'rekəmpens/, *v.,* **-pensed, -pensing,** *n.* ◇*v.t.* **1.** to repay or reward, for service, aid, etc. **2.** to make a return or repayment for. ◇*n.* **3.** a repayment made, as for loss, injury, etc. **4.** reward; remuneration. [ME, from LL, from L]

recompression chamber /rikəm'preʃən 'tʃeɪmbə/, *n.* a room in which a diver suffering from the bends may be placed, in which the air pressure is increased and then slowly brought to normal.

reconcile /'rekənsaɪl/, *v.t.,* **-ciled, -ciling. 1.** to make no longer opposed (fol. by *to*): *to reconcile someone to his fate.* **2.** to win over to friendliness: *to reconcile an angry person.* **3.** to settle (a quarrel, etc.). **4.** to bring into agreement or harmony: *to reconcile differing statements.* [ME, from L] **—reconcilable,** *adj.*

reconciliation /rekənsɪliːˈeɪʃən/, *n.* **1.** the act of reconciling. **2.** *Rom Cath Ch.* the rite of confessing one's sins and obtaining forgiveness; confession.

recondite /rə'kɒndaɪt, 'rekəndaɪt/, *adj.* **1.** dealing with matters that are difficult to understand. **2.** removed from ordinary knowledge or understanding; abstruse. **3.** little known; obscure. [L: put away, hidden]

recondition /rikən'dɪʃən/, *v.t.* to bring back to a good or satisfactory condition; repair; restore; overhaul.

reconnaissance /rə'kɒnəsəns/, *n.* **1.** the act of reconnoitring. **2.** *Mil.* a search made in the field for useful military information. **3.** *Geol.* an examination or survey of the general geological characteristics of an area. [F]

reconnoitre /rekə'nɔɪtə/, *v.,* **-tred, -tring,** *n.* ◇*v.t.* **1.** to study or examine (the enemy's strength or position, etc.) in order to gain information for military purposes. **2.** to examine (an area, etc.) for engineering, geological, or other purposes. ◇*v.i.* **3.** to make a study or examination of (the enemy, an area, etc.). ◇*n.* **4.** the act of reconnoitring; reconnaissance. [F: recognise]

reconsider /rikən'sɪdə/, *v.t., v.i.* to consider again with a view to a change of decision or action. **—reconsideration,** *n.*

reconstitute /ri'kɒnstətjut/, *v.t.,* **-tuted, -tuting.** to create or form again; reconstruct; recompose: *reconstituted milk.*

reconstruct /rikən'strʌkt/, *v.t.* **1.** to rebuild. **2.** to re-create or re-enact past events or another place: *to reconstruct a crime.* **—reconstruction,** *n.*

record /rə'kɔd/, *v.;* /'rekɔd/, *n., adj.,* ◇*v.t.* **1.** to set down in writing, etc., as for later use. **2.** to cause to be set down: *to record one's vote.* **3.** to show or state: *to record a protest by sitting down in the street.* **4.** to set down by marks, cuts, etc., for use on a record-player or tape recorder. ◇*v.i.* **5.** to record something. ◇*n.* **6.** the act of recording. **7.** the state or fact of being recorded, as in writing. **8.** an account in writing, etc., for preserving knowledge. **9.** *Computers.* a self-contained group of data, as a punched card or a line of print. **10.** a report or list of actions or achievements, etc.: *He has a good record at work; He couldn't get a job because of his criminal record.* **11.** any thing or person serving as a memorial. **12.** a marking, etc., made by a recording instrument. **13.** a disc, used for reproducing sound; gramophone record. **14.** the best rate, amount, etc., gained, as in some form of sport. **15.** *Law.* an official written report of the proceedings of a court of justice. **16. off the record,** unofficially. **17. on record,** recorded publicly. ◇*adj.* **18.** making or supplying a record. **19.** above all others: *a record year for sales.* [ME, from OF, from L: call to mind, remember]

recorder /rə'kɔdə/, *n.* **1.** someone who records, esp. as an official duty. **2.** a recording apparatus or device. **3.** **→tape recorder. 4.** a soft-toned flute played in vertical position.

recording /rə'kɔdɪŋ/, *n.* **1.** the act or practice of making a record. **2.** *Elect.* a record of music, speech, etc., made as on magnetic tape for purposes of reproduction; record or tape.

record-player /'rekɔd-pleɪə/, *n.* a machine that reproduces sound from a record; gramophone; phonograph.

recount /rə'kaʊnt/, *v.t.* **1.** to tell in detail; narrate. **2.** to tell one by one; enumerate. [ME, from AF: repeat, relate]

recoup /rə'kup/, *v.;* /'rikup/, *n.,* ◇*v.t.* **1.** to get an equivalent for; compensate for. **2.** to regain or recover. **3.** to pay back; indemnify. ◇*n.* **4.** the act of recouping. [ME, from F: cut again]

recourse /rə'kɔs/, *n.* **1.** a turning to a person or thing for help or protection: *to have recourse to someone.* **2.** a person or thing turned to for help or protection. **3.** *Comm.* the right to turn to a person for monetary repayment. [ME, from OF, from L: a running back]

recover /rə'kʌvə/, *v.t.* **1.** to get again, or regain (something lost or taken away). **2.** to make up for or make good (loss, damage, etc., to oneself). **3.** to regain the strength, balance, etc., of (oneself). **4.** *Law.* **a.** to get by judgment in a court of law: *to recover damages for a wrong.* **b.** to gain title to through legal process: *to recover land.* **5.** to regain from a bad state, practice, etc. ◇*v.i.* **6.** to regain health after sickness, etc. (oft. fol. by *from*): *to recover from an accident.* **7.** to regain a former (and better) state or condition. **8.** to regain one's self-control, balance, etc. [ME, from AF, from L: recuperate] **—recovery,** *n.*

recreant /'rekriənt/, *adj.* **1.** cowardly; craven. **2.** unfaithful; disloyal. ◇*n.* **3.** a

recreant coward. **4.** a traitor. [ME, from OF: yield in a contest] —**recreance, recreancy,** n.

recreation /ˌrekriˈeɪʃən/, n. **1.** relaxation by means of some game, agreeable exercise, etc. **2.** a pastime, game, exercise, etc., giving relaxation and enjoyment. ◇adj. **3.** of or relating to an area, room, etc., set aside for recreation. [ME, from L]

recriminate /rəˈkrɪməneɪt/, v., **-nated, -nating.** ◇v.i. **1.** to bring a countercharge against someone who blames another of wrongdoing. ◇v.t. **2.** to blame another in return. [ML] —**recrimination,** n. —**recriminator,** n.

recruit /rəˈkruːt/, n. **1.** Mil. a newly enlisted member of the armed forces. See Appendix. **2.** a newly created member of any body or class. ◇v.t. **3.** to enlist (someone) for service in the armed forces. ◇v.i. **4.** to enlist someone for service in the armed forces. [F: a new growth] —**recruitment,** n.

rectangle /ˈrektæŋgəl/, n. a parallelogram with all its angles right angles. [LL: right-angled] —**rectangular,** adj.

recti-, a word part meaning 'straight', 'right'. Also, before vowels, **rect-.** [L, combining form of rectus]

rectifier /ˈrektəfaɪə/, n. **1.** someone or something which rectifies. **2.** Elect. an apparatus which changes an alternating current into a direct current, without an intermediate change of energy.

rectify /ˈrektəfaɪ/, v.t., **-fied, -fying. 1.** to make, put, or set right; remedy; correct. **2.** Elect. to change (an alternating current) into a direct current. **3.** to determine the length of (a curve). [ME, from LL] —**rectification,** n.

rectilinear /ˌrektəˈlɪniə/, adj. **1.** formed by or forming a straight line. **2.** moving in a straight line. Also, **rectilineal.**

rectitude /ˈrektətjuːd/, n. **1.** rightness of principle or practice: *the rectitude of one's actions.* **2.** correctness: *rectitude of judgment.* [ME, from LL, from L]

recto /ˈrektoʊ/, n., pl. **-tos.** Print. the right-hand page of an open book or manuscript; the front of a leaf (opposed to verso). [L, short for *recto (folio)* on right-hand (leaf)]

rector /ˈrektə/, n. **1.** *Rom Cath Ch.* an ecclesiastic in charge of a college, religious house, or congregation. **2.** *Anglican Ch.* a clergyman who has the charge of a parish. **3.** a permanent head in certain universities, colleges, and schools. [ME, from L: ruler] —**rectorial,** adj.

rectory /ˈrektəri/, n., pl. **-ries.** a rector's house.

rectum /ˈrektəm/, n., pl. **-ta** /-tə/. the fairly straight final section of the large intestine, ending in the anus. [NL] —**rectal,** adj.

recumbent /rəˈkʌmbənt/, adj. **1.** lying down; reclining; leaning. **2.** inactive; idle. [L] —**recumbency,** n.

recuperate /rəˈkuːpəreɪt/, v.i., **-rated, -rating.** to recover from sickness, tiredness, loss, etc. [L: regained, recovered] —**recuperation,** n. —**recuperative,** adj.

recur /rɪˈkɜː, rə-/, v.i., **-curred, -curring. 1.** to happen again, as an event, experience, etc. **2.** to return in action, thought, conversation, etc. [ME, from L: run back] —**recurrence,** n. —**recurrent,** adj.

recurring decimal, n. Maths. a decimal which has one or more of its digits repeated endlessly. The recurring digits are shown by a bar or dots above them, as in $0.21532 = 0.21\overline{532} = 0.21532532...$

recursion /rəˈkɜːʒən/, n. Maths. the operation of a rule or formula to determine a succession of terms, the rule being obtained by analysis of the preceding terms.

recursive /rəˈkɜːsɪv/, adj. **1.** of or relating to recursion. **2.** allowing or relating to an operation that may be repeated indefinitely.

recycle /riːˈsaɪkəl/, v.t., **-cycled, -cycling.** to treat (waste) so that new products can be made from it. —**recyclable,** adj.

red /red/, adj., **redder, reddest,** n. ◇adj. **1.** of a hue beyond orange in the spectrum. **2.** (oft. cap.) politically extreme, esp. communist. ◇n. **3.** any of the hues beyond orange in the spectrum, such as scarlet, vermilion, etc. **4.** something red. **5.** red wine. **6.** (oft. cap.) someone politically extreme, esp. a communist. **7. see red,** Colloq. to become angry. **8. the red,** a. red ink as used in accounting for recording losses, deficits. **b.** loss or debt: *to be in the red.* [ME red(e), OE rēad]

-red, a noun suffix denoting condition, as in *hatred.* [ME *-rede,* OE *-ræden*]

red alert, n. a state of extreme emergency.

red-back spider, n. a small, very poisonous, Australian spider, colored dark brown to black, usu. with a red or orange streak on the body.

Red Baron, n. →Baron Manfred von Richthofen.

red-bellied black snake, n. a poisonous snake of eastern Australian forests and scrubs, shiny black above and pale pink to red below.

red blood cell, n. a red blood corpuscle. See **corpuscle.**

red-blooded /ˈred-blʌdəd/, adj. strong; virile.

redbreast /ˈredbrest/, n. the European robin, so called from the color of the breast feathers.

red cabbage, n. a purplish variety of cabbage.

red carpet, n. **1.** a strip of red carpet laid for important persons to walk on when entering or leaving a building, etc. **2.** highly favored treatment.

red cedar, n. **1.** a tree, native to the island of NG and eastern Australia, with easily worked red timber valued for cabinet work. **2.** any of several coniferous trees, as a juniper, found in North America, with sweet-smelling reddish wood used for making pencils, etc.

Redcliffe /ˈredklɪf/, n. a city on the periphery of the metropolitan area of Brisbane, Qld, on a peninsula north of Brisbane. Pop. 44 933 (1986).

redcoat /ˈrɛdkout/, *n.* (formerly) a British soldier.

Red Crescent, *n.* the Muslim organisation functioning as the Red Cross, esp. in Turkey.

Red Cross, *n.* 1. an international philanthropic organisation (**Red Cross Society**) established by the Geneva Convention of 1864, to care for the sick and wounded in war, and relieve suffering caused by floods, fire, and other calamities. 2. a branch of it: *the Australian Red Cross*.

redden /ˈrɛdn/, *v.t., v.i.* to make or become red.

redeem /rəˈdim/, *v.t.* 1. to buy or pay off: *to redeem a debt*. 2. to recover (something pledged or mortgaged) by payment, etc.: *to redeem a pawned watch*. 3. to convert (bonds, etc.) into cash. 4. to carry out (a pledge, promise, etc.). 5. to make up for: *He redeemed his lie by later telling the truth*. 6. to cause to be saved from dishonor: *He redeemed himself; a redeeming feature*. 7. to obtain the release of, as from captivity, by paying a ransom. [ME, from L: buy back] **—redeemable**, *adj.*

redeemer /rəˈdimə/, *n.* 1. someone who redeems. 2. (*cap.*) Jesus Christ.

redemption /rəˈdɛmpʃən/, *n.* 1. the act or result of redeeming. 2. deliverance; rescue. 3. *Theol.* rescue from sin; salvation. [ME, from L: buy back]

red ensign, *n.* the flag carried by all merchant vessels registered in Australia.

redeploy /ridəˈplɔɪ/, *v.t.* 1. to rearrange or reorganise (a person, military unit, etc.), in order to create more effective results. ◇*v.i.* 2. to carry out a rearrangement. **—redeployment**, *n.*

redevelop /ridəˈvɛləp/, *v.t., v.i.* to develop again. **—redevelopment**, *n.*

Redfern /ˈrɛdfən/, *n.* **William**, 1774?–1833, Australian pioneer surgeon, born in England; his recommendations led to improvement of conditions of convict ships.

red flag, *n.* 1. the recognised sign of a socialist or revolutionary party. 2. a danger signal. 3. something certain to create anger, etc.

Redford /ˈrɛdfəd/, *n.* 1. **Harry**, Australian cattle stealer; his exploits are believed to have been the basis for Rolf Boldrewood's *Robbery Under Arms* (1888). 2. **Robert**, born 1936, a US film actor and director; starred in *Butch Cassidy and the Sundance Kid* (1969).

Redgrave family /ˈrɛdgreɪv/, *n.* an English family of actors including 1. **Sir Michael (Scudamore)**, 1908–85, films include *The Dam Busters* (1955). 2. his elder daughter, **Vanessa**, born 1937, films include *Julia* (1977). 3. his younger daughter, **Lynn**, born 1944, films include *Georgy Girl* (1966).

Red Guard, *n.* a member of a Chinese youth movement which supported Mao Zedong in his struggle to effect the Cultural Revolution in 1965–71.

red gum, *n.* Australian gum tree with hard red timber.

red-handed /rɛd-ˈhændəd/, *adj., adv.* in the very act of a crime or other deed.

red herring, *n.* 1. something to distract attention; a false clue. 2. smoked herring.

Red Indian, *n.* an aborigine of North America; American Indian.

redistribute /ridəˈstrɪbjut/, *v.t.*, **-buted, -buting.** 1. to divide or share again in a different way. 2. *Govt.* to change the shape and size of an electorate thereby changing the number of electors in it and surrounding electorates. **—redistribution**, *n.*

red kangaroo, *n.* See **kangaroo**.

red lead, *n.* a heavy, earthy substance, Pb_3O_4, orange to red in color, used in the making of paint and glass.

redolent /ˈrɛdələnt/, *adj.* 1. having a pleasant smell; fragrant. 2. smelling (fol. by *of*). 3. suggestive; reminiscent (fol. by *of*): *stories redolent of mystery*. [ME, from L: giving back a smell] **—redolence**, *n.*

redouble /riˈdʌbl/, *v.*, **-led, -ling.** ◇*v.t.* 1. to double or increase greatly: *to redouble one's efforts*. 2. to repeat: *to redouble an attack*. ◇*v.i.* 3. to be doubled. [ME, from F]

redoubtable /rəˈdautəbəl/, *adj.* 1. that is to be feared; formidable. 2. commanding respect. [ME, from OF: fear]

redoubted /rəˈdautəd/, *adj.* respected; renowned.

redound /rəˈdaund/, *v.i.* 1. to have an effect, as to the advantage or disadvantage of a person or thing. 2. to come back, as upon a person. [ME, from OF, from L: overflow]

redox reaction, *n. Chem.* a reaction using the process of reduction-oxidation.

red pepper, *n.* 1. a flavoring, cayenne, used in food. 2. the pepper plant, the pods of which are used for flavoring, sauces, etc.

red peril, *n. Colloq.* the threatened spread of communism.

redress /rəˈdrɛs/, *n.* 1. the setting right of what is wrong. 2. relief from wrong or injury. ◇*v.t.* 3. to set right or correct (wrongs, injuries, etc.). 4. to adjust evenly again, as a balance. [ME, from F]

Red Sea, *n.* a long narrow arm of the Indian Ocean, extending north-west between Africa and Arabia; connected with the Mediterranean by the Suez Canal, so called because of the reddish algae which appear in it at certain times. About 2333 km long; about 461 020 km²; greatest depth, 2211 m.

red shift, *n.* the shift of spectral lines toward the red end of the visible spectrum in the light given out by a celestial body as it moves further out into the universe.

red tape, *n.* 1. tape of a reddish color, much used for tying up official papers. 2. unnecessary attention to formality and rules.

reduce /rəˈdjus/, *v.*, **-duced, -ducing.** ◇*v.t.* 1. to bring down to a smaller size, amount, number, etc. 2. to lower in degree, strength, etc.: *to reduce speed*. 3. to bring down

reduce to a lower rank, standing, etc. **4.** to lower in price. **5.** to bring to a certain state, condition, etc.: *to reduce glass to powder.* **6.** to bring under control; subdue. **7.** *Photog.* to treat so as to make less dense, as a negative. **8.** *Chem.* **a.** to remove oxygen from. **b.** to add hydrogen to. **c.** to lower the valency of the positively-charged element by the addition of electrons. **9.** *Chem, Metall.* to bring into the metallic state by removing non-metallic constituents; smelt. **10.** *Biol.* to cause (a cell) to undergo meiotic (cell) division. ◇*v.i.* **11.** to become reduced. [ME, from L: bring back, restore, replace] **—reduced, reducible**, *adj.*

reducer /rə'djusə/, *n.* **1.** someone or something that reduces. **2.** *Photog.* **a.** an oxidising solution used to reduce a negative in density. **b.** a developing agent.

reducing agent, *n.* a substance that causes another substance to undergo reduction and is oxidised in the process.

reduction /rə'dʌkʃən/, *n.* **1.** the act or result of reducing. **2.** the amount by which something is reduced. **3.** a copy on a smaller scale. **4.** → **meiosis**. **5.** *Chem.* the opposite of oxidation. [L] **—reductional, reductive**, *adj.*

reduction-oxidation /rə,dʌkʃən-ɒksə-'deɪʃən/, *n. Chem.* the process by which one substance is reduced while the other is oxidised.

redundant /rə'dʌndənt/, *adj.* **1.** more than is usual or natural: *a redundant part.* **2.** using too many words to express ideas: *a redundant style.* **3.** of or relating to a worker who is no longer needed in his job. [L: overflowing] **—redundancy**, *n.*

reduplicate /ri'djuplɪkeɪt/, *v.*, **-cated, -cating.** ◇*v.t.* **1.** to double; repeat. **2.** *Gram.* to form (a new word) by doubling a given syllable or word part, as in *can-can.* ◇*v.i.* **3.** to become doubled. [LL: doubled] **—reduplication**, *n.*

redwood /'rɛdwʊd/, *n.* an American coniferous tree, remarkable for its height, and valued for its wood.

reed /rid/, *n.* **1.** the straight stem of any of various tall grasses, usu. found growing in marshy places. **2.** anything made from such a stem or from something similar, as an arrow. **3.** *Music.* **a.** a simple musical pipe made from a reed, etc. **b.** a small piece of cane or metal, fixed to the mouths of some wind instruments **(reed instruments)**, which is set into vibration by a stream of air and, in turn, sets into vibration the air column inside the tube of the instrument. **4. broken reed**, someone who is too weak to be relied upon. [OE *hrēod*]

Reed /rid/, *n.* **1. John**, 1887–1920, US journalist and poet; author of *Ten Days that Shook the World* (1919). **2. Joseph**, 1823?–1890, Australian architect, born in England; built civic buildings in Melbourne, esp. the Exhibition buildings.

reed organ, *n. Music.* a keyboard instrument like the pipe organ but having the notes produced by small metal reeds.

reedwarbler /'ridwɔblə/, *n.* **1.** a small warbler found in freshwater reedy areas throughout Australia, NG and islands to the north. **2.** a small Old World warbler found in marshy places.

reedy /'ridi/, *adj.*, **reedier, reediest. 1.** full of or like reeds. **2.** made of a reed: *a reedy pipe.* **3.** of or having a tone like that of a reed instrument: *He has a reedy voice.*

reef¹ /rif/, *n.* **1.** a narrow ridge of rocks, sand, and often coral, at or near the surface of water. **2.** *Mining.* **—lode.** [D or LG *rif*, from Scand]

reef² /rif/, *n.* **1.** a part of a sail which is rolled and tied down to reduce the area exposed to the wind. ◇*v.t.* **2.** to shorten (a sail) by tying in one or more reefs. [ME *riff*, from Scand]

reef³ /rif/, *v.t. Colloq.* to remove, usu. by force (fol. by *out*).

reefer /'rifə/, *n. Colloq.* a marijuana cigarette. [same as REEF², in generalised sense of rolled object]

reef knot, *n.* a kind of double knot which does not slip.

reek /rik/, *n.* **1.** a strong, unpleasant smell. **2.** steam; vapor. ◇*v.i.* **3.** to smell strongly and unpleasantly: *That pipe reeks; He reeks of garlic.* **4.** to be strongly and unpleasantly suggestive of: *That letter reeks of insincerity.* **5.** to give off steam, smoke, etc. ◇*v.t.* **6.** to treat with smoke. **7.** to give off (smoke, fumes, etc.). [OE *rēc*]

reel¹ /ril/, *n.* **1.** a cylinder, frame, etc., turning on an axis, on which to wind something. **2.** a turning device fixed to the end of a fishing rod, for winding up or letting out the line. **3.** a quantity of something wound on a reel. **4.** *Films.* **a.** the spool, usu. metal, on which film is wound. **b.** a roll of film to be shown with a film projector. ◇*v.t.* **5.** to wind on a reel, as thread, rope, etc. **6.** to draw with a reel, or by winding. **7.** to say, write, or produce in an easy, continuous way (fol. by *off*). [OE *hrēol*] **—reeler**, *n.*

reel² /ril/, *v.i.* **1.** to sway or rock from a blow, dizziness, etc.; stagger. **2.** to fall back. **3.** to turn round and round; whirl; spin. [ME]

reel³ /ril/, *n.* **1.** a lively dance popular in Scotland. **2.** the music for this.

re-entrant angle, *n. Geom.* an angle directed back inwards, rather than outwards, as an exterior angle of less than 180° in a closed polygon.

re-entry /ri-'entri/, *n., pl.* **-tries. 1.** the act of re-entering. **2.** *Aeron.* the return of a spacecraft, rocket, etc., into the earth's atmosphere. **3.** a surfing action in which the surfer heads up into and comes over with, the breaking part of the wave.

Rees /ris/, *n.* **Lloyd Frederic**, 1895–1988, Australian landscape artist.

reeve¹ /riv/, *n.* **1.** *Hist.* an administrative officer of a town or district. **2.** *Hist.* someone of high rank representing the crown. **3.** a bailiff, steward, or overseer. [OE *gerēfa* high official]

reeve

reeve[2] /riːv/, v.t., **reeved** or **rove, reeving. 1.** to pass (a rope, etc.) through a hole, ring, or the like. **2.** to fasten by placing through or around something. [? D *reven* REEF[2]]

refection /rəˈfɛkʃən/, n. refreshment, esp. with food or drink. [ME, from L]

refectory /rəˈfɛktri/, n., pl. **-ries.** the dining hall in a religious house, university, etc. [ML, from L: restore]

refer /rəˈfɜː/, v., **-ferred, -ferring.** ◇v.t. **1.** to direct the attention or thoughts of. **2.** to direct for information or for anything needed. **3.** to hand over for information, consideration, etc. ◇v.i. **4.** to direct attention. **5.** to direct anyone for information, esp. about one's character, abilities, etc.: *to refer to a former employer*. **6.** to have relation; apply. **7.** to turn, as for aid or information: *to refer to one's notes*. **8.** to direct a remark or mention. [ME, from L: carry back] **— referral,** n.

referee /rɛfəˈriː/, n., v., **-reed, -reeing.** ◇n. **1.** a person to whom something is directed, esp. for decision or settlement; arbitrator; umpire. **2.** → REFERENCE (def. 6). ◇v.t., v.i. **3.** to act as referee (in).

reference /ˈrɛfrəns/, n. **1.** the act or fact of referring. **2.** a directing of attention; allusion. **3.** a source of information: *a book of reference*. **4.** a direction in a book, passage, etc.: *to look up a reference*. **5.** use or availability for purposes of information: *a library for public reference*. **6.** a person or writing referred to as a guide to one's character, abilities, etc. **7.** relation; regard; respect: *all persons, without reference to age*. **8.** See **frame of reference. 9. terms of reference,** the range allowed for the study of something. **10. with reference to,** concerning; with regard to. ◇adj. **11.** (of a library, book, etc.) used to supply information.

referendum /rɛfəˈrɛndəm/, n., pl. **-dums, -da** /-də/. **1.** the principle or manner of referring measures recommended or passed by a lawmaking body to the vote of the public. **2.** one such vote. [L]

referent /ˈrɛfərənt/, the object or idea itself, to which a word, phrase, thought, etc. refers.

refill /ˌriːˈfɪl/, v.; /ˈriːfɪl/, n., ◇v.t. **1.** to fill again. ◇n. **2.** material replacing a used-up product: *a lipstick refill*. **3.** any instance of filling again.

refine /rəˈfaɪn/, v., **-fined, -fining.** ◇v.t. **1.** to bring to a fine or pure state. **2.** to make cultured or elegant. ◇v.i. **3.** to become pure. **4.** to become more elegant or polished. [RE- + FINE[1], v.] **—refinement,** n.

refined /rəˈfaɪnd/, adj. **1.** having or showing nice feeling, taste, etc. **2.** free from coarseness, roughness, etc. **3.** freed from impurities: *refined sugar*. **4.** exact; precise.

refinery /rəˈfaɪnəri/, n., pl. **-eries.** an establishment for refining something, as metal, sugar, petroleum, etc.

reflect /rəˈflɛkt/, v.t. **1.** to throw back (light, heat, sound, etc.). **2.** to give back or show an image of; mirror. **3.** to reproduce; show: *followers reflecting the views of the leader*. **4.** to serve to cast or bring (honor, credit, etc.). ◇v.i. **5.** to be turned back, as light. **6.** to cast back light, heat, etc. **7.** to give back or show an image. **8.** to tend to bring disfavor or blame. **9.** to think; ponder; meditate. [ME, from L: bend back]

reflection /rəˈflɛkʃən/, n. **1.** the act or result of reflecting. **2.** an image; counterpart. **3.** the fixing of the thoughts on something. **4.** an unfavorable remark or observation. **5.** *Phys.* **a.** the casting back, or change of direction, of light, heat, sound, etc., after striking a surface. **b.** something so reflected, as heat, or esp., light. Also, **reflexion.**

reflector /rəˈflɛktə/, n. **1.** a body, surface, or device that reflects light, heat, sound, etc. **2.** a reflecting telescope. **3.** a piece of red glass or metal fixed to the rear of a cycle or motor vehicle, or used to mark the edge of a road near road repairs, etc.

reflex /ˈriːflɛks/, adj., n. ◇adj. **1.** of or relating to an involuntary muscular or other bodily response. **2.** happening in reaction; responsive. **3.** cast back; reflected, as light, etc. **4.** bent or turned back. ◇n. **5.** *Psychol.* an immediate, often unconscious response to a stimulus, as blinking, perspiring, etc. **6.** a reflection or image of an object. **7.** a copy; adaptation. [L: reflected, bent back]

reflex angle, n. an angle greater than 180° but less than 360°

reflex arc, n. the path taken by nerve impulses within the body from stimulus to reflex action.

reflexion /rəˈflɛkʃən/, n. → **reflection.**

reflexive /rəˈflɛksɪv/, adj. *Gram.* **1.** (of a verb) having identical subject and object, as *shave* in *He shaved himself*. **2.** (of a pronoun) showing identity of object with subject, as *himself* in the example above. ◇n. **3.** a reflexive verb or pronoun, as *himself* in *He tricked himself*.

reforest /ˌriːˈfɒrəst/, v.t. → **reafforest.** **—reforestation,** n.

reform /rəˈfɔːm/, n. **1.** improvement or correction of what is wrong, evil, etc. **2.** an instance of this. **3.** improvement of behavior, etc. ◇v.t. **4.** to bring back to a former and better state. **5.** to cause (a person) to give up wrong or evil ways of life. **6.** to put an end to (disorders, etc.). ◇v.i. **7.** to give up evil behavior, etc. [ME, from L]

reformation /rɛfəˈmeɪʃən/, n. **1.** the act or result of reforming. **2.** (*cap.*) the great religious movement in the 16th century which had for its object the reform of the Roman Catholic Church, and which led to the establishment of the Protestant churches.

reformatory /rəˈfɔːmətri/, adj., n., pl. **-ries.** ◇adj. **1.** serving or designed to reform. ◇n. **2.** Also, **reform school.** an institution for the reformation of young offenders.

reformism /rəˈfɔːmɪzəm, ˈrɛfəmɪzəm/, n. *Govt.* a policy of bringing about reform within the means and limitations of the existing system of government, usu. without great change in the political system.

refraction /rə'frækʃən/, *n.* **1.** *Phys.* the change of direction of a ray or wave of light, heat, or sound, in passing at an angle from one medium into another. **2.** the ability of the eye to bend light which enters it so as to form an image on the retina. —**refractive**, *adj.*

refractive index, *n.* a measure of the degree through which light is refracted when passing through a particular material compared to a vacuum; See **Snell's law**.

refractory /rə'fræktəri/, *adj.*, *n.*, *pl.* **-ries.** ◇*adj.* **1.** unmanageable; stubborn: *a refractory child.* **2.** fighting against ordinary methods of treatment. **3.** difficult to fuse, reduce, or work, as an ore or metal. ◇*n.* **4.** any material able to keep its shape and properties at high temperatures.

refrain¹ /rə'freɪn/, *v.i.* to keep oneself back (oft. fol. by *from*). [ME, from OF, from L: to bridle]

refrain² /rə'freɪn/, *n.* **1.** a phrase or verse repeated at intervals in a song or poem; chorus. **2.** a musical setting for the refrain of a poem. [ME, from OF, from L: refract]

refrangible /rə'frændʒəbəl/, *adj.* capable of being refracted, as rays of light. —**refrangibility**, *n.*

refresh /rə'freʃ/, *v.t.* **1.** (*oft. reflexive*) to make fresh and strong again, as by rest, food, etc. **2.** to stimulate (the memory). **3.** to make fresh again. **4.** to take refreshment, esp. food or drink. ◇*v.i.* **5.** to become fresh or strong again; revive. [ME, from OF]

refreshing /rə'freʃɪŋ/, *adj.* **1.** (of food, leisure, etc.) restoring or giving new energy, life, etc. **2.** interesting because of special or unusual qualities.

refreshment /rə'freʃmənt/, *n.* **1.** something that refreshes, esp. food or drink. **2.** (*pl.*) food or drink, esp. for a light meal. **3.** the act or result of refreshing.

refrigerant /rə'frɪdʒərənt/, *adj.* **1.** cooling; refrigerating. ◇*n.* **2.** a refrigerant agent, as in a drug. **3.** a liquid capable of vaporising at a low temperature, as ammonia, used in refrigeration. **4.** a cooling substance, as ice, solid carbon dioxide, etc., used in a refrigerator.

refrigerate /rə'frɪdʒəreɪt/, *v.t.*, **-rated, -rating. 1.** to make or keep cold or cool. **2.** to freeze (food, etc.) for keeping. [L: made cool again]

refrigeration /rəfrɪdʒə'reɪʃən/, *n.* **1.** the process of producing low temperatures. **2.** the resulting state.

refrigerator /rə'frɪdʒəreɪtə/, *n.* **1.** a box, room, or cabinet in which food, drink, etc., are kept cool, as by means of ice or mechanical refrigeration. **2.** an element of a refrigerating system consisting of the space or medium to be cooled.

refuel /ri'fjuəl/, *v.*, **-elled, -elling.** ◇*v.t.* **1.** to supply again with fuel. ◇*v.i.* **2.** to take on a fresh supply of fuel.

refuge /'rɛfjudʒ/, *n.* **1.** shelter or protection from danger, trouble, etc. **2.** a place of shelter, protection, or safety. [ME, from OF, from L]

refugee /rɛfju'dʒi/, *n.* someone who escapes to safety, esp. to a foreign country, as in time of war, etc. [F: take refuge]

refulgent /rə'fʌldʒənt/, *adj.* shining; radiant; glowing. [L] —**refulgence**, *n.*

refund¹ /rə'fʌnd/, *v.*; /'rifʌnd/, *n.* ◇*v.t.* **1.** to give back or restore (esp. money); repay; reimburse. ◇*v.i.* **2.** to make a repayment. ◇*n.* **3.** a repayment. [ME, from L: pour back]

refund² /ri'fʌnd/, *v.t.* **1.** to provide funds for (something) again. **2.** *Comm.* (of a company) **a.** to meet (a matured debt) by new borrowing, esp. by issuing bonds. **b.** to replace (an old issue) with a new, esp. one bearing a lower rate of interest.

refurbish /ri'fɜbɪʃ/, *v.t.* to polish up again; renovate.

refusal /rə'fjuzəl/, *n.* **1.** the act of refusing. **2.** the first right in refusing or taking something; option.

refuse¹ /rə'fjuz/, *v.*, **-fused, -fusing.** ◇*v.t.* **1.** to decline to accept (something offered). **2.** to decline to give. **3.** to express a determination not (to do something). ◇*v.i.* **4.** to decline acceptance. [ME, from OF, from VL, from L: poured back]

refuse² /'rɛfjus/, *n.* material thrown away as worthless or useless; rubbish. [ME, from OF: refused]

refute /rə'fjut/, *v.t.*, **-futed, -futing. 1.** to prove to be false, as an opinion, charge, etc. **2.** to prove (a person) to be in error. [L: repel, refute] —**refutation**, *n.*

reg., *Abbrev.* **1.** registration. **2.** registered.

Reg., *Abbrev.* **1.** Regina. **2.** Regiment.

regain /rə'geɪn/, *v.t.* **1.** to get again; recover. **2.** to succeed in reaching again.

regal /'rigəl/, *adj.* **1.** of, relating to, or like a king; royal. **2.** stately; splendid. [ME, from L]

regale /rə'geɪl/, *v.t.*, **-galed, -galing. 1.** to entertain agreeably; delight. **2.** to entertain with good food or drink. [F, from OF: feast, from *gale* pleasure, from MD: wealth]

regalia /rə'geɪljə/, *n.pl.* **1.** the emblems of royalty, as the crown, sceptre, etc. **2.** the decorations of any office or order. [ML, from L: regal]

regard /rə'gad/, *v.t.* **1.** to look upon or think of with a particular feeling. **2.** to think highly of. **3.** to consider. **4.** to look at; observe. **5.** to relate to; concern. ◇*n.* **6.** reference; relation: *in regard to his education.* **7.** point or particular: *quite satisfactory in this regard.* **8.** thought; attention. **9.** look; gaze. **10.** respect; deference: *due regard to authority.* **11.** kindly feeling; liking. **12.** (*pl.*) feelings of respect or friendship. **13. as regards,** in relation to. **14. with regard to,** concerning. [ME, from F]

regarding /rəˈgadɪŋ/, *prep.* with regard to; respecting; concerning: *He knew nothing regarding the lost watch.*

regardless /rəˈgadləs/, *adj.* **1.** having or showing no regard; heedless; unmindful; careless (oft. fol. by *of*). **2.** without regard to expense, danger, etc. ◇*adv.* **3.** anyway.

regatta /rəˈgætə/, *n.* **1.** a boat race. **2.** an organised series of such races. [It]

regency /ˈridʒənsi/, *n., pl.* **-cies**, *adj.* ◇*n.* **1.** the office, authority, or control of a regent exercising the ruling power while the sovereign is too young, absent, etc. **2.** a body of regents. **3.** the term of office of a regent. **4.** (*cap.*) (in Britain) the period (1811-20) during which George (later, George IV) was regent. ◇*adj.* **5.** (*cap.*) of or relating to the regency or to the styles popular at that time.

regenerate /rəˈdʒenəreɪt/, *v.*, **-rated, -rating**; /rəˈdʒenərət/, *adj.* ◇*v.t.* **1.** to bring about a change for the better in a person's character. **2.** to make over, esp. in a better form or condition. **3.** to bring into existence again. ◇*v.i.* **4.** to come into existence or be formed again. **5.** to become as though a new and better person. ◇*adj.* **6.** remade in a better form. **7.** changed for a better character. [ME, from L: made over, produced anew] —**regeneration**, *n.* —**regenerative**, *adj.*

regent /ˈridʒənt/, *n.* **1.** someone who exercises the ruling power in a kingdom while the sovereign is too young, absent or unfit. **2.** (formerly in some universities) a member of certain governing and teaching bodies. ◇*adj.* **3.** acting as regent of a country. [ME, from L: ruling]

regent bower-bird, *n.* the second largest of the Australian bower-birds, the male being jet black and golden in color.

reggae /ˈregeɪ/, *n.* pop music of Jamaican origin with four beats to the bar, the upbeat being accented.

regicide /ˈredʒəsaɪd/, *n.* **1.** someone who kills a king. **2.** the killing of a king. [*regi-* (combining form representing L *rex* king) + -CIDE] —**regicidal**, *adj.*

regime /reɪˈʒim/, *n.* **1.** a mode or system of rule or government. **2.** the ruling system. **3.** → **regimen**. **4.** the variation in the volume of a river with the season. **5.** the seasonal pattern of a climate. Also, **régime**. [F, from L: direction, government]

regimen /ˈredʒəmən/, *n.* **1.** *Med.* a controlled course of diet, exercise, or manner of living, intended to preserve or restore health or to gain some result. **2.** a particular form or system of government. **3.** the prevailing system. [ME, from L]

regiment /ˈredʒəmənt/, *n.*; /ˈredʒəment/, *v.* ◇*n.* **1.** *Mil.* a unit of ground forces, consisting of two or more battalions, a headquarters unit, and certain supporting units. ◇*v.t.* **2.** to form into an organised body or group. **3.** to group together and treat in a uniform manner. [ME, from LL: rule] —**regimental**, *adj.* —**regimentation**, *n.*

regina /rəˈdʒinə/, *n.* (*oft. cap.*) a reigning queen. [L]

region /ˈridʒən/, *n.* **1.** any more or less continuous part of a surface or space. **2.** a part of the earth's surface (land or sea) of considerable and usu. indefinite extent: *tropical regions.* **3.** one of the divisions into which a territory or country, as Italy, is divided for governing, etc. [ME, from L: line; district] —**regional**, *adj.* —**regionalism**, *n.*

register /ˈredʒəstə/, *n.* **1.** a book in which records of acts, happenings, names are made. **2.** any list of such recordings. **3.** a recording in such a book or list. **4.** a mechanical device by which certain information is automatically recorded, as a cash register. **5.** *Music.* **a.** the range of a voice or an instrument. **b.** (in an organ) a stop. **6.** *Print., etc.* exact correspondence, as of lines, columns, etc., esp. on the two sides of a leaf. ◇*v.t.* **7.** to enter or have entered formally in a register. **8.** to have a car, etc., which has been judged safe for the road and on which the necessary tax has been paid, entered in the register of motor vehicles kept by a public authority. **9.** to record or have recorded the posting of (a letter, parcel, etc.) at the post office on payment of a special fee. **10.** (of a scale, etc.) to indicate or show. **11.** to show (surprise, joy, anger, etc.), usu. by facial expression or by actions. ◇*v.i.* **12.** to enter one's name in an electoral or other register; enrol. **13.** (of surprise, joy, etc.) to be obvious or to show. [ME, from ML, from L: recorded] —**registration**, *n.*

registered /ˈredʒəstəd/, *adj.* **1.** recorded, as in a register or book; enrolled. **2.** *Comm.* (with bonds, etc.) officially listing the owner's name with the offering company and suitably inscribing the certificate. **3.** officially or legally certified by a government officer or board: *a registered patent.* **4.** (of cattle, horses, dogs, etc.) having blood lines checked and recorded by official breeders.

registered nurse, *n.* one who has completed a certified nursing course and is registered with a registration board.

registrar /ˈredʒəstra/, *n.* **1.** someone who keeps a record. **2.** the chief administrative official in a university. **3.** a doctor in a hospital next below a consultant, who is training to be a specialist. **4.** *Law.* the chief administrative officer of an intermediate, superior or federal court.

registration plate, *n.* → **numberplate**.

registry /ˈredʒəstri/, *n., pl.* **-tries**. **1.** the place where a register is kept. **2.** the act of registering; registration.

registry office, *n.* the office where births, marriages and deaths are recorded, and non-religious marriages are performed.

regolith /ˈregəliθ/, *n.* the layer of disintegrated and decomposed rock fragments, including soil, just above the solid rock of the earth's crust. [Gk *rhêgo(s)* blanket covering + -LITH]

regress /riˈgres/, *v.*; /ˈrigres/, *n.* ◇*v.i.* **1.** to move in a backward direction; go back. ◇*n.* **2.** the act of going back; return. **3.** a backward

regress 873 **reinforcement**

movement or course; retrogression. [ME, from L: a going back] —**regressive**, *adj.*

regression /rɪˈgrɛʃən/, *n.* **1.** *Biol.* a return to an earlier or less advanced state or form or to a common or general type. **2.** *Psychol.* a return to an earlier or less effective pattern of behavior and feeling.

regret /rəˈgrɛt/, *v.*, **-gretted, -gretting**, *n.* ◇*v.t.* **1.** to feel sorry about (anything disappointing, unpleasant, etc.). **2.** to think of with a sense of loss: *They regret their vanished youth.* ◇*n.* **3.** a sense of loss, disappointment, dissatisfaction, etc. **4.** a feeling of being sorry for some fault, act, etc., of one's own. **5.** (*pl.*) feelings of sorrow over what is lost, gone, done, etc. **6.** (*pl. or sing.*) a polite and formal expression of regretful feelings. [ME, from OF, from Gmc] —**regretful**, *adj.* —**regrettable**, *adj.*

regular /ˈrɛgjələ/, *adj.* **1.** usual; normal; customary: *Put it in its regular place.* **2.** conforming in form or arrangement; symmetrical: *regular teeth.* **3.** even; steady: *regular breathing.* **4.** happening at fixed times; periodic: *regular meals.* **5.** following a rule or procedure: *Be regular in your diet.* **6.** observing fixed times or habits: *a regular customer.* **7.** orderly; well-ordered: *a regular life.* **8.** properly fitted for an occupation. **9.** *Colloq.* complete; thorough: *a regular thief.* **10.** *Gram.* following the most usual pattern of formation, construction, etc. **11.** *Geom.* having all its angles and sides equal: *a regular polygon.* **12.** *Mil.* indicating or belonging to the permanently organised or standing army of a state. ◇*n.* **13.** a soldier in a regular army. **14.** *Colloq.* a regular customer. [L] —**regularity**, *n.*

regulate /ˈrɛgjəleɪt/, *v.t.*, **-lated, -lating**. **1.** to control or direct by rule, principle, method, etc. **2.** to change (amount, degree, etc.) to some standard or requirement: *It is possible to regulate the temperature of the room.* **3.** to adjust so as to ensure correct operation: *regulate your watch.* [LL, from L: rule] —**regulative, regulatory**, *adj.*

regulation /ˌrɛgjəˈleɪʃən/, *n.* **1.** a rule or order for conduct, made by authority. **2.** the act of regulating. **3.** the state of being regulated. ◇*adj.* **4.** according to regulation: *Regulation shoes must be worn.*

regulator /ˈrɛgjəleɪtə/, *n.* **1.** someone or something that regulates. **2.** a device in a clock or a watch for causing it to go faster or slower. **3.** *Elect.* a device whose work is to keep voltage or current at a given point in a circuit, or vary it in a controlled manner.

regurgitate /rəˈgɜdʒəteɪt/, *v.i., v.t.*, **-tated, -tating**. to (cause to) rush back, esp. from the stomach; vomit: *After swallowing Jonah, the whale regurgitated him.* [ML] —**regurgitant**, *n., adj.* —**regurgitation**, *n.*

rehabilitate /ˌrihəˈbɪləteɪt/, *v.t.*, **-tated, -tating**. **1.** to educate and help (a person affected by an accident or disease) to take up normal activities again. **2.** to re-establish (a person, character, name, etc.) in a position of respect. **3.** to return formally to an earlier position, rank, rights, etc. [ML: restored] —**rehabilitation**, *n.*

rehash /riˈhæʃ/, *v.*; /ˈrihæʃ/, *n.* ◇*v.t.* **1.** to work up (old material) in a new form. ◇*n.* **2.** the act of rehashing. **3.** something rehashed.

rehearse /rəˈhɜs/, *v.*, **-hearsed, -hearsing**. ◇*v.t.* **1.** to perform (a play, part, piece of music, etc.) in private, by way of practice before a public performance. **2.** to train (a person, etc.) by rehearsal, usu. for some performance or part. **3.** to repeat the facts or particulars of; enumerate. ◇*v.i.* **4.** to rehearse a play, part, etc. [ME, from OF: harrow again] —**rehearsal**, *n.*

Reibey /ˈrɪbi/, *n.* **Mary**, 1777–1855, Australian businesswoman, born in England; extensive real estate and shipping interests.

Reich /raɪk/, *n.* **1.** the Holy Roman Empire, until its dissolution in 1806 (**First Reich**). **2.** the Prussian Empire, 1871–1919 (**Second Reich**). **3.** the Nazi state, 1933–45 (**Third Reich**). [G]

Reichstag /ˈraɪkstɑg/, *n.* **1.** *German Hist.* the lower house of the German parliament 1919–45. **2.** the building in Berlin where this assembly met 1919–33; destroyed by fire 1933.

Reid /rid/, *n.* **Sir George Houstoun**, 1845–1918, Australian politician; prime minister 1904–05; premier of NSW 1894–99.

reign /reɪn/, *n.* **1.** the period or term of ruling, as of a king or queen. **2.** royal rule or sway. **3.** controlling power or influence: *the reign of law.* ◇*v.i.* **4.** to possess or exercise sovereign power or authority. **5.** to have first place; predominate: *Disorder reigned in the stricken country.* [ME, from OF, from L]

reimburse /ˌrimˈbɜs/, *v.t.*, **-bursed, -bursing**. **1.** to repay for expense or loss suffered. **2.** to pay back; refund; repay. [RE- + *imburse* (from ML: purse, bag)] —**reimbursement**, *n.*

rein /reɪn/, *n.* **1.** a long, narrow strap fastened to the bridle or bit, by which a rider guides a horse or other animal. **2.** any means of controlling or directing; check; restraint. **3.** (*pl.*) controlling influence and power. **4. give (free) rein**, give complete freedom (fol. by *to*): *Give rein to your imagination.* ◇*v.t.* **5.** to check or guide (a horse, etc.) by pulling at the reins (oft. fol. by *back* or *in*). **6.** to control; restrain. [ME, from OF, from L: hold back]

reincarnation /ˌrinkɑˈneɪʃən/, *n.* **1.** the belief that the soul, upon death of the body, moves to another body or form. **2.** the rebirth of the soul in a new body.

reindeer /ˈreɪndɪə/, *n., pl.* **-deer**, (*occasionally*) **-deers**. a type of deer with branched antlers in both males and females, found in northern or arctic areas. [ME: from Scand]

reinforce /ˌrinˈfɔs/, *v.t.*, **-forced, -forcing**. **1.** to strengthen with some added piece, support, or material. **2.** to strengthen with additional personnel or ships for military or naval purposes.

reinforcement /ˌrinˈfɔsmənt/, *n.* **1.** something that reinforces or strengthens. **2.** (*oft. pl.*) an additional supply of men, ships, etc., for a military or naval force. **3.** *Psychol.* anything

reinstate /rɪnˈsteɪt/, *v.t.*, **-stated, -stating.** to put back or establish again, usu. to a former position. —**reinstatement**, *n.*

reissue /riˈɪʃu, riˈɪsju/, *v.t.* **1.** to give out again, esp. in a different form, at a different price, etc. ◇*n.* **2.** something which is reissued.

reiterate /riˈɪtəreɪt/, *v.t.*, **-rated, -rating.** to repeat; say or do again or repeatedly. [L] —**reiteration**, *n.* —**reiterative**, *adj.*

reject /rəˈdʒɛkt/, *v.*; /ˈridʒɛkt/, *n.* ◇*v.t.* **1.** to refuse to accept, recognise, grant, etc.: *to reject a person; to reject a demand; to reject an offer.* **2.** to throw away or refuse as useless or unsatisfactory. ◇*n.* **3.** something rejected, such as an imperfect article. [L: thrown back] —**rejection**, *n.*

rejoice /rəˈdʒɔɪs/, *v.t., v.i.,* **-joiced, -joicing.** to (cause to) be glad or take delight (*in*). [ME, from OF]

rejoicing /rəˈdʒɔɪsɪŋ/, *n.* **1.** a feeling or expression of joy. **2.** (*oft. pl.*) an occasion for expressing joy; celebration.

rejoin[1] /rəˈdʒɔɪn/, *v.t.* to come again into the company of: *to rejoin a party after a brief absence.*

rejoin[2] /rəˈdʒɔɪn/, *v.t.* **1.** to say in answer. ◇*v.i.* **2.** to answer. [ME, from AF]

rejoinder /rəˈdʒɔɪndə/, *n.* what is said in reply; a response. [ME, from AF]

rejuvenate /rəˈdʒuvəneɪt/, *v.t.*, **-nated, -nating.** to make young again in energy, appearance, etc. [LL: become young again + -ATE[1]] —**rejuvenation**, *n.*

-rel, a noun suffix indicating smallness or badness, as in *dotterel*. Also, **-erel.** [ME, from OF]

relapse /rəˈlæps/, *v.*, **-lapsed, -lapsing.** /ˈrilæps, rəˈlæps/, *n.* ◇*v.i.* **1.** to fall or slip back into a former condition, practice, etc.: *to relapse into silence.* **2.** to fall back into illness, wrongdoing, error, etc. ◇*n.* **3.** the act of relapsing. **4.** the return of an illness after partial recovery. [L: slipped back]

relate /rəˈleɪt/, *v.*, **-lated, -lating.** ◇*v.t.* **1.** to tell; narrate. **2.** to bring into connection or relation. ◇*v.i.* **3.** to have reference (*to*). **4.** to have some relation (*to*). [L: reported, carried back] —**relator**, *n.*

related /rəˈleɪtəd/, *adj.* **1.** connected; associated. **2.** connected by family, either by blood or marriage.

relation /rəˈleɪʃən/, *n.* **1.** a connection; particular way of being related: *the relation between cause and effect.* **2.** (*pl.*) the various connections between peoples, countries, etc.: *commercial relations; foreign relations.* **3.** the kind of connection between one person and another or others: *the relation between husband and wife.* **4.** a relative (def. 1). **5.** reference; regard: *to plan with relation to the future.* **6.** the act of relating or telling; narration: *his relation of the story.* **7.** something which is related or told; narrative. [ME, from L: a bringing back; report]

relationship /rəˈleɪʃənʃɪp/, *n.* **1.** a particular connection. **2.** a connection between people by blood or marriage. **3.** an emotional connection between people, sometimes involving sexual relations.

relative /ˈrɛlətɪv/, *n.* **1.** someone who is connected with another or others by blood or marriage. **2.** something having, or standing in, some relation to something else, esp. in scientific usage (opposed to *absolute*). **3.** *Gram.* a relative pronoun, adjective, or adverb. ◇*adj.* **4.** considered in comparison with something else: *the relative advantages of written and oral tests.* **5.** existing or having meaning only by relation to something else; not absolute or independent. **6.** having relation or connection: *Value is relative to demand.* **7.** having reference or regard (fol. by *to*). **8.** *Gram.* **a.** denoting words which introduce subordinate clauses and refer to some person or thing in the principal clause (the antecedent), as in *He's the man who saw you*. **b.** (of a clause) introduced by such a word. [ME, from LL, from L: carried back]

relative density, *n.* the ratio of the density of any substance (usu. at 20°C) to that of a standard substance (usu. water at 4°C for solids and liquids and hydrogen or air for gases); specific gravity. *Abbrev.* r.d.

relative frequency, *n. Maths.* the ratio of the number of times an event occurs to the number of occasions on which it could occur in the same period.

relative humidity, *n.* the ratio, expressed as a percentage, of the water vapour present in the atmosphere to the amount required to saturate it at the same temperature.

relatively /ˈrɛlətɪvli/, *adv.* comparatively: *a relatively small difference.*

relative pronoun, *n.* a pronoun with a relative use. See **relative** (def. 8a).

relative velocity, *n.* the velocity of a body with respect to another body, either moving or stationary.

relativistic /rɛlətəˈvɪstɪk/, *adj.* **1.** of or relating to relativity. **2.** *Phys.* having, or relating to, something which has a velocity close to that of light: *a relativistic particle; relativistic mass.*

relativity /rɛləˈtɪvəti/, *n.* **1.** the condition or fact of being relative. **2. a. special theory of relativity,** the theory formed by Einstein, based on the experimental fact that the velocity of light remains constant no matter what medium it is moving through or what the source is. Nothing can move faster than light, and as things approach this speed, lengths shorten, time slows down and mass increases. See **space-time** and **mass-energy equation. b. general theory of relativity,** Einstein's theory that the presence of matter in space causes it to curve so that a gravitational field is set up. **3.** (*pl.*) the relative differences in wages between groups of workers.

relax /rəˈlæks/, *v.t.* **1.** to make less tense, rigid, or firm: *to relax the muscles.* **2.** to make less strict or severe: *to relax discipline.* ◇*v.i.* **3.** to become less tense, rigid, or firm. **4.** to

relax become less strict or severe. **5.** to stop mental or bodily effort, etc.; take relaxation. [ME, from L]

relaxation /rɪlækˈseɪʃən/, *n.* **1.** a stopping of bodily or mental effort, etc. **2.** something done for enjoyment or entertainment. **3.** a loosening or slackening. **4.** a reduction of strictness or severity.

relay /ˈriːleɪ/, *n.*; /rəˈleɪ, ˈriːleɪ/, *v.* ◇*n.* **1.** a set of people or animals relieving others or taking turns; a shift: *to work in relays*. **2.** Also, **relay race**. race between two or more teams, each member running, swimming, etc., one of the lengths of the distance. **3.** *Elect.* **a.** a device by means of which a change of current or voltage in one circuit can be made to produce a change in the electrical condition of another circuit. **b.** a device that is able, by a variation in the conditions of one electric circuit, to effect the operation of other devices in the same or another electric circuit. ◇*v.t.* **4.** to carry forward by or as by relays: *to relay a message*. [ME, from OF: leave behind (orig., hounds in reserve along the line of the hunt)]

relay station, *n.* a place from which radio and television programs, etc., are broadcast, after being received from another station.

release /rəˈliːs/, *v.*, **-leased, -leasing**, *n.* ◇*v.t.* **1.** to free from imprisonment, responsibility, pain, etc.; set free. **2.** to allow to be made public: *to release a news story*. **3.** *Law.* give up or relinquish (a right, claim, etc.). ◇*n.* **4.** the act of releasing. **5.** an instrument for releasing. **6.** a statement, news story, etc., released to the public. **7.** *Mech.* a device for starting or stopping a machine, esp. by removing some restrictive apparatus. [ME, from OF, from L: relax]

relegate /ˈrɛləgeɪt/, *v.t.*, **-gated, -gating**. **1.** to send to some lower position, place, or condition. **2.** to hand over (a matter, task, etc.) to someone. [L: sent back] **– relegation,** *n.*

relent /rəˈlɛnt/, *v.i.* to soften in feeling, temper, or determination; become more mild or forgiving. [ME: melt, from L: grow slack or soft]

relentless /rəˈlɛntləs/, *adj.* unrelenting; pitiless: *a relentless enemy*.

relevant /ˈrɛləvənt/, *adj.* connected with the matter in hand; to the purpose; pertinent: *a relevant remark*. [ML, from L: raise up] **– relevance, relevancy,** *n.*

reliable /rəˈlaɪəbəl/, *adj.* able to be relied on; trustworthy: *reliable sources of information*. **– reliability,** *n.*

reliant /rəˈlaɪənt/, *adj.* having or showing trust, confidence or dependence. **– reliance,** *n.*

relic /ˈrɛlɪk/, *n.* **1.** an object surviving from the past and having interest because of this: *historical relics*. **2.** a surviving trace of something: *a custom which is a relic of paganism*. **3.** (*pl.*) remaining parts or fragments. **4.** *Rom Cath Ch*, etc. a part of the body of, or other things related to a saint or holy person, kept as worthy of reverence. [OE, from L]

relict /ˈrɛlɪkt/, *n.* **1.** *Ecol.* a plant or animal group living in an environment which has changed from that which is typical for it. **2.** *Geog.* any soil formed under climatic conditions which no longer exist in that area. [ME, from ML: widow, from L: left behind]

relief /rəˈliːf/, *n.* **1.** (something that brings) deliverance or ease through the removal of pain, distress, anxiety, etc. **2.** something giving a pleasing change from monotony, seriousness, etc. **3.** release from a post of duty by the coming of a replacement. **4.** a person or people coming as a replacement or replacements. **5.** the quality of standing out or having prominence due to contrast. **6.** *Sculpture, etc.* the projection of a figure or part from the ground or plane on which it is formed. **7.** a piece or work made by this method. **8.** *Geog.* the difference in height of the land surface in any area from that of a level surface. [ME, from OF]

relief map, *n.* a map showing the relief of an area, usu. by generalised contour lines.

relieve /rəˈliːv/, *v.t.*, **-lieved, -lieving. 1.** to ease or lessen (pain, distress, anxiety, need, etc.). **2.** to free (someone) from anxiety, fear, pain, need, etc. **3.** to bring help to (a place under attack, etc.). **4.** to take something from (someone): *He relieved him of his suitcase*. **5.** to break or vary the sameness of. **6.** to bring into relief or prominence; heighten the effect of. **7.** to release (someone on duty) by coming as or providing a replacement. [ME, from OF, from L: raise again, assist]

relievo /rəˈliːvoʊ/, *n., pl.,* **-vos, -vi,** /-viː/. → **relief** (def. 6). Also, **rilievo**. [It, from *rilevare* raise, modelled on F *relief*]

religion /rəˈlɪdʒən/, *n.* **1.** belief in a controlling superhuman power entitled to obedience, reverence, and worship. **2.** the feeling or spiritual attitude of those recognising such a controlling power. **3.** something regarded as being of great importance or involving moral duty: *to make a religion of doing something*. [ME, from L: fear of the gods, sacredness, scrupulousness]

religiosity /rəlɪdʒiˈɒsəti/, *n.* the quality of being religious, esp. to an affected or extreme degree.

religious /rəˈlɪdʒəs/, *adj.* **1.** of or relating to religion. **2.** believing in religion; pious; devout. **3.** very conscientious: *to do something with religious care*. ◇*n.* **4.** a member of a religious order, etc.; monk, friar, or nun. [ME, from L]

relinquish /rəˈlɪŋkwɪʃ/, *v.t.* to give up, put aside, or surrender (a possession, right, plan, hope, etc.). [ME, from OF]

relish /ˈrɛlɪʃ/, *n.* **1.** liking for or enjoyment of something, esp. something eaten. **2.** something tasty added to a meal, such as a sauce. **3.** a pleasing taste or flavor. ◇*v.t.* **4.** to take pleasure in; enjoy. **5.** to like the taste or flavor of. [ME, from OF: what is left, remainder]

reluctant /rəˈlʌktənt/, *adj.* unwilling; disinclined. [L: struggling against] **– reluctance,** *n.*

rely /rə'laɪ/, *v.i.*, **-lied, -lying.** to depend confidently; put trust in (fol. by *on* or *upon*). [ME, from OF: bind together, from L: bind back]

remain /rə'meɪn/, *v.i.* **1.** to continue in the same condition or place: *to remain at peace*; *to remain at home*. **2.** to be left after the removal, departure, loss, etc., of others or other parts. **3.** to be left to be done, told, etc. ◇*n.* (*always pl.*) **4.** that which remains or is left: *the remains of a meal*; *the remains of past glory*. **5.** what remains of a person after death; dead body. [ME, from AF, from L]

remainder /rə'meɪndə/, *n.* **1.** that which remains or is left: *the remainder of the day*. **2.** *Maths.* the quantity that remains after subtraction or division. **3.** a copy of a book remaining in the publisher's stock when the sale has almost finished, usu. sold at a reduced price. [ME, from AF]

remand /rə'mænd, -'mand/, *v.t.* **1.** *Law.* (of a court) to send back (a prisoner or accused person) into custody to await further proceedings. ◇*n.* **2.** the act of remanding. **3.** the condition of being remanded. [ME, from LL: to send back word, repeat a command]

remark /rə'mak/, *v.t.* **1.** to say casually in the form of a comment. **2.** to note; perceive. ◇*v.i.* **3.** to make a comment (fol. by *on* or *upon*). ◇*n.* **4.** the act of remarking; notice. **5.** a casual or brief expression of thought or opinion; comment. [F: note, heed]

remarkable /rə'makəbəl/, *adj.* worthy of remark or notice because unusual or extraordinary.

Rembrandt /'rembrænt/, *n.* (*Rembrandt Harmenszoon van Rijn* or *van Ryn*), 1606–69, Dutch painter and etcher; famous for his portraits; largest work *Night Watch* (1642), a group portrait.

remedial /rə'midiəl/, *adj.* **1.** providing a remedy. **2.** (of teaching) designed to meet the needs of children who are disadvantaged or have particular learning problems. [L] —**remediable**, *adj.*

remedy /'remədi/, *n.*, *pl.* **-dies**, *v.*, **-died, -dying.** ◇*n.* **1.** something that cures or relieves a disease or bodily disorder. **2.** something that corrects or removes an evil of any kind. **3.** *Law.* the legal means by which a wrong is redressed; legal redress. ◇*v.t.* **4.** to cure or heal. **5.** to put right: *to remedy a matter*. **6.** to correct or remove: *to remedy an evil*. [ME, from L]

remember /rə'membə/, *v.t.* **1.** to bring back to the mind by an act of memory. **2.** to keep in the memory. **3.** to have (something) come into the mind again. **4.** to keep (a person) in mind as deserving a gift, reward, tip, etc. **5.** to mention to another as sending greetings: *Remember me to your mother*. ◇*v.i.* **6.** to possess or use the faculty or ability of memory. [ME, from OF, from LL, from L: call to mind]

remembrance /rə'membrəns/, *n.* **1.** an impression kept in the memory: *fond remembrance of the past*. **2.** the act or fact of remembering. **3.** an object, such as a gift, that serves to keep someone or something in mind. **4.** (*pl.*) greetings.

remind /rə'maɪnd/, *v.t.* to cause (one) to remember: *Remind me to do the shopping*; *Her face reminds me of you*. —**reminder**, *n.*

reminisce /remə'nɪs/, *v.i.*, **-nisced, -niscing.** to remember or talk about past experiences.

reminiscence /remə'nɪsəns/, *n.* **1.** the remembering of one's past. **2.** something remembered; a recollection. **3.** (*oft. pl.*) a spoken or written account of remembered experiences. [L]

reminiscent /remə'nɪsənt/, *adj.* **1.** awakening memories of something else; suggestive (fol. by *of*): *a perfume reminiscent of violets*. **2.** marked by or given to reminiscence. [L: remembering]

remiss /rə'mɪs/, *adj.* careless in duty, business, etc.; negligent. [ME, from L: sent back] —**remissness**, *n.*

remission /rə'mɪʃən/, *n.* **1.** the act of remitting. **2.** forgiveness of sins, offences, etc.; pardon. **3.** a lessening or abatement, as of labor, the symptoms of a disease, etc. Also, **remittal.**

remit /rə'mɪt/, *v.*, **-mitted, -mitting.** ◇*v.t.* **1.** to send (money, etc.) to a person or place. **2.** to decide not to enforce (a punishment, etc.) or demand (a payment of a debt, etc.). **3.** to pardon or forgive (a sin, offence, etc.). **4.** to lessen; abate: *to remit watchfulness*. ◇*v.i.* **5.** to send money, etc., as payment. **6.** to become less; abate: *Her fever has remitted*. [ME, from L: send back]

remittance /rə'mɪtns/, *n.* **1.** the remitting of money, etc., as payment. **2.** money, etc., sent from one place to another.

remittance man, *n.* (formerly) an Englishman in Australia who was supported by a remittance from his family in England on the understanding that he would not return.

remittent /rə'mɪtnt/, *adj.* (of a fever, etc.) lessening for a time or at intervals. —**remittence, remittency**, *n.*

remnant /'remnənt/, *n.* **1.** a part, fragment, quantity, or number (usu. small) remaining. **2.** a trace; vestige: *remnants of former greatness*. [ME, from OF: remain]

remonstrate /'remənstreɪt/, *v.*, **-strated, -strating.** ◇*v.t.* **1.** to say in objection or protest. ◇*v.i.* **2.** to argue in protest (fol. by *with*). [ML: exhibited] —**remonstration**, *n.* —**remonstrative**, *adj.*

remorse /rə'mɔs/, *n.* deep and painful sorrow or regret for one's wrong doing; compunction. [ME, from L: a biting back] —**remorseful**, *adj.* —**remorseless**, *adj.*

remote /rə'moʊt/, *adj.*, **-moter, -motest.** **1.** far away; far distant in space or time: *a remote village*; *the remote past*. **2.** distant in relationship or connection: *a remote ancestor*. **3.** far removed; alien: *remote from common experience*. **4.** slight: *I do not have the remotest idea of what to do*. **5.** distant in feeling; aloof: *She seemed very remote at their first meeting*. [ME, from L: removed]

remote control, *n.* the control of a system by means of electrical, radio, or mechanical signals from a point outside the system.

removalist /rə'muvəlɒst/, *n.* a person or firm whose work is moving furniture, etc., to a new home, office, etc.

remove /rə'muv/, *v.*, **-moved, -moving,** *n.* ◇*v.t.* **1.** to move from a place or position; take away; take off: *Please remove that book from the table; He removed his tie.* **2.** to displace from a position or office. **3.** to do away with; put an end to: *to remove guilt.* ◇*v.i.* **4.** to move from one place to another, esp. to another home. ◇*n.* **5.** the distance by which one person, place, or thing is separated from another. [ME, from OF, from L] **-removal,** *n.*

removed /rə'muvd/, *adj.* **1.** unconnected; remote; separate: *His way of life is far removed from mine.* **2.** distant, used in expressing degrees of relationship: *A first cousin twice removed is a cousin's grandchild.*

remunerate /rə'mjunəreɪt/, *v.t.*, **-rated, -rating.** to pay or reward for work, trouble, etc. [L: given back] **-remuneration,** *n.* **-remunerative,** *adj.*

Remus /'riməs/, *n. Rom Legend.* the twin brother of **Romulus.**

renaissance /rə'neɪsəns, rə'næsəns/, *n.* **1.** a new birth; revival. **2.** (*cap.*) **a.** the activity, spirit, or time of the great rebirth of art, literature, architecture and learning in Europe during the 14th, 15th, and 16th centuries, usu. taken as marking the change from the medieval to the modern world. **b.** any similar revival in the world of art and learning. [F: be born again]

renal /'rinəl/, *adj.* of or relating to the kidneys or the surrounding area. [LL, from L: kidney]

rend /rend/, *v.t.*, **rent, rending. 1.** to tear apart with force or violence. **2.** to pull or tear violently (fol. by *away, off, up,* etc.). [OE]

render /'rendə/, *v.t.* **1.** to cause to be or become: *to render someone helpless.* **2.** to do; perform: *to render a service.* **3.** to give: *to render aid; to render obedience.* **4.** to present for consideration, approval, payment, action, etc.: *to render an account.* **5.** to pay as due (a tax, etc.). **6.** to reproduce in another language; translate. **7.** to represent in painting, etc. **8.** to cover (brickwork, stone, etc.) with a first coat of plaster. ◇*n.* **9.** the mixture of sand, cement, etc., used to render (def. 8). [ME, from OF, from Rom: give back] **-rendering,** *n.*

rendezvous /'rɒndeɪvu, rɒndeɪ'vu/, *n., pl.* **-vous** /-vuz/, *v.*, **-voused** /-vud/, **-vousing** /-vuɪŋ/. ◇*n.* **1.** an appointment made between two or more people to meet at a fixed place and time. **2.** a place fixed for a meeting, esp. of troops, ships, or spacecraft. ◇*v.i., v.t.* **3.** to meet at an appointed place. [F: present or betake yourself (yourselves)]

rendition /ren'dɪʃən/, *n.* **1.** a performance. **2.** a translation. **3.** an interpretation, as of a role or a piece of music. [F, from L]

Rene /rɪn/, *n.* **Roy** (*Henry Van der Sluys*), 1892-1954, Australian vaudeville performer, known for his portrayal of the clown Mo.

renegade /'rɛnəgeɪd/, *n.* **1.** someone who deserts one party or cause for another; traitor. ◇*v.i.* **2.** to become a renegade. [Sp: renounce, from ML, from L: deny]

renege /rə'neg, -'nɪg/, *v.i.*, **-neged, -neging. 1.** *Cards.* to fail to follow suit when one can and should do so; revoke. **2.** *Colloq.* to go back on one's word. [ML, from L] **-reneger,** *n.*

renew /rə'nju/, *v.t.* **1.** to begin or take up again: *to renew a friendship; to renew a lease.* **2.** to restore or replenish: *to renew a stock of goods.* **3.** to make, say, or do again: *She renewed her demands.* **-renewal,** *n.*

rennet /'rɛnət/, *n.* **1.** the lining membrane of the fourth stomach of a calf, or of the stomach of certain other young animals, containing rennin. **2.** a preparation of the rennet membrane, used to curdle milk during the making of cheese, junket, etc. [ME]

rennin /'rɛnən/, *n.* the enzyme found in rennet, that curdles milk.

Renoir /'rɛnwa/, *n.* **1. Jean** /ʒɒ̃/, 1894-1979, French film director; films include *La Grande Illusion* (1937). **2.** his father, **Pierre Auguste** /pi,ɛə ou'gyst/, 1841-1919, French impressionist painter; paintings include *The Luncheon of the Boating-Party* (1881).

renounce /rə'naʊns/, *v.t.*, **-nounced, -nouncing. 1.** to give up or put aside by one's own decision. **2.** to give up by formal declaration: *to renounce a claim.* **3.** to disown; repudiate. [ME, from F, from L: make known, report] **-renouncement,** *n.*

renovate /'rɛnəveɪt/, *v.t.*, **-vated, -vating.** to restore to good condition; repair. [L] **-renovation,** *n.* **-renovator,** *n.*

renown /rə'naʊn/, *n.* fame. [ME, from AF, from OF: name over again, from L] **-renowned,** *adj.*

rent¹ /rent/, *n.* **1.** a payment made regularly for the use of land or building, or other property. **2.** the return gained from any business in excess of production costs. ◇*v.t.* **3.** to allow the possession and use of (property) in return for regular payments. ◇*v.i.* **4.** to be let for rent: *This flat rents for $100 a week.* [ME, from OF, from Rom, from L]

rent² /rent/, *n.* **1.** an opening made by rending or tearing; tear. **2.** a break or split in relations or union. ◇*v.* **3.** past tense and past participle of **rend.**

rental /'rɛntl/, *n.* an amount received or paid as rent. [ME]

renunciation /rənʌnsi'eɪʃən/, *n.* **1.** the act of renouncing. **2.** a formal declaration renouncing something. **-renunciative, renunciatory,** *adj.*

rep /rɛp/, *n. Colloq.* a representative, esp. a travelling salesman or trade union delegate. [abbrev.]

rep., *Abbrev.* **1.** report. **2.** reporter. **3.** repeat. **4.** representative.

Rep

Rep, *Abbrev.* Republic.

repair[1] /rə'peə/, *v.t.* **1.** to restore to a good or sound condition after decay or damage; mend. **2.** to put right; remedy: *to repair damage.* ◇*n.* **3.** the act, process, or work of repairing: *the repair of a building.* **4.** a part that has been repaired or an addition made in repairing: *The repairs to the table were badly done.* **5.** condition in relation to need for repairing: *in good repair; in bad repair.* [ME, from L: put in order]

repair[2] /rə'peə/, *v.i.* **1.** to go (to a place): *He soon repaired to Adelaide.* ◇*n.* **2.** the act of repairing or going: *to make repair to Adelaide.* [ME, from OF: return, from LL: return to one's country]

reparable /'repərəbəl, 'reprəbəl/, *adj.* able to be repaired or put right. Also, **repairable.** [L]

reparation /repə'reɪʃən/, *n.* **1.** the making up for wrong or injury done; compensation: *a wrong for which there can be no reparation.* **2.** (*usu. pl.*) compensation in money, material, labor, etc., paid by a defeated nation for damage to the civilian population and property during war. [ME, from L]

repartee /repɑ'ti/, *n.* **1.** a quick and clever or witty reply. **2.** talk marked by quickness and wittiness of reply. [F: an answering thrust]

repast /rə'pɑst/, *n.* a meal. [ME, from OF, from LL: feed regularly]

repatriate /ri'pætrieɪt/, *v.,* **-ated, -ating.** /ri'pætriət/, *n.* ◇*v.t.* **1.** to bring or send back (a person) to their own country: *to repatriate prisoners of war.* ◇*n.* **2.** someone who has been repatriated. [LL]

repatriation /ˌripætri'eɪʃən/, *n.* **1.** the act of repatriating. **2.** assistance given to ex-servicemen returning to civilian life, in the form of pensions, medical care, allowances for dependents, etc.

repay /ri'peɪ/, *v.t.,* **-paid, -paying. 1.** to pay back (money, etc.). **2.** to make return for in any way: *I can only repay your goodness with thanks.* **3.** to return: *to repay a visit.* —**repayment,** *n.*

repeal /rə'pil/, *v.t.* **1.** to put an end to formally or officially; revoke; annul: *to repeal a law; to repeal a tax.* ◇*n.* **2.** the act of repealing; revocation. [ME, from AF]

repeat /rə'pit/, *v.t.* **1.** to say again (something already spoken by oneself or another): *Please repeat that sentence.* **2.** to do, make, perform, etc., again: *to repeat an action; to repeat a passage of music.* ◇*v.i.* **3.** to do or say something again. **4.** (of food eaten) to be tasted again when the eater belches: *The onions are repeating on me.* **5.** (of a firearm) to fire several times without reloading. ◇*n.* **6.** the act of repeating. **7.** something repeated. **8.** an order for goods the same as a previous order. **9.** a radio or television program that has been broadcast at least once before. [ME, from L: do or say again] —**repeated,** *adj.*

repeater /rə'pitə/, *n.* **1.** a repeating firearm. **2.** *Elect.* an amplifier used in telephone circuits to make good losses of power. **3.** → **recurring decimal.**

repel /rə'pel/, *v.,* **-pelled, -pelling.** ◇*v.t.* **1.** to drive or force back (an attack, attacker, etc.). **2.** to keep off or out; fail to mix with: *Water and oil repel each other.* **3.** to turn away; refuse to have to do with; reject: *to repel temptation.* **4.** to cause feelings of distaste or disgust: *Her dirty appearance repels me.* ◇*v.i.* **5.** to act with a force that drives or keeps away something. **6.** to cause distaste or disgust. [ME, from L: drive back]

repellent /rə'pelənt/, *adj.* **1.** causing distaste or disgust; repulsive. **2.** repelling; driving back. ◇*n.* **3.** Also, **repellant.** something that repels: *an insect repellent.* —**repellence,** *n.*

repent /rə'pent/, *v.i.* **1.** to feel sorrow or regret for one's past behavior: *She repented of what she had done; You will be forgiven if you repent.* ◇*v.t.* **2.** to feel sorry for; regret: *He repented his words.* [ME, from OF] —**repentance,** *n.* —**repentant,** *adj.*

repercussion /ripə'kʌʃən/, *n.* **1.** the indirect effect or result of some event or action: *The repercussions of the plan were very widely felt.* **2.** the condition of being driven or thrown back. **3.** a springing back or rebounding of something, such as an echo. [ME, from L] —**repercussive,** *adj.*

repertoire /'repətwɑ/, *n.* **1.** a list of plays, operas, parts, pieces, etc., which a company, actor, singer, etc., is prepared to perform. **2.** the store of things of a particular kind possessed by a person or group: *She has a large repertoire of jokes.* [F, from L: inventory, catalogue]

repertory /'repətri/, *n., pl.* **-ries. 1.** → **repertoire. 2.** a type of theatrical company, which prepares several plays, operas, etc., and produces them in turn, for a limited run only. **3.** a store of things available. [L]

repetition /repə'tɪʃən/, *n.* **1.** the act of repeating. **2.** something made by or resulting from repeating. [L] —**repetitious, repetitive,** *adj.*

repine /rə'paɪn/, *v.i.,* **-pined, -pining.** to be discontented; fret; complain.

replace /rə'pleɪs/, *v.t.,* **-placed, -placing. 1.** to fill or take the place of; substitute for (a person or thing): *Electricity has replaced gas as a means of lighting.* **2.** to provide something to take the place of: *I must replace this broken dish.* **3.** to put back in place: *Please replace the book where you found it.*

replacement /rə'pleɪsmənt/, *n.* **1.** someone or something that replaces another. **2.** *Mil.* a reinforcement. **3.** *Geol.* the process of removal and deposition happening at almost the same time by which a new mineral of partly or wholly differing chemical composition appears in the body of an old mineral.

replay /'ripleɪ/, *n.* **1.** (in sport) a game, contest, etc., which is played again, esp. to decide a draw. **2.** (in television coverage of sport) the playing again of an important part of a game, often immediately after it has happened.

replenish /rə'plenɪʃ/, *v.t.* to make full or complete again: *to replenish a glass with wine;*

replenish 879 **reprisal**

replenish a fire with wood. [ME, from OF, from L] —**replenishment**, n.

replete /rə'plit/, adj. 1. fully supplied or provided (fol. by with). 2. having had enough food and drink. [ME, from L: filled] —**repletion**, n.

replica /'replikə/, n. a copy or reproduction, esp. of a work of art. [It]

reply /rə'plaɪ/, v., -plied, -plying, n., pl. -plies. ◇v.i. 1. to make answer in words or writing; respond. 2. to respond by some action, performance, etc.: to reply to the enemy's fire. ◇v.t. 3. to return as an answer: He replied that nothing would make him accept. ◇n. 4. an answer or response. [ME, from OF: fold again, turn back, reply, from L: unfold, reply]

report /rə'pɔt/, n. 1. an account brought back or presented, esp. containing information that is the result of investigation. 2. an account of a speech, meeting, etc., esp. as taken down for publication. 3. a written account of a school pupil's academic progress, behavior, attendance, etc., sent home to his or her parents. 4. a story or information generally known; rumor: The surf here is very dangerous according to report. 5. a loud explosive noise, esp. from a gun. ◇v.t. 6. to carry and repeat as an answer or message. 7. to tell what has been learned by examination or investigation. 8. to give a formal account or statement of. 9. to lay a charge against (a person): to be reported to the police. 10. to present (oneself) to a person in authority. 11. to take down (a speech, etc.) in writing, as for publication in a newspaper, etc. ◇v.i. 12. to make a report. 13. to act as a reporter for a newspaper, etc. 14. to present or give an account of oneself to someone in authority: to report to the boss; report sick. 15. to present oneself at an appointed place, etc. [ME, from OF, from L]

reported speech, n. the speech or writing of another, not quoted exactly, but changed in person, tense, etc., so that the hearer or reader knows that the statements made are at second hand; indirect speech (opposed to *direct speech*).

reporter /rə'pɔtə/, n. 1. someone employed to gather and report news for a newspaper, broadcasting organisation, etc. 2. someone who prepares official reports of legal or legislative proceedings, etc.

repose[1] /rə'pouz/, n., v., -posed, -posing. ◇n. 1. a condition of peaceful resting. 2. calmness of behavior, appearance, etc. ◇v.i. 3. to lie at rest; be peaceful. 4. to lie or rest: to repose on a park bench. ◇v.t. 5. (oft. used reflexively) to lay to rest: I will repose myself here. [ME, from F, from L] —**reposeful**, adj. —**reposal**, n.

repose[2] /rə'pouz/, v.t., -posed, -posing. to put (confidence, trust, etc.) in a person or thing. [L]

repository /rə'pɔzətri/, n., pl. -tories. 1. a container or place where things are put, stored, or offered for sale, such as a warehouse. 2. someone to whom something is entrusted or confided. [L]

repossess /ripə'zɛs/, v.t. 1. to regain possession of, as goods not paid for. 2. to put again in possession of something: They repossessed him of his land. —**repossession**, n.

reprehensible /reprɪ'hɛnsəbəl/, adj. deserving to be rebuked; blameworthy: reprehensible conduct. —**reprehensibility**, n.

represent /reprə'zɛnt/, v.t. 1. (of a word, symbol, etc.) to serve to express, show, stand for, or mark; symbolise: C represents common time in music. 2. to express or show by some term, character, symbol, etc.: to represent musical sounds by notes. 3. to stand, act or speak in the place of, as a substitute, proxy, or agent: to represent his government in a foreign country. 4. to act for (a constituency, etc.) by elected right in parliament or government. 5. (of a picture, image, etc.) to present the likeness or outward appearance of; portray; depict. 6. to present in words; set forth; describe; state: The novel represents life in 19th century England. 7. to describe as having a particular character (fol. by *as*, *to be*, etc.): Superman is represented as a man of steel. 8. to be an example or type of; exemplify. 9. to be the equivalent of; correspond to. [ME, from L] —**representation**, n. —**representational**, adj.

representative /reprə'zɛntətɪv/, adj. 1. serving to represent; representing. 2. typical; exemplifying a class: a representative selection of Australian verse. 3. representing a constituency or community or the people generally, in the making and passing of laws or in government: a representative assembly. 4. marked by, founded on, or relating to representation of the people in government: representative government. ◇n. 5. someone or something that represents another or others, esp. an agent, travelling salesman or elected member of parliament. 6. an example; specimen; type.

repress /rə'prɛs/, v.t. 1. to keep under control, check, or suppress (desires, feelings, action, tears, etc.). 2. to put down or stamp out (disorder, rebellion, etc.). 3. to reduce (people) to subjection. 4. *Psychol.* to reject (unacceptable thoughts, feelings, memories, etc.) from one's own consciousness. [ME, from L] —**repressed**, adj. —**repression**, n. —**repressive**, adj.

reprieve /rə'priv/, v., -prieved, -prieving, n. ◇v.t. 1. to relieve (someone) from impending punishment, esp. to allow a delay of a sentence of execution. 2. to relieve temporarily from any evil. ◇n. 3. a delay (for a time) of punishment. 4. a warrant making such an action legal. 5. any rest or temporary relief. [ME: reprove, apparently taken in literal sense of test again (involving postponement)]

reprimand /'reprəmand, -mænd/, n. 1. a severe statement of disapproval, esp. a formal one by a person in a position of power. ◇v.t. 2. to address words of severe disapproval to (a person, etc.), esp. in a formal way; reprove. [F: repress, reprove]

reprint /ri'prɪnt/, v.; /'riprɪnt/, n. ◇v.t. 1. to print again; print a new impression of. ◇n. 2. a new impression, without change, of any printed work.

reprisal /rə'praɪzəl/, n. hurt or damage caused to (a person, army, etc.) in return for

reprisal damage received; retaliation. [ME, from AF: taken back]

reprise /rə'praɪz, -'priːz/, n. Music. a return to the first theme or subject. [ME, from F: take back, from L]

reproach /rɪ'proʊtʃ/, v.t. **1.** to find fault with (a person, etc.); blame; censure. **2.** to blame in a sharp way (fol. by *with*). ◇n. **3.** blame or strong disapproval expressed by reproaching: *a term of reproach.* **4.** an expression of blame, strong disapproval or scolding. **5.** disgrace, discredit, or blame: *to bring reproach on one's family.* **6.** a cause or occasion of disgrace or discredit: *a man beyond reproach.* [late ME, from F, from L: reprove] —**reproachful**, adj.

reprobate /'rɛprəbeɪt/, n., adj., v., -bated, -bating. ◇n. **1.** an unprincipled, immoral or wicked person. ◇adj. **2.** bad; morally depraved; unprincipled. ◇v.t. **3.** to disapprove of; condemn; censure. [ME, from LL: reproved] —**reprobation**, n.

reproduce /riprə'djuːs/, v., -duced, -ducing. ◇v.t. **1.** to make a copy, representation, or strong likeness of. **2.** to produce again or anew by natural process: *to reproduce a broken claw.* **3.** to produce young or offspring. **4.** to produce again or anew in any manner. ◇v.i. **5.** to reproduce its kind, as an animal or plant; propagate. **6.** to turn out (well, etc.) when copied. —**reproducer**, n. —**reproducible**, adj.

reproduction /riprə'dʌkʃən/, n. **1.** the act or process of reproducing. **2.** the state of being reproduced. **3.** something that is made by reproducing; a copy or duplicate, esp. of a picture, etc., made by photoengraving or some similar process. **4.** the natural process among animals and plants by which new members are generated and the species carried on. —**reproductive**, adj.

reproof /rɪ'pruːf/, n. the act or an example of blaming, finding fault with or scolding in a sharp way.

reprove /rɪ'pruːv/, v., -proved, -proving. ◇v.t. **1.** to address words of disapproval to (a person, etc.); rebuke; blame. **2.** to express disapproval of (actions, words, etc.). ◇v.i. **3.** to speak in reproof; administer a reproof. [ME, from OF, from L]

reptile /'rɛptaɪl/, n. **1.** any of a class of cold-blooded animals with back-bones, including the lizards, snakes, turtles, and alligators, together with various types which have now died out. ◇adj. **2.** creeping or crawling like a reptile. [ME, from LL] —**reptilian**, adj., n.

republic /rɪ'pʌblɪk/, n. **1.** a state in which the total power rests in the body of the citizens entitled to vote and is exercised by representatives chosen directly or indirectly by them. **2.** any body of people, etc., viewed as a commonwealth. **3.** a state, esp. a democratic state, in which the head of the government is an elected or appointed president, not a hereditary ruler. [L: public matter]

republican /rɪ'pʌblɪkən/, adj. **1.** of, relating to, or of the nature of a republic. **2.** favoring a republic. ◇n. **3.** someone who favors a republican form of government. **4.** *US Politics.* (*cap.*) a member of the Republican Party. —**republicanism**, n.

Republican Party, n. **1.** one of the two major political parties of the US, originated (1854–56) to combat slavery. **2.** any of a number of political parties in other countries; usu. in opposition to the monarchy in that country.

repudiate /rɪ'pjuːdieɪt/, v.t., -ated, -ating. **1.** to refuse to recognise as having power or binding force. **2.** to throw off or disown: *to repudiate a son.* **3.** to reject with disapproval, esp. a belief, etc. **4.** to refuse to accept as true, esp. a charge, etc.; deny. **5.** to refuse to accept knowledge of and pay, esp. a debt, etc. [LL: rejected, divorced] —**repudiation**, n.

repugnant /rɪ'pʌgnənt/, adj. **1.** distasteful or objectionable. **2.** making opposition; objecting; averse. **3.** opposed or different from, as in nature or character. [L: fighting against] —**repugnance**, n.

repulse /rɪ'pʌls/, v., -pulsed, -pulsing, n. ◇v.t. **1.** to drive or force back, (an attacker, etc.); repel. **2.** to drive back with coldness, rudeness, etc.; refuse or reject. ◇n. **3.** the act of driving back. **4.** a refusal; rejection. [L: repelled]

repulsion /rɪ'pʌlʃən/, n. **1.** the act of driving back. **2.** the condition of being driven back. **3.** a feeling of being driven away; distaste, repugnance, or aversion. **4.** *Phys.* a situation in which objects are repelled from each other (opposed to *attraction*).

repulsive /rɪ'pʌlsɪv/, adj. **1.** causing strong dislike, repugnance or aversion. **2.** tending to drive back by coldness, rudeness, etc.

reputable /'rɛpjətəbəl/, adj. having a good name, etc.; honorable; respectable.

reputation /rɛpjə'teɪʃən/, n. **1.** the regard in which a person or thing is held, esp. by the public generally; repute: *a man of good reputation.* **2.** favorable or good name: *to ruin one's reputation by misconduct.*

repute /rɪ'pjuːt/, n., v., -puted, -puting. ◇n. **1.** regard in the view of others; reputation: *a person of good repute.* ◇v.t. **2.** to consider or regard (a person or thing) to be as stated (commonly in the passive): *He was reputed to be a millionaire.* [ME, from L: reckon, think]

reputed /rɪ'pjuːtəd/, adj. accounted or supposed to be such: *the reputed author of a book.*

request /rɪ'kwɛst/, n. **1.** the act of asking for something to be given or done, esp. as a favor or kindness; solicitation or petition. **2.** something that is asked for: *to obtain one's request.* **3.** the condition of being asked for; demand: *to be in great request as an after-dinner speaker.* ◇v.t. **4.** to ask for (something), esp. politely or formally. **5.** to ask or beg (used with a clause or an infinitive): *to request that he leave; to request to be excused.* **6.** to ask (a person, etc.) to do something: *He requested me to go.* [ME, from OF, from Gallo-Rom: (things) asked for, from LL: seek]

requiem /'rɛkwiəm/, *n. (oft. cap.)* **1.** *Rom Cath Ch.* a mass for the rest and peace of the souls of the dead. **2.** any musical service, hymn, or funeral song for the peaceful resting of the souls of the dead. [ME, from L: rest, the first word of the Latin mass for the dead]

requiescat /ˌrɛkwi'ɛskæt/, *n.* a wish or prayer that the dead may rest in peace. [L: short for *requiescat in pāce* may he (or she) rest in peace]

require /rə'kwaɪə/, *v.*, **-quired, -quiring.** ◇*v.t.* **1.** to have need of; need: *He requires medical care.* **2.** to call on from a position of power; order or enjoin (a person, etc.) to do something: *to require an agent to account for money spent.* **3.** to place under a sense of duty or necessity. ◇*v.i.* **4.** to make a demand; impose an obligation or need: *to do as the law requires.* [ME, from L: search for, require]

requirement /rə'kwaɪəmənt/, *n.* **1.** something that is required; a thing required or obligatory: *A knowledge of Spanish is among the requirements.* **2.** an act or an example of demanding.

requisite /'rɛkwəzət/, *adj.* **1.** needed or demanded by the nature of things or by conditions; indispensable: *He has the requisite qualifications.* ◇*n.* **2.** a necessary thing; something requisite. [late ME, from L: sought for]

requisition /ˌrɛkwə'zɪʃən/, *n.* **1.** the act of demanding, or the demand made. **2.** the demanding formally or from a position of power that something be done, given, etc. **3.** the form on which such a demand is written. ◇*v.t.* **4.** to demand or to take for official use; press into service, esp. for military purposes, public needs, etc.: *to requisition supplies.*

requite /rə'kwaɪt/, *v.t.*, **-quited, -quiting.** to make repayment or return for (service, kindness, etc.) or for (a wrong, damage, hurt, etc.). [RE- + *quite*, obs. var. of QUIT, v.] **—requital,** *n.*

rescind /rə'sɪnd/, *v.t.* **1.** to withdraw formally; annul; revoke; repeal; abrogate. **2.** to cause (an act, measure, etc.) to have no legal force, by a later action or a higher power. [L: cut off, annul] **—rescindable,** *adj.* **—rescission,** *n.*

rescue /'rɛskju/, *v.*, **-cued, -cuing.** *n.* ◇*v.t.* **1.** to free or deliver from confinement, violence, danger, or evil. ◇*n.* **2.** the act of rescuing. [ME, from OF, from L *re-* RE- + *excutere* shake out or off] **—rescuer,** *n.*

research /rə'sɜtʃ, 'risɜtʃ/, *n.* **1.** painstaking and systematic enquiry or careful examination into a subject in order to discover facts or principles: *research in nuclear physics.* ◇*v.t.* **2.** to examine carefully; research: *to research one's family history.* ◇*adj.* **3.** of or relating to research. [F]

resemble /rə'zɛmbəl/, *v.t.*, **-bled, -bling.** to be like or similar to. [ME, from OF, from L: simulate, imitate, copy] **—resemblance,** *n.*

resent /rə'zɛnt/, *v.t.* to feel or show displeasure or anger at, from a sense of hurt or rude treatment. [F, from L: feel] **—resentful,** *adj.* **—resentment,** *n.*

reservation /ˌrɛzə'veɪʃən/, *n.* **1.** a keeping back, withholding, or setting apart. **2.** the making of some objection or limitation. **3.** the objection or limitation made, inwardly or openly: *a mental reservation.* **4.** a piece of public land set apart for a special purpose, as (in the US) for the use of an Indian tribe. **5.** the setting aside or the making sure of accommodation at a hotel, on a train or boat, etc., esp. for a traveller: *to write for reservations.*

reserve /rə'zɜv/, *v.*, **-served, -serving,** *n., adj.* ◇*v.t.* **1.** to keep back or save for future use, arrangement, treatment, etc. **2.** to set aside or book in advance, esp. a place to stay, theatre seats, etc. **3.** to set apart for a particular use, purpose, service, etc.: *ground reserved for a garden.* **4.** *Law.* to delay handing down (a judgment or decision), esp. to give time for better consideration of the matters involved. ◇*n.* **5.** something reserved, usu. for some purpose or in case of accident, etc.; a store or stock. **6.** *Sport.* **a.** a player kept in readiness to take the place of a team member who may drop out through being hurt, etc. **b.** *(pl.)* a club's second team. **7.** a piece of public land set apart for recreation, etc., as a public reserve, or for a special purpose, as a nature reserve. **8.** a piece of public land to be lived on and used by the aboriginal people of a country, allowing them to keep their traditional lifestyle. **9.** a limitation; reservation, exception, or qualification. **10.** the act of reserving. **11.** the condition of being reserved, esp. for future use or for some purpose or person: *money in reserve.* **12.** *Mil.* **a.** a part of a military force held in readiness to support the attack or defence made by the rest of the force. **b.** the part of a country's fighting force not in active service, but used as a further means of defence in case of necessity. **13.** the quality or habit of avoiding close friendships and familiarity; self-restraint in action or speech; reticence. **14.** → **reserve price.** ◇*adj.* **15.** kept in reserve; forming a reserve: *a reserve fund; a reserve supply.* [ME, from L: keep back]

reserve bank, *n.* the national banking organisation of a country, which carries out the monetary policy of a government, receives tax and other revenue, pays government costs and issues money, both paper and coin, as legal tender.

reserved /rə'zɜvd/, *adj.* **1.** set apart for a particular use or purpose; kept in reserve. **2.** kept by special arrangement for some person or people: *a reserved seat.* **3.** keeping oneself back in action or speech; disposed to keep one's feelings, thoughts, or affairs to oneself.

reserve price, *n.* the lowest price at which a person is willing that his or her property shall be sold at auction. Also, **reserve.**

reservoir /'rɛzəvwɑː/, *n.* **1.** a natural or man-made place where water is collected and stored for use. **2.** a container for holding a liquid or fluid, esp. oil or gas. **3.** *Biol.* a space or part which holds some fluid or secretion. **4.** a great supply, or store, of something. [F: keep, reserve]

reshuffle /ˌri'ʃʌfəl/, *v.*, **-fled, -fling,** *n.* ◇*v.t.* **1.** to shuffle again. **2.** to make a new arrangement of jobs, esp. within a government or cabinet. ◊*n.* **3.** a rearrangement or reorganisation; a shake-up.

reside /rə'zaɪd/, *v.i.*, **-sided, -siding. 1.** to live for a considerable time; have one's abode: *He resided in Box Hill.* **2.** (of things, qualities, etc.) to stay with, lie, or be present habitually; exist or be inherent (fol. by *in*). **3.** to rest or be vested in, as powers, rights, etc. (fol. by *in*). [ME, from L]

residence /'rezədəns/, *n.* **1.** a place, esp. the house, in which one lives; dwelling place. **2.** a large house. **3.** the act or fact of living in (a place). **4.** the time during which one lives in a place. **– residency,** *n.*

resident /'rezədənt/, *n.* **1.** someone who lives in a place. **2.** a bird, animal, etc., that does not travel from place to place according to the season. ◊*adj.* **3.** living in a place; residing. **4.** living or staying at a place in discharge of one's duty: *a resident representative; the resident engineer.* **5.** (of qualities) existing; intrinsic. [ME, from L]

resident medical officer, *n.* → RMO.

residential /rezə'denʃəl/, *adj.* **1.** of or relating to housing or houses. **2.** used for housing: *a residential district.* **3.** (of a hotel, etc.) providing for guests who stay all the time or for lengthy periods.

residual /rə'zɪdʒuəl/, *adj.* **1.** remaining; left over. **2.** formed by the subtraction of one quantity from another: *a residual quantity.* ◊*n.* **3.** a residual quantity; remainder.

residuary /rə'zɪdʒuəri/, *adj.* **1.** entitled to the remainder of an estate or property: *a residuary legatee.* **2.** relating to or of the nature of a remainder, or something left over.

residue /'rezədʒu/, *n.* **1.** the part which remains after something is taken, disposed of, or gone; remainder. **2.** *Chem.* the matter remaining after evaporation, combustion, etc. [ME, from F, from L]

residuum /rə'zɪdʒuəm/, *n., pl.* **-sidua** /-'zɪdʒuə/. the remainder, or rest of something; residue. [L]

resign /rə'zaɪn/, *v.i.* **1.** to give up an office or position (oft. fol. by *from*). **2.** to give in to; yield; submit. ◊*v.t.* **3.** to give up (an office, position, right, claim, etc.) formally; relinquish. **4.** to yield (oneself, one's mind, etc.) without resistance. **5.** to hand or sign over; surrender, as to the care or control of another: *to resign a child to foster-parents.* [ME, from OF, from L: unseal, annul]

resignation /rezɪg'neɪʃən/, *n.* **1.** the act of giving up. **2.** the formal statement, letter, etc., stating that one gives up an office, position, etc. **3.** a condition of yielding; submission; unresisting acquiescence. [ME, from ML]

resigned /rə'zaɪnd/, *adj.* **1.** giving in to or yielding; submissive; acquiescent: *He is resigned to his fate.* **2.** marked by or showing signs of giving up or giving in to: *His face has a resigned expression.*

resilient /rə'zɪliənt, -'zɪljənt/, *adj.* **1.** returning to the original form or position after being bent, compressed, or stretched. **2.** readily recovering, esp. from sickness, depression, etc.; buoyant; cheerful. [L: rebounding] **– resilience, resiliency,** *n.*

resin /'rezən/, *n.* **1.** any of a class of semisolid organic substances obtained from certain plant secretions, and used in medicine and varnishes, e.g. rosin and shellac. **2.** substances made synthetically by polymerisation, used in plastics. ◊*v.t.* **3.** to treat or rub with resin, as the bow of a violin, etc. [ME, from L] **– resinous,** *adj.*

resist /rə'zɪst/, *v.t.* **1.** to withstand, fight against, or oppose: *to resist infection.* **2.** to withstand the action or effect of: *Gold resists corrosion.* **3.** to keep oneself back from; refrain; abstain: *to resist a smile.* ◊*v.i.* **4.** to make a stand or make efforts in opposition; act in opposition; offer resistance. ◊*n.* **5.** a substance applied to a surface to enable it to withstand rust, etc. [ME, from L: withstand] **– resistant,** *adj., n.* **– resistive,** *adj.*

resistance /rə'zɪstəns/, *n.* **1.** the act or power of resisting, opposing, or withstanding. **2.** *Elect.* **a.** that property of a device which opposes the flow of an electric current. **b.** a measure of the ability of a device to oppose the flow of an electric current. **3.** (*oft. cap.*) a secret organisation in an enemy-occupied country working to keep fighting unofficially after a formal surrender, esp. that in France during World War II. [ME, from F]

resistivity /rizɪs'tɪvəti/, *n.* **1.** the power or property of resistance. **2.** *Elect.* a measure of the ability of a material to oppose the flows of an electric current (the reciprocal of *conductivity*).

resistor /rə'zɪstə/, *n.* a device, the most important purpose of which is to introduce resistance into an electric circuit.

resolute /'rezəlut/, *adj.* **1.** firmly fixed or determined; set in purpose or opinion. **2.** marked by firmness and determination, esp. of the temper, spirit, actions, etc. [ME, from L: resolved]

resolution /rezə'luʃən/, *n.* **1.** a formal determination, or expression of opinion, of a meeting or other body of people brought together to make decisions, etc. **2.** firmness of purpose or determination. **3.** the act of settling on or determining, as to action, etc. **4.** the mental state or quality of being determined or firm; firmness of purpose. **5.** the act or process of determining or separating into the basic or elementary parts; reduction to a simpler form; conversion. **6.** the resulting condition. **7.** a solution or explanation, esp. of a problem, a doubtful point, etc. **8.** *Music.* the progression of harmony from a dissonance (unfinished and harsh chord) to a consonance (sweet-sounding chord), esp. the tonic chord, or sometimes to a less violent dissonance. **9.** (in a novel, drama, etc.) the concluding part, where any problems are resolved and harmony is restored. [ME, from L]

resolve /rə'zɒlv/, *v.*, **-solved, -solving,** *n.* ◊*v.t.* **1.** to fix or settle on by choice and will; determine (to do something). **2.** to

resolve   883   **respite**

separate into basic or elementary parts; separate or break up (fol. by *into*); analyse. **3.** *Phys.* (of forces, velocities, etc.) to divide into components, usu. perpendicular to each other in direction. **4.** to change into something different (often reflexive). **5.** to settle, determine, or state formally in a vote, etc. **6.** to deal with (a question, a matter of uncertainty, etc.) once and for all; explain; solve (a problem). **7.** to clear away (doubts, etc.), as by explanation. ◇*v.i.* **8.** to come to a determination; make up one's mind; determine (oft. fol. by *on* or *upon*). **9.** *Music.* to achieve a resolution (def. 8). ◇*n.* **10.** determination; firmness of purpose, esp. to follow some course of action. [ME, from L: loosen, dissolve] —**resolvable**, *adj.*

resonance /ˈrɛzənəns/, *n.* **1.** the condition or quality of being resonant. **2.** the amplification of the voice by the bones of the head and upper chest, and by the air cavities of the pharynx, mouth, and nasal passages. **3.** *Phys.* (in a mechanical or electrical system) the increase of the amplitude vibrations as the frequency of an external periodic stimulus approaches the natural frequency of the system. **4.** *Chem.* the condition shown by a molecule when the arrangement of its valency electrons is between two or more arrangements having nearly the same energy, as in a benzene ring.

resonant /ˈrɛzənənt/, *adj.* **1.** resounding or re-echoing, usu. of sounds, places, etc. **2.** deep and full of resonance: *a resonant voice.* **3.** relating to resonance. **4.** having the property of increasing the intensity of sound by sympathetic vibration. [L: resounding]

resonate /ˈrɛzəneɪt/, *v.i.*, **-nated, -nating. 1.** to resound or act as something that resounds. ◇*v.t.* **2.** to cause to resound; to amplify. [L: resounded] —**resonation**, *n.* —**resonator**, *n.*

resort /rəˈzɔːt/, *v.i.* **1.** to turn to a person or thing for use, service, or help: *to resort to drugs.* **2.** to go, esp. frequently or customarily: *a beach to which many people resort.* ◇*n.* **3.** a place frequented, esp. by the public generally: *a summer resort.* **4.** a resorting to some person or thing for help, service, etc.; recourse: *to have resort to reference books.* **5.** someone or something resorted to for help, service, etc. **6. last resort,** the means to which one turns when all others have failed. [ME, from OF: go out again]

resound /rəˈzaʊnd/, *v.i.* **1.** to re-echo or ring with sound. **2.** to make an echoing sound, or sound loudly. **3.** to be echoed, or ring. ◇*v.t.* **4.** to re-echo (a sound). **5.** to make known loudly (praises, etc.); proclaim. [ME re- RE- + soun(en) SOUND¹]

resounding /rəˈzaʊndɪŋ/, *adj.* **1.** ringing or re-echoing as a sound or its cause or location; reverberating. **2.** outstanding; great: *a resounding success.* **3.** (of actions) firmly carried out and often noisy: *a resounding blow.*

resource /rəˈzɔːs, rəˈsɔːs/, *n.* **1.** a source of supply, support, or aid. **2.** (*pl.*) the collective wealth of a country, or its means of producing wealth. **3.** (*oft. pl.*) money, or any property which can be changed into money; assets. **4.** the means at hand afforded by the mind or personal abilities. **5.** any action or measure which one may turn to in an emergency; expedient. **6.** the ability to deal with a situation or difficulty. [F, from OF, from L: rise again]

resourceful /rəˈzɔːsfəl, rəˈsɔːsfəl/, *adj.* skilful in overcoming difficulties; full of resource; ingenious.

respect /rəˈspɛkt/, *n.* **1.** a particular, detail, or point (in phrases prec. by *in*): *to be defective in some respect.* **2.** relation or direction of the attention to (prec. by *in* or *with*): *inquiries with respect to a route.* **3.** high and respectful regard felt or shown; esteem; deference. **4.** the condition of being highly regarded or honored. **5.** (*pl.*) respectful or friendly words of praise, as paid when making a call on a person: *to pay one's respects.* **6.** consideration or regard, as to something that might influence a choice. ◇*v.t.* **7.** to hold in high regard or honor: *to respect one's elders.* **8.** to show high regard, or consideration for: *to respect someone's wishes.* **9.** to treat with consideration; refrain from interfering with: *to respect a person's privacy.* [ME, from L: having been regarded]

respectable /rəˈspɛktəbəl/, *adj.* **1.** worthy of respect or high regard; estimable; worthy: *a respectable citizen.* **2.** of good social standing, name, etc.: *a respectable neighborhood.* **3.** having socially accepted standards of moral behavior; virtuous: *a respectable girl.* **4.** of a presentable appearance; decently clothed. **5.** of a passable standard; fairly good; fair: *a respectable performance.* —**respectability**, *n.*

respective /rəˈspɛktɪv/, *adj.* relating to each one or several of a number of people, things, etc.; particular: *the respective merits of the candidates.*

respectively /rəˈspɛktɪvli/, *adv.* with respect to each of a number in the stated or corresponding order: *A, B, and C correspond to blue, yellow, and red respectively.*

respiration /ˌrɛspəˈreɪʃən/, *n.* **1.** the act of breathing; inhalation and exhalation of air. **2.** (in living organisms) the process by which oxygen and sugars, starches, etc. are absorbed into the system and the products (carbon dioxide and water) are given off.

respirator /ˈrɛspəreɪtə/, *n.* **1.** a device worn over the mouth, or nose or mouth, to prevent the breathing in of poisonous or harmful substances, etc., e.g. a gasmask. **2.** an apparatus to induce artificial respiration.

respiratory /ˈrɛsprətri, rɛsˈpɪrətri/, *adj.* relating to or serving for respiration.

respire /rəˈspaɪə/, *v.i.*, **-spired, -spiring.** to draw in and let out air for the purpose of continuing life; breathe. [ME, from L]

respite /ˈrɛspət, ˈrɛspaɪt/, *n., v.*, **-pited, -piting.** ◇*n.* **1.** a delay or discontinuance for a time, esp. of anything upsetting or trying; an interval of relief: *to work without respite.* **2.** a temporary putting off of the execution of a person condemned to death; reprieve. ◇*v.t.* **3.** to set free temporarily, esp. from anything upsetting or trying; give an interval of relief from. [ME, from OF, from LL: delay, from L: look for, wait for]

resplendent /rə'splendənt/, *adj.* shining brightly; gleaming; splendid: *resplendent in white uniforms*. [L: shining] —**resplendence**, *n.*

respond /rə'spɒnd/, *v.i.* **1.** to answer; give a reply in words: *to respond briefly to a question*. **2.** to make a return by some action as if in answer: *to respond generously to a charitable appeal*. **3.** to show some reaction or effect as if in answer; react: *Nerves respond to a stimulus*. ◇*v.t.* **4.** to say in answer; reply. [ME, from L]

respondent /rə'spɒndənt/, *n.* **1.** *Law.* a defendant, esp. in divorce cases and those relating to appeals. ◇*adj.* **2.** answering; responsive. [L: answering]

response /rə'spɒns/, *n.* **1.** an answer or reply, in words, action, etc. **2.** *Biol.* any behavior of a living organism which results from stimulation. **3.** *Elect.* the proportional relation (ratio) of the output level to the input level of an electrical apparatus or transmission line, at a given frequency. **4.** *Church.* a verse, sentence, phrase, or word said or sung by the choir or people in reply to the priest, etc., during public worship. [L]

responsibility /rəspɒnsə'bɪlətɪ/, *n., pl.* **-ties. 1.** the condition or fact of being responsible. **2.** an example of being responsible. **3.** a particular load of care placed on someone who is responsible: *to feel the responsibilities of one's position*. **4.** something for which someone is responsible: *A child is a responsibility to its parents*.

responsible /rə'spɒnsəbəl/, *adj.* **1.** answerable or accountable, esp. for something within one's power, control, or management (oft. fol. by *to* or *for*). **2.** having to account or answer for one's actions, etc. **3.** chargeable with being the cause of something (fol. by *for*). **4.** having the ability to make moral decisions and therefore accountable; capable of rational thought or action. **5.** able to discharge promises or pay debts. **6.** reliable in business or other dealings; showing reliability.

responsible government, *n.* a system under which the government must account for its actions to some representative body of the people.

responsive /rə'spɒnsɪv/, *adj.* **1.** making answer or reply. **2.** reacting readily to influences, efforts, etc. **3.** *Biol.* acting in response, esp. to some stimulus.

rest[1] /rest/, *n.* **1.** the refreshing quiet or peace of sleep: *a good night's rest*. **2.** refreshing ease or inactivity after exercise or hard work: *to allow an hour for rest*. **3.** relief or freedom, esp. from anything that tires, troubles, or upsets. **4.** the ceasing or absence of movement: *to bring a machine to rest*. **5.** a pause or break. **6.** *Music.* (a mark or sign showing) an interval of silence between notes. **7.** a thing or apparatus that supports something: *an elbow rest*. ◇*v.i.* **8.** to refresh oneself, esp. by sleeping, lying down, or relaxing. **9.** to be at peace; have tranquillity or ease. **10.** to have peace in death. **11.** to cease from motion, come to rest, or stop. **12.** to remain without further action or notice: *to let a matter rest*. **13.** to lie, sit, lean, or be set: *His arm rested on the table*. **14.** *Agric.* to lie unworked; lie fallow: *to let land rest*. **15.** to be placed upon as a weight or responsibility (fol. by *on* or *upon*). **16.** to rely (fol. by *on* or *upon*). **17.** to be based or founded (fol. by *on* or *upon*). **18.** to be found or be (where stated): *The blame rests with them*. **19.** to be present; dwell; linger (fol. by *on* or *upon*): *The torch beam rested upon the desk*. **20.** to be a weight or burden such as something to be done (fol. by *in* or *with*): *It rests with you to complete the job*. **21.** to be fixed or directed on something, as the gaze, eyes, etc. ◇*v.t.* **22.** to give rest to; refresh with rest: *to rest oneself*. **23.** to lay or place for rest, ease, or support: *to rest one's back against a tree*. **24.** to direct (the eyes, etc.): *to rest one's eyes on someone*. **25.** to base, or let depend: *to rest your case on the evidence of this witness*. **26.** to bring to rest; halt; stop. [OE]

rest[2] /rest/, *n.* **1.** the part that is left or remains; the remainder: *The rest of the money is his*. **2.** the others; those who are left; everyone else: *All the rest are going*. ◇*v.i.* **3.** to continue to be; remain (as specified): *rest assured*. [ME, from F, from L: remain]

restaurant /'restərɒnt/, *n.* a shop where meals are served to customers. [F: restore]

restaurateur /restərə'tɜ:/, *n.* the owner or manager of a restaurant. Also, **restauranteur** /restərɒn'tɜ:/.

restful /'restfəl/, *adj.* **1.** full of, or giving, rest. **2.** being at rest; quiet; tranquil; peaceful. —**restfulness**, *n.*

restitution /restə'tjuʃən/, *n.* **1.** repayment made by giving back a similar or equal amount in money or goods to that lost, damaged or harmed; indemnification. **2.** the giving back of property or rights previously taken, carried away, or given up. **3.** the bringing back to the former or original condition or position. [ME, from L: a restoring]

restive /'restɪv/, *adj.* **1.** restless; uneasy. **2.** hard to control; unmanageable. [REST[2] + -IVE]

restless /'restləs/, *adj.* **1.** marked by or showing inability to remain at rest: *a restless mood*. **2.** unquiet or uneasy. **3.** never at rest, or still; never ceasing. **4.** without rest; without restful sleep: *a restless night*. **5.** marked by unceasing activity.

restoration /restə'reɪʃən/, *n.* **1.** the act of restoring, reviving, or re-establishing. **2.** the condition or fact of being renewed. **3.** a bringing or putting back to a former, original, normal, or unmarked condition or position. **4.** the bringing or giving back of something taken away or lost. **5.** something which is renewed. **6.** the representation or reconstruction of an ancient building, extinct animal, etc. **7. the Restoration, a.** the re-establishment of the monarchy in England with the return of Charles II in 1660. **b.** the period of the reign of Charles II (1660–85), sometimes extended to include the reign of James II (1685–88). ◇*adj.* **8.** (*cap.*) marking, relating to, or produced during the period of the restoration (def. 7), esp. a type of play: *Restoration comedy*.

restore /rə'stɔr/, *v.t.*, **-stored, -storing. 1.** to bring back into existence, use, etc.; re-establish: *to restore order.* **2.** to bring back to a former, original, or normal condition, as a building, statue, or painting. **3.** to bring back to a condition of health, soundness, or life. **4.** to put back to a former place, or to a former position, rank, etc. **5.** to give back (anything taken away or lost). **6.** to reproduce, rebuild, or represent (an ancient building, extinct animal, etc.). [ME, from OF, from L: restore, repair] **–restorer,** *n.*

restrain /rə'streɪn/, *v.t.* **1.** to hold back from action; keep in check or under control; keep down; repress. **2.** to take away a person's freedom, etc. [ME, from OF, from L: restrain]

restraining order, *n.* an order made by a court, such as one to stop a husband from visiting his wife during divorce proceedings.

restraint /rə'streɪnt/, *n.* **1.** restraining action or influence: *freedom from restraint.* **2.** a means of restraining. **3.** the act of restraining, controlling, or checking. **4.** the condition or fact of being restrained; deprivation of liberty; confinement. **5.** a holding back of feelings. [ME, from OF: restrain]

restrict /rə'strɪkt/, *v.t.* to confine or keep within limits. [L: restrained, restricted] **–restricted,** *adj.* **–restrictive,** *adj.*

restriction /rə'strɪkʃən/, *n.* **1.** something that limits; a restrictive condition or regulation. **2.** the act or result of restricting.

restrictive clause, *n.* a relative clause, usu. not set off by commas, which identifies the person or object named by the antecedent. In 'The man *who went out the door* is my brother' the italicised part is a restrictive clause, (opposed to *descriptive clause*).

result /rə'zʌlt/, *n.* **1.** the outcome or effect of some action, etc. **2.** *Maths.* a quantity, value, etc., obtained by calculation. ◇*v.i.* **3.** to arise, or proceed as an effect from actions, circumstances, etc.; be the outcome. **4.** to end in a particular manner or thing: *The affair resulted in marriage.* [late ME, from L: spring back]

resultant /rə'zʌltənt/, *adj.* **1.** following as a result or outcome. **2.** resulting from the combination of two or more agents: *resultant force.* ◇*n.* **3.** something that results.

resume /rə'zjum/, *v.*, **-sumed, -suming.** ◇*v.t.* **1.** to take up or go on with again after interruption: *to resume a journey.* **2.** to go back to: *to resume one's seat.* **3.** to take, or take on, again: *She resumed her maiden name.* ◇*v.i.* **4.** to go on or continue after interruption. **5.** to begin again. [late ME, from L: take up again] **–resumable,** *adj.*

résumé /'rezjəmeɪ/, *n.* a summing up; summary. [F]

resumption /rə'zʌmpʃən/, *n.* **1.** a taking up or going on with again, esp. of something interrupted. **2.** a taking, or taking on, again, esp. of something given up or lost. [late ME, from L]

resurgent /rə'sɜdʒənt/, *adj.* rising or tending to rise again. **–resurgence,** *n.*

resurrect /ˌrezə'rekt/, *v.t.* **1.** to raise from the dead; bring to life again. **2.** to bring back into use, practice, etc.: *to resurrect an ancient custom.*

resurrection /ˌrezə'rekʃən/, *n.* **1.** the act of rising again from the dead. **2.** *Church.* (*cap.*) the rising again of Christ after His death and burial. **3.** *Church.* (*cap.*) the rising again of mankind on the Judgment Day. **4.** a rising again, as from decay, disuse, etc.; revival. [ME, from LL]

resuscitate /rə'sʌsəteɪt/, *v.t., v.i.,* **-tated, -tating.** to bring back to life, esp. from seeming death or from unconsciousness. [L: revived] **–resuscitation,** *n.* **–resuscitator,** *n.*

retail /'riteɪl/ *for defs 1–4, 6*; /ri'teɪl/ *for def. 5*, *n.* **1.** the sale of goods directly to the people who use them, usu. in small quantities (opposed to *wholesale*). ◇*adj.* **2.** relating to, having to do with, or taking part in sale at retail: *the retail price.* ◇*adv.* **3.** at a retail price or in a retail quantity; at retail. ◇*v.t.* **4.** to sell directly to the user. **5.** to relate or repeat in detail to others: *to retail scandal.* ◇*v.i.* **6.** to be sold at retail: *It retails at a dollar.* [ME, from AF: cut, clip, pare] **–retailer,** *n.*

retain /rə'teɪn/, *v.t.* **1.** to keep possession of. **2.** to continue to use, practise, etc.: *to retain an old custom.* **3.** to keep in mind; remember. **4.** to hold in place or position. **5.** to engage, esp. by the payment of a preliminary fee, as a lawyer. [ME, from OF, from Rom]

retainer[1] /rə'teɪnə/, *n.* **1.** someone or something that retains. **2.** *Hist.* someone attached to a noble household or owing it service. **3.** any servant, esp. a personal or family servant of long standing. [RETAIN + -ER[1]]

retainer[2] /rə'teɪnə/, *n.* **1.** the act or fact of keeping in one's service. **2.** a fee paid to make certain of services, as to a lawyer. [F]

retaining wall, *n.* a wall built to hold back a mass of earth, etc.

retaliate /rə'tæliˌeɪt/, *v.i.,* **-ated, -ating.** to return like for like (esp. for harm done); take reprisals: *to retaliate for an injury.* [LL: requited] **–retaliation,** *n.*

retard /rə'tad/, *v.t.* **1.** to make slow; hinder; impede. **2.** to slow down or limit (a person's development). [L]

retardation /ˌritɑ'deɪʃən/, *n.* **1.** the act of slowing down. **2.** the condition of being retarded. **3.** something that retards; a hindrance. **4.** *Phys.* the rate of decrease of velocity; deceleration. Also, **retardment.**

retarded /rə'tadəd/, *adj.* (of a person) slow in mental development, esp. having an IQ of 70–85; backward.

retch /retʃ/, *v.i.* **1.** to make efforts to vomit. ◇*n.* **2.** the act or a case of retching. [OE: clear the throat]

retention /rə'tenʃən/, *n.* **1.** the act of retaining. **2.** the condition of being retained. **3.** the power to retain. **4.** the act or power of remembering things; memory. [ME, from L]

retentive /rə'tentɪv/, *adj.* **1.** tending or serving to retain something. **2.** having the power or ability to retain. **3.** having the power or ability to remember; having a good memory.

reticent /'retəsənt/, *adj.* tending to be silent; not inclined to speak freely; reserved. [L: keeping silent] —**reticence**, *n.*

reticulate /rə'tɪkjəlɪt/, *adj.*; /rə'tɪkjəleɪt/, *v.* **-lated, -lating.** ◇*adj.* **1.** netted; covered with a network. **2.** like a network or net. ◇*v.t., v.i.* **3.** to form (into) a network. [L: made like a net] —**reticulation**, *n.*

reticule /'retəkjul/, *n.* a small purse or bag, originally of network but later of silk, etc. [F, from L: little net]

reticulum /rə'tɪkjələm/, *n., pl.* **-la** /-lə/. **1.** a network; any reticulated system or structure. **2.** *Zool.* the second stomach of animals which chew their cud. [L: little net]

retina /'retənə/, *n., pl.* **-nas, -nae** /-ni/. the innermost coat of the back part of the eyeball, which receives the image. [ME, from L: net] —**retinal**, *adj.*

retinue /'retənju/, *n.* a body of servants in attendance upon an important person. [ME, from OF: retain]

retire /rə'taɪə/, *v.,* **-tired, -tiring.** ◇*v.i.* **1.** to go away from others, as to a place of shelter. **2.** to go to bed. **3.** to withdraw from office, business, or active life: *I will retire at the age of 60.* **4.** *Sport.* to leave the field, ring, etc., before completion of the contest, usu. because of injury. ◇*v.t.* **5.** to remove from active service or the usual field of activity. [F: withdraw] —**retirement**, *n.*

retired /rə'taɪəd/, *adj.* withdrawn from or no longer busy with one's business or profession, usu. because of age: *a retired sea-captain.*

retiring /rə'taɪərɪŋ/, *adj.* withdrawing from relations with others; reserved; shy.

retort[1] /rə'tɔt/, *v.i.* **1.** to make a retort, often quickly and sharply. ◇*n.* **2.** a severe, cutting, or witty reply, esp. one that goes against a first speaker's statement, argument, etc. [L: twisted back]

retort[2] /rə'tɔt/, *n. Chem.* a vessel, usu. a glass bulb with a long neck, used for distilling substances, etc. [ML: twisted back]

retrace /rə'treɪs/, *v.t.,* **-traced, -tracing. 1.** to go back over: *to retrace one's steps.* **2.** to go back over with the memory. [F] —**retraceable**, *adj.*

retract[1] /rə'trækt/, *v.t.* to draw back or in. [ME, from L: drawn back] —**retractor**, *n.*

retract[2] /rə'trækt/, *v.t.* to withdraw (a statement, opinion, promise, etc.). [L: recall] —**retractable**, *adj.* —**retraction**, *n.*

retractile /rə'træktaɪl/, *adj.* able to be drawn back or in, as the head of a tortoise. —**retractility**, *n.*

retread /,ri'trɛd/, *v.,* **-treaded, -treading.** /'ritrɛd/, *n.* ◇*v.t.* **1.** to recondition (a worn motor-vehicle tyre) by moulding a new tread on to it. ◇*n.* **2.** a retreaded tyre.

retreat /rə'trit/, *n.* **1.** the forced or planned withdrawal of an armed force before an enemy, or the withdrawing of a ship or fleet from action. **2.** the act of withdrawing, esp. into safety or privacy; retirement; seclusion. **3.** a place of shelter, seclusion, or privacy. **4.** a withdrawal, or a period of withdrawal, for religious exercises and prayer. ◇*v.i.* **5.** to make a retreat. [ME]

retrench /rə'trɛntʃ/, *v.t.* **1.** to cut down or make smaller; curtail (expenses); reduce; diminish. **2.** to dismiss (an employee), as part of an effort to save money. ◇*v.i.* **3.** to save money; reduce expenses: *They retrenched by cutting down staff.* [F] —**retrenchment**, *n.*

retribution /rɛtrə'bjuʃən/, *n.* repayment for one's actions, esp. evil. [ME, from L]

retrieve /rə'triv/, *v.,* **-trieved, -trieving**, *n.* ◇*v.t.* **1.** to recover or regain. **2.** to bring back to a former and better condition; restore: *to retrieve one's fortunes.* **3.** to make good; repair (a loss, error, etc.). **4.** to find and bring back. **5.** to save. ◇*n.* **6.** the act of retrieving; recovery. [ME, from OF: find again] —**retrievable**, *adj.* —**retrieval**, *n.*

retriever /rə'trivə/, *n.* a type of dog bred for retrieving game, as the golden retriever.

retro-, a prefix meaning 'backwards' in space or time, as *retrogression, retrospect*. [L, prefix representing *retrō*, *adv.*, backward, back, behind]

retroactive /rɛtroʊ'æktɪv/, *adj.* (of a statute, etc.) effective or operative with respect to the past; retrospective. —**retroactivity**, *n.*

retroflex /'rɛtrəflɛks/, *adj.* bent backwards. [L: bent back] —**retroflexion**, *n.*

retrograde /'rɛtrəgreɪd/, *adj., v.,* **-graded, -grading.** ◇*adj.* **1.** moving backwards; having a backward motion or direction; retiring or retreating. **2.** returning to an earlier and lesser state: *a retrograde step.* **3.** *Chiefly Biol.* showing a breaking down or moving backwards. ◇*v.i.* **4.** to move or go backwards; retire or retreat. **5.** *Chiefly Biol.* to go down to a worse condition; degenerate. [ME, from L: going backwards]

retrogress /rɛtrə'grɛs/, *v.i.* to go backwards, esp. into a worse or earlier condition. —**retrogression**, *n.*

retro-rocket /'rɛtroʊ-rɒkət/, *n.* **1.** a braking rocket used for slowing down a spacecraft and preparing it for re-entry. **2.** a rocket used to slow down one part of a spacecraft from another. Also, **retrograde rocket.**

retrospect /'rɛtrəspɛkt/, *n.* contemplation of the past; a survey of past time, events, etc. —**retrospection**, *n.*

retrospective /rɛtrə'spɛktɪv/, *adj.* **1.** looking or directed to the past or backwards. **2.** (of a law, pay rise, etc.) taking effect from a past date. ◇*n.* **3.** an exhibition of an entire phase or representative examples of an artist's lifework.

retroversion /rɛtrə'vɜʒən/, *n.* **1.** a looking or turning back. **2.** the resulting state or condition. **3.** *Pathol.* the tilting or turning backwards of an organ or part: *retroversion of the uterus.* [L: turned back + -ION]

return /rə'tɜn/, *v.i.* **1.** to go or come back, (to a former place, position, condition, etc.). **2.** to go or come back in thought or speech: *to return to an idea.* **3.** to reply; retort. ◊*v.t.* **4.** to put, bring, take, give, or send back: *to return a book to its shelf.* **5.** to send or give back in answer to someone; repay: *to return shot for shot; to return compliments.* **6.** *Law.* to give (a verdict, etc.). **7.** to yield (a profit, revenue, etc.), as a result of labor or expense: *to return profits.* **8.** to turn back or in the reverse direction. ◊*n.* **9.** a going or coming back; a bringing, sending, or giving back. **10.** a recurrence: *Many happy returns of the day.* **11.** repayment: *profits in return for outlay; cruelty in return for kindness.* **12.** response or reply. **13.** (*oft. pl.*). yield or profit from labor, land, business, investment, etc. **14.** a report, esp. formal or official: *tax returns; election returns.* **15. by return**, by the next post. ◊*adj.* **16.** relating to return or returning: *a return trip.* **17.** sent, given, or done in return: *a return shot.* **18.** done or occurring when returning: *a return performance of the opera.* [ME, from OF]

returning officer, *n.* an official responsible for the organisation of an election, the accuracy of the count, the reading of the results, etc.

reunion /ri'junjən/, *n.* **1.** the act or state of uniting again. **2.** a gathering of relatives, friends, or associates after a period of separation: *a family reunion.*

Reuters /'rɔɪtəz/, *n.* a British news agency, founded in London in 1851 by Baron Paul Julius von Reuter.

rev /rev/, *n., v.,* **-revved, revving.** ◊*n.* **1.** a revolution (def. 4) (in an engine etc.). ◊*v.t.* **2.** to press down the accelerator pedal of a motor vehicle to make (the engine) run faster. ◊*v.i.* **3.** to undergo revving. [short for REVOLUTION]

Rev, *Abbrev.* **1.** *Bible.* Revelation. **2.** Reverend.

revalue /ri'vælju/, *v.,* **-valued, -valuing.** ◊*v.t.* **1.** to value again, esp. to raise the legal value of (a currency). See **devalue. 2.** to reconsider; review. ◊*v.i.* **3.** (of a currency) to increase in legal value. —**revaluation,** *n.*

reveal /rə'vil/, *v.t.* **1.** to uncover or make known; disclose; divulge: *to reveal a secret.* **2.** to lay open to view; display; exhibit. [ME, from L: unveil, reveal]

reveille /rə'væli/, *n.* a signal (of a drum or bugle) sounded at a certain hour, to waken soldiers or sailors for the day's duties. [F: awaken, from *re-* again + L: keep watch]

revel /'revəl/, *v.,* **-elled, -elling.** ◊*v.i.* **1.** to take great pleasure or delight: *to revel in good food.* **2.** to have a wild party. ◊*n.* **3.** a wild party or festivity; merrymaking. **4.** (*oft. pl.*). an occasion of merrymaking or noisy festivity with dancing, etc. [ME, from OF: to make noise, rebel, from L] —**reveller,** *n.*

revelation /revə'leɪʃən/, *n.* **1.** the act of revealing; disclosure. **2.** something revealed, esp. causing astonishment. **3.** *Theol.* God's revealing of Himself and of His will to His creatures. **4.** Also, **Revelations, Revelation of St John the Divine.** (*cap.*) the last book in the New Testament; the Apocalypse. [ME, from L]

revelry /'revəlri/, *n., pl.* **-ries.** the act of revelling: *The sound of their revelry could be heard across the river.*

revenge /rə'vendʒ/, *n., v.,* **-venged, -venging.** ◊*n.* **1.** retaliation for injuries or wrongs; vengeance. ◊*v.t.* **2.** to make (someone) suffer in return for a wrong done; pay back. [ME, from OF]

revenue /'revənju/, *n.* **1.** the income of a government from taxation, excise duties, customs, or other sources, taken to pay public expenses. **2.** the government department which collects such income. **3.** (*pl.*) the income of a person, a state, etc. [ME, from F: return]

reverberate /rə'vɜbəreɪt/, *v.i.,* **-rated, -rating. 1.** to re-echo or resound; rebound; recoil. **2.** *Phys.* (of soundwaves from a surface) to be reflected many times, within a closed space. [L: beaten back] —**reverberation,** *n.* —**reverberatory,** *adj.* —**reverberative,** *adj.* —**reverberator,** *n.*

revere /rə'vɪə/, *v.t.,* **-vered, -vering.** to regard with reverence and respect; venerate. [L: feel awe of, fear, revere]

Revere /rə'vɪə/, *n.* **Paul,** 1735–1818, American patriot, famous for his night horseback ride to warn Massachusetts colonists of the coming of British troops.

reverence /'revərəns, 'revrəns/, *n., v.,* **-renced, -rencing.** ◊*n.* **1.** a feeling or attitude of deep respect combined with a sense of wonder at someone's greatness and goodness; veneration. **2.** a gesture showing this feeling; an obeisance, bow, or curtsy. ◊*v.t.* **3.** to regard or treat with reverence; venerate. [ME, from L]

Reverend /'revrənd, 'revərənd/, *n.* (*sometimes l.c.*) a title of respect applied to, or prefixed to the name of, a clergyman: *Reverend Smith.* [L: revere]

reverent /'revrənt, 'revərənt/, *adj.* feeling, showing, or marked by reverence; deeply respectful. [L: feeling awe of] —**reverential,** *adj.* —**reverently,** *adv.*

reverie /'revəri/, *n.* **1.** a daydream. **2.** *Music.* an instrumental composition of a vague and dreamy character. Also, **revery.** [F: to dream]

revers /rə'vɪə/, *n., pl.* **-vers** /-'vɪəz/. a part of a garment turned back to show the lining or facing, e.g. a lapel. [F]

reverse /rə'vɜs/, *adj., n., v.,* **-versed, -versing.** ◊*adj.* **1.** opposite in position, direction, order, or character: *He held the reverse view.* **2.** producing a backward motion: *reverse gear.* ◊*n.* **3.** the opposite or contrary of anything. **4.** the back or rear of anything. **5.** a turning back of events to a worse situation; a check, or defeat: *to meet with an unexpected reverse.* **6.** *Motor Vehicles.* the gear which drives a car backwards. ◊*v.t.* **7.** to turn back or in an opposite position or order; transpose: *to reverse the usual order.* **8.** to revoke or annul (a decree, judgment, etc.). **9.** to drive (a motor

reverse

vehicle) backwards: *He reversed the car into a parking space.* ◇*v.i.* **10.** to turn or move in the opposite direction, as in dancing. **11.** (of an engine) to reverse the action of the mechanism. **12.** to drive a vehicle backwards: *He reversed into the garage.* ◇*v.* **13. reverse charges,** to make a telephone call or send a telegram for which the receiver pays. [ME, from L: turned about] — **reverser,** *n.* — **reversal,** *n.*

reversible reaction /rəˌvɜːsəbəl riˈækʃən/, *n.* a chemical reaction which, under suitable conditions, may proceed in either direction.

reversion /rəˈvɜːʒən/, *n.* **1.** the act or result of turning something the reverse way. **2.** the act of returning to a former practice, belief, condition, etc. **3.** *Biol.* the reappearance of ancestral qualities that have been absent in intervening generations. [ME, from L: a turning about] — **reversionary,** *adj.*

revert /rəˈvɜːt/, *v.i.* to return, as to a former habit, belief, condition, subject, etc. [ME, from OF, from LL] — **revertible,** *adj.*

review /rəˈvjuː/, *n.* **1.** a report in a newspaper or magazine of a book, concert, art exhibition, play, etc.; critique. **2.** a magazine, journal, etc., containing articles on current events or affairs, books, art, etc.: *a literary review.* **3.** a looking again; a second view of something. **4.** inspection, or examination by looking, esp. a formal inspection of any military or naval force. **5.** a general report or account of something. ◇*v.t.* **6.** to look over again. **7.** to inspect, esp. formally or officially. **8.** to discuss (a book, etc.) in a critical review. **9.** *Law.* to re-examine judicially. ◇*v.i.* **10.** to write reviews; review books, etc.: *to review for a journal.*

revile /rəˈvaɪl/, *v.t., v.i.* **-viled, -viling.** to speak strongly with contempt and abuse (to someone). [ME, from OF: treat or regard as vile]

revise /rəˈvaɪz/, *v.,* **-vised, -vising.** ◇*v.t.* **1.** to alter after examining: *to revise one's opinion; revise a manuscript.* **2.** to study (a subject, book, etc.) again in order to make it fresh in the mind. ◇*v.i.* **3.** to study a subject again. [F, from L: go to see again, look back on] — **revision,** *n.*

revival /rəˈvaɪvəl/, *n.* **1.** the act of reviving. **2.** the condition of being revived. **3.** the production again of an old play, song, etc. **4.** renewal of interest in a religion. **5.** a religious service or a series of services for renewing interest in a religion: *to hold a revival.* — **revivalism,** *n.* — **revivalist,** *n.*

revive /rəˈvaɪv/, *v.,* **-vived, -viving.** ◇*v.t.* **1.** to set going or in activity again: *to revive old feuds.* **2.** to bring back into notice or use: *to revive a subject of discussion.* **3.** to restore to life, energy or consciousness. ◇*v.i.* **4.** to return to life, consciousness, vigor. **5.** to return to notice or use. [ME, from L: live again]

revoke /rəˈvoʊk/, *v.t.,* **-voked, -voking.** to take back or withdraw; annul, cancel, or reverse; rescind or repeal: *to revoke a decree.* [ME, from L: call back] — **revocation,** *n.*

revolt /rəˈvoʊlt/, *v.i.* **1.** to break away from or rise against authority, esp. violently; rebel;

Reynella

mutiny. **2.** to turn away mentally, as in disgust. ◇*v.t.* **3.** to affect with disgust or abhorrence: *Cruelty revolts me.* ◇*n.* **4.** an act of revolting; an insurrection or rebellion. **5.** disgust or loathing; aversion. **6.** the condition of those revolting: *to be in revolt.* [F, from It: revolt, turning, from L: overturn, revolve]

revolting /rəˈvoʊltɪŋ/, *adj.* **1.** rebellious. **2.** disgusting; repulsive.

revolution /ˌrɛvəˈluːʃən/, *n.* **1.** the complete overthrow of an established government or political system. **2.** a complete or marked change in something. **3.** *Mech.* **a.** a turning round or rotating on an axis, esp. in a motor car engine. **b.** a single cycle in such a course. **4.** *Astron.* **a.** (of a heavenly body) the action or fact of going round in an orbit: *the earth's revolution around the sun.* **b.** a single course of such movement. [ME, from L]

revolutionary /ˌrɛvəˈluːʃənəri, -ʃənri/, *adj., n., pl.* **-ries.** ◇*adj.* **1.** relating to a revolution: *revolutionary violence; revolutionary ideas.* **2.** revolving. ◇*n.* **3.** someone who supports or takes part in a revolution; revolutionist.

revolutionise or **revolutionize** /ˌrɛvəˈluːʃənaɪz/, *v.t.,* **-nised, -nising.** to bring about a revolution in; effect a radical change in: *to revolutionise car production.*

revolve /rəˈvɒlv/, *v.,* **-volved, -volving.** ◇*v.i.* **1.** to turn round or rotate on an axis. **2.** to move in an orbit. **3.** to go in a cycle: *The seasons revolve.* **4.** to turn over in the mind. ◇*v.t.* **5.** to cause to turn round on an axis. **6.** to cause to move in a curving course around a central point. **7.** to think about; consider. [ME, from L: roll, turn]

revolver /rəˈvɒlvə/, *n.* a pistol with a revolving cylinder with chambers for holding a number of cartridges which may be fired one after the other without reloading.

revue /rəˈvjuː/, *n.* **1.** a form of theatrical entertainment in which recent events, popular fashions, etc., are parodied. **2.** any group of skits, dances, and songs. [F]

revulsion /rəˈvʌlʃən/, *n.* a sudden and violent change of feeling against someone or something. [L: a plucking away]

reward /rəˈwɔːd/, *n.* **1.** something given or received in return for service, merit, hardship, etc.; recompense; requital. **2.** a sum of money offered for the detection or capture of a criminal, the recovery of lost or stolen property, etc. ◇*v.t.* **3.** to give something to in return for service, etc.: *to reward a person.* **4.** to make return for (service, merit, etc.): *to reward hard work.* [ME, from OF]

rewarding /rəˈwɔːdɪŋ/, *adj.* giving such satisfaction that the effort made was worthwhile: *Growing your own vegetables can be very rewarding.*

rex /rɛks/, *n., pl.* **reges** /ˈriːdʒiːz/. king. [L]

Reykjavik /ˈreɪkjəvɪk/, *n.* a seaport in and the capital of Iceland, in the south-western part. Pop. 130 175 (1984 est.).

Reynella /rəˈnɛlə/, *n.* a town in south-eastern SA, south of Adelaide; important wine-

Reynella producing area. Pop. 7578 (1986). [named after John *Reynell*, 1809–73, pioneer wine-maker]

Reynolds /ˈrɛnəldz/, n. **Sir Joshua**, 1723–92, English portrait painter; works include *Samuel Johnson* (1772); wrote *Discourses* (1769–78) on the principles of art.

r.h., *Abbrev.* right hand.

Rh, 1. *Chem. Symbol.* rhodium. 2. See **Rh factor**.

-rhagia, a word part meaning 'bursting forth'. Also, **-rhage**, **-rhagy**, **-rrhagia**, **-rrhage**, **-rrhagy**. [Gk]

rhapsody /ˈræpsədi/, n., pl. **-dies**. 1. an exaggerated expression of enthusiasm: *to go into rhapsodies about something*. 2. (a part of) an epic poem, suitable for recitation at one time. 3. an unusually emotional or irregular poem or piece of prose. 4. *Music.* an instrumental composition irregular in form and suggesting improvisation: *Liszt's Hungarian Rhapsodies*. [L, from Gk: epic recital] —**rhapsodical**, *adj.*

rhea /ˈriə/, n. a flightless bird of South America, with three toes. [L, from Gk]

rhenium /ˈriniəm/, n. a hard, grey metallic element with a high melting point. *Symbol:* Re; *at. no.:* 75; *at. wt:* 186.20. [L *Rhēnus* the Rhine + -IUM]

rheo-, a word part meaning 'something flowing', 'a stream', 'current'. [combining form representing Gk *rhéos*]

rheostat /ˈriəstæt/, n. a variable electrical resistor. —**rheostatic**, *adj.*

rhesus /ˈrisəs/, n. a macaque monkey common in India, much used in experimental medicine. [L, from Gk *Rhēsos*, mythological king of Thrace]

Rhesus factor, n. → **Rh factor**.

rhetoric /ˈrɛtərɪk/, n. 1. the art or science of all specially literary uses of language in prose or verse, including the figures of speech. 2. exaggeration or display in writing or speech. 3. (in classical oratory) the art of influencing the thought of one's hearers. [ME, from L, from Gk: the rhetorical (art)]

rhetorical /rəˈtɒrɪkəl/, *adj.* 1. concerned only with style or effect. 2. exaggerated in style; bombastic.

rhetorical question, n. a question which does not seek an answer but is designed to produce an effect.

rheumatic /ruˈmætɪk/, *adj.* 1. relating to rheumatism. 2. having rheumatism. ◇n. 3. someone who has rheumatism. [ME, from L, from Gk]

rheumatic fever, n. a disease usu. afflicting children and marked by fever, inflammation of the joints and muscle pains.

rheumatism /ˈrumətɪzəm/, n. any of various painful diseases with stiffness and inflammation of the joints or muscles. [LL, from Gk: a suffering from a bodily discharge]

rheumatoid arthritis /ˌrumətɔɪd əˈθraɪtəs/, n. a chronic disease marked by inflammation of the joints, often with marked deformities.

Rh factor, n. a substance often present in human blood. Mixing of **Rh positive** blood (containing this substance) with **Rh negative** blood (lacking it), may cause the formation of antibodies and the destruction of red blood cells, as during pregnancy. In full, **Rhesus factor**. [so called because first found in the blood of the RHESUS]

Rhine /raɪn/, n. a river flowing from south-eastern Switzerland through Germany and the Netherlands into the North Sea; branches off into the **Waal**, **Lek**, and **IJssel** in its lower course. About 1320 km. German, **Rhein**. French, **Rhin**. Dutch, **Rijn**.

Rhineland /ˈraɪnlænd/, n. that part of Germany west of the Rhine. German, **Rheinland**.

rhinestone /ˈraɪnstoʊn/, n. an artificial gem made of paste (def. 6). [translation of F *caillou du Rhin* pebble of the Rhine]

rhino /ˈraɪnoʊ/, n., pl. **-nos**. *Abbrev.* → **rhinoceros**.

rhino-, a word part meaning 'nose'. Also, **rhin-**. [Gk, combining form of *rhís*]

rhinoceros /raɪˈnɒsərəs, raɪˈnɒsrəs/, n., pl. **-roses**, (*esp. collectively*) **-ros**. any of various large, heavy, thick-skinned mammals, found in Asia and Africa, and having one or two upright horns on the snout. [ME, from LL, from Gk *rhíno-* RHINO- + *-kerōs* horned]

rhizo-, a word part meaning 'root'. [Gk, combining form of *rhíza*]

rhizome /ˈraɪzoʊm/, n. a rootlike underground stem, growing horizontally, which produces roots below and sends up shoots along the upper surface. [Gk: mass of roots] —**rhizomatous**, *adj.*

Rh negative, *adj.* See **Rh factor**.

Rhode Island /roʊd ˈaɪlənd/, n. a state of the north-eastern US, on the Atlantic coast; a part of New England; the smallest state in the US. Pop. 975 000 (1986 est.); 3144 km². *Cap.*: Providence. —**Rhode Islander** n.

Rhodes[1] /roʊdz/, n. **Cecil John**, 1853–1902, British colonial capitalist and government administrator in southern Africa.

Rhodes[2] /roʊdz/, n. 1. an island in the Aegean, off the south-western coast of Turkey; the largest of the Dodecanese Islands. Pop. 87 831 (1981); 1404 km². 2. **Colossus of**, a huge bronze statue of Apollo that stood (c. 280 BC – 224 BC) at the entrance of Rhodes harbor; one of the Seven Wonders of the World. Ancient Greek, **Rhodos**. Modern Greek, **Ródhos**.

Rhodesia /roʊˈdiʒə/, n. former name of **Zimbabwe**.

Rhodes scholarship, n. one of a number of scholarships at Oxford University established by the will of Cecil Rhodes, for selected students (**Rhodes scholars**) from the countries of the British Commonwealth, and from the US. [named after Cecil RHODES]

rhodium /ˈroʊdiəm/, n. a silvery white metallic element similar to platinum, used in

rhodium alloys and catalysts. *Symbol:* Rh; *at. no.:* 45; *at. wt:* 102.905. [NL]

rhodo-, **rhod-.** a word part meaning 'rose'. Also, **rhod-.** [Gk, combining form of *rhódon*]

rhododendron /roudə'dendrən/, *n.* the name of various evergreen and deciduous shrubs and trees with handsome pink, purple, or white flowers, much cultivated for ornament. [NL, from Gk: rose tree]

-rhoea, a word part meaning 'flow', 'discharge', as in *gonorrhoea*. Also, **-rrhoea.** [Gk: to flow]

rhombus /'rɒmbəs/, *n., pl.* **-buses, -bi** /-baɪ/. an oblique-angled equilateral parallelogram. [L, from Gk] — **rhombic,** *adj.*

Rhone /roun/, *n.* a river flowing from the Alps in southern Switzerland through Lake Geneva and south-eastern France into the Mediterranean. 811 km. French, **Rhône.**

Rh positive, *adj.* See **Rh factor.**

rhubarb /'rubab/, *n.* **1.** a garden plant with edible leafstalks, or a related plant with a medicinal rhizome. **2.** the edible fleshy leafstalks of any of the plant species, used in making desserts. [ME, from OF, from ML, from Gk: foreign rhubarb]

rhyme /raɪm/, *n., v.,* **rhymed, rhyming.** ◇*n.* **1.** agreement in the sounds at the end of lines of verse, or of words. **2.** a word agreeing with another in terminal sound. **3.** verse or poetry with rhyme. **4. rhyme or reason,** logic; explanation; meaning: *There was no rhyme or reason in her behavior.* ◇*v.t.* **5.** to say or write in rhyme. **6.** to use (a word) as a rhyme to another word. ◇*v.i.* **7.** to make rhyme or verse; versify. **8.** to use rhyme in writing verse. **9.** to be composed with rhymes: *This verse rhymes.* Also, **rime.** [ME, from OF: to rhyme, from Gallo-Rom.: put in a row, from OHG: series, row]

rhythm /'rɪðəm/, *n.* **1.** movement in a (regular) pattern of time, esp. with beat, accent, etc. **2. a.** a pattern of regular or irregular pulses caused in music or speech by the occurrence of strong and weak beats. **b.** a particular form of this: *duple rhythm, triple rhythm.* **3.** *Art.* the proper relation of parts to each other and to an artistic whole. **4.** a pattern of regularity in changing elements or conditions: *The rhythm of the seasons.* [L, from Gk]

rhythm and blues, *n.* a commercialised style of popular music of the early 1960s, based on the guitar and derived from the Negro blues style but with a quicker tempo and more complex rhythms.

rhythmical /'rɪðmɪkəl/, *adj.* **1.** (of motion, etc.) happening with a particular pattern of timing. **2.** having a flowing rhythm. **3.** of or relating to rhythm: *an excellent rhythmical sense.* Also, **rhythmic.**

rhythm method, *n.* a method of avoiding conception by confining sexual intercourse to the infertile phases of the menstrual cycle.

rib¹ /rɪb/, *n., v.,* **ribbed, ribbing.** ◇*n.* **1.** one of a series of long, slender, curved bones, occurring in pairs, partly enclosing the chest cavity, and fitting into the vertebrae. **2.** something like a rib in form, position, or use, as a supporting or strengthening part. **3.** the primary vein of a leaf. **4.** *Knitting, Sewing, etc.* a raised pattern or ridge. ◇*v.t.* **5.** to strengthen or enclose with ribs. **6.** to mark with rib-like ridges or markings. [OE] — **ribbed,** *adj.*

rib² /rɪb/, *v.t.,* **ribbed, ribbing.** *Colloq.* to tease; ridicule; make fun of. [short for *ribtickle*]

ribald /'rɪbəld, 'raɪ-/, *adj.* **1.** coarsely mocking or abusive in speech, language, etc.; scurrilous. ◇*n.* **2.** a ribald person. [ME, from OF: dissipate, from MHG: be on heat, or from MD: whore] — **ribaldry,** *n.*

ribbon /'rɪbən/, *n.* **1.** a woven strip or band of fine material, used for ornament, tying hair, etc. **2.** anything like a ribbon. **3.** a band of material soaked with ink that the keys of a typewriter hit to make a mark. **4.** a badge of an order of knighthood or other distinction: *the red ribbon of the French Legion of Honor.* [ME, from OF]

ribbonfish /'rɪbənfɪʃ/, *n., pl.* **-fishes,** (*esp. collectively*) **-fish.** a type of deep-sea fish with a long, flat body, occasionally found along the eastern coast of Australia and in NZ waters.

riboflavin /raɪbəˈfleɪvən/, *n.* one of the vitamins included in the vitamin B complex, found in green vegetables, fish, milk, etc. Also, **riboflavine** /raɪbəˈfleɪvɪn/. [RIBOSE + *flavin* yellow pigment]

ribonucleic acid /raɪbouˌnjukliik 'æsəd/, *n.* → **RNA.**

ribose /'raɪbouz, -ous/, *n.* a simple sugar, $C_5H_{10}O_5$, present in RNA.

ribosome /'raɪbəsoum/, *n.* one of the tiny granules present in living cells, containing ribonucleic acid and protein; the site of protein synthesis.

rice /raɪs/, *n.* **1.** the starchy seeds or grain of a species of grass cultivated in warm climates and used as an important food. **2.** the plant itself. [ME, from OF, from It, from Gk, of Eastern orig.]

rice paper, *n.* **1.** thin paper made from the straw of rice, which can be eaten. **2.** Chinese paper consisting of the pith of certain plants cut and pressed into thin sheets.

rich /rɪtʃ/, *adj.* **1.** having more money and possessions than is necessary for living comfortably: *a rich family; a rich nation.* **2.** having many natural resources such as good soil, minerals, etc.: *a rich territory.* **3.** having much of anything: *a nation rich in traditions.* **4.** of great value or worth; valuable: *a rich harvest.* **5.** expensively elegant or fine: *rich clothes.* **6.** having much fat and sugar or spice: *rich food.* **7.** (of color) showing a deep, shining warmth. **8.** (of sound, the voice, etc.) full and deep in tone. **9.** (of smell) strongly scented. ◇*n.* **10. the rich,** rich people collectively. [OE]

Richard I /'rɪtʃəd/, *n.* ('*Richard the Lion-Heart*', '*Richard Coeur de Lion*'), 1157-99, king of England 1189-99; leader of the third crusade (1191).

Richard II, *n.* 1367-1400, king of England 1377-99 successor and grandson of Edward III; son of the Black Prince; forced to abdicate in favor of his cousin Henry Bolingbroke who became Henry IV.

Richard III, *n.* (*Duke of Gloucester*), 1452-85, king of England 1483-85; suspected murderer of his two nephews; killed at the battle of Bosworth Field in 1485.

Richards /'rɪtʃədz/, *n.* (**Isaac**) **Viv(ian)**, born 1952, West Indian cricketer; a noted batsman.

Richardson /'rɪtʃədsən/, *n.* **1. Henry Handel** (*Ethel Florence Lindesay Robertson*, née *Richardson*), 1870-1946, Australian novelist; author of *The Getting of Wisdom* (1910) and the novel trilogy *The Fortunes of Richard Mahony* (1917-29). **2. Samuel**, 1689-1761, English writer; one of the first English novelists; works include *Pamela* (1740) and *Clarissa* (1747).

Richelieu /'rɪʃəljə/, *n.* **Armand Jean du Plessis** /ˌɑːmb̃ ʒb̃ dy plɛ'siː/, **Duc de**, 1585-1642, French cardinal and statesman; reorganised internal French politics and established the absolute control of the crown.

riches /'rɪtʃəz/, *n.pl.* many and valuable possessions; wealth. [ME, from OF: wealth]

Richmond /'rɪtʃmənd/, *n.* **1.** a town in eastern NSW, west of Windsor. Pop. (with Windsor) 17 088 (1986). **2.** a coastal river on the North Coast of NSW, rising in the McPherson Range and flowing south then east to the Pacific near Ballina. About 260 km.

Richter scale /ˌrɪktə 'skeɪl/, *n.* an open ended logarithmic scale used to measure the energy of disturbances in the earth, such as earthquakes. [named after Charles F *Richter*, 1900-85, US seismologist]

Richthofen /'rɪktəfən/, *n.* **Baron Manfred von**, 1892-1918, German aviator in World War I; became known as the Red Baron; credited with shooting down eighty allied planes.

rick[1] /rɪk/, *n.* a stack of hay, straw, etc. [OE]

rick[2] /rɪk/, *v.t.* to sprain or strain (one's neck, back, etc.).

rickets /'rɪkəts/, *n.* **1.** *Med.* a disease of children, marked by softening of the bones from lack of vitamins and calcium. **2.** an incurable disease of cattle caused by eating certain poisonous plants common in Qld cattle country. [orig. uncert.]

rickety /'rɪkəti/, *adj.* weak in structure; liable to fall or collapse; shaky: *a rickety chair*; *a rickety old man*.

rickshaw /'rɪkʃɔ/, *n.* a small two-wheeled vehicle drawn by one or more men, used in the East. Also, **ricksha**.

ricochet /'rɪkəʃeɪ/, *n., v.,* **-cheted** /-ʃeɪd/, **-cheting** /-ʃeɪŋ/ ◇*n.* **1.** the motion of an object, such as a bullet, when it hits a surface, bounces off, and keeps travelling, but in another direction. ◇*v.i.* **2.** (of a bullet, etc.) to move in this way. [F; orig. uncert.]

rid /rɪd/, *v.t.,* **rid** or **ridded, ridding. 1.** to clear or free of something unwanted: *to rid a house of cockroaches; to rid the mind of doubt.* ◇*adj.* **2. rid of,** free of: *We are now rid of the problem.* [OE: clear (land)]

riddance /'rɪdns/, *n.* **1.** a clearing away of anything unwanted. **2. good riddance,** a welcome deliverance.

ridden /'rɪdn/, *v.* past participle of **ride**.

riddle[1] /'rɪdl/, *n., v.,* **-dled, -dling.** ◇*n.* **1.** a question or statement put so that a person has to use cleverness in answering it; conundrum. **2.** a puzzling thing or person. ◇*v.i.* **3.** to speak in riddles; to speak enigmatically. [OE: enigma]

riddle[2] /'rɪdl/, *v.,* **-dled, -dling,** *n.* ◇*v.t.* **1.** to pierce with many holes, like those of a sieve: *the floorboards were riddled with bullets.* ◇*n.* **2.** a coarse sieve, such as one for sifting sand in a foundry. [OE]

ride /raɪd/, *v.,* **rode** or (*old form*) **rid; ridden** or (*old form*) **rid; riding;** *n.* ◇*v.i.* **1.** to sit on and control a horse or other animal in motion; be carried on the back of an animal. **2.** to sit on or be carried along on or in a bicycle, car, etc. **3.** to float. ◇*v.t.* **4.** to sit on and control (a horse, bicycle, etc.). **5.** to be carried along on something: *to ride the waves.* **6.** to travel over, along or through: *to ride the boundary.* ◇*v.* **7. ride down, a.** to trample under a horse's hooves. **b.** to chase and catch up with. **8. ride out,** to survive through a difficulty by keeping in control: *to ride out a storm.* **9. ride up,** (of clothing) to move up the body when worn. ◇*n.* **10.** a journey by horse or vehicle. **11.** a way, road, etc., made esp. for riding. **12. take for a ride,** to deceive. [OE]

rider /'raɪdə/, *n.* **1.** someone who rides a horse, bicycle, etc. **2.** an addition or amendment to a document, etc.

ridge /rɪdʒ/, *n., v.,* **ridged, ridging.** ◇*n.* **1.** a long, narrow, high part of land, or a chain of hills or mountains. **2.** a long and narrow high part or crest of something, as of an animal's back, a wave, etc. **3.** any raised narrow strip, as on cloth, etc. **4.** the horizontal line in which the tops of the rafters of a roof meet. **5.** *Weather.* a band of relatively high pressure usu. joining two anticyclones. **6.** the earth thrown up by a plough between furrows. **7.** a strip of arable land, usu. between furrows. ◇*v.t.* **8.** to provide with or form into a ridge or ridges. **9.** to mark with ridges. ◇*v.i.* **10.** to form ridges. [OE: spine, crest] —**ridgy,** *adj.*

ridgepole /'rɪdʒpoʊl/, *n.* **1.** the horizontal timber at the top of a roof, to which the upper ends of the rafters are fastened. **2.** the horizontal pole at the top of a tent.

ridicule /'rɪdəkjul/, *n., v.,* **-culed, -culing.** ◇*n.* **1.** words or actions meant to excite contemptuous laughter at a person or thing; derision. ◇*v.t.* **2.** to deride; make fun of. [F, from L: laughable (thing)]

ridiculous /rə'dɪkjələs/, *adj.* **1.** having the quality of making people laugh, usu. with contempt; funny; absurd. ◇*n.* **2.** that which is ridiculous: *from the sublime to the ridiculous.*

Ridley /'rɪdli/, n. John, 1806-87, Australian inventor, born in England; constructed the first workable stripper-harvester.

Riesling /'rizlɪŋ, 'rislɪŋ/, n. (also l.c.) a dry, white wine.

rife /raɪf/, adj. common or frequent; abundant; prevalent. [late OE]

riffraff /'rɪfræf/, n. the worthless or disreputable part of society; the rabble: *the riffraff of the city*. [ME *rif* and *raf* every particle, things of small value, from OF *rifler* spoil, *raffler* ravage, snatch away]

rifle[1] /'raɪfl/, n. a shoulder firearm with spiral grooves cut in the inner surface of the gun barrel to give the bullet a rotatory motion to make its flight more accurate. [LG: to groove]

rifle[2] /'raɪfl/, v.t., v.i., **-fled, -fling**. to search through (a place) quickly, leaving it in a mess: *to rifle through drawers; to rifle the house*. [ME, from OF: scrape, graze, plunder, from D: scrape]

rift /rɪft/, n. **1.** an opening made by splitting; fissure; cleft; chink. **2.** a break in the friendly relations between two people, countries, etc. [ME, from Scand]

rift valley, n. part of the earth's crust that has sunk down between two faults (def. 5).

rig /rɪg/, v., **rigged, rigging**, n. ◇v.t. **1.** to put (a ship, mast, etc.) in proper order for use by fitting with the necessary shrouds (def. 3), stays, etc. **2.** to put anything in proper working order; equip: *to rig up a tent*. **3.** to prepare or put together, esp. as a makeshift: *to rig up a platform for the speeches*. **4.** to control or handle dishonestly: *to rig an election*. ◇n. **5.** the arrangement of the masts, spars, sails, etc., on a boat or ship. **6.** an apparatus for some purpose; equipment; outfit. **7.** the structure and equipment used in drilling an oil or gas well. [probably from Scand] **–rigger**, n.

rigging /'rɪgɪŋ/, n. the ropes, wires, chains, etc., used to support and work the masts, yards, sails, etc., on a ship.

right /raɪt/, adj. **1.** in accordance with rules for what is just or good: *right conduct*. **2.** in accordance with fact, reason, or some standard or principle; correct: *the right solution*. **3.** correct in judgment, opinion, or action. **4.** sound or normal; sane: *in his right mind*. **5.** in a satisfactory state; in good order: *to put things right*. **6.** supplied with or ready: *Are you right for food?* **7.** principal, front, or upper: *the right side of the cloth*. **8.** fitting; appropriate: *to say the right thing*. **9.** belonging to the side of a person or thing which is turned towards the east when the face is towards the north (opposed to *left*). **10.** belonging or relating to the political right (def. 18): *the right wing*. **11.** *Geom.* having the axis perpendicular to the base: *a right cone*. **12. right as rain**, *Colloq.* safe; okay; in good health. ◇n. **13.** a just claim or title to anything: *a right to land; the right to strike*. **14.** something which is due to anyone by just claim: *to give someone his right*. **15.** something which is good and proper according to the moral law. **16.** something which is in accordance with fact or reason. **17.** the right side or what is on the right side: *to turn to the right*. **18. the Right**, (oft. l.c.) a body of people, political party, etc., holding conservative views. **19. by rights**, in all fairness. **20. to rights**, into proper order: *to set a room to rights*. ◇adv. **21.** in a straight line; straight: *right to the bottom; a hole right through the wall*. **22.** immediately: *right after dinner*. **23.** exactly, precisely: *right here*. **24.** properly or fittingly: *to behave right; it serves you right*. **25.** towards the right hand; to the right: *to turn right*. ◇v.t. **26.** to bring to an upright or the proper position. **27.** to set in order or put right. **28.** to do justice to. ◇v.i. **29.** to take an upright or the proper position. [OE]

right angle, n. the angle formed at the interception of two perpendicular lines, and equal to half a straight angle, or approx. 1.57 radians; an angle of 90°.

right-angled triangle, n. a triangle in which one of the angles is a right angle. Also, **right triangle**.

righteous /'raɪtʃəs/, adj. **1.** marked by opinions and behavior which are correct according to moral law: *a righteous act; a righteous person*. **2.** having true cause; justifiable: *righteous indignation*. [OE from *riht* RIGHT + *wis* WISE[2]]

rightful /'raɪtfəl/, adj. **1.** having a right, or just claim, to some possession or position: *the rightful owner*. **2.** belonging by right: *her rightful property*. **3.** just; equitable: *a rightful cause*.

right-hand /'raɪt-hænd/, adj. **1.** on or to the right: *a right-hand drive vehicle*. **2.** of, for, or with the right hand. **3.** most useful as a helper: *his right-hand man*.

right-handed /raɪt-'hændəd/, adj. **1.** having the right hand or arm more useful than the left; preferring to use the right hand. **2.** fitted to or performed by the right hand: *a right-handed racquet; a right-handed shot*.

right of way, n. **1.** the legal or customary right of a person, motor car or vessel to go on ahead of another in particular circumstances. **2.** a path or route which may lawfully be used, esp. over another's land.

right wing, n. **1.** the members of a conservative or reactionary political party or section of a party. **2.** such a group, party, or a group of such parties. **–right-wing**, adj. **–right-winger**, n.

rigid /'rɪdʒəd/, adj. **1.** stiff; not pliant or flexible; hard. **2.** unbending, strict, or severe: *rigid discipline; rigid views*. [L] **–rigidity**, n.

rigmarole /'rɪgməroʊl/, n. **1.** a series of confused or foolish statements; incoherent or rambling discourse. **2.** a long and complicated process. [from obs. *ragman roll* a roll, list, or catalogue]

rigor or **rigour** /'rɪgə/, n. **1.** strictness. **2.** severity of life; hardship. **3.** severity of the weather or climate: *the rigors of winter*. [ME, from OF, from L]

rigor mortis /rɪgə 'mɔtɪs/, n. the stiffening of the body after death. [L: stiffness of death]

rigorous /ˈrɪgərəs/, *adj.* **1.** marked by rigor; unbending; severe or harsh: *rigorous laws; rigorous discipline.* **2.** severely exact or accurate.

rig-out /ˈrɪg-aʊt/, *n.* **1.** apparatus; equipment. **2.** dress; clothes, esp. when conspicuous.

Rig-Veda /rɪgˈveɪdə/, *n. Hinduism.* the Veda of Verses, or Psalms (totalling 1028), the oldest document among the sacred scriptures of the world's living religions dating not later than the second millennium BC. See **Veda**. [Skt, from *ric* praise + *veda* knowledge]

rile /raɪl/, *v.t.*, **riled, riling.** *Colloq.* to irritate or vex.

rill /rɪl/, *n.* a small stream.

rim /rɪm/, *n.* **1.** the outer edge, border, or margin, esp. of a circular object. **2.** any edge or margin, often a raised one. **3.** the circular part of a wheel, farthest from the axle. [OE]

Rimsky-Korsakov /ˌrɪmskiˈkɔːsəkɒf/, *n.* **Nikolai Andreevich** /nɪkɒˌlaɪ anˈdreɪjɪvɪtʃ/, 1844–1908, Russian composer; works include *Scheherazade* (1888).

rind /raɪnd/, *n.* a thick and firm coat or covering of fruits, cheeses, etc.

ring[1] /rɪŋ/, *n., v.*, **ringed, ringing.** ◇*n.* **1.** a circular band, esp. one of gold or other precious metal, often set with gems, for wearing on the finger as an ornament, a sign of engagement or marriage, etc. **2.** anything with the form of a circular band. **3.** a circular line or mark. **4.** a circular course: *to dance in a ring.* **5.** a number of persons or things placed in a circle. **6.** an enclosed circular or other area, for sport or exhibition: *the ring of a circus; a boxing ring.* **7.** a group of people working together, esp. for illegal purposes: *a drug ring.* **8.** *Chem.* a number of atoms linked in a circular form, as in benzene. **9. run rings round,** *Colloq.* to be very superior to; easily surpass. ◇*v.t.* **10.** to surround with a ring; encircle. **11.** →**ringbark.** ◇*v.* **12. ring the board (shed),** to shear more sheep than anyone else in the shearing shed. ◇*v.i.* **13.** to form or move in a ring or rings. [OE]

ring[2] /rɪŋ/, *v.*, **rang, rung, ringing,** *n.* ◇*v.i.* **1.** to give forth a clear sound when set in sudden vibration by a blow or otherwise: *The bells are ringing.* **2.** to have the sound or meaning of: *His words ring true.* **3.** to cause a bell to sound, esp. to call someone: *to ring for a messenger.* **4.** to be filled with sound: *The hills rang with laughter.* ◇*v.t.* **5.** to cause to ring: *to ring the bell.* **6.** to telephone. ◇**7.** Some special uses are:
ring a bell, to arouse a memory; sound familiar.
ring down (up) the curtain, to give a direction to lower (raise) a theatre curtain at the end (beginning) of a performance.
ring in, to put in instead of, often dishonestly.
ring the changes, to vary the way of doing an action.
ring up, 1. to telephone. **2.** to record (the cost of an item) on a cash register.
◇*n.* **8.** a ringing sound: *the ring of sleighbells.* **9.** a resonant sound or note: *There was a ring in his voice.* **10.** a telephone call: *Give me a ring tomorrow.* **11.** a characteristic quality: *His words had the ring of truth.* [OE]

ringbark /ˈrɪŋbɑːk/, *v.t.* to cut away the bark in a ring around a tree trunk or branch, in order to kill the tree or the affected part. Also, **bark.** –**ringbarked,** *adj.*

ringer[1] /ˈrɪŋə/, *n.* a station hand, esp. a stockman or drover.

ringer[2] /ˈrɪŋə/, *n.* **1.** the fastest shearer of a group. **2.** any person who is the fastest or best at anything. [Brit d.: anything superlatively good]

ring finger, *n.* the third finger of the left hand, where wedding rings, etc., are usu. worn.

ring-in /ˈrɪŋ-ɪn/, *n. Colloq.* **1.** a person or thing taking the place of another at the last moment. **2.** someone belonging to a group only in appearance.

ringleader /ˈrɪŋliːdə/, *n.* someone who leads others in opposition to authority, law, etc. [from phrase *to lead the ring* to be first]

ringlet /ˈrɪŋlət/, *n.* a curled lock of hair.

ringmaster /ˈrɪŋmɑːstə/, *n.* the person in charge of the performances at a circus.

ringtail possum /ˈrɪŋteɪl/, *n.* any of various types of tree-living, nocturnal, nest-building possums, with a long prehensile (grasping) tail, the end of which is curled into a ring. Some examples are the **green ringtail** or **toolah,** of north-eastern Qld rainforests, with golden-green fur and two stripes down the back, the **mongan,** with very dark brown fur, also of Qld rainforests, and the **wogoit** or **rock possum,** of north-western savanna areas, with a short thick tail and a stripe down the back. Also, **ring-tailed possum.**

ringworm /ˈrɪŋwɜːm/, *n.* any of certain skin diseases due to fungi and characterised by ring-shaped patches.

rink /rɪŋk/, *n.* **1.** a sheet of ice prepared for skating. **2.** a smooth floor for roller-skating. [Scot]

rinse /rɪns/, *v.*, **rinsed, rinsing,** *n.* ◇*v.t.* **1.** to wash lightly, usu. by pouring water into or over or by dipping in water. **2.** to put through clean water, as a final stage in cleaning. ◇*n.* **3.** an act or instance of rinsing. **4.** any liquid preparation used for coloring the hair. [ME, from OF, from Rom: make fresh, from L: fresh, recent]

Rio de Janeiro /ˌriːoʊ di dʒəˈnɪərəʊ/, *n.* a seaport in and the former capital of Brazil, in the south-eastern part. Pop. 5 615 100 (1985 est.). Also, **Rio.**

Rio Grande /ˌriːoʊ ˈgrænd/, *n.* a river flowing from south-western Colorado through central New Mexico and along the Texas-Mexico boundary into the Gulf of Mexico. About 2897 km. Mexican, **Rio Bravo.**

riot /ˈraɪət/, *n.* **1.** any disturbance of the peace by a group of people. **2.** *Law.* the carrying-out of a violent and unlawful act by three or more people acting together, causing terror to people. **3.** violent or wild disorder or confusion. **4.** a brilliant show: *a riot of color.* **5.** *Colloq.* someone or something that causes

riot great amusement, enthusiasm, etc. **6. run riot, a.** to act without control; disregard all limits. **b.** to grow strongly or wildly. ◇*v.i.* **7.** to take part in a disorderly public outbreak. **8.** to live or act in a wild, uncontrolled way. [ME, from OF: to quarrel, from L: roar] — **rioter**, *n*. — **riotous**, *adj*.

rip¹ /rɪp/, *v.*, **ripped, ripping**, *n*. ◇*v.t.* **1.** to cut or tear apart or off in a rough or violent manner; slash; slit. ◇*v.i.* **2.** to become torn apart or split open. **3.** *Colloq.* to move along with great speed. ◇*v.* **4. let it rip**, to allow an engine, etc., to go as fast as possible. **5. let rip**, to give way to anger, passion, etc. **6. rip into**, to begin rapidly, eagerly: *Let's rip into the housework.* **7. rip off**, to charge too much; swindle. ◇*n*. **8.** a tear made by ripping. [ME]

rip² /rɪp/, *n*. **1.** a disturbance in the sea caused by opposing currents or by a fast current passing over an uneven bottom. **2.** a fast current, esp. one at a beach which can take swimmers out to sea. **3.** → **rip-tide**.

RIP /ar ar 'pi/, may he or she (or they) rest in peace. [L REQUIESCAT (or *requiescant*) *in pace*]

ripcord /'rɪpkɔd/, *n*. a cord or ring which opens a parachute during a descent.

ripe /raɪp/, *adj.*, **riper, ripest**. **1.** (of grain, fruits, etc.) complete in natural growth and ready for gathering or reaping. **2.** (of cheese, beer, etc.) advanced to the point of being in the best condition for use. **3.** having a bad smell: *That dead fish is really ripe!* **4.** arrived at a high point of development or excellence; mature. **5.** characterised by full development of body or mind: *of ripe years*. **6.** fully prepared or ready to do or undergo something, or for some action, purpose, or end. **7.** (of time) fully or sufficiently advanced. [OE] — **ripeness**, *n*.

ripen /'raɪpən/, *v.t., v.i.* to make or become ripe. [OE]

rip-off /'rɪp-ɒf/, *n*. a price or charge that is too much.

riposte /rə'pɒst/, *n., v.*, **-posted, -posting**. ◇*n*. **1.** *Fencing.* a quick thrust given after turning aside a thrust from an opponent. **2.** a quick, sharp return in speech or action. ◇*v.i.* **3.** to make a riposte. [F, from It: response, from L]

ripper /'rɪpə/, *n*. *Colloq.* something or someone causing much admiration.

ripple /'rɪpəl/, *v.*, **-pled, -pling**, *n*. ◇*v.i.* **1.** to have or form small waves on the surface. **2.** (of sound) to go on or proceed with an effect like that of water flowing in ripples. ◇*v.t.* **3.** to form small waves on. ◇*n*. **4.** a small wave, as on water. **5.** any similar movement or appearance. **6.** a sound like water flowing in ripples: *a ripple of laughter.* [orig. uncert.] — **ripply**, *adj*.

rip-roaring /'rɪp-rɔrɪŋ/, *adj. Colloq.* wild and noisy; boisterous; riotous: *a rip-roaring party.*

rip-tide /'rɪp-taɪd/, *n*. a fast-flowing tide such as might be associated with a rip. Also, **rip-current**.

Risdon Cove /'rɪzdən/, *n*. an inlet in central southern Tas, on the east bank of the Derwent River; site of the first settlement in Tas. [named after William *Risdon*, second officer of one of the vessels of a 1793 expedition]

rise /raɪz/, *v.*, **rose, risen, rising**, *n*. ◇*v.i.* **1.** to get up from a lying, sitting, or kneeling position. **2.** to get up from bed. **3.** (of hair, etc.) to become erect and stiff. **4.** to become active in opposition or resistance; rebel. **5.** to be built up or constructed. **6.** to become noticeable on a surface, as a blister. **7.** to come into existence; appear. **8.** to originate or be derived: *Understanding rises from experience.* **9.** to move from a lower to a higher position. **10.** to extend directly upwards: *The tower rises to the height of 20 metres.* **11.** to advance to a higher rank, importance, etc. **12.** to prove oneself equal to a demand, emergency, etc.: *She will rise to the occasion.* **13.** (of spirits, etc.) to become cheerful. **14.** to become stirred up: *His temper would rise.* **15.** (of dough from the action of yeast) to swell or puff up. **16.** to increase in amount, force, etc. **17.** (of the voice, etc.) to become louder or of higher pitch. **18.** to end a session, as of an official body. **19.** to return from the dead. ◇*n*. **20.** an upward movement. **21.** advance in rank, position, fortune, etc.: *the rise and fall of ancient Rome.* **22.** an increase in amount, height, loudness, degree of intensity, etc. **23.** (of wages, salary, etc.) an increase in amount. **24.** the vertical height of any of various things as a stair step, a flight of steps, a roof, an arch, etc. **25.** the origin, source, or beginning. **26.** upward slope, as of ground or a road. **27. get (take) a rise out of**, to provoke to anger, annoyance, etc., by teasing, etc. **28. give rise to**, cause, produce. [OE]

rising /'raɪzɪŋ/, *adj*. **1.** that rises; advancing, ascending, or mounting. **2.** growing, or advancing to adult years: *the rising generation.* ◇*n*. **3.** an uprising; revolt.

rising damp, *n*. dampness in the walls of a house coming up from the foundations.

risk /rɪsk/, *n*. **1.** the state of being open to the chance of injury or loss: *Don't run risks.* **2.** *Insurance.* **a.** the chance of loss. **b.** the type of loss, as life, fire, theft, etc., against which insurance policies are drawn. **3. no risk!** (an exclamation of confidence or approval). ◇*v.t.* **4.** to lay open to the chance of injury or loss: *He risked his life to save another.* **5.** to take or run the risk of: *You will risk a fall by climbing.* [F, from It: to risk, dare, ? from Gk: cliff (through meaning of to sail around a cliff)] — **risky**, *adj*.

Risorgimento /rɪsɔdʒə'mentoʊ/, *n*. the period of and the movement for the liberation and reunification of Italy in the 19th century.

risqué /'rɪskeɪ, rɪs'keɪ/, *adj*. daringly close to being improper or indelicate: *a risqué story.* [F: risk]

rissole /'rɪsoʊl/, *n*. a small fried ball or patty of minced meat or fish mixed with breadcrumbs, egg, etc. [F, ? from VL: reddish]

rit., *Abbrev.* ritardando. Also, **ritard**.

ritardando /rɪtə'dændoʊ/, *adv.* (a musical direction) gradually more slowly. [It: retard]

rite /raɪt/, *n.* **1.** a formal or ceremonial act or procedure followed by custom in religious or other solemn use: *rites of baptism.* **2.** a particular form or system of religious or other ceremonial practice: *the Roman rite.* [ME, from L: ceremony]

ritual /'rɪtʃuəl/, *n.* **1.** an established or set procedure, code, form, system, etc., for a religious or other rite. **2.** the act of following of set forms in public worship. **3.** a ritual service: *the ritual of the dead.* **4.** any solemn or customary action, code of behavior, etc., determining social conduct. [L]

rival /'raɪvəl/, *n., v.,* **-valled, -valling.** ◇*n.* **1.** someone who wishes to gain the same object as someone else, or tries to equal or outdo another person; competitor. **2.** someone or something that is in a position to argue superiority with another: *a theatre without a rival.* ◇*v.t.* **3.** to compete with in an attempt to equal or outdo. **4.** to prove to be a worthy rival of: *He soon rivalled the others in skill.* [L: one living by or using the same stream as another] — **rivalry,** *n.*

rive /raɪv/, *v.t.,* **rived, rived** or **riven, riving. 1.** to tear apart. **2.** to strike into parts; split; cleave. [ME, from Scand]

river /'rɪvə/, *n.* **1.** a large natural stream of water flowing in a definite course or channel or series of channels. **2.** any large stream or flow: *rivers of lava; rivers of blood.* **3. sell down the river,** *Colloq.* to deceive; betray. [ME, from OF, from L: bank] — **riverine,** *adj.*

Rivera /ri'veɪrə/, *n.* **Diego** /'djeɪɡoʊ/, 1886-1957, Mexican painter, esp. of murals which are greatly influenced by Aztec art.

river basin, *n.* the area drained by a river and its branches.

rivergum /'rɪvəɡʌm/, *n.* →**river red gum.**

Riverina /rɪvə'rinə/, *n.* a district in southern NSW, covering the area between the Lachlan River in the north and north-west and the Murray River in the south with the eastern border roughly extending from Albury to Condobolin; one of Australia's most productive rural districts.

river red gum, *n.* a large tree, with white smooth bark on the upper trunk and branches, found lining the banks of Australian inland rivers. Also, **rivergum.**

rivet /'rɪvət/, *n.* **1.** a metal pin or bolt for passing through holes in two or more plates or pieces to hold them together, usu. made with a head at one end, the other end being hammered into a head after being put through the plates. ◇*v.t.* **2.** to fasten with a rivet or rivets. **3.** to hammer or spread out the end of (a pin, etc.), in order to form a head and secure something; clinch. **4.** to fasten or fix firmly: *Fear riveted me to the spot.* **5.** to hold (the eye, attention, etc.) firmly: *The scene riveted his eyes.* [ME, from OF: fix, clinch, from Rom: make firm, come to shore, from L: shore] — **riveter,** *n.*

Riviera /rɪvi'ɛərə/, *n.* a resort region on the Mediterranean coast extending from Marseilles, in south-eastern France, to La Spezia, in north-western Italy.

rivulet /'rɪvjələt/, *n.* a small stream; streamlet; brook. [It, from L: small stream]

Riyadh /ri'jad/, *n.* a city in central Arabia; the capital of Saudia Arabia. Pop. 1 000 000 (1981).

rm, *Abbrev.* room.

RMO /ɑr ɛm 'oʊ/, *n.* a medical officer who has graduated recently and who is appointed to and resident in a hospital. Also, **resident medical officer.** [abbrev.]

r.m.s., *Abbrev.* root mean square

Rn, *Chem. Symbol.* radon.

RNA /ɑr ɛn 'eɪ/, *n. Biochem.* one of a class of large molecules (ribonucleotides) found in all living cells and some viruses, which translates the genetic code (DNA) during protein synthesis. Also, **ribonucleic acid.** [abbrev.]

RNZAF /ɑr ɛn zɛd eɪ 'ɛf/, *Abbrev.* Royal New Zealand Air Force.

RNZN /ɑr ɛn zɛd 'ɛn/, *Abbrev.* Royal New Zealand Navy.

roach[1] /roʊtʃ/, *n., pl.* **roaches,** (*esp. collectively*) **roach.** a European freshwater fish, of the carp family, introduced into Australia. [ME, from OF]

roach[2], *n.* →**cockroach.**

road /roʊd/, *n.* **1.** a way, usu. open to the public, for the passage of vehicles, people and animals. **2.** a way or course: *the road to peace.* **3. on the road, a.** travelling. **b.** (of a theatrical company) on tour. **4. take to the road, a.** to begin a journey. **b.** to move around with no regular place of living or sleeping. [OE: a riding, journey on horseback]

roadblock /'roʊdblɒk/, *n.* anything placed across a road by police, soldiers, etc., to stop or slow down traffic for inspection, slow the progress of an enemy, etc.

road gang, *n.* (formerly) a party of convicts, usu. in irons, employed in roadmaking.

road show, *n.* a public entertainment, esp. a popular band, which travels from town to town.

road toll, *n.* the tally of traffic accident deaths.

road train, *n.* a group of motor vehicles, consisting of a prime mover joined to one or more trailers, used esp. for carrying cattle.

roam /roʊm/, *v.i.* **1.** to walk, go, or travel about without fixed purpose or direction; ramble; wander; rove. ◇*v.t.* **2.** to wander over or through: *They roam the bush often.* ◇*n.* **3.** the act of roaming; ramble. [ME]

roan /roʊn/, *adj.* **1.** (chiefly of horses) of a reddish brown color with splashes of grey or white. ◇*n.* **2.** a roan horse or other animal. **3.** a soft sheepskin leather, used in bookbinding. [ME, from F, from Sp, from L: yellow-grey]

roar /rɔ/, *v.i.* **1.** to utter a loud, deep sound, esp. of excitement, distress, or anger. **2.** to laugh loudly or in high spirits. **3.** to make a loud noise or din, as thunder, cannon, waves, wind, etc. ◇*v.* **4. roar (someone) up,** *Colloq.* to scold angrily. ◇*n.* **5.** a loud, deep sound, as of a person, lion or other large animal. **6.** a loud outburst of laughter. **7.** a loud noise, as of thunder, waves, etc.: *the roar of the surf.* [OE]

roaring /'rɔrɪŋ/, *n.* **1.** a loud, deep cry or sound. ◇*adj.* **2.** that roars, as a person, thunder, etc. **3.** *Colloq.* (of trade, etc.) fast-moving or highly successful.

roaring forties, *n.pl.* **1.** (treated as sing.) the area of ocean below 40° S in which strong westerly winds blow. **2.** such winds, esp. those useful to sailing ships.

roast /roʊst/, *v.t.* **1.** to bake (meat or other food) by dry heat, as in an oven. **2.** to prepare by exposure to heat, as coffee. **3.** to heat (any material) more or less violently. **4.** *Colloq.* to criticise, scold or make fun of severely. ◇*v.i.* **5.** to undergo the process of becoming roasted. ◇*n.* **6.** a piece of roasted meat. ◇*adj.* **7.** roasted: *roast beef.* [ME, from OF, from Gmc]

rob /rɒb/, *v.*, **robbed, robbing.** ◇*v.t.* **1.** to take something from by unlawful force or threat of violence. **2.** to steal from (a house, etc.). **3.** to leave without something: *The shock robbed him of speech.* ◇*v.i.* **4.** to practise robbery. **5. rob Peter to pay Paul,** to do good for one person at the expense of another. [ME, from OF, OHG] **–robber,** *n.*

robbery /'rɒbəri/, *n.* the action, practice, or an instance of robbing.

Robbia /'rɒbjə/, *n.* **1. Luca della** /'luka delə/, 1400?–82, Italian artist, chiefly in enamelled terracotta; best known work is *Cantoria,* a marble relief. **2.** his nephew, **Andrea della** /an'dreɪə/, 1435–1525, Florentine sculptor, best known for his polychrome reliefs.

robe /roʊb/, *n., v.*, **robed, robing.** ◇*n.* **1.** a long, loose or flowing gown or outer garment worn by men or women, esp. for formal occasions. ◇*v.t., v.i.* **2.** to dress in a robe or robes. [ME, from OF]

Roberts /'rɒbəts/, *n.* **1. Nigel,** born 1941 in NZ, Australian poet. **2. Tom** (*Thomas William Roberts*), 1856–1931, Australian artist, born in England; impressionist painter.

Robertson /'rɒbətsən/, *n.* **George,** 1860–1933, Australian bookseller and publisher, born in England; one of the founders of Angus and Robertson Ltd.

Robeson /'roʊbsən/, *n.* **Paul Le Roy** 1898–1976, US bass singer and actor; leader in civil rights movement.

Robespierre /'roʊbzpiɛə/, *n.* **Maximilien François Marie Isidore de** /maksi,miljæ frɔ̃,swa ma,ri izi'dɔə də/, 1758–94, French lawyer and revolutionary leader; established the Reign of Terror in France 1793–94; guillotined after a coup d'etat in 1794.

robin /'rɒbən/, *n.* **1.** any of a group of Australian birds resembling European robins but more brightly and variously colored. **2.** any of several small Old World birds having a red or reddish breast. [ME *Robyn,* from OF *Robin,* little Robert]

Robin Hood /rɒbən 'hʊd/, *n.* a legendary English medieval outlaw, a popular hero in many ballads, who robbed the rich to give to the poor.

robin redbreast, *n.* the scarlet robin, widely distributed in eastern Australia, usu. seen in pairs, and building a nest of dry vegetation matted together with cobwebs.

Robinson /'rɒbənsən/, *n.* **1. George Augustus,** 1788–1866, Australian Methodist lay preacher, born in London; employed to rehabilitate Aborigines on islands in Bass Strait. **2. Roland Edward,** 1912–92 Irish-born Australian poet, literary critic and editor; a member of the Jindyworobak movement.

robot /'roʊbɒt/, *n.* a device designed to do some of the work of a human being. [first used in the play *R.U.R.* by Karel Capek, 1890–1938, Czech dramatist and novelist; apparently from Czech *robotnik* serf]

Rob Roy /rɒb 'rɔɪ/, *n.* (*Robert Macgregor*), 1671–1734, Scottish outlaw; Jacobite hero of legends.

robust /'roʊbʌst, rə'bʌst/, *adj.* **1.** strong, healthy and hardy. **2.** strongly or solidly built: *his robust frame.* [L]

roc /rɒk/, *n.* (in Arabian myths) a bird of enormous size and strength. [Ar, probably from Pers]

rock[1] /rɒk/, *n.* **1.** a large mass of stone. **2.** *Geol.* mineral matter of variable composition, assembled in masses in nature, as by the action of heat (**igneous rock**) or of water, air, or ice (**sedimentary rock**), or by the change in structure of either of these two types by pressure and heat (**metamorphic rock**). **3.** something suggesting a rock, esp. as a foundation or support: *He was a rock of strength in our trouble.* **4.** a hard sweet made in various flavors, as peppermint, usu. long and cylindrical in shape. **5.** *Colloq.* a jewel, esp. a diamond. **6.** a stone of any size. **7. on the rocks, a.** *Colloq.* into or in a state of ruin. **b.** (of drinks) with ice-cubes: *Scotch on the rocks.* **8. the Rock, a.** Ayers Rock. **b.** Gibraltar. [OE, from ML] **–rocky,** *adj.*

rock[2] /rɒk/, *v.i.* **1.** to move or sway to and fro or from side to side. **2.** to dance to rock-'n'roll music. ◇*v.t.* **3.** to move or sway to and fro or from side to side, esp. gently and soothingly. **4.** to move or sway powerfully with emotion, etc. **5.** to shake or disturb violently. ◇*v.* **6. rock the boat,** *Colloq.* to make difficulties, usu. by raising awkward questions, etc. ◇*n.* **7.** → **rock music. 8.** → **rock'n'roll** (defs 1 and 2). ◇*adj.* **9.** of or relating to rock music. [OE] **–rocky,** *adj.*

rock-and-roll /rɒk-ən-'roʊl/, *n.* → **rock'n'roll.**

rock cod, *n.* **1.** a common sea fish of southern Australian waters. **2.** any of a number of fishes of various families, usu. distinctively colored or marked, found in rocky offshore areas around the northern half of Australia.

rock-crystal /'rɒk-krɪstl/, n. transparent quartz, esp. of the colorless kind.

Rockefeller family /'rɒkəfelə/, n. a family of US industrialists and philanthropists, including **1. John Davison**, 1839–1937, founder of the Standard Oil Company. **2.** his grandson, **Nelson Aldrich** /'ɔldrɪtʃ/, 1908–79, US philanthropist; governor of New York State 1958–74; vice president 1974–76.

rocker /'rɒkə/, n. **1.** one of the curved pieces on which a cradle or a rocking chair rocks. **2.** a rocking chair. **3.** any of various devices that operate with a rocking motion. **4. off one's rocker**, *Colloq.* crazy; mad; demented: *You must be off your rocker to suggest such a thing.*

rockery /'rɒkəri/, n., pl. **-ries.** an arrangement of rocks and earth for growing rock plants.

rocket /'rɒkət/, n. *Aeron.* a structure propelled by the emission of heated gas from the rear. **2.** a type of firework which shoots into the air and explodes forming colored stars of light. **3. go like a rocket**, *Colloq.* **a.** to move fast. **b.** (of a machine) to work well. ◊*v.i.* **4.** to move like a rocket. **5.** (of prices, etc.) to increase rapidly. [F]

Rocket /'rɒkət/, n. **the**, an early steam locomotive, designed and built in 1829 by George and Robert Stephenson.

Rockhampton /rɒk'hæmptən/, n. the principal city of central Qld, on the Fitzroy River, about 60 km from the coast. Pop. 54 362 (1986).

Rockingham[1] /'rɒkɪŋəm/, n. **Charles Watson-Wentworth, 2nd Marquess of,** 1730–82, British politician; prime minister 1765–66, 1782; opposed war with American colonists.

Rockingham[2] /'rɒkɪŋəm/, n. a satellite town of Perth, WA, a port on the Cockburn Sound. Pop. 30 635 (1986).

rocking horse, n. a toy horse, usu. of wood, set on rockers, for children.

rockmelon /'rɒkmelən/, n. a round fruit usu. with netted rind whose orange-colored flesh is refreshing to eat; cantaloupe.

rock music, n. a form of popular music derived largely from Negro blues and gospel music. It has a strong, persistent rhythm, is generally loud, and features electronically amplified sound.

rock'n'roll /rɒk ən 'roʊl/, n. **1.** a form of popular music which has a 12 bar blues form, and a heavily accented rhythm. **2.** a dance performed to this music. Also, **rock-and-roll**.

Rocks /rɒks/, n. **The,** a district of Sydney, NSW, on Sydney Cove, noted for its historic buildings and associations.

rock-salt /'rɒk-sɒlt/, n. common salt (sodium chloride), occurring in nature as rock.

rock-wallaby /'rɒk-wɒləbi/, n. any of several small wallabies having long, cylindrical, hairy tails and thickly padded and roughened feet, which live in rocky areas of Australia, e.g. the **yellow-footed rock-wallaby** with yellowish feet and ears, and a banded tail.

Rocky Mountains /'rɒki maʊntənz/, n. pl. the chief mountain system in North America, extending from northern Mexico to Alaska. Highest peak, Elbert Peak, 4399 m. Also, **Rockies**.

rococo /rə'koʊkoʊ/, n. **1.** a style of art, architecture and decoration of the 18th century, with use of ornate scrolls and curves. ◊*adj.* **2.** in the rococo style. **3.** over-elaborately decorated. [F: rockwork, pebblework or shellwork]

rod /rɒd/, n. **1.** a stick or the like, of wood, metal, or other material. **2.** a pole used in fishing. **3.** a measure in the imperial system, of 5½ yards or 16½ feet, equal to 5.0292 m. **4.** a staff carried to stand for office, authority, power, etc. **5.** any micro-organism which is shaped like a rod. **6.** *Anat.* one of the rodlike cells in the retina of the eye which responds to dim light. [OE]

rode /roʊd/, v. past tense of **ride**.

rodent /'roʊdnt/, adj. belonging to the order of gnawing or nibbling mammals, that includes rats, mice, squirrels, etc. [L: gnawing]

rodeo /roʊ'deɪoʊ, 'roʊdioʊ/, n., pl. **-deos.** a display of the skills of cowboys, riding horses, steers, etc., for public entertainment. [Sp: cattle ring, from L]

Rodin /rɔ'dæ/, n. **Auguste** /oʊ'gyst/, 1840–1917, French sculptor; known for portrayal of the human form in anatomical detail; works include *The Kiss* (1886) and *The Thinker* (1905).

roe /roʊ/, n. **1.** the mass of eggs within the ovary of the female fish (**hard roe**). **2.** the sperm of the male fish (**soft roe**). [ME]

Roe /roʊ/, n. **John Septimus,** 1797–1878, Australian explorer, born in England; surveyor-general of WA 1828–70.

roedeer /'roʊdɪə/, n. a small lively deer of Europe and parts of Asia, the grown male of which has three-pointed antlers. [OE]

roentgen /'rɒntgən/, n. the amount of radiation or X-rays producing ions carrying 0.258×10^{-3} coulombs per kilogram. *Symbol:* R [named after WK ROENTGEN]

Roentgen /'rɒntgən, -tjən, 'rʌntgən/, n. **Wilhelm Konrad,** 1845–1923, German physicist; discovered X-rays in 1895; Nobel prize for physics 1901. Also, **Röntgen**.

roger /'rɒdʒə/, *interj.* **1.** message received and understood (used in signalling and telecommunications). **2.** (an expression of agreement understanding, etc.). [*Roger* (personal name) used in telecommunications as a name for *r*, used as an abbrev. for *received*]

Roget /'rɒʒeɪ, 'roʊʒeɪ/, n. **Peter Mark,** 1779–1869, English physician and lexicographer; wrote a *Thesaurus of English Words and Phrases* (1852).

rogue /roʊg/, n. **1.** a dishonest person. **2.** a person who carries out playful tricks; rascal; scamp. **3.** an animal of fierce character which travels alone. [apparently short for obs. *roger*

begging vagabond, b. *roamer* and BEGGAR]
–**roguery**, *n*. –**roguish**, *adj*.

Roland /ˈroʊlənd/, *n*. Charlemagne's greatest legendary paladin, killed at the battle of Roncesvalles (AD 778); also famous for his five days combat with Oliver, another paladin, in which neither gained the advantage.

role /roʊl/, *n*. **1.** the part or character which an actor presents in a play. **2.** a proper or customary position or function: *the teacher's role in society.* Also, **rôle**. [F: the roll (as of paper) containing an actor's part]

roll /roʊl/, *v.i.* **1.** (of a ball, wheel, etc.) to move along a surface by turning over and over. **2.** (of a vehicle, etc.) to move or be moved on wheels (oft. fol. by *along*). **3.** (of water, waves, smoke, etc.) to advance in a stream or with a wavy movement. **4.** (of land, etc.) to spread out in a wave-like appearance. **5.** (of time) to move (fol. by *on*, etc.) or pass (oft. fol. by *away*, etc.). **6.** (of seasons) to move in a cycle (fol. by *round*). **7.** (of thunder, etc.) to have a deep, prolonged sound. **8.** *Colloq.* to abound (in wealth, etc.). **9.** (of the eyes) to turn in a circular movement. **10.** (of a ship) to sway or rock from side to side (opposed to *pitch*). **11.** to walk with a rolling or swaying movement. **12.** to spread out from being rolled up; unroll (fol. by *out*, etc.). **13.** to spread out as under a roller. ◇*v.t.* **14.** to cause to move along a surface by turning over and over: *Roll the ball to me.* **15.** to move along on wheels or rollers. **16.** to utter or give forth with a full, flowing, continuous sound. **17.** to trill: *Can you roll your r's?* **18.** to cause to turn (usu. the eyes) in a circular motion. **19.** to cause to sway or rock from side to side. **20.** to wrap into a roll, ball, or the like. **21.** to make by forming a roll: *They roll cigarettes.* **22.** to spread out from being rolled up; unroll (fol. by *out*, etc.). **23.** to wrap, enfold, or envelope, as in some covering. **24.** to operate upon with a roller, rollers or rolling pin, so as to spread out, level, or the like. ◇*v.* **25. roll up, a.** to form a roll. **b.** *Colloq.* to arrive. **c.** *Colloq.* to gather round. **26. roll in,** to arrive or appear in large numbers. ◇*n.* **27.** a piece of paper, or the like, as for writing, etc., which is or may be rolled up; scroll. **28.** a list, register, or catalogue. **29.** a list containing the names of the people belonging to any company, class, society, etc. **30.** anything rolled up in cylindrical form, as cloth, wallpaper, a number of papers, etc. **31.** a quantity of something in this form, used as a definite measure: *a roll of wallpaper.* **32.** a rounded mass of something: *rolls of fat.* **33.** a small cake of bread, often doubled on itself before baking. **34.** food which is rolled up, used of meat, cake, pastry, etc. **35.** a wavy surface: *the roll of a field of wheat.* **36.** deep-throated or rhythmical flow of words. **37.** a deep, continuing sound: *a roll of thunder.* **38.** the trill of certain birds. **39.** the continuous sound of a drum rapidly beaten. **40.** a rolling movement, as of a ship, person, etc. **41.** *Aeron.* a movement. **41.** *Aeron.* a single complete turn of an aeroplane around its long axis. **42.** (in the high jump and pole vault) the near horizontal position, used by competitors to roll over the bar. [ME, from OF, from L: little wheel]

rollcall /ˈroʊlkɔl/, *n*. **1.** the calling of a list of names, to find out who is absent. **2.** a military signal for this, as one given by a drum.

roller /ˈroʊlə/, *n*. **1.** a cylinder, wheel, or the like, upon which something is rolled along. **2.** a cylinder around which something is rolled: *a hair roller.* **3.** a cylindrical body for rolling over something to be spread out, levelled, crushed, linked, etc. **4.** any of various other revolving cylindrical bodies, as the barrel of a musical box. **5.** a long, swelling wave advancing steadily.

roller-skate /ˈroʊlə-skeɪt/, *n., v.,* -**skated,** -**skating.** ◇*n.* **1.** a form of skate running on small wheels or rollers, for use on a smooth floor, footpath, etc. ◇*v.i.* **2.** to move on roller-skates.

rollick /ˈrɒlɪk/, *v.i.* to move or act in a careless, gay manner. –**rollicking**, *adj*.

rolling /ˈroʊlɪŋ/, *n*. **1.** the action, movement, sound or appearance of anything that rolls. ◇*adj.* **2.** that rolls, as by rising and falling in gentle slopes, moving in waves, rocking, turning over, etc. **3.** *Colloq.* drunk. **4.** Also, **rolling in money** or **rolling in it.** *Colloq.* very rich.

rolling pin, *n*. a cylinder of wood or other material for rolling out pastry, etc.

rolling stock, *n*. the wheeled vehicles of a railway, including engines and carriages.

Rolling Stones, *n.pl.* **the,** British rock'n'roll group, formed in 1963; original members Mick Jagger, Keith Richard, Brian Jones, Bill Wyman, and Ian Stewart; later members Mick Taylor and Ron Wood. See also, Mick **Jagger**.

rolling strike, *n*. industrial action against an employer in which groups of employees go on strike one after the other without interruption.

rollmop /ˈroʊlmɒp/, *n*. a marinated fillet of herring wrapped around an onion, etc. [G]

roll of honor *or* **roll of honour,** *n*. the list of those who are in some way honoured, esp. those who have fought for their country. Also, **honor roll.**

Rolls /roʊlz/, *n*. **1. Charles Stewart,** 1877–1910, English motor-car manufacturer (with Sir FH Royce) and pioneer flyer. **2. Eric C,** born 1923, Australian poet and prose writer; author of the novel *Celebration of the Senses* (1984).

roll-up /ˈroʊl-ʌp/, *n*. (the number attending) an assembly, gathering.

roly-poly /ˌroʊli-ˈpoʊli/, *adj., n., pl.* -**lies.** ◇*adj.* **1.** fat and fleshy. ◇*n.* **2.** a roly-poly person or thing. **3.** a strip of pastry spread with jam, fruit, or the like, rolled up, and steamed or boiled as a pudding.

Rom, *Abbrev.* **1.** Roman. **2.** Romance. **3.** Romanic. **4.** *Bible.* Romans.

Roma /ˈroʊmə/, *n*. a town in south-eastern Qld; agricultural centre; natural gas fields. Pop. 6069 (1986).

Roman /ˈroʊmən/, *adj.* **1.** of or relating to Rome, ancient or modern, or those living there. **2.** (*usu. l.c.*) indicating or relating to the upright style of printing types most commonly

Roman used in modern books, etc. **3.** indicating or relating to Roman numerals. ◇*n.* **4.** someone born or living in ancient or modern Rome. [OE, from L]

Roman Catholic, *adj.* **1.** of or relating to the Roman Catholic Church. ◇*n.* **2.** a member of the Roman Catholic Church. –**Roman Catholicism,** *n.*

Roman Catholic Church, *n.* → **Catholic Church** (def. 2). Also, **Church of Rome.** [the name (oft. used by non-Catholics) emphasises that the members of the Church acknowledge the supremacy of the Pope in Rome]

romance /rə'mæns, 'roumæns/, *n.*; /rə'mæns/, *v.* **-manced, -mancing,** *adj.* ◇*n.* **1.** a tale of brave or wonderful achievements, colorful events or experiences, chivalrous behavior, or other matters of a kind to appeal to the imagination. **2.** a made-up story; fanciful invention. **3.** romantic spirit or character. **4.** a romantic affair or experience; a love affair. ◇*v.i.* **5.** to invent or tell fanciful stories. **6.** to think or talk romantically. ◇*adj.* **7.** (*cap.*) relating to the languages which are derived from Latin, such as French. [ME, from OF, from VL: in Romance (i.e., in one of the Romance languages), from L: Romanic]

Romance language, *n.* any of the group of languages which have developed out of Latin, in their historical or modern forms, principally, Sardinian, Dalmatian (extinct), Romanian, Italian, Rhaeto-Romanic, French, Provençal, Catalan, Spanish, and Portuguese. [OF: from the phrase *langue romance* (now *langue romane*), lit., Romantic language]

Roman Empire, *n.* **1.** the lands and peoples subject to the authority of ancient Rome. **2.** a later empire, as that of Charlemagne or the Byzantine Empire, regarded as a restoration or continuation of the ancient Roman empire or one of its branches.

Romanesque /roumə'nɛsk/, *adj.* indicating the style of European architecture of the late 10th until the 13th century, characterised by towers, heavy walls, small windows, and the use of open timber roofs.

Romania /rə'meɪniə/, *n.* a republic in south-eastern Europe on the Black Sea, bordered by Ukraine, Moldova, Hungary, Yugoslavia and Bulgaria. Pop. 22 913 000 (1987 est.); 237 500 km². *Language:* Romanian. *Currency:* leu. *Cap.:* Bucharest. Also, **Roumania, Rumania.**

Roman numerals, *n.pl.* the numerals used by the ancient Romans, and still used for some purposes. The common basic symbols are I(= 1), V(= 5), X(= 10), L(= 50), C(= 100), D(= 500), and M(= 1000). See Appendix.

Romanov /'roumənɒf/, *n.* **1.** a member of the imperial dynasty which ruled Russia from 1613 to the abdication of Nicholas II in 1917. **2. Mikhail Feodorovich** /mɪka'il fi'ɔdərəvɪtʃ/, 1596–1645, tsar of Russia 1613–45. Also, **Romanoff.**

Romans /'roumənz/, *n.* (in the New Testament) one of the most important doctrinal epistles of Paul, written to the Christian community at Rome.

romantic /rə'mæntɪk/, *adj.* **1.** of, relating to, or of the nature of romance: *a romantic adventure.* **2.** suited to romance rather than to real or practical life; fanciful; unpractical; quixotic: *romantic ideas.* **3.** showing or expressing love, strong affection, etc. **4.** (*sometimes cap.*) of or relating to a style of literature, art, and music of the late 18th and 19th centuries, characterised by freedom of treatment, a viewing of form as less important than matter, imagination, experimentation with form, etc. (opposed to *classical*). **5.** imaginary or made-up. ◇*n.* **6.** a romantic person. [F: romance, novel] –**romanticism,** *n.* –**romanticist,** *n.*

romanticise *or* **romanticize** /rə'mæntəsaɪz/, *v.*, **-cised, -cising.** ◇*v.t.* **1.** to give a romantic character to: *She romanticised her work as an actress.* ◇*v.i.* **2.** to have romantic ideas.

Romany /'rɒməni/, *n., pl.* **-nies,** *adj.* ◇*n.* **1.** a Gipsy. **2.** the language of the Gipsies. ◇*adj.* **3.** relating to the Gipsies, their language, or customs. [Gipsy *Rom* man, husband]

Rome /roum/, *n.* the capital of Italy, in the central part, on the Tiber; the ancient capital of the Roman Empire; the site of Vatican City, seat of authority of the Roman Catholic Church. Pop. 2 823 927 (1986 est.).

Rommel /'rɒməl/, *n.* **Erwin,** 1891–1944, German field marshal; commander of German forces in North Africa in World War II; involved in a plot to overthrow Adolf Hitler in 1944 and later committed suicide.

Romney /'rɒmni/, *n.* a breed of sheep popular in Australia, suitable for high rainfall areas, having long wool, and developed for both wool and meat. Also, **Romney Marsh.** [from *Romney Marsh,* district in SE England]

romp /rɒmp/, *v.i.* **1.** to play or have fun in a lively manner. **2.** to run or go rapidly and without effort, as in racing. ◇*v.* **3. romp home** *or* **in,** to win easily. ◇*n.* **4.** a lively time of fun. **5.** a fast, effortless pace. [obs. *ramp* rough woman]

Romulus /'rɒmjʊləs/, *n. Rom Legend.* the founder of Rome (753 BC) and its first king; he and his twin brother Remus (whom he eventually killed) were abandoned as infants and suckled by a wolf. He was deified by the Romans who identified him with Quirinus, an early god of war.

rondeau /'rɒndoʊ/, *n., pl.* **-deaux** /-doʊ, -doʊz/. a short poem of fixed form, consisting of thirteen (or ten) lines with two rhymes and having the opening words or phrase used in two places as a non-rhyming repeated phrase.

rondo /'rɒndoʊ/, *n., pl.* **-dos.** a musical work or movement, having one main subject which is stated at least three times in the same key and to which a return is made after the introduction of each lesser theme. [It, from F]

roneo /'rouniou/, *v.t.* **1.** to make a copy or copies of by cutting a stencil and reproducing it on a fluid-containing copier. ◇*n.* **2.** a copy made in this way. [Trademark]

roo /ru/, *n. Colloq.* → **kangaroo.**

roo bar, *n.* → **kangaroo-bar.**

rood /rud/, *n.* **1.** a cross as used in crucifixion. **2.** a unit of land measure in the imperial system, equal to 40 square rods or $\frac{1}{4}$ acre. [OE]

roof /ruf/, *n., pl.* **roofs** /rufs, ruvz/. **1.** the outer upper covering of a house or other building. **2.** something which in form or position is like the roof of a house, as the top of a car, the upper part of the mouth, etc. **3. hit the roof,** *Colloq.* to become very angry. **4. raise the roof,** to make a loud noise, esp. in complaint. ◇*v.t.* **5.** to provide or cover with a roof. [OE]

roof-rack /'ruf-ræk/, *n.* a system of bars attached to the roof of a car and used to carry luggage, etc. Also, **luggage-rack**.

rook[1] /ruk/, *n.* a black European crow which nests in groups in trees about buildings. ◇*v.t.* **2.** *Colloq.* to cheat; fleece; swindle. [OE]

rook[2] /ruk/, *n.* a chess piece having the power to move any distance in a straight line if no other pieces are in the way; a castle. [ME, from OF, from Pers]

rookery /'rukəri/, *n., pl.* **-ries**. **1.** (a place housing) a colony of rooks. **2.** a breeding place or colony of other birds or animals, as penguins, seals, etc. **3.** an example of cheating, sharp practice, etc.

rookie /'ruki/, *n. Colloq.* someone new, originally in the army, and hence in any service, sporting team, etc. Also, **rooky**.

room /rum/, *n.* **1.** a part of a building, separated by walls from other parts: *a dining room*. **2.** (*pl.*) a place to live or work, as in a house or building. **3.** the space or amount of space, available for something: *The desk takes up too much room*. **4.** opportunity: *room for improvement*. **5. room to move,** possibility of choice or freedom of movement. ◇*v.i.* **6.** to occupy a room or rooms; lodge. [OE]

Roosevelt /'rouzəvɛlt/, *n.* **1. (Anna) Eleanor,** 1884–1962, US diplomat and writer (wife of FD Roosevelt); delegate to the UN 1945–52. **2. Franklin Delano,** 1882–1945, 32nd president of the US, 1933–45; instituted major economic reforms in the 1930s. **3. Theodore,** 1858–1919, 26th president of the US, 1901–09; organised the building of the Panama Canal in 1903; Nobel Peace prize 1906.

roost /rust/, *n.* **1.** a branch or piece of timber on which fowls rest at night. **2.** a house or place for fowls or birds to sleep in. **3.** a place for sitting, resting, or staying. **4. rule the roost,** to be in charge; dominate. ◇*v.i.* **5.** to sit or rest on a roost, etc. **6.** to settle or stay, esp. for the night. ◇*v.* **7. come home to roost,** (usu. of something unfavorable) to come back to the person who has caused a problem; recoil. [OE]

rooster /'rustə/, *n.* the male of the domestic fowl; cock.

root[1] /rut/, *n.* **1.** a part of a plant which, typically, develops from the radicle and grows downwards into the soil, fixing the plant and taking up food and moisture. **2.** any underground part of a plant, as a rhizome. **3.** the most basic part: *the root of a matter*. **4.** the source or origin of a thing: *Love of money is the root of all evil*. **5.** (*pl.*) **a.** a person's real home and environment: *Though he's lived in the city for ten years his roots are still in the country*. **b.** those elements, as personal relationships, a liking for the area, customs, etc., which make a place someone's true home: *He lived in Darwin for five years but never established any roots there*. **6.** *Maths.* **a.** a quantity which, when multiplied by itself a certain number of times, produces a given quantity: *2 is the square root of 4, the cube root of 8, and the fourth root of 16*. **b.** a quantity which, when used instead of the unknown quantity in an algebraic equation, satisfies the equation. **7.** *Gram.* a basic word or element which can be used by itself, or upon which other words can be built. *Dance* is the root of *dancer* and *dancing*, and *law* is the root of *unlawful*. **8.** *Music.* the note on which a chord is based. **9. take (or strike) root, a.** to send out roots and begin to grow. **b.** to become fixed or established. ◇*v.i.* **10.** to send out roots and begin to grow. **11.** to become fixed or established. ◇*v.t.* **12.** to fix by, or as if by, roots. **13.** to establish deeply. **14.** to pull, tear, or dig (fol. by *up, out*, etc.) by the roots. **15.** to remove totally; exterminate (with *up, out*, etc.). **16.** *Colloq.* **a.** to tire out. **b.** to break; ruin. [OE, from Scand] —**rooted,** *adj.*

root[2] /rut/, *v.i.* **1.** to turn up the soil with the snout, as pigs. **2.** to search as if to find something (fol. by *around*). ◇*v.t.* **3.** to turn over with the snout (oft. fol. by *up*). **4.** to bring to light (fol. by *up*, etc.). [OE]

root beer, *n. US.* a drink containing the juices of various roots, as of dandelion, sarsaparilla, etc.

root hair, *n.* a thin tubular extension of the root serving to absorb water and minerals from the soil.

root mean square, *n.* the square root of the arithmetic mean of the squares of a set of values. *Abbrev.*: r.m.s.

rope /roup/, *n., v.,* **roped, roping.** ◇*n.* **1.** a strong, thick line or cord, usu. of twisted hemp, flax, etc., or of wire or other material. **2.** a noose for hanging a person. **3.** death by hanging as a punishment. **4.** a quantity of material or a number of things strung together in the form of a thick cord: *a rope of beads*. **5.** (*pl.*) methods; procedure; operations of a business, etc.: *to know the ropes*. ◇*v.t.* **6.** to tie, bind, or fasten with a rope. **7.** *Colloq.* to draw or persuade into something (fol. by *in*). [OE]

ropeable /'roupəbəl/, *Colloq.* angry; bad-tempered. Also, **ropable**.

Roper /'roupə/, *n.* a river in the NT, rising east of Katherine and flowing east into the Gulf of Carpentaria. 400 km.

roquefort /'roukfət/, *n.* a semi-soft ripened cheese, with a strong flavor, veined with mould. [orig. made at *Roquefort*, town in S France]

rorqual /'rɔkəl/, *n.* any of the whalebone whales, some being very large but slender and streamlined, able to swim very quickly and having a dorsal fin. [F, from Norw]

Rorschach test /'rɔʃak/, *n. Psychol.* a test using the interpretation of ink blots and drawings to analyse someone's personality. [named after Hermann *Rorschach*, 1884–1922, Swiss psychiatrist]

rort /rɔt/, *n. Colloq.* **1.** a trick; lurk; scheme. **2.** a wild party. ◇*v.t.* **3.** to gain control over (an organisation, as a branch of a political party) esp. by changing its records. [orig. uncert.]

rosaceous /rou'zeɪʃəs/, *adj.* **1.** belonging to the rose family of plants, which includes also the blackberry, strawberry, etc. **2.** like a rose. [L]

rosary /'rouzəri/, *n., pl.* **-ries. 1.** *Rom Cath Ch.* (a string of beads used for counting) a series of prayers. **2.** (among other religious bodies) a string of beads similarly used in praying. **3.** a rose garden; a bed of roses. [ME, from L: rose garden]

rose[1] /rouz/, *n.* **1.** (the flower of) a type of wild or cultivated shrub, usu. prickly-stemmed and bearing showy, often fragrant, flowers. **2.** an ornament shaped like, or suggesting, a rose; a rosette of ribbon, etc. **3.** the traditional reddish color of the rose, varying from a purplish red through different shades to a pale pink. **4.** pinkish red color in the cheek. **5.** a cap or plate with evenly spaced holes punched in it at the end of a water pipe or the spout of a watering-can, etc., to break a flow of water into a spray. **6. bed of roses**, an easy and highly agreeable position or situation. ◇*adj.* **7.** of the color rose. [ME and OE, from L]

rose[2] /rouz/, *v.* past tense of **rise**.

rosé /rou'zeɪ/, *n.* a light wine of an almost transparent pale red color. [F]

Rosebery /'rouzbəri, -brɪ/, *n.* **Archibald Philip Primrose, Earl of,** 1847–1929, British politician and author; prime minister 1894–95.

rosella /rou'zɛlə/, *n.* **1.** any of a number of brilliantly colored parrots all having red brows, e.g. the **eastern rosella,** a common bird of eastern Australia. **2.** *Colloq.* a sheep that has lost wool, esp. through disease and is showing patches of bare skin. [from *Rosehill*, an early settlement in NSW]

rosella bush, *n.* an annual shrub with yellow hibiscus-like flowers, and fruit which is often picked when young and used to make jam. Also, **rosella.**

rosemary /'rouzməri/, *n., pl.* **-maries.** an evergreen shrub, native to the Mediterranean region, used as a herb in cooking and yielding a fragrant oil. It is, by custom, a symbol of remembrance. [ME *rose mary*, from L: dew of the sea]

Rosetta stone /rou'zɛtə stoun/, *n.* a stone slab, found in 1799 near Rosetta, in northern Egypt, bearing parallel inscriptions in Greek and in Egyptian hieroglyphic characters, making possible the decipherment of ancient Egyptian hieroglyphics.

rosette /rou'zɛt/, *n.* **1.** any arrangement, part, object, or shape more or less like a rose. **2.** a rose-shaped arrangement of ribbon or other material, used as an ornament or badge. [F: ROSE[1]]

rose window, *n.* a circular window with a roselike pattern or radiating bars of wood or stone.

rosewood /'rouzwʊd/, *n.* a type of reddish wood used for making fine furniture and yielded by trees such as the **rose mahogany** of Australia and some other tropical trees.

Rosh Hashana, /rɒʃ hə'ʃanə/ *n.* the Jewish New Year. [Heb]

Rosicrucian /rouzə'kruʃən/, *n.* **1.** a member of any of several societies claiming magical powers and secret knowledge of the supernatural. ◇*adj.* **2.** of, relating to, or characteristic of the Rosicrucians. [Latinised form of G *Rosenkreuz*, name of supposed founder]

rosin /'rɒzən/, *n.* a hard, brittle resin made from pine resin, used in making varnish, for rubbing on violin bows, etc. [ME, from OF: RESIN]

Ross /rɒs/, *n.* **Sir James Clark,** 1800–62, British naval officer and explorer of the Arctic and Antarctic; discovered the Ross Sea (1841) and named Mt Erebus.

Rossetti /rɒ'sɛti/, *n.* **1. Christina Georgina,** 1830–94, British poet; major works include *The Prince's Progress* (1866). **2.** her brother, **Dante Gabriel,** 1828–82, British poet and painter; major paintings include *Ecce Ancilla Domini* (1850).

Ross Ice Shelf, *n.* the world's largest body of floating ice; in the southern part of the Ross Sea. Also, **Ross Barrier, Ross Shelf Ice.**

Rossini /rɒ'sini/, *n.* **Gioacchino Antonio** /dʒouə'kinou an'tɒnjou/, 1792–1868, Italian composer; major operas include *The Barber of Seville* (1816).

roster /'rɒstə/, *n.* **1.** a list of people or groups with their turns or periods of duty. **2.** any list, roll, or register. [D: list]

rostrum /'rɒstrəm/, *n., pl.* **-trums, -tra** /-trə/. any platform, stage, or the like, as for public speaking. [L: beak, in pl., speakers' platform]

rosy /'rouzi/, *adj.,* **rosier, rosiest. 1.** pink or pinkish red. **2.** (of people, the cheeks, lips, etc.) having a fresh, healthy redness. **3.** bright, cheerful, or promising: *a rosy future.* **4.** made or consisting of roses.

rot /rɒt/, *v.,* **rotted, rotting,** *n.* ◇*v.i.* **1.** to decay; decompose. **2.** to become morally evil or offensive. ◇*v.t.* **3.** to cause to rot. ◇*n.* **4.** the process of rotting. **5.** rotting or rotten matter. **6.** any of various plant or animal diseases or forms of decay. **7.** *Colloq.* nonsense. [ME, from Scand]

rotary /'routəri/, *adj.* **1.** (of an object) turning round as on an axis. **2.** (of motion) taking place round an axis. **3.** (of a machine) having a part or parts that turn like a wheel. **4.** of or relating to a rotary engine. [LL, from L: wheel]

rotary hoe, *n.* a machine with many fingerlike wheels, pulled over the ground for early crop farming and killing of weeds.

rotate /roʊˈteɪt/, *v.i., v.t.* **-tated, -tating. 1.** to turn or cause to turn round like a wheel on its axis. **2.** to go, or cause to go, through a round or routine of changes: *The seasons rotate; to rotate crops.* [L: swung round, revolved] **–rotatory,** *adj.* **–rotator,** *n.*

rotation /roʊˈteɪʃən/, *n.* **1.** the act of rotating; a turning round as on an axis. **2. a.** the turning of the earth or other body in space about its own axis. **b.** one complete turning or revolution of such a body. **3.** a regularly recurring succession, as of parliaments or other regularly elected bodies. **4.** *Agric.* the process or method of varying, in a definite order, the crops grown on the same ground.

rote /roʊt/, *n.* **1.** *Obs.* a routine; fixed or mechanical course of procedure. **2. by rote,** in a mechanical way without thought of the meaning: *to learn by rote.* [ME; orig. uncert.]

Rothbury /ˈrɒθbəri/, *n.* a colliery near Maitland in central eastern NSW; site of a serious dispute between police and miners in 1929.

rotisserie /roʊˈtɪsəri/, *n.* **1.** Also, **roasting spit.** a spit, driven by a clockwork mechanism or electricity, on which meat, poultry, and game can be cooked. **2.** a restaurant, cafe, etc., where such a spit is used. [F: roasting place]

rotor /ˈroʊtə/, *n.* **1.** *Elect.* the rotating part of a machine. **2.** *Aeron.* a system of rotating flaps, usu. horizontal, as those of a helicopter. **3.** *Mech.* the rotating assembly of blades in a turbine. [short for *rotator*]

Rotorua /roʊtəˈruə/, *n.* **1.** a town in NZ, on North Island; nearby steaming lakes, geysers and mudpools. Pop. 48 314 (1981). **2. Lake,** a large, circular lake on North Island, NZ, with the town of Rotorua on its southern shore. 69 km².

rotten /ˈrɒtn/, *adj.* **1.** in a condition of decomposition or decay; putrid; tainted, foul, or ill-smelling. **2.** dishonest or offensive morally, politically, or otherwise. **3.** *Colloq.* pitifully bad, unsatisfactory, or unpleasant: *to feel rotten; rotten work.* **4.** disgusting; vile; worthless: *a rotten little mob.* **5.** (of soil, rocks, etc.) soft, yielding, or easily broken up as the result of decomposition. **6.** *Colloq.* extremely drunk. [ME, from Scand]

Rotterdam /ˈrɒtədæm/, *n.* a seaport in the south-western Netherlands; one of the world's largest and busiest ports. Pop. 571 372 (1986 est.).

Rottnest Island /ˌrɒtnɛst ˈaɪlənd/, *n.* a small island lying about 20 km north-west of Fremantle, WA, opposite the mouth of the Swan River. Pop. 1297 (1986); about 11 km by 5 km.

rotund /roʊˈtʌnd/, *adj.* **1.** rounded; plump. **2.** full-toned or sonorous: *a rotund baritone voice.* [L] **–rotundity, rotundness,** *n.*

rotunda /rəˈtʌndə/, *n.* a round building or room, esp. one with a dome. [L: rotund]

Rouen /ˈruːɒn, ruˈɒ̃/, *n.* a city in northern France, capital of Seine-Maritime department, on the Seine; cathedral; execution of Joan of Arc, 1431. Pop. 100 696 (1982).

rouge /ruːʒ/, *n., v.,* **rouged, rouging.** ◇*n.* **1.** a type of red cosmetic for coloring the cheeks. **2.** a reddish powder, chiefly ferric oxide, used for polishing metal, etc. ◇*v.t.* **3.** to color with rouge. [F: properly adj., red, from L]

rough /rʌf/, *adj.* **1.** uneven, because of bumps, irregularities, or breaks in the surface; not smooth: *rough boards; a rough road.* **2.** (of ground) covered with scrub, rocks, etc. **3.** shaggy: *a dog with a rough coat.* **4.** acting with or characterised by violence. **5.** (of the sea, weather, etc.) violent. **6.** (of motion) violently irregular: *a rough ride.* **7.** sharp or harsh: *a rough temper.* **8.** disorderly; riotous. **9.** *Colloq.* hard or unpleasant. **10.** (of sounds) harsh to the ear; grating. **11.** harsh to the taste; sharp: *rough cider.* **12.** (of cloth, materials, etc.) coarse. **13.** (of people or their behavior) rude or lacking culture or refinement. **14.** without ordinary comforts or conveniences: *Camping is rough, but fun.* **15.** needing strength rather than skill: *rough work.* **16.** (of language, style, etc.) not perfected or corrected: *a rough draft.* **17.** not exact; approximate: *a rough guess.* **18.** not worked or treated or prepared; crude: *a rough diamond; rough timber.* **19. rough on, a.** severe treatment. **b.** unfortunate for (someone). ◇*n.* **20.** any piece of work, esp. a work of art, in an unfinished condition or early stage. **21.** *Golf.* any part of the course beside the fairway on which the grass, weeds, etc., are not cut. **22.** the rough, hard, or unpleasant side or part of anything. ◇*adv.* **23.** in a rough way; roughly. ◇*v.t.* **24.** to make rough; roughen. **25.** to treat roughly or harshly (oft. fol. by *up*). **26.** to put through a rough first stage of preparation (oft. fol. by *up*). **27.** to cut, shape, or sketch roughly (fol. by *in* or *out*): *to rough out a plan.* ◇*v.* **28. rough it,** to live without even basic comforts. [ME; OE *ruh*]

roughage /ˈrʌfɪdʒ/, *n.* the coarser kinds or parts of animal or human food, of little nutritive value, but assisting digestion, as distinguished from those supplying more concentrated food value.

rough-and-ready /rʌf-ənˈrɛdi/, *adj.* **1.** rough, or crude, but good enough for the purpose: *in a rough-and-ready way.* **2.** showing rough vigor rather than refinement or delicacy: *a rough-and-ready person.*

rough-and-tumble /rʌf-ənˈtʌmbəl/, *adj., n.* (characterised by) violent, uncontrolled behavior.

rough diamond, *n.* **1.** an uncut diamond. **2.** *Colloq.* person without polished manners but having a basically good or likeable character.

roughen /ˈrʌfən/, *v.t., v.i.* to make or become rough.

roughly /ˈrʌfli/, *adv.* **1.** in a crude, harsh or violent manner. **2.** not exactly; without precision or care: *The shirt was roughly ironed.* **3.** approximately; about: *roughly four o'clock.*

Roughsey /ˈrʌfsi/, *n.* **Dick** (*Goobalathaldin*), 1924–85, Australian artist and writer; author and illustrator of children's books including *The Rainbow Serpent* (1975).

roughshod /ˈrʌʃɒd/, *adj.* **1.** shod with horseshoes which have nails or points jutting out. **2. ride roughshod over**, to rudely disregard (someone's) opinions, ideas or feelings; treat without consideration.

roulette /ruˈlet/, *n.* **1.** a game of chance, in which players bet on which of the compartments of a turning wheel will be the resting-place of a ball circling it in the opposite direction. **2.** a small wheel, set in a handle, for making lines of marks, dots, or small holes. [F: round slice]

round /raʊnd/, *adj.* **1.** circular or spherical. **2.** free from angles. **3.** completed by returning to the place of starting: *a round trip.* **4.** full, complete; entire: *a round dozen.* **5.** expressed by an integer or whole number (with no fraction). **6.** approximate: *in round numbers.* **7.** (of a literary character) described in depth, rather than in a stereotyped way. **8.** (of sound) full and rich. **9.** plain; honest. ◇*n.* **10.** something round, e.g. circle, ring, curve, etc. **11.** any complete course or series. **12.** (*sometimes pl.*) a circuit of any place or places: *the postman on his rounds.* **13.** a completed course or spell of activity, in some game, sport, etc. **14.** a continually repeated group of events, duties, etc.: *the daily round.* **15.** a single outburst, as of applause, etc. **16.** a single discharge of shot by each of a number of guns, etc. **17.** a charge of ammunition for a single shot. **18.** a supplying of drink, etc., to all members of a group. **19.** a cut of beef from the lower part of the hind leg. **20.** a slice of bread. **21.** *Music.* a part-song in which the several voices follow one another at equal periods of time. ◇*adv.* **22.** in a circle, ring, etc. **23.** on all sides, or about. **24.** in all directions from a centre. **25.** in circumference: *a tree 40 centimetres round.* **26.** through a circuit, or series, as of places or people: *to show a person round.* **27.** from beginning to end: *all the year round.* **28.** by a roundabout course. **29.** with change to another or opposite direction, course, opinion, etc.: *to sit without looking round.* ◇*prep.* **30.** so as to surround: *to tie paper round a parcel.* **31.** on the border, or outer part of. **32.** around; about. **33.** to all or various parts of: *to wander round the country.* **34.** throughout (a period of time): *a place visited all round the year.* **35.** here and there in: *people standing round a room.* **36.** to the other side of: *to sail round a headland.* **37.** on the far side of: *the church round the corner.* **38.** so as to circle or rotate about (a centre etc.): *The hands went round the clockface.* ◇*v.t.* **39.** to make round. **40.** to finish (oft. by *off*). **41.** to encircle or surround. **42.** to make a turn or part circle about: *to round the bend.* ◇*v.i.* **43.** to become round. **44.** to make a turn about something. ◇*v.* **45. round on** or **upon**, to attack suddenly, usu. with words. **46. round out**, to add more detail to. **47. round up**, to collect (cattle, people, etc.) in a particular place. [ME, from OF, from L: wheel-shaped]

roundabout /ˈraʊndəbaʊt/, *n.* **1.** → **merry-go-round.** **2.** a road junction at which the traffic moves one way in a circular direction. ◇*adj.* **3.** (of a road, statement, etc.) indirect; circuitous. ◇*adv.* **4.** approximately.

roundelay /ˈraʊndəleɪ/, *n.* a song in which a phrase, line, etc., is continually repeated.

rounders /ˈraʊndəz/, *n.* (*pl. treated as sing.*) a game played with bat and ball, in which points are scored by running between bases.

Roundhead /ˈraʊndhed/, *n.* a member or adherent of the Parliamentary or Puritan party during the English Civil War of the 17th century (so called by the Cavaliers because they wore their hair cut short).

roundly /ˈraʊndli/, *adv.* strongly; briskly.

round robin, *n.* **1.** a letter, paper, etc., having the signatures arranged in a circular form, so as to hide the order of signing. **2.** a sporting competition in which each player or team plays against all other participants.

roundsman /ˈraʊndzmən/, *n., pl.* **-men.** a newspaper reporter covering a given area: *a police roundsman.*

round table, *n.* a number of people gathered for a discussion, considered as meeting on equal terms. [from the celebrated table in Arthurian legend, about which King ARTHUR[1] and his knights sat, made round to avoid quarrels as to precedence]

round-up /ˈraʊnd-ʌp/, *n.* **1.** the driving together of cattle, etc., into a herd for branding, etc. **2.** any similar driving or bringing together, as of people, facts, etc.

roundworm /ˈraʊndwɜm/, *n.* a worm which can live in the intestine of humans and other mammals.

rouse[1] /raʊz/, *v.*, **roused, rousing.** ◇*v.t.* **1.** to bring out of a state of sleep, unconsciousness, etc. **2.** to stir to anger. ◇*v.i.* **3.** to come out of a state of sleep, unconsciousness, etc. [orig. uncert.]

rouse[2] /raʊs/, *v.i.* scold, upbraid (fol. by *on*, *at*). [Scot: to shout]

rouseabout /ˈraʊsəbaʊt/, *n.* a handyman on a farm, in a hotel, etc. [ROUSE[1] + ABOUT]

rousing /ˈraʊzɪŋ/, *adj.* **1.** that rouses; stirring: *a rousing song.* **2.** strong; vigorous: *a rousing fire.*

Rousseau /ruˈsoʊ/, *n.* **1. Henri** /ɒˈriː/, ('Le Douanier'), 1844–1910, French painter; major works include *The Sleeping Gypsy* (1897). **2. Jean Jacques** /ʒɒ̃ ˈʒak/, 1712–78, French philosopher and writer, born in Switzerland; writings had great influence on political thought in the French Revolution; major works include *Du contrat social* (1762). **3. (Pierre Etienne) Théodore** /piˌɛə eɪtiˌɛn teɪoʊˈdɔ/, 1812–1867, French landscape painter; leader of the Barbizon school and precursor of Impressionism.

rout /raʊt/, *n.* **1.** a defeat resulting in total disorder: *to put an army to rout.* **2.** a defeated and scattering army. **3.** a noisy or disorderly crowd. ◇*v.t.* **4.** to scatter in defeat: *to rout an army.* **5.** to defeat completely. [ME, from AF, from L: broken]

route /rut/, *n., v.*, **routed, routeing** or **routing.** ◇*n.* **1.** a way or road taken or planned for travel. **2.** a regular line of travel. ◇*v.t.* **3.** to fix the route of. **4.** to send by a

route 904 **rub**

particular route. [ME, from F, from L: broken (road)]

routine /ru'tin/, n. **1.** a regular course of action or conduct: *the routine of an office.* **2.** regular, unvarying, or mechanical way of doing something. **3.** rehearsed, habitual, persuasive talk: *a salesman's routine.* ◇*adj.* **4.** of the nature of, going by, or keeping to routine: *routine duties.* [F: ROUTE]

roux /ru/, n. a mixture of fat and flour which forms the basis of most sauces. [F: browned, reddish, from L]

rove[1] /rouv/, v., **roved, roving.** ◇*v.i.* **1.** to wander. ◇*v.t.* **2.** to wander over or through; traverse: *to rove the world.* [ME, from Scand]

rove[2] /rouv/, v. a past tense and past participle of **reeve**[2].

rover /'rouvə/, n. **1.** someone who roves; wanderer. **2.** a senior boy scout, of 18 years or above. **3.** *Aust Rules.* one of the players in a ruck. [ROVE[1] + -ER[1]]

row[1] /rou/, n. a number of people or things arranged in a line. [OE *rāw*]

row[2] /rou/, v.i. **1.** to use oars, etc., for moving a boat. ◇*v.t.* **2.** to move (a boat, etc.) as by the use of oars. **3.** to carry in a boat, etc., using oars. **4.** to row against in a race: *We row Easts next week.* ◇*n.* **5.** an act of rowing. **6.** a trip in a rowing boat: *to go for a row.* [ME; OE *rōwan*]

row[3] /rau/, n. **1.** a noisy quarrel; commotion. **2.** *Colloq.* noise; clamour. ◇*v.i.* **3.** *Colloq.* to make a noisy quarrel. [orig. uncert.]

rowdy /'raudi/, adj., **-dier, -diest.** noisy and disorderly. [orig. obscure] —**rowdily,** adv. —**rowdiness,** n.

rowel /'rauəl/, n. a small wheel with sharp points, forming the end of a horseman's spur. [ME, from OF, from L: wheel]

rowlock /'rolək/, n. a device on a boat's gunwale in or on which the oar rests and swings. [var. of OARLOCK, by association with ROW[2]]

Roxby Downs /,roksbi 'daunz/, n. an area in central southern SA, with large deposits of copper and uranium.

royal /'rɔɪəl/, adj. **1.** of or relating to a king or queen, or their family **2.** established or existing under the support of a king or queen: *a royal society.* **3.** beyond the usual in size, quality, etc. ◇*n.* **4.** a traditional size of paper in imperial systems. See Appendix. **5.** *Colloq.* a member of a royal family (esp. British). [ME, from OF, from L]

Royal Academy, n. a society founded in 1768 by George III of England to encourage the visual arts by the establishment of a school of design and the holding of an annual exhibition of the works of living artists. Also, **Royal Academy of Arts.**

royal blue, adj., n. (of) a rich deep blue color.

royal commission, n. a person or persons chosen by the government to enquire into and report on some area of public concern.

Royal Flying Doctor Service, n. an aerial medical service providing medical and, in some States, dental relief to people in remote areas of Australia; originated by John Flynn and supported by the Australian Inland Mission; first flight made in 1927. *Abbrev.*: RFDS

royalist /'rɔɪələst/, n. **1.** a supporter of a monarchy, esp. in times of rebellion or civil war. ◇*adj.* **2.** of or relating to royalists. —**royalism,** n.

royal jelly, n. a substance, produced by worker honeybees to be fed to very young larvae and to those chosen as queens, used as a medicine, tonic, etc.

Royal Society, n. a society founded under the patronage of Charles II in 1662 for the advancement of science; membership is by election.

Royal Society for the Prevention of Cruelty to Animals, n. →RSPCA

royalty /'rɔɪəlti/, n., pl. **-ties. 1.** royal people as a group. **2.** royal rank or power; sovereignty. **3.** character proper to a king or queen; nobility. **4.** an agreed share of the proceeds from his work, paid to an author, inventor, etc. **5.** (a payment made for) royal right, as over minerals, given by a sovereign to a person or company. [ME, from OF]

Royce /rɔɪs/, n. **Sir Frederic Henry,** 1863–1933, English motor-car manufacturer (with CS Rolls).

r.p.m. /a pi 'ɛm/, *Abbrev.* revolutions per minute.

r.p.s. /a pi 'ɛs/, *Abbrev.* revolutions per second.

RSL /ar ɛs 'ɛl/, n. an organisation established in Australia in 1916 to provide assistance to those who have served in the armed forces and to their dependents. Formerly, (1916–40) **Returned Sailors' and Soldiers' Imperial League of Australia;** (1940–65) **Returned Sailors', Soldiers' and Airmen's Imperial League of Australia.** Also, **Returned Services League.** [abbrev.]

RSPCA /,ar ɛs pi si 'eɪ/, n. a society founded in England in 1824 and in Australia in 1871; campaigns for the humane treatment of animals. Also, **Royal Society for the Prevention of Cruelty to Animals.** [abbrev.]

RSVP /,ar ɛs vi 'pi/, *Abbrev.* please reply. [F *répondez s'il vous plaît*]

Rt Hon, *Abbrev.* Right Honorable.

Rt Rev, *Abbrev.* Right Reverend.

Ru, *Chem. Symbol.* ruthenium.

rub /rʌb/, v., **rubbed, rubbing,** n. ◇*v.t.* **1.** to subject (an object) to pressure and friction, esp. in order to clean, smooth, polish, etc. **2.** to move, spread, or apply (something) with pressure and friction over something else. **3.** to move (things) with pressure and friction over each other (fol. by *together*, etc.). **4.** to remove by rubbing (fol. by *off, out,* etc.). ◇*v.i.* **5.** to apply pressure and friction, to something. **6.** to move with pressure along the surface of something. **7.** to admit of being rubbed (*off,*

rub etc.): *That stain will rub off.* ◇*v.* **8.** Some special uses are:
rub down, 1. to rub (the surface of something) as to smooth, clean, etc. **2.** to massage, dry or clean (an animal, athlete, etc.) by rubbing.
rub off, to be passed on, esp. as a result of repeated close contact: *His rudeness rubbed off on her.*
rub shoulders or **elbows with,** to meet socially; associate with.
rub (up) the wrong way, to annoy.
rub up, 1. to polish. **2.** to refresh one's memory (fol. by *on*).
rub it in, to remind someone repeatedly of their mistakes.
◇*n.* **9.** the act of rubbing. **10.** a difficulty: *There's the rub.* [ME; of uncert. orig.]

Rubáiyát /'rubaɪæt/, *n.* the best-known work of Omar Khayyám, familiar in English through the version by Edward FitzGerald, published in 1859. [Pers from Ar, fem. pl. of *rubā'ī* quatrain]

rubber[1] /'rʌbə/, *n.* **1.** an elastic material, coming from the latex of certain tropical plants; indiarubber (**natural rubber**). **2.** synthetically-produced rubber. **3.** a piece of indiarubber for removing pencil marks, etc. **4.** an instrument, tool, etc., used for rubbing something. [RUB + -ER[1]] —**rubbery,** *adj.*

rubber[2] /'rʌbə/, *n.* Bridge, etc., a set of games, usu. three or five, the winner being the team to win a majority of games.

rubber band, *n.* a thin, continuous loop of highly elastic rubber, used for holding small objects, etc., together; elastic band.

rubber plant, *n.* a plant with oblong, shining, leathery leaves, often grown as a house plant.

rubber stamp, *n.* **1.** a device of rubber for printing dates, etc., by hand. **2.** *Colloq.* someone who gives approval without thought or objection.

rubber tree, *n.* a large shrub, native to Asia and northern Africa, which has been used for fibre and for mattress-filling.

rubbidy /'rʌbədi/, *n. Colloq.* a pub. Also, **rubbity, rubbidy-dub.** [rhyming slang, *rub-a-dub*, pub]

rubbing /'rʌbɪŋ/, *n.* a reproduction of a grooved or sculptured surface made by laying paper, etc., upon it and rubbing with some marking substance.

rubbish /'rʌbɪʃ/, *n.* **1.** waste material; debris; litter. **2.** worthless stuff; trash. **3.** nonsense. ◇*v.t.* **4.** to find fault with; criticise. [ME; orig. obscure] —**rubbishy,** *adj.*

rubble /'rʌbəl/, *n.* rough pieces of broken stone, brick, concrete, etc. [ME; orig. obscure]

rubella /ru'belə/, *n.* → **German measles.** [NL: reddish]

Rubens /'rubənz/, *n.* **Peter Paul,** 1577–1640, Flemish painter; major works include *The Judgment of Paris* (1625).

Rubicon /'rubɪkən/, *n.* **1.** the river in northern Italy forming the southern boundary of Caesar's province of Cisalpine Gaul, by crossing which, in 49 BC, he began a civil war with Pompey. Present name, **Fiumicino. 2. pass (cross) the Rubicon,** to take a decisive, irrevocable step.

rubicund /'rubəkənd/, *adj.* **1.** red or reddish. **2.** of a high color, as from good living. [L]

rubidium /ru'bɪdiəm/, *n.* a silvery-white metallic element like potassium, with no commercial uses. *Symbol:* Rb; *at. no.:* 37; *at. wt:* 85.47.

rubric /'rubrɪk/, *n.* **1.** a title, heading, direction, or the like, in a book, etc., written or printed in red or otherwise made different from the rest of the text. **2.** a direction for the conduct of divine service or the organisation of the sacraments, found in books of church worship. [L: red earth]

ruby /'rubi/, *n., pl.* **-bies. 1.** a red variety of corundum, highly prized as a precious stone. **2.** a piece of this stone. **3.** a deep red color; carmine. ◇*adj.* **4.** of a ruby color. **5.** made from or containing a ruby. [ME, from OF, from L: red]

ruck /rʌk/, *n.* **1.** the great mass of unimportant people or things. **2.** a crowd; throng. **3.** *Aust Rules.* a group of three players, a rover and two ruckmen, who do not have fixed positions but follow the play with the purpose of winning possession of the ball. **4.** *Rugby Football.* a group of players struggling for the ball in no set pattern of play; scrimmage. ◇*v.i.* **5.** to play as a member of a ruck. **6.** to form a ruck (def. 4). [ME, probably from Scand]

rucksack /'rʌksæk/, *n.* a bag carried on the back by hikers, etc. [G: lit., back sack]

ruction /'rʌkʃən/, *n. Colloq.* a noisy interruption, quarrel or row.

Rudd /rʌd/, *n.* **Steele** (*Arthur Hoey Davis*), 1868–1935, Australian writer; creator of the Dad and Dave characters; author of the collection of sketches *On Our Selection* (1899).

rudder /'rʌdə/, *n.* **1.** a board of wood or metal placed vertically at the back of a boat as a means of steering. **2.** a device like a ship's rudder for steering an aeroplane, etc. [OE *rōthor*]

ruddy /'rʌdi/, *adj.,* **-dier, -diest,** *adv.* ◇*adj.* **1.** of or having a fresh, healthy red color. **2.** reddish. ◇*adv.* **3.** *Colloq.* very; extremely: *I've a ruddy good mind to hit him.* [OE *rudig,* from *rudu* redness] —**ruddiness,** *n.*

rude /rud/, *adj.,* **ruder, rudest. 1.** impolite: *a rude reply.* **2.** without learning, or good taste. **3.** rough; harsh. **4.** roughly built, or formed: *a rude house.* [ME, from L] —**rudeness,** *n.*

rudiments /'rudəmənts/, *n.pl.* **1.** the elements or first principles of a subject: *the rudiments of grammar.* **2.** a beginning; first slight appearance, or undeveloped form of something. [L: beginning] —**rudimentary,** *adj.*

rue[1] /ru/, *v.t.,* **rued, ruing.** to feel sorrow over; repent of; regret bitterly. [OE *hrēowan*]

rue[2] /ru/, *n.* a strongly scented herb with yellow flowers and evergreen leaves, formerly

rue

much used in medicine. [ME from OF and F, from L, from Gk]

rueful /'ruːfəl/, *adj.* **1.** causing sorrow or pity; deplorable: *a rueful plight.* **2.** feeling, showing, or expressing sorrow or pity; mournful.

ruff /rʌf/, *n.* **1.** a neckpiece or collar of lace, etc., gathered into deep, full, regular folds, much worn in the 16th century. **2.** a collar, or set of lengthened or specially marked hairs or feathers, on the neck of an animal. [? n. use of ROUGH adj.]

ruffian /'rʌfiən/, *n.* **1.** a violent, lawless person. ◊*adj.* **2.** characteristic of a ruffian; lawless. [earlier *rufian*, from F]

ruffle /'rʌfəl/, *v.*, **-fled**, **-fling**, *n.* ◊*v.t.* **1.** to destroy the smoothness of. **2.** to make (feathers) stand up, as in anger. **3.** to annoy; disturb. **4.** to turn over (the pages of a book) rapidly. **5.** to pass (cards) through the fingers rapidly. **6.** to draw up (cloth, lace, etc.) into a ruffle by gathering along one edge. ◊*v.i.* **7.** to be ruffled. ◊*n.* **8.** a break in the smoothness of some surface. **9.** a strip of cloth, lace, etc., gathered along one edge, and used as a trimming on a dress, etc. **10.** some object like this, as the ruff of a bird. [ME]

rufous /'ruːfəs/, *adj.* reddish. [L: red, reddish]

rug /rʌg/, *n.*, *v.*, **rugged**, **rugging**. ◊*n.* **1.** a small, often thick, carpet, used as a floor covering or a hanging, and made of woven or tufted wool, cotton, etc. **2.** a thick, warm blanket used as a coverlet or wrap, etc. ◊*v.* **3. rug (oneself) up**, to make or keep (oneself) warm with thick clothing. [Scand]

Rugby football /'rʌgbi/, *n.* **1.** → **Rugby Union**. **2.** → **Rugby League**. [invented at *Rugby* school, Warwickshire, England]

Rugby League, *n.* one of the two forms of Rugby football, played by teams of thirteen players each, differing from Rugby Union in certain details of the rules and in allowing professionalism. Also, **League**.

Rugby Union, *n.* one of the two forms of Rugby football, played by teams of fifteen players each, differing from Rugby League in certain details of the rules and in using only amateurs. Also, **Union**.

rugged /'rʌgəd/, *adj.* **1.** roughly broken; rocky; hilly: *rugged ground.* **2.** roughly irregular, heavy, or hard in outline or form. **3.** rough, harsh, or severe. **4.** uncultivated, but strong: *rugged individualism.* **5.** *Colloq.* unpleasant; unfair. [ME, from Scand]

ruin /'ruːən/, *n.* **1.** (*pl.*) the remains of a fallen building, town, etc. **2.** a ruined building, town, etc. **3.** a fallen or decayed state: *A building falls to ruin.* **4.** the total loss of wealth, social position, etc. **5.** (something that causes) downfall, destruction, or decay: *Gambling will be his ruin.* **6.** a person as the wreck of his or her former self. ◊*v.t.* **7.** to reduce (someone or something) to ruin; destroy. [ME, from OF, from L: overthrow, ruin] – **ruination**, *n.* – **ruined**, *adj.* – **ruinous**, *adj.*

906

rummage

rule /ruːl/, *n.*, *v.*, **ruled**, **ruling**. ◊*n.* **1.** a principle or regulation controlling or governing behavior, action, etc. **2.** something which normally happens: *the rule rather than the exception.* **3.** control, government, or reign: *in the rule of George VI.* **4.** *Printing.* a thin, type-high strip of metal, for printing a line. ◊*v.t.* **5.** to control or direct. **6.** to govern. **7.** to decide legally. **8.** to mark with lines, using a ruler. ◊*v.i.* **9.** to exercise power. **10.** to make a formal decision or ruling. ◊*v.* **11. rule off**, to mark the end (of something written) by ruling a line beneath. **12. rule out**, to declare (something) out of the question. [ME, from OF, from L: straight stick, pattern]

rule of thumb, *n.* **1.** a rule based on experience or practice rather than on scientific knowledge. **2.** a rough, practical method of procedure.

ruler /'ruːlə/, *n.* **1.** someone or something that rules or governs. **2.** a strip of wood, metal, etc., with a straight edge, used in drawing lines, measuring, etc.

ruling /'ruːlɪŋ/, *n.* **1.** an authoritative decision, as by a judge. ◊*adj.* **2.** governing; predominating: *the ruling party.*

rum[1] /rʌm/, *n.* an alcoholic spirit made from molasses or some other sugar-cane product. [? short for obs. *rumbullion*. See F *rebouillir* boil again]

rum[2] /rʌm/, *adj. Colloq.* odd; strange. [earlier *rome*, *room*, great, of unknown orig.]

rumba /'rʌmbə/, *n.* a dance, originally from Cuba. [Sp, probably of Afr orig.]

rumble /'rʌmbəl/, *v.*, **-bled**, **-bling**, *n.* ◊*v.i.* **1.** to make a deep, heavy, continuous, echoing sound, as thunder, etc. **2.** to move or travel with such a sound: *The train rumbled on.* ◊*n.* **3.** a rumbling sound, as of thunder or a heavy vehicle. **4.** a rear part of a carriage containing a seat. **5.** *Colloq.* a fight. [ME; probably imitative]

rumen /'ruːmən/, *n.*, *pl.* **-mina** /-mənə/. **1.** the first stomach of ruminating animals. **2.** the cud of a ruminant. [L: throat, gullet]

Rum Hospital, *n.* the hospital built in 1810 in Macquarie Street, Sydney, NSW; contractors were remunerated by being given exclusive right to import 200 000 litres of rum over a three year period, for sale in the colony.

ruminant /'ruːmənənt/, *n.* **1.** any of a group of four-legged, cloven-hoofed, cud-chewing animals, as cattle, deer, sheep, etc. ◊*adj.* **2.** chewing the cud. **3.** given to or characterised by meditation; meditative. [L]

ruminate /'ruːmənert/, *v.*, **-nated**, **-nating**. ◊*v.i.* **1.** to chew the cud, as a ruminant. **2.** to meditate; ponder. ◊*v.t.* **3.** to chew again. **4.** to meditate on; ponder. [L] – **ruminative**, *adj.* – **ruminator**, *n.*

Rum Jungle, *n.* a mine and mining area in northern NT, south of Darwin; early mining of gold, tin and lead; uranium discovered 1949.

rummage /'rʌmɪdʒ/, *v.*, **-maged**, **-maging**, *n.* ◊*v.t.* **1.** to search thoroughly or actively through (a place, bag, etc.). **2.** to find (fol. by

rummage *out* or *up*) by searching. ◇*v.i.* **3.** to search actively, as in a place or bag, etc. ◇*n.* **4.** a rummaging search. [F: stow goods in hold of ship; orig. uncert.]

rummy /'rʌmi/, *n.* a card game in which the object is to match cards into sets and ordered groups. [orig. uncert.]

rumor *or* **rumour** /'rumə/, *n.* **1.** a story or statement widely spread, without proof as to facts. ◇*v.t.* **2.** to spread or report by a rumor. [ME, from OF, from L]

rump /rʌmp/, *n.* **1.** the hind part of the body of an animal. **2.** a cut of beef from this part of the animal, behind the loin and above the round. **3.** → **buttocks**. [ME, from Scand]

rumple /'rʌmpəl/, *v.*, **-pled, -pling,** *n.* ◇*v.t.* **1.** to draw or crush into wrinkles; crumple. ◇*v.i.* **2.** to become wrinkled or crumpled. ◇*n.* **3.** an irregular fold; wrinkle. [MD, or from MLG]

rumpus /'rʌmpəs/, *n. Colloq.* a disturbing noise; uproar; commotion.

Rum Rebellion, *n.* the deposing of Governor William Bligh on 26 January 1808 by the New South Wales Corps led by Lieutenant-Colonel George Johnston. [so-called because Corps' officers were involved in illegal trafficking of liquor]

run /rʌn/, *v.*, **ran, run, running,** *n.* ◇*v.i.* **1.** to move quickly on foot, so as to go faster than in walking. **2.** to hurry. **3.** to move easily or swiftly. **4.** to flee. **5.** to make a short, quick journey (oft. fol. by *up, over, round,* etc.): *I'll just run up to the shop.* **6. a.** to take part in a race. **b.** to finish a race in a certain position: *He ran second.* **7.** to stand as a candidate for election: *He ran for president.* **8.** (of fish) to pass upstream or inshore in order to spawn. **9.** to sail or be driven (ashore, into rocks, etc.), as a ship. **10.** *Naut.* to sail before the wind. **11.** to travel a route continually: *The buses run every hour.* **12.** to go without restriction (oft. fol. by *about*). **13.** to flow, as a liquid, or as sand, grain, etc. **14.** to discharge mucus, pus, etc. **15.** to overflow or leak (oft. fol. by *over*). **16.** (of vines, etc.) to creep or climb. **17.** to pass through or continue in the mind: *A tune ran through his head.* **18.** to repeat continually; be inherent: *Madness runs in the family.* **19.** (of stitches or a fabric) to come undone; ladder. **20.** (of a machine) to be in operation. **21.** (of time) to pass or go by. **22.** (of a play) to continue to be performed over a period. **23.** to stretch; extend: *The crack runs down the wall.* ◇*v.t.* **24.** to cause (an animal, etc.) to move quickly on foot: *We run the dog each morning.* **25.** to cause (a vehicle, etc.) to move: *to run the car into the garage.* **26.** to cover (a distance, etc.) by running: *He ran a kilometre.* **27.** to perform by or as by running: *to run a race.* **28.** to enter (a horse, etc.) in a race. **29.** to run or get past or through: *to run a blockade.* **30.** to bring into a certain condition by running: *She ran herself out of breath.* **31.** to chase; hunt (game, etc.). **32.** to drive (cattle, etc.), esp. to an area for food. **33.** to graze (cattle, etc.). **34.** to cause to move, esp. quickly: *He ran his fingers through her hair; She ran her eyes over the letter.* **35.** to cause to go regularly between places: *to run a train service between two cities.* **36.** to carry or transport, as in a car, etc.: *I will run you to the station.* **37.** to keep (a machine) operating. **38.** to have and use (a car). **39.** to leave oneself open to (a risk, etc.). **40.** to bring, lead, or force into some condition, action, etc.: *to run oneself into debt.* **41.** to fill (a bath, etc.) with water. **42.** to drive, force, or push. **43.** to draw or trace (a line). **44.** to conduct or manage (a business, experiment, etc.). **45.** (of a newspaper) to publish (a story). ◇*v.* **46.** Some special uses are:

run across, to meet or find unexpectedly.
run (around) with, to keep company with.
run away with, 1. to elope with. **2.** to steal. **3.** to win easily: *He ran away with the contest.* **4.** to get out of control: *The horse ran away with me.*
run down, 1. to slow up before stopping, as a clock. **2.** to knock down and injure. **3.** to criticise. **4.** to find, esp. after general searching. **5.** to pass quickly over; review.
run in, 1. to cause (new machinery) to run at a reduced load and speed for a period, so that the machine gradually becomes ready for full operation without damage: *She ran her car in for a week.* **2.** *Colloq.* → **arrest**.
run into, 1. to meet unexpectedly. **2.** to collide with. **3.** to amount to: *an income running into five figures.*
run off, 1. to go quickly. **2.** to produce by a printing process. **3.** to write, etc., quickly. **4.** to steal (fol. by *with*). **5.** → **elope**. **6.** to determine the result of (a tied contest, etc.) by a run-off.
run on, 1. to have as a subject: *The conversation ran on politics.* **2.** to continue, as talking, at length.
run out, 1. to go quickly. **2.** to use up completely: *We've run out of peanuts.* **3.** to be completely used up: *The food has run out.* **4.** *Cricket.* to put (a batsman) out by hitting the wicket with the ball while neither the batsman nor the bat are touching the ground within the crease. **5.** *Naut.* to pass out (a rope). **6.** *Orig. US.* to drive out.
run out on, to leave; abandon.
run over, 1. to knock down and injure. **2.** to go beyond (a time-limit, etc.). **3.** to read, practise or repeat.
run rings (a)round (someone), to perform with far greater success than (someone).
run short, 1. to become scarce or nearly used up. **2.** to use up almost completely: *We're running short of walnuts, too.*
run through, 1. to practise or reread. **2.** to use up (money, etc.). **3.** to pass a sword, etc., through (somebody): *The pirate ran him through.*
run to, 1. to be enough for: *The money doesn't run to a car.* **2.** to include: *The books don't run to pictures.* **3.** to go towards: *to run to fat.*
run up, 1. to climb quickly. **2.** to put up (a sail, flag, etc.). **3.** to collect or incur (bills, etc.). **4.** to make (clothes, etc.), esp. quickly. ◇*n.* **47.** an act, or period of running: *to go for a run.* **48.** a running speed. **49.** an act of escaping. **50.** an act or period of moving rapidly, as in a car, etc. **51.** a quick, short trip. **52.** a period of causing a machine, etc., to operate. **53.** the amount of something produced at one period. **54.** a line in knitted

or sewn work where stitches have come undone; ladder. **55.** the direction of something: *the run of the grain of timber.* **56.** the particular course of something: *in the normal run of events.* **57.** freedom to use: *the run of the house.* **58.** any fast or easy course of progress. **59.** a continuous series of something. **60.** any continued or large demand, call, etc.: *a run on heaters.* **61.** a series of urgent demands for payment, as on a bank. **62.** a kind or class, esp. of an ordinary kind. **63.** an enclosure within which animals may move about. **64.** a course for a particular service or activity, etc.: *a milk run; paper run.* **65.** a large area of grazing land. **66.** a number of fish or other animals moving together. **67.** *Music.* a rapid ordered pattern of notes. **68.** *Cricket.* the score unit, made by running from one wicket to the other. **69. on the run,** escaped. **70. in the long run,** finally. [OE *rinnan*]

runabout /'rʌnəbaʊt/, *n.* **1.** a small car, used for errands, etc. **2.** a small boat, usu. with an outboard motor.

run-around /'rʌn-əraʊnd/, *n. Colloq.* speech or action intending to trick or mislead: *He gave me the run-around.*

runaway /'rʌnəweɪ/, *n.* **1.** someone who runs away; a fugitive. **2.** a horse or vehicle which has broken away from control. ◇*adj.* **3.** having run away. **4.** (of a horse, etc.) out of control. **5.** (of a win in a race, etc.) easy.

Runcie /'rʌnsi/, *n.* **Robert Alexander Kennedy,** born 1921, English churchman who became Archbishop of Canterbury in 1980.

run-down /rʌn-'daʊn/, *adj.*; /'rʌn-daʊn/, *n.* ◇*adj.* **1.** in a poor state of health; depressed, sick or tired. **2.** in need of repair. ◇*n.* **3.** a short review or summary: *to give a run-down of events.*

rune /ruːn/, *n.* any of the characters of an alphabet used by the ancient Germanic-speaking peoples. [Icel] —**runic,** *adj.*

rung[1] /rʌŋ/, *v.* past participle of **ring**[2].

rung[2] /rʌŋ/, *n.* **1.** one of the crosspieces forming the steps of a ladder. **2.** a rounded or shaped stick, rod, etc., as between the legs of a chair. [ME; OE *hrung*]

run-in /'rʌn-ɪn/, *n. Colloq.* a disagreement; argument.

runnel /'rʌnəl/, *n.* **1.** a small stream or rivulet. **2.** a small channel, as for water. [OE *rynel(e)*]

runner /'rʌnə/, *n.* **1.** a competitor in a race. **2.** a messenger. **3.** something in or on which something else moves, as the strips of wood that guide a drawer, etc. **4.** either of the long pieces of wood or metal on which a sledge, etc., slides. **5.** the blade of a skate. **6.** a long, narrow rug, used in a hall or staircase. **7.** a long, narrow strip of linen, lace, etc., for placing across a table. **8.** *Bot.* a slender stem lying flat on the ground, which sends out roots, thus producing new plants. **9.** → **sandshoe.**

runner bean, *n.* a climbing herb, commonly grown for the long green pods, which are used for food; string bean; green bean.

runner-up /rʌnər-'ʌp/, *n.* the competitor, player, or team finishing in second place.

running /'rʌnɪŋ/, *n.* **1.** the act of someone or something that runs. **2.** smuggling: *gun-running.* **3.** managing; directing: *the running of a business.* **4. in (out of) the running,** having a chance (no chance) of success. ◇*adj.* **5.** going at a run. **6.** (of plants) climbing. **7.** moving easily or smoothly. **8.** (of a rope) moving when pulled. **9.** (of a knot) slipping easily. **10.** (of a machine) operating. **11.** (of measurement) straight-line; linear. **12.** (of handwriting) → **cursive. 13.** (of a stream) flowing. **14.** liquid; fluid. **15.** current: *the running expenses.* **16.** going on continuously: *a running commentary.* **17.** (of a pattern) repeated continuously. **18.** following one after the other (placed after the noun): *for three nights running.* **19.** performed with, by, or during a run: *a running jump.* **20.** (of a sore, etc.) discharging fluid.

running stitch, *n.* a small, even stitch made by passing the thread up and down through the cloth.

runny /'rʌni/, *adj.* **1.** (of matter) fluid or tending to flow. **2.** tending to flow with liquid: *a runny nose.*

Runnymede /'rʌnimiːd/, *n.* a meadow on the southern bank of the river Thames, west of London in Surrey; the supposed place of the signing of the Magna Carta by King John, 1215.

run-off /'rʌn-ɒf/, *n.* **1.** a final contest held after a principal one. **2.** something which runs off, as rain which flows off from the land in streams.

run-of-the-mill /'rʌn-əv-ðə-mɪl/, *adj.* ordinary; mediocre.

run-on /'rʌn-ɒn/, *adj.* **1.** of text which is run on without setting back from the margin: *a run-on entry in a dictionary.* ◇*n.* **2.** run-on text matter.

runt /'rʌnt/, *n.* **1.** an undersized animal, person, or thing. **2.** the smallest in a litter, as of pigs. **3.** (*offensive*) a puny person. [OE *hrunta (in *Hrunting* name of sword in *Beowulf*)]

runway /'rʌnweɪ/, *n.* a paved or cleared strip on which aeroplanes land and take off; airstrip.

Runyon /'rʌnjən/, *n.* (**Alfred**) **Damon,** 1880–1946, US writer and journalist; best known work *Guys and Dolls* (1932).

rupee /ruː'piː/, *n.* **1.** the unit of currency of India. **2.** any of various similar units, as the currencies of Pakistan, Sri Lanka, Mauritius, and Muscat and Oman. *Abbrev.:* R, Re [Hind, from Skt: wrought silver]

rupiah /'ruːpiə/, *n.* the unit of currency of Indonesia. [Malay, from Hind: RUPEE]

rupture /'rʌptʃə/, *n., v.,* **-tured, -turing.** ◇*n.* **1.** the act or result of breaking or bursting. **2.** a loss of friendly or peaceful relations. **3.** *Med.* → **hernia.** ◇*v.t.* **4.** to break or burst (a blood vessel, etc.). **5.** to cause a loss of (good relations, etc.). ◇*v.i.* **6.** to suffer a break or rupture. [L]

rural /ˈrurəl/, *adj.* **1.** of, relating to, or characteristic of the country (as distinguished from the city). **2.** of or relating to agriculture: *rural economy.* [ME, from L]

ruse /ruz/, *n.* a trick; stratagem. [ME, n. use of obs. *ruse* to detour, from F]

Ruse /ˈrus/, *n.* **James,** 1760-1837, Australian convict and pioneer farmer, born in England; first emancipist to receive a land grant.

rush[1] /rʌʃ/, *v.i.* **1.** to move or go with speed, thoughtlessness, or violence. ◇*v.t.* **2.** to send or drive with speed or violence. **3.** to perform or complete (some process or activity) very or too quickly: *He rushed his dinner.* **4.** to attack with a rush: *He rushed his opponent and knocked him down.* **5.** *Colloq.* to put pressure on someone: *Don't rush me.* ◇*n.* **6.** the act of rushing. **7.** an unfriendly attack. **8. a.** a sudden movement, as in a particular direction: *He made a rush for the gun.* **b.** an eager rushing of people to some area: *He joined the gold rush.* **9.** a sudden coming or appearance: *a rush of blood to his face.* **10.** hurried activity: *the rush of city life.* **11.** a hurried condition: *to be in a rush.* **12.** a great demand for a type of goods, etc. (fol. by *on*): *There was a rush on coffee.* **13.** (*pl.*) *Films.* the first prints made after shooting a scene. ◇*adj.* **14.** requiring or done with haste: *a rush order.* **15.** characterised by a rush or press of work, traffic, etc.: *rush hour traffic.* [ME, from AF, from LL: push back, L refuse]

rush[2] /rʌʃ/, *n.* **1.** a grass-like plant with a hollow stem, found in wet or marshy places. **2.** a stem of such a plant, used for making chair bottoms, mats, baskets, etc. [OE *rysc(e)*]

Rushdie /ˈrʌʃdi/, *n.* **Salman** /ˈsalmən/, born 1947, Indian writer living in England; centre of a controversy over his novel *The Satanic Verses* (1988).

Rushmore /ˈrʌʃmɔ/, *n.* **Mount,** a mountain in the Black Hills of south-western South Dakota; a national memorial with sculptures of the heads of US presidents Washington, Jefferson, Lincoln and Roosevelt carved into its side by Gutzon Borglum between 1927 and 1941. 1841 m.

rusk /rʌsk/, *n.* **1.** a piece of bread or cake crisped in the oven. **2.** a similar factory-made product, given esp. to babies when teething. [Sp or Pg: twist of bread, lit., screw]

Ruskin /ˈrʌskən/, *n.* **John,** 1819-1900, English author, art critic, and social reformer; wrote *Modern Painters,* a five-volume work published between 1843 and 1860.

Russell /ˈrʌsəl/, *n.* **1. Bertrand, 3rd Earl,** 1872-1970, English philosopher, mathematician, pacificist, and writer; Nobel prize for literature 1950. **2. John, 1st Earl** (*Lord John Russell*), 1792-1878, British statesman; prime minister 1846-52 and 1865-66.

russet /ˈrʌsət/, *n.* **1.** a reddish brown color. **2.** a coarse, reddish brown, home-made cloth formerly in use. **3.** a winter apple with a rough brownish skin. ◇*adj.* **4.** reddish brown. [ME, from OF: red, from L]

Russia /ˈrʌʃə/, *n.* a republic in eastern Europe and central and northern Asia, extending from the Gulf of Finland to the Pacific Ocean, the largest country in the world; a member of the CIS; the centre of the tsarist **Russian Empire** from the 15th century to the Revolution of 1917; the largest constituent republic of the Soviet Union 1922-91, known as the **Russian Soviet Federated Socialist Republic.** Pop. 147 400 000 (1989); 17 075 400 km². *Language:* Russian and many minority languages. *Currency:* rouble. *Cap.:* Moscow. Also, **Russian Federation.** Russian, **Rossija.** –**Russian,** *n.,* *adj.*

Russian Revolution /ˌrʌʃən revəˈluʃən/, *n.* **1.** the uprising of 12 March 1917 (**February Revolution**), by which the tsar's government was abolished and replaced by a constitutional government. **2.** the overthrow of this provisional government by a coup d'état on 7 November 1917 (**October Revolution**), which led to the establishment of the Soviet Union.

Russian roulette, *n.* a deadly game of chance, as formerly played by Russian army officers, in which each player in turn spins the cylinder of a revolver containing only one bullet, points it at his head, and pulls the trigger.

Russo-, a word part representing 'Russia'.

rust /rʌst/, *n.* **1.** the red or orange coating which forms on the surface of iron when exposed to air and water, consisting chiefly of ferric hydroxide and ferric oxide. **2.** any film or coating on metal due to oxidation, etc. **3.** a stain like iron rust. **4.** *Bot.* any of the various plant diseases caused by fungi, in which the leaves and stems become spotted and turn a red to brown color. **5.** a rust color. ◇*v.i.* **6.** to grow or become rusty. ◇*v.t.* **7.** to affect with or as if with rust. [ME and OE]

rustic /ˈrʌstɪk/, *adj.* **1.** of, relating to, or living in the country as distinguished from the city; rural. **2.** simple; unsophisticated. **3.** rude; uncouth. **4.** made of rough timber, as garden seats, etc. **5.** *Masonry.* having the surface rough or irregular, or the joints deeply sunk. ◇*n.* **6.** a country person, esp. of simple tastes. [late ME, from L]
–**rusticity,** *n.*

rustle /ˈrʌsəl/, *v.,* **-tled, -tling,** *n.* ◇*v.t.* **1.** to make a series of slight, soft sounds, as leaves, papers, etc., rubbing gently together. **2.** to cause such sounds by moving something. ◇*v.t.* **3.** to move so as to cause a rustling sound. **4.** to steal (cattle, etc.). **5.** *Colloq.* to move, bring, get, etc., by energetic action (oft. fol. by *up*): *to rustle up breakfast.* ◇*n.* **6.** the sound made by anything that rustles. [ME; OE *hrūxlian* make a noise] –**rustler,** *n.*

rusty /ˈrʌsti/, *adj.,* **-tier, -tiest. 1.** covered or affected with rust. **2.** consisting of or produced by rust. **3.** of the color of rust. **4.** faded or shabby. **5.** faulty through disuse or neglect: *My Latin is rusty.* [ME; OE *rustig*]

rut[1] /rʌt/, *n.,* *v.,* **rutted, rutting.** ◇*n.* **1.** a groove or track in the ground, esp. one made by a vehicle. **2.** any furrow, groove, etc. **3.** a fixed way of life: *to get into a rut.* ◇*v.t.* **4.**

to make a rut in; furrow. [orig. uncert.; ? var. of ROUTE]

rut² /rʌt/, *n., v.*, **rutted, rutting.** ◇*n.* **1.** the periodically occurring sexual excitement of the deer, goat, sheep, etc. ◇*v.i.* **2.** to be in the condition of rut. [ME, from OF, from L: a roaring]

ruthenium /ruˈθiniəm/, *n.* a steel-grey, rare metallic element, difficult to fuse, similar to platinum. *Symbol:* Ru; *at. no.:* 44; *at. wt:* 101.07. [NL, from ML *Ruthenia* Russia (so named because it was first found in ores from the Ural Mountains)]

Rutherford /ˈrʌðəfəd/, *n.* **1. Ernest Rutherford, 1st Baron,** 1871–1937, British physicist, born in NZ; formulated the first explanation of radioactivity; won the Nobel prize for chemistry (1908); discovered the nuclear structure of the atom in 1909. **2. Dame Margaret,** 1892–1972, British character actor.

ruthless /ˈruθləs/, *adj.* without pity; merciless. —**ruthlessness**, *n.*

rutile /ˈrutaɪl/, *n.* a common mineral, titanium dioxide, having a bright metallic shine and usu. of a reddish brown color. [F, from G, from L: red]

-ry, a suffix of abstract nouns of condition, practice (*heraldry, dentistry*), and of collectives (*peasantry, Jewry*). [short form of -ERY]

rye /raɪ/, *n.* **1.** a widely grown cereal grass with flowered spikes, producing grain used for making wholemeal flour. **2.** an American whisky containing rye grain. [ME; OE *ryge*]

rye-grass /ˈraɪ-gras/, *n.* any of a number of grasses many of which are valuable pasture grasses, as perennial rye, Wimmera rye, and Italian rye.

Ss

S, s, *n., pl.* **S's** or **Ss, s's** or **ss. 1.** the 19th letter of the English alphabet. **2.** something like the letter S in shape.

-s[1], a suffix forming adverbs, as *always, evenings, needs, unawares.* See **-ways.** [ME and OE *-es*, orig. gen. sing. ending]

-s[2], an ending which marks the third person sing. indicative active of verbs, as in *hits.* [northern ME and OE *-(e)s* (orig. ending of second person)]

-s[3], **1.** an ending which marks the regular plural of nouns, as in *dogs.* **2.** a quasi-plural ending occurring in nouns for which there is no proper singular, as in *trousers, shorts, scissors.* [OE *-as*, nom. and acc. pl. of certain classes of strong nouns]

s., *Symbol.* **1.** second. **2.** shilling [L *solidus*]; shillings [L *solidi*]. ◇*Abbrev.* **3.** singular. **4.** son. **5.** south.

's[1], an ending which marks the possessive singular of nouns, as in *man's.* [ME and OE *-es*]

's[2], an ending which marks the possessive plural of nouns, as in *men's.* [pl. use of poss. sing. ending]

's[3], a colloquial reduction of **1.** is: *he's here.* **2.** has: *he's just gone.* **3.** does: *what's he do now?* **4.** us: *let's go.*

S, *Abbrev.* **1.** Sea. **2.** South. **3.** Society. **4.** Summer. ◇*Symbol.* **5.** *Chem.* sulfur. **6.** *Phys.* entropy. **7.** *Phys.* siemens.

SA, *Abbrev.* **1.** South Australia. **2.** Salvation Army.

Sabah /'sabɑ/, *n.* an independent state of Malaysia, in north-eastern Borneo. Pop. 1 222 718 (1985 est.); 73 711 km². *Cap.*: Jesselton. Formerly, **North Borneo**.

Sabbath /'sæbəθ/, *n.* **1.** the seventh day of the week (Saturday) as the day of rest and worship among the Jews and certain Christian sects. **2.** the first day of the week (Sunday), similarly observed by most Christians. [ME and OE *sabat*, from L, from Gk, from Heb]

sabbatical /sə'bætɪkəl/, *adj.* **1.** of or relating to the Sabbath. **2.** bringing a period of rest. ◇*n.* **3.** Also, **sabbatical leave**. (in certain universities, etc.) a year, term, or other period, of freedom from teaching given to a teacher, as for study or travel.

Sabine /'sæbaɪn/, *n.* a member of an ancient people of central Italy who lived chiefly in the Apennines to the north-east of Rome and who were conquered by the Romans about 290 BC.

Sabin vaccine /ˌseɪbɪn væk'sin/, *n.* a vaccine taken by mouth, to protect against poliomyelitis. [from Albert B *Sabin*, b. 1906, US virologist, who developed it]

sackbut

sable /'seɪbəl/, *n.* **1.** a weasel-like mammal of cold areas, valued for its dark brown fur. **2.** a marten. **3.** the fur of the sable. **4.** *Heraldry.* the color black. ◇*adj.* **5.** made of the hair of the sable. **6.** *Poetic.* black; very dark. [ME, from OF, from Slavic]

sabot /'sæboʊ/, *n.* **1.** a wooden shoe made of a single piece of wood hollowed out, worn traditionally by farmers in France, Belgium, etc. **2.** a shoe with a thick wooden sole and sides, and a top of coarse leather. **3.** a class of small sailing boats, intended for children. [F: boot]

sabotage /'sæbətɑʒ/, *n., v.,* **-taged, -taging.** ◇*n.* **1.** deliberate injury to, or interference with, work, machinery, business, etc., by enemy agents, by workers during a trade argument, etc. **2.** any deliberate attack on or interference with a cause. ◇*v.t.* **3.** to injure or attack by sabotage. [F: make a noise with sabots; do work badly]

saboteur /sæbə'tɜ/, *n.* someone who practises sabotage. [F]

sabre /'seɪbə/, *n.* **1.** a heavy one-edged sword, usu. slightly curved. **2.** a light sword for fencing. [F, from G, from Hung]

sabre-toothed /'seɪbə-tuθt/, *adj.* having long and curved teeth, as some extinct mammals of the cat family.

sac /sæk/, *n.* a baglike structure in an animal or plant, one containing fluid. [L]

racchar-, a word part referring to sugar or saccharine. Also, **saccharo-** before consonants. [combining form representing Gk: sugar]

saccharide /'sækəraɪd/, *n.* any sugar or other carbohydrate, esp. a simple sugar.

saccharin /'sækərən, -krən/, *n.* a synthetic crystalline compound 400 times as sweet as cane sugar and used as a sweetener by diabetics and slimmers. Also, **saccharine**.

saccharine /'sækərən, -krən/, *adj.* **1.** of a sugary sweetness: *a saccharine smile.* ◇*n.* **2.** → **saccharin**.

sacerdotal /sæsə'doʊtl, sækə-, sætʃə-/, *adj.* of priests; priestly. [L *sacerdōtālis*]

sachet /'sæʃeɪ/, *n.* **1.** a small sealed bag used for packaging foodstuffs, cosmetics, etc. **2.** a small bag, case, pad, etc., containing perfumed substances for placing among clothing. [F, from L]

sack[1] /sæk/, *n.* **1.** a large bag of strong woven material, as for grain, potatoes, coal, etc. **2.** the amount which a sack will hold. **3.** a woman's loose-fitting, unbelted dress. **4. hit the sack,** *Colloq.* to go to bed. **5. the sack,** *Colloq.* dismissal, as from employment. ◇*v.t.* **6.** *Colloq.* to dismiss as from employment. [OE *sacc*, from L: bag, sackcloth, from Gk, from Heb]

sack[2] /sæk/, *v.t.* **1.** to rob, using violence after capture; plunder: *to sack a city.* ◇*n.* **2.** the violent robbing of a captured place; pillage: *the sack of Troy.* [F, from It: SACK[1]]

sackbut /'sækbət/, *n.* a medieval form of the trombone. [F: pull-push]

sackcloth /'sækklɒθ/, *n.* **1.** sacking. **2.** coarse cloth worn as a sign of sorrow for one's sins or another's death.

sacking /'sækɪŋ/, *n.* strong or coarse woven material of hemp, jute, or the like, used for making sacks, etc.

Sackville-West /ˌsækvəl-'wɛst/, *n.* **Victoria Mary** ('*Vita*'), 1892-1962, English novelist and poet; best known for her long poems including *The Land*.

sacral /'seɪkrəl/, *adj.* of or relating to sacred ceremonies. [L: sacred rite]

sacrament /'sækrəmənt/, *n.* **1.** *Church.* an outward or visible sign of grace given to believers. In the various Christian churches, the sacraments include some or all of the following: baptism; confirmation; the Eucharist or Lord's Supper; matrimony; penance; holy orders; and the anointing of the sick (extreme unction). **2.** (*oft. cap.*) the Eucharist, or Lord's Supper. **3.** something regarded as having a sacred character. **4.** a sign or token; symbol. **5.** an oath; solemn pledge. [ME, from L: oath, solemn engagement] —**sacramental**, *adj.*

sacred /'seɪkrəd/, *adj.* **1.** set aside or dedicated to a god or to some religious purpose; consecrated. **2.** worthy of religious respect; holy. **3.** relating to or connected with religion (opposed to *profane* and *secular*): *sacred music*. **4.** respectfully dedicated to some person or object: *a monument sacred to her memory*. **5.** regarded with deep respect: *the sacred memory of a dead hero*. **6.** not to be broken, damaged, violated, etc.: *sacred promises*. [ME, from L] —**sacredness**, *n.*

sacred cow, *n. Colloq.* something or somebody that escapes critical examination by virtue of popular respect, high office, etc.

sacrifice /'sækrəfaɪs/, *n., v.,* **-ficed, -ficing.** ◇*n.* **1.** the offering of life or some material possession, etc., to a god. **2.** the giving up or destroying of something prized for the sake of something considered as having a higher claim. **3.** something sacrificed. **4.** a loss suffered in selling something below its value. **5.** *Theol.* Christ's offering of His death to God for the sins of mankind. ◇*v.t.* **6.** to make a sacrifice of. ◇*v.i.* **7.** to offer or make a sacrifice. [ME, from F, from L] —**sacrificial**, *adj.*

sacrilege /'sækrəlɪdʒ/, *n.* **1.** violation or treating with disrespect of anything sacred or held sacred. **2.** an instance of this. [ME, from OF, from L] —**sacrilegious**, *adj.*

sacristy /'sækrəsti/, *n., pl.* **-ties.** a room in, or a building connected with, a church, etc., in which the sacred vessels, robes, etc., are kept. [ML *sacristia*]

sacro-, a word part **1.** meaning 'holy'. **2.** referring to the sacrum. [L: holy]

sacrosanct /'sækrəsæŋkt/, *adj.* especially sacred; inviolable. [L] —**sacrosanctity**, *n.*

sacrum /'seɪkrəm/, *n., pl.* **-cra** /-krə/. a bone composed (usu.) of five joined vertebrate and forming the back wall of the pelvis. [NL, from L: sacred (bone); so-called because used in sacrifices] —**sacral**, *adj.*

sad /sæd/, *adj.,* **sadder, saddest. 1.** sorrowful; mournful: *to feel sad*. **2.** expressing or showing sorrow: *sad looks*. **3.** causing sorrow: *a sad disappointment*. **4.** shocking; deplorable: *a sad state of affairs*. [ME; OE *sæd*] —**sadness**, *n.*

Sadat /sə'dæt/, *n.* **(Mohammed) Anwar El** /'ænwɑ el/, 1918-81, Egyptian statesman; president from 1970 until his assassination in 1981.

sadden /'sædn/, *v.t., v.i.* to make or become sad.

saddle /'sædl/, *n., v.,* **-dled, -dling.** ◇*n.* **1.** a seat for a rider on the back of a horse, etc. **2.** a similar seat on a bicycle, machine, etc. **3.** that part of an animal's back on which the saddle is placed. **4.** something like a saddle in shape or position, as a ridge between two mountains. **5.** (of mutton, venison, etc.) a cut including part of the backbone and both loins. **6. in the saddle,** in control. ◇*v.t.* **7.** to put a saddle upon (a horse, etc.). **8.** to load, as with a burden. ◇*v.i.* **9.** to put a saddle on a horse (oft. fol. by *up*). [OE *sadol*]

saddleback /'sædlbæk/, *n.* **1.** a type of animal or bird having marks on the back like a saddle. **2.** *Geog.* a saddle-shaped surface, as a ridge between two peaks. ◇*adj.* **3.** having a shape like a saddle.

saddler /'sædlə/, *n.* someone who makes or deals in saddlery.

saddlery /'sædləri/, *n., pl.* **-ries. 1.** saddles and other articles relating to the equipment of horses, etc. **2.** the work or shop of a saddler.

sadism /'sædɪzəm, 'seɪ-/, *n.* **1.** sexual satisfaction gained through inflicting pain and shame. **2.** any unhealthy enjoyment in causing mental or physical pain. [F *sadisme*, from the Marquis de Sade, 1740-1814, French soldier and novelist, notorious for the mixture of sex and cruelty in his books] —**sadist**, *n.,* *adj.* —**sadistic**, *adj.*

sadomasochism /ˌseɪdoʊ'mæsəkɪzəm, ˌsædoʊ-/, *n.* a disturbed condition of the mind shown by tendencies to inflict mental and physical pain on oneself and others. —**sadomasochist**, *n.*

safari /sə'fɑri/, *n., pl.* **-ris.** a journey, esp. for hunting. [Swahili, from Ar]

safe /seɪf/, *adj.,* **safer, safest,** *n., adv.* ◇*adj.* **1.** free from harm, injury, danger, or risk: *a safe place*. **2.** involving no risk of error, etc.: *a safe bet*. **3.** dependable; trustworthy: *a safe guide*. **4.** careful in avoiding danger; cautious: *a safe player; a safe driver*. **5.** placed beyond the power of doing harm: *a criminal safe in gaol*. **6. be on the safe side,** *Colloq.* to leave nothing to chance. ◇*n.* **7.** a steel or iron box for money, jewels, papers, etc. **8.** any structure, etc., for the storage or safe-keeping of articles: *a meat safe*. ◇*adv.* **9. play safe,** to act carefully. [ME, from OF, from L: uninjured]

safe-conduct /seɪf-'kɒndʌkt/, *n.* (an official paper allowing) safe passage through a region, esp. in time of war.

safeguard /'seɪfgɑd/, n. **1.** something serving as a protection or defence. **2.** a permit for safe travel through (politically) dangerous areas. ◇v.t. **3.** to guard; protect. [ME, from OF. See SAFE, GUARD]

safekeeping /seɪf'kipɪŋ/, n. protection; care.

safety /'seɪfti/, n., pl. **-ties. 1.** the state of being safe. **2.** the quality of protecting against hurt, injury, danger, or risk.

safety belt, n. **1.** → seat belt (def. 1). **2.** a belt or strap fastening a person working at a height to a fixed object, to prevent a fall.

safety catch, n. a locking or cut-off device, as one that prevents a gun from being fired accidentally.

safety fuse, n. **1.** a fuse in an electrical circuit which prevents overloading which might cause damage or fire in the circuit. **2.** a fuse for lighting explosives which burns slowly, allowing those who have lit it to move safely away.

safety pin, n. **1.** a pin bent back on itself to form a spring, with a guard to cover the point. **2.** a locking device on grenades, mines, etc., to keep them safe until required for use.

safety valve, n. **1.** a valve in a steam boiler, etc., which allows steam to escape if the pressure becomes too great. **2.** a harmless way for emotion to be let out.

safflower /'sæflaʊə/, n. a thistle-like herb, native to the Old World, with large orange-red flower heads, grown for seed-oil. [D, from OF, from It; ult. orig. uncert.]

saffron /'sæfrən/, n. **1.** a crocus with handsome purple flowers. **2.** an orange-colored product consisting of its dried stigmas, used to color food. **3.** Also, **saffron yellow**. a yellow-orange color. [ME, from F, from Ar]

sag /sæg/, v., **sagged, sagging**, n. ◇v.i. **1.** to sink or bend downwards by weight or pressure, esp. in the middle. **2.** to droop; hang loosely: *his shoulders sagged; his trousers sagged*. **3.** to drop or become less: *Prices sagged*. ◇n. **4.** the act, degree or place of sagging: *The sag in that pipeline needs repairing*. **5.** a drop in prices. [ME]

saga /'sɑgə/, n. **1.** a medieval Icelandic or Norse prose story about a person or family. **2.** a form of long novel, in French or English, about the members or generations of a family or social group. **3.** any long story about interesting events: *the saga of a voyage*. [Icel: story, history]

sagacious /sə'geɪʃəs/, adj. having good judgment and understanding; shrewd. [L] — **sagacity**, n.

sage[1] /seɪdʒ/, n., adj., **sager, sagest**. ◇n. **1.** a very wise man: *the seven sages of ancient Greece*. ◇adj. **2.** wise; judicious; prudent: *sage behavior*. [ME, from OF, from L: wise]

sage[2] /seɪdʒ/, n. a perennial plant whose greenish grey leaves are used for seasoning in cookery. [ME, from OF, from L]

Sagittarius /sædʒə'tɛəriəs/, n. a constellation and sign of the zodiac, represented by the Archer (a centaur drawing a bow). [L]

sago /'seɪgoʊ/, n. a starchy food from the soft inside of the trunk of various palms. [Malay]

sago grass, n. **1.** Also, **shot grass**. a hardy native grass common in north-western NSW, used as a stock feed. **2.** Also, **small burr grass**. a grass found in inland Australia, used as a stock feed.

Sahara /sə'hɑrə/, n. a desert in northern Africa, extending from the Atlantic to the Nile valley. About 9 065 000 km^2.

sahib /sɑb, 'sɑ-ɪb/, n. (in India) a term of respect used after a man's name. [Hind, from Ar: master, lit., friend]

said /sɛd/, v. **1.** past tense and past participle of **say**. ◇adj. **2.** named or mentioned before: *the said witness; the said amount*.

Saigon /saɪ'gɒn/, n. former name of **Ho Chi Minh City**.

sail /seɪl/, n. **1.** a sheet of canvas or nylon, etc., spread to the wind to make a ship or boat move through the water. **2.** something like this, as the part of an arm of a windmill which catches the wind. **3.** a voyage or trip in a ship or boat. **4.** a sailing ship or boat. **5.** sails taken as a whole: *to take in sail*. **6. set sail**, to begin a voyage. **7. under sail**, with sails set. ◇v.i. **8.** to travel in a ship or boat: *We are sailing to Britain*. **9.** to move along or be carried by wind, steam, etc.: *steamships sailing to Fremantle*. **10.** to manage a boat, esp. for sport: *He sails every Saturday*. **11.** to begin a journey by water: *We're sailing at dawn*. **12.** to move along in a fast or free manner: *clouds sailing overhead; She sailed into the room*. ◇v.t. **13.** to sail upon, over, or through: *to sail the seven seas*. **14.** to cause (a ship, etc.) to move along. [ME]

sailboard /'seɪlbɔd/, n. **1.** a lightweight, polyurethane surfboard with a mast and sail, on which the rider stands to manage the sail. ◇v.i. **2.** to ride on a sailboard. — **sailboarding**, n.

sailcloth /'seɪlklɒθ/, n. **1.** strong canvas or other material used for making sails. **2.** lightweight canvas material used for making clothing, curtains, etc.

sailfish /'seɪlfɪʃ/, n., pl. **-fishes**, (esp. collectively) **-fish**. a type of large sea fish with a very large dorsal fin like a sail, and related to the swordfish.

sailor /'seɪlə/, n. **1.** someone who makes a living by sailing; mariner; seaman. **2.** someone on the crew of a ship, who is not an officer. **3.** someone who sails, with reference to their tendency to become seasick: *a good sailor; a bad sailor*. [ME]

sailplane /'seɪlpleɪn/, n., **-planed, -planing**, v. ◇n. **1.** a glider designed for continuous flight using ascending air currents. ◇v.i. **2.** to soar in a sailplane.

saint /seɪnt/, n. **1.** someone formally recognised by the Christian Church, esp. Roman Catholic Church, as being of great holiness; a

saint canonised person. 2. any person of great holiness. 3. someone who makes a show of being holy. [ME, from OF, from L: consecrated] – **sainthood**, *n.* – **saintly**, *adj.*

St Andrews /sənt 'ændruz/, *n.* a town in eastern Scotland, in Fife, on the North Sea; famous golf links and the oldest university in Scotland. Pop.: 11 302 (1981).

St Andrew's Cross spider, *n.* a large reddish-colored spider, with white and yellow bands crossing its body, which constructs a white silken cross in the centre of its web.

Saint Bernard /sənt 'bɜnəd/, *n.* one of a breed of large dogs with a huge head, noted for their intelligence. [named after the hospice of *St Bernard*, on the pass of the Great St Bernard in the Alps, between Switzerland and Italy, where the dogs are kept by the monks for rescuing travellers from the snow]

sainted /'seɪntɪd/, *adj.* 1. listed among the saints. 2. saintly.

St Helena /sənt hə'linə/, *n.* a British island in the South Atlantic; Napoleon's place of exile, 1815–1821. Pop. 6000 (1986 est.); 121 km².

St Kilda /sənt 'kɪldə/, *n.* a city in southern Vic, within the Melbourne metropolitan area. Pop. 45 889 (1986).

St Lawrence /sənt 'lɒrəns/, *n.* a river in south-eastern Canada, flowing north-east from Lake Ontario, draining the five Great Lakes into the Gulf of St Lawrence. 1224 km.

St Lawrence Seaway, *n.* a waterway system developed jointly by the US and Canada to permit the passage of large ships from the Atlantic Ocean up the St Lawrence river through a series of canals and locks.

St Louis /sənt 'lui, 'luəs/, *n.* a city in the US, in eastern Missouri; a port on the Mississippi. Pop. 429 296 (1984).

St Nicholas /sənt 'nɪkələs/, *n.* a fourth-century bishop of Asia Minor, protector of children; the traditional Father Christmas.

St Paul's /sənt 'pɔlz/, *n.* a cathedral in London, built 1675–1711, designed by Sir Christopher Wren, in place of an earlier cathedral destroyed in 1666.

St Peter's /sənt 'pitəz/, *n.* the great metropolitan church of the see of Rome, one of the finest examples of Renaissance architecture, and especially noted for the structure of its dome.

St Petersburg /sənt 'pitəzbɜg/, *n.* a seaport in north-western Russia; capital of the Russian Empire 1703–1917. Pop. 4 359 000 (1986 est.). Formerly, (1914–24) **Petrograd**, (1924–91) **Leningrad**.

St Vincent /sənt 'vɪnsənt/, *n.* Gulf, an indentation of the Great Australian Bight on the SA coast east of the Yorke Peninsula. About 160 km long and 65 km wide.

St Vincent de Paul Society, *n.* a charitable organisation associated with the Roman Catholic Church; originated in Paris in 1833, founded in Australia in 1854.

St Vitus dance /sənt ˌvaɪtəs 'dæns/, *n.* a disease esp. common among children, characterised by irregular and uncontrollable movements. Also, **St Vitus's dance**. [from *St Vitus*, legendary martyr, venerated for his gift of healing, effected esp. on those who danced before his image at his festival]

saith /sɛθ/, *v. Archaic or Poetic.* third person singular present of **say**.

sake¹ /seɪk/, *n.* 1. cause or advantage; behalf: *for my sake.* 2. purpose or end: *for the sake of appearances.* [ME; OE *sacu* lawsuit, cause]

sake² /'sɑki/, *n.* a Japanese alcoholic drink made from rice. [Jap]

Sakharov /'sɑkərɒf/, *n.* **Andrei** /'ɑndreɪ/, 1921–89, Russian nuclear physicist and dissident; awarded the Nobel Peace prize in 1975.

sal /sæl/, *n. Chiefly Pharm.* salt. [L]

salaam /sə'lɑm/, *n.* 1. (in the East) a greeting meaning 'peace'. 2. a very low bow, esp. with the palm of the right hand placed on the forehead. ◊*v.i.* 3. to greet with a salaam. 4. to perform a salaam. ◊*v.t.* 5. to greet (someone) with a salaam. [Ar: peace]

salacious /sə'leɪʃəs/, *adj.* 1. lustful or lecherous. 2. (of writings, etc.) obscene; titillating. [L: lust] – **salacity**, *n.*

salad /'sæləd/, *n.* 1. a dish of raw vegetables, usu. served with a savory dressing. 2. raw or cooked foods served cold, usu. cut up and mixed with a dressing: *fruit salad; potato salad.* [ME, from OF, from OPr.: to salt, from L: salt]

salamander /'sæləmændə/, *n.* 1. a type of tailed amphibian, usu. living in water when very young, but later on land. 2. a mythical lizard or other reptile supposed to be able to live in fire. 3. someone or something able to live in great heat. 4. *Metall.* a mass of slag or metal remaining on the walls of a blast furnace. 5. a small portable stove used on building sites to keep materials dry. [ME, from OF, from L, from Gk] – **salamandrine**, *adj.*

salami /sə'lɑmi/, *n.* a type of sausage, originally Italian, with a strong or salty taste. [It (pl.), from L: salt]

salary /'sæləri/, *n., pl.* **-ries**. a payment made at fixed intervals for regular work, esp. work of fairly high skill or status. See **pay**. [ME, from AF, from L: orig., money allowed to soldiers for the purchase of salt] – **salaried**, *adj.*

sale /seɪl/, *n.* 1. the act of selling: *the sale of the house.* 2. a quantity sold: *to make a large sale.* 3. an opportunity to sell; demand: *slow sale.* 4. a special selling of goods, usu. at a lower price. 5. **for sale** or **on sale**, offered to be sold; offered to purchasers. [ME; late OE *sala*]

Sale /seɪl/, *n.* a city in Gippsland, Vic, north-east of Traralgon, on the Thomson River; administrative centre for the Bass Strait oil and gas fields. Pop. 13 559 (1986).

Salem /'seɪləm/, *n.* a seaport in the US, in north-eastern Massachusetts; execution of witches, 1692. Pop. 38 220 (1980).

salesperson /'seɪlzpɜsən/, *n.* a person who sells goods.

sales tax, *n.* a tax added to the retail price of goods.

salicylic acid /sæli'sılık/, *n.* an acid used as an antiseptic, in the manufacture of aspirin, and for rheumatic and gout conditions.

salient /'seıliənt/, *adj.* **1.** standing out or easily seen: *salient features*. **2.** jutting or pointing outwards, as an angle. [L: leaping forth] – **salience, saliency**, *n.*

salify /'sæləfaı/, *v.t.*, **-fied, -fying. 1.** to change into a salt, as by chemical combination. **2.** to mix or combine with a salt. [NL, from L: salt]

saline /'seılaın, -lin/, *adj.* **1.** salty or salt-like; containing or tasting like common table salt: *a saline solution*. **2.** of or relating to a salt of sodium, potassium, magnesium, etc. ◇*n.* **3.** a saline health drink or medicine. **4.** *Chem.* an isotonic solution of distilled water and sodium chloride. [L: salt] – **salinity**, *n.*

Salinger /'sælındʒə/, *n.* **J(erome) D(avid)**, born 1919, US author; noted for his novel *The Catcher in the Rye* (1951).

Salisbury[1] /'sɔlzbəri, -bri/, *n.* **Robert Gascoyne Cecil, 3rd Marquess of**, 1830–1903, British politician; Conservative prime minister 1885–86, 1886–92, 1895–1902.

Salisbury[2] /'sɔlzbəri, -bri/, *n.* **1.** a city in southern England in Wiltshire; cathedral has highest spire in England. Pop. 100 929 (1981). **2.** a city in the metropolitan area of Adelaide, SA; site for research into long-range weapons. Pop. 96 618 (1986).

Salisbury Plain, *n.* an extended elevated region in southern England, north of Salisbury; the site of Stonehenge.

saliva /sə'laıvə/, *n.* a watery fluid secreted in the mouth, which begins the process of digesting food; spittle. [ME, from L] – **salivary**, *adj.*

salivate /'sæləveıt/, *v.i.*, **-vated, -vating.** to produce saliva. [L: spat out, salivated] – **salivation**, *n.*

Salk /sɔlk/, *n.* **Jonas Edward**, born 1914, US bacteriologist; developed anti-poliomyelitis vaccine (**Salk vaccine**).

sallow[1] /'sæloʊ/, *adj.* of a yellowish, sickly color: *sallow skin*. [OE *salo*] – **sallowish**, *adj.*

sallow[2] /'sæloʊ/, *n.* → **willow**. [ME; OE *sealh*]

sally[1] /'sæli/, *n., pl.* **-lies**, *v.,* **-lied, -lying.** ◇*n.* **1.** a sudden rushing forth, esp. of soldiers upon an enemy; sortie; dash. **2.** a going out; excursion; expedition. **3.** a lively or clever remark. ◇*v.i.* **4.** to rush or set out: *The soldiers sallied forth from the ruined tower; to sally forth on a shopping spree.* [F: issuing forth, outrush, from L]

sally[2] /'sæli/, *n., pl.* **-lies.** any of various Australian trees thought to look like the willow, esp. wattles and gums, as the **black sally** of NSW and Vic.

salmon /'sæmən/, *n., pl.* **-mons**, (*esp. collectively*) **-mon**, *adj.* ◇*n.* **1.** → **Australian salmon**. **2.** a sea and freshwater food fish, introduced into Australia, with pink flesh, common in the northern Atlantic Ocean near the mouths of large rivers, or in lakes. **3.** any of various important food fishes of the North Pacific similar to the salmon. **4.** Also, **salmon pink**. a light yellowish-pink color. ◇*adj.* **5.** Also, **salmon pink**. of the color salmon. [ME, from AF, from L]

salmonella /sælmə'nelə/, *n., pl.* **-nellae** /-'neli/. a type of bacteria causing sickness in humans and animals, by food poisoning, etc. [named after Daniel E *Salmon*, 1850–1914, US pathologist]

Salome /sə'loʊmi/, *n. Bible*. the daughter of Herodias, whose dancing so pleased Herod that he gave her the head of John the Baptist at her request, as dictated by her mother. [LL, from Gk, from Heb *shālōm* peace]

salon /'sælɒn/, *n.* **1.** a living room in a large house; drawing room. **2.** an assembly of guests in such a room, esp. consisting of leaders in fashion, art, politics, etc. (common during the 17th and 18th centuries). **3.** a place used for the showing of works of art. **4.** a fashionable shop: *beauty salon; a dress salon*. [F, from It: hall, from Gmc]

saloon /sə'lun/, *n.* **1.** large public or dining room on a ship. **2.** → **saloon bar**. [F: SALON]

saloon bar, *n.* a well-appointed bar in a hotel.

salt /sɔlt, sɒlt/, *n.* **1.** a crystalline compound, sodium chloride, NaCl, occurring as a mineral, a part of sea water, etc., and used for seasoning and preserving food. **2.** *Chem.* an ionic compound formed when an inorganic acid and alkali react with (or neutralise) each other. **3.** (*pl.*) any of various salts used as purgatives: *Epsom salts*. **4.** anything which gives liveliness or sharpness: *His wit gives salt to the conversation*. **5.** *Colloq.* an experienced sailor: *an old salt*. **6. rub salt into the wound**, to make things worse; add insult to injury. **7. the salt of the earth**, (of people) the best kind. **8. take with a grain of salt**, to have little belief in; be sceptical. **9. worth one's salt**, capable; efficient; deserving one's pay. ◇*v.t.* **10.** to season with salt. **11.** to cure, preserve, or treat with salt. **12.** to provide with salt: *to salt cattle*. **13.** *Chem.* to add common salt to (a solution) in order to precipitate out a dissolved substance (fol. by *out*). **14.** to introduce a rich ore or other valuable matter, information, etc., to create a false appearance of value: *to salt a mine*. ◇*v.* **15. salt away** or **down**, *Colloq.* to lay or store away: *to salt a lot of money away*. ◇*adj.* **16.** containing or tasting of salt: *salt water*. **17.** cured or preserved with salt: *salt cod*. [ME; OE *sealt*] – **salty**, *adj.*

SALT /sɔlt/, *n.* Strategic Arms Limitation Talks, a series of negotiations between the US and the USSR, resulting in two treaties, SALT I (1972) and SALT II (1979), neither of which affected nuclear weapons. [abbrev.]

saltbush /'sɔltbʊʃ/, *n.* **1.** a type of drought-resistant grazing plant found in dry,

saltbush

saline and alkaline parts of Australia, North America and southern Africa. **2. the saltbush**, regions where saltbush is the main vegetation.

saltcellar /'sɒltselə/, n. a shaker or small dish, etc., for salt. [ME, from OF: salt, from L]

salt flat, n. **1.** a wide expanse of flat country in which the soil is very salty. **2.** → **saltpan**.

Salt Lake City, n. a city in the US, the capital of Utah, in the northern part, near Great Salt Lake; world capital of the Mormon Church. Pop. 158 440 (1986 est.).

salt-lick /'sɒlt-lɪk/, n. **1.** a place to which wild animals go to lick salt found naturally there. **2.** Agric. a block of salt, and sometimes minerals, etc., given to grazing animals to lick.

saltpan /'sɒltpæn/, n. a small basin flooded by salt deposits, the remains of an evaporated salt lake which may have entirely disappeared. Also, **salt flat**.

saltpetre /'sɒlt'piːtə/, n. → **nitre**. [ME, from ML: salt of the rock]

salt tablet, n. a tablet of common salt used to prevent muscular cramps when working in heat.

salubrious /sə'luːbriəs/, adj. (esp. of air, climate, etc.) healthy; health-giving. [L] **– salubrity**, n.

salutary /'sæljətri/, adj. **1.** health-giving; healthful. **2.** doing good; wholesome; beneficial: *a salutary shock*. [L, from *Salus*, Roman goddess of health and prosperity]

salutation /sæljə'teɪʃən/, n. **1.** the act of saluting or greeting. **2.** something said, written, or done as a greeting. **– salutatory**, adj.

salute /sə'luːt/, v., **-luted, -luting**, n. ◇v.t. **1.** to greet with words or movements of goodwill, respect, etc. **2.** *Mil., Navy.* to pay respect to or honor by some formal act, as raising the right hand to the side of the head, presenting arms, firing cannon, dipping colors, etc. ◇v.i. **3.** *Mil., Navy.* to give a salute. ◇n. **4.** the act of saluting; salutation; greeting. **5.** Also, **Australian salute, Barcoo salute**. (*joc.*) the movement of hand and arm to brush away flies from one's face. [ME, from L: greet]

salvage /'sælvɪdʒ/, n., v., **-vaged, -vaging**. ◇n. **1.** the act of saving property, such as a ship or aircraft or their cargo, from some peril. **2.** the saving of anything from loss or danger. **3.** property or a thing so saved. ◇v.t. **4.** to save from shipwreck, fire, etc. **5.** to recover or save: *to salvage his self-respect*. [ML, from L: save] **– salvager**, n.

salvation /sæl'veɪʃən/, n. **1.** the act of saving or condition of being saved. **2.** a source, cause, or means of deliverance: *to be the salvation of a friend*. **3.** *Theol.* deliverance from the power and punishment of sin; redemption. [ME, from LL]

Salvation Army /sæl'veɪʃən 'ami/, n. a quasi-military organisation, founded in 1865 by William Booth; renowned for its charitable work among the poor and homeless.

salvation Jane, n. → **Paterson's curse**.

salve /sælv, sav/, n., v., **salved, salving**. ◇n. **1.** a healing ointment. **2.** anything that soothes. ◇v.t. **3.** to soothe as if with salve: *to salve one's conscience*. [ME; OE *sealf*]

salver /'sælvə/, n. a tray. [Sp, from L]

salvo /'sælvoʊ/, n., pl. **-vos, -voes**. **1.** a discharge of guns in regular succession, oft. as a salute. **2.** a round of cheers, applause, etc. [It, from OF, from L: be in good health]

sal volatile /sæl və'lætəli/, n. volatile ammonium carbonate used as an inhalant to relieve faintness, dizziness, etc.; smelling salts.

Salzburg /'sæltsbəg, 'zaltsbʊəg/, n. a historic city in western Austria, near the German border; birthplace of Mozart; noted for its annual music festival. Pop. 139 426 (1981).

SAM /sæm/, Abbrev. surface-to-air missile.

samarium /sə'mɛəriəm/, n. a rare-earth metallic element. *Symbol:* Sm; *at. no.:* 62; *at. wt:* 150.35.

samba /'sæmbə/, n. a ballroom dance of Brazilian (orig. African) origin.

sambo /'sæmboʊ/, n., pl. **-bos**. (*usu. cap.*) (*offensive*) a Negro. [probably from Sp]

same /seɪm/, adj. **1.** being the very one just mentioned; identical: *the very same man*. **2.** being one or identical, though having different names, etc. **3.** agreeing in kind, amount, etc.; corresponding: *two boxes of the same size*. **4.** unchanged: *She has the same kind face she always had*. ◇pron. **5.** the same person or thing: *She's the same as ever*. **6. the same**, in the same manner (used as an adverb): *If you do it the same you can't go wrong*. **7. all the same, a.** even so; nevertheless. **b.** unimportant; immaterial: *Whether you come or not is all the same to me*. **8. just the same, a.** in the same way. **b.** even so; nevertheless. [ME and OE]

Samoa /sə'moʊə/, n. a group of islands in the southern Pacific. See **Western Samoa** and **American Samoa**.

samovar /'sæməva/, n. a metal urn used in Russia and elsewhere for heating the water for making tea. [Russ: self-boiler]

Samoyed /'sæmɔɪd/, n. one of a breed of Russian dogs, medium in size, with a coat of long, thick, white hair. [Russ: self-eater]

sampan /'sæmpæn/, n. a small Chinese boat, with one oar at the stern. [Chinese: three boards]

sample /'sæmpəl/, n., adj., v., **-pled, -pling**. ◇n. **1.** a small part of anything or one of a number, meant to show the quality, style, etc., of the whole; specimen. ◇adj. **2.** serving as a specimen: *a sample copy*. ◇v.t. **3.** to take a sample or samples of; test or judge by a sample. [ME]

sampler /'sæmplə/, n. **1.** someone who samples. **2.** a piece of embroidery showing a beginner's skill in needlework. [ME, from OF, from L: EXAMPLE]

Samson /'sæmsən/, n. *Old Testament*. a performer of herculean exploits, the fifteenth of the 'judges' of Israel. [see Judges 13–16]

Samuel /'sæmjuəl/, n. Old Testament. 1. a Hebrew judge and prophet. 2. either of the two Old Testament books bearing his name. [see I Samuel 1-3, 8-15]

samurai /'sæmjəraɪ/, n., pl. -rai. (in feudal Japan) 1. a member of the military class. 2. a servant of a Japanese feudal noble, holding land or receiving a payment in rice or money. [Jap]

San Andreas Fault /sæn æn'dreɪəs/, n. a major fracture in the earth's crust running through western California; site of many tremors and earthquakes, including the San Francisco earthquake in 1906; about 960 km long.

sanatorium /sænə'tɔriəm/, n., pl. -toriums, -toria /-'tɔriə/. an establishment for the treatment of sick people who need to rest and live for a time in a healthy climate: *a tuberculosis sanatorium*. Also, **sanitarium**. [NL, from L: healed]

sanctify /'sæŋktəfaɪ/, v.t., -fied, -fying. 1. to make holy. 2. to make acceptable; sanction: *a practice sanctified by use*. [L: make holy] —**sanctification**, n. —**sanctifier**, n. —**sanctifiable**, adj.

sanctimonious /sæŋktə'moʊniəs/, adj. making a show of holiness; affecting sanctity. —**sanctimony**, n.

sanction /'sæŋkʃən/, n. 1. acceptance or approval; authorisation; ratification: *The plans now have the sanction of the Council*. 2. powerful feelings or agreement among people about what is right or wrong: *social sanctions against crime*. 3. *Internat. Law*. action by one or more countries towards another designed to force it to keep certain laws: *trade sanctions*. ◊v.t. 4. to approve or authorise; ratify: *We will sanction its use*. [L]

sanctity /'sæŋktəti/, n., pl. -ties. holiness. [L]

sanctuary /'sæŋktʃəri, 'sæŋktʃuəri/, n., pl. -ries. 1. a sacred or holy place. 2. the part of a church around the altar; chancel. 3. a. (formerly) a church or other holy place where people running away from the law or from oppression were safe from arrest; asylum. b. the protection given by this. 4. a place protected by law where plants and animals are left in peace; reserve. [ME, from L]

sanctum /'sæŋktəm/, n., pl. -tums, -ta /-tə/. 1. a sacred or holy place. 2. an especially private place; retreat: *inner sanctum*. [L (neut.): holy]

sand /sænd/, n. 1. coarse or fine grains from rocks that have been broken up or worn away. 2. (*usu. pl.*) a region made up mainly of sand. 3. a dull reddish yellow color. ◊v.t. 4. to smooth or polish with sand or sandpaper. 5. to sprinkle, fill or mix with, or as with, sand. [ME and OE] —**sandy**, adj.

Sand /sænd, sɒd/, n. **George** (*Madame Amandine Lucile Aurore Dudevant*), 1804-76, French novelist.

sandal /'sændl/, n. a kind of shoe, made of a sole fastened to the foot by straps. [F]

sandalwood /'sændlwʊd/, n. a sweet-smelling wood of certain Asian and Australian trees, used for ornamental carving and burnt as incense. Also, **santal**. [*sandal* (from ML, from Skt) + WOOD]

sandbag /'sændbæg/, n., v., -bagged, -bagging. ◊n. 1. a bag filled with sand, used to form supporting or protecting walls. ◊v.t. 2. to provide with sandbags.

sandbank /'sændbæŋk/, n. a bank of sand in the sea or a river, formed by currents and often uncovered at low tide. Also, **sandbar**.

sandblast /'sændblast/, n. 1. (a machine giving out) a blast of air or steam loaded with sand, used to clean, grind, cut, or decorate hard surfaces. ◊v.t. 2. to clean, etc., with a sandblast.

sandfly /'sændflaɪ/, n., pl. -flies. a small bloodsucking fly, carrier of several human diseases.

sandman /'sændmæn/, n. a man in a fairytale who makes children sleepy by putting sand in their eyes.

sandmining /'sændmaɪnɪŋ/, n. the mining of quartz sands for minerals, as rutile and zircon.

sandpaper /'sændpeɪpə/, n. 1. strong paper coated with a layer of sand, used for smoothing or polishing. ◊v.t. 2. to smooth or polish with or as with sandpaper.

sandpiper /'sændpaɪpə/, n. a type of shorebird that migrates to Australia from the Northern Hemisphere.

sandshoe /'sænʃu, 'sændʃu/, n. a rubber-soled canvas shoe, worn esp. for sport.

sandsoap /'sændsoʊp/, n. an abrasive soap for removing stains.

sandstone /'sændstoʊn/, n. a type of rock formed by the consolidation of sand, the grains being held together by a cement of silica, lime, gypsum, or iron salts.

sand trout, n. → **congolli**.

sandwich /'sænwɪtʃ, -wɪdʒ/, n. 1. two slices of bread with a layer of meat, cheese, etc., between. 2. anything formed by putting a layer of something between two others. **3. the meat in the sandwich**, *Colloq*. a person caught between two opposing parties. ◊v.t. 4. to put between two other things: *The child was sandwiched between two adults in the crush*. [named after the 4th Earl of *Sandwich*, 1718-92]

sandworm /'sændwɜm/, n. a worm found in the sandy mud in estuaries or brackish waters of Australia

sandy blight, n. → **trachoma**.

sane /seɪn/, adj., **saner**, **sanest**. 1. free from madness or mental illness: *a sane person*. 2. sensible or reasonable: *a sane decision*. [L: sound, healthy]

San Francisco /sæn frən'sɪskoʊ/, n. a seaport in western California, on San Francisco Bay; earthquake and fire, 1906. Pop. 749 000 (1986 est.).

sang /sæŋ/, v. past tense of **sing**.

sangfroid

sangfroid /sɒŋ'frwa/, *n.* coolness of mind; calmness; composure. [F: cold blood]

sanguine /'sæŋgwən/, *adj.* **1.** naturally cheerful and hopeful: *a sanguine temperament*. **2.** hopeful or confident: *sanguine expectations*. **3.** ruddy: *a sanguine complexion*. [ME, from L: blood]

sanitarium /sænə'teəriəm/, *n., pl.* **-tariums, -taria** /-'teəriə/. → **sanatorium**. [NL, from L: health]

sanitary /'sænətri/, *adj.* **1.** of or relating to health or the conditions affecting health, esp. cleanliness, care in preventing disease, etc. **2.** free from dirt, germs, etc. [L: health]

sanitary can, *n.* a tarred can or tin in an outside toilet used to hold excreta for collection and emptying.

sanitary cart, *n.* a truck used to collect and empty full sanitary cans. Also, **sanitary wagon**.

sanitary napkin, *n.* an absorbent pad worn during menstruation to absorb the flow from the womb. Also, **sanitary pad**.

sanitation /sænə'teɪʃən/, *n.* **1.** the study and work of protecting public health by proper sewerage and drainage. **2.** a drainage system.

sanity /'sænəti/, *n.* **1.** the condition of being sane; soundness of mind. **2.** soundness of judgment. [L]

sank /sæŋk/, *v.* past tense of **sink**.

Sanskrit /'sænskrɪt/, *n.* an extinct Indic language, the ancient classical literary language of India; one of the oldest recorded Indo-European languages. Also, **Sanscrit**. [Skt *samskrita* prepared, cultivated] —**Sanskritic**, *adj.* —**Sanskritist**, *n.*

sans serif /sæn 'serəf/, *n. Printing*. a style of type without serifs.

Santa Claus /'sæntə klɔz/, *n.* the patron saint of children, giver of gifts on Christmas Eve; Father Christmas; Saint Nicholas. [d. D *Sante Klaas* St Nicholas]

Santa Gertrudis /ˌsæntə gə'trudəs/, *n., pl.* **-dis** /-dəz/. a breed of beef cattle developed in the US from crossbreeding Brahmans and Shorthorns. They are found in tropical areas of northern Australia where they are noted for their heat tolerance and resistance to parasites. [named after *Santa Gertrudis*, an area in Texas, US, where the breed was developed]

Santa Maria /ˌsæntə mə'riə/, *n.* the flagship of Columbus in his voyage of 1492.

Santiago /sænti'agoʊ/, *n.* the capital of Chile, in the central part. Pop. 4 804 000 (metropolitan) (1986 est.). Also, **Santiago de Chile**.

Santo Domingo /ˌsæntoʊ də'mɪŋgoʊ/, *n.* the capital of the Dominican Republic on the southern coast; the first European settlement in America (1496). Pop. 1 410 000 (1983 est.).

Santos-Dumont /sɒtɒs-dymɔ̃/, *n.* **Alberto** /al'beətoʊ/, 1873–1932, Brazilian inventor of dirigibles and aeroplanes, in France.

São Paulo /saʊ paʊ'loʊ/, *n.* the largest city in Brazil, in the southern part; the capital of São Paulo state. Pop. 31 263 000 (1987 est.).

918

Sarajevo

sap[1] /sæp/, *n.* **1.** juice circulating in a plant, carrying water, food, etc. **2.** → **sapwood**. **3.** *Colloq.* a fool or weak person. [ME; OE *sæp*]

sap[2] /sæp/, *n., v.*, **sapped, sapping.** ◇*n.* **1.** a deep trench for approaching an enemy position. ◇*v.t.* **2.** to weaken; undermine: *Exhaustion sapped their strength.* [earlier *zappe*, from It: spade, hoe]

sapient /'seɪpiənt/, *adj.* wise; sage. [late ME, from L: being wise] —**sapience**, **sapiency**, *n.*

sapling /'sæplɪŋ/, *n.* **1.** a young tree. **2.** a young person.

saponify /sə'pɒnɪfaɪ/, *v.t.*, **-fied, -fying.** *Chem.* **1.** to change (a fat) into soap by treating with an alkali. **2.** to decompose (an ester), forming the corresponding alcohol and salt. [NL, from L: soap] —**saponification**, *n.*

sapper /'sæpə/, *n. Mil.* a private in the Royal Australian Engineers. See Appendix. [SAP[2] + -ER[1]]

sapphire /'sæfaɪə/, *n.* **1.** a variety of corundum, esp. a transparent blue kind valued as a gem. **2.** a deep blue color. ◇*adj.* **3.** deep blue. [L, from Gk] —**sapphirine**, *adj.*

Sappho /'sæfoʊ/, *n.* fl. c. 600 BC, Greek lyric poet, living on Lesbos. —**Sapphic**, *adj.*

Sapporo /'sapɒroʊ, 'sæp-/, *n.* a city in northern Japan, on Hokkaido island. Pop. 1 567 724 (1986 est.).

sapro-, a word part meaning 'rotten' or 'saprophytic', as in *saprogenic*. Also, before vowels, **sapr-**. [Gk, combining form of *saprós* putrid]

saprogenic /sæprə'dʒɛnɪk/, *adj.* **1.** producing decay, as certain bacteria. **2.** formed by decay. Also, **saprogenous** /sæ'prɒdʒənəs/.

saprophyte /'sæprəfaɪt/, *n.* any plant that lives on dead organic matter, as certain fungi and bacteria. —**saprophytic**, *adj.*

sapwood /'sæpwʊd/, *n.* in a woody plant, the softer part of the wood between the inner bark and the hard central wood.

saraband /'særəbænd/, *n.* **1.** a popular and vigorous Spanish castanet dance. **2.** (a piece of music for) a slow, stately Spanish dance in triple time. [F, from Sp; probably of Oriental orig.]

Saracen /'særəsən/, *n.* **1.** (among the later Romans and Greeks) a member of the nomadic tribes on the Syrian borders of the Roman Empire. **2.** (in later use) an Arab. **3.** any Muslim or Mohammedan, esp. those who opposed the Crusades. [LL *Saracēnus*, from LGk]

Sarah /'seərə/, *n. Old Testament.* the wife of Abraham and mother of Isaac. [see Genesis 17:15–22, etc.]

Sarah Island, *n.* an island in Macquarie Harbor, western Tas, used as a convict settlement 1822–34.

Sarajevo /særə'jeɪvoʊ/, *n.* the capital city of Bosnia – Herzegovina in the central part;

Sarajevo / satellite

the assassination of the Austrian archduke Franz Ferdinand here 28 June 1914, precipitated World War I. Pop. 319 017 (1981). Also, **Serajevo** /særə'jeɪvou/.

Sarawak /'særəwæk, sə'rawək/, n. a former British colony in north-western Borneo; now an independent state in the Federation of Malaysia. Pop. 1 477 428 (1985 est.); about 129 500 km². *Cap.:* Kuching.

sarc-, a word part meaning 'flesh', as in *sarcous*. Also, before consonants, **sarco-**. [Gk *sark-*, combining form of *sárx*]

sarcasm /'sakæzəm/, n. harsh or bitter words intended to hurt another person, esp. by saying the opposite of what is meant. [LL, from LGk: sneer]

sarcastic /sa'kæstɪk/, adj. 1. marked by, of the nature of, or relating to sarcasm: *a sarcastic reply*. 2. using, or given to the use of, sarcasm.

sarcophagus /sa'kɒfəgəs/, n., pl. **-gi** /-gaɪ/, **-guses**. 1. a stone coffin, esp. a decorated one. 2. (among the ancient Greeks) a type of stone supposed to consume the flesh of corpses, used for coffins. [L, from Gk: orig. adj., flesh-eating]

sard /sad/, n. brownish red chalcedony, or a piece of it, used in jewellery, etc. [ME *saarde*, from L *sarda*]

sardine /sa'din/, n., pl. **-dines**, (esp. collectively) **-dine**. 1. the young of the common pilchard, oft. preserved in oil and canned for food. 2. any of various similar fishes used in this way. [ME, from It, from L: type of fish]

Sardinia /sa'dɪniə/, n. 1. Italian, **Sardegna**. a large island in the Mediterranean, west of Italy; with small nearby islands it comprises a region of Italy. Pop. 1 638 172 (1986 est.); 24 089 km². *Cap.:* Cagliari. 2. a former kingdom (1720–1860), including this island and Savoy, Piedmont, and Genoa (after 1815) in north-western Italy; ruled by the House of Savoy. *Cap.:* Turin.

sardonic /sa'dɒnɪk/, adj. sarcastic or scornfully superior: *a sardonic smile*. [F, from L, from Gk: Sardinian, from a Sardinian plant said to bring on convulsions resembling laughter]

sardonyx /'sadənɪks/, n. a type of onyx containing layers or bands of sard. [ME, from L, from Gk. See SARD, ONYX]

Sargasso Sea /sa,gæsoʊ 'si/, n. a part of the North Atlantic, between the Azores and the West Indies. [named after the floating masses of *sargassum* seaweed found in this area]

sari /'sari/, n., pl. **-ris**. a long piece of cotton or silk, the main outer garment of Hindu women, worn round the body with one end over the head or shoulder. [Hind]

Sarich /'særɪtʃ/, n. **Ralph**, born 1938, Australian engineer; inventor of the orbital engine in the early 1970s.

sarking /'sakɪŋ/, n. sheet material laid under tiles, etc., for insulation or waterproofing.

sarong /sə'rɒŋ/, n. the main garment for both sexes in the Malay Archipelago, etc.,

consisting of a piece of cloth wrapped around the lower part of the body like a skirt. [Malay]

sarsaparilla /saspə'rɪlə/, n. 1. any of various climbing or trailing plants with a root much used medicinally. 2. an extract or other preparation made of it. [Sp]

sartorial /sa'tɔriəl/, adj. of or relating to clothes or dress, usu. men's: *sartorial splendor*. [L: of a tailor]

Sartre /'satrə/, n. **Jean Paul** /ʒɒ̃ 'poʊl/, 1905–80, French writer and philosopher; exponent of existentialism; works include the play *Huis Clos* (1944).

sash¹ /sæʃ/, n. a long band or scarf of silk, etc., worn over one shoulder or round the waist. [Ar: turban]

sash² /sæʃ/, n. 1. a movable window framework in which panes of glass are set. ◇v.t. 2. to provide with sashes or with windows having sashes. [ME; alteration of CHASSIS]

sassafras /'sæsəfræs/, n. 1. an American tree known for the aromatic bark of its root, oft. used medicinally and for flavoring. 2. any of several Australian trees with sweet-smelling bark, as the canary sassafras, or the southern sassafras. [Sp; orig. uncert.]

Sassenach /'sæsənæk/, n. an Englishman (a name applied by the Scottish inhabitants of the British Isles). [Gaelic *Sasunnach* Englishman, from *Sasunn* Saxon]

sat /sæt/, v. past tense and past participle of *sit*.

Sat, *Abbrev.* Saturday.

Satan /'seɪtn/, n. the chief evil spirit; the great enemy of man; the devil. See **Lucifer**. [ME and OE, from L, from Gk, from Heb: adversary]

satanellus /sætə'nɛləs/, n. → **native cat**. [NL: little devil]

satanic /sə'tænɪk/, adj. 1. of Satan. 2. typical of or suitable to Satan; extremely wicked; diabolical. Also, **satanical**.

Satanism /'seɪtənɪzəm/, n. 1. worship of Satan. 2. a form of such worship which copies Christian ceremonies in a debased form. – **Satanist**, n.

satay /'sateɪ/, n. cubes of spiced meat grilled on a skewer and covered with a hot peanut or soya-based sauce. [Malay]

satchel /'sætʃəl/, n. a bag with shoulder-straps for carrying school books, usu. on the back. [ME, from OF: sack, from L]

sate¹ /seɪt/, v.t., **sated**, **sating**. 1. to satisfy (any appetite or desire) to the full. 2. to fill uncomfortably full; surfeit; glut. [b. obs. *sade* satiate (OE *sadian*) and L *sat* enough]

sate² /sæt, seɪt/, v. *Archaic*. past tense and past participle of *sit*.

satellite /'sætəlaɪt/, n., v., **-lited**, **-liting**. ◇n. 1. a small body which moves around a planet; moon. 2. someone or something which depends on, or is dominated by, another. 3. Also, **artificial satellite**. an object, usu. containing recording and transmitting instruments,

satellite

for launching into orbit round the earth or another planet, for purposes of communication, research, etc. ◇*v.t.* **4.** to send (pictures, messages, etc.) by satellite. [L: attendant, guard]

satellite town, *n.* a small town or city dependent on local industry but having economic links with a large city from which it is separated by open country.

satiate /'seɪʃɪeɪt/, *v.t.*, **-ated, -ating. 1.** to supply with too much of something, so as to disgust or weary; surfeit; cloy. **2.** to satisfy the full; sate. [L: filled full] — **satiation**, *n.*

satin /'sætn/, *n.* **1.** a very smooth, shiny cloth, usu. rayon or silk. ◇*adj.* **2.** of or like satin; smooth; glossy. [ME, from OF, from It, from L: silk] — **satiny**, *adj.*

satin stitch, *n.* an embroidery stitch in close parallel lines, which gives a satiny finish.

satinwood /'sætnwʊd/, *n.* any of several small Australian trees, as the scented satinwood or coachwood.

satire /'sætaɪə/, *n.* **1.** the use of irony, sarcasm, ridicule, etc.; the showing up of something as very silly, or as evil, by representing it in a laughable way. **2.** a literary work which does this. [L: medley] — **satiric, satirical**, *adj.*

satirise or **satirize** /'sætəraɪz/, *v.t.*, **-rised, -rising.** to make (someone or something) the object of satire. — **satirist**, *n.*

satisfaction /sætəs'fækʃən/, *n.* **1.** the act of satisfying or condition of being satisfied. **2.** the cause of being satisfied. **3.** the making good of a wrong; reparation. **4.** payment as for a debt or the fulfilling of obligations. [ME, from L]

satisfactory /sætəs'fæktəri, -tri-/, *adj.* giving satisfaction; fulfilling all demands or requirements: *a satisfactory answer.*

satisfy /'sætəsfaɪ/, *v.*, **-fied, -fying.** ◇*v.t.* **1.** to fulfil the desires, expectations or needs of (a person, etc.); gratify; content. **2.** to fulfil (a desire, expectation, need, etc.): *to satisfy hunger.* **3.** to convince; assure: *He satisfied himself that all had gone well.* **4.** to pay back (a debt, etc.). ◇*v.i.* **5.** to give satisfaction. [ME, from OF, from L: do enough] — **satisfier**, *n.*

satrap /'sætræp/, *n.* the governor of a province in ancient Persia. [ME, from L, from Gk, from OPers: lit., country-protector]

saturate /'sætʃəreɪt/, *v.t.*, **-rated, -rating. 1.** *Chem.* to cause (a substance) to unite with the greatest possible amount of another substance, through solution, chemical combination, or the like. **2.** to fill or load fully: *The market is saturated with goods.* **3.** to soak thoroughly; impregnate; imbue. [L: satisfied, saturated] — **saturated, saturable**, *adj.*

saturated compound, *n.* a compound whose molecules contain no double or triple bonds and which therefore has no free valency electrons.

saturation /sætʃə'reɪʃən/, *n.* **1.** the act or process of saturating. **2.** the resulting condition. **3.** *Weather.* a condition in the atmosphere corresponding to 100 per cent rela-

-saur

tive humidity. **4.** (of colors) the degree of purity or freedom from mixture with white.

Saturday /'sætədeɪ, -di/, *n.* the seventh day of the week, following Friday. [ME; OE *Sæterdæg, Sætern(es)dæg:* day of Saturn]

Saturn /'sætn/, *n.* **1.** *Rom Myth.* the god of agriculture and vegetation, whose reign was characterised by happiness and virtue. **2.** the second largest planet, the sixth in order from the sun.

saturnalia /sætə'neɪlɪə/, *n.pl.* any period of wild merrymaking; orgy. [from *Saturnalia*, the festival of SATURN, celebrated in ancient Rome with general feasting and unrestrained merrymaking] — **saturnalian**, *adj.*

saturnine /'sætənam/, *adj.* of an inactive, gloomy temperament; sullen; taciturn. [SATURN + -INE[1], the planet being supposed to give a gloomy nature to those born under its sign]

satyr /'sætə, 'seɪtə/, *n.* **1.** *Class Myth.* a woodland god, part human and part goat, who waits on Bacchus, the god of wine. **2.** a man with very strong, uncontrolled sexual desires. [ME, from L, from Gk] — **satyric**, *adj.*

sauce /sɔs/, *n., v., sauced, saucing.* ◇*n.* **1.** a cooked thick liquid put on, or eaten with, food to make it taste better: *chocolate sauce; chilli sauce.* **2.** something that adds sharpness or interest. **3.** *Colloq.* cheekiness; impertinence; impudence. ◇*v.t.* **4.** to prepare with sauce; season: *meat well sauced.* **5.** to give sharpness or interest to. **6.** *Colloq.* to speak cheekily to. [ME, from OF, from VL: salted]

saucepan /'sɔspən/, *n.* a metal container usu. having a long handle and a lid, for boiling, stewing, etc.

saucer /'sɔsə/, *n.* **1.** a small, round, shallow dish used under a cup. **2.** any saucer-shaped thing: *a flying saucer.* [ME, from OF: vessel for holding sauce]

saucy /'sɔsi/, *adj.*, **-cier, -ciest. 1.** cheeky; impertinent; insolent: *a saucy remark; a saucy child.* **2.** smart; pert: *a saucy hat.*

Saudi Arabia /saʊdi ə'reɪbɪə/, *n.* a kingdom in south-western Asia, occupying most of the Arabian peninsula with a long coastline on the Red Sea. Pop. 12 483 000 (1987 est.); 2 240 000 km². *Language:* Arabic. *Currency:* riyal. *Cap.:* Riyadh. — **Saudi Arabian**, *n., adj.*

sauerkraut /'saʊəkraʊt/, *n.* cabbage cut fine, salted, and allowed to ferment until sour. [G]

Saul /sɔl/, *n. Bible.* **1.** the first king of Israel. [see I Samuel 9] **2.** the original name of the apostle Paul. [see Acts 9:1–30, etc.]

sauna /'sɔnə/, *n.* (a room with) a type of steam bath in which the bather is cleansed by perspiring. [Finnish]

saunter /'sɔntə/, *v.i.* **1.** to walk in an unhurried, carefree way; stroll. ◇*n.* **2.** an unhurried walk; ramble; stroll. [late ME; orig. uncert.] — **saunterer**, *n.*

-saur, a word part meaning 'lizard'. [see SAURO-]

saurian /'sɔriən/, *adj.* **1.** of, like, or relating to lizards. ◇*n.* **2.** a saurian animal, such as a dinosaur or lizard. [NL: an order of reptiles]

sauro-, a word part meaning 'lizard'. [combining form of Gk *saûros*]

-saurus, a Latinised variant of **-saur**.

sausage /'sɒsɪdʒ/, *n.* finely minced meat, with seasonings and preservatives, packed into a special skin, formerly made from the intestines of pigs or oxen, but now often synthetic. [ME, from ONF, from LL, from L: salted]

sausage dog, *n. Colloq.* → **dachshund**.

sauté /'souteɪ/, *adj.*, *v.*, **-téed**, **-téeing**. ◇*adj.* **1.** cooked or browned in a pan with a little fat; gently fried. ◇*v.t.* **2.** to cook in a small amount of fat; pan fry. [F: tossed, from L]

sauterne /sou'tɜn, sə-/, *n.* a rich sweet white table wine. Also, **sauternes**. [named after the district *Sauternes*, near Bordeaux, where it is made]

savage /'sævɪdʒ/, *adj.*, *n.*, *v.*, **savaged**, **savaging**. ◇*adj.* **1.** wild; rugged: *savage wilderness.* **2.** uncivilised; barbarous: *savage tribes.* **3.** fierce or cruel; untamed: *savage beasts.* **4.** furiously angry. ◇*n.* **5.** an uncivilised human being. **6.** a fierce or cruel person. **7.** a rude person. ◇*v.t.* **8.** to attack violently; maul. [ME, from OF, from LL: of the woods, wild]

savagery /'sævɪdʒri, -dʒəri/, *n., pl.* **-ries. 1.** an uncivilised condition; barbarism. **2.** a savage nature, type of behavior or act; barbarity.

savanna /sə'vænə/, *n.* a grassland region with scattered trees, usu. in subtropical or tropical regions. Also, **savannah**. [Sp from Carib]

savant /'sævənt/, *n.* a learned person. [F, from L: be wise]

save[1] /seɪv/, *v.*, **saved**, **saving**, *n.* ◇*v.t.* **1.** to rescue from danger, harm, or loss: *to save someone from drowning; to save the game.* **2.** to keep safe; safeguard: *God save the Queen.* **3.** (in soccer, etc.) to prevent (a goal) being scored by stopping the ball from entering the net. **4.** to avoid the spending, using up, or waste of: *to save money; to save electricity.* **5.** to put aside for future use (oft. fol. by *up*): *I have saved (up) $1000.* **6.** to treat carefully in order to preserve: *To save her eyes, she doesn't sew much.* **7.** to prevent or make unnecessary; obviate: *A stitch in time saves nine.* **8.** *Theol.* to deliver from sin: *to save mankind from hell.* ◇*v.i.* **9.** to put aside money (oft. fol. by *up*): *to save up for a new car.* **10.** *Theol.* to deliver from sin: *Jesus saves.* ◇*n.* **11.** the act of saving, esp. in sports. [ME, from OF, from LL]

save[2] /seɪv/, *prep.* **1.** except; but. ◇*conj.* **2.** except; but. **3.** *Archaic.* unless. [ME; var. of SAFE, *adj.*, in obs. sense of reserving, making exception of]

saveloy /'sævəlɔɪ/, *n.* → **frankfurt**. [F, from It: brain, from L]

Savery /'seɪvri/, *n.* Henry ('Simon Stukeley'), 1791–1842, Australian convict and writer, born in England; author of the first novel to be written, published and printed in Australia, *Quintus Servinton* (1831).

saving /'seɪvɪŋ/, *adj.* **1.** that saves; rescuing; preserving. **2.** making acceptable in spite of other bad qualities; redeeming: *He's a coward, but he has a saving sense of humor.* **3.** making an exception: *a saving clause.* ◇*n.* **4.** a lessening of expense: *a saving of 10 per cent.* **5.** something that is saved. **6.** (*pl.*) sums of money saved and put aside. ◇*prep.* **7.** except: *Everyone came, saving Mark.* **8.** with all due respect to or for: *saving your presence.* ◇*conj.* **9.** save; except; but.

savings bank, *n.* a bank which mainly accepts deposits from individual customers and which lends money for housing. Compare **trading bank**.

savior *or* **saviour** /'seɪvjə/, *n.* **1.** someone who saves, rescues, or delivers: *the savior of the country.* **2.** (*cap.*) a title of God, esp. of Christ. [ME, from OF, from LL]

savoir-faire /,sævwɑː'fɛə, ,sʌv-/, *n.* knowledge of what to do in any situation. [F: lit., to know how to act]

Savonarola /,sævənə'roulə/, *n.* **Girolamo** /dʒɪ'rɒləmoʊ/, 1452–98, Italian monk, reformer, and martyr.

savor *or* **savour** /'seɪvə/, *n.* **1.** a taste or smell: *The savor of mushrooms came down the hall.* **2.** a noticeable quality: *His poems have a strong savor of sadness.* **3.** the power to excite or interest: *The party soon lost its savor for her.* ◇*v.i.* **4.** to have taste or smell. **5.** to show peculiar qualities; smack (fol. by *of*): *His talk savored of a certain nastiness.* ◇*v.t.* **6.** to taste or smell, esp. with pleasure. **7.** to enjoy. [ME, from OF, from L: taste, savor]

savory[1] *or* **savoury** /'seɪvəri/, *adj., pl.* **-vories**. ◇*adj.* **1.** delicious: *a savory smell.* **2.** having the taste of meat, fish, etc., rather than something sweet: *a savory filling.* **3.** pleasing or wholesome: *He is not such a savory character as I first thought.* ◇*n.* **4.** an unsweet, usu. salty, bite-sized piece of food on a small biscuit or piece of toast; canapé. [ME, from OF]

savory[2] /'seɪvəri/, *n., pl.* **-vories**. a European herb used in cookery. [OE *sætheríe*, *saturēge*, from L]

savoy /sə'vɔɪ/, *n.* a variety of cabbage with a firm head and wrinkled leaves. [named after *Savoy*, a district in SE France]

Savoy /sə'vɔɪ/, *n.* **1.** French **Savoie**. a region in south-eastern France, near the Swiss-Italian border; formerly a duchy. **2. House of**, the rulers of the former duchy of Savoy, and since 1862 comprising the royal house of Italy; prior to the dissolution of the Italian monarchy (1946) it was the oldest reigning dynasty of Europe. –**Savoyard**, *n., adj.*

savvy /'sævi/, *v.*, **-vied**, **-vying**. *Colloq.* to know; understand. [Sp]

saw[1] /sɔ/, *n., v.*, **sawed**, **sawn** *or* **sawed**, **sawing**. ◇*n.* **1.** a tool for cutting, typically a thin blade of metal with a series of sharp teeth.

saw

2. any similar tool, as a circular saw. ◇*v.t.* 3. to cut or shape with a saw: *to saw logs.* 4. to make movements as if using a saw: *to saw the air with one's hands.* ◇*v.i.* 5. to use a saw: *He is out the back sawing.* 6. to make sawing movements or sounds like a saw: *to saw away at a violin.* 7. to cut as a saw does. [OE *saga, sagu*]

saw² /sɔ/, *v.* past tense of **see**¹.

saw³ /sɔ/, *n.* a short, wise saying; maxim; proverb: *He could find an old saw for almost every occasion.* [ME; OE *sagu*]

sawfish /'sɔfɪʃ/, *n., pl.* **-fishes**, (*esp.* collectively) **-fish**. a large ray of tropical coasts and lowland rivers, with a bladelike snout and strong teeth.

sawmill /'sɔmɪl/, *n.* a factory where timber is sawn into planks, boards, etc., by machinery.

sawpit /'sɔpɪt/, *n.* a pit in the ground over which trees are placed for sawing up.

Saxe-Coburg-Gotha /ˌsæks-'koubəg-'gouθə/, *n.* **House of,** the name of the British royal family from 1902 until 1917, when it became the House of Windsor.

saxhorn /'sækshɔn/, *n.* a brass instrument similar to the cornet and tuba. [named after Adolphe *Sax*, 1814–94, a Belgian, who invented the instrument]

Saxon /'sæksən/, *n.* 1. a person of the English race or of English descent. 2. an Anglo-Saxon. 3. someone who lives in Saxony in modern Germany. 4. a member of the Germanic people who came to Britain in the fifth and sixth centuries. ◇*adj.* 5. English. 6. of or relating to the early Saxons (def. 4) or their language. 7. of or relating to Saxony in modern Germany. [ME, from L, from Gmc]

Saxony /'sæksəni/, *n.* a medieval and later division of northern Germany with varying boundaries; at its height it extended from the Rhine to east of the Elbe. German, **Sachsen**. French, **Saxe**.

saxophone /'sæksəfoun/, *n.* a wind instrument with a curved brass body and a clarinet mouthpiece. [*sax* (as in SAXHORN) + -O- + -PHONE] — **saxophonist,** *n.*

say /seɪ/, *v.*, **said, saying,** *n.* ◇*v.t.* 1. to speak; utter or pronounce: *What were you saying just now?* 2. to express in words: *He said that he was afraid.* 3. to suppose; estimate: *to learn in, say, ten lessons.* 4. to report; allege; maintain: *People say he will resign.* ◇*v.i.* 5. to speak; declare; express an opinion. ◇*v.* 6. **I say,** an exclamation to attract attention or to express surprise, protest, joy, etc. ◇*n.* 7. one's turn to say something: *Joe hasn't had a say yet.* 8. *Colloq.* a right or opportunity to say, speak or decide: *The workers want a say in running the factory.* 9. **have the last say,** to have the final authority: *The treasurer has the last say on a budget of this size.* [ME; OE *secgan*]

saying /'seɪɪŋ/, *n.* 1. something said; proverb; adage; maxim. 2. **go without saying,** to be completely obvious.

say-so /'seɪ-sou/, *n., Colloq.* 1. a personal statement without proof; assertion: *It's only her say-so.* 2. power to decide; authority: *She has the final say-so on who will be there.*

sb., *Abbrev.* substantive.

Sb, *Chem. Symbol.* antimony. [L *stibium*]

S-bend /'ɛs-bend/, *n.* an S-shaped bend, as in a pipe or road.

sc., *Abbrev.* 1. scilicet (namely). 2. scene.

s.c., *Abbrev.* 1. self-contained. 2. small capitals.

Sc, *Symbol.* 1. *Chem.* scandium. ◇*Abbrev.* 2. Science.

scab /skæb/, *n., v.,* **scabbed, scabbing.** ◇*n.* 1. a crust which forms over a sore during healing. 2. *Vet. Sci.* a mangy disease in animals, esp. sheep; scabies. 3. someone who goes on working during a strike, takes a striker's place or refuses to join a union; blackleg. 4. *Colloq.* a contemptible person. ◇*v.i.* 5. to become covered with a scab. 6. to act or work as a scab. [ME, from Scand] — **scabby,** *n.*

scabbard /'skæbəd/, *n.* 1. a holder for the blade of a sword, dagger, etc.; sheath. ◇*v.t.* 2. to put into a scabbard; sheathe. [ME, from AF; probably of Gmc orig.]

scabies /'skeɪbiz, -biiz/, *n.* an infectious skin disease in sheep and cattle, and in humans, caused by parasitic mites; itch. [L: roughness, the itch] — **scabietic,** *adj.*

scaffold /'skæfəld, -oʊld/, *n.* 1. a temporary structure for supporting workers and materials during work on a building. 2. a raised platform or stage, as that on which a criminal is executed. ◇*v.t.* 3. to furnish with a scaffold. 4. to support by or place on a scaffold. [ME, from OF, from LL]

scaffolding /'skæfəldɪŋ/, *n.* 1. a system of scaffolds. 2. materials for scaffolds.

scalar /'skeɪlə/, *Maths. adj.* 1. representable by position on a line; having only magnitude: *a scalar variable.* ◇*n.* 2. a quantity possessing only magnitude (contrasted with a vector). [L]

scald /skɔld/, *v.t.* 1. to burn or hurt with, or as with, hot liquid or steam. 2. to put quickly into boiling water: *to scald vegetables.* 3. to heat to just below boiling point: *to scald milk.* ◇*v.i.* 4. to be or become scalded. ◇*n.* 5. a burn caused by hot liquid or steam. [ME, from ONF: burn, scald, from LL: wash in hot water]

scale¹ /skeɪl/, *n., v.,* **scaled, scaling.** ◇*n.* 1. one of the thin, flat, horny or hard plates that form the covering of certain animals, such as fishes. 2. any thin platelike piece or flake that peels off from a surface. 3. → **scale insect.** 4. an encrustation caused in various ways: *The inside of the kettle is covered with scale.* ◇*v.t.* 5. to remove the scales from: *to scale fish.* 6. to remove in scales or thin layers: *to scale off paint.* ◇*v.i.* 7. to come off in scales: *The burnt skin scaled off.* 8. to become coated with scale, as the inside of a boiler. [ME, from OF; of Gmc orig.] — **scaly,** *adj.*

scale² /skeɪl/, *n., v.,* **scaled, scaling.** ◇*n.* 1. (*usu. pl.*) an apparatus for weighing; a balance. ◇*v.t.* 2. to weigh in or as in scales. 3. to have a weight of: *The jockey scaled 50 kilograms.* [ME, from Scand]

scale³ /skeɪl/, *n., v.,* **scaled, scaling.** ◇*n.* **1.** a succession of steps or degrees; graduated series. **2.** set of marks along a line, for measuring: *the scale of a thermometer.* **3. a.** marked line on a map showing the size of the map in proportion to what it represents. **b.** the ratio of distances shown in this way. **4.** a set of degrees giving relative quantities, etc.: *the wage scale; a scale of exam marks.* **5.** the proportion which the representation of an object has to the object: *a model on a scale of one centimetre to a metre.* **6.** relative or proportionate size: *The house was rebuilt on a larger scale.* **7.** *Maths.* a system of numerical notation: *the decimal scale.* **8.** *Music.* a series of notes going up or down according to fixed intervals, esp. one beginning on a particular note: *the major scale of C.* ◇*v.t.* **9.** to climb by, or as by, a ladder; climb up or over: *to scale a wall; to scale a mountain.* **10.** to arrange according to a scale: *to scale exam marks.* **11.** to lessen according to a fixed proportion (oft. fol. by *down*): *to scale down wages; to scale down marks.* ◇*v.i.* **12.** to climb; ascend; mount. **13.** to go forward in a graduated series. [ME, from L: staircase, ladder]

scaled score, *n.* the score of a candidate, etc., adjusted to make it comparable to scores obtained by other candidates (opposed to *raw score*).

scale insect, *n.* a type of small plant-destroying insect, the female having the body and eggs covered by a large scale formed by secretions.

scalene /'skeɪliːn/, *adj.* (of a triangle) having three unequal sides. [LL, from Gk]

scallop /'skɒləp/, *n.* **1.** a type of mollusc having two fluted shell valves that can be opened and shut in order to swim. **2.** the large muscle of certain kinds of such molluscs, valued as a food. **3.** one of a series of curves along the edge of pastry, a garment, cloth, etc. ◇*v.t.* **4.** to finish (an edge) with scallops. [ME, from OF: shell; of Gmc orig.]

scallywag /'skæliwæg/, *n.* (*oft. used playfully of children*) a scamp; rascal. Also, **scalawag, scallawag.** [orig. uncert.]

scalp /skælp/, *n.* **1.** the skin of the upper part of the head, usu. including the associated structures just beneath the skin. **2.** part of this skin with its hair, taken from a slain enemy as a victory prize by certain North American Indians. ◇*v.t.* **3.** to cut or tear the scalp from. **4.** *Colloq.* to buy (tickets) and resell them unofficially at a higher rate. [ME, from Scand] **– scalper,** *n.*

scalpel /'skælpəl/, *n.* a small, light, very sharp knife used in surgical operations. [L]

scamp /skæmp/, *n.* a mischievous person; rascal. [special use of obs. *scamp,* v., go (on highways), apparently from D, from OF: DECAMP]

scamper /'skæmpə/, *v.i.* **1.** to run or go hurriedly. ◇*n.* **2.** the act of scampering. [obs. *scamp,* v., go + -ER⁶. See SCAMP]

scan /skæn/, *v.,* **scanned, scanning,** *n.* ◇*v.t.* **1.** to examine closely; scrutinise. **2.** to look through quickly: *to scan a page.* **3.** to analyse the metrical structure of (verse). **4.** *TV.* to go over (a surface) with a beam of light or electrons in order to reproduce or transmit a picture. **5.** *Radar.* to go over (an area) with a beam from a radar transmitter. ◇*v.i.* **6.** (of verse) to be in accordance with the rules of metre. ◇*n.* **7.** the act of scanning. [ME, from LL: scan verse, from L: climb] **– scanner,** *n.*

Scand, *Abbrev.* **1.** Scandinavia. **2.** Scandinavian.

scandal /'skændl/, *n.* **1.** a disgraceful action, happening, etc.: *It was a scandal that the murderer was set free.* **2.** displeasure or offence caused by such an action. **3.** talk or gossip that does harm to someone's reputation. **4.** *Colloq.* gossip in general. **5.** a person whose behavior brings disgrace or offence. [LL: cause of offence, from Gk: trap] **– scandalous,** *adj.*

scandalise or **scandalize** /'skændəlaɪz/, *v.t.,* **-lised, -lising.** to shock or horrify by something considered immoral or improper.

scandalmonger /'skændlmʌŋgə/, *n.* someone who spreads scandal.

Scandinavia /skændə'neɪviə/, *n.* **1.** the collective name of Norway, Sweden, Denmark, and sometimes also Finland and Iceland. **2.** the peninsula of Norway and Sweden. [L (Pliny), of Gmc orig.; cf. OE *Scedenig*]

scandium /'skændiəm/, *n.* a silvery white, trivalent metallic element. *Symbol:* Sc; *at. no.:* 21; *at. wt.:* 44.956. [NL]

scansion /'skænʃən/, *n.* the analysis of the metre of verse. [L: a climbing]

scant /skænt/, *adj.* **1.** barely enough in amount or quantity; inadequate: *He received scant justice.* **2.** barely as much as the amount indicated: *a scant two hours.* **3.** having a limited supply (fol. by *of*): *scant of breath.* [ME, from Scand] **– scanty,** *adj.*

-scape, a suffix meaning a view of the particular location indicated, as in *landscape, streetscape, cityscape.* [from (LAND)SCAPE]

scapegoat /'skeɪpgoʊt/, *n.* someone who is made to bear the blame for others or to suffer in their place. [(E)SCAPE, *v.* + GOAT; orig. with ref. to the goat, in ancient Jewish ritual, sent into the wilderness after the chief priest on the Day of Atonement had symbolically laid the sins of the people upon it (see Leviticus 16)]

scapula /'skæpjələ/, *n., pl.* **-lae** /-liː/. **1.** *Anat.* either of two flat, triangular bones, each forming the back part of a shoulder; shoulder-blade. **2.** *Zool.* the bone forming the back part of the pectoral arch. [NL: shoulder blade (in L only in pl.)]

scar¹ /skɑː/, *n., v.,* **scarred, scarring.** ◇*n.* **1.** a mark left by a healed wound, sore, or burn. **2.** any blemish remaining as a trace or result: *scars upon one's good name.* ◇*v.t.* **3.** to mark with a scar. ◇*v.i.* **4.** to heal with a resulting scar. [ME, from OF, from LL: scab, from Gk: lit., hearth]

scar² /skɑː/, *n.* a steep rocky place; cliff. [ME, from Scand]

scarab /'skærəb/, *n.* **1.** a type of beetle, regarded as sacred by the ancient Egyptians. **2.** the image of this beetle, much used in jewellery, etc. [L]

scarce /skeəs/, *adj.*, **scarcer, scarcest. 1.** not enough for the need or demand; not plentiful: *Coffee is scarce in wartime.* **2.** rarely seen or found: *a scarce book.* **3. make oneself scarce,** *Colloq.* to go or keep away. [ME, from ONF: scanty, stingy, from LL] —**scarceness, scarcity,** *n.*

scarcely /'skeəsli/, *adv.* **1.** barely; hardly; not quite. **2.** definitely not. **3.** probably not.

scare /skeə/, *v.*, **scared, scaring,** *n.* ◇*v.t., v.i.* **1.** to frighten or become frightened. ◇*n.* **2.** a sudden fright or alarm, sometimes with little or no cause. **3.** a condition of widespread fear, worry, etc. [ME, from Scand]

scarecrow /'skeəkrou/, *n.* **1.** an object, usu. a figure of a man in old clothes, set up to frighten birds away from crops. **2.** someone who looks like a scarecrow because of untidiness, thinness, etc.

scarf /skaf/, *n.*, *pl.* **scarfs, scarves** /skavz/. a long, broad piece of material worn about the neck, shoulders, or head for ornament or warmth. [? ONF: sash, sling for arm, probably var. of OF: a pilgrim's bag hung round the neck]

scarify /'skærəfaɪ, 'skeər-/, *v.t.*, **-fied, -fying. 1.** to make scratches or small cuts on the surface of. **2.** to hurt by severe criticism. **3.** to loosen (soil) with a type of cultivator. [late ME, from LL, from Gk: scratch an outline] —**scarification,** *n.*

Scarlatti /ska'læti/, *n.* **1. Alessandro** /ale'sændrou/, 1659–1725, Italian composer. **2.** his son, **Domenico** /də'menikou/, 1685–1757, composer, esp. of harpsichord sonatas.

scarlet /'skalət/, *n.* **1.** a bright red color tending towards orange. **2.** cloth or garments of this color. ◇*adj.* **3.** of this color. [ME, from OF, ? from Pers: a rich cloth]

scarlet fever, *n.* an infectious disease, now chiefly of children, marked by fever and a scarlet rash.

scarp /skap/, *n.* **1.** a steep face on the side of a hill. ◇*v.t.* **2.** to form into a scarp. [It]

scarper /'skapə/, *v.i. Colloq.* to run away; depart suddenly, esp. leaving behind debts, etc. [orig. unknown]

scary /'skeəri/, *adj.*, **scarier, scariest.** *Colloq.* **1.** causing fright. **2.** easily frightened; timid.

scat /skæt/, *v.t.*, **scatted, scatting.** *Colloq.* to go off hastily (usu. as a command).

scathing /'skeɪðɪŋ/, *adj.* intended to hurt the feelings; scornful; severely critical: *a scathing remark.* [ME, from Scand: harm]

scatology /skæ'tɒlədʒi/, *n.* (extreme interest in) the use of images of physical filth (esp. excrement) in literature. [*skato-*, combining form of G', *skôr* dung + -LOGY] —**scatological,** *adj.*

scatter /'skætə/, *v.t.* **1.** to throw loosely about. **2.** to separate and drive off in various directions; disperse. ◇*v.i.* **3.** to separate and go in different directions; disperse. ◇*n.* **4.** the act of scattering. **5.** something which is scattered. [ME: orig. uncert.]

scatterbrain /'skætəbreɪn/, *adj.* someone unable to think logically or seriously. —**scatterbrained,** *adj.*

scattering /'skætərɪŋ/, *n.* **1.** a scattered number or quantity. **2.** *Phys.* the process by which any beam of radiation, electromagnetic or particle, is deflected into random directions when it strikes matter.

scatty /'skæti/, *adj.* scatterbrained; thoughtless; foolish.

scavenge /'skævəndʒ/, *v.*, **-enged, -enging.** ◇*v.t.* **1.** to search for and take (anything useable) from rubbish or material that is no longer being used. ◇*v.i.* **2.** to search amongst rubbish or disused material for anything useable, such as food, clothing, etc. [backformation from *scavenger*, from OF: to inspect] —**scavenger,** *n.*

scenario /sə'nariou/, *n.*, *pl.* **-narios. 1.** an outline of a dramatic work, giving details about scenes, characters, situations, etc. **2.** an outline or script of a film, giving the action in the order in which it takes place, description of scenes and characters, etc. **3.** an outline of a general situation or plan. [It, from LL: relating to stage scenes]

scene /sin/, *n.* **1.** the place where any action happens. **2.** any view or picture. **3.** an event or situation, real or imaginary, esp. as described in writing. **4.** a show of excited or violent feeling before others. **5.** a division of a play, usu. representing what passes between certain of the actors in one place. **6.** → **scenery** (def. 2). **7.** the setting of a story, play, film, etc. **8.** *Colloq.* any field of activity or interest: *the pop scene; the fashion scene.* **9. behind the scenes, a.** out of sight of the audience. **b.** secretly; privately. [L, from Gk: tent, stage]

scenery /'sinəri/, *n.*, *pl.* **-neries. 1.** the total of the natural features that give character to a landscape. **2.** hangings, paintings, structures, etc., placed on the stage to represent the place in which the action is meant to happen.

scenic /'sinɪk/, *adj.* **1.** having beautiful scenery. **2.** of or relating to the stage or stage scenery.

scent /sent/, *n.* **1.** a particular smell, esp. when agreeable. **2.** a smell left in passing, by means of which an animal or person may be tracked. **3.** → **perfume. 4.** the sense of smell. ◇*v.t.* **5.** to become aware of or recognise by the sense of smell. **6.** to become aware of or discover in any way: *to scent trouble.* **7.** to put perfume on or into. [ME, from F: perceive, from L]

sceptic /'skeptɪk/, *n.* **1.** someone who habitually questions accepted knowledge or belief. **2.** someone who habitually has a mistrustful attitude towards people, plans, ideas, etc. **3.** (*cap.*) *Philos.* a member of a philosophical school of ancient Greece, or any later thinker, who believed that real knowledge of things is impossible. [L: inquiring, reflective, from Gk] —**sceptical,** *adj.* —**scepticism,** *n.*

sceptre /'septə/, *n.* **1.** a rod or staff carried in the hand as a symbol of royal or imperial

sceptre   925   **school**

power. **2.** royal or imperial power; sovereignty. [ME, from OF, from L, from Gk]

schedule /'ʃɛdʒul/, *n., v.,* **-uled, -uling.** ◇*n.* **1.** a plan for a particular project setting out the order of operations, time given for each part, etc. **2.** a list of things needed to be dealt with or undertaken: *He has a full schedule tomorrow.* **3.** a written or printed statement of details, often attached to another document. ◇*v.t.* **4.** to make a schedule of; enter in a schedule. **5.** to plan for a certain date: *to schedule publication for June.* [LL, from L: leaf of paper, probably from L: split]

Scheele /'ʃilə/, *n.* **Karl Wilhelm** /kal 'vilhelm/, 1742–86, Swedish chemist; discovered various chemical elements and compounds, including oxygen and chlorine.

scheelite /'ʃilaɪt/, *n.* calcium tungstate, CaWO$_4$, an important ore of tungsten, usu. occurring in crystals. [named after KW SCHEELE + -ITE[1]]

schema /'skimə/, *n., pl.* **-mata** /-mətə/. a diagram, plan, or scheme. [Gk: form]

schematic /ski'mætɪk/, *adj.* **1.** relating to or of the nature of a plan, diagram, or scheme. ◇*n.* **2.** a schematic drawing or diagram. –**schematically,** *adv.*

scheme /skim/, *n., v.,* **schemed, scheming.** ◇*n.* **1.** a plan or design; program of action; project. **2.** a secret plan; plot; intrigue. **3.** any system of connected things, parts, beliefs, etc., or the manner of its arrangement: *a color scheme.* ◇*v.i., v.t.* **4.** to make a scheme (for); plan; plot. [ML, from Gk] –**schemer,** *n.*

scheming /'skimɪŋ/, *adj.* given to forming plans, esp. secret ones; crafty.

Schepisi /'skɛpɪsi/, *n.* **Frederick Thomas,** born 1941, Australian film director; films include *The Chant of Jimmie Blacksmith* (1978).

scherzo /'skɛətsoʊ, 'skɛət-/, *n., pl.* **-zos, -zi** /-si/. (in music) a movement or passage of lively, playful character, esp. as second or third division of a sonata or a symphony. [It: sport, jest, from G]

schism /'skɪzəm, 'sɪzəm/, *n.* a division into opposed parties, esp. within a church. [L, from Gk] –**schismatic,** *adj.*

schist /ʃɪst/, *n.* any of a class of crystalline rocks whose minerals have a more or less parallel arrangement, due mostly to metamorphic action. [F, from L: fissile, readily splitting, from Gk]

schizo-, a word part meaning division. Also, before vowels, **schiz-.** [Gk: parted]

schizoid /'skɪtsɔɪd/, *adj.* related to, tending to, or having schizophrenia.

schizophrenia /skɪtsə'friniə/, *n.* **1.** a mental disorder marked by disconnected thought, behavior and personality functioning, withdrawal from reality, emotional dullness and distortion. **2.** *Colloq.* → **split personality.** –**schizophrenic,** *n., adj.*

Schleiden /'ʃlaɪdən/, *n.* **Matthias Jakob** /ma'tiæs 'jakɒb/, 1804–81, German botanist; with Schwann, formulated the theory that living organisms are composed of cells.

Schlesinger /'ʃlɛsɪndʒə/, *n.* **Arthur Meier,** born 1917, US historian; awarded Pulitzer Prize for *A Thousand Days*, a history of JF Kennedy's presidency.

Schleswig-Holstein /ˌʃlɛzvɪg-'hɒlstaɪn/, *n.* two duchies of Denmark that were a centre of international tension in the 19th century; annexed by Prussia, 1864 (Schleswig) and 1866 (Holstein).

Schliemann /'ʃliman/, *n.* **Heinrich** /'haɪnrɪk/, 1822–90, German archaeologist, best known for excavations of Troy and Mycenae.

schlieren /'ʃliərən/, *n.pl. Geol.* streaks or irregularly-shaped masses in an igneous rock, which differ in texture or composition from the main mass. [G: streaks]

schmalz /ʃmɔlts, ʃmælts/, *n. Colloq.* sickly sentimentality. Also, **schmaltz.** [G: lit., dripping fat] –**schmalzy,** *adj.*

Schmidt /ʃmɪt/, *n.* **Helmut** /'hɛlmʊt/ (*Heinrich Waldemar Schmidt*), born 1918, German Social Democrat political leader; chancellor of West Germany 1974–82.

schnapper /'ʃnæpə/, *n.* → **snapper.**

schnapps /ʃnæps/, *n.* a type of gin[1]. [G: dram, nip]

scholar /'skɒlə/, *n.* **1.** a learned person. **2.** a student; pupil. **3.** a student who has been given a scholarship (def. 2). [LL] –**scholarly,** *adj.*

scholarship /'skɒləʃɪp/, *n.* **1.** learning; academic knowledge gained by study. **2.** a sum of money or other help given to a student on the basis of merit, etc., to allow the continuation of studies.

scholastic /skə'læstɪk/, *adj.* **1.** Also, **scholastical.** of or relating to schools, students, or education: *scholastic attainments.* **2.** of or relating to scholasticism. ◇*n.* **3.** (*sometimes cap.*) a supporter of scholasticism. [L, from Gk: studious, learned]

scholasticism /skə'læstəsɪzəm/, *n.* a medieval system of Christian thought based on the Church fathers and Aristotle.

Schönberg /'ʃɜnbəg/, *n.* **Arnold,** 1874–1951, Austrian composer in the US; originated the twelve-note technique. Also, **Schoenberg.**

school[1] /skul/, *n.* **1.** a place or establishment where instruction is given, esp. one for children. **2.** all the students attending a school. **3.** a session of teaching at a school: *school starts tomorrow.* **4.** a department or faculty in a university, etc. **5.** any instructive place, situation, etc. **6.** a group of students, artists, writers, etc., who have been taught by the same master, or who are united by a similarity of method, style, principles, etc. **7.** *Colloq.* a group of people settled into a session of drinking or gambling. ◇*adj.* **8.** of or connected with a school or schools. ◇*v.t.* **9.** to educate; teach; train. [OE *scōl*, from L, from Gk: orig., leisure, hence employment of leisure, study]

school[2] /skul/, *n.* a large group of fish, porpoises, whales, etc., feeding or migrating together. [ME, from D: troop, multitude]

schooling /'skuliŋ/, *n.* education, esp. that received in a school; training.

school of arts, *n.* a public hall, usu. in a country town, where working people may study and attend educational lectures; mechanics' hall.

School of the Air, *n.* an educational service for children in isolated areas of Australia, which supplements their correspondence courses; first broadcast in 1951, it uses the radio network of the Royal Flying Doctor Service.

school prawn, *n.* a common commercial prawn, pale olive green in color.

school shark, *n.* a small shark of eastern and southern Australian coasts.

schooner /'skunə/, *n.* 1. a sailing ship with two or more masts and fore-and-aft rig. 2. a large glass, usu. for beer. [orig. uncert.; said to be from New England (US) d. verb *scoon* skim along]

Schubert /'ʃubət/, *n.* **Franz** /frants/, 1797–1828, Austrian composer, remembered esp. for his lieder.

Schumann /'ʃumən/, *n.* 1. **Clara**, 1819–96, German pianist, composer and teacher. 2. her husband, **Robert**, 1810–56, German Romantic composer and pianist.

schwa /ʃwa/, *n.* 1. the neutral vowel sound of most unstressed syllables of English, as the sound of *a* in *alone*, *e* in *system*, *i* in *terrible*, *o* in *gallop*, *u* in *circus*. 2. the phonetic symbol for this: /ə/. [G, from Heb]

Schweitzer /'ʃwaɪtsə/, *n.* **Albert**, 1875–1965, Franco-German musician, doctor, and missionary in Africa, born in Alsace; founded medical mission at Lambaréné, in Gabon; Nobel Peace prize, 1952.

sci., *Abbrev.* 1. science. 2. scientific.

sciatic /saɪ'ætɪk/, *adj.* of the back of the hip: *sciatic nerve*. [ML, from L]

sciatica /saɪ'ætɪkə/, *n.* pain and tenderness at some points of the sciatic nerve, which extends from the hip down the back of the thigh. [late ME, from ML, properly fem. of adj.: SCIATIC]

science /'saɪəns/, *n.* 1. **a.** a systematic study of man and the physical world based on reproducible observations, measurements and experiments. **b.** the knowledge so gained. 2. a particular branch of knowledge. 3. skill; proficiency. [ME, from OF, from L: knowledge]

science fiction, *n.* a form of fiction which uses imaginatively scientific knowledge and theory in its plot, setting, etc.

scientific /saɪən'tɪfɪk/, *adj.* 1. of, relating to, or concerned with science or the sciences: *scientific studies*. 2. in accordance with the principles of exact science: *a scientific method*. 3. systematic or accurate. [LL]

scientist /'saɪəntɪst/, *n.* someone skilled in or working in the field of science, esp. physical or natural science.

sci-fi /saɪ'faɪ/, *n. Colloq.* science fiction.

scilicet /'sɪləset, 'saɪl-/, *adv.* that is to say; namely. [L; it is permitted to know]

Scilly Isles /,sɪli 'aɪlz/, a group of about 140 small islands in the Atlantic Ocean, south west of Land's End. Pop. 2628 (1981); 17 km[2]. *Cap.:* Hugh Town. Also, **Scilly Islands**, **Scillies**.

scimitar /'sɪmətə/, *n.* a curved, single-edged sword of Oriental origin. Also, **scimiter**. [It]

scintillate /'sɪntəleɪt/, *v.i.* **-lated, -lating.** 1. to give out sparks; flash. 2. to twinkle, as the stars do. 3. to be bright and amusing in conversation. [L]

scintillation /,sɪntə'leɪʃən/, *n.* 1. the act of scintillating. 2. a spark or flash. 3. *Astron.* the twinkling of the light of the stars. 4. *Phys.* a flash of light produced by a phosphor when it is hit by an electron, apha particle, photon, etc.

scion /'saɪən/, *n.* 1. a descendant or young member of a family, esp. a noble or ancient one. 2. a shoot, esp. one cut for grafting or planting; a cutting. [ME, from OF, from L]

Scipio /'skɪpioʊ/, *n.* 1. **Publius Cornelius Scipio Africanus Major** /,pʌblɪəs kɔ,nilɪəs ,skɪpiou æfrɪ,kænəs 'meɪdʒə/ ('*Scipio the Elder*'), 237–183 BC, Roman general, victor over Hannibal. 2. his adopted grandson, **Publius Cornelius Scipio Aemilianus Africanus Minor** /ɪ,milɪənəs æfrɪ,kænəs 'mɪnə/ ('*Scipio the Younger*'), c. 185–129 BC, Roman general, besieger and destroyer of Carthage.

scissors /'sɪzəz/, *n.pl.* a cutting instrument consisting of two blades (with handles) so joined together that their edges work against each other (often called *a pair of scissors*). [ME, from OF, from LL, from L: cut, slain]

sclera /'sklɪərə/, *n.* the thick, white, fibrous membrane forming, with the cornea, the outer covering of the eyeball. [NL, from Gk: hard]

sclerophyll /'sklɛrəfɪl, 'sklɪə-/, *n.* a type of plant, usu. found in low rainfall areas, having tough leaves which help to reduce water loss.

sclerosis /sklə'roʊsəs/, *n., pl.* **-ses** /-siz/. *Med.* a hardening of a tissue or part. [ML, from Gk: hardening] – **sclerosal**, *adj.*

scoff[1] /skɒf/, *n.* 1. an expression of mockery or scorn; jeer. ◇*v.i.* 2. to speak mockingly; jeer (oft. fol. by *at*). [ME, from Scand]

scoff[2] /skɒf/, *v.t., v.i. Colloq.* to eat greedily and quickly. [Afrikaans: meal, from D: quarter (of the day)]

scold /skoʊld/, *v.t.* 1. to find fault with; chide. ◇*v.i.* 2. to find fault; reprove. 3. to use harsh language. ◇*n.* 4. someone, esp. a woman, who habitually scolds. [ME, from Scand]

scolex /'skoʊlɛks/, *n., pl.* **scoleces** /skoʊ'lisɪz/. the front segment or head of a tapeworm, provided with the organs by which it is attached to the tissues of the host. [NL, from Gk: worm]

scollop /'skɒləp/, *n., v.t.* → **scallop**.

scone /skɒn/, *n.* **1.** a light plain cake, usu. eaten split open and spread with butter, etc. **2.** *Colloq.* the head. [MD: fine bread]

Scone /skun, skoʊn/ for def. 1; /skoʊn/ for def. 2, *n.* **1. The Stone of**, a famous stone, formerly at Scone, Scotland, upon which medieval Scottish kings sat at coronation, now beneath the coronation chair in Westminster Abbey. **2.** a town and shire in central eastern NSW, in the upper Hunter Valley. Pop. 4272 (1986).

scoop /skup/, *n.* **1.** a small ladle-like instrument for taking up flour, sugar, etc. **2.** the bucket of a dredge, shovel (def. 2), etc. **3.** a place scooped out; hollow. **4.** the act of scooping; a movement like that of scooping. **5.** the quantity taken up by a scoop. **6.** *Colloq.* a big profit. **7.** a news story published or broadcast in advance of other newspapers, etc. ◇*v.t.* **8.** to take up or out with or as with a scoop (oft. fol. by *up*). **9.** to form a hollow in (oft. fol. by *out*). **10.** *Journalism Colloq.* to get the better of (another newspaper, etc.) by publishing a news story first. [ME, from MLG or MD: container for drawing or bailing water]

scoot /skut/, *v.i. Colloq.* to go or move quickly; dart. [of Scand orig.]

scooter /'skutə/, *n.* a child's toy with two wheels, one in front of the other, and a board between them for the feet, steered by a handlebar and ridden by pushing against the ground with one foot.

scope /skoʊp/, *n.* **1.** the extent or range of view, outlook, use, operation, effectiveness, etc.: *an investigation of wide scope; He gave his imagination full scope.* **2.** extent in space; area. **3.** a short form of *microscope*, *telescope*, etc. [It, from Gk: mark, aim]

-scope, a word part meaning an 'instrument for viewing', as in *telescope*. [NL, from Gk: look at]

scorbutic /skɔ'bjutɪk/, *adj.* relating to, of the nature of, or having scurvy. Also, **scorbutical**. [NL, from ML: scurvy, apparently from D]

scorch /skɔtʃ/, *v.t.* **1.** to change the color, taste, etc., of by burning slightly. **2.** to dry up with heat. **3.** to criticise severely. ◇*v.i.* **4.** to be or become scorched. ◇*n.* **5.** a slight burn. [Scand]

scorcher /'skɔtʃə/, *n. Colloq.* a very hot day.

score /skɔ/, *n., v.,* **scored, scoring.** ◇*n.* **1.** a point made by a competitor in a game, contest, etc. **2.** the total of points made by a person or team. **3.** *Educ.* the performance of someone in an examination or test, expressed by a letter, number, etc. **4.** a scratch, stroke or line. **5.** an amount recorded as due; debt. **6.** group or set of twenty: *three score years and ten.* **7.** (*pl.*) a great many. **8.** an account, reason, or ground: *to complain on the score of low pay.* **9.** a successful action, remark, etc. **10.** *Music.* **a.** a written or printed piece of music with all the vocal and instrumental parts arranged on staves, one under the other. **b.** the background music to a film, play, etc. **11.** *Colloq.* the latest news or state of progress: *What's the score on our building plans?* ◇*v.t.* **12.** to make (points, etc.) in a game, etc. **13.** to make a score of. **14.** to be worth (as points): *Four aces score one hundred.* **15.** *Music.* **a.** to orchestrate. **b.** to write out in score. **c.** to compose the music for (a film, play, etc.). **16.** to make scratches, cuts, or lines in or on. **17.** *Colloq.* to gain or win: *to score a great success; to score a lot of birthday presents.* ◇*v.i.* **18.** to make a point or points in a game, etc. **19.** to keep the score of a game, etc. **20.** to gain an advantage or a success. ◇*v.* **21. score off**, to gain an advantage over. [ME; late OE *scoru*, from *Scand*]

scoria /'skɔriə/, *n., pl.* **scoriae** /'skɔrii/. **1.** refuse left after smelting or melting metals; slag. **2.** clinker-like cellular lava. [L, from Gk: slag]

scorn /skɔn/, *n.* **1.** open lack of respect; contempt; disdain. ◇*v.t.* **2.** to treat or regard with scorn. **3.** to reject or refuse with scorn. [ME, from OF: mockery, derision; of Gmc orig.] **–scornful**, *adj.*

Scorpio /'skɔpioʊ/, *n.* a constellation and sign of the zodiac, represented by a scorpion. [ME, from L]

scorpion /'skɔpiən/, *n.* a type of arachnid from the warmer parts of the world, having a long narrow tail ending in a curved, poisonous sting. [ME, from L, from Gk] **–scorpioid**, *adj.*

Scot /skɒt/, *n.* **1.** a native or inhabitant of Scotland; a Scotsman. **2.** one of an ancient Gaelic people from northern Ireland who settled in the north-western part of Great Britain in the sixth century, and after whom Scotland was named. [ME; OE *Scottas* (pl.), from LL. *Scotti* the Irish; of unknown orig.]

Scot, *Abbrev.* **1.** Scotland. **2.** Scottish. **3.** Scotch.

scotch /skɒtʃ/, *v.t.* **1.** to injure so as to make harmless. **2.** to put an end to: *Her mother soon scotched her plans for going out.* [b. SCORE and NOTCH]

Scotch /skɒtʃ/, *adj.* **1.** (not usu. used by Scots) Scottish. ◇*n.* **2.** Also, **Scotch whisky.** whisky made in Scotland.

scot-free /skɒt-'fri/, *adj.* free from punishment, payment or harm: *to get off scot-free.*

Scotland /'skɒtlənd/, *n.* a country in north-western Europe, part of the UK; a division of Great Britain in the northern part. Pop. 5 121 000 (1986 est.); 78 775 km². *Cap.:* Edinburgh.

Scotland Yard, *n.* **1.** a short street in London, formerly the site of the London police headquarters. **2.** the London police, esp. the branch engaged in criminal investigation.

Scott /skɒt/, *n.* **1. Charles William Anderson,** 1903–46, English aviator, co-winner of 1934 Melbourne Centenary Air Race, London to Melbourne. **2. Robert Falcon,** 1868–1912, British naval officer and antarctic explorer; reached the South Pole, 1912. **3. Sir Walter,** 1771–1832, Scottish romantic novelist and poet.

Scottish Martyrs /ˌskɒtɪʃ 'mɑːtəz/, *n.pl.* five political activists advocating parliamentary reform who were sentenced to transportation to NSW at trials held in 1793–94 in Scotland.

Scottish terrier /ˌskɒtɪʃ 'terɪə/ *n.* a breed of terrier with short legs and wiry hair, orig. from Scotland. Also, **Scottie**.

scoundrel /'skaʊndrəl/, *n.* a dishonorable man; villain. [orig. uncert.]

scour[1] /'skaʊə/, *v.t.* **1.** to clean or polish by hard rubbing: *to scour pots and pans.* **2.** to clear out (a channel, drain, etc.). **3.** to clear or remove what is dirty or undesirable. ◊*v.i.* **4.** to rub a surface in order to clean or polish it. **5.** to remove dirt, etc. ◊*n.* **6.** the act of scouring. **7.** the place scoured. [ME, probably from MD or MLG, probably from OF, from L: care for, clean] **—scourer**, *n.*

scour[2] /'skaʊə/, *v.i.* **1.** to move or range about rapidly, esp. in search or chase. ◊*v.t.* **2.** to range or pass over, in search, etc.: *He scoured the countryside for her.* [ME]

scourge /skɜːdʒ/, *n., v.*, **scourged, scourging**. ◊*n.* **1.** a whip or lash, esp. for punishment or torture. **2.** any means of punishment. **3.** a cause of severe suffering: *the scourge of disease.* ◊*v.t.* **4.** to whip with a scourge. **5.** to punish or cause to suffer severely. [ME, from AF, from LL: strip off the hide]

Scouse /skaʊs/, *n.* **1.** a person who lives in Liverpool, England. **2.** the dialect of English spoken in Liverpool, England.

scout[1] /skaʊt/, *n.* **1.** a soldier, warship, aeroplane, etc., employed in finding out information about the enemy by spying, etc. **2.** someone sent to search out information, new talent, etc. **3.** the act of searching out information, etc. **4.** (cap.) a member of an organisation (the Scout Association) which aims to develop character, self-reliance, and usefulness to others. **5.** *Colloq.* a fellow: *a good scout.* ◊*v.i.* **6.** to act as a scout; reconnoitre. ◊*v.t.* **7.** to examine or watch for the purpose of obtaining information; reconnoitre: *to scout the enemy's defences.* **8.** *Colloq.* to find by searching (usu. fol. by *out* or *up*). [ME, from OF: action of listening, from L]

scout[2] /skaʊt/, *v.t., v.i.* to reject (an idea, etc.) as being ridiculous. [Scand]

scow /skaʊ/, *n.* a large, flat-bottomed, unpowered boat used chiefly for carrying mud, coal, etc. [D: ferryboat]

scowl /skaʊl/, *v.i.* **1.** to have an angry, sullen or threatening look on the face. ◊*n.* **2.** a scowling expression or look. [ME, from Scand]

SCR, *Abbrev.* silicon-controlled rectifier.

scrabble /'skræbəl/, *v.*, **-bled, -bling**, *n.* ◊*v.i.* **1.** to scratch or scrape, with the claws, hands, etc. **2.** to scribble. **3.** to struggle to gain possession of something. ◊*n.* **4.** a scramble. [D: scratch]

scrag /skræg/, *n., v.*, **scragged, scragging**. ◊*n.* **1.** a thin person or animal. **2.** the thin end of a neck of mutton, etc. ◊*v.t.* **3.** *Colloq.* to wring the neck of. [probably akin to CRAG]

scraggly /'skrægli/, *adj.*, **-glier, -gliest**. irregular; ragged; straggling.

scraggy /'skrægi/, *adj.*, **-gier, -giest**. **1.** thin or bony. **2.** lacking in quantity; meagre: *a scraggy meal.*

scram /skræm/, *v.i.*, **scrammed, scramming**. *Colloq.* to leave quickly; go away. [alteration of SCRAMBLE]

scramble /'skræmbəl/, *v.*, **-bled, -bling**, *n.* ◊*v.i.* **1.** to make one's way hurriedly by use of the hands and feet: *to scramble over rough ground.* **2.** to struggle with others for possession of something. **3.** *Mil., Navy, etc.* (of the crew of an aircraft, submarine, etc., or the craft itself) to prepare for immediate action. ◊*v.t.* **4.** to collect in a hurried or disorderly manner (fol. by *up*, etc.). **5.** to mix together confusedly. **6.** to cook (eggs) by mixing whites and yolks with butter, milk, etc. **7.** *Elect.* to send (a radio signal) in a confused form, so that it can be made intelligible only by a special receiver, and not by a normal instrument. ◊*n.* **8.** a climb or progression over rough, irregular ground, etc. **9.** a form of motorcycle race over very rough, uneven ground. **10.** a disorderly struggle for possession. [nasalised var. of SCRABBLE] **—scrambler**, *n.*

scrap[1] /skræp/, *n., adj., v.*, **scrapped, scrapping**. ◊*n.* **1.** a small piece; fragment: *scraps of paper; scraps of poetry.* **2.** (*pl.*) bits of food, such as those left over after a meal. **3.** →**scrap metal**. **4.** anything put aside as useless, unwanted or worn-out. ◊*adj.* **5.** consisting of scraps: *scrap heap.* **6.** thrown away or left over. ◊*v.t.* **7.** to make into scrap; break up. **8.** to put aside as useless or worthless. [ME, from Scand]

scrap[2] /skræp/, *n., v.*, **scrapped, scrapping**. *Colloq.* ◊*n.* **1.** a fight or quarrel. ◊*v.i.* **2.** to fight or quarrel. [var. of SCRAPE (See defs 5, 7)]

scrape /skreɪp/, *v.*, **scraped, scraping**, *n.* ◊*v.t.* **1.** to remove an outer layer, as of paint, dirt, etc., from (a surface) by drawing or rubbing something sharp or rough over it. **2.** to remove (an outer layer, additional matter, etc.) in this way. **3.** to scratch or produce by scratching. **4.** to collect with difficulty and slowly (fol. by *up* or *together*): *to scrape together enough money.* **5.** to rub harshly on or across (something). ◊*v.i.* **6.** to scrape something. **7.** to rub against something harshly. **8.** to produce a harsh and unmusical tone from a string instrument. **9.** to draw back the foot in making a bow. **10.** to gather or save (money, goods, etc.) with difficulty. ◊*v.* **11. scrape through,** to manage to succeed with difficulty: *We managed to scrape through with very little money.* ◊*n.* **12.** the act of scraping. **13.** a scraping sound. **14.** a scraped place. **15.** an awkward situation. **16.** a fight; scrap. [ME, from Scand] **—scraper**, *n.*

scrap metal, *n.* pieces of metal that can be reworked, esp. scrap iron.

scrappy /'skræpi/, *adj.*, **-pier, -piest**. made up of scraps; fragmentary; disconnected.

scratch /skrætʃ/, *v.t.* **1.** to break or mark slightly with something sharp or rough. **2.** to dig, scrape, or tear (*out, off,* etc.) with the claws, nails, etc. **3.** to rub lightly with the fingernails, etc., to lessen itching. **4.** to rub with a grating sound. **5.** to remove or strike out (writing, etc.). **6.** to withdraw (a horse, contestant, etc.) from list of entries in a race or competition. ◇*v.i.* **7.** to use the nails, claws, etc., for tearing, digging, etc. **8.** to lessen itching by rubbing with the nails, etc. **9.** to make a slight grating noise, as a pen. **10.** to manage with difficulty: *scratch along on very little money.* **11.** to withdraw from a contest. ◇*n.* **12.** a mark produced by scratching. **13.** the act of scratching. **14.** the sound produced by scratching. **15.** the starting place or starting time of a competitor in a race, etc., who has no handicap. **16. from scratch**, from the beginning or from nothing. **17. up to scratch**, of a satisfactory standard. ◇*adj.* **18.** (of a competitor) starting without handicap. **19.** *Colloq.* gathered hastily and without careful selection: *a scratch crew.* [b. obs. *scrat* and *cratch*, both meaning scratch] —**scratchy**, *adj.*

scrawl /skrɔl/, *v.t., v.i.* **1.** to write or draw in an untidy awkward manner. ◇*n.* **2.** something scrawled, as a letter or note. **3.** awkward or careless handwriting. [special use of obs. *scrawl* sprawl, influenced by SCRIBBLE, etc.]

scrawny /ˈskrɔni/, *adj.*, **-nier, -niest.** thin; bony; scraggy: *a long scrawny neck.* [var. of *scranny*]

scream /skrim/, *v.i.* **1.** to make a loud, sharp cry or sound. **2.** to laugh loudly. **3.** to be very noticeable, used esp. of colors. ◇*v.t.* **4.** to say with a scream or screams. ◇*n.* **5.** a loud, sharp cry or sound. **6.** *Colloq.* someone or something that is very funny. [ME; orig. uncert.]

scree /skri/, *n.* a steep mass of broken rocks on the side of a mountain. [Scand]

screech /skritʃ/, *v.i.* **1.** to make a harsh, high-pitched cry. ◇*v.t.* **2.** to say with a screech. ◇*n.* **3.** a harsh, high-pitched cry. [var. of archaic *scritch;* probably imitative]

screech owl, *n.* any owl with a harsh cry.

screed /skrid/, *n.* a long speech or piece of writing; harangue. [OE *scrēade* SHRED]

screen /skrin/, *n.* **1.** a covered frame, curtain, etc., serving as a shelter, partition, etc. **2.** a surface for showing films, slides, etc. **3.** films collectively. **4.** (in a television set) the end of a cathode-ray tube on which the visible image is formed. **5.** anything that shelters, protects, or hides: *a screen of secrecy.* **6.** a frame covered with wire mesh giving protection against insects, etc. **7.** a sieve for grain, sand, etc. ◇*v.t.* **8.** to shelter, protect, or hide with, or as if with, a screen. **9.** to sift by passing through a screen. **10.** to show (pictures, etc.) on a screen. **11.** to provide with a screen. **12.** to examine the loyalty, character, ability, etc., of (job applicants, employees, etc.). [ME, from OF, from OHG]

screenplay /ˈskrinpleɪ/, *n.* the story of a film in written form, including the details of camera positions and movement, action, speech, lighting, etc.

screw /skru/, *n.* **1.** a metal device having a slotted head and a body which narrows to a point with a spiralling ridge, usu. driven into wood with a screwdriver to put together and fix parts of a building, furniture, etc. **2.** a mechanical device consisting of a cylinder with a spiralling ridge winding round it (**external** or **male screw**). **3.** a corresponding part into which such a device fits when turned (**internal** or **female screw**). **4.** something having a spiral form. **5.** a twisting movement; a turn of a screw. **6. have a screw loose**, *Colloq.* to be slightly odd; have crazy ideas. **7. put the screws on**, *Colloq.* to put pressure on; intimidate. ◇*v.t.* **8.** to force, press, hold fast, stretch tight, etc., with, or as with, a screw. **9.** to operate or change position of by a screw. **10.** to turn. **11.** to twist; contort; distort: *The child screwed up her face.* **12.** to force: *screw up one's courage.* **13.** to force (a seller) to lower a price (oft. fol. by *down.*). **14.** *Colloq.* to obtain (something) from a person, sometimes by violence; extract; extort. **15.** *Colloq.* to make a mess of; frustrate (oft. fol. by *up*). ◇*v.i.* **16.** to turn in the same manner as a screw. **17.** to be made for being joined together or taken apart by means of screws (fol. by *on, together, off,* etc.). [ME]

screwball /ˈskrubɔl/, *n. Colloq.* an odd or unconventional person.

screwdriver /ˈskrudraɪvə/, *n.* a tool fitting into the slotted head of a screw, turned to drive the screw in or withdraw it.

screwy /ˈskrui/, *adj.*, **-ier, -iest.** *Colloq.* odd; strange.

scribble /ˈskrɪbəl/, *v.*, **-bled, -bling,** *n.* ◇*v.t.* **1.** to write hastily or carelessly: *to scribble a letter.* ◇*v.i.* **2.** to write literary matter in a hasty, careless way. **3.** to make meaningless marks. ◇*n.* **4.** a hasty or careless piece of writing or drawing. [ME, from ML] —**scribbler**, *n.*

scribbly gum, *n.* any type of eucalypt with smooth bark marked by insects with thin curving lines that look like scribbling.

scribe /skraɪb/, *n.* **1.** (of former times) a penman or copyist who made copies of manuscripts and carried out other clerical duties before the invention of printing. **2.** *Jew. Hist.* one of a class of teachers who taught and explained the Jewish law to the people. **3.** a writer or author. [ME, from L: writer] —**scribal**, *adj.*

scrim /skrɪm/, *n.* cotton or linen cloth of open weave, used for curtains, as a back-drop in the theatre, for cleaning and polishing, etc. [orig. uncert.]

scrimmage /ˈskrɪmɪdʒ/, *n., v.*, **-maged, -maging.** ◇*n.* **1.** a rough or lively struggle. **2.** *Rugby Football.* the action of a number of players struggling for the ball in no set pattern of play. ◇*v.i.* **3.** to take part in a scrimmage. Also, **scrummage**. [var. of *scrimish*, var. of SKIRMISH]

scrimp /skrɪmp/, *v.t.* **1.** to be sparing of or in; stint. **2.** to keep on short allowance, esp.

scrimp of food. ◇*v.i.* **3.** to use severe economy: *They scrimped on butter to save a few cents.* —**scrimpy**, *adj.*

scrip /skrɪp/, *n.* **1.** a written certificate or receipt. **2.** *Finance.* (a certificate representing) shares or stock, sent out to existing shareholders where the purchase price is paid in parts according to agreed terms.

script /skrɪpt/, *n.* **1.** handwriting; handwritten letters or lettering; the characters used in handwriting. **2.** the working text of a play, film, television program, etc. **3.** a manuscript or document in original form. **4.** *Printing.* a typeface made to look like handwriting. [L: (something) written]

Scripture /'skrɪptʃə/, *n.* **1.** the holy writings of the Old and the New Testaments, or of either of them (often called **Holy Scripture** or **the Scriptures**); Holy Writ; the Bible. **2.** (*l.c.*) any writing or book, esp. of a holy nature. [ME, from L: writing] —**scriptural**, *adj.*

scrivener /'skrɪvnə/, *n. Archaic.* **1.** a professional or public writer; a clerk. **2.** → **notary**. [ME]

scrofula /'skrɒfjələ/, *n.* a tuberculous disorder in the body, marked chiefly by swelling of the lymphatic glands, esp. of the neck, and by inflammation of the joints, etc. [ML: glandular swelling] —**scrofulous**, *adj.*

scroll /skroʊl/, *n.* **1.** a roll of parchment or paper, esp. one with writing on it. **2.** something, usu. ornamental, looking like a partly unrolled sheet of paper or having a spiral or coiled form, as at the head of violins, etc. [ME, from AF, of Gmc orig.]

scrooge /skrudʒ/, *n.* a mean, ill-tempered person; miser. [after Ebenezer *Scrooge*, a character in Dickens's story *A Christmas Carol* (1843)]

scrotum /'skroʊtəm/, *n., pl.* **-ta** /-tə/. a pouch of skin that contains the testicles of most male mammals. [L]

scrounge /skraʊndʒ/, *v.t.*, **scrounged**, **scrounging**. *Colloq.* to obtain by borrowing, begging, or stealing. [? var. of d. *scringe* to glean] —**scrounger**, *n.*

scrub[1] /skrʌb/, *v.*, **scrubbed**, **scrubbing**, *n.* ◇*v.t.* **1.** to rub hard with a brush, cloth, etc., or against a rough surface, in washing. **2.** *Colloq.* to get rid of; cancel. ◇*v.i.* **3.** to clean things by hard rubbing. ◇*n.* **4.** the act of scrubbing. [ME, apparently from MD: scratch, rub, scrub]

scrub[2] /skrʌb/, *n.* **1.** low trees or shrubs, collectively. **2.** a large area covered with scrub. **3.** tall, thick rainforest in eastern Australia. **4.** a person, animal or thing which is smaller than usual and therefore considered of common or inferior breeding or status. **5. the scrub**, *Colloq.* country areas in general, as opposed to the city. [var. of SHRUB]

scrubber /'skrʌbə/, *n.* a farm animal, such as a horse, cow, etc., which has taken to the bush and run wild, thus losing condition.

scrubby /'skrʌbi/, *adj.*, **-bier**, **-biest**. **1.** consisting of or covered with stunted trees, etc., or scrub. **2.** undersized or stunted. **3.** unfortunate; shabby; wretched.

scrub turkey, *n.* → **brush turkey**.

scruff /skrʌf/, *n.* the back of the neck; nape. [D: horse's withers]

scruffy /'skrʌfi/, *adj. Colloq.* uncared for or dirty; shabby; unkempt.

scrum /skrʌm/, *n. Rugby Football. n.* **1.** a method of restarting play after a rule has been broken, in which the opposing forwards pack together and push in formation, heads down, in an attempt to gain ground, while the ball is thrown in and the hookers try to kick it back to their team-mates. **2.** the formation. [short for SCRUMMAGE]

scrummage /'skrʌmɪdʒ/, *n.* **1.** → **scrum**. **2.** → **scrimmage**.

scrumptious /'skrʌmpʃəs/, *adj. Colloq.* very tasty, fine, or nice; splendid: *to have a scrumptious meal.* [orig. used, meaning 'stingy', from SCRIMP]

scrunch /skrʌntʃ/, *v.t., v.i.* **1.** to crunch; crush. ◇*n.* **2.** the act or sound of scrunching. [var. of CRUNCH]

scruple /'skrupəl/, *n.* **1.** a doubt stemming from conscience, etc., relating to making decisions between right and wrong. **2.** very small part or amount. **3.** unit of weight in the imperial system, equal to 20 grams or approx. 1.3×10^{-3} kg. [L: small sharp stone, fig., doubt]

scrupulous /'skrupjələs/, *adj.* **1.** having or showing a strict regard for what is right; having scruples. **2.** careful down to the last detail; precise; exact. —**scrupulosity**, **scrupulousness**, *n.*

scrutineer /skrutə'nɪə/, *n.* **1.** someone who inspects the counting of votes by electoral officers. **2.** an official in a race, contest, etc., who checks that the rules are obeyed.

scrutinise or **scrutinize** /'skrutənaɪz/, *v.t.*, **-nised**, **-nising**. to examine closely or critically.

scrutiny /'skrutəni/, *n., pl.* **-nies**. **1.** a searching examination; minute inquiry. **2.** a searching look. [LL]

scuba /'skubə/, *n.* a type of breathing apparatus for free-swimming divers, consisting of a mouthpiece joined by hoses to a tank or tanks of compressed air. [s(*elf*-)c(*ontained*) u(*nderwater*) b(*reathing*) a(*pparatus*)]

scud /skʌd/, *v.*, **scudded**, **scudding**, *n.* ◇*v.i.* **1.** to run or move quickly or hurriedly. **2.** *Naut.* to run before a gale with little or no sail set. ◇*n.* **3.** clouds, spray, etc., driven by the wind. [Scand]

scuff /skʌf/, *v.t.* **1.** to scrape with the feet. **2.** to make a mark on (shoes, furniture, etc.) by scraping or hard use. ◇*v.i.* **3.** to walk without raising the feet; shuffle. ◇*n.* **4.** the act or sound of scuffing. **5.** a type of soft shoe without a back. [? short for SCUFFLE]

scuffle /'skʌfəl/, *v.*, **-fled**, **-fling**, *n.* ◇*v.i.* **1.** to struggle or fight in a scrambling, confused manner. ◇*n.* **2.** a confused struggle or fight. [? of Scand orig.]

scull /skʌl/, *n.* **1. a.** an oar worked from side to side over the stern of a boat as a means of moving forwards. **b.** one of a pair of oars operated, one on each side, by one person. ◇*v.t., v.i.* **2.** to move by means of a scull or sculls. [ME; orig. unknown]

scullery /'skʌləri/, *n., pl.* **-leries.** a small room where rough, dirty work or the washing of pots, etc., is done. [ME, from OF: dish, from L: salver]

Scullin /'skʌlən/, *n.* **James Henry**, 1876-1953, Australian federal Labor politician; prime minister of Australia 1929-32 and a close adviser to John Curtin during World War II.

scullion /'skʌljən/, *n. Archaic.* a kitchen servant. [ME, ? from OF: dishcloth]

sculpt /skʌlpt/, *v.t., v.i.* to carve (a sculpture). [F, from L] —**sculptor**, *n.*

sculpture /'skʌlptʃə/, *n., v.,* **-tured, -turing.** ◇*n.* **1.** the fine art of forming figures or designs in relief (standing out from the background), or in the round (standing independently) by cutting marble, wood, granite, etc., by fashioning clay or plastic materials, or by making moulds for casting in bronze or other metal. **2.** a piece or pieces of such work. ◇*v.t.* **3.** to carve or make (a figure, design, etc.); represent in sculpture. **4.** *Geog.* (of water, wind, etc.) to change the form of (the land surface) by erosion. [ME, from L] —**sculptural**, *adj.*

Sculthorpe /'skʌlθɔp/, *n.* **Peter Joshua**, born 1929, Australian composer; works include *Sun Music* (1968).

scum /skʌm/, *n., v.,* **scummed, scumming.** ◇*n.* **1.** a film of impurities on a liquid. **2.** refuse or rubbish. **3.** (*offensive*) low, worthless people. ◇*v.i.* **4.** to form scum; become covered with scum. [ME, from MD] —**scummy**, *adj.*

scungy /'skʌndʒi/, *adj. Colloq.* mean; dirty; unpleasant. [Brit d.]

scupper /'skʌpə/, *n. Naut.* an opening in the side of a ship at or just below the deck, to allow water to run off. [orig. uncert.]

scurf /skɜf/, *n.* **1.** → **dandruff**. **2.** any dry, scaly matter forming crust-like flakes on a surface. [OE, from Scand]

scurrilous /'skʌrələs/, *adj.* **1.** coarsely rude and nasty: *a scurrilous attack.* **2.** marked by or using a low joking manner; coarsely jocular or derisive: *a scurrilous jest.* —**scurrility**, *n.*

scurry /'skʌri/, *v.,* **-ried, -rying,** *n., pl.* **-ries.** ◇*v.i.* **1.** to go or move quickly or in haste. ◇*n.* **2.** a scurrying rush: *We heard the scurry of little feet down the stairs.*

scurvy /'skɜvi/, *n., adj.,* **-vier, -viest.** ◇*n.* **1.** *Med.* a disease marked by swollen and bleeding gums, dull blue spots on the skin, inability to stand, etc., due to a diet lacking in vitamin C. ◇*adj.* **2.** low, mean, or worthless: *a scurvy trick.* —**scurvily**, *adv.* —**scurviness**, *n.*

scut /skʌt/, *n.* a short tail, esp. that of a hare, rabbit, or deer. [Scand]

scuttle[1] /'skʌtl/, *n.* a large container, esp. for holding coal. [OE: a dish or platter, from L]

scuttle[2] /'skʌtl/, *v.,* **-tled, -tling,** *n.* ◇*v.i.* **1.** to run with quick, hasty steps; hurry. ◇*n.* **2.** a quick pace.

scuttle[3] /'skʌtl/, *n., v.,* **-tled, -tling.** ◇*n.* **1.** a small opening in a ship's deck or side, with a lid or cover. ◇*v.t.* **2.** to sink (a boat) by cutting a hole below the waterline or opening the valves in the hull. [ME: hatchway lid, apparently from D: to shut]

scuttlebutt /'skʌtlbʌt/, *n.* **1.** *Naut.* a cask with a hole cut in it through which a cup can be filled, used to hold drinking water. **2.** *Colloq.* rumor; gossip.

scythe /saɪð/, *n.* a tool consisting of a long, curved blade fastened at an angle to a handle, for cutting grass, etc., by hand. [OE *sīthe*]

se-, a prefix applied mainly to stems not used as words, having a general meaning of setting apart or taking away, as in *seclude, seduce.* [L]

Se, *Chem. Symbol.* selenium.

SE, *Abbrev.* **1.** south-east. **2.** south-eastern. See Appendix.

sea /si/, *n.* **1.** the salt waters that cover most of the earth's surface. **2.** a division of these waters, marked off in most cases by land boundaries: *the Tasman sea.* **3.** a large lake or land-locked body of water. **4.** the movement on the surface of the ocean or other body of water, usu. caused by the wind; the waves. **5.** one of the unclear areas on the surface of the moon, formerly thought to be areas of water. **6.** a huge quantity: *a sea of faces; a sea of troubles.* **7. at sea, a.** out on the ocean. **b.** in a state of uncertainty. **8. put to sea,** to set out from port or land. **9. the high seas,** the sea well away from land. ◇*adj.* **10.** of, relating to, or made suitable for the sea. [E *sǣ*]

sea-anemone /'si-əˌnɛməni/, *n.* a common sea animal, a type of coelenterate, which stays in one place and catches food by means of one or more circles of tentacles on a disc on top of a tube-shaped body.

seaboard /'sibɔd/, *n.* the line where land and sea meet.

sea-cow /'si-kaʊ/, *n.* a plant-eating mammal which lives in the water, e.g. dugong.

sea-dog /'si-dɒg/, *n.* a sailor, esp. one of long experience.

sea-eagle /'si-igəl/, *n.* a type of eagle which feeds on fish, e.g. the **white-breasted sea-eagle** of Australia and certain areas of Asia.

sea elephant, *n.* a type of large, earless seal of Antarctic areas and North America.

seafarer /'sifɛərə/, *n.* **1.** a sailor. **2.** a traveller on the sea. —**seafaring**, *adj.*

seafood /'sifud/, *n.* any saltwater fish or shellfish which is used for food.

seagoing /'sigoʊɪŋ/, *adj.* **1.** (of a ship, etc.) designed or fit for sailing in the open sea. **2.** going to sea; seafaring.

seagrass matting

seagrass matting /ˌsigras 'mætɪŋ/, n. matting made using certain grass fibres.

seagull /'sigʌl/, n. a gull, esp. any of the type which lives by or on the sea.

seahorse /'sihɔs/, n. 1. a small fish with a prehensile (grasping) tail and a beaked head that is turned at right angles to the body. 2. a fabled sea animal with the front of a horse and the tail of a fish.

seal[1] /sil/, n. 1. a design pressed onto a piece of wax or paper, or which is itself put onto a document as evidence that the document is official and/or authentic. 2. a stamp engraved with such a design. 3. an impression made with such a stamp. 4. a piece of wax or similar substance, fixed onto a document, envelope, etc., which then cannot be opened without breaking the seal. 5. anything that effectively closes something. 6. a mark, etc., serving as evidence of something. 7. *Plumbing.* a small amount of water left standing in a trap to prevent the escape of foul air from below. 8. a road surface of hard material, such as tar, bitumen, etc. 9. **set one's seal on** or **to**, to approve; endorse. ◇v.t. 10. to fix a seal to a document, etc. 11. to approve, authorise, or confirm: *to seal an agreement.* 12. to fasten or close by or as if by a seal. 13. to decide finally: *to seal someone's fate.* 14. to surface a road with tar, etc. [ME, from OF, from LL]

seal[2] /sil/, n., pl. **seals**, (esp. collectively for def. 1) **seal**, v. ◇n. 1. a type of sea-dwelling, meat-eating mammal, with smooth fur, large flippers, and a long, rounded body, e.g. the eared sea-lion and **fur seal**, and the earless or **hair seals**. 2. (leather made from) the skin of the seal. ◇v.i. 3. to hunt or take seals. [OE *seolh*]

sealant /'silənt/, n. a type of fluid, chemical preparation, etc., used to give a tough, watertight coating to a surface, usu. on timber, concrete, etc. Also, **sealer.**

sea-legs /'si-legz/, n.pl. *Colloq.* 1. the ability to walk with steadiness or ease on a rolling ship. 2. the ability to resist seasickness.

sea leopard, n. a large black-spotted, Southern Hemisphere seal that lives alone and feeds on penguins and other sea birds. Also, **leopard seal.**

sea-level /'si-levəl/, n. the level of the surface of the sea when halfway between mean high and low water, used as a reference point when recording the height of mountains, etc.

sea lion, n. 1. the Australian white-naped hair seal. 2. a type of large eared seal of the northern Pacific and the Pacific Pacific coast of North America.

seam /sim/, n. 1. the line formed by sewing together pieces of cloth, leather, etc. 2. any line between two edges; crack or fissure; groove. 3. *Geol.* a comparatively thin layer or stratum; a bed, as of coal. ◇v.t. 4. to join with a seam; sew the seams of. 5. to mark with wrinkles, scars, etc.; furrow. ◇v.i. 6. to become cracked, scarred, or furrowed. [ME *seme*, OE *sēam*]

season

seaman /'simən/, n., pl. **-men.** 1. a sailor, or someone skilled in handling a boat. 2. *Mil.* the lowest rank in the Royal Australian Navy. See Appendix. — **seamanship**, n.

seamstress /'simstrəs/, n. a woman whose job is sewing. Also, **sempstress.**

seamy /'simi/, adj., **-mier, -miest.** bad; sordid: *the seamy side of life.*

seance /'seɪɒns/, n. *Occult.* a meeting of people seeking to receive messages from spirits. Also, **séance.** [F: a sitting, from OF, from L: sit]

sea perch, n. any of a number of Australian, usu. tropical, fishes, e.g. the **scarlet sea perch**, of northern reef waters.

seaplane /'siplem/, n. an aeroplane that can land on water, being provided with floats instead of landing wheels.

sear /sɪə/, v.t. 1. to burn or blacken the surface of. 2. to harden or make unfeeling. 3. to dry up or wither. [OE *sēar*]

search /sɜtʃ/, v.t. 1. to go or look through carefully in seeking to find something. 2. to examine (a person) for hidden objects by going through his pockets, etc. 3. to probe. 4. to bring or find (*out*) by a search: *to search out all the facts.* ◇v.i. 5. to seek; make examination or investigation. ◇v. 6. **search me**, *Colloq.* I don't know. ◇n. 7. the act of searching; careful examination or investigation. 8. *Law.* an examination (for a buyer) of records and registers at the Land Titles Office to find claims affecting title to a property. [ME, from OF, from LL, from L: circle]

searching /'sɜtʃɪŋ/, adj. keen; penetrating.

searchlight /'sɜtʃlaɪt/, n. 1. an apparatus, usu. consisting of a light and a reflector, for throwing a beam of light in any direction. 2. a beam of light thrown in this way: *caught in the searchlight.*

search-warrant /'sɜtʃ-wɒrənt/, n. a court order allowing the searching of a house, etc., usu. for stolen goods.

Sears Tower /'sɪəz taʊə/, n. the tallest building in the world, erected in Chicago between 1970–74. 443 m.

seascout /'si-skaʊt/, n. a Scout receiving training in seamanship, etc.

sea-shell /'si-ʃɛl/, n. the shell of any sea-dwelling soft-bodied mollusc.

seasickness /'sisɪknəs/, n. nausea, vomiting, or other discomfort caused by the movement of a vessel at sea. — **seasick**, adj.

sea-snake /'si-sneɪk/, n. a poisonous snake with a fin-like tail found in tropical seas.

season /'sizən/, n. 1. one of the four periods of the year (spring, summer, autumn, and winter), astronomically beginning each at an equinox or a solstice, but geographically at different dates in different climates. 2. a period of the year marked by particular conditions of weather, temperature, etc. 3. the period of the year when something is best or easily obtained: *the avocado season.* 4. the period of the year marked by certain conditions, festivities, activities, etc.: *the cricket season*; /a dull season in trade. **5.** any period of time. **6.** a suitable, proper, fitting, or right time. **7.** *Agric.* a fertile period in female stock; time for mating. **8. in good season,** early enough. **9.** (of female animals) a period of fertility or sexual arousal: *The bitch is in season.* ◊*v.t.* **10.** to increase or improve the flavor of (food) by adding salt, pepper, spices, herbs, etc. **11.** to give a certain character to: *Her conversation was seasoned with wit.* **12.** to mature, ripen, or condition by exposure to suitable conditions or treatment. **13.** to lessen; moderate; temper: *to season his anger.* ◊*v.i.* **14.** to become seasoned, matured, hardened, etc. [ME, from OF, from L: (time of) sowing]

seasoning /'sizənɪŋ/, *n.* **1.** something that flavors or seasons, esp. salt, spices, herbs, or other condiments. **2.** → **stuffing** (def. 3).

seat /sit/, *n.* **1.** something for sitting on, such as a chair or bench; the place on or in which one sits. **2.** the part of a chair, etc., on which one sits. **3.** the part of the body on which one sits; buttocks. **4.** a manner of sitting, as on horseback. **5.** the part on which the base of anything rests. **6.** the base itself. **7.** an established place or centre: *the seat of government; a seat of learning.* **8.** place to live, esp. a large country house with parkland. **9.** the (elected) right to sit as a member in a legislative or similar body such as the House of Representatives. **10.** a parliamentary electorate (area represented by a member). **11.** membership in a stock exchange, etc. **12.** a directorship of a limited company. **13. take a seat,** to sit down. ◊*v.t.* **14.** to place on a seat or seats; cause to sit down. **15.** to find seats for; accommodate with seats: *a hall that seats 1000 people.* **16.** to fix firmly in a particular place. [ME, from Scand]

seat belt, *n.* a belt attached to the frame of a motor vehicle, or to a seat in an aeroplane, etc., for holding a person safely in place against sudden turns, stops, collision, etc. Also, **safety belt.**

SEATO /'sitoʊ/, *n.* a former defence alliance of anti-Communist nations, including Australia, Britain, France, New Zealand, Pakistan, the Philippines, Thailand and the US; dissolved 1977. Also, **South-East Asia Treaty Organisation.** [abbrev.]

Seattle /si'ætl/, *n.* a seaport in the US, in western Washington. Pop. 486 200 (1986 est., city).

sea-urchin /'si-ɜtʃən/, *n.* a small globe-shaped sea creature with a spiny shell.

seaward /'siwəd/, *adj.* **1.** facing or tending towards the sea: *their seaward course.* **2.** (of a wind) coming from the sea. ◊*adv.* **3.** seawards.

seawards /'siwədz/, *adv.* towards the sea. Also, **seaward.**

sea wasp, *n.* a type of box jellyfish with a highly poisonous sting, esp. one found in tropical Australian waters.

sea water, *n.* the water which makes up the seas of the earth, consisting of about 96.4 per cent water, 2.8 per cent common salt, and various other chemicals in small quantities. **–seawater,** *adj.*

seaweed /'siwid/, *n.* any plant or plants growing in the ocean, esp. algae.

seaworthy /'siwɜði/, *adj.* (of a ship) adequately and safely built and fitted out to sail at sea. **–seaworthiness,** *n.*

sebaceous /sə'beɪʃəs/, *adj.* **1.** relating to or like tallow or fat; fatty; greasy. **2.** secreting a fatty substance. [NL, from L: tallow]

Sebastopol /sə'bæstəpɒl/, *n.* → **Sevastopol.**

sebum /'sibəm/, *n.* the fatty secretion of the sebaceous glands. [L: tallow, grease]

sec /sɛk/, *n.* *Maths.* the ratio of the hypotenuse (the side opposite the right angle) to the base in a right-angled triangle; the reciprocal of the cosine of an angle. Also, **secant.** [abbrev.]

sec., *Abbrev.* **1.** second. **2.** secretary.

secant /'sikənt/, *n.* *Maths.* **1.** a straight line which cuts a circle or other curve. **2.** → **sec.** [L: cutting]

secateurs /'sɛkətəz, sɛkə'tɜz/, *n.pl.* a scissor-like instrument for pruning or cutting back shrubs, etc. [F, from L: cut]

secede /sə'sid/, *v.i.* **-ceded, -ceding.** to withdraw formally from a friendship, alliance or association, as from a political or religious organisation. [L: go back, withdraw] **–secession,** *n.*

seclude /sə'klud/, *v.t.* **-cluded, -cluding.** to shut off or keep apart. [L] **–secluded,** *adj.*

seclusion /sə'kluʒən/, *n.* **1.** the condition of being secluded; retirement; solitude: *He found seclusion in the country, where he could study undisturbed.* **2.** a quiet or secluded place. **–seclusive,** *adj.*

Secombe /'sikəm/, *n.* **Sir Harry,** born 1921, Welsh comedian and singer; one of the Goons.

second[1] /'sɛkənd/, *adj.* **1.** next after the first in order, place, time, rank, value, quality, etc.; the ordinal of two; 2nd. **2.** alternate: *every second Monday.* **3.** *Music.* the lower of two parts for the same instrument or voice: *second alto.* **4.** additional; further: *to get a second chance.* ◊*n.* **5.** someone or something that comes next to or after the first, in order, quality, rank, etc.: *King Charles the second.* **6.** *Music.* **a.** the interval between two successive notes. **b.** → **alto. 7.** a helper or assistant, esp. to a boxer, duellist, etc. ◊*v.t.* **8.** to support; assist. **9.** to express support of (a motion, etc.) as a necessary step before further discussion of the motion or voting on it. ◊*adv.* **10.** in the second place, group, etc. [ME, from F, from L]

second[2] /'sɛkənd/, *n.* **1.** a sixtieth part of a minute of time; the basic SI unit of time. **2.** *Geom., etc.* the sixtieth part of a minute of a degree equivalent to 4.848 136 8 x 10^{-6} radians. **3.** a moment or instant. [ME, from F, from ML *secunda (minūta)*, i.e., the result of the second division of the hour into sixty]

second³ /səˈkɒnd/, *v.t.* to move (a military officer, etc.) for a limited time to another post, organisation, or responsibility.

secondary /ˈsekəndri/, *adj., n., pl.* **-aries**. ◇*adj.* **1.** next after the first in order, place, time, importance, etc. **2.** belonging or relating to a second order, division, stage, period, rank, etc. **3.** of or taken from something else; derived; not primary or original: *He used too many secondary sources in his essay.* **4.** of or relating to the processing of primary products: *a secondary industry.* **5.** of minor or lesser importance; subordinate; auxiliary. **6.** *Chem.* **a.** involving, or obtained from replacement of, two atoms or radicals. **b.** containing a carbon atom united to two other carbon atoms in a chain or ring molecule. **7.** *Elect.* relating to the induced circuit, coil, or current in an induction coil, etc. **8.** *Geol.* relating to a rock or mineral derived from another, by decay, alteration, etc. **9.** *Birds.* relating to any of a set of flight feathers on the second segment of a bird's wing. ◇*n.* **10.** someone or something that is secondary. [ME, from L] —**secondarily**, *adv.*

secondary cell, *n.* a voltaic cell which can be charged by passing a current through it in the opposite direction to the electromotive force, and which can therefore be used as a convenient apparatus for storing electrical energy.

secondary color *or* **secondary colour**, *n.* a color produced by mixing two or more primary colors, e.g. orange, green, or violet.

secondary consumer, *n.* a carnivore that eats herbivores. See **primary consumer, tertiary consumer**.

secondary emission, *n. Phys.* an emission of electrons (**secondary electrons**) from a metal which is struck by a beam of fast-moving electrons (**primary electrons**) or ions from another source.

secondary industry, *n.* an industry involved in the production of manufactured goods.

secondary school, *n.* a school providing education after the finish of primary school.

secondary stress, *n. Linguistics.* a stress accent weaker than the primary or main stress, but stronger than a lack of stress.

second-class /ˈsekənd-klas/, *adj.* **1.** of or belonging to the class below the highest, esp. of travelling conditions. **2.** second-rate; inferior. **3.** treated as if inferior or of less importance: *Women were second-class citizens.*

second cousin, *n.* See **cousin**.

second-degree /ˈsekənd-dəgri/, *adj.* of a degree which is next in seriousness to the first-degree, either more serious, such as *second-degree burns* or less serious, such as *second-degree murder.*

second fiddle, *n.* **1.** (in a musical score) the part written to be played by the second violin or violins. **2.** someone who plays such a part. **3. play second fiddle**, to take a minor or secondary part.

Second Fleet, *n.* the name given to the second company of vessels to arrive in Australia carrying convicts, supplies and the first detachment of the New South Wales Corps.

second-hand /ˈsekənd-hænd/, sekənd-ˈhænd/, *adj.; /sekənd-ˈhænd/, adv.,* ◇*adj.* **1.** obtained from another; not original: *second-hand knowledge.* **2.** used or owned before, by someone else: *second-hand clothes.* **3.** dealing in used goods: *a second-hand bookseller.* ◇*adv.* **4.** after having been owned by another person: *to buy goods second-hand.*

Second International, *n.* See **International** (def. 2).

second nature, *n.* a habit, tendency, etc., so long practised that it is firmly fixed in one's character: *Correcting other people's grammar is second nature to him.*

Second Reich, *n.* See **Reich** (def. 2).

seconds /ˈsekəndz/, *n.pl.* **1.** *Colloq.* **a.** a second helping at a meal. **b.** a second course, esp. dessert. **2.** goods with some slight manufacturing imperfections.

second sight, *n.* clairvoyance.

second wind, *n.* **1.** the return of more comfortable breathing and the lessening of muscular strain, which occurs if exertion continues. **2.** a return of interest, enthusiasm, etc.

Second World War, *n.* → **World War II**.

secrecy /ˈsikrəsi/, *n., pl.* **-cies**. **1.** the condition of being secret or hidden: *a meeting in strict secrecy.* **2.** privacy; retirement; seclusion. [obs. *secre(e)* SECRET + -CY]

secret /ˈsikrət/, *adj.* **1.** done, made, or carried out without the knowledge of others: *secret negotiations.* **2.** faithful or careful in keeping secrets; close-mouthed. **3.** designed to escape notice or knowledge: *a secret drawer.* **4.** beyond ordinary human understanding. ◇*n.* **5.** something secret, hidden, or concealed. **6.** a mystery: *the secrets of nature.* **7.** a method or art known only to the chosen or the few: *the secret of happiness.* **8. in secret**, with no-one else knowing. [ME, from F, from L: divided off]

secret agent, *n.* a spy.

secretariat /sekrəˈtɛəriət/, *n.* the officials or office entrusted with keeping records and carrying out secretarial duties, esp. for an international organisation, government, etc. [F, from ML: the office of a secretary]

secretary /ˈsekrətri, ˈsekrətəri/, *n., pl.* **-taries**. a person who writes letters, makes telephone calls, keeps records, etc., for a single person or an organisation. [ML: confidential officer, from L: (something) secret] —**secretarial**, *adj.*

secrete /səˈkrit/, *v.t.,* **-creted, -creting**. **1.** *Biol.* to separate off, prepare, or chemically convert from the blood, as in the process of secretion. **2.** to hide or keep secret. [L: put apart] —**secretor**, *n.*

secretion /səˈkriʃən/, *n.* **1.** the process or function of cells, esp. in the glands, by which various substances, such as bile, milk, etc., are separated and chemically converted from blood. **2.** the product secreted. [L] —**secretionary, secretory**, *adj.*

secretive /ˈsikrətɪv/, /səˈkritɪv/, *for def. 2., adj.* **1.** having or showing a tendency to secrecy; reticent: *He seemed secretive about his new job.* **2.** relating to secretion.

secret police, *n.* a police force whose activities are kept secret from the general public, and whose job is to deal with those people suspected of working against the government.

secret service, *n.* **1.** the department of government concerned with national security, esp. with espionage. **2.** official service of a secret nature; espionage.

sect /sɛkt/, *n.* **1.** a group of people following a particular religious faith. **2.** a group regarded as breaking away from the general religious tradition or as heretical. [ME, from L: following]

-sect, a word part meaning 'cut', as in *intersect*. [L]

sectarian /sɛkˈtɛəriən/, *adj.* of or relating to sects. —**sectarianism**, *n.*

section /ˈsɛkʃən/, *n.* **1.** a part cut off or separated. **2.** one of a number of parts that go together to make a whole: *sections of a fishing rod; a section in a book.* **3.** the act of cutting; separation by cutting. **4.** a thin slice of a tissue, mineral, etc., esp. for examination under a microscope. **5.** the representation of an object as it would appear if cut by a plane, showing the structure inside; cross-section. **6.** *Mil.* a small unit, which may consist of two or more squads. **7.** *Surg.* a type of operation in which it is necessary to cut open the skin, etc., esp. a caesarean section. **8.** a division of a bus route, etc., with a fixed fare. **9.** Also, **section mark**. a mark (§) used to mark a section of a book, chapter, etc., or as a mark of reference to a footnote, etc. ◇*v.t.* **10.** to cut or divide into sections. [L: a cutting]

sectional /ˈsɛkʃənəl/, *adj.* **1.** relating to a particular section; local; partisan: *full of sectional pride.* **2.** made up of several separate sections.

sector /ˈsɛktə/, *n.* **1.** *Geom.* a plane figure bounded by two radii and the included arc of a circle, ellipse, etc. **2.** a mathematical instrument consisting of two flat rulers hinged together at one end. **3.** (a division of) a field or area of activity. [LL, special use of L *sector* cutter] —**sectoral**, *adj.*

secular /ˈsɛkjələ/, *adj.* **1.** of or relating to the world, or to things not religious, holy, or spiritual; temporal; worldly. **2.** (of literature, music, etc.) not relating to or connected with religion. **3.** (of education, etc.) dealing with non-religious subjects, or, esp., excluding religious instruction. **4.** happening or celebrated once in an age or century: *the secular games of Rome.* **5.** going on from age to age; continuing through long ages. ◇*n.* **6.** → **layman**. **7.** one of the clergy not belonging to a religious order. [LL: worldly, from L: belonging to an age] —**secularise**, *v.*

secularism /ˈsɛkjələrɪzəm/, *n.* **1.** secular spirit or tendencies, esp. a system of political or social philosophy which refuses to accept all forms of religious faith and worship. **2.** the view that public education and other matters of state or government policy should be carried out without the introduction of a religious element. —**secularist**, *n.* —**secularistic**, *adj.*

secure /səˈkjuə/, *adj., v.,* **-cured, -curing.** ◇*adj.* **1.** free from or not open to danger; safe. **2.** not likely to fall, give in, become displaced, etc. **3.** affording safety, usu. of a place. **4.** in safe keeping. **5.** free from care; without anxiety. **6.** sure; certain: *to be secure of victory.* ◇*v.t.* **7.** to get hold or possession of; obtain. **8.** to make secure from danger or harm; make safe. **9.** to make sure or certain; ensure. **10.** to make firm or fast. **11.** to confine or close in. **12.** to make not able to be entered, or nearly so, as a military position. **13.** to make someone to whom money is owed certain of payment by the pledge or mortgaging of property. ◇*v.i.* **14.** to be safe; get security: *to secure against danger.* [L: free from care]

security /səˈkjuərəti/, *n., pl.* **-ties.** **1.** freedom from danger, risk, etc.; safety. **2.** freedom from care, worry, or doubt; confidence. **3.** something that secures or makes safe; protection; defence. **4.** protection from or measures taken against the giving away of state secrets, theft, infiltration, damage, etc. **5.** an assurance; guarantee. **6.** *Law.* something given or left as surety for the fulfilment of a promise, the payment of a debt, etc. **7.** (*usu. pl.*) stocks and shares, etc. [ME, from L]

Security Council, *n.* the body of the UN mainly responsible for the maintenance of international peace and security, consisting of five permanent members with the right of veto and ten elected members serving for two years.

Security Force, *n.* a body of troops sent by the UN Security Council to encourage peaceful settlements in cases of international dispute. Official name, **United Nations Peacekeeping Force.**

sedan /səˈdæn/, *n.* **1.** a four-door passenger car seating four to six people. **2.** a covered seat carried by two people, much used in the 17th and 18th centuries. [? from It, from L: seat]

sedate /səˈdeɪt/, *adj., v.,* **-dated, -dating.** ◇*adj.* **1.** calm, quiet, or composed; sober; undisturbed by passion or excitement. ◇*v.t.* **2.** to calm or put to sleep by means of sedatives or tablets that relax the body. [L: calmed] —**sedateness**, *n.*

sedation /səˈdeɪʃən/, *n.* **1.** the condition of lessened pain or anxiety, usu. brought on by a sedative. **2.** the act or fact of soothing or lowering irritability or pain.

sedative /ˈsɛdətɪv/, *adj.* **1.** tending to calm or soothe. **2.** *Med.* reducing irritability or excitement; easing pain. ◇*n.* **3.** a sedative drug.

sedentary /ˈsɛdəntri/, *adj.* **1.** marked by or needing a sitting position: *a sedentary occupation.* **2.** used to sitting a great deal and taking little exercise. **3.** *Chiefly Zool.* **a.** staying in one place; not migratory. **b.** (of animals) not often moving about, or joined to an object that does not move. **4.** *Geol.* marking or relating to a soil formed directly from the solid rocks under it. [L] —**sedentariness**, *n.*

sedge /sedʒ/, *n.* any of the rush or grass-like plants often growing in wet places. [OE *secg*]

sediment /'sedəmənt/, *n.* 1. matter which settles to the bottom of a liquid; lees; dregs. 2. *Geol.* mineral or organic matter left or put down by water, air, or ice. [F, from L: a setting] —**sedimentary**, *adj.* —**sedimentation**, *n.*

sedition /sə'dɪʃən/, *n.* 1. the urging to discontent or rebellion against the government. 2. action or language promoting such discontent or rebellion. [ME, from L: a going apart] —**seditious**, *adj.*

seduce /sə'djus/, *v.t.*, **-duced, -ducing.** 1. to persuade to have sexual intercourse. 2. to lead away from what is right; entice away from duty; corrupt. 3. to lead or draw away, esp. from principles, faith, etc. 4. to win over; entice. [ME, from L: lead aside] —**seducer**, *n.* —**seduction**, *n.*

seductive /sə'dʌktɪv/, *adj.* tending to seduce; enticing; captivating: *a seductive smile*; *a seductive dress.* —**seductiveness**, *n.*

sedulous /'sedʒələs/, *adj.* 1. hardworking and careful; persevering; painstaking. 2. carefully worked at: *sedulous flattery.* [L: busy, careful] —**sedulity**, *n.*

see[1] /si/, *v.*, **saw, seen, seeing.** ◇*v.t.* 1. to observe, be aware of, or perceive, with the eyes. 2. to look at. 3. to imagine or remember: *I see the house as it used to be; I cannot see her as a teacher.* 4. to be aware of with any or all of the senses: *I hate to see a good man turn to crime.* 5. to have experience of: *He's seen a lot of life.* 6. to view or visit as a spectator: *Have you seen the old part of town?* 7. to sense with the mind; understand: *Do you see where we went wrong?* 8. to recognise; appreciate: *I don't see the use of that.* 9. to consider; interpret: *I see the problem this way.* 10. to find out; ascertain: *See who is knocking.* 11. to meet socially: *We are seeing friends tonight.* 12. to visit formally; consult: *to see a doctor.* 13. to receive as a visitor: *The doctor will see you now.* 14. to accompany or escort: *May I see you home?* 15. to make sure: *See that the work is done.* ◇*v.i.* 16. to have or use the power of sight. 17. to understand. 18. to find out; enquire. 19. to give attention or care: *Go and see to it now.* 20. to think; deliberate: *I'll see whether you may go.* ◇*v.* 21. Some special uses are: **see about**, to deal with or attend to.
see in, to greet; celebrate: *to see in the new year.*
see off, to be with someone as he is leaving, esp. as a courtesy.
see out, 1. to continue in (a job) until it is finished. 2. to live until the end of (a period) or outlive (a person).
see things, to imagine things; hallucinate.
see through, 1. to detect: *to see through a disguise.* 2. to remain until the finish of: *to see a project through.* 3. to help or support in finishing something: *His family saw him through university.* [ME; OE *sēon*]

see[2] /si/, *n.* the office or jurisdiction of a bishop. [ME, from OF, from L]

seed /sid/, *n., pl.* **seeds, seed,** *v.* ◇*n.* 1. the part of a plant that has the power to grow new plants, esp. as preserved for growing a new crop, including tubers, bulbs, etc. 2. such parts all together: *to sow seed.* 3. *Bot.* a structure containing an embryo plant (the germ) and food reserves (starch), formed from an ovule after it has been fertilised. 4. any small, seed-like part or fruit, e.g. a grain of wheat. 5. (*usu. pl.*) the beginning of anything: *the seeds of friendship.* 6. children; offspring; progeny. 7. semen or sperm. 8. the ovum or ova of certain animals. 9. **go** or **run to seed, a.** (of plants) to pass to the stage of yielding seed. **b.** to come near the end of vigor, usefulness, prosperity, etc. ◇*v.t.* 10. to sow (land) with seed. 11. to sow or scatter (seed). 12. *Chem.* to add a small crystal to (a super-saturated solution, to cause crystallisation. 13. to sow or scatter (clouds) with crystals or particles, e.g. of solid carbon dioxide, etc., to induce precipitation. 14. to remove the seeds from (fruit). ◇*v.i.* 15. to sow seed. 16. to produce or shed seed. [ME; OE *sēd* (Anglian), *sǣd*]

seed leaf, *n.* → **cotyledon.**

seedling /'sidlɪŋ/, *n.* a young plant developed from the embryo after germination of a seed.

seedy /'sidi/, *adj.*, **-dier, -diest.** 1. having much seed. 2. looking rather untidy, with worn out clothes; shabby. 3. *Colloq.* not feeling well.

seeing /'siɪŋ/, *conj.* in view of the fact (that); considering.

seek /sik/, *v.*, **sought, seeking.** ◇*v.t.* 1. to try to find: *to seek a solution.* 2. to try to get: *to seek fame.* 3. to try: *to seek to convince a person.* ◇*v.i.* 4. to make search or inquiry. ◇*v.* 5. **be sought after,** to be desired or in demand: *He is much sought after as an entertainer.* [OE *sēcan*]

seem /sim/, *v.i.* 1. to appear to be; appear (to be, feel, do, etc.): *You seem well this morning.* 2. to appear to oneself (to be, do, etc.): *I seem to hear someone calling.* 3. to appear to exist: *There seems no need to go now.* 4. to appear to be true or the case: *It seems likely to rain.* [ME, from Scand]

seeming /'simɪŋ/, *adj.* apparent; appearing to be such (whether truly or falsely): *a seeming advantage.*

seemly /'simli/, *adj.*, **-lier, -liest.** 1. looking or behaving according to good taste; becoming; decent; decorous. 2. of pleasing appearance; handsome. [ME, from Scand]

seen /sin/, *v.* past participle of **see**[1].

seep /sip/, *v.i.* 1. to pass gradually; ooze: *Water seeped through the wall.* ◇*n.* 2. moisture that seeps out. [? var. of d. *sipe,* OE *sīpian*] —**seepage**, *n.*

seer /sɪə/, *n.* 1. someone who foretells future events; prophet. 2. magician, clairvoyant, etc., claiming to have occult powers. [SEE[1] + -ER[1]]

seersucker /'sɪəsʌkə/, *n.* a fabric, usu. striped cotton, with every second stripe crinkled in the weaving. [Hind, from Pers: milk and sugar]

seesaw /'si,sɔ/, *n.* **1.** a plank balanced at the middle so that its ends may rise and fall in turn, used by children in play. **2.** a moving up and down or back and forth. ◇*v.i.* **3.** to move like a seesaw. ◇*v.t.* **4.** to cause (something) to move like a seesaw. [varied reduplication suggested by SAW¹]

seethe /sið/, *v.i.* **seethed, seething. 1.** to surge or foam, as a boiling liquid does. **2.** to be excited or agitated: *to seethe with anger.* [ME; OE *sēothan*]

segment /'segmənt/, *n.;* /seg'ment/, *v.,* ◇*n.* **1.** one of the parts into which anything is divided; division; section. **2.** *Geom.* **a.** apart cut off from a figure (esp. a circular or spherical one) by a line or a plane. **b.** a finite section of a straight line or curve. **3.** *Zool.* any one of the rings that compose the body of an arthropod, or similar animal, or one of the sections of a limb between the joints. ◇*v.t., v.i.* **4.** to separate or divide into segments. [L] — **segmental,** *adj.* — **segmentation,** *n.*

Segovia /sə'gouviə/, *n.* **Andrés** /an'dreɪs/, 1893–1987, Spanish classical guitarist.

segregate, /'segrəgeɪt/, *v.,* **-gated, -gating;** /'segrəgət/, *adj.* ◇*v.t.* **1.** to separate from the others; isolate. **2.** to impose a policy of segregation on (a particular racial, religious, group). **3.** to impose a policy of segregation on (a place, community, or state). ◇*v.i.* **4.** to separate or go apart. **5.** *Biol.* (of allelomorphic characters) to separate according to Mendel's laws. ◇*adj.* **6.** set apart. [ME, from L: separated from the flock]

segregation /segrə'geɪʃən/, *n.* **1.** the act or result of segregating. **2.** (a set of laws ordering) the policy or practice of providing separate schools, hospitals, etc., for different racial groups living in the same area and preventing contact between such racial groups. **3.** *Biol.* the separation of allelomorphs into different gametes at meiosis, and the resulting separation of their hereditary characters as seen in the progeny of hybrids. — **segregationist,** *n.*

Seidler /'saɪdlə/, *n.* **Harry,** born 1923, Australian architect, born in Vienna.

seif-dune /'seɪf-djun/, *n. Geog.* a ridge of blown sand, sometimes several kilometres long, stretching across the desert in the direction of the prevailing wind. [*seif* from Ar: sword]

seine /seɪn/, *n.* a fishing net which hangs vertically in the water, with floats at the upper edge and sinkers at the lower. [OE *segne,* from L, from Gk: fishing net]

Seine /seɪn/, *n.* a river flowing from eastern France north-west through Paris to the English Channel. About 770 km.

seismic /'saɪzmɪk/, *adj.* relating to, like, or caused by an earthquake. [Gk]

seismo-, a word part meaning 'seismic', as in *seismology.* [Gk: earthquake]

seismograph /'saɪzməgræf, -graf/, *n.* an instrument for measuring and recording vibrations within the earth, as earthquakes.

seismology /saɪz'mɒlədʒi/, *n.* the science or study of earthquakes and their phenomena. — **seismologic,** *adj.* — **seismologist,** *n.*

seize /siz/, *v.,* **seized, seizing.** ◇*v.t.* **1.** to take hold of suddenly or by force; grasp: *to seize a weapon;* or as if by force: *to seize enemy ships; Panic seized her.* **3.** (of police, etc.) to take possession of; confiscate: *to seize smuggled goods.* **4.** to take advantage of quickly: *to seize an opportunity.* ◇*v.i.* **5.** to lay hold suddenly or forcibly: *to seize on a rope.* **6.** to become jammed or stuck solid: *The car's engine seized.* [ME, from OF, from VL: set, put (in possession), from Gmc] — **seizer,** *n.*

seizure /'siʒə/, *n.* **1.** the act of seizing. **2.** a sudden attack of disease.

seldom /'seldəm/, *adv.* not often; rarely; infrequently. [ME; OE *seldum*]

select /sə'lekt/, *v.t.* **1.** to choose; pick out. ◇*adj.* **2.** chosen; selected. **3.** of special value or excellence; choice. **4.** carefully chosen; exclusive: *a select party.* [L: chosen]

select committee, *n.* a committee chosen from either the Senate or the House of Representatives to inquire into and report on a specific matter.

selection /sə'lekʃən/, *n.* **1.** the act of selecting or the fact of being selected; choice: *His selection for the team pleased him.* **2.** the thing or things selected: *Take your selection to the counter.* **3.** a range of goods, etc. to choose from: *a wide selection of hats.* **4.** *Aust Hist.* a block of land acquired under the system of free selection. **5.** a farm (usu. small). **6.** *Biol.* the singling out of certain forms of animal and vegetable life for reproduction and continuing the species, either by natural causes (**natural selection**) which result in the survival of the fittest, or by man's action (**artificial selection**) as in breeding animals and in growing fruits, vegetables, etc.

selective /sə'lektɪv/, *adj.* **1.** making selection. **2.** choosing the best in anything; discriminating. **3.** marked by selection. — **selectivity,** *n.*

selector /sə'lektə/, *n.* **1.** someone or something which selects. **2.** → **free selector.**

selenium /sə'liniəm/, *n.* a non-metallic element chemically like sulfur, occurring in several allotropic forms, and having electrical resistance which varies under the effect of light. *Symbol:* Se; *at. no.:* 34; *at. wt.:* 78.96. [NL, from Gk: moon]

seleno-, a word part meaning 'moon', as in *selenology.* [combining form of Gk: moon]

self /self/, *n., pl.* **selves,** *adj., pron., pl.* **selves.** ◇*n.* **1.** a person or thing referred to as an individual; one's own person. **2.** someone's nature, character, etc.: *his better self.* **3.** personal interest; selfishness. **4.** *Philos.* the ego as opposed to the non-ego; the unifying condition of all one's knowing, feeling, and willing, as opposed to what one knows, feels, and wills. ◇*adj.* **5.** being the same throughout; uniform. **6.** of the same material as the rest: *a dress with* *self facings.* ◇*pron.* **7.** myself, himself, etc.: *to make a cheque payable to self.* [ME and OE]

self-, prefixal use of *self*, appearing in various parts of speech, expressing mainly reflexive action, e.g., subject identical with direct object, as in *self-control, self-government, self-help*; with indirect-object or adverbial-type relations, as in *self-conscious, self-centred, self-evident.*

self-addressed /ˈsɛlf-ədrɛst/, *adj.* addressed to oneself: *a self-addressed letter.*

self-aggrandisement *or* **self-aggrandizement** /sɛlf-əˈgrændəzmənt/, *n.* the increase of one's own power, wealth, etc., usu. aggressively.

self-appointed /ˈsɛlf-əpɔɪntəd/, *adj.* acting or speaking as if having authority, without being appointed to do so by someone else.

self-assurance /sɛlf-əˈʃɔrəns/, *n.* → **self-confidence.** —**self-assured**, *adj.*

self-centred /sɛlf-ˈsɛntəd/, *adj.* interested in oneself too much; selfish.

self-confessed /ˈsɛlf-kənfɛst/, *adj.* known to be such because one has said so: *a self-confessed murderer.*

self-confidence /sɛlf-ˈkɒnfədəns/, *n.* confidence, or sometimes over-confidence, in one's own judgment, ability, power, etc. —**self-confident**, *adj.*

self-conscious /sɛlf-ˈkɒnʃəs/, *adj.* **1.** too aware of oneself as an object of other people's notice. **2.** conscious of oneself or one's own thoughts, etc.

self-contained /ˈsɛlf-kənteɪnd/, *adj.* **1.** containing in oneself or itself all that is necessary; independent. **2.** (of a flat or house) having its own kitchen, bathroom, and toilet. **3.** keeping one's feelings to oneself; reserved.

self-defence /sɛlf-dəˈfɛns/, *n.* **1.** the act of defending one's own person, reputation, etc. **2.** *Law.* the use of reasonable force against an attacker, which counts as a defence in criminal law and tort.

self-denial /sɛlf-dəˈnaɪəl/, *n.* the giving up of one's own desires; unselfishness. —**self-denying**, *adj.*

selfdestruct /sɛlfdəˈstrʌkt/, *v.*; /ˈsɛlf-dəstrʌkt/, *n., adj.* ◇*v.i.* **1.** to explode as a result of interference or according to some preset internal mechanism. ◇*n.* **2.** a selfdestructing device. ◇*adj.* **3.** of or relating to, an aeroplane, missile, etc., equipped with a self-destruct. Also, **autodestruct.**

self-determination /sɛlf-dətɜməˈneɪʃən/, *n.* the choosing by a people or nationality of the form of government it shall have, without reference to the wishes of any other nation.

self-employed /ˈsɛlf-əmplɔɪd/, *adj.* getting one's income directly from one's own work, profession, or business, and not as a salary from an employer.

self-evident /sɛlf-ˈɛvədənt/, *adj.* evident in itself without proof; axiomatic. —**self-evidence**, *n.*

self-expression /sɛlf-əksˈprɛʃən/, *n.* the free expression or putting forward of one's own personality by writing poetry, playing music, etc., or by one's own behavior.

self-fertilisation *or* **self-fertilization** /ˌsɛlf-fɜtəlaɪˈzeɪʃən/, *n.* the fertilisation of a flower by its own pollen (opposed to *cross-fertilisation*).

self-government /sɛlf-ˈgʌvənmənt/, *n.* **1.** government of a state or community by its own members; democratic government. **2.** political independence of a country, people, region, etc. **3.** the condition of being self-governed. **4.** self-control. —**self-governed**, *adj.*

self-image /sɛlf-ˈɪmɪdʒ/, *n.* the picture one has of oneself in one's own mind.

self-important /sɛlf-ɪmˈpɔtnt/, *adj.* showing too great an opinion of one's own importance; conceited or pompous. —**self-importance**, *n.*

self-interest /sɛlf-ˈɪntrəst/, *n.* regard for one's own advantage, esp. with disregard of others. —**self-interested**, *adj.*

selfish /ˈsɛlfɪʃ/, *adj.* **1.** caring only for oneself. **2.** marked by caring only for oneself: *selfish motives.*

selfless /ˈsɛlfləs/, *adj.* unselfish.

self-made /ˈsɛlf-meɪd/, *adj.* having succeeded in life, without help from inheritance, class background, or other people: *a self-made man.*

self-opinionated /sɛlf-əˈpɪnjəneɪtəd/, *adj.* **1.** vain; conceited. **2.** giving one's own opinion often.

self-pollinated /sɛlf-ˈpɒləneɪtəd/, *adj.* having the pollen transferred from the anthers to the stigmas of the same flower, or another flower on the same plant. —**self-pollination**, *n.*

self-possessed /sɛlf-pəˈzɛst/, *adj.* showing control of one's feelings, behavior, etc. —**self-possession**, *n.*

self-raising flour /sɛlf-ˈreɪzɪŋ/, *n.* wheat flour with baking powder already added.

self-respect /sɛlf-rəˈspɛkt/, *n.* proper esteem or regard for the dignity of one's own character. —**self-respecting**, *adj.*

self-righteous /sɛlf-ˈraɪtʃəs/, *adj.* thinking that one is right or righteous, and often blaming others; pharisaic.

self-rule /sɛlf-ˈrul/, *n.* achievement of independence by a former colony or dependent territory. —**self-ruling**, *adj.*

self-sacrifice /sɛlf-ˈsækrəfaɪs/, *n.* a giving up of one's interests, desires, etc., for the good of another. —**self-sacrificing**, *adj.*

self-service /sɛlf-ˈsɜvəs/, *adj.* (of a restaurant, lift or other service) operating on the principle that the customers, passengers, etc., serve themselves. Also, **self-serve.**

self-sown /sɛlf-ˈsoʊn/, *adj.* **1.** sown by anything other than humans, as by birds, the wind, etc. ◇*n.* **2.** a plant grown from a self-sown seed.

self-starter /self-'statə/, n. a device which starts an internal combustion engine without cranking by hand.

self-sufficient /self-sə'fiʃənt/, adj. 1. able to supply one's own needs. 2. having too much confidence in one's own abilities, powers, etc. —**self-sufficiency**, n.

self-willed /self-'wɪld/, adj. demanding to get one's own way; intractable.

sell /sel/, v., **sold, selling,** n. ◇v.t. 1. to give up (something) for a price: *I sold my car to him.* 2. to deal in; keep for sale: *Do you sell spare parts here?* 3. to act as a dealer in or seller of: *He sells insurance.* 4. to make easy or help the sale of: *The package sells the product.* 5. to try to make people buy: *He is selling soap on television.* 6. to cause to be accepted: *to sell an idea to the public.* ◇v.i. 7. to sell something; engage in selling. 8. to be on sale; find purchasers: *This soap sells well.* ◇v. 9. **be sold on**, *Colloq.* to like or admire very much. 10. **sell off,** to sell at reduced prices, in order to get rid of. 11. **sell out, a.** to sell all of something so that there is none left. **b.** *Colloq.* to betray. 12. **sell up,** to close down (a business, etc.) by selling all stock and assets. ◇n. 13. *Colloq.* the act of selling or salesmanship. See **hard sell, soft sell.** [OE *sellan*]

Sellers /'seləz/, n. **Peter,** 1925–80, English comedian and character actor, best known for *The Goon Show*, and films including the *Pink Panther* series.

sell-out /'sel-aʊt/, n. *Colloq.* 1. a betrayal. 2. a play, show, etc., for which all seats are sold.

selvedge /'selvɪdʒ/, n. the edge of woven fabric finished to prevent fraying. [late ME]

selves /selvz/, n. plural of **self**.

semantic /sə'mæntɪk/, adj. relating to signs or meaning. [Gk: significant]

semantics /sə'mæntɪks/, n. *Linguistics.* the systematic study of the meanings of words and changes in them.

semaphore /'seməfɔ/, n., v., **-phored, -phoring.** ◇n. 1. an apparatus for sending information by means of signals. 2. a system of signalling by hand, in which a flag is held in each hand at arm's length in various positions. ◇v.t., v.i. 3. to signal by semaphore. [Gk] —**semaphoric,** adj.

Semarang /'seməræŋ/, n. a seaport in Indonesia, in northern Java. Pop. 1 077 000 (1984 est.). Also, **Samarang.**

semblance /'sembləns/, n. 1. an outward appearance or likeness. 2. an unreal appearance; a mere show. [ME, from OF: be like, seem, from L]

semen /'simən/, n. the fluid produced by male reproductive organs; seed; sperm. [L: seed]

semester /sə'mestə/, n. (in educational institutions) one of the two divisions of the academic year. See **term**. [G, from L: six monthly] —**semestral,** adj.

semi /'semi/, n. *Colloq.* 1. a semidetached house. 2. a semitrailer. 3. *Sport.* a semifinal.

semi-, a prefix modifying the latter part of the word, meaning 'half' in its precise and less precise meanings, as in *semicircle, semidetached.* [L]

semibreve /'semibriv/, n. the longest note in common use, half the length of a breve, and worth four crotchets.

semicircle /'semisɜkəl/, n. 1. the half of a circle. 2. anything having, or arranged in, the form of a half of a circle. —**semicircular,** adj.

semicolon /semi'koʊlən, 'semikoʊlən/, n. a mark of punctuation (;) used to show a more distinct separation between parts of a sentence than that shown by a comma.

semiconductor /,semikən'dʌktə/, n. 1. a substance whose electrical conductivity at normal temperatures is halfway between that of a metal and an insulator, and whose conductivity increases with a rise in temperature over a certain range, e.g. germanium and silicon. 2. a device, such as a transistor, which is based on the electronic properties of such substances. ◇adj. 3. of or relating to such a substance or device: *a semiconductor diode.* —**semiconducting,** adj.

semidetached /,semidə'tætʃt/, adj. partly detached (used esp. of a pair of houses joined by a common wall but detached from other buildings).

semifluid /semi'fluəd/, adj. 1. having both fluid and solid characteristics. ◇n. 2. a semifluid substance. Also, **semiliquid** /semi'lɪkwəd/.

seminal /'semənəl/, adj. 1. of, relating to, or of the nature of semen. 2. *Bot.* of or relating to seed. 3. highly original and influential. 4. undeveloped; rudimentary; embryonic. [ME, from L: seed]

seminar /'semɑnɑ/, n. 1. a meeting of students, as in a university, engaged in advanced study and original research under a professor, lecturer, etc. 2. a course or subject of study for advanced students. 3. a meeting organised to discuss a specific topic: *a public seminar on uranium mining.* [G, from L: of or for seed]

seminary /'semənri/, n., pl. **-naries.** 1. *Rom Cath Ch.* a college for the education of men for the priesthood. 2. a school, esp. one of higher level. 3. (formerly) a school for young ladies. [late ME, from L: nursery] —**seminarian,** n.

semipermeable /semi'pɜmiəbəl/, adj. permeable to some substances more than to others: *a semipermeable membrane.*

semipolar bond /semi'poʊlə/, n. *Chem.* a valency bond in which two electrons are donated by one atom to another atom which needs both of them to complete its octet. Also, **coordinate covalent bond.**

semiprecious /semi'preʃəs/, adj. (of a gem such as amethyst, garnet, etc.) having value, but not classified as precious.

semiquaver /'semikweɪvə/, n. a note equivalent to $\frac{1}{16}$ of a semibreve; half a quaver.

Semite /'simaɪt/, n. a Jew, Arab, or Assyrian. [NL, from L: Shem, from Gk] —**Semitic,** adj.

semitone /'sɛmɪtoʊn/, *n.* the smallest interval in the chromatic scale of Western music.

semitrailer /ˈsɛmɪˈtreɪlə/, *n.* a truck consisting of a trailer joined to a prime mover.

semivowel /ˈsɛmɪvaʊəl/, *n.* a speech sound of vowel quality used as a consonant, such as *w* in *wet* and *y* in *yet*.

semolina /sɛməˈliːnə/, *n.* the large, hard parts of wheat grains kept back in the sifting machine after the fine flour has passed through it, used in puddings, etc. [It: bran, from L: fine flour]

sempstress /ˈsɛmpstrəs, ˈsɛmstrəs/, *n.* → **seamstress**.

Sen, *Abbrev.* 1. Senate. 2. Senator. 3. Senior.

senate /ˈsɛnət/, *n.* 1. an assembly or council of citizens having the highest decision-making functions in the government. 2. (*cap.*) the upper and smaller house of the Australian Parliament consisting of 76 senators, twelve from each of the six States, two from the NT and two from the ACT. 3. a similar body in certain other countries. 4. the supreme council of state in ancient Rome. 5. a governing, advisory, or disciplinary body, as in certain universities. [ME, from L] — **senator**, *n.* — **senatorial**, *adj.*

send /sɛnd/, *v.*, **sent**, **sending**. ◇*v.t.* 1. to cause to go; direct or order to go: *to send a messenger*. 2. to cause to be carried somewhere: *to send a letter*. 3. to drive or throw: *He sent down a fast ball*. 4. to cause to become: *to send somebody mad*. ◇*v.i.* 5. to send a message, messenger, etc. 6. *Naut.* to lurch forward from the force of a wave. ◇*v.* 7. **send down**, **a.** to expel from a university. **b.** to imprison. 8. **send off**, *Colloq.* **a.** to cause to depart. **b.** to be present at (someone's) departure. 9. **send packing**, *Colloq.* to dismiss; send away. 10. **send up**, *Colloq.* to mock or ridicule; satirise. [OE *sendan*] — **sender**, *n.*

seneschal /ˈsɛnəʃəl/, *n.* an officer in the household of a medieval prince or dignitary, who had full charge of domestic arrangements, ceremonies, administration of justice, etc.; steward. [ME, from OF, from ML, from Gmc]

senile /ˈsiːnaɪl, ˈsɪnaɪl/, *adj.* 1. of or relating to old age. 2. mentally or physically weak due to old age. [L] — **senility**, *n.*

senior /ˈsiːnjə/, *adj.* 1. older or elder (often used after the name of the older of two people bearing the same name). *Abbrev.*: **Sr** or **Sen** 2. of higher rank or standing; esp. because of longer service. ◇*n.* 3. a person who is older than another. 4. someone of higher rank or standing. 5. a senior barrister, esp. Queen's Counsel. [ME, from L: old]

seniority /siːnɪˈɒrəti/, *n.*, *pl.* **-ties**. the condition or fact of being senior, in age or position.

senna /ˈsɛnə/, *n.* 1. a cathartic drug made of dried leaves of some types of cassia. 2. any plant yielding this drug. [NL, from Ar]

sensation /sɛnˈseɪʃən/, *n.* 1. the working of the senses. 2. a mental condition produced through an organ of sense or a physical feeling: *a sensation of fear*; *a sensation of cold*. 3. *Physiol.* the ability to pick up stimuli. 4. a mental feeling, esp. of excitement. 5. a state of excited feeling among people, caused by some event, etc. 6. a cause of such feeling or interest. [ML, from LL: having sense]

sensational /sɛnˈseɪʃənəl/, *adj.* 1. able to produce a sensation. 2. (of a book, film, etc.) sensationalised. 3. *Colloq.* very pleasing, exciting or excellent: *His stage performance was sensational*.

sensationalise or **sensationalize** /sɛnˈseɪʃənəlaɪz/, *v.t.*, **-ised**, **-ising**. to highlight shocking or thrilling aspects, esp. sex or violence, in (a newspaper story, novel, film, etc.).

sensationalism /sɛnˈseɪʃənəlɪzəm/, *n.* the producing of cheap emotional excitement by popular newspapers, novels, etc. — **sensationalist**, *n.*

sense /sɛns/, *n.*, *v.*, **sensed**, **sensing**. ◇*n.* 1. each of the special powers or faculties connected with bodily organs by which man and other animals notice external objects and their own bodily changes (commonly reckoned as sight, hearing, smell, taste, and touch). 2. these powers together. 3. their operation or function; sensation. 4. a physical feeling: *to have a sense of coldness*. 5. an ability of the mind like sensation: *the moral sense; a sense of duty*. 6. any special ability of the personality: *a sense of humor*. 7. any vague feeling: *a sense of security*. 8. practical intelligence; common sense: *He has no sense*. 9. what is sensible or reasonable: *to talk sense*. 10. the meaning of a word, statement, or a passage. 11. *Maths.* one of two opposite directions in which a vector may point. 12. **in a sense**, according to one way of looking at (something). 13. **make sense**, **a.** to be able to be understood: *That word doesn't make sense.* **b.** to understand: *Can you make sense of that book?* ◇*v.t.* 14. to pick up with the senses; become aware of; perceive. 15. to perceive without certainty: *to sense that someone may be unhappy*. [ME, from L]

sense organ, *n.* a specialised structure which receives impressions, such as one of the tastebuds or the eye.

sensibility /sɛnsəˈbɪləti/, *n.*, *pl.* **-ties**. 1. the ability to feel; responsiveness to sensory stimuli. 2. sharpness of emotion and fine feeling.

sensible /ˈsɛnsəbəl/, *adj.* 1. having, using, or showing good sense or sound judgment. 2. knowing; keenly aware: *sensible of his fault*. 3. able to be felt by the senses: *the sensible universe*. 4. conscious: *speechless but still sensible*. [ME, from LL]

sensitise or **sensitize** /ˈsɛnsətaɪz/, *v.t.*, **-tised**, **-tising**. to make sensitive. — **sensitisation**, *n.* — **sensitiser**, *n.*

sensitive /ˈsɛnsətɪv/, *adj.* 1. having sensation. 2. easily influenced or affected. 3. having sharp mental or emotional sensibility. 4. arousing strong feelings or reaction: *a sensitive issue*. 5. (of a body part, etc.) having a low

sensitive

threshold of feeling. **6.** highly affected by certain agents, as photographic plates, films, or paper are to light. **7.** *Radio.* easily affected by outside influences, esp. by radio waves. [ME, from ML, from L: sense] **–sensitivity,** *n.*

sensor /'sensə/, *n.* a device which detects a variable quantity and converts it into a signal for measuring, recording, etc.

sensorimotor /sensəri'moutə/, *adj.* of or relating to sensation and motor activity: *sensorimotor skills.*

sensory /'sensəri/, *adj.* **1.** relating to sensation. **2.** *Anat.* (of a structure) carrying an impulse which results in sensation, such as a nerve. Also, **sensorial** /sen'sɔriəl/.

sensual /'senʃuəl/, *adj.* **1.** of or relating to the senses, or to physical sensation. **2.** overly concerned with the pleasing of the senses. [late ME, from LL] **–sensualist,** *n.* **–sensuality,** *n.*

sensuous /'senʃuəs/, *adj.* **1.** of or relating to the senses. **2.** perceived by or affecting the senses: *the sensuous qualities of music.* **3.** aware of the physical senses: *a sensuous temperament.*

sent /sent/, *v.* past tense and past participle of **send.**

sentence /'sentəns/, *n., v.,* **-tenced, -tencing.** ◊*n.* **1.** a linguistic form (a word or a sequence of words arranged in a grammatical construction) which is complete in itself, expressing statement, inquiry, command, etc., as in, *Fire!* or *Summer is here* or *Who's there?* **2.** *Law.* **a.** a decision made in law to punish a convicted criminal. **b.** the punishment itself. ◊*v.t.* **3.** to give sentence; condemn to punishment. [ME, from F, from L: opinion] **–sentential,** *adj.*

sententious /sen'tenʃəs/, *adj.* **1.** having many pithy sayings or maxims: *a sententious style of writing.* **2.** arrogant and judgmental in speech; moralising; self-righteous. **3.** of the nature of a maxim; pithy. [late ME, from L]

sentient /'sentiənt, 'senʃənt/, *adj.* **1.** having the power of perception by the senses. **2.** marked by sensation. ◊*n.* **3.** someone or something that is sentient. **4.** the mind. [L: feeling] **–sentience,** *n.*

sentiment /'sentəmənt/, *n.* **1.** a mental attitude to something; opinion. **2.** a mental feeling; emotion: *a sentiment of pity.* **3.** refined or tender emotion. **4.** a showing of feeling or sensibility in literature, art, or music. [LL, from L: feel]

sentimental /sentə'mentl/, *adj.* **1.** showing or appealing to the tender emotions: *a sentimental song.* **2.** relating to or dependent on sentiment: *sentimental reasons.* **3.** weakly emotional: *a sentimental schoolgirl.* **4.** marked by or showing sentiment. **–sentimentalism,** *n.* **–sentimentality,** *n.* **–sentimentalist,** *n.*

sentinel /'sentənəl/, *n.* **1.** someone or something that watches, or stands as if watching. **2.** a soldier who stands as guard: *to stand sentinel.* [F, from It, from LL: avoid danger, from L: perceive]

sentry /'sentri/, *n., pl.* **-tries.** a soldier stationed at a place to keep guard and prevent the passage of unauthorised persons, watch for fires, etc.; sentinel. [? short for obs. *centrinel,* var. of SENTINEL]

Seoul /soul/, *n.* the capital of South Korea, in the western part. Pop. 9 645 932 (1985).

Sep, *Abbrev.* September.

sepal /'sipəl/, *n.* any of the individual leaves or parts of the calyx of a flower. [NL, from Gk]

separate /'sepəreit/, *v.,* **-rated, -rating;** /'seprət/, *adj., n.* ◊*v.t.* **1.** to keep apart or divide. **2.** to put apart; part: *to separate people fighting.* **3.** to disconnect; disunite: *to separate church and state.* ◊*v.i.* **4.** to part company; withdraw from personal association (oft. fol. by *from*). **5.** to draw or come apart. **6.** (of a married couple) to stop living together but without becoming divorced. ◊*adj.* **7.** separated or disconnected. **8.** unconnected or distinct: *two separate questions.* ◊*n.* **9.** (*pl.*) articles of women's clothing that can be worn in a variety of combinations. [ME, from L] **–separable,** *adj.* **–separator,** *n.*

separation /sepə'reiʃən/, *n.* **1.** the act of separating. **2.** the condition of being separated. **3.** the place, line, or point of parting. **4.** *Law.* an arrangement by which a husband and wife live apart.

separatist /'seprətəst, 'sepərə-/, *n.* **1.** someone who separates or withdraws as from an established church. **2.** formerly, someone who wanted the separation from England of the administrative and judicial functions of the colonies in Australia, and their independence of each other. **–separatism,** *n.*

sepia /'sipiə/, *n.* **1.** a brown coloring matter obtained from the ink-like substance produced by various cuttlefish, and used in drawing. **2.** a drawing made with sepia. **3.** a dark brown. **4.** *Photog.* a photograph in sepia colors. ◊*adj.* **5.** of a brown like that of sepia ink. [L, from Gk]

Sepik /'sipɪk/, *n.* a river in northern PNG, flowing north-west then generally north-east to the Pacific Ocean east of Wewak. About 982 km.

sepsis /'sepsəs/, *n.* a poisoning of some body part by bacterial organisms: *dental sepsis.* [NL, from Gk]

sept-, a prefix meaning 'seven', as in *septet.* Also, **septem-, septe-, septi-**[1]. [L, combining form of *septem*]

Sept, *Abbrev.* September.

September /sep'tembə/, *n.* the ninth month of the year, containing thirty days. [OE, from L, the seventh month in the early Roman calendar]

septennial /sep'teniəl/, *adj.* **1.** happening every seven years. **2.** of or for seven years.

septet /sep'tet/, *n.* **1.** any group of seven people or things. **2.** *Music.* (a musical composition for) seven voices or instruments. [G. See SEPT-, -ET]

septi-, variant of **sept-,** before most consonants.

septic /'sɛptɪk/, *adj.* **1.** infected, usu. by a pus-forming microbe. **2.** relating to, of the nature of, poisoning by bacterial organisms. ◇*n.* **3.** an agent which causes poisoning. **4.** → **septic tank.** [L, from Gk]

septicaemia *or* **septicemia** /sɛptə-'simiə/, *n.* the entry of disease-producing bacteria into the bloodstream. [NL, from Gk. See SEPTIC, -AEMIA] — **septicaemic,** *adj.*

septic tank, *n.* a tank in which solid waste matter is broken down by anaerobic bacteria.

septum /'sɛptəm/, *n., pl.* **septa** /'sɛptə/. **1.** *Biol.* a dividing wall, membrane, etc., esp. between the nostrils. **2.** a membrane which allows osmosis. [L: enclosure]

septuple /sɛp'tjupəl/, *adj., v.,* **-pled, -pling.** ◇*adj.* **1.** sevenfold; seven times as great. ◇*v.t., v.i.* **2.** to make or become seven times as great. [LL]

sepulchral /sə'pʌlkrəl/, *adj.* **1.** of, relating to, or serving as a tomb. **2.** of or relating to burial. **3.** dismal; gloomy; funereal.

sepulchre /'sɛpəlkə/, *n.* a tomb, grave, or burial place. [ME, from OF, from L]

sequel /'sikwəl/, *n.* **1.** a literary work, film, etc., complete in itself, but continuing a previous work. **2.** an event or circumstance following something. **3.** a result; consequence. [ME, from L]

sequence /'sikwəns/, *n.* **1.** the following of one thing after another; succession. **2.** the order of following one after the other: *a list of books in alphabetical sequence.* **3.** a continuous or connected series: *a poetic sequence.* **4.** something that follows; result; consequence. **5.** *Music.* a pattern of notes or chords repeated at different pitches. **6.** *Films.* a part of a story set in the same place and time, and without breaks of any kind. **7.** *Maths.* a finite or countable set of numbers, arranged in order. [ME, from L: following] — **sequent, sequential,** *adj.*

sequester /sə'kwɛstə, sɪ-/, *v.t.* **1.** to withdraw away or into retirement; seclude. **2.** to remove or separate. **3.** *Law.* to remove (property) for a time from the owner until legal claims are satisfied. [ME, from LL: separate, from L: trustee] — **sequestered,** *adj.*

sequestration /sɛkwəs'treɪʃən/, *n.* **1.** a removal or separation. **2.** withdrawal; retirement or seclusion. **3.** *Law.* the sequestering of property. **4.** *Chem.* the formation of a coordination compound by adding material, so preventing metallic ions in solution from showing their usual properties.

sequin /'sikwən/, *n.* a small shiny disc used to ornament a dress, etc. [F, from It *zecchino*, a Venetian coin] — **sequined,** *adj.*

seraph /'sɛrəf/, *n., pl.* **-aphs, -aphim** /-əfɪm/. **1.** one of the heavenly beings placed above God's throne in Isaiah's vision. (Isa. 6.) **2.** a member of the highest order of angels, often represented as a child's head with wings above, below, and on each side. [from *seraphim* (pl.), from LL, from Heb] — **seraphic,** *adj.*

Serbia /'sɜbiə/, *n.* a former kingdom in southern Europe; from 1918 (with revised boundaries) a constituent republic of Yugoslavia; following the 1991–92 secession of four republics; the dominant state of the new Yugoslavia. Pop. 5 803 000 (1986 est.); about 90 650 km². *Cap.:* Belgrade. Formerly, **Servia.** — **Serbian,** *n. adj.*

Serbo-Croat /sɜboʊ-'kroʊæt/, *n.* a Slavic language, usu. written with Cyrillic letters in Serbia but with Roman letters in Croatia. Also, **Serbo-Croatian** /ˌsɜboʊ-kroʊ'eɪʃən/.

sere[1] /sɪə/, *adj.* dry; withered. [var. of SEAR]

sere[2] /sɪə/, *n.* the set of stages in an ecological sequence. [from SERIES]

serenade /sɛrə'neɪd/, *n., v.,* **-naded, -nading.** ◇*n.* **1.** a musical performance, sung or played in the open air at night, as by a lover under the window of his lady. ◇*v.t.* **2.** to entertain with a serenade. ◇*v.i.* **3.** to perform a serenade. [F, from It]

serendipity /sɛrən'dɪpəti/, *n.* the ability to make desirable but accidental discoveries. [*Serendip,* former name of Sri Lanka (Ceylon) + -ITY; coined by Horace Walpole, 1717–97, English author, from the Persian fairytale *The Three Princes of Serendip,* in which the heroes have this faculty]

serene /sə'rin/, *adj.* **1.** calm; peaceful; tranquil: *a serene old age.* **2.** clear; fair: *serene weather.* **3.** (oft. cap.) a term used in titles of princes, etc.: *His Serene Highness.* [L] — **serenity,** *n.*

serf /sɜf/, *n. Hist.* (esp. in the feudal system) a person forcibly kept in the services of a lord, and transferred, with the land, from one owner to another. [ME, from F, from L: slave] — **serfdom, serfhood,** *n.*

serge /sɜdʒ/, *n.* **1.** a strong twilled woollen cloth used esp. for clothing. **2.** cotton, rayon, or silk in a twill weave. [F]

sergeant /'sadʒənt/, *n.* **1.** *Mil.* See Appendix. **2.** a police officer ranking between constable and inspector. [ME, from OF, from L: serving]

sergeant major, *n. Mil.* → **warrant officer.**

Sergt, *Abbrev.* Sergeant.

serial /'sɪəriəl/, *n.* **1.** anything published, broadcast, etc., in parts at regular intervals. ◇*adj.* **2.** published in parts: *a story in serial form.* **3.** of, relating to, or arranged in a series. [NL, from L: series]

serial number, *n.* an individual number given to a particular person, article, etc., for identification.

series /'sɪəriz/, *n., pl.* **-ries.** ◇*n.* **1.** a number of things, events, etc., ranged or happening in a given order; sequence. **2.** *Radio, TV.* a presentation of a single story, subject area, etc., in successive parts over a number of days or weeks. **3.** a set, esp. of coins, stamps, etc. **4.** *Maths.* the formal sum of the elements of a sequence. **5.** *Music.* an arrangement of 12 notes in a particular order, taken as the basis of a composition. **6.** *Geol.* a division of a system of rocks, marked by sedimentary deposits formed during a geological age. **7.** *Elect.* an arrangement of conductors or cells such that the same current flows through each. The components are said to be **in series** (opposed to **in parallel**). [L]

serif /'serɪf/, *n.* a smaller line used to finish off a main stroke of a letter, as at the top and bottom of M. Also, **seriph**. [probably from D: write]

serious /'sɪərɪəs/, *adj.* **1.** of solemn manner or character; thoughtful. **2.** being sincere; earnest. **3.** demanding serious thought or action: *serious reading; serious music.* **4.** important; weighty: *a serious matter.* **5.** giving cause for concern; critical: *a serious illness.* [ME, from LL, from L]

sermon /'sɜmən/, *n.* **1.** a talk, usu. religious, based on a text of Scripture and delivered in church. **2.** any similar serious talk. **3.** a long, boring speech. [ME, from OF, from L: discourse]

sero-, a word part representing 'serum'.

serous /'sɪərəs/, *adj.* **1.** of a watery nature. **2.** containing or giving off serum. **3.** relating to or like serum. [L] — **serosity**, *n.*

serpent /'sɜpənt/, *n.* **1.** a snake. **2.** a cunning, untrustworthy or evil person. **3.** Satan. [ME, from L: creeping thing]

serpentine¹ /'sɜpəntaɪn/, *adj.* **1.** of or relating to a serpent. **2.** moving in a winding course; tortuous. **3.** having the qualities of a serpent; subtle or cunning. [ME, from L]

serpentine² /'sɜpəntaɪn/, *n.* a common mineral, usu. oily green and sometimes spotted, used for architectural and ornamental purposes. [ME, from ML]

serrate /'sereɪt, -rət/, *adj.;* /sə'reɪt/, *v.*, **-rated, -rating.** ◇*adj.* **1.** haying notches or teeth along the edge: *a serrate leaf; a serrate coin.* ◇*v.t.* **2.** to make serrate. [L: saw-shaped] — **serration**, *n.* — **serrated**, *adj.*

serried /'serid/, *adj.* crowded closely together. [F from L]

serum /'sɪərəm/, *n., pl.* **sera** /'sɪərə/, **serums. 1.** a clear, pale yellow liquid that separates from clotted blood. **2.** fluid of this kind taken from the blood of an immunised animal and used as an antitoxin. **3.** any watery animal fluid. **4.** (of milk) **a.** that part left after butterfat, casein, and albumin have been removed. **b.** that part left after the manufacture of cheese. [L: whey]

serum hepatitis, *n.* a form of hepatitis passed on by means of an infected hypodermic needle or by the transfusion of infected blood.

servant /'sɜvənt/, *n.* **1.** a person employed to carry out home duties. **2.** a person in the service of another. [ME, from OF: serving]

serve /sɜv/, *v.*, **served, serving,** *n.* ◇*v.i.* **1.** to act as a servant. **2.** to wait at table. **3.** to give assistance; help. **4.** to go through a term of service, as in the army, etc. **5.** to be of use: *That tree will serve as a shelter from the rain.* **6.** to answer the purpose: *That will serve to explain my actions.* **7.** *Tennis, etc.* to put the ball in play. ◇*v.t.* **8.** to work for. **9.** to give service to; help. **10.** to go through (a term of service, imprisonment, etc.). **11.** to give obedience to (God, king, etc.). **12.** to answer the needs of: *It serves my purpose well.* **13.** to contribute to; promote: *to serve the needs of the hungry.* **14.** to wait upon: *He served the guests.* **15.** to set (food) on a table. **16.** (of a male animal) to mate with (a female). **17.** *Tennis, etc.* to put (the ball) in play. **18.** *Law.* to make legal delivery of (a process or writ). ◇*n.* **19.** the act, manner, or right of serving, as in tennis: *It's your serve.* [ME, from OF, from L]

server /'sɜvə/, *n.* **1.** something used in serving food, as a salver, serving spoon, etc. **2.** *Church.* an attendant who assists the priest at a religious service. **3.** *Tennis, etc.* a player who puts the ball in play.

servery /'sɜvəri/, *n.* a room or area near the kitchen in which food is set out on plates.

service /'sɜvəs/, *n., adj., v.,* **-viced, -vicing.** ◇*n.* **1.** an act of helpful activity: *to perform a service for someone.* **2.** the supplying of articles, commodities, activities, etc., required or demanded, esp. by the public. **3.** the organised system of facilities, appliances, employees, etc., for meeting public needs: *a transport service; a telegraphic service.* **4.** the performance of duties as a servant: *She gives good service as a maid.* **5.** employment in any duties or work for a person, government, etc. **6.** a department of public employment, or the body of public servants in it: *the diplomatic service.* **7.** *Mil.* (*pl.*) the armed forces: *in the services.* **8.** the act of servicing a piece of machinery, esp. a motor vehicle. **9.** public religious worship or its ceremonies: *divine service; a marriage service.* **10.** a set of dishes, utensils, etc., for a particular use: *a dinner service.* **11.** *Tennis, etc.* the act of putting the ball in play. **12.** the insemination of a female animal by the male. **13. at someone's service**, ready to help; at one's disposal: *My driver will be at your service.* **14. be of service**, to be helpful or useful: *Can I be of service?* ◇*adj.* **15.** of service; useful. **16.** of, relating to, or used by, servants, tradesmen, etc.: *service stairs.* **17.** of or relating to the armed forces. ◇*v.t.* **18.** to make fit for service: *to service a car.* **19.** (of a male animal) to inseminate (a female animal). [OE *serfise*, from OF, from L]

serviceable /'sɜvəsəbəl/, *adj.* **1.** being of service; useful. **2.** able to do good service. **3.** wearing well; durable: *serviceable cloth.* — **serviceability**, *n.*

service industry, *n.* an industry providing services such as transport or entertainment (opposed to *manufacturing industry*).

serviceman /'sɜvəsmən/, *n., pl.* **-men.** a member of the armed forces. — **servicewoman**, *n. fem.*

service station, *n.* a place selling petrol, oil, etc., for motor vehicles, and sometimes offering mechanical repairs. Also, **petrol station**.

serviette /sɜvi'et/, *n.* a piece of cloth or paper, used during a meal to wipe the lips and hands and to protect the clothes. Also, **table napkin, napkin**. [F: serve]

servile /'sɜvaɪl/, *adj.* **1.** weakly allowing another to have control; obsequious: *servile*

servile manners. **2.** of or relating to slaves; abject: *servile obedience*. [ME, from L] —**servility**, *n.*

serving /'sɜvɪŋ/, *n.* **1.** the act of someone or something that serves. **2.** a portion of food or drink; a helping. ◇*adj.* **3.** used for dishing out food at the table: *a serving spoon*. **4.** of or relating to a person still in office: *a serving vice-president*.

servitude /'sɜvətjud/, *n.* **1.** slavery; bondage: *political servitude*. **2.** forced service or labor as a punishment for criminals: *penal servitude*. [ME, from L]

servomechanism /'sɜvoʊˌmɛkənɪzəm/, *n.* a mechanism which is used to change a low-powered mechanical motion into one which requires far greater power. Also, **servosystem** /'sɜvoʊˌsɪstəm/.

sesame /'sɛsəmi/, *n.* a tropical herb, whose small oval seeds are used for food and oil. [Gk]

sesqui-, a word part meaning 'one and a half', as in *sesquicentenary*. [L, contraction of *sēmis* a half + *-que* besides]

sessile /'sɛsaɪl/, *adj. Biol.* **1.** attached by the base without a stalk, as a leaf growing directly from the stem. **2.** permanently attached. [L: sitting down]

session /'sɛʃən/, *n.* **1.** the sitting together of a court, council, etc., for a conference or business affairs: *Parliament is now in session*. **2.** a single continuous sitting, or period of sitting, of people so assembled. **3.** a single continuous period of lessons, study, etc.: *two afternoon sessions a week*. **4.** a part of the year into which teaching is organised at a college, etc. **5.** a period of time for any given activity: *a dancing session*. **6.** *Qld, WA.* the hours on Sunday during which a hotel may open. [ME, from L] —**sessional**, *adj.*

sestet /sɛs'tɛt/, *n.* **1.** the last six lines of a sonnet. **2.** → **sextet** (def. 2). [It]

set /sɛt/, *v.*, **set, setting,** *n., adj.* ◇*v.t.* **1.** to put in a particular place, position, or condition: *to set a vase on a table; to set a house on fire*. **2.** to cause to begin: *to set someone thinking*. **3.** to estimate or fix the value of (something) at a certain amount or rate: *I would set that painting at $500*. **4.** to urge to attack: *to set the dogs on the robber*. **5.** to fix or appoint: *to set a limit*. **6.** to present for others to follow: *to set an example*. **7.** to give or assign (a task): *to set homework for the class*. **8.** to choose for study: *The examiners have set 'King Lear' this year*. **9.** to make up (an examination, etc.): *He set the maths exam*. **10.** to arrange; order for use. **11.** to cover with a cloth and/or arrange cutlery, crockery, etc., on; lay: *to set the table*. **12.** to adjust; regulate: *to set a clock*. **13.** to fix (a gem, etc.) in gold, etc. **14.** to cause (a hen) to sit on eggs in order to hatch them. **15.** to put (muscles, the face, etc.) into a fixed state: *She set a smile on her face*. **16.** to cause to become hard or solid. **17.** to fix (hair, etc.) in a desired shape, style, etc. **18.** *Med.* to put (a broken bone) back in position. **19.** to pitch (a tune). **20.** *Music.* **a.** to fit (words) to music. **b.** to arrange (music) for certain voices or instruments. **21.** to spread (a sail) so as to catch the wind. **22.** *Printing.* to arrange (type) in the order needed for printing. ◇*v.i.* **23.** to pass below the horizon; sink: *The sun sets every evening*. **24.** (of the face, muscles, etc.) to become fixed or rigid. **25.** (of jelly, etc.) to become firm. **26.** (of hair) to take on a desired shape or style. **27.** *Bot.* (of the ovary of a flower) to develop into fruit. ◇*v.* **28.** Some special uses are:
set about, 1. to begin. **2.** to attack.
set against, to cause to be hostile towards.
set back, 1. to delay; hinder. **2.** *Colloq.* to cost (someone): *It set him back $10*.
set down, 1. to put down in writing. **2.** to allow (passengers) to get off a bus, etc.
set eyes on, to see.
set forth, to start.
set in, to begin: *Darkness set in*.
set off, 1. to explode: *They set the bomb off at noon*. **2.** to start (someone doing something). **3.** to begin, as on a journey. **4.** to intensify or improve by contrast: *That jumper set off her red hair to perfection*.
set out, 1. to arrange: *The books were neatly set out on the table*. **2.** to explain carefully: *The answer was set out in writing*. **3.** to start, as on a journey.
set (someone) up, *Colloq.* to arrange a situation so as to make (another) look guilty, wrong, etc.
set store by, to consider worthy or important: *She sets little store by money*. **set up, 1.** to build; erect. **2.** to start (a business, etc.). **3.** to provide (with): *His parents set him up with money*. **4.** to claim to be: *to set up as an expert*. ◇*n.* **29.** the act or result of setting. **30.** a number of things usu. used together or forming a complete range, outfit, or collection: *a set of dishes*. **31.** a group of people classed together: *the smart set*. **32.** a feeling of ill-will (fol. by *against* or *on*): *to have a set on someone*. **33.** posture; bearing: *the set of his shoulder*. **34.** a radio or television receiving apparatus. **35.** *Tennis.* a group of games, as a unit in a match. **36.** a number of pieces of scenery arranged together, used for a play or film. **37.** *Mech.* the bending out of the points of alternate teeth of a saw in opposite directions. **38.** *Maths.* any collection of numbers or objects which have some common property. ◇*adj.* **39.** fixed beforehand: *a set time; set rules*. **40.** customary: *set phrases*. **41.** fixed; rigid: *a set smile*. **42.** fixed by habit or determination: *to be set in one's opinions*. **43.** ready; prepared: *all set to go*. **44.** formed, built, or made (as stated): *a heavily-set man*. **45.** *Colloq.* **a.** determined (fol. by *on*): *She was set on going to England*. **b.** not in favor of (fol. by *against*): *She was set against housework*. [ME *sette(n)* to set, place, from OE *settan*]

Set /sɛt/, *n. Egypt Myth.* the god of evil, deadly opponent of Osiris, and represented with a beast's head and snout; called by the Greeks Typhon. Also, **Seth**. [Gk *Seth*, from Egyptian *Setesh*]

setback /'sɛtbæk/, *n.* a check to progress; hindrance.

seti-, a word part meaning 'bristle'. [combining form representing L *sēta*]

setscrew /'sɛtskru/, *n.* a screw holding two machine parts firmly together, to prevent movement.

set square, *n.* a flat piece of wood, plastic, etc., in the shape of a right-angled triangle, used in technical drawing.

settee /sɛ'ti, sə'ti/, *n.* a seat for two or more people, with a back and sometimes with arms. [? from SEAT]

setter /'sɛtə/, *n.* **1.** someone or something that sets. **2.** a long-haired hunting dog trained to stand stiffly and point its nose towards the animal being hunted.

setting /'sɛtɪŋ/, *n.* **1.** the act of someone or something that sets. **2.** the surroundings of anything. **3.** something in which an object, as a jewel, is set. **4.** a combined group of articles, as of cutlery, china, etc., used for setting a table. **5.** the period or place in which the action of a play, film, etc., takes place. **6.** *Music.* a piece of music composed for certain words.

settle /'sɛtl/, *v.,* **-tled, -tling.** ◇*v.t.* **1.** to agree upon (a time, price, conditions, etc.). **2.** to place in a desired position or in order. **3.** to pay (a bill, etc.). **4.** to close (an account) by payment. **5.** to establish (a place) with settlers; colonise. **6.** to establish (someone) in a way of life, business, etc.: *He settled his family in Tasmania.* **7.** to quiet (the nerves, stomach, etc.). **8.** to end or resolve (an argument, disagreement, etc.). **9.** to calm or pacify (someone). **10.** to cause (particles, dregs, etc.) to sink. **11.** to dispose of finally: *to settle an estate.* **12.** *Law.* **a.** to give (property, title, etc.) to a person by legal process, esp. by a will: *He settled his estate on his son.* **b.** to end (legal proceedings) by agreement of both parties: *They settled out of court.* ◇*v.i.* **13.** to decide; arrange (oft. fol. by *on* or *upon*): *to settle on a plan of action.* **14.** to pay off a debt (oft. fol. by *up*). **15.** to come to live in a new country or place. **16.** to come to rest. **17.** to sink down gradually: *The dust slowly settled.* ◇*v.* **18. settle down, a.** to come to a rest; become calm. **b.** to put (children) to bed. **c.** to begin to do serious work. **d.** to begin a regular way of life, esp. after marrying. [OE *setlan* from *setl* a seat]

settlement /'sɛtlmənt/, *n.* **1.** the act or result of settling. **2.** arrangement; adjustment. **3.** a colony. **4.** a small village, esp. in an area with few people.

settler /'sɛtlə/, *n.* someone who settles in a new country, esp. one who is freeborn and who takes up part of the land for farming.

set-up /'sɛt-ʌp/, *n.* **1.** organisation; arrangement: *The set-up of the library is simple.* **2.** *Survey.* the station or point at which a surveying instrument is set up for taking a number of readings. **3.** *Colloq.* a contest or undertaking which has been arranged so as to present no real challenge or problems. **4.** *Colloq.* a dishonest scheme; swindle. **5.** *Colloq.* a trap. ◇*adj.* **6.** of or pertaining to a set-up.

Seurat /sɜ'ra/, *n.* **Georges** /ʒɔʒ/, 1859–91, French post-impressionist painter.

Sevastopol /sə'væstəpɒl/, *n.* a fortified seaport on the Crimean peninsula of Ukraine; famous for its heroic resistance during sieges of 349 days in 1854–55, and 245 days in 1941–42. Pop. 345 000 (1986 est.). Also, **Sebastopol.**

seven /'sɛvən/, *n.* **1.** a cardinal number, six plus one (6 + 1). **2.** the symbol for this number, as 7 or VII. ◇*adj.* **3.** amounting to seven in number. [OE *seofon*]

Seven Hills of Rome, *n. pl.* the seven hills (the Aventine, Caelian, Capitoline, Esquiline, Palatine, Quirinal, and Viminal) on and about which the ancient city of Rome was built.

seventeen /sɛvən'tin/, *n.* **1.** a cardinal number, ten plus seven (10 + 7). **2.** the symbol for this number, as 17 or XVII. ◇*adj.* **3.** amounting to seventeen in number. [OE *seofontene*] **–seventeenth,** *adj., n.*

seventh /'sɛvənθ/, *adj.* **1.** next after the sixth. **2.** being one of seven equal parts. ◇*n.* **3.** a seventh part, esp. of one ($\frac{1}{7}$). **4.** the seventh member of a series. **5.** *Music.* note on the seventh degree from a given note.

Seventh-Day Adventist /ˌsɛvənθ-deɪ ˈædvəntəst/, *n.* a member of a Christian sect which makes Saturday the main day of rest and worship.

seventh heaven, *n.* a state of great or perfect happiness. [orig. with ref. to the highest heaven in Talmudic literature, where God and the most exalted angels dwell]

seventy /'sɛvənti/, *n., pl.* **-ties,** *adj.* ◇*n.* **1.** cardinal number, ten times seven (10 × 7). **2.** symbol for this number, as 70 or LXX. **3.** (*pl.*) the numbers from 70 to 79 of a series, esp. with reference to the years of a person's age, or the years of a century. ◇*adj.* **4.** amounting to seventy in number. [OE *seofontig*] **–seventieth,** *adj., n.*

Seven Wonders of the World, *n. pl.* the seven most remarkable structures of ancient times: the Egyptian pyramids, the Mausoleum erected by Artemisia at Halicarnassus, the Temple of Artemis at Ephesus, the walls and Hanging Gardens of Babylon, the Colossus of Rhodes, the statue of Zeus by Phidias at Olympia, and the Pharos or lighthouse at Alexandria.

sever /'sɛvə/, *v.t.* **1.** to put apart; separate. **2.** to divide into parts, esp. with force; cut. **3.** to break off (ties, relations, etc.). [ME, from AF, from LL] **–severance,** *n.*

several /'sɛvrəl/, *adj.* **1.** being more than two or three, but not many. **2.** individual; respective: *They went their several ways.* **3.** various: *the several steps in solving a problem.* ◇*n.* **4.** a few people or things; some: *Several were there.* [ME, from AF, from L: distinct] **–severally,** *adv.*

severance pay /'sɛvərəns peɪ/, *n.* money paid by a firm to workers or directors to make up for the loss of their jobs.

severe /sə'vɪə/, *adj.,* **-verer, -verest. 1.** harsh; extreme: *severe punishment.* **2.** unsmiling; stern: *a severe face.* **3.** serious; grave: *a severe illness.* **4.** simple; plain: *She wears severe clothes.* **5.** hard to endure, perform, achieve, etc.: *a severe test.* **6.** extremely strict,

severe /sɪ'vɪə/, *adj.* accurate, or methodical: *He lives by severe standards.* [L] — **severity**, *n.*

Severn /'sevən/, *n.* a river flowing from central Wales, through Shropshire, Hereford and Worcester, and Gloucestershire into the Bristol Channel; the longest river in Great Britain. 354 km.

Seville /sə'vɪl/, *n.* a port in south-western Spain on the river Guadalquivir; site of the Alcazar; cathedral. Pop. 651 299 (1986 est.). Spanish, **Sevilla**.

sew /soʊ/, *v.*, **sewed**, **sewn** or **sewed**, **sewing**. ◇*v.t.* **1.** to join by a thread, etc., as with a needle. **2.** to make, repair, etc., (clothing) by such means. **3.** to close or fasten with stitches: *to sew a wound up.* ◇*v.i.* **4.** to work with a needle and thread, or with a sewing machine. ◇*v.* **5. sew up**, *Colloq.* to complete (arrangements, talks, etc.) successfully. [OE *siw(i)an*] — **sewing**, *n.*

sewage /'suːɪdʒ/, *n.* waste matter which passes through sewers.

Sewell /'suəl/, *n.* **1. Anna**, 1820–78, English novelist, author of *Black Beauty*. **2. Henry**, 1807–79, NZ statesman, born in England; first prime minister of NZ (1856).

sewer /'suə/, *n.* a man-made pipeline, usu. underground, for carrying off waste water and matter, as from a town. [ME, from OF: channel from a fishpond, from Rom, from L]

sewerage /'suərɪdʒ/, *n.* **1.** the removal of waste water and matter by means of sewers. **2.** the pipes and fittings carrying sewage.

sewn /soʊn/, *v.* a past participle of **sew**.

sex /seks/, *n.* **1.** the condition of being either male or female. **2.** *Biol.* the total of physical differences by which the male and the female are distinguished. **3.** the natural desire or attraction drawing one sex towards the other. **4.** — **sexual intercourse**. **5.** men or women seen as a group: *the fair sex.* ◇*v.t.* **6.** to find out the sex of. [ME, from L *sexus* sex, ? orig., division]

sex-, a word part meaning '6'. [L]

sexist /'seksəst/, *adj.* **1.** of an attitude which judges a person by sex rather than by individual qualities. **2.** of or relating to unfair practices based on over-simplified and usu. negative attitudes of one sex to the other, esp. in advertising, job opportunities, etc. ◇*n.* **3.** a person who shows sexist attitudes. — **sexism**, *n.*

sextant /'sekstənt/, *n.* an astronomical instrument used in measuring angular distances, esp. the altitudes of sun, moon, and stars, used at sea to find one's latitude and longitude. [L: sixth part]

sextet /seks'tet/, *n.* **1.** any group or set of six. **2.** (a musical composition for) six voices or instruments. Also, **sestet**, **sextette**. [alteration of SESTET, from L *sex* six]

sexton /'sekstən/, *n.* a church officer whose job it is to take care of the church, its contents, and the graveyard, etc. [ME, from AF, from ML: sacristan]

sextuple /'sekstəpəl/, *adj.* consisting of six parts; sixfold. [L *sextus* sixth + *-uple*, as in QUINTUPLE] — **sextuplet**, *n.*

sexual /'sekʃuəl/, *adj.* **1.** of or relating to sex. **2.** involving the two sexes. **3.** *Biol.* having sex or sexual organs, or reproducing by processes involving both sexes. **4.** having a strong sex drive or sexual appeal. [LL] — **sexuality**, *n.*

sexual intercourse, *n.* the insertion of the penis into the vagina followed by ejaculation; coitus; copulation.

sexually transmitted disease, *n.* any disease that is transmitted principally by sexual contact with an infected person. Also, **STD**

sexy /'seksi/, *adj.* **-ier**, **-iest**. **1.** having or involving a great or intense concern with sex: *a sexy novel.* **2.** having sex appeal.

Seychelles /seɪ'ʃelz/, *n.* a republic consisting of more than one hundred islands in the western Indian Ocean, including the Seychelles archipelago. Pop. 65 967 (1987 est.); 444 km². *Languages:* Creole, also English and French. *Currency:* rupee. *Cap.:* Victoria.

Seymour[1] /'siːmɔː/, *n.* **1. Alan**, born 1927, Australian playwright; noted for *The One Day of the Year* (first produced 1960; published 1962). **2. Jane**, c. 1510–37, third wife of Henry VIII of England, and mother of Edward VI.

Seymour[2] /'siːmɔː/, *n.* a town and shire in central Vic, on the Goulburn River. Pop. 6510 (1986).

SF, *Abbrev.* science fiction.

sforzando /sfɔt'sændoʊ/, *adv. Music.* with force (used as a direction for the playing of a note or chord). *Abbrev.:* sf., sfz. [It: force]

s.g., *Abbrev.* specific gravity.

Sgt, *Abbrev.* Sergeant.

sh /ʃ/, *interj.* (an exclamation requesting or demanding silence.)

Shaanxi /ʃɑ'ɑnʃi/, *n.* a province in northern China. Pop. 30 020 000 (1986 est.); 195 800 km². *Cap.:* Xian. Formerly, **Shensi**.

shabby /'ʃæbi/, *adj.*, **-bier**, **-biest**. **1.** having the appearance of being greatly worn, used, etc.: *shabby clothes*. **2.** wearing worn clothes; seedy: *a shabby dresser*. **3.** making a poor appearance or impression. **4.** meanly ungenerous or unfair. [*shab* (ME; OE *sceabb* scab) + -Y¹] — **shabbily**, *adv.* — **shabbiness**, *n.*

shack /ʃæk/, *n.* **1.** a rough cabin; shanty. ◇*v.* **2. shack up**, **a.** to live at a place (fol. by *with*): *You can come and shack up with us.* **b.** to live in a sexual relationship (fol. by *with*). [short for *shackle* in same sense, itself short for RAMSHACKLE]

shackle /'ʃækəl/, *n.*, *v.*, **-led**, **-ling**. ◇*n.* **1.** a ring of iron or the like for binding the wrist, ankle, etc.; a fetter. **2.** a hobble or fetter for a horse, etc. **3.** anything that serves to prevent freedom of action, thought, etc.: *the shackles of ignorance*. ◇*v.t.* **4.** to put a shackle on; confine. [ME *shackle*, OE *sceacel* fetter]

Shackleton /ˈʃækəltən/, *n.* **Sir Ernest Henry**, 1874–1922, British antarctic explorer.

Shadbolt /ˈʃædboʊlt/, *n.* **Maurice**, born 1932, NZ novelist.

shade /ʃeɪd/, *n., v.*, **shaded, shading.** ◇*n.* **1.** the slight darkness caused by the blocking of rays of light. **2.** an area of slight darkness; shady place. **3.** anything used for protection against light, heat, etc. **4.** (*pl.*) the spirits of the dead. **5.** a degree of darkening of a color. **6.** the dark part of a picture. **7.** a slight variation, amount, or degree: *There is not a shade of difference between them.* **8. cast** or **put in the shade**, to make less important, clever, etc., by comparison. ◇*v.t.* **9.** to produce shade in or on. **10.** to dim or darken. **11.** to block or hide from view. **12.** to protect from light, heat, etc., as by a screen. **13.** to partly darken (a picture) for effects of light and shade. ◇*v.i.* **14.** to pass gradually, as one color or one thing into another. [OE *sceadu*]

shadow /ˈʃædoʊ/, *n.* **1.** a dark figure cast on the ground, etc., by a body blocking a light source. **2.** shade or slight darkness. **3.** a slight suggestion: *not a shadow of a doubt.* **4.** a ghost: *pursued by shadows.* **5.** a faint resemblance: *He is a shadow of his former self.* **6.** a reflected image. **7.** the dark part of a picture. **8.** a constant or powerful threat, influence, etc.: *under the shadow of the atomic bomb.* **9.** a constant companion. **10.** someone who keeps close watch upon another, as a spy, etc. ◇*v.t.* **11.** to shade. **12.** to cast a gloom over. **13.** to protect from light, heat, etc. **14.** to follow (a person) about secretly, in order to keep watch over their movements. [OE *scead(u)we*, form of *sceadu* SHADE] **– shadowy**, *adj.*

shadow-boxing /ˈʃædoʊˌbɒksɪŋ/, *n.* boxing carried on with an imaginary partner, as for exercise.

shadow cabinet, *n. Govt.* the group of members of the chief opposition party who speak on behalf of the party on major issues.

shadow ministry, *n. Govt.* the members of the opposition party each of whom acts as party spokesperson for a portfolio held by a government minister.

shady /ˈʃeɪdi/, *adj.*, **-dier, -diest. 1.** in the shade. **2.** giving shade. **3.** *Colloq.* questionable; of doubtful character or honesty: *a shady deal.*

Shaffer /ˈʃæfə/, *n.* **Peter**, born 1926, British playwright; author of *Equus* (1973).

shaft /ʃɑft/, *n.* **1.** a long pole or rod forming the body of some weapons, as a spear, arrow, etc. **2.** something directed as in sharp attack: *shafts of criticism.* **3.** a ray; beam: *a shaft of sunlight.* **4.** the handle of a hammer, axe, golf club, etc. **5.** a revolving bar serving to transmit motion, as from an engine to various machines. **6.** the body of a column between the base and the top. **7.** either of the parallel bars between which an animal drawing a vehicle is placed. **8.** any well-like passage or vertical or sloping enclosed space, as in a building: *a lift shaft; mine shaft.* **9.** *Bot.* the trunk of a tree. **10.** *Zool.* the main stem of a feather. [OE *sceaft*]

Shaftesbury /ˈʃɑftsbəri, -bri/, *n.* **Anthony Ashley Cooper, 7th Earl of**, 1801–85, English factory reformer and philanthropist.

shag[1] /ʃæg/, *n.* **1.** rough, matted hair, wool, etc. **2.** a heavy or rough woollen cloth, with short, fuzzy fibres. **3.** coarse tobacco cut into fine shreds. [OE *sceacga* wool, etc.]

shag[2] /ʃæg/, *n.* **1.** → **cormorant** (def. 1). **2.** → **darter. 3. like a shag on a rock**, *Colloq.* alone; deserted. [? from the shaggy crest]

shaggy /ˈʃægi/, *adj.*, **-gier, -giest. 1.** covered with or having long, rough hair. **2.** untidy: *a shaggy appearance.* **3.** rough and matted. **4.** having rough end fibres, as cloth. **– shagginess**, *n.*

shagreen /ʃəˈgriːn/, *n.* **1.** a kind of untanned leather with a coarse surface, prepared from the skin of the horse, shark, seal, etc. **2.** the rough skin of certain sharks. [formerly *chagrin*, from F, from Turk: the rump of a horse]

shah /ʃɑ/, *n.* a king, esp. used (*usu. cap.*) as a title of the former rulers of Iran. [Pers]

shake /ʃeɪk/, *v.*, **shook, shaken, shaking,** *n.* ◇*v.i.* **1.** to move or sway with short, quick, irregular movements. **2.** to tremble with fear, cold, etc. **3.** to fall (fol. by *down, off,* etc.) by such motion: *Sand shakes off easily.* **4.** to become unsteady. **5.** to clasp a person's hand in greeting, agreement, etc. ◇*v.t.* **6.** to move to and fro with short, quick, forcible movements. **7.** to bring, throw, rouse, etc., by or as if by some strong movement to and fro. **8.** to cause to become unsettled: *to shake the foundations of society.* **9.** to disturb, unsettle, or weaken. **10.** *Colloq.* to get rid of; escape from (fol. by *off*): *The robber shook off the police.* ◇*v.* **11. shake hands**, to clasp hands in greeting, agreement, etc. **12. shake one's head**, to turn the head from side to side to show refusal, disapproval, disbelief, etc. ◇*n.* **13.** the act or result of shaking. **14.** a trembling motion; tremor. **15.** a disturbing blow; shock. **16.** a drink made by shaking ingredients together: *a milk shake.* **17.** (*pl.*) *Colloq.* a condition of trembling. **18.** a dance in which the body is shaken violently in time to music. **19.** *Colloq.* a moment: *just a shake.* **20. no great shakes**, *Colloq.* of no particular importance. [OE *sceacan*]

Shakespeare /ˈʃeɪkspɪə/, *n.* **William**, 1564–1616, English poet and dramatist. Also, **Shakspere, Shakspeare.**

shaky /ˈʃeɪki/, *adj.*, **-kier, -kiest. 1.** shaking; trembling. **2.** likely to break down or give way; insecure: *a shaky ladder; a shaky friendship.* **– shakiness**, *n.*

shale /ʃeɪl/, *n.* a rock of layered or easily split structure formed by the consolidation of clay or very tiny particles. [special use of obs. *shale* scale (of a fish, etc.)] **– shaly**, *adj.*

shall /ʃæl/; *weak form* /ʃəl/, *auxiliary verb, pres. sing.* and *pl.* **shall**; *past sing.* and *pl.* **should;** *old forms* thou **shalt;** thou **shouldst** or **shouldest;** with no imperative, infinitive, or participle forms. **1.** (used, generally, in the first person to show simple future time): *I shall*

shall *go today.* **2.** (used, generally in the second and third persons, to show promise or determination): *You shall do it.* **3.** (used in questions that allow the use of *shall* in the answer): *Shall he be told? He shall.* **4.** (used conditionally in all persons to show future time): *if he shall come.* [OE *sceal*]

shallot /ʃəˈlɒt/, *n.* **1.** → **spring onion. 2.** a plant of the lily family, whose bulb forms smaller bulbs which are used for flavoring in cookery and as a vegetable. [var. of *eschalot*, from OF]

shallow /ˈʃæloʊ/, *adj.* **1.** not deep: *shallow water.* **2.** lacking depth; superficial: *a shallow mind.* ◇*n.* **3.** (*usu. pl.*) a shallow part of a body of water; shoal. [ME *schalowe*] –**shallowness,** *n.*

shalt /ʃælt/, *v. Archaic.* second person singular of **shall.**

sham /ʃæm/, *n., adj., v.,* **shammed, shamming.** ◇*n.* **1.** something that is not what it appears to be. ◇*adj.* **2.** pretended; counterfeit: *sham attacks.* ◇*v.t.* **3.** to take on the appearance of: *to sham illness.* ◇*v.i.* **4.** to pretend. [special use of Brit d. *sham*, northern var. of SHAME]

shamble /ˈʃæmbəl/, *v.,* **-bled, -bling,** *n.* ◇*v.i.* **1.** to walk or go with a dragging movement; shuffle. ◇*n.* **2.** a shambling walk. [v. use of *shamble*, adj., awkward]

shambles /ˈʃæmbəlz/, *n.* (usu. treated as sing.) **1.** a place for slaughtering animals. **2.** any place of loss of life, as a battlefield. **3.** any place or thing in confusion or disorder. [OE *sc(e)amel* stool, table, later counter for selling meat, later slaughtering place]

shame /ʃeɪm/, *n., v.,* **shamed, shaming.** ◇*n.* **1.** a painful feeling following the realisation that one has said or done something dishonorable, improper, stupid, etc. **2.** the ability to have this feeling: *to be without shame.* **3.** disgrace; ignominy. **4.** an unfortunate situation or state of affairs: *It's a shame you had to wait in the rain.* **5. put to shame, a.** to disgrace. **b.** to do better than; surpass. ◇*v.t.* **6.** to cause to feel shame. **7.** to force by causing a feeling of shame: *He shamed me into helping him.* [OE *sc(e)amu*] –**shameful, shameless,** *adj.*

Shamir /ʃəˈmɪə/, *n.* Yitzhak (*Yitzhak Jazernicki*), born 1915 in Poland, Israeli politician; prime minister 1986–92.

shampoo /ʃæmˈpuː/, *v.,* **-pooed, -pooing,** *n.* ◇*v.t.* **1.** to wash (the hair), esp. with a cleaning preparation. **2.** to clean (carpets, etc.), with a special preparation. ◇*n.* **3.** the act of shampooing. **4.** a preparation used for shampooing. [Hind: to shampoo, lit., to press, squeeze]

shamrock /ˈʃæmrɒk/, *n.* a plant with three leaflets believed to have been used by St Patrick to symbolise the Trinity. [Irish *seamróg*, little clover]

Shandong /ʃænˈdʊŋ/, *n.* a province in north-eastern China. Pop. 76 950 000 (1986 est.); 153 300 km². *Cap.*: Jinan. Formerly, **Shantung.**

shandy /ˈʃændi/, *n.* a mixed drink of beer with ginger beer or lemonade.

Shang /ʃʌŋ/, *n.* a Chinese dynasty ruling from the 18th to the 12th century BC; the first Chinese dynasty whose existence can be verified.

shanghai[1] /ˈʃæŋhaɪ, ʃæŋˈhaɪ/, *v.t.,* **-haied, -haiing. 1.** *Naut.* to unlawfully obtain (a man) for the crew of a ship, as by force, etc. **2.** *Colloq.* to involve someone in an activity, usu. without their knowledge or against their wishes: *to be shanghaied into washing the car.* **3.** *Colloq.* to steal. [apparently short for 'to ship to SHANGHAI']

shanghai[2] /ˈʃæŋhaɪ/, *n., v.,* **-haied, -haiing.** ◇*n.* **1.** a child's catapult; sling (def. 1). ◇*v.t.* **2.** to shoot with a catapult. [Brit d. *shangan* a cleft stick for putting on a dog's tail]

Shanghai /ʃæŋˈhaɪ/, *n.* a seaport and industrial municipality in eastern China, near the mouth of the Chang. Pop. 6 980 000 (1986 est.); 5800 km².

Shangri-la /ʃæŋgriˈlɑː/, *n.* a hidden paradise in *Lost Horizon* (1933) by James Hilton, 1900–54, English novelist. Also, **Shangrilla.**

shank /ʃæŋk/, *n.* **1.** the whole leg. **2.** a cut of meat from the top part of the leg, from the front (**fore shank**) or back (**hind shank**). **3.** that part of an instrument, tool, etc., connecting the acting part with the handle. [OE *sc(e)anca*]

Shankar /ˈʃæŋkə/, *n.* Ravi /ˈrɑːvi/, born 1920, Indian sitarist.

Shannon /ˈʃænən/, *n.* the largest river in Ireland, rising in County Cavan and flowing south-west to the Atlantic. 386 km.

shan't /ʃɑnt/, *v. Colloq.* a shortened form of *shall not.*

shantung /ʃænˈtʌŋ/, *n.* **1.** a heavy silk cloth made of rough, spun wild silk. **2.** a fabric like this made of rayon or cotton. [from *Shantung*, maritime province in NE China]

shanty[1] /ˈʃænti/, *n., pl.* **-ties.** a roughly built hut, cabin, or house. [probably from Canadian F *chantier* log hut, from F: shed, from L: framework]

shanty[2] /ˈʃænti/, *n., pl.* **-ties.** a sailors' song, esp. one sung in rhythm to work. [F *chanter* sing]

Shanxi /ˈʃænʃi/, *n.* a province in northern China. Pop. 26 270 000 (1986 est.); 157 100 km². *Cap.*: Taiyuan. Formerly, **Shansi.**

shape /ʃeɪp/, *n., v.,* **shaped, shaping.** ◇*n.* **1.** the way something appears from its outline or outer surface. **2.** the form of a particular thing or person. **3.** an imaginary form; phantom. **4.** a pretended appearance; guise. **5.** a particular form or kind: *the shape of things to come.* **6.** proper form; orderly arrangement: *The house is in shape for the guest's arrival.* **7.** condition: *affairs in bad shape.* **8.** something used to give form, e.g. a mould or pattern. ◇*v.t.* **9.** to give definite form, shape, or character to. **10.** to alter; adapt: *to shape one's ideas to fit one's income.* **11.** to plan or define: *to shape one's future.* ◇*v.i.* **12.** to develop (oft. fol. by *up*): *The new worker is shaping up well.*

shape — **sheath**

13. to stand ready to fight (fol. by *up*). ◇*v.* **14. shape up or ship out,** to perform as needed or leave. [ME] —**shapeless,** *adj.*

shapely /'ʃeɪpli/, *adj.,* **-lier, -liest.** having a pleasing shape; well-formed.

shard /ʃad/, *n.* **1.** a small piece, esp. of broken earthenware. **2.** *Zool.* **a.** a scale. **b.** a shell, as of an egg or snail. **c.** one of the pair of hard forewings of a beetle. Also, **sherd.** [OE *sceard*]

share /ʃeə/, *n., v.,* **shared, sharing.** ◇*n.* **1.** the part given, belonging to, offered or owed by, an individual or group. **2.** one of the equal parts into which the capital stock of a limited company is divided. See **ordinary, deferred,** and **preference share.** ◇*v.t.* **3.** to divide and give in shares: *to share a cake with others.* **4.** to use, participate in, enjoy, etc., jointly: *to share the car.* ◇*v.i.* **5.** to have a share or part (oft. fol. by *in*): *to share in the fun.* [OE *scearu* cutting, division]

sharefarmer /'ʃeəfamə/, *n.* a farmer who lives on and works the land of another, with whom he shares the profits from his farming.

shark[1] /ʃak/, *n.* any of a group of marine fishes, certain types of which are large, fierce, and destructive to other fishes and sometimes man. [orig. obscure]

shark[2] /ʃak/, *n.* **1.** a person who dishonestly profits from others, as through false or unfair money dealings. ◇*v.t.* **2.** to obtain by trickery; steal. [G: *rascal*]

sharp /ʃap/, *adj.* **1.** having a thin cutting edge or a fine point. **2.** ending in an edge or point. **3.** sudden; abrupt: *a sharp rise in the road; a sharp bend.* **4.** (of a person's features) composed of hard, angular lines. **5.** clearly outlined; distinct: *a sharp picture on TV.* **6.** marked; noticeable: *a sharp distinction.* **7.** strong or biting in taste. **8.** piercing or shrill in sound. **9.** very cold: *a sharp wind.* **10.** very painful; distressing. **11.** angry; harsh: *sharp words.* **12.** alert; vigilant: *a sharp watch.* **13.** mentally quick and alert: *a sharp mind.* **14.** wise; shrewd; astute. **15.** cunning to the point of dishonesty: *sharp practice.* **16.** *Music.* **a.** above an intended pitch; too high. **b.** (of a note) raised a semitone in pitch: *F sharp.* ◇*adv.* **17.** precisely: *at one o'clock sharp.* **18.** watchfully; alertly: *Look sharp!* **19.** quickly; briskly. **20.** *Music.* above the true pitch. ◇*n.* **21.** *Music.* **a.** a note one semitone above a given note. **b.** (in notation) the symbol (#) showing this. [OE *scearp*] —**sharpness,** *n.*

Sharp /ʃap/, **Martin,** born 1941, Australian graphic artist.

sharpen /'ʃapən/, *v.t., v.i.* to make or become sharp or sharper. —**sharpener,** *n.*

shashlik /'ʃæʃlɪk/, *n.* → **shish kebab.** Also, **shashlick, shaslick.** [Russ. *shashlyk*, of Turkic orig.]

shasta daisy /ˌʃæstə 'deɪzi/, *n.* a plant with large white flowers oft. 10 cm in diameter and usu. growing singly on a long leafless stems.

shatter /'ʃætə/, *v.t.* **1.** to break in pieces, as by a blow. **2.** to weaken; destroy (health, nerves, etc.). ◇*v.i.* **3.** to break suddenly into pieces. [ME]

shave /ʃeɪv/, *v.,* **shaved, shaved** or **shaven, shaving,** *n.* ◇*v.i.* **1.** to remove hair with a razor. ◇*v.t.* **2.** to remove hair from (the face, legs, etc.) by cutting it close to the skin. **3.** to cut off (hair, esp. the beard) close to the skin (oft. fol. by *off* or *away*): *He shaved his beard off.* **4.** to take thin slices from, esp. in order to smooth: *to shave wood.* **5.** to come very near to; graze: *to shave a corner.* ◇*n.* **6.** the act or process of shaving. **7.** a narrow miss or escape: *a close shave.* [OE *sceafan*]

shaving /'ʃeɪvɪŋ/, *n.* **1.** (oft. pl.) a very thin piece, esp. of wood. **2.** the act of someone or something that shaves.

Shaw /ʃɔ/, *n.* **George Bernard,** 1856–1950, Irish dramatist, critic, and novelist.

shawl /ʃɔl/, *n.* a piece of material, worn as a covering for the shoulders, head, etc. [Pers]

she /ʃi/, *pron., poss.* **her,** *obj.* **her,** *pl.* **they;** *n., pl.* **shes;** *adj.* ◇*pron.* **1.** the female in question or last mentioned. **2.** used (instead of *it*) of ships, etc., to which female characteristics are attributed. **3.** used (instead of *it*) in phrases: *She'll be right; She's apples.* ◇*n.* **4.** any female person or animal (opposed to *he*). ◇*adj.* **5.** female or feminine, esp. of animals: *a she cat.* [ME, modified form of ME *ghe*, OE *hēo.* See HE]

sheaf /ʃif/, *n., pl.* **sheaves.** *n.* **1.** one of the bundles in which cereal plants, as wheat, rye, etc., are bound after they are cut in the field. **2.** any bundle, group, or collection: *a sheaf of papers.* [OE *scēaf*]

shear /ʃɪə/, *v.,* **sheared** or (*old form*) **shore; sheared** or **shorn; shearing;** *n.* ◇*v.t.* **1.** to remove by cutting with a sharp instrument: *to shear wool from sheep.* **2.** to cut the hair, fleece, wool, etc., from: *to shear sheep.* **3.** to strip or take away (fol. by *of*): *shorn of its legal powers.* ◇*v.i.* **4.** *Phys.* to become fractured by a shear or shears (def. 6). ◇*n.* **5.** (*pl.*) large scissors or other cutting tool. **6.** *Phys.* (the force causing) a form of deformation in a body in which parallel sections or planes slide over one another. [OE *sceran*]

shearer /'ʃɪərə/, *n.* **1.** someone who shears sheep. **2.** someone who uses shears on metal, cloth, leather, etc. **3.** a sheep that is fit and ready for shearing, or that has a good quality wool: *That sheep is a good shearer.*

Shearers' Strike, *n.* the strike in Queensland in 1891 by shearers protesting about pastoralists' attempts to employ cheaper non-union labor; a further strike in 1894 was for 'the recognition of unionism'.

shearing /'ʃɪərɪŋ/, *n.* **1.** the act of shearing sheep. **2.** the time or season of shearing sheep.

shearwater /'ʃɪəwɔtə/, *n.* a long-winged seabird, related to the petrel, appearing, when flying low, to cut the water with its wings. [SHEAR, *v.* + WATER, *n.*]

sheath /ʃiθ/, *n., pl.* **sheaths** /ʃiðz, ʃiθs/. *n.* **1.** a covering for the blade of a sword, dagger, etc. **2.** any similar covering. **3.** *Biol.* a closely

sheath enveloping part or structure, as in an animal or plant. **4.** *Elect.* the covering of a cable. **5.** → **condom**. **6.** a close-fitting dress which follows the shape of the body. [OE *scēath*]

sheathe /ʃið/, *v.t.*, **sheathed, sheathing. 1.** to put (a sword, etc.) into a sheath. **2.** to enclose in or as in a covering. **3.** to cover with a protective layer: *to sheathe a roof with copper.* [ME *shethe*, from SHEATH]

sheave /ʃiv/, *v.t.*, **sheaved, sheaving.** to gather, collect, or bind into sheaves. [from SHEAF]

sheaves /ʃivz/, *n.* plural of **sheaf**.

Sheba /ˈʃibə/, *n.* **Queen of,** the queen who visited Solomon to verify what she had heard of his wisdom. [see I Kings 10:1-13]

shed[1] /ʃed/, *n.* **1.** a simple or rough structure built for shelter, storage, etc. **2.** a large, strongly built structure, often open at the sides or end. **3.** → **outhouse**. ◇*v.t.* **4.** to place or keep (animals) under cover. [OE *scead, sced* shelter, SHADE]

shed[2] /ʃed/, *v.t.*, **shed, shedding. 1.** to pour forth (water, etc.). **2.** to let fall (tears). **3.** to give or send out (light, sound, fragrance, etc.): *The lamp sheds soft light.* **4.** to throw off readily: *cloth that sheds water.* **5.** to cast off or let fall by natural process: *to shed leaves; to shed hair; to shed skin.* [OE]

she'd /ʃid/, a shortened form of: **1.** she had. **2.** she would.

sheen /ʃin/, *n.* brightness; lustre. [OE *scēne* beautiful, bright] —**sheeny,** *adj.*

sheep /ʃip/, *n., pl.* **sheep. 1.** a cud-chewing mammal, closely related to the goat, and kept for its meat and thick wool. **2.** a shy, timid, or stupid person. **3. separate the sheep from the goats,** to separate the good or better people or things from the rest. [OE *scēp* (Anglian), *scēap*]

sheep dip, *n.* a (deep trough containing) a liquid which kills vermin on the fleece or skin as sheep are driven through it.

sheepdog /ˈʃipdɒg/, *n.* a dog trained to guard and muster sheep.

sheepish /ˈʃipɪʃ/, *adj.* awkwardly shy; bashful or embarrassed.

sheep strike, *n.* a disease of the flesh of a living sheep caused by the maggots of a blowfly, esp. the blue blowfly. Also, **blowfly strike.**

sheer[1] /ʃɪə/, *adj.* **1.** (of fabrics) transparently thin; diaphanous. **2.** unmixed with anything else; utter; downright: *a sheer waste of time; sheer luck.* **3.** very steep: *a sheer cliff.* ◇*adv.* **4.** very steeply: *The rock rises sheer from the sea.* [ME *schere*]

sheer[2] /ʃɪə/, *v.i.* **1.** to go aside from a course; deviate; swerve: *The ship sheered off (from) the rocks.* ◇*n.* **2.** a going aside; swerve. **3.** the line of a ship's deck as seen from the side. [special use of SHEAR, *v.*]

sheet[1] /ʃit/, *n.* **1.** a large piece of cloth used on a bed, usu. one of a pair spread immediately above and below the sleeper. **2.** any broad stretch, layer, or covering: *a sheet of water; a sheet of flame.* **3.** a broad, thin piece of iron, glass, ice, etc. **4.** an oblong or square piece of paper to be written on. ◇*v.t.* **5.** to wrap in a sheet: *the sheeted dead.* **6.** to cover with a layer of something: *sheeted with ice.* [OE *scēat* lap]

sheet[2] /ʃit/, *n.* **1.** *Naut.* a rope or chain fastened to the lower corner of a sail to hold it in place or control it. ◇*v.t.* **2.** *Naut.* to hold in place or control by a sheet or sheets. [OE *scēata* rope tied to lower corner of a sail]

sheet anchor, *n.* **1.** a large anchor used only in an emergency. **2.** a person or thing used as a main or sole support in a crisis. [ME *shute anker;* orig. uncert.]

sheet lightning, *n.* lightning appearing as a general flash of brightness over a whole area.

Sheffield Shield /ˈʃefild ʃild/, *n.* a trophy awarded in an annual cricket competition between the states of Australia.

sheikh /ʃik, ʃeɪk/, *n.* (in Arab and other Muslim use) a chief or head, as of a religious group, village, or tribe. [Ar: old man]

sheila /ˈʃilə/, *n. Colloq.* a girl or woman. [probably from *Sheila*, Irish girl's name]

shekel /ˈʃekəl/, *n.* **1.** the monetary unit of Israel. **2.** a silver coin or unit of weight used by the ancient Hebrews. **3.** (*pl.*) Also, **sheckles,** *Colloq.* money. [Heb]

shelf /ʃelf/, *n., pl.* **shelves. 1.** a slab of wood, etc., fixed horizontally to a wall, or in a frame, for supporting objects. **2.** the contents of a shelf: *a shelf of sporting trophies.* **3.** a ledge: *a shelf of rock.* **4. on the shelf,** *Colloq.* (of a woman) unattached to a man; unlikely or too old to get married. [ME]

shell /ʃel/, *n., pl.* **shells** or (*for defs 5, 6*) **shell. 1.** a hard outer covering of an animal, as of a mollusc, turtle, etc. **2.** the material making this up: *sand full of broken shells.* **3.** the hard outer covering of an egg, nut, etc. **4.** something like a shell, in shape, or in being concave or hollow. **5.** a hollow projectile for a cannon, etc., filled with an explosive charge arranged to explode during flight or upon impact. **6.** *Colloq.* a cartridge. **7.** *Phys.* a class of electron orbits in an atom, all of which have almost the same energy. **8.** *Rowing.* a light racing boat. **9.** the walls or outer structure of an unfinished or destroyed building, ship, etc.: *After the fire only the shell of the factory remained.* **10. come out of one's shell,** to come out of a state of shyness or timidity. ◇*v.t.* **11.** to take out of the shell; remove the shell of: *to shell peanuts.* **12.** to fire shells on; bombard. ◇*v.* **13. shell out,** *Colloq.* to hand over; pay up. [OE *scell* (Anglian), *sciell*]

she'll /ʃil/; *weak form* /ʃəl/, contraction of: **1.** she will. **2.** she shall.

shellac /ʃəˈlæk/, *n., v.*, **-lacked, -lacking.** ◇*n.* **1.** a natural resin purified and used for making varnish, polish, and sealing wax, and in electrical insulation. ◇*v.t.* **2.** to coat or treat with shellac. [SHELL + *lac* resin]

Shelley /ˈʃeli/, *n.* **1. Mary Wollstonecraft (Godwin)** /ˈwʊlstənkrɑːft/, 1797–1851, English novelist; author of *Frankenstein.* **2.** her husband, **Percy Bysshe** /bɪʃ/, 1791–1822, English poet.

shellfish /'ʃelfiʃ/, *n., pl.* **-fishes,** (*esp. collectively*) **-fish.** an animal (not a fish) that lives in water and has a shell, e.g. oyster, lobster, etc. [OE *scilfisc*]

shell shock, *n.* a nervous or mental illness, marked by loss of self-command, memory, speech, sight, etc., at first supposed to be brought on by the explosion of shells in battle, but now explained as the result of the strain of modern warfare; battle fatigue. — **shell-shocked,** *adj.*

Shelta /'ʃeltə/, *n.* a tinkers' jargon of Ireland and parts of Britain, based on deliberately altered Gaelic. [orig. obscure]

shelter /'ʃeltə/, *n.* **1.** (something which gives) protection from bad weather, bombing, etc.; (a place of) refuge or safety. **2.** housing: *the right to food and shelter.* ◇*v.t.,* **3.** to give or take shelter: *to shelter a homeless child; to shelter under a tree.* [orig. uncert.]

sheltered workshop, *n.* a factory or workshop set up to provide work for handicapped people.

shelve[1] /ʃelv/, *v.t.,* **shelved, shelving. 1.** to place on a shelf or shelves. **2.** to stop considering: *to shelve the question.* **3.** to dismiss; cease to employ. **4.** to furnish with shelves. [from *shelves,* pl. of SHELF]

shelve[2] /ʃelv/, *v.i.,* **shelved, shelving.** to slope gradually. [orig. uncert.]

shemozzle /ʃə'mɒzl/, *n. Colloq.* **1.** a confused state of affairs; muddle. **2.** an uproar; row. [Yiddish, from Heb: bad luck]

shenanigan /ʃə'nænəgən/, *n.* (*oft. pl.*) *Colloq.* nonsense; deceit; trickery. [orig. uncert.]

Shenyang /'ʃɛnjʌŋ/, *n.* a town in northeastern China, the capital of Liaoning province. Pop. 3 173 200 (1985 est.). Formerly, **Mukden.**

she-oak /'ʃi-oʊk/, *n.* → **casuarina.**

Shepard /'ʃɛpəd/, *n.* **Alan Bartlett Jr,** born 1923, US naval officer; first US astronaut in space.

shepherd /'ʃɛpəd/, *n.* **1.** a person who looks after sheep. **2.** a person who looks after a group of people: *The priest minister is the shepherd of his flock.* ◇*v.t.* **3.** to care for or guard as a shepherd. **4.** to move (a person or people) along: *The police shepherded the crowd away from the accident.* [OE *scēphyrde*] — **shepherdess,** *n. fem.*

Shepparton /'ʃɛpətn/, *n.* a city in northern central Vic, east of Kyabram. Pop. (with Mooroopna) 30 238 (1986).

sherbet /'ʃɜbət/, *n.* **1.** a sweet powder eaten dry or used to make a fizzy drink. **2.** → **sorbet** (def. 2). [Turk and Pers, from Ar: a drink]

Sheridan /'ʃɛrədn/, *n.* **Richard Brinsley** /'brɪnzli/, 1751–1816, Irish dramatist and political leader.

sheriff /'ʃɛrəf/, *n. Law.* an officer of the Supreme Court with duties relating to the service and carrying out of processes, summoning of juries, etc. **2.** *Brit.* the chief officer of the Crown in a county, appointed every year. **3.** *US.* a law enforcement officer of a county or other civil subdivision of a state. [OE *scīrgerēfa*]

Sherpa /'ʃɜpə/, *n.* one of a Tibetan people living on the south side of the Himalayas. [Tibetan *shar* east + *pa* inhabitant]

sherry /'ʃɛri/, *n., pl.* **-ries.** a strong sweet or dry wine, orig. of southern Spain. [earlier *sherris,* taken as pl., from Sp (*vino de*) *Xeres* (wine of) Xeres, now Jerez in S Spain]

Sherwood Forest /ʃɜwʊd 'fɒrəst/, *n.* an ancient royal forest in central England, chiefly in Nottinghamshire; the traditional haunt of Robin Hood.

Shetland pony /ʃɛtlənd 'poʊni/, *n.* a pony of a small, sturdy, rough-coated breed. Also, **sheltie.** [from the *Shetland Islands,* a Scottish island group NE of the mainland, where the ponies were orig. bred]

Shevardnadze /ʃɛvəd'nadzə/, *n.* **Eduard Amvrosiyevich** /ˌɛdwad amvroʊ'sjɛɪəvɪtʃ/, born 1928, Soviet and Georgian politician; foreign minister of the Soviet Union 1985–90; became chairman of the State Council of Georgia in 1992.

shew /ʃoʊ/, *v.t., v.i.,* **shewed, shewn, shewing,** *n. Archaic.* → **show.**

shibboleth /'ʃɪbəlɛθ/, *n.* **1.** a habit, or an odd way of speaking, dressing, etc., which sets a particular group of people apart from others. **2.** a test word or pet phrase of a party, sect, etc. [Heb: stream in flood; a word used by Jephthah as a test word by which to distinguish the fleeing Ephraimites (who could not pronounce the *sh*) from his own men, the Gileadites (Judges 12:4–6.)]

shickered /'ʃɪkəd/, *adj. Colloq.* drunk; intoxicated. Also, **shicker.** [Yiddish, from Heb: to be drunk]

shied /ʃaɪd/, *v.* past tense and past participle of **shy.**

shield /ʃild/, *n.* **1.** a flat piece of metal, leather, or wood, carried to protect the body in battle. **2.** something shaped like or used as a shield. **3.** *Phys.* a screen used to prevent the escape of radiation esp. from a reactor. **4.** *Zool.* a protective plate, etc., on the body of an animal. **5.** *Geol.* a large, exposed mass of preCambrian rocks forming a stable part of the earth's crust. ◇*v.t., v.i.* **6.** to protect with or as with a shield. [OE *sceld*]

shift /ʃɪft/, *v.i.* **1.** to move from one place, position, etc., to another: *He shifted uneasily in his chair.* **2.** to manage to get along or succeed: *She'll shift for herself.* **3.** to change gear in a car: *to shift down.* ◇*v.t.* **4.** to replace by another; change: *to shift house.* **5.** to put or carry from one place, person, etc., to another; transfer: *to shift the blame on to someone else.* ◇*n.* **6.** a change or move: *a shift of emphasis; a shift in the wind.* **7. a.** the part of the day seen as a day's work when a factory, etc., operates continuously during the 24 hours: *night shift.* **b.** the people working during this time: *The day shift takes over now.* **8.** a woman's loose-fitting dress or, formerly, undergarment. **9. make shift,** to manage to get along or do one's best, esp. with difficulty. See **makeshift**. [ME; OE *sciftan*, c. G *schichten* arrange]

shiftless /'ʃɪftləs/, *adj.* lazy; lacking in resource or ambition; inefficient.

shifty /'ʃɪfti/, *adj.*, **-tier, -tiest.** deceitful; furtive; evasive.

Shiite /'ʃiaɪt/, *n.* a member of one of the two great religious divisions of Islam, the Shiah which regards Ali (the son-in-law of Mohammed) as the latter's legitimate successor, and rejects the first three Caliphs. See **Sunnite**.

shilling /'ʃɪlɪŋ/, *n.* **1.** (formerly) a silver coin equal to 1/20 of a pound. ◇*adj.* **2.** of the price or value of a shilling. *Abbrev.*: s., sh. [OE *scilling*]

shillyshally /'ʃɪli,ʃæli/, *v.i.*, **-lied, -lying.** to be unable to make up one's mind; waver; vacillate. [var. of repeated question *Shall I? Shall I?*]

shimmer /'ʃɪmə/, *v.i.* **1.** to shine with a dim, wavering light. ◇*n.* **2.** a dim, wavering light or gleam. [OE *scimerian*, from *scīmian* shine] —**shimmery**, *adj.*

shimmy /'ʃɪmi/, *n.*, *pl.* **-mies**, *v.*, **-mied, -mying.** ◇*n.* **1.** *US.* ragtime dance, marked by shaking of the hips or shoulders. ◇*v.i.* **2.** to dance the shimmy. **3.** to shake; vibrate. [alteration of CHEMISE]

shin /ʃɪn/, *n.*, *v.*, **shinned, shinning.** ◇*n.* **1.** the front part of the leg from the knee to the ankle. **2.** (meat from) the lower part of the foreleg in cattle. ◇*v.i.* **3.** to climb by holding fast with the hands or arms and legs and pulling oneself up (fol. by *up*). [OE *scinu*]

shindig /'ʃɪndɪg/, *n. Colloq.* **1.** a noisy dance or party, etc. **2.** a row; quarrel; disturbance. Also, **shindy**.

shine /ʃaɪn/, *v.*, **shone** or (esp. for def. 5) **shined, shining,** *n.* ◇*v.i.* **1.** to give forth, or glow with, light; shed or cast light. **2.** to be bright with reflected light; glisten; sparkle. **3.** to be very good at; excel: *to shine at sports*. ◇*v.t.* **4.** to direct the light of (a lamp, etc.): *Shine the torch over here.* **5.** to polish or make shiny: *to shine silver; to shine shoes.* ◇*n.* **6.** light; radiance. **7.** polish; lustre. **8.** sunshine; fair weather: *come rain or shine*. **9.** *Colloq.* liking; fancy: *to take a shine to*. [OE *scīnan*] —**shiny**, *adj.*

shiner /'ʃaɪnə/, *n.* **1.** someone or something that shines. **2.** *Colloq.* a black eye.

shingle¹ /'ʃɪŋgəl/, *n.*, *v.*, **-gled, -gling.** ◇*n.* **1.** a thin piece of wood, slate, etc., usu. oblong and with one end thicker than the other, used in overlapping rows to cover the roofs and sides of houses. **2.** a woman's close-cropped haircut. ◇*v.t.* **3.** to cover (a roof, etc.) with shingles. **4.** to cut (hair) close to the head. [ME; var. of *shindle*, from L]

shingle² /'ʃɪŋgəl/, *n.* small, water-worn stones or pebbles lying in masses on the seashore. [earlier *chingle*; ? of imitative orig.] —**shingly**, *adj.*

shingles /'ʃɪŋgəlz/, *n. sing.* or *pl.* a painful skin disease caused by an infection of nerves; herpes zoster. [ME, from ML: girdle, used to translate Gk *zōnē* or *zōstēr*, name of the disease]

shining /'ʃaɪnɪŋ/, *adj.* **1.** bright; radiant; gleaming. **2.** outstandingly good; brilliant: *shining talents; a shining example.*

Shinto /'ʃɪntoʊ/, *n.* one of earliest religions of Japan, mainly a system of nature and ancestor worship. Also, **Shintoism**. [Jap, from Chinese: way of the gods] —**Shintoist**, *n.*, *adj.*

ship /ʃɪp/, *n.*, *v.*, **shipped, shipping.** ◇*n.* **1.** a large vessel for carrying people or goods over deep water. ◇*v.t.* **2.** to send or have carried by ship, rail, etc. **3.** *Naut.* to take in (water) over the side, as a ship or boat does when waves break over it. **4.** to bring on board and fix in place: *to ship a lifeboat; to ship oars.* [OE *scip*]

-ship, a noun suffix indicating condition, character, office, skill, etc., as in *kingship, friendship, statesmanship*. [OE *-scipe*]

shipment /'ʃɪpmənt/, *n.* **1.** the act of shipping goods, etc. **2.** a load of goods sent at one time; consignment.

shipping /'ʃɪpɪŋ/, *n.* **1.** the action or business of sending goods, etc., by ship, rail, etc. **2.** ships taken as a whole: *The harbor was crowded with shipping.*

shipshape /'ʃɪpʃeɪp/, *adj.* in good order; neat; tidy.

shipwreck /'ʃɪprek/, *n.* **1.** the destruction or loss of a ship, by sinking or being broken up on rocks. **2.** the remains of a ship. ◇*v.t.* **3.** to cause to suffer shipwreck.

shipwright /'ʃɪpraɪt/, *n.* someone who works at building or repairing ships.

shiralee /ʃɪrə'li, 'ʃɪrə,li/, *n.* → **swag** (def. 1). [orig. unknown]

Shiraz /ʃə'ræz/, *n.* (a wine made from) a red grape variety grown in Australia. [from *Shiraz*, city in Iran]

shire /'ʃaɪə/, *n.* **1.** an area of land marked out for the purposes of local government, usu. larger than a town, municipality or borough. **2.** *Brit.* one of the counties of Britain. [OE *scīr*]

shirk /ʃɜk/, *v.t.*, *v.i.* to get out of doing (work, duty, etc.); evade. [? G: parasite, sharper] —**shirker**, *n.*

shirr /ʃɜ/, *v.t.* to draw up or gather (cloth) on parallel threads. [orig. uncert.]

shirt /ʃɜt/, *n.* **1.** a garment for the upper part of the body, usu. with buttons down the front, a collar and long or short sleeves. **2. keep one's shirt on**, to keep one's temper or be patient. [OE *scyrte*]

shirty /'ʃɜti/, *adj. Colloq.* bad-tempered; annoyed.

shish kebab, /'ʃɪʃ kəbæb/, *n.* a dish consisting of cubes of meat, marinated, and grilled on a skewer, often with onion, tomato, green pepper, etc. Also, **kebab**. [Turk *şiş* skewer + *kebap* roast meat]

shit /ʃɪt/, *v.*, **shitted, shat** or **shit; shitted; shitting;** *n. Colloq.* (*offensive*) ◇*v.i.* **1.** to defecate. ◇*n.* **2.** faeces; dung; excrement. **3.** the

shits, a. diarrhoea. **b.** a period of anger or annoyance.

Shiva /'ʃivə/, *n.* the third member of the Hindu trinity, known also as 'the Destroyer'. Also, **Siva.** See **Brahma** and **Vishnu.** [Hind, from Skt *çiva* propitious] —**Shivaism**, *n.* —**Shivaist**, *n.* —**Shivaistic**, *adj.*

shiver[1] /'ʃivə/, *v.i.* **1.** to shake or tremble with or as if with cold, fear, excitement, etc. ◇*n.* **2.** a shivering movement; quiver. [ME *chivere;* orig. uncert.] —**shivery**, *adj.*

shiver[2] /'ʃivə/, *v.t., v.i.* **1.** to break or split into fragments. ◇*n.* **2.** a fragment; splinter. [ME *schivere*, n., splinter] —**shivery**, *adj.*

shoal[1] /ʃoʊl/, *n.* **1.** a sandbank or sandbar in a body of shallow water. ◇*adj.* **2.** (of water) shallow. ◇*v.i.* **3.** to become (more) shallow. ◇*v.t.* **4.** to cause to become shallow. [OE *sceald* shallow]

shoal[2] /ʃoʊl/, *n.* **1.** a group of fish crowded fairly close together. Compare **school**[2]. ◇*v.i.* **2.** to collect in a shoal; throng. [OE *scolu* shoal (of fishes), multitude, troop]

shock[1] /ʃɒk/, *n.* **1.** a sudden and violent upset or fright. **2.** *Med.* a sudden collapse of the nervous mechanism caused by physical injury or strong emotional upset: *to be in shock*. **3.** a sudden collision. **4.** the physiological effect produced by the passage of an electric current through the body. ◇*v.t.* **5.** to strike with intense surprise, horror, disgust, etc. **6.** to give an electric shock to. ◇*v.i.* **7.** to come into violent contact; collide. [F: strike against, shock, from MD]

shock[2] /ʃɒk/, *n.* a thick, bushy mass, as of hair. [? var. of **SHAG**[1]]

shock absorber, *n. Mech.* an apparatus for deadening shock, esp. one on the springs of a car.

shocking /'ʃɒkɪŋ/, *adj.* **1.** causing intense surprise, disgust, horror, etc. **2.** *Colloq.* very bad: *shocking weather.*

shock treatment, *n.* Also, **shock therapy**. a method of treating certain mental disorders, as schizophrenia, in which an electric shock is administered to the brain.

shock wave, *n.* a region of sudden change of pressure and density moving in a gas or liquid at or above the speed of sound.

shod /ʃɒd/, *v.* past tense and past participle of **shoe**.

shoddy /'ʃɒdi/, *n., pl.* -**dies**, *adj.,* -**dier**, -**diest**. ◇*n.* **1.** fibrous material made by shredding woollen rags or waste. ◇*adj.* **2.** of poor quality or badly made: *shoddy workmanship*. **3.** contemptible; base: *a shoddy trick*. [orig. uncert.]

shoe /ʃu/, *n., pl.* **shoes**, (*old form*) **shoon**; *v.,* **shod, shoeing**. ◇*n.* **1.** an external covering, usu. of leather, for the human foot. **2.** a thing or part looking like a shoe in form, position, or use. **3.** an iron tip on a staff, pole, etc.; ferrule. **4. in someone's shoes**, in the position or situation of another: *I shouldn't like to be in his shoes.* ◇*v.t.* **5.** to provide or fit (a horse) with shoe(s). **6.** to protect or arm at the point, edge, or face with a ferrule, metal plate, etc. [OE *scōh*]

shoehorn /'ʃuhɔn/, *n.* a shaped piece of metal, plastic, etc., put into a shoe at the heel to make it slip on more easily.

shoestring /'ʃustrɪŋ/, *n.* **1.** a string or lace for fastening a shoe. **2. on a shoestring**, with a very small amount of money.

shogun /'ʃoʊgən/, *n. Jap Hist.* **1.** a military commander. **2.** (later) a hereditary military dictator. [Jap, from Chinese: a general]

shone /ʃɒn/, *v.* past tense and past participle of **shine**.

shook /ʃʊk/, *v.* past tense of **shake**.

shoot /ʃut/, *v.,* **shot** /ʃɒt/, **shooting**, *n.* ◇*v.t.* **1.** to hit, wound, or kill with a bullet, arrow, etc.. **2.** to send forth (arrows, bullets, etc.) from a bow, gun, etc. **3.** to send forth like an arrow or bullet: *to shoot questions*. **4.** to fling; throw; hurl. **5.** to pass rapidly along with: *to shoot rapids*. **6.** to variegate by threads, streaks, etc., of another color. **7.** *Football, Hockey, etc.* to kick or drive (the ball, etc.) as at the goal. **8.** to gain by kicking or driving the ball, etc.: *to shoot a goal*. **9.** to take (photographs of film). **10.** to slide (a bolt, etc.) into or out of its fastening. **11.** to inject (a drug) into the veins (oft. fol. by *up*). ◇*v.i.* **12.** to send forth bullets, etc. from a gun, etc. **13.** to move suddenly or quickly; dart. **14.** (of a seed) to put out shoots or germinate. **15.** to grow, esp. quickly (oft. fol. by *up*). **16.** *Photog.* to take photographs or film. **17.** *Films.* to begin to film a scene. **18.** to jut; extend: *a cape shooting out into the sea*. **19.** to throw or push a ball, etc., in a particular direction or way, as in games. **20.** to kill animals with a gun for sport. **21.** *Colloq.* to begin, esp. to begin to talk. ◇*v.* **22. shoot down**, **a.** to bring down (an aircraft) by gunfire. **b.** to defeat decisively (an argument or person putting forward an argument). **23. shoot off one's mouth**, *Colloq.* **a.** to talk wildly or unwisely. **b.** to boast; exaggerate. **24. shoot through**, *Colloq.* to go away, usu. when one is supposed to stay: *Instead of going to the exam, he shot through.* ◇*n.* **25.** an expedition for shooting animals: *to organise a shoot*. **26.** a match or contest at shooting. **27.** a new or young growth which shoots off from some part of a plant. [OE *scēotan*]

shop /ʃɒp/, *n., v.,* **shopped, shopping**. ◇*n.* **1.** a building where goods are sold. **2.** → **workshop** (def. 1). **3. talk shop**, to discuss one's trade, profession, or business. ◇*v.i.* **4.** to go looking for and buying goods. **5. shop around**, to visit a number of shops comparing quality and price before buying. [OE *sceoppa* booth] —**shopper**, *n.*

shoplift /'ʃɒplɪft/, *v.t., v.i.* to steal (goods) from a shop while appearing to be an ordinary shopper. —**shoplifter**, *n.*

shopping /'ʃɒpɪŋ/, *n.* **1.** the act of someone who shops. **2.** the goods bought: *Please help me carry in the shopping.*

shop steward, *n.* a trade-union official representing workers in a factory, workshop, etc.

shore¹ /ʃɔ/, n. 1. the land along the edge of a sea, lake, large river, etc. 2. some particular country: *my native shore.* 3. land, as opposed to the sea: *marines serving on shore.* ◇adj. 4. of or relating to land: *shore leave.* [ME *schore*, probably from MLG]

shore² /ʃɔ/, n., v., **shored, shoring.** ◇n. 1. a supporting post or beam used as a prop; strut. ◇v.t. 2. to support by a shore or shores; prop (usu. fol. by *up*).

shore³ /ʃɔ/, v. *Archaic.* past tense and past participle of **shear.**

shorn /ʃɔn/, v. past participle of **shear.**

short /ʃɔt/, adj. 1. having little length; not long. 2. having little height; not tall; low. 3. reaching or extending only a little way. 4. brief; not extensive: *a short speech.* 5. rudely brief; curt; brusque: *He was short with her.* 6. small in amount; scanty: *short rations.* 7. not reaching a mark: *a short throw; short of the mark.* 8. below a standard: *short measure.* 9. less than; inferior to (fol. by *of*): *little short of the best.* 10. not having enough; deficient in: *We are short of money; short on sense.* 11. (of pastry) crumbly and made with a lot of butter. 12. (of metals) brittle; friable. 13. **make short work of,** to finish or get rid of quickly. 14. **short for,** being a shorter form of: *'phone' is short for 'telephone'.* ◇adv. 15. suddenly; abruptly: *to stop short.* 16. on the nearer side of an intended or particular point: *to fall short.* 17. without going to the length (fol. by *of*): *to stop short of actual crime.* 18. *Comm.* not possessing at the time of sale the goods sold: *to sell short.* 19. **be caught short,** *Colloq.* to discover an inconvenient lack of something, as money. 20. **cut short,** to end suddenly; curtail; interrupt. 21. **sell oneself short,** *Colloq.* to think too poorly of one's abilities or achievements. ◇n. 22. *Elect. Colloq.* a short circuit. 23. *Films.* (usu. *pl.*) a short film made up of parts of a film soon to be shown; trailer. 24. **for short,** as an abbreviation: *A telephone is called a 'phone' for short.* 25. **in short,** in a few words; in brief; briefly. ◇v.i., v.t. 26. *Colloq.* to cause a short circuit in, or to cut off by a short circuit. [OE *sc(e)ort*] — **shortness,** n.

shortage /ˈʃɔtɪdʒ/, n. 1. lack in quantity: *a shortage of food.* 2. an amount lacking: *a shortage of six men.*

shortbread /ˈʃɔtbrɛd/, n. a thick, crisp biscuit, rich in butter, often baked in one piece and cut into pieces when cool.

shortcake /ˈʃɔtkeɪk/, n. a rich biscuit dough, baked as a cake, and when cool, split, and filled with fruit, esp. strawberries, and topped with cream.

short-change /ʃɔt-ˈtʃeɪndʒ/, v.t., **-changed, -changing.** *Colloq.* 1. to give less than proper change to. 2. to cheat. — **short-changer,** n.

short circuit, n. a faulty connection between two points of relatively low resistance in an electrical circuit, causing an excessive flow of current between them.

shortcoming /ˈʃɔtkʌmɪŋ/, n. a failure or fault in condition, behavior, etc.; defect.

shorten /ˈʃɔtn/, v.t. to make or become short or shorter.

shortening /ˈʃɔtnɪŋ/, n. butter, fat, margarine, etc., used to make pastry, etc., short (def. 11).

shortfall /ˈʃɔtfɔl/, n. an amount by or extent to which production or output falls short of what is expected.

shorthand /ˈʃɔthænd/, n. 1. a method of fast handwriting using a system of simple strokes and dots instead of letters. ◇adj. 2. able to use shorthand: *a shorthand typist.* 3. written in shorthand.

Shorthorn /ˈʃɔthɔn/, n. (one of) a breed of dairy or beef cattle, with white, red, or roan markings.

Shortland /ˈʃɔtlənd/, n. **John,** 1769–1810, naval officer, sailed with the First Fleet; discovered the Hunter River in 1797.

short leg, n. *Cricket.* (the fielder in) the on-side position close to the batsman.

short list, n. a list of specially favored candidates for a position, who have been chosen from a larger group.

shortly /ˈʃɔtli/, adv. 1. in a short time; soon. 2. briefly; concisely: *Write it as shortly as possible.* 3. curtly; abruptly.

shorts /ʃɔts/, n.pl. short trousers, not going beyond the knee.

shortsheet /ʃɔtˈʃit/, v.t. to make (a bed) using only one sheet folded in half from the bottom up, as a practical joke.

short-sighted /ˈʃɔt-saɪtəd/, adj. 1. (of a person) not able to see clearly things that are far away; myopic. 2. lacking in foresight.

short story, n. a piece of prose fiction, usu. confined to a small group of characters and a single main event, and much shorter than a novel.

short wave, n. an electromagnetic wave 60 metres or less in length. — **short-wave,** adj.

Shostakovich /ˌʃɒstəˈkoʊvɪtʃ/, n. **Dimitri Dimitrievich** /dɪˈmitri dɪˈmitrijəvɪtʃ/, 1906–75, Russian composer.

shot¹ /ʃɒt/, n., pl. **shots** or (for def 3) **shot;** v., **shotted, shotting.** ◇n. 1. the firing or shooting of a gun, bow, etc. 2. a small ball or pellet of lead, or these taken as a whole, used in a shotgun: *a charge of shot.* 3. bullets, or a bullet. 4. a person who shoots: *a good shot.* 5. a heavy metal ball which competitors throw as far as possible in shot-putting contests. 6. an aimed stroke, throw, etc., in sports. 7. an attempt or try: *Have a shot.* 8. a remark aimed at some person or thing: *She was having a shot at me.* 9. a guess at something. 10. *Colloq.* an injection of a drug, vaccine, etc. 11. *Photog., Films.* **a.** (the making of) a photograph. **b.** a length of cinefilm taken without stopping or cutting. 12. *Mining, etc.* an explosive charge in place for detonation. 13. **big shot,** *Colloq.* important person. 14. **call the shots, a.** to direct camera angles, etc., in a television production. **b.** *Colloq.* to be in command. 15. **like a shot,** *Colloq.* instantly; very

shot quickly. **16. that's the shot!** (an exclamation of approval). ◇*v.t.* **17.** to load or supply with shot. [OE *sc(e)ot, gesceot*]

shot² /ʃɒt/, *v.* **1.** past tense and past participle of **shoot**. ◇*adj.* **2.** woven so as to present a play of colors: *shot silk*.

shotgun /'ʃɒtgʌn/, *n.* a smoothbore gun for firing small shot to kill small game, though often used with buckshot to kill larger animals.

shotgun wedding, *n.* a wedding hastened or forced by the pregnancy of the bride.

shot-put /'ʃɒt-pʊt/, *n.* **1.** the sport of throwing a heavy metal ball as far as possible. See **shot¹** (def. 5) and **put** (def. 18). **2.** one throw of the shot in this sport. —**shot-putter**, *n.* —**shot-putting**, *n.*

should /ʃʊd/, *v.* **1.** past tense of **shall**. **2.** (specially used) **a.** to indicate obligation, duty, etc.: *You should not do that.* **b.** to make a more polite statement: *I should hardly say that.* **c.** to express uncertainty in conditional and hypothetical clauses: *if it should be true; He should come soon.* [OE *sc(e)olde*]

shoulder /'ʃəʊldə/, *n.* **1.** either of two parts of the human body joining the neck and trunk to the arms. **2.** (*pl.*) these two parts together with the part of the back joining them, forming a place where loads may be carried. **3.** the corresponding part in animals. **4.** (the meat of) the upper foreleg and nearby parts of a sheep, etc. **5.** something jutting out like a shoulder: *shoulder of a hill.* **6.** the part of a garment which covers, or fits over the shoulder. **7.** either of two strips of land at the edge of a road, on which cars, etc., can be parked in an emergency. **8.** the unbroken, tapering part of the wave, away from the curl. **9. give the cold shoulder to**, *Colloq.* to treat coldly; ignore; snub. **10. put one's shoulder to the wheel**, to work hard. **11. shoulder to shoulder**, with united action and support. **12.** straight from the shoulder, openly; without evasion. ◇*v.t.* **13.** to push, as with the shoulder, esp. roughly: *to shoulder a person out of the way.* **14.** to take upon or support with the shoulder. **15.** to take upon oneself as a burden or responsibility: *to shoulder the expense.* ◇*v.* **16. shoulder arms**, to perform a movement in arms drill, in which a rifle is brought to rest vertically against the shoulder. [OE *sculdor*]

shoulder-blade /'ʃəʊldə-bleɪd/, *n.* → **scapula**.

shouldst /ʃʊdst/, *v. Archaic.* second person singular of **should**. Also, **shouldest**.

shout /ʃaʊt/, *v.i.* **1.** to call or cry out loudly and strongly. **2.** to speak noisily or wildly. ◇*v.t.* **3.** to express by a shout or shouts. **4.** *Colloq.* **a.** to stand (the company) a round of drinks. **b.** to pay for something for another person; treat: *I'll shout you to the pictures; I'll shout you a new dress.* ◇*v.* **5. shout down**, to drown (another's words) by shouting or talking loudly. ◇*n.* **6.** a loud call or cry. **7.** a loud burst, as of laughter. **8.** one's turn to pay for drinks. [ME] —**shouter**, *n.* —**shouting**, *n.*

shove /ʃʌv/, *v.*, **shoved, shoving.** ◇*v.t., v.i.* **1.** to push (someone or something) roughly along by force from behind. ◇*v.* **2. shove off**, **a.** to push a boat off. **b.** *Colloq.* to leave; start. ◇*n.* **3.** an act of shoving. ◇*interj.* **4. shove it!** *Colloq.* (an expression of dismissal, contempt, etc.). [OE *scūfan*]

shovel /'ʃʌvəl/, *n., v.,* **-elled, -elling.** ◇*n.* **1.** a tool with a broad blade or scoop attached to a handle. **2.** a machine for shovelling, removing matter, etc. ◇*v.t.* **3.** to take up and throw or remove with a shovel. **4.** to push or put carelessly or quickly: *to shovel food into one's mouth.* **5.** to dig or clear with a shovel: *to shovel a path.* ◇*v.i.* **6.** to work with a shovel. [OE *scofl*] —**shovelful**, *n.* —**shoveller**, *n.*

shoveler /'ʃʌvələ/, *n.* **1.** Also, **blue-winged shoveler.** an Australian duck with a broad, flat, olive-brown bill. **2.** Also, **shovel-bill.** a similar Northern Hemisphere bird; spoonbill.

show /ʃəʊ/, *v.*, **showed, shown** or **showed, showing**, *n.* ◇*v.t.* **1.** to cause to be seen or allow to be seen; exhibit; display; present. **2.** to point out: *to show the way.* **3.** to guide; escort: *He showed me to my room.* **4.** to make clear; make known; explain: *Can you show me what you mean?* **5.** to prove; demonstrate: *Can you show that it is true?* **6.** to indicate; register: *The thermometer showed 10 degrees below zero.* **7.** to give (favor, mercy, etc.); grant; bestow. ◇*v.i.* **8.** to be seen; be or become visible: *Your petticoat is showing.* **9.** to look or appear: *to show to advantage.* **10.** *Colloq.* to give an exhibition, display, or performance: *The painter is showing next month.* ◇*v.* **11. show off,** to show (one's abilities, possessions, etc.) in order to get attention or praise. **12. show up, a.** to reveal or expose (faults, etc.): *She showed up my weakness.* **b.** to stand out in a certain way; appear: *Blue shows up well against that background.* **c.** to appear at a certain place: *Bill showed up later.* ◇*n.* **13.** a display: *a show of freedom.* **14.** a display in order to get attention: *It's all done for show.* **15.** any kind of public exhibition: *an art show.* **16.** appearance: *to make a sorry show.* **17.** a false appearance: *He was bored, but he made a show of interest.* **18.** *Med.* (in pregnancy) a discharge of blood and mucus indicating the start of labor. **19.** *Colloq.* a theatrical performance or company. **20.** a competitive exhibition of farm produce, animals, etc.: *the Royal Easter show.* **21. a show of hands**, a method of voting in which people raise their hands to show agreement or disagreement with a motion or proposal. **22. give the show away,** to make known all the details of a plan, etc. **23. steal the show,** to attract the most attention. ◇*adj.* **24.** of or relating to an animal bred or trained to be entered into a show (def. 20). [OE *scēawian* look at]

showboat /'ʃəʊbəʊt/, *n.* **1.** *US.* a boat, esp. a paddlewheel steamer, used as a travelling theatre. **2.** a boat which takes people on a short cruise in sheltered waters and on which food and entertainment are provided.

show business, *n.* the entertainment industry. Also, **show biz.**

showdown /'ʃəʊdaʊn/, *n.* **1.** the laying down of one's cards, face upwards, in a card

showdown 956 **shrub**

game, esp. poker. **2.** an open airing of disagreements, etc., to bring matters to a climax.

shower /ˈʃauə/, n. **1.** a brief fall of rain. **2.** a similar fall, as of sparks or bullets. **3.** anything coming in a large quantity: *a shower of questions*. **4. a.** a washing apparatus which sends fine streams of water over the body. **b.** a washing done in this way: *Have you had your shower yet?* **5.** *Colloq.* a dust storm: *Wilcannia shower*. **6.** *Phys.* a group of high-energy particles which come from one fast particle, cosmic radiation, or an accelerator. ◊v.t. **7.** to wet with a shower. **8.** to pour (something) down in a shower. **9.** to give generously: *to shower presents on a person*. ◊v.i. **10.** to rain in a shower. **11.** (of a person) to take a shower (def. 4). [OE *scūr*] **—showery**, adj.

shower tea, n. a party for a bride-to-be to which the guests, usu. other women, bring a present for her future home.

showjumping /ˈʃoudʒʌmpɪŋ/, n. (a competition of) horseriding to display skill in jumping obstacles. **—showjumper**, n.

showman /ˈʃoumən/, n., pl. **-men.** someone who presents things well or is a good performer. **—showmanship**, n.

shown /ʃoun/, v. past participle of **show.**

show-off /ˈʃou-ɒf/, n. *Colloq.* someone who says or does things to get attention or praise.

showy /ˈʃoui/, adj., **showier, showiest. 1.** of a very striking appearance, esp. large or colorful: *showy flowers*. **2.** attracting attention; ostentatious; gaudy.

shrank /ʃræŋk/, v. past tense of **shrink.**

shrapnel /ˈʃræpnəl/, n. **1.** a hollow shell (def. 5) filled with small bullets which scatter upon explosion. **2.** a bomb, mine or shell fragments. **3.** *Colloq.* small change, esp. silver. [named after the inventor, H *Shrapnel*, 1761-1842, an officer in the British army]

shred /ʃred/, n., v., **shredded** or **shred, shredding.** ◊n. **1.** a piece cut or torn off, esp. in a narrow strip. **2.** a bit; scrap. ◊v.t., v.i. **3.** to tear or be torn into small pieces, esp. small strips. [OE *scrēade*] **—shredder**, n.

shrew /ʃru/, n. **1.** a kind of small, insect-eating mammal, with a long, sharp snout and mouselike appearance. **2.** a woman of violent temper and speech. [OE *scrēawa*; of unknown orig.] **—shrewish**, adj.

shrewd /ʃrud/, adj. sharp or clever in practical matters; astute: *a shrewd politician*; *a shrewd businessman*. [ME *shrewed*, pp. of *shrew* curse (now obs.), v. use of SHREW, n.] **—shrewdness**, n.

shriek /ʃrik/, n. **1.** a loud, sharp, shrill cry or other sound: *a shriek of fright*; *a shriek of laughter*; *the shriek of a whistle*. ◊v.i. **2.** to utter a loud, sharp, shrill cry. **3.** to make loud, high-pitched sounds in laughing. **4.** (of a musical instrument, a whistle, the wind, etc.) to give forth a loud, shrill sound. ◊v.t. **5.** to cry in a shriek: *to shriek defiance*. [ME *schriche*]

shrift /ʃrɪft/, n. *Archaic.* **1.** a confession of sins to a priest. **2. short shrift,** little consideration in dealing with someone; summary treatment. [OE *scrift* from SHRIVE]

shrike /ʃraɪk/, n. **1.** a European bird of various kinds, with a strong hooked and toothed beak, which feeds on insects and sometimes on small birds and other animals. **2.** any of various Australian birds similar in appearance, e.g. the butcher birds. [OE *scrīc*]

shrike-thrush /ˈʃraɪk-θrʌʃ/, n. any of several Australian singing birds, that eat mainly insects.

shrill /ʃrɪl/, adj. **1.** high-pitched and piercing: *a shrill cry*. ◊v.t., v.i. **2.** to cry shrilly. ◊n. **3.** a shrill sound. [ME *shrille*] **—shrillness**, n. **—shrilly**, adv.

shrimp /ʃrɪmp/, n. **1.** a small, long-tailed, shellfish greatly valued as food; prawn. **2.** *Colloq.* a small or unimportant person. [ME *shrimpe*]

shrine /ʃraɪn/, n. **1.** a container for sacred relics. **2.** a place of worship and pilgrimage, usu. the tomb of a saint. **3.** any place or object made holy by its history or associations. [OE *scrīn* from L: case for books and papers]

shrink /ʃrɪŋk/, v., **shrank** or **shrunk, shrunk** or **shrunken, shrinking.** ◊v.i. **1.** to draw back: *The frightened child shrank into a corner*. **2.** to become smaller with heat, cold, moisture, etc.; contract. **3.** to become less in extent or compass: *Business is shrinking these days*. ◊v.t. **4.** to cause to shrink or contract. ◊n. **5.** a shrinking; shrinkage. **6.** a shrinking movement. **7.** *Colloq.* Also, **headshrinker.** → **psychiatrist.** [OE *scrincan*] **—shrinkable**, adj. **—shrinkage**, n.

shrive /ʃraɪv/, v.t., **shrove** or **shrived, shriven** or **shrived, shriving.** *Archaic.* (of a priest) to hear the confession of (someone) and give absolution. [OE *scrīfan* from L: write]

shrivel /ˈʃrɪvəl/, v.t., v.i., **-elled, -elling. 1.** to shrink and wrinkle, as from great heat or cold. **2.** to wither; make or become powerless or ashamed. [orig. unknown]

shroud /ʃraud/, n. **1.** a cloth in which a corpse is wrapped for burial. **2.** something which covers or hides like a garment: *a shroud of rain*. **3.** (*usu. pl.*) *Naut.* one of a set of strong ropes running from a masthead to the side of a ship to help support the mast. **4.** *Mech.* **a.** circular webs used to stiffen the sides of gear teeth. **b.** a strip used to strengthen turbine blades. ◊v.t. **5.** to wrap or clothe for burial. **6.** to cover; hide from view. **7.** to veil; wrap in darkness or mystery. [OE *scrūd*]

shrove /ʃrouv/, v. past tense of **shrive.**

Shrove Sunday, n. the Sunday before Ash Wednesday.

Shrovetide /ˈʃrouvtaɪd/, n. the three days before Ash Wednesday, once a time of confession and absolution.

Shrove Tuesday, n. the last day of Shrovetide, long observed as a season of merrymaking before Lent; Pancake Day.

shrub /ʃrʌb/, n. a woody perennial plant smaller than a tree, usu. having permanent stems branching from or near the ground. [OE *scrybb* brushwood] **—shrubby**, adj.

shrubbery /'ʃrʌbəri/, *n.*, *pl.* **-beries.** a group of shrubs or a garden area where they are grown.

shrug /ʃrʌg/, *v.*, **shrugged, shrugging,** *n.* ◇*v.t.*, *v.i.* **1.** to raise and lower (the shoulders), expressing lack of interest, contempt, etc. ◇*v.* **2. shrug off,** to take no notice of; disregard: *to shrug off an insult.* ◇*n.* **3.** the act of shrugging. [ME]

shrunk /ʃrʌŋk/, *v.* a past participle and a past tense of **shrink.**

shrunken /'ʃrʌŋkən/, *v.* a past participle of **shrink.**

shudder /'ʃʌdə/, *v.i.* **1.** to tremble with a sudden movement, as from horror, fear, or cold. ◇*n.* **2.** a sudden, trembling movement of the body. [ME *shodder, shuder* from OE *scūdan* move, shake]

shuffle /'ʃʌfəl/, *v.*, **-fled, -fling,** *n.* ◇*v.i.* **1.** to walk clumsily without lifting the feet; shamble. **2.** to make small continual movements; fidget. **3.** to get (*into,* etc.) clumsily: *to shuffle into one's clothes.* **4.** to mix up cards in a pack so as to change their order. ◇*v.t.* **5.** to move (the feet, etc.) clumsily along the ground without lifting them. **6.** to move (things) around: *to shuffle papers on a desk.* **7.** to mix up (cards in a pack). ◇*n.* **8.** a scraping movement; dragging gait. **9.** the act of shuffling. **10.** a dance in which the feet are shuffled along the floor. [LG: walk clumsily or with dragging feet] — **shuffler,** *n.*

shun /ʃʌn/, *v.t.*, **shunned, shunning.** to keep away from (a place, person, etc.), from dislike, caution, etc. [OE *scunian;* orig. obscure]

shunt /ʃʌnt/, *v.t.*, *v.i.* **1.** to move or turn aside or out of the way. **2.** *Trains.* to move from one line of rails to another or from the main track to a siding. ◇*n.* **3.** the act of shunting; a move. **4.** *Elect.* a conducting element bridged across (part of) a circuit, establishing a second current path. **5.** a railway siding. [ME; orig. obscure, ? from SHUN]

shush /ʃʊʃ/, *interj.* **1.** (a command to be quiet or silent); hush. ◇*v.t.*, *v.i.* **2.** to make or become silent.

shut /ʃʌt/, *v.*, **shut, shutting,** *adj.* ◇*v.t.* **1.** to put (a door, lid, etc.) in position to cover the opening for which it is made. **2.** to close the doors of (oft. fol. by *up*): *Shut up the shop.* **3.** to close by bringing together or folding: *to shut a book.* **4.** to enclose; confine: *to shut a bird into a cage.* **5.** to bar; exclude: *to shut a person (out) from one's house.* **6.** to close down; stop normal work: *They decided to shut the office during redecoration.* ◇*v.i.* **7.** to become shut or closed: *The doors shut with a clang.* ◇*8.* Some special uses are:
shut away, to hide or confine.
shut down, 1. to close (a lid, etc.) by lowering. **2.** to close down or stop (a factory, machine, etc.), esp. temporarily.
shut in, to imprison; confine; enclose.
shut off, 1. to stop the flow of (water, electricity, etc.). **2.** to keep separate; isolate.
shut one's eyes to, to refuse to notice; ignore.
shut out, to keep out; exclude.
shut up, 1. to imprison; confine; hide from view. **2.** *Colloq.* to stop talking; become silent. **3.** *Colloq.* to stop (someone) from talking; silence (someone).
◇*adj.* **9.** closed; fastened up. [OE *scyttan* bolt (a door)]

Shute /ʃut/, *n.* Nevil (*Nevil Shute Norway*), 1899-1960, English novelist, emigrated to Australia; best known for *A Town Like Alice* (1950).

shut-eye /'ʃʌt-aɪ/, *n. Colloq.* sleep.

shutter /'ʃʌtə/, *n.* **1.** a movable, usu. hinged, cover for a window. **2.** *Photog.* an apparatus for opening and closing the aperture of a camera lens to expose a plate or film. ◇*v.t.* **3.** to close or provide with shutters.

shuttle /'ʃʌtl/, *n.*, *v.*, **-tled, -tling.** ◇*n.* **1.** a piece of wood used on a loom for passing the weft thread through the warp thread. **2.** a sliding container that carries the lower thread in a sewing machine. **3.** Also, **shuttle service.** a frequent transport service running directly between two points. ◇*v.t.*, *v.i.* **4.** to move quickly to and fro like a shuttle. [OE *scytel* dart, arrow]

shuttlecock /'ʃʌtlkɒk/, *n.* **1.** a piece of cork, or similar light material, with feathers stuck in one end, used in the games of badminton and battledore. **2.** a game of battledore.

shy[1] /ʃaɪ/, *adj.*, **shyer, shyest** or **shier, shiest,** *v.*, **shied, shying,** *n.*, *pl.* **shies.** ◇*adj.* **1.** not relaxed with other people; bashful; retiring. **2.** easily frightened away; timid. **3.** suspicious; distrustful; wary. **4.** short: *shy of money.* **5. fight shy of,** to avoid; keep away from. ◇*v.i.* **6.** (esp. of a horse) to start back or aside, as in fear. ◇*n.* **7.** a sudden movement aside, as in fear. [OE *scēoh*] — **shyness,** *n.*

shy[2] /ʃaɪ/, *v.*, **shied, shying,** *n.*, *pl.* **shies.** ◇*v.t.* **1.** to throw with a sudden swift movement: *to shy a stone.* ◇*n.* **2.** a sudden swift throw. [orig. uncert.]

Shylock /'ʃaɪlɒk/, *n.* a merciless moneylender. [after the character in W Shakespeare's play *The Merchant of Venice*]

shyster /'ʃaɪstə/, *n. Colloq.* a dishonest person, esp. a lawyer. [apparently alteration of *Scheuster,* an unscrupulous 19thC New York lawyer]

si /si/, *n. Music.* See **solfège.** [see GAMUT]

Si, *Chem. Symbol.* silicon.

SI /ɛs 'aɪ/, *n.* → **International System of Units.** [F S(*ystème*) I(*nternational*) (*d'* Unit*és*)]

Siam /saɪ'æm/, *n.* former name of Thailand.

Siamese cat /saɪə,miz 'kæt/, *n.* a shorthaired cat, originating in Siam or Thailand, with blue eyes, a small head, and colored fawn or grey with dark ears, legs and tail.

Siamese twins *n.pl.* twins who are born physically joined together. [from two Chinese men, Chang and Eng (1811–74), who were born in *Siam* joined together at the waist by a short, tubular, cartilaginous band]

Sibelius /sə'beɪlɪəs/, *n.* **Jean Julius Christian** /ʒan/, 1865–1957, Finnish composer, noted for symphonic poem *Finlandia* (1900).

Siberia /saɪˈbɪəriə/, n. a part of Russia, in northern Asia, extending from the Ural mountains to the Pacific Ocean. —**Siberian**, adj.

sibilant /ˈsɪbələnt/, adj. 1. hissing. ◇n. 2. *Phonet.* a hissing sound, as *s* in *this, rose, pressure, pleasure*. [L] —**sibilance**, **sibilancy**, n.

sibling /ˈsɪblɪŋ/, n. a brother or sister. [OE]

sibyl /ˈsɪbəl/, n. a woman fortuneteller, esp. of the ancient world. [ME, from L, from Gk] —**sibylline**, adj.

sic[1] /sɪk/, adv. so; thus (often used in brackets to show that something has been copied exactly from the original). [L]

sic[2] /sɪk/, v.t., **sicked, sicking**. 1. to attack (esp. of a dog). 2. to urge to attack. [var. of SEEK]

Sichuan /sɑːˈtʃwan/, n. a province in central China. Pop. 101 880 000 (1986); 569 000 km². *Cap.*: Chengdu. Formerly, **Szechuan**, **Szechwan**.

Sicily /ˈsɪsəli/, n. the largest island in the Mediterranean, comprising a region of Italy; separated from the south-western tip of the Italian mainland by the Strait of Messina. Pop. 15 084 311 (1986 est.); 25 703 km². *Cap.*: Palermo. Italian, **Sicilia**. —**Sicilian**, n., adj.

sick /sɪk/, adj. 1. affected with nausea or vomiting. 2. affected with any disorder of health; ill; unwell; ailing. 3. of or attended with sickness: *a sick headache*. 4. of or appropriate to sick people: *on sick leave*. 5. deeply affected with some feeling: *sick at heart*; *sick with love*. 6. morbid; macabre: *sick humor*; *a sick joke*. 7. **be sick of**, to feel fed up with; have had enough of: *He was sick of his employer's complaints about his work*. 8. **sick as a dog**, *Colloq.* very sick. ◇n. 9. **the sick**, sick people. 10. vomit. ◇v. 11. **sick up**, to vomit. [OE *sēoc*] —**sickness**, n.

sicken /ˈsɪkən/, v.t., v.i. to make or become sick. —**sickening**, adj.

sickie /ˈsɪki/, n. *Colloq.* a day taken off work with pay, because of genuine or feigned illness.

sickle /ˈsɪkəl/, n. a tool for cutting grain, grass, etc., consisting of a curved, hook-like blade mounted in a short handle. [OE *sicol*, from L]

sickle-cell anaemia or **sickle-cell anemia**, n. an hereditary type of anaemia, occurring mainly in Negroes, where many of the red blood cells become crescent-shaped.

sickly /ˈsɪkli/, adj., **-lier, -liest**. 1. not strong; unhealthy; ailing. 2. of, connected with, or resulting from ill health: *a sickly complexion*. 3. (of food) too sweet; rich. 4. weak or nauseating: *sickly sentimentality*. 5. (of light, color, etc.) faint or feeble. —**sickliness**, n.

side /saɪd/, n., adj., v., **sided, siding**. ◇n. 1. one of the surfaces or lines forming the limits of a thing. 2. either of the two surfaces of paper, cloth, etc. 3. one of the two surfaces of an object other than the front, back, top, and bottom. 4. either of the two lateral (right and left) parts of a thing: *the footpath on the side of the road*. 5. either lateral half of the body of a person or an animal, esp. of the trunk: *The heart is in the left side of the body*. 6. the space immediately beside someone or something: *The girl stood at his side*. 7. an aspect; phase: *all sides of a question*. 8. a region, direction, or position relative to a centre: *the east side of a city*. 9. a division, as of teaching in a school: *the science side*. 10. a slope, as of a hill. 11. one of two or more parties concerned in a case, contest, etc. 12. a line of descent through either the father or the mother: *his mother's side*. 13. **on the side, a.** separate from the main subject. **b.** *Colloq.* as an addition, esp. secretly. 14. **on the ... side**, tending towards the quality or condition stated: *This coffee is a little on the weak side*. 15. **side by side**, next to one another; together; in close proximity. 16. **take sides**, to show support for one person in an argument, contest, etc. ◇adj. 17. being at or on one side: *the side aisles of a theatre*. 18. coming from or directed towards one side: *a side glance; a side blow*. 19. of lesser importance: *a side issue*. ◇v. 20. **side with / against**, to place oneself with / against a side or party to support / oppose an issue. [ME and OE]

sideboard /ˈsaɪdbɔd/, n. 1. a piece of furniture, usu. in a dining room, often with shelves, drawers, etc., for holding plates, etc. 2. (*pl.*) → **sideburns**.

sideburns /ˈsaɪdbɜnz/, n.pl. whiskers extending from the hairline down to below the ears. Also, **sidelevers**, **sideboards**. [alteration of name of AE *Burnside*, 1824–81, a general in the American Civil War]

sidecar /ˈsaɪdka/, n. 1. a small car attached on one side to a motorcycle and supported on the other by a wheel of its own, used for a passenger, etc. ◇adv. 2. in a sidecar: *He rode sidecar*.

sidelevers /ˈsaɪdlivəz/, n.pl. → **sideburns**.

sidelight /ˈsaɪdlaɪt/, n. 1. a light coming from the side. 2. incidental information. 3. either of the two small lights at the front of a vehicle used at night for showing the width of the vehicle to other road-users, and for parking. 4. a window at the side of a door or another window.

sideline /ˈsaɪdlaɪn/, n. 1. a line at the side of something. 2. an additional line of goods or of business. 3. *Sport.* a line or mark fixing the limit of play on the side of the field.

sidelong /ˈsaɪdlɒŋ/, adj. 1. directed to one side. ◇adv. 2. towards the side; obliquely.

sidero-, a word part meaning 'iron', 'steel'. Also, before vowels, **sider-**. [Gk: iron]

side-saddle /ˈsaɪd-sædl/, n. 1. a saddle on which the rider sits with both feet on the same (usu. the left) side of the horse. ◇adv. 2. seated on or as if on a side-saddle: *to ride sidesaddle*.

sideshow /ˈsaɪdʃoʊ/, n. 1. a small show, entertainment, contest, etc., in connection with a larger fair, circus, etc. 2. any secondary or unimportant event or matter.

sidestep /'saɪdstɛp/, v., **-stepped, -stepping**. v.i. **1.** to step to one side, as in avoidance. **2.** to try to avoid making a decision, solving a problem, etc. ◇v.t. **3.** to avoid by or as if by stepping to one side: *I sidestepped the puddle.*

sidestroke /'saɪdstroʊk/, n. a swimming stroke in which the body is turned sideways in the water, the hands pulling alternately, and the legs doing a scissors kick.

sidetrack /'saɪdtræk/, v.t., v.i. **1.** to pull or move away from the main subject or course. ◇n. **2.** an act of sidetracking; diversion; distraction. **3.** a temporary road; detour.

sideways /'saɪdweɪz/, adv. **1.** with the side going first or forwards: *A crab moves sideways.* **2.** facing or leaning to the side. **3.** towards or from one side. ◇adj. **4.** (moving) towards or from one side. Also, **sidewise**.

siding /'saɪdɪŋ/, n. **1.** a short side track or branch off a railway track, used for moving, loading, unloading, and storing goods trucks. **2.** the timber, metal or other material forming the outside surface of a framed building.

Siding Spring Observatory, n. an observatory near Coonabarabran, NSW, built in the late 1960s; one of the world's major astronomical sites.

sidle /'saɪdl/, v., **-dled, -dling**, n. ◇v.i. **1.** to move sideways or at an angle. **2.** to edge along hoping not to be noticed. ◇n. **3.** a sidling movement. [backformation from *sideling* SIDELONG]

SIDS /sɪdz/, n. →**sudden infant death syndrome**.

siege /sidʒ/, n. **1.** the operation of capturing a defended place by surrounding it, cutting off supplies, bombing, and other offensive operations. **2.** any lengthy or determined attempt to overcome opposition. **3. lay siege to**, to place a siege on (a town, enemy, etc.); besiege. [ME, from OF, from L: sit]

Siegfried /'sigfrid/, n. *German Legend*. the hero of the Nibelungenlied, a prince of a region on the lower Rhine. He captured the treasure of the Nibelungs, slew a dragon, and won Brunhild for King Gunther. The hero of a cycle of operas by Wagner.

Siegfried line, n. a zone of fortifications in western Germany facing the Maginot line, constructed in the years preceding the invasion of France, 1940.

siemens /'simənz/, n., pl. **siemens**. the SI unit of electrical conductance, formerly called the mho; the conductance of a conductor that has an electrical resistance of one ohm. Symbol: S [named after EW von *Siemens*, 1816–92, German electrical engineer and inventor]

sienna /si'ɛnə/, n. **1.** an earth containing iron used as a yellowish brown pigment (**raw sienna**) or, after roasting in a furnace, as a reddish brown pigment (**burnt sienna**). **2.** the color of such a pigment. [from *Siena*, town in central Italy]

sierra /si'ɛərə/, n. a chain of hills or mountains, the tops of which look like the teeth of a saw. [Sp: lit., saw, from L]

Sierra Leone /si,ɛərə li'oʊn/, n. a republic on the west coast of Africa, bordered by Guinea and Liberia. Pop. 3 803 000 (1987 est.); 71 740 km². *Languages*: English, also tribal languages. *Currency*: leone. *Cap*.: Freetown. –**Sierra Leonean**, n., adj.

siesta /si'ɛstə/, n. a midday or afternoon rest. [Sp, from L: sixth (hour), midday]

sieve /sɪv/, n., v., **sieved, sieving**. ◇n. **1.** a device with mesh or holes in the bottom, used for separating coarse from fine particles, for straining liquids, etc. ◇v.t. **2.** to put or force through a sieve; sift. [OE *sife*]

sift /sɪft/, v.t. **1.** to separate the coarse parts of (flour, ashes, etc.) with a sieve. **2.** to scatter by means of a sieve: *to sift sugar on to cake*. **3.** to separate by or as if by a sieve. **4.** to examine or question closely. ◇v.i. **5.** to use a sieve. **6.** to pass through a sieve. [OE *siftan*]

sigh /saɪ/, v.i. **1.** to let out one's breath slowly and with a drawn-out sound, as from sorrow, tiredness, relief, etc. **2.** to yearn or long (usu. fol. by *for*). **3.** to make a sound like that of sighing: *The wind was sighing*. ◇v.t. **4.** to express with a sigh. ◇n. **5.** an act or sound of sighing. [OE *sīcan*, of unknown orig.]

sight /saɪt/, n. **1.** the power or ability of seeing; vision. **2.** an act or fact of seeing. **3.** range of vision: *in sight of land*. **4.** a view; glimpse. **5.** a mental view: *In my sight she is perfect*. **6.** something seen or to be seen; spectacle: *the sights of the town*. **7.** *Colloq*. something that looks odd or unpleasing: *She looks a sight in her new hat*. **8.** *Colloq*. a great deal: *It's a sight better here than at the last hotel*. **9.** a measurement taken with a surveying or other instrument. **10.** (usu. pl.) a device on, or used with, a surveying instrument, gun, etc., serving to guide the eye. ◇**11.** Some special uses are: **raise / lower one's sights**, to be more / less ambitious.

at sight, on presentation: *a bill of exchange payable at sight*.

catch sight of, to glimpse; see, esp. briefly or momentarily.

know by sight, to recognise (somebody or something).

on sight, as soon as one sees a thing.

sight unseen, without any examination or interview.

◇v.t. **12.** to get sight of: *to sight a ship*. **13.** to take a sight or observation of, esp. with an instrument. **14.** to direct (a gun, etc.) by a sight or sights. ◇v.i. **15.** to take a sight, as in shooting. [ME; OE *gesiht*]

sightseeing /'saɪtsiɪŋ/, n. the act of visiting or seeing places and things of interest. –**sightseer**, n.

sigma /'sɪgmə/, n. **1.** the 18th letter (Σ, σ, ς = English S, s) of the Greek alphabet. **2.** *Maths*. capital sigma, Σ, is the summation sign. $Σ_n$ means the sum of all the values n may take under the given conditions.

sign /saɪn/, n. **1.** anything which suggests or indicates some other thing; quality, etc.;

token; indication: *Clouds are a sign of rain; Shiny hair is a sign of good health.* **2.** an accepted mark, figure, abbreviation, or symbol used in a particular art, science, or trade, instead of the word or words which it represents. **3.** *Maths.* the plus or minus sign (+ or −), which indicates a positive or negative value for a number. **4.** a movement or gesture meant to express an idea or attitude. **5.** a board, space, etc., which (with writing or pictures) gives information, displays an advertisement, warning, etc., on a building, along a street, etc. **6.** a trace; vestige. **7.** an omen; portent. **8.** *Astrol.* any of the 12 divisions of the zodiac, each known by the name of a group of stars or its symbol. ◊*v.t.* **9.** to affix a signature to: *He signed the document.* **10.** to write as a signature: *She signed her name.* **11.** to employ by written agreement: *to sign a new player.* **12.** to indicate; betoken. **13.** to mark with a sign. ◊*v.i.* **14.** to write one's signature, as a token of agreement, obligation, receipt, etc. **15.** to make a sign or signal. ◊*v.* **16.** Some special uses are:
sign away, to dispose of by affixing one's signature to a document.
sign off, 1. to stop broadcasting a radio or television program, as at the end of the day. **2.** to withdraw from some responsibility, project, etc.
sign on, 1. to employ; hire. **2.** to bind oneself to employment.
sign up, 1. to enlist, esp. for the armed services. **2.** to bind a person to a contract by having them sign it. [ME, from OF, from L: mark, signal]

signal /'sɪgnəl/, *n., adj., v.,* **-nalled, -nalling.** ◊*n.* **1.** a gesture, act, light, etc., serving to warn, direct, command, etc. **2.** anything seen as the occasion for action: *Her success was the signal for a party.* **3.** a token; indication. **4.** *Radio, etc.* **a.** the impulses, waves, sounds, etc., sent or received. **b.** the wave which controls and varies the carrier wave. ◊*adj.* **5.** serving as a sign: *a signal flag.* **6.** remarkable or notable: *a signal failure.* ◊*v.t.* **7.** to make a signal to. **8.** to make known by a signal. ◊*v.i.* **9.** to exchange information by a signal or signals. [ME, from ML, from L: SIGN]

signal box, *n.* a raised cabin above a railway line, from which railway signals, points, etc., are worked.

signalman /'sɪgnəlmən/, *n. Mil.* a private in the Royal Australian Signals Corps. See Appendix.

signatory /'sɪgnətri/, *adj., n., pl.* **-ries.** ◊*adj.* **1.** signing, or joining in signing, a document: *the signatory powers to a treaty.* ◊*n.* **2.** someone who signs, or has the power to sign, a document, cheque, etc.

signature /'sɪgnətʃə/, *n.* **1.** a person's name, or a mark representing it, written by himself or herself. **2.** the act of signing a document. **3.** *Music.* a sign or set of signs at the beginning of a stave to indicate the key or the time of a piece. [ML]

signet /'sɪgnət/, *n.* **1.** a small seal (def. 1), as in a finger ring. **2.** a small official seal. [ME, from ML, from L: SIGN]

significance /sɪg'nɪfɪkəns/, *n.* **1.** importance; consequence. **2.** meaning; import. **3.** the quality of being important or having a special meaning. Also, **significancy**. —**significant,** *adj.*

significant figures /sɪg,nɪfɪkənt 'fɪgəz/, *n.pl.* the figures in a number excluding the zeros after a whole number or before a decimal fraction (except those added to signify accuracy). In 0.0352 and in 35 200 the significant figures, are 3, 5, 2.

signification /sɪgnəfə'keɪʃən/, *n.* **1.** meaning; import; sense. **2.** the act or fact of signifying; indication.

signify /'sɪgnəfaɪ/, *v.,* **-fied, -fying.** ◊*v.t.* **1.** to make known by signs, speech, or action. **2.** to be a sign of; mean; portend. ◊*v.i.* **3.** to be of importance or consequence. [ME, from L: show by signs] —**signifier,** *n.*

sign language, *n.* a system of hand signs instead of speech, esp. that used by deaf-mutes or between speakers of different languages, etc.

Sihanouk /'sɪənʊk/, *n.* Prince Norodom /'nɒrədɒm/ born 1922, Cambodian statesman; king 1941–55; prime minister 1955–60; head of state 1960–70, 1975–76.

Sikh /siːk/, *n.* **1.** a member of a religious sect begun in the early 16th century in north-western India by a Hindu reformer. ◊*adj.* **2.** of or relating to the Sikhs. [Hind: lit., disciple] —**Sikhism,** *n.*

silage /'saɪlɪdʒ/, *n.* green fodder preserved in a silo, silage pit, or mound. [F]

silence /'saɪləns/, *n., v.,* **-lenced, -lencing,** *interj.* ◊*n.* **1.** the absence of any sound or noise; stillness. **2.** the condition or fact of being silent; muteness. **3.** lack of mention: *to pass over a matter in silence.* **4.** secrecy. ◊*v.t.* **5.** to put or bring to silence; still. **6.** to put to rest (doubts, etc.); quieten. ◊*interj.* **7.** be silent! [ME, from OF, from L]

silencer /'saɪlənsə/, *n.* **1.** someone or something that silences. **2.** a device fitted to the exhaust pipe of an internal-combustion engine to reduce the noise made by the exhaust gases; muffler. **3.** a device for deadening the report of a firearm.

silent /'saɪlənt/, *adj.* **1.** making no sound; quiet; still. **2.** not speaking; refraining from speech. **3.** marked by absence of speech or sound: *a silent prayer; a silent film.* **4.** not sounded or pronounced: *a silent letter,* such as 'b' in 'doubt'. [L: being silent]

silent cop, *n. Colloq.* a piece of metal set into the middle of an intersection to stop traffic making too narrow a turn.

silent number, *n.* a telephone number left out of a directory and not given to enquirers.

silent partner, *n.* a partner taking no active or public part in the conduct of a business.

silhouette /sɪlu'ɛt, sɪlə'wɛt/, *n., v.,* **-etted, -etting.** ◊*n.* **1.** an outline drawing, uniformly filled in with black, like a shadow. **2.** a dark image outlined against a lighter background. ◊*v.t.* **3.** to show in, or as in, a silhouette. [named after Etienne de *Silhouette,* 1709–67, French author and politician]

silic-, a word part meaning 'flint', 'silica', 'silicon'. Also, **silici-**, **silico-**. [combining form representing L: flint]

silica /ˈsɪlɪkə/, n. silicon dioxide, SiO₂, appearing as quartz, sand, flint, and agate. [NL, from L: flint] —**siliceous**, adj.

silicate /ˈsɪlɪkət, -keɪt/, n. any salt derived from silica. See **-ate**².

silico-, a variant of *silic-*, before consonants.

silicon /ˈsɪlɪkən/, n. a non-metallic element, having amorphous and crystalline forms, occurring in the combined state in minerals and rocks, and constituting more than one quarter of the earth's crust; used in steel-making, etc. Symbol: Si; at. no.: 14; at. wt: 28.086. [SILIC- + -ON, modelled on BORON, CARBON]

silicone /ˈsɪlɪkoʊn/, n. any of a large group of synthetic polymers containing silicon and oxygen, and stable at extreme temperatures. Among the silicones are oils, greases, resins, and a group of synthetic rubbers. [SILIC- + -ONE]

silicosis /sɪləˈkoʊsəs/, n. a disease of the lungs due to breathing in silica dust, as by stonecutters. [SILIC- + -OSIS]

silk /sɪlk/, n. 1. the fine, soft, shining fibre obtained from the cocoon of the silkworm. 2. the thread or cloth made of this fibre. 3. the gown of such material, worn distinctively by a Queen's or King's Counsel in a court. 4. any fibre or very fine threaded matter resembling silk. 5. **to take silk**, to become a Queen's or King's Counsel. ◇adj. 6. made of silk. 7. resembling silk. 8. of or relating to silk. [ME; OE *sioloc*, *seoloc*, from Baltic or Slavic] —**silky**, adj.

silken /ˈsɪlkən/, adj. 1. made of or like silk. 2. smooth; soft. 3. clothed in silk.

silks /sɪlks/, n. pl. the shirt and cap worn by a jockey in a race.

silk-screen /ˈsɪlk-skrin/, n. 1. the process of printing from stencils, which may be photographically made or cut by hand, through a fine mesh of silk, metal or other material. ◇v.t. 2. to print using this process.

silkworm /ˈsɪlkwɜm/, n. a caterpillar of certain moth families which spins a fine, soft fibre (silk) to form a cocoon, in which it is enclosed while in the pupal stage, esp. the **Chinese silk-worm**. [OE *seolcwyrm*]

silky oak, n. a very tall native tree, the largest of the grevilleas, with golden flowers, and silvery, oak-like timber.

sill /sɪl/, n. 1. a horizontal timber, block, etc., serving as a foundation of a wall, house, etc. 2. a horizontal piece of building material beneath a window, door, or other opening. 3. *Geol.* a table-like body of rock which was once molten and in that state was forced between beds of sedimentary rocks or layers of volcanic matter. [OE *syl*, *syll(e)*]

silly /ˈsɪli/, adj., **-lier**, **-liest**, n., pl. **-lies**. ◇adj. 1. lacking good sense; foolish; stupid. 2. absurd or ridiculous. 3. *Colloq.* stunned. 4. *Cricket*. (of a fielding position) close in to the batsman's wicket: *silly mid-off*. ◇n. 5. *Colloq.* a silly person. [OE *sælig* (Anglian), *sælig*] —**silliness**, n.

silo /ˈsaɪloʊ/, n., pl. **-los**, v., **-loed**, **-loing**. ◇n. 1. a tower-like structure, made resistant to weather and rats, mice etc., for storing grain. 2. a similar structure in which fermenting green fodder is preserved for future use as silage. 3. an underground launching site for a ballistic missile. ◇v.t. 4. to put into or preserve in a silo. [Sp from L, from Gk: pit to keep grain in]

silt /sɪlt/, n. 1. earthy matter, fine sand, etc., carried by moving or running water and then left behind as a sediment. ◇v.i. 2. to become filled or choked up with silt. ◇v.t. 3. to fill or choke up with silt. [ME]

Silurian /saɪˈljʊəriən/, adj. 1. relating to an early Palaeozoic geological period or system of rocks. ◇n. 2. the Silurian period or system of rocks. [named after the *Silures*, an ancient British people who lived chiefly in SE Wales at the time of the Roman conquest of Britain]

Silvanus /sɪlˈveɪnəs/, n. the Roman god of forests and fields; Greek counterpart, Pan.

silver /ˈsɪlvə/, n. 1. *Chem.* a white ductile metallic element, used for making mirrors, coins, ornaments, table utensils, etc. Symbol: Ag (for argentum); at. no.: 47; at.wt: 107.87. 2. coin made of silver or of a metal resembling silver; money. 3. silverware; meal-table articles made of or plated with silver. 4. something looking like this metal in colour, lustre, etc. 5. a shiny whitish-grey color. ◇adj. 6. consisting or made of silver; plated with silver. 7. of or relating to silver. 8. (of coins) made of a metal or alloy resembling silver, as cupronickel. 9. producing or yielding silver. 10. having the color silver, or tinted with silver: *a silver dress*; *silver blue*. 11. clear and soft: *silver sounds*. 12. persuasive; eloquent: *a silver tongue*. 13. indicating the 25th event of a series, as a wedding anniversary. ◇v.t. 14. to coat with silver or some silver-like substance. 15. to give a silver color to. ◇v.i. 16. to become a silver color. [ME; OE *siolfor*]

silver age, n. See **age** (def. 10).

silver beet, n. a type of beet with large, firm, strongly-veined, green leaves and a long fleshy stalk, used as a vegetable.

silver birch, n. a widely-distributed Old World tree, having a whitish, papery bark.

silver bromide, n. a light-sensitive compound, AgBr, which is of basic importance in photography.

silver-eye /ˈsɪlvər-aɪ/, n. any of various birds known also as white-eyes, mainly of yellow or olive coloring, as the **grey-breasted silver-eye**, of eastern and south-eastern Australia and Tas, the **western silver-eye**, of south-western Australia, the **yellow silver-eye**, of northern Australia, and the **pale silver-eye**, of north-eastern Australia.

silverfish /ˈsɪlvəfɪʃ/, n., pl. **-fishes**, (*esp. collectively*) **-fish**. 1. a small white or silvery fish, useful only for bait. 2. a small, wingless insect, with a bristle-like tail, which damages books, wallpaper, etc.

silver plate, n. 1. a thin silver coating put on the surface of another metal, usu. by elec-

silver plate / **since**

trolysis. **2.** tableware plated with such a coating.

silver screen, *n.* **1.** motion pictures collectively. **2.** a special type of screen for a picture theatre.

silverside /'sɪlvəsaɪd/, *n.* a cut of beef from the outside top part of a hind leg.

silversmith /'sɪlvəsmɪθ/, *n.* someone who makes and repairs articles of silver.

silvery /'sɪlvəri/, *adj.* **1.** like silver; of a shining greyish-white color. **2.** having a clear, ringing sound like that of silver. **3.** containing or covered with silver.

sim., *Abbrev.* **1.** similar(ly). **2.** simile.

Simbu /'sɪmbu/, *n.* → Chimbu.

simian /'sɪmiən/, *adj.* (relating to or like) an ape or monkey. [L: ape]

similar /'sɪmələ/, *adj.* **1.** having likeness, esp. in a general way. **2.** *Geom.* (of figures) having corresponding sides proportional and corresponding angles equal. [L: like] —**similarity,** *n.*

simile /'sɪməli/, *n.* a figure of speech directly expressing a likeness, of one thing to another, as *a man like an ox.* [ME, from L: like]

simmer /'sɪmə/, *v.i.* **1.** (of food) to cook in a liquid just below the boiling point. **2.** to be in a state of controlled anger, excitement, etc. **3. simmer down,** *Colloq.* to become calm or calmer. ◇*v.t.* **4.** to cook (food) in a liquid just below the boiling point. ◇*n.* **5.** a state or process of simmering. [earlier *simber,* ME *simper;* orig. unknown]

Simon /'saɪmən/, *n.* the original name of Peter the apostle. Also, **Simon Peter.** [see Mark 3:16]

simpatico /sɪm'pætɪkoʊ/, *adj.* **1.** of like mind or personal feelings; compatible. **2.** having attractive qualities; pleasing. [It: sympathy]

simper /'sɪmpə/, *v.i.* **1.** to smile in a silly, self-conscious way. ◇*n.* **2.** a silly, self-conscious smile. [orig. uncert.]

simple /'sɪmpəl/, *adj.*, **-pler, -plest. 1.** easy to understand, deal with, use, etc.: *a simple matter; simple tools.* **2.** not having complicated or unnecessary elements: *a simple style.* **3.** not having or offering the best in comfort and luxury. **4.** plain and open in behavior; unaffected. **5.** lacking mental acuteness or sense. **6.** considered alone; mere; bare: *the simple truth or fact.* **7.** sincere; innocent. **8.** common or ordinary: *a simple soldier.* **9.** unlearned; ignorant. **10.** *Chem.* **a.** made of one substance or element: *a simple substance.* **b.** not mixed. **11.** *Zool.* not compound. [ME, from OF, from L]

simple harmonic motion, *n.* a form of vibratory motion which may be represented by projecting on to the diameter of a circle the uniform motion of a point round its circumference. *Abbrev.:* SHM

simple interest, *n.* interest which is not compounded, that is, payable only on the principal amount of a debt.

simple sentence, *n.* a sentence with only one clause.

simple time, *n. Music.* a musical rhythm in which the basic beat can be divided by two.

simpleton /'sɪmpəltən/, *n.* a foolish or stupid person; fool. [SIMPLE + -TON]

simplicity /sɪm'plɪsəti/, *n., pl.* **-ties. 1.** the condition or quality of being simple. **2.** freedom from complexity or division into parts. **3.** absence of luxury, ornament, etc.; plainness. **4.** naturalness; sincerity; artlessness. **5.** lack of sharp or quick understanding. [ME, from L]

simplify /'sɪmpləfaɪ/, *v.t.,* **-fied, -fying.** to make plainer or easier. [F, from ML] —**simplification,** *n.*

simplistic /sɪm'plɪstɪk/, *adj.* characterised by too much simplification; oversimplified. —**simplistically,** *adv.*

simply /'sɪmpli/, *adv.* **1.** in a simple manner. **2.** plainly; unaffectedly. **3.** not deceitfully or craftily. **4.** merely; only. **5.** unwisely; foolishly. **6.** absolutely: *simply irresistible.* [ME]

Simpson /'sɪmsən/, *n.* **Bob** (*Robert Baddeley Simpson*), born 1936, Australian cricketer, noted as a batsman.

Simpson Desert, *n.* a large arid area covering about 77 000 km² in the south-eastern NT and parts of Qld and SA.

Simpson's Donkey, *n.* See **Kirkpatrick.**

simulate /'sɪmjəleɪt/, *v.t.,* **-lated, -lating. 1.** to make a pretence or likeness of. **2.** to have the appearance of. [L: made like] —**simulative,** *adj.* —**simulation,** *n.*

simulator /'sɪmjəleɪtə/, *n.* a training or experimental device that simulates movement, flight, or some other condition.

simultaneous /sɪməl'teɪniəs/, *adj.* existing, happening, or operating at the same time: *simultaneous movements; simultaneous announcements.* [ML: simulated]

simultaneous equations, *n.pl.* algebraic equations which must each be satisfied by the same values of the unknowns.

sin¹ /sɪn/, *n., v.,* **sinned, sinning.** ◇*n.* **1.** an act of breaking God's law. **2.** an act regarded as a sin, esp. a wilful or deliberate breaking of some religious or moral principle. ◇*v.i.* **3.** to do a sinful act. [OE *syn(n)*] —**sinful,** *adj.* —**sinless,** *adj.* —**sinner,** *n.*

sin² /saɪn/, *Maths. Abbrev.* → **sine.**

Sinai /'saɪnaɪ/, *n.* **1.** Also, **Sinai Peninsula.** a peninsula in north-eastern Egypt at the northern end of the Red Sea between the Gulfs of Suez and Aqaba. About 370 km long. **2. Mount,** the mountain, of uncertain identity, from which the law was given to Moses. See Exodus 19. —**Sinaitic,** *adj.*

Sinatra /sə'nɑtrə/, *n.* **Frank** (*Francis Albert Sinatra*), born 1917, US singer and actor.

since /sɪns/, *adv.* **1.** from then until now (oft. prec. by *ever*). **2.** between a particular past time and the present; subsequently: *He at first refused, but has since agreed.* **3.** ago; before now:

since 963 **sink**

long since. ◇*prep.* **4.** continuously from or counting from: *since noon*. **5.** between a (past time or event) and the present: *changes since the war*. ◇*conj.* **6.** in the period following the time when: *He has written once since he left.* **7.** continuously from or counting from the time when: *busy since he came.* **8.** because. [ME *syns, synnes*, from OE *siththan* then]

sincere /sɪn'sɪə, sən-/, *adj.*, **-cerer, -cerest.** free from any element of deceit or pretence of being something which one is not. [L] **—sincerity,** *n.*

sine /saɪn/, *n. Maths.* a trigonometric function defined for an acute angle in a right-angled triangle as the ratio of the side opposite the angle to the hypotenuse. [L: curve]

sinecure /'saɪnəkjʊə, 'saɪnə-/, *n.* an office requiring little or no work, esp. one yielding profitable returns. [short for L phrase (*beneficium*) *sine cūrā*]

sinew /'sɪnju/, *n.* **1.** a cord of tough tissue connecting a muscle with a bone or part; tendon. **2.** something which supplies strength. **3.** strength; vigor. [OE *sinu* (nom.), *sinuwe* (gen.)] **—sinewy,** *adj.*

sine wave, *n.* a periodic oscillation which can be shown as a curve having an equation of the form $y = a \sin x$.

sing /sɪŋ/, *v.*, **sang, sung, singing.** ◇*v.i.* **1.** to utter words or sounds one after the other with musical regulations of the voice. **2.** to perform a song or voice composition. **3.** (of birds, insects, etc.) to produce melodious sounds. **4.** to give out a ringing, whistling, murmuring, or sound of musical quality, as a kettle, a brook, etc. **5.** (of the ear) to have the sensation of a ringing or humming sound. ◇*v.t.* **6.** to utter with musical changes of the voice, as a song. **7.** to proclaim, as if by song: *They sing his praises.* **8.** to bring, send, put, etc., with or by singing: *She will sing the child to sleep.* **9.** (in Aboriginal magic) to direct at (a wrongdoer) a chant which is believed to have the power to kill. ◇*v.* **10. sing out,** *Colloq.* to call out in a loud voice; shout. [OE *singan*] **—singer,** *n.*

sing., *Abbrev.* singular.

Singapore /'sɪŋəpɔ/, *n.* **1.** a republic in South-East Asia, consisting of one main island and several smaller islands, off the southern tip of the Malay Peninsula; British colony until 1946; part of Malaysia 1963–65; an independent republic since 1965. Pop. 2 616 000 (1987 est.); 618 km². *Languages*: English, Malay, Mandarin Chinese and Tamil. *Currency*: Singapore dollar. *Cap.*: Singapore. **2.** the capital of the republic of Singapore, a seaport and naval base. Pop. 2 616 000 (1987 est.). **—Singaporean** *n., adj.*

singe /sɪndʒ/, *v.*, **singed, singeing,** *n.* ◇*v.t.* **1.** to burn slightly. **2.** to burn the ends of (hair, etc.). **3.** to subject to flame in order to remove hair, etc. ◇*n.* **4.** a slight burn. **5.** the act of singeing. [OE *sencgan*]

Singhalese /'sɪŋə'liz/, *adj.* relating to Sri Lanka, formerly Ceylon. Also, **Sinhalese**. [Skt *Sinhala* Ceylon]

single /'sɪŋgəl/, *adj.*, *v.*, **-gled, -gling,** *n.* ◇*adj.* **1.** one only; separate; individual. **2.** of or for one person, family, etc.: *a single room*. **3.** alone; solitary. **4.** unmarried. **5.** (in fighting) of one against one. **6.** consisting of one part, element, or member. **7.** (of a flower) having one set of petals. ◇*v.t.* **8.** to pick or choose out from others (usu. fol. by *out*): *I must single out her generosity for special mention.* ◇*n.* **9.** something single or separate; a single one. **10.** a ticket for a train, bus, etc., for a one-way journey only. **11.** a gramophone record which contains only one short musical piece on each side. **12.** (*pl.*) Tennis, etc. a game or match played with one person on each side. **13.** Cricket. a hit for which one run is scored. [ME, from OF, from L] **—singly,** *adv.*

single bond, *n.* a single covalent bond between two atoms.

single file, *n.* a line of people or things arranged one behind the other; Indian file.

single-handed /sɪŋgəl-'hændəd/, *adj.* **1.** acting or working alone or unaided. **2.** performed or completed by one person alone. **3.** having, using, or requiring the use of but one hand or one person.

single-minded /sɪŋgəl-'maɪndəd/, *adj.* **1.** having or showing undivided purpose. **2.** having or showing a sincere mind; steadfast.

singlet /'sɪŋlət, 'sɪŋglət/, *n.* a short garment, with or without sleeves, usu. worn next to the skin on the upper part of the body.

Singleton /'sɪŋgəltən/, *n.* a town and shire in eastern NSW, on the Hunter River. Pop. 10 990 (1986).

singsong /'sɪŋsɒŋ/, *n.* **1.** (a piece of) verse of a jingling or monotonous character. **2.** an informal gathering at which the company sings; community singing. ◇*adj.* **3.** characterised by a regular rising and falling intonation and rhythm.

singular /'sɪŋgjələ/, *adj.* **1.** out of the ordinary; remarkable: *singular success.* **2.** unusual or strange; odd; eccentric. **3.** being the only one of the kind; unique. **4.** *Gram.* indicating one person, thing, or collection, as English *man, thing, he, goes.* ◇*n.* **5.** *Gram.* the singular number, or a form of it. [ME, from L] **—singularity,** *n.*

sinister /'sɪnəstə/, *adj.* **1.** threatening evil; ominous. **2.** bad; evil; base. **3.** on the left side of a shield (in relation to the bearer). [ME, from L; orig. referring to omens observed on the left (the unlucky) side]

sinistral /'sɪnəstrəl/, *adj.* of or relating to the left side; left (opposed to *dextral*).

sink /sɪŋk/, *v.*, **sank, sunk** or **sunken, sinking,** *n.* ◇*v.i.* **1.** (of water, flames, etc.) to descend gradually to a lower level. **2.** to go down towards or below the horizon. **3.** (of ground) to slope downwards. **4.** to go under or to the bottom. **5.** (of a heavy structure) to settle or fall gradually. **6.** to fall slowly from weakness, fatigue, etc. **7.** to pass gradually (into sleep, silence, etc.). **8.** to pass or fall into some lower state, as of fortune, etc. **9.** to enter the mind; become understood (fol. by *in, into,*

sink

etc.): *That idea will sink in slowly.* **10.** (of the cheeks) to become hollow. **11.** to sit or lie down in a slow, relaxed manner: *He would sink back into the old chair with pleasure.* ◇*v.t.* **12.** to cause to sink, fall or descend. **13.** to make (a hole, well, etc.) as by digging out. **14.** to put down or lay (a pipe, post, etc.), as into the ground. **15.** *Golf, Billiards, etc.* to cause (the ball) to run into a hole. **16.** to bring to a worse state or ruin. **17.** to lower (the voice, etc.). **18.** to invest (money), now esp. unprofitably. ◇*v.* **19. sink or swim**, to make a desperate attempt to succeed, knowing that otherwise complete failure will result. ◇*n.* **20.** a basin with a water supply and outlet, esp. in a kitchen. **21.** Also, **sinkhole**. a low-lying area where waters collect or where they disappear by sinking down into the ground or by evaporation. **22.** a place of evil character. **23.** a drain or sewer. [OE *sincan*]

sinker /'sɪŋkə/, *n.* a weight of lead, etc., for sinking a fishing line, fishing net, or the like in the water.

sinkhole /'sɪŋkhoʊl/, *n.* **1.** Also, **pothole, swallow-hole**. a hole formed in soluble rock by the action of water, serving to conduct surface water to an underground passage. **2.** → sink (def. 23).

sinking fund, *n.* a fund set up by periodic payments, e.g. for the purpose of paying off a debt.

Sinn Fein /ʃɪn 'feɪn/, *n.* a political organisation in Ireland, advocating the advancement of Ireland along national lines and its complete political separation from Great Britain. [Irish: we ourselves]

Sino-, a word part meaning 'Chinese', as in *Sino-Tibetan*. [NL, combining form representing L *Sīnae* the Chinese (from Gk)]

sinuous /'sɪnjuəs/, *adj.* **1.** having many curves, bends, or turns; winding. **2.** indirect; devious. [L] **—sinuosity, sinuousness,** *n.*

sinus /'saɪnəs/, *n., pl.* **-nuses**. *Anat.* one of the hollow cavities in the skull connecting with the nose cavities. [L]

sinusitis /saɪnə'saɪtəs/, *n.* inflammation of a sinus or sinuses.

sinusoidal /saɪnə'sɔɪdl/, *adj. Phys.* having a characteristic which can be represented geometrically by a sine wave, as a *sinusoidal current*.

-sion, a suffix having the same function as **-tion**, as in *compulsion*. [L]

Sioux /su/, *n.* a group of North American Indian tribes.

sip /sɪp/, *v.*, **sipped, sipping**, *n.* ◇*v.t., v.i.* **1.** to drink a little at a time. ◇*n.* **2.** an act of sipping. **3.** a small quantity taken by sipping. [OE *sypian* drink in]

siphon /'saɪfən/, *n.* **1.** a tube in the form of an upside-down U through which liquid flows from a higher container to a lower container by atmospheric pressure. **2.** a bottle filled with carbonated water which is forced out by pressure when a lever is pressed. **3.** a tube-like part of some animals, through which water enters or leaves the body. ◇*v.t., v.i.* **4.** to pass through a siphon. Also, **syphon**. [L, from Gk: pipe, tube]

sippet /'sɪpət/, *n.* a small piece of bread served with soup, etc.; crouton. [alteration of SOP + -ET]

sir /sɜ/, *n.* **1.** a respectful term of address used to a man. **2.** (*cap.*) the title belonging to a knight or baronet: *Sir Walter Scott.* [weak var. of SIRE]

sire /saɪə/, *n., v.*, **sired, siring**. ◇*n.* **1.** the male parent of an animal, esp. of an animal kept by man. **2.** a respectful term of address, now used only to a king. **3.** *Poetic.* a father or forefather. ◇*v.t.* **4.** to be the father of. [ME, from OF, from L: senior]

siren /'saɪrən/, *n.* **1.** *Class. Myth.* one of several sea nymphs, part woman and part bird, supposed to lead seamen to destruction by their irresistible singing. **2.** any dangerously attractive woman. **3.** a device used as a whistle, fog signal, warning sound on an ambulance, fire-engine, etc. [ME, from L, from Gk: sea nymph]

Sirius /'sɪriəs/, *n.* **1.** the brightest star in the sky; the Dog Star; Canicula. **2. HMS**, an escorting vessel to the First Fleet, arriving in NSW in 1788, wrecked in 1790.

sirloin /'sɜlɔɪn/, *n.* the part of the loin of beef in front of the rump. [earlier *surloyn*, from OF *surlonge*, from *sur* over, above + *longe* loin]

sirrah /'sɪrə/, *n. Archaic.* a term of address used to a person in impatience, etc. [unexplained var. of SIR]

sisal /'saɪsəl/, *n.* a fibre yielded by a Mexican plant used for making ropes, etc. Also, **sisal hemp**. [named after *Sisal*, port in Yucatan, a peninsula in S Mexico]

Sisley /'sɪsli/, *n.* **Alfred**, 1833–99, French impressionist painter.

sissy /'sɪsi/, *n. Colloq.* **1.** man or boy with mannerisms of the opposite sex. **2.** a fearful or cowardly person. Also, **cissy**. [from SISTER]

sister /'sɪstə/, *n.* **1.** a daughter of the same parents as another person (**full sister** or **sister german**); female sibling. **2.** member of the same kinship group, nationality, profession, etc.: *She addressed her sister lawyers.* **3.** a female member of a religious group, which observes the simple vows of poverty, chastity, and obedience; nun: *a sister of Charity*. **4.** → **registered nurse**. ◇*adj.* **5.** related by, or as by, sisterhood: *sister ships*. [ME, from Scand] **—sisterly,** *adj.* **—sisterhood,** *n.*

sister-in-law /'sɪstər-ɪn-lɔ/, *n., pl.* **sisters-in-law**. **1.** a husband's or wife's sister. **2.** a brother's wife. **3.** a husband's or wife's brother's wife.

Sistine Chapel /ˌsɪstin 'tʃæpəl/, *n.* the chapel of the pope in the Vatican at Rome, built for Pope Sixtus IV, and decorated with frescoes by Michelangelo and others. [*Sistine* adj. from name *Sixtus*]

sit /sɪt/, *v.*, **sat** or (*old form*) **sate, sitting**. ◇*v.i.* **1.** to rest on the lower part of the body; be seated. **2.** to be situated; dwell. **3.** to rest

or lie (in a certain way): *Wealth sits comfortably on him.* **4.** to place oneself in position for an artist, etc.: *Would you sit for a portrait?* **5.** to remain quiet or inactive. **6.** to cover eggs until the young come out. **7.** (of a garment) to fit. **8.** (of a judge, bishop, etc.) to occupy a seat in an official capacity. **9.** to be an elected representative, as in parliament. **10.** (of a meeting) to be in process. **11.** to act as a babysitter. **12.** to take an examination. ◇*v.t.* **13.** to cause to sit; seat (oft. with *down*). **14.** to sit upon (a horse, etc.). **15.** to provide seating room for; seat: *a table which sits eight people.* ◇*v.* **16.** Some special uses are:
be sitting pretty, *Colloq.* to be comfortably established; be at an advantage.
sit down, to take a seat.
sit in, (of a performer) to attach oneself for a time to a band.
sit in for, to take the place of for a short time: *He'll be out for an hour so I'll sit in for him.*
sit in on, take part in as an observer or visitor: *We were allowed to sit in on the discussion.*
sit on or **upon**, **1.** to have a place (on a committee, etc.): *He has sat on several committees.* **2.** *Colloq.* to check; rebuke; repress. **3.** *Colloq.* to prevent (a document) from becoming public knowledge: *The government will sit on the report.*
sit out, **1.** to stay till the end of: *Though the film was boring, we had to sit it out.* **2.** to take no part in: *She sat out the last few dances because she was tired.*
sit pat, *Colloq.* to stick to one's decision.
sit tight, to take no action: *I'll sit tight till I know what the decision is.*
sit up, **1.** to raise oneself from a lying to a sitting position. **2.** to stay up later than usual. **3.** to sit upright. **4.** to become alert: *The speaker's next announcement made us sit up.* [OE *sittan*]

sitar /'sɪtə, 'sɪtɑ/, *n.* a guitar-like instrument of India, having a long neck and usu. three strings. Also, **sittar**. [Hind] —**sitarist**, *n.*

site /saɪt/, *n., v.,* **sited, siting.** ◇*n.* **1.** the position of a town, building, etc., esp. in relation to its environment. **2.** the area on which anything is, has been or is to be situated: *the site of a open-air concert.* ◇*v.t.* **3.** to place; provide with a site: *They will site the hospital here.* [L: position]

sit-in /'sɪt-ɪn/, *n.* an organised non-violent protest in which people occupy places where they are normally not allowed, and refuse to move.

sittella /sə'tɛlə/, *n.* a highly active bird of very sociable habits, found in dry forests throughout mainland Australia, which builds a cleverly camouflaged cup-shaped nest. [L, from Gk: woodpecker]

sitter /'sɪtə/, *n.* **1.** a person who sits, esp. for a portrait. **2.** a baby-sitter.

sitting /'sɪtɪŋ/, *n.* **1.** a period of remaining seated, as for a portrait. **2.** an unbroken period of sitting, as to read a book. **3.** (of a court, etc.) a session. **4.** an occasion of serving a meal to a group, etc.: *We should feed the group in two sittings.*

Sitting Bull, *n.* 1843–90, a noted Sioux Indian warrior and tribal leader.

situate /'sɪtʃueɪt/, *v.,* **-ated, -ating.** to give a site to; locate. [LL: located] —**situated**, *adj.*

situation /sɪtʃu'eɪʃən/, *n.* **1.** a location or position with reference to environment. **2.** a place; locality. **3.** condition; case; plight. **4.** the state of affairs: *We can meet the demands of the situation.* **5.** a position of employment.

sit. vac., *Abbrev.* situation vacant.

Sitwell family /'sɪtwəl/, *n.* a family of English literary figures including **Edith**, 1887–1964, poet and critic.

SI unit /ɛs 'aɪ junət/, *n.* a unit of the International System of Units (Système International d'Unités). See Appendix.

Siva /'ʃivə/, *n.* →**Shiva.**

six /sɪks/, *n.* **1.** a cardinal number, five plus one (5 + 1). **2.** a symbol for this number, as 6 or VI. **3.** *Cricket.* a hit scoring six runs, the ball reaching the boundary without touching the ground. **4. at sixes and sevens,** in confusion. **5. go for six,** to suffer a major setback. **6. hit for six,** to dispose of completely. ◇*adj.* **7.** amounting to six in number. [ME and OE]

Six-Day War, *n.* a war fought for six days in June 1967 in which Israel defeated Egypt, Jordan and Syria and occupied the Gaza Strip, the Sinai, Jerusalem, the West Bank of the Jordan and the Golan Heights.

six-shooter /'sɪks-ʃutə/, *n. Colloq.* a revolver with which six shots can be fired without reloading.

sixteen /sɪks'tin/, *n.* **1.** a cardinal number, ten plus six (10 + 6). **2.** a symbol for this number, as 16 or XVI. ◇*adj.* **3.** amounting to 16 in number. [ME *sixtene*, OE *sixtēne*] —**sixteenth**, *adj.*

sixth /sɪksθ/, *adj.* **1.** next after the fifth. **2.** being one of six equal parts. ◇*n.* **3.** a sixth part, esp. of one ($\frac{1}{6}$). **4.** the sixth member of a series. **5.** sixth class or form. **6.** *Music.* a note on the sixth degree from a given note (counting the first).

Sixtus /'sɪkstəs/, *n.* the name of five popes.

sixty /'sɪksti/, *n., pl.* **-ties,** *adj.* ◇*n.* **1.** a cardinal number, ten times six (10 × 6). **2.** a symbol for this number as 60 or LX. **3.** (*pl.*) the numbers from 60 to 69 of a series, esp. with reference to the years of a person's age, or the years of a century. ◇*adj.* **4.** amounting to sixty in number. [OE *sixtig*]

size¹ /saɪz/, *n., v.,* **sized, sizing.** ◇*n.* **1.** the characteristics of a thing determining how much space it takes up. **2.** considerable or great size: *It is foolish to seek size rather than quality.* **3.** one of a series of graded measures for articles of manufacture: *children's sizes of shoes.* ◇*v.t.* **4.** to separate or sort according to size. ◇*v.* **5. to size up,** to form an idea of. [ME, from OF: assize]

size² /saɪz/, *n., v.,* **sized, sizing.** ◇*n.* **1.** Also, **sizing.** a sticky or jelly-like preparation made from glue, starch, etc., used for coating paper, cloth, etc. ◇*v.t.* **2.** to coat or treat with size. [ME *syse*; ? special use of SIZE¹]

sizeable /ˈsaɪzəbəl/, *adj.* of considerable size; fairly large: *He won a sizeable sum.*

sizzle /ˈsɪzəl/, *v.*, **-zled, -zling,** *n.* ◇*v.i.* **1.** to make a hissing sound, as in frying or burning. ◇*n.* **2.** a sizzling sound. [imitative] **–sizzler,** *n.*

Skara Brae /ˌskærə ˈbreɪ/, *n.* a Stone Age village in the Orkney Islands in Scotland, preserved under sand dunes until uncovered in 1850.

skate[1] /skeɪt/, *n., v.,* **skated, skating.** ◇*n.* **1.** a steel blade attached to the bottom of a shoe, enabling a person to move easily over ice. **2.** a shoe with such a blade attached. **3.** → **roller-skate.** ◇*v.i.* **4.** to move easily over ice, the ground, etc., on skates. **5.** to move or slide smoothly along. **6.** to avoid, as in conversation (fol. by *round* or *over*). ◇*v.* **7. skate on thin ice,** to place oneself in a delicate situation. [D, from ONF: stilt] **–skater,** *n.*

skate[2] /skeɪt/, *n., pl.* **skates,** (*esp. collectively*) **skate.** any of certain rays usu. having a pointed snout and spines down the back but a tail with no spines. [ME, from Scand]

skateboard /ˈskeɪtbɔd/, *n.* a short piece of wood on roller-skate wheels, ridden usu. standing up.

skein /skeɪn/, *n.* **1.** a length of thread or yarn wound in a coil. **2.** a group of geese or similar birds in flight formation. [ME, from OF]

skeleton /ˈskelətn/, *n.* **1.** the bones of a human or other animal body considered together, or assembled or fitted together as a framework. **2.** *Colloq.* a very thin person or animal. **3.** a supporting framework, as of a leaf, building, or ship. **4.** mere lifeless, dry, or small remains. **5.** (of a literary work) basic essentials: *the skeleton of the plot.* **6. skeleton in the cupboard,** some shameful fact in the history of a family which is kept secret. ◇*adj.* **7.** of, like or relating to a skeleton. **8.** reduced to the smallest possible amount: *skeleton staff.* [NL, from Gk: dried up] **–skeletal,** *adj.*

skeleton key, *n.* a key with nearly the whole substance of the bit filed away, so that it may open various locks.

skerrick /ˈskerɪk/, *n.* a very small quantity; a scrap: *not a skerrick left.* [Brit d.; orig. obscure]

sketch /sketʃ/, *n.* **1.** a simply or hastily done drawing or painting, giving the important features without the details. **2.** a rough design, plan, or outline. **3.** a short and usu. light literary work, as a story, essay or short play. ◇*v.i., v.t.* **4.** to make a sketch (of). [D, from It, from L: extemporaneous poem, from Gk: extempore] **–sketcher,** *n.*

sketchy /ˈsketʃi/, *adj.,* **sketchier, sketchiest. 1.** giving only outlines. **2.** slight; imperfect; incomplete; superficial. **–sketchily,** *adv.* **–sketchiness,** *n.*

skew /skju/, *v.i.* **1.** to turn aside or twist. ◇*v.t.* **2.** to give a sloping direction to. **3.** to describe unfairly; distort. ◇*adj.* **4.** having a sloping direction or position; slanting. **5.** *Geom.* not lying in the same plane. ◇*n.* **6.** a twisting or sloping movement, direction, or position. [ME, from ONF: escape]

skewbald /ˈskjubɔld/, *adj.* **1.** (of horses, etc.) having patches of different colors, esp. of white and brown. ◇*n.* **2.** a skewbald horse or pony. See **piebald.** [obs. E *skewed* skewbald (orig. uncert.)]

skewer /ˈskjuə/, *n.* **1.** a long pin of wood or metal for putting through meat to hold it together while being cooked. **2.** any similar pin for some other purpose. ◇*v.t.* **3.** to fasten with, or as with, skewers. [earlier *skiver,* of unknown orig.]

ski /ski/, *n., pl.* **skis, ski,** *v.,* **ski'd** or **skied, skiing.** ◇*n.* **1.** one of a pair of long, thin pieces of hard wood, metal, or plastic, one fastened to each shoe, used for travelling over snow. **2.** a water-ski. ◇*v.i.* **3.** to travel on or use skis. [Norw, var. of *skid,* akin to OE *scid* thin slip of wood] **–skier,** *n.* **–skiing,** *n.*

skid /skɪd/, *n., v.,* **skidded, skidding.** ◇*n.* **1.** a plank, bar, log, or the like, esp. one of a number on which something heavy may be supported, slid or rolled along. **2.** a device for preventing the wheel of a vehicle from revolving, as when descending a hill. **3.** a runner on the underpart of some aeroplanes, enabling the machine to slide along the ground when landing. **4.** an act of skidding: *The car went into a skid on the icy road.* **5. on the skids,** getting worse fast. **6. put the skids under,** to place (someone) in a dangerous position. ◇*v.i.* **7.** (of a wheel) to slide along without turning. **8.** (of a vehicle) to slide forward under its own momentum when the wheels have lost friction with the road surface. ◇*v.t.* **9.** to cause (a vehicle, etc.) to skid. [orig. uncert.; ? irregularly from Scand]

skid row, *n. Orig. US.* a district lived in by people with no means of support and often no home.

skiff /skɪf/, *n.* any of various types of small boat, usu. propelled by oars or sails. [F, from It, from OHG: ship]

skilful /ˈskɪlfəl/, *adj.* **1.** having or exercising skill. **2.** showing or using skill: *a skilful display of fancy diving.*

skill /skɪl/, *n.* **1.** the ability that comes from knowledge, practice, aptitude, etc., to do something well. **2.** efficiency and excellence in performance; expertness; dexterity. [ME, from Scand] **–skilled,** *adj.*

skillet /ˈskɪlət/, *n.* a frying pan. [orig. obscure]

skillion /ˈskɪljən/, *n.* an outer building sometimes leaning against a wall, with a roof sloping in one direction. Also, **skilling.** [Brit d. *skeeling* outhouse]

skim /skɪm/, *v.,* **skimmed, skimming.** ◇*v.t.* **1.** to take up or remove (floating matter) from a liquid with a spoon, etc.: *to skim the fat from the gravy.* **2.** to clear (liquid) thus: *to skim the gravy to remove the fat.* **3.** to move lightly over or along the surface of (the ground, water, etc.). **4.** to go over in reading, treatment, etc., without giving full attention. ◇*v.i.* **5.** to pass lightly along over or near a surface. **6.** to go,

skim pass, glance, etc., over something in a superficial way (usu. fol. by *over*). ◇*n.* **7.** the act of skimming. [d. var. of obs. *scum*, v., skim]

skim milk, *n.* milk from which the cream has been removed. Also, **skimmed milk.**

skimp /skɪmp/, *v.t.* **1.** to do hastily or without attention; scamp. **2.** to allow only little; scrimp. ◇*v.i.* **3.** to be very careful in management (oft. fol. by *on*). [orig. uncert.]

skimpy /'skɪmpi/, *adj.*, **skimpier, skimpiest. 1.** lacking in size, fullness, etc.; scanty. **2.** too concerned with careful management of money, etc.; stingy. —**skimpily,** *adv.* —**skimpiness,** *n.*

skin /skɪn/, *n.*, *v.*, **skinned, skinning.** ◇*n.* **1.** the external covering of an animal body, esp. when soft and flexible. **2.** this cover stripped from the body of an animal; pelt. **3.** any surface layer, as the rind or peel of fruit, or a film on liquid. **4.** a container made of animal skins, used for holding liquids. **5. by the skin of one's teeth,** scarcely; just; barely. **6. get under one's skin,** to annoy someone. **7. save one's skin,** to escape harm. ◇*v.t.* **8.** to strip (animal) of skin; flay; peel. [ME, from Scand]

skindiving /'skɪndaɪvɪŋ/, *n.* underwater swimming for which the diver is equipped with a mask, snorkel, and foot fins. —**skindiver,** *n.*

skinflint /'skɪnflɪnt/, *n.* a mean, stingy person.

skinhead /'skɪnhed/, *n. Colloq.* a member of a gang of young men with close-cropped hair or shaven heads, characteristic (usu. black) clothing and oft. violent behavior.

skink /skɪŋk/, *n.* a harmless, generally smooth-scaled lizard. [L, from Gk]

skinny /'skɪni/, *adj.*, **-nier, -niest.** lean; emaciated. —**skinniness,** *n.*

skip¹ /skɪp/, *v.*, **skipped, skipping,** *n.* ◇*v.i.* **1.** to spring, jump, or leap lightly; gambol. **2.** to pass from one point, thing, subject, etc., to another, taking no notice of or leaving out what is in between. **3.** *Colloq.* to leave hastily; abscond. **4.** to use a skipping-rope. ◇*v.t.* **5.** to jump lightly over: *skip the puddle.* **6.** to miss out (one of a series). **7.** to pass over without reading, notice, mention, action, etc. **8.** to send (a missile) ricocheting along a surface. **9.** *Colloq.* to leave (a place) hastily. ◇*n.* **10.** a movement in which one foot jumps lightly and then the other. [ME]

skip² /skɪp/, *n.* **1.** a large rubbish bin on a building site. **2.** a truck used in an underground railway system for carrying coal, minerals, etc. [OE: a basket]

ski-pole /'ski-poul/, *n.* one of two slender poles with a sharp metal tip, used by a skier for balance and to increase speed. Also, **pole.**

skipper /'skɪpə/, *n.* **1.** the master or captain of a ship, esp. of a small vessel. **2.** a captain or leader, as of a team. ◇*v.t.* **3.** to act as the skipper of. [ME, from MD: ship]

skipping-rope /'skɪpɪŋ-roup/, *n.* a rope, usu. having handles at the ends, which is swung in a loop so that the holder or others jump over it.

skirmish /'skɜmɪʃ/, *n.* **1.** *Mil.* a fight between small bodies of soldiers, esp. those situated away from the main fighting. **2.** any short, lively meeting. ◇*v.i.* **3.** to engage in a skirmish. [ME, from OF, from OHG: shield]

skirt /skɜt/, *n.* **1.** the lower part of a dress, coat, etc., hanging from the waist. **2.** a separate garment (outer or under) worn by women and girls, hanging from the waist downwards. **3.** some part suggesting the skirt of a garment. **4.** a cut of beef from the flank. ◇*v.t.* **5.** to lie on or along the border of. **6.** to pass along or around the border or edge of: *They will skirt the town.* **7.** to remove ragged pieces from (fleeces). ◇*v.i.* **8.** to be, lie, live, pass, etc., on or along the edge of something. [ME, from Scand]

skirting /'skɜtɪŋ/, *n.* **1.** material for making skirts. **2.** (*pl.*) the trimmings of a fleece.

skirting board, *n.* a line of boarding protecting an interior wall next to the floor. **2.** Also, **skirting table.** the table on which a fleece is trimmed.

Skirving /'skɜvɪŋ/, *n.* **William,** died 1796, Scottish political reformer, one of the five Scottish Martyrs transported to Australia in 1794.

skit /skɪt/, *n.* a slight dramatic or literary piece making fun or light of a person, institution, etc. [ME: harlot]

skite /skaɪt/, *Colloq.* ◇*v.i.* **1.** to boast; brag. ◇*n.* **2.** a boast; brag. **3.** Also, **skiter.** a boaster. [Scot and northern d. *skite* (derog.)]

skittish /'skɪtɪʃ/, *adj.* **1.** tending to take fright or be shy. **2.** restlessly lively. **3.** uncertain; fickle. [ME; orig. uncert.] —**skittishness,** *n.*

skittle /'skɪtl/, *n.*, *v.*, **skittled, skittling.** ◇*n.* **1.** (*pl.*) ninepins. ◇*v.t.* **2.** to knock over or send flying, in the manner of skittles. [Scand]

skivvy /'skɪvi/, *n.* a close-fitting garment with long sleeves and a high, close-fitting neck, usu. made of machine-knitted cotton.

skol /skɒl/, *interj.*, *v.*, **skolled, skolling.** ◇*interj.* **1.** to your health. ◇*v.t.* **2.** *Colloq.* to finish (a drink) at one draught. Also, **skoal** /skoul/. [Scand]

skua /'skjuə/, *n.* a gull-like seabird which chases weaker birds in order to make them give up what they have caught. [NL, from ON: tassel]

skulduggery /skʌl'dʌgəri/, *n.* mean dishonesty or trickery. Also, **skullduggery.** [orig. obscure]

skulk /skʌlk/, *v.i.* **1.** to lie or keep in hiding, as for some evil reason. **2.** to avoid duty; malinger. **3.** to move or go in a secretive manner; sneak; slink. [ME, from Scand]

skull /skʌl/, *n.* **1.** the bony framework of the head, enclosing the brain and supporting the face. **2.** (*usu. offensive*) the head as the seat of knowledge. [ME, from Scand]

skull and crossbones, *n.* a representation of a front view of a human skull above two crossed bones, used as a warning sign.

skullcap

skullcap /ˈskʌlkæp/, *n.* a brimless cap of silk, velvet, etc., fitting closely to the head.

skunk /skʌŋk/, *n.* 1. a small, striped, fur-bearing, bushy-tailed, North American mammal, of the weasel family, which lets out a foul-smelling fluid when attacked. 2. *Colloq.* a thoroughly unlikeable person. [Amer Ind]

sky /skaɪ/, *n.* 1. (*oft. pl.*) the area of the clouds or the upper air. 2. (*oft. pl.*) the heavens, appearing as a great arch. 3. (*oft. pl.*) weather; climate: *cloudy skies*. 4. **the sky's the limit**, *Colloq.* There is no limitation. 5. **to the skies**, highly; extravagantly. [ME, from Scand]

skydiving /ˈskaɪdaɪvɪŋ/, *n.* the sport of free-falling from an aeroplane for a great distance, controlling one's course by changes in body position, before opening a parachute. – **skydiver**, *n.*

Skye /skaɪ/, *n.* an island in the Inner Hebrides, off the west coast of Scotland. Pop. 11 327 (1981); 1735 km².

Skylab /ˈskaɪlæb/, *n.* the first US manned orbiting space laboratory, launched in 1973.

skylark¹ /ˈskaɪlɑːk/, *n.* 1. →**lark¹**. 2. any of several native Australian birds known for singing in flight.

skylark² /ˈskaɪlɑːk/, *v.i.* to sport or play about, esp. in high spirits; play tricks.

skylight /ˈskaɪlaɪt/, *n.* an opening in a roof or ceiling, fitted with glass, for letting in daylight.

skyline /ˈskaɪlaɪn/, *n.* 1. the line seeming to divide earth and sky. 2. the outline of something, as city buildings, seen against the sky.

skyrocket /ˈskaɪrɒkət/, *n.* 1. a firework that rises into the air and explodes at a height. ◊*v.i.* 2. to move like a skyrocket. 3. to rise rapidly in amount, position, reputation, etc.

skyscraper /ˈskaɪskreɪpə/, *n.* a tall building of many storeys, esp. one for office or commercial use.

sl., *Abbrev.* (in knitting) slip.

slab /slæb/, *n.* 1. a broad, flat, somewhat thick piece of stone, wood, or other solid material. 2. a thick slice of anything: *a slab of bread*. 3. a rough outside piece cut from a log, as in sawing it into boards. 4. *Colloq.* a mortuary table. [ME; orig. uncert.]

slack /slæk/, *adj.* 1. not stretched tight; loose: *slack rope*. 2. lazy; negligent; remiss. 3. lacking in activity; dull; not brisk: *slack times for business*. 4. (of the water, tide or wind) slow-moving. 5. in a slack manner; slackly. ◊*n.* 6. a slack condition, interval, or part. 7. a part of a rope, sail, or the like, that hangs loose, without strain upon it. ◊*v.t.* 8. to be wanting in respect to (some matter, duty, right, etc.); shirk. 9. to make or allow (effort, labor, etc.) to become less active or strong. 10. to make (rope, etc.) loose; loosen. ◊*v.i.* 11. to avoid one's duty or part. 12. to become less active, rapid, etc. 13. to moderate; slacken. 14. (of a rope, etc.) to ease off. [OE *sleac*, *slæc*]

slapdash

slacken /ˈslækən/, *v.t.*, *v.i.* 1. to make or become less active, intense, etc. 2. to make or become looser or less taut.

slacks /slæks/, *n.pl.* long trousers, worn by men or women.

slag /slæg/, *n.*, *v.*, **slagged, slagging.** ◊*n.* 1. the fused and vitrified matter separated during the smelting or refining of a metal from its ore. 2. the scoria from a volcano. ◊*v.i.* 3. to form slag. [MLG *slagge*] – **slaggy**, *adj.*

slain /sleɪn/, *v.* past participle of **slay**.

slake /sleɪk/, *v.t.*, **slaked, slaking.** 1. to lessen (thirst, desire, anger, etc.) by satisfying. 2. to treat (lime) with water or moist air, causing it to change into calcium hydroxide (**slaked lime**). [OE *slacian*, from *slæc* slack]

slalom /ˈsleɪləm/, *n.* 1. a downhill skiing race over a winding course. 2. similar race for canoes. [Norw]

slam¹ /slæm/, *v.*, **slammed, slamming**, *n.* ◊*v.t.* 1. to shut with force and noise. 2. to hit, throw, etc., with violent and noisy force. 3. *Colloq.* to criticise severely. ◊*v.i.* 4. to shut so as to produce a loud noise. 5. to hit or fall against something with force; crash. ◊*n.* 6. a violent and noisy closing or hitting together. 7. the noise made. [orig. uncert.]

slam² /slæm/, *n. Bridge.* the winning of all the tricks (**grand slam**), or all but one (**little slam**) in one deal. [orig. obscure]

slander /ˈslændə/, *n.* 1. the making of a false statement or report that is damaging to a person's reputation; defamation. 2. such a statement or report; calumny. ◊*v.t.* 3. to speak slander concerning (someone); defame. ◊*v.i.* 4. to speak or spread slander. [ME, from AF, from L: cause of offence] – **slanderer**, *n.* – **slanderous**, *adj.*

slang /slæŋ/, *n.* 1. language that is more informal than standard or written speech in vocabulary and construction, and sometimes regarded as being in some way inferior. 2. language used specially by a particular class, profession, etc.; jargon. [orig. uncert.] – **slangy**, *adj.*

slant /slænt, slɑnt/, *v.i.* 1. to slope. ◊*v.t.* 2. to cause to slope. 3. to present (a piece of writing, story, etc.) in such a way that it emphasises a particular point of view or attracts a particular class of people. ◊*n.* 4. a slanting direction; slope: *the slant of a roof*. 5. a slanting line, surface, etc. 6. attitude or point of view, esp. unusual or unfair; bias. [Scand] – **slanting**, *adj.*

slap /slæp/, *n.*, *v.*, **slapped, slapping**, *adv.* ◊*n.* 1. a smart blow, esp. with the open hand or with something flat. 2. the sound of such a blow. ◊*v.t.* 3. to strike smartly, esp. with the open hand or with something flat. 4. **a.** to put on or apply carelessly or in large quantities: *He slapped paint onto the fence.* **b.** to put or throw forcibly: *She slapped her suitcase down.* ◊*v.* 5. **slap down**, to criticise; crush the enthusiasm of. ◊*adv.* 6. smartly; suddenly. 7. *Colloq.* directly; straight. [LG; imitative]

slapdash /ˈslæpdæʃ/, *adv.* 1. in a hasty, careless manner. ◊*adj.* 2. carelessly hasty.

slapstick /'slæpstɪk/, n. **1.** comedy featuring horseplay and clowning. ◇adj. **2.** marked by the use of slapstick.

slash /slæʃ/, v.t. **1.** to cut with a violent sweeping movement. **2.** to whip; lash. **3.** to reduce greatly; to slash prices. **4.** to make ornamental cuts in (a garment) to show an underlying material. ◇v.i. **5.** to make a sweeping, cutting stroke. ◇n. **6.** a sweeping stroke. **7.** a cut or wound made with such a stroke; gash. [ME, ? from OF: break]

slat /slæt/, n. a long, thin, narrow piece of wood, metal, etc., used as part of a blind, etc. [ME, from OF: piece broken or split off]

slate[1] /sleɪt/, n., v., **slated, slating.** ◇n. **1.** a fine-grained rock formed by the compression of mudstone (a clayey rock), that tends to split along parallel planes, usu. at an angle to the planes of stratification. **2.** a thin piece of this rock or a similar material, used esp. for roofing, or (when framed) for writing on. **3.** a dull, dark bluish grey color. **4. clean slate,** a good record. ◇v.t. **5.** to cover with slate. [ME, from OF: piece broken off]

slate[2] /sleɪt/, v.t., **slated, slating.** Colloq. to criticise severely, esp. in a newspaper review, etc. [special use of SLATE[1]]

slater /'sleɪtə/, n. any of various small crustaceans having a flattened, segmented body, usu. pale brown or greyish in color and found under stones or logs.

slather /'slæðə/, v.t. **1.** to use thickly or in large quantities. ◇n. **2.** a large quantity. **3. open slather, a.** complete freedom; free rein. **b.** an argument or fight in which anyone may join. [Brit d. *slather* to slip, slide, related to *slidder* slippery, *sludder* mud] —**slathering,** n.

slattern /'slætn/, n. a careless, untidy woman or girl. [Brit d. *slatter* to spill] —**slatternly,** adj.

slaughter /'slɔtə/, n. **1.** the killing of cattle, sheep, etc., esp. for food; butchering. **2.** the violent killing of a person. **3.** the killing by violence of great numbers of people. ◇v.t. **4.** to kill (animals), esp. for food; butcher. **5.** to kill (a person) in a violent manner. **6.** to kill (people) in great numbers; massacre. **7.** Colloq. to defeat thoroughly. [ME, from Scand]

Slav /slav/, n. one of a race of people widely spread over eastern, south-eastern, and central Europe, including the Russians and Ruthenians (**Eastern Slavs**), the Serbs, Croats, Slavonians, Slovenes, etc. (**Southern Slavs**), and the Poles, Czechs, Moravians, Slovaks, etc. (**Western Slavs**). [ML *Slavus*. See SLAVE]

slave /sleɪv/, n., v., **slaved, slaving.** ◇n. **1.** someone who is the property of another. **2.** someone who works without payment and is the prisoner of another. **3.** someone who is completely under the influence of another person, a habit, etc.: *She is a slave to her child; a slave to smoking.* **4.** someone who works very hard; a drudge. ◇v.i. **5.** to work like a slave; drudge. [ME, from OF, from ML: slave; SLAV; from the fact that many Slavs were reduced to slavery] —**slavery,** n.

Slave Coast, n. the coast of western equatorial Africa, north of the Gulf of Guinea and between the Benin and Volta Rivers; a centre of slave traffic, 16th—19th centuries.

slaver /'slævə/, v.i. **1.** to let saliva run from the mouth; slobber. **2.** to express great desire by or as if by slavering. ◇n. **3.** saliva coming from the mouth. [ME, from Scand]

Slavic /'slævɪk, 'slɑvɪk/, n. **1.** one of the principal groups of Indo-European languages, usu. divided into **West Slavic** (Polish, Czech, Slovak, Serbian), **East Slavic** (Russian, Ukrainian), and **South Slavic** (Old Church Slavonic, Bulgarian, Serbo-Croat, and Slovene). ◇adj. **2.** of or pertaining to the Slavs, or their languages.

slay /sleɪ/, v.t., **slew, slain, slaying. 1.** to kill by violence. **2.** Colloq. to amuse (someone) greatly. [OE *slēan*]

sleazy /'slizi/, adj., **-zier, -ziest.** untidy and dirty; shabby; sordid. [orig. uncert.]

sled /slɛd/, n., v., **sledded, sledding.** ◇n. **1.** a vehicle on runners for travelling or carrying loads over snow, ice, rough ground, etc. **2.** →**toboggan.** ◇v.t., v.i. **3.** to carry, be carried, or travel on a sled. Also, **sledge.** [ME, from MFlemish or MLG]

sledge /slɛdʒ/, n. →**sled.** [MD]

sledge-hammer /'slɛdʒhæmə/, n. **1.** a large heavy hammer, often held with both hands. ◇v.t. **2.** to strike or knock down with, or as if with, a sledge-hammer. Also, **sledge.**

sleek /slik/, adj. **1.** smooth and shiny: *sleek hair.* **2.** well-fed or well-cared for in appearance. **3.** smooth in manners, speech, etc. ◇v.t. **4.** to make sleek. [var. of SLICK]

sleep /slip/, n., v., **slept, sleeping.** ◇v.i. **1.** to take the rest given by the stopping of bodily activity, closing of the eyes and the natural suspension, complete or partial, of consciousness. **2.** to be in a restful, inactive or inattentive state. ◇v.t. **3.** to take rest in (a particular kind of sleep): *to sleep the sleep of the just.* **4.** to have beds, etc., for: *a caravan that sleeps four.* **5.** to spend or pass (time, etc.) in sleep (fol. by *away* or *out*): *to sleep the hours away.* **6.** to get rid of (a headache, etc.) by sleeping (fol. by *off* or *away*). ◇v. **7. sleep around,** to have many sexual relationships. **8. sleep in,** to sleep later than usual. **9. sleep on it,** to put off a decision, etc. overnight. ◇n. **10.** the condition of being asleep or sleeping. **11.** a period of sleeping. **12.** a state of inactivity. [OE *slēpan, slǣpan*]

sleeper /'slipə/, n. **1.** a wooden, concrete, or steel beam forming part of a railway track, serving as a support for the rails. **2.** →**sleeping car. 3.** a bed in a sleeping-car. **4.** a small ring, bar, etc., worn in the ear after piercing to prevent the hole from closing. **5.** Colloq. someone or something that unexpectedly gains success or fame.

sleeping car, n. a carriage on a passenger train with provision for sleeping overnight.

sleeping sickness, n. a form of inflammation of the brain marked by extreme weakness

sleeping sickness or sleepiness, usu. with paralysis of some cerebral nerves.

sleep-out /'slip-aʊt/, *n.* an enclosed verandah, used as a bedroom.

sleepy /'slipi/, *adj.,* **sleepier, sleepiest. 1.** ready to sleep; drowsy. **2.** quiet: *a sleepy village.*

sleet /slit/, *n.* **1.** rain and snow or hail falling together. ◇*v.i.* **2.** to fall as sleet. [ME]

sleeve /sliv/, *n.* **1.** that part of a garment that covers the arm. **2.** *Mech.* a tube-like piece of metal, fitting over a rod, etc. **3.** a cover for a gramophone record. **4. up one's sleeve,** secretly ready or at hand. [OE *slēfe* (Anglian)] —**sleeved,** *adj.*

sleigh /sleɪ/, *n.* **1.** a vehicle on runners, drawn by horses, dogs, etc., and used for travelling on snow or ice. **2.** →**toboggan.** ◇*v.i.* **3.** to travel or ride in a sleigh. [D]

sleight /slaɪt/, *n.* **1.** skill; dexterity. **2. sleight of hand,** (performance with) skill in using hands quickly in tricks, etc.; legerdemain. [ME, from Scand]

slender /'slɛndə/, *adj.* **1.** thin; slim: *a slender column; a slender girl.* **2.** small in size, amount, etc.: *a slender income.* **3.** having little value or justification: *slender hopes.* [ME; orig. uncert.] —**slenderness,** *n.*

slept /slɛpt/, *v.* past tense and past participle of **sleep.**

Slessor /'slɛsə/, *n.* **Kenneth Adolf,** 1901–71, influential Australian poet and journalist; poems include *Five Bells.*

sleuth /sluθ/, *n.* **1.** *Colloq.* a detective. ◇*v.t., v.i.* **2.** to track or trail as a detective does. [ME, from Scand]

slew[1] /slu/, *v.* past tense of **slay.**

slew[2] /slu/, *v.t., v.i.* **1.** to (cause to) swing or twist round. ◇*n.* **2.** a slewing movement. **3.** a position reached by slewing. [orig. uncert.]

slice /slaɪs/, *n., v.,* **sliced, slicing.** ◇*n.* **1.** a thin, broad, flat piece cut from something: *a slice of bread.* **2.** a part; portion; share: *a slice of the profits.* **3.** a type of tool with a thin, broad blade or part for turning food in a frying pan, or taking up printing ink, etc. **4.** *Sport.* a slicing stroke, kick, hit, etc. ◇*v.t.* **5.** to cut into slices. **6.** to cut through like a knife: *The ship sliced the sea.* **7.** to cut (*off, away, from,* etc.) as or like a slice. **8.** *Sport.* to hit or kick (the ball) so that it does not travel along the line of force of the stroke. [ME, from OF: splinter, sliver of wood, from Gmc]

slick /slɪk/, *adj.* **1.** smooth or smart in appearance; sleek; glossy. **2.** clever and smooth, but not sincere, in manners, speech, etc.: *a slick salesman.* **3.** cleverly worked out or performed: *a slick plan.* ◇*n.* **4.** a smooth place or spot, such as an oil-covered area on the sea. ◇*v.t.* **5.** to make smooth or sleek. [ME]

slide /slaɪd/, *v.,* **slid, slid** or **slidden, sliding,** *n.* ◇*v.i.* **1.** to move along in continuous contact with a smooth or slippery surface: *to slide down a snow-covered hill.* **2.** to slip, as by loosing hold or grip, etc.: *She slid on the uneven ground; The book slid from his hand.* **3.** to pass smoothly onwards; glide. **4.** to go or pass easily, quietly, or unnoticed (fol. by *in, out, away,* etc.): *They slid out the back door; The information has slid from my mind.* **5.** to go unregarded or neglected: *to let things slide.* **6.** to pass or fall gradually into a particular condition, practice, etc.: *to slide into despair.* ◇*v.t.* **7.** to cause to slide. **8.** to put (something) easily or quietly (fol. by *in, into,* etc.). ◇*n.* **9.** an act of sliding. **10.** a framed piece of film for showing in a projector; transparency (def. 2). **11.** a plate of glass or other material on which objects are placed for microscopic examination. **12.** Also, **hair slide.** a pin for holding a woman's hair in place. **13.** something which slides, as part of a machine. **14.** *Music.* **a.** an ornament consisting of an upward or downward series of three or more notes, the last of which is the main note. **b.** (in the trombone, etc.) a section of the tube, usu. U-shaped, which can be pushed in or out to alter the length of the air column and thus the pitch of the notes. [OE *slīdan*] —**slider,** *n.*

slide rule, *n.* an instrument for rapid calculation, consisting of a rule with a sliding piece moving along it, both marked with graduated logarithmic scales.

slight /slaɪt/, *adj.* **1.** small in amount, degree, etc.: *a slight increase; a slight smell.* **2.** of little weight, or importance. **3.** slender; slim. **4.** lacking strength or solidity; frail; flimsy. ◇*v.t.* **5.** to treat as of slight importance; treat with indifference. ◇*n.* **6.** (an instance of) slighting treatment. [OE *sliht* smooth (in *eorthslihtes* close to earth)] —**slightness,** *n.*

slim /slɪm/, *adj.,* **slimmer, slimmest,** *v.,* **slimmed, slimming.** ◇*adj.* **1.** slender; slight in build or structure. **2.** poor; barely enough; meagre: *a slim chance; a slim excuse.* ◇*v.i.* **3.** to make oneself slim, by dieting, exercise, etc. [D or LG]

slime /slaɪm/, *n.* **1.** thin, sticky mud. **2.** any similar liquid matter, esp. of an offensive kind. [OE *slīm*]

slime mould, *n.* a group of primitive organisms showing characteristics of both the animal and plant kingdoms.

slimy /'slaɪmi/, *adj.,* **slimier, slimiest,** *n.* ◇*adj.* **1.** of, like or covered with slime. **2.** offensive; repulsive. **3.** *Colloq.* unpleasantly humble or servile. ◇*n.* **4.** a worm found on the southern and eastern coast of Australia, greenish in color and commonly used for bait. Also, **slimey.** —**slimily,** *adv.* —**sliminess,** *n.*

sling /slɪŋ/, *n., v.,* **slung, slinging.** ◇*n.* **1.** Also, **slingshot.** an instrument for throwing stones, etc., by hand, consisting of a piece of leather for holding the object to be thrown, and two strings, the ends of which are held while the whole is whirled rapidly before throwing out the stone, etc. **2.** →**catapult** (def. 1). **3.** a piece of cloth looped around the neck and used to hold an injured arm or hand. **4.** a rope, strap, band, etc., forming a loop by which something is raised, lowered, carried, or allowed to hang. **5.** *Colloq.* money given as a bribe. ◇*v.t.* **6.** to throw; fling. **7.** to raise, lower, etc., by means of a sling. **8.** to hang in a sling or

sling so as to swing loosely: *He slung his rifle over his shoulder.* ◇*v.i.* **9.** to give money as a bribe. ◇*v.* **10. sling off,** *Colloq.* to make fun of someone; jeer (fol. by *at*). [ME, from Scand]

slingshot /'slɪŋʃɒt/, *n.* → **sling** (def. 1).

slink /slɪŋk/, *v.i.*, **slunk, slinking.** to move in a secretive or humble manner, from fear, shame, etc. [OE *slincan* creep, crawl]

slinky /'slɪŋki/, *adj. Colloq.* **1.** graceful, slender and flowing; sinuous. **2.** secretive in movement; stealthy.

slip[1] /slɪp/, *v.*, **slipped, slipping,** *n.* ◇*v.i.* **1.** to pass or go smoothly or easily; slide (fol. by *along, away, down, off, over, through,* etc.): *Water slips off a smooth surface.* **2.** to lose one's footing and fall: *He slipped on the polished floor.* **3.** to move or slide from position, fastening, the hold, etc.: *The glass slipped from her hand.* **4.** to go, come, get, etc., easily or quickly (fol. by *into* or *out of*): *to slip into a dress.* **5.** to pass quietly or without notice; steal: *Time slips by.* **6.** to become reduced or weaker: *My memory is slipping.* **7.** to make a mistake (oft. fol. by *up*). ◇*v.t.* **8.** to cause to slip, pass, put, draw, etc., with a smooth, easy, or sliding movement: *to slip a letter into a drawer.* **9.** to put (*on*) or take (*off*) easily or quickly: *to slip on a coat.* **10.** to let slip from fastenings, the hold, etc. **11.** to get free or escape from: *The dog slipped his leash.* **12.** to untie or undo (a knot). **13.** to pass over or omit, as in speaking, writing or thought. **14.** to escape (one's memory, notice, knowledge, etc.): *That fact slipped my mind.* **15.** (of animals) to bring forth (offspring) prematurely. ◇*v.* **16. let slip,** to say or reveal without intending to. ◇*n.* **17.** a slipping of the feet, as on slippery ground. **18.** a mistake. **19.** a woman's sleeveless underdress. **20.** a pillowcase. **21.** → **slipway. 22.** *Cricket.* (the position of) a fielder who stands behind and to the offside of the wicket-keeper. **23.** *Geol.* **a.** a smooth joint or crack where the strata have moved upon each other. **b.** the relative displacement of formerly adjacent points on opposite sides of a fault, measured in the fault plane. **c.** a form of landslide caused by the downhill movement of a mass of soil when saturated. **24. give (someone) the slip,** to escape from (someone). [ME, from MLG]

slip[2] /slɪp/, *n.* **1.** a piece cut from a plant for planting or grafting; a cutting. **2.** any long, narrow piece, as of wood, paper, land, etc. **3.** a young person, esp. one of slender form: *a slip of a girl.* [ME, from MD or MLG: cut, slit, strip, etc.]

slipknot /'slɪpnɒt/, *n.* a knot which slips easily along the cord or line round which it is made.

slipped disc, *n.* the displacement of a disc between two vertebrae, often responsible for pain in the back radiating down the back of the leg.

slipper /'slɪpə/, *n.* a light indoor shoe into which the foot may be easily slipped.

slippery /'slɪpəri, 'slɪpri/, *adj.*, **-perier, -periest. 1.** tending to slip or cause slipping: *slippery soap; slippery ground.* **2.** not to be depended on; fickle; unstable. [OE *slipor*] **– slipperiness,** *n.*

slippery dip, *n.* a structure with a smooth slope for children to slide down for amusement. Also, **slippery slide.**

sliprail /'slɪpreɪl/, *n.* one of a number of movable rails in a fence which can be taken out in order to make a gateway.

slipshod /'slɪpʃɒd/, *adj.* untidy; careless or negligent.

slipstream /'slɪpstrim/, *n. Aeron.* an air current forced back by a moving object, esp. an aircraft propeller or jet.

slipway /'slɪpweɪ/, *n.* a sloping plane or ramp, esp. one serving as a landing place for boats or a place on which boats are built or repaired.

slit /slɪt/, *v.*, **slit, slitting,** *n.* ◇*v.t.* **1.** to cut apart or open along a line; make a long cut in. **2.** to cut or tear into long thin pieces. ◇*n.* **3.** a straight, narrow cut or opening. [OE *-slittan* (Nthn d.)]

slither /'slɪðə/, *v.i.* **1.** to slide down or along a surface, esp. unsteadily. **2.** to go with a sliding movement, as a snake. ◇*n.* **3.** a slithering movement. [ME; var. of d. *slidder,* from OE *slīdan* SLIDE]

sliver /'slɪvə/, *n.* **1.** a small, thin piece of wood, etc., broken, or cut off; splinter. ◇*v.i., v.t.* **2.** to break or cut into slivers. [OE *slīfan* split]

slob /slɒb/, *Colloq.* a stupid, coarse, dirty, or untidy person. [Irish *slab* mud, from obs. E *slab* thick in consistency]

slobber /'slɒbə/, *v.i.* **1.** to let saliva, etc., run from the mouth; dribble. **2.** to behave with sickly sentimentality. ◇*n.* **3.** saliva running from the mouth; dribble. [var. of *slabber.* See SLOB] **– slobbery,** *adj.*

sloe-eyed /'sloʊ-aɪd/, *adj.* having attractively dark, narrow eyes.

slog /slɒg/, *v.*, **slogged, slogging,** *n. Colloq.* ◇*v.t.* **1.** to hit hard. ◇*v.i.* **2.** to give heavy blows. **3.** to walk steadily and firmly; plod. **4.** to work hard. ◇*n.* **5.** a strong, rough blow. **6.** a period of hard work or walking. [var. of SLUG[1], *v.*]

slogan /'sloʊgən/, *n.* a striking phrase used to advertise a product or sum up the aims, beliefs, etc., of a political party or other group; catchword. [Gaelic *sluagh-ghairm* army cry]

sloop /slup/, *n.* a single-masted sailing vessel carrying fore-and-aft sails. [D]

slop /slɒp/, *v.*, **slopped, slopping,** *n.* ◇*v.t.* **1.** to spill or splash (liquid). ◇*v.i.* **2.** to spill or splash liquid (sometimes fol. by *about*). **3.** (of liquid) to spill over. **4.** *Colloq.* (of people, etc.) to be too sentimental; gush (fol. by *over*). **5.** to walk or go through mud, water, etc. ◇*n.* **6.** a quantity of liquid spilled or splashed about. **7.** (*oft. pl.*) unattractive liquid or half liquid food. **8.** (*oft. pl.*) the dirty water, liquid waste, etc., of a household, etc. [ME *sloppe* mudhole, OE *-sloppe* (in *cusloppe* cowslip, lit., cow slime)]

slope /sloʊp/, v., **sloped, sloping**, n. ◇v.t., v.i. **1.** to (cause to) have a slanting direction. ◇n. **2.** a downwards or upwards slant; inclination. **3.** a slanting surface. **4.** (oft. pl.) an area of sloping ground. [from *aslope*, adv., on a slant]

sloppy /'slɒpi/, adj., **-pier, -piest. 1.** muddy, or very wet; slushy. **2.** (of food, etc.) watery and unattractive. **3.** *Colloq.* sentimental; maudlin. **4.** *Colloq.* loose, careless, or untidy: *to use sloppy English.* — **sloppily**, adv. — **sloppiness**, n.

slosh /slɒʃ/, n. **1.** → slush. **2.** *Colloq.* a heavy blow. ◇v.i. **3.** to splash in mud, water, etc. ◇v.t. **4.** to pour, stir, spread, etc., a liquid (oft. fol. by *in, on, round*, etc.). **5.** to hit or punch. [b. SLOP and SLUSH]

slot /slɒt/, n., v., **slotted, slotting**. ◇n. **1.** a long, narrow opening or hollow, esp. one to receive something: *Put a coin in the slot.* **2.** a position within a system: *He soon found his slot in the organisation.* ◇v.t. **3.** to make a slot in. **4.** to put into a slot (usu. fol. by *in*). [ME, from OF: hollow between breasts]

sloth /sloʊθ/, n. **1.** habitual dislike of work, activity, etc.; laziness. **2.** *Zool.* either of two kinds of slow-moving mammals of tropical America that live in trees: **the two-toed sloth**, and **the three-toed sloth**. [ME *slowth* (SLOW + -TH¹)] — **slothful**, adj.

slouch /slaʊtʃ/, v.i. **1.** to sit, stand or move in an awkward, drooping manner. ◇v.t. **2.** to cause to droop or bend down: *to slouch the shoulders.* ◇n. **3.** an awkward drooping or bending forward of the head and shoulders. **4.** a drooping or hanging down of the brim of a hat, etc. **5.** *Colloq.* an awkward, unskilful person. [orig. uncert.]

slouch hat, n. **1.** an army hat of soft felt, having a brim which can be joined to the crown on one side to allow a rifle to be carried on the shoulder. **2.** such a hat regarded in Australia as a symbol of courage, or national feeling (particularly associated with Australian soldiers in World War I).

slough¹ /slaʊ/, n. **1.** a piece of soft, muddy ground; swamp. **2.** a condition of despair, helplessness, etc. [OE *slōh*]

slough² /slʌf/, n. **1.** the skin of a snake, esp. the outer skin which is shed periodically. **2.** *Med.* a layer of dead tissue which separates from the surrounding or underlying tissue. ◇v.i. **3.** to be shed or thrown off, as the slough of a snake. ◇v.t. **4.** to shed or throw (sometimes fol. by *off*): *He decided to slough off his bad habits*; *The snake sloughed its skin.* [ME]

Slovakia /sloʊ'vækiə, -'vɑkiə/, n. a republic in central Europe, bordered by the Czech Republic, Poland, Ukraine, Hungary and Austria; a constituent republic of Czechoslovakia before becoming an independent nation in 1993. Pop. 5 268 935 (1991); 48 667 km². *Language:* Slovak. *Currency:* koruna. *Cap.:* Bratislava. Official name, **Slovak Republic**. Slovak, **Slovenská Republika**.

sloven /'slʌvən/, n. someone who is dirty, careless, or untidy. [ME] — **slovenly**, adj., adv. — **slovenliness**, n.

slow /sloʊ/, adj. **1.** taking or needing a comparatively long time for moving, going, acting, happening, etc.; not fast or rapid; inactive; sluggish. **2.** (of a person, the mind, etc.) dull of understanding. **3.** having low heat: *a slow fire*; *a slow oven*. **4.** slack, as trade. **5.** (of a clock, etc.) showing a time earlier than the correct time. **6.** dull, uninteresting or tedious. **7.** *Sport.* (of a pitch, track, court, etc.) tending to prevent fast movement. ◇v.t., v.i. **8.** to make or become slow or slower (oft. fol. by *up, down*, etc.). [OE *slāw* sluggish, dull] — **slowness**, n.

slowcoach /'sloʊkoʊtʃ/, n. *Colloq.* a slow or dull person.

slow-motion /'sloʊ-moʊʃən/, adj. relating to films in which the images move more slowly than their originals, due to having been photographed at a greater number of frames per second than normal, or being projected more slowly than normal.

sludge /slʌdʒ/, n. **1.** soft mud; slush. **2.** any of various mudlike deposits or mixtures. **3.** sediment deposited during the treatment of sewage. [ME *slich* slime; ? imitative] — **sludgy**, adj.

slug¹ /slʌg/, n. **1.** any of various small, slimy molluscs related to the land snails, but having no shell or only a rudimentary one. **2.** a piece of metal for firing from a gun. **3.** *Print.* **a.** a thick strip of type metal less than type-high. **b.** a line of type in one piece, as produced by a linotype machine. [ME, from Scand]

slug² /slʌg/, v., **slugged, slugging**, n. ◇v.t. **1.** to hit hard, esp. with the fist; slog. **2.** *Colloq.* to charge heavy payment: *He slugged you for this car.* ◇n. **3.** a heavy blow, esp. with the fist. **4.** *Colloq.* a high price or tax. [? orig., hit with a slug (piece of lead)]

sluggard /'slʌgəd/, n. **1.** someone who is habitually inactive or lazy. ◇adj. **2.** lazy. [ME *slogard*(e), from obs. *sluggy* sluggish + -ARD] — **sluggardly**, adv.

sluggish /'slʌgɪʃ/, adj. inactive, slow, or of little energy or vigor.

sluice /slus/, n., v., **sluiced, sluicing**. ◇n. **1.** a channel built for carrying water, fitted with a gate for controlling the flow. **2.** a body of water held back or controlled by a sluicegate. **3.** any device for controlling a flow from or into a container. **4.** any channel, esp. one carrying off extra water; drain. **5.** *Mining.* a long, sloping trough into which water is directed to separate gold from gravel or sand. ◇v.t. **6.** to let out (water, etc.) or draw off the contents of (a pond, etc.) by, or as if by, the opening of a sluice. **7.** to wash with running water. ◇v.i. **8.** to flow or pour through or as if through a sluice. [ME, from OF, from LL: shut out]

slum /slʌm/, n., v., **slummed, slumming**. ◇n. **1.** (oft. pl.) an overpopulated part of a city, with low-standard housing, lived in by the poorest people. **2.** a dirty, low-standard street, place, house, etc. ◇v.i. **3.** to visit slums, esp. for reasons of curiosity or charity. ◇v. **4.**

slum it, *Colloq.* to live in conditions below one's usual or expected standard of living. [first occurs as slang word for room; orig. obscure] — **slummy**, *adj.*

slumber /ˈslʌmbə/, *v.i.* **1.** to sleep, esp. deeply. **2.** to be in a state of inactivity, calm, etc. ◊*v.t.* **3.** to spend (time) in slumbering (fol. by *away*, etc.). ◊*n.* **4.** (*oft. pl.*) sleep, esp. deep sleep. **5.** a state of calm, inactivity, etc. [OE *slūma*] — **slumberous, slumbrous**, *adj.*

slump /slʌmp/, *v.i.* **1.** to drop heavily and loosely: *She slumped into a chair.* **2.** to sink heavily: *His spirits slumped at the bad news.* **3.** to slow down markedly in progress, growth, etc.: *The share market slumped.* ◊*n.* **4.** an act of slumping. **5.** a marked slowing down in the growth of the economy, market, prices, etc. [v. use of Brit d. *slump* bog]

slung /slʌŋ/, *v.* past tense and past participle of **sling**.

slunk /slʌŋk/, *v.* past tense and past participle of **slink**.

slur /slɜ/, *v.*, **slurred, slurring**, *n.* ◊*v.t.* **1.** to pass over without due mention or consideration (oft. fol. by *over*). **2.** to pronounce (a syllable, word, etc.) unclearly, as in hurried or careless speech. **3.** *Music.* to sing in a single breath, or play without a break (two or more notes of different pitch). **4.** to speak of (someone) so as to harm their reputation, etc. ◊*n.* **5.** slurred speech or sound. **6.** *Music.* **a.** a combination of two or more notes of different pitch, sung to a single syllable or played without a break. **b.** a curved mark indicating this. **7.** a remark that is harmful to reputation, etc. **8.** harm done to reputation, etc.; discredit: *a slur on his good name.* [Brit d. *slur* fluid mud]

slurp /slɜp/, *v.i.*, *v.t.* **1.** to eat or drink (something) with a lot of noise. ◊*n.* **2.** the noise thus produced. [MD *slorpen* to sip]

slurry /ˈslʌri/, *n.* a half fluid mixture of clay, or cement, etc., and water.

slush /slʌʃ/, *n.* **1.** snow in a partly melted state. **2.** watery mud. **3.** *Colloq.* sentimental, or weakly emotional writing, talk, etc. [Scand] — **slushy**, *adj.*

slush fund, *n.* money for use in political campaigns, etc., esp. secretly or illegally, as in bribery.

slut /slʌt/, *n.* **1.** a dirty, untidy woman. **2.** a sexually immoral woman. [ME] — **sluttish**, *adj.*

sly /slaɪ/, *adj.*, **slyer, slyest** or **slier, sliest**. **1.** cunning or deceitful: *a sly person; a sly plan.* **2.** playfully mischievous; roguish: *sly humor.* **3. on the sly**, secretly. [ME, from Scand]

Sm, *Chem. Symbol.* samarium.

SM, *Abbrev.* stipendiary magistrate.

smack¹ /smæk/, *n.* **1.** a slight taste or flavor, esp. one that is suggestive of something. **2.** a trace or suggestion of something. ◊*v.i.* **3.** to have a trace or suggestion (fol. by *of*). [OE *smæc*]

smack² /smæk/, *v.t.* **1.** to hit smartly, esp. with the open hand or anything flat. **2.** to bring, put, throw, send, etc., with a smart blow or stroke that produces a sharp sound. **3.** to separate (the lips) smartly so as to produce a sharp sound, often as a sign of pleasure. ◊*n.* **4.** a smart blow, esp. with something flat, producing a sharp sound. **5.** a loud kiss. **6.** a smacking of the lips. **7.** *Colloq.* heroin. **8. smack in the eye**, **a.** a snub. **b.** a disappointment. ◊*adv.* **9.** *Colloq.* with a smack; suddenly and sharply. **10.** *Colloq.* directly; straight. [of imitative orig.]

smack³ /smæk/, *n.* a sailing boat, usu. rigged as a sloop, used in fishing, etc. [D *smak*]

small /smɔl/, *adj.* **1.** of comparatively limited size; not big; little. **2.** not great in amount, degree, extent, duration, value, etc. **3.** not great in numbers. **4.** having only little land, capital, investment, etc.: *a small businessman.* **5.** marked by littleness of mind or character; ungenerous. **6.** ashamed or embarrassed: *to feel small.* **7.** (of sound or the voice) gentle, soft, or low. ◊*adv.* **8.** in a small manner or on a small scale: *to start small.* **9.** into small pieces: *to slice small.* ◊*n.* **10.** the lower central part of the back. [OE *smæl*]

small change, *n.* **1.** coins of small value. **2.** something which is ordinary, common or of little value.

small circle, *n.* a circle on a sphere, whose plane does not pass through the centre of the sphere.

small end, *n.* the end of a connecting rod in an engine which is connected to the piston or the piston rod.

smallgoods /ˈsmɔlɡʊdz/, *n.pl.* goods sold in a delicatessen, esp. meats such as sausages.

small intestine, *n.* See **intestine**.

smallpox /ˈsmɔlpɒks/, *n.* an acute, highly infectious disease marked by fever and pustular sores which often leave permanent scars.

small talk, *n.* light, unimportant talk; chitchat.

small-time /ˈsmɔl-taɪm/, *adj. Colloq.* of little importance.

smarmy /ˈsmami/, *adj.* falsely charming or flattering.

smart /smat/, *v.i.* **1.** to be a cause of sharp, surface pain, as a wound, blow, etc. **2.** to feel a sharp pain, as in a wounded surface. **3.** to suffer from keen emotion, such as hurt, anger, etc. ◊*adj.* **4.** sharp or keen: *a smart slap on the arm.* **5.** sharply active or vigorous: *a smart walk.* **6.** intelligent; clever. **7.** cleverly ready or effective: *a smart reply.* **8.** effectively neat in appearance. **9.** stylish; fashionable. ◊*adv.* **10.** in a smart manner. ◊*n.* **11.** a feeling of smarting. [OE *smeortan*]

smart alec /ˈsmat ælək/, *n. Colloq.* someone who likes to show their own knowledge or cleverness. Also, **smart aleck**.

smarten /ˈsmatn/, *v.t.* (sometimes fol. by *up*) **1.** to make smarter in appearance. **2.** to quicken (the pace, etc.).

smash /smæʃ/, *v.t.* **1.** to break to pieces with violence and often with a crashing sound; shatter. **2.** to defeat, ruin or destroy. **3.**

smash

Tennis. to hit (the ball) hard and fast with an overhead stroke. ◇*v.i.* **4.** to break to pieces. **5.** to move with great violence; crash (fol. by *against*, *into*, *through*, etc.). ◇*n.* **6.** a smashing, or the sound of it. **7.** a violent and destructive collision. **8.** a process or condition of failure, ruin, or destruction, esp. in financial affairs. **9.** Also, **smash-hit.** a play, film, etc., that is immediately very successful. **10.** *Tennis.* a forceful overhead stroke. [? b. SMACK² and MASH]

smashed /smæʃt/, *adj. Colloq.* completely under the influence of a drug, alcohol, etc.

smashing /ˈsmæʃɪŋ/, *adj. Colloq.* extremely good; excellent.

smattering /ˈsmætərɪŋ/, *n.* a slight knowledge: *I have only a smattering of French.* [ME, from Scand]

smear /smɪə/, *v.t.* **1.** to rub or spread with oil, grease, paint, dirt, etc. **2.** to spread (oil, grease, etc.) on or over something. **3.** to rub something over (a thing) so as to cause a blurred mark or smudge. **4.** to harm (someone's reputation); defame. ◇*n.* **5.** a mark or stain made by smearing. **6.** something smeared on a thing, as a glaze for pottery, or a substance put on a slide for microscopic examination. **7.** an act of defamation; slander. [OE *smeoru*]

smear test, *n.* → **Pap smear.**

smell /smɛl/, *v.*, **smelled** or **smelt, smelling,** *n.* ◇*v.i.* **1.** to sense through the nerves of the nose; be aware of the odor of. **2.** to test by sensing through the nose: *to smell food to tell if it's bad.* **3.** to be aware of by sense or instinct: *smell danger.* **4.** to search or find as if by smelling (fol. by *out*). ◇*v.i.* **5.** to have the sense of smell. **6.** to search, as if by using the sense of smell (usu. fol. by *around*). **7.** to give out an odor: *Those flowers smell sweet.* **8.** to have the odor (fol. by *of*): *This room smells of medicine.* **9.** to seem or be unpleasant or bad. ◇*n.* **10.** the sense of smelling. **11.** that quality of a thing which is or may be smelled; odor. **12.** the act of smelling. [ME; orig. uncert.]

smelling salts, *n.pl.* a preparation of ammonium carbonate with some agreeable scent, smelled to relieve faintness, headache, etc.

smelly /ˈsmɛli/, *adj.*, **smellier, smelliest.** giving out a strong or offensive smell.

smelt¹ /smɛlt/, *v.t.* **1.** to fuse or melt (ore) in order to separate the metal contained. **2.** to obtain or refine (metal) in this way. [MD or MLG] — **smelter,** *n.*

smelt² /smɛlt/, *n., pl.* **smelts,** (*esp. collectively*) **smelt.** a small silvery food fish of Europe. [ME and OE]

smidgin /ˈsmɪdʒən/, *n.* very small quantity; bit. Also, **smidgen, smidgeon.** [Brit d.]

smile /smaɪl/, *v.*, **smiled, smiling,** *n.* ◇*v.i.* **1.** to widen the mouth usu. with an upward turn of the lips, to show pleasure, favor, kindliness, amusement, etc. **2.** to look with such an expression, esp. (fol. by *at*, *on*, or *upon*) in a pleasant or kindly way, or (fol. by *at*) in amusement. ◇*v.t.* **3.** to express by a smile: *to smile approval.* ◇*n.* **4.** the act of smiling; a

smiling expression of the face. **5.** a favoring look or regard: *fortune's smile.* [ME]

smirch /smɜtʃ/, *v.t.* **1.** to discolor or soil with some substance, as soot, dust, dirt, etc. **2.** to harm (a reputation, etc.); smear; tarnish. ◇*n.* **3.** a dirty mark or smear. **4.** a stain or smear, as on reputation. [ME]

smirk /smɜk/, *v.i.* **1.** to smile in an affected, would-be agreeable, or offensively familiar way. ◇*n.* **2.** the smile or the facial expression of one who smirks. [OE *sme(a)rcian*]

smite /smaɪt/, *v.*, **smote** or (*old form*) **smit; smitten** or **smit; smiting.** **1.** to strike or hit hard, as with the hand, a stick or weapon, etc. **2.** to strike down or kill. **3.** to affect mentally with a sudden feeling: *His conscience smote him.* **4.** to affect suddenly and strongly with a specified feeling: *smitten with terror.* **5.** to impress favorably; charm; enamor: *smitten by her beauty.* [OE *smītan*]

smith /smɪθ/, *n.* **1.** someone who works in metal. **2.** → **blacksmith.** [ME and OE]

Smith /smɪθ/, *n.* **1. Sir Charles Edward Kingsford** → Sir Charles **Kingsford Smith.** **2. Sir Keith (MacPherson),** 1890–1955, Australian pioneer aviator. **3. Maria Ann** ('*Granny Smith*'), c. 1801–70, Australian pioneer; first cultivated the Granny Smith apple at Eastwood, Sydney. **4. Sir Ross,** 1892–1922, brother of Sir Keith, Australian pioneer aviator.

Smith Family, *n.* an Australian welfare organisation established in Sydney in 1922 by five businessmen who chose to remain anonymous and so assumed the name of Smith; operating also in Vic and the ACT.

Smithsonian Institution /smɪθˌsouniən ɪnstɪˈtjuʃən/, *n.* a group of US scientific and cultural institutes, many in Washington, DC, founded in 1846 with a grant left by James Smithson.

Smith's Weekly /smɪθs ˈwikli/, *n.* a newspaper published first in 1919 in Sydney; preserved the 'digger' image and was renowned for its cartoons; ceased publication in 1950. [named after JJJ *Smith*, founder and principal proprietor]

smithy /ˈsmɪθi, ˈsmɪði/, *n., pl.* **smithies.** the workshop of a smith, esp. a blacksmith; forge.

smitten /ˈsmɪtn/, *adj.* **1.** struck, as with a hard blow. **2.** stricken with disease, etc. **3.** *Colloq.* very much in love. ◇*v.* **4.** past participle of **smite.**

smock /smɒk/, *n.* **1.** any loose overgarment, esp. one worn to protect the clothing while at work: *an artist's smock.* ◇*v.t.* **2.** to draw together (a fabric) by needlework into a honeycomb pattern. [OE *smocc*; orig. name of garment with a hole for the head]

smog /smɒg/, *n.* a mixture of smoke and fog. — **smoggy,** *adj.*

smoke /smouk/, *n., v.,* **smoked, smoking.** ◇*n.* **1.** a white, grey, brown or blackish cloud given off by a burning substance such as wood, coal, peat, paper, tobacco, etc. **2.** an act of smoking tobacco, etc. **3.** something which is smoked, as a cigar or cigarette. **4. go**

or **end up in smoke**, **a.** to be burnt up completely. **b.** to have no solid result; end or disappear without coming to anything. **5. go into smoke**, *Colloq.* to disappear. ◇*v.i.* **6.** to give off or emit smoke: *the chimney smoked.* **7.** to draw into the mouth and puff out the smoke of tobacco, etc., as from a pipe, cigar, or cigarette. ◇*v.t.* **8.** to draw into the mouth and puff out the smoke of (tobacco, etc.). **9.** to use (a pipe, cigarette, etc.) in this process. **10.** →**fumigate. 11.** to color or darken by smoke. **12.** to cure (meat, fish, etc.) with smoke. **13.** to drive by means of smoke, as an animal or a person from a hiding place (fol. by *out*, etc.). [OE *smoca*]

smokescreen /'smoʊkskrin/, *n.* **1.** a mass of dense smoke produced to hide an area, vessel, or aeroplane from the enemy. **2.** any device or trick used for hiding the truth, as an unnecessarily long explanation.

smokestack /'smoʊkstæk/, *n.* a pipe for the escape of the smoke or gases of burning fuel, as on a steamship, railway engine, or building, esp. a factory.

smoko /'smoʊkoʊ/, *n. Colloq.* a rest from work; tea-break. Also, **smoke-o, smoke-oh.**

smoky /'smoʊki/, *adj.*, **smokier, smokiest. 1.** giving off smoke, or much smoke, as a fire, a torch, etc. **2.** hazy; darkened or grimy with smoke. **3.** having the character, appearance or color of smoke.

smooch /smutʃ/, *Colloq.* ◇*v.i.* **1.** to kiss; cuddle; behave lovingly. ◇*n.* **2.** the act of smooching. [orig. unknown]

smoodge /smudʒ/, *v.i. Colloq.* **1.** to kiss; caress. **2.** to praise insincerely; curry favor. Also, **smooge**. [probably from Brit *d.*]

smooth /smuð/, *adj.* **1.** free from roughness or unevenness of surface: *Satin is a smooth fabric; a tyre worn smooth; a smooth road.* **2.** free from hairs or hairy growth. **3.** generally flat or unruffled, as a calm sea. **4.** of uniform consistency; free from lumps, as a sauce, etc. **5.** free from unevenness or roughness: *smooth driving.* **6.** easy and uniform, as an outline, motion, the working of a machine, etc. **7.** free from hindrances or difficulties: *a smooth path in life.* **8.** easy, flowing, elegant, or polished, as speech, a speaker, etc. **9.** pleasant, agreeable, or insincerely polite, as manner, people, etc.; bland or suave. **10.** *Tennis.* of or relating to the back of a racquet (from the texture of the strings on that side). ◇*adv.* **11.** in a smooth manner; smoothly. ◇*v.t.* **12.** to make smooth of surface, as by scraping, planing, pressing, stroking, etc. (sometimes fol. by *down*). **13.** to remove (lumps, etc.) in making something smooth (oft. fol. by *away* or *out*). **14.** to calm or soothe, as the feelings. **15.** to ease or improve, as something unpleasant or wrong (usu. fol. by *over*): *Her kindness smoothed over the waiter's accident.* ◇*n.* **16.** that which is smooth; a smooth part or place: *Take the rough with the smooth.* [OE *smōth*]

smorgasbord /'smɔgəzbɔd/, *n.* a buffet meal of various hot and cold hors d'oeuvres, salads, meat dishes, etc. [Swed. *smörgås* sandwich + *bord* table]

smote /smoʊt/, *v.* past tense of **smite**.

smother /'smʌðə/, *v.t.* **1.** to stifle or suffocate, esp. by smoke or by cutting off the air necessary for life. **2.** to put out or deaden (fire, etc.) by covering so as to keep out air. **3.** to cover closely or thickly (oft. fol. by *up, in*). **4.** to surround with love, kindness, etc., to such an extent that it prevents personal development. **5.** to repress, as feelings, impulses, etc.; stifle: *to smother laughter.* ◇*v.i.* **6.** to be prevented from breathing freely. ◇*n.* **7.** dense, stifling smoke. [OE *smorian* suffocate]

smoulder /'smoʊldə/, *v.i.* **1.** to burn or smoke without flame. **2.** to exist or continue in a suppressed state or without outward appearance: *Unrest continued to smoulder despite police action.* **3.** to display repressed feelings, esp. of indignation: *His eyes smouldered.* ◇*n.* **4.** dense smoke resulting from slow or suppressed burning. **5.** a smouldering fire. [ME *smoulder* smoky vapor]

smudge /smʌdʒ/, *n.*, *v.*, **smudged, smudging.** ◇*n.* **1.** a dirty mark or smear. ◇*v.t., v.i.* **2.** to mark or become marked with dirty streaks or smears. [ME; orig. uncert.]

smug /smʌg/, *adj.*, **smugger, smuggest.** complacently proper, righteous, clever, etc.; self-satisfied. [? D: neat]

smuggle /'smʌgəl/, *v.*, **-gled, -gling.** ◇*v.t.* **1.** to import or export (goods) secretly or illegally, without payment of duty. **2.** to bring, take, put, etc., secretly: *She smuggled the gun into prison.* ◇*v.i.* **3.** to smuggle goods. [LG] –**smuggler**, *n.*

smut /smʌt/, *n.*, *v.*, **smutted, smutting.** ◇*n.* **1.** a tiny piece of soot; sooty matter. **2.** a black or dirty mark; a smudge. **3.** offensive talk or writing; obscenity. **4.** a fungous disease of plants, esp. cereals, in which the affected parts are converted into a black powdery mass of spores. **5.** the fungus itself. ◇*v.i.* **6.** to become affected with smut, as a plant. [OE *smitte*] –**smutty**, *adj.*

Sn, *Chem. Symbol.* tin. [L *stannum*]

snack /snæk/, *n.* **1.** a small amount of food or drink; light meal. **2.** *Colloq.* anything easily done. [n. use of *snack*, v., snap]

snaffle[1] /'snæfəl/, *n.* a slender, jointed bit used on a bridle. [? D: beak, mouth]

snaffle[2] /'snæfəl/, *v.t.*, **-fled, -fling.** *Colloq.* to steal.

snag /snæg/, *n.*, *v.*, **snagged, snagging.** ◇*n.* **1.** a short, projecting stump, as of a branch broken or cut off. **2.** any sharp or rough projection. **3.** a tree or part of a tree held fast in the bottom of a river or other water which is a danger to navigation. **4.** any obstacle or impediment: *to strike a snag in carrying out plans.* **5.** a pulled thread in a stocking. **6.** *Colloq.* a sausage. ◇*v.t.* **7.** to ladder (def. 2); catch upon, or damage by, a snag. **8.** to obstruct or impede, as a snag does. [Scand]

snagger /'snægə/, *n. Colloq.* a shearer who works roughly or inexpertly.

snail /sneɪl/, *n.* **1.** a small, slow-moving animal, with a spirally coiled shell and a muscular foot, usu. found in gardens and living on

snail

leaves of plants. **2.** a slow or lazy person; sluggard. [OE *snegel*]

snake /sneɪk/, *n., v.,* **snaked, snaking.** ◇*n.* **1.** a scaly, limbless, usu. slender reptile, poisonous or non-poisonous, found in most countries in numerous classes and kinds; serpent. **2.** a disloyal person; a cunningly deceitful enemy. **3.** something like a snake in form or manner. **4.** a type of easily bent coil spring used for clearing drains, threading wires, etc., through tubes, etc. **5. snake in the grass,** a very deceitful or disloyal person; hidden enemy. ◇*v.i.* **6.** to move, twist, or wind in the manner of a snake: *The path snakes through the field.* ◇*v.t.* **7.** to follow (a course) in the shape of a snake: *He snaked his way through the jungle.* [OE *snaca*]

snakebird /ˈsneɪkbɜd/, *n.* →**darter**.

snake-charmer /ˈsneɪk-tʃɑmə/, *n.* (esp. in Eastern countries) someone who entertains by making apparently dangerous snakes sway to the music of a flute.

snake-lizard /ˈsneɪk-lɪzəd/, *n.* a smooth-scaled, elongated skink, with very small limbs.

snaky /ˈsneɪki/, *adj.,* **snakier, snakiest.** **1.** of or relating to a snake or snakes. **2.** snake-like; twisting, winding, or sinuous. **3.** venomous; treacherous or cunningly deceitful. **4.** *Colloq.* annoyed; angry or spiteful.

snap /snæp/, *v.,* **snapped, snapping,** *n., adj., adv.* ◇*v.t., v.i.* **1.** to make or cause to make a sudden, sharp sound. **2.** to move, strike, shut, catch, etc., with a sharp sound. **3.** to break suddenly, esp. with a sharp, cracking sound. **4.** to move smartly. **5.** *Photog.* to take snapshots of (someone). **6.** to bite or snatch suddenly. **7.** to speak or say sharply or angrily: *She snapped at him; She snapped her reply.* ◇*v.* **8. snap one's fingers at,** to disregard; scorn. **9. snap (someone's) head off,** to speak angrily and sharply to. **10. snap up,** to take advantage of (a bargain, etc.). ◇*n.* **11.** a sharp, crackling or clicking sound, or a movement or action causing such a sound: *a snap of the fingers.* **12.** a sudden breaking, or a sharp, crackling sound caused by it: *There was a snap as the branch broke.* **13.** a quick or sudden bite or snatch, as at something: *The fish made a snap at the bait.* **14.** a short spell, as of cold weather. **15.** →**snapshot**. **16.** a type of simple card game. **17.** *Colloq.* an easy or agreeable position, etc.: *The job's a snap.* ◇*adj.* **18.** describing devices closing by pressure on a spring catch. **19.** made, done, taken, etc., suddenly or offhand: *a snap judgment.* ◇*adv.* **20.** in a brisk, sudden manner. [D or LG]

snapdragon /ˈsnæpdrægən/, *n.* a plant cultivated for its spikes of showy flowers, of various colors, with a petal formation that is supposed to look like the mouth of a dragon.

snapper /ˈsnæpə/, *n.* a sea food fish of the bream family widely distributed in Australian and NZ coastal waters, known as cockney bream when very young, then with increasing age as red bream, squire and 'old man'. Also, **schnapper.**

snappy /ˈsnæpi/, *adj.,* **-pier, -piest.** **1.** Also, **snappish.** likely to speak sharply or irritably. **2.** Also, **snappish.** likely to bite or snap, as a dog. **3.** quick or sudden in action or performance. **4.** *Colloq.* crisp, smart, lively, brisk, etc.

snapshot /ˈsnæpʃɒt/, *n.* a photograph taken quickly without any formal arrangement of the subject.

snare¹ /snɛə/, *n., v.,* **snared, snaring.** ◇*n.* **1.** a device, usu. consisting of a noose, for capturing birds or small animals. **2.** anything serving to entrap, entangle, or catch unawares; a trap. ◇*v.t.* **3.** to catch with a snare; entrap; entangle. **4.** to catch or make to take part in (some action or plan) by trickery or wile. [ME, from Scand]

snare² /snɛə/, *n.* one of the strings of gut wound with metal which are stretched across the skin of the lower side of a side-drum.

snarl¹ /snɑl/, *v.i.* **1.** to growl angrily or fiercely, as a dog. **2.** to speak in a savagely sharp, angry, or quarrelsome manner. ◇*v.t.* **3.** to utter or say with a snarl. ◇*n.* **4.** a snarling sound or utterance. [obs. *snar* snarl] —**snarly,** *adj.*

snarl² /snɑl/, *n.* **1.** a tangle, as of thread or hair. **2.** a complicated or confused condition or matter, as a traffic snarl. **3.** a knot in wood. ◇*v.t.* **4.** to tangle. **5.** to make complicated or confused. ◇*v.i.* **6.** to become tangled. [ME *snarle* snare, from Scand]

snatch /snætʃ/, *v.i.* **1.** to make a sudden effort to seize something, as with the hand (usu. fol. by *at*). ◇*v.t.* **2.** to seize by a sudden or hasty grasp (oft. fol. by *up, from, out of, away,* etc.). **3.** to rescue or save by prompt action. ◇*n.* **4.** a sudden motion to seize something. **5.** a bit, scrap, or fragment of something: *snatches of conversation.* **6.** a brief spell of effort, activity, or any experience: *to work in snatches.* [ME; orig. uncert.]

sneak /snik/, *v.,* **sneaked** or *Colloq.* **snuck, sneaking,** *n.* ◇*v.i.* **1.** to go in a secret or sly manner; slink; skulk (fol. by *about, along, in, off, out,* etc.). **2.** to act in a sly, underhand, or mean way. **3.** *Colloq.* to leave quickly and quietly (fol. by *out, off, away,* etc.). ◇*v.t.* **4.** to move, put, pass, etc., in a stealthy or sly manner. **5.** *Colloq.* to steal; take surreptitiously. ◇*n.* **6.** a person who sneaks; a sneaking, underhand, or contemptible person. **7.** a telltale. [akin to OE *snīcan* sneak along] —**sneaky,** *adj.*

sneaker /ˈsnikə/, *n. Colloq.* a shoe with a rubber or other soft sole, used esp. in gymnasiums.

sneer /snɪə/, *v.i.* **1.** to smile, or curl the lip in a manner that shows scorn, contempt, etc. **2.** to speak or write in a manner expressing mockery, scorn, or contempt. ◇*v.t.* **3.** to utter or say in a sneering manner. ◇*n.* **4.** a look or expression suggesting mockery, scorn, or contempt. **5.** a derisive or scornful utterance or remark, esp. one disguised, half hidden or slyly suggestive. [ME *snere*]

sneeze /sniz/, *v.,* **sneezed, sneezing.** ◇*v.i.* **1.** to expel air or breath suddenly, forcibly, and more or less noisily through the nose and mouth as an uncontrollable reaction to an irritation in the nostrils. ◇v. **2. not to be sneezed at**, worth consideration. ◇n. **3.** an act or sound of sneezing. [OE *fnēosan*]

Snell's law /snelz 'lɔ/, n. a law stating that the ratio of the sine of the angle of incidence of a light ray passing between two media to the sine of the angle of refraction is a constant. [named after Willebrod *Snell* van Royen, d. 1626, Dutch mathematician]

snib /snɪb/, n., v., **snibbed, snibbing**. ◇n. **1.** a mechanism which is usu. part of a lock and which can be operated from only one side of a door. It holds the lock in position without using a key. **2.** →**latch** (def. 1). ◇v.t. **3.** to hold (a lock) by means of a snib.

snick /snɪk/, v.t. **1.** to cut, snip, or nick. **2.** to strike sharply. **3.** *Cricket*. to hit (the ball), esp. accidentally, with the edge of the bat. ◇n. **4.** a small cut; a nick. **5.** *Cricket*. a glancing blow given to the ball. [orig. uncert.]

snicker /'snɪkə/, v.i. **1.** (of a horse) to make a low, snorting neigh. **2.** →**snigger**. ◇v.t. **3.** →**snigger**. [orig. unknown]

snide /snaɪd/, adj. insulting in a nasty, insinuating manner: *snide remarks about the Mayor*. [Brit d. *snidy* treacherous]

sniff /snɪf/, v.i. **1.** to draw air through the nose in a short, audible inhalation. **2.** to clear the nose by so doing; sniffle. **3.** to smell by short inhalations. **4.** to show disdain, contempt, etc., by a sniff (oft. fol. by *at*). ◇v.t. **5.** to draw in through the nose by sniffing, as air, smells, liquid, powder, etc.; inhale. **6.** to become aware of (something) by, or as if by, smelling. ◇n. **7.** a single short, audible inhalation. **8.** the sound made. [ME; from SNIVEL]

sniffle /'snɪfəl/, v., **-fled, -fling**, n. ◇v.i. **1.** to sniff repeatedly, as from a cold in the head or in holding back tears. ◇n. **2.** an act or sound of sniffling. **3. the sniffles**, a cold, or other condition marked by sniffling. [from SNIFF]

snigger /'snɪgə/, v.i. **1.** to laugh in a half-suppressed, often improper manner. ◇v.t. **2.** to utter with a snigger. ◇n. **3.** a sniggering laugh. [imitative]

snip /snɪp/, v., **snipped, snipping**, n. ◇v.t., v.i. **1.** to cut with a small, quick stroke, or a number of such strokes, as with scissors, etc. ◇n. **2.** a small cut, notch, slit, etc., made by snipping. **3.** the sound made by snipping. **4.** a small piece or amount snipped off. [D and LG: snatch, clip]

snipe /snaɪp/, n., v., **sniped, sniping**. ◇n. **1.** any of a genus of small shorebird with plump body, striped head and long, straight bill, found in swamps and wet grasslands. **2.** a bird rather similar in appearance but having a down-curved tip to its bill, as the **painted snipe**, of Australia, Africa and southern Asia. ◇v.i. **3.** to shoot or hunt snipe. **4.** to shoot at individual soldiers, etc., from a concealed or long-range position. **5.** to make critical or damaging comments about (someone) without entering into open conflict. [ME, from Scand]

sniper /'snaɪpə/, n. a person who snipes, esp. a military gunman.

snippet /'snɪpət/, n. a small piece snipped off; a small bit, scrap, or fragment.

snitch[1] /snɪtʃ/, v.t. *Colloq*. to snatch or steal. [? var. of SNATCH]

snitch[2] /snɪtʃ/, *Colloq*. ◇v.i. **1.** to tell tales. ◇n. **2.** Also, **snitcher**. an informer. [orig. uncert.]

snivel /'snɪvəl/, v., **-elled, -elling**, n. ◇v.i. **1.** to weep or cry with sniffling. **2.** to put on or pretend a tearful state; whine. **3.** to draw up mucus noisily through the nose. ◇n. **4.** a light sniff, as in weeping. **5.** mucus running from the nose. [OE *snofl* mucus]

snob /snɒb/, n. **1.** someone who admires, copies, or seeks association with those with social rank, wealth, etc., and is condescending to others. **2.** someone who pretends social or intellectual importance and superiority. [orig. uncert.] —**snobbery**, n. —**snobbish**, adj.

snoek /snuk/, n. (in Australia) usu. the barracouta. [Afrikaans]

snood /snud/, n. **1.** a band or bag-like net for the hair. **2.** the fleshy protuberance at the base of the throat of a turkey. [OE *snōd*]

snook /snuk/, n. →**barracuda**.

snooker /'snukə/, n. **1.** a game played on a billiard table with 15 red balls and six balls of other colors, the object being to pocket them. ◇v.t. **2.** *Colloq*. to try to stop (someone), esp. from reaching some object, aim, etc. [orig. unknown]

snoop /snup/, *Colloq*. ◇v.i. **1.** to prowl or pry in a mean, sly manner. ◇n. **2.** someone who snoops. [D: take and eat (food or drink) on the sly] —**snoopy**, adj.

snooze /snuz/, v., **snoozed, snoozing**, n. *Colloq*. ◇v.i. **1.** to sleep; slumber; doze; nap. ◇n. **2.** a rest; nap. [orig. uncert.]

snore /snɔ/, v., **snored, snoring**, n. ◇v.i. **1.** to breathe during sleep with hoarse or harsh sounds. ◇v.t. **2.** to spend or pass (time) in snoring (fol. by *away* or *out*): *He snored the hours away*. ◇n. **3.** an act of snoring, or the sound made. [ME; ? b. SNIFF and ROAR]

snorkel /'snɔkəl/, n. **1.** a device on a submarine consisting of two vertical tubes for the intake and exhaust of air. **2.** a tube enabling a person swimming face downwards in the water to breathe. ◇v.i. **3.** to swim using such a device, usu. in order to look at the seabed, fish, etc. Also, **schnorkel**. [G]

snort /snɔt/, v.i. **1.** to force the breath violently through the nostrils with a loud, harsh sound, as a horse, etc. **2.** to express contempt, indignation, etc., by such a sound. ◇v.t. **3.** to utter with a snort. ◇n. **4.** the act or sound of snorting. [ME]

snout /snaʊt/, n. **1.** the part of an animal's head projecting forward and containing the nose and jaws; muzzle. **2.** anything that resembles or suggests an animal's snout in shape, function, etc. [ME]

snow /snoʊ/, n. 1. water vapor partly frozen in the atmosphere and falling to the earth in white flakes. 2. a layer of these flakes on the ground, etc. 3. the fall of these flakes. 4. something resembling snow. 5. *Poetic.* the white color of snow. 6. *Chem.* carbon dioxide solidified under great pressure. 7. white spots on a television screen caused by a weak signal. ◇v.i. 8. (of snow) to fall. ◇v.t. 9. to let fall as or like snow. 10. to cover, obstruct, isolate, etc., with snow (fol. by *in*, *over*, *under*, *up*, etc.). ◇v. 11. **be snowed under**, to be overcome by something, as work. [OE *snaw*] – **snowy**, *adj.*

snowball /ˈsnoʊbɔl/, n. 1. a ball of snow pressed or rolled together. ◇v.i. 2. to accumulate or grow larger at an increasing rate.

snow cap, n. a cap of snow on the top of a mountain, over a polar region, etc.

snowdrop /ˈsnoʊdrɒp/, n. a low spring-blooming plant with drooping white flowers.

snowflake /ˈsnoʊfleɪk/, n. one of the small feathery masses or flakes in which snow falls.

snow gum, n. a type of gum tree found in mountain regions in Australia.

snowline /ˈsnoʊlaɪn/, n. 1. the level on mountains, etc., above which snow never completely disappears. 2. the lower limit of snow at a particular time.

snowman /ˈsnoʊmæn/, n., pl. **-men.** a human-like figure made out of packed snow.

snowplough /ˈsnoʊplaʊ/, n. 1. a machine for clearing away snow from roads, railways, etc. 2. a technique for skiing slowly with the skis in a V position.

snowshoe /ˈsnoʊʃu/, n. a light racquet-like frame laced across with leather and attached to the foot for walking on deep snow.

Snowy Mountains /ˌsnoʊi ˈmaʊntənz/, *n.pl.* a series of mountains in south-eastern NSW; part of the Australian Alps. Highest peak, Mt Kosciusko, 2228 m.

Snowy Mountains Hydro-Electric Scheme, n. a hydro-electricity and irrigation scheme in south-eastern NSW, supplying the peak power demands of NSW, Vic and the ACT with its chief storage at Lake Eucumbene; completed in 1972.

Snowy River, n. a river rising on the eastern slopes of the Snowy Mountains, NSW and flowing south to enter the sea south of Orbost, Vic. About 435 km.

snr, *Abbrev.* senior.

snub /snʌb/, v., **snubbed, snubbing,** n., *adj.* ◇v.t. 1. to treat with disdain or contempt, esp. by ignoring. 2. to rebuke sharply. ◇n. 3. an act of snubbing; rebuke or slight. ◇*adj.* 4. (of the nose) short, and turned up at the tip. [ME, from Scand]

snuff[1] /snʌf/, v.t. 1. to breathe in. 2. to examine by smelling, as an animal does. ◇v.i. 3. to smell out something (oft. fol. by *around*). 4. to sniff powdered tobacco; take snuff. ◇n. 5. an act of snuffing; a sniff. 6. a preparation of powdered tobacco, usu. sniffed. [MD]

snuff[2] /snʌf/, n. 1. the burnt part of a candle wick. ◇v.t. 2. to cut off the snuff of (a candle, etc.). 3. to put out (a candle). [ME; orig. uncert.]

snuffle /ˈsnʌfəl/, v., **-fled, -fling,** n. ◇v.i. 1. (of pigs, etc.) to breathe in, in a noisy manner. 2. to speak through the nose or with a nasal twang. 3. to sniff; snivel. ◇v.t. 4. to speak in a snuffling or nasal tone. ◇n. 5. an act or sound of snuffling. 6. **the snuffles**, *Colloq.* a nasal condition, as from a cold. [D or Flemish]

snug /snʌg/, adj., **snugger, snuggest,** adv. ◇*adj.* 1. (of a place, etc.) comfortable or cosy. 2. (of a ship, etc.) neat or compactly arranged, esp. if limited in size. 3. (of a garment) fitting closely, but comfortably. 4. (of people, etc.) comfortably situated. ◇*adv.* 5. in a snug manner. [MD: smart, ship-shape]

snuggle /ˈsnʌgəl/, v., **-gled, -gling,** n. ◇v.i. 1. to lie or press closely, for warmth, comfort and affection; nestle; cuddle (oft. fol. by *up*, *in*, etc). ◇n. 2. a cuddle; embrace. [from SNUG, v.]

so[1] /soʊ/, adv. 1. in the way or manner shown or stated: *Do it so.* 2. as stated or reported: *Is that so?* 3. to that extent: *Do not walk so fast.* 4. very: *You are so kind.* 5. (used in the expression *so ... as*, showing comparison) to such a degree or extent: *so far as I know.* 6. for a given reason; hence. 7. about that amount or number: *a day or so ago.* ◇**8.** Some special uses are:

and so, 1. (used to emphasise a previous statement): *I said I would come, and so I will.* 2. likewise or correspondingly: *He is going, and so am I.* 3. therefore: *She is ill, and so cannot come.*

and so forth / on, continuing in the same way; et cetera.

just so, in perfect order.

quite so, exactly as you have just stated.

so as, with the result or purpose (fol. by an infinitive).

so much, an unspecified amount.

so much for, an expression showing disappointment: *So much for your childhood ideals.*

so-so, only fair: *I'm feeling so-so today.*

so that, 1. with the effect or result that. 2. in order that: *He wrote so that they might expect him.*

so to speak, in a manner of speaking.

so what? *Colloq.* What does that matter? ◇*conj.* 9. *Colloq.* consequently; with the result that. ◇*interj.* 10. (a general exclamation expressing many kinds of feeling as surprise, doubt, etc.). [OE *swā*]

so[2] /soʊ/, n. *Music.* See **solfa**. [See GAMUT]

soak /soʊk/, v.i. 1. to lie in a liquid and become totally wet or saturated. 2. (of a liquid) to pass through pores (usu. fol. by *in*, *through*, *out*, etc.). 3. to become known slowly: *The facts soaked into his mind.* ◇v.t. 4. to put and keep in liquid in order to make thoroughly wet; steep. 5. to wet thoroughly or drench. 6. (of liquid, etc.) to permeate thoroughly. 7. to take in or up by absorption (oft. fol. by *up*): *Blotting paper soaks up ink.* 8. to draw (*out*) by or as by soaking. ◇n. 9. the act of soaking. 10.

soak the condition of being soaked. **11.** *Colloq.* a heavy drinker of alcohol. [OE *socian*]

so-and-so /'sou-ən-sou/, *n.*, *pl.* **-sos. 1.** someone not definitely named: *So-and-so told me.* **2.** *Colloq.* an unpleasant or unkind person: *He really is a so-and-so.*

soap /soup/, *n.* **1.** a substance used for washing and cleansing purposes, usu. made by treating a fat with an alkali (as sodium or potassium hydroxide). **2.** any metallic (usu. sodium) salt of a fatty acid. ◇*v.t.* **3.** to rub, cover or treat with soap. [OE *sāpe*] **–soapy,** *adj.*

soapbox /'soupbɒks/, *n.* **1.** a box, usu. wooden, used as a platform by street speakers. **2.** any place, means, etc., used by a person to make a speech, voice opinions, etc.

soap opera, *n. Colloq.* a radio or television serial, usu. dealing with domestic problems, esp. in a highly emotional manner. Also, **soapy, soapie, soap.** [so called because orig. sponsored on US radio networks by soap manufacturers]

soapstone /'soupstoun/, *n.* a variety of talc with a soapy or greasy feel, used to make hearths, tabletops, etc.; steatite.

soar /sɔ/, *v.i.* **1.** to fly upwards, as a bird. **2.** to fly at a great height, without visible wing movements, as a bird. **3.** *Aeron.* to fly without engine power, esp. in a glider. **4.** to rise to a height, as a mountain. **5.** to rise to a higher level, as hopes, spirits, etc. ◇*n.* **6.** the act of soaring. [ME, from OF: fly up, soar, from LL]

sob /sɒb/, *v.*, **sobbed, sobbing,** *n.* ◇*v.i.* **1.** to weep with a sound caused by sharp intakes of breath. **2.** to make a sound like this. ◇*v.t.* **3.** to utter with sobs. ◇*n.* **4.** the act or sound of sobbing. [ME: imitative]

sober /'soubə/, *adj.* **1.** not drunk. **2.** habitually moderate in drinking alcohol. **3.** (of people) quiet, serious, and controlled in manner. **4.** subdued in tone, as color; not gay or showy, as clothes. **5.** not exaggerated: *sober facts.* ◇*v.i., v.t.* **6.** to make or become sober. [ME, from OF, from L]

sobriety /sə'braɪəti/, *n.* **1.** the state or quality of being sober. **2.** temperance or moderation, esp. in the use of alcohol. **3.** seriousness or solemnity. [ME, from L]

sobriquet /'soubrəkeɪ/, *n.* a nickname. [F; orig. uncert.]

Soc, *Abbrev.* **1.** society. **2.** socialist.

so-called /'sou-kɔld/, *adj.* **1.** called or known as such. **2.** incorrectly regarded as such: *so-called friend.*

soccer /'sɒkə/, *n.* a form of football where the use of hands and arms is forbidden except to the goalkeeper; association football. [(AS)SOC(IATION) + -ER²]

sociable /'souʃəbəl/, *adj.* **1.** tending to be in the company of others. **2.** friendly or agreeable; companionable. **3.** noted for or relating to companionship with others. [L] **–sociability, sociableness,** *n.*

social /'souʃəl/, *adj.* **1.** relating to or marked by friendly companionship or relations: *a social club; a social gathering.* **2.** (of people, disposition, etc.) friendly or sociable. **3.** relating to fashionable society: *a social column.* **4.** (of people or animals) tending to live with others, rather than alone. **5.** of or relating to human society, esp. as being divided into classes according to status: *social rank.* **6.** of or relating to the life of people in a community: *social problems.* ◇*n.* **7.** a social gathering or party. [L]

social class, *n.* a group, within a hierarchical society, usu. classified by occupation, and having the same economic, cultural or political status.

socialise *or* **socialize** /'souʃəlaɪz/, *v.*, **-lised, -lising.** ◇*v.t.* **1.** to educate to fit in with society. **2.** to establish or regulate according to socialist theories. ◇*v.i.* **3.** to be sociable and mix freely, as at a social gathering. **–socialisation,** *n.*

socialism /'souʃəlɪzəm/, *n.* a theory or system of social organisation based on public ownership and control of means of production, capital, land, etc., rather than on private enterprise. **– socialist,** *n., adj.* **– socialistic,** *adj.*

socialite /'souʃəlaɪt/, *n.* someone who goes to exclusive society functions.

social sciences, *n.pl.* a broad group of subjects, including economics, social history, sociology, etc., relating to people as social beings.

social security, *n.* money and services provided by the state for disadvantaged members of the public by means of old-age pensions, sickness and unemployment benefits.

social studies, *n.pl.* social sciences, as taught in schools.

social welfare, *n.* a system of community services set up by a state to help disadvantaged people.

social work, *n.* **1.** organised work directed towards improving social conditions. **2.** the study of methods by which this can be done. **– social worker,** *n.*

society /sə'saɪəti/, *n., pl.* **-ties. 1.** people regarded collectively: *human society.* **2.** people seen as members of a culturally related community: *Western society.* **3.** the structure and organisation of the above as divided into classes, etc.: *the lower classes of society.* **4.** an organisation of people associated together because of common interests, employment, etc. **5.** companionship or company: *She enjoyed his society.* **6.** the wealthy and their social relations, activities, etc. **7.** *Ecol.* a group of organisms of the same species held together by mutual dependence, and showing division of labor. ◇*adj.* **8.** of or relating to society (def. 6): *a society party.* [L]

Society Islands, *n.pl.* a group of islands in the South Pacific, a part of French Polynesia; largest island, Tahiti. Pop. 117 700 (1977); 1173 km².

Society of Friends, *n.* a pacifist Christian sect which does not have a formal creed or ministers; Quakers.

socio-, a word part representing 'social', 'sociological', as in *socioeconomic*. [combining form representing L *socius* companion]

socioeconomic /ˌsousiouˌekəˈnɒmɪk, ˌsouʃiou-, -ˌiːk-/, *adj.* of or relating to both social and economic considerations.

sociol., *Abbrev.* **1.** sociological. **2.** sociologist. **3.** sociology.

sociolinguistics /ˌsousiouˌlɪŋˈgwɪstɪks/, *n.* the study of language as relating to social structures and attitudes.

sociology /ˌsousiˈɒlədʒi/, *n.* the science or study of the origin, development, organisation and social relations of human society. **–sociologist**, *n.*

sock¹ /sɒk/, *n.* **1.** a garment covering the foot and ankle, and sometimes reaching up to the knee. **2. pull one's socks up**, *Colloq.* to make more effort. [OE *socc*]

sock² /sɒk/, *Colloq.* ◇*v.t.* **1.** to strike or hit hard. ◇*n.* **2.** hard blow. [orig. uncert.]

socket /ˈsɒkət/, *n.* **1.** a hollow part for holding some part or thing: *an eye socket*. **2.** one of a set of different-sized circular heads for use with a ratchet spanner. **3.** *Elect.* a device, usu. on a wall, to plug electrical power leads into. [ME, from AF: little ploughshare; of Celtic orig.]

sockeye /ˈsɒkaɪ/, *n.* →**salmon**. [Salishan (an Amer Ind language)]

Socrates /ˈsɒkrətiːz/, *n.* 469?–399 BC, Athenian philosopher whose ideas profoundly influenced the work of Plato.

sod¹ /sɒd/, *n.* **1.** a piece (usu. square or oblong) of grass cut or torn, containing its roots, etc. **2.** a surface of grassy area; turf. [ME, from MD or MLG: turf]

sod² /sɒd/, *n. Colloq.* a disagreeable person.

soda /ˈsoudə/, *n.* **1.** sodium hydroxide, NaOH; caustic soda. **2.** oxide of sodium, Na₂O. **3.** sodium (in phrases): *carbonate of soda*. **4.** soda-water. **5.** a drink made with soda-water, and fruit or other syrups, ice-cream, etc. [ML, from It, from Ar]

soda-water /ˈsoudəˌwɔːtə/, *n.* a bubbly drink consisting of water charged with carbon dioxide.

sodden /ˈsɒdn/, *adj.* **1.** soaked with or as if with liquid. **2.** (of food) heavy or soggy. **3.** expressionless, dull, or stupid. [ME *sothen*, pp. of SEETHE]

sodium /ˈsoudiəm/, *n.* a soft, silver-white metallic element oxidising rapidly in air, found in nature only in combined state, the commonest being salt (**sodium chloride**). *Symbol*: Na (for *natrium*); *at. no.*: 11; *at. wt*: 22.9898. [SOD(A) + -IUM]

sodium bicarbonate, *n.* a white, crystalline compound, NaHCO₃, used in cooking, medicine, etc. Also, **sodium hydrogen carbonate**.

sodium chloride, *n.* common salt, NaCl.

sodium hydroxide, *n.* a white corrosive solid, NaOH, strongly alkaline, used in making soap, rayon, etc.; caustic soda.

Sodom /ˈsɒdəm/, *n. Bible.* one of the 'cities of the plain' destroyed by God for their wickedness. [see Genesis 18–19]

sodomy /ˈsɒdəmi/, *n.* sexual intercourse using the anus, esp. of one man with another. [ME, from OF; from SODOM] **–sodomite**, *n.*

sofa /ˈsoufə/, *n.* a long couch with a back and two arms or raised ends. [Ar: raised floor for use as seat]

Sofia /ˈsoufiə/, *n.* the capital of Bulgaria, in the western part. Also, **Sofiya**. Pop. 1 114 962 (1986 est.).

soft /sɒft/, *adj.* **1.** yielding readily to touch or pressure; easily cut, or altered in shape; not hard. **2.** smooth and pleasant to touch: *soft skin*. **3.** low in sound. **4.** not harsh or glaring, as light or color. **5.** (of outlines) not hard or sharp. **6.** gentle or mild, as wind, rain, climate, etc. **7.** gentle, mild, lenient, or compassionate. **8.** sentimental, as language. **9.** not strong or robust; delicate; incapable of great endurance or exertion. **10.** *Colloq.* not hard, trying, or severe: *a soft job*. **11.** (of water) relatively free from calcium salts that interfere with the action of soap. **12.** *Photog.* having delicate gradations of tone. **13.** (of drinks) not containing alcohol. **14.** (of *c* and *g*) pronounced as in *cent* and *gem*. **15.** (of drugs) non-addictive, as marijuana and LSD. **16.** *Colloq.* easily influenced or swayed, as a person, the mind, etc.; easily imposed upon. **17. a soft touch**, *Colloq.* someone who gives money too easily. **18. be soft on someone**, *Colloq.* **a.** to be sentimentally or romantically inclined towards someone. **b.** to act towards someone less harshly than expected. **19. have a soft spot for (someone or something)**, to be especially fond of (someone or something). **20. soft in the head**, *Colloq.* stupid; insane. ◇*adv.* **21.** in a soft manner. [OE *softe*] **–softness**, *n.*

softball /ˈsɒftbɔːl/, *n.* a form of baseball played with a larger and softer ball, which is bowled underarm.

soft drink, *n.* a drink which is not alcoholic.

soften /ˈsɒfən/, *v.t., v.i.* to make or become soft or softer.

soft palate, *n.* See **palate** (def. 1).

soft pedal, *n.* a pedal, as on a piano, for lessening the volume.

soft-pedal /sɒft-ˈpedl/, *v.t.*, **-alled**, **-alling**. **1.** to soften the sound (of a piano) by means of the soft pedal. **2.** *Colloq.* to tone down; make less strong or harsh.

soft sell, *n.* a method of advertising or selling which is quietly persuasive and indirect. See **hard sell**.

soft-soap /ˈsɒft-soup/, *v.t. Colloq.* to persuade (someone) with smooth words; cajole; flatter.

software /ˈsɒftweə/, *n.* a collection of programs, usu. stored on disk or magnetic tape, that controls the operations of a computer (opposed to *hardware*).

softwood /ˈsɒftwʊd/, *n.* a coniferous tree or its wood.

soggy /'sɒgi/, *adj.*, **-gier, -giest. 1.** soaked; thoroughly wet. **2.** damp and heavy, as under-baked bread. [Brit d. *sog* bog]

soh /soʊ/, *n. Music.* See **solfa.**

soil[1] /sɔɪl/, *n.* **1.** the uppermost surface layer of the earth, containing inorganic and organic material, where plants grow. **2.** a country, land, or region: *on foreign soil.* **3.** ground or earth. [ME, from AF, from L]

soil[2] /sɔɪl/, *v.t.* **1.** to make dirty or stain, esp. on the surface: *to soil one's clothes.* **2.** to tarnish or disgrace (someone or someone's reputation). ◇*v.i.* **3.** to become soiled. ◇*n.* **4.** a spot, mark or stain due to soiling. **5.** manure; sewage. [ME, from OF, from L: pig]

soil creep, *n. Geol.* the slow, almost unnoticeable movement of soil down a slope.

soiree /swɑ'reɪ, 'swɑreɪ/, *n.* an evening social gathering, often for a particular purpose: *a musical soiree.* Also, **soirée.** [F: evening, from L: late]

sojourn /'soʊdʒɜn, 'sɒdʒɜn, 'sʌdʒ-, -ən/, *v.i.* **1.** to stay for a time in a place. ◇*n.* **2.** a temporary stay. [ME, from OF, from L]

sol[1] /sɒl/, *n. Music.* See **solfège.** [ME, from L. See GAMUT]

sol[2] /sɒl/, *n.* a fluid colloidal suspension of a solid in a liquid. See **gel.** [from (HYDRO)SOL]

solace /'sɒləs/, *n., v.,* **-aced, -acing.** ◇*n.* **1.** (something that gives) comfort in sorrow or trouble. ◇*v.t.* **2.** to comfort, console, or cheer. [ME, from OF, from L]

Solander /sə'lændə/, *n.* **Daniel Carl,** 1733–82, Swedish naturalist; accompanied James Cook on his first voyage to Australia in 1768.

solar /'soʊlə/, *adj.* **1.** of or relating to the sun: *solar phenomena.* **2.** coming from the sun, as light or heat. **3.** operated by the light or heat of the sun: *solar heating.* [L]

solar cell, *n.* an electric cell that converts sunlight into electrical energy.

solar day, *n.* See **day** (def. 3).

solar energy, *n.* energy derived from the sun, as for home heating, industrial use, etc.

solarium /sə'lɛəriəm/, *n., pl.* **-laria** /-'lɛəriə/. **1.** a room, glassed-in veranda, etc., exposed to the sun's rays, as at a seaside hotel or hospital. **2.** a room in which people lie under a sunlamp. [L]

solar month, *n.* See **month** (def. 1).

solar plexus, /soʊlə 'plɛksəs/, *n.* **1.** *Anat.* a network of nerves in the upper part of the abdomen, behind the stomach and in front of the aorta. **2.** *Colloq.* a point on the body, just below the sternum, where a blow will affect this nerve centre.

solar system, *n.* the sun together with all the planets, moons, asteroids, etc., revolving around it.

solar year, *n.* See **year** (def. 5).

sold /soʊld/, *v.* past tense and past participle of **sell.**

solder /'sɒldə/, *n.* **1.** any of various metal alloys, heated and used to join metal surfaces, joints, etc. **2.** anything that joins or unites. ◇*v.t., v.i.* **3.** to unite or become united with, or as if with, solder. [ME, from OF: to solder, from L: make firm]

soldier /'soʊldʒə/, *n.* **1.** someone who serves in an army for pay. **2.** someone of the rank and file in such service, as distinct from an officer. **3.** someone who fights or serves in any cause. **4.** *Zool.* (in certain ants and termites) an individual with powerful jaws, etc., for protecting the colony. ◇*v.i.* **5.** to act or serve as a soldier. ◇*v.* **6. soldier on,** to continue, persist. [ME, from OF: pay, from L] –**soldierly,** *adj.*

soldier bird, *n.* → **noisy miner.**

soldier crab, *n.* a small pale blue Australian crab which gathers together in large numbers, giving the impression of soldiers marching.

sole[1] /soʊl/, *adj.* **1.** being the only one; only. **2.** belonging or relating to a person or group to the exclusion of all others: *the sole right to something.* [L: alone]

sole[2] /soʊl/, *n.* the bottom or under surface of a foot or shoe. [ME and OE, from L: sandal, shoe]

sole[3] /soʊl/, *n., pl.* **soles,** (esp. collectively) **sole,** any of several flatfishes, esp. those with a hooklike snout, oft. used as food. [ME, from F, from L]

solecism /'sɒləsɪzəm/, *n.* **1.** a lapsing into incorrect grammar as in *they was.* **2.** a breach of good manners or etiquette. [L, from Gk] –**solecistic,** *adj.*

solemn /'sɒləm/, *adj.* **1.** (of a person, face, mood, tone, etc.) humorless. **2.** causing serious thoughts or a grave mood: *solemn music.* **3.** serious or earnest: *solemn assurances.* **4.** marked by formality. **5.** marked or observed with ritual, esp. of a religious nature. [ME, from L] –**solemnity,** *n.*

solemnise *or* **solemnize** /'sɒləmnaɪz/, *v.t.,* **-nised, -nising.** to observe or perform rites or ceremonies, esp. that of marriage.

solenoid /'sɒlənɔɪd/, *n.* a coil of wound wire around which a magnetic field is induced when electricity flows. [Gk: channel, pipe, shellfish] –**solenoidal,** *adj.*

solfa /sɒl'fɑ/, *n. Music.* **1.** the set of syllables *doh, ray, me, fah, soh, lah* and *te,* used to represent the notes of the scale. **2.** the system of singing notes to these syllables, where *doh* changes to match the tonic of the key. See **solfège.** [SOL[1] + FA. See GAMUT]

solfège /sɒl'fɛɪʒ, -'fɛʒ/, *n. Music.* **1.** the set of syllables *do, re, mi, fa, sol, la* and *si,* used to represent the notes of the scale. **2.** the system of singing notes to these syllables, where *do* always remains as C. See **solfa.**

soli-[1], a word part meaning 'alone', 'solitary'. [L, combining form of *solus*]

soli-[2], a word part meaning 'sun'. [L, combining form of *sōl*]

solicit /sə'lɪsət/, *v.t.* **1.** to seek seriously and respectfully: *to solicit funds.* **2.** (of a prosti-

solicit tute, etc.) to seek the custom of. **3.** to try to get (orders or trade) for business. ◇*v.i.* **4.** to solicit something or someone. [ME, from L: disturb, incite] —**solicitation**, *n.*

solicitor /səˈlɪsɪtə/, *n.* a lawyer who advises clients, represents them before the lower courts, and prepares cases for barristers to try in the higher courts.

solicitous /səˈlɪsɪtəs/, *adj.* **1.** anxious or concerned over something: *solicitous about a person's health.* **2.** anxiously wanting: *solicitous of the esteem of others.* [L] —**solicitude**, *n.*

solid /ˈsɒlɪd/, *adj.* **1.** (of a geometrical body or figure) having three dimensions (length, breadth, and thickness). **2.** of or relating to figures of three dimensions: *solid geometry.* **3.** having the inside completely filled up: *a solid ball.* **4.** without gaps or breaks; continuous: *a solid wall.* **5.** firm, hard, or compact in substance or appearance: *solid ground; solid cloud.* **6.** of matter that is not liquid or gaseous, whose particles stick closely together: *solid particles floating in a liquid.* **7.** relating to such matter: *Ice is water in a solid state.* **8.** having substance; not flimsy: *solid buildings; solid furniture.* **9.** whole or entire: *one solid hour.* **10.** forming the whole; being the only substance or material: *solid gold.* **11.** sound or good: *solid reasons; solid arguments.* **12.** full of common sense: *She is such a solid person.* **13.** financially sound or strong. **14.** *Obs.* cubic: *A solid foot contains 1728 solid inches.* **15.** thorough, vigorous, great, big, etc. (with emphatic force, often after *good*): *a good solid blow.* **16.** united in opinion, policy, etc.; unanimous. ◇*n.* **17.** a body or magnitude having three dimensions (length, breadth, and thickness). **18.** a solid substance or body. **19.** (*pl.*) food that is not in liquid form: *milk solids.* [ME, from L] —**solidity**, *n.*

solid angle, *n.* an angle formed by three or more planes intersecting at a common point. See **steradian**.

solidarity /sɒləˈdærəti/, *n., pl.* **-ties. 1.** union or fellowship arising from common responsibilities and interests, such as between members of a group or between classes, peoples, etc. **2.** community of interests, feelings, purposes, etc. **3.** (*cap.*) a Polish organisation of independent trade unions, formed in 1980. [F, from L: solid]

solidify /səˈlɪdəfaɪ/, *v.t., v.i.,* **-fied, -fying. 1.** to make or become solid. **2.** to form into crystals. —**solidification**, *n.*

solid solution, *n.* a solid homogeneous mixture of two or more substances, such as some alloys, glasses, etc.

solid-state /ˈsɒlɪd-steɪt/, *adj.* **1.** *Phys.* of or relating to the structure and properties of solids. **2.** *Elect.* of or relating to electronic devices which are composed of components in the solid state such as transistors, semiconductor diodes, integrated circuits, etc.

solidus /ˈsɒlɪdəs/, *n., pl.* **-di** /-daɪ/. a sloping line [/] generally used as a dividing line, as in dates, fractions, etc.; diagonal. [LL]

solifluction /ˌsɒlɪˈflʌkʃən/, *n.* **1.** a slow, downward movement of rock debris or soil saturated with water melting from snow and ice over permanently frozen subsoil in tundra regions. **2.** →**soil creep. 3.** a down-slope movement of soil, faster than soil creep. Also, **solifluxion**.

soliloquy /səˈlɪləkwi/, *n., pl.* **-quies.** the act of talking when alone or as if alone. [LL]

solitaire /ˈsɒlɪtɛə/, *n.* **1.** a game played by one person, with marbles or pegs on a board with holes. **2.** *US.* →**patience** (def. 4). **3.** a single precious stone, esp. a diamond, set in a ring, brooch, etc. [F, from L: alone]

solitary /ˈsɒlɪtri/, *adj., n., pl.* **-ries.** ◇*adj.* **1.** quite alone; without companions; unattended. **2.** being the only one or ones: *a solitary exception.* **3.** (of a place) marked by solitude; unfrequented, secluded, or lonely. **4.** *Zool.* (of certain wasps) not social. ◇*n.* **5.** someone who lives alone. [ME, from L]

solitude /ˈsɒlɪtjud/, *n.* **1.** the condition of being or living alone; seclusion. **2.** a lonely place. [ME, from L]

solmisation *or* **solmization** /ˌsɒlməˈzeɪʃən/, *n.* the act, process, or system of using syllables to represent the notes of the musical scale. See **solfa.** [F *sol* SOL¹ + *mi* MI]

solo /ˈsoʊloʊ/, *n., pl.* **-los, -li** /-li/ *adj., adv.* ◇*n.* **1.** a musical composition for one singer or player, with or without accompaniment. **2.** any performance by one person. **3.** *Cards.* any of certain games in which one person plays alone against others. ◇*adj.* **4.** *Music.* performing alone. **5.** performed alone: *a solo flight.* ◇*adv.* **6.** alone: *He made his first flight solo.* [It, from L: alone]

soloist /ˈsoʊloʊəst/, *n.* someone who performs a solo or solos.

Solomon /ˈsɒləmən/, *n.* a tenth century BC king of Israel, famous for his wisdom. [L, from Gk, from Heb *Sh'lōmōh*]

Solomon Islands, *n.* **1.** an archipelago in the south-western Pacific Ocean, east of New Guinea, extending for almost 1450 km. **2.** a parliamentary state in the south-western Pacific Ocean consisting of most of the Solomon Islands (the northern islands of Buka and Bougainville are part of PNG) and several other islands. Pop. 244 000 (1982); 27 556 km². *Languages:* English, pidgin English and more than 80 local languages. *Currency:* Solomon Islands dollar. *Cap.:* Honiara.

Solon /ˈsoʊlɒn/, *n. c.* 638–*c.* 558 BC, Athenian statesman noted for his political reforms and his wisdom.

solstice /ˈsɒlstɪs/, *n.* **1.** *Astron.* either of the two times in the year when the sun is at its greatest distance from the celestial equator and apparently does not move either north or south, about June 21 when it enters the sign of Cancer, and about December 22, when it enters the sign of Capricorn (called respectively, in the Southern Hemisphere, *winter solstice* and *summer solstice*). **2.** either of the two points in the ecliptic farthest from the equator. [ME, from OF, from L] —**solstitial**, *adj.*

solubility /ˌsɒljəˈbɪlɪti/, *n., pl.* **-ties. 1.** the property of being able to be dissolved. **2.** the extent to which a substance will dissolve in

solubility a solvent, shown as grams of solute per 100 grams of solvent, at a specified temperature.

solubility product, *n.* the product of the concentrations of the ions of dissolved electrolyte when in equilibrium with undissolved electrolyte.

soluble /'sɒljəbəl/, *adj.* **1.** able to be dissolved or made liquid. **2.** able to be solved or explained. [ME, from L]

solute /'sɒljut/, *n.* a substance dissolved in a given solution. [L]

solution /sə'luʃən/, *n.* **1.** the act of solving a problem, etc., or the state of being solved. **2.** a particular instance or method of solving; explanation or answer. **3.** *Maths.* **a.** the act of determining the answer to a problem. **b.** the answer. **4.** the act by which a gas, liquid, or solid is spread out evenly in a gas, liquid, or solid without chemical change. **5.** the fact of being dissolved; dissolved state: *salt in solution.* **6.** a mixture of two or more substances when the molecules are perfectly mixed. [ME, from L]

solve /sɒlv/, *v.t.*, **solved, solving. 1.** to clear up or explain; find the answer to. **2.** to work out the answer to (a mathematical problem). [ME, from L: loosen, dissolve]
–solvable, *adj.*

solvent /'sɒlvənt/, *adj.* **1.** able to pay all one's debts. **2.** having the power of dissolving; causing solution. ◊*n.* **3.** a substance, usu. liquid, that can dissolve other substances in it: *Water is a solvent for sugar.* [L: dissolving]
–solvency, *n.*

Solzhenitsyn /sɒlʒə'nɪtsən/, *n.* **Aleksandr Isayevich** /ɪ'seɪjəvɪtʃ/ born 1918, Russian novelist; Nobel prize for literature 1970.

soma /'soumə/, *n., pl.* **-mata** /-mətə/. the body of an organism as contrasted with its germ cells.

Somalia /sə'maliə/, *n.* a republic on the north-eastern coast of Africa, bordered by Ethiopia, Kenya and Djibouti; formed by the uniting of the former protectorates of British Somaliland and Italian Somaliland in 1960. Pop. 6 160 000 (1987 est.); 637 657 km². *Languages:* Somali, also Arabic, English and Italian. *Currency:* Somali shilling. *Cap.:* Mogadishu. Official name, **Somali Democratic Republic**.
–Somalian, *n., adj.*

Somare /sə'mari/, *n.* **Michael Thomas**, born 1936, PNG politician; prime minister 1975–80, 1982–85.

somatic /sou'mætɪk/, *adj.* of the body; bodily; physical. [Gk: of the body]

sombre /'sɒmbə/, *adj.* **1.** gloomily dark, shadowy, or dimly lit. **2.** dark and dull, of color, or of things in respect to color. **3.** gloomy, depressing, or dismal. [Fr, from VL: to shade, from L]

sombrero /sɒm'brɛəroʊ/, *n., pl.* **-ros.** a broad-brimmed hat, usu. of felt, worn in Spain, Mexico, the south-western US, etc. [Sp: shade]

some /sʌm/; *weak form* /səm/, *adj.* **1.** being one thing or person not named: *some poor fellow.* **2.** certain (with plural nouns): *some friends of mine.* **3.** of a certain unspecified number, amount, degree, etc.: *some variation.* **4.** unspecified but fairly large in number, amount, degree, etc.: *He was here for some weeks.* **5.** (used to show an approximate amount): *some four or five of us; some little value.* **6.** *Colloq.* great or important: *That was some storm!* ◊*pron.* **7.** certain people, instances, etc., not named: *Some think he is dead.* **8.** an unstated number, amount, etc., as distinguished from the rest: *Some of this is useful.* [OE *sum*]

-some¹, a suffix found in some adjectives showing a tendency, as in *quarrelsome, burdensome.* [OE *-sum*]

-some², a collective suffix used with numerals, as in *twosome, threesome, foursome.* [special use of SOME]

-some³, a word part meaning 'body', as in *chromosome.* [see SOMA]

somebody /'sʌmbɒdi, 'sʌmbədi/, *pron., n., pl.* **-bodies.** ◊*pron.* **1.** some person. ◊*n.* **2.** a person of some importance: *He thinks he is somebody.*

somehow /'sʌmhaʊ/, *adv.* in some way not specified, apparent, or known.

someone /'sʌmwʌn/, *pron.* somebody.

somersault /'sʌməsɒlt, -sɒlt/, *n.* **1.** an acrobatic movement of the body in which one turns completely, heels over head. ◊*v.i.* **2.** to perform a somersault. [OF, from Pr: leap above, from L]

Somerset /'sʌməset/, *n.* **1.** Also, **Somersetshire** /'sʌməsətʃɪə, -ʃə/. a county in south-western England. Pop. 448 900 (1986 est.); 3540 km². *Administrative Centre:* Taunton. **2.** a town on the north-western coast of Tas, adjoining Burnie. Pop. (with Burnie) 20 665 (1986).

something /'sʌmθɪŋ/, *pron.* **1.** some thing; a certain unnamed thing. ◊*n.* **2.** a thing or person of some value or importance: *His skill is really something.*

sometime /'sʌmtaɪm/, *adv.* **1.** at some indefinite point of time: *He will arrive sometime next week.* **2.** at an indefinite future time: *Come over sometime.* ◊*adj.* **3.** having been formerly; former: *sometime professor of history at Sydney.*

sometimes /'sʌmtaɪmz/, *adv.* on some occasions; at times; now and then.

somewhat /'sʌmwɒt/, *adv.* in some measure or degree; to some extent.

somewhere /'sʌmwɛə/, *adv.* **1.** in, at, or to some place not specified or known. **2.** at or to some point in amount, degree, etc.: *He is somewhere about sixty.* **3.** at some point of time: *This happened somewhere between three o'clock and five o'clock.*

Somme /sɒm/, *n.* **1.** a river in northern France, flowing north-west to the English Channel; battles, 1916, 1918, 1944. 225 km. **2.** a department in northern France. Pop. 549 500 (1986 est.); 6175 km². *Cap.:* Amiens.

somnambulism /sɒm'næmbjəlɪzəm/, *n.* the fact or habit of walking about, and often of

somnambulism   984   **soppy**

doing other things, while asleep. —**somnambulist**, *n.* —**somnambulistic**, *adj.*

somnolent /ˈsɒmnələnt/, *adj.* **1.** sleepy; drowsy. **2.** tending to cause sleep. [late ME, from L] —**somnolence, somnolency**, *n.*

son /sʌn/, *n.* **1.** a male child or person in relation to his parents. **2.** someone adopted legally as a son. **3.** a male descendant. **4.** someone related as if by ties of sonship. **5.** a male person looked upon as the product or result of particular agencies, forces, influences, etc.: *sons of liberty.* **6.** (a familiar term of address to a man or boy from an older person). **7. the Son**, the second person of the Trinity; Jesus, the Christ. [OE *sunu*] —**sonship, sonhood**, *n.*

sonar /ˈsoʊnɑ/, *n.* any device or method for finding depth by sound echoes. [*so*(*und*) *n*(*avigation*) *a*(*nd*) *r*(*anging*)]

sonata /səˈnɑtə/, *n.* an instrumental composition, usu. in several (commonly three or four) movements. [It]

sonata form, *n. Music.* a formal structure, usu. of the first movement of a sonata or symphony, consisting of a division into three parts known as exposition, development and recapitulation.

sonatina /sɒnəˈtinə/, *n., pl.* **-nas, -ne** /-neɪ/. a short or simplified sonata. [It]

song /sɒŋ/, *n.* **1.** a short metrical composition combining words and music; ballad; lyric. **2.** a poetical composition. **3.** the act or art of singing; vocal music. **4.** musical or tuneful sounds produced by certain birds, insects, etc. **5. for a song**, at a very low price. **6. make a song (and dance) about**, *Colloq.* to make a fuss about. [OE]

songster /ˈsɒŋstə/, *n.* **1.** a singer. **2.** a writer of songs or poems; poet. **3.** a songbird. [OE *sangestre*] —**songstress**, *n.fem.*

sonic /ˈsɒnɪk/, *adj.* **1.** having to do with sound waves. **2.** having to do with the speed at which sound travels.

sonic boom, *n.* a sudden loud sound caused by the shock waves generated by an aircraft, or other object, travelling at or above the speed of sound.

son-in-law /ˈsʌn-ɪn-lɔ, -ən-/, *n., pl.* **sons-in-law.** the husband of one's daughter.

sonnet /ˈsɒnət/, *n.* **1.** *Poetry.* a poem of 14 lines, usu. with a single complete thought, idea, or sentiment. **2.** *Obs.* a short, usu. love poem. [F, from It, from OPr: sound, from L]

sonny /ˈsʌni/, *n., pl.* **-nies.** a little boy; young man (often used as a familiar term of address).

sonorous /ˈsɒnərəs/, *adj.* **1.** giving out, or able to give out, sound, esp. deep resonant sound. **2.** loud, deep, or resonant: *a sonorous chime of bells.* **3.** rich and full in sound: *sonorous language; sonorous verse.* [L] —**sonority**, *n.*

-sonous, a word part used in adjectives to refer to sounds. [L *-sonus*]

sook /sʊk/, *n.* (usu. of children) a timid, shy, cowardly person. [orig. uncert.] —**sooky**, *adj.*

soon /sun/, *adv.* **1.** within a short period after this (or that) time, event, etc.: *We shall soon know; He soon realised.* **2.** quickly; promptly. **3.** willingly; readily: *I would as soon walk as ride.* [OE *sōna* at once]

soot /sʊt/, *n.* **1.** a fine black powder containing carbon, produced during the imperfect burning of coal, wood, oil, etc., rising and sticking to the sides of a chimney, etc. ◇*v.t.* **2.** to mark, cover, or treat with soot. [OE *sōt*] —**sooty**, *adj.*

sooth /suθ/, *n. Archaic.* truth, reality, or fact. [OE *sōth*]

soothe /suð/, *v.,* **soothed, soothing.** ◇*v.t.* **1.** to make (someone) calm; relieve, comfort, or refresh. **2.** to lessen or soften; assuage; mitigate: *to soothe pain.* ◇*v.i.* **3.** to bring calm, ease, or comfort. [OE *sōth* SOOTH] —**soothing**, *adj.*

soothsayer /ˈsuθseɪə/, *n.* someone who claims to tell the future. [ME] —**soothsaying**, *n.*

sop /sɒp/, *n., v.,* **sopped, sopping.** ◇*n.* **1.** piece of bread, etc., dipped in milk, soup, etc. **2.** anything thoroughly soaked. **3.** something given to pacify or quieten, or as a bribe. **4.** *Colloq.* a weak or cowardly person. ◇*v.t.* **5.** to dip or soak. **6.** to take or soak up (water, etc.) (usu. fol. by *up*): *The cloth will sop up the water.* [ME; OE *sopp*]

sophism /ˈsɒfɪzəm/, *n.* a clever but false argument. [L, from Gk: clever device, argument]

sophist /ˈsɒfəst/, *n.* (oft. cap.) a person who is concerned more with cleverness than with the soundness of an argument. [L, from Gk: wise person, teacher]

sophisticate /səˈfɪstəkeɪt/, *v.,* **-cated, -cating;** /səˈfɪstəkət/, *n.* ◇*v.t.* **1.** to make sophisticated. ◇*n.* **2.** a sophisticated person. [ML, from L]

sophisticated /səˈfɪstəkeɪtəd/, *adj.* **1.** (of a person, ideas, tastes, manners, etc.) changed by education, experience, etc., to be worldly-wise; refined; artificial. **2.** showing a high degree of skill, intelligence, etc.; subtle: *sophisticated music.* **3.** (of machinery, etc.) complex; intricate. —**sophistication**, *n.*

sophistry /ˈsɒfəstri/, *n., pl.* **-ries. 1.** a subtle, tricky, clever, but generally false method of reasoning. **2.** a false argument; sophism.

Sophocles /ˈsɒfəkliz/, *n.* 495?–406? BC, Greek tragic dramatist, author of *King Oedipus.* —**Sophoclean**, *adj.*

-sophy, a word part referring to systems of thought, as in *theosophy.* [Gk *-sophia*, combining form of *sophía* skill, wisdom]

soporific /sɒpəˈrɪfɪk/, *adj.* **1.** causing or tending to cause sleep. **2.** relating to or marked by sleep or sleepiness; sleepy; drowsy. ◇*n.* **3.** something causing sleep, as a drug. [L *sopor* sleep + -I- + -FIC]

sopping /ˈsɒpɪŋ/, *adj.* extremely wet.

soppy /ˈsɒpi/, *adj.,* **-pier, -piest. 1.** soaked, drenched, or very wet: *soppy ground;*

soppy weather. **2.** *Colloq.* too sentimental; mawkish; silly. —**soppiness**, *n.*

soprano /sə'prɑːnoʊ/, *n., pl.* **-pranos, -prani** /-'prɑːni/. *Music.* **1.** the uppermost part or voice. **2.** the highest singing voice in women and boys. [It: above, from L]

sorbet /'sɔːbeɪ, 'sɔːbət/, *n.* **1.** an iced dessert made with fruit and liqueurs or heavy wines. **2.** a frozen fruit-flavored mixture, made with egg whites, gelatine, etc. [F: water-ice, from Turk and Pers]

Sorbonne /sɔː'bɒn/, *n.* the seat of the faculties of letters, arts, and science of the University of Paris. [F, named after Robert de Sorbon founder of a theological college in Paris in 1257]

sorcery /'sɔːsəri/, *n., pl.* **-ceries.** the art, practices, or spells of a sorcerer; magic, esp. black magic in which supernatural powers are exercised through evil spirits; witchcraft. [ME, from ML, from L: lot] —**sorcerer**, *n.* —**sorceress**, *n. fem.*

sordid /'sɔːdəd/, *adj.* **1.** dirty or filthy; squalid. **2.** morally mean; ignoble: *sordid gains.* [L: dirty, base]

sore /sɔː/, *adj.*, **sorer, sorest**, *n., adv.* ◊*adj.* **1.** (of a wound, diseased part, etc.) painful or sensitive to the body. **2.** (of a person) suffering bodily pain from wounds, bruises, etc. **3.** suffering mental pain; grieved, distressed, or sorrowful: *to be sore at heart.* **4.** causing great mental pain: *a sore bereavement.* **5.** *Colloq.* annoyed or offended: *What are you sore about?* **6.** causing annoyance: *a sore subject.* ◊*n.* **7.** a sore spot or place on the body or mind. ◊*adv.* **8.** *Archaic or Poetic.* painfully or extremely: *He was sore distressed.* [OE *sār*]

sorghum /'sɔːgəm/, *n.* a cereal grass of many varieties, used as food for humans and animals, and for making brooms. [NL, from It, from L: Syrian]

sorority /sə'rɒrəti, -'rɔː-/, *n., pl.* **-ties.** *US.* a society or club of women or girls, as in a college. [ML]

sorrel[1] /'sɒrəl/, *n.* **1.** a light reddish brown color. **2.** a horse of this color. ◊*adj.* **3.** of the color sorrel. [ME, from OF: yellowish brown, from Gmc]

sorrel[2] /'sɒrəl/, *n.* **1.** a type of plant with sour-tasting leaves. **2.** a type of oxalis with acid juice. [ME, from OF, from Gmc: SOUR]

sorrow /'sɒroʊ/, *n.* **1.** mental pain caused by loss, pain, disappointment, etc.; grief, sadness, or regret. **2.** a cause or occasion of grief or regret: *My son is a sorrow to me.* ◊*v.i.* **3.** to feel sorrow; grieve. [OE *sorg*] —**sorrowful**, *adj.*

sorry /'sɒri/, *adj.*, **-rier, -riest. 1.** feeling sadness at having done something wrong; regretful: *I'm sorry I said that.* **2.** causing pity; miserable; deplorable; wretched: *to come to a sorry end; a sorry-looking horse.* **3.** sorrowful or sad; grieved. [OE *sār* SORE]

sort /sɔːt/, *n.* **1.** particular kind, type, variety, class or group, as distinguished by character or nature: *to discover a new sort of mineral.* **2.** a type or example of something: *He's some sort of friend.* **3. of sorts**, of a mediocre, indefinite or poor kind: *He is a friend of sorts.* **4. out of sorts**, not in good health, spirits, or temper. **5. sort of**, to a certain extent; in some way; as it were. ◊*v.t.* **6.** to arrange according to sort, kind, or class; classify: *to sort letters.* **7.** to separate from: *to sort the sheep from the goats.* **8.** *Agric.* to arrange (wool) into types to go into separate bales. [ME, from OF, from L: lot, condition, LL: class, order] —**sorter**, *n.*

sortie /'sɔːti/, *n.* **1.** an attack by troops from a besieged place. **2.** the flying of a military aircraft on a mission. [F: go out]

SOS /ɛs oʊ 'ɛs/, *n.* **1.** the letters represented by the radio telegraphic signal used by ships in distress, etc., to call for help. **2.** any call for help. [said to stand for *Save Our Souls*]

so-so /'soʊ-soʊ, soʊ-'soʊ/, *adj.* **1.** neither very good nor very bad; indifferent. ◊*adv.* **2.** in an indifferent or passable manner.

sot /sɒt/, *n.* a confirmed drunkard. [OE *sott*, from VL]

sotto voce /sɒtoʊ 'voʊtʃeɪ/, *adv.* in a low voice meant not to be overheard. [It: under (normal) voice (level)]

sou' /saʊ/, *n., adj., adv. Chiefly Naut.* south.

soubrette /su'brɛt/, *n.* **1.** a maidservant or lady's maid in a play or opera, esp. one who flirts with men and makes intrigues. **2.** any lively young woman character. [F, from Pr: coy, reserved, from Pr: be left over, from L]

soufflé /'suflеɪ/, *n.* a light baked dish of fish, cheese, etc., made fluffy with beaten egg-whites. [F, from L: blow up]

sough /saʊ/, *v.i.* **1.** to make a rushing, rustling, or murmuring sound. ◊*n.* **2.** such a sound. [OE *swōgan* make a noise]

sought /sɔːt/, *v.* past tense and past participle of **seek.**

soul /soʊl/, *n.* **1.** the principle of life, feeling, thought, and action in humans, believed to be separate in existence from the body, and living after death; the spiritual part of man as distinct from the physical. **2.** highmindedness; noble warmth of feeling, spirit or courage, etc. **3.** a leader or inspirer of some movement; moving spirit: *He was the soul of the Resistance.* **4.** the spirit of a dead person. **5.** a human being; person: *She was a kindly soul.* [OE *sāwl*]

soul music, *n.* commercial American Negro music which combines gospel music with a blues style.

sound[1] /saʊnd/, *n.* **1.** a sensation produced in the organs of hearing when certain vibrations (**soundwaves**) are caused in the surrounding air. **2.** the vibrations in the air producing this sensation. **3.** the effect on the ears from a particular source: *the sound of music.* **4.** noise, speech, music, etc. ◊*v.i.* **5.** to make a sound. **6.** to give forth a sound as a call or summons: *The trumpet sounds.* **7.** to give a certain feeling when heard or read: *to sound strange.* ◊*v.t.* **8.** to cause (an instrument, etc.) to make a sound: *to sound the trumpet.* **9.** to announce, order,

sound or direct by a sound: *to sound a retreat*. **10.** to speak clearly, pronounce, or express: *to sound each letter*. ◊*v.* **11. sound off**, *Colloq.* to complain angrily. [ME, from OF, from L]

sound² /saʊnd/, *adj.* **1.** whole or free from injury, damage, disease, etc.; in good condition; healthy; robust: *a sound heart*. **2.** financially strong, secure, or reliable: *a sound business*. **3.** sure; reliable: *sound judgment*; *sound advice*. **4.** unbroken and deep: *sound sleep*. **5.** vigorous, hearty, or thorough: *a sound beating*. **6. sound as a bell**, in perfect health or condition. ◊*adv.* **7.** in a sound manner. [OE *gesund*]

sound³ /saʊnd/, *v.t.* **1.** to measure or try the depth of (water, a deep hole, etc.) by letting down a lead weight at the end of a line. **2.** to seek the views or feelings of (a person) by indirect ways: *to sound out someone's views*. ◊*v.i.* **3.** to use the lead and line for measuring depth. **4.** to go down or touch bottom: *The lead sounded*. **5.** to plunge downwards or dive: *The whale sounded*. [OE *sundgyrd* sounding pole, from Scand] —**sounder**, *n.*

sound⁴ /saʊnd/, *n.* a narrow channel joining larger bodies of water or between the mainland and an island: *Milford sound*. [OE *sund* channel, sea]

sound barrier, *n.* a point near the speed of sound at which an aircraft or missile meets a sudden increase in air resistance and creates a shock wave.

soundbox /'saʊndbɒks/, *n.* an enclosed space in a musical instrument, such as the body of a violin, for making the tone fuller.

sounding-board /'saʊndɪŋ-bɔd/, *n.* **1.** a thin plate of wood in a musical stringed instrument, to make the tone better. **2.** a structure over, or behind and above, a speaker, orchestra, etc., to reflect the sound towards the audience. **3.** a person or group who listens to and comments on new ideas.

sound mixer, *n.* (a person who operates) a piece of electronic equipment which unites sound signals from various sources, such as several microphones, tape recorders, etc., to make a good complete sound.

soundproof /'saʊndpruːf/, *adj.* **1.** not letting sound through. ◊*v.t.* **2.** to cause to be soundproof: *He soundproofed the walls of the music room*.

sound system, *n.* → **audio system**.

soundtrack /'saʊndtræk/, *n.* **1.** a strip at the side of a cinema film which carries the sound recording. **2.** such a recording, esp. when transferred on to a gramophone record, compact disc, etc.

soundwave /'saʊndweɪv/, *n.* a longitudinal wave by which sound is transmitted.

soup /suːp/, *n.* **1.** liquid food made by boiling meat, fish, or vegetables, with various added ingredients. **2. in the soup**, *Colloq.* in trouble. ◊*v.* **3. soup up**, *Colloq.* to modify (an engine, esp. of a motor car) in order to increase its power. [F: *sop*, broth, of Gmc orig.]

soupçon /'suːpsɒn/, *n.* a very small amount. [F, from LL]

soup kitchen, *n.* a place where food, usu. soup, is served free or at little charge to the poor.

sour /'saʊə/, *adj.* **1.** having an acid taste, such as that of vinegar, lemon juice, etc.; tart. **2.** fermented: *sour milk*. **3.** harsh in spirit or temper; austere; morose; embittered; peevish. **4.** *Agric.* (of soil) having excessive acidity. ◊*v.i., v.t.* **5.** to become or make sour. [OE *sūr*] —**sourish**, *adj.*

source /sɔs/, *n.* **1.** any thing or place from which something comes, arises, or is obtained; origin. **2.** a spring of water from the earth, etc.; the beginning or place of origin of a river, etc. **3.** a book, statement, person, etc., supplying information: *sources for ancient history*. [ME, from OF: spring up, from L: rise]

sourdough /'saʊədoʊ/, *n.* a rising agent, esp. fermented dough kept from one baking to start the next instead of beginning each time with fresh yeast.

souse /saʊs/, *v.*, **soused**, **sousing**, *n.* ◊*v.t., v.i.* **1.** to plunge into water or other liquid. **2.** to soak or become soaked with water, etc. ◊*n.* **3.** the act of sousing. [ME, from OF, from OHG: brine]

south /saʊθ/, *n.* **1.** a cardinal point of the compass directly opposite to the north. See Appendix. **2.** the direction in which this point lies. **3.** (*l.c.* or *cap.*) an area or territory situated in this direction: *news from the south*. ◊*adj.* **4.** lying towards or situated in the south. **5.** directed or going towards the south. **6.** coming from the south: *the south wind*. **7.** (*cap.*) describing the southern part of a region, country, etc.: *South Pacific*. ◊*adv.* **8.** towards or in the south: *to go south*. [OE *sūth*]

South Africa, *n.* a republic in the southernmost part of Africa, bordered by Namibia, Botswana, Zimbabwe, Mozambique and Swaziland; former British dominion (1910); independent since 1934 and a republic outside the Commonwealth of Nations since 1961; apartheid system coming to power of the National Party in 1948; referendum to dismantle this system approved in 1992. Pop. 28 881 000 (1985 est.). 1 123 226 km². *Languages*: Afrikaans, English and African languages. *Currency*: rand. *Caps*.: Pretoria (administrative), Cape Town (legislative) and Bloemfontein (judicial). Formerly, **Union of South Africa**.

Southall /'sʌðɔːl/, *n.* **Ivan**, born 1921, Australian writer of books for young people; works include *Ash Road* (1965).

South America, *n.* a continent in the southern part of the Western Hemisphere. 17 871 000 km². —**South American** *n., adj.*

Southampton /saʊθ'hæmptən/, *n.* a seaport in England, in Hampshire. Pop. 214 802 (1981).

South Australia, *n.* a state in central southern Australia. Pop. 1 345 945 (1986); 984 400 km². *Cap*.: Adelaide.

South Australian Company, *n.* a company formed in 1835, with GF Angas as director, to encourage investment and colonisation in SA; contributed significantly to SA's early development.

South Carolina, *n.* a state in the southeastern US, on the Atlantic coast. Pop. 3 378 000 (1986 est.); 80 582 km². *Cap.:* Columbia. *Abbrev.:* SC —**South Carolinian**, *n., adj.*

South Coast, *n.* a district in NSW, commencing south of the Shoalhaven River and extending to the Vic border, with the coast as its eastern boundary and the Great Dividing Range roughly being its western boundary.

South Dakota, *n.* a state in the northern central US; a part of the Middle West. Pop. 708 000 (1986 est.); 199 730 km². *Cap.:* Pierre. *Abbrev.:* S Dak —**South Dakotan**, *n., adj.*

Southdown /'saʊθdaʊn/, *n.* one of the purest strains of the British short wool breeds of sheep, particularly suited for production of export fat lambs, and now common in Australia. [from the *South Downs* of England, where the sheep were orig. reared]

south-east /saʊθ-'ist/, *n.* **1.** a point or direction midway between south and east. See Appendix. ◊*adj.* **2.** in, going to, or coming from the south-east. —**south-eastern**, *adj.*

South-East Asia, *n.* the area which includes Brunei, Burma, Indonesia, Cambodia, Laos, Malaysia, the Philippines, Thailand and Vietnam; the south-eastern corner of Asia. —**South-East Asian**, *adj.*

south-easter /saʊθ-'istə/, *n.* a wind, gale, or storm from the south-east. Also, *esp. Naut,* **sou'-easter** /saʊ-'istə/.

southerly /'sʌðəli/, *adj.* **1.** moving, directed, or situated towards the south. **2.** coming from the south: *a southerly wind.* ◊*adv.* **3.** towards or from the south. ◊*n.* **4.** a wind from the south.

southerly buster, *n.* a violent, cold southerly wind blowing on the south-eastern coast of Australia.

southern /'sʌðən/, *adj.* **1.** in, towards, or from the south. **2.** of or relating to the south. [OE *sūtherne*]

Southern Alps, *n.pl.* a mountain range in NZ, on South Island. Highest peak, Mt Cook, 3764 m.

Southern Cross[1], *n.* the constellation Crux, whose four chief stars are in the form of a cross, seen in the Southern Hemisphere and particularly associated with Australia and NZ.

Southern Cross[2], *n.* the three-engined Fokker plane used by Sir Charles Kingsford Smith to make the first Pacific crossing in 1928; now an exhibit at Brisbane's Eagle Farm airport.

Southern Hemisphere, *n.* the half of the earth between the South Pole and the equator.

Southern Highlands, *n.* a province in western central PNG. Pop. 259 500 (1986 est.); 23 800 km². *Administrative Centre:* Mendi.

Southern Ocean, *n.* the ocean south of Australia and NZ, extending to Antarctica; contains much sea ice.

Southey /'sʌði, 'saʊði/, *n.* **Robert**, 1774–1843, English poet and prose writer; poet laureate 1813–43.

South Island, *n.* the largest island of NZ, separated from the North Island by Cook Strait. About 150 460 km².

South Korea, *n.* a republic in north-eastern Asia, occupying the southern part of the Korean peninsula; established in 1948; separated from North Korea by a UN supervised demilitarised zone established at the end of the Korean War (1953). Pop. 42 082 000 (1987 est.); 98 966 km². *Language:* Korean. *Currency:* won. *Cap.:* Seoul. Official name, **Republic of Korea**. See **Korea**. —**South Korean**, *n., adj.*

South Pacific, *n.* the southern part of the Pacific Ocean.

South Pole, *n.* that end of the earth's axis of rotation marking the southernmost point of the earth.

South Sea Bubble, *n.* a financial and political scandal in Great Britain, resulting from the collapse in 1720 of the South Sea Company, sponsored by the king and government after it had taken over the national debt.

South Vietnam, *n.* a region of Vietnam which was an independent republic 1955–1976. —**South-Vietnamese**, *n., adj.*

southward /'saʊθwəd/; *Naut.* /'sʌðəd/, *adj.* **1.** moving, bearing, facing, or situated towards the south. ◊*n.* **2.** the southward part, direction, or point. ◊*adv.* **3.** Also, **southwards**. towards the south.

south-west /saʊθ-'west/, *n.* **1.** a point or direction midway between south and west. See Appendix. ◊*adj.* **2.** in, towards, or from the south-west. —**south-western**, *adj.*

south-wester /saʊθ-'westə/, *n.* a wind, gale, or storm from the south-west. Also, *esp. Naut,* **sou'-wester** /saʊ-'westə/.

souvenir /suvə'nɪə/, *n.* something given or kept to remember a place, event, or person; memento. [F: remember, from L: come to mind]

sou'wester /saʊ'westə/, *n.* **1.** a waterproof hat, usu. of oiled cloth, worn esp. by seamen. **2.** *Chiefly Naut,* a south-wester.

sovereign /'sɒvrən/, *n.* **1.** a king or queen; monarch. **2.** someone who has the highest power or authority. **3.** a former British gold coin. ◊*adj.* **4.** having supreme rank, power, or authority. **5.** being above all others in character, importance, excellence, etc. [ME, from OF, from L: above] —**sovereignty**, *n.*

soviet /'souviət, 'sɒv-/, *n.* **1.** formerly, a local governing council in the Soviet Union. **2.** any similar socialist assembly. ◊*adj.* **3.** of a soviet. [Russ: council]

Soviet Union, *n.* formerly, a federation of socialist republics in eastern Europe and western, central and northern Asia; formed from the territories of the Russian Empire following the Revolution of 1917; the Union formally established in 1922; after its dissolution in 1991, most republics became members of the CIS. Official name, **Union of Soviet Socialist Republics (USSR)**.

sow¹ /sou/, *v.t.*, **sowed, sown** or **sowed, sowing. 1.** to scatter (seed) over land, earth, etc., for growth; plant: *to sow seed in the ground.* **2.** to scatter seed over (land, earth, etc.) for the purpose of growth: *to sow a field with lucerne.* **3.** to introduce for development: *to sow distrust.* [OE *sāwan*]

sow² /sau/, *n.* **1.** an adult female pig. **2.** *Metall.* a mould for molten iron. [ME, from OE *sugu*]

Soweto /sə'wεtou, -'weɪ-/, *n.* a black African township south-west of Johannesburg, South Africa. Pop. 864 400 (1980).

sown /soun/, *v.* past participle of **sow¹**.

soya bean /'sɔɪjə biːn/, *n.* **1.** a bushy, leguminous plant of south-east Asia. **2.** the seed of this plant which is used as food, etc., and which yields an oil used as a food and in the manufacture of soap, candles, etc. Also **soy, soybean.**

soya sauce *n.* a salty, dark brown sauce, made by fermenting soya beans in brine. Also, **soy sauce.** [Jap, from Chinese: bean oil]

sp., *Abbrev.* species.

SP, *Abbrev.* starting price.

spa /spɑ/, *n.* **1.** a mineral spring, or place where such springs exist. **2.** an enclosed section of a swimming pool through which heated, aerated water is pumped at pressure. [from *Spa*, town in E Belgium, famous for its mineral springs]

space /speɪs/, *n., v.,* **spaced, spacing.**
◇*n.* **1.** the immeasurably great expanse, commonly thought of as extending in all directions (or having three dimensions), in which all material objects are situated. **2.** a part of this in a particular instance: *the space occupied by a body.* **3.** that part of the universe which lies outside the earth's atmosphere, in which the density of matter is very low; outer space. **4.** an extent or area; a particular extent of surface: *to fill in blank spaces in a document.* **5.** linear distance: *trees set at equal spaces apart.* **6.** extent of time: *a space of two hours.* **7.** an interval of time; a while: *After a space he continued his story.* **8.** *Music.* one of the degrees or intervals between the lines of the stave. ◇*v.t.* **9.** to divide into spaces. **10.** to set some distance apart. [ME, from OF, from L]

space capsule, *n.* a container for instruments or astronauts which is capable of being sent into space and which can be recovered on its return.

spacecraft /'speɪskrɑft/, *n.* a vehicle which can travel outside the earth's atmosphere.

spaced-out /speɪst-'aut/, *adj.* in a pleasantly dreamy state, as if under the influence of a drug. Also, *esp. after a verb,* **spaced out.**

Spacelab /'speɪslæb/, *n.* a science workshop used inside the US space shuttle in the 1970s and 1980s.

spaceship /'speɪsʃɪp/, *n.* a spacecraft carrying and operated by humans.

space shuttle, *n.* a rocket-propelled spacecraft designed to carry equipment and people between earth and a satellite, and which can be used more than once.

space-time /speɪs-'taɪm/, *n.* **1.** a four-dimensional continuum in which time is seen as another dimension, like length, width and depth. See **relativity.** ◇*adj.* **2.** of or relating to such a system.

spacious /'speɪʃəs/, *adj.* **1.** containing much space; ample: *a spacious house.* **2.** broad; large; great. [ME, from L]

spade¹ /speɪd/, *n., v.,* **spaded, spading.**
◇*n.* **1.** a tool for digging, with an iron blade that is driven into the ground with the foot, and a long handle usu. with a grip or crosspiece at the top. **2.** any tool or part like this. **3. call a spade a spade,** to call a thing by its real name; speak plainly or bluntly. ◇*v.t.* **4.** to dig, cut, or remove with a spade. [OE *spadu*]

spade² /speɪd/, *n.* **1.** a black figure shaped like an upside-down heart with a short stem at the cusp, used on playing cards (♠). **2.** a card of the suit bearing such figures. **3.** (*pl.*) the suit of cards bearing this figure. [Lit: orig., sword, later mark on cards, from L, from Gk: wooden blade]

spadework /'speɪdwɜk/, *n.* work, esp. laborious or boring, done to prepare for further work.

spaghetti /spə'gεti/, *n.* a type of pasta of Italian origin, made from wheat flour, in long, thin, solid strips or tubes, and cooked by boiling. [It: little cords]

Spain /speɪn/, *n.* a kingdom in south-western Europe, forming most of the Iberian peninsula between the Mediterranean Sea and the Atlantic, bordered by Portugal and France; a republic from 1931 until the restoration of the monarchy in 1975. Pop. 38 832 000 (1987 est.); 504 782 km². *Language:* Spanish, mostly Castilian but also Catalan, Basque and Galician. *Currency:* peseta. *Cap.:* Madrid. Spanish, **España.**

span /spæn/, *n., v.,* **spanned, spanning.**
◇*n.* **1.** the distance between the tip of the thumb and the tip of the little finger when the hand is fully stretched out. **2.** a unit of length corresponding to this distance, commonly taken as 9 inches or 23 cm. **3.** the distance or space between two supports of a bridge, beam, or arch. **4.** the full stretch of anything: *the span of memory.* **5.** to measure by the span of a hand. ◇*v.t.* **6.** to extend over or across (a space, a river, etc.): *The bridge spans the river.* [OE]

spangle /'spæŋgəl/, *n., v.,* **-gled, -gling.**
◇*n.* **1.** a small, thin piece of glittering material, such as metal, for decorating clothes, etc. **2.** any small, bright drop, object, spot, etc. ◇*v.t., v.i.* **3.** to sprinkle or glitter with small, bright pieces. [ME, from MD]

spaniel /'spænjəl/, *n.* a dog of small or medium size, usu. with a long, silky coat and drooping ears, used in hunting and as a pet. [ME, from OF: Spanish (dog), from L]

Spanish /'spænɪʃ/, *adj.* **1.** of or relating to Spain. ◇*n.* **2.** the language of Spain, standard also in Latin America (except Brazil).

Spanish—American War, *n.* a war between the US and Spain in 1898 marking the beginning of US imperialism.

Spanish Civil War, *n.* the civil war in Spain, lasting from 1936–39, in which the republican government (supported by the Comintern and other left-wing and anarchist groups) was overthrown by the army led by General Franco (aided by fascist and other right-wing groups).

Spanish Inquisition *n.* a state tribunal that defended Roman Catholic orthodoxy in Spain, particularly in its ruthless persecution of heretics in the 15th to 17th centuries.

Spanish mackerel *n.* **1.** Also, **Queensland kingfish.** a valuable commercial fish of Qld waters. **2.** any of several related marine food fishes.

Spanish Main *n.* **1.** (formerly) the mainland of America adjacent to the Caribbean Sea. **2.** the Caribbean Sea, the route of the Spanish treasure galleons, a former haunt of pirates.

spank /spæŋk/, *v.t.* **1.** to strike (a person, usu. a child) with the open hand, a slipper, etc., esp. on the buttocks, as a punishment. ◇*n.* **2.** a blow given in spanking; a smart slap. [imitative]

spanking /'spæŋkɪŋ/, *adj.* **1.** moving quickly and smartly. **2.** *Colloq.* unusually fine, great, large, etc. [orig. uncert.]

spanner /'spænə/, *n.* **1.** a tool for gripping and turning the head of a bolt, nut (def. 10), pipe, etc., usu. consisting of a bar of metal with fixed or moving jaws. **2. a spanner in the works,** *Colloq.* any cause of confusion or interruption. [G]

spar[1] /spɑ/, *n. Naut.* a strong pole used for masts, etc.; a mast, yard, boom, gaff, etc. [ME]

spar[2] /spɑ/, *v.*, **sparred, sparring,** *n.* ◇*v.i.* **1.** *Boxing.* to make the movements of attack and defence with the arms and fists. **2.** to argue vigorously but not very seriously. ◇*n.* **3.** a motion of sparring. [ME; orig. meaning thrust (n. and v.)]

spar[3] /spɑ/, *n.* a type of shiny, transparent or translucent, easily cleavable minerals, such as fluorspar. [from *spar-stone* spar, OE *spærstan* gypsum]

spare /spɛə/, *v.*, **spared, sparing,** *adj.*, **sparer, sparest,** *n.* ◇*v.t.* **1.** to stop oneself from harming or destroying: *to spare a fallen enemy.* **2.** to deal gently with; show consideration for: *to spare a person's feelings.* **3.** to save from effort, discomfort, etc.: *to spare oneself trouble.* **4.** to stop oneself from using, as some instrument, means, aid, etc.: *to spare the rod.* **5.** to part with or let go: *Can you spare a few cents?* **6.** to have left over or unused: *We have room to spare.* ◇*v.i.* **7.** to stop oneself from action; forbear. ◇*adj.* **8.** kept as an extra, for possible use: *a spare tyre.* **9.** free for extra use: *spare time.* **10.** not rich; frugal: *a spare diet.* **11.** lean or thin: *a spare person.* ◇*n.* **12.** an extra thing, part, etc.: *to carry a spare for emergencies.* [OE *sparian*]

spare part, *n.* a part which replaces a faulty, worn, or broken part of a machine, esp. a motor vehicle. Also, **spare.**

spare ribs, *n.pl.* a cut of meat, esp. beef or pork, of ribs with little meat attached. [var. of *ribspare,* from MHG: rib cut]

sparing /'spɛərɪŋ/, *adj.* **1.** using in small amounts; frugal: *Be sparing with the sugar.* **2.** showing mercy.

spark /spɑk/, *n.* **1.** a burning particle that is thrown off by burning wood, etc., or produced by one hard body striking against another. **2.** *Elect.* **a.** a light produced by a sudden discontinuous discharge of electricity through air or another non-conductor. **b.** the discharge itself. **c.** any electric arc of relatively small energy content. **3.** a small amount or trace of something: *a spark of intelligence*; *a spark of life.* ◇*v.i.* **4.** to emit or produce sparks. **5.** to send forth gleams or flashes. ◇*v.t.* **6.** *Colloq.* to set going: *to spark conversation; to spark off interest.* [OE *spearca*]

sparkle /'spɑkəl/, *v.*, **-kled, -kling,** *n.* ◇*v.i.* **1.** (of fire, light, etc.) to come out in or as if in little sparks. **2.** to shine with little gleams of light: *A diamond sparkles.* **3.** to have bubbles of air: *wine sparkling in the glass.* **4.** to be brilliant, lively, or vivacious: *His eyes sparkled.* ◇*n.* **5.** a little spark. **6.** sparkling appearance or shine: *the sparkle of a diamond.* **7.** brilliance; liveliness or vivacity: *the sparkle in your eyes.* [from SPARK]

sparkler /'spɑklə/, *n.* **1.** someone or something that sparkles. **2.** hand-held firework that burns slowly and gives off a shower of sparks.

spark plug, *n.* a device put into the cylinder of an internal-combustion engine, containing two terminals between which passes the electric spark for igniting the explosive gases. Also, **sparking plug.**

sparrow /'spærou/, *n.* a small, hardy, bold passerine bird of Europe, introduced into Australia, America, etc., as a destroyer of insects, but now commonly regarded as a pest. [OE *spearwa*]

sparrowhawk /'spærouhɔk/, *n.* **1.** a small, brownish, square-tailed hawk of Australia and NG which hunts smaller birds. **2.** → **nankeen kestrel.**

sparse /spɑs/, *adj.*, **sparser, sparsest.** **1.** thinly scattered or distributed: *a sparse population.* **2.** thin: *sparse hair.* **3.** of small amount; scanty; meagre. [L: scattered] —**sparsity,** *n.*

Sparta /'spɑtə/, *n.* an ancient city in southern Greece, the capital of Laconia and the chief city of the Peloponnesus, famous for strict discipline and training of soldiers. Also, **Lacedaemon.**

Spartacus /'spɑtəkəs/, *n.* died 71 BC, a Thracian who became a slave and gladiator in Italy, and leader of an insurrection of slaves.

Spartan /'spɑtn/, *adj.* **1.** of or relating to Sparta. **2.** (*l.c.*) unbendingly simple in lifestyle; sternly disciplined. ◇*n.* **3.** a citizen of Sparta. **4.** a person of spartan (def. 2) characteristics. [from SPARTA] —**Spartanism,** *n.*

spasm /'spæzəm/, *n.* **1.** *Pathol.* a sudden, unusual, uncontrolled muscular contraction. **2.** any sudden, short spell of great energy, activity, feeling, etc. [ME, from L, from Gk

spasmodic /spæz'mɒdɪk/, *adj.* **1.** marked by spasms. **2.** like a spasm; sudden and violent, but short, and happening only from time to time; intermittent: *spasmodic efforts*. [ML, from Gk]

spastic /'spæstɪk/, *adj.* **1.** relating to, or marked by spasm. **2.** (*usu. offensive*) idiotic; clumsy. ◇*n.* **3.** a person suffering from spasms, esp. someone who has cerebral palsy. [L, from Gk]

spat[1] /spæt/, *n., v.,* **spatted, spatting.** ◇*n.* **1.** a light blow; slap; smack. **2.** a small quarrel. ◇*v.i.* **3.** to slap. **4.** to splash; spatter. [? imitative]

spat[2] /spæt/, *v.* past tense and past participle of **spit**.

spat[3] /spæt/, *n.* (*usu. pl.*) a short covering worn over the instep, usu. fastened under the foot with a strap. [short for *spatterdash*, kind of gaiter]

spat[4] /spæt/, *n.* the spawn or young of an oyster or similar shellfish. [orig. uncert.]

spate /speɪt/, *n.* a sudden outpouring: *a spate of words*; *a spate of rain*. [ME]

spatial /'speɪʃəl/, *adj.* of or relating to space. — **spatiality**, *n.*

spatio-, a word part meaning 'space'. [L *spatium* SPACE + -O-]

spatter /'spætə/, *v.t.* **1.** to scatter or splash in small particles or drops: *to spatter mud*. ◇*v.i.* **2.** to send out small particles or drops. ◇*n.* **3.** the act or sound of spattering: *the spatter of rain on a roof*. **4.** splash or spot of something spattered. [D and LG: burst, spout]

spatula /'spætjələ/, *n.* a tool with a broad, flat, bending blade, used for mixing foods, drugs, spreading plasters and paints, etc. [L] — **spatular, spatulate**, *adj.*

spawn /spɔn/, *n.* **1.** *Zool.* a mass of sex cells of fishes, amphibians, molluscs, crustaceans, etc., after being shed from the body. **2.** (*usu. offensive*) a large number of children. ◇*v.i.* **3.** to shed eggs and sperm, esp. into water. ◇*v.t.* **4.** to produce (spawn). **5.** to give birth to; give rise to. **6.** (*usu. offensive*) to produce (children) in large numbers. [ME, from AF: spill, from L: expand]

spay /speɪ/, *v.t.* to remove the ovaries of (a female animal). [ME, from AF: cut with a sword]

SP bookmaker /ˌɛs piː 'bʊkmeɪkə/, *n.* an unlicensed bookmaker operating off racetracks and paying the starting price odds.

speak /spik/, *v.,* **spoke** or (*old form*) **spake**; **spoken** or (*old form*) **spoke**; **speaking.** ◇*v.i.* **1.** to give out the sounds of words with the ordinary (talking) voice. **2.** to communicate in this way: *to speak to a person about something*. **3.** to make something known by any means: *The Prime Minister speaks to the people through the press*. **4.** to have a conversation. **5.** to deliver an address, discourse, etc.: *to speak in Parliament*. **6.** to make a sound: *The trumpet speaks*. ◇*v.t.* **7.** to utter or express: *to speak words of praise*. **8.** to make known with the voice: *to speak the truth*. **9.** to be able to use a language: *to speak French*. ◇*v.* **10.** Some special uses are:
so to speak, to use a certain way of speaking; as one might say.
speak for, **1.** to put someone's case forward; recommend. **2.** to put aside; reserve; bespeak: *This dress is already spoken for*.
speak out, to express one's views openly.
speak up, to speak loudly and clearly.
to speak of, worth mentioning: *He has no money to speak of*.
[OE *sprecan*] — **speakable**, *adj.*

-speak, a suffix used to indicate a particular variety of spoken language as in *newspeak*.

speaker /'spikə/, *n.* **1.** someone who speaks, esp. formally before an audience; orator. **2.** (*usu. cap.*) the presiding officer of the lower house of a parliament, as in the House of Representatives.

spear[1] /spɪə/, *n.* **1.** a weapon for thrusting or throwing, being a long staff with a sharp head, of iron or steel. **2.** a man armed with a spear. ◇*v.t.* **3.** to pierce with a spear. [OE *spere*]

spear[2] /spɪə/, *n.* **1.** a sprout or shoot of a plant; head of grain; blade of grass, grain, etc. ◇*v.i.* **2.** to sprout; shoot; send up or rise in a spear or spears. [var. of SPIRE]

spear grass, *n.* a type of native grass, resistant to dry weather, some varieties of which can cause damage to stock.

spear gun, *n.* a gun, propelling a spear, powered by compressed air, a powerful spring, etc., used in underwater fishing.

spearmint /'spɪəmɪnt/, *n.* a garden herb much used for flavoring.

Spears /spɪəz/, **Steve J**, born 1951, Australian playwright; wrote *The Elocution of Benjamin Franklin* (1977).

spec /spɛk/, *Colloq.* ◇*n.* **1.** speculation. **2. on spec**, as a guess, risk, or gamble: *to buy shares on spec*. ◇*adj.* **3.** speculative.

spec builder, *n.* someone who builds houses, etc., in the hope of selling them, rather than under contract.

special /'spɛʃəl/, *adj., n., v.,* **specialled, specialling.** ◇*adj.* **1.** of a distinct or particular character or purpose. **2.** being a particular one; particular, individual, or certain: *I have kept a special place for you*. **3.** different from what is ordinary or usual: *a special occasion*. **4.** extraordinary; exceptional: *special importance*; *a special friend*. ◇*n.* **5.** a special person or thing. **6.** an item sold at a special (usu. bargain) price. **7. on special**, *Colloq.* available at a bargain price. **8.** a special edition of a newspaper. ◇*v.t.* **9.** (of a nurse) to care for (a patient) as a special responsibility. [ME, from L]

specialise or **specialize** /'spɛʃəlaɪz/, *v.,* **-lised, -lising.** ◇*v.i.* **1.** to concentrate on some special line of study, work, etc. **2.** *Biol.* to develop characteristics for special purposes. ◇*v.t.* **3.** *Biol.* to change (an organism or one of its organs) to fit it for a special function or environment. — **specialisation**, *n.* — **specialist**, *n.*

speciality /spɛʃɪˈæləti/, *n., pl.* **-ties. 1.** a special or particular character. **2.** an article of unusual or superior design or quality. **3.** → **specialty**. [ME, from OF, from LL]

specialty /ˈspɛʃəlti/, *n., pl.* **-ties. 1.** a special point or item; particular detail. **2.** a special study, line of work, or manufacture, etc. **3.** → **speciality**. **4. specialty of the house,** a dish by which a restaurant claims to be distinguished from other places. [ME, from OF: speciality]

specie /ˈspiʃi/, *n.* **1.** coin; coined money. **2. in specie, a.** in kind. See **kind**² (def. 6a). **b.** (of money) in actual coin. [L]

species /ˈspiːsɪz, -ʃɪz/, *n., pl.* **-cies. 1.** a group of individuals having some common characteristics or qualities; distinct sort or kind. **2.** a basic category of biological classification, meant to describe a single type of animal or plant. Individual variations are thought of as not affecting the essential sameness which distinguishes them from all other organisms. [L: appearance, sort]

specific /spəˈsɪfɪk/, *adj.* **1.** being particular or definite, describing one type: *specific mention*. **2.** *Zool., Bot.* of or relating to a species: *specific characters*. **3.** *Phys.* indicating a physical quantity which has been divided by mass, i.e. quantity per unit mass, as specific activity, specific charge, specific heat, etc. ◇*n.* **4.** something particular; an item; detail. **–specifically,** *adv.* **–specificity,** *n.*

specification /spɛsəfəˈkeɪʃən/, *n.* **1.** the act of specifying. **2.** a detailed description setting out the dimensions, materials, etc., for a proposed building, engineering work, etc.

specific gravity, *n.* → **relative density**. *Abbrev.*: s.g.

specific heat, *n.* the heat required to raise unit mass of a substance through one degree of temperature, expressed in joules per kilogram per kelvin (SI units), calories per gram per degree C, or BTUs per pound per degree F; specific heat capacity. *Symbol:* c

specify /ˈspɛsəfaɪ/, *v.t.*, **-fied, -fying. 1.** to state in detail; mention or name specifically or definitely. **2.** to give a particular character to. **3.** to name or state (something) as a condition. [ME, from ML: specific, from L: sort, kind]

specimen /ˈspɛsəmən/, *n.* **1.** a typical animal, plant, mineral, part, etc.; a part or individual taken as representing a whole mass or number. **2.** *Med.* a sample of a substance, esp. urine, to be examined or tested for a particular purpose. [L]

specious /ˈspiʃəs/, *adj.* **1.** seemingly good or right but without real worth; superficially pleasing: *specious arguments*. **2.** pleasing to the eye, but deceptive or not really so. [ME, from L: fair, fair-seeming] **–speciosity,** *n.*

speck /spɛk/, *n.* **1.** a small spot, oft. different in quality, color, etc., from its background. **2.** a very little bit or particle. **3.** something appearing small by comparison or by distance. ◇*v.t.* **4.** to mark with, or as if with, a speck or specks. [OE *specca*]

speckle /ˈspɛkəl/, *n., v.,* **-led, -ling.** ◇*n.* **1.** a small speck, spot, or mark. **2.** speckled coloring or marking. ◇*v.t.* **3.** to mark with, or as if with, speckles. [from SPECK]

spectacle /ˈspɛktəkəl/, *n.* **1.** anything presented to the sight or view, esp. something of a striking kind. **2.** (a large) public show or display. **3.** (*pl.*) a device to aid faulty eyesight or to protect the eyes from light, dust, etc., consisting usu. of two glass lenses set in a frame (often called a **pair of spectacles**). **4. make a spectacle of oneself,** to draw attention to oneself by foolish behavior. [ME, from L] **–spectacled,** *adj.*

spectacular /spɛkˈtækjələ/, *adj.* **1.** marked by or given to great display. **2.** dramatic; thrilling. ◇*n.* **3.** an expensively produced film, television show, etc.

spectator /spɛkˈteɪtə, ˈspɛkteɪtə/, *n.* **1.** someone who looks on. **2.** someone who is present at and views a public show, sporting match, etc. [L]

spectra /ˈspɛktrə/, *n.* plural of **spectrum**.

spectral /ˈspɛktrəl/, *adj.* **1.** relating to, like, or typical of a ghost, spectre, etc. **2.** of, relating to, or produced by a spectrum (defs 1a and 1b). **–spectrality,** *n.*

spectre /ˈspɛktə/, *n.* **1.** a spirit that can be seen, esp. one of a frightening nature; ghost; apparition. **2.** some object or source of great fear. [L: apparition]

spectro-, a word part representing 'spectrum'.

spectroscope /ˈspɛktrəskoʊp/, *n.* an optical instrument for producing and examining the spectrum of light or other forms of electromagnetic radiation. **–spectroscopic,** *adj.* **–spectroscopy,** *n.*

spectrum /ˈspɛktrəm/, *n., pl.* **-tra. 1.** *Phys.* **a.** the band of colors, each with a different wavelength (red, orange, yellow, green, blue, indigo, violet), which is seen when white light passes through a prism. **b.** a similar band of other wavelengths or frequencies (as in infrared spectrum, radio-frequency spectrum, etc.). **2.** a range of interrelated values, objects, opinions, etc.: *the spectrum of Australian English speech varieties*. [L: appearance, form]

speculate /ˈspɛkjəleɪt/, *v.i.*, **-lated, -lating. 1.** to think or reflect, esp. with incomplete evidence; meditate or conjecture (oft. fol. by *on*, *upon*, or a clause): *She speculated that she would do well in the exams*. **2.** *Comm.* to buy and sell goods, shares, etc., in the hope of profit or gain through a change in their market value. [L: observed, examined] **–speculation,** *n.* **–speculative,** *adj.* **–speculator,** *n.*

sped /spɛd/, *v.* past tense and past participle of **speed**.

speech /spitʃ/, *n.* **1.** the ability or power of speaking; oral communication; expression of human thought and emotion by speech sounds. **2.** something that is spoken; utterance, remark, or declaration. **3.** a series of remarks or statements in spoken language, made by a speaker before an audience. **4.** the form of speech typical of a particular people or area;

speech

language or dialect. **5.** manner of speaking, usu. of a person. [OE *spǣc*]

speed /spid/, *n., v.,* **sped** or **speeded, speeding.** ◇*n.* **1.** quickness or rapidity in moving, going, travelling, or in any undertaking or performance; swiftness; celerity. **2.** the ratio of the distance covered by a moving body to the time taken. **3.** *Motor Vehicles.* a transmission gear-ratio. **4.** *Archaic.* success; prosperity. **5.** *Colloq.* → **amphetamine.** ◇*v.t.* **6.** to help the success of (an affair, undertaking, etc.); further; forward. **7.** to cause to move, go, or carry on, with speed. **8.** *Archaic.* to cause to succeed or prosper: *God speed you.* ◇*v.i.* **9.** to move, go, pass, or keep on with speed or rapidity. **10.** to drive a vehicle at a rate over the limit allowed by law. **11.** *Archaic.* to succeed or prosper. ◇*v.* **12. speed up, a.** to move faster. **b.** to increase (production). [OE *spēd*] – **speeder, speedster,** *n.* – **speedy,** *adj.*

speedometer /spiˈdɒmətə/, *n.* an apparatus attached to a motor vehicle, etc., to record the rate of travel.

speedway /ˈspidweɪ/, *n.* **1.** a racing track for motor vehicles, esp. motorcycles. **2.** a road on which more than the ordinary speed is allowed.

speleology /spiliˈɒlədʒi/, *n.* the exploration and study of caves. [Gk] – **speleologist,** *n.*

spell[1] /spɛl/, *v.,* **spelt** or **spelled, spelling.** ◇*v.t.* **1.** to name, write, or otherwise give in order, the letters of (a word, etc.). **2.** (of letters) to form (a word). **3.** to mean; amount to: *This delay spells disaster for us.* ◇*v.i.* **4.** to name, write, or give the letters of words, etc. ◇*v.* **5. spell out, a.** to read (something) with difficulty. **b.** to make completely clear; explain. [ME, from OF, from Gmc orig.] – **spelling,** *n.*

spell[2] /spɛl/, *n.* **1.** a form of words supposed to possess magic power; charm; incantation; enchantment. **2.** any overpowering or irresistible influence; fascination. [OE *spell* discourse]

spell[3] /spɛl/, *n.* **1.** a period of work or other activity: *to take a spell at the wheel.* **2.** a turn, bout, fit, or period of anything: *a spell of coughing.* **3.** *Colloq.* (a short) interval or space of time. **4.** a period of weather of a particular kind: *a hot spell.* **5.** an interval or period of rest. ◇*v.t.* **6.** to take the place of or relieve (a person, etc.) for a time while they rest. [OE *spelian* represent]

spellbound /ˈspɛlbaʊnd/, *adj.* bound or held by, or as if by, a spell; enchanted or fascinated: *a spellbound audience.*

spelt[1] /spɛlt/, *v.* a past tense and past participle of **spell**[1].

spelt[2] /spɛlt/, *n.* a type of wheat used in developing improved varieties of wheat. [OE, from LL]

Spence /spɛns/, *n.* **William Guthrie,** 1846–1926, Australian labor leader and politician, born in Scotland.

spencer /ˈspɛnsə/, *n.* a woman's singlet, worn for extra warmth. [named after George John *Spencer,* 1758–1834, 2nd Earl Spencer]

Spencer Gulf, *n.* an inlet on the coast of SA, separating the Eyre and Yorke peninsulas; extends for some 320 km from north to south and is 85 km wide at its entrance. [named in 1802 in honor of Earl *Spencer,* chairman of the British Board of Admiralty]

spend /spɛnd/, *v.,* **spent, spending.** ◇*v.t.* **1.** to pay out (money, wealth, resources, etc.); expend; disburse. **2.** to use (labor, thought, words, time, etc.) on some object, in some business, etc. **3.** to pass (time) in a particular manner, place, etc. **4.** to use up; consume; exhaust: *The storm had spent its fury.* **5.** to give (one's blood, life, etc.) for some cause. ◇*v.i.* **6.** to spend money, etc. [OE *spendan,* from L: expend] – **spender,** *n.*

spendthrift /ˈspɛndθrɪft/, *n.* **1.** someone who spends their possessions or money unnecessarily or wastefully; prodigal. ◇*adj.* **2.** wasteful; extravagant.

Spenser /ˈspɛnsə/, *n.* **Edmund,** c. 1552–99, English poet, wrote *The Faerie Queene.*

spent /spɛnt/, *v.* **1.** past tense and past participle of **spend.** ◇*adj.* **2.** used up or exhausted.

sperm /spɜm/, *n.* **1.** → **semen.** **2.** the male reproductive cell; spermatozoon. [ME, from L, from Gk] – **spermatic, spermous,** *adj.*

sperm-, a word part representing 'sperm'. Also, **spermo-, spermato-, spermat-.**

-sperm, an ending combining form of 'sperm', as in *angiosperm.*

-spermal, a word part used to form adjectives related to 'sperm'.

spermatozoon /ˌspɜmətoʊˈzoʊɒn/, *n., pl.* **-zoa** /-ˈzoʊə/. one of the tiny, usu. actively moving, gametes (male reproductive cells) in semen, which serve to fertilise the ovum; mature male reproductive cell. – **spermatozoal, spermatozoan, spermatozoic,** *adj.*

sperm whale, *n.* a large, square-headed whale, valuable for oil and a white, wax-like substance used in making cosmetics; cachalot.

spew /spju/, *v.i.* **1.** → **vomit.** ◇*v.t.* **2.** to shoot out or discharge violently. [OE *spīwan*]

sp. gr., *Abbrev.* specific gravity.

sphagnum /ˈsfægnəm/, *n.* any of the bog mosses found chiefly in temperate areas of high rainfall and little sun, where they may build up deep layers of peat; used esp. by gardeners in potting plants. [NL, from Gk: a moss]

sphalerite /ˈsfælərʌɪt, ˈsfeɪlə-/, *n.* a very common mineral, zinc sulfide, ZnS, usu. containing some iron and a little cadmium; blende; blackjack. [Gk: deceptive, uncertain]

sphere /sfɪə/, *n.* **1.** a round body whose surface is at all points of equal distance from the centre. **2.** anything shaped like a sphere, as a tennis ball. **3.** a heavenly body; planet or star. **4.** → **celestial sphere. 5.** *Ancient Astron.* any of the transparent, spherical shells sharing a common centre, or 'heavens', in which the planets, fixed stars, etc., were supposed to be set. **6.** the place or environment within which a person or thing exists: *He was out of his sphere.* **7.** a particular level of society or walk of life. **8.** a field of something particular: *a sphere of influence.* [ME, from L, from Gk]

-sphere, a word part representing 'sphere', having a special use in the names of the layers of gases, etc., surrounding the earth and other heavenly bodies, as in *ionosphere.*

spherical /'sferəkəl/, *adj.* **1.** having the form of a sphere; globular. **2.** formed in or on a sphere. **3.** of or relating to a sphere or spheres: *spherical trigonometry.* **—sphericity,** *n.*

spherical aberration, *n.* variation in focal length of a lens from centre to edge due to its spherical shape.

spheroid /'sfɪərɔɪd/, *n.* **1.** a solid of revolution obtained by turning an ellipse about either of its axes; body that looks like a slightly flattened ball or sphere. ◇*adj.* **2.** Also, **spheroidal.** relating to or shaped like a spheroid.

sphincter /'sfɪŋktə/, *n.* a circular band of muscle around an opening of the body or one of its hollow organs. [L, from Gk: band]

Sphinx /sfɪŋks/, *n., pl.* **sphinxes, sphinges** /'sfɪndʒiːz/. **1.** *Egypt Antiq.* the colossal stone figure of a creature with the head of a man or an animal and the body of a lion, situated near the pyramids of El Giza. **2.** *Gk Myth.* a monster with the head and breast of a woman, the body of a lion or a dog, and wings, which killed all who were unable to guess her riddle. [L, from Gk]

sp. ht, *Abbrev.* specific heat.

spice /spaɪs/, *n., v.,* **spiced, spicing.** ◇*n.* **1.** any of a class of strongly or sweetly smelling substances of vegetable origin, such as pepper, cinnamon, cloves, etc., used as seasoning or preservatives. **2.** something that gives interest; a piquant element or quality. ◇*v.t.* **3.** to prepare or season with a spice or spices. **4.** to give flavor or interest to by something added. [ME, from OF, from L: species]

Spice Islands, *n.pl.* the former name of the Moluccas.

spick-and-span /spɪk-ən-'spæn/, *adj.* **1.** neat and clean. **2.** perfectly new; fresh. Also, **spick and span.** [var. of *span-new*, from Scand]

spicy /'spaɪsi/, *adj.,* **spicier, spiciest. 1.** seasoned with or containing spice. **2.** typical or suggestive of spice in flavor or smell. **3.** strongly or sweetly smelling; aromatic; fragrant. **4.** smart, racy or biting: *spicy criticism.* **5.** of a slightly improper, scandalous, or sensational nature. **—spiciness,** *n.*

spider /'spaɪdə/, *n.* **1.** any of the eight-legged wingless, insectlike arachnids, most of which spin webs that serve as nests and as traps for prey. **2.** any vehicle, apparatus, tool, etc., looking like or suggesting a spider. [OE *spīthra*] **—spidery,** *adj.*

spiel /spiːl, ʃpiːl/, *n. Colloq.* **1.** smooth or reasonable-sounding talk, esp. for the purpose of selling, persuasion, cheating, seduction, etc. **2.** any talk or speech. [G: play] **—spieler,** *n.*

spier /'spaɪə/, *n.* someone who spies, watches, or discovers. Also, **spyer.**

spigot /'spɪgət/, *n.* **1.** a small peg or plug for closing the outlet of a cask, etc. **2.** the end of a pipe which enters the enlarged end of another pipe to form a joint. [ME, from SPIKE[1]]

spike[1] /spaɪk/, *n., v.,* **spiked, spiking.** ◇*n.* **1.** a large, strong nail or pin, esp. made of iron. **2.** a stiff, sharp-pointed piece or part. **3. a.** a sharp metal projection on the bottom of a shoe, as that of a golf player, to prevent slipping. **b.** (*pl.*) running shoes having spikes. ◇*v.t.* **4.** to fasten or make firm with a spike or spikes. **5.** to provide or set with a spike or spikes. **6.** to pierce with a spike. **7.** to make ineffective: *to spike a rumor.* **8.** *Colloq.* to add alcohol to (a drink). **9.** to increase the impact, interest or attractiveness of a speech, conversation, etc. [ME, from Scand] **—spiky,** *adj.*

spike[2] /spaɪk/, *n.* **1.** an ear, esp. of wheat or other grain. **2.** *Bot.* a cluster or group of blossoms in which the flowers are joined at the base along a lengthened, unbranched stalk. [ME, from L: ear of grain]

spill[1] /spɪl/, *v.,* **spilt** or **spilled, spilling,** *n.* ◇*v.t.* **1.** to cause or allow (liquid, or any matter in grains or loose pieces) to run out or fall from a container, esp. accidentally or wastefully. **2.** to shed (blood), esp. in killing or wounding. **3.** to cause to fall from a horse, vehicle, etc. **4.** *Colloq.* to disclose, or tell (a secret, etc.). ◇*v.i.* **5.** (of a liquid, loose particles, etc.) to run or escape from a container. ◇*n.* **6.** Also, **spillage.** an act of spilling. **7.** Also, **spillage.** the quantity spilt. **8.** a throw or fall from a horse, vehicle, etc. **9.** the leaving empty of positions of political leadership before new ballots, appointments, etc. [OE *spillan*]

spill[2] /spɪl/, *n.* a slender piece of wood or twisted paper, for lighting candles, lamps, etc. [ME]

spin /spɪn/, *v.,* **spun** or (*old form*) **span; spun; spinning;** *n.* ◇*v.t.* **1.** to make (yarn) by drawing out, twisting, and winding fibres. **2.** to form (any material) into thread. **3.** (of spiders, silkworms, etc.) to produce (a cobweb, silk, etc.) by letting out from the body a long, slender moist thread that hardens in the air. **4.** to cause to turn round rapidly, as if on an axis; twirl; whirl: *to spin a coin on a table.* **5.** to produce or make up in a manner suggestive of spinning thread, such as a story. **6. a.** *Cricket.* (of a bowler) to cause (the ball) to turn on its axis so that on bouncing it changes direction or speed. **b.** *Tennis, etc.* to hit (the ball) so that it behaves in this way. **7.** *Two-up.* to toss the coins. ◇*v.i.* **8.** to turn round rapidly, as if on an axis, as the earth, a top, etc. **9.** to produce a thread from the body, such as spiders, silkworms, etc. **10.** to move, go, run, ride, or travel rapidly. **11.** to be affected with a feeling of whirling. ◇*v.* **12. spin out, a.** to draw out; prolong: *to spin out a story.* **b.** to make (money) last. ◇*n.* **13.** the act of causing a spinning or whirling motion. **14.** a spinning motion given to a ball, etc., when thrown or struck. **15.**

Aeron. a condition of stalled flight in which the aircraft spirals downwards, nose first. **16.** a moving or going rapidly along. **17.** a rapid run, ride, drive, etc., as for exercise or enjoyment. **18.** *Colloq.* a condition of confusion or excitement. **19.** *Colloq.* an experience or chance generally: *a rough spin; a fair spin.* **20.** *Phys.* (of a sub-atomic particle, such as an orbital electron) the energy of the spin around the particle's own axis. [OE *spinnan*]

spina bifida /spaɪnə 'bɪfədə/, *n.* a defect existing from birth in the development of the spinal column in which it fails to join up properly.

spinach /'spɪnɪtʃ/, *n.* **1.** (the leaves of) a large herb grown for its juicy, edible leaves. **2.** → **silver beet.** [OF, from ML, from Sp, from Ar]

spinal /'spaɪnəl/, *adj.* relating or belonging to the spine or backbone. [LL]

spinal column, *n.* the vertebrae forming the axis of the skeleton and protecting the spinal cord; spine; backbone.

spinal cord, *n.* the cord of nervous tissue extending through the spinal column.

spindle /'spɪndl/, *n., adj., v.,* **-dled, -dling.** ◇*n.* **1.** a rod, usu. of wood, used to twist or wind the thread in spinning by hand, wheel or machine. **2.** any rod or peg suggestive of a spindle used in spinning, usu. one which turns round or on which something turns; axle, axis, or shaft. **3.** either of the two shaft-like parts in a lathe which support the work to be turned, one (**live spindle**) turning and giving movement to the work, and the other (**dead spindle**) not turning. **4.** *Biol.* fine threads of material arranged within the cell, during mitosis (a method of cell-division), in a spindle-shaped manner. **5.** a short turned or circular ornament, such as in a stair rail. ◇*adj.* **6.** of or looking like spindles. ◇*v.i.* **7.** to grow tall and slender. [OE *spinnan* SPIN]

spin-dry /spɪn-'draɪ/, *v.t.,* **-dried, -drying.** to dry (washing) by spinning it in a tub so that the moisture is taken out by centrifugal force.

spine /spaɪn/, *n.* **1.** the vertebral or spinal column; backbone. **2.** any backbone-like part. **3.** a pointed process or projection, usu. of a bone. **4.** a stiff, pointed process or part on an animal, such as a quill of a porcupine, or a sharp, bony ray in a fish's fin. **5.** a ridge, usu. of ground, rock, etc. **6.** a sharp-pointed, hard or woody outgrowth on a plant; thorn. **7.** *Bookbinding.* the part of a book's cover that holds the front and back together, and which usu. shows title and author. [ME, from L]

spinebill /'spaɪnbɪl/, *n.* either of two Australian honeyeaters having long, very slender, down-curved bills.

spinel /spə'nɛl/, *n.* **1.** any of a group of minerals made up mainly of oxides of magnesium, aluminium, iron, manganese, chromium, etc., marked by their hardness and eight-faced crystals. **2.** a mineral of this group, mainly magnesium aluminate, $MgAl_2O_4$, and having varieties used as ornamental stones in jewellery. [F, from It: thorn, from L]

spinet /'spɪnət/, *n.* a small keyboard instrument rather like the harpsichord, the main difference being that the strings run across the instrument more or less in the direction of the keyboard, not at right angles to it. [F, ? named after Giovanni *Spinetti*, fl. 1500, Venetian inventor]

spinifex /'spɪnəfɛks/, *n.* **1.** a spiny grass chiefly of Australia, often useful for binding sand on the seashore. **2.** a type of spiny-leaved, tussock-forming grass of inland Australia. [NL: spine maker]

spinifex bird, *n.* a wren-like bird living in the spinifex and low scrubs of Australian dry areas.

spinnaker /'spɪnəkə/, *n.* a large triangular sail with a light boom (**spinnaker boom**), carried by yachts on the side opposite the mainsail when running before the wind, or with the wind behind the beam. [supposedly from *Sphinx* (mispronounced *spinks*), name of yacht on which this sail was first regularly used]

spinner /'spɪnə/, *n.* **1.** someone or something that spins, such as a spider. **2.** a bait with blades that turn when pulled through the water, used in fishing. **3.** *Cricket, etc.* **a.** a type of delivery in which the bowler gives a sideways spin to the ball, making it change course upon pitching. **b.** a bowler specialising in such deliveries.

spinneret /'spɪnərɛt/, *n.* an organ or part by means of which a spider, insect larva, etc., spins a silky thread for its web or cocoon. [from SPINNER]

spinney /'spɪni/, *n., pl.* **-neys.** *Brit.* a thicket or copse. [ME, from OF: thorny place]

spinning /'spɪnɪŋ/, *n.* **1.** a method or act of changing fibrous substances into yarn or thread. **2.** *Angling.* a technique or act of casting and drawing back the bait in such a way as to copy the movement of a live fish.

spinning jenny, *n.* a type of spinning machine with more than one spindle allowing one person to spin several yarns at the same time.

spinning wheel, *n.* a device for spinning wool, flax, etc., into yarn or thread consisting mainly of a single spindle driven by a large wheel operated by hand or foot.

spin-off /'spɪn-ɒf/, *n.* **1.** an object, product or undertaking developed from or because of a larger development: *The non-stick frying pan is a commercially valuable spin-off of space research.* **2.** *Econ.* the formation of a new company by an existing company, with shareholders in the existing company entitled to subscribe for shares in the new company.

spinster /'spɪnstə/, *n.* a woman who remains unmarried. [ME, from SPIN + -STER]

spiny /'spaɪni/, *adj.,* **spinier, spiniest. 1.** having many spines; thorny, as a plant. **2.** covered with or having sharp-pointed processes, as an animal. **3.** in the form of a spine; resembling a spine; spinelike. **4.** worrying or troublesome: *a spiny problem.*

spiny anteater, *n.* → **echidna.**

spiracle /'spaɪrəkəl, 'spɪrəkəl/, n. an opening to admit or discharge air. [ME, from L]

spiral /'spaɪrəl/, n., adj., v., **-ralled**, **-railing**. ◇n. **1.** a plane curve traced by a point which runs continuously round and round a fixed point or centre while constantly going away from or approaching it. **2.** a single circle or ring of a spiral curve or object. **3.** a spiral object, formation, or form. **4.** → **helix**. **5.** *Econ.* the mutual interaction of price and cost changes forming an overall economic change upwards (**inflationary spiral**) or downwards (**deflationary spiral**). ◇adj. **6.** like or arranged in a spiral or spirals. **7.** (of a curve) like a spiral. **8.** → **helical**. ◇v.i., v.t. **9.** to take or cause to take a spiral form or course. [ML]

spire /spaɪə/, n. **1.** a tall, tapering structure, generally a lengthened, upright cone or pyramid built on a tower, roof, etc. **2.** such a structure forming the upper part of a steeple, or the whole steeple. **3.** a tapering, pointed part of something, such as the shoot of a plant. **4.** the highest point or summit of something, esp. the peak of a mountain, etc. [OE *spīr*]

spirit /'spɪrət/, n. **1.** the principle of conscious life, originally related to the breath; vital principle animating a person's life and actions. **2.** a vital, unseen part of a person: *present in spirit though absent in body*. **3.** the soul as separable from the body at death. **4.** any supernatural being. **5.** a life-giving principle: *a spirit of reform*. **6.** → **Holy Spirit**. **7.** (*pl.*) feelings with respect to mood: *in low spirits*; *in high spirits*. **8.** temper or nature: *meek in spirit*. **9.** mental or moral attitude; mood: *Take my advice in the right spirit*. **10.** the main tendency or character of anything: *the spirit of the age*; *team spirit*. **11.** *Chem.* **a.** a distilled aqueous solution of ethyl alcohol. **b.** a distilled liquid extract. **12.** (*oft. pl.*) strong distilled alcoholic liquor. **13.** *Pharm.* an alcohol solution of an essential or volatile principle. ◇adj. **14.** relating to something which works by burning alcoholic spirits: *a spirit lamp*. **15.** of or relating to spiritualist bodies or activities. ◇v.t. **16.** to carry (*away, off*, etc.) mysteriously or secretly. [ME, from L: breathing]

spirited /'spɪrətəd/, adj. **1.** having a spirit, or spirits, as mentioned: *low-spirited*. **2.** having or showing courage, strength, liveliness, etc.

spirit level, n. a type of level consisting of a glass tube containing an oil or spirit, with a movable bubble which is only in the centre of the tube if the spirit level is horizontal.

spiritual /'spɪrətʃuəl, -tʃəl/, adj. **1.** of or consisting of the spirit or soul. **2.** standing in a relationship of the spirit; non-material: *a spiritual attitude*; *a spiritual father*. **3.** of or relating to the spirit as the centre of the moral or religious nature. **4.** of or relating to holy things; belonging to the church; religious; devotional; sacred. ◇n. **5.** a traditional religious song, esp. of American Negroes. [L] —**spirituality**, n.

spiritualism /'spɪrətʃəlɪzəm/, n. **1.** a belief or doctrine that the spirits of the dead keep living after the mortal life, and communicate with the living, esp. through a person (a medium) particularly open to their influence. **2.** the practices or phenomena associated with this belief. **3.** a belief that all or some reality is immaterial and therefore spiritual. **4.** *Metaphys.* any belief that claims the separate but related existence of God, human (or other thinking) beings, and physical nature. **5.** a spiritual quality or tendency. **6.** a firm belief in the spiritual side of things, usu. in philosophy or religion. —**spiritualist**, n., adj.

spirituous /'spɪrətʃuəs/, adj. **1.** of the nature of, or relating to alcohol; alcoholic. **2.** (of liquors) distilled, as opposed to fermented.

spiro-[1], a word part referring to 'respiration'. [combining form representing L *spīrāre* breathe]

spiro-[2], a word part meaning 'coil', 'spiral', as in *spirochaete*. [Gk *speiro-*, combining form of *speira*]

spirochaete /'spaɪrəkit/, n. a slender, corkscrew-like bacterial micro-organism found on man, animals, and plants, and in soil and water. [SPIRO-[2] + Greek: hair]

spit[1] /spɪt/, v., **spat** or **spit**, **spitting**, n. ◇v.i. **1.** to eject saliva from the mouth; expectorate. **2.** to do this at or on a person, etc., to express hatred, contempt, etc. **3.** to fall in scattered drops or flakes, usu. rain or snow. **4.** to make a noise like spitting. ◇v.t. **5.** to eject (saliva, etc.) from the mouth. **6.** to throw or give out; say violently. ◇v. **7. spit chips**, *Colloq.* to be very annoyed or angry. **8. spit it out**, *Colloq.* speak up. ◇n. **9.** saliva, esp. when ejected. **10.** the act of spitting. **11.** a frothy or spitlike secretion given out by various insects; spittle. **12.** Also, **dead spit**. *Colloq.* the image, likeness, or counterpart of a person, etc. [OE *spittan*] —**spitter**, n.

spit[2] /spɪt/, n., v., **spitted**, **spitting**. ◇n. **1.** a sharply pointed, slender rod or bar for thrusting into meat to be roasted at a fire or grilled. **2.** a narrow point of land projecting into the water and attached at one end; cape. See **bar**. ◇v.t. **3.** to pierce, stab, or hold, as if with a spit; impale on something sharp. [OE *spitu*]

spite /spaɪt/, n., v., **spited**, **spiting**. ◇n. **1.** a keen, ill-natured desire to humiliate, annoy, or hurt another; venomous ill will. **2.** a grudge. **3. in spite of**, in disregard or defiance of; notwithstanding. ◇v.t. **4.** to direct one's spite or evil intention on. **5.** to annoy, out of spite. [ME] —**spiteful**, adj.

spitfire /'spɪtfaɪə/, n. a person of fiery temper, easily moved to outbursts.

spitting image, n. → **spit**[1] (def. 12).

spittle /'spɪtl/, n. **1.** saliva; spit. **2.** a frothy protective secretion given out by some insects. [OE *spātl*]

spittoon /spɪ'tun/, n. a bowl, etc., for spitting into.

splade /spleɪd/, n. a spoon-shaped fork with a cutting edge. [Trademark]

splash /splæʃ/, v.t. **1.** to wet or soil by dashing masses or particles of water, mud, etc.,

splash   996   **splutter**

spatter. **2.** to fall upon (something) in scattered masses or particles, as a liquid does. **3.** to cause to appear spattered. **4.** to dash (water, etc.) about in scattered masses or particles. **5.** to make (one's way) with splashing. **6.** *Colloq.* to display or print very noticeably, as in a newspaper. ◇*v.i.* **7.** to fall, move, strike, scatter or go with a splash. **8.** *Colloq.* to spend money freely (oft. fol. by *out*). ◇*n.* **9.** the act or sound of splashing. **10.** a quantity of some liquid or semiliquid substance, like mud, etc., splashed upon or in a thing. **11.** a spot or mark caused by something splashed. **12.** a patch, esp. of color or light. **13.** a striking show or display; sensation or excitement. **14. make a splash**, to be noticed; make an impression on people. [from OE, ? imitative] —**splashy**, *adj.*

splashdown /'splæʃdaʊn/, *n.* the landing of a spacecraft on a body of water.

splatter /'splætə/, *v.i., v.t.* to splash.

splay /spleɪ/, *v.t.* **1.** to spread out, expand, or extend. **2.** to make slanting; bevel. ◇*v.i.* **3.** to have a sloping or slanting direction. **4.** to spread or flare. ◇*n.* **5.** *Archit.* Also, **reveal.** a surface which makes a slanting or sloping angle with another. ◇*adj.* **6.** spread out; wide and flat; turned outwards. **7.** slanted or twisted to one side. [var. of DISPLAY]

spleen /splin/, *n.* **1.** a vascular, glandlike organ in which blood is modified. It is found at the end of the stomach nearest the heart. **2.** bad temper or spite: *venting his spleen on his unfortunate wife.* [ME, from L, from Gk]

splendid /'splendəd/, *adj.* **1.** gorgeous; magnificent. **2.** glorious, such as a name, reputation, victory, etc. **3.** strikingly admirable or fine: *splendid talents.* [L]

splendor or **splendour** /'splendə/, *n.* **1.** a brilliant or gorgeous appearance, coloring, etc.; magnificence, grandeur, or pomp: *the splendor and pomp of his coronation.* **2.** glory; brilliant distinction: *the splendor of ancient Roman architecture.* **3.** great brightness; brilliant light or lustre. [ME, from L]

splice /splaɪs/, *v.,* **spliced, splicing,** *n.* ◇*v.t.* **1.** to join together or unite, such as two ropes or parts of a rope, by the interweaving of strands. **2.** to join or unite, usu. two pieces of timber, etc., by overlapping. ◇*n.* **3.** a joining of two ropes or parts of a rope by splicing. **4.** the union so effected. **5.** a joining or meeting of two pieces of timber, etc., by overlapping and fastening the ends. [MD] —**splicer,** *n.*

splint /splɪnt/, *n.* **1.** a thin piece of wood or other rigid material used to hold still a fractured or dislocated bone, or to keep any part of the body in a fixed position. **2.** one of a number of thin strips of wood woven together to make a chair seat, basket, etc. **3.** one of a number of overlapping bands or strips of metal in armor for protecting the body and limbs. ◇*v.t.* **4.** to secure, hold in position, or support by means of a splint, as a fractured bone. **5.** to support as if with splints. [ME, from MLG: metal pin]

splinter /'splɪntə/, *n.* **1.** a rough piece of wood, bone, etc., usu. fairly long, thin, and sharp, split or broken off from a main body. **2.** fragment or small piece of metal resulting from the explosion of a bomb or shell. ◇*v.t.* **3.** to split or break into splinters. **4.** to break off in splinters. ◇*v.i.* **5.** to be split or broken into splinters. **6.** to break off in splinters. [ME, from MD or MLG]

split /splɪt/, *v.,* **split, splitting,** *n., adj.* ◇*v.t.* **1.** to separate or part from end to end or between layers, often forcibly or by cutting. **2.** to separate off lengthwise: *to split a piece from a block.* **3.** to tear, break or burst apart. **4.** to divide into separate parts or pieces. **5.** to divide (people) into different groups, parties, etc., usu. by disagreement, etc. **6.** *Stock Exchange.* to divide (a company's shares) into smaller units. **7.** *Colloq.* to share between two or more people, etc.: *to split a bottle of wine.* **8.** to separate into parts by putting something in between: *to split an infinitive.* ◇*v.i.* **9.** to break or part lengthways or in any other way. **10.** to break apart; to part by striking on a rock, by the violence of a storm, etc., as a ship. **11.** to break up or separate through disagreement, etc. **12.** *Colloq.* to leave hurriedly. ◇*v.* **13. split one's sides,** to laugh heartily. **14. split up,** *Colloq.* to part; leave each other; become separated. ◇*n.* **15.** the act of splitting. **16.** a crack or tear caused by splitting. **17.** a break or division in a party, etc., or between people. **18.** (*usu. pl.*) a skilful act of separating the legs while sinking to the floor, until they stretch out at right angles to the body, as in stage performances, ballet, gymnastics, etc. **19.** *Colloq.* a share, of money. ◇*adj.* **20.** parted lengthwise; cleft. **21.** divided. [MD]

split infinitive, *n.* a simple infinitive with a word between the *to* and the verb, as *to readily understand.*

split-level /'splɪt-levəl/, *adj.* **1.** marking or relating to a building having certain floors at other than main storey level, or a room with a floor at more than one level. ◇*n.* **2.** a house, etc., built like this.

split personality, *n. Psychiatry.* a nervous state marked by dissociation of mental processes, such as the taking on of many personalities.

splitting /'splɪtɪŋ/, *adj.* **1.** that splits. **2.** overpoweringly noisy, as if to split the ears. **3.** violent or severe, as a headache.

splurge /splɜdʒ/, *n., v.,* **splurged, splurging,** *Colloq.* ◇*n.* **1.** an open and showy display, esp. of wealth. ◇*v.t.* **2.** to spend (money) carelessly or unnecessarily. ◇*v.i.* **3.** to be careless in the spending of money, etc.: *We splurged and bought champagne.* [? b. SPLASH and SURGE]

splutter /'splʌtə/, *v.i.* **1.** to talk hastily, confusedly or unintelligently, esp. in excitement or embarrassment. **2.** to give out particles of something explosively, as something frying or a pen scattering ink: *The fat was spluttering in the pan.* **3.** to fly or fall in particles or drops; spatter, as a liquid. ◇*n.* **4.** spluttering speech or talk; dispute; noise or fuss. **5.** the sputtering or spattering of liquid, etc. [b. SPLASH and SPUTTER] —**splutterer,** *n.*

Spock /spɒk/, n. **Benjamin**, born 1903, US paediatrician.

Spode /spoʊd/, n. **Josiah**, 1754–1827, English potter.

spoil /spɔɪl/, v., **spoiled** or **spoilt**, **spoiling**, n. ◇v.t. **1.** to damage (a thing) so that it can never return to its former excellence, value, usefulness, etc.: *to spoil a sheet of paper*. **2.** (of a person) to damage in character or nature by unwise treatment, benefits, etc., esp. by giving way too much to demands, temper, etc. ◇v.i. **3.** to become spoiled, bad, or unfit for use, usu. food or other substances which go bad easily or quickly; become tainted or putrid. **4.** to plunder or rob; pillage. ◇v. **5. be spoiling for**, to be eager for (a fight, action, etc.). ◇n. **6.** (*oft. pl.*) booty, loot, or plunder taken in war or robbery. **7.** (*usu. pl.*) the advantages associated with a powerful or important position: *the spoils of office*. **8.** treasures won or built up. **9.** waste materials, such as those thrown up in mining, excavating, quarrying, etc. [ME, from OF, from L] –**spoilage**, n.

spoilsport /'spɔɪlspɔt/, n. someone who interferes with the pleasure of others.

spoke[1] /spoʊk/, v. past tense and old past participle of **speak**.

spoke[2] /spoʊk/, n. **1.** one of the bars, rods, or rungs radiating or spreading out from the hub or middle of a wheel and supporting the rim or outside edge. **2.** one of a number of pins or handles projecting from a cylinder or wheel, or joining hub and rim, as on a steering wheel. **3.** a rung of a ladder. [OE *spāca*]

spoken /'spoʊkən/, v. **1.** past participle of **speak**. ◇adj. **2.** expressed by speaking; oral (opposed to *written*). **3.** (in compounds) speaking, or using speech, as indicated: *fair-spoken, plain-spoken*.

spokesperson /'spoʊkspɜsən/, n. **1.** someone who speaks for another or others. **2.** the principal supporter or practitioner (of a movement, organisation, etc.), considered as speaking on its behalf. **3.** a public speaker. –**spokeswoman**, n.fem. –**spokesman**, n.masc.

spondee /'spɒndi/, n. a metrical foot consisting of two long syllables or two heavy beats. [ME, from L, from Gk] –**spondaic**, adj.

sponge /spʌndʒ/, n., v., **sponged**, **sponging**. ◇n. **1.** any of a group of water-dwelling (mostly marine) animals marked by a porous structure and (usu.) a horny, sandy, or chalky skeleton or framework, and which occur in large, often plant-like colonies. **2.** the light, yielding, porous, fibrous skeleton of certain animals, or colonies of this group marked by readily absorbing water, and becoming soft when wet while keeping toughness, used in bathing, cleaning, etc. **3.** any other type of spongelike substances. **4.** someone who usually lives at the expense of others; parasite. **5.** *Cookery*. **a.** dough raised with yeast, esp. before kneading, usu. for bread. **b.** a light sweet pudding of spongy texture, made with gelatine, eggs, fruit juice or other flavoring material, etc. **c.** → **sponge cake**. **6. throw in (up) the sponge**, *Colloq*. to give up; abandon hope or one's efforts. ◇v.t. **7.** to wipe or rub with a wet sponge, in order to clean or moisten. **8.** to remove with a wet sponge (fol. by *off, away*, etc.). **9.** to wipe out with or as if with a sponge (oft. fol. by *out*). **10.** to take up or absorb with a sponge, etc. (oft. fol. by *up*): *to sponge up water*. **11.** to get from another or at another's expense by indirect pressure, trading on good-nature, etc.: *to sponge a dinner*. **12.** *Colloq.* to live at the expense of others. [ME and OE, from L, from Gk] –**spongy**, adj. –**sponger**, n. –**sponginess**, n.

sponge cake, n. a very light kind of sweet cake, made with a large amount of eggs and very little shortening.

sponson /'spɒnsən/, n. **1.** a structure projecting from the side of a ship, such as a gun platform, or a platform for handling gear. **2.** that part at the upper edge on the side of a canoe which tends to float and keeps it from tipping over. [var. of EXPANSION]

sponsor /'spɒnsə/, n. **1.** someone who is responsible for a person or thing. **2.** someone who makes an engagement or promise on behalf of another; a surety. **3.** someone who answers for an infant at baptism, making the required professions and promises; a godfather or godmother. **4.** a person, firm, or other organisation that finances a radio or television program in return for advertisement of a commercial product, service, etc. **5.** *Parl Proc.* a member of a legislative assembly responsible for the introduction of a particular bill (usu. with reference only to private bills). ◇v.t. **6.** to act as sponsor for; promise, vouch, or answer for. [L] –**sponsorship**, n.

spontaneity /spɒntə'niəti, -'neɪəti/, n., pl. **-ties**. the condition, quality, or fact of being spontaneous.

spontaneous /spɒn'teɪniəs/, adj. **1.** proceeding from a personal impulse or action, without effort or thought; natural and unconstrained: *a spontaneous action; a spontaneous remark*. **2.** (of impulses, motion, activity, natural processes, etc.) arising from internal forces or energy. **3.** growing naturally or without cultivation, as plants, fruits, etc. **4.** produced by a natural process. [L]

spontaneous combustion, n. the lighting of a substance or body from the rapid oxidation of its own parts, without heat from any outside source.

spontaneous generation, n. → **abiogenesis**.

spoof /spuf/, n., v.t., v.i., adj. *Colloq.* parody; hoax. [coined by Robert Arthurs, 1852–1933, British comedian] –**spoofer**, n.

spook /spuk/, n. *Colloq.* **1.** a ghost; spectre. ◇v.t. **2.** to frighten. [D] –**spooked**, adj. –**spooky**, adj.

spool /spul/ n. **1.** any cylindrical piece or appliance on which something is wound. **2.** a device for holding film, magnetic tape, etc., which is stopped from slipping off by a disc on each side. **3.** a small cylindrical piece of wood or other material on which yarn is wound in spinning, for use in weaving; bobbin. **4.** →

spool 998 **spot**

reel[1] (def. 3). ◇v.t. **5.** to wind on a spool. [ME, from MD or MLG]

spoon /spun/, n. **1.** a utensil consisting of a handle attached to a bowl-shaped end, used for taking up or stirring liquid or other food, etc. **2.** any of various implements, objects, or parts looking like a spoon. ◇v.t. **3.** to take up or transfer in or as if in a spoon. ◇v.i. **4.** Colloq. to show affection, esp. in an openly sentimental manner. [ME and OE *spōn*]

spoonbill /'spunbɪl/, n. any of several wading birds closely related to the ibis and having a long, flat bill with a spoon-like tip, as the **royal spoonbill**, of Australia and certain islands to the north.

spoonerism /'spunərɪzəm/, n. (a deliberate) slip of the tongue where sounds of words are transposed, as in 'our queer old dean' for 'our dear old queen'. [named after Rev WA Spooner, 1844–1930, of New College, Oxford, noted for such slips]

spoon-feed /'spun-fid/, v.t., **-fed**, **-feeding. 1.** to give food by means of a spoon. **2.** to treat with too much care.

spoor /spɔ/, n. a track or trail, esp. that of a wild animal chased as game. [Afrikaans, from D]

spor-, a variant of **sporo-**, before vowels, as in *sporangium*.

sporadic /spə'rædɪk/, adj. **1.** appearing or happening at intervals in time; occasional: *sporadic rainfall.* **2.** appearing in scattered or separate instances, as a disease, etc. [ML, from Gk]

sporangium /spə'rændʒiəm/, n., pl. **-gia** /-dʒiə/. (in ferns, mosses and fungi) the case within which asexual reproductive cells (spores) are produced. Also, **spore case**. [NL] — **sporangial**, adj.

spore /spɔ/, n., v., **spored**, **sporing**. ◇n. **1.** Biol. a walled body that contains or produces one or more single-nucleus organisms that develop into an adult individual, esp.: **a. asexual spore**, produced asexually, as in ferns. **b. sexual spore**, produced sexually (by the union of two sex cells). **2.** a germ, germ cell, seed, etc. ◇v.i. **3.** to bear or produce spores. [NL, from Gk: seed] — **sporiferous**, adj.

sporo-, a word part meaning 'seed' or 'spore'. Also, **spor-**. [combining form representing Gk *sporá* seed]

sporophore /'spɔroʊfɔ, 'spɒ-/, n. Bot. **1.** a simple or branched fungal hypha specialised to bear spores. **2.** Bot. the whole spore-producing structure of a gill-bearing fungus; toadstool. **3.** Bot. a spore-bearing organ in some other plants.

sporophyte /'spɔrəfaɪt, 'spɒ-/, n. Bot. the asexual form of a plant in the alternation of generations (opposed to *gametophyte*).

sporozoan /spɔrə'zoʊən, spɒ-/, n. a member of the class within the protozoan phylum, which consists of parasites that increase by dividing into reproductive bodies.

sporran /'spɒrən/, n. (in Scottish dress) a large pouch, commonly of fur, worn hanging from the belt over the front of the kilt. [Gaelic]

sport /spɔt/, n. **1.** an activity pursued for exercise or pleasure, usu. requiring some degree of physical skill, as golf, fishing, racing, etc. **2.** a particular form of pastime. **3.** (pl.) a meeting for athletic competition. **4.** a pleasant pastime; recreation. **5.** playful joking: *to do or say a thing in sport.* **6.** an object of laughter: *He is the sport of his jokes.* **7.** Colloq. an informal form of address, usu. between males: *G'day, sport.* **8. a good sport**, Colloq. **a.** person of admirable qualities. **b.** someone who is good-natured and agreeable. **9. be a sport**, Colloq. **a.** to play fair. **b.** to be agreeable. ◇v.i. **10.** to amuse oneself with some pleasant pastime: *I like to sport.* **11.** to play, as a child or an animal: *The children were sporting in the garden.* **12.** to deal lightly; trifle: *He sported with the idea.* ◇v.t. **13.** to have or wear, esp. in an attention-seeking or proud way: *She sported a new hat.* **14.** Colloq. to display freely or obviously: *to sport a roll of money.* [ME]

sporting /'spɔtɪŋ/, adj. **1.** taking part in, given to, or interested in sport. **2.** concerned with or suitable for such sport: *a sporting glove.* **3.** sportsmanlike. **4.** willing to take a chance: *a sporting fellow.* **5.** even or fair: *a sporting chance.*

sportive /'spɔtɪv/, adj. **1.** playful; jesting. **2.** done in fun, rather than seriously: *a sportive action.*

sports /spɔts/, adj. **1.** of, relating to, or concerned with sport or sports: *the sports department of a store.* **2.** (of clothes, etc.) casual: *a sports coat.*

sports car, n. a high-powered car with modern lines, usu. a two-seater.

sportsman /'spɔtsmən/, n., pl. **-men**. **1.** a man who engages in sport, esp. an open-air sport such as hunting, fishing, etc. **2.** someone who shows qualities highly valued in those who play sport, such as fairness, courage, etc. — **sportsmanship**, n.

sportswoman /'spɔtswʊmən/, n. a woman who engages in sport.

sporty /'spɔti/, adj., **sportier**, **sportiest**. Colloq. **1.** flashy; vulgarly showy. **2.** stylish. **3.** like or suited to a sportsman. — **sportiness**, n.

sporulate /'spɒrəleɪt/, v.i., **-lated**, **-lating**. to divide many times resulting in the production of spores.

spot /spɒt/, n., v., **spotted**, **spotting**. ◇n. **1.** a mark made by foreign matter, as mud, blood, paint, etc.; stain, blot, or speck. **2.** a blemish, as a pimple. **3.** a rather small, usu. roundish, part of a surface differing from the rest in appearance or character: *The leopard has spots on its skin.* **4.** a moral stain; flaw: *There was no spot on his reputation.* **5.** a place: *A monument marks the spot.* **6.** advertising time (usu. short) on radio or television: *They booked a 20-second spot each night.* **7.** → **spotlight**. **8. change one's spots**, to alter one's basic character. **9. on the spot**, **a.** instantly: *You'll be fired on the spot if you come late again.* **b.**

at the place in question: *The ambulance was quickly on the spot.* **c.** obliged to deal with a situation: *Her question put him on the spot.* **10. soft spot**, special sympathy or affection: *She has a soft spot for small animals.* **11. tight spot**, a serious problem or difficulty. **12.** to stain with spots. **13.** to stain; blemish: *to spot one's reputation.* **14.** to mark or change with spots, as of color. **15.** *Colloq.* to recognise; detect. ◇*v.i.* **16.** to make a spot. **17.** to become spotted, as clothing, etc. [ME]
– **spotted, spotty**, *adj.*

spot check, *n.* **1.** an inspection made without warning, as of motor vehicles, etc. **2.** a check made on a random sample, as in a factory, etc.

spotlight /'spɒtlaɪt/, *n.* **1.** (in theatrical use) a strong light with a narrow beam used on stage to bring special attention to some object, person, etc. **2.** a lamp producing such light. **3.** a lamp fixed to a car. **4.** the centre of public attention. ◇*v.t.* **5.** to direct a spotlight on.

spouse /spaʊs, spaʊz/, *n.* one's husband or wife. [ME, from OF, from L: betrothed]

spout /spaʊt/, *v.t.*, *v.i.* **1.** to discharge or emit (a liquid, etc.) in a stream with some force. **2.** *Colloq.* to say or speak in a self-important manner. ◇*n.* **3.** a pipe, tube, or liplike structure, by which liquid is discharged or poured. **4.** a trough or chute for discharging or conveying grain, flour, etc. **5.** Also, **spouting**. → **downpipe**. [ME]

spp., *Abbrev.* species (*pl.*).

sprain /spreɪn/, *v.t.* **1.** to overstrain or twist (the ankle, wrist, or similar joint) so as to injure without dislocating or breaking. ◇*n.* **2.** a violent straining or twisting of the parts around a joint, without dislocation. **3.** the condition of being sprained. [orig. uncert.]

sprang /spræŋ/, *v.* past tense of **spring**.

sprat /spræt/, *n.* a small, herring-like marine fish of European waters. [ME and OE *sprott*]

sprawl /sprɔl/, *v.i.* **1.** to be stretched out in ungraceful movements, as the limbs. **2.** to lie or sit with the limbs stretched out in a careless or ungraceful way. **3.** to fall in such a manner. **4.** to spread out in an untidy or irregular manner, as buildings, handwriting, etc. ◇*v.t.* **5.** to stretch out (the limbs) as in sprawling. ◇*n.* **6.** the act of sprawling. **7.** a scattered or irregular grouping of something. [OE *sprēawlian*]

spray¹ /spreɪ/, *n.* **1.** water or other liquid broken up into small particles and blown or falling through the air: *the sea spray.* **2.** a jet of fine particles of liquid coming from an atomiser or other appliance. **3.** an appliance for sending out such a jet. **4.** a quantity of small objects, flying through the air: *a spray of bullets.* ◇*v.t.* **5.** to scatter in the form of fine particles. **6.** to apply as a spray: *to spray perfume on the wrist.* **7.** to direct a spray of particles, bullets, etc., upon. ◇*v.i.* **8.** to scatter spray. **9.** to come forth as spray.

spray² /spreɪ/, *n.* **1.** a single slender shoot, twig, or branch with its leaves, flowers, or berries. **2.** an ornament, decorative figure, etc., with a similar form. **3.** a single flower or small bouquet of flowers: *He pinned the spray on her dress.* [ME; orig. uncert.]

spread /sprɛd/, *v.*, **spread, spreading**, *n.* ◇*v.t.* **1.** to draw or stretch out to the full width, as a cloth, wings, etc. (oft. fol. by *out*): *He spread out the map on the table.* **2.** to extend over a rather large area, space, or period (oft. fol. by *out*): *to spread out handwriting.* **3.** to force apart, as walls, rails, etc., under pressure. **4.** to flatten out: *to spread the dough with a rolling pin.* **5.** to apply in a thin layer or coating: *to spread butter.* **6.** to cover with a thin layer or coating: *to spread bread with jam.* **7.** to send or scatter abroad, as knowledge, news, disease, etc. ◇*v.i.* **8.** to become stretched out, as a flag in the wind, etc. **9.** to extend over a large area or period. **10.** to be able to be spread or applied in a thin layer, as a soft substance. **11.** to become extended over an area, as people, animals, plants, etc. **12.** to become scattered, as light, rumors, ideas, etc. ◇*n.* **13.** expansion; extension; diffusion. **14.** the total area of spreading: *to measure the spread of branches.* **15.** the widening of an area or of size: *middle-age spread.* **16.** a stretch; expanse. **17.** a cloth-covering for a bed, table, etc., esp. a bedspread. **18.** *Colloq.* a meal set out, esp. a feast. **19.** *Colloq.* a showy display made. **20.** any food made for spreading on bread, etc., as jam, etc. [OE *sprǣdan*]

spread-eagle /sprɛd-'igəl/, *adj.*, *v.*, **-gled, -gling**. ◇*adj.* **1.** having the arms and legs stretched out widely. ◇*v.t.* **2.** to stretch out in this manner.

spree /spri/, *n.* **1.** a lively period of fun. **2.** a bout or spell of drinking, esp. of too much alcohol. **3.** a session or period of satisfying personal desires: *a spending spree.* [orig. uncert.]

sprig /sprɪɡ/, *n.*, *v.*, **sprigged, sprigging**. ◇*n.* **1.** a shoot, twig, or small branch: *sprig of holly.* **2.** an ornament having this form. **3.** (*joc.*) a person, usu. young, as a descendant or offshoot of a family. **4.** → **spike¹** (def. 3). ◇*v.t.* **5.** to decorate (cloth, pottery, etc.) with a design of sprigs. [ME; orig. uncert.]

sprightly /'spraɪtli/, *adj.*, **-lier, -liest**. lively; animated; vivacious. [from *spright*, var. of SPRITE]

spring /sprɪŋ/, *v.*, **sprang** or **sprung**, **sprung, springing**, *n.*, *adj.* ◇*v.i.* **1.** to rise or move suddenly and lightly as by some inbuilt power: *to spring into the air.* **2.** to go or come suddenly; leap. **3.** to fly back or away in escaping from a forced position: *The trap sprang open.* **4.** (of water, blood, fire, etc.) to pour or leap suddenly (oft. fol. by *forth*, *out*, or *up*). **5.** to rise or arise (oft. fol. by *up*): *Industries spring up.* **6.** to come, as from a source or cause: *to spring from convict stock.* **7.** to rise upwards, as a tower. **8.** to become bent or warped, as boards. ◇*v.t.* **9.** to cause to shut or close as by a spring. **10.** to cause to fly back, move, or act by elastic force, etc.: *to spring a trap.* **11.** to cause to split, bend, warp, etc. **12.** to produce, make, etc., suddenly: *to spring a surprise.* **13.** to leap over: *to spring the fence.* **14.** *Colloq.* to catch out; to come upon unex-

spring

pectedly. **15.** *Colloq.* to cause or enable (someone) to escape from prison. ◇*v.* **16. spring a leak,** to begin to leak. ◇*n.* **17.** a leap, jump, or bound. **18.** a flying back from a forced position. **19.** elasticity or springiness. **20.** a flow of water from the earth: *mineral springs.* **21.** the source or origin of something. **22.** a season of the year, between winter and summer; in the Southern Hemisphere, September, October, and November. **23.** the first and freshest period: *the spring of life.* **24.** a spiral coil of wire, etc., which returns to its shape after being pressed, pulled, etc. ◇*adj.* **25.** of, relating to, like, suitable for the season of spring: *spring flowers.* **26.** young: *spring chicken.* **27.** resting on or containing springs: *a spring bed.* [ME; OE *springan*]

spring balance, *n.* a balance in which weight is determined by the amount to which a coiled spring is extended.

springboard /'sprɪŋbɔd/, *n.* a board, having some movement or flexibility, used in diving, vaulting, tumbling, etc.

springbok /'sprɪŋbɒk/, *n., pl.* **-boks,** (*esp. collectively*) **-bok.** a gazelle of southern Africa which has a habit of springing upwards in play or when frightened. Also, **springbuck.** [Afrikaans]

spring-clean /sprɪŋ-'klin/, *v.t.* **1.** to clean (house, etc.) thoroughly and completely, as formerly done to homes in the spring of each year. ◇*n.* **2.** such a cleaning. —**spring-cleaning,** *n.*

spring-loaded /'sprɪŋ-loʊdəd/, *adj.* (of a machine part) held in or returned to position by means of a spring.

spring onion, *n.* a type of onion having a small bulb, chiefly used raw as a salad vegetable.

spring tide, *n.* the large rise and fall of the tide at or soon after the new or the full moon. Also, **king tide.**

Springvale /'sprɪŋveɪl/, *n.* a city in Vic, south-east of the Melbourne city centre. Pop. 83 385 (1986).

sprinkle /'sprɪŋkəl/, *v.,* **-kled, -kling,** *n.* ◇*v.t.* **1.** to scatter, as a liquid or a powder, in drops or particles. **2.** to give or place here and there: *His speech was sprinkled with jokes.* ◇*v.i.* **3.** to scatter a liquid, powder, etc., in drops or particles. **4.** to be sprinkled. **5.** to rain slightly. ◇*n.* **6.** an act or result of sprinkling. **7.** light rain. [ME]

sprinkler /'sprɪŋklə/, *n.* a device which sprinkles, esp. one attached to a hose, which sprinkles water over grass, plants, etc.

sprinkling /'sprɪŋklɪŋ/, *n.* **1.** a small quantity or number scattered here and there. **2.** a small quantity sprinkled.

sprint /sprɪnt/, *v., n.* ◇*v.i.* **1.** to race at full speed, esp. for a short distance, as in running, rowing, etc. ◇*v.t.* **2.** to cover by sprinting: *to sprint 100 metres.* ◇*n.* **3.** a short race at full speed. **4.** a brief period of great activity. [Scand] —**sprinter,** *n.*

1000

sprit /sprɪt/, *n.* a small pole crossing a fore-and-aft sail diagonally from the mast to the upper aftermost corner of a sailing vessel, thus serving to extend the sail. [OE *sprēot*]

sprite /spraɪt/, *n.* an elf, fairy, or goblin. [ME, from OF]

sprocket /'sprɒkət/, *n. Mach.* one of a set of projections on the rim of a wheel which engage the links of a chain. [from *sprock* (of obscure orig.]

sprout /spraʊt/, *v.i.* **1.** to begin to grow, esp. quickly. **2.** (of a seed, plant, the earth, etc.) to put forth buds or shoots. ◇*v.t.* **3.** to cause to sprout. ◇*n.* **4.** the shoot of a plant. **5.** new growth from a germinating seed, or from a tuber, bud, etc., often used in salads. **6.** Also, **brussels sprout.** a vegetable with small edible heads or sprouts which look like miniature cabbage heads. [OE *sprūtan*]

spruce[1] /sprus/, *n.* an evergreen cone-bearing tree with short needle-shaped leaves. [ME, var. of *Pruce* Prussia]

spruce[2] /sprus/, *adj.,* **sprucer, sprucest,** *v.,* **spruced, sprucing.** ◇*adj.* **1.** smart in dress or appearance. ◇*v.t.* **2.** to make spruce or smart (oft. fol. by *up*): *to spruce the room up with new wallpaper.* ◇*v.i.* **3.** to make oneself spruce (usu. fol. by *up*): *to spruce up for the visitors.* [? special use of SPRUCE[1] through (obs.) *Spruce leather,* a leather from Prussia used in jerkins, etc.]

sprung /sprʌŋ/, *v.* past tense and past participle of **spring.**

sprung rhythm, *n.* **1.** a system of poetic writing in which the accent always falls on the first syllable of every foot (def. 6) followed by some unaccented syllables, all feet being given equal time length. **2.** a type of poetic metre based on speech rhythm, with the strong beat on the first syllable of each foot, and the number of weak syllables being variable.

spry /spraɪ/, *adj.,* **spryer, spryest** or **sprier, spriest.** active; nimble; brisk. [orig. obscure]

spud /spʌd/, *n.* **1.** a spade-like instrument, used for digging up or cutting the roots of weeds. **2.** *Colloq.* a potato. [ME *spudde* kind of knife]

spume /spjum/, *n., v.,* **spumed, spuming.** ◇*n.* **1.** foam; froth; scum. ◇*v.i.* **2.** to foam; froth. ◇*v.t.* **3.** to send forth as or like foam. [ME, from L]

spun /spʌn/, *v.* **1.** past tense and past participle of **spin.** ◇*adj.* **2.** formed by or as if by spinning: *spun rayon.*

spunk /spʌŋk/, *n. Colloq.* **1.** courage; spirit; mettle. **2.** a good-looking person. **3.** semen. [b. SPARK and obs. *funk* spark, touchwood] —**spunky,** *adj.*

spur /spɜ/, *n., v.,* **spurred, spurring.** ◇*n.* **1.** a pointed device fixed to a horseman's boot heel, for goading a horse onwards, etc. **2.** anything that goads, impels, or urges to action or speed. **3.** something looking like or suggesting a spur. **4.** a stiff, usu. sharp, horny process on the leg of various birds, esp. the domestic male

spur fowl. **5.** a short branch or shoot, as of a tree. **6.** *Bot.* a thin, usu. hollow, projection from some part of a flower, as from the calyx of the larkspur or the corolla of the violet. **7.** *Phys Geog.* a ridge rising up to the main body of a mountain or mountain range. **8.** *Railways.* a siding. **9. on the spur of the moment,** suddenly, without preparation. ◇*v.t.* **10.** to prick with, or as if with, spurs. ◇*v.i.* **11.** to go hurriedly. [ME; OE *spura*]

spurious /ˈspjʊəriəs/, *adj.* **1.** not real or true; counterfeit. **2.** *Bot.* having an outward likeness but having structural differences. [L: false]

spurn /spɜːn/, *v.t.* to find unworthy of notice; scorn; despise. [ME; OE *spurnan*]

spurt /spɜːt/, *v.i.* **1.** to rush suddenly in a stream, as a liquid. **2.** to show marked activity or energy for a short period. ◇*v.t.* **3.** to throw out suddenly in a stream, as a liquid. ◇*n.* **4.** a forcible rush of water, etc.: *a spurt of water from the tap.* **5.** a sudden outburst, as of feeling: *a spurt of words.* **6.** a sudden, short increase of effort as in running, rowing, etc. Also, **spirt**. [OE *spryttan* come forth]

spur wheel, *n. Mach.* a wheel with projecting teeth on the outside, which are placed radially about and parallel to the axis.

sputnik /ˈspʌtnɪk, ˈspʊtnɪk/, *n.* a man-made satellite, esp. an early Soviet one. [Russ: companion]

sputter /ˈspʌtə/, *v.i.* **1.** to give off particles of anything in an explosive manner, as a candle does in burning. **2.** to spit particles of saliva, food, etc., from the mouth in a similar manner. **3.** to utter words or sounds in an explosive, meaningless manner. ◇*n.* **4.** the act, process, or sound of sputtering. **5.** explosive, meaningless sound. [frequentative of SPOUT]

sputum /ˈspjuːtəm/, *n., pl.* **-ta** /-tə/. saliva, esp. mixed with mucus. [L]

spy /spaɪ/, *n., pl.* **spies**, *v.,* **spied, spying.** ◇*n.* **1.** someone who keeps a secret watch on the actions of others, esp. to obtain secret information for a government. ◇*v.i.* **2.** to watch secretly, esp. as in war. ◇*v.t.* **3.** to keep secret watch on (a place) for unfriendly purposes (now usu. fol. by *out*): *He was spying out the land.* **4.** to find (*out*) by looking closely: *to spy out the reason for the secret meetings.* **5.** to catch sight of; see. [ME, from OF: ESPY]

sq., *Abbrev.* **1.** the following one. [L *sequens*] **2.** square.

Sqn Ldr, *Abbrev.* Squadron Leader.

squabble /ˈskwɒbəl/, *v.,* **-bled, -bling,** *n.* ◇*v.i.* **1.** to quarrel. ◇*n.* **2.** a petty quarrel. [? imitative]

squad /skwɒd/, *n.* **1.** any small group of people involved in a common activity, etc. **2.** a group of sportsmen, esp. one selected for a tour. [F, from It: SQUARE]

squadron /ˈskwɒdrən/, *n.* **1.** a part of a naval fleet, or a group of warships employed on a particular service. **2.** an armored cavalry unit consisting of two or more troops (companies), a headquarters, and certain supporting units. **3.** the basic administrative and tactical unit of an air force, made up of two or more flights. [It: SQUARE]

squalid /ˈskwɒlɪd/, *adj.* **1.** dirty; filthy: *squalid conditions.* **2.** sordid: *a squalid theme in the novel.* [L]

squall[1] /skwɔːl/, *n.* **1.** *Weather.* a sudden strong wind. **2.** *Colloq.* a disturbance; commotion. ◇*v.i.* **3.** to blow in a squall. [? akin to SQUALL[2]]

squall[2] /skwɔːl/, *v.i., v.t.* **1.** to cry out or scream loudly. ◇*n.* **2.** the act or sound of squalling. [imitative]

squalor /ˈskwɒlə/, *n.* filth and misery. [L]

squamate /ˈskweɪmeɪt/, *adj.* provided or covered with scales; scaly. [L] —**squamous,** *adj.*

squander /ˈskwɒndə/, *v.t.* to spend (money, time, etc.) wastefully (oft. fol. by *away*). [orig. obscure]

square /skweə/, *n., v.,* **squared, squaring,** *adj.,* **squarer, squarest,** *adv.* ◇*n.* **1.** a four-sided plane figure having all its sides equal and all its angles right angles. **2.** anything having this shape. **3.** an open area in a town, as at the meeting point of streets, often planted with grass, trees, etc. **4.** an L-shaped or T-shaped instrument for drawing and checking right angles. **5.** *Maths.* the second power of a number or quantity: *the square of 4 is 4 x 4, or 16.* **6.** *Bldg Trades.* a former unit of surface measurement equal to 100 square feet. **7.** *Colloq.* someone who is unaware of or uninterested in the latest fashions and ideas. ◇*v.t.* **8.** to make into square, rectangular, or cubic form. **9.** to mark out in squares or rectangles. **10.** to test for any alteration from a right angle, straight line, or plane surface. **11.** *Maths.* to multiply (a number or quantity) by itself. **12.** to set (the shoulders, arms, etc.) so as to present a rectangular outline. **13.** to make straight, level, or even: *to square the edges of the paper.* **14.** to adjust satisfactorily; balance; settle: *to square a debt.* ◇*v.i.* **15.** to agree (oft. fol. by *with*): *His theory does not square with the facts.* ◇*v.* **16. square off, a.** to apologise (fol. by *with*). **b.** to get revenge (fol. by *with*). **17. square up,** to pay a full, debt, etc. **18. square up to,** to face, esp. courageously. ◇*adj.* **19.** of the form of a right angle: *a square corner.* **20.** cubical or approximately so: *a square box.* **21. a.** of a unit representing an area in the form of a square: *a square metre.* **b.** relating to such units: *square measure.* **22.** of a given length on each side of a square: *an area two metres square.* **23.** straight, level, or even, as a surface: *Is the painting square?* **24.** leaving no balance of debt on either side: *to make sure the accounts are square.* **25.** just, fair, or honest: *a square deal.* **26.** *Colloq.* full; complete: *a square meal.* **27.** *Colloq.* unadventurous in manners, dress, or behavior. ◇*adv.* **28.** so as to be square. **29.** at right angles. **30.** *Colloq.* solidly or directly: *to hit a nail square on the head.* [ME, from OF, from L: to square, QUADRATE]

square bracket, *n.* either of the two parenthetical marks: [ ].

square dance, *n.* a dance by couples arranged in a square or some other set form.

square leg, *n.* (in cricket) a fielding position on the leg side at right angles to the pitch and opposite the batter's wicket.

square-rigged /ˈskwɛə-rɪgd/, *adj. Naut.* having square sails as the principal sails.

square root, *n. Maths.* a quantity of which a given quantity is the square: *4 is the square root of 16.*

squash[1] /skwɒʃ/, *v.t.* **1.** to press into a flat mass; crush. **2.** to put down; quash: *to squash an uprising.* **3.** *Colloq.* to silence, as with a crushing reply. ◇*v.i.* **4.** to be pressed into a flat mass. ◇*n.* **5.** the act or result of squashing. **6.** something squashed or crushed. **7.** Also, **squash racquets.** a game for two players, played in a small walled court with light racquets and small rubber ball. **8.** a drink typical of a fruit juice, with soda, etc., added. [OF, ? partly imitative]

squash[2] /skwɒʃ/, *n.* a plant similar to a marrow, bearing a fruit that is usu. round in shape, with paler flesh and softer skin than the pumpkin. [Algonquian: vegetables eaten green]

squat /skwɒt/, *v.*, **squatted** or **squat**, **squatting,** *adj., n.* ◇*v.i.* **1.** to rest in a posture close to the ground with the knees bent and the back more or less straight, resting on the balls of the feet; crouch. **2.** (formerly) to settle on land without government permission. **3.** to occupy a building without title or right. ◇*adj.* **4.** short and thickset or thick: *a squat body.* ◇*n.* **5.** the act or fact of squatting. **6.** the position or posture in which one squats. [ME, from OF] —**squatness,** *n.*

squatter /ˈskwɒtə/, *n.* **1.** someone or something that squats. **2.** (formerly) someone who settled on Crown land to run sheep, etc., first without government permission, but later with a lease or licence. **3.** one of a group of rich and powerful rural landowners. **4.** someone who lives in a building without right or title.

squattocracy /skwɒˈtɒkrəsi/, *n.* long-established and wealthy landowners who see themselves as a privileged class. [SQUAT(TER) + (ARIS)TOCRACY]

squaw /skwɔ/, *n.* a North American Indian woman, esp. a wife. [Algonquian: woman]

squawk /skwɔk/, *v.i.* **1.** to utter a loud, unpleasant cry, as a duck or other fowl when frightened. **2.** *Colloq.* to complain loudly and with feeling. ◇*n.* **3.** a loud, unpleasant cry. **4.** *Colloq.* a loud, emotional complaint. [b. SQUALL[2] and CROAK]

squeak /skwik/, *n.* **1.** a short, sharp, high-pitched cry. ◇*v.i.* **2.** to utter a squeak. **3.** *Colloq.* to confess or turn informer. ◇*v.t.* **4.** to utter or produce with a squeak or squeaks. [ME, apparently from Scand] —**squeaky,** *adj.*

squeal /skwil/, *n.* **1.** a sharp, high-pitched cry, as of pain, fear, etc. **2.** *Colloq.* a complaint; protest. ◇*v.i.* **3.** to utter a squealing sound. **4.** *Colloq.* to give information (to police, etc.) against another. **5.** *Colloq.* to complain; protest. ◇*v.t.* **6.** to utter or produce with a squeal. **7.** *Colloq.* to tell (something secret): *He squealed the information to the police.* [imitative]

squeamish /ˈskwimɪʃ/, *adj.* **1.** easily sickened. **2.** easily shocked by anything slightly improper; prudish. [late ME; orig. unknown]

squeeze /skwiz/, *v.*, **squeezed**, **squeezing,** *n.* ◇*v.t.* **1.** to press forcibly together; compress. **2.** to apply pressure to in order to remove something: *to squeeze a lemon.* **3.** to force by pressure; cram: *to squeeze clothes into a suitcase.* **4.** to force out, by or as if by pressure (usu. fol. by *out* or *from*): *to squeeze juice from an orange; He was squeezed out of business.* **5.** to hug; embrace. **6.** to press (someone's hand, arm, etc.) as an expression of friendship, concern, etc. ◇*v.i.* **7.** to apply a pressing force: *He squeezed hard.* **8.** to force a way through some narrow or crowded place. ◇*n.* **9.** the act or result of squeezing. **10.** *Colloq.* a difficult situation: *in a tight squeeze.* **11.** a crowded gathering. **12.** control or pressure, as enforced by a government: *a credit squeeze.* **13.** a small quantity of anything obtained by squeezing: *a squeeze of lemon.* [OE *cwȳsan*]

squelch /skwɛltʃ/, *v.t.* **1.** to crush down; squash: *to squelch a strawberry between the teeth.* **2.** *Colloq.* to silence, as with a crushing reply. ◇*v.i.* **3.** to make a splashing sound: *Water squelched in her shoes.* **4.** to tread heavily in water, mud, etc., with such a sound. ◇*n.* **5.** a squelched mass of anything. **6.** a squelching sound. **7.** *Elect.* a circuit which cuts off the output of a radio receiver until a signal begins. [var. of *quelch*]

squib /skwɪb/, *n., v.*, **squibbed**, **squibbing.** ◇*n.* **1.** a short witty or sarcastic saying or writing. **2.** a firework which burns with a hissing noise and ends in a slight explosion. **3.** Also, **damp squib.** any plan, project, etc., which does not eventuate. **4.** a mean or cowardly fellow. ◇*v.i.* **5.** to write squibs. **6.** *Colloq.* to behave in a cowardly manner. **7.** to desert (someone) in order to avoid harm to oneself (fol. by *on*). ◇*v.t.* **8.** to withdraw from, usu. through fear: *to squib the meeting.* [orig. uncert.]

squid /skwɪd/, *n., pl.* **squids,** (*esp. collectively*) **squid.** a type of mollusc, esp. any of certain small species having thin bodies and tail fins, much used for bait; cephalopod. [orig. uncert.]

squiggle /ˈskwɪgəl/, *n.* a short twist or curve, as in drawing or writing. [b. SQUIRM and WRIGGLE] —**squiggly,** *adj.*

squint /skwɪnt/, *v.i.* **1.** to look with the eyes partly closed: *to squint at the sun.* **2.** to be cross-eyed. **3.** to look or glance sideways. ◇*v.t.* **4.** to close (the eyes) partly. ◇*n.* **5.** *Med.* a condition where the muscles of the eyes do not work in coordination. **6.** *Colloq.* a secret glance: *to take a quick squint at something.* ◇*adj.* **7.** looking with a side glance. **8.** affected with poor muscle coordination in the eyes.

squire /ˈskwaɪə/, *n., v.*, **squired**, **squiring.** ◇*n.* **1.** (in England) a country gentleman, esp. the chief landowner in a district. **2.** *Hist.* a

squire   1003   **staff**

young man of noble birth who waits upon a knight. ◇*v.t.* **3.** to attend as or in the manner of a squire. [ME, from OF]

squirm /skwɜːm/, *v.i.* **1.** to wriggle; writhe. **2.** to feel or show discomfort or disgust as from an embarrassing or unpleasant circumstance. ◇*n.* **3.** a squirming or wriggling movement. [b. SKEW and WORM *v.*]

squirrel /ˈskwɪrəl/, *n.* **1.** a tree-climbing, bushy-tailed rodent found throughout Europe, Asia and North America. **2.** *Colloq.* a person who collects and keeps objects of little value. [ME, from AF, from LL, from Gk]

squirt /skwɜːt/, *v.i.* **1.** to force out liquid in a jet from a narrow opening. **2.** (of a liquid) to pour in a jetlike stream. ◇*v.t.* **3.** to force (liquid) in a jet from a narrow opening: *to squirt water from a hose.* **4.** to wet with a liquid so forced out: *to squirt someone with water.* ◇*n.* **5.** the act of squirting. **6.** a jet, as of water. **7.** an instrument for squirting, as a syringe. **8.** a small quantity of liquid squirted. **9.** *Colloq.* **a.** an unimportant fellow, who places too much value on his own opinions. **b.** a short person. [orig. obscure]

squish /skwɪʃ/, *Colloq.* ◇*v.t.* **1.** to squeeze or squash. ◇*v.i.* **2.** (of water, soft mud, etc.) to make a squashing sound. ◇*n.* **3.** the noise made by squishing.

squiz /skwɪz/, *v.,* **squizzed, squizzing,** *n.,* *pl.* **squizzes.** *Colloq.* ◇*v.t.* **1.** to look at quickly but closely. ◇*n.* **2.** a quick but close look.

Sr, *Abbrev.* **1.** Senior. ◇*Symbol.* **2.** *Chem.* strontium.

Sri Lanka /ʃri ˈlaŋkə, ˈlæŋkə/, *n.* a republic in southern Asia, consisting of one large island and several smaller ones in the Indian Ocean, east of the southern tip of India; a British colony (Ceylon) before independence. Pop. 16 353 000 (1987); 65 610 km^2. *Languages:* Sinhalese, also Tamil and English. *Currency:* rupee. *Cap.:* Colombo. *Cap. designate:* Sri Jayawardenapura. Official name, **Democratic Socialist Republic of Sri Lanka.** Formerly, **Ceylon.** – **Sri Lankan,** *n., adj.*

SS, *n.* an elite military unit of the Nazi party which served as Hitler's bodyguard and as a special police force. [G S(*chutz*)s(*taffel*) protection squad]

SSE, *Abbrev.* south-south-east. See Appendix.

SSW, *Abbrev.* south-south-west. See Appendix.

st., *Abbrev.* **1.** stitch. **2.** *Cricket.* stumped.

St, *Abbrev.* **1.** Saint (entries beginning with the abbreviation **St** are sorted with entries beginning with **Saint**). **2.** Strait. **3.** Street.

stab /stæb/, *v.,* **stabbed, stabbing,** *n.* ◇*v.t.* **1.** to wound with, or as with, a pointed weapon. **2.** to push (a knife, etc.) forcefully into something. ◇*v.i.* **3.** to push forcefully with or as with a pointed weapon: *to stab at an enemy.* ◇*v.* **4. stab (someone) in the back,** *Colloq.* to harm (someone), esp. by disloyalty. ◇*n.* **5.** a thrust or blow with, or as with, a pointed weapon. **6.** a sudden, usu. painful feeling: *a stab of pain.* **7.** *Colloq.* an attempt; try: *to take a stab at the answer.* [ME]

stabilise or **stabilize** /ˈsteɪbəlaɪz/, *v.,* **-lised, -lising.** ◇*v.t.* **1.** to make firm and steady. **2.** to keep at a given or unchanging level, quantity, condition. ◇*v.i.* **3.** to become firm and steady. – **stabilisation,** *n.* – **stabiliser,** *n.*

stability /stəˈbɪləti/, *n., pl.* **-ties. 1.** firmness in position. **2.** continuance without change; permanence. **3.** dependability, as of character or purpose.

stable^1 /ˈsteɪbəl/, *n., v.,* **-bled, -bling.** ◇*n.* **1.** a building for the keeping and feeding of horses. **2.** a collection of animals belonging in such a building. **3.** *Racing.* **a.** an establishment where racehorses are kept and trained. **b.** the horses belonging to, or people connected with, such an establishment. **4.** a group of people associated in some way with a centre of production, as a group of newspapers, car factories, studios, etc. ◇*v.t.* **5.** to put or keep in or as in a stable. [ME, from OF, from L]

stable^2 /ˈsteɪbəl/, *adj.* **1.** not likely to fall or give way; firm; steady. **2.** able or likely to continue or last; enduring: *a stable government.* **3.** not changeable, as a person, the mind, etc. **4.** *Phys.* having or showing an ability or tendency to maintain or re-establish position, form, etc.: *a stable nucleus.* **5.** *Chem.* not readily decomposing. [ME, from F, from L]

staccato /stəˈkɑːtoʊ/, *adj. Music.* having a short pause between one note and the next; detached. [It: DETACH]

stack /stæk/, *n.* **1.** a more or less orderly pile. **2.** a single chimney or funnel for smoke, or a vertical pipe inside or outside a building for passing waste products down, circulating heat, etc. **3.** *Geol.* a column of rock, no longer attached to the shore by the erosive action of waves. **4.** *Colloq.* a great quantity or number: *a stack of people.* **5.** a measure for coal and wood, equal to 108 cubic feet or 3.06 cubic metres. **6.** that part of a library not for general public use, in which the main holdings of the library are kept. ◇*v.t.* **7.** to pile or arrange in a stack: *to stack hay.* **8.** to cover or load with things in piles: *I'll stack the trailer with bricks.* **9.** to arrange (playing cards in the pack) in an unfair manner. **10.** to bring a large number of one's own supporters to (a meeting) to influence decisions made. ◇*v.i.* **11.** to add up; accumulate (fol. by *up*): *My work stacked up while I was away.* [ME, from Scand]

stadium /ˈsteɪdiəm/, *n., pl.* **-dia** /-diə/, **-diums. 1.** a building for sporting activities, often enclosed and having a playing field, seats for spectators, parking space, etc. **2.** an ancient Greek course for races, typically semicircular. [L, from Gk]

staff /stɑːf/, *n.* **1.** a stick, pole, or rod for use in walking, climbing, fighting, etc. **2.** a rod used as a sign of office or authority. **3.** something which serves to support: *Bread is the staff of life.* **4.** a body of people charged with carrying out the work of an office, business, etc. **5.** the teachers of a school, college, etc. **6.** *Mil., Navy.* **a.** a body of officers without command

staff authority, chosen to help a commanding officer. **b.** the parts of any army concerned with administrative matters, planning, etc., instead of with actual fighting. **7.** *Music.* → **stave** (def. 3). ◇*adj.* **8.** of, or being a member of, a military, naval or teaching staff: *staff officer.* ◇*v.t.* **9.** to provide with a staff: *to staff a new company.* [ME; OE *stæf*]

Staffordshire /'stæfədʃɪə, -ʃə/, *n.* a county in central England. Pop. 1 021 000 (1986 est.); 2716 km². *Administrative Centre:* Stafford.

stag /stæg/, *n.* **1.** an adult male deer. **2.** the male of various other animals. **3.** *Colloq.* a man, esp. one at a social gathering only for men. **4.** an animal castrated after full development of the sex organs. ◇*adj.* **5.** *Colloq.* for or of men only: *a stag party.* [OE (unrecorded) *stagga*]

stage /steɪdʒ/, *n., v.,* **staged, staging.** ◇*n.* **1.** a single step or degree in a process. **2.** a raised floor, as for speakers, performers, etc. **3.** the theatre, drama, or the acting profession: *a life on the stage.* **4.** → **section** (def. 8). **5.** *Zool.* any one of the major time periods in the development of an insect, the embryonic, larval, pupal, and adult stages. **6.** *Geol.* a division of stratified rocks next in rank to a series, representing deposits formed during the part of an epoch that is called an age. **7.** a powered section of a rocket which can be dropped off after firing. **8. by/in easy stages,** without rushing. **9. hold the stage,** to be the centre of attention. ◇*v.t.* **10.** to put, represent, or show on or as on a stage: *to stage a performance.* **11.** to plan or carry out (an action) in which each person has a special task to perform: *to stage a riot.* [ME, from OF, from L: stand]

stagecoach /'steɪdʒkoʊtʃ/, *n.* a coach that runs regularly over a fixed route with passengers, parcels, etc.

stagflation /stæg'fleɪʃən/, *n. Econ.* a situation in which there is no economic growth, but inflation is occurring.

stagger /'stægə/, *v.i.* **1.** to walk, move, or stand unsteadily; sway. ◇*v.t.* **2.** to cause to stagger. **3.** to shock (usu. in passive): *I was staggered by the price.* **4.** to arrange a series so that the beginnings and ends of its component parts are at different positions, times, etc.: *to stagger lunch hours.* ◇*n.* **5.** the act of staggering. [ME, from Scand]

staghorn fern /'stæghɔn 'fɜn/, *n. Bot.* any of various tropical and subtropical ferns, having large leaves looking like the horns of a stag.

stagnant /'stægnənt/, *adj.* **1.** (of water, air, etc.) not running or flowing. **2.** (of a pool of water) unclean from standing. **3.** not developing: *The economy was stagnant.* [L] –**stagnancy,** *n.*

stagnate /'stægneɪt, stæg'neɪt/, *v.i.,* **-nated, -nating. 1.** (of water, air, etc.) to cease to run or flow. **2.** (of a pool of water) to become unclean from standing. **3.** to become inactive; dull. **4.** to stop developing: *The economy stagnated.* [L] –**stagnation,** *n.*

staid /steɪd/, *adj.* of settled or calm character. [var. of *stayed,* pp. of STAY¹] –**staidness,** *n.*

stain /steɪn/, *n.* **1.** a discoloration; spot: *The wine made a stain on his tie.* **2.** a cause of dishonor; blemish: *a stain on one's reputation.* **3.** a mixture of coloring matter in water, spirit, or oil, used to color but not hide a surface. **4.** a dye made into a mixture and used to color cloth, biological specimens, etc. ◇*v.t.* **5.** to cause a stain in. **6.** to color with stain. **7.** to treat (a microscopic specimen) with a reagent or dye in order to color the whole or parts and so give distinctness, contrast of tissues, etc. ◇*v.i.* **8.** to produce a stain: *Red wine stains.* **9.** to become stained: *The wood stained easily.* [ME, from Scand]

stainless steel /ˌsteɪnləs 'stil/, *n.* a hard steel mixed with chromium, which resists rust and stains.

stair /stɛə/, *n.* **1.** one of a series of steps forming a means of passing from one level to another, as in a building. **2.** (*oft. pl.*) such steps collectively. [OE *stæger*]

staircase /'stɛəkeɪs/, *n.* a flight of stairs with its framework, handrails, etc., or a series of such flights.

stairwell /'stɛəwɛl/, *n.* a vertical shaft or opening containing a flight of stairs.

stake¹ /steɪk/, *n., v.,* **staked, staking.** ◇*n.* **1.** a stick or post pointed at one end used as part of a fence, support for a plant, etc. **2. the stake,** the punishment of death by burning. ◇*v.t.* **3.** to mark with stakes (oft. fol. by *off* or *out*). **4.** to take or lay claim to a share of (land, profit, etc.) (sometimes fol. by *out* or *off*): *to stake a claim.* **5.** to protect, separate, or close off by a series of stakes. **6.** to support with a stake, as a plant. **7.** to tie up to a stake, as an animal. **8.** to surround (a building, etc.) for the purposes of arrest or of keeping watch (fol. by *out*): *They staked out the house where the criminal was hiding.* [ME; OE *staca*]

stake² /steɪk/, *n., v.,* **staked, staking.** ◇*n.* **1.** that which is bet in a game, race, or contest. **2.** a financial interest held in a business, etc. **3.** *Colloq.* a personal concern, interest, involvement, etc.: *He had a stake in the boy's future.* **4.** (*oft. pl.*) a prize in a race or contest. **5.** (*pl.* treated as *sing.*) a race in which equal amounts are given by all the owners of the competing horses for prize money. **6.** (*pl.* treated as *sing.*) (*joc.*) an imaginary race or contest: *She'd win any beauty stakes.* **7. at stake,** at risk: *Our jobs are at stake if we lose this deal.* ◇*v.t.* **8.** to wager: *I'll stake two dollars on the game.*

stalactite /'stæləktaɪt/, *n.* a deposit, usu. of calcium carbonate, shaped like an icicle, hanging from the roof of a cave, etc., and formed by the dripping of water containing calcium carbonate. [NL]

stalag /'stælæg/, *n.* a German camp for prisoners of war. [G: group camp]

stalagmite /'stæləgmaɪt/, *n.* a deposit, usu. of calcium carbonate, like an upward facing stalactite, formed on the floor of a cave, etc., by the dripping of water containing calcium carbonate. [NL]

stale /steɪl/, *adj.*, **staler, stalest,** *v.*, **staled, staling.** ◇*adj.* **1.** (of food) not fresh. **2.** having lost interest; trite: *a stale joke.* ◇*v.t., v.i.* **3.** to make or become stale. [ME, ? from AF: stop]

stalemate /'steɪlmeɪt/, *n., v.*, **-mated, -mating.** ◇*n.* **1.** *Chess.* the position of the pieces in which, though the king is not in check, any move would put him in check, the result being a draw. **2.** any position in which no action can be taken; deadlock. ◇*v.t.* **3.** to subject to stalemate. [OF *estal* standstill + *mat* checkmated (from Ar)]

Stalin /'stɑlən/, *n.* **Joseph** (*Iosif Vissarionovich Dzugashvili*), 1879–1953, Soviet marshal and statesman, born in Georgia; general secretary of the Soviet Communist Party 1922–53; premier of the Soviet Union 1941–53.

stalk[1] /stɔk/, *n.* **1.** the stem of a plant. **2.** any thin supporting or connecting part, esp. of a plant. [ME, from OE *stæla* stalk]

stalk[2] /stɔk/, *v.i.* **1.** to follow or approach game, etc., quietly and carefully. **2.** to walk in a slow, stiff, or proud manner. **3.** to go with a slow, relentless and often evil movement: *Hunger stalked through the land.* ◇*v.t.* **4.** to follow (game, a person, etc.) quietly and carefully. ◇*n.* **5.** the act of stalking game, etc. **6.** a slow, stiff walk. [OE *-stealcian* move stealthily]

stall[1] /stɔl/, *n.* **1.** an enclosed space in a stable or shed, for keeping one animal. **2.** a booth, bench, table, or stand on which goods are shown for sale. **3.** → **carrel. 4.** a seat in a theatre, separated from others by armrests. **5.** (*pl.*) the front section on the ground floor of a theatre. **6.** the fact of an engine stopping, as through an incorrect fuel supply. ◇*v.t.* **7.** to put or keep in a stall, as animals. **8.** to bring (a vehicle) to a standstill, esp. by mismanagement. ◇*v.i.* **9.** to come to a standstill. **10.** (of a vehicle or aeroplane engine) to stop. [ME; OE *steall*]

stall[2] /stɔl/, *Colloq.* ◇*n.* **1.** anything used to gain time, or to deceive. ◇*v.i.* **2.** to act in a way that intends to deceive. ◇*v.t.* **3.** to put off, avoid, or deceive: *Stall the visitors until next week.* [ME, from AF, from OE *stæl*]

stallion /'stæljən/, *n.* an uncastrated male horse, esp. one kept for breeding. [ME, from OF; of Gmc orig.]

stalwart /'stɔlwət/, *adj.* **1.** strong and brave; valiant. **2.** firm, dependable, or unyielding. ◇*n.* **3.** a stalwart person. [ME]

stamen /'steɪmən/, *n., pl.* **stamens, stamina** /'stæmənə/. the pollen-bearing organ of a flower, consisting of the filament and the anther. [L: thread, warp in the upright loom] **– staminiferous,** *adj.* **– staminate,** *adj.*

stamina[1] /'stæmənə/, *n.* the strength of one's physical make-up; power to withstand disease, fatigue, etc. [L: threads (specifically, those spun by the Fates determining length of life)]

stamina[2] /'stæmənə/, *n.* a plural of **stamen.**

stammer /'stæmə/, *v.i.* **1.** to speak with uncontrollable breaks and pauses or with occasional repetitions of syllables or sounds. ◇*v.t.* **2.** to say with a stammer (oft. fol. by *out*): *to stammer a reply.* ◇*n.* **3.** a stammering manner of speech: *to have a stammer.* [ME; OE *stamerian*]

stamp /stæmp/, *v.t.* **1.** to strike with a forcible downward push of the foot. **2.** to bring (the foot) down forcibly or smartly on the ground, floor, etc. **3.** to force, drive, etc., by or as by beating down with the foot (usu. fol. by *out* or *on*): *to stamp out a fire.* **4.** to press with a particular mark, as to show genuineness, approval, ownership, etc.: *to stamp a passport.* **5.** to mark with any characters, words, designs, etc.: *to stamp a pattern on the cloth.* **6.** to fix (a letter, etc.) with a sticky paper stamp. **7.** to characterise, distinguish, or reveal: *He was stamped a hero by his actions.* ◇*v.i.* **8.** to bring the foot down forcibly as in crushing something, expressing anger, etc. **9.** to walk with forcible or heavy steps: *to stamp out of a room in anger.* ◇*n.* **10.** an act or an occasion of stamping. **11.** a die, engraved block, etc., for pressing in a design, characters, words, or marks: *a date stamp.* **12.** an official mark showing genuineness, legal correctness, etc., or payment of a tax or charge. **13.** a special character or mark: *a story which bears the stamp of truth.* **14.** a small sticky piece of paper printed with a special design, issued by a government for a fixed sum, for attaching to letters, documents, etc.: *a duty stamp; a postage stamp.* **15.** a similar piece of paper given privately for various purposes: *a trading stamp.* **16.** an instrument or tool for stamping, crushing, or pounding. [early ME]

stamp duty, *n.* a tax placed on certain legal documents, as cheques, receipts, etc., payment of which is shown by a stamp.

stampede /stæm'pid/, *n., v.*, **-peded, -peding.** ◇*n.* **1.** a sudden scattering or headlong flight of a group of cattle, horses, etc., in fright. **2.** any headlong general flight or rush: *a stampede of people.* ◇*v.i.* **3.** to scatter or run in a stampede. ◇*v.t.* **4.** to cause to stampede: *to stampede the cattle.* [Mex Sp: press, of Gmc orig.]

stance /stæns/, *n.* **1.** the position of the body while standing: *a boxer's stance.* **2.** an emotional or intellectual attitude to something: *an unfriendly stance towards modern poetry.* [F, from It *stanza* station, stopping place, room, from L: standing]

stanchion /'stæntʃən, 'stænʃən/, *n.* **1.** an upright bar, beam, post, or support, as in a window, ship, etc. ◇*v.t.* **2.** to hold in place by or to a stanchion. [ME, from OF: STANCE]

stand /stænd/, *v.*, **stood, standing,** *n.* ◇*v.i.* **1.** to take or keep an upright position on the feet (opposed to *sit, lie,* etc.). **2.** to have a given height when in this position: *He stands two metres in his socks.* **3.** to stop moving; halt: *Stand and deliver!* **4.** to take a position: *to stand aside; to stand for racial equality.* **5.** to represent: *The symbol x stands for an unknown quantity.* **6.** (of things) to be in an upright position (opposed to *lie*). **7.** to be placed or situated: *The house stands at the end of the street.* **8.** to be at a certain degree: *The temperature stands at 25°C.* **9.** to continue in force: *The law still stands.* **10.** (of people or things) to be or remain in a specified condition, relation, etc. **11.** to become a candidate: *to stand for parliament.* ◇*v.t.* **12.** to cause to stand: *Stand the box there.* **13.** to endure or undergo: *to stand trial; He cannot stand the sun.* **14.** to tolerate: *I cannot stand him.* ◇*v.* **15.** Some special uses are:

stand a chance, to have a chance, esp. of winning.

stand by, 1. to wait in a state of readiness: *Stand by for further news.* **2.** to aid or uphold: *I'll stand by him.* **3.** to keep to (an agreement, promise, etc.).

stand down, 1. to go off duty. **2.** to withdraw, as from a contest. **3.** to put off (employees) through effects of a strike.

stand in, to act in place of another: *to stand in for the leading player.*

stand one's ground, to be unyielding.

stand up for, to defend the cause of.

stand up to, 1. to remain in good condition in spite of: *to stand up to hard wear.* **2.** to oppose, esp. bravely.

◇*n.* **16.** the act of standing: *to have a stand for a while.* **17.** determined opposition to or support for some cause, etc.: *to take a strong stand against smoking.* **18.** the place where a person or thing stands. **19.** a witness box. **20.** a raised platform, as for spectators. **21.** a simple framework or stall for display of goods in a show, sale, etc.: *a stand at the markets.* **22.** a single performance on a tour: *a one-night stand.* [ME; OE *standan*]

standard /'stændəd/, *n.* **1.** anything taken by general agreement as a basis for comparing other things of a similar nature. **2.** a certain commodity (such as gold or silver) in which the basic money unit is stated. **3.** a grade or level of excellence or achievement: *a high standard of living.* **4.** (*usu. pl.*) behavior, beliefs, etc., thought of as socially acceptable (moral standards). **5.** a flag, emblem, etc., raised on a pole to represent a particular king, army, fleet of ships, etc. **6.** *Heraldry.* long narrowing flag, as of a king or nation. **7.** an upright timber, bar, or rod. **8.** a piece of music, etc., of lasting popularity: *a jazz standard.* ◇*adj.* **9.** serving as a basis of weight, measure, value, etc.: *a standard length of wood.* **10.** of recognised excellence, authority: *a standard author.* **11.** normal, acceptable, or average: *a standard fitting.* [ME, from OF: modification of *estandard,* from Gmc]

standard atmosphere, *n. Phys.* the standard unit of atmospheric pressure that will support a column of mercury 760mm high at 0°C at sea level, equal to 101.325 kilopascals. *Symbol:* atm

standard deviation, *n. Stats.* the square root of the average of the squares of a set of deviations about an arithmetic mean.

Standard English, *n.* **1.** that form of written English characterised by the spelling, syntax and morphology which educated writers of all English dialects adopt with only minor variation. **2.** (loosely) **a.** the pronunciation of educated speakers of the south-eastern English dialect. **b.** the pronunciation of the educated speakers of other dialects of English which resemble it.

standardise *or* **standardize** /'stændədaɪz/, *v.t.*, **-dised, -dising. 1.** to bring to or make of an established standard size, weight, quality, etc.: *to standardise manufactured parts.* **2.** to compare with or test by a standard. —**standardisation,** *n.*

standard lamp, *n.* a lamp having a tall support, standing on the floor of a room.

standard temperature and pressure, *n.* →STP

standard time, *n.* the time officially used in a country or region.

stand-by /'stænd-baɪ/, *n., pl.* **-bys. 1.** something that is kept in readiness to be used when needed or in an emergency. **2.** someone who is on standby; a reliable supporter. **3. on stand-by, a.** (of doctors, etc.) available for duty at short notice. **b.** (of travellers) in readiness to take up a cancelled booking on an aeroplane.

stand-in /'stænd-ɪn/, *n.* **1.** someone used for a short period of time to act in place of another, esp. a film actor during the making of a film. **2.** any substitute.

standing /'stændɪŋ/, *n.* **1.** position, as to rank, credit, reputation, etc.: *men of good standing.* **2.** length of existence, membership, experience, etc.: *a member of long standing.* ◇*adj.* **3.** that stands upright. **4.** performed in or from a stationary or upright position: *a standing start.* **5.** still; not flowing, as water. **6.** continuing without stopping or changing: *a standing rule.* **7.** out of use; idle: *a standing engine.*

standing committee, *n. Govt.* a committee, the members of which are chosen at the beginning of each parliamentary session and which has a continuing responsibility for a general area of government activity.

standing wave, *n. Phys.* a wave produced by the interaction of a transmitted wave and a reflected one having the same amplitude along its axis, as in vibrations of strings, etc. Also, **stationary wave.**

stand-offish /stænd-'ɒfɪʃ/, *adj.* unfriendly; aloof; reserved. —**stand-offishness,** *n.*

standstill /'stændstɪl/, *n.* the condition of standing still; a halt, pause or stop.

Stanislavsky /stænɪs'lavski/, *n.* **Konstantin,** 1863–1938, Russian producer and actor; originator of Method acting.

stank /stæŋk/, *v.* past tense of **stink.**

Stanley /'stænli/, *n.* **1. Sir Henry Morton** (orig. *John Rowlands*), 1841–1904, English explorer in Africa. **2. Owen,** 1811–50, English naval officer and marine surveyor in northern Australia and PNG.

stannic /'stænɪk/, *adj.* of or containing tin, esp. in the tetravalent state.

stannite /'stænaɪt/, *n.* a mineral, copper iron tin sulfide, containing tin, iron-black to steel-grey in color, with a metallic lustre; tin pyrites.

stannous /ˈstænəs/, *adj.* containing tin with a valency of two.

stannum /ˈstænəm/, *n.* → **tin**. Symbol: Sn [LL: tin, in L, alloy of silver and lead]

stanza /ˈstænzə/, *n.* a group of lines of verse, commonly four or more, forming a regularly repeated metrical division of a poem. [It, from L: standing] —**stanzaic**, *adj.*

staphylococcus /stæfələˈkɒkəs/, *n., pl.* **-cocci** /-ˈkɒksaɪ/. any of a certain common group of bacteria in which the individual organisms form irregular clusters, causing boils, septic infections of wounds, etc. [Gk *staphylē* bunch of grapes + COCCUS] —**staphylococcal, staphylococcic**, *adj.*

staple¹ /ˈsteɪpəl/, *n., v.*, **-pled, -pling**. ◇*n.* **1.** a bent piece of wire used to bind papers, sections of a book, etc., together. **2.** a U-shaped or other piece of metal with pointed ends for driving into a surface to hold a hasp, flex, etc. ◇*v.t.* **3.** to fasten by a staple or staples. [ME; OE *stapol* support]

staple² /ˈsteɪpəl/, *n.* **1.** an item, esp. of food, which is used or needed continually: *All kitchens need staples such as flour, sugar, etc.* **2.** a main item, thing, feature, element, or part. **3.** the fibre of wool, cotton, etc., considered with reference to length and fineness. ◇*adj.* **4.** most important among the products exported or produced by a country or district. **5.** (of industries) chief or principal. **6.** principally used: *staple subjects of conversation*. [late ME, from MD: mart, orig. support]

stapler /ˈsteɪplə/, *n.* a small, usu. hand-held, instrument which joins papers with staples. [STAPLE¹ + -ER¹]

star /sta/, *n., adj., v.*, **starred, starring**. ◇*n.* **1.** any of the heavenly bodies appearing as apparently fixed points of light in the sky at night. **2.** *Astron.* any of the light-radiating bodies outside the solar system, as opposed to planets, comets, and meteors. The sun is considered as a star and appears to be a typical member of the galaxy. **3.** *Astrol.* **a.** a heavenly body, esp. a planet, thought to influence mankind and events. **b.** (*pl.*) → **horoscope**. **4.** a figure having rays (usu. five or six) coming from a central point, and considered as representing a star of the sky. **5.** a person who is considered foremost in some field, esp. acting. **6. see stars**, to seem to see bright flashes of light, usu. after a heavy blow on the head. ◇*adj.* **7.** brilliant, best-known or distinguished; chief. ◇*v.t.* **8.** to set with, or as with, stars; spangle. **9.** to present or feature (an actor, etc.) as a star. **10.** to mark (words, etc.) with a star or asterisk, as for special notice. ◇*v.i.* **11.** (of an actor, etc.) to appear as a star. [OE *steorra*] —**starry, starred**, *adj.*

starboard /ˈstabəd/, *n. Naut.* the side of a ship to the right of a person looking towards the bow (opposed to *port*). [OE *stēorbord*, from *stēor* steering + *bord* side (of a ship)]

starch /statʃ/, *n.* **1.** a white, tasteless solid, a carbohydrate, $(C_6H_{10}O_5)_n$, found as small storage granules in the seeds and other parts of plants. It is a major constituent of rice, corn, wheat, beans, potatoes, and many other vegetable foods. **2.** a preparation of this substance used to stiffen linen, etc. **3.** (*pl.*) foods rich in starch. **4.** stiffness or formality of manner. ◇*v.t.* **5.** to treat with starch. [OE *stercean* make stiff or resolute] —**starchy**, *adj.*

Star Chamber, *n.* an English court of law, a tool of the monarchy in Tudor and early Stuart times; abolished 1641.

star-crossed /ˈsta-krɒst/, *adj.* having much bad luck, as if brought about by the influence of the stars: *Romeo and Juliet were star-crossed lovers.*

stardom /ˈstadəm/, *n.* the status of a film star.

stare /stɛə/, *v.*, **stared, staring**, *n.* ◇*v.i.* **1.** to gaze fixedly, esp. with the eyes wide open. ◇*v.t.* **2.** to put, bring, etc., by staring: *She would scare her class into silence.* ◇*v.* **3. stare one in the face**, to be totally obvious. ◇*n.* **4.** a fixed look with the eyes wide open. [ME; OE *starian*]

starfish /ˈstafɪʃ/, *n., pl.* **-fishes**, (*esp. collectively*) **-fish**. a sea animal with a distinctive body, usu. in the form of a star, with five or more rays or arms radiating from a flat, circular centre.

stargaze /ˈstageɪz/, *v.i.*, **-gazed, -gazing. 1.** to gaze at or observe the stars. **2.** to daydream. —**stargazing**, *n.* —**stargazer**, *n.*

stark /stak/, *adj.* **1.** complete, total or utter: *stark madness*. **2.** rigid in death. **3.** (of places, etc.) harsh or forbidding to the view. ◇*adv.* **4.** utterly, absolutely, or quite: *stark naked; stark mad*. [ME; OE *stearc* stiff] —**starkly**, *adv.*

starkers /ˈstakəz/, *adj. Colloq.* **1.** totally naked. **2.** absolutely mad; insane.

starling /ˈstalɪŋ/, *n.* any of a family of sociable, noisy birds, esp. the common European starling introduced into and now common in Australia. [ME; OE *stærling*]

Star of Bethlehem, *n.* the star which is said to have guided the three Magi ('wise men') from the East to the manger of the infant Jesus in Bethlehem. [see Matthew 2, 9, 10]

Star of David, *n.* a figure resembling a six-pointed star, used as a symbol of Judaism.

Starr /sta/, *n.* Ringo /ˈrɪŋgoʊ/ (*Richard Starkey*), born 1940, British pop drummer, singer and composer; drummer for the Beatles.

Stars and Stripes, *n.* the national flag of the US, consisting of 13 horizontal stripes, alternately red and white, equal to the number of the original states, with a blue union marked with white stars equal in number to the whole number of states.

start /stat/, *v.i.* **1.** to begin to move, go, or act: *to start on a journey*. **2.** to begin; esp.: *When did you start on your career? When did your career start?* **3.** to come suddenly into activity, life, view, etc. **4.** to spring or move suddenly from a position or place: *He started from his seat*. **5.** to move with a sudden jerk, as from a shock. **6.** to stick out: *eyes starting from their sockets*. **7.** (of timbers, etc.) to spring, slip, or work loose from place or fastenings. **8.** to be

start   1008   stationary

among the starters in a race, contest, etc. ◇*v.t.* **9.** to set moving, going, or acting: *He will start the engine.* **10.** to set in operation; establish: *The company will start another newspaper.* **11.** to enter upon or begin: *Will you start the letter?* **12.** to cause or help (a person, etc.) to begin a journey, a career, etc.: *He started his son in business.* ◇*n.* **13.** a beginning. **14.** a signal to start, as on a course or in a race. **15.** the first part of anything. **16.** a sudden, involuntary jerking movement of the body: *I woke with a start.* **17.** a lead or advance of a certain amount, as over competitors, etc.: *I had a start of half a lap.* **18.** a chance or opportunity of starting on a course or career. **19.** a spurt of activity: *She works in fits and starts.* [ME]

starter /ˈstɑːtə/, *n.* **1.** someone or something that starts. **2.** someone who gives the signal for starting, as in a race. **3.** any competitor who begins a race, contest, or the like. **4.** (*pl.*) the first course of a meal. **5.** (*pl.*) a first stage in anything: *That'll do for starters.*

startle /ˈstɑːtl/, *v.*, **-tled, -tling.** ◇*v.t.* **1.** to disturb suddenly by a surprise, alarm, or the like. ◇*v.i.* **2.** to move with a sudden jerk, as from a surprise or alarm. [OE *steartlian* kick, struggle] —**startling,** *adj.*

starve /stɑːv/, *v.*, **starved, starving.** ◇*v.i.* **1.** to die from hunger. **2.** to be suffering severely from hunger. **3.** to suffer for lack of something in particular (fol. by *for*). ◇*v.t.* **4.** to cause to die from hunger; to weaken or reduce by lack of food. **5.** to force to some condition or action, by hunger: *The army will starve the town into surrender.* **6.** to cause to suffer for lack of something needed: *to starve children of love.* [OE *steorfan* die] —**starvation,** *n.*

Star Wars, *n.* (in popular usage) a proposed US strategic defence system against nuclear attack, partly space-based.

stash /stæʃ/, *v.t.* **1.** to put away, as for safekeeping or in a prepared place. ◇*n.* **2.** a place where things are hidden. [b. STOW and CACHE]

stat-, a prefix attached to the name of electrical units to indicate the corresponding electrostatic unit.

-stat, a word part meaning 'standing', 'not moving', as in *thermostat*. [Gk *-statēs* that stands]

state /steɪt/, *n., adj., v.,* **stated, stating.** ◇*n.* **1.** the condition of a person or thing with respect to circumstances: *a state of unhappiness.* **2.** condition with respect to structure, form, phase, or the like: *a liquid state.* **3.** (high) social rank. **4.** a ceremonious display of dignity, wealth, pomp, etc.: *a hall used on occasions of state.* **5.** a particularly tense, nervous, or excited condition: *She is in quite a state over the matter.* **6.** a body of people occupying a definite territory and organised under one government. **7.** (*sometimes cap.*) any of the territories, each more or less independent as regards internal affairs, which together make up a federal union, as in the Commonwealth of Australia. **8.** (*oft. cap.*) a system of civil rule and government (often contrasted with the Church). **9. lie in state,** (of a body) to be publicly displayed in honor before burial. **10. the States.** the United States of America. ◇*adj.* **11.** of or relating to the highest-ranking civil government. **12.** (*oft. cap.*) of or relating to one of the territories which make up a federal union. **13.** characterised by or involving ceremony: *a state dinner.* **14.** used on or reserved for occasions of ceremony: *the state rooms.* ◇*v.t.* **15.** to declare definitely or with detail: *to state your views.* **16.** to set forth formally in speech or writing. **17.** to say. [ME]

stately /ˈsteɪtli/, *adj.,* **-lier, -liest.** formal or grand: *a stately palace.* —**stateliness,** *n.*

statement /ˈsteɪtmənt/, *n.* **1.** something stated. **2.** a communication or declaration in speech or writing setting forward facts, particulars, etc. **3.** *Comm.* the summary of an account.

stateroom /ˈsteɪtruːm/, *n.* **1.** a private room or cabin on a ship. **2.** any magnificent room for use on state occasions.

state school, *n.* a school kept at public expense for the education of the children and youth of a district.

statesman /ˈsteɪtsmən/, *n., pl.* **-men. 1.** someone whose work is the management of affairs of state. **2.** someone who shows ability of the highest kind in directing the affairs of a government or in dealing with important public issues. [from *state*'s, gen. of STATE + MAN] —**stateswoman,** *n.fem.* —**statesmanship,** *n.*

static /ˈstætɪk/, *adj.* Also, **statical. 1.** relating to or characterised by a fixed or non-changing condition. **2.** *Elect.* indicating or relating to electricity at rest, as that produced by friction. **3.** relating to atmospheric electricity interfering with the sending and receiving of radio messages, etc. **4.** *Phys.* acting by weight without producing motion: *static pressure.* ◇*n. Elect.* **5.** static or atmospheric electricity. **6.** Also, **atmospherics.** *Radio.* unwanted noises, crackling, etc., caused by electrical currents from storms, etc. [NL, from Gk]

station /ˈsteɪʃən/, *n.* **1.** the place in which anything stands. **2.** (the buildings at) a place at which a train, etc., regularly stops. **3.** the end of a bus or coach route; terminus. **4. a.** (formerly) a government-run farm establishment employing convicts. **b.** a privately-owned country establishment for raising sheep or cattle. **5.** (of people) social standing; rank. **6.** place or position of duty. **7.** a place or position to which a warship, fleet, sailor, etc. is assigned for duty. **8.** a place equipped for some particular kind of work, service, etc.: *a power station; a police station.* **9.** *Radio, TV.* (an organisation which manages) studios, recording and transmitting equipment, buildings, etc., used for producing and sending out programs. **10.** the wave-length on which a radio or television program is broadcast. ◇*v.t.* **11.** to place or post in a station or position. [ME, from L]

stationary /ˈsteɪʃənri, ˈsteɪʃənəri/, *adj.* **1.** standing still; not moving. **2.** having a fixed position; not movable. **3.** remaining in the

stationary

same condition or state; not changing. [ME, from L]

stationary wave, *n.* → **standing wave**.

stationer /'steɪʃənə/, *n.* someone who sells the materials used in writing, as paper, pens, pencils, ink, etc. [ME, from L: stationary, in ML applied to a tradesman who had a shop, as contrasted with a travelling vendor]

stationery /'steɪʃnri, 'steɪʃənəri/, *n.* **1.** writing paper. **2.** writing materials, as pens, pencils, paper, etc.

station wagon, *n.* a car having extra space behind the back seat, and a door or tailgate at the back.

statism /'steɪtɪzəm/, *n.* belief in the state or central government holding economic power. —**statist**, *n.*

statistics /stə'tɪstɪks/, *n.* **1.** (*treated as sing.*) the science which deals with the collection, classification, and use of numerical facts. **2.** (*treated as pl.*) the numerical facts or data themselves. [pl. of *statistic*, from G, from NL: orig., pertaining to a statist] —**statistician**, *n.* —**statistical**, *adj.*

statue /'stætʃu/, *n.* a representation of a person or an animal carved in stone or wood, moulded in a plastic material, or cast in bronze, etc. [ME, from F, from L]

Statue of Liberty, *n.* a giant statue, on Liberty Island, New York harbor, of a woman, sculpted by Frédéric Bartholdi, given to the US by France.

statuesque /stætʃu'ɛsk/, *adj.* like or suggesting a statue, as in dignity, grace, beauty, etc.

stature /'stætʃə/, *n.* **1.** the height of an animal body, esp. of man. **2.** the degree of development or achievement attained. [ME, from OF, from L]

status /'steɪtəs/, *n.* **1.** social, professional or other condition, position, rank, or importance. **2.** the relative standing, position, or condition of anything: *What status does this document have?* **3.** state or condition of affairs. **4.** *Law.* the position of a person before the law. [L]

status quo /ˌsteɪtəs 'kwoʊ/, *n.* (a previously) existing state or condition. [L: state in which]

statute /'stætʃut/, *n.* **1.** *Law.* **a.** a law made by a law-making body and expressed in a formal document. **b.** the document in which the law is expressed. **2.** a rule established by an organisation, etc., for the conduct of its own affairs. [ME, from F, from L: decreed, set up]

Statute of Westminster, *n.* a statute passed in 1931 which formally ratified the independent status of the dominions within the British Empire and Commonwealth.

statutory /'stætʃətri, 'stætʃətəri/, *adj.* **1.** required or fixed by statute. **2.** (of an offence) recognised by statute; legally punishable.

statutory authority, *n.* a government agency created by act of parliament, having the legal status of a corporate body, with independent legal existence.

statutory declaration, *n.* a written statement taken, declared and witnessed by an authorised official, as a justice of the peace, etc., but not sworn on oath and therefore not recognised as evidence in a court of law.

staunch¹ /stɔntʃ/, *v.t.* **1.** to stop the flow of (a liquid, esp. blood). **2.** to stop the flow of blood from (a wound).

staunch² /stɔntʃ/, *adj.* **1.** (of a person) firm in principle, loyalty, etc. **2.** strong; substantial. **3.** able to resist water or other liquids; watertight. Also, **stanch**. [late ME, from OF] —**staunchness**, *n.*

stave /steɪv/, *n., v.,* **staved** or **stove**, **staving**. ◇*n.* **1.** one of the thin, narrow, shaped pieces of wood which form the sides of a cask, tub, or similar vessel. **2.** a verse of a poem or song. **3.** *Music.* Also, **staff.** a set of horizontal lines, now five in number, with the corresponding four spaces between them, music being written on both the lines and spaces. ◇*v.t.* **4.** to break a hole in (oft. fol. by *in*). **5.** to break to pieces, etc. **6.** to furnish with a stave or staves. ◇*v.* **7. stave off**, to put or keep off, as by force or avoidance. [ME; back-formation from *staves*, pl. of STAFF]

Stawell /stɔl/, *n.* a town and shire in the Wimmera region of Vic, north west of Ararat. Pop. 6252 (1986) [named after Sir William Foster *Stawell*, Chief Justice of Vic 1857–86]

Stawell Gift, *n.* an Australian footrace, held annually in Stawell, Vic, since 1878, and claiming to be the oldest in the world. Also, **Stawell Easter Gift**.

stay¹ /steɪ/, *v.,* **stayed** or **staid, staying**, *n.* ◇*v.i.* **1.** to remain in a place, situation, company, etc.: *We cannot stay at home.* **2.** to continue to be (in a particular condition, etc.): *Children cannot stay clean.* **3.** to hold out, as in a contest. **4.** to pause or wait, as for a moment, before continuing. ◇*v.t.* **5.** to stop or hold back. **6.** to satisfy for a time the desires of (the stomach, appetite, etc.). **7.** to remain through or during (a period of time, etc.). **8.** to remain to the end of; endure. ◇*v.* **9. stay put**, to remain where placed. ◇*n.* **10.** the act of stopping. **11.** a time of living somewhere: *We had a short stay in Queensland.* **12.** *Law.* a stoppage of action. [late ME, probably OF: stand, from L]

stay² /steɪ/, *n., v.,* **stayed, staying.** ◇*n.* **1.** something used or serving to support or steady a thing. **2.** a flat strip of steel, plastic, etc., for stiffening corsets, etc. **3.** (*pl.*) a corset. ◇*v.t.* **4.** to support or hold up (sometimes fol. by *up*). [apparently same as STAY³]

stay³ /steɪ/, *n. Chiefly Naut.* a strong rope, now commonly of wire, used to support a mast. [OE *stæg*]

STD¹ /ɛs ti 'di/, *n.* a system for making long distance calls in which the person ringing is automatically connected. Also, **subscriber trunk dialling**. [abbrev.]

STD² /ɛs ti 'di/, *n.* → **sexually transmitted disease**. [abbrev.]

stead /stɛd/, *n.* **1.** the place of a person or thing as occupied by another person: *Since he* *could not come, his brother came in his stead.* **2. stand in good stead**, to be useful or advantageous to. [ME and OE *stede*]

Stead /sted/, *n.* **1. Christina Ellen**, 1902–83, Australian novelist and short-story writer; widely regarded as one of Australia's greatest writers; works include *The Man Who Loved Children* (1941). **2.** her father, **David George**, 1877–1957, Australian naturalist and humanitarian; founder of a wildlife preservation society and of a world peace campaign in 1936.

steadfast /'stedfast, -fəst/, *adj.* **1.** fixed in direction: *a steadfast gaze.* **2.** (of a person) firm in purpose, faith, attachment, etc. **3.** (of faith, loyalty, etc.) unchanging. [OE]

steady /'stedi/, *adj.*, **steadier, steadiest,** *interj.*, *n.*, *pl.* **steadies,** *v.*, **steadied, steadying,** *adv.* ◊*adj.* **1.** firmly placed or fixed; even or regular in movement: *a steady ladder.* **2.** constant or regular: *steady drinkers.* **3.** free from excitement or upset: *steady nerves.* **4.** (of people, principle, etc.) firm or unchanging. **5.** (of a person, habits, etc.) settled or reliable. ◊*interj.* **6.** be calm! control yourself! ◊*n.* **7.** *Colloq.* a regular boyfriend or girlfriend. ◊*v.t., v.i.* **8.** to make or become steady, as in position, movement, action, character, etc. ◊*adv.* **9.** in a firm or steady manner. **10. go steady,** *Colloq.* to go about regularly with the same boyfriend or girlfriend. [STEAD + -Y¹] **– steadily,** *adv.* **– steadiness,** *n.*

steady state, *n.* a state of equilibrium of a system or process that tends to persist once it has been reached.

steak /steɪk/, *n.* **1.** a slice of meat, usu. cut thick and across the grain of the muscle. **2.** a thick slice of a large fish cut across the body. [ME, from ON]

steal /stil/, *v.,* **stole, stolen, stealing,** *n.* ◊*v.t.* **1.** to take or take away dishonestly or wrongfully, esp. secretly. **2.** to take for oneself (ideas, credit, words, etc.) without right. **3.** to take, get, or win by sly, secret or subtle means: *to steal a nap during the lesson.* **4.** to move, bring, or put secretly or quietly (fol. by *away, from, in, into,* etc.). **5.** (in various games) to gain (a point, etc.) by skill or chance. **6.** to obtain more than one's share: *The new baby will steal everybody's attention.* ◊*v.i.* **7.** to practise theft. **8.** to move, go, or come secretly, quietly, or unobserved. **9.** to pass, come, spread, etc., without being noticed: *The years steal by.* ◊*v.* **10. steal a march on,** to obtain an advantage over, esp. by secret means. **11. steal someone's thunder,** to take or use another's idea, plan, etc. **12. steal the show,** (of an actor in a play, etc.) to achieve great success. ◊*n.* **13.** *Colloq.* something acquired at a cost well below its true value. [OE *stelan*] **– stealer,** *n.* **– stealing,** *n., adj.*

stealth /stelθ/, *n.* a secret or hidden procedure. [ME] **– stealthy,** *adj.*

steam /stim/, *n.* **1.** water in the form of a colorless gas or vapor. **2.** water changed to this form by boiling, and used for the making of mechanical power, for heating purposes, etc. **3.** a mist formed when the gas or vapor from boiling water condenses in the air. **4.** *Colloq.* power or energy. **5. let off steam,** *Colloq.* to let go stored-up feelings, by behaving in an uncontrolled manner. ◊*v.i.* **6.** to give off steam. **7.** to rise or pass off in the form of steam, as vapor. **8.** (of a surface) to become covered with condensed steam. **9.** to move or travel by means of steam. ◊*v.t.* **10.** to treat with steam, in order to heat, cook, soften, etc. ◊*adj.* **11.** heated by or heating with steam: *a steam radiator.* **12.** propelled by or propelling with a steam-engine: *a steam train.* **13.** operated by steam. **14.** conducting or carrying steam. [OE *stēam*] **– steamy,** *adj.*

steam-engine /'stim-endʒən/, *n.* an engine in which a sliding piston in a cylinder is moved by the expanding action of the steam made in a boiler.

steamer /'stimə/, *n.* **1.** something driven or operated by steam, e.g. a steamship. **2.** a container in which something is cooked by steam.

steamroller /'stimroulə/, *n.* **1.** a heavy, originally steam-powered vehicle, having a roller or rollers, for crushing or levelling materials in road-making. **2.** an overpowering force, esp. one that crushes opposition with disregard of rights. ◊*v.t.* **3.** to go over or crush as with a steamroller or with a steamroller.

stearate /'stɪəreɪt/, *n.* See **-ate²**.

stearic /stɪ'ærɪk/, *adj. Chem.* of or derived from stearic acid.

stearic acid, *n.* a monobasic organic acid (fatty acid), $C_{17}H_{35}$ COOH, a major component of animal fats, used to make soap, etc.

stearin /'stɪərən/, *n. Chem.* any of three glyceryl esters of stearic acid found in many natural fats. Also, **stearine.** [F, from Gk]

steatite /'stɪətaɪt/, *n.* **→ soapstone.** [L, from Gk: doughlike (stone)] **– steatitic,** *adj.*

steed /stid/, *n. Chiefly Poetic.* a horse, esp. one for fast riding. [OE *stēda* stallion]

steel /stil/, *n.* **1.** iron containing a certain amount of carbon and other metals, and having hardness, elasticity, strength, etc., which vary with composition and heat treatment. **2.** something made of steel, as a knife-sharpener, etc. ◊*adj.* Also, **steely. 3.** relating to or made of steel. **4.** like steel in color, hardness, or strength. ◊*v.t.* **5.** to make unfeeling, unyielding, determined, etc. [ME and d. OE *stēle*]

steel guitar, *n.* **1.** Also, **pedal steel guitar.** an electric guitar developed from the **Hawaiian guitar,** consisting of a flat board horizontal to the floor, with steel strings which are played with a slide. Pitch changes can also be made by means of pedals controlling string tension. **2.** an acoustic guitar with steel strings.

steel wool, *n.* fine threads or shavings of steel, rolled into a small pad, and used for scrubbing, polishing, etc.

steep¹ /stip/, *adj.* **1.** (of a hill, stairs, rise, etc.) having a sharp slope. **2.** *Colloq.* (of a price or amount) too high. **3.** *Colloq.* (of a statement)

steep extreme or extravagant. ◇*n.* **4.** a steep place. [OE *stēap*] —**steepness**, *n.*

steep² /stiːp/, *v.t.* **1.** to soak in water or other liquid, as for the purpose of softening, cleaning, or extracting something. **2.** to wet thoroughly in or with any liquid, or as a liquid does. **3.** to be filled with some absorbing influence: *a mind steeped in romance.* ◇*v.i.* **4.** to lie soaking in a liquid. ◇*n.* **5.** the act or process of steeping. **6.** a liquid in which something is steeped. [ME] —**steeper**, *n.*

steeple /'stiːpəl/, *n.* a tall tower attached to a church, temple, etc., and often with a spire on top. [OE *stēpel*]

steeplechase /'stiːpəltʃeɪs/, *n.* **1.** a horse-race over a course having ditches, hedges, and other obstacles. **2.** a race run on foot by people across country or over a course having obstacles, as ditches, jumps, etc. ◇*v.i.* **3.** to ride or run in a steeplechase.

steer¹ /stɪə/, *v.t.* **1.** to guide the course of (anything in motion) by a rudder, helm, wheel, etc. **2.** to follow (a particular course). **3.** *Colloq.* to direct the course of. ◇*v.i.* **4.** to direct the course of a vessel, vehicle, aeroplane, or the like by the use of a rudder or other means. **5.** to direct the course, or follow a particular course. **6.** (of a vessel, etc.) to be steered or guided in a particular direction. ◇*v.* **7. steer clear of,** to avoid. [OE *stēoran*]

steer² /stɪə/, *n.* a desexed male of the cattle family, esp. one raised for beef. [ME; OE *stēor*]

steerage /'stɪərɪdʒ/, *n.* **1.** a part or division of a ship, originally that containing the steering apparatus, later varying in use. **2.** (in a passenger ship) the part given to the passengers who travel at the cheapest rate.

steering committee, *n.* a committee, esp. one of a law-making body, which prepares the order in which business will be dealt with in meetings.

stegosaur /'stɛɡəsɔː/, *n.* a huge plant-eating dinosaur, with a heavy and bony armor. [Gk *stégos*, var. of *stégē* roof + -SAUR]

Stein /staɪn/, *n.* **Gertrude**, 1874–1946, US author in France.

Steinbeck /'staɪnbɛk/, *n.* **John (Ernst)**, 1902–68, US novelist; won Nobel prize for literature 1962; works include *The Grapes of Wrath* (1939).

Steiner /'staɪnə/, *n.* **Rudolf**, 1861–1925, Austrian philosopher; the methods of the Steiner schools are based on his ideas.

stele /'stiːli/, *n., pl.* **-lae** /-liː/, **-les** /-liːz/. **1.** *Archaeol.* an upright pillar of stone bearing an inscription, design, or the like. **2.** (in ancient Greece and Rome) a burial stone. **3.** *Bot.* the central cylinder of food and water-conducting tissue, etc., in the stem or root of a plant. Also, **stela** (for defs 1–2). [Gk: standing block (of stone)]

stellar /'stɛlə/, *adj.* of, relating to, containing, or like a star or stars. [LL, from L: star] —**stellate, stelliform**, *adj.*

stem¹ /stɛm/, *n., v.,* **stemmed, stemming.** ◇*n.* **1.** the central stalk of a plant which grows upwards in an opposite direction to the root. **2.** a stalk which supports a leaf, flower, or fruit. **3.** a long, thin part: *the stem of a pipe; the stem of a wineglass.* **4.** the line of descent, of a family. **5.** *Gram.* any morpheme or combination of morphemes to which an affix can be added. In English *blackbirds* is made up of the stem *blackbird* (composed of two roots, *black* and *bird*), and the affix *-s.* **6.** a main or relatively thick stroke of a letter in printing, etc. ◇*v.i.* **7.** to originate (usu. fol. by *from*). [ME; OE *stemn*]

stem² /stɛm/, *v.t.,* **stemmed, stemming. 1.** to stop or check (a flow) esp. by damming. **2.** to plug or make tight, as a hole or a joint. [ME, from Scand]

stem³ /stɛm/, *n. Naut.* **1.** an upright at the front of a ship into which the side timbers or plates are jointed. **2.** the forward part of a ship: *from stem to stern.* [OE *stefn, stemn* prow, stern (special use of STEM¹)]

stench /stɛntʃ/, *n.* an offensive smell; stink. [ME; OE *stenc*]

stencil /'stɛnsəl/, *n., v.,* **-cilled, -cilling.** ◇*n.* **1.** a thin sheet of paper, cardboard or metal cut through so as to reproduce a design, letters, etc., when color is rubbed through it. **2.** the letters, designs, etc., produced. ◇*v.t.* **3.** to mark or paint (a surface) or produce (letters, etc.) by means of a stencil. [apparently from ME, from OF, from L: spark]

steno-, a word part meaning 'little', 'narrow', referring especially to shorthand, as in *stenography*. [combining form representing Gk *stenós* narrow, close]

stenographer /stə'nɒɡrəfə/, *n.* someone who is skilled in taking dictation in shorthand. Also, **stenographist**. —**stenography**, *n.*

Stentor /'stɛntɔː/, *n.* a Greek herald in the Trojan war, whose voice was as loud as the voices of fifty men.

stentorian /stɛn'tɔːriən/, *adj.* very loud or powerful in sound: *a stentorian voice.*

step /stɛp/, *n., v.,* **stepped, stepping.** ◇*n.* **1.** a movement made by lifting the foot and setting it down again in a new position, as in walking, running, marching, or dancing. **2.** the space passed over or measured by one such movement: *Move a step nearer.* **3.** a manner of walking; gait. **4.** (*pl.*) the movements or course in stepping or walking: *Retrace your steps.* **5.** a move or proceeding, as towards some end or in the general course of action: *the first step towards peace.* **6.** a degree on a scale. **7.** a support for the foot in ascending or descending: *a step of a ladder; a step of a stair.* **8.** a repeated pattern or unit of movement in a dance formed by a combination of foot and body movements. **9.** (*pl.*) a stepladder. **10. break step,** to stop marching or walking in step. **11. in/out of step, a.** moving at the same/different pace as others. **b.** in agreement/disagreement. **12. watch one's step,** to go, behave, etc., with caution. ◇*v.i.* **13.** to move, go, etc., by lifting the foot and setting it down again in a new position, or by using the feet one after the other in this manner. **14.** to walk, or go on foot, esp. for a few steps or a short distance: *Please step* *this way.* **15.** to come easily as if by a step of the foot: *She was lucky enough to step into a fortune.* **16.** to put the foot down, as on the ground, a support, etc.; tread (*on* or *upon*), by intention or accident: *How could you step on a worm?* ◊*v.t.* **17.** to measure (a distance, ground, etc.) by steps (sometimes fol. by *off* or *out*). **18.** to make or arrange in the manner of a series of steps. ◊*v.* **19.** Some special uses are:

step along, to go fast or briskly.
step down, 1. to decrease. **2.** to resign.
step in, to become involved.
step on it, *Colloq.* to hasten; hurry.
step out, 1. to leave a place or building, esp. for a short time. **2.** to walk briskly.
step up, to increase. [ME; d. OE *steppe*]

step-, a prefix indicating connection between members of a family by the remarriage of a parent, and not by blood, as in *stepmother*, a woman, not one's mother, who marries one's natural father. [ME; OE *stēop-*]

Stephen[1] /'stivən/, *n.* **1. Saint,** the first martyr; stoned to death. [see Acts 6, 7] **2. Saint,** c. 975–1038, first king of Hungary. **3.** 1097?–1154, king of England 1135–54.

Stephen[2] /'stivən/, *n.* **Sir Ninian** /'nɪniən/ **Martin,** born 1923, Australian judge, born in England; governor-general of Australia 1982–89.

Stephenson /'stivənsən/, *n.* **George,** 1781–1848, English inventor and engineer, designer of the 'Rocket' locomotive.

stepladder /'stɛplædə/, *n.* a ladder having flat steps in place of rungs and a hinged support to keep it upright.

steppe /stɛp/, *n.* **1.** a large plain, esp. one without trees. **2. the Steppes,** the extensive plains of Eurasia, mainly in the USSR. [Russ: *step*]

stepping stone *n.* **1.** a stone, or one of a line of stones, in shallow water, etc., used for stepping on in crossing. **2.** any means of advancing or rising.

-ster, a suffix of personal nouns referring esp. to occupation or habit, as in *songster, gamester, trickster,* also having less clear associations, as in *youngster.* [ME; OE *-estre, -istre*]

steradian /stə'reɪdiən/, *n.* a unit of measurement of solid angle, being the solid angle which, having its vertex in the centre of a sphere, cuts off an area of the surface of the sphere equal to that of a square with sides equal to the radius of the sphere. *Symbol:* sr

stereo /'stɛrioʊ, 'stɪərioʊ/, *n., pl.* **stereos,** *adj.* ◊*n.* **1.** (any system equipped for) stereophonic sound reproduction. **2.** a stereoscopic photograph or photography. ◊*adj.* **3.** relating to stereophonic sound, stereoscopic photography, etc.

stereo-, a word element referring to hardness, solidity, and three dimensionality. Also, before some vowels, **stere-.** [combining form representing Gk *stereós* solid]

stereogram /'stɛrioʊgræm, 'stɪə-/, *n.* a record-player with stereophonic sound production. Also, **stereo.**

stereophonic /stɛriə'fɒnɪk, stɪə-/, *adj.* **1.** of or relating to the multi-channel reproduction or broadcasting of sound in which two channels are used and reproduction is from two speakers placed apart in front of the listener. **2.** of or relating to the discs, tapes, equipment, etc., used in creating stereophonic effects. See **monophonic, quadraphonic.** [STEREO- + PHONIC] **—stereophony,** *n.*

stereoscope /'stɛriəskoʊp, 'stɪə-/, *n.* an optical instrument through which two pictures of the same object, taken from slightly different angles, are viewed, one by each eye, producing the effect of a single picture of the object, with the appearance of depth. **—stereoscopy,** *n.*

stereotype /'stɛriətaɪp, 'stɪə-/, *n., v.,* **-typed, -typing.** ◊*n.* **1.** a process of making metal plates to use in printing, by taking a mould of composed type, and then taking from this mould a cast (plate) in type metal. **2.** a plate made by this process. **3.** an oversimplified and conventional idea or image, used to label or define people, etc.: *The common stereotype of a professor is an absent-minded, impractical person.* ◊*v.t.* **4.** to make a stereotype of. **5.** to think of (someone) in terms of a stereotype; categorise.

sterile /'stɛraɪl/, *adj.* **1.** free from living germs or micro-organisms: *a sterile bandage.* **2.** unable to reproduce; barren. **3.** unproductive of results; fruitless. [L: barren] **—sterility,** *n.*

sterilise or **sterilize** /'stɛrəlaɪz/, *v.t.,* **-lised, -lising. 1.** to destroy micro-organisms in (something) usu. by bringing it to a high temperature. **2.** to make permanently unable to reproduce young, esp. by surgery. **—steriliser,** *n.* **—sterilisation,** *n.*

sterling /'stɜlɪŋ/, *adj.* **1.** consisting of or relating to British money. **2.** (of silver) being of standard quality, 92½% pure silver. **3.** made of sterling silver: *sterling cutlery.* **4.** thoroughly excellent: *a man of sterling worth.* ◊*n.* **5.** silver having the sterling fineness. **6.** manufactured goods of sterling silver. [ME]

stern[1] /stɜn/, *adj.* **1.** firm, strict, or unbending: *stern discipline.* **2.** hard, harsh, or severe: *a stern warning.* **3.** grim or forbidding in appearance: *a stern face.* [ME; OE *styrne*] **—sternness,** *n.*

stern[2] /stɜn/, *n.* **1.** the back part of a ship or boat (often opposed to *stem*). **2.** the back part of anything. [ME, ? from Scand]

Stern /stɜn/, *n.* **Isaac,** born 1920, US violinist born in the USSR.

sternum /'stɜnəm/, *n., pl.* **-na** /-nə/, **-nums.** (in humans) a flat, narrow bone connected with the clavicles and the true ribs; the breastbone. [NL, from Gk: chest, breast] **—sternal,** *adj.*

steroid /'stɛrɔɪd, 'stɪə-/, *n.* any of a large group of lipids, most having a particular physiological action, e.g. the sterols, bile acids, and many hormones.

sterol /'stɛrɒl/, *n.* any of a group of steroid alcohols derived from plants or animals, e.g. cholesterol. [abstracted from (CHOLE)STEROL]

stertorous /'stɜːtərəs/, *adj.* characterised by heavy breathing or snoring.

stet /stet/, *v.*, **stetted, stetting.** ◇*v.i.* **1.** let it stand (a direction on a printer's proof, a manuscript, or the like to keep material previously cancelled). ◇*v.t.* **2.** to mark with the word 'stet'. [L: let it stand]

stetho-, a word part meaning 'chest'. Also, before vowels, **steth-**. [combining form representing Gk *stēthos*]

stethoscope /'steθəskoʊp/, *n.* an instrument used to carry sounds in the chest or other parts of the body to the ear of the examiner. — **stethoscopic**, *adj.*

stetson /'stetsən/, *n.* a man's hat having a broad brim and a wide crown, as worn by cowboys. [named after the designer, John Stetson, 1830–1906, US hatmaker]

stevedore /'stivədɔː/, *n.* a firm or individual engaged in the loading or unloading of ships. [Sp: pack, stow, from L: press]

Stevenson /'stivənsən/, *n.* **Robert Louis (Balfour)**, 1850–94, Scottish novelist, essayist, and poet.

stew /stjuː/, *v.t.* **1.** to cook by slow boiling. ◇*v.i.* **2.** to undergo slow boiling. **3.** *Colloq.* to worry or fuss. ◇*v.* **4. stew in one's own juice**, to suffer, without help, one's own misfortunes or the results of one's own actions. ◇*n.* **5.** a preparation of meat, fish or other food cooked by stewing. **6.** *Colloq.* a condition of uneasiness or worry. [ME, from OF, from VL: perspire]

steward /'stjuəd/, *n.* **1.** someone who manages another's property or financial affairs. **2.** someone who has charge of the household of another, providing for the table, directing the servants, etc. **3.** an employee who has charge of the table, the servants, etc., in a club or other establishment. **4.** any person on a ship or aircraft who waits on passengers. **5.** someone responsible for arranging the details and conduct of a public meeting, race meeting, public entertainment, etc. [ME; OE *stīweard*, *stigweard*] — **stewardess**, *n. fem.* — **stewardship**, *n.*

Stewart /'stjuət/, *n.* **1.** the spelling used, prior to the reign of Mary Queen of Scots (Mary Stuart), for the British royal house of **Stuart**. **2. Douglas Alexander**, 1913–85, Australian poet, playwright and critic, born in NZ; author of the verse-drama *The Fire on the Snow* (1939).

sth, *Abbrev.* south. Also, **Sth**

sthn, *Abbrev.* southern. Also, **Sthn**

-stichous, *Bot, Zool.* a word part referring to rows. [Gk]

stick¹ /stɪk/, *n.* **1.** a branch or shoot of a tree or shrub cut or broken off. **2.** a relatively long and thin piece of wood, e.g. a rod, walking stick, club, etc. **3.** an elongated piece of wood for burning, for carpentry, or for any special purpose. **4.** any long, thin piece: *a stick of celery*. **5. the sticks**, *Colloq.* **a.** an area regarded as lacking in the comforts of city life. **b.** → **back country**. **6.** a piece of furniture. [OE *sticca*]

stick² /stɪk/, *v.*, **stuck, sticking**, *n.* ◇*v.t.* **1.** to pierce (something) with a pointed instrument, as a dagger, spear, or pin; stab. **2.** to thrust (something pointed) in, into, through etc.: *If you stick a pin into a balloon, it will burst.* **3.** to fix upon something pointed: *to stick a potato on a fork.* **4.** to set with things piercing the surface: *to stick a cushion full of pins.* **5.** to fasten in position by piercing, gluing, etc.: *to stick a nail in a wall*; *to stick a stamp on a letter.* **6.** to provide with things attached: *to stick a wall with posters.* **7.** to poke into a place or position indicated: *Just stick your head out of the window.* **8.** to place in a particular position: *stick your books on the table.* **9.** to prevent from moving (*usu.* in passive): *The car was stuck in the muddy road.* **10.** to endure; tolerate. **11.** to force an unpleasant task upon. ◇*v.i.* **12.** to have the point piercing into something. **13.** to stay attached as if by glue; cling: *The mud sticks to his shoes*; *He sticks to his old ideas.* **14.** to remain firm in opinion, attachment, etc.: *I will stick to my word.* **15.** to keep steadily at a task, duty, or the like (fol. by *at* or *to*): *He will stick at the job.* **16.** to become fastened, checked, or stationary by some obstruction. **17.** to hesitate (usu. fol. by *at*): *She would stick at actual disloyalty.* **18.** to extend, project, or protrude (fol. by *through, from, out, up,* etc.). **19.** to remain or stay, usu. for a considerable time: *I can't bear to stick indoors all day.* ◇*v.* **20.** Some special uses are: **stick around**, *Colloq.* to stay nearby; linger. **stick by/to/with**, to remain loyal to. **stick out**, **1.** to stand out or in the way; protrude. **2.** to be obvious, conspicuous, etc.: *The facts stick out a mile.* **3.** to endure; stand one's ground. **stick (something) out**, to put up with until the very end: *They were bored by the film but stuck it out for two hours.* **stick together**, to remain friendly, loyal, etc., to one another. **stick up**, **1.** to project or protrude upwards. **2.** *Colloq.* to rob, esp. at gunpoint. **stick up for**, to speak or act in favor of; defend; support. ◇*n.* **21.** a thrust with a pointed instrument; a stab. **22.** the quality of adhering or of causing things to adhere. **23.** *Mil.* a number of bombs fired rapidly from a single aircraft. [ME *stike(n)*, OE *stician*]

sticker /'stɪkə/, *n.* **1.** an adhesive label, usu. with an advertisement or other message printed on it. **2.** someone who, despite difficulties, keeps trying to succeed.

stick insect, *n.* any of certain insects, many wingless, with long, thin, twig-like bodies.

stickleback /'stɪkəlbæk/, *n.* a type of small, aggressive, spiny-backed fish found in fresh waters and sea inlets of the northern hemisphere. [ME, from OE *sticol* scaly + *bæc* back]

stickler /'stɪklə/, *n.* someone who unbendingly insists on something (fol. by *for*): *My teacher is a stickler for correct spelling.*

stick-nest rat, *n.* a primitive Australian rodent which lives in colonies and builds nests or houses of sticks and twigs.

stick-up /ˈstɪk-ʌp/, *n. Colloq.* a hold-up or robbery.

sticky /ˈstɪki/, *adj.*, **stickier, stickiest. 1.** having the quality of adhering, as glue; adhesive: *sticky tape.* **2.** covered with gluey or adhesive matter: *sticky hands.* **3.** *Cricket.* (of a wicket) affected by rain, causing the ball to bounce in an unexpected manner. **4.** (of the weather, etc.) humid: *an unbearably sticky day.* **5.** *Colloq.* difficult to deal with; awkward; troublesome: *a sticky situation.* — **stickily,** *adv.* — **stickiness,** *n.*

stickybeak /ˈstɪkibik/, *v.i.* **1.** to inquire into matters that do not concern one; pry; meddle. ◇*n.* **2.** someone who pries.

stiff /stɪf/, *adj.* **1.** hard or firm in substance; not flexible, pliant, or easily bent: *a stiff collar.* **2.** not moving or working easily: *a stiff hinge.* **3.** (of a person, etc.) moving only with difficulty, as from cold, age, tiredness, etc. **4.** *Colloq.* unfortunate; unlucky: *That's stiff luck, mate.* **5.** blowing violently, strongly, or with steady force: *stiff winds.* **6.** firm in purpose or determination; unyielding; stubborn. **7.** stubbornly continued or kept up, as a struggle, etc. **8.** unbendingly formal, as persons, manners, proceedings, etc. **9.** lacking ease and grace; awkward: *a stiff style of writing.* **10.** excessively regular, as a design. **11.** laborious or difficult, as a task. **12.** severe, as a penalty. **13.** excessive; unusually high or great, as a price, demand, etc. **14.** firm from tension; taut: *to keep a stiff rein.* **15.** relatively firm in consistency, as semisolid matter: *a stiff jelly.* ◇*n.* *Colloq.* **16.** a dead body; corpse. ◇*adv.* **17.** in a hard, unbending state: *The clothes were frozen stiff.* **18.** completely; utterly: *We were all scared stiff.* [ME; OE *stīf*] — **stiffness,** *n.*

stiffen /ˈstɪfən/, *v.t.*, *v.i.* to make or become stiff or tense.

stifle /ˈstaɪfəl/, *v.*, **-fled, -fling.** ◇*v.t.* **1.** to kill by preventing breathing; smother. **2.** to keep back or repress: *to stifle a yawn.* **3.** to suppress, crush, or stop: *to stifle a revolt.* ◇*v.i.* **4.** to become stifled or suffocated. **5.** to suffer from difficulty in breathing, as in a hot or humid atmosphere. [Scand] — **stifling,** *adj.*

stigma /ˈstɪɡmə/, *n.*, *pl.* **stigmata** /stɪɡˈmatə/, **stigmas** (*esp. defs 3 and 4*). **1.** a mark of shame; a stain, as on one's reputation. **2.** a characteristic mark or sign of a fault or imperfection, disease, etc. **3.** *Zool.* a small mark, spot, pore, or the like, on an animal or organ, as: **a.** the eyespot, usu. red, of a protozoan. **b.** (in insects) the entrance into the respiratory system. **4.** *Bot.* that part of a pistil which receives the pollen. **5.** (*pl.*) *Rom Cath Ch.* marks said to have been supernaturally produced upon certain persons in the likeness of the wounds on the crucified body of Christ. [L, from Gk] — **stigmatic,** *adj.*

stigmatise or **stigmatize** /ˈstɪɡmətaɪz/, *v.t.*, **-tised, -tising. 1.** to mark with a stigma or brand. **2.** to set some mark of disgrace or public shame upon.

stilboestrol /stɪlˈbiːstrɒl/, *n.* a synthetic hormone, $C_{18}H_{20}O_2$, the parent substance of a group of oestrogenic agents, some of which are more active than those of the human body.

stile /staɪl/, *n.* **1.** a series of steps for climbing over a fence where there is no gate. **2.** → **turnstile.** [ME; OE *stigel*]

stiletto /stəˈlɛtoʊ/, *n.*, *pl.* **-tos. 1.** a dagger having a narrow, tapered blade. **2.** Also, **stiletto heel.** a high, very narrow, heel on a woman's shoe. [It: dagger, from L: pointed instrument]

still[1] /stɪl/, *adj.* **1.** remaining in place or at rest; motionless; stationary: *to stand still.* **2.** free from sound or noise, as a place, time, etc.; silent: *a still night.* **3.** quiet or low in sound; hushed: *a still, small voice.* **4.** free from movement of any kind; quiet; tranquil; calm: *still water.* **5.** not bubbling or sparkling, as wine. **6.** *Photog.* denoting or relating to a still (photograph). ◇*n.* **7.** *Poetic.* stillness or silence: *in the still of the night.* **8.** a single photographic picture, esp. a print of one of the frames of a moving film. ◇*adv.* **9.** up to or at this time; as previously: *points still unsettled; Is she still here?* **10.** even or yet (with comparatives, etc.): *still more complaints.* **11.** even then; yet; nevertheless: *to be rich and still crave for more.* **12.** without sound or movement. **13.** *Poetic.* steadily; constantly; always. ◇*conj.* **14.** and yet; but yet; nevertheless: *It was futile, still they fought.* ◇*v.t.* **15.** to silence or hush (sounds, etc.). **16.** to calm, quieten; appease; allay. ◇*v.i.* **17.** to become still or quiet. [ME and OE *stille*] — **stillness,** *n.*

still[2] /stɪl/, *n.* **1.** a distilling apparatus, consisting of a container, in which the substance is heated and turned into gas, and a cooling device or coil for bringing the gas back to liquid form. **2.** → **distillery.** [var. of DISTIL]

stillbirth /ˈstɪlbɜθ/, *n.* the birth of a dead child or organism. — **stillborn,** *adj.*

still life, *n.*, *pl.* **still lifes** /stɪl ˈlaɪfs/. a picture representing inanimate objects, such as fruit, flowers, etc. — **still-life,** *adj.*

stilt /stɪlt/, *n.* **1.** one of two poles, each with a support for the foot at some distance above the ground, used for walking on by circus clowns, etc. **2.** one of several high posts underneath any structure built above land or over water. **3.** a type of shore-living bird, with very long legs, long neck, and a slender bill, and living esp. in marshes. [ME]

stilted /ˈstɪltəd/, *adj.* **1.** stiffly dignified or formal, as speech, literary style, etc.; pompous. **2.** *Archit.* (of an arch) having some height between the upright supports and the beginning of the curve.

stilton /ˈstɪltən/, *n.* a rich, waxy, white cheese, veined with blue mould. [after *Stilton* in Huntingdonshire, England]

stimulant /ˈstɪmjələnt/, *n.* **1.** *Med.* something that for a short time quickens some vital process or the necessary activity of some organ or part. **2.** any drink or food that increases activity or wakefulness. ◇*adj.* **3.** stimulating. [L: stimulating, inciting]

stimulate /ˈstɪmjəleɪt/, *v.*, **-lated, -lating.** ◇*v.t.* **1.** to bring to action or effort; spur on;

stimulate

incite: *to stimulate production*. **2.** to excite (a body organ, etc.) to its normal activity. **3.** to make energetic by an alcoholic or other stimulant. ◇*v.i.* **4.** to act as a stimulus or stimulant. [L: goaded on] —**stimulator**, *n.* —**stimulation**, *n.* —**stimulative**, *n.*

stimulus /'stɪmjələs/, *n., pl.* **-li** /-li/, **-lai**/, **-luses. 1.** something that stirs to action, effort, or thought. **2.** anything which causes a response to be made. **3.** something that excites an organism or part to activity. [NL, special use of L: goad, sting]

sting /stɪŋ/, *v.*, **stung, stinging,** *n.* ◇*v.t.* **1.** to prick or wound with some sharp-pointed, often poison-bearing organ, which certain animals have: *A bee has stung me*. **2.** to affect painfully, esp. as a result of contact with certain plants: *to be stung by nettles*. **3.** to cause (someone) mental or moral suffering: *to be stung with remorse*; *Her unkind words stung me*. **4.** to drive or goad as by sharp irritation: *He stung me into answering back*. ◇*v.i.* **5.** (of bees, etc.) to use a sting. **6.** to cause a sharp, smarting physical or mental pain: *Nettles sting; Sarcasm aims to sting*. **7.** to feel sharp physical or mental pain or irritation. ◇*n.* **8.** the act or power of stinging or causing pain. **9.** a wound or pain caused by a sting. **10.** any sharp or smarting wound, hurt, or pain (physical or mental). **11.** *Bot.* a type of hair on certain plants, esp. nettles, which gives off an irritating fluid. **12.** *Zool.* a sharp-pointed, often poison-bearing, organ of insects and other animals, able to cause painful or dangerous wounds. [OE *stingan*]

stingray /'stɪŋreɪ/, *n.* any of the rays (fish), having a long, flexible tail armed near the base with a strong, saw-like bony spine with which they can inflict severe and very painful wounds.

stingy /'stɪndʒi/, *adj.*, **-gier, -giest. 1.** unwilling to give or spend; niggardly; penurious. **2.** scanty or meagre. [orig. meaning 'having a sting', 'bad-tempered'] —**stingily**, *adv.* —**stinginess**, *n.*

stink /stɪŋk/, *v.*, **stank** or **stunk, stunk, stinking,** *n.* ◇*v.i.* **1.** to give off a strong offensive smell. **2.** to be very badly thought of. **3.** *Colloq.* to be very inferior in quality. **4.** *Colloq.* to have a large quantity of something, esp. money (usu. fol. by *of* or *with*). ◇*v.* **5. stink out, a.** to cause to stink. **b.** to drive out, repel, etc., by an offensive smell. ◇*n.* **6.** a strong offensive smell; stench. **7.** *Colloq.* a fuss; commotion; scandal: *kick up a stink*. [ME; OE *stincan*]

stinker /'stɪŋkə/, *n.* **1.** someone or something that stinks. **2.** *Colloq.* a dishonest or disgusting person. **3.** *Colloq.* a difficult task, problem, etc. **4.** something unpleasant, esp. a very hot day.

stinkhorn /'stɪŋkhɔn/, *n.* any of various bad-smelling fungi.

stinking /'stɪŋkɪŋ/, *adj.* **1.** offensive-smelling. **2.** *Colloq.* offensive; disgusting; disgraceful. ◇*adv.* **3.** *Colloq.* (an intensifier, with the sense of 'very'): *stinking hot; stinking rich*.

stinking wattle, *n.* → **gidgee** (def. 1).

1015

stirrup

stint[1] /stɪnt/, *v.t.* **1.** to limit to a certain amount, number, share, or allowance, often unreasonably; set limits to; restrict. ◇*v.i.* **2.** to be limited in spending or frugal; get along on a very small allowance. ◇*n.* **3.** limitation or restriction, esp. as to amount: *to give without stint*. **4.** a limited or stated quantity, share, rate, etc.: *to exceed one's stint*. **5.** a set amount or piece of work: *to do one's daily stint*. [ME; OE *styntan* make blunt, dull]

stint[2] /stɪnt/, *n.* any of various small shore-birds, as the red-necked stint.

stipe /staɪp/, *n. Bot, Zool.* a stalk or thin support. Also, **stipes**. [F, from L: log, post]

stipend /'staɪpɛnd/, *n.* fixed or regular pay; a periodic payment; salary. [ME, from L]

stipendiary /staɪ'pɛndəri/, *adj., n., pl.* **-ries.** ◇*adj.* **1.** receiving a stipend. **2.** relating to or paid by a stipend. ◇*n.* **3.** someone who receives a stipend.

stipple /'stɪpəl/, *v.*, **-pled, -pling,** *n.* ◇*v.t.* **1.** to paint, engrave, or draw by means of dots or small touches. ◇*n.* Also, **stippling. 2.** the method of painting, engraving, etc., by stippling. **3.** a painting, engraving, etc., made by means of dots or small spots. [D: dot, speckle]

stipulate /'stɪpjəleɪt/, *v.*, **-lated, -lating.** ◇*v.i.* **1.** to make a stated demand or arrangement as a condition of agreement. ◇*v.t.* **2.** to arrange specially or state clearly in terms of agreement: *to stipulate a price*. **3.** to require as necessary condition in making an agreement. [L] —**stipulation,** *n.*

stir[1] /stɜ/, *v.*, **stirred, stirring,** *n.* ◇*v.t.* **1.** to disturb (a liquid, etc.) in order to mix it by moving a spoon, etc., around in it: *to stir coffee*. **2.** to move, esp. in some slight way: *The breeze stirred the leaves*. **3.** to move briskly; bestir: *to stir oneself*. **4.** to disturb (someone) from inactivity, quiet, contentment, lack of interest, etc. (oft. fol. by *up*). **5.** to excite, prompt or instigate (oft. fol. by *up*): *to stir up people to rebellion*. **6.** to intentionally upset (people, a meeting, etc.). **7.** to affect strongly; excite: *to stir the heart*. ◇*v.i.* **8.** to move, esp. slightly or lightly: *Not a leaf stirred*. **9.** (of a person) to move about, esp. briskly. **10.** to become active, as from some rousing or quickening impulse. **11.** to have one's feelings moved or strongly affected. **12.** to mention subjects likely to cause argument in a deliberate attempt to involve others in an angry discussion. ◇*n.* **13.** the act of stirring or moving, or the sound made. **14.** a condition or occasion of general excitement; a commotion. [ME; OE *styrian*]

stir[2] /stɜ/, *n. Colloq.* prison. [orig. unknown]

Stirling /'stɜlɪŋ/, *n.* **Sir James**, 1791–1865, Scottish naval officer; lieutenant-governor of WA 1828–32; first governor 1839–39.

stirring /'stɜrɪŋ/, *adj.* **1.** able to stir; moving, active, bustling, or lively. **2.** rousing, exciting, or thrilling: *a stirring speech*.

stirrup /'stɪrəp/, *n.* a loop, ring, or other device of metal, wood, leather, etc., hung from the saddle of a horse to support the rider's foot. [ME; OE *stigrāp*]

stitch /stɪtʃ/, *n.* **1.** one complete movement of a threaded needle through a material, so as to leave behind it a single loop or portion of thread, as in sewing, embroidery, surgical closing of wounds, etc. **2.** a particular type of stitch or the style of work produced: *blanket stitch*. **3.** (a loop of wool or thread made by) one complete movement of the needle in knitting or crocheting. **4.** a thread or bit of any material or of clothing, etc.: *every stitch of clothing*. **5.** a sudden, sharp pain, esp. in the muscles between the ribs. **6. in stitches,** laughing uncontrollably. ◇*v.t.* **7.** to work upon, join, fasten, or ornament with stitches; sew. ◇*v.i.* **8.** to make stitches; sew (by hand or machine). [OE *stice*]

Stivens /'stɪvənz/, *n.* **Dal(las George),** born 1911, Australian short-story writer and novelist; wrote the novel *A Horse of Air* (1970).

stoat /stoʊt/, *n.* a type of weasel found in Europe, Asia and North America, called stoat when in its brown summer coat, and known as ermine in its white winter coat. [ME; orig. unknown]

stock /stɒk/, *n.* **1.** the total quantity of goods kept on hand by a merchant, business firm, manufacturer, etc., for the supply of customers. **2.** a quantity of something gathered and kept, as for future use: *a stock of provisions*. **3.** →**livestock**. **4.** *Bot.* **a.** a stem, tree, or plant from which one can obtain slips or cuttings. **b.** a stem in which a graft (def. 5) is inserted and which is its support. **5.** the type from which a group of animals or plants has been developed or bred. **6.** a race or other related group of animals or plants. **7.** a line of descent; tribe, race, or ethnic group. **8.** a major division of mankind, esp. Caucasoid, Mongoloid, Negroid. **9.** the handle of a whip, etc. **10.** (*pl.*) an instrument of punishment (no longer in use), made of a framework with holes for the ankles and (sometimes) the wrists and neck of an offender. **11.** *Cookery.* a liquid or broth prepared by boiling meat, fish, vegetables, etc., used esp. as the base for soups and sauces. **12.** a common, spring-flowering garden plant of varying height and color, with fragrant, four-petal flowers. **13.** *Finance.* **a.** the capital of a company converted from fully paid shares. **b.** the shares of a particular company. **c.** →**capital stock**. **14.** (*oft. pl.*) repute; standing: *His stocks are high*. **15. take stock,** to make a judgment or survey of resources, prospects, etc.: *to take stock of a situation*. ◇*adj.* **16.** kept regularly in store, as for sale or use; staple; standard: *stock articles*. **17.** in common use; ordinary: *a stock argument*. **18.** designating or relating to livestock raising: *stock farming*. **19.** *Comm.* of or relating to the stock of a company: *stock records*. ◇*v.t.* **20.** to provide with a stock or supply. **21.** to provide (a farm) with horses, cattle, etc. **22.** to collect and store, as for future use. ◇*v.i.* **23.** to collect a supply (oft. fol. by *up*). [ME; OE *stoc(c)*]

stockade /stɒ'keɪd/, *n., v.*, **-aded, -ading.** ◇*n.* **1.** a defensive barrier made of strong posts fixed upright in the ground. **2.** (formerly) an enclosure in which convict laborers employed in road gangs, etc., were held at night. ◇*v.t.* **3.** to protect, strengthen against attack, or surround with a stockade. [F, from OPr: stake, of Gmc orig.]

stockbroker /'stɒkbroʊkə/, *n.* an agent or broker who buys and sells stocks and shares for customers for a commission.

stock-car /'stɒk-kɑ/, *n.* a type of car, adapted to take collisions, used in racing.

stock exchange, *n.* **1.** (*oft. caps*) a building or place where stocks and shares are bought and sold. **2.** an association of brokers, jobbers and dealers in stocks and bonds, who meet to transact their business.

Stockhausen /'ʃtɒkhaʊzən/, *n.* **Karlheinz** /'kalhaɪnts/, born 1928, German composer of electronic music.

Stockholm /'stɒkhoʊm/, *n.* the capital and chief seaport of Sweden, in the southeastern part. Pop. 663 217 (1987 est.).

stocking /'stɒkɪŋ/, *n.* **1.** a close-fitting covering for the foot and leg, usu. knitted (by hand or machine) of wool, cotton, nylon, silk, etc. **2.** something resembling this.

stockman /'stɒkmən/, *n.* a man employed to tend livestock, esp. cattle.

stockpile /'stɒkpaɪl/, *n., v.* **-piled, -piling.** ◇*n.* **1.** a supply of material. **2.** a large supply of materials which cannot be done without, held in reserve for use during a period of shortage, etc. **3.** a supply of munitions, weapons, etc., gathered together for possible future use. ◇*v.t.* **4.** to gather for future use. ◇*v.i.* **5.** to gather in a stockpile.

stocktaking /'stɒkteɪkɪŋ/, *n.* **1.** the examination and listing of goods, assets, etc., in a shop, business, etc. **2.** a reconsideration or reassessment of one's position, progress, prospects, etc.

stockwhip /'stɒkwɪp/, *n.* a long, bullock-hide whip used in handling stock.

stocky /'stɒki/, *adj.*, **-ier, -iest. 1.** of solid and strong form or build; thickset, often short. **2.** having a strong, stout stem, as a plant.

stodgy /'stɒdʒi/, *adj.*, **-ier, -iest. 1.** heavy, dull, or uninteresting. **2.** (of food, etc.) thick, semisolid, and heavy. —**stodge,** *n.* —**stodgily,** *adv.* —**stodginess,** *n.*

Stoic /'stoʊɪk/, *adj.* **1.** of or relating to the school of philosophy founded by Zeno, fl. c. 475 BC, who taught that men should be free from strong feelings, unmoved by joy or grief, and bear without complaint whatever happens to them. **2.** (*l.c.*) stoical. ◇*n.* **3.** a member or adherent of the Stoic school of philosophy. **4.** (*l.c.*) someone who is always mentally strong, patient and uncomplaining. [ME, from L, from Gk: a porch, specifically the porch in Athens where Zeno lectured] —**stoicism,** *n.*

stoical /'stoʊɪkəl/, *adj.* noted for calm or silent strength and courage; impassive: *a stoical sufferer*.

stoichiometry /ˌstɔɪki'ɒmətri/, *n. Chem.* the calculation of the quantities of chemical elements or compounds involved in chemical reactions. Also, **stoechiometry, stoicheiometry.**

stoichiometry 1017 **stoop**

[Gk *stoicheio-* (combining form of *stoicheîon* component) + -METRY] **-stoichiometric,** *adj.*

stoke /stouk/, *v.*, **stoked, stoking.** ◇*v.t.* **1.** to poke, stir up, and feed (a fire). **2.** to look after the fire of (a furnace); supply with fuel. ◇*v.i.* **3.** to shake up the coals of a fire. **4.** to tend a fire or furnace; act as a stoker. [back-formation from STOKER]

stoker /'stoukə/, *n.* **1.** someone employed to tend a furnace used in generating steam, as on a steamship. **2.** a mechanical device for supplying solid fuel to a furnace. [D: feed a fire]

stokes /stouks/, *n.* a non-SI unit of kinematic viscosity, equal to 0.1×10^{-3} square metres per second. *Symbol:* St

Stokes /stouks/, *n.* **John Lort,** 1812–85, Australian naval officer and marine surveyor, born in England; his explorations led him to Port Darwin and the Plains of Promise, Qld.

stole[1] /stoul/, *v.* past tense of **steal.**

stole[2] /stoul/, *n.* **1.** a narrow scarf-like strip worn by clergymen during a service. **2.** a woman's scarf of fur or cloth, usu. worn over the shoulders with the ends hanging down in front. [ME and OE, from L, from Gk: clothing, robe]

stolen /'stoulən/, *v.* past participle of **steal.**

stolid /'stɒlɪd/, *adj.* not easily moved or stirred; dull; unimaginative. [L]

stoma /'stoumə/, *n., pl.* **stomata** /'stoumətə, 'stɒm-/. **1.** *Bot.* a type of small opening, esp. one of the minute orifices or slits in the outer skin or layer of leaves, etc. **2.** *Zool.* a mouth or opening through which food or nutriment is taken, esp. when in the form of a small or simple aperture. [NL, from Gk: mouth] **-stomatal,** *adj.*

stomach /'stʌmək/, *n.* **1.** (in man and other vertebrates) a sac-like enlargement of the alimentary canal, forming an organ of storage, dilution, and digestion. **2.** any similar digestive cavity or tract in invertebrates. **3.** appetite for food. **4.** desire, inclination, or liking: *no stomach for fighting.* ◇*v.t.* **5.** to take into or retain in the stomach. **6.** to endure or tolerate. [ME, from OF, from L, from Gk: throat, gullet, stomach] **-stomachic,** *adj.*

stomatic /stou'mætɪk/, *adj.* **1.** relating to the mouth. **2.** acting as a cure for diseases of the mouth, as a drug.

stomato-, a word part referring to the mouth. Also, **stomat-, -stome.** [Gk, combining form of *stóma* mouth]

-stomy, combining form used in the names of surgical operations for making an artificial opening, as *colostomy*. [Gk: mouth]

stone /stoun/, *n., pl.* **stones** (*except* **stone** for def. 7), *adj., v.,* **stoned, stoning.** ◇*n.* **1.** the hard substance of which stones consist. **2.** a particular kind of rock. **3.** *Mining.* opal-bearing material. **4.** a piece of rock of definite size, shape, etc., for any particular purpose, e.g. a gravestone, building block, etc. **5.** a piece of rock of small or moderate size. **6.** a precious stone; gem. **7.** a unit of mass in the imperial system, equal to 14 lb, or approx. 6.35 kg. **8.** any hard, stone-like mass, esp. as produced abnormally in some bodily organs. **9.** *Bot.* the hard seed of a soft fruit, e.g. peach, cherry, etc. **10.** a light grey or beige color. ◇*adj.* **11.** made of or relating to stone. **12.** made of stoneware: *a stone jug or bottle.* ◇*v.t.* **13.** to drive away by hitting with stones. **14.** to put to death by hitting with stones. **15.** to take the stone(s) out of (fruit). [ME; OE *stān*]

Stone /stoun/, *n.* **1. Emma Constance,** 1856–1902, Australian physician; first woman registered as a medical practitioner in Australia (1890). **2. Louis,** 1871–1935, Australian novelist and playwright; wrote the novel *Jonah* (1911).

Stone Age, *n.* the time during which early humans lived and made tools of stone, mainly flint. It corresponds to the Pleistocene and Holocene epochs up to the beginning of the Bronze Age.

stoned /stound/, *adj. Colloq.* under the influence of drugs or alcohol.

stonefish /'stounfɪʃ/, *n.* a type of highly poisonous, tropical fish, looking like weathered coral or rock, and having spines able to give a very painful, and sometimes deadly sting.

Stonehenge /stoun'hendʒ/, *n.* a prehistoric monument in southern England, in Wiltshire, north of Salisbury, consisting of a large circle of megalithic posts and lintels.

stonemason /'stounmeɪsən/, *n.* a dresser of or builder in stone. **-stonemasonry,** *n.*

stoneware /'stounweə/, *n.* a more or less vitrified type of pottery.

stony /'stouni/, *adj.,* **stonier, stoniest. 1.** full of or having many stones or rocks. **2.** relating to or typical of stone. **3.** like or suggesting stone, esp. hard like stone. **4.** unfeeling; merciless; obdurate: *a stony heart.* **5.** unmoving or rigid; without expression: *a stony look.*

stood /stud/, *v.* past tense and past participle of **stand.**

stooge /studʒ/, *n. Colloq.* **1.** an entertainer who feeds lines to a comedian and is often the object of his or her jokes. **2.** someone who acts on behalf of another, esp. in a flattering, dishonest, corrupt, or secretive fashion. [orig. uncert.]

stool /stul/, *n.* **1.** a seat, usu. without arms or a back, and for one person. **2.** a low support for resting the feet on, etc. **3.** (*pl.*) →**faeces.** [ME; OE *stōl*]

stool pigeon, *n.* **1.** a pigeon used as a decoy. **2.** a spy; informer, esp. for the police.

stoop /stup/, *v.i.* **1.** to bend the head and shoulders, or the body generally, forwards and downwards from an upright position: *to stoop over a desk.* **2.** to carry the head and shoulders habitually bowed forwards: *to stoop from age.* **3.** to descend from one's level of dignity; condescend; deign. **4.** to lower oneself by undignified or unworthy behavior: *How could he stoop so low?* **5.** to swoop down, as a hawk at prey. ◇*v.t.* **6.** to bend (oneself, one's head, etc.) for-

stoop wards and downwards. ◇*n.* **7.** the act of stooping; a stooping movement. **8.** a stooping position or carriage of body. **9.** a downward swoop, as of a hawk. [OE *stūpian*]

stop /stɒp/, *v.*, **stopped** or (*Poetic*) **stopt**, **stopping**, *n.* ◇*v.t.* **1.** to cease from, leave off, or discontinue: *to stop running.* **2.** to cause to cease; put an end to: *to stop noise in the street.* **3.** to interrupt, arrest, or check (a course, proceeding, process, etc.). **4.** to cut off, intercept, or withhold: *to stop supplies.* **5.** to prevent, restrain, or hinder, (fol. by *from*): *to stop a person from doing something.* **6.** to prevent from proceeding, acting, operating, continuing, etc.: *to stop a speaker; to stop a car.* **7.** to block, obstruct, or close (a passageway, channel, opening, duct, etc.) (oft. fol. by *up*). **8.** to fill the hole or holes in (a wall, a decayed tooth, etc.). **9.** to close (a container, tube, etc.) with a cork, plug, etc. **10.** to close the external opening of (the ears, nose, mouth, etc.). **11.** *Banking.* to inform a banker not to pay (a cheque) on presentation. **12.** *Music.* **a.** to close (a fingerhole, etc.) in order to produce a particular note from a wind instrument. **b.** to press down (a string of a violin, etc.) in order to alter the pitch of the note produced from it. **c.** to insert the hand in (the bell of a horn) in order to alter the pitch and quality of the note. **d.** to produce (a particular note) by so doing. ◇*v.i.* **13.** to come to a stand still, as in a course or journey; halt. **14.** to cease moving, proceeding, speaking, acting, operating, etc.; to pause; desist. **15.** to cease; come to an end: *The noise stopped.* **16.** to stay: *I stopped there for dinner.* ◇*v.* **17. stop by**, to call somewhere for a short time on the way to another place. **18. stop off at**, to halt for a short stay in (a place) before leaving for another place. **19. stop over**, to make a brief stop during a long plane flight. ◇*n.* **20.** the act of stopping. **21.** a pause or arrest of movement, action, operation, etc.; end. **22.** a stay made at a place, as in the course of a journey: *a short stop in Canberra.* **23.** a place where buses or other vehicles pick up and set down passengers. **24.** a blocking or obstructing, as of a passage or way. **25.** a plug for sealing off an opening. **26.** a bar, obstacle, impediment, or hindrance. **27.** any piece or device that serves to check or control movement or action in a mechanism. **28.** *Music.* **a.** the act of closing a finger hole, etc., or of pressing down a string of an instrument in order to produce a particular note. **b.** a device or contrivance, as on an instrument, for doing this. **c.** (in an organ) a graduated set of pipes of the same kind and giving tones of the same quality. **29.** *Phonet.* **a.** an act of pronunciation in which the flow of air from the lungs is interrupted. **b.** a consonant sound resulting from such an interruption: *p, b, t, d, k,* and *g* are the English stops. **30.** → **full stop**. **31.** the word 'stop' spelt out, and used instead of a full stop in telegrams. **32. pull out all (the) stops**, *Colloq.* **a.** to speak with great emotion. **b.** to push oneself or a machine to the utmost. [OE *stoppian*, from VL]

stopcock /'stɒpkɒk/, *n.* a valve used to control the flow of a liquid or gas from a container or through a pipe.

stope /stoʊp/, *n.* any excavation made in a mine to remove ore from shafts, etc. [akin to STEP, *n.*]

stopgap /'stɒpgæp/, *n.* **1.** something that fills the place of something lacking; a temporary substitute; makeshift. ◇*adj.* **2.** makeshift.

stoppage /'stɒpɪdʒ/, *n.* **1.** an act of stopping or state of being stopped: *The ship is idle because of a waterfront stoppage.* **2.** an amount of anything stopped.

Stoppard /'stɒpəd/, *n.* **Tom**, born 1937, English dramatist, born in Czechoslovakia.

stopped /stɒpt/, *adj.* **1.** having come to a standstill; halted; checked. **2.** closed or filled up; obstructed. **3.** *Music.* **a.** having the upper end plugged or closed, as an organ pipe. **b.** (of a string, etc.) acted upon by stopping. **c.** produced by the stopping of a string, etc. **d.** muffled, as by putting the hand in the bell of a French horn.

stopping /'stɒpɪŋ/, *n.* **1.** the act of someone or something that stops. **2.** *Mining.* a barrier set up to stop the passage of air, gas, fire, or an explosion. **3.** *Bldg Trades.* material used to fill holes in timber, etc., before finishing with paint, etc.

stop press, *n.* (a space for) extra news put into a newspaper after printing has begun.

stopwatch /'stɒpwɒtʃ/, *n.* a watch with a hand that can be stopped or started at any fraction of a second (used for timing races, etc.).

storage /'stɔrɪdʒ/, *n.* **1.** the act of storing or the state or fact of being stored. **2.** a space for storing. **3.** *Computers.* the capacity to hold information. **4.** a place where something is stored. **5.** the price charged for storing goods.

store /stɔ/, *n., v.*, **stored**, **storing**. ◇*n.* **1.** a large shop with many departments or branches. **2.** a supply or stock (of something), esp. for future use. **3.** (*pl.*) supplies of food, clothing, etc., for a household, armed forces, etc. **4. the stores**, (formerly) government rations. **5.** a storehouse or warehouse. **6.** a measure of importance or value: *to set little store by a thing.* **7.** quantity; abundance; plenty: *a great store of jokes.* **8.** computer memory. **9. in store**, **a.** kept in readiness for future use. **b.** coming in the future: *She did not know what was in store for her.* **c.** put in a warehouse until needed. ◇*adj.* **10.** of or relating to sheep, cattle, etc., bought to be fattened for market. ◇*v.t.* **11.** to supply or stock with something, as for future use. **12.** to lay up or put away, as a supply for future use (oft. with *up* or *away*). **13.** to put in a warehouse, etc., for keeping. [ME, from OF: build, furnish, stock, from L: renew, restore]

storey /'stɔri/, *n., pl.* **-reys**. (a set of rooms on) a complete horizontal section of a building; floor. [ME, from OF: build]

stork /stɔk/, *n.* a long-legged, long-necked, long-billed wading bird, esp. the European white stork or the jabiru of Australia. [OE *storc*]

storm /stɔm/, *n.* **1.** an upset of the normal condition of the atmosphere, shown by strong winds and often rain, snow, hail, thunder and lightning, or flying sand or dust. **2.** a heavy fall of rain, snow, or hail, or a violent outbreak of thunder and lightning without strong wind. **3.** a violent attack on a fortified place, enemy position, etc. **4.** a heavy fall of missiles, blows, etc. **5.** a violent upset in civil, political, social, or domestic affairs. **6.** a violent outburst or outbreak: *a storm of applause*. **7. storm in a teacup**, a lot of fuss about something unimportant. **8. take by storm**, **a.** to take by military attack. **b.** to be a great success in: *The pop singer took Sydney by storm*. ◇*v.i.* **9.** to blow with unusual force, or to rain, snow, hail, etc., esp. with violence (used impersonally): *It stormed all day*. **10.** to rage or complain with violence or great anger. **11.** to rush with angry violence: *to storm out of a room*. ◇*v.t.* **12.** to make a sudden, strong attack on (a fortified place). [ME and OE] — **stormy,** *adj*.

storm-petrel /ˈstɔm-petrəl/, *n.* a type of small, dark, swallow-like seabird.

storm-trooper /ˈstɔm-trupə/, *n.* **1.** a member of a body of soldiers especially selected, trained and equipped for sudden attacks. **2.** a soldier in Hitler's private army before and during World War II.

story /ˈstɔri/, *n., pl.* **-ries**. **1.** a series of facts or events, either true or made up, told about a person or thing, or event or period; tale; narrative: *the story of Napoleon*; *a story about our neighbor's cat*. **2.** a made-up story, shorter and simpler than a novel. **3.** a report or account of a matter, esp. a news item in the newspapers, television or radio: *We are having trouble with that film and will go on to the next story*. **4.** *Colloq.* a lie; fib: *That's just your story, I want the facts*. **5.** *Archaic.* history: *celebrated in story and song*. [ME, from AF, from L]

stout /staʊt/, *adj.* **1.** thick or bulky in figure; solidly built; thickset; corpulent. **2.** bold; fearless; dauntless: *a stout heart*. **3.** firm; stubborn: *stout resistance*. **4.** strong; sturdy: *a stout fence*; *stout fellows*. ◇*n.* **5.** a beer, darker and heavier than ale, getting its color and taste from the roasted malt used in the brewing process. [ME, from OF: brave, proud, from Gmc]

Stout /staʊt/, *n.* **Sir Robert**, 1844–1930, NZ statesman, born in Scotland; prime minister 1884–87.

stove[1] /stoʊv/, *n., v.,* **stoved, stoving**. ◇*n.* **1.** an apparatus for giving heat, for warmth, cooking, or mechanical purposes, usu. using coal, oil, gas, or electricity. **2.** a heated space for some special purpose, as a drying room, or a kiln for firing pottery. ◇*v.t.* **3.** to apply heat to (metalware, etc.) in a kiln to fuse paint to its surface. [OE *stofa* hot air bathroom]

stove[2] /stoʊv/, *v.* past tense and past participle of **stave**.

stow /stoʊ/, *v.t.* **1.** *Naut.* to place or pack (cargo, etc.) in the hold of a ship or elsewhere. **2.** (of a place or container) to have room for; hold. **3.** to pack (fol. by *away*): *to stow away climbing gear until the next trip*. ◇*v.* **4. stow away**, to hide on a ship, etc., in order to get a free trip. [ME, from *stowe* place, OE *stow*]

Stow /stoʊ/, *n.* (**Julian**) **Randolph**, born 1935, Australian novelist and poet; works include the novel *To the Islands* (1958).

stowaway /ˈstoʊəweɪ/, *n.* someone who hides on a ship, etc., to get a free trip.

Stowe /stoʊ/, *n.* **Harriet Elizabeth Beecher**, 1811–96, US writer; author of *Uncle Tom's Cabin* (1852).

STP /ɛs ti ˈpi/, *n.* standard temperature and pressure; temperature of 0° C and a pressure of 101 325 pascals. Also, **NTP**.

strabismus /strəˈbɪzməs/, *n.* a disorder of vision where both eyes cannot be focused on the same point or object at the same time; squint. [NL, from Gk]

Stradbroke /ˈstrædbrʊk, -brʊk/, *n.* two islands located east of Brisbane, in Moreton Bay. **North Stradbroke** is about 38 km long and 11 km wide and **South Stradbroke** is about 22 km long and 2.5 km wide. [named after the Earl of *Stradbroke* by his son, the Hon HJ Rous, who commanded the first warship to enter Moreton Bay]

straddle /ˈstrædl/, *v.,* **-dled, -dling,** *n.* ◇*v.i.* **1.** to walk, stand, or sit with the legs wide apart; stand or sit astride. **2.** (of the legs) to stand wide apart. ◇*v.t.* **3.** to walk, stand, or sit with one leg on each side of; stand or sit astride of. **4.** to spread (the legs) wide apart. **5.** *Mil.* to cover (an area) with bombs. ◇*n.* **6.** the act of straddling. **7.** *Athletics.* a style of high jumping in which the athlete crosses the bar horizontally and face down, rolling forward to land on the back. [Brit d., from STRIDE]

Stradivari /strædəˈvɑri/, *n.* **Antonio**, c. 1644–1737, Italian violin-maker of Cremona. Also, **Stradivarius**.

strafe /straf, strerf/, *v.t.,* **strafed, strafing**. **1.** to attack (a target on the ground) by aircraft with machine-gun fire. **2.** to bombard heavily. [G; from the phrase *Gott strafe England* God punish England]

straggle /ˈstrægəl/, *v.i.,* **-gled, -gling**. **1.** to stray from the road, course, or line of march. **2.** to wander about in a scattered way; ramble. **3.** to go, come, or spread in a scattered, untidy way: *Lank hair straggled down her back*. **4.** to drop behind companions on a journey. [ME; b. STRAY and *draggle*] —**straggler,** *n.* —**straggly,** *adj.*

straight /streɪt/, *adj.* **1.** without a bend, crook, or curve; not curved; direct: *a straight road*. **2.** flat; horizontal: *A straight surface is needed for playing tennis*. **3.** *Cricket.* (of a stroke) playing the ball down the wicket past the bowler: *a straight drive*. **4.** evenly formed or set: *straight shoulders*. **5.** delivered with the arm extended straight from the shoulder, as a blow: *a straight left*. **6.** plain; frank; candid: *a straight answer*. **7.** honest, honorable, or upright; not criminal. **8.** *Colloq.* conforming to conventional forms of behavior. **9.** *Colloq.* (of reports, information, etc.) reliable. **10.** (of thinking, reasoning, etc.) right or correct. **11.** continuous or unbroken: *in straight succession*. **12.** without water added; undiluted; neat: *straight gin*. **13.** not laughing; serious: *a straight face*.

straight — **14.** *Theat.* (of a play, acting style, etc.) serious; without music or dancing. **15. play a straight bat**, *Colloq.* to act in a straightforward and honest fashion. ◇*adv.* **16.** in a straight line: *to walk straight.* **17.** in an even form or position: *pictures hung straight.* **18.** directly: *to go straight to a place.* **19.** plainly (oft. fol. by *out*). **20.** honestly, honorably, or virtuously; not criminally: *to live straight.* **21.** continuously: *to keep straight on.* **22.** at once; immediately; without delay: *I'll come straight over.* **23.** in proper order: *to set a room straight.* **24. set (put) someone straight**, to point out a mistake to someone. **25. go straight**, to lead an honest life, esp. after being in prison. ◇*n.* **26.** the condition of being straight. **27. the straight and narrow**, a way of life according to strict moral principles. **28.** the straight part of a racecourse or a railway. **29.** someone who is straight (def. 7, 8). **30.** *Poker.* a sequence of five cards of various suits. See **sequence**. [ME, orig. pp. of STRETCH]

straight angle, *n.* an angle of 180°

straightaway /ˈstreɪtəˈweɪ/, *adv.* immediately; at once; right away.

straighten /ˈstreɪtn/, *v.t., v.i.* to make or become straight.

straightforward /streɪtˈfɔwəd/, *adj.* **1.** plain; direct; open: *straightforward work.* **2.** free from crookedness or deceit; honest: *straightforward in one's dealings.* **3.** without difficulty; uncomplicated: *The subject set was very straightforward.*

straightjacket /ˈstreɪtdʒækət/, *n.* → **straitjacket**.

straight man, *n.* an entertainer who plays his or her part straight, usu. as a foil for a comedian.

strain¹ /streɪn/, *v.t.* **1.** to pull tight or taut; stretch tightly: *to strain a rope.* **2.** to use to the utmost: *to strain one's ears to catch a sound.* **3.** to damage by overuse: *to strain a muscle.* **4.** to stretch beyond the proper limit: *to strain resources.* **5.** to pass (liquid matter) through a filter, sieve, etc. ◇*v.i.* **6.** to pull forcibly: *a dog straining at a leash.* **7.** to stretch one's muscles, nerves, etc., to the utmost. **8.** to ooze; filter; percolate. ◇*n.* **9.** any force or pressure that may alter shape, cause breakage, etc. **10.** any strong or great effort. **11.** damage to a muscle, tendon, etc., from overuse; a sprain. **12. a.** damage to any body or structure resulting from stress. **b.** *Phys.* the amount of such deformation to a structure resulting from stress expressed as the ratio of the change to the original unstrained dimension (length, area, or volume). **13.** the condition of being strained or stretched: *The strain on the rope brought it near breaking point.* **14.** great pressure that wears down; stress: *the strain of hard work.* **15.** great demand on resources, feelings, a person, etc.: *a strain on hospitality.* **16.** (*sing.* or *pl.*, *oft. collective pl.*) the sound of music or song: *the strains of a violin.* **17.** a passage or piece of poetry. **18.** tone, style, or spirit in expression: *a humorous strain.* [ME, from OF: bind tightly, clasp, squeeze, from L: draw tight]

strain² /streɪn/, *n.* **1.** stock; ancestry; lineage: *There are few people left now of her father's strain.* **2.** a variety of a species of domestic animal or cultivated plant. **3.** a variety of micro-organism. **4.** a quality that tends to be passed down through generations: *a strain of madness in a family.* [OE *gestrēon* acquisition]

strainer /ˈstreɪnə/, *n.* **1.** someone or something that strains. **2.** a filter, sieve, etc. **3.** an apparatus for tightening wire in a fence. **4.** Also, **strainer post**. a solid post against which the wires in a post and wire fence are tightened.

strait /streɪt/, *n.* **1.** (*oft. pl.* with *sing.* sense) a narrow passage of water connecting two large bodies of water. **2.** (*oft. pl.*) a position of difficulty, distress, or need. **3.** *Archaic.* a narrow passage, space, or area. **4.** *Rare.* → **isthmus**. ◇*adj.* **5.** *Archaic.* narrow. [ME, from OF: tight, narrow, from L: bound]

straitened /ˈstreɪtnd/, *adj.* pinched; difficult; restricting: *in straitened circumstances.*

straitjacket /ˈstreɪtdʒækət/, *n.* a type of coat for holding down the arms of violently mad people, etc. Also, **straightjacket**.

straitlaced /ˈstreɪtleɪst/, *adj.* **1.** overstrict in behavior or morality; puritanical; prudish. **2.** *Archaic.* tightly laced, or wearing tightly laced clothes.

strand¹ /strænd/, *v.t.* **1.** to drive aground on a beach. **2.** (*usu. in the passive*) to bring into a helpless position: *He is stranded in Darwin without money.* ◇*v.i.* **3.** to be driven or run ashore, as a ship, etc.; run aground. ◇*n.* **4.** *Poetic.* the shore of the sea or a river. [ME and OE]

strand² /strænd/, *n.* **1.** each of a number of strings or yarns twisted together to form a rope, cord, wire, etc. **2.** a single thread in cloth. **3.** a lock of hair; tress. **4.** a string of pearls, beads, etc. [ME]

strange /streɪndʒ/, *adj.*, **stranger, strangest**. ◇*adj.* **1.** unusual, extraordinary, or curious; odd; queer; peculiar: *a strange remark to make.* **2.** distant, foreign: *to move to a strange place.* **3.** unfamiliar; so far unknown: *I saw a strange bird this morning.* **4.** unacquainted (with); unaccustomed (to) or inexperienced (at). **5.** *Colloq.* slightly mad: *She is a little strange.* [ME, from OF, from L: external, foreign]

stranger /ˈstreɪndʒə/, *n.* **1.** someone not met or known before. **2.** someone who is new to a place; newcomer. **3.** someone or something unaccustomed or new (fol. by *to*): *He is no stranger to poverty.*

strangle /ˈstræŋɡəl/, *v.*, **-gled, -gling**. ◇*v.t.* **1.** to kill by squeezing the windpipe with the hands or by a rope. **2.** to kill by stopping the breath in any way; choke; stifle; suffocate. **3.** to stop something arising, growing, or working; suppress. ◇*v.i.* **4.** to be choked, stifled, or suffocated. [ME, from OF, from L, from Gk] — **strangler**, *n.*

stranglehold /ˈstræŋɡəlhoʊld/, *n.* **1.** *Wrestling.* a hold by which the opponent's

stranglehold breathing is stopped. **2.** anything which prevents movement or development.

strangulate /ˈstræŋgjəleɪt/, *v.t.*, **-lated, -lating.** **1.** *Med.* to squeeze (a duct, intestine, vessel, etc.) so as to prevent circulation or stop functioning. **2.** to strangle. [L: strangled] —**strangulation**, *n.*

strap /stræp/, *n., v.*, **strapped, strapping.** ◇*n.* **1.** a narrow strip of some material that will bend, esp. leather, for tying or holding things together, etc. **2.** a strop for a razor. **3.** a straplike ornament, as a watch-strap. **4.** a beating with a leather strap. ◇*v.t.* **5.** to fasten or secure with a strap or straps. **6.** to beat with a strap. [var. of STROP]

strapper /ˈstræpə/, *n.* someone employed to attend and groom racehorses in the stables.

strapping /ˈstræpɪŋ/, *adj. Colloq.* tall and strongly built; robust.

strasbourg /ˈstræzbɜg/, *n.* **1.** a spiced sausage of pork, veal, etc. **2.** → **devon.** Also, **stras** /stræz/. [from *Strasbourg*, city in NE France]

strata /ˈstrɑtə/, *n.* plural of **stratum.**

stratagem /ˈstrætədʒəm/, *n.* **1.** a plan, scheme, or trick for deceiving an enemy. **2.** any trick; artifice; ruse. [F, from L, from Gk]

strata title, *n.* title to property under a scheme which registers separate ownership of units or lots in a property such as a multistorey building, block of home units, etc.

Strategic Arms Limitation Talks *n.* → **SALT.**

strategy /ˈstrætədʒi/, *n., pl.* **-gies.** **1.** the science or art of combining and using the means of war in planning and directing large military movements and operations. **2.** (a particular) use of this science or art. **3.** skilful management of any kind, esp. by using stratagems. [Gk: generalship] —**strategist**, *n.* —**strategic**, *adj.*

Stratford-on-Avon /ˈstrætfəd-ɒn-ˈeɪvən/, *n.* a town in central England, on the river Avon, in Warwickshire; Shakespeare's birthplace. Pop. 19 449 (1971). Also, **Stratford-upon-Avon.**

strati-, a word part representing **stratum,** as in *stratify.*

stratification /ˌstrætəfəˈkeɪʃən/, *n.* **1.** the act of stratifying. **2.** arrangement in layers: *the stratification of medieval society.* **3.** *Geol.* **a.** the formation of strata; deposition or occurrence in strata. **b.** → **stratum** (def. 3).

stratiform /ˈstrætəfɔm/, *adj.* **1.** *Geol.* occurring as a bed or beds; arranged in strata. **2.** *Weather.* having the appearance or character of a stratus.

stratify /ˈstrætəfaɪ/, *v.*, **-fied, -fying.** ◇*v.t.* **1.** to form in strata or layers. **2.** to preserve or germinate (seeds) by placing them between layers of earth. ◇*v.i.* **3.** to form strata. **4.** *Geol.* to lie in beds or layers. **5.** *Sociol.* to develop horizontal status groups in society. [NL]

stratigraphy /strəˈtɪgrəfi/, *n.* that branch of geology dealing with the classification, naming, correlation, and interpretation of stratified rocks. —**stratigraphic**, *adj.*

strato-, a word part meaning 'low and horizontal', as in *stratosphere.* [NL, combining form representing L *strātus*, a spreading out]

stratosphere /ˈstrætəsfɪə/, *n.* **1.** the region of the earth's atmosphere outside the troposphere but within the ionosphere. **2.** *Archaic.* all of the earth's atmosphere lying outside the troposphere. —**stratospheric**, *adj.*

stratum /ˈstrɑtəm/, *n., pl.* **strata** /ˈstrɑtə/, **stratums.** **1.** a horizontal layer of any material. **2.** one of a number of portions likened to layers or levels. **3.** *Geol.* a single bed of sedimentary rock. **4.** *Biol.* a layer of tissue; lamella. **5.** a layer of the ocean or the atmosphere within natural or arbitrary limits. **6.** *Sociol.* a level or grade of a people or population with reference to social position or education: *the lowest stratum of society.* [NL; L: something spread out] —**stratal**, *adj.*

stratus /ˈstreɪtəs/, *n., pl.* **-ti** /-taɪ/. a continuous horizontal sheet of cloud, like fog, usu. of even thickness and lying fairly low.

Strauss family /straʊs/, *n.* a family of Austrian composers, including **1. Johann** /ˈjouhan/, 1804–49, noted for his waltzes. **2.** his son, **Johann**, 1825–99, remembered esp. for his waltzes and the opera *Die Fledermaus* (1874).

Stravinsky /strəˈvɪnski/, *n.* **Igor Feodorovich** /ˈfjɔdərəvɪtʃ/, 1882–1971, US composer born in Russia, noted for ballet scores including *The Rite of Spring.* Also, **Stravinski.**

straw /strɔ/, *n.* **1.** dried stalks of grain used as bedding for animals and as material for hats, etc. **2.** a hollow paper tube, plant stem, etc., used to suck up drinks. **3.** anything of little value or importance: *not to care a straw.* **4.** any frail thing that appears to be a help in a difficult situation: *to clutch at a straw.* **5. the last straw,** a final fact, circumstance, etc., which makes a situation unbearable. ◇*adj.* **6.** of, relating to, or made of straw. [OE *strēaw*]

strawberry /ˈstrɔbəri, -bri/, *n., pl.* **-ries.** **1.** (a low-growing plant with runners bearing) a red fleshy fruit which has small seeds arranged on its surface. ◇*adj.* **2.** of the color of a strawberry.

straw vote, *n.* an unofficial vote taken at a casual gathering or in a particular district, to get some idea of the general opinion. Also, **straw poll.**

stray /streɪ/, *v.i.* **1.** to wander from the proper course or place or beyond the proper limits, esp. aimlessly; ramble; roam. **2.** to turn away from the right course; go astray; get lost. **3.** to turn aside from a subject of talk or writing; digress. ◇*n.* **4.** a domestic animal found wandering without an owner. **5.** any homeless or friendless creature or person. ◇*adj.* **6.** (of a domestic animal) straying, or having strayed. **7.** found apart from others, or as a single or casual instance. [ME, from OF, from L: wander outside] —**strayer**, *n.*

streak /strik/, *n.* **1.** a long, narrow mark, smear, band of color, etc.: *a streak of mud; a*

streak *streak of lightning*. **2.** a part or layer of something, different in color or nature from the rest; vein or stratum: *streaks of fat in meat*. **3.** a vein; strain; admixture: *a streak of humor*. **4.** *Mining.* rock which shows good color opal. ◇*v.t.* **5.** to mark with streaks: *to streak a wall with paint; streaked with mud*. ◇*v.i.* **6.** to go very quickly: *The man streaked across the paddock*. [OE *strica*] —**streaky,** *adj.*

stream /strim/, *n.* **1.** a small body of water flowing in a channel or bed; creek, rivulet, or brook. **2.** a steady current in water: *to row against the stream.* **3.** a current of air, gas, etc.; beam or trail of light. **4.** a continuous flow of anything: *a stream of words; a stream of abuse.* **5.** drift; prevailing direction: *the stream of opinion; a stream of traffic.* **6.** *Educ.* a division of children of similar ability in one class. ◇*v.i.* **7.** to flow, pass, or come out in a stream, as water, tears, blood, etc. **8.** to run or flow (fol. by *with*): *eyes streaming with tears.* **9.** to flow or float like a stream. ◇*v.t.* **10.** *Educ.* to divide into streams. [OE *strēam*]

streamer /'strimə/, *n.* **1.** a long, narrow flag; pennant. **2.** a long, narrow strip of colored paper, thrown on special public occasions, or strung across streets or rooms.

streamlined /'strimlaind/, *adj.* **1.** indicating, relating to, or having a shape designed to offer the least possible resistance in passing through air or water. **2.** designed to be more efficient.

stream of consciousness, *n.* (esp. in a novel) a continuous flow of thoughts.

street /strit/, *n.* **1.** a public road in a town or city running between houses or public buildings, and usu. with a pavement on either side. **2.** such a road with the buildings opening on to it. **3.** a main way or thoroughfare, as distinct from a lane, alley, etc. **4.** the people who live in a particular street: *Our street mainly votes Liberal.* **5. on the streets, a.** earning one's living as a prostitute. **b.** homeless; destitute. **6. the man in the street,** the average person; typical citizen. **7. streets ahead,** a long way ahead. [OE *strǣt*]

Street family /strit/, *n.* an Australian family, prominent in the public sphere in NSW, including **1. Sir Kenneth Whistler,** 1890–1972, administrator and judge, Lieutenant-Governor 1950–72 and Chief Justice of NSW 1950–60. **2. Jessie Mary Grey,** 1889–1970, wife of Sir Kenneth Whistler, feminist, reformer and writer; initiated the movement which gained the referendum granting legal citizenship to Aborigines. **3.** their son, **Sir Laurence Lillingston Whistler,** born 1926, administrator and judge, Lieutenant-Governor of NSW 1974–89.

streetcar /'stritka/, *n.* US. → **tram**.

Streeton /'stritn/, *n.* **Sir Arthur Ernest,** 1867–1943, Australian landscape painter; one of the founders of the Heidelberg School.

Strehlow /'streɪloʊ/, *n.* **T(heodor) G(eorge) H(enry),** 1908–78, Australian linguist and writer; recorded Aboriginal myths, ceremonies, and songs.

strength /strɛŋθ/, *n.* **1.** the quality or state of being strong; bodily or muscular power; vigor; robustness. **2.** mental or moral power or force. **3.** power from influence, authority, resources, numbers, etc. **4.** number, as of men in an army: *a regiment of a strength of 3000.* **5.** effectiveness: *the strength of her argument.* **6.** toughness; durability. **7.** potency, as in drugs, liquor, etc. **8.** intensity, as in light, color, smell, etc. **9.** something that makes strong; support or stay. **10. on the strength of,** relying on; on the basis of. [OE *strength(u)*]

strengthen /'strɛŋθən/, *v.t., v.i.* to make or grow stronger. —**strengthener,** *n.*

strenuous /'strɛnjuəs/, *adj.* needing or marked by great effort or energy. [L]

streptococcus /strɛptə'kɒkəs/, *n., pl.* **-cocci** /-'kɒksaɪ/. any of a group of bacteria typically forming chains which may cause scarlet fever and other infectious diseases. —**streptococcal,** *adj.*

streptomycin /strɛptə'maɪsən/, *n.* a type of antibiotic, used in the treatment of tuberculosis.

stress /strɛs/, *v.t.* **1.** to give special importance to; emphasise: *to stress the need for safety.* **2.** *Linguistics.* to pronounce strongly: *You should stress the second syllable in 'pronounce'.* **3.** to put pressure or strain on, esp. on a piece of machinery. ◇*n.* **4.** importance; significance; emphasis: *to lay stress upon the need for safety.* **5.** an accent or emphasis on a syllable in speech, esp. so as to form a metrical pattern. **6.** an emphasis in music, rhythm, etc. **7.** the physical pressure, pull, etc., of one thing on another. **8.** *Phys.* **a.** the forces or system of forces, load, etc., on a body which produce a strain. **b.** a measure of the amount of stress, expressed as a force per unit area. **c.** the internal resistance or reaction of an elastic body to the external forces applied to it. **9.** the state of being under great mental or emotional pressure. [var. of DISTRESS]

-stress, the feminine equivalent of **-ster,** as in *seamstress.*

stretch /strɛtʃ/, *v.t.* **1.** to draw out to the full length; extend: *He stretched himself (out) on the ground.* **2.** to hold out or reach forth (fol. by *out*): *to stretch out the head; to stretch out the hand.* **3.** to spread: *to stretch a tarpaulin across a truck.* **4.** to widen or enlarge by tension: *to stretch shoes.* **5.** to draw out beyond the proper limit: *a jumper stretched at the elbows; to stretch the facts.* ◇*v.i.* **6.** to lie down at full length (fol. by *out*): *to stretch out on a couch.* **7.** to be spread over an area, period of time, etc.: *The forest stretches as far as the eye can see; to stretch into the remote past.* **8.** to ease the body by drawing out the limbs, straining the muscles, etc.: *He stretched and yawned.* **9.** to become stretched: *My shoes have stretched.* ◇*v.* **10. stretch a point,** to go beyond the usual limits; make concessions. **11. stretch one's legs,** to take a walk. ◇*n.* **12.** the act of stretching or state of being stretched. **13.** the ability to be stretched: *This wool has a good stretch.* **14.** a continuous length or expanse: *a stretch of bush.* **15.** the straight part of a racecourse, esp.

between the last turn and the winning post. **16.** a period of time: *a stretch of ten years.* **17.** *Colloq.* a term of imprisonment. ◇*adj.* **18.** made to stretch in order to fit different sizes: *stretch socks.* [OE *streccan*] —**stretchy,** *adj.*

stretcher /ˈstretʃə/, *n.* **1.** a light, folding bed; camp stretcher. **2.** a light frame covered with canvas, for carrying the sick or dead. **3.** any instrument for stretching. **4.** *Bldg Trades.* a brick or stone laid horizontally, with its long side facing outward.

strew /struː/, *v.t.*, **strewed, strewed** or **strewn, strewing. 1.** to let fall in separate pieces or particles over a surface; scatter; sprinkle: *to strew seed in a garden bed.* **2.** to cover or overspread: *to strew a floor with rushes.* [OE *strēowian*]

stria /ˈstraɪə/, *n., pl.* **striae** /ˈstraɪiː/. **1.** a small furrow or stripe. **2.** (*pl.*) *Geol.* scratches on the surface of a rock, resulting from glacial action. [L: furrow, channel]

striate /ˈstraɪeɪt/, *v.*, **-ated, -ating;** /ˈstraɪət/, *adj.* ◇*v.t.* **1.** to mark with striae; furrow; stripe; streak. ◇*adj.* **2.** Also, **striated.** marked with striae; furrowed; striped. —**striation,** *n.*

stricken /ˈstrɪkən/, *v.* a past participle of **strike.**

strict /strɪkt/, *adj.* **1.** severe; stringent: *a strict upbringing; strict laws.* **2.** exact; precise: *a strict statement of facts.* **3.** narrowly or carefully limited: *a strict interpretation.* **4.** complete; absolute: *told in strict confidence.* [L: drawn together, tight, severe]

stricture /ˈstrɪktʃə/, *n.* **1.** strong criticism; censure. **2.** the narrowing of any passage of the body as a result of disease. [ME, from L]

stride /straɪd/, *v.*, **strode, stridden, striding,** *n.* ◇*v.t., v.i.* **1.** to walk with long bold steps. **2.** to pass over or across by one long step: *to stride (over) a fallen log.* ◇*n.* **3.** a striding gait. **4.** a long step in walking. **5.** a complete set of movements of an animal's feet, making one step forward. **6.** the distance covered by such a movement. **7.** a regular or steady course, pace, etc.: *to take it in one's stride.* **8.** a step forward in development or progress: *John made rapid strides in mastering algebra.* **9.** (*pl.*) *Colloq.* trousers. [OE *strīdan*]

strident /ˈstraɪdnt/, *adj.* making or having a harsh sound; grating; creaking. [L: creaking] —**stridence,** *n.*, **stridency,** *n.*

stridulate /ˈstrɪdjəleɪt/, *v.i.*, **-lated, -lating.** (of a cricket) to produce a shrill grating sound by rubbing together certain parts of the body; shrill. —**stridulous,** *adj.*

strife /straɪf/, *n.* **1.** a state of conflict or disagreement: *to be at strife.* **2.** a quarrel; struggle; clash. **3. in strife,** *Colloq.* in trouble. [ME, from OF]

strike /straɪk/, *v.*, **struck, struck** or (*esp.* for defs 13–14) **stricken, striking,** *n.* ◇*v.t.* **1.** to give a blow with the hand, a weapon, etc.: *to strike a man; to strike a blow for freedom.* **2.** to produce (fire, sparks, light, etc.) by beating or rubbing: *to strike a match; to strike a light.* **3.** to attack; smite or blast: *struck by lightning.* **4.** to put or come into forcible contact with; hit: *to strike the hands together; The ship struck a rock.* **5.** (of light, sound, etc.) to fall upon (something). **6.** to enter the mind of; occur to: *A happy thought struck him.* **7.** to come across or find: *to strike the name of a friend in a newspaper; to strike trouble; to strike oil.* **8.** (of a plant or cutting) to send down or put forth (a root). **9.** *Naut.* to lower or take down (a sail, mast, etc.). **10.** to blot out or cancel with, or as with, the stroke of a pen (fol. by *off, out,* etc.). **11.** to forbid (someone) to continue practising a profession because of unprofessional behavior (fol. by *off*): *The doctor was struck off for advertising.* **12.** (of a clock) to show (the hour of day) by a stroke or strokes: *to strike twelve.* **13.** to affect deeply with a feeling: *His words struck her with terror.* **14.** to make (blind, dumb, etc.) suddenly, as if by a blow. **15.** to take up (an attitude or posture). **16.** to make (usu. fol. by *up*): *to strike up a friendship; to strike a bargain.* ◇*v.i.* **17.** to aim a blow; make an attack: *The snake struck suddenly.* **18.** to knock; rap; tap. **19.** to hit against something; collide. **20.** (of light, sound, etc.) to fall (fol. by *on* or *upon*). **21.** to make an impression. **22.** to come across or find suddenly (fol. by *on* or *upon*). **23.** to make a stroke in swimming or rowing: *He struck out towards the shore.* **24.** to begin to play: *to strike up a tune.* **25.** (of a cutting) to take root. **26.** to go, esp. in a new direction (fol. by *out*). **27.** to take part in a strike (def. 29). ◇*n.* **28.** the act of striking. **29.** an organised stopping of work as a protest or in order to force an employer to give higher pay or better conditions. **30.** *Tenpin Bowling.* the knocking down of all the pins with the first bowl. **31.** *Geol.* **a.** the direction of the line formed by the intersection of the bedding plane of a bed or stratum of sedimentary rock with a horizontal plane. **b.** the direction or trend of a structural feature, as an anticlinal axis or the lineation resulting from metamorphism. **32.** the discovery of a rich vein of ore, or of oil. [OE *strīcan*] —**striker,** *n.*

strike pay, *n.* an allowance paid by a trade union to members on strike. Also, **strike benefit.**

striking /ˈstraɪkɪŋ/, *adj.* **1.** that strikes: *a striking snake.* **2.** attractive; impressive; noticeable. **3.** being on strike, as workmen.

Strindberg /ˈstrɪndbɜg/, *n.* (**Johan**) **August** /ˈjuːhan ˈɒgʊst/, 1849–1912, Swedish dramatist.

strine /straɪn/, *n. Colloq.* **1.** Australian English, esp. its colloquial words. **2.** the form of it which appeared in the books of Alastair Morrison, pen-name 'Afferbeck Lauder', where it was written in scrambled form to suggest extreme omission of sounds, running of words into each other, etc., as in *Gloria Soame* for *glorious home, muncer go* for *months ago.*

string /strɪŋ/, *n., v.*, **strung, stringing.** ◇*n.* **1.** line, cord, or thread, used for tying parcels, etc. **2.** a narrow strip of cloth, leather, etc., for tying parts together: *strings of a bonnet.* **3.** anything looking like a string or thread. **4.** a number of objects, as beads or pearls, threaded or arranged on a cord. **5.** any series of things arranged or connected in a line or following closely one after another: *a string of islands; a string of questions.* **6.** (in musical instruments) a tightly stretched cord or wire which produces a note when made to vibrate. **7.** (*pl.*) (the players of) stringed musical instruments, esp. those played with a bow. **8.** a bundle of tough fibres in beans, celery, etc. **9.** *Colloq.* limitation; qualification: *a proposal with no strings attached.* **10. keep on a string,** to have someone under one's control, esp. emotionally: *She kept him on a string and then agreed to marry him.* **11. pull strings,** *Colloq.* to seek one's own advancement by using undue influence. **12. two strings to one's bow,** two choices or plans. ◇*v.t.* **13.** to provide with strings. **14.** to draw (a cord, etc.) across from one point to another. **15.** to thread on, or as on, a string: *to string beads.* **16.** to provide or adorn with something suspended or slung: *a room strung with colored lights.* **17.** to remove the strings of (beans). **18.** to make tense, as the sinews, nerves, mind, etc. (*usu. in the passive*): *Her nerves were strung to the highest pitch.* **19.** to kill by hanging (fol. by *up*). ◇*v.i.* **20.** to form into or move in a string or series: *to string along behind.* ◇*v.* **21. string along** *or* **on,** *Colloq.* to deceive (someone) in a series of falsehoods; con. **22. string along with,** *Colloq.* to go along with; accompany; cooperate with; agree with. **23. string out, a.** to spread out at intervals. **b.** to spread over a period of time; prolong. [OE *streng*]

string-course /'strɪŋ-kɔs/, *n.* a horizontal band or course of stone, etc., often moulded and sometimes richly carved.

stringent /'strɪndʒənt/, *adj.* **1.** strict; narrowly binding; rigorously exacting: *stringent laws.* **2.** urgent; compelling; constraining: *stringent necessity.* **3.** (of the money market) tight. [L: drawing tight] **—stringency,** *n.*

stringer /'strɪŋə/, *n.* **1.** a longitudinal timber, metal rod, etc., which is fitted to frames or ribs in the construction of a boat, the fuselage or wing of an aeroplane, etc. **2.** *Bldg Trades.* a long horizontal timber connecting upright posts, supporting a floor, etc.

string quartet, *n.* (a piece of music played by) a group of four stringed instruments, usu. two violins, a viola and a cello.

stringy /'strɪŋi/, *adj.*, **stringier, stringiest.** tough, wiry or fibrous. **—stringiness,** *n.*

stringy-bark /'strɪŋi-bak/, *n.* **1.** a type of gum tree with a typical tough fibrous bark. ◇*adj.* **2.** rustic, uncultured: *a stringy-bark settler.*

stringy-bark cockatoo, *n.* a cockatoo farmer, who farms the poorest land, on which only stringy-bark gums will grow.

strip¹ /strɪp/, *v.*, **stripped, stripping.** ◇*v.t.* **1.** to take away a covering from: *to strip a fruit of its rind.* **2.** to make bare or naked. **3.** to take away; remove: *to strip pictures from a wall.* **4.** to take from; deprive or divest: *to strip a tree of its fruit.* **5.** to rob, plunder, or dispossess: *to strip a man of his possessions; to strip someone of their position.* **6.** *Mech.* to tear off the thread of (a screw, bolt, etc.) or the teeth of (a gear, etc.), by using too much force on it. **7.** *Agric.* to harvest part of a plant, as grains of wheat, using a specially built machine. **8.** to remove old paint, etc., from a surface before redecorating. ◇*v.i.* **9.** to take off one's clothes. [OE *-strӯpan*]

strip² /strɪp/, *n.* **1.** a long narrow piece of anything. **2.** *Colloq.* a sporting uniform. **3.** a continuous series of pictures, as in a newspaper, illustrating a story, conversation, etc. See **comic strip. 4. —airstrip.** [ME]

stripe¹ /straɪp/, *n., v.*, **striped, striping,** *adj.* ◇*n.* **1.** a relatively long, narrow band of a different color or appearance from the rest of a surface or thing: *the stripes of a zebra.* **2.** (*pl.*) a number or combination of strips of braid worn on a uniform as a badge of rank, etc. **3.** a long, narrow piece of anything. **4.** a streak or layer of a different nature within a substance. ◇*v.t.* **5.** to give a stripe or stripes to. ◇*adj.* **6.** furnished with racing stripes: *stripe swimwear.* [MD]

stripe² /straɪp/, *n.* a stroke with a whip, rod, etc. [ME]

stripling /'strɪplɪŋ/, *n.* a youth just passing from boyhood to manhood.

stripper /'strɪpə/, *n.* **1.** a striptease dancer. **2.** an appliance, machine or chemical for stripping.

striptease /'strɪptiz/, *n.* **1.** an act in which a person, usu. a woman, takes off her clothes slowly before an audience. ◇*adj.* **2.** of or relating to such an act.

strive /straɪv/, *v.i.*, **strove, striven, striving. 1.** to try hard: *to strive for success.* **2.** to fight or struggle: *to strive against fate.* [ME, from OF: quarrel, contend] **—striver,** *n.*

strobe /stroʊb/, *n.* a high-intensity flash device used in stroboscopic photography or a similar electronic system. [short for STROBOSCOPE]

strobe lighting, *n.* **1.** a flashing light of great intensity, as at a theatre, dance, etc., obtained by using a strobe. **2.** lighting designed to be similar in effect to that of a strobe.

stroboscope /'stroʊbəskoʊp/, *n.* an instrument used in studying the movement of a body by lighting it up at frequent intervals, or by viewing it through openings in a revolving disc. [Gk: a twisting + -SCOPE] **—stroboscopic,** *adj.*

strode /stroʊd/, *v.* past tense of **stride.**

stroke¹ /stroʊk/, *n., v.*, **stroked, stroking.** ◇*n.* **1.** an act of striking; blow. **2.** (the sound made by) a striking of one thing upon another, as a clapper on a bell. **3.** an attack of apoplexy or paralysis. **4.** a sudden event, etc., befalling one: *a stroke of good luck.* **5.** a single complete, repeated, movement as in swimming, bowing a violin, etc. **6.** *Mech.* one of a series of repeated back and forth movements. **7.** a style of swimming: *The crawl is a rapid stroke.* **8.** an act, feat or achievement: *a stroke of genius.* **9.** (a mark made by) the movement of a pen,

stroke pencil, etc. **10.** *Rowing.* **a.** the manner or style of moving or pulling the oars. **b.** the oarsman nearest to the stern of the boat, to whose strokes those of the other oarsmen must conform. ◇*v.t.* **11.** to row as stroke oarsman of (a boat or crew). ◇*v.i.* **12.** to row as stroke in a race. [ME]

stroke² /strouk/, *v.*, **stroked, stroking,** *n.* ◇*v.t.* **1.** to pass the hand or an instrument over (something) lightly and gently. ◇*n.* **2.** a stroking movement. [OE *strācian*]

stroll /stroul/, *v.i.* **1.** to walk in an unhurried way; ramble; saunter. **2.** to wander or rove from place to place; roam: *strolling minstrels.* ◇*n.* **3.** an unhurried walk; ramble; saunter: *a short stroll before dinner.* [orig. uncert.]

stroller /'stroulə/, *n.* **1.** a person taking a walk or a stroll. **2.** a light collapsible chair on wheels, used for carrying small children.

strong /strɒŋ/, *adj.* **1.** having or showing great bodily or muscular power; physically vigorous or robust. **2.** mentally powerful or energetic: *a strong mind.* **3.** able to stand up to hardship or stress. **4.** esp. powerful or able (oft. fol. by *on* or *in*): *strong in maths.* **5.** of great moral power, firmness, or courage: *strong under temptation.* **6.** powerful in influence or resources: *a strong nation.* **7.** of great force or effectiveness: *strong arguments.* **8.** able to resist force or stand strain, wear, etc.: *strong walls; strong cloth.* **9.** moving or acting with force or energy: *strong wind.* **10.** intense: *strong color.* **11.** (of language, speech, etc.) **a.** forceful; forthright. **b.** indecent; vulgar. **12.** having a large proportion of the effective or essential ingredients: *strong drink; strong tea.* **13.** having a high degree of smell or taste: *strong perfume; strong cheese.* ◇*adv.* **14.** in a strong manner; powerfully; forcibly; vigorously. **15.** in number: *The army was 20 000 strong.* **going strong,** continuing in vigorous good health: *He is very old but still going strong.* [OE]

stronghold /'strɒŋhould/, *n.* **1.** a strong or well-fortified place; fortress. **2.** a place where anything, as an ideology, opinion, etc., is strong.

strontium /'strɒntiəm/, *n.* a bivalent metallic element whose compounds are like those of calcium. Radioactive isotope **strontium-90,** produced in nuclear reactions and present in fall-out, is extremely dangerous to mammals as it replaces calcium in bones. Symbol: Sr; *at. no.:* 38; *at. wt:* 87.62. – **strontic,** *adj.*

strop /strɒp/, *n., v.*, **stropped, stropping.** ◇*n.* **1.** a strip of leather or other material that will bend, or a long, narrow piece of wood with its faces covered with leather or an abrasive, used for sharpening razors. ◇*v.t.* **2.** to sharpen on, or as on, a strop. [OE *strop*]

strophe /'stroufi/, *n.* that part of an ancient Greek choral ode sung by the chorus when moving from right to left. [Gk: a turning] – **strophic,** *adj.*

stroppy /'strɒpi/, *adj. Colloq.* **1.** difficult to control; awkward. **2.** annoyed, angry. [from OBSTREPEROUS]

strove /strouv/, *v.* past tense of **strive.**

struck /strʌk/, *v.* past tense and a past participle of **strike.**

structure /'strʌktʃə/, *n., v.*, **-tured, -turing.** ◇*n.* **1.** the arrangement of parts to make up a whole: *the structure of the atom.* **2.** something built, as a building, bridge, dam, etc. **3.** anything made up of parts arranged together in some way; an organisation. **4.** *Biol.* the construction and arrangement of tissues, parts, or organs. **5.** *Geol.* **a.** the attitude of a bed or stratum of sedimentary rocks, as indicated by the dip and strike. **b.** the coarser features of rocks as contrasted with their texture. **6.** *Chem.* the manner by which atoms in a molecule are joined to each other, esp. in organic chemistry where it is represented by a diagram of the molecular arrangement; configuration. ◇*v.t.* **7.** to give form or organisation to. [L] – **structural,** *adj.*

structural formula /strʌktʃərəl 'fɔmjələ/, *n. Chem.* a formula showing the arrangement of atoms and bonds in a molecule.

strudel /'strudəl/, *n.* a very thin sheet of pastry, spread with a sweet filling, rolled up and baked: *apple strudel.* [G]

struggle /'strʌgəl/, *v.*, **-gled, -gling,** *n.* ◇*v.i.* **1.** to make violent movements or effort: *He struggled for an hour, but could not break his bonds.* **2.** to fight with an enemy, esp. without weapons. **3.** to make a great effort for or against something: *to struggle for existence.* ◇*n.* **4.** a violent movement. **5.** a fight. **6.** a strong effort against any bad conditions. [ME] – **struggler,** *n.*

strum /strʌm/, *v.*, **strummed, strumming,** *n.* ◇*v.t., v.i.* **1.** to play (chords, etc., esp. on a guitar) by sweeping the hand across the strings. **2.** to play chords on a guitar, etc., unskilfully or as a simple accompaniment. ◇*n.* **3.** the act of strumming. [b. STRING and THUMB] – **strummer,** *n.*

strumpet /'strʌmpət/, *n.* a prostitute; harlot; whore.

strung /strʌŋ/, *v.* past tense and past participle of **string.**

strut¹ /strʌt/, *v.*, **strutted, strutting,** *n.* ◇*v.i.* **1.** to walk in a pompous way, as with the head erect and chest thrown out. ◇*n.* **2.** the act of strutting; a strutting walk or gait. [OE *strūtian* stand stiffly] – **strutter,** *n.* – **strutting,** *adj.*

strut² /strʌt/, *n., v.*, **strutted, strutting.** ◇*n.* **1.** a piece of wood or metal designed to support weight in a building or other structure. ◇*v.t.* **2.** to brace or support by a strut or struts. [akin to STRUT¹]

Strutt /strʌt/, *n.* **William,** 1825–1915, English painter and draughtsman in Australia 1850–62; one of the first artists on the Ballarat goldfields.

strychnine /'strɪknin, -nən/, *n.* a colorless crystalline poison, $C_{21}H_{22}N_2O_2$; a powerful stimulant to the central nervous system. [F, from L, from Gk: kind of nightshade]

Strzelecki /strɛz'lɛki/, *n.* **Sir Paul Edmund de,** 1797–1873, Polish-born explorer

Strzelecki   1026   **stuffing**

and scientist in Australia 1839–42; explored the Snowy Mountains.

Stuart /'stjuət/, *n.* **1.** Also, **Stewart.** the royal house which reigned in Scotland from Robert II to James VI (1371–1603) and in England and Scotland from James I (previously James VI of Scotland) to Anne (1603–1714). **2. Charles Edward Louis Philip Casimir** (*'the Young Pretender'* or *'the Young Chevalier'* or *'Bonnie Prince Charlie'*) 1720–88, claimer of the British throne whose landing in Scotland precipitated the Jacobite rebellion of 1745 **3. John McDouall,** 1815–66, Scottish-born Australian explorer; the first European to cross the continent south to north.

stub /stʌb/, *n., v.,* **stubbed, stubbing.** ◇*n.* **1.** a short remaining piece, as of a pencil, cigarette, etc. **2.** something unusually short: *a dog with a stub of a tail.* **3.** the part of a chequebook, etc., on which particulars of cheques, etc., are noted. ◇*v.t.* **4.** to strike (one's toe) against something. **5.** to put out (a cigarette) by pressing the lighted end against a hard surface (fol. by *out*). [OE]

stubble /'stʌbəl/, *n.* **1.** stumps of grain stalks left in the ground when the crop is cut. **2.** any short, rough growth, as of beard. [ME, from OF, from LL] —**stubbled, stubbly,** *adj.*

stubborn /'stʌbən/, *adj.* **1.** refusing to give way; obstinate. **2.** fixed or set in purpose or opinion; resolute. **3.** hard to deal with or manage: *a stubborn machine.* **4.** hard, tough, or stiff, as stone or wood. [ME, from OE *stybb* STUB]

stucco /'stʌkoʊ/, *n., pl.* **-coes, -cos.** plaster used for interior mouldings or as a coating for outside walls. [It, from Gmc]

stuck /stʌk/, *v.* **1.** past tense and past participle of **stick**[2]. **2. get stuck into,** *Colloq.* **a.** to set about with great energy. **b.** to attack energetically.

stuck-up /'stʌk-ʌp/, *adj. Colloq.* proud; conceited; haughty.

stud[1] /stʌd/, *n., v.,* **studded, studding.** ◇*n.* **1.** a small knob or boss sticking out from a surface, esp. as an ornament. **2.** a nail-like metal piece fixed to the sole of a sporting shoe, to give better grip. **3.** an upright post in the frame of a building, to which panels of lining material are fixed. **4.** any pin, lug, etc., sticking out on a machine. **5.** a kind of small button or fastener on a shirt. ◇*v.t.* **6.** to set with or as with studs, knobs, etc. **7.** to scatter or be scattered over with things set at intervals: *Stars studded the sky.* [OE *studu*]

stud[2] /stʌd/, *n.* **1.** a number of horses, for racing, etc., belonging to one owner. **2.** a farm where horses, cattle, etc., are kept for breeding. **3.** *US.* →**stallion. 4.** a young man of obvious sexual power. **5. at stud,** (of an animal) available for breeding. ◇*adj.* **6.** of, associated with, or relating to a stallion. **7.** kept for breeding purposes: *a stud bull.* [OE *stōd*]

student /'stjudnt/, *n.* **1. a.** someone following a course of study and instruction at a university, technical college, etc. **b.** a pupil at a secondary school. **2.** someone who studies a subject with persistence or depth: *a student of firearms.* [ME, from L: being eager, studying]

studied /'stʌdid/, *adj.* **1.** marked by or suggesting effort, rather than natural or spontaneous: *studied simplicity.* **2.** carefully prepared or thought about: *a studied speech.*

studio /'stjudioʊ/, *n., pl.* **-dios. 1.** the workroom of an artist, esp. a painter or sculptor; atelier. **2.** a room or place in which some form of art is followed: *a music studio.* **3.** a room or set of rooms specially equipped for broadcasting radio or television programs or making recordings. **4.** (*oft. pl.*) all the buildings occupied by a company that makes films. [It, from L: zeal, study, LL a place for study]

studious /'stjudiəs/, *adj.* **1.** eager or given to study: *a studious boy.* **2.** concerned with, marked by, or relating to study: *studious tastes.* **3.** painstaking; zealous; assiduous: *studious care.* [ME, from L]

study /'stʌdi/, *n., pl.* **studies,** *v.,* **studied, studying.** ◇*n.* **1.** the putting of the mind to gaining knowledge, by reading, searching, and thinking. **2.** a branch of learning: *the study of law.* **3.** a subject or subjects studied: *to spend more time at his studies.* **4.** (a written account of) any thorough examination: *to publish a study of the NSW railways.* **5.** deep thought; reverie. **6.** a room set apart for private study, reading, writing, etc. **7.** *Music.* a piece of music written to give a performer exercise in technical matters, but with artistic value also. **8.** *Art.* something produced as an exercise, or as a record of observations, or as a guide for a finished work. ◇*v.i.* **9.** to give oneself to gaining knowledge, by reading, searching, thinking, making notes, etc. ◇*v.t.* **10.** to give oneself to gaining a knowledge of a subject, esp. systematically: *to study science.* **11.** to examine carefully and in detail: *to study the political situation.* **12.** to think deeply about. [ME, from L: zeal, application, study, LL: a place for study]

stuff /stʌf/, *n.* **1.** the material of which anything is made. **2.** matter or material indefinitely: *cushions filled with some soft stuff.* **3.** cloth; fabric. **4.** *Colloq.* personal belongings, luggage, etc.: *Go and put your stuff in the car.* **5.** inward character, qualities, or abilities: *the stuff of which heroes are made.* **6.** *Colloq.* actions, performances, talk, etc.: *to cut out the rough stuff.* **7.** worthless matter or things; rubbish: *some old stuff I don't want.* **8.** worthless or foolish ideas, talk, or writing: *stuff and nonsense.* ◇*v.t.* **9.** to fill (a container), esp. by packing the contents closely together; cram full. **10.** to fill (an opening) by forcing something into it; plug. **11.** to fill (a chicken, etc.) with something. **12.** to fill or cram (oneself, one's stomach, etc.) with food. **13.** to fill the skin of (a dead animal) with material, etc., esp. for a museum. **14.** to fill (the mind) with details, facts, etc. [ME, from OF: provide, from Gmc, from LL: tow]

stuffing /'stʌfɪŋ/, *n.* **1.** the act of someone or something that stuffs. **2.** material or fabric used to fill cushions, mattresses, etc.: *the stuffing of an old sofa.* **3.** a filling used to stuff a

stuffing chicken, etc., before cooking. **4. knock or beat the stuffing out of,** *Colloq.* to defeat the self-confidence of or defeat utterly.

stuffy /'stʌfi/, *adj.*, **stuffier, stuffiest. 1.** badly ventilated; close: *a stuffy room; a stuffy train.* **2.** self-important; conceited; pompous. **3.** easily shocked; straitlaced; prim. **4.** old-fashioned or dull. —**stuffiness,** *n.*

stultify /'stʌltəfaɪ/, *v.t.*, **-fied, -fying. 1.** to make stupid or dull. **2.** to make useless or ineffectual. [LL, from L: foolish] —**stultifying,** *adj.*

stumble /'stʌmbəl/, *v.*, **-bled, -bling,** *n.* ◇*v.i.* **1.** to strike the foot against something in walking, running, etc., so as to stagger or fall; trip. **2.** to walk or go unsteadily. **3.** to make a mistake esp. in words. **4.** to act or speak in a hesitating way. **5.** to come accidentally or unexpectedly (fol. by *on, upon, across,* etc.). ◇*n.* **6.** the act of stumbling. **7.** a mistake; slip; blunder. [ME] —**stumbler,** *n.*

stump /stʌmp/, *n.* **1.** a short part remaining after the main part has been cut off or used up: *stump of a tree; the stump of a pencil; the stump of a leg.* **2.** *Old.* one of the piles on which a house is raised above the ground. **3.** *Cricket.* each of the three upright sticks which, with the two bails laid on the top of them, form a wicket. **4.** (*pl.*) *Cricket.* the end of a day's play: *at stumps.* **5.** *Colloq.* union dues. **6. beyond (back of) the black stump,** *Colloq.* in the far outback; in country areas beyond the reach of civilised comforts and facilities. **7. draw stumps,** *Cricket.* to stop play. ◇*v.t.* **8.** to make (someone) completely at a loss; nonplus. **9.** *Cricket.* (of the wicket-keeper) to put (a batsman) out by knocking down a stump or by dislodging a bail with the ball held in the hand, at a moment when the batsman is out of his or her ground. ◇*v.i.* **10.** to walk heavily or clumsily. [ME *stomp*]

stump-jump plough, *n.* a plough designed to rise and fall over roots and stumps in newly cleared ground.

stump-tailed skink, *n.* a common Australian lizard with a stout body, wedge-shaped head, stumpy tail and large, rough scales on the upper surface. Also, **stump-tail lizard.**

stun /stʌn/, *v.t.*, **stunned, stunning. 1.** to make senseless or unconscious: *The blow stunned him; He stunned him with a blunt weapon.* **2.** to strike with astonishment; astound; amaze. **3.** to daze or bewilder by noise, light, etc. [OE *stunian* resound, crash]

stung /stʌŋ/, *v.* **1.** past tense and past participle of **sting.** ◇*adj.* **2.** *Colloq.* drunk. **3.** *Colloq.* tricked; cheated.

stunner /'stʌnə/, *n. Colloq.* a person or thing of unusual excellence or beauty.

stunning /'stʌnɪŋ/, *adj.* **1.** that stuns. **2.** *Colloq.* of striking excellence, beauty, etc.

stunt[1] /stʌnt/, *v.t.* to slow down the growth or development (of): *to stunt his ambition; Sickness stunted her until she was 12.* [v. use of *stunt,* adj. (now d.), dwarfed, stubborn (in ME and OE foolish)] —**stunted,** *adj.*

stunt[2] /stʌnt/, *n.* **1.** a performance serving as a display of strength, skill, or daring. **2.** anything done to attract publicity. [orig. uncert.]

stuntman /'stʌntmæn/, *n.* someone who is paid to perform dangerous or acrobatic acts, esp. a person who replaces a film actor in scenes requiring such acts.

stupefy /'stjupəfaɪ/, *v.t.*, **-fied, -fying. 1.** to put into a state of stupor; dull the faculties of. **2.** to stun as with a narcotic, a shock, strong emotion, etc. **3.** to overcome with amazement; astound. [L] —**stupefier,** *n.* —**stupefactive,** *adj.*

stupendous /stju'pɛndəs/, *adj.* **1.** causing amazement; astounding; marvellous. **2.** amazingly large; immense: *a stupendous mass of information.* [L: to be wondered at]

stupid /'stjupəd/, *adj.* **1.** dull of mind; not clever; very silly. **2.** marked by or coming from mental dullness: *a stupid act.* **3.** boring; uninteresting: *a stupid book.* —**stupidity,** *n.*

stupor /'stjupə/, *n.* a state where the mind or senses are deadened or not working, as from drugs, shock, etc. [ME, from L] —**stuporous,** *adj.*

sturdy /'stɜdi/, *adj.*, **-dier, -diest. 1.** strongly built; stalwart; robust. **2.** firm, unbeatable. **3.** of strong or hardy growth, as a plant. [ME, from OF: dazed, reckless, from LL: deafen (with chatter), from *turdus* turtledove] —**sturdily,** *adv.* —**sturdiness,** *n.*

sturgeon /'stɜdʒən/, *n.* a large fish found in fresh and salt waters of the northern temperate zone, valued for its flesh and as a source of caviar. [ME, from AF, var. of OF, from VL, from Gmc]

Sturt /stɜt/, *n.* **Charles,** 1795–1869, Australian explorer, born in India; his explorations of eastern Australia, 1828–30, led him to the Darling River, and the inland river system of south-eastern Australia.

Sturt's desert pea, *n.* an Australian plant with brilliant scarlet and black flowers, found in inland desert country; floral emblem of SA. [named after Charles Sturt]

Sturt's desert rose, *n.* a shrub of inland Australia with attractive mauve flowers; the floral emblem of the NT. [named after Charles Sturt]

stutter /'stʌtə/, *v.t., v.i.* **1.** to utter (words, phrases, etc.) in which the rhythm of speech is interrupted by blocks or spasms. ◇*n.* **2.** a speech defect marked by stuttering. [Brit d. *stut,* ME *stutte(n)*] —**stutterer,** *n.* —**stutteringly,** *adv.*

Stuyvesant /'staɪvəsənt/, *n.* **Peter,** c. 1610–72, Dutch colonial administrator of New Netherland (later New York).

sty[1] /staɪ/, *n., pl.* **sties. 1.** a pen for pigs. **2.** any filthy place where someone lives. [OE *stig*]

sty[2] /staɪ/, *n., pl.* **sties.** an inflamed swelling on the edge of the eyelid. Also, **stye.** [ME *styan* (OE *stīgend* sty, lit., rising)]

stygian /'stɪdʒɪən/, *adj.* **1.** *Class Myth.* of or relating to the river Styx. **2.** dark; gloomy. **3.** hellish; infernal. [L, from Gk]

style /staɪl/, *n., v.*, **styled**, **styling**. ◇*n.* **1.** a particular kind, sort, or type, as relating to form, appearance, or character. **2.** a particular way of doing things: *a style of singing*. **3.** a way of living, as relating to expense, possessions, etc.: *They live in a simple style*. **4.** an elegant or fashionable way of living: *Since winning the lottery, they live in style*. **5. a.** (good) design, as in dress; elegance. **b.** an admired and distinctive personal expression: *She writes letters with style*. **6.** a particular manner of writing or speaking, depending on historical period, literary form, personality, etc., rather than on content: *the style of Henry Lawson; the Baroque style*. **7.** a particular, characteristic, method or form of construction in any art or work. **8.** a legal, official, or business title: *a firm under the style of Smith, Jones and Co.* **9.** → **stylus** (def. 1). **10.** *Bot.* a narrow tube sometimes coming from the ovary, having the stigma at the top. ◇*v.t.* **11.** to call by a particular style or specific name. **12.** to design in a particular or new style: *to style an evening dress*. [ME, from OF, from L] —**stylistic**, *adj.*

stylise *or* **stylize** /'staɪlaɪz/, *v.t.*, **-lised**, **-lising**. to make (something) match or conform with a particular and usu. simplified style or form; conventionalise. —**stylisation**, *n.* —**stylised**, *adj.*

stylish /'staɪlɪʃ/, *adj.* smart; elegant.

stylist /'staɪləst/, *n.* **1.** a person who designs or arranges a style: *a hair stylist*. **2.** a person who has a good style of writing.

stylus /'staɪləs/, *n.* **1. a.** a pointed instrument for writing on wax or other suitable surfaces. **b.** a pointed instrument for drawing, etching, or writing. **2.** a needle-shaped tool, used to cut grooves in the making of gramophone records. **3.** a needle tipped with diamond, sapphire, etc., for reproducing the sound of such a record. [L]

stymie /'staɪmi/, *n., v.*, **-mied**, **-mieing**. ◇*n.* **1.** *Golf.* the position when an opponent's ball lies (on the green) directly between one's own ball and the hole. **2.** any problem which is difficult to work out. ◇*v.t.* **3.** to block; thwart; frustrate. Also, **stymy**.

styptic /'stɪptɪk/, *n., adj.* (a drug) stopping bleeding. [ME; from L, from Gk]

styrene /'staɪrin/, *n.* a colorless liquid hydrocarbon, $C_6H_5CH:CH_2$, with a fragrant, aromatic smell, used in making synthetic rubber. [L]

Styx /stɪks/, *n.* Gk Myth. a river of the lower world, across which the souls of the dead were ferried.

suave /swav/, *adj.* (of people or their manner, speech, etc.) smooth, agreeable or polite; urbane. [L: gentle] —**suavity**, *n.*

sub /sʌb/, *n. Colloq.* **1.** subaltern. **2.** subeditor. **3.** submarine. **4.** subscription. **5.** substitute.

sub-, **1.** a prefix meaning 'under', 'not quite', or 'somewhat', used as a formative (*subarctic*, *substandard*), also attached to stems not used independently (*subject, subtract, subvert*). **2.** *Chem.* a prefix indicating a basic compound, as in *subcarbonate, subnitrate*. [L, representing *sub*, prep., under, close to]

subaltern /'sʌbəltən/, *n. Mil.* a commissioned officer below the rank of captain.

subatomic /ˌsʌbə'tɒmɪk/, *adj. Phys.* **1.** relating to a particle which is smaller than an atom. **2.** relating to any process which occurs within an atom.

subclimax /sʌb'klaɪmæks/, *n. Ecol.* the imperfect development of a stable plant community because of some factor (such as repeated fires in a forest).

subconscious /sʌb'kɒnʃəs/, *n., adj.* (the mental processes and reactions) existing or operating below the level of consciousness.

subcontinent /sʌb'kɒntənənt/, *n.* a large land mass, smaller than a continent: *the Indian subcontinent*.

subcontract /sʌb'kɒntrækt/, *n.*; /ˌsʌbkən'trækt/, *v. Law.* ◇*n.* **1.** a contract to do, or provide materials for, one section of a larger job or contract. ◇*v.t.* **2.** to make a subcontract for. —**subcontractor**, *n.*

subculture /'sʌbkʌltʃə/, *n.* a network of behavior, beliefs and attitudes existing within and different from a larger culture.

subcutaneous /ˌsʌbkju'teɪniəs/, *adj.* **1.** (of tissues) situated or lying under the skin. **2.** (of an injection, etc.) given under the skin.

subdivide /'sʌbdəvaɪd, sʌbdə'vaɪd/, *v.t., v.i.*, **-vided**, **-viding**. to divide into smaller parts after a first division. —**subdivision**, *n.*

subdominant /sʌb'dɒmənənt/, *n. Music.* the fourth note of a scale, next below the dominant.

subdue /səb'dju/, *v.t.*, **-dued**, **-duing**. **1.** to win control over, usu. by force; conquer; overcome. **2.** to put down or repress (feelings, etc.). **3.** to reduce the amount or force of (sound, light, color, etc.); soften. [ME, from OF: seduce, from L: remove by stealth] —**subdued**, *adj.*

subeditor /sʌb'ɛdətə/, *n.* **1.** *Journalism.* one who prepares material written by others for printing. **2.** an assistant editor.

subgroup /'sʌbgrup/, *n.* **1.** a division of a group. **2.** *Chem.* a vertical division of a group in the periodic table; family.

subheading /'sʌbhɛdɪŋ/, *n.* the title or heading of a section in a chapter, essay, newspaper article, etc.

subhuman /sʌb'hjumən/, *adj.* **1.** below or less than human. **2.** almost human.

subj., *Abbrev.* **1.** subject. **2.** subjective. **3.** subjunctive.

subject /'sʌbdʒɛkt/, *n., adj.*; /səb'dʒɛkt/, *v.* ◇*n.* **1.** something that may become a matter of thought, discussion, investigation, etc.: *a subject of conversation*. **2.** a branch of knowledge organised as a course of study. **3.** a reason, or cause: *a subject for complaint*. **4.** the underlying idea of a sermon, book, story, etc.; theme. **5.**

an object, scene, incident, etc., chosen by an artist or shown in a work of art. **6.** someone who is under the rule of a sovereign, state, or government: *a British subject.* **7.** *Gram.* (in English and other languages) the word or words of a sentence about which something is said. **8.** a person used for medical, surgical, or psychological treatment or experiment. ◇*adj.* **9.** being under control or influence (oft. fol. by *to*). **10.** being under rule or authority; owing loyalty or obedience (*to*). **11.** open or exposed (fol. by *to*): *subject to ridicule.* **12.** being dependent or conditional upon something (fol. by *to*): *His consent is subject to your approval.* **13.** likely or sure to undergo something (fol. by *to*): *Everyone is subject to death; I am subject to headaches.* ◇*v.t.* **14.** to bring under control, rule, or influence (usu. fol. by *to*). **15.** to cause to undergo or experience something (fol. by *to*): *to subject metal to intense heat.* **16.** to lay open, or expose (fol. by *to*): *He subjected himself to ridicule.* [L: placed under] —**subjection**, *n.*

subjective /səbˈdʒɛktɪv/, *adj.* **1.** existing in the mind; belonging to the thinker rather than to the object of thought (opposed to *objective*). **2.** relating to, caused by, or typical of a particular person's ideas, feelings and prejudices; personal; individual. **3.** *Philos.* of or relating to thought itself. —**subjectivity, subjectiveness**, *n.*

subjective case, *n. Gram.* See **case**[1] (def. 8) and Appendix.

subjectivism /səbˈdʒɛktəvɪzəm/, *n.* a philosophical theory that there is no objective truth, everything being dependent on the mind's perceptions. See **idealism** (def. 4).

sub judice /sʌb ˈdʒuːdəsi/, *adv.* before a judge or court of law for consideration. [L]

subjugate /ˈsʌbdʒəgeɪt/, *v.t.*, **-gated, -gating.** to bring under complete control or into subjection; subdue; conquer. [L: brought under the yoke] —**subjugation**, *n.* —**subjugator**, *n.*

subjunctive /səbˈdʒʌŋktɪv/, *adj., n. Gram.* (naming or relating to) a verb mood expressing possible or desirable action. For example, in the sentence *Were I but king, things would alter,* the verb *were* is in the subjunctive mood. See **indicative**. [LL, from L: subjoined]

sublimate /ˈsʌbləmeɪt/, *v.*, **-mated, -mating**; /ˈsʌbləmət/, *n.* ◇*v.t.* **1.** *Psychol.* to redirect (sexual energies, etc.) into socially constructive or creative activities. **2.** *Chem., etc.* → **sublime** (def. 7). **3.** to make nobler. ◇*n.* **4.** *Chem.* the crystals, deposit, etc. obtained when a substance is sublimated. [L: elevated] —**sublimation**, *n.*

sublime /səˈblaɪm/, *adj., n., v.,* **-limed, -liming.** ◇*adj.* **1.** elevated or lofty in thought, language, bearing, etc.: *sublime poetry.* **2.** impressing the mind with a sense of greatness or power; awe-inspiring: *sublime scenery.* **3.** perfect or supreme: *a sublime moment.* **4.** *Poetic.* haughty or proud. ◇*n.* **5.** that which is sublime: *from the sublime to the ridiculous.* ◇*v.t.* **6.** to make higher, nobler, or purer. **7.** *Chem., etc.* to change (a solid) by heat directly into a vapor, which on cooling condenses back to solid form, without becoming liquid first. ◇*v.i.* **8.** *Chem., etc.* to change from solid state to a gas, and then condense as a solid without becoming liquid. [ME, from L: elevate] —**sublimeness, sublimity**, *n.*

subliminal /səbˈblɪmənəl/, *adj. Psychol.* (of stimuli, etc.) being at a level below the threshold of consciousness or perception; subconscious.

submarine /ˈsʌbmərin, sʌbməˈrin/, *n.* **1.** a type of vessel that can travel under water, esp. one used in warfare. ◇*adj.* **2.** situated, occurring, or living under the surface of the sea.

submerge /səbˈmɜdʒ/, *v.*, **-merged, -merging.** ◇*v.t.* **1.** to put under water, etc. **2.** to cover with or as if with water; immerse: *He was submerged in his studies.* ◇*v.i.* **3.** to sink or plunge under the surface of water, etc. [L] —**submergence**, *n.*

submission /səbˈmɪʃən/, *n.* **1.** the act or result of submitting. **2.** submissive behavior. **3.** anything which is submitted, e.g. an official report, application for funds, etc. [ME, from L]

submissive /səbˈmɪsɪv/, *adj.* tending to yield; unresisting and obedient. —**submissiveness**, *n.*

submit /səbˈmɪt/, *v.*, **-mitted, -mitting.** ◇*v.t.* **1.** to yield (something) in surrender or obedience. **2.** to give over (esp. oneself) to conditions imposed, treatment, etc. **3.** to take advice from the decision or judgment of another. **4.** to state or urge with deference (usu. fol. by *that*): *I submit that full proof should be required.* **5.** to offer (a report, newspaper article, etc.) for acceptance, etc. ◇*v.i.* **6.** to yield in surrender, compliance, or obedience: *to submit to a conqueror.* **7.** to allow oneself to be subjected to something: *He submitted to the unfair punishment.* **8.** to give way or defer to the opinion, judgment, etc., of another. [ME, from L: lower; put under] —**submission**, *n.* —**submissible**, *adj.*

subnormal /sʌbˈnɔməl/, *adj.* **1.** less than or inferior to the normal. **2.** lacking in one or more important psychological traits, as intelligence, personality, etc. ◇*n.* **3.** a subnormal person.

subordinate /səˈbɔdənət/, *adj., n.;* /səˈbɔdəneɪt/, *v.,* **-nated, -nating.** ◇*adj.* **1.** placed in or belonging to a lower order or rank. **2.** of lesser importance; secondary. **3.** subject to or under the authority of a superior. ◇*n.* **4.** a subordinate person or thing. ◇*v.t.* **5.** to place in a lower order or rank. **6.** to make secondary (fol. by *to*). **7.** to make (someone) subject, obedient, or dependent (fol. by *to*). [late ME, from ML: subordinated] —**subordination**, *n.* —**subordinative**, *adj.*

subordinate clause, *n.* (in grammar) a clause that modifies and is dependent upon a main clause, as *'when I came'* in the sentence *'They were glad when I came'.*

suborn /səˈbɔn/, *v.t.* to bribe (a person) to do some wrong or unlawful act, usu. perjury. [L: equip secretly]

subpoena /səˈpinə/, *n., v.,* **-naed, -naing.** *Law.* ◇*n.* **1.** a legal document ordering a

subpoena person to appear in court (usu. as a witness). ◇*v.t.* **2.** to send (someone) a subpoena. [ME, from L: under penalty, the first words of the writ]

sub rosa /sʌb 'rouzə/, *adv.* privately; confidentially. [L: under the rose; the rose being the symbol of the Egyptian god Horus, identified by the Greeks with Harpocrates, god of silence]

subscribe /səb'skraɪb/, *v.*, **-scribed**, **-scribing**. ◇*v.t.* **1.** to promise (usu. by signature) to give or pay (a sum of money) as a contribution, payment, share, etc. **2.** to give or pay (money) in fulfilment of such a promise. **3.** to express agreement to (a contract, etc.) by signing one's name. **4.** to write (something) beneath or at the end of a thing; sign (one's name) to a document, etc. ◇*v.i.* **5.** to promise to give or pay money for some special purpose. **6.** to obtain a subscription to a magazine, newspaper, etc.: *I subscribe to several magazines*. **7.** to give or pay money. **8.** to sign one's name to something. **9.** to agree, esp. by signing one's name. [ME, from L] **–subscriber**, *n.*

subscriber trunk dialling *n.* →STD

subscript /'sʌbskrɪpt/, *n., adj.* **1.** (something) written below. **2.** (something) placed low on the line, as the '2' in 'H$_2$O'. [L]

subscription /səb'skrɪpʃən/, *n.* **1.** a contribution of money towards some object or a payment for shares, a periodical, club membership, etc. **2.** a sum of money given. **3.** agreement, assent, or approval expressed by, or as if by, signing one's name. [late ME, from L]

subsection /'sʌbsekʃən/, *n.* **1.** a part or division of a section. **2.** a division within a part of an Aboriginal tribe with its own totem, as a hunting group.

subsequent /'sʌbsəkwənt/, *adj.* occurring later or coming in order after: *subsequent events; subsequent section in a treaty*. [late ME, from L] **–subsequence**, *n.*

subservient /səb'sɜviənt/, *adj.* **1.** serving or acting as a helper; subordinate. **2.** (of persons, their conduct, etc.) very submissive; servile; obsequious. [L] **–subservience**, *n.*, **subserviency**, *n.*

subset /'sʌbset/, *n.* Maths. a set whose elements belong to another particular set; subordinate set.

subside /səb'saɪd/, *v.i.*, **-sided**, **-siding**. **1.** to sink to a low or lower level. **2.** to become quieter, or less active: *The laughter subsided*. [L: settle down] **–subsidence**, *n.*

subsidiary /səb'sɪdʒəri/, *adj., n., pl.* **-ries**. ◇*adj.* **1.** serving to help or add to; auxiliary; supplementary, as a stream. **2.** secondary; subordinate. ◇*n.* **3.** a subsidiary thing or person. [L: belonging to a reserve]

subsidise *or* **subsidize** /'sʌbsədaɪz/, *v.t.*, **-dised**, **-dising**. **1.** to give or aid with a subsidy. **2.** to buy the help of by the payment of a subsidy. [SUBSID(Y) + -ISE^1]

subsidy /'sʌbsədi/, *n., pl.* **-dies**. **1.** direct financial aid given by a government to a private company, a cultural organisation, etc. **2.** a sum paid, as determined by a treaty, by one government to another, to obtain some service in return. **3.** a grant or contribution of money.

subsist /səb'sɪst/, *v.i.* **1.** to exist, or continue in existence. **2.** to continue alive; live, as on food, resources, etc., esp. when these are very limited. [L: stand firm, be adequate to] **–subsistence**, *n.* **–subsistent**, *adj.*

subsistence farming /səb,sɪstəns 'famɪŋ/, *n.* farming in which the produce is eaten by the farmer and his or her family leaving little or none to sell at market.

subsoil /'sʌbsɔɪl/, *n.* the bed or layer of earth just below the surface soil.

substance /'sʌbstəns/, *n.* **1.** anything of which a thing consists or is made; matter; material. **2.** a type of matter of definite chemical composition. **3.** the matter or subject of thought, discussion, study, etc. **4.** the actual matter of a thing, as opposed to its appearance; reality. **5.** solid character or quality: *claims without substance*. **6.** body: *soup without much substance*. **7.** the meaning or gist, as of speech or writing. **8.** possessions or wealth: *He squandered his substance*. **9. in substance, a.** mainly; substantially. **b.** actually; really. [ME, from OF, from L]

substandard /sʌb'stændəd/, *adj.* below standard; inadequate; inferior.

substantial /səb'stænʃəl/, *adj.* **1.** of a bodily or material nature; real or actual. **2.** of a considerable amount, size, etc.: *a substantial sum of money*. **3.** of a solid nature; firm, stout, or strong. **4.** being such with respect to basic parts: *two stories in substantial agreement*. **5.** wealthy: *one of the substantial men of the town*. **6.** relating to the substance, or essence of a matter. **7.** being a substance; having independent existence. [ME, from LL] **–substantiality**, **substantialness**, *n.*

substantiate /səb'stænʃieɪt/, *v.t.*, **-ated**, **-ating**. to establish by proof or evidence: *to substantiate a charge*. **–substantiation**, *n.*

substantive /sʌb'stæntɪv, 'sʌbstəntɪv/, *n.* **1.** Gram. a noun, pronoun, or other word or phrase which acts like a noun. ◇*adj.* **2.** having independent existence; independent. **3.** real or actual. **4.** of considerable amount or quantity. [ME, from LL: standing by itself, from L: substance]

substation /'sʌbsteɪʃən/, *n.* **1.** a subsidiary station. **2.** Elect. an installation in an electrical distribution system, between the generating station and the low-tension network, in which transformation or switching takes place.

substitute /'sʌbstətjut/, *n., v.*, **-tuted**, **-tuting**. ◇*n.* **1.** a person or thing acting in place of another. ◇*v.t.* **2.** to put (one person or thing) in the place of another. **3.** to take the place of; replace. ◇*v.i.* **4.** to act as a substitute. [ME, from L] **–substitution**, *n.*

subsume /səb'sjum/, *v.t.*, **-sumed**, **-suming**. **1.** to consider or include (an idea, term, etc.) as part of a larger group. **2.** to show (a case, instance, etc.) to be under a rule. [NL] **–subsumption**, *n.*

subtend /səb'tɛnd/, *v.t. Geom, etc.* to extend under; be opposite to: *a chord subtending an arc.* [L: stretch under]

subter-, a prefix meaning 'position underneath', with figurative uses, as in *subterfuge*. [L, combining form of *subter*, prep. and adv.]

subterfuge /'sʌbtəfjudʒ/, *n.* something, as a plan, trick, etc., used to hide or avoid something or to escape an argument. [LL, from L: flee secretly]

subterranean /sʌbtə'reɪnɪən/, *adj.* 1. existing, situated, or operating below the earth's surface; underground. 2. hidden or secret. [L: below the earth]

subtitle /'sʌbtaɪtl/, *n.* 1. a secondary, usu. explanatory, title of a literary work. 2. *Films.* **a.** one of a series of captions shown on the lower part of the screen, being a translation of the dialogue of foreign language films. **b.** (in silent films) a title giving dialogue or an explanation to a following scene. ◇*v.t.* 3. to give a subtitle or subtitles to.

subtle /'sʌtl/, *adj.* 1. fine or delicate, often when likely to escape perception or understanding: *subtle irony.* 2. delicate or faint and mysterious: *a subtle smile.* 3. needing mental sharpness: *a subtle point.* 4. characterised by mental acuteness or penetration: *a subtle understanding.* 5. cunning; crafty. 6. not easily noticed, as poison, etc. 7. skilful, clever; ingenious. [ME, from OF, from L: fine, delicate] —**subtleness, subtlety,** *n.*

subtract /səb'trækt/, *v.t.* 1. to withdraw or take away (a part from a whole). 2. *Maths.* to take (one number or quantity) from another; deduct. ◇*v.i.* 3. to take away something or a part, from a whole. [L: carried away] —**subtraction,** *n.*

subtropical /sʌb'trɒpɪkəl/, *adj.* relating to a region between tropical and temperate.

suburb /'sʌbɜb/, *n.* 1. an area where people live, usu. quite far from the city centre, having its own facilities, as schools, shopping centres, etc. 2. an outlying part. [ME, from L]

suburban /sə'bɜbən/, *adj.* 1. relating to, inhabiting, or being in a suburb or the suburbs of a city or town. 2. characteristic of a suburb or suburbs. 3. narrow-minded; conventional in outlook.

suburbia /sə'bɜbɪə/, *n.* 1. (people living in) the suburbs as a group, esp. as they seem to represent the middle range of community standards and values. 2. the characteristic life of people in suburbs.

subvert /səb'vɜt/, *v.t.* 1. to overthrow (something established or existing). 2. to cause the downfall, or destruction of. 3. to undermine the principles of; corrupt. [ME, from L] —**subversion,** *n.* —**subversive,** *n., adj.*

subway /'sʌbweɪ/, *n.* 1. a pedestrian tunnel underneath a street, railway line, etc. 2. *US.* an underground railway.

suc-, a variant of **sub-** before *c*.

succeed /sək'sid/, *v.i.* 1. to have the desired result. 2. to do or accomplish what is attempted. 3. to have success in a particular field. 4. to follow or replace another by descent, election, appointment, etc. (oft. fol. by *to*): *He succeeded to the throne.* 5. to come next after something else. ◇*v.t.* 6. to come after and take the place of: *I succeeded my father in the family business.* 7. to come next after in a series or in the course of events; follow. [ME, from L: go up, be successful]

success /sək'sɛs/, *n.* 1. a favorable or desired end to attempts or endeavors. 2. the gaining of wealth, position, etc. 3. a successful performance or achievement. 4. a thing or a person that is successful. [L] —**successful,** *adj.*

succession /sək'sɛʃən/, *n.* 1. the coming of one after another in order, or in the course of events; sequence. 2. a number of people or things following one another in order. 3. the right, act or process, by which one person succeeds to the office, rank, estate, etc., of another. 4. the order or line of those entitled to succeed. 5. *Ecol.* the gradual replacement of one community by another in development towards a stable community of vegetation. [ME, from L] —**successional,** *adj.*

successive /sək'sɛsɪv/, *adj.* 1. following uninterrupted or in a regular order: *three successive days.* 2. marked by or involving succession.

successor /sək'sɛsə/, *n.* someone or something that succeeds or follows. [L; replacing ME *successour*, from AF]

succinct /sək'sɪŋkt/, *adj.* expressed or expressing in few words; concise. [ME, from L: girded up]

succor or **succour** /'sʌkə/, *n.* 1. (someone or something that gives) help, relief, or aid. ◇*v.t.* 2. to help or relieve in difficulty, need, or distress. [ME, from AF, OF: to help, from L]

succulent /'sʌkjələnt/, *adj.* 1. full of juice; juicy. 2. rich in desirable qualities. 3. (of plants, etc.) having thick, fleshy tissues. ◇*n.* 4. a succulent plant, as a cactus. [L] —**succulence, succulency,** *n.*

succumb /sə'kʌm/, *v.i.* 1. to give way to a superior force; yield. 2. to yield to disease, wounds, old age, etc.; die. [late ME, from L]

such /sʌtʃ/, *adj.* 1. of the kind, type, degree, extent, etc., shown or suggested: *Such a man is dangerous.* 2. of that particular kind or type: *The food, such as it was, was plentiful.* 3. similar: *tea, coffee, and such goods.* 4. of so extreme a kind; so great, good, bad, etc.: *He is such a liar.* 5. being as stated or shown: *such is the case.* 6. being the person(s) or thing(s) referred to: *If any member be behind in his payments, such member shall be suspended.* 7. Also, **such and such.** being particular but not named: *It happened in such and such a place.* ◇*pron.* 8. a similar, or previously indicated person(s) or thing(s): *A car is useful, but we cannot afford such.* 9. **as such, a.** in that position or capacity: *The leader, as such, is entitled to respect.* **b.** in itself or themselves: *Wealth, as such, does not appeal to him.* 10. **such as, a.** of the kind named: *People such as these are*

such | 1032 | **suffuse**

not to be trusted. **b.** for example: *He likes outdoor sports such as tennis and football.* [ME; OE *swulc*]

suck /sʌk/, *v.t.* **1.** to draw into the mouth by action of the lips and tongue which make a partial vacuum: *to suck lemonade through a straw.* **2.** to draw (water, air, etc.) by any process like this: *Plants suck up moisture from the earth.* **3.** to draw or suck liquid, etc., from: *to suck the breast; suck an orange.* **4.** to take into the mouth and absorb by licking, etc.: *to suck toffee.* **5.** to hold and moisten in the mouth: *Don't suck your thumb.* ◇*v.i.* **6.** to suck something: *The baby sucked noisily; to suck on a pipe.* **7.** to draw or be drawn by, or as if by, suction: *The air sucked up the pipe.* ◇*n.* **8.** the act or sound of sucking with the mouth, etc. **9.** a sucking force; suction. [OE *sūcan*]

sucker /'sʌkə/, *n.* **1.** someone or something that sucks. **2.** a baby or a young animal that is suckled. **3.** a part or organ of an animal adapted for sucking nourishment, or for sticking to an object as by suction. **4.** *Colloq.* a person easily deceived or taken advantage of; dupe. **5.** *Bot.* a shoot rising from an underground stem or a root.

suckle /'sʌkəl/, *v.*, **-led**, **-ling**. ◇*v.t.* **1.** to nurse or give milk to at the breast. ◇*v.i.* **2.** to suck at the breast. [frequentative of SUCK]

sucrose /'sukroʊz, -oʊs/, *n.* a crystalline disaccharide (sugar), $C_{12}H_{22}O_{11}$, obtained from sugar cane, sugar beet, etc.

suction /'sʌkʃən/, *n.* **1.** the act, process, or condition of sucking. **2.** a tendency to suck something into the inside space when the pressure is reduced there. **3.** a reduction of pressure in order to cause such a sucking. [L] — **suctorial**, *adj.*

Sudan /su'dæn/, *n.* **1.** a republic in north-eastern Africa on the Red Sea. Pop. 25 562 000 (1987); 2 505 813 km². *Languages:* Arabic, also tribal languages. *Currency:* Sudanese pound. *Cap.:* Khartoum. Formerly, **Anglo-Egyptian Sudan, the Sudan**. French, **Soudan**. **2.** a region of northern Africa, south of the Sahara, extending from the Atlantic to the Red Sea. — **Sudanese**, *n., adj.*

sudden /'sʌdn/, *adj.* **1.** happening, coming, or done quickly, without warning or unexpectedly: *a sudden attack.* **2.** sharp; abrupt: *a sudden turn.* ◇*n.* **3. all of a sudden**, suddenly; quite unexpectedly. [ME, from AF, from L] — **suddenness**, *n.*

sudden infant death syndrome, *n.* the sudden unexplained death of an apparently healthy baby, usu. while asleep. Also, **cot death, SIDS**.

Sudetenland /su'deɪtnlænd/, *n.* a mountainous region in the northern and north-western part of the Czech Republic; part of Czechoslovakia when annexed by Germany 1938; returned to Czechoslovakia 1945. Also, **Sudeten**.

suds /sʌdz/, *n.pl.* soapy water; foam; lather. [MD: marsh] — **sudsy**, *adj.*

sue /su/, *v.*, **sued**, **suing**. ◇*v.t.* **1.** *Law.* to start a civil action against (someone). **2.** to appeal to. ◇*v.i.* **3.** to begin legal proceedings. **4.** to make petition or appeal (oft. fol. by *for*). [ME, from AF, from VL]

suede /sweɪd/, *n.* (a fabric like) leather finished with a soft, napped surface. [F: lit., Sweden]

suet /'suət/, *n.* a hard fatty tissue about the loins and kidneys of cattle, sheep, etc., used in cookery, etc., and prepared as tallow. [ME, from AF]

Suetonius /swi'toʊniəs, sweɪ-/, *n.* (*Gaius Suetonius Tranquillus*), AD 75-150, Roman biographer.

Suez /'suəz/, *n.* **1.** a seaport in north-eastern Egypt, near the south end of the Suez Canal. Pop. 265 000 (1986 est.). **2. Gulf of**, a north-western arm of the Red Sea, west of the Sinai Peninsula. **3. Isthmus of**, an isthmus in north-eastern Egypt, joining Africa and Asia. 116 km wide.

Suez Canal, *n.* a canal across the Isthmus of Suez, connecting the Mediterranean and the Red Sea. About 160 km long.

suf-, a variant of **sub-** before *f*.

suffer /'sʌfə/, *v.i.* **1.** to experience or feel pain or distress. **2.** to experience injury, disadvantage or loss. **3.** to endure patiently or bravely. ◇*v.t.* **4.** to undergo, experience, or be forced to experience (pain, distress, injury, loss, or anything unpleasant). **5.** to undergo (any action, process, etc.): *to suffer change.* **6.** to allow; tolerate. [L] — **suffering**, *n.*

sufferance /'sʌfərəns, 'sʌfrəns/, *n.* **1.** (of a person or thing) tolerance; tacit permission. **2. on sufferance**, reluctantly tolerated.

suffice /sə'faɪs/, *v.i., v.t.,* **-ficed**, **-ficing**. to be enough or adequate (for). [L]

sufficient /sə'fɪʃənt/, *adj.* enough or adequate: *sufficient proof.* [ME, from L: sufficing] — **sufficiency**, *n.*

suffix /'sʌfɪks/, *n.* **1.** *Gram.* an affix added to the end of a word, e.g. *-ly* in *kindly*, and *-er* in *heater*. **2.** something added to the end. ◇*v.t.* **3.** to attach at the end of something. [NL: fastened on]

suffocate /'sʌfəkeɪt/, *v.*, **-cated**, **-cating**. ◇*v.t.* **1.** to kill by preventing air entering the lungs or gills. **2.** to restrict the free breathing of. **3.** to cause discomfort to through lack of cool or fresh air. **4.** to overcome; suppress. ◇*v.i.* **5.** to die from lack of air; smother. **6.** to feel uncomfortable through lack of cool or fresh air. [L: choked] — **suffocation**, *n.*

Suffolk /'sʌfək/, *n.* a county of eastern England, on the North Sea. Pop. 628 600 (1986 est.); 3797 km². *Administrative Centre:* Ipswich.

suffrage /'sʌfrɪdʒ/, *n.* the right of voting, esp. in political elections. [ME, from L]

suffragette /sʌfrə'dʒɛt/, *n.* one of an association of women in the early 20th century who argued and worked for women's suffrage.

suffuse /sə'fjuz/, *v.t.,* **-fused**, **-fusing**. to lightly spread with or as if with a liquid, color, etc. (*oft. in passive*): *Her face was suffused with pink.* [L: overspread] — **suffusion**, *n.* — **suffusive**, *adj.*

sug-, a variant of **sub-** before g.

sugar /ˈʃugə/, n. **1.** a sweet crystalline substance, sucrose, $C_{12}H_{22}O_{11}$, obtained chiefly from sugar cane or sugar beet, used to sweeten food. **2.** a member of the same class of carbohydrates. ◇v.t. **3.** to cover, sprinkle, mix, or sweeten with sugar. **4.** to make more agreeable. [ME, from ML, from Ar] —**sugary**, adj.

sugar beet, n. a variety of beet with a white root, grown for its sugar.

sugarcane /ˈʃugəkeɪn/, n. a tall grass, of tropical and warm areas, having a stout, jointed stalk, being the chief source of sugar. Also, **sugar cane**.

sugar glider, n. See **gliding possum**.

suggest /səˈdʒɛst/, v.t. **1.** to offer (an idea, proposition, plan, etc.) to someone for consideration. **2.** to name (a person or thing) as suitable or possible. **3.** (of things) to cause the consideration, making, doing, etc., of. **4.** to give the idea of (something) indirectly or through association; hint: *To me, his appearance suggests illness.* [L: placed under, added]

suggestible /səˈdʒɛstəbəl/, adj. easily influenced. —**suggestibility**, n.

suggestion /səˈdʒɛstʃən/, n. **1.** the act or result of suggesting. **2.** something suggested, e.g. a plan, etc. **3.** a slight trace: *just a suggestion of a foreign accent*. **4.** the calling up in the mind of one idea by another by some association between the two. [ME, from L]

suggestive /səˈdʒɛstɪv/, adj. **1.** that suggests thoughts, ideas, etc. **2.** relating to hypnotic suggestion. **3.** suggesting something improper or indecent. —**suggestiveness**, n.

Suharto /suˈhatoʊ, sə-/, n. born 1921, Indonesian statesman and general; became acting president 1967, president in 1968. Also, **Soeharto**.

suicide /ˈsuəsaɪd/, n. v., **-cided, -ciding**. ◇n. **1.** someone who takes their own life. **2.** the taking of one's own life. **3.** the deliberate destruction of one's own interests or prospects. ◇v.i. **4.** to kill oneself. [NL] —**suicidal**, adj

suit /sut/, n. **1.** a set of clothes, armor, etc., intended to be worn together. **2.** a set of clothes of the same material, consisting of jacket, and trousers or skirt. **3.** *Law*. a civil action. **4.** *Cards*. **a.** one of the sets (usu. four: spades, clubs, hearts, and diamonds) into which playing cards are divided. **b.** the total number of cards belonging to one of these sets held in a player's hand at one time: *I have a strong suit in diamonds.* **5.** a number of things forming a series or set. **6.** the courting of a woman. **7.** the act of making a petition or appeal. **8. follow suit, a.** to play a card of the suit led. **b.** to follow another's example. **9. strong suit**, something one is very good at; one's forte. ◇v.t. **10.** to provide with a suit of clothes; clothe. **11.** to adapt or fit (one thing) to another: *I will suit my plans to yours.* **12.** to be appropriate, fitting, or becoming to: *That color suits you.* **13.** to satisfy or please: *That suits me!* ◇v.i. **14.** to be satisfactory, appropriate, or acceptable: *Tomorrow will suit quite well.* ◇v. **15. suit oneself**, to do what one chooses, regardless of the interests or advice of others. [ME, from AF: follow]

suitable /ˈsutəbəl/, adj. fitting; appropriate; becoming. —**suitability**, **suitableness**, n.

suitcase /ˈsutkeɪs/, n. a rectangular travelling bag for carrying clothes, etc.

suite /swit/, n. **1.** a company of followers or attendants; train; retinue. **2.** a number of things forming a series or set. **3.** a connected series of rooms to be used together by one or more people. **4.** a set of furniture of similar design and function: *A three-piece suite consists of a couch and two armchairs.* **5.** *Music*. an ordered series of instrumental movements or dances. [F]

suitor /ˈsutə/, n. **1.** someone who courts or woos a woman. **2.** *Law*. someone who sues or petitions for anything; plaintiff.

Sukarno /suˈkanoʊ, sə-/, n. **Achmed** /ˈakmed/, 1901–1970, Indonesian statesman; president 1949–67. Also, **Soekarno**.

Sukarno Peak, n. a former name of Mount Jaya.

Sulawesi /suləˈweɪsi/, n. a large island of eastern Indonesia. Pop. 11 803 100 (1986 est.); 189 216 km². Also, **Celebes**.

sulfa drugs /ˈsʌlfə drʌgz/, n.pl. a group of compounds used as antibacterials in the treatment of various diseases, wounds, burns, etc.

sulfate /ˈsʌlfeɪt/, n. *Chem*. a salt of sulfuric acid. See **-ate²**. [NL]

sulfide /ˈsʌlfaɪd/, n. See **-ide**.

sulfite /ˈsʌlfaɪt/, n. See **-ite¹** (def. 4).

sulfur /ˈsʌlfə/, n. **1.** *Chem*. Also, *Obsolesc.*, **sulphur**. A non-metallic element which exists in several forms, usu. yellow crystalline solid, and which burns with a blue flame and a suffocating smell; used esp. in making gunpowder, matches, rubber, medicine, etc. Symbol: S; at. no.: 16; at. wt: 32.064. **2.** US → **sulphur** (def. 1). [ME, from L]

sulfur dioxide, n. a colorless, strong-smelling gas or liquid, non-combustible, soluble in water, ether and alcohol and used as a preservative for beer and wine, a disinfectant, a bleaching agent, and for various other industrial uses.

sulfureous /sʌlˈfjuriəs/, adj. consisting of, containing, relating to, or like sulfur.

sulfuric /sʌlˈfjurɪk, -ˈfjuə-/, adj. of, relating to, or containing sulfur, esp. in the hexavalent stage.

sulfuric acid, n. a dibasic acid of sulfur, H_2SO_4, a colorless, corrosive, oily liquid, made from sulfur trioxide and used industrially; oil of vitriol.

sulfurous /ˈsʌlfərəs/, adj. **1.** *Chem*. relating to sulfur. **2.** of the yellow color of sulfur. **3.** *Chem*. containing tetravalent sulfur.

sulfurous acid, n. an acid, H_2SO_3, formed by dissolving sulfur dioxide in water, known mainly by its salts (sulfites).

sulk /sʌlk/, *v.i.* **1.** to be in a sullen, bad mood, refusing to talk. ◇*n.* **2.** Also, **the sulks.** a conditon or fit of sulking: *to have the sulks.* **3.** Also, **sulker.** someone who sulks. [backformation from SULKY]

sulky /'sʌlki/, *adj.*, **sulkier, sulkiest,** *n., pl.* **sulkies.** ◇*adj.* **1.** sullenly ill-humored or resentful. ◇*n.* **2.** a light two-wheeled one-horse carriage. [? from OE *-solcen* slothful, remiss] —**sulkiness,** *n.*

Sulla /'sʊlə/, *n.* **Lucius Cornelius** /,lusiəs kəˈniliəs/ (*'Felix'*), 138–78 BC; Roman general and dictator.

sullage /'sʌlɪdʒ/, *n.* **1.** filth; refuse; scum. **2.** *Bldg Trades.* dirty water, as from bathrooms, laundries, kitchens, etc., excluding sewage.

sullen /'sʌlən/, *adj.* **1.** showing a bad mood by a gloomy silence. **2.** silently ill-humored; morose. [ME, from AF: SOLE[1]] —**sullenness,** *n.*

Sullivan /'sʌləvən/, *n.* **Sir Arthur Seymour,** 1842–1900, English composer; collaborator with Sir WS Gilbert in operettas.

sully /'sʌli/, *v.*, **-lied, -lying.** ◇*v.t.* **1.** to soil, stain, or tarnish. **2.** to spoil the purity of; disgrace; defile. ◇*v.i.* **3.** to become stained, soiled, or tarnished. [OE (ā)*solian* become dirty]

sulphur /'sʌlfə/, *n.* **1.** a pale yellow color with a greenish tinge. **2.** *Obsolesc.* —**sulfur** (def. 1).

sulphur-crested cockatoo, *n.* a large common Australian parrot, mainly white, with yellow under the wings and tail, and a forward curving yellow crest. Also, **white cockatoo.**

sultan /'sʌltən/, *n.* the head of a Muslim country. [ML, from Ar: king, ruler, power] —**sultanic,** *adj.* —**sultanship, sultanate,** *n.*

sultana /sʌl'tanə, səl-/, *n.* **1.** a wife or any close female relative of a sultan. **2.** a small, green, seedless grape. **3.** the dried fruit made from such a grape. [It: fem. of *sultano* SULTAN]

sultry /'sʌltri/, *adj.*, **-trier, -triest. 1.** unpleasantly hot, close and humid; sweltering. **2.** marked by or arousing temper or passion. [*sulter* (var. of SWELTER) + -Y[1]] —**sultriness,** *n.*

sum /sʌm/, *n., v.*, **summed, summing,** *adj.* ◇*n.* **1.** *Maths.* the total of two or more numbers, sizes, quantities, or particulars: *The sum of 5 and 7 is 12.* **2.** a quantity or amount, esp. of money: *to lend small sums.* **3.** a series of numbers or quantities to be added up. **4.** any arithmetical problem to be solved. **5.** the total amount. **6.** the substance or gist of a matter: *The letter contains the sum of his opinions.* **7.** → **summary.** ◇*v.t.* **8.** to combine into a total by addition. ◇*v.* **9. sum up, a.** to calculate. **b.** to make a summary of (something already said or done). **c.** to form a quick judgment or opinion of: *to sum someone up.* ◇*adj.* **10.** relating to a sum: *the sum total.* [L: highest]

sum-, an occasional variant of **sub-** before *m*.

Sumatra /sə'matrə/, *n.* a large island in the western part of Indonesia. Pop. 19 105 900 (1986 est.); 425 140 km². Indonesian, **Sumatera.** —**Sumatran,** *n., adj.*

Sumer /'sumə/, *n.* a region in southern Mesopotamia, containing the sites of many ancient cities and a civilisation which flourished perhaps as early as 5000 BC.

Sumerian /su'mɪəriən/, *adj.* **1.** of or relating to Sumer. **2.** the language of the Sumerians, preserved in very ancient cuneiform inscriptions.

summarise *or* **summarize** /'sʌməraɪz/, *v.t.*, **-rised, -rising. 1.** to make a summary of; state or express in a short, clear form. **2.** to be a summary of. —**summarisation,** *n.* —**summariser,** *n.*

summary /'sʌməri/, *n., pl.* **-ries,** *adj.* ◇*n.* **1.** a short presentation of facts or statements covering all the main points; an abstract. ◇*adj.* **2.** short, but giving the important points; concise. **3.** direct and hasty. **4.** (of legal proceedings, etc.) conducted without or exempt from various steps and delays of full proceedings. [ME, from ML, from L: sum] —**summarily,** *adv.*

summation /sʌ'meɪʃən/, *n.* **1.** the process of summing up. **2.** the result of this; aggregate or total.

summer /'sʌmə/, *n.* **1.** the warmest season of the year, between spring and autumn; in the Southern Hemisphere, December, January, and February. **2.** a whole year as represented by this season: *a child of eight summers.* **3.** a period of the finest development, perfection, beauty: *the summer of life.* [OE *sumor*] —**summery,** *adj.*

summerhouse /'sʌməhaʊs/, *n.* a simple, open structure in a park or garden, intended to provide a shady, cool place in summer.

summit /'sʌmɪt/, *n.* **1.** the highest point or part; apex: *the summit of a hill; That discovery was the summit of his achievements.* **2.** Also, **summit meeting.** a meeting between heads of state or other top level officials. [late ME, from F, from L: highest]

summon /'sʌmən/, *v.t.* **1.** to call with authority to some duty, or performance: *She summoned him to work; He summoned her to help him.* **2.** to call or send for the presence of (fol. by *to, away, from,* etc.). **3.** to call together (an assembly, etc.) by authority: *to summon a parliament.* **4.** to call into action; rouse (oft. fol. by *up*): *He summoned up all his courage.* [L: suggest]

summons /'sʌmənz/, *n., pl.* **-monses,** *v.* ◇*n.* **1.** a command, message, or signal by which one's presence is called for. **2.** a call to do something: *a summons to surrender.* **3.** an order to appear at a particular place, esp. before a court of law, or the document by which the order is made. **4.** an order for the meeting of an assembly or parliament. ◇*v.t.* **5.** to serve with a summons; summon. [ME, from AF, OF: SUMMON]

sumo /'sumoʊ/, *n.* a style of Japanese wrestling. [Jap]

sump /sʌmp/, *n.* **1.** a pit, well, etc., in which water or other liquid is collected. **2.** *Mech.* a container situated at the lowest point in a

sump 1035 **Sun Zhong-shan**

circulating system, such as an internal-combustion engine, which collects oil. [ME, from MLG or MD]

sumptuous /'sʌmptʃuəs/, *adj.* 1. involving great cost, as from fine workmanship, materials, etc. 2. luxurious; splendid: *a sumptuous residence*. [late ME, from L: expensive]

sun /sʌn/, *n., v.,* sunned, sunning. ◊*n.* 1. the star which is the central body of the solar system, around which the planets revolve, and from which they receive light and heat. 2. this star with regard to its appearance in the sky, etc. 3. any heavenly body that gives out its own light. 4. sunshine: *to sit in the sun.* 5. something likened to the sun in brightness, splendor, etc. 6. **a place in the sun,** a pleasant or advantageous situation. 7. **under the sun,** anywhere on earth. ◊*v.t.* 8. to expose to the sunshine, so as to warm, dry, tan, etc. [ME and OE *sunne*]

Sun, *Abbrev.* Sunday.

sunbake /'sʌnbeɪk/, *v.i.,* -baked, -baking. to expose one's body to the sun in order to become tanned or relaxed. Also, **sunbathe.** –**sunbaker,** *n.*

sunburn /'sʌnbɜn/, *n., v.,* -burnt or -burned, -burning. ◊*n.* 1. inflammation of the skin, caused by too much or too sudden exposure to the sun's rays. ◊*v.t., v.i.* 2. to affect or be affected with sunburn.

Sunbury /'sʌnbri/, *n.* a town in southern central Vic, north-west of Melbourne. Pop. 15 297 (1986).

sundae /'sʌndeɪ/, *n.* a portion of ice-cream with flavored syrup, chopped nuts, etc., on it. [orig. uncert.]

Sunda Islands /ˌsʌndə 'aɪləndz, ˌsun-/, *n.pl.* an island chain in the Malay Archipelago, including Sumatra, Java, and the **Lesser Sunda Islands,** those smaller islands extending from Java east to Timor.

Sunday /'sʌndeɪ, -di/, *n.* the first day of the week, observed as a day of rest or worship by most Christian churches. [ME; OE *sunnandæg*]

sundeck /'sʌndɛk/, *n.* a flat roof or platform built on to a house, hotel, etc., used for sunbathing.

sunder /'sʌndə/, *v.t., v.i.* to separate or become separated; break apart. [ME; late OE *sundrian*]

sundial /'sʌndaɪəl/, *n.* an instrument for showing the time of day by the position of a shadow thrown by the sun on a plate or surface marked in hours.

sundown /'sʌndaʊn/, *n.* sunset.

sundowner /'sʌndaʊnə/, *n.* a swagman who arrives at a station at nightfall, too late for work, but is given shelter for the night.

sundries /'sʌndriz/, *n.pl.* sundry things or items.

sundry /'sʌndri/, *adj.* 1. various; miscellaneous: *sundry persons*. ◊*n.* 2. Cricket. (*usu. pl.*) a score not made by hitting the ball with the bat, as a bye or wide; an extra. ◊*pron.* 3. **all and sundry,** everyone. [ME; OE *syndrig* private, separate]

sunfish /'sʌnfɪʃ/, *n., pl.* -fishes, (*esp. collectively*) -fish. a huge fish, the **ocean sunfish,** found in Australian waters and elsewhere, having a compressed, deep body and long, pointed fins.

sunflower /'sʌnflaʊə/, *n.* a tall plant with yellow-rayed, showy flowers, and seeds which are used as food and as the source of an oil.

sung /sʌŋ/, *v.* past tense and past participle of **sing.**

Sung /sʊŋ/, *n.* a Chinese dynasty, AD 960–1279, under which culture, esp. art and Confucian philosophy, flourished in the Chang region, until overthrown by the Mongols.

sunglasses /'sʌnglasəz/, *n.pl.* spectacles having darkened, or polaroid lenses to protect the eyes from the glare of the sun.

sunk /sʌŋk/, *v.* a past tense and past participle of **sink.**

sunken /'sʌŋkən/, *v.* 1. a past participle of **sink.** ◊*adj.* 2. sunk or having been sunk beneath the surface; submerged: *a sunken ship.* 3. having settled down to a lower level: *sunken walls.* 4. lying below the general level: *a sunken garden.* 5. hollow: *sunken cheeks.*

Sun King, *n.* →**Louis XIV.**

sunlamp /'sʌnlæmp/, *n.* a lamp which gives out ultraviolet rays, used as a means of producing an artificial suntan, etc.

Sunnite /'sʌnaɪt/, *n.* a member of one of the two great religious divisions of Islam, the Sunni, which regards the first four Caliphs as the legitimate successors of Mohammed. See **Shiite** [Ar: *sunna* form, way, path]

sunny /'sʌni/, *adj.,* -nier, -niest. 1. having plenty of sunshine: *a sunny day; a sunny room.* 2. relating to or like the sun. 3. cheerful: *a sunny nature.* –**sunnily,** *adv.* –**sunniness,** *n.*

Sunraysia /sʌn'reɪziə/, *n.* the name given to the area in north-western Vic, around Mildura, which produces dried fruits.

sunshine, /'sʌnʃaɪn/, *n.* 1. the shining of the sun; direct light of the sun. 2. brightness; cheerfulness or happiness.

Sunshine /'sʌnʃaɪn/, *n.* a city within the Melbourne metropolitan area; important industrial centre. Pop. 94 413 (1986).

sunspot /'sʌnspɒt/, *n.* one of the relatively dark patches which appear periodically on the surface of the sun, and which have a certain effect on some of the earth's phenomena, such as magnetism.

sunstroke /'sʌnstroʊk/, *n.* a condition caused by too much exposure to the sun, marked by weakness, fever, etc.

suntan /'sʌntæn/, *n.* brownness of the skin caused by exposure to the sun, cultivated by some as a mark of health or beauty. Also, **tan.** –**suntanned,** *adj.*

Sun Zhong-shan /ˌsʊn dʒʊŋ-'ʃan/, *n.* 1867–1925, Chinese revolutionary and

Sun Zhong-shan statesman; became first president of the Republic of China in 1911; founded Guomindang. Formerly, **Sun Yat-sen.**

sup[1] /sʌp/, v.i., **supped, supping.** to eat the evening meal; take supper. [ME, from OF]

sup[2] /sʌp/, v.t., **supped, supping.** → **sip.** [OE *suppa*]

sup-, a variant of **sub-** (by assimilation) before *p*.

super /'supə/, n. *Colloq.* **1.** high-octane petrol. **2.** → **superannuation. 3.** → **superintendent. 4.** → **supernumerary. 5.** → **superphosphate.** ◇*adj.* **6.** of a superior quality, grade, size, etc. **7.** extremely good, pleasing, etc.

super-, **1.** a prefix meaning 'superior to' or 'over-', as of quality (*superman*), size (*supermarket*), degree (*supersensitive*), space (*superstructure*), etc. **2.** *Chem.* a prefix having the same sense as 'per-'. [L, combining form of *super*, adv. and prep., above, beyond, in addition]

superannuate /supər'ænjueɪt/, v.t., **-ated, -ating. 1.** to allow to retire on a pension, on account of age or illness. **2.** to set aside as being out of date or too old. [ML: over a year old (said of cattle)] —**superannuated,** *adj.*

superannuation /ˌsupəræniuˈeɪʃən/, n. **1.** a pension or allowance paid to a person, esp. someone who has retired from work on account of age and infirmity. **2.** a sum of money paid regularly by an employee to a superannuation fund.

superb /sə'pɜb, su-/, adj. **1.** admirably fine or excellent: *a superb performance.* **2.** of noble or grand appearance or kind: *superb beauty.* [L: proud, distinguished]

supercharge /'supətʃɑdʒ/, v.t., **-charged, -charging. 1.** to supply air to (an internal-combustion engine) at greater than atmospheric pressure; boost. **2.** to pressurise (a gas or liquid).

supercilious /supə'sɪliəs/, adj. proudly contemptuous: *a supercilious person; a supercilious look.* [L] —**superciliousness,** n.

supercool /'supəkul/, v.t. to cool (a liquid) below its freezing point without it becoming solid.

superconductivity /ˌsupəˌkɒndʌk'tɪvəti/, n. the phenomenon of greatly increased electrical conductivity shown by certain substances at temperatures approaching absolute zero. —**superconductor** /supəkən'dʌktə/, n. —**superconducting,** adj.

superego /supər'igou/, n. (in Freudian theory) a personification of the development of the ego, which is similar to 'conscience', but is largely unconscious, causing guilt or anxiety to be felt when the ego is influenced by primitive impulses.

superficial /supə'fɪʃəl/, adj. **1.** of or relating to the surface: *superficial measurement.* **2.** being at, on, or near the surface: *a superficial wound.* **3.** on the surface only; apparent, rather than real or deep: *a superficial resemblance; superficial piety.* **4.** concerned with only what is on the surface or obviously shallow; not profound: *a superficial observer; a superficial writer.* [ME, from LL, from L] —**superficiality,** n.

superfluous /su'pɜfluəs/, adj. being more than what is enough or needed; unnecessary. [ME, from L: overflowing] —**superfluity,** n.

superheat /'supəhit/, v.t. **1.** to heat (a liquid) above its boiling point without bubbles of vapor forming. **2.** to heat (a gas, such as steam not in contact with water) to such a degree that its temperature may then be lowered or its pressure increased without it turning back into liquid.

superhuman /'supəhjumən/, adj. **1.** having a higher nature or greater powers than man. **2.** of more than ordinary human power, achievement, etc.: *a superhuman effort.*

superimpose /supərɪm'pouz/, v.t., **-posed, -posing. 1.** to place, or set on or over something else. **2.** to put or join as an addition (fol. by *on* or *upon*).

superintendent /supərɪn'tɛndənt, suprɪn-/, n. **1.** someone who supervises work, a business, establishment, institution, house, etc.; supervisor. **2.** a police officer ranking above chief inspector.

superior /sə'pɪəriə, su-/, adj. **1.** higher in position, rank, degree, or grade: *a superior officer.* **2.** of higher grade or quality: *superior intelligence.* **3.** greater in quantity or amount: *superior numbers.* **4.** showing a feeling of being better than others: *a superior manner.* **5.** not yielding or giving way (fol. by *to*): *to be superior to temptation.* ◇*n.* **6.** someone superior to another or others. **7.** *Church.* the head of a monastery, convent, etc. [ME, from L: above] —**superiority,** n.

Superior /sə'pɪəriə/, n. **Lake,** the northernmost of the Great Lakes, between the US and Canada; the largest body of fresh water in the world. About 644 km long; about 82 390 km^2; greatest depth 393 m; 184 m above sea-level.

superlative /su'pɜlətɪv/, adj. **1.** of the highest kind or order; supreme: *superlative wisdom.* **2.** being more than is proper or normal; exaggerated: *a superlative style of writing.* **3.** *Gram.* indicating the highest degree of the comparison of adjectives and adverbs, as English *smoothest* in contrast to *smooth* and *smoother.* ◇*n.* **4.** the highest degree. **5.** *Gram.* the superlative degree, or a form or word in this degree. [ME, from LL, from L: carried beyond]

superman /'supəmæn/, n., pl. **-men. 1.** a man seeming to have more than human powers. **2.** an ideal being, of superior strength, will, etc., thought of by the philosopher, Nietzsche, as the product of human evolution. [G]

supermarket /'supəmakət/, n. a large, usu. self-service, store selling food and other domestic goods.

supernatural /supə'nætʃrəl, -'nætʃərəl/, adj. **1.** being above or beyond what is natural;

supernatural

not able to be explained by known natural laws. **2.** greater than normal; extraordinary: *a man of supernatural intelligence.* ◇*n.* **3.** supernatural forces, effects, and beings collectively. **4.** a supernatural being.

supernumerary /supə'njumərəri/, *adj., n., pl.,* **-aries.** ◇*adj.* **1.** in addition to the usual, proper, or required number; extra. ◇*n.* **2.** a supernumerary person or thing. [LL: in excess]

superphosphate /supə'fɒsfeɪt/, *n.* an artificial fertiliser consisting of calcium sulfate and calcium dihydrogen phosphate.

superpose /supə'pouz/, *v.t.,* **-posed, -posing. 1.** to place above or upon something else. **2.** *Geom.* to place (one figure) in the space occupied by another, so that the two figures coincide throughout their whole extent. [F] — **superposition,** *n.*

superpower /'supəpauə/, *n.* an extremely powerful and influential nation.

supersaturate /supə'sætʃəreɪt/, *v.t.,* **-rated, -rating.** to increase the concentration of (a solution) beyond saturation; saturate abnormally.

superscript /'supəskrɪpt/, *n.* a letter or symbol written after and slightly above a figure, letter or symbol: *i, j,* are superscripts in *b*^{ij}.

supersede /supə'sid/, *v.t.,* **-seded, seding. 1.** to replace in power, office, effectiveness, acceptance, use, etc.; supplant: *Electricity has superseded gas as a means of lighting.* **2.** to set aside as useless or out of date. [L: sit above] — **supersession,** *n.*

supersonic /supə'sɒnɪk/, *adj.* **1.** greater than the velocity or frequency of sound; ultrasonic. **2.** (of velocities) above the velocity of sound in the medium.

superstition /supə'stɪʃən/, *n.* **1.** a belief or idea, not based on reason or knowledge, about the meaning or significance of a particular thing, happening, etc. **2.** any unthinkingly accepted belief or idea. **3.** a system or collection of superstitions and customs. [ME, from L: a standing over, as in wonder or awe] — **superstitious,** *adj.*

superstructure /'supəstrʌktʃə/, *n.* **1.** all of a structure above the basement or foundation. **2.** any structure built on something else. **3.** *Naut.* the parts of a ship built above the main deck.

supervene /supə'vin/, *v.i.,* **-vened, -vening.** to come or happen as something additional (sometimes fol. by *on* or *upon*). [L: follow] — **supervention,** *n.*

supervise /'supəvaɪz/, *v.t.,* **-vised, -vising.** to direct (a process, work, workers, students, etc.); have the direction of (a place, institution, etc.); oversee; superintend. [ML] — **supervision,** *n.* — **supervisor,** *n.* — **supervisory,** *adj.*

supine /'supaɪn/, *adj.* **1.** lying on the back, with the face or front upwards. **2.** inactive or passive, esp. from laziness or lack of interest. [L]

support

supper /'sʌpə/, *n.* **1.** a very light meal, as of a biscuit and a cup of tea taken at night. **2.** *Chiefly Brit and US.* the last main meal of the day, taken in the evening. **3.** any late evening meal, often one served at a social entertainment. [ME, from OF: SUP^1]

supplant /sə'plænt/, *v.t.* **1.** to take the place of (another thing or person); supersede. **2.** to replace (one thing) with something else. [ME, from L: trip up, overthrow]

supple /'sʌpəl/, *adj.,* **-pler, -plest. 1.** bending readily without breaking or suffering harm; pliant: *a supple rod; a supple body.* **2.** marked by ease in bending; lithe: *supple movements.* **3.** adapting or yielding easily: *a supple mind.* [ME, from OF, from L: bending under]

supplement /'sʌpləmənt/, *n.;* /'sʌpləment/, *v.* ◇*n.* **1.** something added to extend a thing, supply a lack, or correct mistakes, etc.: *a supplement to a book.* **2.** a special feature of a newspaper, etc., put out as an additional part: *an educational supplement.* **3.** *Maths.* the quantity by which an angle or an arc falls short of 180° or a semicircle. ◇*v.t.* **4.** to add to, or extend by a supplement; form a supplement or addition to. [ME, from L] — **supplementation,** *n.* — **supplementary,** *adj.*

supplementary angle /sʌplə,mentri 'æŋgəl/, *n.* either of two angles whose sum is 180°.

suppliant /'sʌpliənt/, *n.* **1.** someone who supplicates. ◇*adj.* **2.** supplicating. Also, **supplicant.** [ME, from F, from L: supplicate]

supplicate /'sʌpləkeɪt/, *v.,* **-cated, -cating.** ◇*v.i.* **1.** to pray or ask humbly. ◇*v.t.* **2.** to pray humbly to; entreat. **3.** to ask for humbly. [late ME, from L: begged] — **supplication,** *n.* — **supplicatory,** *adj.*

supply /sə'plaɪ/, *v.,* **-plied, -plying,** *n., pl.* **-plies.** ◇*v.t.* **1.** to provide (a person, place, etc.) with what is lacking or needed: *to supply a community with electricity.* **2.** to provide (something wanted or needed): *to supply electricity to a community.* **3.** to make up for (a loss, lack, absence, etc.); satisfy (a need, demand, etc.). ◇*v.i.* **4.** to fill the place of another; serve as a substitute. ◇*n.* **5.** the act of supplying. **6.** a quantity of something provided or on hand, as for use; stock or store. **7.** (*usu. pl.*) a provision, stock, or store. **8.** money granted by parliament for the expenses of government. **9.** *Econ.* the quantity of a commodity, etc., that is in the market and available for buying, or for buying at a particular price. **10.** *Elect.* a source of electrical energy. **11.** (*pl.*) *Mil.* articles and materials used by an army or navy, such as food, clothing, equipment, and fuel. [ME, from OF, from L: fill up] — **supplier,** *n.*

Supply /sə'plaɪ/, *n.* the ship on which Captain Arthur Phillip arrived at Botany Bay in 1788, as part of the First Fleet; later used for shipping cattle to the colony.

support /sə'pɔt/, *v.t.* **1.** to bear or hold up (a weight, load, structure, part, etc.). **2.** to bear, esp. with patience or humility; endure; tolerate. **3.** to give help, strength, courage, etc., to: *His kindness supported her in her grief.* **4.** to supply (a person, family, establishment, etc.) with things necessary to existence; provide for. **5.** to help to show the truth or validity of (a statement, argument, etc.). **6.** to act in a secondary part with (a leading actor). **7.** to form a secondary part of a program with: *The main film will be supported by two documentaries.* ◇*n.* **8.** the act of supporting. **9.** the state of being supported. **10.** the provision of necessities, money, etc., to a person, family, etc. **11.** a thing or a person that supports. **12.** the part of a structure that carries its weight. **13.** a device, usu. of elastic material, for holding up some part of the body. **14.** an actor or actress, who play secondary roles. [ME, from OF: bear, from L: convey] —**supporter,** *n.* —**supportive,** *adj.*

suppose /sə'pouz/, *v.*, **-posed, -posing.** ◇*v.t.* **1.** to take as a fact, for the sake of argument, etc.: *suppose the distance to be one kilometre.* **2.** to consider as a possibility or idea suggested: *suppose we wait till tomorrow.* **3.** to think or believe, in the absence of positive knowledge: *I supposed that it was an accident; What do you suppose he will do?* **4.** → **presuppose. 5.** to expect (*used in the passive*): *You are supposed to be at work on time.* [ME, from OF] —**supposable,** *adj.* —**supposer,** *n.*

supposed /sə'pouzd/, *adj.* **1.** accepted as true, without positive knowledge: *the supposed site of an ancient temple.* **2.** only thought to be such: *to sacrifice real for supposed gains.*

supposing /sə'pouzɪŋ/, *conj.* in the event that; if.

supposition /sʌpə'zɪʃən/, *n.* **1.** the act of supposing. **2.** something which is supposed; an assumption. [late ME, from ML, used as translation of Gk: HYPOTHESIS] —**suppositional, suppositive,** *adj.*

suppository /sə'pɒzətri/, *n., pl.* **-ries.** a solid medicinal substance put into the rectum or vagina where it dissolves. [LL, from L: placed under]

suppress /sə'prɛs/, *v.t.* **1.** to put an end to the activities of (a person, group of people, etc.). **2.** to put an end to (a practice, etc.), abolish; prohibit. **3.** to keep in or repress (a feeling, smile, groan, etc.). **4.** to keep (truth, evidence, a book, names, etc.) from being known or published. **5.** to stop (a flow of blood, etc.). **6.** to put an end to (a revolt, etc.) by force; quell; subdue. [ME, from L: put down] —**suppression,** *n.* —**suppressor,** *n.* —**suppressive,** *adj.*

suppurate /'sʌpjəreɪt/, *v.i.*, **-rated, -rating.** (of a wound, etc.) to produce or discharge pus. [L: caused to secrete pus] —**suppuration,** *n.* —**suppurative,** *adj.*

supremacy /sə'prɛməsi, su-/, *n.* **1.** the state of being supreme. **2.** supreme authority or power.

supreme /su'prim, sə-/, *adj.* **1.** highest in rank or power: *the supreme commander.* **2.** of the highest quality, character, etc.: *supreme courage.* **3.** greatest, or extreme: *supreme disgust.* **4.** last (with reference to the end of life): *the supreme moment.* [L: that is above]

Supreme Court, *n.* the highest State court.

Supreme Soviet, *n.* formerly, the supreme legislative body of the Soviet Union, consisting of two houses, one house representative on the basis of population, the other assuring every nationality, however small, some representation.

Supt, *Abbrev.* superintendent. Also, **supt**

sur-, a prefix meaning 'above', 'over', as in *surcharge, surmount,* or having a figurative meaning, as in *survive, surname.* [late ME, from F, from L *super-* SUPER-]

Surabaya /suərə'baɪə/, *n.* a seaport in north-eastern Java; second largest city of Indonesia. Pop. 2 289 000 (1983 est.).

surcharge /'sɜtʃadʒ/, *n.*; /'sɜtʃadʒ, sɜ'tʃadʒ/, *v.*, **-charged, -charging.** **1.** an additional charge for payment, tax, etc. **2.** an excessive sum or price charged. **3.** *Philately.* a mark printed over a stamp which alters or restates its face value. ◇*v.t.* **4.** to charge an additional sum (for payment). **5.** to overcharge. **6.** to overload. [ME, from OF]

surcingle /'sɜsɪŋgəl/, *n.* a band going around the body of a horse or other animal, esp. to keep in place a blanket, pack, etc.; girth. [ME, from OF]

surd /sɜd/, *n. Maths.* a quantity not able to be expressed in rational numbers, e.g. $\sqrt{3}$. [L: deaf, indistinct]

sure /ʃɔ/, *adj.*, **surer, surest,** *adv.* ◇*adj.* **1.** free from doubt as to the reliability, truth, character, action, etc., of something (oft. fol. by *of*): *I am sure of my facts.* **2.** confident, as of something expected: *sure of success.* **3.** absolutely certain; assured: *Man is sure of death.* **4.** worthy of confidence; reliable: *a sure messenger; a sure cure.* **5.** firm: *to stand on sure ground.* **6.** never missing, slipping, etc.: *a sure aim.* **7.** certain or bound (to do, happen, etc.): *He is sure to come soon.* **8. be sure,** be certain or careful (to do or be as stated): *Be sure to close the windows.* **9. for sure,** as a certainty; surely. **10. make sure, a.** to be certain (that something is done): *Make sure that you close the windows.* **b.** to be confident in the support or possession (*of*): *I have made sure of his friendship.* **11. to be sure,** surely; certainly. ◇*adv.* **12.** *Colloq.* surely, certainly. [ME, from OF, from L: secure]

surely /'ʃɔli/, *adv.* **1.** firmly; unerringly; without missing, slipping, etc. **2.** undoubtedly, or certainly. **3.** (to give emphasis to statements, etc., that are not necessarily supported by fact) assuredly: *Surely you are mistaken.* **4.** without fail; inevitably: *Slowly but surely the end approached.*

surety /'ʃɔti, 'ʃuəti/, *n., pl.* **-ties.** **1.** security against loss, damage, non-fulfilment of an obligation, non-payment of a debt, etc.; bond. **2.** a certainty. **3.** something which gives confidence or safety. **4.** someone who is legally answerable for the debt, etc., of another. [ME, from OF, from L]

surf /sɜf/, *n.* **1.** foamy water caused by the breaking of the sea upon a shore, etc. ◇*v.i.* **2.** to engage in surfing. [earlier *suff,* ? var. of SOUGH] —**surfy,** *adj.*

surface /'sɜfəs/, *n., adj., v.,* **-faced, -facing.** ◇*n.* **1.** the outer face, or outside, of a thing. **2.** the area of such a face. **3.** any face or side of a thing: *the six surfaces of a cube.* **4.** outward appearance, esp. as opposed to inner nature: *to look below the surface of a matter.* **5.** *Geom.* any figure having only two dimensions; part or all of the boundary of a solid. ◇*adj.* **6.** of, on, or relating to the surface. **7.** apparent, rather than real; superficial. **8.** of, on, or relating to land or sea: *surface travel; surface mail.* ◇*v.t.* **9.** to give a particular kind of surface to; make even or smooth. ◇*v.i.* **10.** to rise to the surface. **11.** *Colloq.* to appear in public, as by arriving at one's job, rising from sleep, etc. [F]

surface structure, *n. Gram.* See **transformational grammar.**

surface tension, *n.* the elastic film-like nature of a liquid surface due to the attraction between molecules.

surfboard /'sɜfbɔd/, *n.* a long, narrow board, slightly rounded, used to ride waves towards the shore.

surf club, *n.* a group of lifesavers who are responsible for one particular beach, together with their organisation, equipment and clubhouse.

surfeit /'sɜfət/, *n.* **1.** too great an amount; excess. **2.** a disorder of the bodily system due to too much eating or drinking. **3.** disgust caused by too much of anything. ◇*v.t.* **4.** to supply with too much of anything; satiate. [ME, from OF: excess]

surfie /'sɜfi/, *n. Colloq.* someone whose main interest is surfboard riding.

surfing /'sɜfɪŋ/, *n.* **1.** Also, **surfboard riding.** a sport in which a person attempts to ride on or with a wave towards the shore, standing on a surfboard. **2.** Also, **body-surfing.** the sport of swimming in the surf, and esp. of riding waves, by allowing oneself to be carried along by the force of the water. **—surfer,** *n.*

surg., *Abbrev.* **1.** surgeon. **2.** surgery. **3.** surgical.

surge /sɜdʒ/, *n., v.,* **surged, surging.** ◇*n.* **1.** a strong forward or upward movement, like that of swelling or rolling waves: *the onward surge of an angry crowd.* **2.** a wave-like rush of something: *a surge of anger; a surge of energy.* **3.** the rolling swell of the sea. **4.** a large swelling or sudden wave. **5.** *Mech.* unevenness of action in an engine. ◇*v.i.* **6.** to rise and fall, or move along, on the waves: *The ship surged at anchor.* **7.** to rise or roll in waves, or like waves: *The crowd surged around the mounted policeman; Blood surged to his face.* [orig. uncert]

surgeon /'sɜdʒən/, *n.* a medical practitioner or physician qualified to practise surgery. [ME, from OF]

surgeonfish /'sɜdʒənfɪʃ/, *n., pl.* **-fishes,** (*esp. collectively*) **-fish.** a type of tropical coral-reef fish, with one or more spines near the base of the tail fin.

surgery /'sɜdʒəri/, *n., pl.* **-geries. 1.** the art, practice, or work of treating diseases, injuries, etc., by operations done with the hands or instrumental appliances, usu. including cutting into the body. **2.** the branch of medicine concerned with such treatment. **3.** an operation, etc., performed by a surgeon. **4.** a room or place for such operations. **5.** the room of a doctor, dentist, etc., which is visited for treatment by patients. [ME, from OF] **—surgical,** *adj.*

surly /'sɜli/, *adj.,* **-lier, -liest.** unfriendly and ill-tempered: *a surly voice; a surly expression.* [var. of obs. *sirly* lordly]

surmise /sə'maɪz/, *v.,* **-mised, -mising;** /sə'maɪz, 'sɜmaɪz/, *n.* ◇*v.i., v.t.* **1.** to think (something) without certain or strong evidence; conjecture; guess. ◇*n.* Also, **surmisal.** something surmised; a conjecture. **2.** the act of surmising. [ME from OF: accuse]

surmount /sə'maʊnt/, *v.t.* **1.** to mount upon; get on the top of: *The walkers surmounted the hill.* **2.** to get over or across (barriers, obstacles, problems, etc.); overcome. **3.** to be on top of or above: *a statue surmounting a pillar.* **4.** to furnish with something placed on top or above: *to surmount a tower with a spire.* [ME, from OF]

surname /'sɜneɪm/, *n.* the family name of a person, as distinguished from the given or first name. [ME, from F]

surpass /sə'pas/, *v.t.* **1.** to go beyond in amount, extent, or degree; exceed. **2.** to go beyond in quality or achievement; excel. **3.** to be beyond the range or capacity of; transcend: *Misery that surpasses description.* [F] **—surpassing,** *adj.*

surplice /'sɜpləs/, *n.* a loose-fitting, broad-sleeved, white outer garment, worn by certain clergymen and choir singers. [ME, from AF, from OF: over-fur (garment)] **—surpliced,** *adj.*

surplus /'sɜpləs/, *n.* **1.** a quantity which remains above what is used or needed. **2.** the amount of assets (of a business, etc.) above what is needed to meet liabilities. ◇*adj.* **3.** being a surplus; excess. [ME, from OF]

surprise /sə'praɪz/, *v.,* **-prised, -prising,** *n.* ◇*v.t.* **1.** to come upon suddenly and unexpectedly. **2.** to attack, or capture suddenly or without warning. **3.** to strike with a sudden feeling of wonder at something unexpected, extraordinary, etc. **4.** to lead or bring (a person, etc.) into doing something not intended, esp. by a surprise. ◇*n.* **5.** the act of surprising. **6.** a sudden attack, or capture. **7.** a sudden and unexpected event, action, gift, etc. **8.** the condition or feeling of being surprised. **9. take by surprise, a.** to come upon suddenly and unexpectedly. **b.** to cause to feel wonder; astonish. [late ME, from F: surprise] **—surprising,** *adj.*

surrealism /sə'rɪəlɪzəm/, *n.* a movement in literature and art from about 1919, based on the expression of imagination uncontrolled by reason, in order to suggest the activities of the subconscious mind. [F] **—surrealist,** *n., adj.* **—surrealistic, surreal,** *adj.*

surrender /sə'rendə/, *v.t.* **1.** to yield (something) to the possession or power of another: *to surrender weapons; to surrender office*. **2.** to give (oneself) up, esp. as a prisoner or to some emotion, course of action, etc. **3.** to give up (comfort, hope, etc.); relinquish. ◇*v.i.* **4.** to give oneself up, esp. as a prisoner or to an emotion, course of action, etc. ◇*n.* **5.** the act of surrendering. [late ME, from AF]

surreptitious /sʌrəp'tɪʃəs/, *adj.* **1.** obtained, done, made, etc., in a secret, stealthy way: *a surreptitious glance*. **2.** acting in a secret, stealthy way. [late ME, from L: snatched away secretly]

Surrey /'sʌri/, *n.* a county in south-eastern England. Pop. 1 011 400 (1986 est.); 1678 km^2. *Administrative Centre:* Kingston-upon-Thames.

surrogate /'sʌrəgət/, *n.* **1.** someone appointed to act for another; deputy. **2.** something that takes the place of another thing; a substitute. [L: put in another's place]

surround /sə'raʊnd/, *v.t.* **1.** to enclose on all sides; encompass. ◇*n.* **2.** a border which surrounds. **3.** (*pl.*) surroundings. [late ME, from AF, from LL: overflow]

surroundings /sə'raʊndɪŋz/, *n.* the circumstances, conditions, etc., surrounding a person, thing or place; environment.

surtax /'sɜːtæks/, *n.* **1.** one of a graded series of additional taxes placed on incomes over a certain amount. **2.** an additional tax on something already taxed.

surveillance /sɜː'veɪləns/, *n.* a watch kept over a person, etc., esp. a suspect, prisoner, etc. [F] —**surveillant**, *adj.*

survey /sɜː'veɪ, 'sɜːveɪ/, *v.*; /'sɜːveɪ/, *n.*, *pl.* **-veys**. ◇*v.t.* **1.** to take a general or overall view of. **2.** to view in detail, esp. in order to determine the overall situation, condition, value, etc., for official reasons. **3.** to determine the form, boundaries, position, extent, etc., of (an area of land) by measurements and the use of the principles of geometry and trigonometry. ◇*v.i.* **4.** to survey land, etc. ◇*n.* **5.** the act of surveying; an overall view. **6.** a formal or official examination of the particulars of something made in order to determine an overall situation, condition, character, etc. **7.** the act of surveying land. **8.** a plan or description resulting from this. [ME, from OF, from L] —**surveyor**, *n.*

survive /sə'vaɪv/, *v.*, **-vived**, **-viving**. ◇*v.i.* **1.** to remain alive or in existence after the death of someone, the ending of something, or the occurrence of some event: *Many were killed in the war, but a few survived*. ◇*v.t.* **2.** to continue to live or exist after the death, ending, or occurrence of; outlive: *Two people survived the accident*. [late ME, from AF] —**survivor**, *n.* —**survival**, *n.* —**surviving**, *adj.*

susceptible /sə'septəbəl/, *adj.* **1.** able to receive, or undergo, something (fol. by *of*): *susceptible of a high polish; susceptible of various interpretations*. **2.** easily affected by something; liable (fol. by *to*): *susceptible to disease; susceptible to flattery*. **3.** able to be affected easily by emotions; impressionable. [ML, from L: taken up] —**susceptibility**, *n.*

suspect /sə'spekt/, *v.*; /'sʌspekt/, *n.*, *adj.* ◇*v.t.* **1.** to think to be guilty, false, bad, etc., with little or no proof: *They suspected him of being a thief*. **2.** to think to be likely; surmise: *I suspect his knowledge did not amount to much*. ◇*n.* **3.** a person suspected, esp. of a crime, offence, etc. ◇*adj.* **4.** open to suspicion. [ME, from L]

suspend /sə'spend/, *v.t.* **1.** to hang by being joined to something above or to something that allows free movement, as a hinge. **2.** to keep from falling or sinking, as if by hanging: *solid particles suspended in a liquid*. **3.** to put off until a later time; defer or postpone, as sentence on a convicted person, judgment, etc. **4.** to cause to stop happening or being effective for a time: *to suspend payment; to suspend a rule*. **5.** to remove for a time from office, position, membership, etc.: *The headmaster suspended the pupil for bad behavior*. [ME, from L] —**suspensive**, **suspensory**, *adj.*

suspended animation, *n.* a temporary stopping of the vital functions of the body.

suspender /sə'spendə/, *n.* **1.** an elastic strap with fastenings to hold up women's stockings, joined to a belt, etc. **2.** (*pl.*) *US.* → **brace** (def. 7).

suspense /sə'spens/, *n.* **1.** a state of mental uncertainty, as in awaiting a decision or outcome, usu. with anxiety. **2.** a state of mental indecision. **3.** an undecided or doubtful condition: *For a few days matters hung in suspense*. [ME, from AF: in suspense, from L: suspended]

suspension /sə'spenʃən/, *n.* **1.** the act of suspending. **2.** the condition of being suspended. **3.** *Chem.* the state in which particles of a solid are mixed in a liquid but are undissolved. **4.** *Chem.* a substance in such a state. **5.** *Phys Chem.* a system consisting of small particles kept dispersed by shaking (in **mechanical suspension**), or by molecular motion in liquid (in **colloidal suspension**). **6.** something on or by which something else is hung. **7.** the arrangement of springs, etc., that support the body of a motor vehicle, railway carriage, etc., and protect it from shock from the movement of the wheels. **8.** *Music*. the continuing of a note in one chord into the following chord, usu. producing a temporary dissonance. [LL]

suspension bridge, *n.* a bridge in which the roadway is suspended from cables which are usu. hung between towers and fastened at each end.

suspicion /sə'spɪʃən/, *n.* **1.** the act of suspecting. **2.** the state of mind or feeling of someone who suspects. **3.** a condition of being suspected. **4.** a slight trace: *a suspicion of a smile*. [late ME, from L]

suspicious /sə'spɪʃəs/, *adj.* **1.** causing or exciting suspicion. **2.** tending to suspect, esp. evil, etc.; distrustful. **3.** feeling suspicion. **4.** expressing or showing suspicion.

Sussex /'sʌsəks/, *n.* a former county of south-eastern England, now divided into East Sussex and West Sussex.

sustain /sə'steɪn/, *v.t.* **1.** to hold up from below; bear the weight of; be the support of. **2.** to bear (a burden, charge, etc.). **3.** to undergo, experience, or suffer (injury, loss, etc.); endure without giving way. **4.** to keep up or keep going an action or process: *to sustain a conversation.* **5.** to supply (a person) with food and drink, or the necessities of life. **6.** to confirm or support; uphold. [ME, from OF, from L]

sustenance /'sʌstənəns/, *n.* **1.** the means of sustaining life; food; nourishment. **2.** money, a job, etc., that makes living possible.

Sutherland /'sʌðələnd/, *n.* **Dame Joan**, born 1926, Australian soprano opera singer and prima donna.

sutra /'sutrə/, *n.* (*also cap.*) a body of rules and teachings in Hindu and Buddhist literature.

suttee /sʌ'ti, 'sʌti/, *n.* **1.** a former Hindu custom in which a widow was burnt on the funeral pyre of her husband. **2.** the widow herself.

Sutton Hoo /sʌtn 'hu/, *n.* an archaeological site in Suffolk where an Anglo-Saxon ship and various precious ornaments, etc., were discovered.

suture /'sutʃə/, *n., v.,* **-tured, -turing.** ◇*n.* **1.** *Surg.* **a.** joining of the edges of a wound, etc., by stitching or some similar process. **b.** one of the stitches used. **2.** *Anat.* the line where two bones meet, esp. in the skull. ◇*v.t.* **3.** to join by or as if by a suture. [L]

Suva /'suvə/, *n.* a seaport in and the capital of Fiji, on Viti Levu island. Pop. 69 481 (1986).

Suvla Bay /ˌsuvlə 'beɪ/, *n.* a bay on the western coast of Gallipoli Peninsula in European Turkey; landing of Anzacs and battle, August 1915.

suzerain /'suzəreɪn/, *n.* **1.** a ruler or state having political control over a dependent state. ◇*adj.* **2.** of the quality of, or being, a suzerain. [F] **—suzerainty,** *n.*

svelte /svelt, sfelt/, *adj.* slender, esp. gracefully slender in figure; lithe. [F, from It: plucked]

SW, *Abbrev.* **1.** south-west(ern). See Appendix. **2.** short wave.

swab /swɒb/, *n., v.,* **swabbed, swabbing.** ◇*n.* **1.** a large mop used on ships for cleaning decks, etc. **2.** *Med, Vet Sci.* a piece of sponge, cloth, cottonwool, etc., often on a stick, for cleaning the mouth of a sick person or animal, or for putting in medicine, taking specimens of discharges and secretions, etc. **3.** the material collected with a swab. ◇*v.t.* **4.** to clean with or as if with a swab. **5.** to test (a racehorse) for possible drugging by taking a saliva sample with a swab. Also, **swob.**

swaddle /'swɒdl/, *v.,* **-dled, -dling,** *n.* ◇*v.t.* **1.** to bind (a new baby) with long, narrow strips of cloth to prevent free movement; wrap tightly with clothes. **2.** to wrap (anything) round with bandages. ◇*n.* **3.** a long, narrow strip of cloth used for swaddling or bandaging. [OE *swæthel* swaddling band]

swag /swæɡ/, *n., v.,* **swagged, swagging.** ◇*n.* **1.** Also, **shiralee, bluey.** a bundle or roll usu. carried across the shoulders, and containing the personal belongings of a swagman, miner, etc. **2.** *Colloq.* an unnamed but large number or quantity: *a swag of people.* ◇*v.i.* **3.** to travel about carrying a bundle of personal belongings. [Brit d.]

swagger /'swæɡə/, *v.i.* **1.** to walk with a vain and bold air; strut. **2.** to boast noisily. ◇*n.* **3.** a swaggering walk, bearing, or air; arrogant show of superiority.

swagman /'swæɡmən/, *n.* a man who travels about the country on foot with a swag on his back, living on his earnings from occasional jobs, or gifts of money or food. See **sundowner.**

Swahili /swɑ'hili/, *n., pl.* **-lis,** (*esp. collectively*) **-li. 1.** a member of a Bantu people with a large amount of Arab blood, who inhabit Zanzibar and the neighboring coast of Africa. **2.** their language, a lingua franca in eastern and central Africa. [Ar: coastal] **—Swahilian,** *adj.*

swain /sweɪn/, *n.* *Chiefly Poetic.* **1.** a country lad. **2.** a lover. [early ME, from Scand]

swallow¹ /'swɒloʊ/, *v.t.* **1.** to take (food) into the stomach through the throat or gullet. **2.** to take in so as to enclose; withdraw from sight; absorb; consume (oft. fol. by *up*): *Darkness swallowed the distant walkers; Household expenses swallow up most of our income.* **3.** *Colloq.* to accept without question or suspicion: *Don't swallow all you read in the papers.* **4.** to put up with: *to swallow an insult.* **5.** to take back (one's words, etc.); retract. ◇*v.i.* **6.** to perform the act of swallowing. ◇*n.* **7.** the act of swallowing. **8.** the quantity swallowed at one time; mouthful. [OE *swelgan*]

swallow² /'swɒloʊ/, *n.* a type of small, swift, migratory bird with long slender wings and a forked tail. [OE *swealwe*]

swallowtail /'swɒloʊteɪl/, *n.* **1.** a swallow's tail, or a deeply forked tail like that of a swallow. **2.** a type of butterfly with the back parts of the wings lengthened, so as to suggest the tail of a swallow.

swam /swæm/, *v.* past tense of **swim.**

swami /'swɑmi/, *n., pl.* **-mis.** a title for a Hindu religious teacher. [Hind: master, from Skt]

swamp /swɒmp/, *n.* **1.** an area of wet, spongy land; marsh. ◇*v.t.* **2.** to flood with water, etc. **3.** to flood over; cover; overwhelm: *to be swamped with work.* ◇*v.i.* **4.** (of a boat) to fill with water and sink. [ME] **—swampy,** *adj.*

swamphen /'swɒmphen/, *n.* a large black waterbird of the rail family, with a rich purple breast and bright red beak and shield, found in Australia and many other parts of the world.

swan /swɒn/, *n.* **1.** a large, grand-looking waterbird found in most parts of Australia

swan which has a long, slender neck: either the native **black swan**, known for its trumpet-like calls, or the white or **mute swan**, seen widely in lakes and rivers in parkland areas. **2.** a person or thing of unusual beauty, excellence, purity, etc. [ME and OE]

Swan /swɒn/, *n.* a river in south-western WA, on which Perth is situated; this name applies to the lower course of the river, 60 km from Upper Swan to its mouth at Fremantle; the upper course is called the **Avon**.

Swan Hill, *n.* a city in north-western Vic, on the Murray River; commercial centre for a productive irrigation district. Pop. 8831 (1986).

swank /swæŋk/, *Colloq.* ◇*n.* **1.** dashing smartness in bearing, appearance, etc.; style; swagger. ◇*v.i.* **2.** to show off. — **swanky**, *adj.*

Swan River Colony, *n.* the original official name for the colony founded in WA in 1829.

swan song, *n.* the last appearance, work, achievement, etc., of someone, esp. composer, writer, or actor, before retirement or death. [fabled last song of the dying swan]

swap /swɒp/, *v.*, **swapped**, **swapping**, *n.* ◇*v.t.* **1.** to exchange, barter, or trade: *I swapped my old car for some sound gear.* ◇*v.i.* **2.** to make an exchange. ◇*n.* **3.** an exchange. [ME]

sward /swɔd/, *n.* **1.** a grassy surface of land; turf. **2.** a stretch of grass. [ME; OE *sweard* skin]

swarm /swɔm/, *n.* **1.** a body of honeybees which emigrate from a hive and fly off together under the direction of a queen, to start a new colony. **2.** a great number of things or people, esp. in motion. ◇*v.i.* **3.** (of bees) to fly off together in a body from a hive to start a new colony. **4.** to move about, or occur, in great numbers: *The soldiers swarmed over the hill; Ants tend to swarm in this area.* **5.** to be covered or overrun; teem (fol. by *with*): *This place is swarming with tourists.* [ME; OE *swearm*]

swarthy /'swɔːði/, *adj.*, **-thier**, **-thiest**. (of a person's skin, complexion, etc.) dark-colored. [var. of *swarty*] — **swarthiness**, *n.*

swash /swɒʃ/, *n. Geog.* a channel of water through or behind a sandbank. [probably imitative]

swashbuckler /'swɒʃˌbʌklə/, *n.* a swaggering swordsman or bully. [*swash* (i.e., strike swords against shields) + BUCKLER] — **swashbuckling**, *adj.*, *n.*

swastika /'swɒstɪkə/, *n.* **1.** an ancient symbol or ornament in the form of a cross with arms of equal length, each continuing at right angles, and all pointing in the same direction, clockwise or anticlockwise. **2.** this figure adapted with clockwise arms as the official emblem of the Nazi Party and the Third Reich. [Skt: well-being]

swat /swɒt/, *v.*, **swatted**, **swatting**, *n.* *Colloq.* ◇*v.t.* **1.** to hit with a sharp blow. ◇*n.* **2.** a sharp blow. [orig. var. of SQUAT]

swathe[1] /sweɪð/, *v.*, **swathed**, **swathing**, *n.* ◇*v.t.* **1.** to wrap with bands of material: *to be swathed in bandages.* **2.** to enfold or envelop, as wrappings do. ◇*n.* **3.** a band of cloth in which something is wrapped. [ME; late OE *swathian*]

swathe[2] /sweɪð/, *n.* **1.** Also, **swath**. the space covered by the stroke of a scythe or the cut of a mowing machine. **2.** a strip or belt of anything: *to cut a swathe through the crowd.* [ME; OE *swæth*]

sway /sweɪ/, *v.i.* **1.** to move, usu. gently, from side to side. **2.** to move or incline to one side or in a particular direction. **3.** to incline in opinion, sympathy, tendency, etc.: *to sway towards radicalism.* ◇*v.t.* **4.** to cause to sway. **5.** to cause (the mind, etc., or a person) to turn in a particular way: *to sway the voters towards another point of view.* **6.** to cause to turn aside: *I swayed him from his idea.* ◇*n.* **7.** the act of swaying; a swaying movement. **8.** control; rule; dominion. [ME, from Scand]

Swaziland /'swɑːzɪlænd/, *n.* a kingdom in southern Africa, bordered by South Africa and Mozambique. Pop. 716 000 (1987); 17 364 km². *Languages:* English and Swazi. *Currency:* lilangeni. *Caps:* Mbabane (administrative), Lobamba (royal and legislative).

swear /sweə/, *v.*, **swore**, **sworn**, **swearing**. ◇*v.i.* **1.** to make a serious statement calling on God as a witness that what is done or said is right or true. **2.** to promise in a serious or formal manner; vow: *I swear to keep the secret.* **3.** to use (unacceptable) language often referring to God, sex, etc.; to curse or blaspheme. ◇*v.t.* **4.** to state or declare by swearing by a god, some sacred object, etc. **5.** to say with great emphasis. **6.** to promise; vow: *to swear allegiance.* **7.** to bind by an oath; administer an oath to (usu. fol. by *to*): *to swear someone to secrecy.* ◇*v.* **8. swear by, a.** to name (some sacred being or thing, etc.) as one's witness for an action or statement. **b.** to rely on; have confidence in. **9. swear in**, to admit to office or service by administering an oath. [OE *swerian*]

sweat /swɛt/, *v.*, **sweat** or **sweated**, **sweating**, *n.* ◇*v.i.* **1.** to give out salty, watery fluid through the pores of the skin, from heat, effort, etc.; perspire, esp. freely. **2.** to condense moisture on a surface. **3.** *Colloq.* to work hard. **4.** *Colloq.* to feel upset from worry, impatience, anger, etc. ◇*v.t.* **5.** to give out (any moisture) in drops or small particles. **6.** to get rid of with or by perspiration: *to sweat out an illness.* **7.** to cause (people, etc.) to work hard. ◇*v.* **8. sweat blood**, *Colloq.* to be under a strain, of worry or effort. **9. sweat it out**, *Colloq.* to hold out; endure until the end. ◇*n.* **10.** the process of sweating or perspiring, from heat, effort, worry, disease, etc. **11.** the fluid secreted by the sweat glands; the product of sweating. **12.** the condition or a period of sweating. **13.** moisture given out from something or gathered on a surface in drops. **14.** *Colloq.* a state of worry or impatience. **15.** *Colloq.* hard work. [OE *swǣtan*] — **sweaty**, *adj.*

sweater /'swɛtə/, *n.* a knitted jumper, usu. of wool.

sweatshop /'swɛtʃɒp/, *n.* a workshop, etc., employing workers at low wages during overlong hours, under bad conditions.

swede /swiːd/, *n.* a turnip with a large yellowish root. [MLG or MD]

Sweden /ˈswiːdn/, *n.* a kingdom in northwestern Europe, in the eastern part of the Scandinavian peninsula, bordered by Finland and Norway. Pop. 8 387 000 (1987 est.); 448 661 km^2. *Language:* Swedish. *Currency:* krona. *Cap.:* Stockholm. Swedish, **Sverige.** – **Swede,** *n.* – **Swedish,** *n., adj.*

sweep /swiːp/, *v.,* **swept, sweeping,** *n.* ◊*v.t.* **1.** to move (something) by pushing it with a broom or brush: *to sweep dust away.* **2.** to move (something) by or as if by a steady, driving stroke: *The wind sweeps the snow into drifts.* **3.** to pass or draw (something) over a surface with a continuous movement: *to sweep a brush over a table.* **4.** to clear or clean (a floor, room, chimney, etc.) of dirt, litter, etc., with a broom, etc. **5.** to clear (a surface, place, etc.) of something on or in it: *to sweep the sea of enemy ships.* **6.** to pass over (a surface, region, etc.) with a steady course: *Fire swept the countryside.* **7.** to win a great victory, as in an election: *The Labor Party swept the polls in the 1972 election.* ◊*v.i.* **8.** to clean a floor, room, etc., with a broom, or as a broom does. **9.** to move steadily and strongly or swiftly: *to sweep down on the enemy.* **10.** to pass in a swift but stately manner: *The procession swept by.* **11.** to move over a wide stretch: *His glance swept about the room.* **12.** to extend in a continuous stretch: *The mountains sweep down to the sea.* ◊*v.* **13. sweep under the carpet,** to refuse to consider (a problem, etc.). ◊*n.* **14.** an act of sweeping, esp. clearing, etc., by or as if by a broom: *to abolish all class distinctions at one sweep.* **15.** the steady, driving motion of something moving with force: *the sweep of the wind; the sweep of the waves.* **16.** a swinging or curving movement or stroke: *the sweep of the oars.* **17.** a continuous extent or stretch: *a broad sweep of sand.* **18.** someone who sweeps, esp. a chimneysweep. **19.** *Phys.* the motion of the spot across the screen of a cathode-ray tube. **20.** → **sweepstake. 21. make a clean sweep of,** to get rid of completely. [ME]

sweeping /ˈswiːpɪŋ/, *adj.* **1.** of wide range or scope; far-reaching: *sweeping reforms.* **2.** moving or passing about over a wide area: *a sweeping glance.* **3.** moving, driving, or passing steadily or forcibly on: *sweeping rain.* **4.** without limitations; disregarding details: *a sweeping statement.* **5.** decisive; overwhelming: *a sweeping victory.* ◊*n.* **6.** the act of someone that sweeps. **7.** (*pl.*) matter swept out or up, as dust, refuse, etc.: *Put the sweepings in this box.*

sweepstake /ˈswiːpsteɪk/, *n.* a type of lottery in which participants buy tickets giving them the chance of drawing the name of a competitor in a race or other contest, the outcome of the lottery depending on the result of the race. [SWEEP + STAKE^2]

sweet /swiːt/, *adj.* **1.** pleasing to the taste, esp. having the flavor characteristic of sugar, honey, etc. **2.** fresh; not stale. **3.** (of water) fresh as opposed to salt. **4.** pleasing to the ear: *sweet sounds.* **5.** of pleasing smell; fragrant. **6.** pleasing in any way; delightful: *a sweet person; a sweet face.* **7.** dear; beloved; precious. **8.** done well or without effort. **9.** (of soil) free from sourness or acidity. ◊*n.* **10.** something which is sweet. **11.** Also, **sweetie.** a pleasant tasting confection made mostly of sugar; a lolly. **12.** (*oft. pl.*) any sweet dish, such as a pudding, tart, etc., served at the end of a meal; dessert. **13.** a beloved person; darling; sweetheart: *my sweet.* [ME and OE *swēte*]

sweetbread /ˈswiːtbrɛd/, *n.* the pancreas or thymus gland of an animal, esp. a calf or a lamb, used for food.

sweeten /ˈswiːtn/, *v.t.* **1.** to make sweet. **2.** to make mild or kind; soften. **3.** to make (the breath, air, etc.) sweet or fresh, as with a mouthwash, spray, etc. ◊*v.i.* **4.** to become sweet. – **sweetener, sweetening,** *n.*

sweetheart /ˈswiːthɑːt/, *n.* **1.** one of a pair of lovers. **2.** a beloved person (often used as a form of affectionate address).

sweet pea, *n.* an annual climbing plant bearing sweet-scented flowers.

sweet potato, *n.* a tropical plant with a tuberous root which can be eaten as a vegetable.

swell /swɛl/, *v.,* **swelled, swollen** or **swelled, swelling,** *n., adj.* ◊*v.i.* **1.** to grow in size, by taking in water or air or by addition of material in growth. **2.** (of the sea) to rise in waves. **3.** (of tears, etc.) to rise or well up. **4.** (of a sail, sides of a cask, etc.) to bulge out. **5.** to grow in amount, degree, force: *The music swelled and then died away.* **6.** to become proud. ◊*v.t.* **7.** to make (someone or something) swell. ◊*n.* **8.** the act of swelling: *the swell of the waves.* **9.** increase in size, amount, degree, etc.; inflation. **10.** a part that bulges out. **11.** a wave, esp. when long and unbroken, or such waves together: *There is a big swell today.* **12.** *Music.* **a.** a gradual increase (crescendo) followed by a gradual decrease (diminuendo) in the loudness or force of a musical sound. **b.** the sign (< >) for indicating this. **13.** *Colloq.* **a.** a fashionably dressed person. **b.** a person of high social standing. ◊*adj.* **14.** *Colloq.* (of things) stylish; elegant; grand: *a swell hotel.* [ME; OE *swellan*]

swelling /ˈswɛlɪŋ/, *n.* **1.** the act of someone or something that swells. **2.** the condition of being swollen. **3.** a swollen part on a body; protuberance.

swelter /ˈswɛltə/, *v.t., v.i.* **1.** to (cause to) suffer badly from heat, esp. damp heat. ◊*n.* **2.** a sweltering condition. [OE *sweltan*] – **sweltering,** *adj.*

swept /swɛpt/, *v.* past tense and past participle of **sweep.**

swerve /swɜːv/, *v.,* **swerved, swerving,** *n.* ◊*v.t., v.i.* **1.** to (cause to) turn aside suddenly in movement or direction; deviate. ◊*n.* **2.** the act of swerving; a deviation. [ME; OE *sweorfan* rub, file]

swift /swɪft/, *adj.* **1.** moving with great speed; fleet; rapid: *a swift ship.* **2.** quick or prompt in action, etc.: *swift to act.* **3.** a fast-flying bird like a swallow, which migrates to Australia. **4.** any of various small lizards, which run swiftly. [ME and OE]

Swift /swɪft/, n. **Jonathan** (*Dean Swift*), 1667–1745, English satirist, born in Ireland; works include *Gulliver's Travels* (1726).

swill /swɪl/, n. **1.** liquid or partly liquid food for animals, esp. kitchen waste given to pigs. **2.** any liquid matter; slops. ◇*v.i.* **3.** to drink greedily or too much. ◇*v.t.* **4.** to drink (something) greedily or too much; guzzle. **5.** to wash or clean by flooding with water. [OE *swilian*; orig. unknown]

swim /swɪm/, v., **swam**, **swum**, **swimming**, n. ◇*v.i.* **1.** to move along or in water by movements of the limbs, fins, tail, etc. **2.** to float on the surface of water or other liquid. **3.** to move, glide, or go smoothly over a surface. **4.** to be sunk in, or flooded with, a liquid: *food swimming in gravy*. **5.** to be dizzy or giddy; seem to whirl: *My head is swimming*. ◇*v.t.* **6.** to move along, across, on or in by swimming: *I swam the river*. **7.** to perform (a particular stroke) in swimming: *to swim breaststroke*. ◇*n.* **8.** an act, instance, or period of swimming: *That was a great swim*. **9. in the swim**, involved in current affairs, social activities, etc. [OE *swimman*] —**swimmer**, n. —**swimming**, n., adj.

swimsuit /'swɪmsut/, n. a garment or garments worn for swimming.

Swinburne /'swɪnbən/, n. **Algernon Charles**, 1837–1909, English poet and critic.

swindle /'swɪndl/, v., **-dled**, **-dling**, n. ◇*v.t.* **1.** to cheat (a person) out of money, etc. **2.** to obtain by deceiving. ◇*n.* **3.** the act of swindling. **4.** anything that deceives; a fraud. [backformation from *swindler*] —**swindler**, n.

swine /swaɪn/, n., pl. **swine**. **1.** → **pig**. **2.** a coarse, gross person, who is concerned only with sensual needs. **3.** a bad, nasty person. [ME; OE *swīn*]

swing¹ /swɪŋ/, v., **swung**, **swinging**, n. ◇*v.t.* **1.** to cause to move to and fro; sway; oscillate: *ladies swinging their umbrellas*. **2.** to cause to move backwards and forwards, or in either direction, from a fixed point: *He swung open the door*. **3.** to move (something held) with a roundabout movement: *to swing a club around one's head*. **4.** to hang so as to move freely: *to swing a door*; *to swing a hammock*. **5.** to sway, influence, or control: *to swing the voters in an election*. ◇*v.i.* **6.** to move to and fro: *lamps swinging from the ceiling*. **7.** to move on a swing (def. 18) for amusement. **8.** to move in alternate directions, or in either direction, from a fixed point: *The door swung open*. **9.** to move quickly in a curve as if about a central point: *The car swung around the corner*. **10.** *Colloq.* to suffer death by hanging. **11.** to change or shift one's opinion, interest, etc.; fluctuate: *swinging voters*. ◇*n.* **12.** the act or way of swinging: *the swing of the pendulum*. **13.** the amount of such movement. **14.** a curving movement or course. **15.** a moving of the body with a free, swaying motion: *to walk with a swing*. **16.** a steady, marked rhythm or movement in verse or music. **17.** active operation: *to get into the swing of things*. **18.** a seat hung from a tree, etc., in which people sit and swing to and fro for amusement. **19.** the degree by which voters turn to or away from a political party: *a heavy swing to Labor*. **20. in full swing**, *Colloq.* fully active. [ME; OE *swingan*]

swing² /swɪŋ/, n., v., **swung**, **swinging**. ◇*n.* **1.** Also, **swing music**. a smooth, orchestral type of jazz popular in the 1930s, often arranged for big bands. ◇*v.i.* **2.** *Colloq.* to have a lively, modern attitude to life. [special use of SWING¹] —**swinger**, n.

swinging voter, n. a person who does not consistently support one political party.

swipe /swaɪp/, n., v., **swiped**, **swiping**. *Colloq.* ◇*n.* **1.** a sweeping stroke; a stroke with a full swing of the arms, as in cricket or golf. ◇*v.t.* **2.** to strike with a sweeping blow. **3.** to steal. ◇*v.i.* **4.** to make a sweeping stroke. [akin to SWEEP]

swirl /swɜl/, v.t., v.i. **1.** to (cause to) move about or along with a whirling motion; whirl; eddy. ◇*n.* **2.** a swirling movement; whirl; eddy. **3.** a curling piece of hair, etc. [? imitative] —**swirly**, adj.

swish /swɪʃ/, v.i. **1.** to move with or make a hissing sound: *The slender rod swished through the air*. **2.** to cause to move with a swishing movement or sound: *The horse swished its tail*. **3.** to bring, take, etc., with such a movement or sound: *to swish the tops off plants with a cane*. ◇*n.* **4.** a swishing movement or sound. **5.** a cane or rod for whipping, or a stroke with this. [imitative]

Swiss /swɪs/, adj. of or relating to Switzerland. [F *Suisse*, from MHG *Swîz*]

switch /swɪtʃ/, n. **1.** a thin, bendable cane or rod, etc., used esp. in whipping, beating, etc. **2.** the act of beating with a switch. **3.** *Elect.* a device for turning on or off an electric current. **4.** a turning, shifting, or changing: *a switch of votes to another candidate*. **5.** a tuft of hair at the end of the tail of some animals. **6.** → **switchboard** (def. 2). ◇*v.t.* **7.** to whip or beat lightly with a switch: *He switched the lad with a cane*. **8.** to move, swing, or whisk (a cane, fishing line, etc.). **9.** to change; shift. **10.** to turn or shift; divert: *to switch conversation from a painful subject*. ◇*v.i.* **11.** to strike with or as if with a switch. **12.** to change direction; turn, shift, or change. ◇*v.* **13. switch off / on**, **a.** to cause an electric current or appliance to stop / start. **b.** *Colloq.* to lose / gain interest. [cf. LG *swutsche*]

switchboard /'swɪtʃbɔd/, n. *Elect.* **1.** an apparatus with switches, instruments, and / or meters necessary for the control of electrical energy. **2.** an arrangement of switches, plugs, and jacks mounted on a board or frame used by an operator to connect telephone users.

Switzerland /'swɪtsələnd/, n. a federal republic in western central Europe, in the Alps and the Jura Mountains, bordered by Austria, Italy, Germany, Liechtenstein and France; present borders fixed by treaty in 1815 since when it has been internationally recognised as a neutral country. Pop. 6 586 000 (1987); 41 293 km². *Languages:* German, French, Italian, also Rhaeto-Romanic. *Currency:* Swiss franc. *Cap.:* Berne. German, **Schweiz**. French, **Suisse**. Italian, **Svizzera**.

swivel /'swɪvəl/, n., v., **-elled**, **-elling**. ◇*n.* **1.** a fastening device which allows the

swivel thing fastened to turn round freely upon it. ◇*v.t.* **2.** to turn on or as if on a swivel. **3.** to fasten by a swivel. ◇*v.i.* **4.** to turn on or as if on a swivel: *He swivelled around to have a look.* [ME, from Scand]

swollen /'swoulən/, *v.* past participle of **swell**.

swoon /swun/, *v.i.* **1.** to faint; lose consciousness. **2.** to be so enthusiastic that one faints or almost faints: *to swoon over a pop star.* ◇*n.* **3.** a faint or fainting fit; syncope. [OE *geswōgen* in a swoon]

swoop /swup/, *v.i.* **1.** to sweep down through the air, as a bird or a bat does, esp. in hunting. **2.** to come down in a sudden swift attack: *The enemy troops swooped down on the town.* ◇*n.* **3.** an act of swooping; sudden, swift descent. **4. at one fell swoop**, all at once. [OE *swāpan* sweep]

sword /sɔd/, *n.* **1.** a weapon in various forms, but typically with a long, straight or slightly curved sharp-edged blade, with one end pointed and the other fixed in a hilt or handle. **2.** this weapon as the symbol of military power, punishing justice, authority, etc. **3.** a cause of death or destruction. **4.** war, fighting, or killing; military force or power: *The Huns brought fire and sword.* **5. cross swords, a.** to join in fighting. **b.** to argue; disagree violently. **6. put to the sword**, to kill; slaughter; massacre. [ME; OE *sweord*]

swordfish /'sɔdfɪʃ/, *n.* a large marine sport fish with the upper jaw lengthened into a swordlike weapon.

swore /swɔ/, *v.* past tense of **swear**.

sworn /swɔn/, *v.* **1.** past participle of **swear**. ◇*adj.* **2.** having taken an oath; bound by or as if by an oath. **3.** determined; confirmed; avowed: *a sworn enemy*.

swot /swɒt/, *v.*, **swotted**, **swotting**, *n. Colloq.* ◇*v.i., v.t.* **1.** to study (a subject) hard. ◇*n.* **2.** someone who studies hard. [d. var. of SWEAT]

swum /swʌm/, *v.* past participle of **swim**.

swung /swʌŋ/, *v.* past tense and past participle of **swing**.

sy-, a variant of **syn-**, before *s* followed by a consonant, and before *z*, as in *systaltic*.

sybarite /'sɪbəraɪt/, *n.* someone devoted to luxury and pleasure; a voluptuary. [from *Sybaris*, an ancient Greek city in S Italy, destroyed 510 BC, famed for its wealth and luxury] —**sybaritic**, *adj.*

sycamore /'sɪkəmɔ/, *n.* **1.** (in Europe) a maple, grown as a shady ornamental tree and for its wood. **2.** a tree of Egypt and southwestern Asia, related to the common fig and bearing an edible fruit. [ME, from LL, from Gk]

sycophant /'sɪkəfənt, 'saɪ-, -fænt/, *n.* a self-seeking flatterer; a fawning, servile parasite. [from Gk: slanderer, false accuser] —**sychophancy**, *n.* —**sycophantic**, *adj.*

Sydney /'sɪdni/, *n.* a seaport in eastern Australia, the capital of NSW. Pop. 3 364 858 (1986). [named by Captain Arthur Phillip after 1st Viscount *Sydney*, Secretary for the Home Department at the time of the foundation of NSW]

Sydney blue gum, *n.* a tall forest gum tree found in coastal areas of NSW, with an attractive pale, smooth, straight trunk and useful timber.

Sydney Gazette, *n.* Australia's first newspaper, published between 1803–42; its full name was *The Sydney Gazette and New South Wales Advertiser*.

Sydney Harbor Bridge or **Sydney Harbour Bridge**, *n.* a bridge spanning Sydney harbor, officially opened in 1932; design and construction was carried out by the English firm Dorman Long and Co Ltd with JJC Bradfield as supervising engineer; one of Australia's main landmarks.

Sydney Morning Herald, *n.* the oldest surviving Australian newspaper, founded in Sydney, NSW, in 1831 as a weekly publication and becoming a daily in 1840; currently published by John Fairfax and Sons.

Sydney Opera House, *n.* an opera house designed by Danish architect, Joern Utzon, located on Bennelong Point, NSW; officially opened in 1973.

Sykes /saɪks/, *n.* **Roberta** (*'Bobbi'*), 1943, Australian writer and Aboriginal activist.

syl-, a variant of **syn-** before *l*.

syllabi /'sɪləbaɪ/, *n.* a plural of **syllabus**.

syllabic /sə'læbɪk/, *adj.* **1.** of, relating to, or consisting of a syllable or syllables. **2.** of or relating to poetry based on the number of syllables as distinct from poetry depending on stresses or quantities.

syllable /'sɪləbəl/, *n.* **1.** *Linguistics*. a segment of speech said with a single impulse of air-pressure from the lungs. For example, *wonderful* has three syllables. **2.** (in writing systems) a character or a set of characters representing (more or less exactly) such an element of speech. **3.** the least part or amount of speech or writing; the least mention: *Do not breathe a syllable of all this.* [ME, from AF, from L, from Gk]

syllabus /'sɪləbəs/, *n., pl.* **-buses**, **-bi** /-baɪ/. **1.** an outline or summary of a course of studies, lectures, etc. **2.** the subjects to be studied on a particular course, at a school, etc. **3.** a list: *the syllabus of errors.* [NL]

syllogism /'sɪlədʒɪzəm/, *n.* **1.** *Logic.* an argument with two premises and a conclusion. For example, *all men are mortal* (major premise), *Socrates is a man* (minor premise), therefore *Socrates is mortal* (conclusion). **2.** deductive reasoning. [L, from Gk] —**syllogistic**, *adj.*

sylph /sɪlf/, *n.* **1.** a slender, graceful, lightly moving woman or girl. **2.** one of a race of imaginary beings, supposed to live in the air. [NL]

sylvan /'sɪlvən/, *adj.* **1.** of, relating to, or living in forests. **2.** having many trees, like a forest. ◇*n.* **3.** a fabled god or spirit of the woods. Also, **silvan**. [L: forest]

sylvite /'sɪlvaɪt/, *n.* a common mineral, potassium chloride, KCl, in various colors, bitter in taste, and the most important source of potassium. Also, **sylvin, sylvine**.

sym-, a variant of **syn-**, before *b*, *p*, and *m*, as in *sympathy*.

symbiosis /sɪmbɪ'oʊsəs, -baɪ-/, *n.* the living together of two types of organisms (animals or plants), usu. where this is an advantage to both, as in the case of the fungus and alga which together make up the lichen; mutualism. [NL, from Gk] —**symbiotic**, *adj.*

symbol /'sɪmbəl/, *n.* **1.** something that stands for or represents something else, esp. a material thing representing something immaterial; emblem; token: *Black is a symbol of death; The dove is a symbol of peace.* **2.** a letter, figure, or other character or mark, or a combination of letters, etc., used to represent something: *the algebraic symbol, x; the chemical symbol, Au; the symbol for a diamond,* ◊. [LL, from Gk: mark, token, ticket] —**symbolic**, *adj.*

symbolic logic /sɪm,bɒlɪk 'lɒdʒɪk/, *n.* a system of logic that has been reduced to a set of precise rules, used in mathematical proofs and also in constructing digital computers.

symbolise *or* **symbolize** /'sɪmbəlaɪz/, *v.t.*, **-lised, -lising. 1.** to be a symbol of; stand for, or represent, as a symbol does. **2.** to represent by a symbol or symbols.

symbolism /'sɪmbəlɪzəm/, *n.* **1.** the practice of representing things by symbols, or of giving things a symbolic meaning. **2.** a set or system of symbols. **3.** symbolic meaning or character.

symbolist /'sɪmbəlɪst/, *n.* **1.** someone who uses symbols or symbolism. **2.** *Lit.* a writer or artist who seeks to express or suggest ideas, emotions, etc., by using symbols.

Syme /saɪm/, *n.* **David**, 1827–1908, newspaper proprietor and spokesman for tariff protection, born in Scotland; responsible for increasing the circulation and influence of the Melbourne *Age*.

symmetry /'sɪmətri/, *n., pl.* **-tries. 1.** the correspondence in size, shape and arrangement of parts on opposite sides of a plane, line or point, or around a central point of a circle or sphere. **2.** the proper relationship of the parts of a body or whole to one another with regard to size and form; good proportion. [LL, from Gk] —**symmetrical, symmetric**, *adj.*

sympathetic /sɪmpə'θɛtɪk/, *adj.* **1.** marked by or showing sympathy; compassionate. **2.** having a natural feeling for; congenial. **3.** agreeing with or liking something: *He is sympathetic to the project.* **4.** *Phys.* (of vibrations, sounds, etc.) produced by vibrations coming from a body already vibrating. See **resonance** (def. 3). —**sympathetically**, *adv.*

sympathise *or* **sympathize** /'sɪmpəθaɪz/, *v.i.*, **-thised, -thising. 1.** to share in a feeling, esp. of sorrow, etc., with someone. **2.** to express sympathy; condole (oft. fol. by *with*). **3.** to see the reason for; understand: *to sympathise with a person's aims.* [F: SYMPATHY]

sympathy /'sɪmpəθi/, *n., pl.* **-thies. 1.** a feeling shared between people. **2.** the shared feeling naturally existing between people of similar tastes or opinion, etc. **3.** the fact or power of entering into the feelings of another, esp. in sorrow or trouble; fellow feeling, compassion, or commiseration. **4.** favorable or approving agreement. [L, from Gk: feeling with another]

symphony /'sɪmfəni/, *n., pl.* **-nies. 1.** *Music.* an instrumental composition, usu. in several movements, similar in form to a sonata but written for full orchestra, and usu. grander and more varied. **2.** any rich combination of parts: *a symphony of colors.* **3.** *Archaic or Poetic.* the harmony of sounds. [ME, from L, from Gk: lit., a sounding together] —**symphonic**, *adj.*

symposium /sɪm'poʊziəm/, *n., pl.* **-siums, -sia** /-ziə/. **1.** a meeting or conference for discussion. **2.** a collection of opinions or articles by several people on a subject. **3.** (among the ancient Greeks) a meeting, usu. following a dinner, for drinking, conversation, and intellectual discussion. [L, from Gk]

symptom /'sɪmptəm/, *n.* **1.** any appearance or sign showing that something is happening; indication. **2.** *Med.* an outward appearance showing that disease is present: *The symptoms of flu are sore throat, runny nose, etc.* [LL, from Gk]

symptomatic /sɪmptə'mætɪk/, *adj.* **1.** relating to a symptom or symptoms. **2.** of the nature of or being a symptom; indicative: *It is symptomatic of flu that you get a runny nose.* **3.** according to symptoms: *a symptomatic classification of disease.* Also, **symptomatical**.

syn-, a prefix having the same function as **co-** (def. 1), as in *synthesis, synoptic.* Also, **sy-, syl-, sym-, sys-**. [Gk, combining form of *sýn*, prep., with, and adv., together]

synagogue /'sɪnəgɒg/, *n.* **1.** a Jewish house of worship, usu. also giving religious instruction. **2.** an assembly or congregation of the Jews for worship. [ME, from LL, from Gk: meeting, assembly] —**synagogical, synagogal**, *adj.*

synapse /'saɪnæps/, *n. Biol.* the region of contact between the processes of two or more nerve cells, across which an impulse passes. [Gk *sýnapsis* connection] —**synaptic**, *adj.*

synchromesh /'sɪŋkroʊmɛʃ/, *Motor Vehicles.* ◊*adj.* **1.** of, relating to or fitted with a system of small friction clutches, by means of which the speeds of the driven and driving gears in a gearbox are automatically synchronised before they engage, to help gear changing and reduce wear. ◊*n.* **2.** such a system. [SYNCHRO(NOUS) + MESH]

synchronise *or* **synchronize** /'sɪŋkrənaɪz/, *v.*, **-nised, -nising.** ◊*v.i.* **1.** to happen at the same time; coincide. **2.** to go on at the same rate or speed. ◊*v.t.* **3.** to cause (one clock, etc.) to show the same time as another. **4.** to cause to go on at the same rate. [Gk: be contemporary with] —**synchronisation**, *n.* —**synchronistic**, *adj.*

synchronous /'sɪŋkrənəs/, *adj.* **1.** happening at the same time; coinciding; simultaneous. **2.** going on at the same rate. **3.** *Phys, Elect, etc.* having the same frequency and no phase difference. [LL, from Gk]

synclinal /sɪŋ'klaɪnəl/, *adj.* **1.** sloping downwards from opposite directions, so as to meet in a common point or line. **2.** *Geol.* **a.** sloping upwards on both sides from a middle line or axis, as in a fold of rock strata. **b.** relating to such a fold. [Gk: lean together]

syncline /'sɪŋklaɪn/, *n. Geol.* a synclinal fold.

syncopate /'sɪŋkəpeɪt/, *v.t.*, **-pated, -pating.** *Music.* **1.** to place (the accents) on beats which are normally unaccented. **2.** to use syncopated accents in (a musical composition). [LL: cut short] **—syncopation,** *n.*

syncope /'sɪŋkəpi/, *n.* **1.** *Gram.* the shortening of a word by leaving out one or more sounds from the middle, as in the reduction of *never* to *ne'er*. **2.** *Med.* brief loss of consciousness; fainting. [ME, from L, from Gk: a cutting up] **—syncopic,** *adj.*

syndicalism /'sɪndɪkəˌlɪzəm/, *n.* a form of trade unionism, originating in France, which aims at controlling production and distribution, and ultimately society, by the federated bodies of industrial workers, using such means as general strikes, violence, etc. **—syndicalist,** *adj.*, *n.* **—syndicalistic,** *adj.*

syndicate /'sɪndɪkət/, *n.*; /'sɪndɪkeɪt/, *v.*, **-cated, -cating.** ◇*n.* **1.** a combination of people, such as business associates, commercial firms, etc., formed to carry out some project, esp. one needing a lot of capital. **2.** any agency which buys and supplies articles, stories, etc., for publication in a number of newspapers, etc., at the same time. ◇*v.t.* **3.** to combine into a syndicate. **4.** to publish in different newspapers at the same time. [F *syndicat*] **—syndication,** *n.*

syndrome /'sɪndroʊm/, *n.* a pattern of symptoms in a disease, condition, etc. [NL, from Gk: a running together] **—syndromic,** *adj.*

synergy /'sɪnədʒi/, *n.*, *pl.* **-gies.** **1.** combined action. **2.** the action of two or more bodily organs, etc., working together. **3.** Also, **synergism.** the action of two or more stimuli or drugs increasing each other's effect. [NL, from Gk] **—synergic, synergetic,** *adj.*

syngamy /'sɪŋgəmi/, *n.* (of plants and animals) the union of gametes, as in fertilisation or conjugation; sexual reproduction. **—syngamic,** *adj.* **—syngamous,** *adj.*

synod /'sɪnəd/, *n.* **1.** an assembly of church officials to discuss and decide church affairs. **2.** any council. [ME, from LL, from Gk: assembly] **—synodal,** *adj.*

synonym /'sɪnənɪm/, *n.* **1.** a word having the same, or nearly the same, meaning as another in the language, e.g. *joyful, elated, glad.* **2.** a word or expression accepted as another name for something, e.g. *Arcadia* for *pastoral simplicity*. [ME, from LL, from Gk: synonymous]

synonymous /sə'nɒnəməs/, *adj.* having the same meaning or quality as: *Eucalypt is synonymous with gumtree.* [ML, from Gk]

synopsis /sə'nɒpsɪs/, *n.*, *pl.* **-ses** /-siz/. **1.** a short statement giving a general view of some subject. **2.** a summary of headings or short paragraphs giving a view of the whole. **3.** the outline of the plot of a novel, play, film, etc. [LL, from Gk: general view]

synoptic /sə'nɒptɪk/, *adj.* **1.** relating to or forming a synopsis; taking a general view of the whole subject. **2.** (*oft. cap.*) taking a common view (applied to the first three Gospels, Matthew, Mark, and Luke, from their similarity in contents, order, and statement). **3.** (*oft. cap.*) relating to the synoptic Gospels. [NL, from Gk]

synoptic chart, *n.* a chart showing the distribution of meteorological conditions over a region at a given moment.

synovia /saɪ'noʊviə, sə-/, *n.* a lubricating liquid like the white of an egg, secreted by certain membranes, such as those of the joints. [SYN- + L *ovum* egg; NL coined by Paracelsus 1493?–1541, Swiss-German physician and alchemist] **—synovial,** *adj.*

syntax /'sɪntæks/, *n.* **1.** *Gram.* **a.** the patterns of formation of sentences and phrases from words in a particular language. **b.** the study and description of these. **2.** the rules governing the order or structure (as opposed to the meaning) of symbols or expressions used in a computer language. [LL, from Gk: arrangement] **—syntactic, syntactical,** *adj.*

synthesis /'sɪnθəsɪs/, *n.*, *pl.* **-ses** /-siz/. **1.** the grouping together of parts or elements, such as material substances or objects of thought, into a complex whole (opposed to *analysis*); combination. **2.** a complex whole made up of parts or elements combined. **3.** *Chem.* the forming or building up of a more complex compound by the combination of elements, simpler compounds, or radicals. [L, from Gk: lit., a taking together]

synthesise or **synthesize** /'sɪnθəsaɪz/, *v.t.*, **-sised, -sising.** **1.** to make up by combining parts or elements. **2.** to combine into a complex whole. **3.** to treat synthetically. **4.** *Chem.* to make (a complex product) by combining simple substances. **—synthesisation,** *n.*

synthesiser or **synthesizer** /'sɪnθəsaɪzə/, *n.* **1.** someone or something that synthesises. **2.** Also, **music synthesiser.** a machine which creates speech or music by combining the controlled outputs of a number of electronic circuits.

synthetic /sɪn'θɛtɪk/, *adj.* Also, **synthetical.** **1.** of or relating to synthesis (opposed to *analytic*). **2.** produced artificially; not of natural origin: *synthetic rubber; synthetic fibre.* ◇*n.* **3.** something made by a synthetic (chemical) process. [NL, from Gk] **—synthetically,** *adv.*

syphilis /'sɪfələs/, *n.* a chronic, infectious venereal disease, caused by a micro-organism and communicated by contact or heredity. [NL, from *Syphilus*, name of shepherd suffering

syphilis from the disease in L poem of 16thC by G Fracastoro] —**syphilitic**, *adj., n.*

syphon /ˈsaɪfən/, *n., v.t., v.i.* → **siphon**.

Syracuse /ˈsɪrəkjuːz/, *n.* **1.** a seaport in Italy, in south-eastern Sicily; the ancient city here was founded by the Carthaginians in 734 BC; battles 413 BC, 212 BC. Pop. 121 286 (1986 est.). Italian, **Siracusa**. **2.** a town in the US, in central New York State; university. Pop. 160 750 (1986 est.). —**Syracusan**, *n., adj.*

Syria /ˈsɪriə/, *n.* **1.** a republic in western Asia on the Mediterranean Sea. Pop. 10 969 000 (1987 est.); 185 180 km². *Languages:* Arabic, also Kurdish, Armenian, Turkish, Kabardian and Syriac. *Currency:* Syrian pound. *Cap.:* Damascus. Official name, **Syrian Arab Republic**. **2.** Biblical name, **Aram**. an ancient country in south-west Asia, including what is now Syria, Lebanon, Israel and adjacent areas; a part of the Roman Empire. —**Syrian**, *n., adj.*

syringe /səˈrɪndʒ, ˈsɪrɪndʒ/, *n., v.,* **-ringed, -ringing**. ◇*n.* **1.** *Med.* a small instrument consisting of a glass, metal, rubber, or plastic tube, with a narrow outlet, and either a piston or a rubber bulb for drawing in fluid and squirting it out, used for cleaning wounds, injecting fluids into the body, etc. **2.** any similar device for pumping and spraying liquids through a small opening. ◇*v.t.* **3.** to clean, wash, inject, etc., with a syringe. [from Gk: pipe]

syrup /ˈsɪrəp/, *n.* **1.** a sweet, sticky liquid, made of fruit juices, water, etc., boiled with sugar. **2.** → **molasses**. **3.** a thick sweet liquid for use in cooking, medicines, etc., prepared from molasses, glucose, etc., water, often with a flavoring: *chocolate syrup*. **4.** *Colloq.* sickly sweetness or sentimentality. [ME, from OF, from Ar: beverage] —**syrupy**, *adj.*

sys-, a variant of **syn-**, before *s*.

systaltic /sɪsˈtæltɪk/, *adj.* **1.** rhythmically contracting. **2.** of the nature of contraction. [LL, from Gk: contractile]

system /ˈsɪstəm/, *n.* **1.** a combination of things or parts forming a complex whole: *a mountain system; a railway system.* **2.** any set of correlated members: *a system of currency; a system of shorthand characters.* **3.** an ordered and wide grouping of facts, principles, doctrines, etc., in a particular field of knowledge or thought: *a system of philosophy.* **4.** an ordered body of methods; scheme or plan: *a system of marking, numbering, or measuring.* **5.** an orderly way of doing something: *to have system in one's work.* **6.** *Biol.* **a.** a grouping of parts of organs of the same or similar tissues, or with the same function: *the nervous system; the digestive system.* **b.** the entire human or animal body: *to get rid of poison from the system.* **7.** (*also pl.*) *Computers.* (in data-processing) the working together of personnel, procedure, hardware, and software. **8.** *Geol.* a major division of rocks comprising sedimentary deposits and igneous masses formed during a geological period. **9.** *Colloq.* society generally or an organisation within it: *to buck the system.* [LL, from Gk: organised whole]

systematic /sɪstəˈmætɪk/, *adj.* **1.** having, showing, or involving a system, method, or plan: *a systematic course of reading; systematic efforts.* **2.** arranged in or marking an ordered system: *systematic theology.* **3.** concerned with classification: *systematic botany.* Also, **systematical**.

systematise or **systematize** /ˈsɪstəmətaɪz/, *v.t.,* **-tised, -tising**. to arrange in or according to a system. Also, **systemise**. —**systematisation**, *n.*

systemic /sɪsˈtɛmɪk, sɪsˈtiːmɪk/, *adj.* **1.** of or relating to a system. **2.** *Physiol, Pathol.* **a.** relating to or affecting the whole bodily system. **b.** relating to a particular system of parts or organs of the body.

systems analysis, *n.* the analysis of an activity or project, usu. with the help of a computer, to find out its aims, methods and effectiveness. —**systems analyst**, *n.*

systole /ˈsɪstəli, ˈsɪstoʊl/, *n.* the normal rhythmical contraction of the heart. See **diastole**. [NL, from Gk: contraction] —**systolic**, *adj.*

Tt

T, t, *n., pl.* **T's** or **Ts, t's** or **ts**. **1.** the twentieth letter of the English alphabet. **2.** something shaped like the letter T. **3. to a T,** exactly.

t, *Symbol.* tonne.

t-, *Chem. Abbrev.* tertiary (def. 2a).

-t, a suffix forming the past tense or past participle of certain verbs; an equivalent of **-ed**.

t., *Abbrev.* **1.** temperature. **2.** time. **3.** transitive.

't, a shortened form of *it*, before or after a verb, as in *'twas, 'tis, do't, see't*.

T, *Abbrev.* **1.** Tenor. **2.** Tuesday. **3.** Tenor. ◇*Symbol.* **4.** *Physics.* absolute temperature. **5.** *Physics.* (surface) tension.

ta /tɑ/, *interj. Colloq.* thankyou. [shortened and altered form of *thankyou*]

Ta, *Chem. Symbol.* tantalum.

TAA /ti eɪ 'eɪ/, Trans-Australia Airlines; former name of **Australian Airlines**.

tab /tæb/, *n., v.,* **tabbed, tabbing**. ◇*n.* **1.** a small flap, strap, loop, etc., on a garment, etc. **2.** a tag or label. **3. keep tabs on,** *Colloq.* to keep account of or a check on: *Keep tabs on your expenses.* ◇*v.t.* **4.** to supply with a tab or tabs. [orig. uncert.]

tab., *Abbrev.* tablet.

TAB /tæb, ti eɪ 'bi/, *n.* a government-run betting shop. [*T*(*otalisator*) *A*(*gency*) *B*(*oard*)]

tabard /'tæbəd/, *n.* **1.** a loose outer garment with short sleeves, or without sleeves, worn by knights over their armor and usu. emblazoned with the arms of the bearer. **2.** the official garment of a herald emblazoned with the arms of his ruler. [ME, from OF]

tabasco /tə'bæskoʊ/, *n.* a tasty sauce used as a condiment, prepared from the fruit of a variety of capsicum. [named after *Tabasco*, state of Mexico]

tabby /'tæbi/, *n., pl.* **-bies,** *adj.* ◇*n.* **1.** a cat with a striped or brindled coat. **2.** a fabric with a stripe woven in; watered fabric. ◇*adj.* **3.** striped or brindled. [ME, from OF, from Ar: rich watered silk, from *'Attābīya* quarter of Baghdad where first made]

tabernacle /'tæbənækəl/, *n.* **1.** a tent used by the Jews as a portable sanctuary before their final settlement in Palestine. **2.** any place of worship, esp. one for a large congregation. **3.** *Church.* an ornamental container for the reserved Eucharist. [ME, from L: tent; booth]

tabi song /'tabi sɒŋ/, *n.* an Aboriginal solo song telling a story, performed at a corroborree.

tablature /'tæblətʃə/, *n. Music.* a system of writing music showing positions on the fingerboard of a stringed instrument, rather than the usual notes on the stave. [F, from It, from L: table]

table /'teɪbəl/, *n., v.,* **-bled, -bling**. ◇*n.* **1.** an article of furniture consisting of a flat top resting on legs or on a central pillar. **2.** food placed on a table to be eaten. **3.** the people at a table for a meal, game, or business: *The whole table laughed.* **4.** a flat surface; level area. **5.** *Archit.* a flat, vertical, usu. rectangular surface forming a distinct feature in a wall, often ornamental. **6.** (*pl.*) tablets on which certain laws were written in ancient times by the Romans, Hebrews, etc. **7.** an arrangement of words, numbers, or signs, e.g. the multiplication tables, to show a set of facts in a definite form; synopsis or scheme. **8. turn the tables,** to cause a complete reversal of circumstances. **9. under the table,** drunk so that one cannot stand up. ◇*v.t.* **10.** to enter in or form into a table or list. **11.** *Parl Proc.* to place (a proposal, resolution, etc.) on the table of an assembly for discussion. [ME; OE *tablu*, from L: board]

tableau /'tæbloʊ/, *n., pl.* **-leaux, -leaus**. a grouping of people to form a picture, or scene. [F: a table, picture]

tableland /'teɪbəllænd/, *n.* a high and generally level region of a wide area; plateau.

Table Mountain, *n.* a mountain in South Africa, near Cape Town. 1082 m.

tablespoon /'teɪbəlspun/, *n.* **1.** a spoon larger than a dessertspoon, used for serving food and as a standard measuring unit in recipes. **2.** a unit of capacity or volume, equal to three household teaspoons.

tablet /'tæblət/, *n.* **1.** a small, flat slab or surface, esp. one that can be carved or written on. **2.** a number of sheets of writing paper, etc., fastened together at the edge; pad. **3.** a small, flat or flattish piece of some solid substance, such as a drug, chemical, soap, etc. [ME, from F]

table tennis, *n.* a small-scale tennis game usu. played indoors on a table with small bats and a hollow plastic ball; ping-pong.

tabloid /'tæblɔɪd/, *n.* a newspaper, about one half the ordinary page size, emphasising pictures and short, rather than detailed, articles. [TABL(ET) + -OID]

taboo /tə'bu, tæ-/, *adj., n., pl.* **-boos,** *v.,* **-booed, -booing**. ◇*adj.* **1.** forbidden to general use; placed under a prohibition or ban. **2.** (among the Polynesians and other peoples of the southern Pacific) separated or set apart as sacred or unclean. ◇*n.* **3.** a prohibiting from use or practice. **4.** (among Polynesians, etc.) a system, practice, or act, whereby things are set apart as holy, forbidden to general use, or placed under a ban. ◇*v.t.* **5.** to put under a taboo; prohibit; forbid. Also, **tabu**. [Tongan *tabu*]

tabulate /'tæbjəleɪt/, *v.t.,* **-lated, -lating**. to put or form into a table, plan, etc. [L: boarded, planked] —**tabulation,** *n.* —**tabular,** *adj.*

tacho-, a word part meaning 'swift'. [Gk, combining form of *táchos* speed]

tachometer /tæˈkɒmətə/, *n.* an instrument for measuring the number of revolutions per minute made by a revolving shaft, as in a car. [TACHO- + -METER[1]]

tachy-, a word part meaning 'swift'. [Gk, combining form of *tachýs*]

tacit /ˈtæsɪt/, *adj.* not openly expressed, but understood; implied or inferred. [L]

taciturn /ˈtæsɪtɜːn/, *adj.* tending to remain silent; not inclined to conversation. [L] –**taciturnity**, *n.*

Tacitus /ˈtæsətəs/, *n.* **Publius Cornelius** /ˈpʊbliəs kəˈniliəs/, AD c. 55–c. 120, Roman historian, noted for his concise style. –**Tacitean**, *adj.*

tack[1] /tæk/, *n.* **1.** a short, sharp-pointed nail or pin, usu. with a flat, large head. **2.** a stitch, esp. a long stitch used in fastening seams, etc., before permanent sewing. **3.** the quality of being sticky. **4.** *Naut.* **a.** the direction or course of a ship in relation to the position of its sails. **b.** a course slanting against the wind. **c.** one of the series of straight runs which make up the zigzag course of a ship travelling to windward. **5.** a course of action or behavior, esp. one of an unusual nature. **6.** all the equipment for the saddling and harnessing of horses; saddlery. ◇*v.t.* **7.** to fasten by a tack or tacks: *to tack a rug to the floor.* **8.** to join by some slight or temporary fastening. **9.** to attach as something extra; append; annex (usu. fol. by *on* or *onto*). **10.** *Naut.* to change the course of (a ship) to the opposite course or direction. ◇*v.i.* **11.** *Naut.* to change the course of a ship by bringing its head into the wind, so changing its position relative to the set of its sails. **12.** to change one's course of action or behavior. [ME, from AF: a fastening, clasp, nail, from Gmc]

tack[2] /tæk/, *n. Colloq.* food; fare: *hard tack.* [orig. obscure]

tackle /ˈtækəl/, *n., v.,* **-led, -ling.** ◇*n.* **1.** apparatus or gear, esp. for fishing. **2.** a mechanism or apparatus, such as a rope and block or a combination of ropes and blocks, for lifting, lowering, moving objects or materials. **3.** *Naut.* the gear and rigging used in handling a ship, esp. that used in working the sails, etc. **4.** the act of tackling, as in football. ◇*v.t.* **5.** to undertake to deal with, master, solve, etc. **6.** *Soccer, Hockey, etc.* to (attempt to) get the ball from (an opponent). **7.** *Rugby, etc.* to seize and pull down (an opponent having the ball). [ME: gear, from MLG] –**tackler**, *n.*

tacky /ˈtæki/, *adj.,* **-ier, -iest.** sticky, as paint, etc., when partly dry.

taco /ˈtakoʊ, ˈtækoʊ/, *n.* a tortilla, usu. fried, and folded around a tasty filling. [Mex Sp]

tact /tækt/, *n.* a keen sense of what to say or do to avoid giving offence; skill in dealing with difficult or delicate situations. [L: sense of touch] –**tactful**, *adj.* –**tactless**, *adj.*

tactic /ˈtæktɪk/, *n.* a plan for gaining a desired end. [NL, from Gk: ordered] –**tactical**, *adj.*

tactics /ˈtæktɪks/, *n.pl.* **1.** (*treated as sing.*) the art or science of placing and moving military or naval forces for and during battle. **2.** such placements and movements; manoeuvres. **3.** a method for gaining advantage or success. –**tactician**, *n.*

tactile /ˈtæktaɪl/, *adj.* **1.** of or relating to the organs or sense of touch; endowed with the sense of touch. **2.** noticeable to the touch; tangible. [L: tangible] –**tactility**, *n.*

Tadzhikistan /tadˈzɪkəstan/, *n.* a republic in western Asia, north of Afghanistan; a member of the CIS; a constituent republic of the Soviet Union 1929–91, known as the **Tadzhik Soviet Socialist Republic.** Pop. 5 109 000 (1989 est.); 143 100 km². *Language:* Iranian dialects. *Cap.:* Dushanbe. Also, **Tajikistan.** –**Tadzhik**, *n., adj.*

tadpole /ˈtædpoʊl/, *n.* the larva or young form of frogs, toads, etc., which lives in water. [ME, from *tadde* TOAD + *pol* POLL (head)]

TAFE /teɪf/, *Abbrev.* Technical and Further Education.

taffeta /ˈtæfətə/, *n.* a shiny silk or rayon fabric of plain weave. [ME, from ML, from Pers: silken or linen cloth]

Taffy /ˈtæfi/, *n. Colloq.* a Welshman. [Welsh form of *Davy*, shortened form of *David*, proper name and name of patron saint of Wales]

Taft /tæft/, *n.* **William Howard**, 1857–1930, 27th president of the US 1909–13 and chief justice of the Supreme Court 1921–30.

tag[1] /tæg/, *n., v.,* **tagged, tagging.** ◇*n.* **1.** a piece or strip of strong paper, leather, etc., attached to something as a label. **2.** any small hanging or loosely joined part or piece. **3.** a point or binding of metal, plastic, or some other hard substance at the end of a cord, lace, etc. **4.** anything on the end of something else. **5.** a word or phrase used as typical of a person or group: *I hate the tag 'trendy' being used of my friends.* **6.** a matted lock of wool on a sheep. ◇*v.t.* **7.** to join a label or tag to. **8.** to apply a word or phrase to (a person or group), as a label: *They tagged us as being 'rude and noisy'.* **9.** *Colloq.* to follow closely. ◇*v.i.* **10.** to go along or about as a follower (usu. fol. by *along*). [ME]

tag[2] /tæg/, *n., v.,* **tagged, tagging.** ◇*n.* **1.** a children's game in which one player chases the others till he or she touches one of them, who then becomes the pursuer. ◇*v.t.* **2.** Also, **tig.** to touch in or as if in the game of tag.

Tagalog /təˈgalɒg/, *n., pl.* **-logs** or **-log.** **1.** one of a Philippine people, living mainly around Manila. ◇*adj.* **2.** of or relating to this people or their language.

Tahiti /taˈhiti/, *n.* the principal island of the Society Islands, in the southern Pacific. Pop. 95 604 (1977). *Cap.:* Papeete.

Taibei /taɪˈbeɪ/, *n.* the capital of Taiwan, in the northern part of the island. Pop. 2 507 620 (1986 est.). Japanese, **Taihoku.** Formerly, **Taipei.**

taiga /ˈtaɪgə/, *n. Geog.* the evergreen conifer forests which cover huge areas of subarctic lands in the Northern Hemisphere. See **tundra** and **steppe.** [Russ]

tail /teɪl/, *n.* **1.** the end part of an animal, esp. when forming a long, flexible, part attached to the main body. **2.** something like or suggesting this in shape or position: *the tail of a kite.* **3.** the end, bottom, or final part of anything: *the tail of a shirt; the tail of a coat.* **4.** the leftover or inferior part of anything. **5.** *Astron.* the shining stream of gas and dust particles extending from the head of a comet. **6.** *Colloq.* (*pl.*) the reverse of a coin (opposed to *head*). **7.** a downward stroke, usu. of a printed or written letter, the stem of a musical note, etc. **8.** (*pl.*) full-dress or formal wear for men. **9.** *Colloq.* the buttocks. **10.** *Colloq.* someone employed to follow or watch another. **11. turn tail**, to run away; flee. **12. with one's tail between one's legs**, in a state of complete defeat or shame. ◇*adj.* **13.** coming from behind: *a tail wind.* **14.** being at the back or rear: *a tail-light.* ◇*v.t.* **15.** to form or provide with a tail. **16.** to form or make up the tail or end of (a procession, etc.). **17.** to dock the tail of (lambs, etc.). **18.** *Colloq.* to follow in order to prevent escape or to watch: *to tail a suspect.* ◇*v.* **19. tail away/off**, to decrease gradually; decline. [OE]

tailgate /ˈteɪlɡeɪt/, *n.* the board at the back of a truck, wagon, etc., which can be removed or let down for ease in loading and unloading.

tailor /ˈteɪlə/, *n.* **1.** someone whose business it is to make or mend clothes, esp. men's suits. **2.** Also, **tailer, taylor.** an Australian sport fish (named because of the scissor-like meshing of its teeth). ◇*v.i.* **3.** to do the work of a tailor. ◇*v.t.* **4.** to make or sew (clothes). **5.** to fit or provide (someone) with clothing. **6.** to design for a particular need or taste: *to tailor prices for the market.* [ME, from OF: cutter] – **tailor-made**, *adj.*

tailplane /ˈteɪlpleɪn/, *n.* a horizontal surface at the rear of an aircraft for providing stability.

taint /teɪnt/, *n.* **1.** a touch of something unpleasant or harmful. **2.** a trace of infection, dishonour, etc. ◇*v.t.* **3.** to affect as if by a touch of something unpleasant or harmful. **4.** to make bad or evil; infect or corrupt. **5.** to spoil; tarnish. ◇*v.i.* **6.** to become tainted. [ME]

taipan /ˈtaɪpæn/, *n.* a long-fanged, highly poisonous snake of northern Australia and New Guinea, brown, with a long head and slender body, about two metres long. [Aboriginal]

Taipei /taɪˈpeɪ/, *n.* → **Taibei.**

Tait /teɪt/, *n.* **Sir Thomas**, 1864–1940, Australian commissioner of railways, born in Canada; introduced many improvements including the sliding-door cars known as 'Tait' cars to the Vic rail system.

Taiwan /taɪˈwɑn, -ˈwɒn/, *n.* an island separated from south-eastern China by the Formosa Strait; home of the Nationalist Chinese since 1949. Pop. 19 630 000 (1987); 36 002 km². *Cap.:* Taibei. Former name, **Formosa.** Also called **Nationalist China.**

Taiyuan /taɪjuˈɑn/, *n.* a walled city in northern China; capital of Shanxi province. Pop. 1 355 900 (1985 est.).

Taj Mahal /tɑʒ məˈhɑl, tɑdʒ/, *n.* a white marble mausoleum built at Agra, India, by the Mogul emperor Shah Jahan (fl. 1628–58) for his favorite wife. [Urdu, from Pers: crown of buildings]

take /teɪk/, *v.*, **took, taken, taking,** *n.* ◇*v.t.* **1.** to get (something) into one's hands, control, or possession (sometimes by force or trickery). **2.** to pick out from a number; choose: *We took the wrong road.* **3.** to receive (money) by way of payment or charge: *We took $500 at the cake stall.* **4.** to obtain by making payment; rent or buy: *to take a house in Paddington.* **5.** to get from a source; derive: *We take oil from olives; I take my name from my grandmother.* **6.** to receive by eating, drinking or breathing: *to take food; to take medicine.* **7.** to eat or use by habit: *Do you take sugar in tea?* **8.** to carry off or remove (fol. by *away*, etc.). **9.** to subtract; deduct: *to take 2 from 5.* **10.** to carry, convey, or transport: *take your lunch with you; I took him to the station.* **11.** to travel on: *to take a bus to the shops; take the new road west.* **12.** to lead or conduct: *Where will this road take me?* **13.** to (attempt to) get over, through, round, etc.: *The horse took the fence with an easy jump.* **14.** (of a disease, etc.) to attack or affect: *He was taken with a fit.* **15.** to receive or adopt (a person) into some particular relation: *to take a woman in marriage.* **16.** to proceed to occupy: *to take a seat.* **17.** to receive in a particular manner: *She took his remarks too personally.* **18.** to make use of (an opportunity, etc.). **19.** to have, experience, enjoy, etc.: *to take a bath.* **20.** to occupy, use up, or consume (space, material, time, etc.). **21.** to attract and hold (one's attention, eye, etc.). **22.** to assume or adopt: *to take the veil.* **23.** to write down (notes, a copy, etc.). **24.** to make (a picture or photograph). **25.** to make a picture or photograph of (a person or thing). **26.** to make or perform (a measurement, observation, etc.). **27.** to experience or feel (delight, pride, etc.). **28.** to form and hold in the mind: *to take a gloomy view.* **29.** to understand, regard, or consider: *He was taken to be wealthy.* **30.** to say and accept the obligation of (a vow, etc.). **31.** to claim or adopt as one's own: *to take the credit for something; I took his side in the argument.* **32.** to accept and act in accordance with (advice, etc.). **33.** to require: *It takes courage to do that.* **34.** *Cards, Chess, etc.* to capture or win (a trick, piece, etc.). **35.** *Gram.* to have or require by usage (a particular form, case, mood, etc.): *A noun following a preposition takes the objective case.* ◇*v.i.* **36.** (of a mechanical device) to catch or engage. **37.** (of a plant) to strike root, or begin to grow. **38.** (of ink, etc.) to stick; adhere. **39.** (of a medicine, etc.) to have the intended result or effect. **40.** to become: *He took ill suddenly.* ◇*v.* **41.** Some special uses are:

take aback, to surprise; disconcert.

take after, to be, look, or act like (one's parent, etc.).

take for, to believe (someone) to be, esp. mistakenly: *I took him for the postman.*

take for a ride, *Colloq.* to deceive; con.

take for granted, to accept or assume without question.

take in, 1. to provide lodging for. **2.** to change

(a garment, etc.) in order to make it smaller. **3.** to include; encompass. **4.** to understand. **5.** to deceive, trick, or cheat.
take it, 1. *Colloq.* to put up with pain, misfortune, etc., with strength. **2.** to react in a manner shown or described: *When I told him the news, he took it very badly.* **3.** to suppose; assume: *I take it from your silence that this is true.*
take it out on, to release one's anger, etc. on (another, uninvolved person).
take off, 1. to remove (a piece of clothing). **2.** to set off; leave. **3.** (of an aeroplane) to leave the ground. **4.** to become popular: *Surfing took off as a national sport.* **5.** to rise quickly; escalate: *Prices took off.* **6.** *Colloq.* to imitate; mimic.
take on, 1. to hire (a worker). **2.** to agree to do or handle. **3.** to get or acquire: *to take on a new aspect.* **4.** *Colloq.* to stand up to; oppose or quarrel with. **5.** *Colloq.* to become popular.
take out, 1. to remove; extract: *to take out a tooth.* **2.** to treat (someone) to dinner, a film, etc. **3.** to obtain; apply for and get: *to take out an insurance policy.* **4.** to release; vent: *to take out one's rage on the dog.*
take over, to get or seize control of.
take part, to be involved.
take to, 1. to devote or addict oneself to: *to take to drink.* **2.** to respond well to: *I did not take to the new boss.* **3.** to go to: *to take to bed.*
take up, 1. to lift; pick up. **2.** to begin or adopt the practice or study of: *to take up Greek; to take up tennis.* **3.** to occupy (time, space, etc.). **4.** to continue; resume: *to take up where we left off.*
take upon oneself, to assume the responsibility for.
take up with, to spend time or make friends with.
◇*n.* **42.** a quantity of anything taken at one time. **43.** *Films, etc.* (a part of) a scene shot at one time without any break. **44.** *Colloq.* a deception; swindle. [OE, from Scand]

takeover /'teɪkouvə/, *n.* **1.** the gaining of control of something, esp. of a business company, by buying more than half of its shares. **2.** the act of taking control over another country, usu. by force.

Takeshita /tæ'keʃtə/, *n.* **Noboru,** born 1924, Japanese statesman; prime minister 1987–89.

talc /tælk/, *n.* a soft greenish grey mineral, hydrous magnesium silicate, oily to the touch, and used in making talcum powder, electrical insulation, etc. Also, **talcum.** [ML, from Ar]

talcum powder /'tælkəm paʊdə/, *n.* powdered talc or soapstone, usu. perfumed for toilet use.

tale /teɪl/, *n.* **1.** a story about some real or imaginary event, happening, or case; narrative. **2.** a falsehood; lie. **3.** a rumor or piece of gossip, esp. when intended to be harmful. [OE: reckoning, speech]

talent /'tælənt/, *n.* **1.** a special natural ability; aptitude: *a talent for drawing.* **2.** capacity for achievement or success; natural ability: *young men of talent.* **3.** people of ability. **4.** an ancient unit of weight. **5.** *Colloq.* (at a party, dance, etc.) women or men viewed as possible sexual partners. [OE, from L, from Gk] —**talented,** *adj.*

tali-, a word part meaning 'ankle'. [L]

talisman /'tælɪzmən/, *n.*, *pl.* **-mans. 1.** any charm; amulet. **2.** anything of almost magic power. [Ar, from LGk: talisman, (earlier) religious rite, performance, completion]

talk /tɔk/, *v.i.* **1.** to perform the act of speaking. **2.** to make known or interchange ideas, information, etc., by means of spoken words. **3.** to consult; confer. **4.** to gossip. **5.** to chatter; prate. **6.** to reveal information: *to make a spy talk.* **7.** to communicate ideas by other means than speech, usu. by writing, signs, or signals. ◇*v.t.* **8.** to express in words; utter: *to talk sense.* **9.** to use as a spoken language; speak: *He can talk three languages.* **10.** to discuss: *to talk politics.* **11.** to persuade, bring, put, influence, etc., by talk: *to talk a person into buying something.* ◇*v.* **12.** Some special uses are:
talk (someone or something) down, 1. to override in an argument by speaking in a loud, continuous manner. **2.** *Aeron.* to radio landing instructions to (an aircraft or pilot) when landing is difficult.
talk down to, to speak to (someone) in a way which suggests that one is superior.
talk into, to persuade someone to take some course, esp. against his or her original intention.
talk out, to find a solution to (differences) by discussion.
talk over, to discuss.
talk round, 1. to discuss generally without coming to the main point. **2.** to persuade; bring around to one's own way of thinking.
◇*n.* **13.** the act of talking; speech; conversation, esp. of a familiar or informal kind. **14.** a lecture or informal speech. **15.** a conference. **16.** a report or rumor; gossip. **17.** a subject or an occasion of talking, esp. of gossip. **18.** mere empty speech. **19.** a way of talking: *baby talk.* [ME]

talkative /'tɔkətɪv/, *adj.* inclined to talk a great deal.

talkback /'tɔkbæk/, *n.* a radio program in which members of the public take part by telephone.

tall /tɔl/, *adj.* **1.** of more than average height: *tall grass.* **2.** having a particular height: *a man 1.9 metres tall.* **3.** *Colloq.* difficult to believe; extravagant: *a tall story.* **4.** *Colloq.* difficult to carry out: *a tall order.* [OE: prompt]

tallboy /'tɔlbɔɪ/, *n.* a tall chest of drawers supported on a low stand.

tallow /'tæloʊ/, *n.* the fatty tissue of animals, esp. sheep, cattle, etc., used to make candles, soap, etc. [ME] —**tallowy,** *adj.*

tallowwood /'tæloʊwʊd/, *n.* a large eucalypt tree, of NSW and Qld, growing in coastal forests and yielding a strong timber and nectar much prized by bee-keepers.

tally /'tæli/, *n.*, *pl.* **-lies,** *v.,* **-lied, lying.** ◇*n.* **1.** (formerly) a stick of wood with notches cut to show the amount of a debt or payment.

tally   1053   **tangible**

2. an account or reckoning; a record of debit and credit, of the score of a game, etc. **3.** the number or group of objects recorded, such as the number of sheep shorn in a given period. ◇*v.t.* **4.** to mark or enter on a tally; register; record. **5.** to count or reckon up. ◇*v.i.* **6.** to agree or accord: *Does his story tally with John's?* [ME, from AF, from L: rod]

Talmud /'tælmʊd/, *n.* the writings which form the basis of Jewish law and tradition. [Heb: study, instruction] **– Talmudic**, *adj.*

talon /'tælən/, *n.* a claw, esp. of birds which hunt smaller animals for food. [ME, from OF: heel, from L: talon]

Tamar /'teɪma/, *n.* a river in northern Tas, formed by the joining of the North and South Esk Rivers and flowing north to Bass Strait. 64 km.

tamarind /'tæmərənd/, *n.* the fruit of a large tropical tree, a pod containing seeds in a juicy acid pulp that is used in drinks and food. [ML, from Ar: date of India]

Tambo /'tæmboʊ/, *n.* **Oliver**, 1922–93, South African politician and anti-apartheid activist; president of the African National Congress 1967–91.

tambourine /tæmbə'rin/, *n.* a small hand-held drum consisting of a circular wooden frame with a skin stretched over it and several pairs of metal discs in the frame, played by hitting, shaking, etc. [F: little drum]

tame /teɪm/, *adj.*, **tamer, tamest**, *v.*, **tamed, taming**. ◇*adj.* **1.** changed from the wild state; domesticated: *a tame bear*. **2.** (of an animal) gentle, fearless, or without shyness. **3.** easily lead or controlled; tractable; docile; submissive. **4.** lacking in life or spirit; dull; insipid: *a tame existence*. ◇*v.t.* **5.** to make tame; domesticate; subdue. **6.** to take away courage, eagerness, or interest from. **7.** to soften; tone down. **8.** to bring under control or make manageable, esp. for domestic or human use: *to tame the natural resources of a country*. [OE] **– tameable, tamable**, *adj.* **– tameness**, *n.* **– tamer**, *n.*

Tamerlane /'tæmərleɪn/, *n.* (*Timour* or *Timur*), 1336?–1405, Mongol conqueror of most of southern and western Asia; ruler of Samarkand 1369–1405. Also, **Tamburlaine**.

Tamil /'tæməl/, *n.* **1.** one of a people living in southern India and Sri Lanka. **2.** their language, spoken chiefly to the south of Madras. ◇*adj.* **3.** of or relating to the Tamils or their language.

tammar /'tæmə/, *n.* See **wallaby**. [Aboriginal]

Tammuz /'tæmʊz, -ʊz/, *n.* a Babylonian god of the springtime and of vegetation, whose return to life from the underworld symbolised the rebirth of earth at spring. Also, **Thammuz**. [Heb]

tam-o'-shanter /tæm-ə-'ʃæntə/, *n.* a cap, of Scottish origin, with a flat top larger in diameter than the headband. Also, **tam, tammy**. [named after *Tam O'Shanter*, the hero of a poem by Robert BURNS]

tamper /'tæmpə/, *v.i.* to meddle, esp. in order to change, damage, misuse, wrongly influence, etc. (fol. by *with*): *to tamper with a lock*; *to tamper with a witness*. **– tamperer**, *n.*

tampon /'tæmpɒn/, *n.* **1.** a plug of cotton, put into an opening, wound, etc., to stop severe bleeding. **2.** a similar device used inside the vagina to absorb menstrual flow. ◇*v.t.* **3.** to fill or plug with a tampon. [F]

Tamworth /'tæmwəθ, -wɜθ/, *n.* a city in north-eastern NSW, on the Peel River; centre for an extensive rural district. Pop. 30 729 (1986).

tan[1] /tæn/, *v.*, **tanned, tanning**, *n.*, *adj.* ◇*v.t.* **1.** to change (a hide) into leather, esp. by soaking in a bath prepared from wattle bark, etc., or synthetically. **2.** to make brown by exposure to ultraviolet rays, esp. of the sun. **3.** *Colloq.* to beat or thrash: *I'll tan your hide!* ◇*v.i.* **4.** to become tanned: *She tans easily.* ◇*n.* **5.** the brown color given to the skin by exposure to the sun; suntan. **6.** a yellowish brown color. ◇*adj.* **7.** of the color of tan; yellowish brown. **8.** used in or relating to tanning processes, materials, etc. [OE, from ML] **– tanner**, *n.*

tan[2] /tæn/, *n. Maths.* a trigonometric function, defined for an acute angle in a right-angled triangle as the ratio of the opposite side to the adjacent side. Also, **tangent**. [abbrev.]

tanbark /'tænbak/, *n.* **1.** bark used in tanning hide. **2.** such bark broken up in chips and used as a ground-cover, usu. in playgrounds, landscape gardening, etc.

tandem /'tændəm/, *adv.* **1.** one behind another; in single file: *to drive horses tandem*. ◇*adj.* **2.** having animals, seats, parts, etc., arranged tandem, or one behind another: *a tandem bicycle*. ◇*n.* **3.** a bicycle for two riders, having twin seats, pedals, etc. **4.** a team of horses harnessed in tandem. [L: at length (in time), probably at first humorously used]

tang /tæŋ/, *n.* **1.** a strong taste or flavor. **2.** the characteristic flavor or quality of a thing. **3.** a strong, biting or characteristic smell. **4.** a smack, touch, or suggestion of something. [ME, from Scand] **– tangy**, *adj.*

Tang /tʌŋ/, *n.* a Chinese dynasty, AD 618–907, noted for territorial expansion (esp. cultural contact with central Asia), first development of printing, the political as well as religious importance of Buddhism, and the highest development of Chinese poetry.

tangent /'tændʒənt/, *adj.* **1.** touching. **2.** *Geom.* touching, esp. of a straight line in relation to a curve or surface. **3.** *Geom.* in contact along a single line or element, such as a plane with a cylinder. ◇*n.* **4.** *Geom.* a tangent line or plane. **5.** *Maths.* → **tan**[2]. **6.** a sudden new direction: *to fly off at a tangent*. [L: touching] **– tangency**, *n.* **– tangential**, *adj.*

tangerine /tændʒə'rin/, *n.* **1.** a small, loose-skinned type of mandarin. See **mandarin** (def. 4). **2.** a deep reddish orange color. [TANGIER + -INE[1]]

tangible /'tændʒəbəl/, *adj.* **1.** able to be touched or felt by touch; material; substantial. **2.** real or actual, rather than imaginary. **3.**

tangible definite; not vague: *no tangible grounds for suspicion.* [L]

Tangier /tæn'dʒɪə/, *n.* a seaport in northern Morocco, near the Strait of Gibraltar. Pop. 266 346 (1982). Also, **Tangiers**.

tangle /'tæŋgəl/, *v.*, **-gled, -gling**, *n.* ◇*v.t.* **1.** to bring together into a mass of confusedly interlaced or intertwisted threads, strands, etc.; snarl. **2.** to catch and hold in, or as if in, a net or snare. ◇*v.i.* **3.** to become tangled. **4.** *Colloq.* to conflict, quarrel, or argue (usu. fol. by *with*). ◇*n.* **5.** a tangled or confused mass or gathering of something. [ME: entangle, from Scand] **—tangler**, *n.*

tango /'tæŋgoʊ/, *n.*, *pl.* **-gos**, *v.*, **-goed, -going**. ◇*n.* **1.** a ballroom dance of Spanish-American origin. **2.** the music for this dance. ◇*v.i.* **3.** to dance the tango. [Amer Sp]

tank /tæŋk/, *n.* **1.** a large container or structure for holding water or other liquid or gas: *tanks for storing oil.* **2.** an artificial pond formed by building walls of earth either dug up from or carried to the site. **3.** *Mil.* an armored, self-propelled fighting vehicle, armed with cannon and machine-guns and moving on endless tracks. [? Indian: pool]

tankard /'tæŋkəd/, *n.* a large drinking cup, now usu. with a handle and (sometimes) a hinged cover. [ME]

tanker /'tæŋkə/, *n.* a ship, aircraft, or road or rail vehicle designed to carry oil or other liquid in bulk.

Tank Stream, *n.* the name given to a small stream and several storage tanks bearing the main water supply for the first settlers at Sydney Cove, NSW.

tannin /'tænən/, *n.* any of a group of harsh and bitter vegetable substances, such as that which gives the tanning properties to wattle bark, or that which in grape skins, stalks and seeds gives a characteristic tannin taste to some wines. [ML]

tantalise *or* **tantalize** /'tæntəlaɪz/, *v.t.*, **-lised, -lising**. to torment, tease or disappoint with, or as if with, the sight of something desired but out of reach. [from TANTALUS]

tantalum /'tæntələm/, *n.* a rare hard, greyish-white element used in chemical manufacturing equipment because of its resistance to strong acids. *Symbol:* Ta; *at. no.:* 73; *at. wt:* 780.948. [NL]

Tantalus /'tæntələs/, *n. Gk Myth.* a son of Zeus and the nymph Pluto, who for revealing secrets of the gods, was condemned to stand, hungry and thirsty, in water up to his chin, under a tree laden with fruit.

tantamount /'tæntəmaʊnt/, *adj.* equivalent, usu. in value, force, effect, or meaning. [F]

Tantra /'tæntrə, 'tʌn-/, *n.* **1.** *Hinduism.* one of several books in dialogue form setting out the requirements of ritual, discipline, etc. **2.** one of a similar series of Buddhist devotional books. [Skt: loom]

tantrum /'tæntrəm/, *n.* a sudden burst of ill humor; fit of ill temper or passion. [orig. uncert.]

Tanzania /tænzə'nɪə/, *n.* a republic in eastern Africa, consisting of Tanganyika on the mainland and the islands of Zanzibar and Pemba; formed in 1964 by the union of the independent states Tanganyika and Zanzibar. Pop. 23 217 000 (1987); 945 050 km². *Languages:* Kiswahili and English. *Currency:* Tanzanian shilling. *Cap.:* Dar es Salaam (administrative cap. being transferred to Dodoma). **—Tanzanian**, *n., adj.*

Taoism /'taʊɪzəm, 'daʊɪzəm, 'teɪoʊˌɪzəm/, *n.* a Chinese philosophy advocating non-interference with nature, and absolute sincerity and honesty. [Chinese *tao* path or way (i.e. way of belief) + -ISM] **—Taoist**, *n., adj.* **—Taoistic**, *adj.*

tap¹ /tæp/, *v.*, **tapped, tapping**, *n.* ◇*v.t.* **1.** to strike with slight blows. **2.** to make, put, etc., by tapping. **3.** to strike (the hand, foot, etc.) lightly upon or against something. ◇*v.i.* **4.** to tap lightly so as to attract attention. **5.** to strike light blows. ◇*n.* **6.** a light, fast blow that can be heard. **7.** the sound made by this. **8.** the smallest amount; skerrick: *No one had done a tap of work.* [ME, from F: strike, slap; of Gmc orig.] **—tapper**, *n.*

tap² /tæp/, *n., v.*, **tapped, tapping**. ◇*n.* **1.** any apparatus for controlling the flow of liquid from a pipe, etc. by opening or closing an opening; cock. **2.** a cylindrical stick, long plug, or stopper for closing an opening through which liquid is drawn, such as in a cask; spigot. **3.** a hole made in tapping, such as one in a pipe to furnish connection for a branch pipe. **4. on tap, a.** ready to be drawn off and served, usu. drink, esp. beer, in a cask. **b.** ready for immediate use. ◇*v.t.* **5.** to draw off (liquid) by drawing out or opening a tap, or by piercing the container. **6.** to draw liquid from (any vessel or reservoir). **7.** to draw the tap or plug from, or pierce (a cask, etc.). **8.** to get through, reach, etc., for the purpose of drawing something off: *to tap one's resources.* **9.** *Colloq.* to take or borrow money from, esp. in a crafty manner. **10.** to make a secret connection with: *to tap telephone wires to hear conversations.* [OE]

tap dance, *n.* a dance in which the rhythm or rhythmical variation is tapped out by the toe or heel. **—tap-dance**, *v.* **—tap-dancer**, *n.*

tape /teɪp/, *n., v.*, **taped, taping**. ◇*n.* **1.** a long narrow strip of linen, cotton, etc., used for tying garments, etc. **2.** a long narrow strip of paper, metal, etc. **3.** → **tape measure**. **4.** → **magnetic tape**. **5.** a string, etc., stretched across the finishing line in a race and broken by the winner. ◇*v.t.* **6.** to furnish with a tape or tapes. **7.** to tie up or bind with tape. **8.** to measure with, or as if with a tape measure. **9.** to record on a tape recorder. ◇*v.* **10. have (someone) taped**, *Colloq.* to understand thoroughly, esp. a person's weakness, etc. **11. have (something) taped**, *Colloq.* to be in complete control of or be easily able to do (something). [ME]

tape deck, *n.* a tape recorder without built-in amplifiers or speakers.

tape measure, *n.* a long strip or ribbon, usu. of linen or steel, marked with subdivisions of the foot or metre for measuring.

taper /'teɪpə/, *v.t., v.i.* **1.** to make or become gradually thinner towards one end. **2.** to gradually make or grow thin. ◇*n.* **3.** a gradual decrease of width, thickness, power, force or capacity. **4.** a very thin candle. [ME: candle]

tape recorder /'teɪp rəkɔdə/, *n.* an apparatus for recording sound on magnetic tape.

tapestry /'tæpəstri/, *n., pl.* **-tries.** a heavy fabric upon which colored threads are woven by hand to produce a design, often pictorial, and used for wall hangings, furniture coverings, etc [ME, from F: maker of tapestry]

tapeworm /'teɪpwɜm/, *n.* any of various flat or tapelike parasitic worms which live in the digestive passage of humans and other vertebrates.

tapioca /tæpi'oʊkə/, *n.* a granular floury food substance prepared from cassava starch, used for making puddings, thickening soups, etc. [Pg, from Brazilian (Tupi-Guarani) *tipioca*, from *tipi* residue + *og, ók* squeeze out]

tappet /'tæpət/, *n.* (in a machine or engine) a projecting part, arm, etc. which at intervals comes in contact with another part from which it receives movement.

taproot /'tæprut/, *n.* the main root descending downwards giving off small lateral or branch roots.

tar¹ /ta/, *n., v.,* **tarred, tarring.** ◇*n.* **1.** any of various dark-colored sticky products obtained by processing substances such as coal, wood, etc. **2.** coal tar pitch. ◇*v.t.* **3.** to smear or cover with, or as if with, tar. ◇*v.* **4. tar and feather,** to punish or have revenge on (someone) by covering with tar and feathers. [OE]

tar² /ta/, *n. Colloq.* a sailor. [said to be short for TARPAULIN]

tarantella /tærən'tɛlə/, *n.* (the music for) a rapid, whirling southern Italian dance in very quick time, usu. performed by a single couple. [from *Taranto*, a seaport in SE Italy, where *tarantism*, a nervous disorder, characterised by an uncontrollable impulse to dance, was common]

tarantula /tə'ræntʃələ/, *n., pl.* **-las, -lae** /-li/. **1.** in Australia, the huntsman spider which often seeks shelter in houses during rain. **2.** a large spider of southern Europe, whose bite was formerly supposed to cause an uncontrollable desire to dance. [ML, from It, from *Taranto* sea-port in SE Italy, where the European spider is common]

tardy /'tadi/, *adj.,* **-dier, -diest. 1.** moving or acting slowly; slow; sluggish. **2.** late or behindhand. **3.** delaying through reluctance. [ME, from F, from L: slow] —**tardily,** *adv.* —**tardiness,** *n.*

tare /tɛə/, *n.* **1.** the weight of the wrapping or the container holding goods. **2.** the unloaded weight of a vehicle, esp. a truck. [ME, from ML, from Ar: deduction]

Taree /ta'ri/, *n.* a city on the North Coast of NSW, on the Manning River. Pop. 15 994 (1986). [Aboriginal *tareebit* name given to a fig-tree found in the area]

target /'tagət/, *n.* **1.** an object, usu. marked with concentric circles, to be aimed at in shooting practice or contests. **2.** anything fired at or aimed at. **3.** a goal to be reached. **4.** the object of attack, scorn, laughter, etc.; butt. **5.** *Hist.* a small round shield or buckler. [ME, from F]

tariff /'tærəf/, *n.* **1.** an official list or table showing the duties or customs placed by a government on exports or, esp., imports. **2.** any duty in such a list or system. **3.** any table of charges, as of a transport undertaking. **4.** (a list of) the prices charged for rooms, meals, etc., at a hotel or restaurant. [It, from Ar: notification, information]

tarmac /'tamæk/, *n., adj., v.,* **-macked, -macking.** ◇*n.* **1.** a road-surfacing mixture of gravel and tar. **2.** a road or airport runway made of tarmac. ◇*adj.* **3.** made of or surfaced with tarmac. ◇*v.t.* **4.** to surface (a road, runway, etc.) with tarmac.

tarmacadam /tamə'kædəm/, *n.* a road-surfacing mixture made up of small stones or gravel bound together with tar or a mixture of tar and bitumen. [TAR¹ + MACADAM]

tarn /tan/, *n.* a small mountain lake or pool. [ME, from Scand]

tarnish /'tanɪʃ/, *v.t.* **1.** to dull or change the surface shine of (metal) by contact with the air; discolor. **2.** to lessen or destroy the purity of; stain; sully. ◇*v.i.* **3.** to grow dull or discolored; lose lustre. **4.** to become stained. ◇*n.* **5.** a tarnished coating. **6.** a tarnished condition; discoloration; alteration of the lustre. **7.** a stain or mark; blemish. [F: dull, dark, probably of Gmc orig.]

tarot /'tærou/, *n.* **1.** one of a pack of 78 playing cards. **2.** a trump card in such a pack, bearing a symbolic or mythological character, now chiefly used in fortune telling, etc. [F, from It]

tarpaulin /ta'pɔlən/, *n.* (a protective covering of) canvas or other material waterproofed with tar, paint, or wax. [earlier *tarpauling*, from TAR¹ + PALL¹ + -ING¹]

Tarquin /'takwɪn/, *n.* one of a famous family of kings of early Rome. The last (*Lucius Tarquinius Superbus*, 'the Proud') died c. 510.

tarragon /'tærəgən/, *n.* an Old World plant with strongly smelling leaves used for flavoring. [Sp, from Ar, probably from Gk]

tarry /'tæri/, *v.i.,* **-ried, -rying. 1.** to remain or stay, as in a place; sojourn. **2.** to delay or be slow in acting, starting, coming, etc.; linger; loiter. **3.** to wait. [ME]

tarsus /'tasəs/, *n., pl.* **-si** /-saɪ/. the collection of bones in the foot, between the tibia and the metatarsus. [NL, from Gk: flat of the foot] —**tarsal,** *adj.*

tart¹ /tat/, *adj.* **1.** sharp to the taste; sour or acid: *tart apples.* **2.** sharp in character, spirit, or expression; cutting; caustic: *a tart remark.* [OE: sharp, rough] —**tartness,** *n.*

tart[2] /tat/, *n.* **1.** a saucer-shaped shell of pastry, filled with cooked fruit, custard, etc., and having no top crust. **2.** *Colloq.* a girl or woman thought to be sexually immoral. [ME, from OF, from L] —**tarty**, *adj.*

tartan /'tatn/, *n.* **1.** a woollen cloth woven with stripes of different colors and widths crossing at right angles, worn chiefly by the Scottish Highlanders, each clan having its own particular pattern. **2.** a design of such a plaid known by name of the clan wearing it. **3.** any plaid. ◇*adj.* **4.** of, relating to, or looking like tartan. **5.** made of tartan. [apparently from F: linsey-woolsey, a coarse fabric of cotton or linen woven under wool]

tartar[1] /'tatə/, *n.* **1.** a hard substance deposited on the teeth by the saliva. **2.** a potassium salt forming a deposit in wines. **3.** a partially purified product which when further purified becomes cream of tartar. [ML, from Gk] —**tartaric**, *adj.*

tartar[2] /'tatə/, *n.* **1.** a savage person who cannot be reasoned with. **2.** (*cap.*) a member of a Mongolian people, who, under the leadership of Genghis Khan, overran Asia and eastern Europe during the Middle Ages. [ME, from ML *Tartarus*, from Pers *Tatar* Mongolian race]

tartare sauce /,tatɛə 'sɔs, ,tata/, *n.* a mayonnaise dressing usu. with capers, olives, green herbs, etc., added, often served with fish. Also, **tartar sauce**. [F]

tartaric acid /ta,tærɪk 'æsəd/, *n.* an organic colorless, crystalline acid, (CHOH-COOH)$_2$ found in grapes and being one of the main acids in wine.

tartrate /'tatreɪt/, *n. Chem.* See -ate[2]. [F]

Tas, *Abbrev.* Tasmania.

Tashkent /tæʃ'kɛnt/, *n.* a city in western Asia; the capital of Uzbekistan. Pop. 2 077 000 (1986 est.). Russian, **Taškent**.

task /task/, *n.* **1.** a definite piece of work given or falling to a person; duty. **2.** a matter of considerable labor or difficulty. **3. take to task**, to call to account, usu. for fault; blame or censure. ◇*v.t.* **4.** to put a strain upon (powers, resources, etc.). [ME, from ML]

taskmaster /'taskmastə/, *n.* someone whose function it is to assign tasks to others, esp. burdensome tasks.

Tasman[1] /'tæzmən/, *n.* **Abel Janszoon** /,eɪbəl 'jansun/, 1602?–59, Dutch navigator, European discoverer of Tas, NZ, and other southern Pacific islands.

Tasman[2] /'tæzmən/, *n.* **Mount**, a mountain on South Island, NZ, in the Southern Alps. 3498 m.

Tasman Bridge, *n.* a bridge spanning the estuary of the Derwent River at Hobart, Tas, opened in 1964; in 1975 the bulk carrier, *Lake Illawarra*, hit the bridge and sank with the loss of at least 12 lives.

Tasman Glacier, *n.* the largest glacier in NZ, rising on Mt Cook in the Southern Alps and flowing about 29 km with a width of nearly 3 km.

Tasmania /tæz'meɪniə/, *n.* an island state off the south-eastern coast of mainland Australia; one of the six states of Australia. Pop. 436 353 (1986); 67 800 km^2. *Cap.*: Hobart. Formerly, **Van Diemen's Land**. [named, in 1855, after Abel TASMAN]

Tasmanian blue gum, *n.* a tall smooth-barked gum tree, native to Tas and Vic; floral emblem of Tas.

Tasmanian devil, *n.* a fierce meat-eating marsupial of Tas having a black coat with white markings.

Tasmanian wolf, *n.* →**thylacine**. Also, **Tasmanian tiger**.

Tasman Sea, *n.* a sea within the South Pacific Ocean, located between Australia and NZ. [named after Abel TASMAN]

Tass /tæs/, *n.* **Itar-Tass**. [Russ T(*elegrafnoye*) A(*genstvo*) S(*ovyetskovo*) S(*ovuza*) Telegraphic Agency of the Soviet Union]

tassel /'tæsəl/, *n.* **1.** a hanging ornament, usu. a bunch of threads or small cords hanging from a roundish knob or head. **2.** something like this, e.g. the flower of certain plants, esp. that at the top of a stalk of sugarcane, maize, etc. [ME, from OF: fastening for a cloak]

taste /teɪst/, *v.*, **tasted, tasting**, *n.* ◇*v.t.* **1.** to try the flavor or quality of (something) by taking some into the mouth. **2.** to sense or distinguish the flavor of: *I can taste wine in this sauce.* **3.** to have or get experience of: *to taste freedom.* ◇*v.i.* **4.** to try the flavor or quality of something. **5.** to have a particular flavor: *The milk tastes sour.* **6.** to have the flavor (usu. fol. by *of*): *This ice-cream tastes of caramel.* ◇*n.* **7.** the act of tasting food, drink, etc. **8.** the sense by which the flavor of things is perceived when they are brought into contact with the special organs (tastebuds) of the tongue. **9.** flavor or quality as perceived by the tastebuds: *This has a sweet taste.* **10.** a small quantity; morsel: *Have just a taste of wine.* **11.** a liking for something: *a taste for music.* **12.** the sense and enjoyment of what is good or beautiful in the arts, literature, etc. **13.** manner, style, or general character as showing a sense of what is fitting or beautiful: *I can see from his clothes that he has no taste.* **14.** a slight experience or sample: *her first taste of freedom.* **15. to one's taste**, agreeable or pleasing to one: *He couldn't find a tie to his taste.* [ME, from OF: try by touching]

tastebud /'teɪstbʌd/, *n.* any of a number of small bodies on the surface of the tongue, etc., which perceive taste.

tasty /'teɪsti/, *adj.*, **tastier, tastiest. 1.** pleasing to the taste; savory; appetising. **2.** *Colloq.* having or showing good taste.

tatters /'tætəz/, *n.pl.* torn or ragged pieces, esp. of clothing.

tatting /'tætɪŋ/, *n.* **1.** the process or work of making a type of knotted lace, with a shuttle. **2.** such lace. [orig. unknown]

tattle /'tætl/, *v.*, **-tled, -tling**, *n.* ◇*v.i.* **1.** to let out secrets. **2.** to chatter or gossip. ◇*n.*

3. idle talk; chatter; gossip. [ME, apparently from M Flemish]

tattoo[1] /'tætu/, n., pl. **-toos. 1.** a signal on a drum, trumpet, etc., at night, for soldiers, etc., to retire to their quarters. **2.** any similar beating or rhythm. **3.** an outdoor military display or pageant. [D: the tap (is) to, i.e. the bar is shut]

tattoo[2] /tæ'tu/, n., pl. **-toos**, v., **-tooed**, **-tooing.** ◇n. **1.** the act or practice of marking the skin with patterns, pictures, etc., which cannot be washed off, by making punctures in it and inserting colors. **2.** a pattern, picture, word, etc., so made. ◇v.t. **3.** to mark with tattoos. **4.** to put (pictures, etc.) on the skin. [earlier *tattow*, from Polynesian] —**tattooist**, n.

tatty /'tæti/, adj. untidy; shabby.

taught /tɔt/, v. past tense and past participle of **teach**.

taunt /tɔnt/, v.t. **1.** to mock (someone) in an insulting or sarcastic manner. ◇n. **2.** an insulting reproach or challenge. [orig. uncert.] —**taunting**, adj.

Taurus /'tɔrəs/, n. a constellation and sign of the zodiac, represented by a bull. [L: bull]

taut /tɔt/, adj. **1.** tightly drawn; tense. **2.** in good order or condition; tidy. [ME]

tauto-, a word part meaning 'same'. [Gk *tò autó* the same]

tautology /tɔ'tɒlədʒi/, n., pl. **-gies. 1.** the needless repetition of an idea, usu. in the same sentence, without giving extra clearness, as in *to descend down*. **2.** *Logic.* a proposition that can be shown to be true because it includes every possibility: *Either Smith owns a car or he doesn't own a car.* [LL, from Gk] —**tautological**, adj.

tavern /'tævən/, n. a building where food and alcoholic drink are served, but where no accommodation is provided.

taw /tɔ/, n. **1.** a favored or fancy marble with which to shoot. **2.** (*pl.*) the game of marbles. [? Scand]

tawdry /'tɔdri/, adj., **-drier, -driest.** (of clothes, etc.) gaudy; showy and cheap. [short for (*Sain*)*t Audrey lace*, i.e. lace bought at her fair in the Isle of Ely]

tawny /'tɔni/, adj., **-nier, -niest**, n. (of) a dark yellowish or yellowish brown color. [ME, from OF: tanned]

tawny frogmouth, n. a medium-sized frogmouth with variously colored, mottled feathers and a low but penetrating call, found throughout Australia.

tax /tæks/, n. **1.** a compulsory contribution of money, demanded by a government for its support, and imposed on incomes, property, goods purchased, etc. **2.** a heavy or unwanted charge, duty, or demand. ◇v.t. **3.** to put a tax on (income, people, etc.). **4.** to lay a burden on; make serious demands: *This job taxes my skills.* **5.** to scold; censure; reprove. [ME, from L: reprove, appraise] —**taxable**, adj.

taxation /tæk'seɪʃən/, n. **1.** the act of taxing. **2.** the fact of being taxed. **3.** a tax imposed. **4.** money raised by taxes.

tax-deductible /'tæks-dədʌktəbəl/, adj. (of an expense, loss, etc.) able to be legally claimed as a deduction from taxable income.

taxi /'tæksi/, n., pl. **taxis**, v., **taxied**, **taxiing** or **taxying**. ◇n. **1.** Also, **taxicab**. a motor car for public hire, esp. one fitted with a device which automatically calculates the fare due. ◇v.i. **2.** (of an aeroplane) to move over the surface of the ground or water under its own power, esp. when preparing to take off or just after landing. [short for *taxicab*]

taxidermy /'tæksədɜmi/, n. the art of preparing and preserving the skins of animals, and stuffing and mounting them in lifelike form. [Gk: arrangement of skin] —**taxidermist**, n.

tax indexation, n. the indexing of tax scales in agreement with certain economic variables such as the consumer price index.

taxis /'tæksəs/, n. **1.** arrangement, order, as in one of the physical sciences. **2.** *Biol.* the movement of an organism in a particular direction in response to an outside stimulus. [NL, from Gk: arrangement]

-taxis, a word part meaning 'arrangement'. [Gk]

taxonomy /tæk'sɒnəmi/, n. (the science dealing with) the classification of types of plants, animals, etc. [F, from Gk] —**taxonomic**, adj. —**taxonomist, taxonomer**, n.

tax return, n. a statement of personal income required every year by tax authorities, used in calculating the amount of tax to be paid.

-taxy, a variant of **-taxis**.

Taylor /'teɪlə/, n. **1. A(lan) J(ohn) P(ercivale)**, 1906-90, English historian; noted for his works on modern European history. **2. Sir (Patrick) Gordon**, 1896-1966, Australian pioneer aviator and author. **3. Headlie Shephard**, 1883-1957, Australian inventor of agricultural machinery, most notably the header harvester. **4. Zachary**, 1784-1850, US statesman and general; 12th president of the US, 1849-50.

Tb, *Chem. Symbol.* terbium.

TB /ti 'bi/, n. tuberculosis. [abbrev.]

Tbilisi /dbɪ'lisi/, n. the capital of Georgia (def. 1) in the southern part. Pop. 1 174 000 (1986 est.). Russian, **Tiflis**.

tbs., *Abbrev.* tablespoon(s). Also, **tbsp.**

Tc, *Chem. Symbol.* technetium.

Tchaikovsky /tʃaɪ'kɒfski/, n. **Peter Ilyich** /ˌpitə ɪl'jitʃ/, 1840-93, Russian composer of symphonies, ballets, operas, piano works, etc., noted for their expressive melody.

tchurunga /tʃə'rʌŋgə/, n. → **churinga**.

te /ti/, n. *Music.* Also, **ti**. See **solfa**.

Te, *Chem. Symbol.* tellurium.

tea /ti/, n. **1.** a shrub, related to the camellia, and widely grown in China, Japan, India, etc.,

tea

with fragrant white flowers. **2.** the dried and prepared leaves of the shrub, from which a bitter, aromatic beverage is made by infusion in boiling water. **3.** any kind of leaves, flowers, etc., so used, or any plant yielding them. **4.** the drink so prepared. **5.** a light meal taken in the late afternoon. **6.** the main evening meal. **7. cup of tea,** *Colloq.* anything well suited to one's experience, taste, or liking: *That show wasn't my cup of tea.* [Chinese *ch'a*]

Tea and Sugar, *n.* a supply train running between Port Augusta, SA, and Kalgoorlie, WA. [so called because it supplies groceries to the settlements along its route]

teach /titʃ/, *v.*, **taught, teaching.** ◇*v.t.* **1.** to give knowledge of or skill in: *He teaches mathematics.* **2.** to give knowledge or skill to; instruct: *She teaches a large class.* ◇*v.i.* **3.** to give knowledge, skill or instruction. [OE] —**teachable,** *adj.* —**teacher,** *n.*

tea-chest /'ti-tʃɛst/, *n.* **1.** a large wooden box or crate in which tea is packed. **2.** a similar crate used for packing and storage.

tea-chest bass, *n.* a musical instrument, used in bush bands, consisting of a pole standing in a large hollow box, and a string, stretched tightly from the edge of the box to the top of the pole, which is plucked to produce a bass note.

teaching /'titʃɪŋ/, *n.* **1.** the work or profession of a teacher. **2.** something which is taught; doctrine; precept.

teacup /'tikʌp/, *n.* **1.** a cup in which tea is served, usu. of small or moderate size. **2. a storm in a teacup,** *Colloq.* a great fuss about nothing very much.

teal /til/, *n.*, *pl.* **teals,** (*esp. collectively*) **teal.** any of various small freshwater ducks, e.g. the **grey teal,** a wide-ranging bird of Australia, Indonesia, NZ, and Pacific islands.

team /tim/, *n.* **1.** a number of people associated in some joint action, activity, etc.: *a team of football players.* **2.** two or more horses, oxen, etc., harnessed together to pull a vehicle, plough, etc. ◇*v.t., v.i.* **3.** to join together in a team. ◇*v.* **4. team up with,** to work together with; collaborate with. [OE]

teamster /'timstə/, *n.* someone who drives a team (def. 2).

teapot /'tipɒt/, *n.* a container with a lid, spout, and handle, in which tea is made and from which it is poured.

tear[1] /tɪə/, *n.* **1.** a drop of the clear fluid appearing in or flowing from the eye, as a result of grief, pain, etc. **2.** something resembling or suggesting a tear. **3.** (*pl.*) grief; sorrow. **4. in tears,** weeping. [OE *tēar*]

tear[2] /tɛə/, *v.*, **tore, torn, tearing,** *n.* ◇*v.t.* **1.** to pull apart or in pieces by force, esp. so as to leave irregular edges. **2.** to pull or grab violently or with force: *to try to tear the newspaper from the dog.* **3.** to split or divide: *a country torn by civil war.* **4.** to wound or hurt by, or as by, pulling apart; lacerate. **5.** to produce by tearing: *She will tear a hole in her coat.* **6.** to remove by force: *How could you tear yourself from this place?* ◇*v.i.* **7.** to become torn. **8.** to make a tear. ◇*v.* **9. tear into,** to attack violently, either physically or verbally. **10. tear off,** **a.** to pull violently. **b.** to leave hurriedly. **11. tear strips off,** to scold severely. ◇*n.* **12.** the act of tearing. **13.** a torn section. [OE *teran*]

tear duct /'tɪə dʌkt/, *n.* a short tube in the inner corner of the lower eyelid which drains tears away into the nose.

tearful /'tɪəfəl/, *adj.* **1.** full of tears; weeping. **2.** causing tears. —**tearfulness,** *n.*

tear gas /'tɪə gæs/, *n.* a gas used in warfare or in riots, which makes the eyes sting and water, producing short-term blindness.

tease /tiz/, *v.*, **teased, teasing,** *n.* ◇*v.t.* **1.** to worry or disturb by continual, annoying requests, light-hearted but embarrassing remarks, or the like. **2.** to pull apart or separate the fibres of, as in combing wool. **3.** to raise the short ends of fibres on (cloth). **4.** to give height and body to (hair) by combing it from the end towards the scalp. **5.** to flirt with. ◇*v.i.* **6.** to worry or disturb a person, etc., with actions or words designed to annoy. ◇*n.* **7.** the act of teasing. **8.** someone or something that teases or annoys. [OE *tæsan* tear up]

teaspoon /'tispun/, *n.* **1.** a small spoon commonly used to stir tea, coffee, etc. **2.** as much as a teaspoon can hold, about 5 mls.

teat /tit/, *n.* **1.** a part which sticks out from the breast or udder in female mammals where the milk-carrying tubes discharge; nipple; mamilla. **2.** something resembling a teat, esp. for feeding a baby from a bottle. [ME *tete,* OF]

tea-tree /'ti-tri/, *n.* any of several small-leaved shrubs of Australia and NZ, frequently developed as an ornamental with white, pink, or red flowers. Also, **ti-tree** (by confusion with **ti**[1]). [so called from its use as a tea substitute in the early days of the colony in Aust]

tech /tɛk/, *n. Colloq.* a technical college or school.

technetium /tɛk'nɪʃəm/, *n.* the first element artificially made, present in the fission products of uranium. *Symbol:* Tc; *at. no.:* 43. The most stable isotope has *at. wt.:* 99. Also, *Obs.,* **masurium.** [Gk: artificial]

technical /'tɛknɪkəl/, *adj.* **1.** belonging or relating to an art, science, or the like. **2.** (of a book, writer, etc.) using terms or treating a subject in a manner used only in a particular field. **3.** (of a person) skilled in, or familiar in a practical way with, a particular art, trade, etc. **4.** relating to or connected with the mechanical or industrial arts and the applied sciences, as motor mechanics, wool classing, industrial electronics, etc. **5.** considered as such only from a strictly legal point of view or a strict following of the rules: *a military exercise ending in a technical defeat.*

technical drawing, *n.* the study of the drawing of plans and designs for use in manufacture, building, construction, etc.

technicality /tɛknə'kæləti/, *n.*, *pl.* **-ties.** **1.** technical character. **2.** something that is technical; a technical point or detail. **3.** an exact, often narrow-minded following of a rule,

technicality

law, etc.: *He was ruled unable to apply on a technicality.*

technician /tek'nıʃən/, *n.* **1.** someone skilled in the technical side of a subject. **2.** someone skilled in the technique of an art, as music or painting.

technicolor or **technicolour** /'teknıkʌlə, -nə-/, *n.* **1.** the process of making cinema films in color. ◇*adj.* **2.** bright, striking, esp. of colors. [Trademark *Technicolor*]

technics /'teknıks/, *n.* **1.** technique. **2.** the study or science of an art or of arts in general, esp. of the mechanical or industrial arts.

technique /tek'nik/, *n.* **1.** a way of doing or performing. **2.** practical skill, esp. in artistic work. [F]

techno-, a word part referring to 'technology'. [Gk, combining form of *téchnē* art, skill]

technocracy /tek'nɒkrəsi/, *n.* **1.** a system of government and economic management controlled by technologists and scientists. **2.** the people who occupy senior positions in various technical fields, as engineering, science, economics, etc., considered as a class exercising a strong influence over society as a whole. —**technocrat**, *n.* —**technocratic**, *adj.*

technology /tek'nɒlədʒi/, *n.* that branch of knowledge that deals with science and engineering, or its practice, as applied to industry; applied science. [Gk: systematic treatment] —**technologist**, *n.* —**technological**, *adj.* —**technologically**, *adv.*

tectonic /tek'tɒnık/, *adj.* **1.** of or relating to building; architectural. **2.** *Geol.* **a.** relating to the structure of the earth's crust. **b.** referring to the forces or conditions within the earth that cause movements of the crust, such as earthquakes, folds, faults, etc. **c.** indicating the results of such movements: *tectonic valleys.* [LL, from Gk]

tedious /'tidiəs/, *adj.* **1.** long and boring: *a tedious task; a tedious journey.* **2.** (of a speaker) wordy and boring. [ME, from LL] —**tedium**, *n.*

tee[1] /ti/, *n.* **1.** the letter T, t. **2.** something shaped like a T, as a three way joint used in fitting pipes together. ◇*adj.* **3.** shaped like a T.

tee[2] /ti/, *n., v.*, **teed, teeing.** ◇*n.* **1.** *Golf.* Also, **teeing ground.** the starting place, at the beginning of each fairway. **2.** *Golf.* a small heap of sand, or a shaped holder, on which the ball is placed and from which it is driven at the beginning of a hole. ◇*v.t.* **3.** *Golf.* to place (the ball) on a tee. **4.** to organise, plan (fol. by *up*). ◇*v.i.* **5.** *Golf.* to strike the ball from a tee (fol. by *off*). [orig. uncert.]

teem[1] /tim/, *v.i.* to be full of or rich in (fol. by *with*): *a river teeming with fish.* [OE *tēman, tīeman* produce (offspring)] —**teeming**, *adj.*

teem[2] /tim/, *v.i.* **1.** to empty or pour out; discharge. **2.** to rain very hard. [ME, from Scand]

telegraph

-teen, an ending forming the cardinal numerals from 13 to 19. [ME and OE *-tēne*, combining form of TEN]

teenager /'tineidʒə/, *n.* someone in his or her teens. —**teenage**, *adj.*

teens /tinz/, *n.pl.* the period of a person's life between the ages of 12 and 20.

teeny /'tini/, *adj.*, **-nier, -niest.** tiny.

teeny-bopper /'tini-bɒpə/, *n.* a young teenager who follows the latest, most popular style in dress, music, etc. [TEEN(AGER) + *bop* + -ER[1]]

tee-shirt /'ti-ʃɜt/, *n.* → T-shirt.

teeter /'titə/, *v.i.* to move or hang unsteadily. [var. of *titter*, from Scand]

teeth /tiθ/, *n.* **1.** plural of **tooth.** **2.** power or effectiveness: *to give a law teeth.* **3. get one's teeth into**, to start to manage effectively. **4. in the teeth of**, in defiance of. **5. to the teeth**, fully: *armed to the teeth.*

teethe /tið/, *v.i.*, **teethed, teething.** to grow teeth; cut one's teeth. —**teething**, *n.*

teetotal /'titoutl, ti'toutl/, *adj.* of, relating to, supporting, or promising total non-use of alcohol. [from TOTAL, with reduplication of initial *t-* for emphasis] —**teetotalism**, *n.* —**teetotaller**, *n.*

teflon /'teflɒn/, *n.* a lining for saucepans, frying pans, etc., to which food does not stick. [Trademark]

Teheran /teiə'ran/, *n.* the capital of Iran, in the northern part; wartime conference of Roosevelt, Churchill, and Stalin, 1943. Pop. 5 751 500 (1985). Also, **Tehran.**

tektite /'tektaɪt/, *n.* a small glasslike body, whose chemical nature is not related to the geological formation in which it is found, believed to be of meteoric origin. [Gk: molten]

tel-, a variant of **tele-**.

Tel-Aviv /tel-ə'viv/, *n.* a city in western Israel. Pop. (with Jaffa) 330 400 (1983 est.).

tele-, **1.** a word part meaning 'distant', esp. 'sent over a distance', as in *telegraph.* Also, **tel-, telo-.** a word part referring to 'television' or 'telephone'. [combining form representing Gk *tēle* far]

telecast /'telǝkast, 'teli-/, *v.*, **-cast** or **-casted, -casting,** *n.* ◇*v.i., v.t.* **1.** to broadcast by television. ◇*n.* **2.** a television broadcast.

telecommunication /ˌtelǝkǝmjunǝ'keıʃǝn, ˌteli-/, *n.* **1.** (*pl.*) the study and practice of the passing of information by line or radio waves. **2.** a message sent this way.

telegram /'telǝgræm/, *n.* a message sent by telegraph.

telegraph /'telǝgræf, -graf/, *n.* **1.** an apparatus, system, or process for sending messages or signals over a distance. **2.** a telegraphic message. ◇*v.t.* **3.** to send (a message, etc.) by telegraph: *We must telegraph a message to his family.* **4.** to send a message to (a person) by telegraph: *I will telegraph my aunt immedi-*

telegraph 1060 **temper**

ately. ◇*v.i.* **5.** to send a message by telegraph. —**telegraphy,** *n.* —**telegrapher, telegraphist,** *n.* —**telegraphic,** *adj.*

teleology /ˌtiliˈɒlədʒi, ˌtɛl-/, *n.* the study of evidence for the idea of design or purpose in nature. [NL, from Gk] —**teleological,** *adj.*

telepathy /təˈlɛpəθi/, *n.* the communication of one mind with another by some means other than the normal use of the senses. —**telepathic,** *adj.* —**telepathist,** *n.*

telephone /ˈtɛləfoʊn/, *n., v.,* **-phoned, -phoning.** ◇*n.* **1.** an apparatus, system, or process for sending sound or speech to a distant point, esp. by an electrical device. ◇*v.t.* **2.** to speak to or call (a person) by telephone. **3.** to send (a message, etc.) by telephone. ◇*v.i.* **4.** to send a message by telephone. —**telephonic,** *adj.* —**telephonically,** *adv.*

telephonist /təˈlɛfənəst/, *n.* someone who operates a system making connections possible between telephone users.

telephoto lens /ˌtɛləfoʊtoʊ ˈlɛnz/, *n.* a camera lens for producing a larger image of a distant object.

teleprinter /ˈtɛlɪprɪntə, ˈtɛlə-/, *n.* an instrument having a typewriter keyboard which sends and receives messages by changing the keyboard information into electrical signals.

telescope /ˈtɛləskoʊp/, *n., adj., v.,* **-scoped, -scoping.** ◇*n.* **1.** an instrument using lenses contained within tubes, for making distant objects appear nearer and larger to the view. ◇*adj.* **2.** consisting of parts which fit and slide one within another. ◇*v.t.* **3.** to force together, one into another, or force into something else, in the manner of the sliding tubes of a jointed telescope. **4.** to shorten; condense. ◇*v.i.* **5.** to slide together, or into something else in the manner of the tubes of a jointed telescope. **6.** to be driven one into another, as railway carriages in a collision. [NL, from Gk: far-seeing] —**telescopic,** *adj.*

televise /ˈtɛləvaɪz/, *v.t.,* **-vised, -vising.** to broadcast by television.

television /ˈtɛləvɪʒən/, *n.* **1.** the broadcasting of a still or moving image, by means of radio waves, to receivers which project it on a picture tube for viewing at a distance from the point of origin. **2.** the field of broadcasting by television: *He works in television.* **3.** a television receiver; television set.

telex /ˈtɛlɛks/, *n.* **1.** an international service provided by postal authorities in which teleprinters are rented to businesses, etc., for use in direct communications. **2.** a message received or sent by teleprinter. ◇*v.i.* **3.** to send a message by telex. ◇*v.t.* **4.** to send (someone) a message by telex. **5.** to send (a message) by telex.

tell /tɛl/, *v.,* **told, telling.** ◇*v.t.* **1.** to give an account of; narrate; relate (a story, tale, etc.). **2.** to make known by speech or writing (a fact, news, information, etc.); communicate. **3.** to utter (the truth, a lie, etc.). **4.** to express in words: *Tell your grievance.* **5.** to inform (someone): *Tell me about your plans.* **6.** to recognise or make out: *You could hardly tell the difference between them; Can you tell who that is?* **7.** to state definitely to: *I won't, I tell you!* **8.** to order or command: *Tell him to stop.* ◇*v.i.* **9.** to give an account or report: *He will tell about his experience.* **10.** to give evidence or be an indication (fol. by *of*): *The cargo from the islands told of the riches that lay there.* **11.** to know; be certain: *How can we tell if there is a life after death?* **12.** to have force or effect: *a race in which every step tells.* **13.** to produce a marked or severe effect: *The strain will tell on his health.* ◇*v.* **14. tell off,** *Colloq.* to scold severely. **15. tell on,** to inform (someone) against (someone): *I'll tell Mummy on you.* **16. tell tales (out of school),** to report the faults or errors of someone. [OE *tellan*]

Tell /tɛl/, *n.* **William** or (*Ger*) **Wilhelm** /ˈvɪlhɛlm/, (? fl. 1307) a legendary Swiss patriot said to have been forced by the Austrian governor to shoot an apple off his son's head with a bow and arrow.

Tell el Amarna /ˌtɛl ɛl əˈmɑːnə/, *n.* a set of ruins and tombs below Asyut on the Nile in Upper Egypt; includes tomb of Amenhotep IV.

teller /ˈtɛlə/, *n.* **1.** a person employed in a bank to receive or pay out money over the counter. **2.** a person appointed to count votes.

Teller, *n.* **Edward,** born 1908, Hungarian-born US nuclear physicist; a major worker in the development of the hydrogen bomb (1952).

telltale /ˈtɛlteɪl/, *n.* **1.** Also, **telltale-tit.** someone who thoughtlessly and sometimes cruelly reveals private matters; tattler. ◇*adj.* **2.** that reveals what is not intended to be known: *a telltale blush.*

tellurium /tɛlˈjʊriəm, təˈlʊ-/, *n.* a rare silver-white, semi-metallic element of the sulfur family occurring in nature with gold and silver, etc. Used in alloys and electrolytic refining of zinc. *Symbol:* Te; *at. no.:* 52; *at. wt:* 127.60. [NL, from L *tellūs* earth + *-ium* -IUM]

Telstar /ˈtɛlstɑː/, *n.* either of two communications satellites in low, elliptical orbits launched by the US in 1962 and 1963, used for transmission of television, telephone, etc.

temerity /təˈmɛrəti/, *n.* foolish boldness; rashness. [late ME, from L]

temp /tɛmp/, *n. Colloq.* → **temporary** (def. 3).

temp., *Abbrev.* **1.** temperature. **2.** temporary.

temper /ˈtɛmpə/, *n.* **1.** a particular state of mind or feelings: *to be in a good temper; to be in a bad temper.* **2.** a habit of mind, esp. with respect to annoyance or impatience, etc.: *He has an even temper.* **3.** heat of mind or feeling, shown in sudden appearance of anger, resentment, etc.: *He's in a temper.* **4.** a calm state of mind: *out of temper.* **5.** a particular degree of hardness and elasticity of steel, etc. ◇*v.t.* **6.** to moderate or make less severe. **7.** to bring to a proper, suitable, or desirable state by, or as if by, blending. **8.** to heat and cool (metal) to bring to the proper degree of hardness, elasticity, etc. **9.** to toughen (glass) by sudden cooling from low red heat. [ME; OE *temprian,* from L: divide or proportion duly, temper]

tempera /ˈtempərə/, *n.* paint made from coloring matter ground in water and mixed with egg yolk or some similar substance. [It: paint in distemper, from L]

temperament /ˈtemprəmənt/, *n.* **1.** the individual character of a person as shown by his or her manner of thinking, feeling, and acting; make-up; disposition. **2.** an unpredictable or moody nature: *He has quite a temperament.* **3.** *Music.* a system of tuning a keyboard instrument, as the piano, organ, etc., so that it is able to be played in all keys. [late ME, from L: due mixture] —**temperamental**, *adj.*

temperance /ˈtempərəns, ˈtemprəns/, *n.* **1.** control of oneself in action, statement, etc.; self-control. **2.** habitual moderation in the enjoyment of a natural appetite, esp. in the drinking of alcohol. **3.** total abstinence from alcohol. [ME, from AF, from L: moderation]

temperate /ˈtempərət, ˈtemprət/, *adj.* **1.** controlled or moderate in opinion, etc. **2.** moderate in enjoyment of appetite or passion, esp. in the drinking of alcohol. **3.** (of things, qualities, etc.) not excessive. **4.** of moderate temperature or climate. [ME, from L] —**temperateness**, *n.*

Temperate Zone, *n.* either of two regions, the North Temperate Zone, between the Arctic Circle and the tropic of Cancer, and the South Temperate Zone, between the Antarctic Circle and the tropic of Capricorn.

temperature /ˈtemprətʃə/, *n.* **1.** a measure of the degree of hotness or coldness of a body or substance which determines the rate at which heat will pass to or from it. **2. a.** the degree of heat of a living body. In adult humans, normal temperature is about 37°C, or about 98.4°F. **b.** a temperature above the normal: *He had a headache and a temperature.* [L]

tempest /ˈtempəst/, *n.* **1.** a large current of wind rushing with great speed and violence, esp. with rain, hail, or snow; violent storm. **2.** a violent disturbance or upset. [ME, from OF, from Rom: time, storm, from L: season] —**tempestuous**, *adj.*

template /ˈtemplət, -leɪt/, *n.* **1.** a pattern or mould(s) usu. consisting of a thin plate of wood, metal or plastic, used as a guide in mechanical work or for putting a design onto a work surface, etc. **2.** *Bldg Trades.* a horizontal piece of timber, stone, or the like, in a wall, to receive and distribute the pressure of a beam, etc. [orig. uncert.; ? from F: stretcher, from L: small timber]

temple[1] /ˈtempəl/, *n.* **1.** a place, esp. a large building, given over to the service or worship of a god or gods. **2.** any place or object regarded as a shrine which God's spirit occupies. [OE *templ*, from L]

temple[2] /ˈtempəl/, *n.* the flattened area on either side of the forehead. [ME, from OF, from Rom]

tempo /ˈtempoʊ/, *n.*, *pl.* **-pos**, **-pi** /-pi/. **1.** *Music.* a relative rate of movement (usu. indicated by such terms as adagio, allegro, etc., or by reference to the metronome). **2.** a characteristic rate, rhythm, or pattern of work or activity: *the tempo of city life.* [It, from L: time]

temporal[1] /ˈtempərəl, ˈtemprəl/, *adj.* **1.** of or relating to time. **2.** relating to or concerned with the present life or this world; not spiritual. [ME, from L: relating to or enduring for a time]

temporal[2] /ˈtempərəl, ˈtemprəl/, *adj. Anat.* of, relating to, or situated near the temple: *temporal bone.* [L]

temporary /ˈtempri, -prəri/, *adj.* **1.** lasting, existing, serving, or effective for a short time only: *a temporary need.* **2.** (of someone employed) not on the permanent staff and therefore not enjoying job certainty or extra advantages, esp. superannuation. ◇*n.* Also, **temp**. **3.** *Colloq.* a temporary member of an office staff, esp. a secretary. —**temporarily**, *adv.*

temporise *or* **temporize** /ˈtempəraɪz/, *v.i.*, **-rised**, **-rising**. **1.** to avoid making a decision in order to gain time or delay matters. **2.** to yield for the moment to the demands of a situation. [ML: delay] —**temporisation**, *n.*

tempt /tempt/, *v.t.* **1.** to persuade by promising pleasure; entice: *He tempted her to have another cake.* **2.** to attract, appeal strongly to, or invite: *The offer tempts me.* **3.** to make (someone) strongly inclined (to do something). **4.** to put to the test in a daring way; provoke: *to tempt fate.* [ME, from L: touch, test] —**temptation**, *n.* —**tempter**, *n.* —**temptress**, *n. fem.* —**tempting**, *adj.*

ten /ten/, *n.* **1.** a cardinal number, nine plus one (9 + 1). **2.** the symbol for this number, as 10 or X. ◇*adj.* **3.** amounting to ten in number. [ME; OE *tēn*]

tenable /ˈtenəbəl/, *adj.* able to be held, supported, or defended, as against attack or objection: *a tenable theory.* [F, from L: hold, keep] —**tenability**, *n.*

tenacious /təˈneɪʃəs/, *adj.* **1.** holding fast; characterised by keeping a firm hold (oft. fol. by *of*). **2.** (of memory) able to store many details. **3.** (of a person, will, etc.) being of a determined or stubborn nature. **4.** holding together; not easily pulled apart; tough. [TENACI(TY) + -OUS] —**tenacity**, *n.*

tenant /ˈtenənt/, *n.* **1.** a person who pays rent to hold the land, house, etc., of another (the landlord). **2.** a person living in or occupying any place. ◇*v.t.* **3.** to hold as a tenant; dwell in; inhabit. [ME, from F: hold, from L] —**tenancy**, *n.*

Tench /tentʃ/, *n.* **Watkin**, c. 1759–1833, Australian officer of marines, born in England; explorer of the Nepean River; author of *A Complete Account of the Settlement at Port Jackson in New South Wales* (1793).

Ten Commandments, *n.pl.* the precepts spoken by God to Israel, delivered to Moses on Mount Sinai, the Decalogue. [see Exodus 20:24; 12:34 and Deuteronomy 5]

tend[1] /tend/, *v.i.* **1.** to move towards a particular action, operation, or effect: *The particles tend to unite.* **2.** to feel moved towards a state of mind, emotion, quality, etc. **3.** to lead (to some result or resulting condition): *measures tending to improve working conditions.* [ME, from F, from L: stretch, go, strive]

tend² /tend/, v.t. **1.** to attend to by work or services, care, etc.: *to tend a fire*. **2.** to watch over and care for. ◇v.i. **3.** to attend by action, care, etc. (usu. fol. by *to*): *The hospital will tend to her needs*. [ME, var. of ATTEND]

tendency /ˈtendənsi/, n., pl. **-cies.** a natural movement in some direction or towards some point, end, or result. [ML, from L: TEND¹]

tendentious /tenˈdenʃəs/, adj. presented so as to influence in a desired direction or present a particular point of view: *a tendentious novel*.

tender¹ /ˈtendə/, adj. **1.** soft or delicate in substance: *a tender steak*. **2.** not strong or hardy; weak or delicate. **3.** young; immature: *children of tender age*. **4.** delicate, soft, or gentle: *the tender touch of her hand*. **5.** (of a person, feelings, etc.) easily touched or affected. **6.** affectionate or loving. **7.** (of a wound, etc.) painfully sensitive. **8.** requiring careful handling: *a tender subject*. [ME, from F, from L: soft, delicate, tender]

tender² /ˈtendə/, v.t. **1.** to present formally or offer for acceptance: *to tender one's resignation*. **2.** *Law.* to offer (money or goods) in payment of a debt or other claim. ◇n. **3.** an offer of something for acceptance. **4.** *Comm.* an offer made in writing by one party to another to carry out certain work, supply certain goods, etc., at a given cost. **5.** *Law.* an offer, as of money or goods, in payment of a debt, etc. [AF, from L]

tender³ /ˈtendə/, n. **1.** someone who attends to or takes charge of something. **2.** a ship attending one or more other ships, esp. for supplying provisions. **3.** an open truck attached to a steam engine, for carrying coal, water, etc. [late ME]

tenderfoot /ˈtendəfʊt/, n., pl. **-foots, -feet** /-fiːt/. *Colloq.* a person with little experience; a novice.

tendon /ˈtendən/, n. a cord or band of dense, tough, non-elastic, fibrous tissue, joining a muscle with a bone or part; sinew. [ML, from Gk: sinew]

tendril /ˈtendrəl/, n. a threadlike leafless organ of climbing plants, often spiral, which supports the plant by attaching itself round some other body. [F: tender shoot, from LL: tender]

tenebrous /ˈtenəbrəs/, adj. dark; gloomy; obscure. [late ME, from L: dark]

tenement /ˈtenəmənt/, n. a house divided into flats, esp. one in the poorer, crowded parts of a large city. [ME, from OF, from L]

tenet /ˈtenət/, n. any opinion, principle, teaching, etc., held as true. [L: he holds]

Tennant /ˈtenənt/, n. **Kylie** /ˈkaɪli/, 1912–88, Australian novelist and biographer; author of *The Battlers* (1941).

Tennant Creek, a goldmining town in the central NT, midway between Alice Springs and Darwin; formerly, one of the largest producers of bismuth in the world. Pop. 3505 (1986).

Tennessee /tenəˈsiː/, n. a state in the south-eastern US. Pop. 4 803 000 (1986 est.); 109 417 km². *Cap.*: Nashville. *Abbrev.*: Tenn – **Tennessean**, n., adj.

tennis /ˈtenɪs/, n. a game played on a court, in which two players, or two pairs of players, hit a ball over a central net with racquets. [ME, from OF: hold, take]

Tennyson /ˈtenəsən/, n. **Alfred, 1st Baron,** 1809–92, English poet who voiced the moral and philosophical concerns of the Victorian age; poet laureate 1850–92.

tenon /ˈtenən/, n. a piece shaped to stick out on the end of a piece of wood, etc., to fit into a mortise (corresponding cavity) in another piece. [ME, from OF: hold, from L]

tenor /ˈtenə/, n. **1.** the course of thought or meaning which runs through something written or spoken; purport; drift. **2.** a continuous course, progress, or movement. **3.** *Music.* **a.** the highest natural male voice. **b.** a part sung by or written for this voice, usu. the second lowest part in four-part harmony. **c.** a singer with such a voice. [ME, from (M)L: course, etc.]

tenor clef, n. (in music) a sign placing middle C on the next to the top line of the stave.

tenpin bowling, n. a game played with ten wooden pins at which a ball is bowled to knock them down.

tense¹ /tens/, adj., **tenser, tensest,** v., **tensed, tensing.** ◇adj. **1.** stretched tight; rigid. **2.** (of a person) in a condition of mental or nervous strain. **3.** placing a strain upon the nerves or feelings: *a tense moment*. ◇v.t., v.i. **4.** to make or become tense. [L: stretched, taut]

tense² /tens/, n. **1.** the form of a verb which shows the time and duration of the action or state expressed by the verb. **2.** the meaning of such a form. There are three basic tenses indicated in English, past tense, as in *I was*, present tense, as in *I am*, future tense, as in *I will be*. See Appendix. [ME, from OF, from L: time]

tensile /ˈtensaɪl/, adj. **1.** of or relating to tension: *tensile stress*. **2.** able to be stretched or drawn out; ductile. [NL, from L: stretch]

tension /ˈtenʃən/, n. **1.** the act of stretching or straining. **2.** the condition of being stretched or strained. **3.** a strained feeling of anxiety or excitement. **4.** a strained relationship between individuals, groups, countries, etc. **5.** *Mech.* a condition in which a body is stretched in size in one direction with a decrease in size in the perpendicular direction. **6.** voltage. **7.** a device to hold the proper tension on the material being woven in a loom. [LL: act of stretching]

tent /tent/, n. an easily-movable shelter of skins or coarse cloth, esp. canvas, supported by one or more poles and ropes fastened to ground pegs. [ME, from OF, from L: stretched]

tentacle /ˈtentəkəl/, n. *Zool.* any of various thin, easily-bent, arm-like growths in animals, esp. invertebrates, which serve to touch, grasp, etc. [NL, from L]

tentative /'tentətɪv/, *adj.* **1.** of the nature of, or made or done as, a test or attempt to see what will happen; experimental. **2.** unsure; cautious; diffident; hesitant. [ML, from L: try]

tenterhooks /'tentəhʊks/, *n.* in the phrase **on tenterhooks**, in a condition of anxious waiting.

tenth /tenθ/, *adj.* **1.** next after the ninth. **2.** being one of ten equal parts. ◇*n.* **3.** a tenth part, esp. of one ($\frac{1}{10}$). **4.** the tenth member of a series.

tenuous /'tenjuəs/, *adj.* **1.** thin or slight in form. **2.** thinned out; not dense. **3.** of slight importance; unsubstantial. **4.** lacking a firm or sound basis; weak; vague; flimsy. [L: slender]

tenure /'tenjə/, *n.* **1.** the holding or possession of anything: *the tenure of an office.* **2.** *Hist.* the holding of property, esp. real property, in return for services. **3.** the time for which something is held. [ME, from OF, from L: hold]

Tenzing /'tenzɪŋ/, *n.* **Norgay** /'nɔːgeɪ/ (*Namgyal Wangdi*), 1914–86, Nepalese mountaineer; climbed Mt Everest 1953.

tepee /'tiːpiː/, *n.* a tent of the North American Indians. Also, **teepee, tipi.** [Dakota Siouan]

tepid /'tepəd/, *adj.* moderately warm; lukewarm. [ME, from L]

tequila /tə'kiːlə/, *n.* a strong Mexican alcoholic drink. [named after *Tequila*, district of Mexico]

terbium /'tɜːbiəm/, *n.* a rare-earth, metallic element having colorless salts. *Symbol:* Tb; *at. no.:* 65; *at. wt:* 158.924. [(*Yt*)*terb*(*y*), name of Swedish town where found]

terbium metals, *n.pl.* See **rare-earth elements**.

Teresa /tə'reɪzə/, *n.* **Mother** (*Agnes Gonxha Bojaxhiu*), born 1910, Albanian-born Roman Catholic missionary; noted for her work with the poor in India; 1979 Nobel Peace prize.

Tereshkova /tɪrɪʃ'kəʊvə/, *n.* **Valentina Vladimirovna** /vælən'tiːnə vlɑːdɪ'mɪrəvnə/, born 1937, Russian cosmonaut; first woman in space.

term /tɜːm/, *n.* **1.** any word or group of words naming something, esp. as used in some particular field of knowledge. **2.** any word or group of words considered as a member of a written or spoken expression. **3.** the time through which something lasts or is planned or determined to last. **4.** each of certain periods of the year into which teaching is regularly organised in schools, etc. **5.** a set time or date, as for the payment of rent, interest, wages, etc. **6.** (*pl.*) conditions with regard to payment, price, charge, rates, wages, etc.: *The loan carries heavy terms.* **7.** (*pl.*) conditions indicating what is proposed to be granted or done: *the terms of a treaty.* **8.** (*pl.*) footing or standing: *on good terms with a person.* **9.** *Maths.* each of the parts making up an expression, a series of quantities, etc. **10.** the normal completion of the period of pregnancy. **11.** *Archaic.* end or conclusion. **12. come to terms, a.** to reach agreement. **b.** to become accustomed. ◇*v.t.* **13.** to apply a particular term or name to; name; call; designate. [ME, from OF, from L: boundary, limit, end]

termagant /'tɜːməgənt/, *n.* **1.** a violent, stormy or quarrelsome woman. ◇*adj.* **2.** violent; turbulent; brawling; shrewish. [ME, from OF *Tervagan* a supposed Muslim deity, represented in some medieval morality plays, etc., as a violent, overbearing person]

terminal /'tɜːmənəl/, *adj.* **1.** situated at or forming the end of something. **2.** relating to or lasting for a term or definite period. **3.** relating to, situated at, or forming the end of a bus or rail route. **4.** happening at or causing the end of life: *a terminal illness.* ◇*n.* **5.** a terminal part or structure. **6.** the end of a railway line, shipping route, etc., at which large scale loading and unloading of passengers, goods, etc., takes place. **7.** *Elect.* **a.** a mechanical device by means of which an electrical connection to an apparatus is established. **b.** the point at which current enters or leaves any conducting part in an electric circuit. **8.** → **computer terminal.** [L: pertaining to an end or boundary]

terminal velocity, *n. Phys.* the maximum velocity reached by a body falling through a resisting medium, as under gravity.

terminate /'tɜːməneɪt/, *v.*, **-nated, -nating.** ◇*v.t.* **1.** to bring to an end. **2.** to form the end of. ◇*v.i.* **3.** to end, conclude, or cease. **4.** (of a train, bus, etc.) to complete a scheduled journey at a certain place. [L: ended, limited] –**termination,** *n.*

terminology /tɜːmə'nɒlədʒi/, *n., pl.* **-gies.** the system of terms belonging to a science, art, or subject; nomenclature: *the terminology of physics.* [G] –**terminological,** *adj.*

terminus /'tɜːmənəs/, *n., pl.* **-ni** /-naɪ/, **-nuses. 1.** the end of anything. **2.** (a station or town at) either end of a railway line, bus route, etc. **3.** the point to which anything tends; goal or end. [L: boundary, limit]

termite /'tɜːmaɪt/, *n.* any of an order of pale-colored, soft-bodied, social insects, some being destructive to buildings, furniture, etc.; white ant. [NL: termite]

tern /tɜːn/, *n.* a gull-like water bird with a slender body and beak, small feet, a long and deeply forked tail, and graceful flight. [Scand]

ternary /'tɜːnəri/, *adj.* **1.** consisting of or involving three; triple. **2.** third in order or rank. **3.** based on the number three. [ME, from LL: made up of three]

ternary form, *n.* a musical form consisting of three parts, where the third is an exact or close repetition of the first. It can be represented as ABA.

terpene /'tɜːpiːn/, *n.* any of certain unsaturated hydrocarbons occurring in essential oils of many plants. [G: TURPENTINE]

terrace /'terəs/, *v.*, **-raced, -racing.** ◇*n.* **1.** a raised bank of earth with a level top, esp. one of a series formed across a slope, mountain side, etc. **2.** *Geol.* a nearly level strip of land (once a floodplain) with a more or less sudden descent along the edge of a sea, lake or river. **3.** an open area connected with a house

terrace and serving as an outdoor living area. **4.** (a house in) a row of identical houses, each usu. sharing a side wall with the next, often of two storeys. **5.** a city street. ◇*v.t.* **6.** to form into or supply with a terrace or terraces. [OF: terrace, pile of earth, from F: earth, from L]

terracotta /ˌterəˈkɒtə/, *n.* **1.** hard, usu. unglazed baked clay used for pots, pipes, etc. **2.** a brownish orange colour. ◇*adj.* **3.** made or having the color of terracotta. [It: baked earth, from L]

terra firma /ˌterə ˈfɜːmə/, *n.* firm or solid earth. [L: solid earth]

terrain /təˈreɪn/, *n.* a section of land, esp. as considered with reference to its natural features, military advantages, etc. [F: earth, from L]

terrarium /təˈreəriəm/, *n., pl.* **-rariums**, **-raria** /-ˈreəriə/. **1.** a closed glass container in which moisture-loving plants are grown. **2.** a container in which small animals, as lizards, turtles, etc., are kept. [NL: earth]

terrazzo /təˈrɑːtsoʊ, -ˈræz-/, *n.* a type of floor material of chippings of broken stone and cement, polished when in place. [It: terrace, balcony]

terrestrial /təˈrestriəl/, *adj.* **1.** relating to, consisting of, or representing the earth: *a terrestrial globe.* **2.** of or relating to the land as separate from the water. **3.** *Zool.* living on the ground. [ME, from L: pertaining to earth]

terrible /ˈterəbəl/, *adj.* **1.** causing great fear; dreadful. **2.** very bad: *a terrible performance.* [ME, from L]

terrier /ˈteriə/, *n.* a type of dog, typically small, formerly bred to chase animals into burrows, e.g. **fox terrier**, **Irish terrier**, **Australian terrier**. [ME, from F: a hunting dog to start badgers, etc., from their earth or burrow]

terrific /təˈrɪfɪk/, *adj.* **1.** causing terror; terrifying. **2.** *Colloq.* very great, intense, etc.: *terrific speed.* **3.** *Colloq.* very good: *terrific food.* [L: frightening] —**terrifically**, *adv.*

terrify /ˈterəfaɪ/, *v.t.*, **-fied, -fying**. to fill with terror. [L]

terrine /təˈriːn/, *n.* **1.** an earthenware cooking dish. **2.** pâté served in such a dish. [F]

territorial /ˌterəˈtɔːriəl/, *adj.* **1.** of or relating to territory or land. **2.** of, relating to, associated with, or limited to a particular territory or district; local.

territory /ˈterətri, -təri/, *n., pl.* **-ries**. **1.** any area of land; region or district: *enemy territory.* **2.** the land and waters belonging to or under the control of a state, king, etc. **3.** (*oft. cap.*) an area controlled by a government in which it is not fully represented. **4. the Territory**, the Northern Territory. **5.** a field of action, thought, etc.: *Giving legal advice is not in my territory.* **6.** an area which an animal claims as its own and defends against intruders. [ME, from L: land round a town, district]

terror /ˈterə/, *n.* **1.** sharp, overpowering fear. **2.** a feeling, occasion or cause of great fear: *to be a terror to evildoers.* **3.** (*cap.*) a period when a political group uses violence to keep or gain control. **4.** *Colloq.* a person or thing that is a particular nuisance: *Their child is a little terror.* [L]

terrorise *or* **terrorize** /ˈterəraɪz/, *v.t.*, **-rised, -rising**. **1.** to fill or overcome with terror. **2.** to control or force by the use of terror. —**terrorisation**, *n.*

terrorism /ˈterərɪzəm/, *n.* **1.** the use of terrorising methods: *The enemy gained control by terrorism.* **2.** a method of fighting a government or of governing by acts of armed violence. —**terrorist**, *n., adj.*

terry towelling, *n.* a cotton pile fabric with loops on both sides.

terse /tɜːs/, *adj.*, **terser, tersest**. **1.** neatly or effectively brief: *a terse speech.* **2.** impolitely brief or bad-tempered, esp. in one's speech. [L: polished]

tertiary /ˈtɜːʃəri/, *adj., n., pl.* **-ries**. ◇*adj.* **1.** of the third order, rank, formation, etc. **2.** *Chem.* **a.** indicating or containing a carbon atom with three other carbon atoms attached. **b.** (of a salt) formed by replacement of three hydrogen ions in an acid, as a phosphate. **3.** (*cap.*) *Geol.* relating to a geological period, or a system of rocks, which comes before the Quaternary and forms the earlier main division of the Cainozoic era. ◇*n.* **4.** (*cap.*) *Geol.* a period or system representing geological time from about 2 to 60 million years ago and made up of the Palaeocene to Pliocene periods or series. [L: of third part or rank]

tertiary consumer *n.* a carnivore that eats carnivores. See **primary consumer**, **secondary consumer**.

tertiary education, *n.* all forms of formal education beyond secondary education, including education at a university, or college.

terylene /ˈterəliːn/, *n.* a synthetic polyester fibre, used in clothing manufacture. [Trademark]

tesla /ˈteslə/, *n.* the SI derived unit of magnetic flux density, or magnetic intensity, defined as the magnetic flux of one weber per square metre (Wb/m^2). *Symbol*: T

tessellate /ˈtesəleɪt/, *v.*, **-lated, -lating**; /ˈtesələt, -leɪt/, *adj.* ◇*v.t.* **1.** to form into small squares or blocks, as floors, paths, etc. ◇*adj.* **2.** like a mosaic; tessellated. [LL: formed in mosaic] —**tessellation**, *n.*

test[1] /test/, *n.* **1.** a trial by which the presence, quality, or genuineness of anything is determined. **2.** a particular process or method of doing this: *This was a difficult test to carry out.* **3.** *Educ.* a form of examination for determining the performance and abilities of a student or class. **4.** *Chem.* **a.** a process of detecting the presence of an element in a compound, etc., or of determining the nature of a substance, usu. by addition of a reagent. **b.** the reagent used. **c.** the result of the above process. **5.** a cup-like vessel for examining or refining metals. **6.** *Sport*. → **test match**.

test 1065 **textual**

◇*v.t.* **7.** to subject to a test of any kind; try: *to test the water for heat.* **8.** to examine or refine in a test. ◇*v.i.* **9.** to conduct a test. [ME, from OF, from L: tile, earthen vessel, pot]

test² /test/, *n.* **1.** *Zool.* the hard covering of certain invertebrates, as molluscs, arthropods, etc.; shell. **2.** *Bot.* a testa. [L]

testa /'testə/, *n., pl.* **-tae** /-tiː/. *Bot.* the outer, usu. hard, coat of a plant seed. [L]

testament /'testəmənt/, *n.* **1.** *Law.* a formal statement, usu. in writing, of a person's wishes as to the ownership of their property after their death. **2.** an agreement, esp. between God and man; covenant. **3.** (*cap.*) either of the two main divisions of the Bible, the **Old Testament** and the **New Testament**. [ME, from L: will] —**testamentary**, *adj.*

testes /'testiz/, *n.* plural of **testis**.

testicle /'testɪkə/, *n.* the male sex gland, either of the two oval glands situated in the scrotum. [L: TESTIS] —**testicular**, *adj.*

testify /'testəfaɪ/, *v.,* **-fied**, **-fying**. ◇*v.i.* **1.** to give evidence; bear witness. **2.** *Law.* to give a statement under solemn promise as to its truth, usu. in court. ◇*v.t.* **3.** to state as fact or truth: *I testify that he lied.* **4.** to give evidence of in any manner: *The barren land testifies to a hard winter.* **5.** to declare, claim, or acknowledge openly. **6.** *Law.* to state under solemn oath, usu. in court. [ME, from L: bear witness]

testimonial /testə'moʊniəl/, *n.* **1.** a written statement giving information about a person's character, conduct, or job skills, or a thing's value, excellence, etc. **2.** something given or done as an expression of admiration, or thanks: *He was given a watch as a testimonial.* ◇*adj.* **3.** relating to or serving as testimony.

testimony /'testəməni/, *n., pl.* **-nies**. **1.** *Law.* the statement of a witness under solemn oath, usu. in court. **2.** evidence in support of a fact or statement; proof. **3.** an open declaration, as of faith. [late ME, from L: evidence, attestation]

testis /'testəs/, *n., pl.* **-tes** /-tiːz/. → **testicle**. [L]

test match, *n.* a match or one of a series of matches, esp. in cricket, between two teams of different nations.

testosterone /tes'tɒstəroʊn/, *n.* a male sex hormone, secreted by the testes, which stimulates development of masculine characteristics. [*testo-* TESTIS + STER(OL) + -ONE]

test tube, *n.* a hollow glass cylinder with one end closed, used in chemical tests.

test-tube baby, *n. Med.* a child conceived artificially outside a mother's body, under conditions suitable for its survival, and then implanted in the womb.

testy /'testi/, *adj.,* **-tier**, **-tiest**. touchy; irritably impatient. [ME, from AF: headstrong, from OF: head, from L: potsherd]

tetanus /'tetənəs/, *n. Med.* (a microorganism causing) an infectious, oft. fatal disease, which enters the body through wounds, and which causes violent sustained muscle spasms esp. in the muscles of the neck and lower jaw. See **lockjaw**. [L, from Gk: spasm (of muscles)] —**tetanoid**, *adj.*

tete-a-tete /tet-a-'tet, teɪt-a-'teɪt/, ◇*n.* **1.** a private conversation or meeting, usu. between two people. ◇*adv.* **2.** (of two people) together in private: *to sit tete-a-tete.* [F: head to head]

tether /'teðə/, *n.* **1.** a rope, chain, etc., tied to an animal to limit its movement. **2. the end of one's tether**, the limit of one's possibilities, patience, etc. ◇*v.t.* **3.** to fasten or hold with or as if with a tether. [ME, apparently from Scand]

tetra-, a word part meaning 'four' as in *tetrahedron*. [Gk, combining form of *téttares*]

tetrachord /'tetrəkɔd/, *n. Music.* a diatonic series of four notes, the first and last separated by a perfect fourth. [Gk: having 4 strings]

tetracycline, *n. Biochem.* any of a group of broad-spectrum antibiotics.

tetrad /'tetræd/, *n.* **1.** a group of four. **2.** the number four. [Gk: group of 4]

tetragon /'tetrəgən, -gɒn/, *n.* a plane figure having four angles; quadrangle; quadrilateral. [Gk: quadrangle]

tetrahedron /tetrə'hidrən/, *n., pl.* **-drons**, **-dra** /-drə/. a solid contained by four plane faces; a triangular pyramid. [LGk: 4-sided]

tetravalent /tetrə'veɪlənt/, *adj.* having a valency of four.

Teuton /'tjutən/, *n.* **1.** a member of a Germanic people or tribe first mentioned in the fourth century BC and supposed to have dwelt in Jutland. **2.** a native of Germany or a person of German origin. **3.** a member of any people speaking a Germanic language. [L *Teutonēs*, *Teutonī* (pl.) tribal name] —**Teutonic**, *n., adj.*

Texas /'teksəs/, *n.* a state in the southern US on the Gulf of Mexico; second largest US state; chief US producer of gas and oil. Pop. 16 682 000 (1986 est.); 691 027 km². *Cap.*: Austin. *Abbrev.*: Tex —**Texan**, *n., adj.*

text /tekst/, *n.* **1.** the main body of matter in a book or manuscript, not including notes, appendixes, etc. **2.** the original words of an author as opposed to a translation, paraphrase, commentary, etc. **3.** the actual wording of anything written or printed. **4.** → **textbook**. **5.** a short passage of Scripture, esp. one chosen as the subject of a sermon, etc. [ME, from ML: wording (of the Gospel), L: structure (of a discourse), orig. texture]

textbook /'tekstbʊk/, *n.* a book used by students as a standard work for a particular branch of study.

textile /'tekstaɪl/, *n.* **1.** any material that is woven. **2.** any material suitable for weaving. ◇*adj.* **3.** woven or able to be woven: *textile fabrics.* **4.** of or relating to weaving: *the textile industries.* [L: woven]

textual /'tekstʃuəl/, *adj.* of, relating to, or contained in a text: *textual mistakes; textual criticism.* [ME, from ML]

texture /'tekstʃə/, *n.* **1.** the characteristic arrangement of the interwoven threads, etc., which make up a textile fabric. **2.** the characteristic appearance or basic quality of something, esp. as sensed by touch: *the rough texture of concrete*. [late ME, from L: weaving] – **textural**, *adj.*

-th[1], a noun suffix referring to condition, quality, or action, added to words (*warmth*) and to stems related to words (*depth, length*). [OE *-thu, -tho, -th*]

-th[2], the suffix of ordinal numerals (*fourth, tenth, twentieth*), added to the cardinal number, and in some cases, to altered stems of the cardinal (*fifth, twelfth*). [OE *-tha, -the*]

Th, *Abbrev.* **1.** Thursday. ◇*Symbol.* **2.** *Chem.* thorium.

Thackeray /'θækərei, -ri/, *n.* **William Makepeace**, 1811–63, English novelist, born in India; satirised social pretensions in such novels as *Vanity Fair* (1848).

Thailand /'tailænd/, *n.* a kingdom in south-east Asia, on the Gulf of Thailand and bordered by Burma, Laos, Cambodia and Malaysia. Pop. 53 722 000 (1987); 513 115 km². *Language:* Thai. *Currency:* baht. *Cap.:* Bangkok. Formerly, **Siam**.

thalidomide /θə'lɪdəmaɪd/, *n.* a drug, formerly used as a sedative until it was found to affect normal growth of the foetus if taken during pregnancy. [*thal(ic)* + *(im)ido-* + *(glutari)mide* (from GLUT(EN) + *(tart)ar(ic)* + *imide*)]

thallium /'θæliəm, 'θeɪ-/, *n.* a soft, malleable, rare, metallic element, used in alloys. Its salts are used in rat poisons. *Symbol:* Tl; *at. no.:* 81; *at. wt:* 204.37. [NL, from Gk: green shoot]

thallus /'θæləs/, *n., pl.* **thalli** /'θælaɪ/, **thalluses**. *Bot.* a simple plant body undifferentiated into true leaves, stem, and root. [NL, from Gk: young shoot, twig]

Thames /temz/, *n.* the second longest river of Great Britain, rising in Gloucestershire and flowing through London to the North Sea. 338 km.

than /ðæn/; *weak form* /ðən/, *conj.* **1.** a particle used after comparative adjectives, adverbs and certain other words, such as *other, otherwise, else,* etc., to introduce the second member of a comparison: *He is taller than I am.* ◇*prep.* **2.** in comparison with: *He is taller than me.* [ME and OE]

thane /θeɪn/, *n.* *Scot. Hist.* a person, ranking with an earl's son, holding lands belonging to the king. [late ME, OE *thegn*]

thank /θæŋk/, *v.t.* **1.** to give thanks to. ◇*n.* **2.** (*usu. pl.*) the expression in words, etc., of grateful feeling, for some benefit or favor: *to return a borrowed book with thanks.* **3.** (*pl.*) a common expression used in expressing a favor, service, etc. **4. thanks to,** as a result of: *thanks to the rain, the game was cancelled.* [ME; OE *thanc* gratitude] – **thankful**, *adj.*

thankless /'θæŋkləs/, *adj.* **1.** not such as to be rewarded with thanks: *a thankless task.* **2.** ungrateful: *a thankless person.*

thanksgiving /θæŋks'gɪvɪŋ, 'θæŋksgɪvɪŋ/, *n.* **1.** the act of giving thanks. **2.** an expression of thanks, esp. to God. **3.** (*cap.*) *US.* Also, **Thanksgiving Day**, an annual festival in acknowledgment of divine favor, usually held on the fourth Thursday of November.

thankyou /'θæŋkju/, *interj.* **1.** (an expression of thanks.) ◇*n.* **2.** the act of expressing thanks: *Have you said your thankyous?* ◇*adj.* **3.** expressing thanks: *a thankyou letter.*

that /ðæt/; *weak form* /ðət/, *pron. and adj., pl.* **those**; *adv., conj.* ◇*pron.* **1.** a demonstrative pronoun used to show: **a.** a person, thing, idea, etc., as pointed out, mentioned, or suggested: *That is my husband.* **b.** one of two or more people, things, etc., already mentioned, referring to the one further away in place, time, or thought (often opposed to *this*): *That is riper than this.* **2.** a relative pronoun used: **a.** as the subject or object of a relative clause: *How old is the car that was stolen?* **b.** in various special forms: *fool that he is.* **3. at that,** additionally; besides: *It's an idea, and a good one at that.* **4. that is,** more exactly and precisely: *I see him often, well that is, once a week.* **5. that's that,** that is the end of the matter: *I've lost it, so that's that.* ◇*adj.* **6.** a demonstrative adjective used to show: **a.** a person, place, thing, idea, etc., as pointed out, mentioned, or suggested: *That man is my husband.* **b.** one of two or more people, things, etc., already mentioned, referring to the one further away in place, time, or thought (often opposed to *this*): *It was that book I wanted, not this one.* ◇*adv.* **7.** an adverb used with adjectives and adverbs of quality or extent to show precise degree or extent: *that much; that far.* ◇*conj.* **8.** a conjunction used to introduce a noun clause: *That he will come is certain.* [ME; OE *thæt* that, the]

thatch /θætʃ/, *n.* **1.** material (straw, rushes, leaves, etc.), used to cover roofs, haystacks, etc. **2.** a covering of such a material. **3.** *Colloq.* the hair covering the head. ◇*v.t.* **4.** to cover with or as if with thatch. [OE *thæc* roof, thatch]

Thatcher /'θætʃə/, *n.* **Lady Margaret (Hilda),** born 1925, English politician; became Conservative Party leader in 1975; prime minister 1979–90.

thaw /θɔ/, *v.i.* **1.** to pass from a frozen to a liquid or semi-liquid state; melt: *The ice thawed.* **2.** to be freed from the physical effect of frost or great cold (oft. fol. by *out*): *My cold fingers thawed out.* **3.** (of the weather) to become warm enough to melt ice and snow: *It will probably thaw today.* **4.** to become less cold or formal in manner: *He thawed out and began talking about himself.* **5.** to become less unfriendly or quarrelsome: *Relations between the Soviet Union and the US have thawed.* ◇*v.t.* **6.** to cause to thaw. ◇*n.* **7.** a reduction in unfriendliness, esp. in international relations: *a thaw in diplomatic relations.* **8.** the condition of the weather caused by the rise of the temperature above freezing point. [OE *thawian*]

the[1] /ði/ *before a vowel;* /ðə/ *before a consonant, def. art.* a word used esp. before nouns **1.** with a limiting or specifying effect (opposed to *a* or *an*). **2.** with or as part of a title or name: *the Duke of Wellington; the Alps.* **3.** to mark a noun as being used to identify a class or type etc.: *the dog is a quadruped.* **4.** in place of a possessive pronoun, to show a part of the body or a personal belonging: *to hang the head and weep.* **5.** to show a class or type: *I saw it on the TV.* **6.** to show that there is enough of something: *I don't have the money to buy a car.* [ME and OE]

the² /ðɪ/ *before a vowel;* /ðə/ *before a consonant,* , *adv.* a word used **1.** to modify an adjective or adverb in the comparative degree: *He is taking more care of himself, and looks the better for it.* **2.** in pairs, to show relationship between two adjectives or adverbs: *Come, the sooner the better.* [ME and OE]

theatre /ˈθɪətə/, *n.* **1.** a building or room built or fitted for the presentation of dramatic performances, stage entertainments, etc. **2.** any area used for dramatic presentations, etc., as one in the open air. **3.** a cinema. **4.** dramatic works collectively, as of a nation, period, or author. **5.** a room or hall, fitted with tiers of seats rising like steps, used for lectures, etc. **6.** a room in a hospital in which surgical operations are performed: *an operating theatre.* **7.** a place of action: *theatre of war.* [ME, from L, from Gk: seeing place, theatre]

theatre of the absurd, *n.* a modern dramatic style which expresses the belief that the human condition is essentially absurd.

theatrical /θɪˈætrəkəl/, *adj.* Also, **theatric**. **1.** of or relating to the theatre: *theatrical performances.* **2.** suggestive of the theatre or of acting: *a theatrical display of grief.* ◇*n.* **3.** (*pl.*) dramatic performances, now esp. as given by amateurs. —**theatricality,** *n.*

Thebes /θiːbz/, *n.* **1.** an ancient ruined city in Upper Egypt, on the Nile; a former capital of Egypt. **2.** a city of ancient Greece, in Boeotia; a rival of ancient Athens. —**Thebaic,** *adj.* —**Theban** *n., adj.*

thee /ðiː/, *pron. Archaic.* the objective case of **thou**: *With this ring, I thee wed.* [ME; OE *thē*]

theft /θɛft/, *n.* the act of stealing; larceny. [ME; OE *thēoft*]

their /ðɛə/, *adj.* **1.** the possessive form of *they* used before a noun: *The boys are in their rooms.* **2.** *Colloq.* (sometimes considered to be bad usage) a possessive adjective with singular force used in place of 'his' or 'her' when the sex of the subject is not stated: *Who has left their pen on my desk?* [ME, from Scand]

theirs /ðɛəz/, *pron.* **1.** a form of the possessive *their* (used after a verb, or without a noun following): *This umbrella is theirs.* **2.** *Colloq.* (sometimes considered to be bad usage) a possessive pronoun with singular force, used in place of 'his' or 'hers' when the sex of the subject is not known: *Does anybody recognise this pen as theirs?*

theism /ˈθiːɪzəm/, *n.* belief in the existence of a God or gods (as opposed to *atheism*). [Gk: god] —**theist,** *n., adj.* —**theistic,** *adj.*

them /ðɛm/; *weak form* /ðəm/, *pron.* **1.** the objective case of **they.** ◇*adj.* **2.** *Colloq.* (usu. considered to be bad usage) those: *Take them things out of here.* [ME, from Scand]

theme /θiːm/, *n.* **1.** a subject of conversation, discussion, thought, or composition; a topic. **2.** a short, informal essay, esp. a school composition. **3.** *Music.* the main subject in a musical composition from which variations may be developed. [ME, from L, from Gk] —**thematic,** *adj.*

Themistocles /θəˈmɪstəkliːz/, *n.* 527?–460? BC, Athenian statesman.

themselves /ðəmˈsɛlvz/, *pron. pl.* **1.** the reflexive form of **them:** *They hurt themselves.* **2.** an emphatic form of **them** or **they** used **a.** as object: *They used it for themselves.* **b.** in apposition to a subject or object: *They themselves did it.* **3.** their proper or normal selves: *They are themselves again.* **4.** Also, **themself.** *Colloq.* (usu. considered to be bad usage) a reflexive pronoun with singular force, used in place of 'himself' or 'herself' when the sex of the person in the sentence is not known: *Someone is deceiving themselves.*

then /ðɛn/, *adv.* **1.** at that time: *Prices were lower then.* **2.** immediately or soon afterwards: *He stopped, and then began again.* **3.** next in order of time: *He unlocked the door, then walked inside.* **4.** at another time. **5.** next in order of place: *Down the road there's a shop, then a garage.* **6.** in addition; besides: *She gave me ten dollars, then another three dollars.* **7.** in that case: *If it gets hot then I'll wear a hat.* **8.** since that is so; therefore: *He doesn't like chocolate, so then I never buy any.* **9. but then,** but at the same time: *She isn't pretty, but then she can sing.* ◇*adj.* **10.** being at that time: *the then prime minister.* ◇*n.* **11.** that time: *till then.* [OE *thænne*]

thence /ðɛns/, *adv.* **1.** from that place: *Julius Caesar marched to Gaul and thence to Spain.* **2.** from that time; thenceforth: *The bill was passed in parliament and thence became law.* **3.** for that reason; therefore: *He had the jewels in his possession, and thence the police believed him to be the robber.* [OE *thanone* thence]

thenceforth /ðɛnsˈfɔθ/, *adv.* from that time or place onwards. Also, **thenceforward, thenceforwards.**

theo-, a word part meaning 'relating to the gods', 'divine'. Also, before vowels, **the-.** [Gk, combining form of *theós* god]

theocracy /θiˈɒkrəsi/, *n., pl.* **-cies. 1.** a form of government in which God or a deity is recognised as the supreme ruler of the people. **2.** a system of government by priests claiming a divine power. [Gk] —**theocrat,** *n.*

theodolite /θiˈɒdəlaɪt/, *n. Surveying.* an instrument for measuring horizontal or vertical angles. [coined word; orig. unknown]

Theodorakis /θiədəˈrakɪs/, *n.* **Mikos** /ˈmikɒs/ born 1925, Greek composer; best known for music in the film *Zorba the Greek* (1965).

theology /θiˈɒlədʒi/, *n., pl.* **-gies. 1.** the science of religion and religious ideas or beliefs; divinity. **2.** a particular form, system, or

theology

branch of this science or study. [ME, from L, from Gk] −**theologian**, *n.* −**theological**, *adj.*

theorem /ˈθɪərəm/, *n.* **1.** *Maths.* a statement containing something to be proved. **2.** a rule or law, esp. one expressed by an equation or formula. **3.** *Logic.* a proposition which can be deduced from the premises of a system. [LL, from Gk: spectacle, theory, thesis (to be proved)]

theoretical /θɪəˈretɪkəl/, *adj.* **1.** of, relating to, or consisting in theory; not practical. **2.** existing only in theory; hypothetical. **3.** given to, forming, or dealing with theories; speculative. Also, **theoretic**.

theoretician /θɪərəˈtɪʃən/, *n.* someone who deals with or is skilled in the theoretical side of a subject.

theorise *or* **theorize** /ˈθɪəraɪz/, *v.i.*, **-rised, -rising. 1.** to form a theory. **2.** to engage in thought; speculate. −**theorisation**, *n.* −**theorist**, *n.*

theory /ˈθɪəri/, *n., pl.* **-ries. 1.** a logical group of statements used as principles to explain something: *Newton's theory of gravitation.* **2.** a suggested explanation not yet established as fact: *a theory about ghosts.* **3.** that part of a science or art which deals with principles and methods rather than with practice. **4.** opinion; conjecture. [LL, from Gk: contemplation, theory]

theosophy /θiˈɒsəfi/, *n.* **1.** any of various forms of philosophical or religious thought which claim to have special understanding of or contact with divine reality. **2.** a system of belief and theory, based largely on Brahmanic and Buddhistic ideas, of the **Theosophical Society** (founded in New York in 1875). [ML, from LGk] −**theosophic, theosophical**, *adj.* −**theosophist**, *n.*

therapeutic /θerəˈpjutɪk/, *adj.* relating to the treating or curing of disease; curative. Also, **therapeutical**. [NL, from Gk: one who treats medically]

therapy /ˈθerəpi/, *n., pl.* **-pies. 1.** treatment of a disease, disorder, etc., as by means of medical aid, exercise, etc. **2.** a power or quality that cures: *Your kind words are a therapy to me.* [NL, from Gk: healing] −**therapist**, *n.*

there /ðeə/, *adv.* **1.** in or at that place: *The book is there, on the top shelf.* **2.** at that point in time, action, speech, etc.: *He finished there, ready to start again later.* **3.** in that matter, particular, or respect: *I must agree with you there.* **4.** into or to that place: *Go in there.* **5.** (used to call attention to something): *there they go.* ◇*adj.* **6.** (used for emphasis): *that man there.* **7. all there**, *Colloq.* of sound mind: *He's not all there.* ◇*pron.* **8.** that place: *He comes from there too.* **9.** (used to introduce a sentence or clause in which the verb comes before its subject): *There is no hope.* **10.** (used in interjectional phrases): *There's a good boy.* ◇*interj.* **11. a.** (an exclamation used to express satisfaction, etc.): *There! It's done!* **b.** (an exclamation used to give sympathy): *There, there, don't cry.* **c.** (an exclamation used to draw attention to something): *There! The jug's broken.* [ME; OE *thǽr*]

thermometer

there-, a word part meaning 'that (place)', 'that (time)', etc., used in combination with certain adverbs and prepositions, as in *thereabouts*. [special use of THERE, demonstrative adv.]

thereabouts /ˌðeərəˈbauts, ˈðeərəbauts/, *adv.* **1.** about or near that place or time. **2.** about that number, amount, etc. Also, **thereabout**.

thereby /ðeəˈbaɪ, ˈðeəbaɪ/, *adv.* **1.** by means of that: *She studied hard, and thereby passed her exams.* **2.** in that connection or relation: *Thereby hangs a tale.* **3.** by or near that place.

therefore /ˈðeəfɔ, ðeəˈfɔ/, *adv.* as a result; consequently. [ME]

therein /ðeərˈɪn/, *adv.* **1.** in that place or thing. **2.** in that matter, circumstance, etc.: *Therein lies the problem.*

thereof /ðeərˈɒv/, *adv.* **1.** of that or it. **2.** from or out of that, as a source or origin.

thereon /ðeərˈɒn/, *adv.* **1.** on that or it: *I received the letter with no date thereon.* **2.** immediately after that; thereupon.

thereupon /ˌðeərəˈpɒn, ˈðeərəpɒn/, *adv.* **1.** immediately following that. **2.** as a result of that. **3.** with reference to that.

therewith /ðeəˈwɪθ, -ˈwɪð/, *adv.* **1.** with that. **2.** in addition to that. **3.** following upon that; thereupon.

therm /θɜm/, *n.* a unit of heat in the imperial system, used as a basis for the selling of gas; about 105.5×10^6 J. [Gk: heat]

therm-, a word part representing 'thermal'. Also, **thermo-**. [Gk, combining form of *thermós* hot, *thérmē* heat]

thermal /ˈθɜməl/, *adj.* **1.** Also, **thermic**. of or relating to heat or temperature: *thermal energy.* ◇*n.* **2.** a rising current of air caused by local heating, used by glider pilots, birds, etc., to go higher. [Gk: heat]

thermal radiation *n.* **1.** the heat and light produced by a nuclear explosion. **2.** electromagnetic radiations emitted from a heat or light source as a consequence of its temperature; it consists essentially of ultraviolet, visible and infra-red radiation.

thermal springs, *n.pl.* natural hot-water springs.

thermocouple /ˈθɜmoukʌpəl/, *n.* two conductors of different metals joined at their ends and producing a thermoelectric current when there is a difference in temperature between the ends. Also, **thermoelectric couple**.

thermodynamics /ˌθɜmoudaɪˈnæmɪks/, *n.* the science concerned with processes involving heat changes and conversion of energy. −**thermodynamic, thermodynamical**, *adj.* −**thermodynamically**, *adv.*

thermodynamic temperature scale, *n.* See **absolute temperature**. *Abbrev:* T

thermometer /θəˈmɒmətə/, *n.* an instrument for measuring temperature; a marked glass tube in which a column of liquid such as mercury expands and rises as the temperature

thermometer

increases, and contracts and falls as the temperature decreases. **—thermometric, thermometrical,** *adj.* **—thermometrically,** *adv.*

thermoplastic /θəmoʊˈplæstɪk/, *adj.* **1.** soft and pliable whenever heated, as some plastics, without any change in properties. ◇*n.* **2.** such a plastic.

Thermopylae /θəˈmɒpəli/, *n.* a narrow pass in eastern Greece; heroic defence by the Spartans against the Persians 480 BC.

thermos /ˈθɜːmɒs, -məs/, *n.* a double-walled container, usu. made of silvered glass and having a vacuum between the two walls, used to keep substances at a constant temperature. [Trademark; Gk: hot]

thermostat /ˈθɜːməstæt/, *n.* a device which establishes and holds a desired temperature automatically, or signals a change in temperature. **—thermostatic,** *adj.* **—thermostatically,** *adv.*

-thermy, a word part referring to 'heat'. [combining form representing Gk *thérmē*]

Therry /ˈteri/, *n.* **John Joseph,** 1790–1864, Australian pioneer Roman Catholic priest, born in Ireland.

thesaurus /θəˈsɔːrəs/, *n., pl.* **-sauruses** /-ˈsɔːrəsəz/. a dictionary, encyclopedia, etc., esp. a dictionary of synonyms and antonyms. [L, from Gk: treasure, treasury]

these /ðiːz/, *pron., adj.* plural of **this.** [ME]

Theseus /ˈθiːsiəs/, *n.* Gk Legend. the chief hero of Attica, son of Aegeus, said to have organised a constitutional government and united the separate states at Athens. Among his many exploits he found his way through the Cretan labyrinth, slew the Minotaur, fought the Amazons, and was one of the Argonauts. **—Thesean,** *adj.*

thesis /ˈθiːsəs/, *n., pl.* **-ses** /-siːz/. **1.** a statement of a theory, esp. one to be discussed and proved. **2.** a subject for a composition or essay. **3.** a written essay, particularly one presented by a candidate for a diploma or degree, esp. a postgraduate degree. [ME, from Gk: setting down, something set down]

Thespian /ˈθɛspiən/, *adj.* **1.** relating to tragedy or to dramatic art in general; tragic; dramatic. ◇*n.* **2.** an actor or actress. [from *Thespis,* a poet (flourished 6th C BC)]

Thessaly /ˈθɛsəli/, *n.* a region in eastern Greece; a former division of ancient Greece. Pop. 695 654 (1981); 13 488 km². **—Thessalian,** *n., adj.*

theta /ˈθiːtə/, *n.* the eighth letter (θ, Θ) of the Greek alphabet.

they /ðeɪ/, *pron. pl., poss.* **theirs,** *obj.* **them.** **1.** subjective plural of *he, she* and *it*: *they sang.* **2.** people in general: *They say he is rich.* **3.** *Colloq.* (sometimes regarded as bad usage) a person (used in place of a singular pronoun where the sex of the person is not determined): *If anybody moves they will get a bullet in their head.* [ME; from Scand]

they'd /ðeɪd/, the shortened form of **1.** they had. **2.** they would.

they'll /ðeɪl/, the shortened form of **1.** they will. **2.** they shall.

they're /ðɛə, ˈðeɪə/, the shortened form of 'they are'.

they've /ðeɪv/, the shortened form of 'they have'.

thi-, a variant of **thio-,** as in *thiazine.*

thiamine /ˈθaɪəmin/, *n.* vitamin B₁, part of vitamin B complex, needed by the nervous system, the absence of which causes beri-beri, etc. Also, **thiamin.** [THI(O)- + (VIT)AMIN]

thiazine /ˈθaɪəziːn, -zaɪn/, *n.* any of a class of compounds containing a ring made of one atom each of sulfur and nitrogen and four atoms of carbon. Also, **thiazin** /ˈθaɪəzən/.

thick /θɪk/, *adj.* **1.** having a relatively great extent from one surface or side to its opposite; not thin: *a thick slice.* **2.** measuring as stated between opposite surfaces: *a board one centimetre thick.* **3.** set close together; dense: *a thick forest.* **4.** abundant; plentiful: *thick hair.* **5.** filled or covered (fol. by *with*): *tables thick with dust.* **6.** not runny; viscous: *a thick syrup.* **7.** (of darkness, etc.) dense, deep, or extreme. **8.** not clear in sound; husky; hoarse: *a thick voice.* **9.** (of an accent or dialect) very pronounced. **10.** containing much solid matter in suspension or solution. **11.** (of mist, smoke, etc.) dense. **12.** heavy-headed; sluggish, as from lack of sleep. **13.** stupid; dull. **14.** *Colloq.* close in friendship; intimate. **15.** *Colloq.* unpleasantly great: *His demands are a bit thick.* ◇*adv.* **16.** in a thick way. **17.** closely; near together: *flowers growing thick beside a wall.* ◇*n.* **18.** anything which is thick. **19.** the thickest, densest, or most crowded part: *in the thick of the fight.* **20. through thick and thin,** under all circumstances; unwaveringly. [ME; OE *thicce*]

thicken /ˈθɪkən/, *v.t., v.i.* **1.** to make or become thick or thicker. **2.** to make or grow more mysterious, complex, intense, etc.: *The plot thickens.* **—thickener,** *n.* **—thickening,** *n.*

thicket /ˈθɪkət/, *n.* a thick growth of shrubs, bushes, or small trees. [OE *thiccet*]

thickness /ˈθɪknəs/, *n.* **1.** the condition or quality of being thick. **2.** the third dimension of a solid, as distinct from length and breadth. **3.** a thick part or body of something. **4.** a layer.

thickset /ˈθɪksɛt/, *adj.* **1.** set thickly or in close arrangement; dense: *a thickset hedge.* **2.** (of a person) with thick form or build.

thief /θiːf/, *n., pl.* **thieves.** someone who steals, esp. secretly or without force. [ME; OE *theof*] **—thievish,** *adj.*

Thiele /ˈtiːli/, *n.* **Colin Milton,** born 1920, Australian poet and writer of children's books, such as *Storm Boy* (1963).

thieve /θiːv/, *v.,* **thieved, thieving.** ◇*v.t.* **1.** to take by theft; steal. ◇*v.i.* **2.** to act as a thief; steal. [OE *thēofian*]

thigh /θaɪ/, *n.* **1.** that part of the leg between the hip and the knee in man. **2.** a similar part of the hind limb of other animals. **3.** → **femur.** [ME; OE *thēoh*]

thimble /ˈθɪmbəl/, *n.* a small cap, usu. of metal, worn on the finger to push the needle in sewing. [OE *thȳmel*]

thin /θɪn/, *adj.*, **thinner, thinnest,** *adv., v.,* **thinned, thinning.** ◊*adj.* **1.** having relatively little extent from one surface or side to its opposite; not thick: *thin ice.* **2.** of small cross-section or diameter in comparison with the length; slender: *a thin wire.* **3.** (of a person, animal, etc.) having little flesh; lean. **4.** not dense; sparse; scanty: *thin hair.* **5. a.** (of a liquid) having a relatively slight consistency. **b.** (of air, etc.) rare or rarefied. **6.** without solidity or substance; unsubstantial: *thin trails of smoke.* **7.** easily seen through; transparent: *a thin excuse.* **8.** (of sound) lacking fullness or volume. **9.** (of color), light in tint. ◊*adv.* **10.** in a thin manner. ◊*v.t.* **11.** to make thin or thinner (oft. fol. by *down, out,* etc.). ◊*v.i.* **12.** to become thin or thinner (fol. by *down, off, away,* etc.). [ME and OE *thynne*] —**thinness,** *n.*

thine /ðaɪn/, *pron., adj. Archaic.* the possessive form of *thou* used after a verb or without a noun following, or before a noun beginning with a vowel or *h.* See **thy.** [ME; OE *thīn*]

thing /θɪŋ/, *n.* **1.** a material object without life or consciousness. **2.** some object, or creature which is not or cannot be precisely described: *The stick had a brass thing on it.* **3.** that which is an object of thought. **4.** a matter or affair: *Things are going well now.* **5.** a fact or circumstance: *It is a curious thing.* **6.** an action, deed, or performance: *to do great things.* **7.** a way; aspect: *perfect in all things.* **8.** what is desired or needed: *just the thing.* **9.** (*pl.*) clothes, personal belongings, utensils, tools and other articles, etc.: *Gather up your things.* **10.** the actual object, as separate from the word, symbol or idea representing it. **11.** a living person or creature: *She looked a poor thing.* **12.** *Colloq.* a strong attitude or feeling about something: *I have a thing about minced meat.* **13. do one's (own) thing,** *Colloq.* to act in a manner pleasing to oneself and which expresses one's own character. **14. on (to) a good thing, a.** backing a likely winner at favorable odds. **b.** involved in a project which promises to be successful. [ME and OD]

think /θɪŋk/, *v.,* **thought, thinking,** *n.* ◊*v.t.* **1.** to form or conceive in the mind: *to think pleasant thoughts.* **2.** to turn over in the mind; meditate: *He was thinking what he could mean.* **3.** to have the mind full of: *She thinks horses all day long.* **4.** to form or have an idea or conception of; imagine: *Think what it would be like to be rich.* **5.** to bear in mind or remember: *I can't think what I have done with it.* **6.** to have in mind, intent, or purpose: *They thought they might have lunch.* **7.** to hold as an opinion; believe: *They thought that the earth was flat.* **8.** to consider (something) to be (as stated): *He thought the film was very interesting.* **9.** to expect: *I did not think to find you here.* **10.** to bring by thinking: *We must think our way out of the problem.* ◊*v.i.* **11.** to use the mind actively; to think hard. **12.** to form or have an idea (fol. by *of*): *to think of a plan.* **13.** to reflect upon the matter in question: *Think carefully before you begin.* **14.** to remember (usu. fol. by *of*): *I can't think of his name.* **15.** to have consideration or regard (usu. fol. by *of*): *to think of others first.* **16.** to form or have a plan (usu. fol. by *of*): *He thought of it first.* **17.** to have a certain opinion of a person or thing (fol. by *of*): *to think well of a person.* **18.** to have an expectation (fol. by *of*): *I'm thinking of going overseas soon.* **19.** to have an opinion: *He thought fit to act alone.* ◊*v.* **20.** Some special uses are:

think aloud, to speak one's thoughts as they come to mind.

think better of, to decide against an original intention.

think little of, to have a low opinion of.

think nothing of, a. to have a very low opinion of: *I think nothing of him as he is so rude.* **b.** to not be worried or hesitant about: *Please, think nothing of asking for my help.*

think over, to consider carefully and unhurriedly.

think up, to form (something) as a concept; invent; devise.

◊*n.* **21.** *Colloq.* the act or process of thinking: *Go away and have a good think.* [ME; OE *thencan*]

think-tank /ˈθɪŋk-tæŋk/, *n.* a group, usu. of specialists, working to solve particular problems and to create useful ideas.

thinner /ˈθɪnə/, *n.* a volatile liquid added to paints or varnishes to aid application and penetration by making them less thick.

thio-, a word part used to indicate replacement of part or all of the oxygen atoms in a compound by sulfur. Also, **thi-.** [combining form representing Gk *theion* sulfur]

thiol /ˈθaɪɒl/, *n.* any of a group of organic compounds containing the radical -SH.

thionic /θaɪˈɒnɪk/, *adj.* of or relating to sulfur. [Gk: sulfur]

third /θɜd/, *adj.* **1.** next after the second in order, time, value, quality, etc. (the ordinal of 3). **2.** one out of every three: *every third Monday.* ◊*n.* **3.** someone or something that comes next after the second. **4.** a third part, esp. of one ($\frac{1}{3}$). **5.** (usu. *pl.*) *Law.* the third part of the personal property of a dead husband, which in certain circumstances goes totally to the widow. **6.** *Music.* the third note in a scale from a given note (counted as the first): *E is a third above C.* [OE (North) *thrida*]

third degree, *n. Colloq.* intensive interrogation to gain information or a statement of guilt: *to give someone the third degree.*

third-degree /ˈθɜd-dəɡri/, *adj.* of a degree which is at the extreme end of a scale, either as the lowest (*third-degree murder*) or the highest (*third-degree burns*).

Third Fleet, *n.* the third group of vessels that brought convicts to Australia, arriving 1791; consisted of ten ships.

Third International, *n.* →**International** (def. 3).

third man, *n. Cricket.* (a player in) a fielding position near the boundary on the off side behind the batsman's wicket.

third party, *n.* any person other than those directly involved in some agreement, business affair, etc.

third-party /'θɜd-pati/, *adj.* relating to an insurance policy against liability caused by the insurer or his servants to the property or person of others.

third person, *n. Gram.* See **person** (def. 6).

Third Reich, *n.* →**Reich** (def. 4).

third world, *n.* (*sometimes cap.*) developing countries collectively, esp. in Africa, South America and SE Asia.

thirst /θɜst/, *n.* **1.** an uneasy or painful sensation of dryness in the mouth and throat caused by need of drink. **2.** the physical condition resulting from this need. **3.** a strong or eager desire; craving: *a thirst for knowledge.* ◇*v.i.* **4.** to feel thirst. **5.** to have a strong desire. [OE *thyrstan*] –**thirsty**, *adj.*

thirteen /θɜ'tin/, *n.* **1.** a cardinal number, ten plus three (10 + 3). **2.** a symbol for this number, e.g. 13 or XIII. ◇*adj.* **3.** amounting to thirteen in number. [OE *thrēotēne*] –**thirteenth**, *adj.*, *n.*

thirty /'θɜti/, *n., pl.* **-ties**, *adj.* ◇*n.* **1.** a cardinal number, ten times three (10 x 3). **2.** a symbol for this number, e.g. 30 or XXX. **3.** (*pl.*) the numbers from 30 to 39 of a series, esp. with reference to the years of a person's age, or the years of a century. ◇*adj.* **4.** amounting to thirty in number. [OE *thrītig*] –**thirtieth**, *adj.*

this /ðɪs/, *pron.* and *adj., pl.* **these**; *adv.* ◇*pron.* **1.** a demonstrative pronoun used to show: **a.** a person, thing, idea, etc., as pointed out, present, or near, as before mentioned or suggested: *This is your seat.* **b.** one of two or more people, things, etc., already mentioned, referring to the one nearer in place, time, or thought (oft. opposed to *that*): *This is a prettier hat than that.* **2. with this**, immediately after this: *John picked up his book and glasses, and with this went into the garden to read.* ◇*adj.* **3.** a demonstrative adjective used to show: **a.** a person, place, thing, idea, etc., as pointed out, present, or near, before mentioned or suggested: *This book is very interesting.* **b.** one of two or more people, things, etc., already mentioned, referring to the one nearer in place, time, or thought (oft. opposed to *that*): *This way is quicker than that.* ◇*adv.* **4.** an adverb used with adjectives and adverbs of quantity or extent: *Do you like this much milk in your tea?* [ME and OE]

thistle /'θɪsəl/, *n.* a plant with prickly leaves and purple, yellow or white flowers. [ME and OE *thistel*]

thistledown /'θɪsəldaʊn/, *n.* tufted, feathery thistle seeds that float in the wind.

thither /'ðɪðə/, *adv.* to or towards that place or point: *The path runs thither.* Also, **thitherwards, thitherward.** [ME; OE *thider*]

tho /ðoʊ/, *conj., adv.* a shortened form of 'though'. Also, **tho'**.

Thomas /'tɒməs/, *n.* an apostle who demanded proof of Christ's resurrection. [See John 20:24–29]

Thomas à Becket /tɒməs ə 'bɛkət/, *n.* **Saint.** →**Becket.**

Thompson /'tɒmsən, 'tɒmp-/, *n.* **Jack** (*John Payne Thompson*), born 1940, Australian television and film actor.

thong /θɒŋ/, *n.* **1.** a narrow strip of leather, etc., used as a fastening, as the lash of a whip, etc. **2.** a sandal held loosely on the foot by two strips of leather, rubber, etc.

Thor /θɔ/, *n.* the ancient Scandinavian god of thunder, represented as wielding a mighty hammer.

thorax /'θɔræks/, *n., pl.* **thoraces** /'θɔrəsiz, θə'reɪsɪz/, **thoraxes. 1.** (in humans and the higher vertebrates) the part of the trunk between the neck and the abdomen, containing the cavity in which the lungs, heart, etc., are placed; the chest. **2.** a similar part in other animals. **3.** (in insects) the part of the body between head and abdomen. [ME, from L, from Gk: breastplate, chest] –**thoracic**, *adj.*

Thoreau /'θɔroʊ/, *n.* **Henry David**, 1817–62, US naturalist and author.

thorium /'θɔriəm/, *n.* a radioactive metallic element used in gas mantles, electrodes and nuclear fuel. *Symbol:* Th; *at. no.:* 90; *at. wt:* 232.038. [NL, from THOR]

thorn /θɔn/, *n.* **1.** a sharp outgrowth on a plant, esp. an incompletely developed, sharp-pointed branch; spine; prickle. **2.** a type of horny shrub or tree, often planted for hedges. **3.** something that wounds or causes discomfort. **4.** the runic character Þ for *th* (once in the English alphabet; still used in Iceland). **5. thorn in one's flesh/side**, a source of continual annoyance, etc. [ME and OE]

thornbill /'θɔnbɪl/, *n.* a type of small, finch-like bird with a small, strong, sharp bill.

thorny /'θɔni/, *adj.*, **-nier, -niest. 1.** covered in thorns; spiny; prickly. **2.** painful; vexatious: *a thorny problem.* **3.** full of points to be argued; difficult: *a thorny question.*

thorough /'θʌrə/, *adj.* **1.** carried out through the whole of something; complete or perfect: *a thorough search.* **2.** being fully or completely (such): *a thorough fool.* **3.** leaving nothing undone: *a thorough clean of the house.* [ME; OE *thuruh*] –**thoroughness**, *n.*

thoroughbred /'θʌrəbrɛd/, *adj.* **1.** (of a horse, etc.) of pure or unmixed breed, stock, or race. **2.** (of human beings) having qualities characteristic of pure breeding. ◇*n.* **3.** a thoroughbred animal.

thoroughfare /'θʌrəfɛə/, *n.* **1.** a road, street, etc., open at both ends, esp. a main road. **2.** a passage or way through: *no thoroughfare.* **3.** a strait, river, etc., giving open passage.

those /ðoʊz/, *pron., adj.* plural of **that.** [ME; OE *thās* these]

Thoth /θoʊθ, toʊt/, *n.* (in Egyptian mythology) the god of learning, wisdom and magic.

thou /ðaʊ/, *pron., sing.*, as subject **thou**, as object **thee**, as possessive **thy** or **thine**; *pl.*, as subject or object **you** or **ye**, as possessive **your** or **yours.** a personal pronoun of the second

thou person, in the singular number and nominative case, used to indicate the person (or thing) spoken to; formerly in general use, but now replaced by *you*. [ME; OE *thū*]

though /ðou/, *conj.* **1.** in spite of the fact that; even if: *Though he had no money, we had a good time.* **2.** yet, still, or nevertheless: *I will go though I fear it will be useless.* **3.** if (usu. in as though): *It poured as though it would never stop.* ◇*adv.* **4.** for all that; however. [ME, from Scand]

thought[1] /θɔt/, *n.* **1.** the product of mental activity; result of thinking. **2.** a single act of thinking; an idea or notion: *to collect one's thoughts.* **3.** the act or process of thinking. **4.** the ability to think: *Man has the power of thought.* **5.** consideration; reflection: *Give it thought before accepting.* **6.** continued mental activity: *lost in thought.* **7.** intention, or purpose: *We had some thought of going.* **8.** expectation: *I had no thought of seeing you here.* **9.** consideration, attention or care: *taking no thought for her appearance.* **10.** a judgment, opinion, or belief: *my thoughts on the subject.* **11.** the ideas, opinions, etc., of a particular place, class, or time: *Greek thought.* **12. second thoughts**, reconsideration. [OE *thoht*]

thought[2] /θɔt/, *v.* past tense and past participle of **think**.

thoughtful /'θɔtfəl/, *adj.* **1.** occupied with or given to thought: *The bad news made him thoughtful.* **2.** marked by thought: *a thoughtful essay.* **3.** careful or mindful: *to be thoughtful of one's safety.* **4.** considerate: *a thoughtful act.*

thoughtless /'θɔtləs/, *adj.* **1.** unthinking, careless: *a thoughtless action.* **2.** showing lack of thought: *a thoughtless essay.* **3.** lacking in consideration for others: *a thoughtless person.*

thousand /'θauzənd/, *n.* **1.** a cardinal number, ten times one hundred (10 × 100). **2.** a symbol for this number, as 1000 or M. **3.** a great number or amount: *a thousand pardons.* **4. one in a thousand**, very good; outstanding. ◇*adj.* **5.** amounting to one thousand in number. [ME; OE *thūsend*] —**thousandth**, *adj., n.*

Thrace /θreɪs/, *n.* an ancient region of varying extent in the eastern part of the Balkan Peninsula, later a Roman province; now in Bulgaria, Turkey, and Greece.

thrall /θrɔl/, *n.* **1.** someone who is in bondage or enslaved; slave. **2.** the state of being in bondage. [ME; OE *thræl*]

thrash /θræʃ/, *v.t.* **1.** to beat soundly by way of punishment. **2.** to defeat completely. ◇*v.i.* **3.** to beat or toss about wildly. ◇*v.* **4. thrash out**, to discuss (a matter) fully. [var. of THRESH]

thread /θred/, *n.* **1.** a fine cord of cotton, etc., spun out to great length, esp. such a cord made of two or more strands twisted together. **2.** twisted fibres of any kind used for sewing. **3.** one of the lengths of yarn forming the warp and woof of a woven fabric. **4.** a strand or fibre of glass or other substance, able to be drawn into thin lengths. **5.** the ridge of a screw. **6.** that which runs through the whole course of something: *the thread of the story.* **7. hang by a thread**, to be in a dangerous position. ◇*v.t.* **8.** to pass the end of a thread through the eye of (a needle). **9.** to fix (beads, etc.) upon a thread; string. **10.** to make (a way) through (a story, a forest, a crowd, etc.). **11.** to form a thread (def. 5) on or in (a bolt, hole, etc.). ◇*v.i.* **12.** to thread one's way, through a passage, etc. **13.** to move in a threadlike course; wind. [OE *thrǣd*]

threadbare /'θredbeə/, *adj.* **1.** (of a cloth, dress, etc.) having the threads worn very thin. **2.** poor; meagre: *a threadbare existence.* **3.** commonplace; hackneyed: *threadbare arguments.* **4.** wearing threadbare clothes; shabby: *a threadbare little old man.*

threadworm /'θredwɜm/, *n.* a type of nematode worm, esp. a pinworm.

threat /θret/, *n.* **1.** a statement of an intention to cause pain or loss to someone; menace. **2.** a sign of possible evil to come: *a threat of war.* [OE *thrēat* throng, threat, distress]

threaten /'θretn/, *v.t.* **1.** to speak a threat against; menace. **2.** to be a source of danger to: *The drought is threatening our crops.* **3.** to offer (a punishment, injury, etc.) by way of a threat: *They are threatening a strike if they are not heard.* **4.** to give a sign of: *The clouds threaten rain.* ◇*v.i.* **5.** to speak or use threats. **6.** to signal possible evil or mischief. [OE *thrēatnian*] —**threatening**, *adj.*

three /θri/, *n.* **1.** a cardinal number, two plus one (2 + 1). **2.** a symbol for this number, e.g. 3 or III. **3.** a set of this many people or things. ◇*adj.* **4.** amounting to three in number. [ME; OE *thrēo*]

3-D /θri-'di/, *adj.* **1.** three-dimensional: *3-D films.* ◇*n.* **2.** a three-dimensional form or appearance.

three-dimensional /'θri-daɪ'menʃənəl, -də'men-/, *adj.* **1.** having, or seeming to have, the dimension of depth as well as length and breadth; solid. **2.** realistic; lifelike.

threepence /'θrɪpəns/, *n.* **1.** a former silver coin valued at three pennies. **2.** a similar coin of other countries. —**threepenny**, *adj.*

three-quarter /θri-'kwɔtə, -'kɔtə/, *adj.* **1.** consisting of or involving three quarters of a whole. ◇*n.* **2. Rugby.** one of the four players (two wings and two centres) stationed between the five-eighth and full-back.

three R's, *n.pl.* reading, (w)riting, and (a)rithmetic, traditionally regarded as the basic subjects of education.

threesome /'θrisəm/, *n.* **1.** three forming a group. **2.** something in which three people participate. [ME]

threnody /'θrenədi/, *n., pl.* **-dies.** a song of sorrow, esp. for the dead; a dirge or funeral song. [Gk]

thresh /θreʃ/, *v.t., v.i.* **1.** to separate grain or seeds from (a cereal plant, etc.) by beating with a flail or by the action of a threshing machine. **2.** to beat, as if with a flail. [OE *threscan*. See THRASH]

thresher /ˈθrɛʃə/, n. **1.** someone or something that separates grain or seeds from wheat, etc., by beating with a flail, using a machine, etc. **2.** Also, **thrasher, thresher shark**. a large shark found off the coast of Australia whose long tail threshes the water to drive together the small fish on which it feeds.

threshold /ˈθrɛʃhould/, n. **1.** the sill of a doorway. **2.** the entrance to a house or building. **3.** any place or point of entering or beginning: *the threshold of a new career*. **4.** *Psychol, Med.* the point at which a stimulus becomes noticeable, or strong enough to produce an effect: *the threshold of pain*. **5.** *Phys.* the lowest value of any signal, stimulus, etc., which will produce a particular effect, as a threshold frequency. [OE *threscold*, *-wold*]

threw /ruː/, v. past tense of **throw**.

thrice /θraɪs/, adv. three times; on three occasions. [OE *thriga*]

thrift /θrɪft/, n. **1.** careful management of one's money; economy. **2.** strong growth, as of a plant. [ME, from THRIVE] —**thrifty**, adj.

thrill /θrɪl/, v.t. **1.** to affect with a sudden wave of strong emotion, so as to produce a tingling sensation through the body. **2.** to cause to vibrate or quiver: *The wind thrilled the leaves*. ◇v.i. **3.** to produce a thrill. **4.** to be stirred by a thrill of emotion or excitement. ◇n. **5.** a tingling sensation passing through the body as the result of sudden strong emotion or excitement: *Hang-gliding gives me a thrill*. **6.** a thrilling quality: *I love the thrill of hang-gliding*. **7.** a vibration or quivering. [ME, from OE *thyrlian*] —**thrilling**, adj.

thriller /ˈθrɪlə/, n. a book, play, or film, dealing with crime, mystery, etc., in an exciting manner.

thrips /θrɪps/, n., pl. **thrips**. a type of small, sap-sucking insect with long, narrow wings fringed with hairs. [L, from Gk: woodworm]

thrive /θraɪv/, v.i., **throve** or **thrived**, **thrived** or **thriven**, **thriving**. **1.** to be fortunate or successful; grow rich. **2.** to grow or develop strongly; flourish. [ME, from Scand]

thro /θruː/, prep., adv., adj. → **through**. Also, **thro'**.

throat /θroʊt/, n. **1.** the passage from the mouth to the stomach or to the lungs. **2.** some similar narrowed part or passage. **3.** the front of the neck below the chin and above the collarbones. **4. jump down someone's throat**, to deliver a strong, spoken attack on. **5. stick in one's throat**, **a.** to be difficult to express. **b.** to be difficult to accept in one's mind. [ME and OE *throte*]

throb /θrɒb/, v., **throbbed**, **throbbing**, n. ◇v.i. **1.** (of the heart, etc.) to beat with increased force or speed; palpitate. **2.** to feel or show emotion: *to throb with excitement*. **3.** to beat; pulsate: *His head began to throb with pain*. ◇n. **4.** the act of throbbing. **5.** a violent beat, as of the heart. **6.** any beat or pulsation: *the throb of the engines*. [ME; orig. unknown] —**throbbingly**, adv.

throe /θroʊ/, n. **1.** a violent spasm or pang; paroxysm. **2.** (*pl.*) any violent disturbance or struggle. **3. in the throes of**, fully involved and struggling with: *She was in the throes of writing her latest novel*. [ME]

thrombosis /θrɒmˈboʊsəs/, n. a clotting of the blood within the blood vessels. [NL, from Gk: curdling, clotting]

throne /θroʊn/, n. **1.** the chair occupied by a king, queen, bishop, or other important personage on ceremonial occasions. **2.** the office or power of a sovereign. **3.** the person who occupies a throne; king or queen. **4.** the office or authority of a bishop. [ME, from L, from Gk: high seat]

throng /θrɒŋ/, n. **1.** a crowd. **2.** a great number of things crowded or considered together. ◇v.i. **3.** to collect or go in large numbers; crowd. ◇v.t. **4.** to crowd or press upon; jostle: *They thronged the royal car*. **5.** to fill by crowding or pressing into: *They thronged the room*. [ME; OE *gethrang*]

Throsby /ˈθrɒzbi/, n. **Charles**, 1777–1828, Australian surgeon and explorer, born in England.

throttle /ˈθrɒtl/, n., v., **-tled**, **-tling**. ◇n. **1.** a lever, pedal, or other device to control the amount of fuel being fed to an engine. ◇v.t. **2.** to strangle. **3.** to stop the breath of in any way; choke. **4.** to silence or check as if by choking. **5.** *Mach.* to block the flow of (steam, etc.) by means of a throttle valve, etc. [late ME]

through /θruː/, prep. **1.** in at one end, side, or surface, and out at the other, of: *The bullet went through his body*. **2.** past: *The car went through the traffic lights without stopping*. **3.** between or among the parts of: *to swing through the trees*. **4.** over the surface or within the limits of: *to travel through a country*. **5.** during the whole period of; throughout: *to work through the night*. **6.** having reached the end of: *to be through one's work*. **7.** successfully to the end of: *to get through an examination*. **8.** by means of: *It was through him that they found out*. **9.** because of: *to run away through fear*. ◇adv. **10.** in at one end, side, or surface and out at the other: *to push a needle through*. **11.** all the way: *This train goes through to Flinders St.* **12.** throughout: *wet through*. **13.** from the beginning to the end: *to read a letter through*. **14.** to the end: *to carry a matter through*. **15.** having completed an action, process, etc.: *He is not yet through*. **16. go through**, to wear out: *He's gone through ten pairs of shoes*. **17. through and through**, in every way; thoroughly. **18. through with**, finished or done with. ◇adj. **19.** passing from one end, side, or surface to the other. **20.** going through the whole of a long distance with no stopping: *a through train*. Also, **thro**, **thro'**, **thru**. [ME; var. of *thourgh*, OE *thurh*]

throughout /θruːˈaʊt/, prep. **1.** in or to every part of; everywhere in. **2.** from the beginning to the end of. ◇adv. **3.** in every part: *In this building there are lifts throughout*. **4.** at every moment or point.

throve /θroʊv/, v. past tense of **thrive**.

throw /θroʊ/, v., **threw, thrown, throwing,** n. ◇v.t. **1.** to drive through the air by a sudden movement of the arm; propel; hurl; cast. **2.** to drive (a missile) through the air, as a gun does. **3.** to cast (light, a shadow, etc.). **4.** to send; direct (words, a look, etc.). **5.** to cause to reach far; project: *to throw the voice to the back of the room.* **6.** to cause to go or come into some place, position, condition, etc., as if by throwing: *to throw a man into prison.* **7.** to put quickly: *to throw a shawl over one's shoulders.* **8.** *Mech.* to move (a lever, etc.) in order to connect or disconnect parts of a mechanism. **9.** to make on a potter's wheel. **10.** to give (a blow or punch). **11.** to cause to fall to the ground. **12.** to cast (dice). **13.** (of domestic animals) to give birth to (young). **14.** *Colloq.* to astonish; confuse; disconcert. **15.** to arrange (a social event): *She threw a party last Saturday.* ◇v.i. **16.** to cast, fling, or hurl something. ◇v. **17.** Some special uses are:
throw back, to show characteristics found in one's ancestors.
throw in, to add as an extra.
throw in one's hand, *Colloq.* to admit defeat; surrender.
throw off, to free oneself from.
throw oneself at (someone), to try to get (someone's) attention, esp. in love.
throw oneself into, to work enthusiastically at.
throw open, to open up (a place) for people to come in.
throw out, 1. to say casually or indirectly (a remark, hint, etc.). **2.** to refuse to accept; reject. **3.** to cause to make a mistake. **4.** to expel.
throw over, to leave behind; abandon; desert.
throw together, to put together in a quick or casual manner.
throw up, 1. to build quickly. **2.** to vomit. ◇n. **18.** the act of throwing or casting; a cast or fling. **19.** *Colloq.* a turn in a ball game. **20.** the distance to which anything is or may be thrown: *a stone's throw.* **21.** *Mech.* **a.** the movement of a reciprocating part from its central position to its extreme position in either direction, or the distance covered (equal to ½ the travel or stroke). **b.** the arm or the radius of a crank, etc. **c.** the complete movement of a reciprocating part, etc., in one direction, or the distance covered (equivalent to the travel or stroke). [ME; OE *thrāwan* turn, twist] –**thrower,** n.

throwing stick, n. an Aboriginal wooden instrument with which a spear or dart is thrown.

thrown /θroʊn/, v.t. past participle of **throw**.

thrum /θrʌm/, v., **thrummed, thrumming,** n. ◇v.i. **1.** to play on a stringed instrument, such as a guitar, by plucking the strings, esp. in a monotonous manner. **2.** to sound when thrummed on: *The guitars thrummed.* **3.** to make any monotonous, drumming sound: *to thrum on a table with the fingers.* ◇v.t. **4.** to thrum (a stringed instrument). ◇n. **5.** the act or sound of thrumming. [imitative]

thrush¹ /θrʌʃ/, n. a type of migratory bird, of medium size, not brightly colored, noted for its song, e.g. the European **song thrush,** introduced into Australia, or the native **ground thrush** of eastern and southern Australia. [OE *thrȳsce*]

thrush² /θrʌʃ/, n. *Med.* a disease caused by a parasitic fungus and characterised by whitish spots and ulcers on the membranes of the mouth, throat, vagina, etc.

thrust /θrʌst/, v., **thrust, thrusting,** n. ◇v.t. **1.** to push with force; shove: *He thrust a dagger into her back.* **2.** to put with force into some position, condition, etc.: *to thrust someone into danger.* ◇v.i. **3.** to push against something. **4.** to push or force one's way: *to thrust through the crowd.* **5.** to make a stab at something; lunge. ◇n. **6.** the act of thrusting; a push; a lunge. **7.** *Mech.* the driving force generated by an engine. **8.** *Geol.* a pressure in the crust of the earth, which produces a fault. [ME; OE from Scand]

Thucydides /θjuːˈsɪdədiːz/, n. c. 460–c. 400 BC, Greek historian; his *History of the Peloponnesian War* is noted for its impartiality and literary style.

thud /θʌd/, n., v., **thudded, thudding.** ◇n. **1.** a dull sound, as of a heavy blow or fall. **2.** a blow causing such a sound. ◇v.i., v.t. **3.** to beat or strike with a dull sound of a heavy blow or fall. [ME; OE *thyddan,* v.]

thug /θʌg/, n. a brutal, vicious, or destructive person; ruffian. [from *Thugs,* a former body of professional robbers and murderers in India who strangled their victims; Hind *thag*] –**thuggery,** n. –**thuggish,** adj.

thulium /ˈθjuːliəm/, n. a rare-earth, silver-grey, metallic element. Its isotope Tm-170 is used in X-ray units. *Symbol:* Tm; *at. no.:* 69; *at. wt:* 168.934. [NL, from L]

thumb /θʌm/, n. **1.** the short, thick inner digit of the human hand, next to the forefinger. **2.** the corresponding digit in other animals. **3.** that part of a glove, etc., which covers the thumb. **4. all thumbs,** clumsy; awkward. **5. under the thumb of,** under the power of. ◇v.t. **6.** to dirty or wear in handling: *to thumb the pages of a book.* **7.** to run through quickly. **8.** (of a hitchhiker) to try to get (a ride) by pointing the thumb in the direction in which one wishes to travel. ◇v. **9. thumb one's nose,** to show defiance or contempt. [ME; OE *thūma*]

thumbscrew /ˈθʌmskruː/, n. an ancient instrument of torture by which thumbs were squashed in a screw device.

thump /θʌmp/, n. **1.** a heavy blow. **2.** the sound made by such a blow. ◇v.t. **3.** to strike or beat with something thick and heavy so as to make a dull sound; pound: *to thump a drum.* **4.** to strike against (something) heavily and noisily. **5.** *Colloq.* to punch. ◇v.i. **6.** to strike or beat heavily, with a dull sound; pound. **7.** to walk with heavy-sounding steps. **8.** (of the heart) to beat violently. [imitative]

thunder /ˈθʌndə/, n. **1.** the loud noise which happens with a flash of lightning, due to a violent disturbance of the air by a discharge of electricity. **2.** any loud, booming noise: *the thunder of applause.* ◇v.i. **3.** to give forth

thunder: *It thundered last night.* **4.** to make a loud noise like thunder: *The horses thundered down the track.* **5.** to make a loud, threatening speech: *The preacher thundered from the pulpit.* [ME; OE *thunor*] –**thunderous**, *adj.* –**thundery**, *adj.*

thunderbolt /ˈθʌndəboʊlt/, *n.* **1.** a flash of lightning with thunder. **2.** (in legend) a weapon that the sky god hurls at the earth in a flash of lightning. **3.** something very destructive, terrible, sudden, or startling.

Thunderbolt /ˈθʌndəboʊlt/, *n.* Captain. → Frederick **Ward**.

thunderclap /ˈθʌndəklæp/, *n.* a crash of thunder.

thunder egg, *n.* a fossil, stone, etc., supposed to have been cast to earth by lightning, esp. a hollow stone with chalcedony inside.

thunder stick, *n.* → **bullroarer**.

thunderstorm /ˈθʌndəstɔm/, *n.* a storm of thunder and lightning and often rain.

thunderstruck /ˈθʌndəstrʌk/, *adj.* astonished; amazed: *He was thunderstruck by the news of his promotion.*

Thur, *Abbrev.* Thursday. Also, **Thurs**

thurible /ˈθjʊərəbəl/, *n.* → **censer**. [ME, from L: censer]

Thursday /ˈθɜzdeɪ, -di/, *n.* the fifth day of the week, following Wednesday. [ME, from Scand]

Thursday Island, *n.* an island in Torres Strait, north-east of Prince of Wales Island; administrative and commercial headquarters of Torres Strait. 3 km². Pop. 2646 (1986).

thus /ðʌs/, *adv.* **1.** in the way just shown; in this way. **2.** in the following manner. **3.** as a result; consequently. **4.** to this extent or degree: *thus far.* [ME and OE]

thwart /θwɔt/, *v.t.* **1.** to oppose successfully; prevent; hinder; frustrate. ◇*n.* **2.** a seat across a boat, esp. one used by an oarsman. ◇*adj.* **3.** passing or lying across; cross; transverse. ◇*prep., adv.* **4.** across; athwart. [ME *thwert*, adv., from Scand]

thy /ðaɪ/, *pron.*, the possessive form corresponding to **thou** and **thee**, used before a noun. See **thine**. [ME, var. of THINE]

thylacine /ˈθaɪləsɪn/, *n.* a rare, meat-eating wolf-like marsupial of Tas, tan-colored, with black stripes across the back. Also, **cynocephalus**, **Tasmanian tiger**, **Tasmanian wolf**. [NL from Gk]

thyme /taɪm/, *n.* a type of plant of the mint family, with scented leaves used in cooking and medicine. [ME, from L, from Gk]

thyr-, a combining form of **thyroid**, as in *thyroxine*. Also, before consonants, **thyro-**.

thyroid /ˈθaɪrɔɪd/, *adj.* **1.** indicating or relating to the thyroid gland. **2.** indicating or relating to the principal cartilage of the larynx, known in men as the Adam's apple. ◇*n.* **3.** → **thyroid gland**. **4.** a preparation made from the thyroid glands of certain animals, used in treating an underactive thyroid. [var. of *thyreoid*, from Gk: shield-shaped]

thyroid gland, *n.* a two-lobed ductless gland lying on either side of the windpipe or trachea and connected below the larynx by a thin link of tissue. It secretes thyroxine which regulates metabolism and growth.

thyroxine /θaɪˈrɒksin/, *n.* a hormone of the thyroid gland. Also, **thyroxin** /θaɪˈrɒksɪn/.

ti /ti/, *n.* → **te**.

Ti, *Chem. Symbol.* titanium.

tiara /tiˈɑrə/, *n.* **1.** an ornamental piece of jewellery like a small crown, worn by women. **2.** a headdress or turban worn by the ancient Persians and others. [L, from Gk]

Tiber /ˈtaɪbə/, *n.* a river in central Italy, flowing through Rome into the Mediterranean. 393 km. Italian, **Tevere**.

Tiberius /taɪˈbɪəriəs/, *n.* (*Tiberius Claudius Nero Caesar*), 42 BC – AD 37, Roman emperor from AD 14 to 37.

Tibet /təˈbɛt/, *n.* → **Xizang Autonomous Region**.

tibia /ˈtɪbiə/, *n., pl.* **tibiae** /ˈtɪbii/, **tibias**. *Anat.* the shinbone; the inner of the two bones of the lower leg, from knee to ankle. [L: shinbone, flute] –**tibial**, *adj.*

tic /tɪk/, *n. Med.* a sudden, painless muscular twitching in the face or hand. [F, from It; of Gmc origin]

tick¹ /tɪk/, *n.* **1.** a slight, sharp click or beat, as of a clock. **2.** *Colloq.* a moment or instant: *Hang on just a tick.* **3.** a small mark (✓) used to show that something is done or is correct. ◇*v.i.* **4.** to make a tick, like that of a clock. **5.** to pass as if with ticks of a clock: *The hours ticked by.* ◇*v.t.* **6.** to mark (an item, etc.) with a tick. ◇*v.* **7. tick off**, to scold; rebuke. **8. tick over**, **a.** (of an internal-combustion engine) to run slowly with the gears disengaged. **b.** to be inactive, often in preparation for action. [late ME]

tick² /tɪk/, *n.* **1.** a type of blood-sucking animal like a mite. **2.** a small insect like a fly, parasitic on certain animals, such as sheep, camels, bats, pigeons. [OE *ticia*]

ticker tape /ˈtɪkə teɪp/, *n.* the paper tape on which a tape machine prints its information.

ticket /ˈtɪkət/, *n.* **1.** a small piece of paper or cardboard which shows that the person holding it has the right to some service: *a railway ticket; a theatre ticket.* **2.** a small piece of paper or cardboard fixed to something to show its nature, price, etc.; a label or tag. **3.** a list of candidates put forward by a political party, faction, etc.: *the Labor ticket.* **4.** a piece of paper given to a motorist by (parking) police to show that a fine must be paid for a traffic or parking offence. **5. have tickets on oneself**, *Colloq.* to be vain. [F: ticket, label]

ticket-of-leave /ˈtɪkət-əv-ˈliv/, *n.* (formerly) a document which allowed convicts to live where they wanted and do the work they wanted within a certain district of a colony until the original sentence ended or they obtained a pardon. Also, **ticket of leave**.

ticking /ˈtɪkɪŋ/, n. a strong cotton fabric, usu. twilled, used for mattress covers. [*tick* cloth case of a mattress, etc. + -ING¹]

tickle /ˈtɪkəl/, v., -led, -ling, n. ◇v.t. 1. to touch or stroke lightly with the fingers, a feather, etc. so as to make a tingling or itching sensation w; titillate. 2. to poke some sensitive part of the body so as to excite a spasm of laughter. 3. to excite pleasantly; gratify: *to tickle someone's vanity*. ◇n. 4. the act of tickling. 5. a tickling sensation. [ME]

ticklish /ˈtɪklɪʃ/, adj. 1. sensitive to tickling. 2. needing careful handling; risky; difficult: *a ticklish situation*.

tidal /ˈtaɪdl/, adj. 1. of, relating to, or marked by tides. 2. coming or going according to whether the tide is high or low: *a tidal steamer*.

tidal wave, n. 1. a large, destructive ocean wave produced by an earthquake, etc. 2. any strong, widespread movement, opinion, etc.

tiddler /ˈtɪdlə/, n. 1. a very small fish, esp. a stickleback or minnow. 2. *Colloq*. an unusually small child.

tiddlywinks /ˈtɪdliwɪŋks/, n. a game, the object of which is to flick small discs into a cup placed some distance away. Also, **tiddleywinks**.

tide /taɪd/, n., v., **tided**, **tiding**. ◇n. 1. the daily rise and fall of the waters of the ocean and its inlets, about every 12 hours and 26 minutes, due to the attraction of the moon and sun. 2. the inflow, outflow, or current of water resulting from this. 3. anything that alternately rises and falls, increases and decreases, etc. 4. a movement; tendency; trend: *the tide of public opinion*. ◇v. 5. **tide over**, to get (a person, etc.) over a period of difficulty, lack, etc. [ME; OE *tīd*, c. G *Zeit* time; akin to TIME]

tidings /ˈtaɪdɪŋz/, n.pl. (*sometimes treated as sing.*) news; information: *sad tidings*. [ME; OE *tīdung*]

tidy /ˈtaɪdi/, adj., -dier, -diest, v., -died, -dying, , pl. -dies. ◇adj. 1. having everything in ts place; trim; orderly: *a tidy room*. 2. *Colloq* quite tidy: *a tidy sum of money*. ◇v.t., v.i. 3. to make tidy or neat (oft. fol. by *up*). ◇n. 4. a container for keeping things tidy. 5. a rubbish tin or wastepaper basket. [ME] —**tidily**, adv. —**tidiness**, n.

tie /taɪ/, v., **tied**, **tying**, n. ◇v.t. 1. to bind or fasten with a cord, string, etc., drawn together and knotted. 2. to draw together the parts of with a knotted string, etc.: *to tie a bundle*. 3. to form by looping a rope or string, etc., around itself: *to tie a knot*. 4. to fasten, join, or connect in any way. 5. to bind or limit (someone); restrict: *His sense of duty ties him to his job*. ◇v.i. 6. to make a tie, bond, or connection. 7. to make the same score; be equal in a contest. ◇v. 8. **tie up**, **a**. to fasten securely by tying: *to tie up a ship to the wharf*. **b**. to bind or wrap up: *to tie up a parcel*. **c**. to block or hinder. **d**. to be busy: *I can't do it because I'm tied up today*. 9. **tie in**, (of a fact, belief, etc.) to relate to; fit in: *His behavior ties in with his sad childhood*. ◇n. 10. something with which anything is tied. 11. a narrow strip of any material, worn round the neck, usu. under a collar, and tied in front. 12. a knot. 13. anything that ties. 14. a link or bond: *to make firm ties of friendship*. 15. a state of equality in points, votes, etc., among competitors: *The game ended in a tie*. 16. *Music*. a curved line connecting two notes on the same line or space to show that the sound is to be held on for the value of both notes, rather than played again. [ME; OE *tīgan* bind]

tie-dye /ˈtaɪ-daɪ/, v.t., -dyed, -dyeing. to create a pattern on (a fabric) by tying it in bunches so that the dye cannot stain the whole area during dyeing.

Tien Shan /tjen ˈʃæn/, n. a mountain system of central Asia. Highest peak, Pik Pobedy, about 7439 m. Also, **Tian Shan**.

tier /tɪə/, n. 1. a row or rank; layer: *three tiers in the wedding cake*. 2. one of a series of rows or ranks rising one behind and above another: *tiers of seats in a theatre*. 3. (*pl*.) (esp. Tas) a range of mountains. [F: sequence]

Tierra del Fuego /tiˈɛrə del ˈfweɪgoʊ/, n. a group of islands at the southern tip of South America, separated from the mainland by the Strait of Magellan, and belonging partly to Argentina (2091 km²), and partly to Chile (50 251 km²).

tiff /tɪf/, n. 1. a slight quarrel. 2. a slight fit of bad temper. [orig. uncert.]

tiffin /ˈtɪfən/, n. (in India and some other countries) lunch.

tiger /ˈtaɪgə/, n. 1. a large, meat-eating cat of Asia, tawny-colored, striped with black, ranging in several types from India and the Malay Peninsula to Siberia. 2. someone who is like a tiger in fierceness, courage, etc. [OE *tīgras* (pl.), from L, from Gk] —**tigress**, n. fem.

tiger cat, n. See **native cat**.

tiger lily, n. a lily with orange flowers spotted with black, and small bulbs in the axils of the leaves.

tiger moth, n. a type of moth with spotted or striped wings.

tiger's-eye /ˈtaɪgəz-aɪ/, n. a stone used for jewellery with a golden band flashing in dark brown.

tiger snake, n. any of several highly venomous snakes found in southern Australia, Tas and Bass Strait islands, of various shades of brown, tan, olive or grey, and about 1.5 metres long.

tight /taɪt/, adj. 1. firmly fixed in place; secure: *a tight knot*. 2. drawn or stretched; taut. 3. fitting closely, esp. too closely: *tight trousers*. 4. difficult to deal with: *to be in a tight corner*. 5. strict; firm; rigid: *tight discipline*. 6. closely packed; full. 7. *Colloq*. close; nearly even: *a tight race*. 8. *Colloq*. mean in giving or spending; stingy; parsimonious. 9. *Colloq*. drunk; tipsy. ◇adv. 10. in a tight manner; firmly; securely: *to draw a knot tight*. [ME, var. of *thight* dense, solid] —**tightness**, n.

-tight, a suffix meaning 'not letting through', as in *watertight*.

tightrope /'taɪtroʊp/, n. **1.** a rope or wire stretched tight, on which acrobats perform acts of balancing. **2. walk a tightrope,** to be in an unsafe situation.

tights /taɪts/, n.pl. a close-fitting stocking-like garment covering the body from the waist to the feet.

Tigris /'taɪgrəs/, n. a river flowing from south-eastern Turkey south-east through Iraq, joining the Euphrates to empty into the Persian Gulf through the Shatt-al-Arab. About 1850 km.

tiki /'tiki/, n. a carved image representing an ancestor, worn as a charm in some Polynesian cultures. [Maori]

tilde /'tɪldə/, n. a diacritical mark (-) placed over a letter, as over the letter *n* in Spanish to indicate a palatal nasal sound, as in *señor*. [Sp, from ML: TITLE]

tile /taɪl/, n., v., **tiled, tiling.** ◇n. **1.** a thin slab or shaped piece of baked clay, sometimes glazed and decorated, used for covering roofs, lining walls, paving floors, in ornamental work, etc. **2.** any of various similar slabs or pieces, such as of stone, metal, cork or plastic. ◇v.t. **3.** to cover with tiles. [ME; OE *tīgele*]

till[1] /tɪl/, *prep. and conj.* → **until.** [ME; OE (Northern) *til*, from Scand]

till[2] /tɪl/, v.t., v.i. to work (land) by ploughing, etc., to raise crops; cultivate. [OE *tilian* strive, get] —**tillable,** adj.

till[3] /tɪl/, n. (in a shop, etc.) a container such as a box or drawer, etc., usu. with compartments for coins and notes of different denominations, for keeping enough cash for daily business. [OE *tyllan*]

till[4] /tɪl/, n. **1.** Geol. a glacial drift consisting of a mixture of clay, sand, gravel, and stones. **2.** a stiff clay. [orig. uncert.]

tiller /'tɪlə/, n. a bar or lever fitted to a boat's rudder, used in steering. [ME, from OF: weaver's beam, from L: web]

tilt /tɪlt/, v.t. **1.** to cause to lean, incline, slope or slant. ◇v.i. **2.** to move into a sloping position or direction. **3.** to strike, thrust, or charge with a lance (fol. by *at*). **4.** to fight in a joust or tournament, etc. ◇n. **5.** the act or result of tilting. **6.** a slope. **7.** a joust or any other contest. **8. full tilt,** with full force or speed. [ME, from OE *tealt* unsteady]

timber /'tɪmbə/, n. **1.** wood cut for building and carpentry, joinery, etc. **2.** wood of growing trees suitable for use in building. **3.** the trees themselves. **4.** *Naut.* (in a ship's frame) a curved piece of wood; a rib. [ME and OE; orig. building, material for building] —**timbering,** n. —**timbered,** adj.

timber line, n. the height above sea-level or distance beyond which trees stop growing.

timbre /'tɪmbə, 'tæmbə/, n. **1.** the characteristic quality of a sound, apart from pitch and loudness. The saxophone and the clarinet have different timbres, and so do the vowels of *bait* and *boat*. **2.** *Music.* the characteristic quality of sound produced by a particular kind of instrument or voice; tone color. [F: quality of sound, orig., kind of tambourine, from L, from Gk: timbrel, kettledrum]

timbrel /'tɪmbrəl/, n. →**tambourine.** [ME]

Timbuktu /tɪmbʌk'tu/, n. French, **Tombouctou.** a town in central Mali, near the river Niger; terminus of Saharan caravan route and Muslim centre between the 14th and 16th centuries. Pop. 10 500 (1975).

time /taɪm/, n., adj., v., **timed, timing.** ◇n. **1.** the system of relationship of events to each other, as past, present, or future, in which events are taken to follow one another. **2.** the series of days, months, years, etc., measured as having limits, as opposed to eternity. **3.** a system or method of measuring the movement and passing of time. **4.** a limited extent of time, such as between two events: *a long time.* **5.** a particular period considered as distinct from other periods: *for the time being.* **6.** (*oft. pl.*) a period in the history of the world: *ancient or modern times.* **7.** (*oft. pl.*) a period considered with reference to what is happening in it: *hard times; good times.* **8.** a certain period of time given, for death, birth, payment of a debt, etc.: *Your time is up.* **9.** a particular period with a certain quality of personal experience: *to have a good time.* **10.** a period of work of an employee, or the pay for it. **11.** the period necessary for something: *to ask for time to consider.* **12.** leisure or spare time: *to have no time.* **13.** a particular or definite point in time: *What time is it?* **14.** a particular part of a year, day, etc.: *Christmas time; opening time.* **15.** a fit, due, or proper time: *There is a time for everything.* **16.** an indefinite period in the future: *Time will tell.* **17.** the period in which an action is completed, esp. in a race: *The winner's time was just under four minutes.* **18.** each occasion of an action done again and again: *to do a thing four times.* **19.** (*pl.*) (used in multiplication: *4 times 5.*) **20.** *Drama.* one of the three unities. See **unity** (def. 6). **21.** *Poetry.* a unit or a group of units in the measurement of metre. **22.** *Music,* **a.** relative speed of movement; tempo. **b.** the metrical length of a note or rest. **c.** the general movement of a particular kind of musical composition, relating to its rhythm, metrical structure, and tempo: *common time; triple time.* ◇**23.** Some special uses are: **against time,** to try to finish something within a limited period.

ahead of one's time, having ideas more advanced than those of the age in which one lives.

at the same time, nevertheless.
behind the times, old-fashioned.
do time, to serve a prison sentence.
for the time being, temporarily.
from time to time, occasionally.
in good time, early; with time to spare.
in no time, very quickly.
in time, 1. soon or early enough. **2.** eventually; after some time. **3.** following the correct rhythm or tempo.
kill time, to occupy oneself so as to make the time pass quickly.
on time, punctually.

pass the time of day, to have a short conversation.
take one's time, to be slow or leisurely.
take time out, to spare the time; to make the effort (to do something).
time after time, often; repeatedly.
◇*adj.* **24.** of, relating to, or showing the passage of time. **25.** (of an explosive device) set to explode: *a time bomb.* **26.** of or relating to purchases with payment postponed: *time payments.* ◇*v.t.* **27.** to find out or record the time, duration, or rate of: *to time a race.* **28.** to fix the duration of: *to time the roast for two hours.* **29.** to choose the moment or occasion for: *He timed his entrance perfectly.* **30.** *Music.* to group (notes or syllables) according to metre, accent, rhythm, etc. [ME; OE *tīma*]

time and motion study, *n.* a systematic examination of methods of working, esp. in industrial organisations, in order to improve efficiency.

time exposure, *n.* the process of keeping the camera shutter open for a second or so in dim or light light conditions giving a long exposure of film to light.

timekeeper /'taɪmkipə/, *n.* **1.** (in a sports contest, etc.) someone who watches and records the time taken by competitors in a race, etc. **2.** → **timepiece**. **3.** a person employed to keep account of the hours of work done by others.

timeless /'taɪmləs/, *adj.* **1.** eternal; unending. **2.** referring to no particular time.

timely /'taɪmli/, *adj.*, **-lier, -liest.** happening at a suitable or right time; opportune; well-timed: *a timely warning.* —**timeliness**, *n.*

time payment, *n.* → **hire-purchase**.

timepiece /'taɪmpis/, *n.* **1.** an apparatus for measuring and recording time; a chronometer. **2.** a clock or a watch.

time signature, *n.* a sign, usu. in the form of a fraction, showing the rhythm of a piece of music, as $\frac{3}{4}$ being waltz time.

timetable /'taɪmteɪbl/, *n.* **1.** a plan showing the times at which railway trains, buses, aeroplanes, etc., arrive and depart. **2.** a plan of times of classes, lectures, etc., in a school, university, etc.

time zone, *n.* a region of the globe that has the same standard time.

timid /'tɪməd/, *adj.* easily frightened; shy. [L: frightened] —**timidity**, *n.*

timing /'taɪmɪŋ/, *n.* the control of events so that they happen together or in a desired pattern: *the timing of a car engine; This actor's timing is perfect.*

Timor /'timɔ/, *n.* an island in the Malay Archipelago, divided into West Timor and East Timor. 30 775 km².

timorous /'tɪmərəs/, *adj.* full of or subject to fear; fearful; timid. [late ME, from ML: fearful, frightened]

Timor Sea, *n.* an arm of the Indian Ocean between Timor and north-western Australia.

Timothy /'tɪməθi/, *n. Bible.* a disciple and companion of the apostle Paul, to whom Paul is supposed to have addressed the two New Testament epistles bearing his name. [L from Gk: God-honoring]

timpani /'tɪmpəni/, *n.pl., sing.* **-no** /-noʊ/. a set of kettledrums. [It, from L, from Gk]

tin /tɪn/, *n., adj., v.,* **tinned, tinning.** ◇*n.* **1.** a low-melting, silver-colored, metallic element used in making alloys and plating. *Symbol:* Sn (for *stannum*); *at. no.:* 50; *at. wt:* 118.69. **2.** thin sheet iron or sheet steel coated with tin. **3.** any shallow metal pan, esp. one used in baking. **4.** a sealed container for food, esp. one made of tin plate; can. **5.** any container made of tin plate. **6.** the contents of a tin; can. ◇*adj.* **7.** made of tin or tin plate. ◇*v.t.* **8.** to cover or coat with a thin layer of tin. **9.** to pack or preserve in tins: *to tin fruit.* [ME and OE]

tincture /'tɪŋktʃə/, *n., v.,* **-tured, -turing.** ◇*n.* **1.** *Pharm.* a solution of a medicinal substance in alcohol. **2.** a trace; a smattering; tinge. ◇*v.t.* **3.** to give a dye or color to; tinge. [ME, from L: dyeing, tingeing] —**tinctorial**, *adj.*

tinder /'tɪndə/, *n.* **1.** a material or preparation formerly used for catching the spark from a flint and steel struck together for fire or light. **2.** any dry substance that easily catches fire from a spark. [ME; OE *tynder*]

tinderbox /'tɪndəbɒks/, *n.* a place or situation that is likely to explode or become dangerous.

tine /taɪn/, *n.* a sharp projecting point or prong, as of a fork, etc. [ME *tyne*, var. of ME and OE *tind*, c. MHG *zint*]

tinea /'tɪniə/, *n.* any of several skin diseases caused by fungi. [NL, in L: gnawing worm]

tinge /tɪndʒ/, *v.,* **tinged, tingeing** or **tinging**, *n.* ◇*v.t.* **1.** to give a small amount of color to; tint. **2.** to give a small amount of anything to: *His acceptance was tinged with distrust.* ◇*n.* **3.** a small amount of color. **4.** a small amount of anything: *The meat had a tinge of garlic.* [late ME, from L: dye, color]

tingle /'tɪŋgəl/, *v.,* **-gled, -gling,** *n.* ◇*v.i.* **1.** to have prickly feelings: *to tingle with cold; to tingle with excitement.* ◇*n.* **2.** a tingling feeling. [ME; apparently var. of TINKLE] —**tingling**, *adj.*

tin god, *n.* an unworthy person who is mistakenly revered and respected.

tinker /'tɪŋkə/, *n.* **1.** a person who mends pots, kettles, pans, etc., usu. a wanderer. **2.** someone who enjoys doing minor kinds of mechanical work. ◇*v.i.* **3.** to do the work of a tinker. **4.** to busy oneself with something, esp. a machine or an appliance, usu. without useful results. [syncopated var. of earlier *tinekere* worker in tin]

tinkle /'tɪŋkəl/, *v.,* **-kled, -kling,** *n.* ◇*v.i.* **1.** to make a succession of short, light, ringing sounds; jingle. ◇*v.t.* **2.** to cause to tinkle. ◇*n.* **3.** a tinkling sound. [ME: imitative] —**tinkling**, *n., adj.*

tinnie /'tɪni/, *n. Colloq.* a can of beer. Also, **tinny**.

tinny /'tɪni/, *adj.*, **-nier, -niest. 1.** of or like tin. **2.** sounding thin and hollow. **3.** not strong or lasting.

tin-pot /'tɪn-pɒt/, *adj. Colloq.* worthless; petty; inferior.

tinsel /'tɪnsəl/, *n.* **1.** a cheap glittering metallic substance, as copper, brass, etc., used in pieces, strips, threads, etc., to produce a sparkling effect. **2.** anything showy or attractive with little or no real worth. ◇*adj.* **3.** made of or containing tinsel. **4.** showy; gaudy; tawdry. [F: spark flash, from L] **—tinselly,** *adj.*

tint /tɪnt/, *n.* **1.** a color, or a variety of a color. **2.** a color diluted with white (as opposed to a *shade*, which is produced by adding black). **3.** a delicate or pale color. **4.** a dye for the hair. ◇*v.t.* **5.** to apply a tint or tints to; color slightly; tinge. [L *tinctus* colored, tinged]

tintack /'tɪntæk/, *n.* **1.** a short nail made of tin-plated steel. **2. get down to tintacks,** to deal with essentials.

tintinnabulation /,tɪntənæbjə'leɪʃən/, *n.* the ringing or sound of bells.

Tintoretto /tɪntə'retoʊ/, *n.* **Il** /il/ (*Jacopo Robusti*), 1518-94, Venetian painter.

tiny /'taɪni/, *adj.*, **-nier, -niest.** very small; minute; wee. [obs. *tine* very small (of unknown orig.)]

-tion, a suffix used to form abstract nouns expressing actions (*revolution, commendation*), states or conditions (*contrition, starvation*), or associated meanings (*relation, temptation*). Also, **-ation, -cion, -ion, -sion, -xion.** [L *-tio* (from *-t-*, pp. stem ending, + *-io*, noun suffix)]

tip¹ /tɪp/, *n., v.,* **tipped, tipping.** ◇*n.* **1.** a slender or pointed end of something: *the tips of the fingers.* **2.** the top; summit or apex. ◇*v.t.* **3.** to put a tip on to: *to tip shoes with metal.* **4.** to mark or form the tip of: *Snow tipped the mountains.* [ME]

tip² /tɪp/, *v., n.,* **tipped, tipping,** *n.* ◇*v.t.* **1.** to cause to slope or slant; incline; tilt. **2.** to cause to fall over; upset. **3.** to take off or lift (the hat) in greeting. **4.** to get rid of (rubbish, etc.) by dumping. ◇*v.i.* **5.** to slope or slant. **6.** to be overturned or upset. ◇*n.* **7.** the act and result of tipping. **8.** a rubbish dump. [ME; orig. uncert.]

tip³ /tɪp/, *n., v.,* **tipped, tipping.** ◇*n.* **1.** a small present of money given to someone for a service; a gratuity. **2.** a piece of private or secret information, such as for use in betting, money speculation, etc. **3.** a useful hint or idea. ◇*v.t.* **4.** to give a small present of money (to). ◇*v.* **5. tip off** or **tip the wink to,** *Colloq.* **a.** to give private or secret information about. **b.** to warn of trouble, danger, etc. [orig. unknown]

Tipperary /tɪpə'reəri/, *n.* a county in the southern Republic of Ireland in Munster province. Irish, **Tiobraid Árann.**

Tippett /'tɪpət/, *n.* **Sir Michael (Kemp),** born 1905, English composer; his works include operas and symphonies.

tipple /'tɪpəl/, *v.t., v.i.,* **-pled, -pling.** to drink (wine, spirits, etc.), esp. repeatedly, in small quantities. [orig. uncert.]

tipsy /'tɪpsi/, *adj.*, **-sier, -siest.** slightly drunk. [apparently from TIP² in obs. sense of intoxicate] **—tipsily,** *adv.* **—tipsiness,** *n.*

tiptoe /'tɪptoʊ/, *n., v.,* **-toed, -toeing,** *adj., adv.* ◇*n.* **1.** the tip or end of a toe. **2. on tiptoe, a.** on the tips of all the toes: *to walk on tiptoe.* **b.** eagerly waiting. **c.** careful; cautious; stealthy. ◇*v.i.* **3.** to move or go on tiptoe; to go quietly and carefully. ◇*adj.* **4.** marked by being on tiptoe. ◇*adv.* **5.** on tiptoe.

tiptop /'tɪptɒp/, *n.* **1.** the extreme top or summit. **2.** *Colloq.* the highest point or degree of excellence. ◇*adj.* **3.** placed at the very top. **4.** *Colloq.* of the highest quality: *in tiptop condition.* [TIP¹ end + TOP¹ highest point; or varied reduplication of TOP¹]

tirade /taɪ'reɪd, tə'reɪd/, *n.* a long speech, full of strong feeling, esp. of anger. [F: draught, shot, from It: volley]

tire /taɪə/, *v.,* **tired, tiring.** ◇*v.t.* **1.** to reduce the strength of; make weary; fatigue (sometimes fol. by *out*). **2.** to reduce the interest, patience of: *A long, boring film tires me.* ◇*v.i.* **3.** to lose strength or interest: *to tire easily.* [ME *tyre*, OE *tyrian*; of unknown orig.]

tired /taɪəd/, *adj.* **1.** weary from effort, work. **2.** bored with: *I'm tired of eating stew all the time.* **3.** *Colloq.* impatient; disgusted: *You make me tired!* **4.** lacking originality; trite; hackneyed: *You're giving me those tired old ideas again.* [TIRE + -ED²]

tiresome /'taɪəsəm/, *adj.* **1.** causing tiredness or boredom. **2.** annoying.

'tis /tɪz/, a short form of *it is.*

tissue /'tɪʃu/, *n.* **1.** *Biol.* **a.** a substance of which (part of) an organism is made. **b.** a group of cells and cell products forming a type of structural material in an animal or plant: *muscular tissue.* **2.** a light, woven fabric. **3.** any mass of connected things: *a tissue of lies.* **4.** soft, thin paper. **5.** a paper handkerchief. [ME, from OF: rich kind of cloth, from L]

tit¹ /tɪt/, *n.* any of various small Australian birds, esp. a thornbill, bluetit, etc. [ME]

tit² /tɪt/, *n.* **1.** a nipple. **2.** *Colloq.* a female breast. [ME and OE]

titan /'taɪtn/, *n.* **1.** (*also cap.*) a person or thing of enormous size, strength, etc. **2.** *Gk Myth.* (*cap.*) one of a family of primordial deities, conceived as lawless beings of gigantic size and enormous strength. **—titanic,** *adj.*

Titania /tə'taniə/, *n.* **1.** the queen of the fairies and the wife of Oberon. **2.** a poetic name used in classical antiquity to refer to Circe, Diana, Latona, or Pyrrha.

Titanic /taɪ'tænɪk/, *n.* a British passenger liner which was claimed to be unsinkable, but which sank on its maiden voyage in 1912 after striking an iceberg off southern Newfoundland.

titanium /taɪ'tiniəm/, *n.* a dark grey, metallic element used in metallurgy to remove oxygen and nitrogen from steel and to toughen

titanium it. *Symbol:* Ti; *at. no.:* 22; *at. wt.:* 47.90. [TITAN + -IUM]

titbit /'tɪtbɪt/, *n.* **1.** a delicate bit of food. **2.** a choice or pleasing bit of anything. [from *tidbit*, from Brit d. *tyd* nice + BIT²]

tithe /taɪð/, *n., v.,* **tithed, tithing.** ◇*n.* **1.** (oft. pl.) the tenth part of the yearly produce of agriculture, etc., due or paid as a tax to the church. **2.** a tenth part of anything. ◇*v.t.* **3.** to give or pay a tithe. **4.** to make (someone) pay a tithe. [OE te(o)g(o)thian]

titian /'tɪʃən, 'ti-/, *n.* a deep reddish or reddish brown color, esp. of hair. [made famous by the Italian painter TITIAN]

Titian /'tɪʃən/, *n.* (*Tiziano Vecellio*), ?1490–1576, Venetian painter; major works include *Venus of Urbino* (1538).

titillate /'tɪtəleɪt/, *v.t.,* **-lated, -lating. 1.** to tickle; excite a tingling sensation in. **2.** to excite pleasantly: *to titillate the fancy.* [L: tickled] **—titillation,** *n.* **—titillative,** *adj.*

titivate /'tɪtɪveɪt/, *v.t., v.i.,* **-vated, -vating.** *Colloq.* to spruce (oneself) up. [earlier *tiddivate*, ? from TIDY] **—titivation,** *n.* **—titivator,** *n.*

title /'taɪtl/, *n., v.,* **-tled, -tling.** ◇*n.* **1.** the name of a book, poem, picture, piece of music, etc. **2.** a descriptive heading of a chapter, or other part of a book. **3.** a name given to a person describing occupation, qualifications, rank, etc., e.g. Doctor, Mr, Reverend, Lady. **4.** *Sport.* the championship: *He lost the title.* **5.** an established right to something. **6.** *Law.* the legal right to the possession of property, esp. houses, land: *He holds the title to our house.* ◇*v.t.* **7.** to give a title to; entitle. [ME, from OF, from L] **—titled,** *adj.*

Tito /'titoʊ/, *n.* **Marshal** (*Josip Broz*), 1892–1980, prime minister of Yugoslavia 1945–53; elected president in 1953, and then made president for life in 1974.

titrate /'taɪtreɪt/, *v.t., v.i.,* **-trated, -trating.** to find the quantity of a given substance present in solution by accurately measuring the volume of a liquid reagent of known strength needed to completely react with an unknown solution (usu. acid-base reaction). [F] **—titration,** *n.*

titre /'taɪtə, 'ti-/, *n.* **1.** the amount of a substance needed to complete reaction exactly in a titration. **2.** the concentration of a standard solution used in titration. [F: fineness, strength, from L: title]

titter /'tɪtə/, *v.i.* **1.** to laugh in a low, half-restrained way, from nervousness or as if trying to cover it up; giggle. ◇*n.* **2.** a tittering laugh.

Titterton /'tɪtətn/, *n.* **Sir Ernest William,** born 1916 in England, Australian nuclear physicist and academic.

tittle /'tɪtl/, *n.* **1.** a dot or other small mark in writing or printing. **2.** a very small part or quantity; a particle, jot, or whit. [ME, from ML: mark over letter or word]

tittle-tattle /'tɪtl-tætl/, *n., v.,* **-tled, -tling.** ◇*n.* **1.** gossip; telltale. ◇*v.i.* **2.** to talk about other people's private affairs; gossip. [varied reduplication of TATTLE]

titular /'tɪtʃələ/, *adj.* **1.** of or relating to a title. **2.** having a title, esp. of rank. **3.** being such in title only: *a titular prince.* [L]

Tiwi /'tiwi/, *n.* an Australian Aboriginal language, used by about one thousand speakers on Bathurst and Melville Islands, off the coast of the NT.

tizz /tɪz/, *n. Colloq.* a state of confused activity where nothing really gets done: *Don't get in a tizz.* Also, **tizzy.**

tjuringa /tjə'rɪŋɡə/, *n.* → **churinga.**

Tl, *Chem. Symbol.* thallium.

Tm, *Chem. Symbol.* thulium.

TM /ti 'ɛm/, *n.* transcendental meditation. [abbrev.]

Tn, *Chem. Symbol.* thoron.

TNT /ti ɛn 'ti/, *n. Chem.* trinitrotoluene, a high explosive set off by detonators, but not affected by ordinary friction or shock. [abbrev.]

to /tu/; *weak form* /tə/, *prep.* **1.** expressing motion or direction towards something: *from east to west.* **2.** showing limit of movement or extent: *rotten to the core.* **3.** expressing contact: *Apply varnish to the surface.* **4.** expressing a point or limit in time: *to this day.* **5.** expressing time until and including: *Monday to Friday.* **6.** expressing aim, purpose, or intention: *going to the rescue.* **7.** expressing destination or appointed end: *sentenced to death.* **8.** indicating result: *to his dismay; to my surprise.* **9.** indicating state or condition: *He tore it to pieces.* **10.** indicating the object of inclination or desire: *They drank to his health.* **11.** expressing the object of a right or claim: *claimants to an estate.* **12.** expressing limit in degree or amount: *punctual to the minute; goods to the value of $100.* **13.** indicating addition or amount: *adding insult to injury.* **14.** expressing attachment: *The paper stuck to the wall; He held to his opinions.* **15.** expressing comparison or opposition: *The score was nine to five.* **16.** expressing agreement or accordance: *a position to one's liking.* **17.** expressing reference or relation: *What will he say to this?* **18.** expressing relative position: *one line parallel to another.* **19.** indicating proportion or ratio: *one teacher to every thirty students.* **20.** used as the ordinary sign or accompaniment of an infinitive verb, as in the verb *to be.* ◇*adv.* **21.** to a contact point or closed position: *Pull the door to.* **22. to and fro, a.** to and from some place or thing. **b.** in opposite or different directions alternately. [ME and OE *tō*]

toad /toʊd/, *n.* **1.** a tailless amphibian like a frog, but bigger, living on land. **2.** a disgusting person or thing. [OE *tādige*; orig. unknown]

toadfish /'toʊdfɪʃ/, *n.* in Australia, the toado.

toado /'toʊdoʊ/, *n.* a type of poisonous fish that can puff itself out, found in warm seas around Australia and elsewhere. [TOAD + -O]

toadstool /'toʊdstul/, *n.* a fleshy fungus like a mushroom, but often poisonous.

toady /'toʊdi/, *n., pl.* **toadies.** someone who flatters another, hoping to win favor; a

toady sycophant. [shortened form of obs. *toadeater*, a mountebank's assistant who pretended to eat toads from which his master had supposedly removed the poison; hence a servile hanger-on]

toast[1] /toust/, *n.* **1.** bread in slices browned on both surfaces by heat. ◇*v.t., v.i.* **2.** to brown or become brown by heat. **3.** to heat or become thoroughly warm at a fire. [ME, from OF, from L: dry, parch] —**toaster,** *n.*

toast[2] /toust/, *n.* **1.** a person or thing to whose health others drink. **2.** a call on another or others to drink to some person or thing. **3.** the act of drinking in this way. **4.** words of congratulation, etc., spoken before drinking. **5.** a person who is suddenly very popular or famous: *She was the toast of the town.* ◇*v.t.* **6.** to propose as a toast. **7.** to drink to the health of, or in honor of. ◇*v.i.* **8.** to propose or drink a toast. [fig. use of TOAST[1], *n.*, with ref. to a piece of toast being put into a beverage to flavor it]

toastmaster /'toustmastə/, *n.* **1.** someone who acts as master of ceremonies at a dinner and introduces the after-dinner speakers. **2.** someone who proposes or announces toasts. —**toastmistress,** *n. fem.*

tobacco /tə'bækou/, *n., pl.* **-cos, -coes. 1.** a tall, bushy plant with long leaves (containing nicotine) which are prepared for smoking or chewing or as snuff. **2.** the leaves so prepared. [Sp, from Arawak (from Guarani): pipe for smoking, or roll of leaves smoked, or plant]

tobacconist /tə'bækənəst/, *n.* someone who sells tobacco, cigarettes, and other items connected with smoking.

Tobago /tə'beigou/, *n.* → **Trinidad and Tobago.**

toboggan /tə'bɒgən/, *n.* **1.** a light sledge with low runners, used in the sport of tobogganing. **2.** a long, narrow, flat-bottomed sledge made of a thin board curved upwards and backwards at the front end, used originally for transport over snow. ◇*v.i.* **3.** to use, or coast on, a toboggan. [Canadian F, from Abnaki (Algonquian): (what is) used for dragging] —**tobogganer, tobogganist,** *n.*

Tobruk /tə'bruk/, *n.* a seaport in eastern Libya; the scene of much fighting, 1940–42. Pop. 28 061 (1973).

toccata /tə'katə/, *n.* a composition in the style of an improvisation, for the piano, organ, or other keyboard instrument, meant to show the player's technique. [It: (pp. fem.) touched]

today /tə'dei/, *n.* **1.** this present day. **2.** this present time or age. ◇*adv.* **3.** on this present day. **4.** at the present time; in these days. [ME; OE *to dæg*]

Todd[1] /tɒd/, *n.* **Sir Charles,** 1826–1910, Australian astronomer, born in England; government astronomer of SA from 1855 and postmaster-general 1870–1905; responsible for construction of Overland Telegraph Line.

Todd[2] /tɒd/, *n.* a river in the NT, rising in the MacDonnell Ranges and extending east and south-east until disappearing in the Simpson Desert near the SA border. About 320 km. [named after Sir Charles Todd]

toddle /'tɒdl/, *v.,* **-dled, -dling,** *n.* ◇*v.i.* **1.** (of a child or an old person) to go with short, unsteady steps. ◇*n.* **2.** the act of toddling. **3.** an unsteady walk. [b. TOTTER and WADDLE] —**toddler,** *n.*

toddy /'tɒdi/, *n., pl.* **-dies. 1.** a drink made of spirits and hot water, sweetened and sometimes spiced. **2.** the sap, esp. when fermented, of various species of palm (**toddy palms**), used as a drink. [Hindi: palm tree]

to-do /tə-'du/, *n., pl.* **-dos.** *Colloq.* bustle; fuss.

toe /tou/, *n., v.,* **toed, toeing.** ◇*n.* **1.** (in man and other animals) one of the end members or digits of the foot. **2.** a part of a stocking or shoe, to cover the toes. **3.** a part like a toe. **4. on one's toes,** prepared to act; wide-awake. **5. tread on someone's toes,** to offend, esp. by acting in another person's area of responsibility. ◇*v.t.* **6.** to kick or strike with the toe: *to toe the ground.* ◇*v.* **7. toe the line,** *Colloq.* to behave according to the rules; conform. [ME; OE *tā*]

toey /'toui/, *adj. Colloq.* keen or anxious; ready to go.

toff /tɒf/, *n. Colloq.* rich, upper-class, usu. well-dressed person. —**toffy,** *adj.*

toffee /'tɒfi/, *n.* a sweet made of sugar or treacle boiled down, often with butter, nuts, etc. Also, **toffy.** [earlier *taffy, tuffy,* of unknown orig.]

tog /tɒg/, *n., v.,* **togged, togging.** *Colloq.* ◇*n.* **1.** (*usu. pl.*) clothes: *football togs; swimming togs.* ◇*v.t.* **2.** to clothe; dress (oft. fol. by *out* or *up*). [apparently short for obs. cant term *togeman(s)* cloak, coat]

toga /'tougə/, *n., pl.* **-gas.** loose outer garment of the citizens of ancient Rome. [L]

together /tə'geðə/, *adv.* **1.** into or in one place, gathering, company, mass, or body: *to call the people together.* **2.** into or in union, contact, or collision, as two or more things: *to sew things together.* **3.** into or in relationship, association: *to bring strangers together.* **4.** taken or considered collectively: *This one cost more than all the others together.* **5.** (of a single thing) into or in a condition of unity, compactness, or coherence: *to squeeze a thing together; The argument does not hang together well.* **6.** at the same time; simultaneously: *You cannot have both together.* **7.** without interruption; continuously: *for days together.* **8.** with united action; in cooperation: *to undertake a task together.* ◇*adj. Colloq.* **9.** capable and calm: *He is quite together these days.* [OE *tōgædere*] —**togetherness,** *n.*

toggle /'tɒgəl/, *n., v.,* **-gled, -gling.** ◇*n.* **1.** a pin, bolt, or rod placed through an eye of a rope, the link of a chain, etc., for various purposes. **2.** a small wooden bar around which a loop is passed, to fasten the front of some coats. ◇*v.t.* **3.** to furnish or fasten with a toggle or toggles. [? akin to TACKLE]

toil /tɔɪl/, *n.* **1.** hard and continuous work; exhausting labor or effort. ◇*v.i.* **2.** to work

toil hard and long. **3.** to move or travel with difficulty, weariness, or pain: *to toil up a hill.* [ME, from AF: strive, dispute, wrangle, from L: stir]

toilet /'tɔɪlət/, *n.* **1.** (a room fitted with) a disposal apparatus of any type used for urination and defecation, esp. one which flushes the waste away with water; water-closet. **2.** the act or process of dressing, including bathing, arranging the hair, etc. [F: cloth]

toiletry /'tɔɪlətri/, *n., pl.* **-tries.** an article or substance used in dressing or washing, e.g. a soap, deodorant, shaving lotion.

toilet-train /'tɔɪlət-treɪn/, *v.t.* to train (a baby) to use a toilet. —**toilet-training,** *n.*

token /'toʊkən/, *n.* **1.** something used to represent or show some fact, event, feeling, etc.; sign: *to wear black as a token of mourning.* **2.** a characteristic mark or indication; symbol. **3.** something given as a way of remembering (a person, place, etc.); memento. **4.** a ticket, metal disc, etc., used in place of money for ferry fares, etc. **5. by the same token,** in the same way; similarly. **6. in token of,** as a sign or evidence of. [ME; OE *tācen*]

Tokyo /'toʊkioʊ/, *n.* a seaport in and the capital of Japan, on **Tokyo Bay,** an inlet of the Pacific in south-eastern Honshu Island, one of the world's three largest cities; destructive earthquake and fire, 1923. Pop. 8 348 000 (1987). Also, **Tokio.** Formerly, **Yeddo** or **Yedo.**

Tokyo Rose, *n.* a nickname given by US troops to a number of women who broadcast music and propaganda from Japan during World War II.

told /toʊld/, *v.* **1.** past tense and past participle of **tell. 2. all told,** in all.

Toledo /tə'leɪdoʊ/, *n.* a city in central Spain, on the river Tagus; the capital of Spain under the Romans. Pop. 57 769 (1981).

tolerable /'tɒlərəbəl/, *adj.* **1.** bearable; endurable. **2.** fairly good; not bad. [ME, from L: bearable]

tolerance /'tɒlərəns/, *n.* **1.** the state of mind of accepting other people's different opinions or practices; freedom from bigotry. **2.** the ability to put up with unpleasant circumstances. **3.** *Med.* the increasing resistance of a body to the effects of a drug, etc., such as morphine, requiring increased doses to give the same effect. **4.** *Mech.* an allowable variation in the dimensions of a machined article or part.

tolerate /'tɒləreɪt/, *v.t.*, **-rated, -rating. 1.** to allow; permit: *to tolerate bad behavior.* **2.** to put up with; endure: *to tolerate hardship.* [L: endured] —**tolerant,** *adj.* —**toleration,** *n.*

Tolkien /'tɒlkən/, *n.* **John Ronald Reuel** /'ruəl/, 1892–1973, British medievalist, writer, and critic, born in South Africa; best-known works include *The Hobbit* (1937) and the trilogy *The Lord of the Rings* (1954–55).

toll[1] /toʊl/, *v.t.* **1.** to make (a bell) sound with single, slow, and regular strokes. **2.** to sound (the hour, a death knell, etc.) by such strokes. ◇*v.i.* **3.** (of a bell) to sound with single, slow and regular strokes. ◇*n.* **4.** the act or sound of tolling. [ME]

toll[2] /toʊl/, *n.* **1.** Also, **tollage.** a payment made to a government or authority for the right to go on a certain road, or over a bridge, etc. **2.** a tax or duty. **3.** the cost, esp. of death or loss: *The accident took a heavy toll of lives.* [ME and OE, from L, from Gk: tollhouse]

Tolpuddle Martyrs /'tɒlpʌdl matəz/, *n.pl.* a name given to six men from the village of Tolpuddle in England who were transported to Australia in 1834 for unlawfully administering oaths of loyalty to a union which they had formed. Also, **Dorchester Laborers.**

Tolstoy /'tɒlstɔɪ/, *n.* **Count Lev** (*Eng.* **Leo**) **Nikolaevich** /ljef nɪkə'lajəvɪtʃ/, 1828–1910, Russian novelist and social reformer; major works include *War and Peace* (1865–69) and *Anna Karenina* (1875–77). Also, **Tolstoi.**

Toltec /'tɒltek/, *n.* (*pl.*) an Indian people who flourished in central Mexico before the advent of the Aztecs, and who, according to tradition, laid the foundation of Aztec culture.

tom /tɒm/, *n.* the male of various animals, esp. of the cat. Also, **tomcat.** [short for *Thomas*]

tomahawk /'tɒməhɔk/, *n.* **1.** a small, short-handled axe; hatchet. **2.** a light axe used by the North American Indians. ◇*v.t.* **3.** to strike, cut, or kill with or as if with a tomahawk. [Algonquian: war club, ceremonial object]

tomato /tə'matoʊ/, *n., pl.* **-toes.** a widely cultivated plant bearing a slightly acid, pulpy, red fruit. [Sp, from Nahuatl]

tomb /tum/, *n.* **1.** a grave or vault for the dead. **2.** an ornamental structure enclosing the body of an important person; mausoleum. [ME, from OF, from LL, from Gk]

tomboy /'tɒmbɔɪ/, *n.* a spirited girl who likes to play or act like a boy.

tombstone /'tumstoʊn/, *n.* a stone at the head of a grave, with the name, dates, etc. of the dead person cut into it.

tome /toʊm/, *n.* **1.** a single book forming a part of a larger work; volume. **2.** a heavy or learned book. [F, from L, from Gk: volume, section of book]

-tome, a word part referring to cutting, used esp. in scientific terms. [combining form representing Gk *tomē* a cutting, section]

tomfoolery /tɒm'fuləri/, *n., pl.* **-eries.** foolish or silly behavior.

tomography /tə'mɒgrəfi/, *n.* the technique of getting an X-ray picture of a particular layer in an object. [Gk *tómos* slice + -GRAPHY]

tomorrow /tə'mɒroʊ/, *n.* **1.** the day after the present day (today). **2.** some future day or time. ◇*adv.* **3.** on the day after the present day (today): *Come tomorrow.* Also, **to-morrow.** [OE *tō morgen(ne)* on the morrow, in the morning]

Tom Price /tɒm 'praɪs/, *n.* a town in western central WA, in the Hamersley Range; residential and service centre for nearby iron ore mine. Pop. 3435 (1986). [named after

Thomas Moore *Price*, vice-president of Kaiser Steel Ltd]

Tompson /'tɒmsən/, *n.* **Charles**, 1807–83, Australian poet; noted for *Wild Notes, from the Lyre of a Native Minstrel* (1826), the first volume of poetry written by an Australian-born writer, published in Australia.

tom-tom /'tɒm-tɒm/, *n.* **1.** a drum of Africa, India, etc. **2.** a dull repeated drumbeat or similar sound. [Hind or other East Ind vernacular; imitative]

-tomy, a noun ending meaning a 'cutting', esp. relating to a surgical operation, as in *appendectomy*, or sometimes a division, as in *dichotomy*. [Gk *-tomia*]

ton[1] /tʌn/, *n.* **1.** a unit of mass in the imperial system equal to 2240 lb (**long ton**), or approx. 1016 kg, and, in the US, 2000 lb (**short ton**), or approx. 907 kg. **2.** a unit of freight equal to 1000 kg or, formerly, 40 cubic feet (**freight ton**). **3.** a unit of displacement of ships in the imperial system equal to 35 cubic feet of salt water (**displacement ton** or **shipping ton**), or approx. 0.99 cubic metres. **4.** a unit of internal capacity of ships in the imperial system, equal to 100 cubic feet, or approx. 2.83 cubic metres (**gross ton**). **5.** → **tonne**. **6.** *Colloq.* heavy weight: *That book weighs a ton.* **7.** (*pl.*) *Colloq.* very many; a good deal: *tons of things to see.* [ME]

ton[2] /tʌn/, *n. Colloq.* **1.** a score of a hundred. **2.** a speed of 100 mph or 100 km/h, esp. on a motorcycle.

-ton, a noun suffix, as in *simpleton*. [Brit d.]

tonal /'toʊnəl/, *adj.* **1.** *Music.* relating to tonality (opposed to *atonal* and *modal*). **2.** relating to tone. —**tonally,** *adv.*

tonality /toʊnˈælɪtiː/, *n., pl.* **-ties. 1.** *Music.* all the relations, melodic and harmonic, existing between the notes of a scale or musical system; key. **2.** *Painting, etc.* the system of tones or colors of a picture; etc.

tone /toʊn/, *n., v.*, **toned, toning.** ◇*n.* **1.** any sound considered with regard to its quality, pitch, strength, source, etc.: *shrill tones.* **2.** the quality or character of sound: *The cello has a mellow tone.* **3.** the particular quality or pitch of the voice; intonation: *a tone of command.* **4.** *Music.* an interval equal to two semitones; whole tone. **5. a.** the degree of lightness or darkness of a color, or of black, grey or white. **b.** a small variation produced in a given color by the addition of another color or of white, grey or black. **6.** the state of firmness proper to the organs or tissues of the body: *good muscle tone.* **7.** normal healthy condition of the mind. **8.** general character or style: *Bad behavior lowers the tone of the school.* **9.** the quality of style in literature, esp. as showing the author's attitude: *a serious tone; an ironic tone.* ◇*v.* **10. tone down, a.** *Painting.* to make less bright; subdue. **b.** to soften or make less; moderate: *to tone down efforts.* **11. tone in,** to match; harmonise: *Those shoes will tone in with your new dress.* **12. tone up,** to make stronger or more healthy: *Walking tones up the muscles.* [ME, from ML, from Gk: tension, pitch, key]

tone row, *n.* a sequence of intervals which involves all the twelve tones of an octave without repetition, used in twelve-tone music.

Tonga /'tɒŋə, 'tɒŋɡə/, *n.* a kingdom in the south-western Pacific Ocean, consisting of 169 islands divided into the Vava'u, Ha'apai and Tongatapu groups; a British protectorate before independence in 1970. Pop. 94 800 (1987); 747 km^2. *Languages:* English and Tongan. *Currency:* pa'anga. *Cap.:* Nuku'alofa. Also, **Friendly Islands.** —**Tongan,** *n., adj.*

tongs /tɒŋz/, *n.pl.* a tool consisting of two arms fastened or hinged together, for taking hold of something: *fire tongs.* [ME; OE *tang*]

tongue /tʌŋ/, *n., v.*, **tongued, tonguing.** ◇*n.* **1.** a movable organ in humans and most vertebrates occupying the floor of the mouth, being the main organ of taste, and, in humans, speech. **2.** this organ in an animal, such as the ox, etc., used as food. **3.** the power of speech: *to lose your tongue.* **4.** a manner or character of speech: *a flattering tongue.* **5.** a language or dialect: *the Hebrew tongue.* **6.** *Bible.* a people as known by its language: *all nations and tongues.* **7.** a strip of leather under the lacing of a shoe. **8.** a piece of hanging metal inside a bell that produces a sound when it strikes against the side; clapper. **9.** *Carp.* a strip jutting out along the centre of the edge of a board, for fitting into a groove in another board. **10.** a narrow strip of land stretching out into a body of water. ◇**11.** Some special uses are:

hold one's tongue, to be quiet.

mind one's tongue, to be careful what one says.

on the tip of one's tongue, almost able to be remembered.

slip of the tongue, an unintended remark.

(with) tongue in cheek, not seriously; facetiously; ironically.

◇*v.t., v.i.* **12.** to sound (the notes of a flute, trumpet, etc.) separately by strokes of the tongue. **13.** to touch with the tongue. [ME and OE *tunge*] —**tongued,** *adj.*

tongue twister, *n.* a word, phrase or sentence which is difficult to say quickly because of repeated similar sounds, as in: *She sells sea shells by the sea shore.*

tonic /'tɒnɪk/, *n.* **1.** a medicine that gives health and strength. **2.** anything that gives new strength or energy: *His success was a tonic to his spirits.* **3.** *Music.* the first note or degree of the scale. ◇*adj.* **4.** giving health, strength, or energy. **5.** *Med.* **a.** relating to tension, as of the muscles. **b.** marked by continued muscular tension: *a tonic spasm.* **6.** relating to tone or accent in speech. **7.** *Music.* relating to or founded on the tonic of a scale: *a tonic chord.* [Gk: pertaining to tone] —**tonicity,** *n.*

tonic solfa, *n.* → **solfa.**

tonic water, *n.* bubbly water with quinine, often added to spirits: *gin and tonic water.*

tonight /tə'naɪt/, *n.* **1.** the night of this present day. ◇*adv.* **2.** on the night of this present day. [ME; OE *tō niht*]

tonnage /'tʌnɪdʒ/, *n.* **1.** the amount in tons a ship or boat can carry. **2.** ships taken as a whole measured by how much they can

tonnage 1084 **top dressing**

carry or together with their cargoes. **3.** a duty on ships or boats at so much per ton of cargo. Also, **tunnage.**

tonne /tɒn/, *n.* a unit of mass equal to 1000 kilograms. *Symbol:* t

tonsil /'tɒnsəl/, *n.* either of two oval masses of lymphoid tissue at the back of the mouth cavity. [L] —**tonsillar,** *adj.*

tonsillectomy /tɒnsə'lɛktəmi/, *n., pl.* **-mies.** the operation of cutting out one or both tonsils. [L]

tonsillitis /tɒnsə'laɪtəs/, *n.* inflammation of the tonsils. [NL, from L]

tonsure /'tɒnʃə/, *n.* **1.** the act of shaving the hair on top of the head, esp. formerly as a sign of becoming a priest or monk. **2.** the shaved top of the head. [ME, from L: shearing] —**tonsured,** *adj.*

too /tu/, *adv.* **1.** also; in addition; moreover: *young, clever, and rich too.* **2.** beyond what is wanted, fitting, or right; excessively: *too long.* **3.** more than should be: *too many pupils.* **4.** very; extremely (esp. after *only* or a negative): *only too glad to help you; not too bad.* **5.** *Colloq.* indeed (used for emphasis): *I did so too!* **6. too right,** *Colloq.* (emphatic expression of agreement). [var. of TO, adv.]

took /tʊk/, *v.* past tense of **take.**

tool /tul/, *n.* **1.** something held in the hand, for doing some mechanical work, e.g. a hammer, saw, file. **2.** (part of) a machine which cuts, grinds, drills, etc. **3.** anything used like a tool to do work or cause some result. **4.** a person used by another for his own ends. ◊*v.t., v.i.* **5.** to work or shape with a tool. ◊*v.* **6. tool up,** to fit out (a workshop) for a particular job. [ME: OE *tol*]

toolache /'tuleɪtʃi/, *n.* See **wallaby.**

toolah /'tulə/, *n.* See **ringtail possum.**

Toongabbie /tun'gæbi/, *n.* a western suburb of Sydney, NSW; site of early land grants to settlers and of the government farm, established 1792. [Aboriginal: near the water]

toot /tut/, *v.t., v.i.* **1.** to (cause to) sound in short blasts, as a horn, whistle, etc. ◊*n.* **2.** the act or sound of tooting. [late ME]

tooth /tuθ/, *n., pl.* **teeth** /tiθ/, *v.* **1.** (in most vertebrates) one of the hard outgrowths set in rows in the jaws, used for eating or catching food, or for attacking enemies. **2.** a toothlike part of a comb, rake, saw, cogwheel, etc. **3.** something effective or giving force: *to give teeth to the law.* **4. a sweet tooth,** a liking for sweet things. **5. long in the tooth,** old. ◊*v.t.* **6.** to provide with teeth. **7.** to cut teeth upon. ◊*v.i.* **8.** (of cogwheels) to interlock. [ME; OE *tōth*] —**toothed,** *adj.*

toothcomb /'tuθkoʊm/, *n.* **1.** a comb with very fine teeth, usu. at each edge. **2. with a (fine) toothcomb,** in great detail; very painstakingly.

toothless /'tuθləs/, *adj.* **1.** having no teeth. **2.** having no real power: *toothless legislation.*

toothpick /'tuθpɪk/, *n.* a small pointed piece of wood for removing food stuck between the teeth.

toothy /'tuθi/, *adj.* **1.** having prominent teeth. **2.** showing the teeth: *a toothy grin.* —**toothily,** *adv.*

tootle /'tutl/, *v.*, **-tled, -tling,** *n.* ◊*v.i.* **1.** to toot gently or repeatedly on a flute, etc. ◊*n.* **2.** the sound itself. [frequentative of TOOT]

Toowoomba /tə'wʊmbə/, *n.* a city in south-eastern Qld, on the Great Dividing Range; commercial and industrial centre for the Darling Downs. Pop. 71 362 (1986).

top[1] /tɒp/, *n., adj., v.,* **topped, topping.** ◊*n.* **1.** the highest point or part of anything; apex; summit. **2.** the upper part or surface of anything. **3.** a part thought of as higher: *the top of a street.* **4.** the part of a plant above ground, as different from the root: *carrot tops.* **5.** the highest point, pitch, or degree: *to speak at the top of one's voice.* **6.** (someone or something in) the highest or leading position: *She is (at) the top of her class.* **7.** a covering or lid, as of a box, car, carriage, etc. **8.** the head. **9.** the crown of the head. **10.** an outer garment that covers the upper part of the body. ◊**11.** Some special uses are:
blow one's top, *Colloq.* to lose one's temper.
off the top of one's head, without preparation or thought; impromptu.
from the top, from the beginning.
on top, successful; victorious; dominant.
on top of, 1. upon. **2.** following very closely upon.
the tops, 1. peaks or ridges of a high mountain range: *Barrington Tops.* **2.** Also, **tops.** *Colloq.* the very best: *That book really is the tops.* ◊*adj.* **12.** highest; uppermost; upper: *the top shelf.* **13.** greatest: *to pay top prices.* **14.** foremost; chief; principal: *to win top honors in a competition.* **15.** *Colloq.* the best; excellent: *He's a top bloke.* **16.** of or relating to the highest forward gear on a car, etc. ◊*v.t.* **17.** to give a top to; put a top on. **18.** to be at or form the top of. **19.** to reach the top of. **20.** to rise above: *The sun had topped the horizon.* **21.** to be or do more or better than: *Your story tops even Jack's funniest ones.* **22.** to remove the top of; crop; prune. **23.** to get or leap over the top of (a fence, etc.). **24.** *Golf, etc.* to hit the ball above the centre. **25.** to top-dress (land). ◊*v.i.* **26.** *Golf, etc.* to hit the ball above the centre. ◊*v.* **27. top off,** to complete by adding a finishing touch (fol. by *with*): *to top off his dinner with a glass of port.* **28. top up,** to fill up (a partly filled container). [ME and OE]

top[2] /tɒp/, *n.* a conical toy, with a point on which it is made to spin. [ME and OE]

top-, variant of **topo-,** before vowels.

topaz /'toʊpæz/, *n.* **1.** a mineral, a type of silicate of aluminium, usu. occurring in crystals of various colors, and used as a gem (**true topaz** or **precious topaz**). **2.** a yellow variety of sapphire (**oriental topaz**). **3.** a yellow variety of quartz (**false topaz** or **common topaz**). [L, from Gk]

top dressing, *n.* **1.** a layer of manure, soil, fertiliser, etc. spread on the surface of lawns, crops, etc. **2.** the action of someone who top-dresses. **3.** the top layer of gravel, crushed rock, etc., on a roadway. **4.** any treatment or covering that does not go very deep. —**top-dress,** *v.*

topee /'toupi/, *n.* → **pith helmet.** Also, **topi.** [Hind: hat]

top hat, *n.* a man's tall silk hat.

topiary /'toupiəri/, *adj., n., pl.* **-aries.** ◇*adj.* **1.** (of hedges, trees, etc.) clipped or trimmed into (ornamental) shapes. ◇*n.* **2.** (a garden containing) topiary work. [L] —**topiarian,** *adj.*

topic /'tɒpɪk/, *n.* **1.** a subject of conversation or discussion: *to provide a topic for discussion.* **2.** the subject or theme of a speech or piece of writing. [sing. of *topics,* from L, from Gk]

topical /'tɒpɪkəl/, *adj.* **1.** relating to or dealing with matters of present or local interest: *Energy is a topical matter these days.* **2.** of a place; local: *topical history.*

topknot /'tɒpnɒt/, *n.* **1.** a tuft of hair or feathers growing on top of the head. **2.** a knot of hair arranged on the top of the head.

topless /'tɒpləs/, *adj.* **1.** without a top. **2.** allowing the breasts to be shown: *a topless dress; a topless waitress.*

topmast /'tɒpmast/; *Naut.* /-məst/, *n.* the second section of the mast above the deck, just above the lower mast.

topo-, a word part meaning 'place', as in *topography.* Also, **top-.** [Gk, combining form of *tópos*]

topography /tə'pɒgrəfi/, *n., pl.* **-phies.** (a detailed description and analysis of) the geographical features of a fairly small area. [ME, from LL, from Gk] —**topographer,** *n.* —**topographic, topographical,** *adj.*

topology /tə'pɒlədʒi/, *n.* the study of those properties of geometric forms that are considered to be unchanged even when bent, stretched, etc. For example, in topology, a sphere and a spheroid are considered equal. [TOPO- + -LOGY]

topper /'tɒpə/, *n. Colloq.* **1.** a top hat. **2.** anything excellent.

topple /'tɒpəl/, *v.,* **-pled, -pling.** ◇*v.i.* **1.** to fall forwards; pitch or tumble down. **2.** to lean over or jut, as if about to fall. ◇*v.t.* **3.** to cause to topple: *to topple a government from power.* [frequentative of *top* topple]

topsail /'tɒpseɪl/; *Naut.* /-səl/, *n.* **1.** a square sail next above the lowest or chief square sail on a square-rigged ship. **2.** in a fore-and-aft rig, a square or triangular sail set above the gaff.

topside /'tɒpsaɪd/, *n.* the top section of a butt of beef, without bone, below the rump.

topsoil /'tɒpsɔɪl/, *n.* **1.** the valuable upper part of the soil where most plants grow. ◇*v.t.* **2.** to cover (land) with topsoil.

topsy-turvy /tɒpsi-'tɜvi/, *adv.* **1.** upside down. **2.** backwards. **3.** confused; disordered.

tor /tɔ/, *n.* **1.** *Geol.* rock (usu. granite) shaped by erosion into slabs or boulders. **2.** a hill. [ME; OE *torr,* from Celtic. See Gael *torr,* Welsh *twr* protuberance]

Torah /'tɔrə/, *n.* the Jewish law, as found in the Pentateuch (the first five books of the Bible). Also, **Tora.** [Heb: instruction, law]

torch /tɔtʃ/, *n.* **1.** a small portable electric lamp powered by dry batteries. **2.** a burning substance carried or set on a post to give light; flare. **3.** something considered as a source of knowledge, guidance, etc.: *the torch of learning.* **4.** a lamplike instrument which produces a hot flame and is used for soldering, burning off paint, etc.; oxyacetylene burner. **5. carry a torch for,** to love, esp. without being loved in return. [ME, from OF]

tore /tɔ/, *v.* past tense of **tear**[2].

toreador /'tɔriədɔ/, *n.* a Spanish bullfighter. [Sp: fight bulls]

torment /tɔ'mɛnt/, *v.;* /'tɔmɛnt/, *n.* ◇*v.t.* **1.** to give great bodily or mental suffering to; torture: *to be tormented with violent headaches.* **2.** to worry or annoy greatly: *She tormented him with questions.* **3.** to stir into violent movement: *The wind tormented the trees.* ◇*n.* **4.** a state of great bodily or mental suffering; agony; misery. **5.** something that causes great bodily or mental pain or suffering. **6.** a source of trouble, worry, or annoyance. [ME, from OF: torment, from L: torment, instrument operated by twisting] —**tormentor,** *n.* —**tormenting,** *adj.*

torn /tɔn/, *v.* **1.** past participle of **tear**[2]. **2. that's torn it,** everything is ruined. **3. torn between,** unable to choose between (conflicting desires, duties, etc.).

tornado /tɔ'neɪdoʊ/, *n., pl.* **-does, -dos.** **1.** *Weather.* a violent whirlwind, advancing over the land, in which winds of destructive force circulate round a centre. It is marked by strong upward currents and is usu. seen as a funnel-shaped cloud. **2.** a violent outburst, as of emotion or activity. [Sp] —**tornadic,** *adj.*

Toronto /tə'rɒntoʊ/, *n.* a city in south-eastern Canada, on Lake Ontario; the capital of Ontario. Pop. 3 427 168 (1986).

torpedo /tɔ'pidoʊ/, *n., pl.* **-does,** *v.,* **-doed, -doing.** ◇*n.* **1.** a self-propelled cigar-shaped missile containing explosives, which is launched from a tube in a submarine, torpedo-boat, or aircraft, and explodes when it hits a ship. ◇*v.t., v.i.* **2.** to attack or destroy (a ship) with a torpedo or torpedoes. [L: crampfish or electric ray, which disables its prey by electric discharge]

torpor /'tɔpə/, *n.* **1.** a state where physical powers are not active. **2.** sluggish inactivity or inertia; lethargy. **3.** dormancy, as of a hibernating animal. [L: numbness] —**torpid,** *adj.*

torque /tɔk/, *n.* **1.** *Mech.* something which produces or tends to produce torsion or rotation; the moment of a system of forces which tends to cause rotation. **2.** *Mech.* the turning power of a shaft. **3.** Also, **torc.** a twisted band of precious metal, worn as a collar or necklace, esp. by the ancient Gauls and Britons. [L: twisted metal necklace]

Torrens /'tɒrənz/, n. **Sir Robert Richard,** 1814-84, Australian state politician, born in Ireland; premier of SA for one month in 1857; introduced a bill simplifying the laws relating to land ownership. See **Torrens title.**

Torrens title, n. the name given to a system by which title to land is established by the official registration of changes in ownership of that land. Also, **Torrens system.** See **strata title.** [introduced by Sir Robert Richard TORRENS]

torrent /'tɒrənt/, n. **1.** a stream of water flowing with great speed and violence. **2.** a violent or plentiful flow of anything: *a torrent of lava*; *a torrent of abuse.* **3.** a violent downpour of rain. [L: torrent, lit., boiling] —**torrential,** *adj.*

Torres /'tɒrəs/, n. **Luis Vaez de,** fl. 1605-07, Spanish navigator who sailed with Pedro Fernandez de Quiros in search of *Terra Australis Incognita* in 1605.

Torres Strait, n. a stretch of water extending between Cape York Peninsula, Qld and PNG's southern coast. [named after Luis Vaez de TORRES in honor of his navigation through it]

torrid /'tɒrəd/, *adj.* **1.** (of regions, etc.) subject to burning heat. **2.** (of climate, weather, etc.) unpleasantly hot. **3.** passionate; ardent. [L]

Torrid Zone, n. *Geog.* the zone which includes the equator, lying between the tropics of Cancer and Capricorn.

torsion /'tɔʃən/, n. **1.** an act of twisting or the state of being twisted. **2.** *Mech.* **a.** the twisting of a body by two equal and opposite torques. **b.** the internal torque so produced. [ME, from LL: twist] —**torsional,** *adj.*

torsion balance, n. an instrument for measuring small forces (as electrical attraction or repulsion) by determining the amount of torsion or twisting they cause in a slender wire or filament.

torso /'tɔsoʊ/, n., pl. **-sos.** the trunk of the human body. Also, **torse.** [It: trunk, stump, stalk, trunk of statue, from L]

tort /tɔt/, n. *Law.* **1.** a civil injury, where legal action is undertaken by a private individual (e.g. trespass, negligence, etc.), as opposed to a criminal wrong, where legal action is undertaken by the state. **2.** (*pl.*) the branch of law concerned with civil injuries. [F: a wrong] —**tortious,** *adj.*

torte /tɔt/, n. a large, rich, decorated cake. [G, from LL]

tortilla /tɔ'tijə/, n. (in Mexico, etc.) a thin, round, unleavened cake made from cornmeal. [Sp: cake, from LL: twisted (bread)]

tortoise /'tɔtəs/, n. **1.** a land or freshwater reptile with toed feet rather than flippers, and a hard shell covering its body. **2.** a very slow person or thing. [ME, from ML, from L: twisted]

tortoiseshell /'tɔtəʃel/, n. **1.** a horny yellow-brown substance making up the plates or scales that cover the marine **tortoiseshell turtle,** formerly used for making combs, etc., or for inlaying. **2.** the shell of a tortoise.

tortuous /'tɔtʃuəs/, *adj.* **1.** twisting, winding, or crooked: *a tortuous mountain road.* **2.** not direct or straightforward: *a tortuous procedure*; *tortuous writing.* [ME, from L: full of turns or twists]

torture /'tɔtʃə/, n., v., **-tured, -turing.** ◇n. **1.** the act of causing severe pain, esp. from cruelty, or to get information from the victim. **2.** a method of causing such pain. **3.** (*oft. pl.*) the pain or suffering caused or undergone. **4.** (a cause of) agony of body or mind. ◇v.t. **5.** to cause severe bodily or mental pain to. **6.** to twist, force, or bring into some unnatural position or form. **7.** to twist or distort (language, etc.). [L: twisting, torment, torture] —**torturer,** n. —**torturous,** *adj.*

torus /'tɔrəs/, n., pl. **tori** /'tɔraɪ/. *Geom.* (the solid shaped by) a closed surface like a doughnut or tyre inner tube. [L: bulge, rounded moulding]

Tory /'tɔri/, n., pl. **-ries. 1.** a member of a political party in Great Britain, in general favoring conservation of the existing order of things in State and Church, evolving into the Conservative Party in the early 19th century. Cf. **Whig** (def. 3). **2.** a member of the Conservative Party. ◇*adj.* **3.** of or relating to the Conservative Party. [Irish *tōraidhe* pursuer]

Toscanini /tɒskə'nini/, n. **Arturo** /a'tuəroʊ/, 1867-1957, Italian musician and conductor of operas and symphonies.

toss /tɒs/, v., **tossed** or (*Poetic*) **tost**; **tossing,** n. ◇v.t. **1.** to throw, pitch, or fling, esp. lightly or carelessly: *to toss a piece of paper into the wastepaper basket.* **2.** to fling or jerk about: *A tree tosses its branches in the wind*; *a ship tossed by the waves.* **3.** to move or turn around; agitate: *to toss a salad.* **4.** to throw, raise, or jerk upwards suddenly: *to toss the head.* **5.** to throw (a coin, etc.) into the air in a toss-up (oft. fol. by *up*). **6.** to drink or eat very quickly (fol. by *off*): *He tossed off a few drinks and then left.* **7.** to produce quickly and easily: *She tossed off a few ideas.* ◇v.i. **8.** to pitch, rock, sway, or move irregularly: *The ship was tossing in heavy seas.* **9.** to fling or jerk oneself or move restlessly about: *He tossed in his sleep.* **10.** to throw something. **11.** to throw a coin, etc., in a toss-up (oft. fol. by *up*). ◇n. **12.** the act of tossing; a throw, etc. **13.** a pitching about or up and down: *the endless toss of the waves.* **14.** →**toss-up. 15.** a sudden fling or jerk of the body: *'No,' she said, with a toss of the head.* **16. argue the toss,** to go on arguing after a dispute has been settled. [apparently from Scand]

toss-up /'tɒs-ʌp/, n. **1.** the tossing up of a coin, etc., to decide something by the side on which it falls. **2.** *Colloq.* an even chance: *It's a toss-up whether he'll make it in time.*

tot[1] /tɒt/, n. **1.** a small child. **2.** a small amount of drink. **3.** a small quantity of anything. [? short for *totterer* child learning to walk]

tot[2] /tɒt/, v.t., **totted, totting.** *Colloq.* to add (oft. fol. by *up*). [L: so much, so many]

total /'toʊtl/, *adj.*, n., v., **-talled, -talling.** ◇*adj.* **1.** making up the whole; entire; whole:

total — *the total expenditure.* **2.** of or relating to the whole of something: *a total eclipse.* **3.** complete; utter; absolute: *a total failure.* ◇*n.* **4.** the sum; aggregate: *to add the several items to find the total; The costs reached a total of $200.* ◇*v.t.* **5.** to bring to a total; add up. **6.** to reach a total of; amount to. ◇*v.i.* **7.** to amount (oft. fol. by *to*). [ME, from ML, from L: entire]

total heat, *n. Phys.* → **enthalpy**.

total internal reflection, *n.* the total reflection of a light ray which occurs when light from one medium strikes another of refractive index or optical density, at an angle of incidence in excess of the critical angle.

totalisator or **totalizator** /ˈtoutəlaɪˌzeɪtə/, *n.* **1.** a machine for registering and indicating the total of operations, measurements, etc. **2.** a form of betting, as on horseraces, in which those who bet on the winners divide the bets or stakes, less a percentage for the management, taxes, etc.

totalitarian /touˌtælɪˈtɛəriən/, *adj.* **1.** of or relating to a centralised state or government which has complete control and does not allow opposition parties to function or opposing opinions to be expressed openly. ◇*n.* **2.** someone who follows totalitarian principles. – **totalitarianism**, *n.*

totality /touˈtælətɪ/, *n., pl.* **-ties. 1.** the state of being total; entirety. **2.** that which is total; total amount; whole.

totally /ˈtoutəli/, *adv.* wholly; entirely; completely: *I agree with you totally.*

tote[1] /tout/, *v.t.*, **toted, toting**, *Colloq.* **1.** to carry: *to tote books around.* **2.** to wear or be armed with: *to tote a gun.* [orig. uncert.]

tote[2] /tout/, *n.* → **totalisator**.

totem /ˈtoutəm/, *n.* **1.** something, often an animal, taken as the token or emblem of a clan or family group, and to which people may see themselves related by blood. **2.** a statue, drawing, etc., of such an object serving as the distinctive mark of the clan or group. [Algonquian (N America): his brother-sister kin] – **totemic**, *adj.* – **totemism**, *n.*

totem pole, *n.* a pole or post carved and painted with totemic figures, set up by Indians of the north-western coast of North America, esp. in front of their houses. Also, **totem post**.

totter /ˈtɒtə/, *v.i.* **1.** to walk unsteadily or weakly. **2.** to sway or rock as if about to fall: *The government is tottering.* **3.** to shake or tremble. ◇*n.* **4.** an unsteady movement or gait. [ME from Scand] – **tottering, tottery**, *adj.*

toucan /ˈtukæn/, *n.* a fruit-eating bird of tropical America, brightly colored and with an enormous beak. [Tupi]

touch /tʌtʃ/, *v.t.* **1.** (of a person) to put the hand, finger, etc., on or into contact with (something) to feel it. **2.** (of the hand, etc.) to come into contact with and feel (something). **3.** to bring (the hand, finger, or something held) into contact with something: *to touch a match to kindling.* **4.** to strike or hit gently or lightly: *She touched him on the shoulder; to touch the strings of a guitar.* **5.** to hurt or harm: *Don't be frightened, I won't touch you.* **6.** to come into or be in contact with. **7.** *Geom.* (of a line or surface) to be tangent to. **8.** to come up to; reach; attain: *Can you touch last year's score?* **9.** to compare with (usu. with a negative): *John doesn't touch Mark as a golfer.* **10.** (of a ship, etc.) to stop at (a place). **11.** to mark or affect; tinge; imbue (usu. in passive): *The music was touched with sadness.* **12.** to affect with an emotion, esp. tenderness, pity, gratitude, etc.: *Their sufferings touched his heart.* **13.** to handle, eat, use, have to do with, etc.: *He won't touch another drink.* **14.** to deal with or treat in speech or writing. **15.** to relate to: *He knows about everything that touches sport.* **16.** to be important to; make a difference to: *Praise doesn't touch her.* **17.** *Colloq.* to ask for money, or succeed in getting money from; beg. ◇*v.i.* **18.** to place the hand, finger, etc., on or in contact with something. **19.** to come into or be in contact: *The two wires are touching.* **20.** (of a ship or passengers) to make a stop or a short call at a place (usu. fol. by *at*). ◇*v.* **21. touch down**, (of an aircraft) to land after a flight. **22. touch on, a.** to talk shortly about: *I can't do more than touch on the subject today.* **b.** to refer to: *At dinner she cruelly touched on his failure.* **23. touch up, a.** to put finishing details to, etc. (see def. 31). **b.** to repair, renew, add points of detail to, as of photographs. ◇*n.* **24.** the act of touching or state or fact of being touched. **25.** the sense or power by which anything material is discovered or perceived by means of the contact with it of some part of the body. **26.** the feeling or effect caused by touching something, seen as a quality of the thing: *a fabric with a smooth touch.* **27.** close communication, agreement, etc.: *to be in touch with public opinion.* **28.** a slight stroke or blow: *My car escaped with a mere touch.* **29.** a slight attack: *a touch of rheumatism.* **30.** a slight added action, effort or thing brought to complete a piece of work: *a finishing touch.* **31.** a detail in any artistic work: *His use of the bird motif is a clever touch.* **32.** a very small amount or degree: *a touch of salt; a touch of sarcasm in his voice.* **33.** a quality which sets something off from another: *the touch of the master.* **34.** *Colloq.* the act of asking for or getting money, or the money itself. [ME, from OF; orig. uncert.]

touchdown /ˈtʌtʃdaʊn/, *n.* **1.** *Rugby.* the act of a player touching the ball down to the ground behind the opponent's goal line, so as to score a try. **2.** the landing of an aeroplane.

touché /tuˈʃeɪ, ˈtuʃeɪ/, *interj.* **1.** *Fencing.* (an expression indicating a touch by the point of a weapon.) **2.** good point! (said in acknowledging a telling remark or reply). [F pp.: touch]

touching /ˈtʌtʃɪŋ/, *adj.* **1.** affecting; moving; pathetic. ◇*prep.* **2.** about; concerning; in reference or relation to.

touchline /ˈtʌtʃlaɪn/, *n.* (in Rugby football, etc.) any of the sidelines bordering the field of play.

touchstone /ˈtʌtʃstoʊn/, *n.* **1.** a black siliceous stone used to test the purity of gold and

touchstone

silver by the color of the streak produced on it by rubbing it with either metal. **2.** a test; criterion.

touch-type /ˈtʌtʃ-taɪp/, *v.i.*, **-typed**, **-typing**. to type without looking at the keys of the typewriter.

touchy /ˈtʌtʃi/, *adj.*, **touchier**, **touchiest**. **1.** easily offended; irritable. **2.** likely to give offence: *His failure is a touchy subject*. **—touchily**, *adv.* **—touchiness**, *n.*

tough /tʌf/, *adj.* **1.** not easily broken or cut: *tough wood; tough rope*. **2.** difficult to chew: *tough meat*. **3.** able to put up with bad conditions; sturdy; hardy. **4.** not easily influenced: *tough-minded*. **5.** hardened; incorrigible. **6.** difficult to deal with; hard, trying, or troublesome: *a tough exam; She is having a tough time*. **7.** severe; violent; vigorous: *a tough struggle*. **8.** rough, disorderly, or aggressive: *tough behavior*. **—adv. 9.** *Colloq.* aggressively; threateningly: *to act tough*. ◇*n.* **10.** an aggressive person; ruffian; thug. [ME; OE *tōh*] **—toughness**, *n.*

Toulouse-Lautrec /tuluz-louˈtrek/, *n.* **Henri Marie Raymond de** /ɒ̃ˌri maˌri reɪˈmɔ̃ də/, 1864–1901, French painter and lithographer; noted for his portrayal of Parisian nightlife.

toupee /ˈtupeɪ/, *n.* a wig or patch of false hair worn to cover a bald spot. Also, **toupée**. [F, from OF: tuft of hair]

tour /tʊə, ˈtuə, tɔ/, *v.t., v.i.* **1.** to travel through (a place) or from place to place, sometimes giving musical or theatrical performances: *to tour Rome; The band is touring this summer*. ◇*n.* **2.** (an organised) journey to or through a place or from place to place: *a tour of Sydney; a tour through the Snowy Mountains*. **3.** *Chiefly Mil.* a period of duty at one place. [ME, from F, from L: tool for making a circle] **—tourer**, *n.*

tourism /ˈtʊərɪzəm, ˈtuə-, ˈtɔ-/, *n.* **1.** the practice of touring, esp. for pleasure. **2.** the work and industry of providing local services, such as entertainment, lodging, food, etc., for tourists.

tourist /ˈtʊərəst, ˈtuə-, ˈtɔ-/, *n.* **1.** someone who travels or goes on tours, esp. for pleasure. **2.** a member of a touring international sporting team. **—touristy**, *adj.*

tournament /ˈtɔnəmənt/, *n.* **1.** a meeting for contests in sports, chess, or bridge. **2.** *Hist.* a contest or warlike sport in which two opposing parties of mounted and armored knights fought for a prize, with blunted weapons and in accordance with certain rules. [ME, from OF]

tourniquet /ˈtɔnəkeɪ, ˈtʊə-/, *n.* a tight bandage, etc., twisted or wrapped around a limb, etc., to stop bleeding. [F, from *tourner* turn]

tousle /ˈtaʊzəl/, *v.t.*, **-sled**, **-sling**. to make untidy or dishevelled: *His hair was tousled*. [ME]

tout /taʊt/, *v.i.* **1.** to try urgently or persistently to get business, employment, votes, etc.

town

2. to spy on a racehorse, etc., to get (and sell) information for betting purposes. ◇*v.t.* **3.** to describe or declare, esp. favorably: *to tout a politician as a friend of the people.* **4.** to watch; spy on. ◇*n.* **5.** someone who touts (see defs. 1 and 2). [ME]

tow[1] /toʊ/, *v.t.* **1.** to drag or pull (a boat, car, etc.) by a rope or chain. ◇*n.* **2.** the act of towing. **3.** the thing being towed. **4.** a rope, chain, etc., for towing. **5. in tow**, **a.** in the condition of being towed. **b.** in one's charge. **c.** following someone around; in attendance. **6. on** or **under tow**, in the condition of being towed. [OE *togian* by force, drag]

tow[2] /toʊ/, *n.* **1.** the coarse and broken parts of flax or hemp separated from the finer parts in combing. ◇*adj.* **2.** pale yellow: *tow-colored hair*. [ME; OE *tōw*]

toward /təˈwɔd, tɔd/, *prep.*; /ˈtoʊəd/, *adj.* ◇*prep.* **1.** towards. **2.** *Archaic*. going on; in progress: *when there is work toward*. [OE *tō*-to + -*weard* -WARD]

towards /təˈwɔdz, tɔdz/, *prep.* **1.** in the direction of (with reference to movement or position): *to walk towards the north*. **2.** with respect to; as regards: *My attitude towards you is unchanged*. **3.** nearly as late as; shortly before: *towards 2 o'clock*. **4.** as a help or contribution to: *to give money towards a gift*. Also, **toward**. [See TOWARD]

towel /ˈtaʊəl, taʊl/, *n., v.*, **-elled, -elling**. ◇*n.* **1.** an absorbent cloth for wiping and drying something wet, esp. one for the hands, face, or body after washing. **2. throw in the towel**, to give up; admit defeat. ◇*v.t.* **3.** to wipe or dry with a towel. **4.** *Colloq.* to give (someone) a beating. [ME, from OF: cloth for washing or wiping, from Gmc]

towelling /ˈtaʊəlɪŋ/, *n.* **1.** a type of absorbent cloth used for making towels, and clothes for the beach, etc. **2.** a rubbing with a towel. **3.** *Colloq.* a thrashing.

tower /ˈtaʊə/, *n.* **1.** a tall narrow structure, usu. part of a building. **2.** such a structure used as a fortress or prison. **3. tower of strength**, a person who is a source of mental and physical support. ◇*v.i.* **4.** to rise or stretch far upwards: *The mountain towers into the sky*. **5.** to be bigger or better than (fol. by *over, above*, etc.): *The man towered over the child; The athelete towered over his companions*. [OE *tūr*, from OF] **—towered,** *adj.* **—tower-like,** *adj.*

towering /ˈtaʊərɪŋ/, *adj.* **1.** very tall; lofty: *a towering oak*. **2.** very great: *a towering success; a towering rage*.

Tower of London, *n.* a historic fortress in London; orig. a royal palace, later a prison, now a group of buildings containing an arsenal and museum.

town /taʊn/, *n.* **1.** a large area of houses, shops, offices, etc., where many people live and work, larger than a village and smaller than a city, and with some degree of self-government. **2.** city life, opposed to country: *I prefer the town to the country*. **3.** the main shopping, business, or entertainment area of a large town or city, contrasted with the suburbs: *I'm going into town*

town

this afternoon. **4.** the people of a town: *The town has voted against daylight saving.* ◊**5.** Some special uses are:
go to town, 1. to do something thoroughly. **2.** to do something enthusiastically; splash out. **3.** to go too far; overindulge or lose one's self-restraint. **4.** to celebrate. **5.** to tell off or scold (usu. fol. by *on*).
man about town, a pleasure-seeking and sociable man.
on the town, looking for entertainment in a town.
talk of the town, the subject of general gossip or rumor.
[ME; OE *tūn*] —**townish,** *adj.*

town clerk, *n.* the appointed official of a council who is in charge of all responsibilities of local government.

town crier, *n.* (formerly) a person who cried news or public announcements in the streets.

town hall, *n.* a large public building belonging to a town, where people can gather, or public business can be carried out.

town house, *n.* **1.** an extra house in a city, owned by someone who lives in the country. **2.** a house built as part of a small block of similar houses, sold under strata title and with its own entrance at ground floor.

town planning, *n.* the planned control of the physical conditions of a town for the good of its people. —**town-planner,** *n.*

township /'taʊnʃɪp/, *n.* **1.** a small town or settlement. **2.** *Chiefly Brit Hist.* one of the local divisions of a large parish, usu. with a church of its own. [OE *tūnscipe*]

Townsville /'taʊnzvɪl, -vəl/, *n.* a city and port on the north-eastern coast of Qld; important transport, commercial, industrial and service centre. Pop. 96 230 (1986). [named after Robert Towns, 1794–1873, merchant and politician, who established Townsville as a port]

tox-, a variant of **toxo-,** before vowels, as in *toxaemia.*

toxaemia or **toxemia** /tɒkˈsimiə/, *n.* the presence in the bloodstream of bacterial poisons which are circulated to all parts of the body. [NL] —**toxaemic,** *adj.*

toxic /'tɒksɪk/, *adj.* **1.** of, relating to, affected with, or caused by a toxin. **2.** poisonous. [ML, poison, from Gk] —**toxically,** *adv.* —**toxicity,** *n.*

toxico-, a combining form of **toxic.** See **toxo-.** [combining form representing Gk *toxikón* poison]

toxic shock syndrome, *n.* a disease caused by toxins produced by certain bacteria in the vagina of women of menstruating age, thought to be associated with the use of tampons.

toxin /'tɒksən/, *n.* **1.** any poison given off by pathogenic micro-organisms, causing diseases such as tetanus, diphtheria, etc. **2.** any of various organic poisons produced in living or dead organisms. Also, **toxine** /'tɒksin, -sən/. [TOX(IC) + -IN(E)^2]

toxo-, a combining form representing **toxin,** or short for **toxico-.**

tracheo-

toy /tɔɪ/, *n.* **1.** an object, often a small imitation of some familiar thing, for children or others to play with; plaything. **2.** something of little value or importance; trifle. **3.** anything very small, esp. a dog of a small breed. ◊*adj.* **4.** of or like a toy, esp. in size. **5.** made as a toy: *a toy train.* ◊*v.* **6. toy with, a.** to handle idly or carelessly: *He sat there toying with his bread.* **b.** to think or act without plan or seriousness; trifle: *to toy with an idea.* [ME; orig. uncert.]

Toynbee /'tɔɪnbi/, *n.* **Arnold Joseph,** 1889–1975, English historian.

TPI /ti pi 'aɪ/, *adj.* (relating to) returned service personnel judged to be totally and permanently incapacitated by their injuries. [T(*otally and*) P(*ermanently*) I(*ncapacitated*)]

tr., *Abbrev.* **1.** *Gram.* transitive. **2.** translated. **3.** *Music.* trill.

Tr, *Chem. Symbol.* terbium.

trace[1] /treɪs/, *n., v.,* **traced, tracing.** ◊*n.* **1.** a mark which shows that something has been present; vestige: *a trace of blood on a dress; They didn't find a trace of the thieves.* **2.** a very small amount: *a trace of iron in the earth.* **3.** (esp. in *pl.*) a footprint or track. ◊*v.t.* **4.** to follow the footprints, track, or traces of. **5.** to follow or make out the course or line of: *to trace a river to its source; to trace the history of the wool trade.* **6.** to find by investigation; discover: *The police traced the missing man.* **7.** to copy (a drawing, plan, etc.) by following the lines of the original on a transparent sheet placed over it. **8.** to draw (a line, outline, figure, etc.). [ME, from OF: delineate, trace, pursue, from L] **traceable,** *adj.*

trace[2] /treɪs/, *n.* **1.** each of the two straps, ropes, or chains by which a carriage, wagon, etc., is drawn by a horse, etc. **2. kick over the traces,** to free oneself from discipline, authority, etc. [ME, from OF: strap for harness, act of drawing, from L]

trace element, *n.* any of some chemical elements found in plants and animals in tiny amounts which are very important in physiological processes.

tracer /'treɪsə/, *n.* ammunition containing a chemical which by burning or smoking makes it visible, to show the path of the projectile and indicate the target to other firers.

tracery /'treɪsəri/, *n., pl.* **-ries. 1.** ornamental work consisting of branching ribs, bars, etc., as in the upper part of a Gothic window, or in panels, screens, etc. **2.** any delicate interlacing pattern: *a tracery of leaves.* —**traceried,** *adj.*

trache-, a variant of **tracheo-** before vowels.

trachea /trəˈkiə/, *n., pl.* **tracheae** /trəˈkiaɪ/. **1.** (in air-breathing vertebrates) the tube stretching from the larynx to the bronchi, serving as the main passage for sending air to and from the lungs; windpipe. **2.** *Bot.* a duct formed by a row of cells which have perforated end walls, as in xylem vessels. [ML, from Gk] —**tracheal,** *adj.*

tracheo-, a combining form representing **trachea.** Also, **trache-.**

trachoma /trəˈkoumə/, n. a painful and contagious inflammation of the inner surface of the eyelids, marked by the formation of granulations, eventually causing blindness. [NL, from Gk: roughness] –**trachomatous**, adj.

track /træk/, n. **1.** a rough path; trail. **2.** a structure of rails, sleepers, etc., on which a train runs; railway line. **3.** a mark, or series of marks, left by anything that has passed along. **4.** (esp. pl.) a footprint or other mark left by an animal, person, car, etc. **5.** a line of travel or movement: *the track of a bird*. **6.** an endless jointed metal band driven by the wheels of a tank, tractor, etc., to enable it to move over rough ground. **7.** a course of action: *to go on in the same track year after year*. **8.** a path or course laid out for racing. **9.** sports which are performed on a track; athletics. **10.** one of the separate sections of a gramophone record. **11.** one of the bands of material recorded lengthwise beside other such bands on magnetic tape. ◇**12.** Some special uses are: **in one's tracks**, just where one is standing: *He was stopped in his tracks*.
in the tracks of, following; pursuing.
keep track of, to keep sight or knowledge of.
lose track of, to fail to stay in touch with.
make tracks, *Colloq.* to leave; depart.
off the beaten track, little known, unusual, or hidden from view.
off the track, away from what is being talked or written about.
on the track of, on the scent of; pursuing.
the right or **wrong track**, *Colloq.* the right (or wrong) idea, plan, interpretation, etc.
◇*v.t.* **13.** to follow the tracks, traces, or footprints of. **14.** to hunt by following the tracks of. **15.** to follow the course of, as by radar. **16.** to catch or find, after hunting for (fol. by *down*). **17.** to follow (a track, course, etc.). ◇*v.i.* **18.** to follow up a track or trail. **19.** (as one gearwheel with another) to be in alignment. **20.** *Films, TV, etc.* (of the camera) to move bodily in any direction while in operation. See **pan²**, **zoom**. ◇*adj.* **21.** *Athletics.* relating to those sports performed on a running track (contrasted with *field*). [late ME, from F *trac*, ? from Gmc] –**tracker**, n.

tracking station /ˈtrækɪŋ steɪʃən/, n. a station used for following an object, esp. a satellite, moving through the atmosphere or space, usu. by means of radio or radar.

track record, n. **1.** an account of a racehorse's successes and defeats on the racecourse. **2.** an account of a person's successes or failures in a particular field: *The Government's track record is good in this area*.

track shoe, n. See **spike¹** (def. 3b).

tracksuit /ˈtræksut/, n. a loose, two-piece overgarment worn by athletes in training, between events, etc.

tract¹ /trækt/, n. **1.** a stretch of land, water, etc.; region. **2.** a space or stretch of time; period. **3.** *Anat.* a system of related parts or organs: *the digestive tract*. [late ME, from L: drawing, stretch, extent, tract]

tract² /trækt/, n. a short piece of writing, usu. on religion; short treatise. Also, **tractate**. [ME *tracte*]

tractable /ˈtræktəbəl/, adj. **1.** (of people) easily managed; docile. **2.** (of metals) easily handled or dealt with; malleable. [L] –**tractability**, n. –**tractably**, adv.

traction /ˈtrækʃən/, n. **1.** the act of drawing or pulling or the state of being drawn. **2.** the pulling of a body, car, etc., along a surface. **3.** a force that prevents a wheel slipping: *These tyres have good traction*. **4.** the medical treatment of applying tension to a limb or bone by means of weights and pulleys. **5.** a form or type of power used for pulling: *steam traction*. [ML: act of drawing, from L: draw] –**tractional**, adj.

tractor /ˈtræktə/, n. a motor vehicle fitted with deeply treaded tyres, used to pull farm machinery, etc. [obs. *tract*, v. draw + -OR²]

trad /træd/, *Colloq.* ◇n. **1.** traditional jazz. ◇adj. **2.** traditional; old-fashioned; conventional.

trade /treɪd/, n., v., **traded**, **trading**. ◇n. **1.** the buying and selling, or exchanging, of goods: *domestic trade; foreign trade*. **2.** some line of skilled manual work: *the trade of a carpenter*. **3.** people who work in a particular line of business: *a magazine for the electrical trade only*. **4.** amount of dealings; traffic: *a brisk trade in bicycles*. **5.** market: *the tourist trade*. ◇v.t. **6.** to give in return; exchange; barter. **7.** to exchange: *to trade seats with a person*. ◇v.i. **8.** to buy and sell: *to trade in wheat*. **9.** to make an exchange. ◇v. **10. trade in**, to give in part exchange: *to trade in an old car when buying a new one*. **11. trade on**, to take advantage of, esp. unfairly; exploit. ◇adj. **12.** of or relating to commerce, a particular trade or occupation, or trade as a whole. [ME, from MLG: a track]

trade-in /ˈtreɪd-ɪn/, n. **1.** goods given in part payment: *I had my old car as a trade-in*. ◇adj. **2.** of or relating to such goods, or to such a method of payment.

trademark /ˈtreɪdmak/, n. **1.** a name, sign, or mark put on or associated with goods to show that they have been made by a particular manufacturer. It is registered by law, and no other manufacturer is allowed to use it. **2.** a particular sign or way of doing things by which someone is recognised. Also, **trade mark**.

trade name, n. **1.** the name under which a firm does business. **2.** a word or phrase used in trade indicating a business or a particular class of goods, but which is not a trademark.

trade price, n. the price at which goods are sold to members of the same trade, or to retail dealers by wholesalers.

trader /ˈtreɪdə/, n. **1.** a merchant or businessman. **2.** a ship used in trade, esp. in a small way, as among a chain of islands.

tradesman /ˈtreɪdzmən/, n., pl. **-men**. a man engaged in trade, as a shopkeeper. –**tradeswoman**, n.fem.

trade union, n. an organisation of employees for mutual aid and protection, and for dealing with employers. Also, **trades union**. –**trade unionism**, n. –**trade unionist**, n.

trade wind, *n.* one of the winds blowing steadily over the oceans from about 30°north latitude to about 30°south latitude, and blowing from north-east to south-west in the Northern Hemisphere, and from south-east to north-west in the Southern Hemisphere towards the equator.

trading bank, *n.* a bank which offers a wide range of services to both individual and corporate customers, e.g. cheque accounts, overdrafts, term loans, etc. See **savings bank**.

trading post, *n.* a type of shop for carrying on trade in a region with few people.

tradition /trə'dɪʃən/, *n.* 1. the handing down of statements, beliefs, legends, customs, etc., from generation to generation, esp. by word of mouth or by practice: *a story that has come down to us by popular tradition*. 2. the customs, teachings, etc., so handed down: *the traditions of the Aborigines*. [ME, from L: delivery, handing down] —**traditional**, *adj.*

traduce /trə'djus/, *v.t.*, **-duced**, **-ducing**. to speak evil or maliciously and falsely of; slander; malign: *to traduce someone's character*. [L: transport, disgrace]

traffic /'træfɪk/, *n., v.,* **-ficked**, **-ficking**. ◇*n.* 1. the coming and going of people, cars, ships, etc., along a way, road or water route: *heavy traffic in a street*. 2. the people, cars, etc., going along such a way. 3. the business done by a railway or other carrier in the transportation of goods or of passengers. 4. trade or dealing in certain things or goods, often against the law: *traffic in drugs*. 5. dealings or exchanges of anything between parties, people, etc. ◇*v.i.* 6. to carry on traffic, trade, or commercial dealings, esp. of an illegal kind. [F, from It, ult. orig. uncert.] —**trafficker**, *n.* —**trafficable**, *adj.*

trafficator /'træfəkeɪtə/, *n.* (in a car, etc.) a flashing light or lighted arm which indicates a driver's intention to turn left or right.

traffic light, *n.* (usu. *pl.*) one of a set of colored lights used to direct or control road traffic at intersections, pedestrian crossings, etc.

tragedian /trə'dʒidiən/, *n.* 1. a writer of tragedy. 2. (*fem.* **tragedienne**) an actor of tragedy.

tragedy /'trædʒədi/, *n., pl.* **-dies**. 1. a sad or serious play, with an unhappy ending: *Shakespeare's tragedy of 'Hamlet'*. 2. that branch of drama concerned with this kind of play. 3. any literary work, such as a novel, dealing with a sad and serious theme. 4. the tragic element of drama, of literature generally, or of life. 5. any very sad, dreadful, or fatal event or affair; disaster or calamity. [ME, from L, from Gk: goat song (reason for name variously explained)]

tragic /'trædʒɪk/, *adj.* 1. typical of or suggesting tragedy: *tragic solemnity*. 2. very mournful or pathetic: *a tragic expression*. 3. dreadful or fatal: *a tragic death*. 4. relating to tragedy: *the tragic drama*. Also, **tragical**. [L, from Gk: of tragedy]

tragicomedy /trædʒɪ'kɒmədi/, *n., pl.* **-dies**. 1. a play or other literary work combining elements of both tragedy and comedy. 2. an event or situation of mixed tragic and comic character. [LL] —**tragicomic, tragicomical**, *adj.*

trail /treɪl/, *v.t.* 1. to drag or let drag along the ground or behind. 2. to bring or have floating behind: *to trail clouds of dust*. 3. to follow the track or trail of; track. 4. *Colloq.* to follow along behind (others), as in a race. ◇*v.i.* 5. to be drawn or dragged along the ground: *Her long gown trailed over the floor*. 6. to hang down loosely from something. 7. (of dust, smoke, etc.) to stream or float from and after something moving. 8. to follow: *The little girl trailed after her sister.* 9. to go slowly, lazily, or wearily along; straggle. 10. to become weaker, slower, etc.; diminish (fol. by *off*): *Her voice trailed off*. 11. to fall behind the leaders, in a race or activity. 12. to grow along the ground, as a plant. ◇*n.* 13. a path or track made across wild or rough country: *to follow the trail*. 14. the footprints, smell, etc., left by a hunted animal, etc. 15. a stream of dust, smoke, light, people, etc., behind something moving. [ME, from AF: trail, OF: tow (a boat), from L: dragnet]

trail bike, *n.* a motorbike designed for cross-country conditions, built with a high engine and exhaust system, often of light construction.

trailblazer /'treɪlbleɪzə/, *n.* someone who is the first to do something.

trailer /'treɪlə/, *n.* 1. a vehicle, made to be towed by a car or truck, used to carry loads. 2. *Films.* an advertisement for a coming film, usu. made up of scenes from it.

train /treɪn/, *n.* 1. a set of railway carriages joined together and driven by electric or diesel power, or pulled by a locomotive. 2. → **locomotive** (def. 1). 3. a line of people, cars, etc., travelling together. 4. *Mil.* a crowd of vehicles, animals, and people accompanying an army, to carry supplies. 5. *Mech.* a series of connected parts, as wheels and pinions, through which movement is carried. 6. something that is drawn along; a trailing part. 7. a group of followers or attendants; retinue: *The king and his train entered*. 8. a series of proceedings, events, circumstances, etc. 9. a series of connected ideas; course of reasoning: *a train of thought*. 10. aftermath: *War brings misery in its train*. ◇*v.t.* 11. to teach (a person or animal) to know or do something; educate; drill. 12. to make (a person, etc.) fit by proper exercise, diet, etc., for some sport or contest. 13. to bring (a plant, branch, etc.) into a particular shape or position, by bending, pruning, etc. 14. to bring (a gun, camera, glance, etc.) to bear on some object or point. ◇*v.i.* 15. to give or undergo teaching, drill, practice, etc. 16. to get oneself into condition by exercise, etc. [ME from OF, from L: draw] —**trainable**, *adj.*

trainee /treɪ'ni/, *n., adj.* (someone) receiving training: *a trainee designer*.

trainer /'treɪnə/, *n.* 1. someone who prepares racehorses for racing. 2. someone who trains athletes in a sport.

traipse /treɪps/, *v.i.*, **traipsed, traipsing**. *Colloq.* to walk tiredly; trudge. [orig. uncert]

trait /treɪ, treɪt/, *n.* that feature or quality that sets something apart from others; characteristic: *bad trait of character*. [late ME, from F: draught, from L]

traitor /'treɪtə/, *n.* someone who betrays a person, a cause, or a country. [ME, from OF, from L: betrayer] —**traitorous,** *adj.*

Trajan /'treɪdʒən/, *n.* (*Marcus Ulpius Nerva Trajanus*), AD 53?–117, Roman emperor 98–117.

trajectory /trə'dʒɛktəri/, *n., pl.* **-ries.** the curved flight path of a bullet or other body. [ML: casting over]

tram /træm/, *n.* a passenger vehicle running on rails laid in the street, usu. powered by electricity from an overhead wire. [MLG or MD: beam, rung, etc.]

trammel /'træməl/, *n., v.,* **-melled, -melling.** ◇*n.* **1.** (*usu. pl.*) anything that stops or gets in the way of free action; restraint: *the trammels of custom.* **2.** a three-layered fishing net. **3.** a net for catching birds. ◇*v.t.* **4.** to involve or hold in trammels; hamper; restrain. **5.** to catch or entangle in or as if in a net. [ME, from OF: net with 3 layers of meshes, from L]

tramp /træmp/, *v.i.* **1.** to tread or walk steadily with a firm, heavy step; march; trudge. **2.** to tread heavily or trample (fol. by *on* or *upon*): *to tramp on someone's toes.* ◇*v.t.* **3.** to walk heavily or steadily through or over: *to tramp Sydney looking for a hotel.* **4.** to tread or trample underfoot: *to tramp it in.* ◇*n.* **5.** the act of tramping: *a tramp over the hills.* **6.** (the sound of) a firm, heavy tread. **7.** a person who travels about on foot from place to place, esp. a homeless person living on occasional jobs or gifts of money or food. **8.** *Colloq.* a socially unacceptable woman, often promiscuous. **9.** a cargo boat which does not run regularly between ports, but goes wherever shippers want. [ME]

trample /'træmpəl/, *v.,* **-pled, -pling,** *n.* ◇*v.t., v.i.* **1.** to tread heavily, roughly, or crushingly (on), esp. repeatedly. **2.** to treat with contempt. **3.** to crush or treat cruelly (fol. by *on, upon,* etc.): *to trample on an oppressed people.* ◇*n.* **4.** the act or sound of trampling. [ME, frequentative of TRAMP]

trampoline /'træmpəlin, træmpə'lin/, *n., v.,* **-lined, -lining.** ◇*n.* **1.** a canvas springboard attached to a horizontal frame, on which people jump for pleasure or sport. ◇*v.i.* **2.** to jump on a trampoline. [It: springboard]

trance /træns, trans/, *n.* **1.** a half-conscious or dazed state. **2.** the condition of being completely lost in thought. **3.** *Occult.* a temporary state of unconsciousness in which a medium is controlled by an intelligence from without and used as a means of communication with the dead. [ME, from OF: passage, esp. from life to death, deadly suspense or fear, from L]

tranquil /'træŋkwəl/, *adj.* peaceful; quiet; calm. [earlier *tranquill*, from L] —**tranquillity,** *n.*

tranquilliser or **tranquillizer** /'træŋkwəlaɪzə/, *n.* a drug that has a calming effect without inducing sleepiness.

Tranquillity /træŋ'kwɪləti/, *n.* **Sea of,** a plain, *Mare Tranquillitatis,* in the first quadrant of the face of the moon, site of man's first landing on the moon, 20 July 1969.

trans-, a prefix meaning 'across', 'beyond', freely applied in geographical terms (*transcontinental, trans-Australian*), also found attached to stems not used as words, and in figurative meanings, as *transpire, transport, transcend.* [L, combining form of *trans*, prep.]

trans., *Abbrev.* **1.** transaction. **2.** transcript. **3.** transitive. **4.** translated. **5.** translation. **6.** transport.

transact /trænz'ækt/, *v.t., v.i.* to carry through (affairs, business, negotiations, etc.) to a conclusion or settlement. [L: carried out, driven through, accomplished] —**transactor,** *n.* —**transaction,** *n.*

Trans-Australia Airlines, *n.* former name of **Australian Airlines.** *Abbrev.:* TAA

Trans Australian, *n.* **the,** a train running between Adelaide and Perth.

transceiver /træn'sivə/, *n.* a radio set able both to transmit and receive.

transcend /træn'sɛnd/, *v.t., v.i.* to go or be above or beyond (a limit, something with limits, etc.); surpass or exceed. [ME, from L: climb over or beyond]

transcendent /træn'sɛndənt/, *adj.* **1.** going beyond ordinary limits; surpassing or extraordinary. **2.** *Theol.* being beyond matter, and having a continuing existence therefore outside the created world. ◇*n.* **3.** *Philos.* that which is beyond experience. —**transcendence,** *n.*

transcendental /trænsen'dentl/, *adj.* **1.** transcendent, surpassing, or superior. **2.** going beyond ordinary experience, thought, or belief; supernatural; metaphysical. **3.** abstract. **4.** *Philos.* belonging to every kind of thing, transcending all other distinctions. **5.** *Maths.* (of a number) not algebraic; not able to be produced by the algebraic operations of addition, subtraction, multiplication, division, and the extraction of roots. For example, *pi* and *e* are transcendental numbers.

transcendentalism /trænsen'dentəlɪzəm/, *n.* **1.** transcendental character, thought, or language. **2.** a philosophy based upon the doctrine that the principles of reality are to be discovered by the study of the processes of thought, rather than of material objects. —**transcendentalist,** *n., adj.*

transcendental meditation, *n.* a type of meditation which aims to relax and quieten the mind, and to increase awareness. Also, **TM**

transcribe /træn'skraɪb/, *v.t.,* **-scribed, -scribing. 1.** to make a copy of in writing: *to transcribe a letter.* **2.** to reproduce in writing or print from speech. **3.** to write out in other characters: *to transcribe shorthand notes.* **4.** *Music.* to arrange (a piece) for a different instrument or voice: *to transcribe a violin piece for piano.* [L: copy across] —**transcription,** *n.* —**transcript,** *n.*

transducer /trænz'djusə/, *n.* any device which receives energy from one system, and

transducer   1093   **transitory**

supplies related energy to another system. [from L: transport]

transept /'trænsept/, n. the two arms of a cross-shaped church, at right angles to the nave. [Anglo-L, from L]

transfer /træns'fɜ/, v., **-ferred, -ferring**; /'trænsfɜ/, n., ◇v.t. **1.** to carry or send from one place, person, etc., to another. **2.** *Law.* to make over; convey: *to transfer a title to land.* **3.** to take (a drawing, design, pattern, etc.) over from one surface to another. ◇v.i. **4.** to change over or be carried. ◇n. **5.** the act or means of transferring. **6.** the fact of being transferred. **7.** a drawing, pattern, etc., which may be put on to another surface, esp. by direct contact. **8.** *Law.* a making over, by sale or gift, of real or personal property to another. **9.** *Econ.* the act of having the ownership of a stock or registered bond transferred upon the books of the issuing company or its agent. **10.** *Econ.* a form filled in when stocks and shares change hands; share transfer. [ME, from L: carry across] **—transferability,** n. **—transferral,** n. **—transference,** n.

transfiguration /ˌtrænsfɪgəˈreɪʃən/, n. **1.** the act of transfiguring or condition of being transfigured. **2.** (*cap.*) the change in the appearance of Christ when glorified in the presence of three chosen disciples. **3.** (*cap.*) the church festival commemorating this, observed on 6 August.

transfigure /træns'fɪgə/, v.t., **-ured, -uring**. **1.** to change in outward form or appearance; transform, change, or alter. **2.** to change so as to glorify, exalt, or idealise. [ME, from L]

transfix /træns'fɪks/, v.t. **1.** to pierce through with or as if with a pointed weapon. **2.** to fix fast with or on something sharp. **3.** to cause to be unable to move, with amazement, terror, etc. [L: pierced, transfixed]

transform /træns'fɔm/, v.t. **1.** to change in form. **2.** to change in appearance, condition, nature, or character, esp. completely or deeply: *to transform a desert into productive land.* **3.** *Chem.* to change (one substance, element, etc.) into another. **4.** *Maths.* to change the form of (a figure, expression, etc.) without changing the value. **5.** *Phys.* to change (one form of energy) into another. ◇v.i. **6.** to change in form, appearance, or character; become transformed. [ME, from L: change form] **—transformable,** *adj.* **—transformation,** n. **—transformational,** *adj.*

transformational grammar /trænsfə-ˌmeɪʃənəl 'græmə/, n. a way of understanding language which assumes that it has two levels. The **deep structure** contains only simple statements in the active voice, which are transformed, according to rules, into a **surface structure** (the form in which something is spoken or written).

transformer /træns'fɔmə/, n. *Elect.* an electric device which by electromagnetic induction transforms electric energy from circuit(s) to circuit(s) at the same frequency, usu. with the aim of changing the voltage and current.

transfuse /træns'fjuz/, v.t., **-fused, -fusing**. **1.** to pour in or spread through. **2.** *Med.* **a.** to take (blood) from the blood vessels of one person or animal and inject it into those of another. **b.** to inject (a saline solution, etc.) into a blood vessel. [ME, from L: poured across] **—transfusion,** n.

transgress /trænz'grɛs/, v.t. **1.** to pass over or go beyond (a limit, etc.): *to transgress the bounds of prudence.* **2.** to go beyond the limits laid down by (a law, command, etc.); break; violate; infringe. ◇v.i. **3.** to break a law, command, etc.; offend or sin (fol. by *against*). [L: having stepped across] **—transgression,** n. **—transgressor,** n.

transient /'trænzɪənt/, *adj.* **1.** passing with time; not lasting; ephemeral; transitory: *a transient feeling of loneliness.* **2.** lasting or remaining only for a time; temporary: *a transient guest at a hotel.* ◇n. **3.** someone or something that is transient. **—transiency,** n.

transistor /træn'zɪstə/, n. **1.** *Elect.* a very small solid-state apparatus for amplifying or switching, using silicon or germanium semiconducting materials. **2.** a radio equipped with transistors. ◇*adj.* **3.** equipped with transistors. [TRANS(FER) + (RES)ISTOR]

transit /'trænzət/, n., v., **-sited, -siting**. ◇n. **1.** the act or fact of passing across or through: *the transit of passengers from Sydney to Perth.* **2.** the state of being carried from one place to another: *The parcel was lost in transit.* **3.** a transition or change. **4.** *Astron.* the passage of a heavenly body across the meridian of a place or through the field of a telescope. **5. in transit,** passing through a place; staying for only a short time. ◇v.t., v.i. **6.** to pass across or through (a place or thing). [ME, from L: act of crossing]

transition /træn'zɪʃən/, n. **1.** a passing from one position, state, stage, etc., to another. **2.** *Music.* **a.** a passing from one key to another; modulation. **b.** a passage serving as a connecting link between two more important passages. **3.** *Phys.* a change in the make up of an atomic nucleus, either by changing to another nuclide by the emission of alpha or beta particles, or by changing its energy state by the emission of gamma rays. [L: act of going across] **—transitionary,** *adj.*

transition element, n. any of the elements which occur in three series in the middle of the periodic table, have incomplete inner electron shells, show variable valencies, and form complexes.

transitive /'trænzətɪv/, *Gram.* ◇*adj.* **1.** (of a verb) regularly having a direct object. ◇n. **2.** a transitive verb. [LL]

transitive verb, n. a verb that has a direct object, as *ate* in *She ate her lunch.*

transit lane, n. a traffic lane which is restricted during peak hours to cars, etc., carrying more than a certain number of people.

transitory /'trænzətri/, *adj.* **1.** passing away; not lasting or eternal. **2.** lasting for a short time; brief; transient.

Transkei

Transkei /træns'kaɪ/, *n.* a Bantu state in the Republic of South Africa; self-governing since 1963, nominally independent since 1976. Pop. 2 186 000 (1976); 41 002 km².

translate /trænz'leɪt/, *v.*, **-lated, -lating.** ◇*v.t.* **1.** to turn (something written or spoken) from one language into another: *to translate Arunta into English.* **2.** to change into another form; transform; convert. **3.** to carry or remove from one place, position, condition, etc., to another; transfer. **4.** to express in other terms; interpret; explain. **5.** *Phys.* to cause (a body) to move without sideways rotation or angular displacement. ◇*v.i.* **6.** to turn or be turned from one language into another. [ME, from L: carried over] **—translatable,** *adj.* **—translator,** *n.* **—translation,** *n.*

translucent /trænz'lusənt/, *adj.* allowing light to come through imperfectly, as in frosted glass. [L: shining through] **—translucence, translucency,** *n.*

transmigrate /trænzmaɪ'greɪt/, *v.i.*, **-grated, -grating. 1.** to pass from one place to another. **2.** to go from one country to another in order to settle there. [ME, from L] **—transmigrator,** *n.* **—transmigration,** *n.* **—transmigratory,** *adj.*

transmission /trænz'mɪʃən/, *n.* **1.** the act of transmitting. **2.** something which is transmitted. **3.** *Mach.* a device for transmitting the force of movement, esp. the mechanism for transmitting power from the revolutions of the engine in a motor vehicle to the driving wheels by gears. **4.** *Radio, TV.* the broadcasting of a radio or television program. [L] **—transmissive,** *adj.*

transmit /trænz'mɪt/, *v.t.*, **-mitted, -mitting. 1.** to send over or along, such as to a person or place. **2.** to pass on or communicate (information, news, etc.). **3.** to pass on or hand down to heirs, successors, etc. **4.** to pass on (a disease, etc.). **5.** to broadcast (a radio or television program). **6.** *Phys.* to cause or permit (light, heat, sound, etc.) to pass through a medium. [ME, from L: send across] **—transmittable, transmittible,** *adj.* **—transmittal, transmittance,** *n.* **—transmissible,** *adj.*

transmitter /trænz'mɪtə/, *n.* **1.** Also, **transmitting set.** *Radio.* that part of the broadcasting apparatus which generates and modulates the radio waves and sends them to the aerial. **2.** that part of a telephonic or telegraphic apparatus that changes soundwaves or mechanical movements into electrical waves or impulses.

transmute /trænz'mjut/, *v.t.*, **-muted, -muting.** to change from one nature, substance, or form into another; transform. [ME, from L] **—transmutation,** *n.*

transom /'trænsəm/, *n.* **1.** a crosspiece separating a door, window, etc., from a window above it. **2.** a window above a door; fanlight. [ME, from L] **—transomed,** *adj.*

transparency /træns'pɛərənsi, -'pær-/, *n.*, *pl.* **-cies. 1.** Also, **transparence.** the state or quality of being transparent. **2.** something which is transparent, esp. a positive photograph image on a transparent material, projected or viewed by light shining through from behind.

transparent /træns'pɛərənt, -'pær-/, *adj.* **1.** having the property of sending rays of light through its substance so that objects situated beyond or behind can be clearly seen (opposed to *opaque*). **2.** (of material) allowing light to pass through. **3.** open, or candid: *transparent honesty.* **4.** obvious. **5.** easily seen through or understood: *transparent excuses.* [ME, from ML, from L]

transpire /træns'paɪə/, *v.*, **-spired, -spiring.** ◇*v.i.* **1.** to happen, or take place. **2.** (of the body, a leaf, etc.) to give off waste matter, etc., through the surface. **3.** (of moisture, smell, etc.) to escape through the surface of the body, etc. **4.** to escape from secrecy; become known. ◇*v.t.* **5.** (of the body, a leaf, etc.) to give off (waste matter, moisture, a smell, etc.) through the surface. [ML, from L] **—transpiration,** *n.* **—transpiratory,** *adj.*

transplant /træns'plænt, -'plant/, *v.*; /'trænsplænt, -plant/, *n.* ◇*v.t.* **1.** to remove (a plant) from one place and plant it in another. **2.** *Surg.* to transfer (an organ or a portion of tissue) from one part of the body to another or from one person or animal to another. **3.** to remove (something) from one place to another. **4.** to bring (people, culture, etc.) from one country to another for settlement. ◇*n.* **5.** the act of transplanting. **6.** something transplanted, such as an organ of the body or a seedling. [late ME, from LL] **—transplantation,** *n.*

transport /træns'pɔt/, 'trænspɔt/, *v.*; /'trænspɔt/, *n.* ◇*v.t.* **1.** to carry from one place to another; convey. **2.** to carry away by strong emotion. **3.** (formerly) to carry or send (a criminal, etc.) to a penal colony. ◇*n.* **4.** an act or method of transporting; conveyance. **5.** a system of transporting passengers or goods: *public transport.* **6.** a ship, truck or aeroplane used for transporting, such as a ship that carries soldiers or military stores. **7.** a large truck. **8.** strong emotion, such as joy, delight, etc. [ME, from L: carry across] **—transporter,** *n.*

transportation /ˌtrænspɔ'teɪʃən/, *n.* **1.** the act of transporting. **2.** the state of being transported. **3.** a means of transport. **4.** (formerly) the sending or carrying of a criminal, etc., to a penal colony.

transpose /træns'pouz/, *v.t.*, **-posed, -posing. 1.** to change the relative position or order of (a thing in a series, or a series of things): *to transpose the words of a sentence.* **2.** to cause (two or more things) to change places; interchange. **3.** *Music.* to reproduce in a different key from the original by raising or lowering in pitch. [ME, from F] **—transposition, transposal,** *n.* **—transpositional,** *adj.*

transsexual /trænz'sɛkʃuəl/, *n.* someone who feels himself or herself, though physically of one sex, to be of the other sex psychologically.

Trans-Siberian Railway /tran-saɪˌbɪəriən 'reɪlweɪ/, *n.* a railway constructed 1891–1916 by the Russian government, crossing Siberia and Manchuria from Kuibyshev to Vladivostok; more than 6437 km.

transubstantiation /ˌtrænsəbˌstænʃiˈeɪʃən/, *n.* **1.** the changing of one substance into another. **2.** *Theol.* the doctrine of the Catholic Church, etc., that, in the Eucharist, the whole substance of the bread and wine are changed into the body and blood of Christ, but still look and taste like bread and wine.

transuranic element /trænzjuˌrænɪk ˈɛləmənt/, *n.* a synthetic, radioactive element with a higher atomic number than uranium.

transversal /trænzˈvɜsəl/, *n. Geom.* a line intersecting two or more lines. [late ME, from ML]

transverse /ˈtrænzvɜs, trænzˈvɜs/, *adj.* **1.** lying or being across or in a crosswise direction. ◇*n.* **2.** something which is transverse. **3.** *Geom.* an axis that passes through the foci of a hyperbola. [L: turned or directed across]

transverse wave, *n.* a wave in which vibrations of the medium (as in a vibrating wire etc., or in an electromagnetic wave) are perpendicular to the direction it is travelling in.

transvestite /trænzˈvɛstaɪt/, *n.* someone who wears the clothing of the opposite sex in order to gain sexual pleasure. —**transvestism,** *n.*

Tranter /ˈtræntə/, *n.* **John,** born 1943, Australian poet; works include *Crying in Early Infancy: 100 Sonnets* (1977).

trap¹ /træp/, *n., v.,* **trapped, trapping.** ◇*n.* **1.** a device for catching animals, such as a cage with a door that springs shut suddenly, a pit, etc. **2.** any means used to trick someone into being taken by surprise. **3.** any of various mechanical devices for preventing the passage of steam, water, air, gases, etc. **4.** (*pl.*) percussion instruments, esp. a drum kit. **5.** a carriage, esp. a light two-wheeled one. **6.** a trapdoor. **7.** *Colloq.* the mouth. ◇*v.t.* **8.** to catch in a trap: *to trap foxes.* **9.** to trick into being taken by surprise; lead by tricking: *She trapped him into telling the truth.* **10.** to supply with a trap or traps. **11.** to stop and hold (water, air, etc.) by a trap. [OE *træppe*] —**trapper,** *n.*

trap² /træp/, *n., v.,* **trapped, trapping.** ◇*n.* **1.** (*pl.*) *Colloq.* personal belongings; luggage. ◇*v.t.* **2.** to decorate with trappings. [ME; orig. uncert.]

trap³ /træp/, *n.* any of various fine-grained dark-colored igneous rocks with a column-like structure, esp. basalt. [Swed: stair (so named from their appearance)]

trapdoor /ˈtræpdɔ/, *n.* **1.** a door, etc., cut into the surface of a floor, ceiling, roof, etc. **2.** the opening which it covers.

trapdoor spider, *n.* a type of spider that digs silk-lined tunnels in the ground, sometimes fitted with a lid, such as the **brown trapdoor spider,** of eastern Australia.

trapeze /trəˈpiz/, *n.* **1.** a short bar joined to the ends of two hanging ropes on which gymnasts and acrobats swing and perform. **2.** (on a small sailing boat) a device similar to this by which one may lean almost completely out of the boat. [F, from L: small table, from Gk]

trapezium /trəˈpiziəm/, *n., pl.* **-ziums, -zia** /-ziə/, a four-sided plane figure in which only one pair of opposite sides is parallel. [NL. See TRAPEZE] —**trapezial,** *adj.*

trappings /ˈtræpɪŋz/, *n.pl.* **1.** articles of equipment or dress, esp. ornamental. **2.** the things, esp. ornamental, which necessarily go with a position, office, etc.: *the trappings of power.* **3.** the coverings, harness, etc., for a horse, esp. ornamental.

Trappist /ˈtræpəst/, *n.* **1.** a member of a monastic body, observing the extremely severe rule of austerity and silence established at the abbey of La Trappe, in Normandy, France, in 1664. ◇*adj.* **2.** of or pertaining to the Trappists. [F: *trappiste*]

Traralgon /trəˈrælgən/, *n.* a city in the Latrobe Valley, Vic, north-east of Morwell. Pop. 19 233 (1986). [Aboriginal: heron or crane feeding on frogs]

trash /træʃ/, *n.* **1.** anything worthless or useless; rubbish. **2.** foolish ideas, talk, or writing; nonsense. **3.** people regarded as worthless. [ME] —**trashy,** *adj.*

trauma /ˈtrɔmə/, *n., pl.* **-mata** /-mətə/, **-mas.** *Med.* **1.** a bodily injury or wound. **2.** an experience which shocks and has a lasting mental effect. [Gk: wound] —**traumatic,** *adj.*

traumatise *or* **traumatize** /ˈtrɔmətaɪz/, *v.t.,* **-tised, -tising. 1.** to injure (tissues of the body). **2.** to shock deeply and lastingly.

travail /ˈtræveɪl/, *n.* **1.** physical or mental hard work. **2.** the labor and pain of childbirth.

travel /ˈtrævəl/, *v.,* **-elled, -elling,** *n.* ◇*v.i.* **1.** to go from one place to another; make a journey. **2.** to move or advance in any way. **3.** to go from place to place as a representative of a business firm. **4.** *Colloq.* to move with speed. **5.** (of a mechanical part, etc.) to move in a fixed course. **6.** (of light, sound, etc.) to pass, or be transmitted. ◇*v.t.* **7.** to journey through or over (a country, area, road, etc.). **8.** to journey (a particular distance). ◇*n.* **9.** (*pl.*) journeys. **10.** *Mech.* a complete movement of a moving part in one direction, or the distance covered; a stroke. **11.** movement or passage in general. [ME; from TRAVAIL] —**traveller,** *n.*

traveller's cheque, *n.* a cheque of fixed amount issued by a bank, company, etc., to a traveller, to save carrying cash.

travelogue /ˈtrævəlɒg/, *n.* a film or illustrated talk describing a country, travels, etc.

traverse /trəˈvɜs, ˈtrævɜs/, *v.,* **-ersed, -ersing,** *n., adj.* ◇*v.t.* **1.** to pass across, over, or through. **2.** to go back and forwards over or along. **3.** to extend across. **4.** to examine or survey carefully. **5.** *Law.* to deny formally. ◇*n.* **6.** the act of traversing, or passing across. **7.** something that traverses or lies across, such as a crossbar or a barrier. **8.** a place where a person may traverse or cross; crossing. **9.** *Naut.* the zigzag course taken by a vessel during tacking. ◇*adj.* **10.** lying, extending, or passing across; transverse. [ME]

travesty /ˈtrævəsti/, *n., pl.* **-ties,** *v.,* **-tied, -tying.** ◇*n.* **1.** any inferior or distorted likeness or imitation: *a travesty of justice.* ◇*v.t.* **2.** to make or be a travesty of. [F: disguised, from It: disguise]

trawl /trɔl/, *n.* Also, **trawl net.** a strong net dragged along the sea bottom to catch fish. ◇*v.t., v.i.* **2.** to catch (fish) with such a net.

trawler /ˈtrɔlə/, *n.* **1.** a type of boat used in fishing with a trawl (def. 1). **2.** someone who trawls.

tray /treɪ/, *n.* **1.** a flat piece of wood, metal, etc., with slightly raised edges used for carrying or holding articles, etc. **2.** a removable object of this shape in a cabinet, box, etc., sometimes forming a drawer. [ME; OE *trēg*]

treacherous /ˈtretʃərəs/, *adj.* **1.** breaking faith or trust; disloyal. **2.** not be to trusted in; unreliable: *treacherous weather.* **3.** dangerously deceptive: *treacherous seas.*

treachery /ˈtretʃəri/, *n., pl.* **-eries.** the act of breaking faith or trust; treason; disloyalty. [ME, from OF: cheat; orig. uncert.]

treacle /ˈtrikəl/, *n.* **1.** the dark, thick syrup obtained in refining sugar. **2.** → **golden syrup. 3.** *Colloq.* sickening sweetness, as in music, behavior, etc. [ME, from OF: antidote, from L, from Gk] —**treacly,** *adj.*

tread /tred/, *v.,* **trod** or (*Archaic*) **trode; trodden** or **trod; treading;** *n.* ◇*v.t.* **1.** to step or walk on, about, in, or along. **2.** to crush underfoot; trample. **3.** to do or perform by walking or dancing: *to tread a measure.* **4.** (of male birds) to copulate with. ◇*v.i.* **5.** to set down the foot or feet in walking; step. ◇*v.* **6. tread water,** *Swimming.* to move the arms and legs in such a way as to keep the body upright with the head above water. ◇*n.* **7.** a treading, or stepping, or the sound of this. **8.** the manner of treading or walking. **9.** any of various things or parts on which a person or thing treads, stands, or moves, such as the sole of the foot or of a shoe, the flat upper surface of a stair, etc. **10.** that part of a wheel or tyre which touches the road. [ME]

treadle /ˈtredl/, *n.* a lever, etc., worked by the foot to give movement to a machine. [ME and OE *tredel*]

treadmill /ˈtredmɪl/, *n.* **1.** an apparatus for producing rotating movement by the weight of people or animals treading on a series of moving steps that form a kind of continuous path, as around the outside of a wheel. **2.** a boring round of repetitive activities; life, work, etc., seen in these terms.

treason /ˈtrizən/, *n.* an act of disloyalty to one's sovereign or country, such as the giving of information to an enemy; high treason. [ME, from AF, from L: act of betraying] —**treasonable, treasonous,** *adj.*

treasure /ˈtreʒə/, *n., v.,* **-ured, -uring.** ◇*n.* **1.** a store of wealth or riches, esp. precious metals or money. **2.** any thing or person greatly valued: *This book was his chief treasure.* ◇*v.t.* **3.** to store up (money, etc.) for future use. **4.** to regard as precious; cherish. [ME, from OF, from L]

treasurer /ˈtreʒərə/, *n.* **1.** the person in charge of the funds of a company, private society, city, etc. **2.** (*cap.*) the government minister responsible for the Treasury.

treasure-trove /ˈtreʒə-troʊv/, *n.* **1.** *Law.* a store of money, precious metal, etc., of unknown ownership, found hidden. **2.** any store of valuable things, ideas, etc.: *She is a treasure-trove of knowledge.* [AF: treasure found]

treasury /ˈtreʒəri/, *n., pl.* **-uries. 1.** a place where public money, or the funds of a company, etc., are kept. **2.** the funds of a state or a public or private company, etc. **3.** (*cap.*) the department of government which controls the collection and management of the public money. **4.** a building, room, box, etc., for the keeping of treasure or valuable objects. **5.** a store or collection of valuable things of any kind.

treat /trit/, *v.t.* **1.** to act or behave towards in some particular way: *to treat someone with respect.* **2.** to regard in a particular way and deal with accordingly: *to treat a matter as unimportant.* **3.** to deal with (a patient, disease, etc.) in order to relieve or cure. **4.** to deal with (a subject, etc.) in speech, writing, or art in a particular way: *to treat a theme realistically.* **5.** to put through some, usu. chemical, process in order to bring about a particular result: *to treat a substance so as to make it fireproof.* **6.** to entertain (another) with food, drink, amusement, etc., at one's own expense. ◇*v.i.* **7.** to deal with in speech, writing, etc. **8.** to discuss terms of settlement, or negotiate. ◇*n.* **9.** an entertainment of food, drink, amusement, etc., given at another's expense. **10.** *Colloq.* anything that gives particular pleasure or enjoyment. **11.** the act of treating. [ME, from OF, from L: drag, handle, treat] —**treatment,** *n.*

treatise /ˈtritəs/, *n.* a book or writing dealing with some particular subject, esp. in a formal or detailed way. [ME, from AF: TREAT]

treaty /ˈtriti/, *n., pl.* **-ties. 1.** (a document containing) a formal agreement between two or more independent states with regard to peace, alliance, trade, or other international relations. **2.** any agreement or compact. [ME, from AF: handled, treated]

treble /ˈtrebəl/, *adj., n., v.,* **-bled, -bling.** ◇*adj.* **1.** threefold; triple. **2.** *Music.* (of a voice part, voice, singer, or instrument) of the highest pitch or range. ◇*n.* **3.** *Music.* a piano part for the right hand. **4.** a high-pitched voice or sound. ◇*v.t., v.i.* **5.** to make or become three times as much or as many; triple. [ME, from OF, from L: triple]

treble clef, *n.* the sign on a music score which indicates the G above middle C, placed on the second line of the stave, counting upwards.

Treblinka /trəˈblɪŋkə/, *n.* a Nazi concentration camp in Poland, near Warsaw.

tree /tri/, *n.* **1.** a plant having a permanent, woody, self-supporting main stem or trunk, usu. growing to a considerable height, and usu. developing branches at some distance from the ground. **2.** any of various shrubs, bushes, etc., such as the banana, similar to a tree in form or size. **3.** something similar to a tree in shape, such as a family tree, etc. **4.** *Maths.* a network with no loops. [ME; OE *trēo(w)*]

tree fern, *n.* any fern, which reaches the size of a tree, sending up a straight trunklike stem with leaves at the top.

tree-kangaroo /tri-kæŋgə,ru/, *n.* any of certain medium-sized kangaroos of northeastern Qld and NG, highly adapted to living in trees.

tree-rat /'tri-ræt/, *n.* any member of a group of native rodents, found mostly in northern Australia, usu. living and nesting in trees.

trefoil /'trɛfɔɪl/, *n.* **1.** any of a group of herbs, usu. having leaves divided into three leaflets, and reddish, purple, yellow, or white flower heads, and including the common clovers. **2.** an ornamental figure or structure shaped like the leaf of such a plant. [ME, from AF, from L: triple leaf]

trek /trɛk/, *v.*, **trekked, trekking,** *n.* ◇*v.i.* **1.** to travel, esp. with difficulty. **2.** to walk over long distances, esp. for recreation: *We trekked for three days in the mountains.* ◇*n.* **3.** a journey, esp. a long and difficult one. [D: draw, travel] **— trekker,** *n.*

trellis /'trɛləs/, *n.* a frame or structure of crossed wooden or metal strips with open spaces between them, used for the support of growing vines, etc.; lattice. [ME, from OF, from LL]

tremble /'trɛmbəl/, *v.*, **-bled, -bling,** *n.* ◇*v.i.* **1.** (of people, the body, the voice, etc.) to shake from fear, excitement, weakness, cold, etc.; quiver. **2.** to be affected by a feeling of fear, etc. **3.** (of things) to shake with short, quick movements; vibrate. ◇*n.* **4.** the act of trembling. **5.** (*pl.*) a condition or disease marked by continued trembling, such as malaria. [ME, from F, from L] **— trembly,** *adj.*

tremendous /trə'mɛndəs/, *Colloq. adj.* **1.** very great in size, amount, degree, etc. **2.** wonderful; remarkable. [L: dreadful]

tremolo /'trɛməloʊ/, *n., pl.* **-los.** a trembling effect produced on certain instruments and in the human voice, expressing emotion, etc. [It: trembling, from L]

tremor /'trɛmə/, *n.* **1.** a shaking of the body or limbs from fear, weakness, etc. **2.** any trembling movement; vibration. **3.** a trembling effect, as of light, sound, etc. [ME, from L: trembling; terror]

tremulous /'trɛmjələs/, *adj.* **1.** (of people, the body, etc.) marked by trembling from fear, nervousness, weakness, excitement, etc. **2.** fearful; timorous. **3.** (of things) trembling or vibratory. [L]

trench /trɛntʃ/, *n.* **1.** a long, narrow ditch dug in the ground, the earth from which is thrown up in front to serve as a shelter from the enemy's fire, etc. **2.** (*pl.*) a system of ditches which formed the front line of battle in Europe in World War I. **3.** a deep ditch, furrow, or cut. ◇*v.t., v.i.* **4.** to dig a trench or trenches (in). [ME, from OF: act of cutting, slice, from L: cut off]

trenchant /'trɛntʃənt/, *adj.* keenly effective; forceful; vigorous: *a trenchant argument; a trenchant policy.* [ME, from OF: cut] **— trenchancy,** *n.*

trencher /'trɛntʃə/, *n.* **1.** → **mortarboard** (def. 2). **2.** *Archaic.* a flat piece of wood, etc., on which meat or other food was formerly served or carved. [ME, from AF: a cutting place, trencher]

trend /trɛnd/, *n.* **1.** a general course, direction, or tendency: *The trend now is towards the use of computers.* **2.** a style; fashion. ◇*v.i.* **3.** (of events, etc.) to have a general tendency. **4.** (of a road, river, etc.) to tend to take a particular direction. [OE *trendan*]

trendy /'trɛndi/, *Colloq.* ◇*adj.* **1.** forming part of or influenced by fashionable trends. ◇*n.* **2.** someone who takes up a very fashionable life-style or set of opinions. **— trendiness,** *n.*

trepidation /trɛpə'deɪʃən/, *n.* fearful alarm or agitation. [L: act of hurrying, or of being alarmed]

Tresillian /trə'sɪljən/, *adj.* **1.** of or relating to a nurse trained in the care of mothers and newborn children according to the principles of the Tresillian organisation. **2.** of or relating to a nursing home or hospital run on those principles. [from *Tresillian* Bridge, village in Cornwall, England, from where the founders of the organisation came]

trespass /'trɛspəs/, *n.* **1.** *Law.* **a.** an unlawful act of interference with a person (e.g. assault, battery, or wrongful imprisonment) or with land (e.g. unauthorised entry). **b.** the action to recover damages for trespass. **2.** an offence or sin. ◇*v.i.* **3.** *Law.* to perform an act of trespass. **4.** to encroach or infringe (usu. fol. by *on* or *upon*): *to trespass on someone's time; to trespass on someone's generosity.* **5.** to do wrong; offend; sin. [ME, from OF, from L] **— trespasser,** *n.*

tress /trɛs/, *n.* (usu. *pl.*) a long lock or curl of hair, esp. of a woman. [ME, from F: plait or braid of hair; orig. uncert.]

-tress, a suffix forming some feminine nouns, corresponding to masculine nouns in *-ter, -tor,* as *actor, actress,* etc. See **-ess.**

trestle /'trɛsəl/, *n.* **1.** a frame used as a support, usu. consisting of a horizontal beam or bar fixed at each end to a pair of spreading legs, to form a table, etc. **2.** *Civ Eng.* a supporting framework consisting chiefly of upright or cross pieces, used for various purposes, such as supporting a bridge across a gap. [ME, from OF: transom, beam, from L]

trevally /trə'væli/, *n.* a type of Australian sport and food fish, usu. fast-swimming and having a forked or crescent-shaped tail.

tri-, a word part meaning 'three', as in *triad, tricycle.* [L, combining form of *trēs, tria* three; or from Gk, combining form of *treîs, tría* three and *trís* thrice]

triad /'traɪæd/, *n.* **1.** a group of three, esp. of three closely connected people or things.

2. *Chem.* an element, atom, or radical having a valency of three. **3.** *Music.* a chord of three notes, esp. one consisting of a given note with its major or minor third and its perfect, augmented, or diminished fifth. **4.** (*cap.*) a secret Chinese organisation, oft. involved in criminal activities. [L, from Gk: group of three.] — **triadic**, *adj.*

trial /ˈtraɪəl, traɪl/, *n.* **1.** *Law.* **a.** the examination in a court of law of the facts of a case. **b.** the judging of a person's guilt or innocence by a court. **2.** an act of trying or testing, or putting to the proof. **3.** a contest or competition. **4.** an experiment. **5.** suffering; affliction: *comfort in the hour of trial.* **6.** a thing, person, or situation that causes suffering, distress, or annoyance: *He is a great trial to me; Life is full of trials.* **7. on trial, a.** undergoing a trial before a court of law. **b.** undergoing a test; on approval. ◇*adj.* **8.** relating to a trial. **9.** done or used by way of test, proof, or experiment. [from AF: TRY]

trial and error, *n.* a way of achieving a desired result, in which various methods are tried until a successful one is found.

triangle /ˈtraɪæŋɡəl/, *n.* **1.** a plane figure formed by three (usu.) straight lines which meet so as to form three angles. **2.** any three-cornered or three-sided figure, object, or piece: *a triangle of land.* **3.** *Music.* a percussion instrument, made of a steel rod bent into the form of a triangle open at one of the corners, and sounded by being struck with a small steel rod. **4.** any group of three; triad. [ME, from L: lit. 3-cornered object] — **triangular**, *adj.*

triangulate /traɪˈæŋɡjələt, -leɪt/, *adj.*; /traɪˈæŋɡjəleɪt/, *v.*, **-lated, -lating.** ◇*adj.* **1.** triangular. ◇*v.t.* **2.** *Survey.* **a.** to survey (a region, etc.) by dividing the area into triangles and measuring the angles of these triangles. **b.** to determine by trigonometry. — **triangulation**, *n.*

Triassic /traɪˈæsɪk/, *adj.*, *n.* (relating to) the period or system marked by widespread land deposits, at the beginning of the Mesozoic era, following the Permian and coming before the Jurassic. [LL: the number 3; so called because deposits are divisible into 3 groups]

tribe /traɪb/, *n.* **1.** any group of people united by descent from a common ancestor, by the sharing of common customs and traditions, by loyalty to the same leaders, etc. **2.** (in the culture of the Aborigines) a social group which claims a religious right to occupy and hunt in a particular area. **3.** *Bot, Zool.* **a.** a classificatory group of animals or plants, ranking between a family and a genus. **b.** any group of plants or animals. **4.** a company, or large number of people or animals. **5.** (*joc.*) **a.** a class or set of people. **b.** a family. [L] — **tribal**, *adj.*

tribo-, a word part meaning 'friction'. [Gk, combining form of *tríbein* to rub]

tribulation /ˌtrɪbjəˈleɪʃən/, *n.* great trouble, trial or sadness. [ME, from L: afflict]

tribunal /traɪˈbjuːnəl/, *n.* **1.** a court of justice. **2.** a special court officially appointed to deal with a specific matter. [L: judgment seat]

tribune[1] /ˈtrɪbjuːn/, *n.* **1.** (in ancient Rome) one of several magistrates whose duty was to protect the interests of the ordinary people. **2.** a person who defends the rights of the people. [ME, from L]

tribune[2] /ˈtrɪbjuːn/, *n.* a raised platform for a speaker; dais; rostrum. [It: tribunal]

tributary /ˈtrɪbjətri/, *n.*, *pl.* **-taries**, *adj.* ◇*n.* **1.** a stream flowing into a larger stream or other body of water. **2.** a ruler or state paying tribute (def. 2). ◇*adj.* **3.** (of a stream) flowing into a larger stream or other body of water. **4.** giving aid; contributory. **5.** paying or required to pay tribute (def. 2). — **tributarily**, *adv.*

tribute /ˈtrɪbjuːt/, *n.* **1.** a gift, speech of praise, etc., made to show gratitude, respect, or regard. **2.** a stated amount of money or other valuables demanded by one ruler or state from another in return for peace, protection, etc. **3.** any enforced payment. [ME, from L] — **tributer**, *n.*

trice /traɪs/, *n.* a very short time; an instant: *I'll be back in a trice.* [ME]

triceps /ˈtraɪsɛps/, *n.* a muscle having three points of origin, esp. the one at the back of the upper arm. [L: 3-headed]

trichina /trəˈkaɪnə/, *n.*, *pl.*, **-nae** /-niː/. a small worm, the adults of which live in the intestines and muscle tissue of man, pigs, etc., causing disease (**trichinosis**).

trick /trɪk/, *n.* **1.** something done in order to deceive; stratagem; a ruse. **2.** a deceptive appearance; an illusion. **3.** a mischievous performance; prank: *to play a trick on someone.* **4.** a clever device or feat: *a trick of literary style; a trick of horsemanship.* **5.** the art or knack of doing something well. **6.** a skilful act performed by a trained animal. **7.** an act of jugglery, magic, etc. **8.** a particular habit or way of acting; characteristic mannerism. **9. do the trick**, to bring about the desired result. **10. to be unable to take a trick**, to have no success or luck at all. ◇*adj.* **11.** relating to or having the nature of a trick or tricks. ◇*v.t.* **12.** to deceive or cheat by a trick. [ME, from OF: deceit; orig. uncert.] — **trickery**, *n.* — **trickster**, *n.*

trickle /ˈtrɪkəl/, *v.*, **-led, -ling**, *n.* ◇*v.i.* **1.** to flow or fall by drops, or in a small, gentle stream: *Tears trickled down her cheeks.* **2.** to come, go, or move slowly and bit by bit: *Replies trickled in.* ◇*v.t.* **3.** to cause to trickle. ◇*n.* **4.** a trickling flow or stream. **5.** a small, slow, or irregular quantity of anything coming, going, or moving: *a trickle of visitors.* [var. of obs. *strickle*, frequentative of STRIKE]

tricky /ˈtrɪki/, *adj.*, **trickier, trickiest. 1.** given to or marked by tricks. **2.** deceptive or difficult to deal with or handle: *a tricky problem.* — **trickily**, *adv.* — **trickiness**, *n.*

tricolor *or* **tricolour** /ˈtrɪkələ, ˈtraɪkʌlə/, *n.* a flag, etc., with three colors. [F, from LL]

tricycle /'traɪsɪkəl/, *n*. a cycle with three wheels (usu. one in front and one on each side behind). [F]

trident /'traɪdnt/, *n*. 1. a three-pronged instrument or weapon. 2. a spear having three prongs. [L: having 3 teeth]

tried /traɪd/, *v*. past tense and past participle of **try**.

triennial /traɪ'ɛnɪəl/, *adj*. 1. lasting three years. 2. happening every three years. ◇*n*. 3. Also, **triennium**. a period of three years. 4. a third anniversary. [L: period of 3 years]

Trieste /tri'ɛst/, *n*. 1. a seaport in northeastern Italy on the **Gulf of Trieste**. Pop. 239 978 (1986 est.). 2. **Free Territory of**, an area surrounding and including the town of Trieste, divided in 1954 between Italy and Yugoslavia.

trifecta /traɪ'fɛktə/, *n*. a form of betting in which the first three placegetters in a particular race must be selected in the correct order. [TRI- + per(*fecta*) a US form of betting]

trifle /'traɪfəl/, *n*., *v*., **-fled, -fling**. ◇*n*. 1. something of small value or importance. 2. a small sum of money. 3. a sweet dish made with sponge cake, sherry or wine, jam, fruit, jelly, etc., and topped with custard. ◇*v.i*. 4. to deal lightly with or without proper seriousness or respect (usu. fol. by *with*): *He was in no mood to be trifled with*. 5. to play by handling or fingering (usu. fol. by *with*): *He sat trifling with a pen*. ◇*v.t*. 6. to pass (time, etc.) in a wasteful way; idle (usu. fol. by *away*). [ME *treoflen*, from OF *trufler* make sport of, deceive; orig. uncert.] –**trifler**, *n*.

trifling /'traɪflɪŋ/, *adj*. 1. of slight importance; trivial: *a trifling matter*. 2. of small value, cost, or amount: *a trifling sum*.

trig., *Abbrev*. 1. trigonometric. 2. trigonometry.

trigger /'trɪɡə/, *n*. 1. (in firearms) a small lever which, when pressed by the finger, fires the weapon. 2. any lever, the pulling or pressing of which releases a catch or spring. 3. *Elect*. any circuit which is used to set a system in operation by the application of a single pulse. ◇*v.t*. 4. to start or set off (something), such as a series of events or a scientific reaction (oft. fol. by *off*). [earlier *tricker*, from D: pull]

trigonometrical function /trɪɡənə,mɛtrɪkəl 'fʌŋkʃən/, *n*. a function relating two sides of a right-angled triangle with one of the acute angles in the triangle, such as tangent, sine, cosine, cotangent, secant, cosecant, or any function based on any of these.

trigonometry /trɪɡə'nɒmətri/, *n*. that branch of mathematics that deals with the relations between the sides and angles of triangles, and the calculations, etc., based on these. [NL, from Gk] –**trigonometric, trigonometrical**, *adj*.

trig station, *n*. a position of importance in the surveying of an area, marked by a fixed post or pole against which a bearing may be taken later. Also, **trig point**. [TRIG(ONOMETRICAL) *station*]

trilby /'trɪlbi/, *n*., *pl*. **-bies**. a man's soft felt hat with a dent in the crown. [named after the heroine of *Trilby*, a novel by G Du Maurier, 1834–96, an English novelist]

trill /trɪl/, *n*. 1. *Music*. a vibrating sound, or a rapid alternation of two consecutive notes, in singing or in instrumental music. 2. a similar sound, or series of sounds, made by a bird, an insect, a frog, a person laughing, etc. 3. the pronunciation, as of the letter 'r' in some languages, performed by the rapid vibration of a speech organ, such as the tongue tip. ◇*v.i*., *v.t*. 4. to sound, sing, etc. with a trill. [It: quaver or warble in singing; of Gmc orig.]

trillion /'trɪljən/, *n*. 1. a million times a million, or 10^{12}. 2. (less commonly in Aust) a million times a billion, or 10^{18}. [F] –**trillionth**, *n*., *adj*.

trilobite /'traɪləbaɪt/, *n*. any of a group of extinct arthropods, with a flattened oval body varying in length from 3 cm to 60 cm, their fossils, widely found in Palaeozoic rocks, being among the earliest known fossils. [NL] –**trilobitic**, *adj*.

trilogy /'trɪlədʒi/, *n*., *pl*. **-gies**. a series or group of three related plays, novels, etc. [Gk]

trim /trɪm/, *v*., **trimmed, trimming**, *n*., *adj*., **trimmer, trimmest**, *adv*. ◇*v.t*. 1. to reduce to a neat or orderly state by cutting, clipping, etc.: *to trim a hedge; to trim hair*. 2. to remove by cutting, clipping, etc. (oft. fol. by *off*): *to trim off loose threads from a ragged edge*. 3. to change (one's opinions, etc.) in order to please others, gain support, etc. 4. *Carp*. to bring (a piece of wood, etc.) to the required smoothness or shape. 5. *Naut*. to adjust (the sails) with regard to the direction of the wind and the course of the ship. 6. to decorate or ornament: *to trim a hat; to trim a Christmas tree*. ◇*n*. 7. proper condition or order: *to find everything out of trim*. 8. material used for decoration. 9. a trimming by cutting, clipping, etc. 10. a haircut which neatens the hair without changing the style. ◇*adj*. 11. pleasingly neat or smart in appearance. 12. in good condition or order. ◇*adv*. 13. Also, **trimly**. in a trim manner. [OE *trymman, trymian* strengthen; prepare]

trimaran /'traɪməræn/, *n*. a boat with a main middle hull and two outer hulls parallel to it acting as floats. [TRI- + (CATA)MARAN]

trimester /traɪ'mɛstə, trə-/, *n*. a term or period of three months. [F, from L: of three months] –**trimestral, trimestrial**, *adj*.

trimmer /'trɪmə/, *n*. *Colloq*. someone or something excellent.

trimming /'trɪmɪŋ/, *n*. 1. anything used to trim or decorate. 2. (*pl*.) *Colloq*. agreeable accompaniments or additions to plain dishes of food. 3. (*pl*.) pieces cut off in trimming, etc.

Trinidad and Tobago /,trɪnədæd ən tə'beɪɡoʊ/, *n*. a republic consisting of two islands at the southern end of the Lesser Antilles group in the Caribbean Sea. Pop. 1 221 000 (1987); 5128 km². *Languages*: English, also French, Spanish, Hindi and Chinese. *Currency*: Trinidad and Tobago dollar. *Cap*.: Port of Spain.

trinitrotoluene /ˌtraɪnaɪtrouˈtɒljuin/, n.
→ TNT

trinity /ˈtrɪnəti/, n., pl. **-ties.** 1. a group of three; triad. 2. the state of being threefold or triple. 3. (*cap.*) *Theol.* the union of three divine persons (Father, Son, and Holy Spirit) as one God. [ME, from OF., from L: triad, trio, trinity]

trinket /ˈtrɪŋkət/, n. any small, ornamental article, such as a piece of jewellery, usu. of little value. [orig. uncert.]

trinomial /traɪˈnoumiəl/, adj. 1. *Alg.* consisting of, or relating to, three terms connected by the sign +, the sign −, or both of these. ◇n. 2. *Alg.* a trinomial expression, as $a + b - c$. [TRI- + (BI)NOMIAL]

trio /ˈtriou/, n., pl. **trios.** 1. (a musical composition for) a group of three voices or instruments. 2. a division of a minuet, scherzo, march, etc., usu. in a contrasted key and style. 3. any group of three people or things. [It: three]

trioxide /traɪˈɒksaɪd/, n. an oxide containing three oxygen atoms.

trip /trɪp/, n., v., **tripped, tripping.** ◇n. 1. a journey or voyage. 2. a journey made for pleasure; excursion. 3. *Colloq.* a period under the influence of a hallucinatory drug. 4. a falling over; stumble. 5. a mistake, or blunder. ◇v.i. 6. to fall over; stumble: *I tripped over that toy.* 7. to make a mistake. ◇v.t. 8. to cause to fall over (oft. fol. by *up*): *The rug tripped him up.* 9. to cause to fail or make a mistake (oft. fol. by *up*): *to trip up a witness by clever questioning.* 10. to operate, start, or set free (a mechanism, weight, etc.) by suddenly releasing a catch, spring, etc. [ME, from OF: strike with the feet, from Gmc]

tripartite /traɪˈpɑtaɪt/, adj. 1. divided into or consisting of three parts. 2. (of a treaty, etc.) involving three parties. [ME, from L: divided into 3 parts]

tripe /traɪp/, n. 1. the first and second divisions of the stomach of an animal of the ox family, prepared for use as food. 2. *Colloq.* anything poor or worthless, esp. written work; nonsense; rubbish. [ME, from OF., ult. from Ar: folds of peritoneum]

triple /ˈtrɪpəl/, adj., n., v., **-pled, -pling.** ◇adj. 1. consisting of three parts; threefold. 2. three times as great. ◇n. 3. an amount, number, etc., three times as great as another. ◇v.t., v.i. 4. to make or become triple. [ME, from L, from Gk: threefold]

Triple Alliance, n. 1. the alliance (1882–1915) between Germany, Austria-Hungary, and Italy. 2. a league (1717) of France, Great Britain and the Netherlands against Spain. 3. a league (1668) of England, Sweden and the Netherlands against France.

triple bond, n. a chemical bond between atoms in a molecule consisting of three covalent bonds, shown in formulas by three lines, as in acetylene (ethyne), CH≡CH.

Triple Entente /ˌtrɪpəl ɒnˈtɒnt/, n. an informal understanding among Great Britain, France, and Russia considered as a counter balance to the Triple Alliance (1882–1915) and terminating when the Bolsheviks came to power in Russia in 1917.

triple point, n. *Phys.* the temperature at which the solid, liquid and vapor phases of a substance all exist in equilibrium. For water, this is 273.16°K.

triplet /ˈtrɪplət/, n. 1. one of three children born at one birth. 2. (*pl.*) three offspring born at one birth. 3. any group of three. 4. a thin bar of opal set between two layers of plastic, or one layer each of potch and crystal. 5. three rhyming lines of poetry, usu. forming a stanza. 6. *Music.* a group of three notes to be performed in the time of two ordinary notes of the same kind. [from TRIPLE]

triple time, n. *Music.* a time or rhythm marked by three beats to the bar with an accent on the first beat. Also, **triple measure.**

triplicate /ˈtrɪpləkeɪt/, v., **-cated, -cating**; /ˈtrɪpləkət/, adj., n. ◇v.t. 1. to make threefold; triple. 2. to make or produce a third time. ◇adj. 3. threefold; triple. ◇n. 4. one of three identical things. [L: tripled] —**triplication,** n.

tripod /ˈtraɪpɒd/, n. 1. a stool, etc., with three legs. 2. a three-legged stand for a camera, etc. [L, from Gk: 3-footed]

Tripoli /ˈtrɪpəli/, n. 1. Also, **Tripolitania.** one of the former Barbary States of northern Africa; later a province of Turkey; now a part of Libya. 2. a seaport in and the capital of Libya, in the north-western part. Pop. 858 500 (1981). Arabic, **Tarābulus el Gharb.** 3. a seaport in northern Lebanon, on the Mediterranean. Pop. 500 000 (1985 est.). Arabic, **Tarābulus esh Sham.** —**Tripolitan,** n., adj.

tripping /ˈtrɪpɪŋ/, adj. (of a step, movement, etc.) light and quick.

triptych /ˈtrɪptɪk/, n. *Art.* a set of three-hinged panels featuring pictures, carvings, etc. [Gk: of three plates]

trireme /ˈtraɪrim/, n. a galley with three rows of oars on each side used chiefly as a warship. [L]

Tristan /ˈtrɪstən/, n. *Arthurian Legend.* one of the knights of the Round Table, whose love for Iseult, wife of King Mark, is the subject of many legends. Also, **Tristram.**

trite /traɪt/, adj., **triter, tritest.** (of a saying, idea, etc.) repeated too often; hackneyed; unoriginal. [L: rubbed, worn]

tritium /ˈtrɪtiəm/, n. a radioactive isotope of hydrogen containing two neutrons and a proton, with a mass number of 3.

triton /ˈtraɪtn/, n. 1. any of various sea molluscs with a large, spiral, oft. beautifully colored shell. 2. the shell of a triton. 3. (*cap.*) *Class Myth.* a sea-god, son of Poseidon and Amphitrite, represented as having the head and trunk of a man and the tail of a fish, and bearing a conch-shell trumpet. [L from Gk]

triumph /ˈtraɪʌmf, ˈtraɪəmf/, n. 1. the act or fact of being victorious; victory. 2. a great success; notable achievement. 3. the joy of victory or success. 4. *Anc Hist.* the ceremonial

triumph entrance into ancient Rome of a victorious commander with his army, spoils, captives, etc. ◇*v.i.* **5.** to gain a victory; be victorious. **6.** to achieve success. **7.** to rejoice over victory or success. [OE *triumpha*, from L] —**triumphal, triumphant,** *adj.*

triumvir /ˈtraɪəmvɪə/, *n.* **1.** *Anc Hist.* one of three officers, etc., sharing the same function. **2.** one of three people associated in any office. [L: of three men] —**triumviral,** *adj.*

triumvirate /traɪˈʌmvərət/, *n.* **1.** *Anc Hist.* the office of a triumvir. **2.** any association, group or set of three people in office or authority. [L]

trivalent /traɪˈveɪlənt, ˈtrɪvələnt/, *adj.* having a valency of three.

trivia /ˈtrɪviə/, *n.pl.* inessential, unimportant, or inconsequential things. [apparently backformation from TRIVIAL] —**triviality,** *n.*

trivial /ˈtrɪviəl/, *adj.* **1.** of little importance; trifling; insignificant. **2.** commonplace; ordinary. [ME, from L: belonging to the crossroads, (hence) common] —**triviality,** *n.*

-trix, a suffix of feminine agent-nouns, as in *executrix.* See -**or**[2]. [L]

trochee /ˈtroʊki/, *n.* (in poetry) a metrical foot of two syllables, a long followed by a short, or an accented followed by an unaccented. [L, from Gk: running]

trod /trɒd/, *v.* past tense and past participle of **tread.**

trodden /ˈtrɒdn/, *v.* past participle of **tread.**

troglodyte /ˈtrɒglədaɪt/, *n.* **1.** a prehistoric caveman or cave-dweller. **2.** *Colloq.* anyone thought to be primitive, unintelligent, or insensitive. [L, from Gk: one who creeps into holes]

troika /ˈtrɔɪkə/, *n.* **1.** a Russian vehicle drawn by a team of three horses abreast. **2.** any group of three acting together. [Russ]

Troilus /ˈtrɔɪləs/, *n. Class and Medieval Legend.* the warrior son of King Priam of Troy, mentioned by Homer and Virgil, and greatly developed in medieval versions of the Troy story as the lover of Cressida.

Trojan Horse /ˈtroʊdʒən ˈhɔs/, *n. Class Legend.* the gigantic, hollow, wooden figure of a horse, filled with armed Greeks, and brought into Troy, which led to the destruction of the city. Also, **Wooden Horse.**

Trojan War, *n. Class Legend.* a ten-year war waged by the Greeks, under king Agamemnon, against the Trojans to avenge the abduction of Helen, wife of the Greek king Menelaus, by Paris, son of the Trojan king Priam, and ending in the destruction of Troy.

troll[1] /troʊl/, *v.i.* **1.** to fish with a moving line, trailing it behind a boat. ◇*n.* **2.** a song whose parts are sung one after the other; a round. [ME from OF, from MHG]

troll[2] /trɒl/, *n.* (in Scandinavian folklore) one of a race of supernatural beings, giants or dwarfs, living in caves or underground dwellings. [Scand]

trolley /ˈtrɒli/, *n., pl.* **-leys. 1.** any of various types of low carts, etc., as used in supermarkets, etc. **2.** a small table on wheels for carrying dishes, serving food, etc. **3.** a low truck running on rails, used on railways, in factories, mines, etc. [probably from TROLL[1]]

trollop /ˈtrɒləp/, *n.* **1.** an untidy or slovenly woman; slattern. **2.** a sexually immoral woman, esp. a prostitute.

Trollope /ˈtrɒləp/, *n.* **Anthony,** 1815–82, English novelist; major novels include *Barchester Towers* (1857).

trombone /trɒmˈboʊn/, *n. Music.* a wind instrument consisting of a cylindrical metal tube widening into a bell and bent twice in a U shape, the pitch being changed by the movement of a slide. [It: trumpet, from OHG] —**trombonist,** *n.*

troop /trup/, *n.* **1.** a group of people, animals or things; a company, band, herd, etc. **2.** a great number. **3.** *Mil.* (*pl.*) a body of soldiers, marines, etc. **4.** a unit of 32 boy scouts, equal to four patrols. ◇*v.i.* **5.** to go or come in great numbers. **6.** to walk as if on a march. ◇*v.t.* **7.** *Mil.* to carry (the flag or colors) in a ceremonial way before troops: *trooping the color.* [F, from LL: flock, from Gmc]

trooper /ˈtrupə/, *n.* **1.** a cavalry soldier. **2.** (formerly) a mounted policeman. **3.** *Mil.* a private in the Royal Australian Armed Corps. See Appendix. [from TROOP]

-trope, a combining form referring to 'turning', as in *heliotrope.* [Gk *-trópos*]

trophic /ˈtroʊfɪk/, *adj.* relating to nutrition; concerned in nutritive processes. [Gk] —**trophically,** *adv.*

trophy /ˈtroʊfi/, *n., pl.* **-phies. 1.** anything taken in war, hunting, etc., esp. when kept as a memento or souvenir; a spoil or prize. **2.** anything serving as a token or evidence of victory, courage, skill, etc. [F, from L, from Gk: putting to flight]

-trophy, a word part indicating 'nourishment', as in *hypertrophy.* [Gk: nutrition]

tropic /ˈtrɒpɪk/, *n.* **1.** *Geog.* **a.** either of two corresponding parallels of latitude on the earth (or celestial sphere), one (**tropic of Cancer**) about 23½° north, and the other (**tropic of Capricorn**) about 23½° south of and parallel to the equator. **b. the tropics,** an area lying between and near these parallels of latitude; the Torrid Zone and neighboring regions. ◇*adj.* **2.** relating to the tropics; tropical. [ME, from L, from Gk: relating to a turn] —**tropical,** *adj.*

-tropic, an adjective combining form corresponding to *-trope, -tropism,* as in *geotropic.*

tropism /ˈtroʊpɪzəm/, *n.* a response of a plant or animal, in its growth, to the influences of external stimuli, such as sunlight, gravity, etc. [separate use of -TROPISM]

-tropism, a word part referring to 'tropism', as in *heliotropism.* Also, **-tropy.** [-TROP(E) + -ISM]

tropo-, a word part referring to 'turning' or 'change'. [Gk, combining form of *trópos*]

troposphere /'trɒpəsfɪə/, *n.* the inner layer of atmosphere, between the heights of about 10 km and 19 km, within which nearly all clouds are formed.

trot /trɒt/, *v.*, **trotted, trotting**, *n.* ◊*v.i.* **1.** (of a horse, etc.) to go at a gait between a walk and a run, in which the legs move in alternating diagonal pairs. **2.** to go at a quick, steady speed; hurry. ◊*v.t.* **3.** to ride at a trot. ◊*v.* **4. trot out**, *Colloq.* **a.** to bring forward for or as if for inspection. **b.** to give voice to in a meaningless or boring way. ◊*n.* **5.** the manner of movement or sound of a horse when trotting. **6.** a type of movement between a walk and a run; jog. **7.** (*pl.*) races for trotting horses; a trotting meeting. **8.** (*pl.*) *Colloq.* diarrhoea. **9. a good (bad) trot**, *Colloq.* a run of good (bad) luck. [ME, from OF, from MHG: run, orig. tread]

troth /troʊθ/, *n. Archaic.* **1.** faithfulness, fidelity, or loyalty: *by my troth*. **2.** truth: *in troth*. **3.** one's word or promise, esp. in engaging oneself to marry: *pledge one's troth*. [OE *trēowth*]

Trotsky /'trɒtski/, *n.* **Leon** (*Lev*, or *Leiba*, *Davidovich Bronstein*), 1879–1940, Russian revolutionary leader and writer; minister of war 1918–25; later exiled. Also, **Trotski**.

trotter /'trɒtə/, *n.* **1.** a horse bred and trained for harness racing. **2.** an animal's foot, esp. of a pig or sheep used as food.

troubadour /'tru:bədɔː/, *n.* a minstrel or ballad singer. [F, from Pr, ? from LL: figure of speech]

trouble /'trʌbəl/, *v.*, **-bled, -bling**, *n.* ◊*v.t.* **1.** to disturb in mind; distress; worry. **2.** to put (someone) to inconvenience, pains, etc.: *May I trouble you to shut the door?* **3.** to annoy or bother. **4.** to disturb or stir up (water, etc.). ◊*v.i.* **5.** to put oneself to inconvenience. ◊*n.* **6.** annoyance or difficulty; harassment: *to make trouble for someone.* **7.** unfortunate position; unhappy circumstances; misfortunes: *to be in trouble.* **8.** disorder; unrest: *industrial trouble; political troubles.* **9.** physical disorder: *heart trouble.* **10.** worry; distress. **11.** inconvenience endured, or accepted, in order to do something. **12.** a personal habit, etc., which is a source of anxiety: *My trouble is I talk too much.* [ME, from OF, from LL] **–troublesome**, *adj.*

troubleshooter /'trʌbəlʃuːtə/, *n.* an expert in finding and fixing or settling the cause of trouble in the operation of something, in disputes, etc. **–troubleshooting**, *n.*

trough /trɒf/, *n.* **1.** an open, boxlike container, usu. long and narrow, for holding water or food for animals, etc. **2.** any receptacle or vessel of similar shape, such as a trough used to wash clothes. **3.** any long depression or hollow, as between two waves. **4.** *Weather.* a trough-like area of relatively low pressure. [ME; OE *trōh*]

trounce /traʊns/, *v.t.*, **trounced, trouncing**. **1.** to beat; thrash. **2.** *Colloq.* to defeat convincingly. [orig. uncert.]

troupe /tru:p/, *n.* a company, band, or group of actors, singers, etc. [F] **–trouper**, *n.*

trousers /'traʊzəz/, *n.pl.* an outer garment covering the body and each leg separately from the waist to the ankles.

trousseau /'tru:soʊ/, *n., pl.* **-seaux, -seaus** /-soʊz/. a bride's outfit of clothes, linen, etc. [F: lit., bundle]

trout /traʊt/, *n., pl.* **trouts**, (*esp. collectively*) **trout**. a freshwater fish related to salmon caught for sport and food. [OE *truht*, from L, from Gk: gnawer, a sea fish]

trowel /'traʊəl/, *n., v.*, **-elled, -elling**. ◊*n.* **1.** a tool having a flat plate, usu. of metal, and a short handle, used for spreading, shaping, or smoothing plaster, mortar, etc. **2.** a similar tool with a curved, scooplike blade, used in gardening. ◊*v.t.* **3.** to apply, shape, or smooth with, or as if with, a trowel. [ME, from OF, from LL]

Troy /trɔɪ/, *n.* an ancient ruined city in north-western Asia Minor; the seventh of nine settlements on the same site; in ancient times besieged for ten years by the Greeks. Latin, **Ilium**. Greek, **Ilion**.

troy weight /trɔɪ/, *n.* (in the imperial system) a measure of the mass of precious metals and gems.

truant /'tru:ənt/, *n.* **1.** a pupil who stays away from school or particular classes without permission. **2.** someone who neglects their duty. **3. play truant**, to be absent from school, etc., without permission. ◊*adj.* **4.** relating to or typical of a truant. [ME, from OF, probably of Celtic orig.] **–truancy**, *n.*

truce /tru:s/, *n.* (an agreement calling for) an end to fighting between enemies for a time; armistice. [OE *trēow* treaty, good faith]

truck[1] /trʌk/, *n.* **1.** any of various, usu. large, motor vehicles with an area at the rear for carrying goods, etc. **2.** a railway goods wagon. ◊*v.t.* **3.** to transport by a truck or trucks. ◊*v.i.* **4.** to drive a truck. [backformation from *truckle* wheel] **–trucking**, *n.*

truck[2] /trʌk/, *n.* **1.** dealings: *to have no truck with someone.* **2.** barter. **3.** payment of wages in goods, etc., instead of money. [ME, from OF; orig. uncert.]

truckie, *n. Colloq.* a truck driver.

truculent /'trʌkjələnt/, *adj.* fierce; aggressive; belligerent. [L] **–truculence**, **truculency**, *n.*

Trudeau /tru:'doʊ/, *n.* **Pierre Elliott** /pɪˌɛə 'elɪət/, born 1921, Canadian statesman; prime minister 1968–79; 1980–84.

trudge /trʌdʒ/, *v.i., v.t.*, **trudged, trudging**. to walk slowly and wearily (along or over). [orig. uncert.]

true /tru:/, *adj.*, **truer, truest**, *adv.* ◊*adj.* **1.** being the actual state of things; not false: *a true story.* **2.** real or genuine: *true gold.* **3.** sincere: *a true interest in someone's welfare.* **4.** loyal; faithful; trusty. **5.** exact, correct, or accurate: *a true balance.* **6.** legitimate or rightful: *the true heir.* **7.** reliable, unfailing, or sure: *a true sign.* **8.** (of a surface, instrument, etc.) exactly or accurately shaped, formed, fitted, or placed. **9.** *Biol.* belonging to a

true — particular group; typical. **10.** (of a bearing) fixed in relation to the earth's axis rather than the magnetic poles: *true north.* ◇*adv.* **11.** in a true manner; truly or truthfully. **12.** exactly or accurately. **13. to come true,** to happen in reality as desired, dreamt, etc.: *if dreams came true.* [ME; OE *trēowe*]

true-blue /'tru-blu /, *adj.* unchanging; true; staunch; loyal.

truffle /'trʌfəl /, *n.* **1.** an edible fungus that grows underground. **2.** a chocolate sweet usu. filled with rum. [F, from Pr or from It ?, from LL]

Truganini /trugə'nɪni /, *n.* 1812?—76, Australian Aborigine; considered to be the last full-blooded Tasmanian Aborigine.

truism /'truzəm /, *n.* a self-evident, obvious truth. —**truistic,** *adj.*

truly /'truli /, *adv.* **1.** in a true manner; exactly; accurately; correctly. **2.** rightly; duly; properly. **3.** genuinely; really.

Truman /'trumən /, *n.* **Harry S,** 1884–1972, 33rd president of the US, 1945–53; carried on the New Deal reform tradition; involved the US in the Korean War (1950).

trump¹ /trʌmp /, *n.* **1.** *Cards.* (any card of) a suit that for the time outranks other suits. ◇*v.t.* **2.** *Cards.* to take with a trump. ◇*v.* **3. trump up,** to invent dishonestly, as an accusation; fabricate. [unexplained var. of TRIUMPH]

trump² /trʌmp /, *Archaic or Poetic. n.* a trumpet. [ME, from F, of Gmc orig.]

trumpery /'trʌmpəri /, *n., pl.* **-ries,** *adj.* ◇*n.* **1.** something showy but worthless. **2.** rubbish; nonsense. ◇*adj.* **3.** showy but useless. [F: deceive]

trumpet /'trʌmpət /, *n.* **1.** *Music.* a wind instrument of the brass family, consisting of a metallic tube curved round upon itself, having a cup-shaped mouthpiece at one end and a flaring bell at the other. **2.** a sound like that of a trumpet. **3.** the loud cry of the elephant. **4.** → **ear trumpet. 5. blow one's own trumpet,** to praise oneself. ◇*v.i.* **6.** to blow a trumpet. **7.** to make a sound like a trumpet, as an elephant. ◇*v.t.* **8.** to sound on or as if on a trumpet. **9.** to announce loudly or widely. [ME, from OF] —**trumpeter,** *n.*

truncate /trʌŋ'keɪt /, *v.t.,* **-cated, -cating. 1.** to shorten by cutting off a part; mutilate. **2.** to cut off the corners or angles of: *a truncated pyramid.* [L: cut] —**truncation,** *n.*

truncheon /'trʌnʃən /, *n.* **1.** a short club carried by a police officer. **2.** a baton or staff showing authority. [ME, from OF: piece cut off, from L: stump]

trundle /'trʌndəl /, *v.,* **-dled, -dling.** ◇*v.t.* **1.** to cause (a ball, hoop, etc.) to roll along; roll. ◇*v.i.* **2.** to move or run on a wheel or wheels. [OE *tryndel* wheel]

trunk /trʌŋk /, *n.* **1.** the main stem of a tree, as distinct from the branches and roots. **2.** a box or chest for holding clothes and other articles, as for use on a journey. **3.** the body of a human being or of an animal, excluding the head and limbs. **4.** → **trunk line. 5.** (*pl.*) shorts worn by swimmers, athletes, etc. **6.** the long, flexible, snout of the elephant. ◇*adj.* **7.** showing or relating to the main line of a railway, road, etc. [late ME, from L]

trunk line, *n.* **1.** a telephone line between two exchanges in different parts of a country or the world, used for making long-distance calls. **2.** a main railway line. Also, **trunkline.**

truss /trʌs /, *v.t.* **1.** to tie, bind (oft. fol. by *up*). **2.** to make fast with skewers, etc., as the wings of a chicken before cooking. **3.** *Bldg Trades, etc.* to supply or support with a truss. ◇*n.* **4.** *Bldg Trades.* a combination of beams, bars, ties, etc., arranged so as to form a rigid framework, used in bridges, roofs, etc. **5.** *Med.* an apparatus for binding a hernia to keep it in place. **6.** bundle; pack. [ME, from OF, from L: bundle]

trust /trʌst /, *n.* **1.** reliance on the honesty, etc., of a person, or on some other quality; confidence. **2.** confident expectation of something; hope. **3.** confidence in the ability or intention of a person to pay at some future time for goods, etc.; credit: *to sell goods on trust.* **4.** the state of being relied on or depended on. **5.** a responsibility required of someone in whom confidence or authority is placed: *a position of trust.* **6.** the condition of being left to another's care: *to leave something in trust with a person.* **7.** *Law.* **a.** a relationship in which one person (the trustee) holds the title to property (**trust estate** or **trust property**) for the benefit of another (beneficiary). **b.** a fund of securities, cash or other assets, held in this way. **8.** *Comm.* a combination of companies having a central committee, controlling most or all of the stock of each company. This arrangement helps to keep costs down, defeat competition, etc. ◇*adj.* **9.** *Law.* of or relating to a trust or trusts. ◇*v.i.* **10.** to have or place trust, reliance, or confidence (usu. fol. by *in*). **11.** to have confidence; hope. ◇*v.t.* **12.** to depend on; rely on (oft. fol. by *to*). **13.** to believe. **14.** to hope (usu. fol. by a clause or infinitive). **15.** to commit with trust or confidence. **16.** to permit to be in some place, care, etc., without fear of loss, theft, etc.: *He will not trust it out of his sight.* **17.** to give credit to (a person) for goods, etc., supplied. [ME, from Scand]

trustee /trʌs'ti /, *n. Law.* **1.** a person, usu. one of a body of people, appointed to manage the affairs of a company, institution, etc. **2.** a person who holds the title to property for the benefit of another.

trustworthy /'trʌstwɜði /, *adj.* worthy of trust or confidence: *a trustworthy friend.* —**trustworthiness,** *n.*

trusty /'trʌsti /, *adj.,* **trustier, trustiest,** *n., pl.* **trusties.** ◇*adj.* **1.** able to be trusted or relied on: *a trusty sword.* ◇*n.* **2.** someone, esp. a convict, who is trusted. —**trustiness,** *n.*

truth /truθ /, *n.* **1.** something which is true or actual: *to tell the truth.* **2.** agreement with fact or reality: *the truth of a statement.* **3.** an indisputable fact, principle, etc.: *mathematical truths.* **4.** genuineness, reality, or actual existence. **5.** honesty or integrity. **6. in truth,** in fact; in reality; truly. [OE *trēowth*] —**truthful,** *adj.*

try /traɪ/, v., **tried, trying,** n., pl. **tries.**
◇v.t. **1.** to attempt to do (something): *It seems easy until you try it.* **2.** to test the effect or result of: *to try a new method.* **3.** to attempt to find out by experiment: *to try one's luck; to try a new product.* **4.** *Law.* to examine by means of a trial. **5.** to put to a severe test; strain the patience, etc., of. ◇v.i. **6.** to make an attempt or effort: *try harder next time.* ◇v. **try it on,** *Colloq.* to attempt to deceive or test the patience of, esp. cheekily. ◇n. **7.** an attempt: *to have a try at something.* **8.** *Rugby.* a score of four points (League) or five points (Union) earned by a touchdown. [ME, from OF: pick, cull]

trying /'traɪɪŋ/, adj. annoying; irritating; testing one's patience.

tryst /trɪst/, n. a planned meeting, esp. between lovers; a rendezvous. [ME, from OF; orig. uncert.]

tsar /zɑ/, n. **1.** an emperor or king. **2.** (*usu. cap.*) the emperor of Russia. **3.** (*oft. cap.*) an absolute ruler; dictator. Also, **czar, tzar.** [Russ, from L *Caesar*] —**tsarina,** n. fem.

tsetse fly /'tsetsi flaɪ, 'setsi/, n. any of the African blood-sucking flies, some of which carry parasites which cause sleeping sickness, etc. [native name]

T-shirt /'ti-ʃɜt/, n. a light, close-fitting, collarless shirt, with short sleeves.

tsp., *Abbrev.* teaspoon.

T square /'ti skweə/, n. a T-shaped ruler used in mechanical drawing to make parallel lines, etc.

tuan /'tjuən/, n. a brush-tailed, meat-eating, rat-sized marsupial that lives in trees; wambenger. [Aboriginal]

tub /tʌb/, n. **1.** a large, round, open, flat-bottomed container made of wood or metal used for bathing, washing clothes, etc. **2.** any container shaped like a tub: *a tub of margarine.* **3.** *Colloq.* a slow, clumsy ship or boat. [ME; orig. unknown]

tuba /'tjubə/, n., pl. **-bas, -bae** /-biː/. a low-pitched wind instrument of the brass family which has a conical bore and a cup-shaped mouthpiece and is equipped with valves. [L: trumpet]

tubal ligation /ˌtjubəl laɪ'geɪʃən/, n. a surgical operation in which the Fallopian tubes are tied off to prevent conception.

tubby /'tʌbi/, adj., **-bier, -biest.** short and fat: *a tubby man.* —**tubbiness,** n.

tube /tjub/, n., v., **tubed, tubing.** ◇n. **1.** a hollow, narrow cylindrical body or pipe made of metal, glass, rubber, etc. used for containing or allowing the flow of liquids and gases. **2.** a small, soft, metal or plastic cylinder, usu. screw-topped, closed at one end, for holding paint, toothpaste, etc., to be squeezed out by pressure. **3.** *Anat, Zool.* any hollow, cylindrical vessel or organ: *the bronchial tubes.* **4.** the hollow formed under the crest of a wave as it breaks. **5.** (*pl.*) → Fallopian tubes. **6.** *Brit.* an underground train system, esp. in London. **7.** *Colloq.* a television set. [L: pipe] —**tubed,** *adj.* —**tubing,** n.

tuber /'tjubə/, n. *Bot.* a fleshy, usu. long or round outgrowth (as the potato) of an underground stem from which new plants may grow. [L: bump, swelling]

tubercle /'tjubəkəl/, n. *Med.* a small, firm, rounded swelling, esp. one typical of tuberculosis. [L: small swelling]

tuberculosis /təbɜkjə'loʊsəs/, n. an infectious bacterial disease, usu. affecting the lungs, and marked by the production of characteristic small rounded nodules or swellings. Also, **TB** [NL, from L: TUBERCLE] —**tuberculous, tubercular,** *adj.*

tuberose /'tjubə'roʊz, 'tjubəroʊz/, n. a bulbous plant grown for its fragrant, creamy white, lily-like flowers. [L: tuberous]

tuberous /'tjubərəs/, *adj.* **1.** covered with or marked by rounded outgrowths or tubers. **2.** of the nature of or looking like such an outgrowth. **3.** *Bot.* bearing tubers. [L]

tubular /'tjubjələ/, *adj.* **1.** of or relating to a tube or tubes. **2.** Also, **tubiform.** having the nature or form of a tube. [NL, from L: little tube]

tuck /tʌk/, *v.t.* **1.** to put into some narrow or hidden place: *tuck this in your pocket.* **2.** to put the edge of (a garment, covering, etc.) closely into place under other things (oft. fol. by *in, up,* etc.): *He tucked his napkin under his chin.* **3.** to cover snugly in or as if in this manner: *to tuck someone up in bed.* **4.** to draw up in a folded manner: *to tuck one's legs under a chair.* **5.** *Sewing.* to sew tucks in. ◇v.i. **6.** *Colloq.* to eat or drink with enthusiasm (oft. fol. by *in, into, away,* etc.). ◇n. **7.** *Sewing.* a flat fold sewn in a garment to give it shape. [OE *tūcian* torment]

tucker /'tʌkə/, n. *Colloq.* food. [TUCK + -ER¹]

Tucker /'tʌkə/, n. **1. Albert,** born 1914, Australian artist; a pioneer of surrealist and symbolist painting. **2. James,** c. 1808–88?, Australian convict, born in England; thought to be the author of several works, including *Ralph Rashleigh, or the Life of an Exile.*

tuckshop /'tʌkʃɒp/, n. a shop, esp. in a school, where sandwiches, cakes, etc., are sold.

-tude, a suffix forming abstract nouns, generally from Latin adjectives or participles, as in *latitude, fortitude.* [L *-tūdo*]

Tudor /'tjudə/, n. **1.** a member of the royal family which ruled England from 1485 to 1603, and which was descended from **Sir Owen Tudor,** a Welshman who married the widow of Henry V. ◇*adj.* **2.** of, relating to, or belonging to the house of Tudor.

Tues, *Abbrev.* Tuesday. Also, **Tue**

Tuesday /'tjuzdeɪ, -di/, n. the third day of the week, following Monday. [OE *Tiwesdæg* Tiw's day (translation of L: day of Mars)]

tuffet /'tʌfət/, n. **1.** a hillock; mound. **2.** a footstool; hassock.

tuft /tʌft/, n. **1.** a bunch of small, usu. soft and flexible things, as feathers, hairs, grass, etc., fixed at the base with the upper part loose.

tuft 1105 **tuning fork**

◇*v.t.* **2.** to provide with or arrange in a tuft or tufts. ◇*v.i.* **3.** to form a tuft or tufts. [ME; orig. uncert.]

tug /tʌg/, *v.*, **tugged, tugging,** *n.* ◇*v.t.* **1.** to pull at with force or effort. **2.** to move by pulling forcibly; drag; haul. **3.** to tow (a vessel, etc.) by means of a tugboat. ◇*v.i.* **4.** to pull with force or effort: *to tug at an oar.* **5.** to strive hard, labor, or toil. ◇*n.* **6.** the act of tugging; a strong pull. **7.** →**tugboat.** [ME]

tugboat /'tʌgbout/, *n.* a strongly built, heavily powered vessel for towing other vessels.

tug of war, *n.* **1.** a contest between two teams at opposite ends of a rope, each trying to drag the other over a line. **2.** a severe or critical struggle.

Tuileries /'twiləriz/, *n.* a former royal residence in Paris, begun by Catherine de' Medici, 1564; burned by supporters of the Paris Commune, 1871.

tuition /tjuˈɪʃən/, *n.* teaching or instruction. [late ME, from L: guardianship]

tula-adze flake /tjulə-ædz 'fleɪk/, *n.* a stone flake attached with resin onto a wooden handle, used by Aborigines of central Australia for chiselling and scraping wood. Also, **tula, tula adze.**

tulip /'tjulɪp/, *n.* a plant with many varieties, growing from a bulb, with sword-shaped leaves, and one stem bearing a large, showy, cup-shaped flower. [earlier *tulipa(n)*, from Turk: TURBAN]

Tull /tʌl/, *n.* **Jethro** /'dʒεθroʊ/, 1674–1741, English agriculturist who developed the seed drill.

tulle /tjul/, *n.* thin silk or nylon net, used in hat-making, dressmaking, etc. [F *Tulle* town in central France]

tumble /'tʌmbəl/, *v.*, **-bled, -bling,** *n.* ◇*v.i.* **1.** to roll or fall over or down as by losing one's footing, etc.: *to tumble down the stairs.* **2.** to fall rapidly, as stock market prices. **3.** to perform leaps, springs, somersaults, etc., for sport, etc. **4.** to roll or toss about. **5.** to stumble or fall (usu. fol. by *over*). ◇*v.t.* **6.** to send falling or rolling; throw over or down. **7.** to put in disorder by or as if by tossing about. ◇*n.* **8.** a fall. **9.** a disordered heap. [OE *tumbian* dance)]

tumbler /'tʌmblə/, *n.* a drinking glass without handle or stem.

tumble-weed, *n.* any of various plants whose upper part comes away from its roots in autumn and is blown about by the wind.

tumbrel /'tʌmbrəl/, *n.* a cart used during the French Revolution to carry victims to the guillotine. [ME, from ML, from OLG: fall]

tumescent /tjuˈmεsənt/, *adj.* swelling; slightly tumid. [L: beginning to swell] —**tumescence,** *n.*

tumid /'tjumɪd/, *adj.* **1.** swollen, as a part of the body. **2.** (of language) pompous; turgid. ◇*n.* **3.** [L: swollen] —**tumidity,** *n.*

tumor or **tumour** /'tjumə/, *n. Med.* an abnormal swelling consisting of tissue which grows within the body, oft. spreading widely at the expense of other healthy tissue. See **benign, malignant.** [L: swollen state] —**tumorous,** *adj.*

tumult /'tjumʌlt/, *n.* **1.** the noisy disturbance of a huge crowd; uproar. **2.** a popular uprising; commotion, or violent disorder. **3.** mental or emotional disturbance. [ME, from L] —**tumultuous,** *adj.*

Tumut /'tjumət/, *n.* a town and shire in south-western NSW; timber-milling and a key point in the Snowy Mountains Hydro-Electric Scheme. Pop. 6099 (1986).

tuna /'tjunə/, *n.* a type of large, fast-swimming sea food fish with red flesh related to the mackerel, found in warmer waters. Also, **tunny.** [Amer Sp]

Tuncurry /tʌnˈkɑri/, *n.* a town on the central coast of NSW, at the entrance to Wallis Lake. Pop. (with Forster) 11 239 (1986). [Aboriginal: plenty fish]

tundra /'tʌndrə/, *n.* one of the vast, nearly level, treeless plains of the arctic regions of Europe, Asia, and North America. [Russ: marshy plain]

tune /tjun/, *n., v.*, **tuned, tuning.** ◇*n.* **1.** a succession of musical sounds forming an air or melody. **2.** the condition of being in the proper pitch: *to be in tune.* **3.** agreement, as of radio instruments or circuits with respect to frequency. **4.** agreement; accord. **5. call the tune,** to be in a position to give orders; command; control. **6. change one's tune,** to change one's opinions, etc. **7. to the tune of,** to the amount of. ◇*v.t.* **8.** to set (a musical instrument) to a correct or given musical pitch (oft. fol. by *up*). **9.** to bring into harmony. **10.** to put (an engine, machine, etc.) into good running order (oft. fol. by *up*). **11.** *Radio.* to adjust (a receiving apparatus) so as to make it able to receive the signals of a sending station. **12.** to put into proper or particular condition, mood, etc. ◇*v.i.* **13.** to put a musical instrument, etc., in tune (oft. fol. by *up*). **14.** to sound or be in harmony: *This guitar does not tune easily.* [ME; unexplained var. of TONE] —**tunable, tuneful,** *adj.*

tuner /'tjunə/, *n.* that part of a radio receiver which picks up any chosen radio frequency and feeds it into an amplifier.

tungoo /'tʌŋgu/, *n.* See **rat-kangaroo.** [Aboriginal]

tungsten /'tʌŋstən/, *n.* a rare, bright grey metallic element having a high melting point (3410° C), used to make high-speed, steel cutting tools, electric-lamp filaments, etc. *Symbol:* W (for *wolframium*); *at. no.:* 74; *at. wt:* 183.85. [Swed: heavy stone]

tunic /'tjunɪk/, *n.* **1.** a coat worn as part of military or other uniform. **2.** a loose, sleeveless dress, esp. as worn by girls as part of a school uniform or for gymnastics, dancing etc. **3.** a garment like a shirt or gown, worn by both sexes among the ancient Greeks and Romans. [OE *tunice*, from L]

tuning fork /'tjunɪŋ fɔk/, *n.* a small steel instrument consisting of two prongs on a stem, designed to produce, when struck, a pure

tuning fork musical note of a particular pitch, and so acting as a standard for tuning musical instruments, etc.

Tunisia /tjuˈnɪsɪə/, *n.* a republic in northern Africa on the Mediterranean Sea, bordered by Algeria and Libya. Pop. 7 636 000 (1987); 154 530 km². *Languages:* Arabic, also French and Berber. *Currency:* dinar. *Cap.:* Tunis. — **Tunisian,** *n., adj.*

tunnel /ˈtʌnəl/, *n., v.,* **-nelled, -nelling.** ◇*n.* **1.** an underground passage. **2.** a passageway, as for trains, motor vehicles, etc., through or under a mountain, town, harbor, etc. **3.** a passage made by an animal; burrow. ◇*v.t.* **4.** to make or form as or like a tunnel: *to tunnel a passage under a river.* ◇*v.i.* **5.** to make a tunnel: *to tunnel through the Snowy Mountains.* [late ME]

tunny /ˈtʌni/, *n., pl.* **-nies,** (*esp. collectively*) **-ny. 1.** a marine food fish of the mackerel family, found in warmer parts of the Atlantic and Pacific oceans, sometimes reaching a weight of 350 kg or more. **2.** → **tuna.** [F, from Pr, from L, from Gk]

tup /tʌp/, *n.* a male sheep; ram.

tupong /ˈtupɒŋ/, *n.* → **congolli.** [Aboriginal]

turban /ˈtɜbən/, *n.* **1.** a headdress of Muslim origin worn by men of northern Africa and southern Asia, consisting of a long piece of silk, linen, cotton, etc., and wound round the head in folds. **2.** any headdress looking like this. [earlier *turband,* from Turk *tülbend,* from Ar *dulband,* from Pers, Hind]

turbid /ˈtɜbəd/, *adj.* **1.** (of liquids) muddy, with stirred-up particles. **2.** not clear; thick, as smoke or clouds; dense. **3.** disturbed; confused; muddled. [L *turbidus* disturbed]

turbine /ˈtɜbaɪn/, *n.* any of a class of hydraulic motors in which a vaned wheel is made to revolve by the pressure of liquid, steam, air or gas. [F, from L: anything that spins]

turbo- /ˈtɜboʊ-/, *adj.* a prefix indicating: **1.** driven by a turbine. **2.** of or relating to a turbine.

turbojet /ˈtɜboʊdʒɛt/, *n.* **1.** an aircraft engine where air is compressed then forced into a combustion chamber and burnt with fuel, the expanding hot gases providing the force for driving the turbine and compressor. **2.** any vehicle, usu. an aircraft, driven by such an engine.

turboprop /ˈtɜboʊprɒp/, *n.* **1.** a gas-turbine engine connected to a propeller forming the powering unit of an aircraft. **2.** an aeroplane driven by one or more such units.

turbot /ˈtɜbət/, *n., pl.* **-bots** (*esp. collectively*) **-bot.** a European flatfish with a diamond-shaped body. [ME, from MD; orig. uncert.]

turbulence /ˈtɜbjələns/, *n.* **1.** a turbulent state. **2.** random secondary motion due to eddies within a moving fluid. **3.** irregular motion of the atmosphere, as shown by gusts and lulls in the wind. Also, **turbulency.** — **turbulent,** *adj.*

tureen /təˈrin, tju-/, *n.* a large deep dish with a cover, for holding soup, etc., at the table. [earlier *terrine,* from F: earthenware dish, from L: earth]

turf /tɜf/, *n., pl.* **turfs, turves** /tɜvz/, *v.* ◇*n.* **1.** a covering or surface of grass, etc., with its matted roots. **2.** a piece of this; a sod. **3.** a block or piece of peat dug for fuel. **4.** peat as a substance for fuel. **5. the turf, a.** a grassy course or other track over which horseraces are run. **b.** the practice of racing horses. ◇*v.t.* **6.** to cover with turf or peat. ◇*v.* **7. turf out,** *Colloq.* to throw out; get rid of. [OE]

turgid /ˈtɜdʒəd/, *adj.* **1.** high-sounding, as language, style, etc.; pompous. **2.** swollen; distended; tumid. [L] — **turgidity, turgidness,** *n.*

turgor /ˈtɜgə/, *n.* **1.** the condition of being swelled or filled out. **2.** *Bot.* the normal rigidity of plant cells, due to internal cell pressure. [L: swell]

Turin /tjuˈrɪn/, *n.* a city in north-western Italy, on the river Po; capital of the Kingdom of Italy 1860–65. Pop. 1 030 011 (1986).

turinga /təˈrɪŋə/, *n.* → **churinga.**

turkey /ˈtɜki/, *n., pl.* **-keys,** (*esp. collectively for def. 1*) **-key. 1.** a large domesticated fowl, originally American. **2.** the flesh of this bird, used as food. **3. talk turkey,** *Colloq.* to talk seriously; talk business.

Turkey /ˈtɜki/, *n.* a republic mostly in western Asia with a European part separated by the Bosporus Straits, the Asian part bordered by Armenia, Georgia, Iran, Iraq and Syria, the European part by Greece and Bulgaria; centre of the Turkish (Ottoman) Empire before its dissolution after World War I; a republic since 1923. Pop. 52 845 000 (1987); 779 452 km². *Languages:* Turkish, also Kurdish. *Currency:* lira. *Cap.:* Ankara.

turkey's-nest tank, *n.* a tank (def. 2) built on flat country with walls above ground level and filled with water, usu. from a bore or nearby creek. Also, **turkey's-nest dam.**

Turkish bath /ˌtɜkɪʃ ˈbɑθ/, *n.* a public bath in which, after perspiring heavily in a heated room, the body is washed, massaged, etc.

Turkish delight, *n.* a fragrant jelly-like sweet cut into cubes and covered with icing sugar. Also, **Grecian delight.**

Turkmenia /tɜkˈminiə/, *n.* a republic in western Asia on the Caspian Sea and bordered by Iran and Afghanistan; a member of the CIS; a constituent republic of the Soviet Union 1924–91, known as the **Turkmen Soviet Socialist Republic.** Pop. 3 534 000 (1989 est.); 488 100 km². *Language:* Turkmen. *Cap.:* Ashkhabad. Also, **Turkmenistan, Turkomen.** — **Turkmen,** *n., adj.*

turmeric /ˈtɜmərɪk/, *n.* **1.** the strongly smelling, root-like underground stem of an East Indian plant. **2.** a yellow powder prepared from it, used as a seasoning, a dye, in medicine, etc. [ML: deserving earth]

turmoil /ˈtɜmɔɪl/, *n.* a condition of uproar or disquiet; tumult; agitation; commotion; disturbance. [apparently from TURN + Brit. d. *moil* confusion]

turn /tɜn/, *v.t.* **1.** to cause to move round about a centre; rotate: *to turn a wheel.* **2.** to cause to move round or partly round, esp. for the purpose of opening, closing, tightening, etc.: *to turn a key.* **3.** to change the position or condition of; reverse; invert: *to turn a page; to turn the soil in ploughing.* **4.** to change the course of; divert; deflect. **5.** to change the nature, character, or appearance of. **6.** to change the color of (leaves, etc.). **7.** to cause to become sour, fermented, etc.: *Warm weather turns milk.* **8.** to cause (the stomach) to vomit food or anything swallowed. **9.** to put to some use or purpose: *to turn a thing to good use.* **10.** to go or pass round or to the other side of: *to turn a street corner.* **11.** to get beyond or pass (a certain age, time, amount, etc.): *He has just turned forty.* **12.** to direct, aim or set going towards or away from a particular person or thing, or in a particular direction: *to turn the ship towards the north.* **13.** to direct (the eyes, face, etc.) another way; avert. **14.** to bring or shape into a rounded or curved form in any way, as on a lathe. **15.** to form, shape or express gracefully: *to turn a sentence.* **16.** to cause to go; send; drive: *to turn someone from the door.* **17.** to curve, bend, or twist. **18.** to carry out (a somersault, etc.) by revolving, etc. **19.** to disturb the mental balance of, or make mad; distract; derange. ◇*v.i.* **20.** to move or revolve about a centre; rotate. **21.** to direct one's thought, attention, desire, etc., towards or away from something. **22.** to hinge or depend (usu. fol. by *on* or *upon*): *The question turns on this point.* **23.** to change or reverse the course, position, or face so as to go in a different or opposite direction: *to turn to the right.* **24.** to take a curved form; bend. **25.** to be affected with a feeling of sickness, as the stomach. **26.** to adopt a different religion, manner of life, etc. **27.** to change or alter, as in nature, character, or appearance. **28.** to become sour, fermented, etc., as milk, etc. **29.** (of leaves, etc.) to change color. **30.** to be changed, or transformed (fol. by *into* or *to*). ◇*v.* **31.** Some special uses are:

turn down, 1. to refuse or reject (a person, request, etc.). **2.** to lessen the strength of; moderate.

turn off, 1. to stop the flow of (water, etc.). **2.** to switch off (a radio, light, etc.). **3.** to awaken strong dislike in: *His bad manners turn me off.* **4.** to lose interest in or sympathy with; develop a dislike for: *I've turned off gardening.*
turn on, 1. to start the flow of: *turn on the water; to turn on the charm.* **2.** to switch on (a radio, light, etc.). **3.** *Colloq.* to excite or interest (a person): *That music really turns me on!*
turn out, 1. to put out (a light, etc.). **2.** to produce as the result of labor; manufacture; make. **3.** to drive out; expel; send away; dismiss; discharge. **4.** to clear or empty (a cupboard, pocket, drawer, etc.) of contents. **5.** to come to be; become ultimately: *the party turned out well.* **6.** *Colloq.* to come or gather together; muster; parade; assemble.
turn over, 1. to move or be moved from one side to another. **2.** (of an engine) to start. **3.** to hand over; transfer. **4.** *Comm.* to buy and then sell (goods, etc.).
turn up, 1. to fold (a garment or hem) esp. so as to shorten. **2.** to find; bring to light; uncover. **3.** to increase the strength of. **4.** to arrive; come.
◇*n.* **32.** a movement of rotation, whether total or partial: *a slight turn of the handle.* **33.** the act of changing position, esp. by a revolving movement: *a turn of the dial.* **34.** a time for action, duty or proceeding which comes in order to each of a number of people, etc.: *It's my turn to pay.* **35.** an act of changing or reversing the course: *to make a turn to the right.* **36.** a place where a road, river, etc., turns. **37.** an act of turning so as to face or go in a different direction. **38.** a change in nature, character, condition, situation, etc. **39.** a single round, usu. of a wound or coiled rope. **40.** a characteristic form or style (of language, etc.): *a strange turn of expression.* **41.** a short walk, ride, etc. **42.** a natural liking for; inclination; bent; aptitude. **43.** a spell or period of work or action. **44.** *Colloq.* a nervous shock, usu. from fright or astonishment. **45.** *Music.* a melodic ornament or grace, commonly consisting of one important note with two lesser notes, one above and the other below it. **46.** a performance of a song, etc., esp. in a music hall, cabaret, etc. **47.** Also, **turnout.** a party; social entertainment: *It was a great turn on Friday.* **48.** Some special uses are:

at every turn, constantly; in every case.
good / bad turn, an act of service / disservice to someone.
in turn, in due order of succession.
out of turn, 1. out of proper order. **2.** at the wrong time; at an unsuitable moment; indiscreetly; tactlessly.
take turns, to do in order or one after another; alternate.
to a turn, to just the proper degree; perfectly.
turn and turn about, by turns; alternately. [ME; OE *turnian,* from L: *turn* (in a lathe)] —**turner,** *n.*

turncoat /ˈtɜnkoʊt/, *n.* someone who changes their party or principles; renegade.

Turner /ˈtɜnə/, *n.* **1. Ethel Sibyl** (née *Burwell*), 1872–1958, Australian novelist and children's writer, born in England; noted for *Seven Little Australians* (1894). **2. Joseph Mallord William** /ˈmælǝd/, 1775–1851, English landscape painter.

turnip /ˈtɜnəp/, *n.* a plant with a thick, fleshy, edible root, such as the common **white turnip,** or the **swedish turnip** or swede. [earlier *turnepe*]

turnkey /ˈtɜnˌki/, *n., pl.* **-keys.** someone who has charge of the keys of a prison; jailer.

turnout /ˈtɜnaʊt/, *n.* **1.** a body of people who come to a meeting, show, concert, etc. **2.** a quantity produced; output. **3.** the act of turning out. **4.** the manner or style in which a person or thing is dressed, equipped, etc. **5.** an outfit. **6.** *Colloq.* a party, show, entertainment, etc.

turnover /ˈtɜnoʊvə/, *n.* **1.** the act or result of turning over; upset. **2.** the total value of worker replacements in a given period in a given business or industry. **3.** the number of times that capital is invested and reinvested in a line of goods during a particular period of

turnover

time. **4.** the total amount of business done in a given time. **5.** the rate at which items are sold or stock used up and replaced. **6.** a small pastry made by putting fruit, preserves, or some other filling on one half of a circular piece of pastry, folding the other half over, and then baking it.

turnpike /'tɜnpaɪk/, *n. Hist.* **1.** a barrier set across a road to stop passage until toll was paid; tollgate. **2.** a road on which a turnpike operated. **3.** *US.* an expressway.

turnstile /'tɜnstaɪl/, *n.* a structure usu. consisting of four arms revolving horizontally on top of a post, and set in a gateway or opening, to allow the passage of people one at a time.

turntable /'tɜnteɪbəl/, *n.* **1.** the turning disc on which the record in a gramophone rests. **2.** *Railways.* a revolving, track-bearing platform pivoted in the centre, used for turning round engines and other rolling stock.

turpentine /'tɜpəntaɪn/, *n.* **1.** any of various natural mixtures extracted from coniferous trees, yielding an oil which evaporates quickly, and a resin. **2.** a tall, rough-barked tree, common in eastern Australia. [ME, from L, from Gk]

Turpin /'tɜpən/, *n.* **Dick**, 1706-39, English highwayman.

turpitude /'tɜpətʃud/, *n.* the condition of being wicked; depravity. [L *turpitūdo* baseness]

turquoise /'tɜkwɔɪz/, *n.* **1.** a sky blue or greenish blue mineral, mainly aluminium phosphate, much used in jewellery. **2.** Also, **turquoise blue**. a greenish blue or bluish green color. [F: Turkish (stone)]

turret /'tʌrət/, *n.* **1.** a small tower at an angle of a building, frequently beginning some distance above the ground. **2.** Also, **turret-head**. a pivoted attachment on a lathe, etc., for holding a number of tools, each of which can be presented to the work in rapid succession by a simple turning movement. [ME, from OF: TOWER] **–turreted**, *adj.*

turtle /'tɜtl/, *n.* **1.** any of various reptiles having the body completely enclosed in a shell from which the head, tail, and four legs protrude. **2.** a type of sea-living turtle, different from freshwater and land-dwelling tortoises in having flippers rather than toed feet. **3. turn turtle**, to tip over; capsize. [Sp, from LL: twisted]

turtledove /'tɜtldʌv/, *n.* **1.** a small, slender dove noted for devotion to its mate. **2.** a type of turtledove, **spotted turtledove**, native to Asia and introduced into Australia, pale brown underneath and dark brown above, with a black neck marked with white spots.

turtleneck /'tɜtlnɛk/, *n., adj.* (of a sweater, etc.) having a high, close-fitting neck.

Tuscany /'tʌskəni/, *n.* a region in western central Italy; formerly a grand duchy. Pop. 3 576 508 (1987); 22 996 km². *Cap.:* Florence. Italian, **Toscana**.

tusk /tʌsk/, *n.* **1.** (in certain animals) a tooth developed to great length, usu. as one of a pair, such as in the elephant, walrus, wild boar, etc.

1108

tuxedo

2. a projecting part looking like the tusk of an animal. ◇*v.t., v.i.* **3.** to dig, tear, or rip with the tusks. [var. of ME and OE *tux*] **–tusked**, *adj.*

Tussaud /ty'sou/, *n.* **Marie**, 1760-1850, Swiss modeller in wax; founder of **Madame Tussaud's** waxworks exhibition in London.

tussle /'tʌsəl/, *v.*, **-sled, -sling**, *n.* ◇*v.i.* **1.** to struggle or fight roughly; wrestle; scuffle. ◇*n.* **2.** a rough struggle, usu. in fighting or wrestling; scuffle. **3.** any lively disagreement or contest. [var. of TOUSLE]

tussock /'tʌsək/, *n.* **1.** a tuft or clump of growing grass, etc. **2.** any of a number of types of grass, rush or grass-like plants, often growing in wet places. **–tussocky**, *adj.*

tut /tʌt/; *or clicked* /t/, *interj.* **1.** (used as an exclamation expressing impatience, etc.). ◇*n.* **2.** an exclamation of 'tut'. Also, **tut-tut**.

Tutankhamen /tutən'kamən/, *n.* 14th century BC, a king of Egypt of the 18th dynasty; his rich tomb discovered in 1922 near Luxor.

tutelage /'tjutəlɪdʒ/, *n.* **1.** the office or function of a guardian; guardianship. **2.** instruction. **3.** the condition of being under a guardian or tutor. [L: watching] **–tutelary**, *adj.*

tutor /'tjutə/, *n.* **1.** someone employed to instruct another in some branch or branches of learning, esp. a private instructor. **2.** a university teacher who oversees the studies of certain undergraduates. **3.** (in some universities and colleges) a teacher of academic rank lower than lecturer. ◇*v.t.* **4.** to act as a tutor to; teach or instruct, esp. privately. ◇*v.i.* **5.** to act as a tutor or private instructor. [ME, from L: protector]

tutorial /tju'tɔriəl/, *adj.* **1.** relating to or exercised by a tutor: *tutorial functions or authority.* ◇*n.* **2.** a period of instruction given by a university tutor to a single student or a small group of students.

tutti /'tuti/, *adj., n., pl.* **-tis.** *Music.* ◇*adj.* **1.** including all the voices or instruments together (used as a direction). **2.** intended for or performed by all (or most of) the voices or instruments together, (opposed to *solo*). ◇*n.* **3.** a tutti passage or movement. [It]

tutu /'tutu, 'tjutju/, *n.* a short, full, ballet skirt, usu. made of several layers of net-like material. [F]

Tutu /'tutu/, *n.* **Desmond Mpilo** /əm'pilou/, born 1931, South African Anglican bishop; noted anti-apartheid activist; Nobel Peace Prize, 1985.

Tuvalu /tuvə'lu/, *n.* a parliamentary state in the south-western Pacific Ocean, consisting of nine small atolls; part of the former British colony of the Gilbert and Ellice Islands. Pop. 8200 (1987); 26 km². *Languages:* Tuvaluan and English. *Currency:* Australian dollar and Tuvaluan dollar. *Cap.:* Funafuti. Formerly, **Ellice Islands**, **Lagoon Islands**. **–Tuvaluan**, *n., adj.*

tuxedo /tʌk'sidou/, *n., pl.* **-dos.** a dinner jacket. [short for *Tuxedo coat*, named after country club at *Tuxedo* Park, in New York State, US]

TV /ti'vi/, *n.* →**television.** [abbrev.]

twaddle /'twɒdl/, *n., v.,* **-dled, -dling.** ◇*n.* **1.** unimportant, feeble, silly or tiring talk or writing. ◇*v.i.* **2.** to talk in a trivial, feeble, silly or tiring manner; prate. [var. of *twattle,* b. TWIDDLE and TATTLE]

twain /twein/, *adj., n. Archaic.* two. [OE *twēgen*]

Twain /twein/, *n.* **Mark** (*Samuel Langhorne Clemens*), 1835–1910, US author and humorist; best known for *The Adventures of Tom Sawyer* (1876) and *The Adventures of Huckleberry Finn* (1885).

twang /twæŋ/, *v.i.* **1.** to give out a sharp, ringing sound, such as that made by the string of a musical instrument when plucked. **2.** to have a sharp, nasal tone, as the human voice. ◇*v.t.* **3.** to cause to make a sharp, ringing sound, like the string of a musical instrument. **4.** to speak with a sharp, nasal tone. ◇*n.* **5.** a sharp, ringing sound produced by plucking or suddenly releasing a tense string. **6.** a sound like this. **7.** a sharp, nasal tone, as of the human voice. [imitative] –**twangy,** *adj.*

'twas /twɒz; *unstressed* /twəz/, contraction of *it was.*

tweak /twik/, *v.t.* **1.** to seize and pull with a sharp jerk and twist: *to tweak someone's ear.* ◇*n.* **2.** an act of tweaking; a sharp pull and twist. [OE *twician*] –**tweaky,** *adj.*

twee /twi/, *adj. Colloq.* too delicate; affected; precious; excessively dainty.

tweed /twid/, *n.* (a garment made of) a coarse wool cloth in a variety of weaves and colors.

Tweed Heads, *n.* a town in north-eastern NSW at the mouth of the Tweed River; fishing and tourism. Pop. 22 280 (1986).

Tweedledum and Tweedledee, *n.pl.* any two persons, things, etc., nominally different but practically the same. [humorous imitative coinage, apparently first applied as nicknames to Handel and Bononcini, with reference to their musical rivalry]

'tween /twin/, *prep. Poetic.* between.

tweet /twit/, *n.* the weak chirp of a young or small bird. [imitative]

tweeter /'twitə/, *n.* a small loudspeaker designed for the reproduction of high-frequency sounds.

tweezers /'twizəz/, *n.pl.* small pincers or nippers for plucking out hairs, taking up small objects, etc.

twelfth /twelfθ/, *adj.* **1.** next after the eleventh. **2.** being one of twelve equal parts. ◇*n.* **3.** a twelfth part, esp. of one ($\frac{1}{12}$). **4.** the twelfth one of a series.

Twelfth day, *n.* the twelfth day after Christmas, 6 January, on which the festival of the Epiphany is celebrated, formerly observed as the last day of the Christmas festivities.

Twelfth night, *n.* **1.** the evening before Twelfth day, formerly observed with various festivities. **2.** the evening of Twelfth day itself.

twelve /twelv/, *n.* **1.** a cardinal number, ten plus two (10 + 2). **2.** a symbol for this number, as 12 or XII. **3.** a set of this many people or things. **4. the Twelve,** the 12 apostles chosen by Christ. ◇*adj.* **5.** amounting to 12 in number. [ME; OE *twelf*]

twelve-string guitar, *n.* a guitar which has six pairs of strings, one member of the four lowest pairs being tuned at an octave above the other.

Twelve Tables, *n.pl.* **the,** the tablets on which were engraved short statements of Roman law most important in the affairs of daily life, drawn up in 451 and 450 BC.

twenty /'twenti/, *n., pl.* **-ties,** *adj.* ◇*n.* **1.** a cardinal number, ten times two (10 × 2). **2.** a symbol for this number, as 20 or XX. **3.** a set of this many people or things. **4.** (*pl.*) the numbers from 20 to 29 of a series, esp. with reference to the years of a person's age, or the years of a century. ◇*adj.* **5.** amounting to twenty in number. [ME; OE *twēntig*] –**twentieth,** *adj., n.*

twice /twais/, *adv.* **1.** two times, as in succession: *Write twice a week.* **2.** on two occasions; in two instances. **3.** in twofold quantity or degree; doubly: *twice as much.*

twiddle /'twidl/, *v.t.* **1.** to turn round and round, esp. with the fingers. ◇*v.* **2. twiddle one's thumbs** or **fingers, a.** to keep turning one's thumbs or fingers idly about each other. **b.** to do nothing; be idle. [b. TWITCH and FIDDLE] –**twiddler,** *n.*

twig[1] /twig/, *n.* **1.** a slender shoot of a tree or other plant. **2.** a small offshoot from a branch or stem. **3.** a small dry, woody piece fallen from a branch: *a fire of twigs.* [ME and OE *twigge*] –**twiggy,** *adj.*

twig[2] /twig/, *v.i., v.t.,* **twigged, twigging.** *Colloq.* to understand (something). [orig. uncert.]

twilight /'twailait/, *n.* **1.** the light from the sky when the sun is below the horizon, esp. in the evening. **2.** the time during which this light persists. **3.** the condition or period coming after full development, glory, etc.; decline. ◇*adj.* **4.** relating to or like twilight: *the twilight hour.* [ME]

twill /twil/, *n.* **1.** fabric woven so as to produce an effect of parallel diagonal lines. **2.** the characteristic weave or pattern of such fabrics. [OE *twili(c),* from L: having double thread] –**twilled,** *adj.*

'twill /twil/, a contraction of *it will.*

twin /twin/, *n., adj., v.,* **twinned, twinning.** ◇*n.* **1.** (*pl.*) two children or animals brought forth at a birth. **2.** one of two such children or animals. **3.** (*pl.*) either of two people or things closely related or closely looking like each other. ◇*adj.* **4.** being two, or one of two, children or animals born at the same birth: *twin sisters.* **5.** consisting of two similar parts or elements joined or connected:

a twin vase. ◇*v.t., v.i.* **6.** to pair or couple or be paired or coupled. [ME; OE (ge)*twinn*]

twine /twaɪn/, *n., v.*, **twined, twining.** ◇*n.* **1.** strong thread or string made up of two or more strands twisted together. ◇*v.t.* **2.** to twist together; intertwine. **3.** to twist (one strand, thread, or thing) with another. **4.** to enfold. ◇*v.i.* **5.** to become twined or twisted together, usu. two things, or one thing with another. **6.** to wind in a smoothly curving or winding course. [ME; OE *twin*] —**twiner,** *n.*

twinge /twɪndʒ/, *n.* a sudden, sharp pain (in the body or mind): *a twinge of rheumatism; twinge of remorse.* [OE *twengan* pinch]

twinkle /ˈtwɪŋkəl/, *v.*, **-kled, -kling,** *n.* ◇*v.i.* **1.** to shine with quick, flickering, gleams of light, as stars, distant lights, etc. **2.** (of the eyes) to be bright with amusement, pleasure, etc. **3.** to appear or move as if with little flashes of light. ◇*v.t.* **4.** to give out (light) in little gleams or flashes. ◇*n.* **5.** a sparkle. **6.** a twinkling brightness in the eyes. **7.** the time needed for a wink; twinkling. **8.** a wink of the eye. [ME; OE *twinclian*] —**twinkler,** *n.*

twinkling /ˈtwɪŋklɪŋ/, *n.* **1.** the act of shining with little gleams of light. **2.** the time needed for a wink; instant.

twin-set /ˈtwɪn-sɛt/, *n.* a cardigan and matching jumper, worn by women.

twirl /twɜl/, *v.t.* **1.** to cause to turn rapidly; spin; whirl; swing circularly. **2.** to wind aimlessly, usu. about something. ◇*v.i.* **3.** to spin rapidly; whirl; rotate. **4.** to turn quickly so as to face or point another way. ◇*n.* **5.** a twirling or a being twirled; spin; whirl; twist. **6.** something twirled; curl; convolution. [b. TWIST and WHIRL] —**twirler,** *n.*

twist /twɪst/, *v.t.* **1.** to combine, as two or more strands or threads, by winding together closely; intertwine. **2.** to form by or as if by winding threads together. **3.** to wind or twine (something) about a thing. **4.** to change in shape, usu. by turning the ends in opposite directions, so that the parts are placed in a spiral curve. **5.** to wring or squeeze out of shape or place; contort or distort. **6.** to turn sharply and put out of place; sprain: *When she fell she twisted her ankle.* **7.** to change the proper form or meaning; pervert. **8.** to cause to move with a turning movement, esp. a ball pitched in a curve. **9.** to turn in another direction. ◇*v.i.* **10.** to be or become twisted together or about something. **11.** to twist the body as if in pain; writhe; squirm. **12.** to take a spiral form or course; wind, curve, or bend. **13.** to turn or rotate, as on an axis; revolve, usu. about something. **14.** to turn so as to face in another direction. **15.** to change shape with a spiral or screwing movement of parts. **16.** to move forward with a turning movement, usu. of a ball pitched in a curve. **17.** to dance the twist. ◇*v.* **18. twist (someone's) arm,** *Colloq.* to persuade. ◇*n.* **19.** a curve, bend, or turn. **20.** a turning or rotating as on an axis; rotary motion; spin. **21.** anything formed by or as if by twisting or twining parts together. **22.** the act or manner of twisting strands together, as in thread, yarn, or rope. **23.** the act of twisting and pulling; wrench. **24.** a changing or differing of meaning. **25.** spiral nature, arrangement, or form. **26.** a peculiar tendency, etc., esp. in the mind or nature. **27.** a changing of the shape of anything by or as if by turning the ends in opposite directions. **28.** a stress causing this change. **29.** a sudden, unexpected change to the course of events, esp. in a play. **30.** a type of tobacco made in the form of a rope or thick cord. **31.** a lively dance performed by couples and marked by strongly rhythmic swings of the body and movements of the arms and legs in time to heavily accented music. [OE *-twist*]

twitch /twɪtʃ/, *v.t.* **1.** to give a short, sudden pull at; jerk. **2.** to pull or draw with a hasty pull. **3.** to move (a part of the body) with a sharp pull. **4.** to pinch and pull sharply; nip. ◇*v.i.* **5.** to move or be moved in a quick, twitchy way. **6.** to give a short, sudden pull; tug (fol. by *at*). ◇*n.* **7.** a short, sudden pull (of the body, etc.); jerk. **8. the twitches,** *Colloq.* a state of the nerves causing sudden tightening of the muscles. [ME *twicchen*] —**twitcher,** *n.* —**twitchy,** *adj.*

twitter /ˈtwɪtə/, *v.i.* **1.** to give out a series of small, trembling sounds, as a bird. **2.** to laugh in a light, uncontrolled manner; giggle. **3.** to tremble with excitement, etc.; be in a flutter. ◇*v.t.* **4.** to express, speak or make sounds by twittering. ◇*n.* **5.** the act or sound of twittering. **6.** a state of trembling or shaky excitement. [ME, G] —**twittery,** *adj.*

'twixt /twɪkst/, *prep. Archaic.* betwixt.

two /tu/, *n.* **1.** a cardinal number, one plus one (1 + 1). **2.** a symbol for this number, as 2 or II. **3.** a set of this many people or things. **4. put two and two together,** to draw an answer or judgment from certain facts, events, etc. ◇*adj.* **5.** amounting to two in number. [ME; OE *twā*]

two-dimensional /tu-daɪˈmɛnʃənəl, tu-də-/, *adj.* having two different planes of measurement, such as height and width.

two-faced /ˈtu-feɪst/, *adj.* dishonest; hypocritical; deceitful.

2, 4, 5-T, /tu fɔ faɪv ˈti/ *n.* a commonly used weed-killer.

twopence /ˈtʌpəns/, *n.* (formerly) a sum of money of the value of two pennies. Also, **tuppence.** —**twopenny,** *adj.*

twostep /ˈtustɛp/, *n.* a dance in duple time, marked by sliding steps.

two-time /ˈtu-taɪm/, *v.t., v.i.*, **-timed, -timing.** *Colloq.* to deceive or doublecross (a friend or lover) by having a similar relationship with another.

two-tooth /ˈtu-tuθ/, *n.* a sheep of either sex from about one year to one and a half years old, and showing two permanent cutting teeth.

'twould /twʊd/, a contraction of *it would.*

two-up /ˈtu-ʌp/, *n.* a gambling game in which two coins are spun in the air and bets are laid on whether they fall heads or tails.

-ty[1], a suffix of numerals marking multiples of ten, as *twenty*. [OE *-tig*]

-ty² , a suffix of nouns marking quality, condition, etc., as *unity, enmity*. [ME -*te(e)*, from OF, from L]

tycoon /taɪˈkuːn/, *n.* a business person having great wealth and power. [Jap, from Chinese]

Tyler /ˈtaɪlə/, *n.* **John**, 1790–1862, tenth president of the US, 1841–45.

tympanic membrane /tɪmˌpænɪk ˈmembreɪn/, *n.* a membrane separating the middle ear from the passage of the outer ear; eardrum.

tympanum /ˈtɪmpənəm/, *n., pl.* **-nums**, **-na** /-nə/. **1.** *Anat., Zool.* the middle ear. **2.** → **tympanic membrane. 3.** a drum or similar instrument. [L, from Gk: drum] —**tympanic**, *adj.*

type /taɪp/, *n., v.*, **typed, typing.** ◇*n.* **1.** a kind, class, or group as marked by a particular characteristic. **2.** a person or thing representing the characteristic qualities of a kind, class, or group; a representative specimen. **3.** the general form, style, or character marking a particular kind, class or group. **4.** *Biol.* **a.** the general form or plan of structure common to a group of animals, plants, etc. **b.** the genus or species which most nearly serves as an example of the main characteristics of a higher group and frequently gives the latter its name. See **genus** and **species**. **5.** a pattern or model from which something is made. **6.** *Print.* **a.** a rectangular piece or block, now usu. of metal, having on its upper surface a letter or character that stands out from its background. **b.** similar pieces or blocks grouped together. **c.** a similar piece or pieces in a typewriter, etc. **d.** a printed character or characters: *a headline in large type*. ◇*v.t.* **7.** to write (a letter, etc.) by means of a typewriter or keyboard. **8.** to represent by a symbol; symbolise. ◇*v.i.* **9.** to write by means of a typewriter or keyboard. [late ME, from L, from Gk: blow, impression]

-type, a word part representing **type**, as in *prototype*, esp. used of photographic processes.

typecast /ˈtaɪpkɑːst/, *v.t.*, **-cast, -casting.** to cast (an actor, etc.) continually in the same kind of part.

typeface /ˈtaɪpfeɪs/, *n.* → **face** (def. 12b).

typescript /ˈtaɪpskrɪpt/, *n.* a typewritten copy of a piece of formal or legal writing.

typeset /ˈtaɪpsɛt/, *v.t.*, **-set, -setting.** *Print.* to set type (def. 6). —**typesetter**, *n.*

typewriter /ˈtaɪpraɪtə/, *n.* a machine with keys which are struck to produce letters and characters on paper.

typhoid fever /ˌtaɪfɔɪd ˈfiːvə/, *n.* an infectious disease, often resulting in death, caused by the **typhoid bacillus** which infects food or drink. Also, **typhoid**.

typhoon /taɪˈfuːn/, *n.* **1.** a tropical cyclone or hurricane esp. in the western Pacific area and the China seas. **2.** a violent storm of India. [Chinese: great wind]

typhus /ˈtaɪfəs/, *n.* an acute infectious disease marked by extreme exhaustion, severe nervous symptoms, and an outbreak of reddish spots on the body, now regarded as due to a particular micro-organism carried by lice and fleas. Also, **typhus fever**. [NL, from Gk: vapor] —**typhous**, *adj.*

typical /ˈtɪpɪkəl/, *adj.* **1.** relating to, of the nature of, or serving as a type or sign; symbolic. **2.** agreeing with the type. **3.** *Biol.* showing most nearly the main elements of a higher group in natural history, and forming the type: *the typical genus of a family*. **4.** relating or belonging to a representative example; characteristic.

typify /ˈtɪpɪfaɪ/, *v.t.*, **-fied, -fying. 1.** to serve as the typical example of. **2.** to serve as a sign of; symbolise; prefigure. **3.** to represent by a type, etc. [L]

typist /ˈtaɪpɪst/, *n.* someone who operates a typewriter.

typography /taɪˈpɒɡrəfi/, *n.* **1.** the art or method of printing with type. **2.** the work of setting and arranging type and of printing from it. **3.** the general character or appearance of printed matter. [NL, from Gk] —**typographical**, *adj.*

tyrannical /təˈrænɪkəl, taɪ-/, *adj.* severely cruel or harsh; arbitrary; despotic; oppressive. Also, **tyrannic**. [L, from Gk]

tyrannise *or* **tyrannize** /ˈtɪrənaɪz/, *v.*, **-nised, -nising.** ◇*v.i.* **1.** to exercise power cruelly or severely. **2.** to rule or govern as a tyrant. ◇*v.t.* **3.** to act as a tyrant towards.

tyrannosaurus /təˌrænəˈsɔːrəs/, *n.* a great meat-eating dinosaur of the later Cretaceous period in North America, which walked upright on its powerful back limbs. Also, **tyrannosaur**.

tyranny /ˈtɪrəni/, *n., pl.* **-nies. 1.** the complete or unchecked exercise of power; despotic abuse of authority. **2.** the government or rule of a tyrant or ruler with total power. **3.** a state ruled by a tyrant or ruler holding total power. **4.** unjustly severe government. **5.** undue severity or cruelty. **6.** a tyrannical act or undertaking. [ME, from ML: TYRANT]

tyrant /ˈtaɪrənt/, *n.* **1.** a ruler who uses power unjustly or oppressively. **2.** a ruler who has seized complete power by force, as in ancient Greece. [ME, from OF, from L, from Gk]

tyre /taɪə/, *n.* a band of metal or rubber fitted round the rim of a wheel as a running surface. [late ME]

Tyre /taɪə/, *n.* an ancient seaport of Phoenicia; one of the great cities of antiquity, famous for its navigators and traders.

tyro /ˈtaɪroʊ/, *n., pl.* **-ros.** a beginner. [L]

Tyrol /ˈtɪrəl, tɪˈroʊl/, *n.* an alpine region in western Austria and northern Italy; a former Austrian crownland.

Tyrone /taɪˈroʊn/, *n.* a former county in western Northern Ireland.

Tyrrell /ˈtɪrəl/, *n.* **Lake**, a salt lake in north-western Vic; saltworks. 18 000 ha.

tzar /zɑː/, *n.* → **tsar**.

tzetze fly, *n.* → **tsetse fly**.

Uu

U, u, *n., pl.* **U's** or **Us, u's** or **us.** the 21st letter of the English alphabet.

u, *Phys. Symbol.* atomic mass unit.

U[1], *Chem. Symbol.* uranium.

U[2] /ju/, *adj. Colloq.* suitable for or characteristic of the upper class. See **non-U**. [initial of UPPER (CLASS)]

U[3] /u, ju/, *n.* a Burmese title of respect for a man (used before the proper name). [Burm: uncle]

UAE /ju eɪ 'i/, *n.* → **United Arab Emirates.** [abbrev.]

Ubangi /juˈbæŋgi/, *n.* a river forming a part of the boundary between Zaire, the Central African Republic, and Congo, flowing into the river Congo. About 1126 km (with the Vele 2253 km). Also, **Mobangi, Mubangi**; French, **Oubangui.**

ubiquity /juˈbɪkwəti/, *n.* the state of being or ability to be everywhere at the same time; omnipresence. [NL, from L: everywhere] – **ubiquitous,** *adj.*

U-boat /ˈju-boʊt/, *n.* a German submarine. [from G: undersea boat]

Uccello /uˈtʃɛloʊ/, *n.* **Paolo** /ˈpaoʊloʊ/, 1396/7–1475, Italian painter; esp. noted for his use of perspective.

UDA /ju di eɪ/, *n.* → **Ulster Defence Association.** [abbrev.]

udder /ˈʌdə/, *n.* a gland for the production of milk, esp. when hanging down and with more than one teat, as in cows. [OE *ūder*]

UFO /ju ɛf 'oʊ, 'jufoʊ/, *n.* an unidentified flying object. – **ufologist,** *n.* [abbrev.]

Uganda /juˈgændə/, *n.* a republic in eastern Africa, bordered by Sudan, Zaire, Kenya, Rwanda, Tanzania and Lake Victoria. Pop. 15 514 000 (1987); 241 139 km^2. *Languages:* English, Swahili, Luo and Luganda. *Currency:* Uganda shilling. *Cap.:* Kampala. – **Ugandan,** *n., adj.*

ugh /ʌg, əg, ʌ/, *interj.* (an exclamation expressing strong or sickening dislike, shock, etc.)

ugh boot, *n. Trademark.* a sheepskin boot with the fleece inside.

ugly /ˈʌgli/, *adj.,* **-lier, -liest. 1.** nasty or displeasing in appearance; offensive to the sense of beauty: *an ugly building.* **2.** morally displeasing: *an ugly sin.* **3.** of a troublesome nature; threatening disadvantage or danger: *ugly symptoms.* **4.** unpleasantly or dangerously rough: *ugly weather.* **5.** ill-natured; quarrelsome; vicious: *an ugly disposition.* [ME, from Scand] – **ugliness,** *n.*

ugly duckling, *n.* an unattractive or unpromising child who becomes a beautiful or much admired adult. [name of a story by Hans Christian Andersen, 1805–1875, Danish author]

u.h.f. /ju eɪtʃ 'ɛf/, *Abbrev.* ultra high frequency. Also, **UHF**

Ujung Pandang /ˈudʒʊŋ pænˈdæŋ/, *n.* a seaport in Indonesia, in south-western Sulawesi. Pop. 888 000 (1983 est.). Formerly, **Macassar, Makasar, Makassar.**

UK /ju keɪ/, *n.* → **United Kingdom.** [abbrev.]

Ukraine /juˈkreɪn/, *n.* a republic in eastern Europe on the northern shores of the Black and Azov seas; the second most populous member of the CIS; a constituent republic of the Soviet Union 1922–91, known as the **Ukrainian Soviet Socialist Republic.** Pop. 51 707 000 (1989 est.); 603 700 km^2. *Language:* Ukrainian. *Cap.:* Kiev. Also, **the Ukraine.** – **Ukrainian,** *n., adj.*

ukulele /jukəˈleɪli/, *n.* a small guitar-like four-stringed musical instrument. Also, **ukelele.** [Hawaiian: lit., flea]

ulcer /ˈʌlsə/, *n. Med.* a sore open either to the surface of the body or to a natural cavity, and accompanied by the breaking down of tissue and formation of pus, etc. [ME, from L] – **ulcerous,** *adj.*

ulcerate /ˈʌlsəreɪt/, *v.t., v.i.,* **-rated, -rating.** to affect or be affected with an ulcer; make or become ulcerous. [ME, from L] – **ulceration,** *n.*

-ule, a suffix of nouns, indicating smallness, as in *globule.* [L]

-ulent, an adjective suffix meaning 'abounding in', as in *fraudulent.* [L: full of]

Ulladulla /ʌləˈdʌlə/, *n.* a town on the south coast of NSW; fishing and tourism. Pop. 7408 (1986). [Aboriginal: safe harbor]

Ulm /ʌlm/, *n.* **Charles Thomas Philippe,** 1898–1934, Australian pioneer aviator and administrator; record-breaking flights with Charles Kingsford-Smith.

ulna /ˈʌlnə/, *n., pl.* **-nae** /-ni/, **-nas. 1.** *Anat.* that one of the two bones of the forearm which is on the side opposite to the thumb. **2.** a similar bone in the forelimb of other vertebrates (animals with backbones). [NL, from L: elbow, arm] – **ulnar,** *adj.*

-ulose, a variant of **-ulous** in scientific terms. [L *-ulōsus*]

-ulous, a suffix forming adjectives meaning 'tending to', as in *credulous, populous.* [L *-ulosus* or *-ulus*]

Ulster /ˈʌlstə/, *n.* **1.** an ancient province in Ireland now comprising Northern Ireland and part of the Republic of Ireland. **2.** a province in the north of the Republic of Ireland, comprising three counties: Cavan, Donegal, and Monaghan. Pop. 230 159 (1981); 8013 km^2. **3.** → **Northern Ireland.** Irish, **Uladh.**

Ulster Defence Association, *n.* (in Northern Ireland) a Protestant paramilitary group. Also, **UDA**

ult., *Abbrev.* **1.** ultimate(ly). **2.** Also, **ulto** ultimo.

ulterior /ʌl'tɪərɪə/, *adj.* **1.** being beyond what is seen or declared openly; intentionally kept concealed: *ulterior motives.* **2.** being or placed beyond, or on the farther side: *ulterior regions.* [L: farther]

ultimate /'ʌltəmət/, *adj.* **1.** coming at the end, as of a course of action, etc.; final; decisive: *his ultimate goal; her ultimate lot in life.* **2.** beyond which it is impossible to proceed; fundamental; elemental: *ultimate principles.* **3.** impossible to go beyond or override: *ultimate weapon.* **4.** last, as in a series. ◇*n.* **5.** the final point or result. **6.** a basic fact or principle. **7. the ultimate,** *Colloq.* the most successful, pleasing, handsome, etc. [LL: ended, from L: last]

ultima Thule /ˌʌltɪmə 'θjul/, *n.* **1.** the furthest limit or point possible. **2.** the furthest north. Also, **Thule.** [L: furthest Thule (supposedly the northernmost point in the world)]

ultimatum /ˌʌltə'meɪtəm/, *n., pl.* **-tums, -ta** /-tə/. a final proposal or statement of conditions. [NL: ULTIMATE]

ultimo /'ʌltəmoʊ/, *adv.* in or of the month coming before the present: *on the 12th ultimo.* *Abbrev.*: ult., ulto See **proximo.** [from L: in the last month]

ultra /'ʌltrə/, *adj.* going beyond what is usual or ordinary; excessive; extreme.

ultra-, a prefix meaning: **1.** beyond (in space or time) as in *ultrasound.* **2.** more than usually; excessively. [L, combining form of *ultrā*, adv., prep., beyond]

ultrabasic rock /ˌʌltrəˌbeɪsɪk 'rɒk/, *n.* rock which contains less silica than basic rock; rock containing less than 45 per cent of silica.

ultra high frequency, *n.* any frequency between 300 and 3000 megahertz. *Abbrev.*: u.h.f.

ultramarine /ˌʌltrəmə'rin/, *adj.* **1.** of a deep blue color. ◇*n.* **2.** blue coloring matter formerly consisting of powdered lapis lazuli. **3.** a deep blue color. [ML]

ultrasound /'ʌltrəsaʊnd/, *n.* pressure waves like soundwaves but whose frequencies, greater than 20 000 hertz, cannot be heard, used esp. in cleaning metallic parts, medical diagnosis and therapy, etc. **-ultrasonic,** *adj.*

ultraviolet /ˌʌltrə'vaɪələt, -'vaɪlət/, *adj.* beyond the violet, as the rays of the spectrum lying outside the violet end which cannot be seen with the eye.

ululate /'juljəleɪt/, *v.i.*, **-lated, -lating. 1.** (of a dog, wolf, etc.) to howl. **2.** to make some similar sound; hoot; wail. **3.** to loudly express deep sorrow. [L]

Uluru /ʊlə'ru/, *n.* a giant sandstone monolith on a plain in the south-west of the NT; first recorded in 1872; an Aboriginal sacred site. 335 m high. Former name, **Ayers Rock.** [Aborig.]

-ulus, a suffix of nouns, indicating smallness, as in *homunculus, calculus.*

Ulverstone /'ʌlvəstən/, *n.* a town on the northern coast of Tas; a port and tourist resort. Pop. 10 055 (1986).

Ulysses /ju'lɪsiz, 'juləsiz/, *n.* the Latin name for **Odysseus.** **-Ulyssean,** *adj.*

umbel /'ʌmbəl/, *n.* an inflorescence (flowering arrangement) in which a number of pedicels (flower stalks), nearly equal in length, spread from a common centre. [L: sunshade, parasol] **-umbellate,** *adj.* **-umbelliferous,** *adj.*

umber /'ʌmbə/, *n.* **1.** earth consisting chiefly of a hydrated oxide of iron and some oxide of manganese, used in its natural state (**raw umber**) as a brown pigment, or after heating (**burnt umber**) as a reddish brown pigment. **2.** a dark dusky brown or dark reddish brown color. ◇*adj.* **3.** of such a color. [It: (earth of) shade]

umbilical cord /ʌm'bɪləkəl kɔd, ˌʌmbə'laɪkəl/, *n. Anat.* a cord connecting the embryo or foetus with the placenta of the mother, and transmitting nourishment from the mother.

umbilicus /ʌm'bɪlɪkəs, ˌʌmbə'laɪkəs/, *n., pl.* **-bilici** /-'bɪləsaɪ, -bə'laɪsaɪ/. **1.** *Anat.* the navel, or central depression in the surface of the abdomen, showing the point of attachment of the umbilical cord. **2.** *Bot, Zool, etc.* a navel-like formation, such as the hilum of a seed. [L] **-umbilical,** *adj.*

umbra /'ʌmbrə/, *n., pl.* **-brae** /-bri/. **1.** a shade; shadow. **2.** *Astron.* a complete shadow of a body that does not let light through. [L] **-umbral,** *adj.*

umbrage /'ʌmbrɪdʒ/, *n.* offence given or taken; resentful displeasure. [late ME, from F, from L: of or in the shade]

umbrella /ʌm'brelə/, *n.* **1.** a shade or screen used for protection from sunlight, rain, etc., in its modern form consisting of a light circular covering of silk, cotton, or other material on a folding frame of bars or strips of steel, cane, etc. **2.** a saucer- or bowl-shaped body of a jellyfish; bell. **3.** any general protection or cover. ◇*adj.* **4.** covering or intended to cover a group or class of things, events, etc.; all-embracing: *Winter sports is an umbrella term for skiing, skating, etc.* [It: shade, from L]

umbrella tree, *n.* an Australian tree with large shiny leaves and small raspberry-like groups of red flowers which are carried at the ends of branches in long radiating combinations of stems shaped like the frame of an umbrella.

Umbria /'ʌmbrɪə/, *n.* an ancient district in central and northern Italy.

umiak /'umiæk/, *n.* an open Eskimo boat consisting of a wooden frame covered with skins and provided with several seats, for transport of goods and passengers. Also, **umiack.** [Eskimo (Eastern d.): large skin boat, or woman's boat]

umlaut /'ʊmlaʊt/, *n.* two dots over a vowel to show a different vowel sound from that of the letter without these, esp. as used in German. [G]

umpire /'ʌmpaɪə/, *n., v.*, **-pired, -piring.** ◇*n.* **1.** a person chosen to see that a game is played in accordance with the rules. **2.** a person to whose decision an argument between parties is referred; arbiter or referee. ◇*v.t.* **3.** to act as umpire in (a game). **4.** to decide or settle (an argument, etc.) as an umpire;

umpire arbitrate. ◇*v.i.* **5.** to act as an umpire. [ME, from OF: uneven, odd]

umpteen /ˈʌmpˈtin, ˈʌmptɪn/, *adj.* of an unknown or immeasurably large number. —**umpteenth**, *adj.*

un-[1], a prefix meaning 'not', freely used as an English formative, giving a negative or opposite force in adjectives and the adverbs and nouns coming from them, as in *unfair, unfairly, unfairness, unseen, unheard-of,* and less freely in certain other nouns, as in *unease, unrest, unemployment*. Note: Of the words in **un-**[1], only a chosen number are separately entered, since in most formations of this class, the meaning, spelling, and pronunciation may easily be seen by looking at the simple word from which each is formed. [ME and OE]

un-[2], a prefix freely used in English to form verbs expressing a reversal of some action or state, or removal, release, etc., as in *unbend, uncork, unfasten,* or to intensify the force of a verb already having such a meaning, as in *unloose*. [OE *un-, on-*]

UN /ju ˈɛn/, *n.* → **United Nations**. [abbrev.]

unable /ʌnˈeɪbəl/, *adj.* not able (to do something); lacking ability or power (to do something); weak; impotent.

unaccompanied /ʌnəˈkʌmpənid/, *adj. Music.* referring to voice(s) or instrument(s) playing or singing alone; without an accompaniment.

unaccountable /ʌnəˈkaʊntəbəl/, *adj.* **1.** not able to be accounted for or explained. **2.** not accountable or answerable.

unaccustomed /ʌnəˈkʌstəmd/, *adj.* **1.** unused: *to be unaccustomed to hardships.* **2.** unusual; unfamiliar.

unanimity /junəˈnɪməti/, *n.* complete agreement or accord.

unanimous /juˈnænəməs/, *adj.* **1.** of one mind; in complete agreement. **2.** marked by or showing complete agreement: *a unanimous vote.* [L]

unapproachable /ʌnəˈproʊtʃəbəl/, *adj.* **1.** not able to be approached; inaccessible. **2.** unfriendly; remote. **3.** unequalled; unrivalled.

unassuming /ʌnəˈsjumɪŋ/, *adj.* modest; unpretentious.

unattached /ʌnəˈtætʃt/, *adj.* **1.** not connected with any particular body, group, etc.; independent. **2.** not engaged, married, or a partner in a stable relationship.

unattended /ʌnəˈtɛndəd/, *adj.* **1.** unaccompanied. **2.** with no-one in charge. **3.** not taken notice of or paid attention to.

unavailing /ʌnəˈveɪlɪŋ/, *adj.* useless; ineffectual.

unaware /ʌnəˈwɛə/, *adj.* not aware; unconscious, as of something: *to be unaware of any change.*

unawares /ʌnəˈwɛəz/, *adv.* **1.** while not aware of a thing oneself; unknowingly; inadvertently. **2.** while another is not aware: *to come upon someone unawares.*

unbalanced /ʌnˈbælənst/, *adj.* **1.** not balanced, or not properly balanced. **2.** lacking steadiness and soundness of judgment. **3.** mentally disordered or deranged. **4.** (of an account) not adjusted; not brought to an equality of debits and credits.

unbecoming /ʌnbəˈkʌmɪŋ/, *adj.* **1.** not becoming; not appropriate; unsuited. **2.** improper; unseemly. **3.** (of clothing, etc.) unattractive.

unbeknown /ʌnbəˈnoʊn/, *adj. Colloq.* unknown; unperceived; without a person's knowledge (usu. fol. by *to*): *Unbeknown to him, she was married already.* Also, **unbeknownst**.

unbelief /ʌnbəˈlif/, *n.* lack of belief, esp. in religion; doubt. —**unbeliever**, *n.* —**unbelieving**, *adj.*

unbend /ʌnˈbɛnd/, *v.t., v.i.,* **-bent** or **-bended, -bending. 1.** to make or become less formal. **2.** to make or become straight.

unbending /ʌnˈbɛndɪŋ/, *adj.* **1.** not bending; rigid; inflexible. **2.** stern; rigorous; resolute.

unbidden /ʌnˈbɪdn/, *adj.* **1.** not commanded; spontaneous. **2.** uninvited. Also, **unbid**.

unblinking /ʌnˈblɪŋkɪŋ/, *adj.* **1.** not blinking. **2.** without any show of response: *an unblinking reaction to a jury's verdict.* **3.** fearless; undismayed.

unblushing /ʌnˈblʌʃɪŋ/, *adj.* shameless.

unborn /ʌnˈbɔn/, *adj.* **1.** (of a baby) still in the womb; not born. **2.** yet to come; future: *ages unborn.*

unbosom /ʌnˈbʊzəm/, *v.t.* to reveal (one's thoughts, feelings, etc.), esp. in confidence.

unbounded /ʌnˈbaʊndəd/, *adj.* **1.** unlimited; boundless: *Her good humor was unbounded.* **2.** unrestrained; uncontrolled: *Her joy on hearing of her son's safety was unbounded.*

unbridled /ʌnˈbraɪdld/, *adj.* **1.** unrestrained or uncontrolled: *the unbridled joy of children at a picnic.* **2.** not having a bridle on, as a horse.

unburden /ʌnˈbɜdn/, *v.t.* **1.** to free from a burden. **2.** to ease (one's mind, conscience, etc., or oneself) by telling or confessing something.

uncalled-for /ʌnˈkɔld-fɔ/, *adj.* unnecessary and improper; unwarranted.

uncanny /ʌnˈkæni/, *adj.* **1.** unnaturally strange; eerie. **2.** almost supernaturally good: *uncanny judgment.* —**uncannily**, *adv.* —**uncanniness**, *n.*

unceremonious /ˌʌnsɛrəˈmoʊniəs/, *adj.* informal; not ceremonious; abrupt or rude.

uncertain /ʌnˈsɜtn/, *adj.* **1.** not definitely or surely known; doubtful. **2.** not confident, assured, or decided: *The applicant's uncertain manner was a point against him.* **3.** not fixed or determined. **4.** doubtful; vague; indistinct. **5.** not to be depended on. **6.** subject to change; variable; capricious: *a person of uncertain temper.* **7.** dependent on chance. **8.** unsteady or fitful, as light. —**uncertainty**, *n.*

uncertainty principle, *n. Phys.* the principle that it is not possible to determine with accuracy both the position and velocity of an atomic particle, such as an electron. Also, **indeterminacy principle**.

uncharitable /ʌn'tʃærətəbəl/, *adj.* **1.** unforgiving; harsh; censorious: *an uncharitable opinion of his character.* **2.** miserly.

uncharted /ʌn'tʃɑtəd/, *adj.* not mapped; unexplored; unknown, as a remote region.

uncial /'ʌnsiəl/, *adj.* **1.** of or relating to large, specially shaped letters used in Greek and Latin manuscripts of the third to eighth centuries. ◇*n.* **2.** an uncial letter. [L: pertaining to an inch]

uncircumcised /ʌn'sɜkəmsaɪzd/, *adj.* **1.** not circumcised. **2.** not Jewish; gentile.

uncle /'ʌŋkəl/, *n.* **1.** a brother of one's father or mother. **2.** an aunt's husband. [ME, from AF, from L: mother's brother]

unclean /ʌn'klin/, *adj.* **1.** morally, spiritually or ritually impure. **2.** (of food) unfit to be eaten; forbidden.

Uncle Sam /ʌŋkəl 'sæm/, *n.* a personification of the government or people of the US. [extension of the initials *US*]

uncomfortable /ʌn'kʌmfətəbəl, -'kʌmftəbəl/, *adj.* **1.** causing discomfort; disquieting: *an uncomfortable chair.* **2.** in a condition of discomfort; uneasy; ill-at-ease: *to be uncomfortable in high society.*

uncommon /ʌn'kɒmən/, *adj.* **1.** not common; unusual or rare. **2.** unusual in amount or degree; above the ordinary: *bravery uncommon in a young child.*

uncommunicative /ʌnkə'mjunəkətɪv/, *adj.* not wanting to give information, express opinions, etc.; reserved; taciturn.

uncompromising /ʌn'kɒmprəmaɪzɪŋ/, *adj.* not prepared to compromise; unyielding; inflexible.

unconcerned /ʌnkən'sɜnd/, *adj.* **1.** not concerned; free from anxiety or care for others; uninterested. **2.** not involved (with) or taking part (in).

unconditional /ʌnkən'dɪʃənəl/, *adj.* not limited by conditions; absolute: *an unconditional promise.*

unconnected /ʌnkə'nɛktəd/, *adj.* **1.** not connected; separate; distinct (sometimes fol. by *with*). **2.** (of a piece of writing) not put together logically; incoherent.

unconscionable /ʌn'kɒnʃənəbəl/, *adj.* **1.** unreasonably overdone or excessive. **2.** not guided by conscience; unscrupulous: *unconscionable behavior.*

unconscious /ʌn'kɒnʃəs/, *adj.* **1.** not conscious; unaware: *He is unconscious of his surroundings when reading.* **2.** temporarily without consciousness: *He was knocked unconscious by the blow.* **3.** unintentional: *an unconscious slight.* **4.** *Psychol.* relating to feelings and ideas which the individual cannot bring into consciousness. ◇*n.* **5. the unconscious,** *Psychol.* the part of the mind containing all the feelings and ideas of which a person is not aware.

unconstitutional /ˌʌnkɒnstə'tjuʃənəl/, *adj.* not authorised by or contrary to the constitution, as of a country.

unconventional /ʌnkən'vɛnʃənəl/, *adj.* not conventional; not according to usual or accepted ways or behavior.

uncouth /ʌn'kuθ/, *adj.* awkward, clumsy, or unmannerly, as persons, behavior, actions, etc. [ME; OE *uncūth* known]

uncover /ʌn'kʌvə/, *v.t.* **1.** to lay bare; disclose; reveal. **2.** to remove the cover or covering from.

unction /'ʌŋkʃən/, *n.* **1.** the act of anointing, esp. for medical purposes or as a religious rite. **2.** something soothing or comforting. [ME, from L]

unctuous /'ʌŋkʃuəs/, *adj.* **1.** like an unguent or ointment; oily; greasy. **2.** marked by an excessively smooth, earnest manner, esp. of an insincere kind. [ME, from ML, from L: ointment]

uncut /ʌn'kʌt/, *adj.* (of drugs, as heroin) not mixed with other substances; pure.

undefined /ʌndə'faɪnd/, *adj.* **1.** not limited in a clearly stated way; indefinite. **2.** not described by a clear statement or explanation; not explained.

undemonstrative /ʌndə'mɒnstrətɪv/, *adj.* not usually showing enthusiasm, affection, etc.; reserved.

undeniable /ʌndə'naɪəbəl/, *adj.* **1.** not able to be proved false; indisputable. **2.** not able to be refused.

under /'ʌndə/, *prep.* **1.** beneath and covered by: *under a table; under a tree.* **2.** below the surface of: *under the sea.* **3.** at a point or position lower than or farther down than: *to stand under a window.* **4.** in the position or condition of bearing, supporting, sustaining, undergoing, etc.: *to sink under a load; a matter under consideration.* **5.** subject to: *under the influence of drink.* **6.** beneath (a head, heading, etc.), as in classification. **7.** as designated, indicated, or represented by: *under a new name.* **8.** below in degree, amount, price, etc.; less than: *under age.* **9.** below in rank, dignity, etc. **10.** subject to the influence, direction, guidance, etc., of: *under supervision; born under Leo; to study under a professor; under these circumstances.* **11.** during the reign or rule of. **12.** with the favor or aid of: *under protection.* **13.** authorised, warranted, or attested by: *under one's hand or seal.* **14.** in accordance with: *under the provisions of the law.* **15.** in the condition or process of: *under repair.* ◇*adv.* **16.** under or beneath something. **17.** beneath the surface. **18.** in a lower degree, amount, etc. **19.** in a subordinate position or condition. **20.** in or into cover or submersion: *to send a boat under.* **21. down under,** *Colloq.* in or to Australia and NZ. ◇*adj.* **22.** beneath; lower in position. [ME and OE]

under-, a prefix meaning **1.** a place or situation below or beneath, as in *underbrush, undertow,* or lower in grade or dignity, as in *understudy.* **2.** lesser in degree, extent, or amount, as in *undersized*. **3.** insufficiency, as in *underfeed*.

under-age /'ʌndər-eɪdʒ/, *adj.* below the customary or required age, esp. legal age, as for entering licensed premises, marrying, etc.

underarm /'ʌndəram/, *adj.* **1.** under the arm: *an underarm seam*. **2.** in the armpit: *underarm odor*. **3.** *Cricket, Tennis, etc.* done with the hand below the shoulder as in bowling, serving, etc. ◇*adv.* **4.** *Cricket, Tennis, etc.* with an underarm action.

undercarriage /'ʌndəkærɪdʒ/, *n.* **1.** the supporting framework beneath the body of a carriage, etc. **2.** the parts of an aeroplane beneath the body, serving as a support when on the ground or water or when taking off and landing.

underclothes /'ʌndəkloʊðz/, *n.pl.* →**underwear**. Also, **underclothing**.

undercoat /'ʌndəkoʊt/, *n.* a coat of paint put on a surface after priming and filling, or after preparation of a previously painted surface, before putting on the finishing coat.

undercover /'ʌndəkʌvə/, *adj.* working or done out of public sight; secret: *an undercover agent*.

undercurrent /'ʌndəkʌrənt/, *n.* **1.** a current below the upper currents or below the surface. **2.** an underlying or hidden condition or tendency.

undercut /ʌndə'kʌt/, *v.*, **-cut, -cutting**; /'ʌndəkʌt/, *n.* ◇*v.t.* **1.** to cut under or beneath. **2.** to sell or work at a lower price than. **3.** *Sport.* to hit (the ball) so as to cause a backspin. **4.** to outwit or outmanoeuvre (a rival); undermine. ◇*n.* **5.** a cut, or a cutting away, underneath.

underdeveloped /ʌndədə'vɛləpt/, *adj.* **1.** (of a country) →**developing**. **2.** less fully developed than average. —**underdevelopment**, *n.*

underdog /'ʌndədɒg/, *n.* **1.** someone who is ill-treated. **2.** the loser or expected loser in a competitive situation, fight, etc.

underdone /ʌndə'dʌn/, *adj.* (of food, esp. meat) cooked lightly or less than completely.

underestimate /ʌndər'ɛstəmeɪt/, *v.*, **-mated, -mating**; /ʌndər'ɛstəmət/, *n.* ◇*v.t.* **1.** to work out or calculate at too low a value, rate, etc. ◇*n.* **2.** a calculation that is too low.

underexpose /ʌndərək'spoʊz/, *v.t.*, **-exposed, -exposing**. to give too little exposure to light, as in photography. —**underexposure**, *n.*

underfoot /ʌndə'fʊt/, *adv.* **1.** under the foot or feet; on the ground. **2.** in the way. ◇*adj.* **3.** lying under the foot or feet.

undergarment /'ʌndəgamənt/, *n.* an article of underwear.

undergo /ʌndə'goʊ/, *v.t.*, **-went, -gone, -going**. **1.** to experience; be subjected to; pass through. **2.** to suffer; endure; sustain.

undergraduate /ʌndə'grædʒuət/, *n.* **1.** a student in a university or college who has not taken a first degree. ◇*adj.* **2.** relating to, typical of, or consisting of undergraduates.

underground /'ʌndəgraʊnd/, *adv.* **1.** beneath the surface of the ground. **2.** secretly; not openly. ◇*adj.* **3.** being or taking place beneath the surface of the ground: *an underground river*. **4.** used, or for use, underground. **5.** hidden or secret; not open. **6.** referring to a group, organisation, etc., that holds radical political views and does not work as part of the establishment, or to the publications, etc., of such a group. ◇*n.* **7.** a place or region beneath the surface of the earth. **8.** a railway running mainly through underground tunnels. **9.** a secret organisation fighting the established government or occupation forces, esp. in World War II.

undergrowth /'ʌndəgroʊθ/, *n.* shrubs or small trees growing beneath or among large trees.

underhand /'ʌndəhænd/, *adj.* **1.** not open and honest; secret and sly. **2.** done or delivered underhand. ◇*adv.* **3.** with the hand below the shoulder, as in pitching or bowling a ball. **4.** secretly; stealthily; slyly.

underlay /ʌndə'leɪ/, *v.*, **-laid, -laying**; /'ʌndəleɪ/, *n.* ◇*v.t.* **1.** to lay (one thing) under or beneath another. **2.** to raise or support with something laid underneath. **3.** to extend beneath. ◇*n.* **4.** something underlaid esp. under a floorcovering.

underlie /ʌndə'laɪ/, *v.t.*, **-lay, -lain, -lying**. **1.** to lie under or beneath; be situated under. **2.** to be at the basis of; form the foundation of. [OE *underlicgan*]

underline /'ʌndəlaɪn/, *v.t.*, **-lined, -lining**. **1.** to mark with a line or lines underneath; underscore. **2.** to draw attention to the importance of.

underling /'ʌndəlɪŋ/, *n.* (usu. derog.) a subordinate. [ME and OE]

underlying /'ʌndəlaɪɪŋ/, *adj.* **1.** fundamental; existing beneath the seeming aspect of: *an underlying problem*. ◇*v.* **2.** present tense and participle of **underlie**.

undermine /ʌndə'maɪn, 'ʌndəmaɪn/, *v.t.*, **-mined, -mining**. **1.** to make unstable by digging into or wearing away supports or foundations. **2.** to harm or weaken by secret or underhand means. **3.** to destroy gradually: *to undermine her confidence*.

underneath /ʌndə'niθ/, *prep.* **1.** under; beneath. ◇*adv.* **2.** beneath; below. ◇*adj.* **3.** lower. ◇*n.* **4.** the under or lowest part or view. [OE *underneothan*]

undernourish /ʌndə'nʌrɪʃ/, *v.t.* to provide with less nourishment than is necessary to maintain normal health. —**undernourished**, *adj.*

underpants /'ʌndəpænts/, *n.pl.* a type of close-fitting undergarment, like short trousers, usu. without legs.

underpass /'ʌndəpas/, *n.* an underground road or pathway, often under a railway, road, etc.

underpin /ʌndə'pɪn/, *v.t.*, **-pinned, -pinning**. **1.** to pin or support underneath. **2.** to support with masonry, stones, etc., as a building. **3.** to support; prop.

underplay /ˌʌndəˈpleɪ/, *v.i., v.t.* **1.** to act (a part) without giving enough detail or finer meaning. **2.** to act (a part) in a subtle or restrained manner.

underprivileged /ˌʌndəˈprɪvəlɪdʒd/, *adj.* not having the normal privileges or rights of a society because of lack of money and low social status.

underproof /ˈʌndəpruːf/, *adj.* containing a smaller proportion of alcohol than proof spirit does.

underscore /ˌʌndəˈskɔː/, *v.t.,* **-scored, -scoring.** to mark with a line or lines underneath; underline.

undersell /ˌʌndəˈsel/, *v.t.,* **-sold, -selling. 1.** to advertise or publicise with restraint. **2.** to sell things at a lower price than (a competitor). ◇*v.* **3. undersell oneself,** to lack confidence in one's own worth.

undershot /ˈʌndəʃɒt/, *adj.* **1.** driven by water passing beneath, as a kind of vertical waterwheel. **2.** having the upper part shorter than the lower, as the jaw.

undersign /ˌʌndəˈsaɪn/, *v.t.* to sign one's name under, or at the end of (a letter or document).

understand /ˌʌndəˈstænd/, *v.,* **-stood, -standing.** ◇*v.t.* **1.** to grasp the idea of; comprehend: *Now I understand your plan.* **2.** to be thoroughly familiar with the character or nature of: *She understands mathematics; She understands her husband well.* **3.** to get the idea of by knowing the meaning of the words used: *Can you understand foreign broadcasts?* **4.** to grasp the possible results or importance of: *Does he understand what war would mean?* **5.** to accept as a fact; learn or hear: *From what I understand, the charge is true.* **6.** to take the meaning of in a particular way: *You are to understand the phrase exactly as written.* **7.** to accept as being present or existing: *His loyalty is understood.* ◇*v.i.* **8.** to see what is meant. **9.** to have knowledge about something: *to understand about a matter.* **10.** to accept sympathetically: *If you go away, I shall understand.* [ME; OE]

understanding /ˌʌndəˈstændɪŋ/, *n.* **1.** the act of one who understands; comprehension. **2.** concerned awareness; intelligence. **3.** great power of recognising the truth: *men of understanding.* **4.** a shared knowing of each other's meaning, thoughts, etc. **5.** a private agreement between people. **6. on the understanding that,** on condition that. ◇*adj.* **7.** having or showing sympathetic concern.

understate /ˌʌndəˈsteɪt/, *v.t.,* **-stated, -stating.** to describe (something) as less than it is. —**understatement,** *n.*

understood /ˌʌndəˈstʊd/, *v.* **1.** past tense and past participle of **understand.** ◇*adj.* **2.** agreed upon by all. **3.** taken to mean; assumed.

understudy /ˈʌndəstʌdi/, *n., v.,* **-studied, -studying.** ◇*n.* **1.** an actor or actress who stands by to replace a person unable to perform. ◇*v.t.* **2.** to act as an understudy to (an actor or actress). **3.** to be the understudy for (a particular role).

undertake /ˌʌndəˈteɪk/, *v.t.,* **-took, -taken, -taking. 1.** to say that one will do (a job, etc.); essay; attempt. **2.** to take on oneself by formal promise or agreement. —**undertaking,** *n.*

undertaker /ˈʌndəteɪkə/, *n.* a person whose business it is to prepare the dead for burial and to take charge of funerals; funeral director.

under-the-counter /ˈʌndə-ðə-kaʊntə/, *adj.* relating to goods kept hidden for sale in some improper way, as on the black market.

undertone /ˈʌndətoʊn/, *n.* **1.** (of speech) a low or quietened tone. **2.** an underlying quality, element, or tendency. **3.** a background color.

undertow /ˈʌndətoʊ/, *n.* **1.** a backward flow of water below the surface of waves breaking on a beach. **2.** any strong current below the surface of water, moving in a direction different from that of the surface current.

underwear /ˈʌndəwɛə/, *n.* clothes worn under outer clothes, esp. those worn next to the skin.

underworld /ˈʌndəwɜːld/, *n.* **1.** the criminal part of human society. **2.** (in myths) the world beneath the earth inhabited by the dead.

underwrite /ˈʌndəraɪt, ˌʌndəˈraɪt/, *v.,* **-wrote, -written, -writing.** ◇*v.t.* **1.** to agree to meet the cost of. **2.** to guarantee the sale of (shares or bonds to be offered to the public for subscription). **3.** *Insurance.* **a.** to write one's name at the end of (a policy of insurance), thereby becoming responsible for payment in case of certain losses. **b.** to take on responsibility up to (a certain sum) by way of insurance. ◇*v.i.* **4.** to carry on the business of underwriting. [ME; OE, from L]

undesirable /ˌʌndəˈzaɪərəbəl/, *adj.* **1.** not having qualities thought good or useful. **2.** not desirable. ◇*n.* **3.** an undesirable person or thing.

undeveloped /ˌʌndəˈvɛləpt/, *adj.* **1.** not fully grown or matured. **2.** (of land) not built on.

undo /ʌnˈduː/, *v.t.,* **-did, -done, -doing. 1.** to unfasten and open (something closed, locked, etc.). **2.** to untie or loose (strings, etc.). **3.** to open (a parcel, sealed letter, etc.). **4.** to cause to be as if never done: *He undid all her good work.* **5.** to bring to ruin; destroy. [ME; OE] —**undoing,** *n.*

undress /ʌnˈdrɛs/, *v., n.* ◇*v.t.* **1.** to remove the clothes from; disrobe. ◇*v.i.* **2.** to take off one's clothes. ◇*n.* **3.** the state of having little or no clothes on. **4.** ordinary or informal dress.

undue /ʌnˈdjuː/, *adj.* **1.** too great; unwarranted; excessive: *undue haste.* **2.** not proper, fitting, or right; unjustified: *to exercise undue influence.*

undulate /ˈʌndʒəleɪt/, *v.,* **-lated, -lating;** /ˈʌndʒələt, -leɪt/, *adj.* ◇*v.t., v.i.* **1.** to (cause to) rise and fall. **2.** to (cause to) have a wavy form or surface. ◇*adj.* **3.** Also, **undulated.** wavy; having a waved form, surface, edge, etc. [L: wavy] —**undulation,** *n.*

unduly /ʌn'djuli/, *adv.* **1.** too much. **2.** improperly; unjustifiably; inappropriately.

undying /ʌn'daɪŋ/, *adj.* deathless; immortal; unending.

unearth /ʌn'ɜθ/, *v.t.* **1.** to dig or get out of the earth. **2.** to uncover or bring to light by digging, searching, or discovery.

unearthly /ʌn'ɜθli/, *adj.* **1.** not of this earth or world. **2.** unnaturally strange; supernatural; weird: *an unearthly scream.* **3.** *Colloq.* unreasonable; absurd: *to get up at an unearthly hour.*

uneasy /ʌn'izi/, *adj.* **-easier, -easiest. 1.** not easy in body or mind; uncomfortable; perturbed. **2.** not easy in manner; constrained. **–uneasily,** *adv.* **uneasiness,** *n.*

uneducated /ʌn'ɛdʒəkeɪtəd/, *adj.* **1.** not educated. **2.** not showing signs of education: *an uneducated handwriting.*

unemployed /ʌnəm'plɔɪd, -ɛm-/, *adj.* **1.** out of work, esp. of someone who wishes to work. **2.** not in use. ◊*n.* *(sing. treated as pl.)* **3.** people who are unemployed. **–unemployment,** *n.*

unemployment benefit, *n.* a regular social security payment made to unemployed persons who are able to work and are actively seeking employment.

unequal /ʌn'ikwəl/, *adj.* **1.** not of the same quantity, value, rank, ability, etc.: *unequal size.* **2.** (of amount, power, ability, etc.) not enough (fol. by *to*): *strength unequal to the task.* **3.** not having the parts alike: *an unequal leaf.* **4.** (of movement, length of time, amount, etc.) not even or regular. **5.** in which the parties are unevenly matched: *an unequal contest.*

unequivocal /ʌni'kwɪvəkəl, -ə'kwɪv-/, *adj.* having a single definite meaning; clear; plain: *an unequivocal reply.*

unerring /ʌn'ɜrɪŋ/, *adj.* without error or mistake; exact; sure.

UNESCO /ju'nɛskou/, *n.* an agency of the UN that promotes educational and cultural programs. [*U(nited)* *N(ations)* *E(ducational)* *S(cientific and)* *C(ultural)* *O(rganization)*]

uneven /ʌn'ivən/, *adj.* **1.** not level or flat; rough; rugged. **2.** not the same throughout; irregular; varying. **3.** not equally balanced; not equal: *an uneven contest.* **4.** (of a number) odd; not able to be divided into two equal integers: *3, 5, and 7 are uneven numbers.* [ME; OE] **–unevenness,** *n.*

unfailing /ʌn'feɪlɪŋ/, *adj.* **1.** not failing or giving way; totally dependable. **2.** never giving out; unceasing; continuous: *an unfailing supply.*

unfair /ʌn'fɛə/, *adj.* **1.** not fair or just; unjust. **2.** marked by dishonest practices. [ME; OE *unfæger*]

unfamiliar /ʌnfə'mɪliə/, *adj.* **1.** not familiar or acquainted: *to be unfamiliar with a subject.* **2.** not well-known; strange: *a subject unfamiliar to me.* **–unfamiliarity,** *n.*

unfeeling /ʌn'filɪŋ/, *adj.* **1.** having no ability to feel; insensible. **2.** unsympathetic; callous; hard-hearted.

unfinished /ʌn'fɪnɪʃt/, *adj.* **1.** not finished; incomplete. **2.** (of wood, metal, etc.) lacking some special finish.

unfit /ʌn'fɪt/, *adj., v.,* **-fitted, -fitting.** ◊*adj.* **1.** not fit; not adapted or suited; unsuitable. **2.** not in good physical condition. ◊*v.t.* **3.** to make unfit or unsuitable; disqualify.

unflagging /ʌn'flægɪŋ/, *adj.* not weakening; strong: *unflagging loyalty.*

unflappable /ʌn'flæpəbəl/, *adj.* not easily upset; imperturbable.

unfold /ʌn'fould/, *v.t.* **1.** to spread or open out: *unfold your arms.* **2.** to develop: *The skills of an artist unfold with experience.* **3.** to reveal, display or explain. ◊*v.i.* **4.** to become unfolded or be revealed. [ME; OE *unfealdan*]

unforeseen /ʌnfɔ'sin, -fə-/, *adj.* not expected.

unformed /ʌn'fɔmd/, *adj.* **1.** not formed; shapeless or formless. **2.** undeveloped; crude. **3.** (of the mind) not trained or educated.

unfortunate /ʌn'fɔtʃənət/, *adj.* **1.** not lucky. **2.** being a misfortune; regrettable; disastrous. **3.** likely to have undesirable results; unpropitious: *an unfortunate decision.* **4.** unsuitable; inept: *an unfortunate choice of words.* **5.** deserving of sympathy; sad. ◊*n.* **6.** an unfortunate person.

unfounded /ʌn'faundəd/, *adj.* without foundation; baseless: *unfounded fears.*

unfrock /ʌn'frɒk/, *v.t.* to take rank or status from (a priest).

unfurl /ʌn'fɜl/, *v.t.* **1.** to spread or shake out (a sail, flag, etc.) from a tightly-rolled condition; unfold. ◊*v.i.* **2.** to become unfurled.

ungainly /ʌn'geɪnli/, *adj.* not graceful or shapely; awkward; clumsy. [ME] **–ungainliness,** *n.*

ungodly /ʌn'gɒdli/, *adj.* **1.** not following God's laws; impious; sinful. **2.** wicked. **3.** *Colloq.* dreadful; outrageous: *an ungodly hour of the morning.* **–ungodliness,** *n.*

ungracious /ʌn'greɪʃəs/, *adj.* lacking in politeness or courtesy.

unguarded /ʌn'gadəd/, *adj.* **1.** not guarded; unprotected; undefended. **2.** marked by carelessness or thoughtlessness; incautious; imprudent: *secrets told in an unguarded moment.* **3.** (of a person) open; guileless; candid.

unguent /'ʌŋgwənt/, *n.* any soft medicated preparation for rubbing or putting on sore places; ointment. [ME, from L]

ungulate /'ʌŋgjələt, -leɪt/, *n., adj.* (a mammal) having hoofs. [L: having claws]

unhappy /ʌn'hæpi/, *adj.,* **-ier, -iest. 1.** sad or miserable. **2.** unfortunate; unlucky: *He was an unhappy choice for the job.* **3.** unsuitable: *an unhappy remark.* **–unhappily,** *adv.* **–unhappiness,** *n.*

unhealthy /ʌn'hɛlθi/, *adj.,* **-healthier, -healthiest. 1.** not in a healthy or sound condition. **2.** hurtful to health; unwholesome: *unhealthy air.* **3.** morally harmful; noxious.

unhealthy 4. of or relating to a diseased condition, esp. mental: *an unhealthy interest in death*. —**unhealthily**, *adv.* —**unhealthiness**, *n.*

unheard-of /ʌnˈhɜːd-ɒv/, *adj.* 1. such as was never known before; unprecedented. 2. (of behavior) totally unacceptable.

unhinge /ʌnˈhɪndʒ/, *v.t.*, **-hinged, -hinging**. 1. to take (a door, etc.) off the hinges. 2. to unbalance (the mind, etc.). 3. to throw into confusion or disorder.

unholy /ʌnˈhoʊli/, *adj.*, **-lier, -liest**. 1. not holy. 2. wicked; sinful; impious. 3. *Colloq.* dreadful; outrageous. [ME; OE *unhālig*]

uni /ˈjuni/, *n. Colloq.* university.

uni-, a word part meaning 'one', 'single', as in *unify*. [L, combining form of *ūnus* one]

unicameral /juniˈkæmərəl/, *adj.* (of a parliament) having a single chamber (law-making body).

UNICEF /ˈjunəsɛf/, *n.* an agency of the UN that assists child health, nutrition, and welfare programs; formed in 1946. [U(nited) N(ations) I(nternational) C(hildren's) E(mergency) F(und)]

unicellular /juniˈsɛljələ/, *adj.* relating to or consisting of a single cell.

unicorn /ˈjunəkɔn/, *n. Myth.* an animal resembling a horse with a single, long horn. [ME, from L: having one horn]

unidirectional /ˌjunidəˈrɛkʃənəl/, *adj.* having, or moving in, only one direction.

uniform /ˈjunəfɔm/, *adj.* 1. having always the same form or character; unvarying. 2. without variation in appearance, color, etc.; unbroken. 3. (of a person, action, rule, etc.) consistent in action, opinion, effect, etc.: *a uniform divorce law*. 4. agreeing with one another in form, character, appearance, etc.; alike. ◇*n.* 5. dress of the same style, materials, and color worn by and setting apart the members of a group, esp. a military body, school, etc. 6. a single suit of such dress. ◇*v.t.* 7. to clothe with a uniform. [L] —**uniformity**, *n.*

unify /ˈjunəfaɪ/, *v.t.*, **-fied, -fying**. to form into one. [ML, from L] —**unification**, *n.*

unilateral /juniˈlætərəl, -ˈlætrəl, junə-/, *adj.* 1. relating to, happening on, or affecting one side only. 2. done by one side only: *unilateral disarmament*. 3. *Law*. (of contracts, etc.) binding one party only.

unimaginable /ˌʌnəˈmædʒənəbəl/, *adj.* 1. impossible to think of or understand. 2. remarkable or out of the ordinary.

unimpeachable /ˌʌnɪmˈpitʃəbəl/, *adj.* 1. not able to be doubted; beyond question. 2. blameless; irreproachable.

unimproved /ˌʌnɪmˈpruvd/, *adj.* 1. not made better, more useful, more efficient, etc. 2. (of land) not built upon or cultivated. 3. (of health) not better.

uninhibited /ˌʌnɪnˈhɪbətəd/, *adj.* not held back by feelings of guilt, worry, etc., esp. with regard to social behavior.

uninspired /ˌʌnɪnˈspaɪəd/, *adj.* lacking imagination or creative spirit; dull. —**uninspiring**, *adj.*

union /ˈjunjən/, *n.* 1. the act or result of making two or more things into one. 2. a number of people, societies, states, etc., associated for some common purpose. 3. a uniting or being united, esp. in marriage. 4. → **trade union**. 5. (*cap*.) *R Union*. 6. a. an organisation of Rugby Union clubs which acts as a law-making body. b. the game, as opposed to (Rugby) League. 6. (*cap*.) a club offering dining and sporting services for the members of certain universities. [ME, from L] —**unionism**, *n.*

union card, *n.* a card showing membership of a trade union.

unionise or **unionize** /ˈjunjənaɪz/, *v.t.*, **-nised, -nising**. 1. to organise into a trade union. 2. to bring into line with the rules of a trade union. —**unionisation**, *n.*

unionist /ˈjunjənəst/, *n.* 1. someone supporting the idea of union. 2. a trade unionist. 3. (*cap*.) Also, **Ulster Unionist**. a member of the party upholding the legislative union of Great Britain and Ireland or (since 1920) Northern Ireland. 4. (*cap*.) an adherent of the federal union of the United States of America, esp. during the Civil War. —**unionistic**, *adj.*

Union Jack, *n.* (the design of) the national flag of the UK, standing for the union of England, Scotland and Ireland.

Union of South Africa, *n.* the former name of the Republic of South Africa. See **South Africa**.

Union of Soviet Socialist Republics, *n.* the official name of the former **Soviet Union**. *Abbrev.:* USSR

unique /juˈnik/, *adj.* 1. having no like or equal; sole. 2. remarkable, rare or unusual: *a unique experience*. [F, from L]

unisex /ˈjunisɛks/, *adj.* (of a style of dress, etc.) suitable for either sex.

unisexual /juniˈsɛkʃuəl/, *adj.* (of an animal or flower) having either male or female organs but not both. —**unisexuality**, *n.*

unison /ˈjunəsən/, *n.* 1. a sounding together of the same note by more than one voice or instrument. 2. agreement; accord. [LL: having one sound, from L]

unit /ˈjunət/, *n.* 1. a person, thing, or group regarded as a single entity. 2. a particular quantity (of length, volume, time, etc.) regarded as a single, undivided amount, esp. when used as a standard against which other quantities are measured. 3. *Maths.* the lowest positive integer; one. 4. *Educ.* a quantity of educational instruction, determined usu. on hours of work and examinations passed: *He has three units towards his degree*. 5. *Med, Pharmacol.* the measured amount of a substance necessary to cause a certain effect: *one hundred units of vitamin E*. 6. → **home unit**. ◇*adj.* 6. of, relating to, equal to, containing, or forming a unit or units. [apparently backformation from UNITY] —**unitary**, *n.*

Unitarian / unlearned

Unitarian /ˌjunəˈtɛəriən/, n. **1.** someone who holds that God is one being and not a Trinity (three beings in one). ◇adj. **2.** relating to ideas held by Unitarians. —**unitarianism**, n.

unite /juˈnaɪt/, v., **united**, **uniting**. ◇v.t. **1.** to join in order to form one connected whole. **2.** to cause to hold together. **3.** to join in marriage. **4.** to join in action, interest, opinion, feeling, etc. ◇v.i. **5.** to become one in action, opinion, feelings, etc.; combine. [ME, from L: joined together, made one] —**united**, adj.

United Arab Emirates /juˌnaɪtəd ˌærəb ˈɛmərəts/, n. **the**, a federation of seven mainly autonomous emirates in the east of the Arabian peninsula on the Persian Gulf; consists of Abu Dhabi, Ajman, Dubai, Fujairah, Ras al-Khaimah, Sharjah and Umm al-Qaiwain. Pop. 1 856 000 (1987); 77 700 km^2. *Language*: Arabic. *Currency*: dirham. *Cap*.: Abu Dhabi. Formerly, **Trucial Oman**, **the Trucial States**. Also, **UAE**

United Australia Party, n. the main conservative political party in Australia from 1931 until its collapse after the 1943 federal elections.

United Kingdom, n. an island kingdom in north-western Europe, consisting mainly of Great Britain and Northern Ireland; included the rest of Ireland before it became autonomous as the Irish Free State in 1922. Pop. 56 878 000 (1987 est.); 244 103 km^2. *Languages*: English, also Welsh and Gaelic. *Currency*: pound sterling. *Cap*.: London. See **Great Britain** and **Northern Ireland**. Also, **UK**

United Nations, n. an international association of states formed in 1945 to promote international peace and cooperation. Also, **United Nations Organisation**, **UNO**

United States of America, n. **the**, a federal republic in North America between Canada and Mexico, also comprising the states of Alaska, north-west of Canada, and Hawaii, in the central Pacific; 13 British colonies declared independence in 1776 and became the United States after the War of Independence. Pop. 243 773 000 (1987 est.); 9 363 123 km^2. *Language*: English. *Currency*: US dollar. *Cap*.: Washington, DC. Also, **United States**, **the States**, **America**, **US**, **USA**

Uniting Church /juˌnaɪtɪŋ tʃɜtʃ/, n. an Australian church formed in 1977, drawing membership from the Presbyterian, Methodist and Congregational churches.

unit trust, n. **1.** an organisation whose management buys shares from a number of companies and manages them on behalf of those who buy units of those shares. **2.** the units put up for sale by such a trust.

unity /ˈjunəti/, n., pl. **-ties**. **1.** the condition or fact of being one; oneness. **2.** something complete in itself, or regarded as being complete. **3.** (of the parts of a whole) the fact or condition of being united or combined into one. **4.** oneness of mind, feeling, etc., as among a number of people; agreement. **5.** *Maths*. the number one. **6.** *Theat*. one of the three principles of dramatic structure: **unity of time** (action within 24 hours); **unity of place** (no large shifts in setting); **unity of action** (a single plot). [ME, from L]

univalent /juniˈveɪlənt/, adj. *Chem*. → **monovalent**. [UNI- + -VALENT]

univalve /ˈjunɪvælv/, adj. **1.** (of a shell) composed of a single piece or valve. ◇n. **2.** a univalve mollusc.

universal /junəˈvɜsəl/, adj. **1.** covering, including, or coming from all or the whole (of something known or understood). **2.** affecting, concerning, or given to all: *universal education*. **3.** used or understood by all: *a universal language*. **4.** existing everywhere. **5.** *Mech*. etc. able to be used for all or various angles, sizes, etc. **6.** (of a joint, etc.) allowing free movement in all directions, within certain limits. ◇n. **7.** something that may be applied throughout the universe to many things, usu. thought of as something which can be in many places at the same time (opposed to *particular*). **8.** a characteristic which can be possessed in common by many different things, such as *mortality*. **9.** *Philos*. (a type referred to by) a general term or concept. **10.** *Mech*. a universal joint, esp. one at the end of the propeller shaft in a motor vehicle. [ME, from L *ūniversālis*] —**universality**, n.

universal suffrage, n. the principle that the right to vote should be given to everyone above a particular age.

universal-wound /ˈjunəvɜsəl-ˌwaʊnd/, adj. (of an electric motor) wound so that it will work with either DC or low frequency AC supply.

universe /ˈjunəvɜs/, n. **1.** all of space, and all the matter and energy which it contains; cosmos. **2.** mankind generally: *The whole universe knows it*. **3.** an area in which something exists or is the case. **4.** a galaxy. [L]

university /junəˈvɜsəti/, n., pl. **-ties**. **1.** a place of higher learning, at which both teaching and research are carried on. **2.** the members (teachers, undergraduates, graduate members, etc.) of a university. **3.** the buildings of a university. **4.** the governing body of a university. [ME, from ML: guild (of teachers and students)]

unkempt /ʌnˈkɛmpt/, adj. **1.** (of the hair) not combed. **2.** having the hair not combed or cared for. **3.** in an uncared-for or untidy condition. [pp. of obs. *kemb* (ME *kembe*, OE *cemban*) comb]

unkind /ʌnˈkaɪnd/, adj. not kind; harsh; cruel; unmerciful. —**unkindly**, adj., adv.

unknown /ʌnˈnoʊn/, adj. **1.** not known; unfamiliar; strange. **2.** not worked out, discovered, explored, or identified. ◇n. **3.** someone or something that is unknown. **4.** *Maths*. (a symbol representing) an unknown quantity.

unlawful /ʌnˈlɔfəl/, adj. **1.** not in keeping with or allowed by the law. **2.** not in keeping with moral rule; immoral; irreligious.

unlearned /ʌnˈlɜnəd/ for def. 1; /ʌnˈlɜnt/ for defs 2 and 3, adj. **1.** → **uneducated**. **2.** not acquired by learning; never learned. **3.**

unlearned known without being learned: *Crying is an unlearned response to pain.* Also (*for defs 2 and 3*), **unlearnt**.

unleash /ʌn'liːʃ/, *v.t.* **1.** to let loose or give way to (rage, violence, etc.). **2.** to set free to run at will; let loose.

unleavened /ʌn'lɛvənd/, *adj.* (of bread, etc.) not made to rise by the addition of yeast or bicarbonate of soda.

unless /ʌn'lɛs, ən-/, *conj.* except on condition that: *I shan't come unless you really want me to.* [ME]

unlettered /ʌn'lɛtəd/, *adj.* without knowledge of books; illiterate.

unlike /ʌn'laɪk/, *adj.* **1.** not like; different; dissimilar. ◇*prep.* **2.** different from. **3.** uncharacteristic of: *It is unlike you to be so cheerful.*

unlikely /ʌn'laɪkli/, *adj.* **1.** not likely to happen or be; improbable. **2.** not likely to be true; doubtful. **3.** holding out little possibility of success; unpromising. —**unlikelihood**, *n.*

unlimited /ʌn'lɪmətəd/, *adj.* **1.** not limited; unrestricted. **2.** without bounds; limitless.

unlimited company, *n.* a company whose members are each responsible for its debts to the full extent of their property.

unload /ʌn'loʊd/, *v.t.* **1.** to take the load from. **2.** to relieve of anything burdensome. **3.** to remove or discharge (a load, etc.). **4.** to get rid of (stock, etc.) by sale. ◇*v.i.* **5.** to unload something; remove or discharge a load.

unlooked-for /ʌn'lʊktfɔː/, *adj.* not looked for; unexpected; unforeseen.

unlucky /ʌn'lʌki/, *adj.* not having good luck; unfortunate or ill-fated. —**unluckily**, *adv.* —**unluckiness**, *n.*

unmade /ʌn'meɪd/, *adj.* **1.** not yet made. **2.** not having been made; uncreated.

unmake /ʌn'meɪk/, *v.t.,* **-made, -making**. **1.** to cause to be as if never made. **2.** to take to pieces; destroy. **3.** to depose from office or authority.

unman /ʌn'mæn/, *v.t.* **1.** to deprive of the character or qualities of a man. **2.** to deprive of the character or qualities of a human being.

unmanageable /ʌn'mænədʒəbəl/, *adj.* **1.** (of a horse, child, etc.) impossible to govern or control; refractory. **2.** (of affairs, objects, etc.) unable to be satisfactorily dealt with; unwieldy.

unmanly /ʌn'mænli/, *adj.* **1.** not manly; not like or expected of a man. **2.** weak; cowardly; ignoble. —**unmanliness**, *n.*

unmannerly /ʌn'mænəli/, *adj.* not polite; ill-bred; rude. —**unmannerliness**, *n.*

unmentionable /ʌn'mɛnʃənəbəl/, *adj.* **1.** not worthy or fit to be mentioned; rude; obscene. ◇*n.* **2.** (*pl.*) (*joc.*) underwear.

unmistakable /ʌnməs'teɪkəbəl/, *adj.* not allowing of any mistake; clear; plain; evident. Also, **unmistakeable**. —**unmistakably**, *adv.*

unmitigated /ʌn'mɪtəgeɪtəd/, *adj.* **1.** not softened or lessened. **2.** total or absolute.

unmoved /ʌn'muːvd/, *adj.* not affected; calm; not emotional: *Although it was a sad story, he was quite unmoved.*

unnatural /ʌn'nætʃərəl, -'nætʃrəl/, *adj.* **1.** having or showing a lack of natural or proper instincts, feelings, etc. **2.** unusual, strange, or abnormal. **3.** artificial or affected; forced or strained. **4.** more than usually cruel or evil.

unnecessary /ʌn'nɛsəsəri, -səsri/, *adj.* not necessary; superfluous; needless. —**unnecessarily**, *adv.*

unnerve /ʌn'nɜːv/, *v.t.*, **-nerved, -nerving**. to deprive of nerve, strength, or physical or mental firmness; break down the self-control of; upset.

UNO, /'juːnoʊ/ *n.* United Nations Organisation. See **United Nations**. [abbrev.]

unobtrusive /ʌnəb'truːsɪv, -zɪv/, *adj.* not obvious; discreet: *The unobtrusive presence of security men ensures the safety of royalty.*

unofficial /ʌnə'fɪʃəl/, *adj.* **1.** (of news) not confirmed by official sources. **2.** *Sport.* (of a time or speed, or a record) not confirmed by an official body.

unorganised or **unorganized** /ʌn'ɔːgənaɪzd/, *adj.* **1.** not organised; without organic structure. **2.** not formed into an organised or systematised whole. **3.** not having membership in a trade union.

unpalatable /ʌn'pælətəbəl/, *adj.* **1.** disagreeable; distasteful. **2.** ill-tasting; not agreeable to the palate.

unparalleled /ʌn'pærəlɛld/, *adj.* unparalleled; having no parallel; unequalled; unmatched.

unpick /ʌn'pɪk/, *v.t.* to undo the stitches of (something sewn, etc.).

unplaced /ʌn'pleɪst/, *adj.* **1.** not put in or assigned to a particular place. **2.** not among the first three (or sometimes four) placegetters in a race or competition.

unpolished /ʌn'pɒlɪʃt/, *adj.* **1.** not smoothed by polishing. **2.** rough or inelegant. **3.** (of rice) unmilled, still having the husk.

unpopular /ʌn'pɒpjələ/, *adj.* not popular; not liked by people generally, or by an individual. —**unpopularity**, *n.*

unprecedented /ʌn'prɛsədɛntəd, -'priː-/, *adj.* having no precedent or preceding instance; never known before.

unprincipled /ʌn'prɪnsəpəld/, *adj.* **1.** (of a person) lacking sound moral principles. **2.** (of an action, etc.) showing want of principle.

unprintable /ʌn'prɪntəbəl/, *adj.* not fit to be printed; offensive.

unprofessional /ʌnprə'fɛʃənəl, -'fɛʃnəl/, *adj.* **1.** not in accordance with professional standards of behavior; unsuitable to the members of a profession. **2.** not professional; not relating to or connected with a profession.

unqualified /ʌn'kwɒləfaɪd/, *adj.* **1.** not qualified; not fitted; not having the necessary qualifications. **2.** not modified, limited, or

unqualified

restricted in any way: *unqualified praise*. **3.** absolute; complete.

unquestionable /ʌnˈkwestʃənəbəl/, *adj.* not questionable; not open to question; beyond argument or doubt; indisputable.

unravel /ʌnˈrævəl/, *v.*, **-elled, -elling.** ◇*v.t.* **1.** to free from a ravelled or tangled condition; disentangle; disengage the threads or fibres of (a woven or knitted fabric, rope, etc.). **2.** to free from complication or difficulty; make plain or clear; solve: *to unravel a mystery.* ◇*v.i.* **3.** to become unravelled.

unread /ʌnˈred/, *adj.* **1.** not having gained knowledge by reading: *Although unread, he was a wise old man*. **2.** not having read (some subject or matter) (fol. by *in*): *a learned scientist unread in literature*.

unreal /ʌnˈril/, *adj.* **1.** not real; not substantial; imaginary; unpractical or visionary. **2.** *Colloq*. **a.** quite awful. **b.** quite wonderful.

unrealistic /ʌnriəˈlɪstɪk/, *adj.* **1.** not closely or accurately like an object or situation represented. **2.** not practical, hard-headed or clear-sighted.

unreasonable /ʌnˈrizənəbəl/, *adj.* **1.** not reasonable. **2.** not guided by reason or good sense. **3.** not agreeable to or willing to listen to reason. **4.** exceeding the bounds of reason; immoderate; exorbitant: *unreasonable expense*.

unrecognised or **unrecognized** /ʌnˈrekəgnaɪzd/, *adj.* not given enough credit or appreciation.

unredeemed /ʌnrəˈdimd, -ri-/, *adj.* **1.** unrelieved or unmodified, as by some good feature: *foolish actions unredeemed by good intentions*. **2.** not recovered from pawn or by ransom.

unrelated /ʌnrəˈleɪtəd/, *adj.* **1.** not connected by blood or marriage; not kin. **2.** having no relationship; unconnected: *The accident was the result of many unrelated causes*.

unrelenting /ʌnrəˈlentɪŋ/, *adj.* **1.** not yielding to feelings of kindness or compassion. **2.** not slackening in severity or determination. **3.** maintaining speed or rate of advance.

unrelieved /ʌnrəˈlivd/, *adj.* **1.** not varied, moderated, or made less monotonous. **2.** not provided with relief or aid: *unrelieved poverty*.

unremitting /ʌnrəˈmɪtɪŋ/, *adj.* not reducing or slackening; not abating for a time; incessant.

unrepeatable /ʌnrəˈpitəbəl/, *adj.* **1.** too rude, offensive or otherwise unpleasant to be repeated. **2.** not able to be repeated: *an unrepeatable offer of goods on sale*.

unrequited /ʌnrəˈkwaɪtəd/, *adj.* (used esp. of affection) not returned or reciprocated: *unrequited love*.

unrest /ʌnˈrest/, *n.* **1.** lack of rest; a restless or uneasy condition; inquietude. **2.** strong, almost rebellious, dissatisfaction and agitation: *unrest among the workers*.

unrivalled /ʌnˈraɪvəld/, *adj.* having no equal, rival, or competitor; peerless.

1122

unskilled

unruffled /ʌnˈrʌfəld/, *adj.* **1.** (of a person) calm; undisturbed. **2.** not physically ruffled or disturbed; not choppy, as the sea.

unruly /ʌnˈruli/, *adj.* not obeying rules; ungovernable; turbulent; lawless.

unsafe /ʌnˈseɪf/, *adj.* **1.** not safe. **2.** not to be trusted; unreliable.

unsaturated /ʌnˈsætʃəreɪtəd/, *adj.* **1.** not saturated; being able to dissolve more of a substance (in solution). **2.** *Chem.* a type of compound containing double or triple bonds and therefore able to bond to other elements, etc., by chemical addition.

unsavory or **unsavoury** /ʌnˈseɪvəri/, *adj.* **1.** unpleasant in taste or smell. **2.** socially or morally unpleasant or offensive.

unscathed /ʌnˈskeɪðd/, *adj.* not hurt; unharmed; uninjured physically or spiritually.

unschooled /ʌnˈskuld/, *adj.* **1.** uneducated; having received no schooling. **2.** not disciplined. **3.** not gained by training; natural.

unscrew /ʌnˈskru/, *v.t.* **1.** to draw the screw or screws from; unfasten by withdrawing screws. **2.** to remove (the lid of a screw-top jar, etc.) by turning.

unseasonable /ʌnˈsizənəbəl, -ˈsiznə-/, *adj.* **1.** unusual at the time of year or the hour. **2.** untimely; ill-timed; inopportune.

unseat /ʌnˈsit/, *v.t.* **1.** to throw from a saddle, as a rider. **2.** to depose from an official seat or from office: *to unseat a minister of the parliament*.

unsecured /ʌnsəˈkjuəd/, *adj.* **1.** not made secure or fastened. **2.** not insured against loss, as by a mortgage, bond, pledge, etc.

unseemly /ʌnˈsimli/, *adj.* not seemly; unfitting; unbecoming; improper; indecorous. —**unseemliness**, *n.*

unseen /ʌnˈsin/, *adj.* **1.** not seen; unperceived; unobserved; invisible. **2.** (of passages of writing or music) not previously seen. ◇*n.* **3.** an unprepared passage for translation, as in an examination.

unselfish /ʌnˈselfɪʃ/, *adj.* not selfish; disinterested; altruistic.

unserviceable /ʌnˈsɜvəsəbəl/, *adj.* **1.** not useful, as for its proper purpose. **2.** not able to be put to use because of wear or damage.

unsettled /ʌnˈsetld/, *adj.* **1.** not settled; not fixed in a place or abode. **2.** not populated, as a region. **3.** not fixed or stable, as conditions, opinions, etc.; without established order, as times. **4.** liable to change, as weather. **5.** undetermined, as a point at issue. **6.** not adjusted, closed, or disposed of finally, as an account.

unshakeable /ʌnˈʃeɪkəbəl/, *adj.* (of opinions, beliefs, positions, etc.) firmly held; not open to dissuasion. Also, **unshakable**.

unsightly /ʌnˈsaɪtli/, *adj.* not pleasing to the sight; forming an unpleasing sight.

unskilled /ʌnˈskɪld/, *adj.* **1.** of or relating to workers lacking specialised training or ability. **2.** not skilled, not requiring or exhibiting skill (in some activity).

unsociable /ʌn'souʃəbəl/, *adj.* not sociable; not having or wanting friendly social relations. **—unsociability**, *n.*

unsolicited /ʌnsə'lɪsətəd/, *adj.* **1.** not asked for: *unsolicited contributions.* **2.** (of people) not asked or solicited (for some purpose).

unsound /ʌn'saund/, *adj.* **1.** not sound; diseased, as the body or mind. **2.** decayed, as timber or fruit; impaired or defective, as goods. **3.** not solid or firm, as foundations. **4.** not well-founded or valid; fallacious: *an unsound argument.* **5.** not financially strong; unreliable: *an unsound business.*

unspeakable /ʌn'spikəbəl/, *adj.* **1.** impossible to express in words; unutterable; inexpressible: *unspeakable horror; unspeakable joy.* **2.** not able to be spoken; not to be spoken (of): *an unspeakable suggestion; unspeakable behavior.*

unspoilt /ʌn'spɔɪlt/, *adj.* not harmed or damaged; not having deteriorated, as the character of a person or place. Also, **unspoiled.**

unstable /ʌn'steɪbəl/, *adj.* **1.** not stable; unsteady. **2.** lacking emotional stability. **3.** *Chem.* indicating compounds which easily decompose.

unsteady /ʌn'stɛdi/, *adj.* **1.** not steady; not firmly fixed; not secure or stable. **2.** varying or wavering; unsteadfast. **3.** irregular or uneven. ◇*v.t.* **4.** to make unsteady.

unstructured /ʌn'strʌktʃəd/, *adj.* **1.** without structural organisation. **2.** not governed by rules: *an unstructured program.*

unstudied /ʌn'stʌdid/, *adj.* not practised or planned; natural; unaffected.

unsubstantial /ʌnsəb'stænʃəl/, *adj.* **1.** not substantial; not solid, firm, or strong; flimsy; slight; unreal; insubstantial: *an unsubstantial structure.* **2.** having no foundation in fact: *unsubstantial rumors.* **3.** immaterial; having no substance: *unsubstantial fears.*

unsung /ʌn'sʌŋ/, *adj.* not praised or made famous in, or as if in, song.

unsure /ʌn'ʃɔ/, *adj.* **1.** not certain; not confident. **2.** not to be relied on: *an unsure method.* **3.** unsafe; dependent on chance.

unswerving /ʌn'swɜvɪŋ/, *adj.* steady; constant; not turning aside: *unswerving loyalty.*

untangle /ʌn'tæŋgəl/, *v.t.*, **-gled, -gling.** **1.** to bring out of a tangled state; disentangle; unsnarl. **2.** to straighten out or clear up (anything confused or perplexing).

untapped /ʌn'tæpt/, *adj.* not drawn on, as resources, potentialities, etc.: *an untapped fund of money; untapped enthusiasm.*

untenable /ʌn'tɛnəbəl/, *adj.* **1.** not able to be held against attack. **2.** not able to be defended against argument, as an opinion, scheme, etc.

unthinkable /ʌn'θɪŋkəbəl/, *adj.* **1.** unimaginable; inconceivable. **2.** not to be considered; utterly out of the question.

unthinking /ʌn'θɪŋkɪŋ/, *adj.* **1.** not thinking; thoughtless; heedless. **2.** indicating lack of thought or reflection. **3.** not given to reflection; uncritical.

untidy /ʌn'taɪdi/, *adj.,* **-tidier, -tidiest,** *v.,* **-tidied, -tidying.** ◇*adj.* **1.** not tidy or neat; slovenly; disordered. ◇*v.t.* **2.** to make untidy; disorder. **—untidily,** *adv.* **—untidiness,** *n.*

untie /ʌn'taɪ/, *v.t.,* **-tied, -tying.** to loosen or unfasten (anything tied); let or set loose by undoing a knot.

until /ʌn'tɪl/, *conj.* **1.** up to the time that or when; till. **2.** (with negatives) before: *He did not come until the meeting was half over.* ◇*prep.* **3.** onward to, or till (a specified time); up to the time of (some occurrence): *He stayed until dawn.* **4.** (with negatives) before: *He did not go until night.* [ME, from Scand]

untimely /ʌn'taɪmli/, *adj.* **1.** not timely; not happening at a suitable time or season; ill-timed or inopportune. **2.** not fully mature or ripe; premature. ◇*adv.* **3.** unseasonably.

unto /'ʌntu/, *prep. Archaic.* **1.** to (in its various uses, except as the accompaniment of the infinitive). **2.** until; till. [ME]

untold /ʌn'toʊld/, *adj.* **1.** not told; not related; not revealed. **2.** more than can be numbered or enumerated; uncounted. **3.** too much to be measured; incalculable: *untold damage.*

untouchable /ʌn'tʌtʃəbəl/, *adj.* **1.** not able to be touched; intangible. **2.** vile or loathsome to the touch. ◇*n.* **3.** a member of the lower castes in India, whose touch is believed to defile a high-caste Hindu.

untoward /ʌntə'wɔd, ʌn'toʊəd/, *adj.* **1.** unfavorable or unfortunate. **2.** unseemly. [UN-¹ + TOWARD]

untrue /ʌn'tru/, *adj.* **1.** unfaithful; false. **2.** incorrect or inaccurate.

untruth /ʌn'truθ/, *n.* **1.** the condition or character of being untrue. **2.** want of truthfulness; divergence from truth. **3.** a falsehood or lie. **—untruthful,** *adj.*

unturned /ʌn'tɜnd/, *adj.* **1.** not having been turned or turned over. **2. leave no stone unturned,** to make a thorough search; do everything possible.

unusual /ʌn'juʒuəl/, *adj.* not usual, common, or ordinary; uncommon in amount or degree; of an exceptional kind.

unutterable /ʌn'ʌtərəbəl, -'trəbəl/, *adj.* **1.** not able to be spoken of or about; not able to be expressed. **2.** too great or remarkable to be described; unspeakable. **3.** unpronounceable.

unveil /ʌn'veɪl/, *v.t.* **1.** to remove a veil from; disclose to view. **2.** to disclose or uncover, as if by removing a veil; reveal. ◇*v.i.* **3.** to remove a veil; reveal oneself; become unveiled.

unveiling /ʌn'veɪlɪŋ/, *n.* **1.** the act of showing a monument, etc., for the first time, as in a ceremonial removal of a covering. **2.** the showing of something for the first time.

unvoiced /ʌn'vɔɪst/, *adj.* not spoken, uttered, or sounded.

unwarranted /ʌn'wɒrəntəd/, *adj.* **1.** not supported, justified, or confirmed: *an unwarranted supposition.* **2.** not authorised, as actions.

unwelcome /ʌn'welkəm/, *adj.* **1.** not welcome, as a person. **2.** not acceptable; unpleasing.

unwholesome /ʌn'hoʊlsəm/, *adj.* **1.** not wholesome; unhealthy; harmful to health or well-being, physically or morally. **2.** not sound in health; suggestive of disease.

unwieldy /ʌn'wildi/, *adj.* **1.** wielded with difficulty; not readily handled or managed in use or action. **2.** ungainly; awkward. —**unwieldiness**, *n.*

unwilling /ʌn'wɪlɪŋ/, *adj.* **1.** not willing; loath; reluctant. **2.** performed or given reluctantly: *unwilling admiration.*

unwind /ʌn'waɪnd/, *v.*, **-wound, -winding.** ◇*v.t.* **1.** to undo (something wound). **2.** to disentangle. ◇*v.i.* **3.** to become unwound. **4.** to calm down.

unwitting /ʌn'wɪtɪŋ/, *adj.* **1.** not knowing; ignorant; unaware. **2.** performed unknowingly; unpremeditated.

unwonted /ʌn'woʊntəd/, *adj.* *Archaic.* not usual or customary. —**unwontedness**, *n.*

unworldly /ʌn'wɜldli/, *adj.* **1.** not seeking material advantage or gain. **2.** having simplicity of nature; naive. **3.** not of this world; unearthly. —**unworldliness**, *n.*

unworthy /ʌn'wɜði/, *adj.* **1.** lacking worth or excellence. **2.** not to be recommended; uncommendable. **3.** of a kind not worthy (with *of*, expressed or understood): *unworthy of praise.* **4.** undeserving: *an unworthy scoundrel.* **5.** not deserved: *That was an unworthy comment.* —**unworthily**, *adv.* —**unworthiness**, *n.*

unwritten /ʌn'rɪtn/, *adj.* **1.** not written. **2.** not actually expressed or given form; customary: *It is an unwritten rule that you take your shoes off at the door.* [OE]

up /ʌp/, *adv., prep., adj., n., v.,* **upped, upping.** Note: *up* is frequently combined with a verb to form a compound as in *set up, dig up, catch up,* etc. The meanings of these compounds can be found in the entry for the main verb. ◇*adv.* **1.** to, towards, or in a higher position: *to climb up to the top of a ladder.* **2.** into the air: *to throw up a ball.* **3.** to or in an upright position. **4.** to or at any point that is considered higher, such as the north, a capital city, etc.: *up to town.* **5.** to or at a higher point in a scale (of rank, size, value, pitch, etc.). ◇*prep.* **6.** towards, or at, a higher place on or in: *up the stairs.* **7.** towards, near, or at a higher rank or condition: *up the ladder of success.* **8.** towards, or at a farther or higher point of: *up the street.* **9.** in a direction opposite to that of: *to sail up wind.* **10.** *Colloq.* towards or at: *up country.* ◇*adj.* **11.** upwards. **12.** travelling towards a particular place: *an up escalator.* **13.** pointing upwards: *The signal is up.* **14.** standing and speaking: *The prime minister was up for three hours.* **15.** out of bed: *I have been up since 6 o'clock.* **16.** risen: *The sun is up.* **17.** at a high point: *The tide is up.* **18.** in the air: *The aeroplane is 2000 metres up.* **19.** well informed or advanced: *to be up in mathematics.* **20.** under consideration; on offer: *a candidate up for election.* **21.** appearing before a court, etc., on some charge: *He is up for speeding again.* **22.** in the process of happening: *They wondered what was up.* **23.** *Games.* winning or ahead: *He is three points up on his partner.* **24. up against,** *Colloq.* faced with: *They are up against enormous problems.* **25. up and about,** active. **26. up to,** *a.* doing: *What are you up to?* *b.* resting upon, as a duty: *It is up to them to make the next move.* *c.* as many as: *It will carry up to eight passengers.* *d.* as far as: *up to their knees in water.* *e. Colloq.* capable of: *not up to the job.* ◇*n.* **27.** a rise of fortune, mood, etc.: *to have one's ups and downs.* **28. on the up and up,** *Colloq.* *a.* having increasing success. *b.* honest; straightforward. ◇*v.t.* **29.** to raise: *to up the bet.* ◇*v.i.* **30.** *Colloq.* to get or start up: *to up and away; He upped and left.* [OE]

up-, a prefix, using *up* to describe or identify, as in *upland, upgrade, upheaval.* [ME and OE]

up-and-coming /'ʌp-ən-kʌmɪŋ/, *adj.* becoming successful, well-known, etc. Also (*esp. after the verb*), **up and coming.**

Upanishad /u'pænɪʃəd, -'pʌn-, -'fæd/, *n. Theol.* the chief religious writings of ancient Hinduism, giving in more detail the mystical knowledge contained in the earlier Vedas.

up-beat /'ʌp-bit/, *n.* **1.** *Music.* **a.** the last beat of a bar, esp. when the piece of music or section or phrase starts with a note on that beat. **b.** the introductory beat of a conductor when bringing in the orchestra. ◇*adj.* **2.** *Colloq.* cheerful; optimistic.

upbraid /ʌp'breɪd/, *v.t.* **1.** to blame for some fault or wrong. ◇*v.i.* **2.** to lay blame. [OE]

upbringing /'ʌpbrɪŋɪŋ/, *n.* the bringing up of a person from childhood.

up-country /'ʌp-kʌntri/, *adj., n.;* /ʌp'kʌntri/, *adv.* ◇*adj.* **1.** being or living far from the coast or border; interior: *an up-country town.* **2.** simple; unsophisticated. ◇*n.* **3.** the interior of a country. ◇*adv.* **4.** towards or in the interior of a country.

update /ʌp'deɪt/, *v.,* **-dated, -dating.** /'ʌpdeɪt/, *n.* ◇*v.t.* **1.** to bring up to date. ◇*n.* **2.** a more recent version; revision: *an update on our earlier news.*

up-end /ʌp-'end/, *v.t.* **1.** to set on end: *up-end the barrel.* **2.** to upset or change greatly: *to up-end the plans.* ◇*v.i.* **3.** to stand on end.

Upfield /'ʌpfild/, *n.* **Arthur William,** 1890–1964, Australian author, born in England; most of his novels feature Bony, a part-Aboriginal detective.

upgrade /ʌp'greɪd/, *v.t.,* **-graded, -grading. 1.** to place (a person, job, etc.) into a position of greater importance, usu. with a larger salary. **2.** to improve: *to upgrade one's marks.*

upheaval /ʌp'hivəl/, *n.* a complete, violent, or revolutionary change or disturbance, esp. in a society.

upheld /ʌp'hɛld/, *v.* past tense and past participle of **uphold.**

uphill /ʌp'hɪl/, *adv.;* /'ʌphɪl/, *adj.* ◇*adv.* **1.** upwards. ◇*adj.* **2.** going upwards on or as

uphill 3. very tiring or difficult. 4. **an uphill battle,** a task to be completed or end to be reached only with great difficulty.

uphold /ʌp'hould/, v.t., **-held, -holding.** 1. to support or keep unchanged or undamaged: *to uphold the old order.* 2. to keep up; support. 3. to support or keep, as by agreement: *to uphold the decision of a lower court.*

upholster /ʌp'houlstə/, v.t. 1. to provide (stools, armchairs, etc.) with coverings, stuffing, springs, etc. 2. to cover in the manner of upholstery. **– upholsterer,** n.

upholstery /ʌp'houlstri, -stəri/, n., pl. **-ries.** 1. the cushions, furniture coverings and other material used to stuff and cover furniture and cushions. 2. the interior padding and lining for the seats, etc., of a car.

upkeep /'ʌpkip/, n. 1. the process of keeping up or maintaining: *the upkeep of a house.* 2. the cost of this, including operating expenses, cost of renewal or repair, etc.

upland /'ʌplənd/, n. 1. an area of high ground. ◇adj. 2. of or relating to uplands.

uplift /ʌp'lɪft/, v.; /'ʌplɪft/, n. ◇v.t. 1. to lift up; raise. 2. to raise socially or morally. 3. to raise emotionally or spiritually. ◇n. 4. the act of lifting up or raising. 5. the work of improving socially or morally. 6. a great emotional or spiritual lift.

up-market /'ʌp-makət/, adj. 1. of or relating to commercial services and goods of high status, quality and price. 2. superior in style or production; pretentious. See **down-market.**

upon /ə'pɒn/, prep. 1. up and on: *to climb upon a table.* 2. in a raised position on: *The hat is upon his head.* 3. on, in any of various senses (usu. in the same way as *on* with no added meanings). [ME]

upper /'ʌpə/, adj. 1. higher or highest, in place, position, class, wealth, etc.: *the upper slopes of a mountain; the upper class.* 2. placed or consisting of high ground, or farther into the interior: *the upper reaches of the Amazon.* 3. forming the higher of a pair of corresponding things or sets. 4. (of a surface) facing upwards. 5. (*cap.*) *Geol.* indicating a later division of a period, system, etc.: *the Upper Devonian.* ◇n. 6. anything which is higher (than another, as of a pair) or highest. 7. the part of a shoe above the sole. 8. *Colloq.* a drug which raises the spirits. 9. *Colloq.* a pleasant or exciting experience. 10. **be on one's uppers,** *Colloq.* to be in need; impoverished.

upper case, n. *Print.* the upper half of a pair of cases, which contains the capital letters of the alphabet. **– upper-case,** adj.

upper chamber, n. → **upper house.**

uppercut /'ʌpəkʌt/, n. a swinging blow directed upwards.

upper hand, n. the controlling position; advantage.

upper house, n. *Govt.* one of two branches of a law-making body (legislature), generally smaller and less representative than the lower branch, usu. acting as a house of review, rarely introducing legislation and lacking the constitutional power to initiate any financial legislation, as the Senate in the Australian Parliament. Also, **upper chamber.**

uppermost /'ʌpəmoust/, adj. 1. highest in place, order, rank, power, etc. 2. topmost; predominant; foremost. ◇adv. 3. in the highest or topmost place, rank, etc.

upright /'ʌpraɪt/, adj. 1. straight upward or vertical, in position or posture. 2. raised or directed vertically. 3. honest or just; righteous. ◇n. 4. the state of being upright or vertical. 5. (of timber, etc.) something standing straight upward. 6. an upright piano. ◇adv. 7. in an upright position or direction. [OE]

uprising /'ʌpraɪzɪŋ, ʌp'raɪzɪŋ/, n. 1. an armed rising against authority; revolt. 2. the act of rising.

uproar /'ʌprɔ/, n. a violent and noisy disturbance; tumultuous noise. [D: tumult] **– uproarious,** adj.

uproot /ʌp'rut/, v.t. 1. to tear up by or as if by the roots. 2. to remove completely. 3. to remove (people) from their usual environment; displace.

upset /ʌp'sɛt/, v., **-set, -setting;** /ʌp'sɛt/, n.; /'ʌpsɛt/, *esp. in predicative use* /ʌp'sɛt/, adj. ◇v.t. 1. to overturn: *to upset the boat.* 2. to spill by knocking over: *to upset the cup.* 3. to throw into disorder: *to upset the pile of papers.* 4. to disturb (someone) mentally or emotionally; distress. 5. to make ill, esp. in the stomach. 6. to make ineffective: *to upset someone's plans.* 7. to defeat a competitor. ◇v.i. 8. to become overturned. ◇n. 9. a physical upsetting or being upset. 10. the act or fact of disordering (ideas, patterns, etc.). 11. a slight illness, esp. of the stomach. 12. an emotional disturbance. 13. a quarrel. 14. a defeat, esp. unexpected. ◇adj. 15. emotionally disturbed. 16. overturned; capsized.

upshot /'ʌpʃɒt/, n. the final issue, conclusion, or result: *the upshot of the argument.* [UP- (in sense of termination) + SHOT¹]

upside down, adv. 1. with the upper part underneath. 2. in complete disorder; topsyturvy. [alteration of ME *up so down*]

upstage /ʌp'steɪdʒ/, adv.; /'ʌpsteɪdʒ/, adj.; /ʌp'steɪdʒ/, v., **-staged, -staging.** ◇adv. 1. on or to the back of the stage. ◇adj. 2. of or relating to the back of the stage. 3. coldly proud; haughty; aloof. ◇v.t. 4. to steal attention from (another) by placing oneself in a more favorable position in word or action.

upstairs /ʌp'stɛəz/, adv.; /'ʌpstɛəz/ adj., n. ◇adv. 1. up the stairs. 2. to or in a higher rank or office. 3. **kick upstairs,** to promote (someone) in order to get them out of the way. ◇adj. 4. on or relating to an upper floor. ◇n. 5. an upper storey or storeys.

upstanding /'ʌpstændɪŋ/, *esp. in predicative use* /ʌp'stændɪŋ/, adj. 1. standing upright; erect. 2. straightforward, open, or independent; honorable. 3. *Colloq.* standing up: *Be upstanding and charge your glasses.*

upstart /'ʌpstat/, n. someone who has risen suddenly from a low position to wealth or

upstart power, esp. one who is self-important and objectionable.

upsurge /'ʌpsədʒ/, n. a strong rising or moving upwards: *an upsurge of anger*.

upswing /'ʌpswɪŋ/, n. 1. an upward swing, as of a pendulum. 2. a marked advance or increase.

uptake /'ʌpteɪk/, n. 1. the action of understanding; mental grasp. 2. the act of taking up. 3. **quick (slow) on the uptake**, quick (slow) to understand or learn new or difficult ideas.

up-tempo /'ʌp-tempoʊ/, n. 1. a fast rhythm. ◇adj. 2. rhythmic; fast.

uptight /'ʌptaɪt/, adj. *Colloq.* tense, nervous, or irritable.

up-to-date /ʌp-tə-'deɪt/, adj. 1. including the latest facts: *an up-to-date record*. 2. in accordance with the newest standards, ideas, or style; modern: *up-to-date clothes*. 3. (of people, etc.) keeping up with the times, as in information, ideas, methods, style, etc.

upturn /ʌp'tɜn/, v.; /'ʌptɜn/, n., ◇v.t. 1. to turn up or over: *to upturn a boat to empty out the water*. 2. to direct upwards. ◇v.i. 3. to turn upwards. ◇n. 4. an upward turn, or a changing and rising movement, as in prices, business, etc.

upward /'ʌpwəd/, adj. 1. directed or moving towards a higher point or level; ascending. ◇adv. 2. upwards. [OE]

upwards /'ʌpwədz/, adv. 1. towards a higher place or position. 2. (of thought, feeling, age, rank, etc.), towards a higher level, degree, or standard. 3. towards the centre, source, most important part, etc.: *fish swimming upwards against the current*. 4. in or facing the highest position: *to look upwards to see the stars*. 5. **upwards of**, **a.** more than; above: *He is upwards of 60 years of age*. **b.** approximately: *There were upwards of 30 people at the meeting*. Also, **upward**.

Ur /ɜ/, n. an ancient Sumerian city and district in southern Babylonia, on the Euphrates, now in south-eastern Iraq.

Urals /'jʊərəlz/, n. a mountain system in Russia, extending north and south from the Arctic Sea to near the Caspian Sea, forming a natural boundary between Europe and Asia. Highest peak, Mt Telpos, 1688 m. Also, **Ural Mountains**.

uranic /jʊ'rænɪk/, adj. of or containing uranium, esp. in the tetravalent state. [URAN(IUM) + -IC]

uranium /jʊ'reɪniəm/, n. a naturally-occurring white, lustrous, radioactive, metallic element, consisting of 99.28 per cent of isotope U-238 and 0.71 per cent of isotope U-235, the latter being the basis of nuclear reactors and weapons. Symbol: U; at. no.: 92; at. wt: 238.03. [NL]

urano-, a word part meaning 'heaven'. [Gk, combining form of *ouranós*]

Uranus /jʊ'reɪnəs/, n. the seventh planet in order from the sun. [in Greek mythology, the personification of Heaven, and the ruler of the world; L, from Gk *Ouranós*]

urban /'ɜbən/, adj. 1. of, in, relating to, or characteristic of a city or town. 2. living in a city. [L] —**urbanise**, v.

urbane /ɜ'beɪn/, adj. 1. having or showing the good taste and manners considered to be characteristic of city-dwellers; civilised; sophisticated. 2. smoothly polite; suave. [L] —**urbanity**, n.

urchin /'ɜtʃən/, n. 1. a small child, esp. one who is mischievous or very poorly dressed. 2. → **sea-urchin**. ◇adj. 3. of the nature of or like an urchin. [ME, from d. OF, from L: hedgehog]

Urdu /'ʊdu/, n. one of the official languages of Pakistan, a dialect used by Muslims, derived from Hindustani but using Arabic characters and drawing on Persian and Arabic vocabulary. [Hind: camp (speech), from Turk *ordū* camp.

-ure, a suffix of abstract nouns showing action, result, and process, as in *legislature*, *pressure*. [representing F -*ure* and L -*ūra*]

urea /jʊ'riə, 'jʊriə/, n. colorless, crystalline substance, $CO(NH_2)_2$, used in fertilisers and in making plastics and adhesives; the main excretory product of mammals, amphibians, etc. [NL, from Gk: urination] —**ureal**, **uric**, adj.

-uret, a noun suffix in names of some chemical compounds, having the same force as **-ide**. [NL]

ureter /jʊ'ritə/, n. *Anat.* one of a pair of muscular tubes carrying the urine from the kidneys to the bladder. [L, from Gk]

urethr-, variant of **urethro-** before vowels.

urethra /jʊ'riθrə/, n., pl. **-thrae** /-θri/ **-thras**. *Anat.* the membranous tube which discharges urine from the bladder. [LL, from Gk] —**urethral**, adj.

urethro-, a word part representing **urethra**. Also, **urethr-**.

urge /ɜdʒ/, v., **urged**, **urging**, n. ◇v.t. 1. to try to persuade, by pleading or recommending: *urge a person to take more care*. 2. to recommend earnestly: *urge a plan of action*. 3. to press (something) upon the attention: *urge a claim*. 4. to insist on or declare with earnestness: *urge the need for haste*. 5. to push, force, or drive along: *urge the horse along*. 6. to force or move to some action: *urged by necessity*. ◇v.i. 7. to make earnest recommendations: *to urge by pleading*. 8. to use a driving force: *Hunger urges*. 9. to press, push, or hurry on (oft. fol. by *on*, *onwards*, *along*, etc.). ◇n. 10. a natural or instinctive impulse: *an urge to eat*. [L: press, drive]

urgent /'ɜdʒənt/, adj. 1. pressing; requiring immediate action or attention: *This is an urgent message, to be sent immediately*. 2. earnest in request; insistent: *an urgent appeal to help the homeless*. [L] —**urgency**, n.

-urgy, a word part meaning 'a technology', as in *metallurgy*. [Gk: work]

-uria, a word part meaning 'urine'. [NL, from Gk: urine]

urinal /'jurənəl, ju'raɪnəl/, *n*. **1**. a fixture, room, or building for discharging urine in. **2**. a glass or metallic container for urine. [ME, from L]

urinate /'jurəneɪt/, *v.i.*, **-nated, -nating**. to pass urine. **—urination**, *n*.

urine /'jurən, -aɪn/, *n*. a substance produced by the kidneys (in mammals, a fluid), which in most mammals is carried to the bladder by the ureter, and from there by the urethra. [ME, from L] **—urinous, —urinary**, *adj*.

urinogenital /jurənoʊ'dʒɛnətl/, *adj*. → **urogenital**.

urn /ɜn/, *n*. **1**. a type of vase, of various forms, esp. one with a foot or base. **2**. such a vase for holding the ashes of the dead after cremation. **3**. a large apparatus with a tap, used for heating water, tea, coffee, etc. [ME, from L]

uro-[1], a word part referring to urine and the urinary tract. [Gk, combining form of *oûron* urine]

uro-[2], a word part meaning 'tail'. [combining form representing Gk *ourá*]

urogenital /jurou'dʒɛnətl/, *adj*. of or relating to the urinary and genital organs. [URO-[1] + GENITAL]

urology /ju'rɒlədʒi/, *n*. the scientific study of the urine and the urogenital tract. [URO-[1] + -LOGY] **—urological**, *adj*. **—urologist**, *n*.

Ursa Major /,ɜsə 'meɪdʒə/, *n*. → **Great Bear**. [L: greater bear]

ursine /'ɜsaɪn/, *adj*. **1**. of or relating to a bear. **2**. bearlike. [L]

urticaria /ɜtə'kɛəriə/, *n*. a skin condition marked by periods of itching or the appearance of swellings, usu. due to contact with something to which one is allergic; nettle rash; hives. [NL, from L: nettle] **—urticarial, urticarious**, *adj*.

Uruguay /'jurəgwaɪ/, *n*. a republic on the south-eastern coast of South America, bordered by Brazil and Argentina; a Spanish colony before independence in 1825. Pop. 3 058 000 (1987); 176 215 km². *Language:* Spanish. *Currency:* peso. *Cap.:* Montevideo. Official name, **Eastern Republic of Uraquay**. **—Uruguayan**, *n*., *adj*.

us /ʌs; *weak forms* /əs, əz/, *pron*. objective case of **we**. [OE]

US /ju 'ɛs/, *n*. United States. See **United States of America**. [abbrev.]

USA /ju ɛs 'eɪ/, *n*. → **United States of America**. [abbrev.]

usable /'juzəbəl/, *adj*. → **useable**. **—usability, usableness**, *n*.

usage /'jusɪdʒ, 'juzɪdʒ/, *n*. **1**. custom or practice: *the usages of the last fifty years*. **2**. the customary or standard manner of using a language or any of its forms: *English usage*. **3**. a particular instance of this: *a usage borrowed from the French*. **4**. the body of rules or customs followed by a particular set of people. **5**. way of using or treating: *hard or rough usage*. [ME, from OF: use, from L]

use /juz/, *v.*, **-used, -using**; /jus/, *n*. ◇*v.t.* **1**. to employ for some purpose: *to use a knife to cut*. **2**. to take in; consume; expend: *His car uses a lot of oil*. **3**. to act or behave towards, or treat (a person) in some manner: *You use him for selfish reasons*. **4**. to utter (words) or speak (a language). **5**. to operate or put into effect: *use a machine*. ◇*v.* **6**. **use up, a**. to take completely; consume: *I've used up the toothpaste*. **b**. to exhaust: *He used up his strength*. ◇*n*. **7**. the act of using: *the use of tools*. **8**. the condition of being used: *This book is in use*. **9**. an instance of using something: *each separate use of the tool*. **10**. a way of being used: *The instrument has different uses*. **11**. the power or right of using something: *to lose the use of the right eye*. **12**. usefulness; utility: *of no practical use*. **13**. occasion or need, for something to be used: *Have you any use for another calendar?* [ME, from OF, from L]

useable /'juzəbəl/, *adj*. **1**. available for use. **2**. in a condition to be used. Also, **usable**.

used[1] /juzd/, *adj*. **1**. that has been made use of, esp. as showing signs of wear. **2**. → **second-hand**. **3**. **used up**, completely consumed or exhausted. [pp. of USE]

used[2] /just/, *adj*. accustomed; habituated (fol. by *to*): *I am used to eating late*. [special use of USE]

useful /'jusfəl/, *adj*. **1**. being of use or service. **2**. of practical use, as for doing work: *the useful arts*. **—usefulness**, *n*.

useless /'juslas/, *adj*. **1**. of no use: *a useless tool*. **2**. without useful qualities: *a useless worker*. **—uselessness**, *n*.

user-friendly /'juzə-frɛndli/, *adj*. (esp. of computer programs or equipment) easy to operate or understand.

usher /'ʌʃə/, *n*. **1**. someone who takes people to their seats in a church, theatre, etc. **2**. an attendant who keeps order in a law court. **3**. *Obs*. an officer having charge of an entrance door; a doorkeeper. ◇*v.t.* **4**. to act as an usher to (fol. by *in, into, out,* etc.). **5**. to attend at the beginning: *Birdsong ushered in the day*. [ME, from AF, from LL: doorkeeper]

usherette /ʌʃə'rɛt/, *n*. a female attendant, esp. one who shows people to their seats in a cinema or theatre.

USSR /ju ɛs ɛs 'a/, *n*. Union of Soviet Socialist Republics. See **Soviet Union**. [abbrev.]

Ustashi /u'staʃi/, *n*. a right-wing terrorist organisation of exiled Yugoslavians dedicated to the overthrow of Communism in their native land.

Ustinov /'justənɒf/, *n*. **Peter**, born 1921, British actor, director, and dramatist of stage and film.

usu., *Abbrev*. **1**. usually. **2**. usual.

usual /'juʒuəl/, *adj*. **1**. normal; habitual; customary: *his usual skill*. **2**. such as is commonly met with in experience; ordinary: *the usual January weather*. **3**. in common use; common: *the usual means of transport*. **4**. **as usual**, as is (or was) usual: *He will come as*

usual

usual. ◇n. 5. something which is usual: *I'll have the usual to eat.* [ME, from L] —**usually,** *adv.*

usurp /ju'zɜp/, *v.t.* 1. to seize and hold (an office, position, power, etc.) by force or without right. 2. to take or make use of (rights, property, etc.) not one's own. ◇v.i. 3. to seize forcibly or illegally, an office, power, etc.; encroach. [ME, from L] —**usurper,** *n.* —**usurpation,** *n.*

usury /'juʒəri/, *n., pl.* **-ries.** 1. a very high rate of interest, esp. in excess of the legal rate. 2. the lending, or practice of lending money at a very high rate of interest. [ME, from ML: interest] —**usurer,** *n.* —**usurious,** *adj.*

Utah /'juta/, *n.* a state in the western US; settled by Mormons in 1847. Pop. 1 665 000 (1986 est.). *Cap.*: Salt Lake City. *Abbrev.*: Ut —**Utahan,** *n., adj.*

ute /jut/, *n.* → **utility** (def. 4).

utensil /ju'tensəl/, *n.* 1. any of the instruments or vessels commonly used in a kitchen, dairy, etc. 2. any instrument, vessel, or implement. [ME, from ML: useful]

uterine /'jutəraɪn/, *adj.* 1. of or relating to the uterus or womb. 2. related through having the same mother. [ME, from LL, from L: uterus]

utero-, a word part representing **uterus.**

uterus /'jutərəs/, *n., pl.* **uteri** /'jutəraɪ/. the organ in which the fertilised ovum implants itself and develops during pregnancy; the womb of mammals. [L]

utilise *or* **utilize** /'jutəlaɪz/, *v.t.,* **-lised, -lising.** to put to use: *to utilise water power for driving machinery.* —**utilisation,** *n.*

utilitarian /ju,tɪlə'tɛəriən/, *adj.* 1. concerning practical or material things: *a utilitarian idea.* 2. having regard to usefulness rather than beauty, etc.: *utilitarian clothes.* 3. *Ethics.* of, relating to, or following the doctrine of utilitarianism. ◇n. 4. a follower of utilitarianism. 5. someone who is only concerned with practical matters, or who takes a practical attitude.

utilitarianism /,jutɪlə'tɛəriə,nɪzəm/, *n. Ethics.* the doctrine that goodness is based on usefulness, and that conduct should be directed towards creating the greatest happiness for the greatest number of people.

utility /ju'tɪləti/, *n., pl.* **-ties.** 1. the state or character of being useful. 2. something useful. 3. a public service, such as a bus or railway service, gas or electricity supply, etc. 4. Also, **ute.** small truck with an enclosed cabin and open body which is sometimes covered with a tarpaulin. 5. *Econ.* the ability of an object to satisfy a human want. ◇adj. 6. provided, designed, bred, or made for usefulness rather than beauty. [ME, from L]

utmost /'ʌtmoust/, *adj.* 1. of the greatest or highest degree, quantity, etc.: *of the utmost importance.* 2. being at the farthest point; farthest: *the utmost boundary of the Roman Empire.* ◇n. 3. the greatest degree or amount: *the utmost that can be said.* 4. the highest, greatest, or best of one's power: *Do your utmost.* 5. the extreme limit: *The runner pushed his strength to the utmost.* Also, **uttermost.** [OE]

Uzbekistan

utopia /ju'toupiə/, *n. (sometimes cap.)* a place or state of ideal perfection. [from *Utopia* by Sir Thomas More, 1478–1535; NL, from Gk *ou* not + *-topia,* from *tópas* place] —**utopian,** *adj.* —**utopianism,** *n.*

utricle /'jutrɪkəl/, *n.* 1. a small baglike body, such as an air-filled cavity in a seaweed. 2. *Bot.* a membranous covering surrounding certain fruit. [L: bag] —**utricular,** *adj.* —**utriculate,** *adj.*

Utrillo /ju'trɪloʊ/, *n.* **Maurice** /mɒ'ris/, 1883–1955, French painter; known for his interpretations of Parisian street scenes.

Uttar Pradesh /ʊtə 'pradɛʃ/, *n.* a state in northern India. Pop. 110 862 013 (1981); 294 411 km². *Cap.*: Lucknow. Formerly, **United Provinces.**

utter[1] /'ʌtə/, *v.t.* 1. to speak or pronounce: *The words were uttered in my hearing.* 2. to give expression to (a subject, etc.): *unable to utter her opinions.* 3. to make publicly known; publish: *utter a libel.* 4. (of coins, notes, etc. and esp. counterfeit money) to place into general use. ◇v.i. 5. to use the power of speech. [ME]

utter[2] /'ʌtə/, *adj.* 1. complete; total; absolute: *She has an utter horror of spiders.* 2. unconditional; unqualified: *utter surrender.* [OE: outer]

utterance /'ʌtrəns, 'ʌtərəns/, *n.* 1. the act of uttering. 2. manner of speaking. 3. something uttered, such as a word, cry, call, etc. [ME]

utterly /'ʌtəli/, *adv.* completely; absolutely.

uttermost /'ʌtəmoust/, *adj., n.* → **utmost.** [ME]

U-turn /'ju-tɜn/, *n.* a turn made by a motor vehicle within the width of a road to face the way it has just come.

Utzon /'ʊtzən/, *n.* **Joern** /'jɜn/, born 1918, Danish architect; designed the Sydney Opera House.

UV, /ju 'vi/ *Abbrev.* ultraviolet.

uvula /'juvjələ/, *n., pl.* **-las, -lae** /-li/. the small, fleshy, cone-shaped body projecting downwards from the middle of the soft palate. [ME, from ML, from L: little grape] —**uvular,** *adj.*

uxorious /ʌk'sɔriəs/, *adj.* greatly or foolishly fond of one's wife. [L] —**uxoriousness,** *n.*

Uzbekistan /ʊz'bekəstan, ʌz-/, *n.* a republic in central Asia on the Aral Sea; a member of the CIS; a constituent republic of the Soviet Union 1924–91, known as the **Uzbek Soviet Socialist Republic.** Pop. 19 905 000 (1989 est.); 447 400 km². *Language*: Uzbek. *Cap.*: Tashkent. —**Uzbek,** *n., adj.*

Vv

V, v, *n., pl.* **V's** or **Vs, v's** or **vs.** 1. the 22nd letter of the English alphabet. 2. (*sometimes l.c.*) the Roman numeral for 5. 3. something shaped like the letter V.

v, *Symbol.* velocity.

v., *Abbrev.* 1. *Bot.* variety (of). 2. vector. 3. verb. 4. verse. 5. versus (against). 6. very.

V, *Symbol.* 1. *Chem.* vanadium. 2. *Phys.* velocity. 3. *Elect.* volt.

V-, a prefix meaning that the cylinders of a given number in an internal-combustion engine are arranged in a V shape: *V-twin, V-6, V-8.*

vac., *Abbrev.* 1. vacant. 2. vacancy. 3. vacation. 4. vacuum.

vacancy /ˈveɪkənsi/, *n., pl.* **-cies.** 1. emptiness; unoccupied state. 2. a gap or opening. 3. an unfilled office or position: *There is a vacancy in this department.* 4. lack of thought or intelligence; vacuity.

vacant /ˈveɪkənt/, *adj.* 1. empty; void. 2. (of a chair, position, house, etc.) not occupied. 3. free from work, business, etc.: *a vacant hour.* 4. characterised by, showing, or coming from lack of thought or intelligence. [ME, from L]

vacant possession, *n.* the right to move into a house or property, the former occupant having left.

vacate /vəˈkeɪt, veɪˈkeɪt/, *v.t.*, **-cated, -cating.** 1. to make empty. 2. to give up (an office, position, house, etc.). [L: freed, emptied]

vacation /vəˈkeɪʃən, veɪˈkeɪʃən/, *n.* 1. that part of the year when law courts, universities, etc., are closed. 2. *Chiefly US.* a holiday. 3. the act of vacating. [ME, from L]

vaccinate /ˈvæksəneɪt/, *v.t.*, **-nated, -nating.** to administer a vaccine to (someone), to prevent illness. [VACCINE + -ATE¹] **—vaccination,** *n.* **—vaccinator,** *n.*

vaccine /ˈvæksin, vækˈsin/, *n.* the altered virus of various diseases used for inoculation against illness, esp. smallpox. [L: pertaining to cows]

vacillate /ˈvæsəleɪt/, *v.i.*, **-lated, -lating.** 1. to sway unsteadily; waver; stagger. 2. to change continually from one course, position, etc., to another; fluctuate. 3. to be indecisive or hesitant. [L] **—vacillation,** *n.*

vacuity /vəˈkjuəti/, *n., pl.* **-ties.** 1. the condition of being empty. 2. an empty space; vacuum. 3. absence or lack of something in particular. 4. absence of ideas, thought, or intelligence. 5. something stupid or senseless. [L]

vacuole /ˈvækjuoʊl/, *n.* 1. a space within a cell containing fluid. 2. a tiny space in organic tissue. [NL: VACUUM]

vacuous /ˈvækjuəs/, *adj.* empty, esp. of ideas or intelligence. [L] **—vacuousness,** *n.*

vacuum /ˈvækjum/, *n., pl.* **vacuums, vacua** /ˈvækjuə/, *v.* ◇*n.* 1. a space completely free of matter (**perfect** or **complete vacuum**). 2. an enclosed space from which air (or other gas) has been removed, as by an air pump (**partial vacuum**). 3. emptiness. ◇*v.t.* 4. to clean with a vacuum cleaner. [L: empty]

vacuum cleaner, *n.* an apparatus for cleaning carpets, floors, etc., by sucking in dust.

vacuum flask, *n.* → **thermos.** Also, **vacuum bottle.**

vacuum-packed /ˈvækjum-pækt/, *adj.* packed with little or no air in an airtight container, so as to keep freshness, flavor, etc. Also, **vacuum-sealed.**

vacuum pump, *n.* a pump or device by which a partial vacuum can be produced.

vagabond /ˈvægəbɒnd/, *adj.* 1. wandering from place to place without being settled; nomadic. 2. good-for-nothing; worthless: *vagabond friends.* ◇*n.* 3. someone who is without a fixed home and who wanders from place to place, esp. one thought to be idle or worthless; tramp; vagrant. [ME, from L: strolling about]

vagary /ˈveɪgəri/, *n., pl.* **-ries.** 1. an unusual, quaint, or extravagant idea. 2. a wild, fanciful, or fantastic action; freak. [apparently from L: wander] **—vagarious,** *adj.*

vagina /vəˈdʒaɪnə/, *n., pl.* **-nas, -nae** /-ni/. 1. *Anat.* the passage leading from the uterus to the vulva in a female mammal. 2. *Bot.* a sheath formed by the base of certain leaves where they join the stem. [L: sheath] **—vaginal,** *adj.* **—vaginate,** *adj.*

vagrant /ˈveɪgrənt/, *n.* 1. someone who wanders from place to place and has no settled home or means of support; a tramp. ◇*adj.* 2. wandering from place to place; nomadic. [late ME, from L] **—vagrancy,** *n.*

vague /veɪg/, *adj.*, **vaguer, vaguest.** 1. not clear or certain in statement or meaning: *vague promises.* 2. (of ideas, feelings, etc.) not clear or exact. 3. not clear or sharp to the senses: *vague forms seen through mist.* 4. not definitely fixed or known; uncertain: *vague plans.* 5. (of people, etc.) not clear in thought or understanding. [L: wandering] **—vagueness,** *n.*

vain /veɪn/, *adj.* 1. without real value or importance; idle; worthless: *a vain promise.* 2. futile; useless: *vain attempts.* 3. having enormous pride in one's own appearance, qualities, gifts, etc.; conceited. 4. coming from or showing personal vanity: *vain boasts.* ◇*adv.* 5. **in vain, a.** to no purpose: *He tried in vain to save her.* **b.** improperly; blasphemously: *to take God's name in vain.* [ME, from OF, from L: empty, idle]

vainglory /veɪnˈglɔri/, *n.* 1. very great pride in one's achievements, abilities, etc. 2. vain display or show. [ME; translation of ML] **—vainglorious,** *adj.*

vale /veɪl/, *n. Chiefly Poetic.* a valley. [ME, from OF, from L]

valediction /ˌvælə'dɪkʃən/, n. **1.** a saying goodbye. **2.** a speech, etc., made at the time of or by way of leave-taking. [L: bidden goodbye] — **valedictory**, adj., n.

Valencia /vəˈlensiə/, n. **1.** a region in eastern Spain; formerly a Moorish kingdom. 23 530 km². **2.** a seaport in eastern Spain, capital of Valencia province. Pop. 751 734 (1981).

valency /'veɪlənsi/, n., pl. **-cies.** (the quality determining) the combining power of an atom or radical compared with the hydrogen atom: *a valency of one* (the ability to combine with or replace one atom of hydrogen). Also, *Chiefly US*, **valence**. [L: strength]

valency bond, n. a chemical bond between two atoms in a molecule.

valency electron, n. an electron from an outer shell of an atom able to take part in forming valency bonds. Also, **valence electron**.

-valent, a word part meaning 'having worth or value', used esp. in scientific terminology to refer to valency, as in *quadrivalent*. [L]

valentine /'væləntaɪn/, n. **1.** a card, gift or token, expressing love or warm emotion, sent by one person to another on St Valentine's Day. **2.** a sweetheart chosen on St Valentine's Day, 14 February. [named after St *Valentine*, d. AD c. 270, Christian martyr at Rome]

valerian /vəˈlɪəriən, -'lɪə-/, n. **1.** a plant with white or pink flowers and a medicinal root. **2.** a drug made from the root, used to calm nerves. [ME, from ML, fem., from *Valerius*, personal name]

Valéry /vaˌleɪˈriː/, n. **Paul** /pɒl/, 1871–1945, French poet and philosopher; influenced by the symbolist aesthetics, his poetry is rich in imagery.

valet /'væleɪ, 'væləʔ/, n., v., **-leted, -leting.** ◇n. **1.** a manservant who attends to his employer's personal needs. **2.** someone who performs similar services for guests in a hotel, etc. ◇v.t., v.i. **3.** to serve or act as valet. [F, var. of MF]

Valhalla /vælˈhælə/, n. *Scand Myth.* the hall of immortality where the souls of heroes slain in battle go. Also, **Valhall, Walhalla**. [NL, from Icel *valhöll* hall of the slain]

valiant /'væliənt/, adj. **1.** brave or courageous: *a valiant person.* **2.** marked by or showing bravery: *valiant attempts to save a life.* [ME, from OF: be strong, from L] — **valiance**, n.

valid /'væləd/, adj. **1.** sound, just, or well-founded: *a valid reason.* **2.** having force, weight, or power to convince; authoritative. **3.** legally sound, effective, or binding. **4.** *Logic.* relating to arguments in which the premises imply the conclusion (opposed to *invalid*). [L: strong] — **validity**, n.

validate /'vælədeɪt/, v.t., **-dated, -dating. 1.** to make valid; confirm: *The booking office will validate her ticket.* **2.** to give legal force to; legalise: *to validate a passport.* — **validation**, n.

valise /vəˈliːz, -ˈliːs/, n. a small traveller's case for holding clothes, toilet articles, etc. [F, from I; orig. uncert.]

Valkyrie /vælˈkɪəri/, n. *Scand. Myth.* one of the handmaids of Odin who ride through the air to battle and choose the heroes who are to be slain and taken to Valhalla. Also, **Valkyr, Walkyrie**. [Icel *valkyrja* chooser of the slain] — **Valkyrian**, adj.

valley /'væli/, n., pl. **-leys. 1.** lower land, usu. with an outlet, between hills or mountains. **2.** a large, rather low, flat region drained by a great river system. **3.** any hollow or structure likened to a valley. [ME, from OF, from L]

valor or **valour** /'vælə/, n. boldness or firmness in braving danger. [ME, from OF, from L: be strong, be worth] — **valorous**, adj.

valuable /'væljuəbəl, 'væljubəl/, adj. **1.** of worth, in terms of money. **2.** representing a large market value: *valuable paintings.* **3.** of great use, service, or importance: *valuable information.* ◇n. **4.** (usu. pl.) a valuable article, esp. one of rather small size, such as a piece of jewellery. — **valuably**, adv.

valuation /ˌvæljuˈeɪʃən/, n. **1.** the fixing of the value of a thing. **2.** the value decided or fixed.

value /'vælju/, n., v., **-ued, -uing.** ◇n. **1.** that property of a thing that makes it highly regarded, desirable, or useful; worth; merit: *the value of education.* **2.** the worth of a thing as measured by the amount of other things for which it can be exchanged. **3.** decided worth; valuation. **4.** force or importance: *the value of a word or phrase.* **5.** *Maths.* **a.** the size of a quantity or measurement. **b.** (of a function) the number obtained when particular numbers are substituted for the variables. **6.** (*pl.*) the ideals, customs, institutions, etc. in which the people of a social group believe. **7.** *Music.* the relative length of a note. ◇v.t. **8.** to decide the value of: *to value a ring.* **9.** to consider, with respect to worth, excellence, usefulness, or importance: *to value honesty more than profit.* **10.** to regard highly: *to value a friendship.* [ME, from OF: be worth, from L] — **valuer**, n.

valued /'væljud/, adj. **1.** highly regarded; esteemed: *a valued opinion.* **2.** judged; estimated or appraised: *the valued price of the car.*

value judgment, n. an assessment based on one's personal or social values.

valve /vælv/, n., v., **valved, valving.** ◇n. **1.** any device, esp. a hinge-like part, for closing or altering the passage through a pipe, outlet, etc., in order to control the flow of liquids, gases, etc. **2.** *Music.* a device, as in the trumpet, for changing the length of the air column to alter the pitch of a note. **3.** *Zool.* one of the two or more separable pieces making up certain shells. **4.** *Bot.* one of the parts into which a dry fruit opens to release its seeds. **5.** *Elect.* a device consisting of two or more electrodes in an evacuated or gas-filled cylinder, which can be used for controlling a flow of electricity. ◇v.t. **6.** to provide with a means of control of fluid flow (as gas from a balloon), by supplying with a valve. [ME, from L: leaf of

valve   a door (pl., folding doors)] **—valvate, valvular**, *adj.*

vamoose /və'muːs/, *v.i., v.t.,* **-moosed, -moosing**. *Chiefly US.* to depart quickly. [Sp: let us go]

vamp[1] /væmp/, *n.* **1.** the front part of the upper of a shoe or boot. **2.** anything patched up or pieced together. **3.** *Music.* an accompaniment, usu. improvised, consisting of a succession of simple chords. ◊*v.t.* **4.** to patch up or repair (oft. fol. by *up*): *to vamp up the house.* ◊*v.i.* **5.** *Music.* to improvise an accompaniment, tune, etc. [ME, from OF: forepart of the foot, from L]

vamp[2] /væmp/, *Colloq.* ◊*n.* **1.** a woman who uses her charms to attract and take advantage of men. ◊*v.i., v.t.* **2.** to act as a vamp (towards). [short for VAMPIRE]

vampire /'væmpaɪə/, *n.* **1.** (in common belief) the corpse of a person improperly buried, who comes to life again in order to suck the blood of people while they sleep. **2.** someone who preys cruelly on others; extortionist. **3.** Also, **vampire bat**. any of various South and Central American bats which feed on the blood of animals including man. [F, from G, ? from Turk: witch] **—vampiric, vampirish,** *adj.* **—vampirism,** *n.*

van[1] /væn/, *n.* →**vanguard.**

van[2] /væn/, *n.* **1.** a covered vehicle, usu. large in size, for moving furniture, goods, etc. **2.** a closed railway wagon. [short for CARAVAN]

vanadium /və'neɪdɪəm/, *n.* a rare, light-grey, powdery element used to toughen steel. *Symbol:* V; *at. no.:* 23; *at. wt:* 50.942. [Icel]

Van Buren /væn 'bjʊərən/, *n.* **Martin,** 1782-1862, eighth president of the US, 1837-41.

Vancouver[1] /væn'kuːvə/, *n.* **George,** 1757-98, English navigator; explorer of the Pacific coast of North America; in 1791 explored a large part of the south-west coast of Australia.

Vancouver[2] /væn'kuːvə/, *n.* a seaport in Canada in south-western British Columbia, on Georgia Strait opposite south-eastern Vancouver Island. Pop. 431 137 (1986).

vandal /'vændl/, *n.* **1.** someone who deliberately or ignorantly destroys or damages property, works of art, etc. **2.** (*cap.*) a member of a Germanic people which in the fifth century AD ravaged Gaul and Spain, settled in Africa, and in 455 sacked Rome. ◊*adj.* **3.** characterised by vandalism. **4.** (*cap.*) of or relating to the Vandals. [LL. *Vandalus,* Latinisation of native tribal name] **—vandalism,** *n.*

van der Waals forces /væn də 'wɑːlz/, *n.* weak forces of attraction between atoms or molecules arising as a result of electrons in neighboring atoms or molecules moving in sympathy with each other. [named after JD *van der Waals,* 1837-1923, Dutch physicist]

Van Diemen's Land /væn 'diːmənz/, *n.* the name originally given to Tasmania by Abel Tasman in 1642. [named after Anthony *Van Diemen,* Governor-General of Dutch East Indies 1636]

Van Diemen's Land Company, *n.* an Australian agricultural company formed by a London syndicate in 1825, investing in livestock breeding in northern Tas.

Vandyke /væn'daɪk/, *n.* **Sir Anthony,** 1599-1641, Flemish painter living in England. Also, **Van Dyke, Van Dyct.**

vane /veɪn/, *n.* **1.** a flat piece of metal, etc., fixed upon a roof, etc., which moves with the wind and shows its direction; weathervane. **2.** a sail in the wheel of a windmill, to be moved by the air. **3.** any plate, blade, etc., joined to an axis and moved by or in air or a liquid: *a vane of a screw propeller.* [ME; OE *fana* flag] **—vaned,** *adj.*

Van Eyck /væn 'aɪk/, *n.* →**Eyck.**

Van Gogh /væn 'gɒf, 'gou/, *n.* **Vincent** 1853-90, Dutch post-impressionist painter; his work was influential in the development of Fauvism and German expressionism.

vanguard /'væŋgɑːd/, *n.* **1.** the foremost division or front part of an army. **2.** the leading position in any field. **3.** the leaders of any intellectual or political movement. Also, **van.** [late ME, from OF]

vanilla /və'nɪlə/, *n.* a tropical climbing orchid whose podlike fruit yields a substance used in flavoring food, in perfumery, etc. [NL, from Sp: little pod, from L]

vanish /'vænɪʃ/, *v.i.* **1.** to disappear from sight, or become invisible, esp. quickly. **2.** to cease to exist. **3.** *Maths.* (of a number or quantity) to become zero. [ME, from OF]

vanishing point, *n.* **1.** the point of disappearance. **2.** (in perspective) that point at which receding parallel lines appear to meet.

vanity /'vænəti/, *n., pl.* **-ties. 1.** extreme pride in one's own appearance, qualities, gifts, etc. **2.** an instance or display of this quality or feeling. **3.** something about which one is vain: *Her long hair was her chief vanity.* **4.** futility; uselessness: *It is vanity to expect a child to think the same way as an adult.* **5.** Also, **vanity unit**. a bathroom basin set in a bench. [ME, from OF, from L: emptiness]

Vanity Fair /ˌvænəti 'feə/, *n.* (in John Bunyan's *Pilgrim's Progress*) a fair which goes on perpetually in the town of Vanity. It symbolises worldly ostentation and frivolity.

vanquish /'væŋkwɪʃ/, *v.t.* **1.** to defeat in battle or conflict. **2.** to defeat in any contest. **3.** to overcome or overpower: *to vanquish a fear of the dark.* [ME, from OF from L] **—vanquisher,** *n.* **—vanquishment,** *n.*

vantage /'væntɪdʒ, 'vɑːn-/, *n.* **1.** a position or condition giving a benefit: *With the vantage of height he was able to see above the crowd.* **2.** an opportunity likely to give a benefit. ◊*adj.* **3.** giving or being a vantage: *a vantage point*; *vantage ground.* [ME; short for ADVANTAGE]

Vanuatu /ˌvænə'wɑːtu/, *n.* a republic in the south-western Pacific Ocean, consisting of about 80 islands; an Anglo-French con-

Vanuatu

dominium before independence in 1980. Pop. 145 000 (1987); 12 190 km². *Languages:* Bislama, English and French. *Currency:* vatu. *Cap.:* Vila. Formerly, **New Hebrides**.

vapid /'væpɪd/, *adj.* **1.** having lost sharpness or flavor; insipid; flat. **2.** without spirit; dull or uninteresting: *vapid talk*. [L] **—vapidity, vapidness,** *n.*

vapor *or* **vapour** /'veɪpə/, *n.* **1.** a visible cloud of a gas-like substance, as fog, mist, steam, etc. **2.** a gaseous state of a substance that is normally a liquid or solid. **3.** (*pl.*) *Archaic.* low spirits. [ME, from AF, from L: steam] **—vaporability,** *n.* **—vaporous,** *adj.*

vapor density *or* **vapour density,** *n.* the ratio of the density of a gas to the density of hydrogen at standard temperature and pressure; relative density.

vaporise *or* **vaporize** /'veɪpəraɪz/, *v.t., v.i.,* -**rised,** -**rising.** to change into vapor. **—vaporisable,** *adj.* **—vaporisation,** *n.* **—vaporiser,** *n.*

vapor pressure *or* **vapour pressure,** *n.* the maximum pressure of a vapor at a given temperature in an enclosed space, where a liquid (or solid) is in equilibrium with its vapor; saturated vapor pressure.

var., *Abbrev.* **1.** variant. **2.** variation. **3.** variety.

varan /'værən/, *n.* →**goanna**. [NL]

variable /'veəriəbl/, *adj.* **1.** likely to vary or change; inconsistent; changeable: *variable weather; a variable person.* **2.** capable of being varied or changed; alterable: *The width of the waistband is variable.* **3.** *Biol.* (of a species or a specific character) departing from the usual type. ◇*n.* **4.** something variable. **5.** *Maths.* a symbol, or the quantity or function which it signifies, which may represent any one of a given set of numbers and other objects. [L] **—variability, variableness,** *n.*

variable resistor, *n.* a rheostat.

variance /'veərɪəns/, *n.* **1.** the condition or fact of varying; divergence. **2.** an instance of this; a difference. **3.** *Stats.* the square of the standard deviation. **4.** a disagreement or quarrel. **5. at variance,** not agreeing; differing. [ME, from OF]

variant /'veəriənt/, *adj.* **1.** tending to change or alter; varying. **2.** being an altered form of something: *a variant spelling of a word.* ◇*n.* **3.** a variant form. **4.** *Stats.* →**variate**. [ME, from L: varying]

variate /'veəriət/, *n.* the numerical value of an attribute belonging to a statistical item. Also, **variant.**

variation /veəri'eɪʃən/, *n.* **1.** the act or process of varying. **2.** an instance of this. **3.** amount or rate of change: *A thermometer measures variation in temperature.* **4.** a different form of something; variant: *This recipe is a variation of the one you use.* **5.** *Music.* a transformation of a theme with changes in harmony, rhythm, or melody. [ME, from L]

varicolored *or* **varicoloured** /'veərɪkʌləd/, *adj.* **1.** having various colors; motley. **2.** varied; assorted.

vascular

varicose /'værəkoʊs, -kəs/, *adj.* **1.** abnormally or unusually enlarged or swollen. **2.** relating to or affected with varicose veins, which often affect areas close to the skin in the lower limbs. [L] **—varicosity,** *n.*

varied /'veərid/, *adj.* **1.** characterised by variety: *a varied assortment.* **2.** changed or altered: *a varied form of a word.* **3.** variegated, esp. in color, as an animal.

variegate /'veəriəgeɪt, 'veərə-/, *v.t.,* -**gated,** -**gating. 1.** to make varied in appearance. **2.** to give variety to; diversify. [LL] **—variegated,** *adj.* **—variegation,** *n.*

variety /və'raɪəti/, *n., pl.* -**ties. 1.** the state or character of being various or varied; diversity. **2.** a number of things of different kinds: *a variety of cakes to eat.* **3.** kind or sort: *This variety of wood burns well.* **4.** a different form, condition, or phase of something. **5.** a category within a species, based on some hereditary difference not considered great enough to distinguish species. **6.** *Theat.* entertainment of mixed character, including singing, dancing, etc. [L] **—varietal,** *adj.*

variform /'veərəfɔm/, *adj.* varied in form. [L]

variola /və'raɪələ/, *n.* →**smallpox**. [ML, from L: various, spotted] **—variolous,** *adj.*

various /'veərɪəs/, *adj.* **1.** differing one from another: *many and various.* **2.** several or many: *in various parts of the world.* [L] **—variousness,** *n.*

varlet /'valət/, *n. Archaic.* **1.** a page attached to a knight. **2.** a dishonest man or boy; rascal. [ME, from OF: VALET]

varnish /'vanɪʃ/, *n.* **1.** a resinous preparation dissolved in an oil (**oil varnish**) or in alcohol (**spirit varnish**), which, when put on a surface, esp. of wood, dries and leaves a hard glossy coating. **2.** the sap of certain trees, used for the same purpose (**natural varnish**). **3.** a coating or surface of varnish. **4.** merely external show; veneer. ◇*v.t.* **5.** to lay varnish on. **6.** to cover with a false appearance. [ME, from OF: varnish, from ML: sweet-smelling resin, from MGk]

vary /'veəri/, *v.,* -**ried,** -**rying.** ◇*v.t.* **1.** to change or alter in form, appearance, character, degree, etc.: *She will not vary her opinion.* **2.** to cause to be different, one from another: *She varied the lunches every day.* ◇*v.i.* **3.** to be different; show diversity or variation: *Opinions vary on this issue.* **4.** to undergo change in form, appearance, character, etc.: *The trees vary with the seasons.* **5.** to depart; deviate (usu. fol. by *from*): *The ship varied from its course.* [ME, from L: various] **—varying,** *adj.*

vas /væs/, *n., pl.* **vasa** /'veɪsə/. *Anat., Zool., Bot.* a vessel or duct. [L: vessel]

Vasco da Gama /ˌvæskoʊ də 'gamə/, *n.* →Vasco da Gama.

vascular /'væskjələ/, *adj.* relating to, composed of, or provided with vessels or ducts which carry fluids, like blood, lymph, or sap. Also, **vasculose, vasculous.** [NL, from L: little vessel] **—vascularity,** *n.*

vas deferens /væs 'defərəns/, *n., pl.* **vasa deferentia** /,veɪsə defə'renʃiə/. the duct which carries the sperm from the testis to the urethra. [L: vessel carrying down]

vase /vaz/, *n.* a hollow vessel, made of glass, earthenware, etc., now chiefly used as a flower container or for decoration. [F, from L: vessel]

vasectomy /və'sɛktəmi/, *n., pl.* **-mies.** the cutting of the vas deferens, or of a part of it, as a method of male sterilisation.

vaseline /'væsəlin, væsə'lin/, *n.* a jelly made from petroleum, used medicinally and as a lubricant. [Trademark]

vaso-, a word part meaning 'vessel'. [combining form representing L *vās* vessel]

vassal /'væsəl/, *n.* **1.** (in the feudal system) a person who lived on and used the land of a nobleman, and gave him military and other service in return. **2.** a servant; follower; slave. [ME, from OF, from LL: servant; of Celtic orig.]

vast /vast/, *adj.* **1.** of very great size, bulk, or area; immense; enormous; huge. **2.** very great in number or amount: *a vast army, a vast sum.* **3.** very great in degree: *vast importance.* [L] **—vastness,** *n.*

vat /væt/, *n., v.,* **vatted, vatting.** ◇*n.* **1.** a large container for liquids. ◇*v.t.* **2.** to put into or treat in a vat. [OE]

Vatican /'vætɪkən/, *n.* **1.** the palace of the popes in Rome and their chief residence since 1377; includes a library, art museum, archives, administrative offices, etc. **2.** the papal power or government, as distinguished from the Quirinal (representing the Italian government). [L *Vāticānus (mons)* Vatican (hill)]

Vatican City, *n.* an independent state within the city of Rome, on the right bank of the Tiber; established in 1929, it is ruled by the pope and includes St Peter's church and the Vaticano. Pop. 750 (1987 est.); 44 ha. Italian, **Città del Vaticano.**

vaudeville /'vɔdvɪl, 'vɔdəvɪl/, *n.* **1.** variety entertainment. **2.** a light or funny theatrical piece accompanied by songs and dances. [F, from *chanson du Vau de Vire,* type of satirical song popular in the 15thC in the Valley of Vire, a region in Normandy, France]

Vaughan Williams /vɔn 'wɪljəmz/, *n.* **Ralph,** 1872–1958, English composer of operas, symphonies, and choral music; influenced by British folk music and music of Tudor times.

vault¹ /vɔlt, vɒlt/, *n.* **1.** an arched structure forming a ceiling or roof over a hall, room, sewer, etc. **2.** an arched space, room, or passage, esp. underground. **3.** an underground room, esp. one used as a cellar or strongroom. **4.** a room for burying the dead. **5.** something like an arched roof: *the vault of heaven.* ◇*v.t.* **6.** to build or cover with a vault. [ME, from OF, from Rom] **—vaulted,** *adj.*

vault² /vɔlt, vɒlt/, *v.i.* **1.** to leap or jump: *to vault on to a horse.* **2.** to leap with the hands supported on something: *to vault over a fence.* ◇*v.t.* **3.** to leap or jump over: *to vault a fence.*

◇*n.* **4.** the act of vaulting. [OF, from It, from L: roll]

vaunt /vɔnt/, *v.t.* **1.** to speak boastfully of: *a much-vaunted program.* ◇*n.* **2.** boastful speech. [ME, from LL, from L: vain]

Vaux /vou/, *n.* **James Hardy,** 1782–?, Australian convict, born in England; three times transported for his crimes.

vb, *Abbrev.* verb.

VC /vi 'si/, *Abbrev.* **1.** Vice-Chairman. **2.** Vice-Chancellor. **3.** Vice-Consul. **4.** Victoria Cross.

VD /vi 'di/, *n.* any of those diseases which are spread by sexual intercourse with an infected person, esp. syphilis and gonorrhoea; sexually transmitted disease. Also, **venereal disease.** [abbrev.]

V-Day, *n.* a day nominated to celebrate victory, as in V-E Day or V-J Day in World War II.

VDT /vi di 'ti/, *n.* a visual display terminal. See **VDU.** [abbrev.]

VDU /vi di 'ju/, *n.* a computer terminal which shows information on a screen. Also, **visual display unit, visual display terminal, VDT** [abbrev.]

've, /v/ *v.* short form of have: *I've; you've; I should've gone.*

veal /vil/, *n.* the flesh of a calf used for food. [ME, from OF, from L: little calf]

vector /'vɛktə/, *n. Maths.* a quantity which possesses both magnitude and direction, e.g. velocity, and which may be represented by two sides of a parallelogram. [L: carrier] **—vectorial,** *adj.*

Veda /'veɪdə, 'vidə/, *n. (sometimes pl.)* the ancient sacred scriptures of Hinduism. [Skt: knowledge] **—Vedaic,** *adj.* **—Vedaism,** *n.*

V-E Day /vi-'i deɪ/, *n.* the day of victory in Europe for the Allies in World War II (8 May 1945). [*V(ictory in) E(urope)*]

veer /vɪə/, *v.i.* **1.** to turn or shift to another direction: *The road veers (off) to the left.* **2.** to change; alter: *He veers from excitement to depression.* ◇*n.* **3.** a change of direction. [F, from L]

veg., *Abbrev.* vegetable(s).

vegan /'vigən/, *n.* a person who eats no animal products; a strict vegetarian.

vegemite /'vɛdʒəmaɪt/, *n.* **1.** a yeast extract used as a spread. **2.** (*used affectionately*) small child: *happy little vegemites.* [Trademark]

vegetable /'vɛdʒtəbəl/, *n.* **1.** any herbaceous plant, annual, biennial, or perennial, whose fruits, seeds, roots, tubers, bulbs, stems, leaves, or flower parts are used as food, as tomato, bean, beet, potato, asparagus, cabbage, etc. **2.** the edible part of such plants, as the fruit of the tomato or the tuber of the potato. **3.** any member of the vegetable kingdom; a plant. **4.** *Colloq.* a person who, due to physical injury or mental deficiency, is physically completely helpless or has no mental powers. ◇*adj.* **5.** of, consisting of, or made from vegetables that can be eaten: *a vegetable diet.*

vegetable

6. of or relating to plants: *vegetable kingdom*; *vegetable life*. 7. obtained from plants: *vegetable fibre*; *vegetable oil*; *vegetable dye*. [ME, from LL: vivifying] —**vegetal**, *adj.*

vegetable oil, *n.* any of a group of oils which are obtained from plants or their seeds or fruits.

vegetarian /vedʒə'teəriən/, *n.* 1. someone who on moral principle or from personal choice lives on vegetable food (refusing meat, fish, etc.). ◇*adj.* 2. of or relating to, this practice or principle. 3. consisting solely of vegetables. —**vegetarianism**, *n.*

vegetate /'vedʒəteɪt/, *v.i.*, **-tated**, **-tating**. 1. to grow in the manner of plants. 2. (of people) to be inactive, dull, or unthinking. [L: enlivened]

vegetation /vedʒə'teɪʃən/, *n.* the plant life of a particular region, considered as a whole. —**vegetational**, *adj.*

vegetative /'vedʒəteɪtɪv/, *adj.* 1. growing as or like plants; vegetating. 2. of, or relating to, vegetation or vegetable growth. 3. helping plant growth: *vegetative mould*. Also, **vegetive**. —**vegetativeness**, *n.*

vehement /'viəmənt/, *adj.* 1. eager, impetuous, or impassioned: *vehement personality*. 2. angry or bitter: *vehement opposition*. 3. passionate; strongly emotional: *vehement desire*; *vehement dislike*. 4. (of actions) marked by great energy; forceful. [ME, from L] —**vehemence**, *n.*

vehicle /'viːkəl, 'viːəkəl/, *n.* 1. anything, esp. moving on wheels, on which people or goods may be carried, e.g. a car, truck, bicycle, etc. 2. a means of carrying or sending: *Air is the vehicle of sound*; *Language is a vehicle for thought*. [L: conveyance] —**vehicular**, *adj.*

veil /veɪl/, *n.* 1. a piece of material, usu. light and transparent, worn by women over the head or face. 2. a part of a nun's headdress, falling over the head and shoulders on each side of the face. 3. something that covers, screens, or hides: *a veil of smoke*; *a veil of mist*. 4. a mask, disguise, or pretence. 5. **take the veil**, to become a nun. ◇*v.t.* 6. to cover or conceal with, or as if with, a veil. 7. to hide the real nature of; mask; disguise. [ME, from AF, from L: sail, covering]

vein /veɪn/, *n.* 1. one of the system of branching vessels or tubes carrying blood from various parts of the body to the heart. 2. (loosely) any blood vessel. 3. one of the tubular, riblike thickenings in an insect's wing. 4. one of the strands or bundles of vascular tissue forming the framework of a leaf. 5. any body or stratum of ore, coal, etc., clearly separated or defined. 6. a streak or marking of a different color, running through marble, wood, etc. 7. a strain or quality traceable in character or behavior, writing, etc.: *a vein of stubbornness*; *to write in a poetic vein*. ◇*v.t.* 8. to provide with veins. 9. to mark with lines or streaks suggesting veins. [ME, from OF, from L]

vel., *Abbrev.* velocity.

velar /'viːlə/, *adj.* 1. *Linguistics*. made with the back of the tongue held close to or touching the soft palate. ◇*n.* 2. a velar sound. [L: curtain]

Velázquez /və'læskwəθ/, *n.* **Diego Rodriquez de Silva y** /'djeɪgou rou'driːgəθ də 'silva i/, 1599–1660, Spanish painter; noted esp. for portraits of the court of Phillip IV of Spain. Also, **Velasquez**.

veldt /velt/, *n.* open country, with grass, bushes, or shrubs, or thinly forested, typical of parts of southern Africa. Also, **veld**. [Afrikaans, from D: FIELD]

vellum /'veləm/, *n.* 1. a sheet of calfskin prepared as fine parchment for writing or bookbinding. 2. a texture of paper or cloth like that of fine parchment. ◇*adj.* 3. made of, or looking like, vellum. [ME, from OF: VEAL]

velocity /və'losəti/, *n.*, *pl.* **-ties**. 1. speed. 2. *Phys.* rate of motion in a given direction. [L: swiftness]

velodrome /'velədroum/, *n.* an arena with a banked track for cycle races.

velour /və'luə/, *n.* any of various cloths with a fine, raised finish. Also, **velours**. [F: velvet, from Pr, from L: hair]

velvet /'velvət/, *n.* 1. material of silk, silk and cotton, cotton, etc., with a thick, soft pile formed of loops of the warp thread either cut at the outer end (as in ordinary velvet) or left uncut (as in uncut or terry velvet). 2. anything with the soft, furry quality of velvet. 3. the soft covering of a growing antler. ◇*adj.* 4. Also, **velveted**. made of velvet or covered with velvet. 5. resembling velvet; smooth and soft. [ME, from ML, from L: shaggy hair] —**velvety**, *adj.*

velveteen /velvə'tiːn/, *n.* 1. a cotton material with short pile. 2. (*pl.*) trousers or knickerbockers made of velveteen. ◇*adj.* 3. Also, **velveteened**. made of velveteen.

venal /'viːnəl/, *adj.* open to or marked by, bribery and corruption. [L: for sale] —**venality**, *n.*

venation /və'neɪʃən/, *n.* 1. an arrangement of veins, as in a leaf or an insect's wing. 2. these veins taken as a whole. [NL, from L: vein] —**venational**, *adj.*

vend /vend/, *v.t.*, *v.i.* to sell, esp. small articles; peddle. [L: sell] —**vendor**, *n.*

vendetta /ven'detə/, *n.* 1. a private quarrel in which the relatives of a murdered person try to get revenge by killing the murderer or a member of the murderer's family; blood feud. 2. any long or persistent quarrel, rivalry, etc. 3. *Colloq.* a firm stand taken on a particular issue and strictly enforced: *The police led a vendetta against drunken driving*. [It, from L: vengeance] —**vendettist**, *n.*

vending machine, *n.* a coin-operated machine for selling goods such as snack foods, etc.

veneer /və'nɪə/, *n.* 1. a thin layer of wood or other material used for facing or overlaying wood. 2. one of the several layers of plywood. 3. an outwardly pleasing appearance or show: *a veneer of good manners*. ◇*v.t.* 4. to overlay or face (wood) with thin sheets of some material,

veneer as a fine wood, ivory, tortoiseshell, etc. **5.** to cover (an object) with a thin layer of costly material to give an appearance of superior quality. **6.** to cement (layers of wood veneer) to form plywood. **7.** to give an outwardly pleasing appearance to. [G, from F]

Venera /'vɛnərə/, *n.* a series of unmanned Russian spacecraft designed for the exploration of Venus.

venerable /'vɛnrəbəl, -nərəbəl/, *adj.* (of people or things) worthy of respect or reverence because of age, dignity, high character, etc. [ME, from L *venerābilis*] — **venerability**, *n.*

venerate /'vɛnəreɪt/, *v.t.*, **-rated, -rating.** to have a reverent respect for; revere. [L: having reverenced] — **venerator**, *n.* — **veneration**, *n.*

venereal /və'nɪəriəl/, *adj.* **1.** arising from or connected with sexual intercourse with an infected person: *venereal disease.* **2.** relating to diseases arising in this way. **3.** of or relating to sexual desire or intercourse. [ME, from L: relating to Venus + -AL¹]

venereal disease, *n.* → **VD.**

venetian blind /və,niʃən 'blaɪnd/, *n.* a window blind with overlapping horizontal slats that may be opened or closed.

Venezuela /vɛnə'zweɪlə/, *n.* a republic on the north coast of South America, bordered by Colombia, Guyana and Brazil; Pop. 18 272 157 (1987); 912 050 km². *Language:* Spanish. *Currency:* bolívar. *Cap.:* Caracas. — **Venezuelan,** *n., adj.*

vengeance /'vɛndʒəns/, *n.* **1.** the causing of harm or wrong to someone in return for harm received; revenge. **2.** the desire to cause such harm: *He went off vowing vengeance.* **3.** **with a vengeance, a.** with force or violence. **b.** to a surprising or unusual degree. [ME, from OF]

vengeful /'vɛndʒfəl/, *adj.* desiring, seeking, or taking vengeance; vindictive. — **vengefulness**, *n.*

venial /'viniəl/, *adj.* **1.** *Theol.* (of a sin) not causing spiritual death; not seriously wrong (opposed to **mortal**). **2.** excusable; pardonable. [ME, from L: pardon] — **veniality, venialness**, *n.*

Venice /'vɛnəs/, *n.* a seaport in north-eastern Italy, built on numerous small islands in the **Lagoon of Venice**, an inlet of the Adriatic. Pop. 332 762 (1986 est.). Italian, **Venezia**, *n.* — **Venetian,** *n., adj.*

venin /'vɛnən/, *n.* any of various toxic components of venom.

venison /'vɛnəsən, 'vɛnzən/, *n.* the flesh of a deer or similar animal. [ME, from OF, from L: hunting]

Venn diagram /'vɛn ,daɪəgræm/, *n.* *Maths, Logic.* a diagram which represents sets of elements as circles whose overlap indicates the overlap of the sets. [named after John Venn, 1834–1923, English logician]

venom /'vɛnəm/, *n.* **1.** a poisonous liquid which snakes, spiders, etc., secrete, and inject into the bodies of their victims by biting, stinging, etc. **2.** something like poison, such as spite or malice. [ME, from OF, from L: poison]

venomous /'vɛnəməs/, *adj.* **1.** (of an animal) having a gland or glands for secreting venom; inflicting a poisoned bite, sting, or wound. **2.** full of venom; poisonous. **3.** spiteful or malignant: *a venomous nature; a venomous attack.*

venous /'vinəs/, *adj.* **1.** of, relating to, or of the nature of, a vein or veins. **2.** relating to the blood of the veins. [L]

vent¹ /vɛnt/, *n.* **1.** an opening serving as an outlet for air, smoke, fumes, etc. **2.** *Zool.* an anal or excretory opening of birds, reptiles, and other lower animals. **3.** expression: *to give vent to anger.* ◊*v.t.* **4.** to let out or give expression to: *to vent anger.* **5.** to let out (liquid, smoke, etc.); discharge. **6.** to provide with a vent or vents. [OF, from L]

vent² /vɛnt/, *n.* a slit in the back or sides of a coat. [ME, from OF: slit]

ventilate /'vɛntəleɪt/, *v.t.*, **-lated, -lating. 1.** to provide (a room, mine, etc.) with fresh air in place of stale air. **2.** to introduce fresh air to: *The lungs ventilate the blood.* **3.** to express: *to ventilate opinions.* **4.** to provide (a building, room) with a vent or vents. [L: fanned] — **ventilation**, *n.* — **ventilator**, *n.*

ventral /'vɛntrəl/, *adj.* **1.** of, or relating to, the belly; abdominal. **2.** on the abdominal side of the body. **3.** of or on the lower side or surface, as of an organ or part: *ventral fin.* [L]

ventricle /'vɛntrɪkəl/, *n.* **1.** any of various hollow organs or parts in an animal body. **2.** one of the two main cavities of the heart which receive the blood from the auricles and send it into the arteries. [ME, from L: belly] — **ventricular**, *adj.*

ventriloquism /vɛn'trɪləkwɪzəm/, *n.* the art of speaking with little or no lip movement, so that the voice seems to come not from the speaker but from some other source. Also, **ventriloquy**. [LL: one who apparently speaks from the belly] — **ventriloquial**, *adj.* — **ventriloquist**, *n.*

Ventris /'vɛntrəs/, *n.* **Michael George Francis**, 1922–56, English philologist who deciphered a part of the ancient Mycenaean Greek known as Linear B script.

venture /'vɛntʃə/, *n., v.*, **-tured, -turing.** ◊*n.* **1.** a risky or daring undertaking, esp. in business, where loss is risked in the hope of profit. **2.** something on which risk is taken, as a ship, cargo, merchandise, etc. ◊*v.t.* **3.** to expose to chance; risk: *They ventured all their money on the race.* **4.** to take the risk of; brave the dangers of: *to venture the high seas.* **5.** to dare; presume; be so bold as: *to venture an opinion.* ◊*v.i.* **6.** to go with uncertainty or risk: *to venture into the bush.* **7.** to take a risk; dare or presume (oft. fol. by *on* or *upon* or an infinitive): *to venture on an ambitious project.* [ME, earlier form of ADVENTURE] — **venturesome**, *adj.*

venue /'vɛnju/, *n.* the scene of any action or event, as a hall for a concert, meeting, etc. [ME, from OF: coming]

Venus /ˈviːnəs/, n. **1.** the Roman goddess of love and beauty; Greek counterpart, Aphrodite. **2.** *Astron.* the most brilliant planet, having an orbit next inside the earth's and second from the sun.

Venus de Milo /ˌviːnəs də ˈmaɪloʊ/, n. a Greek statue of antiquity portraying Venus in marble, found in 1820 on Melos and now in the Louvre, Paris. Also, **Venus of Melos.**

Venus's flytrap /ˌviːnəsəz ˈflaɪtræp/, n. a plant native to the south-eastern US, whose leaves have two lobes which close like a trap when an insect touches hairs on them. Also, **Venus flytrap.**

veracity /vəˈræsəti/, n., pl. **-ties. 1.** truthfulness or honesty. **2.** accuracy; precision. [ML, from L: true] **—veracious,** adj.

veranda /vəˈrændə/, n. an open or partly open part on the outside of a house, usu. covered by the main roof. Also, **verandah.** [apparently from Pg and OSp: railing, from L: rod]

verb /vɜːb/, n. **1.** a word which expresses the occurrence of an action, existence of a condition, etc., e.g. *hit, walk, do, exist, be.* **2.** the grammatical class to which such words belong. [ME, from L: word, verb]

verbal /ˈvɜːbəl/, adj. **1.** of or relating to words: *verbal symbols.* **2.** made up of or in the form of words: *a verbal picture of a scene.* **3.** expressed in spoken words rather than writing; oral: *verbal tradition; a verbal message.* **4.** concerned with words only, rather than ideas, facts, or realities: *a purely verbal distinction.* **5.** *Gram.* of, relating to, or coming from a verb. ◇n. **6.** a spoken confession made to police. [ME, from L: word]

verbalise *or* **verbalize** /ˈvɜːbəlaɪz/, v.t., v.i., **-lised, -lising.** to express in (too many) words. **—verbalisation,** n.

verbal noun, n. a noun made from a verb by adding *-ing;* a gerund.

verbatim /vɜːˈbeɪtɪm/, adv., adj. word for word; in exactly the same words. [ML, from L: word]

verbena /vɜːˈbiːnə/, n. a garden plant with flowers of different colors. [L: foliage]

verbiage /ˈvɜːbiɪdʒ/, n. a mass of useless words, in writing or speech; wordiness. [F: gabble, from L: word]

verbose /vɜːˈbous/, adj. expressed in, marked by the use of, or using many or too many words; wordy. [L: full of words] **—verbosity,** n.

verdant /ˈvɜːdnt/, adj. **1.** green with vegetation; covered with growing plants or grass. **2.** green. [VERD(URE)+-ANT] **—verdancy,** n.

Verdi /ˈvɜːdi/, n. **Giuseppe** /dʒəˈsepi/, 1813–1901, Italian composer esp. noted for his dramatic operas.

verdict /ˈvɜːdɪkt/, n. **1.** *Law.* the finding or answer given to the court by a jury. **2.** a judgment or decision: *the verdict of the public.* [b. ML and ME]

Verdun /veəˈdʌn/, n. a fortress town in north-eastern France, on the river Meuse; a German offensive was stopped here in 1916 in the bloodiest fighting of World War I. Pop. 24 120 (1982).

verdure /ˈvɜːdjuə/, n. **1.** greenness, esp. of fresh, flourishing vegetation. **2.** green vegetation, esp. grass or herbage. [ME, from OF: green, from L] **—verdurous,** adj.

verge¹ /vɜːdʒ/, n., v., **verged, verging.** ◇n. **1.** an edge, rim, or margin. **2.** a limit or point beyond which something begins or happens: *to be on the verge of tears.* **3. a.** a narrow strip of grass at the edge of a road, etc. **b.** a cleared, levelled space bordering the edge of a sealed road. ◇v.i. **4.** to come close to; approach (usu. fol. by *on* or *upon*): *silliness verging on madness.* [ME, from F, from L: rod]

verge² /vɜːdʒ/, v.i., **verged, verging.** to incline or tend; slope (usu. fol. by *to* or *towards*). [L: turn, incline]

Verge /vɜːdʒ/, n. **John,** c. 1782–1861, Australian architect and builder, born in England.

verger /ˈvɜːdʒə/, n. **1.** an official who takes care of a church and acts as attendant. **2.** an official who carries the symbol of office before a bishop, etc. [late ME, from F (obs.): rod]

veriest /ˈvɛriɪst/, adj. greatest; utmost: *the veriest stupidity.*

verify /ˈvɛrəfaɪ/, v.t., **-fied, -fying. 1.** to prove (something) to be true; confirm; substantiate. **2.** to find out the truth or correctness of, esp. by examination or comparison: *to verify dates; to verify spelling.* **3.** to state to be true, esp., in legal use, formally or upon oath. [ME, from OF, from L: true] **—verifiable,** adj. **—verification,** n.

verily /ˈvɛrəli/, adv. *Archaic.* in very truth; truly; really; indeed. [ME]

verisimilitude /ˌvɛrəsəˈmɪlətjuːd/, n. **1.** an appearance of truth. **2.** something only seeming to be true. [L: likeness of truth]

veritable /ˈvɛrətəbəl/, adj. being truly such; genuine or real: *a veritable triumph.* [ME, from AF, from L: truth]

verity /ˈvɛrəti/, n., pl. **-ties. 1.** the quality of being true or in accordance with fact or reality. **2.** a truth or true statement, principle, belief, idea, or the like. [ME, from L]

Vermeer /veəˈmɪə/, n. **Jan** /jɒn/ (*Jan van der Meer of Delft*), 1632–75, Dutch genre painter whose few works are admired for effects of light and color.

vermi-, a word part meaning 'worm', as in *vermiform.* [L, combining form of *vermis*]

vermicelli /ˌvɜːməˈseli, -ˈtʃeli/, n. pasta in the shape of thin spaghetti. [It, pl.: little worm, from L]

vermicule /ˈvɜːməkjuːl/, n. any small worm. **—vermicular,** adj.

vermiform /ˈvɜːməfɔːm/, adj. like a worm in form; long and thin. [ML]

vermiform appendix, n. a short, narrow, blind tube protruding from the caecum, situated in the lower right-hand part of the abdomen in humans, and having no known useful function. Also, **appendix.**

vermilion /vəˈmɪljən/, n. **1.** a brilliant scarlet red. **2.** bright red pigment consisting of mercuric sulfide; cinnabar. ◇adj. **3.** of the color of vermilion. [ME, from OF: bright red]

vermin /ˈvɜmən/, n.pl. **1.** harmful, troublesome, or unpleasant animals collectively, such as rats, fleas, mites, etc., which are killed whenever possible. **2.** people who are annoying or unpleasant. [ME, from OF: worm, from L] —**verminous**, adj.

Vermont /vəˈmɒnt/, n. a state of the northeastern US; a part of New England. Pop. 541 000 (1986 est.); 24 887 km². *Cap.*: Montpelier. *Abbrev.*: Vt —**Vermonter**, n.

vermouth /ˈvɜməθ, vəˈmuθ/, n. a fortified white wine flavored by herbs, roots, barks, bitters, etc. [F, from G: wormwood]

vernacular /vəˈnækjələ/, adj. **1.** (of language or words) native or originating in the place of its use (as opposed to *literary* or *learned* language). **2.** expressed or written in the native language: *a vernacular text.* **3.** using such a language: *a vernacular writer.* ◇n. **4.** the native speech or language of a place: *The Catholic liturgy is now in the vernacular instead of Latin.* **5.** the language used by a class or profession: *Punters have their own vernacular.* **6.** everyday language, as opposed to formal or learned language. [L: native + -AR¹] —**vernacularism**, n.

vernal /ˈvɜnəl/, adj. **1.** of or relating to spring. **2.** belonging or relating to youth. [L]

vernal equinox, n. See **equinox**. Also, **vernal point**.

Verne /vɜn/, n. **Jules**, 1828–1905, French novelist; esp. known for his science fiction including *Twenty Thousand Leagues under the Sea* (1870).

vernier /ˈvɜnɪə/, n. **1.** Also, **vernier scale**. a small, movable, graduated scale running parallel with the fixed graduated scale of a sextant, theodolite, barometer, or other instrument, and used for measuring a fractional part of one of the divisions of the fixed scale. ◇adj. **2.** equipped with a vernier: *a vernier barometer.* **3.** *Aeron.* indicating or relating to a low-thrust rocket engine used to achieve fine adjustments of the velocity or altitude of a spacecraft. [F; named after Pierre *Vernier*, 1580–1637, French mathematician]

Verona /vəˈroʊnə/, n. a city in northern Italy, on the river Adige. Pop. 259 636 (1986 est.).

Versailles /veəˈsaɪ/, n. a city in northern France, about 20 km south-west of Paris; palace of Louis XIV; treaty of peace between the Allies and Germany 1919. Pop. 95 240 (1982).

versatile /ˈvɜsətaɪl/, adj. **1.** able to turn with ease from one to another of various tasks, subjects, etc.; many-sided in interests. **2.** variable or changeable, esp. in feeling, purpose, policy, etc. [L: turning about] —**versatility**, n.

verse /vɜs/, n. **1.** (not in technical use) a stanza of a poem: *the first verse of a hymn.* **2.** (in technical use) a single metrical line of a poem: *a stanza of six verses.* **3.** a poem or piece of poetry: *a young man writing verses.* **4.** poetry: *English verse and prose.* **5.** a short division of a chapter in the Bible. ◇adj. **6.** written in poetry: *a verse drama.* [OE, from L: line, row]

versed /vɜst/, adj. experienced; practised; skilled (fol. by *in*): *well versed in a subject.* [L: busied; engaged]

versification /vɜsəfəˈkeɪʃən/, n. **1.** the act of versifying. **2.** a form or style of verse; metrical structure. **3.** a metrical version of something. **4.** the rules or customs of versemaking: *a primer of versification.*

versify /ˈvɜsəfaɪ/, v., **-fied, -fying.** ◇v.t. **1.** to relate or describe in poetry. **2.** to turn into verse or metrical form (from prose). ◇v.i. **3.** to compose verses (def. 3). [ME, from L: put into verse] —**versifier**, n.

version /ˈvɜʒən/, n. **1.** a particular account of some matter, as different from another: *Her version of what happened seemed more likely.* **2.** a translation. **3.** a particular form or variant of anything. [L: turning]

verso /ˈvɜsoʊ/, n., pl. **-sos. 1.** Also, **reverso.** the left-hand page of a book or manuscript (opposed to *recto*). **2.** the back or reverse of a coin, medal, etc. [from L: on the turned leaf]

versus /ˈvɜsəs/, prep. against (used esp. in law with reference to the opposing sides in a case and in sport with reference to the two opposing teams or players). *Abbrev.*: v., vs [L]

vertebra /ˈvɜtəbrə/, n., pl. **-brae** /-bri/, **-bras.** a bone or segment making up the backbone or spinal column. [L] —**vertebral**, adj.

vertebrate /ˈvɜtəbreɪt, -brət/, n., adj. (an animal) having a backbone or spinal column. [L: jointed]

vertex /ˈvɜtɛks/, n., pl. **-tices** /-təsiz/, **-texes. 1.** the highest point of something; apex; top; summit. **2.** *Anat, Zool.* the crown or top of the head. **3.** *Astron. etc.* a point in the celestial sphere towards which a group of stars is directed. **4.** *Maths.* the point farthest from the base. **5.** *Geom.* the point where two sides of an angle, or three or more sides of a solid, meet. [L: whirl, crown of the head, summit]

vertical /ˈvɜtɪkəl/, adj. **1.** at right angles or perpendicular to the horizon; upright; plumb. **2.** of, relating to, or situated at the vertex. ◇n. **3.** a vertical line, plane, etc. **4.** a vertical or upright position. [LL: vertex]

vertical angle, n. *Geom.* **1.** either of the two opposite angles formed by two intersecting lines or planes; vertically opposite angle. **2.** the angle at the vertex of a triangle or polygon.

vertices /ˈvɜtəsiz/, n. a plural of **vertex.**

vertigo /ˈvɜtəgoʊ/, n., pl. **vertigos, vertigines** /vəˈtɪdʒəniz/. a feeling of sickness or dizziness, often caused by looking down from a height. [L: whirling round] —**vertiginous**, adj.

verve /vɜv/, n. spirit, liveliness, or energy: *She spoke with verve; Her novel lacks verve.* [F: enthusiasm, fancy; orig. uncert.]

very /'veri/, *adv., adj.,* **-rier, -riest.** ◇*adv.*
1. in a high degree; extremely; exceedingly.
2. (used as an intensive): *the very best thing to be done; in the very same place.* ◇*adj.* **3.** same or precise: *the very thing you should have done.*
4. even (what is specified): *They grew to fear his very name.* **5.** mere: *The very thought is distressing.* **6.** actual: *caught in the very act.* **7.** true, genuine, or real: *the very President himself.* [ME, from OF, from L: true]

very low frequency, *n.* any radio frequency below 30 kilohertz. *Abbrev.:* v.l.f.

vesicle /'vesɪkəl, 'vi-/, *n.* **1.** a little sac or cyst. **2.** *Med.* a small, raised part of the skin, usu. filled with fluid; blister. **3.** *Bot.* a small bladder or air cavity, esp. in plants which float on water. **4.** *Geol.* a small, usu. spherical cavity in a rock or mineral, due to gas or vapor. [L: little bladder, little blister] —**vesicular,** *adj.*

vesper /'vespə/, *n.* the evening star, esp. Venus; Hesperus. [ME, from L]

vespers /'vespəz/, *n.pl. (sometimes cap.)* (a religious service or prayers for) the sixth canonical hour, held or said in the late afternoon or evening. [ME, from L: evening]

Vespucci /ves'putʃi/, *n.* **Amerigo** /amei'rigou/ (*Americus Vespucius*), 1451–1512, Italian merchant, adventurer, and explorer after whom America was named.

vessel /'vesəl/, *n.* **1.** a craft for travelling on water, now esp. one larger than an ordinary rowing boat; ship or boat. **2.** a hollow article, as a cup, bowl, bottle, etc., for holding liquid, food, etc. **3.** *Anat., Zool.* a tube or duct, as an artery, vein, etc., carrying blood through the body. **4.** *Bot.* a duct formed of connected cells, containing or carrying sap, etc. [ME, from OF, from L: small vase]

vest /vest/, *n.* **1.** a waistcoat. **2.** *Brit.* a short, warm undergarment with sleeves, worn under a shirt; singlet. ◇*v.t.* **3.** to place or settle (property, rights, powers, etc.) in the possession or control of a person or people (usu. fol. by *in*): *He vested the property in his son.* **4.** to invest or endow (a person or group) with powers, functions, etc. (fol. by *with*). ◇*v.i.* **5.** to put on church vestments. **6.** (of a right, etc.) to become vested in a person. [ME, from OF, from L: clothe]

Vesta /'vestə/, *n. Rom Myth.* the goddess of the hearth, worshipped in a temple containing an altar on which a sacred fire was kept burning under the care of the vestal virgins.

vestal /'vestl/, *adj.* **1.** virginal; chaste. ◇*n.* **2.** a virgin; a chaste, unmarried woman. [from the 4 (later 6) virgins, consecrated by the ancient Romans to VESTA]

vested interests, *n.pl.* **1.** personal interests or rights in a system, institution, etc., usu. protected by law or custom. **2.** powerful people, groups, etc., who can control government-policy, big business, etc.

vestibule /'vestɪbjul/, *n.* an entrance hall; antechamber. [L] —**vestibular,** *adj.*

vestige /'vestɪdʒ/, *n.* **1.** a mark, trace, or something that remains to show that something once existed or happened. **2.** a very small amount: *He has not a vestige of wit, but he tries to be funny.* **3.** *Biol.* a degenerate or imperfectly developed organ or structure, now having little or no use. [F, from L: footprint] —**vestigial,** *adj.*

vestment /'vestmənt/, *n.* **1.** an outer garment, esp. a ceremonial one. **2.** *Church.* one of a set of special garments worn by the clergy, etc., at church services. [ME, from OF, from L: clothing] —**vestmental,** *adj.*

vestry /'vestri/, *n., pl.* **-tries. 1.** a room in a church, in which the vestments, sacred vessels, etc., are kept; sacristy. **2.** (in some churches) a room used for Sunday school, parish meetings, etc. **3.** (in the Anglican Church) **a.** a meeting of parishioners held in the vestry for the official business of the parish. **b.** the body of parishioners so meeting; parish council. [ME, from VEST + -RY]

vesture /'vestʃə/, *n. Archaic.* clothing. [ME, from OF: clothe]

Vesuvius /və'suviəs/, *n.* **Mount,** an active volcano in south-western Italy, near Naples; many severe eruptions including the one that buried the ancient cities of Pompeii and Herculaneum in AD 79. About 1220 m.

vet /vet/, *n., v.,* **vetted, vetting.** *Colloq.* ◇*n.* **1.** a veterinary surgeon. ◇*v.t.* **2.** to examine or treat as a veterinary surgeon does. **3.** to examine to see if suitable: *to vet the applicants for the job; to vet a proposal.* ◇*v.i.* **4.** to work as a veterinary surgeon. [short for VETERINARY]

vetch /vetʃ/, *n.* any of various leguminous plants, mostly climbing herbs, such as the common vetch, cultivated for fodder and soil improvement. [ME, from d. OF, from L]

veteran /'vetərən, 'vetrən/, *n.* **1.** someone who has seen long service in any occupation or office. **2.** a soldier who has seen active service: *Vietnam veterans.* ◇*adj.* **3.** experienced through long service or practice. **4.** of or relating to veterans. **5.** indicating or relating to cars built before 1918. [L: old]

veterinary /'vetənri, 'vetərənri/, *n., pl.* **-ries,** *adj.* ◇*n.* **1.** a veterinary surgeon. ◇*adj.* **2.** of the medical and surgical treatment of animals, esp. farm animals and pets. [L: pertaining to cattle]

veterinary science, *n.* that branch of medicine dealing with the study, prevention, and treatment of animal diseases. Also, **veterinary medicine.**

veterinary surgeon, *n.* someone trained to give treatment or surgery to sick animals.

veto /'vitou/, *n., pl.* **-toes,** *v.,* **-toed, -toing.** ◇*n.* **1.** the power or right of preventing action by a vote or an order forbidding it. **2.** such an order or vote directed against some proposed or intended act. ◇*v.t.* **3.** to prevent (a proposal, legislative bill, etc.) being put into action by using the right of veto. **4.** to refuse to agree to; forbid. [L: I forbid]

vex /veks/, *v.t.* **1.** to annoy; irritate: *enough to vex a saint.* **2.** to torment; plague; worry:

vex

Lack of money vexes many people. [ME, from L: agitate] **–vexation,** *n.* **–vexatious,** *adj.* **–vexed,** *adj.* **–vexingly,** *adv.*

VF, *Abbrev.* video frequency.

v.h.f. /ˌviː eɪtʃ 'ef/, *Radio. Abbrev.* very high frequency. Also, **VHF**

v.i., *Abbrev.* verb intransitive.

via /'vaɪə/, *prep.* **1.** by way of; by a route that passes through: *Go to Italy via Singapore.* **2.** by means of: *to reach a conclusion via three logical steps.* [L: way]

viable /'vaɪəbəl/, *adj.* **1.** practicable; workable. **2.** *Med.* **a.** physically fitted to live. **b.** (of a foetus) having reached such a stage of development so as to be able to live outside the womb. **3.** *Bot.* able to live and grow. [F: life, from L] **–viability,** *n.*

Via Dolorosa /ˌviːə dɒləˈroʊsə/, *n.* the route taken by Christ to the place of crucifixion. [L, lit.: sorrowful road]

viaduct /'vaɪədʌkt/, *n.* a bridge consisting of a series of arches with high supporting piers, for carrying a road or railway over a valley, gorge, etc. [L *via* way + *-duct* as in AQUEDUCT]

vial /'vaɪəl/, *n.* →**phial.** [ME, var. of *fiole* PHIAL]

viand /'vaɪənd, 'viːənd/, *n.* **1.** an article of food. **2.** (*pl.*) articles or dishes of food, now usu. of a choice or delicate kind. [ME, from OF, from L: things to be lived on]

viaticum /vaɪˈætɪkəm, viː-/, *n., pl.* **-ca** /-kə/, **-cums.** the Eucharist given to a dying person. [L]

vibes[1] /vaɪbz/, *n.pl. Colloq.* →**vibraphone.**

vibes[2] /vaɪbz/, *n.pl. Colloq.* the quality, mood or atmosphere of a place or person: *The vibes of that town were all wrong.*

vibrant /'vaɪbrənt/, *adj.* **1.** moving to and fro rapidly; vibrating. **2.** (of sounds) resonant. **3.** full of energy and vigor. **4.** exciting; producing a thrill. [L] **–vibrancy,** *n.*

vibraphone /'vaɪbrəfoʊn/, *n.* a xylophone-like musical instrument with electronically operated resonators controlled by a pedal. Also, *US,* **vibraharp.** [L: shake, vibrate + -PHONE] **–vibraphonist,** *n.*

vibrate /vaɪˈbreɪt/, *v.,* **-brated, -brating.** ◇*v.i.* **1.** to move to and fro, as a pendulum; oscillate. **2.** to move to and fro or up and down quickly and repeatedly; quiver; tremble. **3.** (of sounds) to produce or have a quivering or vibratory effect; resound. ◇*v.t.* **4.** to cause to move to and fro. **5.** to cause to quiver or tremble. [L: shaken]

vibration /vaɪˈbreɪʃən/, *n.* **1.** the act or state of vibrating. **2.** *Phys.* the oscillating motion of particles or a solid, as in guitar strings, sound waves, etc. **3.** (*pl.*) *Colloq.* →**vibes**[2].

vibrato /vəˈbrɑːtoʊ/, *n., pl.* **-tos.** the pulsating effect produced in the singing voice or in an instrumental tone by rapid small oscillations in pitch about the given note. [It: vibrate, from L]

vibrator /vaɪˈbreɪtə, 'vaɪbreɪtə/, *n.* something that produces vibrations, esp. for use in massage, etc.

vibrio /'vɪbrioʊ/, *n., pl.* **-rios.** one of a class of bacteria which includes the one causing cholera. [NL, from L: shake] **–vibrioid,** *adj.*

viburnum /vəˈbɜːnəm/, *n.* **1.** one of a group of shrubs or small trees, such as the snowball tree, which are cultivated for ornament. **2.** the dried bark of various kinds of viburnum used in medicine. [L: the wayfaring tree]

Vic, *Abbrev.* Victoria.

vicar /'vɪkə/, *n.* **1.** *Anglican Ch.* a clergyman acting as priest of a parish. **2.** *Rom Cath Ch.* **a.** a priest representing the pope or a bishop. **b.** the pope as Christ's representative on earth. **3.** someone acting in place of another; deputy. [ME, from AF, from L: substitute] **–vicarial,** *adj.*

vicarage /'vɪkərɪdʒ/, *n.* the house of a vicar.

vicarious /vəˈkɛəriəs, vaɪ-/, *adj.* **1.** done or experienced by one person in place of another. **2.** felt at second-hand, by identification with the experiences of another: *vicarious pleasure.* [L: substituted]

Vicars /'vɪkəz/, *n.* Sir William, 1859–1940, Australian manufacturer, born in Scotland; established one of Australia's largest woollen mills in 1894.

vice[1] /vaɪs/, *n.* **1.** wickedness or evil in general. **2.** evil or immoral behavior, esp. in the criminal use of sex, drugs, etc. **3.** a particular example of evil behavior; sin: *the vice of envy.* **4.** a fault; defect; imperfection: *a vice of literary style.* **5.** any bad habit. [ME, from OF, from L: fault]

vice[2] /vaɪs/, *n.* an implement for holding an object tightly so that it can be worked on, usu. having two jaws which can be screwed together. [ME, from OF: screw, from L: vine] **–vice-like,** *adj.*

vice[3] /'vaɪsi/, *prep.* instead of; in the place of. [L: turn]

vice-, a prefix indicating a substitute, deputy, or subordinate: *vice-chairman, viceroy, viceregent.*

vice-chancellor /vaɪs-'tʃænsələ, -'tʃɑːn-/, *n.* the executive head of a university.

vice-president /vaɪs-'prezədənt/, *n.* an officer next in rank to a president and taking his or her place if he or she is ill or absent. **–vice-presidency,** *n.* **–vice-presidential,** *adj.*

viceregal /vaɪsˈriːgəl/, *adj.* **1.** of or relating to a viceroy. **2.** of or relating to the governor-general or a state governor.

viceroy /'vaɪsrɔɪ/, *n.* someone appointed to rule a country or province as the deputy of a king or queen. [F, from VICE- + *roi* king]

vice squad *n.* that section of the police force concerned with enforcement of laws relating to prostitution, gambling, etc.

vice versa /ˌvaɪsə 'vɜːsə, vaɪs, vaɪsi/, *adv.* the order being changed (from that of a preceding statement); conversely: *John distrusts Jack, and vice versa.* [L]

Vichy /ˈvɪʃɪ/, n. a town in central France; the capital of unoccupied France 1940–44; hot springs. Pop. 63 501 (1982). Latin, **Vicus Calidus**.

vicinity /vəˈsɪnətɪ/, n., pl. **-ties. 1.** a region near or about a place; neighborhood. **2.** the condition or fact of being near in place; proximity; propinquity. [L]

vicious /ˈvɪʃəs/, adj. **1.** cruel; spiteful or malignant: *a vicious attack*. **2.** unpleasantly severe: *a vicious headache*. **3.** faulty; defective: *vicious reasoning*. **4.** (of a horse, dog, etc.) having bad habits or a bad temper. [ME, from L: faulty]

vicious circle, n. **1.** a situation in which the solution of one problem creates further difficulties, and usu. makes the original problem worse. **2.** *Logic.* the use of one proposition or definition to establish a second, when the second is in turn used to establish the first.

vicissitude /vəˈsɪsɪtjud/, n. **1.** a change, or something different, occurring in the course of something. **2.** (pl.) changes from good to bad or bad to good; ups and downs: *vicissitudes of life*. [L: change]

victim /ˈvɪktəm/, n. **1.** someone who suffers harm, pain, destruction, etc.: *victims of disease*; *victims of war*. **2.** someone who is taken in, used, or deceived by someone; dupe. **3.** a living creature sacrificed in a religious rite. [L: beast for sacrifice]

victimise or **victimize** /ˈvɪktəmaɪz/, v.t., **-mised, -mising. 1.** to make a victim of. **2.** to punish unfairly or selectively. **3.** to cheat; dupe; swindle. – **victimisation**, n.

victimless crime, n. behavior which has been made illegal because it offends against the moral ideals of a society, even though it involves no threat to the property or person of another, as vagrancy, homosexuality, etc.

victor /ˈvɪktə/, n. **1.** someone who has defeated an enemy; a conqueror. **2.** the winner in any fight, race, etc. [ME, from L]

Victoria[1] /vɪkˈtɔrɪə/, n. 1819–1901, queen of Great Britain and Ireland 1837–1901, and empress of India 1876–1901.

Victoria[2] /vɪkˈtɔrɪə/, n. **1.** a state in south-eastern Australia, the smallest in area of the mainland states. Pop. 4 019 478 (1986). 227 620 km² *Cap.*: Melbourne. *Abbrev.*: Vic [named after Queen VICTORIA]. **2. Mount**, the second highest mountain in PNG, in the Central District on the crest of the Owen Stanley Range. 4084m. **3. Lake**. Also, **Victoria Nyanza**. a lake in eastern Africa; the second largest freshwater lake in the world; principal headwaters of the Nile. 69 485 km².

Victoria Cross, n. a British decoration in the shape of a bronze Maltese cross awarded to members of the armed services for acts of conspicuous bravery in the presence of the enemy, founded by Queen Victoria in 1856. *Abbrev.*: VC

Victoria Falls, n.pl. falls of the river Zambezi in southern Africa between Zambia and Zimbabwe, near Livingstone. About 122 m high; about a kilometre and a half wide.

Victorian /vɪkˈtɔrɪən/, adj. **1.** of or relating to Queen Victoria or her reign or period: *the Victorian age*. **2.** respectable or outwardly pure like Victorian society. **3.** of or relating to the State of Victoria. ◇n. **4.** a person living in the Victorian period. **5.** someone born in or now living in Victoria.

Victoriana /vɪkˌtɔrɪˈɑnə/, n. ornaments, bric-a-brac, etc., of the Victorian period.

victory /ˈvɪktərɪ, -trɪ/, n., pl. **-ries. 1.** a decisive win in a battle, fight, etc. **2.** any success in a struggle or difficulty. [ME, from L] – **victorious**, adj.

victual /ˈvɪtl/, n., v., **-ualled, -ualling.** ◇n. **1.** (pl.) *Colloq.* food. ◇v.t. **2.** to supply or store with victuals. [ME, from OF, from LL: provisions] – **victualler**, n.

vide /ˈvideɪ, ˈvaɪdi/, v. see (used esp. in making reference to parts of a text). *Abbrev.*: vid. [L]

video /ˈvɪdɪoʊ/, adj. **1.** relating to or used in the sending or receiving of a televised image, or to images displayed on television screens as in the video terminal of a computer. **2.** of or relating to a video recording. ◇n. **3.** a video recording. [L: I see]

video clip, n. a short video recording, esp. one showing a performance of a popular song. Also, **clip**.

videophone /ˈvɪdɪoʊfoʊn/, n. a telephone which allows visual, as well as verbal, communication.

videotape /ˈvɪdɪoʊteɪp/, n., v., **-taped, -taping.** ◇n. **1.** a magnetic tape upon which a video-frequency signal is recorded; used for storing a television program or film. ◇v.t. **2.** to record on videotape.

vie /vaɪ/, v.i., **vied, vying.** to compete against someone (fol. by *with*): *He was always vying with his sister in games*. [F: challenge, from L: invite]

vienna /viˈɛnə/, n. **1.** smoked sausage, eaten boiled, usu. made of beef or pork. **2.** Also, **vienna loaf**. a cigar-shaped loaf of white bread. **3.** espresso coffee with whipped cream on top. **4.** (*cap.*) the capital of Austria, in the north-eastern part, which has separate provincial status; a port on the Danube. Pop. 1 531 346 (1981). German, **Wien**.

Vientiane /vientiˈɑn/, n. a city in north-western Laos, on the Mekong river; administrative capital. Pop. 200 000 (1984 est.).

Vietcong /vjetˈkɒŋ/, n. (in the Vietnam war) a communist-led organisation and guerilla army in South Vietnam, supported by North Vietnam, fighting the Americans and South Vietnamese and seeking to overthrow the existing government.

Vietminh /vjetˈmɪn/, n. a revolutionary nationalist organisation in Vietnam which fought first the Japanese, then the French 1941–54.

Vietnam /vjetˈnɑm, -ˈnæm/, n. a republic in south-east Asia on the South China Sea, bordered by Laos and Kampuchea; divided in 1954

Vietnam 1141 **vindictive**

into North Vietnam (under the Vietminh) and South Vietnam (under French control, independent from 1955); Vietnam War from 1959 to eventual defeat of the South in 1975 and reunification in 1976. Pop. 62 468 000 (1987); 329 465 km². *Language:* Vietnamese, French and English. *Currency:* dông. *Cap.:* Hanoi. Official name, **Socialist Republic of Vietnam.** Also, **Viet Nam.**

Vietnam War, *n.* a war, 1959–75, between the Vietcong, supported by North Vietnam, and the South Vietnamese government, supported by the US; withdrawal of US troops from 1973; defeat of South Vietnamese government 1975.

view /vjuː/, *n.* **1.** a seeing or looking at: *a closer view of the problem.* **2.** sight or vision: *exposed to view.* **3.** the range of sight or vision: *The boat came into view.* **4.** something seen from a particular place: *a harbor view; a view over the valley.* **5.** a picture of a scene. **6.** an aspect: *Look at the problem from this view.* **7.** aim, intention, or purpose: *to work with a view to going overseas.* **8.** a hope or likelihood; prospect; expectation: *with no view of success.* **9.** a particular way of thinking about something: *my view of the matter; to take a wider view.* **10. a dim view,** an unfavorable opinion. **11. in view of, a.** in sight of. **b.** in hope of. **c.** in consideration of. **12. on view,** showing or displayed in a public place; on exhibition. ◇*v.t.* **13.** to see, look at, or watch. **14.** to think about in a particular way; consider. ◇*v.i.* **15.** to watch television or a television program. [ME, from AF: see, from L]

viewer /ˈvjuə/, *n.* **1.** someone who watches television or a television program. **2.** an instrument for showing photographic slides.

viewfinder /ˈvjuːfaɪndə/, *n.* an attachment to a camera allowing the photographer to determine what will be included in the picture.

viewpoint /ˈvjuːpɔɪnt/, *n.* **1.** a place giving a view of something. **2.** a point of view; attitude of mind: *the different viewpoints of an artist and a surgeon towards the human body.*

vigil /ˈvɪdʒəl/, *n.* **1.** a keeping awake for any purpose during the normal hours of sleep; watch: *to keep vigil by the bed of a sick person.* **2.** *Church* (*oft. caps.*) a night or evening service before a church festival: *We are singing at the vigil of the Ascension.* [ME, from AF, from L: watch]

vigilance /ˈvɪdʒələns/, *n.* the quality or fact of being vigilant; watchfulness; alertness. –**vigilant,** *adj.*

vigilante /vɪdʒəˈlænti/, *n. Chiefly US.* a member of an unauthorised committee of citizens organised to keep order and punish crime in the absence of regular law enforcement. [Sp: vigilant]

vigneron /ˈvɪnjərɒn/, *n.* wine-grower. [F]

vignette /vɪnˈjɛt/, *n., v.,* **-gnetted, -gnetting.** ◇*n.* **1.** a decorative design or small illustration used on the title-page of a book, or at the beginning or end of a chapter. **2.** an engraving, drawing, photograph, etc., shading off gradually at the edges. **3.** any small, pleasing picture or view. **4.** a small, graceful literary sketch. [F: vine] –**vignettist,** *n.*

vigor *or* **vigour** /ˈvɪgə/, *n.* **1.** active strength or force, of body or mind. **2.** healthy physical or mental energy or power. **3.** energy; energetic activity. **4.** force of healthy growth in any living matter or organism, as a plant. [ME, from OF, from L] –**vigorous,** *adj.* –**vigorousness,** *n.*

vigoro /ˈvɪgəroʊ/, *n.* a team game with 12 players a side, combining elements of baseball and cricket. [? from VIGOR]

Viking /ˈvaɪkɪŋ/, *n.* (*sometimes l.c.*) **1.** a Scandinavian sea-robber of the type that roamed the seas about northern and western Europe during the eighth, ninth, and tenth centuries, making raids upon the coasts. **2.** either of two unmanned US spacecraft designed to explore Mars; landings were effected in 1976. [Icel *vikingr* free-booter, pirate]

vile /vaɪl/, *adj.,* **viler, vilest.** **1.** wretchedly bad: *vile weather; clothes of vile quality.* **2.** highly offensive; obnoxious; objectionable: *vile behavior; vile language.* **3.** morally bad; base; depraved: *vile thoughts.* **4.** low; humiliating; ignominious: *vile servitude; a vile task.* [ME, from AF, from L: cheap, base] –**vileness,** *n.*

vilify /ˈvɪləfaɪ/, *v.t.,* **-fied, -fying.** to speak evil of; defame. [ME, from LL] –**vilification,** *n.* –**vilifier,** *n.*

villa /ˈvɪlə/, *n.* **1.** a country house, usu. a large or important one, esp. in a Mediterranean country. **2.** a suburban house of pseudo-Spanish style. **3.** an ancient Roman country house associated with agriculture, usu. built round a courtyard. [L or It]

village /ˈvɪlɪdʒ/, *n.* **1.** a settlement or small town in a country district. **2.** the people of a village. **3.** a group of small, sometimes fashionable and exclusive shops, in a suburb. [ME, from OF, from L: villa]

villager /ˈvɪlədʒə/, *n.* someone who lives in a village.

villain /ˈvɪlən/, *n.* **1.** a wicked person; scoundrel. **2.** a wicked character in a play, novel, etc.: *Iago is the villain of 'Othello'.* [ME, from OF, from L: farm servant] –**villainy,** *n.* –**villainous,** *adj.*

villein /ˈvɪlən/, *n. Hist.* a member of a class of half-free people under the feudal system, who were serfs with respect to their lord but had the rights of freemen with respect to others. Also, **villain.** [var. of VILLAIN]

vim /vɪm/, *n. Colloq.* energy; vigor. [L]

vinaigrette /vɪnəˈgrɛt/, *n.* a small ornamental bottle or box for holding aromatic vinegar, smelling salts, etc. Also, **vinegarette.** [F: vinegar + -ETTE]

vindicate /ˈvɪndəkeɪt/, *v.t.,* **-cated, -cating.** **1.** to clear from a charge, blame, suspicion, etc. **2.** to show to be right or just; justify: *Later events vindicated his policy.* **3.** to support, or defend (a right, cause, etc.) against opposition. [L] –**vindicator,** *n.* –**vindication,** *n.*

vindictive /vɪnˈdɪktɪv/, *adj.* having or showing a revengeful spirit: *a vindictive person; a vindictive remark.* [L] –**vindictiveness,** *n.*

vine /vaɪn/, *n.* **1.** (a plant with) a long, thin stem that trails on the ground or climbs by winding itself about a support or holding fast with tendrils. **2.** any of various climbing plants with a woody stem and bearing grapes; grapevine. [ME, from OF, from L]

vinegar /ˈvɪnɪɡə, -nə-/, *n.* **1.** a sour liquid consisting of dilute and impure acetic acid, made by fermenting wine, cider, etc. and used as a condiment, preservative, etc. **2.** sour speech, temper, or appearance. [ME, from OF, from *vin* wine + *egre* sour] – **vinegary**, *adj.*

Vinegar Hill, *n.* the former name given to Rouse Hill in eastern NSW, near Sydney; site of the capture of convicts from the Castle Hill Rising in 1804. [named as an ironical allusion to a battleground, known by the same name, in Ireland where rebels were defeated by General Lake in 1798]

vineyard /ˈvɪnjəd/, *n.* an area of land planted with vines producing grapes for winemaking, etc. [ME; from VINE + YARD²]

vino /ˈviːnoʊ/, *n. Colloq.* wine. [It]

vintage /ˈvɪntɪdʒ/, *n.* **1.** a harvest or crop of grapes of a single year. **2.** the wine produced from a particular harvest. **3.** a very fine wine from the crop of a good year, labelled and sold as such. **4.** *Colloq.* the style of a particular period of production of anything: *a hat of last year's vintage.* ◇ *adj.* **5.** (of wines) labelled and sold as the produce of a particular year. **6.** of high quality (oft. from, or in the manner of the past): *The actor gave a vintage performance.* **7.** indicating a motor vehicle built between 1918 and 1930, or a racing car more than ten years old. **8.** from a past period; old-fashioned. [ME, from AF, from L: grape gathering]

vinyl /ˈvaɪnəl/, *n.* **1.** *Chem.* a univalent radical CH₂:CH–, derived from ethylene, compounds of which undergo polymerisation to form plastics and resins. **2.** a type of plastic made from vinyl, used for household objects, toys, floor and seat coverings, etc. [L: wine + -YL]

viol /ˈvaɪəl/, *n.* a six-stringed musical instrument, played with a bow and having frets, common in the 16th and 17th centuries. [OF: instrument]

viola¹ /viˈoʊlə/, *n.* a four-stringed musical instrument of the violin family, slightly larger than the violin. [It]

viola² /ˈvaɪələ, vaɪˈoʊlə/, *n.* any of a group of plants which includes the violet and pansy. [L: violet]

violate /ˈvaɪəleɪt/, *v.t.*, **-lated, -lating. 1.** to break (a law, rule, agreement, promise, etc.). **2.** to break in upon rudely: *to violate privacy; to violate peace.* **3.** to do violence to, esp. by raping. **4.** to deal with or treat (something sacred) in a violent or irreverent way; desecrate; profane. [late ME, from L] – **violator**, *n.* – **violation**, *n.* – **violable**, *adj.*

violence /ˈvaɪələns/, *n.* **1.** rough force: *the violence of the wind.* **2.** rough force that is used to injure or harm: *to die by violence.* **3.** any wrongful use of force or power, as against rights, laws, etc. **4.** intensity of feeling, language, etc.; fury. [ME, from OF, from L: vehemence] – **violent**, *adj.*

violet /ˈvaɪələt/, *n.* **1.** a low, stemless or leafy-stemmed plant with purple, blue, yellow, white, or variegated flowers. **2.** a bluish purple color. ◇ *adj.* **3.** of a bluish purple color. [ME, from OF, from L]

violin /vaɪəˈlɪn/, *n.* a modern four-stringed instrument, played with a bow while being held nearly horizontal with the lower part supported against the shoulder; fiddle. [It: little viol] – **violinist**, *n.*

violoncello /vaɪələnˈtʃɛloʊ/, *n., pl.* **-los, -li** -li/. – **cello.** [It: little bass viol] – **violoncellist**, *n.*

VIP /ˌviː aɪ ˈpiː/, *n. Colloq.* a very important person. [abbrev.]

viper /ˈvaɪpə/, *n.* **1.** any of various highly poisonous snakes of the Old World, including the common vipers, the adders, etc. **2.** a false, treacherous, or spiteful person. [L: bringing forth living young (vipers were formerly thought to be viviparous)] – **viperous**, *adj.*

virago /vəˈrɑːɡoʊ/, *n., pl.* **-goes, -gos.** a violent or bad-tempered woman; shrew. [OE, from L: manlike woman]

viral /ˈvaɪrəl/, *adj.* relating to or caused by a virus.

Virgil /ˈvɜːdʒəl/, *n.* (*Publius Vergilius Maro*), 70–19 BC, Roman poet; his best-known work, the *Aeneid* (30–19) describes the fortunes of Aeneas. Also, **Vergil.** [ML *Virgilius*, misspelling of L *Vergilius*] – **Virgilian**, *adj.*

virgin /ˈvɜːdʒən/, *n.* **1.** a person, esp. a woman, who has never had sexual intercourse. ◇ *adj.* **2.** being a virgin. **3.** like or suggesting a virgin; pure; undefiled: *virgin snow.* **4.** untreated or unprocessed: *virgin gold; virgin wool.* **5.** untouched, untried, or unused: *virgin bush; virgin soil.* [ME, from OF, from L: maiden]

virginal¹ /ˈvɜːdʒənəl/, *adj.* **1.** of, relating to, typical of, or like a virgin. **2.** pure; untouched; fresh. [L *virginālis* maidenly]

virginal² /ˈvɜːdʒənəl/, *n.* a small rectangular harpsichord with the strings parallel to the keyboard, the earlier types placed on a table, common in the 16th and 17th centuries. Also, **virginals, pair of virginals.**

Virginia /vəˈdʒɪniə/, *n.* a state in the eastern US, on the Atlantic coast. Pop. 5 787 000 (1986 est.); 105 710 km². *Cap.:* Richmond. *Abbrev.:* Va – **Virginian**, *n., adj.*

virginity /vəˈdʒɪnəti/, *n.* **1.** the condition of being a virgin; maidenhood. **2.** the condition of being unspoilt or unused.

Virgin Mary, *n.* Mary, the mother of Jesus.

Virgo /ˈvɜːɡoʊ/, *n.* a constellation and sign of the zodiac, represented by a virgin. [L: maiden]

virile /ˈvɪraɪl/, *adj.* **1.** of, relating to, or characteristic of a man, as opposed to a woman or a child; masculine; manly. **2.** having or showing in a marked degree masculine strength, energy, or forcefulness: *a virile attitude; a virile style of writing*. **3.** (of a male) sexually active and capable of procreation. [L, from *vir* man] – **virility**, *n*.

virology /vaɪ'rɒlədʒi/, *n*. the study of viruses and the diseases caused by them. [*viro*- (combining form of VIRUS) + -LOGY] – **virological**, *adj*. – **virologist**, *n*.

virtual /'vɜtʃuəl/, *adj*. being so in force or effect, although not such in fact: *Although his family was rich, he lived in virtual poverty*. [ME, from ML]

virtual image, *n*. *Optics*. an image formed by the apparent convergence of light rays, as the image in a mirror (opposed to *real image*).

virtually /'vɜtʃuəli, 'vɜtʃəli/, *adv*. **1.** in effect, although not in name or in fact: *The deputy was virtually the head of the school*. **2.** *Colloq*. almost.

virtue /'vɜtʃu/, *n*. **1.** moral excellence or goodness. **2.** one particular moral or spiritual excellence: *Faith is a virtue*. **3.** any excellence or good quality: *Silence is often a virtue*. **4.** chastity, esp. in women. **5.** effective force: *There is no virtue in such methods*. **6. by/in virtue of**, by reason of. [ME, from L: manliness] – **virtuous**, *adj*.

virtuoso /vɜtʃu'ousou, -'ouzou/, *n*., *pl*. **-sos**, **-si** /-si, -zi/, *adj*. ◇*n*. **1.** someone who has special skill in any field, esp. in musical performance. **2.** someone who has a cultivated appreciation of artistic excellence; a connoisseur or collector of works or objects of art. ◇*adj*. **3.** characteristic of a virtuoso. [It: learned, skilful] – **virtuosity**, *n*.

virulent /'vɪrələnt/, *adj*. **1.** actively poisonous or deadly. **2.** (of a disease) **a.** rapid in effect; malignant or deadly. **b.** highly infectious. **3.** (of a micro-organism) causing particular or general clinical symptoms. **4.** (of a person) full of bitter enmity or spite; acrimonious. [ME, from L: poisonous. See VIRUS] – **virulence, virulency**, *n*.

virus /'vaɪrəs/, *n*. **1.** an infective agent, esp. one smaller than a common micro-organism, needing living cells for multiplication. **2.** any disease caused by a virus. **3.** any harmful or poisonous influence. [L: slimy liquid, poison]

visa /'vizə/, *n*. a stamp or written notice put in a passport by an official representative of a country, giving the holder of the passport permission to enter that country. [L, short for *carta visa* paper (has been) seen]

visage /'vɪzɪdʒ/, *n*. **1.** a face, esp. of a human being; countenance. **2.** appearance; aspect. [ME, from AF and OF: face, from L: to see]

vis-a-vis /viz-a-'vi/, *adv*., *adj*., *prep*., *n*., *pl*. **-vis**. ◇*adv*., *adj*. **1.** face to face. ◇*prep*. **2.** face to face with; opposite. **3.** regarding; with relation to: *discussions vis-a-vis a new proposal*. ◇*n*. **4.** a person corresponding in position or function to another; opposite number. [F: face to face]

viscera /'vɪsərə/, *n.pl*., *sing*. **viscus**. **1.** the soft interior organs of the body, including the brain, lungs, heart, stomach, intestines, etc. **2.** (in popular use) the intestines or bowels. [L] – **visceral**, *adj*.

viscose /'vɪskouz, -ous/, *n*. *Chem*. **1.** a viscous solution prepared by treating cellulose; used in making rayon or cellophane, etc. ◇*adj*. **2.** relating to or made from viscose. [L]

viscosity /vɪs'kɒsəti/, *n*., *pl*. **-ties**. *Phys*. that property of a fluid which causes it to tend to resist movement or change of shape during flow, or the degree of this property in a particular fluid.

viscount /'vaɪkaʊnt/, *n*. a nobleman ranking below an earl or count and above a baron. [ME, from AF, from *vis* VICE- + *counte* COUNT²]

viscountess /'vaɪkaʊntəs/, *n*. **1.** the wife or widow of a viscount. **2.** a woman holding in her own right a rank the same as that of a viscount.

viscous /'vɪskəs/, *adj*. **1.** Also, **viscid** /'vɪsɪd/. sticky and thick; glutinous. **2.** having the property of viscosity. [ME, from L: birdlime]

Vishnu /'vɪʃnu/, *n*. *Hinduism*. **1.** 'the Preserver', the second member of an important trinity. See **Brahma**, **Shiva**. **2.** a savior, appearing in many incarnations, including that of the Krishna of the Bhagavad-gita. [Skt]

visibility /vɪzə'bɪləti/, *n*., *pl*. **-ties**. **1.** relative ability to be seen under given conditions of distance, light, etc.: *low visibility because of the fog*. **2.** the greatest distance at which a particular object can be seen and identified; visual range.

visible /'vɪzəbəl/, *adj*. **1.** able to be seen by the eye. **2.** *Phys*. (of electromagnetic radiation) having a wavelength between 380 and 780 nanometres. **3.** evident to the mind; perceptible; obvious. [ME, from L]

Visigoth /'vɪzɪgɒθ/, *n*. a member of the westerly division of the Goths, which formed a monarchy about AD 418, maintaining it in southern France until AD 507 and in Spain until AD 711. [LL *Visigothi* (pl.), Latinisation of Gmc tribal name] – **Visigothic**, *adj*.

vision /'vɪʒən/, *n*. **1.** the act of seeing with the eye; power, or sense of sight. **2.** the act or power of perceiving what is not actually present to the eye, either by imagination, or intelligence: *She shows vision in dealing with great problems*. **3.** a mental view or image, either of supernatural origin or imaginary, of what is not actually present in place or time: *visions of the future; visions of God*. **4.** something seen, esp. in a dream, trance, etc. **5.** someone or something of great beauty. [ME, from L: sight]

visionary /'vɪʒənri/, *adj*., *n*., *pl*. **-ries**. ◇*adj*. **1.** given to or concerned with seeing visions. **2.** belonging to or seen in a vision. **3.** unreal or imaginary: *visionary evils*. **4.** given to or based on imagination or theory; ideal; unpractical: *a visionary plan; a visionary thinker*. ◇*n*. **5.** someone who sees visions. **6.** someone who is given to ideas or plans which are not immediately practical; a dreamer, theorist, or enthusiast.

visit /'vɪzət/, *v.t.* **1.** to go or call on to see (a person, family, place, etc.). **2.** to stay with as a guest. **3.** to come upon or afflict: *The plague visited London in 1665.* ◇*v.i.* **4.** to visit someone or something. ◇*n.* **5.** the act of visiting. [ME, from L: go to see] —**visitor,** *n.*

visitant /'vɪzətənt/, *n.* **1.** a visitor; guest. **2.** a supernatural visitor; apparition; ghost.

visitation /ˌvɪzə'teɪʃən/, *n.* **1.** a visit, esp. for the purpose of making an official inspection, etc. **2.** a giving by God of a reward, or punishment, or an event or experience regarded as such.

visor /'vaɪzə/, *n.* **1.** the movable front parts of a helmet, covering the face, esp. the part which protects the eyes. **2.** *Chiefly US.* the front part of a cap, which protects the eyes from sunlight; peak. **3.** a small shade fitted to the inside roof of a car, which may be swung down to protect the driver's eyes from sunlight, etc. [ME, from AF, from *vis* face]

vista /'vɪstə/, *n.* **1.** a view, esp. one seen through a long, narrow passage, as between rows of trees, houses, etc. **2.** a mental view stretching over a long time or over a series of remembered or imagined experiences: *vistas of the past.* [It: view, from L]

Vistula /'vɪstjələ/, *n.* a river in Poland, flowing from the Carpathian Mountains past Warsaw into the Baltic near Danzig. About 1046 km. Polish, **Wisla.** German, **Weichsel.**

visual /'vɪʒuəl/, *adj.* **1.** of or relating to sight. **2.** able to be seen; visible. ◇*n.* **3.** (*pl.*) objects having a visual effect, such as photographs, films, slides, etc. [ME, from LL: belonging to sight]

visual display unit, *n.* → VDU. Also, **visual display terminal.**

visualise *or* **visualize** /'vɪʒuəlaɪz/, *v.t., v.i.,* **-lised, -lising.** to form a mental image or picture (of something). —**visualisation,** *n.*

vital /'vaɪtl/, *adj.* **1.** of or relating to life: *vital functions.* **2.** having life, or living. **3.** having great energy, enthusiasm, etc.: *a vital personality.* **4.** being necessary to life: *the vital organs.* **5.** necessary; indispensable; essential: *It is vital that we act now.* **6.** of basic importance: *vital problems.* ◇*n.* **7.** (*pl.*) the essential parts of anything. [ME, from L]

vitality /vaɪ'tæləti/, *n., pl.* **-ties. 1.** energy, vigor. **2.** the power to live; vital force. **3.** the power of continued existence.

vital statistics, *n.pl.* **1.** statistics concerning human life, population, or the conditions affecting human life. **2.** *Colloq.* the measurements of a woman's figure at the bust, waist, and hips.

vitamin /'vaɪtəmən, 'vɪt-/, *n.* any of a group of organic substances present in food, essential in small amounts for life; the absence of any one results in a particular deficiency disease. [L: life + AMIN(E)]

vitamin A, *n.* a fat-soluble yellow alcohol found in green and yellow vegetables, butter, egg yolk and fish-liver oil, necessary for the prevention of night blindness. Also, **vitamin A$_1$.**

vitamin B$_1$, *n.* → thiamine.

vitamin B$_2$, *n.* → riboflavin.

vitamin B complex, *n.* an important group of water-soluble vitamins containing vitamin B$_1$ (thiamine), vitamin B$_2$ (riboflavin), etc.

vitamin C, *n.* → ascorbic acid.

vitamin D, *n.* any of the several fat-soluble vitamins found in milk and fish-liver oils, or by the action of ultraviolet light on substances in the skin; necessary to prevent rickets.

vitamin E, *n.* a fat-soluble pale yellow compound, found in wheat-germ oil, which is thought to increase fertility in mammals.

vitamin H, *n.* → biotin.

vitamin K, *n.* a group of fat-soluble compounds, found esp. in leafy green vegetables, involved in blood clotting.

vitiate /'vɪʃieɪt/, *v.t.,* **-ated, -ating. 1.** to lower the quality of; make faulty; spoil. **2.** to make legally ineffective; invalidate. [L: spoiled] —**vitiation,** *n.* —**vitiator,** *n.*

viticulture /'vɪtɪkʌltʃə/, *n.* (the study of) the cultivation of the grapevine. [L: vine + CULTURE] —**viticultural,** *adj.* —**viticulturist,** *n.*

vitreous /'vɪtriəs/, *adj.* **1.** of the nature of glass, in transparency, hardness, etc.; glassy: *vitreous china.* **2.** of or relating to glass. **3.** obtained from glass. [L: glass] —**vitreosity,** *n.*

vitreous humor *or* **vitreous humour,** *n. Anat.* the transparent jelly-like substance filling the eyeball behind the lens.

vitri-, a word part meaning 'glass'. [combining form representing L vitri-]

vitrify /'vɪtrəfaɪ/, *v.t., v.i.,* **-fied, -fying. 1.** to change or be changed into glass, so that all the particles of clay, sand, etc., are fused together, becoming waterproof. **2.** to make or become like glass. —**vitrification,** *n.*

vitriol /'vɪtriəl/, *n.* **1.** *Chem.* any of certain glassy metallic sulfates, as of copper (blue vitriol), or iron (green vitriol), etc. **2.** sulfuric acid. **3.** something sharp, bitter, or severe, as criticism, speech, etc. [ME, from ML, from L: glass] —**vitriolic,** *adj.*

vituperate /və'tjupəreɪt, vaɪ-/, *v.t.,* **-rated, -rating.** to find fault with, using rough language; abuse; revile. [L] —**vituperation,** *n.* —**vituperative,** *adj.* —**vituperator,** *n.*

viva[1] /'vivə/, *interj.* long live (the person or idea named)! [It: may he live]

viva[2] /'vaɪvə/, *n. Colloq.* → **viva voce** (def. 2).

vivace /və'vatʃeɪ/, *Music.* ◇*adj.* **1.** lively; vivacious. ◇*adv.* **2.** in a lively manner. [It, from L]

vivacious /və'veɪʃəs/, *adj.* lively; animated; spirited: *a vivacious manner*; *vivacious conversation.* —**vivacity, vivaciousness,** *n.*

Vivaldi /və'vældi/, *n.* **Antonio,** 1680?–1741, Italian composer and violinist; large output of instrumental baroque music.

viva voce /ˌvaɪvə ˈvoʊtʃeɪ/, *adv.* **1.** by word of mouth; orally. ◇*n.* **2.** an examination where questions are asked and answered orally rather than by a written paper. Also, **viva**. [ME: with the living voice]

Vivian /ˈvɪvɪən/, *n. Arthurian Legend.* an enchantress, the mistress of Merlin; known as 'the Lady of the Lake.' Also, **Vivien**.

vivid /ˈvɪvəd/, *adj.* **1.** strikingly bright, as color, light, etc. **2.** lively; full of life: *a vivid personality*. **3.** presenting the appearance, freshness, etc., of life: *a vivid picture*. **4.** strong and clear: *a vivid impression; a vivid memory*. **5.** forming clear and striking mental images: *a vivid imagination*. [L *vividus* animated] **–vividness**, *n.*

viviparous /vəˈvɪpərəs/, *adj. Zool.* bringing forth living young (rather than laying eggs), as most mammals and some reptiles and fishes do. [L: bringing forth living young]

vivisection /ˌvɪvəˈsɛkʃən/, *n.* the practice of cutting up living animals, esp. in order to advance medical knowledge. **–vivisect**, *v.* **–vivisectionist**, *n.*

vixen /ˈvɪksən/, *n.* **1.** a female fox. **2.** an ill-tempered or quarrelsome woman. [southern d. var. of ME: she-fox, from OE]

viz., namely; that is to say. [L, short for *videlicet* that is]

vizier /vəˈzɪə/, *n.* a high government official in various Muslim countries. Also, **vizir**. [Turk, from Ar: bearer of burdens]

V-J Day /vi-ˈdʒeɪ deɪ/, *n.* 15 August 1945 (in the US 2 September 1945), the day of victory over Japan for the Allies in World War II. [from *V(ictory over) J(apan)*]

Vladivostok /ˌvlædəˈvɒstɒk/, *n.* a seaport in south-eastern Russia in Asia, on the Sea of Japan; eastern terminus of the Trans-Siberian Railway. Pop. 608 000 (1986 est.).

v.l.f. /vi el ˈɛf/, *Phys. Abbrev.* very low frequency.

vocabulary /vəˈkæbjələri/, *n., pl.* **-ries**. **1.** the total stock of words used by a person or a particular group or class of people. **2.** a list or collection of the words of a language, book, author, branch of science, etc., usu. in alphabetical order and defined. **3.** all the words of a language. [ML, from L: vocable]

vocal /ˈvoʊkəl/, *adj.* **1.** of or relating to the voice: *the vocal organs*. **2.** spoken with the voice; oral. **3.** sung, or intended for singing: *the vocal score*. **4.** having a voice: *a vocal being*. **5.** able to or inclined to express oneself clearly in speech. ◇*n.* **6.** a vocal sound. **7.** (*usu. pl.*) (in pop, rock, etc.) the musical part written for or performed by a singer. [ME, from L: voice]

vocal cords, *n.pl.* folds of mucous membrane in the larynx, the edges of which are made to vibrate by the passage of air from the lungs, thus producing vocal sound. Also, **vocal folds**.

vocalise[1] or **vocalize** /ˈvoʊkəlaɪz/, *v.,* **-lised, -lising**. ◇*v.t.* **1.** to express with the voice; speak or sing. ◇*v.i.* **2.** to use the voice; speak or sing. **–vocalisation**, *n.*

vocalise[2] /ˌvoʊkəˈliz/, *n.* a piece of vocal music without words. [F]

vocalist /ˈvoʊkələst/, *n.* a singer.

vocation /voʊˈkeɪʃən/, *n.* **1.** a particular occupation, business, or profession. **2.** a calling or summons to a particular activity or career. **3.** a call to God's service or to the Christian life. [ME, from L: calling] **–vocational**, *adj.*

vocative /ˈvɒkətɪv/, *adj.* **1.** *Gram.* (in some inflected languages) denoting a case that indicates the person or thing addressed. ◇*n.* **2.** *Gram.* the vocative case. [ME, from L: call]

vociferous /vəˈsɪfərəs/, *adj.* noisy; clamorous; forcefully expressing feeling, etc.: *a vociferous crowd; a vociferous protest*. **–vociferousness**, *n.*

vodka /ˈvɒdkə/, *n.* an alcoholic drink of Russian origin, made from wheat, or other cereals, and potatoes. [Russ: little water]

vogue /voʊg/, *n.* **1.** the fashion at a particular time: *a style in vogue fifty years ago*. **2.** popular acceptance, or favor: *That book had a great vogue once*. [F: row, go along smoothly, from It, ? from L: call (through use in sailors' shanties)]

voice /vɔɪs/, *n., v.,* **voiced, voicing**. ◇*n.* **1.** sound(s) made through the mouth of living creatures, esp. of human beings in speaking, singing, etc. **2.** the power to make such sounds. **3.** the quality or condition of the voice for singing: *She was in poor voice*. **4.** anything likened to the human voice, either in sound or in power to communicate: *the voice of the wind; the voice of the conscience*. **5.** expression in spoken or written words, or by other means: *He gave voice to his disapproval by a letter*. **6.** an expressed opinion, wish, etc.: *His voice was for peace*. **7.** the right to express an opinion or choice: *I had no voice in the matter*. **8.** a person or other means by which something is expressed. **9.** *Linguistics.* the sound produced by vibration of the vocal cords as air from the lungs is forced through between them. **10.** *Gram.* a verb form showing the relationship between the action expressed and the subject of the sentence. See **active voice** and **passive voice**. **11. with one voice**, in chorus; unanimously. ◇*v.t.* **12.** to express (a feeling, opinion, etc.) with the voice. [ME, from AF, from L]

voice box, *n.* →**larynx**.

void /vɔɪd/, *adj.* **1.** *Law.* without legal force or effect. **2.** useless; ineffectual. **3.** completely lacking; devoid (fol. by *of*). **4.** completely empty; without contents. ◇*n.* **5.** an empty space or opening: *the void of the sky*. **6.** a place without the usual or desired occupant or contents: *His death left a void among us*. **7.** a feeling of emptiness or loss: *a void in my heart*. ◇*v.t.* **8.** to make void or of no effect; nullify. **9.** to empty (contents); discharge (excrement, etc.). [ME, from OF, from L: be empty]

voile /vɔɪl/, *n.* a type of semitransparent dress material of wool, silk, rayon, or cotton. [F: veil]

vol., *Abbrev.* volume.

volatile /'vɒlətaɪl/, *adj.* 1. (of a substance) forming a vapor easily or quickly at relatively low temperatures: *a volatile oil*. 2. changeable of mind or mood; frivolous; flighty. [ME, from L: flying]

volcanic /vɒl'kænɪk/, *adj.* 1. of or relating to a volcano or volcanoes: *volcanic activity; volcanic mud*. 2. like a volcano in violence, etc. 3. *Geol.* denoting a class of igneous rocks which have become solid on the earth's surface.

volcanic plug, *n.* a mass of solid lava filling the vent of an extinct volcano, often the only evidence left after the cone has been eroded away.

volcano /vɒl'keɪnoʊ/, *n., pl.* **-noes, -nos**. 1. an opening in the earth's crust through which molten rock (lava), steam, ashes, etc., burst out, either continuously or at intervals, gradually forming a cone-shaped heap or mountain, commonly with a cup-shaped hollow (crater) about the opening. 2. a mountain or hill having such an opening and formed wholly or partly of its own lava. [It, from L: Vulcan, god of fire]

vole /voʊl/, *n.* a kind of rodent similar to and belonging to the same family as the common rats and mice, and usu. of heavy build with short limbs and tail. [short for *volemouse* field mouse, from Scand]

Volga /'vɒlɡə/, *n.* a river flowing from the Valdai Hills in north-western Russia east then south to the Caspian Sea; the longest river in Europe. 3742 km.

volition /və'lɪʃən/, *n.* 1. the act or power of willing. 2. a determination made by the will. [ML, from L: I wish] —**volitional**, *adj.*

volley /'vɒli/, *n., pl.* **-leys**, *v.,* **-leyed, -leying**. ◇*n* 1. a. the firing of a number of guns or other weapons together. b. the missiles fired. 2. a burst or outpouring of many things at once or close together: *a volley of words; a volley of blows*. 3. *Tennis.* a return of the ball before it touches the ground. ◇*v.t.* 4. to fire in a volley. 5. *Tennis, Soccer, etc.* to return, kick, etc., (the ball) before it strikes the ground. ◇*v.i.* 6. to fly or be fired together. 7. to move, proceed, or sound with great rapidity, as in a volley. [F: flight, from L]

volleyball /'vɒlibɔl/, *n.* 1. a game played by two teams, the object of which is to prevent a large ball from touching the ground by striking it from side to side over a high net with the hands or arms. 2. the ball used in this game.

volt /voʊlt/, *n.* the SI unit of electric potential or electromotive force. *Symbol:* V [named after Count Alessandro *Volta*, 1745–1827, Italian physicist]

Volta /'vɒltə/, *n.* a river in western Africa, in Ghana, flowing into the Bight of Benin. About 320 km long (with its main upper branch, the **Black Volta**, about 1270 km).

voltage /'voʊltɪdʒ/, *n.* electromotive force or potential expressed in volts.

voltaic /vɒl'teɪɪk/, *adj.* indicating or relating to the electricity or electric currents produced by chemical action, or, more broadly, to any electric current; galvanic.

voltaic cell, *n.* See **cell** (def. 5).

Voltaire /vɒl'tɛə/, *n.* **François Marie Arouet de** /frɒ,swa ma,ri a'rweɪ də/, 1694–1778, French philosopher, historian, dramatist, and essayist; his major works include *Lettres philosophiques* (1734) and the satire *Candide* (1759). —**Voltairean, Voltairian**, *adj.*

voltammeter /voʊlt'æmətə/, *n. Elect.* an instrument which can be used for measuring either volts or amperes.

volte-face /vɒlt-'fɑs/, *n.* a complete change of opinion or policy. [F, from It, from *volta* turn + *faccia* face, from L]

voltmeter /'voʊltmitə/, *n.* an instrument for measuring the voltage between two points.

voluble /'vɒljəbəl/, *adj.* marked by a ready and continuous flow of words: *a voluble talker; a voluble speech*. [L: roll, turn] —**volubility**, *n.*

volume /'vɒljum/, *n.* 1. a collection of written or printed sheets bound together and forming a book. 2. a book forming one of a related set or series. 3. the size, measure, or amount of anything in three dimensions; the space occupied by a body or substance measured in cubic units. 4. mass, amount, or quantity, esp. a large quantity, of anything: *volumes of smoke; volumes of abuse; The volume of traffic increases in the evening*. 5. loudness or softness. [ME, from OF, from L: roll (of papyrus or parchment)]

volumetric /vɒljə'mɛtrɪk/, *adj.* relating to, or depending upon measurement by volume. Also, **volumetrical**.

volumetric analysis, *n.* chemical analysis by volume, esp. by titration. See **titrate**.

voluminous /və'lumɪnəs/, *adj.* 1. forming or writing enough to fill a large volume or book, or many volumes: *a voluminous author; voluminous correspondence*. 2. of great volume, size, or extent: *a voluminous flow of water*. 3. large or full: *a voluminous dress*. [LL: full of folds]

voluntary /'vɒlntri, -lntəri/, *adj., n., pl.* **-taries**. ◇*adj.* 1. done, made, brought about, etc., by free will or choice: *a voluntary contribution*. 2. acting of one's own will or choice: *a voluntary helper*. 3. relating to or depending on voluntary action or help. 4. *Biol.* controlled by the will: *voluntary muscles*. 5. having the power of willing or choosing: *a voluntary agent*. ◇*n.* 6. a piece of music, often improvised, esp. a piece of organ music performed before, during, or after a church service. [ME, from L]

volunteer /vɒlən'tɪə/, *n.* 1. someone who enters into any service, or offers to do something, of his or her own free will. ◇*adj.* 2. being a volunteer or consisting of volunteers: *a volunteer soldier; a volunteer force*. ◇*v.i.* 3. to offer to do something. 4. to enter a service, esp. the armed forces, as a volunteer. ◇*v.t.* 5. to offer (one's services, etc., or oneself) for some duty or purpose. 6. to offer to give without being asked: *to volunteer advice; to volunteer an explanation*. [F, from L: VOLUNTARY]

voluptuary /və'lʌptjuəri/, *n., pl.* **-aries**. someone who delights in luxury and the

voluptuary 1147 **V-2**

pleasures of the senses. [L: *voluptuārius*, var. of *voluptārius*, from *voluptas* pleasure]

voluptuous /vəˈlʌptʃuəs/, *adj.* 1. full of, suggesting, or producing sensual, esp. sexual, pleasure: *a voluptuous dance.* 2. arising from enjoyment of the pleasures of the senses: *the voluptuous pleasure of a warm bath.* 3. (of the female figure) full and shapely. [ME, from L: pleasure]

volute /vəˈljut/, *n.* 1. a spiral or twisted formation or object, like that on the capital of an Ionic column. 2. *Zool.* a turn or whorl of a spiral shell. ◇*adj.* 3. in the form of a volute; rolled up. [L: scroll] — **volution**, *n.*

vomit /ˈvɒmət/, *v.i.*, *v.t.* 1. to throw out (the contents of the stomach) by the mouth. 2. to send or be sent out with force or violence. ◇*n.* 3. the act of vomiting. 4. the matter thrown up in vomiting. [late ME, from L]

V-1 /viˈwʌn/, *n.* a flying bomb developed by the Germans in World War II and launched against England. Also, **V-one**. [G: part trans. of *Vergeltungswaffe* retaliation weapon]

Vonnegut /ˈvɒnəgət/, *n.* Kurt, born 1922, US writer; noted for such novels as *Slaughterhouse-Five* (1969).

voodoo /ˈvudu/, *n., pl.* **-doos**, *adj., v.*, **-dooed, -dooing.** ◇*n.* 1. a class of mysterious practices, of the nature of sorcery, witchcraft, and fetishism, common among the Negroes of the West Indies and the southern US, and probably of African origin. 2. a fetish or other object of voodoo worship. ◇*adj.* 3. relating to, or practising voodoo. ◇*v.t.* 4. to affect by or as by voodoo. [Haitian Creole *vodu*, from an African language] — **voodooism**, *n.*

voracious /vəˈreɪʃəs/, *adj.* 1. eating or wanting food in large quantities; ravenous: *a voracious appetite.* 2. eager or greedy in some activity: *a voracious reader.* [L: greediness + -OUS] — **voracity, voraciousness**, *n.*

-vorous, a word part meaning 'eating', as in *carnivorous, herbivorous, omnivorous.* [L: devouring]

vortex /ˈvɔːteks/, *n., pl.* **-texes, -tices** /-təsiz/. 1. a whirling mass of water, air, fire, etc. 2. a state of affairs likened to this for violent activity, irresistible force, etc. [L] — **vortical**, *adj.*

Vostok /ˈvɒstɒk/, *n.* any of six manned Russian spacecraft made to orbit the earth. The first in April 1961 carried Yuri Gagarin, first human in space.

votary /ˈvoʊtəri/, *n., pl.* **-ries.** 1. someone who is bound by a vow to a religious life; monk or nun. 2. someone devoted to some activity, study, etc. Also, **votarist**. [L: vow + -ARY¹] — **votaress, votress**, *n. fem.*

vote /voʊt/, *n., v.*, **voted, voting.** ◇*n.* 1. a formal expression of will, wish, or choice in some matter, indicated by voice, ballot, etc. 2. the means by which such expression is made, such as a ballot, ticket, etc. 3. the right to such expression; suffrage. 4. the decision reached by voting. 5. a certain number of, or the total number of, votes collectively: *the Labor vote;* *The vote has increased this year.* ◇*v.i.* 6. to express choice in a matter for decision, by voice, ballot, etc.: *For whom will you vote at the election?* ◇*v.t.* 7. to establish or determine by vote; bring or put (*in, out, down*, etc.) by vote: *They voted funds for a new school; They voted in a new government.* 8. to support by or as if by one's vote: *I vote that the report be accepted.* 9. to declare by general consent: *They voted the trip a success.* [ME, from L: vow, wish]

votive /ˈvoʊtɪv/, *adj.* 1. done, given, etc., in accordance with a vow: *a votive offering.* 2. of the nature of or expressive of a wish or desire. [L: pertaining to a vow]

vouch /vaʊtʃ/, *v.i.* 1. to answer (*for*) or serve as evidence (*for*) of the truth, certainty, reliability, etc., of something or someone: *These facts vouch for his story.* 2. to make oneself responsible; give one's own assurance or guarantee (fol. by *for*): *I can vouch for him.* [ME, from AF]

voucher /ˈvaʊtʃə/, *n.* 1. a paper, such as a receipt, which proves the truth of a claimed expenditure. 2. a ticket used instead of money: *a gift voucher; a luncheon voucher.*

vouchsafe /vaʊtʃˈseɪf/, *v.*, **-safed, -safing.** ◇*v.t.* 1. to give, by favor, graciousness, etc.: to *vouchsafe a reply.* ◇*v.i.* 2. to condescend; have the graciousness (to do something). [ME: guarantee as safe]

vow /vaʊ/, *n.* 1. a solemn promise or pledge: *marriage vows; a vow of secrecy.* 2. a solemn declaration. 3. **take vows**, to enter a religious order or house. ◇*v.t.* 4. to promise by a vow: *to vow revenge.* 5. to declare solemnly: *She vowed she would go.* 6. to dedicate by a vow: *She vowed herself to the service of God.* ◇*v.i.* 7. to make a vow. [ME, from AF, from L]

vowel /ˈvaʊəl/, *n.* 1. a speech sound made by allowing air from the lungs to pass out through the mouth without friction occurring. 2. a letter which usually represents a vowel, as in English, *a, e, i, o, u,* and sometimes *y.* [ME, from OF, from L: vocal]

vox populi /vɒks ˈpɒpjəlaɪ/, *n.* the voice or opinion of the people. [L]

voyage /ˈvɔɪdʒ/, *n., v.*, **-aged, -aging.** ◇*n.* 1. a journey, by sea or air, esp. to a distant place. 2. (*oft. pl.*) a written account of a voyage. ◇*v.i.* 3. to travel by water, or air. [ME, from OF, from L: provision for a journey]

Voyager /ˈvɔɪədʒə/, *n.* 1. **HMAS**, an Australian navy destroyer, sunk in a collision with HMAS *Melbourne* in 1964. 2. an unmanned US space probe program, for the exploration of Jupiter and Saturn; two spacecraft were launched in 1977.

voyeur /vɔɪˈɜ, vwɑːˈjɜ/, *n.* someone who satisfies sexual desires by looking on at sexual acts. [F: see] — **voyeurism**, *n.*

VP, *Abbrev.* Vice-President. Also, **V Pres**

vs, *Abbrev.* versus.

v.t., *Abbrev.* verb transitive.

V-2 /viˈtu/, *n.* a long-range rocket developed by the Germans in World War II and used as a missile against England. Also, **V-two**.

Vulcan /ˈvʌlkən/, *n.* **1.** the Roman god of fire and metal-working. Cf. **Hephaestus. 2.** an imaginary planet, with a smaller orbit than that of Mercury, which was believed to exist in the 19th century but whose existence has now been disproved.

vulcanise *or* **vulcanize** /ˈvʌlkənaɪz/, *v.t.*, **-nised, -nising.** to treat (substances such as indiarubber) with sulfur and heat to make them solid, hard, long-wearing and able to stretch.

vulcanism /ˈvʌlkənɪzəm/, *n.* phenomena connected with the origin and movement of molten rock material within and at the surface of the earth. Also, **vulcanicity** /vʌlkəˈnɪsəti/.

vulcanite /ˈvʌlkənaɪt/, *n.* hard rubber, easily cut and polished, used for making combs, buttons, etc., and for electrical insulation, and made by vulcanising indiarubber.

vulcanology /vʌlkəˈnɒlədʒi/, *n.* the scientific study of volcanoes. Also, **volcanology.** — **vulcanological,** *adj.* — **vulcanologist,** *n.*

vulgar /ˈvʌlgə/, *adj.* **1.** marked by lack of good taste; coarse; crude: *vulgar manners; vulgar clothes.* **2.** offensively sexual; indecent: *a vulgar joke.* **3.** belonging to the common people of society: *vulgar superstitions.* **4.** spoken by or being in the language spoken by the people generally; vernacular: *a vulgar translation of the Greek text of the New Testament.* [ME, from L: relating to the common people]

vulgar fraction, *n.* → **common fraction.**

vulgarise *or* **vulgarize** /ˈvʌlgəraɪz/, *v.t.*, **-rised, -rising. 1.** to make vulgar. **2.** to put into general use. — **vulgarisation,** *n.*

vulgarism /ˈvʌlgərɪzəm/, *n.* a word or phrase used only in common colloquial, and esp. in coarse, speech.

vulgarity /vʌlˈgærəti/, *n., pl.* **-ties. 1.** the condition or quality of being vulgar; lack of good manners or taste. **2.** a vulgar act or speech.

Vulgate /ˈvʌlgeɪt, -gət/, *n.* **1.** the Latin version of the Scriptures, prepared mainly by St Jerome near the end of the fourth century. ◇*adj.* **2.** of or relating to the Vulgate. [ML, from LL: popular edition]

vulnerable /ˈvʌlnrəbəl, -nərəbəl/, *adj.* **1.** able to be hurt or wounded. **2.** not protected against emotional hurt; highly sensitive. **3.** open to attack by criticism, temptation, influence, etc. **4.** (of a place, fortress, etc.) open to attack. [LL: wounding] — **vulnerability,** *n.*

vulnerary /ˈvʌlnərəri/, *n., pl.* **-ries.** *adj.,* (a plant or remedy) used or useful for healing wounds.

vulpine /ˈvʌlpaɪn/, *adj.* relating to or like a fox. [L]

vulture /ˈvʌltʃə/, *n.* **1.** a large, carrion-eating bird related to the eagles, kites, hawks, falcons, etc., but having less powerful toes and straighter claws and usu. a naked head. **2.** someone or something that cruelly feeds on or uses others. [ME, from L] — **vulturine,** *adj.*

vulva /ˈvʊlvə/, *n., pl.* **-vae** /-viː/, **-vas.** the external female sexual organs, in particular the two pairs of labia and the cleft between them. [L: wrapper] — **vulval, vulvar,** *adj.*

vv., *Abbrev.* verses.

v.v., *Abbrev.* vice versa.

vying /ˈvaɪɪŋ/, *adj.* in competition: *children vying with one another for attention.*

Ww

W, w, *n., pl.* **W's** or **Ws**, **w's** or **ws.** the 23rd letter of the English alphabet.

w., *Abbrev.* **1.** weight. **2.** width.

W, *Abbrev.* **1.** west. **2.** western. **3.** Wednesday. ◇*Symbol.* **4.** *Chem.* wolfram (tungsten). **5.** *Elect.* watt(s).

WA /ˌdʌbəlju 'eɪ/, *Abbrev.* Western Australia.

Wackett /'wækət/, *n.* **Sir Lawrence James,** 1896–1982, Australian pilot and designer of aircraft; responsible for the construction of Australian planes during World War II.

wad /wɒd/, *n.* **1.** a small mass or lump of anything soft. **2.** a ball or mass of something squeezed together: *a wad of folded paper.* **3.** a roll or bundle, esp. of banknotes. **4.** a large quantity of something, esp. money.

wadding /'wɒdɪŋ/, *n.* any soft material for stuffing, padding, packing, etc.

waddle /'wɒdl/, *v.*, **-dled, -dling,** *n.* ◇*v.i.* **1.** to walk with short steps, swaying or rocking from side to side like a duck. ◇*n.* **2.** the act of waddling; a waddling gait. [frequentative of WADE]

waddy /'wɒdi/, *n., pl.* **-dies.** an Aboriginal heavy wooden war club. [Aboriginal]

wade /weɪd/, *v.*, **waded, wading,** *n.* ◇*v.i.* **1.** to walk through any substance, such as water, snow, sand, etc., that prevents free movement. **2.** to make one's way with labor or difficulty: *to wade through a dull book.* ◇*v.t.* **3.** to pass through by wading; ford: *to wade a stream.* ◇*n.* **4.** the act of wading. [OE: go]

wader /'weɪdə/, *n.* **1.** any of various longlegged birds, such as cranes, herons, storks, sandpipers, plovers, etc., that wade in water in search of food. **2.** (*pl.*) high waterproof boots used for wading.

wadi /'wɒdi/, *n., pl.* **-ies.** *Geog.* (in Arabia, Syria, northern Africa, etc.) (a channel of) a watercourse which is dry except during periods of rainfall. [Ar]

wafer /'weɪfə/, *n.* **1.** a thin, crisp cake or biscuit. **2.** a thin disc of unleavened bread, used in the Eucharist. **3.** any other thin, flat cake or sheet, etc. [ME, from OF, from MLG: honeycomb] – **wafery,** *adj.*

waffle[1] /'wɒfəl/, *n.* a crisp batter cake with a pattern of squares left by the hinged appliance in which it is cooked. [D]

waffle[2] /'wɒfəl/, *v.*, **-fled, -fling,** *n. Colloq.* ◇*v.i.* **1.** to speak or write vaguely, to no purpose, and at length. ◇*n.* **2.** lengthy, vague speech or writing. **3.** nonsense; twaddle. [frequentative of Brit d. *waff* to yelp]

Waikato

waft /wɒft/, *v.t.* **1.** to carry or take lightly as if in flight: *He wafted her away.* ◇*v.i.* **2.** to float or be carried, esp. through the air. ◇*n.* **3.** the act of wafting. [from obs. *wafter*, ME: armed escort vessel, from D or LG: guard]

wag[1] /wæg/, *v.*, **wagged, wagging.** ◇*v.t.* **1.** to move from side to side, forwards and backwards, or up and down, esp. quickly and many times: *A dog wagged his tail.* **2.** to move (the tongue) in talking. **3.** to shake (a finger) at someone, esp. in scolding or warning. **4.** to be absent from (school, etc.) without permission. ◇*v.i.* **5.** (of the head or the tail) to be moved from side to side or one way and the other, esp. quickly and many times. **6.** (of the tongue) to move busily, esp. in gossiping. ◇*n.* **7.** the act of wagging. [ME, from Scand]

wag[2] /wæg/, *n.* a humorous person; joker. – **waggish,** *adj.*

wage /weɪdʒ/, *n., v.*, **waged, waging.** ◇*n.* **1.** (*oft. pl.*) money paid for work or services, by the day, week, etc.; hire; pay (opposed to *salary*). **2.** (*usu. pl., sometimes treated as sing.*) result; reward or punishment: *the wages of sin.* ◇*v.t.* **3.** to carry on (a battle, war, conflict, etc.). [ME, from OF: pledge]

wage indexation, *n.* the adjustment of wages in accordance with changes in prices as shown in the consumer price index.

wager /'weɪdʒə/, *n.* **1.** something, such as money, placed as a bet on the outcome of an uncertain event; gamble. **2.** the act of betting. ◇*v.t.* **3.** to risk (something) on the result of a race, fight or any uncertain event; stake; bet. ◇*v.i.* **4.** to make or offer a waggering bet. [ME, from AF]

Wagga Wagga /ˌwɒgə 'wɒgə/, *n.* a city in southern central NSW, on the Murrumbidgee River; agricultural and educational centre. Pop. 37 577 (1986). Also, **Wagga.** [Aboriginal: many crows]

waggle /'wægəl/, *v.*, **-gled, -gling,** *n.* ◇*v.t., v.i.* **1.** to wag with short, quick movements; jiggle. ◇*n.* **2.** a waggling motion. [frequentative of WAG[1]] – **waggly,** *adj.*

Wagner /'vagnə/, *n.* **(Wilhelm) Richard,** 1813–83, German composer of operas such as *The Ring of the Nibelung,* a cycle of four music dramas. – **Wagnerian,** *adj.*

wagon /'wægən/, *n.* **1.** a four-wheeled vehicle, esp. for the transport of heavy loads, delivery, etc. **2.** a railway truck. [D]

wagtail /'wægteɪl/, *n.* a type of small, chiefly Old World bird with a slender body and long, narrow tail which is frequently wagged.

wahine /wa'hini/, *n. NZ.* a girl or woman, usu. Maori. [Maori]

waif /weɪf/, *n.* a person without a home or friends, esp. a child. [ME, from AF, probably from Scand]

Waikato /waɪ'kætoʊ, -'katoʊ/, *n.* the longest river in NZ, in western North Island, flowing north-west then west to the Tasman Sea. About 435 km.

wail /weɪl/, v.i. **1.** to utter a long, mournful cry (in grief or suffering): *The child wailed when he fell over.* ◇v.t. **2.** to wail over; lament: *to wail the dead.* ◇n. **3.** the act of wailing. **4.** a cry of grief or pain. [ME, from Scand]

Wailing Wall /'weɪlɪŋ wɔl/, n. a wall in Jerusalem where Jews assemble on certain occasions for prayers and lamentation; reputedly the remains of the temple built by Herod. Also, **Wailing Wall of the Jews.**

Waimangu Geyser /waɪ,mʌŋu 'gaɪzə/, n. a geyser on the North Island, NZ; now dormant, but formerly one of the greatest geysers in the world; known to have erupted to over 305 m.

wainscot /'weɪnskət, -koʊt/, n. panels of wood used to line the walls of a room, etc. Also, **wainscotting, wainscoting.** [ME, from MLG]

wainwright /'weɪnraɪt/, n. a wagon maker and repairer.

waist /weɪst/, n. **1.** that part of the human body between the ribs and hips. **2.** the part of a garment covering the waist. **3.** the central or middle part of an object: *the waist of a violin; the waist of a ship.* **4.** the narrow part or petiole of the abdomen of certain insects, such as the wasp. [ME]

waistcoat /'weɪstkoʊt/, n. a close-fitting, sleeveless garment which reaches to the waist and buttons down the front, oft. worn under a jacket. —**waistcoated**, adj.

waistline /'weɪstlaɪn/, n. **1.** a line around the body at smallest part of the waist. **2.** that part of a dress, coat, etc., which lies at or close to the waist. **3. watch one's waistline,** to take care not to put on weight.

wait /weɪt/, v.i. **1.** to stay or rest until something happens: *I'm waiting for him to go.* **2.** (of things) to be ready: *Your dinner is waiting for you.* **3.** to remain not done for a time: *a matter that can wait.* **4.** to serve food, drinks, etc., to others: *to wait at a table.* ◇v.t. **5.** to continue inactive until the occurrence of; await: *to wait one's turn in a queue.* ◇v. **6. wait up,** to delay going to bed to wait for someone to come. ◇n. **7.** the act of waiting. **8:** a period of waiting. [ME, OF, from OHG: *watch*]

Waite /weɪt/, n. **Edgar Ravenswood,** 1866–1928, Australian scientist, born in England; member of several expeditions into the subantarctic islands, New Guinea, and central Australia which contributed significantly to scientific knowledge of vertebrates.

Waitemata /waɪtə'mata/, n. a town in the northern part of the North Island, NZ. Pop. 99 000 (1985).

waiter /'weɪtə/, n. **1.** a man who serves food, drink, etc., at table in a restaurant, hotel, etc. **2.** a tray on which dishes, etc., are carried; salver. —**waitress**, n. fem.

waiting list, a list of people waiting for something to become available, as applicants for housing, job, etc.

waive /weɪv/, v.t., **waived, waiving. 1.** to decide not to insist on; relinquish; forgo: *to waive one's rank; to waive a fine.* **2.** to put aside for the time; defer. **3.** to put aside or dismiss from discussion: *He waived my attempts to explain.* [ME, from AF: abandon]

wake¹ /weɪk/, v., **woke, woken, waking,** n. ◇v.i. **1.** to stop being asleep; awake: *to wake up.* **2.** to stop being inactive; become roused. **3.** to become aware of: *to wake to nature.* ◇v.t. **4.** to rouse from sleep; awake (oft. fol. by *up*): *Don't wake the baby.* **5.** to rouse from inactivity, unconsciousness, ignorance, etc. (oft. fol. by *up*): *to wake people up to the dangers of war.* ◇v. **6. wake up to (oneself),** Colloq. to become more sensible and responsible. ◇n. **7.** a solemn watch kept, esp. for a dead person before or after a burial. [OE]

wake² /weɪk/, n. **1.** a track left by a ship or other object moving in the water. **2.** the path of anything that has gone past. [Scand]

Wakefield /'weɪkfild/, n. **Edward Gibbon,** 1796–1862, English-born theorist of systematic colonisation in Australia and NZ; developed the idea of funding emigration, played an important role in the abolition of transportation, and was a staunch advocate of responsible government.

wakeful /'weɪkfəl/, adj. **1.** (of a person) unable to sleep. **2.** marked by lack of sleep: *a wakeful night.* **3.** watchful; vigilant: *a wakeful enemy.*

waken /'weɪkən/, v.t., v.i. to rouse (someone) from sleep; awake. [OE]

Waldheim /'valthaɪm/, n. **Kurt,** born 1918, Austrian politician and diplomat; secretary-general of the UN 1971–81; president of Austria 1986–92; controversy over wartime activities.

Waler /'weɪlə/, n. a horse bred in NSW, orig. for export to the British Indian Army in the late 19th century. [from New South *Wales*]

Wales /weɪlz/, n. a division of the UK; a principality forming the south-western part of Great Britain. Pop. 2 821 000 (1986 est.); 20 761 km². *Cap.*: Cardiff. Welsh, **Cymru.**

Walesa /va'lensə/, n. **Lech** /lɛk/, born 1943, Polish trade union leader; chairman of Solidarity and leader of the 1980 strikes at Gdansk; 1983 Nobel Peace Prize; became president of Poland in 1990.

walk /wɔk/, v.i. **1.** to go or travel on foot by putting one foot in front and moving the other past it. **2.** (of a ghost, etc.) to go about on the earth, or appear to living people. **3.** (of things) to move in a manner like walking. ◇v.t. **4.** to go through, over, or upon by walking: *walking Sydney streets by night.* **5.** to cause to walk; lead, drive, or ride at a walk: *to walk a horse.* **6.** to go with (someone) on a walk: *He walked them to the gate.* ◇v. **7.** Some special uses are: **walk all over (someone),** Colloq. to behave in a bossy and aggressive way towards (someone). **walk away with,** to win easily. **walk off, 1.** to get rid of by walking: *to walk off a headache.* **walk out, 1.** to go on strike. **2.** to leave angrily. **walk out on,** to abandon; forsake; desert. **walk the streets, 1.** to wander about the streets, esp. as a result of being homeless. **2.** to be a prostitute.

walk / **wall-to-wall**

◇*n.* **8.** the act of walking, or going on foot. **9.** walking for exercise or pleasure: *to take a walk.* **10.** a distance walked or to be walked: *The house is a ten minute walk from the station.* **11.** a manner of walking: *It's impossible to mistake her walk.* **12.** a branch of activity, or particular line of work: *in all walks of life.* **13.** a place prepared or set apart for walking: *a forest walk.* **14.** a path or passage. [OE: roll, toss, go] — **walker,** *n.*

walkabout /'wɔkəbaʊt/, *n.* **1.** the periodical, nomadic wandering of an Aborigine into the bush. **2. go walkabout,** to wander around the country on walkabout.

walkathon /'wɔkəθɒn/, *n.* a fund-raising activity in which the people taking part are sponsored for the distance walked.

Walker /'wɔkə/, *n.* **Kath(leen Jean Mary)** → **Oodgeroo Noonuccal.**

walkie-talkie /ˌwɔki-'tɔki/, *n.* a combined radio transmitter and receiver, light enough to be carried by one person, developed originally for military use in World War II and since widely used by police, medical services, etc.

walking /'wɔkɪŋ/, *adj.* **1.** able to walk. **2.** used for or in walking: *walking shoes.* **3.** marked by or consisting of walking: *a walking holiday.* ◇*n.* **4.** the act of walking: *Walking was the best exercise for him.* **5.** a manner or style of walking.

walkout /'wɔkaʊt/, *n.* **1.** a strike by workers. **2.** the act of leaving a conference, meeting, etc., esp. as a protest.

walkover /'wɔkoʊvə/, *n.* an unopposed or easy victory.

wall /wɔl/, *n.* **1.** an upright structure of stone, brick, wood, etc., built for enclosure, division, support, protection, etc., such as one of the sides of a building. **2.** anything which keeps people out, like a wall: *a wall of prejudice.* **3.** a wall-like enclosing part, thing, mass, etc.: *a wall of fire; a wall of troops.* **4.** a bank built to prevent flooding. **5.** *Mountaineering.* a vertical or nearly vertical stretch of unbroken rock. **6. go to the wall, a.** to give way or be defeated. **b.** to fail in business, or become bankrupt. **7. with one's back to the wall,** in a very difficult or desperate situation. ◇*adj.* **8.** of or relating to a wall: *wall tiles.* **9.** placed in or on a wall: *a wall phone.* ◇*v.t.* **10.** to enclose, shut off, divide, protect, etc., with or as if with a wall: *to wall off a room; to wall in one's feelings.* [OE, from L] — **walled,** *adj.*

wallaby /'wɒləbi/, *n., pl.* **-bies,** (*esp. collectively*) **-by. 1.** any of several types of plant-eating marsupial, related and similar to the kangaroo: **a.** large types, e.g. the **agile wallaby** or **jungle kangaroo,** of northern river country, sandy-colored with a white hip and cheek stripe, the **toolache,** very rare, of south-eastern Australia, and the **western brush wallaby,** which each have a white face stripe and black and white ears. **b.** the smaller **parma wallaby,** dark brown, rare, of NSW rainforests and the **tammar,** of south-western Australia, grey-brown and able to survive with little water. **c.** the small **pademelon,** one type found in Tas scrub and two types in eastern mainland rainforests. **d.** the **quokka,** just larger than a cat, with rounded ears and a short face, of swamps and islands of south-western Australia. See **hare-wallaby, nail-tailed wallaby,** and **rock-wallaby. 2. on the wallaby (track),** *Colloq.* on the move as a swagman. [Aboriginal]

wallaby grass, *n.* a hardy native perennial grass used as winter food for animals, growing in clumps in the southern parts of the continent.

Wallace-Crabbe /ˌwɒləs-'kræb/, *n.* **Chris(topher Keith),** born 1934, Australian poet; works include the collection *In Light and Darkness* (1963).

Wallace's line /ˌwɒləsəz 'laɪn/, *n.* an imaginary line passing between the islands of Bali and Lombok, through the Makassar Strait, to the east of the Philippines. It separates the Australian and Oriental biogeographical realms; the term is used to delineate the difference between the Oriental and Australian/New Guinea faunas. [named after AR WALLACE, who first pointed out the sharp break between the two realms]

wallaroo /ˌwɒlə'ruː/, *n.* See **kangaroo.** [Aboriginal]

wallet /'wɒlət/, *n.* **1.** a small, booklike folding case for carrying papers, paper money, etc., in the pocket. **2.** a bag for holding food, clothing, toilet articles, etc. [ME]

walleyed /'wɒlaɪd/, *adj.* **1.** having eyes in which a squint results in an unusual amount of white showing. **2.** having eyes with little or no color. [ME, from Scand]

wallflower /'wɒlflaʊə/, *n.* **1.** a European perennial plant, growing wild on old walls, cliffs, etc., and also cultivated in gardens, with sweet-scented red or yellow flowers. **2.** *Colloq.* a person at a dance, esp. a woman, who is not chosen as a partner.

Walloon /wə'luːn/, *n.* **1.** one of a people living mainly in the southern and south-eastern parts of Belgium and adjacent regions in France. **2.** the French dialect of Belgium, esp. of the south-east. [F *Wallon,* from ML *Wallo,* from Gmc; cf. OHG *walh* foreigner]

wallop /'wɒləp/, *Colloq.* ◇*v.t.* **1.** to beat hard and thoroughly; thrash. **2.** to defeat thoroughly, as in a game. ◇*n.* **3.** a vigorous blow. [ME, from OF]

wallow /'wɒloʊ/, *v.i.* **1.** to roll the body about, or lie, in water, snow, mud, dust, etc.: *Pigs wallow in the mud.* **2.** to live or behave self-indulgently: *to wallow in luxury; to wallow in self-pity.* ◇*n.* **3.** the act of wallowing. **4.** a place to which animals, such as buffaloes, go to wallow. [OE: roll]

wallpaper /'wɒlpeɪpə/, *n.* **1.** paper, usu. with printed decorative patterns in color, for pasting on and covering walls or ceilings of rooms, etc. ◇*v.t.* **2.** to put wallpaper on.

Wall Street, *n.* **1.** a street in New York City, in southern Manhattan; the chief financial centre of the US. **2.** the money market or the financiers of the US.

wall-to-wall /ˌwɔl-tə-'wɔl/, *adj.* covering the whole floor space of a room: *a wall-to-wall carpet.*

walnut /ˈwɔlnʌt/, *n.* **1.** the edible nut of a large deciduous tree of the northern Temperate Zone. **2.** the timber of this tree or other similar timbers. [OE: foreign nuts]

Walpole /ˈwɔlpoʊl/, *n.* **1. Horace** (*4th Earl of Orford*), 1717–97, English Gothic author. **2. Sir Robert** (*1st Earl of Orford*), 1676–1745, British Whig statesman; prime minister 1721–42.

Walpurgis Night /valˈpɜːgəs naɪt/, *n.* the evening preceding the first of May, the feast day of St Walpurgis (an English missionary and abbess in Germany, who died about AD 780), on which, according to German popular superstition, witches ride to some appointed rendezvous, esp. the Brocken, the highest of the Harz Mountains. Also, German, **Walpurgisnacht.**

walrus /ˈwɔlrəs, ˈwɒlrəs/, *n., pl.* **-ruses**, (*esp. collectively*) **-rus.** a large marine mammal of arctic seas, related to the seals, with flippers, a pair of large tusks, and a thick, tough skin. [D: whalehorse]

Walton /ˈwɔltən/, *n.* **1. Ernest Thomas Sinton**, born 1903, Irish physicist; shared Nobel prize for physics 1951 with Sir John D Cockcroft for their work in nuclear physics which included the splitting of the atom (1932). **2. Nancy Bird**, born 1915, Australian aviator; first woman commercial pilot.

waltz[1] /wɔls/, *n.* **1.** a ballroom dance in triple time, in which the dancers move in a series of circles, taking one step to each beat. **2.** a piece of music for, or in the rhythm of, this dance. ◇*adj.* **3.** of, relating to, or of the quality of the waltz: *waltz music; waltz rhythm.* ◇*v.i.* **4.** to dance in the movement of a waltz. **5.** *Colloq.* to take easily: *He waltzed off with the first prize.* ◇*v.t.* **6.** to cause to waltz; accompany in a waltz: *He waltzed her around the floor.* [G: roll, dance a waltz]

waltz[2] /wɔls/, *v.t. in the phrase* **waltz Matilda,** *Colloq.* to wander about as a swagman. [? G *walzen* to move in a circular fashion, as of apprentices travelling from master to master + G *Mathilde*, female travelling companion, bed-roll, from the girl's name; ? taken to goldfields by German speakers from SA]

'Waltzing Matilda' *n.* an Australian popular song; the words written by AB Paterson and the music coming from an old Scottish ballad, it was first sung in public in Winton in 1895.

wambenger /wɒmˈbɛnə/, *n.* →**tuan.** [Aboriginal]

wampum /ˈwɒmpəm/, *n.* cylindrical beads made from shells, pierced and strung, used by North American Indians for money and ornament. [Amer Ind: string of shell beads]

wan /wɒn/, *adj.,* **wanner, wannest. 1.** of an unnatural or sickly paleness; pallid: *His wan face looked miserable.* **2.** pale in color. **3.** showing or suggesting ill health, unhappiness, etc.: *a wan look; a wan smile.* [OE: dark, gloomy]

wand /wɒnd/, *n.* **1.** a slender stick or rod, esp. one used by a conjurer, or supposedly by a magician or fairy to work magic. **2.** a rod or staff carried as a sign of office or authority. **3.** a slender shoot, stem, or branch of a tree. [ME, from Scand]

wanda /ˈwɒndə/, *n. Colloq.* a white man. [Aboriginal: white ghost]

wander /ˈwɒndə/, *v.i.* **1.** to go around without having to be in or go to a particular place; ramble; roam; rove: *to wander over the earth.* **2.** to go without purpose or casually: *He wandered into the next room.* **3.** (of the hand, pen, eyes, mind, etc.) to move or turn idly. **4.** to go away from a path, place, companions, rules, etc.: *He can't have wandered far.* ◇*v.t.* **5.** *Poetic.* to wander over or through: *to wander the hills.* ◇*n.* **6.** a stroll; ramble. [OE] —**wanderer**, *n.*

wandering albatross *n.* a large albatross of southern waters, white with dark markings on the upper parts, that spends most of its life on the wing.

Wandering Jew, *n.* **1.** a legendary character condemned to roam without rest because he struck or mocked Christ on the day of Crucifixion. **2.** Also, **wandering Jew.** a type of trailing or creeping plant.

wanderlust /ˈwɒndəlʌst/, *n.* a great desire to travel about. [G]

wane /weɪn/, *v.,* **waned, waning,** *n.* ◇*v.i.* **1.** (of the moon) to grow smaller after the time of full moon (opposed to *wax*). **2.** to grow less. ◇*n.* **3.** gradual lessening in strength, intensity, power, etc. **4. on the wane,** gradually lessening. [OE: lessen]

Wangaratta /wæŋgəˈrætə/, *n.* a city in north-eastern Vic, at the junction of the Ovens and King Rivers; major producer of tobacco and wine. Pop. 16 598 (1986).

wangle /ˈwæŋgəl/, *v.,* **-gled, -gling,** *n. Colloq.* ◇*v.t.* **1.** to do or get (something) by cunning, trickery, etc.: *I wangled an extra day's holiday.* ◇*v.i.* **2.** to do or get something by trickery. ◇*n.* **3.** an act or instance of wangling. [b. WAG[1] and DANGLE] —**wangler**, *n.*

Wankel engine /ˈwæŋkəl ɛndʒən/, *n.* a form of internal-combustion engine which has one or more elliptical chambers, each swept by a triangular-shaped piston, and which has the same cycles as, but fewer parts than, normal internal-combustion engines. [named after Dr Felix *Wankel*, 1902–88, German engineer]

want /wɒnt/, *v.t.* **1.** to feel a need or a desire for; wish for: *to want one's dinner; always wanting something new.* **2.** to wish or desire (oft. fol. by infinitive): *I want to see you.* **3.** to have none or little of; be deficient in: *He wants commonsense.* **4.** to require or need: *The car wants cleaning.* ◇*v.i.* **5.** to wish; like; feel inclined to: *They can go out if they want.* **6.** to have none or little of something: *He did not want for money.* **7.** to need: *If you want for anything, let him know.* **8.** to be in a condition of need or poverty. ◇*n.* **9.** something wanted or needed; a necessity: *to see to someone's wants.* **10.** an absence or lack of something necessary: *plants dying for want of rain.* **11.** the condition of being without the necessities of life; destitution; poverty: *to live in want.* [ME, from Scand]

wanted /'wɒntəd/, *adj.* (of a suspected criminal, etc.) sought by the police.

wanting /'wɒntɪŋ/, *adj.* **1.** lacking or absent: *an apparatus with some of the parts wanting.* **2.** lacking some part, thing, or respect: *to be wanting in courtesy.* ◇*prep.* **3.** lacking; without.

wanton /'wɒntən/, *adj.* **1.** done or behaving in an uncontrolled, selfish way, with bad results: *wanton attacker; wanton cruelty.* **2.** uncontrolled in sexual behavior; loose; lascivious. **3.** *Poetic.* (of children, young animals, etc.) playful; frolicsome. ◇*n.* **4.** a wanton or lustful person, esp. a woman. [ME: undisciplined]

war /wɔ/, *n., v.,* **warred, warring.** ◇*n.* **1.** fighting or conflict carried on with weapons, in a series of battles, bombings, etc., between nations or states, or between parties within a state; warfare. **2.** any other conflict or quarrelling: *a war of words.* **3.** armed fighting, as a kind of activity, profession, or art: *War is our business.* **4. at war**, in a state of active fighting. **5. in the wars,** *Colloq.* having many small injuries or misfortunes. ◇*v.i.* **6.** to make or carry on a war; fight: *Those two countries are warring; to war with evil.* [ME, from OF, from OHG: strife]

waratah /wɒrəˈta, ˈwɒrətə/, *n.* a shrub or small tree of eastern Australia, the flower emblem of NSW, which has a thick round head of red flowers surrounded by red bracts. [Aboriginal]

waratah anemone, *n.* a small, brownish-red sea anemone with vivid, light red tentacles, common along the Australian coastline; bloodsucker.

warble /'wɔbəl/, *v.,* **-bled, -bling,** *n.* ◇*v.i.* **1.** to sing like a bird with trills, quavers, or other musical ornaments. ◇*n.* **2.** a warbled song. **3.** the act of warbling. [ME, from OF: quaver, from Gmc]

warbler /'wɔblə/, *n.* **1.** a type of small songbird, chiefly from the Old World, with a few species in Australia, such as the **redwarbler.** **2.** a type of small bird found in Australia, NZ, and islands to the north, e.g. the **white-throated warbler.** **3.** a type of small, insect-eating, often brightly-colored bird of the New World.

Warburton /'wɔbətən/, *n.* Peter Egerton, 1813-89, Australian explorer and police commissioner, born in England.

war cry, *n.* a cry or slogan of a party in a contest.

ward /wɔd/, *n.* **1.** a division of a municipality, city or town in administration and politics: *Jones is standing for the East ward.* **2.** a room or division in a hospital, etc., sometimes for a particular class of patients: *a maternity ward.* **3.** a division in a prison. **4.** *Law.* a person, esp. under age, who has been legally placed under the care or control of a guardian: *a state ward.* ◇*v.* **5. ward off,** to turn aside: *to ward off a blow.* [OE]

-ward, an adjectival and adverbial suffix showing direction, as in *onward, seaward, backward.* [OE: towards]

Ward /wɔd/, *n.* **1.** Frederick (*'Captain Thunderbolt'*), 1835-70, Australian bushranger, active in NSW. **2.** Sir Joseph George, 1856-1930, NZ Liberal Party (later United Party) politician, born in Australia; prime minister of NZ 1906-12, 1928-30. **3.** Russel, born 1914, Australian historian; best known work is *The Australian Legend* (1958).

Wardell /wɔˈdel/, *n.* Robert, 1793-1834, Australian editor and barrister, born in England; founded the *Australian* with William Wentworth in 1824 and commenced campaigning for self-government.

warden /'wɔdn/, *n.* **1.** someone who is given the care or responsibility of something; a keeper. **2.** a public official in charge of a place, such as a port, prison, etc. **3.** the head of certain colleges, schools, hospitals, youth hostels, etc. **4.** *Mining.* a government official in charge of a mineral field. [ME, from OF]

warder /'wɔdə/, *n.* **1.** an official in charge of prisoners in a jail; prison officer. **2.** someone who guards something. [ME, from WARD] -**wardress,** *n. fem.*

wardrobe /'wɔdrəʊb/, *n.* **1.** a stock of clothes or costumes, of a person or of a theatrical or film company. **2.** a piece of furniture for holding clothes. **3.** the department responsible for the wardrobe in a film company. [ME, from OF]

-wards, an adverbial suffix showing direction, as in *onwards, seawards, backwards.* [OE]

ware /weə/, *n.* **1.** (*usu. pl.*) articles for sale: *a shopkeeper displaying his wares.* **2.** a particular kind of manufactured article for sale (now chiefly in combination): *tinware; silverware.* **3.** pottery, or a particular kind of pottery: *Delft ware.* [OE]

warehouse /'weəhaʊs/, *n.* **1.** a storehouse for wares or goods. **2.** a building in which a wholesale dealer keeps his stock of goods.

warfare /'wɔfeə/, *n.* **1.** the act of waging war. **2.** armed conflict.

warhead /'wɔhed/, *n.* the front section of a self-propelled missile, bomb, torpedo, etc., containing explosives, etc.

Warhol /'wɔhəʊl/, *n.* Andy, 1931-87, US artist and film-maker; celebrated exponent of pop art.

warlike /'wɔlaɪk/, *adj.* **1.** tending to or ready for war; martial: *warlike tribes.* **2.** threatening war: *a warlike tone.* **3.** of or relating to war: *a warlike expedition; a warlike deed.*

warlock /'wɔlɒk/, *n.* a man who practises magic arts by the aid of the devil; sorcerer; wizard. [OE: oath-breaker, devil]

Warlpiri /'walbri/, *n.* an Australian Aboriginal language from the north of Central Australia, still in full tribal use. Also, **Wailbri, Walbiri, Walpiri.**

warm /wɔm/, *adj.* **1.** having some heat that can be felt. **2.** marked by fairly high temperatures: *a warm climate.* **3.** keeping or making heat: *warm clothes.* **4.** (of color, effects of color, etc.) suggestive of heat; inclining towards red or orange rather than towards green or blue. **5.** marked by or relating to kindly feelings of interest towards others: *a warm heart; a warm welcome.* **6.** lively, brisk, or vigorous; animated: *a warm debate.* **7.** strong or fresh: *a warm scent.* ◇*v.t.* **8.** to make warm; heat: *to warm one's feet; warm up a room.* ◇*v.i.* **9.** to become warm (oft. fol. by *up*). **10.** to become interested, friendly, enthusiastic, etc.: *I warmed to him because of his good manners.* ◇*v.* **11. warm up,** to prepare for performance, as in sport, music, etc. [OE]

warm-blooded /'wɔm-blʌdəd/, *adj.* **1.** indicating or relating to animals, such as mammals and birds, whose blood ranges in temperature from about 36° to 44°C, and stays more or less the same whether the temperature around them is hot or cold. **2.** lively, passionate: *young and warm-blooded valor.*

war memorial, *n.* a public building built as a memorial to those who died in a war.

warm front, *n. Weather.* **1.** the contact surface between two air masses where the warmer mass is advancing against and over the cooler mass. **2.** the line of intersection of this surface with the surface of the earth.

warmonger /'wɔmʌŋgə/, *n.* someone who advises war as the best action to take. — **warmongering,** *n.*

warmth /wɔmθ/, *n.* **1.** moderate or gentle heat. **2.** a feeling of moderate heat. **3.** liveliness of feelings; ardor or fervor; cordiality; enthusiasm or zeal. **4.** rising anger.

warn /wɔn/, *v.t.* **1.** to tell or signal to (a person, etc.) that something, usu. bad, is going to or may happen: *to warn a person of a plot against him.* **2.** to advise to be careful; caution: *to warn a foolish person; I'm warning you that I can't take this much longer.* **3.** to advise about behavior, etc.: *to warn a person to be on time.* ◇*v.i.* **4.** to tell a person that something may happen: *to warn of impending disaster.* [OE]

warning /'wɔnɪŋ/, *n.* **1.** something that is used to warn, give notice, or caution. **2.** the act of warning. ◇*adj.* **3.** relating to or used for warning: *a warning system; a warning look.*

War of American Independence, *n.* the war between Great Britain and its American colonies, 1775–83, in which the colonies won their independence. Also, *US,* **American Revolution.**

warp /wɔp/, *v.t.* **1.** to bend or twist out of shape: *Rain has warped this timber.* **2.** to bend or turn from the natural direction. **3.** to bend from truth or right; bias or pervert: *Hatred warps the mind.* ◇*v.i.* **4.** to become bent or twisted out of shape: *The wood has warped.* **5.** *Geol.* (of the earth's crust) to undergo a slow bending process without forming definite folds or displacements. ◇*n.* **6.** a bend or twist in something. **7.** a twist or bias of the mind. **8.** the lengthwise fibres in weaving, placed across the weft (or woof) and interlaced with it. [OE]

Warragamba Dam /wɒrə,gæmbə 'dæm/, *n.* a dam across the Warragamba River, west of Sydney, completed in 1960; largest source of Sydney's water supply. 116 m high.

Warragul /'wɒrəgəl/, *n.* a town and shire in western Gippsland, Vic, west of Moe. Pop. 8170 (1986). [Aboriginal WARRIGAL wild dog]

warrant /'wɒrənt/, *n.* **1.** a giving of authority to do something: *a treasury warrant.* **2.** something which says formally that something is quite certain; guarantee. **3.** *Law.* a written authority to do some act, e.g. to make an arrest, make a search, etc. **4.** (in the armed forces) a certificate of appointment given to a non-commissioned officer. ◇*v.t.* **5.** to give authority to; authorise. **6.** to show that there is need for; justify: *The circumstances warrant such measures.* **7.** to give one's word for; vouch for: *I'll warrant he did!* **8.** to give a formal promise for; guarantee: *to warrant safe delivery.* [ME from OF: defender, from Gmc] — **warrantor,** *n.*

warrant officer, *n. Mil.* a member of the armed forces holding by warrant an intermediate rank between that of commissioned and non-commissioned officers; sergeant major. See Appendix.

warranty /'wɒrənti/, *n., pl.* **-ties.** **1.** the act of warranting; warrant; assurance. **2.** *Law.* a promise or engagement, stated or implied, relating to a detail in a contract, as of sale: *a warranty of the quality of goods.* [ME, from OF]

warren /'wɒrən/, *n.* **1.** a place where many rabbits live. **2.** a building, district, etc., where many poor people live in crowded conditions. [ME, from AF: game park]

warrigal /'wɒrəgəl/, *n.* **1.** a dingo. ◇*adj.* **2.** wild; untamed. Also, **warragul, warregal.** [Aboriginal]

warrior /'wɒriə/, *n.* a person occupied or experienced in warfare; soldier. [ME, from ONF]

Warrnambool /'wɒnəmbul/, *n.* a coastal city in the Western District of Vic, east of Port Fairy; major distributing and manufacturing centre and popular tourist resort. Pop. 22 706 (1986).

Warsaw /'wɔsɔ/, *n.* the capital of Poland, in the eastern central part, on the river Vistula. Pop. 1 669 400 (1986 est.). Polish, **Warszawa.**

Warsaw Pact, *n.* formerly (1955–91), a military alliance, comprising Bulgaria, Czechoslovakia, East Germany, Hungary, Poland, Romania, and the USSR. Also, **Warsaw Treaty Organisation.**

Wars of the Roses, *n.pl.* the civil struggle between the royal house of Lancaster, whose emblem was a red rose, and the royal house of York, whose emblem was a white rose, beginning in 1455 and ending in the accession of Henry VII and the union of the two houses in 1485.

wart /wɔt/, *n.* a small, usu. hard, lump on the skin, caused by a virus. [OE]

wart-hog /'wɔt-hɒg/, *n.* an African wild pig with large tusks, and lumps like warts on the face.

Warwick /'wɒrɪk/, n. a city in southeastern Qld, on the Condamine River in the Darling Downs. Pop. 9435 (1986).

Warwickshire /'wɔːrɪkʃɪə, -ʃə/, n. a county in central England. Pop. 477 800 (1983); 1981 km². *Administrative Centre:* Warwick. Also, **Warwick**. *Abbrev.:* War, Warks

wary /'wɛəri/, adj., **warier, wariest**. 1. watchful, or on one's guard; on the alert; cautious; careful. 2. marked by watchfulness. – **warily**, adv. – **wariness**, n.

was /wɒz/, v. the first and third person singular past tense indicative of **be**. [OE]

wash /wɒʃ/, v.t. 1. to dip and rub, in or with water and usu. some kind of soap to get rid of dirt; clean; cleanse. 2. to clean by using the action of a liquid in any other way: *a cat washing itself*. 3. to clean or purify. 4. to flow over or against: *a shore or cliff washed by waves*. 5. to carry or bring with water or any liquid: *The storm washed seaweed up on the beach*. 6. to form (a channel, etc.), as flowing water does. 7. *Mining, etc.* to let water flow through earth, rock, etc. in order to separate valuable material. 8. to purify (a gas or gaseous mixture) by passage through or over a liquid. 9. to cover with a watery or thin coat of color. ◇v.i. 10. to wash oneself: *time to wash for dinner*. 11. to wash clothes. 12. to be carried or driven (along, ashore, etc.) by water: *Planks washed in to shore*. 13. to flow or beat with a lapping sound: *The waves washed on the shore*. 14. to be worn by the action of water: *The road washed away in the flood*. ◇v. 15. **wash down**, a. to clean completely by washing. b. to swallow (food) with the help of liquid. 16. **wash out**, a. to remove by washing. b. to cause (an arrangement, sporting event, etc.) to be cancelled: *A storm washed out our match today*. 17. **wash up**, to wash (dishes, saucepans, etc.) after a meal. ◇n. 18. the act of washing. 19. a quantity of clothes, etc., washed, or to be washed, at one time: *Put on another wash*. 20. a liquid with which something is wetted or colored. 21. a flow or sweep of water. 22. the sound made by this: *listening to the wash of the Atlantic*. 23. the rough or broken water left behind a moving ship, etc. 24. any of various liquids for toilet or medicinal purposes: *an eye wash*. 25. an area of land washed by the action of the sea or a river. 26. **come out in the wash**, *Colloq.* to be revealed eventually; become known. [ME]

washboard /'wɒʃbɔːd/, n. 1. (formerly) a board or frame with a ridged surface of metal or wood on which clothes were scrubbed in washing. 2. such an object, used as a musical instrument in certain kinds of folk-music.

washer /'wɒʃə/, n. 1. a machine or apparatus for washing something. 2. a flat ring of leather, rubber, metal, etc., used to give tightness to a joint, to stop water, leaking, and to distribute pressure evenly (under the head of a bolt, nut, etc.). 3. small piece of towelling for washing the face or body.

washing /'wɒʃɪŋ/, n. 1. the act of someone or something that washes; ablution. 2. clothes, etc., washed or to be washed.

washing soda, n. crystalline sodium carbonate, used as a cleaning agent.

Washington¹ /'wɒʃɪŋtən/, n. **George**, 1732–99, US general and first president of the US, 1789–97.

Washington² /'wɒʃɪŋtən/, n. 1. Also, **Washington DC**. the capital of the US on the Potomac between Maryland and Virginia; coextensive with the District of Columbia. Pop. 626 000 (1986 est.). 2. a state in the northwestern US, on the Pacific coast. Pop. 4 463 000 (1986 est.); 176 379 km². *Cap.:* Olympia. *Abbrev.:* Wash

wash-out /'wɒʃ-aʊt/, n. 1. a washing out of earth, etc., by water, such as from an embankment or a roadway by heavy rain. 2. the hole or gap produced. 3. *Colloq.* a failure or fiasco.

wasn't /'wɒzənt/, v. a short form of *was not*.

wasp /wɒsp/, n. 1. any of numerous four-winged, stinging insects, which live alone or in groups. 2. a sharp-tongued person. [OE] – **waspish**, adj.

WASP /wɒsp/, n. *US* 1. a member of the social establishment thought of as being white, Anglo-Saxon and Protestant. ◇adj. 2. of or relating to this establishment and its values. [W(hite) A(nglo-)S(axon) P(rotestant)]

wassail /'wɒsəl, -seɪl/, n. 1. a party, festivity or revel with much festive toasting. ◇v.i. 2. to drink healths; revel with drinking. [ME, from Scand] – **wassailer**, n.

wastage /'weɪstɪdʒ/, n. loss by use, wear, decay, wastefulness, etc.

waste /weɪst/, v., **wasted, wasting**, n., adj. ◇v.t. 1. to use up or spend, without enough result; use to no avail; squander: *to waste time; to waste words*. 2. to fail to use: *to waste an opportunity*. 3. to destroy or wear away gradually. 4. to wear down or reduce in health or strength; emaciate; enfeeble: *to be wasted by disease or hunger*. 5. to destroy, devastate, or ruin: *a country wasted with fire and sword*. ◇v.i. 6. to be used up or spent without enough result. 7. to become physically wasted, lose flesh or strength (oft. fol. by *away*). 8. to diminish gradually: *His wealth is wasting away*. 9. to pass gradually: *Time is wasting*. ◇n. 10. the useless spending or use without enough result: *waste of material; waste of money*. 11. neglect, instead of use: *waste of opportunity*. 12. a gradual destroying; decay: *the waste and repair of bodily tissue*. 13. ruin or devastation, as from war, fire, etc. 14. → **wasteland** (def. 1). 15. anything left over from production: *industrial waste; kitchen waste*. 16. **go to waste**, to fail to be used; be wasted. 17. **lay waste**, to destroy; devastate; ruin. ◇adj. 18. not used or in use: *waste energy*. 19. (of land, regions, etc.) rough, uncultivated and lonely. 20. left over or unnecessary: *waste products of manufacture*. 21. *Physiol.* relating to material unused by or unusable to the organism. 22. carrying waste material. [ME, from ONF, from L: make empty, lay waste] – **wasteful**, adj.

wasteland /ˈweɪstlænd/, n. 1. land which lies waste, barren and uncultivated. 2. a place, time, or group with no intellectual, artistic, or spiritual cultivation.

wastrel /ˈweɪstrəl/, n. 1. a wasteful person; spendthrift. 2. someone who does nothing useful with their time.

watch /wɒtʃ/, v.i. 1. to look around to see what comes, happens, etc.: *to watch while an experiment is performed*. 2. to look or wait attentively and expectantly (usu. fol. by *for*): *to watch for a signal*; *to watch for an opportunity*. 3. to be careful or cautious. 4. to stay awake, esp. for a purpose; keep vigil. ◊v.t. 5. to look at with interest: *to watch a game of cricket*. 6. to regard mentally: *to watch his progress*. 7. to look or wait attentively for: *to watch one's chance*. 8. to guard. 9. to be careful of; pay attention to: *Watch what you're doing*. ◊v. 10. **watch out**, to be on one's guard; be alert or cautious. 11. **watch out for**, **a.** to beware of; avoid. **b.** to look for. 12. **watch over**, to guard; protect. ◊n. 13. a lookout for something expected: *to keep watch*. 14. a guarding. 15. a staying awake for some special purpose: *a watch beside a sickbed*. 16. a period of time for watching or keeping guard: *the night watch*. 17. a device that measures and shows the progress of time, usu. worn on the wrist. 18. one of the periods into which the night was divided by the ancients: *the fourth watch of the night*. 19. a person or group who keeps watch. ◊adj. 20. of or relating to a watch. [OE *wacian* WAKE[1]]

watchdog /ˈwɒtʃdɒg/, n. 1. a dog kept to guard property. 2. someone who guards morals, standards, etc.

watchman /ˈwɒtʃmən/, n., pl. **-men**. 1. someone who keeps guard over a building, usu. at night, to protect it from fire or thieves. 2. (formerly) someone who guarded the streets at night.

watchword /ˈwɒtʃwɜd/, n. 1. a password; countersign. 2. a word or phrase expressing a principle or rule of action: *The watchword is liberty.*

water /ˈwɔtə/, n. 1. a colorless, transparent liquid, being the main constituent of rain, oceans, lakes, rivers, etc., a compound of hydrogen and oxygen, H_2O, freezing at $0°$ C, and boiling at $100°$ C. 2. a special form of this liquid, such as rain. 3. (oft. pl.) liquid obtained from a mineral spring. 4. the water of a river, etc., with reference to its height, from a tide or flood: *high water*; *low water*. 5. the surface of water: *above water*; *below water*; *on the water*. 6. a liquid solution or preparation: *toilet water*. 7. any liquid that is passed out of the body, such as tears, perspiration, urine, etc. 8. a wavy, shining pattern or marking, such as on silk fabrics, metal surfaces, etc. ◊9. Some special uses are:
in deep (hot) water, in trouble; in a difficult situation.
like water, freely: *to spend money like water*.
of the first water, of the finest quality or rank.
throw cold water on, to discourage.
◊v.t. 10. to make wet: *to water a road*; *to water a garden*. 11. to supply with water for drinking: *to water animals*; *to water a ship*. 12. to make less strong by adding water; dilute (oft. fol. by *down*): *to water down soup*. 13. to weaken (fol. by *down*): *to water down an argument*. ◊v.i. 14. to discharge water: *Cutting onions makes the eyes water*. 15. to drink or take in water: *The ship watered at Perth*. ◊adj. 16. of or relating to water. [ME]

waterbed /ˈwɔtəbɛd/, n. a hard-wearing plastic bag filled with water, used as a mattress in a supporting wooden frame.

water-buffalo /ˈwɔtə-bʌfəloʊ/, n. a large buffalo domesticated in India, introduced into Australia and living in great numbers in the NT. Also, **water-ox**.

water-chestnut /ˈwɔtə-ˌtʃɛsnʌt/, n. a water plant with an edible nut.

water-closet /ˈwɔtə-klɒzət/, n. → **toilet**.

watercolor or **watercolour** /ˈwɔtəkʌlə/, n. 1. paint made from pigment dispersed in a water-soluble gum. 2. the art or method of painting with such paint. 3. a painting or design done by this method. ◊adj. 4. of or relating to watercolor or a watercolor painting. **–watercolorist**, n.

water-column /ˈwɔtə-kɒləm/, n. the sea viewed as the living-place of sea creatures, as opposed to the bottom of the ocean, the surface of the water, etc.

watercourse /ˈwɔtəkɔs/, n. 1. a stream of water, such as a river or brook. 2. the bed of such a stream. 3. a natural or man-made channel carrying water.

watercress /ˈwɔtəkrɛs/, n. a perennial cress, usu. growing in clear, running water, eaten in salads, etc.

water cycle, n. the continuous circulation of water on earth, through the process of evaporation from the sea, condensation into clouds, and precipitation (rain) falling on the land and returning to the sea.

water dragon, n. a robust, rough-skinned lizard found throughout Australia, generally close to water. Also, **water goanna**.

waterfall /ˈwɔtəfɔl/, n. a steep fall or flow of water, usu. from a great height; cascade.

waterfowl /ˈwɔtəfaʊl/, n. 1. a waterbird, esp. a swimming bird. 2. such birds collectively.

waterfront /ˈwɔtəfrʌnt/, n. 1. land next to a body of water. 2. the part of a city or town on such land. 3. (the workers in) the industry of cargo movement on the wharves: *unrest on the waterfront*. **–waterfrontage**, n.

Watergate /ˈwɔtəgeɪt/, n. 1. a political scandal during the 1972 US presidential campaign in which five people, employed by President Nixon's re-election committee were caught breaking into the Democrat headquarters in the Watergate building in Washington DC. The investigation and attempted cover-up of White House involvement caused Nixon to resign. 2. (*l.c.*) *Colloq.* a scandal involving a charge of corruption against a political leader. 3. *Colloq.* (*l.c.*) the downfall of a political leader, caused by a scandal.

water goanna, *n.* → **water dragon**.

waterhole /'wɔtəhoul/, *n.* a natural hole or hollow in which water collects, such as a spring in a desert, or a cavity in the dried-up course of a river.

Waterhouse /'wɔtəhaus/, *n.* **Henry**, 1770–1812, British naval officer in Australia; responsible for introducing Merino sheep to Australia.

water hyacinth, *n.* a floating plant of Central and South America which has become a serious pest of rivers in warm countries.

watering /'wɔtərɪŋ/, *n.* **1.** the act of someone or something that waters. **2.** a wavy pattern on silk, etc.

watering-can /'wɔtərɪŋ-kæn/, *n.* a vessel with a spout for watering or sprinkling plants, etc.

watering hole, *n.* **1.** a waterhole where animals drink. **2.** *Colloq.* a hotel. Also, **watering-place.**

waterlily /'wɔtəlɪli/, *n.* a type of aquatic plant with floating leaves and colorful, often fragrant, flowers.

waterlog /'wɔtəlɔg/, *v.t.*, **-logged, -logging.** to soak in or saturate with water. **–waterlogged,** *adj.*

waterloo /wɔtə'lu/, *n.* **1.** a final and complete defeat. **2.** (*cap.*) a village in central Belgium, south of Brussels; Napoleon (Bonaparte) was decisively defeated here by the British, under Wellington, and the Prussians.

watermark /'wɔtəmak/, *n.* **1.** a mark indicating the height to which water rises or has risen, as in a river, etc. **2.** a figure or design impressed into the fabric of paper and visible when the paper is held to the light. ◇*v.t.* **3.** to mark (paper) with a watermark.

watermelon /'wɔtəmɛlən/, *n.* the large, round or elongated fruit of a trailing vine with a hard, green rind and sweet, juicy, pink or red pulp.

water of crystallisation, *n.* water that is chemically combined in crystals of certain compounds. Also, **water of hydration.**

water-pistol /'wɔtə-pɪstl/, *n.* a toy gun that squirts a jet of water or other liquid.

water-polo /'wɔtə-poulou/, *n.* a water game played by two teams, each with seven swimmers, in which the object is to pass a ball over the opponent's goal line.

waterproof /'wɔtəpruf/, *adj.* **1.** not letting water through. ◇*n.* **2.** a rubberised or coated material which will hold water. **3.** an outer garment of waterproof material. ◇*v.t.* **4.** to make waterproof, as by coating or treating with rubber, etc.

water-rat /'wɔtə-ræt/, *n.* a large, aquatic, native rat, with soft thick fur and webbed back feet, found near rivers and streams throughout Australia.

water-repellent /'wɔtə-rəpɛlənt, -ri-/, *adj.* having a finish which does not let water in.

watershed /'wɔtəʃɛd/, *n.* **1.** the ridge line at the top of a hill dividing two drainage areas;
divide. **2.** a turning point; a crucial event or time in a career, venture, etc. **3.** *US.* an area drained by a river, etc.; drainage area.

water-ski /'wɔtə-ski/, *v.i.*, **-ski'd** or **-skied, -skiing.** to be towed across water by a speedboat, wearing a special type of broad ski or skis.

watertable /'wɔtəteɪbəl/, *n.* the limit of the water-soaked section of earth in an aquifer.

watertight /'wɔtətaɪt/, *adj.* **1.** not letting water through. **2.** without fault; irrefutable; flawless: *a watertight argument; a watertight alibi.*

water tortoise, *n.* any of the native tortoises of Australia which are mainly aquatic but have webbed feet rather than turtle flippers and are able to move considerable distances overland.

water-tower /'wɔtə-tauə/, *n.* a tower holding a tank into which water is pumped to obtain the right pressure.

water-vapor or **water-vapour** /'wɔtə-veɪpə/, *n.* gaseous water, esp. when below boiling point, distinguished from steam; mist.

waterway /'wɔtəweɪ/, *n.* a river, canal, or other body of water used as a route or way of travel or transport, esp. for large ships or boats.

waterwheel /'wɔtəwɪl/, *n.* **1.** a wheel turned by water and used to perform mechanical work; water turbine. **2.** a wheel with buckets for raising water.

waterworks /'wɔtəwɜks/, *n.pl.* **1.** (*oft. treated as sing.*) a system made up of apparatus and structures by which water is collected, preserved, and sent out for home use and other purposes, esp. for a town. **2. turn on the waterworks,** *Colloq.* to cry loudly and freely, usu. for the sake of gaining sympathy or getting one's own way.

watery /'wɔtəri/, *adj.* **1.** relating to, like, or in water: *a watery fluid.* **2.** full of or containing too much water: *watery soup.*

Watling /'wɒtlɪŋ/, *n.* **Thomas**, 1762–?, Australian pioneer artist and convict, born in Scotland; noted for his natural-history paintings.

Watson /'wɒtsən/, *n.* **1. James Dewey**, born 1928, US biochemist; contributed to the discovery of the structure of DNA; shared Nobel prize for physiology or medicine (1962) with Francis Crick and Maurice Wilkins. **2. (John) Chris(tian)**, 1867–1941, Australian Labor Party politician, born in Chile; third prime minister of Australia 1904.

watt /wɒt/, *n.* a derived SI unit of power, defined as one joule per second. *Symbol:* W [named after James WATT]

Watt /wɒt/, *n.* **James**, 1736–1819, Scottish engineer and inventor; developed an improved steam engine which was widely applied in industry.

wattage /'wɒtɪdʒ/, *n.* **1.** *Elect.* power, in watts. **2.** the number of watts needed to operate an electrical apparatus.

Watteau /'wɒtou/, *n.* **Jean Antoine** /ʒɒ̃ ɒ̃'twan/, 1684–1721, French painter.

wattle /wɒtl/, *n., v.,* **-tled, -tling,** *adj.* ◇*n.* **1.** any of the many Australian types of acacia, being shrubs or trees with spikes or globe-shaped heads of yellow or cream flowers. **2.** (*pl.* or *sing.*) rods interwoven with twigs or branches of trees, used for making fences, walls, roofs, etc. **3.** a fleshy part or lobe hanging down from the throat or chin of certain birds, such as the hen, turkey, etc., or from the neck of certain breeds of pigs, sheep and goats. ◇*v.t.* **4.** to form (a structure) by interweaving twigs or branches: *to wattle a fence.* ◇*adj.* **5.** built or roofed with wattles. [OE: covering] −**wattled**, *adj.*

wattlebird /'wɒtlbɜd/, *n.* any of several large honeyeaters with hanging wattles on each side of the throat, such as the **red wattlebird**.

Wattle Day, *n.* an Australian commemorative day held either on 1 August or 1 September in which the native flower is utilised as a symbol encouraging national sentiment.

Watts /wɒts/, *n.* **John**, 1755–?, English naval officer and amateur artist; made sketches of the Australian coast during an exploratory expedition in 1788.

Waugh /wɔː/, *n.* **Evelyn Arthur St John** /'sɪndʒən/, 1903–66, English satirical novelist and essayist; author of *The Loved One* (1948).

waul /wɔːl/, *v.i.* to cry like a cat or a newborn baby; squall. Also, **wawl**.

wave /weɪv/, *n., v.,* **waved, waving.** ◇*n.* **1.** a movement of the surface of a liquid body, such as the sea or a lake, in the form of a ridge or swell. **2.** any movement or part like a wave of the sea. **3.** a swell or rush, esp. of feeling, excitement, etc.: *A wave of anger swept over him; a wave of anti-Americanism.* **4.** one of a succession of movements of people moving into an area, country, etc. **5.** an outward curve, or one of a number of such curves, in a surface or line; undulation. **6.** *Phys.* a regular vibrational disturbance travelling through a medium such as air, without corresponding movement forward of the medium itself, as in sound or electromagnetic energy. **7.** a sign made by waving the hand, a flag, etc. ◇*v.i.* **8.** to move loosely to and fro or up and down; flutter. **9.** to curve in a line, etc., like a wave; have an undulating form. **10.** to be moved, esp. first in one direction and then in the opposite: *The lady's handkerchief waved in encouragement.* **11.** to give a signal by waving something: *She waved to me as I left.* ◇*v.t.* **12.** to cause to move loosely to and fro or up and down. **13.** to cause to curve up and down or in and out. **14.** to give a wave or wavy appearance or pattern to (the hair, silk, etc.). **15.** to move, esp. first in one direction and then in the opposite: *to wave the hand.* **16.** to direct by a waving movement: *to wave a train to a halt.* **17.** to express by a waving movement: *to wave a last goodbye.* [OE]

waveband /'weɪvbænd/, *n.* a range of radio waves whose wavelengths and frequencies are very close to each other.

wavefront /'weɪvfrʌnt/, a surface over which all the points just reached by a propagating wave are vibrating in the same phase (def. 7).

wave function, *n. Phys.* a function used in wave mechanics to define the three-dimensional stationary wave system which represents the orbital electrons around an atomic nucleus.

wavelength /'weɪvleŋθ/, *n.* **1.** *Phys.,* etc. the distance between two successive points of a wave at the same phase, as from one crest to the next. **2.** *Radio.* the wavelength of the carrier wave of a particular radio transmitter or station. **3.** a way of thinking or understanding: *The teacher was obviously not on the same wavelength as his pupils.*

wave mechanics, *n.* a development of quantum mechanics in which elementary particles were seen as having wave properties.

wave number, *n.* the number of waves per unit length; the reciprocal of wavelength.

waver /'weɪvə/, *v.i.* **1.** to sway to and fro; flutter: *Leaves wavered in the breeze.* **2.** to become unsteady or begin to fail or give way: *His mind is wavering; His voice is wavering.* **3.** to feel or show doubt or indecision; vacillate: *He wavered in his determination.* [OE: wave]

Waverley /'weɪvəli/, *n.* a city in the eastern suburbs of Melbourne's metropolitan area. Pop. 122 935 (1986).

wave theory, *n.* the theory, proposed by Christian Huygens, 1629–95, Dutch physicist, that light travels in waves.

wavy /'weɪvi/, *adj.,* **-vier, -viest. 1.** curving first in one direction and then in the opposite in movement or form: *a wavy course; wavy hair.* **2.** like or suggesting waves. −**wavily**, *adv.* −**waviness**, *n.*

wax[1] /wæks/, *n.* **1.** any of a group of amorphous solids consisting of esters of alcohols and long-chain, fatty acids, e.g. beeswax. **2.** any of various other similar substances. **3.** something suggesting wax, as being easily worked upon, handled, etc.: *He was helpless wax in their hands.* ◇*v.t.* **4.** to rub, smear, stiffen, polish, etc., with wax; treat with wax: *a waxed moustache; a waxed floor.* ◇*adj.* **5.** made of or like wax. [OE] −**waxy**, *adj.*

wax[2] /wæks/, *v.i.,* **waxed, waxed** or (*Poetic*) **waxen, waxing. 1.** to increase in length, quantity, strength, power, etc.: *The tension waxed daily.* **2.** (of the moon) to increase in the size of its illuminated part before the full moon (opposed to *wane*).

waxen /'wæksən/, *adj.* **1.** made of or covered with wax. **2.** like or suggesting wax: *His face had an unhealthy waxen appearance.*

waxflower /'wæksflaʊə/, *n.* any of various Australian shrubs the flowers of which have thick, waxy petals, such as the **Bendigo waxflower** of south-eastern Australia.

waxplant /'wæksplænt, -plant/, *n.* any of a group of climbing or trailing plants, natives of tropical Asia and Australia, having glossy leaves and groups of pink, white, or yellowish waxy flowers whose stalks are of equal length and come from a common centre.

waxwork /'wækswɜk/, *n.* **1.** figures, ornaments, etc., made of wax, or one such figure. **2.** (*pl. treated as sing.*) a public showing of wax figures, ornaments, etc.

way /weɪ/, *n.* **1.** a manner, method, or fashion: *a new way of looking at a matter; to reply in a polite way.* **2.** usual or habitual manner: *the way of setting the table.* **3.** a course, plan, or means for gaining an end: *to find a way to reduce friction.* **4.** a respect or particular: *a plan defective in several ways.* **5.** direction: *Look this way.* **6.** passage or progress on a course: *to make one's way on foot; to lead the way.* **7.** distance: *a long way off.* **8.** a path or course leading from one place to another. **9.** a road, route, passage, or channel (usu. used in combination): *highway; waterway; doorway.* **10.** (*oft. pl.*) habit or custom: *I don't like his ways at all.* **11.** the course of action which one likes the most or upon which one has decided: *to have one's own way.* **12.** *Colloq.* a condition of health, wealth, etc.: *to be in a bad way.* **13.** range of experience or notice: *the best car that ever came my way.* **14.** course of life, action, or experience: *The way of the poor is hard.* ◇**15.** Some special uses are:
by the way, 1. in the course of one's remarks; incidentally: *By the way, have you received that letter yet?*
by way of, 1. through; by the route of; via. **2.** as a method or means of.
give way, 1. to withdraw; retreat. **2.** to break down; collapse; yield.
go out of one's way, to make a special effort; inconvenience oneself.
on the way out, 1. ready for rest or retirement; becoming obsolete. **2.** losing popularity.
out of the way, 1. so as not to block or keep back. **2.** dealt with; disposed of. **3.** away from the usual route; off the beaten track. **4.** unusual; extraordinary.
under way, 1. (of a ship, etc.) moving along. **2.** (of an event, meeting, etc.) in progress.
◇*adv.* **16.** *Colloq.* very far: *He's way out in the surf.* [OE]

wayang /'waɪæŋ/, *n.* a ritual performance, as with dances or puppet plays, of the religious epics of Java and Bali. [Javanese *wayang* shadow]

waybill /'weɪbɪl/, *n.* **1.** a list of goods sent by a common carrier, such as a railway, with directions. **2.** (on a bus, etc.) a list showing the number of passengers carried or tickets sold.

wayfarer /'weɪfɛərə/, *n.* a traveller, esp. on foot.

waylay /weɪ'leɪ/, *v.t.*, **-laid, -laying. 1.** to fall upon or attack violently from a hidden position, esp. in order to rob, seize, or kill. **2.** to await and come near to unexpectedly, esp. with a greeting or remark. [WAY + LAY¹]

Wayne /weɪn/, *n.* **John** (*Marion Michael Morrison*), 1907–79, US film actor, esp. in Westerns; won an Academy Award for *True Grit* (1969).

way-out /'weɪ-aʊt/, *adj. Colloq.* **1.** advanced in method, style, etc. **2.** unusual; odd; eccentric.

-ways, a suffix of manner forming adverbs, as in *sideways, lengthways.* See **-wise.** [from WAY]

wayward /'weɪwəd/, *adj.* **1.** turned or turning away from what is right or proper; perverse: *a wayward child.* **2.** influenced or caused by a sudden change in thought or action; capricious: *a wayward fancy; a wayward impulse.* **3.** turning or changing irregularly: *a wayward stream; a wayward breeze.* [ME]

Wb, *Phys. Symbol.* weber.

w.c., *Abbrev.* without charge.

WC /,dʌbəlju 'si/, *n. Colloq.* a toilet. Also, **wc.** [*w(ater-)c(loset)*]

we /wi/, *pron. pl.*; *poss.* **our** or **ours**; *obj.* **us. 1.** nominative plural of 'I'. **2.** (used by a speaker or writer to mean people in general, including himself.) **3.** (used by a ruler when referring to himself or herself in formal speech): *We are not amused.* **4.** (used for *I* by newspaper editors): *We deplore the present economic situation.* **5.** (used as a term of encouragement, etc., where the second person sing. is meant): *We really should work a little harder, shouldn't we?* [OE]

WEA /,dʌbəlju i 'eɪ/, *n.* an organisation which aims to make higher education available to working people; founded in England in 1903 and in Australia in 1913. Also, **Workers' Educational Association.** [abbrev.]

weak /wik/, *adj.* **1.** likely to yield, break, or fall down under pressure or strain; fragile; frail; not strong: *a weak spot in the armor.* **2.** lacking in bodily strength or health; feeble; infirm: *a weak old man.* **3.** lacking in political strength, or authority: *a weak ruler.* **4.** lacking in force or effectiveness; impotent, ineffectual, or inadequate: *a weak heart.* **5.** lacking in logical or legal force or soundness: *a weak argument.* **6.** lacking in mental power, intelligence, or judgment: *a weak mind.* **7.** lacking in moral strength: *weak compliance.* **8.** lacking in amount, volume, loudness, strength, etc.; faint; slight: *a weak current of electricity.* **9.** unstressed (of a syllable, word, etc). **10.** (of Germanic verbs) inflected with suffixes, without change of the root or original vowel, as in English *work, worked.* [ME, from Scand] —**weakish,** *adj.*

weaken /'wikən/, *v.t., v.i.* to make or become weak or weaker.

weak ending, *n.* a verse ending in which the metrical stress falls on a word or syllable which would not be stressed in natural speech, such as a preposition whose object is in the next line.

weakling /'wiklɪŋ/, *n.* a weak person or animal (in body or morals).

weakly /'wikli/, *adj.*, **-lier, -liest,** *adv.* ◇*adj.* **1.** weak or infirm in body; not robust; sickly. ◇*adv.* **2.** in a weak manner. —**weakliness,** *n.*

weakness /'wiknəs/, *n.* **1.** the state or quality of being weak; feebleness. **2.** a weak point, such as in a person's character; slight fault or defect. **3.** a self-indulgent liking, usu. for a person, object, food, etc.

weal /wil/, *n.* a mark or ridge raised on the skin, as from a blow. [OE *walu* weal, ridge]

wealth /wɛlθ/, *n.* **1.** a great store of valuable possessions, property, or riches: *the wealth of a city.* **2.** a rich supply or plenty of anything: *a wealth of imagery.* **3.** *Econ.* **a.** all things

wealth having a value in money, in exchange, or in use. **b.** anything having a use and able to be set aside for a particular purpose or exchanged. **4.** rich or valuable contents or produce: *the wealth of the soil.* **5.** the state of being rich; affluence: *people of wealth and standing.* [ME, from *wel* WELL[1] + -TH[1]] — **wealthy**, *adj.* — **wealthiness**, *n.*

wean /wiːn/, *v.t.* **1.** to make (a child or animal) used to food other than its mother's milk. **2.** to withdraw from any object or form of habit or enjoyment (usu. fol. by *from*). [OE]

weaner /'wiːnə/, *n.* a young animal which has been withdrawn from its mother's milk, to live wholly on grass or other types of food.

weapon /'wepən/, *n.* **1.** any instrument for use in attack or defence in fighting or war, such as a sword, rifle, guided missile, etc. **2.** anything used as an instrument for making or resisting an attack: *the deadly weapon of meekness.* [OE]

wear /weə/, *v.*, **wore**, **worn**, **wearing**, *n.* ◇*v.t.* **1.** to carry or have on the body as a covering, equipment, ornament, etc.: *to wear a coat; to wear a watch.* **2.** to show or have in the expression or appearance: *to wear a smile.* **3.** to damage (clothes, books, etc.) by use: *Hard use will wear the shoes quickly.* **4.** to waste or make gradually smaller in size, etc., by rubbing, scraping, washing, etc.: *The waves will wear the rocks.* **5.** to make (a hole, channel, way, etc.) by such action. **6.** to tire or use up; exhaust: *The children wear me down.* **7.** *Colloq.* to accept or be convinced by: *He told me a lie but I wouldn't wear it.* ◇*v.i.* **8.** to undergo gradual loss, reduction, etc., from wear, use, etc. (often fol. by *away*, *down*, *out*, or *off*). **9.** to hold out or last under wear, use, or any continued strain: *materials or colors that will wear well.* **10.** (of time, etc.) to pass, esp. slowly or tiresomely (often fol. by *away* or *on*). ◇*v.t.* **11. wear out, a.** to wear or use until no longer fit for use: *to wear out clothes.* **b.** to use up. **c.** to tire out by continued use, strain, or any gradual process: *to wear out patience.* ◇*n.* **12.** the act of wearing; use of, as a garment: *I have had very good wear from this dress.* **13.** clothing. **14.** style of dress: *evening wear; beach wear.* **15.** gradual damage, wasting, reduction, etc. from use: *The carpet shows wear.* [OE]

wearing /'weərɪŋ/, *adj.* **1.** gradually damaging or wasting. **2.** tiring; exhausting.

weary /'wɪəri/, *adj.*, **-rier**, **-riest**, *v.*, **-ried**, **-rying**. ◇*adj.* **1.** tired out physically or mentally by hard work, etc.; fatigued: *weary eyes.* **2.** marked by or causing tiredness: *a weary journey.* **3.** impatient or dissatisfied at too much or too many of (oft. fol. by *of*): *weary of rich food; weary of excuses.* **4.** marked by or causing impatience or dissatisfaction; tedious; irksome: *a weary wait.* ◇*v.t.*, *v.i.* **5.** to make or become weary; fatigue or tire. **6.** to make or grow impatient or dissatisfied at having too much of something (oft. fol. by *of*). [OE] — **wearisome**, *adj.*

weasel /'wiːzəl/, *n.* any of certain small meat-eating animals, esp. common in Europe and much of northern Asia, with a long, slender body, and feeding largely on small mice, rats, etc. [OE]

weather /'weðə/, *n.* **1.** the state of the atmosphere with respect to wind, temperature, cloudiness, moisture, pressure, etc. **2.** windy or stormy weather. **3. under the weather**, *Colloq.* ill, drunk, or indisposed. ◇*v.t.* **4.** to leave open to the weather, in order to dry, season etc.: *to weather timber.* **5.** to come safely through (a storm, danger, trouble, etc.). ◇*v.i.* **6.** to discolor or break up, from being left open to atmospheric conditions. ◇*adj.* **7.** of or relating to the side or part, as of a ship, that is open to the wind: *the weather bow.* [OE]

weatherboard /'weðəbɔːd/, *n.* **1.** one of a number of thin boards, usu. thicker along one edge than the other, nailed on an outside wall or a roof in overlapping fashion to form a protective covering which will shed water. ◇*v.t.* **2.** to cover or furnish with weatherboards. — **weather-boarded**, *adj.*

weathercock /'weðəkɒk/, *n.* **1.** a vane (def. 1) in the shape of a cock. **2.** a person or thing that changes often.

weathering /'weðərɪŋ/, *n. Geog.* the disintegration of rock in the earth's mantle by the chemical and physical effects of the climate.

weathervane /'weðəveɪn/, *n.* → **vane** (def. 1).

weave /wiːv/, *v.*, **wove** or (*esp. for defs 5 and 9*) **weaved**; **woven** or **wove**; **weaving**; *n.* ◇*v.t.* **1.** to interlace (threads, yarns, strips, fibrous material, etc.) so as to form a fabric or material. **2.** to form by interlacing threads, yarns, strands, or strips of some material: *to weave a basket, to weave cloth.* **3.** to form by combining various elements or details into a connected whole: *to weave a tale; to weave a plot.* **4.** to introduce as an element or detail into a connected whole: *to weave a melody into a musical composition.* **5.** to follow in a winding course; to move from side to side: *to weave one's way through traffic.* ◇*v.i.* **6.** to weave cloth, etc. **7.** to become woven or interwoven. **8.** to move from side to side. **9.** to wind in and out of or through: *She weaved through the crowd.* ◇*v.* **10. get weaving**, *Colloq.* to make a start, esp. hurriedly. ◇*n.* **11.** a manner of interlacing yarns: *plain, twill, or satin weave.* [OE]

web /web/, *n.*, *v.*, **webbed**, **webbing**. ◇*n.* **1.** a thin silken net spun by spiders, and also by the larvae of some insects, as caterpillars, etc.; cobweb. **2.** a woven material or something like this, esp. a whole piece of cloth in the course of being woven or after it comes from the loom. **3.** a confused, puzzling state of conditions, events, etc.: *a web of intrigue.* **4.** *Zool.* a membrane which joins together the fingers and toes of an animal, esp. for swimming. ◇*v.t.* **5.** to cover with or as if with a web; envelop. [OE]

Webb /web/, *n.* **1. Beatrice Potter**, 1858–1943, English writer on economic and social problems. **2. Francis Charles**, 1925–73, Australian writer; widely considered one of Australia's most original and influential poets; works include the poem sequence 'Ward

Webb Two' (1964). **3. Sidney James** (*Lord Passfield*), 1859-1947, husband of Beatrice, English economist and sociologist.

webbing /'wɛbɪŋ/, *n*. **1.** a woven material of hemp, cotton, or jute, in bands of various widths, for use where strength is needed. **2.** such woven bands nailed on furniture under springs or upholstery, for support. **3.** *Zool.* the membrane forming a web or webs.

weber /'veɪbə, 'weɪbə/, *n*. the SI unit of magnetic flow. Symbol: Wb [named after Wilhelm WEBER]

Weber /'veɪbə/, *n*. **1. Baron Carl Maria von,** 1786-1826, German composer and conductor. **2. Wilhelm Eduard,** 1804-91, German physicist; noted for work on magnetism and electricity. **3. Max,** 1864-1920, German sociologist and economist.

webfoot /'wɛbfʊt/, *n., pl.* **-feet.** a foot with the toes joined by a web. — **web-footed,** *adj.*

wed /wɛd/, *v.,* **wedded** or **wed, wedding.** ◇*v.t.* **1.** to take (someone) as a husband or wife. **2.** to unite (a couple) or join (one person to another) in marriage; marry. **3.** to bind by close or lasting ties; attach firmly: *to be wedded to a theory.* ◇*v.i.* **4.** to marry. **5.** to become united as if in marriage. [OE: pledge] — **wedded,** *adj.*

we'd /wid/, the shortened form of *we had, we should* or *we would.*

Wed, *Abbrev.* Wednesday.

wedding /'wɛdɪŋ/, *n*. **1.** the act or ceremony of marrying; marriage; nuptials. ◇*adj.* **2.** relating to a wedding [OE]

wedge /wɛdʒ/, *n., v.,* **wedged, wedging.** ◇*n.* **1.** a piece of hard material tapered for forcing into a narrow opening and used for splitting, securing or levering. **2.** a piece of anything with a shape like this: *a wedge of pie; a wedge of cheese.* **3.** something that parts or divides, etc.: *The tariff issue was a wedge that divided the party members.* **4. thin end of the wedge,** something small or of little importance which is likely to lead to something large and important. ◇*v.t.* **5.** to break up or split with or as if with a wedge. **6.** to pack or fix tightly by driving in a wedge or wedges. **7.** to thrust, drive, or fix (in, between, etc.) like a wedge: *to wedge oneself into a narrow opening.* [OE] — **wedgy,** *adj.*

wedge-tailed eagle, *n*. a very large, dark, long-tailed eagle of plains and forests throughout Australia and PNG; the largest of Australian birds of prey. Also, **wedgetail eagle, wedgie.**

Wedgwood /'wɛdʒwʊd/, *n*. **Josiah,** 1730-95, English potter.

wedlock /'wɛdlɒk/, *n*. the state of marriage; matrimony. [OE]

Wednesday /'wɛnzdeɪ, -di, 'wɛdn-/, *n*. the fourth day of the week, following Tuesday. [OE: Woden's day, (translation of L: day of mercury)]

wee /wi/, *adj.,* **weer, weest.** little; very small. [ME: (small) quantity, OE: weight, amount]

weed[1] /wid/, *n*. **1.** a useless or troublesome plant growing wild, esp. in cultivated ground and harming or keeping the desired crop from growing. **2.** *Colloq.* a cigar or cigarette. **3.** *Colloq.* a thin or weakly person, esp. one regarded as stupid or childish. **4.** an animal in poor condition, esp. a horse unfit for racing or breeding purposes. ◇*v.t.* **5.** to free from weeds or other troublesome plants: *to weed a garden.* **6.** to remove ideas, people, etc., who are undesirable or unnecessary (oft. fol. by *out*): *to weed out undesirable members.* ◇*v.i.* **7.** to remove weeds, etc. [OE]

weed[2] /wid/, *n*. **1.** (*pl.*) garments (oft. black or dark in color) worn to express sorrow at a death: *widow's weeds.* **2.** a band of black crepe or cloth, usu. on a man's hat or coat sleeve, worn as an expression of mourning. [OE: garment]

weedy /'widi/, *adj.,* **-dier, -diest. 1.** full of weeds. **2.** consisting of or relating to weeds. **3.** thin and weakly (of a person or animal). — **weediness,** *n.*

week /wik/, *n*. **1.** a period of seven days, one following another, commonly understood as beginning with Sunday, followed by Monday, Tuesday, Wednesday, Thursday, Friday, and Saturday. **2.** the working days or working part of the seven-day period: *a working week of forty hours.* **3.** seven days after a particular day: *I shall come Tuesday week.* **4. week in, week out,** continuously; incessantly. [OE]

weekday /'wikdeɪ/, *n*. **1.** any day of the week except Saturday and Sunday. ◇*adj.* **2.** of or on a weekday: *weekday occupations.*

weekend /wik'ɛnd/, *n.;* /'wikɛnd/, *adj.* ◇*n.* **1.** the end of the working week, esp. the period from Friday night or Saturday to Monday morning, as a time for sporting activities, visiting, etc. ◇*adj.* **2.** of, for, or on a weekend.

weekender /wik'ɛndə/, *n*. a holiday cottage used at weekends or during holidays.

weekly /'wikli/, *adj., adv., n., pl.* **-lies.** ◇*adj.* **1.** done, happening, appearing, etc., once a week, or every week. **2.** continuing or staying for a week: *a weekly boarder.* ◇*adv.* **3.** once a week. **4.** by the week. ◇*n.* **5.** a magazine, paper, etc. appearing once a week.

weep /wip/, *v.,* **wept, weeping,** *n.* ◇*v.i.* **1.** to show grief, sorrow, or any strong emotion by tears; cry. **2.** to let fall drops of water or liquid; drip. **3.** to pass or let out water or liquid, (of soil, rock, a plant stem, a sore, etc.). ◇*v.t.* **4.** to shed (tears, etc.). ◇*n.* **5.** *Colloq.* a weeping, or a fit of weeping. [OE: wail]

weeping /'wipɪŋ/, *adj.* **1.** passing out liquid (of soil, a wound, etc.). **2.** expressing sorrow by shedding tears. **3.** (of trees, etc.) having narrow, graceful branches that hang down.

weeping willow, *n*. a commonly cultivated willow with long branches that hang down freely to the ground.

weevil /'wivəl/, *n*. a type of beetle which destroys nuts, grain, fruit, the stems of leaves, etc. [OE]

weft /weft/, *n.* **1.** (in weaving) the horizontal thread which crosses the lengthwise-running warp; woof. **2.** a woven piece. [OE]

Wehrmacht /'veəmakt/, *n.* the armed forces of Germany (1935–45), prior to and during World War II. [G: defence force]

weigh /weɪ/, *v.t.* **1.** to find out the weight of by a balance, scale, or other mechanical apparatus: *to weigh gold.* **2.** to hold up or balance, usu. in the hand, in order to form an opinion of the weight of. **3.** to measure (a certain quantity of something) according to weight (usu. fol. by *out*): *to weigh out 5 kg of sugar.* **4.** to press (down) by weight, heaviness, etc.: *weighed down with parcels; weighed down with care.* **5.** to balance in the mind; consider carefully (sometimes fol. by *up*): *to weigh the pros and cons.* ◇*v.i.* **6.** to have weight or heaviness: *to weigh little.* **7.** to have importance or effect: *Wealth weighs little in this case.* **8.** to press down as a weight or load: *Such responsibility weighed upon him.* ◇*v.* **9.** Some special uses are:
weigh anchor, to raise the anchor of a ship; set out on a voyage.
weigh in, 1. (of a boxer or wrestler) to be weighed before a fight. **2.** (of a jockey) to be weighed after a race.
weigh into, to attack, physically or verbally.
weigh one's words, to consider and choose one's words carefully in speaking or writing. [OE: carry, weigh]

weight /weɪt/, *n.* **1.** amount of heaviness; the amount a thing weighs. **2.** the gravitational force upon a body, varying with geographical position. It is often taken as a measure of the mass, which does not vary, and is equal to the mass times the acceleration due to gravity. **3.** a system of units for expressing weight or mass: *avoirdupois weight.* **4.** a unit of weight or mass. **5.** a piece of metal, etc., of a certain mass, used on a balance or scale to measure the opposing mass of an object, substance, etc. **6.** any heavy mass or object, esp. an object used because of its heaviness, e.g. a paperweight. **7.** a load of care or responsibility: *to remove a weight from my mind.* **8.** importance: *an opinion of great weight.* ◇**9.** Some special uses are:
by weight, according to weight measurement.
carry weight, to have influence or importance.
pull one's weight, to do one's fair share of work.
throw one's weight around or **about, 1.** to behave in a quarrelsome or selfish way. **2.** to use one's influence, authority, etc., unnecessarily.
◇*v.t.* **10.** to add weight to. **11.** to load down with or as if with weight: *to be weighted with years.* [OE] –**weighty**, *adj.* –**weightiness**, *n.*

weight density, *n.* weight per unit volume.

weightlessness /'weɪtləsnəs/, *n.* a state of being without apparent weight as experienced in free fall, due to the absence of any apparent gravitational pull; zero gravity.

Weimar Republic /ˌvaɪma rə'pʌblɪk/, *n.* the German Republic from 1919 to 1933; founded at Weimar, a city in central eastern Germany.

Weipa /'wipə/, *n.* a town on the north-west coast of Cape York Peninsula, Qld; Aboriginal community; bauxite mining. Pop. 2480 (1986).

weir /wɪə/, *n.* **1.** a dam in a river or stream to stop and raise the water, for directing it to a mill, for watering crops, etc. **2.** a blockage placed across a stream causing the water to pass through a particular opening or notch, thus measuring the quantity flowing. [OE]

Weir /wɪə/, *n.* **Peter Lindsay**, born 1944, Australian film director

weird /wɪəd/, *adj.* **1.** relating to or suggesting the supernatural; unearthly or uncanny: *a weird howling.* **2.** *Colloq.* startlingly or extraordinarily odd, or strange: *weird clothes.* [OE: fate]

WEL /wɛl/, *n.* → **Women's Electoral Lobby.** [abbrev.]

welch /wɛlʃ/, *v.t., v.i. Colloq.* → **welsh.**

welcome /'wɛlkəm/, *interj., n., v.,* **-comed, -coming,** *adj.* ◇*interj.* **1.** (a word of kindly greeting to a friend): *Welcome, friends!* ◇*n.* **2.** a kindly greeting or reception: *to give one a warm welcome.* ◇*v.t.* **3.** to greet the coming of (a person, etc.) with pleasure or kindly politeness. **4.** to receive or regard, usu. with pleasure: *to welcome a change.* ◇*adj.* **5.** gladly received: *a welcome visitor.* **6.** pleasing, such as something coming, happening, or experienced: *a welcome letter; a welcome rest.* **7.** given full right by the friendly consent of others: *He's welcome to anything he can find.* **8.** free to enjoy politeness, favors, etc., without being indebted (used in conventional response to thanks): *You are quite welcome.* [OE, from *wil-* pleasure + *cuma* guest]

'Welcome Stranger' nugget, *n.* a gold nugget discovered on the Dunolly goldfield in 1869; was the largest nugget known to exist; gross weight 78 381 grams.

welcome swallow, *n.* a swallow with a swift, swooping flight, widely spread throughout Australia, except in the north-west and the NT.

weld /wɛld/, *v.t.* **1.** to join (pieces of metal, etc.) by hammering, compression, etc., esp. after making soft or pasty by heat, and sometimes with the addition of fusible material like or unlike the pieces to be joined. **2.** to join anything firmly. ◇*v.i.* **3.** to undergo welding; be capable of being welded. ◇*n.* **4.** a welded joint. **5.** the act of welding. [var. of WELL²] –**welder**, *n.*

welfare /'wɛlfɛə/, *n.* the state of being well; well-being: *physical or moral welfare of society.* [ME]

welfare state, *n.* a state (def. 8) in which the well-being of the people in social security, health, education, housing, and working conditions is the responsibility of the government.

welfare work, *n.* work devoted to the well-being of people in a community, esp. the aged, sick, poor, etc.

well¹ /wɛl/, *adv., adj., compar.* **better**, *super.* **best**, *interj.* ◇*adv.* **1.** in a satisfactory, favorable, or advantageous manner; fortunately or happily: *Affairs are going well.* **2.** in a good or proper manner: *He behaved very well.* **3.** in a manner worthy of praise, deserving reward; excellently: *a good work well done.* **4.** with good reason: *I could not well refuse.* **5.** enough; satisfactorily; adequately: *Think well before you act.* **6.** thoroughly or soundly: *Shake well before using.* **7.** easily; clearly: *I can see it very well.* **8.** to a considerable extent or degree: *a sum well over the amount fixed.* **9. as well**, in addition: *She is bringing a friend as well.* **10. as well as**, in addition to; no less than: *He was handsome as well as rich.* ◇*adj.* **11.** in good health, or sound in body and mind: *I am well again.* **12.** satisfactory or good: *All is well with us.* **13.** proper or fitting. **14.** in a satisfactory position; well-off: *I am very well as I am.* ◇*interj.* **15.** (used to express surprise, agreement): *Well, who would have thought it?* **16.** (used as an introduction to further speech): *Well, as I was saying.* [OE]

well[2] /wel/, *n.* **1.** a hole drilled into the earth, generally by boring, to obtain water, petroleum, natural gas, etc. **2.** a spring or natural source of water. **3.** a fountain, fountainhead, or source. **4.** a vessel, etc. for holding a liquid: *an inkwell.* **5.** any sunken or deep enclosed space, esp. a shaft for air or light, or for stairs, a lift, etc., extending in an upright direction through the floors of a building. ◇*v.i.* **6.** to rise, spring, or gush from the earth or some source (oft. fol. by *up*, *out*, or *forth*): *Tears welled up in his eyes.* ◇*v.t.* **7.** to send welling up or out: *a fountain welling its pure water.* [OE]

we'll /wil/, a shorter form of *we will* or *we shall*.

well-appointed /ˈwɛl-əpɔɪntəd/, *adj.* (of a hotel, house, etc.) comfortably and well equipped, decorated, furnished, etc. Also (*esp. after a verb*), **well appointed** /wɛl əˈpɔɪntəd/.

well-balanced /ˈwɛl-bælənst/, *adj.* **1.** rightly balanced. **2.** sensible; sane. Also (*esp. after a verb*), **well balanced** /wɛl ˈbælənst/.

well-being /ˈwɛl-biɪŋ/, *n.* good or satisfactory condition of existence; welfare.

well-born /ˈwɛl-bɔn/, *adj.* of good birth or family. Also (*esp. after a verb*), **well born** /wɛl ˈbɔn/.

well-bred /ˈwɛl-brɛd/, *adj.* **1.** (of people) well brought up. **2.** showing good breeding, with regard to behavior, manners, etc. **3.** (of a domestic animal) of good breed. Also (*esp. after a verb*), **well bred** /wɛl ˈbrɛd/.

well-connected /ˈwɛl-kənɛktəd/, *adj.* **1.** having important, powerful, or influential relatives. **2.** having useful connections with influential people. Also (*esp. after a verb*), **well connected** /wɛl kəˈnɛktəd/.

well-disposed /ˈwɛl-dəspoʊzd/, *adj.* **1.** well-meaning. **2.** having favorable or kind feelings towards: *well-disposed hearts.* Also (*esp. after a verb*), **well disposed** /wɛl dəsˈpoʊzd/.

well-grounded /ˈwɛl-graʊndəd/, *adj.* **1.** based on good grounds or reasons. **2.** well or thoroughly instructed in the first principles of a subject. Also (*esp. after a verb*), **well grounded** /wɛl ˈgraʊndəd/.

well-heeled /ˈwɛl-hild/, *adj. Colloq.* wealthy; prosperous. Also (*esp. after a verb*), **well heeled** /wɛl ˈhild/.

well-informed /ˈwɛl-ɪnfɔmd/, *adj.* **1.** having reliable or full information on a subject. **2.** having information on a variety of subjects: *a well-informed person.* Also (*esp. after a verb*), **well informed** /wɛl ɪnˈfɔmd/.

Wellington[1] /ˈwɛlɪŋtən/, *n.* **Arthur Wellesley, 1st Duke of**, 1769–1852, British general and statesman, prime minister 1828–30; fought against Napoleon at Waterloo.

Wellington[2] /ˈwɛlɪŋtən/, *n.* **1.** the capital city of NZ, on the southern coast of North Island at an inlet of Cook Strait. Pop. 137 495 (1986). **2.** a town and shire in eastern central NSW, on the junction of the Macquarie and Bell Rivers. Pop. 5277 (1986). **3. Mount**, a mountain in southern Tas, behind and to the west of Hobart. 1270 m.

wellington boot, *n.* a gumboot. Also, **wellington**. [named after the Duke of WELLINGTON]

well-known /ˈwɛl-noʊn/, *adj.* **1.** clearly or fully known. **2.** familiar: *a well-known face.* **3.** generally or widely known: *the well-known sculptor.* Also (*esp. after a verb*), **well known** /wɛl ˈnoʊn/.

well-meaning /ˈwɛl-minɪŋ/, *adj.* **1.** meaning or intending well: *a well-meaning but tactless person.* **2.** coming from or being a result of good intentions but not necessarily having good results. Also (*esp. after a verb*), **well meaning** /wɛl ˈminɪŋ/.

wellnigh /ˈwɛlnaɪ/, *adv.* very nearly; almost.

well-off /ˈwɛl-ɒf/, *adj.* **1.** in a satisfactory, favorable, or good position or condition. **2.** comfortably rich. Also (*esp. after a verb*), **well off** /wɛl ˈɒf/.

well-preserved /ˈwɛl-prəzɜvd/, *adj.* **1.** having been kept in good condition. **2.** keeping a young or youthful appearance. Also (*esp. after a verb*), **well preserved** /wɛl prəˈzɜvd/.

well-read /ˈwɛl-rɛd/, *adj.* **1.** having read much: *well-read in science.* **2.** having a wide-ranging and intelligent knowledge of books or literature. Also (*esp. after a verb*), **well read** /wɛl ˈrɛd/.

well-rounded /ˈwɛl-raʊndəd/, *adj.* **1.** having an agreeable, rounded shape. **2.** full and varied, esp. of a person's life. **3.** put together well, and sounding full, deep and rich, esp. a phrase or sentence. Also (*esp. after a verb*), **well rounded** /wɛl ˈraʊndəd/.

Wells /wɛlz/, *n.* **H(erbert) G(eorge)**, 1866–1946, English novelist and writer on social and political problems; one of the first authors of science fiction; author of *The Time Machine* (1895).

well-spoken /ˈwɛl-spoʊkən/, *adj.* **1.** having a carefully developed, refined way of speaking. **2.** speaking well, fittingly, or pleasingly. **3.** polite in speech. Also (*esp. after a verb*), **well spoken** /wɛl ˈspoʊkən/.

well-to-do /'wel-tə-du/; *esp. after a verb* /wel-tə-'du/, *adj.* having enough money to be able to enjoy comfortable living; well-off; prosperous; wealthy.

welsh /welʃ/, *v.t., v.i. Colloq.* **1.** to cheat by escaping payment, esp. of a gambling debt (sometimes fol. by *on*). **2.** to inform or tell on someone. Also, **welch**. [orig. obscure]

welt /welt/, *n.* **1.** a ridge or raised mark on the surface of the body, usu. from the stroke of a stick or whip. **2.** strip of leather set in between the edges of the inner sole and upper and the outer sole of a shoe. **3.** a strengthening or ornamental finish along a seam, the edge of a garment, etc. **4.** a type of seam in which one edge is cut close to the stitching line and covered by the other edge which is stitched over it. ◊*v.t.* **5.** to beat soundly with a stick or whip. **6.** to supply with a welt or welts. [ME]

welter /'weltə/, *v.i.* **1.** *Archaic.* to lie bathed or be soaked in something, esp. blood. ◊*n.* **2.** a rolling or tumbling about: *in the welter of the sea*. **3.** an uproar or state of confusion; chaos: *the welter of our changing world*. **4.** a race in which the horses carry weights which are not less than 51 kg. [ME, frequentative of obs. *welt* roll]

welterweight /'weltəweɪt/, *n.* a boxer weighing between 63.5 and 67 kg (in the amateur ranks) and 63.503 and 66.678 kg (in the professional ranks). [*welter* heavyweight rider or boxer + WEIGHT]

wen /wen/, *n.* a harmless swelling of the skin, found esp. on the scalp. [OE]

Wenceslaus /'wensəsləs/, *n.* **Saint** (*Good King Wenceslaus*), c. 907–929, prince of Bohemia; patron saint of the Czech Republic. Also, **Wenceslas**. German, **Wenzel**.

wench /wentʃ/, *n.* **1.** a girl or young woman. **2.** a country or working girl. **3.** *Archaic.* a prostitute. [OE: child]

wend /wend/, *v.t.*, **wended, wending.** to direct or make (one's way, etc.): *He wended his way to the riverside*. [OE]

went /went/, *v.* past tense of **go**.

Wentworth /'wentwəθ/, *n.* **William Charles**, 1790–1872, Australian explorer and politician; active in gaining self-government for NSW.

wept /wept/, *v.* past tense and past participle of **weep**.

were /wɜ/, *v.* past tense indicative plural and subjunctive singular and plural of **be**. [OE]

we're /wɪə, wɜ, weə/, a shortened form of *we are*.

weren't /wɜnt/, a shortened form of *were not*.

werewolf /'wɪəwʊlf, 'wɜ-, 'weə-/, *n., pl.* **-wolves** /-wʊlvz/. (in old folk tales, etc.) a human being turned by supernatural forces into a wolf. Also, **werwolf**. [OE, from *wer* man + WOLF]

Werribee /'werəbi/, *n.* a town and shire in southern Vic, near the western shores of Port Phillip Bay. Pop. 52 458 (1986).

wert /wɜt/, *v. Archaic.* second person singular past tense indicative and subjunctive of **be**.

Wesley /'wezli/, *n.* **1. Charles,** 1707–88, English Methodist preacher and hymn-writer. **2.** his brother, **John,** 1703–91, English preacher, founder of Methodism. –**Wesleyan,** *adj., n.*

Wessex /'wesəks/, *n.* **1.** an Anglo-Saxon kingdom, later an earldom, in southern England. *Cap.:* Winchester. **2.** (in recent times) a region principally in Dorset, described in Hardy's novels.

Wessex saddleback, *n.* a breed of pig, black with a white saddle over its shoulder, reared for pork and bacon.

west /west/, *n.* **1.** a principal point of the compass (90° to the left of north) corresponding to the point where the sun is seen to set. **2.** the direction in which this point lies. **3.** (*l.c.* or *cap.*) land situated in this direction. **4. the West, a.** the western part of the world as separate from the East or Orient; the Occident. **b.** the countries of Western Europe, the Americas, Australia, etc., not under Communist government. ◊*adj., adv.* **5.** in, towards or coming from the west. ◊*adv.* **6. go west,** *Colloq.* **a.** to die. **b.** to disappear; be lost. [OE]

West /west/, *n.* **Dame Rebecca** (*Dame Cicily Isabel Fairfield Andrews*), 1892–1983, English novelist and critic.

West Bank, *n.* an area on the western bank of the river Jordan, between Israel and Jordan; Arab-Israeli dispute over sovereignty.

West Berlin, *n.* formerly, a city and state, administratively part of, but isolated from West Germany, formed by the western part of Berlin (the former **western sector** occupied by the US, Britain and France). See **Berlin**.

westerly /'westəli/, *adj., adv., n., pl.* **-lies**. ◊*adv., adj.* **1.** towards or from the west. ◊*n.* **2.** a westerly wind.

western /'westən/, *adj.* **1.** in, towards, or from the west. **2.** (*usu. cap.*) of or relating to the West (def. 4): *the Western Church*. ◊*n.* **3.** (*usu. cap.*) a story or film about life in the American west during the latter half of the 19th century. [OE] –**westernmost,** *adj.*

Western /'westən/, *n.* a province in southwestern PNG. Pop. 91 700 (1986 est.); 99 300 km². *Administrative Centre:* Daru.

Western Australia *n.* a state in western Australia, the largest of the six states. Pop. 1 406 929 (1986); 2 525 500 km². *Cap.:* Perth. *Abbrev.:* WA

Western Church, *n.* **1.** the Roman Catholic Church, sometimes with the Anglican Church, or, more broadly, the Christian Churches of western Europe and those churches elsewhere which are connected with or have sprung from them. **2.** the Christian Church in those countries once part of the western part of the Roman Empire and in countries evangelised from these countries, or that part of the Christian Church which acknowledged the popes after the split between Greek and Latin Christianity.

Western Desert, *n.* a major Australian Aboriginal language spoken over a wide area of central western Australia.

Western District, *n.* an area in the south-western corner of Vic, extending west from Port Phillip Bay to the SA border and from the south coast north to the Grampians.

Western Hemisphere, *n.* **1.** a hemisphere of the earth cut along a meridian so chosen as to include all of North and South America, but no part of any other continent. **2.** that half of the earth traversed in passing westwards from the prime meridian to 180° longitude.

Western Highlands, *n.* a province in western PNG. Pop. 300 200 (1986 est.); 8500 km². *Administrative Centre:* Mount Hagen.

Westernise *or* **Westernize** /'westənaɪz/, *v.t.,* **-nised, -nising.** to make Western (def. 2) in ideas, character, ways, etc.

Western red cedar, *n.* → **red cedar.**

Western Samoa *n.* a monarchy in the southern Pacific Ocean, consisting of two large and seven smaller islands Pop. 161 300 (1987); 2831 km². *Languages:* Samoan and English. *Currency:* tala. *Cap.:* Apia. –**Western Samoan,** *n., adj.*

Western Standard Time, *n.* a time zone lying on the 120th meridian in WA, eight hours ahead of Greenwich Mean Time, two hours behind Eastern Standard Time, and one and a half hours behind Central Standard Time.

Westgarth /'westgaθ/, *n.* **William,** 1815–89, Australian merchant, politician and historian, born in Scotland; prominent in the development of Vic.

West Germany, *n.* formerly, a republic in northern central Europe; formed in 1949 from the British, American and French occupied zones of Germany; became part of reunified Germany in 1990. *Cap.:* Bonn. Official name: **Federal Republic of Germany.** –**West German,** *n., adj.*

West Indies /west 'ɪndiz/, *n.pl.* **1.** an archipelago in the northern Atlantic between North and South America, enclosing the Caribbean Sea and the Gulf of Mexico; divided into the Greater Antilles, the Lesser Antilles, and the Bahamas. **2. Federation of the,** a former federation (1958–62) of British islands in the Caribbean, comprising Barbados, Jamaica, Trinidad and Tobago, and the Windward and Leeward Island colonies. –**West Indian,** *n., adj.*

Westinghouse /'westɪŋhaʊs/, *n.* **George,** 1846–1914, US inventor, esp. of a type of air-brake.

West Irian /west 'ɪriən/, *n.* → **Irian Jaya.**

Westminster /'westmɪnstə/, *n.* **1.** Also, **City of Westminster.** a central borough (officially a city) in London; Westminster Abbey; Houses of Parliament; Buckingham Palace. Pop. 190 661 (1981). **2. Statute of** → **Statute of Westminster.**

Westminster Abbey, *n.* a church in London founded in 1065 by King Edward the Confessor; the place of coronation of every English king and queen, of most royal marriages, and of many national ceremonies.

Westminster system, *n.* a system of bicameral parliamentary government originating in Britain, in which ministers are members of parliament and are responsible to it, and in which the head of state is not also head of government, and the judiciary is independent of the executive and legislature. [so named because the British Houses of Parliament are situated in WESTMINSTER]

West New Britain, *n.* a province of PNG, comprising part of New Britain and several small islands. Pop. 107 700 (1986 est.); 21 000 km². *Administrative Centre:* Kimbe.

Weston /'westən/, *n.* a town within the City of Greater Cessnock, NSW. Pop. (with Kurri Kurri) 13 411 (1986).

West Sepik /west 'sipɪk/, *n.* a province of PNG, in the north-west. Pop. 128 300 (1986 est.); 36 300 km². *Administrative Centre:* Vanimo. Also, **Sandaun.**

West Timor, *n.* the western part of the island of Timor; part of the Indonesian province of Nusa Tenggara Timur. Until 1950, **Netherlands Timor;** until 1976, **Indonesian Timor.**

West Virginia, *n.* a state in the eastern US. Pop. 1 919 000 (1986 est.); 62 629 km². *Cap.:* Charleston. *Abbrev.:* W Va –**West Virginian,** *n., adj.*

westward /'westwəd/, *adj.* **1.** moving, bearing, facing, or placed towards the west. ◊*adv.* **2.** westwards. ◊*n.* **3.** the westward part, direction, or point. –**westwardly,** *adj., adv.*

westwards /'westwədz/, *adv.* towards the west; west. Also, **westward.**

wet /wet/, *adj.,* **wetter, wettest,** *n., v.,* **wet** *or* **wetted, wetting.** ◊*adj.* **1.** covered or soaked, wholly or in part, with water or some other liquid: *wet hands; a wet sponge.* **2.** moist, damp, or not yet dry: *wet ink; wet paint.* **3.** marked by the presence or use of water or other liquid. **4.** rainy; having a rainy climate. **5.** *Colloq.* weak; feeble; spiritless. **6. wet behind the ears,** *Colloq.* lacking experience, etc.; naive. ◊*n.* **7.** anything that makes something wet, such as water or other liquid; moisture. **8.** a wet state, condition, or place. **9.** rain. **10. the wet,** the rainy season in central and northern Australia, from December to March. ◊*v.t.* **11.** to make wet. **12.** to make wet by urinating: *The child wet the bed.* ◊*v.i.* **13.** to become wet. [OE: to wet] –**wettish,** *adj.*

wet blanket, *n.* a person or thing that has a discouraging or depressing effect.

wet cell, *n.* an electric cell whose electrolyte is in liquid form and free to flow.

wet dream, *n.* a sexually exciting dream, resulting in the emission of semen while or just after being asleep.

wether /'weðə/, *n.* a ram castrated or gelded when young. [OE]

wetlands /'wetlændz/, *n.pl.* an area in which the soil is frequently or permanently under water, as a swamp, marsh, etc.

wet nurse, *n.* a woman hired to give another's baby milk from her own breast.

wetsuit /'wetsuːt/, *n.* a set of tight-fitting upper and lower garments made of rubber, worn by divers, etc., to keep in body heat while under water.

wettex /'weteks/, *n.* a small cloth of spongy, absorbent material used for cleaning. [Trademark]

we've /wiv/; *unstressed* /wəv/, a shortened form of *we have*.

Wewak /'wiwæk/, *n.* a coastal town in East Sepik province, PNG. Pop. 23 000 (1988 est.).

whack /wæk/, *Colloq.* ◇*v.t., v.i.* **1.** to strike with a sharp, resounding blow. ◇*n.* **2.** a sharp, resounding blow: *a whack with his hand.* **3.** a trial or attempt: *to take a whack at a job.* **4.** a part or share. [? imitative; ? var. of *thwack*]

whacko /'wækoʊ/, *interj.* (an expression indicating pleasure, delight, etc.) Also, **whacko-the-diddle-oh** /ˌwækoʊ-ðə-'dɪdl-oʊ/.

whale /weɪl/, *n., pl.* **whales,** (esp. collectively) **whale,** *v.,* **whaled, whaling.** ◇*n.* **1.** *Zool.* a large sea mammal with fishlike body, flippers and a horizontally flattened tail. **2.** *Colloq.* something very big, great, or fine of its kind: *a whale of a time.* ◇*v.i.* **3.** to carry on the work of catching whales. [OE] **–whaler,** *n.*

whaleboat /'weɪlboʊt/, *n.* a boat designed for quick turning and use in rough sea, formerly used in whaling, now mainly for sea rescue.

whalebone /'weɪlboʊn/, *n.* **1.** an elastic horny substance growing in place of teeth in the upper jaw of certain whales; baleen. **2.** a thin strip of this material, used for stiffening corsets, etc.

whaler shark, *n.* a large dangerous shark of eastern Australian waters.

wham /wæm/, *n., v.,* **whammed, whamming.** ◇*n.* **1.** a forceful stroke or blow. ◇*v.i., v.t.* **2.** to hit forcefully, esp. with a single loud noise.

wharf /wɔf/, *n., pl.* **wharves, wharfs,** *v.* ◇*n.* **1.** a structure built on the shore of, or sticking out into, a harbor, stream, etc., at which ships load or unload; quay; pier. ◇*v.t.* **2.** to place or store on a wharf. [OE: dam]

wharfie /'wɔfi/, *n. Colloq.* someone employed to load and unload ships in port.

what /wɒt/, *interrog. pron.* **1.** (asking for something to be named or stated): *What is your name? What did he do?* **2.** (asking about the nature, character, class, origin, etc., of a thing or person): *What is that animal?* **3.** (asking about the worth, usefulness, force, or importance of something): *What is wealth without health?* **4.** (asking for repetition or explanation of some word or words used as by an earlier speaker): *You need five what?* **5.** (oft. used to give force in exclamatory phrases): *What luck! What an idea!* **6. so what?** (an exclamation showing the attitude that something is not serious, worthwhile, etc.). **7. what for?** for what reason or purpose. **8. what of it?** what does it matter? ◇*relative pron.* **9.** the thing that; that which: *This is what he says.* **10.** anything that; whatever: *Say what you please.* **11.** something that: *She went, and, what is more surprising, gained a hearing.* **12. what it takes,** the necessary ability, personality, etc.: *He's got what it takes to make a great foreman.* **13. what's what, a.** the true position. **b.** the correct procedure: *He knows what's what.* ◇*adj.* **14.** whatever: *Take what time and help you need.* ◇*adv.* **15.** to what degree?; how much?: *what does it matter?* ◇*interj.* **16.** (to express surprise, disbelief, anger, etc.): *What! Did you do that painting yourself?* [OE]

whata /'wɒtə/, *n. NZ.* a Maori storehouse on raised posts. [Maori]

whatever /wɒt'evə/, *pron.* **1.** *indef. relative pron.* **a.** anything that: *Do whatever you like.* **b.** no matter what: *Do it, whatever happens.* **2.** *interrog. pron. Colloq.* what ever? what? (used to give force): *Whatever do you mean?* ◇*adj.* **3.** any ... that: *Whatever worth the work has is to John's credit.* **4.** no matter what: *Whatever blame he might receive, he'll still carry on.* **5.** what (who) ... it may be: *For whatever reason, he is unwilling; any person whatever.* Also, *Poetic,* **whate'er.**

whatnot /'wɒtnɒt/, *n.* **1.** a stand with shelves for books, small articles, etc. **2.** *Colloq.* anything; no matter what; what you please: *Bring food, drink and whatnot to the party.*

whatsoever /wɒtsoʊ'evə/, *pron., adj.* a strong form of **whatever.** Also, *Poetic,* **whatsoe'er.**

wheat /wit/, *n.* **1.** the grain of a widely spread cereal grass, esp. one type much used in the form of flour for bread, cakes, pastry, etc. **2.** a plant which bears the grain in dense spikes. [OE] **–wheaten,** *adj.*

wheat germ, *n.* the centre of the wheat grain, rich in vitamins.

wheatmeal /'witmil/, *n.* grains of wheat crushed into a coarse powder.

wheedle /'widl/, *v.,* **-dled, -dling.** ◇*v.t.* **1.** to try to influence (a person) by smooth and persuasive words. **2.** to get by clever persuasions: *to wheedle money from them.* ◇*v.i.* **3.** to use clever persuasions.

wheel /wil/, *n.* **1.** a circular frame or solid disc arranged to turn on an axis, as in vehicles, machinery, etc. **2.** any instrument, machine, apparatus, etc., shaped like this, or having such a structure as an important feature: *a potter's wheel.* **3.** a circular frame with an axle connecting with the rudder, for steering a ship. **4.** an old instrument of torture in the form of a circular frame on which the victim was stretched. **5.** anything like or suggesting a wheel in shape, movement, etc. **6.** Also, **wheel of Fortune.** *Myth.* a wheel turned by a personification of fortune, symbolising change in human affairs. **7.** (*pl.*) the forces controlling something: *the wheels of trade; the wheels of government.* **8.** (*pl.*) *Colloq.* a motor vehicle: *Have you got wheels?* **9.** *Colloq.* someone of much importance or influence: *a big wheel.* **10. put one's shoulder to the wheel,** to put in a great deal of effort to achieve some end. ◇*v.t.*

wheel 11. to move, roll, or push on wheels, etc.: *The maid wheels the trolley.* ◇*v.i.* 12. to turn on or as if on an axis or about a centre; rotate; revolve. 13. *Mil.* to change direction while marching: *to wheel to the left.* 14. to move in a circular or curving course: *birds wheeling above.* 15. to turn or change in course or opinion (oft. fol. by *about* or *round*). ◇*v.* 16. **wheel and deal**, to act as a wheeler-dealer. [OE] **—wheeled**, *adj.*

wheelbarrow /ˈwɪlbærou/, *n.* a frame or box for carrying a load, usu. supported at one end by a wheel and at the other by two legs above which are two long handles.

wheelchair /ˈwiltʃeə/, *n.* a chair moved by large wheels, and used esp. by those people unable to walk.

Wheeler /ˈwilə/, *n.* **Sir (Robert Eric) Mortimer**, 1890–1976, Scottish archaeologist.

wheeler-dealer /wilə-ˈdilə/, *n.* someone who actively advances their position by moving constantly from one profitable business deal to another.

wheeze /wiz/, *v.*, **wheezed, wheezing**, *n.* ◇*v.i.* 1. to breathe with difficulty and with a whistling sound. ◇*n.* 2. a wheezing breath or sound. [ME *whese*, probably from Scand; compare Icel *hvæsa* hiss] **—wheezy**, *adj.*

whelk /welk/, *n.* any of a family of large, spiral-shelled sea snails. [OE]

whelp /welp/, *n.* 1. the young of the dog, wolf, bear, lion, tiger, seal, etc. 2. (*offensive*) a youth. ◇*v.t., v.i.* 3. (of a bitch, lioness, etc.) to bring forth (young). [OE]

when /wen/, *adv.* 1. at what time?: *When are you coming?* ◇*conj.* 2. at what time: *I know when he is coming.* 3. at the time that: *When we are ready we will go.* 4. at any time: *He is impatient when he is kept waiting.* 5. while on the contrary, or whereas: *You covered up the wound when you should have cleaned it first.* ◇*pron.* 6. what time: *Since when have you known this?* 7. which time: *They left on Monday, since when we have heard nothing.* ◇*n.* 8. the time of anything: *the when and the where of an act.* [OE]

whence /wens/, *adv. Archaic.* 1. from what place, source or origin? ◇*conj.* 2. from what place, source, cause, etc.: *He told them whence he came.* [ME]

whenever /wenˈevə/, *conj.* 1. at any time when: *Come whenever you like.* ◇*adv.* 2. *Colloq.* when? (used to give force): *Whenever did he say that?* Also, *Poetic,* **whene'er**.

where /weə/, *adv.* 1. in or at what place?: *Where is he?* 2. in what position?: *Where do you stand on this question?* 3. in what particular respect, way, etc.?: *Where does this affect us?* 4. to what place, point, or end?: *Where are you going?* 5. from what source: *Where did you get such an idea?* ◇*conj.* 6. in, at, or to what place, part, point, etc.: *Find where the trouble is; Find out where he's gone.* 7. in or at the place, part, point, etc., in or at which: *The book is where you left it.* 8. in a position, case, etc., in which: *There are times where it is better not to know the truth.* 9. in or at which place: *They came to the town, where they stayed for the night.* 10.*Colloq.* that: *I read where they are going to increase taxes.* ◇*pron.* 11. what place: *Where have you come from?* 12. the place in which: *This is where we live.* [OE]

where-, a word part meaning 'what' or 'which', as in *whereby, whereat.* [special use of WHERE]

whereabouts /ˈweərəbauts/, *interrogatively* /weərəˈbauts/, *adv.* 1. about where?; where? ◇*conj.* 2. near or in what place: *seeing whereabouts in the world we were.* ◇*n.pl.* 3. (sometimes treated as sing.) the place where a person or thing is: *no clue as to his whereabouts.*

whereas /weərˈæz/, *conj.* 1. while on the other hand: *Peter came, whereas the others didn't.* 2. it being the case that (used esp. in legal documents).

wherefore /ˈweəfɔ/, *adv.* 1. for what?; why? ◇*conj.* 2. for what or which cause or reason? ◇*n.* 3. the cause or reason: *the whys and wherefores.* [ME; from WHERE + *fore* because of, FOR]

wheresoever /weəsouˈevə/, *adv., conj.* in or to whatsoever place; wherever. Also, *Poetic,* **wheresoe'er**.

whereupon /weərəˈpɒn/, *conj.* 1. at or after which. 2. upon what or upon which.

wherever /weərˈevə/, *conj.* 1. in, at, or to, whatever place. ◇*adv.* 2. *Colloq.* where? (used to give force): *Wherever did you find that?* Also, *Poetic,* **where'er**.

wherewithal /ˈweəwɪðɔl, -θɔl/, *n.* the means or supplies for the purpose or need, esp. money: *the wherewithal to pay my rent.*

whet /wet/, *v.t.*, **whetted, whetting**. 1. to sharpen (a knife, tool, etc.) by rubbing on a stone, etc. 2. to make keen or eager: *to whet the appetite.* [OE]

whether /ˈweðə/, *conj.* 1. a word introducing the first of two or more possible happenings, and sometimes repeated before the second one (used together with *or*): *It matters little whether we go or whether we stay.* 2. used to introduce a single happening (the other being understood): *See whether he has come* (or *not*). 3. **whether or no**, in any case: *He threatens to go, whether or no.* [OE]

whetstone /ˈwetstoun/, *n.* a stone for sharpening knives or tools.

whew /hwju/, *interj.* (a whistling exclamation or sound expressing surprise, etc.)

whey /wei/, *n.* a watery liquid separating from the thickened mass of milk curd, formed in cheese-making. [OE]

which /wɪtʃ/, *interrog. pron.* 1. what one (of a certain number)?: *Which of these do you want?* ◇*relative pron.* 2. (used as the subject or object of a relative clause): *How old is the car which was stolen?* 3. what particular one or any one that: *She knows which she wants; Choose which you like.* 4. a thing that: *And, which is worse, your work is wrong.* ◇*adj.* 5. what one (of a certain number)?: *Which book do you want?* 6. any ... that: *Go which way you please.* 7. being previously mentioned: *It stormed all day, during which time the ship broke up.* [OE]

whichever /wɪtʃˈevə/, *pron.* **1.** any one (of those in question) that: *Take whichever you like.* **2.** no matter which: *Whichever you choose, the others will be hurt.* ◇*adj.* **3.** no matter which: *whichever day; whichever person.*

whiff /wɪf/, *n.* **1.** a slight movement or puff: *a whiff of fresh air.* **2.** a slight smell. ◇*v.i.* **3.** (of wind, smoke, etc.) to blow lightly. [? b. WHIP and PUFF]

Whig /wɪg/, *n.* a member of one of the two major political parties in England in the 18th and early 19th centuries, associated with attempts to limit royal authority and increase parliamentary power, generally favoring various political and social reforms, and finally evolving into the Liberal Party. Cf. **Tory** (def. 1). [prob. short for *whiggamore*, one of a body of rebels who marched on Edinburgh, 1648] —**Whiggery, Whiggism,** *n.* —**Whiggish,** *adj.*

while /waɪl/, *n., conj., v.,* **whiled, whiling.** ◇*n.* **1.** a space of time: *a long while.* **2.** once in a while, occasionally. **3. worth one's while,** worth time, pains, or expense. ◇*conj.* Also, **whilst. 4.** during or in the time that: *Stay here while I'm out.* **5.** although: *While he loved her, he was unable to marry her.* ◇*v.t.* **6.** to cause (time) to pass, esp. in some easy or pleasant manner (usu. fol. by *away*): *to while the day away in the sun.* [OE]

whilst /waɪlst/, *conj.* while.

whim /wɪm/, *n.* an odd or fanciful idea or desire. [probably from Scand]

whimper /ˈwɪmpə/, *v.i., v.t.* **1.** to cry with low, sorrowful, broken sounds. ◇*n.* **2.** a whimpering cry or sound. [frequentative of *whimp* (now Brit d.) whine]

whimsical /ˈwɪmzɪkəl/, *adj.* **1.** given to odd ideas. **2.** (of thoughts, actions, etc.) of the nature of or coming from a whimsy. **3.** of an odd, quaint, or comical kind. —**whimsicality,** *n.*

whimsy /ˈwɪmzi/, *n., pl.* **-sies. 1.** an odd or fanciful notion. **2.** a product of playful fancy, such as a small written piece. Also, **whimsey.**

whine /waɪn/, *v.,* **whined, whining,** *n.* ◇*v.i.* **1.** to utter a high-pitched, complaining cry or sound, from discontent, annoyance, etc. **2.** to complain continually, often causing annoyance. **3.** (of machines, etc.) to give out a high-pitched, continuous sound. ◇*v.t.* **4.** to utter with a whine. ◇*n.* **5.** a whining complaint, sound, or tone. [OE] —**whiny,** *adj.*

whinge /wɪndʒ/, *v.i.,* **whinged, whingeing.** to complain; whine.

whinny /ˈwɪni/, *v.,* **-nied, -nying,** *n., pl.* **-nies. 1.** (of a horse) to utter its characteristic cry; neigh. ◇*n.* **2.** the sound produced. [from WHINE in (now obs.) sense 'whinny']

whip /wɪp/, *v.,* **whipped** or **whipt, whipping,** *n.* ◇*v.t.* **1.** to strike with quick, repeated strokes of something long, thin and flexible; lash. **2.** to beat with a whip, etc., esp. to punish; flog; thrash. **3.** to drive (*on, out, in,* etc.) by strokes. **4.** to bring (*in, into line, together,* etc.), as a party whip (def. 15). **5.** to pull, grab, seize, put, etc., with a sudden movement (fol. by *away, out, up, into,* etc.): *to whip out a gun.* **6.** to take, steal (fol. by *off*). **7.** to cover (rope, etc.) with cord, thread, etc. wound about it. **8.** to gather by sewing a turned edge with small stitches and drawing up the thread. **9.** to beat (eggs, cream, etc.) with a fork, etc. ◇*v.i.* **10.** to move or go quickly and suddenly (*away, off, out, in,* etc.); dart; whisk. **11.** to beat about, as a flag does in the wind. ◇*v.* **12. whip up, a.** to create quickly: *I will whip up a meal in no time.* **b.** to move to strong anger, excitement, etc.: *That speech will whip up the crowd.* ◇*n.* **13.** an instrument to strike with, usu. for driving animals or for punishing, typically consisting of a flexible lash attached to a rod. **14.** a whipping strike or movement. **15.** *Govt.* Also, **party whip.** a party manager in a parliament, who supplies information to members about government business, organises their attendance for voting, etc. [ME]

whipbird /ˈwɪpbɜd/, *n.* a bird whose call ends with a sound like the crack of a whip, esp. the **eastern whipbird,** of coastal and mountain forests from northern Qld to Vic.

whipcord /ˈwɪpkɔd/, *n.* **1.** a fabric of firmly-twisted wool yarn with a diagonally ribbed surface. **2.** a type of strong, hard-twisted cord, sometimes used for the lashes of whips.

whiplash /ˈwɪplæʃ/, *n.* **1.** the lash of a whip. **2.** an injury to the spine, usu. in the neck area, caused by sudden movement forwards or backwards, esp. in a motor accident.

whippersnapper /ˈwɪpəsnæpə/, *n.* a person, usu. young and unimportant, who pretends to be important.

whippet /ˈwɪpət/, *n.* a dog like a greyhound, used esp. in rabbit hunting and racing. [n. use of obs. v., to frisk, orig. in the phrase *whip it* move briskly]

whipping /ˈwɪpɪŋ/, *n.* **1.** a beating given with a whip, etc., usu. for punishment; flogging. **2.** an arrangement of cord, etc., whipped or wound about a thing.

whipping boy, *n.* → scapegoat (def. 1).

whip-round /ˈwɪp-raʊnd/, *n. Colloq.* a collection of money taken without notice, usu. to buy a present for someone leaving, etc.

whip snake, *n.* any of a group of thin snakes in which the scaling of the tail is like a braided whip.

whirl /wɜl/, *v.i.* **1.** to turn round, spin, or revolve rapidly. **2.** to move, travel, or be carried rapidly along on wheels. ◇*v.t.* **3.** to cause to turn round, spin, or rotate rapidly. **4.** to drive, send, or carry along with great speed. ◇*n.* **5.** the act of whirling. **6.** a quick turn or swing. **7.** a short drive, run, walk, etc. **8.** rapid movement in events, affairs, feelings, etc. **9. give it a whirl,** *Colloq.* to make an attempt. [ME, from Scand]

whirligig /ˈwɜlɪgɪg/, *n.* something that whirls, revolves, or goes round, esp. a toy such as a top. [from WHIRL. See GIG[1]]

whirlpool /ˈwɜlpul/, *n.* a whirling movement of water, formed by the meeting of

whirlpool opposing currents, by the acting together of winds and tides, etc.

whirlwind /'wɜlwɪnd/, *n.* **1.** a mass of air rotating rapidly round and towards a more or less vertical axis, and moving over the surface of the land or sea. **2.** anything like a whirlwind in violent activity. [ME, from Scand. See WHIRL, WIND¹]

whirr /wɜ/, *v.*, **whirred, whirring**, *n.* ◊*v.i.* **1.** to go, fly, revolve, or otherwise move quickly with a vibrating or buzzing sound. ◊*n.* **2.** the act or sound of whirring: *the whirr of wings*. Also, **whir**. [ME, from Scand]

whisk¹ /wɪsk/, *v.t.* **1.** to draw, grab, move, carry, etc., lightly and quickly. ◊*v.i.* **2.** to sweep, pass, or go lightly and quickly. ◊*n.* **3.** a quick, sweeping stroke; light, rapid movement. [ME, from Scand: wipe]

whisk² /wɪsk/, *v.t.* **1.** to whip (eggs, cream, etc.) to a froth with a beating device. ◊*n.* **2.** a small bunch of grass, straw, hair, etc., used as a brush. **3.** a kitchen tool, in one form a bunch of loops of wire held together in a handle, for beating or whipping eggs, cream, etc. [ME, from Scand: wisp]

whisker /'wɪskə/, *n.* **1.** a single hair of the beard. **2.** (*pl.*) the beard or moustache. **3.** one of the long, stiff, bristly hairs growing about the mouth of certain animals, such as the cat, rat, etc. **4. by a whisker**, *Colloq.* by a very small amount. [ME]

whisky /'wɪski/, *n., pl.* **-kies**. ◊*n.* **1.** a distilled spirit made from grain, such as barley, rye, oats, etc. **2.** a single drink of whisky. Also, *US and Irish,* **whiskey**. [short for *whiskybae*, from Gaelic: water of life]

whisper /'wɪspə/, *v.i.* **1.** to speak with soft, low sounds, using the breath, lips, etc., without vibration of the vocal cords. **2.** to talk softly and privately (often in telling tales, plotting, etc.). **3.** (of trees, water, breezes, etc.) to make a soft, rustling sound. ◊*v.t.* **4.** to utter (soft, low sounds), using the breath, lips, etc. **5.** to tell privately or secretly. ◊*n.* **6.** the type of utterance, or the voice, of one who whispers. **7.** a sound, word, remark, etc. made by whispering. **8.** a soft, rustling sound. **9.** private information; rumor. [OE]

whist, *n.* a card game played by four players, two against two, with 52 cards. [earlier *whisk*, ? special use of WHISK¹, altered by confusion with *whist* silence!]

whistle /'wɪsl/, *v.*, **-tled, -tling**, *n.* ◊*v.i.* **1.** to make a kind of clear musical sound, by the forcing of breath through a small opening formed by shaping the lips, or through the teeth, together with the help of the tongue. **2.** to make such a sound by passing air or steam through a particular device. **3.** (of birds) to give out similar sounds from the mouth. **4.** (of a bullet) to move, go, pass, etc., with a high-pitched sound. ◊*v.t.* **5.** to produce by whistling: *to whistle a tune*. **6.** to call, direct, or signal by or as if by whistling: *to whistle the children to come home*. ◊*v.* **7. whistle for**, to ask or wish for (something) without result. ◊*n.* **8.** a small wooden or tin pipe, for producing whistling sounds by the breath, steam, etc. **9.** a sound produced by or as if by whistling. **10. wet one's whistle**, *Colloq.* to satisfy one's thirst, usu. with alcohol. [OE] —**whistling**, *n.*

whistler /'wɪslə/, *n.* **1.** any of a large number of birds found in Australia which have loud tuneful calls. **2.** any of various birds whose wings whistle in flight.

Whistler /'wɪslə/, *n.* **James Abbott McNeill**, 1845–1903, US painter and etcher, living in England and France after 1855.

whit /wɪt/, *n.* (*used esp. in negative phrases*) a bit; jot: *not a whit better*.

white /waɪt/, *adj.*, **whiter, whitest**, *n.* ◊*adj.* **1.** of the color of pure snow, reflecting all or nearly all the rays of sunlight; achromatic. **2.** light or relatively light in color: *white wine; white coffee*. **3.** relating to the Caucasian race. **4.** controlled by or for white people only. **5.** pale, from fear, pain, etc. **6.** (used of hair) silvery or grey. **7.** snowy: *a white Christmas*. **8.** kindly or good: *white magic*. **9.** pure or innocent. ◊*n.* **10.** a white color. **11.** the quality or condition of being white. **12.** (*sometimes cap.*) a member of the white or Caucasian race. **13.** something white, or a white part of something: *white of the eye*. **14.** the clear, sticky fluid which surrounds the yolk of an egg; albumen. **15.** (*pl.*) white or off-white clothing worn for sports, esp. cricket. [OE]

White /waɪt/, *n.* **Patrick Victor Martindale**, 1912–90, born in England, Australian novelist, playwright, short-story writer, and poet; Nobel prize for literature 1973; works include the novel *The Tree of Man* (1955).

white ant, *n.* a wood-eating insect, not related to a true ant but like ants having social organisation and often forming very large colonies which destroy trees, wooden fences, etc.; termite.

White Australia Policy, *n.* an unofficial term which referred to the Australian government's restricted immigration policy; began in the 1850s with restrictions being placed on the number of Chinese on the goldfields and later spreading to include other races. The term was eliminated from all government documents in 1945.

whitebait /'waɪtbeɪt/, *n., pl.* **-bait**. any small delicate fish cooked and eaten whole.

white blood cell, *n.* → leucocyte.

white-breasted sea-eagle, *n.* an eagle, skilled at hunting fish, other birds and small mammals, of Australian coasts and some inland waters, and certain areas of Asia.

whitecap /'waɪtkæp/, *n.* a wave with a broken white top.

white cedar, *n.* a large rainforest tree of eastern Australia, frequently planted in dry inland areas.

white cockatoo, *n.* → sulphur-crested cockatoo.

white-collar /'waɪt-kɒlə/, *adj.* belonging or relating to workers in professional or clerical positions, who traditionally wear a suit, white shirt and tie.

white elephant, *n.* **1.** an annoyingly useless possession. **2.** a possession of great value but which causes even greater expense.

white ensign, *n.* the flag carried by ships of the Royal Australian Navy.

white-eye /'waɪt-aɪ/, *n.* any of a family of small, chiefly tropical, singing birds of Australia, most species of which have a ring of white feathers round the eye, e.g. the silver-eye.

white feather, *n.* a symbol of cowardice.

whitefish /'waɪtfɪʃ/, *n., pl.* **-fishes**, (*esp. collectively*) **-fish**. a fish for eating, of any kind except herring, any of the salmon species or any species of migratory trout.

white flag, *n.* an all-white flag, used to indicate surrender or truce.

white gold, *n.* any of several gold alloys with a white color due to the presence of nickel or platinum.

Whitehall /'waɪthɒl/, *n.* the British government or its policies. [from *Whitehall* a street in central London flanked by government offices]

white heat, *n.* **1.** great heat, under which a substance, usu. metal, glows with white light. **2.** a state of great activity, excitement, feeling, etc.: *to work at white heat.*

white hope, *n.* someone who is expected to bring glory, etc., to a country, team, etc.

White House, *n.* **the, 1.** the official residence of the president of the US, at Washington, DC. **2.** the US president's office; the executive branch of the Federal government.

white lead, *n.* basic white powdered lead carbonate, used as a pigment, in putty, and in ointments for burns.

white leghorn, *n.* a pure white fowl raised for eggs and flesh.

Whiteley /'waɪtli/, *n.* Brett, 1939–92, Australian painter; Archibald Prize winner.

white lie, *n.* a lie made for polite, friendly or pardonable reasons.

white light, *n.* light which contains all the wave-lengths of the visible spectrum.

white man's burden, *n.* the supposed duty of the white race to care for and educate peoples of other races. [coined by Rudyard KIPLING]

white noise, *n.* an electronically produced noise in which all audible frequencies are equally represented.

white paper, *n.* an official report or policy proposal of a government on a particular subject.

white pointer, *n.* → **white shark**.

white shark, *n.* the largest of the man-eating sharks, growing to a length of 13 metres. Also, **white pointer**.

white slave, *n.* a white woman who is sold or forced to serve as a prostitute, esp. outside her native land. — **white slavery**, *n.*

white spirit, *n.* a mixture of petroleum hydrocarbons used as a solvent for paints and varnishes and as a substitute for turpentine.

white tie, *n.* (a white bow tie worn with) the most formal style of evening dress for men, which includes a coat with tails (distinguished from *black tie*).

whitewash /'waɪtwɒʃ/, *n.* **1.** a mixture of lime or chalk and water, used for whitening walls, ceilings, etc. **2.** anything used to cover up faults or errors, or give an incorrect appearance of respectability, honesty, etc. **3.** *Colloq.* (in various games) a defeat in which the loser fails to score. ◇*v.t.* **4.** to whiten with whitewash. **5.** to cover up faults, errors, etc., of by some means. **6.** *Colloq.* (in various games) to subject to a whitewash.

white water, *n.* water with a broken foaming surface, as shallow water rushing over rocks.

whither /'wɪðə/, *Archaic; now replaced by* **where**. ◇*adv.* **1.** to what place or to what? ◇*conj.* **2.** to what, whatever, or which place, point, end, etc. [OE]

whiting[1] /'waɪtɪŋ/, *n.* **1.** in Australia, any of many species of fish of estuary and sea, highly prized for sport and table. **2.** elsewhere, any of several European species of the cod family. [ME, ? alteration of OE: kind of fish]

whiting[2] /'waɪtɪŋ/, *n.* pure white chalk (calcium carbonate) which has been ground and washed, used in making putty, whitewash, etc.; calcite.

Whitlam /'wɪtləm/, *n.* **(Edward) Gough**, born 1916, Australian Labor politician, prime minister 1972–75; Australian ambassador to UNESCO 1983–86.

whitlow /'wɪtloʊ/, *n.* an inflammation of the deeper tissues of a finger or toe. [ME, from WHITE + FLAW[1]]

Whitman /'wɪtmən/, *n.* **Walt(er)**, 1819–92, US poet; author of the collection *Leaves of Grass* (1855).

Whit Sunday /wɪt 'sʌndeɪ/, *n.* the seventh Sunday after Easter, celebrated as a festival in commemoration of the descent of the Holy Spirit on the day of Pentecost. [ME *whytsonenday*, OE *Hwīta Sunnandæg*, lit., white Sunday, from the white (baptismal) robes worn on that day]

Whittington /'wɪtɪŋtən/, *n.* **Richard** (**'Dick'**), died 1423, lord mayor of London 1398, 1406–07, and 1419–20, about whom many legends survive.

whittle /'wɪtl/, *v.*, **-tled, -tling**. ◇*v.t.* **1.** to cut, trim, or shape (a stick, piece of wood, etc.) by taking off bits with a knife. **2.** to cut off (a bit or bits). **3.** to make less (esp. fol. by *down*): *to whittle down expenses.* ◇*v.i.* **4.** to cut bits or chips from wood, etc., with a knife. [alteration of ME: knife, from OE: whittle]

Whittle /'wɪtl/, *n.* **Sir Frank**, born 1907, English aircraft designer; developed the jet engine.

Whitton /'wɪtn/, *n.* **John**, 1820–98, Australian railway engineer, born in England; responsible for the main lines linking Sydney to the Qld and Vic borders.

whiz[1] /wɪz/, *v.*, **whizzed, whizzing**, *n.* ◇*v.i.* **1.** (of something passing quickly through

whiz /wɪz/, *n. Colloq.* **3.** a fast movement producing such a sound. Also, **whizz**. [imitative]

whiz[2] /wɪz/, *n. Colloq.* a person who shows great ability in a particular field; expert: *a whiz at maths*. [? abbreviation of WIZARD]

who /huː/, *pron.; poss.* **whose**; *obj.* **whom**. ◇*interrog. pron.* **1.** what person?: *Who told you so?* **2.** (of a person) what? (as to character, origin, position, importance, etc.): *Who is the man in uniform?* ◇*relative pron.* **3.** the person that: *I know who did it.* **4.** (as a simple relative, linked with person(s) stated): *We saw men who were at work.* **5. who's who**, the people who carry influence or importance in society. [OE]

WHO /dʌbəlju eɪtʃ 'oʊ/, *n.* → **World Health Organisation**. [abbrev.]

whoa /woʊ/, *interj.* stop! (used esp. to horses).

who'd /huːd/, shortened form of *who would*.

whodunit /huː'dʌnɪt/, *n. Colloq.* a novel, play, etc., dealing with a murder and the finding of the criminal.

whoever /huː'ɛvə/, *pron.; possessive* **whosever**; *objective* **whomever**. ◇*indef. rel. pron.* **1.** whatever person, or anyone that: *Whoever wants it may have it.* ◇*interrog. pron.* **2.** *Colloq.* who ever?; who? (used to give force): *Whoever is that?* Also, *Poetic*, **whoe'er**.

whole /hoʊl/, *adj.* **1.** making up the full quantity, amount, number, etc.; entire, full, or total. **2.** containing all the elements properly belonging; complete: *a whole set.* **3.** in one piece: *to swallow a thing whole.* **4.** *Maths.* integral: *a whole number.* **5.** undamaged or unbroken; intact. **6.** sound; healthy. **7.** fully developed and balanced in all areas: *educated to be a whole person.* **8.** being fully or entirely such: *a whole brother.* ◇*n.* **9.** the entire quantity, amount, or number. **10.** a thing complete in itself. **11.** a group of parts seen together as one thing. **12. on the whole**, in general. [OE]

wholegrain /'hoʊlɡreɪn/, *adj.* → **wholemeal**.

wholehearted /'hoʊlhɑːtəd/, *adj.* sincere; earnest.

wholemeal /'hoʊlmiːl/, *adj.* (of flour or bread) prepared with the complete wheat grain.

whole note, *n. US Music.* → **semibreve**.

whole number, *n.* an integer without fractions, such as 0, 1, 2, 3, 4, 5, etc.

wholesale /'hoʊlseɪl/, *n., adj., adv., v.,* **-saled, -saling**. ◇*n.* **1.** the sale of goods in large quantities, usu. to shop owners, etc., rather than direct to the public (opposed to *retail*). ◇*adj.* **2.** of, relating to, or employed in sale by wholesale. **3.** on a large scale: *wholesale slaughter.* **4.** with no exception: *wholesale discharge of workers.* ◇*adv.* **5.** in a wholesale way: *He will refuse it wholesale.* ◇*v.t., v.i.* **6.** to sell by wholesale.

wholesome /'hoʊlsəm/, *adj.* **1.** leading to moral or general well-being; salutary; beneficial: *wholesome advice.* **2.** good for bodily health; healthful; salubrious: *wholesome food; wholesome air.* **3.** suggestive of health, esp. in appearance. **4.** healthy or sound. [ME, from *hol* WHOLE + *-sum* -SOME[1]]

who'll /huːl/, shortened form of *who will* or *who shall*.

wholly /'hoʊlli, 'hoʊli/, *adv.* entirely; totally; altogether; quite.

whom /huːm/, *pron.* the objective case of **who**. [OE]

whoop /wuːp/, *n.* **1.** a loud cry or shout, usu. made by children, etc. **2.** the sound characteristic of whooping cough. ◇*v.i., v.t.* **3.** to utter with or as if with a whoop or whoops. [OE: threaten]

whoopee /'wuːpi/ *for defs 1 and 2*; /wuː'piː/ *for def. 3*, *Colloq.* ◇*n.* **1.** uproarious festivity. **2. make whoopee**, to enjoy wild merry-making. ◇*interj.* **3.** (a shout of 'whoopee'.) [extended var. of WHOOP]

whooping cough /'huːpɪŋ kɒf/, *n.* an infectious disease of the air passages, esp. of children, marked by a series of short, sharp coughs followed by the taking-in of a deep breath accompanied by a whooping sound.

whoops /wʊps/, *interj.* (an exclamation of mild surprise, upset, etc.). Also, **whoops-a-daisy**.

whoosh /wʊʃ/, *n.* a loud rushing noise, usu. of water or air.

whop /wɒp/, *v.t.,* **whopped, whopping**. *Colloq.* **1.** to strike with force. **2.** to defeat soundly. [orig. uncert.]

whopper /'wɒpə/, *n. Colloq.* **1.** something unusually large of its kind. **2.** a big lie.

whore /hɔː/, *n., v.,* **whored, whoring**. ◇*n.* **1.** a woman who is paid for sex; prostitute. ◇*v.i.* **2.** to act as a whore. **3.** to have sexual relations with whores. [OE]

who're /'huːə/, shortened form of *who are*.

whorl /wɜːl/, *n.* **1.** a circular arrangement of like parts, as in leaves, flowers, etc., round a point. **2.** one of the turns of a spiral shell. **3.** one of the principal ridge-shapes of a fingerprint, forming at least one complete circle. [ME] —**whorled**, *adj.*

who's /huːz/, shortened form of *who is* or *who has*.

whose /huːz/, *pron.* **1.** the possessive case of the relative and interrogative pronoun *who*: *the man whose book I borrowed.* **2.** possessive case of the relative pronoun *which*: *the pen whose point is broken.* [OE]

whosoever /huːsoʊ'ɛvə/, *pron., possessive* **whosesoever**; *objective* **whomsoever**. whoever; whatever person. Also, *Poetic*, **whosoe'er**.

who've /huːv/, shortened form of *who have*.

why /waɪ/, *adv., conj., n., pl.* **whys**, *interj.* ◇*adv.* **1.** for what?; for what cause, reason, or purpose? ◇*conj.* **2.** for what cause or reason. **3.** for which (after *reason*, etc., to introduce a relative clause): *the reason why he refused.* **4.**

why   1172   **wild**

the reason for which: *That is why I raised this question again.* ◇*n.* **5.** the cause or reason: *the whys and wherefores.* ◇*interj.* **6.** (an expression of surprise, hesitation, etc.): *Why, it is all gone!* [OE]

Whyalla /waɪˈælə/, *n.* a city in SA, on the north-western shore of Spencer Gulf; iron and steel. Pop. 26 900 (1986).

wick /wɪk/, *n.* a bundle or loose twist of soft threads, often cotton, which in a candle, etc., draws up the melted wax to be burned at its top end. [OE]

wicked /ˈwɪkəd/, *adj.* **1.** evil or morally bad in principle or practice; iniquitous; sinful. **2.** playfully naughty. **3.** *Colloq.* ill-natured: *a wicked horse.* [ME] **—wickedness**, *n.*

wicker /ˈwɪkə/, *n.* **1.** a slender, but strong, flexible twig of willow easily bent or woven. **2.** Also, **wickerwork**. articles made of plaited or woven twigs. ◇*adj.* **3.** consisting of or made of wicker. [ME, from Scand]

wicket /ˈwɪkət/, *n.* **1.** a small door or gate, esp. one beside, or forming part of, a larger one. **2.** a gate by which a flow of water is controlled, often to turn a waterwheel. **3.** *Cricket.* **a.** either of the two frameworks, each consisting of three stumps with two bails across their tops, at which the bowler aims the ball. **b.** an area between the wickets, esp. with reference to the state of the ground. **c.** the period during which two players bat together. **d.** the achievement by the fielding side of dismissing a batsman. **4. a good wicket**, *Colloq.* profitable or lucky circumstances: *to be on a good wicket.* [ME, from AF, from Scand]

wicket-keeper /ˈwɪkət-kipə/, *n. Cricket.* the player on the fielding side who stands behind the wicket to stop balls that pass it.

wide /waɪd/, *adj.*, **wider**, **widest**, *adv.*, *n.* ◇*adj.* **1.** having great extent from side to side; broad; not narrow. **2.** having a certain extent from side to side: *three metres wide.* **3.** of great range. **4.** open to the full or a great extent; expanded; distended: *to stare with wide eyes.* **5.** too far or too much to one side: *a wide ball in cricket.* ◇*adv.* **6.** to a great, or relatively great, extent from side to side. **7.** over a large space or area: *scattered far and wide.* **8.** to the full extent of opening: *to open the eyes wide.* **9.** fully: *to be wide awake.* **10.** away from or to one side of a point, mark, purpose, etc.; aside; astray: *The shot went wide.* ◇*n.* **11.** *Cricket.* a bowled ball that passes outside the batter's reach, and counts as a run for the side batting. [OE]

wide-angle /ˈwaɪd-æŋgəl/, *adj.* (in photography) relating to a camera lens with a wide angle of view and a short focal length.

widely /ˈwaɪdli/, *adv.* **1.** over a wide area. **2.** through or by many people: *He is widely known.* **3.** in many subjects, etc.: *She has read widely.* **4.** greatly; very: *two widely different cases.*

widen /ˈwaɪdn/, *v.t., v.i.* to make or become wide or wider; expand.

widespread /ˈwaɪdsprɛd/, *adj.* **1.** spread over a wide space. **2.** happening in many places or among many people.

widgie /ˈwɪdʒi/, *n. Colloq.* a female bodgie[2].

widow /ˈwɪdoʊ/, *n.* **1.** a woman whose husband has died and has not married again. **2.** (used in combination) a woman whose husband is often absent, because of his devotion to work, sport, etc.: *a golf widow.* ◇*v.t.* **3.** to make (someone) a widow (us. in passive): *She is widowed.* [OE] **—widowhood**, *n.*

widower /ˈwɪdoʊə/, *n.* a man whose wife has died and has not married again.

widow's peak, *n.* a point formed by the hair growing down in the middle of the forehead.

width /wɪdθ/, *n.* **1.** extent from side to side; breadth; wideness. **2.** a piece of the full wideness: *a width of cloth.*

wield /wild/, *v.t.* **1.** to exercise (power, authority, influence, etc.), usu. in ruling or controlling. **2.** to handle (a weapon, instrument, etc.). [ME *welde(n)*, OE *wieldan* control, from *wealdan* rule, govern, c. G *walten*]

wife /waɪf/, *n., pl.* **wives** /waɪvz/. **1.** a woman joined in marriage to a man (her husband). **2.** a woman (*archaic* except in compounds): *housewife, midwife.* [OE: woman, wife]

wig /wɪg/, *n., v.*, **wigged**, **wigging**. ◇*n.* **1.** an artificial covering of hair for the head. **2.** the wool on a sheep's face and head. ◇*v.t.* **3.** to supply with a wig. **4.** *Agric.* to remove wool from around the eyes (of a sheep) so that it does not become wool blind. [short for *periwig*, from F]

wiggle /ˈwɪgəl/, *v.*, **-gled**, **-gling**, *n.* ◇*v.i.* **1.** to move or go with short, quick, irregular movements from side to side. ◇*v.t.* **2.** to cause to wiggle. ◇*n.* **3.** a wiggling movement. **4.** a wavy line. [ME, frequentative of *wig* (now Brit d.) wag] **—wiggly**, *adj.*

wigwam /ˈwɪgwɒm/, *n.* an American Indian hut, usu. of rounded or oval shape, formed of poles overlaid with bark, mats, or skins. [NAmer Ind: dwelling]

Wik-Munkan /wɪk-ˈmʊŋkən/, *n.* an Australian Aboriginal language of Cape York, Qld.

Wilberforce /ˈwɪlbəfɔs/, *n.* **William**, 1759–1833, British statesman, philanthropist, and religious writer; campaigned successfully against slavery.

wilco /ˈwɪlkoʊ/, *interj.* message received and will be obeyed (used in signalling and telecommunications). [shortened form of *will comply*]

wild /waɪld/, *adj.* **1.** living in a state of nature, as animals that have not been tamed or domesticated. **2.** (of plants, fruit, honey, etc.), growing or produced without the care of humans. **3.** (of land), not used by humans. **4.** (of certain tribes, etc.) uncivilised; barbarous. **5.** violent; furious: *wild fighting.* **6.** crazy; frantic: *to drive someone wild.* **7.** lawless; undisciplined; unruly: *wild children.* **8.** uncontrolled; unrestrained: *wild gaiety.* **9.** lacking reason or judgment: *wild schemes*. **10.** disorderly; dishevelled: *wild hair*. **11.** *Colloq.* intensely eager: *He is wild about going.* **12. wild and woolly,** *Colloq.* **a.** rough; untidy. **b.** uncontrolled; uncivilised. ◇*adv.* **13.** in a wild manner; wildly. **14. run wild, a.** to grow without care or control. **b.** to behave in an uncontrolled manner. ◇*n.* **15.** (*oft. pl.*) a waste; wilderness; desert. **16. in the wild,** in natural surroundings, far from the influence of civilisation. [OE]

wildcat /'waɪldkæt/, *n., adj., v.,* **-catted, -catting.** ◇**1.** a large undomesticated cat. **2.** a quick-tempered or fierce person. **3.** an exploratory well drilled in an effort to discover deposits of oil or gas. ◇*adj.* **4.** marked by or proceeding from irresponsible or unsafe business methods: *wildcat companies.* **5.** of or relating to an unauthorised undertaking or product. ◇*v.i.* **6.** to search for oil, minerals, etc., as an independent prospector.

wildcat strike, *n.* a strike which has not been called or approved by officials of a trade union.

Wilde /waɪld/, *n.* **Oscar (Fingal O'Flahertie Wills)** /fɪŋgəl oʊ'flɛətɪ/, 1854–1900, Irish dramatist, poet, novelist, essayist, and critic.

wildebeest /'wɪldəbist/, *n., pl.* **-beests.** → **gnu.** [Afrikaans: wild beast]

wilderness /'wɪldənəs/, *n.* **1.** a wild region, as of forest, desert, etc.; area inhabited by wild animals only. **2.** a part of a garden set apart for plants growing unchecked. **3.** a confusing mass or collection. [OE: of wild beasts]

wildfire /'waɪldfaɪə/, *n.* **1.** a substance which burns easily, and is difficult to put out when lit. **2.** something that runs or spreads with great rapidity: *The news spread like wildfire.* **3.** sheet lightning, not followed by thunder.

wild flower, *n.* the flower of a plant that grows in a wild or uncultivated state. Also, **wildflower.**

wildfowl /'waɪldfaʊl/, *n.* **1.** a game bird, esp. a wild duck or goose. **2.** game birds collectively.

wild-goose chase, *n.* **1.** a wild or pointless chase after something non-existent or unobtainable. **2.** any senseless attempt to gain an object or end.

wildlife /'waɪldlaɪf/, *n.* animals living in their natural surroundings.

wild oat, *n.* **1.** Also, **black oat.** a common grass or weed which looks like the cultivated oat. **2. sow one's wild oats,** to live a wild life, esp. in one's youth.

wild rose, *n.* any uncultivated species of rose, usu. having a single flower with the corolla consisting of one circle of roundish spreading petals.

Wild West, *n.* the western frontier region of the US before the establishment of settled government, esp. as used as a setting for cowboy films and stories.

wile /waɪl/, *n.* **1.** (*oft. pl.*) an artful or misleading procedure. **2.** trickery; deceitful cunning. [ME, probably from Scand]

wilful /'wɪlfəl/, *adj.* **1.** done purposely; intentional: *wilful murder.* **2.** self-willed; headstrong: *a wilful child.* [OE: willing. See WILL[2], -FUL]

Wilhelm /'wɪlhɛlm/, *n.* **Mount,** a peak in the Western Highlands province of PNG. About 4694 m.

Wilkes /wɪlks/, *n.* **1. Charles,** 1798–1877, US rear admiral and Antarctic explorer. **2. John,** 1727–97, English politician, journalist, and writer.

Wilkins /'wɪlkənz/, *n.* **1. Sir George Hubert,** 1888–1958, Australian explorer and pioneer of polar aviation. **2. Maurice Hugh Frederick,** born 1916, NZ-born British biochemist; contributed to the discovery of the structure of DNA; shared Nobel prize for physiology or medicine (1962) with Francis Crick and James Watson.

wilkintie /wɪl'kɪntɪ/, *n.* See **hopping-mouse.** [Aboriginal]

will[1] /wɪl/; *weak forms* /wəl, l/, *v. pres. sing. and pl.* **will**; *past sing. and pl.* **would**; *old forms* **thou wilt; thou wouldst.** *There is no imperative or infinitive.* ◇*aux. v.* **1.** am (is, are, etc.) about or going to: *I will cut his hair.* **2.** am (is, are, etc.) willing to: *I will help you.* **3.** am (is, are, etc.) expected or required to: *They will have me arrive on time.* **4.** may be expected or supposed to: *This will be right.* **5.** am (is, are, etc.) determined or sure to (used emphatically): *People will talk.* **6.** am (is, are, etc.) accustomed to: *He would write for hours at a time.* ◇*v.t., v.i.* **7.** to wish; desire; like: *as you will.* [OE *wyllan*]

will[2] /wɪl/, *n., v.,* **willed, willing.** ◇*n.* **1.** the power of choosing one's own actions. **2.** the act or process of using this power. **3.** wish or desire: *to give in against one's will.* **4.** purpose or determination: *to have the will to succeed.* **5.** attitude (good or ill) towards another. **6.** *Law.* **a.** a person's declaration of intention, spoken or written, concerning arrangements to take effect after their death. **b.** the document containing such a declaration. **7. at will,** at one's choice: *to wander at will.* **8. a will of one's own,** a strong power to act according to one's own wishes. ◇*v.t.* **9.** to give by will or testament. **10.** to influence or control by force of will: *We willed the rain to stop.* **11.** to decide by act of will. ◇*v.i.* **12.** to exercise the will. **13.** to determine or decide, as by act of will. [OE *willa*]

Willandra Lakes /wɪˌlændrə 'leɪks/, *n.pl.* a series of dry lakebeds and river courses in south-western NSW; important archaeological site.

William I /'wɪljəm/, *n.* **1.** (*William the Conqueror*), Duke of Normandy, 1027–87; king of England 1066–87, first Norman king.

William III, *n.* (*Prince of Orange*), 1650–1702, king of Great Britain and Ireland 1689–1702 (successor to and nephew of James II, and husband of Mary II). Also, **William of Orange.**

Williams /'wɪljəmz/, *n.* **Tennessee** (*Thomas Lanier Williams*), 1911–83, US dramatist; plays such as *A Streetcar Named Desire* (1947) examine frustration and tension, esp. in the southern US.

Williamson /ˈwɪljəmsən/, n. **1. David**, born 1942, Australian playwright and scriptwriter; plays include *Don's Party* (1973). **2. J(ames) C(assius)**, 1845–1913, Australian actor and theatrical entrepreneur, born in the US; co-founder of The Firm which changed its name to JC Williamson Ltd in 1911.

Williamstown /ˈwɪljəmztaʊn/, n. a suburb of Melbourne, Vic, on Port Phillip Bay; important in the 1800s for its port facilities. Pop. 23 287 (1986).

William Tell, n. →Tell.

William the Conqueror, n. →William I (def. 1).

Willie wagtail, n. a common black and white Australian fantail bird. Also, **Willy wagtail**.

willing /ˈwɪlɪŋ/, adj. **1.** able or agreeing (without any great desire): *willing to take a risk.* **2.** cheerfully agreeing or ready: *a willing worker.* **3.** done, given, used, etc., with cheerful readiness: *The waiter gave us willing service.* **4.** of or relating to someone who overcharges or makes great demands: *That salesman is a bit willing.* —**willingness**, n.

will-o'-the-wisp /ˈwɪl-ə-ðə-wɪsp/, n. **1.** flitting phosphorescent light seen at night, mainly over marshy ground, and supposed to be caused by spontaneous combustion of gas from decomposed organic matter. **2.** anything that tricks or misleads by attracting.

willow /ˈwɪloʊ/, n. **1.** (the wood of) a tree or shrub which has tough but easily bent branches used for basketwork, etc. **2.** *Colloq.* a cricket bat. [OE]

willowy /ˈwɪloʊi/, adj. **1.** easily bent; pliant. **2.** gracefully slender.

willpower /ˈwɪlpaʊə/, n. **1.** control over one's desires and actions. **2.** strength of will: *He has great willpower.*

Wills /wɪlz/, n. **William John**, 1834–61, Australian explorer, born in England; with Robert O'Hara Burke undertook an expedition to explore central Australia in 1860; both men died of starvation.

willy-nilly /ˈwɪli-ˈnɪli/, adv. **1.** regardless of whether one is willing or not: *He did his own thing willy-nilly.* **2.** without order: *His clothes were thrown willy-nilly about the room.* [from phrase *will I (he, ye), nill I (he, ye); nill* be unwilling]

willy-willy /ˈwɪli-wɪli/, n. a spiralling wind, often collecting dust, waste matter, etc. [Aboriginal]

Wilpena Pound /ˌwɪlpinə ˈpaʊnd/, n. a large natural rock basin and national park in the Flinders Ranges, SA. [Aboriginal: place of bent fingers]

Wilson /ˈwɪlsən/, n. **1. Sir (James) Harold**, born 1916, British Labour statesman; prime minister 1964–70. **2. Thomas) Woodrow** /ˈwʊdroʊ/, 1856–1924, 28th president of the US, 1913–21; Nobel Peace prize 1919.

Wilsons Promontory, n. a mountainous peninsula in Vic; the southernmost point of the Australian mainland. [named by Governor Hunter after Thomas *Wilson*, a London merchant trading with Australia]

wilt¹ /wɪlt/, v.i. **1.** to lose stiffness and firmness; wither: *The flower wilted.* **2.** to lose strength, confidence, etc. ◇v.t. **3.** to cause to wilt. [d. var. of *wilk* wither]

wilt² /wɪlt/, n. *Bot.* any of various plant diseases in which the leaves lose their firmness and then dry, usu. because water cannot pass through the plant. [special use of WILT¹]

Wiltshire /ˈwɪltʃɪə, -ʃə/, n. a county in southern England. Pop. 545 200 (1986 est.); 3478 km². *Administrative centre:* Trowbridge. *Abbrev.:* Wilts

wily /ˈwaɪli/, adj., **-lier, -liest.** sly; crafty; cunning. [ME, from WIL(E) + -Y¹] —**wiliness**, n.

Wimmera /ˈwɪmərə/, n. a district in western Vic, extending from the Grampians in the south to the Mallee district in the north, and from the SA border in the west to St Arnaud in the east; important pastoral area.

wimp /wɪmp/, n. *Colloq.* a timid, weak or ineffectual person. [? from *Wimpy* the timid character in the comic strip *Popeye*]

wimple /ˈwɪmpəl/, n. a woman's headcloth drawn in folds about the chin, formerly worn out of doors, and still in use by some nuns. [OE]

win /wɪn/, v., **won, winning**, n. ◇v.i. **1.** to succeed by effort (sometimes fol. by *out*). **2.** to gain a victory. ◇v.t. **3.** to get by effort; gain: *to win honor.* **4.** to be successful in (a game, battle, etc.). **5.** to reach (a point, goal, etc.): *to win the shore in a storm.* **6.** to bring (*over*) to favor, agreement, etc.; persuade: *He was won over by her charm.* **7.** to persuade to love or marriage. ◇n. **8.** an act of winning; success; victory. [OE: work, fight, bear] —**winner**, n.

wince /wɪns/, v., **winced, wincing**, n. ◇v.i. **1.** to shrink, as in pain or from a blow; start; flinch. ◇n. **2.** a shrinking movement; a slight start. [ME]

winch /wɪntʃ/, n. **1.** the handle of a revolving machine. **2.** a windlass turned by a crank, for hoisting, etc. **3.** any one of a number of contrivances for cranking. ◇v.t. **4.** to lift or move by means of a winch. [OE]

wind¹ /wɪnd/, n. **1.** air in natural motion. **2.** a gale; storm; hurricane. **3.** any stream of air, as that produced by a fan, etc. **4.** air containing the scent of an animal. **5.** a hint or slight sign: *get wind of the scandal.* **6.** breath or breathing: *He needed good wind for playing the flute.* **7.** empty talk: *Your opinion is just wind.* **8.** gas coming from the stomach and bowels. **9.** See **second wind**. **10.** *Music.* a wind instrument or wind instruments collectively. **11.** Some special uses are:
break wind, to expel air through the anus.
close to the wind, 1. *Naut.* sailing as near as possible to the direction from which the wind is blowing. **2.** taking a knowing risk. **3.** breaking or nearly breaking rules of taste, etc.
get the wind up, *Colloq.* to take fright.

in the wind, 1. likely to happen: *A marriage is in the wind.* **2.** spreading as a rumor: *His promotion is in the wind.*
take the wind out of one's sails, to defeat, discomfit, or rob of an advantage.
◇*v.t.* **12.** to make short of wind or breath: *to be winded by the exercise.* **13.** to remove the breath momentarily, as by a blow. **14.** to let recover breath: *We'll rest and wind the animals.* [OE]

wind[2] /waɪnd/, *v.*, **wound, winding,** *n.*
◇*v.i.* **1.** to change direction; bend; turn: *The path winds through the forest.* **2.** to have a circular or spiral course or direction: *The stairs wind up to an attic.* **3.** to proceed in an indirect or roundabout way: *Her explanation wound on.* ◇*v.t.* **4.** to roll (thread, etc.) into a ball, etc. **5.** to remove or take off by unwinding (fol. by *off*). **6.** to tighten the spring of (oft. fol. by *up*): *to wind a clock.* **7.** to make (one's or its way) in a winding or bending course. ◇*v.* **8. wind down, a.** to relax after a period of tension or activity. **b.** (of a clock) to run down. **c.** to reduce the size or force of (an operation). **d.** to lower by winding. **e.** to end action, speech, etc. **9. wind up,** *Colloq.* **a.** to end: *He'll wind up in trouble; to wind up a project.* **b.** to bring to a condition of great tension. ◇*n.* **10.** a winding; a bend or turn. [OE]

windbag /ˈwɪndbæg/, *n.* **1.** *Colloq.* someone who is full of empty talk. **2.** the bag of a bagpipe.

windbreak /ˈwɪndbreɪk/, *n.* a growth of trees, structure of boards, etc., serving as a shelter from the wind.

windcheater /ˈwɪntʃitə/, *n.* any close-fitting garment for the upper part of the body, worn to give protection against the wind.

Windermere /ˈwɪndəmɪə/, *n.* Lake, a lake in north-western England in Cumbria; the largest lake in England. 17 km long; 14.5 km[2].

windfall /ˈwɪndfɔl/, *n.* **1.** something, such as fruit, blown down by the wind. **2.** an unexpected piece of good fortune.

wind gauge /ˈwɪnd ˌgeɪdʒ/, *n.* → anemometer.

windhover /ˈwɪndhɒvə/, *n.* → nankeen kestrel. [WIND[1] + HOVER]

winding /ˈwaɪndɪŋ/, *n.* **1.** the act of someone or something which winds. **2.** a bend or turn. **3.** a coiling, folding, or wrapping. **4.** something that is wound or coiled. **5.** *Elect.* **a.** a symmetrically laid, electrically conducting current path in any device. **b.** the manner of such coiling: *a series winding.* ◇*adj.* **6.** bending or turning; sinuous. **7.** (of stairs, etc.) spiral.

winding sheet, *n.* **1.** a sheet in which a body is wrapped for burial. **2.** a mass of wax that has run down and hardened on the side of a candle.

wind instrument /ˈwɪnd ˌɪnstrəmənt/, *n.* a musical instrument sounded by the player's breath or any current of air.

windjammer /ˈwɪndʒæmə/, *n.* a large sailing ship.

windlass /ˈwɪndləs/, *n.* **1.** a device for raising weights, etc., usu. consisting of a horizontal cylinder or barrel turned by a crank, lever, etc., upon which a cable or the like winds. ◇*v.t.* **2.** to raise or move by means of a windlass. [ME. from *windel* to wind + *-as* pole (from Scand)]

windmill /ˈwɪndmɪl, ˈwɪn-/, *n.* **1.** a mill or machine for grinding or pumping, operated usu. by the wind acting on a set of revolving arms or sails. **2. tilt at windmills,** to fight imaginary enemies (in allusion to Cervantes' *Don Quixote*).

window /ˈwɪndoʊ/, *n.* **1.** an opening in the wall of a building, the cabin of a boat, etc., for the admission of air and light, commonly fitted with a frame containing panes of glass. **2.** anything like a window in appearance or function. [ME, from Scand]

window-dressing /ˈwɪndoʊˌdrɛsɪŋ/, *n.* **1.** the act or fact of preparing a display in a shop-window. **2.** the presentation of the most favorable aspect of something, esp. when unpleasant facts are hidden.

window-shop /ˈwɪndoʊʃɒp/, *v.i.*, **-shopped, -shopping.** to look at articles in shop windows instead of actually buying. —**window-shopper,** *n.* —**window-shopping,** *adj.*, *n.*

windpipe /ˈwɪndpaɪp, ˈwɪn-/, *n.* the trachea.

windrow /ˈwɪndroʊ, ˈwɪnroʊ/, *n.* a row, as of hay, leaves, timber, etc., raked or swept together. [WIND + ROW[1]]

windscreen /ˈwɪndskrɪn, ˈwɪn-/, *n.* the sheet of glass which forms the front window of a motor vehicle.

windsock /ˈwɪndsɒk, ˈwɪn-/, *n.* a wind-direction indicator, used at airports and elsewhere, consisting of a long cone of textile material, flown from a mast. Also, **airsock, wind cone, wind sleeve.**

Windsor[1] /ˈwɪnzə/, *n.* **1.** Formerly, **Guelph.** the British royal house since 1917; comprises the kings George V, Edward VIII, George VI, and Queen Elizabeth II. **2. Duchess of** (*Wallis Warfield Simpson*), 1896–1986, US divorced socialite, whose marriage to Edward VIII forced his abdication. **3. Duke of.** →**Edward VIII.**

Windsor[2] /ˈwɪnzə/, *n.* **1.** a town in England, in Berkshire, on the Thames; site of **Windsor Castle**, a residence of English sovereigns since William the Conqueror. Pop. 30 054 (1981). **2.** a town in central eastern NSW, on the Hawkesbury River, just west of Sydney; one of the Five Towns founded by Governor Macquarie in 1810. Pop. (with Richmond) 17 088 (1986).

windsurf /ˈwɪndsəf/, *v.i.* to ride a windsurfer.

windsurfer /ˈwɪndsəfə/, *n.* **1.** → **sailboard.** **2.** a person who windsurfs. [Trademark]

wind-tunnel /ˈwɪnd-tʌnəl, ˈwɪn-/, *n.* a tunnel-like device through which a controlled

wind-tunnel

airstream can be drawn at various speeds, in order to subject scale models of aircraft, parts of aircraft, or complete aircraft, to air motion tests.

windvane /'wɪndveɪn/, *n.* a device using a moving arm with a vertical vane to show the direction of the wind.

windward /'wɪndwəd/, *adv.* **1.** towards the wind. ◇*adj.* **2.** relating to, situated in, or moving towards the direction from which the wind blows (opposed to *leeward*). ◇*n.* **3.** the point from which the wind blows. **4.** the side towards the wind. **5. get to the windward of**, to get the advantage of.

Windward Islands, *n.pl.* an island group in the West Indies, comprising the southern part of the Lesser Antilles; includes Dominica, Martinique, St Lucia, St Vincent, and Grenada.

windy /'wɪndi/, *adj.*, **windier**, **windiest**. **1.** accompanied by wind: *windy weather*. **2.** swept by the wind: *a windy hill*. **3.** towards the wind; windward. **4.** empty; unsubstantial. **5.** characterised by or causing flatulence. **6.** *Colloq.* frightened; nervous. [OE]

wine /waɪn/, *n.*, *adj.*, *v.*, **wined**, **wining**. ◇*n.* **1.** the fermented juice of the grape, in many varieties (red, white, sweet, dry, still, sparkling, etc.) used as a drink, and in cookery, religious rites, etc. **2.** a particular variety of such fermented grape juice: *port and sherry wines*. **3.** the juice, fermented or unfermented, of various other fruits or plants, used as a drink, etc.: *gooseberry wine*. **4.** a dark reddish color. **5.** something that cheers, or makes light-headed like wine. ◇*adj.* **6.** wine-colored. ◇*v.t.* **7.** to entertain with wine. ◇*v.i.* **8.** to drink wine. [OE]

wine-tasting /'waɪn-teɪstɪŋ/, *n.* a social gathering to try various wines.

wing /wɪŋ/, *n.* **1.** either of the two front forelimbs of birds and bats which are used for flight. **2.** either of two corresponding parts in certain flightless birds, such as emus and penguins. **3.** (in insects) one of the thin, flat, movable extensions from the back of the thorax by means of which the insects fly. **4.** a similar structure with which gods, angels, demons, etc., are thought to fly. **5.** flight; departure: *to take wing*. **6.** something likened to a wing, such as a sail of a windmill. **7.** *Aeron.* the part of the main supporting surface placed to one side of an aeroplane. **8.** *Archit.* a part of a building placed on one side of a central or main part. **9.** (in the RAAF and certain other air-forces) a number of squadrons, operating together as a tactical unit. **10.** (*pl.*) an emblem worn by a trained pilot. **11.** *Hockey*, *Rugby*, *Soccer*, *etc.* (a player in) either of the two areas of the pitch near the touchline, known as the left and right wings. **12.** *Theat.* the part hidden from the audience on the right or left of the stage proper. **13.** a group within a political party: *right wing of the ALP*. **14. in the wings**, quietly ready to take action when needed. **15. on the wing**, in flight; flying. **16. under one's wing**, in or into one's care. **17.** to supply with wings. **18.** to make (one's way) by or as by flying: *He winged his way home*. **19.** to wound (a bird, person, etc.) in the wing, arm, or other non-vital part. ◇*v.i.* **20.** to travel on or as on wings; fly. [ME, from Scand]

wing chair, *n.* a large upholstered chair, with winglike parts projecting from the back above the arms.

Winged Victory /wɪŋd 'vɪktəri/, *n.* a marble statue (c. 200 BC) of the Greek goddess Nike, found at Samothrace and now in the Louvre, Paris.

winger /'wɪŋə/, *n. Hockey*, *Rugby*, *Soccer*, *etc.* a player on the wing.

wing nut, *n.* a nut (def. 10) which has two flat projecting wings allowing it to be turned by thumb and forefinger. Also, **butterfly nut**.

wingspan /'wɪŋspæn/, *n.* the distance between the wingtips of an aeroplane, bird, or insect. Also, **wingspread**.

wink /wɪŋk/, *v.i.* **1.** to close and open the eyes quickly; blink. **2.** to close and open one eye quickly, often as a signal. **3.** to shine with little flashes of light; twinkle. ◇*v.t.* **4.** to close and open (an eye) quickly. **5.** to signal by a wink. ◇*n.* **6.** the act of winking. **7.** the time taken for a wink; twinkling: *The accident happened in a wink*. **8.** a little flash of light; twinkle. **9. forty winks**, *Colloq.* a short sleep. [OE]

winkle /'wɪŋkəl/, *n.*, *v.*, **-kled**, **-kling**. ◇*n.* **1.** any of various marine gastropods; periwinkle. ◇*v.t.* **2.** *Colloq.* to get (something) out with effort, as a winkle from its shell (fol. by *out*): *to winkle out the information*. [short for PERIWINKLE¹]

winning /'wɪnɪŋ/, *n.* **1.** the act of someone or something that wins. **2.** (*usu. pl.*) something won. ◇*adj.* **3.** that wins: *the winning entry*. **4.** charming (of a person, manners, qualities, ways, etc.): *a winning smile*.

winnow /'wɪnoʊ/, *v.t.* **1.** to free (grain, etc.) from chaff, dirt, etc., by means of wind or driven air; fan. **2.** to blow upon, as the wind does upon grain in this process. **3.** to subject to some process of separating or distinguishing; analyse critically: *to winnow a mass of statements*. ◇*v.i.* **4.** to free grain from chaff by wind or driven air. ◇*n.* **5.** a device for winnowing grain, etc. **6.** the act of winnowing. [OE, from WIND¹] —**winnower**, *n.*

winsome /'wɪnsəm/, *adj.* pleasing or charming: *a winsome smile*. [OE, from *wyn* joy + -*sum* -SOME¹] —**winsomeness**, *n.*

winter /'wɪntə/, *n.* **1.** the coldest season of the year. **2.** a whole year as represented by this season: *a man of sixty winters*. **3.** a period of decline, decay, inactivity, hardship, etc.: *the winter of life*. ◇*adj.* **4.** of, relating to, or characteristic of winter. **5.** suitable for wear or use in winter. ◇*v.i.* **6.** to spend the winter: *planning to winter in Cairns*. ◇*v.t.* **7.** to keep, feed, or manage (plants, cattle, etc.) during the winter. [OE] —**wintry**, *adj.*

wipe /waɪp/, *v.*, **wiped**, **wiping**, *n.* ◇*v.t.* **1.** to rub lightly with or on a cloth, towel, paper, the hand, etc., to clean or dry. **2.** to remove by rubbing with or on something (usu. fol. by *away*, *off*, *out*, etc.). **3.** to remove as if by rubbing: *Wipe the smile off your face*. ◇*v.*

wipe **4. wipe out**, to destroy completely. **5. wipe the floor with**, *Colloq.* to defeat completely. ◊*n.* **6.** the action of wiping. **7.** a rub, as of one thing over another. [OE]

wipe-out /'waɪp-aʊt/, *n. Colloq.* **1.** *Surfing.* a fall from a surfboard because of loss of balance. **2.** a failure; fiasco. **3.** a blotting out of radio signals by atmospherics, jamming, etc.

wire /'waɪə/, *n., adj., v.,* **wired, wiring.** ◊*n.* **1.** flexible metal, round in section, ranging from a thickness that can just be bent by the hand down to a fine thread. **2.** a length of such material used as a conductor of electricity. **3.** a barbed-wire fence. **4.** a long wire used in a telegraph, telephone, or cable system. **5.** a telegram. **6.** (*pl.*) a system of wires by which puppets are moved. **7. have (get) one's wires crossed**, *Colloq.* to become confused. ◊*adj.* **8.** made of wire. ◊*v.t.* **9.** to supply, fasten or string with a wire. **10.** to set up an electric system of wiring, as for lighting, etc. **11.** *Colloq.* to send (a message) by telegraph. ◊*v.i.* **12.** *Colloq.* to send a telegraphic message. [OE]

wireless /'waɪələs/, *adj.* **1.** having no wire. **2.** of or relating to any of various devices which are operated with or set in action by electromagnetic waves. **3.** of or relating to radio. ◊*n.* **4.** a radio. **5.** a wireless telegraph or telephone, etc. ◊*v.t., v.i.* **6.** to telegraph or telephone by wireless.

wirrah /'wɪrə/, *n.* an Australian rock fish, usu. dull brown with blue spots, or sometimes with bands across the body. Also, **peppermint cod**. [Aboriginal]

wiry /'waɪəri/, *adj.,* **wirier, wiriest,** *n.* ◊*adj.* **1.** like wire in form, stiffness, etc.: *wiry grass.* **2.** thin and muscular. ◊*n.* **3.** a beachworm, growing up to 100 cm long and 1 cm wide, and found in northern NSW and Qld.

Wisconsin /wɪs'kɒnsən/, *n.* a state in the northern central US; a part of the Midwest. Pop. 4 785 000 (1986 est.); 145 439 km². *Cap.*: Madison. *Abbrev.*: Wis or Wisc

wisdom /'wɪzdəm/, *n.* **1.** the quality or condition of being wise. **2.** scholarly knowledge: *the wisdom of the ages.* **3.** wise sayings or teachings. [OE]

wisdom tooth, *n.* the third molar tooth, appearing usu. between the ages of 17 and 25.

wise[1] /waɪz/, *adj.,* **wiser, wisest,** *v.* ◊*adj.* **1.** having the power of judging properly what is true or right. **2.** characterised by or showing such power; shrewd; judicious. **3.** having or characterised by scholarly knowledge; learned; erudite: *wise in the law.* **4.** having information about facts, circumstances, etc.: *We are wiser for his explanations.* **5.** *Colloq.* in the know (about something); alerted; cognisant (oft. fol. by *to*): *I'm wise to your tricks.* **6. none the wiser**, still in ignorance: *Although I've read the book I'm none the wiser about the topic.* **7. put wise**, *Colloq.* **a.** to explain something to. **b.** to warn. ◊*v.* **8. wise up**, *Colloq.* to become aware or informed. [OE]

wise[2] /waɪz/, *n. Archaic.* **1.** a way of proceeding; manner; fashion. **2.** respect; degree: *in no wise.* [OE]

-wise, suffixal use of **wise**[2] in adverbs meaning: **1.** attitude or direction: *lengthwise, clockwise.* **2.** *Colloq.* with reference to: *moneywise.*

wisecrack /'waɪzkræk/, *Colloq. n.* **1.** a smart or amusing remark. ◊*v.i.* **2.** to make wisecracks. —**wisecracker**, *n.*

Wiseman /'waɪzmən/, *n.* **Solomon**, 1777–1838, Australian pioneer, transported from England to NSW in 1806; began Wiseman's Ferry across the Hawkesbury River in 1827.

wish /wɪʃ/, *v.t.* **1.** to want; desire; long for: *I wish to see him.* **2.** to desire (a person or thing) to be: *I wish myself elsewhere; to wish him dead.* **3.** to have wishes of something, good or bad, for: *to wish someone well.* **4.** to bid, as in greeting: *to wish someone a good morning.* **5.** to command; request; entreat: *I wish him to come.* **6.** to force or impose (fol. by *on*): *That was a hard job they wished on me.* ◊*v.i.* **7.** to have a desire or longing. **8.** to express a desire for something: *Blow out the candles and wish.* ◊*v.* **9. wish on** or **upon**, to wish, using something like a charm: *to wish on a lucky coin.* ◊*n.* **10.** a desire, felt or expressed: *Ignore the wishes of others.* **11.** an expression of a wish: *I send my best wishes.* **12.** something wished for: *to get one's wish.* **13.** act of wishing: *to make a wish.* [OE]

wishbone /'wɪʃboʊn/, *n.* a forked bone in front of the breastbone in most birds. [from the superstition that when two people pull the bone apart, the one getting the longer piece will have a wish fulfilled]

wishful /'wɪʃfəl/, *adj.* **1.** having or showing a wish; desirous; longing. **2. wishful thinking**, a belief that a thing will happen or be so, based on one's hopes rather than on reality.

wishy-washy /'wɪʃi-wɒʃi/, *adj.* **1.** washy or watery, as a liquid; thin and weak. **2.** without strength or force; weak.

wisp /wɪsp/, *n.* **1.** a handful of straw, hay, etc. **2.** any small or thin bunch, lock, mass, etc.: *wisps of hair.* **3.** a thin column or trail of smoke, etc. **4.** a small or thin person. [ME] —**wisplike**, *adj.*

wist /wɪst/, *v.* past tense and past participle of **wit**[2].

wisteria /wɪs'tɪəriə/, *n.* a climbing shrub, with handsome bunches of purple or white flowers, much used to cover verandas and walls. [after Caspar *Wistar*, 1761–1818, US anatomist]

wistful /'wɪstfəl/, *adj.* **1.** thoughtful or sad. **2.** showing longing touched with sadness; melancholy; regretful. [obs. *wist* attentive] —**wistfulness**, *n.*

wit[1] /wɪt/, *n.* **1.** the ability to make clever connections between ideas, and so give pleasure and amusement. **2.** a person having such wit. **3.** understanding; intelligence: *wit enough to come in out of the rain.* **4.** (*pl.*) mental abilities; powers of intelligent reasoning: *He has his wits about him.* **5. at one's wits'** (or **wit's**) **end**, at the end of one's mental powers; utterly perplexed. [OE]

wit[2] /wɪt/, v. pres. sing. I **wot**, thou **wost**, he, she, it **wot**, pl. **wit**; past tense and past part. **wist**; pres. part. **witting**. Archaic. ◇v.t., v.i. **1.** to know. ◇v. **2. God wot**, God knows (used to emphasise a statement). **3. to wit**, that is to say; namely. [OE]

witan /ˈwɪtən/, n.pl. Early Eng Hist. the members of the national council. [OE: men of knowledge, councillors]

witch /wɪtʃ/, n. **1.** a person, now esp. a woman, who claims to practise magic, esp. evil magic; a sorceress. **2.** an ugly or dangerous old woman; a hag. **3.** a fascinatingly attractive woman. [OE: practise sorcery]

witchcraft /ˈwɪtʃkrɑːft/, n. the art or practices of a witch; sorcery; magic.

witchdoctor /ˈwɪtʃdɒktə/, n. (in various primitive societies) a person supposed to have magical powers of healing or harming; medicine man.

witchetty grub /ˈwɪtʃəti grʌb/, n. any of various large, white, edible, wood-boring grubs that are the larvae of certain Australian moths and beetles. Also, **witchety grub**. [Aboriginal]

witch-hazel /ˈwɪtʃ-heɪzəl/, n. a shrub of eastern North America, whose bark and leaves are made into medicinal preparations used for swellings, bruises, etc.

witch-hunt /ˈwɪtʃ-hʌnt/, n. **1.** Hist. the searching out of people to be accused of, and killed for, witchcraft. **2.** a strong effort to discover and accuse people of disloyalty, dishonesty, etc., usu. based on slight, doubtful, or unimportant evidence. —**witch-hunting**, n., adj.

with /wɪð, wɪθ/, prep. **1.** in the company of: I will go with you. **2.** in some particular relation to: to mix water with milk; to talk with a friend. **3.** (expressing similarity or agreement): in harmony with him. **4.** (expressing equality or identity): to be level with someone. **5.** on the side of: Are you with us or against us? **6.** Colloq. understanding the train of thought of: Are you with me? **7.** in the same direction as: with the stream. **8.** by the use or means of: to cut with a knife. **9.** in proportion to: Their power increased with their number. **10.** at the same time as: to rise with the dawn. **11.** in regard to: to be pleased with a thing. **12.** according to: It's always the way with him. **13.** by: racked with pain. **14.** against: to fight with evil. **15.** in the care or keeping of: Leave it with me. **16. be (get) with it**, Colloq. **a.** to be (become) aware of a situation: Get with it. He's already married. **b.** to concentrate: I can't get with it today. **c.** to be (become) fashionable: You are with it in that outfit. [OE]

with-, limited prefixal use of *with*, indicating separation or opposition, as in *withdraw*, *withstand*. [ME and OE. See WITH]

withdraw /wɪðˈdrɔː, wɪθ-/, v., **-drew**, **-drawn**, **-drawing**. ◇v.t. **1.** to draw back or away; remove. **2.** to take back; retract: to withdraw a charge. ◇v.i. **3.** to retire; retreat: to withdraw into the kitchen. **4.** to take back a statement or expression. —**withdrawal**, n.

withdrawal symptom /wɪðˈdrɔːəl ˈsɪmptəm, wɪθ-/, n. any upsetting or painful symptom experienced by an addict due to the giving up of an addictive drug.

withdrawn /wɪðˈdrɔːn, wɪθ-/, v. **1.** past participle of **withdraw**. ◇adj. **2.** shy; retiring; modest.

wither /ˈwɪðə/, v.i. **1.** to dry up; shrivel; fade. **2.** to lose freshness (often fol. by *away*). ◇v.t. **3.** to make drooping, shrunken, or dry, from loss of moisture. **4.** to embarrass by a scornful glance. [ME; ? var. of WEATHER] —**withering**, adj.

withers /ˈwɪðəz/, n. pl. the highest part of a horse's or other animal's back, behind the neck.

withhold /wɪðˈhoʊld, wɪθ-/, v., **-held**, **-holding**. ◇v.t. **1.** to hold back; restrain. **2.** to keep from giving: to withhold payment. [ME] —**withholder**, n.

within /wɪðˈɪn, wɪθˈɪn/, adv. **1.** in or into the inner part; inside. **2.** in the mind, heart, or soul; inwardly: He rejoiced within. ◇prep. **3.** in or into the interior of: within a city. **4.** not beyond: within view; within one's lifetime. **5.** at or to some amount not greater than: within two degrees of freezing. **6.** in the sphere or scope of: within the family; within the law. [OE]

without /wɪðˈaʊt, wɪθ-/, prep. **1.** not with; lacking: without help. **2.** free from; excluding: without pain. **3.** beyond the limits, range, etc., of (now used chiefly in opposition to *within*): whether within or without the law. ◇adv. **4.** Archaic. outside. **5.** lacking: We must take this or go without. ◇adj. **6.** lacking money, goods, etc.; destitute: to be without. [OE]

withstand /wɪðˈstænd, wɪθ-/, v., **-stood**, **-standing**. ◇v.t. **1.** to stand or hold out against; resist. ◇v.i. **2.** to stand in opposition. [OE]

witness /ˈwɪtnəs/, v.t. **1.** to see or know by personal presence. **2.** to be present at (an occurrence) as a formal witness or otherwise: He witnessed the shooting. **3.** to bear witness to; testify to: She witnessed that he was the killer. **4.** to declare true by one's signature. **5.** to be the scene of: This room witnessed many former parties. ◇v.i. **6.** to bear witness; testify; (also fol. by *to*). ◇n. **7.** someone who, being present, personally sees or perceives a thing. **8.** a person or thing that gives evidence. **9.** someone who gives testimony in a court of law. **10.** someone who signs a document to declare the genuineness of other signatures on it. **11.** testimony or evidence: to bear witness to the truth of a statement. [OE *witnes*. See WIT[1], n., -NESS]

witticism /ˈwɪtəsɪzəm/, n. a joke; witty remark. [from WITTY; modelled on CRITICISM]

witty /ˈwɪti/, adj., **-tier**, **-tiest**. amusingly clever in expression. [OE, from WIT[1]]

wives /waɪvz/, n. plural of **wife**.

wizard /ˈwɪzəd/, n. **1.** someone who claims to practise magic; magician; sorcerer. **2.** a person of outstanding or great accomplishment (esp. in a particular field). [ME, from *wys* WISE[1] + -ARD] —**wizardry**, n.

wizened /'wɪzənd/, *adj.* dried-up; withered; shrivelled.

wk, *pl.* **wks**. *Abbrev.* **1.** week. **2.** work.

wkt, *pl.* **wkts**. *Abbrev.* wicket.

WNW, *Abbrev.* west-north-west. See Appendix.

wobbegong /'wɒbɪgɒŋ/, *n.* a shark, of the eastern Australian coast, having a flattened body and mottled skin and living on the bottom of the sea. [Aboriginal]

wobble /'wɒbəl/, *v.*, **-bled, -bling,** *n.* ◇*v.i.* **1.** to move from one side and then to the other, because not properly balanced. **2.** to show unsteadiness; tremble; quaver: *His voice wobbled.* ◇*v.t.* **3.** to cause to wobble. ◇*n.* **4.** the act or fact of wobbling. [LG] —**wobbling, wobbly,** *adj.*

wobble board, *n.* a thin rectangular sheet of hardboard approx. 90 cm by 60 cm which is held in both hands and shaken, thus producing a low-pitched booming sound.

Wobbly /'wɒblɪ/, *n., pl.* **-blies.** *Colloq.* a member of the Industrial Workers of the World (trade union).

Woden /'woʊdn/, *n.* the chief Anglo-Saxon god, identical with the Scandinavian Odin. Also, **Wodan, Wotan.**

Wodonga /wə'dɒŋgə/, *n.* →**Albury-Wodonga.** Formerly (1852–76), **Belvoir.**

woe /woʊ/, *n.* **1.** great unhappiness, sorrow, or trouble. **2.** a cause of pain, distress, or sorrow. ◇*interj.* **3.** (an exclamation of grief, or unhappiness). [OE]

woebegone /'woʊbəgɒn/, *adj.* sad or miserable: *He had a woebegone look on his face.*

woeful /'woʊfəl/, *adj.* **1.** full of woe; unhappy. **2.** of poor quality; pitiful: *in woeful condition.* —**woefulness,** *n.*

wog[1] /wɒg/, *n. Colloq. (offensive)* **1.** a native of North Africa or the Middle East, esp. an Arab. **2.** a person of Mediterranean origin, or of similar coloring and appearance. [? short for GOLLIWOG]

wog[2] /wɒg/, *n. Colloq.* **1.** a small insect. **2.** a germ leading to a minor disease.

wogoit /'woʊgɔɪt/, *n.* See **ringtail possum.**

wok /wɒk/, *n.* a large, shallow, round-bottomed, metal bowl used for frying, esp. in Chinese cooking. [Cantonese: cooking pot]

woke /woʊk/, *v.* past tense of **wake.**

woken /'woʊkən/, *v.* past participle of **wake.**

wolf /wʊlf/, *n., pl.* **wolves** /wʊlvz/, *v.* ◇*n.* **1.** a large, wild, flesh-eating mammal of Europe, Asia, and North America, belonging to the dog family. **2.** a cruelly greedy person. **3.** *Colloq.* a man who boldly pursues women. **4. cry wolf,** to give false alarms continually. **5. keep the wolf from the door,** to keep away poverty or hunger. **6. lone wolf,** a person or animal who prefers to be and act alone. ◇*v.t.* **7.** *Colloq.* to eat hungrily. [OE] —**wolfish,** *adj.*

Wolfe /wʊlf/, *n.* **James,** 1727–59, English general, killed at the Battle of Quebec.

wolfhound /'wʊlfhaʊnd/, *n.* a dog of various breeds formerly used in hunting wolves, such as the borzoi.

wolfram /'wʊlfrəm/, *n.* **1.** →**tungsten. 2.** →**wolframite.**

wolframite /'wʊlfrəmaɪt/, *n.* a mineral, iron manganese tungstate, (Fe, Mn)WO$_4$, occurring in heavy, greyish to brownish black tabular or bladed crystals (*sp. gr.*: 7.0–7.5), an important ore of tungsten. Also, **wolfram.** [G]

wolf spider, *n.* the most common ground-tunnelling Australian spider, often mistaken for a funnel-web spider but regarded as harmless to humans.

wolf-whistle /'wʊlf-wɪsəl/, *n., v.,* **-led, -ling.** ◇*n.* **1.** a whistle in approval of an attractive person, typically sliding up to a high note and then sliding down to a low one. ◇*v.t.* **2.** to make such a whistle at (someone). ◇*v.i.* **3.** to whistle in this manner.

Wollongong /'wʊləŋgɒŋ/, *n.* a city on the South Coast of NSW, in the Illawarra district. Pop. 206 803 (1986). [Aboriginal: see, the monster comes]

Wolsey /'wʊlzɪ/, *n.* **Thomas,** 1475?–1530, English cardinal and statesman; lord chancellor 1515–29; adviser to Henry VIII, he was arrested for high treason after his inability to obtain papal consent for Henry's divorce from Catherine of Aragon.

wolves /wʊlvz/, *n.* plural of **wolf.**

woman /'wʊmən/, *n., pl.* **women** /'wɪmən/ *adj.* ◇*n.* **1.** the female human being (distinguished from *man*). **2.** an adult female person (distinguished from *girl*). **3.** a female servant, esp. one who cleans, cooks, etc. **4. kept woman,** a woman maintained as a mistress by one man. **5. old woman,** a man who tends to fuss, gossip, etc. **6. scarlet woman,** a woman known for her frequent sexual relations with men. ◇*adj.* **7.** female: *a woman doctor.* **8.** of, characteristic of, or belonging to women: *woman talk.* [OE from *wīf* female + *man* human being] —**womanly,** *adj.* **womanish,** *adj.*

womanise or **womanize** /'wʊmənaɪz/, *v.i.* **-nised, -nising.** (of a man) to have many casual affairs; philander. —**womaniser,** *n.*

womb /wum/, *n.* **1.** the uterus of the human female and of some of the higher four-legged mammals. **2.** a place of origin, conception, etc. [OE]

wombat /'wɒmbæt/, *n.* **1.** any of several species of large, burrowing marsupials, heavily built with short legs and looking somewhat like small bears. **2. blind as a wombat,** *Colloq.* very blind. [Aboriginal]

women /'wɪmən/, *n.* plural of **woman.**

Women's Electoral Lobby, *n.* an Australian feminist, non-party, political lobby group founded in Melbourne in 1972 and now located throughout Australia. Also, **WEL**

women's liberation, *n.* a movement seeking to end inequality between the sexes. Also, **women's lib.**

womera /ˈwʊmərə/, *n.* →**woomera**.

wompoo pigeon /ˈwɒmpuː ˈpɪdʒən/, *n.* a large, strikingly-colored pigeon of eastern Australia and NG, having deep gurgling notes in its call. [Aboriginal]

won /wʌn/, *v.* past tense and past participle of **win**.

wonder /ˈwʌndə/, *v.i.* **1.** to think curiously: *to wonder about something.* **2.** to be affected with wonder; marvel (oft. fol. by *at*). ◇*v.t.* **3.** to be curious about: *to wonder what happened.* **4.** to feel surprise; marvel at: *I wonder that you went.* ◇*n.* **5.** something strange and surprising: *It is a wonder he refused.* **6.** the emotion created by what is strange and surprising. **7. no wonder,** (it is) not at all surprising (that). [OE] —**wonderment,** *n.*

wonderful /ˈwʌndəfəl/, *adj.* **1.** excellent; delightful. **2.** of a kind to excite wonder; marvellous. [OE] —**wonderfulness,** *n.*

wondrous /ˈwʌndrəs/, *adj.* **1.** wonderful; marvellous. ◇*adv.* **2.** in a wonderful or surprising degree; remarkably. [var. of ME: wonderful]

wonga pigeon /ˈwɒŋɡə ˌpɪdʒən/, *n.* a large ground-dwelling bird, living in heavily timbered areas of eastern Australia. Also, **wonga-wonga**. [Aboriginal]

wonky /ˈwɒŋki/, *adj. Colloq.* **1.** shaky; unsound. **2.** to one side; askew. **3.** unwell; upset. [var. of Brit d. *wanky*, from OE: shaky, unsteady]

wont /woʊnt/, *adj.* **1.** accustomed; used: *She is wont to speak her mind.* ◇*n.* **2.** custom; habit: *She spoke her mind, as is her wont.* [OE: be accustomed]

won't /woʊnt/, *v.* shortened form of **will not**.

Wonthaggi /wɒnˈθæɡi/, *n.* a town in southern Vic, west of Inverloch; formerly a major supplier of coal for the state. Pop. 5346 (1986).

woo /wuː/, *v.t.* **1.** to try to win the favor or love of, esp. with a view to marriage. **2.** to try to win: *to woo fame.* **3.** to invite (an outcome) by one's own action: *to woo one's own destruction.* ◇*v.i.* **4.** to try to win another's love. [OE] —**wooer,** *n.*

wood /wʊd/, *n.* **1.** the hard, fibrous substance making up most of the stem and branches of a tree or shrub, and lying beneath the bark; xylem. **2.** the trunks of trees used for building, etc.; timber. **3.** firewood. **4.** the cask, barrel, or keg in which wine, beer, etc., are stored: *aged in wood.* **5.** *Music.* a wooden wind instrument. **6.** (*oft. pl.*) a large and thick collection of growing trees. **7.** *Golf.* a club with a wooden head. ◇*adj.* **8.** made of wood. **9.** used to store, carry, cut, or shape wood. **10.** living or growing in woods: *a wood owl.* [OE]

woodblock /ˈwʊdblɒk/, *n.* **1.** *Print.* **a.** a block of wood engraved in relief, for printing from; woodcut. **b.** a print from such a block. **2.** a wooden block, used for flooring, road making, etc.; sett. **3.** *Music.* a hollow block used in the percussion section of an orchestra.

woodchip /ˈwʊdtʃɪp/, *n.* **1.** (*pl.*) small pieces of wood, made by mechanically reducing trees to fragments for later industrial use. ◇*adj.* **2.** of or relating to an industry, company, etc., which deals in woodchips.

wood coal, *n.* →**lignite**.

woodcut /ˈwʊdkʌt/, *n.* →**woodblock** (def. 1).

wooden /ˈwʊdn/, *adj.* **1.** consisting or made of wood. **2.** stiff; ungainly; awkward: *a wooden manner of walking.* **3.** without spirit: *a wooden stare.* **4.** (of a sound) as if coming from a hollow wooden object when struck. **5.** (of a wedding anniversary, etc.), showing the fifth event of a series. —**woodenness,** *n.*

wooden leg, *n.* an artificial leg, esp. one made of wood.

Woodfull /ˈwʊdfəl/, *n.* **William Maldon** (*'Bill'*), 1897–1965, Australian cricketer; Test captain in 1932–33 'Bodyline' series.

woodpecker /ˈwʊdpɛkə/, *n.* a stiff-tailed climbing bird, having a hard, chisel-like bill for digging into wood after insects.

wood pulp, *n.* wood reduced to pulp through mechanical and chemical treatment and used in the manufacture of paper.

woodsman /ˈwʊdzmən/, *n., pl.* **-men. 1.** someone used to life in the woods and skilled in hunting, trapping, etc. **2.** someone who works in the woods, esp. a timbergetter.

wood stove, *n.* a type of fuel stove designed to burn wood.

wood tar, *n.* a dark sticky product obtained from wood, which, when distilled, yields creosote, oils, and a final product called **wood pitch.**

Woodward /ˈwʊdwəd/, *n.* **Roger Robert,** born 1943, Australian pianist.

woodwind /ˈwʊdwɪnd/, *n.* (*sing.*, sometimes treated as *pl.*) the group of wind instruments made up of the flutes, clarinets, oboes, and bassoons.

woodwork /ˈwʊdwɜk/, *n.* **1.** objects or parts made of wood. **2.** the interior wooden fittings of a house, etc. **3.** the art or craft of working in wood; carpentry.

woody /ˈwʊdi/, *adj.*, **woodier, woodiest. 1.** covered with woods. **2.** belonging or relating to the woods; sylvan. **3.** consisting of or containing wood; ligneous. **4.** like wood, in hardness, texture, etc.

woof[1] /wʊf/, *n.* **1.** threads which travel from selvage to selvage in a loom, interlacing with the warp; weft. **2.** texture; fabric. [OE]

woof[2] /wʊf/, *n.* **1.** the sound of a dog barking, esp. deeply and loudly. ◇*v.i.* **2.** to make such a sound. [imitative]

woofer /ˈwʊfə/, *n.* a loudspeaker designed for the reproduction of low-frequency sounds.

wool /wʊl/, *n.* **1.** the fine, soft, curly hair that forms the fleece of sheep and certain other animals. **2.** a fibre produced from sheep's fleece, etc., that may be spun into threads, or made into felt, upholstery materials, etc. **3.** cloth made from sheep's wool. **4.** a woollen thread used for knitting, crocheting, etc. **5.** any of various substances used in place of

wool. **6.** any fine thread-like matter resembling the wool of sheep: *steel wool.* **7. dyed in the wool,** firmly established; inveterate: *He's a dyed in the wool opera lover.* **8. pull the wool over one's eyes,** to trick or deceive someone. [OE]

wool classing, *n.* the trade or job of grading wool. —**wool classer,** *n.*

woolclip /'wulklɪp/, *n.* the amount of wool yielded from the yearly shearing season (by a farm, district, etc.). Also, **clip.**

Woolf /wulf/, *n.* **Virginia,** 1882–1941, English novelist and critic; developed the stream-of-consciousness technique in works such as *To the Lighthouse* (1927).

wool-gathering /'wul-gæðərɪŋ/, *n.* daydreaming; absent-mindedness. —**wool-gatherer,** *n.*

woolgrower /'wulgrouə/, *n.* a farmer who raises sheep for wool. —**wool-growing,** *n.*

woollen /'wulən/, *n.* **1.** a cloth made from wool, esp. a soft loose one. **2.** (*pl.*) knitted woollen clothing, esp. jumpers. ◇*adj.* **3.** made or consisting of wool. **4.** of or relating to wool, products made of wool, or their manufacture.

Woolley /'wuli/, *n.* **Sir (Charles) Leonard,** 1880–1960, English archaeologist and explorer.

woolly /'wuli/, *adj.*, **-lier, -liest,** *n., pl.* **-lies.** ◇*adj.* **1.** consisting of or like wool. **2.** clothed or covered with wool or something like it. **3.** not clear or firm: *woolly thinking; a woolly outline.* ◇*n.* **4.** *Colloq.* an article of clothing made of wool. **5.** *Colloq.* a sheep. —**woollily,** *adv.* —**woolliness,** *n.*

woolly butt, *n.* **1.** a type of gum tree with thick fibrous bark found only on the lower part of the trunk. **2.** a tussocky native perennial plant growing in low rainfall areas.

wool press, *n.* a hydraulic press for ramming wool into a wool bale. Also, **wool screw.**

woolshed /'wulʃɛd/, *n.* a large shed for shearing and baling wool.

wool-stapler /'wul-steɪplə/, *n.* a dealer in wool, esp. a person who sorts it according to the staple or fibre, before selling it to the manufacturer. —**wool-stapling,** *adj.*

woomera /'wumərə/, *n.* **1.** Also, **womera.** a type of throwing stick with a notch at one end for holding a dart or spear, used by Australian Aborigines. **2.** (*cap.*) a town in southern SA, west of Lake Torrens; established as a base for the Weapons Research Establishment in 1948 and for the Joint Australian US Defence Space Communications Station at Nurrungar, 16 km south-west, in 1969. Pop. 1805 (1986). [Aboriginal]

Woop Woop, *n. Colloq.* (*joc.*) (*also l.c.*) any remote or backward town or district.

Wootten /'wutn/, *n.* **Sir George Frederick,** 1893–1970, Australian military officer and solicitor; while serving as a major-general during World War II he accepted the Japanese surrender in Borneo in 1945.

woozy /'wuzi/, *adj. Colloq.* **1.** muddled, or stupidly confused. **2.** dizzy, nauseous, etc. **3.** slightly or rather drunk. —**woozily,** *adv.* —**wooziness,** *n.*

wop /wɒp/, *n. Colloq.* (*offensive*). ◇*n.* **1.** an Italian. ◇*adj.* **2.** of or relating to any Latin country, its culture, or inhabitants. [? from It: dandy]

Worcestershire /'wustəʃɪə, -ʃə/, *n.* a former county in western central England; now part of Hereford and Worcester.

word /wɜd/, *n.* **1.** a sound or combination of sounds, or the written or printed letters standing for them, used in any language as the sign of an idea. **2.** *Gram.* such a sign which can stand alone and complete, as *boy* and *boyish,* but not *-ish,* which is less than a word, nor *boy scout,* which is more. **3.** (*oft. pl.*) speech or talk: *Can I have a word with you?* **4.** an utterance or expression, usu. short: *a word of praise; a word of warning.* **5.** (*pl.*) the text of a song as different from the music; lyrics. **6.** (*pl.*) angry speech; a quarrel. **7.** a promise; assurance: *to give or keep one's word.* **8.** news; tidings: *to get word of an accident.* **9.** a password. **10.** command: *His word was law.* **11.** (*cap.*) *Theol.* **a.** the Scriptures, or Bible (oft. **the Word of God**). **b.** the second person of the Trinity; the Logos (oft. **the Word made Flesh**). [transl. of Greek *Logos*] **12.** *Computers.* a unit of information, usu. consisting of a number or a group of alphanumeric characters, in the memory of a computer. **13.** *Archaic.* a proverb; motto. ◇**14.** Some special uses are:
as good as one's word, dependable; reliable.
eat one's words, *Colloq.* to take back something said or written.
have a word with, to speak briefly to.
have words with, to argue with; remonstrate with.
in a word, 1. in short; briefly. **2.** as a summary.
in so many words, openly; plainly; explicitly; unequivocally.
my word! 1. (an expression of agreement). **2.** (an expression of surprise, mild annoyance, etc.)
of one's word, reliable; dependable: *He is a man of his word.*
play on words, the use or arrangement of words that shows up their peculiarities, esp. ambiguities of spelling or pronunciation, such as a pun.
put in a (good) word for, to mention (someone) in a favorable way.
suit the action to the word, to do what one has said one would do.
take one at one's word, to act on the belief that someone means what he says literally.
take the words out of one's mouth, to say exactly what another was about to say.
the last word, 1. a remark that closes an argument. **2.** the very latest or best: *This machine is the last word in automation.*
word for word, 1. (of a repetition, report, etc.) using exactly the same words as the original; verbatim. **2.** translated by means of exact verbal equivalents rather than by general sense.
word of honor, promise.
word perfect, knowing (a lesson, part in a play, formula, etc.) completely and correctly; by rote: *Study this until you are word perfect.*
◇*v.t.* **15.** to express in words; phrase; choose

words to express: *He words his speeches carefully to avoid giving offence.* **16.** *Colloq.* (oft. fol. by *up*) to speak to, esp. when informing beforehand: *He worded up the magistrate.* [OE]

worded /'wɜdəd/, *adj.* expressed by words chosen in a particular way: *a carefully worded report.*

wording /'wɜdɪŋ/, *n.* the form of words in which a thing is expressed; phrasing: *careful wording.*

wordless /'wɜdləs/, *adj.* **1.** speechless; silent; mute. **2.** not put into words; unexpressed.

word processor, *n.* a computer, usu. with keyboard and visual display unit, designed esp. for storing and editing text.

Wordsworth /'wɜdzwɜθ/, *n.* **1.** Dorothy, 1771–1855, English writer. **2.** her brother, **William**, 1770–1850, English romantic poet.

wordy /'wɜdi/, *adj.*, **-dier, -diest.** marked by or given to the use of many, or too many, words; verbose. **—wordily,** *adv.* **—wordiness,** *n.*

wore /wɔ/, *v.* past tense of **wear**.

work /wɜk/, *n., adj., v.,* **worked** or **wrought, working.** ◇*n.* **1.** the physical or mental effort made to make or do something; labor; toil: *Digging a garden is hard work.* **2.** something to be made or done; task; undertaking: *Bring some work home from school.* **3.** productive activity: *to be hard at work.* **4.** the manner of working or quality of workmanship. **5.** *Phys.* **a.** the product of the force acting upon a body and the distance through which it is moved by this force. Derived SI unit is the joule. **b.** the transference of energy from one body or system to another. **6. a.** a job, esp. that by which one earns a living; employment: *to find work.* **b.** a trade or profession: *My work is teaching.* **7.** the materials, things, etc., on which one is working, or is to work: *Bring your work in here where it is warm.* **8.** a product of effort or activity: *a work of art; literary works.* **9.** an engineering structure, such as a building, bridge, dock, etc. **10.** (*pl. oft. treated as sing.*) a place for carrying on some form of labor or industry: *iron works.* **11.** a piece being cut, formed, ground, etc., in a machine tool, grinder, punching machine, etc. **12.** (*pl.*) *Theol.* acts performed in obedience to the law of God; righteous deeds. ◇**13.** Some special uses are:

at work, 1. at one's place of employment. **2.** engaged in working: *Danger, men at work.* **3.** operating; functioning: *Strange forces have been at work in the neighborhood.*

have one's work cut out, to be pressed; have a difficult task.

make short work of, to deal with or finish quickly.

out of work, unemployed.

set to work, to start; begin.

the works, everything there is; the whole lot. ◇*adj.* **14.** of, for, or concerning work: *work clothes.* ◇*v.i.* **15.** to do work, or labor; make efforts (contrasted with *play*): *You should be working, not listening to music.* **16.** to be employed, for one's livelihood: *He works in a laundry.* **17.** (of a machine) to operate; function. **18.** to act or operate effectively: *The plan is working.* **19.** to get or become by continuous effort, friction, etc.: *to work round a difficulty; The screw has worked loose.* **20.** to have an effect or influence (fol. by *on*): *He worked on him for a whole week before he agreed.* **21.** *Mech.* to move improperly, as from defective fitting of parts or from wear. **22.** to undergo treatment by labor in a given way: *This dough works slowly.* ◇*v.t.* **23.** to use or manage (a machine, etc.). **24.** to bring, put, get, make, etc., by effort, or action (fol. by *in, off, out,* etc.): *to work off a debt; to work up a case.* **25.** to get, or cause (something or someone) to go or be (*in, into, up,* etc.) gradually, carefully, or with difficulty: *to work a broom up the chimney.* **26.** to bring about; effect: *to work a change.* **27.** to treat by handling, etc.; manipulate: *to work butter; to work clay.* **28.** to make (a mine, farm, etc.) function in producing. **29.** to act or operate in (an area). **30.** to arrange; contrive: *It'll be difficult but I think I can work it for you.* **31.** to keep (a person, horse, etc.) at work: *to work him hard.* **32.** to move, stir, or excite in feeling, etc. (oft. fol. by *up*): *He worked himself into a frenzy.* **33.** to sew, embroider or knit: *to work a design; to work three rows.* ◇*v.* **35.** Some special uses are:

work a point, *Colloq.* to take an unfair advantage.

work at, to make continuous efforts to achieve or master (something): *Skating isn't easy, you've got to work at it.*

work back, to work after hours at one's place of employment.

work in, 1. to introduce, insert, or cause to penetrate, esp. gradually: *to work in the butter and sugar; He managed to work in the question of money.* **2.** to find room for or fit in, as into a program.

work into, to get (something) into (somewhere) slowly, or with difficulty: *He worked his feet into his boots.*

work off, 1. to get rid of by working: *to work off energy.* **2.** to pay back (a debt) by working.

work one's passage, to pay for one's fare on a sea journey, etc., by working as a member of the crew.

work out, 1. to effect or achieve by effort: *to work out his own salvation.* **2.** to solve: *to work out a mathematical problem.* **3.** to find by thinking: *to work out the answer.* **4.** to calculate (the best way of doing something, etc.): *to work out a plan of action.* **5.** to amount to a total: *It works out at $10 a metre.* **6.** to turn out; prove (good, effective or suitable). **7.** to develop; elaborate: *He doesn't always work out his plots.* **8.** to exhaust (a mine, etc.).

work up, 1. to excite or arouse (feelings, etc.): *to work up an appetite; to work up anger; to get worked up.* **2.** to make (something) bigger and better organised: *to work up notes into an essay.* **3.** to (cause to) move gradually upwards: *to work up to the top of the firm; to work up to a climax.* **4.** to get gradually to something considered as important: *I was working up to that topic.* [OE: act, deed]

workable /'wɜkəbəl/, *adj.* **1.** practicable; feasible. **2.** suitable for being worked.

workaday /ˈwɜkədeɪ/, *adj.* **1.** working; practical; everyday. **2.** dull and ordinary; commonplace; humdrum: *a workaday mind.*

workaholic /wɔkəˈhɒlɪk/, *n.* a person who is addicted to work. [modelled on ALCOHOLIC]

workbench /ˈwɜkbentʃ/, *n.* a bench or table at which someone works.

workbox /ˈwɜkbɒks/, *n.* a box to hold sewing materials.

worker /ˈwɜkə/, *n.* **1.** someone or something that works: *He's a good steady worker.* **2.** someone employed in manual or industrial labor (as opposed to an employer). **3.** someone who works in a particular occupation: *office workers; research workers.* **4.** *Zool.* the sterile or infertile female of bees, wasps, ants, or termites, which does the work of the colony.

workers' compensation, *n.* **1.** a compulsory insurance scheme for employers to cover payments made to employees as compensation for injuries incurred at work or on the way to or from work. **2.** a payment made under such a scheme.

Workers' Educational Association, *n.* → WEA

work force, *n.* all the people in a country, city, etc., who are employed.

workhorse /ˈwɜkhɔs/, *n.* **1.** a horse used for pulling loads, riding after stock, etc., rather than for recreation or sport. **2.** *Colloq.* a person who works very hard.

workhouse /ˈwɜkhaʊs/, *n. Hist.* a publicly supported institution where very poor people lived and worked without pay.

working /ˈwɜkɪŋ/, *n.* **1.** the act of someone or something that works. **2.** the operation; action: *There's something wrong with the working of this machine.* **3.** (*usu. pl.*) a part of a mine or quarry, in which work is being or has been carried on. **4.** (*pl.*) the intermediate stages of a calculation, esp. in mathematics. **5.** disturbed or twisting movements: *the working of his face.* ◇*adj.* **6.** performing work or labor, esp. of a manual, mechanical or industrial kind, (as different from owners, managers, etc.): *a working man.* **7.** (of a machine, etc.) functional or operative. **8.** allowing work of a particular kind to go on: *a working majority; working knowledge of chemistry.* **9.** relating to, connected with, or used in operating or working.

working capital, *n.* **1.** the amount of capital needed to carry on a business. **2.** *Accounting.* current assets minus current liabilities.

working class, *n., pl.* **classes.** the class of people made up mainly of manual workers and laborers; proletariat.

working model, *n.* a model of a machine, etc., with a moving mechanism which reproduces that of the original.

working party, *n.* **1.** a group, committee, etc., appointed to study a problem in detail. **2.** a group of soldiers, prisoners, etc., who are appointed to carry out a special task.

workman /ˈwɜkmən/, *n., pl.* **-men.** **1.** a man employed or skilled in some form of manual, mechanical, or industrial work. **2.** a male worker.

work-out /ˈwɜk-aʊt/, *n.* **1.** a trial match, race, etc. **2.** energetic physical exercise: *He has a work-out in the gym once a week.*

works committee, *n.* **1.** an elected body of employee representatives which consult with management about grievances, working conditions, wages, etc. **2.** a joint council or committee representing employer and employees concerned with similar matters within a factory or office. Also, **works council.**

workshop /ˈwɜkʃɒp/, *n.* **1.** a room or building in which work, esp. mechanical work, is carried on (considered as smaller than a factory). **2.** a group meeting to exchange ideas and study techniques, skills, etc.: *a theatre workshop.*

work-to-rule /wɜk-tə-ˈrul/, *n.* **1.** the deliberate cutting back of output by workers, by strict observation of rules, as a form of industrial action. **2.** → **go-slow.**

world /wɜld/, *n.* **1.** the earth or globe. **2.** (*oft. cap.*) a particular division of the earth: *the New World.* **3.** the earth, with its people, affairs, etc., during a particular period: *the ancient world.* **4.** (*oft. cap.*) a particular section of the world's people: *the Third World.* **5.** mankind; humanity. **6.** the public generally: *The whole world knows it.* **7.** the class of people active in or concerned with the affairs or interests of this life (as opposed to a spiritual life or the afterlife): *The world worships success.* **8.** social or fashionable life, with its ways and interests; society: *to withdraw from the world.* **9.** a particular class of mankind, with common interests, ways, etc.: *the fashionable world; the academic world.* **10.** any area of life, with all that belongs to it: *the world of dreams; the insect world; the world of high finance.* **11.** an entire system of created things; universe; macrocosm. **12.** any complex whole thought of as being like the universe (See **microcosm**): *The living cell is a world in itself.* **13.** someone's private, individual mental life: *She withdrew into her own world.* **14.** one of the three general groupings of physical nature, as the **animal world, mineral world, vegetable world.** **15.** any period or state of existence: *this world; the world to come.* **16.** a very great amount or extent: *A holiday will do you the world of good.* **17.** any indefinitely great expanse or amount: *Whole worlds opened up to him as he dreamed of his business prospects.* **18.** *Colloq.* all that is important, agreeable, or necessary to one's happiness: *You're the world to me.* **19.** any heavenly body: *the starry worlds.* ◇**20.** Some special uses are: **a world of one's own**, the state of being out of touch with other people.

bring into the world, to give birth to or deliver (a child).

come into the world, to be born.

dead to the world, *Colloq.* **1.** sleeping heavily. **2.** totally drunk.

for all the world, **1.** for any consideration, no matter how great: *He wouldn't come for all the world.* **2.** in every respect; exactly: *He looks for all the world like a drug addict.*

for the world or **for worlds**, on any account.

world 1184 **worship**

in the world, at all; ever: *Nothing in the world will make me change my mind*; *Where in the world did you get that hat?*

on top of the world, delighted; elated; exultant.

out of this world, excellent; supremely or sublimely good.

set the world on fire, to be a great success.

think the world of, to think very highly of.

world without end, through all eternity; forever. [OE]

World Bank, *n.* an international bank set up by the UN in 1944 to economically assist developing countries, esp. by loans. Official name, **International Bank for Reconstruction and Development**.

world-class /'wɜld-klas/, *adj.* good enough to be acceptable anywhere in the world.

World Health Organisation, *n.* an agency of the UN, formed in 1948 to improve the health of all countries and control disease by training, the collection of information, and guidance of all kinds. Also, **WHO**.

worldly /'wɜldli/, *adj.*, **-lier**, **-liest**. **1.** concerned or connected with the affairs, interests, or pleasures of this world. **2.** secular (as opposed to *ecclesiastic*, *religious*, etc.). **– worldliness**, *n.*

World War I, *n.* the war, conducted mainly in Europe and the Middle East, between the Triple Entente (Great Britain, France, and Russia, aided by the US, Belgium, Japan, and others) and the Central Powers (Germany and Austria-Hungary, aided by Turkey and Bulgaria) from 28 July 1914, until the Central Powers' surrender on 11 November 1918. Also, **First World War**, **Great War**. *Abbrev.:* WW I

World War II, *n.* the war, conducted mainly in Europe and the Far East, between the Allies (Great Britain and France and later the USSR and the US) and the Axis (Germany, Italy, and Japan), from 3 September 1939, until the surrender of Germany on 8 May 1945, and of Japan on 14 August 1945. Also, **Second World War**. *Abbrev.:* WW II

worm /wɜm/, *n.* **1.** *Zool.* a long, thin, soft-bodied invertebrate. **2.** (in popular use) any small creeping animal with a more or less long, thin body, and without limbs or with very short ones, such as a grub, maggot, etc. **3.** something like a worm in appearance, movement, etc. **4.** a screw or screw thread. **5.** an endless screw (a shaft on which one or more helical grooves are cut), or an apparatus in which this is the main feature. **6.** an endless screw which engages with a worm wheel. **7.** a wretched or miserable person. **8.** something that eats away or destroys slowly. **9.** (*pl.*) *Med.* any disease arising from the presence of parasitic worms in the intestines or other tissues. **10.** (*pl.*) **a can of worms**, *Colloq.* a difficult and complicated situation. ◇*v.i.* **11.** to move or act like a worm; creep, crawl, etc.: *to worm along under a wall*. **12.** to get by roundabout ways (fol. by *out*, etc.): *to worm into the boss's favor*. ◇*v.t.* **13.** to get by persistent, roundabout efforts (esp. fol. by *out* or *from*): *to worm a secret out of a person*. **14.** to free from worms (def. 9). [OE: worm, serpent] **– wormy**, *adj.*

wormcast /'wɜmkast/, *n.* a coil of earth excreted by some worms, such as earthworms and lugworms.

wormhole /'wɜmhoʊl/, *n.* a hole made by a worm in timber, nuts, etc.

Worms /wɜmz/, *n.* **1.** a town in south-western Germany, on the Rhine. Pop. 73 000 (1983). **2. Diet of**, an assemblage held here (1521), at which Luther was condemned as a heretic.

worm wheel, *n. Mech.* a toothed wheel which engages with a revolving worm, or endless screw, in order to receive or give motion. Also, **worm gear**.

wormwood /'wɜmwʊd/, *n.* **1.** a bitter, aromatic herb native to the Old World, formerly much used as a medicine, but now mainly in making absinth. **2.** something bitter or extremely unpleasant; bitterness: *It was gall and wormwood to her to hear her sister praised*. [OE *wermōd*]

worn /wɔn/, *v.* **1.** past participle of **wear**[1]. ◇*adj.* **2.** damaged by wear or use: *worn clothing*. **3.** made very tired: *worn shoulders*.

worn-out /'wɔn-'aʊt/, *adj.* **1.** worn or used until no longer fit for use. **2.** made very tired by use, strain, etc.

worrisome /'wʌrɪsəm/, *adj.* worrying or annoying; causing worry.

worry /'wʌri/, *v.*, **-ried**, **-rying**, *n.*, *pl.* **-ries**. ◇*v.i.* **1.** to feel uneasy or anxious; fret. ◇*v.t.* **2.** to cause to feel uneasy or anxious; trouble; torment; plague, pester, or bother. **3.** to seize (originally by the throat) with the teeth and shake or mangle, as an animal does. **4.** to chase and bite at: *a dog worrying sheep*. ◇*n.* **5.** a cause, feeling or condition of uneasiness or anxiety. [OE: strangle] **– worrier**, *n.*

worse /wɜs/, *adj.*, used as *compar.* of **bad**. **1.** bad, evil, unfavorable, etc., in a greater or higher degree; less good. **2.** in less good condition; in poorer health. **3.** **none the worse for**, not harmed by. **4. the worse for wear**, **a.** showing signs of being worn out; shabby. **b.** *Colloq.* drunk. ◇*n.* **5.** someone or something which is worse. **6. for the worse**, in a worse condition: *a change for the worse*. **7. go from bad to worse**, to become extremely bad. ◇*adv.* **8.** in a more unpleasant, evil, severe, or unfavorable manner. **9.** with more severity, intensity, etc. **10. worse off**, in worse circumstances; poorer; less fortunate or well placed. [OE *wyrsa*]

worsen /'wɜsən/, *v.t.*, *v.i.* to make or become worse.

worship /'wɜʃəp/, *n.*, *v.*, **-shipped**, **-shipping**. ◇*n.* **1.** deeply respectful honor paid to God, or to any person or thing regarded as sacred; adoration. **2.** the giving of such honor in formal ceremony, prayer, etc. **3.** great love or adoration; infatuation: *hero worship*. **4.** (*cap.*) (with *Your*, *His*, *Her*, etc.) a title of honor used esp. in addressing or mentioning certain magistrates in court. ◇*v.t.* **5.** to give religious adoration to (God). **6.** to feel great love or adoration for (any person or thing). ◇*v.i.* **7.** to give religious adoration. **8.** to go to religious

worship services of worship; pray. **9.** to feel great love or adoration. [OE *weorth* WORTH + *-scipe* -SHIP] — **worshipful**, *adj.* — **worshipper**, *n.*

worst /wɜst/, *adj.*, used as superl. of **bad**. **1.** bad, evil, unfavorable, etc., in the greatest or highest degree: *worst behavior; the worst weather.* **2.** most faulty or unsatisfactory: *The worst novel I've ever read.* ◇*n.* **3.** someone or something that is worst or the worst part. **4. come off worst** or **get the worst (of)**, to be beaten (in a competition, fight, etc.). **5. if (the) worst comes to (the) worst,** if the very worst happens. **6. one's worst,** the most harm that a person is able to do: *Let him do his worst.* ◇*adv.* **7.** in the most evil or unfavorable way: *They behave worst when the teacher is away.* **8.** in the greatest degree: *It's hurting worst in my arm.* **9.** in the least satisfactory manner: *the worst-dressed girl in the room.* ◇*v.t.* **10.** to beat (someone) in a competition, fight, etc. [OE *wurresta*]

worsted[1] /ˈwʊstəd/, *n.* **1.** a firmly twisted yarn or thread spun from combed wool, used for weaving, etc. **2.** wool cloth woven from such yarns, having a hard, smooth surface, and no nap. ◇*adj.* **3.** consisting or made of worsted. [named after ME *Worsted*, parish in Norfolk, England (now Worstead)]

worsted[2] /ˈwʊstəd/, *v.* past participle of **worst**.

wort /wɜt/, *n.* a plant; herb; vegetable (now used mainly in combination, as in *liverwort*, etc.). [OE: root, plant]

worth /wɜθ/, *adj.* **1.** good or important enough to deserve (what is specified): *advice worth taking; a place worth visiting.* **2.** equal in value to: *It's worth far more than that.* **3.** having property to the value of: *a man worth millions.* ◇*n.* **4.** excellence: *people of worth.* **5.** usefulness, importance or value: *He has shown the worth of his skill.* **6.** a quantity of something: *a dollar's worth of sausages.* **7.** wealth; value of one's property: *What is his mother worth in shares?* **8. for all one's worth,** with all one's might; to one's utmost. **9. for what it is worth,** even if it is not very good, much use, or true: *I tell you this for what it is worth.* [OE]

worthless /ˈwɜθləs/, *adj.* of no use, importance, or value.

worthwhile /wɜθˈwaɪl/, *adj.* good enough to repay one's time, attention, interest, work, trouble, etc.: *a worthwhile book.*

worthy /ˈwɜði/, *adj.*, **-thier, -thiest**, *n., pl.* **-thies**. ◇*adj.* **1.** of adequate merit or character. **2.** so good as to deserve (oft. fol. by *of*, or an infinitive): *worthy of a better job; worthy to take her place.* ◇*n.* **3.** admirable or respected person: *She is one of the worthies of Ballarat.* **4.** (*oft. joc.*) a person: *There were the three worthies up in the front pew.* — **worthily**, *adv.* — **worthiness**, *n.*

Wotan /ˈvoʊtæn/, *n. Germanic Myth.* the chief of the gods, corresponding to the Anglo-Saxon Woden, and the Scandinavian Odin. [G]

would /wʊd/, *weak forms* /wəd, d/, *v.* past tense of **will**[1] used: **1.** specially in expressing a wish: *I would it were true.* **2.** to express condition: *I would have come had you asked me.* **3.** often in place of *will*, to make a statement or question less direct or blunt: *That would scarcely be fair; Would you be so kind?* [OE *wolde*]

would-be /ˈwʊd-bi/, *adj.* **1.** wishing or pretending to be: *a would-be wit.* **2.** intended to be: *a would-be kindness.*

wouldn't /ˈwʊdənt/, *v.* **1.** short form of *would not.* **2. wouldn't it!** (an exclamation indicating dismay, disapproval, disgust, etc.): *Oh, wouldn't it rain today!*

wound[1] /wund/, *n.* **1.** an injury in which the skin, flesh, an organ, etc., is cut or broken by external violence, not disease. **2.** a similar injury to the tissue of a plant. **3.** an injury to feelings, reputation, etc. ◇*v.t., v.i.* **4.** to hurt by a physical or emotional wound. [OE *wund*]

wound[2] /waʊnd/, *v.* past tense and past participle of **wind**[2] and **wind**[3].

wove /woʊv/, *v.* past tense and occasional past participle of **weave**.

woven /ˈwoʊvən/, *v.* usual past participle of **weave**.

wowser /ˈwaʊzə/, *n. Colloq.* a prudish teetotaller; killjoy. [? Brit d. *wow* to make a complaint; whine; popularly supposed to be an acronym of W(e) O(nly) W(ant) S(ocial) E(vils) R(emedied), a slogan invented by John Norton, Aust journalist and politician, 1862–1916]

wpm, *Abbrev.* words per minute.

WRAAC, *Abbrev.* Women's Royal Australian Army Corps.

WRAAF, *Abbrev.* Women's Royal Australian Air Force.

wrack /ræk/, *n.* **1.** a type of brown seaweed. **2.** a wreck or wreckage. **3.** ruin or destruction; disaster; rack. [ME: wreck, from MD or MLG]

wraith /reɪθ/, *n.* **1.** a ghostlike appearance of a living person, supposed to be seen just before, or as a sign of, that person's death. **2.** a ghost. **3.** someone or something pale, thin, and not solid. [orig. uncert.]

Wran /ræn/, *n.* **Neville Kenneth**, born 1926, Australian state Labor politician, premier of NSW 1976–86.

wrangle /ˈræŋgəl/, *v.*, **-gled, -gling**. ◇*v.i.* **1.** to argue or quarrel, esp. in a noisy or angry manner. ◇*n.* **2.** a noisy or angry quarrel; altercation. [LG: struggle, make uproar] — **wrangler**, *n.*

WRANS, *Abbrev.* Womens Royal Australian Naval Service.

wrap /ræp/, *v.*, **wrapped** or **wrapt, wrapping**, *n.* ◇*v.t.* **1.** to fold material, a covering, around (someone or something) (oft. fol. by *up*): *He wrapped the child (up) in a blanket; to wrap up a parcel.* **2.** to wind, fold, or bind (something) about as a covering: *to wrap a blanket round a child.* **3.** to protect with coverings, garments, etc.: *She wrapped him (up) well against the cold.* **4.** to surround; enfold; envelop; shroud; wreathe. ◇*v.i.* **5.** to become wrapped

wrap about something; fold. ◇*v.* **6. wrap up**, *Colloq.* **a.** to conclude or settle: *to wrap up (a money deal)*. **b.** to put on warm outer garments. ◇*n.* **7.** a scarf, shawl, etc. **8.** (*pl.*) outdoor garments, furs, etc. [b. obs. *wry*, to cover and LAP²]

wrapper /'ræpə/, *n.* **1.** a covering esp. of a sweet, ice cream, etc. **2.** a book jacket. **3.** someone or something that wraps.

wrasse /ræs/, *n.* any of various sea fishes with thick, fleshy lips, powerful teeth, and usu. a brilliant color, certain species being valued as food fishes, such as the **hump-headed wrasse** of the Great Barrier Reef. [Cornish *wrach*, var. of *gwrach*]

wrath /roθ/, *n.* **1.** anger; ire. **2.** punishment or vengeance, as the result of anger: *the day of God's wrath*. [OE: wroth] — **wrathful**, *adj.*

wreak /rik/, *v.t.* to carry out; inflict; execute: *to wreak havoc*; *He wreaked his anger on his son.* [OE *wrecan*]

wreath /riθ/, *n., pl.* **wreaths** /riðz/. **1.** an ornamental circular band of flowers, leaves, etc., esp. as worn on the head as a sign of honor, or placed on a grave as a sign of respect; garland; chaplet. **2.** any ringlike, curving, or curling mass or formation: *a wreath of cloud*. [OE *wræth*]

wreathe /rið/, *v.*, **wreathed; wreathed** or (*Archaic*) **wreathen; wreathing**. ◇*v.t.* **1.** to encircle or adorn with or as if with a wreath. **2.** to surround in curving or curling masses or form: *Mist wreathed the valley*. **3.** to cover: *a face wreathed in smiles*. ◇*v.i.* **4.** to move in curving or curling masses, as smoke.

wreck /rek/, *n.* **1.** the ruin or destruction of a ship or aircraft in the course of navigation. **2.** any ship or aircraft in a state of ruin from disaster. **3.** anything brought to a state of ruin: *My car is just a wreck*. **4.** the ruin or destruction of anything: *the wreck of my hopes*. **5.** someone in very bad physical or mental health. ◇*v.t.* **6.** to cause the loss of (a ship, etc.); shipwreck. **7.** to involve in a wreck (usu. pass.): *The sailors were wrecked on a strange coast*. **8.** to ruin or destroy. [ME, from Scand] — **wrecker**, *n.*

wreckage /'rekɪdʒ/, *n.* **1.** the remains or fragments of something that has been wrecked. **2.** act of wrecking or state of being wrecked.

wrecked /rekt/, *v.* **1.** past tense and past participle of **wreck**. ◇*adj.* **2.** ill or weak because of tiredness or eating or drinking too much: *I'm wrecked after that party last night*.

wren /ren/, *n.* **1.** any of a large number of small birds with long legs and long, almost upright tails, esp. the brightly colored kinds, e.g. the **superb blue wren**, and related kinds, e.g. the **emu-wren** and the **grass-wren**. **2.** any of the European or North American wrens of similar shape. [OE *wrenna*]

Wren /ren/, *n.* **John**, 1871-1953, Australian sports promoter, financier and gambler; said to be the model for Frank Hardy's novel *Power Without Glory*.

wrench /rentʃ/, *v.t.* **1.** to pull, jerk, or force by a violent twist. **2.** to overstrain or injure (the ankle, etc.) by a sudden, violent twist. **3.** to affect distressingly as if by a wrench: *wrenched by sorrow*. ◇*v.i.* **4.** to pull at something with a violent, twisting movement: *He wrenched at the door*. ◇*n.* **5.** a sudden, violent twist. **6.** a sharp, distressing strain to the feelings. **7.** a twisted or forced meaning. **8.** an adjustable spanner. **9.** a spanner. [OE: twist; turn]

wrest /rest/, *v.t.* **1.** to twist or turn; pull, jerk, or force by a violent twist. **2.** to take away by force. **3.** to get by effort: *to wrest a living from the soil*. **4.** to twist or turn from the proper course, use, meaning, etc. ◇*n.* **5.** a wresting; twist; wrench. [OE *wræstan*] — **wrester**, *n.*

wrestle /'resəl/, *v.*, **-tled, -tling**, *n.* ◇*v.i.* **1.** to engage someone in wrestling. **2.** to struggle in a fight for mastery; grapple. **3.** to deal (with a subject) as a difficult task or duty. ◇*v.t.* **4.** to struggle with in wrestling. ◇*n.* **5.** an act of or bout at wrestling. **6.** a struggle. [ME, frequentative of WREST] — **wrestler**, *n.*

wrestling /'reslɪŋ/, *n.* **1.** an exercise or sport in which two people struggle hand to hand, each trying to throw or force the other to the ground. **2.** the act of someone who wrestles.

wretch /retʃ/, *n.* **1.** a very unfortunate or unhappy person. **2.** a person of contemptible character. [OE: exile; adventurer]

wretched /'retʃəd/, *adj.* **1.** very unfortunate in condition or circumstances; miserable; pitiable. **2.** mean or contemptible; despicable. **3.** poor, sorry, or pitiful; worthless: *That wretched sound she makes is meant to be singing*.

wrick /rɪk/, *v.t.* **1.** to wrench or strain; rick. ◇*n.* **2.** a strain. [ME: jerk]

wriggle /'rɪgəl/, *v.*, **-gled, -gling**, *n.* ◇*v.i.* **1.** to twist to and fro, writhe, or squirm. **2.** to move along by twisting and turning the body, as a worm or snake does. **3.** to make one's way by shifts or tricks; worm: *to wriggle out of a difficulty*. ◇*v.t.* **4.** to cause to wriggle. **5.** to bring, get, make, etc., by or as if by wriggling: *He wriggled his way into the tunnel*. ◇*n.* **6.** the act of wriggling; wriggling movement. **7.** a wavy formation or course. **8. get a wriggle on**, to hurry. [MLG] — **wriggler**, *n.* — **wriggly**, *adj.*

wright /raɪt/, *n.* a maker or worker (now mainly in *wheelwright, playwright*, etc.). [OE: worker]

Wright /raɪt/, *n.* **1. Frank Lloyd**, 1869-1959, US architect. **2. Judith Arundel**, born 1915, Australian poet; works include the collections *Woman to Man* (1949), and *Five Senses* (1963). **3. Orville**, 1871-1948, and his brother, **Wilbur**, 1867-1912, US aeronautical inventors; made first powered aeroplane flight, 1903.

wring /rɪŋ/, *v.*, **wrung** or (*Rare*) **wringed; wringing**; *n.* ◇*v.t.* **1.** to twist forcibly: *to wring a chicken's neck*. **2.** to twist and squeeze in order to force out moisture (oft. fol. by *out*): *to wring clothes out*. **3.** to draw out by force: *to wring a confession out of a murderer*. **4.** to

wring affect painfully; torment. **5.** to clasp (another's hand) warmly. **6.** to clasp (one's hands) together in sorrow, etc. **7.** to force (*off*, etc.) by twisting. ◇*v.i.* **8.** to perform the action of wringing something. ◇*n.* **9.** a wringing; forcible twist or squeeze. [OE *wringan*]

wringer /ˈrɪŋə/, *n.* an apparatus or machine which wrings water out of wet clothes; mangle.

wringing /ˈrɪŋɪŋ/, *v.* **1.** present participle of **wring**. ◇*adv.* **2. wringing wet**, very wet; soaked.

wrinkle /ˈrɪŋkəl/, *n., v.,* **-kled, -kling.** ◇*n.* **1.** a ridge or furrow on a usu. smooth surface. ◇*v.t.* **2.** to form a wrinkle or wrinkles in; corrugate; crease. ◇*v.i.* **3.** to become drawn together into wrinkles. [OE *gewrinclod* serrate] – **wrinkly**, *adj.*

wrist /rɪst/, *n.* **1.** the part of the arm between the forearm and the hand. **2.** the joint between the radius and the carpus. [OE]

wristpin /ˈrɪstpɪn/, *n.* a stud or pin sticking out from the side of a crank, wheel, etc., and attaching it to a connecting rod leading to some other part of the mechanism.

writ /rɪt/, *n.* **1.** *Law.* a written order issued in connection with a judicial proceeding. **2.** *Archaic.* something written: *Holy writ* (the Bible). [OE]

write /raɪt/, *v.,* **wrote** or (*Archaic*) **writ; written, writing.** ◇*v.t.* **1.** to trace or form (letters, words) on the surface of some material with a pen, pencil, etc.; inscribe. **2.** to express in writing; give a written account of. **3.** to fill in the blank spaces of (a form, etc.) with writing: *to write a cheque.* **4.** to compose and produce in words or characters: *to write a letter to a friend.* **5.** to produce or create: *to write books; to write music.* **6.** to set down the marks of (usu. in passive): *Honesty is written on his face.* **7.** *US.* to write a letter to (someone): *Write your aunt every week.* ◇*v.i.* **8.** to trace or form words, etc. **9.** (of a pen, etc.) to produce letters, words, etc., in a particular manner: *This pen writes well.* **10.** to be an author of books, articles, poems, etc. **11.** to write a letter, or communicate by letter: *Will you promise to write?* ◇*v.* **12.** Some special uses are:
write down, 1. to set down in writing. **2.** to harm by writing against. **3.** to write in a simple way to be easily understood (fol. by *to*).
write for, to ask or apply for by letter.
write in, to write a letter to a newspaper, business firm, etc.
write off, 1. to cancel, as an entry in an account. **2.** to treat as a nonrecoverable loss: *to write off a ship.* **3.** to consider as dead.
write out, 1. to put into writing. **2.** to write in full form. **3.** to write so much that there is nothing left to write.
write up, 1. to write out in full or in detail: *to write up an essay from notes.* **2.** to bring (a diary, etc.) up to date. **3.** to bring to public notice by writing. **4.** to praise in writing. **5.** *Accounting.* to make an excessive valuation of (an asset).
write oneself off, *Colloq.* **1.** to get very drunk. **2.** to have a car accident. **3.** to give a poor account of oneself. [OE *wrītan*]

write-off /ˈraɪt-ɒf/, *n.* **1.** *Accounting.* something written off from the books. **2.** *Colloq.* something damaged too badly to be repaired, such as a car after an accident. **3.** *Colloq.* an incompetent person; no-hoper.

writer /ˈraɪtə/, *n.* **1.** someone who writes poems, plays, novels, etc. **2.** someone who writes as a full-time occupation.

writhe /raɪð/, *v.,* **writhed; writhed** or (*Archaic or Poetic*), **writhen; writhing;** *n.* ◇*v.i.* **1.** to twist or squirm, as in pain, violent effort, etc. **2.** to shrink mentally, as in discomfort, embarrassment, etc.: *Her rudeness makes me writhe.* ◇*v.t.* **3.** to twist or bend out of shape or position; distort; contort. **4.** to twist (oneself, the body, etc.) about, as in pain. ◇*n.* **5.** a writhing movement. [OE: twist, wind]

writing /ˈraɪtɪŋ/, *n.* **1.** the act of someone or something that writes: *The writing took him a long time.* **2.** the state of being written; written form: *Put it in writing.* **3.** written characters: *We can't read the writing.* **4.** written matter seen in its style, kind, quality, etc.: *There's some fierce writing in that pamphlet.* **5.** handwriting. **6.** an inscription: *some old writing on a tombstone.* **7.** any written or printed paper, document, etc. **8.** literary matter or work, seen in its style, kind, quality, etc.: *It takes time to learn fine writing.* **9.** literary composition or production: *the writings of Shakespeare.* **10. writing on the wall**, an event foretelling disaster, etc.

written /ˈrɪtn/, *v.* past participle of **write**.

wrong /rɒŋ/, *adj.* **1.** not morally right or good; evil; sinful: *Stealing is wrong.* **2.** going aside from truth or fact; erroneous: *wrong information.* **3.** (of a person) not correct in action, opinion, method, etc.; in error: *You are wrong to think she did it.* **4.** not in accordance with a set of rules; not proper: *the wrong way to behave at a table.* **5.** not in accordance with needs or expectations: *to take the wrong road; the wrong way to hold a golf club.* **6.** out of order; awry; amiss: *Something is wrong with this machine.* **7.** not suitable or appropriate: *to say the wrong thing.* **8.** (of a fabric, etc.) relating to or being the side that is less finished, which forms the inner side of a garment, etc. **9. get on the wrong side of**, to incur the anger or disfavor of. **10. get the wrong end of the stick**, to misunderstand. **11. get up on the wrong side (of bed)**, to be bad-tempered. ◇*n.* **12.** that which is not in accordance with morality, goodness, justice, truth, etc.; evil. **13.** an unjust act; injury: *to do a person (a) wrong.* **14.** *Law.* a violation of a right. **15. in the wrong, a.** guilty; worthy of blame. **b.** mistaken; in error. **16. in wrong with**, in disfavor with. ◇*adv.* **17.** in a wrong manner; wrongly; awry or amiss. **18. get (someone) wrong**, to misunderstand (someone). ◇*v.t.* **19.** to treat unfairly or unjustly; injure or harm. **20.** to blame someone unjustly. **21.** to seduce. [OE *wrang*, from Scand] –**wrongly**, *adv.*

wrongdoing /ˈrɒŋduɪŋ/, *n.* evil action or behavior.

wrote /rout/, *v.* past tense of **write**.

wroth /roʊθ, rɒθ/, *adj.* angry; wrathful (used after a verb). Also, *Archaic,* **wrath.** [OE *wrāth*]

wrought /rɔt/, *v.* **1.** *Archaic.* past tense and past participle of **work.** ◊*adj.* **2.** made or formed by manufacture. **3.** produced or shaped by beating with a hammer, etc.: *wrought iron.* **4.** ornamented or elaborated: *a highly wrought design.*

wrought iron, *n.* a fairly pure form of iron (as that produced by treating pig-iron) which contains almost no carbon, which is easily forged, welded, etc., and does not harden when suddenly cooled.

wrung /rʌŋ/, *v.* past tense and past participle of **wring.**

wry /raɪ/, *adj.* **wryer, wryest** or **wrier, wriest. 1.** (of a facial expression) showing dislike or discomfort: *She made a wry face when he suggested a picnic.* **2.** ironically or bitterly amusing: *wry humor.* **3.** abnormally bent or turned to one side; twisted or crooked: *a wry nose.* [OE *wrigian* swerve]

WST, *Abbrev.* Western Standard Time.

WSW, *Abbrev.* west-south-west. See Appendix.

wt, *Abbrev.* weight.

Wuhan /wu'hæn/, *n.* a city in central eastern China, capital of Hubei province, at the junction of the rivers Han and Chang; formed by the union of the cities Hanyang, Wuchang and Hankou. Pop. 2 899 000 (1985 est.).

wuhl-wuhl /'wʊl-wʊl/, *n.* See **jerboa** (def. 1). [Aboriginal]

wurley /'wɜli/, *n.* an Aboriginal hut or shelter made of boughs, leaves and plaited grass. Also, **wurlie.** [Aboriginal]

wurlitzer /'wɜlɪtsə/, *n.* a large electric organ designed mainly for theatres, etc., and with a large number of sound effects which try to reproduce the sounds of an orchestra. [Trademark]

wurrung /'wʌrʌŋ/, *n.* See **nail-tailed wallaby.** [Aboriginal]

wurrup /'wʌrəp/, *n.* See **hare-wallaby.** [Aboriginal]

WWI, *Abbrev.* World War I.

WWII, *Abbrev.* World War II.

Wycherley /'wɪtʃəli/, *n.* **William,** c. 1640–1716, English Restoration dramatist; comedies include *The Country Wife* (1675) and *The Plain Dealer* (1676).

Wyclif /'wɪklɪf/, *n.* **John,** 1320?–1384, English religious reformer and theologian. Also, **Wyclife, Wickliffe, Wiclif.**

wye /waɪ/, *n., pl.* **wyes.** the letter Y, or something having a similar shape.

Wylie /'waɪli/, *n.* an Aborigine who accompanied EJ Eyre on an expedition from SA to the west coast in 1840–41.

Wyndham[1] /'wɪndəm/, *n.* **John** (*John Beynon Harris*), 1903–69, English science fiction writer; author of *The Day of the Triffids* (1951).

Wyndham[2] /'wɪndəm/, *n.* a town in north-western WA, on the Cambridge Gulf; the most northerly port in WA. Pop. 1329 (1986).

Wynne Prize /'wɪn praɪz/, *n.* a prize awarded annually since 1897 for an oil or water-color Australian landscape painting or a figure sculpture in any medium. [named after Richard *Wynne,* 1822–95, whose bequest funded the award]

Wyoming /waɪ'oʊmɪŋ/, *n.* a state in the north-western US. Pop. 507 000 (1986 est.); 253 597 km^2. *Cap.:* Cheyenne. *Abbrev.:* Wyo or Wy —**Wyomingite,** *n.*

Xx

X, x, *n., pl.* **X's** or **Xs, x's** or **xs. 1.** the 24th letter of the English alphabet. **2.** a term used to indicate a person or thing whose true name is unknown or withheld: *The missing Mr X.* **3.** the Roman numeral for 10. **4.** anything shaped like an X.

x, /ɛks/ *Maths. Symbol.* an unknown quantity or a variable.

X, *Symbol.* cross.

xanthic /'zænθɪk/, *adj. Chiefly Bot.* yellow.

Xanthippe /zæn'θɪpi/, *n.* c.469–c.399 BC, the wife of Socrates, known as a nagging, scolding woman. Also, **Xantippe.**

xantho-, a word part meaning 'yellow'. Also, **xanth-.** [Gk, combining form of *xanthós*]

xanthorrhoea /zænθə'riə/, *n.* any plant belonging to the Australian genus which includes the grasstree.

Xavier /'zeɪviə/, *n.* St Francis (*Francisco Javier, 'the Apostle of the Indies'*), 1506–52, Spanish Jesuit missionary, esp. in India and Japan. Also, **Zavier.**

X-axis /'ɛks-æksəs/, *n.* the horizontal axis in a two-dimensional Cartesian coordinate system.

X chromosome, *n.* one of two sex chromosomes controlling sex determination, often paired with a Y chromosome. In humans and most mammals the XX pairing controls femaleness and XY maleness; in poultry and some insects the opposite is true. See **Y chromosome.**

Xe, *Chem. Symbol.* xenon.

xeno-, a word part meaning 'alien', 'strange', 'foreign'. Also, (before a vowel), **xen-.** [Gk, combining form of *xénos*, stranger, guest and *xénos*, foreign, alien]

xenon /'zɛnɒn/, *n.* a heavy, colorless, chemically unreactive monatomic gaseous element present in the atmosphere. *Symbol:* Xe; *at. no.:* 54; *at. wt:* 131.3. See **rare gas.** [Gk: strange]

xenophobia /zɛnə'foʊbiə/, *n.* the fear or hatred of foreigners or strangers. **–xenophobe,** *n.* **–xenophobic,** *adj.*

Xenophon /'zɛnəfən/, *n.* c.434–c.355 BC, Greek historian, writer and soldier; a follower of Socrates.

xero-, a word part meaning 'dry', as in *xerophyte.* Also, before a vowel, **xer-.** [combining form representing Gk *xērós*]

xerography /zɪə'rɒgrəfi/, *n.* a method of dry photographic copying of printed material in which charged ink particles stick to an electrostatic image formed by a photoelectric beam and are fixed by heating. [Gk *xēró(s)* dry + *graphē* writing] **–xerograph,** *n.* **–xerographic,** *adj.*

xerophyte /'zɪərəfaɪt/, *n.* a plant adapted for growth under dry conditions. **–xerophytic,** *adj.*

xerox /'zɪərɒks/, *n.* **1.** (a copy obtained by) a xerographic process. ◇*v.t., v.i.* **2.** to obtain copies (of) by this process. [Trademark]

Xerxes I /'zɜksiz/, *n.* c. 519–465 BC, king of Persia 486?–465, son of Darius I and Atossa.

Xi'an /ʃi'æn/, *n.* a city in central China; capital of Shaanxi province. Pop. 2 276 500 (1984). Formerly, **Sian, Hsian, Siking, Singan, Changan.**

-xion, variant of **-tion,** as in *inflexion, flexion.*

Xizang Autonomous Region /ʃi'zɑŋ/, *n.* an administrative division of south-western China, north of the Himalayas; former theocracy and centre of Buddhism; part of China since 1951. Pop. 1 970 000 (1985 est.); 1 221 600 km^2; elevation about 4880 m. *Cap.:* Lhasa. Formerly, **Sitsang AR.** Also, **Tibet.**

Xmas /'ɛksməs, 'krɪsməs/, *n.* Christmas.

XP /kaɪ'roʊ/, *n.* the Christian monogram made from the first two letters of the Greek word for Christ. [Gk, representing *chi* and *rho*]

X-ray /'ɛks-reɪ, ɛks-'reɪ/, *n.* **1.** *Phys.* (*oft. pl.*) electromagnetic radiation of very short wavelength (5 x 10^{-9} to 6 x $^{-12}$ m) which can penetrate solids, ionise gases, and expose photographic plates; roentgen ray. **2.** the examination of the inside of a person's body or something opaque by an X-ray machine. **3.** the photograph taken using the process. ◇*v.t.* **4.** to examine by means of X-rays. **5.** to make an X-ray of. **6.** to treat with X-rays. [so called because their nature was not known]

X-ray crystallography, *n.* the study of a crystalline substance by observing diffraction patterns which occur when a beam of X-rays is passed through it.

X-ray tube, *n. Phys.* a tube with a vacuum inside in which a heavy metal target is bombarded with a high-velocity stream of electrons to produce X-rays.

xylem /'zaɪləm/, *n. Bot.* the woody cells in a plant that conduct water and minerals and give its structure support; woody tissue. See **phloem.** [Gk]

xylo-, a word part meaning 'wood'. Also, **xyl-.** [Gk, combining form of *xýlon*]

xylography /zaɪ'lɒgrəfi/, *n.* the art of engraving on wood, or of printing from such engravings. [F] **–xylographic, xylographical,** *adj.*

xylophone /'zaɪləfoʊn/, *n.* a musical instrument consisting of a series of wooden bars, the largest having the lowest pitch and the smallest having the highest pitch, usu. sounded by striking with small wooden hammers. **–xylophonist,** *n.*

Yy

Y, y, *n., pl.* **Y's** or **Ys**, **y's** or **ys**. **1.** the 25th letter of the English alphabet. **2.** anything shaped like the letter Y.

y /waɪ/, *Maths. Symbol.* an unknown quantity, or a variable.

-y[1], an adjective suffix meaning 'marked by or tending to', as in *juicy, dreamy, chilly*. Also, **-ey**[1]. [OE *-ig*]

-y[2], a suffix, meaning 'little', often used affectionately, common in names, as in *Billy, pussy*. Also, **-ey**[2], **-ie**. [ME; often through Scot influence]

-y[3], a suffix forming action nouns from verbs, as in *enquiry*, and also found in other abstract nouns, as *carpentry, infamy*. [L]

y., *Abbrev.* year.

Y, *Chem. Symbol.* yttrium.

yabber /ˈjæbə/, *Colloq.* ◇*v.i.* **1.** to talk; converse. ◇*n.* **2.** a talk; conversation. [Aboriginal]

yabby /ˈjæbi/, *n.* a small Australian freshwater crayfish. [Aboriginal]

yacht /jɒt/, *n.* **1.** a sailing boat used for cruising, racing, or other non-commercial purposes. ◇*v.i.* **2.** to sail or race in a yacht. [early mod. D short for *jaghtschip* ship for chasing] —**yachting**, *n., adj.*

Yagan /ˈjʌgan/, *n.* died 1833, Australian outlaw and leader of an Aboriginal tribe involved in a series of conflicts with European settlers in the early years of white settlement in Perth, WA.

yahoo /ˈjahu, jaˈhu/, *n.* **1.** a rough, coarse, or uncouth person. ◇*v.i.* **2.** to behave in a rough, uncouth manner (fol. by *around*). ◇*interj.* **3.** (an exclamation expressing enthusiasm or delight). [from *Yahoo*, one of a race of brutes having the form of man and all his degrading passions, in *Gulliver's Travels* (1726) by Jonathan SWIFT]

Yahweh /ˈjaweɪ/, *n.* the name of God in the Hebrew text of the Old Testament, commonly written as Jehovah. Also, **Yahve**, **Yahveh** /ˈjaveɪ/, **Jahveh**, **Jahve**.

yak[1] /jæk/, *n.* the long-haired wild ox of the Tibetan highlands. [Tibetan]

yak[2] /jæk/, *n., v.,* **yakked, yakking.** *Colloq.* ◇*n.* **1.** empty talk. ◇*v.i.* **2.** to talk or chatter, esp. pointlessly and continuously. Also, **yakety-yak**. [imitative]

yakka /ˈjækə/, *n. Colloq.* work. Also, **yacker, yakker**. [Aboriginal]

Yale /jeɪl/, *n.* a university in New Haven, Connecticut, US, founded in 1701.

Yalta /ˈjæltə/, *n.* a seaport on the Crimean peninsula of Ukraine, on the Black Sea; wartime conference of Roosevelt, Churchill, and Stalin, February 1945. Pop. 77 000 (1977). Russian, **Jalta**.

Yalu /ˈjalu/, *n.* a river forming part of the boundary between North Korea and the north-eastern provinces of China, flowing south-west to the Yellow Sea. About 480 km. Also, **Amnok-kang**.

yam /jæm/, *n.* **1.** the starchy, tuberous root of a type of climbing vine much used for food in the warmer parts of the world. **2.** any of several other plants with such roots, such as **blackfellow's yam**. [Sp, ultimately of African orig.]

yam stick, *n.* a long, pointed stick used by Aboriginals in digging for yams.

yandy /ˈjændi/, *n.* a long shallow dish used to separate minerals from alluvial soil by rocking. [Aboriginal]

Yang /jæŋ/, *n.* (in Chinese philosophy) one of the two basic principles of the universe, regarded as positive, masculine, active, and assertive. See **Yin**.

yank /jæŋk/, *Colloq.* ◇*v.t., v.i.* **1.** to pull or move with a sudden jerking motion; tug sharply. ◇*n.* **2.** a jerk or tug. [orig. uncert.]

Yank /jæŋk/, *n., adj. Colloq.* American. [short for *Yankee*, from D *Jan Kees* John Cheese, a nickname]

yap /jæp/, *v.,* **yapped, yapping,** *n.* ◇*v.i.* **1.** to bark with short, high sounds; yelp. **2.** *Colloq.* to talk snappishly, noisily, or foolishly. ◇*n.* **3.** an act or instance of yapping. [imitative]

yard[1] /jad/, *n.* **1.** a common unit of linear measure in the imperial system equal to 3 ft or 36 in., defined as 0.9144 metres. **2.** *Naut.* a long round pole tapering towards each end, slung crosswise to a mast and suspending a sail. [OE *gerd*]

yard[2] /jad/, *n.* **1.** a piece of enclosed ground next to or around a house or other building, often used for animals, as a garden, etc. **2.** any outside area, with fence or wall, within which any work or business is carried on: *a brickyard; a shipyard*. ◇*v.t.* **3.** to put into a yard. [OE *geard* enclosure]

yardarm /ˈjadam/, *n.* either end of the yard of a square sail.

yardstick /ˈjadstɪk/, *n.* **1.** a measuring stick one yard long. **2.** any standard of measurement.

yarn /jan/, *n.* **1.** a thread made by twisting fibres, such as nylon, cotton or wool, and used for knitting and weaving. **2.** *Colloq.* a story, esp. a long one about unlikely events. **3.** a talk; chat. ◇*v.i.* **4.** *Colloq.* to tell stories. **5.** to talk; chat. [OE *gearn*]

Yarra /ˈjærə/, *n.* a river in central southern Vic, rising near Mt Baw Baw in the Great Dividing Range and flowing generally west and south-west through Melbourne to Port Phillip Bay; once an important source of the city's water supply, its upper reaches continue to contribute to the needs of the metropolitan area. About 250 km. [Aboriginal]

Yarralumla /ˈjærəˈlʌmlə/, *n.* the official residence in Canberra, ACT, of the Australian governor-general.

yarran /ˈjærən/, *n.* a small tree, a type of acacia, found in inland eastern Australia and useful as fodder, for firewood and fence posts. [Aboriginal]

Yass /jæs/, *n.* a town and shire in south-eastern NSW, north of Canberra; noted for its merino wool. Pop. 4529 (1986). [Aboriginal *Yarh* or *Yahr* running water]

yaw /jɔ/, *v.i.* **1.** (of a ship, etc.) to move temporarily back and forth from a straight course. **2.** (of an aircraft, rocket, etc.) to swing around its vertical axis. ◇*n.* **3.** a yawing movement. [orig. uncert.]

yawl /jɔl/, *n.* a sailing boat with a large mainmast forward and a much smaller mast set far back. [D: kind of boat; orig. unknown]

yawn /jɔn/, *v.i.* **1.** to open the mouth involuntarily with a long, deep intake of breath, as from sleepiness or boredom. **2.** to open wide like a mouth. **3.** to extend wide, as an open, deep space. ◇*n.* **4.** the act of yawning. [OE *geonian*]

yaws /jɔz/, *n. pl.* an infectious disease, common in certain tropical areas and marked by a rash of raspberry-like sores.

Y-axis /ˈwaɪˌæksəs/, *n.* the vertical axis in a two-dimensional Cartesian coordinate system.

Yb, *Chem. Symbol.* ytterbium.

Y chromosome, *n.* one of a pair with the X chromosome in the male of many animals including humans. See **X chromosome**.

yd, *Abbrev.* yard(s).

ye[1] /ji/, *pron. Archaic.* you. [OE *gē*]

ye[2] /ði/; *spelling pron.* /ji/, *def. art.* an archaic spelling of **the**[1]. [var. of THE[1] due to misreading of ME symbol]

yea /jeɪ/, *adv.* **1.** yes (used esp. in a vote, etc.). **2.** *Archaic.* indeed or truly. ◇*n.* **3.** a reply or vote of 'yes'. [OE *gēa*]

yeah /jɛə/, *adv. Colloq.* yes.

year /jɪə/, *n.* **1.** a period of 365 or 366 days, divided into 12 months, now reckoned from 1 January to 31 December (**calendar year**). **2.** a period of about the same length in other calendars. **3.** the same period starting from any point: *He'll be away for a year from 15 May.* **4.** a period consisting of 12 lunar months (**lunar year**). **5.** (in scientific use) the period during which the earth makes one complete revolution around the sun, being equal to about 365 days, 5 hours, 48 minutes, 46 seconds (**tropical year**, **solar year**, **astronomical year**). **6.** a period out of every 12 months, during which a certain activity, etc., takes place: *the school year.* **7.** a level or grade in an education program, usu. indicating one full year's study: *He's in 4th year science.* **8.** a group of students in a high school, university, etc., who enrolled at the beginning of the same year and move up through the school, etc., together: *She was in my year.* **9.** (*pl.*) age, esp. of a person: *I could not judge his years.* **10.** (*pl.*) time, esp. a long time. **11. year in, year out,** happening regularly year after year; monotonously. [OE *gēar*]

yearbook /ˈjɪəbʊk/, *n.* a book published each year, containing information, statistics, etc., about that year.

yearling /ˈjɪəlɪŋ/, *n.* an animal one year old or in the second year of its age.

yearly /ˈjɪəli/, *adj., adv., n., pl.* **-lies.** ◇*adj.* **1.** done, made, happening, appearing, etc., once a year, or every year. **2.** continuing for a year. ◇*adv.* **3.** once a year; annually. ◇*n.* **4.** a publication appearing once a year.

yearn /jɜn/, *v.i.* **1.** to have a strong desire; long. **2.** to be moved to tenderness. [OE *giernan*] **–yearning**, *n.*

year of grace, *n.* any year or date as counted from the birth of Christ; AD.

yeast /jist/, *n.* **1.** a type of fungus which is able to ferment sugar, used in the making of alcoholic drink, esp. beer, and as a leavening in baking bread, etc. **2.** a commercial substance made from yeast, used to make dough rise for bread, etc. [OE *gist*] **–yeasty**, *adj.*

Yeats /jeɪts/, *n.* **William Butler**, 1865–1939, Irish nationalist poet, dramatist, and essayist; won the Nobel prize for literature, 1923.

yell /jɛl/, *v.i.* **1.** to call out loudly; shout. **2.** to cry out loudly with pain, fright, etc. ◇*v.t.* **3.** to tell by yelling. ◇*n.* **4.** a cry made by yelling. [OE *gellan*]

yellow /ˈjɛloʊ/, *adj.* **1.** of a bright color like that of butter, lemons, etc.; between green and orange in the spectrum. **2.** having the almost yellow skin of the Mongoloid peoples. **3.** *Colloq.* cowardly. ◇*n.* **4.** a yellow color. **5.** a yellow pigment or dye. ◇*v.t., v.i.* **6.** to make or become yellow. [OE *geolu*] **–yellowish**, *adj.*

yellow-belly /ˈjɛləˌbɛli/, *n. Colloq.* coward.

yellow box, *n.* a large spreading type of gum tree, common on the western slopes in eastern Australia, and valued as a source of honey.

yellowcake /ˈjɛloʊkeɪk/, *n.* uranium oxide in an unprocessed form, which has low radioactivity.

yellow fever, *n.* an infectious disease of warm climates, due to a virus carried by a mosquito, and marked by fever, jaundice, vomiting of blood, etc., often causing death.

yellow flag, *n.* a flag indicating a state of quarantine, esp. on a ship.

yellow Monday, *n. Colloq.* a large, yellow cicada, a color variant of the greengrocer.

yellow pages, *n.pl.* (*sometimes treated as sing.*) a telephone book listing businesses, professional people, organisations, etc.

yellow peril, *n. Colloq.* **1.** the danger, claimed by some, of the 'yellow' race, with its enormous numbers, gaining power over the white race and Western civilisation generally. **2.** the danger, claimed by some, of a Chinese invasion of Australia.

yellow press, *n.* publications that distort or exaggerate news to create sensations and attract readers. [said to be an allusion to the *Yellow Kid*, cartoon (1895) in the *New York World*, which was noted for sensationalism and vulgarity]

Yellow River, *n.* →**Huang He**.

yellows /ˈjelouz/, *n.* **1.** *Bot.* one of various plant diseases, the main symptom being loss of green pigment in the leaves. **2.** jaundice, esp. in animals.

Yellow Sea, *n.* an arm of the Pacific between north-eastern China and Korea. Chinese, **Huang Hai** (formerly, **Hwang Hai**).

Yellowstone /ˈjeloustoun/, *n.* a river in the US, flowing from north-western Wyoming through Yellowstone Lake (32 km long; about 360 km²) in Yellowstone National Park, and north-east through Montana into the Missouri river in western North Dakota; two falls; deep canyon. 1080 km.

yellowtail /ˈjelouteɪl/, *n.* any of various fishes with yellowish fins, found in southern Australian and NZ waters.

yelp /jelp/, *v.i.* **1.** to give a quick, sharp cry, as dogs, foxes, etc., do. ◇*n.* **2.** a quick, sharp bark or cry. [OE *gelpan* boast]

Yeltsin /ˈjeltzɪn/, *n.* **Boris**, born 1931, Russian politician; a Soviet Communist Party leader 1985–87; president of the Russian parliament within the Soviet Union 1990–91; became president of the Russian republic in 1991.

Yemen /ˈjemən/, *n.* a republic in the southern part of the Arabian peninsula, bordered by Oman and Saudi Arabia; formed in 1990 by the uniting of South Yemen (the People's Democratic Republic of Yemen, formerly the British colony of Aden) and North Yemen (the Yemen Arab Republic). Pop. 11 546 000 (1990 est.); 531 869 km². *Languages*: Arabic and English. *Currency*: dinar and rial. *Cap.*: San'a. Official name, **Republic of Yemen**.

yen[1] /jen/, *n., pl.* **yen**. the unit of currency in Japan. [Jap, from Chinese: a round thing, a dollar]

yen[2] /jen/, *n., v.,* **yenned, yenning**. *Colloq.* ◇*n.* **1.** a desire; longing. ◇*v.i.* **2.** to desire; yearn. [? from YEARN]

yeo /jou/, *n. Colloq.* ewe. [Brit d. var. of EWE]

yeoman /ˈjoumən/, *n., pl.* **-men**. **1.** *Brit.* a countryman who cultivates his own land. **2.** a petty officer in the Royal Australian Navy. **3.** *Hist.* a servant or official in a royal or other great household. [ME *yeman, yoman,* from *ye, yo* (of uncert. orig.) + MAN]

yeoman service, *n.* good, useful, or loyal service. Also, **yeoman's service**.

Yeppoon /jəˈpun/, *n.* a coastal town in central eastern Qld, north-east of Rockhampton. Pop. 6452 (1986).

yes /jes/, *adv., n., pl.* **yeses**. ◇*adv.* **1.** (used to express agreement or assent, or to mark the addition of something emphasising a previous statement.) ◇*n.* **2.** a reply of 'yes'. [OE *gēse*; ? from *gēa* yes + *sī* be it]

yes-man /ˈjes-mæn/, *n. Colloq.* someone who always agrees with his superiors.

yesterday /ˈjestədeɪ, -di/, *adv.* **1.** on the day before this day. **2.** a short time ago. ◇*n.* **3.** the day before this day. **4.** a time in the recent past. [OE *geostrandæg*]

yet /jet/, *adv.* **1.** at the present time: *Don't go yet.* **2.** up to a particular time; thus far: *He had not yet come.* **3.** in the time still remaining: *There is yet time.* **4.** in addition: *yet once more.* **5.** even: *He won't do it for you nor yet for me.* **6.** nevertheless: *strange and yet true.* **7. as yet**, up to the present time. ◇*conj.* **8.** nevertheless: *It is good, yet it could be improved.* [OE *giet*]

yeti /ˈjeti/, *n.* the abominable snowman, a manlike creature supposed to live in the snows of Tibet. [Tibetan]

Yevtushenko /jevtəˈʃeŋkou/, *n.* **Yevgeny Aleksandrovich** /jɪvˈgjeɪni əlɪkˈsandrəvɪtʃ/, born 1933, Russian poet.

yew /ju/, *n.* an evergreen, cone-bearing tree, of medium height, native to the Old World, western North America, and Japan, having dense, dark leaves and a fine-grained elastic wood. [OE *īw, ēow*]

Yiddish /ˈjɪdɪʃ/, *n.* **1.** a language consisting of a group of closely similar High German dialects, with some vocabulary from Hebrew and Slavic, written in Hebrew letters, spoken mainly by Jews in countries east of Germany and by Jewish emigrants from these regions, and now the official language of Birobidzhan, an autonomous Jewish region in south-eastern Russia in Asia. ◇*adj.* **2.** Jewish. [G: Jewish]

yield /jild/, *v.t.* **1.** to give forth or produce by natural means or after cultivation. **2.** to produce or furnish as payment, profit, or interest. **3.** to give up or surrender; relinquish: *They yielded their land to the conqueror.* **4.** to give up or surrender (oneself) (oft. fol. by *up*): *He yielded himself up to despair.* ◇*v.i.* **5.** to produce or bear. **6.** to give up or surrender to a stronger power, etc. **7.** to give way to influence, demand, argument, etc. **8.** to give place (fol. by *to*). **9.** to give way to force, etc., so as to move, bend, fall, etc. ◇*n.* **10.** the quantity or amount of something yielded. **11.** *Chem.* the ratio of a product actually formed in a chemical process to that theoretically possible, usu. expressed as a percentage. [OE *g(i)eldan* pay]

yielding /ˈjildɪŋ/, *adj.* willing to yield; compliant; obedient.

Yin /jɪn/, *n.* (in Chinese philosophy) one of the two basic principles of the universe, regarded as feminine, passive, and yielding. See **Yang**.

yippee /jɪˈpi/, *interj.* (an exclamation expressing joy, pleasure, etc.)

-yl, a word part used in names of chemical radicals, as in *ethyl*. [combining form representing Gk *hýlē* wood, matter]

YMCA /ˌwaɪ em si 'eɪ/, Young Men's Christian Association. [abbrev.]

yob /jɒb/, *n. Colloq.* a rude, uncultivated or aggressive young man. Also, **yobbo** /'jɒboʊ/. [? *boy* spelt backwards]

yodel /'joʊdl/, *v.*, **-delled, -delling**, *n.* ◇*v.t., v.i.* **1.** to sing with frequent changes between the natural voice and falsetto, in the manner of Swiss and Tyrolean mountaineers. ◇*n.* **2.** a song, etc., so sung. Also, **yodle**. [G] **–yodeller**, *n.*

yoga /'joʊɡə/, *n.* (*also cap.*) (in Hindu religious philosophy) the union of the human soul with the Universal Spirit; a practice aiming to effect such union through mental concentration, often using exercises or postures, controlled breathing, etc. [Hind, from Skt: union] **–yogic**, *adj.*

yoghurt /'joʊɡət, 'jɒɡət/, *n.* a food in the form of a thick liquid, sometimes flavored, made from milk curdled by the action of enzymes, etc. Also, **yoghourt, yogurt.** [Turk]

yogi /'joʊɡi/, *n., pl.* **-gis** /-ɡiz/. someone who is a master of yoga.

Yogyakarta /dʒɒɡdʒə'kɑtə/, *n.* a city in Indonesia in southern central Java. Pop. 398 727 (1980). Formerly, **Djokjakarta, Jokyakarta, Jogjakarta.**

yoke /joʊk/, *n., v.,* **yoked, yoking.** ◇*n.* **1.** a device for joining a pair of oxen, etc., usu. consisting of a crosspiece with a bow-shaped piece at each end, each bow enclosing the head of an animal. **2.** a pair of animals fastened together by a yoke. **3.** something like a yoke, such as a frame fitting the neck and shoulders of a person, for carrying a pair of buckets, etc. **4.** a shaped piece in a garment, fitted about the neck, shoulders, or hips, from which the rest of the garment hangs. **5.** something that binds; bond or tie: *the yoke of servitude.* ◇*v.t.* **6.** to put a yoke on; join by means of a yoke. **7.** to harness (a draught animal) to a plough or vehicle. **8.** to harness a draught animal to (a plough or vehicle). **9.** to join, link, or unite. ◇*v.i.* **10.** to be or become joined, linked, or united. [OE *ġeoc*]

yokel /'joʊkəl/, *n.* (*offensive*) a countryman or rustic. [orig. uncert.]

Yokohama /joʊkə'hɑmə/, *n.* a seaport in central Japan, in south-eastern Honshu island, on Tokyo Bay. Pop. 3 049 782 (1986 est.).

yolk /joʊk/, *n.* **1.** the yellow part of an egg. **2.** *Biol.* that part of the contents of the egg of an animal which enters directly into the formation of the embryo, together with any material which nourishes the embryo during its formation. [OE *ġeolca*, from *ġeolu* yellow]

Yom Kippur /jɒm 'kɪpə/, *n.* Day of Atonement, a yearly Jewish fast day. [Heb: Day of Atonement]

yonder /'jɒndə/, *adj.* **1.** being the more distant. **2.** being in that place or over there. ◇*adv.* **3.** at, in, or to that place; over there. [ME]

yoo-hoo /'ju-hu/, *interj.* (a call used to attract someone's attention.)

yore /jɔ/, *n.* time long past, now only in the phrase **of yore**: *in days of yore.* [OE *ġeāra*, ? from *ġēar* YEAR]

York[1] /jɔk/, *n.* an English royal house, 1461–85; comprised three kings: Edward IV, Edward V, and Richard III. See also, **Wars of the Roses.**

York[2] /jɔk/, *n.* **Cape,** the northernmost point of Australia, at the tip of the Cape York Peninsula. [named by James COOK in 1770 after the Duke of *York*, brother of King George II]

Yorke Peninsula /jɔk pə'nɪnsələ/, *n.* a large peninsula in SA, lying between Gulf St Vincent and Spencer Gulf; principal product is grain with three deep-sea ports for its transportation. [named by Matthew Flinders in 1802 after Charles Philip *Yorke*, First Lord of the Admiralty]

yorker /'jɔkə/, *n.* (in cricket) a ball bowled in such a way that it pitches directly under the bat. [? from YORKSHIRE]

Yorkshire /'jɔkʃɪə, -ʃə/, *n.* a former county in northern England; was divided for administrative purposes into the East Riding, West Riding, and North Riding; now divided into the counties North, West, and South Yorkshire.

Yorkshire pudding, *n.* a batter baked and served with roast beef. [from YORKSHIRE]

you /ju/; *weak form* /jə/, *pron., poss.* **your** or **yours**, *obj.* **you. 1.** the ordinary pronoun of the second person, with either plural or singular meaning; the person or people being addressed. **2.** one; anyone; people in general: *You never know what will happen next.* [OE *ēow*]

you'd /jud/; *weak form* /jəd/, short form of *you had* or *you would.*

you'll /jul/; *weak form* /jəl/, short form of *you will* or *you shall.*

young /jʌŋ/, *adj.* **1.** being in the first or early stage of life or growth; not old. **2.** having the appearance, freshness, energy, etc., of youth. **3.** of or relating to youth: *in his young days.* **4.** inexperienced: *He is young in that job.* **5.** not far advanced in years in comparison with another or others; junior. **6.** being in an early stage generally; new: *The year is still young; a young nation.* **7.** representing new or progressive tendencies, policies, etc. ◇*n.* **8.** (of animals) young offspring. **9.** young people collectively. **10. with young,** pregnant. [OE *ġeong*]

Young /jʌŋ/, *n.* a town and shire in south-western NSW; scene of Lambing Flat riots 1860–61. Pop. 6797 (1986). Formerly, **Lambing Flat.** [named after Sir John *Young*, 1807–76, governor of NSW 1861–67]

youngster /'jʌŋstə/, *n.* a child or young person.

your /jɔ/, *weak form* /jə/, *pron.* **1.** the possessive form of *you*, used before a noun; belonging to or done by you. **2.** *Colloq.* (used to indicate all members of a particular group): *your typical housewife.* See **yours.** [OE *ēower*]

you're /jɔ/, short form of *you are*.

yours /jɔz/, *pron.* a form of *your* used after a verb or without a noun following: *These books are yours; Yours are very good.*

yourself /jɔˈself/, *pron., pl.* **-selves. 1.** the reflexive form of *you: You've cut yourself.* **2.** an emphatic form of *you: You took it for yourself; You yourself did it.* **3.** your proper or normal self: *You'll soon be yourself again.*

youth /juθ/, *n., pl.* **youths** /juðz/, (*collectively*) **youth. 1.** the condition of being young; youngness. **2.** the appearance, freshness, energy, etc., that marks someone who is young. **3.** the time of being young, esp. period of adolescence. **4.** the first or early period of anything. **5.** young people collectively. **6.** a young man. [OE *geoguth*] **–youthful,** *adj.* **–youthfulness,** *n.*

youth hostel, *n.* a place for young travellers to stay overnight at little expense.

you've /juv/, short form of *you have*.

yowie /ˈjaui/, *n.* an ape-like man, believed by some to wander about in certain parts of Australia, esp. southern NSW.

yowl /jaul/, *v.i.* **1.** to make a long distressed cry; howl. ◇*n.* **2.** a yowling cry; howl. [? from OE *gēoh-* in *gēohthu* care, sorrow]

yoyo /ˈjoujou/, *n., pl.* **-yos.** a toy, consisting of a round, flat-sided block of wood, plastic, etc., with a groove in the middle, which is made to spin up and down on an attached string. [Trademark]

Ypres /ˈiprə/; *Colloq.* /ˈwaɪpəz/, *n.* a town in Belgium, in western Flanders; the scene of many battles, 1914–18. Pop. 34 426 (1981). Flemish, **Ieper.**

yr, *Abbrev.* **1.** year. **2.** your.

ytterbium /ɪˈtɜbiəm/, *n.* a rare metallic element of the rare earth series. *Symbol:* Yb; *at. no.:* 70; *at. wt:* 173.04. [NL] **–ytterbic,** *adj.*

yttrium, a rare trivalent metallic element, *Symbol:* Y; *at. no.:* 39; *at. wt:* 88.905.

yuan /ˈjuan/, *n.* the unit of currency of China. [see YEN[1]]

Yucatán /jukəˈtæn/, *n.* a peninsula comprising parts of south-eastern Mexico, northern Guatemala, and Belize.

yucca /ˈjʌkə/, *n.* a kind of plant of the warmer areas of America, having pointed, usu. stiff leaves, and whitish flowers. [NL, from Sp]

yucky /ˈjʌki/, *adj. Colloq.* disgusting; unpleasant. Also, **yukky.**

Yugoslavia /jugəˈslaviə/, *n.* a federal republic in south-eastern Europe, on the Adriatic Sea; formed in 1918 to unite the southern Slav peoples by joining the kingdoms of Serbia and Montenegro with regions of the former Austro-Hungarian Empire; four of its constituent republics seceded in 1991–92 leaving the republics of Serbia and Montenegro and the autonomous provinces of Kosovo and Vojvodina. Pop. 10 469 000 (based on 1989 est. for the former Yugoslavia); 102 173 km². *Language:* Serbo-Croat. *Currency:* dinar. *Cap.:* Belgrade. Also, **Jugoslavia. –Yugoslavian,** *n., adj.*

Yukon /ˈjukɒn/, *n.* a river flowing from north-western Canada generally west through central Alaska to the Bering Sea. About 3700 km.

yule /jul/, *n.* Christmas, or the Christmas season. Also, **yuletide.** [OE *gēōl(a)*]

yummy /ˈjʌmi/, *adj. Colloq.* (esp. of food) very good; delicious. Also, **yum.**

YWCA /ˌwaɪ dʌbəlju si ˈeɪ/, Young Women's Christian Association. [abbrev.]

Zz

Z, z, *n., pl.* **Z's** or **Zs, z's** or **zs.** the 26th letter of the English alphabet.

z, *Maths. Symbol.* an unknown quantity or a variable.

Z, *Chem. Symbol.* atomic number.

Zacharias /zækəˈraɪəs/, *n. New Testament.* father of John the Baptist. Also, **Zachariah, Zachary.** [see Luke 1:5]

zack /zæk/, *n. Colloq.* **1.** (formerly) sixpence. **2.** a five cent piece.

Zagreb /ˈzɑgrɛb/, *n.* the capital city in the central western part of Croatia. Pop. 649 586 (1981). German, **Agram.**

Zaire /zɑˈɪə/, *n.* **1.** a republic in central Africa in the basin of the Zaire River with a short Atlantic coastline. Pop. 31 804 000 (1987 est.); 2 344 885 km². *Languages:* French, also over 400 Sudanese and Bantu dialects. *Currency:* zaire. *Cap.:* Kinshasa. Formerly, the **Belgian Congo,** the **Democratic Republic of the Congo. 2.** → **Congo** (def. 2). – **Zairean, Zairese,** *n., adj.*

Zambezi /zæmˈbizi/, *n.* a river in southern Africa, rising in Zambia, flowing through eastern Angola, Zimbabwe and Mozambique into the Indian Ocean; Victoria Falls. About 1050 km long. Also, **Zambesi.**

Zambia /ˈzæmbiə/, *n.* a land-locked republic in southern central Africa. Pop. 7 135 000 (1987 est.); 752 614 km². *Languages:* English and Bantu languages. *Currency:* kwacha. *Cap.:* Lusaka. Formerly, **Northern Rhodesia.** – **Zambian,** *n., adj.*

zany /ˈzeɪni/, *adj.,* **-nier, -niest. 1.** funny or comical in a crazy way. **2.** slightly crazy. [F, from d. It (Venetian): clown, lit., Johnny (It *Giovanni* John)]

zap /zæp/, *v.,* **zapped, zapping,** *n. Colloq.* ◇*v.t.* **1.** to destroy with a sudden burst of violence; annihilate. ◇*v.i.* **2.** to move quickly. ◇*n.* **3.** energy; liveliness; force.

Zapata /səˈpɑtə/, *n.* **Emiliano** /eɪmiˈljɑnoʊ/, 1877?–1919, Mexican political leader; revolutionary 1911–16.

zeal /zil/, *n.* enthusiasm for a person, cause, or object; eager desire or activity. [ME, from L, from Gk: boil]

Zealand /ˈzilənd/, *n.* the largest island of Denmark; Copenhagen is situated here. Pop. 2 129 846 (1970); 7016 km². Also, **Seeland.** Danish, **Sjælland.**

zealot /ˈzɛlət/, *n.* **1.** someone who shows zeal. **2.** someone carried away by too much zeal, esp. for a religious cause; fanatic. [LL, from Gk: zeal] – **zealotry,** *n.*

zealous /ˈzɛləs/, *adj.* full of, marked by, or due to zeal.

zebra /ˈzɛbrə/, *USA.* /ˈzibrə/, *n.* a wild, horselike, African animal, with dark stripes on a light colored body, occurring in three different species. [It or Pg; orig. uncert.] – **zebrine,** *adj.*

zebra crossing, *n.* a street crossing marked with broad black and white or black and yellow stripes.

zebra finch, *n.* a small finch having black and white striped feathers on the hind part.

zebu /ˈzibu/, *n.* an animal of the ox family having a large hump over the shoulders and a very large dewlap, widely domesticated in India, China, eastern Africa, etc., and used for crossbreeding in Australia. [F; orig. uncert.]

Zen /zɛn/, *n.* a Buddhist sect, popular in Japan, believing in self-contemplation as the key to the understanding of the universe. [Jap, from Chinese, from Skt: religious meditation]

zenith /ˈzɛnəθ/, *n.* **1.** the point of the celestial sphere vertically above any place or observer. See **nadir. 2.** the highest point or state; culmination. [ME, from ML, from Ar] – **zenithal,** *adj.*

Zeno of Citium /ˌzinoʊ əv ˈsɪtiəm/, *n.* c. 336–c.264 BC, Greek philosopher and founder of the Stoic school.

zephyr /ˈzɛfə/, *n.* **1.** a soft, mild breeze. **2.** (*cap.*) *Poetic.* the west wind personified. [L, from Gk]

zeppelin /ˈzɛpələn/, *n.* a large airship consisting of a long, covered framework containing compartments filled with gas, and of various structures for holding the engines, passengers, etc. [named after F von *Zeppelin,* 1838–1917, German general and airship builder]

zero /ˈzɪəroʊ/, *n., pl.* **-ros, -roes,** *v.,* **-roed, -roing.** ◇*n.* **1.** the figure or symbol 0, standing for the absence of quantity. **2.** the starting point of any kind of measurement; the line or point from which all divisions of a scale (as a thermometer) are measured in either a positive or a negative direction. **3.** naught or nothing. **4.** the lowest point or degree. ◇*v.* **5. zero in on, a.** to adjust the sight settings of a rifle, etc., so as to aim directly at: *I zeroed in on the target.* **b.** to focus attention on. [It, from Ar: cipher]

zero gravity, *n.* → **weightlessness.**

zero hour, *n.* **1.** *Mil.* the time set for the beginning of an attack. **2.** *Colloq.* the time at which any planned action is to begin.

zero population growth, *n.* the belief that population increase should be limited to the number of children needed to maintain the existing level of population, calculated to be 2.11 children per family. Also, **ZPG**

zest /zɛst/, *n.* **1.** anything added to give flavor or enjoyment. **2.** an agreeably sharp flavor. **3.** a quality that excites or awakens sharp interest; piquancy. **4.** keen enjoyment; gusto. **5.** the peel of citrus fruits, used as a flavoring. [F: orange or lemon peel (used for flavoring)] – **zestful,** *adj.*

zeugma /ˈzjugmə/, *n.* a figure of speech in which a verb is associated with two subjects or

zeugma objects, or an adjective with two nouns, although connected in sense to only one of the two, as in 'to wage war and peace'. [NL, from Gk: yoking] —**zeugmatic**, *adj.*

Zeus /zjus/, *n.* **1.** the chief god of the ancient Greeks, ruler of the heavens, Roman counterpart, Jupiter. **2.** his statue, by Phidias at Olympia is one of the Seven Wonders of the World.

Zeuxis /'zjuksəs/, *n.* fl. late fifth century BC, Greek painter, noted for his naturalism.

Zhao Ziyang /'dʒau 'zijʌŋ/, *n.* born 1919, Chinese communist statesman; premier 1980–89.

Zhengzhou /'dʒʌŋ'dʒou/, *n.* a city in China; capital of Henan province. Pop. 962 500 (1985 est.). Formerly, **Chengchow**.

Zhou /dʒou/, *n.* a Chinese dynasty, beginning in legendary times and continuing into historical times. The traditional date for its foundation, 1122 BC, cannot be verified; it ended c. 249 BC. Formerly, **Chou**.

Zhou Enlai /dʒou en'laɪ/, *n.* 1898–1976, premier of the People's Republic of China 1949–76; important in Chinese Communist movement. Formerly, **Chou En-lai**.

ziggurat /'zɪgəræt/, *n.* (among the ancient Babylonians and Assyrians) a temple in the form of a pyramidal tower, having a broad ascent winding round the outside of the structure and presenting the appearance of a series of terraces or steps. Also, **zikkurat, zikurat**. [Assyrian: pinnacle]

zigzag /'zɪgzæg/, *n., adj., adv., v., -zagged, -zagging.* ◇*n.* **1.** a line, course, or progression marked by sharp turns first to one side and then to the other. ◇*adj.* **2.** moving or formed in a zigzag. ◇*adv.* **3.** with frequent sharp turns from side to side. ◇*v.i., v.t.* **4.** to move (something) in a zigzag course. [F, from G, reduplication of *Zacke* point, tooth]

zillion /'zɪljən/, *n. Colloq.* an unimaginably large number. [the letter *z*, the last in the alphabet + (m)*illion*]

Zimbabwe /zɪm'bɑbwi/, *n.* a land-locked republic in southern Africa bordered by Mozambique, Zambia, Botswana, South Africa; a British protectorate, then colony, before unilateral declaration of independence by government of Ian Smith in 1965; election for internationally recognised independent republic in 1980. Pop. 8 640 000 (1987 est.); 390 759 km^2. *Languages:* English and Bantu languages. *Currency:* Zimbabwe dollar. *Cap.:* Harare. Formerly, **Southern Rhodesia, Rhodesia**. —**Zimbabwean**, *n., adj.*

zinc /zɪŋk/, *n., v., **zincked, zincking** or **zinced** /zɪŋkt/, **zincing** /'zɪŋkɪŋ/. ◇*n.* **1.** *Chem.* a bluish-white metallic element chemically like magnesium and used in making galvanised iron, alloys such as brass, etc., in voltaic cells, etc. *Symbol:* Zn; *at. no.:* 30; *at. wt.:* 65.37. ◇*v.t.* **2.** to coat or cover with zinc. [G]

zinc oxide, *n.* a compound of zinc and oxygen, ZnO, mildly antiseptic, used in ointments, etc., for treatment of certain skin diseases, and as a white pigment.

zing /zɪŋ/, *n.* **1.** a sharp singing sound. **2.** *Colloq.* energy; enthusiasm. [imitative]

zinnia /'zɪniə/, *n.* a cultivated annual plant with colorful flowers, native to Mexico. [NL, named after JG *Zinn*, 1727–59, German botanist]

Zion /'zaɪən/, *n.* **1.** a hill in Jerusalem, on which, in the ancient city, stood the Temple of Jehovah. **2.** the Jewish people. **3.** Israel as the national home of the Jews. **4.** heaven as the final gathering place of true believers. Also, **Sion**. [OE *Sion*, from LL, from Gk, from Heb]

Zionism /'zaɪənɪzəm/, *n.* a worldwide movement founded with the purpose of establishing a national home for the Jews in Palestine, which now provides support to the state of Israel. —**Zionist**, *n., adj.* —**Zionistic**, *adj.*

zip /zɪp/, *n., v.,* **zipped, zipping**. **1.** Also, **zip-fastener**. a fastener consisting of two edges which are interlocked (or separated) when an attached piece sliding between them is pulled up (or down). **2.** *Colloq.* a short, sudden hissing sound, as of a bullet. **3.** energy; vim. ◇*v.i.* **4.** *Colloq.* to move with energy. ◇*v.t.* **5.** to fasten with a zip (fol. by *up*). [imitative] —**zippy**, *adj.*

zipper /'zɪpə/, *n.* → **zip** (def. 1).

zircon /'zɜkɒn/, *n.* a common mineral, zirconium silicate, ZrSiO$_4$, occurring in various colors, used industrially as a refractory when opaque and as a gem when transparent. [? from Pers: gold-colored]

zirconium /zɜ'kouniəm/, *n.* a metallic element like titanium chemically, used in steel metallurgy, etc. *Symbol:* Zr; *at. no.:* 40; *at. wt.:* 91.22. [NL. See ZIRCON]

zither /'zɪðə/, *n.* a folk musical instrument consisting of a flat soundbox with numerous strings stretched over it, played with a plectrum and the fingertips. [G, from L]

Zn, *Chem. Symbol.* zinc.

-zoa, plural combining form naming zoological groups. [NL]

zodiac /'zoudiæk/, *n.* **1.** an imaginary belt of the heavens, within which are the apparent paths of the sun, moon, and principal planets. It contains 12 constellations and hence 12 divisions (called *signs*). **2.** a diagram representing this belt, and usu. containing pictures of the animals, etc., which are associated with the constellations and signs. [ME, from L, from Gk: (circle) of the signs, little animals] —**zodiacal**, *adj.*

zombie /'zɒmbi/, *n.* **1.** *Occult.* a dead body brought to life by a supernatural force. **2.** a person thought to be like the walking dead in having no independent judgment, intelligence, etc. Also, **zombi**. [WAfrican: good-luck fetish] —**zombiism**, *n.*

zone /zoun/, *n., v.,* **zoned, zoning**. ◇*n.* **1.** any continuous area, which differs in some

zone respect, or is marked off for some purpose, from surrounding areas, or within which certain special circumstances exist: *a military zone; an industrial zone.* **2.** *Geog.* any of the five divisions of the earth's surface, bounded by imaginary lines parallel to the equator, and named according to the prevailing temperature (the Torrid Zone, the North Temperate Zone, the South Temperate Zone, the North Frigid Zone, and the South Frigid Zone). **3.** *Ecol.* an area lived in by a particular set of organisms, which is determined by a particular set of environmental conditions. **4.** *Geol.* a geological horizon. ◇*v.t.* **5.** to divide into zones, according to existing characteristics, or for some purpose, use, etc. [L, from Gk: girdle] —**zonal**, *adj.*

zoning /ˈzoʊnɪŋ/, *n.* (of land) the marking out of an area of land with respect to its use.

zoo /zuː/, *n.* park or other large enclosure in which live animals are kept for public viewing. [from *zoological garden*]

zoo-, a word part meaning 'living animal', as in *zoology.* [Gk *zōio-*, combining form of *zōion* animal]

zoogamy /zoʊˈɒɡəmi/, *n.* reproduction by means of gametes; sexual reproduction.

zoology /zoʊˈɒlədʒi/, *n.*, *pl.* **-gies.** the science that deals with animals or the animal kingdom. [NL or NGk] —**zoologist**, *n.* —**zoological**, *adj.*

zoom /zuːm/, *v.i.* **1.** to make a continuous humming sound. **2.** to move quickly with this sound: *He zooms along in his new car.* **3.** (of prices) to rise rapidly. **4.** *Aeron.* to gain height in an aircraft in a sudden climb. **5.** *Films, TV, etc.* to use a zoom lens so as to make an object appear to approach (oft. fol. by *in*) or move away from the viewer. ◇*n.* **6.** the act of zooming. [imitative]

zoom lens, *n.* (in a camera or projector) a lens system which can be adjusted so as to give continuously varying close-up or distance views of an image without loss of focus.

zoomorphic /zoʊəˈmɔːfɪk/, *adj.* attributing animal form or behavior to beings or things not animals, such as gods. —**zoomorphism**, *n.*

-zoon, a combining form referring to a single individual in a compound organism.

zoophyte /ˈzoʊəfaɪt/, *n.* any of various animals resembling a plant, such as coral, a sea anemone, etc. [NL, from Gk] —**zoophytic**, **zoophytical**, *adj.*

Zoroastrianism /zɒroʊˈæstriənɪzəm/, *n.* a strongly moral religious system, originating in ancient Persia, which teaches a continuous struggle between the spirit of Good and the spirit of Evil. Also, **Zoroastrism**. [after *Zoroaster* (also Zarathustra), fl. c. 600 BC, Persian religious teacher] —**Zoroastrian**, *adj., n.*

zot /zɒt/, *v.*, **zotted, zotting.** *Colloq.* ◇*v.i.* **1.** to depart quickly (usu. fol. by *off*). ◇*v.t.* **2.** to knock, or kill: *Quickly, zot that fly.*

zounds /zaʊndz, zʊndz/, *interj. Archaic.* (exclamation of surprise, anger, etc.) [short for *by God's wounds*]

ZPG /zed piː ˈdʒiː/, → **zero population growth.** [abbrev.]

Zr, *Chem. Symbol.* zirconium.

zucchini /zəˈkiːni, zuː-/, *n., pl.* **-ni, -nis.** a small vegetable marrow, usu. harvested when very young; courgette. [It]

Zulu /ˈzuːluː/, *n., pl.* **-lus, -lu.** *n.* a Bantu people of south-eastern Africa, occupying the coastal region between Natal and Lourenço Marques.

Zurich /ˈzjʊərɪk/, *n.* **1.** a canton in northern Switzerland. Pop. 1 131 100 (1987 est.); 1729 km². **2.** the capital of this canton, on **Lake Zurich** (40 km long; 88 km²). Pop. 351 545 (1986). German, **Zürich**.

zygo-, a word part meaning 'yoke', 'joining' or 'pairing', as in *zygosis*. Also, before vowels, **zyg-**. [Gk, combining form of *zygón*]

zygosis /zaɪˈɡoʊsəs, zɪ-/, *n.* the coming together of two apparently identical cells to allow the fusion of two similar gametes; conjugation.

zygospore /ˈzaɪɡəspɔː, ˈzɪɡə-/, *n.* a cell formed by the fusion of two similar gametes, as in certain algae and fungi.

zygote /ˈzaɪɡoʊt, ˈzɪɡoʊt/, *n.* a cell produced by the union of two gametes. [Gk: yoked] —**zygotic**, *adj.*

zymurgy /ˈzaɪmədʒi/, *n.* the branch of chemistry dealing with fermentation, as in winemaking, brewing, distilling, preparation of yeast, etc.

zzz /zɪz/, *n. Colloq.* a sleep. [from the convention used, esp. by cartoonists, to represent sleep or the sound of snoring]

APPENDIXES

Grammar

Tense

of the English verb system
(shown in the irregular verb **swim** /swIm/, *v.*, **swam, swum, swimming**)

	Past tense	Present tense	Future tense
Simple	I swam[1]	I swim	I will swim
Continuous[2]	I was swimming	I am swimming	I will be swimming
Perfect	I had swum[3]	I have swum	I will have swum
Perfect continuous	I had been swimming	I have been swimming	I will have been swimming

1. *Past simple:* also called *preterite*.
2. *Continuous:* also called *imperfect*.
3. *Past perfect:* also called *pluperfect*.

Case

as shown in English pronouns

Number	Person	Subjective case	Objective case	Possessive case	
Singular	I	I	me	my	(mine)
	II	you	you	your	(yours)
	III	he, she, it	him, her it	his, her, its	(his, hers, —)
Plural	I	we	us	our	(ours)
	II	you	you	your	(yours)
	III	they	them	their	(theirs)

Note: *Subjective* case (also called *nominative*) marks the subject of a verb.

Objective case (also called *accusative*) marks the object of a verb.

Possessive case (also called *genitive*) marks possession, ownership, origin, etc.

Metric conversion

Quantity	Metric unit	Imperial unit	Conversion factors (approximate) Metric to Imperial units	Imperial to metric units
LENGTH	millimetre (mm) or centimetre (cm)	inch (in)	1 cm = 0.394 in	1 in = 25.4 mm
	centimetre (cm) or metre (m)	foot (ft)	1 m = 3.28 ft	1 ft = 30.5 cm
	metre (m)	yard (yd)	1 m = 1.09 yd	1 yd = 0.914 m
	kilometre (km)	mile	1 km = 0.621 mile	1 mile = 1.61 km
MASS	gram (g)	ounce (oz)	1 g = 0.0353 oz	1 oz = 28.3 g
	gram (g) or kilogram (kg)	pound (lb)	1 kg = 2.20 lb	1 lb = 454 g
	tonne (t)	ton	1 tonne = 0.984 ton	1 ton = 1.02 tonne
AREA	square centimetre (cm^2)	square inch (in^2)	1 cm^2 = 0.155 in^2	1 in^2 = 6.45 cm^2
	square centimetre (cm^2) or square metre (m^2)	square foot (ft^2)	1 m^2 = 10.8 ft^2	1 ft^2 = 929 cm^2
	square metre (m^2)	square yard (yd^2)	1 m^2 = 1.20 yd^2	1 yd^2 = 0.836 m^2
	hectare (ha)	acre (ac)	1 ha = 2.47 ac	1 ac = 0.405 ha
	square kilometre (km^2)	square mile (sq. mile)	1 km^2 = 0.386 sq. mile	1 sq. mile = 2.59 km^2

VOLUME	cubic centimetre (cm³)	cubic inch (in³)	1 cm³ = 0.0610 in³
	cubic decimetre (dm³) or cubic metre (m³)	cubic foot (ft³)	1 m³ = 35.3 ft³
	cubic metre (m³)	cubic yard (yd³)	1 m³ = 1.31 yd³
	cubic metre (m³)	bushel (bus)	1 m³ = 27.5 bus
VOLUME (fluids)	millilitre (mL)	fluid ounce (fl oz)	1 mL = 0.0352 fl oz
	millilitre (mL) or litre (L)	pint (pt)	1 litre = 1.76 pint
	litre (L) or cubic metre (m³)	gallon (gal)	1 m³ = 220 gallons
FORCE	newton (N)	pound-force (lbf)	1 N = 0.225 lbf
PRESSURE	kilopascal (kPa)	pound per square inch (psi)	1 kPa = 0.145 psi
(for meteorology)	millibar (mb)	inch of mercury (inHg)	1 mb = 0.0295 inHg
ANGULAR VELOCITY	radian per second (rad/s)	revolution per minute (r/min, rpm)	1 rad/s = 9.55 r/min
VELOCITY	kilometre per hour (km/h)	mile per hour (mph)	1 km/h = 0.621 mph
TEMPERATURE	Celsius temp (°C)	Fahrenheit temp (°F)	°F = $\frac{9}{5}$ × °C + 32
ENERGY	kilojoule (kJ)	British thermal unit (Btu)	1 kJ = 0.948 Btu
	megajoule (MJ)	therm	1 MJ = 9.48 × 10³ therm
POWER	kilowatt (kW)	horsepower (hp)	1 kW = 1.34 hp

1 in³ = 16.4 cm³		
1 ft³ = 28.3 dm³		
1 yd³ = 0.765 m³		
1 bus = 0.0364 m³		
1 fl oz = 28.4 mL		
1 pint = 568 mL		
1 gal = 4.55 litre		
1 lbf = 4.45 N		
1 psi = 6.89 kPa		
1 inHg = 33.9 mb		
1 r/min = 0.105 rad/s		
1 mph = 1.61 km/h		
°C = $\frac{5}{9}$ × (°F − 32)		
1 Btu = 1.06 kJ		
1 therm = .106 MJ		
1 hp = 0.746 kW		

Paper sizes

International paper sizes

The following tables show the range of sizes which can be obtained by the progressive subdivision of the basic sizes A0 and B0:

A series

millimetres

A0	1189 × 841
A1	841 × 594
A2	594 × 420
A3	420 × 297
A4	297 × 210
A5	210 × 148
A6	148 × 105
A7	105 × 74
A8	74 × 52
A9	52 × 37
A10	37 × 26

B series

millimetres

B0	1414 × 1000
B1	1000 × 707
B2	707 × 500
B3	500 × 353
B4	353 × 250
B5	250 × 176
B6	176 × 125
B7	125 × 88
B8	88 × 62
B9	62 × 44
B10	44 × 31

In stationery A4 replaces the traditional foolscap folio and large post quarto.

(By courtesy of the Australian Library Promotion Council)

Traditional British paper sizes

The most common names are:

Crown	20″ × 15″
Demy	22½″ × 17½″
Medium	23″ × 18″
Royal	25″ × 20″
Large post	21″ × 16½″
Foolscap	17″ × 13½″

The basic sizes (as shown above) are known as broadsheets. The normal subdivisions are folio, quarto (4to), octavo (8vo) and sixteenmo (16mo). Multiples of the broadsheet are called 'doubles' and 'quads' (see figure).

The regular subdivision of a quad sheet.

Military ranks, armed forces of Australia

NAVY

Commissioned officers
Admiral
Vice Admiral
Rear Admiral
Commodore
Captain
Commander
Lieutenant Commander
Lieutenant
Sub Lieutenant

Warrant and non-commissioned officers
Warrant Officer
Chief Petty Officer
Petty Officer
Leading Seaman
Able Seaman

ARMY

Commissioned officers
General
Lieutenant General
Major General
Brigadier
Colonel
Lieutenant Colonel
Major
Captain
Lieutenant
Second Lieutenant

Warrant and non-commissioned officers
Warrant Officer Class 1
Warrant Officer Class 2
Staff Sergeant
Sergeant
Corporal or Bombardier
Lance Corporal or Lance Bombardier
Private, including Craftsman, Gunner, Sapper, Signalman, Trooper

AIR FORCE

Commissioned officers
Air Chief Marshal
Air Marshal
Air Vice Marshal
Air Commodore
Group Captain
Wing Commander
Squadron Leader
Flight Lieutenant
Flying Officer
Pilot Officer

Warrant and non-commissioned officers
Warrant Officer
Flight Sergeant
Sergeant
Corporal
Leading Aircraftman
Aircraftman

Roman numerals

Number	Roman numeral	Number	Roman numeral
1	I	43	XLIII
2	II	50	L
3	III	54	LIV
4	IV	60	LX
5	V	65	LXV
6	VI	70	LXX
7	VII	76	LXXVI
8	VIII	80	LXXX
9	IX	87	LXXXVII
10	X	90	XC
11	XI	98	XCVIII
12	XII	100	C
13	XIII	101	CI
14	XIV	115	CXV
15	XV	150	CL
16	XVI	200	CC
17	XVII	300	CCC
18	XVIII	400	CD
19	XIX	500	D
20	XX	600	DC
21	XXI	700	DCC
30	XXX	800	DCCC
32	XXXII	900	CM
40	XL	1000	M

Abbreviations for common academic qualifications

BA	Bachelor of Arts
BAdmin	Bachelor of Administration
BAgr	Bachelor of Agriculture
BAgrSc	Bachelor of Agricultural Science
BA,LLB	Bachelor of Arts and Bachelor of Laws
BArch	Bachelor of Architecture
BBA	Bachelor of Business Administration
BCE	1. Bachelor of Chemical Engineering 2. Bachelor of Civil Engineering
BCh	Bachelor of Surgery
BChD	Bachelor of Dental Surgery
BChE	Bachelor of Chemical Engineering
BCom	Bachelor of Commerce
BD	Bachelor of Divinity
BDS	Bachelor of Dental Surgery
BDSc	Bachelor of Dental Science
BE	Bachelor of Engineering
BEcon	Bachelor of Economics
BEd	Bachelor of Education
BEE	Bachelor of Electrical Engineering
BEng	Bachelor of Engineering
BL	Bachelor of Law
BLitt	Bachelor of Letters
BLL	Bachelor of Laws
BM	Bachelor of Medicine
BMechE	Bachelor of Mechanical Engineering
BMedSc	Bachelor of Medical Science
BMus	Bachelor of Music
BN	Bachelor of Nursing
BPharm	Bachelor of Pharmacy
BS	Bachelor of Surgery
BSc	Bachelor of Science
BSocSc	Bachelor of Social Science
BSocWk	Bachelor of Social Work
BTh	Bachelor of Theology
BVetSc	Bachelor of Veterinary Science
ChB	Bachelor of Surgery
ChD	1. Doctor of Chemistry 2. Doctor of Surgery
ChM	Master of Surgery
DAgr	Doctor of Agriculture
DAgrSc	Doctor of Agricultural Science
DArch	Doctor of Architecture
DCh	Doctor of Surgery
DD	Doctor of Divinity
DDS	Doctor of Dental Surgery
DE	Doctor of Engineering
DEcon	Doctor of Economics
DEd	Doctor of Education
DEng	Doctor of Engineering
DipEd	Diploma of Education

DLitt	1. Doctor of Letters
	2. Doctor of Literature
DMus	Doctor of Music
DPh	Doctor of Philosophy
DPhil	Doctor of Philosophy
DSc	Doctor of Science
DSocSc	Doctor of Social Science
DSocWk	Doctor of Social Work
DTh	Doctor of Theology
DVetSc	Doctor of Veterinary Science
LD	Doctor of Letters
LitD	Doctor of Letters
LittB	Bachelor of Letters
LittD	Doctor of Letters
LLB	Bachelor of Laws
LLD	Doctor of Laws
LLM	Master of Laws
MA	Master of Arts
MAdmin	Master of Administration
MAgr	Master of Agriculture
MAgrSc	Master of Agricultural Science
MArch	Master of Architecture
MB	Bachelor of Medicine
MBA	Master of Business Administration
MCE	Master of Civil Engineering
MChD	Master of Dental Surgery
MChemE	Master of Chemical Engineering
MD	Doctor of Medicine
MEcon	Master of Economics
MEd	Master of Education
MEE	Master of Electrical Engineering
MEng	Master of Engineering
MLitt	Master of Letters
MMechE	Master of Mechanical Engineering
MMed	Master of Medicine
MMus	Master of Music
MSc	Master of Science
MSocSc	Master of Social Science
MSocWk	Master of Social Work
MTh	Master of Theology
MusB	Bachelor of Music
MusD	Doctor of Music
MusM	Master of Music
MVSc	Master of Veterinary Science
PhD	Doctor of Philosophy

The Periodic Table

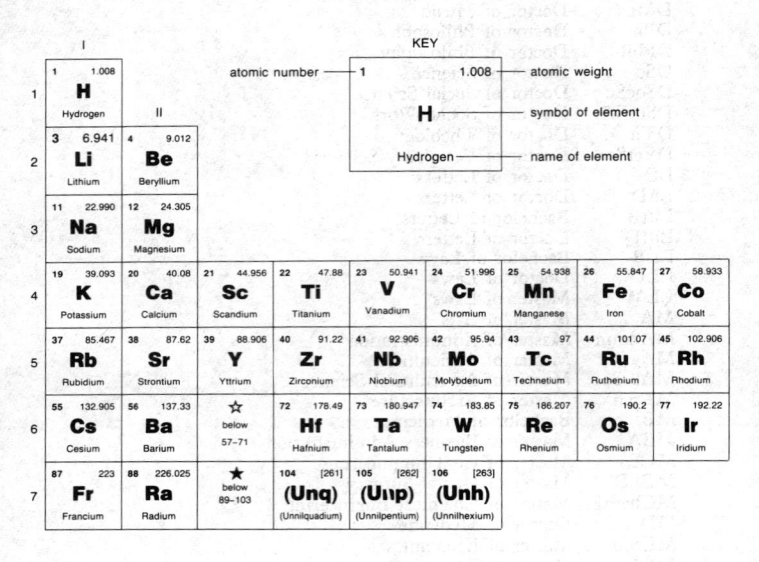

KEY: atomic number — 1 | 1.008 — atomic weight; H — symbol of element; Hydrogen — name of element

	I	II							
1	1 1.008 **H** Hydrogen								
2	3 6.941 **Li** Lithium	4 9.012 **Be** Beryllium							
3	11 22.990 **Na** Sodium	12 24.305 **Mg** Magnesium							
4	19 39.093 **K** Potassium	20 40.08 **Ca** Calcium	21 44.956 **Sc** Scandium	22 47.88 **Ti** Titanium	23 50.941 **V** Vanadium	24 51.996 **Cr** Chromium	25 54.938 **Mn** Manganese	26 55.847 **Fe** Iron	27 58.933 **Co** Cobalt
5	37 85.467 **Rb** Rubidium	38 87.62 **Sr** Strontium	39 88.906 **Y** Yttrium	40 91.22 **Zr** Zirconium	41 92.906 **Nb** Niobium	42 95.94 **Mo** Molybdenum	43 97 **Tc** Technetium	44 101.07 **Ru** Ruthenium	45 102.906 **Rh** Rhodium
6	55 132.905 **Cs** Cesium	56 137.33 **Ba** Barium	☆ below 57–71	72 178.49 **Hf** Hafnium	73 180.947 **Ta** Tantalum	74 183.85 **W** Tungsten	75 186.207 **Re** Rhenium	76 190.2 **Os** Osmium	77 192.22 **Ir** Iridium
7	87 223 **Fr** Francium	88 226.025 **Ra** Radium	★ below 89–103	104 [261] **(Unq)** (Unnilquadium)	105 [262] **(Unp)** (Unnilpentium)	106 [263] **(Unh)** (Unnilhexium)			

☆ **LANTHANIDE SERIES**

57 138.905 **La** Lanthanum	58 140.12 **Ce** Cerium	59 140.908 **Pr** Praseodymium	60 144.24 **Nd** Neodymium	61 145 **Pm** Promethium	62 150.36 **Sm** Samarium	63 151.96 **Eu** Europium

★ **ACTINIDE SERIES**

89 227.027 **Ac** Actinium	90 232.038 **Th** Thorium	91 231.036 **Pa** Protactinium	92 238.029 **U** Uranium	93 237.048 **Np** Neptunium	94 [244] **Pu** Plutonium	95 [243] **Am** Americium

						VIII
						2 4.003 **He** Helium
	III	IV	V	VI	VII	
	5 10.81 **B** Boron	6 12.011 **C** Carbon	7 14.007 **N** Nitrogen	8 15.999 **O** Oxygen	9 18.998 **F** Fluorine	10 20.179 **Ne** Neon
	13 26.982 **Al** Aluminum	14 28.085 **Si** Silicon	15 30.974 **P** Phosphorus	16 32.06 **S** Sulfur	17 35.453 **Cl** Chlorine	18 39.948 **Ar** Argon
28 58.89 **Ni** Nickel	29 63.546 **Cu** Copper	30 65.38 **Zn** Zinc	31 69.72 **Ga** Gallium	32 72.59 **Ge** Germanium	33 74.922 **As** Arsenic	34 78.96 **Se** Selenium	35 79.904 **Br** Bromine	36 83.80 **Kr** Krypton
46 106.42 **Pd** Palladium	47 107.868 **Ag** Silver	48 112.41 **Cd** Cadmium	49 114.82 **In** Indium	50 118.69 **Sn** Tin	51 121.75 **Sb** Antimony	52 127.60 **Te** Tellurium	53 126.905 **I** Iodine	54 131.29 **Xe** Xenon
78 195.08 **Pt** Platinum	79 196.967 **Au** Gold	80 200.59 **Hg** Mercury	81 204.383 **Tl** Thallium	82 207.2 **Pb** Lead	83 208.980 **Bi** Bismuth	84 209 **Po** Polonium	85 210 **At** Astatine	86 222 **Rn** Radon

64 157.25 **Gd** Gadolinium	65 158.925 **Tb** Terbium	66 162.5 **Dy** Dysprosium	67 164.930 **Ho** Holmium	68 167.26 **Er** Erbium	69 168.934 **Tm** Thulium	70 173.04 **Yb** Ytterbium	71 174.967 **Lu** Lutetium
96 [247] **Cm** Curium	97 [247] **Bk** Berkelium	98 [251] **Cf** Californium	99 [252] **Es** Einsteinium	100 [257] **Fm** Fermium	101 [258] **Md** Mendelevium	102 [259] **No** Nobelium	103 [260] **Lr** Lawrencium

[ ] Values given in square brackets are the atomic mass number of the isotope of the element with the longest half-life.

( ) Names and symbols in parentheses are those recommended by the International Union of Pure and Applied Chemists (IUPAC).

The International System of Units (SI)

1. Base SI units

Basic physical quantity	SI unit	Symbol
length	metre	m
mass	kilogram	kg
time	second	s
electric current	ampere	A
thermodynamic temperature	kelvin	K
amount of substance	mole	mol
luminous intensity	candela	cd

2. Supplementary units

plane angle	radian	rad
solid angle	steradian	sr

3. Some derived SI units with special names

Physical quantity	SI unit	Symbol
frequency	hertz	Hz
energy	joule	J
force	newton	N
power	watt	W
electrical charge	coulomb	C
potential difference	volt	V
resistance	ohm	Ω
capacitance	farad	F
conductance	siemens	S
magnetic flux	weber	Wb
inductance	henry	H
magnetic flux density	tesla	T
luminous flux	lumen	lm
illumination	lux	lx

4. Prefixes for SI units

Fraction	Prefix	Symbol	Multiple	Prefix	Symbol
10^{-1}	deci	d	10	deka	da
10^{-2}	centi	c	10^2	hecto	h
10^{-3}	milli	m	10^3	kilo	k
10^{-6}	micro	μ	10^6	mega	M
10^{-9}	nano	n	10^9	giga	G
10^{-12}	pico	p	10^{12}	tera	T
10^{-15}	femto	f	10^{15}	peta	P
10^{-18}	atto	a	10^{18}	exa	E

Points of the compass

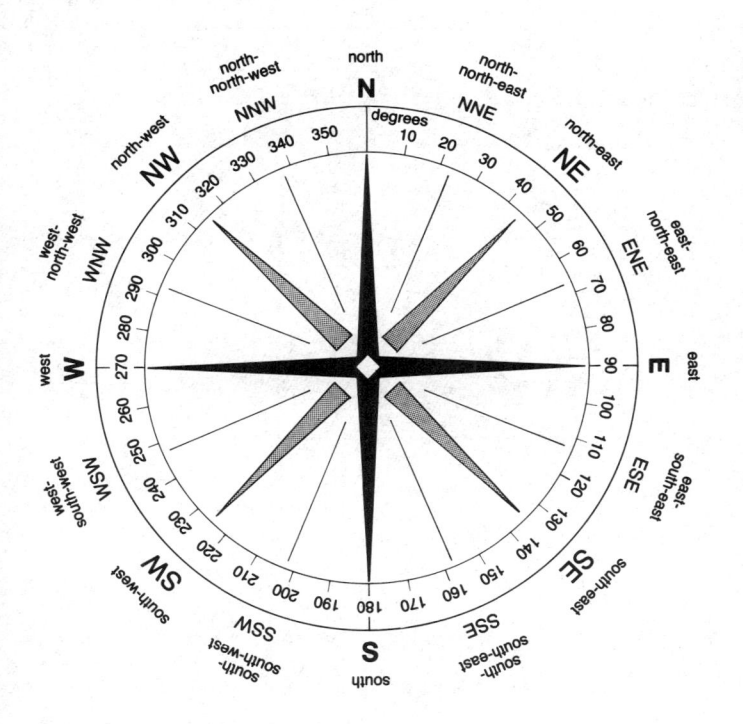

Notes